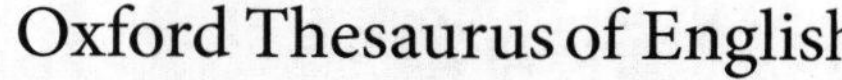
Oxford Thesaurus of English

Oxford Thesaurus of English

THIRD EDITION

OXFORD
UNIVERSITY PRESS

OXFORD
UNIVERSITY PRESS

Great Clarendon Street, Oxford OX2 6DP

Oxford University Press is a department of the University of Oxford.
It furthers the University's objective of excellence in research, scholarship,
and education by publishing worldwide in

Oxford New York
Auckland Cape Town Dar es Salaam Hong Kong Karachi
Kuala Lumpur Madrid Melbourne Mexico City Nairobi
New Delhi Shanghai Taipei Toronto

With offices in

Argentina Austria Brazil Chile Czech Republic France Greece
Guatemala Hungary Italy Japan Poland Portugal Singapore
South Korea Switzerland Thailand Turkey Ukraine Vietnam

First edition 2000
Second edition 2004
Second edition, revised 2006
Third edition 2009

British Library Cataloguing in Publication Data
Data available

Library of Congress Cataloging in Publication Data
Data available

Typeset in Parable, Frutiger, and Argo by Asiatype, Inc.
Printed in China via Golden Cup Printing Co., Ltd.

ISBN 978-0-19-956081-3

10 9 8 7 6 5 4 3

Contents

Editorial staff

Editor
Maurice Waite

assisted by
Juliet Field
Lucy Hollingworth
Jane Horwood

For the first edition

Chief Editor
Patrick Hanks

Maurice Waite
Sara Hawker
Catherine Bailey
Martin Coleman
Chris Cowley
Lucinda Coventry
David Edmonds
Muriel Summersgill
Valerie Fairhurst

Preface

The word *thesaurus* comes from the Greek word *thesauros*, meaning 'storehouse' or 'treasure'. This is an apt description, because a thesaurus is a kind of treasure trove of the language, allowing you to explore its richness and variety. By listing groups of words that have similar meanings to each other, a thesaurus offers a choice of alternative words (synonyms) that can be used in place of one that you already have in mind.

A thesaurus thus helps you to express yourself more accurately and in more interesting and varied ways. It is an invaluable tool for anyone who writes, whether for memos and reports at work, essays and dissertations at school and college, letters to business contacts, friends, or potential employers, or creative writing for a living or for pleasure. A thesaurus can provide the answer when a word is on the tip of your tongue, or it can expand your vocabulary to help you find new ways of saying what you want to. A thesaurus can also help in solving crossword puzzles and with many other word games.

The *Oxford Thesaurus of English*, first published in 2000 and now in its third edition, contains an unrivalled number of alternative and opposite words: well over 600,000 in total. It is the most comprehensive one-volume thesaurus available, including not only everyday words but also unusual and colourful words, specialist terms, and archaic and historical terms. There are approximately 16,000 entries, arranged A–Z, which means that there is no bulky index to consult first. For each of those 16,000 entries, there is an average of 38 alternatives, carefully chosen and arranged to help you find the word you need as quickly as possible.

For this edition, several hundred more phrasal entries have been added, so you can now find synonyms for expressions such as *gear oneself up* and *the whip hand*.

In addition to the standard entries, the *Oxford Thesaurus of English* offers an array of special features designed to make it more useful and accessible. Three different types of panel attached to selected entries explore the differences between similar words, based on sophisticated computational analysis of how these words are used in real English, giving the user the fullest and most accurate account available. Then there are over 1300 Word Links, at over 700 entries, to words which are not synonyms but which have another kind of relation to the headword: for example, at *cat* there are terms for the male and female cat (*tom*, *queen*) as well as the adjective relating to cats (*feline*).

Lastly, the central Wordfinder section offers hundreds of lists covering everything from types of cheese to species of bird and names of dances, ideal for crossword and word-game enthusiasts. These lists are organized into thematic groups so that they are interesting to browse, and they have an index to make the information quickly accessible. They are supplemented by lists of imitative, archaic, foreign, and other fascinating words drawn from the resources of Oxford Dictionaries.

For a quick tour of the main features of the *Oxford Thesaurus of English*, look at the Guide on pp. xi–xii. The Introduction starting overleaf gives more details on the contents and organization of the thesaurus and how to get the most out of it.

Introduction

The *Oxford Thesaurus of English* (*OTE*) has been compiled using new evidence in new ways, in order to create an original work of reference that will be most useful to a wide range of users for many different purposes. It is an independent resource in its own right, but it may also be viewed as a companion volume to the *Oxford Dictionary of English*, Oxford's ground-breaking one-volume dictionary which, based on systematic analysis of hundreds of millions of words of real English, presents the most accurate picture of the language available. *OTE* draws on the same data to give sets of words compiled according to their similarity in meaning and checked for actual usage against the evidence in the Oxford English Corpus.

All thesauruses contain lists of words that are linked by having a similar or related meaning, but this thesaurus also contains:

- antonyms (i.e. opposites such as, for the different senses of **smart**: *scruffy*, *unfashionable*, *stupid*, *slow*, and *gentle*).
- word links (e.g. words related to **horse**, such as *stallion*, *mare*, and *equine*)
- studies of synonyms with similar meanings, entitled 'Choose the right word' (e.g. *brusque*, *abrupt*, *curt*, and *terse*)
- word toolkits to help you choose the best adjective to use (e.g. *defiant*, *rebellious*, or *unruly*)
- advice on pairs of confusable words (e.g. *militate* and *mitigate*)
- a central Wordfinder section of thematic word lists (e.g. **herbs**: *angelica*, *anise*, *basil*, *bay leaf*, *bergamot*, etc.)

For more information on these features, see p. x.

Selection of entries

The primary purpose of *OTE* is to give synonyms for the common everyday words of English: words with roughly the same meaning as the entry word (headword). Some words, especially those for animals, plants, and physical objects, do not have synonyms, so you will not find entries for *gerbil* or *geranium*. There is, however, an entry for *squirrel* because of the phrasal verb *squirrel something away*, which has synonyms such as *save*, *put aside*, and *stash away*.

The words selected as headwords are general words that non-specialists are likely to want to look up. It is the job of a dictionary, not a thesaurus, to explain the meanings of unusual words, such as *supererogatory*, so such words do not get an alphabetical entry here. However, *supererogatory* is given as a synonym at entries for the more familiar words *inessential*, *needless*, and *unnecessary*. A thesaurus can thus lead you from the familiar to the unfamiliar, improving your word power.

Homonyms

Homonyms are words that have the same spelling but different and unrelated meanings, such as the *bank* of a river or lake and a *bank* that looks after people's money. Each has its own numbered entry, thus:

bank[1] *... the banks of Lake Michigan...*
bank[2] *... I paid the money into my bank...*

Synonyms

It is sometimes argued that no two words have exactly the same meaning. Even words as similar in meaning as *close* and *shut* may have slightly different nuances. *Closing* a shop implies that the shop is no longer open for business, so no one can come in. On the other hand, *shutting* a shop implies that the shop is being made secure, so that nothing can be taken out. A similar distinction is found between *strong* and *powerful*: *powerful enemies* may threaten from outside, but a *strong defence* on the inside will deter them from attacking. However, these are unusually subtle distinctions: for most practical purposes, *close* and *shut* have the same meaning. Other synonyms are more distant, or emphasize different aspects of the meaning. For example, another close synonym of *strong* is *muscular*, but it places much more emphasis on physical strength. By contrast, *stalwart* and *staunch* are synonyms that emphasize more abstract aspects of this meaning of *strong*. *Forceful*, *secure*, *durable*, *loud*, *intense*, *bright*, and *alcoholic* are other close synonyms of *strong*, but all in quite different senses. They are not, of course, synonyms of each other.

In this book, the broadest possible definition of the term 'synonym' has been adopted, as being the one that will be most useful to users. Even words whose meaning is quite distantly related to that of the headword are supplied if they can be used to get the same message across in some contexts or if they are synonymous with a part of the meaning of the headword.

The synonyms in each entry are grouped together in synonym sets. Major synonym sets correspond roughly to different senses of a word in a dictionary, but the divisions are also governed by the matches between headwords and synonyms. Each major synonym set is numbered, and many have finer subdivisions, which are marked by semicolons.

At the start of almost every synonym set is a 'core synonym': the term which is closest in meaning to the headword in that particular sense. Core synonyms are printed in **bold**. If no one synonym is particularly close, there may be no bold core synonym. Some synonym sets have more than one core synonym; for example at *avant-garde* (adjective), both *innovative* and *advanced* are very close in meaning to the headword, so both are given as core synonyms. Two different core synonyms within the same sense group may emphasize slightly different aspects of the meaning of the headword. For example, at *dutiful*, the first core synonym given is *conscientious*, followed by a group of words closely related to this aspect of its meaning. Then, after a semicolon, a second core synonym, *obedient*, is given, with a further group of synonyms related to that aspect.

Synonyms whose usage is restricted in some way, such as regional expressions and informal or very formal words, are placed at the end of each major synonym set and labelled accordingly. See **Register** below.

Illustrative examples

Almost every synonym set in *OTE* is illustrated with a carefully chosen example of the word in use in the relevant sense. These are authentic examples of natural usage taken from the Oxford English Corpus (see **Linguistic evidence** below). The examples can therefore be trusted for guidance on using unfamiliar words in an idiomatic way, but it does not follow that each synonym given could be used in the example, in place of the headword.

Where part of an example is printed in ***bold italic*** type, this indicates that some or all of the synonyms can be substituted for that particular phrase, not just for the headword alone. Thus at *attached*, the example given is:

> *she was very **attached to** her brother*

because the synonyms are equivalent to *attached to*:

> **fond of**, devoted to, full of regard for, full of admiration for; affectionate towards, tender towards, caring towards; informal mad about, crazy about, nuts about.

Linguistic evidence

OTE was compiled using the Oxford English Corpus, a huge collection of written English amounting currently to over two billion words, held in Oxford's computers and made available for computational and lexicographical analysis. This body of language (or 'corpus') is drawn from a very diverse range of sources (from scholarly journals to internet chatrooms, via novels and newspapers) and from all parts of the English-speaking world.

The Oxford English Corpus allows lexicographers to sort and analyse thousands of examples in context and thereby see more clearly than ever before how words are actually used. The editors of this thesaurus have been able to:

- confirm whether a word has senses for which there are suitable synonyms
- check the sense of words being selected as synonyms
- actively find synonyms which have not previously been recorded
- compare and contrast close synonyms using computational methods of analysis

The Corpus is also used to obtain the sentences and phrases given as examples of usage.

Idiomatic phrases and phrasal verbs

English is full of idiomatic expressions—phrases whose meaning is more than the sum of their parts. For example, *a shot in the dark* means 'a guess', while *a shot in the arm* means 'a boost'. The origin of each is apparent, but neither entire phrase has very much to do with more literal meanings of *shot*. Phrasal verbs are expressions such as *book in* and *turn out*, consisting of a verb plus a particle. The meaning of a phrasal verb is also often quite idiomatic; for example, the meanings of *take off* are quite distinct from the meanings of *take*. This thesaurus includes a rich selection of both kinds of idiomatic expression, and provides synonyms for each. If a word is used as both a noun and a verb, the idiomatic expressions are entered as subentries under the part of speech in which the word is used. Thus, *by the book* is given under the noun senses of *book*, while *book in* is given under the verb senses.

Register: standard vs. informal and regional English

Informal usage becomes ever more prevalent. Expressions once considered slang are now used in writing and more formal contexts, while the use of swear words and taboo words is on the increase. This thesaurus therefore includes a rich selection of informal and vulgar synonyms, but users should treat the vulgar slang labels as warning notices.

Most of the synonyms given are part of standard English; that is, they are in normal use everywhere in the English-speaking world, at many different levels of formality, ranging from official documents to casual conversation. These general synonyms are given first in each synonym set. Some words, however, are appropriate only in particular contexts, and these are placed after the standard expressions and labelled accordingly. The technical term for these differences in levels of usage is 'register'. The register labels used in this thesaurus are:

informal: normally used only in contexts such as conversations or letters between friends, e.g. *swig* as a synonym for *drink*.

formal: normally used only in writing such as official documents, e.g. *dwelling* as a synonym for *home*.

dated: no longer used by the majority of English speakers, but still encountered occasionally, especially among the older generation, e.g. *measure one's length* as a synonym for *fall down*.

archaic: very old-fashioned language, not in ordinary use at all today, but sometimes used to give a deliberately old-fashioned effect, or found in works of the past that are still widely read, e.g. *aliment* as a synonym for *food*.

historical: still used today, but only to refer to some practice or article that is no longer part of the modern world, e.g. *ruff*, the type of collar.

humorous: used with the intention of sounding funny or playful, e.g. *terminological inexactitude* as a synonym for *lie*.

derogatory: intended to express a low opinion or to insult someone, e.g. *brat* as a synonym of *child*.

offensive: likely to cause offence, especially racial offence, whether the person using it means to or not.

vulgar slang: very informal language that is likely to cause offence, usually because it refers to sexual activity or bodily functions.

euphemistic: used instead of a more direct or rude term, e.g. *asleep* as a synonym for *dead*.

technical: normally used only in technical and specialist language, though not necessarily restricted to any specific field, e.g. *littoral* as a synonym for *beach*. Words used in specific fields are given appropriate labels, e.g. Medicine, Christianity.

literary: found only or mainly in literature written in an 'elevated' style, e.g. *ambrosial* as a synonym for *delicious*.

rare: not in common use, e.g. *acclivitous* as a synonym for *steep*.

World English

English is a world language, so particular care has been taken to include synonyms from every variety of English; and when these are exclusively or very strongly associated with a region of the world they are labelled as such.

The main regional standards are British (abbreviated to *Brit.*), North American (*N. Amer.*), Australian and New Zealand (*Austral./NZ*), South African (*S. African*), Indian (in the sense of the variety of English found throughout the subcontinent), and West Indian (*W. Indian*). If a finer distinction is apparent, more precise labelling may be used, as with *beer parlour*, a Canadian synonym for *bar*.

Scottish, Irish, and Northern English are varieties within the British Isles containing distinctive vocabulary items of their own. The main synonyms found as regional terms of this kind are entered and labelled accordingly.

The term for something found mainly or exclusively in a particular country or region (although it may be mentioned in any variety of English) is identified by an indication such as in the Caribbean. An example is *key* (as a synonym for *island*).

Many regionally restricted terms are informal, rather than being part of the standard language. Writers in the northern hemisphere in search of local colour may be delighted to learn that an Australian synonym for *sordid* is *scungy*, while Australian writers may find it equally useful to be given the equivalent British terms as *manky* and *grotty*.

Words that are used in English but still generally regarded as foreign are labelled with their language of origin. For example, among the synonyms for *hotel* are: French pension, auberge; Spanish posada, parador; Portuguese pousada; Italian pensione; German Gasthaus.

Antonyms

Many synonym sets are followed by one or more antonyms—words that have the opposite meaning to the headword. There are several different kinds of antonym. *True* and *false* are absolute antonyms, with no middle ground, because, logically, a statement is either true or false: it cannot be slightly true or rather false. *Hot* and *cold*, on the other hand, are antonyms with gradations of meaning: it makes perfectly good sense to say that something is rather hot or very cold, and there are a number of words (*warm*, *tepid*, *cool*) which represent intermediate stages, so *hot* and *cold* are at opposite ends of a continuum, rather than being absolutes.

For many words, such as *senile*, there is no single word that serves as an antonym, but the phrase *in the prime of life* does the job. In this book the broadest possible definition has been adopted, giving the maximum amount of information to the user. In some cases, a phrasal antonym is given for a phrasal subentry, e.g. *bottle things up* as an antonym of *let off steam*.

The antonyms given in this book are not the only possibilities, but they are usually the furthest in meaning from the headword. By looking up the antonym as an entry in its own right, you will generally find a much larger range to choose from. For example, the entry for *delete* includes:

▷**ANTONYMS** add, insert.

Both *add* and *insert* are entries in their own right and give synonyms such as *include*, *append*, and *interpolate*.

Word links

The 'Word links' panels at the end of certain entries supply words which are not actual synonyms but have a different kind of relation to the headword. For example, at *milk*, the adjective relating to milk is given (*lactic*); at *town*, the related adjectives *urban*, *municipal*, and the rarer *oppidan*. Examples of other types of relation include collective nouns (e.g. *school* at *dolphin*, or *charm* at *finch*); the male, female, or young of an animal (e.g. *levret* at *hare*, or *tom*, *queen*, and *kitten* at *cat*); phobias (e.g. *arachnophobia* at *spider*); the study of a particular subject (e.g. *bryology* at *moss*); and a geometric figure with a given number of sides (e.g. *pentagon* at *five*).

Some word links are prefixes or suffixes related to the headword, such as *photo-* at *light*, *-metry* at *measurement*, and *cerebro-* at *brain*: knowledge of prefixes and suffixes helps the user to understand many new or unfamiliar words, such as *photometry* and *cerebrospinal*.

'Choose the right word' panels

No two synonyms are exactly the same: they may have subtly different meanings or be used in different contexts. For instance, the words *blunt*, *candid*, *forthright*, *frank*, and *outspoken* are all synonyms of each other because they all have roughly the same meaning, but there are subtle differences. The 'Choose the right word' panels are devoted to explaining the differences in meaning between such groups of close synonyms. The distinctions are based on careful analysis of actual usage as recorded in the Oxford English Corpus (see **Linguistic evidence** above). This analysis involved the most up-to-date computational techniques to sift large amounts of data, as well as traditional lexicographical analysis.

Confusable words

Further panels explain the difference between pairs of words such as *militate* and *mitigate*, *flaunt* and *flout*, or *principal* and *principle*, that may cause difficulty because they are written or pronounced similarly but have different meanings.

Word toolkits

New to this third edition are a selection of 'Word toolkit' panels, each of which compares three partly synonymous adjectives by means of the nouns that they commonly qualify. These have been derived directly from the Oxford English Corpus (see **Linguistic evidence** above).

Wordfinder

The centre section of the *Oxford Thesaurus of English* contains word lists to supplement the main entries. While the main entry for, say, *sport* gives synonyms for *sport—game*, *recreation*, etc.—the list entitled 'Sports' in the centre section gives the names of particular sports—*archery*, *badminton*, *curling*, *dressage*, etc. There is a thorough index to these lists at the start of the section. There are also fascinating lists of imitative, archaic, foreign, and other words. These lists all make *OTE* an invaluable aid to crossword-solving and a fascinating source of encyclopedic information on subjects as diverse as clouds, cocktails, marsupials, and martial arts.

Guide to thesaurus entries

Synonym entries

part of speech of the headword

headword

core synonym, the closest synonym to the headword

example of use, to help identify the sense you want

noun phrase entered under the noun section

form of the headword for which synonyms are given

number for each sense treated separately

label indicating the currency of the following synonyms

phrasal verb entered under the verb section

book noun **1** *he published his first book in 1610*: **volume**, tome, work, printed work, publication, title, opus, treatise; novel, storybook; manual, handbook, guide, companion, reference book; paperback, hardback, softback; historical yellowback.
2 *he scribbled a few notes in his book*: **notepad**, notebook, pad, memo pad, exercise book, binder; ledger, record book, log, logbook, chronicle, journal, diary, daybook; Brit. jotter, pocketbook; N. Amer. scratch pad; French cahier.
3 (**books**) *the council had to balance its books*: **accounts**, records, archives; account book, record book, ledger, log, balance sheet, financial statement.
□ **by the book** *he does all his police work by the book*: **according to the rules**, in accordance with the rules, within the law, abiding by the law, lawfully, legally, legitimately, licitly; honestly, fairly, openly; informal on the level, on the up and up, fair and square.
▸ verb **1** *Steven booked a table at their favourite restaurant*: **reserve**, make a reservation for, arrange in advance, prearrange, arrange for, order; charter, hire; informal bag; dated engage, bespeak.
2 *we booked a number of events in the Wellington Festival*: **arrange**, programme, schedule, timetable, line up, secure, fix up, lay on; N. Amer. slate.
□ **book in** *he booked in at the St Francis Hotel*: **register**, check in, enrol, record/log one's arrival.

Word links **book**
bibliography list of books **bibliophile, bibliomane** book enthusiast **antiquarian** relating to rare books

homonym number showing that there are other entries for *lead*

pronunciation, to help identify the word you want

lead[2] (rhymes with 'bed') **noun** *he was removing the lead from the man's chest*: **bullet**, pellet, ball, slug; shot, buckshot, ammunition.

words, prefixes, or suffixes with meanings related to that of the headword

Word links **lead**
plumbic, plumbous relating to lead **plumb-**: *plumbate* related prefix

semicolon marking a subdivision of the synonym set

label indicating the origin of the following synonym

words meaning the opposite of the headword

label indicating that the following synonyms are used in informal language

label indicating that this sense of *peculiar* is used in informal language

label indicating that the following synonyms are used in a particular region of the world

phrase for which synonyms are given

peculiar adjective **1** *something even more peculiar began to happen*: **strange**, unusual, odd, funny, curious, bizarre, weird, uncanny, queer, unexpected, unfamiliar, abnormal, atypical, anomalous, untypical, different, out of the ordinary, out of the way; exceptional, rare, extraordinary, remarkable; puzzling, mystifying, mysterious, perplexing, baffling, unaccountable, incongruous, uncommon, irregular, singular, deviant, aberrant, freak, freakish; suspicious, dubious, questionable; eerie, unnatural; Scottish unco; French outré; informal fishy, creepy, spooky; Brit. informal rum; N. Amer. informal bizarro.
▷ ANTONYMS normal, ordinary.
2 *his peculiar behaviour at the airport*: **bizarre**, eccentric, strange, odd, weird, queer, funny, unusual, abnormal, idiosyncratic, unconventional, outlandish, offbeat, freakish, quirky, quaint, droll, zany, off-centre; informal wacky, freaky, kooky, screwy, kinky, oddball, cranky; N. Amer. informal off the wall, wacko; Austral./NZ informal, dated dilly.
3 informal *I still feel a bit peculiar*: **unwell**, ill, poorly, bad, out of sorts, indisposed, not oneself, sick, queasy, nauseous, nauseated, peaky, liverish, green about the gills, run down, washed out; Brit. off, off colour; informal under the weather, below par, not up to par, funny, rough, lousy, rotten, awful, terrible, dreadful, crummy, seedy; Brit. informal grotty, ropy; Scottish informal wabbit, peely-wally; Austral./NZ informal crook; rare peaked, peakish.
4 *attitudes and mannerisms peculiar to the islanders*: **characteristic of**, typical of, representative of, belonging to, indicative of, symptomatic of,

Other features

article explaining the differences between a group of close synonyms

Choose the right word **strange, odd, curious, peculiar**

These words are all applied to things that are unusual or unfamiliar; they generally also suggest that something is in some way surprising.

Strange is the most neutral term for something that is not expected or is hard to understand or explain (*this is strange behaviour for a left-wing party | he looked at her with a strange expression*). This is the only word of the four that can be used in the expression *strange to say*, as in *I went to see 'Fallen Angels', which, strange to say, is a hit*.

Odd gives a stronger sense that the speaker or writer is perplexed (*do you think* . . .

article explaining the difference between a confusable pair of words

Easily confused words **flaunt or flout?**

It is a common error to use **flaunt** as though it meant the same as **flout**. *Flaunt* means 'display ostentatiously', as in *tourists flaunting their wealth*. *Flout*, on the other hand, means 'defy or disobey (a rule)', as in *timber companies are continuing to flout environmental laws*. Saying that someone *flaunts the rules* is an error due to similarity in sound and to the element of ostentation involved in *flouting* a regulation.

article comparing the nouns used with a set of similar adjectives

Word toolkit

organic	**biological**	**living**
food	weapons	organisms
vegetables	warfare	creatures
waste	father/mother	cells
fertilizer	diversity	people
chemistry	clock	plants

centre section containing thematic lists of words

Wordfinder

Wordfinder

index to thematic lists in Wordfinder section

Index to thematic lists

thematic section heading

Music

list of types of wind instrument

Wind instruments

alpenhorn *or* alphorn
bagpipes
barrel organ
basset horn
bassoon
bombarde
clarinet
contrabassoon
cor anglais
cornetto
didgeridoo
fife
fipple flute
flageolet
flute
harmonica
heckelphone
kazoo
krummhorn

aback adverb
□ **take someone aback** *Joanna was taken aback by the violence of his reaction*: **surprise**, shock, stun, stagger, astound, astonish, startle, take by surprise; dumbfound, daze, nonplus, stop someone in their tracks, stupefy, take someone's breath away; shake (up), jolt, throw, unnerve, disconcert, disturb, disquiet, unsettle, discompose, bewilder; informal flabbergast, knock for six, knock sideways, knock out, floor, strike dumb.

abandon verb **1** *the party has abandoned policies which made it unelectable*: **renounce**, relinquish, dispense with, forswear, disclaim, disown, disavow, discard, wash one's hands of; give up, drop, do away with, jettison; informal ditch, scrap, scrub, axe, junk.
▷**ANTONYMS** keep, claim.
2 *by that stage, she had abandoned painting*: **give up**, stop, cease, drop, forgo, desist from, have done with, abjure, abstain from, discontinue, break off, refrain from, set/lay aside; informal cut out, kick, jack in, pack in, quit.
▷**ANTONYMS** continue; take up.
3 *he abandoned his wife and children*: **desert**, leave, leave high and dry, turn one's back on, cast aside, break (up) with; jilt, strand, leave stranded, leave in the lurch, throw over; informal run/walk out on, dump, ditch; archaic forsake.
▷**ANTONYMS** stick by.
4 *the skipper gave the order to abandon ship*: **vacate**, leave, quit, evacuate, withdraw from.
5 *an attempt to persuade businesses not to abandon the area to inner-city deprivation*: **relinquish**, surrender, give up, cede, yield, leave.
6 *she abandoned herself to the sensuousness of the music*: **indulge in**, give way to, give oneself up to, yield to, lose oneself to/in.
▷**ANTONYMS** control oneself.
▶ noun *reckless abandon*: **uninhibitedness**, recklessness, lack of restraint, lack of inhibition, unruliness, wildness, impulsiveness, impetuosity, immoderation, wantonness.
▷**ANTONYMS** self-control.

abandoned adjective **1** *an abandoned child*: **deserted**, forsaken, cast aside/off; jilted, stranded, rejected; informal dumped, ditched.
2 *an abandoned tin mine*: **unused**, disused, neglected, idle; deserted, unoccupied, uninhabited, empty.
3 *a wild, abandoned dance*: **uninhibited**, reckless, unrestrained, unruly, wild, unbridled, impulsive, impetuous; immoderate, wanton.

abandonment noun **1** *she will be charged with child abandonment*: **desertion**, neglect, stranding; jilting, betrayal.
2 *the buildings were used as rubbish pits after abandonment*: **disuse**, evacuation, neglect.
3 *abandonment of the reform plan would probably result in hyperinflation*: **renunciation**, relinquishment, rejection, withdrawal, dropping, cessation, discontinuation, termination, stopping, surrender, dispensation.
▷**ANTONYMS** adoption.

abase verb *I watched my colleagues* **abasing themselves** *before the dean*: **humble**, humiliate, belittle, demean, lower, degrade, disgrace, disparage, debase, cheapen, discredit, mortify, bring low, demote, reduce; grovel, kowtow, bow and scrape, toady, fawn; informal crawl, suck up to someone, lick someone's boots.

abasement noun *the dog flattened himself at Mark's feet, tail thumping in abject abasement*: **humility**, humbleness, humiliation, belittlement, lowering, degradation, disgrace, mortification.
▷**ANTONYMS** pride.

abashed adjective *the boy looked down, abashed*: **embarrassed**, ashamed, shamefaced, remorseful, mortified, conscience-stricken, humiliated, humbled, taken aback, disconcerted, nonplussed, discomfited, discomposed, distressed, chagrined, perturbed, confounded, dismayed, dumbfounded, crestfallen, sheepish, red-faced, blushing, confused, put out of countenance, discountenanced, with one's tail between one's legs; informal floored.
▷**ANTONYMS** unabashed, undaunted.

abate verb **1** *thankfully, the storm had abated | the recession showed no signs of abating*: **subside**, die down/away/out, drop off/away, lessen, ease (off), let up, decrease, diminish, moderate, decline, fade, dwindle, slacken, recede, cool off, tail off, peter out, taper off, wane, ebb, relent, desist, weaken, become weaker, come to an end; archaic remit.
▷**ANTONYMS** intensify.
2 *energy efficiency may be the quickest way to abate emissions of carbon dioxide*: **decrease**, lessen, diminish, reduce, lower, moderate, ease, soothe, relieve, dampen, calm, tone down, alleviate, mitigate, mollify, allay, assuage, palliate, temper, appease, attenuate.
▷**ANTONYMS** increase.

abatement noun **1** *the storm still rages with no sign of abatement*: **subsiding**, dying down/away/out, dropping off/away, lessening, easing (off), decrease, diminishing, moderation, decline, declining, fade, dwindling, cooling off, tailing off, petering out, tapering off, wane, waning, ebb, relenting, desisting, weakening.
▷**ANTONYMS** intensification.
2 *as though sensing some abatement of my ferocity, she spoke to me gently*: **lessening**, decrease, moderation, easing, softening, soothing, relief, blunting, deadening, alleviation, mitigation, mollification, allaying, assuagement, palliation, tempering, appeasement, attenuation.
▷**ANTONYMS** intensification.
3 formal *the prospective purchaser demanded an abatement on the purchase price*: **decrease**, reduction, lowering.
▷**ANTONYMS** increase.

abattoir noun **slaughterhouse**; Brit. butchery, knacker's yard; archaic shambles, butcher-row.

abbey noun *there was a Benedictine abbey here in the Middle Ages*: **monastery**, **convent**, priory, cloister, friary, nunnery, religious house, religious community; historical charterhouse, cell; rare coenobium, coenoby.

> *Word links* **abbey**
>
> **abbatial** relating to an abbey

abbot noun

> *Word links* **abbot**
>
> **abbatial** relating to an abbot

abbreviate verb *they called the phenomenon long-term potentiation, soon abbreviated to LTP*: **shorten**, reduce, cut, cut short/down, contract, condense, compress, abridge, truncate, clip, crop, pare down, prune, shrink,

constrict, telescope, curtail; summarize, abstract, precis, synopsize, digest, edit.
▷ANTONYMS lengthen, expand, elongate.

Choose the right word **abbreviate, shorten, abridge, truncate, curtail**

See **shorten**.

abbreviated adjective *an abbreviated version of the declaration*: **shortened**, reduced, cut, cut short/down, contracted, condensed, compressed, abridged, truncated, concise, compendious, compact, succinct, clipped, cropped, pared down, pruned, shrunk, constricted, telescoped; summary, thumbnail, summarized, synoptic, abstracted, edited (down).
▷ANTONYMS expanded, long.

abbreviation noun **1** *the abbreviation 'mAh' stands for milliamp hours*: **shortened form**, short form, contraction, elision, acronym, initialism, symbol, diminutive.
▷ANTONYMS full form.
2 *she felt a slight irritation at the abbreviation of her name*: **shortening**, reduction, cutting, cutting short/down, contraction, condensation, compression, abridgement, truncation, clipping, cropping, paring down, pruning, shrinking, constricting, telescoping.
▷ANTONYMS expansion.

abdicate verb **1** *in 1936, Edward VIII abdicated in favour of George VI*: **resign**, retire, quit, stand down, step down, bow out, renounce the throne; archaic demit.
▷ANTONYMS be crowned.
2 *Napoleon compelled Ferdinand to abdicate the throne*: **resign from**, relinquish, renounce, give up, hand over, turn over, deliver up, surrender, vacate, forswear, abjure, cede; Law disclaim.
▷ANTONYMS accede to.
3 *the state virtually abdicated all responsibility for their welfare*: **disown**, turn down, spurn, reject, renounce, give up, avoid, refuse, abnegate, relinquish, abjure, repudiate, waive, yield, forgo, abandon, surrender, deliver up, disgorge, cast aside, drop, turn one's back on, wash one's hands of; informal shirk; archaic forsake.
▷ANTONYMS accept, take on.

abdication noun **1** *the monarchy is facing its biggest crisis since Edward VIII's abdication in 1936*: **resignation**, retirement; relinquishment, renunciation, giving up, surrender, abjuration, vacation, ceding, cession; archaic demission.
▷ANTONYMS coronation.
2 *an abdication of responsibility*: **disowning**, renunciation, rejection, refusal, avoidance, abnegation, relinquishment, abjuration, repudiation, waiving, yielding, forgoing, abandonment, surrender, disgorgement, casting aside.
▷ANTONYMS acceptance.

abdomen noun *I woke in the middle of the night with pains in my abdomen*: **stomach**, belly, gut, middle, midriff, intestines; informal tummy, tum, insides, guts, corporation, maw, breadbasket, pot, paunch; Austral. informal bingy.

Word links **abdomen**

abdominal, **ventral**, **coeliac** relating to the abdomen
laparotomy surgical incision of the abdomen

abdominal adjective *abdominal pain can be produced by too much caffeine*: **stomach**, gastric, intestinal, stomachic, enteric, duodenal, visceral, coeliac, ventral.

abduct verb *she was abducted by two men and held for 36 hours*. See **kidnap**.

aberrant adjective *Mrs Casper seems to be responsible for Billy's aberrant behaviour*. See **deviant** (adjective).

aberration noun **1** *economists said the figure was an aberration*: **anomaly**, deviation, divergence, abnormality, irregularity, variation, digression, freak, rogue, rarity, quirk, oddity, curiosity, mistake.
2 *it is possible that, in a moment of aberration, the parent may strike the child*: **abnormality**, irregularity, eccentricity, deviation, transgression, straying, lapse, aberrancy.
3 *the experience might have been no more than a temporary aberration of an exhausted mind*: **disorder**, defect, disease, irregularity, instability, derangement, vagary.

abet verb *several villagers are accused of aiding and abetting the smugglers*: **assist**, aid, help, lend a hand, support, back, encourage; cooperate with, collaborate with, work with, connive with, collude with, go along with, be in collusion with, be hand in glove with, side with; second, endorse, boost, favour, champion, sanction, succour; promote, further, expedite, push, give a push to, connive at, participate in.
▷ANTONYMS hinder.

abeyance noun *the project was left* ***in abeyance*** *for the time being*: **suspension**, a state of suspension, a state of dormancy, a state of latency, a state of uncertainty, suspense, remission, reserve; pending, suspended, deferred, postponed, put off, put to one side, unattended, unfinished, incomplete, unresolved, undetermined, up in the air, betwixt and between; informal in cold storage, on ice, on the back burner, hanging fire.
▷ANTONYMS in hand, under way, continuing.
□ **hold something in abeyance** *the application was held in abeyance whilst legal advice was sought*: **suspend**, adjourn, interrupt, break off, postpone, delay, defer, shelve, arrest, put off, intermit, prorogue, hold over, put aside, pigeonhole; reschedule; cut short, bring to an end, cease, discontinue, dissolve, disband, terminate, call a halt to; N. Amer. table; informal put on ice, put on the back burner, mothball; N. Amer. informal take a rain check on.
▷ANTONYMS continue, resume.

abhor verb *Walter abhorred sexism in every form*. See **detest**.

abhorrence noun *my husband had an abhorrence of show and pomp*. See **hatred**.

abhorrent adjective *the rack and thumbscrew are abhorrent to any civilized society*: **detestable**, detested, hateful, hated, loathsome, loathed, despicable, despised, abominable, abominated, execrable, execrated, repellent, repugnant, repulsive, revolting, disgusting, distasteful, horrible, horrid, horrifying, awful, heinous, reprehensible, obnoxious, odious, nauseating, offensive, contemptible.
▷ANTONYMS admirable, loved.

abide verb **1** informal *he cannot abide lies*: **tolerate**, bear, stand, put up with, endure, suffer, accept, cope with, live with, brook, support, take, countenance, face, handle; informal stick, swallow, stomach, hack, wear.
2 *at least one memory will abide*: **continue**, remain, survive, last, persist, stay, hold on, live on.
▷ANTONYMS fade, disappear.
□ **abide by** *he expected everybody to abide by the rules*: **comply with**, obey, observe, follow, keep to, hold to, conform to, adhere to, stick to, stand by, act in accordance with, uphold, heed, pay attention to, agree to/with, consent to, accede to, accept, acquiesce in, go along with, acknowledge, respect, defer to.
▷ANTONYMS flout, reject.

abiding adjective *his collections reflect his abiding interest in Italy*: **enduring**, lasting, persisting, long-lasting, lifelong, continuing, remaining, surviving, standing, fixed, durable, everlasting, perpetual, eternal, unending, constant, permanent, stable, unchanging, steadfast, immutable.
▷ANTONYMS short-lived, ephemeral, transitory.

ability noun **1** *he was proud of his daughter's ability to read and write*: **capacity**, capability, potential, potentiality, power, faculty, aptness, facility, propensity, wherewithal, means, preparedness.
▷ANTONYMS inability, incapacity.
2 *they are taught French in sets based on their ability | they criticized the president's leadership abilities*: **talent**, skill, expertise, expertness, adeptness, aptitude, skilfulness, prowess, mastery, artistry, calibre, accomplishment; competence, competency, proficiency; dexterity, adroitness, deftness, cleverness, smartness, flair, finesse, gift, knack, brilliance, genius; qualification, resources; French savoir faire; informal know-how.

ab initio adverb & adjective Latin *the transactions were void ab initio*: **from the beginning**, from the start, initially, originally, from first principles, to begin with, to start with, primarily; Music da capo; informal from scratch, from the word go.

abject adjective **1** *many such families are living in abject poverty*: **wretched**, miserable, hopeless, pathetic, pitiful, pitiable, piteous, stark, sorry, forlorn, woeful, lamentable, degrading, appalling, atrocious, awful.
2 *an abject sinner*: **contemptible**, base, low, vile, worthless, debased, degraded, despicable, ignominious, mean, unworthy, sordid, ignoble, shabby.
▷ANTONYMS proud, respected.
3 *an abject apology*: **obsequious**, grovelling, crawling, creeping, fawning, toadyish, servile, cringing, snivelling, ingratiating, toadying, sycophantic, submissive, craven, humiliating.
▷ANTONYMS proud.

abjure verb *I have abjured all stimulants*: **renounce**, relinquish, reject, dispense with, forgo, forswear, disavow, abandon, deny, gainsay, disclaim, repudiate, give up, spurn, abnegate, wash one's hands of, drop, do away with; eschew, abstain from, refrain from; informal kick, jack in, pack in; Law disaffirm; archaic forsake.

ablaze adjective **1** *rioters overturned cars and set them ablaze*: **alight**, aflame, on fire, in flames, flaming, burning, blazing, raging, fiery, lit, lighted, ignited; literary afire.
▷ANTONYMS extinguished.
2 *every window was ablaze with light*: **lit up**, alight, gleaming, glowing, aglow, illuminated, brilliant, bright, shining, radiant, shimmering, sparkling, flashing, dazzling, luminous, lustrous, incandescent.
▷ANTONYMS dark.

3 *his piercing eyes were ablaze with fury*: **passionate**, impassioned, aroused, excited, stimulated, eager, animated, incensed, intense, heated, ardent, fervent, frenzied, feverish.

able adjective *the university attracts able students from across the UK*: **intelligent**, clever, brilliant, talented, skilful, skilled, accomplished, gifted, masterly, virtuoso, expert; proficient, apt, good, adroit, adept, qualified, fit, suited, suitable; capable, competent, efficient, effective.
▷ANTONYMS incompetent, incapable, inept.
□ **able to** *visitors will be able to buy some of the articles on display*: **allowed to**, free to, in a position to; capable of, qualified to, competent to, equal to, up to, fit to, prepared to.

Choose the right word **able, competent, capable, efficient**

See **competent**.

able-bodied adjective *every able-bodied man was required to serve in the armed forces*: **healthy**, **fit**, in good health, robust, strong, sound, sturdy, vigorous, hardy, hale and hearty, athletic, muscular, strapping, tough, powerful, mighty, rugged, burly, brawny, stalwart, lusty, staunch; in good shape, in good trim, in tip-top condition, in fine fettle, fighting fit, as fit as a fiddle, as fit as a flea, as strong as an ox; informal husky.
▷ANTONYMS infirm, frail; disabled.

ablutions plural noun formal or humorous *she took up water ready for the morning ablutions*: **washing**, cleansing, bathing, showering, scrubbing, purification; wash, bath, shower, toilet, soak, dip, douche; rare lavage, lavation.

abnegate verb *he cannot abnegate the responsibility which the choice confers on him*: **renounce**, reject, refuse, abandon, spurn, abdicate, give up, relinquish, abjure, repudiate, forswear, disavow, cast aside, drop, turn one's back on, wash one's hands of, eschew; archaic forsake.
▷ANTONYMS accept.

abnegation noun **1** *to ignore these issues would be a serious abnegation of their responsibilities*: **renunciation**, rejection, refusal, abandonment, abdication, surrender, giving up, relinquishment, abjuration, repudiation, denial, eschewal, disavowal, casting aside.
▷ANTONYMS acceptance.
2 *such people are capable of abnegation and unselfishness*: **self-denial**, self-sacrifice, abstinence, temperance, continence, asceticism, abstemiousness, austerity, renunciation, resignation.
▷ANTONYMS self-indulgence.

abnormal adjective *the laboratory investigations often yielded abnormal results*: **unusual**, uncommon, atypical, untypical, non-typical, unrepresentative, rare, isolated, irregular, anomalous, deviant, deviating, divergent, wayward, aberrant, freak, freakish; **strange**, odd, peculiar, curious, bizarre, weird, queer; eccentric, idiosyncratic, quirky; unexpected, unfamiliar, unconventional, surprising, unorthodox, singular, exceptional, extraordinary, out of the ordinary, out of the way; unnatural, perverse, perverted, twisted, warped, corrupt, unhealthy, distorted, malformed; Brit. out of the common; informal funny, oddball, off the wall, wacky, wacko, way out, freaky, kinky.
▷ANTONYMS normal, typical, common.

abnormality noun **1** *he was born with numerous abnormalities*: **malformation**, deformity, irregularity, flaw; oddity, peculiarity, deviation, aberration, divergence, anomaly, idiosyncrasy, singularity, rarity.
2 *if the test shows any abnormality you may need further treatment*: **unusualness**, uncommonness, strangeness, waywardness, oddness, unexpectedness, irregularity, singularity, atypicality, anomalousness, deviation, divergence, aberrance, aberration, freakishness, peculiarity, curiousness, eccentricity, idiosyncrasy, quirkiness, unorthodoxy.

abode noun formal *you are most welcome to my humble abode*: **home**, house, place of residence/habitation, accommodation, habitat, base, seat; quarters, lodgings, rooms; address, location, place, whereabouts; informal pad, digs, diggings; formal dwelling, dwelling place, residence, habitation.
□ **of no fixed abode** *Salter, of no fixed abode, admitted causing grievous bodily harm*: **without a roof over one's head**, on the streets, vagrant, sleeping rough, living rough; destitute, down and out, derelict, itinerant.

abolish verb *a bill to abolish the council tax*: **put an end to**, do away with, get rid of, scrap, end, stop, terminate, eradicate, eliminate, exterminate, destroy, annihilate, stamp out, obliterate, wipe out, extinguish, quash, expunge, extirpate; annul, cancel, invalidate, nullify, void, dissolve, erase, delete; rescind, repeal, revoke, overturn; discontinue, remove, withdraw, retract, countermand, excise, drop, jettison, vitiate, abrogate; informal axe, ditch, junk, scrub, dump, chop, give something the chop, knock something on the head; rare deracinate.
▷ANTONYMS retain, create.

abolition noun *the abolition of free eye tests*: **scrapping**, ending, stopping, doing away with, termination, eradication, elimination, extermination, destruction, annihilation, obliteration, quashing, extirpation; annulment, cancellation, invalidation, nullification, dissolution; revocation, repeal, rescindment, overturning, discontinuation, removal, withdrawal, retraction, countermanding, excising, vitiation, abrogation; informal axing, ditching, junking, scrubbing, dumping, chopping; rare deracination, rescission.
▷ANTONYMS retention; creation.

abominable adjective *the abominable slave trade*: **loathsome**, detestable, hateful, odious, obnoxious, despicable, contemptible, damnable, cursed, accursed, diabolical; disgusting, revolting, repellent, repulsive, offensive, repugnant, abhorrent, reprehensible, atrocious, horrifying, execrable; foul, vile, wretched, base, miserable, horrible, awful, dreadful, appalling, abysmal, brutal, nauseating; horrid, nasty, disagreeable, unpleasant, distasteful; informal terrible, shocking, God-awful, beastly; Brit. informal chronic.
▷ANTONYMS good, admirable.

abominably adverb *I treated her abominably*: **reprehensibly**, badly, dreadfully, appallingly, brutally, abysmally, nauseatingly, horridly, nastily; atrociously, horrifyingly, execrably, foully, vilely, wretchedly, miserably, horribly, awfully; disagreeably, unpleasantly, distastefully; hatefully, loathsomely, detestably, odiously; despicably, contemptibly, damnably, diabolically, disgustingly, revoltingly, repellently, repulsively, repugnantly, abhorrently; informal terribly, shockingly.
▷ANTONYMS well, admirably.

abominate verb *most New Yorkers abominate the countryside*. See **detest**.

abomination noun **1** *in both wars, internment was an abomination*: **atrocity**, disgrace, horror, obscenity, outrage, curse, torment, evil, crime, monstrosity, violation, bugbear, anathema, bane; French bête noire.
2 *he had a Calvinist abomination of indulgence*: **detestation**, loathing, hatred, aversion, antipathy, revulsion, repugnance, abhorrence, odium, execration, disgust, horror, hostility, disdain, contempt, distaste, dislike.
▷ANTONYMS liking, love.

aboriginal adjective *the area's aboriginal inhabitants*: **indigenous**, native; original, earliest, first, initial; ancient, primitive, primeval, primordial; rare autochthonous, autochthonic.
▶ noun *the social structure of the aboriginals*: **native**, indigene, aborigine, local, original inhabitant; rare autochthon.

aborigine noun See **aboriginal**.

abort verb **1** *I decided not to abort the pregnancy*: **terminate**, end; have an abortion.
2 *this organism infects sheep and can cause pregnant ewes to abort*: **miscarry**, have a miscarriage.
3 *the 'escape' key is used to abort the program*: **halt**, stop, end, call off, cut short, discontinue, terminate, arrest, suspend, check, nullify; informal scrub, axe, pull the plug on.
▷ANTONYMS continue, complete.
4 *there are times when the mission aborts*: **fail**, come to a halt, end, terminate, miscarry, go wrong, not succeed, fall through, break down, be frustrated, collapse, founder, come to grief, fizzle out, flop.
▷ANTONYMS succeed, complete.

abortion noun *she had an abortion*: **termination**, miscarriage; rare feticide.

abortive adjective *the rebels who led the abortive coup were shot*: **failed**, unsuccessful, non-successful, vain, thwarted, futile, useless, worthless, ineffective, ineffectual, to no effect, inefficacious, fruitless, unproductive, unavailing, to no avail, sterile, nugatory; archaic bootless.
▷ANTONYMS successful, fruitful.

abound verb *omens and prodigies abound in his work*: **be plentiful**, be abundant, be numerous, proliferate, superabound, thrive, flourish, be thick on the ground; informal grow on trees; Brit. informal be two/ten a penny.
▷ANTONYMS be scarce.
□ **abound in/with** *a beautiful stream which abounded with trout and eels*: **be full of**, overflow with, teem with, be packed with, be crowded with, be thronged with, be jammed with; be alive with, be overrun with, swarm with, bristle with, be bristling with, be infested with, be thick with; informal be crawling with, be lousy with, be stuffed with, be jam-packed with, be chock-a-block with, be chock-full of; rare pullulate with.

abounding adjective *Ruth had abounding strength and energy*: **abundant**, plentiful, superabundant, considerable, copious, ample, lavish, luxuriant, profuse, boundless, munificent, bountiful, prolific, inexhaustible, generous; galore; literary plenteous.
▷ANTONYMS meagre, scanty.

about preposition **1** *a book about ancient Greece*: **regarding**, concerning, with reference to, referring to, with regard to, with respect to, respecting, relating to, on, touching on, dealing with, relevant to, with relevance to, connected with, in connection with, on the subject of, in the matter of, apropos, re; Scottish anent.
2 *two hundred people were milling about the room*: **around**, round, throughout, over, through, all over, in all parts of, on every side of, encircling, surrounding; here and there, everywhere.
3 *they aren't seen about here very often*: **near**, nearby, close to, not far (away) from, a short distance from, in the vicinity of, in the neighbourhood

of, within reach of, adjacent to, beside, around, a stone's throw away from; informal within spitting distance of, {a hop, skip, and a jump away from}.
4 *while I am about it, I had better apologize for what happened*: **occupied with**, concerned with, busy with, taken up with, employed in, involved in, absorbed in, in the process of, in the course of, in the midst of, in the throes of; conducting, pursuing, following, practising.
□ **about to** *I was about to climb into bed when the bell rang*: **going to**, ready to, all set to, preparing to, intending to, soon to; on the point of, on the verge of, on the brink of, within an ace of.
▶ **adverb 1** *there were babies crawling about in the grass*: **around**, here and there, to and fro, back and forth, from place to place, hither and thither, in every direction, in all directions, abroad.
2 *although I hadn't seen him for two years, I knew he was about somewhere*: **near**, nearby, around, about the place, hereabouts, not far off/away, close by, in the vicinity, in the neighbourhood, at hand, within reach, on the doorstep, (just) around the corner.
3 *we think the explosion has caused about £15,000 worth of damage*: **approximately**, roughly, around, round about, in the neighbourhood/region of, in the area of, of the order of, something like; or so, or thereabouts, there or thereabouts, more or less, give or take a few, not far off; Brit. getting on for; Latin circa; informal as near as dammit; N. Amer. informal in the ballpark of.
▷**ANTONYMS** exactly, precisely.
4 *he gave orders to turn about*: **in the opposite direction**, in the reverse direction, around, backwards, to face the other way.
5 *there was a lot of flu about*: **around**, in circulation, in existence, current, going on, prevailing, prevalent, widespread, pervasive, endemic, happening, in the air, abroad.

about-turn Brit. **noun 1** *he saluted, did an about-turn, and marched out of the tent*: **about-face**, volte-face, turnaround, turnround, turnabout, U-turn; informal U-ey, one-eighty.
2 *the government was forced to make an embarrassing about-turn over the bill*: **reversal**, retraction, backtracking, swing, shift, swerve, U-turn, volte-face, turnaround, turnround; change of heart, change of mind, sea change.
▶ **verb** *suddenly he about-turned and saluted again*: **about-face**, turn around, turn round, turn about, do a U-turn, reverse.

above preposition 1 *light filtered through a tiny window above the door*: **over**, higher (up) than, overlooking; on top of, atop, on, upon.
▷**ANTONYMS** below, under, beneath.
2 *no one above the rank of Colonel was willing to compromise himself*: **superior to**, senior to, over, higher than, higher up than, more powerful than, more responsible than, ahead of; in charge of, commanding.
▷**ANTONYMS** below, beneath, junior to.
3 *you must be above suspicion of any impropriety*: **beyond**, not subject to, insusceptible to, not liable to, not open to, not vulnerable to, not exposed to, not in danger of, superior to, out of reach of, immune to, exempt from.
4 *I have always valued culture above technology*: **more than**, over, before, rather than, in preference to, in favour of, instead of, sooner than.
5 *the increase is above the rate of inflation*: **greater than**, more than, higher than, exceeding, in excess of, over, over and above, beyond, surpassing, upwards of.
▷**ANTONYMS** less than, below.
6 *the river above the bridge*: **upstream from**.
7 *they live above the Arctic Circle*: **north of**, northward(s) from.
□ **above all** *the job offered wider horizons, higher status, and, above all, a valuable source of income*: **most importantly**, before everything, beyond everything, first of all, most of all, chiefly, primarily, in the first place, first and foremost, mainly, principally, predominantly, especially, essentially, basically, elementally, in essence, at bottom; informal at the end of the day, when all is said and done.
□ **above and beyond** *you might consider giving employees an extra day or two off each quarter, above and beyond sick days*: **in addition to**, as well as, over and above; N. Amer. informal outside of; archaic forbye.
□ **above oneself** *ever since her promotion she'd been getting above herself*: **conceited**, proud, arrogant, self-important, haughty, disdainful, snobbish, snobby, supercilious, imperious; informal stuck-up, cocky, high and mighty, snooty, uppity, uppish, big-headed, swollen-headed, too big for one's boots.
▶ **adverb 1** *in the darkness above, something moved*: **overhead**, on/at the top, on/at a higher place, high up, on high, up above, (up) in the sky, high above one's head, aloft, (up) in the heavens.
2 *we will return to some of the issues raised above*: **earlier**, previously, before, formerly, further back.
▶ **adjective** *the above example was chosen to illustrate the underlying problem*: **preceding**, precedent, previous, earlier, former, foregoing, prior, antecedent, above-stated; aforementioned, aforesaid; rare anterior, prevenient, precursive, supra.

above board adjective *he had set up a chain of more or less above-board casinos*: **honest**, fair, open, frank, straight, overt, candid, forthright, unconcealed, trustworthy, unequivocal; legal, legitimate, lawful, licit; informal legit, kosher, pukka, by the book, fair and square, square, on the level, on the up and up, upfront.
▷**ANTONYMS** dishonest, shady.
▶ **adverb** *it's imperative that you play it all above board*: **honestly**, fairly, openly, frankly, overtly, candidly, forthrightly, unequivocally; legally, legitimately, lawfully.
▷**ANTONYMS** dishonestly, shadily.

ab ovo adverb Latin *he was a great man ab ovo*: **from the beginning**, from the start, from the first; from the egg; informal from the word go.

abracadabra exclamation hocus-pocus, open sesame; mumbo-jumbo.

abrade verb *the paintwork had been abraded over the years by the weather*: **wear away/down**, wear, erode, scrape away, corrode, eat away at, gnaw away at, bite into, scour, rasp, strip, flay.

abrasion noun 1 *diamond's extreme resistance to abrasion*: **wearing away/down**, wearing, erosion, scraping, corrosion, being eaten away, chafing, rubbing, stripping, flaying, excoriation.
2 *he had abrasions to his forehead*: **graze**, scrape, scratch, cut, gash, laceration, tear, rent, slash, injury, contusion; sore, ulcer; Medicine trauma, traumatism.

abrasive adjective 1 *don't use abrasive kitchen cleaners*: **grinding**, rubbing, polishing, coarse, caustic, harsh, mordant; corrosive, corroding, erosive, eroding.
2 *she was a tough girl with an abrasive manner*: **caustic**, cutting, grating, biting, acerbic, vitriolic; rough, harsh, hard, tough, sharp, curt, brusque, stern, severe; wounding, nasty, cruel, callous, insensitive, unfeeling, unsympathetic, inconsiderate; N. Amer. acerb.
▷**ANTONYMS** kind, gentle.

abreast adverb *the roads were full of bicycles, three or more abreast*: **in a row**, side by side, alongside, level, abeam, on a level, beside each other, shoulder to shoulder, cheek by jowl.
□ **abreast of** *it can be a good idea to keep children abreast of current affairs*: **up to date with**, up with, in touch with, informed about, familiar with, acquainted with, knowledgeable about, conversant with, au courant with, au fait with; informal plugged into.
▷**ANTONYMS** out of touch with.

abridge verb *the editor reserves the right to abridge letters to fit the space available*: **shorten**, cut, cut short/down, curtail, truncate, lessen, trim, crop, clip, pare down, prune; abbreviate, condense, contract, compress, reduce, decrease, diminish, shrink; summarize, give a summary of, sum up, abstract, give an abstract of, precis, give a precis of, synopsize, give a synopsis of, digest, give a digest of, outline, give an outline of, sketch, put in a nutshell, edit; rare epitomize.
▷**ANTONYMS** lengthen, expand on, pad out.

> *Choose the right word* **abridge, shorten, abbreviate, truncate, curtail**
>
> See **shorten**.

abridged adjective *an abridged version of his inaugural lecture*: **shortened**, cut, cut short, cut down, concise, condensed, contracted, compressed, abbreviated, reduced, decreased, diminished, curtailed, truncated, lessened, trimmed, cropped, clipped, pared down, pruned, shrunk; summarized, summary, abstracted, precised, synoptic, synopsized, digest, outline, thumbnail, sketch, edited; censored, bowdlerized, expurgated; informal potted.
▷**ANTONYMS** lengthened, expanded.

abridgement, abridgment noun *an abridgement of a book*: **summary**, abstract, synopsis, precis, outline, résumé, sketch, truncation, digest, recapitulation, recap, summing-up, rundown, round-up, review, shortening, shortened version, abridged version, concise version, condensation; rare conspectus.
▷**ANTONYMS** expansion.

abroad adverb 1 *a valid passport is essential when travelling abroad*: **overseas**, out of the country, to/in foreign parts, to/in a foreign country/land, over the sea, beyond the seas.
2 *rumours of his intention to visit a holy shrine were spread abroad*: **widely**, far and wide, everywhere, {here, there, and everywhere}, in all directions; about, around, forth; publicly, extensively; informal every which way.
3 *the Christmas spirit was abroad*: **at large**, current, in circulation, circulating, in the air, about, afoot, around, astir.

abrogate verb *the government has formally abrogated the 1977 treaty*: **repudiate**, revoke, repeal, rescind, overturn, overrule, override, do away with, annul, cancel, break off, invalidate, nullify, void, negate, dissolve, countermand, veto, declare null and void, discontinue; renege on, go back on, backtrack on, reverse, retract, remove, withdraw, abolish, put an end to, get rid of, suspend, end, stop, quash, scrap; Law disaffirm, avoid, vacate, vitiate; informal axe, ditch, dump, chop, give something the chop, knock something on the head; rare deracinate.
▷**ANTONYMS** institute, introduce.

abrogation noun *the abrogation of the Net Book Agreement*: **repudiation**, revocation, repeal, rescinding, rescindment, overturning, overruling, overriding, annulment, cancellation, invalidation, nullification, voiding,

negation, dissolution, countermanding, vetoing, discontinuation, reversal, retraction, removal, withdrawal, abolition, suspension, ending, stopping, quashing, scrapping; Law rescission, disaffirmation, avoidance, vitiation; informal axing, ditching, dumping, chopping; rare deracination.
▷ANTONYMS institution, introduction.

abrupt adjective 1 *the car came to an abrupt halt | he was grumbling at the abrupt change of weather*: **sudden**, immediate, instantaneous, hurried, hasty, quick, swift, rapid, speedy, precipitate; **unexpected**, surprising, startling, unanticipated, unforeseen, without warning; violent, headlong, breakneck, meteoric.
▷ANTONYMS gradual, unhurried.
2 *an abrupt manner*: **curt**, brusque, blunt, short, sharp, terse, brisk, crisp, gruff, snappish, snappy, unceremonious, offhand, cavalier, rough, harsh; rude, discourteous, uncivil, surly, churlish; bluff, no-nonsense, to the point, laconic; informal off.
▷ANTONYMS friendly, polite, expansive.
3 *he tends to write in abrupt, epigrammatic paragraphs*: **jerky**, uneven, irregular, disconnected, discontinuous, broken, rough, inelegant.
▷ANTONYMS smooth, flowing.
4 *an abrupt slope*: **steep**, sheer, precipitous, bluff, sharp, sudden, acute; perpendicular, vertical, dizzy, vertiginous; rare declivitous.
▷ANTONYMS gradual, gentle.

Choose the right word **abrupt, brusque, curt, terse**

See **brusque**.

abscess noun *a rabbit with a large abscess on its cheek*: **ulcer**, ulceration, cyst, boil, blister, sore, pustule, carbuncle, pimple, papule, wen, whitlow, vesication, furuncle, canker; inflammation, infection, eruption.

abscond verb *he had absconded from a Borstal*: **run away**, **escape**, bolt, clear out, flee, make off, take flight, take off, fly, decamp; make a break for it, take to one's heels, make a quick getaway, beat a hasty retreat, show a clean pair of heels, run for it, make a run for it; disappear, vanish, slip away, steal away, sneak away; informal do a bunk, do a moonlight flit, cut and run, skedaddle, skip, do a runner, head for the hills, do a disappearing/vanishing act, fly the coop, take French leave, scarper, vamoose; N. Amer. informal take a powder, go on the lam.

absence noun 1 *Derek gave Carol a flimsy excuse for his absence*: **non-attendance**, non-appearance, absenteeism; **truancy**, playing truant, truanting; leave, holiday, vacation, sabbatical; Brit. informal skiving, bunking off; N. Amer. informal playing hookey, goofing off, ditching; Austral./NZ playing the wag, wagging.
▷ANTONYMS presence, attendance.
2 *the absence of a clear candidate was likely to result in civil war*: **lack**, want, non-existence, unavailability, deficiency, deprivation, dearth; omission, exclusion, default; need, privation, famine, drought, poverty.
▷ANTONYMS presence, availability.
□ **in the absence of** *in the absence of glass, the traditional material was rice paper glued to a fine grille of wood*: **failing**, in default of, lacking, wanting, notwithstanding, without.

absent adjective (stress on the first syllable) 1 *she was absent from work | an absent parent*: **away**, off, out, not present, non-attending, truant; not working, not at work, off duty, on holiday, on leave; gone, missing, lacking, unavailable, non-existent; Latin in absentia; informal AWOL; Brit. informal bunking off, skiving; Austral./NZ informal wagging.
▷ANTONYMS present.
2 *his eyes had an absent, dreaming look*: **distracted**, preoccupied, inattentive, vague, absorbed, abstracted, unheeding, oblivious, distrait, absent-minded; daydreaming, dreamy, dreaming, far away, somewhere else, musing, wool-gathering, with one's head in the clouds, in a world of one's own, lost in thought, in a brown study; blank, empty, vacant, vacuous; informal miles away, not with us.
▷ANTONYMS attentive, alert.
▶ verb (stress on the second syllable)
□ **absent oneself** *it might be advisable for Jenny to absent herself during my visit*: **stay away**, keep away, be absent, withdraw, retire, take one's leave, remove oneself, slip away, take oneself off, abscond; informal slope off.
▷ANTONYMS attend, be present.

absently adverb *Hilary absently took the glass he was holding out*: **distractedly**, inattentively, abstractedly, unheedingly, carelessly, absent-mindedly, on automatic pilot; dreamily, with one's head in the clouds, in a world of one's own, lost in thought; blankly, vacuously.
▷ANTONYMS attentively.

absent-minded adjective *an absent-minded boffin*: **forgetful**, **distracted**, preoccupied, inattentive, vague, absorbed, abstracted, unheeding, oblivious, distrait, in a brown study, wool-gathering; lost in thought, pensive, thoughtful, brooding; informal scatterbrained, miles away, with a mind/memory like a sieve.
▷ANTONYMS alert, observant.

absent-mindedness noun *there are endless stories about his idiosyncrasies and absent-mindedness*: **forgetfulness**, amnesia, poor memory, tendency to forget, lapse of memory; **distractedness**, preoccupation, inattentiveness, inattention, vagueness, abstraction, absence, absorption, engrossment, heedlessness, obliviousness; pensiveness, thoughtfulness, musing, brooding; humorous blonde moment.
▷ANTONYMS alertness.

absolute adjective 1 *there was absolute silence in the house | an absolute disgrace*: **complete**, total, utter, out-and-out, outright, entire, perfect, pure, decided; thorough, thoroughgoing, undivided, unqualified, unadulterated, unalloyed, unmodified, unreserved, downright, undiluted, solid, consummate, unmitigated, sheer, arrant, rank, dyed-in-the-wool; plenary; Law peremptory.
▷ANTONYMS partial, qualified.
2 *everything I have told you is the absolute truth*: **definite**, certain, positive, unconditional, categorical, unquestionable, undoubted, unequivocal, decisive, conclusive, confirmed, manifest, infallible.
▷ANTONYMS partial, qualified.
3 *the parliament was only consultative, with absolute power remaining with the king*: **unlimited**, unrestricted, unrestrained, unbounded, unbound, boundless, infinite, ultimate, total, supreme, unconditional, full, utter, sovereign, omnipotent.
▷ANTONYMS conditional.
4 *an absolute monarch*: **autocratic**, despotic, dictatorial, tyrannical, tyrannous, authoritarian, arbitrary, imperious, domineering, high-handed, draconian, autonomous, sovereign, autarchic, autarchical.
▷ANTONYMS constitutional.
5 *absolute moral standards*: **universal**, fixed, independent, non-relative, non-variable, absolutist; **rigid**, established, set, settled, definite, decided, irrevocable, unalterable, unquestionable, authoritative, incontrovertible, in black and white.
▷ANTONYMS relative, flexible.

absolutely adverb 1 *the honourable gentleman is absolutely right*: **completely**, totally, utterly, perfectly, entirely, wholly, fully, quite, thoroughly, unreservedly; definitely, certainly, positively, unconditionally, categorically, unquestionably, no doubt, undoubtedly, without (a) doubt, without question, surely, unequivocally; exactly, precisely, decisively, conclusively, manifestly, in every way/respect, one hundred per cent, every inch, to the hilt; informal dead.
▷ANTONYMS partially.
2 *she ruled absolutely in her own department and dealt summarily with opposition*: **autocratically**, despotically, dictatorially, tyrannically, tyrannously, in an authoritarian manner, arbitrarily, imperiously, domineeringly, high-handedly, with draconian powers, autonomously; **unrestrictedly**, supremely, fully, utterly, unconditionally, totally, omnipotently, without challenge, without check, without checks and balances, without let or hindrance.
□ **absolutely no/none** *there was absolutely no room for it*: **no ... whatever**, no ... whatsoever, no ... at all; none whatever, none whatsoever, none at all.
▶ exclamation *'Have I made myself clear?' 'Absolutely!'*: **certainly**, yes, indeed, of course, definitely, quite, positively, naturally, without (a) doubt, without question, unquestionably; affirmative, by all means.

absolution noun Christianity *she had been given absolution for her sins*: **forgiveness**, pardoning, exoneration, remission, dispensation, indulgence, purgation, clemency, mercy; pardon, reprieve, discharge, amnesty, delivery, acquittal, clearing; freedom, liberation, deliverance, release; condoning, vindication, exculpation; informal let-off, letting off; archaic shrift, shriving.
▷ANTONYMS punishment.

absolve verb 1 *the fact that a criminal offence occurred a long time ago does not absolve the wrongdoer from guilt*: **exonerate**, discharge, acquit, exculpate, vindicate; release, relieve, liberate, free, deliver, clear, spare, exempt; informal let off.
▷ANTONYMS blame, condemn.
2 Christianity *I absolve you from all your sins*: **forgive**, pardon, excuse, give amnesty to, give dispensation to, give indulgence to; reprieve, have mercy on, show mercy to.
▷ANTONYMS punish.

absorb verb 1 *when wood gets wet, it absorbs water and expands*: **soak up**, suck up, draw up/in, take up/in, blot up, mop up, sponge up, sop up.
▷ANTONYMS exude, give out.
2 *patience is needed to absorb all this information*: **assimilate**, digest, ingest, take in, imbibe, drink in, familiarize oneself with; comprehend, grasp, learn, understand, master.
3 *the company was absorbed into the new concern*: **incorporate**, assimilate, integrate, appropriate, take in, subsume, include, co-opt, swallow up.
4 *these roles absorb most of his time and energy*: **use (up)**, consume, take up, occupy; waste, squander, go through, deplete, drain, exhaust, swallow up.
5 *the inner lining will absorb some of the sound*: **deaden**, soften, cushion; reduce, decrease, lessen; soak up.
▷ANTONYMS reflect; increase.

a

6 *she was absorbed in a letter when Mervyn came into the room*: **preoccupy**, engross, captivate, occupy, engage; rivet, grip, hold, interest, intrigue, immerse, involve, enthral, spellbind, fascinate, arrest, monopolize; distract, divert, entertain, amuse.

absorbent adjective *a piece of absorbent cotton wool*: **porous**, spongy, sponge-like, permeable, pervious, absorptive, penetrable, assimilative, receptive, soaking, blotting; technical spongiform; rare sorbefacient.
▷ANTONYMS impermeable, waterproof.

absorbing adjective *an absorbing and informative book*: **fascinating**, interesting, captivating, gripping, engrossing, compelling, compulsive, enthralling, riveting, spellbinding, entrancing, preoccupying, overwhelming, intriguing, thrilling, exciting; informal unputdownable.
▷ANTONYMS boring, uninteresting.

absorption noun **1** *the absorption of water*: **soaking up**, sucking up, drawing up/in, taking up/in, blotting up, mopping up, sponging up, sopping up; technical osmosis.
2 *by 1543, Scottish fears of absorption by England seemed to have been allayed*: **incorporation**, assimilation, integration, appropriation, taking in, subsuming, inclusion, co-opting, swallowing up.
3 *shock absorption*: **reduction**, decrease, lessening, softening, deadening, cushioning; soaking up.
4 *she returned to her absorption in the game show on TV*: **immersion**, intentness, raptness, involvement, engrossment, occupation, engagement, preoccupation, captivation, monopolization; fascination, enthralment, interest.

abstain verb **1** *during Lent, Benjamin **abstained from** wine*: **refrain**, desist, hold back, forbear, keep; **renounce**, avoid, shun, eschew, abandon, abjure, forgo, go without, do without; refuse, decline; give up, have done with; informal cut out, kick, quit, jack in, pack in.
▷ANTONYMS indulge in.
2 *our advice is about sensible drinking, not about abstaining*: **be teetotal**, be a teetotaller, take the pledge; deny oneself; informal be on the wagon.
▷ANTONYMS drink.
3 *262 voted against, 38 abstained*: **not vote**, decline/refuse to vote; informal sit on the fence.
▷ANTONYMS vote.

abstemious adjective *he seems to have led an abstemious, not to say ascetic life*: **temperate**, abstinent, austere, moderate, self-disciplined, self-denying, restrained, self-restrained, non-indulgent, sober, ascetic, puritanical, spartan, strict, severe, self-abnegating, hair-shirt.
▷ANTONYMS self-indulgent, intemperate.

abstemiousness noun *the traditional belief in the virtues of abstemiousness*: **temperance**, abstinence, austerity, moderation, plain/simple living, self-discipline, self-denial, renunciation, restraint, self-restraint, self-deprivation, sobriety, asceticism, puritanism, severity, self-abnegation, continence.
▷ANTONYMS self-indulgence, intemperance.

abstention noun **1** *the election was marked by a high rate of abstention*: **refusal to vote**, abstaining, non-voting; informal sitting on the fence.
2 *the rights and wrongs of alcohol consumption versus abstention*. See **abstinence**.

abstinence noun **1** *he took a pledge of abstinence*: **teetotalism**, temperance, sobriety, abstemiousness, abstention; rare nephalism.
2 *only one per cent use abstinence to reduce the risk of unwanted fatherhood*: **celibacy**, chastity, singleness, continence, virginity, bachelorhood, spinsterhood, self-restraint, self-denial.
▷ANTONYMS promiscuity.
3 *a three-day period of **abstinence from** food and drink*: **refraining**, desisting, holding back, forbearing, keeping, withholding; **renunciation of**, refusal of, declining, avoidance of, eschewal of, abjuration of; shunning, forgoing, going without, doing without.

abstract adjective (stress on the first syllable) **1** *abstract concepts such as love and beauty*: **theoretical**, conceptual, notional, intellectual, metaphysical, philosophical, academic; hypothetical, speculative, conjectural, conjectured, suppositional, putative; rare suppositious, suppositive, ideational.
▷ANTONYMS actual, concrete.
2 *abstract art*: **non-representational**, non-realistic, non-pictorial, symbolic, impressionistic.
▷ANTONYMS representational.
▶ **verb** (stress on the second syllable) **1** *staff who index and abstract material for an online database*: **summarize**, write a summary of, precis, abridge, condense, compress, shorten, cut down, abbreviate, synopsize; rare epitomize.
2 *they want to abstract water from the river*: **extract**, pump, draw (off), tap, suck, withdraw, remove, take out/away; separate, detach, isolate, dissociate.
3 *his pockets contained all he had been able to abstract from the flat*: **steal**, purloin, thieve, take, take for oneself, help oneself to, loot, pilfer, abscond with, run off with, appropriate, carry off, shoplift; embezzle, misappropriate; have one's fingers/hand in the till; informal walk off/away with, run away/off with, rob, swipe, nab, rip off, lift, 'liberate', 'borrow', filch, snaffle, snitch, souvenir; Brit. informal nick, pinch, half-inch, whip, knock off, nobble, bone, scrump, blag; N. Amer. informal heist, glom; Austral. informal snavel; W. Indian tief; archaic crib, hook; rare peculate, defalcate.
▶ **noun** (stress on the first syllable) *an abstract of her speech*: **summary**, synopsis, precis, résumé, outline, recapitulation, abridgement, condensation, digest, summation; French aperçu; N. Amer. wrap-up; archaic argument; rare epitome, conspectus.
▷ANTONYMS complete version, full text.

abstracted adjective *she seemed abstracted and unaware of her surroundings*: **absent-minded**, distracted, preoccupied, absorbed, engrossed, far away, somewhere else, not there, not with us, in a world of one's own, with one's head in the clouds, daydreaming, dreamy, inattentive, thoughtful, pensive, lost in thought, deep in thought, immersed in thought, wool-gathering, in a brown study, musing, brooding, absent, distrait, heedless, oblivious; informal miles away.
▷ANTONYMS attentive.

abstraction noun **1** *his style of writing focuses on facts rather than abstractions*: **concept**, idea, notion, thought, generality, generalization, theory, theorem, formula, hypothesis, speculation, conjecture, supposition, presumption.
▷ANTONYMS fact; material consideration.
2 *she sensed his momentary abstraction*: **absent-mindedness**, distraction, preoccupation, daydreaming, dreaminess, inattentiveness, inattention, wool-gathering, absence, heedlessness, obliviousness; thoughtfulness, pensiveness, musing, brooding, absorption, engrossment, raptness.
▷ANTONYMS attention.
3 *the abstraction of metal from ore*: **extraction**, removal, separation, detachment.

abstruse adjective *he was unable to follow the abstruse arguments put forward*: **obscure**, arcane, esoteric, little known, recherché, rarefied, recondite, difficult, hard, puzzling, perplexing, enigmatic, inscrutable, cryptic, Delphic, complex, complicated, involved, over/above one's head, incomprehensible, unfathomable, impenetrable, mysterious; rare involute, involuted.
▷ANTONYMS clear, obvious.

absurd adjective *what an absurd idea!* **preposterous**, ridiculous, ludicrous, farcical, laughable, risible; idiotic, stupid, foolish, silly, inane, imbecilic, insane, hare-brained; unreasonable, irrational, illogical, nonsensical, pointless, senseless; outrageous, shocking, astonishing, monstrous, fantastic, incongruous, grotesque; unbelievable, incredible, unthinkable, implausible; informal crazy; Brit. informal barmy, daft.
▷ANTONYMS reasonable, sensible.

absurdity noun *Duncan laughed at the absurdity of the situation*: **preposterousness**, ridiculousness, ludicrousness, absurdness, farcicality, risibility; idiocy, stupidity, foolishness, folly, silliness, inanity, insanity; unreasonableness, irrationality, illogicality, nonsensicality, pointlessness, senselessness, incongruity; informal craziness.
▷ANTONYMS reasonableness, sense.

absurdly adverb *that is an absurdly optimistic claim*: **preposterously**, ridiculously, ludicrously, farcically, laughably, risibly; idiotically, stupidly, foolishly, inanely, insanely, madly, wildly, fantastically, grotesquely; completely, absolutely, entirely, totally, wholly, thoroughly, utterly, quite, altogether, downright, perfectly; unbelievably, incredibly, unthinkably, implausibly; extremely, exceedingly, excessively, exorbitantly, unduly, inordinately, immoderately, unreasonably, irrationally, illogically, impossibly; offensively, unspeakably, intolerably, maddeningly, outrageously, shockingly; informal crazily, barmily.
▷ANTONYMS reasonably, sensibly; somewhat.

abundance noun *the area is famous for its abundance of wildlife*: **profusion**, plentifulness, profuseness, copiousness, amplitude, affluence, lavishness, bountifulness, infinity, opulence, exuberance, luxuriance; host, plenitude, cornucopia, riot; plenty, a lot, mass, quantities, scores, millions, multitude; informal sea, ocean(s), wealth, lots, heap(s), mass(es), stack(s), pile(s), load(s), bags, mountain(s), ton(s), oodles; Brit. informal shedload; N. Amer. informal slew, gobs, scads; Austral./NZ informal swag; vulgar slang shitload; rare nimiety.
▷ANTONYMS lack, scarcity.

abundant adjective *there is abundant rainfall during the summer*: **plentiful**, copious, ample, profuse, rich, lavish, liberal, generous, bountiful, large, huge, great, bumper, overflowing, superabundant, infinite, inexhaustible, opulent, prolific, teeming; in plenty, in abundance; informal a gogo, galore; S. African informal lank; literary bounteous, plenteous.
▷ANTONYMS scarce, sparse.
□ **be abundant abound**, be plentiful, be numerous, exist in abundance, proliferate, be thick on the ground; informal grow on trees; Brit. informal be two/ten a penny.

abundantly adverb **1** *the plant grows abundantly in the wild*: **copiously**, plentifully, amply, profusely, exuberantly, prolifically, luxuriantly, in

profusion, in abundance, in great quantity, in large quantities, in plenty, aplenty, in huge numbers, freely, extensively, everywhere, all over the place; literary bounteously, plenteously.
▷ANTONYMS sparsely.
2 *she made her wishes abundantly clear*: **extremely**, exceedingly, exceptionally, especially, extraordinarily, extra, tremendously, immensely, vastly, hugely, singularly, significantly, distinctly, outstandingly, uncommonly, unusually, decidedly, particularly, eminently, supremely, highly, remarkably, really, truly, mightily, thoroughly; all that, to a great extent, most, so; sufficiently, ... enough; Scottish unco; French très; N. English right; informal terrifically, awfully, terribly, devilishly, majorly, seriously, mega, ultra, oh-so, stinking, mucho, damn, damned; Brit. informal ever so, well, dead, bloody, dirty, jolly, fair; N. Amer. informal real, mighty, powerful, awful, plumb, darned, way, bitching; S. African informal lekker; informal, dated devilish, hellish, frightfully; archaic exceeding.
▷ANTONYMS scarcely; moderately.

abuse verb **1** *the judge abused his power by imposing the fines*: **misuse**, misapply, misemploy, mishandle; exploit, pervert, take advantage of.
2 *he was accused of abusing children*: **mistreat**, maltreat, ill-treat, treat badly, ill-use, misuse; handle/treat roughly, knock about/around, manhandle, mishandle, maul, molest, interfere with, indecently assault, sexually abuse, sexually assault, grope, assault, hit, strike, beat; injure, hurt, harm, damage; wrong, bully, persecute, oppress, torture; informal beat up, rough up, do over.
▷ANTONYMS look after.
3 *the referee was abused by players from both teams*: **insult**, be rude to, swear at, curse, call someone names, taunt, shout at, scold, rebuke, upbraid, reprove, castigate, inveigh against, impugn, slur, revile, smear, vilify, vituperate against, slander, libel, cast aspersions on, offend, slight, disparage, denigrate, defame; Brit. informal slag off; N. Amer. informal trash-talk; archaic miscall.
▷ANTONYMS compliment, flatter.
▶noun **1** *this law is not going to stop the abuse of power*: **misuse**, misapplication, misemployment, mishandling; exploitation, perversion.
2 *the abuse of children is a major social problem*: **mistreatment**, maltreatment, ill-treatment, ill-use, misuse; rough treatment, manhandling, mishandling, molestation, interference, indecent assault, sexual abuse, sexual assault, assaulting, hitting, striking, beating; injury, hurt, harm, damage; wronging, bullying, persecution, oppression, torture; informal beating up, roughing up, doing over.
▷ANTONYMS care.
3 *the scheme is open to political control and administrative abuse*: **corruption**, injustice, wrongdoing, wrong, misconduct, delinquency, misdeed(s), offence(s), crime, fault, sin.
4 *torrents of abuse*: **insults**, curses, jibes, slurs, expletives, swear words; swearing, cursing, name-calling, scolding; rebukes, upbraiding, reproval, invective, castigation, revilement, vilification, vituperation, slander, libel, slights, disparagement, denigration, defamation; informal slanging, a slanging match, mud-slinging, disrespect; Brit. informal verbal(s); N. Amer. informal trash talk; archaic contumely.
▷ANTONYMS compliments, flattery.

abusive adjective *he was fined for making abusive comments to officials*: **insulting**, rude, vulgar, offensive, disparaging, belittling, derogatory, disrespectful, denigratory, uncomplimentary, pejorative, vituperative; disdainful, derisive, scornful, contemptuous; defamatory, slanderous, libellous, scurrilous, blasphemous; scolding, castigatory, reproving, reproachful; informal bitchy; archaic contumelious.

Word toolkit

abusive	pejorative	slanderous
relationship	term	comment
language	connotation	allegation
father/mother	meaning	campaign
treatment	label	remark
partner	description	accusation
situation	phrase	testimony

abut verb *one of my pastures abuts your garden*: **adjoin**, be adjacent to, border, butt up against/to, be next to, neighbour, verge on, join, touch, meet, reach, impinge on, be contiguous with.

abysmal adjective **1** informal *some of the teaching was abysmal*: **very bad**, dreadful, awful, terrible, frightful, atrocious, disgraceful, deplorable, shameful, woeful, hopeless, lamentable, laughable, substandard, poor, inadequate, inferior, unsatisfactory; informal rotten, appalling, crummy, pathetic, pitiful, useless, lousy, shocking, dire, poxy, the pits; Brit. informal duff, chronic, a load of pants, pants; N. Amer. vulgar slang chickenshit.
▷ANTONYMS superb.
2 *abysmal ignorance*: **profound**, extreme, utter, complete, thorough, deep, endless, immeasurable, boundless, incalculable, unfathomable, bottomless.

abyss noun *a rope led down into the dark abyss*: **chasm**, gorge, ravine, canyon, fissure, rift, crevasse, gap, hole, gulf, pit, depth, cavity, void, bottomless pit.

academic adjective **1** *an academic institution*: **educational**, scholastic, instructional, pedagogical; school, college, collegiate, university.
2 *he has a distinctly academic turn of mind*: **scholarly**, studious, literary, well read, intellectual, clever, erudite, learned, educated, cultured, bookish, highbrow, pedantic, donnish, cerebral, serious; informal brainy; dated lettered.
3 *the debate has been largely academic*: **theoretical**, conceptual, notional, philosophical, unpragmatic, hypothetical, speculative, conjectural, conjectured, suppositional, putative; indefinite, abstract, vague, general; impractical, unrealistic, ivory-tower, irrelevant, useless; rare suppositious, suppositive, ideational.
▷ANTONYMS practical.
▶noun *a group of Russian academics is researching this phenomenon*: **scholar**, lecturer, don, teacher, educator, instructor, trainer, tutor, professor, fellow, man/woman of letters, highbrow, thinker, bluestocking; informal egghead, bookworm; archaic pedagogue.

academy noun **educational institution**, training establishment, centre of learning; school, college, university, institute, seminary, conservatory, conservatoire; historical polytechnic.

accede verb **1** *the authorities did not* **accede to** *the strikers' demands*: **agree to**, consent to, accept, assent to, acquiesce in, endorse, comply with, go along with, concur with, allow, recognize, grant, surrender to, yield to, give in to, give way to, defer to; relent, back down.
▷ANTONYMS refuse, deny.
2 *Elizabeth I* **acceded to** *the throne in 1558*: **succeed to**, assume, attain, come to, come into, inherit, take over, be elevated to.
▷ANTONYMS abdicate, renounce.
3 *Albania* **acceded to** *the IMF in 1990*: **join**, become a member of, become (a) party to, sign up to, enrol in.
▷ANTONYMS leave, secede.

accelerate verb **1** *the car accelerated down the hill*: **speed up**, hurry up, get faster, move faster, go faster, drive faster, get a move on, put on a spurt, open it up, gain momentum, increase speed, pick up speed, gather speed; informal step on the gas, step on it, get cracking, get moving; N. Amer. informal get a wiggle on; Austral. informal get a wriggle on.
▷ANTONYMS decelerate, slow down.
2 *inflation started to accelerate*: **increase**, rise, go up, advance, leap, surge, speed up, escalate, spiral, get worse.
▷ANTONYMS slow down, drop.
3 *the University has accelerated its planning process*: **hasten**, expedite, precipitate, speed, speed up, hurry up, make faster, step up, advance, further, forward, promote, boost, give a boost to, stimulate, spur on; aid, assist, help along, facilitate, ease, make easier, simplify; informal crank up.
▷ANTONYMS delay, slow down.

acceleration noun **1** *the car's acceleration is sensational*: **speeding up**, increasing speed, increase in speed, gain in momentum, gathering speed, opening up; technical rate of change of velocity.
▷ANTONYMS deceleration, slowing down.
2 *there was some acceleration of the process*: **hastening**, speeding up, quickening, stepping up, advancement, furthering, furtherance, forwarding, promotion, boosting, boost, stimulation, spur, aid, assistance, facilitation, easing, simplification, expedition, precipitation.
3 *an acceleration in the divorce rate*: **increase**, rise, advance, leap, surge, escalation, spiralling, worsening.

accent noun (stress on the first syllable) **1** *a Scottish accent*: **pronunciation**, intonation, enunciation, elocution, articulation, inflection, tone, modulation, cadence, timbre, utterance, manner of speaking, speech pattern, speech, diction, delivery; brogue, burr, drawl, twang; rare orthoepy.
2 *the accent is on the first syllable*: **stress**, emphasis, accentuation, force, prominence; primary stress, secondary stress; beat, rhythm, pulse; technical tone, ictus.
3 *the accent is on comfort*: **emphasis**, stress, priority; importance, prominence.
4 *an acute accent*: **mark**, diacritic, diacritical mark, accent mark, sign.
▶verb (stress on the second syllable) **1** *both versions of this chant accent the last syllable*: **stress**, put/lay/place the stress on, emphasize, put/lay/place the emphasis on, give emphasis to, put the force on, accentuate.
2 *fabrics which accent the background colours in the room*: **focus attention on**, bring/call/draw attention to, point up, underline, underscore, accentuate, highlight, spotlight, foreground, feature, give prominence to, make more prominent, make more noticeable, play up, bring to the fore, heighten, stress, emphasize, put/lay emphasis on.
▷ANTONYMS mask, divert attention from.

accentuate verb **1** *the simple outfit accentuated her long legs*: **focus attention on**, bring/call/draw attention to, point up, underline, underscore, accent, highlight, spotlight, foreground, feature, give prominence to, make more prominent, make more noticeable, play up, bring to the fore, heighten, stress, emphasize, put/lay emphasis on.
▷ANTONYMS mask, divert attention from.
2 *that characteristic thump which accentuates the first beat of the bar*:

a

emphasize, stress, put/lay/place the stress on, put/lay/place the emphasis on, give emphasis to, put the force on, accent.

accept verb **1** *he accepted a pen as a present*: **receive**, agree to receive, welcome, take, take receipt of, get, gain, obtain, acquire, come by.
▷ANTONYMS refuse, reject, turn down.
2 *he accepted the job immediately*: **take on**, take up, undertake, tackle, take on oneself, shoulder, bear, assume, manage, take responsibility for, be responsible for, engage in, become involved in, take part in, participate in, devote oneself to, concentrate on, address oneself to, go about, set about, approach, handle, get down to, deal with, get to grips with; launch into, enter on, begin, start, embark on, venture on, turn one's hand to; informal get cracking on, have a crack/go/shot/stab at, give something a whirl; formal commence.
3 *she accepted an invitation to lunch*: **say yes to**, reply in the affirmative, agree to, comply with.
4 *she was accepted as one of the family*: **welcome**, greet, let in, receive, receive favourably, embrace, offer friendship to, adopt, integrate.
5 *he grudgingly accepted Ellen's explanation*: **believe**, trust, give credence to, credit, give credit to, put confidence in, be convinced of, have faith in, count on, rely on, depend on; informal go for, buy, fall for, swallow, {swallow something hook, line, and sinker}, take something as gospel.
6 *we have agreed to accept his decision*: **go along with**, accede to, agree to, consent to, acquiesce in, concur with, assent to, endorse, comply with, abide by, follow, adhere to, conform to, act in accordance with, defer to, yield to, surrender to, bow to, give in to, submit to, respect, recognize, acknowledge, cooperate with, adopt.
▷ANTONYMS defy.
7 *she will just have to accept the consequences*: **tolerate**, endure, put up with, suffer, bear, take, stand, support, submit to, stomach, undergo, swallow; become reconciled to, reconcile oneself to, become resigned to, get used to, become accustomed to, adjust to, accommodate oneself to, acclimatize oneself to; learn to live with, make the best of; face up to; Scottish thole; Brit. informal wear.

acceptable adjective **1** *an acceptable substitute for champagne*: **satisfactory**, adequate, reasonable, quite good, fair, decent, good enough, sufficient, sufficiently good, fine, in order, up to scratch, up to the mark, up to standard, up to par, competent, not bad, all right, average, tolerable, passable, middling, moderate; presentable; suitable, convenient; informal OK, so-so, fair-to-middling; N. Amer. & Austral./NZ informal jake.
▷ANTONYMS unacceptable, unsatisfactory.
2 *a most acceptable present*: **welcome**, appreciated; **pleasing**, agreeable, delightful, desirable, satisfying, gratifying, to one's liking.
▷ANTONYMS unwelcome, unsuitable, undesirable.
3 *the risk had seemed acceptable at the time*: **bearable**, tolerable, allowable, admissible, supportable, sustainable, justifiable, defensible, defendable.
▷ANTONYMS unacceptable, undesirable.

acceptance noun **1** *the acceptance of an award*: **receipt**, receiving, taking, obtaining, acquiring.
2 *the acceptance of responsibility*: **undertaking**, taking on, assumption, tackling.
3 *acceptances to an invitation*: **yes**, affirmative reply, affirmation, confirmation, ratification.
4 *she greatly valued her acceptance as one of the family*: **welcome**, welcoming, favourable reception, embracing, embrace, approval, adoption, integration.
5 *his instant **acceptance of** Matilda's explanation | the idea soon gained complete acceptance*: **credence (in)**, belief (in), trust (in), confidence (in), faith (in), reliance (on), dependence (on); swallowing.
6 *their acceptance of the decision must be final*: **compliance with**, endorsement of, accession to, agreement with, consent to, acquiescence in, concurrence with, assent to, abidance by, adherence to, conformity with, deference to, surrender to, submission to, respect for, recognition of, acknowledgement of, adoption of; rare accedence to.
7 *the acceptance of pain*: **toleration**, endurance, sufferance, forbearance; putting up with.

accepted adjective *it is accepted practice | an accepted authority*: **recognized**, acknowledged, traditional, orthodox, habitual, confirmed, set, fixed, settled; **usual**, customary, common, normal, general, prevailing, accustomed, familiar, wonted, popular, expected, routine, regular, typical, conventional, established, mainstream, standard, stock.

access noun **1** *the building has a side access*: **entrance**, entry, way in, means of entry, ingress; approach, means of approach.
2 *they were denied **access to** the stadium*: **admission**, admittance, entry, entrée, ingress, right of entry, permission to enter, the opportunity to enter.
3 *students have **access to** a photocopier*: **(the) use of**, the opportunity to use, permission to use.
4 *an access of rage*: **fit**, attack, bout, outpouring, eruption, explosion, outburst, burst, outbreak, flare-up, blow-up, blaze, spasm, paroxysm, seizure, rush; gale, flood, storm, hurricane, torrent, surge, upsurge; spurt, effusion, outflow, outflowing, welling up; informal splurt; rare ebullition, boutade.
▶ verb *the program that is used to access the data*: **retrieve**, gain, gain access to, acquire, obtain; read, examine.

accessibility noun **1** *security concerns have to be balanced with public accessibility*: **ease of access**, availability, approachability, obtainability; nearness, convenience, handiness, readiness; rare attainability, reachability.
▷ANTONYMS inaccessibility.
2 *the accessibility of this type of music*: **comprehensibility**, intelligibility, understandability, penetrability, approachability.
▷ANTONYMS incomprehensibility.
3 *journalists loved his accessibility*: **approachability**, availability, easy-going manner, informality, friendliness, hospitable manner, agreeableness, obliging nature, congeniality, affability, cordiality.
▷ANTONYMS unapproachability.

accessible adjective **1** *the village is only accessible on foot | the tools should be stored in a place where they are easily accessible*: **reachable**, attainable, approachable, within reach, available, on hand, obtainable; nearby, ready, convenient, handy; informal get-at-able.
▷ANTONYMS inaccessible.
2 *he set out to write accessible music*: **understandable**, comprehensible, easy to understand, easy to appreciate, intelligible, penetrable, fathomable, graspable, approachable.
▷ANTONYMS incomprehensible.
3 *he is more accessible than most tycoons*: **approachable**, available, easy-going, informal, friendly, welcoming, hospitable, pleasant, agreeable, obliging, congenial, affable, cordial.
▷ANTONYMS unapproachable.

accession noun **1** *the Queen's **accession to** the throne*: **succession**, elevation; assumption of, attainment of, inheritance of.
2 *the accession of Spain and Portugal to the EC*: **joining**, signing up, enrolment.
3 ***accession to** the Treaty of Rome was effected in 1971*: **assent**, consent, agreement; acceptance of, acquiescence in, endorsement of, compliance with, concurrence with, recognition of.
4 *among recent accessions to the museum are some Victorian watercolours*: **addition**, acquisition, new item, gift, purchase, adjunct, add-on, gain.

accessorize verb *there was no hat to accessorize this dress*: **complement**, supplement, add to, augment; enhance, set off, show off; go with, suit; beautify, pretty (up), dress up, decorate, adorn, grace, ornament, embellish, trim, garnish, bedeck, deck (out), festoon; literary bedizen, furbelow.

accessory noun **1** *camera accessories such as tripods and flashguns*: **attachment**, extra, addition, add-on, retrofit, adjunct, appendage, appurtenance, (additional) component, fitment, supplement.
2 *Paula wore each suit with perfectly matching accessories*: **adornment**, embellishment, finery, trimming, ornament, ornamentation, decoration, complement, fashion detail, frill; trappings; handbag, shoes, gloves, hat, belt, jewellery.
3 *she was charged as an accessory to murder*: **accomplice**, partner in crime, abetter, associate, confederate, collaborator, fellow conspirator, henchman, conniver.
▶ adjective *functionally the maxillae are a pair of accessory jaws*: **additional**, extra, supplementary, supplemental, auxiliary, ancillary, secondary, subsidiary, supportive, assisting, reserve, complementary, further, more, add-on.

accident noun **1** *he was involved in an accident at work*: **mishap**, misfortune, misadventure, mischance, unfortunate incident, injury, disaster, tragedy, catastrophe, contretemps, calamity, blow, trouble, problem, difficulty; technical casualty.
2 *there was an accident on the motorway*: **crash**, collision, smash, bump, car crash, car accident, road accident, traffic accident, road traffic accident, RTA, multiple crash, multiple collision; rail accident, derailment; air accident, air crash; N. Amer. wreck; informal smash-up, pile-up, shunt; Brit. informal prang.
3 *it is no accident that there is a similarity between them*: **chance**, mere chance, coincidence, twist of fate, freak, hazard; piece of good fortune, (bit of) luck, (bit of) good luck, fluke, happy chance; serendipity, fate, fortuity, fortune, providence; N. Amer. happenstance.
□ **by accident** *we met purely by accident*: **fortuitously**, accidentally, coincidentally, by chance, by coincidence, by a fluke, unintentionally, inadvertently; unwittingly, unknowingly, unawares, unconsciously; by mistake, mistakenly.
▷ANTONYMS intentionally.

accidental adjective **1** *accidental damage | an accidental meeting*: **fortuitous**, **chance**, occurring by chance/accident, adventitious, fluky, coincidental, casual, serendipitous, random, aleatory; unexpected, unforeseen, unanticipated, unlooked-for; **unintentional**, unintended, inadvertent, involuntary, unplanned, unpremeditated, unthinking, unmeant; unwitting, unknowing, unconscious, subconscious; mistaken, misguided.
▷ANTONYMS intentional, planned.
2 *the location is accidental and contributes nothing to the poem*: **incidental**,

unimportant, by the way, by the by, supplementary, subsidiary, subordinate, secondary, marginal, minor, lesser, accessory, peripheral, tangential, extraneous, extrinsic, parenthetical, irrelevant, immaterial, beside the point, of little account, unnecessary, non-essential, inessential.
▷ANTONYMS essential, central.

accidentally adverb *we met accidentally | they accidentally set off a smoke alarm*: **fortuitously**, by accident, by chance, by a mere chance, by a twist of fate, adventitiously, as luck would have it, by a fluke, flukily, coincidentally, by coincidence, serendipitously; by a happy chance, by good fortune, by a piece of luck; unexpectedly; **unintentionally**, inadvertently, involuntarily, unpremeditatedly, unthinkingly; unwittingly, unknowingly, unconsciously, subconsciously, unawares; by mistake, mistakenly, misguidedly; N. Amer. by happenstance.

acclaim verb **1** *the booklet has been widely acclaimed by teachers*: **praise**, applaud, cheer, commend, express approval of, approve, express admiration for, welcome, pay tribute to, speak highly of, eulogize, compliment, congratulate, celebrate, sing the praises of, praise to the skies, rave about, go into raptures about/over, heap praise on, wax lyrical about, say nice things about, make much of, pat on the back, take one's hat off to, salute, throw bouquets at, lionize, exalt, admire, hail, toast, flatter, adulate, vaunt, extol, glorify, honour, hymn, clap; informal crack someone/something up; N. Amer. informal ballyhoo; black English big someone/something up; dated cry someone/something up; archaic emblazon; rare laud, panegyrize.
▷ANTONYMS criticize.
2 *Eardwulf was acclaimed king of Northumbria in 796*: **proclaim**, announce, declare, pronounce, hail as.
▶ **noun** *she has won acclaim for her commitment to democracy*: **praise**, applause, cheers, ovation, tribute, accolade, acclamation, salutes, plaudits; approval, admiration, approbation, congratulations, commendation, welcome, flattery, kudos, adulation, homage; compliment, a pat on the back, eulogy, encomium, panegyric, bouquets, laurels, testimonial; rare extolment, laudation, eulogium.
▷ANTONYMS criticism.

acclaimed adjective *an acclaimed public figure*: **celebrated**, admired, highly rated, lionized, revered, honoured, esteemed, exalted, lauded, vaunted, much touted, well thought of, well received, acknowledged; eminent, venerable, august, great, renowned, distinguished, prestigious, illustrious, pre-eminent, estimable, of note, noted, notable, of repute, of high standing, considerable.
▷ANTONYMS criticized; unsung; obscure.

acclamation noun **1** *the proposal was received with considerable acclamation*: **praise**, applause, cheers, ovation, tribute, accolade, acclaim, salutes, plaudits; approval, admiration, approbation, congratulations, commendation, welcome, flattery, kudos, adulation, homage; compliment, a pat on the back, eulogy, encomium, panegyric, bouquets, laurels, testimonial; rare extolment, laudation, eulogium.
▷ANTONYMS criticism.
2 *he was elected **by acclamation***: **shouting**, calling out, oral vote, non-ballot; shouts; without a vote, without a ballot, with overwhelming vocal approval, by popular demand.

acclimatization noun *you should not rush your acclimatization when you arrive*: **adjustment**, adaptation, attunement, accommodation, habituation, familiarization, acclimation, acculturation, inurement, hardening, seasoning, conditioning; assimilation, integration, domestication, naturalization.

acclimatize verb *the need to **acclimatize to** life at 3,000 metres | I lowered the bag into the tank to acclimatize the fish*: **adjust**, adapt, attune, accustom, get (someone) accustomed, get (someone) used, accommodate, habituate, assimilate, acculturate, become inured, harden, condition, reconcile, become resigned, resign oneself; familiarize someone/oneself with, find one's way around, come to terms with, come to accept, learn to live with; integrate, domesticate; find one's feet, get one's bearings, become naturalized, become seasoned; N. Amer. acclimate.

accolade noun **1** *he received the accolade of knighthood*: **honour**, recognition, privilege, award, gift, title; prize, laurels, bays, palm.
2 *his role in the game earned him this accolade from his manager*: **tribute**, commendation, acclaim, applause, ovation, acclamation, approval, admiration, approbation, testimonial, praise, welcome, flattery, kudos, adulation, homage, compliment, pat on the back, eulogy, encomium, panegyric; cheers, salutes, plaudits, congratulations, bouquets; informal rave; rare extolment, laudation, eulogium.
▷ANTONYMS criticism.

accommodate verb **1** *backpacking tourists can be accommodated in dormitories*: **lodge**, house, put up, billet, quarter, board, take in, provide shelter for, shelter, give a bed to, give someone a roof over their head, provide a roof over someone's head, harbour, make room for, give accommodation to, provide with accommodation, provide accommodation for.
2 *the cottages accommodate up to six people*: **hold**, take, fit, seat, have room for.
3 *the company altered the launch date in order to accommodate a major customer*: **help**, fit in with, allow for, assist, aid, lend a hand to, oblige, serve, do someone a service, meet the needs/wants of, do someone a good turn, favour, do someone a favour, cater for, indulge, pander to, humour, gratify, satisfy.
▷ANTONYMS hinder.
4 *she was desperately trying to **accommodate herself** to her new position*: **adjust**, adapt, attune, accustom, get (someone) accustomed, get (someone) used, habituate, acclimatize, assimilate, acculturate; familiarize someone/oneself with, find one's way around, come to terms with, come to accept, learn to live with; integrate, domesticate; find one's feet, get one's bearings, become naturalized, become seasoned; N. Amer. acclimate.
5 *the bank would be glad to accommodate you with a loan*: **provide**, supply, furnish, serve, grant.
▷ANTONYMS deny, refuse.

accommodating adjective *we always found our local branch most accommodating*: **obliging**, cooperative, helpful, eager to help/please, adaptable, amenable, pliable, compliant, complaisant, indulgent, considerate, unselfish, generous, civil, willing, polite, kindly, hospitable, neighbourly, kind, friendly, pleasant, agreeable; Brit. informal decent.
▷ANTONYMS unobliging, disobliging.

accommodation noun **1** *they were living in temporary accommodation*: **housing**, lodging(s), living quarters, quarters, rooms, chambers; place, place to stay, billet; shelter, board; a roof over one's head; informal digs, pad; formal abode, residence, place of residence, dwelling, dwelling place, habitation.
2 *there was lifeboat accommodation for 1,178 people*: **space**, room, seating; places.
3 *the prime minister was seeking an accommodation with the Social Democrats*: **arrangement**, **understanding**, settlement, accord, deal, bargain, compromise.
4 *their capacity for accommodation to novelty is very limited*: **adjustment**, adaptation, attunement, fitting in, habituation, acclimatization, acclimation, acculturation, inurement, hardening, seasoning, conditioning, familiarization, assimilation, integration, domestication, naturalization.

accompaniment noun **1** *a musical accompaniment*: **backing**, support, background, soundtrack, comp; ripieno, obbligato, organum.
2 *the wine makes a superb accompaniment to cheese*: **complement**, supplement, addition, adjunct, appendage, trimming, companion, accessory.

accompany verb **1** *his wife accompanied him on overseas trips | the driver accompanied her to the door*: **go with**, go along with, travel with, keep someone company, tag along with, partner, escort, chaperone, attend, follow, conduct, lead, take, show, see, guide, steer, usher, pilot, convoy, help, assist, show someone the way; lead the way; Scottish chum; rare company, bear someone company, companion.
2 *the illness is often accompanied by nausea*: **occur with**, co-occur with, coincide with, coexist with, go with, go along with, go together with, go hand in hand with, appear with; be associated with, be connected with, be linked with, attend, be concomitant with, supplement, complement, belong to; be caused by, result from, arise from, follow, be a consequence of.
3 *he accompanied the choir on the piano*: **back**, play a musical accompaniment for, play with, play for, support.

accomplice noun *he was arrested as an accomplice to murder*: **abetter**, accessory, partner in crime, associate, confederate, collaborator, fellow conspirator, co-conspirator; henchman; rare conniver.

accomplish verb *the planes accomplished their mission*: **fulfil**, achieve, succeed in, realize, attain, manage, bring about, bring off, carry out, carry off, carry through, execute, conduct, effect, fix, engineer, perform, do, perpetrate, discharge, complete, finish, consummate, conclude; rare effectuate.
▷ANTONYMS fail in; give up.

accomplished adjective *an accomplished pianist*: **expert**, skilled, skilful, masterly, virtuoso, master, consummate, proficient, talented, gifted, adept, adroit, deft, dexterous, able, good, competent, capable, efficient, experienced, seasoned, trained, practised, professional, polished, well versed, versed, smart, clever, ingenious, ready, apt, handy, artful; magnificent, brilliant, splendid, marvellous, impressive, excellent, formidable, outstanding, first-class, first-rate, fine; deadly; informal great, mean, wicked, nifty, crack, ace; Brit. informal a dab hand at; N. Amer. informal crackerjack; Brit. dated, informal wizard; vulgar slang shit-hot; archaic or humorous compleat; rare habile.
▷ANTONYMS incompetent.

accomplishment noun **1** *the reduction of inflation was a remarkable accomplishment*: **achievement**, act, deed, exercise, exploit, performance, attainment, effort, feat, manoeuvre, operation, move, stunt, stratagem, coup, master stroke, stroke of genius, triumph.
2 *typing was another of her accomplishments*: **ability**, **talent**, skill, gift, attainment, achievement, aptitude, faculty, capability, proficiency, forte, knack.

3 *a poet of considerable accomplishment*: **expertise**, skill, skilfulness, expertness, adeptness, adroitness, deftness, dexterity, ability, prowess, mastery, achievement, competence, competency, capability, proficiency, efficiency, aptitude, artistry, art, finesse, flair, virtuosity, experience, professionalism, talent, cleverness, smartness, ingenuity, versatility; informal know-how.

accord noun **1** *the two countries were about to sign an economic cooperation accord*: **pact**, treaty, agreement, settlement, deal, entente, concordat, concord, protocol, compact, contract, convention.
2 *the two sides failed to reach accord*: **agreement**, consensus, unanimity, harmony, unison, unity, concord, concert, like-mindedness, rapport, conformity, congruence, settlement.
□ **of one's own accord** *Matthew went to sea of his own accord*: **voluntarily**, of one's own free will, of one's own volition, of one's own choice, of one's own choosing, by choice, by preference; willingly, readily, freely, intentionally, deliberately, on purpose, purposely, spontaneously, without being asked, without being forced, without hesitation, without reluctance; gladly, with pleasure, with good grace, eagerly, enthusiastically.
▷ANTONYMS reluctantly, under duress.
□ **with one accord** *the association is acting with one accord in this matter*: **unanimously**, in complete agreement, with one mind, unitedly, concertedly, without exception, as one, of one voice, to a man.
▷ANTONYMS separately; in disarray.
▸ verb **1** *the national assembly accorded the General more power*: **give**, grant, tender, present, award, hand, vouchsafe, concede, yield, cede; confer on, bestow on, vest in, put in someone's hands; invest with, endow with, entrust with, favour with.
▷ANTONYMS withhold; remove.
2 *such an idea appears to accord with the known state of affairs*: **correspond**, agree, tally, match up, concur, coincide, be in agreement, be consistent, equate, harmonize, be in harmony, be compatible, be consonant, be congruous, be in tune, dovetail, correlate; conform to; suit, fit, match, parallel; informal square; N. Amer. informal jibe.
▷ANTONYMS disagree, contrast.

accordance noun *the accordance of a suitable welcome to a visiting dignitary*: **granting**, conferring, bestowal, tendering.
□ **in accordance with** *they had acted in accordance with their orders*: **in agreement with**, in conformity with, in line with, commensurate with, in compliance with, true to, in fulfilment of, in obedience to, in the spirit of, following, honouring, heeding, observing.

according adjective
□ **according to 1** *she had had a narrow escape, according to the doctors*: **as stated by**, as maintained by, as claimed by, on the authority of, on the report of, in the opinion of. **2** *cook the rice according to the instructions*: **as specified by**, as per, in accordance with, in compliance with, in agreement with, in line with, in keeping with, commensurate with, in harmony with, in conformity with, in obedience to, true to, in fulfilment of, following, honouring, heeding, observing. **3** *salary will be fixed according to experience*: **in proportion to**, proportional to, commensurate with, in relation to, relative to, corresponding to, dependent on, based on.

accordingly adverb **1** *they appreciate the danger and act accordingly*: **appropriately**, correspondingly, suitably, fitly, duly, consistently, properly, correctly.
▷ANTONYMS inappropriately.
2 *they needed each other and accordingly made an effort to conceal their mutual distrust*: **therefore**, for that reason, consequently, so, as a result, as a consequence, in consequence, hence, thus, then, that being so, that being the case, on that account; Latin ergo; formal whence; archaic wherefore, thence.

accost verb *the police accosted him in the street*: **speak to**, talk to, call to, shout to, hail, initiate a discussion with; address, approach, waylay, take aside, detain, stop, halt, grab, catch, confront, importune, solicit; informal buttonhole, collar; Brit. informal nobble.

account noun **1** *the police officer then gave his account of the incident*: **description**, report, version, story, narration, narrative, statement, news, explanation, exposition, interpretation, communiqué, recital, rendition, sketch, delineation, portrayal, tale; chronicle, history, record, archive, annal, minute, transaction, proceeding, transcript, diary, journal, weblog, blog, moblog, memoir, review, register, log, relation, rehearsal, side, view, impression; Military, informal sitrep.
2 *a sensitive account of the Debussy Sonata*: **performance**, interpretation, rendering, rendition, reading, recital, playing, singing, execution.
3 (usually **accounts**) *the firm's accounts are in good order*: **financial record**, book, ledger, journal, balance sheet, financial statement, results.
4 *departing guests pay their accounts at the office*: **bill**, invoice, statement, list of charges, reckoning, tally; debt, amount due; N. Amer. check; informal tab; archaic score.
5 *he has accounts with several banks*: **bank account**; current account, deposit account, savings account.
6 *the casualties they suffer will be of no account*: **importance**, import, significance, consequence, moment, momentousness, substance, note, mark, prominence, value, weightiness, weight, concern, interest, gravity, seriousness.
□ **by all accounts** *by all accounts Hayes was a man of taste and cultivation*: **reputedly**, supposedly, according to popular belief, so the story goes, so I'm told, so people say, by repute, allegedly, putatively, apparently, seemingly, ostensibly.
□ **on account of** *they had closed early on account of the snow*: **because of**, owing to, due to, as a consequence of, thanks to, through, by reason of, by/in virtue of, on grounds of, in view of; after, following, in the wake of, at a time of.
□ **on no account** *on no account sign any document without reading it*: **never**, certainly not, absolutely not, definitely not, not in any event, by no means; not under/in any circumstances, under/in no circumstances, not for any reason, not for a moment; informal no way, not on your life, not in a million years, not for love or money; Brit. informal not on your nelly.
▷ANTONYMS definitely.
□ **take something into account** (or **take account of something**) *let's look at the factors you should take into account*: **consider**, take into consideration, make allowances for, respect, bear in mind, be mindful of, have regard to, reckon with, remember, mind, mark, heed, note, not forget, make provision for, take to heart, pay/have regard to, be guided by.
▷ANTONYMS ignore.
▸ verb *her visit could not be accounted a success*: **consider**, regard as, reckon, hold to be, think, think of as, look on as, view as, see as, take for, judge, adjudge, count, deem, rate, gauge, interpret as.
□ **account for 1** *they must account for the delay*: **explain**, give an explanation, come up with an explanation, explain away, answer for, give reasons for, rationalize, provide a rationale for, show grounds for, elucidate, illuminate, clear up; defend, vindicate, justify, excuse, make excuses for, make acceptable; rare extenuate. **2** *excise duties account for over half the price of Scotch*: **constitute**, make up, comprise, form, compose, be responsible for, represent, supply, provide, give. **3** *its awe-inspiring whirlpool has accounted for many sailors' lives*: **dispose of**, finish off, make an end of, deal with, put paid to, take care of, clear up, mop up, eliminate, kill, destroy, dispatch, put out of action, incapacitate.

accountability noun **1** *there must be clear accountability for the expenditure of public money*: **responsibility**, liability, answerability.
▷ANTONYMS unaccountability.
2 *ministers' accountability to parliament*: **answerability**, responsibility, reporting, obedience.

accountable adjective **1** *the government was held accountable for the food shortage*: **responsible**, liable, answerable, chargeable; to blame.
▷ANTONYMS unaccountable.
2 *ministers are **accountable to** parliament*: **answerable**, responsible, reporting, subject; under the charge of, bound to obey, obeying, bound by.
3 *the game's popularity is barely accountable*: **explicable**, explainable; understandable, comprehensible, intelligible, definable, reasonable, unsurprising.

accoutrements plural noun *all the alarming accoutrements of modern medicine*. See **paraphernalia**.

accredit verb **1** *he was **accredited with** being one of the world's fastest sprinters*: **recognize as**, credit with; have something ascribed to one, have something attributed to one, receive the credit for, be given the credit for.
2 *the discovery of distillation is usually **accredited to** the Arabs*: **ascribe**, attribute, chalk up; lay at the door of.
3 *professional bodies accredit these research degrees*: **recognize**, license, authorize, approve, certify, warrant, empower, depute, endorse, sanction, vouch for, put one's seal of approval on, appoint.
▷ANTONYMS ban.

accredited adjective *the UK accredited representative*: **official**, appointed, legal, recognized, licensed, authorized, approved, certified, warranted, empowered, deputed, endorsed, sanctioned, vouched for.

accretion noun **1** *the accretion of sediments in coastal mangroves*: **accumulation**, collecting, gathering, amassing, cumulation, accrual, growth, formation, enlargement, increase, gain, augmentation, rise, mushrooming, snowballing; rare amassment.
2 *the city has a historic core surrounded by recent accretions*: **addition**, extension, growth, appendage, add-on, supplement.

accrue verb **1** *financial benefits will **accrue from** restructuring*: **result**, arise, follow, ensue, emanate, stem, spring, flow; be caused by, be brought about by, be produced by, originate in, attend, accompany, be consequent on.
2 *interest is added to the account as it accrues | the funds accrue interest*: **accumulate**, collect, gather, build up, mount up, amass, grow, increase, augment, be added.

accumulate verb *he accumulated considerable wealth | the drug accumulates in the heart muscles*: **gather**, collect, assemble; amass, stockpile, pile up, heap up, rack up, run up, scrape together, store (up), hoard, cumulate, lay in/up, garner; mass, increase, multiply, accrue, snowball; Brit. tot up; informal stash (away).
▷ANTONYMS dissipate.

accumulation noun **1** *the accumulation of money*: **amassing**, building up, build-up, collection, gathering, assembling, assembly, stockpiling, hoarding, cumulation, accrual; rare amassment.
▷ANTONYMS dissipation.
2 *an accumulation of rubbish*: **mass**, build-up, pile, heap, stack, collection, gathering, stock, store, stockpile, reserve, hoard, bank, pool, fund, mine, reservoir, cumulation, accrual, aggregation, accretion, agglomerate, agglomeration.

accuracy noun **1** *we have confidence in the accuracy of the statistics*: **correctness**, precision, exactness, rightness, perfection, validity, unambiguousness, authority, reliability.
▷ANTONYMS inaccuracy, inexactness.
2 *the accuracy of his description was remarkable*: **factuality**, literalness, correctness, fidelity, faithfulness, exactness, closeness, truth, truthfulness, veracity, authenticity, realism, verisimilitude, fairness; carefulness, strictness, conscientiousness, punctiliousness, thoroughness, scrupulousness, rigour; rare veridicality, scrupulosity.
▷ANTONYMS inaccuracy, looseness.
3 *she hit the ball with great accuracy*: **precision**, carefulness, meticulousness.
▷ANTONYMS inaccuracy, waywardness.

accurate adjective **1** *accurate information*: **correct**, precise, exact, right, errorless, error-free, without error, faultless, perfect, valid, specific, detailed, minute, explicit, clear-cut, word for word, unambiguous, meticulous, authoritative, reliable, canonical; Brit. informal spot on, bang on; N. Amer. informal on the money.
▷ANTONYMS inaccurate, inexact.
2 *an accurate description*: **factual**, fact-based, literal, correct, faithful, exact, close, true, truthful, veracious, true to life, telling it like it is, as it really happened, lifelike, authentic, realistic, fair; convincing, careful, word-perfect, strict, conscientious, punctilious, painstaking, thorough, scrupulous, rigorous; informal on the mark, on the beam, on the nail, on the button; Brit. informal spot on, bang on; rare verisimilar, veristic, veridical.
▷ANTONYMS inaccurate, loose.
3 *an accurate shot*: **well aimed**, precise, on target, unerring, deadly, lethal, sure, true, on the mark, careful, meticulous, painstaking, precision; Brit. informal spot on, bang on.
▷ANTONYMS inaccurate, wayward.

Choose the right word **accurate, precise, exact**

All these words apply to information or statements that are correct.

An **accurate** statement or representation has been put together with great care and corresponds to the facts (*he gave a frighteningly accurate description of her life | an accurate and intelligible technical drawing*). Both *accurate* and *exact* can be used to mean 'providing a faithful representation' (*an accurate description | an exact copy*).

Precise denotes minute attention to detail and implies that something can be measured or quantified. It draws a contrast with something that may be correct (or 'accurate') but is more vague or approximate (*we have no precise figures for possible job losses | he gave her precise directions on the route*). The common idiom *to be precise* is used to narrow the focus of a topic and give more detail (*my parents live abroad—in North Borneo, to be precise*).

Exact emphasizes that something has been definitely identified, with no margin for vagueness or error (*we may never know the exact number of deaths*), and an *exact statement* is one that is both precise and truthful. Unlike *precise*, *exact* is an adjective that cannot generally be modified by an adverb (one cannot say that something is *'very exact'*), which underlines the sense of absoluteness and pinpoint detail. Both *precise* and *exact* are used for emphasis (*at that precise moment | you can show me the exact spot*).

accurately adverb **1** *they need to assess the age and numbers of whale stocks accurately*: **correctly**, precisely, exactly, right, without error, faultlessly, perfectly, validly, specifically, in detail, minutely, explicitly, word for word, unambiguously, meticulously, authoritatively, reliably; Brit. informal spot on, bang on; N. Amer. informal on the money.
▷ANTONYMS inaccurately, inexactly.
2 *the Minister has accurately described the position*: **factually**, literally, correctly, faithfully, exactly, closely, truly, truthfully, veraciously, like it is, as it really happened, authentically, realistically, fairly; convincingly, carefully, strictly, conscientiously, punctiliously, painstakingly, thoroughly, scrupulously, rigorously; rare veridically.
▷ANTONYMS inaccurately, loosely.
3 *the gun can shoot accurately at moving targets*: **precisely**, with precise aim, on target, unerringly.
▷ANTONYMS inaccurately, waywardly.

accursed adjective **1** informal *that accursed woman*: **hateful**, detestable, loathsome, foul, abominable, damnable, odious, obnoxious, despicable, execrable, horrible, horrid, ghastly, awful, dreadful, terrible; annoying, irritating, infuriating, exasperating; informal damned, damn, blasted, beastly, pesky, pestilential, infernal; archaic scurvy, loathly.
▷ANTONYMS pleasant, nice.
2 literary *he and his line are accursed*. See **cursed**.

accusation noun *the man's lawyer said the accusation was groundless*: **allegation**, charge, claim, assertion, asseveration, attribution, incrimination, imputation, denouncement, indictment, arraignment, citation, inculpation, blame, condemnation, criticism, complaint; suit, lawsuit; Brit. plaint; N. Amer. impeachment, bill of indictment; N. Amer. informal beef.

accuse verb **1** *four people were* ***accused of*** *assault*: **charge with**, indict for, arraign for, take to court for, put on trial for, bring to trial for, prosecute for; summons, cite, make accusations about, lay charges against, file charges against, prefer charges against; N. Amer. impeach for; archaic inculpate.
▷ANTONYMS absolve, clear, exonerate.
2 *the companies have been* ***accused of*** *causing job losses*: **blame for**, hold responsible for, lay the blame on someone for, hold accountable for, hold answerable for, condemn for, criticize for, denounce for; impute blame to, assign guilt to, attribute liability to, declare guilty; informal lay at the door of, point the finger at, stick on, pin on.
▷ANTONYMS defend, hold blameless.

accustom verb *she could not* ***accustom herself*** *to an altered way of life*: **adapt**, adjust, acclimatize, attune, habituate, accommodate, assimilate, acculturate, inure, harden, condition, reconcile, become resigned, resign; get used to, come to terms with, come to accept, learn to live with, make familiar with, become acquainted with; find one's feet, get one's bearings, blend in, fit in; N. Amer. acclimate.

accustomed adjective **1** *the money would not have kept Nicholas in his accustomed lifestyle*: **customary**, usual, normal, habitual, familiar, regular, routine, ordinary, typical, traditional, conventional, established, common, general, standard, prevailing, confirmed, fixed, set, settled, stock; literary wonted.
▷ANTONYMS unusual, unaccustomed.
2 *she is* ***accustomed to*** *being told what to do*: **used to**, adapted, adjusted, habituated, hardened, no stranger to; familiar with, acquainted with, at home with, in the habit of, experienced in, versed in, conversant with.
▷ANTONYMS unfamiliar, unused to.

ace informal noun *a rowing ace*: **expert**, master, genius, virtuoso, maestro, professional, adept, past master, doyen, champion, star, winner; German wunderkind; informal demon, pro, wizard, hotshot, whizz, wiz; Brit. informal dab hand; N. Amer. informal maven, crackerjack.
▷ANTONYMS amateur.
▶ adjective *an ace tennis player*: **excellent**, very good, first-rate, first-class, marvellous, wonderful, magnificent, outstanding, superlative, formidable, virtuoso, masterly, expert, champion, fine, consummate, skilful, adept; informal great, terrific, tremendous, superb, smashing, fantastic, stellar, sensational, fabulous, fab, crack, hotshot, A1, mean, demon, awesome, magic, wicked, tip-top, top-notch; Brit. informal brilliant, brill; vulgar slang shit-hot.
▷ANTONYMS mediocre, amateurish.

acerbic adjective **1** *he was renowned for his abrasive manner and acerbic tongue*: **sharp**, sarcastic, sardonic, satirical, scathing, cutting, razor-edged, incisive, penetrating, piercing, biting, stinging, searing, keen, caustic, trenchant, bitter, acrimonious, astringent, harsh, severe, devastating, abrasive, wounding, hurtful, unkind, cruel, vitriolic, virulent, mordant, venomous, waspish, poisonous, spiteful, vicious, malicious; N. Amer. acerb; informal bitchy, catty; Brit. informal sarky; N. Amer. informal snarky; rare mordacious, acidulous.
▷ANTONYMS mild, kind.
2 *a yellowy acerbic fluid came out of the tap*: **sour**, acid, acidic, acidulated, tart, bitter, unsweetened, sharp, acetic, acetous, vinegary, pungent, acrid; unpleasant, distasteful; N. Amer. acerb; rare acidulous.
▷ANTONYMS sweet.

ache noun **1** *an extremely bad stomach ache*: **pain**, dull pain, pang, twinge, throb; gnawing, stabbing, sting, stinging, spasm, muscular spasm, cramp, convulsion; smarting, soreness, tenderness, irritation, discomfort.
2 *his absence was a constant nagging ache in her heart*: **sorrow**, sadness, misery, grief, anguish, suffering, pain, agony, torture, wretchedness, distress, hurt, affliction, woe, mourning.
▷ANTONYMS joy.
3 *his unrelenting ache for his homeland*: **longing**, yearning, craving, desire, pining, hankering, hunger, hungering, thirst, itch, burning; informal yen.
▷ANTONYMS disinclination.
▶ verb **1** *the box was so heavy that it made his shoulders ache*: **hurt**, be sore, be painful, be in pain, throb, pound, twinge; smart, gnaw, burn, tingle, sting, be uncomfortable, be tender, give someone trouble; informal play up, give someone gyp.
2 *her heart ached unbearably*: **grieve**, sorrow, be sorrowful, be sad, be distressed, be in distress, be miserable, mourn, be mournful, lament, agonize, anguish, be in anguish, suffer, bleed; eat one's heart out, weep and wail.
▷ANTONYMS rejoice.

3 *the whole world seemed to **ache for** summer's coming*: **long for**, yearn for, hunger for, thirst for, hanker for, hanker after, pine for, pine after, itch for, be desperate for, be unable to wait for; crave, desire, covet; informal have a yen for, yen for, be dying for; archaic be athirst for, suspire for.

achieve verb *we hope that our goals will be achieved | he achieved distinction as an artist*: **attain**, reach, arrive at; realize, carry off, bring off, pull off, bring about, accomplish, carry through, fulfil, execute, perform, engineer, carry out, bring to fruition, conclude, complete, finish, consummate; earn, win, gain, find, establish, acquire, obtain, procure, come by, get, secure, clinch, seize, wrest, hook, net; informal wrap up, polish off, bag, wangle, swing; rare effectuate, reify.

achievement noun 1 *the achievement of a high rate of economic growth*: **attainment**, reaching, gaining, winning, acquirement, procurement; realization, accomplishment, fulfilment, fulfilling, carrying out, carrying through, effecting, implementation, execution, performance, engineering; conclusion, concluding, completion, completing, close, closing, finishing, consummation, success, fruition; informal winding up; rare effectuation, reification.
2 *they felt justifiably proud of their achievement*: **accomplishment**, attainment, feat, performance, undertaking, act, action, deed, effort, exploit, manoeuvre, operation, enterprise; work, handiwork, creation; **triumph**, success, positive result, coup, master stroke, stroke of genius.

achiever noun *he will go down in financial history as a great achiever*: **performer**, doer, worker, succeeder, high achiever, activist, man of action, woman of action, entrepreneur; success; informal **high-flyer**, go-getter, success story, whizz kid, powerhouse, fireball, human dynamo, wheeler-dealer, live wire, tiger, giant.
▷ANTONYMS loser; failure.

Achilles heel noun *the cost of the process may prove to be its Achilles heel*: **weak spot**, weak point, weakness, vulnerable spot, soft underbelly, shortcoming, failing, imperfection, flaw, defect, deficiency, fault, foible, chink in one's armour; downfall, undoing, nemesis, Waterloo.
▷ANTONYMS strength.

aching adjective 1 *he had a stiff neck and an aching back*: **painful**, achy, sore, stiff, hurt, tender, uncomfortable, troublesome; hurting, in pain, throbbing, pounding, twingeing; smarting, gnawing, burning, tingling, stinging, agonizing, searing, feeling tender, feeling uncomfortable, giving someone trouble; informal killing, playing someone up, giving someone gyp.
2 *she's nursing an aching heart*: **sorrowful**, sad, mournful, miserable, upset, distressed, anguished, heavy with grief, grief-stricken, wretched, heavy; **grieving**, sorrowing, mourning, lamenting, in distress, in anguish, suffering, bleeding.
▷ANTONYMS cheerful, light.

acid adjective 1 *a very juicy fruit with a slightly acid flavour*: **acidic**, **sour**, tart, bitter, unsweetened, sharp, biting, acrid, pungent, acerbic, vinegary, vinegarish, acetic, acetous; rare acidulous, acidulated.
▷ANTONYMS sweet.
2 *she was prone to making acid remarks*: **acerbic**, **sarcastic**, sharp, sardonic, satirical, scathing, cutting, razor-edged; incisive, penetrating, piercing, biting, stinging, searing; keen, caustic, trenchant, mordant, bitter, acrimonious, astringent; harsh, severe, abrasive, wounding, hurtful, unkind, cruel, vitriolic, virulent, venomous, poisonous, waspish, spiteful, vicious, malicious; N. Amer. acerb; informal bitchy, catty; Brit. informal sarky; N. Amer. informal snarky; rare mordacious, acidulous.
▷ANTONYMS kind, pleasant, complimentary.

acknowledge verb 1 *the government acknowledged the need to begin talks*: **admit**, accept, grant, allow, concede, confess, own, appreciate, recognize, realize, be aware of, be conscious of; subscribe to, approve (of), agree to, accede to, concur with, acquiesce in, go along with, respect, cooperate with, bow to; informal take on board, be wise to; rare cognize.
▷ANTONYMS reject, deny.
2 *he did not acknowledge Colin, but hurried on past*: **greet**, salute, address, hail, accost; nod to, wave to, signal to, raise one's hat to, say hello to, smile at; recognize, notice.
▷ANTONYMS ignore.
3 *few people acknowledged my letters*: **answer**, return, reply to, respond to, react to; write back to someone, come back to someone.
▷ANTONYMS overlook.
4 *Douglas was glad to acknowledge her help*: **express gratitude for**, show appreciation for, give thanks for, thank someone for, pay tribute to someone for, salute someone for, toast someone for; honour, celebrate, praise, speak highly of.

acknowledged adjective *he is the acknowledged leader of the Turkish community*: **recognized**, admitted, accepted, approved, accredited, confirmed, declared, proclaimed, confessed, sworn, avowed; undisputed, undoubted, unquestioned, unchallenged; rightful, true, proper, correct, genuine, authorized, sanctioned, just.

acknowledgement noun 1 *there was **acknowledgement of** the need to take new initiatives*: **acceptance**, admission, granting, allowing, concession, confession, appreciation, recognition, realization, awareness, cognizance, knowledge; approval of, acquiescence in, agreement with, concurrence with, respect for, cooperation with.
▷ANTONYMS denial.
2 *Travis gave a smile of acknowledgement*: **greeting**, welcome, salutation, saluting, hailing, address, hello, hallo; recognition, notice, heed, consideration.
3 *I sent off the application form but there was no acknowledgement*: **answer**, reply, response, reaction; answering; receipt; informal comeback.
4 *their land has been exploited without acknowledgement or compensation*: **thanks**, gratitude, appreciation, praise, commendation, credit, recognition, regard, respect; expression of appreciation, expression of gratitude, mention, honourable mention; a pat on the back, a round of applause; informal bouquets, brownie points; rare laudation.
▷ANTONYMS ingratitude.

acme noun *she was at the acme of her power*. See **peak** (sense 4 of the noun).

acolyte noun *he found himself surrounded by eager acolytes*: **assistant**, helper, attendant, retainer, servant, minion, underling, lackey, henchman; **follower**, disciple, supporter, votary, satellite, shadow; informal sidekick, man/girl Friday, running dog, groupie, hanger-on; archaic liegeman, pursuivant; Hinduism chela; rare janissary.
▷ANTONYMS leader, master, mistress.

acquaint verb *it is sensible to **acquaint** yourself **with** some basic facts | they were getting **acquainted with** each other's work*: **familiarize**, make familiar, make conversant, get/keep up to date; accustom to, make known to, make aware of, inform of, advise of, apprise of, brief as to, give information about; enlighten, keep posted, let know; prime on, ground in, instruct in, teach in, educate in, school in, indoctrinate in, initiate into; informal give the gen about, give the low-down on, give a rundown of, fill in on, gen up on, clue up about, clue in on, put in the picture about, keep up to speed with.

acquaintance noun 1 *Mr Barnet was no more than a business acquaintance*: **contact**, associate, connection, ally, colleague; French confrère.
2 *she had prospered from her acquaintance with the sergeant*: **association**, relationship, contact, social contact; fellowship, companionship.
3 *the critical reader must have some **acquaintance with** poetry already*: **familiarity**, conversance, conversancy, contact, acquaintanceship; knowledge of, experience of, awareness of, understanding of, comprehension of, cognizance of, grasp of; proficiency in, skill in, expertise in, insight into; informal know-how.

acquainted adjective 1 *she was well **acquainted with** Gothic literature*: **familiar**, conversant, at home, up to date, up; well versed in, knowledgeable about, well informed about, cognizant in, apprised of, abreast of, no stranger to; French au fait, au courant; informal well up on, in the know about, plugged in to, genned up on, clued in on, wise to, hip to.
▷ANTONYMS unfamiliar; ignorant.
2 *I am not personally **acquainted with** him*: **known to**; familiar, friendly, on friendly terms, on good terms, on a sociable footing.

acquiesce verb *he **acquiesced in** his sister's marriage with a divorced man*: **permit**, consent to, agree to, allow, assent to, give one's consent to, accept, concur with, give one's assent to, give one's blessing to, say yes to, give the nod to, give one's approval to; comply with, conform to, abide by, respect, stand by, cooperate with, tolerate, brook; give in to, bow to, yield to, submit to; informal go along with, give the go-ahead to, give the thumbs up to, OK, okay, give the green light to, say the word; archaic suffer.
▷ANTONYMS forbid.

> *Choose the right word* **acquiesce, agree, consent, assent**
>
> See **agree**.

acquiescence noun *the tsar secured the acquiescence of the nobility*: **consent**, agreement, acceptance, accession, concurrence, approval, seal of approval, approbation, assent, leave, permission, blessing, sanction; compliance, conforming, conformity, adherence, respect, accord, accordance; conceding, concession, deference, yielding, bowing, submission, surrender, obedience; informal OK, say-so, go-ahead, green light, thumbs up, nod; archaic abidance; rare permit.
▷ANTONYMS refusal.

acquiescent adjective *the masses are generally apolitical and acquiescent*: **compliant**, complying, consenting, cooperative, willing, obliging, agreeable, amenable, tractable, persuadable, easily persuaded, pliant, flexible, easy, unprotesting, resigned; **submissive**, servile, subservient, obsequious, ingratiating, toadying, Uriah Heepish, self-effacing, unassertive, yielding, biddable, docile, deferential, respectful; informal bootlicking; rare obeisant, persuasible, suasible, convincible, susceptive, longanimous, resistless.

acquire verb *she acquired a collection of fine art prints | I rapidly acquired the confidence of the leadership*: **obtain**, come by, come to have, get, receive, gain, earn, win, come into, come in for, take possession of, take receipt of, be given; buy, purchase, procure, possess oneself of, secure; gather, collect, pick up, appropriate, amass, build up, hook, net, land; achieve, attain;

informal get one's hands on, get one's mitts on, get hold of, grab, bag, score, swing, nab, collar, cop.
▷ANTONYMS lose; part with.

acquirement noun **1** *her husband praised her acquirements*: **attainment**, achievement, accomplishment, skill, art, talent, capability, qualification; proficiency, mastery.
2 *they lived for the acquirement of money*: **acquisition**, acquiring, obtaining, gaining, earning, winning, securing, procuring, procurement; collecting, collection, appropriation, amassing.
▷ANTONYMS loss.

acquisition noun **1** *the gallery's Bronze Room will house a new acquisition*: **purchase**, **accession**, addition, asset; buy, investment, possession, accretion; property, goods.
2 *the acquisition of funds for the war effort*: **obtaining**, acquiring, gaining, gain, procuring, procurement, collecting, collection, attainment, appropriation, amassing.

acquisitive adjective *he had the acquisitive instinct of a magpie*: **greedy**, **hoarding**, covetous, avaricious, possessive, grasping, grabbing, predatory, avid, rapacious, mercenary, materialistic, money-oriented; informal money-grubbing, money-grabbing, on the make; N. Amer. informal grabby; Austral. informal hungry; rare quaestuary, Mammonish, Mammonistic.

acquisitiveness noun *the grasping acquisitiveness of an affluent society*: **greed**, greediness, covetousness, cupidity, possessiveness, grasping, graspingness, grabbing, avarice, avidity, predatoriness, rapaciousness, rapacity, voracity, voraciousness, mercenariness, materialism; informal money-grubbing, money-grabbing; N. Amer. informal grabbiness; rare Mammonism.

acquit verb **1** *the jury acquitted her of attempted arson*: **absolve**, clear, exonerate, exculpate, declare innocent, find innocent, pronounce not guilty; discharge, release, liberate, emancipate, free, set free, deliver, spare, exempt, dismiss; vindicate; informal let someone off (the hook).
▷ANTONYMS convict.
2 *the boys **acquitted themselves** exceedingly well*: **conduct oneself**, bear oneself; perform, act, behave; rare comport oneself, deport oneself.
3 archaic *they **acquitted** themselves **of** their important duty*: **discharge**, execute, perform, do, carry out, effect, implement, bring about, bring off, accomplish, achieve, fulfil, complete; informal pull off; rare effectuate.

acquittal noun **1** *we make every effort to secure the acquittal of our clients*: **absolution**, clearing, exoneration, exculpation, declaration of innocence; discharge, release, freeing, liberation, deliverance; vindication; informal let-off, letting off.
▷ANTONYMS conviction.
2 archaic *we received no guidance for the acquittal of these duties*: **discharge**, execution, performance, doing, carrying out, effecting, implementation, implementing, bringing off, accomplishment, achievement, fulfilment, fulfilling, completion, completing; informal pulling off; rare effectuation.

acrid adjective *the acrid smell of smoke clung about the building*: **pungent**, bitter, sharp, sour, tart, harsh, acid, acidic, acidulated, vinegary, acerbic, acetic, acetous; stinging, burning, irritating, nauseating; noxious, strong, malodorous, odorous, burnt, sooty; literary mephitic; rare acidulous, miasmic, miasmal.
▷ANTONYMS sweet.

acrimonious adjective *they had a heated and acrimonious discussion*: **bitter**, rancorous, caustic, acerbic, scathing, sarcastic, acid, harsh, sharp, razor-edged, cutting, astringent, trenchant, mordant, virulent; spiteful, vicious, crabbed, vitriolic, savage, hostile, hate-filled, venomous, poisonous, nasty, ill-natured, mean, malign, malicious, malignant, waspish, pernicious, splenetic, irascible, choleric; informal bitchy, catty, slashing; rare acidulous, mordacious, envenomed, squint-eyed.

acrimony noun *the meeting ended with acrimony on both sides*: **bitterness**, rancour, resentment, ill feeling, ill will, bad blood, animosity, hostility, enmity, antagonism, irascibility, waspishness, spleen; malice, spitefulness, crabbedness, causticity, sarcasm, venom, poison, viciousness, nastiness, harshness, sharpness, acerbity, virulence, astringency; grudge, grievance.
▷ANTONYMS goodwill.

acrobat noun *the acrobat performed a back somersault*: **tumbler**, gymnast; rope walker, tightrope walker, wire walker, balancer, trapeze artist; stuntman, stuntwoman; rare equilibrist, aerialist, funambulist.

acrobatics plural noun **1** *they performed staggering feats of acrobatics*: **gymnastics**, gymnastic feats, gymnastic skills, tumbling, balancing, nimbleness; tightrope walking, rope walking, wire walking; stunts, agility, skill; rare funambulism.
2 *the acrobatics required to negotiate major international contracts*: **agility**, skill, mental agility, quick thinking, alertness, inventiveness, nimbleness.

across preposition **1** *I ran across the street*: **to the other side of**, from one side of ... to the other, over, throughout the width/expanse of, covering, everywhere on, on all parts of.
2 *they lived across the river from us*: on the other side of, over, beyond, past.

> *Word links* **across**
>
> **trans-** related prefix, as in *transfer, transatlantic*

act verb **1** *the Government must act to remedy the situation*: **take action**, take steps, take measures, take the initiative, move, make a move, react, do something, proceed, go ahead; make progress, make headway, be active, be employed, be busy; informal get moving.
▷ANTONYMS do nothing.
2 *over dinner Alison began to act oddly*: **behave**, function, react, perform; conduct oneself, acquit oneself, bear oneself; rare comport oneself, deport oneself.
3 *the scents act as a powerful aphrodisiac*: **operate**, work, take effect, function, serve, be efficacious.
4 *he acted in a highly successful film*: **perform**, play, play a part, take part, be an actor, be an actress, be one of the cast, appear; informal tread the boards.
5 *we laughed, but most of us were just acting*: **pretend**, play-act, sham, fake, feign, put it on, bluff, pose, posture, masquerade, dissemble, dissimulate; informal kid.
□ **act for** *the estate agent was acting for a prospective buyer*: **represent**, act on behalf of, speak on behalf of; **stand in for**, fill in for, deputize for, cover for, substitute for, be a substitute for, replace, take the place of, act in place of, do/be a locum for, sit in for, understudy; hold the fort, step into the breach; informal sub for, fill someone's shoes/boots; N. Amer. informal pinch-hit for.
□ **act on/upon 1** *the drug acted directly on the blood vessels*: **affect**, have an effect on, influence, exert influence on, work on, have an impact on, impact on, alter, change, modify, transform, condition, control.
▷ANTONYMS have no effect on.
2 *he was merely acting on the orders of the party leader*: **comply with**, act in accordance with, follow, go along with; **obey**, take heed of, heed, conform to, abide by, adhere to, stick to, stand by, uphold, fulfil, meet, discharge.
▷ANTONYMS flout.
□ **act up 1** *the pupils are past masters at acting up in class*: **misbehave**, give someone trouble, cause someone trouble, act badly, get up to mischief, get up to no good, be bad, be naughty, forget oneself, misconduct oneself; clown about/around, fool about/around, act the clown, act the fool, act the goat, act foolishly; informal carry on, mess about/around; Brit. informal muck about/around, play up.
2 *the computers are always acting up*: **malfunction**, crash, develop a fault, go wrong, break down, give out, stall, be defective, be faulty, fail, cease to function, cease to work, stop working; informal conk out, go kaput, go phut, go on the blink, be on the blink; Brit. informal pack up, play up.
▶ **noun 1** *a life filled with acts of kindness* | *a criminal act*: **deed**, action, gesture, feat, exploit, move, performance, undertaking, manoeuvre, stunt, operation, venture, effort, enterprise, achievement, accomplishment.
2 *the Act raised the tax on tobacco*: **law**, decree, statute, bill, Act of Parliament, edict, fiat, dictum, dictate, enactment, resolution, ruling, rule, judgement, canon, ordinance, proclamation, command, commandment, mandate, measure, stipulation, direction, requirement; legislation; in Tsarist Russia ukase; in Spanish-speaking countries pronunciamento.
3 *I have written one act of a play*: **division**, section, subsection, portion, part, segment, component, bit; passage, episode, chapter.
4 *a marvellous music hall act*: **performance**, turn, routine, number, item, piece, sketch, skit, playlet, dance, song; show, production, presentation, entertainment; informal gig.
5 *my mother thinks crying is simply putting on an act*: **pretence**, false display, show, front, facade, masquerade, charade, guise, posture, pose, affectation, appearance; sham, fake, bluff, hoax; make-believe, play-acting, feigning, shamming, posturing, posing, counterfeit, subterfuge, dissimulation, dissemblance, fabrication, falsification; informal a put-on, a put-up job.

acting noun **1** *she studied the theory and practice of acting*: **drama**, the theatre, the stage, the performing arts, dramatic art, dramatics, dramaturgy, stagecraft, theatricals, theatrics, the thespian art, show business; performing, performance, portraying, portrayal, playing a role, appearing on stage; informal the boards, treading the boards, show biz; rare thespianism, histrionics.
2 *EC law prevents the ministers from acting*: **taking action**, taking steps, taking measures, doing something, moving, making a move, reacting, functioning, working, performing.
3 *he looks angry but we know it's all just acting*: **pretending**, pretence, play-acting, make-believe, illusion, masquerade, feigning, shamming, hoaxing, bluffing, posture, posturing, posing, affectation, counterfeit, subterfuge, dissimulation, dissemblance, falsification, humbug; sham, hoax, bluff, show, front, facade, charade, guise, pose; Brit. false colours; informal a put-on, a put-up job.
▶ **adjective** *the acting governor of the bank*: **substitute**, deputy, reserve, fill-in, stand-in, caretaker; **temporary**, short-term, provisional, interim, intervening, pro tem, improvised, surrogate, stopgap, transitional,

a

changeover; Latin pro tempore, ad interim; informal second-string; N. Amer. informal pinch-hitting.
▶ANTONYMS permanent.

action noun **1** *there can be no excuse for their actions*: **deed**, act, activity, move, gesture, undertaking, exploit, manoeuvre, achievement, accomplishment, venture, enterprise, endeavour, effort, exertion; work, handiwork, doing, creation, performance, behaviour, conduct; reaction, response.
2 *they recognized the need for local community action*: **steps**, measures, activity, movement, work, working, effort, exertion, operation.
3 *he was a patriot and a man of action*: **energy**, vitality, vigour, forcefulness, drive, push, ambition, motivation, initiative, spirit, liveliness, vim, pep; activity; informal get-up-and-go, punch, zip, pizzazz.
4 *they observed the action of hormones on the pancreas*: **effect**, influence, power, working, work; result, consequence.
5 *he missed all the action while he was away*: **excitement**, activity, bustle; happenings, occurrences, proceedings, events, incidents, episodes, eventualities, chain of events; informal goings-on.
6 *the men saw action in World War II | twenty-nine men died in the action*: **fighting**, hostilities, battle, conflict, armed conflict, combat, warfare, war, bloodshed; engagement, clash, encounter, confrontation, skirmish, affray.
7 *he won his action but the damages awarded were nominal*: **lawsuit**, legal action, suit, suit at law, case, cause, prosecution, litigation, legal dispute, legal contest; proceedings, legal proceedings, judicial proceedings.
□ **in action** *the company has worked on the plan for about two years and says it should be in action by April 1*: **functioning**, working, running, up and running, operative, in use, going.
□ **out of action** *the group's Utah power station is out of action at the moment*: **not working**, not in working order, not functioning, broken, broken-down, out of order, out of service, out of commission, acting up, unserviceable, faulty, defective, non-functional, in disrepair; down; informal conked out, bust, (gone) kaput, gone phut, on the blink, gone haywire, shot.
▶ANTONYMS operative, working.
□ **take action** *still, there is pressure to take action regarding food labels*: **act**, take steps, take measures, take the initiative, move, make a move, react, do something.
▶ANTONYMS do nothing.

activate verb *Mark pressed the button which activated the machine*: **operate**, switch on, turn on, start, start off, start up, set going, get going, trigger off, trigger, trip, set in motion, actuate, initiate, initialize, energize, animate.
▶ANTONYMS switch off.

active adjective **1** *they located the area of brain tissue that was active | the active ingredient of tobacco*: **operative**, working, functioning, functional, operating, operational, in action, in operation, in force, live; **effective**, effectual, powerful, potent, non-passive, non-inert; informal up and running.
▶ANTONYMS inactive; inert.
2 *despite her illness she remained quite active*: **mobile**, **energetic**, agile, sporty, nimble, vigorous, vital, dynamic, sprightly, spry, lively, animated, bouncy, bubbly, perky, frisky, zestful, spirited; busy, bustling, occupied, involved; informal on the go, on the move, full of get-up-and-go, full of vim and vigour, full of beans, sparky, zippy, peppy, bright-eyed and bushy-tailed; N. Amer. informal go-go.
▶ANTONYMS listless.
3 *he was an active member of the union*: **hard-working**, busy, industrious, diligent, tireless, contributing, enterprising, influential; occupied, engaged, involved; **enthusiastic**, keen, committed, devoted, determined, zealous, militant, radical; informal go-getting, go-ahead.
▶ANTONYMS passive; indifferent.

> *Choose the right word* **active, busy, occupied, engaged**
>
> See **busy**.

activity noun **1** *there was a lot of activity around the orchard*: **bustle**, hustle and bustle, busyness, action, liveliness, movement, life, stir, animation, commotion, flurry, tumult, hubbub, excitement, agitation, fuss, whirl; happenings, occurrences, proceedings, events, incidents; informal toing and froing, comings and goings, to-do; archaic hurry scurry, pother.
▶ANTONYMS calm.
2 *Members of Parliament engage in a wide range of activities*: **pursuit**, occupation, venture, undertaking, enterprise, project, scheme, business, job, affair, task, campaign; interest, hobby, pastime, recreation, diversion, entertainment; act, action, deed, doing, exploit, manoeuvre; informal thing, lark, caper.
3 *they often experience restricted activity due to illness*: **functioning**, effectiveness, mobility, motion, movement; vitality, vigour, energy, strength, potency, dynamism; informal get-up-and-go, bounce, oomph, vim, vim and vigour.
▶ANTONYMS inactivity.

actor, actress noun **performer**, player, trouper, theatrical, dramatic artist, thespian, member of the cast, artist, artiste; Indian filmi; Brit. informal luvvy; archaic histrionic, stager.

> *Word links* **actor**
>
> **histrionic, theatrical, thespian** relating to actors

actual adjective *they suffered actual physical harm*: **real**, true, genuine, authentic, verified, attested, confirmed, definite, hard, plain, clear, clear-cut, undeniable, veritable; existing, existent, manifest, substantial, non-fictional, factual, unquestionable, indisputable; effective, realistic; Latin de facto, bona fide; informal real live, honest-to-goodness, your actual; rare unimaginary.
▶ANTONYMS notional; non-existent.
□ **in actual fact** *the sale of shares, which had been criticized for not having been adequately publicized, was in actual fact over-subscribed*: **really**, in fact, in actuality, in point of fact, as a matter of fact, in reality, actually, in truth, if truth be told, to tell the truth; dated indeed, truly; archaic in sooth, verily; rare in the concrete.

actuality noun *dissatisfaction occurs when actuality falls short of expectation*: **reality**, fact, truth, the real world, real life, existence, living.
□ **in actuality** *the journey seemed a thousand miles though in actuality it was only five*: **really**, in fact, in actual fact, in point of fact, as a matter of fact, in reality, actually, in truth, if truth be told, to tell the truth; dated indeed, truly; archaic in sooth, verily; rare in the concrete.

actually adverb **1** *I looked upset but actually I was terribly excited*: **really**, in fact, in actual fact, in point of fact, as a matter of fact, in reality, in actuality, in truth, if truth be told, to tell the truth; dated indeed, truly; archaic in sooth, verily; rare in the concrete.
2 *he had actually conspired against his friends*: **literally**, to all intents and purposes, in effect; **even**, though it may seem strange, believe it or not, surprisingly, as it happens; archaic forsooth.

actuate verb **1** *the sprinkler system was actuated by the fire*: **activate**, operate, switch on, turn on, start up, set going, get going, start off, trigger off, trigger, trip, set in motion, initiate, initialize, energize, animate.
2 *they proved that the defendant was actuated by malice*: **motivate**, stimulate, move, drive, rouse, stir, stir up, fire, fire up, arouse; **prompt**, incite, spark off, influence, impel, spur on, urge, goad; rare activate.

acumen noun *a gullible young man with little or no business acumen*: **astuteness**, awareness, shrewdness, acuity, sharpness, sharp-wittedness, cleverness, brightness, smartness; judgement, understanding, sense, common sense, canniness, discernment, wisdom, wit, sagacity, perspicacity, ingenuity, insight, intuition, intuitiveness, perception, perspicuity, penetration; capability, enterprise, initiative, resourcefulness, flair, vision; brains, powers of reasoning; French savoir faire; informal nous, savvy, know-how, horse sense, gumption, grey matter; Brit. informal common; N. Amer. informal smarts; rare sapience, arguteness.
▶ANTONYMS witlessness.

acute adjective **1** *Emily had an acute ear for instrumental sounds*: **keen**, sharp, good, penetrating, discerning, perceptive, sensitive, subtle.
▶ANTONYMS poor.
2 *he has an exceptionally acute mind*: **astute**, shrewd, sharp, sharp-witted, razor-sharp, rapier-like, quick, quick-witted, agile, nimble, ingenious, clever, intelligent, bright, brilliant, smart, canny, intuitive, discerning, perceptive, perspicacious, penetrating, insightful, incisive, piercing, discriminating, sagacious, wise, judicious; informal on the ball, quick off the mark, quick on the uptake, brainy, streetwise, savvy; Brit. informal suss; Scottish & N. English informal pawky; N. Amer. informal heads-up; dated, informal long-headed; rare argute, sapient.
▶ANTONYMS slow-witted.
3 *the acute food shortages of post-war England*: **severe**, critical, drastic, dire, dreadful, terrible, awful, grave, bad, serious, profound; urgent, pressing, desperate; all-important, vital, dangerous, hazardous, perilous, precarious; life-threatening, life-and-death; archaic parlous; rare egregious.
▶ANTONYMS negligible.
4 *the meal gave us acute pains in our stomachs*: **stabbing**, shooting, penetrating, piercing, sharp, keen, racking, searing, burning, consuming; fierce, ferocious; **intense**, severe, extreme, excruciating, agonizing, grievous, hellish, torturous, tormenting, unbearable, insufferable, unendurable, more than one can bear, more than flesh and blood can stand; literary exquisite.
▶ANTONYMS dull; mild.
5 *the patient had acute colitis*: **severe**, intense, short-lasting; Medicine peracute; informal short and sharp.
▶ANTONYMS chronic.

> *Choose the right word* **acute, keen, penetrating**
>
> See **keen**[1].

acutely adverb *Lucy looked acutely embarrassed*: **extremely**, exceedingly, very, markedly, severely, intensely, in the extreme, deeply, profoundly, keenly, sharply, painfully, desperately, awfully, terribly, tremendously,

enormously, thoroughly, heartily; informal well, seriously, majorly, oh-so; informal, dated jolly, devilish; N. Amer. informal mighty, plumb; S. African informal lekker.
▷ANTONYMS slightly.

adage noun *it is vital for every pilot to remember the old adage 'safety first'*: **saying**, maxim, axiom, proverb, aphorism, saw, dictum, precept, epigram, epigraph, motto, truism, platitude, cliché, commonplace; words of wisdom, pearls of wisdom; expression, phrase, formula, slogan, quotation; rare apophthegm, gnome.

adamant adjective *scientists are adamant about the absence of risk*: **unshakeable**, immovable, inflexible, unwavering, uncompromising, resolute, resolved, determined, firm, rigid, steadfast; unswerving, stubborn, unrelenting, unyielding, unbending, obdurate, inexorable, intransigent, dead set, iron-willed, strong-willed, steely; N. Amer. rock-ribbed; informal stiff-necked; rare indurate.
▷ANTONYMS unsure.

adapt verb **1** *we've adapted the hotels to suit their needs*: **modify**, alter, make alterations to, change, adjust, make adjustments to, convert, transform, redesign, restyle, refashion, remodel, reshape, revamp, rework, redo, reconstruct, reorganize; customize, tailor; improve, make improvements to, amend, refine; informal tweak.
▷ANTONYMS preserve.
2 *he has **adapted** well **to** his new home*: **adjust**, acclimatize, accommodate, attune, habituate, acculturate, conform; familiarize oneself with, habituate oneself to, become habituated to, get used to, orient oneself in, condition oneself to; reconcile oneself to, resign oneself to, become resigned to, come to terms with, find one's way around; become naturalized, become seasoned, get one's bearings, find one's feet, blend in, fit in; N. Amer. acclimate.

adaptable adjective **1** *a conservatory is the most adaptable room in your home*: **versatile**, variable, convertible, alterable, modifiable, adjustable, changeable; multi-purpose, all-purpose.
▷ANTONYMS limited.
2 *an adaptable workforce capable of acquiring new skills*: **flexible**, adjustable, pliant, compliant, malleable, versatile, resilient, conformable; easy-going, accommodating, obliging, cooperative, amenable; informal easy.
▷ANTONYMS inflexible.

adaptation noun **1** *the adaptation of old buildings to new uses*: **converting**, conversion, alteration, modification, adjustment, changing, transformation; remodelling, revamping, reshaping, reconstruction; tailoring, customizing.
2 *her daughters' remarkable adaptation to life in Britain*: **adjustment**, conformity, acclimatization, accommodation, attunement, familiarization, habituation, orientation, conditioning, inurement, hardening, seasoning, acculturation, assimilation, integration, domestication, naturalization; blending in, fitting in, settling in, settling down; N. Amer. acclimation.

add verb **1** *the front porch was added in 1751*: **attach**, build on, add on, put on, put in, append, adjoin, join, affix, connect, annex; include.
▷ANTONYMS remove.
2 *the calculating machine could store and add 23-digit numbers*: **add up**, add together, total, count, count up, figure up, compute, calculate, reckon, tally, enumerate, find the sum of; Brit. tot up; dated cast up.
▷ANTONYMS subtract.
3 *she added that she had every confidence in Laura*: **go on to say**, state further, continue, carry on; informal tack on, tag on.
□ **add to** *her decision just added to his woe*: **increase**, magnify, amplify, augment, intensify, heighten, deepen, enhance, boost, inflate, escalate; **exacerbate**, aggravate, inflame, worsen, make worse, compound, reinforce; add fuel to the fire/flames, fan the flames, put salt on the wound.
▷ANTONYMS lessen.
□ **add up 1** *the subsidies **added up to** £1700*: **amount to**, come to, run to, number, make, total, equal, be equal to, be equivalent to, count as; Brit. tot up to. **2** *the recent riots **add up to** a severe and deepening crisis*: **amount to**, constitute, comprise, equal, be equivalent to, approximate to; signify, signal, mean, indicate, suggest, denote, point to, be evidence of, be symptomatic of; informal spell, spell out; literary betoken. **3** *the situation just didn't add up*: **make sense**, seem reasonable, seem plausible, stand to reason, stand up, hold up, hold water, bear examination, bear investigation, be verifiable, ring true, be convincing.
□ **add something up** *I added up all the subtotals*: **total**, add together, count, count up, figure up, compute, calculate, reckon, tally, enumerate, find the sum of; Brit. tot up; dated cast up.
▷ANTONYMS subtract.

addendum noun *each chapter ends with a short addendum entitled 'Further Reading'*: **appendix**, codicil, postscript, afterword, tailpiece, rider, coda, supplement, accompaniment; adjunct, appendage, addition, add-on, attachment, extension; rare postlude, subscript, allonge.

addict noun **1** *her brother was a heroin addict*: **abuser**, user; informal **junkie**, druggy, druggie, space cadet, -freak, -head, -fiend, tripper, hype, hypo, cokey, pill-popper, metho; N. Amer. informal hophead, hoppy, needleman, schmecker, snowbird; informal, dated drugger; N. Amer. informal, dated dope, dopester, junker, muggler, snifter; rare narcotist, morphinist, morphiomaniac, etheromaniac, viper.
2 *the resort is a must for all skiing addicts*: **enthusiast**, **fan**, fanatic, lover, devotee, aficionado, master, wizard; adherent, follower, admirer; informal buff, freak, nut, fiend, maniac, ace; N. Amer. informal geek, jock; S. African informal fundi.

addicted adjective **1** *he was seriously **addicted to** tranquillizers | he had the occasional bet, but he was never addicted*: **dependent on**, given to using, given to abusing, in the habit of using; dependent, obsessive, obsessional; informal hooked on.
2 *she became **addicted to** the theatre*: **devoted to**, dedicated to, fond of, partial to, keen on, enthusiastic about, enamoured of, in love with, infatuated with, obsessed with, fixated on, fanatical about; informal hooked on, gone on, wild about, nuts about, potty about, dotty about, crazy about.
▷ANTONYMS indifferent.

> *Word links* **addicted**
>
> **-holic** person addicted to something, as in *alcoholic, chocoholic*

addiction noun **1** *he blamed Murray for his heroin addiction*: **dependency**, dependence, craving, habit, weakness, compulsion, fixation, enslavement; informal monkey; N. Amer. informal jones.
2 *a slavish **addiction to** fashion*: **devotion**, dedication; obsession with, infatuation with, passion for, love of, fondness for, weakness for, penchant for, predilection for, appetite for, mania for; informal thing about, yen for; rare appetency for.
▷ANTONYMS indifference.

addictive adjective *crack cocaine is highly addictive*: **habit-forming**, causing addiction, causing dependency; compelling, compulsive; Brit. informal moreish.

addition noun **1** *the soil is greatly improved by the addition of compost*: **inclusion**, adding, adding in, incorporation, introduction, insertion.
2 *an improved machine for the addition of numbers*: **adding up**, counting, totalling, computation, calculation, reckoning, tallying, summation; informal totting up; informal, dated casting up.
3 *he proposes a number of additions to existing taxation*: **supplement**, appendage, adjunct, addendum, add-on, extra, accompaniment, extension, rider; increase, increment, augmentation.
□ **in addition 1** *conditions were harsh and in addition some soldiers fell victim to snipers*: **additionally**, as well, what's more, besides, furthermore, moreover, also, into the bargain, to boot. **2** *there were eight presidential candidates **in addition to** the General*: **besides**, as well as, on top of, along with, plus, over and above; other than, apart from, excepting, with the exception of, excluding, not including, barring, bar, save (for), omitting, leaving out, not to mention, to say nothing of.

additional adjective *beach towels are provided without additional charge*: **extra**, added, supplementary, supplemental, further, auxiliary, ancillary, subsidiary, secondary, attendant, accessory; more, other, another, new, fresh.

additionally adverb *the organization relied additionally on a vast network of informers*: **also**, in addition, as well, too, besides, on top (of that), moreover, further, furthermore, what's more, over and above that, into the bargain, to boot; archaic withal, forbye.

additive noun *the marmalade is free from any artificial additives*: **added ingredient**, addition, extra, add-on, supplement, accompaniment; preservative, flavour enhancer, colouring; Brit. informal E-number.

addled adjective *her brains were irretrievably addled*: **muddled**, confused, fuddled, befuddled, bewildered, dazed, dizzy, disoriented, disorientated, stupefied, unbalanced, unhinged, demented, deranged; informal discombobulated, woolly, muzzy, woozy, dopey, not with it, bamboozled, fazed.

address noun **1** *Juliet looked at the scribbled address on the envelope*: **inscription**, label, mark, superscription; directions.
2 *she wondered if she had come to the wrong address*: **location**, locality, place, situation, whereabouts; house, flat, apartment, home, residence; formal dwelling, dwelling place, habitation, abode, domicile.
3 *the president's address received lukewarm applause*: **speech**, lecture, talk, monologue, dissertation, discourse, oration, peroration; sermon, homily, lesson; N. Amer. salutatory; informal spiel; rare disquisition, allocution, predication.
▸ **verb 1** *I addressed the envelope by hand*: **label**, direct, inscribe, superscribe.
2 *the preacher addressed a crowded congregation*: **talk to**, give a talk to, give an address to, speak to, make a speech to, lecture, give a lecture to, hold forth to, give a discourse to, give a dissertation to, give an oration to, declaim to; **preach to**, deliver a sermon to, give a sermon to, sermonize; informal speechify to, preachify to, spout to, jaw to, sound off to, spiel to, drone on to.
3 *she is always uncertain how to address her boss*: **greet**, hail, salute, speak to, write to, talk to, make conversation with, approach; name, call, describe, designate; formal denominate.

4 *any correspondence should be addressed to the Banking Ombudsman*: **send**, direct, post, mail, communicate, convey, forward, remit.
5 *hold the putter off the ground as you address the ball*: **take aim at**, aim at, face.
6 *the minister failed to address the issue of subsidies | he* ***addressed himself to*** *the composition of a letter*: **attend to**, tackle, see to, deal with, confront, grapple with, attack, buckle down to, get to grips with, embark on, settle down to, direct one's attention to, turn to, get down to, concentrate on, focus on, apply oneself to, devote oneself to; turn one's hand to, try to deal with, try to sort out, take up, take in hand, undertake, engage in, become involved in; informal get stuck into, get cracking on, get weaving on, have a crack at, have a go at, have a shot at, have a stab at.

adduce verb *facts and figures have been adduced to bolster the argument*. See **cite** (sense 2).

adept adjective *the Minoans were adept at sculpting figures from ivory*: **expert**, proficient, accomplished, skilful, talented, gifted, masterly, virtuoso, consummate, peerless; adroit, dexterous, deft, nimble-fingered, handy, artful, able, capable, competent; brilliant, very good, splendid, marvellous, formidable, outstanding, first-rate, first-class, excellent, impressive, fine; informal great, top-notch, top-drawer, top-hole, tip-top, A1, wizard, magic, ace, fab, smashing, mean, crack, nifty, deadly, slick; Brit. informal brill, a dab hand at; N. Amer. informal crackerjack; archaic or humorous compleat; rare habile.
▷ANTONYMS inept; mediocre.
▸ noun *adepts at kung fu and karate can smash through stacks of roofing tiles*. See **expert** (noun).

adequacy noun 1 *questions were raised about the adequacy of the firm's audit procedures*: **acceptability**, reasonableness, passableness, tolerableness, satisfactoriness, fairness; sufficiency, ampleness; appropriateness, suitability, suitableness, pertinence, appositeness, effectiveness, efficacy, usefulness, helpfulness.
2 *he had deep misgivings about his own adequacy*: **capability**, competence, competency, ability, aptitude, skill, skilfulness, adeptness; effectiveness, efficacy, productiveness; qualifications, fitness, suitability; value, worth, merit.

adequate adjective 1 *he lacked adequate financial resources*: **sufficient**, enough, ample, requisite, apposite, appropriate, suitable.
▷ANTONYMS insufficient.
2 *the company provides an adequate but not top-notch service*: **acceptable**, passable, reasonable, satisfactory, tolerable, fair, fairly good, pretty good, goodish, middle-of-the-road, mediocre, unexceptional, unexceptionable, undistinguished, unremarkable, ordinary, commonplace, indifferent, average, not bad, all right, good enough, so-so, minimal, medium, moderate, run-of-the-mill, forgettable; informal OK, okay, fair-to-middling, nothing to write home about, nothing to shout about, no great shakes, (plain) vanilla, bog-standard; Austral./NZ informal half-pie.
▷ANTONYMS inadequate.
3 *the workstations were small but seemed* ***adequate to*** *the task*: **equal to**, up to, capable, of, suited to, suitable for, able to do, qualified for, fit for, good enough for, sufficient for; informal up to scratch.
▷ANTONYMS unequal to.

adhere verb 1 *a little dollop of cream adhered to her nose*: **stick**, stick fast, cling, hold fast, cohere, bond, attach; be stuck, be fixed, be pasted, be glued.
2 *they* ***adhere*** *scrupulously* ***to*** *Judaic law*: **abide by**, stick to, hold to, comply with, stand by, be faithful to, act in accordance with, pay attention to, pay regard to, go along with, cooperate with, conform to, submit to; take to heart, bear in mind, be guided by; follow, obey, heed, observe, respect, uphold, fulfil.
▷ANTONYMS flout, ignore.
3 *most of the county* ***adhered to*** *the episcopal church*: **be attached to**, be connected with, be affiliated to, be a member of; follow, support, give support to, cleave to, be loyal to, be faithful to, remain true to; informal stick with.

adherent noun *an adherent of the Catholic religion | adherents of the grunge music scene*: **follower**, supporter, upholder, defender, advocate, disciple, votary, partisan, member, friend, stalwart; fanatic, zealot; believer, worshipper, attender; **fan**, admirer, enthusiast, devotee, lover, addict, aficionado; informal hanger-on, groupie, buff, freak, fiend, nut, maniac; N. Amer. informal booster, cohort, rooter; rare janissary, sectary.
▷ANTONYMS opponent.
▸ adjective *the colon has an adherent layer of mucus gel*: **adhesive**, sticky, sticking, adhering, clinging, tacky, gluey, gummy, gummed, cohesive, viscous, viscid, glutinous, mucilaginous; Brit. claggy; Scottish & N. English clarty; informal gooey, gloopy, cloggy, gungy, icky; N. Amer. informal gloppy; rare tenacious, viscoid.

adhesion noun 1 *pressure will help the adhesion of the gum strip to the paper fibres*: **sticking**, adherence, gluing, fixing, fastening, union.
2 *the front tyres were struggling for adhesion*: **traction**, grip, purchase, friction, resistance.

adhesive noun *fix the stencil in place with a spray adhesive*: **glue**, fixative, gum, paste, cement, bonding, binder, sealer, sealant; superglue, epoxy resin; N. Amer. mucilage; N. Amer. informal stickum.
▸ adjective *a special adhesive mortar suitable for outdoor use*: **sticky**, sticking, adhering, adherent, clinging, tacky, gluey, gummy, gummed, cohesive, viscous, viscid, glutinous, mucilaginous; Brit. claggy; Scottish & N. English clarty; informal gooey, gloopy, cloggy, gungy, icky; N. Amer. informal gloppy; rare tenacious, viscoid.

ad hoc Latin adjective *discussions were held on an ad hoc basis*: **impromptu**, extempore, extemporary, extemporaneous, expedient, emergency, improvised, rough and ready, makeshift, make-do, cobbled together, thrown together; Nautical jury-rigged, jury; informal quick and dirty.
▸ adverb *committees of enquiry can be set up ad hoc*: **as the need arises**, when necessary, when needed.

adieu noun & exclamation *I whispered a fond adieu | I bid you adieu, but I will return*. See **goodbye**.

ad infinitum adverb Latin *the tradition will be maintained ad infinitum*: **forever**, for ever and ever, evermore, always, for all time, till the end of time, in perpetuity; perpetually, eternally, endlessly, interminably, unceasingly, unendingly, everlastingly; Brit. for evermore, forever more; N. Amer. forevermore; Latin in perpetuum; informal until the cows come home, until the twelfth of never, until hell freezes over, until doomsday, until kingdom come; archaic for aye.

adjacent adjective *a railway museum* ***adjacent to*** *the Moat House Hotel*: **adjoining**, neighbouring (on), next door to, abutting, close to, near to, next to, by, close by, by the side of, bordering (on), beside, alongside, abreast of, contiguous with, proximate to, attached to, touching, joining; cheek by jowl with; rare conjoining, approximate to, vicinal.
▷ANTONYMS remote from.

adjoin verb *my office adjoined the doctor's surgery*: **be next to**, be adjacent to, border (on), neighbour, verge on, abut, butt up against, butt up to, bound on, be contiguous with, be connected to, communicate with, link up with, extend as far as, extend to; join, conjoin, connect with/to, touch, meet.

adjoining adjective *the two women had adjoining bedrooms*: **connecting**, connected, interconnecting, adjacent, abutting, neighbouring, bordering, next-door; contiguous, proximate; attached, joining, touching, meeting; rare conjoining, approximate, vicinal.
▷ANTONYMS remote.

adjourn verb 1 *the hearing was adjourned for a week | the opening session adjourned after barely thirty minutes*: **suspend**, break off, discontinue, interrupt, postpone, put off, put back, defer, delay, hold over, hold in abeyance, shelve, pigeonhole, stay, prorogue, dissolve, terminate, bring to an end, halt, call a halt to; pause, suspend proceedings, take a break, recess, break up, end, come to an end; N. Amer. put over, table, lay on the table, take a recess; informal put on ice, put on the back burner, put in cold storage, mothball, take a breather, let up, knock off, take five; N. Amer. informal take a rain check; N. Amer. Law continue; rare remit, respite.
2 *they adjourned to the sitting room for liqueurs and brandy*: **withdraw**, retire, retreat, beat a retreat, take oneself, decamp, depart, go out, go off, go away, exit; formal repair, remove; literary betake oneself; rare abstract oneself.

adjournment noun *opposition parties forced the adjournment of the parliament*: **suspension**, breaking off, discontinuation, interruption, postponement, rescheduling, deferment, deferral, delay, shelving, stay, pigeonholing, prorogation, dissolution, dissolving, disbandment, termination, halting; break, pause, suspension of proceedings, temporary cessation, recess, rest, time out, stoppage; N. Amer. tabling; informal let up, breather, mothballing, knocking off, taking five; Law moratorium; N. Amer. Law continuation; rare put-off.

adjudge verb *he was adjudged guilty of the offence of obstruction*. See **judge** (sense 3 of the verb).

adjudicate verb *the case was adjudicated in the High Court*: **judge**, adjudge, try, hear, examine, arbitrate, decide on, decide, settle, resolve, determine, pronounce on, give a ruling on, sit in judgement on, pass judgement on, give a verdict on, make a ruling on; referee, umpire.

adjudication noun *matters were ultimately settled by adjudication | the jury's verdict is a final adjudication*: **arbitration**, refereeing, umpiring; judging, judgement, decision, pronouncement, ruling, settlement, resolution, finding, verdict, conclusion, sentence, decree, order; Law determination; N. Amer. resolve; rare arbitrament.

adjudicator noun *their application for asylum is being considered by an adjudicator*: **arbitrator**, arbiter, mediator, referee, umpire, judge.

adjunct noun *the compound is still used by some practitioners as an adjunct to penicillin therapy*: **supplement**, addition, accompaniment, complement, companion, extra, add-on, additive, accessory, appurtenance; attachment, appendage, addendum, affix, auxiliary.

adjust verb 1 *Kate had adjusted to her new life at boarding school*: **adapt**, become accustomed, get used, accommodate, acclimatize, attune, orient

oneself, reconcile oneself, habituate oneself, assimilate, conform; come to terms with, familiarize oneself with, acquaint oneself with, blend in with, fit in with, find one's feet in; N. Amer. acclimate.
2 *he adjusted the brakes after I found them inefficient*: **modify**, alter, regulate, tune, fine-tune, calibrate, balance; adapt, rearrange, change, rejig, rework, revamp, remodel, reshape, convert, transform, tailor, improve, enhance, customize; repair, fix, correct, rectify, make good, put in working order, overhaul, put right, set right, set to rights, standardize, normalize; informal jigger, tweak, twiddle, patch up, see to.

adjustable adjective *the pilots sit on adjustable seats*: **modifiable**, alterable, adaptable, convertible, variable, multiway, versatile, accommodating; movable, mobile.
▷ANTONYMS fixed, immovable.

adjustment noun **1** *new teachers face a challenging period of adjustment*: **adaptation**, adapting, accustoming, accommodation, accommodating, acclimatization, reconciliation, inurement, habituation, habituating, familiarization, acculturation, naturalization, assimilation, assimilating, harmonization; settling in, settling down; N. Amer. acclimation.
2 *the car will run on unleaded petrol with no adjustment*: **modification**, modifying, alteration, adaptation, regulation, regulating, rearrangement, change, converting, conversion; remodelling, revamping, restyling, reshaping, reconstruction, transformation, variation, customization, tailoring, refinement, refining; fixing, mending, repair, correction, correcting, amendment, amending, rectifying, overhauling, overhaul, improvement; informal jiggering, tweaking, twiddling, patching up.

ad lib verb *I never work from a script—I just ad lib the whole programme*: **improvise**, extemporize, speak impromptu, make it up as one goes along, think on one's feet, take it as it comes; informal speak off the cuff, speak off the top of one's head, play it by ear, busk it, wing it.
▶ adverb *she spoke ad lib*: **impromptu**, extempore, without preparation, without rehearsal, extemporaneously, spontaneously, offhand; Latin ad libitum; informal off the cuff, off the top of one's head, on the spur of the moment, just like that, at the drop of a hat.
▶ adjective *they gave a live, ad lib commentary as the film was shown*: **impromptu**, extempore, extemporaneous, extemporary, improvised, improvisational, improvisatory, improvisatorial, unprepared, unarranged, unplanned, unrehearsed, unscripted, unpremeditated, spontaneous, on-the-spot; informal **off-the-cuff**, spur-of-the-moment.
▷ANTONYMS planned.

administer verb **1** *the union is administered by a central executive*: **manage**, direct, control, operate, regulate, conduct, handle, run, orchestrate, organize, supervise, superintend, oversee, preside over, boss, be the boss of, govern, rule, lead, head, guide, steer, pilot; exercise control over, be in control of, be in charge of, be in command of, take care of, look after, be responsible for, be at the helm of, hold sway over; informal head up, call the shots, call the tune, pull the strings, run the show, be in the driving seat, be in the saddle.
2 *the lifeboat crew administered first aid to the fisherman | a gym shoe was used to administer punishment*: **dispense**, deliver, issue, give, provide, apply, discharge, allot, distribute, apportion, deal, hand out, mete out, measure out, dole out, disburse, bestow; inflict, impose, enforce, deal out, serve out, exact.

administration noun **1** *the administration of the army was divided between a number of bodies*: **management**, managing, direction, directing, command, commanding, control, controlling, charge, conduct, conducting, operation, regulation, regulating, handling, running, leadership, government, governing, superintendence, supervision, supervising, overseeing, oversight, orchestration, orchestrating, guidance, care; archaic regiment.
2 *the ministers had also been part of the previous Labour administration*: **government**, cabinet, ministry, regime, executive, authority, directorate, council, leadership, management; parliament, congress, senate; rule, term of office, incumbency; informal top brass.
3 *the administration of anti-inflammatory drugs | a framework for the administration of criminal justice*: **dispensation**, dispensing, delivering, issuing, giving, provision, providing, application, applying, discharge, allotment, distribution, apportionment, apportioning, dealing out, handing out, meting out, measuring out, doling out, disbursement, disbursing, bestowal; infliction, inflicting, imposition, imposing, enforcement, enforcing, exacting, execution, exercise, effectuation.

administrative adjective *he demonstrated his excellent administrative skills*: **managerial**, management, directorial, directing, executive, organizational, controlling, governmental, supervisory, regulatory; rare gubernatorial.

administrator noun *he became football's top administrator in 1973*: **manager**, director, managing director, executive, chief executive, controller, chair, chairperson, chairman, chairwoman, head, boss, chief, principal, official, leader, governor, premier, president, superintendent, supervisor, employer, proprietor; informal gaffer, kingpin, top dog, bigwig, numero uno, Mister Big, honcho, head honcho; N. Amer. informal big wheel.

admirable adjective *the player has done an admirable job for the team*: **commendable**, worthy of admiration, worthy of commendation, praiseworthy, laudable, estimable, meritorious, creditable, exemplary, exceptional, notable, honourable, worthy, deserving, respectable, worthwhile; excellent, good, sterling, superb, superlative, brilliant, outstanding, first-rate, first-class, second to none, of the first order, of the highest order, of the first water, supreme, prime, great, fine, masterly, marvellous, wonderful, magnificent; informal A1, wicked, stellar, super, splendiferous, top-notch, fab, ace, tip-top; Brit. informal smashing, brill, champion, grand; N. Amer. informal bully; Austral./NZ informal beaut; Brit. dated, informal top-hole; rare applaudable.
▷ANTONYMS deplorable, abominable.

admiration noun **1** *his patience and good nature commanded widespread admiration*: **commendation**, acclaim, applause, approbation, approval, appreciation, regard, high regard, respect, praise, esteem, veneration, adulation, extolment; compliments, tributes, accolades, plaudits, pats on the back; rare laudation.
▷ANTONYMS disgust.
2 *their garden was the admiration of the village*: **object of admiration**, **pride**, pride and joy, joy, wonder, delight, marvel, sensation.

admire verb **1** *she was admired for her cheerful efficiency*: **applaud**, praise, express admiration for, commend, approve of, express approval for, favour, look on with favour, think highly of, appreciate; **respect**, rate highly, hold in high regard, hold in high esteem, look up to, acclaim; compliment, speak highly of, put on a pedestal.
▷ANTONYMS disapprove of.
2 *Simon had admired her from afar for a long time*: **worship**, adore, love, cherish, dote on, be enamoured of, be infatuated with, be taken with, be attracted to, find attractive; idolize, lionize; informal carry a torch for, be mad about, be crazy about, be potty about, be wild about, have a crush on, have a thing about, have a pash on, have the hots for, be soft on, take a shine to; Brit. informal fancy.
▷ANTONYMS loathe.

admirer noun **1** *he was a great admirer of Churchill*: **fan**, enthusiast, devotee, addict, aficionado, supporter, adherent, follower, disciple, votary, fanatic, zealot; informal hanger-on, groupie.
2 *a handsome admirer from her Cambridge days*: **suitor**, wooer, worshipper, beau, sweetheart, lover, love, beloved, lady love, boyfriend, girlfriend, young man, young lady, man friend, lady friend, escort; catch, conquest; Italian inamorato, inamorata; informal fancy man, fancy woman, toy boy, sugar daddy; literary swain; archaic gallant, paramour, leman.

admissible adjective *an admissible claim for damages*: **allowable**, allowed, permissible, permitted, acceptable, passable, tolerable, satisfactory, justifiable, defensible, supportable, well founded, tenable, sound, sensible, reasonable; legitimate, lawful, legal, licit, within the law, above board, valid, recognized, sanctioned; informal OK, okay, legit, kosher, pukka, by the book.
▷ANTONYMS inadmissible.

admission noun **1** *membership entitles you to free admission | they had the necessary ability for admission to grammar school*: **admittance**, entry, entrance, right of entry, permission to enter, access, means of entry, ingress, entrée, acceptance.
2 *admission to the fête is fifty pence*: **entrance fee**, admission fee, entry charge, ticket.
3 *a written admission of liability for the accident*: **acknowledgement**, acceptance, recognition, concession, profession, expression, declaration, confession, revelation, disclosure, divulgence, avowal, claim, unbosoming, owning up; rare asseveration, divulgation.

admit verb **1** *he unlocked the door to admit her | he was admitted as a scholar to Winchester College*: **let in**, allow entry, permit entry, grant entrance to, give right of entry to, give access to, give admission to, accept, take in, usher in, show in, receive, welcome; take on, enrol, enlist, register, sign up.
▷ANTONYMS exclude, bar, expel.
2 *he admitted three offences of reckless driving | Paul admitted that he was angry with his father*: **acknowledge**, confess, reveal, make known, disclose, divulge, make public, avow, declare, profess, own up to, make a clean breast of, bring into the open, bring to light, give away, blurt out, leak; concede, accept, accede, grant, agree, allow, own, concur, assent, recognize, realize, be aware of, be conscious of, appreciate; informal get something off one's chest, spill the beans about, tell all about, blow the lid off, squeal about; Brit. informal blow the gaff on; archaic discover.
▷ANTONYMS deny, conceal.

admittance noun *they refused me admittance on the grounds that I wasn't a member*: **entry**, right of entry, permission to enter, admission, entrance, access, right of access, ingress, entrée, acceptance.
▷ANTONYMS exclusion.

admonish verb **1** *he was severely admonished by his father*: **reprimand**, rebuke, scold, reprove, upbraid, chastise, chide, censure, castigate, lambaste, berate, reproach, lecture, criticize, take to task, pull up, read the Riot Act to, give a piece of one's mind to, haul over the coals; informal tell

off, give someone a telling-off, dress down, give someone a dressing-down, bawl out, pitch into, lay into, lace into, blow up, give someone an earful, give someone a roasting, give someone a rocket, give someone a rollicking, rap over the knuckles, slap someone's wrist, send someone away with a flea in their ear, let someone have it, give someone hell; Brit. informal tick off, have a go at, carpet, tear someone off a strip, monster, give someone a mouthful, give someone what for, give someone some stick, give someone a wigging; N. Amer. informal chew out, ream out; Brit. vulgar slang bollock, give someone a bollocking; dated trim, rate, give someone a rating; rare reprehend, objurgate.
▷ANTONYMS praise.
2 *she admonished him to drink no more than one glass of wine*: **advise**, recommend, urge, caution, warn, counsel, exhort, implore, beseech, entreat, encourage, bid, enjoin, adjure, push, pressure.
▷ANTONYMS discourage.

admonition noun 1 *Palmerston sent him a blunt admonition over the mistake*: **reprimand**, rebuke, reproof, remonstrance, reproach, admonishment, stricture, lecture, criticism, recrimination, tirade, diatribe, philippic, harangue, attack; scolding, chastisement, castigation, upbraiding, berating, reproval, censure, condemnation; informal telling-off, dressing-down, talking-to, tongue-lashing, bashing, blast, rap, rap over the knuckles, slap on the wrist, flea in one's ear, earful, roasting, rollicking, caning, blowing-up; Brit. informal rocket, wigging, slating, ticking-off, carpeting; Austral./NZ informal serve; Brit. vulgar slang bollocking; dated rating.
▷ANTONYMS commendation, pat on the back, praise.
2 *the frequent admonitions of his anxious parents*: **exhortation**, warning, caution, caveat, piece of advice, admonishment, recommendation; injunction, monition, enjoinment, instruction, direction, suggestion, lesson, lecture, precept; advice, counsel, guidance, urging, encouragement, persuasion, pressure.

ado noun *she decided to take matters in hand without further ado*: **fuss**, trouble, bother, upset, agitation, commotion, stir, hubbub, confusion, excitement, tumult, disturbance, hurly-burly, uproar, flurry, to-do, palaver, rigmarole, brouhaha, furore; N. Amer. fuss and feathers; Indian tamasha; informal hassle, hoo-ha, ballyhoo, hoopla, rumpus, flap, tizz, tizzy, stew, song and dance, performance, pantomime; Brit. informal carry-on, kerfuffle.

adolescence noun *they spent their adolescence hanging out together*: **teenage years**, teens, youth, young adulthood, young days, early life; pubescence, puberty; rare juvenescence, juvenility.

adolescent noun *an awkward adolescent beset with self-doubt*: **teenager**, youngster, young person, young adult, young man, young woman, young lady, young one, youth, juvenile, minor; schoolboy, schoolgirl, boy, girl, lad, lass, stripling, fledgling, whippersnapper; Scottish & N. English bairn; informal teen, teeny-bopper, kid, young 'un, shaver; archaic hobbledehoy.
▷ANTONYMS adult; infant.
▶ adjective 1 *adolescent boys are more likely to join gangs*: **teenage**, teenaged, pubescent, youthful, young, juvenile; informal teen.
▷ANTONYMS adult.
2 *his colleagues have to cope with his adolescent mood swings*: **immature**, childish, babyish, infantile, juvenile, puerile, jejune, inane, silly, fatuous; undeveloped, unsophisticated, inexperienced, callow.
▷ANTONYMS mature.

adopt verb 1 *a republican constitution was adopted in 1971*: **embrace**, take on, acquire, affect, espouse, assume, appropriate, arrogate; approve, endorse, agree to, consent to, accede to, accept, ratify, validate, rubber-stamp, sanction, support, back, vote for; informal give something the go ahead, give something the green light, give something the thumbs up, OK, okay.
▷ANTONYMS abandon.
2 *the people adopted him as their patron saint*: **choose**, select, pick, pick out, vote for, elect, settle on, decide on, single out, plump for, opt for, name, nominate, designate, appoint.
▷ANTONYMS reject.

adoption noun 1 *the consultants recommended the adoption of a new housing policy*: **assumption**, assuming, taking on, acquiring, acquisition, affecting, affectation, espousal, advocacy, promotion, appropriation, arrogation; approval, endorsement, acceptance, ratification, validation, rubber-stamping, authorization, sanctioning, support, backing.
▷ANTONYMS abandonment.
2 *the election campaign will begin with the formal adoption of a candidate*: **selection**, choosing, choice, voting in, election, electing, naming, nominating, nomination, designation, designating, appointment, appointing.
▷ANTONYMS rejection.

adorable adjective *I have four adorable Siamese cats*: **lovable**, appealing, charming, cute, sweet, enchanting, bewitching, captivating, engaging, endearing, dear, darling, precious, delightful, lovely, beautiful, attractive, gorgeous, winsome, winning, fetching, pleasing; chocolate-box; Scottish & N. English bonny; dated taking.
▷ANTONYMS hateful.

adoration noun 1 *they regarded him with an almost breathless adoration*: **love**, devotion, care, fondness, warmth, affection; **admiration**, regard, high regard, awe, reverence, idolization, lionization, worship, hero-worship, adulation, deification.
2 *the Mass begins our day of prayer and adoration*: **worship**, worshipping, glory, glorification, glorifying, praise, praising, thanksgiving, homage, paying homage, exaltation, exalting, extolment, veneration, venerating, revering, reverence; rare laudation, lauding, magnification, magnifying.

adore verb 1 *the boy had lost the father he adored*: **love dearly**, love, be devoted to, dote on, care for, hold dear, cherish, treasure, prize, think the world of, set great store by; **admire**, hold in admiration, hold in high regard, regard highly, have a high opinion of, look up to, stand in awe of, revere, reverence, idolize, lionize, worship, deify; informal put on a pedestal.
▷ANTONYMS hate, loathe, detest.
2 *the people had come to pray and adore God*: **worship**, glorify, praise, revere, reverence, exalt, laud, extol, esteem, venerate, pay homage to, pay tribute to; archaic magnify.
3 *I adore oysters*: **like**, love, have a liking for, be fond of, be keen on, be partial to, have a taste for, have a weakness for, enjoy, delight in, revel in, take pleasure in, relish, savour, rate highly, regard highly; informal be crazy about, be wild about, be potty about, have a thing about, get a kick out of, get a charge out of, get a buzz from, get a thrill from, be hooked on, go a bundle on; N. Amer. informal be nutso about; Austral./NZ informal be shook on.
▷ANTONYMS hate, loathe, detest.

adorn verb *the public rooms are adorned with tapestries*: **embellish**, decorate, furnish, ornament, add ornament to, enhance; beautify, prettify, grace, enrich, bedeck, deck (out), dress (up), trick out, trim, swathe, wreathe, festoon, garland, array, garnish, emblazon, gild, set off; informal get up, do up, do out; literary bejewel, bedizen, caparison, furbelow.
▷ANTONYMS strip; disfigure.

adornment noun *her drawings needed some adornment*: **embellishment**, embellishing, decorating, decoration, ornamentation, ornament, enhancement, enhancing; beautification, beatifying, prettification, prettifying, dressing up, trimming, emblazoning, elaboration, enrichment, garnishing, gilding; frills, accessories, trimmings, finishing touches; rare fallalery.

adrift adjective 1 *the pipe of my breathing apparatus came adrift*: **loose**, free, astray; detached, unsecured, unhitched, unfastened, untied, untethered, unknotted, undone.
2 *their empty boat was spotted adrift in the water*: **drifting**, unmoored, unanchored.
3 *he was adrift in a strange country*: **lost**, off course, off track, off the right track, having lost one's bearings, disorientated, disoriented, confused, bewildered, (all) at sea; unsettled, drifting, rootless, directionless, aimless, purposeless, without purpose, without goal, at a loose end.
4 Brit. informal *his instincts were not entirely adrift*: **wrong**, mistaken, inaccurate, wide of the mark, off target, awry, amiss, astray, off course, off the right track.

adroit adjective *an adroit shot from a bunker enabled him to finish well | he showed himself to be an adroit politician*: **skilful**, adept, dexterous, deft, agile, nimble, nimble-fingered, handy; able, capable, competent, skilled, expert, masterly, masterful, master, practised, polished, slick, proficient, accomplished, gifted, talented, peerless; quick-witted, quick-thinking, quick, clever, intelligent, brilliant, bright, smart, sharp, cunning, artful, wily, resourceful, astute, shrewd, canny, ingenious, inventive; informal nifty, nippy, crack, mean, wicked, wizard, demon, ace, A1, on the ball, savvy; N. Amer. informal crackerjack; archaic compleat, rathe.
▷ANTONYMS clumsy, incompetent.

adroitness noun *there in an undeniable adroitness in his economic plan*: **skill**, skilfulness, prowess, expertise, expertness, adeptness, handiness, nimbleness, dexterity, dexterousness, deftness; ability, capability, competence, competency, mastery, virtuosity, proficiency, accomplishment, artistry, art, knack, bent, faculty, facility, aptitude, flair, finesse, talent, gift, giftedness; quick-wittedness, cleverness, intelligence, wisdom, brilliance, brightness, sharpness, cunning, artfulness, astuteness, diplomacy, discretion, shrewdness, resourcefulness, ingenuity, inventiveness, imagination, imaginativeness; French savoir faire; informal niftiness, nippiness, know-how, savvy.
▷ANTONYMS clumsiness; incompetence.

adulation noun *he is remarkably unspoilt by all the adulation he has received*: **hero-worship**, worship, admiration, admiring, high regard, respect, lionization, lionizing, idolization, idolizing, veneration, awe, devotion, adoration, exaltation, honour, homage, glorification, glory, praise, praising, commendation, flattery, applause; blandishments, compliments, tributes, accolades, plaudits, eulogies, pats on the back; rare laudation, eulogiums, magnification, magnifying.

adulatory adjective *he wrote back to Lewis in adulatory terms*: **flattering**, complimentary, highly favourable, commendatory, enthusiastic, glowing, appreciative, praising, worshipping, worshipful, reverential, lionizing, blandishing, acclamatory, rhapsodic, eulogistic, laudatory, fulsome; honeyed, sugary, saccharine, cloying; nauseating, ingratiating, obsequious, unctuous, sycophantic, servile, fawning; informal bootlicking, smarmy, rave;

rare encomiastic, encomiastical.
▷ANTONYMS disparaging, unflattering.

adult adjective 1 *the adult population of Great Britain*: **mature**, grown-up, fully grown, full-grown, fully developed, fully fledged, of age, having reached one's majority; in one's prime, in full bloom.
▷ANTONYMS infant, juvenile.
2 *an adult movie*: **sexually explicit**, obscene, pornographic, hard-core, soft-core, lewd, smutty, dirty, filthy, vulgar, crude, rude, racy, risqué, ribald, naughty, arousing, earthy, Rabelaisian, erotic, carnal, sensual, sexy, suggestive, titillating, spicy, raw, taboo, off colour, indecent, improper; informal porn, porno, blue, raunchy, steamy, X-rated, full-frontal, skin; Brit. informal fruity, saucy, near the knuckle, near the bone; N. Amer. informal gamy; rare rank, ithyphallic, Fescennine, Cyprian.
▷ANTONYMS family.
▶ noun *the tent is just large enough for three adults*: **grown person**, grown man, grown woman, grown-up person, grown-up, mature person, mature man, mature woman, person of mature age; man, woman, gentleman, lady.

adulterate verb *the brewer was accused of adulterating his beer*: **make impure**, degrade, debase, spoil, taint, defile, contaminate, pollute, foul, sully; doctor, tamper with, mix, lace, dilute, water down, thin out, weaken; bastardize, corrupt; informal cut, spike, dope; rare vitiate.
▷ANTONYMS refine.

adulterer noun *an adulterer cheating with someone else's wife*: **philanderer**, deceiver, womanizer, ladies' man, playboy, Don Juan, Casanova, Lothario, Romeo, seducer, libertine, rake, reprobate, wanton, profligate, lecher, debauchee, sinner; informal cheat, love cheat, love rat, skirt-chaser, ladykiller, lech, goat, wolf, stud; dated gay dog, rip, blood; rare fornicator, rakehell, dissolute.

adulterous adjective *British women are the most adulterous in Europe | an adulterous relationship*: **unfaithful**, faithless, disloyal, untrue, inconstant, fickle, flighty, unreliable, untrustworthy, false, false-hearted, deceiving, deceitful, treacherous, traitorous; extramarital; informal cheating, two-timing.
▷ANTONYMS faithful.

adultery noun *she divorced me because of my adultery*: **unfaithfulness**, infidelity, falseness, disloyalty, unchastity, cuckoldry, extramarital sex, extramarital relations; affair, liaison, intrigue, amour, entanglement, flirtation; informal cheating, two-timing, fooling around, playing around, playing the field, carryings-on, hanky-panky, a bit on the side; formal fornication.
▷ANTONYMS faithfulness, fidelity.

advance verb 1 *the battalion advanced on Rawlinson's orders | the tide was advancing*: **move forward**, proceed, move along, press on, push on, push forward, make progress, make headway, forge on, forge ahead, gain ground, approach, come closer, move closer, move nearer, draw nearer, near; dated draw nigh.
▷ANTONYMS retreat.
2 *the court may advance the date of the hearing*: **bring forward**, put forward, move forward, make earlier.
▷ANTONYMS postpone.
3 *their firm was to be advanced at the expense of others*: **promote**, further, forward, help, aid, assist, facilitate, boost, strengthen, improve, make better, benefit, foster, cultivate, encourage, support, back.
▷ANTONYMS impede, hinder.
4 *our technology has advanced in the last few years*: **progress**, make progress, make headway, develop, improve, become better, thrive, flourish, prosper, mature; evolve, make strides, move forward (in leaps and bounds), move ahead, get ahead; informal go places, get somewhere.
5 *they advanced a claim of imperial sovereignty*: **put forward**, present, come up with, submit, suggest, propose, introduce, put up, offer, proffer, adduce, moot.
▷ANTONYMS retract.
6 *he had inadequate funds but a relative advanced him some money*: **lend**, loan, credit, pay in advance, supply on credit; pay out, put up, come up with, contribute, give, donate, hand over; informal dish out, shell out, fork out, cough up; Brit. informal sub.
▷ANTONYMS borrow.
7 dated *they apologized for advancing the subscription to one guinea per copy*. See **increase** (sense 2 of the verb).
▶ noun 1 *alarm over the advance of the aggressors was spreading*: **progress**, headway, moving forward, forward movement; approach, nearing, coming, arrival.
2 *the treatment would be a significant medical advance | the rapid post-war advance of science*: **breakthrough**, **development**, step forward, step in the right direction, leap, quantum leap, find, finding, discovery, invention, success; headway, progress, advancement, evolution, improvement, betterment, furtherance.
3 *the bank was engaged in the task of restraining the pound's advance*: **increase**, rise, upturn, upsurge, upswing, growth, boom, boost, elevation, escalation, augmentation; informal hike.
4 *the writer is going to be given a huge advance*: **down payment**, advance against royalty, deposit, retainer, prepayment, front money, money up front.
5 (usually **advances**) *my tutor made unwelcome sexual advances to me in his office*: **sexual approaches**, overtures, moves; a pass, proposal, proposition, offer, suggestion, appeal; informal come-on.
□ **in advance** *ski equipment may be hired in advance*: **beforehand**, before, ahead of time, earlier, previously, in readiness.
▶ adjective 1 *an advance party of settlers*: **preliminary**, leading, forward, foremost, at the fore, sent (on) ahead, first, exploratory, explorative, pilot, vanguard, test, trial.
2 *the new weather monitor gives plenty of advance warning*: **early**, previous, prior, beforehand.

advanced adjective 1 *advanced manufacturing techniques*: **state-of-the-art**, new, modern, up to date, up to the minute, the newest, the latest, recently developed, newly discovered, newfangled, ultra-modern, futuristic; **progressive**, forward, highly developed, avant-garde, ahead of the times, pioneering, groundbreaking, trailblazing, revolutionary, innovatory; sophisticated, complex, complicated, elaborate, intricate, ingenious; informal flash, snazzy, nifty; rare new-fashioned.
▷ANTONYMS primitive, backward.
2 *there were 14,000 students on advanced courses*: **higher-level**, higher, tertiary, third-level.
▷ANTONYMS foundation, elementary.

advancement noun 1 *the company has benefited greatly from the advancement of computer technology*: **development**, progress, evolution, growth, improvement, advance, furtherance, forwarding, expansion, extension, spread; headway.
2 *employees must be offered appropriate opportunities for advancement*: **promotion**, preferment, career development, elevation, upgrading, being upgraded, progress, improvement, betterment, growth, rise, moving up; a step up the ladder, a step up, a move up; aggrandizement; informal a kick upstairs.

advantage noun 1 *the advantages of belonging to a union*: **benefit**, value, reward, merit, good point, strong point, asset, plus, bonus, boon, blessing, virtue, privilege, perk, fringe benefit, additional benefit, added extra; attraction, desirability, beauty, usefulness, helpfulness, convenience, advantageousness, expedience, expediency, profit, profitability, advisability; formal perquisite.
▷ANTONYMS disadvantage, drawback, handicap.
2 *they appeared to be gaining the advantage over their opponents*: **upper hand**, edge, lead, head, whip hand, trump card; **superiority**, dominance, ascendancy, supremacy, primacy, precedence, power, mastery, control, sway, authority; N. Amer. informal the catbird seat; Austral./NZ informal the box seat.
3 *they exploit natural resources to their own advantage | there is no advantage to be gained from delaying the process*: **benefit**, profit, gain, good, interest, welfare, well-being, enjoyment, satisfaction, comfort, ease, convenience; help, aid, assistance, use, utility, service, purpose, effect, object, reason, worth; informal mileage, percentage.
▷ANTONYMS detriment.
□ **take advantage of 1** *you are trying to take advantage of my staff and my friends*: **exploit**, abuse, impose on, prey on, play on, misuse, ill-treat, bleed, suck dry, squeeze, wring, enslave, treat unfairly, withhold rights from; manipulate, cheat, swindle, fleece, victimize, live off the backs of; informal walk (all) over, take for a ride, put one over on, cash in on, rip off.
2 *we encourage farmers to take advantage of this free service*: **make use of**, utilize, put to use, use, use to good advantage, turn/put to good use, make the most of, capitalize on, benefit from, turn to account, draw on; profit from/by, make capital out of; informal cash in on, milk.

advantageous adjective 1 *at the end of the war, farmers were in a relatively advantageous position*: **superior**, dominant, powerful, important, commanding, excellent, good, fine, fortunate, lucky, privileged, favourable, preferable, preferred, favoured, more desirable, most desirable.
▷ANTONYMS inferior.
2 *the arrangement is advantageous to both sides*: **beneficial**, of benefit, helpful, of assistance, useful, of use, valuable, of value, of service, profitable, fruitful, rewarding, gainful, lucrative; suitable, convenient, expedient, appropriate, fitting, favourable, auspicious, propitious, fortuitous, lucky; in everyone's interests.
▷ANTONYMS disadvantageous, detrimental.

advent noun *operative techniques greatly improved with the advent of anaesthesia | the inevitable advent of his death*: **arrival**, appearance, emergence, materialization, surfacing, occurrence, dawn, origin, birth, rise, development; approach, coming, looming, nearing, advance.
▷ANTONYMS departure, disappearance.

adventitious adjective 1 *he felt that the conversation was not entirely adventitious*: **unplanned**, unpremeditated, accidental, unintentional, unintended, unexpected, unforeseen, involuntary, chance, fortuitous, serendipitous, coincidental, casual, random, fluky, unlooked-for, unhoped-for, not bargained for, out of the blue, without warning; rare aleatory.
▷ANTONYMS planned.

a

2 *some rural parishes recorded high adventitious populations*: **foreign**, alien, non-native, outside, external, extraneous, extrinsic.
▷ANTONYMS native, indigenous.

adventure noun **1** *stories of astonishing miracles and heroic adventures*: **exploit**, escapade, deed, feat, trial, experience, incident, occurrence, event, happening, episode, affair; stunt, caper, romp, antic; quest, crusade, campaign, venture.
2 *they set off in search of adventure*: **excitement**, exciting experience, thrill, stimulation; risk, riskiness, danger, dangerousness, hazard, hazardousness, peril, perilousness, uncertainty, precariousness; informal a kick, a buzz; N. Amer. informal a charge.

adventurer noun *a tough adventurer who had sailed around the world*: **daredevil**, seeker of adventures, hero, heroine, swashbuckler, knight errant, crusader, venturer, traveller, voyager, wanderer; buccaneer, mercenary, soldier of fortune; Argonaut, Ulysses; French beau sabreur.

adventurous adjective **1** *as a child he was always adventurous*: **daring**, daredevil, intrepid, venturesome, bold, audacious, fearless, brave, unafraid, unshrinking, undaunted, dauntless, valiant, valorous, heroic, dashing; confident, enterprising; rash, reckless, heedless; informal gutsy, spunky, peppy, pushy; rare adventuresome, venturous.
▷ANTONYMS cautious, unadventurous.
2 *they needed someone to finance their more adventurous activities*: **risky**, dangerous, perilous, hazardous, precarious, uncertain.
▷ANTONYMS tame, unadventurous.

adversary noun *he parried the strokes of his adversary with almost contemptuous ease*: **opponent**, rival, enemy, foe, antagonist, combatant, challenger, contender, competitor, opposer, fellow contestant; opposition, competition; rare corrival.
▷ANTONYMS ally, supporter.

adverse adjective **1** *the plane crashed into a lake in adverse weather conditions*: **unfavourable**, disadvantageous, inauspicious, unpropitious, unfortunate, unlucky, untimely, untoward; disagreeable, unpleasant, bad, poor, terrible, dreadful, dire, wretched, nasty, hostile.
▷ANTONYMS favourable.
2 *the company knew of the drug's adverse side effects*: **harmful**, dangerous, injurious, detrimental, hurtful, deleterious, destructive, pernicious, disadvantageous, unfavourable, unfortunate, unhealthy.
▷ANTONYMS beneficial.
3 *the military feared an adverse response from the American public*: **hostile**, **unfavourable**, antagonistic, unfriendly, ill-disposed, negative, opposing, opposed, contrary, dissenting, inimical, antipathetic, at odds.
▷ANTONYMS positive, friendly.

adversity noun *they remain steadfast in the face of adversity | it helps to laugh about life's adversities*: **misfortune**, ill luck, bad luck, trouble, difficulty, hardship, distress, disaster, misadventure, suffering, affliction, sorrow, misery, heartbreak, heartache, wretchedness, tribulation, woe, pain, trauma, torment, torture; mishap, stroke of ill luck, stroke of bad luck, accident, shock, upset, reverse, reversal, reversal of fortune, setback, crisis, catastrophe, tragedy, calamity, trial, cross, burden, blow, buffet, vicissitude; hard times, dire straits, trials and tribulations; informal hell, hell on earth, hassle, stress; literary dolour, travails.
▷ANTONYMS good times.

advertise verb *the booklets are designed to advertise the hotel*: **publicize**, make public, make known, give publicity to, bill, post, announce, broadcast, proclaim, trumpet, shout from the rooftops, give notice of, call attention to, promulgate; promote, market, merchandise, peddle, display, tout, build up, beat/bang the drum for, trail, trailer; informal push, plug, hype, hype up, give a plug to, puff, give a puff to, boost, flog; N. Amer. informal ballyhoo, flack, huckster, blurb; Austral./NZ informal spruik.

advertisement noun **1** *an advertisement for toothpaste | she placed an advertisement in a Canadian newspaper*: **notice**, announcement, bulletin; **commercial**, promotion, blurb, write-up, display; poster, leaflet, pamphlet, flyer, bill, handbill, handout, circular, brochure, sign, placard; N. Amer. folder, dodger; French affiche; informal ad, push, plug, puff, bumf; Brit. informal advert.
2 *they showed no desire for advertisement of their intellectual achievements*: **publicizing**, publicization, advertising, promotion, touting, broadcasting, declaration, notification, promulgation; informal plugging, pushing, puffing; literary blazoning.

advice noun *the charity offers support and advice to people with mental illness*: **guidance**, advising, counselling, counsel, help, direction, instruction, information, enlightenment; recommendations, guidelines, suggestions, hints, tips, pointers, ideas, opinions, views, facts, data; informal info, gen, dope, the low-down, the inside story.

advisability noun *the advisability of sticking to a low-fat diet*: **preferability**, preferableness, desirability, wisdom, soundness, prudence, sensibleness, sense, appropriateness, aptness, fitness, suitability, judiciousness, expediency, expedience, helpfulness, effectiveness, advantageousness, advantage, benefit, merit, value, profit, profitability, gain.

advisable adjective *it is advisable to book a table in advance*: **wise**, desirable, preferable, well, best, sensible, commonsensical, sound, prudent, proper, appropriate, apt, suitable, fitting, judicious, recommended, recommendable, suggested, expedient, politic, helpful, useful, effective, advantageous, beneficial, valuable, profitable, gainful; in one's (best) interests.
▷ANTONYMS inadvisable, unwise.

advise verb **1** *her grandmother advised her about marriage*: **counsel**, give counsel, give counselling, give guidance, guide, make recommendations, offer suggestions, offer opinions, give hints, give tips, give pointers, direct, give direction(s), instruct, give instruction, illuminate, educate.
2 *he goes on to advise an effective means of achieving this goal*: **advocate**, suggest, recommend, commend, urge, admonish, bid, encourage, enjoin, push for, press for, subscribe to, endorse, champion, back, support, speak for, call for, campaign for, argue for, promote, prompt.
3 *club members will be **advised of** the outcome of this meeting*: **inform**, notify, give notice, apprise, brief, give intelligence, send word, keep posted, warn, forewarn; acquaint with, make familiar with, make known to, let know, enlighten as to, give information about, keep up to date with, update about; informal give the gen, give the low-down, give the rundown, fill in on, gen up on, clue up about, clue in on, put in the picture about, put wise about, keep up to speed with.

adviser noun *he is the president's personal adviser*: **counsellor**, mentor, guide, consultant, consultee, confidant, confidante, guide, right hand man, right hand woman, aide, helper; instructor, coach, trainer, teacher, tutor, guru; Italian consigliere; informal main man; N. Amer. informal Dutch uncle.

advisory adjective *she agreed to serve the central committee in an advisory role*: **consultative**, consultatory, consulting, advising, counselling, recommendatory, recommending, assisting, helping, aiding.
▷ANTONYMS executive.

advocacy noun *he incurred opprobrium for his **advocacy of** contraception*: **support for**, argument for, arguing for, calling for, pushing for, pressing for; defence, espousal, espousing, approval, approving, endorsement, endorsing, recommendation, recommending, advising in favour, backing, supporting, favouring, promotion, promoting, championship, championing, sanctioning, acceptance; N. Amer. informal boosterism.

advocate noun **1** *she was a powerful **advocate of** children's rights*: **champion**, upholder, supporter, backer, promoter, proponent, exponent, protector, patron; spokesman for, spokeswoman for, spokesperson for, speaker for, campaigner for, fighter for, battler for, crusader for; missionary, reformer, pioneer, pleader, propagandist, apostle, apologist; N. Amer. booster; informal plugger.
▷ANTONYMS critic.
2 Scottish Law *he studied law and became an advocate at twenty-one*: **barrister**, lawyer, counsel, counsellor, professional pleader, legal practitioner; N. Amer. attorney; N. Amer. & Irish counsellor-at-law; informal brief.
▶verb *heart disease specialists advocate a diet low in cholesterol*: **recommend**, prescribe, commend, advise, favour, approve of, support, back, uphold, subscribe to, champion, campaign on behalf of, stand up for, speak for, argue for, plead for, press for, lobby for, urge, promote, espouse, endorse, sanction, vouch for; informal plug, push.
▷ANTONYMS reject.

aegis noun *there are many societies run under the aegis of the Students' Union*: **patronage**, sponsorship, backing, protection, shelter, umbrella, charge, keeping, care, supervision, guidance, guardianship, trusteeship, support, agency, safeguarding, defence, protectorship, championship, aid, assistance, guaranty; auspices; archaic ward.

aeon noun *the age of piracy was stamped out aeons ago.* See **age** (sense 4 of the noun).

aesthetic adjective *the law applies to both functional and aesthetic objects*: **decorative**, ornamental, graceful, elegant, exquisite, beautiful, attractive, pleasing, lovely, stylish, artistic, tasteful, in good taste.

affability noun *a caring doctor blessed with a natural ease and affability*: **friendliness**, amiability, geniality, congeniality, cordiality, warmth, warmness, pleasantness, niceness, charm, agreeableness, good humour, good nature, kindliness, kindness, courtesy, courteousness, civility, graciousness, approachability, approachableness, accessibility, amenability, sociability, gregariousness, conviviality, clubbability, neighbourliness, hospitable manner, obliging nature, easy-going manner, informality, lack of reserve, naturalness, relaxedness, ease, easiness; informal chumminess, palliness; N. Amer. informal clubbiness.
▷ANTONYMS unfriendliness.

affable adjective *Murray was in a most affable mood*: **friendly**, amiable, genial, congenial, cordial, warm, pleasant, pleasing, nice, likeable, personable, charming, agreeable, sympathetic, benevolent, benign, good-humoured, good-natured, kindly, kind, courteous, civil, gracious, approachable, accessible, amenable, sociable, outgoing, gregarious, convivial, jovial, clubbable, comradely, neighbourly, welcoming, hospitable, obliging, easy-going, informal, open, communicative, unreserved, uninhibited, natural, relaxed, easy; informal chummy, pally; Brit.

informal matey, decent; N. Amer. informal clubby, buddy-buddy; rare conversable.
▷ANTONYMS unfriendly, prickly.

affair noun 1 *what my mum does in her spare time is her affair*: **business**, concern, matter, responsibility, province, preserve, interest; problem, worry, lookout; informal pigeon, funeral, headache, baby, bailiwick.
2 (**affairs**) *they aren't worried about their financial affairs*: **transactions**, concerns, matters, activities, dealings, undertakings, ventures, proceedings; business, field, sphere; informal goings-on, doings.
3 *this is a truly shocking affair*: **event**, incident, happening, occurrence, phenomenon, eventuality, episode, interlude, circumstance, set of circumstances, adventure, experience, case, matter, business, thing; proceedings.
4 *I heard there were to be fireworks—it'll be a grand affair*: **party**, celebration, function, reception, gathering, soirée, event, social event, occasion, social occasion; informal do, rave, bash, get-together, blowout; Brit. informal rave-up, thrash, knees-up, beanfeast, beano, bunfight, jolly.
5 *the director and his secretary were having an affair*: **relationship**, love affair, romance, fling, flirtation, dalliance, liaison, entanglement, romantic entanglement, involvement, attachment, affair of the heart, intrigue; relations; French affaire, affaire de/du cœur, amour; informal hanky-panky; Brit. informal carry-on.

affect[1] verb 1 *the climate was likely to be affected by greenhouse gas emissions*: **influence**, exert influence on, have an effect on, act on, work on, condition, touch, have an impact on, impact on, take hold of, attack, infect, strike, strike at, hit; change, alter, modify, transform, form, shape, control, govern, determine, decide, guide, sway, bias.
▷ANTONYMS be unaffected.
2 *she had been deeply affected by her parents' divorce*: **upset**, trouble, hit hard, overwhelm, devastate, damage, hurt, pain, grieve, sadden, distress, disturb, perturb, agitate, shake, shake up, stir; move, touch, tug at someone's heartstrings; make an impression on; informal knock for six, knock back, bowl over, throw, faze, get to.
▷ANTONYMS be unaffected, be indifferent to.

affect[2] verb 1 *he deliberately affected a republican stance*: **assume**, put on, take on, adopt, like, have a liking for, embrace, espouse.
2 *she affected a small frown of concentration*: **pretend**, feign, fake, counterfeit, sham, simulate, fabricate, give the appearance of, make a show of, make a pretence of, play at, go through the motions of; informal put on; N. Amer. informal make like.

Easily confused words **affect or effect?**

Affect and **effect** are quite different in meaning, though frequently confused. *Affect* is primarily a verb meaning either 'make a difference to', as in *their gender need not affect their career* (**affect**[1]), or 'pretend to have or feel', as in *I affected a supreme unconcern* (**affect**[2]). *Effect*, on the other hand, is commonly used both as a noun and as a verb, meaning 'something brought about' as a noun (*move the cursor until you get the effect you want*) or 'bring about (a result)' as a verb (*growth in the economy can only be effected by stringent economic controls*).

affectation noun 1 *she has no affectation | the affectations of a prima donna*: **pretension**, pretentiousness, affectedness, artificiality, insincerity, posturing, posing, pretence, ostentation, grandiosity, snobbery, superciliousness; airs, airs and graces, pretensions; informal snootiness, uppishness, humbug; Brit. informal side.
▷ANTONYMS naturalness.
2 *nothing would shake his affectation of calm*: **facade**, front, show, appearance, false display, pretence, simulation, posture, pose, sham, fake, act, masquerade, charade, mask, cloak, veil, veneer, guise; make-believe, play-acting, feigning, shamming.

affected adjective *he was talking in the rather affected boom he used with strangers*: **pretentious**, high-flown, ostentatious, pompous, grandiose, over-elaborate, overblown, overworked, overdone; contrived, forced, laboured, strained, stiff, posed, stagy, studied, mannered, hollow, insincere, unconvincing; artificial, unnatural, assumed, pretended, feigned, false, fake, faked, counterfeit, sham, simulated, spurious, pseudo, mock, imitation; informal la-di-da, hoity-toity, highfalutin, fancy-pants, posey, pseud, phoney, pretend, put on; Brit. informal poncey, posh, toffee-nosed.
▷ANTONYMS natural, unpretentious, genuine.

affecting adjective *their fumbling onstage shyness is oddly affecting*: **touching**, moving, emotive, powerful, stirring, impressive, telling, soul-stirring, uplifting, heart-warming; poignant, pathetic, pitiful, piteous, plaintive, emotional, tear-jerking, heart-rending, heartbreaking, disturbing, distressing, upsetting, saddening, sad, painful, agonizing, harrowing, tragic, haunting.
▷ANTONYMS unaffecting, unmoving.

Choose the right word **affecting, moving, touching**

See **moving**.

affection noun *they greeted each other with obvious affection*: **fondness**, love, liking, endearment, feeling, sentiment, tenderness, warmth, warmness, devotion, care; caring, attentiveness, closeness, attachment, affinity, friendliness, friendship, intimacy, familiarity; amity, favour, regard, respect, admiration; warm feelings.

affectionate adjective *an affectionate hug | Thomas is such an affectionate child*: **loving**, fond, adoring, devoted, caring, doting, tender, warm, warm-hearted, big-hearted, soft-centred, soft-hearted, soft, unselfish, kind, kind-hearted, kindly, comforting; sympathetic, solicitous, supportive, attentive, friendly, demonstrative, cuddly, amicable, cordial, welcoming, good-natured; brotherly, sisterly, motherly, fatherly, maternal, paternal, maternalistic, paternalistic; informal touchy-feely, lovey-dovey, chummy, pally; Brit. informal matey; N. Amer. informal buddy-buddy.
▷ANTONYMS cold, unfeeling.

affianced adjective *Edward was affianced to Lady Eleanor*. See **engaged** (sense 2).

affiliate verb *the college is **affiliated with** the University of Wisconsin | the society is not **affiliated to** any political party*: **associate with**, be in league with, unite with, combine with, join with, join up with, join forces with, ally with, form an alliance with, align with, amalgamate with, merge with, coalesce with, federate with, confederate with, form a federation with, form a confederation with, team up with, band together with, cooperate with; **annex to**, attach to, yoke to, incorporate into, integrate into.

affiliated adjective *the committee comprised two delegates from each affiliated club*: **associated**, allied, related, integrated, amalgamated, incorporated, federated, confederated, unified, connected, linked, joined, bound, belonging; in league, in partnership.

affiliation noun *it rejected affiliation to the current left-wing parties | an economist with no party political affiliation*: **annexing**, attaching, connecting, joining, bonding, uniting, combining, associating, aligning, allying, amalgamation, amalgamating, merging, incorporation, incorporating, integration, integrating, federating, federation, confederating, confederation, coupling, fusion; connection, relationship, fellowship, partnership, association, coalition, union, alliance, alignment, attachment, link, bond, tie, yoke; communication, rapport, sympathy, cooperation, collaboration, belonging; rare consociation.

affinity noun 1 *she has a natural **affinity with** animals and birds*: **empathy**, rapport, sympathy, accord, harmony, like-mindedness; closeness to, fellow feeling for, understanding of; **liking for**, fondness for, inclination towards, partiality for, penchant for, predilection towards, attraction towards; informal chemistry.
▷ANTONYMS dislike, aversion.
2 *there is a semantic affinity between the two words*: **similarity**, resemblance, likeness, kinship; correspondence, relationship, association, link, analogy, similitude, agreement, compatibility, congruity, parallelism, consonance; identity, identicalness, uniformity, equivalence.
▷ANTONYMS dissimilitude.
3 *despite their different backgrounds, an affinity grew and developed*: **relationship**, bond, connection, propinquity.
▷ANTONYMS antipathy; blood relationship.

affirm verb 1 *he affirmed that they would lend military assistance*: **declare**, state, assert, aver, proclaim, pronounce, attest, swear, avow, vow, guarantee, promise, certify, pledge, give one's word, give an undertaking; rare asseverate.
▷ANTONYMS deny.
2 *the charter affirmed the right of national minorities to use their own language*: **uphold**, support, defend, maintain, confirm, ratify, endorse, approve (of), agree to, consent to, assent to, sanction.

affirmation noun 1 *an affirmation of faith*: **assertion**, declaration, statement, proclamation, pronouncement, attestation, assurance; oath, vow, swearing, avowal, guarantee, promise, certification, pledge; deposition; rare asseveration, averment.
▷ANTONYMS denial, refutation.
2 *the poem ends with an affirmation of pastoral values*: **confirmation**, ratification, endorsement, defence.

affirmative adjective *an affirmative answer*: **positive**, assenting, consenting, agreeing, concurring, corroborative, favourable, approving, encouraging, supportive, in the affirmative.
▷ANTONYMS dissenting, negative.
▶ noun *Penelope took his grunt as an affirmative*: **agreement**, acceptance, approval, confirmation, assent, ratification, acquiescence, concurrence; OK, yes.
▷ANTONYMS disagreement.

affix verb 1 *he affixed a stamp to the envelope*: **attach**, stick, fasten, bind, fix, post, secure, join, connect, couple; clip, tack, pin; glue, paste, gum, tape; trademark Sellotape.
▷ANTONYMS detach, remove.
2 formal *affix your signature to the document*: **append**, add, add on, attach.

afflict verb *he was afflicted with chilblains*: **trouble**, bother, burden, distress, cause trouble to, cause suffering to, beset, harass, worry, oppress,

a

annoy, vex, irritate, exasperate, strain, stress, tax; torment, plague, blight, bedevil, pursue, rack, smite, curse, harrow, grip, visit, take; rare discommode, ail.
▷ANTONYMS comfort.

affliction noun **1** *the herb is reputed to cure a variety of afflictions*: **disorder**, disease, malady, complaint, ailment, illness, indisposition, scourge, plague, trouble, menace, evil, visitation.
2 *he bore his affliction with great dignity*: **suffering**, distress, pain, trouble, misery, wretchedness, hardship, misfortune, adversity, sorrow, torment, tribulation, woe, cross to bear, thorn in one's flesh/side; bane, trial, calamity, ordeal; (**afflictions**) ills.

affluence noun *the affluence of the higher social classes*: **wealth**, prosperity, opulence, fortune, richness, luxury, plenty; riches, money, cash, lucre, resources, assets, possessions, property, substance, means.
▷ANTONYMS poverty.

affluent adjective *a residence in the affluent part of Montreal*: **wealthy**, rich, prosperous, opulent, well off, moneyed, with deep pockets, well-to-do, comfortable; propertied, substantial, of means, of substance, with deep pockets, in clover, plutocratic; N. Amer. silk-stocking; informal well heeled, rolling in it/money, in the money, made of money, filthy rich, stinking rich, loaded, flush, on easy street, quids in, worth a packet/bundle.
▷ANTONYMS poor, impoverished.

afford verb **1** *they cannot afford a holiday this year*: **pay for**, bear/meet the expense of, spare the price of, have the money for, be rich enough for, have the wherewithal for; run to, stretch to, manage.
2 *we can no longer afford the luxury of complacency*: **bear**, sustain, stand, carry; allow oneself.
3 *this highway affords stunning views of California's coastline*: **provide**, supply, present, purvey, make available, offer, give, impart, bestow, furnish, render, grant, yield, produce, bear.

affray noun *his men became involved in a violent affray with a band of archers*: **fight**, brawl, battle, engagement, encounter, confrontation, melee, clash, skirmish, scuffle, tussle, fracas, altercation; disturbance, commotion, breach of the peace, riot; informal scrap, dust-up, punch-up, set-to, shindy, shindig, free-for-all.

affront noun *the paintings, in his view, were an affront to public morality*: **insult**, offence, indignity, slight, snub, slur, aspersion, provocation, injury, put down, humiliation; outrage, atrocity, scandal, injustice, abuse, desecration, violation; informal slap in the face, kick in the teeth.
▷ANTONYMS compliment.
▸ verb *she was affronted by his familiarity*: **insult**, offend, outrage, mortify, provoke, slight, hurt, pique, wound, put out, irk, displease, distress, bother, rankle, needle, vex, gall, scandalize, disgust, disgruntle, put someone's back up, ruffle someone's feathers, make someone's hackles rise, raise someone's hackles.
▷ANTONYMS compliment.

aficionado noun *an aficionado of fine wines*: **connoisseur**, expert, authority, specialist, pundit, one of the cognoscenti, cognoscente, devotee, appreciator, fan, fanatic, savant; enthusiast, lover, addict; informal buff, freak, nut, fiend, maniac, a great one for.

aflame adjective *most of the city was aflame*. See **ablaze** (sense 1).

afloat adverb & adjective *a swimmer fighting to stay afloat*: **buoyant**, floating, buoyed up, non-submerged, suspended, drifting, on/above the surface, (keeping one's head) above water.
▷ANTONYMS sunk, sinking.

afoot adjective & adverb *evil plans are afoot*: **going on**, happening, around, about, abroad, circulating, current, stirring, in circulation, at large, going about, in the air, in the wind; brewing, looming, on the way, in the offing, on the horizon; informal on the go, doing the rounds, on the cards, in the pipeline; literary astir.

aforesaid adjective *the insurer undertakes to insure the aforesaid items against all risks*: **previously mentioned**, aforementioned, aforenamed, previously described, above, above-stated, foregoing, preceding, precedent, earlier, previous, same, selfsame.
▷ANTONYMS subsequent.

afraid adjective **1** *I'm afraid of dogs | they ran away because they were afraid*: **frightened**, scared, scared stiff, terrified, fearful, petrified, nervous, scared to death; apprehensive (about), intimidated (by), alarmed (at); uneasy, tense, worried, panicky, terror-stricken, terror-struck, horror-stricken, horror-struck, frightened/scared out of one's wits, scared witless, beside oneself, frantic, hysterical, with one's heart in one's mouth, shaking in one's shoes, shaking like a leaf; timid, timorous, faint-hearted, cowardly, cowering, cowed, pusillanimous, daunted; Brit. nervy; informal in a (blue) funk, in a cold sweat, in a flap, in a fluster, in a state, in a tizzy/tizz, yellow, chicken, jittery, jumpy; dialect frit; Scottish feart; N. Amer. informal spooked; vulgar slang shit scared; archaic afeared, affrighted.
▷ANTONYMS unafraid, brave, confident.
2 *don't be **afraid to** ask awkward questions*: **reluctant**, unwilling, disinclined, loath, slow; hesitant about, chary of, shy of, averse to.
▷ANTONYMS keen, confident.
3 *I'm afraid that your daughter is ill*: **sorry**, sad, distressed, regretful, apologetic, unhappy, remorseful, rueful.

> **Word links afraid**
>
> **-phobic** afraid of someone/something, as in *claustrophobic, xenophobic*
> **-phobe** person who is afraid of someone/something, as in *Anglophobe, technophobe*

afresh adverb *we should go back to the drawing board and start afresh*: **anew**, again, over again, once again, once more, a second time, another time.

after preposition **1** *he made a speech on stage after the performance*: **following**, subsequent to, succeeding, at the close/end of, in the wake of, later than; rare posterior to.
▷ANTONYMS before, preceding.
2 *Guy shut the door after them*: **behind**, following, in the rear of.
▷ANTONYMS before, in front of.
3 *after the way he treated my sister I never want to speak to him again*: **because of**, as a result of, as a consequence of, in view of, owing to, on account of, on grounds of, by dint of, in the wake of.
4 *he's still going to marry her, after all that's happened?* **despite**, in spite of, regardless of, notwithstanding, in defiance of, in the face of, for all.
5 *the policeman ran after him*: **in pursuit of**, in someone's direction, following, on the track of, in the tracks of, in someone's footsteps.
▷ANTONYMS away from; in front of.
6 *I'm after information, and I'm willing to pay for it*: **in search of**, in quest of, on a quest for, in pursuit of, trying to find, looking for, on the lookout for, hunting for.
7 *their next most accessible source after books is television*: **next to**, beside, besides, following, nearest to, below, immediately inferior to.
▷ANTONYMS before.
8 *we asked after Pop and were glad to hear that he was well*: **about**, concerning, regarding, with regard to, with respect to, with reference to, referring to, in connection with, on the subject of, in the matter of, apropos, re.
9 *the village is thought to have been named after a Roman officer*: **in honour of**, as a tribute to, as a mark of respect to, the same as; N. Amer. for.
10 *the exhibition includes some chalk animal studies after Bandinelli*: **in the style of**, in the manner of, in imitation of, on the model of, following the pattern of, after the fashion of, along/on the lines of, influenced by; similar to, like, characteristic of.
□ **after all** *I had to come—after all, I am your cousin*: **most importantly**, above all, beyond everything, most of all, ultimately, first and foremost, essentially, basically, elementally, at bottom, when you get right down to it; informal when all's said and done, at the end of the day, when push comes to shove.
▸ adverb **1** *the week after, we went to Madrid*: **later**, following, afterwards, after this/that, subsequently; next, ensuing; formal thereafter.
▷ANTONYMS previously, before.
2 *porters were following on after with their bags*: **behind**, in the rear, at the back, in someone's wake, at the end.
▷ANTONYMS ahead, in front.

> **Word links after**
>
> **post-:** *postscript, post-date* related prefix

after-effect noun *she was suffering from the after-effects of a hip injury*: **repercussion**, aftermath, consequence, spin-off, sequel, follow-up, aftershock, trail, wake, offshoot; informal hangover; Medicine sequela.

afterlife noun (**the afterlife**) *they were inspired by their belief in the afterlife*: **life after death**, immortality, everlasting life; heaven, paradise, nirvana, the next world, the hereafter; afterworld, world without end.

aftermath noun *the bleak aftermath of war*: **repercussions**, after-effects, by-product, fallout, backwash, trail, wake, corollary; reverberations, consequences, effects, results, fruits; end result, outcome, upshot, issue, end; informal follow-up.

afterwards adverb *we all celebrated afterwards at a little pub near the church*: **later**, later on, subsequently, then, after, after this/that, following this/that, at a later time/date, next, eventually, after a period of time, in due course; formal thereupon.

again adverb **1** *her spirits lifted again*: **once more**, one more time, another time, a second time, afresh, anew.
2 *a full set of business software can add half as much again to the price of the machine*: **extra**, in addition, additionally, over and above, on top, also, too, as well, besides, furthermore, moreover, yet, to boot.
3 *again, evidence was not always consistent*: **also**, furthermore, further; **moreover**, besides.
□ **again and again** *I read this book again and again*: **repeatedly**, over and over (again), time and (time) again, many times, many a time, on several occasions, often, frequently, recurrently, habitually, continually, persistently, constantly.

against preposition **1** *a number of delegates opened by saying that they were against the motion*: **opposed to**, in opposition to, hostile to, averse to, antagonistic towards, inimical to, unsympathetic to, resistant to, at odds with, in disagreement with, contra; in defiance of, versus, counter, at cross purposes with, dead set against; informal anti, con, agin.
▷ANTONYMS in favour of, pro.
2 *he was swimming against the tide*: **in opposition to**, counter to, contrary to, in the opposite direction to, not in accord with; resisting.
▷ANTONYMS with, in the same direction as.
3 *his age is against him*: **disadvantageous to**, unfavourable to, damaging to, detrimental to, prejudicial to, deleterious to, harmful to, injurious to, hurtful to, inconvenient for, adverse to, unfortunate for, a drawback for.
▷ANTONYMS advantageous to.
4 *it is advisable to insure all oriental rugs against theft*: **in case of**, in/as provision for, in preparation for, in anticipation of, in expectation of.
5 *she had to put up her umbrella against the rain*: **to protect oneself from**, in resistance to.
6 *a group of men huddled round a fire, silhouetted against the orange flames*: **in contrast to**, as a foil to.
7 *the exchange rate of the dollar against the yen*: **in exchange for**, in return for, in compensation for.
8 *she leaned against the wall*: **touching**, in contact with, close up to, up against, abutting, on, adjacent to.

> *Word links* **against**
>
> **anti-** related prefix, as in *anti-aircraft, antidote*

age noun **1** *he retired at the age of 36 | he has a girlfriend of the same age*: **number of years**, lifetime, duration, length of life; stage of life, generation, age group, peer group; years, summers, winters.
2 *her hearing had deteriorated with age*: **elderliness**, old age, oldness, seniority, maturity, dotage, senility; one's advancing/advanced years, one's declining years, the winter/autumn of one's life; formal senescence; archaic eld; rare caducity.
▷ANTONYMS youth, childhood.
3 *the Elizabethan age | an age of computers and fax machines*: **era**, epoch, period, time, aeon, span.
4 informal *you haven't been in touch with me for **an age** | I've wanted to do this **for ages***: **a long time**, a lifetime, an eternity, seemingly forever; hours, days, months, years, aeons, hours/days/months on end, ages and ages, a month of Sundays; Brit. informal yonks, donkey's years; N. Amer. informal, dated a coon's age.
▸ verb *Cabernet Sauvignon ages well, especially in oak | I assume Mother Nature will age me along with everyone else*: **mature**, ripen, mellow, become/make mellow, season, condition, soften, sweeten, grow up, come of age; **grow/become/make old**, weather, (cause to) decline, wither, fade.

aged adjective *she treated him with the respect one might give to an aged relative*: **elderly**, old, mature, older, senior, ancient, venerable; advanced in years, getting on; in one's dotage, long in the tooth, as old as the hills; grey, grey-haired, grey-bearded, grizzled, hoary; past one's prime, not as young as one was, not as young as one used to be; decrepit, doddering, doddery, not long for this world, senile, superannuated; septuagenarian, octogenarian, nonagenarian, centenarian; informal past it, over the hill, no spring chicken; formal senescent; rare longevous.
▷ANTONYMS young.

agency noun **1** *an advertising agency*: **business**, organization, company, firm, office, bureau, concern, service; branch, representative.
2 *there are many diseases in which infection is caused by the agency of insects*: **action**, activity, effect, influence, force, power, work; **means**, vehicle, medium, instrument, mechanism, route, channel, mode, technique, expedient.
3 *regional policy was introduced through the agency of the Board of Trade*: **intervention**, intercession, involvement, mediation, arbitration, interposing, instrumentality, good offices; auspices, aegis.

agenda noun *a meeting with a fixed agenda*: **list of items**, schedule, programme, timetable, line-up, list, listing, to-do list, plan, scheme, syllabus, bill, card, directory, table; Computing menu.

agent noun **1** *my agent told me that someone wanted to make a film out of my novel*: **representative**, negotiator, business manager, emissary, envoy, factor, go-between, proxy, surrogate, trustee, liaison, broker, delegate, spokesperson, spokesman, spokeswoman, mouthpiece; informal rep.
2 *a travel agent*: **agency**, business, organization, company, firm, office, bureau, concern, service.
3 *a CIA agent*: **spy**, secret agent, undercover agent, operative, fifth columnist, Mata Hari; informal mole, spook, snooper, G-man; archaic intelligencer, beagle, lurcher.
4 *the agents of destruction*: **doer**, performer, author, executor, perpetrator, operator, operative, mover, producer; cause, origin, root, source, instrument, catalyst.
5 *a cleansing agent*: **medium**, means, instrument, vehicle; power, force.

agglomeration noun *the suburb is an agglomeration of houses, shops, and offices*: **collection**, mass, cluster, lump, clump, pile, heap, bunch, stack, bundle, quantity, hoard, store, stockpile; accumulation, aggregate, build-up; miscellany, jumble, hotchpotch; informal mixed bag.

aggravate verb **1** *according to some, the new law will aggravate the situation*: **worsen**, make worse, exacerbate, inflame, compound; intensify, increase, heighten, magnify, add to, amplify, augment; add fuel to the fire/flames, add insult to injury, rub salt in the wound.
▷ANTONYMS alleviate, improve.
2 informal *you don't have to aggravate people to get what you want*. See **annoy**.

> *Choose the right word* **aggravate, annoy, irritate, vex, peeve**
>
> See **annoy**.

aggravation noun **1** *the recession led to the aggravation of unemployment problems*: **worsening**, exacerbation, compounding; intensification, increase, heightening, magnification, amplification, augmentation.
▷ANTONYMS improvement.
2 informal *she decided that no amount of money is worth the aggravation*. See **nuisance**.

aggregate noun **1** *the specimen is an aggregate of rock and mineral fragments*: **collection**, mass, cluster, lump, clump, pile, heap, bundle, quantity; accumulation, build-up, agglomeration, concentration, assemblage; mixture, mix, combination, blend, compound, alloy, amalgam, conjunction, synthesis, marriage; miscellany, jumble, hotchpotch; informal mixed bag.
2 *he won with a 90-hole aggregate of 325*: **total**, sum total, sum, whole amount, grand total, totality, entirety, summation, gross, result, final figure.
▸ adjective *an aggregate score of 3–2*: **total**, combined, whole, gross, accumulated, added, entire, complete, full, comprehensive, overall, composite.

aggression noun **1** *an act of aggression*: **hostility**, aggressiveness, belligerence, bellicosity, antagonism, truculence; pugnacity, pugnaciousness, combativeness, militancy, warmongering, warlikeness, hawkishness, force, violence; attack, assault, encroachment, offence, invasion, infringement.
▷ANTONYMS meekness.
2 *he played the game with unceasing aggression*: **confidence**, self-confidence, boldness, audacity, self-assertion, assertion, assertiveness, self-assertiveness, determination, forcefulness, vigour, energy, dynamism, zeal.
▷ANTONYMS diffidence.

aggressive adjective **1** *an aggressive, grubby schoolkid*: **hostile**, belligerent, bellicose, antagonistic, truculent; pugnacious, combative, violent, macho; confrontational, quarrelsome, argumentative.
▷ANTONYMS meek, friendly.
2 *an aggressive foreign policy*: **warmongering**, warlike, warring, hawkish, violent, combative, attacking; jingoistic, militaristic, flag-waving, sabre-rattling; offensive, expansionist, invasive, intrusive; informal gung-ho.
▷ANTONYMS peaceful.
3 *an aggressive promotional drive*: **assertive**, forceful, competitive, insistent, vigorous, energetic, dynamic, driving, bold, audacious, enterprising, go-ahead, zealous, pushing; informal pushy, in-your-face, feisty.
▷ANTONYMS submissive, diffident.

aggressor noun *England fought a succession of wars in which she was the aggressor*: **attacker**, assaulter, assailant, invader; **instigator**, provoker, initiator, warmonger, offender.
▷ANTONYMS victim; retaliator.

aggrieved adjective **1** *the manager looked aggrieved at the suggestion*: **resentful**, affronted, indignant, disgruntled, discontented, angry, distressed, unhappy, disturbed, anguished, hurt, pained, upset, offended, piqued, in high dudgeon, riled, nettled, vexed, irked, irritated, annoyed, put out, chagrined; informal peeved, miffed, in a huff; Brit. informal cheesed off; N. Amer. informal sore, steamed; vulgar slang pissed off; N. Amer. vulgar slang pissed.
▷ANTONYMS pleased.
2 *the aggrieved party*: **wronged**, injured, abused, harmed, mistreated, ill-used, offended, maltreated, ill-treated, maligned.

aghast adjective *she winced, aghast at his cruelty*: **horrified**, appalled, astounded, amazed, dismayed, thunderstruck, stunned, shocked, in shock, flabbergasted, staggered, taken aback, speechless, awestruck, open-mouthed, wide-eyed; informal floored, gobsmacked.

agile adjective **1** *the little girl was as agile as a monkey*: **nimble**, lithe, spry, supple, limber, sprightly, acrobatic, dexterous, deft, willowy, graceful, light-footed, nimble-footed, light on one's feet, fleet-footed; active, fit, in good condition; lively, vigorous, quick-moving; informal nippy, twinkle-toed; literary fleet, lightsome.
▷ANTONYMS clumsy, stiff.
2 *his agile mind was forever seeking new ways of conserving energy*: **alert**,

sharp, acute, clever, shrewd, astute, intelligent, quick-witted, perceptive, penetrating, piercing, active, nimble, quick off the mark, finely honed, rapier-like; informal smart, on the ball.
▷ANTONYMS slow, dull.

agitate verb **1** *I must warn you that any mention of Clare agitates your grandmother*: **upset**, perturb, fluster, ruffle, disconcert, unnerve, disquiet, disturb, distress, unsettle, bother, concern, trouble, cause anxiety to, make anxious, alarm, work up, flurry, worry; inflame, incite, provoke, stir up; informal rattle, faze, discombobulate.
▷ANTONYMS calm.
2 *she urged us to agitate for the appointment of more women to cabinet posts*: **campaign**, strive, battle, fight, struggle, crusade, push, press; argue, debate, dispute, wrangle.
3 *they were used as stirrers to help to agitate the vast masses of fermenting vegetation*: **stir**, whisk, beat, churn, shake, toss, blend, whip (up), fold, roil, jolt, disturb.

agitated adjective *I could see that he was agitated and edgy*: **upset**, perturbed, flustered, ruffled, disconcerted, unnerved, disquieted, disturbed, distressed, unsettled, bothered, concerned, troubled, anxious, alarmed, worked up, worried, harassed; nervous, jittery, jumpy, on edge, tense, overwrought, frantic, keyed up, in a panic; inflamed, stirred up; informal rattled, fazed, discombobulated, in a dither, in a flap, in a state, in a lather, in a tizz/tizzy, all of a dither, beside oneself, hot and bothered, hot under the collar; Brit. informal having kittens, in a (flat) spin.
▷ANTONYMS calm, relaxed.

agitation noun **1** *Freddie gritted his teeth in agitation*: **anxiety**, perturbation, disquiet, distress, concern, trouble, alarm, worry, upset; nervous excitement; rare disconcertment.
▷ANTONYMS calmness, relaxation.
2 *there was an upsurge in nationalist agitation*: **campaigning**, striving, battling, fighting, struggling, crusading; arguing, argument, wrangling, debate, discussion; rabble-rousing, provocation, stirring up, commotion.
3 *the solutions were prepared by vigorous agitation of the components*: **stirring**, whisking, beating, churning, shaking, turbulence, tossing, blending, whipping, folding, rolling, jolting.

agitator noun *a left-wing agitator*: **troublemaker**, rabble-rouser, demagogue, soapbox orator, incendiary; revolutionary, firebrand, rebel, insurgent, revolutionist, subversive; instigator, inciter, provoker, fomenter, dissentient; French agent provocateur; informal stirrer.

agnostic noun *he was an agnostic, but his notebooks reveal a kind of religious attitude to the universe*: **sceptic**, doubter, questioner, doubting Thomas, challenger, scoffer, cynic; unbeliever, disbeliever, non-believer; rationalist; rare nullifidian.
▷ANTONYMS believer, theist.
▶ adjective *a group of prominent agnostic scientists*: **sceptical**, doubting, questioning, unsure, cynical, unbelieving, disbelieving, non-believing, faithless, irreligious; rationalist; rare nullifidian.
▷ANTONYMS theist.

ago adverb *a few days ago they had a long discussion*: **in the past**, before the present, before, earlier, back, in time gone by, since, formerly, previously; formal heretofore.

agog adverb *everyone was agog to hear what on earth he would say*: **eager**, excited, impatient, in suspense, on tenterhooks, on the edge of one's seat, on pins and needles, keen, anxious, longing; curious, expectant, enthralled, enthusiastic, avid, breathless, open-mouthed, waiting with bated breath; informal itching.
▷ANTONYMS uninterested, incurious.

agonize verb *all the way home she **agonized about** what she should do*: **worry**, fret, fuss, upset oneself, rack one's brains, wrestle with oneself, be worried, be anxious, feel uneasy, exercise oneself, brood, muse; mull over, dwell on, contemplate, ruminate, chew over, puzzle over, speculate, weigh up, turn over in one's mind; be indecisive; informal stew; archaic pore on.

agonizing adjective *he died after suffering months of agonizing pain*: **excruciating**, harrowing, racking, painful, acute, severe, intense, extreme, grievous, hellish, killing, searing, torturous, tormenting, piercing; insufferable, unbearable, unendurable, more than one can bear, more than flesh and blood can stand; literary exquisite.

agony noun *he was screaming in agony*: **pain**, hurt, suffering, torture, torment, anguish, affliction, trauma; misery, distress, grief, woe, wretchedness, heartbreak, heartache; pangs, throes; rare excruciation.

agrarian adjective *Brazil is diversifying its agrarian economy*.
See **agricultural**.

agree verb **1** *I agree with you | officials agreed that it has good potential*: **concur**, be of the same mind/opinion, see eye to eye, be in sympathy, sympathize, be united, be as one man, accord; acknowledge, admit, concede, grant, own, confess.
▷ANTONYMS disagree, differ.
2 *they had **agreed to** a ceasefire*: **consent**, assent, accede; acquiesce in, accept, approve (of), allow, admit, grant, comply with, undertake, go along with, say yes to, give one's approval to, give something the nod, recognize, acknowledge.
▷ANTONYMS reject.
3 *the plan and the drawing of the church do not agree with each other*: **match**, match up, accord, correspond, conform, coincide, fit, tally, harmonize, be in harmony, be in agreement, be consistent, be compatible, be consonant, be congruous, be in tune, equate, be equivalent, dovetail, chime, correlate, be parallel; informal square.
▷ANTONYMS differ, contradict.
4 *they **agreed on** a price*: **settle**, decide, shake hands; arrange, arrive at, negotiate, work out, thrash out, hammer out, reach an agreement on, come to terms about, reach terms on; strike a bargain, make a deal.
5 *she's probably eaten something that didn't agree with her*: **be agreeable to**, be good for, be healthy for, be acceptable to, suit.

> *Choose the right word* **agree, consent, assent, acquiesce**
>
> More than one party is needed for an agreement, but the contributions made by each may be different.
>
> **Agree** is the only word of the four that describes being of one mind with others over something (*we'll have to decide what compromise we can agree on | they agree a currency price and payment terms*), but all of them can be used for giving one's permission. When someone agrees *to* something, the parties to the agreement may be on an equal footing (*the company and the shareholders agreed to a lock-out clause*), but it may depend on the willingness of one party who is in a position of superior power (*the owner has refused to say whether he'll agree to the rescue plan*).
>
> Someone who **consents** to something proposed to them also has the power to decide on it and typically has some reservations or initial opposition. Many uses are concerned with legal considerations (*the Attorney General has to consent to any prosecution under the Act*). People also consent, for example, to medical *treatment* of various kinds, to *testing* for genetic susceptibility to various disorders, and to *sex*: the phrase *consenting adult* is used exclusively with reference to sexual activity. One can also consent *to do something* (*Loretta was hoping that Koogan would consent to lend them a key*).
>
> Someone who **assents** to a proposal is generally a person whose approval is required, although they may feel quite indifferent to it. They are free to accept or reject the proposal, but have played no part in working it out: they merely accept what is presented to them (*the inspector assented to the remark with a nod*).
>
> To **acquiesce** is to accept something by default through failing to resist. Often what is accepted is not something that the person really wants, and their acquiescence is due to exhaustion, attrition, or lack of real bargaining power (*the authorities believed that most refugees would acquiesce and not resist attempts to send them back*). Acquiescence can easily slip into passive connivance in something bad (*the oil company was accused of acquiescing in the pollution of the people's lands*).

agreeable adjective **1** *a village atmosphere which we find rather agreeable*: **pleasant**, pleasing, enjoyable, pleasurable, nice, to one's liking, appealing, engaging, satisfying, fine, charming, delightful.
▷ANTONYMS disagreeable, unpleasant.
2 *the policeman was an agreeable fellow*: **likeable**, charming, amiable, affable, pleasant, nice, friendly, good-natured, sociable, genial, congenial, appealing, sympathetic, benign, benevolent.
▷ANTONYMS disagreeable, unpleasant.
3 *we should get together for a talk, if you're agreeable*: **willing**, amenable, compliant, complying, consenting, assenting, in accord/agreement, disposed, accommodating, acquiescent, tractable, obliging, complaisant.
▷ANTONYMS unwilling.

agreement noun **1** *all heads nodded in agreement*: **accord**, concurrence, consensus, harmony, accordance, unity, unison, concord, like-mindedness, rapport, sympathy; **assent**, acceptance, consent, acquiescence, endorsement, confirmation.
▷ANTONYMS disagreement.
2 *the defence minister signed an agreement on military cooperation*: **contract**, compact, treaty, covenant, pact, accord, deal, bargain, settlement, concordat, protocol, entente, arrangement, understanding, pledge, promise, bond.
3 *there is some agreement between my view and that of the author*: **correspondence**, consistency, compatibility, conformity, coincidence, harmony, concord, accord, accordance, congruity; similarity, resemblance, likeness, identity, uniformity, relationship, association, similitude.
▷ANTONYMS discord.

agricultural adjective **1** *an agricultural labourer*: **farm**, farming, agrarian; rural, countryside, country, rustic, pastoral, bucolic; literary georgic, sylvan, Arcadian, agrestic.
▷ANTONYMS urban.
2 *agricultural land*: **farmed**, farm, agrarian, cultivated, tilled, productive.
▷ANTONYMS wild.

agriculture noun *the mechanization of agriculture is reducing work opportunities*: **farming**, cultivation, tillage, tilling, husbandry, land

management, farm management, crofting; agribusiness, agronomics, agronomy.
▷ANTONYMS industry.

> *Word links* **agriculture**
>
> **agri-** related prefix, as in *agribusiness, agriscience*
> **agro-** related prefix, as in *agroforestry, agro-industry*
> **agrarian** relating to agriculture

aground adverb & adjective *a year later, the tanker was still aground*: **foundered**, ashore, beached, grounded, stuck, shipwrecked, wrecked, high and dry, on the rocks, on the ground/bottom; marooned, stranded.
▷ANTONYMS afloat.

ahead adverb **1** *he peered ahead, but could see nothing*: **forward(s)**, towards the front, frontwards; onwards, on, forth.
▷ANTONYMS behind.
2 *he had ridden on ahead*: **in front**, at the head, in the lead, at the fore, to the fore, in the vanguard, in the van, in advance, at the head of the queue.
▷ANTONYMS behind, at the back.
3 *she was preparing herself mentally for what lay ahead*: **in the future**, in time, in time to come, in the fullness of time, at a later date, after this, henceforth, subsequently, later on, in due course, next, from now on, from this day/time on, from this day forth/forward.
▷ANTONYMS in the past.
4 *a poll showed them ahead by six points*: **leading**, winning, in the lead, (out) in front, to the fore, first, coming first; informal up front.
▷ANTONYMS losing.
□ **ahead of 1** *she stood back to allow Blanche to go ahead of her*: **in front of**, before. ▷ANTONYMS behind.
2 *we have a demanding trip ahead of us*: **in store for**, waiting for, in wait for.
3 *the motorway was finished two months ahead of schedule*: **in advance of**, before, earlier than, prior to, previous to. ▷ANTONYMS behind.
4 *in terms of these amenities, Britain was ahead of other European countries*: **more advanced than**, further on than, superior to, outdistancing, outstripping, surpassing, exceeding, better than, prevailing over.
▷ANTONYMS behind; inferior to.

aid noun **1** *with the aid of his colleagues he prepared a manifesto*: **assistance**, support; help, backing, abettance, encouragement, cooperation, succour; a helping hand.
▷ANTONYMS hindrance.
2 *we have provided valuable economic and humanitarian aid*: **donations**, funding, contributions, subsidies, benefits, welfare, gifts, grants, relief, charity, financial assistance, subvention, alms, offerings, handouts, largesse; patronage, sponsorship, backing; scholarships, bursaries; debt remission; informal a leg up, shot in the arm.
3 *a hospital aid*: **helper**, assistant; informal girl/man Friday.
▶ verb **1** *he was liable to provide an army to aid the King of England*: **help**, assist, abet, come to the aid of, give assistance to, lend a hand to, be of service to; avail, succour, sustain; support, back, back up, second, stand by, uphold.
▷ANTONYMS hinder.
2 *essences can be added to your bath to aid restful sleep*: **facilitate**, promote, encourage, help, speed up, hasten, accelerate, expedite, further, boost, give a boost/lift/push to, spur on, smooth/clear the way for.
▷ANTONYMS discourage, hinder.

> *Choose the right word* **aid, help, assist, support**
>
> See **help**.

aide noun *a presidential aide*: **assistant**, helper, adviser, right-hand man, attaché, adjutant, deputy, second, second in command, acolyte, auxiliary, companion, confidante; subordinate, junior, underling, lackey, flunkey, henchman; N. Amer. cohort; informal main man, man/girl Friday.

ail verb archaic *what ails you, Elizabeth?* See **afflict**.

ailing adjective **1** *her husband was away visiting his ailing mother*: **ill**, unwell, not well, sick, sickly, poorly, weak, indisposed, in poor/bad health, infirm, debilitated, delicate, off colour; languishing, valetudinarian; dying, at death's door; informal under the weather, below par, laid up.
▷ANTONYMS healthy.
2 *a government programme to rescue the country's ailing economy*: **failing**, in poor condition, weak, poor, inadequate, deficient, imperfect, substandard, flawed.
▷ANTONYMS strong, successful.

ailment noun *the doctor diagnosed a common stomach ailment*: **illness**, disease, disorder, sickness, affliction, malady, complaint, infection, upset, condition, infirmity, indisposition, malaise, trouble; informal bug, virus; Brit. informal lurgy.

aim verb **1** *he aimed the rifle*: **point**, direct, train, sight, focus, level, line up, position; turn something on someone.
2 *she aimed at the target*: **take aim at**, fix on, zero in on, draw a bead on.
3 *undergraduates aiming for a first degree*: **work towards**, be after, set one's sights on, try for, strive for, pursue, seek, aspire to, endeavour to achieve, have in view, have designs on, wish for, want; formal essay.
4 *this system is* **aimed at** *the home entertainment market*: **intend for**, mean for, address to, destine for; target at, direct towards, market at, design for, tailor to, orient towards, pitch to/towards.
5 *the course aims to educate children to cope with dangerous situations*: **intend**, plan, resolve, propose, purpose, design, mean, have in mind/view.
▶ noun *our aim is to develop gymnasts to the top level*: **objective**, object, goal, end, target, grail, holy grail, design, desire, desired result, intention, intent, plan, purpose, idea, point, object of the exercise; ambition, aspiration, wish, dream, hope; resolve; French raison d'être.

aimless adjective **1** *Flavia set out on an aimless walk*: **purposeless**, pointless, goalless, undirected, objectless, unfocused, without purpose, without goal; meaningless, senseless, futile, hollow, frivolous, barren, profitless, fruitless.
▷ANTONYMS purposeful.
2 *the huddles of aimless men standing outside the bars*: **unambitious**, purposeless, undirected, apathetic, goalless; drifting, wandering, adrift; unoccupied, idle, at a loose end, with time to kill.
▷ANTONYMS determined.

air noun **1** *hundreds of birds hovered in the air*: **sky**, heavens, ether; **atmosphere**, aerosphere, airspace.
2 *I was opening the windows to get some air into the room*: **breeze**, draught, wind; breath of air, gust of air, flurry of air, waft of air, puff of wind, whiff of air, blast of air.
3 *he upended his glass with an air of defiance*: **expression**, appearance, look, impression, aspect, manner, bearing, mien, countenance; mood, quality, ambience, aura, feeling, flavour, tone; informal vibe.
4 (**airs**) *he'd no patience with women putting on airs*: **affectations**, pretension, pretentiousness, affectedness, posing, posturing, pretence; **self-importance**, superiority, condescension, ostentation, snobbery, superciliousness, pomposity, arrogance, haughtiness, hauteur, pride, conceit, airs and graces; informal swank, snootiness, uppishness, side.
5 *a traditional Scottish air*: **tune**, melody, song, theme, strain, refrain, piece, aria; literary lay.
□ **in the air** *lots of exciting things are in the air here*: **going on**, happening, afoot, around, about, abroad, circulating, current, stirring, in circulation, at large, going about, in the wind; brewing, looming, on the way, in the offing, on the horizon; informal on the go, doing the rounds, on the cards, in the pipeline; literary astir.
□ **up in the air** *it's still up in the air whether he is going to join us*: **uncertain**, unknown, undetermined, unsettled, unresolved, unsure, pending, in the balance, in limbo, debatable, open to question, in doubt; informal dicey, hairy, iffy; Brit. informal dodgy.
▷ANTONYMS certain, settled.
▶ verb **1** *this is a chance for you to air your views*: **express**, voice, make public, vent, ventilate, articulate, state, declare, give expression to, give voice to; make known, publicize, publish, disseminate, circulate, communicate, spread, promulgate, broadcast; reveal, announce, proclaim, divulge, submit, raise, moot, propose; discuss, debate; have one's say.
2 *the windows were opened regularly to air the room*: **ventilate**, aerate, freshen, refresh, cool, air-condition.
3 *the film was aired nationwide*: **broadcast**, transmit, beam, send/put out, televise, show, telecast, relay, put on the air/airwaves, disseminate; informal screen.

> *Word links* **air**
>
> **aero-** related prefix, as in *aeroplane, aerosol*
> **aerial** relating to air
> **aerodynamics** study of moving air

airborne adjective *the shuttle was airborne*: **flying**, in flight, in the air, on the wing, winging; gliding, hovering, soaring.

aircraft noun

> *Word links* **aircraft**
>
> **aero-** related prefix, as in *aerospace, aeromodelling*
> **aeronautics** science of aircraft flight
> **aviation** commercial operation of aircraft

airily adverb *the doctor had dismissed his troubles airily*: **lightly**, breezily, flippantly, casually, nonchalantly; readily, heedlessly, without consideration, uncaringly, indifferently, unthinkingly; light-heartedly, gaily, blithely, jauntily, cheerfully.
▷ANTONYMS seriously, thoughtfully.

airing noun **1** *we should give the place a good airing before we go*: **ventilating**, ventilation, aerating, aeration, freshening, refreshing, cooling, air conditioning.

a

2 *the governess took them out to the park for an airing*: **stroll**, walk, saunter, turn, jaunt, amble; outing, excursion, trip, expedition; formal promenade; dated constitutional.
3 *the media has to be a forum for the airing of different views*: **expression**, voicing, venting, ventilation, articulation, statement, declaration; publicizing, publication, dissemination, circulation, communication, spreading, promulgation, broadcast, broadcasting; revelation, announcement, proclamation, divulgence, submission, raising, mooting, proposal; discussion, debate.
4 *I hope the BBC gives the play another airing very soon*: **broadcast**, transmission, televising, showing, relaying, telecast, dissemination; informal screening.

airless adjective *a hot, airless room*: **stuffy**, close, stifling, suffocating, breathless, sultry, muggy, fuggy, stale, humid, oppressive; unventilated, badly/poorly ventilated; smoky.
▷ANTONYMS airy, ventilated.

airport noun airfield, airstrip, landing strip, runway; heliport, helipad; Military air station; Brit. aerodrome; N. Amer. airdrome; informal, dated drome.

airtight adjective **1** *an airtight container*: **sealed**, closed, shut tight, tight, impermeable, hermetically sealed; watertight, waterproof.
▷ANTONYMS leaky.
2 *he had an airtight alibi*: **indisputable**, unquestionable, incontrovertible, undeniable, incontestable, irrefutable, unassailable, beyond dispute, beyond question, beyond doubt; foolproof, sound, flawless, watertight, conclusive, without loopholes.
▷ANTONYMS flawed.

airy adjective **1** *the conservatory is light and airy*: **well ventilated**, fresh; **spacious**, open, uncrowded, uncluttered; light, well lit, bright.
▷ANTONYMS stuffy.
2 *he rested his face against his airy pillow*: **delicate**, soft, fine, feathery, floaty, insubstantial, flimsy, wispy.
▷ANTONYMS heavy, solid.
3 *'It was obvious,' said Robyn with an airy gesture*: **nonchalant**, casual, breezy, flippant, insouciant; heedless, unconsidered, uncaring, indifferent, unthinking, unworried, untroubled; light-hearted, blithe, jaunty, cheerful, unserious, insubstantial.
▷ANTONYMS serious.

airy-fairy adjective informal *an airy-fairy principle of political philosophy*: **impractical**, unrealistic, idealistic; unfocused, vague, fanciful, insubstantial, without substance, unconvincing.
▷ANTONYMS matter of fact, solid.

aisle noun *she wandered round the aisles, filling up her trolley*: **passage**, passageway, corridor, gangway, walkway, path, lane, alley.

ajar adjective & adverb *a door further down the wall stood ajar*: **slightly open**, half open, agape; unfastened, unlatched, unlocked, unsecured, off the latch.
▷ANTONYMS closed; wide open.

akin adjective *walking through the streets of Hong Kong is an experience* ***akin to*** *a rugby match*: **similar**, related, close, near, corresponding, comparable, parallel, equivalent; allied with, connected with, like; alike, matching, analogous, cognate, of a piece.
▷ANTONYMS unlike.

alacrity noun *she accepted with alacrity*: **eagerness**, willingness, readiness; enthusiasm, ardour, fervour, keenness, joyousness, liveliness, zeal; promptness, haste, briskness, swiftness, dispatch, speed; dated address.
▷ANTONYMS apathy.

alarm noun **1** *the girl spun round in alarm*: **fear**, anxiety, apprehension, trepidation, nervousness, unease, distress, agitation, consternation, disquiet, perturbation, fright, panic, dread, horror, shock, terror.
▷ANTONYMS calmness, composure.
2 *a smoke alarm*: **siren**, warning sound, alarm signal, danger signal, distress signal, alert; warning device, alarm bell, bell, horn, whistle; red light, red flag; archaic tocsin.
▶ verb *the news had alarmed her*: **frighten**, scare, panic, startle, unnerve, distress, agitate, upset, fluster, ruffle, disconcert, shock, daunt, dismay, disturb, work up, terrify, terrorize, petrify, make someone's blood run cold; informal put the wind up someone, rattle, spook, scare the living daylights out of.

alarming adjective *infant mortality is rising at an alarming rate*: **frightening**, startling, unnerving, shocking, hair-raising; distressing, upsetting, disconcerting, perturbing, dismaying, disquieting, daunting, disturbing, harrowing; fearsome, dreadful, monstrous, forbidding, appalling, chilling, terrifying, petrifying; informal scary.
▷ANTONYMS reassuring.

alarmist noun *this problem is purely a fabrication by alarmists*: **scaremonger**, gloom-monger, doom-monger, voice of doom, doomster, doomsayer, doom merchant, Cassandra; fatalist, pessimist, killjoy, misery; informal doom and gloom merchant, wet blanket.
▷ANTONYMS optimist, Pollyanna.

alchemy noun *they were involved with the quest for immortality through alchemy*: **chemistry**; **magic**, sorcery, witchcraft, enchantment.

alcohol noun *I don't even smoke cigarettes or touch alcohol*: **liquor**, intoxicating liquor, alcoholic drink, strong drink, drink, spirits, intoxicants; informal booze, hooch, the hard stuff, firewater, gut-rot, rotgut, moonshine, tipple, the demon drink, the bottle, juice, bevvy, grog, Dutch courage, John Barleycorn; technical ethyl alcohol, ethanol.

Word links **alcohol**

alcoholism, dipsomania addiction to alcohol
temperance, teetotalism refusal to drink alcohol

alcoholic adjective *you should moderate your consumption of alcoholic drinks*: **intoxicating**, inebriating, containing alcohol; strong, hard, potent, stiff; brewed, distilled, fermented; rare spirituous, vinous.
▶ noun *he took the crucial step of admitting that he was an alcoholic*: **dipsomaniac**, drunk, drunkard, heavy/hard/serious drinker, problem drinker, drinker, alcohol-abuser, alcohol addict, person with a drink problem; tippler, sot, toper, inebriate, imbiber; informal boozer, lush, alky, dipso, soak, tosspot, wino, sponge, barfly; Austral./NZ hophead, metho; vulgar slang pisshead, piss artist.

alcove noun *an old brick fireplace set back in a spacious alcove*: **recess**, niche, nook, opening, bay, hollow, cavity, corner, indentation, booth; apse; inglenook.

alert adjective **1** *police have asked neighbours to be alert after a spate of burglaries in the area*: **vigilant**, wide awake, aware, watchful, attentive, observant, circumspect, wary, chary, heedful, canny; on the lookout, on one's guard, on one's toes, all ears, keeping one's eyes open/peeled, keeping a weather eye open, on the qui vive.
▷ANTONYMS inattentive.
2 *she continued to paint in old age in order to remain mentally alert*: **quick-witted**, sharp, bright, quick, keen, perceptive, wide awake, responsive, agile, acute, astute; informal on the ball, on one's toes, quick off the mark, quick on the uptake, all there, with it, bright-eyed and bushy-tailed.
▷ANTONYMS slow.
▶ noun **1** *the army called for a state of alert*: **vigilance**, watchfulness, carefulness, attentiveness, guardedness, care, caution, cautiousness, wariness, chariness, alertness, circumspection, prudence, heedfulness, heed, mindfulness.
▷ANTONYMS carelessness.
2 *a flood alert has been issued*: **warning**, caution, notification, notice, exhortation, injunction; siren, alarm, signal, danger signal, distress signal.
▶ verb *police were alerted by a phone call from the house*: **warn**, notify, apprise, caution, put on one's guard, forewarn, put on the qui vive, arouse; informal tip off, clue in, put in the picture, put wise.

alertness noun **1** *he had the supernatural alertness of the hunted*: **vigilance**, awareness, watchfulness, attentiveness, attention, circumspection, wariness, chariness, heedfulness, canniness, discretion, prudence.
▷ANTONYMS inattentiveness.
2 *work is unquestionably one of the most important factors in preserving mental alertness and bodily health*: **quick-wittedness**, quick thinking, quickness of mind, sharpness, quickness, keenness, perceptiveness, responsiveness, agility, acuteness, acuity, shrewdness, astuteness, intelligence, insight, presence of mind.
▷ANTONYMS slowness.

alias noun *he is known under several aliases by Interpol*: **assumed name**, false name, pseudonym, sobriquet, incognito, nickname; pen name, stage name; French nom de plume, nom de guerre; rare allonym, anonym.
▶ adverb *Cassius Clay, alias Muhammad Ali*: **also known as**, aka, also called, otherwise known as, otherwise.

alibi noun *luckily we've both got a very good alibi for last night*: **defence**, defending evidence, plea; justification, explanation, reason, vindication; excuse, pretext; informal story, line.
▶ verb informal *her brother had reluctantly agreed to alibi her*: **cover for**, give an alibi to, provide with an alibi, shield, protect.

alien adjective **1** *the study of alien cultures promotes self-awareness*: **foreign**, overseas, non-native, external, distant, remote.
▷ANTONYMS native.
2 *emerging from the station in the City, they found themselves in an alien landscape*: **unfamiliar**, unknown, unheard of, foreign; strange, peculiar, odd, bizarre, outlandish; remote, exotic, novel.
▷ANTONYMS familiar.
3 *he has been asked to adopt a vicious role* ***alien to*** *his nature*: **incompatible with**, unusual for, opposed to, conflicting with, contrary to, adverse to, in conflict with, at variance with, antagonistic to; unacceptable to, repugnant to, hostile to, inimical to; rare oppugnant to.
▷ANTONYMS familiar.
4 *alien beings have landed on Earth*: **extraterrestrial**, other-worldly, unearthly; Martian, Venutian, Jovian.
▷ANTONYMS earthly.

▶ **noun 1** *he was deported as an illegal alien*: **foreigner**, non-native, immigrant, emigrant, émigré, incomer, newcomer, visitor, outsider, stranger.
▷ANTONYMS native.
2 *the alien's spaceship has crashed*: **extraterrestrial**, ET; Martian, Venutian, Jovian; informal little green man.

alienate **verb 1** *his homosexuality* ***alienated*** *him* ***from*** *his conservative father*: **estrange**, turn away, set apart, drive apart, isolate, detach, distance, put at a distance; set against, part, separate, cut off, sever, divide, divorce, disunite, set at variance/odds, make hostile to, drive a wedge between, sow dissension.
▷ANTONYMS unite.
2 *they approached the government for aid in preventing the land from being alienated*: **transfer**, convey, pass on, hand over, devolve.

alienation **noun 1** *she shared my deep sense of alienation from our environment*: **isolation**, detachment, estrangement, distance, separation, severance, parting, division, divorce, cutting off, turning away, withdrawal; variance, difference, schism.
2 *most leases contain restrictions against alienation*: **transfer**, conveyance, passing on, handing over, devolution.

alight[1] **verb 1** *he was the only passenger to* ***alight from*** *the train*: **get off**, step off, get down; dismount, disembark, descend, exit; detrain, deplane; informal pile out.
▷ANTONYMS get on, board.
2 *a swallow alighted on a branch*: **land**, come down, come to rest, touch down, light, arrive, descend; settle, perch, roost, sit, rest.
▷ANTONYMS fly off.

alight[2] **adjective 1** *bales of hay were set alight | he kept the fire alight*: **on fire**, ablaze, aflame, in flames, flaming, burning, blazing, raging, fiery, lit, lighted, ignited; literary afire.
▷ANTONYMS extinguished.
2 *her face was suddenly alight with laughter*: **lit up**, gleaming, glowing, aglow, ablaze, illuminated, brilliant, bright, shining, radiant, shimmering, sparkling, flashing, dazzling, luminous, incandescent.
▷ANTONYMS dark.

align **verb 1** *desks are typically aligned in straight rows facing forwards*: **line up**, range, arrange in line, put in order, put in rows/columns, straighten (up); marshal, orient, place, position, dispose, situate, set.
2 *he* ***aligned himself with*** *the workers*: **ally**, affiliate, associate, join, side, sympathize, be in league, unite, combine, join (up), join forces, form an alliance, team up, band together, cooperate, collaborate, throw in one's lot, make common cause.

alike **adjective** *all the doors looked alike*: **similar**, the same, indistinguishable, identical, uniform, interchangeable, undifferentiated, homogeneous, much the same, of a piece, cut from the same cloth; resembling, corresponding, like, parallel, analogous, cognate; informal like (two) peas in a pod, much of a muchness, (like) Tweedledum and Tweedledee.
▷ANTONYMS different.
▶ **adverb** *great minds think alike*: **similarly**, the same, just the same, in the same way/manner/fashion, in like manner, identically, uniformly.
▷ANTONYMS differently.

alimony **noun** N. Amer. *his ex-wife has been trying to track him down for alimony*: **financial support**, maintenance, support, provision, allowance, keep, upkeep, sustenance, livelihood, subsistence, living expenses; child support; Scottish aliment.

alive **adjective 1** *he was last seen alive on Boxing Day*: **living**, live, having life, not dead; breathing, moving; vital, vigorous, flourishing, dynamic, energetic, functioning; animate, organic, biological, sentient; existing, existent; informal in the land of the living, among the living, alive and kicking; archaic quick.
▷ANTONYMS dead; extinct; inanimate.
2 *the synagogue has kept the Jewish faith alive throughout the centuries*: **active**, existing, in existence, existent, extant, functioning, in operation, ongoing, going on, continuing, surviving, persisting, remaining, abiding; prevalent, current, contemporary, present; informal on the map, on the agenda.
▷ANTONYMS inactive; obsolete.
3 *the thrills of life that kept him really alive*: **animated**, lively, full of life, alert, active, energetic, vigorous, spry, sprightly, vital, vibrant, vivacious, buoyant, exuberant, ebullient, zestful, spirited, enthusiastic, eager, bouncy, bubbly, perky, sparkling; informal full of beans, bright-eyed and bushy-tailed, bright and breezy, sparky, chirpy, chipper, peppy, full of vim and vigour, (still) going strong; N. Amer. informal peart.
▷ANTONYMS lethargic, lifeless.
4 *teachers need to be* ***alive to*** *cultural differences between their pupils' backgrounds*: **alert to**, awake to, aware of, sensitive to, conscious of, mindful of, heedful of, watchful of, responsive to; familiar with, cognizant of, apprised of, sensible of; informal wise to, hip to.
▷ANTONYMS unaware, blind.
5 *the place was probably* ***alive with*** *mice*: **teeming**, swarming, thronged, overflowing, overrun, bristling, bustling, rife, infested, thick, crowded, packed; full of, abounding in; informal crawling, lousy, hopping, stuffed, jam-packed, chock-a-block, chock-full of, buzzing, jumping; Scottish hotching; rare pullulating.

all **determiner 1** *all the children went | all creatures need sleep*: **each of**, each one of the, every one of the, every single one of the; every, each and every, every single.
▷ANTONYMS no.
2 *the sun shone all week | did you believe all that?* **the whole of the**, every bit of the, the complete, the entire, the totality of the; in its entirety.
▷ANTONYMS none of the.
3 *in all honesty | with all speed*: **complete**, entire, total, full, utter, perfect, all-out, greatest (possible), maximum.
▷ANTONYMS no, little.
▶ **pronoun 1** *all are welcome*: **everyone**, everybody, each/every person, the (whole) lot.
▷ANTONYMS none, nobody.
2 *all of the cups were broken*: **each one**, each thing, the sum, the total, the whole lot.
▷ANTONYMS none.
3 *they took all of it*: **everything**, every part, the whole amount, the total amount, the (whole) lot, the entirety, the sum total, the aggregate.
▷ANTONYMS none, nothing.
□ **all and sundry** *they walk out and decry what they've seen to all and sundry*: **everyone**, everybody, every person, each person, each one, each and every one, all, one and all, the whole world, the world at large, the public, the general public, people everywhere; informal {every Tom, Dick, and Harry}, every man jack, every mother's son.
▶ **adverb** *he was dressed all in black*: **completely**, fully, entirely, totally, wholly, absolutely, utterly, outright, thoroughly, altogether, quite, in every respect, in all respects, without reservation, without exception.
▷ANTONYMS partly; not at all.
□ **all but** *the entire nation was limited to three weekly gallons, making long-distance travel by car all but impossible*: **nearly**, almost, just about, about, more or less, practically, virtually, as good as, next to, close to, near, nigh on, not far from, not far off, to all intents and purposes, approaching, bordering on, verging on, nearing; roughly, approximately; not quite; informal pretty nearly, pretty much, pretty well; literary well-nigh.
□ **all for** *I'm all for genetic engineering to remove diseases*: **in favour of**, pro, for, giving support to, giving backing to, right behind, encouraging of, approving of, sympathetic to.
▷ANTONYMS against.
□ **all in all** *all in all, I think this is a thorough report*: **all things considered**, considering everything, on the whole, taking everything into consideration/account, at the end of the day, when all's said and done.

> *Word links* **all**
>
> **omni-** related prefix, as in *omnivorous, omnipresent*
> **pan-** related prefix, as in *pan-European, pansexual*
> **panto-** related prefix, as in *pantograph, pantomime*

allay **verb** *this should help to allay your fears*: **reduce**, diminish, decrease, lessen, assuage, alleviate, ease, relieve, soothe, soften, take the edge off, dull, cushion, mollify, moderate, calm, lull, temper, mitigate, palliate, blunt, deaden, abate, tone down; **dispel**, banish, dismiss, dissipate, drive away, drive off, chase away, put to rest, quell, check, eliminate; rare lenify.
▷ANTONYMS increase, intensify.

allegation **noun** *he rejected the allegation that he had lied*: **claim**, assertion, declaration, statement, proclamation, contention, argument, affirmation, averment, avowal, attestation, testimony, certification, evidence, witness, charge, accusation, suggestion, implication, hint, insinuation, indication, intimation, imputation, plea, pretence, profession; informal making out; technical deposition, representation; rare asseveration.

allege **verb** *she alleged that the boy had hit her*: **claim**, assert, declare, state, proclaim, maintain, advance, contend, argue, affirm, aver, avow, attest, testify, swear, certify, give evidence, bear witness, charge, accuse, suggest, imply, hint, insinuate, indicate, intimate, impute, plead, pretend, profess; technical depose, represent; informal make out; rare asseverate.

alleged **adjective** *the place where the alleged offences were committed*: **supposed**, so-called, claimed, professed, purported, ostensible, apparent, putative, unproven, rumoured, reputed, presumed, assumed, reported, declared, stated, avowed, described.

allegedly **adverb** *he allegedly stabbed the girl*: **reportedly**, supposedly, reputedly, purportedly, ostensibly, apparently, by all accounts, so the story goes, putatively, presumedly, presumably, assumedly, declaredly, avowedly; be accused of being/doing, be alleged to be/have, be said to be/have, be rumoured to be/have.

allegiance **noun** *the warriors quickly swore allegiance to the new king*: **loyalty**, faithfulness, fidelity, obedience, fealty, adherence, homage, devotion, bond; trueness, true-heartedness; trustiness, trustworthiness; steadfastness, fastness, staunchness, dependability, reliability, duty, constancy, dedication, commitment; patriotism; archaic troth.
▷ANTONYMS disloyalty, treachery.

allegorical adjective *an allegorical painting*: **symbolic**, metaphorical, figurative, representative, emblematic, imagistic, mystical, parabolic, symbolizing; rare tropical.
▷ANTONYMS literal.

allegory noun *'Pilgrim's Progress' is an allegory of the spiritual journey*: **parable**, analogy, metaphor, symbol, emblem; story, tale, myth, legend, saga, fable, apologue.

allergic adjective **1** *she was allergic to nuts*: **hypersensitive**, sensitive, susceptible, sensitized.
2 informal *boys are allergic to washing*: **averse**, opposed, hostile, inimical, antagonistic, antipathetic, resistant, unsympathetic; (dead) set against; archaic indisposed.
▷ANTONYMS receptive, in favour of.

allergy noun **1** *she developed an allergy to feathers*: **hypersensitivity**, sensitivity, susceptibility; allergic reaction.
2 informal *their allergy to free enterprise*: **aversion**, antipathy, opposition, hostility, antagonism; dislike of, hate for, distaste for; archaic indisposition.
▷ANTONYMS affinity, liking.

alleviate verb *he couldn't prevent her pain, only alleviate it*: **reduce**, ease, relieve, take the edge off, deaden, dull, diminish, lessen, weaken, lighten, attenuate, allay, assuage, palliate, damp, soothe, help, soften, temper, control, still, quell, quieten, quiet, tone down, blunt, dilute, moderate, mitigate, modify, abate, lull, pacify, placate, mollify, sweeten; rare extenuate.
▷ANTONYMS aggravate.

alley noun **passage**, passageway, alleyway, back alley, backstreet, lane, path, pathway, walk; corridor, aisle, arcade; N. English ginnel, snicket, twitten; Scottish vennel; Scottish & N. English wynd; Indian gully; French allée.

alliance noun **1** *a defensive alliance between Australia and New Zealand*: **association**, union, league, treaty, pact, compact, entente, concordat; bloc, confederation, federation, confederacy, coalition, consortium, combine, syndicate, affiliation, partnership; fraternity, brotherhood, sorority, team, ring, society, club, guild, group, organization.
2 *an alliance between medicine and morality*: **relationship**, affinity, association, connection, closeness, kinship, propinquity.
▷ANTONYMS distance, separation.

allied adjective **1** *a group of allied nations*: **federated**, confederated, federal, associated, in alliance, in league, in partnership, cooperating; unified, united, amalgamated, integrated.
▷ANTONYMS independent; hostile.
2 *agricultural and allied industries*: **associated**, related, connected, interconnected, linked, coupled; similar, like, kindred, comparable, parallel, equivalent, corresponding, cognate, analogous, homologous.
▷ANTONYMS unrelated, dissimilar.

all-important adjective *the town's all-important tourist industry*: **vital**, essential, indispensable, crucial, key, necessary, needed, required, requisite, important, vitally important, of the utmost importance, of great consequence, of the essence, critical, life-and-death, imperative, mandatory; urgent, pressing, burning, compelling, acute; paramount, pre-eminent, high-priority, significant, consequential.
▷ANTONYMS inessential.

allocate verb *the funds will be **allocated to** various projects*: **allot**, assign, issue, award, grant, administer, devote; **share out**, apportion, portion out, distribute, hand out, deal out, dole out, give out, parcel out, ration out, divide out, divide up, dispense, measure out, mete out; earmark for, designate for, set aside for, appropriate for, budget for; informal divvy up, dish out.

allocation noun **1** *more efficient allocation of resources*: **allotment**, assignment, issuing, issuance, awarding, grant, granting, administration; earmarking, designation, setting aside, budgeting; **sharing out**, apportionment, distribution, handing out, dealing out, doling out, giving out, parcelling out, rationing out, dividing out, dividing up, dispensation, measuring out, meting out; informal divvying up, dishing out.
2 *the Ministry spent more than its annual allocation of funds*: **allowance**, allotment, quota, share, ration, grant, limit, portion, helping, slice, stint, lot, measure, proportion, percentage; informal cut, whack.

allot verb *an extra £3 billion has been **allotted to** the health service*: **allocate**, assign, issue, award, grant, administer, devote; earmark for, designate for, set aside for, appropriate for, budget for; **share out**, apportion, portion out, distribute, hand out, deal out, dole out, give out, parcel out, ration out, divide out, divide up, dispense, measure out, mete out; informal divvy up, dish out.

allotment noun **1** Brit. *he grows vegetables on his allotment*: rented plot/land/garden.
2 *the allotment of shares by a company*: **allocation**, assignment, issuing, issuance, awarding, grant, granting, administration, earmarking, designation, setting aside, budgeting; **sharing out**, apportionment, distribution, handing out, dealing out, doling out, giving out, parcelling out, rationing out, dividing out, dividing up, dispensation, measuring out, meting out; informal divvying up, dishing out.
3 *each member received an allotment of new shares*: **quota**, share, ration, grant, limit, portion, allocation, allowance, helping, batch, slice, stint, lot, measure, proportion, percentage; informal cut, whack.

all out adverb *I'm working all out to finish my novel*: **strenuously**, energetically, vigorously, hard, mightily, with all one's might (and main), heartily, with vigour, with great effort, fiercely, intensely, eagerly, enthusiastically, industriously, diligently, assiduously, conscientiously, sedulously, with application, earnestly, with perseverance, persistently, indefatigably; informal like billy-o, like mad, like crazy.
▷ANTONYMS lackadaisically.
▶ adjective *an all-out attack on the enemy*: **strenuous**, energetic, vigorous, powerful, potent, forceful, forcible; spirited, mettlesome, plucky, determined, resolute, aggressive, eager, keen, enthusiastic, zealous, ardent, fervent, vehement, intense, intensive, passionate, fiery; wild, unrestrained, uncontrolled, unbridled; tough, blunt, hard-hitting, pulling no punches; informal punchy, in-your-face.
▷ANTONYMS half-hearted.

allow verb **1** *the police allowed him to go home*: **permit**, let, authorize, give someone permission to, give authorization to, give leave to, sanction, grant, grant someone the right, license, empower, enable, entitle, qualify; **consent to**, assent to, give one's consent/assent to, give one's blessing to, give someone/something the nod, acquiesce in, agree to, accede to, approve of, tolerate, countenance, suffer, brook, admit of; legalize, legitimatize, legitimate; informal give the go-ahead to, give the thumbs up to, OK, give the OK to, give the green light to, say the word.
▷ANTONYMS prevent, forbid.
2 *allow an hour or so for driving*: **set aside**, allocate, allot, earmark, designate, spare, devote, give, afford, apportion, assign.
3 *the house was demolished to **allow for** road widening*: **provide for**, plan for, make plans for, get ready for, cater for, take into consideration, take into account, make provision for, make preparations for, prepare for, accommodate, make allowances for, make concessions for, arrange for; bargain for, reckon with.
▷ANTONYMS discount.
4 *she allowed that all people had their funny little ways*: **admit**, acknowledge, recognize, agree, accept, concede, grant, own, confess, accede.
▷ANTONYMS deny.

allowable adjective *the maximum allowable number of users*: **permissible**, permitted, allowed, admissible, acceptable, legal, lawful, legitimate, licit, within the law, authorized, sanctioned, sanctionable, approved, above board, within accepted bounds, passable, tolerated, tolerable, proper, all right, in order; excusable, pardonable, venial; informal OK, legit, kosher, pukka, by the book.
▷ANTONYMS forbidden.

allowance noun **1** *your baggage allowance*: **permitted amount/quantity**, allocation, allotment, quota, share, ration, grant, limit, portion, helping, slice, lot.
2 *her father gave her an allowance*: **payment**, pocket money, sum of money, remittance, contribution, consideration, handout, grant, subsidy, maintenance, financial support, subsistence, benefit, stipend, pension, annuity, keep, upkeep, expenses.
3 *a tax allowance*: **concession**, reduction, decrease, deduction, discount, weighting, rebate, refund, repayment.
□ **make allowance(s) for 1** *you must make allowances for delays*: **take into consideration**, take into account, bear in mind, keep in mind, not lose sight of, have regard to, provide for, plan for, make plans for, foresee, anticipate, get ready for, cater for, allow for, make provision for, make preparations for, prepare for, accommodate, make concessions for; bargain for, reckon with, remember. **2** *she made allowances for his faults*: **excuse**, make excuses for, forgive, pardon, overlook, pass over, treat leniently, condone; rare remit.

alloy noun (stress on the first syllable) *bronze is an alloy of copper and tin*: **mixture**, mix, amalgam, fusion, meld, blend, compound, combination, admixture, composite, union.
▶ verb (stress on the second syllable) *copper and tin are alloyed to make bronze*: **mix**, amalgamate, fuse, meld, blend, compound, combine, unite, intermix, intermingle; rare admix.

all-powerful adjective *an all-powerful ruler*: **omnipotent**, almighty, supreme, most high, pre-eminent; dictatorial, despotic, totalitarian, autocratic, autarchic; invincible, unconquerable.
▷ANTONYMS powerless.

all right adjective **1** *the tea was all right*: **satisfactory**, acceptable, adequate, good enough, fairly good, fine, passable, reasonable, unobjectionable, suitable; informal OK, so-so.
▷ANTONYMS unsatisfactory.
2 *are you sure you're all right?* **unhurt**, uninjured, unscathed, in one piece, undamaged, safe, safe and sound, unharmed, alive and well, well, fine, out of danger, out of the wood(s); informal OK.
▷ANTONYMS hurt, in danger.

3 *it's all right for you to go now*: **permissible**, permitted, allowed, allowable, admissible, acceptable; legal, lawful, legitimate, licit, within the law, authorized, sanctioned, sanctionable, approved, above board, within accepted bounds; passable, tolerated, tolerable, proper, in order; excusable, pardonable, venial; informal OK, legit, kosher, pukka.
▷ANTONYMS forbidden, unacceptable.
▸**adverb 1** *the system works all right*: **satisfactorily**, adequately, well enough, fairly well, fine, passably, acceptably, reasonably, unobjectionably, suitably; informal OK.
▷ANTONYMS unsatisfactorily.
2 *it's him all right*: **definitely**, certainly, unquestionably, undoubtedly, positively, without (a) doubt, beyond any doubt, beyond doubt, beyond question, unmistakably, indubitably, undeniably, beyond the shadow of a doubt, surely, assuredly; in truth, truly, really, in reality, actually, in fact; archaic forsooth, in sooth, verily.
▷ANTONYMS possibly.
▸**exclamation** *all right, I'll go*: **very well (then)**, fine, good, right, right then, yes, agreed; informal wilco, OK, oke, okey-dokey, okey-doke, roger; Brit. informal righto, righty-ho; Indian informal acha.
▷ANTONYMS no.

allude verb *the Vice-Chancellor* ***alluded to*** *the same idea*: **refer to**, suggest, hint at, imply, mention, touch on, mention in passing, mention en passant, speak briefly of, make an allusion to, cite; rare advert to.

allure noun *the nostalgic allure of Paris in the fifties*: **attraction**, lure, draw, pull, appeal, glamour, allurement, enticement, temptation, bewitchment, enchantment, charm, seduction, persuasion, fascination, magnetism.
▷ANTONYMS repulsion.
▸**verb** *melody is the element with the most power to allure the listener*: **attract**, lure, entice, tempt, appeal to, whet the appetite of, make someone's mouth water, captivate, draw, beguile, bewitch, enchant, win over, charm, seduce, persuade, lead on, tantalize; intrigue, fascinate; informal give the come-on to.
▷ANTONYMS repel.

alluring adjective *the old town offers alluring shops and restaurants*: **enticing**, tempting, attractive, appealing, fetching, inviting, glamorous, captivating, seductive; enchanting, beguiling, charming, fascinating, intriguing, tantalizing, magnetic; irresistible; informal, dated come-hither.

allusion noun *the bird's name is doubtless an* ***allusion to*** *its raucous call*: **reference to**, mention of, comment on, remark about, citation of, quotation of, hint at, intimation of, suggestion of; implication, insinuation.

ally noun *he was forced to dismiss his closest political ally*: **associate**, colleague, friend, confederate, partner, supporter, accomplice, helper, accessory, abetter.
▷ANTONYMS enemy, opponent.
▸**verb 1** *he allied his racing experience with his father's business acumen*: **combine**, marry, couple, merge, amalgamate, join, pool, fuse, weld, knit.
▷ANTONYMS split.
2 *the Catholic powers in France had allied with Philip II | Bruce once more* ***allied himself*** *with the English*: **unite**, join, join up, join forces, band together, go into partnership, team up, combine, collaborate, side, align oneself, league, go into league, affiliate, confederate, form an alliance, throw in one's lot, make common cause.
▷ANTONYMS split.

almanac noun *a nautical almanac*: **yearbook**, calendar, register, annual, manual, handbook, compendium; annal(s), archive(s), chronicle(s).

almighty adjective **1** *I swear by almighty God*: **all-powerful**, omnipotent, supreme, most high, pre-eminent; invincible, unconquerable.
▷ANTONYMS powerless.
2 informal *an almighty explosion*. See **huge**.

almost adverb *lunch is almost ready*: **nearly**, just about, about, more or less, practically, virtually, all but, as good as, next to, close to, near, nigh on, not far from, not far off, to all intents and purposes, approaching, bordering on, verging on, nearing; roughly, approximately; not quite; informal pretty nearly, pretty much, pretty well; literary well-nigh.

alms plural noun historical *a beggar held out a hand for alms*: **gift(s)**, donation(s), charity, handout(s), bounty, benefaction, subsidy, offering(s), contribution(s), endowment, favour(s), largesse; in parts of the Middle & Far East baksheesh; Islam zakat; rare donative.

aloft adjective & adverb **1** *he hoisted the Cup aloft*: **upwards**, up, high, higher, into the air, into the sky, skyward, on high, heavenward.
▷ANTONYMS down.
2 *the airships were able to stay aloft for many hours*: **in the air**, in the sky, high up, up, high, up above, on high, overhead, above.
▷ANTONYMS down.

alone adjective & adverb **1** *she was alone in the house | he lived alone*: **by oneself**, on one's own, all alone, solo, lone, solitary, single, singly; **unescorted**, without an escort, unattended, unchaperoned, partnerless, companionless; Latin solus; Brit. informal on one's tod, on one's lonesome, on one's jack, on one's Jack Jones; Austral./NZ informal on one's pat, on one's Pat Malone.
▷ANTONYMS accompanied, in company.
2 *he managed alone*: **unaided**, unassisted, without help, without assistance, by one's own efforts, under one's own steam, independently, single-handedly, solo, on one's own, all alone, off one's own bat, on one's own initiative.
▷ANTONYMS with help.
3 *she felt terribly alone*: **lonely**, isolated, solitary, deserted, abandoned, forsaken, forlorn, friendless, desolate.
▷ANTONYMS loved, wanted.
4 *a house standing alone*: **apart**, by itself/oneself, separate, detached, isolated, to one side, unconnected.
▷ANTONYMS among others.
5 *you alone can inspire me*: **only**, solely, just, uniquely, exclusively; and no one else, and nothing else, to the exclusion of everyone/everything else, no one but, nothing but.

along preposition **1** *she walked along the corridor*: **down**, throughout the length of, from one end of ... to the other, through, across.
2 *trees grew along the river bank*: **beside**, by the side of, on the edge of, alongside, next to, adjacent to, close by, in a line by, one after the other by.
3 *they'll have to stop somewhere along the way*: **on**, at a point on, in the middle of; in the course of, during.
▸**adverb 1** *Maurice moved along past the other exhibits*: **onwards**, on, ahead, forward(s), further.
2 *I invited a friend along*: **as company**, with one, to accompany one, as a partner, in company.
□ **along with** *he spent three weeks at Etna along with two colleagues*: **together with**, accompanying, accompanied by, in company with; at the same time as; as well as, in addition to, plus, coupled with, added to, besides, on top of.

aloof adjective *I used to be aloof because I didn't want people becoming too familiar*: **distant**, detached, unresponsive, remote, unapproachable, forbidding, stand-offish, formal, impersonal, stiff, austere, stuffy, withdrawn, reserved, unforthcoming, uncommunicative, indifferent; **unfriendly**, unsympathetic, unsociable, antisocial, cool, cold, chilly, frigid, frosty; haughty, supercilious, disdainful.
▷ANTONYMS familiar, friendly.

aloud adverb *he read the letter aloud*: **audibly**, out loud, for all to hear, clearly, distinctly, plainly, intelligibly.
▷ANTONYMS silently.

alphabet noun *can you say the alphabet backwards?* **ABC**, letters; symbols, icons, writing system, syllabary; rare signary.

already adverb **1** *Anna had suffered a great deal already*: **by this/that time**, by now/then, thus far, so far, hitherto, before, before now/then, previously, earlier, earlier on, until now/then, up to now/then; rare heretofore.
2 *is it 3 o'clock already?* **as early as this/that**, as soon as this/that, so soon, so early, even now/then.

also adverb *he's also very good at sport*: **too**, as well, besides, in addition, additionally, furthermore, further, moreover, into the bargain, on top (of that), over and above that, what's more, to boot, else, then, equally; informal and all; archaic withal, forbye.

alter verb **1** *he altered his theories a number of times*: **change**, make changes to, make different, make alterations to, adjust, make adjustments to, adapt, amend, improve, modify, convert, revise, recast, reform, reshape, refashion, redesign, restyle, revamp, rework, remake, remodel, remould, redo, reconstruct, reorganize, reorder, refine, reorient, reorientate, vary, transform, transfigure, transmute, evolve; customize, tailor; informal tweak; technical permute.
▷ANTONYMS preserve.
2 *the state of affairs has altered*: **change**, become different, undergo a change, undergo a sea change, turn, adjust, adapt, convert, vary, transform, metamorphose, evolve, improve.
▷ANTONYMS stay the same.

alteration noun *he made an alteration to the text*: **change**, adjustment, adaptation, modification, variation, conversion, revision, amendment; remodelling, reshaping, remoulding, redoing, reconstruction, rebuilding, recasting, reorganization, rearrangement, reordering, reshuffling, restyling, rejigging, reworking, renewal, renewing, revamping, renovation, remaking; metamorphosis, transformation, transfiguration, translation, evolution, mutation, sea change; humorous transmogrification.
▷ANTONYMS preservation.

altercation noun *I had an altercation with the ticket collector*: **argument**, quarrel, squabble, fight, shouting match, contretemps, disagreement, difference of opinion, dissension, falling-out, dispute, disputation, contention, clash, acrimonious exchange, war of words, wrangle; Irish, N. Amer., & Austral. donnybrook; informal tiff, set-to, run-in, spat, scrap, dust-up; Brit. informal row, barney, slanging match, ding-dong, bust-up, bit of argy-bargy, ruck; Scottish informal rammy; N. Amer. informal rhubarb; archaic broil, miff; Scottish archaic threap, collieshangie.

alternate verb **1** *stands of trees alternate with dense shrubby tundra*: **be interspersed**, follow one another, be staggered, take turns, take it in turns, work/act in sequence, occur in turn, occur in rotation; rotate, oscillate, see-saw, yo-yo, chop and change, fluctuate.
2 *we could alternate the groups so that no one felt they had been left out*: **give turns to**, take in turn, rotate, take in rotation; intersperse, stagger, swap, exchange, interchange, switch, vary.
▸ **adjective 1** *she was asked to attend on alternate days*: **every other**, every second.
2 *place the leeks and noodles in alternate layers*: **alternating**, in rotation, rotating, occurring in turns, interchanging, following in sequence, sequential.
3 N. Amer. *an alternate plan of action*: **alternative**, other, another, second, different, possible, substitute, replacement, deputy, relief, proxy, surrogate, cover, fill-in, stand-in, standby, emergency, reserve, backup, auxiliary, fallback; N. Amer. informal pinch-hitting.

alternative adjective **1** *an alternative route | an alternative government*: **different**, other, another, second, possible, substitute, replacement; deputy, relief, proxy, surrogate, cover, fill-in, stand-in; standby, emergency, reserve, backup, auxiliary, fallback; N. Amer. alternate; N. Amer. informal pinch-hitting.
2 *alternative medicine | an alternative lifestyle*: **unorthodox**, unconventional, non-standard, unusual, uncommon, unwonted, out of the ordinary, radical, revolutionary, nonconformist, unconforming, irregular, offbeat, avant-garde; original, new, novel, fresh; eccentric, exotic, Bohemian, idiosyncratic, abnormal, extreme, divergent, aberrant, anomalous, bizarre, outlandish, perverse; informal off the wall, oddball, way-out, cranky, zany; rare heteroclite.
▸ **noun** *we have no alternative but to go | an acceptable alternative to tropical hardwood*: **option**, choice, other possibility; substitute, replacement, proxy, reserve, surrogate, stand-in; possible course of action, resort, way out.

alternatively adverb *alternatively, you can build your own barbecue*: **on the other hand**, as an alternative, or, as another option, as a substitute, as a replacement; otherwise, instead, if not, then again, but; N. Amer. alternately.

although conjunction *although the sun was shining it wasn't that warm*: **in spite of the fact that**, despite the fact that, notwithstanding the fact that, notwithstanding that, even though, even if, for all that, while, whilst; granted that, even supposing, despite the possibility that, albeit, however, yet, but.

altitude noun *we are now flying at an altitude of 40,000 feet*: **height**, elevation, distance above the sea/ground; loftiness.
▷ANTONYMS depth.

> *Word links* **altitude**
>
> **altimetry**, **hypsometry** measurement of altitude

altogether adverb **1** *he wasn't altogether happy*: **completely**, totally, entirely, absolutely, wholly, fully, thoroughly, utterly, quite, one hundred per cent, downright, unqualifiedly, in all respects, unconditionally, perfectly, unrestrictedly, consummately, undisputedly, unmitigatedly, wholeheartedly; {lock, stock, and barrel}, in toto; at all, very, terribly.
▷ANTONYMS partially.
2 *we have five offices altogether*: **in all**, all told, in toto, taken together, in sum, counting them all.
3 *altogether it was a great evening*: **on the whole**, overall, all in all, all things considered, taking everything into consideration/account, on balance, on average, for the most part, mostly, mainly, in the main, in general, generally, generally speaking, largely, by and large, to a large extent, to a great degree.
▷ANTONYMS relatively.

altruism noun *they supported the measures not out of altruism but out of self-interest*: **unselfishness**, selflessness, self-sacrifice, self-denial; consideration, compassion, kindness, goodwill, decency, nobility, public-spiritedness; generosity, magnanimity, liberality, open-handedness, free-handedness, big-heartedness, lavishness, benevolence, beneficence, philanthropy, humanitarianism, charity, charitableness; literary bounty, bounteousness.
▷ANTONYMS selfishness.

altruistic adjective *a wholly altruistic desire to help*: **unselfish**, selfless, self-sacrificing, self-denying; considerate, compassionate, kind, decent, noble, public-spirited; generous, magnanimous, ungrudging, unstinting, charitable, benevolent, beneficent, liberal, open-handed, free-handed, philanthropic, humanitarian; literary bounteous.
▷ANTONYMS selfish.

always adverb **1** *he's always late*: **every time**, each time, at all times, all the time, on every occasion, on all occasions, consistently, invariably, without fail, without exception, regularly, repeatedly, habitually, unfailingly, infallibly, inevitably.
▷ANTONYMS never; seldom; sometimes.
2 *she's always complaining*: **continually**, continuously, constantly, forever, repeatedly, perpetually, incessantly, ceaselessly, unceasingly, endlessly, interminably, eternally, the entire time, permanently; informal 24-7.
3 *the place will always be dear to me*: **forever**, permanently, for always, for good, for good and all, perpetually, ever, (for) evermore, for ever and ever, for all (future) time, until the end of time, eternally, for eternity, in perpetuity, everlastingly, endlessly; N. Amer. forevermore; informal for keeps, until hell freezes over, until the cows come home, until doomsday; archaic for aye.
4 *you can always take it back to the shop*: **as a last resort**, whatever the circumstances, no matter what, in any event, in any case, come what may.

amalgam noun *a curious amalgam of the traditional and the modern*: **combination**, union, merger, blend, mixture, mingling, compound, fusion, marriage, weave, coalescence, synthesis, composite, composition, concoction, amalgamation; informal mash-up.

amalgamate verb *the two departments were amalgamated | various companies amalgamated*: **combine**, merge, unite, integrate, fuse, blend, mingle, coalesce, consolidate, meld, intermingle, mix, intermix, incorporate, affiliate; join (together), join forces, band (together), club together, get together, link (up), team up, go into partnership, pool resources; unify; informal gang up, gang together; literary commingle.
▷ANTONYMS separate.

amalgamation noun *the Queen's Regiment is an amalgamation of several others*: **combination**, union, merger, blend, mixture, mingling, compound, fusion, marriage, weave, coalescence, synthesis, composite, composition, concoction, amalgam; informal mash-up.

amass verb *he amassed a large fortune*: **gather**, collect, assemble; accumulate, stockpile, pile up, heap up, rack up, run up, scrape together, store (up), hoard, cumulate, accrue, lay in/up, garner; informal stash (away).
▷ANTONYMS dissipate.

amateur noun **1** *the crew were all amateurs who had paid £15,000 apiece for the trip*: **non-professional**, non-specialist, layman, layperson; dilettante, dabbler, potterer, trifler; enthusiast, devotee, fan, ... lover; informal buff, ham.
▷ANTONYMS professional.
2 *what a bunch of amateurs*: **bungler**, blunderer, incompetent, bumbler; Brit. informal bodger.
▷ANTONYMS expert.
▸ **adjective 1** *it is still largely an amateur sport*: **non-professional**, non-specialist, lay; dilettante; enthusiasts'.
2 *they may scoff at others' amateur efforts*: **incompetent**, inept, useless, unskilful, inexpert, clumsy, maladroit, gauche, blundering, bungling, bumbling, amateurish, botched, crude; Brit. informal bodged.

amateurish adjective *he dismissed the tape as an amateurish hoax*: **incompetent**, inept, useless, unskilful, inexpert, amateur, clumsy, maladroit, gauche, blundering, bungling, bumbling, botched, crude; Brit. informal bodged.
▷ANTONYMS professional.

amatory adjective *his amatory exploits*: **sexual**, erotic, amorous, romantic, sensual, libidinous, passionate, ardent, hot-blooded, sexy; torrid; informal randy, steamy, naughty.
▷ANTONYMS platonic; frigid.

amaze verb *it never ceases to amaze me*: **astonish**, astound, surprise, bewilder, stun, stagger, flabbergast, nonplus, shock, startle, shake, stop someone in their tracks, stupefy, leave open-mouthed, leave aghast, take someone's breath away, dumbfound, daze, benumb, perplex, confound, dismay, disconcert, shatter, take aback, jolt, shake up; informal bowl over, knock for six, floor, blow someone's mind, strike dumb; (**amazed**) thunderstruck, at a loss for words, speechless; Brit. informal gobsmacked.

amazement noun *they stared in amazement*: **astonishment**, surprise, bewilderment, shock, stupefaction, dismay, consternation, devastation, confusion, perplexity, incredulity, disbelief, bafflement, speechlessness, awe, wonder, wonderment.

amazing adjective *yet another amazing coincidence*: **astonishing**, astounding, surprising, bewildering, stunning, staggering, shocking, startling, stupefying, breathtaking, perplexing, confounding, dismaying, disconcerting, shattering; awesome, awe-inspiring, sensational, remarkable, spectacular, stupendous, phenomenal, prodigious, extraordinary, incredible, unbelievable; wonderful, marvellous; thrilling, exciting; informal mind-blowing, flabbergasting; literary wondrous; rare dumbfounding.
▷ANTONYMS everyday.

ambassador noun **1** *the American ambassador to London*: **envoy**, diplomat, ambassador extraordinary, ambassador plenipotentiary, plenipotentiary, consul, attaché, chargé d'affaires, emissary, legate, (papal) nuncio, representative, deputy; dated ambassadress.
2 *a great ambassador for the sport*: **campaigner**; **representative**, exponent, promoter, proponent, advocate, champion, supporter, backer, upholder, protagonist; N. Amer. booster.

ambience noun *the relaxed ambience of the cocktail lounge*: **atmosphere**, air, aura, climate, mood, feel, feeling, vibrations, echo, character, quality, complexion, impression, flavour, look, tone, tenor, spirit; **setting**, milieu, background, backdrop, frame, element; environment, conditions, circumstances, situation, context; vicinity, locality, habitat; informal vibes.

ambiguity noun *the plot revolves around the ambiguity in the title*: **ambivalence**, equivocation; obscurity, vagueness, abstruseness, doubtfulness, uncertainty; puzzle, enigma; archaic equivocacy; rare dubiety; (**ambiguities**) doublespeak, doubletalk.
▷ANTONYMS unambiguousness, transparency.

ambiguous adjective *the judge agreed that the law was ambiguous*: **equivocal**, ambivalent, open to debate, open to argument, arguable, debatable; Delphic, cryptic, enigmatic, gnomic, paradoxical, misleading; obscure, unclear, vague, abstruse, puzzling, perplexing, riddling, doubtful, dubious, uncertain; double-edged, backhanded.
▷ANTONYMS unambiguous, clear.

ambit noun *a select committee can review any matter that falls within its ambit*. See **scope** (sense 1).

ambition noun **1** *young people with ambition*: **drive**, determination, desire, enterprise, initiative, eagerness, motivation, enthusiasm, zeal, commitment, a sense of purpose, longing, yearning, hankering; informal get-up-and-go.
2 *her ambition was to become a model*: **aspiration**, intention, goal, aim, objective, object, purpose, intent, plan, scheme, mission, calling, vocation, desire, wish, design, target, end, dream, hope.

ambitious adjective **1** *he was an exceptionally energetic, ambitious, and intelligent politician*: **aspiring**, determined, forceful, pushy, enterprising, pioneering, progressive, eager, motivated, enthusiastic, energetic, zealous, committed, go-ahead, go-getting, purposeful, assertive, aggressive, hungry, power-hungry; informal on the make.
▷ANTONYMS unambitious, lazy.
2 *he was ambitious to make it to the top*: **eager**, determined, enthusiastic, desirous, anxious, hungry, impatient, striving, yearning, longing, wishing, itching, dying, hoping, avid, hankering; intent on; informal raring.
3 *an ambitious task*: **difficult**, exacting, demanding, formidable, challenging, hard, arduous, onerous, tough, stiff, strenuous; **bold**, grandiose, extravagant, monumental; informal killing, hellish; Brit. informal knackering; archaic toilsome.
▷ANTONYMS unambitious, easy; modest.

ambivalence noun *there is ambivalence over whether cars should be encouraged into the countryside*: **equivocation**, uncertainty, unsureness, doubt, indecision, inconclusiveness, irresolution, irresoluteness, hesitation, hesitancy, fluctuation, vacillation, shilly-shallying, tentativeness; conflict, contradiction, clash, confusion, dilemma, quandary; muddle, vagueness, haze, haziness, unclearness; informal iffiness; archaic equivocacy.
▷ANTONYMS certainty, decisiveness.

ambivalent adjective *the public has a rather ambivalent attitude toward science*: **equivocal**, uncertain, unsure, doubtful, indecisive, inconclusive, irresolute, in two minds, undecided, unresolved, in a dilemma, on the horns of a dilemma, in a quandary, on the fence, torn, hesitating, fluctuating, wavering, vacillating, equivocating, mixed; opposing, conflicting, contradictory, clashing; confused, muddled, vague, hazy, unclear; informal iffy, blowing hot and cold.
▷ANTONYMS unequivocal, certain.

amble verb *they ambled along the river bank*: **stroll**, saunter, wander, meander, ramble, dawdle, promenade, walk, go for a walk, take a walk, roam, traipse, stretch one's legs, get some exercise, get some air, take the air; Scottish & Irish stravaig; informal mosey, tootle; Brit. informal pootle, mooch, swan; N. Amer. informal putter; rare perambulate, peregrinate.
▷ANTONYMS stride.

> *Choose the right word* **amble, stroll, saunter**
>
> See **stroll**.

ambush noun *seven members of a patrol were killed in an ambush*: **surprise attack**, **trap**, snare, pitfall, lure; dated ambuscade.
▸ verb *a gang of twenty youths ambushed their patrol car*: **attack by surprise**, **trap**, surprise, pounce on, lay a trap for, set an ambush for, lie in wait for, waylay, entrap, ensnare; N. Amer. bushwhack; archaic ambuscade.

ameliorate verb *any move that ameliorates the situation is welcome*. See **improve** (sense 1).

amelioration noun *a decided amelioration in the status of women*. See **improvement**.

amenable adjective **1** *an easy-going, amenable child*: **compliant**, acquiescent, biddable, manageable, controllable, governable, persuadable, tractable, responsive, pliant, flexible, malleable, complaisant, accommodating, docile, submissive, obedient, tame, meek, easily handled; rare persuasible.
▷ANTONYMS uncooperative.
2 *many cancers of this kind are* ***amenable to*** *treatment*: **susceptible**, receptive, responsive, reactive, vulnerable; defenceless against; rare susceptive.
▷ANTONYMS resistant.

amend verb *the government may amend the law*: **revise**, alter, change, modify, qualify, adapt, adjust; edit, copy-edit, rewrite, redraft, recast, rephrase, reword, rework, reform, update, revamp; **correct**, remedy, fix, set right, put right, repair, emend, improve, ameliorate, better, enhance, clarify.

amendment noun *Parliament approved an amendment to the Constitution*: **revision**, alteration, change, modification, qualification, adaptation, adjustment; edit, editing, rewrite, rewriting, redraft, redrafting, recasting, rephrasing, rewording, reworking, reform; update, revamp, reshaping; **correction**, emendation, improvement, enhancement, clarification.

amends plural noun *I wanted to* ***make amends for*** *the way I treated his mother*: **compensation**, recompense, reparation, restitution, restoration, redress, indemnity, indemnification, atonement, expiation, requital; atone for, make up for, make good, do penance for, expiate, pay the price for; redeem oneself, redress the balance.
□ **make amends to** *we want to make amends to them for the hurt we have caused*: **compensate**, recompense, indemnify, make it up to, repay, reimburse, pay back.

amenity noun **1** *the older type of housing lacks basic amenities*: **facility**, service, convenience, resource, utility, system, appliance, aid, advantage, comfort, benefit, arrangement, opportunity; (**amenities**) equipment, provision, assistance.
2 *gravel working means lorries, dust, noise, and a general loss of amenity*: **pleasantness**, agreeableness, pleasurableness, enjoyableness, niceness.

America noun See **United States of America**.

amiability noun *she was now all amiability*: **friendliness**, affability, cordiality; warmth, warm-heartedness, good nature, niceness, pleasantness, agreeableness, likeability, lovableness, geniality, amicableness, amicability, sociableness; good humour, charm, kindness, kindliness; neighbourliness, hospitality, companionableness, sociability, gregariousness, conviviality, clubbability, clubbableness, personableness; Scottish couthiness; Brit. informal chumminess, mateyness.
▷ANTONYMS unfriendliness.

amiable adjective *this amiable young man greeted me enthusiastically*: **friendly**, affable, amicable, cordial; warm, warm-hearted, good-natured, nice, pleasant, agreeable, pleasing, likeable, lovable, genial, good-humoured, charming, winning, engaging, delightful, easy to get on/along with, obliging, kind, kindly; neighbourly, hospitable, companionable, sociable, gregarious, convivial, clubbable, personable; Scottish couthy; Brit. informal chummy, matey; N. Amer. informal regular; rare conversable.
▷ANTONYMS unfriendly, disagreeable.

amicable adjective *we have always enjoyed a very amicable relationship*: **friendly**, good-natured, cordial, civil, courteous, polite, easy, easy-going, neighbourly, brotherly, fraternal, harmonious, cooperative, civilized; non-hostile, peaceable, peaceful.
▷ANTONYMS unfriendly, hostile.

amid preposition **1** *the jeep was concealed amid pine trees*: **in the middle of**, surrounded by, among, amongst, between, in the thick of; literary amidst, in the midst of.
▷ANTONYMS surrounding.
2 *the truce collapsed amid fears of an army revolt*: **at a time of**, in an atmosphere of, against a background of, during; as a result of.

amiss adjective *an inspection revealed nothing amiss*: **wrong**, awry, faulty, out of order, defective, unsatisfactory, incorrect, untoward, adrift, astray, inappropriate, improper, unsuitable.
▷ANTONYMS right, in order.
□ **not come/go amiss** *an apology wouldn't go amiss*: **be welcome**, be appropriate, be useful.
□ **take something amiss** *they would take it amiss if they were left out*: **be offended by**, take offence at, be upset by.

amity noun *this will bring greater amity between our peoples*: **friendship**, friendliness, peace, peacefulness, peaceableness, harmony, harmoniousness, understanding, accord, concord, concurrence, cooperation, amicableness, goodwill, cordiality, warmth, geniality, fellowship, fraternity, brotherhood, brotherliness; rare comity.
▷ANTONYMS animosity, enmity.

ammunition noun **1** *police seized arms and ammunition*: **bullets**, **shells**, projectiles, missiles, rounds, shot, slugs, cartridges, rockets, bombs, stores; munitions, materiel; informal ammo.
2 *the report could provide ammunition for legal action*: **arguments**, considerations, points, pointers, material, information, evidence, testimony, facts, data, input; fuel, encouragement.

amnesty noun *an amnesty for political prisoners*: **pardon**, pardoning, reprieve; release, discharge, liberty, freedom; absolution, forgiveness, dispensation, remission, indulgence, clemency, mercy; informal let-off, letting off.

▸ verb *the guerrillas were amnestied and allowed to return to civilian life*: **pardon**, grant an amnesty to, reprieve; release, discharge, liberate, free; forgive, excuse, exempt, spare, deliver; deal leniently with, be lenient on/to, be merciful to, show mercy to, have mercy on; informal let off, let off the hook, go easy on.

amok, amuck adverb
□ **run amok** *the army had run amok in the town, killing and looting*: **go berserk**, get out of control, rampage, run riot, riot, rush wildly/madly about, go on the rampage; storm, charge; behave like a maniac, behave wildly, behave uncontrollably; become violent, become destructive; go mad, go crazy, go insane; informal steam, raise hell; N. Amer. informal go postal.

among, amongst preposition **1** *you're among friends*: **surrounded by**, in the company of, amid, in the middle of, between, in the thick of; literary amidst, in the midst of.
2 *a child was among the injured*: **included in**, one of, some of, in the group of, in the number of, out of.
3 *you'll have to decide **among yourselves***: **jointly**, with one another, together, mutually, reciprocally; by the joint action of, by all of, by the whole of.
4 *he had to distribute the proceeds among his creditors*: **between**, to each of.

amoral adjective *without society we are amoral beings*: **unprincipled**, without standards, without morals; unethical, without scruples, unscrupulous.
▷ANTONYMS moral, principled.

Easily confused words **amoral or immoral?**

Amoral means 'not concerned with or affected by morality', so that something described as *amoral* cannot appropriately be criticized for failure to conform to accepted moral standards (*the client pays for the amoral expertise of the lawyer*). **Immoral**, on the other hand, means 'not conforming to accepted standards of morality', and implies condemnation (*they felt it was immoral to accept a loan that they could not hope to repay*).

amorous adjective *she rejected his amorous advances*: **lustful**, sexual, erotic, amatory, ardent; passionate, impassioned; romantic; affectionate, fond, loving, tender, doting; in love, enamoured, lovesick; informal lovey-dovey, spoony, kissy, smoochy, goo-goo, hot; Brit. informal slap-and-tickle, randy; archaic sportive.
▷ANTONYMS unloving, cold.

amorphous adjective *an amorphous grey mass which proved to be mashed potato*: **shapeless**, formless, unformed, unshaped, structureless, unstructured, indeterminate, indefinite, vague, nebulous.
▷ANTONYMS shaped; definite.

amount noun *a substantial amount of money | the same amount of people as last year*: **quantity**, **number**, total, aggregate, sum, quota, group, size, mass, weight, volume, bulk, load, consignment; proportion, portion, part, dose, dosage; technical quantum.
□ **the full amount the grand total**, the total, the aggregate; informal the whole caboodle, the whole shebang, the full nine yards.
▸ verb
□ **amount to 1** *the bill amounted to £50*: **add up to**, come to, run to, number, be, make, total, equal, be equal to, be equivalent to, represent, count as; Brit. tot up to. **2** *the delays amounted to maladministration*: **constitute**, comprise, be equivalent to, be tantamount to, approximate to, add up to, come down to, boil down to; signify, signal, mean, indicate, suggest, denote, point to, be evidence of, be symptomatic of; informal spell, spell out; literary betoken. **3** *her relationships had never amounted to anything significant*: **become**, grow into, develop into, mature into, prove to be, turn out to be, progress to, advance to.

amphibian noun

Word links **amphibian**

batrachophobia fear of amphibians

ample adjective **1** *there is ample time for discussion*: **enough**, sufficient, adequate, plenty of, abundant, more than enough, enough and to spare; suitable, satisfactory, passable, allowable, tolerable; informal plenty, decent.
▷ANTONYMS insufficient.
2 *an ample supply of wine*: **plentiful**, abundant, copious, profuse, rich, lavish, liberal, generous, bountiful, large, huge, great, bumper, flush, overflowing, superabundant, infinite, inexhaustible, opulent, prolific, teeming; informal a gogo, galore; S. African informal lank; literary bounteous, plenteous.
▷ANTONYMS meagre.
3 *he leaned back in his ample chair | his ample tunic*: **spacious**, commodious, capacious, roomy, sizeable, substantial, generous, big, large, broad, wide, extensive; voluminous, loose-fitting, baggy, slack, sloppy, full; rare spacey.
▷ANTONYMS cramped; tight-fitting.

amplify verb **1** *many frogs amplify the sound of their voices*: **louden**, make louder, turn up, increase, boost, step up, raise, magnify, intensify, escalate, swell, heighten; add to, augment, supplement.
▷ANTONYMS reduce, quieten.
2 *the notes amplify information contained in the statement*: **expand**, enlarge on, elaborate on, add to, develop, flesh out, add flesh to, add detail to, go into detail about, embroider, supplement, augment, reinforce.
▷ANTONYMS condense.

amplitude noun *the amplitude of the output signal*: **magnitude**, size, volume, proportions, dimensions; extent, range, scope, compass; breadth, width.

amputate verb *they had to amputate his leg*: **cut off**, sever, remove (surgically), saw off, chop off, lop off, hack off, dock, cleave, hew off, shear off, slice off; separate, part, detach, disconnect; rare dissever, abscise.

amulet noun *they wore amulets to ward off the plague*: **lucky charm**, charm, talisman, fetish, mascot, totem, idol, juju, phylactery; archaic periapt.

amuse verb **1** *her annoyance simply amused him*: **entertain**, make laugh, delight, divert, gladden, cheer (up), please, charm, tickle, convulse, beguile, enliven, regale; informal tickle someone pink, crack someone up, wow, be a hit with; Brit. informal crease someone up.
▷ANTONYMS bore, depress.
2 *he amused himself by writing poetry*: **occupy**, engage, busy, employ, distract, absorb, engross, preoccupy, hold, hold someone's attention, immerse, interest, involve, entertain, divert, beguile.

amusement noun **1** *we looked with amusement at the cartoon*: **mirth**, merriment, light-heartedness, hilarity, glee, delight, laughter, levity, gaiety, joviality, fun, jocularity; enjoyment, pleasure, high spirits, mirthfulness, cheerfulness, cheeriness, cheer; dated sport.
▷ANTONYMS boredom, depression.
2 *I read the book for amusement*: **entertainment**, pleasure, leisure, relaxation, fun, enjoyment, interest, occupation, refreshment, restoration, distraction, diversion, divertissement, play; informal R and R, jollies; Brit. informal beer and skittles; N. Amer. informal rec; dated sport; archaic disport.
3 *the camp site offers a wide range of amusements*: **activity**, entertainment, diversion, distraction, interest, recreation, game, sport, pastime, hobby.

amusing adjective *they are very colourful and amusing characters*: **entertaining**, funny, comical, humorous, light-hearted, jocular, witty, mirthful, hilarious, chucklesome, ludicrous, laughable, rollicking, facetious, droll, whimsical, novel, interesting, diverting, engaging, beguiling; informal wacky, side-splitting, rib-tickling.
▷ANTONYMS boring, solemn.

anaemic adjective **1** *his naturally anaemic face became even paler*: **colourless**, bloodless, pale, pallid, wan, ashen, white, white as a ghost/sheet, grey, jaundiced, waxen, chalky, chalk-white, milky, pasty, pasty-faced, whey-faced, peaky, sickly, tired-looking, washed out, sallow, drained, drawn, sapped, ghostly, deathly, deathlike, bleached; rare etiolated.
▷ANTONYMS ruddy.
2 *'attraction' was an anaemic description of her feelings*: **feeble**, weak, insipid, pallid, pale, wishy-washy, vapid, bland, poor, puny, flat, inadequate; lame, tame, uninspired, unimaginative, lacklustre, spiritless, half-hearted, vigourless, lifeless, powerless, impotent, ineffective, ineffectual, enervated, bloodless; informal pathetic; rare etiolated.
▷ANTONYMS punchy.

anaesthetic noun *the use of chloroform as an anaesthetic*: **narcotic**, soporific, stupefacient, painkiller, sedative, anodyne, analgesic, opiate; general, local.
▸ adjective *an anaesthetic drug*: **narcotic**, numbing, deadening, dulling, soporific, stupefacient, painkilling, sedative, analgesic, anodyne, opiate.

analgesic adjective *an analgesic drug*: **painkilling**, anodyne, pain-relieving; rare palliative.
▸ noun *aspirin is an analgesic*: **painkiller**, painkilling drug, anodyne, pain reliever; rare palliative.

analogous adjective *sport is in some ways analogous to life*: **comparable**, parallel, similar, like, corresponding, related, kindred, matching, cognate, equivalent, symmetrical, homologous.
▷ANTONYMS dissimilar, unrelated.

analogy noun *an analogy between the workings of nature and those of human societies*: **similarity**, parallel, parallelism, correspondence, likeness, resemblance, correlation, relation, kinship, equivalence, similitude, symmetry, homology.
▷ANTONYMS dissimilarity.

analyse verb **1** *DNA can be analysed by various methods*: **break down**, resolve, separate, reduce, decompose, disintegrate, dissect, divide, assay, test; rare fractionate.
▷ANTONYMS synthesize.
2 *the results of the experiment were analysed*: **examine**, inspect, survey, scan, study, scrutinize, look over, peruse; search, investigate, explore, probe, research, enquire into, go over, go over with a fine-tooth comb, check, sift, dissect; audit, judge, review, evaluate, interpret; rare anatomize.

analysis noun **1** *analysis of the pottery fragments confirmed their Mediterranean origin*: **dissection**, assay, testing; breaking down,

separation, reduction, decomposition; rare fractionation.
▷ANTONYMS synthesis.
2 *an analysis of popular culture*: **examination**, investigation, inspection, survey, scanning, study, scrutiny, perusal; exploration, probe, research, enquiry, anatomy, audit, review, evaluation, interpretation; rare anatomization.

analytical, analytic adjective *a more analytical approach was needed*: **systematic**, logical, scientific, inquisitive, investigative, enquiring, methodical, organized, well organized, ordered, orderly, meticulous, rigorous, searching, critical, interpretative, diagnostic, exact, precise, accurate, mathematical, regulated, controlled, rational.
▷ANTONYMS unsystematic.

anarchic adjective *an authority was needed which could restore peace to an anarchic country*: **lawless**, without law and order, unruly, in disorder, disordered, disorganized, chaotic, in turmoil, turbulent; rebellious, mutinous.
▷ANTONYMS ordered.

anarchist noun *perhaps he was just some form of anarchist, suspicious of all government*: **nihilist**, insurgent, agitator, subversive, guerrilla, terrorist, bioterrorist, narcoterrorist, ecoterrorist, cyberterrorist, agroterrorist, freedom fighter, resistance fighter, rebel, revolutionary, revolutionist, Bolshevik, mutineer; rare insurrectionist; French, rare frondeur.

anarchy noun *the country is threatened with anarchy*: **lawlessness**, absence of government, nihilism, mobocracy, revolution, insurrection, riot, rebellion, mutiny, disorder, disorganization, misrule, chaos, tumult, turmoil, mayhem, pandemonium.
▷ANTONYMS government; order.

anathema noun **1** *racial hatred was anathema to her*: **abhorrent**, hateful, odious, repugnant, repellent, offensive; **abomination**, abhorrence, aversion, monstrosity, outrage, evil, disgrace, bane, bugbear, bête noire, pariah.
2 *the Vatican Council expressed their view without an anathema*: **curse**, ban, excommunication, damnation, proscription, debarment, denunciation, malediction, execration, imprecation.

anatomy noun **1** *descriptions of the cat's anatomy and behaviour | the anatomy of a town*: **structure**, make-up, composition, constitution; construction, layout, organization, arrangement, pattern, plan, mechanisms, framework, form, fabric.
2 *he conducted an anatomy of his society*: **analysis**, examination, inspection, survey, study, scrutiny, perusal; investigation, exploration, probe, research, enquiry, dissection, audit, review, evaluation, interpretation; rare anatomization.

ancestor noun **1** *he could trace his ancestors back to King James I*: **forebear**, forefather, predecessor, progenitor, antecedent; rare primogenitor.
▷ANTONYMS descendant, successor.
2 *the instrument is an ancestor of the lute*: **forerunner**, precursor, predecessor; prototype.

ancestral adjective *the family's ancestral home*: **inherited**, hereditary, familial; rare lineal.

ancestry noun *his Irish ancestry*: **ancestors**, forebears, forefathers, progenitors, antecedents; family tree; **lineage**, line, descent, family, parentage, extraction, origin, derivation, genealogy, heredity, pedigree, blood, bloodline, stock, strain, roots; rare filiation, stirps.

anchor noun **1** *the Liberals are the anchor of the new coalition*: **mainstay**, cornerstone, bulwark, chief support, main source of stability/security, foundation, prop, linchpin.
2 *a CBS news anchor*: **presenter**, announcer, anchorman, anchorwoman, newsreader, newscaster, broadcaster, reporter.
▸ verb **1** *the ship was anchored in the lee of the island*: **moor**, berth, harbour, be at anchor, tie up; cast anchor, drop anchor.
2 *the tail is used as a hook with which the fish anchors itself to the coral*: **secure**, fasten, attach, make fast, connect, bind, affix, fix.

anchorage noun **moorings**, harbour, port, roads; marina; rare moorage, harbourage, roadstead.

anchorite noun See **hermit**.

ancient adjective **1** *the ancient civilizations of the Mediterranean | ancient history*: **of long ago**, earliest, first, early, past, former, bygone; prehistoric, primeval, primordial, primitive; classical; literary olden, of yore, foregone.
▷ANTONYMS recent, contemporary.
2 *an ancient custom*: **old**, very old, age-old, antediluvian, time-worn, time-honoured, immemorial, long-lived; atavistic.
▷ANTONYMS new, recent, modern.
3 *you make me feel positively ancient*: **antiquated**, archaic, antediluvian, medieval, obsolete, obsolescent, superannuated, anachronistic, old-fashioned, out of date, outmoded; aged, elderly, venerable, hoary, decrepit; French démodé, passé; informal fossilized, as old as the hills, cobwebby, in one's dotage, out of the ark, creaky, mouldy; Brit. informal past its/one's sell-by date; N. Amer. informal mossy, clunky, horse and buggy.
▷ANTONYMS youthful, up to date.

> *Word links* **ancient**
>
> **archaeo-** related prefix, as in *archaeology, archaeoastronomy*
> **palaeo-** related prefix, as in *palaeography, Palaeozoic*

> *Word toolkit* **ancient**
>
> See **prehistoric**.

ancillary adjective *ancillary staff | ancillary benefits*: **additional**, auxiliary, supporting, helping, assisting, extra, supplementary, supplemental, accessory, contributory, attendant; subsidiary, secondary, subordinate; Medicine adjuvant; rare adminicular.

> *Word links* **ancillary**
>
> **para-** related prefix, as in *paramedic, paramilitary*

and conjunction **together with**, along with, with, as well as, in addition to, including, also, too; besides, furthermore, moreover; informal plus, what's more.

anecdotal adjective **1** *the evidence is merely anecdotal*: **informal**, unreliable, based on hearsay; **unscientific**.
▷ANTONYMS experimental, scientific.
2 *her book is anecdotal and chatty*: **narrative**, full of stories, packed/crammed with incident.
▷ANTONYMS abstract, austere.

anecdote noun **story**, tale, narrative, sketch; urban myth; reminiscence; informal yarn, shaggy-dog story.

anew adverb *tears filled her eyes anew*: **again**, once more, once again, a second time, afresh, over again.

angel noun **1** *God sent an angel to talk to Gideon*: **messenger of God**, divine/heavenly messenger, divine being, spirit.
▷ANTONYMS devil.
2 informal *she's been an absolute angel*: **paragon of virtue**, saint, gem, treasure, nonpareil; darling, dear; informal star, brick, one in a million.
3 informal *a financial angel*: **backer**, sponsor, supporter, benefactor, subsidizer, promoter, patron; guarantor, underwriter; rare Maecenas.

angelic adjective **1** *angelic beings*: **divine**, heavenly, celestial, holy; seraphic, cherubic, ethereal, spiritual; rare empyrean.
▷ANTONYMS demonic, satanic, infernal.
2 *Sophie's angelic appearance*: **innocent**, pure, as pure as the driven snow, virtuous, good, saintly, wholesome, exemplary; **beautiful**, adorable, lovely, lovable, enchanting.

> *Word toolkit* **angelic**
>
> See **heavenly**.

anger noun *his face darkened with anger*: **annoyance**, vexation, exasperation, crossness, irritation, irritability, indignation, pique, displeasure, resentment; **rage**, fury, wrath, outrage, temper, irascibility, ill temper, dyspepsia, spleen, ill humour, tetchiness, testiness, waspishness; informal aggravation; literary ire, choler, bile.
▷ANTONYMS pleasure, good humour.
▸ verb *she was angered by his terse reply*: **annoy**, irritate, exasperate, irk, vex, put out, provoke, pique, gall, displease; **enrage**, incense, infuriate, madden, inflame, antagonize, make someone's blood boil, make someone's hackles rise, rub up the wrong way, ruffle someone's feathers, ruffle, peeve; informal drive mad/crazy, drive up the wall, make someone see red, get someone's back up, get someone's dander up, get someone's goat, get under someone's skin, get up someone's nose, rattle someone's cage; aggravate, get someone, needle, bug, nettle, rile, miff, hack off; Brit. informal wind up, get at, nark, get across, get on someone's wick; N. Amer. informal tee off, tick off, burn up, gravel; vulgar slang piss off; informal, dated give someone the pip; rare empurple.
▷ANTONYMS pacify, placate.

angle[1] noun **1** *the wall is sloping at an angle of 33° to the vertical*: **gradient**, slant, inclination; geometrical relation.
2 *the right-hand angle of the goal*: **corner**, intersection, point, apex, cusp; nook, niche, recess, crook; projection.
3 *we need to consider the problem from a different angle*: **perspective**, way of looking at something, point of view, viewpoint, standpoint, position, side, aspect, slant, direction, approach, outlook, light.
□ **at an angle** *he has inserted 6-foot-long, clear plastic tubes deep into the soil, at an angle*: **at a slant**, on the slant, not straight, sloping, slanting, slanted, slantwise, slant, oblique, leaning, inclining, inclined, angled, cambered, canted; askew, skew, lopsided, crooked, tilting, tilted, atilt, dipping, out of true, out of line; Scottish squint; rare declivitous, declivous,

a

acclivitous, acclivous.
▷ANTONYMS straight; perpendicular.
▸verb 1 *Anna angled her camera towards the tree*: **tilt**, slant; point, direct, aim, turn.
2 *angle your answer so that it is relevant to the job for which you are applying*: **present**, slant, give a particular slant to, orient; skew, distort, twist, bias.

> *Word links* **angle**
>
> **goniometry** measurement of angles

angle[2] verb *she smiled, realizing he was **angling for** an invitation*: **try to get**, seek to obtain, make a bid for, aim for, cast about/around/round for, solicit, hope for, look for; informal fish for, be after.

angler noun **fisherman**; informal rod; archaic fisher; rare piscator.

angry adjective 1 *Vivienne got angry and started shouting | she shot him an angry look*: **irate**, annoyed, cross, vexed, irritated, exasperated, indignant, aggrieved, irked, piqued, displeased, provoked, galled, resentful; **furious**, enraged, infuriated, in a temper, incensed, raging, incandescent, wrathful, fuming, ranting, raving, seething, frenzied, in a frenzy, beside oneself, outraged, in high dudgeon; irascible, bad-tempered, hot-tempered, choleric, splenetic, dyspeptic, tetchy, testy, crabby, waspish; hostile, antagonistic, black, dark, dirty, filthy; informal mad, hopping mad, wild, livid, as cross as two sticks, boiling, apoplectic, aerated, hot under the collar, riled, on the warpath, up in arms, with all guns blazing, foaming at the mouth, steamed up, in a lather, in a paddy, fit to be tied, aggravated, snappy, snappish; Brit. informal shirty, stroppy, narky, ratty, eggy; N. Amer. informal sore, bent out of shape, soreheaded, teed off, ticked off; Austral./NZ informal ropeable, snaky, crook; W. Indian informal vex; Brit. informal, dated in a bate, waxy; vulgar slang pissed off; N. Amer. vulgar slang pissed; literary ireful, wroth.
▷ANTONYMS calm; pleased.
2 *an angry debate erupted*: **heated**, hot, passionate, furious, fiery, stormy, tempestuous, lively; bad-tempered, ill-tempered, acrimonious, bitter.
▷ANTONYMS good-humoured, peaceful.
3 *he had an angry spot on the side of his nose*: **inflamed**, red, swollen, sore, painful.
□ **get angry lose one's temper**, become enraged, go into a rage, rant and rave, go berserk, fume, seethe, flare up, bristle; informal go/get mad, go crazy, go wild, go bananas, hit the roof, go through the roof, go up the wall, jump up and down, see red, go off the deep end, fly off the handle, blow one's top, blow a fuse/gasket, lose one's rag, go ape, burst a blood vessel, breathe fire, flip, flip one's lid, foam at the mouth, get all steamed up, get worked up, have a fit, explode, have steam coming out of one's ears, gnash one's teeth, go non-linear, go ballistic, go into orbit, go psycho; Brit. informal go spare, go crackers, do one's nut, get one's knickers in a twist, throw a wobbly; N. Amer. informal flip one's wig, blow one's lid/stack, have a cow, go postal, have a conniption fit; vulgar slang go apeshit.

angst noun **anxiety**, fear, dread, apprehension, worry, perturbation, foreboding, trepidation, malaise, distress, disquiet, disquietude, unease, uneasiness; rare inquietude.

anguish noun *a cry of anguish*: **agony**, pain, torment, torture, suffering, distress, angst, misery, sorrow, grief, heartache, heartbreak, wretchedness, unhappiness, woe, desolation, despair; the dark night of the soul, purgatory, hell on earth; literary dolour.
▷ANTONYMS happiness, contentment.

anguished adjective *an anguished cry | her anguished face*: **agonized**, tormented, racked with pain/suffering, tortured, harrowed; **miserable**, unhappy, sad, broken-hearted, heartbroken, grief-stricken, wretched, sorrowful, sorrowing, distressed, desolate, devastated, despairing; informal cut up; literary dolorous.
▷ANTONYMS happy, contented.

angular adjective 1 *a dark, angular shape*: **sharp-cornered**, pointed, V-shaped, Y-shaped; forked, bifurcate.
▷ANTONYMS rounded, curving.
2 *an angular girl with prominent cheekbones*: **bony**, raw-boned, skin-and-bones; **lean**, rangy, spare, thin, lanky, spindly, skinny, gaunt, scrawny, scraggy; informal looking like a bag of bones, anorexic, anorectic; dated spindle-shanked; rare gracile, macilent.
▷ANTONYMS plump, curvy.

animal noun 1 *rare and endangered animals and plants*: **creature**, beast, living thing, being, brute; informal critter; (**animals**) wildlife, fauna.
2 *the man was an animal*: **brute**, beast, monster, savage, devil, demon, fiend, villain, sadist, barbarian, ogre; informal swine, bastard, pig.
▸adjective 1 *the evolution of animal life*: **zoological**, animalistic; rare zoic, theriomorphic.
2 *his grunt of animal passion*: **carnal**, fleshly, bodily, physical, sensual; instinctive, instinctual; brutish, unrefined, uncultured, coarse, gross, inhuman, subhuman; rare appetitive.
▷ANTONYMS spiritual.

> *Word links* **animal**
>
> **zoo-** related prefix, as in *zoogeography, zooplankton*
> **faunal, zoological** relating to animals
> **zoology** study of animals
> **veterinary medicine** branch of medicine to do with animals

animate verb *a sense of excitement animated the whole school*: **enliven**, vitalize, give (new) life to, breathe (new) life into, energize, invigorate, revive, vivify, liven up, light up, cheer up, gladden; encourage, hearten, inspire, exhilarate, thrill, excite, fire, arouse, rouse, stir, stimulate, galvanize, electrify; informal buck up, pep up, give someone a buzz, ginger up; N. Amer. informal light a fire under; rare inspirit.
▷ANTONYMS depress, inhibit.
▸adjective *an animate being*: **living**, alive, live, breathing, sentient, conscious; organic; archaic quick.
▷ANTONYMS inanimate.

animated adjective *an animated discussion | Simon became quite animated*: **lively**, spirited, high-spirited, energetic, full of life, excited, enthusiastic, eager, alive, active, vigorous, vibrant, vital, vivacious, buoyant, exuberant, ebullient, effervescent, bouncy, bubbly, perky, sparkling, sprightly, zestful; fiery, passionate, impassioned, heated, dynamic, forceful, fervent, ardent; informal bright-eyed and bushy-tailed, full of beans, bright and breezy, sparky, chirpy, go-go, chipper, peppy, zippy, zappy, full of vim and vigour; N. Amer. informal peart.
▷ANTONYMS lethargic, apathetic, lifeless.

animation noun *he had always admired her animation*: **liveliness**, spirit, high spirits, spiritedness, high-spiritedness, energy, enthusiasm, eagerness, excitement, vigour, vivacity, vivaciousness, vitality, vibrancy, exuberance, ebullience, buoyancy, bounciness, bounce, perkiness, sprightliness, verve, zest, sparkle, dash, elan, brio; fire, fieriness, passion, dynamism, forcefulness, intensity, ardour, fervour; informal chirpiness, pep, vim, zing, go, get-up-and-go.
▷ANTONYMS lethargy, sluggishness, inertia.

animosity noun *there was considerable animosity between him and his brother*: **antipathy**, hostility, friction, antagonism, enmity, animus, opposition, aversion, acrimony, bitterness, rancour, resentment, dislike, ill feeling, bad feeling, ill will, bad blood, hatred, hate, loathing, detestation, abhorrence, odium; malice, spite, spitefulness, venom, malevolence, malignity; grudges, grievances; archaic disrelish.
▷ANTONYMS goodwill, friendship.

annals plural noun **records**, archives, chronicles, accounts, registers, journals; history; rare muniments.

annex verb (stress on the second syllable) 1 *the first ten amendments were annexed to the constitution in 1791*: **add**, append, attach, join; informal tack on, tag on.
2 *Charlemagne annexed northern Italy, Saxony, and Bavaria*: **take over**, take possession of, appropriate, expropriate, arrogate, seize, conquer, occupy, garrison; usurp.
▷ANTONYMS relinquish.
▸noun (stress on the first syllable) (also **annexe**) *a school annex*: **extension**, supplementary building, addition; wing; N. Amer. informal ell.

annexation noun *the annexation of Austria*: **seizure**, occupation, invasion, conquest, takeover, appropriation, expropriation, arrogation; usurping.

annihilate verb *this was an attempt to annihilate an entire people*: **destroy**, wipe out, obliterate, wipe off the face of the earth, wipe off the map, kill, slaughter, exterminate, eliminate, liquidate, eradicate, extinguish, finish off, erase, root out, extirpate; informal take out, rub out, snuff out, zap, waste.
▷ANTONYMS create, build, establish.

anniversary noun **jubilee**, commemoration.

annotate verb *the text was annotated with explanatory notes*: **comment on**, add notes/footnotes to, gloss; explain, interpret, elucidate, explicate; rare footnote, margin, marginalize.

annotation noun *Coleridge's marginal annotations*: **note**, notation, comment, gloss; footnote; commentary, explanation, interpretation, observation, elucidation, explication, exegesis.

announce verb 1 *the company's financial results were announced on May 12*: **make public**, make known, report, issue a statement about, declare, state, set forth, give out, put out, post, notify, give notice of, publicize, broadcast, publish, advertise, circulate, proclaim, promulgate, trumpet, noise abroad; disclose, reveal, divulge, intimate; informal shout something from the rooftops; literary blazon abroad; rare preconize.
▷ANTONYMS conceal, suppress.
2 *Victor announced their guests*: **introduce**, present, name; usher in.
3 *strains of music announced her arrival in the church*: **signal**, indicate, be an indication of, signify, give notice of, herald, proclaim; warn of, foretell, augur, portend; literary betoken, harbinger.

announcement noun **1** *an announcement by the Minister is expected this afternoon*: **statement**, report, declaration, proclamation, pronouncement; bulletin, communiqué, dispatch, message; information, word, news; N. Amer. advisory; in Tsarist Russia ukase; in Spain & Spanish-speaking countries pronunciamento; Latin ipse dixit; rare rescript, asseveration.
2 *the announcement of the decision*: **declaration**, notification, report, reporting, publishing, broadcasting, proclamation, promulgation; disclosure, revelation, intimation, divulging; archaic annunciation.

announcer noun **presenter**, anchorman, anchorwoman, anchor; newsreader, newscaster, broadcaster, reporter, commentator; master of ceremonies, MC, compère, host; informal talking head, emcee.

annoy verb *such remarks never failed to annoy him*: **irritate**, vex, make angry, make cross, anger, exasperate, irk, gall, pique, put out, displease, get/put someone's back up, antagonize, get on someone's nerves, rub up the wrong way, ruffle, ruffle someone's feathers, make someone's hackles rise, raise someone's hackles; enrage, infuriate, madden, make someone's blood boil, drive to distraction, goad, provoke; informal aggravate, peeve, hassle, miff, rile, nettle, needle, get, get to, bug, hack off, get under someone's skin, get in someone's hair, get up someone's nose, put someone's nose out of joint, get someone's goat, give someone the hump, rattle someone's cage, drive mad/crazy, drive round the bend/twist, drive up the wall, make someone see red; Brit. informal wind up, nark, get across, get on someone's wick; N. Amer. informal tee off, tick off, burn up, rankle, ride, gravel; vulgar slang piss off; Brit. vulgar slang get on someone's tits; informal, dated give someone the pip, get someone's dander up; rare exacerbate, hump, rasp.
▷ANTONYMS please, gratify.

Choose the right word **annoy, irritate, aggravate, vex, peeve**

Someone or something that **annoys** a person displeases them and makes them moderately angry (*his tone of joking superiority annoyed me*).

Irritate suggests a trifling but long-lasting cause of annoyance (*nothing irritated him more than to be kept waiting*).

Some people believe that **aggravate** is properly used to mean only 'make worse', but the sense 'annoy or exasperate' is widespread and represents no greater a departure from an older meaning than many others that have long been accepted without comment. An action that *aggravates* someone else is quite often deliberate or at least easily avoidable (*he hummed under his breath, which aggravated her*).

Vex is a more formal or literary word used of something that irritates or worries someone, especially when they are unable to do anything about it (*I'm vexed at that girl—she ruined Christmas for the family*).

Peeve is an informal word, generally used when someone feels that they have been unfairly treated (*Birkitt was looking distinctly peeved, aware that Banks had upstaged him*). It generally expresses relatively mild annoyance.

All these words, apart from *peeve*, are widely used as adjectives (*it's so irritating having to constantly stop and put your kagoul on etc.*).

annoyance noun **1** *much to his annoyance, Louise didn't even notice*: **irritation**, exasperation, vexation, indignation, anger, crossness, displeasure, chagrin, pique; informal aggravation; literary ire.
▷ANTONYMS pleasure.
2 *the council found him an annoyance*: **nuisance**, source of irritation, pest, bother, trial, irritant, inconvenience, menace, thorn in one's flesh; informal pain, pain in the neck, bind, bore, headache, hassle; Scottish informal nyaff, skelf; N. Amer. informal pain in the butt, nudnik, burr in/under someone's saddle; Austral./NZ informal nark; Brit. vulgar slang pain in the arse.

annoyed adjective *Maureen was beginning to look annoyed*: **irritated**, cross, angry, vexed, exasperated, irked, piqued, displeased, put out, fed up, disgruntled, in a bad mood, in a temper, testy, in high dudgeon, huffy, in a huff, resentful, aggrieved; furious, irate, infuriated, incensed, enraged, wrathful, choleric; informal aggravated, peeved, nettled, miffed, miffy, mad, riled, hacked off, peed off, hot under the collar, foaming at the mouth; Brit. informal browned off, cheesed off, brassed off, narked, ratty, shirty, eggy; N. Amer. informal teed off, ticked off, sore, bent out of shape; Austral./NZ informal snaky, crook; W. Indian informal vex; vulgar slang pissed off; N. Amer. vulgar slang pissed; literary ireful; archaic snuffy, wrath.

annoying adjective *he really was the most annoying man she'd ever met*: **irritating**, infuriating, exasperating, maddening, trying, tiresome, troublesome, bothersome, irksome, vexing, vexatious, galling, provoking, displeasing; awkward, difficult, inconvenient; informal aggravating, pesky, cussed, confounded, infernal, pestiferous, plaguy, pestilent.
▷ANTONYMS pleasant, agreeable.

annual adjective **1** *an annual report*: **yearly**, once-a-year, every twelve months.
2 *an annual subscription*: **year-long**, lasting a year, twelve-month.

annually adverb *subscriptions are payable annually*: **yearly**, once a year, each year, by the year, per annum, per year; every year.

annul verb *the European Court annulled the decision*: **declare invalid**, declare null and void, nullify, invalidate, void; **repeal**, reverse, rescind, revoke, set aside, cancel, abolish, undo, abrogate, countermand, dissolve, withdraw, cast aside, quash; Law vacate; rare disannul, negate, recall.
▷ANTONYMS restore; enact.

annular adjective *the city grew much like the annular rings of a tree*: **circular**, ring-shaped, disk-shaped, round; technical discoid.

Word toolkit **annular**

See **circular**.

annulment noun *the annulment of the commission's decision*: **invalidation**, nullification, voiding; **repeal**, cancellation, rescinding, reversal, revocation, setting aside, abolition, abrogation, rescindment, withdrawal, countermanding, quashing; rare rescission, disannulment, negation, recall.
▷ANTONYMS restoration, enactment.

anodyne noun **painkiller**, painkilling drug, analgesic, pain reliever, palliative.
▶ adjective *she tried to keep the conversation as anodyne as possible*: **bland**, inoffensive, innocuous, neutral, unobjectionable, unexceptionable, unremarkable, commonplace, dull, tedious, run-of-the-mill.

anoint verb **1** *during the public baptism, the head of the infant was anointed*: **smear with oil**, rub with oil, apply oil to, spread oil over; archaic anele.
2 *he was anointed and crowned in Charlemagne's basilica*: **consecrate**, sanctify, bless, ordain, hallow.

anomalous adjective *nuclear weapons testing may have been responsible for the anomalous weather conditions*: **abnormal**, atypical, non-typical, irregular, aberrant, exceptional, freak, freakish, odd, bizarre, peculiar, unusual, out of the ordinary, inconsistent, incongruous, deviant, deviating, divergent, eccentric; rare, singular.
▷ANTONYMS normal, typical, regular.

anomaly noun *there are a number of anomalies in the present system*: **oddity**, peculiarity, abnormality, irregularity, inconsistency, incongruity, deviation, aberration, quirk, freak, exception, departure, divergence, variation; rarity, eccentricity.

anon adverb archaic or informal *I'll see you anon*: **soon**, shortly, in a little while, in a short time, presently, before long, in the near future; S. African just now; dated directly; literary by and by, ere long.

anonymous adjective **1** *an anonymous donor*: **unnamed**, of unknown name, nameless, incognito, unidentified, unknown, unspecified, undesignated, unacknowledged, mystery; unsung; rare innominate.
▷ANTONYMS known, identified.
2 *an anonymous letter*: **unsigned**, unattributed, unattested, uncredited.
▷ANTONYMS signed.
3 *an anonymous London housing estate*: **characterless**, unremarkable, nondescript, impersonal, faceless, colourless, grey.

another determiner **1** *have another drink | I've got another umbrella*: **one more**, a further, an additional, a second; an extra, a spare.
2 *she left him for another man*: **a different**, some other, not the same, an alternative.
▷ANTONYMS the same.

answer noun **1** *her answer was swift and unequivocal*: **reply**, response, rejoinder, return, reaction; acknowledgement; retort, riposte; informal comeback.
▷ANTONYMS question, query.
2 *the answer is 150*: **solution**, explanation, resolution; key.
3 *simply increasing the number of troops is not the answer*: **solution**, remedy, way of solving the problem, way out; informal quick fix.
4 *his answer to the charge*: **defence**, plea, refutation, rebuttal; Law counterstatement, surrejoinder, rebutter, surrebutter, replication.
▶ verb **1** *Steve was about to answer, but Hazel spoke first | 'Of course I can,' she answered*: **reply**, respond, speak/say in response, make a rejoinder, rejoin; retort, come back, fling back, hurl back; acknowledge, write back; informal get back to; rare riposte.
2 *he has yet to answer the charges made against him*: **rebut**, refute, defend oneself against.
3 *the police had a tip-off about a man answering this description*: **match**, fit, correspond to, be similar to, conform to, correlate to.
4 *we're looking at new types of programmes to answer the needs of our audience*: **satisfy**, meet, fulfil, fill, serve, suit, measure up to, match up to; fit/fill the bill.
5 *I* ***answer to*** *the Assistant Commissioner of Specialist Operations*: **report**, be accountable, be answerable, be responsible; work for, work under, be subordinate to, be supervised by, be managed by.
□ **answer someone back respond cheekily to**, be cheeky to, be impertinent to, talk back to; contradict, argue with, disagree with; retaliate, retort, counter; informal cheek; N. Amer. informal sass, be sassy to.
□ **answer for 1** *no one has been made to answer for the crime*: **pay for**, be punished for, suffer the consequences of, suffer for; make amends for,

make reparation for, atone for. **2** *the present government has a lot to answer for*: **be accountable for**, be responsible for, be liable for, take the blame for; vouch for; informal take the rap for.

answerable adjective *the Attorney General is answerable only to Parliament for his decisions*: **accountable**, responsible, liable; subject.

ant noun

> *Word links* **ant**
>
> **formic, myrmeco-** relating to ants
> **myrmecology** study of ants

antagonism noun *the overt antagonism between her and Susan*: **hostility**, friction, enmity, antipathy, animus, opposition, dissension, rivalry, feud, conflict, discord, contention; acrimony, bitterness, rancour, resentment, aversion, dislike, ill feeling, bad feeling, ill will, bad blood, hatred, hate, loathing, detestation, abhorrence, odium; malice, spite, spitefulness, venom, malevolence, malignity; grudges, grievances; Brit. informal needle; archaic disrelish.
▷ANTONYMS rapport, friendship.

antagonist noun **adversary**, opponent, enemy, foe, rival, competitor, contender; (**antagonists**) opposition, competition, the other side; rare corrival.
▷ANTONYMS ally, friend, supporter.

antagonistic adjective **1** *he was increasingly* ***antagonistic to*** *the government's reforms*: **hostile**, **opposed**, inimical, antipathetic, unsympathetic, ill-disposed, resistant, averse; against, (dead) set against, at odds with, at variance with, in disagreement with, dissenting from; informal anti, agin.
▷ANTONYMS pro, sympathetic.
2 *an antagonistic group of bystanders*: **hostile**, **aggressive**, belligerent, bellicose, pugnacious, combative, contentious, truculent, confrontational, quarrelsome, argumentative; rare oppugnant.

antagonize verb *he seemed to be deliberately trying to antagonize her*: **arouse hostility in**, alienate, set someone against someone else, estrange, disaffect; **anger**, annoy, provoke, vex, irritate, offend; informal aggravate, rile, needle, get someone's back up, make someone's hackles rise, rub up the wrong way, ruffle someone's feathers, rattle someone's cage, get up someone's nose, get in someone's hair, get someone's dander up, get under someone's skin; Brit. informal nark, get on someone's wick.
▷ANTONYMS pacify, placate.

antecedent noun **1** (**antecedents**) *her early life and antecedents have been traced*: **ancestors**, ancestry, forefathers, forebears, predecessors, progenitors, family, family tree, stock; descent, genealogy, roots, extraction, birth; history, past, background, record; rare filiation, stirps.
▷ANTONYMS descendant.
2 *music composed for vihuela (the guitar's lute-like antecedent)*: **precursor**, forerunner, predecessor.
▶ adjective *antecedent events*: **previous**, earlier, prior, foregoing, preceding, precursory; pre-existing; rare anterior.
▷ANTONYMS later, subsequent.

antedate verb *a civilization that antedated the Roman Empire*: **precede**, predate, come/go before, be earlier than, anticipate.

antediluvian adjective **1** *gigantic bones of antediluvian animals*: **before the flood**, **prehistoric**, primeval, primordial, primal, earliest, ancient, early; rare primigenial.
2 *his antediluvian attitudes*: **out of date**, outdated, outmoded, old-fashioned, ancient, antiquated, archaic, antique, superannuated, anachronistic, outworn, behind the times, primitive, medieval, quaint, old-fangled, obsolescent, obsolete, prehistoric; French passé; informal out of the ark, fossilized, as old as the hills, old hat, creaky, mouldy; Brit. informal past its/one's sell-by date; N. Amer. informal horse and buggy, mossy, clunky.
▷ANTONYMS modern, up to date.

antelope noun

> *Word links* **antelope**
>
> **buck** male
> **doe** female
> **calf** young

anteroom noun **antechamber**, outer room, vestibule, lobby, waiting room, reception area; foyer; in churches narthex.

anthem noun *the choir sang two anthems*: **hymn**, song, song of praise, chorale, psalm, paean, plainsong, chant, canticle.

anthology noun *an anthology of European poetry*: **collection**, selection, compendium, treasury, compilation, miscellany, pot-pourri; archaic garland; rare analects, collectanea, florilegium.

anticipate verb **1** *the police did not anticipate any trouble*: **expect**, foresee, predict, think likely, forecast, prophesy, foretell, contemplate the possibility of, allow for, be prepared for; count on, bank on, look for, bargain on; informal reckon on; N. Amer. informal figure on; archaic apprehend.
2 *Elaine tingled with excitement as she anticipated her meeting with Will*: **look forward to**, await, count the days until; informal lick one's lips over.
▷ANTONYMS dread.
3 *warders can't always anticipate the actions of prisoners*: **pre-empt**, forestall, intercept; second-guess; informal beat someone to it, beat someone to the draw, beat someone to the punch.
4 *she wrote plays for all-women casts, which anticipated her film work*: **foreshadow**, precede, antedate, come/go before, be earlier than.

> *Choose the right word* **anticipate, expect, foresee**
>
> These words all mean 'regard as probable', but they all have other meanings that can colour the general sense.
>
> **Anticipate** is used especially when someone takes action or makes plans to prepare for what they think will happen (*the police anticipated trouble and drafted in reinforcements*). It is often used for looking forward to something desirable, and when used as an adjective it is frequently modified by an adverb such as *eagerly* (*it was the most eagerly anticipated show in town*) and, with the same approving sense, *highly* (*one of the year's most highly anticipated video games*). *Anticipate* is less commonly used in a passive construction than the other two words.
>
> **Expect** is the most general word (*sales are expected to drop next year* | *over 20,000 visitors are expected*). *Expect* may also be used of something that is required or demanded, whether or not one thinks it is likely (*the firm expected its employees to be prepared to move*). While all these words can be used with a direct object or a *that*-clause (*I expect that she knew too*), only *expect* can be used with an object and an infinitive (*you expect me to believe you?*).
>
> **Foresee** can imply certainty, as its meaning verges on 'prophesy, predict', and the objects with which it is used are typically undesirable (*we foresee enormous problems for local authorities*). Only *foresee* and *anticipate* can be used with a present participle (*Cleo had anticipated having to apologize for him*).

anticipation noun **1** *my anticipation is that we will see a rise in rates on Monday*: **expectation**, prediction, forecast; rare prolepsis.
2 *her eyes sparkled with anticipation*: **expectancy**, expectation, hope, hopefulness; excitement, suspense.
□ **in anticipation of** *they manned the telephones in anticipation of a flood of calls*: **in the expectation of**, in preparation for, in case of, ready for, against.

anticlimax noun **let-down**, disappointment, comedown, non-event; disillusionment; bathos; Brit. damp squib; informal washout, not what it was cracked up to be.
▷ANTONYMS triumph, climax.

antics plural noun *she laughed, recalling her son's antics*: **capers**, amusing behaviour, pranks, larks, escapades, high jinks, skylarking, stunts, tricks, horseplay, romps, frolics; silliness, foolish behaviour, tomfoolery, foolery, clowning, buffoonery; Brit. informal monkey tricks; N. Amer. informal didoes; archaic harlequinades.

antidote noun **1** *there is no known antidote to this poison*: **antitoxin**, antiserum; cure, remedy; neutralizer, neutralizing agent, counteragent; rare mithridate, antivenin, antivenene, theriac.
2 *laughter is a good antidote to stress*: **remedy**, cure, corrective, nostrum, countermeasure, counteragent; solution.

antipathetic adjective *French nationalists became vehemently* ***antipathetic to*** *all things German*: **hostile**, opposed, antagonistic, averse, ill-disposed, unsympathetic; against, (dead) set against; informal anti, agin, down on.
▷ANTONYMS pro.

antipathy noun *she felt a violent antipathy to Emily*: **hostility**, antagonism, animosity, aversion, animus, opposition, enmity, dislike, distaste, ill will, ill feeling, hatred, hate, abhorrence, loathing, repugnance, odium; grudge; informal allergy; archaic disrelish.
▷ANTONYMS liking, affinity, rapport.

antiquated adjective *antiquated attitudes* | *an antiquated cash register*: **outdated**, out of date, outmoded, behind the times, old-fashioned, archaic, anachronistic, superannuated, outworn, ancient, antediluvian, primitive, medieval, quaint, old-fangled, obsolescent, obsolete, prehistoric; French passé, démodé, vieux jeu; informal out of the ark, fossilized, as old as the hills, creaky, mouldy; Brit. informal past its/one's sell-by date; N. Amer. informal horse and buggy, mossy, clunky.
▷ANTONYMS current, modern, up to date.

antique noun *the chair's an antique*: **collector's item**, period piece, museum piece, antiquity, object of virtu; heirloom; treasure, relic, curio; French objet d'art; rare bygone.
▶ adjective **1** *antique furniture*: **old**, antiquarian, collectable; vintage, classic.
▷ANTONYMS new, modern, state-of-the-art.
2 *statues of antique gods*: **ancient**, of long ago; classical; literary of yore.
3 *antique work practices*: **out of date**, outdated, outmoded, old-fashioned, archaic, antiquated, anachronistic, ancient, antediluvian, superannuated,

outworn, behind the times, primitive, medieval, quaint, old-fangled, obsolescent, obsolete, prehistoric; French passé; informal out of the ark, fossilized, as old as the hills, old hat, creaky, mouldy; Brit. informal past its/one's sell-by date; N. Amer. informal horse and buggy, mossy, clunky.
▷ANTONYMS current, modern, up to date.

antiquity noun 1 *the great civilizations of antiquity*: **ancient times**, the ancient past, classical times, former times, the distant past, times gone by; literary the olden days, days of yore, yesteryear; archaic the eld.
2 *a collection of Islamic antiquities*: **antique**, period piece, museum piece; treasure, relic, curio; rare bygone.
3 *a church of great antiquity*: **age**, oldness, elderliness, ancientness.

antiseptic adjective 1 *an antiseptic substance*: **disinfectant**, germicidal, bactericidal; medicated.
2 *antiseptic bandages*: **sterile**, aseptic, germ-free, uncontaminated, unpolluted; disinfected, sanitized.
▷ANTONYMS dirty, contaminated.
3 *the antiseptic surroundings of the conference centre*: **characterless**, colourless, soulless, bland, nondescript, uninspiring; clinical, institutional.
▷ANTONYMS colourful.
▶noun *a mild antiseptic*: **disinfectant**, germicide, bactericide.

antisocial adjective 1 *antisocial behaviour*: **objectionable**, offensive, beyond the pale, unacceptable, unsocial, asocial, distasteful; disruptive, disorderly, lawless, rebellious; sociopathic.
2 *I'm feeling a bit antisocial*: **unsociable**, misanthropic, unwilling to mix with other people, unfriendly, uncommunicative, unforthcoming, reserved, withdrawn, retiring, reclusive.
▷ANTONYMS sociable, gregarious.

Easily confused words **antisocial, unsocial, or unsociable?**

See **unsociable**.

antithesis noun 1 *love is the antithesis of selfishness*: **(direct) opposite**, converse, reverse, reversal, inverse, obverse; the other extreme, the other side of the coin; informal the flip side.
2 *the antithesis between sin and grace*: **contrast**, opposition.

antithetical adjective *an administration packed with people holding policy views **antithetical to** his own*: **(directly) opposed to**, contrary to, contradictory to, conflicting with, incompatible with, irreconcilable with, inconsistent with, at variance with, at odds with, contrasting with, different from/to, differing from, divergent from, unlike; opposing, poles apart, polar, obverse; rare oppugnant.
▷ANTONYMS same, identical, like.

anxiety noun 1 *his anxiety grew as his messages were all left unanswered*: **worry**, concern, apprehension, apprehensiveness, consternation, uneasiness, unease, fearfulness, fear, disquiet, disquietude, perturbation, fretfulness, agitation, angst, nervousness, nerves, edginess, tension, tenseness, stress, misgiving, trepidation, foreboding, suspense; informal butterflies (in one's stomach), the willies, the heebie-jeebies, the jitters, the shakes, the jumps, the yips, collywobbles, jitteriness, jim-jams, twitchiness; Brit. informal the (screaming) abdabs; Austral. rhyming slang Joe Blakes; N. Amer. archaic worriment.
▷ANTONYMS calmness, serenity.
2 *her anxiety to please*: **eagerness**, keenness, desire, impatience, longing, yearning.

anxious adjective 1 *I'm very anxious about her welfare | anxious relatives waited for news*: **worried**, concerned, apprehensive, fearful, uneasy, ill at ease, perturbed, troubled, disquieted, bothered, disturbed, distressed, fretful, fretting, agitated, in a state of agitation, nervous, in a state of nerves, edgy, on edge, tense, overwrought, worked up, keyed up, strung out, jumpy, afraid, worried sick, with one's stomach in knots, with one's heart in one's mouth, on pins and needles, stressed, under stress, in suspense, flurried; informal uptight, a bundle of nerves, on tenterhooks, with butterflies in one's stomach, like a cat on a hot tin roof, jittery, twitchy, in a state, in a stew, all of a dither, in a flap, in a sweat, in a tizz/tizzy, all of a lather, het up, in a twitter; Brit. informal strung up, windy, having kittens, in a (flat) spin, like a cat on hot bricks; N. Amer. informal antsy, spooky, spooked, squirrelly, in a twit; Austral./NZ informal toey; dated overstrung, unquiet.
▷ANTONYMS carefree, unconcerned.
2 *she was anxious for news of him*: **eager**, keen, desirous, impatient, itching, longing, yearning, aching, dying.

any determiner 1 *is there any ginger cake left?* **some**, a piece of, a part of, a bit of.
2 *it doesn't make any difference*: **the slightest bit of**, the smallest amount of, a scrap of, a shred of, a particle of, an atom of, an iota of, a jot of, a whit of.
3 *any job will do, to begin with*: **whichever**, whichever comes to hand, no matter which, never mind which; informal any old.
▶pronoun 1 *you don't know any of my friends*: **a single one**, one, even one.
2 *they ceased payments to any but the aged*: **anyone**, anybody.
▶adverb *is your father any better?* **at all**, in the least, to any extent, to some extent, somewhat, in any degree, to some degree.

anyhow adverb 1 *anyhow, it doesn't really matter now*: **anyway**, in any case, in any event, at any rate, at all events, no matter what, regardless; however, be that as it may; informal still and all; N. Amer. informal anyways.
2 *her clothes were strewn about anyhow*: **haphazardly**, carelessly, heedlessly, negligently, in a muddle, in a disorganized manner; informal all over the place, every which way; Brit. informal all over the shop; N. Amer. informal all over the lot.

apace adverb literary *things are moving on apace*: **quickly**, fast, swiftly, rapidly, speedily, briskly, without delay, post-haste, expeditiously, at full speed, at full tilt; informal at warp speed; Brit. informal at a rate of knots.
▷ANTONYMS slowly.

apart adverb 1 *the villages are only two miles apart*: **away from each other**, distant from each other.
2 *Isabel stepped away from Joanna and stood apart*: **to one side**, aside, to the side; separately, alone, by oneself/itself; distant, isolated, cut off.
3 *his parents are now living apart*: **separately**, not together, independently, on one's own; separated, divorced.
4 *he leapt out of the car just before it was blown apart*: **to pieces**, to bits, in pieces; up; in two; literary asunder.
□ **apart from** *he was unhurt apart from a huge bump on his head*: **except for**, but for, aside from, with the exception of, excepting, excluding, not including, not counting, disregarding, save, bar, barring, besides, other than; informal outside of.

apartment noun 1 *a rented apartment in New York*: **flat**; penthouse; Austral. home unit; N. Amer. informal crib.
2 *the royal apartments*: **suite (of rooms)**, set of rooms, rooms, chambers; living quarters, accommodation.

apathetic adjective *the workforce was described as apathetic and demoralized*: **uninterested**, **indifferent**, unconcerned, unmoved, unresponsive, impassive, passive, detached, uninvolved, disinterested, unfeeling, unemotional, emotionless, dispassionate, lukewarm, cool, uncaring, half-hearted, lackadaisical, non-committal; listless, lethargic, languid, phlegmatic, torpid, supine, inert; bored, unmotivated, unambitious; informal couldn't-care-less; Brit. vulgar slang half-arsed; rare Laodicean, poco-curante.
▷ANTONYMS enthusiastic, eager, passionate.

apathy noun *there were reports of widespread apathy amongst the electorate*: **indifference**, lack of interest, lack of enthusiasm, lack of concern, unconcern, uninterestedness, unresponsiveness, impassivity, passivity, passiveness, detachment, dispassion, dispassionateness, lack of involvement, phlegm, coolness; listlessness, lethargy, languor, lassitude, torpor; boredom, ennui, accidie; rare acedia, mopery.
▷ANTONYMS enthusiasm, interest, passion.

ape noun **primate**, simian; monkey; technical anthropoid.
▶verb *he aped Barbara's accent*: **imitate**, mimic, copy, do an impression of, echo, parrot; take off, mock, parody, caricature; informal send up; archaic monkey.

Word links **ape**

simian relating to apes
shrewdness collective noun

aperture noun **opening**, hole, gap, space, slit, slot, vent, passage, crevice, chink, crack, fissure, perforation, breach, eye, interstice; technical orifice, foramen.

apex noun 1 *the apex of a pyramid*: **tip**, peak, summit, pinnacle, top, highest point/part, crest, vertex; rare fastigium.
▷ANTONYMS bottom.
2 *the apex of his career*: **climax**, culmination, culminating point, apotheosis; peak, pinnacle, summit, zenith, acme, apogee, high point, highest point, height, crowning moment, high water mark.
▷ANTONYMS nadir.

Word links **apex**

apical relating to an apex

aphorism noun See **saying**.

aphrodisiac noun **love potion**, philtre; stimulant.
▶adjective **erotic**, sexy, sexually arousing, stimulative, stimulant; rare venereous.

apiece adverb *the largest stones weigh over fifty tons apiece*: **each**, respectively, per item; individually, separately; informal a throw; formal severally.

aplenty adjective *the town has museums and galleries aplenty*: **in abundance**, in profusion, galore, in large quantities, in large numbers, by the dozen; everywhere, all over; to spare; informal a gogo, by the truckload, by the shedload.

a

aplomb noun *he handled the crisis with surprising aplomb*: **poise**, self-assurance, assurance, self-possession, self-confidence, calmness, composure, collectedness, presence of mind, level-headedness, sangfroid, equilibrium, equanimity, nerve, nonchalance; French savoir faire, savoir vivre; informal cool, unflappability.
▷ANTONYMS gaucheness.

apocryphal adjective *an apocryphal story*: **fictitious**, made-up, untrue, fabricated, false, spurious; imaginary, mythical, legendary; dubious, doubtful, debatable, questionable, unverified, unauthenticated, unsubstantiated, unsupported.
▷ANTONYMS authentic, true.

apologetic adjective *she was very apologetic about the whole incident*: **regretful**, full of regret, sorry, contrite, remorseful, penitent, repentant, rueful, deprecatory, self-reproachful; conscience-stricken, red-faced, shamefaced, sheepish, hangdog, ashamed, in sackcloth and ashes; rare compunctious.
▷ANTONYMS unrepentant, impenitent; defiant.

Word toolkit

apologetic	contrite	penitent
response	heart	man/woman
letter	spirit	thief
gesture	expression	sinner
statement	tone	saints
explanation	apology	silence

apologia noun *Norbrook offers a spirited apologia for his methodology*: **defence**, justification, vindication, explanation, apology; argument, case; plea.

apologist noun *an apologist for hard-line government policies*: **defender**, supporter, upholder, advocate, proponent, exponent, propagandist, apostle, champion, backer, promoter, campaigner, spokesman, spokeswoman, spokesperson, speaker, arguer, enthusiast.
▷ANTONYMS critic.

apologize verb **say sorry**, express regret, be apologetic, make an apology, ask forgiveness, beg (someone's) forgiveness, ask for pardon, beg (someone's) pardon; informal eat humble pie, eat one's words.

apology noun **1** *I owe you an apology*: **expression of regret**, one's regrets; French amende honorable; Austral./NZ informal beg-pardon.
2 *a dire **apology for** a decent flat*: **travesty of**, excuse for, inadequate example of, poor imitation of, poor substitute for, pale shadow of, mockery of, caricature of.
3 *the Acts of the Apostles is in fact an apology for the Church*: **defence**, apologia, justification, vindication.

apoplectic adjective informal *Mark was apoplectic with rage at the decision*: **furious**, enraged, overcome with anger, infuriated, in a temper, incensed, raging; **incandescent**, wrathful, fuming, ranting, raving, seething, frenzied, in a frenzy, beside oneself, outraged, in high dudgeon; informal mad, hopping mad, wild, livid, as cross as two sticks, boiling, aerated, with all guns blazing, foaming at the mouth, fit to be tied.

apostasy noun **renunciation of belief**, abandonment of belief, recantation; treachery, perfidy, faithlessness, disloyalty, betrayal, defection, desertion; heresy; rare tergiversation, recreancy.
▷ANTONYMS loyalty.

apostate noun *after 50 years as an apostate, he returned to the faith*: **dissenter**, heretic, nonconformist; defector, deserter, traitor, turncoat; schismatic; archaic recusant, recreant, renegade, tergiversator.
▷ANTONYMS follower, disciple.

apostle noun **1** *the 12 apostles of Jesus*: **disciple**; follower.
2 *the apostles of the faith*: **missionary**, evangelist, evangelical, proselytizer, spreader of the faith/word, preacher, teacher; reformer.
3 *an apostle of capitalism*: **advocate**, apologist, proponent, exponent, promoter, propagandist, spokesperson, spokesman, spokeswoman, supporter, upholder, champion; campaigner, crusader, pioneer; adherent, believer; N. Amer. booster.
▷ANTONYMS opponent, critic.

apotheosis noun *his appearance as Hamlet was the apotheosis of his career*: **culmination**, climax, crowning moment, peak, pinnacle, summit, zenith, apex, acme, apogee, high point, highest point, height, high water mark.
▷ANTONYMS nadir.

appal verb *civil-rights activists were appalled by the police brutality*: **horrify**, **shock**, dismay, distress greatly, outrage, scandalize, alarm; make someone's blood run cold, make someone's hair stand on end; disgust, repel, revolt, sicken, nauseate, offend.

Choose the right word **appal, dismay, horrify**

See **dismay**.

appalling adjective **1** *appalling injuries | an appalling crime*: **shocking**, **horrific**, horrifying, horrible, terrible, awful, dreadful, ghastly, hideous, horrendous, frightful, atrocious, abominable, abhorrent, outrageous, hateful, loathsome, odious, gruesome, grisly, monstrous, nightmarish, heinous, harrowing, dire, vile, shameful, unspeakable, unforgivable, unpardonable; abject; disgusting, revolting, repellent, repulsive, repugnant, sickening, nauseating; rare egregious.
2 informal *your school work is appalling*: **dreadful**, very bad, awful, terrible, frightful, atrocious, disgraceful, deplorable, shameful, hopeless, lamentable, laughable, substandard, poor, inadequate, inferior, unsatisfactory; informal rotten, woeful, crummy, pathetic, pitiful, useless, lousy, God-awful, shocking, abysmal, dire, poxy, the pits; Brit. informal duff, chronic, pants; N. Amer. informal hellacious.
▷ANTONYMS admirable, excellent.

apparatus noun **1** *laboratory apparatus | an apparatus for distilling seawater*: **equipment**, gear, rig, tackle, gadgetry, paraphernalia; appliance, instrument, tool, utensil, machine, mechanism, device, contraption; hardware, plant, machinery; informal things, stuff; Brit. informal gubbins.
2 *the apparatus of government*: **structure**, system, framework, organization, set-up, network; hierarchy, chain of command.

apparel noun formal **clothes**, clothing, garments, dress, attire, wear, garb, wardrobe; outfit, costume; robes, vestments; informal gear, get-up, togs, duds, garms; Brit. informal clobber, kit, rig-out; N. Amer. informal threads; literary raiment, habit, habiliments.

apparent adjective **1** *their relief was all too apparent*: **evident**, plain, obvious, clear, manifest, visible, discernible, perceptible, perceivable, noticeable, detectable, recognizable, observable; unmistakable, crystal clear, as clear as crystal, transparent, palpable, patent, distinct, pronounced, marked, striking, conspicuous, overt, blatant, as plain as a pikestaff, staring someone in the face, writ large, written all over someone, as plain as day, beyond (a) doubt, beyond question, self-evident, indisputable; informal as plain as the nose on one's face, standing/sticking out like a sore thumb, standing/sticking out a mile.
▷ANTONYMS unclear, obscure.
2 *his apparent lack of concern*: **seeming**, ostensible, outward, superficial, surface, supposed, presumed, so-called, alleged, professed, avowed, declared, claimed, purported, pretended, feigned; rare ostensive.
▷ANTONYMS genuine.

apparently adverb *apparently he had a mild heart attack | she sipped her tea, apparently content with his answer*: **seemingly**, evidently, it seems (that), it would seem (that), it appears (that), it would appear (that), as far as one knows, by all accounts, so it seems; ostensibly, outwardly, on the face of it, to all appearances, to all intents and purposes, on the surface, so the story goes, so I'm told; allegedly, supposedly, reputedly; rare ostensively.

apparition noun **1** *a monstrous apparition*: **ghost**, phantom, spectre, spirit, wraith, shadow, presence; vision, hallucination; Scottish & Irish bodach; German Doppelgänger; W. Indian duppy; informal spook; literary phantasm, shade, revenant, visitant, wight; rare eidolon, manes.
2 *he was startled by the apparition of a strange man*: **appearance**, manifestation, materialization, emergence; visitation; arrival, advent.

appeal verb **1** *police are **appealing for** information*: **ask urgently/earnestly**, request urgently/earnestly, make an urgent/earnest request, call, make a plea, plead, beg; sue.
2 *Andrew **appealed to** me to help them*: **implore**, beg, beseech, entreat, call on, plead with, ask, request, petition, pray to, apply to, solicit, exhort, adjure, invoke; lobby; rare obtest, obsecrate, impetrate.
3 *the thought of travelling **appealed to** me*: **attract**, be attractive to, interest, be of interest to, please, take someone's fancy, charm, engage, fascinate, intrigue, tempt, entice, allure, beguile, lure, invite, draw, whet someone's appetite; informal float someone's boat, tickle someone's fancy.
▷ANTONYMS bore, leave someone cold.
▶noun **1** *an emotional appeal for help*: **plea**, urgent/earnest request, entreaty, cry, cry from the heart, call, petition, prayer, supplication, solicitation, application, overture, suit; French cri de cœur; Latin de profundis; archaic orison; rare imploration, adjuration, obtestation, impetration, obsecration.
2 *the cultural appeal of the island | her lack of sophistication was part of her appeal*: **attraction**, attractiveness, interest, allure, charm, enchantment, fascination, beauty, charisma, magnetism, temptation, seductiveness, drawing power, enticement; informal pull.
3 *on 13 March 1992, the Court allowed the appeal*: **retrial**, reconsideration, re-examination.

appealing adjective **1** *men found her trim figure and neat little face very appealing*: **attractive**, engaging, alluring, enchanting, captivating, bewitching, fascinating, winning, winsome, likeable, lovable, charming, delightful; beautiful, pretty, good-looking, prepossessing, striking, fetching, delectable, desirable; irresistible; Scottish & N. English bonny; Brit. informal tasty; dated taking.
▷ANTONYMS off-putting.
2 *flying off to the Bahamas was an appealing prospect*: **inviting**, attractive, tempting, appetizing, enticing, seductive; agreeable, to one's liking,

pleasant, pleasing, pleasurable; interesting, intriguing, irresistible; informal juicy, sexy.
▷ANTONYMS disagreeable, unappealing.

Word toolkit appealing

See **enchanting**.

appear verb **1** *a cloud of dust appeared on the horizon*: **become visible**, come into view, come into sight, materialize, take shape; informal pop up, bob up.
▷ANTONYMS disappear, vanish.
2 *by now, fundamental differences between them were beginning to appear*: **be revealed**, be seen, emerge, manifest itself, become apparent, become evident, surface, come to light, arise, crop up, occur, develop, enter into the picture.
3 informal *by ten o'clock Bill still hadn't appeared*: **arrive**, turn up, put in an appearance, make an appearance, come, get here/there, present oneself; informal show up, show, show one's face, pitch up, fetch up, roll in, blow in.
4 *he and Charlotte appeared to be completely devoted*: **seem**, look, give the impression of being, have the appearance/air of being, come across as being, look as though one is, look to be, strike someone as.
5 *the paperback edition didn't appear for another two years*: **become available**, come on the market, go on sale, come out, be published, be produced; come into existence.
6 *he appeared on Broadway | O'Hara* **appeared as** *Captain Hook*: **perform**, play, act; take the role of, take the part of.

appearance noun **1** *she was conscious of her slightly dishevelled appearance*: **look(s)**, air, aspect, mien, outward form.
2 *Martha took care to keep up an appearance of respectability*: **impression**, air, (outward) show, image; semblance, facade, veneer, guise, pretence, front, illusion.
3 *the sudden appearance of her daughter startled her*: **arrival**, advent, coming, coming into view, emergence, materialization, surfacing.
▷ANTONYMS disappearance, departure.
4 *the appearance of these symptoms*: **occurrence**, manifestation, development.
□ **to all appearances** *to all appearances, Tom is a steadfast family man with an adoring wife*: **outwardly**, externally, on the outside, on the surface, superficially, on the face of it, at first sight/glance, to the casual eye/observer, as far as one can see/tell/judge, to all intents and purposes, apparently, ostensibly, seemingly, evidently.

appease verb **1** *his action was seen as an attempt to appease critics of his regime*: **conciliate**, **placate**, pacify, make peace with, propitiate, palliate, allay, reconcile, win over; calm (down), mollify, soothe, quieten down, subdue, soften, content, still, quieten, silence, tranquillize, humour; informal sweeten.
▷ANTONYMS provoke, inflame.
2 *I'd wasted a lot of money to appease my vanity*: **satisfy**, fulfil, gratify, meet, fill, serve, provide for, indulge; assuage, relieve, take the edge off, deaden, dull, blunt, quench, slake, sate, diminish.
▷ANTONYMS frustrate.

appeasement noun **1** *the National Government's policy of appeasement*: **conciliation**, **placation**, pacification, propitiation, palliation, allaying, reconciliation; **acquiescence**, acceding, concession, accommodation, peace offering, peacemaking, peace-mongering, dovishness; calming, mollification, soothing; informal sweetening.
▷ANTONYMS provocation, aggression.
2 *this was a cop-out, designed to provide appeasement for battered male consciences*: **satisfaction**, fulfilment, gratification, indulgence, provision; assuagement, relief, deadening, tempering, quenching, slaking, satiation.

appellation noun formal *the city fully justifies its appellation 'the Pearl of the Orient'*: **name**, **title**, designation, denomination, honorific, tag, epithet, label, sobriquet, byname, nickname; informal moniker, handle; formal cognomen.

append verb *the head teacher has the right to append comments to the final report*: **add**, attach, affix, adjoin, include, put in/on; informal tack on, tag on; formal subjoin, conjoin.

appendage noun **1** *I am a person in my own right, instead of an appendage to the family*: **addition**, attachment, adjunct, addendum, appurtenance, accessory, accompaniment, affix, extra, add-on, supplement, accretion, peripheral.
2 *this species has a pair of feathery appendages through which oxygen is absorbed*: **protuberance**, projection, extremity, limb, organ; tail, tailpiece, arm, leg; technical process; archaic member.

appendix noun *the list was published as an appendix to the report*: **supplement**, addendum, postscript, codicil; addition, extension, continuation, adjunct, appendage; coda, epilogue, afterword, rider, sequel, tailpiece, back matter; rare postlude.

Word links appendix

appendectomy, appendicectomy surgical removal of appendix

appertain verb
□ **appertain to** *in those days, the laws appertaining to hygiene were much slacker*: **pertain to**, relate to, concern, be concerned with, have to do with; be relevant to, have relevance to, apply to, be pertinent to, have reference to, have a bearing on, bear on, be connected with, be about, affect, involve, cover, deal with, touch; be part of, belong to; archaic regard.

appetite noun **1** *a walk before lunch sharpens the appetite*: **hunger**, ravenousness, hungriness, need for food; taste, palate; desire, relish; voracity, greed, gluttony, stomach; rare edacity, esurience.
2 *my appetite for learning was insatiable*: **craving**, longing, yearning, hankering, hunger, thirst, passion, relish, lust, love, zest, gusto, avidity, ardour; need, demand, urge, addiction, itch, ache; enthusiasm, keenness, eagerness; desire, liking, fancy, inclination, propensity, proclivity, partiality; informal yen; formal appetency.
▷ANTONYMS aversion.

appetizer noun *don't miss the appetizer of fried whitebait*: **starter**, canapé, first course, finger food, titbit, savoury, snack; French hors d'oeuvre, amuse-gueule; Italian antipasto.

appetizing adjective **1** *an appetizing ploughman's lunch was served*: **mouth-watering**, inviting, tempting; **tasty**, succulent, delicious, palatable, delectable, choice, flavoursome, luscious, toothsome; informal scrumptious, scrummy, yummy, yum-yum, moreish, lush; literary ambrosial, ambrosian.
▷ANTONYMS bland, off-putting.
2 *party political broadcasts are often regarded by voters as the least appetizing part of election campaigns*: **appealing**, attractive, inviting, enticing, alluring, tempting, seductive, enchanting, beguiling.
▷ANTONYMS unappealing, off-putting.

applaud verb **1** *the audience applauded*: **clap**, cheer, whistle, give a standing ovation to, put one's hands together; hail, acclaim, hurrah, hurray, shout at; show one's appreciation; ask for an encore; informal give someone a big hand, bring the house down.
▷ANTONYMS boo, hiss.
2 *police have applauded members of the public whose information has led to a series of arrests*: **praise**, commend, acclaim, salute, extol, laud, admire, welcome, celebrate, express admiration for, express approval of, look on with favour, favour, approve of, sing the praises of, pay tribute to, speak highly of, take one's hat off to, pay homage to, express respect for.
▷ANTONYMS criticize.

applause noun **1** *everyone broke out in a massive round of applause*: **clapping**, handclapping, cheering, whistling, (standing) ovation, acclamation, cheers, whistles, bravos; curtain calls, encores.
▷ANTONYMS booing, hissing.
2 *the museum's sloping design won general applause*: **praise**, acclaim, acclamation, admiration, commendation, adulation, favour, approbation, approval, éclat, extolment, respect, eulogy; compliments, accolades, plaudits, tributes; informal brownie points, kudos; rare laudation.
▷ANTONYMS criticism.

appliance noun **1** *domestic appliances like microwave ovens*: **device**, machine, instrument, gadget, contraption, apparatus, utensil, implement, tool, mechanism, contrivance, labour-saving device, amenity, aid; informal gizmo, mod con.
2 *the belief that Utopia is attainable through the appliance of science*: **application**, use, exercise, employment, implementation, administration, utilization, practice, applying, discharge, exertion, execution, prosecution, enactment, carrying out, accomplishment, putting into operation/practice; formal praxis.

applicable adjective *there is no consensus on the laws* **applicable to** *the dispute*: **relevant**, appropriate, pertinent, apposite, germane, material, felicitous, significant, related, connected; apropos of; fitting, suitable, apt, befitting, to the point, to the purpose, useful, helpful, of use; formal ad rem, appurtenant.
▷ANTONYMS inappropriate, irrelevant.

applicant noun *admissions tutors vet applicants for places at university*: **candidate**, interviewee, competitor, contestant, contender, entrant; claimant, suppliant, supplicant, petitioner, suitor, postulant, prospective student/employee, aspirant, possibility, possible; job-seeker, job-hunter; auditioner.

application noun **1** *an application for an overdraft*: **request**, appeal, petition, entreaty, plea, solicitation, supplication, requisition, suit, approach, enquiry, claim, demand.
2 *the application of anti-inflation policies caused many unforeseen problems*: **implementation**, use, exercise, employment, administration, utilization, practice, applying, discharge, exertion, execution, prosecution, enactment, carrying out, accomplishment, putting into operation/practice; formal praxis.
3 *the argument is clearest in its application to the theatre*: **relevance**, relevancy, bearing, significance, pertinence, aptness, appositeness, germaneness, importance.
4 *her face was scrubbed prior to the application of make-up*: **putting on**, rubbing in, spreading, smearing.
5 *an application to relieve muscle pain*: **ointment**, lotion, cream, rub, salve,

a

emollient, preparation, liniment, embrocation, balm, poultice, unguent.
6 *a degree shows that you have the intelligence and application needed to hold down a job*: **diligence**, industriousness, industry, assiduity, commitment, dedication, devotion, conscientiousness, perseverance, persistence, tenacity, doggedness, sedulousness; concentration, intentness, attention, attentiveness, steadiness, patience, endurance; effort, hard work, labour, striving, endeavour.
7 *a vector graphics application*: **program**, software, routine, use.

apply verb **1** *more than 3,000 people had **applied for** the jobs*: **put in an application**, put in, try, bid, appeal, petition, make an entreaty, sue, register, audition; enquire after, request, seek, solicit, claim, ask for, try to obtain.
2 *the Act did not **apply to** Scotland*: **be relevant**, have relevance to, have a bearing on, bear on, appertain, pertain, relate, concern, be concerned with, have to do with; be pertinent, be significant, be apt, be apposite, be appropriate, be fitting, be germane; affect, involve, cover, deal with, touch.
3 *she applied ointment to the survivors' burns and bruises*: **put on**, rub in, spread, smear, cover with, work in.
4 *a firm, steady pressure should be applied*: **exert**, administer, implement, use, exercise, employ, utilize, practise, put into practice, execute, prosecute, enact, carry out, put to use, bring into effect/play, bring to bear.
□ **apply oneself** *if he applied himself he could be the best in the world*: **be diligent**, be industrious, be assiduous, show commitment, show dedication; work hard, study hard, exert oneself, make an effort, spare no effort, try hard, do one's best, give one's all, buckle down/to, put one's shoulder to the wheel, keep one's nose to the grindstone; strive, endeavour, struggle, labour, toil; pay attention, be attentive, commit oneself, devote oneself; persevere, persist; informal put one's back in it, knuckle down, use some elbow grease, get stuck in.

appoint verb **1** *he was appointed Environment Secretary*: **nominate**, name, designate, install as, commission, engage, adopt, co-opt; select, choose, elect, vote in; Military detail.
▷ANTONYMS reject.
2 *the arbitrator shall appoint a date for the preliminary meeting*: **specify**, determine, assign, designate, allot, set, fix, arrange, choose, decide on, establish, settle, authorize, ordain, prescribe, decree.

appointed adjective **1** *I reported to HQ at the appointed time*: **scheduled**, arranged, prearranged, specified, decided, agreed, determined, assigned, designated, allotted, set, fixed, chosen, established, settled, preordained, authorized, ordained, prescribed, decreed.
2 *a well appointed room with private facilities*: **furnished**, decorated, outfitted, fitted out, rigged out, provided, supplied.

appointment noun **1** *she failed to keep a six o'clock appointment*: **meeting**, engagement, interview, arrangement, consultation, session; date, rendezvous, assignation; commitment, fixture; literary tryst.
2 *the appointment of non-executive directors*: **nomination**, naming, designation, designating, installation, commissioning, engagement, adoption, co-option; selection, choosing, election, voting in; Military detailing.
▷ANTONYMS rejection.
3 *he held an appointment at the University of Sheffield*: **job**, post, position, situation, employment, engagement, place, office, station.

apportion verb *in many households, domestic work is not apportioned equally between partners*: **share out**, divide out, allocate, distribute, allot, assign, dispense; give out, hand out, mete out, deal out, dole out; ration, parcel out, measure out; split, carve up, slice up; informal divvy up, dish out.

apportionment noun *the apportionment of costs*: **sharing**, division, allocation, distribution, allotment, assigning, dispensation; ration; splitting, carving up, parcelling out, slicing up; informal divvying up.

apposite adjective *each chapter is prefaced by an apposite quotation*: **appropriate**, suitable, fitting, apt, befitting; **relevant**, pertinent, to the point, to the purpose, applicable, germane, material, congruous, felicitous; Latin ad rem; formal appurtenant.
▷ANTONYMS inappropriate.

appraisal noun **1** *my review was an objective appraisal of the book*: **assessment**, evaluation, estimation, judgement, rating, gauging, sizing up, summing-up, consideration.
2 *the price of the work leapt from $6,000, an appraisal offered in 1972, to $60,000*: **valuation**, pricing, estimate, estimation, quotation, estimated price/value/cost; survey.

appraise verb **1** *the men stepped back to appraise their handiwork*: **assess**, evaluate, estimate, judge, rate, gauge, sum up, review, consider; informal size up.
2 *his goods were appraised at £1,800*: **value**, price, set a price on, estimate, quote; survey.

appreciable adjective *tea and coffee both contain appreciable amounts of caffeine*: **considerable**, substantial, significant, sizeable, goodly, fair, reasonable, tidy, marked; **perceptible**, noticeable, measurable, detectable, visible.
▷ANTONYMS negligible.

> *Word toolkit* **appreciable**
>
> See **perceptible**.

appreciably adverb *white-collar unionization is appreciably lower in the United States*: **considerably**, substantially, significantly, markedly; noticeably, measurably, perceptibly, detectably, visibly, ascertainably; greatly, much, a great deal; sizeably, fairly, reasonably, tidily.
▷ANTONYMS negligibly.

appreciate verb **1** *I'd appreciate any advice you can give*: **be grateful for**, be thankful for, give thanks for, be obliged for, be indebted for, be beholden for, be in your debt for, be appreciative of.
▷ANTONYMS disparage.
2 *by this time, the college appreciated me rather more*: **value**, respect, prize, cherish, treasure, admire, hold in high regard, hold in esteem, rate highly, think highly of, think much of, have a high opinion of, set (great) store by.
3 *I appreciate the problems of administration that would make this scheme impractical*: **acknowledge**, recognize, realize, know; be aware of, be conscious of, be cognizant of; be alive to, be sensitive to, be alert to; sympathize with, understand, comprehend, perceive, discern; informal take on board, be wise to.
▷ANTONYMS be unaware of.
4 *with good advice a couple can buy a home that will appreciate in value*: **increase**, gain, grow, build up, rise, go up, mount, inflate, escalate, soar, rocket; improve, enhance.
▷ANTONYMS depreciate, decrease.

appreciation noun **1** *he expressed his appreciation for the large amount of work done*: **gratitude**, thanks, gratefulness, thankfulness, recognition, sense of obligation; indebtedness, obligation.
▷ANTONYMS ingratitude.
2 *appreciation of literature comes only from first-hand study of the works of great writers*: **valuing**, respect, prizing, cherishing, treasuring, admiration, regard, esteem, high opinion.
3 *he gained an appreciation of the significance of teamwork*: **acknowledgement**, recognition, realization, knowledge; awareness, consciousness, cognizance; sensitivity, alertness; sympathy, understanding, comprehension, perception, discernment.
▷ANTONYMS unawareness.
4 *the appreciation of the franc against the pound*: **increase**, gain, growth, rise, mounting, inflation, escalation; improvement, enhancement.
▷ANTONYMS depreciation, decrease.
5 *an appreciation of the professor's life and work*: **review**, critique, criticism, critical analysis, commentary, write-up, notice; assessment, evaluation, judgement, rating, report; praise, acclamation; Brit. informal crit.

appreciative adjective **1** *my colleagues and I are **appreciative of** all your efforts*: **grateful for**, thankful for, obliged for; indebted for, beholden for; in someone's debt, obligated.
▷ANTONYMS ungrateful.
2 *they played in front of an appreciative audience*: **supportive**, encouraging, sympathetic, responsive, enthusiastic, sensitive.
3 *Harper took a step back and gave Lucille an appreciative smile*: **admiring**, approving, complimentary, flattering, praising, congratulatory, laudatory.

> *Choose the right word* **appreciative, grateful, thankful**
>
> See **grateful**.

apprehend verb **1** *the thieves were quickly apprehended*: **arrest**, catch, capture, seize; take prisoner, take into custody, detain, put in jail, throw in jail, put behind bars, imprison, incarcerate; informal collar, nab, nail, run in, pinch, bust, pick up, pull in, haul in, do, feel someone's collar; Brit. informal nick.
2 *language is the only tool we have at our disposal for apprehending reality*: **understand**, comprehend, realize, recognize, appreciate, discern, perceive, fathom, penetrate, catch, follow, grasp, make out, take in; informal get the picture, get the drift of, get the hang of, make head or tail of; Brit. informal twig, suss (out).

apprehension noun **1** *he had been filled with apprehension at having to report his failure*: **anxiety**, angst, alarm, worry, uneasiness, unease, nervousness, misgiving, disquiet, concern, agitation, restlessness, edginess, fidgetiness, nerves, tension, trepidation, perturbation, consternation, panic, fearfulness, dread, fear, shock, horror, terror; foreboding, presentiment; informal butterflies in the stomach, the willies, the heebie-jeebies.
▷ANTONYMS confidence.
2 *she was popular because of her quick apprehension of the wishes of the people*: **understanding**, grasp, comprehension, realization, recognition, appreciation, discernment, perception, awareness, cognizance, consciousness, penetration.
3 *police activity centred around the apprehension of a perpetrator*: **arrest**, capture, seizure, catching; detention, imprisonment, incarceration; informal collaring, nabbing, nailing, pinching, bust, busting; Brit. informal nick.

apprehensive adjective *many of the pupils were very apprehensive about their first visit to the new school*: **anxious**, alarmed, worried, uneasy, nervous, concerned, agitated, restless, edgy, on edge, fidgety, tense, strained, stressed, neurotic, panicky, afraid, scared, frightened, fearful, terrified; informal on tenterhooks, trepidatious.
▷ANTONYMS confident.

Word toolkit

apprehensive	tense	neurotic
knock	situation	behaviour
expression	silence	disorder
glance	atmosphere	passion
face	relationship	tendencies
voice	game	personality
parents	stand-off	individual
approach	encounter	patterns
steps	drama	obsession

apprentice noun *on leaving school Herbert joined his father as an engineering apprentice*: **trainee**, learner, probationer, tyro, novice, mentee, neophyte, raw recruit, fledgling, new boy/girl, novitiate; pupil, student; beginner, starter; N. Amer. informal rookie, greenhorn, tenderfoot.
▷ANTONYMS veteran.

apprenticeship noun *he served an apprenticeship to a master blacksmith*: **traineeship**, training period, studentship, novitiate; initiation, probationary period, trial period; historical indentureship.

apprise verb *he continued to keep them apprised of all that was going on in Salzburg*: **inform**, notify, tell, let know, advise, brief, intimate, make aware of, send word to, update, keep posted, keep up to date, keep up to speed, enlighten; informal clue in, fill in, put wise, tip off, put in the picture.

approach verb **1** *she approached the altar with her head bowed*: **proceed towards**, come/go towards, advance towards, go near/nearer, come near/nearer, draw near/nearer, come close/closer, go close/closer, draw close/closer, move near/nearer, edge near/nearer, near, draw near; close in on, centre on, focus on, converge on; catch up on, gain on; creep up on, loom; reach, arrive at.
▷ANTONYMS leave.
2 *the trade deficit is now approaching £20 million*: **border on**, approximate, verge on, resemble; be comparable/similar to, compare with; touch, nudge, get on for; near, come near to, come/be close to; informal be not a million miles away from.
3 *the publishing tycoon approached him about leaving his job*: **speak to**, talk to, make conversation with, engage in conversation; take aside, detain; greet, address, salute, hail, initiate a discussion with; broach the matter to, make advances to, make overtures to, make a proposal to, sound out, proposition, solicit, appeal to, apply to; informal buttonhole.
4 *he had approached the whole business in the best way*: **set about**, tackle, begin, start, commence, embark on, make a start on, address oneself to, undertake, get down to, launch into, go about, get to grips with; informal get cracking on.
▸ noun **1** *the traditional British approach to air pollution control*: **attitude**, slant, perspective, point of view, viewpoint, outlook, line of attack, line of action; **method**, procedure, process, technique, MO, style, strategy, stratagem, way, manner, mode, tactic, tack, path, system, means; Latin modus operandi.
2 *doctors are considering an approach to the High Court*: **proposal**, proposition, submission, motion, offer, application, appeal, plea.
3 (**approaches**) dated *he found all his approaches repulsed*: **advances**, overtures, suggestions, attentions; suit.
4 *at the approach of any intruder, she would raise her wings and screech*: **advance**, coming near/nearer, coming, nearing, advent; **arrival**, entrance, appearance.
5 *this department is our nearest approach to a Ministry of Justice*: **approximation**, likeness, semblance, correspondence, parallel.
6 *two riders turned in at the approach to the castle*: **driveway**, drive, access road, road, avenue, street, passageway.

approachable adjective **1** *most students said that they found the staff approachable*: **friendly**, welcoming, pleasant, agreeable, congenial, affable, cordial, well disposed, obliging, communicative, open, hospitable, helpful; informal, easy-going, accessible, available, easy to get on/along with; informal unstuffy.
▷ANTONYMS aloof, unapproachable.
2 *the south landing is approachable by boat*: **accessible**, attainable, reachable, obtainable; informal get-at-able, come-at-able.
▷ANTONYMS inaccessible.

approbation noun *he yearned for popular approbation*: **approval**, acceptance, assent, endorsement, encouragement, recognition, appreciation, support, respect, admiration, commendation, congratulations; **praise**, acclamation, adulation, regard, esteem, veneration, kudos, applause, ovation, accolades, salutes, plaudits; rare laudation.
▷ANTONYMS criticism.

appropriate adjective *refer to the appropriate page of the atlas | this isn't the appropriate time or place*: **suitable**, proper, fitting, apt; **relevant**, connected, pertinent, apposite, applicable, germane, material, significant, right, congruous, to the point, to the purpose; convenient, expedient, favourable, auspicious, propitious, opportune, felicitous, timely, well judged, well timed; seemly, befitting, deserved; Latin ad rem; formal appurtenant; archaic meet, seasonable.
▷ANTONYMS inappropriate; irrelevant.
▸ verb **1** *he acquired resources by appropriating local church lands*: **seize**, commandeer, expropriate, annex, arrogate, sequestrate, sequester, take possession of, take over, assume, secure, acquire, wrest, usurp, claim, lay claim to, hijack.
2 *allegations that he had appropriated £40,000 had led to his dismissal*: **steal**, take, misappropriate; thieve, pilfer, pocket, purloin, make off with; embezzle; informal swipe, nab, rip off, lift, filch, snaffle, snitch, bag, walk off/away with, 'abstract', 'borrow', 'liberate'; Brit. informal pinch, nick, half-inch, whip, knock off; rare peculate, defalcate.
3 *there can be constitutional problems in appropriating funds for these expenses*: **allocate**, assign, allot, earmark, set apart/aside, devote, apportion, budget.
4 *his images have been appropriated by advertisers*: **plagiarize**, copy, reproduce; poach, steal, 'borrow', bootleg, infringe the copyright of; informal pirate, rip off, crib, lift.

Choose the right word **appropriate, suitable, proper, fitting**

Something that is **appropriate** suits a particular situation (*she searched for an appropriate word | we need care packages appropriate to people's needs*). The word may convey pleasure or satisfaction at the particular relevance of something (*it is appropriate that healing should still be important in the village where the Red Cross was born*), or it can be used if you want to persuade others, by slight subterfuge, to agree with you that something is desirable (*we consider it is now appropriate to consult interested individuals and agencies*). *Appropriate* is often used for something that is socially acceptable (*society seems to think it is appropriate for little girls to shed tears*).

Suitable is a more general word for things that are right for a particular purpose or occasion, and they need not be the only correct or possible ones (*he may be able to find suitable alternative work | the site isn't suitable for residential use*).

A **proper** person or thing may well be the only correct person or thing for a purpose or a job (*inquiries should be addressed to the proper officer | medium-sized and larger building firms should carry out proper training*). In this sense, *proper* is always used before the noun it qualifies. *Proper* is also used to mean 'socially acceptable' (*her parents' view of what was proper for a well-bred girl*).

Something that is **fitting** (the least common word of this group) is particularly apposite, and usually desirable (*his election as president of the society was a fitting tribute | it was very fitting that the late Sgt Day's brother and sister were among the guests*).

approval noun **1** *proposals for the licensing system will now go forward to the ministry for approval*: **acceptance**, agreement, consent, assent, acquiescence, compliance, concurrence; blessing, imprimatur, seal/stamp of approval, rubber stamp; sanction, endorsement, ratification, authorization, mandate, licence, validation; confirmation, support, backing; permission, leave; informal the go-ahead, the green light, the OK, the thumbs up, the nod, say-so.
▷ANTONYMS refusal.
2 *Lily looked at him with approval*: **approbation**, appreciation, favour, liking, encouragement, support, acceptance; admiration, regard, esteem, respect, commendation, applause, acclaim, acclamation, praise.
▷ANTONYMS disapproval.
□ **on approval** *we would be happy to send you a selection on approval*: **on trial**, under probation; on sale or return; Brit. informal on appro.

approve verb **1** *his boss doesn't **approve of** his party-boy lifestyle*: **agree with**, hold with, endorse, support, back, uphold, subscribe to, recommend, advocate, second, express one's approval of, be in favour of, favour, think well of, like, look on with favour, give one's blessing to, tolerate, appreciate, countenance, take kindly to; be pleased with, admire, hold in regard/esteem, commend, embrace, applaud, acclaim, praise; informal go along with.
▷ANTONYMS condemn, disapprove.
2 *the government has approved proposals for a new waste law*: **accept**, agree to, consent to, assent to, acquiesce in, concur in, accede to, give one's blessing to, bless, give one's seal/stamp of approval to, rubber-stamp, say yes to; ratify, sanction, endorse, authorize, mandate, license, warrant, validate, pass; confirm, support, back; give one's permission/leave; informal give the go-ahead to, give the green light to, give the OK to, OK, give the thumbs up to, give the nod, say the word, buy.
▷ANTONYMS refuse.

approving adjective *Gina paused to pass her approving gaze around the rest of the room*: **admiring**, appreciative, appreciating, favourable, respectful,

a

esteeming, commendatory, commending, applauding, acclamatory, acclaiming, praising, flattering, congratulatory, rapturous; formal encomiastic, eulogistic, laudatory, panegyrical.
▷ANTONYMS critical.

approximate adjective *all measurements are approximate and for guidance only*: **estimated**, rough, imprecise, inexact; near, close; indefinite, broad, loose, general, vague, hazy, fuzzy, woolly; N. Amer. informal ballpark.
▷ANTONYMS precise.
▸ verb *research shows that this scenario probably* ***approximates to*** *the truth*: **be close to**, be near to, come close to, come near to, approach, border on, verge on, equal roughly; be similar to, resemble, correspond to, compare with, be tantamount to, be not dissimilar to, be not unlike; touch, nudge, get on for.
▷ANTONYMS be nothing like.

approximately adverb *approximately £1 million*: **roughly**, about, around, just about, round about, or so, or thereabouts, more or less, in the neighbourhood of, in the region of, in the area of, in the vicinity of, of the order of, something like, or thereabouts, give or take (a few), in round numbers, rounded up/down; near to, close to, nearly, not far off, almost, approaching; Brit. getting on for; Latin circa; informal pushing, as near as dammit; N. Amer. informal in the ballpark of; archaic nigh.
▷ANTONYMS precisely.

approximation noun **1** *a general approximation is that a ten degree rise in temperature doubles the rate of reaction*: **estimate**, estimation, guess, conjecture, rough calculation, rough idea, surmise; guesswork; informal guesstimate; N. Amer. informal **ballpark figure**.
2 *we can only look for an approximation to the truth about these matters*: **semblance**, outward appearance, likeness, resemblance, similarity, correspondence, comparison.

appurtenances plural noun *the corrupting appurtenances of modern civilization*: **accessories**, trappings, appendages, accoutrements, extras, additions, adjuncts, conveniences, incidentals; equipment, paraphernalia, impedimenta, belongings, bits and pieces; informal things, stuff.

appurtenant adjective formal *the lands appurtenant to his forestership*. See **pertinent**.

a priori adjective *he argued that Conservatism was based on an observation of life, and not a priori reasoning*: **theoretical**, deduced, deductive, inferred, scientific; postulated, suppositional, self-evident.
▷ANTONYMS empirical.
▸ adverb *the words were not necessarily the ones which would have been predicted a priori*: **theoretically**, from theory, deductively, scientifically.
▷ANTONYMS empirically.

apron noun *a striped butcher's apron*: **pinafore**, overall; informal pinny.

apropos preposition *value judgements* ***apropos of*** *particular works of art* | *he was asked a question apropos the recent resignation*: **with reference to**, with regard to, with respect to, regarding, concerning, respecting, on the subject of, in the matter of, touching on, dealing with, connected with, in connection with, about, re; Scottish anent.
□ **apropos of nothing** *suddenly, apropos of nothing, he asked, 'What made you decide your engagement was a mistake?'*: **irrelevantly**, arbitrarily, at random, for no reason, illogically.
▸ adjective *the word 'conglomerate' was decidedly apropos*: **appropriate**, pertinent, relevant, apposite, apt, applicable, suitable, germane, material, becoming, befitting, significant, to the point/purpose; opportune, felicitous, timely.
▷ANTONYMS inappropriate.

apt adjective **1** *this is an apt place to celebrate the end of a great walk*: **suitable**, fitting, appropriate, befitting, relevant, felicitous, congruous, fit, applicable, judicious, apposite, apropos, to the purpose, to the point; perfect, ideal, right, just right, made to order, tailor-made; convenient, expedient, useful, timely; informal spot on.
▷ANTONYMS inappropriate.
2 *men left to themselves are apt to get a mite slipshod about meals*: **inclined**, given, likely, liable, disposed, predisposed, prone, ready, tending, subject, of a mind, capable.
▷ANTONYMS unlikely.
3 *an apt pupil*: **clever**, quick, bright, sharp, quick to learn, smart, intelligent; able, gifted, talented, adept, proficient, competent, astute.
▷ANTONYMS slow.

aptitude noun *he showed an aptitude for skiing*: **talent**, gift, flair, bent, skill, knack, facility, finesse, genius; ability, proficiency, competence, capability, potential, capacity, faculty; expertise, expertness, adeptness, prowess, mastery, artistry; propensity, inclination, natural ability, suitability, fitness; head, mind, brain; informal know-how.

aptness noun *he was surprised at the aptness of the comparison*: **suitability**, appropriateness, relevance, fitness, felicity, congruity, applicability, pertinence, judiciousness, appositeness, becomingness; convenience, expedience, usefulness, timeliness; correctness, rightness.
▷ANTONYMS inappropriateness.

aquatic adjective *aquatic plants*: **water**; sea, marine, maritime, saltwater, seawater, oceanic; freshwater, river, fluvial; rare pelagic, thalassic.

aqueduct noun **conduit**, race, channel, watercourse, waterway, sluice, sluiceway, spillway; bridge, viaduct.

aquiline adjective *he had an aquiline nose*: **hooked**, curved, hook-shaped, hook-like, bent, bowed, angular; technical falcate, falciform.
▷ANTONYMS straight.

arable adjective *acres of arable land*: **farmable**, cultivable, cultivatable, ploughable, tillable; fertile, productive, fruitful, fecund, lush.
▷ANTONYMS infertile.

arbiter noun **1** *he believed that Britain could play a major role as arbiter between Moscow and Washington*. See **arbitrator**.
2 *the great arbiter of fashion*: **judge**, **authority**, determiner, controller, director, governor, master, expert, pundit, critic.

arbitrary adjective **1** *an arbitrary decision from the top*: **capricious**, whimsical, random, chance, erratic, unpredictable, inconsistent, wild, hit-or-miss, haphazard, casual; **unmotivated**, motiveless, unreasoned, unreasonable, unsupported, irrational, illogical, groundless, unjustifiable, unjustified, wanton; discretionary, personal, subjective; rare discretional.
▷ANTONYMS rational, reasoned.
2 *the arbitrary power of a prince*: **despotic**, tyrannical, tyrannous, peremptory, summary, autocratic, dictatorial, authoritarian, draconian, autarchic; oppressive, repressive, undemocratic, illiberal; imperious, domineering, high-handed; absolute, uncontrolled, unlimited, unrestrained.
▷ANTONYMS democratic, accountable.

arbitrate verb *James II offered to arbitrate in the dispute*: **adjudicate**, judge, adjudge, referee, umpire, sit in judgement, pass judgement, pronounce judgement, give a verdict, make a ruling; **mediate**, negotiate, conciliate, intervene, intercede, interpose, step in, make peace, act as peacemaker; settle, decide, determine, resolve.

arbitration noun *the council called for arbitration to settle the dispute*: **adjudication**, **mediation**, mediatorship, negotiation, conciliation, intervention, interceding, interposition, peacemaking; judgement; rare arbitrament.

arbitrator noun *the facts of the case were put to an independent arbitrator*: **adjudicator**, arbiter, judge, referee, umpire; mediator, conciliator, intervenor, intercessor, go-between, negotiator, peacemaker.

arbour noun *behind the orange blossom was a little arbour with a stone bench*: **bower**, alcove, grotto, recess, pergola, gazebo, summer house; shady place, shelter, hideaway, retreat, sanctuary.

arc noun *the arc of a circle*: **curve**, bend, bow, arch; crescent, semicircle, circular section/line, half-moon; curvature, convexity, curling.
▸ verb *I sent the ball arcing out over the river*: **curl**, curve, swerve, spin, turn; **soar**, sail, fly, ascend, mount, climb.

arcade noun **1** *they walked on, past a classical arcade*: **gallery**, colonnade, cloister, loggia, portico, forum, peristyle, stoa.
2 *she went to a cafe in an arcade*: **shopping centre**, shopping precinct, shopping complex; N. Amer. plaza, mall, strip mall, shopping mall.

arcane adjective *the arcane world of the legal profession*: **mysterious**, secret, hidden, concealed, covert, clandestine, enigmatic, dark; esoteric, obscure, abstruse, recondite, little known, recherché, inscrutable, impenetrable, opaque, incomprehensible, cryptic, occult.
▷ANTONYMS well known, open.

> *Word toolkit* **arcane**
>
> See **secret**.

arch[1] noun **1** *a stone arch was built at the entrance*: **archway**, vault, span, dome; bridge.
2 *the arch of the spine*: **curve**, bow, bend, arc, semicircle, sweep; curvature, convexity, curving, curling, bending, flex; hunch, crook.
▸ verb *she arched her eyebrows and shrugged*: **curve**, bow, bend, arc, curl.

arch[2] adjective *'I wonder for how long!' he said in a somewhat arch tone*: **knowing**, **playful**, mischievous, puckish, roguish, impish, elfin, devilish, naughty, wicked, cheeky, teasing, saucy, flippant, tongue-in-cheek; artful, sly, cunning, affected; archaic frolicsome.

arch- combining form *archbishop* | *arch-enemy*: **chief**, principal, foremost, leading, main, pre-eminent, cardinal, major, prime, premier, elite, star, outstanding, ultra-, super-; top, highest, greatest, best, first, head; out-and-out, complete, utter, total; informal number-one, numero uno.
▷ANTONYMS minor, pseudo-.

archaic adjective *an archaic word* | *archaic conventions*: **obsolete**, obsolescent, out of date, anachronistic, old-fashioned, outmoded, behind the times, bygone, antiquated, antique, superannuated, antediluvian, past its prime, having seen better days, olde worlde, old-fangled; **ancient**, very old, aged, prehistoric, primitive, of yore; extinct, defunct, discontinued,

a

discarded, fossilized, dead; French passé, démodé; informal old hat, out of the ark.
▷ANTONYMS new, modern.

archbishop noun

Word links **archbishop**

archiepiscopal relating to an archbishop

arched adjective *a great arched ceiling*: **vaulted**, curved, domed, rounded, bowed; formal embowed.

archer noun **bowman**.

Word links **archer**

toxophily archery

archetypal adjective *Blackpool is the archetypal British seaside resort*: **most typical**, most characteristic, representative, standard, conventional, classic, model, exemplary, quintessential, prime, textbook, copybook; stock, stereotypical, prototypical, paradigmatic, illustrative; average, clichéd, trite, hackneyed.
▷ANTONYMS atypical, unique.

Word toolkit

archetypal	consummate	exemplary
story	professional	work
characters	politician	fashion
hero	performer	service
model	showman	behaviour
narrative	artist	leadership
imagery	storyteller	conduct
symbolism	gentleman	lives
role	liar	student

archetype noun *an archetype of the old-style football-club chairman*: **typification**, type, prototype, representative, stereotype; original, pattern, model, standard, mould; embodiment, exemplar, essence, quintessence, textbook example, paradigm, ideal, idea.

architect noun **1** *the great Norman architect of Durham Cathedral*: **designer**, planner, builder, building consultant, draughtsman.
2 *Aneurin Bevan, architect of the National Health Service*: **originator**, author, creator, instigator, founder, father, mother, founding father, prime mover; engineer, designer, deviser, planner, shaper, inventor, maker, producer, contriver, mastermind; cause, agent; literary begetter.

architecture noun **1** *schools of architecture and design*: **building design**, planning, building, construction; formal architectonics.
2 *an example of modern architecture*: **building style**, design, structure, construction, framework.
3 *the architecture of a computer system*: **structure**, construction, form, formation, shape, composition, organization, layout, design, build, anatomy, make-up, constitution; informal set-up.

Word links **architecture**

architectonic relating to architecture
architectonics study of architecture

archive noun **1** **(archives)** *if you delve into the family archives you'll find that their marriage was a very happy one*: **records**, annals, chronicles, registers, accounts; papers, documents, rolls, dossiers, files, deeds, ledgers; history, information, evidence; documentation, paperwork; formal muniments.
2 *more and more museums, archives, and libraries are becoming independent*: **record office**, registry, repository, museum, chancery.
▸ verb *these videos are archived for future use*: **file**, log, catalogue, pigeonhole; **store**, record, register, chronicle, cache; document, put on record, post.

arctic adjective **1** **(Arctic)** *iceberg movement in Arctic waters*: **polar**; **far northern**, northern, northerly; rare boreal, hyperborean.
▷ANTONYMS Antarctic.
2 *February brought arctic conditions*: **(bitterly) cold**, intensely cold, frosty, wintry; freezing, frigid, frozen, icy, ice-cold, glacial, sub-zero, polar, Siberian; bitter, biting, piercing, cutting, raw, extreme; rare gelid, brumal, rimy, algid.
▷ANTONYMS tropical.
▸ noun **(the Arctic)** **the far north**, the North Pole, the Arctic circle.
▷ANTONYMS the Antarctic.

ardent adjective *an ardent feminist*: **passionate**, avid, impassioned, fervent, fervid, zealous, wholehearted, eager, vehement, intense, fierce, fiery, flaming, emotional, hot-blooded; earnest, sincere; enthusiastic, keen, committed, dedicated, assiduous; informal mad keen.
▷ANTONYMS half-hearted.

ardour noun *she was unaccustomed to being kissed with such ardour*: **passion**, avidity, fervour, zeal, wholeheartedness, eagerness, vehemence, intensity, fierceness, zest, gusto, energy, animation, fire, fieriness, emotion, emotionalism, feeling, hot-bloodedness; earnestness, sincerity; enthusiasm, keenness, dedication, devotion, assiduity, readiness; archaic empressement.

arduous adjective *she was now faced with an arduous journey into a remote country*: **onerous**, taxing, difficult, hard, heavy, laborious, burdensome, strenuous, vigorous, back-breaking, stiff, uphill, relentless, Herculean; demanding, trying, tough, challenging, formidable, exacting; exhausting, wearying, fatiguing, tiring, punishing, gruelling, grinding; intolerable, unbearable, murderous, harrowing; informal killing, no picnic; Brit. informal knackering; archaic toilsome; rare exigent.
▷ANTONYMS easy, effortless.

Word toolkit

arduous	challenging	onerous
journey	problem	responsibility
process	task	regulations
training	question	tax
climb	environment	debt

area noun **1** *an inner-city area*: **district**, region, zone, sector, quarter; locality, locale, neighbourhood, community, domain, realm, sphere, environment, territory; part, section, parish, spot, patch; tract, stretch, sweep, belt; informal neck of the woods; Brit. informal manor; N. Amer. informal turf.
2 *most of these attainments relate to specific areas of scientific knowledge*: **domain**, sector, department, province, territory, compartment, line; field, sphere, discipline, realm.
3 *the dining area*: **section**, space, sector, part, portion.
4 *he climbed over the area railings*: **(sunken) enclosure**, yard.
5 *the area of a circle varies with the square of its radius*: **expanse**, extent, size, scope, compass; measurements, dimensions, proportions; square footage, acreage.

Word links **area**

planimetry measurement of area

arena noun **1** *an ice-hockey arena*: **stadium**, amphitheatre, theatre, coliseum; ground, field, ring, rink, pitch, court, stage, platform; in ancient Rome circus, hippodrome; N. Amer. bowl; informal park; rare cirque.
2 *not all interest groups are able to compete in the political arena*: **area**, scene, sphere, realm, province, domain, sector, forum, territory, theatre, stage, world; battleground, battlefield, area/field of conflict, sphere of action/activity, lists.

argot noun *the argot of CB radio*: **jargon**, slang, idiom, cant, dialect, parlance, patter, speech, vernacular, patois, terminology, language, tongue, -speak; informal lingo.

arguable adjective **1** *it seems to me arguable that both courts had jurisdiction*: **tenable**, maintainable, assertable, defendable, defensible, supportable, sustainable, able to hold water; reasonable, rational, viable, workable, credible, believable, feasible, conceivable, acceptable, imaginable.
▷ANTONYMS untenable.
2 *it is arguable whether such conditions existed anyway*: **debatable**, disputable, questionable, open to question, controversial, contentious, open to debate, doubtful, open to doubt, dubious, uncertain, unsure, moot.
▷ANTONYMS certain.

arguably adverb *these criteria are exceedingly vague and arguably provide too much scope for judicial interpretation*: **possibly**, conceivably, feasibly, plausibly, probably, maybe, perhaps, potentially; debatably, contestably, controversially.

argue verb **1** *critics argued that the government had been to blame for the country's economic problems*: **contend**, assert, declare, maintain, state, proclaim, advance, insist, hold, claim, aver, avow, reason, attest, expostulate, testify, swear, certify; propound, submit, posit, postulate, adduce, move, advocate, opine, allege; make a case for, give reasons for, defend, explain, vindicate, justify; technical depose, represent; rare asseverate.
2 *the children are always arguing*: **quarrel**, disagree, row, squabble, bicker, fight, wrangle, dispute, feud, have a row, bandy words, have words, cross swords, lock horns, be at each other's throats; dissent, clash, differ, be at odds; informal fall out, scrap, argy-bargy, argufy, spat, go at it hammer and tongs, fight like cat and dog; archaic altercate.
3 *it is hard to argue the point*: **dispute**, debate, discuss, controvert.
□ **argue someone into something** *it would be better to argue her into going back home*: **persuade to**, convince to, prevail on to, coax into; talk someone round.

a

◻ **argue someone out of something** *Vivienne had argued Malcolm out of one of his crazier ideas*: **dissuade from**, persuade against, talk out of.

> *Choose the right word* **argue, quarrel, wrangle, dispute, bicker**
>
> See **quarrel**.

argument noun **1** *he had a long argument with Tony*: **quarrel**, disagreement, squabble, fight, difference of opinion, dispute, wrangle, clash, altercation, feud, dissension, war of words, contretemps, exchange of views; debate, discussion, discourse, disputation, controversy; informal tiff, barney, set-to, dust-up, bust-up, shouting/slanging match, spat, ding-dong, falling-out; Brit. informal row; Scottish informal rammy.
2 *his arguments for the existence of God*: **reasoning**, line of reasoning, logic, case; defence, justification, vindication, apology, explanation, rationalization; evidence, reasons, grounds; argumentation, polemic; assertion, declaration, claim, plea, contention, expostulation, demonstration.
3 archaic *the argument of the book*: **theme**, topic, subject matter; gist, outline, summary, synopsis, abstract, precis; plot, storyline.

argumentative adjective *he was argumentative, opinionated, and outspoken*: **quarrelsome**, disputatious, bickering, wrangling, captious, contrary, cantankerous, contentious, litigious, dissentient, polemical; belligerent, bellicose, combative, antagonistic, aggressive, truculent, pugnacious; rare oppugnant.
▷ANTONYMS compliant.

arid adjective **1** *an arid landscape*: **dry**, dried up, waterless, as dry as a bone, moistureless, parched, scorched, baked, thirsty; dehydrated, desiccated; **barren**, desert, waste, desolate; infertile, non-fertile, unfruitful, unproductive, uncultivatable, sterile; rare infecund, droughty, torrefied.
▷ANTONYMS wet; fertile.
2 *this town has an arid, empty feel*: **dreary**, dull, drab, dry, sterile, banal, colourless, monochrome, unstimulating, uninspiring, flat, boring, uninteresting, monotonous, lifeless, tedious, vapid, jejune, soul-destroying.
▷ANTONYMS interesting, vibrant.

aright adverb dated *I can't believe that I'm hearing you aright*. See **correctly** (sense 1).

arise verb **1** *if any problems arise, go to the Citizens' Advice Bureau*: **come to light**, become apparent, make an appearance, appear, emerge, crop/turn up, come about, surface, spring up, enter into the picture; **occur**, ensue, set in, transpire, come into being/existence, begin, commence; literary befall, come to pass.
2 *manufacturers are liable for all losses* ***arising from*** *defective products*: **result**, proceed, follow, ensue, derive, stem, accrue; originate, emanate, spring, flow; be caused by, be brought about by, be produced by.
3 formal *the beast stretched his legs and arose*: **stand up**, rise, get to one's feet, get up, jump up, leap up, spring up; become erect, straighten up.
▷ANTONYMS sit down, lie down.

aristocracy noun (**the aristocracy**) **the nobility**, the peerage, the gentry, the upper class, the ruling class, the privileged class, the elite, high society, the establishment, the patriciate, the haut monde, the beau monde; aristocrats, lords, ladies, peers, peers of the realm, nobles, noblemen, noblewomen, titled men/women/people, patricians; informal the upper crust, the jet set, the beautiful people, the crème de la crème, the top drawer, aristos; Brit. informal nobs, toffs.
▷ANTONYMS the working class, the common people, the masses.

aristocrat noun *a decadent old blue-blooded aristocrat*: **nobleman**, noblewoman, lord, lady, peer, peeress, peer of the realm, patrician, grandee, titled man/woman/person; informal aristo, top person, member of the upper crust; Brit. informal toff, nob, chinless wonder; rare optimate.
▷ANTONYMS commoner.

aristocratic adjective **1** *an aristocratic family*: **noble**, titled, upper-class, blue-blooded, high-born, well born, patrician, elite; grand, distinguished, respectable; born with a silver spoon in one's mouth, silver-spoon; informal posh, upper crust, upmarket, top drawer; archaic gentle, of gentle birth.
▷ANTONYMS plebeian, working-class.
2 *he had a stately, aristocratic manner*: **well bred**, dignified, courtly; refined, polished, elegant, stylish; decorous, gracious, fine, polite, well mannered, civil, courteous, chivalrous, gallant, gentlemanly, ladylike, urbane, suave, debonair; haughty, proud; informal snobbish.
▷ANTONYMS vulgar, coarse.

arm[1] noun **1** *she flapped her arms like wings*: **upper limb**, forelimb, appendage; archaic member.
2 *a jacket with the arms hacked off*: **sleeve**.
3 *an arm of the sea*: **inlet**, creek, cove, fjord, bay, voe; estuary, firth; branch, strait(s), neck, narrows, sound, channel, passage, stretch of water, waterway.
4 *the political arm of the separatist group*: **branch**, section, department, division, subdivision, wing, sector, chapter, lodge, detachment, agency, office, bureau, offshoot, satellite, extension.
5 *the long arm of the law*: **reach**, power, force, authority, strength, might, potency.
◻ **keep someone/something at arm's length** *she is wise enough to keep him at arm's length until he proposes marriage*: **avoid**, keep away from, stay away from, steer clear of, circumvent, give a wide berth to.

> *Word links* **arm**
>
> **brachial** relating to an arm

arm[2] verb **1** *he had armed himself with a revolver*: **provide**, supply, equip, furnish, issue, fit out, fit up, outfit, rig out, accoutre, gird, provision, stock.
2 *one has to arm oneself against criticism*: **prepare**, forearm, make ready, brace, steel, fortify; archaic gird one's loins.

armada noun *an armada of forty-five warships*: **fleet**, flotilla, squadron, navy, naval force, (naval) task force.

armaments plural noun **arms**, weapons (of war), weaponry, firearms, guns, ordnance, cannon, artillery, munitions, instruments of war, war machines, military supplies, materiel.

armistice noun *an armistice was concluded between all the warring countries*: **truce**, ceasefire, suspension of hostilities, cessation of hostilities, peace; break, respite, lull, moratorium; treaty, peace treaty; informal let-up.
▷ANTONYMS declaration of war; hostilities.

armour noun *a suit of armour*: **protective covering**, armour plate; covering, protection, sheathing, shield; historical chain armour, chain mail, coat of mail, panoply.

armoured adjective *an armoured vehicle*: **armour-plated**, steel-plated, ironclad, mailed; bulletproof, bombproof, mineproof, reinforced, protected, toughened.

armoury noun **arsenal**, arms depot, arms cache, ordnance depot, magazine, ammunition dump.

arms plural noun **1** *arms and ammunition*: **weapons (of war)**, weaponry, firearms, guns, ordnance, cannon, artillery, armaments, munitions, instruments of war, war machines, military supplies, materiel.
2 *the family arms*: **crest**, emblem, heraldic device, coat of arms, armorial bearing, insignia, escutcheon, shield, heraldry, blazonry.
◻ **take up arms** *he was eventually forced to take up arms when his sister and mother were charged with attempted murder*: **fight**, do battle, give battle, wage war, go to war, make war; attack, mount an attack; combat, engage, meet, clash, skirmish; be a soldier, fight for Queen/King and country; crusade.

army noun **1** *the invading army*: **armed force**, fighting force, defence force, military force, the military, land force, soldiery, infantry, militia, horde; troops, soldiers, land forces; informal, dated thin red line; archaic host.
2 *an army of tourists*: **crowd**, swarm, multitude, horde, host, mob, gang, throng, stream, mass, body, band, troop, legion, flock, herd, pack, drove, sea, array; literary myriad.

> *Word links* **army**
>
> **military, martial** relating to armies

aroma noun *the tantalizing aroma of fresh coffee*: **smell**, odour, fragrance, scent, perfume, whiff, redolence, tang, savour, bouquet, nose.

aromatic adjective *an aromatic herb*: **fragrant**, scented, sweet-scented, sweet-smelling, perfumed, fragranced, odoriferous; piquant, spicy, savoury, pungent; literary redolent; rare aromatized, balmy.
▷ANTONYMS foul-smelling.

> *Word toolkit* **aromatic**
>
> See **pungent**.

around adverb **1** *there were houses scattered around*: **on every side**, on all sides, in all directions, throughout, all over, all over the place, everywhere, about, here and there.
2 *he turned around to face her*: **in the opposite direction**, in the reverse direction, to face the other way, backwards, to the rear.
3 *there was no one around*: **nearby**, near, about, close by, close, at hand, close at hand, in the vicinity, in the neighbourhood, on the doorstep, (just) round the corner, within (easy) reach, at close range, hard by; accessible, handy, convenient.
▶ preposition **1** *the palazzo is built around a courtyard*: **on every side of**, on all sides of, about, circling, encircling, surrounding, encompassing, framing.
2 *they drove around town*: **all over**, about, here and there in, everywhere in, in/to all parts of.
3 *around three miles*: **approximately**, about, round about, roughly, in the region of, something like, in the area of, in the neighbourhood of, of the order of, or so, or thereabouts, there or thereabouts, more or less, give or take a few, plus or minus a few; nearly, close to, as near as dammit, not far

off, approaching; Brit. getting on for; S. African plus-minus; Latin circa; N. Amer. informal in the ballpark of.

> *Word links* **around**
>
> **amphi-** related prefix, as in *amphitheatre*

arouse verb **1** *they had aroused his hostility and suspicion*: **cause**, induce, prompt, set off, trigger, stir up, inspire, call forth, call/bring into being, draw forth, bring out, excite, evoke, pique, whet, stir, engender, generate, kindle, fire, touch off, spark off, provoke, foster, whip up, sow the seeds of; literary enkindle.
▷**ANTONYMS** allay.
2 *an ability to influence the audience and to arouse the masses*: **stir up**, rouse, excite, galvanize, electrify, stimulate, inspire, move, fire up, fire the enthusiasm of, fire the imagination of, get going, whip up, inflame, agitate, goad, provoke, spur on, urge, encourage, animate, incite, egg on; N. Amer. light a fire under; rare inspirit.
▷**ANTONYMS** pacify.
3 *his touch aroused her*: **excite**, arouse sexually, stimulate, make feel sexually excited, make feel sexy, titillate; please, attract; informal turn on, get going, give someone a thrill, float someone's boat, do it for someone, light someone's fire, tickle someone's fancy.
▷**ANTONYMS** turn off.
4 *she was aroused from her sleep by her mother*: **wake**, wake up, waken, awaken, bring to, bring around, rouse; Brit. informal knock up.
▷**ANTONYMS** send to sleep.

arraign verb **1** *he was* ***arraigned for*** *murder*: **indict**, prosecute, put on trial, bring to trial; denounce, sue, take to court, bring an action against, lay charges against, file charges against, prefer charges against, summons, cite; accuse of, charge with; N. Amer. impeach; informal have the law on, do; archaic inculpate.
▷**ANTONYMS** clear, acquit.
2 *the soldiers bitterly arraigned the government for failing to keep its word*: **criticize**, censure, attack, condemn, castigate, chastise, lambaste, pillory, find fault with, reprimand, rebuke, admonish, remonstrate with, take to task, haul over the coals, berate, reproach, reprove; informal knock, slam, hammer, lay into, roast, give someone a roasting, cane, blast, bawl out, dress down, rap over the knuckles, give someone hell; Brit. informal carpet, slate, slag off, monster, rollick, give someone a rollicking, give someone a rocket, tear someone off a strip; N. Amer. informal chew out, ream out, pummel, cut up; Austral./NZ informal bag; dated rate; archaic slash; rare excoriate, objurgate, reprehend.
▷**ANTONYMS** praise.

arraignment noun *he awaited his arraignment in his cell*: **indictment**, accusation, denunciation, prosecution, trial, charge, summons, citation; Brit. plaint; N. Amer. impeachment, bill of indictment; N. Amer. informal beef; archaic inculpation.
▷**ANTONYMS** acquittal.

arrange verb **1** *she had just finished arranging the flowers*: **put in order**, order, set out, lay out, spread out, array, present, put out, display, exhibit, group, sort, organize, tidy, position, dispose; marshal, range, align, line up, rank, file; classify, categorize, systematize, methodize; Medicine triage.
▷**ANTONYMS** disturb.
2 *they hoped to arrange a meeting*: **organize**, fix, plan, schedule, pencil in, devise, contrive; make arrangements for, fix up, prepare for, make preparations for; settle on, decide, determine, agree, come to an agreement, come to terms about.
▷**ANTONYMS** cancel.
3 *Toscanini arranged the piece for full string orchestra*: **adapt**, set, score, orchestrate, instrument, harmonize.

arrangement noun **1** *the arrangement of the furniture in the room*: **positioning**, disposition, marshalling, ranging, ordering; order, array, presentation, display, exhibition, grouping; sorting, organization, system, alignment; filing, classification, categorization.
2 (usually **arrangements**) *how are the arrangements for your trip going?* **preparations**, plans; planning, preparing, groundwork, provision.
3 *we had an arrangement to meet at 10*: **agreement**, appointment, engagement, deal, understanding, settlement, bargain, compact, pact, contract, covenant, compromise, gentleman's agreement; Latin modus vivendi.
4 *an arrangement of Beethoven's symphonies for piano duet*: **adaptation**, setting, scoring, orchestration, instrumentation, reduction, harmonization.

arrant adjective archaic *what arrant nonsense!* **utter**, downright, thoroughgoing, absolute, complete, thorough, through and through, total, unmitigated, outright, out-and-out, real, perfect, consummate, surpassing, sheer, rank, pure, unqualified, inveterate, positive, undiluted, unalloyed, unadulterated, in every respect, unconditional; blatant, flagrant, overt, naked, barefaced, brazen; N. Amer. full-bore; informal deep-dyed; Brit. informal right; Austral./NZ informal fair; rare right-down.

array noun **1** *a huge array of cars met our eyes*: **arrangement**, assembling, assemblage, line-up, formation, ordering, disposition, marshalling, muster, amassing; show, display, exhibition, presentation, exposition, spectacle; agglomeration, collection, aggregation, raft, range, variety, assortment, diversity, mixture, selection.
2 *she arrived in silken array*: **dress**, attire, apparel, clothing, garb, finery; garments; informal garms.
▶ verb **1** *a wonderful buffet was arrayed on the table*: **arrange**, assemble, draw up, group, order, range, place, position, set out, set forth, dispose, marshal, muster; **lay out**, display, exhibit, put on show, put on display, put on view, expose to view, unveil, present, uncover, reveal.
2 *the boy was arrayed in a neat grey flannel suit*: **dress**, attire, clothe, robe, garb, deck, deck out, drape, accoutre, outfit, fit out, costume, get up, turn out, trick out/up; informal doll up; archaic apparel, bedizen, caparison, invest, habit, trap out.

arrears plural noun **1** *council house rent arrears amounted to over £1m*: **money owing**, outstanding payment(s), debt(s), liabilities, indebtedness, dues; balance, deficit.
2 *there are huge arrears of work after the holidays*: **backlog**, logjam, accumulation, pile-up, reserve, stockpile.
□ **in arrears** *the tenants were in arrears with their rent*: **behind**, behindhand, late, overdue, in the red, in default, in debt.
▷**ANTONYMS** in credit.

arrest verb **1** *police arrested him for possession of marijuana*: **apprehend**, take into custody, seize, take in, take prisoner, detain, put in jail, throw in jail; informal pick up, run in, pull in, haul in, pinch, cop, bust, nab, nail, do, collar, feel someone's collar; Brit. informal nick.
▷**ANTONYMS** release.
2 *the spread of the disease can be arrested*: **stop**, halt, end, bring to a standstill, check, block, hinder, hamper, delay, hold up, hold back, restrict, limit, interrupt, prevent, obstruct, inhibit, impede, interfere with, thwart, baulk, curb, put a brake on, slow, slow down, retard, nip in the bud; literary stay.
▷**ANTONYMS** start.
3 *she put out a hand to arrest his attention | it was not the mere words which arrested him*: **attract**, capture, catch, catch hold of, hold, grip, engage; absorb, occupy, rivet, engross, fascinate, mesmerize, hypnotize, spellbind, bewitch, captivate, entrance, enthral, enrapture.
▶ noun **1** *I have a warrant for your arrest*: **detention**, apprehension, seizure, capture, taking into custody.
2 *he suffered a cardiac arrest*: **stoppage**, halt, interruption.

arresting adjective *this is certainly an arresting image*: **striking**, eye-catching, conspicuous, noticeable, dramatic, impressive, imposing, spectacular, breathtaking, dazzling, amazing, astounding, astonishing, surprising, staggering, stunning, sensational, awesome, awe-inspiring, engaging; remarkable, notable, noteworthy, distinctive, extraordinary, outstanding, incredible, phenomenal, unusual, rare, uncommon, out of the ordinary.
▷**ANTONYMS** inconspicuous, unexceptional.

arrival noun **1** *they awaited Ruth's arrival*: **coming**, advent, appearance, entrance, entry, materialization, approach.
▷**ANTONYMS** departure.
2 *hotel staff greeted the late arrivals*: **comer**, entrant, newcomer, new boy, new girl, incomer; visitor, caller, guest, immigrant; archaic visitant.
3 *the arrival of democracy*: **emergence**, (first) appearance, advent, coming, materialization, surfacing, occurrence, dawn, origin, birth, rise, springing up, development, start, onset, inauguration.
▷**ANTONYMS** demise.

arrive verb **1** *more police arrived*: **come**, get here/there, reach one's destination, make it, appear, put in an appearance, make an appearance, come on the scene, come up, approach, enter, present oneself, turn up, be along, come along, materialize; W. Indian reach; informal show up, show, roll in, roll up, blow in, show one's face.
▷**ANTONYMS** depart.
2 *we* ***arrived at*** *his house*: **reach**, get to, get as far as, come to, make, make it to, set foot on, gain, attain; end up at, land up at, fetch up at; informal hit, wind up at.
▷**ANTONYMS** leave.
3 *they did* ***arrive at*** *a tentative agreement*: **achieve**, attain, reach, gain, accomplish; work out, draw up, put together, strike, negotiate, thrash out, hammer out; settle on, sign, endorse, ratify, sanction; informal clinch.
4 *the moment finally arrived*: **happen**, occur, take place, come about, transpire, ensue, present itself, crop up; literary come to pass, befall.
▷**ANTONYMS** go.
5 *quadraphony had arrived*: **emerge**, appear, make an appearance, surface, dawn, be born, come into being, arise, spring up, be developed, start.
6 informal *their Rolls Royce and gold jewellery proved that they had arrived*: **succeed**, achieve success, be successful, be a success, do well, get ahead, reach the top, make good, prosper, flourish, thrive, advance, triumph, be victorious, break through, become famous, achieve recognition; informal make it, make the grade, cut it, crack it, make a name for oneself, make

a

one's mark, get somewhere, do all right for oneself, bring home the bacon, find a place in the sun.

arriviste noun *he regarded trade as a haven for arrivistes*: **social climber**, status seeker, would-be, go-getter, self-seeker, adventurer, adventuress; newcomer, upstart, parvenu, parvenue, vulgarian; (**arrivistes**) the nouveau riche, the new rich, new money.

arrogance noun *to dismiss all the academic work on the subject displays breathtaking arrogance*: **haughtiness**, conceit, hubris, self-importance, egotism, sense of superiority; pomposity, high-handedness, swagger, boasting, bumptiousness, bluster, condescension, disdain, contempt, imperiousness; pride, vanity, immodesty; loftiness, lordliness, snobbishness, snobbery, superciliousness, smugness; pretension, pretentiousness, affectation; scorn, mocking, sneering, scoffing; presumption, insolence; informal uppitiness, big-headedness.
▷ANTONYMS humility, modesty.

arrogant adjective *he's too arrogant to know when he's lost*: **haughty**, conceited, hubristic, self-important, opinionated, egotistic, full of oneself, superior; overbearing, pompous, high-handed, swaggering, boastful, bumptious, blustering, patronizing, condescending, disdainful, contemptuous, imperious; proud, vain, immodest; lofty, lordly, snobbish, snobby, overweening, supercilious, smug; pretentious, affected; scornful, mocking, sneering, scoffing; informal hoity-toity, high and mighty, uppity, snooty, stuck-up, toffee-nosed, fancy-pants, snotty, jumped up, too big for one's boots, big-headed.
▷ANTONYMS humble, modest.

arrogate verb *the Church **arrogated to itself** the power to create kings*: **assume**, take, take on, take over, secure, acquire, seize, expropriate, take possession of, help oneself to, make free with, appropriate, steal, wrest, usurp, commandeer, hijack, annex, claim, lay claim to.
▷ANTONYMS renounce.

arrow noun **1** *he could shoot a bow and arrow*: **shaft**, bolt, dart; literary reed; historical quarrel.
2 *the arrow on the sign pointed to the right*: **pointer**, indicator, marker, needle, hand, index.

> *Word links* **arrow**
>
> **fletcher** maker or seller of arrows

arsenal noun **1** *Britain's nuclear arsenal*: **weapons**, weaponry, arms, armaments.
2 *the mutineers broke into the arsenal*: **armoury**, arms depot, arms cache, ordnance depot, magazine, ammunition dump.
3 *there is an arsenal of penalties for insider trading*: **array**, battery, range, line-up, assortment, collection.

arson noun *the fire is being treated as arson*: **incendiarism**, pyromania, firebombing; Brit. fire-raising.

arsonist noun *an arsonist is thought to have caused the blaze*: **incendiary**, pyromaniac, firebomber; Brit. fire-raiser; informal firebug, pyro; N. Amer. informal torch.

art noun **1** *he studied art*: **fine art**, artwork, creative activity.
2 *the art of writing*: **skill**, craft, technique; aptitude, talent, flair, gift, genius, knack, facility, ability, capability, competence; artistry, mastery, dexterity, dexterousness, craftsmanship, expertness, expertise, proficiency, skilfulness, adroitness, adeptness, deftness, cleverness, ingenuity, virtuosity; informal know-how.
3 *she knows how to use art to achieve her objectives*: **cunning**, artfulness; deceit, deception, wiliness, slyness, craft, craftiness, guile, trickery, duplicity, artifice; wiles.

artery noun *all the arteries taking people out of town are busy*: **main/trunk route**, main/trunk road, main/trunk line, high road, highway.

> *Word links* **artery**
>
> **arteriotomy** surgical incision of artery

artful adjective *an artful political ruse*: **sly**, crafty, cunning, wily, scheming, devious, Machiavellian, sneaky, guileful, tricky, conniving, designing, calculating; **shrewd**, astute, sharp-witted, sharp, acute, intelligent, clever, alert, canny; deceitful, deceptive, duplicitous, cheating, dishonest, disingenuous, underhand, untrustworthy, unscrupulous, double-dealing; informal dirty, foxy, shifty, smart; Brit. informal fly; Austral./NZ informal shonky; S. African informal slim; rare vulpine, carny, subtle.
▷ANTONYMS ingenuous, honest, dull.

article noun **1** *small household articles*: **object**, thing, item, unit, artefact, piece of merchandise, commodity, product; device, gadget, contrivance, instrument, utensil, tool, implement; informal whatsit, what-d'you-call-it, what's-its-name, whatchamacallit, thingummy, thingy, thingamabob, thingamajig, oojamaflip, oojah, gizmo; Brit. informal gubbins, doodah, doobry; N. Amer. informal doodad, doohickey, doojigger, dingus.
2 *he wrote an article on the subject*: **essay**, report, account, story, write-up, feature, item, piece (of writing), composition, column, paper, tract, study, review, commentary, treatise, analysis, disquisition, discourse; N. Amer. theme.
3 *the crucial article of the treaty*: **clause**, section, subsection, point, item, paragraph, division, subdivision, heading, part, bit, passage, portion, segment; provision, proviso, stipulation.

articulate adjective *an articulate speaker | an articulate speech*: **eloquent**, fluent, communicative, effective, persuasive, coherent, lucid, vivid, expressive, silver-tongued, vocal; cogent, illuminating, intelligible, comprehensible, understandable.
▷ANTONYMS inarticulate, hesitant, unintelligible.
▸verb *they were unable to articulate their emotions*: **express**, give expression to, voice, give voice to, vocalize, put in words, give utterance to, communicate, declare, state, set forth, bring into the open, make public, assert, divulge, reveal, proclaim, announce, raise, table, air, ventilate, vent, give vent to, pour out, mention, talk of, point out, go into; utter, say, speak, enunciate, pronounce, mouth; informal come out with.
▷ANTONYMS bottle up.

articulated adjective *an articulated lorry*: **hinged**, jointed, segmented; coupled, attached, joined, connected, interlocked; flexible, bending; that bends; technical articulate.
▷ANTONYMS fixed.

articulation noun *the formal articulation of theories of linguistic knowledge*: **expression**, voicing, utterance, uttering, communication, declaration, statement, setting forth, assertion, revelation, proclamation, announcement, raising, tabling, airing, ventilation, venting, mention, talk; enunciation, pronunciation, mouthing; rare divulgement, divulgation.

artifice noun **1** *an industry dominated by artifice*: **trickery**, deviousness, deceit, deception, dishonesty, cheating, duplicity, guile, cunning, artfulness, wiliness, craft, craftiness, evasion, slyness, chicanery, intrigue, subterfuge, strategy, bluff, pretence; fraud, fraudulence, sophistry, sharp practice; informal monkey business, funny business, hanky-panky, jiggery-pokery, every trick in the book.
2 *the artifice of couching autobiography in the form of a novel did not really work*: **device**, **trick**, stratagem, ploy, tactic, ruse, scheme, move, manoeuvre, contrivance, machination, expedient, wile, dodge; swindle, hoax, fraud, confidence trick; informal con, con trick, set-up, game, scam, sting, gyp, flimflam; Brit. informal wheeze; N. Amer. informal bunco, grift; Austral. informal lurk, rort; S. African informal schlenter; Brit. informal, dated flanker; archaic shift, fetch, rig.

artificial adjective **1** *artificial flowers*: **synthetic**, fake, false, imitation, mock, simulated, faux, ersatz, substitute; pseudo, sham, bogus, spurious, counterfeit, forged, pretended, so-called; plastic; **man-made**, manufactured, unnatural, fabricated; replica, reproduction, facsimile; informal phoney, pretend.
▷ANTONYMS natural.
2 *an artificial smile*: **feigned**, **insincere**, false, affected, mannered, unnatural, stilted, contrived, pretended, put-on, exaggerated, overdone, forced, laboured, strained, hollow, spurious; informal pretend, phoney, hammy, ham, campy.
▷ANTONYMS genuine, sincere.

Word toolkit

artificial	synthetic	man-made
intelligence	chemical	structure
chromosome	hormone	lake
reef	peptide	canal
turf	fiber	waterfall
sweetener	rubber	disaster
limb	dye	catastrophe
heart	fertilizer	warming
flowers	pesticide	pollutant
nails	pyrethroid	emission

artillery noun **(big) guns**, **ordnance**, cannon(s), cannonry, heavy weapons, heavy weaponry, battery.

artisan noun *each guild organized the artisans of a particular craft*: **craftsman**, craftswoman, craftsperson, skilled worker, mechanic, technician, operative, maker, smith, wright, journeyman; archaic artificer; rare handicraftsman, handicraftswoman.

artist noun **1** *their first exhibition devoted to a single artist*: **creator**, originator, designer, producer, fine artist; old master; literary begetter.
2 *a surgeon who is an artist with the scalpel*: **expert**, master, maestro, past master, adept, virtuoso, genius, old hand, skilled person; informal pro, ace, whizz, wizard, hotshot; Brit. informal dab hand; N. Amer. informal maven, crackerjack; rare proficient.
▷ANTONYMS novice, amateur.

artiste noun *a cabaret artiste*: **entertainer**, performer, trouper, showman, artist; player, musician, singer, dancer, actor, actress, Thespian; comic, comedian, comedienne, clown, impressionist, mime artist, conjuror, magician, acrobat; star, superstar; rare executant.

artistic adjective **1** *he's very artistic*: **creative**, imaginative, inventive, original; expressive, inspired; poetic, eloquent, aesthetic, cultivated; sensitive, perceptive, discerning.
▷ANTONYMS unimaginative.
2 *Bali's people are noted for their artistic dances*: **aesthetic**, aesthetically pleasing, beautiful, fine, attractive, decorative, ornamental, lovely, moving, emotional, tasteful, graceful, stylish, elegant, subtle, exquisite, expressive.
▷ANTONYMS inelegant.

artistry noun *all four perform with innate artistry*: **creative skill**, creativity, art, skill, ability, accomplishment, talent, genius, brilliance, expertness, flair, proficiency, virtuosity, finesse, style, touch, expressiveness, perception, sensitivity, inspiration, poetry, eloquence; craftsmanship, workmanship.

artless adjective *she described her characters with apparently artless sincerity*: **natural**, naive, simple, innocent, childlike, pure, ingenuous, guileless, candid, open, honest, sincere, frank, straightforward, unaffected, unpretentious, modest, unassuming; N. Amer. on the up and up.
▷ANTONYMS scheming.

Choose the right word **artless, naive, ingenuous**

See **naive**.

as conjunction **1** *she caught a glimpse of him as he disappeared*: **while**, just as, even as, at the (same) time that, at the moment that, during the time that, just when; simultaneously.
2 *there were some who felt as Frank did*: **in the (same) way that**, the (same) way, in the (same) manner that; informal like.
3 *do as you're told*: **what**; archaic that which.
4 *the athletes were free to compete again, as the case against them had not been proved*: **because**, since, seeing that, seeing as, considering that, on account of the fact that, in view of the fact that, owing to the fact that; informal on account of; literary for; archaic forasmuch.
5 *try as she did, she couldn't laugh*: **although**, though, even though/if, in spite of the fact that, despite the fact that, notwithstanding the fact that, notwithstanding that, for all that, while, whilst, albeit, however.
6 *trains compete successfully with the airlines over short distances, as Paris to Lyons*: **such as**, like, for instance, for example, e.g., to give an instance, to give an example, by way of illustration, as an illustration.
7 *I'm away a lot, as you know*: **which**, a fact which, something which.
□ **as against** *37 per cent said yes, as against 64 per cent in 1994*: **compared to/with**, by contrast with, next to, against, beside.
□ **as for/as to** *as for composts, he recommends peat-free varieties*: **concerning**, respecting, with respect to, on the subject of, as regards, regarding, with reference to, re, in/with regard to, apropos, in the matter of, in connection with; French vis-à-vis; Latin in re.
□ **as it were** *the street plan evolved, as it were, by natural selection*: **so to speak**, in a manner of speaking, in a way, in some way or other, to some extent, so to say; informal sort of.
□ **as yet** *there is no sign of them as yet*: **so far**, thus far, yet, still, even now, up till now, up to now, until now, up to the present time.
▶ **preposition 1** *he was dressed as a policeman*: **in the guise of**, with the appearance of, in the character of, so as to appear to be.
2 *I'm speaking to you as your friend*: **in the role of**, being, acting as, functioning as.

ascend verb *she ascended the stairs | the lift ascended to the eighteenth floor*: **climb (up)**, come/go/move up, make one's/its way up, come/go/move upwards, rise (up), arise; mount, scale, conquer, clamber up, scramble up, shin up; levitate, fly up, take to the air, take off, soar; slope upwards, loom, tower.
▷ANTONYMS descend.

ascendancy noun *the ascendancy of good over evil*: **dominance**, domination, supremacy, superiority, predominance, pre-eminence, primacy, dominion, hegemony, authority, mastery, control, command, power, sway, rule, sovereignty, lordship, leadership, influence; the upper hand, the whip hand, the edge, advantage; rare predomination, paramountcy, prepotence, prepotency, prepollency.
▷ANTONYMS subordination.

ascendant adjective *by the late 1990s liberal ideas were ascendant in much of the developed world*: **rising (in power)**, in the ascendant, on the up and up, on the way up, up-and-coming, on the rise, growing, increasing, flourishing, prospering, burgeoning, developing, budding.
▷ANTONYMS declining.

ascent noun **1** *the first ascent of the Matterhorn*: **climb**, scaling, conquest, scramble, clamber, trek.
▷ANTONYMS descent.
2 *a balloon ascent*: **rise**, upward movement, take-off, lift-off, launch, blast-off, climb, levitation, soaring; jump, leap; Christianity Ascension.
▷ANTONYMS descent, drop.
3 *the ascent grew steeper*: **(upward) slope**, incline, ramp, rise, bank, tilt, slant, upward gradient, inclination, acclivity.
▷ANTONYMS descent, drop.

ascertain verb *we ascertained the exact location of the vehicle*: **find out**, discover, get/come to know, work out, make out, fathom (out), become aware of, learn, ferret out, dig out/up, establish, fix, determine, settle, decide, verify, make certain of, confirm, deduce, divine, intuit, diagnose, discern, perceive, see, realize, appreciate, identify, pin down, recognize, register, understand, grasp, take in, comprehend; informal figure out, get a fix on, latch on to, cotton on to, catch on to, tumble to, get; Brit. informal twig, suss (out); N. Amer. informal savvy; rare cognize.

ascetic adjective *an ascetic life of prayer, fasting, and manual labour*: **austere**, self-denying, abstinent, abstemious, non-indulgent, self-disciplined, frugal, simple, rigorous, strict, severe, hair-shirt, spartan, monastic, monkish, nunlike; reclusive, solitary, cloistered, eremitic, anchoritic, hermitic; celibate, continent, chaste, puritanical, self-abnegating, other-worldly, mortified.
▷ANTONYMS sybaritic.
▶ **noun** *St Paul the Egyptian was a desert ascetic*: **abstainer**, recluse, hermit, solitary, anchorite, anchoress, desert saint, celibate, puritan, nun, monk; Islam fakir, Sufi, dervish; Hinduism yogi, rishi, sannyasi; in India sadhu, muni; rare gymnosophist, marabout, santon, self-denier, eremite, stylite, pillar saint, pillar hermit, pillarist, aerialist, coenobite.
▷ANTONYMS sybarite.

asceticism noun *countless dictators have pointed out the asceticism of their private lives*: **austerity**, self-denial, abstinence, abstemiousness, non-indulgence, self-discipline, frugality, simplicity, rigour, strictness, severity; a hair shirt, a spartan life, monasticism, monkishness, reclusiveness, solitude, hermitism, celibacy, continence, chastity, puritanism, self-abnegation, other-worldliness, self-mortification; archaic anchorism.
▷ANTONYMS sybaritism.

ascribe verb *he ascribed Jane's short temper to her upset stomach*: **attribute**, assign, put down, set down, accredit, credit, give the credit for, chalk up, impute; lay on, pin on, blame on, lay at the door of; connect with, associate with.

ash noun *the fire had gone, leaving only ash*: **cinders**, ashes, embers, clinker.

Word links **ash**

cinerary relating to ash

ashamed adjective **1** *she was ashamed of the way she had behaved*: **sorry**, shamefaced, abashed, sheepish, guilty, conscience-stricken, guilt-ridden, contrite, remorseful, repentant, penitent, hangdog, regretful, rueful, apologetic; **embarrassed**, mortified, red-faced, chagrined, humiliated, uncomfortable, discomfited, distressed; in sackcloth and ashes; informal with one's tail between one's legs; rare compunctious; (**be ashamed of**) blush to think of.
▷ANTONYMS proud, unabashed.
2 *he was ashamed to admit it*: **reluctant**, loath, unwilling, disinclined, hesitant, indisposed, slow, afraid; averse.
▷ANTONYMS pleased.

ashen adjective *his ashen face*: **pale**, wan, pasty, grey, leaden, colourless, sallow, pallid, white, waxen, ghostly; pale-faced, ashen-faced, grey-faced, anaemic, bloodless; rare etiolated, lymphatic.

ashore adverb *the seals come ashore to breed*: **on to (the) land**, on to the shore; towards the shore, shorewards, landwards; on the shore, on the beach, on (the) land, on dry land.

aside adverb **1** *they stood aside to let a car pass*: **to one side**, to the side; on one side, alongside; apart, away, separately, alone, by oneself/itself, distant, detached, in isolation.
2 *that aside, he seemed a nice man*: **apart**, notwithstanding.
□ **aside from** *aside from his London office he has property in several African capitals*: **apart from**, besides, in addition to, over and above, beyond, not counting, leaving aside, barring, other than, but (for), excluding, not including, without, with the exception of, except, except for, excepting, omitting, leaving out, short of, save (for).
▶ **noun** *'Both her parents died a couple of years back,' said Mrs Manton in an aside to Betty*: **whispered remark**, confidential remark, stage whisper; soliloquy, monologue, apostrophe; casual remark, throwaway line; digression, parenthetic remark, incidental remark, obiter dictum, deviation, departure, red herring, excursus; archaic excursion.

asinine adjective *another asinine bit of advertising*: **stupid**, **foolish**, pointless, brainless, mindless, senseless, doltish, idiotic, imbecilic, imbecile, insane, lunatic, ridiculous, ludicrous, absurd, preposterous, nonsensical, fatuous, silly, childish, infantile, puerile, immature, juvenile, inane, witless, half-baked, empty-headed, unintelligent, half-witted, slow-witted, weak-minded; informal crazy, dumb, cretinous, moronic, gormless, damfool; Brit. informal divvy, daft; Scottish & N. English informal glaikit; N. Amer.

informal dumb-ass, chowderheaded; S. African informal dof; W. Indian informal dotish.
▷ANTONYMS intelligent.

ask verb **1** *ask her what she did | he asked what time we opened*: **enquire (of)**, query, want to know, question, put a question to, interrogate, quiz, cross-question, cross-examine, catechize; informal grill, pump, give the third degree to.
▷ANTONYMS answer.
2 *they just want to ask a few questions*: **put**, put forward, pose, raise, submit, propose, seek/get the answer to.
▷ANTONYMS answer.
3 *I asked him to call the manager | don't be afraid to ask for advice*: **request**, demand, appeal to, apply to, petition, call on, entreat, beg, implore, exhort, urge, enjoin, importune, pray, solicit, beseech, plead with, sue, supplicate; seek, put in for, call for, crave.
4 *let's ask them to dinner*: **invite**, bid, have someone over/round, summon; request the pleasure of someone's company.

askance adverb **1** *she looked askance at her neighbour*: **obliquely**, sideways, indirectly, out of the corner of one's eye.
2 *they **look askance at** almost anything foreign*: **suspiciously**, with suspicion, sceptically, with misgivings, cynically, mistrustfully, distrustfully, with distrust, doubtfully, dubiously, with doubt; **disapprovingly**, with disapproval, with disfavour, contemptuously, scornfully, disdainfully; **suspect**, mistrust, distrust; **disapprove of**, frown on, be hostile towards.
▷ANTONYMS welcomingly, approvingly.

askew adverb & adjective *her hat was slightly askew | the picture is hanging askew*: **crooked(ly)**, lopsided(ly), tilted, angled, at an angle, oblique(ly), at an oblique angle, skew, skewed, slanted, aslant, awry, out of true, out of line, to one side, on one side, uneven(ly), off balance, off centre, asymmetrical(ly), unsymmetrical(ly); Scottish agley, squint, thrawn; informal cock-eyed; Brit. informal skew-whiff, wonky, wonkily, squiffy, squiffily.
▷ANTONYMS straight, symmetrical(ly).

asleep adjective & adverb **1** *she was still asleep in bed*: **sleeping**, fast asleep, sound asleep, in a deep sleep, slumbering, napping, catnapping, dozing, resting, reposing, drowsing, dormant, comatose; informal snoozing, dead to the world, flat out, kipping, out like a light, in the land of Nod; literary in the arms of Morpheus.
▷ANTONYMS awake.
2 *my leg's asleep*: **numb**, without feeling, numbed, benumbed, dead, deadened, desensitized, insensible, insensate, senseless, unfeeling; anaesthetized; rare torpefied.
▷ANTONYMS sensitive.

aspect noun **1** *the photographs depict every aspect of life on a kibbutz*: **feature**, facet, side, characteristic, particular, detail, point, ingredient, strand; angle, slant, sense, respect, regard.
2 *the black patch hiding one eye gave his face a sinister aspect*: **appearance**, look, air, bearing, cast, manner, mien, demeanour, deportment, expression, countenance, features, semblance, guise, impression, effect; atmosphere, mood, quality, ambience, feeling, flavour.
3 *a summer house with a southern aspect*: **outlook**, view, exposure, direction, situation, position, location.
4 *the front aspect of the hotel was unremarkable*: **face**, elevation, facade, side.

asperity noun *'How should I know?' he replied with some asperity*: **harshness**, sharpness, roughness, abrasiveness, severity, acerbity, astringency, bitterness, acidity, tartness, edge, acrimony, virulence, sarcasm.
▷ANTONYMS mildness.

aspersions plural noun *he claimed he could prove the aspersions groundless*: **vilification**, disparagement, denigration, defamation, defamation of character, abuse, vituperation, condemnation, criticism, censure, castigation, denunciation, flak, deprecation, opprobrium, obloquy, derogation, slander, revilement, reviling, calumny, calumniation, slurs, smears, execration, excoriation, lambasting, upbraiding, bad press, character assassination, attack, invective, libel, insults, slights, curses; informal mud-slinging, bad-mouthing, tongue-lashing; Brit. informal stick, verbal, slagging off; archaic contumely; rare animadversion, objurgation.
□ **cast aspersions on** *I don't think anyone is casting aspersions on you*: **vilify**, disparage, denigrate, defame, run down, impugn, revile, berate, belittle, abuse, insult, slight, attack, speak badly of, speak ill of, speak evil of, pour scorn on, criticize, censure, condemn, decry, denounce, pillory, lambaste; fulminate against, rail against, inveigh against, malign, slander, libel, conduct a smear campaign against, spread lies about, blacken the name/reputation of, sully the reputation of, give someone a bad name, bring into disrepute, discredit, stigmatize, traduce, calumniate, slur; informal bad-mouth, do a hatchet job on, take to pieces, pull apart, throw mud at, drag through the mud, slate, have a go at, hit out at, jump on, lay into, tear into, knock, slam, pan, bash, hammer, roast, skewer, bad-mouth, throw brickbats at; Brit. informal rubbish, slag off; N. Amer. informal pummel, dump on; Austral./NZ informal bag, monster; archaic contemn; rare derogate, vituperate, asperse, vilipend.

asphyxiate verb *they were asphyxiated by the carbon monoxide fumes*: **choke (to death)**, suffocate, smother, stifle; kill; throttle, strangle, strangulate, constrict.

aspiration noun *the jobs created do not match the aspirations of local residents*: **desire**, hope, longing, yearning, hankering, urge, wish; **aim**, ambition, expectation, inclination, objective, goal, target, end, object, dream; informal yen, itch.

aspire verb *a more prosperous Britain can **aspire to** excellence in the arts | they **aspire to** emulate their heroes*: **desire (to)**, **aim for/to**, hope for/to, long for/to, yearn for/to, hanker after/for/to, set one's heart on, wish for/to, want (to), expect (to), have the objective of, dream of, hunger for/to, seek (to), pursue, have as one's goal/aim, set one's sights on; be ambitious; literary thirst for/after; archaic be desirous of.

aspiring adjective *advice to aspiring writers*: **would-be**, intending, aspirant, hopeful, optimistic, budding, wishful; potential, possible, prospective, likely, future; ambitious, eager, keen, striving, determined, enterprising, pioneering, progressive, motivated, enthusiastic, energetic, zealous, committed, go-ahead, go-getting, purposeful; informal wannabe, on the make; archaic expectant.
▷ANTONYMS feckless.

ass noun **1** *he rode on an ass*: **donkey**; jackass, jenny; Scottish cuddy; Brit. informal moke, neddy.
2 *don't be a silly ass*: **fool**, nincompoop, clown, dolt, simpleton; informal idiot, ninny, dope, dimwit, chump, goon, dumbo, dummy, halfwit, dum-dum, loon, jackass, cretin, imbecile, jerk, nerd, fathead, blockhead, numbskull, dunderhead, dunce, dipstick, bonehead, chucklehead, clod, goop, knucklehead, lamebrain, pea-brain, pudding-head, thickhead, wooden-head, pinhead, airhead, birdbrain, dumb-bell, donkey, stupe, noodle; Brit. informal nit, nitwit, twit, numpty, clot, plonker, berk, prat, pillock, wally, git, wazzock, divvy, nerk, dork, twerp, charlie, mug, muppet; Scottish informal nyaff, balloon, sumph, gowk; Irish informal gobdaw; N. Amer. informal schmuck, bozo, boob, lamer, turkey, schlepper, chowderhead, dumbhead, goofball, goof, goofus, galoot, lummox, klutz, putz, schlemiel, sap, meatball, gink, cluck, clunk, ding-dong, dingbat, wiener, weeny, dip, simp, spud, coot, palooka, poop, squarehead, yo-yo, dingleberry; Austral./NZ informal drongo, dill, alec, galah, nong, bogan, poon, boofhead; S. African informal mompara; dated tomfool, muttonhead, noddy; archaic clodpole, loggerhead, spoony, mooncalf.

> *Word links* **ass**
>
> **herd**, **pace** collective noun

assail verb **1** *the army moved down the slope to assail the enemy*: **attack**, assault, make an assault on, launch an attack on, pounce on, set upon, set about, launch oneself at, weigh into, fly at, let fly at, turn on, round on, lash out at, hit out at, beset, belabour, fall on, accost, mug, charge, rush, storm, besiege; informal lay into, tear into, lace into, sail into, pitch into, get stuck into, wade into, let someone have it, beat up, jump; Brit. informal have a go at; N. Amer. informal light into.
2 *she was **assailed by** doubts*: **trouble**, disturb, worry, plague, beset, torture, torment, rack, bedevil, nag, vex, harass, pester, dog; be prey to, be the victim of.
3 *critics assailed the policy*: **criticize**, censure, attack, condemn, castigate, chastise, berate, lambaste, lash, pillory, find fault with, abuse, revile, give someone a bad press; informal knock, slam, hammer, lay into, give someone a roasting, cane, blast, give someone hell, bite someone's head off, jump down someone's throat; Brit. informal slate, slag off, monster; N. Amer. informal pummel, cut up; Austral./NZ informal bag; dated rate; archaic slash; rare excoriate, objurgate, reprehend.

assailant noun *she escaped from her assailant after kicking him*: **attacker**, mugger; rare assaulter, assailer.

assassin noun *his presidency was cut short by an assassin's bullet*: **murderer**, killer, executioner, gunman, butcher, slaughterer, liquidator, exterminator, terminator; informal hit man, contract man, hired gun; N. Amer. informal button man; literary slayer; dated homicide.

assassinate verb *John F. Kennedy was assassinated in 1963*: **murder**, kill, execute, slaughter, butcher, liquidate, eliminate, exterminate, terminate; informal hit; literary slay.

assassination noun *the assassination of John F. Kennedy*: **murder**, killing, political execution, slaughter, butchery, homicide, liquidation, elimination, extermination, termination, putting/doing to death, martyrdom; informal hit; literary slaying.

assault verb **1** *he pleaded guilty to assaulting a police officer*: **hit**, strike, physically attack, aim blows at, slap, smack, beat, thrash, spank, thump, thwack, punch, cuff, swat, knock, rap; pummel, pound, batter, pelt, welt; cane, lash, whip, club, cudgel, box someone's ears; informal clout, wallop, belt, whack, bash, clobber, bop, biff, sock, deck, slug, plug, knock about/around, knock into the middle of next week, lay into, do over, rough up; Austral./NZ informal quilt; literary smite.

2 *they left their position to assault the hill*: **attack**, make an assault on, launch an attack on, assail, pounce on, set upon, launch oneself at, strike at, fall on, swoop on, rush, storm, besiege.
3 *police believe that he first assaulted then murdered her*: **rape**, sexually assault, molest, interfere with.
▸ **noun 1** *he was charged with assault*: **(physical) violence**, battery, mugging, actual bodily harm, ABH; violent act, physical attack; sexual assault, sexual misconduct, molesting, sexual interference, rape; Brit. grievous bodily harm, GBH.
2 *troops began an assault on the city*: **attack**, strike, onslaught, offensive, storming, charge, drive, push, thrust, invasion, bombardment, sortie, sally, foray, incursion, raid, act of war, act of aggression, blitz, campaign.

assay noun *new plate was taxed when it was brought for assay*: **evaluation**, assessment, analysis, examination, test, trial, check, inspection, appraisal, investigation, scrutiny, probe.
▸ **verb** *silver and gold is assayed to determine its purity*: **evaluate**, assess, analyse, examine, test, check, inspect, appraise, investigate, scrutinize, probe.

assemblage noun *the most varied assemblage of plants in the world*: **collection**, accumulation, conglomeration, gathering, group, cluster, aggregation, raft, mass, medley, assortment, selection, jumble, series, complete series, batch, number, combination, grouping, arrangement, array.

assemble verb **1** *a crowd had assembled*: **come together**, get together, gather, collect, meet, muster, rally, congregate, convene, flock together; rare foregather.
▹ANTONYMS disperse.
2 *he assembled the suspects in the lounge*: **bring together**, get together, call together, gather, collect, round up, marshal, muster, summon, rally, convene, accumulate, mass, amass; formal convoke.
▹ANTONYMS disperse.
3 *how to assemble the kite*: **construct**, build, fabricate, manufacture, erect, set up, join up, fit together, put together, piece together, connect, join, unite, patch up, sew (up).
▹ANTONYMS dismantle.

assembly noun **1** *the Council of Nicaea was the largest assembly of bishops hitherto*: **gathering**, meeting, congregation, convention, rally, convocation, congress, council, synod, audience, assemblage, turnout, group, body, crowd, throng, company; informal get-together.
2 *the amount of labour needed in assembly is reduced*: **construction**, building, fabrication, manufacture, erection, setting up, putting together, fitting together, piecing together, connection, joining.
▹ANTONYMS dismantling.

assent noun *a loud murmur of assent*: **agreement**, acceptance, approval, approbation, consent, acquiescence, compliance, concurrence; blessing, imprimatur, seal/stamp of approval, rubber stamp; sanction, endorsement, ratification, authorization, mandate, licence, validation; confirmation, support, backing; permission, leave; informal the go-ahead, the green light, the OK, the thumbs up, the nod, say-so.
▹ANTONYMS dissent; refusal.
▸ **verb** *the Prime Minister* ***assented to*** *the change*: **agree to**, accept, approve, consent to, acquiesce in, concur in, accede to, give one's blessing to, bless, give one's seal/stamp of approval to, rubber-stamp, say yes to; ratify, sanction, endorse, authorize, mandate, license, warrant, validate, pass; confirm, support, back; give one's permission/leave; informal give the go-ahead to, give the green light to, give the OK to, OK, give the thumbs up to, give the nod, say the word, buy.
▹ANTONYMS dissent from; refuse.

Choose the right word **assent, agree, consent, acquiesce**

See **agree**.

assert verb **1** *he asserted that the day of the cottage industry was over*: **declare**, maintain, contend, argue, state, claim, propound, submit, posit, postulate, adduce, move, advocate, venture, volunteer, aver, proclaim, announce, pronounce, attest, affirm, protest, profess, swear, insist, avow; formal opine; rare asseverate.
2 *elderly people find it increasingly difficult to assert their rights*: **insist on**, stand up for, uphold, defend, contend, establish, press/push for, stress.
□ **assert oneself** *a large government majority can encourage backbenchers to assert themselves*: **behave confidently**, speak confidently, be assertive, put oneself forward, make one's presence felt, exert one's influence, make people sit up and take notice, make people sit up and listen; informal put one's foot down.

assertion noun **1** *I questioned his assertion that little risk is involved*: **declaration**, contention, statement, claim, submission, postulation, averment, opinion, proclamation, announcement, pronouncement, assurance, attestation, affirmation, protestation, profession, swearing, insistence, avowal; rare maintenance, asseveration.
2 *the demonstration was a principled* ***assertion of*** *the right to march*: **defence**, upholding; insistence on.

assertive adjective *the job may call for assertive behaviour*: **confident**, **forceful**, self-confident, positive, bold, decisive, assured, self-assured, self-possessed, believing in oneself, self-assertive, authoritative, strong-willed, insistent, firm, determined, commanding, bullish, dominant, domineering, assaultive; informal feisty, not backward in coming forward, pushy; rare pushful.
▹ANTONYMS retiring.

assess verb **1** *frequent patrols were made to assess the enemy's strength*: **evaluate**, judge, gauge, rate, estimate, appraise, form an opinion of, check out, form an impression of, make up one's mind about, get the measure of, determine, weigh up, analyse; informal size up.
2 *the damage was assessed at £5 billion*: **value**, put a value on, calculate, compute, work out, determine, fix, cost, price, estimate.

assessment noun **1** *I endorse your assessment of the quality*: **evaluation**, judgement, gauging, rating, estimation, appraisal, opinion, analysis.
2 *some assessments valued the estate at between £2 million and £7 million*: **valuation**, calculation, computation, costing, pricing, estimate.

asset noun **1** *his strong sense of humour was a great asset*: **benefit**, advantage, blessing, good point, strong point, strength, forte, talent, gift, strong suit, long suit, virtue, recommendation, attraction, attractive feature, selling point, resource, beauty, boon, value, merit, bonus, aid, help; saving grace, redeeming feature, compensating feature; informal plus, pro.
▹ANTONYMS liability, handicap.
2 (usually **assets**) *the company can use its own assets as the security for credit*: **property**, resources, estate, holdings, possessions, effects, goods, valuables, belongings, chattels, worldly goods, worldly possessions; capital, funds, wealth, principal, money, riches, means, fortune, finance, reserves, savings, securities.
▹ANTONYMS liability.

assiduous adjective *she was assiduous in pointing out every feature*: **diligent**, careful, meticulous, thorough, sedulous, attentive, industrious, laborious, hard-working, conscientious, ultra-careful, punctilious, painstaking, demanding, exacting, persevering, unflagging, searching, close, elaborate, minute, accurate, correct, studious, rigorous, particular; religious, strict; pedantic, fussy.

assign verb **1** *a young physician was assigned the task of solving this problem*: **allocate**, allot, give, set; charge with, entrust with.
2 *he was then* ***assigned to*** *another public relations post*: **appoint**, promote, delegate, commission, post, nominate, vote, elect, adopt, co-opt; make, create, name, designate, dub; decide on for, select for, choose for, install in, induct in, institute in, invest in, ordain in; Military detail for.
3 *managers happily* ***assign*** *large sums of money* ***to*** *travel budgets*: **earmark**, appropriate, designate, set aside, set apart, keep, reserve; allot, allocate, apportion; fix, appoint, decide on, determine, specify, stipulate; rare hypothecate.
4 *he decided to* ***assign*** *the opinion* ***to*** *the Prince*: **ascribe**, attribute, put down, set down, accredit, credit, give the credit for, chalk up, impute; lay on, pin on, blame on, lay at the door of; connect with, associate with.
5 *the depositor may assign the money in his account to a third party*: **transfer**, make over, give, pass, hand over, hand down, convey, consign, alienate; Law demise, devise, attorn.

assignation noun *he and Jane arranged a secret assignation in town*: **rendezvous**, date, appointment, meeting; literary tryst.

assignment noun **1** *I'm going to finish this assignment tonight*: **task**, piece of work, piece of business, job, duty, chore, charge, labour, function, commission, mission, errand, engagement, occupation, undertaking, exercise, business, office, responsibility, detail, endeavour, enterprise; piece of research, project, homework, prep.
2 *the effective assignment of tasks*: **allocation**, allotment, issuing, issuance, awarding, grant, granting, administration, earmarking, designation, setting aside, budgeting; **sharing out**, apportionment, distribution, handing out, dealing out, doling out, giving out, dishing out, parcelling out, rationing out, dividing out, dividing up, dispensation, measuring out, meting out; informal divvying up.
3 *the assignment of property*: **transfer**, making over, giving, passing on, handing down, conveyance, consignment, alienation; Law demise, devise, attornment.

assimilate verb **1** *there are limits to the amount of information he can assimilate | the plants do not assimilate nitrates fast enough*: **absorb**, take in, acquire, pick up, grasp, comprehend, understand, learn, master; digest, ingest, imbibe, drink in, soak in; informal get the hang of, get.
2 *many tribes disappeared, having been assimilated by the Russian or Turkic peoples*: **subsume**, incorporate, integrate, absorb, engulf, swallow up, take over, co-opt, naturalize, adopt, embrace, accept, admit; rare acculturate.

assist verb **1** *I spend much of my time assisting the chef*: **help**, aid, abet, lend a (helping) hand to, give assistance to, be of use to, oblige, accommodate, serve, be of service to, do someone a service, do someone a favour, do someone a good turn, bail someone out, come to someone's rescue; cooperate with, collaborate with, work with; succour, encourage, support,

a

back, back up, second, be a tower of strength to; informal pitch in with, get someone out of a tight spot, save someone's bacon, save someone's skin, give someone a leg up; Brit. informal muck in with, get stuck in with.
▷ANTONYMS hinder.
2 *the exchange rates assisted the massive expansion of trade*: **facilitate**, aid, ease, make easier, expedite, spur, promote, boost, give a boost to, benefit, foster, encourage, stimulate, precipitate, accelerate, advance, further, forward, help along, contribute to, be a factor in, smooth the way for, clear a path for, open the door for, oil the wheels of; informal jack up, hike, hike up.
▷ANTONYMS impede.

> *Choose the right word* **assist, help, aid, support**
>
> See **help**.

assistance noun *they said that they could manage and did not need assistance*: **help**, aid, abettance, support, backing, succour, encouragement, reinforcement, relief, intervention, cooperation, collaboration; a helping hand, a hand, a good turn, a favour, a kindness; ministrations, offices, services; informal a break, a leg up; rare easement.
▷ANTONYMS hindrance.

assistant noun **1** *he spent three years as a photographer's assistant*: **subordinate**, deputy, auxiliary, second, second in command, number two, right-hand man, right-hand woman, aide, personal assistant, PA, attendant, mate, apprentice, junior; henchman, underling, hired hand, hired help, servant; **helper**, aider, colleague, associate, partner, confederate, accomplice, collaborator, accessory, abetter, supporter, backer; informal vice, man/girl Friday, sidekick, skivvy, running dog, gofer, gopher; Brit. informal dogsbody, poodle.
2 *Judy was an assistant in the local shop*: **sales assistant**, shop assistant, retail assistant, salesperson, saleswoman, salesman, saleslady, salesgirl, server, checkout girl, checkout person, checkout operator; seller, vendor; N. Amer. clerk, sales clerk; informal counter-jumper, sales rep, pusher; dated shop boy, shop girl, shopman.

> *Word links* **assistant**
>
> **sub-** related prefix, as in *subdirector*
> **vice-** related prefix, as in *vice-principal*

associate verb **1** *elegance was not a concept I associated with nuns*: **link**, connect, couple, relate, identify, equate, bracket, think of together; think of in connection with, draw a parallel with, mention in the same breath as, set side by side with.
2 *Simon had been known to associate with anarchist groups*: **mix**, keep company, mingle, socialize, get together, go around, rub shoulders, fraternize, consort, have dealings; N. Amer. rub elbows; informal hobnob, run around, hang out, hang around/round, knock about/around, pal up, pal around, chum around, be thick with; Brit. informal hang about.
3 *the firm is associated with a local non-profit-making organization*: **affiliate**, align, connect, join, join up, join forces, attach, combine, team up, band together, be in league, ally, form an alliance, syndicate, federate, consolidate, incorporate, conjoin, merge, integrate.
▸ noun *the bank was run by his business associate*: **partner**, colleague, co-worker, fellow worker, workmate, compatriot, comrade, friend, ally, supporter, confederate, connection, contact, acquaintance; accomplice, accessory, abetter, partner in crime, collaborator, colluder, fellow conspirator, henchman; French confrère; informal crony, pal, chum, buddy; Brit. informal mate, oppo; Austral./NZ informal offsider; archaic compeer; rare conniver, consociate.

associated adjective **1** *salaries and associated costs have risen this year*: **related**, connected, linked, correlated, analogous, similar, alike, kindred, corresponding; attendant, accompanying, auxiliary, accessory, incidental; formal cognate.
▷ANTONYMS unrelated.
2 *they share in the results and net assets of their associated company*: **affiliated**, allied, integrated, amalgamated, incorporated, federated, confederated, syndicated, unified, connected, interconnected, related, linked, joined, bound; in league, in partnership, in alliance.

association noun **1** *the industry has established a trade association*: **alliance**, consortium, coalition, union, league, guild, syndicate, corporation, federation, confederation, confederacy, conglomerate, cooperative, partnership, amalgamation, merger; body, group, ring, circle, trust, company, organization, affiliation, society, club, band, brotherhood, fraternity, sorority, clique, cartel; rare consociation, sodality.
2 *they study the association between man and environment*: **relationship**, relation, interrelation, connection, interconnection, link, bond, tie, attachment, interdependence, union; communication, interchange, contact, affiliation, cooperation; dealings.

assorted adjective *assorted artefacts were recovered from the site*: **mixed**, varied, variegated, varying, various, miscellaneous, diverse, diversified, eclectic, manifold, multifarious, multitudinous, motley, sundry, heterogeneous, disparate, different, differing, dissimilar; literary divers; rare farraginous.
▷ANTONYMS similar, identical.

assortment noun *the alcove held an assortment of books*: **mixture**, variety, array, mixed bag, mix, miscellany, random selection, motley collection, selection, medley, melange, diversity, mishmash, hotchpotch, hodgepodge, ragbag, pot-pourri, jumble, mess, confusion, conglomeration, farrago, patchwork, hash; rare gallimaufry, omnium gatherum, olio, olla podrida, salmagundi, macédoine, motley.

assuage verb **1** *an aching pain that could never be assuaged*: **relieve**, ease, alleviate, soothe, mitigate, dampen, allay, calm, palliate, abate, lull, temper, suppress, smother, stifle, subdue, tranquillize, mollify, moderate, modify, tone down, attenuate, dilute, lessen, diminish, decrease, reduce, lower; put an end to, put a stop to, take the edge off; informal kill; rare lenify.
▷ANTONYMS aggravate.
2 *her physical hunger could be quickly assuaged*: **satisfy**, fulfil, gratify, appease, indulge, relieve, slake, sate, satiate, quench, quell, overcome, check, keep in check, dull, blunt, allay, take the edge off, diminish.
▷ANTONYMS intensify.

assume verb **1** *I assumed he wanted me to keep the book*: **presume**, suppose, take it, take for granted, take as read, take it as given, presuppose, conjecture, surmise, conclude, come to the conclusion, deduce, infer, draw the inference, reckon, reason, guess, imagine, think, fancy, suspect, expect, accept, believe, be of the opinion, understand, be given to understand, gather, glean; N. Amer. figure; formal opine; archaic ween.
2 *he had assumed a stage Southern accent*: **feign**, fake, put on, simulate, counterfeit, sham, affect, adopt, impersonate.
3 *the disease may assume epidemic proportions*: **acquire**, take on, adopt, come to have.
4 *the children are to assume as much responsibility as possible*: **accept**, shoulder, bear, undertake, take on, take up, take on oneself, manage, handle, deal with, get to grips with, turn one's hand to.
5 *Edward I used the conflict to assume control of Scotland*: **seize**, take, take possession of, take over, take away, appropriate, commandeer, expropriate, confiscate, requisition, hijack, wrest, usurp, pre-empt, arrogate to oneself, help oneself to, claim, lay claim to.

assumed adjective *he may have travelled under an assumed name*: **false**, fictitious, invented, made-up, concocted, feigned, pretended, faked, fake, bogus, sham, spurious, counterfeit, pseudo, make-believe, improvised, affected, adopted; informal pretend, phoney, pseud; Brit. informal, dated cod; rare pseudonymous.
▷ANTONYMS real, genuine.

assumption noun **1** *the statistic is only an informed assumption*: **supposition**, presupposition, presumption, premise, belief, expectation, conjecture, speculation, surmise, guess, theory, hypothesis, postulation, conclusion, deduction, inference, thought, suspicion, notion, impression, fancy; guesswork, guessing, reckoning; informal guesstimate.
2 *Theresa shrugged with an assumption of ease*: **pretence**, simulation, affectation; feigning, faking, shamming, pretending.
3 *there is an early assumption of community obligation in the tribe*: **acceptance**, shouldering, handling, managing, tackling, taking on; undertaking, entering on, setting about, embarkation on.
4 *no one had foreseen the assumption of power by the revolutionaries*: **seizure**, seizing, taking, taking over, taking away, appropriation, appropriating, commandeering, expropriation, expropriating, confiscation, confiscating, requisition, requisitioning, hijack, hijacking, wresting, usurping, pre-empting, arrogation, claiming.

assurance noun **1** *nothing could shake her calm assurance*: **self-confidence**, confidence, self-assurance, belief in oneself, faith in oneself, positiveness, assertiveness, self-possession, self-reliance, nerve, poise, aplomb, presence of mind, phlegm, level-headedness, cool-headedness; coolness, calmness, composure, collectedness, sangfroid, equilibrium, equanimity, imperturbability, impassivity, nonchalance, serenity, tranquillity, peace of mind; informal cool, unflappability.
▷ANTONYMS self-doubt; nervousness.
2 *you have my assurance that I shall write to you*: **word of honour**, word, guarantee, promise, pledge, vow, avowal, oath, bond, affirmation, undertaking, commitment; archaic troth, parole.
3 *there is no assurance of getting one's money back*: **certainty**, guarantee, sureness, certitude, confidence; hope, expectation.
▷ANTONYMS uncertainty.
4 *they required him to take out life assurance*: **insurance**, indemnity, indemnification, protection, security, surety, cover, coverage; guarantee, safeguard, warranty, provision.

assure verb **1** *we need to assure him of our loyal support | I can assure all our consumers that the water is safe to drink*: **reassure**, convince, satisfy, persuade, guarantee, promise, tell; prove to, certify to, attest to, confirm to, affirm to, pledge to, swear to, give one's word to, give one's assurance to, vow to, declare to.
2 *he made some changes in his cabinet to assure a favourable vote*: **ensure**, make certain, make sure; **secure**, guarantee, seal, set the seal on, clinch,

confirm, establish; informal sew up.
3 *they guarantee to assure your life for £750,000*: **insure**, provide insurance for, cover, indemnify, guarantee, warrant.

assured adjective **1** *the guide spoke in an assured voice*: **self-confident**, confident, self-assured, sure of oneself, positive, assertive, self-possessed, self-reliant, poised, filled with aplomb, phlegmatic, level-headed, cool-headed; calm, collected, {cool, calm, and collected}, composed, nonchalant, unperturbed, imperturbable, unruffled, impassive, serene, tranquil, relaxed, at ease; informal unflappable, together, unfazed, laid-back; rare equanimous.
▷ANTONYMS doubtful; nervous.
2 *the British wanted an assured supply of weapons*: **guaranteed**, certain, sure, secure, reliable, dependable, solid, sound, established; infallible, unerring, unfailing, impeccable, faultless; informal sure-fire, in the bag.
▷ANTONYMS uncertain.

astonish verb *I was astonished at how much he had learned*: **amaze**, astound, stagger, surprise, startle, stun, confound, dumbfound, stupefy, daze, nonplus; throw, shake, unnerve, disconcert, discompose, bewilder; take someone's breath away, take by surprise, take aback, shake up, stop someone in their tracks, strike dumb, leave open-mouthed, leave aghast, catch off balance; informal flabbergast, floor, knock for six, knock sideways, knock out, knock the stuffing out of, bowl over, blow someone's mind, blow away.

astonished adjective *his tricks attracted crowds of astonished bystanders*: **amazed**, filled with astonishment, filled with amazement, astounded, staggered, surprised, startled, stunned, thunderstruck, aghast, taken aback, confounded, dumbfounded, stupefied, dazed, nonplussed, dumbstruck, open-mouthed, agape, lost for words, wide-eyed, awed, filled with awe, filled with wonder, awestruck, wonderstruck; shaken, shaken up, unnerved, disconcerted, discomposed, bewildered, bemused; informal flabbergasted, flummoxed, floored, knocked for six, bowled over, blown away, unable to believe one's eyes/ears; Brit. informal gobsmacked.

astonishing adjective *she has read an astonishing number of books*: **amazing**, astounding, staggering, shocking, surprising, breathtaking, striking, impressive, bewildering, stunning, stupefying; unnerving, unsettling, disturbing, disquieting; awe-inspiring, remarkable, notable, noteworthy, extraordinary, outstanding, incredible, unbelievable, phenomenal, uncommon, unheard of; informal mind-boggling, mind-blowing, hard to swallow.

astonishment noun *she stared at him in astonishment*: **amazement**, surprise, shock, stupefaction, bafflement, bewilderment, confusion, perplexity, incredulity, disbelief, dismay, consternation, speechlessness, awe, wonder, wonderment.

astound verb *Kate was astounded by his arrogance*: **amaze**, astonish, stagger, surprise, startle, stun, confound, dumbfound, stupefy, daze, nonplus; throw, shake, unnerve, disconcert, discompose, bewilder; take someone's breath away, take by surprise, take aback, shake up, stop someone in their tracks, strike dumb, leave open-mouthed, leave aghast, catch off balance; informal flabbergast, floor, knock for six, knock someone sideways, knock out, knock the stuffing out of, bowl over, blow someone's mind, blow away.

astounding adjective *his speed and fitness were astounding*: **amazing**, astonishing, staggering, shocking, surprising, breathtaking, striking, impressive, bewildering, stunning, stupefying; unnerving, unsettling, disturbing, disquieting; awe-inspiring, remarkable, notable, noteworthy, extraordinary, outstanding, incredible, unbelievable, phenomenal, uncommon, unheard of; informal mind-boggling, mind-blowing, hard to swallow.

astray adverb **1** *the gunman claimed that the shots had gone astray*: **off target**, wide of the mark, wide, awry; **off course**, off track, off the right track, adrift; informal off beam.
2 *they were accused of leading young girls astray*: **into wrongdoing**, into error, into sin, into iniquity, away from the straight and narrow, away from the path of righteousness; informal off the rails.

astringent adjective **1** *the lotion has a mildly astringent effect on open pores*: **constricting**, contracting, constrictive, constringent, styptic.
2 *her godmother's astringent words had the desired effect*: **severe**, sharp, stern, harsh, rough, acerbic, austere, caustic, mordant, trenchant; sarcastic, sardonic, scathing, cutting, incisive, penetrating, piercing, stinging, searing; wounding, hurtful, unkind, cruel, spiteful, waspish, poisonous, vicious; N. Amer. acerb; informal bitchy, catty; Brit. informal sarky; N. Amer. informal snarky; rare acidulous, mordacious.

astrology noun **horoscopy**, stargazing; horoscopes; rare astromancy.

astronaut noun **spaceman**, **spacewoman**, cosmonaut, space traveller, space pilot, space flyer, space cadet; N. Amer. informal jock.

astronomical adjective **1** *they studied Stonehenge in terms of astronomical alignments*: **celestial**, planetary, stellar, astronomic, heavenly.
2 informal *the sums he has paid out are astronomical*. See **huge**.

astronomy noun

> *Word links* **astronomy**
>
> **Urania** the Muse of astronomy

astute adjective *he had a reputation as an astute businessman* | *an uncomfortably astute remark*: **shrewd**, sharp, sharp-witted, razor-sharp, acute, quick, quick-witted, ingenious, clever, intelligent, bright, brilliant, smart, canny, intuitive, discerning, perceptive, perspicacious, penetrating, insightful, incisive, piercing, discriminating, sagacious, wise, judicious; cunning, artful, crafty, wily, calculating; informal on the ball, quick off the mark, quick on the uptake, brainy, streetwise, savvy; Brit. informal suss; Scottish & N. English informal pawky; N. Amer. informal heads-up; dated, informal long-headed; rare argute, sapient.
▷ANTONYMS stupid.

asunder adverb literary *the very fabric of society may be torn asunder*: **apart**, up, in two; into pieces, to pieces, to bits, to shreds.

asylum noun **1** *he appealed to Germany for political asylum* | *the refugees had to find another asylum*: **refuge**, sanctuary, shelter, safety, safe keeping, protection, security, immunity; haven, safe haven, retreat, sanctum, harbour, port in a storm, oasis; safe house, fastness, hideaway, hideout, bolt-hole, foxhole, hiding place, den.
2 *his father went mad and was confined to an asylum*: **psychiatric hospital**, mental hospital, mental institution, mental asylum, institution; informal madhouse, nuthouse, loony bin, funny farm; N. Amer. informal bughouse, booby hatch; dated lunatic asylum; archaic bedlam.

asymmetrical adjective *it was an engagingly asymmetrical church* | *the asymmetrical division of labour*: **lopsided**, unsymmetrical, crooked; **uneven**, unbalanced, off-balance, off-centre, to one side, awry, askew, skew, skewed, squint, tilted, tilting, misaligned, sloping, slanted, aslant, out of true, out of line; disproportionate, unequal, misproportioned, ill-proportioned, ill-shaped, misshapen, irregular, distorted, out of shape, malformed, formless; Scottish agley, thrawn; informal cock-eyed; Brit. informal skew-whiff, wonky, squiffy.
▷ANTONYMS symmetrical.

atheism noun *atheism is virtually unknown in rural societies*: **non-belief**, disbelief, unbelief, scepticism, doubt, agnosticism, irreligion, godlessness, ungodliness, profaneness, impiety, heresy, apostasy, paganism, heathenism, freethinking, nihilism.
▷ANTONYMS belief, faith.

atheist noun *he was an intellectually fulfilled atheist*: **non-believer**, disbeliever, unbeliever, heretic, sceptic, doubter, doubting Thomas, agnostic, infidel, irreligious person, heathen, pagan, freethinker, libertine, nihilist; archaic paynim; rare nullifidian.
▷ANTONYMS believer.

athlete noun *she is a superbly gifted all-round athlete*: **sportswoman**, **sportsman**, sportsperson; runner, racer, player, games player, gymnast, team member; competitor, contestant, contender; informal keep-fit buff, keep-fit freak; N. Amer. informal jock, jockstrap.

athletic adjective **1** *his shirt did not hide his athletic physique*: **muscular**, muscly, sturdy, strapping, well built, powerfully built, strong, powerful, robust, able-bodied, vigorous, hardy, lusty, hearty, hale and hearty, brawny, burly, broad-shouldered, thickset, Herculean; **fit**, fighting fit, as fit as a fiddle, as fit as a flea, in good shape, in good trim, in trim, in tip-top condition, aerobicized, healthy, in good health, bursting with health, in fine fettle, as strong as an ox, as strong as a horse, as strong as a lion; Brit. in rude health; informal sporty, husky, hunky, beefy; dated stalwart; literary thewy, stark; technical mesomorphic.
▷ANTONYMS weak, frail.
2 *they were banned from the athletic events*: **sporting**, sports, games, gymnastic; competitive.

athletics plural noun *he dropped out of athletics after a season without a win*: **track and field events**, sporting events, sports, games, organized games, matches, races, contests, competitions; exercises, gymnastics; archaic palaestra.

atmosphere noun **1** *ozone-depleting gases are present in the atmosphere*: **air**, aerosphere, airspace, sky; literary the heavens, the firmament, the vault of heaven, the blue, the wide blue yonder, the azure, the ether, the welkin, the empyrean, the upper regions, the sphere.
2 *the hotel has a friendly and relaxed atmosphere*: **ambience**, aura, climate, air, mood, feel, feeling, character, tone, overtone, undertone, tenor, spirit, quality, aspect, element, undercurrent, flavour, colour, colouring, look, impression, suggestion, emanation; environment, milieu, medium, background, backdrop, setting, context; surroundings, environs, conditions, circumstances, vibrations; informal vibe, vibes; rare subcurrent.

> *Word links* **atmosphere**
>
> **meteorology**, **aerology** (dated) study of the atmosphere
> **aeronomy** study of the upper atmosphere

a

atom noun *they build tiny circuits atom by atom | there wasn't an atom of truth in the allegations*: **particle**, molecule, bit, little bit, tiny bit, tiny piece, fragment, fraction, grain, granule, crumb, morsel, mite, mote, speck, spot, dot; **iota**, jot, whit, scrap, shred, trace, tinge, ounce, modicum, scintilla, vestige; Irish stim; informal smidgen, smidge, tad; archaic scantling, scruple.

atone verb *what would you have me do to* ***atone for*** *my sin?* **make amends**, make reparation, make restitution, make recompense, make redress, make up for, compensate, pay, pay the penalty, pay the price, recompense, answer; expiate, make good, offset; do penance, redeem oneself, redress the balance; formal requite.

atonement noun *I was making a pilgrimage in atonement for my sins*: **reparation**, compensation, recompense, payment, repayment, redress, restitution, indemnity, indemnification, expiation, penance, redemption; amends; formal requital; rare solatium.

atrocious adjective **1** *atrocious cruelties were committed in the name of religion*: **brutal**, barbaric, barbarous, brutish, savage, vicious, wicked, cruel, nasty, ruthless, merciless, villainous, murderous, heinous, nefarious, monstrous, base, low, low-down, vile, inhuman, infernal, dark, black, black-hearted, fiendish, hellish, diabolical, ghastly, horrible; abominable, outrageous, offensive, hateful, disgusting, despicable, contemptible, loathsome, odious, revolting, repellent, repugnant, abhorrent, harrowing, nightmarish, gruesome, grisly, sickening, nauseating, horrifying, hideous, unspeakable, unforgivable, intolerable, beyond the pale, scandalous, flagrant, execrable; informal horrid, gross, sick-making, sick; Brit. informal beastly; archaic disgustful, loathly, scurvy; rare egregious, flagitious, cacodemonic, facinorous.
▷ANTONYMS admirable; kindly.
2 *the weather was atrocious*: **appalling**, dreadful, terrible, very bad, unpleasant, lamentable, woeful, miserable, poor, inadequate, unsatisfactory; informal abysmal, dire, rotten, crummy, lousy, poxy, yucky, God-awful, the pits; Brit. informal shocking, duff, beastly, chronic, pants, a load of pants, rubbish, rubbishy, ropy; vulgar slang crap, crappy, chickenshit; archaic direful.
▷ANTONYMS superb.

atrocity noun **1** *press reports detailed a number of atrocities*: **act of barbarity**, act of brutality, act of savagery, act of wickedness, cruelty, abomination, enormity, outrage, horror, monstrosity, obscenity, iniquity, violation, crime, transgression, wrong, wrongdoing, offence, injury, affront, scandal, injustice, abuse; Law malfeasance, tort.
2 *he observed conflict and atrocity around the globe*: **barbarity**, barbarism, brutality, savagery, inhumanity, cruelty, wickedness, badness, baseness, evil, iniquity, horror, heinousness, villainy, lawlessness, crime, transgression, wrong, wrongdoing, injustice, abuse; Law malfeasance; rare malefaction.

atrophy verb **1** *the body parts which are no longer required gradually atrophy*: **waste away**, waste, become emaciated, wither, shrivel, shrivel up, shrink, become shrunken, dry up, decay, wilt; decline, deteriorate, degenerate, grow weak, weaken, become debilitated, become enfeebled.
▷ANTONYMS strengthen.
2 *in the final few days, the Labour campaign atrophied*: **peter out**, taper off, tail off, dwindle, deteriorate, decline, wane, fade, fade away, fade out, give in, give up, give way, crumble, disintegrate, collapse, slump, go downhill, draw to a close, subside; be neglected, be abandoned, be disregarded, be forgotten.
▷ANTONYMS flourish.
▶ noun *they located the gene that causes muscular atrophy*: **wasting**, wasting away, emaciation, withering, shrivelling, shrivelling up, shrinking, drying up, wilting, decaying, decay; declining, deteriorating, deterioration, degenerating, degeneration, weakening, debilitation, enfeeblement.
▷ANTONYMS strengthening.

attach verb **1** *his ankles were attached by chains to the wall*: **fasten**, fix, affix, join, connect, couple, link, secure, make fast, tie, tie up, bind, fetter, strap, rope, tether, truss, lash, hitch, moor, anchor, yoke, chain; stick, tape, adhere, glue, bond, cement, fuse, weld, solder; pin, peg, screw, bolt, rivet, batten, pinion, clamp, clip; add, append, annex, subjoin.
▷ANTONYMS detach.
2 *he* ***attached*** *himself* ***to*** *the radical section of the Liberal Party*: **affiliate with**, associate with, align with, ally with, unite with, combine with, integrate into, join to; join up with, join forces with, band together with, team up with, latch on to, cooperate with, be in league with, form an alliance with, make a pact with; informal tag along with.
▷ANTONYMS break away from.
3 *they* ***attached*** *great importance* ***to*** *research*: **ascribe**, assign, attribute, accredit, apply, impute; invest with, put on, place on, lay on.
4 *he is the medical officer attached to Brigade Headquarters*: **assign**, allot, allocate, detail, appoint; relocate, reassign, transfer, move, send, second, lend.
▷ANTONYMS separate.
5 Law *the state attached criminals' property*: **seize**, confiscate, commandeer, requisition, appropriate, expropriate, take possession of, take away, take, sequester, sequestrate; Law distrain, disseize; Scottish Law poind.

attached adjective **1** *the young couple are now attached*: **married**, wed, wedded, joined in marriage, joined in matrimony, united in wedlock; **engaged**, affianced, pledged, promised, promised in marriage, going out, spoken for, involved; united, bound, contracted; informal hitched, spliced, yoked, shackled, going steady, boyfriend and girlfriend; dated betrothed; archaic espoused, plighted.
▷ANTONYMS unattached, single.
2 *she was very* ***attached to*** *her brother*: **fond of**, devoted to, full of regard for, full of admiration for; affectionate towards, tender towards, caring towards; informal mad about, crazy about, nuts about.

attachment noun **1** *he had a strong* ***attachment to*** *his mother*: **bond**, closeness, devotion, loyalty; **fondness for**, love for, liking for, affection for, affinity for, tenderness for, feeling for, sentiment for, regard for, respect for, admiration for, reverence for; relationship with, friendship with, intimacy with.
2 *the shower had a soothing massage attachment*: **accessory**, fitting, fitment, extension, supplementary part, supplementary component, extra, extra part, adjunct, addition, add-on, appurtenance, appendage, accoutrement, auxiliary.
3 *all cars have points for the attachment of safety restraints*: **fixing**, fastening, affixing, linking, coupling, clamping, connection, connecting; addition, adding, incorporation, introduction, insertion.
4 *he was on attachment from another regiment*: **assignment**, detail, appointment, allocation, secondment, transfer, relocation.
5 *he maintained his family's Conservative attachment*: **affiliation**, association, alliance, alignment, union, bond, liaison, coalition, partnership, fellowship, belonging; links, ties, connections, sympathies.
6 Law *the attachment of criminals' property*: **seizure**, confiscation, appropriation, expropriation, sequestration, taking away, commandeering; Law distrainment, disseizin; Scottish Law poinding.

attack verb **1** *Christopher had been brutally attacked*: **assault**, beat, beat up, batter, thrash, pound, pummel, assail, set upon, fall upon, set about, strike at, let fly at, tear into, lash out at; ambush, mug, pounce on; informal jump, paste, do over, work over, knock about/around, rough up, lay into, lace into, sail into, pitch into, get stuck into, beat the living daylights out of, let someone have it; Brit. informal have a go at, duff someone up; N. Amer. informal beat up on, light into.
2 *by eight o'clock the French had still not attacked*: **begin an assault**, charge, pounce, strike, begin hostilities, ambush; bombard, shell, blitz, strafe, fire on/at; rush, storm.
▷ANTONYMS defend.
3 *the clergy have consistently attacked government policies*: **criticize**, censure, condemn, castigate, chastise, lambaste, pillory, savage, find fault with, fulminate against, abuse; berate, reprove, rebuke, reprimand, admonish, remonstrate with, reproach, take to task, haul over the coals, impugn, harangue, blame, revile, vilify, give someone a bad press; informal knock, slam, take to pieces, pull apart, crucify, bash, hammer, lay into, tear into, sail into, roast, give someone a roasting, cane, blast, bawl out, dress down, rap over the knuckles, have a go at, give someone hell; Brit. informal carpet, slate, slag off, rubbish, monster, rollick, give someone a rollicking, give someone a rocket, tear someone off a strip, tear a strip off someone; N. Amer. informal chew out, ream out, pummel, cut up; Austral./NZ informal bag; Brit. vulgar slang bollock, give someone a bollocking; dated rate; archaic slash; rare excoriate, objurgate, reprehend.
▷ANTONYMS praise.
4 *they have started to attack the problem of threatened species*: **attend to**, address, see to, deal with, grapple with, confront, direct one's attention to, focus on, concentrate on, apply oneself to; buckle down to, get to work on, go to work on, set to work on, set about, get started on, undertake, embark on; informal get stuck into, get cracking on, get weaving on, have a crack at, have a go at, have a shot at, have a stab at.
5 *the virus attacks the liver, heart, and lungs*: **affect**, have an effect on, strike, strike at, take hold of, infect; **damage**, injure.
▷ANTONYMS protect.
▶ noun **1** *they were killed in an attack on their home*: **assault**, onslaught, offensive, strike, blitz, raid, sortie, sally, storming, charge, rush, drive, push, thrust, invasion, incursion, inroad; act of aggression; historical razzia; archaic onset.
2 *she wrote a ferociously hostile attack on him*: **criticism**, censure, rebuke, admonition, admonishment, reprimand, reproval; condemnation, denunciation, revilement; invective, vilification; tirade, diatribe, rant, polemic, broadside, harangue, verbal onslaught, stricture; informal knocking, telling-off, dressing-down, rap over the knuckles, earful, roasting, rollicking, caning; Brit. informal rocket, wigging, slating, ticking-off, carpeting, bashing, blast; Brit. vulgar slang bollocking; dated rating; rare philippic.
▷ANTONYMS commendation, defence.
3 *she had suffered an acute asthmatic attack*: **fit**, seizure, spasm, convulsion, paroxysm, outburst, flare-up; bout, spell, dose; rare access.

attacker noun *she was punched in the face by the attacker*: **assailant**, assaulter, aggressor, striker; mugger, rapist, killer, murderer; informal slasher.

attain verb *they help the child attain his or her full potential*: **achieve**, accomplish, reach, arrive at, come by, obtain, gain, procure, secure, get, grasp, hook, net, win, earn, acquire, establish, make; realize, fulfil, succeed in, bring off, bring about, bring to fruition, carry off, carry through, effect; informal hit, clinch, bag, wangle, wrap up, polish off; rare effectuate, reify.

attainable adjective *a challenging but attainable target*: **achievable**, obtainable, accessible, within reach, at hand, reachable, winnable, securable, realizable; practicable, workable, manageable, realistic, reasonable, viable, feasible, possible, within the bounds/realms of possibility, potential, conceivable, imaginable; informal doable, get-at-able, up for grabs; rare accomplishable.
▷ANTONYMS unattainable.

attainment noun **1** *they are making progress towards the attainment of common goals*: **achievement**, accomplishment, realization, realizing, fulfilment, fulfilling, effecting, completion, consummation; success, fruition; securing, gaining, gain, procurement, procuring, acquiring, acquisition; rare effectuation, reification.
2 *a low standard of educational attainment*: **proficiency**, competence, mastery, accomplishment, achievement, qualification; art, skill, talent, gift, aptitude, faculty, ability, capability.

attempt verb *I attempted to answer the question | he attempted a takeover bid*: **try**, strive, aim, venture, endeavour, seek, set out, do one's best, do all one can, do one's utmost, make an effort, make every effort, spare no effort, give one's all, take it on oneself; have a go at, undertake, embark on, try one's hand at, try out; informal give it a whirl, give it one's best shot, go all out, pull out all the stops, bend over backwards, knock oneself out, bust a gut, break one's neck, move heaven and earth, have a crack at, have a shot at, have a stab at; Austral./NZ informal give it a burl, give it a fly; formal essay; archaic assay.
▶ noun *an attempt to put the economy to rights*: **effort**, endeavour, try, bid, venture, trial, experiment; informal crack, go, shot, stab, bash, whack; formal essay; archaic assay.

attend verb **1** *they attended a carol service | she attended evening classes*: **be present at**, be at, be there at, sit in on, take part in; appear at, put in an appearance at, make an appearance at, present oneself at, turn up at, visit, pay a visit to, go to; frequent, haunt, patronize; informal show up at, pop up at, show one's face at, hang out at, take in, catch.
▷ANTONYMS miss.
2 *he had not **attended** sufficiently **to** the regulations*: **pay attention**, pay heed, be attentive, listen, lend an ear; concentrate on, take note of, bear in mind, give thought to, take into consideration, be heedful of, heed, respect, follow, observe, notice, mark; informal tune in to, get a load of, check out, be all ears for; archaic hearken, give ear, regard.
▷ANTONYMS disregard, ignore.
3 *the wounded could be **attended to** at a nearby village*: **care for**, look after, take care of, minister to, administer to, keep an eye on, see to; tend, treat, nurse, help, aid, assist, succour, nurture, mind; informal doctor.
4 *their father **attended to** the boy's education*: **deal with**, cope with, see to, address, manage, organize, orchestrate, make arrangements for, sort out, handle, take care of, take charge of, take responsibility for, take in hand, take up, undertake, tackle, give one's attention to, apply oneself to.
▷ANTONYMS neglect.
5 *the queen was attended by a liveried usher*: **escort**, accompany, guard, chaperone, squire, convoy, guide, lead, conduct, usher, shepherd, follow, shadow; **assist**, help, serve, wait on.
6 *her giddiness **was attended with** a fever*: **be accompanied by**, be associated with, be connected with, be linked with, go hand in hand with; occur with, co-occur with, coexist with, be produced by, be brought about by, originate from, originate in, stem from, result from, be a result of, arise from, follow on from, be a consequence of.

attendance noun **1** *you requested the attendance of a doctor*: **presence**, appearance, attending, being there; informal turning up, showing up, showing.
▷ANTONYMS absence.
2 *their gig attendances grew at an alarming rate*: **audience**, turnout, number present, house, gate; crowd, throng, congregation, assembly, gathering; Austral./NZ informal muster.
□ **in attendance** *his wife is in labour with three obstetricians in attendance*: **present**, here, there, near, nearby, at hand, by one's side, available; assisting, giving assistance, helping, aiding; supervising, monitoring, on guard.

attendant noun **1** *a sleeping-car attendant delivered hot-water bottles*: **steward**, waiter, waitress, porter, servant, menial, auxiliary, assistant, helper; caretaker, keeper, concierge, warden; N. Amer. waitperson, tender; French garçon.
2 *he prospered as a royal attendant*: **escort**, companion, retainer, aide, assistant, personal assistant, right-hand man, right-hand woman, lady in waiting, equerry, squire, chaperone, guard, bodyguard, minder, custodian; servant, manservant, valet, gentleman's gentleman, maidservant, maid, butler, footman, page, usher, lackey, flunkey; N. Amer. houseman; informal sidekick, skivvy; Military, dated batman.
▶ adjective *we crave new discoveries and the attendant excitement*: **accompanying**, associated, related, connected, concomitant, accessory; resultant, resulting, consequent.

attention noun **1** *the issue clearly needs further attention*: **observation**, attentiveness, intentness, notice, concentration, heed, heedfulness, mindfulness, regard, scrutiny; contemplation, consideration, deliberation, thought, thinking, studying, investigation, action.
2 *he was likely to attract the attention of a policeman*: **awareness**, notice, observation, consciousness, heed, recognition, regard, scrutiny, surveillance, attentiveness; curiosity, inquisitiveness.
3 *they failed to give adequate medical attention*: **care**, treatment, therapy, ministration, succour, relief, support, aid, help, assistance, service.
4 *the parson was effusive in his attentions*: **courtesy**, civility, politeness, respect, gallantry, urbanity, deference; compliment, flattery, blandishment; overture, suggestion, approach, suit, pass, wooing, courting.
□ **pay attention** *an assortment of motivational tools is necessary to keep them in class and paying attention*: **listen**, be attentive, attend, concentrate on, concentrate on hearing, give ear to, lend an ear to; hang on someone's words.

attentive adjective **1** *she was a bright and attentive scholar*: **alert**, awake, watchful, wide awake, observant, perceptive, percipient, acute, aware, noticing, heeding, heedful, mindful, vigilant, on guard, on one's guard, on one's toes, on the qui vive, on the lookout; concentrating, intent, absorbed, engrossed, focused, committed, studious, diligent, scrupulous, rigorous, earnest, interested; informal all ears, beady-eyed, not missing a trick, on the ball; rare regardful.
▷ANTONYMS inattentive.
2 *I haven't been the most attentive of husbands*: **conscientious**, considerate, thoughtful, kind, kindly, caring, tender, solicitous, understanding, sympathetic, obliging, accommodating, gallant, chivalrous; polite, well mannered, courteous, gracious, civil, respectful, reverential, dutiful, responsible; Brit. informal decent; dated mannerly; rare regardful.
▷ANTONYMS inconsiderate.

attenuated adjective **1** *he rippled his attenuated fingers in the air*: **thin**, slender, slim, skinny, spindly, bony, gaunt, skeletal; narrow, thread-like, thinned down, stretched out, drawn out; rare extenuated, attenuate.
▷ANTONYMS plump; broad.
2 *radiation from the sun is attenuated by the earth's atmosphere*: **weakened**, reduced, lessened, decreased, diminished, impaired, enervated.
▷ANTONYMS strengthened.

attest verb *previous experience is attested by a certificate | I can **attest to** his tremendous energy*: **certify**, corroborate, confirm, verify, substantiate, document, authenticate, give proof of, provide evidence of, evidence, demonstrate, evince, display, exhibit, show, manifest, prove, endorse, back up, support, guarantee; affirm, aver, swear to, testify to, bear witness to, bear out, give credence to, vouch for; Law depose to; informal stick up for, throw one's weight behind; rare asseverate.
▷ANTONYMS disprove.

attic noun *a short flight of rickety steps led to the attic*: **loft**, roof space, cock loft; garret, mansard, loft conversion; informal, dated sky parlour.

attire noun *Thomas preferred formal attire for dinner*: **clothing**, clothes, garments, dress, wear, outfit, turnout, garb, ensemble, costume, array, finery, regalia; wardrobe, accoutrements, trappings; Brit. kit, strip; informal gear, togs, garms, duds, glad rags, get-up; Brit. informal clobber, rig-out; N. Amer. informal threads; formal apparel; archaic raiment, habiliments, habit, vestments.
▶ verb *the widow was correctly attired in black crêpe*: **dress**, clothe, dress up, fit out, garb, robe, array, deck, deck out, turn out, trick out, trick up, costume, accoutre; drape, swathe, adorn; informal doll up, get up; Brit. informal rig out; formal apparel; literary bedizen, caparison, furbelow; archaic invest, habit, trap out.

attired adjective *he was always impeccably attired*: **dressed**, clothed, dressed up, fitted out, garbed, arrayed, decked out, turned out, tricked up, costumed; informal dolled up, got up, got out; Brit. informal rigged out; archaic apparelled, invested, habited, trapped out.

attitude noun **1** *you seem oddly ambivalent in your attitude*: **point of view**, view, viewpoint, vantage point, frame of mind, way of thinking, way of looking at things, school of thought, outlook, angle, slant, perspective, reaction, stance, standpoint, position, inclination, orientation, approach; opinion, ideas, belief, convictions, feelings, sentiments, persuasion, thoughts, thinking, interpretation.
2 *they knelt around her bed in attitudes of prayer*: **position**, posture, pose, stance, stand; bearing, deportment, comportment, carriage.

attorney noun N. Amer. *the defendant will have trouble finding an attorney*: **lawyer**, legal practitioner, legal executive, legal adviser, legal representative, agent, member of the bar, advocate, counsel, counsellor, intercessor, defending counsel, prosecuting counsel; Brit. barrister, Queen's Counsel, QC; N. Amer. & Irish counsellor-at-law; informal brief.

attract verb **1** *positively charged hydrogen ions are attracted to the negatively charged terminal*: **draw**, pull, magnetize.
▷ANTONYMS repel.
2 *he was immediately attracted by her friendly smile*: **entice**, allure, lure, tempt, charm, win over, woo, engage, enchant, entrance, mesmerize,

hypnotize, spellbind, captivate, beguile, bewitch, seduce, dazzle, tantalize, inveigle, lead on; interest, fascinate, enthral, absorb, rivet; excite, titillate, arouse, stimulate; informal tickle someone's fancy, turn on, light someone's fire, float someone's boat, make someone's mouth water.
▷ANTONYMS repel.

attraction noun 1 *the stars are held close together by mutual gravitational attraction*: **pull**, draw; magnetism.
▷ANTONYMS repulsion.
2 *she felt that she had lost whatever attraction she had ever had | he felt the attraction of the literary life*: **appeal**, attractiveness, desirability, seductiveness, seduction, allure, allurement, magnetism, animal magnetism, sexual magnetism, charisma, charm, beauty, good looks, glamour, magic, spell; pull, draw, lure, enticement, entrancement, temptation, inducement, interest, fascination, enchantment, captivation; informal come-on.
▷ANTONYMS repulsion.
3 *the fair offers sideshows, stalls, and other attractions*: **entertainment**, activity, diversion, interest, feature, crowd-pleaser.

attractive adjective 1 *they wanted to make military service a more attractive career*: **appealing**, agreeable, pleasing, inviting, tempting, interesting, fascinating, irresistible.
▷ANTONYMS unattractive, uninviting.
2 *I'm sure she has no idea how attractive she is*: **good-looking**, nice-looking, beautiful, pretty, as pretty as a picture, handsome, lovely, stunning, striking, arresting, gorgeous, prepossessing, winning, fetching, captivating, bewitching, beguiling, engaging, charming, charismatic, enchanting, appealing, delightful, irresistible; sexy, sexually attractive, sexual, seductive, alluring, tantalizing, ravishing, desirable, sultry, sensuous, sensual, erotic, arousing, luscious, lush, nubile; Scottish & N. English bonny; informal fanciable, beddable, tasty, hot, smashing, knockout, drop-dead gorgeous, out of this world, easy on the eye, come-hither, come-to-bed; Brit. informal fit; N. Amer. informal cute, foxy, bootylicious; Austral./NZ informal spunky; literary beauteous; dated taking, well favoured; archaic comely, fair; rare sightly, pulchritudinous.
▷ANTONYMS unattractive, ugly.

attribute verb (stress on the second syllable) *they **attributed** the success of the expedition entirely **to** one man*: **ascribe**, assign, accredit, credit, impute, allot, allocate; put down to, set down to, chalk up to, lay at the door of, hold responsible for, pin something on, lay something on, place something on; connect with, associate with; informal stick something on.
▶ noun (stress on the first syllable) 1 *he has all the attributes of a top midfield player*: **quality**, feature, characteristic, trait, element, aspect, property, hallmark, mark, distinction, sign, telltale sign, sure sign; idiosyncrasy, peculiarity, quirk.
2 *the hourglass was depicted as the attribute of Father Time*: **symbol**, indicator, mark, sign, hallmark, trademark, status symbol.

attrition noun 1 *the strike developed into a bitter war of attrition*: **wearing down**, wearing away, weakening, debilitation, enfeebling, sapping, attenuation; harassment, harrying.
2 *the attrition of the edges of the teeth*: **abrasion**, friction, rubbing, chafing, corroding, corrosion, erosion, eating away, grinding, scraping, wearing away, wearing, excoriation, deterioration, damaging; rare detrition.

attune verb *she was **attuned to** the refinements of Cambridge society*: **accustom**, adjust, adapt, acclimatize, assimilate, condition, accommodate, tailor; (**be attuned to**) be in tune with, be in harmony with, be in accord with; N. Amer. acclimate.

atypical adjective *a lack of social relationships is atypical*: **unusual**, untypical, non-typical, uncommon, unconventional, unorthodox, anomalous, irregular, abnormal, aberrant, deviant, divergent; strange, odd, peculiar, curious, bizarre, weird, queer, freakish, freak, eccentric, quirky, alien; exceptional, singular, rare, unique, isolated, unrepresentative, out of the way, out of the ordinary, extraordinary; Brit. out of the common; informal funny, oddball, off the wall, wacko, wacky, way out, freaky, kinky, something else; Brit. informal rum.
▷ANTONYMS typical.

auburn adjective *she had a head of flowing auburn hair*: **reddish-brown**, red-brown, dark red, Titian, Titian red, tawny, russet, chestnut, chestnut-coloured, copper, coppery, copper-coloured, rust-coloured, rufous, henna, hennaed; rare rufescent.

au courant adjective French *he is **au courant with** the twists and turns of all major events*: **up to date**, up with, in touch, familiar, at home, acquainted, conversant; abreast of, apprised of, in the know about, well informed about, knowledgeable about, well versed in, enlightened about, aware of, no stranger to; French au fait; informal clued up about, genned up about, clued up on, well up on, plugged into, wise to, hip to; Brit. informal switched on to; black English down.
▷ANTONYMS out of touch.

audacious adjective 1 *the audience were left gasping at his audacious exploits*: **bold**, daring, fearless, intrepid, brave, unafraid, unflinching, courageous, valiant, valorous, heroic, dashing, plucky, daredevil, devil-may-care, death-or-glory, reckless, wild, madcap; adventurous, venturesome, enterprising, dynamic, spirited, mettlesome; informal game, gutsy, spunky, ballsy, have-a-go, go-ahead; rare venturous, temerarious.
▷ANTONYMS timid.
2 *Des made some audacious remark to her*: **impudent**, impertinent, insolent, presumptuous, forward, cheeky, irreverent, discourteous, disrespectful, insubordinate, ill-mannered, bad-mannered, unmannerly, rude, crude, brazen, brazen-faced, brash, shameless, pert, defiant, bold, bold as brass, outrageous, shocking, out of line; informal brass-necked, cocky, lippy, mouthy, fresh, flip; Brit. informal saucy, smart-arsed; N. Amer. informal sassy, nervy, smart-assed; archaic malapert, contumelious; rare tossy, mannerless.
▷ANTONYMS polite.

> *Choose the right word* **audacious, bold, daring**
>
> See **bold**.

audacity noun 1 *he was a traveller of extraordinary audacity*: **boldness**, daring, fearlessness, intrepidity, bravery, courage, courageousness, valour, valorousness, heroism, pluck, recklessness; adventurousness, enterprise, dynamism, spirit, mettle, confidence; informal guts, gutsiness, spunk, grit; Brit. informal bottle, ballsiness; N. Amer. informal moxie, cojones, sand; vulgar slang balls; rare venturousness, temerariousness.
▷ANTONYMS timidity.
2 *he had the audacity to contradict me*: **impudence**, impertinence, insolence, presumption, presumptuousness, forwardness, cheek, cheekiness, impoliteness, unmannerliness, bad manners, rudeness, effrontery, nerve, gall, brazenness, brashness, shamelessness, pertness, defiance, boldness, temerity; informal brass, brass neck, neck, face, cockiness; Brit. informal sauce; Scottish informal snash; N. Amer. informal sass, sassiness, nerviness, chutzpah; informal, dated hide; Brit. informal, dated crust; archaic malapertness; rare procacity, assumption.
▷ANTONYMS politeness.

audible adjective *her voice was weak and barely audible*: **perceptible**, discernible, detectable, hearable, able to be heard, recognizable, appreciable; clear, distinct, loud, carrying.
▷ANTONYMS inaudible, faint.

audience noun 1 *they performed three sketches which went down well with the audience*: **spectators**, **listeners**, viewers, onlookers, patrons; assembly, gathering, crowd, throng, company, assemblage, congregation, turnout; house, gallery, stalls; Brit. informal punters.
2 *the radio station was clearly geared to a teenage audience*: **market**, **public**, following, clientele, patronage, listenership, viewership; followers, fans, devotees, aficionados; informal buffs, freaks.
3 *he had an audience with Pope John Paul II*: **meeting**, consultation, conference, hearing, reception, interview, question and answer session, exchange, dialogue, discussion.

audit noun *he announced an immediate audit of the party accounts*: **inspection**, examination, survey, scrutiny, probe, vetting, investigation, check, assessment, appraisal, evaluation, review, analysis, study, perusal, dissection; informal going-over, once-over, look-see.
▶ verb *we have audited the accounts of the corporation*: **inspect**, examine, survey, look over, go over, go through, scrutinize, probe, vet, investigate, look into, enquire into, check, check into, assess, appraise, evaluate, review, analyse, study, pore over, peruse, sift, dissect, go over with a fine-tooth comb, delve into, dig into; N. Amer. check out; informal give something a/the once-over, give something a going-over.

auditorium noun *the singer's voice carries through the vast auditorium*: **theatre**, hall, concert hall, conference hall, assembly hall, assembly room; chamber, room.

au fait adjective French *she was **au fait with** all the latest technology*: **familiar**, acquainted, conversant, at home, up to date, up with, in touch; abreast of, apprised of, in the know about, well informed about, knowledgeable about, well versed in, enlightened about, aware of, no stranger to; French au courant; informal clued up about, genned up about, clued up on, plugged into, well up on, wise to, hip to; Brit. informal switched on to; black English down.
▷ANTONYMS out of touch.

augment verb *he augmented his meagre income by plying for hire as a ferryman | Aubrey's arrival had augmented their difficulties*: **increase**, make larger, make bigger, make greater, add to, supplement, top up, build up, enlarge, expand, extend, raise, multiply, elevate, swell, inflate; magnify, intensify, amplify, heighten, escalate; worsen, make worse, exacerbate, aggravate, inflame, compound, reinforce; improve, make better, boost, ameliorate, enhance, upgrade; informal up, jack up, hike up, hike, bump up, crank up, step up.
▷ANTONYMS decrease.

augur verb *their recent successes augur well for the future | a new coalition would not augur a new period of social reforms*: **bode**; **portend**, herald, be a sign of, be an indication of, be a warning of, warn of, forewarn of, be an omen of, be a harbinger of, foreshadow, presage, indicate, signify, signal, point to, promise, threaten, spell, denote; foretell, forecast, predict, prophesy, prognosticate, divine, foresee; literary betoken, foretoken, forebode, harbinger; archaic foreshow, previse; Scottish archaic spae; rare vaticinate, auspicate.

▶ **noun** *the augur's skill consisted in reading the omens correctly*: **seer**, soothsayer, fortune teller, crystal-gazer, clairvoyant, psychic, visionary, prognosticator, diviner, prophesier, prophet, prophetess, oracle, sibyl, sage, wise man, wise woman; Scottish spaewife, spaeman; rare oracler, vaticinator, haruspex.

august adjective *she was in august company*: **distinguished**, respected, eminent, venerable, hallowed, illustrious, prestigious, renowned, celebrated, honoured, acclaimed, esteemed, exalted, highly regarded, well thought of, of distinction, of repute; great, important, of high standing, lofty, high-ranking, noble, regal, royal, aristocratic; imposing, impressive, awe-inspiring, magnificent, majestic, imperial, stately, lordly, kingly, grand, dignified, solemn, proud.

aura noun *the Peak District will always retain a magical aura*: **atmosphere**, air, quality, aspect, character, ambience, mood, spirit, feeling, feel, flavour, colouring, colour, complexion, climate, tone, overtone, undertone, tenor, impression, suggestion, emanation; vibrations; informal vibes, vibe.

auspices plural noun *the talks were to be held under the auspices of the UN*: **patronage**, aegis, umbrella, protection, guidance, support, backing, guardianship, trusteeship, sponsorship, supervision, influence, control, charge, responsibility, keeping, care; archaic ward.

auspicious adjective *an auspicious day was chosen for the wedding*: **favourable**, propitious, promising, full of promise, bright, rosy, good, optimistic, hopeful, encouraging; **opportune**, timely, well timed, lucky, fortunate, providential, felicitous, advantageous, beneficial.
▷ANTONYMS inauspicious.

> *Choose the right word* **auspicious, opportune, timely**
>
> See **opportune**.

austere adjective **1** *he was a conscientious and outwardly austere man*: **severe**, stern, strict, harsh, unfeeling, stony, steely, flinty, dour, grim, cold, frosty, frigid, icy, chilly, unemotional, unfriendly, formal, stiff, stuffy, reserved, remote, distant, aloof, forbidding, grave, solemn, serious, unsmiling, unsympathetic, unforgiving, uncharitable; hard, rigorous, stringent, unyielding, unbending, unrelenting, inflexible, illiberal, no-nonsense; informal hard-boiled, hard-nosed; Austral./NZ informal solid.
▷ANTONYMS genial.
2 *I still enjoy this austere and disciplined life*: **strict**, self-denying, self-abnegating, moderate, temperate, sober, simple, frugal, spartan, restrained, self-restrained, self-disciplined, non-indulgent, ascetic, puritanical, self-sacrificing, hair-shirt, abstemious, abstinent, celibate, chaste, continent; moral, upright.
▷ANTONYMS immoderate.
3 *the buildings around me were understated and austere*: **plain**, simple, basic, functional, modest, unadorned, undecorated, unornamented, unembellished, unostentatious, unfurnished, uncluttered, unfussy, without frills, subdued, muted, restrained; **stark**, bleak, bare, bald, clinical, sombre, severe, spartan, ascetic; informal no frills.
▷ANTONYMS ornate.

authentic adjective **1** *the first authentic Rubens in the museum's collection | an authentic document*: **genuine**, original, real, actual, pukka, bona fide, true, veritable; sterling; attested, undisputed, rightful, legitimate, lawful, legal, valid; German echt; informal the real McCoy, the genuine article, the real thing, your actual, kosher, honest-to-goodness; Austral./NZ informal dinkum; rare simon-pure.
▷ANTONYMS fake, spurious.
2 *an authentic depiction of the situation*: **reliable**, dependable, trustworthy, authoritative, honest, faithful; accurate, exact, factual, true, truthful, veracious, true to life; informal straight from the horse's mouth; rare veridical.
▷ANTONYMS unreliable, inaccurate.

authenticate verb **1** *he must produce evidence which will authenticate his claim*: **verify**, validate, prove to be genuine, certify; substantiate, prove, be proof of, give proof of, corroborate, confirm, support, evidence, attest to, bear out, give credence to, back up; document.
2 *a mandate authenticated by an absolute majority of the popular vote*: **validate**, ratify, confirm, seal, sanction, endorse, guarantee.

authenticity noun **1** *the authenticity of the painting*: **genuineness**, originality; rightfulness, legitimacy, legality, validity, bona fides.
▷ANTONYMS spuriousness.
2 *some doubt has been cast on the authenticity of this account*: **reliability**, dependability, trustworthiness, truth, veracity, verity, faithfulness, fidelity, authoritativeness, credibility; accuracy, factualness; historicity; rare veridicality.
▷ANTONYMS unreliability, inaccuracy.

author noun **1** *modern Canadian authors*: **writer**, man/woman of letters, wordsmith; novelist, dramatist, playwright, screenwriter, scriptwriter, poet, essayist, biographer; journalist, columnist, reporter, correspondent; librettist, lyricist, songwriter; French littérateur; informal penman, penwoman, scribe, scribbler, pen-pusher.
2 *the author of the peace plan*: **originator**, creator, initiator, instigator, founder, father, prime mover, architect, engineer, designer, deviser, planner, inventor, maker, producer; cause, agent; literary begetter.

> *Word links* **author**
>
> **auctorial** relating to an author

authoritarian adjective *an authoritarian regime | his authoritarian manner*: **autocratic**, **dictatorial**, totalitarian, despotic, tyrannical, autarchic, draconian, absolute, arbitrary, oppressive, repressive, illiberal, undemocratic; disciplinarian, domineering, doctrinaire, dogmatic, overweening, overbearing, high-handed, bossy, peremptory, imperious, harsh, strict, severe, rigid, inflexible, unyielding.
▷ANTONYMS democratic, liberal; lenient, permissive.

▶ **noun** *the army's high command is dominated by authoritarians*: **autocrat**, despot, dictator, tyrant, absolutist; disciplinarian, martinet.
▷ANTONYMS liberal.

authoritative adjective **1** *authoritative information | an authoritative source*: **reliable**, dependable, trustworthy, good, sound, authentic, valid, well founded, attested, certified, verifiable; accurate, factual, from the horse's mouth.
▷ANTONYMS unreliable.
2 *the authoritative edition*: **definitive**, most reliable, best, most scholarly; classic; authorized, accredited, recognized, accepted, approved, sanctioned.
3 *his authoritative manner*: **self-assured**, assured, self-confident, confident, sure of oneself; **commanding**, imposing, masterful, magisterial, lordly, assertive, dogmatic, peremptory, arrogant, dominating, domineering, imperious, overbearing, bossy, authoritarian.
▷ANTONYMS timid, diffident.

authority noun **1** *he had absolute authority over his subordinates | a rebellion against those in authority*: **power**, jurisdiction, command, control, mastery, charge, dominance, dominion, rule, sovereignty, ascendancy, supremacy, domination; influence, sway, the upper hand, leverage, hold, grip; informal clout, pull, muscle, teeth; N. Amer. informal drag.
2 *military forces have the legal authority to arrest drug traffickers*: **authorization**, right, power, mandate, prerogative, licence; French carte blanche; Law, historical droit.
3 *the money was spent without parliamentary authority*: **authorization**, permission, consent, leave, sanction, licence, dispensation, assent, acquiescence, agreement, approval, seal of approval, approbation, endorsement, imprimatur, clearance; informal the go-ahead, the thumbs up, the OK, the green light, say-so; rare permit.
4 (**authorities**) *the plight of the refugees was acknowledged by the authorities*: **officials**, officialdom, the people in charge, the government, the administration, the establishment, the bureaucracy, the system; the police; informal the powers that be, the (men in) suits, Big Brother.
5 *he was an authority on the stock market*: **expert**, specialist, professional, pundit, oracle, past master, master, maestro, doyen, adept; guru, sage, scholar; connoisseur, aficionado, one of the cognoscenti; informal walking encyclopedia, bible, buff, boffin, ace, pro, whizz, wizard; Brit. informal dab hand; N. Amer. informal maven, crackerjack.
6 *the court cited a series of authorities supporting their decision*: **source**, reference, piece of documentation; citation, quotation, quote, excerpt, passage.
7 *I have it on good authority that you were there*: **evidence**, testimony, witness, attestation, sworn statement, declaration, word, avowal, deposition, profession.

authorization noun *they will require authorization from the Law Society or another regulator*: **permission**, consent, leave, sanction, licence, dispensation, warrant, clearance; assent, acquiescence, agreement, approval, seal of approval, approbation, endorsement, blessing, imprimatur, acceptance, rubber stamp, accreditation; authority, right, power, mandate; Latin nihil obstat; informal the go-ahead, the thumbs up, the OK, the green light, the nod, say-so; rare permit.
▷ANTONYMS refusal, prohibition.

> *Choose the right word* **authorization, permission, consent, leave**
>
> See **permission**.

authorize verb **1** *the government authorized further aircraft production*: **give permission for**, permit, sanction, allow, agree to, approve, give one's consent/assent to, consent to, assent to, accede to, countenance; license, legalize, make legal, legitimize, legitimatize; ratify, endorse, validate, accredit, warrant; informal give the green light to, give the go-ahead for, give the OK to, OK, give the thumbs up to; N. Amer. rare approbate.
▷ANTONYMS forbid, veto.

2 *the Commander-in-Chief authorized him to recruit a further six officers*: **give someone the authority**, give someone permission, mandate, commission, empower; entitle.

authorized adjective *authorized financial institutions | an authorized biography*: **approved**, recognized, sanctioned, commissioned; accredited, licensed, certified, warranted; official, lawful, legal, legitimate, licit.
▷ANTONYMS unofficial.

autobiography noun **memoirs**, life story, account of one's life, personal history; diary, journal.

autocracy noun **absolutism**, absolute power, totalitarianism, dictatorship, despotism, tyranny, monocracy, autarchy; dystopia.
▷ANTONYMS democracy.

autocrat noun **absolute ruler**, dictator, despot, tyrant, monocrat; authoritarian, absolutist.

autocratic adjective *an autocratic government | her autocratic management style*: **despotic**, tyrannical, oppressive, repressive; **dictatorial**, totalitarian, autarchic, absolute, all-powerful, arbitrary; undemocratic, one-party, monocratic; illiberal, domineering, doctrinaire, dogmatic, draconian, overweening, overbearing, bossy, high-handed, peremptory, imperious, harsh, strict, severe, rigid, inflexible, unyielding; dystopian.
▷ANTONYMS democratic, liberal.

> *Choose the right word* **autocratic, despotic, tyrannical**
>
> These words are all more or less critical descriptions of someone's exercise of power.
>
> **Autocratic** is used of a person in sole power (*the autocratic ruler of a vast territory*). It is also typically used to describe a *leader* or *director* or someone's *rule*, *style*, *leadership*, or *management*. *Autocratic* also implies a disregard of the welfare and wishes of the people being ruled and an unwillingness to share power (*autocratic, serf-ridden tsarist Russia*). It is the most technical and objective term of the three and is contrasted with *democratic*, but is also used more commonly than the other two words to describe the character of an ordinary person as well as a political leader (*any second now he would ring the doorbell in his usual autocratic, impatient manner*).
>
> **Despotic** is an emotionally loaded word, used of someone who not only holds great power but also exercises it cruelly and oppressively (*the cruel, corrupt, and despotic Shah*). The noun that it most commonly qualifies is *regime*, which itself has disapproving connotations.
>
> **Tyrannical** refers to cruel exercise of power by a group or individual who cannot be called to account (*he had been devastated by the oppression of the tyrannical landowner*). Nouns that it commonly qualifies include *government*, *master*, *regime*, *rule*, and *despot*.

autograph noun *fans pestered him for his autograph*: **signature**; informal moniker; N. Amer. informal John Hancock.
▶ verb *Jack autographed copies of his book*: **sign**, write one's signature on, sign one's name on.

automatic adjective **1** *automatic garage doors*: **mechanized**, mechanical, automated, push-button, preprogrammed, computerized, electronic, robotic, unmanned; self-activating, self-regulating, self-directing, self-executing.
▷ANTONYMS manual, hand-operated.
2 *an automatic reaction*: **instinctive**, involuntary, unconscious, reflex, knee-jerk, reflexive, instinctual, subconscious, unconditioned; **spontaneous**, impulsive, unthinking, unpremeditated, unintentional, unintended, unbidden, unwitting, inadvertent; mechanical; habitual; informal gut.
▷ANTONYMS conscious, intentional, deliberate.
3 *he is the automatic choice for the senior team*: **inevitable**, unavoidable, inescapable, necessary, ineluctable; certain, definite, undoubted, assured, obvious; mandatory, compulsory.

autonomous adjective *an autonomous republic*: **self-governing**, **independent**, sovereign, free, self-ruling, self-determining, autarchic; self-sufficient.

autonomy noun *Tatarstan demanded greater autonomy within the Russian Federation*: **self-government**, **independence**, self-rule, home rule, sovereignty, self-determination, freedom, autarchy; self-sufficiency, individualism.

autopsy noun **post-mortem**, PM, necropsy.

auxiliary adjective **1** *an auxiliary power source*: **additional**, supplementary, supplemental, extra, reserve, backup, emergency, fallback, spare, substitute, other; subsidiary, accessory, adjunct.
2 *auxiliary nursing staff*: **ancillary**, assistant, support, supporting, helping, assisting, aiding.
▶ noun *a nursing auxiliary*: **assistant**, helper, aide.

> *Word links* **auxiliary**
>
> **para-** related prefix, as in *paramedic*

avail verb **1** *guests paying by credit card can* ***avail themselves of*** *the express checkout service*: **use**, make use of, take advantage of, utilize, employ; resort to, have recourse to, turn to, look to.
2 *even if his arguments are correct, that cannot avail him in this case*: **help**, aid, assist, benefit, be of use to, be useful to, profit, be of advantage to, be of service to.
▶ noun
□ **to no avail** *he searched in several bookshops, but to no avail*: **in vain**, without success, unsuccessfully, vainly, with no result, fruitlessly, to no purpose; for nothing; archaic bootlessly.
▷ANTONYMS successfully.

available adjective **1** *refreshments will be available all afternoon | a few places are still available*: **obtainable**, accessible, to be had, ready for use, at hand, to hand, at one's disposal, at one's fingertips, within easy reach, handy, convenient; on sale, on the market, in stock, in season; untaken, unengaged, unused; informal up for grabs, yours for the asking, on tap, get-at-able, gettable; rare procurable.
▷ANTONYMS unavailable.
2 *hold the line, and I'll see if he's available*: **free**, unoccupied, not busy; present, in attendance; contactable.
▷ANTONYMS unavailable, busy, engaged.

avalanche noun **1** **snowslide**, snow-slip; rockslide, icefall; landslide, landslip.
2 *the publication of the book produced an avalanche of press comment*: **barrage**, volley; **flood**, deluge, torrent, tide, stream, storm, shower, spate, wave.
▷ANTONYMS trickle.

avant-garde adjective *her tastes were too avant-garde for her contemporaries*: **innovative**, **advanced**, innovatory, original, experimental, inventive, ahead of the times, new, forward-looking, futuristic, modern, ultra-modern, state-of-the-art, trendsetting, pioneering, progressive, groundbreaking, trailblazing, revolutionary; unfamiliar, unorthodox, unconventional, eccentric, offbeat, bohemian; N. Amer. left-field; informal go-ahead, way-out; rare new-fashioned, neoteric.
▷ANTONYMS conservative, reactionary.

avarice noun *he had a reputation for ruthlessness and avarice*: **greed**, acquisitiveness, cupidity, covetousness, avariciousness, rapacity, rapaciousness, graspingness, materialism, mercenariness; meanness, miserliness; informal money-grubbing, money-grabbing, an itching palm; N. Amer. informal grabbiness; rare Mammonism, pleonexia.
▷ANTONYMS generosity.

avaricious adjective **grasping**, acquisitive, covetous, greedy, rapacious, mercenary, materialistic, mean, miserly; informal money-grubbing, money-grabbing; N. Amer. informal grabby; rare pleonectic, Mammonish, Mammonistic.
▷ANTONYMS generous.

avenge verb *his determination to avenge the murder of his brother*: **take revenge for**, take vengeance for, exact retribution for, requite; pay someone back for, get even with someone for.

avenue noun **1** *tree-lined avenues*: **road**, street, thoroughfare, boulevard, way, broadway. See also **road**.
2 *three possible avenues of research suggested themselves*: **line**, path, direction, route; method, approach, course of action.

aver verb *he averred that he was innocent of the allegations*. See **declare** (sense 2).

average noun *the price was low compared with the average of the past 25 years*: **mean**, median, mode, midpoint, centre; norm, standard, rule, par; the general run.
□ **on average** *on average, I suppose we watch a couple of hours of television a night*: **normally**, usually, ordinarily, generally, generally speaking, in general, for the most part, in most cases, as a rule, typically; overall, by and large, on the whole, on balance.
▶ adjective **1** *the average temperature in May was 4°C below normal*: **mean**, median, medial, middle.
2 *a woman of average height | the average reader of a newspaper*: **ordinary**, standard, usual, normal, typical, regular, unexceptional.
3 *a very average director making very average movies*: **mediocre**, second-rate, uninspired, undistinguished, ordinary, commonplace, middle-of-the-road, mainstream, unexceptional, unexciting, unremarkable, unmemorable, indifferent, humdrum, nothing special, everyday, bland, run-of-the-mill, not very good, pedestrian, prosaic, lacklustre, forgettable, amateur, amateurish; acceptable, passable, all right, adequate, fair, middling, moderate, tolerable; N. Amer. garden-variety; informal OK, so-so, bog-standard, fair-to-middling, (plain) vanilla, nothing to write home about, nothing to get excited about, a dime a dozen, no great shakes, not so hot, not up to much; Brit. informal common or garden, not much cop, ten a penny; N. Amer. informal bush-league; N. Amer. & Austral./NZ informal jake; NZ informal half-pie.
▷ANTONYMS outstanding, exceptional.

averse adjective *many manufacturing firms remain* ***averse to*** *innovation and risk-taking*: **opposed to**, against, antipathetic to, hostile to, antagonistic to, unfavourably disposed to, ill-disposed to; resistant to; disinclined,

unwilling, reluctant, loath; informal anti, agin.
▷ANTONYMS keen.

aversion noun *their deep-seated* ***aversion to*** *the use of force*: **dislike of**, distaste for, disinclination, abhorrence, hatred, hate, loathing, detestation, odium, antipathy, hostility; disgust, revulsion, repugnance, horror; phobia; resistance, unwillingness, reluctance, avoidance, evasion, shunning; informal allergy; archaic disrelish.
▷ANTONYMS liking, inclination, desire.

avert verb **1** *she averted her head*: **turn aside**, turn away, turn to one side.
2 *an attempt to avert political chaos*: **prevent**, stop, avoid, nip in the bud; stave off, head off, ward off; forestall, preclude.

aviator noun dated See **pilot** (sense 1 of the noun).

avid adjective *an avid reader of science fiction*: **keen**, eager, enthusiastic, ardent, passionate, devoted, dedicated, fervent, fervid, zealous, fanatical, voracious, insatiable; wholehearted, earnest; Brit. informal as keen as mustard.
▷ANTONYMS apathetic, half-hearted.

> *Choose the right word* **avid, eager, keen, enthusiastic**
>
> See **eager**.

avidity noun **enthusiasm**, keenness, eagerness, avidness, ardour, fervour, passion, zeal, zealousness, fanaticism, voracity, voraciousness; appetite, hunger, thirst; rare fervency, ardency, passionateness.
▷ANTONYMS indifference, apathy.

avoid verb **1** *I avoid many of the situations that used to stress me*: **keep away from**, stay away from, steer clear of, circumvent, give a wide berth to, give something a miss, keep at arm's length, fight shy of.
▷ANTONYMS confront.
2 *by resigning today, he is trying to avoid responsibility for the political crisis*: **evade**, dodge, sidestep, skirt round, bypass; escape, run away from; informal duck, wriggle out of, cop out of, get out of; Brit. informal funk; Austral./NZ informal duck-shove; archaic decline.
▷ANTONYMS face up to.
3 *Guy jerked back to avoid a blow to the head*: **duck**, dodge, get out of the way of, body-swerve; Scottish & N. English jouk.
4 *you've been avoiding me all evening*: **shun**, stay away from, evade, keep one's distance from, hide from, elude; ignore; informal, dated give someone the go-by; archaic bilk.
▷ANTONYMS seek out.
5 *women planning to become pregnant should avoid drinking alcohol altogether*: **refrain from**, abstain from, desist from, forbear from, eschew.
▷ANTONYMS indulge.

avoidable adjective **preventable**, stoppable, avertible; escapable; needless, unnecessary.
▷ANTONYMS inescapable, inevitable.

avow verb *he avowed that the president had been fully aware of the situation*: **assert**, declare, state, maintain, aver, attest, swear, vow, insist; confess, admit; rare asseverate.

avowed adjective *an avowed golf fanatic*: **declared**, sworn, self-confessed, confessed, self-proclaimed, acknowledged, admitted, open, overt; known.

await verb **1** *Peter was at home, awaiting news*: **wait for**; expect, anticipate, look for, hope for.
2 *many dangers await them*: **be in store for**, lie ahead of, lie in wait for, be waiting for.

awake verb **1** *she awoke late the following morning*: **wake (up)**, awaken, stir, come to, come round, bestir oneself, show signs of life, return to the land of the living.
▷ANTONYMS fall asleep.
2 *the alarm awoke him at 7.30*: **wake (up)**, awaken, waken, rouse, arouse; informal give someone a shout; Brit. informal knock up.
3 *the authorities finally* ***awoke to*** *the extent of the problem*: **realize**, become aware of, become conscious of, become cognizant of, become mindful of; informal get wise to; rare cognize.
▶ adjective **1** *two hours later she was still awake*: **wakeful**, sleepless, wide awake, conscious; tossing and turning, restless, restive; archaic watchful; rare insomnolent.
▷ANTONYMS asleep.
2 *too few are* ***awake to*** *the dangers*: **aware of**, conscious of, cognizant of, mindful of, sensible of, alive to, alert to, sensitive to; archaic ware of.
▷ANTONYMS unaware, ignorant, oblivious.

awaken verb **1** *when she awakened, the sun was streaming through the windows | I was awakened at 2 a.m. by the sergeant*: **wake (up)**. See also **awake**.
▷ANTONYMS go to sleep, put to sleep.
2 *he had awakened strong emotions in her*: **arouse**, rouse, call/bring into being, draw/call forth, bring out, engender, generate, evoke, trigger, stir up, inspire, stimulate, excite, kindle, fire, touch off, spark off; revive; literary enkindle.
▷ANTONYMS allay.

awakening noun *the awakening of her real feelings for him*: **arousal**, rousing, triggering off, stirring up, kindling, stimulation, inspiration, birth; revival.

award verb *a 3.5 per cent pay rise was awarded to staff | the society awarded him a silver medal*: **give**, grant; **confer on**, present to, bestow on, gift with, furnish with, endow with, decorate with; accord, assign, apportion, allot, allocate, allow.
▶ noun **1** *the company's annual award for high-quality service*: **prize**, trophy, medal; reward, honours, decoration; informal gong.
2 *a £200,000 libel award*: **payment**, settlement, compensation, damages.
3 *under its Jazz Bursary Scheme, the Arts Council gave him an award of £1,500*: **grant**, scholarship; subsidy, subvention, endowment; Brit. bursary, bursarship.
4 *the award of an honorary doctorate*: **giving**, granting, conferment, conferral, presentation, bestowal.

aware adjective **1** *most people are* ***aware of*** *the dangers of sunbathing*: **conscious of**, acquainted with, informed of/about, apprised of, cognizant of, mindful of, sensible of, familiar with, conversant with, no stranger to, alive to, awake to, alert to, sensitive to; privy to; informal wise to, well up on, up to speed on, plugged into, in the know about, hip to; archaic ware of; rare seized of, recognizant of, regardful of.
▷ANTONYMS unaware, ignorant, oblivious.
2 *everyone needs to become more environmentally aware*: **well informed**, knowledgeable, up to date, enlightened; French au fait, au courant; informal clued up, genned up; Brit. informal switched-on; black English down.
▷ANTONYMS ignorant.

awareness noun *a growing public* ***awareness of*** *the need to protect the environment*: **consciousness**, recognition, realization, cognizance, perception, apprehension, understanding, grasp, appreciation; acknowledgement, knowledge; sensitivity to, sensibility to, insight into; familiarity with, acquaintance with.
▷ANTONYMS ignorance.

awash adjective **1** *the road was awash and impassable in places*: **flooded**, covered with water, under water; submerged, engulfed, submersed.
2 *the city was* ***awash with*** *journalists*: **inundated**, flooded, deluged, swamped, teeming, heaving, overflowing; overrun by, full of; informal knee-deep in.

away adverb **1** *she began to walk away*: **off**, from here, from there.
2 *stay indoors, away from the trouble*: **at a distance**, apart, isolated.
3 *Bernice pushed him away*: **aside**, off, to one side.
4 *we'll be away for two weeks*: **elsewhere**, abroad, not at home, not here, gone, absent; on holiday, on vacation.

> *Word links* **away**
>
> **ab-** related prefix, as in *abduct*
> **abs-** related prefix, as in *abscond*

awe noun *the sight filled me with awe*: **wonder**, wonderment, amazement, astonishment; admiration, reverence, veneration, respect; dread, terror, fear.
▷ANTONYMS contempt, indifference.
□ **be/stand in awe of** *the cast was in awe of Ned Beatty*: **revere**, worship, pay homage to, venerate, adulate, idolize, put on a pedestal, lionize, hero-worship, honour, love, respect.
▷ANTONYMS despise.

awed adjective *he spoke in an awed whisper*: **filled with wonder**, wonderstruck, awestruck, amazed, filled with amazement, astonished, filled with astonishment, lost for words, open-mouthed; reverential; terrified, afraid, fearful.

awe-inspiring adjective *an awe-inspiring sight*: **breathtaking**, amazing, stunning, stupendous, astonishing, awesome, extraordinary, incredible; magnificent, wonderful, spectacular, sublime, glorious, magical, dazzling, imposing, stirring, impressive; formidable, terrifying, fearsome; informal mind-boggling, mind-blowing, out of this world, sensational; literary wondrous; archaic awful.
▷ANTONYMS uninspiring, unimpressive.

awesome adjective *the scale of the mountains was awesome | an awesome achievement*: **breathtaking**, amazing, stunning, astounding, astonishing, awe-inspiring, stupendous, staggering, extraordinary, incredible, unbelievable; magnificent, wonderful, spectacular, remarkable, phenomenal, prodigious, miraculous, sublime; formidable, imposing, impressive; informal mind-boggling, mind-blowing, out of this world; literary wondrous; archaic awful.

awestruck adjective *Caroline was too awestruck by her surroundings to reply*: **awed**, filled with wonder, filled with awe, wonderstruck, amazed, filled with amazement, astonished, filled with astonishment, lost for words, open-mouthed; reverential; terrified, afraid, fearful.

awful adjective **1** *the place smelled awful*: **very unpleasant**, disgusting, nasty, terrible, dreadful, ghastly, horrid, horrible, vile, foul, abominable,

appalling, atrocious, horrendous, hideous, offensive, objectionable, obnoxious, frightful, loathsome, revolting, repulsive, repellent, repugnant, odious, sickening, nauseating, nauseous; informal gruesome, diabolical, yucky, sick-making, God-awful, gross, from hell, icky; Brit. informal grotty, beastly; N. Amer. informal hellacious, lousy; literary noisome; archaic disgustful, loathly.
▷ANTONYMS lovely, wonderful.
2 *I think it's an awful book*: **very bad**, poor, dreadful, terrible, frightful, atrocious, hopeless, inadequate, inferior, unsatisfactory, substandard, laughable, lamentable, execrable; informal crummy, pathetic, rotten, useless, woeful, lousy, appalling, abysmal, dire, poxy, God-awful; Brit. informal duff, chronic, rubbish, a load of pants; vulgar slang crap, shit, chickenshit; rare egregious.
▷ANTONYMS good, excellent.
3 *Ronnie's awful accident at the crossroads*: **serious**, grave, bad, terrible, dreadful, alarming, critical.
▷ANTONYMS slight, minor.
4 *you look awful—you should go and lie down*: **ill**, unwell, washed out, peaky; sick, queasy, nauseous, nauseated, green about the gills; faint, dizzy, giddy; Brit. off, off colour, poorly; informal rough, lousy, rotten, terrible, dreadful, crummy; Brit. informal grotty, ropy; Scottish informal wabbit, peely-wally; Austral./NZ informal crook; dated queer, seedy; rare peaked, peakish.
5 *I felt awful for being so angry with him*: **remorseful**, conscience-stricken, guilty, guilt-ridden, ashamed, chastened, contrite, sorry, full of regret, regretful, repentant, penitent, shamefaced, self-reproachful, apologetic.
6 archaic *the awful and majestic sights of nature*: **awe-inspiring**, awesome, impressive, amazing; dread, fearful.

awfully adverb **1** *an awfully nice man*: **very**, extremely, really, exceedingly, immensely, thoroughly, decidedly, terribly, frightfully, dreadfully, fearfully, exceptionally, uncommonly, remarkably, eminently, extraordinarily, most, positively, particularly; heartily, profoundly; N. English right; Scottish unco; N. Amer. quite; French très; informal terrifically, tremendously, desperately, devilishly, ultra, too ... for words, mucho, mega, seriously, oh-so, madly, majorly; Brit. informal jolly, ever so, dead, well, fair; N. Amer. informal real, mighty, awful, plumb, powerful; S. African informal lekker; informal, dated devilish, hellish; archaic exceeding, sore.
2 *we played awfully*: **very badly**, atrociously, terribly, dismally, dreadfully, appallingly, execrably, poorly, incompetently, inexpertly; informal abysmally, pitifully, crummily, diabolically, rottenly; rare egregiously.
3 informal, dated *thanks awfully for the tea*: **very much**, a lot; informal a million.

awhile adverb *stand here awhile*: **for a moment**, for a while, for a short time, for a little while; informal for a bit.

awkward adjective **1** *one of the most awkward jobs is painting a ceiling*: **difficult**, tricky; Brit. informal fiddly.
▷ANTONYMS easy, straightforward.
2 *the box was heavy and awkward to carry*: **cumbersome**, unwieldy, unhandy; informal a devil; vulgar slang a bugger, a bastard; rare cumbrous, lumbersome.
3 *I'm sorry to call at such an awkward time*: **inconvenient**, difficult, inappropriate, inopportune, unfortunate; archaic unseasonable.
▷ANTONYMS convenient.
4 *he had put her in a very awkward position*: **embarrassing**, uncomfortable, unpleasant, delicate, ticklish, tricky, sensitive, problematic, problematical, troublesome, perplexing, thorny, vexatious; humiliating, compromising; informal sticky, dicey, hairy, cringeworthy, cringe-making; Brit. informal dodgy; N. Amer. informal gnarly.
5 *she felt awkward alone with him*: **embarrassed**, self-conscious, uncomfortable, ill at ease, uneasy, tense, nervous, edgy, unrelaxed, strained; rare unquiet.
▷ANTONYMS relaxed, at ease.
6 *he was long-legged and rather awkward | his awkward movements*: **clumsy**, ungainly, uncoordinated, maladroit, graceless, ungraceful, inept, inelegant, unskilful, unhandy, gauche, gawky, gangling, blundering, lumbering, cloddish; wooden, stiff; coltish; informal clodhopping, ham-fisted, ham-handed, with two left feet, cack-handed; Brit. informal all thumbs, all fingers and thumbs; archaic lubberly.
▷ANTONYMS graceful, adroit.
7 Brit. *you're being damned awkward*: **unreasonable**, uncooperative, unhelpful, difficult, annoying, obstructive, unaccommodating, refractory, disobliging, contrary, perverse, tiresome, exasperating, trying; stubborn, obstinate; Scottish thrawn; informal cussed, pesky; Brit. informal bloody-minded, bolshie; N. Amer. informal balky; archaic contumacious, froward; rare renitent, pervicacious.
▷ANTONYMS amenable, cooperative.

awkwardness noun **1** *the gesture betrayed his momentary awkwardness*: **embarrassment**, self-consciousness, discomfort, discomfiture, uneasiness, edginess, tension, nervousness.
2 *the adolescent awkwardness of his angular body*: **ungainliness**, clumsiness, lack of coordination, gracelessness, inelegance, ineptness, gaucheness, gawkiness.

awning noun **canopy**, shade, sunshade, shelter, cover, covering; tarpaulin; Brit. blind, sunblind; technical velarium.

awry adjective **1** *I got the impression that something was awry*: **amiss**, wrong, not right; informal up.
2 *his wig awry, he gasped and coughed for air*: **askew**, crooked, lopsided, uneven, asymmetrical, to one side, off-centre, skewed, skew, misaligned; Scottish agley, squint, thrawn; informal cock-eyed; Brit. informal skew-whiff, wonky, squiffy.
▷ANTONYMS straight, symmetrical.

axe noun **hatchet**, cleaver; adze; tomahawk; Brit. chopper; historical battleaxe, poleaxe.
▶verb **1** *the show was axed last month as a result of poor ratings*: **cancel**, withdraw, drop, abandon, end, terminate, put an end to, discontinue; informal scrap, cut, junk, ditch, dump, give something the chop, pull the plug on, knock something on the head.
2 *500 staff were axed as part of a rationalization programme*: **dismiss**, give someone notice, make redundant, throw out, get rid of, lay off, let go, discharge; informal **sack**, fire, kick out, boot out, give someone the sack, give someone the boot, give someone the bullet, give someone the (old) heave-ho, give someone the elbow, give someone the push, give someone their marching orders, show someone the door; Brit. informal give someone their cards.

axiom noun **accepted truth**, general truth, dictum, truism, principle; proposition, postulate; maxim, saying, adage, aphorism; rare apophthegm, gnome.

axiomatic adjective *it was axiomatic that prices and interest rates should be kept down*: **self-evident**, unquestionable, undeniable; accepted, understood, given, granted; rare apodictic, indemonstrable.

axis noun **1** *the earth revolves on its axis once every 24 hours*: **centre line**, vertical, horizontal.
2 *the Anglo-American axis*: **alliance**, coalition, bloc, confederation, confederacy, union, league; agreement, treaty, pact, compact, entente, concordat.

axle noun **shaft**, spindle, rod, arbor, pin, pivot; mandrel.

azure adjective **sky-blue**, deep blue, bright blue, blue, ultramarine; literary cerulean; rare cyanic.

babble verb **1** *Betty babbled away, oblivious to the look on his face*: **prattle**, rattle on, gabble, chatter, jabber, twitter, go on, run on, prate, ramble, burble, blather, blether, blither, maunder, drivel, patter, yap, jibber-jabber; Scottish & Irish slabber; informal gab, yak, yackety-yak, yabber, yatter, yammer, blabber, jaw, gas, shoot one's mouth off; Brit. informal witter, rabbit, chunter, natter, waffle; N. Amer. informal run off at the mouth; Austral./NZ informal mag; archaic twaddle, clack, twattle.
2 *my father **babbled out** the truth*: **blurt out**, blab, reveal, divulge, let slip, let out, give away, come out with; informal spill.
3 *just out of sight a brook babbled gently*: **burble**, murmur, gurgle, purl, tinkle; literary plash.
▸ noun *her soft voice stopped his babble*: **prattle**, gabble, chatter, jabber, prating, rambling, blather, blether; gibbering, gibberish, drivel; informal gab, yak, yackety-yak, yabbering, yatter, twaddle; Brit. informal wittering, waffle, natter, chuntering; archaic clack, twattle.

babe noun **1** literary *a newborn babe*. See **baby**.
2 *just a babe in the world of business*: **ingénue**, innocent, babe in arms, greenhorn, novice, tyro, beginner.

babel noun *the babel of a furious crowd*: **clamour**, din, racket, confused noise, tumult, uproar, hubbub; babble, babbling, shouting, yelling, screaming; commotion, chaos, bedlam, pandemonium, confusion; Scottish & N. English stramash; informal hullabaloo; Brit. informal row; rare charivari.
▷ANTONYMS silence.

baby noun **1** *a newborn baby*: **infant**, newborn, child, tot, little one; Scottish & N. English bairn; informal sprog, tiny; literary babe, babe in arms; technical neonate.
2 *the baby of the family*: **youngest**, junior member; smallest, littlest.
3 informal *baby, please don't cry*: **darling**, sweetheart, dearest, dear; informal honey, sweetie, sugar, babe; archaic sweeting.
▸ adjective *baby carrots*: **miniature**, mini, little, small, small-scale, scaled-down, toy, pocket, midget, dwarf; Scottish wee; N. Amer. vest-pocket; informal teeny, teeny-weeny, teensy, teensy-weensy, weeny, itsy-bitsy, itty-bitty, eensy, eensy-weensy, tiddly, pint-sized, bite-sized; Brit. informal titchy; N. Amer. informal little-bitty.
▷ANTONYMS large.
▸ verb *her aunt babied her*: **pamper**, mollycoddle, spoil, cosset, coddle, indulge, overindulge, pet, wait on someone hand and foot, feather-bed, wrap in cotton wool, nanny; pander to; archaic cocker.

> *Word links* **baby**
>
> **infantile** relating to babies

babyish adjective **childish**, immature, infantile, juvenile, puerile, adolescent, silly, foolish, inane, jejune, naive.
▷ANTONYMS mature.

back noun **1** *they think she's broken her back*: **spine**, backbone, spinal column, vertebral column; technical dorsum, rachis.
2 *the back of the house*: **rear**, rear side, other side; Nautical stern.
▷ANTONYMS front.
3 *the back of the queue*: **end**, tail end, rear end, tail, far end; N. Amer. tag end.
▷ANTONYMS front, head.
4 *the back of a postcard*: **reverse**, reverse side, other side, underside; verso; informal flip side.
▷ANTONYMS front, face.
□ **behind someone's back** **secretly**, without someone's knowledge, on the sly, deceitfully, slyly, sneakily, covertly, surreptitiously, furtively.
□ **get/put someone's back up** *these kinds of questions tend to engage the other party, whereas assertions can put their backs up*: **annoy**, irritate, vex, make angry, make cross, anger, exasperate, irk, gall, pique, put out, displease, antagonize, get on someone's nerves, rub up the wrong way, ruffle, ruffle someone's feathers, make someone's hackles rise, raise someone's hackles; enrage, infuriate, madden, make someone's blood boil, drive to distraction, goad, provoke; informal aggravate, peeve, hassle, miff, rile, nettle, needle, get, get to, bug, hack off, get under someone's skin, get in someone's hair, get up someone's nose, put someone's nose out of joint, get someone's goat, give someone the hump, rattle someone's cage, drive mad/crazy, drive round the bend/twist, drive up the wall, make someone see red; Brit. informal wind up, nark, get across, get on someone's wick; N. Amer. informal tee off, tick off, burn up, rankle, ride, gravel; vulgar slang piss off; Brit. vulgar slang get on someone's tits; informal, dated give someone the pip, get someone's dander up; rare exacerbate, hump, rasp.
▷ANTONYMS please, gratify.
□ **the back of beyond** **the middle of nowhere**, the backwoods, the wilds, the hinterland, a backwater; Austral./NZ the back country, the backblocks, the booay; S. African the backveld, the platteland; N. Amer. informal the boondocks, the boonies, the tall timbers; Austral./NZ informal Woop Woop, beyond the black stump.
□ **turn one's back on** *in 1973, she turned her back on her career*: **abandon**, give up, have done with, throw up; reject, renounce, repudiate; informal quit, pack in, jack in.
▸ adverb **1** *she walked away without looking back | he pushed his chair back*: **backwards**, behind one, to one's rear, rearwards; away, off.
▷ANTONYMS forward.
2 *keep back from the roadside*: **away**, at a distance.
3 *her husband left her a few months back*: **ago**, earlier, previously, before, in the past.
▸ verb **1** *the project was backed by the English Tourist Board*: **sponsor**, finance, put up the money for, fund, subsidize, underwrite, promote, lend one's name to, be a patron of, act as guarantor of, support; informal foot the bill for, pick up the tab for; N. Amer. informal bankroll, stake.
2 *over 97 per cent backed the changes*: **support**, endorse, sanction, approve of, give one's blessing to, smile on, favour, advocate, promote, uphold, champion; vote for, ally oneself with, stand behind, side with, be on the side of, defend, take up the cudgels for; second; informal throw one's weight behind.
▷ANTONYMS oppose.
3 *he backed the horse at 33–1*: **bet on**, place a bet on, gamble on, stake money on.
4 *he backed slowly out of the garage*: **reverse**, move/drive backwards; backtrack, retrace one's steps.
▷ANTONYMS move forwards, advance.
□ **back away** *he took a step towards her and she hurriedly backed away*: **draw back**, step back, move away, back off, retreat, withdraw, pull back, give ground; shrink back, blench, cower, quail, quake.
▷ANTONYMS move forward.
□ **back down** *the government backed down under pressure from the House of Lords*: **give in**, concede defeat, surrender, yield, submit, climb down, concede, reconsider; backtrack, back-pedal.
□ **back out** *Coleman **backed out of** the deal*: **renege on**, go back on, withdraw from, pull out of, retreat from, fail to honour, abandon, default

b

on, repudiate; back-pedal; informal get cold feet about, chicken out of.
□ **back something up** *his statement was backed up by evidence from Mr Eric Bartlett*: **substantiate**, corroborate, confirm, support, bear out, endorse, bolster, reinforce, lend weight to; prove, verify, validate.
▷ANTONYMS contradict, undermine.
□ **back someone up** *her husband's bound to back her up*: **support**, stand by, give one's support to, side with, be on someone's side, take someone's side, take someone's part; vouch for; help, assist, aid.
▶ **adjective 1** *the back garden*: **rear**.
▷ANTONYMS front.
2 *the back row*: **end**, hind, hindmost, rearmost.
▷ANTONYMS front.
3 *the bird's back feathers*: **dorsal**, posterior.
▷ANTONYMS front.
4 *back copies of the journal*: **past**, old, previous, earlier, former, out of date.
▷ANTONYMS future.

Word links **back**

dorsal, lumbar relating to the back
supine lying on one's back
posterior further back

backbiting noun *there is a lot of backbiting in the world of television*: **malicious talk**, spiteful talk, slander, libel, defamation, abuse, character assassination, scandalmongering, disparagement, denigration, vilification, vituperation, calumny, revilement; insults, slurs, aspersions; informal bitching, bitchiness, cattiness, mud-slinging, bad-mouthing; Brit. informal slagging off, rubbishing.
▷ANTONYMS praise.

backbone noun **1** *an injured backbone*: **spine**, spinal column, vertebral column, vertebrae; back; technical dorsum, rachis.
2 *these firms are the backbone of our industrial sector*: **mainstay**, cornerstone, foundation, chief support, buttress, pillar.
3 *he has enough backbone to see us through this difficulty*: **strength of character**, strength of will, firmness of purpose, firmness, resolution, resolve, determination, fortitude, mettle, moral fibre, spine, steel, nerve, spirit, pluck, pluckiness, courage, courageousness, bravery, braveness, valour, manliness; informal guts, spunk, grit; Brit. informal bottle; vulgar slang balls.
▷ANTONYMS weakness.

Word links **backbone**

spinal, vertebral relating to the backbone

back-breaking adjective *a back-breaking task*: **gruelling**, arduous, strenuous, onerous, punishing, murderous, crushing, Herculean, demanding, exacting, taxing, formidable, exhausting, draining, laborious, burdensome, tough, stiff, uphill, heavy; informal killing; Brit. informal knackering; archaic toilsome.
▷ANTONYMS easy, effortless.

backchat noun Brit. informal *don't put up with any backchat from them*: **impudence**, impertinence, cheek, cheekiness, effrontery, sauciness, pertness, insolence, rudeness, rude retorts; answering back, talking back; informal mouth, lip; Scottish informal snash; N. Amer. informal sassiness, sass, smart mouth, back talk; rare malapertness, contumely, procacity.

backer noun **1** *£3 million was provided by the project's backers*: **sponsor**, investor, subsidizer, underwriter, promoter, financier, patron, benefactor, benefactress, guarantor, supporter, friend; informal angel; rare Maecenas.
2 *the backers of the proposition*: **supporter**, upholder, champion, defender, advocate, promoter, proponent, protagonist; seconder, second; N. Amer. booster.

backfire verb **1** *the engine backfired*: **misfire**.
2 *Bernard's plan* ***backfired on*** *him*: **rebound**, boomerang, come back, have an adverse effect; have unwelcome repercussions for, cause one to be hoist with one's own petard, be self-defeating, be counterproductive; fail, miscarry, go wrong; informal blow up in someone's face; archaic redound on.

background noun **1** *the house stands against a background of sheltering trees*: **surrounding(s)**, backdrop, backcloth, framework; scene.
2 *the figures of the saints are shown against a gold background*: **setting**, surround, framework.
3 *the airport may be seen* ***in the background***: **in the distance**, on the horizon.
▷ANTONYMS foreground, front.
4 *after that evening, she remained* ***in the background***: **behind the scenes**, out of the public eye, out of the spotlight, out of the limelight, backstage; inconspicuous, unobtrusive, unnoticed.
5 *a mix of students from many different backgrounds*: **social circumstances**, family circumstances; environment, class, culture, tradition; upbringing, rearing.
6 *her nursing background*: **experience**, record, history, past, training, education, grounding, knowledge; qualifications, credentials; Latin curriculum vitae.
7 *the political background*: **circumstances**, context, conditions, situation, environment, milieu, scene, scenario, framework, atmosphere; factors, influences; lead-up.

backhanded adjective *a backhanded compliment*: **indirect**, ambiguous, oblique, equivocal; **double-edged**, two-edged; tongue-in-cheek, sarcastic, ironic, sardonic.
▷ANTONYMS direct, straightforward.

backing noun **1** *the foreign secretary won the backing of opposition parties*: **support**, help, assistance, cooperation, aid; approval, commendation, endorsement, sanction, blessing; promotion, advocacy, championship, espousal.
2 *they had financial backing from local firms*: **sponsorship**, funding, financing, promotion, patronage; money, investment, funds, finance; grant, contribution, subsidy.
3 *a mix of slick vocals and sophisticated backing*: **musical accompaniment**, orchestration; harmony, obbligato.
4 *the fabric has a special backing for durability*: **lining**, interlining, facing, underlay, reinforcement.

backlash noun *the move provoked a furious backlash from union leaders*: **adverse reaction/response**, counteraction, counterblast, comeback, recoil; retaliation, reprisal; repercussions, reverberations, fallout, backwash.

backlog noun *a backlog of paperwork*: **accumulation**, logjam, pile-up, pile, heap, mountain, excess; arrears.

back-pedal verb **1** *although agreeing at first to the peace plan, they soon began to back-pedal*: **change one's mind**, change one's opinion, go into reverse, do an about-face, do a U-turn, shift one's ground, sing a different song, have second thoughts, reconsider, climb down; Brit. do an about-turn.
2 *the president* ***back-pedalled on*** *his promises to tax foreign companies heavily*: **renege on**, back down on, go back on, back out of, fail to honour, withdraw, backtrack on, take back, abandon, default on.

backslide verb **1** *there are many things that can cause slimmers to backslide*: **relapse**, lapse, regress, retrogress, revert to one's bad habits, weaken, lose one's resolve, give in to temptation, go astray, leave the straight and narrow, go down the primrose path.
▷ANTONYMS persevere.
2 *his only worry was that if she left things would backslide*: **degenerate**, deteriorate, slip, slide, fall off, revert to a former state, regress, retrogress; informal go downhill, go to pot, go to the dogs; rare recidivate.
▷ANTONYMS progress.

backslider noun **recidivist**, regressor; apostate, defector, deserter, turncoat, renegade, fallen angel.

backup noun *no police backup could be expected*: **help**, support, assistance, aid; reinforcements, reserves, additional resources.

backward adjective **1** *a backward look | a backward movement*: **reverse**; to/towards the rear, rearward, to/towards the back; behind one.
▷ANTONYMS forward.
2 *the decision was a backward step*: **retrograde**, retrogressive, regressive, unprogressive, for the worse, in the wrong direction, downhill, negative.
▷ANTONYMS progressive, forward-looking.
3 *an economically backward country*: **underdeveloped**, undeveloped, unsophisticated; primitive, benighted.
▷ANTONYMS advanced, sophisticated.
4 *he was not* ***backward in*** *displaying his talents*: **reticent about**, hesitant about, reluctant to, unwilling to, afraid to, loath to, averse to; shy about, diffident about, unconfident about, bashful about, timid about, coy about; informal backward in coming forward.
▷ANTONYMS confident, bold.
▶ **adverb** *the car rolled slowly backward*. See **backwards**.

Word links **backward**

retro- related prefix, as in *retrograde, retrocede*

backwards adverb **1** *Penny glanced backwards | he took a step backwards*: **towards the rear**, rearwards, backward, behind one.
▷ANTONYMS forwards.
2 *count backwards from twenty to ten*: **in reverse**, from the highest to lowest, in reverse order.
3 *his campaign is* ***going backwards***: **deteriorate**, decline, degenerate, worsen, get worse; informal go downhill, take a nosedive, go to pot, go to the dogs, hit the skids, go down the toilet, go down the tubes.
▷ANTONYMS improve.

backwash noun **1** *a ship's backwash*: **wake**, wash, slipstream, backflow; path, trail.
2 *the backwash of the Cuban missile crisis*: **repercussions**, reverberations, after-effects, aftermath, fallout; upshot, consequences, results, effects, by-products.

b

backwoods plural noun **the back of beyond**, the middle of nowhere, remote areas, the wilds, the hinterlands, a backwater; N. Amer. the backcountry, the backland; Austral. the outback, the bush, the backblocks, the booay; S. African the backveld, the platteland; informal the sticks; N. Amer. informal the boondocks, the boonies, the tall timbers; Austral./NZ informal Woop Woop, beyond the black stump.

bacteria plural noun **micro-organisms**, microbes, germs, bacilli, pathogens; aerobes, anaerobes; informal bugs.

> *Word links* **bacteria**
>
> **bacteriology** study of bacteria
> **bacteriophobia** fear of bacteria
> **bactericide** substance that kills bacteria

bad adjective **1** *bad workmanship*: **substandard**, poor, inferior, second-rate, second-class, unsatisfactory, inadequate, unacceptable, not up to scratch, not up to par, deficient, imperfect, defective, faulty, shoddy, amateurish, careless, negligent; **dreadful**, awful, terrible, abominable, frightful, atrocious, disgraceful, deplorable, hopeless, worthless, laughable, lamentable, miserable, sorry, third-rate, diabolical, execrable; incompetent, inept, inexpert, ineffectual; informal crummy, rotten, pathetic, useless, woeful, bum, lousy, ropy, appalling, abysmal, pitiful, God-awful, dire, poxy, not up to snuff, the pits; Brit. informal duff, chronic, rubbish, pants, a load of pants; vulgar slang crap, shit, chickenshit; rare egregious.
▸ANTONYMS good, excellent, skilled.
2 *the alcohol is having a bad effect on her health*: **harmful**, damaging, detrimental, undesirable, injurious, hurtful, inimical, dangerous, destructive, ruinous, deleterious; unhealthy, unwholesome.
▸ANTONYMS good, beneficial.
3 *she had heard about him and his dissolute, bad life | the bad guys*: **wicked**, sinful, immoral, evil, morally wrong, corrupt, base, black-hearted, reprobate, depraved, degenerate, dissolute, amoral; criminal, villainous, nefarious, iniquitous, dishonest, dishonourable, unscrupulous, unprincipled; informal crooked, bent, dirty; archaic dastardly.
▸ANTONYMS virtuous.
4 *Tilda! You bad girl!* **naughty**, badly behaved, disobedient, wayward, wilful, self-willed, defiant, unruly, insubordinate, undisciplined, unmanageable, uncontrollable, ungovernable, unbiddable, disruptive, rebellious, refractory, recalcitrant; **mischievous**, full of mischief, playful, impish, roguish, puckish, rascally, prankish, tricksy; informal brattish, scampish; Scottish informal gallus; archaic contumacious.
▸ANTONYMS well behaved.
5 *bad news*: **unpleasant**, disagreeable, unwelcome, unfortunate, unfavourable, unlucky, adverse, nasty; terrible, dreadful, awful, grim, distressing, regrettable; archaic or humorous parlous.
▸ANTONYMS good.
6 *a recession is a bad time to try and sell a business*: **inauspicious**, disadvantageous, adverse, difficult, inopportune, unpropitious, inappropriate, unsuitable, unfavourable, unfortunate, untoward; informal disastrous.
▸ANTONYMS good.
7 *a bad accident | a bad head injury*: **severe**, serious, grave, critical, grievous, acute, dreadful, terrible, awful, ghastly, dire, grim, frightful, shocking; life-threatening; Medicine peracute.
▸ANTONYMS minor, slight.
8 *the meat's gone bad*: **rotten**, off, decayed, decomposed, decomposing, putrid, putrefied, putrescent, mouldy, mouldering; sour, rancid, rank, unfit for human consumption; addled; maggoty, worm-eaten, wormy, flyblown; rare putrefactive, putrefacient.
▸ANTONYMS fresh.
9 *if you still feel bad, stay in bed*. See **ill**.
10 *a bad knee*: **injured**, wounded, diseased; Brit. informal gammy, knackered; Austral./NZ informal crook; dated game.
11 *George always felt bad after shouting at her*: **guilty**, conscience-stricken, remorseful, guilt-ridden, ashamed, chastened, contrite, sorry, full of regret, regretful, repentant, penitent, shamefaced, self-reproachful, apologetic.
▸ANTONYMS unrepentant.
12 *a bad cheque*: **invalid**, worthless; counterfeit, fake, false, spurious, fraudulent; informal bogus, phoney, dud.
13 *bad language*: **offensive**, vulgar, crude, foul, obscene, rude, coarse, smutty, dirty, filthy, indecent, indecorous; blasphemous, profane.
□ **not bad** *the bean casserole wasn't bad*: **all right**, quite good, good, adequate, acceptable, good enough, reasonable, fair, decent, average, tolerable, passable, middling, moderate, sufficiently good, fine; informal OK, so-so, fair-to-middling; N. Amer. & Austral./NZ informal jake.
▸ANTONYMS outstanding.

> *Word links* **bad**
>
> **caco-** related prefix, as in *cacophony, cacography*
> **dys-** related prefix, as in *dyspepsia, dysfunctional*

badge noun **1** *a name badge*: **pin**, breastpin, brooch; N. Amer. button.
2 *the badge of the Cheshire regiment*: **emblem**, crest, insignia, device, shield, escutcheon; trademark, logo.
3 *in places like Dallas, Stetsons have long been considered a badge of success*: **sign**, symbol, indication, indicator, signal, mark, token; hallmark, trademark.

badger verb *let me get on with it, instead of badgering me the whole time*: **pester**, harass, bother, plague, torment, hound, nag, chivvy, harry, keep on at, go on at, harp on at, keep after, importune, annoy, trouble; N. English mither; informal hassle, bug; Austral. informal heavy.

> *Word links* **badger**
>
> **boar** male
> **sow** female
> **cub** young
> **sett**, **earth** home
> **cete** collective noun

badinage noun *he engaged in badinage with his guests*. See **banter** (noun).

badly adverb **1** *the job had been badly done*: **poorly**, incompetently, ineptly, inexpertly, inefficiently, imperfectly, deficiently, defectively, unsatisfactorily, inadequately, incorrectly, faultily, shoddily, amateurishly, carelessly, negligently; awfully, terribly, dreadfully, abominably, atrociously, frightfully, miserably, wretchedly, lamentably, deplorably, dismally, execrably; informal abysmally, appallingly, crummily, diabolically, pitifully, woefully; rare egregiously.
▸ANTONYMS well.
2 *try not to think badly of me*: **unfavourably**, ill, critically, with disapproval, with disfavour.
3 *Anna knew she had been behaving badly*: **reprehensibly**, naughtily, mischievously.
4 *many of the animals had been badly treated*: **cruelly**, wickedly, unkindly, harshly, shamefully; unfairly, unjustly, wrongly, improperly.
5 *it's his own fault it turned out badly*: **unsuccessfully**, unfavourably, adversely, unfortunately, unhappily, unluckily.
6 *some of the victims are badly hurt*: **severely**, seriously, gravely, greatly, grievously, acutely, critically, dangerously.
▸ANTONYMS slightly.
7 *the house is badly in need of redecoration*: **very much**, greatly, intensely, desperately, exceedingly, painfully, sorely; informal seriously.

bad manners plural noun **rudeness**, discourtesy, discourteousness, impoliteness, incivility, unmannerliness, boorishness, uncouthness, vulgarity, ungentlemanly behaviour, unladylike behaviour, lack of social grace, lack of refinement.

bad-tempered adjective **irritable**, irascible, tetchy, testy, grumpy, grouchy, crotchety, in a (bad) mood, cantankerous, curmudgeonly, ill-tempered, ill-natured, ill-humoured, peevish, having got out of bed the wrong side, cross, as cross as two sticks; fractious, disagreeable, pettish, crabbed, crabby, waspish, prickly, peppery, touchy, scratchy, crusty, splenetic, shrewish, short-tempered, hot-tempered, quick-tempered, dyspeptic, choleric, bilious, liverish, cross-grained; informal snappish, snappy, chippy, on a short fuse, short-fused; Brit. informal shirty, stroppy, narky, ratty, eggy, like a bear with a sore head; N. Amer. informal cranky, ornery, peckish, soreheaded; Austral./NZ informal snaky; informal, dated waxy, miffy.
▸ANTONYMS good-humoured, affable.

baffle verb **1** *his reaction baffled her*: **perplex**, puzzle, bewilder, mystify, bemuse, confuse, confound, nonplus, disconcert, throw, set someone thinking; informal flummox, discombobulate, faze, stump, beat, fox, make someone scratch their head, be all Greek to, floor, fog; N. Amer. informal buffalo; rare wilder, gravel, maze, cause to be at a stand, pose, obfuscate.
▸ANTONYMS enlighten.
2 *her intention was to baffle their plans*: **thwart**, frustrate, foil, baulk, check, block, hinder, obstruct, bar, prevent, deflect, divert.
▸ANTONYMS further.

> *Choose the right word* **baffle, puzzle, perplex, mystify**
>
> See **puzzle**.

baffling adjective *I found his explanation baffling*: **puzzling**, **bewildering**, perplexing, mystifying, bemusing, confusing, unclear, difficult/hard to understand, beyond one, above one's head; mysterious, enigmatic, obscure, abstruse, unfathomable, inexplicable, incomprehensible, impenetrable, cryptic, opaque; archaic wildering.
▸ANTONYMS clear, comprehensible.

bag noun **1** *he carried a bag filled with sandwiches*: **receptacle**, container; **shopping bag**, string bag, sack; Brit. **carrier bag**, carrier; Scottish poke; N. Amer. dated keister.
2 *I dug around in my bag for my lipstick*: **handbag**, shoulder bag, clutch bag, evening bag, pochette; N. Amer. pocketbook, purse; Brit. informal bumbag; N. Amer. informal fanny pack; historical reticule, scrip.

b

3 *she began to unpack her bags*: **suitcase**, case, valise, portmanteau, holdall, carryall, grip, overnight bag, overnighter, flight bag, travelling bag, Gladstone bag, carpet bag; backpack, rucksack, knapsack, haversack, kitbag, duffel bag; satchel; (**bags**) luggage, baggage; Austral./NZ informal port.
▸ **verb 1** *he bagged three pheasants*: **catch**, capture, trap, snare, ensnare, land; **kill**, shoot, pick off.
2 *I got there early to bag a seat in the front row | he bagged seven League medals during his career*: **get**, secure, obtain, acquire; reserve, commandeer, grab, appropriate, take; win, achieve, attain; informal get one's hands on, get one's mitts on, nab, pick up, land, net.
3 *her trousers bagged at the knee*: **sag**, hang loosely, bulge, swell, balloon.

baggage noun **luggage**, suitcases, cases, bags, trunks; things, belongings, possessions, kit, equipment, effects, goods and chattels, impedimenta, paraphernalia, accoutrements, rig, tackle; informal gear, stuff, traps, dunnage; Brit. informal clobber; S. African informal trek.

baggy adjective *baggy corduroy trousers*: **loose-fitting**, loose, roomy, generously cut, full, ample, voluminous, billowing; oversized, shapeless, ill-fitting, tent-like, sack-like, bagging, sagging, saggy, slack, floppy, ballooning.
▷**ANTONYMS** tight.

bail noun *he has been released on bail*: **surety**, security, collateral, assurance, indemnity, indemnification; **bond**, guarantee, warranty, pledge; archaic gage, earnest.
▸ **verb**
▫ **bail out 1** *the state will not bail out loss-making industries*: **rescue**, save, relieve, deliver, redeem; finance, help (out), assist, aid, come to the aid of, give/lend a helping hand to; informal save someone's bacon, save someone's neck, save someone's skin. **2** *he levelled the plane long enough for his crew to bail out*: **eject**, parachute to safety. **3** *after the strong run, investors bailed out*: **sell up**, sell out, sell; **withdraw**, retreat, beat a retreat, quit, give up.

bait noun **1** *the fish let go of the bait*: **lure**, decoy, fly, troll, jig, plug, teaser.
2 *was she the bait to lure him into a trap?* **enticement**, lure, decoy, snare, trap, siren, carrot, attraction, draw, magnet, incentive, temptation, allurement, incitement, inducement; informal come-on.
▸ **verb** *the other boys revelled in baiting him*: **taunt**, goad, provoke, pick on, torment, torture, persecute, badger, plague, harry, harass, hound, tease, annoy, irritate, get someone's back up; informal hassle, needle, give someone a hard time, wind up, nark.

bake verb **1** *bake the fish for 15–20 mins*: **cook**, oven-bake, dry-roast, roast, spit-roast, pot-roast; rare oven.
2 *the surface of the earth has been baked into a crust*: **scorch**, burn, sear, parch, dry (up), desiccate, wither, shrivel, fire; N. Amer. broil.

balance noun **1** *I tripped and lost my balance*: **stability**, equilibrium, steadiness, footing.
▷**ANTONYMS** instability.
2 *the way to peace and some kind of personal balance*: **composure**, assurance, self-assurance, self-control, calmness, coolness, cool head; ease, tranquillity, serenity, imperturbability, impassivity, equanimity, nonchalance, confidence, self-confidence, self-possession, sureness; poise, dignity, aplomb, presence of mind, nerve, sangfroid, countenance, collectedness, suaveness, urbanity, elegance; informal cool, unflappability.
▷**ANTONYMS** nervousness.
3 *the obligations of political balance in broadcasting*: **fairness**, justice, impartiality, egalitarianism, equal opportunity; **parity**, equity, equilibrium, evenness, symmetry, equipoise, correspondence, uniformity, equality, equivalence, similarity, levelness, parallelism, comparability.
▷**ANTONYMS** imbalance.
4 *this stylistic development provides a balance to the rest of the work*: **counterbalance**, equipoise, counterweight, stabilizer, compensation, recompense, ballast, makeweight; archaic countercheck.
5 *a girl was weighing material on a balance*: **scale(s)**, weighing machine, weighbridge.
6 *the landlord demanded payment of the balance of the rent*: **remainder**, outstanding amount, rest, residue, difference, remaining part/number/quantity.
▫ **in the balance** *the aircraft's future is in the balance after this crash*: **uncertain**, unknown, undetermined, unsettled, unresolved, unsure, pending, in limbo, up in the air, at a turning point, critical, at a critical stage, at a crisis; debatable, open to question, in doubt; unpredictable, unforeseeable, incalculable, speculative, unreliable, untrustworthy, undependable, risky, chancy; informal dicey, hairy, iffy; Brit. informal dodgy.
▫ **on balance** *their allegation is, on balance, substantially correct*: **overall**, all in all, all things considered, taking everything into consideration/account, by and large, on average, for the most part, mostly, mainly, in the main, on the whole, in general, generally, generally speaking, largely, to a large extent, to a great degree.
▸ **verb 1** *she balanced the book on her head*: **steady**, stabilize; **poise**, level, prop, position.
2 *he balanced his radical remarks with more familiar declarations*: **counterbalance**, balance out, cancel, cancel out, offset, even out/up, counteract, counterpoise, countervail, equalize, neutralize, nullify, compensate for, make up for; rare equilibrize.
3 *a country's payments for imports and receipts for exports must balance*: **correspond**, agree, tally, match up, concur, coincide, be in agreement, be consistent, equate, be equal, harmonize, be in harmony, be compatible, be consonant, be congruous, be in tune, dovetail, correlate; informal square; N. Amer. informal jibe.
4 *it is a matter of balancing advantages against disadvantages*: **weigh**, weigh up, compare, evaluate, consider, assess, appraise, estimate.

balanced adjective **1** *a balanced view of the issues involved*: **fair**, equitable, just, unbiased, unprejudiced, objective, impartial, dispassionate, in proportion, that takes everything into account.
▷**ANTONYMS** partial.
2 *a balanced diet*: **mixed**, varied; **healthy**, sensible, well balanced.
▷**ANTONYMS** monotonous, unhealthy.
3 *she would come to terms with her predicament as any balanced individual would do*: **level-headed**, well balanced, well adjusted, sensible, practical, realistic, with one's/both feet on the ground, prudent, circumspect, pragmatic, wise, reasonable, rational, mature, stable, sane, even-tempered, commonsensical, full of common sense, judicious, sound, sober, businesslike, reliable, dependable; **calm**, cool, collected, composed, {cool, calm, and collected}, serene, relaxed, at ease, confident, equable, unworried, unmoved, unemotional, cool-headed, imperturbable; informal together, laid-back, unflappable.
▷**ANTONYMS** neurotic, panicky.

balcony noun **1** *the balcony of a villa*: veranda, terrace, portico, loggia.
2 *the applause was loudest in the balcony*: **gallery**, upper circle; informal the gods.

bald adjective **1** *he had a bald head*: **hairless**, bald-headed, smooth; shaven, depilated; Scottish & Irish baldy; technical glabrous; archaic bald-pated.
▷**ANTONYMS** hairy.
2 *the garden contained a few bald bushes*: **leafless**, bare, uncovered, stark.
▷**ANTONYMS** lush.
3 *such a bald statement requires some elaboration*: **plain**, simple, unadorned, unvarnished, unembellished, undisguised, unveiled, stark, severe, austere, brutal, harsh; **blunt**, direct, forthright, plain-spoken, straight, straightforward, candid, honest, truthful, realistic, true to life, frank, outspoken, downright, outright, straight from the shoulder, explicit, unequivocal, unambiguous, unexaggerated, unqualified; informal upfront, warts and all.
▷**ANTONYMS** exhaustive.

balderdash noun *his story was a load of balderdash*. See **nonsense** (sense 1).

balding adjective *a balding man*: **losing one's hair**, thinning, with receding hair; informal (going) thin on top.

baldness noun *he shaved his head to hide his baldness*: **hair loss**, hairlessness; Medicine alopecia, madarosis; archaic bald-patedness, glabreity.

bale[1] noun *a bale of cotton*: **bundle**, truss, bunch, pack, package, parcel, load.

bale[2] verb
▫ **bale out** See **bail out** at **bail**.

baleful adjective *she gave him a baleful stare*: **menacing**, threatening, unfriendly, hostile, antagonistic, evil, evil-intentioned, wicked, nasty, hate-filled, bitter, acrimonious, malevolent, malicious, malignant, malign, sinister, deadly, harmful, injurious, dangerous, noxious, virulent, pernicious, venomous, poisonous, vitriolic, vindictive; literary malefic, maleficent.
▷**ANTONYMS** benevolent, friendly.

balk verb See **baulk**.

ball[1] noun **1** *a cricket ball | a ball of wool*: **sphere**, globe, orb, globule, spherule, spheroid, ovoid; drop, droplet, bead; informal pill.
2 *a musket ball*: **bullet**, projectile, shot, pellet, slug, lead.
▫ **on the ball** informal *if you are really on the ball, you'll guess the killer*: **alert**, quick-witted, sharp, bright, quick, keen, perceptive, wide awake, responsive, agile, acute, astute; informal on one's toes, quick off the mark, quick on the uptake, all there, with it, bright-eyed and bushy-tailed.
▷**ANTONYMS** slow.

ball[2] noun *a fancy-dress ball*: **dance**, dinner dance, masked ball, masquerade, tea dance; N. Amer. hoedown, prom; French thé dansant; informal hop, disco, bop.
▫ **have a ball** informal **have a good time**, have a great time, have fun, have the time of one's life; enjoy oneself; informal let one's hair down, whoop it up, have a fling, make whoopee, push the boat out, paint the town red, live it up.

ballad noun *a ballad sung in the pubs of Ireland*: **song**, folk song, shanty, ditty, canzone; poem, tale, saga.

balloon noun **hot-air balloon**, fire balloon, barrage balloon, weather balloon; airship, dirigible, Zeppelin, Montgolfier; envelope, gasbag; informal blimp.
▸ **verb 1** *the slack sail was ballooning in the squall*: **swell (out)**, puff out/up, bulge (out), bag, belly (out), fill (out), billow (out); blow up, inflate, distend, expand, dilate.

▷ANTONYMS sag, flap.
2 *the company's debt has ballooned in the last five years*: **increase rapidly**, soar, rocket, shoot up, escalate, mount, surge, spiral, grow rapidly, rise rapidly; informal go through the ceiling, go through the roof, skyrocket.
▷ANTONYMS plummet.

ballot noun *the ballot for the leadership election*: **vote**, poll, election, referendum, plebiscite, general election, local election, popular vote, straw poll, show of hands; voting, polling.

ballyhoo noun informal *after all the ballyhoo, the film was a flop*: **publicity**, advertising, promotion, marketing, propaganda, push, puffery, build-up, boosting; **commotion**, fuss, ado, flurry, excitement, ferment, tumult, hurly-burly, hue and cry, bustle, hustle and bustle; informal hype, spiel, hoo-ha, hullabaloo, flap, song and dance, splash; Brit. informal kerfuffle, carry-on; NZ informal bobsy-die.

balm noun **1** *a skin balm for use after shaving*: **ointment**, lotion, cream, salve, liniment, embrocation, rub, gel, emollient, unguent, balsam, moisturizer; pomade, pomatum; technical demulcent, humectant; archaic unction.
▷ANTONYMS astringent; irritant.
2 *the murmur of the water can provide balm for troubled spirits*: **relief**, comfort, ease, consolation, cheer, solace; alleviation, mitigation, assuagement, healing.
▷ANTONYMS exacerbation.

balmy adjective *the balmy days of late summer*: **mild**, gentle, temperate, summery, calm, tranquil, clement, fine, pleasant, benign, soothing, soft; fragrant, scented, perfumed.
▷ANTONYMS harsh, wintry.

bamboozle verb informal *convicts could bamboozle prison chaplains into believing that they had reformed*. See **trick** (verb).

ban verb **1** *Norway banned all tobacco advertising in 1975*: **prohibit**, forbid, veto, proscribe, disallow, outlaw, make illegal, embargo, place an embargo on, bar, debar, block, stop, put a stop to, put an end to, suppress, interdict; Law enjoin, restrain.
▷ANTONYMS permit.
2 *Gary was banned from the playground*: **exclude**, banish, expel, eject, evict, drive out, force out, oust, remove, get rid of, drum out, thrust out, push out, turn out; prohibit from entering; informal boot out, kick out, give someone the boot; Brit. informal turf out.
▷ANTONYMS admit.
▶ noun **1** *a total ban on smoking*: **prohibition**, veto, proscription, embargo, bar, suppression, stoppage, interdict, interdiction, moratorium, injunction.
▷ANTONYMS permission.
2 *he faced a possible ban from international football*: **exclusion**, banishment, expulsion, ejection, eviction, removal.
▷ANTONYMS admission.

> *Choose the right word* **ban, forbid, prohibit**
>
> See **forbid**.

banal adjective *songs with banal, repeated words*: **trite**, hackneyed, clichéd, platitudinous, vapid, commonplace, ordinary, common, stock, conventional, stereotyped, predictable, overused, overdone, overworked, stale, worn out, time-worn, tired, threadbare, hoary, hack, unimaginative, unoriginal, derivative, uninspired, prosaic, dull, boring, pedestrian, run-of-the-mill, routine, humdrum; informal old hat, corny, played out; N. Amer. informal cornball, dime-store; rare truistic, bromidic.
▷ANTONYMS original.

banality noun **1** *the banality of most sitcoms*: **triteness**, platitudinousness, vapidity, pedestrianism, conventionality, predictability, staleness, unimaginativeness, lack of originality, lack of inspiration, prosaicness, dullness, ordinariness; informal corniness.
▷ANTONYMS originality.
2 *they exchanged banalities for a couple of minutes*: **platitude**, cliché, truism, banal phrase, trite phrase, hackneyed phrase, overworked phrase, stock phrase, commonplace, old chestnut, bromide.
▷ANTONYMS epigram, witticism.

band[1] noun **1** *she wore a scarlet band round her waist*: **belt**, sash, girdle, strap, tape, ring, hoop, loop, circlet, circle, cord, tie, string, thong, ribbon, fillet, strip; literary cincture.
2 *grey socks with a dark red band around their tops*: **stripe**, strip, streak, line, bar, belt, swathe, vein, thread, flash; technical stria, striation, lane.

band[2] noun **1** *a band of robbers*: **group**, gang, mob, pack, troop, troupe, company, party, bevy, crew, body, working party, posse; team, side, selection, line-up, array; gathering, crowd, horde, throng, assembly, assemblage; association, society, club, circle, fellowship, partnership, guild, lodge, order, fraternity, confraternity, brotherhood, sisterhood, sorority, union, alliance, affiliation, institution, league, federation, clique, set, coterie; squad, corps, cadre, contingent, detachment, unit, detail, patrol, army, cohort; informal bunch, gaggle; rare sodality.
2 *he plays the trumpet in a band*: **(musical) group**, pop group, ensemble, orchestra; in Spain & Spanish-speaking countries conjunto; informal combo.
▶ verb *local people **banded together** to fight the company*: **join (up)**, team up, join forces, pool resources, club together, get together, come together; collaborate, cooperate, work together, pull together; amalgamate, unite, form an alliance, form an association, combine, merge, affiliate, federate.
▷ANTONYMS split up.

bandage noun *she had a bandage on her foot*: **dressing**, covering, gauze, lint, compress, plaster, ligature, tourniquet, swathe, strap, sling; trademark Elastoplast, Band-Aid.
▶ verb *she bandaged my knee*: **bind**, bind up, dress, cover, wrap, swaddle, swathe, strap (up), plaster, put a plaster on.

bandit noun *most of the food aid was stolen by bandits*: **robber**, raider, mugger; brigand, freebooter, outlaw, desperado, hijacker, plunderer, pillager, looter, marauder, gangster, gunman, criminal, crook, thief; historical rustler, highwayman, footpad, reaver, snaphance; Scottish historical cateran, mosstrooper.

bandy[1] adjective *bandy legs*: **bowed**, curved, bent, crooked, misshapen, malformed; bow-legged, bandy-legged.
▷ANTONYMS straight.

bandy[2] verb **1** *£40,000 is the figure that has been **bandied about***: **spread (about/around)**, put about, toss about, discuss, rumour; circulate, disseminate, communicate, purvey, diffuse, broadcast, publicize, make public, make known, pass on, propagate, promulgate, announce, give out, repeat; literary bruit about/abroad.
2 *I'm not going to bandy words with you*: **exchange**, swap, trade, interchange, barter, reciprocate, pass back and forth, give and take.

bane noun *scurvy was the bane of seamen two centuries ago*: **scourge**, ruin, death, plague, ruination, destruction; torment, torture, menace, suffering, pain, distress, hardship, cross to bear, burden, thorn in one's flesh/side, bitter pill, affliction, calamity, despair, trouble, misery, woe, tribulation, misfortune, nuisance, pest, headache, trial, blight, curse, nightmare.

bang noun **1** *the door slammed with a bang*: **sharp noise**, crack, boom, clang, peal, clap, pop, snap, knock, tap, slam, bump, thud, thump, clunk, clonk, clash, crash, smash, smack; stamp, stomp, clump, clomp; report, explosion, detonation, shot; informal wham, whump.
2 *a nasty bang on the head*: **blow**, hit, punch, knock, thump, rap, bump, thwack, smack, crack, slap, welt, cuff, box; informal bash, whack, clobber, clout, clip, wallop, belt, tan, biff, bop, sock, lam, whomp; Brit. informal slosh; N. Amer. informal boff, bust, slug, whale; Austral./NZ informal dong; dated buffet.
▶ verb **1** *he began to bang the table with his fist*: **hit**, strike, beat, thump, hammer, knock, rap, pound, thud, punch, bump, thwack, smack, crack, slap, slam, welt, cuff, pummel, buffet; informal bash, whack, clobber, clout, clip, wallop, belt, tan, biff, bop, sock, lam, whomp; Brit. informal slosh; N. Amer. informal boff, bust, slug, whale; Austral./NZ informal dong.
2 *the door banged*: **go bang**, crash, smash, thud.
3 *guns were banging all around them*: **explode**, crack, go off with a bang, detonate, burst, blow up.
▶ adverb informal **1** *bang in the middle of town | the train arrived bang on time*: **precisely**, exactly, right, directly, immediately, squarely, just, dead; **promptly**, prompt, dead on, on the stroke of ..., on the dot of ...; sharp, on the dot; informal spot on, smack, slap, slap bang, plumb; N. Amer. informal on the button, on the nose, smack dab, spang.
2 *the machines will be bang up to date*: **completely**, absolutely, totally, entirely, wholly, fully, thoroughly, utterly, quite, altogether, one hundred per cent, downright, unqualifiedly, in all respects, unconditionally, perfectly, unrestrictedly, undisputedly, to the maximum extent; informal clean, plumb, dead.
3 *the minute something becomes obsolete, bang, it's gone*: **suddenly**, abruptly, immediately, instantaneously, instantly, in an instant, straight away, all of a sudden, at once, all at once, promptly, in a trice, swiftly; **unexpectedly**, without warning, without notice, on the spur of the moment; informal straight off, out of the blue, in a flash, like a shot, before you can say Jack Robinson, before you can say knife, in two shakes (of a lamb's tail).

bangle noun **bracelet**, wristlet, anklet, armlet, slave bangle; Sikhism kara.

banish verb **1** *he was banished for his crime*: **exile**, expel, deport, eject, expatriate, extradite, repatriate, transport; cast out, oust, drive away, evict, throw out, exclude, shut out, ban; Christianity excommunicate; in ancient Greece ostracize.
▷ANTONYMS admit; readmit.
2 *Chris's smile would banish any fear or suspicion*: **dispel**, dismiss, disperse, scatter, dissipate, drive away, drive off, chase away, rout, oust, cast out, shut out, get rid of, quell, allay, eliminate, dislodge.
▷ANTONYMS engender.

banister noun **handrail**, railing, rail, balustrade, banisters; balusters.

bank[1] noun **1** *the banks of Lake Michigan*: **edge**, side, embankment, levee, border, verge, boundary, margin, rim, fringe, fringes, flank, brink, perimeter, circumference, extremity, periphery, limit, outer limit, limits, bound, bounds; literary marge, bourn, skirt.

b

2 *a grassy bank*: **slope**, rise, incline, gradient, ramp, acclivity; mound, ridge, hillock, hummock, knoll, hump, barrow, tumulus, earthwork, parados, berm; elevation, eminence, prominence; bar, reef, shoal, shelf; accumulation, pile, heap, mass, drift; Welsh & West Midlands tump.
3 *a bank of switches*: **array**, row, line, tier, group, series; panel, console, board.
▸ **verb 1** *they **banked up** the earth around their hollow | snows have **banked up** under the evergreens*: **pile (up)**, heap (up), stack (up), make a pile of, make a heap of, make a stack of; accumulate, amass, assemble, put together.
2 *she **banked up** the fire*: **damp (down)**, smother, stifle.
3 *she taught him how to bank the plane | the aircraft banked gently*: **tilt**, **lean**, tip, slant, incline, angle, slope, list, camber, pitch, dip, cant, put/be at an angle.

> *Word links* **bank**
>
> **riparian**, **riverine** relating to a river bank

bank[2] **noun 1** *I paid the money into my bank*: **financial institution**; commercial bank, merchant bank, savings bank, finance company, finance house, lender, mortgagee; Brit. high-street bank, clearing bank, building society; N. Amer. savings and loan (association), thrift.
2 *a blood bank*: **store**, reserve, accumulation, stock, stockpile, inventory, supply, pool, fund, cache, hoard, deposit; storehouse, reservoir, repository, depository; rare amassment.
▸ **verb 1** *I banked the cheque*: **deposit**, pay in; clear; save, save up, keep, keep in reserve, lay by, put aside, set aside, put by, put by for a rainy day, hoard, cache, garner; informal stash (away), salt away, squirrel away.
2 *the family has **banked with** Coutts for generations*: **have an account at**, deposit one's money with, use, be a customer of, deal with, do business with.
□ **bank on** *the prime minister cannot bank on their support*: **rely on**, **depend on**, count on, place reliance on, bargain on, plan on, reckon on, calculate on, presume on; anticipate, expect, pin one's hopes on, hope for, take for granted, take as read, take on trust; be confident of, have (every) confidence in, place (one's) confidence in, be sure of, pin one's faith on, trust in; N. Amer. informal figure on.

banknote noun note; N. Amer. **bill**; N. Amer. informal greenback; N. Amer. & historical Treasury note; (**banknotes**) paper money.
▷**ANTONYMS** coin; plastic.

bankrupt adjective 1 *the company was declared bankrupt*: **insolvent**, bankrupted; failed, ruined, wiped out, gone under; in debt, owing money, in the red, in arrears; Brit. in administration, in receivership; informal bust, belly up, gone to the wall, on the rocks, broke, flat broke; informal, dated smashed; Brit. informal skint, stony broke, cleaned out, in Queer Street; Brit. informal, dated in Carey Street.
▷**ANTONYMS** solvent.
2 *this government is **bankrupt of** ideas*: **completely lacking in**, without, bereft of, exhausted of, devoid of, empty of, depleted of, destitute of, vacant of, bare of, denuded of, deprived of; in need of, wanting; informal minus, sans.
▷**ANTONYMS** teeming with.
▸ **noun** *he was soon a bankrupt*: **insolvent**, bankrupt person; debtor; pauper.
▸ **verb** *the strike nearly bankrupted the union*: **ruin**, make bankrupt, cause to go bankrupt, make insolvent, impoverish, reduce to penury/destitution, bring to ruin, bring someone to their knees, wipe out, break, cripple; rare pauperize, beggar.

bankruptcy noun *many companies were facing bankruptcy*: **insolvency**, liquidation, failure, (financial) ruin, ruination, debt, indebtedness; penury, beggary; Brit. administration, receivership; rare pauperdom.
▷**ANTONYMS** solvency.

banner noun 1 *students waved banners and chanted slogans*: **placard**, sign, poster, notice.
2 *banners fluttered above the waiting troops*: **flag**, standard, ensign, jack, colour(s), pennant, pennon, streamer, banderole; Brit. pendant; Nautical burgee; in ancient Rome vexillum; rare gonfalon, guidon, labarum.

banquet noun *local caterers were providing a farewell banquet*: **feast**, **dinner**, dinner party, formal meal, celebratory meal, treat; informal spread, blowout, binge; Brit. informal nosh-up, scoff, slap-up meal, tuck-in.
▷**ANTONYMS** snack.

banter noun *a brief exchange of harmless banter*: **repartee**, raillery, ripostes, sallies, swordplay, quips, wisecracks, crosstalk, wordplay; badinage, witty conversation, witty remarks, witticism(s), joking, jesting, jocularity, drollery; French bons mots; informal kidding, ribbing, joshing; rare persiflage.
▸ **verb** *a small crowd of sightseers were bantering with the guards*: **joke**, jest, pun, sally, quip; informal josh, wisecrack.

baptism noun 1 *the baptism ceremony*: **christening**, naming, immersion, sprinkling; rare lustration.
2 *this event constituted his baptism as a politician*: **initiation**, debut, introduction, inauguration, launch, beginning, rite of passage; French rite de passage; formal commencement.

baptize verb 1 *he was baptized at the parish church*: **christen**, immerse, sprinkle; rare lustrate.
2 *he had been baptized into the Roman Catholic Church*: **admit**, introduce, initiate, enrol, recruit, convert.
3 *he was baptized with the names John Cyril*: **name**, give a name to, call, dub, nickname; label, style, term, describe as, title, entitle, designate; rare clepe, denominate.

bar noun 1 *an iron bar*: **rod**, pole, stake, stick, batten, shaft, shank, rail, pale, paling, spar, strut, support, prop, spoke, crosspiece, girder, beam, boom.
2 *a bar of chocolate*: **block**, slab, cake, tablet, brick, loaf, wedge, lump, chunk, hunk, cube, ingot, nugget, piece.
3 *please purchase your drinks from the bar*: **counter**, table, buffet, stand.
4 *she went to her favourite bar on West 43rd Street*: **hostelry**, tavern, inn, wine bar, taproom; Brit. **pub**, public house, free house, tied house; Scottish howff; Canadian beer parlour; Austral./NZ hotel; Spanish cantina; German Bierkeller, Weinstube; informal watering hole; Brit. informal local, boozer; N. Amer. informal gin mill; historical alehouse, pot-house, taphouse, beerhouse; N. Amer. historical saloon.
5 *a bar to promotion*: **obstacle**, impediment, hindrance, obstruction, check, stop, block, hurdle, barrier, stumbling block, handicap, restriction, limitation.
▷**ANTONYMS** aid.
6 Brit. *members of the Bar*: **barristers**, advocates, counsel.
7 *he dredged a channel through the bar across the river mouth*: **sandbank**, shoal, bank, shallow, reef, ridge, ledge, shelf.
▸ **verb 1** *they have barred the door*: **bolt**, lock, fasten, padlock, secure, latch, deadlock, block, barricade, obstruct; Scottish & Irish sneck, snib.
▷**ANTONYMS** unbar.
2 *they were barred from entering the country*: **prohibit**, debar, preclude, forbid, ban, interdict, inhibit; exclude, keep out; obstruct, hinder, restrain, check, block, impede, stop; Law enjoin, estop.
▷**ANTONYMS** admit; accept.
▸ **preposition** *all the others, bar one, were killed*: **except (for)**, apart from, but (for), other than, besides, aside from, with the exception of, short of, barring, excepting, excluding, omitting, leaving out, save (for), saving; informal outside of.
▷**ANTONYMS** including.

barb noun 1 *the barb on the hook cut his finger badly*: **spike**, prong, point, projection, spur, thorn, needle, prickle, spine, quill, bristle, tine; technical spicule, spicula, spiculum, spinule.
2 *he ignored the barbs from his critics*: **insult**, sneer, jibe, cut, cutting remark, shaft, affront, slap in the face, slight, rebuff, brickbat, slur, scoff, jeer, taunt; (**barbs**) abuse, disparagement, scoffing, scorn, spite, sarcasm, goading, ridiculing, derision, mockery; informal dig, put-down.

barbarian noun *the city was besieged by barbarians*: **savage**, brute, beast, wild man/woman, troglodyte; ruffian, lout, thug, vandal, hoodlum, hooligan, rowdy; boor, oaf, ignoramus, philistine, vulgarian, yahoo; informal clod, clodhopper, roughneck; Brit. informal yobbo, yob, lager lout, oik; Austral./NZ informal hoon.
▸ **adjective** *the barbarian hordes*: **savage**, uncivilized, barbaric, barbarous, primitive, heathen, wild, brutish, Neanderthal; thuggish, loutish, uncouth, coarse, rough, boorish, oafish, vulgar, gross, philistine, uneducated, uncultured, uncultivated, benighted, unsophisticated, unrefined, unpolished, ill-bred, ill-mannered; informal yobbish; archaic rude.
▷**ANTONYMS** civilized.

barbaric adjective 1 *the regime's barbaric crimes were exposed after the war was over*: **brutal**, barbarous, brutish, bestial, savage, vicious, fierce, ferocious, wicked, cruel, nasty, ruthless, remorseless, merciless, villainous, murderous, heinous, nefarious, monstrous, base, low, low-down, vile, inhuman, infernal, dark, black, black-hearted, fiendish, hellish, diabolical, ghastly, horrible.
▷**ANTONYMS** benevolent.
2 *he tore the raw chicken apart with barbaric strength*: **savage**, barbarian, barbarous, primitive, heathen, wild, brutish, Neanderthal; thuggish, loutish; uncouth, coarse, rough, boorish, oafish, vulgar; archaic rude.
▷**ANTONYMS** civilized.

barbarity noun 1 *the barbarity of slavery*: **brutality**, brutalism, cruelty, bestiality, barbarism, barbarousness, savagery, viciousness, fierceness, ferocity, wickedness, nastiness, ruthlessness, remorselessness, mercilessness, villainy, murderousness, heinousness, nefariousness, monstrousness, baseness, vileness, inhumanity, blackness, fiendishness, black-heartedness, hellishness, ghastliness, horror.
▷**ANTONYMS** benevolence.
2 *the barbarities of the last war*: **atrocity**, act of brutality, act of savagery, evil, crime, outrage, offence, abomination, obscenity, enormity, wrong.
3 *beyond the empire lay barbarity*: **heathendom**, barbarianism, barbarism, barbarousness, primitiveness, wildness; philistinism, benightedness, unsophisticatedness, lack of civilization; archaic rudeness.
▷**ANTONYMS** civilization.

barbarous adjective See **barbaric**.

barbecue noun **1** *there was an evening barbecue*: **meal cooked outdoors**, ... roast; N. Amer. cookout; S. African braaivleis; NZ hangi; informal BBQ; Austral. informal barbie.
2 *she bought a barbecue for the garden*: **grill**, rotisserie; N. Amer. brazier; in Japan hibachi.
▸ verb *they barbecued some steaks*: **cook outdoors**, grill, spit-roast; N. Amer. broil, charbroil.

barbed adjective **1** *barbed wire*: **jagged**, hooked, spiky, spiked, spined, spiny, prickly, thorny, scratchy, bristly, bristled, briary, brambly, sharp, pointed; technical spinose, spinous.
2 *a barbed remark*: **hurtful**, wounding, cutting, biting, stinging, mean, spiteful, nasty, rude, cruel, vicious, unkind, unfriendly, snide, pointed, hateful, ill-natured, bitter, venomous, poisonous, mordant, acid, acerbic, acrimonious, astringent, caustic, sharp, scathing, hostile, rancorous, malicious, malevolent, evil-intentioned, baleful, vindictive, vengeful, vitriolic, splenetic, malign, malignant, pernicious, bilious; informal bitchy, catty; literary malefic, maleficent.
▷ANTONYMS kindly, generous.

> *Word toolkit* **barbed**
>
> See **spiky**.

bard noun archaic or literary *the words of the song are by our national bard*: **poet**, versifier, verse-maker, rhymester, rhymer, sonneteer, lyricist, lyrist, elegist; laureate; balladeer; literary swan; derogatory poetaster; historical troubadour; archaic rhymist, maker; rare metricist, ballad-monger, idyllist, Parnassian, poeticule.

bare adjective **1** *he was bare from the waist up*: **naked**, unclothed, undressed, uncovered, stripped, with nothing on, in a state of nature, disrobed, unclad, undraped, exposed; nude, in the nude, stark naked; French au naturel; informal without a stitch on, in one's birthday suit, in the raw, in the altogether, in the buff, as naked as the day one was born, in the nuddy, mother naked; Brit. informal starkers; Scottish informal in the scud, scuddy; N. Amer. informal bare-assed, buck naked; Austral. informal bollocky; Brit. vulgar slang bollock-naked.
▷ANTONYMS clothed.
2 *a bare room*: **empty**, emptied, unfurnished, vacant, clear, cleared, free, stark, austere, spartan, unadorned, unembellished, unornamented, unfussy, plain.
▷ANTONYMS furnished, embellished.
3 *bare floorboards*: **uncovered**, uncarpeted, unpainted, unvarnished; stripped; polished, sealed.
4 *a cupboard **bare of** food*: **empty of**, emptied of, without, lacking, devoid of, bereft of, wanting, deprived of, destitute of, free from.
▷ANTONYMS containing.
5 *a bare landscape*: **barren**, bleak, exposed, desolate, stark, arid, desert, denuded, lunar; treeless, forestless, without vegetation, defoliated; unsheltered, unprotected, unshielded; rare unwooded.
▷ANTONYMS lush.
6 *Herodotus did not record just the bare facts*: **straightforward**, plain, simple, basic, pure, essential, fundamental, stark, bald, cold, hard; truthful, realistic, true to life; brutal, harsh; explicit, unequivocal, unambiguous, unexaggerated, unadorned, unembellished, undisguised, unveiled, unvarnished, unqualified; informal warts and all.
7 *the bare minimum | a bare majority*: **mere**, no more than, no better than, just a, only a, simple, sheer, very, basic; slim, slight, slender, paltry, skimpy, minimum, trifling.
▷ANTONYMS comfortable.
▸ verb *he bared his arm*: **uncover**, strip, lay bare, undress, unclothe, denude, unveil, unmask; expose, expose to view, reveal; display, put on display, put on show, exhibit.
▷ANTONYMS cover.

> *Choose the right word* **bare, naked, nude**
>
> See **naked**.

barefaced adjective *a barefaced lie*: **flagrant**, blatant, glaring, obvious, undisguised, unconcealed, overt, open, transparent, patent, evident, manifest, palpable, unmistakable; **shameless**, unabashed, unashamed, without shame, impudent, insolent, audacious, unembarrassed, unblushing, brazen, brass-necked, brash, bold, unrepentant; archaic arrant.

barely adverb *we barely got home in time*: **hardly**, scarcely, just, only just, narrowly, by the skin of one's teeth, by a hair's breadth, by a very small margin, by the narrowest of margins, by a nose; almost not; informal by a whisker.
▷ANTONYMS easily.

bargain noun **1** *the Government made some kind of bargain with the Opposition*: **agreement**, arrangement, understanding, deal; contract, pact, compact, covenant, concordat, treaty, entente, accord, concord, protocol, convention; pledge, promise, engagement; transaction, negotiation.
2 *this binder is a bargain at £1.98*: **good buy**, cheap buy; (good) value for money, surprisingly cheap; informal snip, steal, giveaway.
▷ANTONYMS rip-off.
□ **into the bargain** *I'll tell you another thing into the bargain*: **also**, as well, in addition, additionally, besides, furthermore, moreover, yet, on top (of that), over and above that, as a bonus, as an extra, to boot, for good measure; N. Amer. in the bargain.
▸ verb *he bargained with the Council to rent the stadium*: **haggle**, barter, negotiate, discuss terms, hold talks, deal, wheel and deal, trade, traffic; N. Amer. dicker; formal treat; archaic chaffer, palter.
□ **bargain for/on** *this was more than we had bargained for*: **expect**, anticipate, be prepared for, allow for, plan for, reckon with, take into account/consideration, contemplate, imagine, envisage, foresee, predict, look for, hope for, look to; **count on**, rely on, depend on, bank on, plan on, reckon on, calculate on, be sure of, trust in, take for granted, take as read; N. Amer. informal figure on.

barge noun **lighter**, canal boat, flatboat; Brit. narrowboat, wherry; N. Amer. scow.
▸ verb *he barged his way to the front of the queue*: **push**, shove, force, elbow, shoulder, jostle, bludgeon, bulldoze, muscle.
□ **barge in** *I'm sorry for barging in*: **burst in**, break in, butt in, cut in, interrupt, intervene, intrude, encroach; gatecrash; informal horn in.

bark[1] noun *the bark of a dog*: **woof**, yap, yelp, bay; growl, snarl, howl.
▸ verb **1** *the dog barked*: **woof**, yap, yelp, bay; growl, snarl, howl, whine.
2 *'Okay, outside!' he barked*: **say/speak brusquely**, say/speak abruptly, say/speak angrily, snap, snarl, growl; **shout**, bawl, cry, yell, roar, bellow, thunder; N. Amer. informal holler.

bark[2] noun *the bark of a tree*: **rind**, skin, peel, sheath, covering, outer layer, coating, casing, crust; cork; technical cortex, integument, bast.
▸ verb *he barked his shin on a tree stump*: **scrape**, graze, scratch, abrade, scuff, rasp, skin, rub something raw; cut, lacerate, chafe, strip, flay, wound; technical excoriate.

> *Word links* **bark**
>
> **corticate** relating to bark

barmy adjective Brit. informal *I think that's a barmy idea*. See **foolish**.

barn noun **outbuilding**, shed, outhouse, shelter; stable, mews, stall, pound, sty, coop; Dutch barn, byre; SW English linhay; archaic grange, garner.

baron noun **1** historical *the French supported the barons against King John*: **noble**, nobleman, aristocrat, peer, lord.
2 *a press baron*: **magnate**, tycoon, mogul, captain of industry, nabob, grandee, mandarin; industrialist, proprietor, entrepreneur, executive, chief, leader; informal big shot, bigwig, honcho; N. Amer. informal big wheel; derogatory fat cat.
▷ANTONYMS small fry.

baroque adjective **1** *the baroque exuberance of his printed silk shirts*: **ornate**, fancy, very elaborate, over-elaborate, curlicued, extravagant, rococo, fussy, busy, ostentatious, showy, wedding-cake, gingerbread.
2 *a baroque prose style*: **flowery**, florid, flamboyant, high-flown, high-sounding, magniloquent, grandiloquent, orotund, rhetorical, oratorical, bombastic, laboured, strained, overwrought, overblown, overdone, convoluted, turgid, inflated; informal highfalutin, purple; rare tumid, pleonastic, euphuistic, aureate, Ossianic, fustian, hyperventilated.
▷ANTONYMS plain.

barrack verb Brit. & Austral./NZ *Bob Dylan was barracked for using electric instruments*: **jeer**, heckle, taunt, abuse, shout at/down, boo, hiss, interrupt.
▷ANTONYMS cheer, applaud.

barracks plural noun **garrison**, camp, encampment, depot, billet, quarters, fort, cantonment, guardhouse; Spanish cuartel; Nautical, informal stone frigate; archaic, informal lobster box; rare casern.

barrage noun **1** *the artillery began to lay down a barrage*: **bombardment**, gunfire, cannonade, battery, blast, broadside, salvo, volley, fusillade; storm, hail, shower, cascade, rain, stream, blitz; shelling, wall/curtain/barrier of fire.
2 *a barrage of criticism*: **abundance**, mass, superabundance, plethora, profusion; **deluge**, stream, storm, torrent, onslaught, flood, spate, tide, avalanche, hail, burst, blaze; outburst, outpouring.
3 *a barrage across the River Usk*: **dam**, weir, barrier, dyke, defence, embankment, wall, obstruction, gate, sluice.

barrel noun **cask**, keg, butt, vat, tun, tub, drum, tank, firkin, hogshead, kilderkin, pin, pipe, barrique; Spanish solera; historical puncheon, tierce.

barren adjective **1** *barren land*: **unproductive**, infertile, unfruitful, sterile, arid, desert, waste, desolate, uncultivatable; impoverished.
▷ANTONYMS fertile, productive.
2 archaic *a barren woman*: **infertile**, sterile, childless; technical infecund.
▷ANTONYMS fertile.
3 *a barren exchange of courtesies*: **pointless**, futile, worthless, profitless, valueless, unrewarding, purposeless, useless, vain, aimless; uninteresting,

b

boring, dull, drab, dry, arid, flat, lifeless, uninspiring, unstimulating, stale, prosaic, hollow, empty, vacuous, vapid.
▷ANTONYMS stimulating, fruitful.

barricade noun *a brick lorry was overturned and used as a barricade*: **barrier**, obstacle, blockade, bar, fence, obstruction, roadblock, bulwark, stockade, rampart, palisade, hurdle, protection, defence.
▸verb *they barricaded the building*: **blockade**, obstruct, close up, bar, block off, shut off/in, fence in, seal up, defend, protect, fortify, strengthen.

barrier noun 1 *police erected barriers to control the crowd*: **fence**, railing, barricade, hurdle, bar, blockade, roadblock; fencing.
2 *a barrier to international trade*: **obstacle**, obstruction, hurdle, stumbling block, bar, block, impediment, hindrance; snag, catch, drawback, hitch, handicap, deterrent, complication, difficulty, problem, disadvantage, baulk, curb, check, stop; informal fly in the ointment, hiccup, facer; Brit. informal spanner in the works; N. Amer. informal monkey wrench in the works; literary trammel; archaic cumber.

barring preposition *barring accidents, the whole team should be fit for Saturday*: **except for**, with the exception of, excepting, if there is/are no, bar, discounting, short of, apart from, but for, other than, aside from, excluding, omitting, leaving out, save for, saving; informal outside of.

barrister noun **advocate**, lawyer, professional pleader, counsel, Queen's Counsel, QC, defending counsel, prosecuting counsel; N. Amer. attorney, counselor(-at-law); informal brief; Brit. historical serjeant-at-law; (**barristers**) Brit. the Bar.

barter verb 1 *peasants with a surplus of food could barter it for vital equipment*: **trade**, **swap**, trade off, exchange, give in exchange, change, traffic, sell.
2 *you can barter for souvenirs in the flea market*: **haggle**, bargain, negotiate, discuss terms, hold talks, deal, wheel and deal, trade, traffic; N. Amer. dicker; formal treat; archaic chaffer, palter.
▸noun *an economy based on barter*: **trading**, trade, exchange, swapping, trafficking, business, commerce, buying and selling, dealing; haggling, negotiation.

base[1] noun 1 *the base of the tower*: **foundation**, bottom, foot, support, prop, stay, stand, pedestal, plinth, rest, bed, substructure.
▷ANTONYMS top.
2 *early learning will provide a sound base for what follows*: **basis**, bedrock, foundation, core, essence, essential, nitty-gritty, basics, starting point, key component, fundamental, root(s), heart, backbone, theory, principle, rationale; source, origin, spring, well head, fountainhead, fount.
3 *he used the hut as a base for his search*: **headquarters**, centre, starting point, camp, site, station, settlement, post.
4 *add a few drops of the aromatic oil to a vegetable oil base*: **medium**, vehicle, carrier.
▸verb 1 *the legend is based on fact*: **found**, build, construct, form, establish, ground, root; use as a basis; rest, hinge; emanate from, derive from, spring from, stem from, originate in, have its origin in, can be traced back to.
2 *the company was based in London*: **locate**, station, situate, post, position, place, install, deploy, site, establish, garrison.

base[2] adjective *some of these struggles have been inspired by base motives*: **sordid**, improper, low, mean, bad, wrong, evil, wicked, iniquitous, immoral, sinful; unscrupulous, unprincipled, unseemly, unsavoury, shoddy, squalid, vile, foul, vulgar, tawdry, cheap, low-minded, debased, degenerate, depraved, corrupt, reprobate, dissolute, dishonest, dishonourable, disreputable, despicable, discreditable, contemptible, petty, ignominious, ignoble, shameful, wretched, scandalous, infamous, abhorrent, abominable, disgusting.
▷ANTONYMS good, lofty.

baseless adjective *the accusations were found to be baseless*: **groundless**, unfounded, unsubstantiated, unproven, unsupported, uncorroborated, untested, unconfirmed, unverified, unattested, unjustified, unwarranted, foundationless, ill-founded, without basis, without foundation, not backed up by evidence; speculative, conjectural, idle, vain, unsound, unreliable, questionable, misinformed, misguided, spurious, specious, fallacious, erroneous, fabricated, untrue, trumped-up.
▷ANTONYMS well founded, proven.

basement noun **cellar**, vault, crypt, undercroft, underground room, catacomb; garden flat, sub-basement; Brit. lower ground floor; Scottish dunny; Brit. dated below stairs.

baseness noun *the baseness of which humankind is capable*: **meanness**, **sordidness**, evil, wickedness, iniquity, iniquitousness, immorality, sin, wrong; unscrupulousness, unseemliness, unsavouriness, shoddiness, squalidness, vileness, foulness, vulgarity, tawdriness, cheapness, low-mindedness, debasement, degeneracy, depravity, corruption, reprobation, dissolution, dishonesty, dishonour, disreputableness, contemptibility, pettiness, ignominy, wretchedness, infamy; rare turpitude.
▷ANTONYMS nobility.

bash informal verb *she bashed him across the knuckles with her stick*: **strike**, hit, beat, thump, slap, smack, batter, pound, pummel, thrash, rap, buffet, hammer, bang, knock; informal wallop, belt, whack, clout, clip, clobber, bop, biff, sock, deck, swipe, lay one on.
□ **bash into** *they bashed into one another*: **collide with**, hit, crash into, run into, bang into, smash into, knock into, bump into, meet head-on.
▸noun 1 *he got a bash on the head with a golf club*: **blow**, rap, hit, knock, bang, slap, crack, thump, tap, clip; informal clout, whack, wallop.
2 *Harry's birthday bash*. See **party**.
3 Brit. *she'll have a bash at anything*. See **attempt**.

bashful adjective *many men are bashful about discussing their feelings*: **shy**, reserved, diffident, retiring, self-conscious, coy, demure, reticent, reluctant, shrinking, timid, timorous, meek; hesitant, apprehensive, nervous, insecure, doubting, wary, unconfident, inhibited, faint-hearted; embarrassed, shamefaced, sheepish.
▷ANTONYMS bold, confident.

> *Choose the right word* **bashful, shy, diffident, timid**
>
> See **shy**[1].

basic adjective 1 *the basic principles of criminal law | basic human rights*: **fundamental**, rudimentary, primary, principal, cardinal, chief, elementary, elemental, root; central, pivotal, critical, key, focal, salient, staple; essential, quintessential, vital, necessary, indispensable, foundational, intrinsic, underlying, ingrained.
▷ANTONYMS secondary, unimportant.
2 *she got a basic salary plus a commission*: **lowest**, lowest-level, bottom, starting, ground, undermost; without commission.
3 *all the rooms have basic cooking facilities*: **plain**, simple, unsophisticated, straightforward, adequate, unadorned, undecorated, unornamented, without frills; spartan, sparse, stark, severe, austere, limited, meagre, rudimentary, patchy, sketchy, minimal; modest, ordinary, unpretentious, unostentatious, unfussy, homely, homespun; rough, rough and ready, rough-hewn, crude, makeshift; restrained, muted; informal bog-standard.
▷ANTONYMS elaborate.

> *Choose the right word* **basic, fundamental**
>
> *Basic* and *fundamental* are synonymous in many contexts and are both used to describe *principles*, *concepts*, *understanding*, *research*, and *rights*.
>
> Something described as **basic** is seen as a necessary minimum, to which further elaborations may or may not be added. The *basic concept* or *basic design* of something is the essential core of what may be a more complex idea or design, identified for the purpose of better understanding. In examples like *a plain, basic, rock-bottom hatchback* or *teaching basic camera skills*, *basic* denotes a necessary minimum which can then be improved upon or elaborated upon for purposes of luxury or proficiency. This is illustrated by the fact that *basic*, rather than *fundamental*, is more likely to be used with the following nouns: *necessity*, *training*, *information*, and *ingredient*.
>
> **Fundamental** derives from Latin *fundamentum* 'foundation'. Something that is *fundamental* to something else is essential to it, determining its nature. So physics might be called a *fundamental* aspect of the curriculum if it influences and shapes some or all of the other topics taught, but *basic* if it merely provides an elementary educational grounding. A *fundamental* flaw, on the other hand, is one which impairs the whole structure; other nouns which are typically used with *fundamental* include: *change*, *importance*, and *question*.

basically adverb *his disposition is basically peaceful*: **fundamentally**, primarily, principally, chiefly, essentially, elementally, firstly, predominantly; above all, first of all, most of all, first and foremost, in essence, at bottom, at heart; mostly, for the most part, in the main, mainly, on the whole, by and large, substantially, in substance; intrinsically, inherently; French au fond; informal at the end of the day, when all is said and done, when you get right down to it.

basics plural noun informal *having learnt the basics of dinghy sailing, the next stage is to join a sailing club*: **fundamentals**, essentials, rudiments, principles, first principles, foundations, preliminaries, groundwork; essence, basis, core, kernel, nub, marrow, meat, crux, bedrock; facts, hard facts, practicalities, realities; Latin sine qua non; informal nitty-gritty, brass tacks, nuts and bolts, ABC.

basin noun 1 *she poured water into the basin*: **bowl**, dish, pan, pot; container, receptacle, vessel.
2 *the loch is cupped in a shallow basin among low hills*: **valley**, hollow, gully, gorge, ravine, bed, channel, dip, depression, concavity, trough.

basis noun 1 *the factual basis for his criticism*: **foundation**, support, base, footing; reasoning, rationale, defence; reason, grounds, justification, rationalization, motive, motivation, cause.
2 *the White Paper formed the basis of the Consumer Credit Act*: **starting point**, base, point of departure, beginning, premise; fundamental point/principle, principal constituent, main ingredient, cornerstone, core, heart, thrust, essence, kernel, nub, underpinning, groundwork.
3 *those who are studying on a part-time basis*: **footing**, condition, status,

position; **arrangement**, system, method, procedure, way.

bask verb **1** *I sat on the bank, basking in the warm sunshine*: **laze**, lie, lounge, relax, sprawl, loll; sunbathe, sun oneself, warm oneself.
2 *they were still* ***basking in*** *the glory of success*: **revel**, luxuriate, wallow, delight, take pleasure, rejoice, glory, indulge oneself; enjoy, relish, savour, lap up; informal get a kick out of, get a thrill out of, get a charge from.

basket noun *a basket of flowers*: **receptacle**, container, holder, vessel, box, case; wickerwork box, hamper, creel, pannier, punnet, trug.

bass adjective *a bass drum*: **deep-toned**, deep-pitched, deep, low-pitched, low-toned, low, full-toned, resonant, sonorous, powerful, rumbling, booming, resounding; baritone.
▷ANTONYMS high.

bastard noun **1** archaic *he had fathered a bastard*: **illegitimate child**, child born out of wedlock; dated love child, by-blow; archaic natural child/son/daughter.
2 informal *the director's an arrogant bastard*: **scoundrel**, villain, rogue, rascal, brute, animal, weasel, snake, monster, ogre, wretch, devil, good-for-nothing, reprobate, wrongdoer, evil-doer; Spanish picaro; informal scumbag, pig, swine, louse, hound, cur, rat, beast, son of a bitch, s.o.b., low life, skunk, nasty piece of work, ratbag, wrong 'un; Brit. informal git, toerag, scrote; Irish informal spalpeen, sleeveen; N. Amer. informal fink, rat fink; W. Indian informal scamp; Austral./NZ informal dingo; informal, dated cad, heel, rotter, bounder, bad egg, bad lot, dastard, knave, stinker, blighter; archaic blackguard, miscreant, varlet, vagabond, rapscallion, whoreson; vulgar slang sod, bugger, shit, fucker; N. Amer. vulgar slang fuck, motherfucker, mofo, mother.
▸ adjective **1** archaic *a bastard child*: **illegitimate**, born out of wedlock; archaic natural.
2 *a bastard language*: **hybrid**, alloyed; adulterated, impure, inferior.

bastardize verb *he spoke franglais, bastardizing both languages*: **adulterate**, corrupt, contaminate, weaken, dilute, spoil, taint, pollute, foul, defile, debase, degrade, devalue, depreciate, distort; formal vitiate.

bastion noun **1** *he had fortified the stronghold with ditches and bastions*: **rampart**, bulwark, parapet, fortification, buttress, outwork, projection, breastwork, redoubt, barbican, stockade, palisade; rare bartizan.
2 *the last bastion of male-only suffrage in Europe*: **stronghold**, bulwark, defender, support, supporter, guard, protection, protector, defence, prop, mainstay.

batch noun *a batch of fairy cakes*: **group**, quantity, lot, bunch, mass, cluster, raft, set, collection, bundle, series, number; consignment, shipment; pack, crowd, band; accumulation, assemblage, aggregate, aggregation, conglomeration.

bath noun **1** *the bedrooms have their own bath and shower*: **bathtub**, tub, hot tub; hip bath, sitz bath; whirlpool bath, sauna, steam bath, Turkish bath, pool; trademark jacuzzi; archaic slipper bath; in ancient Greece & Rome thermae; rare balneal.
2 *she had a quick bath and got dressed*: **wash**, soak, dip, shower, douche, soaping, sponging, toilet; formal or humorous ablution.
▸ verb *he would bath the baby and put her to bed*: **bathe**, give/have/take a bath, wash, clean, soak, shower, douche, soap, freshen up; literary lave; formal or humorous perform one's ablutions.

> *Word links* **bath**
>
> **balneal, balneary** relating to a bath

bathe verb **1** *she bathed and went down to dinner*. See **bath** (verb).
2 *occasionally I bathed in the local swimming pool*: **swim**, go swimming, take a dip, dip, splash around.
3 *his arm was bathed and the wound was lanced*: **cleanse**, clean, wash, rinse, wet, moisten; soak, immerse; disinfect.
4 *the room was suddenly bathed in light*: **suffuse**, envelop, permeate, cover, pervade, wash, saturate, imbue, fill, load, impregnate, inform, steep, colour; literary mantle.
▸ noun *we would lie together in the sun after a bathe*: **swim**, dip, dive, plunge, paddle.

bathetic adjective *the show begins unpromisingly with a bathetic comedy*: **anticlimactic**, disappointing, disillusioning; **mawkish**, sentimental.

bathing costume noun Brit. **swimsuit**, bathing suit, bathing dress, swimming trunks, trunks, swimwear, bikini; Brit. swimming costume; informal swimming togs, cossie; Austral./NZ informal bathers.

bathos noun *his epic poem has passages of almost embarrassing bathos*: **anticlimax**, let-down, disappointment, disillusionment; **mawkishness**, sentimentality; informal comedown.

baton noun **1** *the conductor stopped the orchestra with a tap of his baton*: **stick**, rod, staff, wand, bar.
2 *riot policemen swinging batons*: **truncheon**, club, cudgel, bludgeon, stick, bat, mace; N. Amer. nightstick, blackjack; in Ireland shillelagh; Brit. informal cosh.

battalion noun **1** *an infantry battalion*: **unit**, regiment, brigade, force, garrison, division, squadron, squad, company, section, detachment, contingent, legion, corps, troop, group; in ancient Rome cohort.
2 *a battalion of women promoting the latest perfumes*: **crowd**, army, mob, throng, horde, swarm, multitude, herd, host, mass, drove, large number.

batten[1] noun *two pieces of hardboard, joined with timber battens*: **bar**, bolt, clamp, rail, shaft; board, strip.
▸ verb *Stephen was busy* ***battening down*** *all the shutters with planks of wood*: **fasten**, fix, secure, clamp, clasp, bolt, rivet, lash, make fast, nail down, seal, tether.

batten[2] verb
□ **batten on** *demons who batten on the helpless*: **flourish at the expense of**, thrive at the expense of, fatten at the expense of, prosper at the expense of, gain at the expense of, be a parasite on.

batter verb **1** *he battered his opponent into submission*: **pummel**, pound, rain blows on, buffet, belabour, thrash, beat up, abuse; hit, strike, beat, smack, assault, attack, thump, lash, aim blows at; informal whack, clout, wallop, bash, clobber, bop, biff, sock, deck, plug, knock about/around, knock into the middle of next week, beat the living daylights out of, give someone a good hiding, lay into, lace into, do over, rough up.
2 *the storm had severely battered the pier*: **damage**, injure, hurt, harm, impair, mar, spoil; destroy, demolish, crush, shatter, smash, ruin; informal total, trash.

battered adjective **1** *a battered wife*: **beaten**, assaulted, thrashed, hit, thumped; **abused**, maltreated, ill-treated, mistreated, misused, victimized, downtrodden, tyrannized.
2 *a battered blue van*: **damaged**, **shabby**, run down, worn out, falling to pieces, falling apart, dilapidated, rickety, ramshackle, crumbling, decayed, antiquated, superannuated, the worse for wear, on its last legs.

battery noun **1** *her car had a flat battery*: **cell**, accumulator, power unit.
2 *anti-aircraft missile batteries*: **gun emplacement**, artillery unit; (**batteries**) artillery, cannonry, ordnance, heavy weapons, heavy weaponry, guns, cannons.
3 *a battery of equipment to monitor blood pressure*: **array**, set, bank, group, row, line, line-up, raft, collection, assortment.
4 *the paediatrician ran a battery of tests*: **series**, sequence, range, set, cycle, chain, string, progression, succession.
5 *I'll have the police on you for assault and battery*: **violence**, assault, mugging; grievous bodily harm, GBH, actual bodily harm, ABH; **beating**, striking, thumping, thrashing, bashing; aggression.

battle noun **1** *the battle raged throughout the night*: **fight**, conflict, armed conflict, clash, struggle, skirmish, engagement, affray, fray, encounter, confrontation; contest, meeting, collision, duel; tussle, scuffle, melee, fracas; war, campaign, crusade; fighting, warfare, combat, action, hostilities; informal scrap, dogfight, shoot-out.
▷ANTONYMS truce, peace.
2 *a legal battle to overturn a music licence ban*: **conflict**, clash, contest, competition, struggle; disagreement, argument, dispute, controversy, debate; dissension, altercation, strife.
▸ verb **1** *he has been* ***battling against*** *illness*: **fight**, combat, contend with; resist, withstand, stand up to, put up a fight against, confront; war, feud; struggle, strive, campaign, work, toil.
▷ANTONYMS give up, give in.
2 *Mark* ***battled his way*** *back to the bar*: **scramble**, struggle, labour; fight, elbow, push.

battleaxe noun **1** *a severe blow from a battleaxe*: **poleaxe**, axe, pike, halberd, tomahawk, war mattock, mace.
2 informal *his mother was a right old battleaxe*: **harridan**, dragon, crone, witch, hag, gorgon, ogress, hellcat, harpy, tartar, martinet, termagant, virago, fury; shrew, nag; informal old bat, old bag, bitch; archaic scold; rare Xanthippe.

battle cry noun **1** *the battle cry of the Imperial Army*: **war cry**, war whoop, rallying call/cry, cry.
2 *'equal pay for equal work' was a battle cry of the feminist movement*: **slogan**, motto, watchword, catchphrase, catchword, byword, shibboleth.

battlefield noun *the battlefields of the Great War*: **battleground**, front, battle front, battle lines, field of operations, field of battle, combat zone, theatre, theatre/arena of war, battle stations; historical lists.

battlement noun *the castle had seven towers and high battlements*: **castellation**, parapet, rampart, balustrade, wall, bulwark, barbican, bastion; fortification, breastwork, crenellation, circumvallation, outwork; in ancient Rome vallum; rare bartizan.

batty adjective informal *she has gone completely batty*. See **mad** (sense 1).

bauble noun *gift-shop baubles*: **trinket**, knick-knack, ornament, toy, novelty, curiosity, gimmick, plaything, trifle, frippery, gewgaw, gimcrack, bagatelle, bibelot, furbelow; informal whatnot; Brit. informal doodah, doobry; N. Amer. informal tchotchke, tsatske; archaic folderol, whim-wham, kickshaw, bijou, gaud.

baulk verb **1** *sensitive gardeners who* ***baulk at*** *using pesticides*: **eschew**, resist, refuse to, be unwilling to, draw the line at, be reluctant to, draw back from, flinch from, shrink from, shy from, recoil from, quail at, demur

from, hesitate over, scruple to, take exception to, not like to, hate to, jib at; scorn, disdain.
▷ANTONYMS accept.
2 *they were baulked by traffic*: **impede**, obstruct, thwart, hinder, prevent, check, stop, curb, halt, bar, block, forestall, frustrate, stall, baffle, foil, defeat, beat, counteract, head off.
▷ANTONYMS assist.

bawdy adjective *they told bawdy jokes*: **ribald**, indecent, risqué, racy, rude, spicy, suggestive, titillating, naughty, improper, indelicate, indecorous, off colour, earthy, broad, locker-room, Rabelaisian; pornographic, obscene, vulgar, crude, coarse, gross, lewd, dirty, filthy, smutty, unseemly, salacious, prurient, lascivious, licentious, X-rated, scatological, near the bone, near the knuckle; erotic, sexy, sexual; informal blue, raunchy, nudge-nudge; euphemistic adult.
▷ANTONYMS clean, innocent.

bawl verb 1 *'Come on, Simon!' he bawled*: **shout**, call out, cry out, cry, yell, roar, bellow, screech, scream, shriek, howl, whoop, bark, growl, snarl, bluster, vociferate, trumpet, thunder; informal yammer; N. Amer. informal holler.
▷ANTONYMS whisper.
2 *the children continued to bawl*: **cry**, sob, weep, shed tears, wail, blubber, snivel, whimper, whine, howl, squall; informal blub; Scottish informal greet; rare ululate.
▸noun *he addressed the class in a terrifying bawl*: **shout**, yell, cry, roar, bellow, screech, scream, howl, whoop; N. Amer. informal holler.
▷ANTONYMS whisper.
□ **bawl someone out** informal *the Brigadier had been bawling him out*: **reprimand**, rebuke, scold, admonish, reprove, upbraid, chastise, chide, censure, castigate, lambaste, berate, lecture, criticize, take to task, read the Riot Act to, give a piece of one's mind to, haul over the coals; informal tell off, give someone a telling-off, dress down, give someone a dressing-down, pitch into, lay into, lace into, blow up at, give someone an earful, give someone a roasting, give someone a rocket, give someone a rollicking; Brit. informal have a go at, carpet, tear someone off a strip, give someone what for, let someone have it; N. Amer. informal chew out, ream out; Brit. vulgar slang bollock, give someone a bollocking.
▷ANTONYMS compliment.

bay[1] noun *the ships were anchored in the bay*: **cove**, inlet, estuary, indentation, natural harbour, gulf, basin, fjord, ria, sound, arm, bight, firth, anchorage; Scottish (sea) loch; Irish lough.

bay[2] noun *there is a bay in the far wall of the living room*: **alcove**, recess, niche, nook, cubbyhole, opening, hollow, cavity, corner, indentation, booth; apse; inglenook.

bay[3] verb 1 *a jackal baying at the moon*: **howl**, bark, yelp, yap, cry, growl, bellow, roar, clamour, snarl; rare ululate.
2 *the crowd* ***bayed for*** *an encore*: **clamour**, shout, call, press, yell, scream, shriek, roar; **demand**, insist on, urge, claim, make a claim for.
▸noun *the bloodhounds' heavy bay*: **baying**, howl, howling, bark, barking, cry, crying, growl, growling, bellow, bellowing, roar, roaring, clamour, clamouring; rare ululation.
□ **at bay** *they lit smoky fires to keep the mosquitoes at bay*: **at a distance**, away, off, aside, at arm's length.

bayonet noun *a man armed with a bayonet*: **blade**, knife, sword, spear, lance, pike, javelin, shaft, harpoon.
▸verb *stragglers were bayoneted where they fell*: **stab**, pierce, spear, knife, gore, spike, stick, impale, run through, transfix, prick, puncture, gash, slash.

bazaar noun 1 *a Turkish bazaar*: **market**, market place, mart, exchange; Arabic souk.
2 *the church bazaar*: **fête**, fair, jumble sale, sale, bring-and-buy sale, car boot sale, carnival; fund-raiser, charity event; N. Amer. tag sale; Dutch kermis.

be verb 1 *there was this boy who lived next door*: **exist**, have being, have existence; live, be alive, have life, breathe, draw breath, be extant, be viable.
2 *what theatres will there be for them to visit?* **be present**, be around, be available, be near, be nearby, be at hand.
3 *the trial is tomorrow*: **occur**, happen, take place, come about, arise, crop up, transpire, fall, materialize, ensue; literary come to pass, befall, betide.
4 *Pat was on the sofa in the living room*: **be situated**, be located, be found, be present, be set, be positioned, be placed, be installed.
5 *after she'd been there a couple of hours she ordered a drink*: **remain**, stay, wait, linger; hold on, hang on; last, continue, survive, endure, persist, prevail, obtain.
6 *I'm at college*: **attend**, go to, be present, take part; frequent, haunt, patronize.
7 *tickets are £15*: **cost**, be priced at, sell for, be valued at, fetch, come to; informal set one back, go for.
8 *one and one is two*: **amount to**, come to, add up to, run to, number, make, total, equal, be equal to, be equivalent to, comprise, represent; Brit. tot up to.

beach noun *a fabulous sandy beach*: **seaside**, seashore, shore, coast, coastline, coastal region, seaboard, foreshore, water's edge, margin; sands, sand, shingle, (sand) dunes; lido; dated plage; technical littoral; literary strand.
▸verb 1 *they checked for places where minor craft could beach*: **land**, reach the shore, run ashore; ground, be grounded, run aground; shipwreck, wreck, run on the rocks, be high and dry.
▷ANTONYMS put to sea, depart.
2 *sixty common dolphins have been beached on Cornish shores*: **make/become stranded**, make/become beached, strand, ground, get stuck.
3 *he managed to beach a fine trout*: **catch**, capture, land, hook, reel in.

beachcomber noun *anything that came ashore would be snatched up at once by thrifty beachcombers*: **scavenger**, scrounger, forager, gatherer, collector, accumulator; tramp, vagrant, wanderer, itinerant, nomad, drifter, transient, homeless person; N. Amer. hobo; informal bum.

beached adjective *a beached whale*: **stranded**, stuck, marooned, high and dry, helpless; ashore, aground, grounded, stuck fast.

beacon noun *an uninhabited island supporting a navigational beacon*: **warning light/fire**, signal light/fire, bonfire, smoke signal, beam, signal, danger signal, guiding light; rocket, flare, Very light; lighthouse, light-tower, pharos, phare, watchtower.

bead noun 1 *a long string of beads*: **ball**, pellet, pill, globule, spheroid, spherule, sphere, oval, ovoid, orb, round, pearl; (**beads**) **necklace**, string of beads; Roman Catholic Church rosary, chaplet.
2 *beads of sweat*: **droplet**, drop, blob, bubble, dot, dewdrop, teardrop; informal glob.
□ **draw/get a bead on** *I drew a bead on the nape of his neck*: **aim at**, fix on, focus on, zero in on, sight.

beak noun *a bird with a caterpillar in its beak*: **bill**, nib, mandible; Scottish & N. English neb.

beaker noun *she was drinking blackcurrant juice from a plastic beaker*: **cup**, tumbler, glass, mug, jug, drinking vessel.

beam noun 1 *there are very fine oak beams in the oldest part of the house*: **joist**, purlin, girder, spar, support, strut, stay, brace, scantling, batten, transom, lintel, stringer, baulk, board, timber, plank, lath, rafter; collar beam, tie beam, summer (tree), hammer beam, cantilever.
2 *a beam of light*: **ray**, shaft, stream, streak, pencil, finger; flash, gleam, glow, glimmer, glint, flare, bar; radiation, emission.
3 *seeing the beam on her face was enough to cheer me up*: **grin**, smile, bright look.
▷ANTONYMS frown.
□ **off beam** informal *you're way off beam on this one*: **mistaken**, incorrect, inaccurate, wrong, erroneous, off-target, out, on the wrong track, wide of the mark, awry; informal (getting) cold.
▷ANTONYMS spot on, on the beam.
□ **on the beam** informal *I've been trying to keep him on the beam*: **correct**, right, accurate, true, on the right track, on the right lines; informal on the straight and narrow, on the money, on the mark, spot on, (getting) warm.
▷ANTONYMS wide of the mark, off beam.
▸verb 1 *satellites for beaming TV to rooftop aerials*: **broadcast**, transmit, relay, send/put out, disseminate; direct, aim; televise, show, telecast, put on the air/airwaves.
2 *golden rays beamed down through the clouds*: **shine**, radiate, glare, glitter, gleam, shimmer, glimmer, twinkle, flash, flare, streak.
3 *she was beaming from ear to ear*: **grin**, smile, dimple, grin like a Cheshire Cat, twinkle, smirk, laugh; informal be all smiles.
▷ANTONYMS frown.

beaming adjective 1 *his beaming face*: **grinning**, smiling, laughing; cheerful, happy, radiant, glowing, sunny, joyful, elated, thrilled, delighted, overjoyed, rapturous, blissful.
▷ANTONYMS frowning.
2 *he greeted her with a beaming smile*: **bright**, **cheery**, sparkling, flashing, brilliant, dazzling, intense, gleaming, radiant.

bear[1] verb 1 *Bill arrived, bearing a large picnic hamper*: **carry**, bring, transport, move, convey, take, fetch, haul, lug, shift; deliver; informal tote.
2 *the letter bore the signature of a local councillor*: **display**, exhibit, show, present, set forth, be marked with, carry, have.
3 *the track has horizontal concrete slabs, which bear the weight of the vehicle*: **support**, carry, hold up, prop up, keep up, bolster up; brace, shore up, underpin, buttress, reinforce.
4 *ratepayers will have to bear the cost of such a move*: **sustain**, carry, support, shoulder, uphold, absorb, take on.
5 *the drugs had been planted by someone who bore a grudge against him*: **harbour**, foster, entertain, cherish, nurse, nurture, brood over, possess, have, hold (on to), cling to, maintain, retain.
6 *such a solution does not bear close scrutiny*: **withstand**, stand up to, stand, put up with, take, cope with, handle, resist, sustain, absorb, accept.
7 *I'm not sure how much longer I can bear the pain*: **endure**, tolerate, put up with, stand, suffer, abide, submit to, experience, undergo, go through, countenance, brook, brave, weather, support; informal stick, stomach, swallow.
8 *I can't bear being dependent on other people*: **tolerate**, stand, put up with, stomach, swallow, brook, undergo, accept, approve of, endorse, allow,

admit, permit; Scottish thole; informal stick, hack, abide; Brit. informal wear, be doing with; archaic suffer.
9 *at seventeen she bore his daughter*: **give birth to**, bring forth, deliver, be delivered of, have, mother, create, produce, spawn; conceive; breed, procreate, reproduce; N. Amer. birth; informal drop; literary beget; archaic engender, be brought to bed of.
10 *the radio bore the news of a policeman shot in Belfast*: **communicate**, carry, spread, disclose, tell, disseminate, circulate, diffuse, pass on, make public, make known; transmit, broadcast, publish.
11 *a squash that bears fruit shaped like cucumbers*: **produce**, yield, give forth, give, provide, supply, generate, afford, furnish, bestow.
12 *you drive to the end of the street, bear left, and go into the car park*: **veer**, curve, swerve, incline, turn, fork, diverge, deviate, bend; go, move; Sailing tack, sheer.
□ **bear oneself** *she bore herself like a queen as she slowly descended the stairs*: **conduct oneself**, carry oneself, acquit oneself, act, behave, perform; rare comport oneself, deport oneself.
□ **bear down on** *at a canter they bore down on the mass of men ahead*: **advance on**, close in on, move in on, converge on, approach, come/move closer/close to, draw near/nearer to, press on towards; attack, set upon, fall upon, assail, set about, let fly at, tear into.
▸ANTONYMS retreat from, move away from.
□ **bear fruit** *plans for power-sharing may be about to bear fruit*: **yield results**, get results, succeed, meet with success, be successful, be effective, be profitable, work, go as planned; informal pay off, come off, pan out, do the trick, do the business.
▸ANTONYMS come to nothing.
□ **bear something in mind** *it is important to bear in mind that different countries have different regimes*: **take into account**, be mindful, remember, consider, mind, mark, heed, take into consideration, not forget; respect, pay/have regard to, make allowances for, be guided by.
▸ANTONYMS forget, ignore.
□ **bear on** *there is a long cultural history which bears on the way these writers express themselves*: **be relevant to**, appertain to, pertain to, relate to, have a bearing on, have relevance to, apply to, be pertinent to, have reference to, concern, be concerned with, have to do with, be connected with.
▸ANTONYMS be irrelevant to.
□ **bear something out** *he has conducted experiments that bear out these ideas*: **confirm**, corroborate, substantiate, endorse, vindicate, give credence to, support, ratify, warrant, uphold, justify, prove, authenticate, verify.
▸ANTONYMS contradict, falsify.
□ **bear up** *she looks fantastic and is bearing up remarkably well*: **cope**, persevere, manage, endure; muddle through/along, get through, get on, carry on, get along, deal with the situation; grin and bear it, weather the storm; informal make out, get by, hack it.
▸ANTONYMS go to pieces.
□ **bear with** *bear with me a moment while I make a telephone call*: **be patient with**, show forbearance towards, make allowances for, tolerate, put up with, endure, suffer.
□ **bear witness/testimony to** *the great cathedrals bore witness to a towering vision of transcendence*: **testify to**, be evidence/proof of, attest to, confirm, evidence, prove, vouch for; demonstrate, show, establish, indicate, reveal, bespeak.

Word links **bear**
-ferous bearing or yielding something, as in *Carboniferous, melliferous*

bear² noun

Word links **bear**
ursine relating to bears
boar male
sow female
cub young
den home
sloth collective noun

bearable adjective *the pain was made more bearable by the fact that their father was in constant touch*: **tolerable**, endurable, supportable, sufferable, brookable, sustainable; acceptable, admissible, passable, manageable.
▸ANTONYMS unbearable, intolerable.

beard noun *he had a black beard*: **facial hair**, whiskers, stubble, designer stubble, five o'clock shadow, bristles; full beard, goatee, imperial, Vandyke, Abe Lincoln, side whiskers, sideboards, sideburns, mutton chops; moustache, moustaches; Brit. informal, dated beaver.
▸ verb *he was afraid to beard the sultan himself*: **confront**, face, challenge, brave, come face to face with, meet head on; defy, oppose, stand up against, square up to, dare, throw down the gauntlet at.

Word links **beard**
pogonophobia fear of beards

bearded adjective *a bearded man*: **unshaven**, whiskered, whiskery, bewhiskered; stubbly, bristly, hairy, hirsute, bushy, shaggy; Brit. informal, dated beavered.
▸ANTONYMS clean shaven.

bearer noun **1** *they went accompanied by lantern-bearers*: **carrier**, porter, conveyor, transporter.
2 *I'm sorry to be the bearer of bad news*: **messenger**, agent, conveyor, emissary, carrier, provider; runner, courier.
3 *the bank's promise to pay the bearer on demand*: **holder**, possessor, owner, payee, consignee, beneficiary.

Word links **bearer**
-fer related suffix, as in *crucifer, Lucifer*
-phore related suffix, as in *carpophore, semaphore*

bearing noun **1** *his greying hair and tanned complexion accentuated his distinguished bearing*: **posture**, comportment, carriage, gait, stance; Brit. deportment.
2 *she has a rather regal bearing*: **demeanour**, manner, air, aspect, attitude, behaviour, mien, countenance, guise, cast, look, feel, style.
3 *being successful in battle has an important bearing on natural selection*: **relevance**, relevancy, significance, pertinence, connection, relation, aptness, appositeness, germaneness, importance, import, application.
4 *the point is on a bearing of 315°*: **direction**, orientation, course, trajectory, heading, tack, path, line, run.
5 *his arrogance goaded her beyond bearing*: **endurance**, endurability, tolerance, tolerability, acceptance, acceptability, sufferance, manageability.
6 (**bearings**) *I lost my bearings in those country lanes*: **orientation**, sense of direction; whereabouts, location, position, situation, track, way.

beast noun **1** *the terrible roaring of caged beasts*: **animal**, creature, brute; N. Amer. informal critter.
2 *a sex beast*: **monster**, brute, savage, barbarian, animal, swine, pig, ogre, fiend, sadist, demon, devil.

beastly adjective **1** Brit. informal *I think politics is a beastly profession.* See **unpleasant** (sense 1).
2 Brit. informal *Karl had been absolutely beastly to her.* See **unkind** (sense 1).

beat verb **1** *before running off, the men beat me with pickaxe handles*: **hit**, strike, batter, thump, hammer, punch, knock, thrash, pound, pummel, slap, smack, crack, thwack, cuff, buffet, maul, pelt, drub, rain blows on; assault, attack, abuse; flay, whip, lash, cudgel, club, birch; informal wallop, belt, bash, whack, clout, clobber, slug, tan, biff, bop, sock, deck, plug, lay into, do over, knock about/around, rough up, fill in, knock into the middle of next week, beat the living daylights out of, give someone a good hiding; dated chastise.
2 *he could hear a drum being beaten*: **bang**, hit, strike, rap, tap, pound, thump, hammer; **play**, sound, perform on, make music on.
3 *the waves beat all along the shore*: **lash**, strike, dash, break against; sweep, lap, wash, splash, ripple, roll, splosh, move against; literary plash, lave.
4 *the metal is beaten into a die*: **hammer**, forge, form, shape, mould, work, stamp, fashion, model, fabricate, make, cast, frame, sculpt, sculpture.
5 *she could hear her own heart beating*: **pulsate**, pulse, palpitate, vibrate, throb, reverberate; pump, pound, thump, thud, hammer, drum; pitter-patter, go pit-a-pat; rare quop.
6 *doves wheel around the rooftops, beating their wings*: **flap**, flutter, move up and down, thresh, thrash, wave, shake, swing, agitate, quiver, tremble, vibrate, oscillate.
7 *beat the cream into the mixture*: **whisk**, mix, blend, whip, stir, fold.
8 *she beat a path through clumps of bushes*: **tread**, tramp, trample, wear, track, groove; crush, flatten, press down, squash.
9 *he played in a team that beat England 2–1 at home*: **defeat**, conquer, win against, get the better of, vanquish, trounce, rout, overpower, overcome, overwhelm, overthrow, subdue, quash, crush; informal lick, thrash, whip, wipe the floor with, clobber.
10 *he cleared 2.68m to beat the previous record of 2.67m*: **surpass**, outdo, exceed, eclipse, transcend, top, trump, cap, better, outperform, outstrip, outshine, outclass, overshadow, put in the shade, be better than, improve on, go one better than.
□ **beat about the bush** *he never beat about the bush when something was annoying him*: **prevaricate**, vacillate, evade/dodge the issue, be non-committal, hedge, hedge one's bets, quibble, parry questions, fudge the issue, mince one's words, stall, shilly-shally, hesitate; Brit. hum and haw; informal pussyfoot around, waffle, flannel, sit on the fence, duck the question; rare tergiversate.
▸ANTONYMS come to the point.
□ **beat a (hasty) retreat** See **retreat** (sense 1 of the verb).
□ **beat it** informal *we beat it as fast as we could.* See **run** (sense 2 of the verb).
□ **beat someone/something off** *we beat off the raiders with sticks*: **repel**, fight off, repulse, drive away/back, force back, beat back, push back, thrust

back, put to flight; hold off, ward off, fend off, stand off, stave off, keep at bay, keep at arm's length.
□ **beat something out** *he beat out the flames*: **extinguish**, put out, quench, smother, douse, snuff out, stifle, choke.
□ **beat someone up** **assault**, attack, mug, batter, thrash, pummel, pound; informal knock about/around, do over, work over, clobber, rough up, fill in, kick in, jump, paste, lay into, lace into, sail into, pitch into, get stuck into, beat the living daylights out of, let someone have it; Brit. informal have a go at, duff someone up; N. Amer. informal beat up on.
▸ **noun 1** *this song has a catchy tune and a good beat*: **rhythm**, pulse, stress, metre, time, measure, cadence, accent, rhythmical flow/pattern.
2 *the beat of hooves*: **pounding**, banging, thumping, thudding, booming, hammering, battering, crashing.
3 *her heart settled to an angry beat*: **pulse**, pulsing, pulsating, vibration, vibrating, throb, throbbing, palpitation, palpitating, reverberation, reverberating; beating, pumping, pounding, thumping, thudding, hammering, drumming; pitter-patter, pit-a-pat.
4 *a policeman on his beat*: **circuit**, round, course, route, way, path, orbit, tour, turn.
▸ **adjective** informal See **exhausted**.

> *Word links* **beat**
>
> **mastigophobia** fear of being beaten

beaten **adjective 1** *the beaten team*: **defeated**, losing, unsuccessful, conquered, bettered, vanquished, trounced, routed, overcome, overwhelmed, overpowered, overthrown, bested, subdued, quashed, crushed, broken, foiled, hapless, luckless; informal licked, thrashed, clobbered.
▷ANTONYMS victorious, winning.
2 *a beaten dog*: **abused**, battered, maltreated, ill-treated, mistreated, misused, downtrodden; **assaulted**, thumped, hit, thrashed, pummelled, smacked, drubbed; informal walloped, belted, bashed, whacked, clobbered, knocked about/around, roughed up.
3 *gradually stir in the beaten eggs*: **whisked**, whipped, stirred, mixed, blended; frothy, foamy.
4 *a beaten copper coffee table*: **hammered**, forged, formed, shaped, moulded, worked, stamped, fashioned, modelled, fabricated, cast, sculpted; dimpled, pockmarked, spotted.
5 *a beaten path*: **trodden**, trampled; well trodden, much trodden, well used, much travelled, worn, well worn.
□ **off the beaten track** *we tried to find locations off the beaten track*: **unfrequented**, isolated, quiet, private, remote, out of the way, outlying, secluded, hidden, backwoods, in the back of beyond, in the middle of nowhere, in the hinterlands; informal in the sticks.
▷ANTONYMS busy, popular.

beatific **adjective 1** *he was beaming a beatific smile*: **rapturous**, joyful, ecstatic, seraphic, blissful, serene, happy, beaming, glad.
2 *the beatific vision of God*: **blessed**, blissful, exalted, sublime, joyful, rapt, heavenly, holy, divine, celestial, paradisical, glorious.

beatify **verb** *he was beatified by Pope Leo XIII*: **canonize**, bless, sanctify, hallow, consecrate, make holy, make sacred; rare macarize.

beating **noun 1** *he received a near fatal beating*: **battering**, thrashing, thumping, pounding, pummelling, drubbing, slapping, smacking, hammering, hitting, striking, punching, knocking, thwacking, cuffing, buffeting, boxing, mauling, pelting, lambasting; assault, attack; flaying, whipping, lashing, cudgelling, clubbing, birching; corporal punishment, chastisement; informal beating-up, duffing-up, doing-over, belting, bashing, pasting, walloping, whacking, clobbering, slugging, tanning, biffing, bopping, hiding.
2 *she could hear the beating of her heart*: **pulsation**, pulsating, pulse, pulsing, palpitating, throb, reverberation, reverberating; pumping, pounding, thumping, thudding, hammering, drumming; pitter-patter, pit-a-pat.
3 *a 5–1 beating at the hands of their rivals*: **defeat**, loss, conquest, vanquishing, trouncing, routing, overthrow, downfall; informal licking, thrashing, clobbering.

beatitude **noun** *the everlasting beatitude that follows the second coming*: **blessedness**, benediction, grace; bliss, ecstasy, exaltation, supreme happiness, heavenly joy, divine rapture, saintliness, sainthood.

beau **noun** dated **1** *she was approached by three potential beaux*: **boyfriend**, sweetheart, lover, fiancé, darling, partner, significant other, escort, young man, admirer, suitor, follower; informal steady, date, toy boy, fancy man, fella; literary swain.
2 *an eighteenth-century beau*: **dandy**, fop, gallant, cavalier, man about town; informal swell, toff; archaic dude, blade, blood, coxcomb, popinjay.

beautiful **adjective** *a beautiful young woman*: **attractive**, pretty, handsome, good-looking, nice-looking, pleasing, alluring, prepossessing, as pretty as a picture; lovely, charming, delightful, appealing, engaging, winsome; ravishing, gorgeous, heavenly, stunning, arresting, glamorous, irresistible, bewitching, beguiling; graceful, elegant, exquisite, aesthetic, artistic, decorative, magnificent; Scottish & N. English bonny; informal tasty, smashing, divine, knockout, drop-dead gorgeous, fanciable, beddable, easy on the eye; Brit. informal fit; N. Amer. informal cute, foxy; Austral./NZ informal beaut, spunky; formal beauteous; archaic comely, fair; rare sightly, pulchritudinous.
▷ANTONYMS ugly.

beautify **verb 1** *he can grow flowers to beautify the garden*: **adorn**, embellish, enhance, decorate, ornament, garnish, gild, smarten, prettify, enrich, glamorize, spruce up, deck (out), trick out, grace; informal get up, do up, do out, tart up.
▷ANTONYMS spoil, uglify.
2 *she started to beautify herself*: **prettify**, glamorize, prink, primp, preen; apply make-up/cosmetics; informal do/doll oneself up.

beauty **noun 1** *a young woman of great beauty* | *the raw beauty of the Australian deserts*: **attractiveness**, prettiness, good looks, pleasingness, comeliness, allure, allurement; loveliness, charm, appeal, heavenliness, voluptuousness; winsomeness, grace, elegance, exquisiteness; splendour, magnificence, grandeur, impressiveness, picturesqueness, artistry, decorativeness; gorgeousness, glamour, irresistibility; Scottish & N. English bonniness; formal beauteousness, pulchritude.
▷ANTONYMS ugliness.
2 *Esther was no beauty*: **beautiful woman**, belle, vision, charmer, enchantress, Venus, goddess, beauty queen, English rose, picture, seductress; French femme fatale; informal looker, good looker, lovely, stunner, knockout, bombshell, dish, cracker, smasher, peach, eyeful, bit of all right.
▷ANTONYMS ugly woman; hag.
3 *the beauty of the system is that the information can be called up instantaneously*: **advantage**, attraction, strength, benefit, asset, draw, lure, pull, strong point, boon, blessing, virtue, merit, selling point, good thing/point, bonus, plus, added extra.
▷ANTONYMS drawback.

beaver **verb**
□ **beaver away** informal *we spent our spare time beavering away in the garage*. See **slog**.

becalmed **adjective** *the wind never arrived, and the boats were left becalmed*: **stranded**, stuck, marooned, motionless, at a halt, still, at a standstill, unmoving.

because **conjunction** *his classmates liked him because he was very friendly*: **since**, as, for the reason that, in view of the fact that, owing to the fact that, seeing that/as.
▷ANTONYMS despite.
□ **because of** *I thought I could not have children because of my age*: **on account of**, as a result of, as a consequence of, owing to, by reason of, on grounds of, by dint of, due to; thanks to, by virtue of, on the strength of; through, after, following, in the wake of.

beckon **verb 1** *the guard beckoned to Benny*: **gesture**, signal, wave, gesticulate, make a gesture, motion, nod, call.
2 *the moorland and miles of coastal path beckon many walkers*: **entice**, invite, tempt, coax, lure, charm, attract, draw, pull (in), bring in, call, allure, interest, fascinate, engage, enchant, captivate, persuade, induce, catch the eye of.

become **verb 1** *she became rich*: **come to be**, get to be, turn out to be, grow, get, turn; literary wax.
2 *he became Foreign Secretary*: **be appointed as**, be assigned as, be nominated, be elected as, be made; be transformed into, be converted into, change into, turn into, transform into.
3 *the dress becomes her*: **suit**, flatter, look good on, look right on; set off, show to advantage, enhance, go well with; embellish, ornament, grace; informal do something for.
4 *it ill becomes him to preach the gospel*: **befit**, behove, suit, be suitable to, be fitting to.
□ **become of** *I asked Harry what had become of the old gang*: **happen to**, be the fate of, be the lot of, overtake, be visited on; literary befall, betide.

becoming **adjective** *her soft curls are very becoming*: **flattering**, fetching, attractive, lovely, pretty, handsome, stylish, elegant, chic, fashionable, comely, tasteful.
▷ANTONYMS unbecoming.

bed **noun 1** *she undressed and climbed into her bed*: **couch**, berth, billet; informal the sack, the hay; Brit. informal one's pit; Scottish informal kip.
2 *a flower bed*: **patch**, plot, area, lot, space, border, strip, row.
3 *the pavement consists of granite blocks set on a bed of cement*: **base**, basis, foundation, support, prop, stay, bottom, core, substructure, substratum; groundwork.
4 *the bed of the stream*: **bottom**, floor, ground, depths.
□ **go to bed** **retire**, call it a day; **go to sleep**, get some sleep, sleep, nap, have/take a nap, catnap, doze, have a doze; informal hit the sack, hit the hay, turn in, snooze, snatch forty winks, get some shut-eye; Brit. informal kip, have a kip, get some kip, hit the pit; N. Amer. informal catch some Zs; literary slumber.
▷ANTONYMS get up, rise.
□ **go to bed with someone** **have sex with**, have sexual intercourse

with, make love to, sleep with, spend the night with; couple with, mate with; informal bed, score with; euphemistic have one's (wicked) way with; formal copulate with; formal fornicate with.

▶ **verb 1** *the tiles are bedded in mortar*: **embed**, set, fix into, insert, inlay, implant, bury, base, plant, settle.
2 *I bedded out a few of the house plants in a prominent position in the garden*: **plant**, plant out, set in beds/soil, put in the ground, set out, transplant.
□ **bed down** See **go to bed**.

> *Word links* **bed**
>
> **clinophobia** fear of beds

bedaub verb literary *their faces were bedaubed with white paint*. See **daub** (verb).

bedclothes plural noun **bedding**, sheets, bed linen, linen, bedcovers, covers, blankets.

bedding noun See **bedclothes**.

bedeck verb *we were in a church bedecked with flowers*: **decorate**, adorn, ornament, trim, deck, enhance, beautify, prettify, embellish, furnish, garnish, grace, enrich, dress up, trick out; swathe, wreathe, festoon, array, bespangle; informal get up, do up, do out; literary furbelow.

bedevil verb *the party was bedevilled by internal dissensions*: **afflict**, torment, beset, assail, beleaguer, plague, blight, harrow, rack, oppress, harry, curse, dog; harass, distress, trouble, worry, torture; frustrate, annoy, vex, irritate, pester, irk, exasperate, strain; informal aggravate.

bedlam noun *there was bedlam in the stadium after he won*: **uproar**, pandemonium, commotion, mayhem, confusion, unrest, furore, upheaval, hubbub, hurly-burly, turmoil, riot, ruckus, tumult, disarray, turbulence; disorder, chaos, anarchy, lawlessness; informal hullabaloo, ructions, rumpus, snafu.
▷**ANTONYMS** calm.

bedraggled adjective *one by one the men reached the shore, weary and bedraggled*: **dishevelled**, disordered, untidy, unkempt, tousled, disarranged, messy, in a mess; dirty, muddy, muddied, soiled, sullied, stained; wet, sodden, soaking, soaking wet, wringing wet, soaked, drenched, saturated, dripping, soggy, splashed; N. Amer. informal mussed.
▷**ANTONYMS** clean, neat.

bedridden adjective *her father was bedridden with arthritis*: **confined to bed**, housebound, out of action/commission; disabled, incapacitated, paralysed, immobilized; informal laid up, flat on one's back.

bedrock noun **1** *there was thirty feet of peat on top of the bedrock*: **substratum**, substructure, understructure, solid foundation, base, basis, underpinning, bed, rock bed.
2 *Labour's traditional bedrock of support is among the working classes*: **core**, basis, base, foundation, root, roots, heart, backbone, essence, nitty-gritty; informal nuts and bolts.

bee noun

> *Word links* **bee**
>
> **apian** relating to bees
> **apiary, hive** home
> **swarm, drive, erst** collective noun
> **apiphobia** fear of bees

beef noun **1** informal *my girl, you'll have to get a bit of beef on you*: **muscle**, muscularity, brawn, bulk, heftiness, burliness, huskiness, physique; strength, powerfulness, robustness, sturdiness, stockiness.
2 informal *our only beef about this car was the colour*: **complaint**, criticism, objection, protestation, cavil, quibble, grievance, grumble, moan, grumbling, carping; informal gripe, griping, grouse, grousing, whinge, whingeing, nit-picking.
□ **beef something up** informal *he noticed that the security was being beefed up*: **toughen up**, strengthen, build up, reinforce, substantiate, consolidate, invigorate, improve, flesh out.
▷**ANTONYMS** weaken.

beefy adjective informal *a beefy tattooed barman*: **muscular**, brawny, hefty, burly, strapping, well built, thickset, solid, strong, powerful, heavy, robust, sturdy, stocky; **fat**, stout, plump, overweight, chubby, obese, flabby, fleshy, rotund, portly, corpulent, paunchy, beer-bellied, dumpy; informal hunky, hulking, husky, tubby, roly-poly; Brit. informal podgy.
▷**ANTONYMS** puny, thin.

beer noun **ale**, beverage, brew; informal jar, pint, booze, wallop, sherbet; Austral./NZ hop.

beetle noun **winged insect**; technical coleopteran.

▶ **verb** informal *I beetled off to the library*: **scurry**, scamper, scuttle, bustle, hurry, hasten, rush, race, dash; informal scoot, tear, pelt, zip, belt.

> *Word links* **beetle**
>
> **coleopteran, coleopterous** relating to beetles

beetling adjective *Marcus glared at him under beetling brows*: **projecting**, protruding, prominent, overhanging, sticking out, jutting out, standing out, bulging, bulbous, pendent.

befall verb literary **1** *a catastrophe befell their grandsons*: **happen to**, overtake, come upon, fall upon, hit, strike, be visited on.
2 *she was to blame for anything that befell*: **happen**, occur, take place, chance to happen, arise, emerge, come about, transpire, materialize, appear, make an appearance, surface, crop up, spring up, present itself; ensue, follow, result, supervene; N. Amer. informal go down; literary come to pass, betide; rare hap, eventuate.

befitting preposition *the gowns were of good material, befitting the bride's status*: **in keeping with**, as befits, fitting, appropriate to, fit for, suitable for, suited to, apt for, proper to, right for, compatible with, consistent with, in character with; archaic meet for.
▷**ANTONYMS** out of keeping with.

befogged adjective *her brain is befogged by lack of sleep*: **confused**, muddled, fuddled, befuddled, addled, groggy, dizzy, muzzy; informal dopey, woozy, not with it.

before preposition **1** *he locked all the doors before going to bed*: **prior to**, previous to, earlier than, preparatory to, in preparation for, preliminary to, in anticipation of, in expectation of; in advance of, ahead of, leading up to, on the eve of; rare anterior to.
▷**ANTONYMS** after.
2 *he was ordered to appear before Sir Robert*: **in front of**, in the presence of, in the sight of; before the very eyes of, under the nose of.
3 *he lived up to the tradition of death before dishonour*: **in preference to**, rather than, sooner than, above, over, instead of.

▶ **adverb 1** *she had never confided in anyone before*: **previously**, before now, before then, until now, until then, up to now, up to then; earlier, formerly, hitherto, in the past, in days gone by; rare heretofore.
2 *a small party went on before*: **ahead**, in front, in advance, in the lead.

> *Word links* **before**
>
> **ante-** related prefix, as in *antenatal, ante-post*
> **pre-** related prefix, as in *prewar, precede*

beforehand adverb *it is important to save any files you have created beforehand*: **in advance**, in readiness, ahead of time; before, before now, earlier, earlier on, previously, already, sooner.

befriend verb *she decided to befriend the new girl*: **make friends with**, make a friend of, look after, protect, keep an eye on, support, back, stand by, side with, encourage, sustain, uphold, succour, advise, guide; help, assist, aid, be of service to, lend a helping hand to.
▷**ANTONYMS** snub, reject.

befuddled adjective *his befuddled brain refused to accept that there was a problem*: **confused**, muddled, addled, bewildered, disoriented, disorientated, all at sea, mixed up, fazed, perplexed, stunned, dazed, dizzy, stupefied, groggy, foggy, fuzzy, fuddled, benumbed, numbed, numb, vague; informal discombobulated, bamboozled, dopey, woolly, woolly-headed, muzzy, woozy, out of it.
▷**ANTONYMS** clear.

beg verb **1** *he scavenged and begged when that was the only way to stay alive*: **ask for money**, solicit money, seek charity, seek alms; informal sponge, cadge, scrounge, bum, touch someone for money; Brit. informal scab; Scottish informal sorn on someone; N. Amer. informal mooch; Austral./NZ informal bludge.
2 *we begged for mercy and he let us live*: **ask for**, request, plead for, appeal for, call for, sue for, solicit, seek, look for, press for; rare impetrate.
3 *he begged her not to leave him*: **beseech**, entreat, implore, adjure, plead with, appeal to, pray to; ask, request, call on, petition, apply to; importune, exhort, enjoin, press; rare obsecrate.

beget verb literary **1** *he married again and begat Alexander*: **father**, sire, engender, generate, spawn, create, give life to, bring into being, bring into the world, have; procreate, reproduce, breed.
2 *we have to make people realize that violence begets more violence*: **cause**, give rise to, lead to, result in, bring about, create, produce, generate, engender, spawn, occasion, effect, bring to pass, bring on, precipitate, prompt, provoke, kindle, trigger, spark off, touch off, stir up, whip up, induce, inspire, promote, foster; literary enkindle; rare effectuate.

beggar noun **1** *he never turned any beggar from his kitchen door*: **tramp**, beggarman, beggarwoman, vagrant, vagabond, down-and-out, homeless person, derelict, mendicant; pauper, poor person; N. Amer. hobo; informal **scrounger**, sponger, cadger, freeloader, bag lady, have-not, crusty; Brit. informal dosser; N. Amer. informal bum, moocher, mooch, schnorrer; Austral./NZ informal bagman, swagman, bludger; rare clochard.
2 informal *he's been on holiday for three weeks, lucky beggar!* **fellow**, thing, individual, soul, character, creature, wretch; person, man, woman, boy, girl;

b

informal guy, fella, devil, bunny, bastard; Brit. informal chap, bloke, bugger, sod, bod; N. Amer. informal dude, hombre; informal, dated body, dog; Brit. informal, dated cove; archaic wight.
▸ verb rare *the latest crisis beggared nearly half the population*: **impoverish**, make poor, reduce to poverty, reduce to penury, reduce to destitution, bankrupt, make bankrupt, make destitute, ruin, wipe out, break, cripple; bring someone to their knees; rare pauperize.

beggarly adjective **1** *a priest's stipend in 1522 was a beggarly 26s 8d*: **meagre**, modest, slight, lean, scant, scanty, skimpy, puny, inadequate, insufficient, insubstantial, miserly, paltry, pitiful, derisory, niggardly, ungenerous, miserable, contemptible, despicable; informal measly, stingy, lousy, pathetic, piddling, piffling, mingy, poxy; rare exiguous.
▷ANTONYMS considerable.
2 *they lived in the most beggarly part of Bethnal Green*: **wretched**, miserable, sordid, squalid, shabby, shoddy, mean, base, vile, foul, despicable, unpleasant; **poor**, poverty-stricken, impoverished, distressed, beggared, needy, penniless, destitute, indigent, impecunious, penurious; informal hard up, on one's uppers.

beggary noun *there is no unemployment pay to stand between them and beggary*: **poverty**, penury, destitution, ruin, ruination, indigence, impecuniousness, impoverishment, need, neediness, privation, want, hardship, distress, difficulties, dire straits, reduced circumstances, straitened circumstances, mendicancy, vagrancy; bankruptcy, insolvency, liquidation, debt, indebtedness, financial ruin; Brit. administration, receivership; Economics primary poverty; rare pauperdom, pauperism, mendicity.

begin verb **1** *he must begin work first thing in the morning*: **start**, set about, go about, embark on, launch into, get down to, take up, turn one's hand to, undertake, tackle; initiate, set in motion, institute, inaugurate, get ahead with; informal get cracking on, get going on; formal commence.
▷ANTONYMS cease.
2 *the interviewer began by asking me what my bad points were*: **open**, lead off, get under way, get going, get off the ground, start, start off, go ahead; informal start the ball rolling, kick off, get the show on the road, get to it, fire away, take the plunge; formal commence.
▷ANTONYMS conclude, finish.
3 *when did the illness actually begin?* **appear**, arise, become apparent, make an appearance, spring up, crop up, turn up, surface, emerge, come into existence, come into being, originate, start, develop, unfold; set in, become established; happen, occur; formal commence; literary come to pass.
▷ANTONYMS disappear.

> *Word links* **begin**
>
> **inceptive**, **initial** relating to a beginning
> **incipient**, **inchoate**, **embryonic** beginning

beginner noun *the book guides the beginner through the basics*: **novice**, starter, learner, student, pupil, trainee, apprentice, probationer; recruit, raw recruit, newcomer, new boy, new girl, tyro, fledgling, neophyte, initiate, fresher, freshman, cub; Christianity postulant, novitiate; N. Amer. tenderfoot; informal rookie, new kid (on the block), newie, newbie; N. Amer. informal greenhorn, probie, punk; Austral./NZ informal new chum.
▷ANTONYMS expert, veteran.

beginning noun **1** *the beginning of the industrial revolution*: **dawn**, birth, inception, conception, origination, genesis, emergence, rise, start, starting point, very beginning, launch, onset, outset, unfolding, development, developing, debut; day one; informal kick-off; formal commencement.
▷ANTONYMS end.
2 *she read the beginning of the book*: **opening**, start, first part, preface, introduction, foreword, preamble, opening statement, opening remarks, prelude, prologue; formal commencement; rare exordium, proem, prolegomenon.
▷ANTONYMS conclusion, end.
3 (**beginnings**) *the therapy has its beginnings in China*: **origin**, source, starting point, basis, birthplace, cradle, spring, mainspring, embryo, germ; genesis, creation, infancy; roots, seeds, early stages; Latin fons et origo; literary fountainhead, fount, well spring.

begrime verb literary *her face and hands had been begrimed with a black substance*. See **dirty** (verb).

begrudge verb **1** *it was plain that she begrudged Brian his affluence*: **envy**, grudge, resent; be jealous of, be envious of, be resentful of.
2 *I don't begrudge the support we've given*: **resent**, feel aggrieved about, feel bitter about, be annoyed about, be angry about, be displeased about, be resentful of, grudge, mind, object to, take exception to, regret; give unwillingly, give reluctantly, give resentfully, give stintingly, be dissatisfied with.

beguile verb **1** *he'll beguile you with his famous smile*: **charm**, attract, enchant, entrance, win over, woo, captivate, bewitch, spellbind, dazzle, blind, hypnotize, mesmerize, seduce, tempt, lead on, lure, entice, ensnare, entrap; **deceive**, mislead, take in, trick, inveigle, dupe, fool, double-cross, hoodwink, take advantage of; informal tickle someone's fancy, float someone's boat, butter up, sweet-talk, soft-soap, bamboozle, con, diddle, shaft, pull a fast one on, put one over on, take for a ride, string along, lead up the garden path, pull the wool over someone's eyes; N. Amer. informal sucker, snooker; Austral./NZ pull a swifty on.
▷ANTONYMS repel; be straight with.
2 *the television programme has been beguiling children for years*: **entertain**, amuse, delight, please, occupy, absorb, engage, distract, divert, interest, fascinate, enthral, engross, preoccupy, hold the attention of.
▷ANTONYMS bore.
3 literary *to beguile some of the time they went to the cinema*: **while away**, pass, spend, use up, take up; kill, waste, fritter, dissipate.

beguiling adjective *he praised her in that soft, beguiling voice*: **charming**, attractive, appealing, pleasing, pleasant, lovely, delightful, enchanting, entrancing, charismatic, captivating, bewitching, spellbinding, hypnotizing, mesmerizing, magnetic, alluring, enticing, tempting, inviting, seductive, irresistible; informal dreamy, heavenly, gorgeous, come-hither.
▷ANTONYMS unappealing.

behalf noun
□ **on behalf of/on someone's behalf 1** *I am writing to you on behalf of my client*: **as a representative of**, as a spokesperson for, for, in the name of, with power of attorney for, in place of, on the authority of, at the behest of; appearing for, representing; in the interests of. **2** *she campaigned on behalf of chimpanzees in the wild*: **in the interests of**, in support of, for, for the benefit of, for the good of, for the sake of, to the advantage of, to the profit of, on account of.

behave verb **1** *the children worked hard and* **behaved themselves**: **act correctly**, act properly, conduct oneself well, act in a polite way, show good manners, mind one's manners, mind one's Ps and Qs; be good, be polite, be well behaved.
▷ANTONYMS misbehave.
2 *she behaved abominably last night*: **conduct oneself**, act, acquit oneself, bear oneself, carry oneself; rare comport oneself, deport oneself.

behaviour noun **1** *we are absolutely disgusted with his behaviour*: **conduct**, way of behaving, way of acting, deportment, bearing, etiquette; actions, exploits, doings, efforts; manners, ways, habits, practices; informal capers; rare comportment.
2 *they examined the structure and behaviour of the chromosomes*: **functioning**, action, performance, operation, working, running, reaction, response; actions, reactions, responses.

> *Word links* **behaviour**
>
> **ethology** science of animal behaviour

behead verb *the axes were used to behead traitors*: **decapitate**, cut off the head of, guillotine; execute, put to death, kill.

behest noun literary *Mary signed away her kingdom at the behest of Henri II*: **instruction**, bidding, request, requirement, wish, desire; command, order, decree, edict, rule, ruling, directive, direction, charge, will, dictate, demand, insistence, injunction, mandate, precept; informal say-so; rare rescript.

behind preposition **1** *he slept in a hut behind their house*: **at the back of**, at the rear of, beyond, on the other side of, on the far side of, on the further side of; N. Amer. in back of.
▷ANTONYMS in front of.
2 *behind her was a small child*: **after**, following, to the rear of, in the wake of, at the back of, close on, hard on the heels of, on the trail of.
3 *you are way behind the rest of the class*: **less advanced than**, slower than, weaker than, inferior to.
4 *work on the car is months behind schedule*: **later than**, late in relation to, after.
5 *he was believed to have been behind a number of bombings*: **responsible for**, at the bottom of, at the back of, the cause of, the source of, the organizer of; to blame for, culpable of, guilty of; causing, instigating, initiating, urging.
6 *the All Blacks have the whole nation behind them*: **supporting**, backing, for, on the side of, in agreement with; financing.
□ **put something behind one** *the team have to put this morning's result behind them*: **consign something to the past**, put something down to experience, forget about something, pay no heed to something, ignore, regard as water under the bridge.
▸ adverb **1** *each plane took off with a glider following on behind*: **after**, afterwards, at the back, in the rear, in the wake, at the end.
▷ANTONYMS ahead, in front.
2 *'I'm off to dance!' he called behind*: **over one's shoulder**, to the rear, to the back, towards the rear, towards the back, backwards.
▷ANTONYMS ahead.
3 *he stayed behind to sign autographs*: **afterwards**, remaining after departure.
4 *we're behind so don't stop*: **running late, late**, behind schedule, behindhand, delayed, not on time, behind time.

▷ANTONYMS ahead.
5 *he was behind with his subscription payments*: **in arrears**, overdue, in debt, in the red; **late**, unpunctual, tardy, behindhand, behind target.
▷ANTONYMS ahead.
▶ **noun** See **bottom** (sense 6 of the noun).

behindhand adjective *I'm awfully behindhand with my work*: **behind**, behind schedule, behind time, delayed; **late**, belated, dilatory, tardy, unpunctual, slow, remiss; running late, not on time.
▷ANTONYMS ahead.

behold verb literary *the orchids are a sight to behold*: **look at**, see, observe, view, watch, survey, gaze at, gaze upon, stare at, scan, witness, regard, contemplate, inspect, eye; catch sight of, glimpse, spot, spy, notice, make out, discern, perceive; take note of, pay attention to, mark, remark, consider, pay heed to; informal clap eyes on, lay eyes on, set eyes on, have/take a gander at, have a squint at, get a load of, check out, gawp at, size up; Brit. informal have/take a dekko at, have/take a butcher's at, have/take a shufti at, clock; N. Amer. informal eyeball; literary espy, descry.
▶ **exclamation** archaic *behold, here I am!* **look**, see, lo; Latin ecce.

beholden adjective *I don't like to be beholden to anybody*: **indebted**, obligated, under an obligation, obliged, bound, duty-bound, honour-bound; owing a debt of gratitude, grateful, thankful, appreciative; in someone's debt, owing someone thanks.

behove verb **1** *my brother-in-law is ill and it behoves me to see him*: **be incumbent on**, be obligatory for, be required of, be appropriate for, be expected of, be advisable for, be sensible for, be wise for.
2 *it ill behoves our national broadcasting channel to be so underhanded*: **befit**, become, suit; be fitting to, be suitable for, be seemly for, be proper for, be decorous for.

beige adjective *David arrived in a beige boiler suit*: **fawn**, brownish-yellow, pale brown, buff, sand, sandy, oatmeal, wheaten, biscuit, coffee, coffee-coloured, café au lait, camel, kasha, ecru, taupe, stone, stone-coloured, mushroom, putty, greige; neutral, natural, naturelle.

being noun **1** *she finds herself warmed by his very being*: **existence**, living, life, animation, animateness, aliveness, reality, actuality, essential nature, lifeblood, vital force, entity; Philosophy esse.
▷ANTONYMS non-existence.
2 *God is alive and working in the being of man*: **soul**, spirit, nature, essence, substance, entity, inner being, inner self, psyche; heart, bosom, breast, core, kernel, marrow; Philosophy quiddity, pneuma.
3 *I wanted to become an enlightened being*: **creature**, life form, living entity, living thing, living soul, soul, individual, person, personage, human being, human, man, woman; life, existence; earthling.

belabour verb **1** *Bernard was belabouring Jed with his fists*: **beat**, hit, strike, smack, batter, pummel, pound, buffet, rain blows on, thrash, bombard, pelt; beat up, assault, attack, set upon, set about, weigh into; N. Amer. beat up on; informal wallop, whack, clout, clobber, bop, biff, sock, deck, plug, knock about/around, knock into the middle of next week, beat the living daylights out of, give someone a good hiding, do over, work over, rough up, lay into, tear into, lace into, sail into, get stuck into; Brit. informal have a go at; N. Amer. informal whale, light into; archaic smite.
2 *I have been dreadfully belaboured in the London Magazine*: **criticize**, attack, berate, censure, condemn, denounce, denigrate, revile, castigate, pillory, flay, lambaste, savage, tear/pull to pieces, find fault with, run down, abuse; informal knock, slam, pan, bash, take apart, crucify, hammer, lay into, roast, skewer, bad-mouth; Brit. informal slate, rubbish, slag off, monster; N. Amer. informal pummel, cut up; Austral./NZ informal bag; rare excoriate.
▷ANTONYMS praise.
3 *there is no need to belabour the point here*: **over-elaborate**, labour, discuss at length, dwell on, harp on about, hammer away at, expound on, expand on; overdo, overplay, overdramatize, make too much of, place too much emphasis on; informal flog to death, drag out, make a big thing of, blow out of all proportion; N. Amer. informal do over.
▷ANTONYMS understate.

belated adjective *he was given a belated birthday cake*: **late**, **overdue**, behindhand, behind time, not on time, behind schedule, delayed, running late, tardy, unpunctual.
▷ANTONYMS early.

belch verb **1** *Laurence belched behind his hand*: bring up wind; Scottish & N. English rift; informal **burp**, gurk; archaic bolk, rout, ruck; rare eruct, eructate.
2 *the blast furnaces belched flames into the sky*: **emit**, issue, vent, gush, discharge, eject, expel, empty, evacuate, give off, give out, pour out, disgorge, spew out, spit out, vomit, cough up, throw up; rare disembogue.
▶ **noun** *he gave a loud belch*: informal **burp**, gurk; archaic bolk, ventosity; Scottish & N. English **rift**; rare eructation.

beleaguered adjective **1** *English forces came to relieve the beleaguered garrison*: **besieged**, under siege, blockaded, surrounded, encircled, hemmed in, under attack.
2 *she mobilized popular support behind her beleaguered government*: **hard-pressed**, troubled, in difficulties, under pressure, under stress, with one's back to the wall, in a tight corner, in a tight spot; informal up against it.

belie verb **1** *the expression in his eyes belied his easy manner*: **contradict**, be at odds with, call into question, give the lie to, show/prove to be false; disprove, debunk, discredit, explode, knock the bottom out of, drive a coach and horses through; informal shoot full of holes, shoot down (in flames); rare controvert, confute, negative.
▷ANTONYMS testify to.
2 *he made a light-hearted speech which belied his deep disappointment*: **conceal**, cover, disguise, misrepresent, falsify, distort, warp, put a spin on, colour; give a false idea of, give a false account of.
▷ANTONYMS reveal.

belief noun **1** *she clung to the belief that Diane was innocent*: **opinion**, view, viewpoint, point of view, attitude, stance, stand, standpoint, position, perspective, contention, conviction, judgement, thinking, way of thinking, thought, idea, theory, hypothesis, thesis, interpretation, assumption, presumption, supposition, surmise, postulation, conclusion, deduction, inference, notion, impression, sense, feeling, fancy, hunch.
2 *I have no real belief in the power of reason*: **faith**, trust, reliance, confidence, credence, freedom from doubt; optimism, hopefulness, hope.
▷ANTONYMS disbelief, doubt.
3 *he opposed traditional religious beliefs*: **ideology**, principle, ideal, ethic, conviction; **doctrine**, teaching, dogma, tenet, canon, article of faith, credence, creed, credo, code of belief.

believable adjective *Dawn's story was not quite believable*: **credible**, plausible, likely, convincing, creditable, probable, possible, feasible, tenable, acceptable, reasonable, sound, rational, logical, within the bounds of possibility, able to hold water, with a ring of truth; conceivable, imaginable, thinkable.
▷ANTONYMS unbelievable.

believe verb **1** *I don't believe you*: **be convinced by**, trust, have confidence in, consider honest, consider truthful.
▷ANTONYMS disbelieve.
2 *if you believe that story you will believe anything*: **regard as true**, accept as true, accept, be convinced by, give credence to, credit, give credit to, trust, put confidence in, count on, rely on, depend on; informal swallow, {swallow something hook, line, and sinker}, fall for, go for, buy, take as gospel.
▷ANTONYMS disbelieve.
3 *police believe they've identified the smuggler | I believe he worked for you*: **think**, be of the opinion that, think it likely that, have an idea that, imagine, feel, have a feeling, hold, maintain, suspect, suppose, assume, presume, conjecture, surmise, postulate that, theorize that, conclude, come to the conclusion that, deduce; understand, be given to understand, take it, gather, fancy, guess, dare say; N. Amer. figure; informal reckon; archaic ween.
▷ANTONYMS doubt.
□ **believe in 1** *Lucy wasn't sure if she believed in God or not*: **be convinced of the existence of**, be sure of the existence of, be persuaded of the existence of, believe in the existence of. **2** *she believed in the benefits of Turkish baths for slimming*: **have faith in**, pin one's faith on, trust in, have every confidence in, cling to, set store by, value, swear by, be convinced by, be persuaded by; subscribe to, approve of, back, support, advocate, champion; informal rate.

believer noun *she was a believer in the Christian religion*: **devotee of**, adherent of, disciple of, follower of, supporter of, upholder of, worshipper in; convert, proselyte, neophyte; Hinduism bhakta; N. Amer. born-again.
▷ANTONYMS infidel; sceptic.

belittle verb *the opposition belittled the government's successes*: **disparage**, denigrate, run down, deprecate, depreciate, downgrade, play down, trivialize, minimize, make light of, treat lightly, undervalue, underrate, underestimate; **scoff at**, **sneer at**, laugh at, laugh off, mock, ridicule, deride, dismiss, scorn, pour scorn on, cast aspersions on, discredit, vilify, defame, decry, criticize, condemn, censure, abuse, malign, revile; N. Amer. slur; informal do down, do a hatchet job on, take to pieces, pull apart, pick holes in, drag through the mud, have a go at, hit out at, knock, slam, pan, bash, bad-mouth, pooh-pooh, look down one's nose at; Brit. informal rubbish, slate, slag off; archaic hold cheap; rare asperse, derogate, misprize, minify.
▷ANTONYMS praise; magnify.

bell noun *the bell rang for the start of school*: **chime**, gong, alarm; peal, knell, toll; signal, warning, alert; archaic tocsin.
□ **give someone a bell** Brit. informal *just give me a bell when you need me.* See **telephone**.

Word links **bell**
campanology bell-ringing

belle noun *a dainty Southern belle from Virginia*: **beauty**, beautiful woman, dream, vision, picture, pin-up, goddess, Venus, siren, charmer, enchantress, seductress; informal looker, good looker, lovely, sensation, stunner, knockout, bombshell, dish, cracker, smasher, bobby-dazzler, peach, honey, eyeful, sight for sore eyes, bit of all right.

bellicose adjective *the extreme right adopted a bellicose attitude*: **belligerent**, aggressive, hostile, threatening, antagonistic, pugnacious,

b

truculent, confrontational, argumentative, quarrelsome, disputatious, contentious, militant, combative; quick-tempered, hot-tempered, ill-tempered, bad-tempered, irascible, captious; informal spoiling for a fight; Brit. informal **stroppy**, **bolshie**; N. Amer. informal **scrappy**; rare **oppugnant**.
▷ANTONYMS peaceable.

belligerent adjective **1** *she stared about her in a belligerent manner*: **hostile**, aggressive, threatening, antagonistic, pugnacious, bellicose, truculent, confrontational, argumentative, quarrelsome, disputatious, contentious, militant, combative; quick-tempered, hot-tempered, ill-tempered, bad-tempered, irascible, captious; informal spoiling for a fight; Brit. informal stroppy, bolshie; N. Amer. informal scrappy; N. Amer. vulgar slang pissy; rare oppugnant.
▷ANTONYMS friendly, peaceable.
2 *he helped to bring peace between two belligerent states*: **warring**, at war, combatant, fighting, battling, contending, conflicting, clashing, quarrelling; militant, militaristic, martial, warlike, warmongering, sabre-rattling, hawkish, gung-ho; informal at each other's throats.
▷ANTONYMS peaceful, neutral.

bellow verb *he cringed as she bellowed in his ear*: **roar**, shout, bawl, thunder, trumpet, boom, bark, bay, yawp, yell, yelp, shriek, howl, scream, screech, call, cry, cry out, sing out, whoop, wail, caterwaul; raise one's voice; N. Amer. informal holler; rare vociferate, ululate.
▷ANTONYMS whisper.
▸ noun *he gave a bellow of pain and rage*: **roar**, shout, bawl, bark, bay, yawp, yell, yelp, shriek, howl, scream, screech, call, cry, whoop, wail, caterwaul; N. Amer. informal holler; rare vociferation, ululation.
▷ANTONYMS whisper.

belly noun **1** *he scratched his hairy belly*: **stomach**, abdomen, paunch, middle, midriff, girth; informal tummy, tum, gut, guts, insides, pot, bread basket, pot belly, beer belly, beer gut, spare tyre, middle-aged spread; Scottish informal kyte; N. Amer. informal bay window; Austral./NZ informal bingy, bingee; dated, humorous corporation.
2 *the aircraft finally came to rest on its belly*: **undercarriage**, underbelly, underside, undersurface, underneath, underpart, lower side, bottom.
▸ verb *her skirt* **bellied out** *in the wind*: **billow (out)**, bulge (out), swell (out), balloon (out), bag (out), fill out, puff out; distend.

belong verb **1** *the plant probably belongs within this broad group*: **have a place**, be located, be situated, be found, lie, stand, be included, be classed, be classified, be categorized.
2 *she is a stranger and doesn't belong here*: **fit in**, be suited to, have a rightful place, have a home, be part of; informal go, click.
□ **belong to 1** *the house they lived in belonged to a German lady*: **be owned by**, be the property of, be the possession of, be in the ownership of, be held by, be at the disposal of, be in the hands of. **2** *I don't belong to a trade union*: **be a member of**, be in, be included in, be affiliated to, be allied to, be associated with, be connected to, be linked to, be an adherent of. **3** *the balcony belonged to a room on the first floor*: **be part of**, be attached to, be an adjunct of, link up with, go with.

belonging noun *the club helps their members maintain a sense of belonging*: **affiliation**, **acceptance**, association, attachment, connection, union, integration, closeness; rapport, fellow feeling, fellowship, kinship, partnership.
▷ANTONYMS alienation.

belongings plural noun *she carried a canvas bag containing all her belongings*: **possessions**, personal possessions, personal effects, effects, goods, worldly goods, chattels, goods and chattels, accoutrements, appurtenances; property, paraphernalia; luggage, baggage; informal gear, tackle, kit, things, stuff, junk, rubbish, bits and pieces, bits and bobs; Brit. informal clobber, gubbins; vulgar slang shit, crap.

beloved adjective **1** *she wrote regularly to her beloved brother*: **darling**, dear, dearest, precious, adored, loved, much loved, favourite, cherished, treasured, prized, esteemed, worshipped, idolized, lionized.
2 *Tuscany is a region much beloved by artists*: **loved**, liked, highly regarded, adored, admired, esteemed, valued, prized, revered, venerated, exalted.
▸ noun *he watched his beloved from afar*: **sweetheart**, loved one, love, true love, lady love, darling, dearest, dear one, lover, girlfriend, boyfriend, young lady, young man, woman friend, lady friend, man friend, beau, admirer, worshipper, inamorata, inamorato; fiancée, fiancé, betrothed, partner, significant other; the love of one's life, the apple of one's eye, the object of one's affections; informal fancy woman, fancy man, flame, steady, baby, angel, honey, pet, bird, WAGs (wives and girlfriends), fella; literary swain; archaic gallant, paramour, leman, doxy.

below preposition **1** *the overcoat had two side pockets below the hips*: **beneath**, under, underneath, further down than, lower than.
▷ANTONYMS above, over.
2 *they have an income below the national average*: **less than**, lower than, under, not as much as, not so much as, smaller than; informal shy of.
▷ANTONYMS above, more than.
3 *the aristocracy ranked below the monarchy*: **lower than**, under, inferior to, subordinate to, secondary to, subservient to; subject to, controlled by, at the mercy of, under the heel of.
▷ANTONYMS above.
▸ adverb **1** *the balcony gave a good view of what was happening down below*: **further down**, lower down, in a lower position, underneath, beneath, downstairs.
2 *please answer yes or no to the statements below*: **underneath**, following, further on, at a later point, in a later place, at the bottom, at the end.

> *Word links* **below**
>
> **hypo-** related prefix, as in *hypodermic, hypogeum*
> **sub-** related prefix, as in *subterranean, subdominant*

belt noun **1** *she wore a plain raincoat tied with a belt*: **girdle**, sash, strap, cummerbund, waistband, band, girth; Japanese obi; archaic zone; rare baldric, cincture, ceinture, cestus, cingulum.
2 *a great wheel driven by a leather belt powered the drill*: **band**, loop, hoop, thong; drive belt, fan belt, conveyor belt.
3 *he made a tour of the cotton belt*: **region**, area, district, zone, sector, province, quarter, pocket, enclave, territory, neighbourhood, locality; tract, stretch, extent; informal neck of the woods, parts; Brit. informal patch.
4 *I saw a belt of silver on the horizon*: **band**, strip, stripe, swathe, bar, line, streak, flash, vein, thread; technical stria, striation.
5 informal *he gave David a belt across the face*: **blow**, punch, smack, crack, slap, bang, thump, knock, rap, thwack, box; informal clout, clip, clobber, bash, biff, whack, wallop, sock, swipe, lam, whomp; Brit. informal slosh; N. Amer. informal boff, bust, slug, whale; Austral./NZ informal dong; dated buffet.
□ **below the belt** *she thinks what they have done is a bit below the belt*: **unfair**, unjust, uncalled for, unjustified, unjustifiable, unacceptable, unreasonable, unsatisfactory, unwarranted, unnecessary, inequitable, off, out of turn; **unethical**, unprincipled, immoral, unscrupulous, treacherous, two-faced, unsporting, sneaky, dishonourable, dishonest, underhand, underhanded; informal a bit much, not on, low-down, dirty; Brit. informal out of order, a bit thick, not cricket; Austral./NZ informal over the fence.
▸ verb **1** *her trousers are belted at precisely the wrong curve of her hip*: **fasten**, tie, bind; **encircle**, gird, encompass, circle.
2 informal *a guy belted him in the face*: **hit**, strike, smack, slap, bang, beat, punch, thump, welt; informal clout, bash, biff, whack, thwack, wallop, sock, slog, clobber, bop, lam, larrup; N. Amer. informal boff, bust, slug, whale; archaic smite.
3 informal *they watched cars belting around oval tracks*. See **speed**.
□ **belt something out** informal *she belted out songs from the Fifties*: **sing loudly**, carol, trill, yodel; perform, render; rare troll.
□ **belt up** informal *belt up and listen out for your names*: **be quiet**, quieten down, be silent, fall silent, hush, stop talking, hold your tongue, keep your lips sealed; informal shut up, shut your face, shut your mouth, shut your trap, button your lip, pipe down, cut the cackle, put a sock in it, give it a rest; Brit. informal shut your gob, wrap it up, wrap up; N. Amer. informal save it.
▷ANTONYMS speak up.

bemoan verb *they were bemoaning the sad decline of moral standards*: **lament**, bewail, deplore, complain about, express regret about; mourn, grieve over, express sorrow about, sorrow for, sigh over, cry over, weep over, shed tears over, wail over, keen over, beat one's breast about; archaic plain over.
▷ANTONYMS applaud.

bemused adjective *they wandered about with bemused expressions*: **bewildered**, confused, puzzled, perplexed, baffled, stumped, mystified, stupefied, nonplussed, muddled, befuddled, fuddled, dumbfounded, at sea, at a loss, at sixes and sevens, thrown (off balance), taken aback, disoriented, disconcerted, discomposed, troubled, discomfited, unnerved, shaken, shaken up, dazed, stunned, astonished, astounded; informal flummoxed, bamboozled, discombobulated, clueless, fazed, floored, beaten; Canadian & Austral./NZ informal bushed; archaic wildered, mazed, distracted.

bemusement noun *Rachel shook her head in bemusement*: **bewilderment**, confusion, puzzlement, perplexity, bafflement, befuddlement, stupefaction, mystification, incomprehension, disorientation, dumbfoundedness, astonishment; informal discombobulation, bamboozlement, cluelessness; rare disconcertment.

bench noun **1** *he sat on a bench at the front of the hall*: **pew**, form, long seat, seat, stall, settle.
2 *in the centre of the laboratory was a huge bench*: **workbench**, work table, table, counter, trestle table, board, work surface, worktop, buffet.
3 *the bench began to hear the evidence*: **judges**, magistrates, judiciary, judicature; **court**, law court, court of justice, bar, courtroom, tribunal, forum.

benchmark noun *the settlement was used as a benchmark in all further negotiations*: **standard**, point of reference, basis, gauge, criterion, specification, canon, convention, guide, guideline, guiding principle, norm, touchstone, yardstick, test, litmus test, barometer, indicator, measure, model, exemplar, classic example, pattern, paradigm, archetype, prototype, ideal.

bend verb **1** *copper pipes should not be bent without support*: **curve**, crook, make crooked, make curved, flex, angle, hook, bow, arc, arch, buckle, warp, contort, distort, deform; twist, spiral, coil, curl, loop.
▷ANTONYMS straighten.
2 *the highway bent to the left up ahead*: **turn**, curve, incline, swing, veer, swerve, deviate, diverge, fork, change course; twist, snake, wind, meander, zigzag, curl, loop; rare divagate, incurvate.
3 *he bent and patted the dog*: **stoop**, bow, crouch, squat, kneel, hunch; bend down, bend over, lean down, lean over, hunker down, bob down, duck down; N. Amer. informal scooch.
▷ANTONYMS straighten up.
4 *they want to bend me to their will*: **mould**, shape, manipulate, direct, force, press, influence, incline, sway, bias, warp, impress, compel, persuade; subdue, subjugate.
5 *he bent his mind to the question*: **direct**, point, aim, turn, train, steer, set.
□ **bend over backwards** informal *they have bent over backwards to ensure a fair trial*: **try one's hardest**, try as hard as one can, do one's best, do one's utmost, do all one can, give one's all, make every effort; strive, struggle, apply oneself, exert oneself, work hard, endeavour, try; informal do one's damnedest, go all out, pull out all the stops, bust a gut, move heaven and earth, give it one's best shot; Austral./NZ informal go for the doctor.
▶ **noun** *he came to a bend in the road*: **curve**, turn, corner, kink, angle, arc, crescent, twist, crook, deviation, deflection, loop; dog-leg, oxbow, zigzag; Brit. hairpin bend, hairpin turn, hairpin; rare incurvation.
▷ANTONYMS straight.

beneath preposition **1** *we sat in the shade beneath the trees*: **under**, underneath, below, at the foot of, at the bottom of; lower than.
▷ANTONYMS above.
2 *they seemed to think that you were beneath them*: **inferior to**, not so important as, lower in status than, lower than, below; secondary to, subordinate to, subservient to.
▷ANTONYMS above.
3 *she thought such an attitude was beneath her*: **unworthy of**, unbefitting for, inappropriate for, unbecoming to, undignified for, degrading to, below.
▷ANTONYMS above.
▶ **adverb** *the floor was parquet with concrete beneath*: **underneath**, below, further down, lower down, in a lower place.
▷ANTONYMS above.

benediction noun **1** *the preacher asked him to come up and give the benediction*: **blessing**, prayer, invocation, dedication; grace, thanksgiving, thanks; archaic orison.
2 *those who receive the sacrament may be filled with heavenly benediction*: **blessedness**, beatitude, bliss, grace, favour.

benefactor noun *they erected a statue to their most generous benefactor*: **patron**, benefactress, supporter, backer, helper, sponsor, promoter, champion; donor, contributor, subscriber, subsidizer; philanthropist, good Samaritan, sympathizer, well-wisher, friend; informal angel, fairy godmother; archaic almsgiver; rare benefactrice, benefactrix, philanthrope, Maecenas.

beneficent adjective *he sees himself as their beneficent saviour*: **benevolent**, charitable, altruistic, humane, humanitarian, neighbourly, public-spirited, philanthropic; **generous**, magnanimous, munificent, unselfish, ungrudging, unstinting, open-handed, free-handed, free, liberal, lavish, bountiful, benign, indulgent, kind; literary bounteous; rare benignant.
▷ANTONYMS unkind, mean.

beneficial adjective *alcohol taken in moderation can be beneficial to health | their relationship was mutually beneficial*: **advantageous**, favourable, helpful, useful, of use, of benefit, of assistance, serviceable, of service, instrumental, valuable, of value, in one's (best) interests, worthwhile, good, positive; **profitable**, rewarding, gainful, fruitful, lucrative, remunerative, productive; propitious, promising.
▷ANTONYMS disadvantageous, detrimental.

beneficiary noun *she was the major beneficiary of her parents' will*: **heir**, heiress, inheritor, legatee; recipient, receiver, payee, donee, assignee; Law devisee, grantee, cestui que trust; Scottish Law heritor.

benefit noun **1** *they improved the station for the benefit of customers*: **good**, sake, interest, welfare, well-being, satisfaction, enjoyment, advantage, comfort, ease, convenience; help, aid, assistance, avail, use, utility, service.
▷ANTONYMS detriment.
2 *the benefits of massage are endless*: **advantage**, reward, merit, good point, strong point, strength, asset, plus, plus point, bonus, boon, blessing, virtue; perk, fringe benefit, additional benefit, added extra; usefulness, helpfulness, convenience, advantageousness, value, profit; formal perquisite.
▷ANTONYMS disadvantage, drawback.
3 *there is new hope for those who are dependent on benefit*: **social security payments**, social security, state benefit, unemployment benefit, government benefit, benefit payments, public assistance allowance, welfare, insurance money, sick pay, pension; charity, donations, gifts, financial assistance; informal the dole; Scottish informal the buroo, the broo.
▶ **verb 1** *they came to a compromise that benefited all parties*: **be advantageous to**, be beneficial to, be of advantage to, be to the advantage of, profit, do good to, be of service to, serve, be useful to, be of use to, be helpful to, be of help to, help, aid, assist, be of assistance to; better, improve, strengthen, boost, advance, further.
▷ANTONYMS damage.
2 *she benefited from a credit and loan scheme*: **profit**, gain, reap benefits, reap financial reward, make money; make the most of, exploit, turn to one's advantage, put to good use, do well out of; informal cash in, make a killing.

benevolence noun *the hospital depended on the benevolence of local businessmen*: **kindness**, kind-heartedness, big-heartedness, goodness, goodwill, benignity, compassion, consideration, thoughtfulness, decency, public-spiritedness, social conscience, charity, charitableness, altruism, humanity, humanitarianism, philanthropism; **generosity**, magnanimity, magnanimousness, munificence, unselfishness, open-handedness, free-handedness, largesse, lavishness, liberality, beneficence, indulgence; historical almsgiving; literary bounty, bounteousness.
▷ANTONYMS spite; miserliness.

benevolent adjective **1** *they thought him a benevolent and conscientious guardian*: **kind**, kindly, kind-hearted, warm-hearted, tender-hearted, big-hearted, good-natured, good, gracious, tolerant, benign, compassionate, caring, sympathetic, considerate, thoughtful, well meaning, obliging, accommodating, helpful, decent, neighbourly, public-spirited, charitable, altruistic, humane, humanitarian, philanthropic; **generous**, magnanimous, munificent, unselfish, ungrudging, unstinting, open-handed, free-handed, free, liberal, lavish, bountiful, beneficent, indulgent; literary bounteous; rare benignant.
▷ANTONYMS unkind; tight-fisted.
2 *a benevolent institution for the aged and infirm*: **charitable**, non-profit-making, non-profit, not-for-profit; historical almsgiving; rare eleemosynary.

> *Word toolkit* **benevolent**
>
> See **generous**.

benighted adjective *he knew what was best for the benighted peasant*: **ignorant**, unenlightened, uneducated, unschooled, untutored, illiterate, unlettered, unlearned, unscholarly, unread, uninformed, backward, simple; primitive, uncivilized, unsophisticated, unrefined, uncouth, unpolished, uncultured, philistine, barbarian, barbaric, barbarous, savage, crude, coarse, rough, vulgar, gross; informal yobbish; literary nescient; archaic rude.
▷ANTONYMS enlightened.

benign adjective **1** *he adopted a benign grandfatherly role*: **kindly**, kind, warm-hearted, good-natured, friendly, warm, affectionate, agreeable, amiable, good-humoured, genial, congenial, cordial, approachable, tender, tender-hearted, soft-hearted, gentle, sympathetic, compassionate, caring, considerate, thoughtful, helpful, well disposed, obliging, accommodating, generous, big-hearted, unselfish, benevolent, gracious, liberal, indulgent; rare benignant.
▷ANTONYMS unfriendly, hostile.
2 *the climate becomes more benign nearer to the Black Sea*: **temperate**, mild, gentle, clement, calm, balmy, pleasant, agreeable, soft, soothing, refreshing; healthy, health-giving, wholesome, salubrious.
▷ANTONYMS harsh; unhealthy.
3 *the lizard has a chance of survival if its environment is benign*: **favourable**, advantageous, beneficial; helpful, propitious, auspicious, lucky, opportune, fortunate, providential, encouraging, benevolent, conducive; right, good.
▷ANTONYMS unfavourable.
4 *he had surgery to remove a benign tumour*: **harmless**, non-malignant, non-cancerous, non-dangerous, innocent; curable, remediable, treatable, removable; technical benignant.
▷ANTONYMS malignant.

> *Word toolkit* **benign**
>
> See **harmless**.

bent adjective **1** *the bucket was dented and had a bent handle*: **twisted**, **crooked**, warped, contorted, deformed, misshapen, out of shape, irregular; bowed, arched, curved, angled, hooked, kinked, kinky; N. Amer. informal pretzeled.
▷ANTONYMS straight.
2 Brit. informal *he hates drug dealers more than he hates bent coppers*: **corrupt**, corruptible, bribable, buyable, venal, fraudulent, swindling, grafting, criminal, lawless, villainous; dishonest, underhand, unprincipled, unscrupulous, amoral, dishonourable, untrustworthy, double-dealing, rotten; Law malfeasant; informal crooked, shady, tricky; Brit. informal dodgy; archaic hollow-hearted.
▷ANTONYMS law-abiding.
3 See **homosexual**.
□ **bent on** *she's bent on going and nothing will stop her*: **intent on**, determined on, set on, insistent on, fixed on, resolved on, hell-bent on, firm about, committed to; single-minded about, obsessive about, obsessed with, fanatical about, fixated on.
▶ **noun** *she has an artistic bent*: **inclination**, predisposition, disposition,

b

instinct, orientation, leaning, tendency, penchant, bias, predilection, proclivity, propensity, talent, gift, flair, ability, knack, aptitude, facility, faculty, skill, capability, capacity, forte, genius; mind, brain, head.

benumbed adjective *my benumbed brain was quickened by the bracing air.* See **numb** (adjective).

bequeath verb **1** *he* ***bequeathed*** *his artworks* ***to*** *the city of Philadelphia*: **leave**, leave in one's will, will, make over, pass on, hand on, hand down, cede, consign, commit, entrust, grant, transfer, convey; **donate**, give, give over, turn over, vouchsafe; bestow on, confer on; Law demise, devise.
2 *they bequeathed their expertise to those who built the railways*: **hand down**, hand on, pass on, impart, transmit.

bequest noun *they received a bequest of over £300,000*: **legacy**, inheritance, endowment, estate, heritage, bestowal, bequeathal, settlement, provision, benefaction, gift, present, contribution, donation; Law devise, hereditament.

berate verb *she had to berate Patsy and Betsy for giggling*: **rebuke**, reprimand, reproach, reprove, admonish, remonstrate with, chastise, chide, upbraid, take to task, pull up, castigate, lambaste, read someone the Riot Act, give someone a piece of one's mind, go on at, haul over the coals, criticize, censure; informal tell off, give someone a talking-to, give someone a telling-off, dress down, give someone a dressing-down, give someone an earful, give someone a roasting, give someone a rocket, give someone a rollicking, rap, rap over the knuckles, slap someone's wrist, let someone have it, send someone away with a flea in their ear, bawl out, give someone hell, come down on, blow up at, pitch into, lay into, lace into, tear into, give someone a caning, put on the mat, slap down, blast, rag, keelhaul; Brit. informal tick off, have a go at, monster, carpet, give someone a carpeting, give someone a mouthful, tear someone off a strip, tear a strip off someone, give someone what for, give someone some stick, wig, give someone a wigging, give someone a row, row; N. Amer. informal chew out, ream out, take to the woodshed; Brit. vulgar slang bollock, give someone a bollocking; N. Amer. vulgar slang chew someone's ass, ream someone's ass; dated call down, rate, give someone a rating, trim; rare reprehend, objurgate.
▷ANTONYMS praise.

bereave verb *she was bereaved of two daughters*: **deprive**, dispossess, rob, divest, strip.

bereaved adjective *they sent condolences to the bereaved family*: **orphaned**, **widowed**; grieving, sorrowful, lamenting; deprived, dispossessed.

bereavement noun **1** *he is slowly getting over his bereavement*: **loss**, deprivation, dispossession, privation; grief, sorrow, sadness, suffering, hurt, trauma.
2 *she suffered three bereavements in quick succession*: **death in the family**, loss, passing, passing away, passing on, demise, decease, end, expiry, expiration; rare quietus.

bereft adjective *the peasantry were* ***bereft of*** *any opportunity for social mobility*: **deprived of**, robbed of, stripped of, denuded of; **cut off from**, parted from, devoid of, destitute of, bankrupt of; wanting, in need of, lacking, without, free from; low on, short of, deficient in; informal minus, sans, clean out of, fresh out of.

berserk adjective *he went berserk when he heard his wife had left him*: **mad**, crazy, insane, out of one's mind, hysterical, beside oneself, frenzied, crazed, demented, maniacal, manic, frantic, wound up, worked up, raving, wild; **enraged**, raging, out of control, uncontrollable, amok, on the rampage; informal off one's head, up the wall, through the roof, off the deep end, ape, bananas, bonkers, mental, barmy, nutty, nuts, bats, batty, hyper; Brit. informal spare, crackers; N. Amer. informal postal; Austral./NZ informal crook; vulgar slang apeshit.

berth noun **1** *she suffers badly from seasickness and keeps to her berth*: **bunk**, bed, bunk bed, cot, couch, hammock; sleeping quarters, sleeping accommodation, cabin, compartment, billet; informal sack; Brit. informal pit; Scottish informal kip.
2 *the vessel left its berth*: **docking site**, anchorage, mooring.
□ **give someone/something a wide berth avoid**, **shun**, keep away from, stay away from, steer clear of, keep at arm's length, fight shy of, have nothing to do with, have no truck with, have no dealings with, have no contact with, give something/someone a miss; eschew, dodge, sidestep, circumvent, skirt round.
▶ **verb 1** *the ship berthed at Wallasey docks*: **dock**, moor, land, tie up, make fast.
2 *the boats berthed two or three*: **accommodate**, sleep, provide beds for, put up, house, shelter, lodge.

beseech verb literary *they beseeched him to stay*: **implore**, beg, entreat, importune, plead with, appeal to, exhort, ask urgently, petition, call on, supplicate, pray to, adjure; crave, appeal for; Scottish archaic prig; rare obsecrate, impetrate, obtest.

beset verb **1** *the social problems which beset the UK*: **plague**, bedevil, attack, assail, beleaguer, afflict, torment, torture, rack, oppress, trouble, worry, bother, harass, hound, harry, dog.
2 *they were beset by enemy forces*: **surround**, besiege, hem in, shut in, fence in, box in, encircle, ring round, enclose.

besetting adjective *the besetting sins of greed and sexual immorality*: **persistent**, constant, recurrent, recurring; inveterate, habitual, compulsive, obsessive, obsessional, uncontrollable, irresistible.

beside preposition **1** *Kate walked beside him*: **alongside**, by the side of, at the side of, next to, parallel to, abreast of, at someone's elbow, with, by; **adjacent to**, next door to, cheek by jowl with, hard by; bordering, abutting, neighbouring, close to, near, overlooking; archaic aside of.
2 *beside Paula, she always felt clumsy*: **compared with**, in comparison with, next to, against, contrasted with, in contrast to/with.
□ **beside oneself** *Ursula was beside herself with worry*: **distraught**, overcome, out of one's mind, frantic, desperate, distracted, not knowing what to do with oneself, at one's wits' end, frenzied, in a frenzy; hysterical, unhinged, mad, crazed, berserk, demented; emotional, wound up, worked up, fraught.
□ **beside the point** See **point**[1].

> *Word links* **beside**
>
> **para-** related prefix, as in *parathyroid, parasite*

besides preposition *who did you ask besides Mary?* **apart from**, other than, aside from, but for, save for, not counting, excluding, not including, except, with the exception of, excepting, bar, barring, leaving aside, beyond; **in addition to**, as well as, over and above, above and beyond; N. Amer. informal outside of; archaic forbye.
▶ **adverb 1** *I'm capable of doing the work and a lot more besides*: **as well**, too, in addition, also, into the bargain, on top of that, to boot; archaic therewithal.
2 *besides, it's nothing to do with you*: **furthermore**, moreover, further; **anyway**, anyhow, in any case, be that as it may; informal what's more; N. Amer. informal anyways.

besiege verb **1** *in 1560 the English army besieged the town of Leith*: **lay siege to**, beleaguer, blockade, surround; shut off, block off; archaic invest.
2 *he was besieged by fans*: **surround**, mob, crowd round, swarm round, throng round, ring round, encircle; hem in, shut in; set upon, fall upon.
3 *guilt besieged him for many years*: **oppress**, torment, torture, rack, plague, afflict, harrow, beset, beleaguer, trouble, bedevil, cause suffering to, prey on, weigh heavily on, lie heavy on, gnaw at, nag at, haunt.
4 *the television station was besieged with calls from worried homeowners*: **overwhelm**, inundate, deluge, flood, swamp, snow under; bombard.

besmirch verb *he had besmirched the good name of his family*: **sully**, tarnish, blacken, drag through the mud/mire, stain, taint, smear, befoul, soil, contaminate, pollute, disgrace, dishonour, bring discredit to, stigmatize, injure, damage, debase, spoil, ruin; slander, defame; literary smirch, besmear; archaic breathe on, spot.
▷ANTONYMS honour, enhance.

besotted adjective *she won't listen to me—she's* ***besotted with*** *him*: **infatuated with**, smitten with, in love with, head over heels in love with, hopelessly in love with, obsessed with, passionate about, consumed with desire for, devoted to, doting on, greatly enamoured of, very attracted to, very taken with, charmed by, captivated by, enchanted by, enthralled by, bewitched by, beguiled by, under someone's spell, hypnotized by; informal bowled over by, swept off one's feet by, struck on, crazy about, mad about, wild about, potty about, nuts about, very keen on, gone on, really into, hung up on, carrying a torch for; literary ensorcelled by.
▷ANTONYMS indifferent.

bespatter verb *his shoes and trousers were bespattered with mud*: **splatter**, spatter, splash, speck, fleck, mark, spot, muddy, dirty, soil, smear, stain, sully, bedaub, begrime, befoul, besmirch; Scottish & Irish slabber; informal splotch, splodge, splosh.

bespeak verb *a room which, without being pretentious, bespoke his new standing in life*: **indicate**, be an indication of, be evidence of, be a sign of, testify to, bear witness to, reflect, demonstrate, show, manifest, display, signify, denote, point to, evince, evidence; reveal, betray; imply, intimate; informal spell (out); literary betoken.
▷ANTONYMS belie.

best adjective **1** *the best hotel in Paris*: **finest**, greatest, top, foremost, leading, pre-eminent, premier, prime, first, chief, principal, supreme, of the highest quality, superlative, unrivalled, second to none, without equal, nonpareil, unsurpassed, unsurpassable, peerless, matchless, unparalleled, unbeaten, unbeatable, unexcelled, optimum, optimal, ultimate, surpassing, incomparable, ideal, perfect; highest, record-breaking; French par excellence; informal star, number-one, one-in-a-million, a cut above the rest, top-drawer; rare unexampled.
▷ANTONYMS worst.
2 *do whatever you think best*: **most advantageous**, most suitable, most fitting, most appropriate, most apt; most prudent, most sensible, most advisable, most desirable.
▶ **adverb 1** *the best-dressed man in Britain*: **to the highest standard**, in the best way.
▷ANTONYMS worst.

2 *the food he liked best*: **most**, to the highest/greatest degree.
▷**ANTONYMS** least.
3 *this is best done at home*: **most sensibly**, most prudently, most wisely, most suitably, most fittingly, most advantageously, most usefully; better.
□ **had best** *I'd best be going*: **ought to**, should.
▶ **noun 1** *people for whom only the best will do*: **finest**, top, cream, choice, choicest, prime, elite, crème de la crème, flower, jewel in the crown, nonpareil; informal the tops, the pick of the bunch.
2 *he always tries to see the best in others*: **most favourable/pleasant aspect**, best point; advantage, asset, virtue, good point.
3 *she dressed in her best*: **best clothes**, finery, Sunday best; informal best bib and tucker, glad rags.
4 *give her my best when you see her*: **best wishes**, regards, kind/kindest regards, greetings, compliments, compliments of the season, felicitations, respects; love.
□ **at one's best** *Lily was not at her best yesterday*: **on top form**, in the pink, in great shape, in the best of health; peak, prime; Brit. informal on song; rare in fine feather.
□ **do one's best** *Caroline had done her best to help him*: **do one's utmost**, try one's hardest, try as hard as one can, make every effort, spare no effort, do all one can, give one's all, be at pains; informal bend/fall/lean over backwards, do one's damnedest, go all out, pull out all the stops, bust a gut, break one's neck, move heaven and earth; N. Amer. informal do one's darnedest/ durnedest; Austral. informal go for the doctor.
▶ **verb** informal *he won't like being bested by a woman*: **defeat**, beat, get the better of, gain the advantage over, get the upper hand over, outdo, outwit, outsmart, worst, be more than a match for, prevail over, conquer, vanquish, trounce, triumph over; surpass, outclass, outshine, put someone in the shade, overshadow, eclipse; informal lick, get one over on.

bestial adjective **1** *Stanley's bestial behaviour*: **savage**, brutish, brutal, barbarous, barbaric, cruel, vicious, violent, inhuman, subhuman; **depraved**, degenerate, unnatural, perverted, corrupt, immoral, amoral, warped, vile, gross, sordid; carnal, lustful, lecherous, licentious, lascivious, goatish, libidinous, lubricious, salacious, prurient, lewd, crude.
▷**ANTONYMS** civilized, humane.
2 *man's bestial ancestors*: **animal**, beast-like, animalistic; rare zoic, theriomorphic, theroid.

bestir verb
□ **bestir oneself** *his friends urged him to bestir himself*: **exert oneself**, make an effort, rouse oneself, get going, get moving, get on with it; informal shake a leg, look lively, get cracking, get weaving, get one's finger out, get off one's backside, get the show on the road; Brit. informal, dated stir one's stumps.

bestow verb *the favours bestowed on him by the new king*: **confer on**, present to, award to, give, grant, vouchsafe, accord to, afford to; vest in, invest in; bequeath to, donate to; allot to, assign to, consign to, apportion to, distribute to, impart to, entrust to, commit to; lavish on, heap on.

bestride verb **1** *he bestrode his horse with the easy grace of a born horseman*: **straddle**, bestraddle, sit/stand astride; mount, get on, get astride, hop on to.
2 *the oilfield bestrides the border of the two countries*: **extend across**, straddle, lie on both sides of; span, bridge.
3 *he stands alone, a colossus bestriding the entire development of modern art*: **dominate**, tower over, be the most important person in.

best-seller noun **success**, brand leader; informal **blockbuster**, chart-topper, chartbuster, hit, smash hit, smash.
▷**ANTONYMS** failure, flop.

best-selling adjective *their best-selling album*: **very successful**, very popular; informal **number-one**, chart-topping, hit, smash.

bet verb **1** *most people would bet their life savings on the prospect*: **wager**, gamble, stake, risk, venture, hazard, chance, lay down, put, place; lay money, put money, lay bets, speculate, try one's luck; informal punt; Brit. informal have a flutter, chance one's arm.
2 informal *I bet it was your idea*: **be certain**, be sure, be convinced, be confident; expect, predict; Brit. informal put one's shirt on.
▶ **noun 1** *a £20 bet*: **wager**, stake, gamble, ante; each-way bet, place bet, ante-post bet, daily double, side bet, Yankee; Brit. accumulator, tricast; N. Amer. perfecta, quinella, trifecta; informal long shot; Brit. informal flutter, punt.
2 informal *my bet is that Liverpool won't win anything*: **prediction**, forecast, guess; opinion, belief, feeling, view, theory.
3 informal *your best bet is to go early*: **option**, choice, alternative, course of action, plan.

bête noire noun **bugbear**, **pet hate**, pet aversion, anathema, abomination, bogey, bugaboo; a thorn in one's flesh/side, the bane of one's life.
▷**ANTONYMS** favourite.

betide verb literary *I waited with beating heart, not knowing what would betide*: **happen**, occur, take place, come about, transpire, arise, chance; result, ensue, follow, develop, supervene; N. Amer. informal go down; literary come to pass, befall, bechance; rare hap, arrive, eventuate.

betoken verb literary **1** *she wondered if his cold, level gaze betokened indifference or anger*: **indicate**, be an indication of, signify, be a sign of, be evidence of, evidence, manifest, mean, denote, represent, show, demonstrate, bespeak; informal spell.
2 *the falling comet betokened the true end of Merlin's powers*: **presage**, portend, augur, be an omen of, be a sign of, be a warning of, warn of, bode, foreshadow, foretell, prophesy, be a harbinger of, herald; literary foretoken, forebode, harbinger.

betray verb **1** *I trusted them and they betrayed me*: **break one's promise to**, **be disloyal to**, be unfaithful to, break faith with, play someone false, fail, let down; double-cross, deceive, cheat; inform on/against, give away, denounce, sell out, stab someone in the back, be a Judas to, give someone a Judas kiss, bite the hand that feeds one; turn traitor, sell the pass; English Law turn Queen's/King's evidence; informal split on, blow the whistle on, rat on, peach on, stitch up, do the dirty on, sell down the river, squeal on, squeak on; Brit. informal grass on, shop, sneak on; N. Amer. informal rat out, drop a/the dime on, finger, job; Austral./NZ informal dob on, pimp on, pool, shelf, put someone's pot on, point the bone at; rare delate.
▷**ANTONYMS** be loyal to.
2 *she hoped her face didn't betray her feelings*: **reveal**, disclose, divulge, give away, leak, lay bare, make known, uncover, unmask, expose, bring out into the open, tell; let slip, let out, let drop, blurt out; give the game away, let the cat out of the bag; informal blab, spill; archaic discover.
▷**ANTONYMS** conceal, hide.

betrayal noun **1** *a cowardly act of betrayal*: **disloyalty**, **treachery**, perfidy, perfidiousness, bad faith, faithlessness, falseness; duplicity, deception, double-dealing; breach of faith, breach of trust, stab in the back, Judas kiss; double-cross, sell-out; French trahison des clercs; rare false-heartedness, Punic faith.
▷**ANTONYMS** loyalty, faithfulness.
2 *the betrayal of a secret*: **revelation**, disclosure, divulging, giving away, leaking, leak, telling; rare divulgation.

betrayer noun **traitor**, back-stabber, Judas, double-crosser; renegade, quisling, fifth columnist, double agent, collaborator, informer, mole, stool pigeon; turncoat, defector, apostate, deserter; fraternizer, colluder, false friend; informal snake in the grass, whistle-blower, grass, supergrass, rat, scab, stoolie, nose; Brit. informal nark; N. Amer. informal fink; rare traditor, renegado, Catilinarian.

betrothal noun dated **engagement**, betrothment, marriage contract; French fiançailles; archaic plighting of one's troth, espousal, affiance, affiancing, handfast; rare sponsalia, subarrhation.

betrothed adjective dated *his youngest son is betrothed to the Count's daughter*. See **engaged** (sense 2).

better adjective **1** *the better player | better facilities*: **superior**, finer, of higher quality, greater, in a different class, one step ahead; more acceptable, preferable, recommended; informal a cut above, streets ahead, head and shoulders above, ahead of the pack/field.
▷**ANTONYMS** worse, inferior.
2 *there couldn't be a better time to take up this job*: **more advantageous**, more suitable, more fitting, more appropriate, more useful, more valuable, more desirable.
▷**ANTONYMS** worse.
3 *is Emma any better today?* **healthier**, fitter, stronger, less ill; well, cured, healed, recovered; convalescent, recovering, on the road to recovery, making progress, progressing, improving; informal on the mend, looking up.
▷**ANTONYMS** worse.
▶ **adverb 1** *I played better today*: **to a higher standard**, in a superior/finer way.
2 *you may find alternatives that suit you better*: **more**, to a greater degree.
3 *the money could be better spent on more urgent cases*: **more wisely**, more sensibly, more suitably, more fittingly, more advantageously.
▶ **verb 1** *a record bettered by only one other non-league side*: **surpass**, improve on, beat, exceed, excel, top, cap, trump, eclipse, outstrip, outdo, outmatch, go one better than; informal best.
2 *musicians will be advised on how to better their work*: **improve**, make better, ameliorate, raise, advance, further, lift, upgrade, enhance; reform, rectify; rare meliorate.
▷**ANTONYMS** worsen.
▶ **noun**
□ **get the better of** *I was going to disagree but impulse got the better of me | he usually gets the better of the bigger and stronger animals*: **defeat**, beat, best, conquer, trounce, thrash, rout, vanquish, overcome, overwhelm, overpower, destroy, drub, triumph over, prevail over, gain a victory over, win over/against, worst, subdue, quash, crush; informal lick, slaughter, murder, kill, clobber, hammer, whip, paste, crucify, demolish, wipe the floor with, make mincemeat of, take to the cleaners, walk (all) over, run rings around; Brit. informal stuff, marmalize; N. Amer. informal shellac, skunk.

betterment noun *the betterment of society as a whole*: **improvement**, amelioration, advancement, change for the better, furtherance, upgrading, enhancement; reform, rectification.

between preposition **1** *Philip stood between his parents*: **in the middle of**, with one ... on either side; archaic betwixt.

b

2 *the bond between her and her mother*: **connecting**, linking, joining; uniting, allying.
□ **between you and me/ourselves** *just between you and me, I think I'm in love with him*: **between us**, entre nous, in (strict) confidence, confidentially, in private, privately, off the record; informal between you and me and the bedpost/gatepost/wall; Latin sub rosa; archaic under the rose.

> *Word links* **between**
>
> **inter-** related prefix, as in *international, inter-agency*

bevel noun **slope**, slant, angle, cant, chamfer, mitre, oblique, diagonal, tilt; rare bezel.

beverage noun **drink**; liquid refreshment; archaic potation; rare libation, potable.

bevy noun *a bevy of beautiful women*: **group**, gang, troop, troupe, party, company, band, body, crowd, pack, army, herd, flock, drove, horde, galaxy, assemblage, gathering; knot, cluster, covey; informal bunch, gaggle, posse, crew.

bewail verb *many bewailed the decline of standards*: **lament**, bemoan, beat one's breast about, wring one's hands over, rue, express regret about, sigh over, deplore, complain about; mourn, grieve over, sorrow for/over, express woe/sorrow for, cry/weep over, wail/keen over; archaic plain over.

beware verb *there are loose rocks in the area so beware!* **be on your guard**, watch out, look out, mind out, be wary, be careful, be cautious, be on the lookout, be on the alert, keep your eyes open, keep a sharp lookout, be on the qui vive; take care, take heed, have a care, take it slowly, look where you're going, tread carefully, proceed with caution; informal watch your step, keep an eye out, keep your eyes peeled/skinned, look before you leap, think twice; Brit. school slang, dated cave; Golf fore; Hunting ware.
▷ANTONYMS ignore.

bewilder verb *his words bewildered Sally*: **baffle**, mystify, bemuse, perplex, puzzle, confuse, confound, nonplus, disconcert, throw, set someone thinking; informal flummox, discombobulate, faze, stump, beat, fox, make someone scratch their head, be all Greek to, make someone's head spin, floor, fog; N. Amer. informal buffalo; archaic wilder, gravel, maze, cause to be at a stand, distract, pose; rare obfuscate.
▷ANTONYMS enlighten.

bewildered adjective *Kate looked completely bewildered*: **baffled**, mystified, bemused, perplexed, puzzled, confused, nonplussed, at sea, at a loss, thrown off balance, disorientated, taken aback; informal flummoxed, bamboozled, discombobulated; Canadian & Austral./NZ informal bushed; archaic wildered, distracted, mazed.

bewildering adjective *the bewildering complexity of world politics*: **baffling**, difficult to understand, perplexing, puzzling, mystifying, mysterious, confusing, disconcerting; unaccountable, inexplicable, impenetrable, unfathomable, above one's head, beyond one; complex, complicated, involved, intricate, convoluted, labyrinthine, Byzantine, Daedalian, Gordian; archaic wildering.
▷ANTONYMS straightforward, comprehensible.

bewitch verb **1** *his relatives were convinced that he had been bewitched*: **cast a spell on**, put a spell on, enchant; possess, witch, curse; N. Amer. hex, hoodoo; Austral. point the bone at; in S. Africa tagati; literary entrance.
2 *she was bewitched by her surroundings*: **captivate**, enchant, entrance, enrapture, charm, beguile, delight, fascinate, enthral, seduce, ravish, spellbind, hold spellbound, mesmerize, hypnotize, transfix; rare rapture.
▷ANTONYMS repel.

beyond preposition **1** *farm buildings were visible beyond the trees*: **on the far side of**, on the farther side of, on the other side of, further on than, behind, past, after; over; Scottish outwith.
2 *nobody ever worked beyond six o'clock*: **later than**, past, after.
3 *matters beyond his understanding*: **outside the range of**, beyond the power/capacity of, outside the limitations of, surpassing.
4 *inflation beyond 10 per cent*: **greater than**, more than, exceeding, in excess of, above, over and above, above and beyond, upwards of.
5 *there was little vegetation beyond scrub and brush growth*: **apart from**, except, other than.
▸ adverb *a view of Hobart with Mount Wellington beyond*: **further on**, far off, far away, in the distance, afar; archaic yonder.
▷ANTONYMS near, close.

> *Word links* **beyond**
>
> **extra-** related prefix, as in *extraterritorial, extracellular*
> **hyper-** related prefix, as in *hypersonic, hyperplasia*
> **para-** related prefix, as in *paranormal, paratyphoid*

bias noun **1** *the chairman accused the media of bias | he did not always hide his pro-British bias*: **prejudice**, partiality, partisanship, favouritism, unfairness, one-sidedness; bigotry, intolerance, racism, racialism, sexism, heterosexism, homophobia, chauvinism, anti-Semitism, discrimination, a jaundiced eye; predisposition, leaning, tendency, inclination, propensity, proclivity, proneness, predilection; French parti pris.
▷ANTONYMS objectivity, fairness, impartiality.
2 *a dress cut on the bias*: **diagonal**, cross, slant, oblique, angle.
▸ verb *witnesses' recollections may be biased by discussions with other people*: **prejudice**, influence, colour, sway, weight, predispose; distort, skew, bend, twist, warp; angle, load, slant.

biased adjective *a biased view of the situation*: **prejudiced**, partial, partisan, one-sided, blinkered, subjective; bigoted, intolerant, discriminatory, racist, racialist, sexist, heterosexist, homophobic, chauvinistic, chauvinist, anti-Semitic; jaundiced, distorted, warped, twisted, skewed; French parti pris.
▷ANTONYMS unbiased, impartial, fair.

> *Choose the right word* **biased, prejudiced, partial**
>
> These words all denote a tendency to be unfairly or irrationally opinionated in favour of or against people or groups.
>
> Someone who is **biased** is predisposed to make judgements in favour of or against someone or something, typically because of some emotional commitment rather than because of any rational consideration. The resulting judgements are generally unfair or inaccurate (*do you think the police in the area are biased against young people? | maybe he was biased, but he thought his daughter was the best player*).
>
> **Prejudiced** describes someone who brings a ready-made opinion, especially a value judgement, to some question or issue, without consideration of the actual facts. This opinion is likely to affect their other judgements and attitudes, too (*William's grandad was prejudiced against Americans*). It is much more common to be *prejudiced against* someone or something than *prejudiced in favour of* them.
>
> **Partial** can be used to mean 'unjustly weighted in favour of one side', but often lacks the implication of injustice (*he was partial only in so far as he took a stand against conservatism*). Although *impartial* is a more common word than *unbiased* or *unprejudiced*, *partial* in this sense is relatively uncommon.

Bible noun **1** *he read the Bible and prayed*: **the (Holy) Scriptures**, Holy Writ, the Good Book, the Book of Books; New English Bible, King James Bible, Authorized Version, Revised Version, Good News Bible, Jerusalem Bible, Geneva Bible; Gideon Bible.
2 informal *the professional electrician's bible*: **handbook**, manual, ABC, companion, guide, primer, essential book, authoritative book; Latin vade mecum; rare enchiridion.

bibliography noun **list of references**, book list, list of books, catalogue, record; rare bibliotheca.

bibliophile noun **book lover**; informal bookworm; rare bibliomaniac, bibliomane, bibliolater, bibliophilist.

bicker verb *couples who bicker over who gets what from the divorce*: **squabble**, argue; **quarrel**, wrangle, fight, fall out, have a disagreement, disagree, dispute, spar, bandy words, have words, be at each other's throats, lock horns; informal scrap, argufy, have a tiff, have a spat, spat; Brit. informal row, have a row, have a barney; archaic altercate, chop logic.
▷ANTONYMS agree.

> *Choose the right word* **bicker, quarrel, argue, wrangle, dispute**
>
> See **quarrel**.

bicycle noun **cycle**, two-wheeler, pedal cycle; mountain bike, racing bike, racer, roadster, shopper; tandem, unicycle, tricycle; informal **bike**, pushbike; historical penny-farthing, velocipede, boneshaker.

bid[1] verb **1** *a consortium of dealers bid a world record price for the painting*: **offer**, make an offer of, put in a bid of, put up, tender, proffer, propose, submit, put forward, advance.
2 *the two forwards are bidding for a place in the England side*: **try to obtain**, try to get, make a pitch for, make a bid for.
▸ noun **1** *I put in a bid of £3,000*: **offer**, tender, proposal, submission; price, sum, amount; advance, ante.
2 *an investigation carried out in a bid to establish what had happened*: **attempt**, effort, endeavour, try; informal go, crack, stab.

bid[2] verb **1** *she turned and bid him farewell*: **wish**.
2 literary *I did as he bade me*: **order**, command, tell, instruct, direct, require, enjoin, charge, demand, call upon.
3 literary *he bade his companions enter*: **invite to**, ask to, request to, tell to.

biddable adjective *a pretty, biddable child*: **obedient**, tractable, amenable, pliable, pliant, complaisant, cooperative, malleable, persuadable, like putty in one's hands, manipulable; docile, compliant, dutiful, meek, unresisting, submissive, passive, yielding; informal, dated milky; rare persuasible.
▷ANTONYMS disobedient, uncooperative.

b

> *Choose the right word* **biddable, obedient, docile, compliant, dutiful**
>
> See **obedient**.

bidding[1] noun *she was here at his bidding*: **command**, order, instruction, dictate, decree, injunction, demand, mandate, direction, charge, summons, call; wish, desire, will; request, invitation; literary behest; archaic hest.

bidding[2] noun **1** *I opened the bidding at £200*: **auction**; making of bids, offering of bids.
2 *the bidding rose to £280,000*: **bids**, offers, tenders.

big adjective **1** *a big garden | big buildings*: **large**, sizeable, of considerable size, substantial, considerable, great, huge, immense, enormous, extensive, colossal, massive, mammoth, vast, prodigious, tremendous, gigantic, giant, monumental, mighty, stupendous, gargantuan, elephantine, titanic, epic, mountainous, megalithic, monstrous, Brobdingnagian; towering, tall, high, lofty; outsize, oversized, overgrown, cumbersome, unwieldy; inordinate, unlimited, goodly; capacious, voluminous, commodious, spacious, good-size(d), fair-size(d); king-size(d), man-size, family-size(d), economy-size(d); informal jumbo, whopping, whopping great, thumping, thumping great, bumper, mega, humongous, monster, astronomical, almighty, dirty great, socking great, tidy; Brit. informal whacking, whacking great, ginormous; literary massy.
▷ANTONYMS small, little.
2 *a big man with a square red face*: **well built**, sturdily built, heavily built, sturdy, brawny, burly, broad-shouldered, muscular, muscly, well muscled, robust, rugged, lusty, Herculean, bulky, strapping, thickset, stocky, solid, hefty, meaty; tall, huge, gigantic; fat, stout, portly, plump, heavy, overweight, oversize, fleshy, paunchy, corpulent, obese, gargantuan, elephantine; informal hunky, hulking, beefy, husky; dated stalwart; literary thewy, stark.
▷ANTONYMS small, slight, short.
3 *you're a big girl now | my big brother*: **grown-up**, adult, mature, grown, full grown; elder, older.
4 *it's a big decision, so don't rush it*: **important**, significant, major, of great import, of significance, momentous, of moment, weighty, consequential, of consequence, far-reaching, key, vital, critical, crucial, life-and-death, high-priority, serious, grave, solemn; no joke, no laughing matter.
▷ANTONYMS minor, unimportant, trivial.
5 informal *a big man in the government*: **powerful**, **important**, prominent, influential, high-powered, leading, pre-eminent, of high standing, outstanding, well known, eminent, distinguished, principal, foremost, noteworthy, notable, noted; N. Amer. major-league.
▷ANTONYMS unimportant, obscure.
6 informal *a small company with big plans*: **ambitious**, far-reaching, on a grand scale; grandiose, unrealistic, overambitious.
▷ANTONYMS modest.
7 *she's got a big heart*: **generous**, **kind**, kindly, kind-hearted, caring, compassionate, loving, benevolent, magnanimous, unselfish, altruistic, selfless, philanthropic.
8 informal *African bands are big in Britain*: **popular**, successful, commercially successful, in demand, sought-after, all the rage; informal hot, in, cool, trendy, now, hip; Brit. informal, dated all the go.
□ **too big for one's boots** informal **conceited**, full of oneself, cocky, boastful, arrogant, cocksure, above oneself, self-important, immodest, swaggering, strutting; vain, self-satisfied, self-congratulatory, pleased with oneself, self-loving, in love with oneself, self-admiring, self-regarding, smug, complacent; informal big-headed, swollen-headed; literary vainglorious; rare peacockish.
▷ANTONYMS modest.

big-headed adjective informal **conceited**, arrogant, boastful, cocky, cocksure, full of oneself, above oneself, self-important, immodest, swaggering, strutting; vain, self-satisfied, self-congratulatory, pleased with oneself, self-loving, in love with oneself, self-admiring, self-regarding, smug, complacent; informal swollen-headed, too big for one's boots; literary vainglorious; rare peacockish.
▷ANTONYMS modest, self-effacing.

big-hearted adjective *thousands of big-hearted readers pledged cash to help the aid effort*: **generous**, magnanimous, munificent, open-handed, bountiful, free-handed, generous to a fault, ungrudging, unstinting, charitable, philanthropic, benevolent, beneficent; kind, kindly, kind-hearted, unselfish, altruistic, selfless; literary bounteous.
▷ANTONYMS mean.

bigot noun **dogmatist**, partisan, sectarian, prejudiced person; racist, racialist, sexist, homophobe, chauvinist, jingoist, anti-Semite; informal male chauvinist pig, MCP.

bigoted adjective *a bigoted group of reactionaries*: **prejudiced**, biased, partial, one-sided, sectarian, discriminatory; **intolerant**, narrow-minded, blinkered, illiberal, inflexible, uncompromising, fanatical, dogmatic, opinionated; racist, racialist, sexist, heterosexist, homophobic, chauvinistic, chauvinist, anti-Semitic, jingoistic; jaundiced, warped, twisted, distorted; French parti pris.
▷ANTONYMS tolerant, liberal.

bigotry noun **prejudice**, bias, partiality, partisanship, sectarianism, discrimination, unfairness, injustice; **intolerance**, narrow-mindedness, fanaticism, dogmatism; racism, racialism, sexism, heterosexism, homophobia, chauvinism, anti-Semitism, jingoism; US Jim Crowism.
▷ANTONYMS tolerance.

bigwig noun informal **VIP**, important person, notable, notability, personage, dignitary, grandee, panjandrum; celebrity; magnate, mogul; informal somebody, heavyweight, hotshot, big shot, big noise, big gun, big cheese, big fish, biggie, big bug, Big Chief, Big Daddy, honcho; Brit. informal brass hat; N. Amer. informal big wheel; Austral./NZ informal joss.
▷ANTONYMS nobody, nonentity.

bijou adjective *a bijou Chelsea flat*: **small**, little, compact, snug, cosy; desirable, sought-after; elegant, stylish, chic, fashionable.

bilge noun informal *a review dismissed the book as bilge*. See **nonsense**.

bilious adjective **1** *I woke up feeling bilious and with a raging headache*: **nauseous**, sick, queasy, nauseated, green about the gills, liverish; N. Amer. informal barfy; rare qualmish.
2 *his bilious disposition*: **bad-tempered**, irritable, irascible, tetchy, testy, grumpy, grouchy, crotchety, cantankerous, curmudgeonly, ill-tempered, ill-natured, ill-humoured, peevish, fractious, disagreeable, pettish, crabbed, crabby, waspish, prickly, peppery, touchy, scratchy, crusty, splenetic, shrewish, short-tempered, hot-tempered, quick-tempered, dyspeptic, choleric, liverish, cross-grained; N. Amer. informal cranky, ornery.
▷ANTONYMS good-humoured.
3 *a bilious green and pink colour scheme*: **lurid**, garish, loud, violent; sickly, nauseating, distasteful, unattractive.
▷ANTONYMS muted, subtle.

bilk verb informal *thousands of investors claimed they had been bilked by his schemes*. See **cheat** (sense 1 of the verb).

bill[1] noun **1** *their bill came to £69*: **invoice**, account, statement, list of charges, tally; amount due; N. Amer. check; informal the damage; N. Amer. informal tab; Brit. informal, dated shot; archaic reckoning, score.
2 *the bill was passed by 189 votes to 108*: **draft law**, proposed legislation, proposal, measure; act, Act of Parliament.
3 *she was top of the bill*: **programme (of entertainment)**, listing, list, line-up; N. Amer. playbill; dated bill of fare.
4 N. Amer. *a ten-dollar bill*: **banknote**, note; N. Amer. greenback.
5 *he had been hard at work posting bills*: **poster**, advertisement, public notice, announcement; flyer, leaflet, circular, handout, handbill; Brit. fly-poster; N. Amer. & Austral. dodger; French affiche; informal ad; Brit. informal advert.
▸ verb **1** *we shall be billing them for the damage caused*: **send an invoice to**, invoice, charge, debit, send a statement to.
2 *Goddard gave assurances that the concert would go ahead as billed*: **advertise**, promote, announce, post, give advance notice of, put up in lights; **schedule**, programme, timetable; N. Amer. slate.
3 *he was* **billed as** *the new Sean Connery*: **describe as**, call, style, label, dub, designate, pronounce; promote as, publicize as, talk up as; informal hype as.

bill[2] noun **1** *a bird's bill*: **beak**; Scottish & N. English neb; technical mandibles.
2 *a view of Portland Bill*: **promontory**, headland, point, head, foreland, cape, peninsula, bluff, ness, naze, horn, spit, tongue; Scottish mull.

billet noun *the troops marched back to their billets*: **living quarters**, quarters, rooms; accommodation, lodging, housing; barracks, cantonment; rare casern.
▸ verb *the farmhouse in which the men were billeted*: **accommodate**, quarter, put up, lodge, house; station, garrison.

billow noun **1** *billows of smoke*: **cloud**, mass.
2 archaic *the billows that break upon the shore*: **wave**, roller, breaker.
▸ verb **1** *her dress* **billowed out** *around her*: **puff up/out**, balloon (out), swell, fill out, bulge out, belly out.
2 *smoke was billowing from the chimney*: **pour**, flow; swirl, spiral, roll, undulate, rise and fall, eddy.

billowing adjective *billowing clouds of dust*: **rolling**, swirling, undulating, rising and falling, billowy, swelling, rippling; rare undulant.

bin noun *flour storage bins*: **container**, receptacle, holder; drum, canister, caddy, box, can, tin, crate; archaic reservatory.

bind verb **1** *bundles of logs bound together with ropes | they bound her hands and feet*: **tie**, tie up, fasten (together), hold together, secure, make fast, attach; rope, strap, lash, truss, tether, hitch, chain, fetter, pinion, shackle, hobble; moor.
▷ANTONYMS untie, release.
2 *Shelley* **bound up** *the wound with a clean dressing*: **bandage**, dress, cover, wrap, swathe, swaddle; strap up, tape up.
3 *the experience had* **bound** *them* **together**: **unite**, join, bond, knit together, draw together, yoke together.
▷ANTONYMS separate.
4 *other OPEC members* **bound themselves** *to return to the quotas of 1984*: **commit oneself**, undertake, give an undertaking, pledge; vow, promise,

swear, give one's word.
5 *clay is made up chiefly of tiny soil particles which bind together tightly*: **stick**, cohere.
6 *a frill with the edges bound in a contrasting colour*: **trim**, hem, edge, border, fringe, rim, band; finish; archaic purfle.
7 *Sarah did not want to be bound by a rigid timetable*: **constrain**, restrict, confine, restrain, tie hand and foot, tie down, shackle; hamper, hinder, inhibit, cramp someone's style; literary trammel.
▶ **noun** informal **1** *I know being disturbed on Christmas Day is a bind*: **nuisance**, annoyance, inconvenience, bore, bother, source of irritation, irritant, problem, trial; informal pain, pain in the neck, pain in the backside, headache, hassle, drag, aggravation, pest; N. Amer. informal pain in the butt; Austral./NZ informal nark; Brit. vulgar slang pain in the arse; dated infliction.
2 *he is in a political bind over the abortion issue*: **predicament**, awkward situation, quandary, dilemma, plight, difficult situation, cleft stick, mess, quagmire; impasse, double bind; informal spot, tight spot, hole.

binding **adjective** *a legally binding agreement*: **irrevocable**, unalterable, unbreakable, indissoluble, permanent; compulsory, obligatory, imperative, mandatory, necessary; conclusive.

binge **noun** informal **1** *after a midweek game in London, the two lads went on a two-day binge*: **drinking bout**, debauch; informal bender, session, sesh, booze-up, beer-up, souse, drunk, blind; Scottish informal skite; N. Amer. informal jag, toot; NZ informal boozeroo; Brit. vulgar slang piss-up; literary bacchanal, bacchanalia; archaic wassail, fuddle, potation.
2 *a shopping binge*: **spree**, unrestrained bout, orgy; informal splurge.

biography **noun** **life story**, life history, life, memoir, profile, account; informal bio, biog; rare prosopography.

biological **adjective** *two conditions are essential to support biological growth: nutrients and moisture*: **biotic**, biologic, organic, living; botanic, botanical, zoologic, zoological.

> *Word toolkit* **biological**
>
> See **organic**.

bird **noun** **fowl**; songbird, warbler, passerine; bird of prey, raptor; chick, fledgling, nestling; (**birds**) avifauna; informal feathered friend, birdie.

> *Word links* **bird**
>
> **ornith-** related prefix
> **avian** relating to birds
> **aviary**, **nest** home
> **flock**, **flight**, **pod** collective noun
> **ornithology** study of birds
> **ornithophobia** fear of birds

birth **noun** **1** *the birth of a child*: **childbirth**, delivery, nativity, birthing; informal the patter of tiny feet; technical parturition; archaic confinement, accouchement, childbed.
▷**ANTONYMS** death.
2 *the birth of a new era*: **beginning(s)**, emergence, genesis, dawn, dawning, rise, start, arrival, advent; origin, source, fountainhead.
▷**ANTONYMS** end, demise.
3 *he is of noble birth*: **ancestry**, descent, origin(s), parentage, lineage, line, line of descent, heritage, family, stock, blood, bloodline, genealogy, breeding, pedigree, house, extraction, derivation, background; rare filiation, stirps.
□ **give birth to** *she gave birth to a son*: **have**, bear, produce, be delivered of, bring into the world; N. Amer. birth; informal drop; dated mother; archaic be brought to bed of, bring forth.

> *Word links* **birth**
>
> **natal** relating to one's birth
> **antenatal** before birth
> **post-natal** after childbirth
> **obstetrics** branch of medicine concerned with birth

birthmark **noun** **naevus**, strawberry mark, port wine stain; mole; blemish, discoloration, patch.

birthright **noun** **patrimony**, inheritance, heritage; right, due, prerogative, privilege; primogeniture.

biscuit **noun** Brit. **cracker**, wafer; N. Amer. cookie; informal bicky.

bisect **verb** *bisect the exterior angle*: **cut in half**, halve, divide/cut/split in two, split down the middle, cleave, separate into two; cross, intersect.

bisexual **adjective** **1** technical **hermaphrodite**, hermaphroditic; androgynous, epicene; technical monoclinous, gynandrous, gynandromorphic.
2 informal **AC/DC**, bi, swinging both ways, ambidextrous, ambisexual; N. Amer. informal switch-hitting.

bishop **noun** **prelate**, diocesan, metropolitan, suffragan, coadjutor; Orthodox Church exarch.

> *Word links* **bishop**
>
> **episcopal** relating to a bishop

bishopric **noun** **diocese**, see; episcopate, episcopacy, primacy.

bit **noun** **1** *a bit of cake | bits of broken glass | add a bit of salt*: **small portion**, small piece, piece, portion, segment, section, part; chunk, lump, hunk, slice; **fragment**, scrap, shred, flake, chip, shaving, paring, crumb, grain, fleck, speck; **spot**, drop, pinch, dash, soupçon, modicum, dollop; morsel, mouthful, spoonful, bite, taste, gobbet, sample; iota, jot, tittle, whit, atom, particle, scintilla, mote, trace, touch, suggestion, hint, tinge; shard, sliver; snippet, snatch, extract, excerpt; informal smidgen, smidge, tad; Austral./NZ informal skerrick; N. Amer. rare smitch.
2 *wait a bit*: **moment**, minute, second, little while, short time; informal sec, jiffy, jiff; Brit. informal mo, tick, two ticks.
□ **a bit** *he came back looking a bit annoyed*: **rather**, a little, fairly, slightly, somewhat, relatively, quite, to some degree/extent, comparatively, moderately; informal pretty, sort of, kind of, kinda, a tad, ish.
▷**ANTONYMS** very, extremely.
□ **bits and bobs/pieces** *there are a number of openings and storage areas for all sorts of bits and bobs*: **odds and ends**, oddments, stuff, paraphernalia, things, miscellanea, bric-a-brac, sundries, knick-knacks, souvenirs, keepsakes, mementoes, lumber, flotsam and jetsam; informal junk; Brit. informal odds and sods, gubbins, clobber; vulgar slang crap, shit; archaic rummage, truck; rare knick-knackery.
□ **bit by bit** *bit by bit the truth started to emerge*: **gradually**, little by little, in stages, step by step, slowly, one step at a time; piecemeal.
□ **do one's bit** *I try to do my bit for the children*: **assist**, help, lend a hand, be of service, give one's support, give one's backing, contribute, chip in, throw in one's lot; participate, take part, join in, get involved; informal pitch in, play ball, tag along, get in on the act; Brit. informal muck in, get stuck in.
□ **in a bit** *I'll see you in a bit*: **soon**, in a (little) while, in a second, in a minute, in a moment, in a trice, in a flash, shortly, in a short time, in (less than) no time, in no time at all, before you know it, before long, directly; N. Amer. momentarily; informal in a jiffy, in two shakes, in two shakes of a lamb's tail; Brit. informal in a tick, in two ticks, in a mo; N. Amer. informal in a snap; archaic or informal anon; literary ere long.

bitch **noun** informal **1** *I was always such a bitch to him*: **shrew**, vixen, she-devil, hellcat; informal cow, cat; archaic grimalkin.
2 *the night shift is a bitch—you're always tired*: **nightmare**; informal bastard, bummer, ... from hell, swine, pig, stinker; vulgar slang bugger, sod.
3 *her number-one bitch is her love life*: **complaint**, moan, grumble, gripe, grouse, grouch; informal beef, whinge, bellyache.
▶ **verb** *she never **bitched about** other members of the team*: **be spiteful about**, criticize, find fault with, run down, cast aspersions on, speak ill of, slander, malign; complain, moan, grumble, grouse, grouch, gripe; informal whinge, knock, pull to pieces, take apart, do a hatchet job on; N. Amer. informal bad-mouth, trash; Brit. informal slag off, rubbish.
□ **bitch something up** informal **make a mess of**, mess up, spoil, ruin, wreck; botch, bungle, mishandle, mismanage; informal make a hash of, screw up, louse up, muck up, muff, fluff, foul up; Brit. informal make a muck of, make a pig's ear of, cock up, make a Horlicks of; N. Amer. informal flub, goof up; vulgar slang fuck up, bugger up, balls up.

bitchy **adjective** informal *bitchy remarks*. See **spiteful**.

bite **verb** **1** *he bit a mouthful from the sandwich*: **sink one's teeth into**, chew, munch, crunch, champ, tear at, masticate, eat; nibble at, gnaw at.
2 *the insect does not bite people*: **puncture**, prick, pierce, sting, wound.
3 *the acid **bites into** the copper plate*: **corrode**, eat into, eat away at, wear away, burn (into), etch, erode, dissolve, destroy, consume.
4 *my boots failed to bite*: **grip**, hold, get a purchase.
5 *there may be popular unrest as free-market measures begin to bite*: **take effect**, have an effect, be effective, be efficacious, work, function, act, have results, take hold; succeed, be successful, work out, go as planned, have the desired effect/result; informal come off, pay off, do the trick, do the business; N. Amer. informal turn the trick.
6 *a hundred or so retailers are expected to bite*: **accept**, go for it, agree, respond; be lured, be enticed, be tempted, be allured; take the bait, rise to the bait.
▶ **noun** **1** *a bite on the ear can be very painful*: **nip**, snap, chew, munch, nibble, gnaw.
2 *an insect bite*: **puncture**, prick, sting, wound.
3 *Stephen ate a hot dog in three bites*: **mouthful**, piece, morsel, bit.
4 *I only have a bite at lunchtime*: **snack**, light meal, something to eat, mouthful, soupçon, nibbles, titbit, savoury, appetizer; refreshments; informal bite to eat, a little something; Brit. informal elevenses.
5 *the appetizer had a fiery bite*: **piquancy**, pungency, spice, spiciness, saltiness, pepperiness, flavour, flavouring, savour, taste, tastiness, relish, tang, zest, sharpness, tartness, interest, edge, effect, potency; informal kick, punch, oomph, zing.

biting adjective **1** *a biting commentary on contemporary life*: **vicious**, harsh, cruel, savage, cutting, sharp, bitter, sarcastic, scathing, incisive, trenchant, caustic, acid, mordant, astringent, acrimonious, acerbic, stinging, blistering, searing, withering; vitriolic, hostile, spiteful, venomous, vindictive, rancorous, abusive, mean, nasty, aggressive, devastating; informal bitchy, catty.
▷ANTONYMS mild.
2 *the biting wind*: **bitterly cold**, freezing, icy-cold, arctic, glacial, frigid, frosty, icy, chilly; bitter, piercing, penetrating, nipping, stinging, sharp, raw, harsh, wintry; informal nippy; Brit. informal parky; literary chill.
▷ANTONYMS balmy.

bitter adjective **1** *very bitter coffee*: **sharp**, acid, acidic, pungent, acrid, tart, sour, biting, harsh, unsweetened, vinegary, acetous; N. Amer. acerb; archaic or technical acerbic.
▷ANTONYMS sweet.
2 *a bitter old woman*: **resentful**, embittered, aggrieved, dissatisfied, disgruntled, discontented, grudge-bearing, grudging, begrudging, indignant, rancorous, splenetic, spiteful, jaundiced, ill-disposed, sullen, sour, churlish, morose, petulant, peevish, with a chip on one's shoulder.
▷ANTONYMS magnanimous; content.
3 *today's decision has come as a bitter blow*: **painful**, unpleasant, disagreeable, nasty, cruel, awful, distressing, disquieting, disturbing, upsetting, harrowing, heartbreaking, heart-rending, agonizing, unhappy, miserable, wretched, sad, poignant, grievous, traumatic, tragic, chilling, mortifying, galling, vexatious; rare distressful.
▷ANTONYMS welcome.
4 *a bitter north wind*: **intensely cold**, bitterly cold, freezing, icy, icy-cold, arctic, glacial, frosty, frigid, chilly; piercing, penetrating, biting, nipping, stinging, sharp, keen, raw, harsh, wintry; informal nippy; Brit. informal parky; literary chill.
▷ANTONYMS warm, balmy.
5 *a bitter row broke out*: **acrimonious**, virulent, angry, rancorous, spiteful, vindictive, vicious, vitriolic, savage, hostile, ferocious, scathing, antagonistic, hate-filled, venomous, poisonous, acrid, bilious, nasty, ill-natured, malign, choleric.
▷ANTONYMS amicable.

bitterness noun **1** *the bitterness of the medicine*: **sharpness**, acidity, pungency, acridity, tartness, sourness, harshness, vinegariness, acerbity.
▷ANTONYMS sweetness.
2 *his bitterness against his parents grew*: **resentment**, resentfulness, embitteredness, dissatisfaction, disgruntlement, discontent, grudge, pique, indignation, sourness, rancour, spite, sullenness, churlishness, moroseness, petulance, peevishness, spleen, acrimony.
▷ANTONYMS magnanimity; contentment.
3 *the bitterness of war*: **trauma**, pain, painfulness, agony, grief; unpleasantness, disagreeableness, nastiness, awfulness; upset, heartache, heartbreak, unhappiness, misery, wretchedness, sorrow, sadness, distress, desolation, despair, desperation, poignancy, tragedy.
▷ANTONYMS delight.
4 *the bitterness of the wind*: **intense cold**, bitter cold, iciness, frostiness, chilliness, chill; penetration, intensity, bite, nip, sting, sharpness, keenness, rawness, harshness, wintriness; Brit. informal parkiness.
▷ANTONYMS warmth, balminess.
5 *there was irreconcilable bitterness between strikers and strike-breakers*: **acrimony**, hostility, antipathy, antagonism, enmity, animus, friction, virulence, anger, rancour, spite, spitefulness, vindictiveness, viciousness, vitriol, savagery, ferocity, hate, hatred, loathing, detestation, venom, poison, bile, nastiness, ill feeling, ill will, bad blood, malignity, malevolence; literary or archaic choler.
▷ANTONYMS goodwill.

bitty adjective informal *the variety of the material leads to the video being rather bitty*: **disjointed**, incoherent, fragmented, fragmentary, scrappy, piecemeal; inconsistent, unsystematic, jumbled; variable, varying, irregular, uneven, erratic, fitful, patchy.
▷ANTONYMS coherent.

bizarre adjective *his behaviour became more and more bizarre*: **strange**, peculiar, odd, funny, curious, offbeat, outlandish, eccentric, unconventional, unorthodox, queer, unexpected, unfamiliar, abnormal, atypical, unusual, out of the ordinary, out of the way, extraordinary; fantastic, remarkable, puzzling, mystifying, mysterious, perplexing, baffling, unaccountable, inexplicable, incongruous, irregular, singular, ludicrous, comical, ridiculous, droll, deviant, aberrant, grotesque, freak, freakish, surreal; French outré; informal weird, wacky, oddball, way out, freaky, off the wall; Brit. informal rum; N. Amer. informal wacko, bizarro.
▷ANTONYMS ordinary, normal.

> *Word toolkit* **bizarre**
>
> See **eccentric**.

blab verb informal **1** *she blabbed to the press*: **talk**, **give the game/show away**, open one's mouth, tell; informal let the cat out of the bag, spill the beans; Brit. informal blow the gaff, cough.
▷ANTONYMS keep quiet.
2 *there's no need to blab the whole story*: **blurt out**, let slip, let out, tell, reveal, betray, disclose, give away, divulge, leak, take/blow the lid off, blow something wide open; informal let on, spill.
▷ANTONYMS keep something to oneself.

blabber verb informal *she blabbered on and on*. See **prattle**.

blabbermouth noun informal *we can't let a blabbermouth loose with information like this*. See **chatterbox**.

black adjective **1** *a black horse*: **dark**, pitch-black, as black as pitch, pitch-dark, jet-black, inky, coal-black, blackish; Heraldry sable; literary Stygian;
▷ANTONYMS white.
2 *a black night*: **unlit**, dark, starless, moonless, unlighted, unilluminated; gloomy, dusky, dim, murky, dingy, shadowy, overcast; literary crepuscular, tenebrous; rare Stygian, Cimmerian, Tartarean, caliginous.
▷ANTONYMS clear, bright.
3 *his hands were black from the gardening*: **dirty**, filthy, grimy, muddy, mud-caked, grubby, mucky, messy, soiled, stained, smeared, smeary, scummy, slimy, sticky, sooty, dusty, unclean, foul, begrimed, bespattered, befouled, polluted; informal cruddy, grungy, yucky, icky, gloopy, crummy; Brit. informal manky, gungy, grotty; Austral./NZ informal scungy; literary besmirched; rare feculent.
▷ANTONYMS clean.
4 *the blackest day of the war*: **tragic**, disastrous, calamitous, catastrophic, cataclysmic, ruinous, devastating, fatal, fateful, wretched, woeful, grievous, lamentable, miserable, dire, unfortunate, awful, terrible; literary direful.
▷ANTONYMS joyful.
5 *Mary was in a black mood*: **miserable**, unhappy, sad, wretched, broken-hearted, heartbroken, grief-stricken, grieving, sorrowful, sorrowing, mourning, anguished, distressed, desolate, devastated, despairing, inconsolable, disconsolate, downcast, down, downhearted, dejected, crestfallen, cheerless, depressed, pessimistic, melancholy, morose, gloomy, glum, mournful, funereal, doleful, dismal, forlorn, woeful, woebegone, abject, low-spirited, long-faced; informal blue, down in the mouth, down in the dumps; literary dolorous.
▷ANTONYMS cheerful.
6 *black humour*: **cynical**, sick, macabre, weird, unhealthy, ghoulish, morbid, perverted, gruesome, sadistic, cruel, offensive.
7 *Rory shot her a black look*: **angry**, cross, annoyed, irate, vexed, irritated, exasperated, indignant, aggrieved, irked, piqued, displeased, provoked, galled, resentful, irascible, bad-tempered, tetchy, testy, crabby, waspish, dark, dirty, filthy, furious, outraged; **threatening**, menacing, unfriendly, aggressive, belligerent, hostile, antagonistic, evil, evil-intentioned, wicked, nasty, hate-filled, bitter, acrimonious, malevolent, malicious, malignant, malign, venomous, poisonous, vitriolic, vindictive; Brit. informal shirty, stroppy, narky, ratty, eggy; literary malefic, maleficent.
▷ANTONYMS pleasant, friendly.
□ **in the black** *the company's in the black again*: **in credit**, in funds, debt-free, out of debt, solvent, financially sound, able to pay one's debts, creditworthy, of good financial standing, solid, secure, profit-making, profitable; rare unindebted.
▷ANTONYMS in debt.
□ **black and white 1** *a black-and-white picture*: **monochrome**, greyscale.
▷ANTONYMS colour.
2 *I wish to see the proposals* ***in black and white***: **in print**, printed, written down, set down, on paper, committed to paper, recorded, on record, documented, clearly/plainly/explicitly defined. ▷ANTONYMS spoken.
3 *they tend to talk around the subject instead of making black-and-white statements*: **categorical**, unequivocal, absolute, uncompromising, unconditional, unqualified, unambiguous, clear, clear-cut, positive, straightforward, definite, definitive; simplistic, shallow, pat, glib, jejune, naive. ▷ANTONYMS equivocal.
4 *children think* ***in black and white****, good and bad*: **in absolute terms**, unequivocally, without shades of grey, categorically, uncompromisingly, unconditionally, unambiguously, clearly, positively, straightforwardly, definitely, definitively; simplistically, shallowly, patly, glibly, jejunely, naively. ▷ANTONYMS equivocally.
▶verb **1** *the steps of the houses were neatly blacked*. See **blacken**.
2 *he broke his nose and blacked his eye*: **bruise**, contuse; hit, punch, injure; make black, discolour.
3 Brit. dated *trade union members blacked the work*: **boycott**, embargo, put/place an embargo on, blacklist, ban, bar, proscribe.
□ **black out** *the pain hit him and he blacked out*: **faint**, lose consciousness, pass out, collapse, keel over; informal flake out, conk out, go out; literary swoon.
□ **black something out 1** *the city was blacked out as an air-raid precaution*: **darken**, make dark/darker, shade, turn off the lights in; keep the light out of. **2** *the report on the incident has over 200 pages blacked out*: **censor**, suppress, withhold, cover up, hide, conceal, obscure, veil, draw/pull a veil over, hush up, sweep under the carpet, whitewash.

b

Choose the right word black

Black has been used to refer to African peoples and their descendants since the 14th century, and has been in continuous use ever since. Other terms have enjoyed prominence too: in the US **coloured** was the term adopted in preference by emancipated slaves following the American Civil War, and *coloured* was itself superseded in the US in the early 20th century by **Negro** as the term preferred by black American campaigners. In Britain, on the other hand, *coloured* was the most widely used and accepted term in the 1950s and early 1960s. With the civil rights and Black Power movements of the 1960s, *black* was adopted in the US to signify a sense of racial pride, and it is the usual word in Britain today. In the US **African American** is the currently accepted term, which first became prominent in the late 1980s.

Word links black

melan- related prefix, as in *melanin, Melanesia*

blackball verb *her husband was blackballed when he tried to join the Country Club*: **reject**, debar, bar, ban, vote against, blacklist, exclude, shut out, leave out in the cold; expel, drum out, oust, cashier, ostracize, repudiate; boycott, snub, shun, spurn, cold-shoulder, give the cold shoulder to; N. Amer. disfellowship.
▷ANTONYMS admit.

blacken verb **1** *you use it to blacken your hair*: **make black**, black, darken, make dark/darker; dirty, make dirty, make sooty, make smoky, stain, grime, begrime, befoul, soil.
▷ANTONYMS whiten, clean.
2 *the sky blackened*: **grow/become black, darken**, dim, grow dim, cloud over.
▷ANTONYMS lighten, brighten.
3 *she won't thank you for blackening her husband's name*: **sully**, tarnish, blot, besmirch, drag through the mud/mire, stain, taint, smear, smudge, befoul, soil, contaminate, pollute, disgrace, dishonour, bring discredit to, injure, damage, spoil; slander, defame, traduce; literary besmear, smirch; archaic spot, breathe on.
▷ANTONYMS clear, enhance.

blacklist verb *workers were blacklisted after being quoted in the newspaper*: **boycott**, ostracize, avoid, embargo, put/place an embargo on, consider undesirable, steer clear of, ignore; refuse to employ; Brit. dated black.

black magic noun *they were found guilty of practising black magic*: **sorcery**, magic, witchcraft, wizardry, necromancy, enchantment, spell-working, incantation, the supernatural, occultism, the occult, the black arts, devilry; malediction, voodoo, hoodoo, witching, witchery, hex, spell, jinx; N. Amer. mojo, orenda; NZ makutu; S. African informal muti; rare sortilege, thaumaturgy, theurgy.

blackmail noun *troops using narcotics could be susceptible to blackmail*: **extortion**, demanding money with menaces, exaction, intimidation; protection racket, bribery; wringing, milking, bleeding, bloodsucking; informal hush money; archaic chantage.
▸ verb **1** *he was going to blackmail the murderers*: **extort money from**, threaten, hold to ransom, milk, bleed; informal demand hush money from.
2 *she had tried to blackmail him into marrying her*: **coerce**, pressurize, pressure, bring pressure to bear on, bulldoze, force, railroad; informal lean on, put the screws on, twist someone's arm.

blackout noun **1** *a generator would power the computer in the event of a blackout*: **power cut**, power failure, electricity failure; trip, blown fuse; brown-out.
2 *the authorities imposed a news blackout*: **suppression**, silence, censorship, reporting restrictions, non-communication, cut-off.
3 *he had a blackout on the street*: **faint**, fainting fit, loss of consciousness, coma, passing out, period of oblivion, swoon, collapse; Medicine syncope.

bladder noun

Word links bladder

cystic, vesical relating to a bladder

blame verb **1** *the inquiry blamed the train driver for the accident*: **hold responsible**, hold accountable, hold liable, place/lay the blame on; censure, criticize, condemn, accuse of, find/consider guilty of; assign fault/liability/guilt to; archaic inculpate.
▷ANTONYMS absolve; forgive.
2 *they **blame** youth crime **on** unemployment*: **ascribe to**, attribute to, impute to, lay at the door of, put down to, set down to; informal pin, stick.
▸ noun *he was cleared of all blame for the incident*: **responsibility**, guilt, accountability, liability, onus, blameworthiness, culpability, fault; censure, criticism, condemnation, recrimination; informal rap.

blameless adjective *he led a blameless life*: **innocent**, guiltless, above reproach, beyond criticism, above suspicion, irreproachable, unimpeachable, in the clear, not to blame, without fault, faultless, exemplary, perfect, virtuous, pure, moral, upright, impeccable, sinless, unblemished, spotless, stainless, untarnished; informal squeaky clean.
▷ANTONYMS blameworthy, guilty.

Choose the right word blameless, innocent, guiltless

See **innocent**.

blameworthy adjective *do you consider him blameworthy?* **culpable**, reprehensible, indefensible, inexcusable, guilty, criminal, delinquent, sinful, wicked, wrong, evil, shameful, discreditable; to blame, at fault, blameable, condemnable, censurable, reproachable, responsible, answerable, offending, erring, errant, in the wrong; rare reprovable.
▷ANTONYMS blameless, innocent.

blanch verb **1** *the moon blanches her hair*: **make/turn pale**, whiten, make/turn pallid, lighten, grey, wash out, fade, blench, etiolate, decolorize, bleach, peroxide.
▷ANTONYMS colour, darken, redden.
2 *his face blanched*: **pale**, go/grow/turn/become pale, go/grow/turn/become white, go/grow/turn/become pallid, lose its colour, lighten, bleach, fade, blench.
▷ANTONYMS colour, darken, blush.
3 *blanch the spinach leaves in boiling water*: **scald**, boil, dunk.

bland adjective **1** *the peppers give the bland turkey a piquant flavour*: **tasteless**, flavourless, insipid, mild, savourless, unflavoured, weak, thin, watery, watered-down, spiceless, unappetizing; informal wishy-washy.
▷ANTONYMS tangy.
2 *a very bland general election campaign*: **uninteresting**, dull, boring, tedious, monotonous, dry, drab, dreary, wearisome; unexciting, unimaginative, uninspiring, uninspired, weak, insipid, colourless, lustreless, lacklustre, vapid, flat, stale, trite, vacuous, feeble, pallid, wishy-washy; limp, lame, tired, lifeless, torpid, unanimated, zestless, spiritless, sterile, anaemic, barren, tame, bloodless, antiseptic; middle-of-the-road, run-of-the-mill, commonplace, mediocre, nondescript, characterless, mundane, inoffensive, humdrum, prosaic.
▷ANTONYMS interesting, stimulating.
3 *bland breezes*: **temperate**, mild, soft, calm, balmy, soothing, benign.
▷ANTONYMS violent, destructive.

blandishments plural noun *consumers have the capacity to resist the blandishments of advertisers*: **flattery**, cajolery, coaxing, wheedling, honeyed words, smooth talk, soft words, blarney; fulsomeness, simpering, fawning, toadying, ingratiating, ingratiation, currying favour, inveiglement; charm offensive; informal sweet talk, soft soap, smarm, spiel, ego massage, buttering up, cosying up, cuddling up; Brit. informal flannel; Austral./NZ informal guyver, smoodging; rare glozing, lipsalve, cajolement.

blank adjective **1** *a blank sheet of paper*: **empty**, unfilled, unmarked, unwritten on, unused, clear, free, bare, clean, plain, spotless, white; vacant, void.
▷ANTONYMS full.
2 *a blank face*: **expressionless**, empty, vacant, deadpan, wooden, stony, impassive, inanimate, poker-faced, vacuous, glazed, fixed, lifeless, uninterested, emotionless, unresponsive, inscrutable.
▷ANTONYMS expressive, mobile.
3 *'What?' said Maxim, looking blank*: **baffled**, nonplussed, mystified, stumped, at a loss, stuck, puzzled, perplexed, bewildered, bemused, ignorant, lost, muddled, uncomprehending, befuddled, fuddled, addled, (all) at sea, at sixes and sevens, confused; informal clueless, flummoxed, bamboozled, discombobulated, fazed, beaten.
4 *a blank refusal*: **outright**, absolute, categorical, unqualified, utter, complete, thorough, flat, straight, positive, certain, explicit, unequivocal, unambiguous, unmistakable, plain, clear, clear-cut.
▸ noun **1** *leave blanks to type in the appropriate names*: **space**, gap, blank space, empty space.
2 *that period is a blank to her now*: **void**, vacuum, emptiness, vacancy.

blanket noun **1** *the bed had a red blanket on it*: **cover**, covering, rug, afghan, quilt, eiderdown, duvet; bedcover, bedspread, throw-over; bedclothes; N. Amer. throw, spread; S. African kaross; in Latin America serape; archaic coverlet, counterpane.
2 *a dense grey blanket of cloud*: **covering**, layer, cover, coat, coating, film, sheet, carpet, veneer, surface, skin, thickness, overlay, cloak, mantle, veil, pall, shroud, screen, mask, cloud, curtain.
▸ adjective *a blanket ban on tobacco advertising*: **wholesale**, across the board, outright, indiscriminate, overall, general, mass, umbrella, inclusive, all-inclusive, all-round, sweeping, total, complete, comprehensive, thorough, extensive, wide-ranging, far-reaching, large-scale, widespread; universal, global, worldwide, international, nationwide, countrywide, coast-to-coast, company-wide.
▷ANTONYMS partial, piecemeal.
▸ verb **1** *snow blanketed the mountains*: **cover**, coat, carpet, overlay, overlie, overspread, extend over, cap, top, crown; conceal, obscure, blot out, hide, mask, cloud, cloak, veil, shroud, swathe, envelop, submerge, surround;

literary mantle, enshroud.
2 *the double glazing blankets the noise a bit*: **muffle**, deaden, soften, mute, silence, quieten, smother, dampen, damp down, tone down, mask, suppress, reduce, abate, kill.
▷ANTONYMS amplify.

blare verb *sirens blared across the town*: **blast**, sound loudly, trumpet, clamour, boom, roar, thunder, bellow, resound, honk, toot, shriek, screech.
▷ANTONYMS murmur, waft.
▸ noun *the blare of trumpets*: **blast**, blasting, clamour, boom, booming, roar, roaring, thunder, thundering, bellow, bellowing, resounding, honk, honking, shriek, shrieking, screech.
▷ANTONYMS murmur.

blarney noun *it took all my Irish blarney to keep us out of court*: **blandishments**, honeyed words, smooth talk, soft words, flattery, cajolery, coaxing, wheedling, compliments; fulsomeness, simpering, fawning, toadying, ingratiation, currying favour, inveiglement; charm offensive; informal sweet talk, soft soap, smarm, spiel, ego massage, buttering up, cosying up, cuddling up; Brit. informal flannel; Austral./NZ informal guyver, smoodging; archaic glozing, lipsalve; rare cajolement.

blasé adjective *she was becoming quite **blasé about** the dangers*: **indifferent to**, unconcerned about, uncaring about, casual about, nonchalant about, offhand about, uninterested in, uninvolved in/with, apathetic towards, unimpressed by, bored by, weary of, unmoved by, unresponsive to, lukewarm about, unenthusiastic about, phlegmatic about; impassive, dispassionate, emotionless, insouciant; jaded, surfeited, glutted, cloyed, satiated; rare poco-curante.
▷ANTONYMS responsive, excited.

blaspheme verb *how could you blaspheme in church?* **swear**, curse, utter oaths, utter profanities, take the Lord's name in vain; informal cuss; archaic execrate, imprecate.

blasphemous adjective *a blasphemous mock communion*: **sacrilegious**, profane, irreligious, irreverent, impious, ungodly, godless, unholy, disrespectful; archaic execratory, execrative; rare desecrative, imprecatory.
▷ANTONYMS reverent.

blasphemy noun *he was condemned for his blasphemy*: **profanity**, profaneness, sacrilege, irreligiousness, irreverence, taking the Lord's name in vain, swearing, curse, cursing, impiety, impiousness, ungodliness, unholiness, desecration, disrespect; formal imprecation; archaic execration.
▷ANTONYMS reverence.

blast noun **1** *the blast blew in dozens of windows*: **shock wave**, pressure wave, bang, crash, crack.
2 *a bomb blast*: **explosion**, detonation, discharge, burst, eruption.
3 *a sudden blast of cold air*: **gust**, rush, blow, gale, squall, storm, wind, draught, waft, puff, flurry, breeze.
4 *a blast of the ship's siren*: **blare**, blaring, honk, bellow, boom, roar, screech, wail.
5 informal *I braced myself for the inevitable blast*: **reprimand**, rebuke, reproof, admonishment, admonition, reproach, reproval, scolding, remonstration, upbraiding, castigation, lambasting, lecture, criticism, censure; informal telling-off, rap, rap over the knuckles, slap on the wrist, flea in one's ear, dressing-down, earful, roasting, tongue-lashing, bawling-out, caning, blowing-up; Brit. informal ticking-off, carpeting, wigging, rollicking, rocket, row; Austral./NZ informal serve; Brit. vulgar slang bollocking; dated rating.
▷ANTONYMS commendation.
▸ verb **1** *fighter-bombers were blasting enemy airfields*: **blow up**, bomb, blow (to pieces), dynamite, explode; break up, demolish, raze to the ground, destroy, ruin, shatter.
2 *heavy Browning machine guns were blasting away*: **fire (away)**, shoot (away), blaze (away), let fly; discharge.
3 *an impatient motorist blasted his horn*: **honk**, sound loudly, trumpet, blare, boom, roar.
4 *radios blasting out pop music*: **blare**, boom, roar, thunder, bellow, pump, shriek, screech.
5 *Fowler was blasted with an air gun*: **shoot (down)**, gun down, mow down, cut down, put a bullet in, pick off, bag, fell, kill; informal pot, pump full of lead, plug, zap, let someone have it; N. Amer. informal smoke; literary slay.
6 literary *frost blasted the plants*: **blight**, kill, destroy, wither, shrivel.
7 *poverty was blasting their hopes*: **destroy**, crush, dash, blight, wreck, ruin, spoil, mar, annihilate, disappoint, frustrate.
8 informal *he blasted the pupils for being late*: **reprimand**, rebuke, criticize, upbraid, berate, castigate, reprove, rail at, flay.
□ **blast off** *a rocket blasted off for a rendezvous with the space station*: **be launched**, take off, lift off, leave the ground, become airborne, take to the air.
▷ANTONYMS touch down.

blasted adjective informal *make your own blasted coffee!* **damned**, damn, blessed, flaming, precious, confounded, pestilential, rotten, wretched; Brit. informal flipping, blinking, blooming, bloody, bleeding, effing, chuffing; N. Amer. informal goddam; Austral./NZ informal plurry; Brit. informal, dated bally, ruddy, deuced; vulgar slang fucking, frigging; Brit. vulgar slang sodding; Irish vulgar slang fecking; dated cursed, accursed, damnable.

blast-off noun *the rocket was ready for blast-off*: **launch**, launching, lift-off, take-off, ascent, firing, flight.
▷ANTONYMS touchdown.

blatant adjective *a blatant lie*: **flagrant**, glaring, obvious, undisguised, unconcealed, overt, open, transparent, patent, evident, manifest, palpable, unmistakable; **shameless**, unabashed, unashamed, without shame, impudent, insolent, audacious, unembarrassed, unblushing, brazen, barefaced, brass-necked, brash, bold, unrepentant; archaic arrant.
▷ANTONYMS inconspicuous, subtle.

blather verb *he just blathered on and on*: **prattle**, babble, chatter, twitter, prate, gabble, jabber, go on, run on, rattle on/away, yap, jibber-jabber, patter, blether, blither, maunder, ramble, drivel; informal yak, yackety-yak, yabber, yatter; Brit. informal witter, rabbit, chunter, natter, waffle; Scottish & Irish informal slabber; Austral./NZ informal mag; archaic twaddle, clack, twattle.
▸ noun *he has to write about all the blather at the town council*: **prattle**, chatter, twitter, babble, talk, prating, gabble, jabber, blether, rambling; **nonsense**, rubbish, balderdash, gibberish, claptrap; informal yackety-yak, yabbering, yatter, rot, tripe, twaddle, hogwash, baloney, drivel, bilge, bosh, bull, bunk, guff, eyewash, piffle, poppycock, phooey, hooey, malarkey, dribble; Brit. informal wittering, nattering, chuntering, cobblers, codswallop, stuff and nonsense, tosh, cack; Scottish & N. English informal havers; N. Amer. informal garbage, flapdoodle, blathers, wack, bushwa, applesauce; informal, dated bunkum, tommyrot, cod, gammon, toffee; vulgar slang shit, bullshit, horseshit, crap, bollocks, balls; Austral./NZ vulgar slang bulldust; archaic clack, twattle.

blaze noun **1** *twenty firemen fought the blaze*: **fire**, flames, conflagration, inferno, holocaust, firestorm.
2 *the blaze of light from the security lamps*: **glare**, gleam, flash, burst, flare, dazzle, streak, radiance, brilliance, beam, glitter.
3 *he left in a blaze of anger*: **outburst**, burst, eruption, flare-up, explosion, outbreak, blow-up; blast, attack, fit, spasm, paroxysm, access, rush, gale, flood, storm, hurricane, torrent, outpouring, surge, upsurge, spurt, effusion, outflow, outflowing, welling up; informal splurt; rare ebullition, boutade.
▸ verb **1** *the fire blazed merrily*: **burn**, be ablaze, be alight, be on fire, be in flames, flame, be aflame, flare up; literary be afire; archaic be ardent.
2 *he drove straight through the crowd, lights blazing*: **shine**, beam, flash, flare, glare, gleam, glint, dazzle, glitter, glisten, be radiant, burn brightly.
3 *soldiers blazed away with sub-machine guns*: **fire (away)**, shoot (away), blast (away), let fly; discharge.

blazon verb **1** *the manufacturer's name is blazoned across sporting events*: **display**, exhibit, show, put on display, draw attention to, present, spread, emblazon, plaster, flaunt, parade, reveal.
2 *the newspapers blazoned the news*: **publicize**, make known, make public, bring to public notice/attention, announce, report, communicate, impart, disclose, reveal, divulge, leak, publish, broadcast, transmit, issue, post, put out, distribute, spread, unfold, disseminate, circulate, air, herald, trumpet, advertise, proclaim, promulgate; informal splatter.

bleach verb **1** *the blinds had been bleached by the sun*: **make/turn white**, whiten, make/turn pale, make/turn pallid, blanch, lighten, fade, wash out, decolour, decolorize, peroxide, etiolate.
2 *they saw bones bleaching in the desert*: **go/grow/turn/become white**, whiten, go/turn/grow/become pale, pale, go/grow/turn/become pallid, blanch, lose its colour, be washed out, lighten, fade, blench.

bleak adjective **1** *a bleak landscape*: **bare**, exposed, desolate, stark, arid, desert, denuded, lunar, open, empty, windswept; treeless, forestless, without vegetation, defoliated; unsheltered, unprotected, unshielded; rare unwooded.
▷ANTONYMS lush, verdant.
2 *a bleak wind had got up*: **cold**, keen, raw, harsh, wintry; piercing, penetrating, biting, nipping, stinging, sharp; freezing, icy, icy-cold, frosty, frigid, chilly; informal nippy; Brit. informal parky; literary chill.
▷ANTONYMS warm, balmy.
3 *the future looks bleak*: **unpromising**, unfavourable, unpropitious, inauspicious, adverse, disadvantageous, uninviting, discouraging, disheartening, depressing, cheerless, joyless, gloomy, sombre, dreary, dismal, wretched, miserable, black, dark, grim, drab, portentous, foreboding, hopeless, ominous.
▷ANTONYMS promising, hopeful.

Word toolkit **bleak**

See **dismal**.

bleary adjective *he tried to focus his bleary eyes*: **blurred**, blurry, unfocused; fogged, clouded, cloudy, dim, dull, filmy; muzzy, tired; moist, misty, watery, rheumy; archaic blear.
▷ANTONYMS clear, limpid.

bleat verb **1** *the sheep were bleating in the field*: **baa**, maa, cry, call; N. Amer. informal blat.

b

2 *don't bleat to me about fairness*: **complain**, moan, mutter, grumble, grouse, groan, grouch, growl, carp, snivel, make a fuss; Scottish & Irish gurn; informal gripe, beef, bellyache, bitch, whinge, sound off, go on; Brit. informal chunter, create, be on at someone; N. English informal mither; N. Amer. informal kvetch; S. African informal chirp; Brit. dated crib, natter.

bleed verb **1** *his arm was bleeding badly*: **lose blood**, haemorrhage.
2 *the doctor bled him*: **draw blood from**; technical phlebotomize, venesect, exsanguinate.
▷ANTONYMS transfuse.
3 *one colour* ***bled into*** *another*: **flow**, run, ooze, seep, trickle, leak, filter, percolate, escape, leach; permeate, merge with.
4 *sap was bleeding from a cut in the trunk*: **flow**, run, ooze, seep, exude, weep, gush, spurt.
5 *the country is being* ***bled dry*** *by poachers*: **drain**, exhaust, sap, deplete, deprive, milk, suck dry, empty, reduce.
6 *my heart* ***bleeds for*** *them*: **grieve**, ache, sorrow, be sorrowful, be sad, mourn, be mournful, be distressed, be in distress, be miserable, lament, feel, suffer, agonize, anguish, be in anguish; sympathize with, pity; eat one's heart out, weep and wail.

blemish noun **1** *not a blemish marred her milky skin*: **imperfection**, fault, flaw, defect, deformity, discoloration, disfigurement; bruise, scar, pit, pockmark, pock, scratch, dent, chip, notch, nick, line, score, cut, incision, gash; **mark**, streak, spot, fleck, dot, blot, stain, smear, patch, trace, speck, speckle, blotch, smudge, smut, smirch, fingermark, fingerprint, impression, imprint; marking, blaze, stripe; birthmark; informal splotch, splodge; technical stigma.
▷ANTONYMS enhancement.
2 *local government is not without blemish*: **defect**, fault, failing, flaw, imperfection, frailty, fallibility, foible, vice; shortcoming, weakness, weak spot, weak point, deficiency, limitation; blot, taint, stain, smirch, dishonour, disgrace.
▷ANTONYMS virtue.
▶ verb **1** *neither bungalow nor caravan blemished the coast*: **mar**, spoil, impair, disfigure, blight, deface, flaw, mark, spot, speckle, blotch, discolour, scar; ruin, destroy, wreck; be a blot on the landscape; rare disfeature.
▷ANTONYMS enhance.
2 *his reign as world champion has been blemished by controversy*: **sully**, tarnish, besmirch, blacken, smirch, stain, blot, taint, soil, befoul, spoil, ruin, dirty, disgrace, mar, damage, defame, calumniate, injure, harm, hurt, undermine, debase, degrade, denigrate, dishonour, stigmatize; informal drag through the mud; rare vitiate.

Choose the right word **blemish, imperfection, flaw**

These words all denote a noticeable feature of something that reduces its value or attractiveness.

A **blemish** is a small mark or injury spoiling the appearance of an otherwise smooth or beautiful surface, especially skin (*your skin hasn't a single blemish*). A blemish may appear unexpectedly on the surface of something that was previously perfect.

Imperfections are shortcomings which tend to be inherent, unlike *blemishes*, which are generally superficial (*the policy has its imperfections | great art is, like religion, concerned with moral imperfections*).

Flaw is derived from a Middle English word for 'fragment' or 'splinter'. *Flaws* are inherent cracks or marks on a surface (*most natural crystals have flaws*). A *flaw* may also be a deep imperfection, one that affects and undermines the whole nature of someone or something (*a flaw at the heart of NATO's deterrent strategy*). Nouns commonly described as having flaws include *security, design, strategy, character*, and *system*. The perception that a flaw is more than skin-deep is reflected in the fact that skin may have *imperfections* or *blemishes* but not *flaws*.

blench verb *she blenched at the size of the bill*: **flinch**, start, shy (away), recoil, shrink, pull back, back away, draw back, cringe, wince, quiver, shudder, shiver, tremble, quake, shake, quail, cower, waver, falter, hesitate, get cold feet, blanch.

blend verb **1** *blend the ingredients until smooth | this allows the flavours to blend together*: **mix**, mingle, combine, put together, stir, whisk, fold in, jumble, merge; fuse, unite, unify, join, amalgamate, incorporate; meld, marry, compound, alloy, coalesce, homogenize, intermingle, intermix, interpenetrate; integrate, emulsify, premix; informal blunge; rare admix, commingle, interflow, commix.
▷ANTONYMS clash.
2 *the recent buildings* ***blend with*** *the older ones*: **harmonize**, go, go well, go together, fit (in), tone, be in tune, dovetail, coordinate, team, accord, be compatible; match, suit, complement, set off.
▶ noun *the chutney is a blend of bananas, raisins, and ginger*: **mixture**, mix, combination, admixture, mingling, commingling, amalgamation, amalgam, union, conjunction, marriage, merging, compound, alloy, fusion, meld, composite, concoction, synthesis, homogenization; miscellany, jumble, hotchpotch; informal mash-up.

bless verb **1** *the chaplain said more prayers and blessed the couple*: **ask God's favour for**, ask God's protection for, give a benediction for, invoke happiness on.
▷ANTONYMS curse.
2 *the Cardinal blessed the memorial plaque*: **consecrate**, sanctify, hallow, dedicate (to God), make holy, make sacred, set apart, devote to God; anoint, ordain, canonize, beatify.
▷ANTONYMS deconsecrate.
3 *let us bless the name of the Lord*: **praise**, worship, glorify, honour, exalt, adore, pay tribute to, pay homage to, give thanks to, venerate, reverence, hallow; archaic magnify, laud.
4 *the gods have* ***blessed us with*** *magical voices*: **endow**, favour, provide, grace, bestow, furnish, entrust, present; grant, vouchsafe, afford, accord, give, donate; confer on, lavish on; literary endue.
▷ANTONYMS trouble.
5 *I bless the day you came here*: **give thanks for**, express gratitude for, be grateful for; thank, appreciate, celebrate.
▷ANTONYMS rue.
6 *the government refused to bless the undertaking*: **sanction**, consent to, give consent for, give assent to, endorse, agree to, concur with, approve, give approval for, give one's blessing to, back, support, be in favour of, smile on; informal give the thumbs up to, give the green light to, OK; N. Amer. rare approbate.
▷ANTONYMS oppose.

blessed adjective **1** *a blessed place*: **holy**, sacred, hallowed, consecrated, sanctified, divine, dedicated, venerated, revered, ordained, canonized, beatified.
▷ANTONYMS cursed.
2 *blessed are the meek*: **favoured**, fortunate, lucky, privileged, select, happy, joyful, joyous, blissful, glad, enviable.
▷ANTONYMS wretched.
3 *the fresh air made a blessed change from the polluted city atmosphere*: **welcome**, pleasant, pleasing, agreeable, refreshing, favourable, cheering, gratifying, heartening, much needed, to one's liking, to one's taste.
▷ANTONYMS unwelcome.
4 informal *never mind the blessed television*. See **damned** (sense 2).

blessing noun **1** *may God continue to give us his blessing*: **protection**, favour.
▷ANTONYMS condemnation.
2 *they received a special blessing from a Catholic priest*: **benediction**, dedication, consecration, invocation, commendation, prayer for someone, intercession; grace, thanksgiving, thanks; Jewish kiddush; archaic orison.
▷ANTONYMS anathema.
3 *he gave the plan his blessing*: **sanction**, consent, assent, endorsement, clearance, agreement, concurrence, approval, seal of approval, stamp of approval, imprimatur, backing, support, favour, good wishes; informal the go-ahead, the thumbs up, the green light, the OK; formal approbation.
4 *it was a blessing that they didn't have very far to go*: **advantage**, benefit, help, boon, good thing, godsend, favour, gift, convenience; bonus, plus point, added attraction, additional benefit, extra, added extra; luck, stroke of luck, piece of luck, good fortune, windfall, gain, profit, virtue, bounty; informal plus, perk; literary benison.
▷ANTONYMS affliction.

blight noun **1** *potato blight*: **disease**, canker, infestation, fungus, mildew, mould, rot, decay.
2 *the government are protecting people from the blight of aircraft noise*: **affliction**, scourge, bane, curse, plague, menace, evil, misfortune, woe, calamity, trouble, ordeal, thorn in one's flesh/side, trial, tribulation, visitation, nuisance, pest, pollution, contamination, cancer, canker.
▷ANTONYMS blessing.
▶ verb **1** *a peach tree blighted by leaf curl*: **infect**, wither, shrivel, blast, mildew, nip in the bud, kill, destroy.
2 *the scandal blighted the careers of several leading politicians*: **ruin**, wreck, spoil, disrupt, undo, mar, play havoc with, make a mess of, put an end to, end, bring to an end, put a stop to, prevent, frustrate, crush, quell, quash, dash, destroy, scotch, shatter, devastate, demolish, sabotage; informal mess up, screw up, louse up, foul up, make a hash of, do in, put paid to, put the lid on, put the kibosh on, stymie, queer, nix, banjax, blow a hole in; Brit. informal scupper, dish, throw a spanner in the works of; N. Amer. informal throw a monkey wrench in the works of; Austral. informal euchre, cruel; archaic bring to naught.

blind adjective **1** *he has been blind since birth*: **visually impaired**, unsighted, sightless, visionless, unseeing, stone blind, eyeless; partially sighted, half blind, purblind; informal as blind as a bat; Austral. informal boko.
▷ANTONYMS sighted.
2 *she was ignorant, but not stupid or blind*: **imperceptive**, unperceptive, slow, obtuse, stupid, uncomprehending, unimaginative, insensitive, thick-skinned, bovine, stolid, unintelligent; informal dense, dim, dim-witted, thick, slow on the uptake, dumb, dopey, not with it; Brit. informal dozy; Scottish & N. English informal glaikit; N. Amer. informal dumb-ass, chowderheaded; S. African informal dof.
▷ANTONYMS perceptive.
3 *you should be* ***blind to*** *failure at your age*: **unmindful of**, mindless of, careless of, heedless of, oblivious to, insensible to, unconcerned about/by,

inattentive to, indifferent to; rare insensitive of, negligent of.
▷ANTONYMS mindful.
4 *a blind acceptance of conventional opinions*: **uncritical**, unreasoned, unthinking, unconsidered, mindless, injudicious, undiscerning, indiscriminate; airy, insouciant; credulous, naive.
▷ANTONYMS discerning.
5 *in a blind rage*: **impetuous**, impulsive, rash, hasty, reckless, uncontrolled, uncontrollable, uninhibited, unrestrained, immoderate, intemperate, wild, unruly, irrational, frantic, violent, furious, unbridled, uncurbed, unchecked, unrepressed.
▷ANTONYMS calm.
6 *a blind alley*: **without exit**, exitless, blocked, closed, barred, impassable; dead end, no through road, cul-de-sac.
▷ANTONYMS through.
□ **turn a blind eye to** *it seems like they all turned a blind eye to the fact that they were creating something truly terrible*: **overlook**, disregard, neglect, ignore, pay no attention/heed to, pass over, omit, skip (over), gloss over, leave out, leave undone, forget.
▶ **verb 1** *he was blinded in a car crash*: **make blind**, deprive of sight, deprive of vision, render unsighted, render sightless, put someone's eyes out, gouge someone's eyes out.
2 *the salt water blinded him temporarily*: **stop someone seeing**, obscure someone's vision, block someone's vision, get in someone's line of vision.
3 *Perdita was blinded by sunshine*: **dazzle**.
4 *scaffolding blinded the windows*: **obscure**, cover, blot out, blanket, mask, shroud, hide, conceal, block, darken, eclipse, obstruct.
▷ANTONYMS reveal.
5 *he was blinded by his faith*: **deprive of understanding**, deprive of perception, deprive of judgement, deprive of reason, deprive of sense.
6 *they try to blind you with science*: **overawe**, awe, intimidate, daunt, deter, cow, abash; disquiet, make anxious, make uneasy, perturb, discomfit, disconcert; **confuse**, nonplus, bewilder, confound, perplex, overwhelm; **unsettle**, discompose, unnerve, discourage, subdue, dismay, frighten, alarm, scare, terrify, terrorize, browbeat, bully, trouble, bother, agitate, fluster, ruffle, jolt, shake (up), throw, put off, take aback, unbalance, destabilize, throw off balance, put off one's stroke, pull the rug (out) from under; informal rattle, faze, psych out.
▶ **noun 1** *a window blind*: **screen**, shade, louvre, awning, canopy, sunshade, curtain, shutter, cover, covering, protection; Venetian blind, Austrian blind, roller blind; French jalousie, persienne.
2 *he'd claim that some crook had sent the card as a blind*: **deception**, camouflage, screen, smokescreen, front, facade, cover, disguise, cloak, pretext, masquerade, mask, feint; trick, stratagem, ploy, ruse, scheme, device, move, manoeuvre, contrivance, machination, expedient, artifice, wile, dodge.

blindly **adverb 1** *he continued to stare blindly ahead*: **sightlessly**, without sight, without vision, unseeingly.
2 *he ran blindly upstairs*: **impetuously**, impulsively, rashly, hastily, recklessly, heedlessly, uncontrolledly, uncontrollably, uninhibitedly, unrestrainedly, wildly, irrationally, frantically, violently, furiously.
▷ANTONYMS cautiously.
3 *the government has blindly followed US policy*: **uncritically**, unthinkingly, mindlessly, injudiciously, indiscriminately; airily, insouciantly; credulously, naively; rare undiscerningly.
▷ANTONYMS critically.

blink **verb 1** *the man's eyes did not blink*: **shut and open**, flutter, flicker, wink, bat; technical nictitate, nictate.
2 *several red lights on the control panel had begun to blink*: **flash**, flicker, twinkle, waver, wink, scintillate, glint, glimmer, glitter, shine (intermittently).
3 *no one even blinks at the 'waitresses' in drag*: **be surprised**, **look twice**, be startled, be shocked; informal boggle.

blinkered **adjective** *blinkered ideological dogma*: **narrow-minded**, limited, restricted, inward-looking, conventional, parochial, provincial, insular, small-town, localist, small-minded, petty-minded, petty, close-minded, short-sighted, myopic, hidebound, dyed-in-the-wool, diehard, set, set in one's ways, inflexible, dogmatic, rigid, entrenched, prejudiced, bigoted, biased, partisan, sectarian, discriminatory; Brit. parish-pump, blimpish; French borné; N. Amer. informal jerkwater; rare claustral.
▷ANTONYMS broad-minded.

bliss **noun 1** *it was sheer bliss to be there*: **joy**, pleasure, delight, happiness, gladness, ecstasy, elation, rapture, euphoria, heaven, paradise, seventh heaven, cloud nine, Eden, Utopia, Arcadia; halcyon days; informal the top of the world.
▷ANTONYMS misery.
2 *religions promise perfect bliss after death*: **blessedness**, blessing, benediction, glory, heaven, paradise, heavenly joy, divine happiness, supreme happiness, divine rapture, beatitude, saintliness, sainthood.
▷ANTONYMS hell.

blissful **adjective** *they spent a blissful week together*: **ecstatic**, rapturous, joyful, joyous, elated, beatific, euphoric, enraptured, on cloud nine, in seventh heaven, transported, in transports, in raptures, beside oneself with joy/happiness, rhapsodic, ravished, enchanted, enthusiastic, delighted, thrilled, overjoyed, happy; informal over the moon, on top of the world, blissed out; Austral. informal wrapped.
▷ANTONYMS miserable.

blister **noun 1** *his heels were covered in blisters*: **bleb**, bulla, pustule, vesicle, vesication, blain.
2 *check for cracks and blisters in sheet roofing felt*: **bubble**, swelling, bulge, bump, lump, protuberance; cavity, hollow, void.

blistering **adjective 1** *the blistering heat of the desert*: **intense**, extreme, ferocious, fierce, acute, strong, very great; **scorching**, searing, flaming, blazing (hot), baking (hot), burning, fiery, torrid, parching, withering; informal boiling, boiling hot, sizzling, roasting, sweltering.
▷ANTONYMS icy.
2 *a blistering attack on the government's transport policy*: **savage**, vicious, fierce, bitter, severe, sharp, harsh, scathing, devastating, mordant, trenchant, caustic, cutting, biting, stinging, searing, withering, virulent, vitriolic.
▷ANTONYMS mild.
3 *Burke set a blistering pace*: **very fast**, breakneck; impressive; informal scorching, blinding.
▷ANTONYMS leisurely.

blithe **adjective 1** *he drove out with blithe disregard for the rules of the road*: **heedless**, uncaring, careless, casual, indifferent, thoughtless, unconcerned, unworried, untroubled; nonchalant, cool, blasé, devil-may-care, irresponsible.
▷ANTONYMS thoughtful.
2 literary *his blithe broadly smiling face*: **happy**, cheerful, cheery, light-hearted, jolly, merry, sunny, joyous, joyful, blissful, ecstatic, euphoric, elated, beatific, gladsome, mirthful; carefree, easy-going, buoyant, airy, breezy, jaunty, in high spirits, without a care in the world; animated, sprightly, vivacious, spirited, frisky; literary blithesome, jocund; dated gay.
▷ANTONYMS sad.

blitz **noun 1** *the 1940 blitz on London*: **bombardment**, battery, bombing, onslaught, barrage, sally; attack, assault, raid, offensive, strike, blitzkrieg; Italian razzia.
2 informal *Katrina and I had a blitz on the cleaning*: **all-out effort**, effort, exertion, endeavour, onslaught, attack, push, thrust, set-to.
▶ **verb** *the town was blitzed in the war*: **bombard**, attack, pound, blast; bomb, shell, torpedo, strafe; destroy, wipe out, wreck, devastate, ravage, smash.

blizzard **noun** **snowstorm**, snow blast, snow squall; white-out.

bloated **adjective** *his once firm stomach was now bloated from stodgy food*: **swollen**, puffed up/out, blown up, distended, inflated, enlarged, expanded, dilated, tumefied, bulging, ballooning (up/out), pumped up/out.
▷ANTONYMS shrunken.

> *Word toolkit* **bloated**
>
> See **puffy**.

blob **noun 1** *a blob of cold gravy*: **drop**, droplet, globule, bead, ball, bubble, pellet, pill, pearl; informal glob.
2 *a blob of ink*: **spot**, dab, splash, daub, blotch, blot, dot, fleck, speck, smudge, smear, streak, mark; informal splotch, splodge.
▶ **verb** *the masking fluid is blobbed on very freely*: **daub**, dab, spot, smear, bedaub, splash, slap, slop.

bloc **noun** *a free-trade bloc*: **alliance**, **association**, coalition, federation, confederation, league, faction, union, partnership, body, group, grouping; ring, syndicate; concordat, entente, axis; party, camp, lobby, wing, cabal, clique, coterie, caucus.

block **noun 1** *a block of cheese | a wall of concrete blocks*: **chunk**, hunk, brick, slab, lump, piece; bar, cake, cube, wedge, mass, wad, slice; Brit. informal wodge.
2 *the convent is likely to be transformed into a block of bedsits*: **building**, complex, structure, development.
3 *a block of shares*: **batch**, group, cluster, set, section, quantity, series.
4 *a sketching block*: **pad**, notebook, jotter, tablet, sketchbook, scratch pad.
5 *imperialism is a block to Third World development*: **obstacle**, obstruction, bar, barrier, impediment, hindrance, check, hurdle, stumbling block; difficulty, problem, snag, disadvantage, complication, drawback, hitch, handicap, deterrent.
▷ANTONYMS assistance, encouragement.
6 *a block in the pipe*: **blockage**, obstruction, stoppage, stopping up, clot, occlusion; impediment, hindrance; congestion.
▶ **verb 1** *weeds can block drainage ditches*: **clog (up)**, stop up, choke, plug, obstruct, gum up, occlude, dam up, congest, jam, close; informal bung up, gunge up.
▷ANTONYMS unblock, open.
2 *picket lines blocked access to the factory*: **hinder**, hamper, obstruct, impede, inhibit, check, arrest, restrict, limit, deter, curb, interrupt; halt, stop, bar, prevent, thwart, baulk, frustrate, foil, scotch, circumvent, stand in the way of; informal fetter.

▷ANTONYMS help, facilitate.
3 *the defender blocked a shot on the goal line*: **parry**, stop, defend against, fend off, stave off, turn aside, deflect, hold off, avert, repel, rebuff, repulse, hold/keep at bay.
□ **block something off** *exits from main roads were blocked off*: **close up**, bar, obstruct, shut off, barricade, seal.
▷ANTONYMS open.
□ **block something out 1** *the towering trees blocked out the light*: **conceal**, hide, screen, keep out, blot out, exclude; eliminate, obliterate, eradicate, erase, rub out, wipe out, blank out, efface, remove all traces of; halt, stop, deny, suppress, repress. **2** *I would block out an area and then sketch in the detail*: **rough (out)**, sketch out, trace out, outline, set out, lay out, delineate, draft.

blockade noun **1** *a naval blockade of the island*: **siege**, beleaguerment, encirclement; rare investment, besiegement.
2 *demonstrators erected blockades in the streets*: **barricade**, barrier, roadblock; obstacle, obstruction, impediment, bulwark, block, hindrance, check, deterrent, hurdle.
▸ verb *rebels blockaded the capital*: **barricade**, close up, block off, shut off, seal, bar; **besiege**, lay siege to, beleaguer, beset, surround; archaic invest.

blockage noun *there's a blockage in the drain*: **obstruction**, stoppage, block, clot, occlusion; impediment, hindrance; congestion.

blockhead noun informal See **idiot**.

bloke noun Brit. informal **man**, boy, male, individual, body; informal chap, fellow, geezer, lad, fella, punter, character, customer, sort, bod; N. Amer. informal guy, dude, hombre; Brit. informal, dated cove.

blonde adjective **1** *her blonde hair tumbled about her face*: **fair**, light, light-coloured, light-toned, yellow, flaxen, tow-coloured, strawberry blonde, yellowish, golden, silver, silvery, platinum, ash blonde; bleached, sun-bleached, peroxide, bottle-blonde.
▷ANTONYMS dark.
2 *a blonde woman*: **fair-haired**, light-haired, golden-haired, tow-headed.
▷ANTONYMS brunette.

blood noun **1** *there was blood streaming from a wound in his head*: **gore**, lifeblood, vital fluid; literary ichor.
2 *a woman of noble blood*: **ancestry**, lineage, line, bloodline, descent, parentage, family, house, dynasty, birth, extraction, derivation, origin, genealogy, heritage, breeding, stock, strain, race, pedigree, roots, kinship, consanguinity.
3 *my daughter defies me—my own flesh and blood! | relations by blood or marriage*: **kin**, kindred, relation, member of one's family, next of kin; blood relationship, relationship, kinship; formal kinsman, kinswoman.

Word links **blood**

haem-, **haemat-** related prefixes
haemal, **haemic**, **haematic**, archaic **sanguineous** relating to blood
haematology branch of medicine to do with the blood
oscillometry, **sphygmomanometry** measurement of blood pressure
haemophobia fear of blood

blood-curdling adjective *a blood-curdling scream*: **terrifying**, frightening, spine-chilling, hair-raising, chilling, horrifying, petrifying, alarming, shocking, scaring; eerie, sinister, fearsome, horrific, horrible, horrendous, fearful, appalling; Scottish eldritch; informal spooky, scary, creepy.

bloodless adjective **1** *a bloodless revolution*: **non-violent**, peaceful, peaceable, pacifistic, strife-free, non-warlike, harmonious; orderly, disciplined.
▷ANTONYMS bloody, violent.
2 *his face was bloodless*: **anaemic**, pale, wan, pallid, ashen, colourless, chalky, chalk-white, milky, waxen, white, grey; pasty, sallow, jaundiced, washed out, sickly, peaked, drained, sapped, drawn, deathly, deathlike, ghostlike, white as a sheet; informal peaky; rare etiolated.
▷ANTONYMS ruddy.
3 *a shrewd and bloodless Hollywood mogul*: **heartless**, unfeeling, cruel; **ruthless**, merciless, pitiless, cold, hard, stony-hearted, stony, with a heart of stone, cold-blooded, cold-hearted; harsh, callous, severe, unmerciful, unpitying, uncaring, unsympathetic, uncharitable.
▷ANTONYMS warm-hearted, charitable.
4 *the bloodless flimsiness of modern fiction*: **feeble**, spiritless, lifeless, passionless, listless, limp, unanimated, languid, half-hearted, unenthusiastic, lukewarm; bland, vapid, wishy-washy.
▷ANTONYMS powerful.

bloodshed noun *the president feared bloodshed and disorder if the demands for reform were not met*: **slaughter**, slaying, killing, carnage, butchery, massacre, murder, bloodletting, bloodbath, gore, pogrom, genocide; violence, fighting, hostilities, conflict, warfare, war, battle; wounding, injury.
▷ANTONYMS peace.

bloodthirsty adjective *a bloodthirsty Viking*: **murderous**, homicidal, violent, sadistic, warlike, bellicose, bloody; vicious, ruthless, callous, heartless, merciless, barbarous, barbaric, savage, brutal, cut-throat; fierce, ferocious, inhuman; archaic sanguinary.
▷ANTONYMS peaceful.

bloody[1] adjective **1** *he wiped his bloody nose*: **bleeding**, shedding blood, emitting blood, unstaunched, raw, gaping.
2 *the disposal of bloody medical waste*: **bloodstained**, bloodsoaked, blood-spattered, gory; archaic sanguinary.
3 *a bloody civil war*: **involving bloodshed**, gory, bloodthirsty; vicious, cruel, ferocious, savage, fierce, brutal, murderous; archaic sanguinary.

bloody[2] adjective informal *what a bloody nuisance!* See **damned** (sense 2).

bloody-minded adjective Brit. informal *a truculent, bloody-minded shop steward*: **uncooperative**, unreasonable, contrary, unhelpful, awkward, obstructive, truculent, recalcitrant, unaccommodating, unyielding, inflexible, uncompromising, unbending, refractory, disobliging, obstinate, stubborn, perverse, not giving an inch; difficult, exasperating, trying; Scottish thrawn; informal pig-headed, cussed; Brit. informal bolshie, stroppy; N. Amer. informal balky.
▷ANTONYMS compliant.

bloom noun **1** *gorgeous orchid-like blooms*: **flower**, blossom, floweret; flowering, blossoming, florescence, efflorescence.
2 *a country girl in the bloom of health and youth*: **prime**, perfection, acme, zenith, peak, height, heyday, flourishing, strength, vigour; salad days.
▷ANTONYMS decline, nadir.
3 *your earrings complement the bloom of your skin to perfection*: **lustre**, sheen, glow, radiance, freshness, perfection; **blush**, flush, rosiness, pinkness, redness, ruddiness, colour.
▸ verb **1** *the geraniums had already bloomed*: **blossom**, flower, be in blossom/flower, come into flower/blossom, open, open out, bud, sprout, burgeon, mature.
▷ANTONYMS wither, fade.
2 *the children had bloomed in the soft Devonshire air*: **flourish**, thrive, be in good health, get on well, get ahead, prosper, succeed, be successful, progress, make progress, make headway, burgeon; informal be in the pink, be fine and dandy, go great guns.

blossom noun *the trees stood flushed with pink blossoms*: **flower**, bloom, floweret; blossoming, inflorescence, florescence, efflorescence.
□ **in blossom** *the cherry trees are out in blossom*: **in flower**, flowering, blossoming, blooming, in (full) bloom, open, out.
▸ verb **1** *the snowdrops have blossomed a month early*: **bloom**, flower, be in flower, come into flower/blossom, open (out), burgeon, bud, sprout, mature, burst forth, unfold.
2 *the idea has now blossomed into a successful business*: **develop**, grow, mature, progress, evolve, burst forth, come to fruition; flourish, thrive, get on well, prosper, succeed, be successful, make headway, bloom, burgeon; informal go great guns.
▷ANTONYMS fade, fail.

blot noun **1** *an ink blot*: **spot**, dot, mark, speck, fleck, blotch, smudge, patch, dab, smut, splash, smear, streak; informal splotch, splodge.
2 *the only blot on an otherwise clean campaign*: **blemish**, taint, flaw, fault, defect, stain, tarnishing, imperfection, blight; disgrace, dishonour, stigma, brand, slur.
3 *a blot on the landscape*: **eyesore**, monstrosity, carbuncle, atrocity, horror, mess; informal sight.
▸ verb **1** *he used a towel to blot excess water*: **soak up**, absorb, take up, suck up, draw up, sponge up, mop up, sop up; dry up, dry out; dab, pat, press.
▷ANTONYMS exude; moisten.
2 *the writing was messy and blotted*: **smudge**, smear, spot, blotch, dot, mark, speckle, bespatter.
3 *he had blotted our name forever by this disgraceful behaviour*: **tarnish**, taint, stain, blacken, sully, smear, mar; **dishonour**, disgrace, bring discredit to, calumniate, traduce, drag through the mud/mire; literary besmear, besmirch; archaic spot, breathe on.
▷ANTONYMS honour, enhance.
□ **blot something out 1** *Mary blotted out her picture*: **erase**, obliterate, delete, efface, rub out, wipe out, blank out, remove all traces of, expunge, eliminate; cancel, cross out, strike out. **2** *clouds were starting to blot out the stars*: **conceal**, hide, obscure, exclude, obliterate, erase; darken, dim, shadow, eclipse, cast a shadow over. ▷ANTONYMS reveal. **3** *he urged her to blot out the memory of what she had seen*: **wipe out**, erase, efface, eradicate, obliterate, expunge, destroy, exterminate.

blotch noun **1** *huge pink flowers with dark blotches*: **patch**, smudge, dot, spot, speck, speckle; blot, stain, smear, streak, dab, daub, splash; informal splotch, splodge.
2 *his face was puffy and covered in dark blotches*: **rash**, blemish, spot, freckle, birthmark, strawberry mark, port wine stain, eruption; patch, mark, discoloration; technical naevus, haemangioma.
▸ verb *her face was blotched and swollen with crying*: **spot**, mark, speck, speckle, smudge, smear, streak, blemish, cover with blotches.

blotchy adjective *her face had become blotchy*: **spotty**, spotted, blemished, blotched, patchy, uneven, smudged, freckled, marked, smeary, streaked, stippled, macular, covered with blotches; reddened, red, inflamed; dappled, mottled, flecked, variegated, particoloured; informal splotchy, splodgy.

Word toolkit

blotchy	**dappled**	**patchy**
skin	shade	coverage
face	sunlight	hair
complexion	shadows	fog
patches	horse	lawn
mess	pattern	beard

blow[1] verb **1** *the icy wind blew around our ankles*: **gust**, puff, flurry, blast, roar, bluster, rush, storm; move, be in motion.
2 *his ship was blown on to the rocks*: **sweep**, carry, pull, drag, drive, buffet, move, whisk, toss, waft, whirl.
3 *leaves blew across the concourse*: **drift**, flutter, waft, flow, stream, whirl, move, wave, flap, undulate, float, glide, travel, be carried.
4 *he blew a series of smoke rings*: **exhale**, breathe out, puff out, emit, expel, discharge, give out, issue, send forth.
5 *Uncle Albert was soon puffing and blowing*: **wheeze**, puff, pant, puff and pant, gasp, huff and puff, breathe hard/heavily, fight for breath, catch one's breath.
6 *he blew a trumpet*: **sound**, play, blast, toot, pipe, trumpet; make a noise with.
7 *a rear tyre had blown*: **burst**, explode, blow out, split, rupture, crack, break, fly open; puncture, get a puncture; get a flat tyre.
8 *the bulb had blown*: **fuse**, short-circuit, burn out, expire, break, go.
9 informal *he blew a lot of his money on gambling*: **squander**, waste, misspend, throw away, fritter away, spend freely, run through, go through, lose, lavish, dissipate; make poor use of, be prodigal with, spend recklessly, spend unwisely, spend like water, throw around like confetti; burn, use up; informal splurge, pour/throw down the drain, spend as if it grows on trees, spend as if there were no tomorrow, spend as if it were going out of style; Brit. informal splash out, blue.
▷ANTONYMS save, spend wisely.
10 informal *if you blow this opportunity you might never get another chance*: **spoil**, ruin, bungle, make a mess of, mess up, fudge, muff; **waste**, lose, squander, throw away; informal botch, make a hash of, screw up, louse up, foul up, bodge, fluff; Brit. informal cock up; vulgar slang fuck up, bugger up.
11 *he was a powerful agent before his cover was blown*: **expose**, reveal, uncover, disclose, divulge, unveil, betray, leak.
□ **blow someone away** informal *the quality blew me away*: **impress**, overwhelm, bedazzle, strike, move, stir, affect, touch, sweep someone off their feet, awe, overawe, leave speechless, take someone's breath away, spellbind, hypnotize, fascinate, take aback, daze, stagger, floor, amaze, astonish; informal bowl over, knock out.
□ **blow hot and cold** informal See **hot**.
□ **blow someone's mind** informal *the music you were playing really blew my mind*. See **blow someone away**.
□ **blow out 1** *the matches are designed not to blow out in a strong wind*: **be extinguished**, go out, be put out, be doused, be quenched, stop burning, fade, die out. ▷ANTONYMS light.
2 *the front tyre blew out*. See **blow**[1] (sense 7 of the verb).
3 *the observation windows blew out in a shower of glass*: **shatter**, rupture, fly into pieces, crack, smash, splinter, disintegrate; burst, explode, blow up, fly apart, break open; informal bust, be smashed to smithereens; rare shiver.
□ **blow something out** *Rosie blew out the candle*: **extinguish**, put out, snuff, douse, quench, smother, stifle, dampen down, choke.
▷ANTONYMS light.
□ **blow over** *the crisis blew over*: **abate**, subside, settle down, drop off/away, lessen, ease (off), let up, diminish, fade, dwindle, slacken, recede, cool off, tail off, peter out, pass away, pass, die down/away/out, be forgotten, fizzle out, sink into oblivion, come to an end; disappear, vanish, cease, terminate; archaic remit. ▷ANTONYMS flare up, get worse.
□ **blow one's top/lid/stack** informal See **blow up** (sense 2).
□ **blow up 1** *a lorryload of mortars and shells blew up*: **explode**, detonate, go off, be set off, ignite, erupt, burst apart, shatter; informal go bang, go boom.
2 *he blows up at whoever's in his way when he's in a bad mood*: **lose one's temper**, get/become angry, become enraged, become furious, go into a rage/fury, rant and rave, go berserk, flare up, erupt, rage, blow/lose one's cool; informal hit the roof, go up the wall, go off the deep end, fly off the handle, go/get mad, go crazy, go wild, go bananas, see red, lose one's rag, go ape, blow a gasket, flip one's lid. ▷ANTONYMS keep one's temper.
3 *a crisis blew up between the two countries in 1967*: **break out**, erupt, flare up, boil over, start/commence/occur suddenly, emerge, arise.
□ **blow something up 1** *they blew the plane up with dynamite*: **explode**, bomb, blast, destroy; detonate, blitz.
2 *his party trick was to blow up balloons and make them into little animals*: **inflate**, pump up, fill up, swell, enlarge, distend, expand, puff up, balloon, aerate. ▷ANTONYMS deflate, let down.
3 *these things get blown up out of all proportion*: **exaggerate**, overstate, overemphasize, hyperbolize, overstress, overestimate, magnify, amplify; embroider, colour, heighten, expand on, aggrandize, dress up, touch up, embellish, elaborate, gild. ▷ANTONYMS understate.
4 *I blew the picture up on a colour photocopier*: **enlarge**, magnify, expand, extend, increase in size, make larger, make bigger. ▷ANTONYMS reduce.
▶ noun **1** *they had lost their storm jib during a severe blow*: **gale**, storm, tempest, hurricane, blast; wind, breeze, gust, puff of wind, draught, flurry; turbulence; literary zephyr.
2 *a blow on the guard's whistle*: **toot**, blare, blast, sound, whistle, shriek.

blow[2] noun **1** *death was due to a blow on the head with a blunt instrument*: **knock**, **bang**, hit, punch, thump, smack, crack, thwack, buffet, jolt, stroke, rap, tap, clip; informal whack, bash, belt, clout, sock, wallop, battering, lick, slosh, bat.
2 *losing his wife must have been a blow to him*: **shock**, surprise, bombshell, bolt from the blue, bolt out of the blue, thunderbolt, jolt, rude awakening; calamity, catastrophe, disaster, upset, misfortune, setback, disturbance, source of distress, disappointment, let-down; informal whammy.

blowout noun **1** *I always leave plenty of time to get to the airport in case I have a blowout or breakdown*: **puncture**, flat tyre, burst tyre; informal flat.
2 informal *this meal may be the last real blowout we have for a while*: **party**, **feast**, banquet, celebration, binge; informal shindig, shindy, do; Brit. informal beanfeast, beano, bunfight, thrash, nosh-up, scoff, slap-up meal, tuck-in.

blowsy adjective *a blowsy old dame*: **untidy**, sloppy, scruffy, messy, dishevelled, slovenly, sluttish, slatternly, tousled, unkempt, frowzy, slipshod, bedraggled, down at heel; coarse-looking; **red-faced**, ruddy, florid, ruddy-complexioned, flushed, raddled, rubicund, rubescent.
▷ANTONYMS tidy, respectable.

blowy adjective *it was a blowy night*: **windy**, windswept, blustery, gusty, breezy, draughty, fresh; wild, stormy, squally, tempestuous, turbulent; rare boisterous.
▷ANTONYMS still.

blubber[1] noun **1** *whale blubber*: **fat**, fatty tissue.
2 informal *she wanted to burn off all of her blubber*: **fat**, excessive weight, fatness, plumpness, bulk; beer belly, beer gut, paunch; informal **flab**, beef.

blubber[2] verb informal *I was blubbering like a baby*. See **cry** (sense 1 of the verb).

bludgeon noun *they were violently assaulted by hooligans wielding bludgeons*: **cudgel**, club, stick, truncheon, baton, bat, heavy weapon, blunt instrument; N. Amer. nightstick, blackjack; Brit. informal cosh.
▶ verb **1** *he was waylaid by four of them and bludgeoned to death*: **batter**, cudgel, club, strike, hit, beat, beat up, hammer, thrash; informal clobber.
2 *there are few things worse than being bludgeoned into reading a book you hate*: **coerce**, force, compel, press, pressurize, pressure, drive, bully, browbeat, hector, badger, dragoon, steamroller; oblige, make, prevail on, constrain; informal strong-arm, railroad, bulldoze, put the screws on, turn/tighten the screws on.

blue adjective **1** *she had bright blue eyes*: sky-blue, azure, cobalt (blue), sapphire, cerulean, navy (blue), saxe (blue), Oxford blue, Cambridge blue, ultramarine, lapis lazuli, indigo, aquamarine, turquoise, teal (blue), cyan, of the colour of the sky, of the colour of the sea.
2 informal *Dad had died that year and Mum was feeling a bit blue*: **depressed**, down, sad, saddened, unhappy, melancholy, miserable, sorrowful, gloomy, dejected, downhearted, disheartened, despondent, dispirited, low, in low spirits, low-spirited, heavy-hearted, glum, morose, dismal, downcast, cast down, tearful; informal down in the dumps, down in the mouth, fed up.
▷ANTONYMS happy, cheerful.
3 *a blue movie*: **indecent**, dirty, rude, coarse, vulgar, bawdy, lewd, racy, risqué, salacious, naughty, wicked, improper, unseemly, smutty, spicy, raw, off colour, ribald, Rabelaisian; pornographic, filthy, obscene, offensive, prurient, sordid, low, profane, foul, vile; erotic, arousing, sexy, suggestive, titillating, explicit; informal near the knuckle/bone, nudge-nudge, porn, porno, X-rated, raunchy, skin; Brit. informal fruity, saucy; euphemistic adult.
▷ANTONYMS clean, family.

Word links **blue**

cyano- related prefix, as in *cyanic, cyanotype*

blueprint noun **1** *the blueprints of the aircraft and its components*: **plan**, design, draft, diagram, drawing, scale drawing, outline, sketch, pattern, map, layout, representation; technical drawing.
2 *the Thai programme provides a blueprint for similar measures in other developing countries*: **model**, plan, template, framework, pattern, design, example, exemplar, guide, prototype, paradigm, sample, pilot, recipe.

blues plural noun informal *a fit of blues bedevilled her*: **depression**, sadness, unhappiness, melancholy, misery, sorrow, gloominess, gloom, dejection, downheartedness, despondency, dispiritedness, low spirits, heavy-heartedness, glumness, moroseness, dismalness, despair; the doldrums; informal the dumps.
▷ANTONYMS happiness.

b

bluff[1] noun *this offer was denounced as a bluff*: **deception**, **subterfuge**, pretence, sham, fake, show, deceit, false show, idle boast, feint, delusion, hoax, fraud, masquerade, charade; trick, stratagem, ruse, manoeuvre, scheme, artifice, machination; humbug, bluster, bombast, bragging; Irish informal codology; informal put-on, put-up job, kidology.
▸ verb **1** *the family are simply bluffing to hide their guilt*: **pretend**, sham, fake, feign, put on an act, put it on, lie, hoax, pose, posture, masquerade, dissemble, dissimulate; informal kid.
2 *I managed to bluff the board into believing that I had a long-term strategy*: **deceive**, delude, mislead, trick, fool, hoodwink, dupe, hoax, take in, beguile, humbug, bamboozle, gull, cheat; informal con, kid, put one over on, have on, pull the wool over someone's eyes; vulgar slang bullshit; archaic cozen.

bluff[2] adjective *a bluff, hearty man*: **plain-spoken**, straightforward, blunt, direct, no-nonsense, frank, open, candid, outspoken, to the point, forthright, unequivocal, downright, hearty; rough, abrupt, curt, gruff, short, brusque, not afraid to call a spade a spade, speaking as one finds; **genial**, approachable, good-natured, friendly; informal straight from the shoulder, upfront.
▷ANTONYMS diplomatic; evasive.

bluff[3] noun *the villa was set high on a bluff overlooking the sea*: **cliff**, ridge, promontory, headland, crag, bank, slope, height, peak, escarpment, scarp, precipice, rock face, overhang; rare eminence.

blunder noun *she stopped, finally aware of the terrible blunder she had made*: **mistake**, error, gaffe, fault, slip, oversight, inaccuracy, botch; debacle, fiasco; French faux pas; informal slip-up, clanger, boob, boo-boo, howler, foul-up; N. Amer. informal blooper; Brit. informal, dated bloomer; vulgar slang fuck-up.
▸ verb **1** *the government admitted that it had blundered in its handling of the affair*: **make a mistake**, be mistaken, err, be in error, misjudge, miscalculate, bungle, trip up, be wrong, get something wrong, be wide of the mark; informal slip up, screw up, blow it, foul up, goof, boob, put one's foot in it, make a boo-boo, drop a brick; vulgar slang fuck up, bugger up.
2 *I heard her blundering about the flat*: **stumble**, lurch, stagger, falter, flounder, muddle, struggle, fumble, grope.

blunt adjective **1** *a blunt knife*: **not sharp**, unsharpened, dull, dulled, worn (down), edgeless.
▷ANTONYMS sharp.
2 *the scale is broad with a blunt tip*: **rounded**, flat, thick, obtuse, stubby, stubbed, unpointed.
▷ANTONYMS pointed.
3 *he had a blunt message for the audience*: **straightforward**, frank, plain-spoken, candid, direct, bluff, to the point, forthright, unequivocal, point-blank, unceremonious, undiplomatic, indelicate; **brusque**, abrupt, curt, short, sharp, terse, crisp, gruff, bald, brutal, harsh, caustic; stark, bare, simple, unadorned, unembellished, undisguised, unvarnished, unqualified, pulling no punches, hard-hitting, outspoken, speaking one's mind, not mincing one's words, not beating about the bush, calling a spade a spade; informal upfront, straight from the shoulder.
▷ANTONYMS subtle, tactful.
▸ verb **1** *ebony blunts tools very rapidly*: **make less sharp**, make blunt, make dull.
▷ANTONYMS sharpen, hone.
2 *age hasn't blunted my passion for the good things in life*: **dull**, deaden, dampen, soften, numb, weaken, take the edge off; calm, cool, temper, muffle, impair, allay, abate; tone down, dilute, sap, water down, thin, reduce, moderate; assuage, alleviate, mollify, ease, relieve, slake, sate, appease; diminish, decrease, lessen, deplete.
▷ANTONYMS intensify, sharpen.

> *Choose the right word* **blunt, candid, forthright, frank, outspoken**
>
> See **candid**.

blur verb **1** *if the ray focus does not fall exactly on the film, the image will be blurred*: **make indistinct**, make vague, unfocus, soften; obscure, dim, fade, make hazy, fog, cloud (over); literary bedim, befog, becloud; archaic blear.
▷ANTONYMS sharpen, focus.
2 *such 'advertorials' blur the distinction between editorial content and advertising*: **make vague**, make unclear, make less distinct; **obscure**, muddy, muddle, mix up, confuse, obfuscate, cloud, befog, garble, lessen, weaken; muddy the waters.
3 *memories of the picnic had blurred*: **become dim**, become less sharp, dull, numb, deaden, lessen, decrease, diminish, reduce, mute, tone down.
▷ANTONYMS sharpen.
▸ noun *a blur on the horizon slowly began to take shape*: **indistinct shape**, hazy shape, vague shape, something indistinct/hazy/vague, haze, cloud, mist, smear, smudge; haziness, indistinctness, fogginess, murkiness, cloudiness.

blurred adjective *a blurred photograph*: **indistinct**, blurry, fuzzy, hazy, misty, foggy, shadowy, smoky, faint; unclear, vague, indefinite, unfocused, obscure, lacking definition, ill-defined, out of focus, nebulous; woolly, muzzy, bleary; archaic blear.
▷ANTONYMS clear, distinct.

blurt verb
□ **blurt something out** *he blurted out his story*: **utter suddenly**, exclaim, ejaculate, tell, babble, jabber, call out, cry out, burst out with, come out with; **divulge**, disclose, reveal, betray, leak, let slip, let out, give away, give the game away, bring to light; informal blab, gush, let on, spill the beans, spill one's guts, let the cat out of the bag, run off at the mouth, spout.
▷ANTONYMS keep quiet.

blush verb *Joan blushed at the unexpected compliment*: **redden**, turn/go pink, turn/go red, turn/go crimson, turn/go scarlet, flush, colour, crimson, tint, burn up; feel shy, feel embarrassment, feel shame, feel embarrassed, feel ashamed, feel sheepish, feel mortified; archaic mantle.
▸ noun *a deep blush spread from her head to her neck*: **flush**, reddening, high colour, colour, rosiness, pinkness, ruddiness, bloom.

> *Word links* **blush**
>
> **erythrophobia** fear of blushing

bluster verb **1** *he's still blustering and saying that he'll never resort to that*: **rant**, thunder; boast, brag, swagger, throw one's weight about/around, be overbearing, lord it, vaunt, bray, crow.
2 *in winter the storms bluster in from the Mediterranean*: **blow fiercely**, blast, gust, storm, roar, rush.
▸ noun *he sought refuge in bluster and bullying*: **ranting**, hectoring, thundering, threatening, threats, bullying, domineering; boasting, bragging, swaggering, throwing one's weight around; bombast, bravado, bumptiousness, imperiousness; empty threats, humbug; literary braggadocio.

blustery adjective *a wet and blustery night*: **stormy**, gusty, gusting, windy, squally, wild, rough, raging, tempestuous, turbulent, violent; howling, roaring; inclement, foul, filthy, dirty, nasty; informal blowy.
▷ANTONYMS calm, still.

board noun **1** *a wooden board*: **plank**, beam, panel, slat, batten, timber, length of timber, piece of wood, lath.
2 *the board of directors*: **committee**, council, panel, directorate, commission, group, delegation, delegates, trustees, panel of trustees, convocation; Brit. quango.
3 *your room and board will be free*: **food**, meals, daily meals, provisions, sustenance, nourishment, fare, diet, menu, table, bread, daily bread, foodstuffs, refreshments, edibles; keep, maintenance, upkeep; Scottish vivas; informal grub, nosh, eats, chow, scoff; formal comestibles, provender; archaic vittles, commons, victuals, viands, aliment.
▸ verb **1** *he had boarded the aircraft*: **get on**, enter, go on board, go aboard, step aboard, climb on, mount, ascend, embark; catch; informal hop on, jump on; formal emplane, entrain, embus.
▷ANTONYMS alight, get off.
2 *a number of his students boarded with him and his wife*: **lodge**, live, reside, have rooms, be quartered, be housed, be settled, have one's home; N. Amer. room; informal put up, have digs.
3 *the old system of boarding young trainees on the farm has virtually disappeared*: **accommodate**, lodge, take in, put up, house, billet, quarter, harbour, provide shelter for, shelter, give a bed to, give someone a roof over their head, make room for, give accommodation to, receive; keep, feed, cater for, cook for.
□ **board something up/over** *both its windows had been boarded up*: **cover up/over**, close up, shut up, seal.

boast verb **1** *his mother had been boasting about how wonderful he was to all her friends*: **brag**, crow, swagger, swank, gloat, show off, blow one's own trumpet, sing one's own praises, congratulate oneself, pat oneself on the back; exaggerate, overstate; preen oneself, give oneself airs; informal talk big, blow hard, lay it on thick, shoot one's mouth off; Austral./NZ informal skite, big-note oneself.
▷ANTONYMS deprecate, belittle.
2 *the museum boasts a breathtaking collection of glassware*: **possess**, have, own, enjoy, pride oneself/itself on, be the proud owner of.
▸ noun **1** *his proud boast is that he started off without any outside financial backing*: **brag**, self-praise; exaggeration, overstatement; bragging, crowing, swaggering; informal swank, swanking; Austral./NZ informal skite; literary fanfaronade; archaic vaunt, rodomontade, gasconade.
2 *the hall is the boast of the county*: **pride**, pride and joy, joy, wonder, delight, darling, treasure, gem, pearl, apple of someone's eye, valued object, source of satisfaction.

boastful adjective *he always seemed to be rather boastful and above himself*: **bragging**, crowing, swaggering, braggart, overweening, overbearing, bumptious, puffed up, vaunting, blowhard, ostentatious, full of oneself; cocky, conceited, proud, arrogant, vain, egotistical; informal swanking, swanky, big-mouthed, big-headed, swollen-headed; formal vainglorious.
▷ANTONYMS modest, unassuming.

boat noun *a small rowing boat*: **vessel**, craft, watercraft, ship; literary keel, barque.
▸ verb *he often went boating*: **sail**, yacht, go sailing, cruise, travel by boat.

bob verb **1** *their yacht bobbed about on the choppy waters*: **bounce**, move up and down, float, spring, toss, skip, hop, dance, jump, jounce; quiver, wobble, jiggle, joggle, jolt, jerk, shake, oscillate.
2 *the bookie's head bobbed*: **nod**, incline, bow, dip, duck; wag, waggle.
3 *the maid bobbed and left the room*: **curtsy**, drop a curtsy, bow, genuflect, prostrate oneself.
▶ noun **1** *he spoke with a bob of his head*: **nod**, inclination, bow, dip, duck; wag, waggle.
2 *the maid scurried away with a bob*: **curtsy**, bow, genuflection, obeisance.

bode verb *the look on her face boded ill for anyone who crossed her path*: **augur**, presage, portend, foretell, prophesy, predict; forebode, foreshadow, herald, be an omen of, warn of; indicate, signify, be a sign of, purport, point to, threaten, promise, spell, mean; rare betoken, foretoken, adumbrate.

bodily adjective *our experience of bodily sensations*: **physical**, corporeal, corporal, mortal, carnal, fleshly, sensual; material, concrete, earthly, real, actual, tangible, substantial; rare somatic.
▷ANTONYMS spiritual, mental.
▶ adverb *she lifted him bodily out of his seat*: **forcefully**, with force, powerfully, forcibly, violently; **wholly**, completely, altogether, entirely, totally.

body noun **1** *the human body*: **anatomy**, figure, frame, form, shape, build, physique, framework, skeleton, bones, flesh and bones; informal bod; rare corse, soma.
2 *he was in a critical condition after he was hit in the head and body*: **torso**, trunk, chest, stomach, middle.
3 *his body was badly charred in the fire*: **corpse**, dead body, cadaver, carcass, skeleton, remains, relics; informal stiff.
4 *the article would fit equally well into the body of the magazine or the supplement*: **main part**, principal part, central part, core, heart, hub, nub, kernel.
5 *the car body*: **bodywork**, hull, fuselage, outer casing.
6 *a body of water*: **expanse**, mass, area, stretch, region, tract, breadth, sweep, extent, aggregate, accumulation, concretion, accretion.
7 *a growing body of evidence reveals discrimination against the old*: **quantity**, amount, volume, collection, proportion, mass, corpus.
8 *the body of parental opinion*: **majority**, preponderance, greater part, major part, main part, best part, better part, lion's share, bulk, mass, generality.
9 *the representative body of the employers*: **association**, organization, group, grouping, party, band, company, society, club, circle, fellowship, partnership, fraternity, syndicate, guild, federation, confederation, bloc, corporation, contingent, coterie, clique.
10 *the earth is a heavenly body circling a larger heavenly body*: **object**, entity, item, piece of matter.
11 *mousse was used to add body and bounce to this feminine style*: **fullness**, solidity, density, thickness, firmness, substance, mass; **shape**, structure.
□ **body and soul** *he seemed ready to dedicate himself to them body and soul*: **completely**, entirely, totally, utterly, fully, thoroughly, wholeheartedly, unconditionally, unrestrictedly, one hundred per cent, in all respects, to the hilt, all the way.
▷ANTONYMS half-heartedly.

Word links **body**

somato- related prefix, as in *somatotype, somatotrophin*
corporal, corporeal, somatic relating to the body
anthropometry measurement of the human body

bodyguard noun *his bodyguards were watching the door*: **minder**, guard, protector, guardian, defender, keeper, escort, companion, chaperone; informal heavy, bouncer, hired gun.

boffin noun Brit. informal *they wore the white coats of the back-room boffin*: **expert**, specialist, authority, genius, mastermind; **scientist**, technician, researcher, inventor; informal egghead, brains, Einstein, whizz, wizard; Brit. informal brainbox, clever clogs; N. Amer. informal maven, rocket scientist, brainiac.

bog noun *a peat bog*: **marsh**, marshland, swamp, swampland, sump, mire, quagmire, quag, morass, slough, fen, fenland, wetland, carr; salt marsh, saltings, salina; N. Amer. bayou, moor; Scottish & N. English moss.
▶ verb
□ **bog someone/something down** *many great ideas got bogged down in bureaucracy*: **mire**, stick, trap, entangle, ensnare, embroil, encumber, catch up; hamper, hinder, obstruct, impede, halt, stop, delay, stall, slow down, detain, hold in check, restrain; swamp, overwhelm, overpower, overburden.

bogey noun **1** *bogies and other denizens of the night*: **evil spirit**, bogle, ghost, spectre, phantom, hobgoblin, ogre, troll, demon, devil, fiend, sprite, witch, warlock, apparition; informal spook.
2 *home taping became the record industry's chief bogey*: **bugbear**, **pet hate**, bane, anathema, abomination, nightmare, horror, dread, curse, thorn in one's flesh/side, bane of one's life, bugaboo; French bête noire; informal peeve.

boggle verb informal **1** *the proliferation of data makes the mind boggle*: **marvel**, wonder, be astonished, be astounded, be amazed, be filled with amazement, be overwhelmed, be shocked, be staggered, be bowled over, be startled; gape, goggle, gawk; informal be flabbergasted.
2 *it boggles my mind that everyone thinks that they can pull the wool over the eyes of record companies*: **astonish**, astound, amaze, fill with amazement, overwhelm, shock, startle, fill with wonder; informal flabbergast, bowl over.
3 *you never **boggle at** plain speaking*: **demur**, jib, shrink from, flinch from, recoil from, hang back from, waver, falter, dither, baulk, vacillate about, think twice about, be reluctant about, have scruples about, scruple about, have misgivings about, have qualms about, be chary of, hesitate to, be shy about, be coy about, shy away from; informal be cagey about, shilly-shally.

b

boggy adjective *trudging through boggy ground*: **marshy**, swampy, miry, fenny, mucky, muddy, waterlogged, wet, soggy, sodden, squelchy, oozy, slimy; clogged, spongy, heavy, sloughy, soft, yielding; Scottish & N. English mossy, clarty; technical paludal, uliginose; archaic quaggy.
▷ANTONYMS dry, hard.

bogus adjective *a bogus insurance claim*: **fake**, faked, spurious, false, fraudulent, sham, deceptive, misleading, pretended; **counterfeit**, forged, feigned, simulated; artificial, imitation, mock, make-believe, fictitious, dummy, quasi-, pseudo, ersatz; informal phoney, pretend, dud, put-on; Brit. informal cod.
▷ANTONYMS genuine, authentic.

bohemian noun *he is a real artist and a real bohemian*: **nonconformist**, unconventional person, beatnik, hippy, avant-gardist, free spirit, dropout, artistic person; informal freak.
▷ANTONYMS conformist, conservative.
▶ adjective *she lived a bohemian student life in Paris*: **unconventional**, nonconformist, unorthodox, avant-garde, offbeat, irregular, original, alternative, experimental, artistic, idiosyncratic, eccentric; informal arty, arty-farty, way-out, off the wall, oddball.
▷ANTONYMS conventional, conservative.

boil[1] verb **1** *boil the potatoes in salted water*: **bring to the boil**, simmer, heat; cook.
▷ANTONYMS freeze.
2 *the stew is boiling*: **simmer**, bubble, seethe, heat, cook, stew.
▷ANTONYMS freeze.
3 *a huge cliff with the sea boiling below*: **be turbulent**, be agitated, froth, foam, churn, seethe, bubble, fizz, effervesce; literary roil.
4 *inwardly, she boiled at his lack of consideration*: **be angry**, be furious, be indignant, rage, fume, seethe, smoulder; lose one's temper, lose control, rant, rave, storm, fulminate, bluster, explode, flare up, go berserk, throw a tantrum; informal blow one's top, fly off the handle, go off the deep end, hit the roof, go up the wall, blow a fuse, see red, get worked up, get steamed up; Brit. informal spit feathers.
▷ANTONYMS keep calm.
□ **boil something down** *continuing to boil down the syrup produces maple sugar crystals*: **condense**, concentrate, reduce, distil, thicken, compress; strengthen.
▷ANTONYMS dilute.
□ **boil down to** *it all boils down to a personality clash*: **come down to**, amount to, be in essence, comprise, add up to.
▶ noun *add the stock and bring it to **the boil***: **boiling point**, 100 degrees Celsius/centigrade.
▷ANTONYMS freezing point.

boil[2] noun *a girl with a boil on her nose*: **swelling**, **spot**, pimple, blister, pustule, eruption, blemish, carbuncle, wen, cyst, abscess, tumour, ulcer, chilblain, gumboil; technical furuncle; rare blain.

boiling adjective **1** *boiling water*: **at boiling point**, at 100 degrees Celsius/centigrade; steaming, bubbling, gurgling, evaporating; very hot, piping (hot), red hot, sizzling.
▷ANTONYMS cold, freezing.
2 informal *it was a **boiling hot** morning*: **very hot**, scorching, roasting, baking, blistering, blazing, sweltering, parching, searing, broiling, sultry, torrid, sweaty, oven-like.
▷ANTONYMS cold, cool.

boisterous adjective **1** *a boisterous game of handball*: **lively**, active, animated, exuberant, spirited, bouncy, frisky, excited, overexcited, in high spirits, high-spirited, ebullient, vibrant, rowdy, unruly, wild, uproarious, unrestrained, undisciplined, uninhibited, uncontrolled, abandoned, rough, romping, rollicking, disorderly, knockabout, riotous, rip-roaring, rumbustious, roistering, tumultuous; noisy, loud, clamorous, clangorous.
▷ANTONYMS quiet, restrained.
2 *a boisterous wind*: **blustery**, gusting, gusty, breezy, windy, stormy, wild, squally, rough, choppy, turbulent, tempestuous, howling, roaring, raging, furious; informal blowy.
▷ANTONYMS calm, quiet.

Word toolkit **boisterous**

See **rowdy**.

bold adjective **1** *Derby's manager made another bold move into the transfer market | bold adventurers*: **daring**, intrepid, courageous, brave,

b

valiant, fearless, unafraid, undaunted, dauntless, valorous; **audacious**, adventurous, dashing, heroic, gallant, swashbuckling, adventuresome, daredevil, venturesome, plucky, unflinching; spirited, confident, positive, decisive, assured, enterprising; rash, reckless, brash, foolhardy; informal gutsy, spunky, ballsy, game, feisty; literary temerarious.
▷ANTONYMS timid, unadventurous.
2 dated *a bold streetwise young girl*: **brazen**, shameless, forward, brash, impudent, audacious, cheeky, saucy, cocky, pert, impertinent, insolent, presumptuous, immodest, unabashed, unreserved, barefaced, unshrinking, defiant, brass-necked, bold as brass; informal brassy, sassy.
▷ANTONYMS retiring.
3 *a bold pattern of yellow and black*: **striking**, vivid, bright, strong, eye-catching, conspicuous, distinct, pronounced, prominent, obvious, outstanding, well marked, showy, flashy, gaudy, lurid, garish.
▷ANTONYMS pale.
4 *cross references are printed in bold type*: **heavy**, thick, clear, conspicuous, distinct, pronounced, outstanding.
▷ANTONYMS light, roman.

Choose the right word **bold, daring, audacious**

These words all refer to someone's bravery or courage and are used to describe either a person or an action.

A **bold** action typically does not involve physical danger and is more likely to be approved of than a *daring* or *audacious* one (*people are looking to their leaders to take bold decisions now*).

A **daring** action involves adventurousness undeterred by physical danger and does not necessarily describe activities that are approved of (*a daring mission to rescue wounded soldiers | one of the most daring crimes of the century*). Other nouns described as *daring* include *adventure, rescue, robbery, raid*, and *escape*. *Daring* can also refer to a readiness to shock (*she smoked in the street, which was considered very daring in those days*) and is also used to mean 'provocative' (*the beaded chiffon dress with its daring low back*).

An **audacious** act is one that goes well beyond the normal boundaries in a readiness to take risks (*ever more audacious and vicious assaults by partisans | he hit the post with an audacious drop goal attempt*). *Audacity* can involve deliberately risking shocking or offending people (*his theatrical roles were funny, audacious, subversive*).

bolshie adjective Brit. informal *with your bolshie attitude, you're riding for a fall*: **uncooperative**, awkward, contrary, truculent, perverse, difficult, unreasonable, obstructive, disobliging, stubborn, obstinate, unhelpful, recalcitrant, mutinous, refractory, annoying, tiresome, exasperating, trying; Scottish thrawn; informal bloody-minded, stroppy, cussed, pesky; N. Amer. informal balky; archaic contumacious, froward.
▷ANTONYMS helpful, cooperative.

bolster noun *most of them were sitting on the floor which was strewn with cushions, bolsters, and rugs*: **pillow**, cushion, pad, support, rest.
▸verb *going away for a few days would bolster her morale*: **strengthen**, support, reinforce, make stronger, boost, fortify, give a boost to; prop up, buoy up, shore up, hold up, maintain, buttress, brace, stiffen, uphold; aid, assist, help; supplement, augment, feed, add to, increase; revitalize, invigorate, renew, regenerate.
▷ANTONYMS undermine.

bolt noun 1 *he managed to slip the bolt on the shed door*: **bar**, **lock**, catch, latch, fastener, hasp, pin.
2 *nuts and bolts*: **rivet**, pin, peg, screw.
3 *I heard the click of a crossbow, and a bolt whirred over my head*: **arrow**, quarrel, dart, shaft, missile, projectile; literary reed.
4 *the house was struck by a bolt of lightning*: **flash**, shaft, streak, burst, discharge, flare, fulmination; archaic levin.
5 *Marco made a bolt for the door*: **dash**, dart, run, sprint, rush, bound, leap, jump, spring, gallop.
6 *a bolt of cloth*: **roll**, reel, spool, bundle, bale, parcel, packet, quantity, amount.
□ **a bolt from the blue/a bolt out of the blue** *it was a bolt out of the blue when Alan resigned*: **shock**, surprise, bombshell, jolt, thunderbolt, revelation, source of amazement; informal turn-up for the books, shocker, whammy.
▸verb 1 *he bolted the door behind us*: **lock**, bar, fasten, latch, secure, seal.
▷ANTONYMS unbolt, open.
2 *the lid was bolted down*: **rivet**, pin, clamp, peg, screw, batten, pinion; fasten, fix, secure.
3 *Anna turned and bolted from the room*: **dash**, dart, run, sprint, hurtle, rush, hurry, fly, shoot, flash, spring, leap, bound, start; flee, abscond, escape, take flight, make a break/run for it, take to one's heels, beat a (hasty) retreat, clear out; informal tear, zoom, skedaddle, scram, beat it, leg it, scoot, make oneself scarce; Brit. informal flit, scarper, do a bunk; N. Amer. informal hightail (it), take a powder, cut and run.
4 *he bolted down his breakfast*: **gobble**, gulp, wolf, guzzle, devour, gorge (oneself) on, eat greedily/hungrily; informal tuck into, put/pack away, demolish, polish off, scoff (down), down, stuff one's face with, pig oneself on, murder, shovel down; Brit. informal **shift**, gollop; N. Amer. informal scarf (down/up), snarf (down/up), inhale; rare ingurgitate.
▸adverb
□ **bolt upright** *Joanna sat bolt upright on her chair*: **straight**, rigidly, stiffly, completely upright.
▷ANTONYMS slouching.

bomb noun 1 *as they approached they saw bombs bursting on the runway*: **explosive**, incendiary device, incendiary, device; missile, projectile, trajectile; dated blockbuster, bombshell.
2 (**the bomb**) *for nearly half a century, the world has lived with the bomb*: **nuclear weapons**, nuclear bombs, atom bombs, A-bombs.
3 (**a bomb**) Brit. informal *building a new superstore will take months and cost a bomb*: **a fortune**, a small fortune, a king's ransom, a huge amount, a vast sum, a large sum of money, a lot, millions, billions; informal a packet, a mint, a bundle, a pile, a wad, a pretty penny, an arm and a leg, a tidy sum, a killing; Brit. informal loadsamoney, shedloads; N. Amer. informal big bucks, big money, gazillions; Austral. informal big bickies.
▸verb 1 *their headquarters were bombed in the blitz*: **bombard**, drop bombs on, explode, blast; shell, torpedo, blitz, strafe, pound; attack, assault, raid; blow up, blow to bits, blow sky-high, destroy, wipe out, level, raze (to the ground), demolish, flatten, topple, wreck, devastate, pulverize, obliterate, ravage, smash; archaic cannonade.
2 Brit. informal *she bombed across Texas at a hundred miles an hour*. See **speed**.
3 informal *the film bombed at the box office*. See **fail**.

bombard verb 1 *gun batteries bombarded the islands*: **shell**, torpedo, pound, blitz, strafe, pepper, fire at/on, bomb; assail, attack, assault, raid, batter, blast, pelt; archaic cannonade, fusillade.
2 *we were bombarded with information and statistics*: **inundate**, swamp, flood, deluge, snow under; besiege, beset, belabour; bother, pester, plague, harass, badger, hound; informal hassle.

bombardment noun *the aerial bombardment of London during World War II*: **shelling**, strafing, pounding, pelting, blitz, air raid, strafe, bombing; barrage, strike, attack, assault, onslaught; archaic cannonade, fusillade.

bombast noun *the articles lead the text into exaggeration and bombast*: **bluster**, **pomposity**, ranting, rant, nonsense, empty talk, humbug, wind, blather, blether, claptrap; turgidity, verbosity, verbiage, periphrasis, euphuism, fustian; pretentiousness, affectedness, ostentation, grandiloquence, magniloquence; informal hot air, bunkum, guff, bosh; literary braggadocio, rodomontade.
▷ANTONYMS plain speaking.

bombastic adjective *Howard really was the most bombastic prig*: **pompous**, blustering, ranting, blathering; **verbose**, wordy, turgid, periphrastic, euphuistic, orotund, pleonastic, high-flown, high-sounding, highfalutin, lofty, overwrought, convoluted; pretentious, affected, ostentatious, grandiloquent, magniloquent, fustian.
▷ANTONYMS straightforward.

bona fide adjective *each partner is entitled to an indemnity for all bona fide expenses*: **authentic**, genuine, real, true, actual, sterling, sound, legal, legitimate, lawful, valid, non-counterfeit, non-fake, unadulterated, unalloyed, proper, straight, fair and square; informal honest-to-goodness, legit, pukka, on the level, the real McCoy.
▷ANTONYMS fake, bogus.

bonanza noun *the conference will bring in an £11 million bonanza for the city*: **windfall**, godsend; stroke/run of luck, boon, bonus, blessing, benefit, advantage; pennies from heaven, manna from heaven; informal jackpot; literary benison.

bond noun 1 *the two women forged a close bond*: **friendship**, relationship, fellowship, partnership, association, affiliation, alliance, coalition; attachment, tie, link, connection, union, nexus.
2 (**bonds**) *the prisoner struggled with his bonds*: **chains**, fetters, shackles, manacles, irons; ropes, cords, ties, fastenings, restraints; rare trammels.
3 *I ran away and I've broken my bond*: **promise**, pledge, vow, avowal, oath, word, word of honour, solemn word, guarantee, assurance; agreement, understanding, engagement, commitment, obligation, contract, pact, transaction, bargain, deal, settlement, covenant, compact, treaty, concordat, accord; **bail**, parole; archaic troth.
▸verb *the extensions are bonded to small sections of your hair*: **join**, connect, fasten, fix, affix, attach, secure, bind, stick, glue, gum, paste, cement, fuse, weld, solder.

bondage noun *the serfs were set free from their bondage*: **slavery**, enslavement, servitude, subjugation, subjection, oppression, domination, exploitation, persecution; captivity, imprisonment, incarceration, confinement, detention; bonds, chains, fetters, shackles, restraints, yoke; literary thraldom, thrall; historical serfdom, vassalage; archaic enthralment, duress.
▷ANTONYMS liberty.

bone noun

Word links bone

osteo- relating to bone
osseous consisting of bone
osteitis inflammation of bone
orthopaedics branch of medicine concerned with bones
osteology study of bones
osteotomy surgical incision into bone
osteometry measurement of bones

bonhomie noun *he radiated an aura of benevolence and bonhomie*: **geniality**, congeniality, conviviality, cordiality, affability, amiability, sociability, friendliness, warmth, warm-heartedness, good nature, good humour, joviality, cheerfulness, good cheer, cheeriness, jollity, happiness.
▷ANTONYMS coldness.

bon mot noun French *he exchanged bon mots and badinage with his guests*: **witticism**, quip, pun, pleasantry, jest, joke, sally; informal wisecrack, one-liner; rare apophthegm, paronomasia, equivoque, Atticism.

bonny adjective Scottish & N. English *did you ever see such a bonny baby?* **beautiful**, attractive, handsome, pretty, gorgeous, good-looking, nice-looking, well favoured, fetching, prepossessing, ravishing, stunning; lovely, nice, sweet, cute, appealing, endearing, adorable, lovable, charming, dear, darling, delightful, winsome, winning; blooming, bouncing, healthy, fine; informal divine, drop-dead gorgeous, easy on the eye; Austral./NZ informal beaut; literary beauteous; archaic fair, comely, taking.
▷ANTONYMS unattractive.

bonus noun **1** *the work's fun and coming back to Ireland is a real bonus*: **benefit**, advantage, boon, blessing, godsend, stroke of luck, asset, attraction, added attraction, fringe benefit, additional benefit, extra, added extra; beauty; informal plus, pro, perk; formal perquisite.
▷ANTONYMS disadvantage.
2 *she's on a good salary and she gets a bonus*: **extra payment**, gratuity, tip, handout, gift, present, honorarium, reward, prize, commission, dividend, premium, percentage; incentive, inducement; informal perk, sweetener, cut; formal perquisite; historical bounty; rare lagniappe.
▷ANTONYMS penalty.

bon viveur, bon vivant noun French *he was a bon viveur, savouring his food and especially his wine*: **hedonist**, pleasure seeker, pleasure lover, sensualist, sybarite, voluptuary; epicure, epicurean, gourmet, gourmand, gastronome, connoisseur; informal foodie.
▷ANTONYMS puritan.

bony adjective *his pale, bony face was half hidden by hair*: **gaunt**, **angular**, hollow-cheeked, skinny, thin, thin as a rake, lean, spare, raw-boned, skin-and-bones, skeletal, cadaverous, size-zero; underfed, underweight, half-starved, emaciated, fleshless; rangy, gangly, gangling, spindly, scraggy, scrawny; informal anorexic, anorectic, like a bag of bones; dated spindle-shanked; rare gracile, macilent, starveling.
▷ANTONYMS plump.

booby noun *it wasn't like him to be such a booby*: **idiot**, fool, stupid person, simpleton, moron, cretin, imbecile, ignoramus, oaf, dunce, dolt, dullard, nincompoop, duffer, jackass; bungler, blunderer; informal dope, chump, clot, clod, nitwit, dimwit, wally, airhead, birdbrain, lamebrain, pea-brain, numbskull, thickhead, fathead, blockhead, bonehead, meathead, dunderhead, chucklehead, knucklehead, pinhead, cloth-head, wooden-head, dipstick, dumb-bell, dumbhead, dumbo, dum-dum, noodle, nerd, ninny, ass, donkey; Brit. informal berk, divvy, nit, numpty, goat, mug, pillock, prat, silly billy, wazzock, muppet; Scottish informal balloon, cuddy, galoot, nyaff; N. Amer. informal doofus, goof, goofball, goofus, putz, bozo, lamer, boob, chowderhead, meatball, lummox, dummy, turkey, clunk, ding-a-ling, dip, palooka, poop; Austral./NZ informal galah, drongo, alec, alick, dingbat, nong; vulgar slang arsehole, dick, dildo, fuckwit; Brit. vulgar slang arse.

book noun **1** *he published his first book in 1610*: **volume**, tome, work, printed work, publication, title, opus, treatise; novel, storybook; manual, handbook, guide, companion, reference book; paperback, hardback, softback; historical yellowback.
2 *he scribbled a few notes in his book*: **notepad**, notebook, pad, memo pad, exercise book, binder; ledger, record book, log, logbook, chronicle, journal, diary, daybook; Brit. jotter, pocketbook; N. Amer. scratch pad; French cahier.
3 (**books**) *the council had to balance its books*: **accounts**, records, archives; account book, record book, ledger, log, balance sheet, financial statement.
□ **by the book** *he does all his police work by the book*: **according to the rules**, in accordance with the rules, within the law, abiding by the law, lawfully, legally, legitimately, licitly; honestly, fairly, openly; informal on the level, on the up and up, fair and square.
▶ verb **1** *Steven booked a table at their favourite restaurant*: **reserve**, make a reservation for, arrange in advance, prearrange, arrange for, order; charter, hire; informal bag; dated engage, bespeak.
2 *we booked a number of events in the Wellington Festival*: **arrange**, programme, schedule, timetable, line up, secure, fix up, lay on; N. Amer. slate.
□ **book in** *he booked in at the St Francis Hotel*: **register**, check in, enrol, record/log one's arrival.

Word links book

bibliography list of books
bibliophile, bibliomane book enthusiast
antiquarian relating to rare books

booking noun *he made a provisional booking for Friday afternoon*: **reservation**, appointment, date; advance booking, prior arrangement, prearrangement; dated engagement.

bookish adjective *he was more bookish than his fellow students*: **studious**, scholarly, academic, literary, intellectual, highbrow, erudite, learned, well read, widely read, educated, well educated, well informed, knowledgeable, cultured, accomplished; pedantic, pedagogical, donnish, bluestocking, cerebral, serious, earnest, thoughtful; impractical, ivory-towerish; informal brainy, egghead; dated lettered; archaic clerkly.
▷ANTONYMS lowbrow.

booklet noun *the information pack includes a free booklet*: **pamphlet**, brochure, leaflet, handout, handbill, circular, flyer, notice, tract; N. Amer. folder, mailer; informal bumf; N. Amer. & Austral./NZ informal dodger.

boom noun **1** *she heard the boom of the waves on the rocks below*: **reverberation**, resonance, resounding; thunder, thundering, roaring, echoing, re-echoing, blasting, crashing, drumming, thrumming, pounding; roar, rumble, bellow, bang, blast, blare, loud noise.
2 *retailers are cashing in on an unprecedented boom*: **upturn**, upsurge, upswing, increase, advance, growth spurt, boost; expansion, escalation, augmentation, improvement, progress, development, success.
▷ANTONYMS recession, slump.
▶ verb **1** *thunder boomed in the sky overhead*: **reverberate**, resound, resonate; rumble, thunder, ring out, sound loudly, blare, echo, fill the air; crack, crash, roll, clap, explode, bang, blast.
2 *a voice boomed at her from a small doorway*: **bellow**, roar, thunder, shout, bawl, yell, bark; N. Amer. informal holler; rare vociferate.
▷ANTONYMS whisper.
3 *the property market continued to boom*: **flourish**, burgeon, thrive, prosper, progress, do well, succeed, be successful, improve, pick up, come on; grow rapidly, develop, expand, balloon, increase, swell, intensify, mushroom, snowball, rocket.
▷ANTONYMS decline, slump.

boomerang verb *misleading consumers about quality will eventually boomerang on a car maker*: **backfire**, recoil, reverse, rebound, come back, bounce back, spring back, return, ricochet; have an adverse effect, have unwelcome repercussions, be self-defeating, cause one to be hoist with one's own petard; informal blow up in one's face; archaic redound.

booming adjective **1** *he had a booming voice that contradicted his physical stature*: **resonant**, sonorous, ringing, resounding, reverberating, reverberative, reverberant, reverberatory, carrying, thundering, thunderous, rumbling, roaring; **very loud**, strident, stentorian, strong, powerful, full, full-toned, rich, deep, deep-toned, baritone, bass; rare canorous, stentorious.
2 *shops are reporting booming business*: **flourishing**, burgeoning, thriving, prospering, prosperous, successful, strong, vigorous, buoyant; productive, profitable, fruitful, lucrative; growing, developing, progressing, improving, expanding, mushrooming, snowballing, ballooning; informal going strong.

boon[1] noun *his offer of rent-free accommodation was such a boon*: **blessing**, godsend, bonus, good thing, benefit, help, aid, advantage, gain, asset, privilege, luxury; windfall, bonanza, stroke of luck, piece of good fortune; informal perk, plus, plus point, pro; formal perquisite; literary benison.
▷ANTONYMS curse, disadvantage.

boon[2] adjective *the two girls soon became boon companions*: **bosom**, close, intimate, confidential, inseparable, faithful, special, dear; favourite, best; informal (as) thick as thieves, pally, matey, chummy, buddy-buddy.

boor noun *he is such a boor when he is intoxicated*: **lout**, oaf, ruffian, hooligan, thug, rowdy, bully boy, brawler, rough, churl, lubber, philistine, vulgarian, yahoo, barbarian, Neanderthal, primitive, savage, brute, beast, monster; Irish bosthoon; informal clodhopper, clod, tough, toughie, roughneck, peasant, pig, bruiser, hard man; Brit. informal yobbo, yob, chav, lager lout, oik, lump, ape, gorilla; N. Amer. informal lummox; Austral./NZ informal hoon.

boorish adjective *they reproached him for his boorish behaviour*: **coarse**, uncouth, rude, discourteous, impolite, ungentlemanly, unladylike, ill-bred, ill-mannered, churlish, gruff, uncivilized, uncultured, uncultivated, unsophisticated, unrefined, common, rough, thuggish, loutish; crude, vulgar, crass, tasteless, unsavoury, gross, lumpen, brutish, bearish, barbaric, barbarous, Neanderthal, philistine; informal clodhopping, cloddish, slobbish, plebby; Brit. informal yobbish; Austral./NZ informal ocker.
▷ANTONYMS refined, sophisticated.

boost noun **1** *it's a boost to one's morale to know that people care*: **uplift**, lift, spur, encouragement, help, inspiration, stimulus, pick-me-up, fillip; support, bolster; informal shot in the arm.

b

2 *the economy will benefit from a boost in sales*: **increase**, expansion, upturn, upsurge, upswing, rise, elevation, escalation, augmentation, improvement, development, advance, growth, boom, spurt; informal hike, step up, jack up.
▷ANTONYMS decrease.
3 *she gave him a boost into the tree*: **lift up**, hoist up, push, thrust, shove, heave; informal a leg up, a hoick up.
▸**verb 1** *he phones her regularly to boost her morale*: **improve**, raise, uplift, increase, augment, magnify, swell, amplify, enhance, encourage, heighten, help, promote, foster, nurture, arouse, stimulate, invigorate, revitalize, inspire, perk up; support, bolster, buttress, shore up; informal buck up, jack up, give a shot in the arm to.
2 *they used radio advertising to boost sales*: **increase**, expand, raise, elevate, escalate, augment, add to, improve, strengthen, amplify, enlarge, inflate, push up, promote, advance, develop, further, foster, stimulate; facilitate, help, assist, aid, support, back, shore up; informal jack up, hike, hike up, beef up, crank up, bump up, step up.
▷ANTONYMS decrease, hinder.
3 *he boosted her over the wall and scrambled up behind her*: **lift**, raise, hoist, push, thrust, shove, heave, elevate; help, aid, assist; informal hoick, give someone a leg up; rare upheave.
4 *they employ an agency to boost their products*: **publicize**, promote, advertise, write up, praise; informal plug, give a plug to.

boot[1] **noun 1** *don't come in here in those muddy boots!* **gumboot**, wellington, wader, walking boot, riding boot, field boot, jackboot, thigh boot, half-boot, ankle boot, pixie boot, Chelsea boot, balmoral, desert boot, moon boot, snow boot; galosh, overshoe; football boot; informal welly, bovver boot; Brit. informal beetle-crusher; trademark Doc Martens; historical buskin, napoleon, top boot.
2 informal *he got a boot in the stomach*: **kick**, blow, knock.
□ **give someone the boot** informal See **dismiss**.
▸**verb 1** *his shot was booted off the line by the goalkeeper*: **kick**, punt, bunt, strike with the foot, tap; propel, drive, knock, send; Scottish blooter.
2 *the menu is ready as soon as you boot up your computer*: **start up**, fire up, prepare, ready, make ready.
□ **boot someone out** informal See **dismiss**.

boot[2] **noun**
□ **to boot** *you're not only a chauvinist, but a voyeur to boot*: **as well**, also, too, besides, into the bargain, in addition, additionally, on top (of that), over and above that, what's more, moreover, furthermore; N. Amer. in the bargain; informal and all; archaic withal, forbye.

booth noun 1 *the market place was covered with booths for different traders*: **stall**, stand, kiosk, trading post; counter, table.
2 *she called headquarters from a phone booth*: **cubicle**, kiosk, box, compartment, enclosure, cupboard, carrel, cubbyhole; cabin, hut; alcove, bay, recess.

bootleg adjective *he had a stall selling bootleg cassette tapes*: **illegal**, illicit, unlawful, unauthorized, unsanctioned, unlicensed, unofficial, pirated; bootlegged, contraband, smuggled, black-market, under the counter.

bootless adjective archaic *remonstrating with him seems to have been a bootless task*. See **ineffective** (sense 1).

bootlicker noun informal *there was a crowd of bootlickers telling him what a star he would be*: **sycophant**, obsequious person, toady, fawner, flatterer, creep, crawler, lickspittle, truckler, groveller, doormat, kowtower, spaniel, Uriah Heep; N. Amer. informal suck-up, brown-nose, brown-noser; Brit. vulgar slang arse-licker, arse-kisser, bum-sucker; N. Amer. vulgar slang ass-kisser, suckhole; archaic toad-eater.

booty noun *the robbers met up and split the booty*: **loot**, plunder, pillage, haul, prize, trophy; **spoils**, stolen goods, gains, ill-gotten gains, profits, pickings, takings, winnings; informal swag, boodle, the goods.

booze informal **noun** *they had a buffet lunch with loads of booze*: **alcohol**, alcoholic drink, liquor, intoxicating liquor, drink, strong drink, spirits, intoxicants; informal grog, firewater, gut-rot, rotgut, mother's milk, tipple, the hard stuff, the demon drink, the bottle, Dutch courage, John Barleycorn, hooch, moonshine; Brit. informal wallop, bevvy; N. English & Irish informal sup; N. Amer. informal juice, the sauce.
▸**verb** *I was boozing with my mates every evening*: **drink**, have a drink, drink alcohol, indulge, tipple, imbibe, swill; informal hit the bottle, take to the bottle, crack a bottle, knock a few back; Brit. informal bevvy; N. Amer. informal bend one's elbow; archaic wassail, tope.

boozer noun 1 informal *he is a notorious boozer and womanizer*. See **drinker**.
2 Brit. informal *I'm off down the boozer for a bottle of the usual*. See **bar** (sense 4 of the noun).

bop informal **noun 1** *this is just the sort of music you want when you fancy a bop*: **dance**; informal boogie, jive.
2 *a college bop*: **discotheque**; informal disco, hop.
▸**verb** *they were bopping around the hall to 1970s disco music*: **dance**, jig, leap, jump, skip, bounce; informal boogie, jive, groove, disco, rock, pogo, mosh, stomp, hoof it; N. Amer. informal get down, shake one's booty, cut a/the rug, slam-dance; dated step it.

bordello noun *he possessed pornographic pictures taken in a high-class bordello*. See **brothel**.

border noun 1 *the designs decorating the border of a medieval manuscript*: **edge**, **margin**, perimeter, circumference, periphery; rim, fringe, verge; sides, bounds, limits, extremities; literary marge, bourn, skirt.
2 *I had to present my passport at the US border*: **frontier**, boundary, partition, borderline, dividing line, bounding line, perimeter; marches, bounds.
▸**verb 1** *the fields were bordered by hedges and trees*: **surround**, enclose, encircle, circle, edge, skirt, fringe, hem, bound, line, flank.
2 *the shoulder straps are bordered with gold braid*: **edge**, fringe, hem; **trim**, pipe, bind, band, decorate, finish.
3 *years ago, Windsor Forest* **bordered on** *Broadmoor*: **adjoin**, abut (on), bound on, butt up against, be adjacent to, lie next to, neighbour, be contiguous with, touch, join, connect, meet, reach, extend as far as.
□ **border on** *he looked at her with something that bordered on contempt*: **verge on**, approach, come close to, come near to, be near to, be comparable to, approximate to, be tantamount to, be not dissimilar to, be not unlike, be similar to, resemble, look like; informal be not a million miles away from.

Choose the right word **border, boundary, frontier**

Border generally denotes a national boundary and, as such, a barrier (*the building of a huge dam on the Thai–Laotian border | a border checkpoint*). It is also used figuratively of the division between concepts (*his mistake in crossing the border between passion and brutality*).

A **boundary** marks the division between two areas, but the emphasis is less on the existence of a barrier than on simply defining the area (*there were frequent disputes between the two counties as to the exact position of the boundary*). The word *boundary* is commonly used in a figurative sense (*technologies which cut across traditional boundaries between industrial sectors*), and the dividing line is seen as more fluid than a border (*literacy campaigns push back the boundaries of ignorance*).

A **frontier** is used of national borders, especially borders between hostile powers (*Germany recognized its frontier with France and Belgium*). A *Europe without frontiers* would be one with no barriers to trade or travel. *Frontier* can also denote the point beyond which no one can go or has yet gone (*extending the frontiers of knowledge*) and is frequently used in the same context as words such as *new*, *explore*, *last*, *push*, and *science*.

borderline noun *the item is on the borderline between being old and antique*: **dividing line**, divide, division, demarcation line, line of demarcation, line, cut-off point; threshold, margin, fringe, limit, border, boundary, periphery.
▸**adjective** *the moderators discussed student grades and borderline cases*: **marginal**, indefinite, uncertain, unsure, unsettled, undecided, up in the air, doubtful, open to doubt, problematic, indeterminate, unclassifiable, ambivalent, equivocal; questionable, open to question, disputable, debatable, arguable, controversial, contentious, moot; informal iffy; Brit. informal dodgy.

bore[1] **verb** *you must bore a hole in the ceiling to pass the cable through*: **drill**, pierce, perforate, puncture, punch, cut; tunnel, burrow, mine, dig (out), gouge (out), sink; make, create, put, drive.
▸**noun 1** *a large amount of water had been pumped from the well bore*: **borehole**, hole, well, shaft, pit, passage, tunnel.
2 *the canon has a bore of 890 millimetres*: **calibre**, diameter, gauge.

bore[2] **verb** *the news bored Philip so he didn't watch it*: **be tedious to**, pall on, stultify, stupefy, weary, tire, fatigue, send to sleep, exhaust, wear out, leave cold; bore to tears, bore to death, bore out of one's mind, bore stiff, bore rigid, bore stupid; informal turn off; rare hebetate.
▷ANTONYMS interest, entertain.
▸**noun** *the poetry reading turned out to be a great bore | you can be such a bore*: **tedious thing**, tiresome thing, nuisance, bother, pest, annoyance, trial, vexation, thorn in one's flesh; tiresome person, tedious person; informal drag, pain, pain in the neck, bind, headache, hassle; N. Amer. informal pain in the butt, nudnik; Austral./NZ informal nark; Brit. informal, dated blighter, blister, pill; Brit. vulgar slang pain in the arse.

boredom noun *his eyes were glassy with boredom*: **weariness**, ennui, lack of enthusiasm, lack of interest, lack of concern, apathy, uninterestedness, unconcern, languor, sluggishness, accidie, malaise, world-weariness; frustration, dissatisfaction, restlessness, restiveness; **tedium**, tediousness, dullness, monotony, repetitiveness, lack of variety, lack of variation, flatness, blandness, sameness, uniformity, routine, humdrum, dreariness, lack of excitement; informal deadliness; Brit. informal sameyness.
▷ANTONYMS interest, entertainment.

boring adjective *his letters are really rather boring*: **tedious**, dull, monotonous; repetitious, repetitive; unrelieved, lacking variety, lacking variation, lacking excitement, lacking interest, unvaried, unimaginative, uneventful, characterless, featureless, colourless, lifeless, soulless, passionless, spiritless, unspirited, insipid, uninteresting, unexciting, uninspiring, unstimulating, unoriginal, derivative, jejune, nondescript, sterile, flat, bland, (plain) vanilla, arid, dry, dry as dust, stale, wishy-

washy, grey, anaemic, tired, banal, lame, plodding, ponderous, pedestrian, lacklustre, stodgy, dreary, mechanical, stiff, leaden, wooden; mind-numbing, soul-destroying, wearisome, tiring, tiresome, irksome, trying, frustrating; humdrum, prosaic, mundane, commonplace, workaday, quotidian, unremarkable, routine, run-of-the-mill, normal, usual, ordinary, conventional, suburban; N. Amer. garden variety; informal deadly, bog-standard, nothing to write home about, a dime a dozen, no great shakes, not up to much; Brit. informal samey, common or garden; N. Amer. informal dullsville, ornery.
▷ANTONYMS interesting.

borrow verb **1** *they borrowed a lot of money from the bank*: **take as a loan**, ask for the loan of, receive as a loan, use temporarily, have temporarily; lease, hire; informal cadge, scrounge, sponge, beg, bum, touch someone for; Brit. informal scab; Scottish informal sorn on someone for; N. Amer. informal mooch; Austral./NZ informal bludge.
▷ANTONYMS lend.
2 informal *his workmates had 'borrowed' all his tools*: **take**, take for oneself, help oneself to, use as one's own, abscond with, carry off, appropriate, commandeer, abstract; steal, purloin, shoplift; informal filch, rob, swipe, nab, rip off, lift, 'liberate', snaffle, snitch; Brit. informal nick, pinch, half-inch, whip, knock off, nobble, bone, scrump, bag, blag; N. Amer. informal heist, glom; Austral./NZ informal snavel; W. Indian informal tief; archaic crib, hook.
3 *adventurous chefs borrow foreign techniques where appropriate*: **adopt**, take on, take in, take over, acquire, embrace.

bosom noun **1** *the gown was set low over her bosom*: **bust**, chest; breasts; technical mammary glands, mammae; informal boobs, boobies, tits, titties, knockers, bazookas, melons, jubblies, bubbies, orbs, globes, jugs; Brit. informal bristols, charlies, baps; N. Amer. informal bazooms, casabas, chichis, hooters; Austral. informal norks; archaic dugs, paps, embonpoint.
2 *the family took Gillian into its bosom*: **protection**, heart, core, midst, centre, circle, shelter, safety, refuge.
3 *love was kindled within his bosom*: **heart**, breast, soul, being, inner being, core, spirit; seat of one's emotions, seat of one's affections.
▸ **adjective** *the two girls had become bosom friends*: **close**, boon, intimate, confidential, inseparable, faithful, constant, devoted, loving; special, dear, good, best, fast, firm, favourite, valued, treasured, cherished; informal (as) thick as thieves, pally, matey, chummy.

boss noun *he is the boss of a large trading company*: **head**, head man/woman, top man/woman, chief, principal, director, president, executive, chief executive, chair, chairperson, chairman, chairwoman, manager, manageress, administrator, leader, superintendent, supervisor, foreman, forewoman, overseer, controller, employer, master, owner, proprietor, patron; informal boss man, number one, kingpin, top dog, bigwig, big cheese, Mister Big, skipper; Brit. informal gaffer, governor, guv'nor; N. Amer. informal honcho, head honcho, numero uno, padrone, sachem, big wheel, big kahuna, big white chief, high muckamuck.
▸ **verb** *you have no right to* **boss** *me* **about**: **order about/around**, give orders to, dictate to, impose one's will on, lord it over, bully, push around/about, domineer, dominate, ride roughshod over, trample on, try to control, pressurize, browbeat, use strong-arm tactics on; throw one's weight about/around, call the shots, lay down the law; informal bulldoze, walk all over, railroad, lean on.

bossy adjective *do you treat all your guests in this bossy manner?* **domineering**, dominating, overbearing, imperious, masterful, autocratic, autarchic, officious, high-handed, high and mighty, authoritarian, dictatorial, strict, harsh, severe, iron-handed, controlling, despotic, tyrannical, draconian, oppressive, subjugating, undemocratic; informal pushy, cocky, throwing one's weight about.
▷ANTONYMS submissive.

botch informal verb *examiners botched the marking of 1,000 A-Level papers*: **bungle**, do badly, do clumsily, make a mess of, mismanage, mishandle, mangle, fumble; informal mess up, make a hash of, hash, muff, fluff, foozle, butcher, bodge, make a botch of, foul up, bitch up, screw up, blow, louse up; Brit. informal make a muck of, make a pig's ear of, cock up, make a Horlicks of; N. Amer. informal flub, goof up, bobble; vulgar slang fuck up, bugger up, balls up.
▸ **noun** *I've probably made a botch of things*: **mess**, fiasco, debacle, blunder, failure, wreck; informal **hash**, bodge, flop, foul-up, screw-up; Brit. informal cock-up, pig's ear; N. Amer. informal snafu; vulgar slang fuck-up, balls-up.
▷ANTONYMS success.

both determiner

> *Word links* **both**
>
> **ambi-** related prefix, as in *ambidextrous, ambiguous*
> **amphi-** related prefix, as in *amphibious, amphipathic*

bother verb **1** *she had her own life and no one bothered her*: **disturb**, trouble, worry, inconvenience, put out, impose on, pester, badger, harass, molest, plague, beset, torment, nag, hound, dog, chivvy, harry, annoy, upset, irritate, vex, provoke, nettle, try someone's patience, make one's hackles rise; informal hassle, bug, give someone a hard time, get in someone's hair, get on someone's case, get up someone's nose, rub up the wrong way, drive up the wall; N. English informal mither; N. Amer. informal ride, devil; Austral./NZ informal heavy; rare discommode.
2 *the incident was too small to bother about*: **concern oneself**, trouble oneself, mind, care, worry oneself, burden oneself, occupy oneself, busy oneself; take the time, make the effort, go to trouble, inconvenience oneself; informal give a damn, give a hoot, give a rap, give a hang.
3 *there was something in her voice that bothered him*: **worry**, trouble, concern, perturb, disturb, disquiet, disconcert, unnerve, fret, upset, distress, alarm, make anxious, cause someone anxiety, work up, agitate, gnaw at, weigh down, lie heavy on; informal rattle, faze, discombobulate.
▷ANTONYMS comfort.
▸ **noun 1** *I don't want to put you to any bother*: **trouble**, effort, exertion, strain, inconvenience, fuss, bustle, hustle and bustle, disruption; pains; informal hassle.
2 *the food was such a bother to cook*: **nuisance**, pest, palaver, rigmarole, job, trial, tribulation, bind, bore, drag, inconvenience, difficulty, trouble, problem, irritation, annoyance, vexation; informal hassle, performance, pantomime, song and dance, headache, pain, pain in the neck, pain in the backside; Scottish informal nyaff, skelf; Austral./NZ informal nark; vulgar slang pain in the arse/ass.
3 *he went to sort out a spot of bother in the public bar*: **disorder**, fighting, trouble, ado, disturbance, agitation, commotion, uproar, furore, brouhaha, hubbub, hurly burly; informal hoo-ha, ballyhoo, hoopla, rumpus, aggro, argy-bargy; Brit. informal kerfuffle; NZ informal bobsy-die.

bothersome adjective *I have had a lot of bothersome letters from students*: **annoying**, irritating, irking, vexing, vexatious, maddening, exasperating, tedious, wearisome, tiresome; troublesome, trying, taxing, awkward, difficult, tricky, thorny, knotty; informal aggravating, pesky, cussed, confounded, infernal, pestiferous, plaguy, pestilent, pestilential.

bottle noun **1** *Gareth opened a bottle of whisky*: **container**; flask, carafe, decanter, pitcher, flagon, carboy, demijohn.
2 Brit. informal *no one had the bottle to stand up to McGregor*: **courage**, courageousness, bravery, valour, intrepidity, boldness, nerve, confidence, daring, audacity, pluck, pluckiness, spirit, mettle, spine, backbone, steel, fibre, stout-heartedness; informal guts, gutsiness, spunk, grit, gumption, gameness; Brit. informal ballsiness; N. Amer. informal moxie, cojones, sand; vulgar slang balls; rare temerariousness, venturousness.
▷ANTONYMS cowardice.
▸ **verb**
▫ **bottle something up** *your feelings have been bottled up for too long*: **suppress**, repress, restrain, withhold, keep back, keep in check, keep in, hold in, rein in, bite back, choke back, swallow, fight back, curb, inhibit, smother, stifle, contain, shut in, conceal, hide; informal keep a lid on, cork up, button up.
▷ANTONYMS express, let out.

bottleneck noun *cars were advised to avoid the bottleneck on Talbot Road*: **traffic jam**, jam, congestion, hold-up, gridlock, queue, tailback; constriction, narrowing, restriction, obstruction, block, blockage, stoppage; informal snarl-up.

bottom noun **1** *she reached the bottom of the stairs*: **foot**, lowest part, lowest point, base, extremity; **foundation**, basis, support, substructure, substratum, groundwork, underpinning.
▷ANTONYMS top.
2 *they examined the bottom of the car*: **underside**, lower side, underneath, undersurface, undercarriage, underpart, belly, underbelly.
3 *the boat sank to the bottom of Lake Ontario*: **floor**, bed, ground, depths.
▷ANTONYMS surface.
4 *there's a little cottage at the bottom of his garden*: **the furthest part**, the farthest point, the far end, the extremity.
▷ANTONYMS top.
5 *Mark was right at the bottom of his class*: **lowest level**, lowest position, least important part, least successful part, least honourable part.
▷ANTONYMS top.
6 Brit. *I've got a tattoo on my bottom*: **rear**, rump, rear end, backside, seat; buttocks, cheeks, hindquarters, haunches; French derrière; German Sitzfleisch; technical nates; informal behind, sit-upon, stern, BTM, tochus; Brit. informal bum, botty, prat, jacksie; Scottish informal bahookie; N. Amer. informal butt, fanny, tush, tushie, tail, duff, buns, booty, caboose, heinie, patootie, keister, tuchis, bazoo, bippy; W. Indian informal batty; humorous fundament, posterior; black English rass, rusty dusty; Brit. vulgar slang arse; N. Amer. vulgar slang ass; archaic breech.
7 *Police got to the bottom of a racket in stolen cars*: **origin**, cause, root, source, starting point, core, centre, heart, kernel, base, basis, foundation; reality, essence, nitty-gritty, substance; essentials.
▫ **from top to bottom** *they had to fumigate the house from top to bottom*: **thoroughly**, fully, to the fullest extent, extensively, completely, comprehensively, rigorously, exhaustively, scrupulously, meticulously, conscientiously, minutely, in close detail.
▸ **adjective** *she sat on the bottom step*: **lowest**, last, bottommost, undermost, ground; technical basal.
▷ANTONYMS highest.

bottomless adjective **1** *you both are doomed to the bottomless pits of hell*: **fathomless**, unfathomable, unfathomed, endless, infinite, immeasurable, measureless; deep, profound, yawning.
▷ANTONYMS shallow.
2 *George's appetite was bottomless*: **unlimited**, limitless, boundless, unbounded, inexhaustible, infinite, incalculable, inestimable, immeasurable, indeterminable, endless, never-ending, everlasting; vast, immense, huge, enormous, great, extensive.
▷ANTONYMS limited.

bough noun *the willows dipped their boughs into the river*: **branch**, limb, arm, twig, sprig, offshoot, spur.

boulder noun *she clambered over some boulders at the water's edge*: **rock**, stone, boulderstone; Austral./NZ gibber, gibber stone.

boulevard noun *they strolled through the parks and boulevards*: **avenue**, street, road, main road, high road, drive, row, lane, parade, promenade, way, roadway, thoroughfare; N. Amer. strip, highway.

bounce verb **1** *the ball hit the ground and bounced*: **rebound**, spring back, bob, recoil, ricochet, jounce; N. Amer. carom; rare resile.
2 *William bounced down the stairs grinning*: **bound**, leap, jump, spring, bob, hop, skip, trip, gambol, dance, prance, romp, caper, cavort, frisk, frolic, sport.
□ **bounce back** *they haven't knocked out our spirit and we will bounce back*: **recover**, revive, rally, make a comeback, take a turn for the better, pick up, be on the mend, be on the road to recovery; perk up, cheer up, brighten up, become livelier, take heart, be heartened, liven up, take on a new lease of life; informal buck up.
▸ noun **1** *he caught the ball after a single bounce*: **rebound**, reflection, ricochet.
2 *the pitch's uneven bounce deceived the batsman*: **springiness**, spring; resilience, elasticity, give, rebound, recoil.
3 *she had lost a good deal of her bloom and bounce*: **vitality**, vigour, energy, vivacity, liveliness, life, animation, sparkle, effervescence, exuberance, verve, spiritedness, spirit, enthusiasm, dynamism, fire, ardour, zeal, push, drive; cheerfulness, cheeriness, happiness, joy, buoyancy, optimism, high spirits, light-heartedness, merriment, jollity, ebullience; informal go, get-up-and-go, pep, oomph, pizzazz, zing, zip, fizz, feistiness.

bouncing adjective *they all have beautiful bouncing babies*: **vigorous**, thriving, flourishing, blooming; **healthy**, strong, robust, sturdy, fine, fit, in good health, in good condition, in good shape, in good trim, aerobicized, in fine fettle; informal bright-eyed and bushy-tailed, in the pink, fit as a fiddle.

bouncy adjective **1** *they crossed a bouncy bridge of wooden planks*: **springy**, flexible, resilient; elastic, stretchy, stretchable, spongy, rubbery; rare tensible.
2 *the car gives a rather bouncy ride*: **bumpy**, jolting, jolty, lurching, jerky, jumpy, jarring, bone-shaking, bone-breaking, turbulent, rough, uncomfortable.
3 *she was always bouncy and rarely lost for words*: **lively**, energetic, perky, frisky, jaunty, zestful, dynamic, vital, vigorous, vibrant, animated, spirited, buoyant, bubbly, bubbling, sparkling, effervescent, vivacious, sunny, breezy, bright and breezy, enthusiastic, upbeat; informal peppy, zingy, zippy, zesty, chirpy, full of beans; N. Amer. informal peart.

bound[1] adjective **1** *he raised his bound ankles and kicked the door down*: **tied**, tied up, roped, tethered, chained, fettered, shackled, hobbled, secured; in irons, in chains.
2 *she was so far ahead that she seemed bound to win*: **certain**, sure, very likely, destined, predestined, fated.
3 *you're bound by the Official Secrets Act to keep this to yourselves*: **obligated**, obliged, under obligation, compelled, required, duty-bound, honour-bound, constrained; pledged, committed.
4 *religion and morality are* **bound up with** *one another*: **connected with**, linked with, tied up with, united with, allied to, attached to, dependent on, reliant on.

bound[2] verb *the hares bound and skip in the warm sunshine*: **leap**, jump, spring, bounce, hop, vault, hurdle; skip, bob, dance, prance, romp, caper, cavort, sport, frisk, frolic, gambol, gallop, hurtle; rare curvet, rollick, capriole.
▸ noun *he crossed the room with a single bound*: **leap**, jump, spring, bounce, hop, vault, hurdle; rare curvet, capriole.

bound[3] verb **1** *corporate freedom of action is bounded by law*: **limit**, restrict, confine, cramp, straiten, restrain, circumscribe, demarcate, delimit, define.
2 *the heath is bounded by a hedge of conifers*: **enclose**, surround, encircle, circle, ring, circumscribe, border; hedge in, wall in, fence in, close in, hem in, lock in, cut off.
3 *the garden was bounded on the east by Swan Lane*: **border**, adjoin, abut, meet, touch; be next to, be adjacent to, be contiguous with, be connected to.

boundary noun **1** *the river Jordan marks the boundary between Israel and Jordan*: **border**, frontier, borderline, partition, dividing line, bounding line.
2 *the boundary between art and advertising*: **dividing line**, divide, division, borderline, demarcation line, line of demarcation, cut-off point, threshold.
3 *he walked the boundary of his estate*: **bounds**, confines, limits, outer limits, extremities, margins, edges, fringes; border, periphery, perimeter, circumference, rim, circuit; literary marge, bourn, skirt.
4 (**boundaries**) *the pupils probed the boundaries of accepted behaviour*: **limits**, parameters, bounds, outer limits, confines, extremities, barriers, thresholds; ambit, compass.

> *Choose the right word* **boundary, border, frontier**
>
> See **border**.

boundless adjective *children have boundless curiosity and enthusiasm*: **limitless**, without limit, unlimited, illimitable, unbounded, untold, bottomless, immeasurable, measureless, incalculable, inestimable, abundant, abounding, great, inexhaustible, no end of; **endless**, unending, never-ending, without end, infinite, undying, interminable, unfailing, unfading, unceasing, ceaseless, everlasting.
▷ANTONYMS limited.

bounds plural noun **1** *landlords are keeping rents within reasonable bounds*: **limits**, confines, restrictions, limitations, demarcations, proportions.
2 *they held land within the forest bounds*: **borders**, boundaries, confines, limits, outer limits, extremities, margins, edges, fringes, marches; periphery, perimeter, circumference, compass, precinct, pale.
□ **out of bounds off limits**, restricted, reserved, closed off; **forbidden**, banned, proscribed, vetoed, interdicted, ruled out, not allowed, not permitted, illegal, illicit, unlawful, impermissible, not acceptable, taboo; German verboten; informal no go; rare non licet.

bountiful adjective **1** *he was exceedingly bountiful to people in distress*: **generous**, magnanimous, munificent, giving, open-handed, free-handed, unselfish, ungrudging, unstinting, unsparing, free, liberal, lavish, indulgent; benevolent, beneficent, charitable, philanthropic, altruistic, kind, kindly; rare eleemosynary, benignant.
▷ANTONYMS mean.
2 *the ocean provided a bountiful supply of fresh food*: **abundant**, plentiful, ample, bumper, superabundant, inexhaustible, prolific, profuse, teeming, copious, prodigal, considerable, vast, immense, great, liberal, lavish, generous, princely, handsome, luxuriant, rich; informal tidy, whopping; S. African informal lank; literary plenteous, bounteous, proliferous.
▷ANTONYMS meagre.

bounty noun **1** *the cartel's leader paid a bounty for each policeman killed*: **reward**, prize, award, recompense, remuneration, commission, consideration, premium, dividend, bonus, endowment, gratuity, tip, favour, donation, handout; incentive, inducement; purse, winnings, money; informal perk, sweetener; formal perquisite; rare guerdon, meed, lagniappe.
2 literary *What shall I render to the Lord for all his bounty to me?* **generosity**, magnanimity, munificence, open-handedness, free-handedness, bountifulness, largesse, liberality, lavishness, indulgence; benevolence, beneficence, charity, charitableness, goodwill, big-heartedness, kindness, kindliness, compassion, care; blessings, favours, gifts; literary bounteousness; historical almsgiving.
▷ANTONYMS meanness.

bouquet noun **1** *she wanted orchids for her bridal bouquet*: **bunch of flowers**, posy, nosegay, spray, sprig; wreath, garland, chaplet, corsage, buttonhole; French boutonnière; rare tussie-mussie.
2 *the Chardonnay has a great depth of flavour and bouquet*: **aroma**, nose, smell, fragrance, perfume, scent, odour, redolence, whiff, tang, savour.
3 *bouquets go to Ann for ensuring a well-planned event*: **compliment**, commendation, tribute, accolade, eulogy, paean, plaudit, panegyric; praise, congratulations, applause, homage, acclaim; a pat on the back; rare laudation.

bourgeois adjective **1** *she came from a bourgeois family*: **middle-class**, property-owning, propertied, shopkeeping; **conventional**, traditional, conservative, conformist; ordinary, commonplace, provincial, parochial, suburban, small-town, parish-pump.
▷ANTONYMS proletarian; unconventional.
2 *foreign ideas were denounced as bourgeois decadence*: **capitalistic**, materialistic, money-oriented, commercial; informal, derogatory yuppie.
▷ANTONYMS communist.
▸ noun *Liebermann was a self-professed and proud bourgeois*: **member of the middle class**, property owner.
▷ANTONYMS communist.

bout noun **1** *a short bout of exercise can ease insomnia*: **spell**, period, time, stretch, stint, turn, run, session, round, cycle; fit, burst, flurry, spurt, streak; informal sesh, spot.
2 *his breathlessness sparked off a coughing bout*: **attack**, fit, spasm, paroxysm, convulsion, eruption, outbreak, outburst, burst, spell, dose; rare access, boutade.
3 *the bout ended when a fighter was knocked to the ground*: **contest**, match, round, heat, competition, tournament, event, meeting, meet, fixture, game; encounter, fight, prizefight, struggle, set-to.

bovine adjective **1** *she gazed at me with her large, bovine eyes*: **cow-like**, cattle-like, calf-like, taurine.

2 *his jaw dropped in an expression of bovine amazement*: **stupid**, slow, dim-witted, dull-witted, ignorant, unintelligent, imperceptive, half-baked, vacuous, mindless, witless, obtuse, doltish, blockish, lumpish, wooden; stolid, phlegmatic, placid, somnolent, sluggish, torpid, lifeless, inert, inanimate; informal thick, thickheaded, thick as two short planks, dumb, dense, dim, dopey, slow on the uptake, dead from the neck up, boneheaded, blockheaded, lamebrained, chuckleheaded, dunderheaded, wooden-headed, log-headed, muttonheaded, pig-ignorant, birdbrained, pea-brained; Brit. informal dozy, divvy, daft, not the full shilling; Scottish & N. English informal glaikit; N. Amer. informal chowderhead, dumb-ass; W. Indian informal dotish; rare hebete.
▷ANTONYMS quick-witted.
▸ noun *the 700-pound bovine bolted back to the herd*: **cow**, heifer, bull, bullock, calf, ox; beef; N. Amer. informal boss, bossy; archaic neat.

bow[1] (rhymes with 'now') verb 1 *the officers bowed and doffed their caps*: **incline the body**, incline the head, make an obeisance, make a bow, nod, curtsy, drop a curtsy, bob, salaam, genuflect, bend the knee, kowtow.
2 *the government reluctantly **bowed to** foreign pressure*: **give in**, give way, yield, submit, surrender, succumb, capitulate, assent, defer, kowtow, truckle, adhere, conform; acquiesce in, concur with, comply with, act in accordance with, cooperate with, accept, heed, observe.
▷ANTONYMS defy.
3 *a footman bowed her into the hallway*: **usher**, conduct, show, lead, guide, direct, steer, take, escort, accompany, walk, shepherd, chaperone.
□ **bow out** *the player **bowed out of** international competition*: **withdraw from**, resign from, retire from, step down from, get out of, pull out of, back out of, stop participating in; give up, quit, leave, abandon; informal pack in, chuck, chuck in, jack in; call it a day, throw in the towel/sponge; archaic forsake, demit.
▷ANTONYMS engage in.
▸ noun *Webster offered the Prince a perfunctory bow*: **inclination**, obeisance, nod, curtsy, bob, salaam, salutation; Indian namaskar; Chinese, historical kowtow; archaic reverence.

bow[2] (rhymes with 'now') noun *the bow of the tanker swept by their stern*: **prow**, front, forepart, stem, rostrum, ram, nose, head, bowsprit, cutwater; informal sharp end; rare fore-end, stem-post, beak, beak-head.

bow[3] (rhymes with 'flow') noun 1 *thread the ribbon through the hole and tie it in a bow*: **loop**, knot; lace, ribbon.
2 *he bent the rod into a bow*: **arc**, arch, crescent, curve, bend; half-moon, oxbow.
3 *swifter than an arrow from an archer's bow*: **longbow**, crossbow, recurve.
▸ verb *the mast quivered and bowed as Trent climbed up it*: **bend**, buckle, stoop, curve, arch, arc, crook, flex, curl, deform.

> *Word links* **bow**
>
> **arcuate** (rare) relating to archers' bows
> **bowyer** seller of archers' bows

bowdlerize verb *he crossed out the expletives in Sheridan and bowdlerized 'Macbeth'*: **expurgate**, censor, blue-pencil, cut, edit, redact; make cuts to, delete parts of, make deletions in; purge, purify, sanitize, make presentable, make acceptable, make palatable, water down, emasculate; informal clean up.

bowel noun 1 *he had trouble with his bowels*: **intestine(s)**, small intestine, large intestine, colon; entrails, viscera; informal guts, insides, innards.
2 (**bowels**) *the skipper emerged from the bowels of the ship*: **interior**, inside, core, belly, cavity, pit; depths, recesses; informal innards; rare penetralia.

bower noun 1 *the garden had a hidden, rose-scented bower*: **arbour**, shady place, leafy shelter, alcove, recess, pergola, grotto, sanctuary; summer house, gazebo, conservatory, pavilion, belvedere; archaic kiosk.
2 literary *the prince looked into the lady's bower*: **boudoir**, bedchamber, chamber, bedroom, dressing room, room.

bowl[1] verb 1 *he got a wicket for every thirty balls he bowled*: **pitch**, throw, propel, hurl, toss, lob, loft, fling, launch, let fly, shy, cast, project, send, deliver; spin, roll; informal chuck, sling, bung, heave, buzz, whang; N. Amer. informal peg; Austral. informal hoy; NZ informal bish.
2 *the car bowled along the country roads*: **hurtle**, speed, career, shoot, streak, sweep, hare, fly, wing; drive, motor, move, travel, go, proceed; informal belt, pelt, tear, scoot, tool; Brit. informal bomb, bucket, shift, go like the clappers; N. Amer. informal clip, boogie, hightail, barrel; archaic post, hie.
□ **bowl someone over** 1 *the explosion bowled us over*: **knock down**, knock over, bring down, fell, floor, prostrate; catch off balance. 2 informal *I have been bowled over by everyone's generosity*: **overwhelm**, astound, amaze, astonish, surprise, impress, overawe, dumbfound, stagger, stun, daze, bewilder, nonplus, shock, startle, shake, take aback, leave open-mouthed, leave aghast; take someone's breath away, strike dumb, catch off balance; informal knock for six, knock sideways, throw, floor, flabbergast, faze, blow someone's mind, blow away.

bowl[2] noun 1 *she cracked two eggs into a bowl*: **dish**, basin, pan, pot, crock, crucible, mortar; container, vessel, receptacle, repository; pudding bowl, soup bowl, fruit bowl, punchbowl, mixing bowl, sugar bowl, finger bowl, rose bowl; in ancient Greece crater; historical jorum, mazer, porringer, reservatory.
2 *the town lay half a mile away in a shallow bowl*: **hollow**, valley, dip, depression, indentation, well, trough, crater, cavity, concavity, sinkhole, hole, pit, excavation; dust bowl; Brit. punchbowl.
3 N. Amer. *they are playing a concert at the Hollywood Bowl next month*: **stadium**, arena, amphitheatre, coliseum, colosseum; enclosure, ground; in ancient Rome circus, hippodrome; informal park; rare cirque.

box[1] noun 1 *a box of Havana cigars*: **carton**, pack, packet, package; case, crate, chest, trunk, coffer, casket, hamper, canteen; bin, drum, canister; container, receptacle, repository, holder, vessel; archaic reservatory.
2 *she left her purse in a telephone box*: **booth**, cubicle, kiosk, cabin, hut; enclosure, compartment, carrel, cupboard, cubbyhole, alcove, bay, recess.
▸ verb *Muriel **boxed up** Christopher's clothes*: **package**, pack, parcel, wrap, bundle, bale, crate; stow, store, put away.
□ **box something/someone in** *he got boxed in by members of the press*: **hem in**, fence in, close in, cage in, shut in, coop up, mew up; trap, confine, restrain, constrain, imprison, intern, hold captive; surround, enclose, encircle, circle, ring, encompass; N. Amer. corral; rare compass.

box[2] verb 1 *he began boxing professionally before his 15th birthday*: **fight**, prizefight, spar; exchange blows, engage in fisticuffs, battle, grapple, brawl; informal scrap.
2 *he boxed both my ears and stalked out*: **cuff**, strike, hit, thump, slap, smack, crack, swat, punch, jab, knock, thwack, bang, wallop, batter, pummel, buffet; assault, aim blows at; Scottish & N. English skelp; informal belt, bop, biff, sock, clout, clobber, whack, plug, slug, slam, whop, lam; Brit. informal slosh, dot, stick one on; N. Amer. informal boff, bust, whale; Austral./NZ informal dong, quilt; literary smite, swinge.
▸ noun *he sent him away with a box on the ear*: **cuff**, hit, thump, slap, smack, crack, swat, punch, fist, jab, hook, knock, thwack, bang, wallop; Scottish & N. English skelp; informal belt, bop, biff, sock, clout, whack, plug, slug, whop; Brit. informal slosh, dot; N. Amer. informal boff, bust, whale; Austral./NZ informal dong, quilt.

boxer noun **fighter**, pugilist, ringster, prizefighter, kick-boxer; sparring partner, counterpuncher; informal bruiser, scrapper.

boxing noun *he believes boxing keeps kids on the straight and narrow*: **pugilism**, fighting, sparring, fisticuffs; kick-boxing, Thai boxing, prizefighting, bare-knuckle boxing/fighting; the ring, the prize ring; archaic the noble art/science (of self defence).

boy noun *as a boy he had been fascinated by architecture*: **lad**, schoolboy, child, little one, young one, youngster, youth, young man, young fellow, young adult, young person, teenager, adolescent, juvenile, minor, junior; stripling, fledgling, whippersnapper; Scottish & N. English bairn, wean, laddie; informal kid, kiddie, kiddiewink, shaver, nipper, tot, tiny, young 'un, teen, teeny-bopper; Brit. informal sprog; N. Amer. informal rug rat; Austral./NZ informal ankle-biter; derogatory brat, chit, urchin, guttersnipe.
▷ANTONYMS man.

boycott verb *the main opposition parties boycotted the elections*: **spurn**, snub, cold-shoulder, shun, avoid, abstain from, stay away from, steer clear of, give a wide berth to, refuse to take part in, turn one's back on, have nothing to do with, wash one's hands of; ban, bar, reject, veto, embargo, place an embargo on, prohibit, debar, outlaw, proscribe, interdict, blackball, blacklist; Brit. dated black.
▷ANTONYMS support, approve of.
▸ noun *they called for a boycott on the use of tropical timbers*: **ban**, bar, veto, embargo, moratorium, prohibition, proscription, interdict, injunction, sanction, restriction, barrier; avoidance, shunning, rejection, refusal; informal thumbs down, red light, knock-back.
▷ANTONYMS approval.

boyfriend noun *she carries round a picture of her boyfriend*: **lover**, sweetheart, loved one, love, beloved, darling, dearest, young man, man friend, man, escort, suitor, wooer, admirer, worshipper, follower; **partner**, significant other, live-in lover, cohabitee, common-law husband, fiancé; the love of one's life, the apple of one's eye, the object of one's affections; Italian inamorato; S. African jong; informal fella, baby, date, flame, fancy man, toy boy, sugar daddy; N. Amer. informal squeeze; informal, dated intended; literary swain; dated beau, steady; archaic gallant, paramour, leman.

boyish adjective *his boyish enthusiasm*: **youthful**, young, childlike, adolescent, teenage, teenaged, fresh-faced; immature, juvenile, infantile, childish, babyish, callow, green, puerile; archaic bread-and-butter.
▷ANTONYMS manly.

brace noun 1 *the saw is best used with a brace*: **vice**, clamp, press; clasp, fastener, hasp, coupling.
2 *power drills run at a higher speed than a brace*: **drill**, drilling tool, boring tool, rotary tool.
3 *the aquarium is supported by wooden braces*: **prop**, beam, joist, batten, rod, post, pole, column, strut, stay, support, truss, reinforcement, buttress, shore, stanchion, bracket; Mining sprag.
4 *he has to wear a brace on his right leg*: **support**, caliper, truss, surgical appliance.

b

5 *he killed a brace of partridges*: **pair**, couple, duo, twosome; two; rare duplet, dyad, duad, doubleton.
6 Printing *the first term is within braces*: **bracket**, parenthesis.
▸**verb 1** *the plane's wing is braced by a system of rods*: **support**, shore up, prop up, hold up, buttress, carry, bear, underpin; strengthen, reinforce, fortify; archaic underprop.
2 *he braced his hand on the railing*: **steady**, secure, stabilize, fix, make fast, prop, poise; tense, tighten, stiffen, strain.
3 *you'd better brace yourself for disappointment*: **prepare**, get ready, make ready, gear up, nerve, steel, galvanize, gird, strengthen, fortify, bolster, buttress; informal psych oneself up.

bracelet noun *she wore a heavy gold bracelet*: **bangle**, band, circlet, armlet, wristlet.

bracing adjective *the sea air is very bracing*: **invigorating**, refreshing, stimulating, energizing, exhilarating, enlivening, reviving, restorative, rejuvenating, revitalizing, vitalizing, rousing, fortifying, strengthening, healthy, healthful, health-giving, salubrious, beneficial, tonic, salutary; **fresh**, brisk, crisp, cool, keen; informal pick-me-up; rare inspiriting.
▹ANTONYMS tiring.

Word toolkit

bracing	**stimulating**	**exhilarating**
walk	environment	feeling
cold air	conversation	ride
wind	discussion	performance
climate	work	rush
drink	reading	speed
tonic	material	sport
swim	challenge	adventure
slap	activity	victory

bracket noun **1** *each speaker is fixed on a separate bracket*: **support**, prop, stay, batten, joist, buttress; rest, mounting, holder, shelf, rack, frame.
2 *put the words in brackets*: **parenthesis**, brace; round bracket, square bracket, angle bracket, curly bracket.
3 *I'm now in a higher tax bracket*: **group**, grouping, category, categorization, grade, grading, classification, class, set, section, division, order, batch, cohort, list.
▸**verb** *women were bracketed with minors for the purpose of wage assessment*: **group**, **classify**, class, categorize, grade, list, sort, set, place, assign; couple, pair, twin, yoke, put together, set side by side, regard as the same, regard as identical, liken, compare.

brackish adjective *the fish lay their eggs in brackish water*: **slightly salty**, slightly briny, saline, salt, salted; S. African brak.
▹ANTONYMS fresh.

brag verb *she listened to him brag about his connections*: **boast**, crow, show off, swagger, swank, bluster, gloat, blow one's own trumpet, sing one's own praises, congratulate oneself, pat oneself on the back, preen oneself, give oneself airs; informal talk big, blow hard, lay it on thick, shoot one's mouth off; N. Amer. informal shoot the bull, speak for Buncombe; Austral./NZ informal skite, big-note oneself; literary vaunt, roister, hyperbolize; archaic rodomontade, gasconade.

braggart noun *he was a prodigious braggart and a liar*: **boaster**, brag, bragger, show-off, blusterer, trumpeter, swaggerer, poser, poseur, poseuse, peacock, egotist, self-publicist; informal blowhard, big mouth, big-head, bag of wind, windbag, gasbag, loudmouth, bull-shooter, swank, swanker; N. Amer. informal showboat; Austral./NZ informal skite; Brit. informal, dated swankpot; vulgar slang bullshitter; archaic blower, bouncer, shaker, puff, rodomont; rare braggadocio, gasconader, fanfaronade, attitudinizer.

braid noun **1** *the shoulder straps were bordered with gold braid*: **cord**, cording, braiding, bullion, thread, twine, yarn, tape, binding, rickrack, ribbon; cordon, torsade, galloon, soutache; military slang scrambled egg.
2 *his hair is in braids*: **plait**, pigtail, twist; cornrows, dreadlocks.
▸**verb 1** *she began to braid her long hair*: **plait**, entwine, intertwine, interweave, interlace, interthread, criss-cross, weave, knit, lace, twist, twine, wind.
2 *the sleeves are braided in scarlet and lined with ermine*: **trim**, edge, border, pipe, hem, fringe, frill; decorate, adorn, ornament, embellish, embroider; rare befrill.

brain noun **1** *the disease attacks certain cells in the brain*: **cerebrum**, cerebral matter; technical encephalon.
2 (also **brains**) *success requires brains as well as brawn | she racked her brain for inspiration*: **intelligence**, intellect, intellectual capacity, mental capacity, brainpower, cleverness, wit, wits, powers of reasoning, reasoning, wisdom, sagacity, acumen, discernment, shrewdness, judgement, understanding, common sense, sense; mind, head; informal nous, grey matter, savvy, braininess, upper storey; Brit. informal loaf; N. Amer. informal smarts; S. African informal kop.
3 (**brains**) informal *Janice is the brains of the family*: **clever person**, intellectual, intellect, bluestocking, thinker, highbrow, mind, scholar, sage; genius, Einstein, polymath, prodigy; mastermind; informal egghead, bright spark; Brit. informal brainbox, clever clogs, boffin; N. Amer. informal brainiac, rocket scientist.
▹ANTONYMS dunce, idiot.

Word links **brain**

cerebro- related prefix, as in *cerebro-spinal*
cerebral, encephalic relating to the brain
encephalitis inflammation of the brain
encephalo- related prefix, as in *encephalopathy*

brainless adjective *they behave as if they are totally brainless*: **stupid**, **foolish**, witless, unintelligent, ignorant, mindless, idiotic, imbecilic, imbecile, half-witted, simple-minded, silly, empty-headed, half-baked; informal dumb, brain-dead, moronic, cretinous, thick, as thick as two short planks, thickheaded, dopey, dozy, birdbrained, pea-brained, pinheaded, dippy, lamebrained, dunderheaded, wooden-headed; Brit. informal divvy; Scottish & N. English informal glaikit; N. Amer. informal dumb-ass, chowderheaded; S. African informal dof; W. Indian informal dotish.
▹ANTONYMS bright, intelligent, clever.

brain-teaser noun informal **puzzle**, problem, riddle, conundrum, puzzler, poser; informal brain-twister.

brainwash verb *women of the nineties have been brainwashed into thinking they should go back to work*: **indoctrinate**, condition, re-educate, persuade, propagandize, influence, inculcate, drill; pressurize.

brainy adjective informal *she was brainy, except for maths*: **clever**, intelligent, bright, brilliant, gifted; **intellectual**, erudite, well read, cultured, highbrow, academic, scholarly, cerebral, studious, bookish, bluestocking; informal smart; Brit. informal swotty.
▹ANTONYMS stupid.

brake noun *constrained resources will act as a brake on research*: **curb**, check, restraint, restriction, constraint, rein, control, damper, impediment, limitation.
▸**verb** *she braked as a Metro pulled out in front of her*: **slow down**, slow, decelerate; reduce speed, put on the brakes, hit the brakes; Brit. informal slam on the anchors.
▹ANTONYMS accelerate.

branch noun **1** *the branches of a tree*: **bough**, limb, arm, offshoot.
2 *a branch of the river*: **tributary**, feeder, side stream.
3 *the judicial branch of government*: **division**, subdivision, section, subsection, department, sector, part, side, wing; area, sphere, discipline, field.
4 *the corporation's New York branch*: **office**, bureau, agency; affiliate, subsidiary, offshoot, satellite; chapter, lodge.
▸**verb 1** *when you get to the place where the road branches, bear right*: **fork**, bifurcate, divide, subdivide, split, separate, go in different directions; technical furcate, divaricate.
2 *several narrow paths* ***branched off*** *the main road*: **diverge from**, deviate from, depart from, turn aside from, shoot off from, split off from, go off at a tangent from; fan out from, ray out from, radiate from; technical ramify.
□ **branch out** *the company is branching out into Europe*: **expand**, spread out, open up, extend; diversify, spread/stretch one's wings, broaden one's horizons.

brand noun **1** *a new brand of margarine*: **make**, line, label, marque; **type**, kind, sort, variety; trade name, trademark, proprietary name, logo; Brit. archaic chop.
2 *her particular brand of humour*: **type**, kind, sort, variety, class, category, species, genre, breed, style, stamp, cast, ilk, kidney; N. Amer. informal stripe.
3 *the brand on a sheep*: **identifying mark**, identification, marker, earmark.
4 *the brand of dipsomania*: **stigma**, shame, disgrace; stain, taint, blot, blot on one's escutcheon, blemish, mark, slur; literary smirch.
▸**verb 1** *the letter M was branded on each animal*: **mark**, stamp, burn, sear; identify.
2 *the scene was branded on her brain*: **fix permanently**, engrave, stamp, etch, imprint, print.
3 *newspapers branded him as a traitor*: **stigmatize**, accuse of being, mark out; denounce, discredit, vilify, besmirch; characterize, label, classify, categorize.

brandish verb *an old man approached me, brandishing a stick*: **flourish**, wave, shake, wield, raise, hold aloft; swing, twirl, wag, swish, flap; display, flaunt, show off.

brash adjective **1** *a brash, noisy man*: **self-assertive**, assertive, cocksure, full of oneself, self-confident, arrogant, thrusting, bold, as bold as brass, audacious, brazen, brazen-faced; forward, impudent, insolent, impertinent, rude, cheeky; informal cocky, pushy, brassy.
▹ANTONYMS meek, diffident.
2 *brash colours*: **garish**, gaudy, loud, over-bright, ostentatious, showy, flamboyant, flashy, vulgar, tasteless, tawdry; informal tacky; N. Amer. informal bling-bling.

brassy adjective *brassy music*: **loud**, blaring, noisy, thundering, booming, deafening, ear-splitting; **raucous**, harsh, dissonant, discordant, cacophonous, jangling, grating, jarring, strident, piercing, shrill, tinny.
▷ANTONYMS soft, dulcet.

brat noun informal **badly behaved child**, spoilt child; rascal, wretch, imp, whippersnapper; minx, chit; informal monster, horror; N. Amer. informal hellion; archaic jackanapes.

bravado noun *despite all his bravado, he was actually a very sensitive man*: **boldness**, bold manner, swagger, swaggering, bluster, swashbuckling; machismo; boasting, boastfulness, bragging, bombast; informal showing off; Austral./NZ informal skite; rare braggadocio, rodomontade, fanfaronade, gasconade.
▷ANTONYMS modesty.

brave adjective **1** *they put up a brave fight*: **courageous**, plucky, fearless, valiant, valorous, intrepid, heroic, lionhearted, manful, macho, bold, daring, daredevil, adventurous, audacious, death-or-glory; undaunted, unflinching, unshrinking, unafraid, dauntless, indomitable, doughty, mettlesome, venturesome, stout-hearted, stout, spirited, gallant, stalwart, resolute, determined; N. Amer. rock-ribbed; informal game, gutsy, spunky, ballsy, have-a-go; rare venturous.
▷ANTONYMS cowardly, fearful.
2 literary *his medals made a brave show*. See **splendid** (sense 1).
▸ verb *around 400 fans braved freezing temperatures to see them play*: **endure**, put up with, bear, withstand, weather, suffer, sustain, go through; face, confront, stand up to, meet head on, face up to, brazen out, defy; literary dare.
▷ANTONYMS get cold feet.

bravery noun *he received a medal for bravery*: **courage**, courageousness, pluck, pluckiness, braveness, valour, fearlessness, intrepidity, intrepidness, nerve, daring, audacity, boldness, dauntlessness, doughtiness, stout-heartedness, hardihood, manfulness, heroism, gallantry; backbone, spine, spirit, spiritedness, mettle, determination, fortitude, resolve, resolution; informal guts, grit, spunk, gutsiness, gameness; Brit. informal bottle, ballsiness; N. Amer. informal moxie, cojones, sand; vulgar slang balls.
▷ANTONYMS cowardice, fear.

bravo exclamation *people kept on clapping and shouting 'bravo!'*: **well done**, good for you, congratulations, take a bow, encore.

bravura adjective *a bravura performance*: **virtuoso**, magnificent, outstanding, exceptional, exceptionally good, excellent, superb, brilliant, dazzling, first-class, masterly, expert; informal out of this world, mean, ace, stellar, crack, A1; vulgar slang shit-hot.

brawl noun *a drunken brawl*: **fight**, fist fight, skirmish, scuffle, tussle, fracas, scrimmage, fray, melee, rumpus, altercation, wrangle, clash, free-for-all, scrum, brouhaha, commotion, uproar; fisticuffs, rough and tumble; Irish, N. Amer., & Austral. donnybrook; Law, dated affray; informal scrap, dust-up, set-to, shindy; Brit. informal punch-up, bust-up, ruck, bit of argy-bargy; Scottish informal rammy, swedge, square go; N. Amer. informal rough house, brannigan; Austral./NZ informal stoush; rare broil, bagarre.
▸ verb *he ended up brawling with photographers*: **fight**, skirmish, scuffle, tussle, exchange blows, come to blows, struggle, grapple, wrestle, scrimmage; informal scrap, have a dust-up, have a set-to; Brit. informal have a punch-up; Scottish informal swedge; N. Amer. informal rough-house; Austral./NZ informal stoush, go the knuckle.

brawn noun *commando work requires as much brain as brawn*: **physical strength**, muscle, muscles, muscular strength, muscularity, muscliness, brawniness, burliness, huskiness, robustness, toughness, powerfulness, might, mightiness, lustiness; informal beef, beefiness; literary thew, thewiness.
▷ANTONYMS weakness, puniness.

brawny adjective *a big brawny man with tattooed arms*: **strong**, as strong as an ox, muscular, well muscled, muscly, muscle-bound, well built, powerfully built, powerful, mighty, Herculean, strapping, burly, robust, sturdy, husky, lusty, sinewy, well knit, rugged; bulky, hefty, meaty, solid, solidly built; informal beefy, hunky, hulking; dated stalwart; literary thewy, stark.
▷ANTONYMS scrawny, puny, weak.

bray verb **1** *a donkey brayed*: **neigh**, whinny, hee-haw; rare hinny.
2 *Billy brayed with laughter*: **roar**, bellow, trumpet.

brazen adjective **1** *brazen defiance*: **bold**, **shameless**, as bold as brass, brazen-faced, forward, presumptuous, brash, immodest, unashamed, unabashed, unembarrassed, unblushing; defiant, impudent, insolent, impertinent, cheeky, pert; barefaced, blatant, flagrant, undisguised; informal brassy, pushy; Brit. informal saucy.
▷ANTONYMS timid, shy.
2 literary *brazen objects*: **brass**, made of brass, metallic.
▸ verb
□ **brazen it out** *there was nothing to do but brazen it out*: **put on a bold front**, put a bold face on it, be defiant, be unrepentant, be impenitent, be unashamed, be unabashed, stand one's ground.

breach noun **1** *a clear breach of the Race Relations Act*: **contravention**, violation, breaking, non-observance, infringement, transgression, neglect, dereliction; failure to observe, non-compliance with; Law infraction, delict.
2 *a widening breach between government and Church*: **rift**, gulf, chasm, division, difference, schism, disunion, estrangement, alienation, discord, dissension, disaffection; separation, split, break, break-up, parting, parting of the ways, severance, rupture; quarrel, falling-out; Brit. informal bust-up; rare scission.
3 *a breach in the sea wall*: **break**, rupture, split, crack, fracture, rent, rift; opening, gap, hole, fissure, cleft, aperture.
▸ verb **1** *the river breached its bank*: **break (through)**, burst (through), rupture, force itself through, split; informal bust.
2 *the proposed changes breached trade union rules*: **break**, contravene, violate, fail to comply with, infringe, transgress against; defy, disobey, flout, fly in the face of; Law infract.

breadth noun **1** *a breadth of about 100 metres*: **width**, broadness, wideness, thickness; span, spread; diameter; Nautical beam.
2 *the breadth of his knowledge*: **range**, extent, scope, width, depth, amplitude, extensiveness, comprehensiveness, all-inclusiveness; spread, sweep, reach, compass, magnitude, scale, degree.
▷ANTONYMS narrowness, limitedness.

break verb **1** *the mirror fell to the floor, where it broke into pieces*: **shatter**, smash, smash to smithereens, crack, snap, fracture, fragment, splinter; disintegrate, fall to bits, fall to pieces; split, burst, blow out; tear, rend, sever, rupture, separate, divide; informal bust; rare shiver.
▷ANTONYMS repair, mend.
2 *she had broken her leg in two places*: **fracture**, crack, smash.
3 *the bite had barely broken the skin*: **pierce**, puncture, penetrate, perforate; cut, graze, make a flesh wound in.
4 *the machine has broken and they can't fix it until next week*: **stop working**, cease to work/function, break down, go wrong, give out, develop a fault, malfunction, be damaged, be unusable; **crash**; informal go kaput, go/be on the blink, die, give up the ghost, conk out, go phut, go haywire, have had it; Brit. informal pack up.
5 *the council will prosecute traders who break the law*: **contravene**, violate, fail to comply with, fail to observe, disobey, infringe, breach, commit a breach of, transgress against; defy, flout, fly in the face of, ignore, disregard; Law infract.
▷ANTONYMS keep, abide by.
6 *his concentration was broken by a sound*: **interrupt**, disturb, interfere with.
7 *at mid-morning they broke for coffee*: **stop**, pause, take/have a break, have a rest; recess, suspend proceedings; informal knock off, take/have a breather, take five.
▷ANTONYMS resume.
8 *he landed on a pile of carpets which broke his fall*: **cushion**, lessen/reduce/soften the impact of, take the edge off, diminish, moderate, mitigate.
9 *the film broke box-office records*: **exceed**, surpass, beat, better, cap, top, trump, outdo, outstrip, go beyond, eclipse, put in the shade; informal leave standing.
10 *deeply established habits are very difficult to break*: **give up**, relinquish, drop, get out of; informal kick, shake, pack in, quit.
11 *the strategies used to break the union*: **destroy**, crush, smash, quash, defeat, vanquish, overcome, overpower, overwhelm, cripple, bring someone to their knees; weaken, enfeeble, sap, suppress, subdue, cow, dispirit, impair, undermine, demoralize, incapacitate, extinguish.
12 *her self-control finally broke*: **give way**, collapse, crack, be overcome, give in, cave in, yield, crumple, go to pieces.
13 *four thousand pounds wouldn't break him*: **bankrupt**, make bankrupt, ruin, reduce to penury, reduce to nothing, pauperize.
14 *he tried to break the news gently*: **reveal**, disclose, divulge, let out; announce, tell, impart, make public, make known, release, proclaim.
15 *Krycek managed to break the encryption code*: **decipher**, decode, decrypt, unravel, solve, work out; informal crack, figure out.
16 *the day broke fair and cloudless*: **dawn**, begin, start, come into being, come forth, emerge, appear.
17 *a political scandal broke in mid-1991*: **erupt**, burst out, break out.
18 *overnight, the weather broke*: **change**, undergo a change, alter, shift, metamorphose.
19 *waves broke against the rocks*: **crash**, dash, beat, pound, lash; batter.
20 *her voice broke as she relived the experience*: **falter**, quaver, quiver, tremble, shake.
□ **break away** **1** *Anna attempted to break away, but he held her tight*: **escape**, get away, run away, make a break for it, make a run for it, run for it, make one's getaway, flee, make off; break free, break loose, get out of someone's clutches; informal leg it, cut and run, hook it. **2** *a group of intellectuals broke away from the Party to form the Democratic Alliance*: **leave**, secede from, break with, split with, split off from, separate (oneself) from, detach oneself from, part company with, disaffiliate from, defect from, desert; form a splinter group.
□ **break down** **1** *his van broke down*: **stop working**, cease to work/function, go wrong, seize up, give out, develop a fault; informal conk out, go kaput, go on the blink, die, give up the ghost, go phut, have had it; Brit. informal pack up. **2** *pay negotiations with management broke down*:

b

fail, collapse, come to nothing, founder, fall through, come to grief, be unsuccessful, not succeed, disintegrate; informal fizzle out. **3** *Vicky broke down, sobbing loudly*: **burst into tears**, dissolve into tears; **lose control**, be overcome, collapse, go to pieces, come apart at the seams, crumble, disintegrate; informal crack up, lose it, lose one's cool.
□ **break something down 1** *they had to get the police to break the door down*: **knock down**, kick down, stave in, smash in, pull down, tear down, demolish, destroy; informal bust. **2** *break big tasks down into smaller, more manageable parts*: **divide**, separate; rare fractionate. **3** *graphs show how the information can be broken down*: **analyse**, categorize, classify, sort out, itemize, organize; dissect; examine, investigate; rare anatomize.
□ **break in 1** *thieves broke in and took her cheque book*: **commit burglary**, break and enter; force one's way in, burst in; Brit. archaic crack a crib. **2** *'I don't want to interfere,' Mrs Hendry broke in*: **interrupt**, butt in, cut in, interject, interpose, intervene, chime in; interfere, put one's oar in, have one's say; Brit. informal chip in.
□ **break someone in** *there was no time to break in a new foreign minister*: **train**, prepare, prime, initiate, condition; informal show someone the ropes.
□ **break into 1** *£1,500 was stolen when thieves broke into a house in Perth Street*: **burgle**, rob; force one's way into, burst into. **2** *Phil broke into the discussion*: **interrupt**, butt into, cut in on, intervene in; Brit. put one's pennyworth in; N. Amer. put one's two cents in. **3** *he broke into a song*: **begin suddenly**, burst into, launch into.
□ **break off** *the fuselage had broken off just behind the pilot's seat*: **snap off**, come off, become detached, become separated, become severed.
□ **break something off 1** *I broke off a branch from one of the trees*: **snap off**, pull off, sever, detach, separate; rare dissever. **2** *Britain threatened to break off diplomatic relations*: **end**, bring to an end, terminate, put an end to, call a halt to, stop, cease, finish, dissolve; **suspend**, discontinue; informal pull the plug on; archaic sunder.
□ **break out 1** *he broke out of jail*: **escape from**, make one's escape from, break loose from, burst out of, abscond from, flee from; get free. **2** *fighting broke out between rival army units*: **flare up**, start/begin suddenly, erupt, burst out, blow up, set in.
□ **break up 1** *after about an hour, the meeting broke up*: **come to an end**, end, finish, stop, terminate; adjourn, recess. **2** *the crowd began to break up*: **disperse**, scatter, go/move in different directions, go separate ways, disband, separate, part company. **3** *Danny and I broke up last year*: **split up**, separate, part, stop living together, part company, reach a parting of the ways, become estranged; divorce, get divorced, get a divorce; Brit. informal bust up. **4** informal *the whole cast broke up*: **burst out laughing**, start to laugh, roar with laughter, dissolve into laughter, shake with laughter, laugh uncontrollably, guffaw, be doubled up, split one's sides, hold one's sides; informal fall about, be in stitches, crack up, crease up, be creased up, be rolling in the aisles, laugh like a drain.
□ **break something up 1** *police tried to break up a crowd of about 10,000 people*: **disperse**, scatter, disband, separate. **2** *I'm not going to let you break up my marriage*: **put an end to**, bring to an end, destroy, wreck, ruin.
▸ **noun 1** *the magazine has been published without a break since 1950*: **interruption**, interval, gap, hiatus, lapse of time, lacuna; discontinuation, discontinuance, discontinuity, suspension, disruption, cut-off; stop, stoppage, cessation; Prosody caesura; archaic surcease.
2 *a break in the weather*: **change**, alteration, variation.
3 *let's have a break and get something to eat*: **rest**, respite, interval, breathing space, lull, recess; stop, pause; tea break, coffee break; intermission, interlude, entr'acte; informal breather, let-up, time out, down time; Austral./NZ informal smoko.
4 *a weekend break*: **holiday**, time off, period of leave; N. Amer. vacation; informal vac.
5 *a break in diplomatic relations*: **rift**, gulf, chasm, division, difference, schism, disunion, estrangement, alienation; separation, split, break-up, parting, parting of the ways, severance, rupture; quarrel, falling-out; Brit. informal bust-up; rare scission.
6 *a break in the wall*: **gap**, opening, space, hole, breach, chink, crack, fissure, cleft, rift, chasm; tear, split, slit, rent, rupture.
7 informal *she got her first break in 1951, with Broadway's 'Gigi'*: **opportunity**, stroke of luck, chance, opening, foot in the door.

Choose the right word **break, holiday, vacation**

See **holiday**.

breakable adjective *bubble wrap is used for breakable items*: **fragile**, delicate, easily broken, easily damaged, destructible, frangible, frail, flimsy, insubstantial; brittle, crumbly, friable.
▷ANTONYMS unbreakable, shatterproof.

breakaway adjective *a radical breakaway group*: **separatist**, secessionist, splinter; rebel, renegade, dissenting, schismatic, apostate.

breakdown noun **1** *the breakdown of the negotiations*: **failure**, collapse, disintegration, foundering, falling through; informal fizzling out.
2 *since her breakdown, Lily has lost all her self-confidence*: **nervous breakdown**, (mental) collapse; informal crack-up.
3 *the breakdown of the new computer system*: **malfunction**, failure, seizing up; **crash**; informal conking out.
4 *a breakdown of the figures*: **analysis**, classification, categorization, itemization, dissection; examination, investigation; rare anatomization, fractionation.

breaker noun *breakers crashed against the cliffs*: **wave**, roller, comber, white horse, white cap; Austral./NZ **bombora**; informal **boomer**; N. Amer. informal kahuna; archaic billow.

break-in noun *police are investigating a series of break-ins in the area*: **burglary**, robbery, theft; raid, breaking and entering, housebreaking, forced entry; informal smash-and-grab.

breakneck adjective *the breakneck pace of technological change*: **extremely fast**, high-speed, lightning, whirlwind, rapid, speedy; **dangerously fast**, reckless, dangerous, excessive, precipitate, headlong.
□ **at breakneck speed dangerously fast**, at full speed, at full tilt, at full pelt, flat out, as fast as one's legs can carry one; French ventre à terre; informal hell for leather, at a lick, like the wind, like a bat out of hell, like a bomb, like greased lightning; Brit. informal like the clappers, at a rate of knots, like billy-o.

breakthrough noun *a major breakthrough in the fight against Aids*: **advance**, development, step forward, leap forward, quantum leap, step in the right direction, success, discovery, find, improvement, innovation, revolution; progress, headway, advancement.
▷ANTONYMS setback.

break-up noun **1** *the break-up of the peace negotiations*: **end**, termination, dissolution, splitting up; breakdown, failure, collapse, foundering, disintegration; Brit. informal bust-up.
2 *their break-up was very amicable*: **separation**, split, split-up, parting, parting of the ways, estrangement, rift, rupture, breach; divorce; Brit. informal bust-up.
3 *the break-up of the Soviet Union*: **division**, splitting up, partition, breaking up.
▷ANTONYMS integration.

breakwater noun **sea wall**, barrier, embankment; jetty, mole, groyne, pier.

breast noun **1** *the curve of her breasts*: technical mammary gland, mamma; (**breasts**) **bosom(s)**, bust, chest; informal boobs, knockers, boobies, bazookas, melons, jubblies, bubbies, orbs, globes; Brit. informal bristols, charlies, baps; N. Amer. informal bazooms, casabas, chichis; Austral. informal norks; vulgar slang tits, titties, jugs; N. Amer. vulgar slang hooters; archaic dugs, paps, embonpoint.
2 *wild feelings of frustration were rising up in his breast*: **heart**, soul, bosom, seat of one's emotions/feelings, innermost being, core.

Word links **breast**

mammo- related prefix, as in *mammogram*
mast- related prefix, as in *mastitis*
mastectomy surgical removal of a breast

breath noun **1** *I took a deep breath*: **gulp of air**, inhalation, inspiration; exhalation, expiration; sigh; pant, gasp, wheeze; technical respiration.
2 *I had barely enough breath left to gasp a reply*: **wind**; informal puff.
3 *the night was still, with hardly a breath of wind*: **puff**, waft, slight stirring, sigh, faint breeze; literary zephyr.
4 *not a breath of scandal was ever associated with his name*: **hint**, suggestion, trace, touch, whisper, suspicion, whiff, undertone.
5 archaic *there was no breath left in him*: **life**, life force, animation, vital force.
□ **take someone's breath away astonish**, astound, amaze, surprise greatly, stun, startle, stagger, shock, shatter, take aback, stop someone in their tracks, leave open-mouthed, leave aghast, dumbfound, jolt, shake up; awe, overawe, thrill; informal knock for six, knock sideways, floor, flabbergast, blow someone's mind, blow away, knock someone out, bowl over, strike dumb.

Word links **breath**

spiro- related prefix, as in *spirometer*
respiratory relating to breath

breathe verb **1** *she breathed deeply*: **inhale and exhale**, **respire**, draw breath; puff, pant, blow, gasp, wheeze; technical inspire, expire; literary suspire.
2 *at least I'm still breathing*: **be alive**, be living, live, have life, continue in existence; informal be in the land of the living, be alive and kicking.
3 *the Prime Minister would breathe new life into his party*: **instil**, infuse, inject, impart, imbue with, transfuse.
4 *'We're together at last,' she breathed*: **whisper**, murmur, purr, sigh, say.
5 *the whole room breathed an air of hygienic efficiency*: **give an impression of**, suggest, indicate, be indicative of, have all the hallmarks of.
6 literary *the wind was breathing through the trees*: **blow softly**, whisper, murmur, sigh.

breather noun informal *reaching the top of the hill, he decided to have a breather*: **break**, **rest**, pause, interval, respite, breathing space, lull, recess, time out; stop, halt.

breathless adjective **1** *Will ran back, arriving flushed and breathless*: **out of breath**, panting, puffing, gasping (for breath), huffing and puffing, puffing and blowing, puffed, puffed out, gulping (for breath), wheezing, wheezy, choking, winded; short of breath, short-winded; exhausted, tired out; informal out of puff.
2 *the crowd waited, breathless with anticipation*: **agog**, all agog, eager, expectant, open-mouthed, waiting with bated breath, on the edge of one's seat, on tenterhooks, in suspense, on pins and needles, on edge, excited, impatient.

breathtaking adjective *the view over the mountains is breathtaking*: **spectacular**, magnificent, wonderful, awe-inspiring, awesome, astounding, astonishing, amazing, stunning, stupendous, incredible; thrilling, exciting; informal sensational, out of this world, fabulous, fantastic; literary wondrous.
▷ANTONYMS unimpressive.

breed verb **1** *Asian elephants breed readily in captivity*: **reproduce**, produce offspring, procreate, bear young, multiply, propagate; mate; literary beget offspring.
2 *these horses are bred for racing*: **rear**, raise, nurture.
3 *she was born and bred in the village*: **bring up**, rear, raise, nurture; educate, teach, train.
4 *the political system bred massive discontent*: **cause**, bring about, give rise to, lead to, create, produce, generate, spawn, foster, occasion, make for, result in; arouse, stir up; literary beget.
▸ noun **1** *a medium-sized breed of cow*: **variety**, stock, strain, line, family; type, kind, sort, class.
2 *a new breed of journalist*: **type**, kind, sort, variety, class, genre, genus, order, calibre, brand, generation, vintage; N. Amer. informal stripe.

breeding noun **1** *individuals pair late in the season for breeding the following year*: **reproduction**, reproducing, procreation, multiplying, propagation; mating.
2 *the breeding of rats and mice for experiment*: **rearing**, raising, nurturing.
3 *her aristocratic breeding*: **upbringing**, rearing; birth, parentage, family, pedigree, blood, stock, lineage.
4 *people of rank and breeding*: **(good) manners**, gentility, refinement, cultivation, culture, polish, civility, urbanity; politeness, courtesy, graciousness; informal class.
▷ANTONYMS bad manners, vulgarity.

breeding ground noun *Arkansas is a breeding ground for progressive politics*: **nursery**, cradle, nest, den; seedbed, hotbed, forcing house.

breeze noun **1** *a slight breeze ruffled the leaves of the trees*: **gentle wind**, breath of wind, puff of air, current of air, flurry of air, gust; informal blow; technical light air; literary zephyr; rare cat's paw.
2 informal *travelling through London was a breeze*: **easy task**, easy job, child's play, nothing, five-finger exercise, gift, walkover, sinecure; informal doddle, walk in the park, piece of cake, picnic, money for old rope, money for jam, cinch, sitter, kids' stuff, cushy job/number, doss, cakewalk, pushover; N. Amer. informal duck soup, snap; Austral./NZ informal bludge, snack; S. African informal a piece of old tackie; Brit. vulgar slang a piece of piss; dated snip.
▸ verb informal *Roger breezed into her office*: **saunter**, stroll, sail, cruise, walk casually; glide, drift, float.

breezy adjective **1** *a bright, breezy day*: **windy**, fresh, brisk, airy; blowy, blustery, gusty; rare blusterous, boisterous.
▷ANTONYMS windless, still.
2 *his breezy manner*: **jaunty**, **cheerful**, cheery, brisk, airy, carefree, free and easy, easy, easy-going, casual, relaxed, informal, light-hearted, lively, spirited, buoyant, sparkling, animated, vivacious, frisky, sprightly, sunny, full of the joys of spring; nonchalant, insouciant, without a care in the world; informal upbeat, bright-eyed and bushy-tailed, sparky; literary blithe, blithesome; dated gay.
▷ANTONYMS serious, lifeless.

brevity noun **1** *the report is notable for its clarity and brevity*: **conciseness**, concision, succinctness, economy of language, compendiousness, shortness, briefness, pithiness, pith, incisiveness, crispness, compactness, compression; laconicism, terseness, pointedness, curtness, abruptness; rare brachylogy.
▷ANTONYMS long-windedness, verbosity.
2 *the brevity of human life*: **shortness**, briefness, transience, transitoriness, ephemerality, impermanence.

brew verb **1** *this beer is brewed in Frankfurt*: **ferment**, make.
2 *I'll brew some tea*: **prepare**, infuse, make.
3 *the tea's brewing*: **infuse**, be in preparation; stew; Brit. informal mash.
4 *there's trouble brewing*: **develop**, gather force, loom, be close, be ominously close, be on the way, be on the horizon, be in the offing, be in the wings, be imminent, be threatening, be impending, impend, be just around the corner.
▸ noun **1** *three pints of his home brew*: **beer**, ale.
2 *she took a sip of the hot reviving brew*: **drink**; tea, coffee; formal beverage.
3 *a dangerous brew of political turmoil and violent conflict*: **mixture**, mix, blend, combination, compound, amalgam, concoction, pot-pourri, melange.

bribe verb *he used his considerable wealth to bribe officials*: **buy off**, pay off, suborn, give an inducement to, corrupt; informal grease someone's palm, give someone a backhander, give someone a sweetener, keep someone sweet, get at, fix, square; Brit. informal nobble.
▸ noun *he accepted bribes from lobbyists*: **inducement**, 'incentive'; N. Amer. payola; informal backhander, pay-off, kickback, sweetener, carrot; Brit. informal bung, dropsy; N. Amer. informal plugola, schmear; Austral. informal sling; rare douceur, drop.

bribery noun *they were charged with bribery and corruption*: **corruption**, subornation; N. Amer. payola; informal palm-greasing, graft, hush money.

bric-a-brac noun **ornaments**, knick-knacks, trinkets, bibelots, baubles, gewgaws, trumpery, curios, gimcracks; bits and pieces, bits and bobs, odds and ends, miscellanea, sundries, things, stuff; N. Amer. kickshaws; informal junk; Brit. informal odds and sods; rare knick-knackery.

brick noun *a brick of ice cream*: **block**, cube, slab, bar, cake.

bridal adjective *her white bridal gown*: **nuptial**, wedding, marriage, matrimonial, marital, connubial, conjugal; literary hymeneal, epithalamic.

bride noun **newly-wed**, honeymooner; marriage partner, wife; blushing bride; war bride, GI bride.

bridge noun **1** *a bridge over the river*: **viaduct**, aqueduct, flyover, overpass; way over.
2 *a bridge between rival party groups*: **link**, connection, means of uniting; bond, tie.
▸ verb **1** *a covered walkway bridged the motorway*: **span**, cross, cross over, go over, pass over, extend across, reach across, traverse, arch over.
2 *an attempt to bridge the gap between European and Eastern cultures*: **join**, link, connect, unite; straddle; overcome, reconcile.
▷ANTONYMS divide, separate.

> *Word links* **bridge**
>
> **pontine** relating to bridges
> **gephyrophobia** fear of bridges

bridle noun archaic *put a bridle on her tongue*: **curb**, check, restraint, control.
▸ verb **1** *she bridled at his tone*: **bristle**, be/become indignant, take offence, take umbrage, be affronted, be offended, get angry, draw oneself up, feel one's hackles rise.
2 *he bridled his indignation*: **curb**, restrain, hold back, bite back, control, keep control of, keep in check, check, keep a tight rein on, rein in/back; govern, master, repress, suppress, subdue, stifle; informal keep a/the lid on.

brief adjective **1** *a brief account of what had happened*: **concise**, succinct, short, thumbnail, to the point, pithy, incisive, short and sweet, crisp, abridged, condensed, compressed, abbreviated, compact, compendious, potted; epigrammatic, aphoristic; laconic, sparing, terse, pointed, curt, clipped, monosyllabic.
▷ANTONYMS lengthy, long-winded.
2 *a brief visit | a brief smile*: **short**, flying, fleeting, hasty, hurried, quick, cursory, perfunctory; temporary, short-lived, momentary, passing, transient, transitory, impermanent, fading, ephemeral, evanescent, fugitive; informal quickie; rare fugacious.
▷ANTONYMS long.
3 *a pair of extremely brief black shorts*: **skimpy**, scanty, revealing, short; low-cut.
4 *the boss was rather brief with him*: **brusque**, abrupt, curt, short, blunt, sharp.
▸ noun **1** *Kirov had received only a vague brief about his current project*: **instructions**, directions, directives, briefing; information, guidelines, guidance; remit, mandate; informal gen, rundown, low-down.
2 *a barrister's brief*: **summary of the facts**, case, argument, contention; dossier.
3 informal *it was only his brief's eloquence that saved him from prison*. See **lawyer**.
4 *supply them with a brief of our requirements*: **outline**, summary, synopsis, abstract, résumé, precis, sketch, abridgement, digest.
▸ verb *council employees were* **briefed about** *the decision*: **inform of**, tell about, bring up to date on, update on, notify of, advise of, acquaint with, apprise of, give information about; prepare, prime, instruct, direct, guide; informal give the gen on, give the rundown on, fill in on, gen up on, put in the picture about, clue in on, clue up about, keep up to speed with.

briefing noun **1** *the daily press briefing*: **press conference**, conference, meeting, question and answer session; N. Amer. backgrounder.
2 *this briefing explains the systems, products, and standards*: **information**, orientation, preparation, rundown; instructions, directions, guidelines, guidance.

briefly adverb **1** *Henry paused briefly*: **momentarily**, temporarily, for a few moments, for a few seconds, for a little while; hurriedly, hastily, quickly, fleetingly.
2 *briefly, the plot is as follows*: **in short**, in brief, to put it briefly, to cut a long story short, in a word, to sum up, in sum, to come to the point,

(to put it) in a nutshell, in essence, in outline.

briefs plural noun **underpants**, pants, Y-fronts; knickers, bikini briefs; informal panties; Brit. informal kecks.

b

brigade noun **1** *a brigade of British soldiers*: **unit**, contingent, battalion, regiment, garrison, division, squadron, company, platoon, section, detachment, legion, corps, troop; in ancient Rome cohort.
2 *it was at this point that the forensic brigade arrived*: **squad**, team, group, band, party, body, crew, force, outfit, section; informal bunch.

brigand noun *they were robbed by brigands*. See **bandit**.

bright adjective **1** *she stood blinking in the bright sunlight | the bright surface of the metal*: **shining**, light, brilliant, vivid, blazing, dazzling, beaming, intense, glaring; sparkling, flashing, glittering, scintillating, gleaming, glowing, aglow, twinkling, flickering, glistening, shimmering; illuminated, lit, lighted, ablaze, luminous, luminescent, radiant, incandescent, phosphorescent, fluorescent; shiny, lustrous, glossy, sheeny, polished, varnished; literary irradiant, lucent, effulgent, refulgent, fulgent, lucid, glistering, coruscating, lambent, fulgurant, fulgurating, fulgurous.
▷ANTONYMS dark, dull.
2 *it had been a cold but bright morning*: **sunny**, sunshiny, cloudless, unclouded, clear, fair, fine.
3 *he loved bright colours*: **vivid**, brilliant, intense, striking, strong, eye-catching, glowing, bold, rich, flamboyant; gaudy, lurid, garish.
4 *bright flowers*: **colourful**, bright-coloured, deep-coloured, vivid, brilliant, rich, vibrant; dated gay.
5 *a bright guitar sound*: **clear**, vibrant, pellucid; high-pitched, high.
6 *a bright young graduate*: **clever**, intelligent, sharp, quick-witted, quick, smart, canny, astute, intuitive, acute, alert, keen, perceptive, ingenious, inventive, resourceful, proficient, accomplished, gifted, brilliant; informal brainy.
▷ANTONYMS stupid.
7 *he felt bright and cheerful | a bright smile*: **happy**, genial, cheerful, cheery, jolly, joyful, glad, merry, sunny, light-hearted, blithe, beaming; **vivacious**, animated, lively, spirited, high-spirited, exuberant, ebullient, buoyant, effervescent, bubbly, bouncy, perky, chirpy, chipper, zippy, peppy, fresh, bright-eyed and bushy-tailed, bright and breezy, full of beans; dated gay.
8 *she had a bright future*: **promising**, rosy, full of promise, optimistic, hopeful, favourable, propitious, auspicious, providential, encouraging, lucky, fortunate, good, excellent, golden.
▶ adverb literary *a full moon shining bright*: **brightly**, brilliantly, vividly, intensely.

brighten verb **1** *the morning sunshine brightened the room | the sky was brightening*: **make/become bright**, make/become brighter, light up, lighten, throw/cast/shed light on, illuminate, illumine, irradiate.
2 *with the right choice of shrubs and plants, you can* **brighten up** *the shadiest of corners*: **enhance**, embellish, make more attractive, enrich, freshen; dress up, ginger up, add some colour to, prettify, beautify, grace; informal jazz up.
3 *Sarah* **brightened up** *considerably as she thought of Emily's words*: **cheer up**, buoy up, perk up, wake up, rally; gladden, enliven, animate, invigorate, hearten, rejuvenate, uplift, encourage, stimulate, arouse, raise someone's spirits, give someone a lift; informal buck up, pep up.

brilliance noun **1** *the brilliance of the sunshine*: **brightness**, vividness, intensity; sparkle, flash, flashing, glitter, glittering, glow, blaze, beam, dazzle, luminosity, lustre, radiance, resplendence; rare effulgence, refulgence.
▷ANTONYMS darkness, gloom.
2 *a philosopher of great brilliance*: **genius**, prowess, mastery, skill, talent, ability, artistry, expertise, adeptness, aptitude, skilfulness, virtuosity, flair, finesse, panache, deftness, excellence, power, greatness, distinction; intelligence, cleverness, wisdom, sagacity, intellect, wit.
▷ANTONYMS stupidity.
3 *the brilliance and beauty of Paris*: **splendour**, splendidness, magnificence, grandeur, glamour, pomp, lustre, resplendence, illustriousness, éclat.

brilliant adjective **1** *a brilliant student*: **gifted**, talented, virtuoso, genius, accomplished, ingenious, masterly, inventive, creative; intelligent, bright, clever, smart, astute, acute, brainy, intellectual, profound; skilful, able, expert, adept, elite, superior, crack, choice, first-class, first-rate, excellent; educated, scholarly, learned, erudite, cerebral; precocious.
▷ANTONYMS stupid, untalented.
2 Brit. informal *we had a brilliant time*: **excellent**, marvellous, superb, very good, first-rate, first-class, wonderful, outstanding, exceptional, magnificent, splendid, superlative, matchless, peerless; informal great, terrific, tremendous, smashing, fantastic, sensational, stellar, fabulous, ace, fab, A1, cool, awesome, magic, wicked, tip-top, top-notch, out of sight, out of this world, way-out, capital; Brit. informal brill, bosting; Austral./NZ informal bonzer; Brit. informal, dated spiffing, topping, top-hole, wizard.
▷ANTONYMS bad.
3 *a shaft of brilliant light*: **bright**, shining, blazing, dazzling, light; vivid, intense, ablaze, beaming, gleaming, glaring, luminous, lustrous, luminescent, radiant, incandescent, phosphorescent, scintillating, resplendent; literary irradiant, lucent, effulgent, refulgent, fulgent, lucid, glistering, coruscating, lambent, fulgurant, fulgurating, fulgurous.
▷ANTONYMS dark, gloomy.
4 *a grassy meadow of brilliant green*: **vivid**, intense, bright, blazing, dazzling.
▷ANTONYMS dark, dull.
5 *a brilliant display*: **superb**, magnificent, splendid, impressive, remarkable, exceptional, glorious, illustrious.

brim noun **1** *the rector fingered the brim of his hat*: **peak**, visor, bill, projection, shield, shade.
2 *the cup was filled to its brim with cocoa*: **rim**, lip, brink, edge, margin.
▶ verb **1** *the pan was brimming with water*: **be full**, be filled up, be filled to the top, be full to capacity, be packed with, overflow, run/well over.
2 *the tears brimmed in her eyes*: **fill**, fill up, fill to capacity, overflow.

brimful adjective *the reservoir is brimful*: **brimming**, **full**, filled, filled up, filled/full to the brim, filled to capacity, overfull, running over; replete, loaded, overloaded, stuffed, chock-full, chock-a-block, bursting, teeming, seething, abounding; informal flush, full to the gunwales.
▷ANTONYMS empty.

brindle, brindled adjective *a brindled cat*: **tawny**, brownish, brown; **dappled**, streaked, stippled, mottled, speckled, flecked, marbled, pied, piebald, pinto.

bring verb **1** *he brought over a tray with coffee on it*: **carry**, **fetch**, bear, take; convey, transport; transfer, move, come carrying; lug, haul, shift.
▷ANTONYMS take, accept.
2 *Philip brought his young bride to his mansion*: **conduct**, **escort**, guide, lead, usher, show, show someone the way, lead the way, pilot, accompany; shepherd, herd, drive, convoy; see, help, assist.
▷ANTONYMS follow.
3 *that evening the wind changed, and brought rain*: **cause**, make happen, bring about/on, give rise to, create, produce, result in, wreak, effect, engender, occasion, generate, lead to, precipitate, kindle, trigger (off), spark (off), touch off, stir up, whip up, promote, contribute to; literary enkindle, beget; rare effectuate.
4 *the police contemplated bringing charges of riot*: **put forward**, prefer, propose, present, submit, lay, initiate, introduce, institute, moot.
▷ANTONYMS drop.
5 *this job brings him a regular salary*: **earn**, make, bring in, fetch, yield, net, gross; command, attract, realize, secure, return, produce.
□ **bring something about 1** *the war brought about a large increase in government debt*: **cause**, create, produce, give rise to; achieve, result in, lead to, effect, provoke, call forth, occasion, bring to pass; generate, originate, engender, precipitate, wreak, kindle; rare effectuate.
2 *he brought the ship about*: **turn**, turn round/around, reverse, reverse the direction of, change the direction of.
□ **bring something back 1** *the smell brought back memories of when she had been younger*: **remind one of**, put one in mind of, bring/call to mind, cause one to recall, make one think of, take one back to, awaken (one's) memories of; conjure up, suggest, evoke, summon up, call up.
2 *the conference renewed its policy to bring back capital punishment*: **reintroduce**, re-establish, reinstall, reinstate, relaunch, revive, resuscitate, resurrect, breathe new life into. ▷ANTONYMS abolish.
□ **bring someone down 1** *he was brought down by a clumsy challenge*: **foul**, trip, knock over.
2 *she was in such a good mood that I couldn't bear to bring her down*: **depress**, sadden, make sad/unhappy, upset, cast down, get down, make desolate, deject, dispirit, dishearten, discourage, weigh down, dampen the spirits of, oppress. ▷ANTONYMS cheer up.
□ **bring something down 1** *an attempt to bring down the price of compact discs*: **decrease**, reduce, lower, cut, drop, diminish, cause to fall; informal slash, knock down. ▷ANTONYMS increase.
2 *the unrest brought down the government*: **overthrow**, depose, oust, unseat, overturn, topple, cause to fall, pull down, lay low.
□ **bring something forward** *we intend to bring forward proposals for new Sunday trading legislation*: **propose**, suggest, advance, raise, put forward, table, offer, present, move, submit, prefer, lodge, adduce, come up with; propound, proffer, posit.
▷ANTONYMS withdraw.
□ **bring someone in** *it was nice of him to bring me in on it*: **involve**, include, count in, take in.
▷ANTONYMS exclude.
□ **bring something in 1** *he brought in a private member's bill*: **introduce**, launch, inaugurate, initiate, put in place, institute, usher in; **propose**, suggest, submit, present, move, moot, file, lodge.
2 *the event brings in an estimated one million pounds each year*. See **bring** (sense 5).
□ **bring something off** *they knew he could bring off brilliant business coups*: **achieve**, accomplish, bring about, succeed in, pull off, carry off, carry through, manage, carry out; execute, realize, perform, discharge, complete, finish, consummate, conclude, attain, engineer; rare effectuate.
▷ANTONYMS fail in/at.
□ **bring something on** *his fatal illness was brought on by severe shock*: **cause**, be the cause of, make happen, bring about, give rise to, begin,

create, produce, originate, occasion, effect, engender, spawn, lead to, result in, precipitate, provoke, trigger (off), spark (off), touch off, stir up, whip up, induce, foster; literary enkindle; rare effectuate.

□ **bring something out 1** *they were bringing out a new magazine called 'Teens Today'*: **launch**, establish, begin, start, found, set up, open, get going, get under way, initiate, instigate, institute, inaugurate, market; **publish**, print, issue, produce; informal churn out, kick off.

2 *the shawl brings out the colour of your eyes*: **accentuate**, call attention to, make evident, highlight, emphasize, give prominence to, underline, accent, foreground, throw into relief. ▷ANTONYMS cover up, play down.

□ **bring someone round 1** *she administered artificial respiration and brought him round*: **wake up**, return to consciousness, rouse, arouse, bring to. ▷ANTONYMS knock out.

2 *we would have brought him round when he got to know the situation a bit better*: **persuade**, convince, talk round, win over, sway, influence, coax, entice.

□ **bring oneself to** *he couldn't bring himself to pull the trigger*: **force oneself to**, make oneself, bear to.

□ **bring something to bear** *the very best science must be brought to bear on the important decisions that will need to be taken in the future*: **apply**, exert, administer, implement, use, exercise, employ, utilize, practise, put into practice, execute, prosecute, enact, carry out, put to use, bring into effect/play.

□ **bring someone up** *she was brought up by her maternal grandparents*: **rear**, raise, care for, take care of, look after, nurture, provide for; develop, mother, parent, foster, breed; educate, train, instruct.

□ **bring something up** *later that evening he casually brought the subject up*: **mention**, allude to, touch on, raise, broach, introduce; voice, suggest, propose, submit, advance, moot, put forward, bring forward, pose, present, table, propound, air, ventilate.

brink noun **1** *the brink of the abyss*: **edge**, verge, margin, rim, lip; extremity, border, boundary, fringe; perimeter, circumference, periphery; limit, limits, bound, bounds; literary marge, bourn, skirt.
▷ANTONYMS middle.

2 *border disputes have brought both countries to the brink of war*: **verge**, edge, threshold, point, dawn; starting point, start.

brio noun *Britain's early film makers set about the business of film production with some brio*: **vigour**, vivacity, vivaciousness, gusto, verve, zest, sparkle, dash, elan, panache, exuberance, ebullience, enthusiasm, eagerness, vitality, dynamism, animation, spirit, energy; informal pep, vim, zing, get-up-and-go.
▷ANTONYMS lethargy.

brisk adjective **1** *he set off at a brisk pace*: **quick**, rapid, fast, swift, speedy, fleet-footed; hasty, hurried, urgent; **energetic**, lively, vigorous, sharp; agile, nimble, spry, sprightly, spirited; informal nippy, snappy; rare alacritous.
▷ANTONYMS sluggish, slow.

2 *the public bar was already doing a brisk trade*: **busy**, bustling, lively, active, vibrant, hectic; good.
▷ANTONYMS quiet.

3 *his tone became brisk and businesslike*: **no-nonsense**, decisive, businesslike; **brusque**, abrupt, short, sharp, curt, crisp, blunt, terse, snappy, snappish, gruff; rude, discourteous, uncivil.

4 *there was a brisk breeze*: **bracing**, fresh, crisp, invigorating, refreshing, reviving, stimulating, rousing, enlivening, exhilarating, energizing; restorative, tonic, vitalizing, healthful, health-giving; sharp, biting, keen, chilly, cold; informal nippy.

bristle noun **1** *Curtis smoothed the bristles on his chin*: **hair**, whisker; (**bristles**) stubble, designer stubble, five o'clock shadow; technical seta.

2 *a hedgehog's bristles*: **prickle**, spine, quill, thorn, barb.

▶ verb **1** *Corbett sensed menace and malevolence, and the hair on the back of his neck bristled*: **rise**, stand up, stand on end; literary horripilate.

2 *she swivelled round, bristling at his tone*: **get angry**, become infuriated, be furious, be maddened, bridle, become indignant, be irritated, get/have one's hackles up, feel one's hackles rise, rear up, draw oneself up, flare up, see red; take offence, take umbrage; be defensive.

3 *the roof bristled with antennae*: **abound**, swarm, teem, crawl, overflow, hum, be alive, be packed, be crowded, be thronged, be jammed, be infested, be full, be covered; informal be thick, be crawling, be lousy, be stuffed, be jam-packed, be chock-a-block, be chock-full.

bristly adjective **1** *the dunes were dotted with bristly little bushes*: **prickly**, spiky, spiked, thorny, scratchy, stiff; briary, brambly.

2 *the bristly skin of his cheek*: **stubbly**, hairy, scratchy, fuzzy, unshaven; whiskered, whiskery, bewhiskered, bearded, hirsute; rough, coarse, prickly; technical hispid.
▷ANTONYMS smooth, clean-shaven.

Britain noun **the United Kingdom**, the UK, Great Britain, the British Isles; Brit. informal Blighty; literary Albion.

brittle adjective **1** *glass is a brittle material*: **breakable**, splintery, shatterable, fragile, frail, delicate, frangible; **rigid**, hard, crisp.
▷ANTONYMS flexible; resilient.

2 *she began to speak in a brittle, staccato voice*: **harsh**, hard, sharp, strident, grating, rasping.
▷ANTONYMS soft.

3 *a brittle young woman*: **edgy**, on edge, nervous, unstable, highly strung, anxious, tense, excitable, jumpy, skittish, neurotic, hysterical; sensitive, insecure; Brit. nervy; informal uptight.
▷ANTONYMS relaxed, cool.

broach verb **1** *I thought it over very carefully before broaching the subject to Nigel*: **bring up**, raise, introduce, talk about, mention, touch on, open, embark on, enter on, air, ventilate; put forward, propound, propose, suggest, submit.

2 *Jeffrey broached a barrel of beer*: **pierce**, puncture, tap; **open**, uncork, start, begin; informal crack (open).

broad adjective **1** *they descended the broad flight of steps*: **wide**, large, big.
▷ANTONYMS narrow.

2 *the leaves are six inches long and two inches broad*: **in breadth**, in width, from side to side, wide, across, thick.
▷ANTONYMS long.

3 *a broad expanse of grass prairie*: **extensive**, vast, immense, great, spacious, expansive, sizeable, sweeping, rambling, rolling, ample, spread out, far reaching, boundless, immeasurable.

4 *they offer a broad range of opportunities for young would-be executives*: **comprehensive**, inclusive, extensive, wide, wide-ranging, broad-ranging, encyclopedic, all-embracing; general, universal, catholic, eclectic, unlimited.
▷ANTONYMS limited.

5 *this report gives only a broad outline of our environmental performance*: **general**, non-specific, unspecific, unfocused, rough, approximate, overall, sweeping, basic, loose, indefinite, vague, hazy, fuzzy, woolly; N. Amer. informal ballpark.
▷ANTONYMS detailed; precise.

6 *he dropped a broad hint*: **obvious**, direct, plain, clear, unsubtle, explicit, straightforward, bald, clear-cut, manifest, patent, conspicuous, transparent, prominent, unmistakable, undisguised, unconcealed, overt, undeniable.
▷ANTONYMS subtle.

7 *the broad humour of the campaign has been toned down*: **indecent**, improper, coarse, unrefined, indelicate, ribald, risqué, racy, rude, spicy, suggestive, naughty, indecorous, off colour, earthy, smutty, dirty, filthy, vulgar, gross; informal blue, near the bone, near the knuckle.

8 *a broad Somerset accent*: **noticeable**, strong, thick, heavy, pronounced.
▷ANTONYMS slight.

9 *he was attacked in broad daylight*: **full**, complete, total, clear, bright, plain, undiminished.

▶ noun N. Amer. informal *the broads will go crazy about his looks*. See **woman**.

> *Word links* **broad**
>
> **platy-** related prefix, as in *platypus, platyhelminth*

broadcast verb **1** *the show will be broadcast on TV worldwide*: **transmit**, relay, air, beam, send/put out, put on the air/airwaves, show, televise, telecast; informal screen.

2 *the result of the match was broadcast far and wide*: **report**, announce, publicize, publish, make public, make known, advertise, proclaim, declare; spread, circulate, air, pass round, disseminate, promulgate, blazon, trumpet; informal shout from the rooftops.

3 *the most common mistake is to broadcast too much seed, resulting in a very heavy crop*: **scatter**, sow, disperse, sprinkle, spread, distribute, disseminate, strew, throw, toss, fling; literary bestrew.

▶ noun *he communicated with the people via radio and television broadcasts*: **programme**, show, production, presentation, performance; transmission, telecast; informal screening, prog.

broaden verb **1** *her smile broadened*: **widen**, become/make broader, become/make wider, expand, fill out, stretch (out), draw out, spread out, deepen, thicken.
▷ANTONYMS narrow.

2 *the government attempted to broaden its political base*: **expand**, enlarge, extend, widen, swell; increase, augment, supplement, add to, amplify, fill out; develop, enrich, enhance, intensify, improve, build on, open up.
▷ANTONYMS diminish.

broadly adverb **1** *the pattern of mortality is broadly similar for men and women*: **in general**, on the whole, as a rule, in the main, mainly, predominantly; loosely, roughly, approximately; chiefly, commonly, usually.
▷ANTONYMS exactly.

2 *he was smiling broadly now*: **widely**, openly.

broad-minded adjective *I like to think that I'm broad-minded, but his language was beyond the pale*: **liberal**, tolerant, open-minded, forbearing, indulgent, receptive, progressive, freethinking, permissive, libertarian, unshockable; unprejudiced, unbiased, unbigoted, impartial, undogmatic, catholic, flexible, dispassionate, just, fair.
▷ANTONYMS narrow-minded, intolerant.

b

broadside noun **1** *the gunners fired broadsides*: **salvo**, volley, cannonade, barrage, blast, bombardment, fusillade, hail of bullets.
2 *a broadside against the economic reforms*: **criticism**, censure, denunciation, harangue, rant, polemic, diatribe, tirade, philippic; attack, assault, onslaught, abuse, battering; informal flak, brickbat; Brit. informal slating.

brochure noun *a travel brochure*: **pamphlet**, booklet, prospectus, catalogue, leaflet, handbill, handout, bill, circular, flyer, notice, advertisement; N. Amer. mailer, folder.

broil verb N. Amer. *he broiled a wedge of sea bass*: **grill**, toast, barbecue, cook, fry, bake.

broiling adjective *the sweaty nights and broiling days*: **hot**, scorching, roasting, baking, boiling (hot), blistering, sweltering, parching, searing, blazing, sizzling, burning (hot), sultry, torrid, tropical, like an oven, like a furnace.
▷ANTONYMS cold, cool.

broke adjective Brit. informal *the worst part of being unemployed is having to be always broke*: **penniless**, moneyless, bankrupt, insolvent, poor, poverty-stricken, impoverished, impecunious, penurious, indigent, in penury, needy, destitute, ruined, down and out, without a penny to one's name, without two pennies to rub together; informal stony broke, flat broke, on one's uppers, cleaned out, strapped (for cash), on one's beam-ends, bust, hard up, without a brass farthing, without a bean, without a sou, as poor as a church mouse; Brit. informal skint, without a shot in one's locker; Brit. rhyming slang boracic (lint); N. Amer. informal stone broke, without a red cent.
▷ANTONYMS rich.

broken adjective **1** *a broken bottle*: **smashed**, shattered, burst, fragmented, splintered, shivered, crushed, snapped, rent, torn, ruptured, separated, severed, in bits, in pieces; destroyed, wrecked, demolished, disintegrated; cracked, split, chipped; informal in smithereens/smithers.
▷ANTONYMS whole, unbroken.
2 *a broken arm*: **fractured**, damaged, injured, maimed, crippled, lame.
3 *his video's broken*: **damaged**, faulty, defective, unsound; not working, not functioning, non-functioning, malfunctioning, in disrepair, inoperative, out of order/commission, not in working order, broken-down, out of kilter, down; informal on the blink, on its last legs, kaput, bust, busted, conked out, acting/playing up, gone haywire, gone phut, finished, done for, wonky, dud, duff; Brit. informal knackered; Brit. vulgar slang buggered.
▷ANTONYMS working, fixed.
4 *never apply a depilatory cream to inflamed or broken skin*: **cut**, pierced, punctured, perforated, ruptured.
5 *a broken marriage*: **failed**, ended.
6 *his broken promises*: **flouted**, violated, infringed, disregarded, ignored, contravened; informal infracted.
▷ANTONYMS kept, obeyed.
7 *it was an enormous humiliation and he was left a broken man*: **defeated**, beaten, vanquished, overpowered, overwhelmed, subdued; **demoralized**, dispirited, discouraged, dejected, crushed, humbled, dishonoured, ruined, crippled.
8 *it was a long, noisy night of broken sleep*: **interrupted**, disturbed, fitful, disrupted, disconnected, discontinuous, fragmentary, intermittent, unsettled, sporadic, spasmodic, erratic, troubled, incomplete.
▷ANTONYMS uninterrupted.
9 *he pressed onwards gingerly over the broken ground*: **uneven**, rough, irregular, bumpy; jagged, ragged, craggy, rutted, pitted, rutty.
▷ANTONYMS flat, smooth.
10 *she spoke in broken English*: **halting**, hesitating, disjointed, faltering, stumbling, stammering, stuttering, imperfect.
▷ANTONYMS perfect.

broken-down adjective **1** *a broken-down hotel*: **dilapidated**, ramshackle, rickety, tumbledown, run down, worn out, in disrepair, battered, decayed, crumbling, deteriorated, falling to pieces, gone to rack and ruin; informal the worse for wear.
▷ANTONYMS smart, chic.
2 *a broken-down car*: **defective**, broken, damaged, faulty, unsound; not working, not functioning, malfunctioning, in disrepair, inoperative, out of order/commission, not in working order, non-functioning, down; informal **kaput**, on the blink, on its last legs, bust, busted, conked out, clapped out, acting/playing up, gone haywire, gone phut, finished, done for, dud; Brit. informal knackered, duff.
▷ANTONYMS working, fixed.

broken-hearted adjective *the boy was broken-hearted and inconsolable*. See **heartbroken**.

broker noun *a top City broker*: **dealer**, broker-dealer, agent, negotiator, trafficker; middleman, intermediary, mediator; factor, trustee, liaison, representative, go-between; stockbroker, insurance broker; informal rep; historical scrivener.
▸verb *an agreement brokered by the Commonwealth Secretariat*: **arrange**, organize, orchestrate, work out, thrash out, hammer out, settle, clinch, contract, pull off, bring off/about; negotiate, mediate, arbitrate, act as go-between; informal sort out, swing.

bronze noun *in the relay, Scotland won the bronze*: **bronze medal**, third prize.
▸adjective *the gleam of his bronze skin*: **bronze-coloured**, copper-coloured, copper, reddish-brown, chestnut, metallic brown, rust-coloured, rust, henna, tan; tanned, suntanned, sunburned, bronzed, browned.

bronzed adjective *the firmness of his bronzed skin*: **tanned**, suntanned, sunburned, bronze, browned, brown, tan.
▷ANTONYMS pale.

brooch noun *an emerald and diamond brooch*: **breastpin**, pin, clasp, clip, fastening, badge.

brood noun **1** *it flew under the bridge to feed its brood*: **offspring**, young, progeny, spawn; family, hatch, clutch, nest, litter; rare progeniture.
2 informal *Gillian was the youngest of the brood*: **family**, household, ménage, clan, tribe; children, offspring, youngsters, little ones, progeny, descendants, issue; informal kids, sprogs.
▸verb **1** *the male takes over once the eggs are laid and broods them*: **incubate**, cover, hatch, sit on.
2 *he slumped in his armchair, **brooding on** how life had let him down*: **worry about**, fret about, agonize over, mope over, moon over, languish over, feel despondent about, grieve over, sulk about, eat one's heart out over; **think about**, ponder, contemplate, pore over, meditate on, muse on, mull over, dwell on, ruminate on/over, chew over, puzzle over, weigh up, turn over in one's mind.

brook[1] noun *they dozed beside the gurgling brook*: **stream**, small river, streamlet, rivulet, rill, brooklet, runnel, runlet, freshet, gill; N. English beck; S. English bourn; Austral./NZ billabong; Scottish & N. English burn; N. Amer. & Austral./NZ creek.

brook[2] verb *the authorities would brook no delay*: **tolerate**, allow, stand, bear, abide, stomach, swallow, put up with, go along with, endure, suffer, withstand, cope with; accept, permit, admit of, countenance; Scottish thole; informal stand for, stick, hack.

brothel noun **bordello**, house of ill repute, house of prostitution; Law disorderly house; French maison close; informal whorehouse, cathouse, drum; Brit. informal knocking shop; N. Amer. informal creepjoint; Austral./NZ informal crib; euphemistic massage parlour; archaic bawdy house, house of ill fame, bagnio, stew.

brother noun **1** *she had a younger brother named William*: **male sibling**; informal bro.
2 *they were brothers in crime*: **colleague**, associate, companion, partner, comrade, comrade-in-arms, co-worker, fellow, friend; French confrère; informal pal, chum; Brit. informal mate; archaic compeer.
3 *a brother of the Order*: **monk**, cleric, friar, religious, regular, monastic, contemplative.

> *Word links* **brother**
>
> **fraternal** relating to a brother
> **fratricide** killing of one's brother or sister

brotherhood noun **1** *we hold the same ideals of justice and brotherhood*: **comradeship**, fellowship, brotherliness, fraternalism, kinship; companionship, camaraderie, friendship, amity, rapport; French esprit de corps.
2 *a Masonic brotherhood*: **society**, association, union, alliance, institution, league, guild, coalition, affiliation, consortium, fraternity, order, body, community, club, syndicate, circle, lodge, clan, set, clique, coterie; rare sodality.

brotherly adjective **1** *brotherly rivalry*: **fraternal**, sibling.
2 *he spoke of brotherly love*: **friendly**, affectionate, amicable, kind, kindly, devoted, loving, loyal, cordial, sympathetic, comradely; philanthropic, charitable, altruistic; informal chummy, pally.

brow noun **1** *the doctor wiped his brow with his handkerchief*: **forehead**, temple; Zoology frons.
2 *his eyes were deep set beneath heavy black brows*: **eyebrow**.
3 *the beagles tumbled over the brow of the hill*: **summit**, peak, top, crest, crown, tip, head, pinnacle, apex, vertex, apogee.
▷ANTONYMS bottom.

browbeat verb *the interrogators browbeat a young witness into changing her story*: **bully**, hector, intimidate, force, coerce, compel, badger, dragoon, cow, bludgeon, persecute, domineer, oppress, pressure, pressurize, tyrannize, terrorize, menace, subjugate, use strong-arm tactics on; harass, harry, hound, nag, goad, boss about/around; informal bulldoze, railroad, lean on.

brown adjective **1** *brown eyes | a brown coat*: hazel, chocolate-coloured, coffee-coloured, cocoa-coloured, nut-brown; brunette, mousy; sepia, mahogany, umber, burnt sienna; beige, buff, tan, fawn, biscuit, camel, café au lait, caramel, mushroom; bay, sorrel, dun, brindle, brindled; auburn, tawny, coppery, chestnut, bronze, russet.

2 *his skin was brown from the wind and the sun*: **tanned**, suntanned, sunburned, browned, bronze, bronzed, dark; swarthy, dusky.
3 *brown bread*: **unbleached**, wholemeal.
▶ verb *the grill browns food evenly as it turns on the turntable*: **singe**, sear, seal, crisp (up); **grill**, toast, barbecue, fry, sauté, bake.

browned off adjective informal *it's this bureaucracy that's getting the older staff browned off*: **fed up**, irritated, annoyed, exasperated, irked, put out, peeved, piqued, disgruntled; discontented, discouraged, disheartened, depressed; bored, weary, tired; informal hacked off, cheesed off, brassed off, narked; vulgar slang pissed off.

browse verb **1** *returning to the main street, I browsed among the many little shops I found there*: **look around/round**, have a look, window-shop, peruse.
2 *Stella **browsed through** the newspaper*: **scan**, skim, glance, look, run one's eye over, have a look at, peruse, give something a/the once-over; thumb, leaf, flip, flick, run, dip into; riffle, speed-read.
3 *three cows were browsing at the far end of the meadow*: **graze**, feed, eat, nibble, crop, pasture, ruminate.
▶ noun *this brochure is well worth a browse*: **scan**, read, skim, leaf, flick through, glance, look.

bruise noun *she had a bruise across her forehead*: **contusion**, lesion, mark, injury, black-and-blue mark, skin discoloration, blackening; swelling, lump, bump, welt; black eye; informal shiner; technical ecchymosis, trauma.
▶ verb **1** *the right side of her face was badly bruised*: **contuse**, injure, mark, make black and blue, discolour, blacken, hurt.
2 *the movement jars the contents, until nearly every apple is bruised*: **mark**, discolour, blemish; damage, spoil, impair, mar.
3 *Eric's ego was bruised when the crowd jeered*: **upset**, offend, insult, affront, hurt, wound, pain, injure, crush, displease, peeve, vex, distress, grieve.

bruiser noun informal *a bruiser standing in the doorway of the pub*. See **thug**.

brunette adjective *a brunette woman*: **brown-haired**, dark, dark-haired, darkish.
▷ANTONYMS blonde.

brunt noun *her two teenage sons bore the brunt of her bitter and depressed spirit*: **full force**, force, impact, shock, burden, pressure, strain, stress, impetus, thrust, weight, violence; effect, repercussions, consequences.

brush[1] noun **1** *a dustpan and brush | a fine camel-hair brush*: **broom**, sweeper, besom, whisk, sweeping brush; hairbrush, clothes brush, scrubbing brush, toothbrush, paintbrush.
2 *he gave the seat a brush with the back of his hand*: **clean**, sweep, wipe, dust, mop.
3 *a fox's brush*: **tail**, tailpiece; scut, dock.
4 *Luke had said goodbye with no more than the lightest brush of his lips against her cheek*: **touch**, stroke, skim, graze, glance, rub, shave, pat, nudge, contact; kiss; informal swipe.
5 *a brush with the law*: **encounter**, clash, confrontation, collision, conflict; altercation, skirmish, wrangle, scuffle, tussle, fight, battle, engagement, feud, quarrel, incident, to-do; informal run-in, scrap, set-to, argy-bargy; Brit. informal spot of bother.
▶ verb **1** *he spent most of his day brushing the floors*: **sweep**, clean, buff, scrub.
2 *she brushed her long auburn hair*: **groom**, comb, neaten, tidy, make neat/tidy, smarten, smooth, arrange, fix, adjust, preen, primp, do, titivate; curry.
3 *she felt his lips lightly brush against her cheek*: **touch**, stroke, caress, skim, sweep, graze, shave, glance, contact, flick, scrape; kiss.
4 *she brushed a wisp of hair away from her face*: **push**, move, sweep, clear, clean, remove.
□ **brush something aside** *she brushed aside his repeated warnings*: **disregard**, ignore, dismiss, shrug off, pass over, put aside, sweep aside, wave aside; overlook, pay no attention to, take no notice of, refuse to acknowledge, neglect, think no more of, forget about, have no time for, shut one's eyes to, turn a blind eye to, turn a deaf ear to; reject, spurn, flout; scoff at, laugh off, make light of, trivialize, belittle, minimize; informal play down, pooh-pooh, cock a snook at.
□ **brush someone off** *he scrambled up to help her, but she brushed him off*: **rebuff**, dismiss, spurn, reject, repudiate, refuse, disown, slight, deny, scorn, disdain; ignore, disregard, snub, cut, cut dead, turn one's back on, give someone the cold shoulder, cold-shoulder, look right through, freeze out; jilt, cast aside, discard, throw over, send off, send away, send packing, drop, leave; informal knock back, give the brush-off, give the heave-ho, give someone their marching orders, give someone their walking papers, tell someone to get lost; archaic forsake.
□ **brush up (on)** *I've been brushing up on my Italian*: **revise**, read up, go over, refresh one's memory of, relearn, cram, study, learn; improve, sharpen (up), polish up, better, enhance; hone, refine, fine-tune, perfect; informal rub up, bone up; Brit. informal swot up (on), gen up on.

brush[2] noun *a haven of open spaces and thick brush*: **undergrowth**, underwood, scrub, scrubland, brushwood, bracken, bushes; wood, thicket, copse; N. Amer. underbrush, chaparral; rare boscage.

brush-off noun informal *she gave him a polite brush-off*: **rejection**, refusal, rebuff, dismissal, spurning, repudiation, repulse, turndown, discouragement; snub, slight, cut, cold-shouldering; informal elbow, knock-back; N. Amer. informal kiss-off.
▷ANTONYMS acceptance.

brusque adjective *he was disliked because of his brusque manners*: **curt**, abrupt, blunt, short, sharp, terse, brisk, crisp, clipped, monosyllabic, peremptory, gruff, bluff; caustic, tart, abrasive; outspoken, plain-spoken, not afraid to call a spade a spade, indelicate, tactless, undiplomatic; discourteous, impolite, rude, uncivil, offhand, snappish, snappy, churlish.
▷ANTONYMS polite, verbose.

Choose the right word **brusque, curt, abrupt, terse**

All these words apply to remarks that are noticeably short and unadorned, or to the people who make them. Unlike *concise* and *succinct* (see **concise**), all usually imply criticism, as shown by the other adjectives with which they typically occur: *overbearing, arrogant, impetuous, rude,* and *sharp*.

Brusque remarks are short in an aggressive, dismissive, or off-putting way; the *brusque* person is trying to get a conversation over and move quickly on to something else (*he sounded nicer now he had dropped his brusque, cold manner*).

A **curt** statement or gesture is excessively businesslike and efficient, having had everything but the absolutely necessary minimum removed (*he led the way with a curt 'Follow me!'*). The absence of any extra polite or friendly remarks may make a *curt* comment or person appear rude.

Suddenness and unexpectedness are central to the meaning of **abrupt**, which is from a Latin word meaning 'broken off'. An *abrupt* remark has no polite or softening introduction or conclusion; an *abrupt* manner appears rude through the speed with which it deals with and dismisses people (*his abrupt question was laced with impatience | you were rather abrupt with that nice young man*).

A **terse** statement or expression has had any dispensable words removed—a brevity that is bald at best and verges on the harsh or unfriendly (*Luke's terse reply forbade further talk*).

brutal adjective **1** *a brutal attack on an elderly man*: **savage**, cruel, bloodthirsty, vicious, ferocious, barbaric, barbarous, wicked, murderous, cold-blooded, hard-hearted, harsh; ruthless, callous, heartless, merciless, pitiless, remorseless, sadistic, unfeeling; inhuman, heinous, monstrous, abominable, atrocious, vile, infernal, uncivilized; bestial, brutish, beastly, animal.
▷ANTONYMS gentle, humane.
2 *he replied with brutal honesty*: **unsparing**, unstinting, unadorned, unembellished, unvarnished, bald, naked, stark, blunt, direct, straight, straightforward, frank, outspoken, forthright, plain-spoken; heartless, severe; complete, total, unequivocal, unambiguous.

brutality noun *the murders were carried out with unbelievable brutality*: **savagery**, cruelty, bloodthirstiness, viciousness, ferocity, barbarity, wickedness, murderousness, cold-bloodedness, hard-heartedness, harshness; ruthlessness, callousness, heartlessness, mercilessness, pitilessness, remorselessness, sadism; inhumanity, heinousness, monstrousness, atrocity, vileness; bestiality, brutishness, beastliness.
▷ANTONYMS gentleness, kindness.

brutalize verb **1** *the men were brutalized by life in the trenches*: **desensitize**, dehumanize, harden, toughen, case-harden, inure, make unfeeling, make callous, degrade.
2 *they were brutalized by the police*: **attack**, abuse, assault, beat, thrash, thump, pummel, pound, batter.

brute noun **1** *he was a callous brute*: **savage**, beast, monster, animal, sadist, barbarian, devil, demon, fiend, ogre; thug, lout, boor, oaf, ruffian, yahoo, rowdy, bully boy; informal swine, bastard, pig; Scottish informal radge.
2 *the Alsatian, a vicious-looking brute, strained at the leash*: **animal**, beast, wild animal, wild beast, creature; informal critter.
▶ adjective *by sheer brute strength he almost reached the top of the incline*: **physical**, crude, fleshly, bodily, violent.

bubble noun **1** *he watched the bubbles rise in his glass of mineral water*: **globule**, bead, blister, drop; air cavity, air pocket; (**bubbles**) sparkle, fizz, effervescence, froth, head, lather, suds; informal glob; technical barm.
2 *a great deal of economic activity had been supported by the bubble of housing wealth*: **illusion**, delusion, fantasy, dream, pipe dream, daydream, chimera, vanity, castle in the air; transient phenomenon, short-lived phenomenon; informal pie in the sky.
▶ verb **1** *two glasses that overflowed with bubbling champagne*: **sparkle**, fizz, effervesce, gurgle, foam, froth, spume.
▷ANTONYMS be flat, be still.
2 *the milk was bubbling above the flame*: **boil**, simmer, seethe, gurgle.
3 *she was **bubbling over** with enthusiasm*: **overflow**, brim over, be filled, run over, gush.

bubbly adjective **1** *a bubbly wine*: **sparkling**, fizzy, carbonated, aerated, effervescent, gassy, frothy, foamy, bubbling; sudsy; French (vin) mousseux, pétillant; Italian spumante, frizzante; German Schaum-, Perl-.
▷ANTONYMS still, flat.
2 *she was bubbly and full of life*: **vivacious**, animated, ebullient, lively, full

of life, spirited, high-spirited, scintillating, vibrant, zestful, energetic, dynamic; bubbling, effervescent, sparkling, bouncy, buoyant, carefree, happy-go-lucky; excited, elated, merry, happy, cheerful, cheery, perky, sunny, airy, breezy, bright, bright and breezy, enthusiastic; informal upbeat, peppy, zingy, zippy, chirpy, full of beans; N. Amer. informal peart.
▷ANTONYMS dull, listless.
▶ noun informal *a bottle of bubbly*: **champagne**, sparkling wine; French mousseux; Italian **spumante**; Spanish **cava**; S. African **perlé**; informal champers, fizz, sparkler.

buccaneer noun *a crew of swashbuckling buccaneers*: **pirate**, marauder, raider, sea rover, freebooter, plunderer, cut-throat, privateer, Viking, bandit, robber, desperado; adventurer, swashbuckler; archaic corsair.

buck verb *it takes guts to buck the system*: **resist**, oppose, contradict, defy, fight (against), go against, kick against.
□ **buck up** informal **1** *buck up, for heaven's sake—there's lots of people in the same boat*: **cheer up**, perk up, take heart, rally, pick up, bounce back; become more cheerful, become livelier. **2** *buck up or you'll be late*: **hurry up**, speed up, make haste, hasten; informal get a move on, step on it, shake a leg.
▷ANTONYMS slow down.
□ **buck someone up** informal **cheer up**, brighten up, buoy up, ginger up, perk up, rally, animate, invigorate, hearten, uplift, encourage, stimulate, enliven, make someone happier, raise someone's spirits, give someone a lift; informal pep up; rare inspirit.

bucket noun *a bucket of cold water*: **pail**, scuttle, can, tub, pitcher, vessel.
□ **buckets** informal *everyone wept buckets*: **floods**, gallons, pints, oceans; Brit. informal lashings.
▶ verb Brit. informal **1** *it began to rain again, and soon it was* ***bucketing down***. See **pour** (sense 3).
2 *the car came bucketing out of a side road*. See **speed** (sense 1 of the verb).

buckle noun *his belt buckle*: **clasp**, clip, catch, fastener, fastening, hasp.
▶ verb **1** *he buckled the belt round his waist*: **fasten**, do up, hook, strap, tie, secure, clasp, catch, clip.
▷ANTONYMS unfasten.
2 *Harry's front axle buckled | he had buckled the front axle*: **warp**, become/make warped, bend, bend out of shape, become/make bent, twist, become/make twisted, curve, become/make curved, distort, become/make distorted, contort, become/make contorted, become/make crooked, deform, become/make deformed, malform, become/make malformed, misshape, become/make misshapen, mangle, become/make mangled, develop a kink/wrinkle/fold, bulge, arc, arch, wrinkle; crumple, collapse, cave in, give way.
▷ANTONYMS straighten.
□ **buckle down** *I just buckled down and got on with playing as well as I could*: **get (down) to work**, set to work, get down to business, roll up one's sleeves, put one's hand to the plough; **work hard**, apply oneself, make an effort, strive, be industrious, be diligent, be assiduous, exert oneself, focus; informal get cracking, pull/get one's finger out, get weaving, get off one's backside; Brit. informal get stuck in.

bucolic adjective *the bucolic scene of a farmer ploughing behind a shire horse*: **rustic**, rural, pastoral, country, countryside, agricultural, agrarian, outdoor, idyllic, unspoilt; literary Arcadian, sylvan; rare georgic, agrestic.
▷ANTONYMS urban.

bud noun *then comes spring, and fresh buds*: **sprout**, shoot, flowerlet, floret; technical plumule; rare burgeon.
▶ verb *trees began to bud*: **sprout**, shoot, form/develop buds, send out shoots, germinate, burgeon, swell, vegetate, mature; technical pullulate.
▷ANTONYMS wither.

budding adjective *a budding artist*: **promising**, up-and-coming, rising, coming, in the making, aspiring, future, prospective, with potential; potential, beginning, fledgling, incipient, embryonic, nascent; developing, growing, burgeoning; informal would-be, wannabe.
▷ANTONYMS veteran, experienced.

budge verb **1** *they tried to lift the cage, but it wouldn't budge*: **move**, shift, change position, stir, give way, go.
2 *I couldn't budge the door*: **move**, dislodge, shift, change the position of, remove, relocate, reposition, get/set going.
3 *they might be prepared to budge on the issue*: **change one's mind**, give way, give in, yield, acquiesce, compromise, adapt, retract, do a U-turn, eat one's words; Brit. do an about-turn.
4 *our customers won't be budged on price alone*: **influence**, sway, convince, persuade, prevail on, coax, induce, entice, tempt, lure, cajole, bring round, coerce, alter, change, shift, bend.
□ **budge up/over** informal **move up/over**, shift up/over, make room, make space.

budget noun **1** *draw up your own personal budget for a typical week*: **financial plan**, financial estimate, financial blueprint, prediction of revenue and expenditure, forecast; **accounts**, statement, spreadsheet.
2 *an announcement of cuts in the defence budget*: **allowance**, allocation, allotment, quota, share, ration, helping, lot, slice; grant, award, funds, means, resources, wherewithal, capital.
▶ verb **1** *you will have to budget at least £7,000 for the most basic system*: **allocate**, allot, assign, allow, earmark, devote, designate, appropriate, set aside; award, grant.
2 *the repayments will be the same for each month—this will help you budget your finances*: **schedule**, plan, cost, cost out, estimate; allocate, ration, apportion.
▶ adjective *a budget hotel*: **cheap**, inexpensive, economy, economic, economical, low-cost, low-price, low-budget, reasonable, reasonably priced, cut-price, cut-rate, discount, discounted, bargain, bargain-basement.
▷ANTONYMS expensive.

buff[1] adjective *a plain buff envelope*: **beige**, straw-coloured, yellowish, yellowish-brown, brownish-yellow, light brown, pale brown, tan, fawn, sand, sandy, oatmeal, wheaten, biscuit, coffee, coffee-coloured, camel, caramel.
▶ verb *Victor buffed the glass until it gleamed*: **polish**, burnish, rub up, rub, smooth, shine, wipe, clean.
▶ noun
□ **in the buff** informal See **naked**.

buff[2] noun informal *an opera buff*: **enthusiast**, fan, fanatic, devotee, addict, lover, admirer; **expert**, connoisseur, aficionado, authority, pundit, cognoscente, one of the cognoscenti, savant; informal freak, nut, fiend, maniac, ham; N. Amer. informal maven, geek, nerd; S. African informal fundi.

buffer noun *their agent became a buffer against the business world*: **cushion**, bulwark; shield, screen, barrier, guard, safeguard, hedge, shock absorber, armour; **intermediary**, middleman, go-between.
▶ verb *the aromatherapy massage was helping to buffer some of the strain*: **cushion**, absorb, soften, lessen, diminish, moderate, mitigate, allay, deaden, muffle, stifle, shield.
▷ANTONYMS intensify.

buffet[1] (rhymes with 'book day') noun **1** *a sumptuous buffet was spread out at the restaurant*: **cold table**, cold meal, self-service, smorgasbord.
2 *a station buffet*: **cafe**, cafeteria, snack bar, canteen, salad bar, refreshment stall/counter, restaurant.
3 *an old-fashioned built-in buffet in the dining room*: **sideboard**, cabinet, china cupboard, counter.

buffet[2] (rhymes with 'tuffet') verb **1** *the car was buffeted by the wind*: **batter**, pound, beat/knock/dash against, push against, lash, strike, hit, bang.
2 *he has been buffeted by bad publicity*: **afflict**, trouble, harm, distress, burden, bother, beset, harass, worry, oppress, strain, stress, tax, torment, blight, bedevil, harrow, cause trouble to, cause suffering to.
▶ noun *all the blows and buffets of this world*: **shock**, jolt, jar, upset, setback, crisis, catastrophe, blow; **misfortune**, trouble, problem, difficulty, hardship, adversity, distress, disaster, misadventure; affliction, sorrow, misery, tribulation, woe, pain, tragedy, calamity, vicissitude; trial, cross, burden.

buffoon noun **1** archaic *Feste the buffoon*. See **fool** (sense 3 of the noun).
2 *he regarded the chaplain as a buffoon*. See **fool** (sense 1 of the noun).

bug noun **1** *bugs were crawling everywhere*: **insect**, flea, mite, midge; informal creepy-crawly, beastie; Brit. informal minibeast.
2 informal *he went down with a stomach bug*: **illness**, ailment, infection, disease, disorder, sickness, affliction, malady, complaint, upset, condition, infirmity, indisposition, malaise; **bacterium**, germ, virus, bacillus, micro-organism, microbe; Brit. informal lurgy.
3 informal *he caught the journalism bug at an early age*: **obsession**, enthusiasm, craze, fad, mania, rage, passion, fixation; hobby, interest, pastime; informal thing.
4 *the bug they planted on O'Brien's phone malfunctioned*: **listening device**, hidden microphone, receiver, transmitter, wire, wiretap, phone tap, tap; informal bugging device.
5 *the program we used developed a bug*: **fault**, error, defect, flaw, imperfection, failing, breakdown; virus; informal glitch, gremlin, snarl-up.
▶ verb **1** *she fears that her conversations were bugged*: **record**, tap, listen in on, eavesdrop on, spy on, overhear; **wiretap**, tap, monitor, phone-tap; informal snoop on.
2 informal *if there's one thing that really bugs me, it's trendy, middle-class liberals*. See **annoy**.

bugbear noun *paperwork is our bugbear*: **pet hate**, hate, bane, irritant, irritation, dislike, anathema, aversion, vexation, thorn in one's flesh/side, bane of one's life; torment, nightmare, horror, dread, curse, bugaboo, bogey; French bête noire; informal peeve, pain, pain in the neck, hang-up.

build verb **1** *a small supermarket had been built*: **construct**, erect, put up, assemble, set up, raise.
▷ANTONYMS demolish.
2 *the kids were building a snowman*: **make**, construct, fabricate, form, manufacture, create, fashion, model, mould, shape, forge; informal knock together.
3 *they are building a business strategy for the next decade*: **establish**, found, set up, originate, institute, start, begin, inaugurate, initiate, put in place, constitute, secure.

□ **build something in/into** *environmental priorities must be built into all economic decision-making*: **incorporate in/into**, include in, embody in, absorb into, subsume into, assimilate into.
□ **build on** *a case study will be undertaken to build on existing research*: **expand on**, enlarge on, develop, elaborate, flesh out, add flesh to, add detail to, embellish, enhance, amplify; refine, improve, polish, perfect.
□ **build up** *the traffic is steadily building up*: **increase**, grow, mount up, intensify, escalate; strengthen, get stronger.
□ **build something up 1** *he built up a huge export business*: **establish**, set up, form, found, institute, start, begin, bring into being, create, inaugurate, organize; **develop**, expand, enlarge. **2** *he built up his stamina by playing football*: **boost**, strengthen, increase, improve, invigorate, augment, raise, intensify, enhance, escalate, multiply, swell; informal beef up. **3** *over the years I have built up a collection of around 1,700 prints*: **accumulate**, accrue, amass, collect, gather, stockpile, heap up, rack up, run up, scrape together, hoard, lay in/up, garner; Brit. tot up.
▸ **noun** *police are looking for a man of slim build*: **physique**, frame, body, figure, form, structure, shape, make-up, formation, stature; proportions; informal chassis, vital statistics.

builder noun **1** *Thomas Telford was a canal builder and road maker*: **designer**, planner, maker, constructor, deviser, contriver, establisher, creator, fabricator, architect, -wright.
2 *by law, builders must finish the job in a proper and workmanlike fashion*: **construction worker**, labourer, ganger, craftsman, bricklayer; housebuilder; Brit. dated navvy.

building noun **1** *the church is a plain red brick building*: **structure**, construction, edifice, erection, pile; property, premises, establishment, place.
2 *a moratorium on the building of new power stations*: **construction**, erection, putting up, raising, establishment, fabrication, production, assembly.

> *Word links* **building**
> **tectonic** relating to building

build-up noun **1** *the build-up of military strength*: **increase**, growth, expansion, spread, enlargement, escalation, development, accumulation, proliferation, multiplication, snowballing, mushrooming.
▷ANTONYMS decrease.
2 *the build-up of carbon dioxide in the atmosphere*: **accumulation**, building up, accretion, gathering, amassing.
3 *the build-up for the World Cup*: **publicity**, promotion, advertising, puff, marketing, propaganda; informal hype, plugging, plug, ballyhoo, hoo-ha.

built-in adjective **1** *a built-in cupboard*: **fitted**, fixed, integral, integrated, incorporated, permanent.
2 *television has built-in advantages for advertisers*: **inherent**, intrinsic, incorporated, inseparable, inbuilt; essential, implicit, basic, fundamental, deep-rooted, rooted, permanent, ingrained, natural, native, radical; rare connatural.

bulb noun *a tulip bulb*: **tuber**, corm, rhizome.

bulbous adjective *he had a large bulbous red nose*: **bulging**, round, fat, rotund, swollen, spherical, swelling, distended, bloated, protuberant, ovoid, convex, pear-shaped, bulb-shaped, balloon-shaped; rare tumid.

bulge noun **1** *the money made a fat bulge in his hip pocket*: **swelling**, bump, lump, protuberance, protrusion, prominence, projection, eruption, convexity; rare intumescence.
2 informal *there will be a bulge in the prison population*: **surge**, upsurge, rise, increase, escalation, jump, leap, boost, intensification, augmentation.
▷ANTONYMS decrease.
▸ **verb** *his eyes were bulging*: **swell**, swell out, puff up/out, stick out, balloon, balloon up/out, fill out, bag, belly; project, protrude, jut (out), stand out, be prominent; expand, inflate, distend, dilate, enlarge, bloat; rare intumesce, tumefy.
▷ANTONYMS contract.

bulk noun **1** *the sheer bulk of the bags*: **size**, volume, dimensions, measurements, proportions, mass, substance, scale, magnitude, immensity, hugeness, vastness, massiveness, bulkiness, largeness, bigness, ampleness, amplitude.
2 ***the bulk** of entrants were British*: **majority**, greater quantity/number, larger part/number, best/better part, main part, major part; most, almost all, more than half; (main) body, lion's share, predominance, preponderance, generality.
▷ANTONYMS minority.
▸ **verb** *some takeaway meals are **bulked out** with fat*: **make bigger**, make larger, expand, pad out, fill out, eke out, add to, augment, increase.
□ **bulk large** *local factors bulked large in the negotiations*: **be important**, loom large, dominate, preponderate, be prominent, be significant, be influential, be of consequence, be of account, be relevant, mean a lot, count, matter, signify, carry weight.
▷ANTONYMS be insignificant.

bulky adjective **1** *bulky items of household refuse*: **large**, big, great, huge, of considerable size, sizeable, substantial, voluminous, immense, enormous, colossal, massive, mammoth, vast, goodly, prodigious, tremendous, gigantic, giant, monumental, stupendous, gargantuan, elephantine, titanic, mountainous, monstrous; mighty, epic, inordinate, unlimited, king-size, king-sized, giant-size, giant-sized, man-size, man-sized, outsize, oversized, overgrown, considerable, major, Brobdingnagian; **cumbersome**, unmanageable, unmanoeuvrable, unwieldy, awkward, ponderous, heavy, weighty; informal jumbo, whopping, whopping great, thumping, thumping great, hulking, mega, humongous, monster, astronomical, dirty great; Brit. informal whacking, whacking great, ginormous; dated incommodious.
▷ANTONYMS small, compact, manageable.
2 *he was a bulky man, not good at climbing*: **heavily built**, stocky, thickset, sturdy, sturdily built, well built, burly, strapping, brawny, muscular, solid, heavy, hefty, meaty; **stout**, fat, fattish, plump, chubby, portly, rotund, roly-poly, pot-bellied, round, dumpy, chunky, broad in the beam, overweight, obese, fleshy, paunchy, corpulent; buxom, well upholstered, well covered, well padded, of ample proportions, ample, rounded, well rounded; cobby; informal hulking, tubby, pudgy, beefy, porky, blubbery, poddy; Brit. informal podgy, fubsy; N. Amer. informal zaftig, corn-fed, lard-assed; Austral./NZ nuggety; technical mesomorphic, pyknic; rare squabby, pursy, abdominous.
▷ANTONYMS slight.

> *Word toolkit* **bulky**
> See **burly**.

bull noun

> *Word links* **bull**
> **taurine** relating to a bull

bulldoze verb **1** *they are planning to bulldoze the park and build workers' flats*: **demolish**, knock down, tear down, pull down, flatten, fell, level, raze, raze to the ground, clear, destroy, lay waste to.
▷ANTONYMS construct.
2 *the forward bulldozed his way through to score*: **force one's way**, push (one's way), shove (one's way), barge (one's way), elbow (one's way), shoulder (one's way), jostle (one's way), muscle, bludgeon one's way, plunge, crash, sweep, bundle, hustle.
▷ANTONYMS ease.
3 informal *she believes that to build status you need to bulldoze everyone else*: **bully**, hector, browbeat, intimidate, coerce, steamroller, badger, boss about/around, dragoon, cow, bludgeon, persecute, domineer, oppress, pressure, pressurize, tyrannize, terrorize, menace, subjugate, strong-arm, use strong-arm tactics on; informal railroad, lean on.

bullet noun ball, shot; informal slug; (**bullets**) lead.

> *Word links* **bullet**
> **ballistophobia** fear of bullets

bulletin noun **1** *a television news bulletin*: **report**, news, news report, newscast, flash, newsflash, headlines, dispatch, piece, story, communiqué, press release, statement, announcement, account, message, communication, notification.
2 *the Society produces a monthly bulletin*: **newsletter**, news-sheet, newspaper, journal, proceedings, digest, gazette, magazine, review, periodical, organ.

bullish adjective *individual employers were bullish about the prospects for their own firms*: **optimistic**, hopeful, buoyant, positive, disposed to look on the bright side, sanguine, confident, cheerful, cheery, bright, assured, animated, spirited; informal upbeat; archaic of good cheer.
▷ANTONYMS pessimistic.

bully noun *you mustn't give in to the village bully*: **persecutor**, oppressor, tyrant, tormentor, browbeater, intimidator, coercer, subjugator; scourge, tough, heavy, bully boy, ruffian, thug.
▸ **verb 1** *the other children used to bully him*: **persecute**, oppress, tyrannize, torment, browbeat, intimidate, cow, coerce, strong-arm, subjugate, domineer; informal push around/about, play the heavy with.
2 *a local man was **bullied into** helping them*: **coerce**, pressure, pressurize, bring pressure to bear on, use pressure on, put pressure on, constrain, lean on, press, push; force, compel, oblige, put under an obligation; hound, harass, nag, harry, badger, goad, prod, pester, browbeat, brainwash, bludgeon, persuade, prevail on, work on, act on, influence, intimidate, dragoon, twist someone's arm, strong-arm; N. Amer. blackjack; informal bulldoze, railroad, put the screws/squeeze on; Brit. informal bounce; N. Amer. informal hustle, fast-talk.

bulwark noun **1** *the inner-city ring road follows the line of the ancient bulwarks*: **wall**, rampart, fortification, parapet, stockade, palisade, barricade, embankment, earthwork, breastwork, berm; Latin vallum; rare circumvallation.

b

2 *a bulwark of liberty*: **protector**, protection, guard, defence, defender, support, supporter, prop, buttress, mainstay, bastion, safeguard, stronghold.

bum[1] noun Brit. informal See **bottom** (sense 6 of the noun).

bum[2] informal **noun 1** N. Amer. *bums would wander up and ask for a sandwich*. See **tramp**[2] (sense 1).
2 *get out of bed, you lazy bum*: **idler**, loafer, good-for-nothing, wastrel, drone, scrounger, cadger, ne'er-do-well, do-nothing, layabout, slob, lounger, shirker, sluggard, laggard, slugabed, malingerer; rogue, rascal, scoundrel, villain; informal waster, loser, skiver, slacker, lazybones.
▸ **verb 1** *he bummed around Florida for a few months*: **loaf**, lounge, idle, laze, languish, moon, stooge, droop, dally, dawdle, amble, potter, wander, drift, meander; informal mooch; N. Amer. informal lollygag, bat.
2 *they tried to bum money off him*: **scrounge**, beg, borrow; informal cadge, sponge, touch someone for; Brit. informal scab; Scottish informal sorn on someone for; N. Amer. informal mooch; Austral./NZ informal bludge.
▸ **adjective** *they have had a bum deal*: **bad**, poor, inferior, second-rate, second-class, unsatisfactory, inadequate, unacceptable, substandard, not up to scratch, not up to par, deficient, imperfect, defective, faulty, shoddy, amateurish, careless, negligent; **dreadful**, awful, terrible, abominable, frightful, atrocious, disgraceful, deplorable, hopeless, worthless, laughable, lamentable, miserable, sorry, third-rate, diabolical, execrable; informal crummy, rotten, pathetic, useless, woeful, lousy, ropy, appalling, abysmal, pitiful, God-awful, dire, poxy, not up to snuff, the pits; Brit. informal duff, chronic, rubbish; vulgar slang crap, shit, chickenshit.
▷ANTONYMS excellent.

bumble verb **1** *they bumbled around the house*: **blunder**, lurch, stumble, wobble, lumber, shamble, shuffle, stagger, totter, teeter, reel, weave, pitch, muddle, flounder, falter.
2 *by comparison all the other speakers bumbled*: **ramble**, babble, burble, drivel, gibber, blather, mumble, mutter, stumble.

bumbling adjective *Sherlock Holmes' bumbling sidekick Watson*: **blundering**, bungling, amateurish, incompetent, inept, unskilful, inexpert, clumsy, maladroit, gauche, awkward, inefficient, muddled, oafish, clodhopping, stumbling, lumbering, foolish, useless; crude, botched; informal ham-fisted, ham-handed, cack-handed.
▷ANTONYMS efficient, expert.

bump noun **1** *I landed with a bump*: **jolt**, collision, crash, smash, smack, crack, thwack, bang, thud, thump, buffet, knock, rap, tap, impact; informal whack, bash, wallop.
2 *I was woken by a bump*: **bang**, sharp noise, crack, boom, clang, peal, clap, pop, snap, knock, tap, slam, thud, thump, clunk, clonk, clash, crash, smash, smack; stamp, stomp, clump, clomp; report, explosion, detonation, shot; informal wham, whump.
3 *the wheels hit a bump in the road*: **hump**, bulge, lump, knob, knot, projection, prominence, eminence, ridge, protuberance.
▷ANTONYMS pothole.
4 *the police would ask him how he got the bump on his head*: **swelling**, lump, bulge, injury, contusion; nodule, node, outgrowth, growth, carbuncle, hunch, excrescence, protuberance, projection; technical process, bulla; rare tumescence, intumescence, tumefaction.
▸ **verb 1** *all those cars **bumped into** each other*: **hit**, ram, bang (into), collide with, be in collision with, strike, knock (into), knock against, crash into/against, smash into, slam into, crack into/against, dash against, run into, plough into; N. Amer. impact.
▷ANTONYMS miss.
2 *the cart bumping along the road*: **bounce**, jolt, jerk, rattle, shake, jounce.
□ **bump into** informal *I bumped into an old friend*: **meet (by chance)**, encounter, meet up with, run into, come across, run across, chance on, stumble on/across, happen on; archaic run against.
□ **bump someone off** informal *he would try and bump the blackmailer off*. See **kill**.

bumper adjective *a bumper crop*: **abundant**, rich, heavy, healthy, bountiful, goodly, large, big, huge, immense, massive, exceptional, unusual, good, excellent, fine, magnificent, lovely, vintage, superabundant, prolific, profuse, copious, profitable; informal whopping; S. African informal lank; literary bounteous, plenteous.
▷ANTONYMS poor, meagre, disastrous.

bumpkin noun *she thought Tom a bit of a country bumpkin*: **yokel**, country cousin, rustic, countryman, countrywoman, country dweller, son/daughter of the soil, peasant, provincial; **oaf**, lout, boor, barbarian; informal clod, clodhopper, yahoo, yob, yobbo; Irish informal culchie, bogman; N. Amer. informal hayseed, hillbilly, hick, rube, schlub; Austral. informal bushy; archaic carl, churl, hind, kern, bucolic.
▷ANTONYMS sophisticate.

bumptious adjective *you're a bumptious little know-all at times*: **self-important**, conceited, arrogant, self-assertive, full of oneself, puffed up, swollen-headed, pompous, overbearing, (self-)opinionated, cocky, swaggering, strutting, presumptuous, forward, imperious, domineering, pontificating, sententious, grandiose, affected, stiff, vain, haughty, overweening, proud, egotistic, egotistical; supercilious, condescending, patronizing; informal snooty, uppity, uppish, pushy.
▷ANTONYMS self-effacing.

bumpy adjective **1** *a bumpy road*: **uneven**, rough, irregular; holed, potholed, holey, rutted, pitted, rutty; lumpy, knobby, knobbly, gnarled; stony, rocky.
▷ANTONYMS smooth, level.
2 *a bumpy ride*: **bouncy**, rough, uncomfortable, choppy, jolting, jolty, lurching, jerky, jumpy, jarring, bone-shaking, bone-breaking, jouncy, jouncing, turbulent.
▷ANTONYMS smooth, comfortable.
3 *the season got off to a bumpy start*: **inconsistent**, variable, varying, changeable, irregular, fluctuating, intermittent, wavering, erratic, patchy; rocky, unsettled, unstable, roller-coaster, stormy, tumultuous, turbulent, tempestuous, explosive, in turmoil, full of upheavals, full of conflict, full of ups and downs, chaotic.
▷ANTONYMS consistent, settled.

bunch noun **1** *a bunch of flowers*: **bouquet**, spray, posy, nosegay, corsage; wreath, garland, chaplet; buttonhole; flower arrangement; French boutonnière; rare tussie-mussie.
2 *a bunch of keys | a bunch of bananas*: **cluster**, clump, knot; group, assemblage, collection.
3 informal *what a wonderful bunch of people*: **group**, set, circle, body, company, troupe, collection, assemblage, gathering, throng, knot, cluster, huddle, multitude, bevy, party, band, horde, pack, drove, flock, swarm, stream, mob; informal gang, crowd, load, crew, gaggle.
4 N. Amer. informal *they did a whole bunch of things*. See **lot**.
▸ **verb 1** *he bunched the reins in his hands*: **bundle**, clump, cluster, group, arrange, gather, collect, assemble; bind, pack, fasten together, truss.
▷ANTONYMS spread out, release.
2 *his trousers bunched around his ankles*: **gather**, ruffle, pucker, shirr, tuck, fold, pleat.
▷ANTONYMS spread out.
3 *he halted, forcing the rest of the runners to **bunch up** behind him*: **cluster**, huddle, gather, concentrate, congregate, collect, accumulate, amass, group, herd, crowd, flock, mass; pack somewhere, cram somewhere.
▷ANTONYMS disperse.

bundle noun *a bundle of clothes*: **bunch**, roll, clump, wad, parcel, packet, package, pack, sheaf, bale, bolt, truss, faggot, fascicle; pile, stack, heap, mass, quantity, armful, collection, accumulation, agglomeration, lot, batch; informal load, wodge.
▸ **verb 1** *she quickly **bundled up** her clothes*: **tie (up)**, tie together, do up, pack (up), pack together, package, parcel (up), packet, wrap (up), roll (up), wind up, fold (up), furl, bind (up), fasten together, bale, truss (up).
▷ANTONYMS undo.
2 *the figure was bundled in furs*: **wrap**, envelop, clothe, cover, muffle, swathe, swaddle, bind, bandage, shroud, drape, wind, enfold, sheathe, enclose, encase; literary lap.
3 informal *he was bundled into a van*: **hustle**, jostle, manhandle, frogmarch, sweep, throw, hurry, rush; shove, push, thrust, propel, impel.

Word links **bundle**

fascicular relating to a bundle

bung noun *the jar is sealed with a rubber bung*: **stopper**, plug, cork, spigot, spile, seal, cap, top, lid, cover; N. Amer. stopple.

bungle verb *the prisoners bungled their escape bid*: **mishandle**, mismanage, mess up, make a mess of, botch, spoil, mar, ruin; informal make a hash of, muff, fluff, foul up, screw up, louse up, bitch up, blow, foozle; Brit. informal make a muck of, make a pig's ear of, cock up, make a Horlicks of; N. Amer. informal flub, goof up, bobble; vulgar slang fuck up, bugger up, balls up, bollix up.
▷ANTONYMS succeed in, manage successfully.

bungler noun *his mistakes have caused him to be branded a bungler*: **blunderer**, incompetent, amateur, bumbler, botcher, clown, hopeless case; informal mutt, butterfingers; Brit. informal bodger, prat; N. Amer. informal jackleg, spud; archaic lurdan; (**bunglers**) Brit. informal shower.
▷ANTONYMS expert.

bungling adjective *the work of a bungling amateur*: **incompetent**, blundering, amateurish, inept, unskilful, inexpert, clumsy, maladroit, gauche, awkward, inefficient, muddled, oafish, clodhopping, bumbling, stumbling, lumbering, foolish, useless; informal ham-fisted, ham-handed, cack-handed.
▷ANTONYMS expert.

bunk[1] noun *the skipper slept in a bunk in the forward cabin*: **berth**, cot, bunk bed, bed.

bunk[2] Brit. informal **verb** *he **bunked off** school*: **play truant from**, truant from, stay away from, not go to, be absent from, skip, avoid, shirk; Brit. informal skive off; Irish informal mitch off; N. Amer. informal play hookey from, goof off, ditch, cut; Austral./NZ informal play the wag from; rare bag, hop the wag from.

▶ noun
▫ **do a bunk** *he'd done a bunk with all our money*: **run off**, run away, make off, take off, take to one's heels, run for it, make a run for it, make a break for it, bolt, beat a (hasty) retreat, make a quick exit, make one's getaway, escape, head for the hills, do a disappearing act; informal beat it, clear off, clear out, vamoose, skedaddle, split, cut and run, leg it, show a clean pair of heels, turn tail, scram; Brit. informal do a runner, scarper, do a moonlight (flit); N. Amer. informal light out, bug out, cut out, peel out, take a powder, skidoo; Austral. informal go through, shoot through; vulgar slang bugger off; archaic fly.

bunk[3] noun informal *that idea is just sheer bunk*. See **nonsense**.

bunkum noun informal, dated *they talk a lot of bunkum*. See **nonsense**.

buoy noun *the channel is marked by red and green buoys*: **marker**, anchored float, navigation mark, guide, beacon, signal.
▶ verb *the party was buoyed by an election victory*: **cheer**, cheer up, brighten up, ginger up, hearten, rally, animate, invigorate, comfort, uplift, lift, encourage, stimulate, raise someone's spirits, give a lift to; support, sustain, give strength to, be a source of strength to, be a tower of strength to, keep someone going, see someone through; informal pep up, perk up, buck up; rare inspirit.
▷ANTONYMS depress.

buoyancy noun **1** *the drum's buoyancy forced it up again*: **ability to float**, tendency to float, lightness; rare floatability.
2 *the buoyancy of the salt water*: **lift**, lifting effect.
3 *the buoyancy of her personality*: **cheerfulness**, cheeriness, happiness, light-heartedness, carefreeness, brightness, gladness, merriment, joy, bounce, effervescence, blitheness, sunniness, breeziness, jollity, joviality, animation, liveliness, life, sprightliness, jauntiness, ebullience, high spirits, vivacity, vitality, verve, sparkle, zest; **optimism**, confidence, hope, bullishness, sanguineness, positiveness; informal pep, zing, zip.
▷ANTONYMS depression, pessimism.
4 *the buoyancy of the market*: **vigour**, strength, high level of activity, burgeoning, resilience, growth, development, progress, improvement, expansion, mushrooming, snowballing, ballooning.
▷ANTONYMS depression.

buoyant adjective **1** *a buoyant substance*: **able to float**, light, floating; rare floatable.
▷ANTONYMS heavy.
2 *they dispersed in a buoyant mood*: **cheerful**, cheery, happy, light-hearted, carefree, bright, glad, merry, joyful, bubbly, bouncy, effervescent, blithe, sunny, breezy, jolly, jovial, animated, lively, sprightly, jaunty, ebullient, high-spirited, vivacious, vital, sparkling, sparky, zestful, perky; **optimistic**, confident, hopeful, sanguine, bullish, positive; informal peppy, zippy, zingy, upbeat; dated gay.
▷ANTONYMS depressed, pessimistic.
3 *car sales were buoyant*: **booming**, strong, vigorous, burgeoning, thriving, growing, developing, progressing, improving, expanding, mushrooming, snowballing, ballooning; informal going strong.
▷ANTONYMS depressed.

burble verb **1** *the exhaust was burbling as only a twin-pipe V8 can burble*: **gurgle**, bubble, murmur, purr, purl, tinkle, whirr, drone, rumble, buzz, hum; literary plash.
2 *he burbled on about annuities*: **prattle**, blather, blether, blither, babble (on), gabble, prate, drivel, rattle on/away, ramble, maunder, go on, run on, talk at length, talk incessantly, talk a lot; chatter, yap, gossip; Brit. talk nineteen to the dozen; Scottish & Irish slabber on; informal jabber, blabber, yatter, jaw, gab, gas, chit-chat, yackety-yak; Brit. informal rabbit, witter, waffle, natter, chunter, talk the hind legs off a donkey; N. Amer. informal run off at the mouth; Austral./NZ informal mag; archaic twaddle, twattle, claver, clack.

burden noun **1** *the porters shouldered their burdens*: **load**, cargo, freight, weight; charge, pack, bundle, parcel.
2 *he took on a huge financial burden*: **responsibility**, onus, charge, duty, obligation, liability; trouble, care, problem, worry, anxiety, tribulation, affliction, trial, difficulty, misfortune, strain, stress, encumbrance, millstone, cross to bear, albatross; archaic cumber.
3 *the burden of his message*: **gist**, substance, drift, implication, intention, thrust, meaning, significance, signification, sense, essence, thesis, import, purport, tenor, message, spirit.
▶ verb **1** *he was burdened with a heavy pack*: **load**, weight, charge; **weigh down**, encumber, hamper, overload, overburden; (**burdened**) laden; rare trammel.
2 *we should avoid burdening parents with too much guilt*: **oppress**, trouble, cause trouble to, cause suffering to; worry, beset, bother, harass, disturb, upset, depress, get someone down; distress, grieve, haunt, nag, torment, harrow, afflict, strain, stress, tax, overwhelm, perturb, plague, bedevil.

burdensome adjective *compliance with the order can be burdensome*: **onerous**, oppressive, troublesome, weighty, worrisome, vexatious, irksome, trying, crushing, inconvenient, awkward, a nuisance; harsh, severe, stiff, stringent, formidable, an imposition; arduous, strenuous, rigorous, uphill, difficult, hard, laborious, Herculean, exhausting, tiring, taxing, demanding, punishing, gruelling, back-breaking, exacting, wearing, stressful, wearisome, fatiguing; rare toilsome, exigent.
▷ANTONYMS easy, light.

bureau noun **1** *a beautiful oak bureau*: **desk**, writing desk, writing table, roll-top desk; Brit. davenport; French secretaire, escritoire.
2 *a marriage bureau*: **agency**, service, office, business, company, firm, organization, operation, concern.
3 *the intelligence bureau*: **department**, division, branch, section.

bureaucracy noun **1** *the higher ranks of the bureaucracy*: **civil service**, administration, government, directorate, the establishment, the system, the powers that be, corridors of power; ministries, authorities, officials, officialdom; informal Big Brother.
2 *the unnecessary bureaucracy in local government*: **red tape**, rules and regulations, etiquette, protocol, officialdom, (unnecessary) paperwork; humorous bumbledom.

bureaucrat noun *the faceless bureaucrats who make the rules*: **official**, administrator, office-holder, office-bearer, civil servant, public servant, government servant, minister, functionary, appointee, apparatchik, mandarin; Brit. jack-in-office.

bureaucratic adjective **1** *the bureaucratic structure of the Council*: **administrative**, official, procedural, red-tape, governmental, ministerial, state, civic, constitutional, political.
2 *the current practice is far too bureaucratic*: **rule-bound**, rigid, inflexible, complicated, red-tape-bound; by the book.
▷ANTONYMS simple, relaxed.

burgeon verb *tourism has burgeoned over the last ten years*: **grow rapidly**, increase rapidly/exponentially, expand, spring up, shoot up, swell, explode, boom, mushroom, proliferate, snowball, multiply, become more numerous, escalate, rocket, skyrocket, run riot, put on a spurt; flourish, thrive, prosper.
▷ANTONYMS shrink.

burglar noun *the burglar stole jewellery worth several thousand pounds*: **housebreaker**, robber, cat burglar, raider, looter, pilferer, picklock, thief, sneak thief, safe-breaker, safe-blower, safe-cracker; kleptomaniac; intruder, trespasser; informal filcher, cracksman; N. Amer. informal second-story man/worker, yegg.

burglary noun **1** *a two-year sentence for burglary*: **housebreaking**, breaking and entering, breaking in, forced entry, theft, thieving, stealing, robbery, robbing, larceny, thievery, pilfering, pilferage, looting; trespassing; informal filching.
2 *a series of burglaries*: **break-in**, theft, robbery, raid, hold-up; informal snatch, smash and grab; N. Amer. informal heist, stick-up.

burgle verb *her house was burgled last night*: **break into**, force (an) entry into, force one's way into; steal from, rob, loot, plunder, rifle, sack, ransack, pillage; informal do.

burial noun *the body was flown home for burial*: **burying**, interment, committal, inhumation; entombment; funeral, obsequies, funerary rites; rare sepulture, exequies.
▷ANTONYMS exhumation.

Word links **burial**

funerary, sepulchral relating to burial

burial ground noun *in the burial ground will be found the graves of many distinguished men*. See **cemetery**.

burlesque noun *the funniest burlesque of music hall there has been*: **parody**, caricature, travesty, pastiche, take-off, skit, imitation, satire, lampoon; informal send-up, spoof; Brit. vulgar slang piss-take; rare pasquinade, pasticcio.

burly adjective *two burly bodyguards stood by him*: **strapping**, well built, sturdy, sturdily built, powerfully built, broad-shouldered, brawny, strong, muscular, muscly, well muscled, athletic, thickset, big, hefty, bulky, robust, rugged, stocky, lusty, Herculean, vigorous; informal hunky, beefy, husky, hulking; literary stalwart, thewy, stark; technical mesomorphic.
▷ANTONYMS puny.

Word toolkit

burly	**sturdy**	**bulky**
guy	boots	sweater
security guard	legs	jacket
soldier	branch	equipment
bouncer	construction	backpack
policeman	cardboard	package
wrestler	chair	shape

burn verb **1** *the house was burning*: **be on fire**, be alight, be ablaze, blaze, go up, go up in smoke, be in flames, be aflame; smoulder, glow, flare, flash, flicker; literary be afire; archaic be ardent.
2 *he burned all the letters*: **set fire to**, set on fire, set alight, set light to,

light, set burning, ignite, touch off, put a match to, kindle, incinerate, reduce to ashes, destroy by fire; informal torch; archaic fire, inflame.
3 *I forgot to turn off the iron and nearly burned his dress shirt*: **scorch**, singe, sear, char, blacken, discolour, brand; scald; technical cauterize, calcine; rare torrefy.
4 *her face burned with humiliation*: **be hot**, be warm, feel hot, be feverish, be fevered, be on fire; **blush**, redden, be red, go red, go pink, turn red, turn crimson, turn scarlet, flush, colour, crimson.
5 *her lip burned where her teeth had pierced it*: **smart**, sting, tingle, prick, prickle, be irritated, be sore, hurt, be painful, throb, ache.
6 *Martha was burning with curiosity*: **be consumed by/with**, be eaten up by/with, be obsessed by/with, be tormented by/with, be bedevilled by.
7 *he was burning with fury*: **seethe**, boil, fume, smoulder, simmer, be boiling over, be beside oneself; informal be livid, be wild, jump up and down, froth/foam at the mouth.
8 *Meredith burned to know what the secret was*: **yearn**, long, have a longing, ache, be aching, itch, be itching, desire, be consumed with the desire, want, want badly, be unable to wait, be eager, be desperate, hanker, have a hankering, wish, crave, lust, pant, hunger, be hungry, be greedy, thirst, be thirsty; informal have a yen, yen, be dying; archaic be athirst, be desirous.
9 *people differ considerably in the energy they burn up*: **use up**, consume, expend, get through, go through, dissipate, eat up, exhaust.
▷ANTONYMS conserve.
□ **burn oneself out** *don't burn yourself out or you won't even feel up to making that once-weekly trip*: **work too hard**, work like a Trojan/horse/slave, work/run oneself into the ground, wear oneself to a shadow, work one's fingers to the bone, drive oneself into the ground, sweat, sweat blood, work day and night, burn the candle at both ends, burn the midnight oil, overtax oneself, overtax one's strength, kill oneself, do too much, overdo it, strain oneself, overburden oneself, overload oneself, drive/push oneself too hard; informal knock oneself out, work one's tail off; vulgar slang work/sweat one's balls off.
▷ANTONYMS be idle.

burning adjective **1** *a burning house*: **blazing**, flaming, aflame, fiery, flaring, ignited, glowing, red-hot, flickering, smouldering; scorching, raging, roaring, live.
▷ANTONYMS extinguished.
2 *the burning desert sands*: **extremely hot**, red-hot, unbearably hot, baking (hot), blazing (hot), flaming, fiery, blistering, scorching, searing, sweltering, torrid, tropical, like an oven, like a furnace, like a blowtorch; parching, withering; N. Amer. broiling; informal baking, boiling (hot), roasting, sizzling.
▷ANTONYMS freezing.
3 *a burning desire to win*: **intense**, passionate, deep-seated, profound, wholehearted, strong, powerful, forceful, vigorous, ardent, urgent, fervent, fierce, earnest, eager, keen, enthusiastic, zealous, fanatical, frantic, consuming, extreme, acute, raging, blazing, uncontrollable; rare fervid, perfervid, passional.
4 *the burning issues of the day*: **important**, crucial, significant, prevalent, pertinent, relevant, topical, current, contemporary, of interest, active, live, controversial, urgent, pressing, compelling, critical, vital, lively, essential, acute, pivotal, climacteric.

burnish verb *marks can be removed by scraping and burnishing the metal*: **polish (up)**, shine, brighten, rub up/down, buff (up), smooth, glaze; archaic furbish.
▷ANTONYMS dull.

burp informal verb *he couldn't help burping*: **belch**, bring up wind; Scottish & N. English rift; informal gurk; archaic bolk, rout, ruck; rare eruct, eructate.
▶ noun *Cranston let out a burp*: **belch**; Scottish & N. English rift; informal gurk; archaic bolk; rare eructation, ventosity.

burrow noun *the rabbits' burrow*: **warren**, tunnel, hole, lair, set, den, earth, retreat, excavation, cave, dugout, hollow, scrape.
▶ verb *the mouse can burrow a hiding place*: **tunnel**, dig (out), excavate, grub, mine, bore, drill, channel; hollow out, gouge out, scoop out, cut out; literary delve.

burst verb **1** *one balloon burst | he's burst my balloon*: **split open**, burst open, break open, tear open, rupture, crack, fracture, fragment, shatter, shiver, fly open; literary tear asunder, rend asunder.
2 *a shell burst a short distance away*: **explode**, blow up, detonate, go off, be set off, land; informal go bang.
3 *smoke, dust, and heat burst through the hole*: **break**, erupt, surge, gush, rush, stream, flow, pour, cascade, spill; sweep, spout, spurt, jet, spew, discharge, roll, whirl.
4 *he burst into the room without knocking*: **plunge**, charge, barge, shove, plough, lurch, hurtle, career, rush, dash, tear.
5 *she **burst into** tears*: **break out in**, launch into, erupt in, have a fit of; suddenly start.
□ **burst out 1** *'Well, I don't care!' she burst out angrily*: **exclaim**, blurt out, ejaculate, cry out, call out, shout, yell. **2** *he burst out crying*: **suddenly start**.
▶ noun **1** *damage to tyres by punctures and bursts*: **rupture**, breach, split, blowout.
2 *the mortar bursts were further away than before*: **explosion**, detonation, blast, discharge, eruption, bang.
3 *a burst of anger | a sudden burst of activity*: **outbreak**, outburst, eruption, flare-up, explosion, blow-up, blast, blaze, attack, fit, spasm, paroxysm, access, rush, gale, flood, storm, hurricane, torrent, outpouring, surge, upsurge, spurt, effusion, outflow, outflowing, welling up; informal splurt; rare ebullition, boutade.
4 *a burst of gunfire*: **volley**, salvo, fusillade, barrage, discharge, shower, spray, hail, rain.

bury verb **1** *all the crew were buried at Stonefall cemetery*: **inter**, lay to rest, consign to the grave, entomb; earth up; informal put six feet under, plant; N. Amer. informal deep-six; literary sepulchre, ensepulchre, inhume, inearth.
▷ANTONYMS exhume.
2 *she buried her face in her hands*: **hide**, conceal, cover, put out of sight, secrete, enfold; submerge, sink, embed, engulf, immerse, enclose, tuck, cup; literary enshroud.
▷ANTONYMS reveal, take out of.
3 *the bullet buried itself in the wood*: **embed**, sink, implant, submerge, insert; drive something into.
▷ANTONYMS extract from.
4 *he buried himself in his work*: **absorb**, engross, occupy, engage, busy, employ, distract, preoccupy, immerse, interest, involve.

Word links **bury**

taphephobia fear of being buried alive

bush noun **1** *a rose bush*: **shrub**, woody plant; (**bushes**) undergrowth, shrubbery, hedge, thicket.
2 *it is easy to become lost in the bush*: **wilds**, remote areas, wilderness; the backwoods, the hinterland(s); N. Amer. the backcountry, the backland; Austral./NZ the outback, the backblocks, the booay; S. African the backveld, the platteland; N. Amer. informal the boondocks, the boonies, the tall timbers; Austral./NZ informal Woop Woop, beyond the black stump.

bushy adjective *a bushy walrus moustache*: **thick**, shaggy, unruly, fuzzy, rough, bristling, bristly, fluffy, woolly, luxuriant, exuberant, spreading; informal jungly.
▷ANTONYMS wispy, straggly.

busily adverb *Sunil was busily getting the machine to work*: **actively**, industriously, purposefully, diligently, dutifully, energetically, vigorously, enthusiastically, strenuously, tirelessly, indefatigably; hard.
▷ANTONYMS idly.

business noun **1** *she had to do a lot of smiling in her business*: **work**, line of work, line, occupation, profession, career, employment, job, position, pursuit, vocation, calling, field, sphere, walk of life, trade, craft; Scottish way; French métier; informal racket, game; Austral. informal grip; archaic employ.
2 *who do you do business with in Manila?* **trade**, trading, commerce, buying and selling, dealing, traffic, trafficking, marketing, merchandising, bargaining; dealings, transactions, negotiations, proceedings.
3 *she was running her own business*: **firm**, company, concern, enterprise, venture, organization, operation, undertaking, industry, corporation, establishment, house, shop, office, bureau, agency, franchise, practice, partnership, consortium, cooperative, conglomerate, group, combine, syndicate; informal outfit, set-up.
4 *that's none of my business | it's our business to know that sort of thing*: **concern**, affair, responsibility, province, preserve, duty, function, task, assignment, obligation, problem, worry, lookout; informal funeral, headache, bailiwick; Brit. informal pigeon, baby.
5 *the odd business with the keys remained unexplained*: **affair**, matter, thing, issue, case, set of circumstances, circumstance, situation, occasion, experience, event, incident, happening, occurrence, phenomenon, eventuality, episode, interlude, adventure.

businesslike adjective *the group was run in a businesslike way*: **professional**, efficient, slick, competent, practised, methodical, disciplined, systematic, orderly, organized, well ordered, planned, structured, practical, pragmatic.
▷ANTONYMS disorganized, inefficient.

businessman, businesswoman noun *he was a shrewd businessman who was also good for the local economy*: **entrepreneur**, business person, industrialist, manufacturer, tycoon, magnate, big businessman, employer; dealer, trader, merchant, wholesaler, buyer, seller, buyer and seller, marketeer, merchandiser, broker, agent, distributor, vendor, tradesman, shopkeeper, retailer, purveyor, supplier, trafficker; French, dated homme d'affaires.

bust[1] noun **1** *a woman with a large bust*: **chest**, bosom, breasts; technical mammary glands, mammae; informal boobs, boobies, tits, titties, knockers, bazookas, melons, jubblies, bubbies, orbs, globes, jugs; Brit. informal bristols, charlies, baps; N. Amer. informal bazooms, casabas, chichis, hooters; Austral. informal norks; archaic dugs, paps, embonpoint.
2 *a bust of Julius Caesar*: **sculpture**, carving, effigy, three-dimensional representation; statue, torso, head.

bust² informal **verb 1** *he had bust the clip that held the lid up | the box has bust*: **break**, crack, snap, fracture, shatter, smash, smash to smithereens, fragment, splinter; disintegrate, fall to bits, fall to pieces; split, burst, rupture; tear, rend, sever, separate, divide; rare shiver.
2 *he promised to bust the mafia*: **overthrow**, destroy, bring about the downfall of, topple, bring down, bring low, ruin, break, overturn, overcome, defeat, purge, get rid of, oust, unseat, dislodge, eject, supplant.
▷ANTONYMS perpetuate; support.
3 *two roadies were busted for drugs*. See **arrest**.
4 N. Amer. *my apartment got busted*: **raid**, search, make a search of, swoop on, make a raid on; informal do over.
▶ **adjective**
□ **go bust** *his haulage business went bust and he owes £120,000*: **fail**, collapse, crash, fold (up), go under, founder, be ruined, cave in; **go bankrupt**, become insolvent, cease trading, go into receivership, go into liquidation, be liquidated, be wound up, be closed (down), be shut (down); informal go broke, go bump, go to the wall, go belly up, come a cropper, flop.

bustle **verb 1** *people clutching clipboards bustled about*: **rush**, dash, scurry, scuttle, scamper, scramble, flutter, fuss; hurry, hasten, make haste, race, run, sprint, tear, shoot, charge, chase, career; Brit. scutter; informal scoot, beetle, whizz, buzz, hare, zoom, zip.
▷ANTONYMS amble.
2 *she bustled us into the kitchen*: **hustle**, bundle, sweep, push, hurry, rush, whisk, whip.
▶ **noun** *the bustle of the market*: **activity**, hustle and bustle, animation, commotion, flurry, tumult, hubbub, busyness, action, liveliness, movement, life, stir, excitement, agitation, fuss, whirl; informal toing and froing, comings and goings, to-do; archaic hurry scurry, pother.
▷ANTONYMS inactivity.

bustling **adjective** *the bustling streets of Kowloon*: **busy**, crowded, swarming, teeming, full, astir, buzzing, hectic, lively, vibrant, thronging, thronged; energetic, active; informal buzzy.
▷ANTONYMS deserted, inactive.

busy **adjective 1** *he's always **busy with** some useful job | the team members are busy raising money*: **occupied (in)**, engaged in, involved in, employed in, working at, labouring at, toiling at, slaving at, hard at work (on), wrapped up (in/with); rushed off one's feet (with), hard-pressed; at work (on), on the job, absorbed in, engrossed in, immersed in, preoccupied with; active (in), lively, industrious, bustling, energetic, tireless; informal busy as a bee, on the go, hard at it; Brit. informal on the hop; **(be busy)** have one's hands full.
▷ANTONYMS idle.
2 *Mr Jenkins is busy at the moment*: **unavailable**, otherwise engaged; **engaged**, occupied, in a meeting, working, at work, on duty, on active service, in harness; informal tied up; **(be busy)** have a prior/previous engagement.
▷ANTONYMS free.
3 *I've had a busy day*: **strenuous**, hectic, energetic, active, lively, exacting, tiring, full, eventful.
▷ANTONYMS quiet.
4 *the town centre was unusually busy*: **crowded**, bustling, swarming, teeming, astir, buzzing, hectic, full, thronged, thronging, lively, vibrant; informal buzzy.
5 *the frame should be fairly plain, to balance the rather busy design*: **excessively ornate**, over-ornate, over-elaborate, over-embellished, over-decorated, overblown, overwrought, exaggerated, overdone, florid, fussy, cluttered, contrived, overworked, over-detailed, strained, laboured, baroque, rococo.
▷ANTONYMS quiet, restrained.
▶ **verb** *a single clerk busied himself with paperwork*: **occupy**, involve, engage, concern, employ, absorb, engross, immerse, preoccupy; interest, entertain, distract, divert, amuse, beguile.

> *Choose the right word* **busy, occupied, engaged, active**
>
> Each of these words has several meanings, but those applied to people have subtle distinctions.
>
> Saying that someone is **busy** means that they have a great deal to do (*if I'm busy, my husband does the cooking*) or are occupied with a specified activity (*Bernard was busy with flying lessons*). Either way, they are likely to have no time for further calls on their attention (*I'm too busy to write letters*).
>
> Someone who is **occupied** has something to do which takes up a good deal of their time or attention. There is a suggestion that this activity is a welcome means of filling empty time, but not unduly onerous (*the children were fully occupied with games and competitions*). In spite of this use of *fully*, neither *occupied* nor *engaged* is often qualified as to degree—someone is either occupied/engaged or they are not, whereas people are frequently described as *very, extremely, really* or *too busy/active*. Both *occupied* and *busy* can be followed by *with* and the relevant activity, as in the examples given.
>
> **Engaged** emphasizes the fact that someone has no time or attention left for any new activities or demands; in this sense it is somewhat formal (*you'll have to wait to see her, she's engaged at present*). *Occupied* and *engaged* (in this sense) always follow the verb *to be*, rather than being used before a noun.
>
> To say that someone is **active** is to say that they are doing a great deal (*she has been active in local politics since 1985*). The context or area in which they are active is often expressed by an adverb, such as *sexually*, *physically*, or *politically*.

b

busybody **noun** *others considered him an interfering busybody*: **meddler**, interferer, mischief-maker, troublemaker, gossip, scandalmonger, muckraker, eavesdropper, intruder, ghoul, gawker; informal nosy parker, snoop, snooper, rubberneck; Brit. informal gawper; N. Amer. informal **buttinsky**; informal, dated Paul Pry; rare pryer, pry.

but **conjunction 1** *he stumbled but didn't fall*: **yet**; **nevertheless**, nonetheless, even so, however, still, notwithstanding, despite that, in spite of that, for all that, all the same, just the same, at the same time, be that as it may; though, although; informal still and all; archaic withal, natheless, howbeit.
▷ANTONYMS and.
2 *I am clean but you are dirty*: **whereas**; **conversely**, but then, then again, on the other hand, by contrast, in contrast, contrarily, on the contrary.
▷ANTONYMS and.
3 *one cannot but sympathize*: **(do) other than**, otherwise than, except.
▶ **preposition** *everyone but him had gone*: **except (for)**, apart from, other than, besides, aside from, with the exception of, short of, bar, barring, excepting, excluding, omitting, leaving out, save (for), saving; informal outside of.
▷ANTONYMS including.
□ **but for** *but for the rain he would have gone*: **if it were not for**, were it not for, except for, without, barring, notwithstanding.
▶ **adverb** *he is but a shadow of his former self*: **only**, just, simply, merely, no more than, nothing but; a mere; N. English informal nobbut.

butch **adjective** informal *a butch guardsman*: **(aggressively) masculine**, manly, all man, virile, red-blooded, swashbuckling; **mannish**, manlike, unfeminine, unladylike, Amazonian; informal macho, dykey; rare viraginous, viragoish.
▷ANTONYMS effeminate, feminine.

butcher **noun 1** *a butcher's shop*: **meat seller**, meat merchant, meat trader; slaughterer, slaughterman; Scottish archaic flesher.
2 *a callous butcher of men*: **murderer**, mass murderer, slaughterer, killer, assassin, serial killer, homicidal maniac, destroyer, terminator, liquidator; literary slayer; dated cut-throat, homicide.
▶ **verb 1** *the goat was then butchered and skinned*: **slaughter**, cut up, carve up, slice up, joint, prepare, dress.
2 *they rounded up and butchered 150 people*: **massacre**, murder, slaughter, kill, put to death, dispatch, dispose of, destroy, exterminate, liquidate, eliminate, terminate, assassinate, put to the sword, cut down, cut to pieces; literary slay.
3 *the film was butchered by the studio*: **spoil**, ruin, mar, mutilate, mangle, cut about, mess up, make a mess of, wreck; informal murder, make a hash of, muck up, screw up, louse up.

butchery **noun 1** *the butchery trade*: **meat selling**, meat retailing.
2 Brit. *the cattle were taken to the butchery*: **abattoir**, slaughterhouse; Brit. knacker's yard; archaic shambles, butcher-row.
3 Brit. *the truck crashed into a butchery and a florist's*: **butcher's**, butcher's shop, meat market, meat counter.
4 *the butchery in the trenches in the First World War*: **slaughter**, massacre, slaying, murdering, murder, mass murdering, homicide, blood shedding.

butt¹ **verb** *she butted him in the chest*: **ram**, headbutt, bunt; bump, buffet, push, thrust, shove, prod, knock; N. English tup.
□ **butt in** *he **butted in on** our conversation*: **interrupt**, break in, cut in, chime in, interject, interpose, intervene; interfere (with), put one's oar in; informal poke one's nose in/into; Brit. informal chip in.
▷ANTONYMS keep out (of).

butt² **noun** *she had just been made the butt of a joke*: **target**, victim, object, subject, recipient, laughing stock, Aunt Sally.

butt³ **noun 1** *the butt of a gun*: **stock**, shaft, shank, end, handle, hilt, haft, grip, helve.
2 *a cigarette butt*: **stub**, end, tail end, stump, remnant, remains, remainder; informal fag end, dog end.
3 N. Amer. informal *he was just sitting on his butt doing nothing*. See **bottom** (sense 6 of the noun).
▶ **verb** *the shop **butted up against** the row of houses*: **adjoin**, abut, butt up to, be next to, be adjacent to, border (on), neighbour, verge on, bound on, be contiguous with, be connected to, communicate with, link up with, extend as far as, extend to; join, conjoin, connect with/to, touch, meet.
▷ANTONYMS be separate from.

butt⁴ **noun** *a butt of brandy*. See **barrel**.

butter **verb**
□ **butter someone up** informal *she was good at buttering up advertisers*: **be obsequious towards**, grovel to, be servile towards, be sycophantic towards, kowtow to, abase oneself to, demean oneself to, bow and scrape to, prostrate oneself to, toady to, truckle to, dance attendance on, fawn on, make up to, play up to, ingratiate oneself with, rub up the right way, curry

favour with; **wheedle**, flatter, court, persuade, blarney, coax, talk into, get round, prevail on; informal suck up to, crawl to, creep to, be all over, lick someone's boots, fall all over, keep someone sweet, sweet-talk, soft-soap; N. Amer. brown-nose; vulgar slang lick/kiss someone's arse; archaic blandish.

butterfly noun

Word links **butterfly**

lepidopteran relating to butterflies

buttocks plural noun *stand with you heels, buttocks, and back touching the wall*: **backside**, behind, seat, rump, rear, rear end; cheeks, hindquarters, haunches; Brit. **bottom**; French derrière; German Sitzfleisch; technical nates; informal sit-upon, stern, BTM, tochus; Brit. informal bum, botty, prat, jacksie; Scottish informal bahookie; N. Amer. informal butt, fanny, tush, tushie, tail, duff, buns, booty, caboose, heinie, patootie, keister, tuchis, bazoo, bippy; W. Indian informal batty; humorous fundament, posterior; black English rass, rusty dusty; Brit. vulgar slang arse; N. Amer. vulgar slang ass; archaic breech.

Word links **buttocks**

natal relating to the buttocks

button noun **1** *he did up his shirt buttons*: **fastener**, stud, link, toggle; hook, catch, clasp.
2 *press the appropriate button to record*: **knob**, switch, on/off switch, push switch, disc, lever, handle, key, control, controller.

buttonhole verb informal *in the pub, I buttonholed the team captain*. See **accost**.

buttress noun **1** *the wall was supported by stone buttresses*: **prop**, support, abutment, shore, pier, reinforcement, stanchion, stay, strut.
2 *a buttress against social collapse*: **safeguard**, defence, defender, protector, protection, guard, support, supporter, prop, mainstay; bulwark, bastion, stronghold.
▸ verb *authority was buttressed by religious belief*: **strengthen**, reinforce, fortify, support, prop up, bolster up, shore up, underpin, cement, brace, uphold, confirm, defend, maintain, back up, buoy up.

buxom adjective *a buxom young woman*: **large-breasted**, big-breasted, full-breasted, heavy-breasted, bosomy, large-bosomed, big-bosomed, full-bosomed; shapely, well covered, well padded, of ample proportions, ample, plump, rounded, well rounded, full-figured, womanly, voluptuous, curvaceous, Junoesque, Rubenesque; informal busty, chesty, stacked, well upholstered, well endowed, curvy, pneumatic.
▷ANTONYMS skinny, petite.

buy verb **1** *they bought a new house*: **purchase**, make a/the purchase of, acquire, obtain, get, pick up, snap up; take, secure, procure, come by, pay for, shop for; invest in, put money into; informal get hold of, get one's hands on, lay one's hands on, get one's mitts on, score.
▷ANTONYMS sell.
2 *here was a man who could not be bought*: **bribe**, buy off, pay off, suborn, give an inducement to, corrupt; informal grease someone's palm, give someone a backhander, give someone a sweetener, keep someone sweet, get at, fix, square; Brit. informal nobble.
▸ noun informal *salmon trimmings are a good buy for making into mousse*: **purchase**, deal, bargain, investment, acquisition, addition, gain, asset, possession, holding.

buyer noun *the typical buyer of this product*: **purchaser**, shopper, customer, consumer, client, patron, investor, user; (**buyers**) clientele, patronage, public, trade, market; Law vendee; rare emptor.
▷ANTONYMS seller.

buzz noun **1** *the buzz of the bees*: **hum**, humming, buzzing, murmur, drone, whirr, whirring, fizz, fizzing, fuzz, hiss, singing, whisper; Brit. informal zizz; Medicine tinnitus; literary bombination, bombilation, susurration, susurrus; rare sibilation.
2 *there was an insistent buzz from her control panel*: **audible warning**, purr, purring, ring, ringing, note, tone, beep, bleep, warble, signal, alarm, alert.
3 informal *I'll give you a buzz*. See **call** (sense 3 of the noun).
4 informal *the buzz is that he's gone*. See **rumour** (sense 2).
5 informal *I got a buzz out of seeing the kids' faces*: **thrill**, feeling of excitement, feeling of euphoria, stimulation, glow, tingle; delight, joy, pleasure, fun, enjoyment; titillation; informal kick; N. Amer. informal charge.
▸ verb **1** *bees buzzed in the clover*: **hum**, drone, bumble, whirr, fizz, fuzz, hiss, sing, murmur, whisper; Brit. informal zizz; literary bombinate, bombilate, susurrate; rare sibilate.
2 *the intercom on her desk buzzed*: **purr**, sound, reverberate, ring, beep, bleep, warble.
3 informal *the director buzzed around checking camera angles*: **bustle**, scurry, scuttle, scramble, scamper, flutter, fuss; hurry, hasten, make haste, rush, race, dash, run, sprint, tear, shoot, charge, chase, career; Brit. scutter; informal scoot, beetle, whizz, hare, zoom, zip.
4 *the club is **buzzing with** excitement*: **have an air of**; be active, be lively, be busy, bustle, be bustling, hum, throb, vibrate, pulse, whirl.

by preposition **1** *he was arrested by the police | I broke it by forcing the lid*: **through the agency of**, **by means of**, under the aegis of, using, utilizing, employing, with the help of, with the aid of, as a result of, because of, by dint of, by way of, by virtue of, via, through.
2 *please be there by midday*: **no later than**, in good time for, at, before.
3 *the house by the lake*: **next to**, beside, next door to, alongside, by/at the side of, abreast of, adjacent to, cheek by jowl with, side by side with; near, close to, hard by, nearest to, neighbouring, adjoining, abutting, bordering, overlooking; connected to, connecting with, contiguous with, attached to.
4 *go by the building*: **past**, in front of, beyond.
5 *anything you do is all right by me*: **according to**, with, as far as ... is concerned, concerning.
▫ **by all means** *take your grandmother to see it by all means but she might not thank you for it!* **certainly**, indeed, of course, definitely, without (a) doubt, without question, unquestionably; affirmative.
▫ **by and large** *by and large, all of the chapters follow the same format*: **largely**, mostly, mainly, to a large extent, to a great extent, to a great degree, on the whole, chiefly, generally, in general, predominantly, substantially, primarily, overall, for the most part, in the main, principally, in great measure, preponderantly, first and foremost, for all intents and purposes, basically; usually, typically, commonly.
▫ **by oneself 1** *reading by oneself was encouraged only when it was raining*: **alone**, all alone, on one's own, in a solitary state, singly, separately, solitarily, unaccompanied, companionless, partnerless, unattended, unescorted, unchaperoned, solo; informal by one's lonesome; Brit. informal on one's tod, on one's lonesome, on one's jack, on one's Jack Jones. **2** *there is no possibility of creating anything either by oneself or in conjunction with others*: **unaided**, unassisted, without help, without assistance, by one's own efforts, under one's own steam, independently, single-handed(ly), solo, on one's own, alone, all alone, off one's own bat, on one's own initiative.
▸ adverb *people hurried by*: **past**, on, along, beyond.
▫ **by and by** *by and by you will learn the ropes*: **eventually**, ultimately, finally, in the end, as time goes on/by, one day, some day, sooner or later, in time, in a while, after a bit, in the long run, in the fullness of time, at a later time, at a later date, at length, at a future time/date, at some point in the future, in the future, in time to come, in due course.

bygone adjective *the values of a bygone age*: **past**, former, earlier, one-time, long-ago, gone by, previous, forgotten, lost, finished, completed, of old, ancient, antiquated, obsolete, departed, dead, extinct, defunct, out of date, outmoded, passé; literary of yore, olden, foregone; rare forepassed.
▷ANTONYMS present, recent.

by-law noun Brit. *a by-law banning public drinking in the town centre*: **local law**, regulation, rule.

bypass noun *a bypass round the city*: **ring road**, detour, diversion, circuitous route, roundabout way, alternative route; Brit. relief road; Brit. informal rat run.
▸ verb **1** *bypass the farm and continue to the road*: **go round**, go past, make a detour round, pass round; avoid, keep out of, don't go near.
2 *crime surveys attempt to bypass the problems of police statistics*: **avoid**, evade, dodge, escape, elude, circumvent, get round, skirt (round), find a way round, give a wide berth to, sidestep, steer clear of, get out of, shirk; informal duck.
3 *the unofficial Workers' Combine bypassed the official union structure*: **ignore**, pass over, miss out, omit, go over the head of, neglect; informal short-circuit.

by-product noun *he saw poverty as the by-product of colonial prosperity*: **side effect**, consequence, entailment, corollary, concomitant; ramification, aftermath, after-effect, repercussion, backlash, ripple, shock wave, spin-off, fallout, heritage, fruits; Brit. knock-on effect; technical externality.

bystander noun *the police had shot dead an innocent bystander*: **onlooker**, passer-by, non-participant, observer, spectator, eyewitness, witness, looker-on, sightseer, watcher, viewer, gaper; informal gawper, rubberneck; literary beholder.
▷ANTONYMS participant.

byword noun **1** *the Court of Chancery had become a **byword for** administrative delay*: **perfect example of**, classic case of, model of, exemplar of, embodiment of, incarnation of, personification of, epitome of, typification of; synonymous with; rare avatar of.
2 *reality was his byword*: **slogan**, motto, maxim, axiom, dictum, mantra, catchword, watchword, formula, cry, battle cry, rallying cry; nickname, middle name; rare apophthegm.

cab noun **1** *she hailed a cab*: **taxi**, taxi cab, minicab, hackney cab; Brit. formal hackney carriage; N. Amer. **hack**; historical **fiacre**.
2 *a truck driver's cab*: **compartment**, driver's compartment, cabin.

cabal noun *a cabal of dissidents*: **clique**, faction, coterie, group, set, band, party, camp, gang, ring, cell, sect, caucus, league, confederacy, junta; pressure group; Brit. **ginger group**; Austral./NZ **push**; historical **junto**; rare camarilla.

cabaret noun **1** *the evening's cabaret*: **entertainment**, show, floor show, performance.
2 *the dance halls and cabarets of Montreal*: **nightclub**, club, boîte, supper club; N. Amer. **cafe**; informal **nightspot**, **hot spot**, **niterie**, **clip joint**; Brit. informal, dated **drum**; N. Amer. informal **honky-tonk**.

cabin noun **1** *a first-class cabin on the liner*: **berth**, stateroom, compartment, room, deckhouse, sleeping quarters; forecabin, outside cabin; historical **roundhouse**.
2 *an aircraft cabin*: **compartment**, passenger area, passenger accommodation.
3 *a cabin by the lake*: **hut**, log cabin, shanty, shack, shed; chalet; Scottish **bothy**, **shieling**, **shiel**, **but and ben**; N. Amer. **cabana**; Canadian **tilt**; Austral. **mia-mia**, **gunyah**, **humpy**; NZ **whare**; S. African **hok**; archaic **cot**; N. Amer. archaic **shebang**.
4 *the driver's cabin*: **cab**, compartment.

cabinet noun **1** *an inlaid walnut cabinet*: **cupboard**; case, container.
2 *the first meeting of the new cabinet*: **senior ministers**, ministry, council, counsellors, administration, executive; inner circle; senate.

cable noun **1** *a thick cable moored the ship to the dock*: **rope**, cord, line, guy, piece of cordage; wire, chain; Nautical **hawser**, **stay**, **bridle**, **topping lift**; N. Amer. **choker**.
2 *electric cables*: **wire**, lead, cord; power line; Brit. **flex**.

cache noun **1** *a cache of arms was seized in North London | a cache of gold coins*: **hoard**, store, stockpile, stock, supply, collection, accumulation, reserve, fund; arsenal; hidden treasure, treasure; nest egg; informal **stash**; rare **amassment**.
2 *a niche in the rocks that could be used for a cache*: **hiding place**, storage place, secret place, hole; hideout; informal **hidey-hole**; informal, dated **stash**.

cachet noun *no other shipping company had quite the cachet of Cunard*: **prestige**, prestigiousness, distinction, status, standing, kudos, snob value, stature, prominence, importance, pre-eminence, eminence; street credibility; merit, value; NZ **mana**; informal **street cred**.

cackle verb **1** *the geese cackled at him*: **squawk**, cluck, clack.
2 *Noel left the room, cackling with glee*: **laugh loudly**, laugh uproariously, guffaw, crow, chortle, chuckle, giggle, tee-hee; informal **laugh like a drain**.

cacophonous adjective *cacophonous rock music blared from the speakers*: **loud**, noisy, ear-splitting, blaring, booming, thunderous, deafening; **raucous**, discordant, dissonant, inharmonious, unmelodious, unmusical, tuneless, harsh, strident, screeching, screechy, grating, jarring, jangling; rare **horrisonant**, **absonant**.
▷ANTONYMS harmonious, sweet.

cacophony noun *despite the cacophony, Rita slept on*: **din**, racket, noise, discord, dissonance, discordance, caterwauling, raucousness, screeching, jarring, stridency, grating, rasping.

cad noun dated *her adulterous cad of a husband*. See **scoundrel**.

cadaver noun See **corpse**.

cadaverous adjective *his cadaverous face | a tall, cadaverous figure*: **(deathly) pale**, pallid, white, bloodless, ashen, ashen-faced, ashy, chalky, chalk-white, grey, white-faced, whey-faced, waxen, waxy, corpse-like, deathlike, ghostly; **very thin**, as thin as a rake, bony, skeletal, emaciated, skin-and-bones, scrawny, scraggy, raw-boned, haggard, gaunt, drawn, pinched, hollow-cheeked, hollow-eyed; informal **like death warmed up**, **like a bag of bones**, **anorexic**; dated **spindle-shanked**; rare **livid**, **etiolated**, **lymphatic**, **exsanguinous**, **starveling**, **macilent**.
▷ANTONYMS rosy, florid; fat, plump.

cadence noun *there is a biblical cadence in the last words he utters*: **rhythm**, tempo, metre, measure, rise and fall, beat, pulse, rhythmical flow/pattern, swing, lilt, cadency; **intonation**, modulation, inflection, speech pattern.

cadge verb informal *can I cadge £5 off you?* **scrounge**, beg, borrow; informal **bum**, **touch someone for**, **sponge**; Brit. informal **scab**; Scottish informal **sorn on someone for**; N. Amer. informal **mooch**; Austral./NZ informal **bludge**.

cadre noun *a cadre of academic specialists*: **small group**, body, team, corps; core, nucleus, key group.

cafe, café noun **snack bar**, cafeteria, buffet; coffee bar, coffee shop, tea room, tea shop; restaurant, bistro, brasserie, wine bar, cafe bar, cybercafe; Brit. **milk bar**; N. Amer. **diner**; informal **greasy spoon**, **eatery**, **noshery**; Brit. informal **caff**; dated **pull-up**, **pull-in**; rare **estaminet**.

cafeteria noun **self-service restaurant**, canteen, cafe, restaurant, buffet; N. Amer. dated **automat**.

cage noun *people are increasingly uneasy about going to see animals in cages*: **enclosure**, pen, pound; coop, hutch, crate; birdcage, aviary, mew; N. Amer. **corral**.
▶verb *many animals are captured and caged in conditions of extreme cruelty*: **confine**, shut in/up, pen, lock up, coop up, immure, incarcerate, imprison, impound; mew; N. Amer. **corral**.

cagey adjective informal *he was rather cagey about his plans*: **secretive**, guarded, non-committal, tight-lipped, reticent, cautious, circumspect, chary, wary, careful, evasive, elusive, equivocal; discreet; informal **playing one's cards close to one's chest**.
▷ANTONYMS frank, open.

cahoots plural noun informal
□ **in cahoots** *politicians accused of being in cahoots with the Mafia*: **in league**, colluding, in collusion, conspiring, conniving, collaborating, hand in glove, allied, in alliance.

cajole verb *he had been cajoled into escorting Nadia to a concert*: **persuade**, wheedle, coax, talk into, manoeuvre, get round, prevail on, beguile, blarney, flatter, seduce, lure, entice, tempt, inveigle, woo; informal **sweet-talk**, **soft-soap**, **butter up**, **twist someone's arm**; archaic **blandish**.
▷ANTONYMS bully.

cajolery noun *it had proved impossible to resist Rose's cajolery*: **persuasion**, **wheedling**, coaxing, inveiglement; blandishments, blarney, beguilement, flattery, honeyed words, flattering; informal **sweet talk**, **sweet-talking**, **soft soap**, **soft-soaping**, **arm-twisting**; Brit. informal **flannel**; Austral./NZ informal **guyver**; archaic **glozing**, **lipsalve**; rare **cajolement**, **suasion**.
▷ANTONYMS bullying.

cake noun **1** *a plate of cream cakes*: **gateau**, kuchen.
2 *a cake of soap*: **bar**, tablet; block, slab, lump, cube, loaf, chunk, brick; piece.
▶verb **1** *a pair of boots caked with mud*: **cover**, coat, encrust, plaster, spread thickly, smother.

2 *the blood under his nose was beginning to cake*: **clot**, congeal, coagulate, thicken; solidify, harden, set, dry; rare inspissate.
▷ANTONYMS liquefy.

> *Word links* **cake**
>
> **patissier** maker or seller of cakes
> **patisserie** shop selling cakes

C

calamitous adjective *the consequences of his decision were calamitous*: **disastrous**, catastrophic, cataclysmic, devastating, dire, tragic, fatal, ruinous, crippling, awful, dreadful, terrible, woeful, grievous; literary direful.
▷ANTONYMS good, advantageous.

calamity noun *the fire was only the latest calamity to strike the area*: **disaster**, catastrophe, tragedy, cataclysm, devastating blow, crisis, adversity, blight, tribulation, woe, affliction, evil; misfortune, misadventure, accident, stroke of bad luck, reverse of fortune, setback, mischance, mishap; archaic bale; Scottish archaic mishanter.
▷ANTONYMS godsend, blessing.

calculate verb **1** *the interest charged is calculated on a daily basis*: **compute**, work out, reckon, figure, enumerate, determine, evaluate, quantify, assess, cost, put a figure on; add up, add together, count up, tally, total, totalize; calibrate, gauge; Brit. tot up; rare cast.
2 *his last words were calculated to wound her*: **intend**, mean, design, plan, aim.
3 *we had* **calculated on** *a quiet Sunday*: **expect**, anticipate; reckon, bargain, rely, depend, count, bank; take as read; N. Amer. informal figure on.

calculated adjective *a vicious and calculated assault* | *a calculated risk*: **deliberate**, **premeditated**, planned, pre-planned, preconceived, intentional, intended, done on purpose, purposeful, purposive, thought out in advance; aforethought; considered, conscious, studied, strategic; Law, dated prepense.
▷ANTONYMS unintentional, spontaneous; reckless.

calculating adjective *a coolly calculating, ruthless man*: **cunning**, crafty, wily, shrewd, scheming, devious, designing, conniving, manipulative, Machiavellian, artful, guileful, slippery, slick, sly, disingenuous, unscrupulous; informal foxy; S. African informal slim; archaic subtle.
▷ANTONYMS ingenuous, artless; thoughtless.

calculation noun **1** *by my calculations, that makes £3,500* | *the calculation of the overall cost*: **computation**, reckoning, adding up, counting up, working out, determining, figuring, estimation, estimate; sum; Brit. totting up.
2 *the government's political calculations*: **assessment**, judgement; forecast, projection, prediction, expectation.

calendar noun **1** **almanac**; archaic ephemeris.
2 *my social calendar's pretty full*: **timetable**, schedule, programme, diary.

calibre noun **1** *they could ill afford to lose a man of his calibre*: **quality**, merit, distinction, character, worth, stature, excellence, superiority, eminence, pre-eminence; **ability**, expertise, talent, capability, capacity, proficiency, competence; gifts, endowments, strengths, qualifications.
2 *if only they could play rugby of this calibre every week*: **standard**, level, grade, quality.
3 *the calibre of a gun*: **bore**, diameter, gauge; size, measure.

call verb **1** *'Wait for me!' she called*: **cry out**, cry, shout, yell, sing out, whoop, bellow, roar, halloo, bawl, scream, shriek, screech; exclaim; informal holler, yoo-hoo, cooee; rare ejaculate, vociferate.
2 *I got so tired, Mum had to call me at least three times every morning*: **wake up**, wake, awaken, waken, rouse; informal give someone a shout; Brit. informal knock up.
3 *I'll call you tomorrow*: **phone**, telephone, get on the phone to, get someone on the phone, dial, make/place a call to, get, reach; Brit. **ring up**, ring, give someone a ring; informal call up, give someone a call, give someone a buzz, buzz; Brit. informal give someone a bell, bell, give someone a tinkle, get on the blower to; N. Amer. informal get someone on the horn.
4 *you'd better call the doctor* | *Rose called a taxi*: **summon**, send for, ask for; order; page.
5 *he* **called at** *Ashgrove Cottage on his way home*: **pay a visit to**, pay a brief visit to, visit, pay a call on, call in on, look in on; informal drop in on, drop by, stop by, pop into.
6 *the prime minister called a meeting of senior cabinet ministers* | *there was no alternative but to call a general election*: **convene**, summon, call together, order, assemble; **arrange**, arrange a time/date for; announce, declare; formal convoke.
7 *they called their daughter Hannah*: **name**; christen, baptize; designate, style, term, dub, label, entitle; archaic clepe; rare denominate; (**be called**) answer to the name of, go by the name of.
8 *he's the only person I would call a friend*: **describe as**, **regard as**, look on as, consider to be, judge to be, think of as, class as, categorize as.
□ **call for 1** *desperate times call for desperate measures*: **require**, need, necessitate, make necessary, demand; be grounds for, justify, warrant, be a justification/reason for; involve, entail. **2** *I'll call for you around seven*: **pick up**, collect, fetch, go/come to get, come for.
□ **call something into question** *the safety of milk was never really called into question*: **doubt**, distrust, mistrust, suspect, lack confidence in, have doubts about, be suspicious of, have suspicions about, have misgivings about, feel uneasy about, feel apprehensive about, cast doubt on, query, question, challenge, dispute, have reservations about; archaic misdoubt.
▷ANTONYMS trust.
□ **call something off** *the proposed tour to Australia was called off*: **cancel**, abandon, shelve, scrap, drop, mothball; informal axe, scrub, scratch, nix; N. Amer. informal redline.
□ **call on 1** *I thought I might call on her later today*: **visit**, pay a visit to, pay a call on, go and see, look in on; N. Amer. visit with, go see; informal look up, drop in on, pop in on. **2** *he called on the government to hold a plebiscite*: **appeal to**, ask, request, apply to, petition; urge; beg, implore, entreat, beseech, plead with. **3** *we are able to call on academic staff with a wide variety of expertise*: **have recourse to**, avail oneself of, turn to, draw on, look to, make use of, use, utilize, bring into play.
□ **call the shots** *directors call the shots and nothing happens on set without their say-so*: **be in charge**, be in control, be in command, be the boss, be at the helm, be in the driving seat, be at the wheel, be in the saddle, pull the strings, hold the purse strings; informal run the show, rule the roost; Brit. informal wear the trousers.
□ **call to mind 1** *the still lifes call to mind Cézanne's works*: **evoke**, put one in mind of, recall, bring to mind, call up, summon up, conjure up; echo, allude to. **2** *I cannot call to mind where I have seen you*: **remember**, recall, recollect, think; Scottish mind; archaic bethink oneself of.
□ **call someone up 1** informal *Roland called me up at the crack of dawn*: **phone**, telephone, call, get on the phone to, get someone on the phone, dial, make/place a call to, get, reach; Brit. **ring up**, ring, give someone a ring; informal give someone a call, give someone a buzz, buzz; Brit. informal give someone a bell, bell, give someone a tinkle, get on the blower to; N. Amer. informal get someone on the horn. **2** *they have called up more than 20,000 reservists*: **enlist**, recruit, sign up; conscript; US draft. **3** *he was called up for England's final Test at the Oval*: **select**, pick, choose; Brit. cap; informal give someone the nod.
▶ noun **1** *I heard calls of 'Come on Steve' from the auditorium*: **cry**, shout, yell, whoop, roar, scream, shriek; exclamation; informal holler; rare vociferation.
2 *the call of the water rail*: **cry**, song, sound.
3 *I'll give you a call tomorrow*: **phone call**, telephone call; Brit. **ring**; informal buzz; Brit. informal bell, tinkle.
4 *later that day, he paid a call on Harold Shoesmith*: **visit**, social call.
5 *the President issued a call for party unity*: **appeal**, request, plea, entreaty; **demand**, order, command.
6 *the last call for passengers on flight BA701*: **summons**, request.
7 *there's no call for that kind of language*: **need**, necessity, occasion, reason, justification, grounds, excuse, pretext; cause.
8 *there's no call for expensive wine here*: **demand**, desire, want, requirement, need; market.
9 *walkers can't resist the call of the Cairngorms*: **attraction**, appeal, lure, allure, allurement, fascination, seductiveness; magic, beauty, spell, pull, draw.
□ **on call** *one of the team will be on call around the clock*: **on duty**, on standby, standing by, ready, available.

call girl noun **prostitute**, whore, sex worker; French fille de joie, demi-mondaine; Spanish puta; N. Amer. sporting girl/woman/lady; informal tart, pro, moll, tail, brass nail, grande horizontale, woman on the game, working girl, member of the oldest profession; N. Amer. informal hooker, hustler, chippy; black English ho; euphemistic model, escort, masseuse; dated woman of the streets, lady/woman of the night, scarlet woman, cocotte; archaic courtesan, strumpet, harlot, trollop, woman of ill repute, lady of pleasure, Cyprian, doxy, drab, quean, trull, wench; rare sing-song girl.

calling noun **1** *those who have a special calling to minister to others' needs*: **vocation**, mission; call, summons.
2 *he considered engineering one of the highest possible callings*: **profession**, occupation, career, work, employment, job, business, trade, craft, line, line of work, pursuit, métier, walk of life, province, field; archaic employ.

callous adjective *his callous disregard for the feelings and wishes of others*: **heartless**, unfeeling, uncaring, cold, cold-hearted, hard, as hard as nails, hard-hearted, with a heart of stone, stony-hearted, insensitive, lacking compassion, hardbitten, cold-blooded, hardened, case-hardened, harsh, cruel, ruthless, brutal; unsympathetic, uncharitable, indifferent, unconcerned, unsusceptible, insensible, bloodless, soulless; informal hard-boiled; rare indurate, indurated, marble-hearted.
▷ANTONYMS kind, compassionate.

callow adjective *a callow youth*: **immature**, **inexperienced**, naive, green, as green as grass, born yesterday, raw, unseasoned, untrained, untried; juvenile, adolescent, jejune; innocent, guileless, artless, unworldly, unsophisticated; informal wet behind the ears.
▷ANTONYMS mature, experienced, sophisticated.

calm adjective **1** *her voice was steady and she seemed very calm*: **serene**, tranquil, relaxed, unruffled, unperturbed, unflustered, undisturbed, unagitated, unmoved, unbothered, untroubled; equable, even-tempered, imperturbable, quiet, steady; **placid**, peaceful, sedate, unexcitable,

impassive, dispassionate, unemotional, phlegmatic, stolid; **composed**, cool, collected, {cool, calm, and collected}, as cool as a cucumber, cool-headed, self-possessed, controlled, self-controlled, poised; informal unflappable, unfazed, together, laid-back; rare equanimous.
▷ANTONYMS excited, upset, nervous.
2 *the night was clear and calm*: **windless**, still, tranquil, quiet, serene, peaceful, pacific, undisturbed, restful, balmy, halcyon.
▷ANTONYMS windy, stormy.
3 *the calm waters of the lake*: **tranquil**, still, like a millpond, smooth, glassy, flat, motionless, waveless, unagitated, storm-free; literary stilly.
▷ANTONYMS rough, stormy.
▶ **noun 1** *in the centre of the storm, calm prevailed*: **tranquillity**, stillness, calmness, quiet, quietness, quietude, peace, peacefulness, serenity, silence, hush; restfulness, repose.
▷ANTONYMS violence, unrest.
2 *his usual calm deserted him*: **composure**, coolness, calmness, self-possession, sangfroid, presence of mind, poise, aplomb, self-control; serenity, tranquillity, equanimity, imperturbability, equability, placidness, placidity, impassiveness, impassivity, dispassion, phlegm, stolidity; informal cool, unflappability; rare ataraxy, ataraxia.
▷ANTONYMS anxiety.
▶ **verb 1** *I took him inside and tried to **calm him down** | he went round to the pub to calm his nerves*: **soothe**, pacify, placate, mollify, appease, conciliate; hush, lull, gentle, tranquillize; quell, allay, alleviate, assuage; Brit. quieten (down); Austral. square off; rare dulcify.
▷ANTONYMS excite, upset.
2 *she took a deep breath and forced herself to **calm down***: **compose oneself**, recover/regain one's composure, control oneself, recover/regain one's self-control, pull oneself together, keep one's head, simmer down, cool down, cool off, take it easy; Brit. quieten down; informal get a grip, keep one's cool, play it cool, keep one's shirt on, wind down, come back down to earth; N. Amer. informal chill out, hang loose, stay loose, decompress.
▷ANTONYMS lose one's temper.

Choose the right word calm, serene, tranquil, placid, peaceful

All these words indicate a freedom from disturbance or agitation, and all are used of people, concrete nouns, such as *water*, and abstract nouns, such as *look*.

Someone who is **calm** remains unperturbed in a worrying or frightening situation (*you were wonderful, coping with all of us and always calm*). *Calm* is often applied to a place where fighting or unrest is normal but is absent or has died down, and is the word most commonly used in connection with weather, to describe the *sea*, *day*, *weather*, or *sky*.

Serene suggests that a person has an inner calm and is used to describe their appearance or behaviour (*the serene beauty of her delicate golden face belied her years | an attitude of serene detachment*). It is also used of places that are relaxed, free from strife, and untouched by human cares (*charming properties of character await—secluded, historic and serene | Cologne is a city of serene parks*).

Tranquil is most commonly used of places that are relaxingly free from noise or disturbance—a *setting*, *scene*, *village*, or *garden*, in particular. It is also used to describe people or their lives (*most people over twenty never have a tranquil moment*).

Someone with a **placid** nature is not easily worried or upset (*a placid, contented family man | her usually placid temper began to stir*). *Placid* can have critical overtones, suggesting that someone is slow to react and rather dull (*moderate voters of placid and unreflective temperament*). *Placid* is also used to describe animals and children with a quiet, docile nature, as well as areas of calm water, such as a *bay*, *sea*, or *canal*.

Peaceful most commonly refers to an absence of conflict or aggression (*a peaceful solution to the Saharan conflict | 400,000 people participated in a peaceful demonstration*).

calumny noun *a bitter struggle marked by calumny and litigation*: **slander**, defamation (of character), character assassination, misrepresentation of character, evil-speaking, calumniation, libel; scandalmongering, malicious gossip, muckraking, smear campaign, disparagement, denigration, derogation, aspersions, vilification, traducement, obloquy, verbal abuse, backbiting, vituperation, revilement, scurrility; lies, slurs, smears, untruths, false accusations, false reports, insults, slights; informal mud-slinging; N. Amer. informal bad-mouthing; archaic contumely.

camaraderie noun *he enjoyed the camaraderie of army life*: **friendship**, **comradeship**, fellowship, good fellowship, companionship, brotherliness, brotherhood, sisterhood, closeness, affinity, togetherness, solidarity, mutual support; sociability; team spirit; French esprit de corps.

camouflage noun **1** *on the trenches were pieces of turf which served for camouflage*: **disguise**, concealment.
2 *an animal may adapt its camouflage to fit into a new environment*: **protective colouring**; technical cryptic colouring, cryptic coloration, mimicry.
3 *much of my apparent indifference was merely protective camouflage*: **facade**, front, false front, smokescreen, cover-up, disguise, mask, cloak, blind, screen, masquerade, concealment, dissimulation, pretence; subterfuge.
▶ **verb** *the caravan was camouflaged with netting and branches*: **disguise**, hide, conceal, keep hidden, mask, screen, veil, cloak, cover, cover up, obscure, shroud.

camp[1] noun **1** *an army camp | they went back to the camp and lit a fire*: **bivouac**, encampment, cantonment, barracks, base; campsite, camping ground; tents; S. African historical laager.
2 *both the liberal and conservative camps were annoyed by his high-handed manner*: **faction**, wing, side, group, party, lobby, caucus, bloc, clique, coterie, set, sect, cabal.
▶ **verb** *that night they camped in a field*: **pitch tents**, set up camp, pitch camp, encamp, bivouac; S. African outspan.

camp[2] informal **adjective 1** *a heavily made-up and highly camp actor*: **effeminate**, effete, foppish, affected, niminy-piminy, mincing, posturing; informal campy; informal, derogatory poncey, limp-wristed, pansyish, queeny, faggy.
▷ANTONYMS macho, virile.
2 *a film full of camp humour and slapstick*: **exaggerated**, theatrical, affected, mannered, flamboyant, extravagant; informal over the top, OTT, camped up.
▶ **verb**
□ **camp it up** *he camped it up a bit for the cameras*: **posture**, behave theatrically, behave affectedly, overact, overdo it, go overboard; informal show off, ham it up; N. Amer. informal cop an attitude.

campaign noun **1** *Napoleon's Russian campaign | the air campaign*: **military operation(s)**, manoeuvre(s); offensive, attack, advance, push, thrust; crusade, war, battle, engagement, action.
2 *the campaign to reduce harmful vehicle emissions | a new campaign against drinking and driving*: **crusade**, drive, push, effort, struggle, move, movement; operation, manoeuvre, course of action, strategy, set of tactics, battle plan; battle, war.
▶ **verb 1** *a movement **campaigning for** political reform*: **crusade**, fight, battle, work, push, press, strive, struggle, agitate; promote, advocate, champion, speak for, lobby for, propagandize.
2 *she campaigned as a political outsider*: **run/stand for office**, throw one's hat in the ring; canvass, electioneer, solicit votes; N. Amer. informal stump, take to the stump.

campaigner noun **crusader**, fighter, battler; champion, advocate, promoter, enthusiast; activist, demonstrator, reformer.

can noun *a can of paint | a petrol can*: **tin**, canister; jerrycan, oilcan; container, receptacle, vessel.

canal noun **1** *brightly painted barges chugged up the canal*: **inland waterway**, channel, watercourse, waterway; ship canal.
2 *the ear canal*: **duct**, tube, passage, vessel.

cancel verb **1** *the match was cancelled due to a frozen pitch*: **call off**, abandon, scrap, drop; postpone, mothball; informal scrub, scratch, axe, nix; N. Amer. informal redline.
2 *his visa had been cancelled | you must inform the bank in writing if you wish to cancel this instruction*: **annul**, invalidate, nullify, declare null and void, render null and void, void; **revoke**, rescind, retract, countermand, set aside, take back, withdraw, recall, repeal, overrule, override, abrogate, quash; extinguish, remit, retire; Law vacate, discharge; rare disannul, negate.
3 *rising unemployment had **cancelled out** the earlier economic gains*: **neutralize**, **counterbalance**, counteract, balance (out), countervail; negate, nullify, wipe out; offset, compensate for, make up for; rare negative, counterweigh.
4 *there is one paragraph that should be cancelled*: **delete**, cross out, strike out, put a line through, blue-pencil, scratch out, obliterate, blot out, cut out, expunge, efface, erase, rub out, eradicate, eliminate; Brit. trademark Tippex out; technical dele.

cancer noun **1** *most skin cancers are curable*: **malignant growth**, cancerous growth, malignant tumour, tumour, malignancy; technical carcinoma, sarcoma, melanoma, lymphoma, myeloma, neoplasm, metastasis, neurofibroma, teratoma, fibroadenoma, meningioma.
2 *racism is a cancer sweeping across Europe*: **evil**, blight, scourge, poison, canker, sickness, disease, pestilence, plague; rot, corruption.

Word links cancer

carcin- related prefix
carcinomatous relating to cancer
carcinogenic causing cancer
carcinophobia fear of cancer
oncology branch of medicine treating cancer

candid adjective **1** *his responses were remarkably candid*: **frank**, outspoken, forthright, blunt, open, honest, truthful, sincere, direct, straightforward, plain-spoken, bluff, unreserved, downright, not afraid to call a spade a spade, straight from the shoulder, unvarnished, bald; heart-to-heart,

intimate, personal, man-to-man, woman-to-woman; informal upfront, on the level; N. Amer. informal on the up and up; archaic round, free-spoken.
▷ANTONYMS secretive, guarded, insincere.
2 *it's better to let the photographer mingle and take candid shots*: **unposed**, informal, uncontrived, unstudied, impromptu; **spontaneous**, extemporary, natural.

C

Choose the right word **candid, frank, outspoken, forthright, blunt**

These words generally show admiration for openness and honesty, although this can be tinged with the feeling that some things are better concealed. They can all describe a person or the things they say or write.

A **candid** person keeps no secrets and does not gloss over distressing or discreditable facts (*he was candid about the difficulties | the head of the information directorate said only that discussions had been candid*). Such total openness is often welcome or unusual, as shown by the frequent accompanying use of *refreshingly*.

Frank, while very close in meaning to *candid*, suggests a greater bluntness and is more often used to describe painful or difficult revelations such as a *confession* or *admission*. It also suggests a down-to-earth openness on matters seen as sensitive or embarrassing (*frank discussion of sexual matters*).

Someone who is **outspoken** is unusually ready to risk unpopularity or even danger by expressing controversial opinions (*an outspoken critic of the military*). It is much more commonly used than the other four words to describe *critics, advocates, opponents, criticism, politicians*, and *leaders*.

Someone who is **forthright** says what they have to say, without fear or favour and in an uncompromising manner (*a forthright rejection of the idea of electoral pacts*).

Someone who is **blunt** may even take a perverse delight in mentioning sensitive issues or giving unwelcome news in an abrupt and unadorned way (*to be blunt, a substantial majority of candidates are not fully literate | blunt warnings about the dangers of smoking*).

candidate noun 1 *candidates applying for this position should be computer-literate*: **applicant**, job applicant, job-seeker, prospective employee; contender, contestant, nominee, aspirant, possibility, possible; interviewee; postulant, suitor, pretender; informal runner.
2 *A-level candidates*: **examinee**, entrant.
3 *the most likely candidate for the title of Designer of the Year*: **prospect**; informal bet.

candle noun **taper**, sconce; tallow candle, wax candle, Christmas candle, votary candle, paschal candle; archaic wax light, glim, rush candle, rushlight; rare bougie, cierge.

Word links **candle**

chandler maker or seller of candles
chandlery shop selling candles

candour noun *he spoke with a degree of candour unusual in political life*: **frankness**, openness, honesty, candidness, truthfulness, sincerity, forthrightness, directness, lack of restraint, straightforwardness, plain-spokenness, plain dealing, plainness, calling a spade a spade, unreservedness, bluffness, bluntness, outspokenness; informal telling it like it is.
▷ANTONYMS guardedness, evasiveness, insincerity.

candy noun N. Amer. See **confectionery**.

cane noun 1 *he carried a silver-topped cane*: **walking stick**, stick, staff; alpenstock, malacca, blackthorn, ashplant, rattan; crook; Austral./NZ waddy; historical ferule.
2 *tie the shoot to a cane if vertical growth is required*: **stick**, stake, rod, upright, pole, beanpole.
3 *he told the court he had been beaten with a cane every week*: **stick**, rod, birch; N. Amer. informal paddle; historical ferule.
▶ verb *Matthew was caned for bullying*: **beat**, strike, hit, flog, thrash, lash, birch, whip, horsewhip, strap, leather, flagellate, scourge; N. Amer. bullwhip; informal tan someone's hide, give someone a hiding, take a strap to, larrup; N. Amer. informal whale; rare yerk, quirt.

canker noun 1 *a plant which is very susceptible to canker*: **fungal disease**, fungal rot, plant rot; blight.
2 *ear cankers in rabbits are caused by a mite*: **ulcer**, ulceration, infection, sore, running sore, lesion, abscess, chancre.
3 *racism remains a canker at the heart of the nation*: **blight**, evil, scourge, poison, cancer, sickness, disease, pestilence, plague; rot, corruption.

cannabis noun **marijuana**, hashish, bhang, hemp, kef, kif, charas, ganja, sinsemilla; informal dope, hash, grass, pot, blow, draw, stuff, Mary Jane, tea, the weed, gold, green, mezz, skunkweed, skunk, reefer, rope, smoke, gage, boo, charge, jive, mootah, pod; Brit. informal wacky backy; N. Amer. informal locoweed; S. African dagga, zol.

cannibal noun **maneater**, people-eater; rare anthropophagite, anthropophagist.

cannon noun **mounted gun**, field gun, gun, piece of artillery, piece of ordnance; mortar, howitzer; informal big gun; historical carronade, bombard, culverin, falconet, long tom, serpentine; Brit. historical pom-pom.
▶ verb *the couple behind almost* **cannoned into** *us*: **collide with**, hit, run into, bang into, crash into, smash into, smack into, crack into, ram into, be in collision with, plough into; N. Amer. impact with; N. Amer. informal barrel into.

cannonade noun *the French troops resumed their cannonade*: **bombardment**, shelling, gunfire, artillery fire, barrage, battery, attack, pounding; volley, salvo, broadside, fusillade.

canny adjective *canny investors*: **shrewd**, astute, sharp, sharp-witted, discerning, acute, penetrating, discriminating, perceptive, perspicacious, clever, intelligent, wise, sagacious, sensible, judicious, circumspect, careful, prudent, cautious; cunning, crafty, wily, artful, calculating; informal on the ball, smart, savvy; Brit. informal suss, sussed; Scottish & N. English informal pawky; N. Amer. informal heads-up, as sharp as a tack; rare long-headed, sapient, argute.
▷ANTONYMS foolish, reckless.

canoe noun **kayak**, dugout, outrigger; in Alaska bidarka; in Central America pirogue; in NZ waka.

canon noun 1 *the appointment violated the canons of fair play and equal opportunity*: **principle**, rule, law, tenet, precept, formula; standard, convention, norm, pattern, model, exemplar; criterion, measure, yardstick, benchmark, test.
2 *a set of ecclesiastical canons*: **law**, decree, edict, statute, dictate, dictum, ordinance; rule, ruling, regulation; Roman Catholic Church decretal.
3 *the Shakespeare canon*: **(list of) works**, writings, oeuvre.

canonical adjective *the canonical method of comparative linguistics*: **recognized**, authoritative, authorized, accepted, sanctioned, approved, received, established, orthodox; standard, normal, usual, ordinary, stock, customary, regular, traditional.
▷ANTONYMS unorthodox, innovative.

canonize verb 1 *the last English saint to be canonized*: **beatify**, declare to be a saint.
2 *we have canonized freedom of speech as an absolute virtue*: **glorify**, acclaim; regard as sacred, deify, idolize, apotheosize; enshrine.

canopy noun **awning**, shade, sunshade, cover, covering; baldachin, tester, half-tester; Judaism chuppah; technical velarium.

cant[1] noun 1 *religious cant*: **hypocrisy**, **sanctimoniousness**, sanctimony, humbug, pietism, affected piety, insincerity, sham, lip service, empty talk, pretence; rare Pharisaism, Tartufferie.
▷ANTONYMS sincerity.
2 *thieves' cant*: **slang**, jargon, idiom, argot, patter, patois, vernacular, speech, terminology, language; informal lingo, -speak, -ese.

cant[2] verb *the deck canted some twenty degrees*: **tilt**, lean, slant, slope, incline, angle, be at an angle; tip, list, bank, heel.
▶ noun *the outward cant of the curving walls*: **slope**, slant, tilt, angle, inclination.

cantankerous adjective *a cantankerous old man*: **bad-tempered**, irascible, irritable, grumpy, grouchy, crotchety, tetchy, testy, crusty, curmudgeonly, ill-tempered, ill-natured, ill-humoured, peevish, cross, as cross as two sticks, fractious, disagreeable, pettish, crabbed, crabby, waspish, prickly, peppery, touchy, scratchy, splenetic, shrewish, short-tempered, hot-tempered, quick-tempered, dyspeptic, choleric, bilious, liverish, cross-grained; argumentative, quarrelsome, uncooperative, contrary, perverse, difficult, awkward; informal snappish, snappy, chippy, on a short fuse, short-fused; Brit. informal shirty, stroppy, narky, ratty, eggy, like a bear with a sore head; N. Amer. informal cranky, ornery, peckish, soreheaded; Austral./NZ informal snaky; informal, dated waxy, miffy.
▷ANTONYMS good-natured, affable.

canteen noun 1 *the staff canteen*: **restaurant**, cafeteria, refectory, mess hall; Brit. Military NAAFI; N. Amer. lunchroom; French popote; Russian stolovaya; S. African informal cafe de move-on.
2 *a canteen of water*: **container**; flask, bottle, skin; French bidon; S. African vatje.

canvass verb 1 *he's canvassing for the Green Party*: **campaign**, electioneer, solicit votes, drum up support; N. Amer. stump; Brit. informal doorstep; N. Amer. informal be a ward heeler.
2 *they promised to canvass all member clubs for their views*: **poll**, question, ask, survey, interview, sound out, ascertain the opinions of.
3 *they're canvassing support among shareholders*: **seek**, try to obtain, go after, make a pitch for.
4 *early retirement was canvassed as a solution to the problem of unemployment*: **propose**, suggest, submit, offer, air; **discuss**, debate, consider.

canyon noun **ravine**, gorge, gully, pass, defile, couloir; chasm, abyss, gulf; N. Amer. gulch, coulee, flume; American Spanish arroyo, barranca, quebrada; Indian nullah, khud; S. African sloot, kloof, donga; rare khor.

cap noun 1 *a small bottle with a white plastic cap*: **lid**, top, stopper, cork, bung, spile; ferrule; cover, covering; N. Amer. stopple.
2 *school leavers in cap and gown*: **mortar board**, academic cap; dated

trencher, trencher cap, square.
3 *he raised the cap on local authority spending*: **limit**, upper limit, ceiling; curb, check.
▶ **verb 1** *mountains capped with snow*: **top**, crown; **cover**, coat, blanket, mantle.
2 *his innings capped a great day for the Australians*: **round off**, crown, be a fitting climax to, put the finishing touch/touches to, perfect, complete.
3 *they tried to cap each other's stories*: **beat**, better, surpass, outdo, outshine, trump, top, upstage; improve on, go one better than; informal best.
4 Brit. *he was capped 22 times for England*: **choose**, select, pick, include; informal give someone the nod.
5 *council budgets will be capped*: **set a limit on**, put a ceiling on, limit, restrict, keep within bounds; curb, control, peg.

capability noun *the company's capability to understand and respond to customer needs | her professional capabilities*: **ability**, capacity, power, potential, potentiality; competence, proficiency, accomplishment, adeptness, aptitude, aptness, faculty, experience, skill, skilfulness, talent, flair; cleverness, intelligence; gift, strong point, forte, knack; informal know-how.
▷ANTONYMS inability, incompetence.

capable adjective *a very capable young woman*: **competent**, able, efficient, effective, proficient, accomplished, adept, apt, practised, experienced, qualified, skilful, skilled, masterly, talented, gifted; clever, intelligent; informal handy, useful; rare habile.
▷ANTONYMS incompetent, inept.
□ **be capable of 1** *I'm quite capable of looking after myself | I don't believe he's capable of murder*: **have the ability to**, have the potential to, be equal to (the task of), be up to; be disposed to, be inclined to, be prone to, be liable to, be likely to, be apt to; informal have what it takes to. **2** *the strange events are capable of rational explanation*: **be open to**, be susceptible of, admit of, allow of.

> *Choose the right word* **capable, competent, efficient, able**
>
> See **competent**.

capacious adjective *the car's capacious boot*: **roomy**, commodious, spacious, ample, big, large, sizeable, generous, extensive, substantial, vast, huge, immense; voluminous; rare spacey.
▷ANTONYMS cramped, small.

capacity noun **1** *the capacity of the freezer is 1.1 cubic feet*: **volume**, cubic measure; size, dimensions, measurements, magnitude, proportions, amplitude; room, space; extent, range, scope, compass.
2 *his capacity to inspire trust in others | the task was beyond my intellectual capacities*: **ability**, power, potential, potentiality; competence, competency, proficiency, accomplishment, adeptness, aptitude, aptness, faculty, skill, skilfulness, talent, flair; cleverness, intelligence; gift, strong point, forte, knack; experience; informal know-how.
▷ANTONYMS inability.
3 *in his capacity as Commander-in-Chief of the Armed Forces*: **position**, post, job, office, appointment; **role**, function.

cape[1] noun *she wore a black cape over a red velvet dress*: **cloak**, mantle, shawl, wrap, stole, tippet; S. American poncho, serape; Ecclesiastical cope, mozzetta, amice; archaic mantlet; rare pelisse, pelerine.

cape[2] noun *we could just make out the island from the cape*: **headland**, promontory, point, head, foreland, neck; bluff, cliff, precipice, prominence, projection, overhang; horn, hook, bill, ness, naze; peninsula; Scottish mull; rare chersonese.

caper verb *children were capering about the room*: **skip**, **dance**, romp, jig, frisk, gambol, cavort, prance, frolic, leap, hop, jump, bound, spring; rare curvet, rollick, capriole.
▶ **noun 1** *she did a little caper*: **dance**, **skip**, hop, leap, jump; rare curvet, gambado, gambade.
2 informal *I'm too old for this kind of caper*: **escapade**, stunt, prank, trick, practical joke, antics, high jinks, mischief, game, sport, fun, jest, jesting, jape; informal shenanigans, lark, skylarking; Brit. informal monkey tricks, monkey business; N. Amer. informal dido.

capital noun **1** *Warsaw is the capital of Poland*: **first city**, most important city, seat of government, centre of administration; metropolis.
2 *by 1977 he had amassed enough capital to pull off the property deal of the century*: **money**, finance(s), funds, the wherewithal, the means, assets, wealth, resources, reserves, stock, principal; working capital, investment capital; informal dough, bread, loot, the ready, readies, shekels, moolah, the necessary, wad, boodle, dibs, gelt, ducats, rhino, gravy, scratch, stuff, oof; Brit. informal dosh, brass, lolly, spondulicks, wonga, ackers; N. Amer. informal dinero, greenbacks, simoleons, bucks, jack, mazuma; Austral./NZ informal Oscar; informal, dated splosh, green, tin; Brit. dated l.s.d.; N. Amer. informal, dated kale, rocks, shinplasters; archaic pelf.
3 *he wrote the name in capitals*: **capital letter**, upper-case letter, block capital; informal cap; technical uncial, uncial letter, majuscule letter.
▶ **adjective** *capital letters*: **upper-case**, block; technical uncial, majuscule.

capitalism noun **private enterprise**, free enterprise, private ownership, privatized industries, the free market, individualism; laissez-faire.
▷ANTONYMS communism.

capitalist noun **financier**, investor, industrialist; magnate, tycoon, mogul, nabob; plutocrat, money man; informal fat cat, yuppie, loadsamoney, moneybags.

capitalize verb *the capacity of mature businesses to capitalize rapidly growing ventures*: **finance**, fund, underwrite, provide capital for, back, sponsor; N. Amer. bankroll; N. Amer. informal stake.
□ **capitalize on** *an attempt by the opposition to capitalize on the government's embarrassment*: **take advantage of**, profit from, turn to account, make capital out of, make the most of, exploit, benefit from, put to advantage; maximize; strike while the iron is hot, make hay while the sun shines; informal cash in on.

capitulate verb *by the end of the month, the rebels had been forced to capitulate*: **surrender**, give in, yield, admit defeat, concede defeat, give up the struggle, submit, back down, climb down, give way, cave in, succumb, crumble, bow to someone/something; relent, acquiesce, accede, come to terms; be beaten, be overcome, be overwhelmed, fall; lay down one's arms, raise/show the white flag; informal throw in the towel, throw in the sponge.
▷ANTONYMS resist, hold out.

capitulation noun *the capitulation of the Republican forces*: **surrender**, submission, yielding, giving in, succumbing, acquiescence, laying down of arms; fall, defeat.
▷ANTONYMS resistance.

caprice noun **1** *his wife's caprices and demands made his life impossible*: **whim**, whimsy, vagary, fancy, notion, fad, freak, humour, impulse, quirk, eccentricity, foible, crotchet, urge.
2 *the staff tired of his tyranny and his caprice*: **fickleness**, changeableness, volatility, inconstancy, capriciousness, fitfulness, unpredictability.
▷ANTONYMS stability.

capricious adjective *the capricious workings of fate*: **fickle**, inconstant, changeable, variable, unstable, mercurial, volatile, erratic, vacillating, irregular, inconsistent, fitful, arbitrary; impulsive, temperamental, wild, ungovernable; whimsical, fanciful, flighty, wayward, quirky, faddish, freakish; unpredictable, random, chance, haphazard.
▷ANTONYMS stable, consistent.

> *Choose the right word* **capricious, inconstant, changeable, fickle**
>
> See **inconstant**.

capsize verb *gale force winds capsized their small craft*: **overturn**, turn over, turn upside down, upset, upend, knock over, flip over, tip over, topple over, invert, keel over, turn turtle; Nautical pitchpole; archaic overset.
▷ANTONYMS right.

capsule noun **1** *he placed a capsule under his tongue*: **pill**, tablet, lozenge, pastille, pilule, drop, caplet, pellet, bolus, troche; informal tab.
2 *the bottle's capsule is lead-free*: **cover**, seal, cap, top.
3 *a space capsule*: **module**, craft, probe; detachable compartment, section.
4 *sow small pots with two or three capsules*: **seed case**, pod, shell, husk, hull, case, sheath; technical pericarp, exocarp, legume, integument.

captain noun **1** *the ship's captain*: **commander**, master, skipper; informal old man.
2 *the cup was presented to the winning team's captain*: **leader**, head, skipper; representative, figurehead; informal boss.
3 *a captain of industry*: **magnate**, tycoon, mogul, grandee, baron, nabob, mandarin, industrialist; chief, head, leader, boss, principal; informal number one, bigwig, big wheel, big cheese, big shot, big gun, big noise, top dog, fat cat; N. Amer. informal honcho, kahuna, top banana, big enchilada, macher.
▶ **verb** *a small vessel captained by a cut-throat*: **command**, skipper, run, be in charge of, have charge of, control, have control of, govern, preside over, direct, rule, manage, supervise, superintend.

caption noun *he designed a series of posters with the caption 'No one is innocent'*: **title**, heading, wording, head, legend, inscription, explanation, description, rubric, label, motto, slogan.

captious adjective *the losers were glum and captious*: **critical**, fault-finding, quibbling, niggling, cavilling, carping, criticizing, disapproving, censorious, judgemental, overcritical, hypercritical, pedantic, hair-splitting, pettifogging; informal nit-picking, pernickety.
▷ANTONYMS forgiving, easy-going.

captivate verb *his audiences found themselves captivated by his energy and enthusiasm*: **enthral**, **charm**, enchant, bewitch, fascinate, beguile, entrance, enrapture, delight, attract, allure, lure; win, ensnare, dazzle, absorb, engross, rivet, grip, hypnotize, mesmerize, spellbind; infatuate, enamour, seduce, woo, ravish.
▷ANTONYMS repel; bore.

captivating adjective *a lively and captivating young girl*: **charming**, **enchanting**, bewitching, fascinating, beguiling, entrancing, alluring, engaging, interesting, winning, delightful; attractive, beautiful,

charismatic; dazzling, engrossing, riveting, gripping, enthralling, spellbinding, seductive.
▷ANTONYMS repellent; boring.

captive noun *the policeman put handcuffs on the captive*: **prisoner**, convict, detainee, inmate; prisoner of war, POW, internee, hostage; slave, bondsman; informal jailbird, con; Brit. informal (old) lag; N. Amer. informal yardbird.
▶ adjective *she was against keeping wild animals captive*: **confined**, caged, incarcerated, locked up, penned up; chained, shackled, fettered, ensnared; restrained, under restraint, restricted, secure; jailed, imprisoned, in prison, interned, detained, in captivity, under lock and key, behind bars, in bondage, taken prisoner; captured.
▷ANTONYMS free.

C

captivity noun *he was weakened by his captivity*: **imprisonment**, confinement, internment, incarceration, custody, detention, restraint, constraint, committal, arrest; bondage, slavery, servitude, enslavement, subjugation, subjection; literary thraldom, thrall; archaic duress, durance.
▷ANTONYMS freedom.

captor noun *he managed to escape from his captors*: **jailer**, guard, incarcerator, custodian, keeper, enslaver; Law detainer.

capture verb **1** *a spy had been captured in Moscow*: **catch**, apprehend, seize, arrest; take prisoner, take captive, take into custody; imprison, detain, put/throw in jail, put behind bars, put under lock and key, incarcerate; lay hold of, abduct, carry off, take; trap, snare, ensnare, net, hook, reel in, land, beach; informal nab, collar, pinch, lift, nail, bust, pick up, bag, run in, haul in, pull in, feel someone's collar; Brit. informal nick.
▷ANTONYMS free.
2 *guerrillas captured a strategic district*: **occupy**, invade, conquer, seize, take, take over, take possession of, annex, subjugate; win, gain, secure.
3 *haunting music captures the atmosphere of a summer morning*: **express**, reproduce, represent, show, encapsulate, record.
4 *tales of pirates have captured the imagination of children through the centuries*: **engage**, attract, draw, gain, catch, grab, arrest, seize, hold.
▶ noun *he's extremely dangerous and will do anything to evade capture*: **arrest**, apprehension, seizure, being trapped, being taken prisoner, being taken captive, being taken into custody, imprisonment, being imprisoned; informal being nabbed, being collared, being pinched, being lifted.
▷ANTONYMS freedom; escape.

car noun **1** *an officer drove up in a car*: **motor car**, automobile, motor, machine; informal wheels, heap, crate, (old) banger, jalopy, limo; N. Amer. informal auto; US informal hooptie; archaic horseless carriage.
2 *they set off up the train to eat in the dining car*: **carriage**, coach; Brit. saloon; Indian bogie.

carafe noun *a carafe of white wine*: **flask**, jug, pitcher, decanter, bottle, flagon, container, vessel, ewer, crock, urn.

caravan noun **1** *they spent a fishing holiday in a caravan*: **mobile home**, camper, caravanette; N. Amer. trailer; informal van; Brit. trademark Dormobile.
2 *a gypsy caravan*: **wagon**, covered cart, van.
3 *the refugee caravan crossed the border*: **convoy**, procession, column, train, cavalcade, fleet, cortège, company, troop, band, group, assemblage.

carbuncle noun *the carbuncle on his neck*: **boil**, blister, sore, abscess, pustule, pimple, wart, papule, wen, whitlow, canker; swelling, lump, growth, outgrowth, eruption, infection, inflammation; technical vesication, furuncle.

carcass noun **1** *a lamb carcass*: **corpse**, cadaver, dead body, body, remains, skeleton, relics; informal stiff; archaic corse.
2 informal *shift your carcass from the seat*: **body**, person, self; backside; N. Amer. informal butt; Brit. vulgar slang arse; N. Amer. vulgar slang ass.

card noun **1** *paste it on a piece of stiff card*: **cardboard**, pasteboard, board, stiff paper.
2 *I'll send her some flowers and a card*: **greetings card**, postcard, Christmas card, birthday card, good luck card, get well card, sympathy card.
3 *she dug into her bag and produced her card*: **identification**, ID, credentials, papers; ID card, identification card, visiting card, business card, calling card.
4 *she paid for the goods with her card*: **credit card**, debit card, cash card, swipe card; informal plastic.
5 *the cards were dealt for the last hand*: **playing card**; plain card, picture card, tarot card; Brit. court card; N. Amer. face card; (**cards**) pack of cards.
□ **give someone their cards** Brit. informal *the firm has just given 74,000 workers their cards*: **dismiss**, give someone their notice, throw out, get rid of, lay off, make redundant, let someone go, discharge, cashier; informal sack, give someone the sack, fire, kick out, boot out, give someone the boot, give someone their marching orders, give someone the bullet, give someone the (old) heave-ho, give someone the elbow, give someone the push, show someone the door, send packing; Brit. informal turf out; dated out.
▷ANTONYMS employ, take on.
□ **on the cards** informal *a decisive victory was on the cards*: **likely**, possible, probable, expected, liable to happen, in the wind, in the air, in the offing, on the horizon, in view, in prospect, in store, to come.
▷ANTONYMS unlikely, out of the question.

cardinal adjective **1** *one of the cardinal principles of the law of trusts*: **fundamental**, basic, main, chief, primary, prime, principal, premier, first, leading, capital, paramount, pre-eminent; important, major, foremost, top, topmost, greatest, highest, key; essential, vital, crucial, intrinsic, integral, elemental, rudimentary, root, radical.
▷ANTONYMS unimportant.
2 *a black dress with cardinal trimmings*: **scarlet**, red, crimson, vermilion, cinnabar, wine, wine-coloured, claret, claret-red, claret-coloured; literary vermeil.

care noun **1** *foster-parents had the care of the child*: **safe keeping**, **supervision**, custody, charge, protection, keeping, keep, control, management, ministration, guidance, superintendence, tutelage, aegis, responsibility; guardianship, wardship, trusteeship, trust; provision of care, looking after; parenting, mothering, fathering.
▷ANTONYMS neglect.
2 *these chemicals need to be handled with care*: **caution**, carefulness, wariness, awareness, heedfulness, heed, attention, attentiveness, alertness, watchfulness, vigilance, circumspection, prudence, guardedness, observance.
▷ANTONYMS carelessness.
3 *she chose her words with care*: **discretion**, judiciousness, forethought, thought, regard, heed, mindfulness; conscientiousness, painstakingness, pains, effort, meticulousness, punctiliousness, fastidiousness; accuracy, precision.
▷ANTONYMS carelessness.
4 *a place where you can escape from the cares of the day*: **worry**, anxiety, trouble, disquiet, disquietude, bother, unease, upset, distress, concern; sorrow, anguish, grief, sadness, affliction, woe, hardship, tribulation, suffering, pain, torment, misery, angst; responsibility, stress, pressure, strain, perturbation, burdens.
▷ANTONYMS happiness.
5 *a life of unblemished virtue and constant care for others*: **concern**, consideration, attention, attentiveness, thought, regard, mind, notice, heed, solicitude, interest, caringness, sympathy, respect; looking after.
▷ANTONYMS disregard.
□ **take care of 1** *raising four children and taking care of two other foster children is no easy task*: **look after**, care for, attend to, tend, mind, minister to, take charge of, supervise, protect, guard; keep an eye on, keep safe, be responsible for, watch, sit with, nurse, babysit, childmind. **2** *the activity of beneficial predators usually takes care of such infestations when they occur*: **deal with**, cope with, handle, manage, attend to, see to, take charge of, take in hand, sort out, tackle.
▶ verb *the teachers didn't seem to* **care about** *our academic work*: **be concerned**, worry (oneself), trouble oneself, bother, mind; concern oneself with, be interested in, interest oneself in, trouble oneself with, have regard for, burden oneself with; informal give a damn, give a hoot, give a rap, give a hang, give a tinker's curse/damn, give a monkey's, lose sleep over, get worked up.
□ **care for 1** *he obviously cares for his children*: **love**, be fond of, feel affection for, cherish, hold dear, treasure, prize, adore, dote on, think the world of, worship, idolize, be devoted to; be in love with. ▷ANTONYMS hate.
2 *would you care for a cup of coffee?* **like**, wish for, want, desire, prefer, fancy, have a fancy for, take a fancy to, feel like; informal have a yen for.
3 *a hospice which cares for the terminally ill*: **look after**, take care of, tend, attend to, mind, minister to, take charge of, nurse, provide for, foster, protect, watch, guard; be responsible for, keep safe, keep an eye on; sit with, babysit, childmind. ▷ANTONYMS neglect.

career noun **1** *he spent three years training for a business career*: **profession**, occupation, vocation, calling, employment, job, line, line of work, walk of life, position, post, sphere; French métier.
2 *these unions had had a chequered career*: **existence**, life, progress, course, progression, passage, path.
▶ adjective *a career politician*: **professional**, permanent, full-time, committed.
▶ verb *he saw the runaway pram careering down the hill*: **rush**, hurtle, streak, shoot, race, bolt, dash, speed, run, gallop, stampede, cannon, careen, whizz, buzz, zoom, flash, blast, charge, hare, fly, wing, pelt, scurry, scud, go like the wind; informal belt, scoot, scorch, tear, skedaddle, zap, zip, whip, burn rubber, go like a bat out of hell; Brit. informal bomb, bucket, shift; N. Amer. informal hightail, clip, boogie.

carefree adjective *a carefree young woman*: **unworried**, untroubled, blithe, airy, nonchalant, insouciant, happy-go-lucky, free and easy, easy-going, blasé, devil-may-care, casual, relaxed, serene; cheerful, cheery, happy, merry, jolly, joyful, gleeful, glad; bright, sunny, buoyant, vivacious, bubbly, bouncy, breezy, jaunty, frisky; informal upbeat, laid back.
▷ANTONYMS anxious, careworn.

careful adjective **1** *be careful when you go up the stairs*: **cautious**, heedful, alert, aware, attentive, watchful, vigilant, wary, on guard, chary, circumspect, prudent, mindful, guarded; unhurried, measured, deliberate; informal leery, cagey.
▷ANTONYMS careless.
2 *Roland was careful of his reputation*: **mindful**, heedful, protective, watchful.
▷ANTONYMS careless.

3 *his mother had always been careful with money*: **prudent**, thrifty, economical, economic, economizing, sparing, frugal, scrimping, abstemious, canny, sensible, cautious; mean, miserly, niggardly, penny-pinching, parsimonious; informal stingy.
▷**ANTONYMS** extravagant.
4 *a careful driver | a careful consideration of the facts*: **attentive**, conscientious, painstaking, meticulous, diligent, assiduous, sedulous, scrupulous, punctilious, fastidious, methodical, orderly, deliberate, judicious, perfectionist; thorough, exhaustive, rigorous; accurate, precise, correct, particular; fussy, finicky; informal pernickety; archaic nice, laborious.
▷**ANTONYMS** inattentive.

careless adjective **1** *careless motorists*: **inattentive**, incautious, negligent, remiss; forgetful, absent-minded; heedless, irresponsible, impetuous, reckless; informal sloppy, couldn't care less, slap-happy.
▷**ANTONYMS** careful, attentive.
2 *an unsatisfactory excuse for incomplete or careless work*: **shoddy**, slapdash, slipshod, scrappy, slovenly, unconsidered, amateurish, negligent, lax, slack, wild, disorganized; hasty, hurried, perfunctory, cursory, thrown together, sketchy, hit-or-miss; inaccurate, imprecise, inexact, incorrect, wrong, erroneous, error-ridden; informal sloppy, slap-happy, scatterbrained; Brit. vulgar slang half-arsed.
▷**ANTONYMS** meticulous.
3 *a careless remark*: **thoughtless**, unthinking, insensitive, indiscreet, unguarded, ill-advised, ill-considered, ill-thought-out, unwise, misguided, incautious, inadvertent, rash, foolhardy; hasty, spur-of-the-moment, hare-brained.
▷**ANTONYMS** judicious.
4 *she was very **careless of** investments and spent too much of her capital*: **negligent in**, mindless of, heedless of, improvident about, unconcerned about, indifferent to, oblivious to; reckless about, remiss in, slapdash about, slipshod about, frivolous about; informal sloppy in, messy in.
5 *she saw him leaning with careless masculine grace against the wall*: **unstudied**, artless, casual, effortless, unconcerned, nonchalant, insouciant, languid, leisurely, informal; informal couldn't-care-less.

> *Choose the right word* **careless, heedless, thoughtless**
>
> Someone who is **careless** is not giving their full attention to what they are doing, typically in a situation where this could result in harm to themselves or to others (*try not to be so careless when you're handling glass | a motorist has been charged with causing death by careless driving*). The word may also be used to indicate that someone is relaxed and casual (*she moved with careless grace*), trying to appear so (*she managed to turn the wince into a careless shrug*), or genuinely unconcerned about something (*he was careless of his own safety*).
>
> **Heedless** indicates that someone is deliberately taking no notice of a factor which might be expected to influence their behaviour, either in their own interests (*she knelt on the floor, heedless of the cold stone*) or in those of others (*she brought him to a halt in the middle of the pavement, heedless of the passers-by*).
>
> **Thoughtless** is generally used to describe something done by a person who is insensitive, either consciously or unconsciously, to the feelings or convenience of others (*the thoughtless actions of a few loud-mouthed oafs*).

carelessness noun *the fire was caused through the carelessness of one of the workmen*: **inattention**, inattentiveness, heedlessness, thoughtlessness, negligence, improvidence, remissness; forgetfulness, absent-mindedness; irresponsibility, impetuosity, recklessness, rashness; laxity, laxness, slackness; clumsiness, ineptitude; oversight, omission, dereliction; informal sloppiness.
▷**ANTONYMS** carefulness.

caress verb *his hands caressed her back*: **stroke**, touch, fondle, brush, skim, pet, pat, nuzzle, kiss; cuddle, embrace, hug.
▶ noun *she enjoyed the light caress of his fingers*: **stroke**, stroking, touch, touching, fondle, fondling, skim, pat, nuzzle, nuzzling, kiss; cuddle, embrace, hug.

caretaker noun *he works as a caretaker for a block of flats*: **janitor**, warden, attendant, porter, custodian, keeper, watchman, steward, curator, concierge; N. Amer. superintendent.
▶ adjective *he has taken over as caretaker manager at Stoke*: **temporary**, short-term, provisional, substitute, acting, interim, pro tem, stand-in, fill-in, supply, stopgap, reserve, deputy; transitional, changeover; emergency, impromptu, rough and ready; Latin pro tempore, ad interim; N. Amer. informal pinch-hitting; rare expediential.
▷**ANTONYMS** permanent.

careworn adjective *his old face looked more haggard and careworn than usual*: **worried**, anxious, harassed, strained, stressed, under pressure, overburdened; tired, drained, drawn, gaunt, grim, haggard, pinched, exhausted, sapped, spent; informal hassled.
▷**ANTONYMS** carefree.

cargo noun *the ship's cargo*: **freight**, load, haul, consignment, delivery, shipment, contents, baggage, burden; goods, merchandise; shipload, boatload, lorryload, truckload, containerload; archaic lading; rare freightage.

caricature noun *a crude caricature of the Prime Minister*: **cartoon**, distorted/exaggerated drawing, distortion; parody, satire, lampoon, burlesque, mimicry, travesty, farce, skit, squib; informal send-up, take-off, spoof; rare pasquinade.
▶ verb *she has turned her acute eye and pen to caricaturing her fellow actors*: **parody**, satirize, lampoon, mimic, ridicule, mock, make fun of, burlesque; distort, exaggerate; informal send up, take off.

C

caring adjective *a caring, approachable employer*: **kind**, kind-hearted, warm-hearted, soft-hearted, tender, feeling; concerned, attentive, thoughtful, solicitous, responsible, considerate; affectionate, loving, doting, fond, warm, benevolent, benign, humane, good-natured, gentle, mild, indulgent, sympathetic, understanding, receptive, compassionate, charitable, gracious; long-suffering, patient.
▷**ANTONYMS** uncaring, cruel.

carnage noun *the carnage and suffering of the trenches*: **slaughter**, massacre, mass murder, mass destruction, butchery, bloodbath, indiscriminate bloodshed, bloodletting, annihilation, destruction, decimation, havoc; holocaust, pogrom, ethnic cleansing; informal shambles.

carnal adjective *the carnal desires of the flesh*: **sexual**, sensual, erotic, lustful, lascivious, libidinous, lecherous, licentious, lewd, prurient, salacious, coarse, gross, lubricious, venereal; **physical**, bodily, corporeal, fleshly, animal; informal sexy.
▷**ANTONYMS** spiritual.

carnival noun **1** *the town's raucous carnival*: **festival**, fiesta, fête, gala, jamboree, holiday, celebration, party; parade, procession, march, tattoo.
2 N. Amer. *he worked at a carnival, climbing Ferris wheels and working 18-hour days*: **funfair**, **circus**, fair, amusement show, sideshows.

carnivorous adjective *a carnivorous lizard*: **meat-eating**, predatory, of prey, hunting, raptorial; rare creophagous, zoophagous.
▷**ANTONYMS** herbivorous; vegetarian.

carol noun *children came from the village school to sing carols*: **Christmas song**, hymn, psalm, canticle; archaic noel.
▶ verb *'Yo heave ho,' carolled Boris happily*: **sing**, trill, chorus, warble, chirp, pipe, quaver, chant, intone; archaic wassail.

carouse verb *a band of sailors had gone ashore to carouse at the grog stalls*: **drink and make merry**, go on a drinking bout, go on a binge, binge, overindulge, drink heavily/freely, go on a pub crawl, go on a spree; have a party, revel, celebrate, feast, enjoy oneself, have a good time, roister, {eat, drink, and be merry}, frolic, romp; informal booze, go boozing, go on a bender, paint the town red, bend one's elbow, party, rave, have a ball, raise hell, make whoopee, live it up, whoop it up, have a fling; Brit. informal go on the bevvy; archaic wassail.

carp verb *broadcasters always found something to **carp about**, even after an undoubted success*: **complain**, cavil, grumble, moan, grouse, grouch, whine, bleat, quibble, niggle, nag; find fault with, criticize, pick on, censure, denounce, condemn, decry, disparage; informal gripe, beef, bellyache, bitch, whinge, nit-pick, pick holes, split hairs, sound off, kick up a fuss, knock; Brit. informal chunter, create, be on at someone; N. English informal mither; N. Amer. informal kvetch.
▷**ANTONYMS** praise.

carpenter noun **woodworker**, joiner, cabinetmaker; Scottish & N. English wright; Brit. informal chippy, Chips.

carpet noun **1** *a genuine Turkish carpet*: **rug**, mat, matting, floor covering, runner, drugget.
2 *a carpet of wild flowers*: **covering**, blanket, layer, cover, coat, coating, sheet, film, overlay, cloak, mantle, canopy, bed, expanse; crust.
▶ verb **1** *the gravel was carpeted in bright green moss*: **cover**, coat, overlay, overspread, blanket, overlie, extend over, pave.
2 Brit. informal *a top fraud officer has been carpeted for leaking information*. See **reprimand**.

carping adjective *she has silenced the carping critics with a massively successful debut tour*: **complaining**, cavilling, grumbling, moaning, grousing, grouching, grouchy, whining, bleating, fault-finding, quibbling, niggling, captious, nagging; critical, criticizing, censorious, condemnatory, disparaging, scathing, slighting, reproachful, deprecatory, hypercritical, overcritical, pedantic, hard/difficult/impossible to please; informal griping, bellyaching, bitching, whingeing, nit-picking, hair-splitting, picky; Brit. informal chuntering; N. English informal mithering; N. Amer. informal kvetching.
▷**ANTONYMS** forgiving; complimentary.

carriage noun **1** *a railway carriage*: **coach**; N. Amer. car; Brit. saloon; Indian bogie.
2 *a horse and carriage*: **wagon**, hackney, hansom, gig, landau, trap, caravan, car.
3 *the carriage of bikes on trains*: **transport**, transportation, conveyance, transfer, transference, delivery, distribution, carrying, transmission, movement, haulage, freight, freightage, portage, cartage, shipment.
4 *she had an erect carriage and a firm step*: **posture**, bearing, stance, gait, comportment; attitude, manner, presence, air, demeanour, mien, appearance; behaviour, conduct; Brit. deportment.

C

carrier noun *the carriers of wood and water came and went*: **bearer**, conveyor, transporter; porter, runner, courier, delivery man, delivery woman, haulier; dated carman.

carry verb **1** *she carried the box of food into the kitchen*: **convey**, transfer, move, take, bring, bear, shift, switch, fetch, transport; informal cart, lug, hump, schlep, tote.
2 *Britain's biggest coach operator carries 12 million passengers a year*: **transport**, convey, transmit, move, handle.
3 *satellites were used to carry the signal over the Atlantic*: **transmit**, conduct, pass on, relay, communicate, convey, impart, bear, dispatch, beam; disseminate, spread, circulate, diffuse.
4 *the dinghy would carry the weight of the baggage easily enough*: **support**, sustain, stand, prop up, shore up, bolster, underpin, buttress.
5 *managers carry as much responsibility as possible*: **undertake**, accept, assume, bear, shoulder, support, sustain; take on, take up, take on oneself; manage, handle, deal with, get to grips with, turn one's hand to.
6 *she told him the baby she was carrying was not his*: **be pregnant with**, bear, expect; technical be gravid with.
7 *she **carried herself** with a certain assurance*: **conduct**, bear, hold; act, behave, perform, acquit; rare comport, deport.
8 *a resolution was carried by an overwhelming majority*: **approve**, vote for, accept, endorse, ratify, authorize, mandate, support, back, uphold; agree to, consent to, assent to, acquiesce in, concur in, accede to, give one's blessing to, bless, give one's seal/stamp of approval to, rubber-stamp, say yes to; informal give the go-ahead to, give the green light to, give the OK to, OK, give the thumbs up to, give the nod to, buy.
▷ANTONYMS reject.
9 *this argument carried the day*: **win**, capture, gain, secure, effect, take, accomplish.
▷ANTONYMS lose.
10 *I spoke for forty minutes and carried the whole audience*: **win over**, sway, prevail on, convince, persuade, influence; affect, have an effect on, have an impact on, impact on, motivate, stimulate, drive, touch, reach.
11 *today's paper carried an article on housing policy*: **publish**, print, communicate, give, release, distribute, spread, disseminate; broadcast, transmit.
12 *we carry a wide assortment of hockey sticks*: **sell**, **stock**, keep, keep in stock, offer, have for sale, have, retail, market, supply, trade in, deal in, traffic in, peddle, hawk.
13 *most common domestic toxins carry poison warnings*: **display**, bear, exhibit, show, present, set forth, be marked with, have.
14 *contempt of court carries a maximum penalty of two years' imprisonment*: **entail**, involve, lead to, result in, occasion, have as a consequence, have; require, demand.
15 *his voice carried across the quay*: **be audible**, travel, reach, be transmitted.
□ **be/get carried away** *I'm afraid I got a bit carried away*: **lose self-control**, get excited, get overexcited, go too far, lose one's sense of proportion, be swept off one's feet; informal flip, lose it.
□ **carry someone off** *his elder brother had been carried off by consumption*: **kill**, kill off, cause the death of, cause to die, take/end the life of, dispatch, finish off; informal polish off, do in.
□ **carry something off 1** *her co-star carried off four awards*: **win**, secure, capture, gain, achieve, attain, earn, obtain, acquire, procure, get, collect, pick up, come away with; informal land, net, bag, bank, pot, scoop, walk off/away with.
2 *against the odds, he has carried it off*: **succeed in**, triumph in, be victorious in, achieve success in, be successful in, be a success in, do well at, make good in; informal crack.
□ **carry on 1** *she didn't have the strength to carry on arguing*: **continue**, keep on, keep, keep at, go on, push on, press on, persist in, persevere in, not stop, maintain; informal stick with/at. ▷ANTONYMS stop.
2 *it's just not the English way of carrying on*: **behave**, act, perform, conduct oneself, acquit oneself, bear oneself, carry oneself; rare comport oneself, deport oneself.
3 Brit. informal *his wife had been carrying on with other men*: **have an affair**, commit adultery, philander, dally, be involved; informal play around, have a fling, mess about/around, play away; N. Amer. informal fool around.
4 *I abused the teachers and was always carrying on*: **misbehave**, behave badly, make mischief, get up to mischief, be mischievous, act up, cause trouble, cause a fuss/commotion, get/be up to no good, be bad, be naughty, clown about/around, fool about/around, mess about/around, act the clown, act the fool, act the goat, act foolishly; informal create; Brit. informal muck about/around, play up. ▷ANTONYMS behave.
□ **carry something on** *a bank carrying on a bona fide business*: **engage in**, conduct, undertake, be involved in, take part in, participate in, carry out, perform, direct.
□ **carry something out 1** *the decision to carry out a Caesarean section*: **conduct**, perform, implement, execute, discharge, bring about, bring off, effect; rare effectuate.
2 *I carried out my promise to her*: **fulfil**, carry through, implement, execute, effect, discharge, perform, honour, redeem, make good; keep, observe, abide by, comply with, obey, respect, conform to, stick to, act in accordance with, act according to, have regard to, heed, follow, pay attention to, defer to, take notice of, be bound by, keep faith with, stand by, adhere to.
▷ANTONYMS break.

carry-on noun Brit. informal *he was not going to stand for any of this carry-on*: **fuss**, commotion, trouble, bother, upset, agitation, stir, excitement, ado, hurly-burly, palaver, rigmarole; nonsense; informal hoo-ha, ballyhoo, song and dance, performance, pantomime, hoopla, rumpus, monkey business, jiggery-pokery; Brit. informal carrying-on, kerfuffle.

cart noun **1** *a horse-drawn cart*: **wagon**, carriage; archaic wain.
2 *a man with a cart took their luggage*: **handcart**, pushcart, trolley, barrow, wheelbarrow.
▸ verb *he had the wreckage carted away*: **transport**, convey, haul, transfer, move, conduct, transmit, shift, fetch, take, ferry; **carry**, lug, tote, heave, heft, drag; informal hump, schlep.

cartilage noun

> *Word links* **cartilage**
>
> **chondro-** related prefix, as in *chondrocyte*

carton noun *a carton of ice cream*: **box**, package, cardboard box, container, case, pack, packet, parcel.

cartoon noun **1** *a cartoon of the Prime Minister*: **caricature**, parody, lampoon, satire, travesty; distorted/exaggerated drawing, distortion; informal take-off, send-up, spoof; rare pasquinade.
2 *he could often be found reading cartoons at this time of day*: **comic strip**, cartoon strip, comic, graphic novel; Japanese manga.
3 *they watched the Saturday morning cartoons on television*: **animated film**, animated cartoon, animation; Japanese anime.
4 *we have detailed cartoons for the production of another full-size portrait*: **sketch**, rough, preliminary drawing, outline, delineation, tracing; technical wireframe, underdrawing, maquette, ébauche, esquisse, croquis.

cartridge noun **1** *the toner cartridge slots neatly into place*: **cassette**, magazine, cylinder, canister, container, capsule, case, pack, packet, package.
2 *a rifle cartridge*: **bullet**, round, shell, charge, shot, casing.

carve verb **1** *he used to carve horn handles for walking sticks*: **sculpt**, sculpture; cut, chisel, hew, whittle, chip, hack, slash; form, shape, fashion.
2 *I carved my initials on the tree*: **engrave**, etch, notch, cut in, incise, score, print, mark.
▷ANTONYMS erase.
3 *he stood carving the roast chicken*: **slice**, cut up, chop, dice.
□ **carve something up** *the Empire was carved up into three kingdoms*: **divide**, partition, parcel out, apportion, subdivide, split up, break up, separate out, segregate, measure out; share out, dole out; informal divvy up.
▷ANTONYMS unify; reunify.

carving noun *a carving of an elephant*: **sculpture**, model, statue, statuette, figure, figurine, effigy; bust, head.

> *Word links* **carving**
>
> **glyptic** relating to carving

cascade noun *a delightful boulder-strewn ravine with a series of cascades*: **waterfall**, falls, water chute, cataract, rapids, torrent, flood, deluge, outpouring, white water, fountain, shower, avalanche; N. English force; Scottish archaic linn.
▸ verb *rain cascaded from the veranda roof*: **pour**, gush, surge, spill, stream, flow, issue, spurt, jet; tumble, descend, fall, drop, plunge, pitch; overflow.

case[1] noun **1** *this moral panic is a classic case of overreaction*: **instance**, occurrence, occasion, manifestation, demonstration, exhibition, exposition, expression; **example**, illustration, specimen, sample, exemplification, type, prototype.
2 (**the case**) *he told me that if that was the case I would have to find somebody else*: **the situation**, the position, the picture, the state of affairs, the state of play, the lie of the land; plight, predicament; event, contingency; circumstances, conditions, facts; how things stand, what's going on; informal kettle of fish, ball game, score, story, set-up.
3 *officers on the case are unable to find a motive*: **investigation**, enquiry, examination, exploration, probe, search, scrutiny, scrutinization, study, inspection, inquest, reconnoitring, sounding; **incident**, event, happening, occurrence, episode, proceeding, matter, affair, set of circumstances.
4 *urgent cases were turned away from the hospital*: **patient**, sick person, invalid, sufferer, victim; client.
5 *he lost his case and was ordered to pay £1.5 million in damages*: **lawsuit**, action, legal action, suit, suit at law, cause, legal cause, trial, proceedings, legal proceeding(s), judicial proceedings, litigation, legal process, legal dispute, indictment.
6 *this book makes a strong case for new research methods*: **argument**, contention, reasoning, logic, defence, justification, vindication, apology, polemic; statement, postulation, explanation, exposition, thesis, presentation, proclamation, expounding, claim; plea, appeal, petition.

7 *the genitive case*: **inflection**, form, ending; morphology; semantic relationship.

case² noun **1** *a monogrammed cigarette case*: **container**, box, canister, cassette, cartridge, receptacle, holder, vessel, repository; dated etui.
2 *a seed case*: **casing**, covering, sheath, sheathing, wrapper, wrapping, cover, envelope, sleeve, housing, jacket, capsule, folder; technical integument.
3 Brit. *she hastily threw some clothes into a case*: **suitcase**, bag, travelling bag, travel bag, valise, grip, holdall, portmanteau; piece of luggage, item of baggage; briefcase, attaché case, Gladstone bag; trunk, chest; (**cases**) luggage, baggage.
4 *a case of wine*: **crate**, box, pack, bin, coffer, casket, chest, basket, hamper.
5 *his art collection sparkled in a glass display case*: **cabinet**, cupboard, chiffonier, bureau, sideboard.
▸ verb **1** *the Lee–Enfield rifle is cased in wood from butt to muzzle*: **cover**, surround, coat, encase, sheathe, wrap, envelop.
2 informal *he went from room to room like a thief casing the joint*: **reconnoitre**, inspect, investigate, examine, scrutinize, survey, scout, explore, make an observation of, take stock of; informal recce, make a recce of, check out.

cash noun **1** *a wallet stuffed with cash*: **money**, ready money/cash, currency, legal tender, hard cash; notes, bank notes; coins, coinage, coin, coin of the realm, change, silver, copper; N. Amer. bills; informal dough, bread, loot, the ready, readies, shekels, moolah, wad, boodle, dibs, gelt, ducats, rhino, gravy; Brit. informal dosh, brass, lolly, spondulicks, wonga, ackers; N. Amer. informal greenbacks, dinero, simoleons, bucks, jack, mazuma; Austral./NZ informal Oscar; informal, dated splosh, green, tin; Brit. dated l.s.d.; N. Amer. informal, dated kale, rocks, shinplasters; formal specie.
▷ANTONYMS cheque, credit.
2 *thousands of hospital beds are closing because of a lack of cash*: **finance**, resources, funds, money, means, assets, wherewithal, capital, investment capital.
▸ verb *the bank cashed her cheque*: **exchange**, change, convert into cash/money, turn into cash/money, encash, realize, liquidate; honour, pay, accept, take.
□ **cash in on** *the band is cashing in on merchandising*: **take advantage of**, turn to one's advantage, exploit; make money from, profit from, do well out of; milk, bleed, suck dry, squeeze, wring; informal make a killing out of.

cashier¹ noun *he hands the day's takings to the cashier*: **clerk**, bank clerk, teller, bank teller, banker, treasurer, bursar, purser; accountant, bookkeeper, controller, money man.

cashier² verb *he was cashiered from the army on charges of insubordination*: **dismiss**, discharge, expel, drum out, throw out, cast out, discard, get rid of; informal sack, fire, give someone the boot, boot out, kick out, send packing, give someone their marching orders, give someone the bullet, give someone the push, show someone the door.

casing noun *the hard disk is safe from damage in its casing*: **cover**, case, shell, envelope, sheath, sheathing, wrapper, wrapping, sleeve, jacket, housing, capsule, folder; technical integument.

casino noun *he enjoyed a flutter at the casino*: **gambling house**, gambling club, gaming club, gambling den; German kursaal; dated gaming house.

cask noun *a cask of cider*: **barrel**, keg, butt, tun, vat, drum, tank, vessel, hogshead, firkin, kilderkin, pipe, pin; archaic puncheon, tierce.

casket noun **1** *a small casket containing four black opals*: **box**, chest, case, container, receptacle, coffer, trunk, crate; rare pyxis.
2 N. Amer. *the casket of a soldier who had died fighting*: **coffin**, box; informal wooden overcoat; historical sarcophagus, cist.

cast verb **1** *he cast the stone into the stream*: **throw**, toss, fling, pitch, hurl, bowl, dash, shy, lob, launch, flip, let fly, direct, discharge, project, propel, send; informal chuck, heave, sling, bung.
2 *fishermen cast their nets into the sea*: **spread**, throw, lay out, open out, unroll, fan out, stretch out.
3 *she cast a fearful glance over her shoulder*: **direct**, shoot, turn, throw, send, dart, bestow, give.
4 *each adult citizen has the right to cast a vote*: **register**, record, enter, file, lodge, post, set down, vote; allot, assign, give.
5 *the fire cast a soft light*: **emit**, give off, send out, send forth, shed, radiate, diffuse, spread out.
6 *the figures cast dancing shadows on the carpet*: **form**, create, make, produce, cause; project, throw.
7 *the stags' antlers are cast each year*: **shed**, discard, slough off, throw off, get rid of, let fall, let drop; moult, peel off; technical exuviate.
8 *until the 1880s printing type was cast by hand*: **mould**, fashion, form, shape, model; sculpt, sculpture, frame, forge, carve; make, create, build, manufacture.
9 *he gave lectures on astrology and cast horoscopes in his spare time*: **calculate**, devise, compute, reckon, determine, assess, work out, formulate, record, write; predict, forecast, foretell, foresee, prophesy.
10 *they were cast as extras in the film*: **choose**, select, pick, name, nominate, assign, appoint, give/assign the part to.
□ **cast aside** *he glanced down at a newspaper that had been cast aside*: **discard**, reject, cast/throw away, cast/throw out, dispense with, get rid of, dispose of, abandon.
□ **cast away** *he returned home three years after being cast away on the island*: **shipwreck**, wreck; strand, leave stranded, maroon, cast ashore, abandon, leave behind, leave; informal leave high and dry; archaic forsake.
□ **cast down** *she could not bear to see him so miserable and cast down*: **depressed**, downcast, unhappy, sad, miserable, gloomy, down, low, blue, melancholy, doleful, mournful; dejected, dispirited, discouraged, disheartened, downhearted, demoralized, daunted, dismayed, desolate, disconsolate, crestfallen, crushed, sapped, shaken, undermined, despondent, weighed down, oppressed, wretched.
▸ noun **1** *a cast of the writer's hand was taken*: **mould**, die, form, matrix, shape, casting, template, pattern, frame; sculpture, model, replica, copy, representation, mock-up, imitation, reproduction, figure.
2 *a cast of the dice*: **throw**, toss, fling, pitch, hurl, shy, lob, flip; informal chuck, heave, sling, bung, go.
3 *a child with an enquiring, ironical cast of mind*: **type**, sort, kind, variety, class, style, stamp, nature, manner, pattern, grain, mould, ilk, kidney, strain, brand, genre; turn, inclination, bent.
4 *he had a pronounced cast in one eye*: **squint**, cross-eyes; Brit. informal boss-eye; technical strabismus.
5 *he joined the cast of 'The Barber of Seville'*: **actors**, performers, players, company, troupe; dramatis personae, characters.

caste noun *prohibitions prevent people from marrying outside their caste*: **class**, social class, order, social order, social division, grade, grading, group, grouping, station, stratum, echelon, rank, level, degree, set; place, standing, position, status; Hinduism varna; archaic estate, sphere.

castigate verb *Leopold castigated his son for leaving the archbishop's service*: **reprimand**, rebuke, admonish, chastise, chide, upbraid, reprove, reproach, scold, remonstrate with, berate, take to task, pull up, lambaste, read someone the Riot Act, give someone a piece of one's mind, haul over the coals, lecture, criticize, censure; punish, discipline, chasten; informal tell off, give someone a telling-off, give someone a talking-to, give someone an earful, dress down, give someone a dressing-down, give someone a roasting, give someone a rocket, give someone a rollicking, rap, rap someone the knuckles, slap someone's wrist, send someone away with a flea in their ear, let someone have it, bawl out, give someone hell, come down on, blow up at, pitch into, lay into, lace into, give someone a caning, put on the mat, slap down, blast, rag, keelhaul; Brit. informal tick off, have a go at, carpet, monster, give someone a mouthful, tear someone off a strip, give someone what for, give someone some stick, wig, give someone a wigging, give someone a row, row; N. Amer. informal chew out, ream out; Brit. vulgar slang bollock, give someone a bollocking; N. Amer. vulgar slang chew someone's ass, ream someone's ass; dated call down, rate, give someone a rating, trim; rare reprehend, objurgate.
▷ANTONYMS praise, commend.

castle noun **fortress**, fort, stronghold, fortification, keep, citadel, fastness, tower, peel, palace, chateau, donjon; in Spain alcazar.

castrate verb *many of these colts are castrated*: **neuter**, geld, cut, emasculate, desex, sterilize, unman, remove the testicles of; N. Amer. & Austral. alter; informal doctor, fix; rare evirate, caponize, eunuchize.

casual adjective **1** *he has a casual attitude to life*: **indifferent**, apathetic, uncaring, uninterested, unconcerned; lackadaisical, blasé, nonchalant, lukewarm, insouciant, offhand, hit-or-miss; easy-going, free and easy, airy, breezy, blithe, carefree; flippant, lax, slack, irresponsible, devil-may-care; informal couldn't-care-less, laid-back; rare poco-curante.
▷ANTONYMS careful, concerned.
2 *a casual remark*: **offhand**, random, impromptu, spontaneous, unpremeditated, unthinking, unstudied, unconsidered, parenthetical, passing, throwaway, trivial; ill-considered, ill-judged, unguarded; informal off-the-cuff.
▷ANTONYMS premeditated.
3 *he threw a casual glance over his shoulder*: **cursory**, perfunctory, superficial, passing, fleeting, summary, desultory, careless; hasty, hurried, rushed, brief, quick.
▷ANTONYMS thorough, careful.
4 *she was no more than a casual acquaintance*: **slight**, superficial, shallow, vague, faint.
▷ANTONYMS intimate, close.
5 *he does casual work on farms*: **temporary**, part-time, impermanent, freelance; irregular, occasional, intermittent; outside, outsourced.
▷ANTONYMS permanent; full-time.
6 *casual sex had never been her scene*: **promiscuous**, recreational, extramarital; liberated, uninhibited, free; informal swinging.
7 *a casual meeting with two students changed his life*: **chance**, accidental, random, unintentional, unplanned, unintended, inadvertent, unexpected, unforeseen, unanticipated, unlooked-for, occurring by chance/accident, fortuitous, coincidental, fluky, serendipitous, adventitious, aleatory.
▷ANTONYMS planned, intentional.
8 *a casual short-sleeved shirt*: **informal**, not formal, relaxed, comfortable, sloppy, leisure, sportif, everyday; Military undress; informal sporty.
▷ANTONYMS formal, smart.
9 *the inn's casual atmosphere*: **relaxed**, friendly, natural, informal, unceremonious, unpretentious, easy-going, free and easy, uninhibited,

open; informal laid-back.
▷ANTONYMS formal.
▸ **noun** *we employ eight full-time staff and ten casuals*: **temporary worker**, part-timer, freelance, freelancer; informal temp.
▷ANTONYMS full-timer.

casualty noun **1** *the shelling caused thousands of casualties*: **victim**, fatality, mortality; loss, MIA; (**casualties**) dead and injured/wounded, missing in action, missing.
2 *the corporation was a casualty of the weak economy*: **victim**, sufferer, loser, loss.

casuistry noun *the usual teenage casuistry about altruism always being ultimately selfish*: **sophistry**, specious reasoning, speciousness, sophism, chicanery, quibbling, equivocation, fallaciousness; informal fudging.

cat noun *their pet cat*: **feline**; tabby, ginger tom, tortoiseshell, marmalade cat, mouser, wild cat, alley cat; informal pussy, pussy cat, puss; Brit. informal moggie, mog; archaic grimalkin.

Word links **cat**

feline relating to cats
tom, tomcat male
queen female
kitten young
clowder, glaring collective noun
ailurophobia fear of cats

cataclysm noun *their homeland was destroyed by a great cataclysm*: **disaster**, catastrophe, calamity, tragedy, act of God, devastation, crisis, holocaust, ruin, ruination, upheaval, convulsion, blow, shock, reverse, trouble, trial, tribulation; misfortune, mishap, accident, mischance, misadventure, woe, affliction, distress; informal meltdown, whammy; archaic bale; Scottish archaic mishanter.
▷ANTONYMS salvation, godsend.

cataclysmic adjective *the cataclysmic Krakatoa eruption of 1883*: **disastrous**, catastrophic, calamitous, tragic, devastating, ruinous, terrible, violent, awful.
▷ANTONYMS fortunate, beneficial.

catacombs plural noun **underground cemetery**, sepulchre, crypt, vault, mausoleum, tomb, ossuary; tunnels, labyrinth, maze.

catalogue noun **1** *a computerized library catalogue*: **directory**, register, index, list, listing, record, archive, inventory, roll, table, calendar, classification, roster.
2 *a mail-order catalogue*: **brochure**, prospectus, guide, magalogue, mailer; N. Amer. informal wish book.
▸ **verb** *it will be some time before the collection is fully catalogued*: **classify**, categorize, systematize, systemize, index, list, archive, make an inventory of, inventory, record, register, file, log, enumerate, alphabetize, itemize, pigeonhole, tabulate.

catapult noun *a 16-year-old boy fired a catapult at a low-flying helicopter*: **sling**; N. Amer. slingshot; Austral./NZ shanghai.
▸ **verb** *Sam felt himself being catapulted into the sea*: **propel**, launch, hurl, hurtle, fling, send flying, send, let fly, let loose, fire, blast, shoot.

cataract noun **1** *the river descends in a succession of spectacular cataracts*: **waterfall**, cascade, falls, rapids, white water; torrent; downpour, shower; N. English force; Scottish archaic linn.
2 *he had cataracts in both eyes*: **opacity**, opaqueness.

catastrophe noun *the bush fires were the latest in a growing list of catastrophes*: **disaster**, calamity, cataclysm, crisis, holocaust, ruin, ruination, tragedy, blow, shock; adversity, blight, trouble, trial, tribulation, mishap, misfortune, mischance, misadventure, accident, failure, reverse, woe, affliction, distress; informal meltdown, whammy; archaic bale; Scottish archaic mishanter.
▷ANTONYMS salvation, godsend.

catastrophic adjective *the catastrophic consequences of a major oil spill*: **disastrous**, calamitous, cataclysmic, ruinous, tragic, fatal, dire, awful, terrible, dreadful, black, woeful, grievous, lamentable, miserable, unfortunate; literary direful.
▷ANTONYMS fortunate, beneficial.

catcall noun *he walked out of the meeting to jeers and catcalls*: **whistle**, **boo**, hiss, jeer, raspberry, hoot, brickbat, taunt, shout of derision; wolf whistle; (**catcalls**) scoffing, abuse, teasing, taunting, derision, ridiculing, mockery; Brit. informal the bird.

catch verb **1** *he caught the ball*: **seize**, grab, snatch, seize/grab/take hold of, lay (one's) hands on, get one's hands on, grasp, grip, clutch, clench, fasten on, pluck, hold, hang on to; receive, acquire, get, come into possession of, intercept.
▷ANTONYMS drop.
2 *we've caught a dangerous thief*: **capture**, seize; apprehend, take, arrest, lay hold of, take prisoner, take captive, take into custody, haul in; trap, snare, ensnare; net, hook, reel in, land, beach, bag; informal nab, collar, run in, pinch, bust, pull in, do, feel someone's collar; Brit. informal nick.
▷ANTONYMS release.
3 *the heel of Gloria's shoe had caught in a hole*: **become trapped**, become stuck, stick, become wedged, become entangled, become snarled up, become snagged, snag.
4 *she caught the 7.45 bus*: **be in time for**, reach in time, make, get to; **board**, get on, enter, go on board, go aboard, step aboard, mount, ascend, embark; informal hop on, jump on; formal embus, entrain, emplane.
▷ANTONYMS miss; alight.
5 *they were caught siphoning petrol from a car*: **discover**, detect, find, come upon/across, stumble on, chance on, light on, bring to light, turn up, expose, find out, unmask; surprise, take by surprise, catch unawares, catch off guard, catch red-handed, catch in the act, catch out, burst in on.
6 *it was the business scheme that had caught his imagination*: **engage**, capture, attract, draw, gain, grab, arrest, seize, hold, win, absorb, engross, rivet, grip, captivate, bewitch.
7 *she caught a faint trace of discreet aftershave*: **perceive**, notice, observe, discern, detect, note, become aware of, make out, spot, see; Brit. informal clock.
▷ANTONYMS miss.
8 *I had to strain my ears to catch what she was saying*: **hear**, perceive, recognize, discern, make out; **understand**, comprehend, grasp, take in, fathom, puzzle out, apprehend, get to the bottom of, unravel, decipher; follow, keep up with; informal get, get the drift of, get the hang of, catch on to, latch on to, make head or tail of, figure out, get the picture, get the message; Brit. informal twig, suss out, suss.
9 *the scenes caught the flavour of London in the sixties*: **evoke**, conjure up, suggest, summon up, call to mind, recall, express, reproduce, represent, show, encapsulate, capture, record; film, photograph, draw, paint.
10 *the blow caught her on the side of her face*: **hit**, strike, slap, smack, crack, bang, connect with, contact.
▷ANTONYMS miss.
11 *he served in Macedonia, where he caught malaria*: **become infected with**, contract, get, take, become ill/sick with, fall ill/sick with, be taken ill with, show symptoms of, succumb to, develop, go/come down with, sicken for, fall victim to, be struck down with, be stricken with; Brit. go down with; informal take ill with; N. Amer. informal take sick with.
▷ANTONYMS shake off; escape.
12 *as the kindling caught he added larger pieces of wood*: **ignite**, become ignited, burn, start burning, flame, catch/take fire, burst into flames, flame up, kindle.
▷ANTONYMS go out.
13 *the generator caught immediately*: **start**, start running, fire, begin working, go, function, operate.
▷ANTONYMS stop.
□ **catch it** informal *I'll catch it if he finds me here*: **be reprimanded**, be scolded, be rebuked, be taken to task, be admonished, be chastised, be castigated, get into trouble, be hauled over the coals; informal **be told off**, be for it, be for the high jump, get into hot/deep water, get into shtook, get a dressing-down, get an earful, get a roasting, get a rocket, get a rollicking, get a rap over the knuckles, get a slap on the wrist.
□ **catch on 1** *as radio caught on, politicians became increasingly aware of the medium's power*: **become popular**, take off, become fashionable, come into fashion/vogue, boom, flourish, thrive; informal become trendy, become all the rage. **2** *it's double Dutch to me at the moment, but I catch on fast*: **understand**, comprehend, learn, realize; find out, see the light, see daylight, work out what's going on, get the point; informal cotton on, tumble, latch on, get the picture, get the message, get the drift, get wise, understand/see what's what; Brit. informal twig.
□ **catch (someone) up** *he stopped and waited for Lily to catch up | you go with Tess and I'll catch you up*: **draw level (with)**; get to, come to, reach; gain on, gain.
▸ **noun 1** *he scooped up the net to inspect the catch*: **haul**, net, bag, take, yield, booty, prize.
2 informal *Giles is a good catch for any girl*: **eligible man/woman**, marriage prospect, match, suitable husband/wife/spouse.
3 *he put a hand inside the window, trying to slip the catch*: **latch**, lock, fastener, fastening, clasp, hasp, hook, bar, clip, bolt; Scottish sneck, snib.
4 *the suspicious customer is always looking for the catch*: **snag**, disadvantage, drawback, stumbling block, hitch, fly in the ointment, joker in the pack, pitfall, complication, problem, hiccup, hindrance, difficulty, setback, hurdle, downside, minus; trap, trick, snare, wile, dodge; informal ploy, con.
5 *there was a catch in her voice*: **tremor**, unevenness, shake, shakiness, quiver, quivering, wobble.

catching adjective informal *Huntington's chorea isn't catching*: **infectious**, contagious, communicable, transmittable, transmissible, transferable, spreading; dated infective.

catchphrase noun *the movie gave the world the catchphrase 'I'm gonna make him an offer he can't refuse'*: **saying**, quotation, quote, sound bite, slogan, catchline, catchword, motto, watchword, mantra; N. Amer. informal tag line.

catchword noun *'variety' will be the catchword at the new venue*: **motto**, watchword, slogan, byword, catchphrase, formula, refrain, maxim, axiom, mantra, shibboleth; informal buzzword.

catchy adjective *a catchy tune*: **memorable**, unforgettable; appealing, captivating, snappy, with instant appeal; popular; singable, melodious, melodic, tuneful.
▷ANTONYMS forgettable.

catechize verb *Mrs Garrowby had catechized her sister about this matter.* See **interrogate**.

categorical adjective *a categorical assurance that the government will not raise VAT*: **unqualified**, unconditional, unequivocal, unreserved, absolute, explicit, unambiguous, definite, certain, direct, downright, outright, complete, thorough, thoroughgoing, total, emphatic, positive, express, point-blank, wholehearted, conclusive, undiluted, unalloyed, unadulterated, unstinting, without reservations, out-and-out, one hundred per cent; formal apodictic.
▷ANTONYMS qualified, equivocal.

categorize verb *half the pupils were categorized by their head teachers as casual or persistent truants*: **classify**, class, group, grade, rate, designate, label, tag, brand; order, arrange, sort, rank, type, break down; file, catalogue, list, tabulate, index, assign, pigeonhole.

category noun *weedkillers fall into five broad categories*: **class**, classification, categorization, group, grouping, bracket, head, heading, list, listing, set; type, sort, kind, variety, species, genre, breed, style, brand, make, model, family, stamp, cast, ilk, kidney; grade, grading, order, rank, status; division, section, department, compartment, pigeonhole.

cater verb
□ **cater for 1** *the hotel is happy to cater for vegetarians*: **provide food for**, feed, serve, cook for, wine and dine, regale, provide for, provision; dated victual. **2** *a seaside resort catering for older holidaymakers*: **serve**, provide for, oblige, meet the needs/wants of, accommodate, entertain, receive; deal with, handle, see to, look after, care for. **3** *he seemed to cater for all tastes in his selection of music*: **take into account**, take into consideration, make allowances for, allow for, consider, bear in mind, make provision for, make preparations for, prepare for, make concessions for, have regard for.
□ **cater to** *Britain's vast number of markets and second-hand shops cater to every whim*: **satisfy**, indulge, pander to, gratify, please, accommodate, pacify, appease, minister to, give in to, fulfil, satiate, pamper, mollycoddle, feather-bed, spoil.

caterwaul verb **howl**, wail, bawl, cry, yell, scream, screech, yelp, yowl, squall, whine; miaow; rare ululate.

caterwauling noun *the caterwauling of an aggressive cat*: **howl**, howling, wail, wailing, screech, screeching, shriek, shrieking, scream, screaming, bawl, bawling, cry, crying, yell, yelling, yelp, yelping, yowl, yowling, squall, squalling, whine, whining, ululating; miaowing, miaow.

catharsis noun *there is a view that violent games can exert a positive effect through catharsis*: **purging**, purgation, purification, cleansing, release, relief, emotional release, freeing, deliverance, exorcism, ridding; Psychoanalysis abreaction; rare depuration, lustration.
▷ANTONYMS repression.

cathartic adjective *writing my first book was a very cathartic experience for me*: **purgative**, purging, purifying, cleansing, cleaning, release-bringing, releasing, relieving, freeing, delivering, exorcizing, ridding; Psychoanalysis abreactive; rare depurative, lustral.
▷ANTONYMS repressive.

catholic adjective *her musical tastes are pretty catholic*: **diverse**, diversified, wide, broad, broad-based, eclectic, indiscriminate; open-minded, broad-minded, liberal, tolerant, undogmatic, flexible, unbigoted, unprejudiced, unsectarian, ecumenical; general, universal, widespread, global, worldwide, comprehensive, all-encompassing all-embracing, all-inclusive, unlimited.
▷ANTONYMS limited; narrow.

cattle plural noun **cows**, bovines, oxen, bulls; stock, livestock; archaic neat, kine.

> *Word links* **cattle**
>
> **bovine** relating to cattle
> **bull** male
> **cow** female
> **calf** young
> **herd**, **drove** collective noun

catty adjective informal *that was a catty remark—she's not a bad sort.* See **spiteful**.

caucus noun **1** in North America & NZ *the Democratic caucus in the House*: **parliamentary party**.
2 in North America & NZ *caucuses will be held in eleven states*: **meeting**, assembly, gathering, congress, conference, convention, rally, conclave, congregation, convocation, synod, council, session, parley; informal get-together.
3 in the UK *the right-wing caucus in the Cabinet*: **faction**, camp, bloc, group, gang, set, band, ring, party, league, cabal, camarilla, clique, coterie, junta, pressure group; Brit. ginger group; historical junto.

cause noun **1** *the cause of the fire has not been found*: **source**, root, origin, beginning(s), starting point, seed, germ, genesis, agency, occasion; mainspring, base, basis, foundation, bottom, seat; originator, author, creator, producer, agent, prime mover, maker; Latin fons et origo; literary fountainhead, wellspring, fount, begetter; rare radix.
▷ANTONYMS effect; result.
2 *there is no cause for alarm*: **reason**, grounds, justification, call, need, necessity, occasion, basis, motive, motivation, inducement, excuse, pretext, purpose, stimulus, provocation.
3 *aid projects must serve the cause of human rights | I am raising money for a good cause*: **principle**, ideal, belief (in), conviction, tenet; object, end, aim, objective, purpose, interest; movement, enterprise, undertaking, charity.
4 *he visited Germany to plead his cause with politicians*: **case**, suit, lawsuit, action, dispute, contention, point of view.
▶ verb *this disease can cause blindness*: **bring about**, give rise to, be the cause of, lead to, result in, create, begin, produce, generate, originate, engender, spawn, occasion, effect, bring to pass, bring on, precipitate, prompt, provoke, kindle, trigger, make happen, spark off, touch off, stir up, whip up, induce, inspire, promote, foster; literary beget, enkindle; rare effectuate.
▷ANTONYMS result from.

> *Word links* **cause**
>
> **-genic**, **-facient** suffixes meaning 'causing something', as in *carcinogenic*, *liquefacient*

caustic adjective **1** *a caustic cleaner*: **corrosive**, corroding, mordant, acid, alkaline, burning, stinging, acrid, harsh, destructive.
2 *a caustic comment*: **sarcastic**, **cutting**, biting, mordant, stinging, sharp, bitter, scathing, derisive, sardonic, ironic, scornful, trenchant, acerbic, vitriolic, tart, acid, pungent, acrimonious, astringent, rapier-like, razor-edged, critical, polemic, virulent, venomous, waspish; Brit. informal sarky; rare mordacious, acidulous.
▷ANTONYMS kind.

> *Choose the right word* **caustic, sarcastic, sardonic, ironic**
>
> See **sarcastic**.

cauterize verb Medicine *the wound needs to be cauterized*: **burn**, sear, singe, scorch; disinfect, sterilize, sanitize, clean, cleanse, decontaminate.

caution noun **1** *you are advised to proceed with caution*: **care**, carefulness, wariness, awareness, heedfulness, heed, attention, attentiveness, alertness, watchfulness, vigilance, circumspection, discretion, prudence, guardedness, chariness, forethought, mindfulness; informal caginess.
▷ANTONYMS incaution, recklessness.
2 *a first offender may receive a caution from the police*: **warning**, admonition, admonishment, injunction, monition; **reprimand**, rebuke, reproof, scolding; exhortation, guidance, caveat, counsel; informal telling-off, dressing-down, talking-to; Brit. informal ticking-off, carpeting.
▶ verb **1** *advisers have cautioned against tax increases*: **advise**, **warn**, recommend, counsel, urge, admonish, exhort.
2 *he was cautioned by the police*: **warn**, admonish, give an injunction to; **reprimand**, rebuke, reprove, scold; informal tell off, give someone a telling-off, give someone a dressing-down, give someone a talking-to; Brit. informal give someone a ticking-off, carpet.

cautious adjective *he's a very cautious driver*: **careful**, wary, aware, heedful, attentive, alert, watchful, vigilant, circumspect, prudent, guarded, on one's guard, chary, mindful; informal cagey.
▷ANTONYMS incautious; reckless.

cavalcade noun *a royal cavalcade proceeded through the city*: **procession**, parade, motorcade, cortège; march, column, troop, file, train, caravan, retinue; Brit. march past; informal crocodile.

cavalier noun **1** (**Cavalier**) historical *Cavaliers dying for King Charles*: **Royalist**, king's man.
▷ANTONYMS Roundhead, parliamentarian.
2 archaic *foot soldiers and cavaliers*: **horseman**, cavalryman, horse soldier, trooper, equestrian, knight, chevalier; dragoon, hussar, lancer, carabineer, cuirassier, sabreur.
▶ adjective *a cavalier disregard for the real dangers | a cavalier attitude to other people's problems*: **offhand**, indifferent, casual, dismissive, insouciant, uninterested, unconcerned; **supercilious**, patronizing, condescending, haughty, arrogant, lofty, lordly, disdainful, scornful, contemptuous, unceremonious, discourteous, uncivil, insolent, rude, glib, ungracious, perfunctory, cursory, curt, abrupt, terse, brusque; informal off, offish, couldn't-care-less, take-it-or-leave-it; rare poco-curante.
▷ANTONYMS thoughtful.

cavalry plural noun *the cavalry charged up the hill*: **mounted troops**, cavalrymen, horse soldiers, troopers, horse; dragoons, lancers, hussars, carabineers, cuirassiers, sabreurs.

C

cave noun *there is a cave at the bottom of the cliff*: **cavern**, grotto, hollow, cavity, pothole, underground chamber, gallery, tunnel, dugout.
□ **cave in 1** *the roof caved in*: **collapse**, fall in, give, give way, crumble, crumple, disintegrate, subside, fall down, sag, slump. ▷ANTONYMS hold up.
2 *the manager caved in to their demands*: **yield**, surrender, submit, succumb, back down, make concessions, capitulate, give up/in, raise/show the white flag; acquiesce, agree, concur, approve, assent; informal throw in the towel, throw in the sponge. ▷ANTONYMS hold out against.

Word links cave

speleology, N. Amer. **spelunking** exploration of caves
speleologist, **potholer** explorer of caves

caveat noun *he added the caveat that the results still had to be corroborated*: **warning**, caution, admonition, monition, red flag, alarm bells; **proviso**, condition, stipulation, provision, clause, rider, qualification, restriction, reservation, limitation, strings.

caveman, cavewoman noun **cave-dweller**, troglodyte, primitive man/woman, prehistoric man/woman.
▶ adjective informal *women resent caveman tactics*: **primitive**, uncivilized, crude, brutal, savage; masterful, domineering, autocratic.
▷ANTONYMS sophisticated.

cavern noun *the cave opens up into a fantastic cavern*: **large cave**, grotto, hollow, cavity, underground chamber, gallery, tunnel, dugout.

cavernous adjective *the cavernous cargo space*: **vast**, huge, large, immense, spacious, roomy, airy, commodious, capacious, voluminous, ample, rambling, extensive, high, deep; hollow, gaping, yawning, unfathomable; dark, gloomy, dismal, sepulchral.
▷ANTONYMS small, poky.

cavil verb *they cavilled at the cost*: **complain**, carp, grumble, moan, grouse, grouch, whine, bleat, find fault with, quibble about, niggle about; criticize, censure, denounce, condemn, decry; informal gripe, beef, bellyache, bitch, whinge, nit-pick, pick holes in, split hairs, sound off, kick up a fuss, knock; Brit. informal chunter, create; N. English informal mither; N. Amer. informal kvetch about.

cavity noun *customs officers found a secret cavity in the car*: **space**, chamber, hollow, hole, pocket, pouch; orifice, aperture; socket, gap, crater, pit; cutting, concavity; Anatomy lacuna, sac, alveolus, ampulla, antrum, archenteron, bulla, bursa, lumen, orbit, sinus, ventricle, vesicle; Zoology calyx; Botany cyst; Geology geode, vug.

cavort verb *two of his companions linked arms and cavorted around him*: **skip**, **dance**, romp, jig, caper, cut capers, frisk, gambol, prance, frolic, play, lark; bounce, trip, leap, jump, bound, spring, hop, bob; dated sport; rare rollick.

cease verb **1** *hostilities had ceased*: **come to an end**, come to a halt, come to a stop, end, halt, stop, conclude, terminate, finish, wind up, draw to a close, be over, come to a standstill; pause, break off; peter out, fizzle out, abate, fade away, die away.
▷ANTONYMS start; continue.
2 *they were asked to cease all military activity*: **bring to an end**, bring to a halt, bring to a stop, end, halt, stop, conclude, terminate, finish, wind up, discontinue, desist from, refrain from, leave off, quit, shut down, suspend, break off, cut short.
▷ANTONYMS start; continue.
▶ noun
□ **without cease continuously**, incessantly, unendingly, unremittingly, without cessation/stopping/let-up, without a pause/break, on and on, time without end.

ceaseless adjective *they kept up a ceaseless flow of questions*: **continual**, constant, continuous; **incessant**, unceasing, unending, endless, never-ending, interminable, non-stop, uninterrupted, unabated, unabating, unremitting, relentless, unrelenting, unrelieved, sustained, persistent, lasting, eternal, perpetual; unfaltering, unflagging, untiring, unwearied, unwavering, unswerving, undeviating, persevering, dogged, tireless, indefatigable.
▷ANTONYMS intermittent; brief.

Choose the right word ceaseless, continual, continuous, constant

See **continual**.

cede verb *Austria ceded the South Tyrol to Italy in 1919*: **surrender**, concede, relinquish, yield, part with, give up; **hand over**, deliver up, turn over, give over, make over, transfer, bequeath, grant, remit, renounce, resign, abandon, forgo, sacrifice, waive; archaic forsake.
▷ANTONYMS keep; gain.

ceiling noun **1** *the ceiling was painted yellow*: **roof**, vault, vaulting; French plafond.
▷ANTONYMS floor.
2 *a ceiling was to be set on prices*: **upper limit**, maximum, limitation, highest permissible level/value.
▷ANTONYMS floor, minimum.

celebrate verb **1** *they were celebrating their wedding anniversary*: **commemorate**, observe, honour, mark, salute, recognize, acknowledge, remember, memorialize, keep, drink to, toast, drink a toast to.
2 *let's open the champagne and celebrate!* **enjoy oneself**, make merry, have fun, have a good/wild time, rave, party, have a party, {eat, drink, and be merry}, revel, roister, carouse, kill the fatted calf, put the flag(s) out; N. Amer. step out; informal go out on the town, paint the town red, whoop it up, make whoopee, junket, have a night on the tiles, live it up, have a ball; Brit. informal push the boat out; S. African informal jol; dated spree, go on a spree; rare rollick.
3 *the priest celebrated mass*: **perform**, observe, officiate at, preside at, solemnize, ceremonialize.
4 *he was celebrated for his achievements*: **praise**, laud, extol, glorify, eulogize, reverence, honour, pay tribute to, pay homage to, salute, hymn, sing; archaic emblazon.

celebrated adjective *a celebrated amateur artist*: **acclaimed**, admired, highly rated, lionized, revered, honoured, esteemed, exalted, lauded, vaunted, much touted, well thought of, well received, acknowledged; eminent, great, distinguished, prestigious, illustrious, pre-eminent, venerable, august, estimable, of note, noted, notable, of repute, of high standing, considerable; famous, renowned, well known.
▷ANTONYMS criticized; unsung; obscure.

Choose the right word celebrated, famous, well known, renowned

See **famous**.

celebration noun **1** *the school's celebration of its 50th birthday*: **commemoration**, observance, honouring, salute to, marking, keeping.
2 *this is a cause for celebration*: **jollification**, merrymaking, carousing, carousal, revelry, revels, enjoying oneself, partying, parties, festivity, festivities; roistering, debauchery, frolics; informal **junketing**.
3 *a birthday celebration*: **party**, function, gathering, event, affair, occasion, festivities, festival, fête, carnival, gala, jamboree; W. Indian jump-up; Jewish simcha; informal do, bash, get-together, blowout, rave; Brit. informal rave-up, thrash, knees-up, jolly, beanfeast, bunfight, beano; S. African informal jol.
4 *the celebration of the Eucharist*: **observance**, performance, officiation, solemnization.

celebrity noun **1** *his prestige and celebrity grew*: **fame**, prominence, renown, eminence, pre-eminence, importance, stardom, popularity, distinction, greatness, note, notability, prestige, stature, standing, position, rank, repute, reputation, illustriousness, glory, acclaim, influence, account, consequence, visibility.
▷ANTONYMS obscurity.
2 *questions are put to a panel of celebrities*: **famous person**, VIP, very important person, personality, name, big name, famous name, household name, star, superstar, celebutante, leading light, giant, great, master, guru; **dignitary**, luminary, worthy, grandee, lion, public figure, pillar of society, notable, notability, personage, panjandrum; informal heavyweight, celeb, somebody, someone, bigwig, biggie, big shot, big noise, big gun, big cheese, big chief, nob, lady muck, lord muck, top brass, honcho, head honcho, top dog, mogul, supremo, megastar, heavy, fat cat; N. Amer. informal big wheel, big kahuna, kahuna, top banana, big enchilada, macher, high muckamuck, high muckety-muck.
▷ANTONYMS nonentity.

celestial adjective **1** *a celestial body*: **(in) space**, heavenly, astronomical, extraterrestrial, stellar, planetary, in the sky, in the heavens; rare superterrestrial.
▷ANTONYMS terrestrial, earthly.
2 *celestial beings*: **heavenly**, holy, saintly, divine, godly, godlike, ethereal, paradisical, Elysian, spiritual, empyrean, superlunary; immortal, angelic, seraphic, cherubic, blessed, beatific, blissful, sublime.
▷ANTONYMS hellish; mundane.

celibacy noun *a priest who had taken a vow of celibacy*: **chastity**, virginity, maidenhood, maidenhead, abstinence, self-denial, self-restraint, abnegation, asceticism; the unmarried state, singleness, bachelorhood, spinsterhood; monkhood, nunhood, monasticism; rare single blessedness, continence.
▷ANTONYMS marriage; sex.

celibate adjective *a celibate priest*: **unmarried**, single, unwed, spouseless, wifeless, husbandless; **chaste**, virginal, virgin, maidenly, maiden, intact, abstinent, self-denying, self-restrained, ascetic; monkish, monklike, nunnish, nunlike, monastic; rare continent.
▷ANTONYMS married; sexually active.

cell noun **1** *a prison cell*: **dungeon**, oubliette, lock-up, prison; room, cubicle, compartment, chamber, stall, enclosure; N. Amer. informal **bullpen**, tank, drunk tank; Austral./NZ informal peter.
2 *each cell of the honeycomb*: **compartment**, cavity, hole, hollow, bay, chamber, slot, niche, section.

3 *terrorist cells*: **caucus**, **unit**, faction, arm, section, nucleus, clique, coterie, group, party, clan, wing.

> *Word links* **cell**
>
> **cyto-** related prefix, as in *cytology, cytotoxic*
> **-cyte**, **-blast** related suffixes, as in *lymphocyte, fibroblast*

cellar noun **basement**, vault, crypt, undercroft, underground room, catacomb; garden flat, sub-basement, lower ground floor; Brit. dated below stairs.
▷ANTONYMS attic.

cement noun *polystyrene cement*: **adhesive**, glue, fixative, gum, paste, bonding, binder, sealer, sealant; superglue, epoxy resin; N. Amer. mucilage; N. Amer. informal stickum.
▸ verb *he cemented the rock sample to a microscope slide*: **stick**, bond, join, connect; **fasten**, fix, affix, attach, secure, bind, glue, gum, paste, fuse, weld, solder.

cemetery noun **graveyard**, churchyard, burial ground, burial place, burying place, burying ground, garden of remembrance; Scottish kirkyard; N. Amer. memorial park; informal boneyard; literary golgotha; historical urnfield, potter's field, catacomb, necropolis; archaic God's acre.

censor noun *the film censors*: **expurgator**, bowdlerizer; **examiner**, inspector, editor.
▸ verb *letters home from the front line were censored*: **cut**, delete, delete parts of, make cuts in, blue-pencil; **examine**, inspect; edit, make changes to; make acceptable, expurgate, bowdlerize, sanitize; informal clean up; rare redact.

censorious adjective *the appointment of censorious watchdogs over the broadcasters*: **hypercritical**, overcritical, severely critical, disapproving, condemnatory, condemning, castigatory, denunciatory, deprecatory, disparaging, unforgiving, reproachful, reproving, censuring, captious, fault-finding, carping, cavilling, full of reproof, vituperative.
▷ANTONYMS complimentary, approving.

censure verb *the commission censured him for his conduct*. See **reprimand**.
▸ noun *his voice took on a note of censure*: **condemnation**, criticism, attack, abuse, revilement; **reprimand**, rebuke, admonishment, admonition, reproof, reproval, upbraiding, castigation, berating, denunciation, disapproval, reproach, scolding, chiding, reprehension, obloquy, vituperation; rare excoriation, objurgation.
▷ANTONYMS approval, commendation.

central adjective **1** *a Roman basilica always occupied a central position*: **middle**, centre, halfway, midway, mid, median, medial, mean, middling, intermediate, intermedial; Anatomy mesial.
▷ANTONYMS side; extreme.
2 *central London*: **inner**, innermost, middle, mid, interior, nuclear.
▷ANTONYMS outer.
3 *their central campaign issue*: **main**, chief, principal, primary, leading, foremost, first, most important, predominant, dominant, (most) prominent, key, crucial, vital, essential, basic, fundamental, core, staple, critical, pivotal, salient, prime, focal, premier, paramount, major, ruling, master, supreme, overriding, cardinal, capital, pre-eminent, ultimate, uppermost, highest, utmost, top, topmost, arch-; informal number-one.
▷ANTONYMS subordinate; minor.

centralize verb *the minister intends to centralize tax collection*: **concentrate**, bring under one roof, consolidate, amalgamate, condense, collect, cluster, compact, unify, incorporate, streamline, focus, rationalize.
▷ANTONYMS disperse, devolve.

centre noun *the centre of the town | the centre of a circle*: **middle**, nucleus, heart, core, hub, pivot, kernel, eye, bosom; middle point, midpoint, halfway point, mean, median; interior; depths, thick, bullseye, focus, focal point, cynosure.
▷ANTONYMS edge.
▸ verb *the story* **centres on** *an eye surgeon working in Paris*: **focus**, concentrate, pivot, hinge, be based; revolve around, have as its starting point.

centrepiece noun *the tower is the centrepiece of the park*: **highlight**, main feature, high point, high spot, best part, climax; focus of attention, focal point, centre of attention/interest, magnet, cynosure; most prominent element, central component, nucleus, heart, core, hub, kernel.

ceramics plural noun **pottery**, pots, china, terracotta.

ceremonial adjective *a ceremonial occasion*: **formal**, official, state, public; ritual, ritualistic, prescribed, set, stately, courtly, solemn, dignified, celebratory, sacramental, liturgical.
▷ANTONYMS informal, unofficial.
▸ noun *there was great sensitivity over diplomatic ceremonial*: **ritual**, ceremony, rite, formality, pomp, solemnity; form, custom, tradition, convention, usage, practice, routine, protocol, office, observance; sacrament, liturgy; formal praxis.

ceremonious adjective *he rose from his desk to take a ceremonious farewell*: **dignified**, **majestic**, imposing, impressive, solemn, stately; awe-inspiring, regal, imperial, elegant, grand, glorious, splendid, magnificent, resplendent, important, august, portentous; formal, courtly, punctilious, courteous, civil, deferential, stiff, rigid, affected; slow-moving, measured, deliberate, precise, scrupulous; informal starchy, just so.
▷ANTONYMS unceremonious.

ceremony noun **1** *a wedding ceremony*: **rite**, ritual, ceremonial, observance; **service**, sacrament, liturgy, worship, mystery, office, celebration; performance, act, practice, order, custom, tradition, convention, institution, formality, procedure, usage, habit, form.
2 *the new Queen was proclaimed with due ceremony*: **pomp**, protocol, formalities, niceties, decorum, etiquette, good form, propriety, conventionality, punctilio, attention to detail, fuss; French politesse.

certain adjective **1** *I'm certain he's guilty*: **sure**, **confident**, positive, convinced, in no doubt, unshaken in one's belief, secure in one's belief, easy in one's mind, satisfied, assured, persuaded; (**be certain**) have no doubt, not question, hold the unwavering view.
▷ANTONYMS doubtful.
2 *it is certain that more changes are in the offing*: **unquestionable**, **sure**, definite, beyond question, not in question, not in doubt, beyond doubt, unequivocal, indubitable, undeniable, irrefutable, indisputable, incontrovertible, incontestable, obvious, patent, manifest, evident, plain, clear, transparent, palpable, unmistakable, conclusive, recognized, confirmed, accepted, acknowledged, undisputed, undoubted, unquestioned, unchallenged, uncontested; there are no two ways about it; informal as sure as eggs is eggs.
▷ANTONYMS unthinkable; doubtful; possible.
3 *they are certain to win*: **sure**, **very likely**, bound, destined, predestined, fated, trusted, assured of doing something.
▷ANTONYMS unlikely.
4 *Pakistan's lead of 380 runs meant certain success*: **inevitable**, assured, destined, predestined, fated; reliable, unavoidable, inescapable, automatic, bound to happen, sure to happen, inexorable, ineluctable, predictable, necessary, out of one's hands; informal in the bag.
5 *there is no certain cure for this*: **reliable**, dependable, trustworthy, sound, foolproof, tested, tried and tested, effective, efficacious, guaranteed, sure, unfailing, infallible, unerring; informal sure-fire; dated sovereign.
▷ANTONYMS unreliable.
6 *a certain sum of money is required*: **determined**, definite, fixed, established, precise, defined, exact, explicit, express.
▷ANTONYMS undefined.
7 ***a certain** lady that you know*: **particular**, specific, individual, special, especial.
▷ANTONYMS nameless; undifferentiated; general.
8 *to **a certain** extent that is true*: **moderate**, modest, medium, middling, unexceptional; tolerable, passable, adequate, fair, decent, acceptable; limited, small.
▷ANTONYMS great.
□ **make certain** *make certain that storage and access areas are of adequate size for any power equipment used*: **make sure**, ensure, see to it; confirm, check, verify, corroborate, establish.

> *Choose the right word* **certain, sure, positive, convinced, definite**
>
> See **sure**.

certainly adverb **1** *this is certainly a late work*: **unquestionably**, surely, assuredly, definitely, beyond question, without question, beyond doubt, unequivocally, indubitably, undeniably, irrefutably, indisputably, incontrovertibly, incontestably, obviously, patently, manifestly, evidently, plainly, clearly, transparently, palpably, unmistakably, conclusively, undisputedly, undoubtedly; there are no two ways about it; informal as sure as eggs is eggs.
▷ANTONYMS possibly.
2 *our revenues are certainly lower than anticipated*: **admittedly**, beyond question, without question, definitely, undoubtedly, without a doubt.
▸ exclamation *'And now, shall we clean the diamonds?' 'Certainly.'*: **yes**, definitely, absolutely, sure, by all means, quite, indeed, of course, positively, naturally, without doubt, without question, unquestionably; affirmative; Brit. dated rather.
▷ANTONYMS no; possibly.

certainty noun **1** *she knew with certainty that he was telling the truth*: **confidence**, sureness, positiveness, conviction, certitude, reliability, assuredness, assurance, validity, conclusiveness, authoritativeness, truth, fact, factualness.
▷ANTONYMS uncertainty; doubt.
2 *he accepted defeat as a certainty | that horse is a certainty for the 2.00 at Newmarket tomorrow*: **inevitability**, necessity, foregone conclusion, predictable result, matter of course; certain winner; informal sure thing, cert, dead cert, sure-fire winner.
▷ANTONYMS possibility; impossibility.

certificate noun *a certificate of motor insurance*: **guarantee**, proof, certification, document, authorization, authentication, verification, credentials, accreditation, testimonial, warrant, licence, voucher, diploma.

C

Word links certificate

scripophily collecting old bond and share certificates

certify verb **1** *the aircraft was certified as airworthy*: **verify**, **guarantee**, attest, validate, ratify, warrant, confirm, corroborate, substantiate, endorse, vouch for, testify to, provide evidence of, authenticate, document; bear witness to, bear out, give proof of, prove, demonstrate, back up, support.
2 *the woman would be taken to a certified hospital for examination*: **accredit**, recognize, license, authorize, approve, warrant; empower, qualify, endorse, sanction, vouch for, put one's seal of approval on, appoint, give a certificate to, give a diploma to.

certitude noun *the question may never be answered with certitude*: **certainty**, confidence, sureness, positiveness, conviction, reliability, assuredness, assurance.
▷ANTONYMS doubt.

cessation noun *the cessation of hostilities*: **end**, ending, termination, stopping, halting, ceasing, finish, finishing, stoppage, closing, closure, close, conclusion, winding up, discontinuation, discontinuance, breaking off, abandonment, interruption, suspension, cutting short; pause, break, respite, let-up.
▷ANTONYMS start; resumption.

cession noun *the cession of this province to the Kingdom of Italy*: **surrender**, surrendering, ceding, conceding, concession, relinquishment, yielding, giving up, handing over, transfer, transference, transferral, granting, grant, bequest; resignation, abdication, abandonment, forgoing, forsaking, sacrifice, waiving, waiver, renunciation.
▷ANTONYMS gain.

chafe verb **1** *the collar chafed his neck*: **abrade**, graze, grate, rub against, rub painfully, gall, skin, scrape, scratch, rasp; inflame; rare excoriate.
2 *I chafed her feet and wrapped the blanket around her*: **rub**, warm, warm up.
3 *material chafed by the rock*: **wear away**, wear down, wear out, wear to shreds, fray, tatter, erode, abrade, scour, rasp, scrape away, gnaw away at, bite into.
4 *the bank chafed at the restrictions imposed on it*: **be impatient**, be angry, be annoyed, be irritated, be incensed, be exasperated, be frustrated; fume, brood, fuss, upset oneself; informal blow one's top, blow a fuse.

chaff[1] noun **1** *a machine that separated the chaff from the grain*: **husks**, hulls, bran, pods, seed cases, shells, capsules, sheaths; N. Amer. shucks.
2 *the proposals were characterized as so much chaff*: **rubbish**, refuse, waste, garbage, litter, discarded matter, debris, detritus, scrap, dross; flotsam and jetsam, lumber; sweepings, leavings, leftovers, remains, scraps, dregs, offscourings, odds and ends; muck; N. Amer. trash; Austral./NZ **mullock**; informal dreck, junk; Brit. informal grot, gash; Archaeology **debitage**; rare **draff**, **raff**, **raffle**, cultch, orts.

chaff[2] noun *we used to come in for a fair amount of good-natured chaff*: **banter**, repartee, raillery, ripostes, sallies, quips, wisecracks, crosstalk, wordplay, teasing, ragging; badinage, witty conversation, witty remarks, witticism(s), joking, jesting, jocularity, drollery; French bons mots; informal kidding, kidology, ribbing, joshing, wisecracking; rare persiflage.
▶ verb *the pleasures of drinking and betting and chaffing your mates*: **tease**, make fun of, poke fun at, rag, mock, laugh at, guy; deride, ridicule, scoff at, jeer at, jibe at; taunt, bait, goad, pick on; informal take the mickey out of, send up, rib, josh, kid, wind up, have on, pull someone's leg, make a monkey out of; N. Amer. informal goof on, rag on, put on, pull someone's chain, razz, fun, shuck; Austral./NZ informal poke mullock at, poke borak at, sling off at, chiack; Brit. vulgar slang take the piss out of; archaic make sport of, twit, quiz, smoke, flout at, rally.

chagrin noun *to his chagrin, his son chose to become an actor*: **annoyance**, irritation, vexation, exasperation, displeasure, pique, spleen, crossness, anger, rage, fury, wrath; dissatisfaction, discontent, indignation, resentment, umbrage, disgruntlement, rankling, smarting, distress, discomposure, discomfiture, disquiet, fretfulness, frustration; embarrassment, mortification, humiliation, shame; informal aggravation; literary ire.
▷ANTONYMS delight.

chagrined adjective *he was chagrined when his friend poured scorn on him*. See **annoyed**.

chain noun **1** (**chains**) *he had been held in chains while he was a prisoner*: **fetters**, shackles, bonds, irons, leg irons, manacles, handcuffs; informal cuffs, bracelets; archaic trammels, gyves, darbies, bilboes.
2 *a chain of events*: **series**, succession, string, sequence, train, trail, run, pattern, progression, course, set, line, row, concatenation.
3 *a chain of shops*: **group**; multiple shop/store, multiple, firm, company.
▶ verb *she chained her bicycle to the railings*: **tie**, secure, fasten, tether, hitch, bind, rope, moor; restrain, shackle, fetter, manacle, handcuff, hobble; confine, imprison; rare trammel, gyve.

chair noun **1** *he sat down on a chair*: **seat**.
2 *he was chair of the union for eight years*: **chairperson**, chairman, chairwoman, president, convener, spokesperson, spokesman, spokeswoman, leader, MC, master/mistress of ceremonies; Brit. shop steward, father/mother of the chapel.
3 *a university chair*: **professorship**.
4 N. Amer. *he was sent to the chair*: **electric chair**; electrocution, execution.
▶ verb *she chairs the economic committee*: **preside over**, take the chair of, be in the chair at, officiate at, moderate; lead, direct, conduct, run, manage, control, be in charge of, be in control of, have control of, supervise, superintend, oversee, guide.

chairman, chairwoman noun *the chairman of the conference*: **chair**, chairperson, president, convener; spokesperson, spokesman, spokeswoman, leader, MC, master/mistress of ceremonies; Brit. shop steward, father/mother of the chapel.

chalk verb
□ **chalk something up 1** *he has chalked up another box-office success*: **achieve**, attain, accomplish, gain, earn, win, succeed in making, reach, make, get, obtain; score, tally, record, register, enter, mark, log; informal clock up, knock up, notch up, turn in, rack up, bag. **2** *I forgot completely—chalk it up to age*: **attribute**, assign, ascribe, put down, set down, accredit, credit, give the credit for, impute; lay on, pin on, blame on, lay at the door of; connect with, associate with.

Word links chalk

calcareous chalky

chalky adjective **1** *Rosaleen's skin was so chalky that her veins showed blue through it*: **pale**, bloodless, pallid, colourless, wan, ashen, white; waxen, chalk-white, milky; pasty, pasty-faced, whey-faced, peaky, sickly, anaemic, tired-looking, washed out, sallow, drained, drawn, sapped, ghostly, deathly, deathlike, blanched, bleached; rare etiolated.
▷ANTONYMS rosy; flushed.
2 *there were some chalky bits at the bottom of the glass*: **powdery**, floury, mealy, dusty, gritty, crumbly, friable, granulated, granular, ground, crushed, pulverized; rare pulverulent, levigated.
▷ANTONYMS smooth.

challenge noun **1** *he accepted the challenge*: **dare**, provocation; summons.
2 *he successfully resisted a **challenge to** his leadership*: **confrontation with**, **dispute with**, stand against, test of, opposition, disagreement with; questioning of, defiance, ultimatum.
3 *getting ready for the visitors was proving quite a challenge*: **problem**, difficult task, test, trial; trouble, bother, obstacle.
▶ verb **1** *you will need to be able to challenge their statistics in an informed way*: **question**, **disagree with**, object to, take exception to, confront, dispute, take issue with, protest against, call into question; demur about/against, dissent from, be a dissenter from.
2 *he challenged one of my men to a duel*: **dare**, summon, invite, bid, throw down the gauntlet to, defy someone to do something.
3 *a new way of life that would challenge them*: **test**, tax, try; strain, make demands on, weary, wear out, drain, sap; **stretch**, stimulate, arouse, inspire, excite, spur on.

challenging adjective *an interesting, worthwhile, and challenging job*: **demanding**, testing, taxing, exacting, exigent, searching; stretching, exciting, stimulating, inspiring, energizing, inspirational; difficult, tough, hard, heavy, stiff, formidable, onerous, arduous, laborious, burdensome, strenuous, gruelling.
▷ANTONYMS easy; uninspiring.

Word toolkit challenging

See **arduous**.

chamber noun **1** *a debating chamber*: **room**, hall, assembly room, auditorium.
2 archaic *we returned to the castle and slept safely in our own chamber*: **bedroom**, bedchamber, boudoir, room; literary bower.
3 *the lower left chamber of the heart*: **compartment**, cavity, hollow, pocket, cell; part; Anatomy auricle, ventricle.

champagne noun informal champers, bubbly.

champion noun **1** *the world snooker champion*: **winner**, title-holder, defending champion, gold medallist; **prizewinner**, cup winner, victor, conqueror; Latin victor ludorum; informal champ, top dog, number one.
2 *a **champion** of change*: **advocate**, proponent, promoter, proposer, supporter, standard-bearer, torch-bearer, defender, protector, upholder, backer, exponent, patron, sponsor, prime mover; pleader for, campaigner for, propagandist for, lobbyist for, fighter for, battler for, crusader for, apologist for; apostle, evangelist, missionary; N. Amer. booster; informal plugger.
▷ANTONYMS opponent, critic.
3 historical *there was little chance of his defeating the King's Champion*: **knight**, man-at-arms, warrior, defender, duellist, paladin, hero.

▶ **verb** *an organization championing the rights of tribal peoples*: **advocate**, promote, plead for, hold a torch for, defend, protect, uphold, support, back, espouse, ally oneself with, stand behind, stand up for, take someone's part, campaign for, lobby for, fight for, battle for, crusade for, take up the cudgels for; propose, sponsor, vouch for, second; informal stick up for, throw one's weight behind, plug.
▷ANTONYMS oppose, criticize.

chance **noun 1** *there was a reasonable chance that he might be released*: **possibility**, prospect, probability, odds, likelihood, likeliness, expectation, anticipation, conceivability, feasibility, plausibility; risk, threat, menace, hazard, danger, fear, peril, liability; hope, opportunity, promise.
▷ANTONYMS unlikelihood.
2 *I gave her a chance to answer*: **opportunity**, opening, occasion, turn, time, moment, window (of opportunity), slot; N. Amer. & Austral./NZ show; Canadian a kick at the can/cat; informal break, shot, look-in.
3 *'Test them,' Nigel said, taking an awful chance*: **risk**, gamble, hazard, venture, speculation, long shot, leap in the dark, pig in a poke, lottery, pot luck.
▷ANTONYMS certainty.
4 *it was pure chance that made me notice the writing*: **accident**, coincidence, serendipity, fate, a twist of fate, destiny, fortuity, fortune, providence, freak, hazard; a piece of good fortune, (a bit of) luck, (a bit of) good luck, a fluke, a happy chance; N. Amer. happenstance.
□ **by chance** *I came across the book by chance*: **fortuitously**, by accident, accidentally, coincidentally, serendipitously, unintentionally, inadvertently; unwittingly, unknowingly, unawares, unconsciously.
▷ANTONYMS intentionally, knowingly.
▶ **adjective** *a chance discovery*: **accidental**, occurring by chance/accident, fortuitous, adventitious, fluky, coincidental, casual, serendipitous, random, aleatory; unexpected, unforeseen, unanticipated, unforeseeable, unlooked-for; unintentional, unintended, inadvertent, involuntary, unplanned, unpremeditated, unthinking, unmeant; unwitting, unknowing, unconscious, subconscious.
▷ANTONYMS intentional, planned.
▶ **verb 1** *I chanced to meet him a year or so later*: **happen**.
2 informal *I waited a few seconds and chanced another look*: **risk**, hazard, venture, try, try one's luck with; formal essay.
3 dated *it so chanced that the king was passing through the village*. See **happen** (sense 1).
□ **chance on/upon** *a passing motorist chanced on the scene*: **come across**, run across, run into, happen on, hit on, light on, come upon, stumble on, blunder on, find by chance, meet (by chance); informal bump into; archaic run against.

chancy **adjective** informal *bookselling is a chancy occupation*: **risky**, **unpredictable**, uncertain, speculative, precarious; problematical, unsettled, unsafe, insecure, exposed, touch-and-go, tricky, treacherous, dangerous, fraught with danger, high-risk, hazardous, perilous; informal dicey, sticky, hairy; Brit. informal dodgy; N. Amer. informal gnarly; archaic or humorous parlous.
▷ANTONYMS safe; predictable.

change **verb 1** *this could change the face of Britain | things have changed since my day*: **alter**, make different, become different, undergo a change, make alterations to, adjust, make adjustments to, adapt, turn, amend, improve, modify, convert, revise, recast, reform, reshape, refashion, redesign, restyle, revamp, rework, remake, remodel, remould, redo, reconstruct, reorganize, reorder, refine, reorient, reorientate, vary, transform, transfigure, transmute, metamorphose, undergo a sea change, evolve; customize, tailor; informal tweak; technical permute.
▷ANTONYMS preserve; stay the same.
2 *he'd changed his job*: **swap**, exchange, interchange, substitute, switch, commute, convert, replace, rotate, alternate, transpose; trade, barter; archaic truck.
▷ANTONYMS keep.
▶ **noun 1** *there has been a change of plan*: **alteration**, modification, variation, conversion, revision, amendment, adjustment, adaptation; remodelling, reshaping, remoulding, redoing, reconstruction, rebuilding, recasting, reorganization, rearrangement, reordering, reshuffling, restyling, rejigging, reworking, renewal, renewing, revamping, renovation, remaking; metamorphosis, transformation, transfiguration, translation, evolution, mutation, sea change; humorous transmogrification.
2 *we need a change of government*: **swap**, exchange, interchange, substitution, switch, commutation, conversion, replacement, rotation, alternation, transposition; trade, barter, bartering; archaic truck.
3 *sorry about the note—I've no change*: **coins**, loose change, small change, cash, petty cash, coinage, coin, coin of the realm, hard cash, silver, copper, coppers, gold; formal specie.
□ **have a change of heart** See **heart**.

> *Word links* **change**
>
> **meta-** related prefix, as in *metamorphosis*
> **-tropic** related suffix, as in *phototropic, psychotropic*

changeable **adjective 1** *the weather will be changeable | she experienced changeable moods and panic attacks*: **variable**, inconstant, varying, changing, shifting, fluctuating, irregular, erratic, wavering, vacillating, inconsistent, fluid, floating, unsteady, unfixed, uneven, unstable, unsettled, turbulent, movable, mutable, chameleon-like; fickle, capricious, temperamental, whimsical, ever-changing, kaleidoscopic, volatile, mercurial, fitful, uncertain, unpredictable, undependable, unreliable; informal up and down, full of ups and downs, blowing hot and cold; rare vicissitudinous, protean, chameleonic, changeful, fluctuant, variational.
▷ANTONYMS unchanging, constant.
2 *the colours on the screen are instantly changeable*: **alterable**, adjustable, modifiable, variable, convertible, mutable, permutable, exchangeable, interchangeable, replaceable, transposable.
▷ANTONYMS unchangeable; inflexible.

> *Choose the right word* **changeable, inconstant, capricious, fickle**
>
> See **inconstant**.

changeless **adjective** *parents are so utterly changeless in their behaviour*: **unchanging**, unvarying, timeless, static, standing, fixed, permanent, constant, unchanged, fast, consistent, uniform, undeviating; stable, steady, unchangeable, unalterable, invariable, immutable; **lasting**, long-lasting, abiding, enduring, persistent, indefinite, continuing, perpetual, everlasting, perennial, unending, endless, never-ending.
▷ANTONYMS variable; fleeting.

channel **noun 1** *the English Channel*: **strait(s)**, sound, neck, arm, narrows, passage, sea passage, stretch of water, waterway.
2 *the clear water from the spring ran down a channel towards the house*: **duct**, gutter, groove, furrow, rut, conduit, trough, trench, culvert, cut, sluice, spillway, race, ditch, drain, watercourse, waterway, canal.
3 *it is hard to find the right* ***channel for*** *extraordinary energy*: **use**, medium, means/mode of expression, vehicle; release, means of release, release mechanism, safety valve, vent; way of harnessing; **course**, direction, path, route.
4 *a channel of communication*: **means**, medium, instrument, mechanism, agency, vehicle, route, avenue, course, method, mode; procedure, technique.
▶ **verb 1** *you need to* ***channel out*** *the plaster where the conduit is to go*: **hollow out**, gouge (out), cut (out), flute; cut a groove in, make a furrow in.
2 *the arches were put up to channel the waters of an underground river | many countries channel their aid through charities*: **convey**, transmit, transport, conduct, direct, guide, bear, carry, relay, pass on, transfer.

chant **noun 1** *a chant of 'Out! Out! Out!' made itself heard*: **shout**, cry, slogan, rallying call, war cry, chorus, chanting.
2 *the melodious chant of the monks intoning the psalm*: **incantation**, intonation, recitation, singing, song, recitative, mantra; rare cantillation.
▶ **verb 1** *protesters were chanting slogans*: **shout**, sing, chorus, carol; repeat.
2 *the choir then chanted Psalm 118*: **sing**, intone, incant, recite; rare cantillate, intonate.

chaos **noun** *there was complete chaos when she entered the classroom*: **disorder**, disarray, disorganization, confusion, mayhem, bedlam, pandemonium, madness, havoc, turmoil, tumult, commotion, disruption, upheaval, furore, frenzy, uproar, hue and cry, babel, hurly-burly; a maelstrom, a muddle, a mess, a shambles, a mare's nest; anarchy, entropy, lawlessness; W. Indian bangarang; informal hullabaloo, all hell broken loose, a madhouse; N. Amer. informal a three-ring circus.
▷ANTONYMS order, orderliness.

chaotic **adjective** *their tall Victorian house was like a chaotic museum*: **disorderly**, disordered, in disorder, in chaos, in disarray, disorganized, topsy-turvy, haywire, confused, in pandemonium, in turmoil, tumultuous, disrupted; frenzied, in uproar, in a muddle, jumbled, in a mess, messy, in a shambles, anarchic, lawless; rare orderless.
▷ANTONYMS orderly.

> *Word toolkit* **chaotic**
>
> See **messy**.

chap[1] **verb** *his skin is very dry and chaps easily*: **become raw**, become sore, redden, become inflamed, chafe, crack, roughen.

chap[2] **noun** Brit. informal *some chap gave it to me*: **man**, boy, male, individual, body; informal fellow, fella, geezer, punter, character, customer, sort, type; Brit. informal **bloke**, guy, lad, bod; N. Amer. informal dude, hombre; Brit. informal, dated cove; archaic wight.

chaperone **noun** *Aunt Millie went with her as chaperone*: **companion**, duenna, protectress, escort, governess, 'aunt', nursemaid, carer, keeper, protector, bodyguard, minder.
▶ **verb** *she was chaperoned at the ball by her mother*: **accompany**, escort, attend, shepherd, watch over, take care of, keep an eye on, protect, defend, guard, safeguard, shield, keep from harm, mind, screen, shelter, mother, nursemaid, nanny.

C

chapter noun **1** *the first chapter of 'Tom Brown's Schooldays'*: **section**, division, part, portion, segment, component, bit; instalment.
2 *it was the start of a new chapter in the country's history*: **period**, time, phase, page, stage, episode, epoch, era.
3 *the mistake sparked a chapter of errors*: **series**, sequence, succession, string, chain, progression, set, course, cycle; spate, wave, stream, rash, outbreak.
4 *a local chapter of the American Cancer Society*: **branch**, division, subdivision, section, department, bureau, agency, lodge, wing, arm, offshoot, subsidiary, satellite.
5 *the cathedral chapter requested consultation with other sees*: **governing body**, council, assembly, convocation, convention, synod, consistory.

char verb *the flames charred his clothes*: **scorch**, burn, singe, sear; blacken, discolour; informal toast; technical carbonize, calcine; rare torrefy.

character noun **1** *Jenny had a forceful character | buildings are important to the character of a town*: **personality**, nature, disposition, temperament, temper, mentality, turn of mind, psychology, psyche, constitution, make-up, make, stamp, mould, cast; persona; attributes, features, qualities, properties, traits; **essential quality**, essence, sum and substance, individuality, identity, distinctiveness, uniqueness, spirit, ethos, complexion, key, tone, tenor, ambience, air, aura, feel, feeling, vibrations; informal kidney; archaic humour, grain.
2 *how could any woman of character live with that man?* **integrity**, honour, moral strength, moral fibre, rectitude, uprightness; fortitude, strength, spine, backbone, toughness, resolve, will power, firmness of purpose; informal grit, guts, gutsiness, gumption; Brit. informal bottle.
3 *no stain will be on his character*: **reputation**, name, good name, standing, stature, position, status, image, credibility, acceptability, prestige, cachet, kudos, eminence; Indian izzat; archaic report.
4 informal *John was a bit of a character*: **eccentric**, oddity, odd fellow, madcap, crank, original, individualist, nonconformist, rare bird; square peg in a round hole; informal oddball, queer fish, odd fish, one; Brit. informal odd bod, oner; informal, dated card, caution, case; rare rara avis.
5 informal *her luncheon companion was a boorish character*: **individual**, person, personage, figure, party, being, human being, fellow, man, woman, mortal, soul, creature; informal fella, sort, type, thing, customer, punter, cookie, bunny, critter; Brit. informal bloke, chap, bod, geezer, gent; N. Amer. informal guy, gal, dame, dude, hombre; informal, dated body, dog; Brit. vulgar slang sod, bugger; archaic wight.
6 *the characters develop greatly throughout the novel*: **persona**, person, role, part; (**characters**) dramatis personae.
7 *the file name must not exceed thirty characters*: **letter**, figure, symbol, sign, mark, type, cipher, device, hieroglyph, rune; technical grapheme.

characteristic noun *these men have some interesting characteristics*: **attribute**, feature; quality, essential quality, property, trait, aspect, element, facet; mannerism, manner, habit, custom, way, mark, trademark, hallmark, distinction; idiosyncrasy, peculiarity, quirk, oddity, foible; penchant, proclivity, bent.
▶ adjective *his characteristic eloquence | poor soils are characteristic of the uplands*: **typical**, usual, normal, predictable, habitual, in character; **distinctive**, distinguishing, particular, special, especial, individual, specific, peculiar, idiosyncratic, singular, unique, exclusive, unmistakable; representative, symbolic, symptomatic, indicative, diagnostic.
▷ANTONYMS unusual.

characterize verb **1** *the period was characterized by rapid scientific advancement*: **distinguish**, make distinctive, mark, set apart, identify, specify, signalize, indicate, denote, designate, stamp; typify, pervade, permeate, suffuse.
2 *the women are typically characterized as prophets of doom*: **portray**, depict, present, represent, describe, outline, delineate, show, draw, sketch; categorize, class, classify, style, brand.

charade noun *the race for the presidential nomination has been a shameless charade*: **farce**, pantomime, travesty, mockery, parody, pretence, act, masquerade, sham, fake, false display, show, front, facade; rare simulacrum.

charge verb **1** *he didn't charge much for her flat*: **ask in payment**, ask, fix a charge, fix a price, impose, levy; expect, demand, exact; bill, invoice.
2 *the subscription price will be* **charged to** *your account annually*: **bill**, put down, debit from, take from.
▷ANTONYMS credit to.
3 *two men from London were* **charged with** *affray*: **accuse of**, indict for, arraign for; prosecute for, try for, bring to trial for, put on trial for; blame for, hold accountable for, implicate in; N. Amer. impeach for; archaic inculpate.
▷ANTONYMS absolve.
4 *they charged him with writing a history of the Ottoman dynasty*: **entrust**; **burden**, encumber, hamper, saddle, tax, weigh, weigh down, load.
5 *their mounted cavalry charged the advancing tanks*: **attack**, storm, rush, assault, assail, open fire on, fall on, set upon, swoop on, descend on, fly at, make an onslaught on, make a raid on; take by storm, attempt to capture; informal lay into, tear into.
6 *riot police charged into the crowd*: **rush**, move quickly, storm, stampede, career, tear, push, plough, swoop, dive, lunge, launch oneself, throw oneself, go headlong; informal steam; N. Amer. informal barrel.
▷ANTONYMS retreat.
7 *please see to it that your glasses are charged | the guns were charged and primed*: **fill**, fill up, fill to the brim, top up, stock; load, load up, pack, plug, arm, prepare to fire.
▷ANTONYMS empty.
8 *his work was charged with a kind of demonic energy*: **suffuse**, pervade, permeate, saturate, infuse, imbue, impregnate, inform, infect, inject, fill, load, instil, inspire, affect.
9 *I charge you to stop this course of action*: **order**, command, direct, instruct, tell, exhort, enjoin, adjure, demand, require; literary bid.
▶ noun **1** *customers pay a charge for the water consumed | all bus rides were free of charge*: **fee**, price, tariff, amount, sum, figure, fare, rate, payment, toll, levy; **cost**, expense, expenditure, outlay, dues.
2 *his client would be pleading not guilty to the charge*: **accusation**, allegation, indictment, arraignment, citation, imputation; blame, incrimination; N. Amer. impeachment; N. Amer. informal beef; archaic inculpation.
3 *Miles mustered the 5th Infantry for a charge*: **attack**, assault, offensive, onslaught, offence, drive, push, thrust, onrush, sortie, sally, swoop, foray, raid, invasion, incursion, campaign; storming; German blitzkrieg; Italian razzia; archaic onset.
▷ANTONYMS retreat.
4 *he put Gabriel in the charge of his daughter*: **care**, protection, safe keeping, keeping, supervision, surveillance, control, handling; custody, guardianship, tutelage, wardship, protectorship, patronage, trusteeship, auspices, aegis; hands, lap; archaic ward.
5 *his charge was to save the paper from bankruptcy*: **duty**, responsibility, task, job, obligation, assignment, mission, business, concern, function, burden, onus; directive, brief, briefing, instruction; Brit. informal pigeon; dated office.
6 *I am concerned for the safety of my charge*: **ward**, protégé, dependant; pupil, trainee, apprentice, mentee; minor.
▷ANTONYMS guardian.
7 *the judge gave a painstakingly careful charge to the jury*: **instruction**, direction, directive, order, command, dictate, injunction, exhortation, mandate.
8 N. Amer. informal *I get a real charge out of working hard*: **thrill**, tingle, glow; excitement, stimulation, fun, enjoyment, amusement, pleasure, gratification; informal **kick**, buzz, high.
□ **in charge of** *he was in charge of his father's printing works*: **responsible for**, in control of, at the helm of, in the driving seat of, at the wheel of; **managing**, running, administering, directing, supervising, overseeing, controlling, commanding, leading, heading up, looking after, taking care of; informal running the show, calling the shots.

charisma noun *some managers acquire authority through their personal charisma*: **charm**, presence, aura, personality, force of personality, strength of character, individuality; magnetism, animal magnetism, drawing power, attractiveness, appeal, allure, pull; magic, spell, mystique, glamour.

charismatic adjective *a charismatic leader*: **charming**, fascinating, full of personality, strong in character; magnetic, mesmerizing, captivating, bewitching, beguiling, attractive, appealing, alluring, hypnotic; magical, glamorous.

charitable adjective **1** *she became involved in local charitable activities*: **philanthropic**, humanitarian, humane, altruistic, benevolent, beneficent, welfare, public-spirited, socially concerned, doing good works; non-profit-making, non-profit, not-for-profit; historical almsgiving; rare eleemosynary.
2 *we were fed by some charitable people*: **big-hearted**, giving, generous, liberal, open-handed, free-handed, magnanimous, munificent, bountiful; literary bounteous; rare benignant.
▷ANTONYMS mean.
3 *he was charitable in his judgements, never censorious*: **magnanimous**, generous, generous to a fault, liberal, tolerant, moderate, easy-going, broad-minded, understanding, considerate, sympathetic, lenient, indulgent, forgiving, kind, kindly, compassionate, kind-hearted, tender-hearted, benign, mild, gracious.
▷ANTONYMS uncharitable.

charity noun **1** *they raised money for an AIDS charity*: **non-profit-making organization**, non-profit organization, not-for-profit organization, voluntary organization, charitable institution; fund, trust, foundation, cause, movement.
2 *we may be poor but we don't need charity*: **financial assistance**, aid, welfare, relief, financial relief, funding; handouts, gifts, presents, largesse, donations, contributions, grants, endowments, scholarships, bursaries, subsidies; patronage; historical alms, almsgiving; rare donatives, benefactions.
3 *his actions are rooted in self-interest rather than charity*: **philanthropy**, humanitarianism, humanity, altruism, public-spiritedness, social conscience, social concern, benevolence, benignity, beneficence, generosity, magnanimity, munificence, largesse; unselfishness, selflessness, self-sacrifice, self-denial.
▷ANTONYMS selfishness.
4 *show a bit of charity to those less fortunate than you*: **goodwill**, compassion, consideration, concern, kindness, kindliness, kind-heartedness, tenderness, tender-heartedness, warm-heartedness, brotherly love, love, sympathy, understanding, fellow feeling, thoughtfulness,

indulgence, tolerance, liberality, decency, nobility, graciousness, lenience, leniency; literary bounty, bounteousness; rare caritas.
▷ANTONYMS meanness.

charlatan noun *they denounced him as a corrupt charlatan*: **quack**, mountebank, sham, fraud, fake, humbug, impostor, pretender, masquerader, hoodwinker, hoaxer, cheat, deceiver, dissembler, double-dealer, double-crosser, trickster, confidence trickster, cheater, swindler, fraudster, racketeer; rogue, villain, scoundrel; informal phoney, sharper, sharp, shark, con man, con artist, hustler, flimflammer, flimflam man; Brit. informal twister; N. Amer. informal grifter, bunco artist, gold brick, chiseller; Austral. informal shicer, magsman, illywhacker; S. African informal schlenter; dated confidence man/woman; rare defalcator, tregetour.

charm noun **1** *people were captivated by her charm | she was resistant to his charms*: **attractiveness**, beauty, glamour, prettiness, loveliness; appeal, allure, desirability, seductiveness, magnetism, sexual magnetism, animal magnetism, charisma; wiles, blandishments, enticement; Scottish & N. English bonniness; informal gorgeousness, pulling power, come-on; formal beauteousness; archaic comeliness.
▷ANTONYMS unattractiveness.
2 *these traditional stories retain a lot of charm*: **appeal**, pull, draw, drawing power, attraction, allure, fascination, captivation, pleasingness, engagingness, delightfulness.
3 *they seek supernatural assistance through magical charms*: **spell**, incantation, conjuration, rune, magic formula, magic word, abracadabra, jinx; sorcery, magic, witchcraft, wizardry; N. Amer. mojo, hex; NZ makutu.
4 *he took the charms from his wife's bracelet*: **ornament**, trinket, bauble; archaic bijou.
5 *he always carries a lucky charm*: **talisman**, fetish, amulet, mascot, totem, idol, juju; archaic periapt; rare phylactery.
▶ verb **1** *he charmed thousands with his singing*: **delight**, please, win, win over, appeal to, attract, captivate, allure, lure, draw, dazzle, fascinate, bewitch, beguile, enchant, enthral, enrapture, enamour, seduce, ravish, hypnotize, mesmerize, spellbind, transfix, rivet, grip; rare rapture.
▷ANTONYMS repel.
2 *he charmed his mother into letting him have his own way*: **coax**, cajole, wheedle; woo; informal sweet-talk, soft-soap; archaic blandish.

charming adjective *he stayed with a French family and their charming daughter*: **delightful**, pleasing, pleasant, agreeable, likeable, endearing, lovely, lovable, adorable, cute, sweet, appealing, attractive, good-looking, prepossessing; striking, alluring, delectable, ravishing, winning, winsome, fetching, captivating, engaging, enchanting, entrancing, fascinating, bewitching, beguiling, spellbinding, hypnotizing, mesmerizing, seductive, desirable, tempting, inviting, irresistible; informal dreamy, heavenly, divine, gorgeous, smashing, easy on the eye, as nice as pie; N. Amer. informal babelicious, bodacious; dated taking; literary beauteous; archaic fair, comely.
▷ANTONYMS repulsive.

chart noun **1** *check your height and ideal weight on the chart*: **graph**, table, tabulation, grid, histogram, diagram, guide, scheme, figure, illustration; bar chart, pie chart, flow chart; map, plan, blueprint; Computing graphic.
2 (**charts**) *the song went straight to the top of the pop charts*: **hit parade**, top twenty; list, listing, league, catalogue, index.
▶ verb **1** *the population increase can be charted fairly accurately*: **tabulate**, plot, graph, delineate, map, map out, draw up, sketch, draft, document, record, register, represent; make a chart of, make a diagram of.
2 *the book charted his passage through Chicago*: **follow**, trace, outline, describe, detail, note, report, record, register, document, chronicle, log, catalogue.

charter noun **1** *the company is operating under Royal charter*: **authority**, authorization, sanction, covenant, dispensation, consent, permission, sufferance; prerogative, privilege, right; Law, historical droit.
2 *they violated the principles of the UN Charter*: **constitution**, code, canon, body of law, system of rules; fundamental principles, rules, laws.
3 *there is a fee for the independent charter of yachts*: **hire**, hiring, lease, leasing, rent, rental, renting, booking, reservation, reserving; dated engaging, engagement; rare bespeaking.
4 *Henry II granted him a charter to hold a market*: **permit**, licence, warrant, warranty, deed, bond, document, indenture; concession, franchise, privilege.
▶ verb *they chartered a train for the trip to Milwaukee*: **hire**, lease, rent, pay for the use of, book, reserve; dated engage; rare bespeak.

chary adjective *he was chary of broaching the subject*: **wary**, cautious, circumspect, heedful, careful, on one's guard, guarded, mindful, watchful; distrustful, mistrustful, doubtful, sceptical, suspicious, dubious, hesitant, reluctant, disinclined, loath, averse, shy, nervous, apprehensive, uneasy, afraid; informal leery, cagey, iffy, on one's toes.
▷ANTONYMS heedless.

chase[1] verb **1** *the attacker chased Mr Lee into an alley | the dogs chased after the fox*: **pursue**, run after, follow, hunt, track, trail; give chase to, be hot on someone's heels; informal tail.
▷ANTONYMS run away from.
2 *Jim had been chasing young girls for years*: **court**, woo, pursue, run after, seek the company of, make advances to, make up to, flirt with, romance; informal chat up, make (sheep's) eyes at, give the come-on to, come on to, be all over; Austral. informal track with, track square with; dated set one's cap at, pay addresses to, pay suit to, pay court to, seek the hand of, make love to; archaic spark.
3 *she* ***chased away*** *some donkeys from her garden*: **drive away**, drive off, drive out, put to flight, send away, scare off, scatter; informal send packing.
4 *she* ***chased away*** *all thoughts of him*: **dispel**, banish, dismiss, drive away, drive off, shut out, put out of one's mind.
▷ANTONYMS conjure up.
5 *photographers chased on to the runway to photograph him*: **rush**, dash, race, speed, streak, shoot, charge, career, scramble, scurry, hurry, make haste, hare, fly, pelt; informal scoot, belt, tear, zip, whip, go like a bat out of hell; N. Amer. informal boogie, hightail, clip; N. Amer. vulgar slang drag/tear/haul ass; informal, dated cut along; archaic post, hie.
▷ANTONYMS amble.
□ **chase someone/something up** *his job includes chasing up slow payers*: **pester**, harass, harry, nag, plague, hound; seek out, find, go after, follow up; informal hassle.
▶ noun *the predator finally gave up the chase*: **pursuit**, hunt, trail; hunting, coursing, course.
□ **give chase to** *they give chase to the bandits*: **chase**, pursue, run after, follow, hunt, track, trail; be hot on someone's heels; informal tail.

chase[2] verb *figures are chased in low relief on the dish*: **engrave**, etch, carve, inscribe, cut, chisel, imprint, impress, print, mark.

chasm noun **1** *the ground dropped away into an awesome chasm*: **gorge**, abyss, canyon, ravine, gully, gulf, pass, defile, couloir, crevasse, cleft, rift, rent; pit, void, crater, cavity, hole, opening, gap, fissure, crevice, hollow; S. English chine, bunny; N. English clough, gill, thrutch; Scottish cleuch, heugh; N. Amer. gulch, coulee, flume; American Spanish arroyo, barranca, quebrada; Indian nullah, khud; S. African sloot, kloof, donga; rare khor.
2 *a chasm between theory and practice*: **breach**, gulf, rift; division, schism, split, severance, rupture, break, break-up, parting of the ways; separation, disunion, estrangement, alienation, difference, dissension, discord, argument, quarrel; rare scission.

chassis noun *rubber tyres help to reduce shocks on the chassis*: **framework**, frame, skeleton, shell, casing, structure, substructure, bodywork, body; fuselage, hull, keel; anatomy, carcass.

chaste adjective **1** *the dress gave her a look of chaste girlhood*: **virginal**, virgin, intact, maidenly, maiden, unmarried, unwed; celibate, abstinent, self-restrained, self-denying, nunlike; **innocent**, pure, pure as the driven snow, guiltless, sinless, free of sin, uncorrupted, incorrupt, uncontaminated, undefiled, unsullied; virtuous, good, decent, moral, proper, decorous, demure, modest, wholesome, upright; informal squeaky clean; Christianity immaculate; literary vestal; rare continent.
▷ANTONYMS promiscuous, immoral.
2 *he gave her a chaste kiss on the cheek*: **non-sexual**, friendly, platonic, innocent.
▷ANTONYMS passionate.
3 *the dark, chaste interior was lightened by tilework*: **plain**, simple, bare, unadorned, undecorated, unornamented, unembellished, restrained, unaffected, unpretentious, unfussy, uncluttered, functional, without frills, spartan, austere, ascetic, monastic; informal no-frills.
▷ANTONYMS ostentatious.

chasten verb *both men were chastened by the bitter lessons of life*: **subdue**, humble, cow, squash, deflate, flatten, bring down, bring low, take down a peg or two, humiliate, mortify; restrain, tame, curb, check; informal cut down to size, put down, put someone in their place, settle someone's hash.

chastise verb **1** *the staff were chastised for arriving late*: **scold**, upbraid, berate, reprimand, reprove, rebuke, admonish, chide, censure, castigate, lambaste, lecture, criticize, pull up, take to task, haul over the coals, bring to book; informal tell off, give someone a telling-off, dress down, give someone a dressing-down, bawl out, blow up at, give someone an earful, give someone a caning, give someone a roasting, give someone a rocket, give someone a rollicking, come down on someone like a ton of bricks, have someone's guts for garters, slap someone's wrist, rap over the knuckles, give someone a piece of one's mind, throw the book at, read someone the Riot Act, let someone have it, give someone hell; Brit. informal carpet, monster, tear someone off a strip, tick off, have a go at, give someone a mouthful, give someone what for, give someone some stick, give someone a wigging; N. Amer. informal chew out, ream out; Brit. vulgar slang bollock, give someone a bollocking; dated trim, rate, give someone a rating; archaic chasten, recompense, visit; rare reprehend, objurgate.
▷ANTONYMS praise.
2 dated *her mistress chastised her with a whip*: **punish**, discipline; **beat**, thrash, flog, whip, horsewhip, strap, belt, cane, lash, birch, scourge, flay, flagellate; informal wallop, thump, clout, tan, tan someone's hide, beat the living daylights out of someone, give someone a good hiding.

chastity noun *the Vestals were sworn to a life of chastity*: **celibacy**, chasteness, virginity, abstinence, self-restraint, self-denial; singleness, maidenhood, the unmarried state; innocence, purity, virtue, goodness, decency, morality, decorum, modesty, wholesomeness; Christianity immaculateness; rare continence.
▷ANTONYMS promiscuity, immorality.

C

chat noun *I popped into Gill's house for a chat*: **talk**, conversation, gossip, chatter, heart-to-heart, tête-à-tête, powwow, blether, blather; conference, discussion, dialogue, exchange; Indian adda; informal jaw, gas, confab; Brit. informal natter, chinwag, rabbit; Scottish & N. English informal crack; N. Amer. informal rap, bull session, gabfest; formal confabulation; rare colloquy.
▶ verb *they sat and chatted with their guests*: **talk**, gossip, chatter, speak, converse, have a conversation, engage in conversation, tittle-tattle, prattle, jabber, jibber-jabber, babble, prate, go on, run on; communicate; Brit. talk nineteen to the dozen; Scottish & Irish slabber; informal gas, have a confab, jaw, chew the rag, chew the fat, yap, yak, yackety-yak, yabber, yatter, yammer, powwow; Brit. informal natter, witter, rabbit, chunter, waffle, have a chinwag, chinwag; N. Amer. informal shoot the breeze, shoot the bull, visit; Austral./NZ informal mag; formal confabulate; archaic twaddle, twattle, clack, claver.
□ **chat someone up** informal *he cornered her in the canteen and tried to chat her up*: **flirt with**, make up to, make advances to, make overtures to, romance; informal come on to, give the come-on to, make (sheep's) eyes at, be all over; dated make love to, set one's cap at.

chatter noun *she had often tired him with her chatter*: **chat**, talk, gossip, chit-chat, chitter-chatter, patter, jabbering, jabber, prattling, prattle, babbling, babble, tittle-tattle, tattle, blathering, blather, blethering, blether, rambling, gibbering; conversation, dialogue, discourse; informal gab, yak, yackety-yak, yabbering, yammering, yattering, yapping, jawing, chewing the fat, chewing the rag, confab; Brit. informal chinwagging, nattering, wittering, waffling, waffle, chuntering, rabbiting on; formal confabulation; archaic clack, claver, twaddle, twattle; rare colloquy.
▶ verb *they chattered excitedly throughout the journey*. See **chat** (verb).

chatterbox noun informal *Nicola was known as a chatterbox at work*: **talker**, chatterer, jabberer, babbler, prattler, blatherer, bletherer, prater; tittle-tattler, tattler, gossip, gossiper, gossipmonger; conversationalist; N. Amer. blatherskite; informal windbag, gasbag, gabber, big mouth, loudmouth, blabbermouth; Brit. informal natterer.

chatty adjective **1** *he was in an unusually chatty mood*: **talkative**, communicative, expansive, forthcoming, open, unreserved, gossipy, gossiping, garrulous, loquacious, voluble, verbose, effusive, gushing, glib; informal mouthy, gabby, windy, gassy; Brit. informal able to talk the hind legs off a donkey; rare multiloquent, multiloquous.
▷ANTONYMS taciturn.
2 *she received a long chatty letter from Ellen*: **conversational**, gossipy, informal, casual, colloquial, familiar, friendly; lively; informal newsy.
▷ANTONYMS formal.

chauvinism noun *they have a tendency towards small-mindedness and chauvinism*: **jingoism**, excessive patriotism, blind patriotism, excessive nationalism, sectarianism, isolationism, excessive loyalty, flag-waving, xenophobia, racism, racialism, racial prejudice, ethnocentrism, ethnocentricity; **partisanship**, partiality, prejudice, bias, discrimination, intolerance, bigotry; male chauvinism, sexism, misogyny.

chauvinist adjective *pamphlets expressing chauvinist and nationalist sentiments*: **jingoistic**, chauvinistic, excessively patriotic, excessively nationalistic, sectarian, isolationist, flag-waving, xenophobic, racist, racialist, ethnocentric; **partisan**, partial, prejudiced, biased, discriminating, discriminatory, intolerant, bigoted; **sexist**, male chauvinist, misogynist, woman-hating, anti-feminist, male supremacist; French parti pris.
▶ noun *he learned to show women some respect, but he's still a chauvinist*: **sexist**, male chauvinist, misogynist, woman-hater, anti-feminist, male supremacist; informal male chauvinist pig, MCP.

cheap adjective **1** *the firm are offering cheap day trips to London*: **inexpensive**, low-priced, low-price, low-cost, economical, economic, competitive, affordable, reasonable, reasonably priced, moderately priced, keenly priced, budget, economy, cheap and cheerful, bargain, cut-rate, cut-price, half-price, sale-price, sale, reduced, on special offer, marked down, discounted, discount, rock-bottom, giveaway; informal bargain-basement, slashed, going for a song, dirt cheap.
▷ANTONYMS expensive.
2 *the dashboard is plain without looking cheap*: **poor-quality**, second-rate, third-rate, substandard, low-grade, inferior, common, vulgar, shoddy, trashy, rubbishy, tawdry, tinny, brassy, worthless, meretricious, cheap and nasty, cheapjack, gimcrack, Brummagem, pinchbeck; informal cheapo, junky, tacky, kitsch, not up to much; Brit. informal naff, duff, ropy, grotty, rubbish, twopenny-halfpenny; N. Amer. informal a dime a dozen, tinhorn, two-bit, dime-store; Brit. vulgar slang crap, crappy; N. Amer. vulgar slang chickenshit; archaic trumpery.
▷ANTONYMS high-class.
3 *I disliked this film and its cheap exploitation of suffering*: **despicable**, contemptible, low, base, immoral, unscrupulous, unprincipled, unsavoury, distasteful, unpleasant, mean, shabby, sordid, vulgar, tawdry, low-minded, dishonourable, discreditable, ignoble, sorry, shameful; Brit. informal beastly; archaic scurvy.
▷ANTONYMS admirable.
4 *he made me feel cheap*: **ashamed**, embarrassed, humiliated, mortified, abashed, debased, degraded.
5 N. Amer. informal *he was so generous he made the other guests look cheap*. See **mean**[2].

cheapen verb **1** *he needed to cheapen the costs of his raw materials*: **reduce**, lower, lower in price, cut, mark down, discount, depreciate, devalue, depress, put down, keep down; informal slash, axe.
▷ANTONYMS raise.
2 *Hetty never compromised or cheapened herself*: **demean**, debase, degrade, lower, humble, devalue, drag down, abase, discredit, disgrace, dishonour, shame, humiliate, mortify, betray, prostitute; belittle, diminish, depreciate, denigrate, derogate; sell out, abandon one's principles, be untrue to oneself.

cheat verb **1** *customers were cheated by unscrupulous retailers*: **swindle**, defraud, deceive, trick, dupe, hoodwink, double-cross, gull; short-change; exploit, take advantage of, victimize; informal do, diddle, rip off, con, bamboozle, rob, fleece, shaft, sting, have, bilk, rook, gyp, finagle, flimflam, put one over on, pull a fast one on, take for a ride, lead up the garden path, sell down the river, pull the wool over someone's eyes; N. Amer. informal sucker, snooker, goldbrick, gouge, stiff, give someone a bum steer; Austral. informal pull a swifty on; Brit. informal, dated rush; archaic cozen, chicane, sell; rare illude, mulct.
2 *she cheated Ryan out of his fortune*: **deprive of**, deny, prevent from gaining, preclude from gaining; rob of, do out of.
3 *a schoolboy cheated death when he was struck by lightning*: **avoid**, escape, evade, elude, steer clear of, dodge, duck, miss, sidestep, bypass, skirt, shun, eschew; foil, frustrate, thwart, baulk, defeat.
4 *sixty per cent of husbands have cheated at least once*: **commit adultery**, be unfaithful, stray, be untrue, be inconstant, be false; informal two-time, play away, play around.
▶ noun **1** *he called the principal witness a liar and a cheat*: **swindler**, cheater, fraudster, trickster, confidence trickster, deceiver, hoaxer, hoodwinker, double-dealer, double-crosser, sham, fraud, fake, crook, rogue, charlatan, quack, mountebank, racketeer; informal con man, con artist, shark, sharper, phoney, hustler, flimflammer, flimflam man; Brit. informal twister; N. Amer. informal grifter, bunco artist, gold brick, chiseller; Austral. informal shicer, magsman, illywhacker; S. African informal schlenter; dated confidence man, confidence woman; rare defalcator, tregetour.
2 *Is there a sure cheat for generating cash?* **swindle**, fraud, deception, deceit, hoax, sham, trick, ruse, dodge, stratagem, blind, wile, Trojan horse; trickery, imposture, artifice, subterfuge; informal con, leg-pull.

check verb **1** *troops set up a road block and checked all vehicles* | *I checked up on your background*: **examine**, inspect, look at, look over, scrutinize, scan, survey; study, investigate, research, probe, dissect, explore, look into, enquire into, go into, go over with a fine-tooth comb; check out, test, monitor, review; informal give something a/the once-over, give something a look-see, give something a going-over.
2 *he checked that the gun was cocked*: **make sure**, confirm, verify, corroborate, validate, substantiate.
3 *two successive defeats checked their progress*: **halt**, stop, arrest, bring to a standstill, cut short; bar, obstruct, hamper, impede, inhibit, frustrate, foil, thwart, stand in the way of, prevent, curb, block, stall, hold up, interfere with, retard, delay, slow down, brake, put a brake on; stem, staunch; archaic stay.
4 *her tears could not be checked*: **suppress**, repress, restrain, contain, control, curb, rein in, bridle, smother, muffle, stifle, keep in check, hold back, swallow, choke back, fight back, bite back, bottle up; informal nip in the bud, keep a lid on.
▷ANTONYMS release.
□ **check in** *at the airport they check in at a special desk*: **report**, report one's arrival, record one's arrival, book oneself in, book in, enrol, register.
□ **check out** *she checked out of the hotel without saying goodbye*: **leave**, vacate, depart from, exit from, take one's leave from; pay the bill, pay up, settle up.
□ **check something out** informal **1** *the police have checked out dozens of leads*: **investigate**, look into, enquire into, probe, research, sound out, examine, go over, go through, vet; assess, weigh up, analyse, evaluate; follow up; informal suss out, recce, give something a/the once-over, give something a going-over; N. Amer. informal scope out; rare anatomize. **2** *she checked herself out in the mirror*: **look at**, observe, survey, gaze at, regard, inspect, contemplate; take note of; informal have a gander at, have a squint at, get a load of; Brit. informal take a dekko at, have a butcher's at, take a shufti at, clock; N. Amer. informal eyeball.
▶ noun **1** *they did an official check of the records*: **examination**, inspection, scrutiny, scrutinization, check-up, perusal, study, investigation, probe, dissection, analysis, assessment, enquiry; test, trial, assay, monitoring; informal once-over, going-over, look-see; rare anatomization.
2 *a permanent check on the abuse of authority*: **control**, restraint, constraint, break, bridle, curb, deterrent, hindrance, impediment, obstruction, inhibition, limitation.
3 N. Amer. *the waitress arrived with the check*: **bill**, account, invoice, statement, list of charges, tally; amount due; informal the damage; N. Amer. informal tab; Brit. informal, dated shot; archaic reckoning, score.
□ **keep something in check** *I strive to keep my temper in check*: **curb**, restrain, hold back, keep under control, keep a tight rein on, bridle, rein in, rein back; control, govern, master, repress, suppress, subdue, stifle, smother, tone down; informal keep a lid on, nip in the bud.

C

check-up noun *you should go to the hospital for a check-up*: **examination**, inspection, assessment, evaluation, analysis, survey, scan, scrutinization, scrutiny, observation, exploration, probe, test, appraisal; check, health check; informal once-over, going-over, overhaul.

cheek noun *he had the cheek to suggest I was too old | less of the cheek, if you don't mind*: **impudence**, impertinence, insolence, cheekiness, audacity, temerity, brazenness, presumption, effrontery, nerve, gall, pertness, boldness, shamelessness, impoliteness, disrespect, bad manners, unmannerliness, overfamiliarity; answering back, talking back; informal brass, brass neck, neck, face, lip, mouth, cockiness; Brit. informal sauce; Scottish informal snash; N. Amer. informal sass, sassiness, nerviness, chutzpah, back talk; informal, dated hide; Brit. informal, dated crust, backchat; archaic malapertness, contumely; rare procacity, assumption.
▷ANTONYMS politeness.
▸ verb informal *they were told off for cheeking the dinner lady*: **answer back to**, talk back to, be cheeky to, be impertinent to; contradict, argue with, disagree with; informal backchat; N. Amer. informal sass, be sassy to.

> *Word links* **cheek**
>
> **buccal**, **malar** relating to the cheek

cheeky adjective *you should have heard the cheeky boy lecturing me*: **impudent**, impertinent, insolent, presumptuous, forward, pert, bold, bold as brass, brazen, brazen-faced, shameless, audacious, overfamiliar, irreverent, discourteous, disrespectful, insubordinate, impolite, bad-mannered, ill-mannered, unmannerly, rude, insulting; informal brass-necked, cocky, lippy, mouthy, fresh, flip; Brit. informal saucy, smart-arsed; N. Amer. informal sassy, nervy, smart-assed; archaic malapert, contumelious, presumptive, assumptive; rare tossy, mannerless.
▷ANTONYMS respectful, polite.

cheep verb *the chicks cheeped loudly and paddled for shelter*: **chirp**, chirrup, twitter, tweet, peep, chitter, chatter, chirr, trill, warble, sing, pipe.
▸ noun *the bird gave a shrill cheep*: **chirp**, chirrup, twitter, tweet, peep, chirr, warble, trill.

cheer noun **1** *she acknowledged the cheers of the onlookers*: **hurrah**, hurray, whoop, bravo, hoot, shout, shriek; hosanna, alleluia; (**cheers**) acclaim, acclamation, shouting, clamour, applause, clapping, ovation; informal holler; rare laudation; archaic huzza.
▷ANTONYMS boo.
2 *Christmas and New Year are a time of cheer*: **happiness**, joy, joyousness, cheerfulness, cheeriness, gladness, merriment, gaiety, hilarity, mirth, glee, blitheness, jubilation, exultation, euphoria, jollity, jolliness, high spirits, joviality, jocularity, conviviality, light-heartedness, buoyancy, optimism, hope, hopefulness; merrymaking, pleasure, enjoyment, rejoicing, revelry, festivity, frolics; informal larking about, living it up; dated sport.
▷ANTONYMS sadness, doom and gloom.
3 *the table was groaning with Christmas cheer*: **fare**, food, foodstuffs, eatables, provisions, rations, sustenance, meat; drink, beverages; informal eats, nibbles, nosh, grub, chow; Brit. informal scoff, scran; N. Amer. informal chuck; archaic viands, victuals, vittles, commons; rare comestibles, provender, aliment, commissariat, viaticum.
▸ verb **1** *they'll all be at Lords to cheer their cricket team*: **acclaim**, hail, salute, praise, congratulate, toast, hurrah, hurray, applaud, clap, shout for, whistle; honour, glorify; express approval of, express admiration for, show one's appreciation of, put one's hands together for; informal root for, holler for, give someone a big hand, bring the house down; N. Amer. informal ballyhoo; black English big someone/something up; archaic emblazon; rare laud, panegyrize.
▷ANTONYMS boo.
2 *the bad weather did little to cheer me*: **raise someone's spirits**, brighten, buoy up, enliven, animate, elate, exhilarate, hearten, gladden, uplift, give a lift to, perk up, encourage, comfort, solace, console; informal buck up; rare inspirit.
▷ANTONYMS depress.
□ **cheer someone on** *knots of spectators were there to cheer me on*: **encourage**, urge on, spur on, drive on, motivate, rally, inspire, fire, fire up; give someone a lift, keep someone going, see someone through; N. Amer. informal root for, light a fire under; rare inspirit.
▷ANTONYMS discourage.
□ **cheer up** *once I got inside the house I began to cheer up*: **perk up**, brighten (up), become more cheerful, pick up, liven up, become livelier, rally, revive, bounce back, take heart, be heartened, take on a new lease of life; informal buck up.
▷ANTONYMS feel depressed.
□ **cheer someone up** *I asked her out to lunch to cheer her up*: **raise someone's spirits**, make happier, make more cheerful, buoy up, perk up, enliven, animate, hearten, gladden, uplift, give a lift to, encourage; comfort, solace, console; informal buck up, pep up; rare inspirit.
▷ANTONYMS depress.

cheerful adjective **1** *he arrived looking relaxed and cheerful*: **happy**, jolly, merry, bright, glad, sunny, joyful, joyous, light-hearted, in good spirits, in high spirits, sparkling, bubbly, exuberant, ebullient, cock-a-hoop, elated, gleeful, breezy, airy, cheery, sprightly, jaunty, animated, radiant, smiling, grinning, laughing, mirthful, frolicsome; jovial, genial, good-humoured; happy-go-lucky, carefree, unworried, untroubled, without a care in the world, full of the joys of spring; buoyant, optimistic, hopeful, full of hope, positive; content, contented; informal upbeat, chipper, chirpy, peppy, smiley, sparky, zippy, zingy, bright-eyed and bushy-tailed, full of beans, full of vim and vigour; N. Amer. informal peart; dated gay; literary jocund, gladsome, blithe, blithesome; archaic of good cheer.
▷ANTONYMS sad.
2 *primary colours make for a cheerful family room*: **pleasant**, attractive, agreeable, cheering, uplifting, bright, sunny, happy, friendly, welcoming, homelike, comfortable; informal comfy.
▷ANTONYMS cheerless.
3 *he supported our scheme with cheerful generosity*: **eager**, keen, enthusiastic, happy, glad, ready, willing, obliging, cooperative, compliant, complying, acquiescent, agreeing, assenting, ungrudging; informal game.
▷ANTONYMS unwilling.

cheerio exclamation Brit. informal *My car's at the door. Cheerio!* See **goodbye**.

cheerless adjective *his office was grey and cheerless*: **gloomy**, dreary, dull, dismal, bleak, drab, grim, sombre, dark, dim, dingy, funereal; austere, stark, bare, desolate, comfortless; miserable, wretched, joyless, unhappy, depressing, disheartening, dispiriting, unwelcoming, uninviting, inhospitable, bland, clinical, institutional, impersonal.
▷ANTONYMS cheerful, cosy.

cheers exclamation **1** informal *he raised his glass and said 'Cheers!'*: **here's to you**, good health, your health, here's health, skol, good luck; Irish slainte; German prost, prosit; French salut; Spanish salud; informal bottoms up, down the hatch; Brit. informal here's mud in your eye; Brit. informal, dated cheerio, chin-chin, here's how.
2 Brit. informal *Cheers, Jack, see you in church!* See **goodbye**.
3 Brit. informal *cheers for listening to me.* See **thanks** (exclamation).

cheery adjective *Gareth was a cheery, ever-smiling boy*: **jolly**, happy, merry, bright, cheerful, glad, sunny, joyful, joyous, light-hearted, in high spirits, sparkling, bubbly, exuberant, ebullient, cock-a-hoop, elated, blissful, ecstatic, euphoric, gleeful, breezy, airy, sprightly, jaunty, animated, radiant, smiling, grinning, laughing, mirthful, frolicsome; happy-go-lucky, in good spirits, carefree, unworried, untroubled, without a care in the world, full of the joys of spring; buoyant, optimistic, hopeful, full of hope, positive, content; informal upbeat, chipper, chirpy, smiley, peppy, sparky, zippy, zingy, bright-eyed and bushy-tailed, full of beans, full of vim and vigour; N. Amer. informal peart; dated gay; literary gladsome, jocund, blithe, blithesome; archaic of good cheer.
▷ANTONYMS gloomy.

cheese noun

> *Word links* **cheese**
>
> **caseous** relating to cheese
> **cheesemonger** seller of cheese

chef noun *he worked as a chef for a catering company*: **cook**, cordon bleu cook, food preparer; head chef, sous chef, commis chef, chef de cuisine, chef de partie; pastry cook, saucier; N. Amer. informal short-order cook.

chef-d'œuvre noun French *his chef-d'œuvre was his biography of George Washington*: **masterpiece**, masterwork, best work, finest work, greatest creation, crowning achievement, work of art; treasure, gem, pearl, jewel, jewel in the crown; Latin magnum opus; French pièce de résistance, tour de force.

chequered adjective **1** *he wore short chequered breeches*: **checked**, multicoloured, many-coloured, harlequin, varicoloured, particoloured.
2 *the corporation has had a chequered history*: **varied**, mixed, eventful, full of ups and downs, up and down, with good and bad parts, with its fair share of rough and tumble; unsettled, unstable, irregular, erratic, inconstant, fluctuating, changeful; diverse, diversified, many-faceted; rare vicissitudinous.

cherish verb **1** *he was cherished by a wide circle of friends*: **adore**, hold dear, love, care very much for, feel great affection for, dote on, be devoted to, revere, esteem, admire, appreciate; think the world of, set great store by, hold in high esteem; **care for**, look after, tend, protect, preserve, shelter, keep safe, support, nurture, cosset, indulge; informal put on a pedestal.
2 *I cherish the letters she wrote*: **treasure**, prize, value highly, hold dear.
▷ANTONYMS neglect.
3 *they cherished dreams of football glory*: **harbour**, have, possess, hold (on to), cling to, entertain, retain, maintain, keep in one's mind, foster, nurture, nurse.
▷ANTONYMS abandon.

cherub noun **1** *she was borne up to heaven by cherubs*: **angel**, seraph.
2 *the picture showed a wistful cherub of 18 months*: **baby**, infant, toddler, little one; **pretty child**, lovable child, well behaved child, innocent child; little angel, little dear, little darling; informal kid, tot, tiny tot, tiny; literary babe, babe in arms.

C

cherubic adjective *his cherubic face creased into a wide grin*: **angelic**; sweet, cute, attractive, adorable, appealing, lovable, lovely; innocent, seraphic, saintly; informal butter-wouldn't-melt.

chest noun **1** *he had several bullet wounds in his chest*: **breast**, upper body, body, torso, trunk; technical thorax, sternum.
2 *the matron had a phenomenally large chest*: **bust**, bosom; archaic embonpoint.
3 *they took logs from a metal-bound oak chest*: **box**, case, casket, crate, trunk, coffer, strongbox; container, receptacle.
□ **get something off one's chest** informal **confess**, disclose, divulge, reveal, make known, make public, own up to, make a clean breast of, bring into the open, tell all about, say what one is thinking; get a load off one's mind, unburden oneself; informal spill the beans about, come out with it; archaic discover.
▷ANTONYMS bottle something up.

> *Word links* **chest**
>
> **pectoral**, **thoracic** relating to the chest
> **thoracotomy** surgical incision of the chest

chew verb *Carolyn chewed a mouthful of toast*: **masticate**, munch, champ, chomp, crunch, bite, nibble, gnaw, grind; eat, consume, devour; technical manducate, triturate; rare chumble.
□ **chew something over** *the doctor chewed over possible responses*: **meditate on**, ruminate on, think about, think over, think through, mull over, contemplate, consider, weigh up, ponder on, deliberate on, reflect on, muse on, cogitate about, dwell on, take stock of, give thought to, turn over in one's mind, consider the pros and cons of; brood over, wrestle with, puzzle over, rack one's brains about; N. Amer. think on; informal kick around/about, bat around/about; archaic pore on; rare cerebrate.
□ **chew the fat/rag** informal *he liked drinking with friends and chewing the fat*: **chat**, talk, converse, speak to each other, discuss things, have a talk, have a chat, have a tête-à-tête, have a conversation; informal have a confab, jaw, rap, yak, yap; Brit. informal natter, rabbit, have a chinwag, chinwag; N. Amer. informal shoot the breeze, shoot the bull, visit; Austral./NZ informal mag; formal confabulate.

chic adjective *she wore a chic black costume and white wrap*: **stylish**, smart, elegant, sophisticated, dapper, debonair, dashing, trim, tasteful, understated, attractive, flattering; **fashionable**, high-fashion, modish, voguish, in vogue, up to date, up to the minute, ultra-modern, contemporary; French à la mode; informal trendy, with it, now, sharp, snappy, snazzy, natty, dressy, swish; N. Amer. informal fly, spiffy, sassy, kicky, tony; archaic trig.
▷ANTONYMS unfashionable.

chicanery noun *political chicanery of all sorts goes on behind closed doors*: **trickery**, deception, deceit, deceitfulness, duplicity, dishonesty, unscrupulousness, underhandedness, subterfuge, fraud, fraudulence, legerdemain, sophistry, sharp practice, skulduggery, swindling, cheating, duping, hoodwinking; deviousness, guile, intrigue, craft, craftiness, artfulness, slyness, wiles; misleading talk; informal crookedness, monkey business, funny business, hanky-panky, shenanigans, flimflam; Brit. informal jiggery-pokery; N. Amer. informal monkeyshines; Irish informal codology; archaic management, knavery.

chicken noun

> *Word links* **chicken**
>
> **cock**, **rooster** male
> **hen** female
> **chick** young

chide verb *he was forever being chided for overfamiliarity*: **scold**, chastise, upbraid, berate, castigate, lambaste, rebuke, reprimand, reproach, reprove, admonish, remonstrate with, lecture, criticize, censure; call to account, take to task, pull up, go on at, read someone the Riot Act, haul someone over the coals, give someone a piece of one's mind; informal tell off, give someone a telling-off, dress down, give someone a dressing-down, give someone an earful, give someone a roasting, give someone a talking-to, give someone a rocket, give someone a rollicking, rap, rap over the knuckles, slap someone's wrist, let someone have it, send someone away with a flea in their ear, bawl out, give someone hell, come down on, blow up at, pitch into, lay into, lace into, tear into, give someone a caning, put on the mat, slap down, blast, rag, keelhaul; Brit. informal tick off, have a go at, carpet, monster, give someone a mouthful, tear someone off a strip, give someone what for, give someone some stick, wig, give someone a wigging, give someone a row, row; N. Amer. informal chew out, ream out, take to the woodshed; Brit. vulgar slang bollock, give someone a bollocking; N. Amer. vulgar slang chew someone's ass, ream someone's ass; dated call down, rate, give someone a rating, trim; rare reprehend, objurgate.
▷ANTONYMS praise.

chief noun **1** *a Highland chief petitioned her father for her hand*: **leader**, chieftain, head, headman, ruler, overlord, master, commander, suzerain, seigneur, liege, liege lord, potentate; among American Indians sachem.
2 *he is the chief of the US central bank*: **head**, principal, chief executive, executive, president, chair, chairman, chairwoman, chairperson, governor, director, administrator, manager, manageress, superintendent, foreman, forewoman, controller, overseer; boss, employer, proprietor; N. Amer. chief executive officer, CEO; informal boss man, kingpin, top dog, big cheese, bigwig, skipper; Brit. informal gaffer, guv'nor; N. Amer. informal numero uno, Mister Big, honcho, head honcho, padrone, sachem, big white chief, big kahuna, big wheel, high muckamuck; informal, derogatory fat cat.
▶ adjective **1** *he had a meeting with the chief rabbi*: **head**, leading, principal, premier, highest, foremost, supreme, grand, superior, arch-; directing, governing; informal number-one.
▷ANTONYMS subordinate.
2 *their chief aim was to remove the invading forces*: **main**, principal, most important, uppermost, primary, prime, first, cardinal, central, key, focal, vital, crucial, essential, pivotal, supreme, predominant, pre-eminent, paramount, overriding, leading, major, ruling, dominant, highest; arch; informal number-one.
▷ANTONYMS minor.

chiefly adverb *the theatre was used chiefly for performances of music*: **mainly**, in the main, primarily, principally, predominantly, above all, mostly, for the most part, first and foremost, especially, particularly, essentially, substantially; usually, customarily, habitually, typically, commonly, generally, on the whole, largely, by and large, as a rule, in most instances, almost always, almost entirely, to a large extent, to a great degree.

child noun *I've known Kate since she was a child | his wife gave birth to their first child*: **youngster**, young one, little one, boy, girl; baby, newborn, infant, toddler; schoolboy, schoolgirl, adolescent, teenager, youth, young man, young woman, young lady, young person, young adult, juvenile, minor, junior; stripling, fledgling, whippersnapper; **son**, **daughter**, son and heir, scion, descendant; (**children**) offspring, progeny, issue; technical neonate; Scottish & N. English bairn, wean, laddie, lassie; informal kid, kiddie, kiddiewink, nipper, tot, tiny, tiny tot, shaver, young 'un, lad, lass, teen, teeny-bopper; Brit. informal sprog; N. Amer. informal rug rat; Austral./NZ informal ankle-biter; derogatory brat, chit, urchin, guttersnipe; literary babe, babe in arms; archaic hobbledehoy.

> *Word links* **child**
>
> **paedo-** related prefix
> **paedophobia** fear of children
> **paediatrics** branch of medicine dealing with children
> **infanticide** killing of a young child

childbirth noun *her mother had major problems during childbirth*: **labour**, delivery, giving birth, birthing; technical parturition; literary travail; archaic confinement, lying-in, accouchement, childbed.

> *Word links* **childbirth**
>
> **obstetric** relating to childbirth
> **obstetrics** branch of medicine to do with childbirth
> **tocophobia** fear of childbirth

childhood noun *she had been writing poems since her childhood*: **youth**, early years, early days, early life, infancy, babyhood, boyhood, girlhood, pre-teens, prepubescence, adolescence, teens, teenage years, young adulthood, immaturity; the springtime of life, one's salad days; Law minority; rare nonage, juvenility, juniority, juvenescence.
▷ANTONYMS adulthood, old age.

childish adjective **1** *it was childish of her to rip up the picture*: **immature**, babyish, infantile, juvenile, puerile; silly, inane, fatuous, jejune, foolish, stupid, irresponsible, naive.
▷ANTONYMS mature.
2 *she had a round childish face*: **childlike**, youthful, young, young-looking, girlish, boyish, children's, child's, adolescent, teenaged, teenage; archaic bread-and-butter.
▷ANTONYMS adult.

childlike adjective **1** *my grandmother looked almost childlike in the big white bed*: **youthful**, young, young-looking, girlish, boyish, adolescent, teenaged, teenage.
2 *geniuses tend to be rather childlike*: **innocent**, artless, guileless, simple, unworldly, unsophisticated, green, inexperienced, naive, ingenuous, trusting, trustful, unsuspicious, unwary, unguarded, credulous, gullible, easily taken in; **unaffected**, without airs, open, frank, uninhibited, natural, spontaneous, down-to-earth; informal wet behind the ears.

chill noun **1** *there was a distinct chill in the air*: **coldness**, chilliness, coolness, iciness, crispness, rawness, bitterness, nip, bite, sting, sharpness, keenness, harshness, wintriness, frigidity; informal nippiness; Brit. informal parkiness; rare gelidity.
▷ANTONYMS warmth.
2 *he took to his bed with a chill*: **cold**, dose of flu, dose of influenza,

respiratory infection, viral infection, virus; archaic grippe.
3 *he tried to end the chill in his relations with the West*: **unfriendliness**, lack of understanding, lack of sympathy, lack of warmth, chilliness, coldness, coolness, frigidity, aloofness, distance, remoteness, unresponsiveness.
▷ANTONYMS friendliness.
▶verb **1** *the dessert is best made ahead and then chilled*: **make cold**, make colder, cool, cool down, cool off; refrigerate, freeze, quick-freeze, deep-freeze, ice.
▷ANTONYMS warm.
2 *his quiet tone chilled Ruth more than if he had shouted*: **scare**, frighten, petrify, terrify, alarm, appal, disturb, disquiet, unsettle; make someone's blood run cold, chill someone's blood, chill to the bone, chill to the marrow, make someone's flesh crawl, give someone goose pimples, scare witless, frighten the living daylights out of, fill with fear, strike terror into, put the fear of God into, throw into a panic; informal scare the pants off; Brit. informal put the wind up, give someone the heebie-jeebies, make someone's hair curl; Irish informal scare the bejesus out of; vulgar slang scare shitless; archaic affright.
▷ANTONYMS comfort, reassure.
□ **chill out** N. Amer. informal *the home should be a place to chill out*. See **relax**.
▶adjective literary *a chill wind came through the open doors*: **cold**, chilly, cool, crisp, fresh, brisk; bleak, wintry, snowy, frosty, icy, ice-cold, icy-cold, glacial, polar, arctic, raw, sharp, bitter, bitterly cold, biting, piercing, penetrating, numbing, freezing, frigid; informal nippy; Brit. informal parky; rare gelid, brumal.

chilly adjective **1** *the weather had turned chilly*: **cold**, cool, crisp, fresh, brisk, bleak, wintry, snowy, frosty, icy, ice-cold, icy-cold, glacial, polar, arctic, raw, sharp, bitter, bitterly cold, biting, piercing, penetrating, freezing, frigid; informal nippy; Brit. informal parky; literary chill; rare gelid, brumal.
▷ANTONYMS warm.
2 *I woke up feeling chilly*: **cold**, frozen, frozen stiff, frozen to the marrow/core/bone, freezing, freezing cold, bitterly cold, shivery, numb, numbed, chilled.
3 *her chilly face splintered into a smile*: **unfriendly**, unsympathetic, unwelcoming, forbidding, cold, cool, frosty, glacial, frigid; haughty, supercilious, disdainful, aloof, distant, remote; reserved, withdrawn, uncommunicative, unresponsive, unemotional, dispassionate, passionless, wooden, impersonal, formal, stiff, austere; informal stand-offish, offish; rare gelid.
▷ANTONYMS friendly.

chime verb **1** *at the stroke of nine, the bells began to chime*: **ring**, peal, toll, sound; ding, dong, clang, boom, resound, reverberate; tinkle, jingle, jangle; archaic knell; rare tintinnabulate.
2 *the clock on the mantelpiece chimed eight o'clock*: **strike**, sound; indicate, mark.
□ **chime in 1** *'Yes, you do that,' Doreen chimed in eagerly*: **interject**, interpose, intervene, interrupt, butt in, cut in, break in, join in, join the conversation; Brit. informal chip in, add one's pennyworth. **2** *some of his remarks chimed in with the ideas of Adam Smith*: **accord**, correspond, be consistent, be compatible, agree, be in agreement, be in accordance, fit in, be in harmony, harmonize, be in tune, be consonant, be similar; informal square.
▶noun *the chimes of the cathedral bells*: **peal**, pealing, ringing, carillon, toll, tolling, sound; ding-dong, clanging; angelus; archaic knell; rare tintinnabulation.

chimera noun *the economic sovereignty she claims to defend is a chimera*: **illusion**, fantasy, delusion, dream, fancy, figment of the imagination, will-o'-the-wisp, phantom, mirage; Latin ignis fatuus.

chimney noun **stack**, smokestack; flue, shaft, funnel, vent; Scottish & N. English lum; rare femerell.

China noun

> *Word links* **China**
>
> **Sino-** related prefix, as in *Sino-American*
> **sinology** study of China

china noun **1** *a china cup*: **porcelain**.
2 *a table laid with the best china and crystal glasses*: **dishes**, plates, cups and saucers, crockery, dinner service, tea service; tableware, ware; N. Amer. dinnerware; Irish delph.

chink[1] noun *the sun had found a chink in the clouds | a chink in the wall*: **opening**, gap, space, hole, aperture, break, breach, crack, fissure, crevice, cranny, cleft, cut, rift, split, slit, slot.

chink[2] verb *I heard her bracelets chinking as she walked away*: **jingle**, jangle, clink, tinkle, rattle, clank.

chip noun **1** *wood chips*: **fragment**, piece, bit; sliver, splinter, spell, spillikin, shaving, paring; scrap, snippet, flake; shard; Scottish skelf; technical gallet, spall.
2 *a glass with a chip in the bottom*: **nick**, crack, snick, scratch; flaw, fault.
3 *fish and chips*: (**chips**) chipped potatoes, potato chips, game chips; Brit. French fried potatoes; N. Amer. French fries.
4 *gambling chips*: **counter**, token, disc, jetton; N. Amer. check.
▶verb **1** *the teacup was chipped and dirty*: **nick**, crack, snick, scratch; damage.
2 *the plaster had chipped and no repairs had been done*: **break (off)**, crack, fragment, crumble.
3 *it required a craftsman to chip the blocks of flint to the required shape*: **whittle**, hew, chisel.
□ **chip in 1** *'He's right,' Gloria chipped in*: **interrupt**, cut in, chime in, break in, interject, interpose, butt in. **2** *parents, pupils, and staff chipped in to help raise the cash | the firm chipped in nearly £100,000 in sponsorship*: **contribute**, donate, give, make a contribution/donation, hand over, pay; club together; informal fork out, shell out, lay out, come across with, cough up; Brit. informal stump up, have a whip-round; N. Amer. informal kick in, pony up.

C

chirp verb *a canary chirped from a cage on the veranda*: **tweet**, twitter, chirrup, cheep, peep, chitter, chatter, chirr; sing, warble, trill, pipe.

chirpy adjective informal *Leonard was in a chirpy mood*. See **cheerful**.

chit-chat noun informal *Lucenzo didn't indulge in idle chit-chat*: **small talk**, chat, chatting, chatter, chitter-chatter, prattling, prattle, gossip, tittle-tattle, tattle; Brit. informal nattering, chuntering.

chivalrous adjective **1** *he was well known for his chivalrous treatment of women*: **gallant**, gentlemanly, honourable, respectful, thoughtful, considerate, protective, attentive; **courteous**, polite, gracious, well mannered, urbane, courtly; dated mannerly; archaic gentle.
▷ANTONYMS rude, boorish, unmannerly.
2 *the prince's taste for chivalrous pursuits and warlike deeds*: **knightly**, noble, chivalric; brave, courageous, bold, valiant, valorous, heroic, daring, intrepid; honourable, high-minded, just, fair, loyal, constant, true, virtuous.
▷ANTONYMS cowardly.

chivalry noun **1** *small but pleasing acts of chivalry that seemed to come so naturally to him*: **gallantry**, gentlemanliness, thoughtfulness, attentiveness, consideration, considerateness; **courtesy**, courteousness, politeness, graciousness, mannerliness, good manners, urbanity, courtliness.
▷ANTONYMS rudeness, boorishness.
2 *Edward III created a court which exemplified the values of chivalry*: **knight errantry**, the knightly code, knighthood, courtly manners, knightliness, courtliness, nobility, magnanimity; bravery, courage, boldness, valour, heroism, daring, intrepidity; honour, integrity, high-mindedness, justice, justness, fairness, loyalty, constancy, trueness, truthfulness, virtuousness.

chivvy verb *she did nothing to help, but constantly chivvied the girls and interfered with their work*: **nag**, badger, hound, harass, harry, keep after, keep on at, go on at, pester, plague, torment, persecute, goad, annoy, bother; urge, prod, pressure, pressurize; informal hassle, bug, breathe down someone's neck, get on someone's case; N. English informal mither; N. Amer. informal ride; Austral. informal heavy.

choice noun **1** *the voters' choice of candidate | an individual's freedom of choice*: **selection**, choosing, picking; election, adoption, nomination; decision, say, vote, preference, pick.
2 *you must trust me—you have no other choice*: **option**, **alternative**, possibility, possible course of action; solution, answer, way out.
3 *an extensive choice of wines, spirits, and beers*: **range**, variety, selection, assortment; array, display.
4 *John would have been the perfect choice*: **appointee**; nominee, candidate, selection.
□ **by choice** *by default, if not by choice, they quickly learn to develop the art of the trickster*: **voluntarily**, of one's own accord, of one's own free will, of one's own volition, of one's own choice, of one's own choosing, by preference; willingly, readily, freely, intentionally, deliberately, on purpose, purposely, spontaneously, without being asked, without being forced, without hesitation, without reluctance; gladly, with pleasure, with good grace, eagerly, enthusiastically.
▷ANTONYMS reluctantly, under duress.
▶adjective **1** *choice plums | a choice property in some of the finest country in the state*: **superior**, first-class, first-rate, prime, premier, grade A, best, finest, excellent, select, quality, high-quality, top, top-quality, high-grade, of the first water, prize, special, exclusive, hand-picked, carefully chosen, vintage, fine; French par excellence; informal tip-top, A1, top-notch, plum.
▷ANTONYMS inferior, mediocre.
2 *she had often rehearsed the choice phrases she would use*: **well chosen**, well put, well expressed; appropriate, apposite, apt, fit, felicitous.
3 *a few choice words that he usually saved for the traffic warden*: **rude**, abusive, insulting, offensive, unprintable.
▷ANTONYMS polite.

choir noun **singers**, chorus, chorale.

> *Word links* **choir**
>
> **choral** relating to a choir

choke verb **1** *Christopher gulped and started to choke*: **gag**, retch, cough, struggle for air, fight for breath, gasp.
2 *thick clouds of dust choked her*: **suffocate**, asphyxiate, smother, stifle; overpower, overcome.

3 *she had been choked to death when her necklace snagged on overhanging branches*: **strangle**, throttle; asphyxiate, suffocate; informal strangulate.
4 *sections of guttering were choked with leaves and other debris*: **clog (up)**, bung up, block, obstruct, stop up, silt up, plug, dam up; congest, jam; informal gunge up; technical occlude, obturate.
□ **choke something back** *he choked back his tears*: **suppress**, hold back, fight back, bite back, gulp back, swallow, check, keep in check, restrain, contain, control, repress, smother, stifle, curb, bridle, rein in; bite one's lip; informal keep a/the lid on.

C

choleric adjective *a choleric, self-important little man*: **bad-tempered**, irascible, irritable, grumpy, grouchy, crotchety, tetchy, testy, crusty, cantankerous, curmudgeonly, ill-tempered, ill-natured, ill-humoured, peevish, cross, fractious, disagreeable, pettish, crabbed, crabby, waspish, prickly, peppery, touchy, scratchy, splenetic, shrewish, short-tempered, hot-tempered, quick-tempered, dyspeptic, bilious, liverish, cross-grained; argumentative, quarrelsome, uncooperative, contrary, perverse, difficult, awkward; informal snappish, snappy, chippy, short-fused; Brit. informal shirty, stroppy, narky, ratty, eggy, like a bear with a sore head; N. Amer. informal cranky, ornery, peckish, soreheaded; Austral./NZ informal snaky; informal, dated waxy, miffy.
▷ANTONYMS good-natured, affable.

choose verb 1 *we chose a quiet country hotel for our honeymoon*: **select**, pick, pick out, opt for, plump for, go for, take, settle on, decide on, fix on, come down in favour of, vote for; single out, hand-pick; set, designate, determine, specify, appoint, name, nominate, adopt, espouse; Brit. pitch on.
▷ANTONYMS reject; decline.
2 *you may choose to stay here all night*: **wish**, want, desire, prefer, feel/be inclined, please, like, see fit; **decide**, elect, make up one's mind.

choosy adjective informal *she's become very choosy about the food she'll eat*: **fussy**, finicky, over-fastidious, over-particular, faddish, difficult/hard to please, dainty, exacting, demanding; discriminating, discerning, selective; informal picky, pernickety; Brit. informal faddy; N. Amer. informal persnickety; archaic nice, overnice; rare finical.
▷ANTONYMS easy to please, indiscriminate.

chop verb 1 *chop the potatoes into bite-sized pieces*: **cut up**, cut into pieces, chop up; cube, dice, mince; N. Amer. hash.
2 *the sound of men chopping wood*: **chop up**, cut up, cut into pieces, hew, split, cleave.
3 *all four fingers of his left hand were* ***chopped off***: **sever**, cut off, hack off, slice off, lop off, saw off, shear off; remove, take off; archaic sunder; rare dissever.
4 *the scheme would mean* ***chopping down*** *large areas of rainforest*: **cut down**, fell, bring down, hack down, saw down.
5 informal *their training courses are to be chopped*: **reduce drastically**, cut; abolish, scrap; informal axe, slash.
□ **the chop** Brit. informal *hundreds of workers have been given the chop*: **notice**, one's marching orders; informal **the sack**, the boot, the (old) heave-ho, the elbow, the push, the bullet; Brit. informal one's cards.

chopper noun Brit. **axe**, cleaver, hatchet; butcher's knife.

choppy adjective *the choppy sea*: **rough**, full of waves, turbulent, heavy, heaving, storm-tossed, stormy, tempestuous, squally; broken, ruffled, uneven.
▷ANTONYMS calm, smooth.

chore noun *daily household chores like shopping and cleaning*: **task**, job, duty, errand, thing to be done, burden; (**chores**) work, domestic work, drudgery.

> *Choose the right word* **chore, task, job, duty**
>
> See **task**.

chortle verb *pleased with his joke, Robert chortled and slapped his thigh*: **chuckle**, laugh, giggle, titter, tee-hee, snigger; guffaw, cackle, crow.

chorus noun 1 *the soloists were good and the chorus sang powerfully*: **choir**, ensemble, choral group, choristers, vocalists, (group of) singers.
2 *they sang the chorus again*: **refrain**, burden, strain; informal hook.
3 *the girls of the chorus*: **chorus line**, **dance troupe**; dancing girls.
□ **in chorus** *'Good Morning,' we replied in chorus*: **in unison**, together, simultaneously, at the same time, as one; in concert, in harmony.

Christ noun **Jesus**, Jesus Christ, Our Lord, the Messiah, the Saviour, the Son of God, the Lamb of God, the Good Shepherd, the Redeemer, the Prince of Peace, the Nazarene, the Galilean.

christen verb 1 *the church in which Jonathan was christened | she was christened Sara*: **baptize**; name, give a name to, give the name of, call; rare lustrate.
2 *a group who were later christened 'The Magic Circle'*: **call**, name, dub, style, term, designate, label, nickname, refer to as, give the name of; rare denominate.
3 informal *Makel christened his new boots with his first goal at the McAlpine Stadium*: **begin using**, use for the first time, break in.

Christmas noun **Xmas**, Noel; Indian Burra Din; Brit. informal Chrimbo, Chrissie; archaic Yule, Yuletide.

chronic adjective 1 *a chronic illness*: **persistent**, long-standing, long-term, constantly recurring; incurable; rare immedicable.
▷ANTONYMS acute.
2 *the chronic shortage of food | chronic economic problems*: **constant**, continuing, continual, ceaseless, incessant, unabating, unending, persistent, perennial, long-lasting, lingering; deep-rooted, deep-seated, ineradicable; severe, serious, acute, grave, dire.
▷ANTONYMS temporary; mild.
3 *a chronic liar*: **inveterate**, confirmed, hardened, dyed-in-the-wool, incorrigible, habitual; compulsive, pathological.
▷ANTONYMS occasional.
4 Brit. informal *the film was absolutely chronic*. See **bad** (sense 1).

chronicle noun *a chronicle of the turbulent years of the region's past*: **record**, written account, history, annals, archive(s), register; log, diary, journal, calendar, chronology; narrative, description, story.
▸ verb *the events that followed have been chronicled by many of those who took part*: **record**, put on record, write down, set down, document, register, report, enter; narrate, relate, recount, describe, tell about, retail.

chronicler noun **annalist**, historian, archivist, diarist, recorder, reporter; narrator; scribe; rare chronologer, chronologist, chronographer.

chronological adjective *a chronological account of the period | the entries are in chronological order*: **sequential**, consecutive, in sequence, in order of time, in order, ordered, progressive, serial; historical.
▷ANTONYMS random.

chubby adjective *a chubby little man with a red face*: **plump**, tubby, roly-poly, rotund, portly, stout, dumpy, chunky, broad in the beam, well upholstered, well covered, well padded, of ample proportions, ample, round, rounded, well rounded; fat, overweight, fleshy, paunchy, pot-bellied, bulky; buxom; informal pudgy, beefy, porky, blubbery, poddy; Brit. informal podgy, fubsy; N. Amer. informal zaftig, corn-fed, lard-assed; archaic pursy; rare abdominous.
▷ANTONYMS skinny, slender.

chuck verb informal 1 *he chucked the letter into the bin*: **throw**, toss, fling, hurl, pitch, cast, lob, launch, flip, catapult, shy, dash, project, propel, send, bowl; let fly with; informal heave, sling, bung, buzz, whang; N. Amer. informal peg; Austral. informal hoy; NZ informal bish.
2 *I kept the personal bits and pieces and chucked the rest*: **throw away**, discard, throw out, dispose of, get rid of, toss out, dump, bin, scrap, jettison; informal ditch, junk, get shut of; Brit. informal get shot of; N. Amer. informal trash.
▷ANTONYMS keep, retain, hold on to.
3 *I've decided to chuck my job*: **give up**, leave, resign from, abandon, relinquish; informal quit, pack in, jack in.
4 *Mary chucked him for another guy*: **leave**, throw over, drop, finish with, stop going out with, break off one's relationship with, desert, abandon, leave high and dry; informal dump, ditch, give someone the elbow, walk out on, run out on, leave flat; Brit. informal give someone the push, give someone the big E; dated jilt; archaic forsake.

chuckle verb *Adam chuckled to himself as he drove away*: **chortle**, giggle, titter, laugh quietly, tee-hee, snicker, snigger; crow.

chum noun informal **friend**, companion, intimate, familiar, confidant, alter ego, second self; playmate, classmate, schoolmate, workmate; informal pal, buddy, bosom pal, sidekick, cully, spar, crony, main man; Brit. informal mate, oppo, china, mucker, butty; NE English informal marrow, marra, marrer; N. Amer. informal amigo, compadre, paisan; N. Amer. & S. African informal homeboy; S. African informal gabba; archaic compeer; rare fidus Achates.
▷ANTONYMS enemy; stranger.

chummy adjective informal *she's become rather chummy with Ted*: **friendly**, on good terms, close, familiar, affectionate, intimate; informal as thick as thieves, thick, matey, pally, buddy-buddy, palsy-walsy, clubby.

chunk noun *chunks of cheese*: **lump**, hunk, wedge, block, slab, square, nugget, nub, brick, cube, bar, cake, loaf; knob, ball; piece, portion, bit; mass; informal wodge; N. Amer. informal gob.

chunky adjective 1 *a chunky young man*: **stocky**, sturdy, thickset, sturdily built, heavily built, well built, burly, bulky, brawny, solid, bull-necked, heavy, hefty, beefy, meaty; short, dumpy, squat, stubby; cobby; Austral./NZ nuggety; Brit. informal fubsy; technical mesomorphic, pyknic.
▷ANTONYMS slight.
2 *a chunky Aran sweater*: **thick**, bulky, heavy-knit, cable-knit.
▷ANTONYMS light, lightweight.

church noun 1 *a village church*: **house of God**, the Lord's house, house of prayer; Scottish & N. English kirk.
2 *the Methodist Church*: **denomination**, sect, creed; faith.

> *Word links* **church**
>
> **ecclesiastical** relating to a church
> **ecclesiology** study of churches
> **ecclesiophobia** fear of church

churchyard noun **graveyard**, cemetery, necropolis, burial ground, burial place, burying place, burying ground, garden of remembrance;

Scottish kirkyard; N. Amer. memorial park; informal boneyard; literary golgotha; historical urnfield; archaic God's acre, potter's field.

churlish adjective *it seemed churlish to refuse her invitation*: **rude**, ill-mannered, discourteous, impolite, ungracious, unmannerly, uncivil, ungentlemanly, ungallant, unchivalrous; ill-bred, boorish, oafish, loutish; mean-spirited, ill-tempered, unkind, inconsiderate, uncharitable; ill-humoured, surly, sullen; informal ignorant.
▷ANTONYMS polite.

churn verb **1** *village girls churned the milk to make butter*: **stir**, agitate; beat, whip, whisk.
2 *beneath the ship the sea churned*: **be turbulent**, heave, boil, swirl, toss, seethe, foam, froth; literary roil.
3 *the twin propellers churned up the water*: **disturb**, stir up, agitate; ruffle; literary roil.
□ **churn something out** *the British film industry has churned out many such films in recent years*: **produce**, make, turn out; informal crank out, bang out.

chute noun **1** *a refuse chute*: **channel**, slide, trough, shaft, funnel, conduit; ramp, runway.
2 *magnificent seawater pools with chutes and waterfalls*: **water slide**, slide, flume, log flume, hydro-slide.

cigarette noun filter tip, king-size; cigar; informal **ciggy**, cig, tab, tube, smoke, cancer stick, coffin nail; Brit. informal **fag**, snout, roll-up; Brit. informal, dated gasper, burn.

cinch noun informal **1** *I've done it before—it's a cinch*: **easy task**, easy job, child's play, five-finger exercise, gift, walkover, nothing; informal doddle, walk in the park, piece of cake, picnic, money for old rope, money for jam, breeze, sitter, kids' stuff, cushy job/number, doss, cakewalk, pushover; N. Amer. informal duck soup, snap; Austral./NZ informal bludge, snack; S. African informal a piece of old tackie; dated snip; Brit. vulgar slang a piece of piss.
See also **easy**.
▷ANTONYMS challenge.
2 *he was a cinch to take a prize*: **certainty**, sure thing; informal cert, dead cert.

cinders plural noun *a cold hearth full of cinders*: **ashes**, ash, embers; clinker, charcoal, slag.

cinema noun **1** *the local cinema*: N. Amer. movie theatre, movie house; N. Amer. trademark cineplex; informal fleapit; dated picture palace, picture theatre; S. African dated bioscope; historical nickelodeon.
2 *I hardly ever go to the cinema*: **the pictures**; N. Amer. the movies; informal the flicks.
3 *one of the giants of British cinema*: **films**, pictures; N. Amer. movies, motion pictures; informal the big screen, the silver screen.

Word links **cinema**

cinematographic relating to the cinema

cipher noun **1** *the information may be given in cipher*: **code**, secret writing; coded message, cryptograph, cryptogram.
2 *he has spent most of his working life as a cipher*: **nobody**, nonentity, nothing, non-person, unimportant person, person of no account.
▷ANTONYMS celebrity.
3 *a row of ciphers*: **zero**, nought, nil, o; archaic naught.
4 *Arabic ciphers*: **numeral**, number, integer, figure, digit; character, symbol, sign.

circa preposition Latin *a survey by questionnaire of circa 100 companies*: **approximately**, about, around, round about, in the region of, roughly, something like, in the area of, in the neighbourhood of, of the order of, or so, or thereabouts, there or thereabouts, more or less, give or take a few, plus or minus a few; nearly, close to, not far off, approaching; Brit. getting on for; S. African plus-minus; informal as near as dammit; N. Amer. informal in the ballpark of.
▷ANTONYMS exactly, precisely.

circle noun **1** *a circle of gold stars on a background of azure blue | the lamp spread a circle of light*: **ring**, round, band, hoop, circlet; halo, disc, wreath; technical annulus.
2 *a new circle of friends*: **group**, set, ring, company, body, coterie, clique; camp, league, faction; crowd, band, crew; informal gang, bunch, pack.
3 *I'm afraid I don't move in such illustrious circles*: **sphere**, world, milieu, arena, domain; society.
▸ verb **1** *seagulls circled above his head*: **wheel**, move round, move round in circles, revolve, rotate, whirl, spiral, gyrate.
2 *Adam circled the building | the satellites circle the earth at tremendous speed*: **go round**, walk round, travel round, circumnavigate; **orbit**, revolve round; rare circumambulate.
3 *the abbey was circled by a huge wall*: **surround**, encircle, ring, ring round, enclose, encompass, bound; hedge in, fence in, hem in; literary gird, girdle.

circuit noun **1** *two circuits of the village green*: **lap**, turn, tour, round, circle, orbit, revolution, loop; beat.
2 Brit. *a racing circuit*: **track**, racetrack, running track, course.
3 *the judge completed his circuit in a matter of weeks*: **tour**, tour of duty, rounds; regular journey; rare peregrination.

circuitous adjective **1** *a circuitous route*: **roundabout**, indirect, winding, meandering, serpentine, tortuous, twisting; rare anfractuous.
▷ANTONYMS direct, straight.
2 *a circuitous discussion*: **indirect**, oblique, roundabout, circumlocutory, periphrastic; meandering, discursive, digressive, long-winded; evasive; rare circumlocutionary, ambagious.
▷ANTONYMS to the point.

circular adjective *a circular window*: **round**, disc-shaped, disk-like; ring-shaped, hoop-shaped, hoop-like, annular; technical cycloidal, discoid, discoidal.
▸ noun *a circular from a local building society*: **leaflet**, pamphlet, handbill; flyer, advertisement, notice; N. Amer. mailer, folder; N. Amer. & Austral. dodger.

Word toolkit

circular	round	annular
motion	table	eclipse
orbit	face	lesion
room	hole	rings
route	ball	disk
path	corners	eruption
driveway	belly	rim

circulate verb **1** *news of the event was widely circulated*: **spread**, spread about/around, pass around, pass on, communicate, disseminate, transmit, make known, air, put about, bandy about; make public, broadcast, publicize, advertise, publish, post, propagate, promulgate, blazon abroad, noise abroad; distribute, give out, issue, purvey; literary bruit about/abroad.
2 *rumours of his arrest circulated*: **spread**, be passed around, get around, go the rounds.
3 *fresh air circulates freely throughout the house*: **flow**, course, move round, go round.
4 *the couple circulated, chatting to their guests*: **socialize**, mingle.

circulation noun **1** *the circulation of fresh air*: **flow**, motion, movement, course, passage.
2 *the circulation of the information*: **dissemination**, spreading, communication, transmission, making known, putting about; broadcasting, publication, propagation, promulgation; distribution, diffusion, issuance.
3 *the magazine had a large circulation*: **distribution**, readership; sales figures.
□ **in circulation** *the term has been in circulation for only a few years*: **around**, about, in existence, current, going on, prevailing, prevalent, widespread, pervasive, endemic, happening, in the air, abroad.

circumference noun **1** *the circumference of the pit | the road which acted as the circumference of the downtown area*: **perimeter**, border, boundary; edge, rim, verge, margin, outline, fringe; bounds, limits, extremity, confines; literary marge, bourn, skirt.
2 *the circumference of his upper arm*: **girth**, width.

circumlocution noun **periphrasis**, circuitousness, indirectness; **tautology**, repetition, repetitiveness, repetitiousness, diffuseness, discursiveness, long-windedness, verbosity, wordiness, prolixity, verbiage, redundancy, superfluity; euphemism; informal beating about the bush; rare pleonasm, perissology.

circumlocutory adjective *his circumlocutory language*: **periphrastic**, circuitous, indirect, roundabout; **tautological**, repetitive, repetitious, diffuse, discursive, long-winded, prolix, verbose, wordy, rambling, wandering, tortuous; rare pleonastic, circumlocutionary, ambagious.

circumscribe verb *the power of the organization has until recently been severely circumscribed*: **restrict**, **limit**, set/impose limits on, keep within bounds, delimit, curb, confine, bound, restrain; regulate, control.

circumspect adjective *she would have to be very circumspect in her dealings with Catherine*: **cautious**, wary, careful, chary, guarded, on one's guard; discreet; watchful, alert, attentive, heedful, vigilant, observant; prudent, judicious, canny, politic; informal softly-softly, cagey, leery, playing one's cards close to one's chest.
▷ANTONYMS unguarded, incautious.

Word toolkit **circumspect**

See **wary**.

circumspection noun *circumspection is required in the day-to-day exercise of administrative powers*: **caution**, carefulness, care, wariness, chariness, guardedness; discretion; watchfulness, alertness, attentiveness, heed, heedfulness, vigilance; prudence, judiciousness; informal caginess; rare precaution.

circumstances plural noun **1** *a combination of favourable political and economic circumstances*: **situation**, conditions, set of conditions, state of affairs, things, position; events, turn of events, incidents, occurrences, happenings, episodes; factors, context, background, environment; informal circs.
2 *Jane explained* ***the circumstances*** *to him*: **the facts**, the details, the

particulars, the picture, how things stand, the lie of the land, how the land lies, the case; Brit. the state of play; N. Amer. the lay of the land; informal what's what, the score, the set-up.
3 *a desire to improve their circumstances*: **financial/material position**, financial/material situation, financial/material status, station in life, lot, lifestyle; resources, means, finances, income; plight, predicament.

C

circumstantial adjective **1** *the prosecution will have to rely on circumstantial evidence*: **indirect**, inferred, inferential, deduced, presumed, conjectural; contingent; inconclusive, unprovable; technical presumptive, implicative.
▷**ANTONYMS** provable.
2 *the picture was so circumstantial that it began to be convincing*: **detailed**, particularized, particular, precise, minute, blow-by-blow; full, comprehensive, thorough, exhaustive; explicit, specific.
▷**ANTONYMS** vague.

circumvent verb *although the law limits individual contributions, it's easy to circumvent*: **avoid**, get round, find a way round, evade, get past, bypass, sidestep, dodge; overcome, outwit, outmanoeuvre, foil; N. Amer. end-run; informal duck.

cistern noun **tank**, reservoir, container; vat, butt.

citadel noun **fortress**, fort, stronghold, fortification, castle, burg, keep, tower, donjon, bunker; fastness; in Spain alcazar; archaic hold.

citation noun **1** *a citation from an eighteenth century text*: **quotation**, quote, extract, excerpt, passage, line, piece; N. Amer. cite.
2 *he made extensive citations to Baynton v. Morgan*: **reference**, allusion.
3 *a citation for gallantry*: **commendation**, award, honour; mention, honourable mention.
4 N. Amer. *a traffic citation*: **summons**, subpoena, writ, court order, process; Latin subpoena ad testificandum.

cite verb **1** *I have cited the passage in full*: **quote**, reproduce.
2 *he cited the case of Leigh v. Gladstone*: **refer to**, make reference to, mention, allude to, adduce, instance, give as an example, point to; specify, name; bring up, advance, invoke, draw attention to.
3 *he has been cited many times for his contributions in this area*: **commend**, pay tribute to, praise, recognize, give recognition to.
4 *the writ cited only four of the signatories of the petition*: **summon**, summons, serve with a summons, subpoena, serve with a writ, call.

citizen noun **1** *a British citizen*: **subject**, national, passport holder, native; taxpayer, voter.
2 *the citizens of Edinburgh*: **inhabitant**, resident, native, townsman, townswoman, householder, local; freeman; humorous denizen, burgher; formal dweller; Brit. archaic burgess; rare residentiary, oppidan.

city noun **town**, municipality, metropolis, megalopolis; **conurbation**, urban area, metropolitan area; Scottish burgh; informal big smoke; N. Amer. informal burg; archaic wen.

> *Word links* **city**
>
> **urban**, **civic**, **metropolitan** relating to cities

civic adjective *civic buildings | the civic life of Swindon*: **municipal**, city, town, urban, metropolitan; **public**, civil, community, local, communal; rare oppidan.

civil adjective **1** *a civil marriage ceremony*: **secular**, non-religious, lay, non-ecclesiastic; rare laic, laical.
▷**ANTONYMS** religious.
2 *civil aviation*: **non-military**, civilian.
▷**ANTONYMS** military.
3 *a civil war | the civil administration*: **internal**, domestic, interior, home; national, state, local.
▷**ANTONYMS** foreign, international.
4 *a sense of civil duty*: **civic**, municipal, public, community, social.
5 *I hope you're going to behave in a civil manner*: **polite**, courteous, well mannered, well bred, gentlemanly, chivalrous, gallant, ladylike, gracious, respectful; refined, urbane, polished, cultured, cultivated, civilized, cordial, genial, pleasant, affable, obliging; Brit. informal decent; dated mannerly.
▷**ANTONYMS** rude, discourteous.

> *Choose the right word* **civil, polite, courteous**
>
> See **polite**.

civilian noun *the slaughter of unarmed civilians*: **non-military person**, non-combatant, ordinary citizen, private citizen; informal civvy.
▶ adjective *civilian casualties | civilian clothes*: **non-military**, non-combatant, civil; informal civvy.

civility noun **1** *he treated me with the utmost civility*: **courtesy**, courteousness, politeness, good manners, mannerliness, gentlemanliness, chivalry, gallantry, graciousness, consideration, respect, gentility; urbanity, cordiality, geniality, pleasantness, affability; French politesse; rare comity.
▷**ANTONYMS** discourtesy, rudeness.
2 *she didn't waste time on civilities*: **polite remark**, politeness, courtesy; formality.

civilization noun **1** *a higher stage of civilization*: **human development**, advancement, progress, enlightenment, edification, culture, cultivation, refinement, sophistication.
2 *the ancient civilizations of the Mediterranean*: **culture**, customs, mores, way of life, attainments, achievements; society, nation, people, community.

civilize verb *he built roads and attempted to civilize the people*: **enlighten**, edify, educate, instruct, refine, cultivate, polish, sophisticate, socialize, humanize; improve, better; archaic reclaim; rare acculturate.

civilized adjective *his civilized behaviour | a civilized society*: **polite**, courteous, well mannered, good mannered, civil, decorous, gentlemanly, ladylike, gracious; cultured, cultivated, refined, polished, sophisticated, urbane; enlightened, educated, advanced, developed; informal couth; dated mannerly.
▷**ANTONYMS** uncivilized, unsophisticated.

civil servant noun **public servant**, government official, government worker, civil-service employee; **bureaucrat**, mandarin, official, administrator, office-holder, functionary; Brit. jack-in-office.

clad adjective *Verity was **clad in** a filmy chiffon dress*: **dressed**, clothed, attired, got up, garbed, rigged out, costumed; **wearing**, sporting; informal dolled up; literary caparisoned, accoutred; archaic apparelled.

claim verb **1** *Davies claimed that she was lying*: **assert**, declare, profess, maintain, state, hold, affirm, avow, aver, protest, insist, swear, attest; argue, contend, submit, move; allege; informal make out; archaic avouch; rare asseverate, represent.
2 *if no one claims the items, they will become Crown property*: **lay claim to**, say that one owns, assert ownership of, formally request; pretend to.
3 *you are entitled to claim compensation*: **request**, ask for, apply for, put in for, put in an application for; sue for; demand, exact.
4 *the fire claimed the lives of five people*: **take**; cause/result in the loss of.
▶ noun **1** *her claims that she was raped*: **assertion**, declaration, profession, affirmation, avowal, averment, protestation, representation; contention, submission, case; allegation; pretence; rare asseveration.
2 *a claim for damages*: **request**, application; demand, petition, call.
3 *they have first **claim on** the assets of the trust*: **entitlement to**, title to, right to, rights to.

claimant noun **applicant**, candidate, supplicant, suppliant, pretender, suitor; petitioner, plaintiff, litigant, appellant; rare pretendant.

clairvoyance noun **second sight**, **psychic powers**, ESP, extrasensory perception, sixth sense; telepathy.

clairvoyant noun *a woman claiming to be a clairvoyant*: **psychic**, fortune teller, forecaster of the future, crystal-gazer, prophet, seer, soothsayer, oracle; medium, spiritualist; telepathist, telepath, mind-reader; palmist, palm-reader, chiromancer; rare chirosophist, spiritist, palmister.
▶ adjective *he didn't tell me about it and I'm not clairvoyant*: **psychic**, with second sight, with a sixth sense, prophetic, visionary, oracular; telepathic, extrasensory; rare second-sighted.

clamber verb *we **clambered up** the hillside*: **scramble**, climb, scrabble, move awkwardly, claw one's way; shin; scale, ascend, mount; N. Amer. shinny.

clammy adjective **1** *his clammy hands*: **moist**, damp, sweaty, perspiring, sweating, sticky; slimy, slippery, slick.
▷**ANTONYMS** dry.
2 *the clammy atmosphere*: **damp**, dank, wet, moisture-laden; humid, close, muggy, heavy, steamy.

clamorous adjective *a crowd of clamorous children*: **noisy**, loud, vocal, vociferous, raucous, rowdy, rackety, tumultuous, shouting, shrieking, screaming; importunate, demanding, insistent, vehement.
▷**ANTONYMS** quiet.

clamour noun **1** *her cold, crisp voice rose above the clamour*: **din**, racket, loud noise, uproar, tumult, babel, shouting, yelling, screaming, baying, roaring, blaring, clangour; commotion, brouhaha, hue and cry, hubbub, bedlam, pandemonium; Scottish & N. English stramash; informal hullabaloo, rumpus; Brit. informal row; rare vociferation, ululation, charivari.
▷**ANTONYMS** silence.
2 *the growing clamour for her resignation*: **demand(s)**, call(s), urging, insistence.
3 *a smaller trade deficit will still the clamour of protectionists*: **protests**, storms of protest, complaints, outcry.
▶ verb **1** *the surging crowds clamoured for attention*: **yell**, shout loudly, bay, scream, shriek, roar.
2 *scientists are **clamouring for** a ban on all chlorine substances*: **demand**, call, bay; press, push, lobby.

clamp noun **1** *a clamp holds the pieces of wood at right angles*: **brace**, vice, press; clasp, fastener, bracket, holdfast; Music mute, capo, capo tasto; Climbing jumar.
2 *clamps had been fitted to the car's back wheels*: **immobilizer**, wheel clamp; N. Amer. boot.
▶ verb **1** *the sander is clamped on to the edge of a workbench*: **fasten**, secure, fix, clip, attach, make fast; screw, bolt.

2 *an empty pipe was clamped between his teeth*: **clench**, grip, hold, press, squeeze; clasp, grasp, clutch.
3 *yesterday, the government clamped a curfew on the city*: **impose**, inflict; informal clap, slap.
4 *he flew into a rage when he found his car was clamped*: **immobilize**, wheel-clamp; N. Amer. boot.
□ **clamp down on** *a new initiative to clamp down on software piracy*: **suppress**, prevent, stop, put a stop to, put an end to, stamp out; crack down on, come down hard on, limit, restrain, restrict, check, keep in check, control, keep under control.

clampdown noun informal *the military regime continued its clampdown on the pro-democracy movement*: **suppression**, prevention, stopping, stamping out; crackdown, limitation, restriction, restraint, curb, check.

clan noun 1 *the Macleod clan*: **group of families**, sept, gens; **family**, house, dynasty, tribe, line; Anthropology sib, kinship group.
2 *this clan of rich and ambitious art collectors*: **group**, set, circle, clique, coterie, in-crowd, fraternity, brotherhood, community, society; crowd, band, ring, crew; faction; informal gang, bunch; rare sodality, confraternity.

clandestine adjective *their clandestine meetings*: **secret**, covert, furtive, surreptitious, stealthy, cloak-and-dagger, hole-and-corner, hole-in-the-corner, closet, behind-the-scenes, backstairs, back-alley, under-the-table, hugger-mugger, concealed, hidden, private; sly, sneaky, underhand; undercover, underground; informal hush-hush.
▷ANTONYMS open, above board.

clang noun *the clang of the church bells*: **reverberation**, ringing, ring, ding-dong, bong, peal, chime, toll; **clank**, clash, crash, clangour; informal boing.
▸ verb *the huge bells clanged*: **reverberate**, resound, ring, bong, peal, chime, toll; **clank**, clash, crash; informal boing; rare tang.

clanger noun Brit. informal See **mistake** (sense 1 of the noun).

clank noun *the clank of rusty chains*: **jangling**, clanging, rattling, clinking, jingling, clunking, clattering; clang, jangle, rattle, clangour, clink, jingle, clunk, clatter.
▸ verb *I could hear the chain clanking as the dog moved around*: **jangle**, rattle, clink, clang, jingle, clunk, clatter.

clannish adjective *he was regarded as an outsider in the clannish community*: **cliquey**, cliquish, insular, exclusive; unfriendly, unwelcoming; narrow, parochial, provincial.

clap verb 1 *the crowd clapped and cheered*: **applaud**, clap one's hands, give someone a round of applause, put one's hands together; give someone a standing ovation, applaud someone to the echo; informal give someone a (big) hand, bring the house down; N. Amer. informal give it up.
▷ANTONYMS boo, jeer.
2 *he clapped Owen on the back*: **slap**, strike, hit, smack, crack, bang, thump, cuff; pat; informal whack, thwack, wallop.
3 *in the old days, they would have clapped you in jail*: **fling**, cast, put, place; informal slap, stick.
4 *the dove clapped its wings*: **flap**, beat, flutter.
▸ noun 1 *everybody gave him a clap*: **round of applause**, hand, handclap; standing ovation.
2 *a clap on the shoulder that almost rattled my teeth*: **slap**, blow, smack, crack, thump, cuff; informal whack, thwack.
3 *a clap of thunder*: **crack**, crash, bang, boom; thunderclap.

claptrap noun *I've had enough of this sentimental claptrap*. See **nonsense**.

clarification noun *please advise us if you require further clarification of these matters*: **explanation**, elucidation, illumination, simplification; exposition, explication, exegesis.
▷ANTONYMS obfuscation.

clarify verb 1 *a meeting was called in order to clarify the situation*: **make clear**, shed light on, throw light on, elucidate, illuminate, make plain, make simple, simplify; **explain**, explicate, define, spell out; clear up, sort out, resolve.
▷ANTONYMS confuse, obscure.
2 *an operation designed to clarify the wine | clarified butter*: **purify**, refine; filter, make clear; melt (down), render; technical fine.

clarity noun 1 *the clarity of his account*: **lucidity**, lucidness, clearness, perspicuity, intelligibility, comprehensibility, coherence; simplicity, plainness, explicitness, lack of ambiguity, precision.
▷ANTONYMS obscurity, vagueness.
2 *the clarity of the original image*: **sharpness**, clearness, crispness, definition, distinctness, precision.
▷ANTONYMS blurriness.
3 *the crystal clarity of the water*: **limpidity**, limpidness, clearness, transparency, translucence, pellucidity, glassiness; purity; rare transpicuousness.
▷ANTONYMS opacity, murkiness.

clash noun 1 *eleven people were killed after clashes between armed gangs and security forces*: **confrontation**, skirmish, brush, encounter, engagement, collision, incident, conflict, fight, battle; hostilities, fighting, warring; archaic rencounter.
2 *a clash between the prime minister and his predecessor*: **argument**, **altercation**, confrontation, angry exchange, shouting match, war of words, battle royal, passage of arms; contretemps, quarrel, difference of opinion, disagreement, dispute; informal run-in; Brit. informal slanging match.
3 *a clash of tweeds and a striped shirt*: **mismatch**, discordance, discord, lack of harmony, incompatibility, jarring.
4 *a clash of dates*: **coincidence**, concurrence, co-occurrence; conflict.
5 *the clash of cymbals*: **striking**, bang, clang, crash, clatter, clank; clangour.
▸ verb 1 *protesters **clashed with** police*: **fight**, skirmish, contend, come to blows, be in conflict, come into conflict, engage, war, grapple; do battle; confront, attack.
2 *the prime minister clashed with other commonwealth leaders*: **disagree**, dissent, differ, wrangle, dispute, cross swords, lock horns, be at odds, be at loggerheads.
3 *her red coat **clashed** violently **with** her auburn hair*: **be incompatible**, not match, not go, be discordant, jar; informal scream at.
▷ANTONYMS match, set off.
4 *the date of this year's conference **clashed with** the director's meeting*: **conflict**, coincide, occur simultaneously, happen at the same time as.
5 *clashing the cymbals together, he began to walk down the road*: **bang**, strike, clang, crash, smash, clank, clatter.

clasp verb 1 *Ruth clasped his hand*: **grasp**, grip, clutch, hold tightly, hang on to, cling to; take hold of, seize, grab.
2 *he clasped Joanne in his arms*: **embrace**, hug, enfold, fold, enclose, envelop, wrap; hold, squeeze; archaic strain.
▸ noun 1 *a gold bracelet with a turquoise clasp*: **fastener**, fastening, catch, clip, pin; hook, hook and eye, buckle, hasp, lock; Archaeology fibula.
2 *his tight clasp*: **embrace**, hug, cuddle, hold, squeeze; grip, grasp.

class noun 1 *it was good accommodation for a hotel of this class*: **category**, grade, rating, classification, group, grouping, bracket, set, division.
2 *a new class of heart drug*: **kind**, sort, type, order, variety, genre, brand; species, genus, family, generation, breed, strain, denomination; stamp, ilk, kidney, style, cast, grain, mould; N. Amer. stripe; technical phylum.
3 *the middle class | there is no discrimination on the basis of sex, class, or ethnic origin*: **social division**, social order, social stratum, rank, level, echelon, group, grouping, set, caste; social status, position/standing in society, social hierarchy, pecking order; Hinduism varna; archaic estate, sphere, condition, degree.
4 *selected pupils act as representatives for the whole class*: **form**, study group, school group, set, stream, band; year; N. Amer. grade.
5 *a maths class*: **lesson**, period, period of instruction; seminar, tutorial, workshop.
6 informal *a woman of class | the place had real class*: **style**, stylishness, elegance, chic, sophistication, taste, refinement; quality, excellence, distinction, merit, prestige; French savoir faire, savoir vivre.
▸ verb *the 12-seater is classed as a commercial vehicle*: **classify**, categorize, group, grade, rate, type; order, sort, codify, file, index; bracket, designate, brand, mark down, label, pigeonhole; characterize; Medicine triage.
▸ adjective informal *a class player*: **excellent**, very good, first-rate, first-class, marvellous, wonderful, magnificent, outstanding, superlative, superb, formidable, virtuoso, masterly, expert, champion, fine, consummate, skilful, adept; informal great, terrific, tremendous, smashing, fantastic, sensational, stellar, fabulous, fab, crack, hotshot, A1, mean, demon, awesome, magic, wicked, tip-top, top-notch; Brit. informal brilliant, brill; vulgar slang shit-hot.

classic adjective 1 *the classic work on the subject*: **definitive**, authoritative; **outstanding**, of the highest quality, first-rate, first-class, best, finest, excellent, superior, masterly, exemplary, consummate; ideal.
2 *a classic example of Norman design*: **typical**, archetypal, quintessential, vintage; model, representative, prototypical, paradigmatic; perfect, prime, copybook, textbook; standard, characteristic, stock, true to form.
▷ANTONYMS atypical, anomalous.
3 *a classic style which never dates*: **simple**, **elegant**, understated, uncluttered, restrained; traditional, time-honoured, timeless, ageless, abiding, enduring, immortal.
▸ noun *a classic of the genre*: **definitive example**, model, epitome, paradigm, exemplar, prototype; outstanding example, paragon, great work, masterpiece, masterwork; established work, standard; French pièce de résistance.

classical adjective 1 *classical mythology | the birthplace of classical architecture*: **ancient Greek**, Grecian, Hellenic, Attic; **Latin**, ancient Roman.
2 *classical ballet | classical music*: **traditional**, long-established; serious, highbrow, heavyweight; symphonic, concert; informal heavy.
▷ANTONYMS modern.
3 *a classical style*: **simple**, pure, restrained, plain, austere; **well proportioned**, harmonious, balanced, symmetrical, elegant, aesthetic; Literature Augustan.

classification noun 1 *the classification of diseases according to symptoms*: **categorization**, categorizing, classifying, classing, grouping, grading, ranking, organization, sorting, codification, systematization, stratification, taxonomy.
2 *a series of classifications into which people are fitted*: **category**, class,

group, grouping, grade, grading, rating, ranking, bracket; kind, sort, type, variety.

classify verb *we can classify the students into two distinct groups*: **categorize**, class, group, put into sets, grade, rank, rate, order, organize, range, sort, type, codify, bracket, systematize, systemize, stratify, catalogue, tabulate, list, file, index; assign, allocate, consign, place, put; brand, label, pigeonhole; archaic assort.

C

classy adjective informal *a classy hotel*: **stylish**, high-class, superior, exclusive, chic, elegant, smart, sophisticated, fancy; expensive; Brit. upmarket; N. Amer. high-toned; informal posh, ritzy, plush, plushy, swanky, snazzy; Brit. informal swish; N. Amer. informal swank, tony; US black English dicty.

clatter verb *an antique fan clattered and whirred in the corner of the office | the coach clattered along the cobbles*: **rattle**, clank, clink, clunk, clang, bang; rare blatter.

clause noun *a new clause had been added to the treaty*: **section**, paragraph, article, subsection, note, item, point, passage, part, heading; stipulation, condition, proviso, provision, rider; specification, requirement.

claw noun **1** *a cat's claw | a bird's claw*: **nail**, **talon**; technical unguis; rare pounce.
2 *a crab's claw*: **pincer**, nipper; technical chela.
▸ verb *her fingers clawed his shoulders*: **scratch**, lacerate, tear, rake, rip, slash, scrape, graze, dig into; maul, savage, mutilate; scrabble at.

Word links **claw**
ungual relating to claws

clay noun **earth**, terracotta, gault, catlinite, pipeclay, pipestone, argil, china clay, kaolin, adobe, ball clay, bole, pug; slip, barbotine; fireclay.

clean adjective **1** *he bared his clean, white teeth in a smile | keep the wound clean*: **washed**, scrubbed, cleansed, cleaned, polished; spotless, unsoiled, unstained, unspotted, unsullied, unblemished, immaculate, pristine, speckless, dirt-free; hygienic, sanitary, disinfected, sterilized, sterile, aseptic, decontaminated, healthy; pure, white, whiter than white; laundered; informal squeaky clean, as clean as a whistle.
▷ANTONYMS dirty.
2 *a clean sheet of paper*: **blank**, empty, bare, clear, plain, white; unused, new, pristine, fresh, unmarked, unfilled, untouched.
▷ANTONYMS used.
3 *he breathed in the sharp, clean air*: **pure**, clear, fresh, crisp, refreshing; unpolluted, uncontaminated, untainted, unmixed, unadulterated; distilled, purified.
▷ANTONYMS polluted.
4 *Kate had envied her mother her nice clean life*: **virtuous**, good, upright, upstanding; honourable, respectable, reputable, decent, righteous, moral, morally correct, ethical, exemplary, honest, just; innocent, pure, chaste, undefiled, guiltless, blameless, irreproachable, unimpeachable, pure as the driven snow, whiter than white; Christianity immaculate, impeccable; informal squeaky clean.
▷ANTONYMS immoral.
5 *the investigation demonstrated that the firm is clean*: **innocent**, guiltless, blameless, clear, in the clear, not to blame, guilt-free, crime-free, above suspicion, unimpeachable, irreproachable; informal squeaky clean.
▷ANTONYMS guilty.
6 *a good clean fight*: **fair**, honest, sporting, sportsmanlike, just, upright, law-abiding, chivalrous, honourable, according to the rules, according to Hoyle; informal on the level.
▷ANTONYMS dirty, unfair.
7 informal *the staff at the facility gave them counselling and taught them to stay clean*: **sober**, teetotal, non-drinking, clear-headed, as sober as a judge; **drug-free**, free of drugs, off drugs; abstinent, self-restrained; informal dry, on the wagon, straight.
8 *these secateurs give a clean cut | he took a clean catch*: **neat**, smooth, crisp, straight, accurate, precise, slick.
▷ANTONYMS ragged.
9 *the clean lines of a good design*: **simple**, elegant, graceful, uncluttered, trim, shapely, unfussy, uncomplicated; streamlined, smooth, well defined, definite, clean-cut; regular, symmetrical.
▷ANTONYMS complex, elaborate.
□ **come clean** informal *I'll have to come clean—that story is only a rumour*: **tell the truth**, be completely honest, tell all, make a clean breast of it; **confess**, own up, admit guilt, admit to one's actions/crimes/sins, accept blame/responsibility, plead guilty; informal get something off one's chest, fess up.
▸ adverb informal *I clean forgot her birthday*: **completely**, entirely, totally, fully, wholly, thoroughly, altogether, quite, utterly, absolutely.
▸ verb **1** *Dad had cleaned the kitchen windows*: **wash**, cleanse, wipe, sponge, scrub, mop, rinse, scour, swab, hose down, sluice (down), flush, polish, disinfect; shampoo; floss; literary lave.
▷ANTONYMS dirty, soil.
2 *I would have to get my clothes cleaned*: **launder**; dry-clean.
3 *she began to clean the fish*: **gut**, eviscerate, remove the innards of, draw, dress.
□ **clean someone out** informal *the fine cleaned him out*: **bankrupt**, ruin, make insolvent, make penniless, wipe out, impoverish, reduce to penury/destitution, bring to ruin, bring someone to their knees, break, cripple; rare pauperize, beggar.

cleanse verb **1** *the wound was then cleansed and redressed aseptically*: **clean**, make clean, clean up, wash, bathe, rinse, disinfect, sanitize, decontaminate, purify; rare deterge.
2 *a plan to cleanse the environment of traces of lead*: **rid**, clear, free, purify, purge, empty, strip, void, relieve.
3 *the monk works to cleanse himself from the sins of the fleshly body*: **purify**, purge, absolve, free; deliver; archaic shrive; rare lustrate.

clear adjective **1** *the book gives clear instructions for carrying out various DIY tasks*: **understandable**, comprehensible, intelligible, easy to understand, plain, direct, uncomplicated, explicit, lucid, perspicuous, coherent, logical, distinct, simple, straightforward, clearly expressed, unambiguous, clear-cut, crystal clear, accessible, user-friendly; in words of one syllable; informal Anglo-Saxon.
▷ANTONYMS vague, unclear.
2 *he made it clear to the team that he was in charge | a clear case of harassment*: **obvious**, evident, plain, apparent, crystal clear, as clear as crystal, transparent; sure, definite, unmistakable, manifest, indisputable, patent, incontrovertible, irrefutable, beyond doubt, beyond question, self-evident; palpable, visible, discernible, noticeable, detectable, recognizable, pronounced, marked, striking, conspicuous, overt, blatant, glaring; as plain as a pikestaff, staring someone in the face, writ large, as plain as day; informal as plain as the nose on one's face, standing/sticking out like a sore thumb, standing/sticking out a mile, as clear as day.
▷ANTONYMS vague, possible.
3 *a beautiful lagoon of clear water*: **transparent**, limpid, pellucid, translucent, crystalline, crystal clear, glassy, glass-like; diaphanous, see-through; unclouded, uncloudy; rare transpicuous.
▷ANTONYMS opaque, murky.
4 *a clear blue sky*: **bright**, cloudless, unclouded, without a cloud in the sky, fair, fine, light, undimmed; sunny, sunshiny, sunlit, starlit, moonlit.
▷ANTONYMS cloudy.
5 *her clear complexion*: **unblemished**, spot-free; fresh.
▷ANTONYMS pimply, spotty.
6 *Rosa's clear voice*: **distinct**, bell-like, as clear as a bell, clarion, pure; unwavering.
▷ANTONYMS muffled.
7 *the road was clear | Christina had a clear view of Stephen's face*: **unobstructed**, unblocked, passable, unimpeded, open, empty, free, unlimited, unrestricted, unhindered.
▷ANTONYMS obstructed; limited.
8 *the algae were* **clear of** *toxins*: **free**, devoid, empty, vacant, void; rid, relieved; without, unaffected by, no longer affected by.
9 *I left the house with a clear conscience*: **untroubled**, undisturbed, unworried, unperturbed, unconcerned, unbothered, with no qualms; peaceful, at peace, tranquil, serene, calm, easy; innocent, guiltless, guilt-free, blameless, clean, sinless, stainless, unimpeachable, irreproachable.
▷ANTONYMS guilty.
10 *two clear days' notice is required*: **whole**, full, entire, complete, total, solid, round, unbroken.
▷ANTONYMS partial.
▸ adverb **1** *an indicator told them to stand* **clear of** *the doors*: **away from**, apart from, beyond, at a distance from, at a safe distance from, out of contact with.
▷ANTONYMS close to.
2 *Tommy's voice came loud and clear from the row behind*: **distinctly**, clearly, as clear as a bell, plainly, audibly, intelligibly, with clarity.
▷ANTONYMS indistinctly.
3 *he will have time to get clear away*: **completely**, entirely, thoroughly, fully, wholly, totally, utterly, quite, altogether; informal clean.
▸ verb **1** *the sky cleared briefly | the weather was clearing*: **brighten**, (up), lighten, become light, light up, break, clear up, become bright/brighter/lighter, become fine, become sunny.
▷ANTONYMS darken.
2 *the drizzle had cleared, leaving the evening fine*: **disappear**, go away, melt away, vanish, end; dwindle, peter out, fade, wear off, decrease, lessen, diminish, recede, withdraw, ebb, wane; disperse.
3 *shops have cleared the shelves of anything that could offend the public | together they cleared the table*: **empty**, void; free, rid, strip, unload, unburden.
▷ANTONYMS fill.
4 *plumbers' tools for clearing drains*: **unblock**, unclog, unstop.
▷ANTONYMS block.
5 *he warned the staff to clear the building*: **evacuate**, empty, make empty, make vacant; leave.
6 *Karen cleared the dirty plates*: **remove**, take away, carry away, move, shift, tidy away/up.
7 *at the moment I'm clearing debts*: **pay off**, pay, repay, settle, discharge, square, make good, honour, defray, satisfy, account for, remit, liquidate.
▷ANTONYMS run up.

8 *I cleared the bar at my first attempt*: **go over**, get past, go above, pass over, sail over; jump (over), vault (over), leap (over), hop (over), hurdle, spring over, bound over, skip (over), leapfrog (over).
9 *he was jailed for possessing drugs, but was later cleared by an appeal court*: **acquit**, declare innocent, find not guilty; absolve, exonerate, exculpate, vindicate; informal let off (the hook).
▷**ANTONYMS** convict.
10 *I was cleared to work on the atomic project*: **authorize**, give permission, permit, allow, pass, accept, endorse, license, sanction, give approval to, give one's seal of approval to, give consent to; informal OK, give the OK, give the thumbs up, give the green light, give the go-ahead.
▷**ANTONYMS** veto.
11 *I hoped to clear £50,000 profit from each match*: **net**, make a profit of, realize a profit of, take home, pocket; gain, earn, make, get, acquire, secure, reap, bring in, pull in, be paid; informal rake in.
▷**ANTONYMS** spend.
□ **clear off** informal *Clear off! You're trespassing!* **go away**, get out, leave; be off with you!, shoo!, make yourself scarce!, on your way!; informal beat it, push off, clear out, shove off, scram, scoot, skedaddle, buzz off; Brit. informal hop it, sling your hook; Austral./NZ informal rack off; N. Amer. informal bug off, take a hike; S. African informal voetsak, hamba; vulgar slang piss off, bugger off; archaic begone.
▷**ANTONYMS** stay.
□ **clear out** informal *get everyone to clear out of the building as quickly as possible*. See **leave**[1] (sense 1).
□ **clear something out 1** *we had to clear out the junk room to make a nursery for James*: **empty**, empty out, void, make vacant; tidy, tidy up, clear up, clean; informal dejunk. **2** *clear out the rubbish as you go*: **get rid of**, throw out/away, discard, dispose of, dump, bin, scrap, do away with, jettison, eject, eliminate, throw on the scrap heap; informal chuck (out/away), ditch, junk, get shut of; Brit. informal get shot of; N. Amer. informal trash.
□ **clear the air** *that conversation cleared the air somehow*: **restore harmony**, make peace, reconcile differences; pour oil on troubled waters.
□ **clear up** *the weather had cleared up*. See **clear** (senses 1 and 2 of the verb).
□ **clear something up 1** *clear up the garden before you go*: **tidy**, tidy up, put in order, straighten up, clean up, put to rights, make shipshape, spruce up. **2** *I'm glad we've cleared up that little problem*: **solve**, resolve, straighten out, find an/the answer to, answer, find the key to, decipher, break, get to the bottom of, make head or tail of, piece together, explain, expound; unravel, untangle, elucidate; informal crack, figure out, suss out.

clearance noun **1** *the dissatisfaction with housing conditions produced schemes for slum clearance*: **removal**, clearing, clear-out, demolition; evacuation, eviction, purge, emptying, depopulation, unpeopling.
2 *to become a regular prison visitor you must have Home Office clearance*: **authorization**, permission, consent, approval, seal of approval, blessing, acceptance, leave, sanction, licence, dispensation, assent, agreement, concurrence, endorsement, imprimatur; permit; informal the green light, the go-ahead, the thumbs up, the OK, the say-so, the nod, the rubber stamp; rare nihil obstat.
▷**ANTONYMS** veto.
3 *the clearance of a debt*: **repayment**, payment, paying, paying off, settling, discharge, squaring, making good, honouring, defrayal, defrayment, defraying, remission, liquidation, reckoning.
4 *adjust the door up or down to ensure equal clearance between door and frame*: **space**, gap, room, room to spare, headroom, margin, leeway, allowance, separation, clearing.

clear-cut adjective *we now had a clear-cut objective*: **definite**, distinct, clear, well defined, sharply defined, precise, specific, explicit, unambiguous, black and white, hard and fast; unequivocal, straightforward; striking, obvious; marked, decided; sharp, crisp, stark; informal cut and dried.
▷**ANTONYMS** blurred, indistinct, vague.

clearing noun *at last the trees gave way to a clearing*: **glade**, dell, space, gap, opening.

clearly adverb **1** *everybody has to be able to write clearly*: **intelligibly**, plainly, distinctly, comprehensibly, understandably, perspicuously, with clarity; legibly, readably; audibly.
2 *clearly, substantial changes are needed*: **obviously**, evidently, patently, unquestionably, undoubtedly, without doubt, indubitably, plainly, decidedly, surely, assuredly, certainly, definitely, undeniably, incontrovertibly, irrefutably, incontestably, unmistakably, doubtless; visibly, demonstrably, noticeably, manifestly, markedly, transparently, palpably; it goes without saying, needless to say, of course.

cleave[1] verb **1** *the axe his father used to cleave wood for the fire*: **split**, split open, crack open, lay open, divide, sever, splinter; cut (up), hew, hack, chop up, slice up, halve, bisect, quarter; literary rend; archaic sunder, rive.
2 *Stan was away, cleaving a path through the traffic*: **plough**, drive, bulldoze, cut, carve, make.

cleave[2] verb
□ **cleave to** literary **1** *her tongue clove to the roof of her mouth*: **stick to**, stick fast to, be stuck to, adhere to, cohere to, be attached to, bond to. **2** *a state formerly criticized for cleaving too closely to Moscow's line*: **adhere to**, hold to, cling to, stand by, abide by, be loyal to, be faithful to, remain true to.

cleaver noun *a meat cleaver*: **chopper**, hatchet, axe, knife; butcher's knife, kitchen knife.

cleft noun **1** *a deep cleft in the rocks*: **split**, slit, crack, fissure, crevice, chasm, opening, rift, break, fracture, rent, breach, gash; cranny, interstice, furrow, indentation; gap, hole, pit, void, crater.
2 *the cleft in his chin*: **dimple**.
▸ adjective *the little gull has a cleft tail*: **split**, divided, cloven, parted, separated.

C

clemency noun *the high court commuted his prison term to five years as an act of clemency*: **mercy**, mercifulness, leniency, lenience, mildness, indulgence, forbearance, quarter; compassion, humanity, pity, sympathy, kindness, magnanimity, benignity, charity, grace, humaneness, humanitarianism, soft-heartedness, tenderness.
▷**ANTONYMS** ruthlessness, strictness.

clench verb **1** *she clenched her teeth, fighting waves of nausea | he stood there, clenching and unclenching his hands*: **squeeze together**, press together, clamp together, close tightly, shut tightly; grit; make into a fist, make into a ball.
2 *the knuckles on his hand were white where he clenched the back of the chair*: **grip**, grasp, grab, clutch, clamp, clasp, hold tightly, seize, press, squeeze, lay (one's) hands on, fasten one's hand on, hang on to.
▸ noun *she felt a clench in her stomach*: **contraction**, tightening, tensing, tension, constricting, cramp.

clergy noun **clergymen**, **clergywomen**, churchmen, churchwomen, clerics, priests, ecclesiastics, men/women of God, men/women of the cloth; ministry, priesthood, holy orders, the church, the cloth, first estate.
▷**ANTONYMS** laity.

Word links **clergy**

clerical relating to clergy

clergyman, clergywoman noun **priest**, churchman, churchwoman, man/woman of the cloth, man/woman of God, cleric, minister, preacher, chaplain, father; ecclesiastic, divine, theologian; Christianity bishop, pastor, vicar, rector, parson, (assistant) curate, deacon, deaconess; Judaism rabbi; Islam imam; Scottish kirkman; French abbé, curé; N. Amer. dominie; informal reverend, padre, Holy Joe, sky pilot; Austral. informal josser; informal, derogatory Bible-basher, God-botherer.

clerical adjective **1** *there are a number of clerical jobs to be done in a media department*: **office**, desk, back-room; **administrative**, secretarial, writing, typing, keyboarding, filing, bookkeeping; white-collar; informal pen-pushing.
2 *a clerical collar*: **ecclesiastical**, church, priestly, pastoral, religious, spiritual, prelatic, apostolic, canonical, parsonical; holy, divine; archaic vicarial; rare sacerdotal, hieratic, rectorial, presbyteral.
▷**ANTONYMS** secular.

clerk noun **office worker**, clerical worker, administrator, administrative officer; bookkeeper, record-keeper, account-keeper; cashier, teller; Indian babu; informal pen-pusher; archaic scrivener.

clever adjective **1** *an extremely clever and studious young woman*: **intelligent**, bright, smart, brilliant; talented, gifted, precocious; capable, able, competent, apt, proficient; educated, learned, erudite, academic, bookish, knowledgeable, wise, sagacious; informal brainy.
▷**ANTONYMS** stupid.
2 *a clever scheme | he had a cruel, clever face*: **shrewd**, astute, sharp, acute, quick, sharp-witted, quick-witted; ingenious, resourceful, canny, cunning, crafty, artful, wily, slick, neat; informal foxy, savvy; Brit. informal fly; Scottish & N. English informal pawky; N. Amer. informal as sharp as a tack, cute.
▷**ANTONYMS** ill-advised, foolish.
3 *Grandma was clever with her hands*: **skilful**, dexterous, adroit, deft, nimble, nimble-fingered, handy, adept; skilled, talented.
4 *a clever remark*: **witty**, quick-witted, amusing, droll, humorous, funny, sparkling, entertaining, scintillating.

Word toolkit **clever**

See **witty**.

cleverness noun **1** *people marvelled at his cleverness*: **intelligence**, brilliance, genius, intellect; precocity, precociousness, talent, ability, capability, competence, proficiency; education, learnedness, erudition, bookishness, knowledgeableness, sagacity, wisdom; informal braininess, brains; N. Amer. informal smarts.
▷**ANTONYMS** stupidity.
2 *the cleverness of his strategy*: **shrewdness**, astuteness, sharp-wittedness, quick-wittedness, acuteness, acuity; ingenuity, ingeniousness, resourcefulness, canniness, cunning, craftiness, artfulness, wiliness.
▷**ANTONYMS** foolishness.

cliché noun *there is plenty of truth in the cliché that a trouble shared is a trouble halved*: **platitude**, hackneyed phrase, commonplace, banality, truism, trite phrase, banal phrase, overworked phrase, stock phrase,

C

bromide; saw, maxim, adage, dictum, saying; tag, aphorism; expression, phrase, formula; informal old chestnut; rare apophthegm.

click noun *the door shut with a click*: **clink**, clack, chink, snick, snap, pop, tick.
▶ verb **1** *the cameras clicked as the oarsmen prepared for the challenge | he clicked his fingers*: **clink**, clack, chink, snick, tick; **snap**, pop.
2 informal *that night it just clicked that this was what I wanted to do*: **become clear**, fall into place, come home to one, make sense, dawn, register, get through, sink in.
3 informal *we just clicked, and very quickly I found myself falling deeper and deeper in love*: **take to each other**, get along/on, warm to each other, be compatible, be in harmony, be like-minded, feel a rapport, see eye to eye; informal **hit it off**, get on like a house on fire, be on the same wavelength.
4 informal *I don't think this issue has clicked with the voters*: **go down well**, prove popular, be/make a hit, get an enthusiastic reception, be successful, be a success, succeed.

client noun *a salesman needs to understand his clients' needs*: **customer**, buyer, purchaser, shopper, consumer, user; patient; patron, regular, habitué, frequenter; (**clients**) clientele, patronage, public; market, trade, business; Brit. informal punter; Law vendee; rare emptor.

clientele noun clients. See **client**.

cliff noun **precipice**, rock face, face, crag, bluff, ridge, escarpment, scar, scarp, overhang; S. African krantz; Geology cuesta; literary steep; Scottish archaic linn.

climactic adjective *the movie's climactic scene*: **final**, culminating, ending, finishing, closing, concluding, ultimate; **exciting**, thrilling, stirring, action-packed, gripping, riveting, dramatic, hair-raising; crucial, decisive, deciding, critical, momentous.
▷ANTONYMS anticlimactic, bathetic.

climate noun **1** *the Channel Islands have an enviably mild climate*: **weather pattern**, weather conditions, weather, atmospheric conditions.
2 *they migrate here from colder climates*: **region**, area, zone, country, place; literary clime.
3 *the political climate of the 1940s*: **atmosphere**, mood, temper, spirit, feeling, feel, ambience, aura, tenor, tendency, essence, ethos, attitude, milieu; informal vibe(s).

> *Word links* **climate**
>
> **climatology** study of climate

climax noun **1** *the climax of his career came when he captained Palace to promotion*: **peak**, pinnacle, height, high point, highest point, summit, top; acme, zenith, apex, apogee, apotheosis; culmination, crowning point, crown, crest; crescendo, finale, denouement; highlight, high spot, best part, high water mark.
▷ANTONYMS nadir; anticlimax.
2 **orgasm**, sexual climax; ejaculation.
▶ verb **1** *the event will climax with a gala concert*: **culminate**, peak, come to a climax, reach a pinnacle, come to a crescendo; result, end, come to a head.
2 **have an orgasm**, reach/achieve orgasm; ejaculate; informal come, feel the earth move, get one's rocks off; Brit. informal come off; literary die.

climb verb **1** *we climbed the hill | Auntie slowly **climbed up** the stairs*: **ascend**, mount, scale, scramble up, clamber up, shin up; go up, move up, walk up, make one's way up, swarm up; conquer; N. Amer. shinny (up).
▷ANTONYMS descend.
2 *the plane climbed to eleven thousand feet*: **rise**, ascend, fly upwards, gain altitude.
▷ANTONYMS dive.
3 *the road climbs steeply from the bay*: **slope upwards**, rise, go uphill, incline upwards.
▷ANTONYMS drop.
4 *the shares opened at 47.5p and climbed to 55p*: **increase**, rise, go up, mount, escalate, shoot up, leap up, soar, spiral, rocket; informal be hiked/jacked up, go through the roof/ceiling.
▷ANTONYMS fall, decrease.
5 *he's climbed through the ranks to become chairman of the association*: **advance**, work one's way up, rise, move up, progress, make progress, make strides, get ahead.
6 *the man climbed out of his car*: **clamber**, scramble; scrabble, claw one's way, crawl.
□ **climb down** **1** *Sandy climbed down the ladder*: **descend**, go down, come down, move down, shin down. **2** *the Government had to climb down over its claim that it was offering the miners a pay increase*: **back down**, admit defeat, concede defeat, surrender, capitulate, yield, give in/up, give way, cave in, submit; retreat, backtrack, back-pedal; admit that one is wrong, retract one's words, eat one's words, eat humble pie; do a U-turn, do an about-face, shift one's ground, sing a different song, have second thoughts; Brit. do an about-turn; N. Amer. informal eat crow.
▶ noun *he was out of breath after his steep climb*: **ascent**, clamber; conquest.
▷ANTONYMS descent.

clinch verb **1** *a salesman eager to clinch a deal*: **secure**, settle, conclude, close, pull off, bring off, complete, confirm, seal, set the seal on, finalize, shake hands on, reach an agreement on; transact; informal sew up, wrap up, string, button up.
2 *these findings clinched the matter*: **settle**, decide, determine, establish; resolve; informal sort out.
3 *his team clinched the title*: **win**, be the victor in, be the winner of, be victorious in, come first in, finish first in, take first prize in, triumph in, achieve success in, be successful in, prevail in.
▷ANTONYMS lose.
4 *they clinch every nail they drive in*: **secure**, fasten, make fast, fix, clamp, bolt, rivet, pinion.
5 *there was heavy sparring, then the figures clinched*: **grapple**, wrestle, struggle with each other, scuffle with each other; grasp each other, clutch each other, grip each other.
▶ noun *a passionate clinch*: **embrace**, hug, cuddle, squeeze, hold, clasp, bear hug.

cling verb *shorter rice grains have a tendency to cling together*: **stick**, adhere, hold, cohere, bond, bind.
□ **cling (on) to** **1** *she clung to him, shuddering with emotion*: **hold on to**, clutch, grip, grasp, clasp, attach oneself to, hang on to, hold tightly, clench; embrace, hug, cuddle, entwine oneself around. **2** *some politicians clung to the belief that peace could be maintained*: **adhere to**, hold to, stick to, stand by, abide by, remain attached to, remain devoted to, cherish, be loyal to, be faithful to, remain true to, have faith in, swear by; informal stick with; literary cleave to.

clinic noun *an orthopaedic clinic*: **medical centre**, health centre, outpatients' department, surgery, doctor's, polyclinic.

clinical adjective **1** *what made it worse was his coldness—he seemed so absolutely serious and clinical*: **detached**, impersonal, dispassionate, objective, uninvolved, distant, remote, aloof, removed, cold, indifferent, neutral, unsympathetic, unfeeling, unemotional, non-emotional, unsentimental; scientific, analytic, rational, logical, hard-headed, sober, businesslike.
▷ANTONYMS emotional.
2 *the room was white and clinical*: **plain**, simple, unadorned, unornamented, unembellished, stark, austere, severe, spartan, ascetic, monastic, bleak, bare, chaste, cheerless; clean; functional, basic, institutional, impersonal, characterless, soulless, colourless, antiseptic; informal no frills.
▷ANTONYMS luxurious.

clip[1] noun **1** *he opened the clip, resting the briefcase on his knee*: **fastener**, clasp, hasp, catch, pin, hook, buckle, lock, coupler, link.
2 *a diamanté clip*: **brooch**, pin, breastpin; badge.
3 *he pulled the trigger twice, but his clip was empty*: **magazine**, cartridge, cylinder.
▶ verb *he clipped the pages together and slipped them into a file*: **fasten**, attach, fix, affix, hold, join, connect, secure; pin, staple, tack.

clip[2] verb **1** *I was clipping the hedges*: **trim**, cut, cut short/shorter, snip, prune, shorten, crop, shear, shave, pare; lop, pollard; mow; neaten, shape, tidy up, even up.
2 *simply clip the coupon below*: **remove**, cut out, snip out, detach, extract, tear out.
3 *his lorry clipped a van as it overturned*: **hit**, strike, make contact with, touch, brush, graze, glance off, tap, run into, bang into, crack into/against.
4 *Maggie clipped his ear, making him yell*: **hit**, strike, cuff, smack, slap, thump, punch, knock, rap, box someone's ears; informal clout, whack, wallop, belt, clobber, bop, biff, sock; Scottish & N. English informal skelp.
▶ noun **1** *I gave him a full clip*: **cut**, trim, crop, haircut, shortening; shear, shearing, pruning.
2 *a clip from an old black-and-white film*: **extract**, excerpt, snippet, selection, cutting, fragment; scene, moment; trailer.
3 informal *if he didn't shut up he might get a clip round the ear*: **smack**, cuff, slap, thump, punch, box, knock, rap; informal clout, whack, wallop, belt, clobbering, bop, biff, sock.
4 informal *the truck was speeding along at a good clip*: **speed**, rate, pace, velocity, tempo, momentum; informal lick, fair old rate.
□ **clip someone's wings** *some MPs are eager to clip the Prime Minister's wings*: **restrict someone's freedom**, check, curb, set/impose limits on, keep within bounds, keep under control, obstruct, impede, frustrate, thwart, stand in the way of, fetter, hamstring.

clipping noun *friends are sending us newspaper clippings from the British press*: **cutting**, extract, excerpt, snippet, fragment, piece; article, passage, column, paragraph.

clique noun *his flat became a haven for a clique of young men of similar tastes*: **coterie**, circle, inner circle, crowd, in-crowd, set, group; pack, band, ring, mob, crew; club, society, fraternity, sorority, fellowship; camp; cartel, cabal, junta, caucus, cell, lobby; Austral./NZ push; informal gang, bunch; rare camarilla.

cloak noun **1** *he threw his cloak over his shoulders*: **cape**, mantle, robe.
2 *ministers tried to cover up the truth by hiding under a cloak of secrecy*: **cover**, screen, mask, blind, front, camouflage, shield, veneer; **veil**, mantle, shroud, blanket; pretext, smokescreen.
▶ verb *the summit was cloaked in thick mist | the brothers were men cloaked in*

mystery: **conceal**, hide, cover, veil, shroud, screen, mask, cloud; envelop, swathe, surround, cocoon; disguise, camouflage, obscure.

clobber[1] noun Brit. informal *the latest designer clobber*. See **clothes**.

clobber[2] verb informal *if he does that I'll clobber him*. See **hit**.

clock noun **1** *he glanced at the clock—it was 10.30*: **timepiece**, timekeeper, timer; chronometer, chronograph.
2 informal *the car was three years old and had over 50,000 miles on the clock*: **milometer**, odometer, counter; speedometer, taximeter.
▸ verb **1** *he finished second in the 100 metres, clocking 11.8 seconds | the UK **clocked up** record exports of £4.3 billion in January*: **register**, record, log; **achieve**, attain, accomplish, gain, earn, win, make; informal do, chalk up, notch up, rack up, bag, turn in, knock up.
2 Brit. informal *Liz was the first to clock the change in her new neighbour*. See **notice**.

clod noun **1** *clods of earth*: **lump**, clump, chunk, mass, piece, hunk, slab, wedge; informal dollop, wodge.
2 informal *you're an insensitive clod!* See **fool**.

clog noun *a pair of wooden clogs*: **sabot**, wooden shoe, wooden-soled shoe.
▸ verb *the drainpipes became clogged with clay and silt*: **block**, obstruct, congest, jam, choke, bung up, dam (up), plug, silt up, stop up, seal, fill up, close; informal gunge up; technical occlude, obturate.
▷ANTONYMS unblock.

cloister noun **1** *the shadowed cloisters of the convent*: **walkway**, covered walk, corridor, aisle, arcade, loggia, gallery, piazza; technical colonnade, ambulatory, stoa.
2 *I was educated in the cloister*: **abbey**, monastery, friary, convent, priory, nunnery, religious house, religious community; historical charterhouse; rare coenobium, coenoby.
▸ verb *the women were all cloistered at home*: **confine**, isolate, shut away, sequester, seclude, closet.

cloistered adjective *his cloistered life was devoted to writing*: **secluded**, sheltered, sequestered, shielded, protected; shut-off, isolated, withdrawn, confined, restricted, insulated, reclusive, retiring, unworldly; solitary, monastic, hermitic, hermit-like; rare eremitic, anchoritic, cloistral.
▷ANTONYMS sociable, gregarious.

close[1] (rhymes with 'dose') adjective **1** *the town is located **close to** Manchester's airport*: **near**, adjacent, in close proximity, close/near at hand; not far from, in the vicinity of, in the neighbourhood of, within reach of, within close range of; neighbouring, hard by, adjoining, abutting, alongside, on the doorstep, within sight, within earshot, a stone's throw away; close by, nearby, at hand, at close quarters, contiguous, proximate; accessible, handy, convenient; informal within spitting distance, {a hop, a skip, and a jump away}, within sniffing distance; archaic nigh.
▷ANTONYMS far, distant, remote.
2 *flying in close formation*: **dense**, compact, tight, close-packed, tightly packed, packed, solid, condensed, compressed, concentrated; crowded, cramped, crammed, congested, crushed, squeezed, jammed.
▷ANTONYMS sparse.
3 *I was **close to** tears in the dressing room*: **on the verge of**, near, on the brink of, on the point of, within an ace of, in danger of.
4 *Essex versus Bedfordshire should be a very close match*: **evenly matched**, even, well matched; neck and neck, side by side, nose to nose, with nothing to choose between them; hard-fought, sharply contested, nip and tuck; informal fifty-fifty, even-steven(s).
▷ANTONYMS one-sided.
5 *not all elderly people have close relatives they might live with*: **immediate**, direct, near.
▷ANTONYMS distant.
6 *they became close friends*: **intimate**, dear, bosom; close-knit, inseparable, attached, loving, devoted, faithful, constant; special, good, best, fast, firm, valued, treasured, cherished; informal matey, chummy, pally, (as) thick as thieves; N. Amer. informal buddy-buddy, palsy-walsy.
▷ANTONYMS casual.
7 *he bears a close resemblance to our school janitor*: **strong**, marked, distinct, pronounced.
▷ANTONYMS slight.
8 *a close examination of the language of a text*: **careful**, detailed, thorough, minute, painstaking, meticulous, assiduous, diligent, rigorous, scrupulous, conscientious, attentive, focused, intent, concentrated, searching, methodical.
▷ANTONYMS casual.
9 *we need to keep a close eye on the project*: **vigilant**, watchful, keen, alert.
10 *a close translation of a French original*: **strict**, faithful, exact, precise, literal; word for word, verbatim.
▷ANTONYMS loose.
11 *Woolley placed her under close arrest for mutiny*: **carefully guarded**, closely guarded, strict, tight.
12 *he's usually pretty close about his clients' deals*: **reticent**, quiet, uncommunicative, unforthcoming, private, secretive, tight-lipped, close-mouthed, close-lipped, guarded, evasive; informal playing one's cards close to one's chest.
13 *Sylvie was close with money*: **mean**, miserly, niggardly, parsimonious, penny-pinching, cheese-paring, ungenerous, illiberal; informal tight-fisted, stingy, tight, mingy.
▷ANTONYMS generous.
14 *the weather was hot and close*: **humid**, muggy, stuffy, airless, fuggy, heavy, sticky, steamy, clammy, sultry, oppressive, stifling, suffocating, like a Turkish bath, like a sauna; unventilated.
▷ANTONYMS fresh.
▸ noun *a small close of semi-detached houses*: **street**, road, cul-de-sac; **courtyard**, quadrangle, enclosure, piazza.

close[2] (rhymes with 'nose') verb **1** *she closed the door*: **shut**, draw to, pull to, push to, slam; fasten, secure, lock, bolt, bar, latch, padlock; put up the shutter.
▷ANTONYMS open; unlock.
2 *close the hole with a plug of cotton wool*: **block (up/off)**, stop up, plug, seal (up/off), shut up/off, cork, stopper, bung (up); make airtight, make watertight; fill (up), pack, stuff; clog (up), choke, obstruct, occlude; N. Amer. stopple.
▷ANTONYMS open, unblock.
3 *there were a group of aircraft about 130 miles away and closing fast*: **catch up**, creep up, near, approach, gain on someone, draw nearer/near, get nearer/near, come nearer/near, draw closer/close, get closer/close, come closer/close.
4 *although unemployment here is still below the national average, the gap is closing*: **narrow**, lessen, grow/become/make smaller, dwindle, diminish, reduce, shrink, contract, constrict, get/become/make narrower; archaic straiten.
▷ANTONYMS widen.
5 *his arms closed around her*: **come together**, join, connect, come into contact, unite, form a circle.
6 *the chairman hastily closed the meeting*: **end**, bring/come to an end, conclude, finish, terminate, wind up, break off, halt, call a halt to, discontinue, dissolve; adjourn, suspend, prorogue, recess.
▷ANTONYMS open, begin.
7 *the factory is to close within two years*: **cease activity**, shut down, close down, cease production, cease operating, come to a halt, cease trading; fail, collapse, go out of business, crash, go under, go bankrupt, become insolvent, go into receivership, go into liquidation, be liquidated, be wound up, be closed (down), be shut (down); informal fold, flop, go broke, go bump, go to the wall, go bust.
▷ANTONYMS open.
8 *it wouldn't be long before he closed a deal with one of the chain stores*: **clinch**, settle, secure, seal, set the seal on, confirm, guarantee, establish, transact, pull off, bring off/about; complete, conclude, fix, agree, finalize, shake hands on; informal wrap up.
□ **close down** *the company closed down some years later*. See **close**[2] (sense 7 of the verb).
▸ noun *a statement was issued at the close of the talks*: **end**, finish, conclusion, termination, cessation, completion; culmination, finale, resolution, climax, denouement; informal wind-up.
▷ANTONYMS beginning.
□ **bring something to a close** *he has now brought this series to a close*: **bring to an end**, finish, conclude, close, wind up, terminate, dissolve; round off; informal wrap up; dated put a period to.
▷ANTONYMS start, begin, open.

closet noun *a clothes closet*: **cupboard**, wardrobe, cabinet, locker; storage room, cubicle.
▸ adjective *a closet gay*: **secret**, covert, unrevealed, undisclosed, private, hidden, concealed, surreptitious, clandestine, underground, furtive.
▷ANTONYMS out, open.
▸ verb *David was closeted in the den with Luther*: **shut away**, sequester, seclude, cloister, insulate, confine, isolate.

closure noun *the closure of rural schools*: **closing down**, shutting down, shutdown, winding up; termination, discontinuation, discontinuance, cessation, finish, finishing, conclusion, concluding, stoppage, stopping, halting, ceasing; failure; informal folding.

clot noun **1** *he had two operations to remove blood clots*: **lump**, clump, mass, curdling; obstruction; informal glob, gob; Medicine thrombus, thrombosis, embolus, embolism.
2 Brit. informal *I felt like a clumsy clot*. See **fool**.
▸ verb *such substances make the blood more likely to clot*: **coagulate**, set, congeal, cake, curdle, thicken, solidify, harden, dry, stiffen.
▷ANTONYMS thin, liquefy.

Word links **clot**

embolectomy, thrombectomy surgical removal of a blood clot

cloth noun **1** *commodities such as wool and cloth*: **fabric**, material, textile, stuff; textiles, dry goods, soft goods.
2 *he fetched a cloth to wipe up the mess*: **rag**, dishcloth, floorcloth, wipe, sponge, duster; flannel, facecloth; towel, paper towel, tea towel, tea cloth;

C

tablecloth; N. Amer. washcloth, washrag; Austral. washer; UK trademark J-cloth.
3 (**the cloth**) *a gentleman of the cloth*: **the clergy**, the church, the priesthood, the ministry, the first estate; clergymen, clerics, priests, ecclesiastics.

> *Word links* **cloth**
>
> **clothier**, **draper** seller of cloth

clothe verb **1** *they were clothed from head to foot in robes of gold*: **dress**, attire, outfit, array, rig (out), turn out, fit out, costume, trick out/up, robe, garb, deck out, drape, accoutre; put clothes on; informal doll up, get up; literary bedizen, caparison; archaic apparel, trap out, habit, invest.
▷ANTONYMS undress.
2 *a long valley clothed in conifers*: **cover**, overlay, overspread, cloak, blanket, carpet; envelop, swathe, swaddle, shroud, wrap, surround; literary enshroud.
▷ANTONYMS uncover.

clothes plural noun *she took off her clothes and crawled into bed*: **clothing**, garments, articles of clothing/dress, attire, garb; dress, wear, wardrobe; outfit, costume, turnout; finery; informal gear, garms, togs, duds, get-up, glad rags; Brit. informal clobber, kit, rig-out; N. Amer. informal threads; formal apparel; literary raiment, habiliments, habit; archaic vestments.

> *Word links* **clothes**
>
> **sartorial** relating to clothes
> **clothier**, **outfitter**, **couturier**, **tailor** maker or seller of clothes

clothing noun *they were wearing dark clothing*. See **clothes**.

cloud noun **1** *a cloud of blue exhaust smoke*: **mass**, billow, pall, shroud, mantle, blanket, layer, sheet, curtain, canopy.
2 *from the elms rose a cloud of rooks*: **swarm**, flock, flight, hive, covey, drove, herd; mass, multitude, host, horde, throng, crowd.
3 *the dark clouds of a recession*: **threat**, menace, shadow, spectre, blight; gloom, darkness, chill, pall; trouble, problem, worry.
□ **on cloud nine/seven ecstatic**, rapturous, joyful, elated, blissful, joyous, beatific, euphoric, enraptured, in seventh heaven, transported, in transports, in raptures, beside oneself with joy/happiness, rhapsodic, ravished, enchanted, delighted, thrilled, overjoyed, very happy; informal over the moon, on top of the world, walking on air, blissed out; Austral. informal wrapped.
▷ANTONYMS depressed.
□ **under a cloud** *they arrive in a rush, having fled New Hampshire under a cloud*: in disgrace, disgraced, discredited, shamed.
▶ verb **1** *the sky clouded*: **become cloudy**, cloud over, become overcast, become gloomy, grow dim, lour, blacken, darken, dim.
▷ANTONYMS clear.
2 *the bottom of the river is churned up, clouding the water*: **make cloudy**, make murky, dirty, darken, blacken; N. Amer. roil, rile.
▷ANTONYMS clear.
3 *anger clouded my professional judgement*: **confuse**, muddle; make unclear, obscure, fog, befog, muddy, blur.
▷ANTONYMS clarify.

> *Word links* **cloud**
>
> **nephophobia** fear of clouds

cloudy adjective **1** *a cloudy sky*: **overcast**, clouded, clouded over, overclouded; dark, darkened, grey, black, leaden, dull, murky; sombre, dismal, dreary, cheerless, heavy, gloomy, dim, louring; sunless, starless; hazy, misty, foggy; threatening, menacing, promising rain.
▷ANTONYMS bright.
2 *the drinking water looked cloudy*: **murky**, muddy, milky, dirty, clouded, dull, opaque, non-transparent, emulsified, opalescent, turbid; N. Amer. riled, roily; literary roiled.
▷ANTONYMS clear.
3 *Alexei's eyes grew cloudy*: **tearful**, teary, weepy, weeping, lachrymose; moist, misty, watery, rheumy; blurred, blurry, unfocused.
▷ANTONYMS dry.
4 *it is important to avoid cloudy phrases, in which the real meaning may be obscured*: **vague**, blurred, fuzzy, indistinct, imprecise, foggy, hazy, confused, muddled, indefinite, lacking definition, nebulous, obscure, unformed.
▷ANTONYMS clear, focused.

clout informal noun **1** *I gave him a clout on the ear*: **smack**, slap, thump, punch, blow, hit, knock, bang, cuff, box, spanking, spank, tap, clip; informal whack, wallop, clobbering, sock.
2 *the negotiating clout of a large business*: **influence**, power, pull, weight, sway, leverage, control, say, mastery, dominance, domination, advantage; authority, prestige, standing, stature, rank; informal teeth, beef, muscle.
▶ verb *he started to clout me around the head*: **hit**, strike, punch, smack, slap, cuff, thump, beat, batter, pound, pummel, thrash, rap, spank, buffet, hammer, bang, knock, box someone's ears; informal wallop, belt, whack, clobber, sock, clip, bop, biff, swipe, tan, lay one on.

cloven adjective *cloven hooves*: **split**, divided, bisected, cleft.

clown noun **1** *a circus clown*: **comic entertainer**, Pierrot, comedian; historical jester, fool, zany, harlequin, merry andrew, Punchinello.
2 *I was always the class clown*: **joker**, comedian, comic, humorist, wag, wit, funny man/woman/girl, prankster, jester, jokester, buffoon, character; informal case, hoot, scream, laugh, kidder, wisecracker, riot, barrel of laughs; Austral./NZ informal hard case; informal, dated card, caution.
3 *the department is staffed with bureaucratic clowns*: **fool**, idiot, dolt, ass, nincompoop, blockhead, dunce, dunderhead, simpleton, ignoramus, donkey, jackass, dullard; **bungler**, blunderer, incompetent, bumbler, botcher, amateur; informal moron, clot, dope, mutt, chump, numbskull, twit, nitwit, halfwit, bonehead, fathead, birdbrain, twerp, berk, ninny; Brit. informal bodger, prat, numpty, berk, nit.
▶ verb *Harvey* ***clowned around****, pretending to be a dog*: **fool around/about**, play the fool, act foolishly, act the clown/fool/goat, play about/around, monkey about/around, play tricks, indulge in horseplay, engage in high jinks; joke, jest; informal mess about/around, lark (about/around), horse about/around; Brit. informal muck about/around; N. Amer. informal cut up; Brit. vulgar slang piss about/around, arse about/around, bugger about/around; dated play the giddy goat.

cloy verb *the piece goes on a little too long and the sweetness can tend to cloy*: **become sickening**, become nauseating, pall, become distasteful, become tedious, become tiresome; be excessive.

cloying adjective *the romance never becomes cloying*: **sickly sweet**, sugary, syrupy, saccharine, honeyed, oversweet; sickening, nauseating, disgusting; mawkish, maudlin, sentimental, over-sentimental; Brit. twee; informal over the top, OTT, mushy, slushy, sloppy, cutesy, cute, gooey, drippy, treacly, cheesy, corny, icky, sick-making; N. Amer. informal cornball, sappy.

club[1] noun **1** *a youth club | a canoeing club*: **society**, association, organization, institution, group; circle, set, clique, coterie, band, body, ring, crew, troupe; affiliation, alliance, league, union, federation, company, coalition, consortium, combine, guild, lodge, order; fraternity, brotherhood, sorority, fellowship; rare sodality.
2 *people crowd the island's amazing bars, clubs, and discos*: **nightclub**, night spot, disco, discotheque, cabaret club, supper club, bar; informal hot spot, nite club, niterie.
3 *the club are struggling at the bottom of the table*: **team**, squad, side, group, line-up.
▶ verb
□ **club together** *some friends have clubbed together to buy an old van*: **pool resources**, make a kitty, join forces, make a joint contribution, divide/share costs; team up, join up, band together, come together, get together, pull together, collaborate, ally; informal have a whip-round, chip in.

club[2] noun *they beat him with a wooden club*: **cudgel**, truncheon, bludgeon, baton, stick, mace, staff, bat; N. Amer. blackjack, billy, billy club, nightstick; in Ireland shillelagh; Indian lathi, danda; S. African kierie, knobkerrie; Brit. informal cosh, life preserver.
▶ verb *he was clubbed with an iron bar*: **cudgel**, bludgeon, bash, beat/strike with a stick; hit, strike, beat, beat up, batter, belabour; informal clout, clobber; Brit. informal cosh; informal, dated baste.

clue noun **1** *give me a clue about what's going on | police are still searching for clues*: **hint**, indication, sign, signal, pointer, guide, suggestion, intimation, trace, indicator; lead, tip, tip-off, piece of evidence, piece of information.
2 *a long-pondered clue in a half-completed crossword*: **question**, problem, puzzle, riddle, poser, conundrum; cryptic clue.
□ **not have a clue** informal *I didn't have a clue what was happening*: **have no idea**, not have any idea, be ignorant, not have an inkling; be puzzled, be perplexed, be bewildered, be baffled, be mystified, be at a loss, be (all) at sea; informal be clueless, not have the faintest.
▶ verb
□ **clue someone in** informal *Stella had* ***clued*** *her* ***in about*** *Peter*: **inform**, let know, notify, make aware, give information, prime; familiarize with, make familiar with, acquaint with; keep up to date, keep posted; informal tip off, give the gen, give the low-down on, give a rundown on/of, fill in on, gen up on, clue up, put in the picture, put wise, keep up to speed.

clump noun **1** *a clump of conifers*: **cluster**, thicket, group, bunch, collection, assembly, assemblage; tuft, tuffet, tussock, mat, tangle.
2 *a clump of earth*: **lump**, clod, mass, gobbet, wad, concentration; agglutination, agglomeration, accumulation, build-up; informal glob, gob.
▶ verb **1** *galaxies tend to clump together in clusters*: **cluster**, group, bunch, collect, gather, assemble, congregate, mass, lump, bundle, pack, pile.
2 *people were clumping around upstairs*: **stamp**, stomp, stump, clomp, tramp, plod, trudge, walk heavily, lumber, stumble; thump, thud, bang; informal galumph.

clumsy adjective **1** *in her haste she was clumsy*: **awkward**, uncoordinated, ungainly, graceless, ungraceful, inelegant, gawky, gauche, gangling, cloddish, blundering, lumbering; bungling, bumbling, fumbling, inept, maladroit, unskilful, inexpert, unhandy, accident-prone, like a bull in a china shop, all fingers and thumbs; informal cack-handed, ham-fisted,

ham-handed, butterfingered, with two left feet, hulking; N. Amer. informal klutzy.
▷ANTONYMS graceful.
2 *a clumsy contraption*: **unwieldy**, unmanageable, cumbersome, bulky, hulking, heavy, solid, awkward, unmanoeuvrable.
▷ANTONYMS elegant.
3 *he said a clumsy farewell*: **gauche**, awkward, graceless, unpolished, unsubtle, crude, uncouth, boorish, crass; tactless, insensitive, thoughtless, inconsiderate, undiplomatic, indelicate, impolitic, injudicious, ill-judged.
▷ANTONYMS tactful.

cluster noun **1** *clusters of berries | a cluster of buildings*: **bunch**, clump, collection, mass, knot, group, clutch, bundle, nest; agglomeration, conglomeration, aggregate; Botany raceme, panicle, inflorescence, truss.
2 *a cluster of spectators*: **crowd**, group, knot, huddle, bunch, gathering, throng, swarm, flock, pack, troupe, party, band, body, collection, assemblage, congregation; informal gang, gaggle.
▶ verb *they clustered around the television set*: **congregate**, gather, collect, group, come together, assemble; huddle; crowd, flock, press, pack, mass, swarm.

clutch[1] verb *he was clutching a pewter tankard*: **grip**, grasp, clasp, cling to, hang on to, clench, hold.
□ **clutch at** *she saved herself from falling further by clutching at a branch*: **reach for**, snatch at, make a grab for, catch at, claw at; **grab**, seize, lay (one's) hands on, get one's hands on, grab/seize/take hold of.

clutch[2] noun **1** *a clutch of eggs*: **group**, batch, nestful.
2 *a clutch of holiday cottages | the film won a clutch of awards*: **group**, collection, set, quantity, raft; handful, fistful, armful; informal load, bunch.

clutches plural noun *we want to rescue the captives from the clutches of the enemy*: **power**, control, domination, command, mastery, rule, tyranny; hands, hold, grip, grasp, claws, jaws, evil embrace; custody, possession, keeping.

clutter noun **1** *a clutter of toys, clothes, and newspapers lay around*: **mess**, jumble, litter, heap, tangle, welter, muddle, hotchpotch, hodgepodge, mishmash, farrago, confusion, medley; rare gallimaufry.
2 *he liked to work amidst clutter*: **disorder**, chaos, disarray, untidiness, mess, muddle, confusion, disorderliness; state of confusion/untidiness; litter, rubbish.
▶ verb *the garden was cluttered with broken appliances and discarded furniture*: **litter**, make untidy, make a mess of, mess up, throw into disorder, disarrange, jumble; be strewn about, be scattered about; informal make a shambles of; literary bestrew.

coach[1] noun **1** *they made their journey by coach*: **bus**, minibus, van; dated motor coach, omnibus, charabanc; N. Amer. trademark greyhound.
2 *a railway coach*: **carriage**, wagon, compartment, van, Pullman; N. Amer. car.
3 *a coach drawn by two horses*: **horse-drawn carriage**, trap, hackney, hansom, gig, landau, brougham, cab.

coach[2] noun *a football coach*: **instructor**, trainer; teacher, tutor, mentor, guru; Brit. crammer; archaic pedagogue.
▶ verb *Philip coached Richard in his school work*: **instruct**, teach, tutor, school, educate, upskill, guide, drill, prime, cram, put someone through their paces; train.

coagulate verb *the heat causes the blood to coagulate*: **congeal**, clot, cake, solidify, thicken, harden, gel, curdle, stiffen, set, dry; rare inspissate.
▷ANTONYMS liquefy.

coal noun

> *Word links* **coal**
>
> **colliery** coal mine
> **collier** coal miner, coal ship

coalesce verb *some of the puddles had coalesced into shallow streams*: **unite**, join together, combine, merge, fuse, mingle, meld, blend, intermingle, knit (together), amalgamate, consolidate, integrate, affiliate, link up, homogenize, synthesize, converge; literary commingle; archaic commix.

coalition noun *the general election saw no change in the ruling four-party coalition*: **alliance**, union, partnership, affiliation, bloc, caucus; federation, league, association, confederacy, confederation, consortium, syndicate, combine, entente, alignment; amalgamation, merger; conjunction, combination, fusion.

coarse adjective **1** *coarse blankets*: **rough**, bristly, scratchy, prickly, hairy, shaggy, wiry.
▷ANTONYMS soft.
2 *his coarse ugly features contorted with rage*: **heavy**, broad, large, rough, rough-hewn, unrefined, inelegant; rugged, craggy.
▷ANTONYMS delicate.
3 *a coarse, common boy*: **oafish**, loutish, boorish, churlish, uncouth, rude, discourteous, impolite, ungentlemanly, unladylike, ill-mannered, uncivil, ill-bred, vulgar, common, rough, uncultured, uncivilized, crass, foul-mouthed; N. Amer. informal trailer-park.
▷ANTONYMS sophisticated, refined.
4 *a coarse innuendo*: **vulgar**, crude, rude, off colour, offensive, dirty, filthy, smutty, obscene, indelicate, improper, indecent, indecorous, unseemly, crass, tasteless, lewd, prurient; **bawdy**, earthy, broad, ribald, salty; informal blue, raunchy, nudge-nudge, farmyard.
▷ANTONYMS inoffensive.

coarsen verb **1** *her hands were coarsened by outside work*: **roughen**, thicken, toughen, harden.
▷ANTONYMS soften.
2 *she felt that I had been coarsened by the army*: **desensitize**, harshen, dehumanize; blunt, dull, deaden; rare indurate.
▷ANTONYMS refine, sensitize.

coarseness noun **1** *the coarseness of her hair*: **roughness**, prickliness, wiriness, bristliness, scratchiness; shagginess.
▷ANTONYMS softness.
2 *he disliked the coarseness of the men around him*: **oafishness**, loutishness, boorishness, churlishness, uncouthness, rudeness, ill manners, discourteousness, ungentlemanliness, vulgarity, roughness, crassness.
▷ANTONYMS sophistication, refinement.
3 *incapable of coarseness himself, he enjoyed listening to it on the lips of others*: **vulgarity**, crudeness, offensiveness, indelicacy, impropriety, indecorousness, unseemliness, crassness, tastelessness, lewdness, prurience; bawdiness, earthiness.

coast noun *the west coast of Africa*: **seaboard**, coastal region, coastline, seashore, shore, shoreline, seaside, beach, sand, sands, foreshore, waterside, water's edge, waterfront; technical littoral; literary strand.
▷ANTONYMS interior.
▶ verb *they were coasting down a long hill | Colchester coasted to victory*: **freewheel**, cruise, taxi, drift, glide, sail, float, skate, slip, skim.
▷ANTONYMS struggle.

> *Word links* **coast**
>
> **littoral** relating to a coast

coat noun **1** *a winter coat*: **overcoat**, tunic.
2 *a dog's coat*: **fur**, hair, wool, fleece; hide, pelt, skin; archaic fell.
3 *a coat of paint*: **layer**, covering, overlay, coating, skin, skim, plating, film, wash, glaze, varnish, veneer, lamination, sheet, finish, dusting, blanket, mantle, daub, smear, topping, crust, patina, lustre, deposit, scale, facing, cladding.
▶ verb *the steel tube was coated with a waxy substance*: **cover**, overlay, paint, glaze, varnish, wash, surface, veneer, inlay, laminate, plate, blanket, mantle, daub, smear, bedaub, cake, plaster, overspread, encrust, face; literary besmear.

coating noun *a coating of ice*: **layer**, covering, overlay, coat, skim, skin, thickness, plating, film, wash, glaze, varnish, veneer, lamination, sheet, finish, dusting, blanket, mantle, daub, smear, topping, crust, patina, lustre, deposit, scale, facing, cladding.

coax verb *you have to coax some of the children to speak*: **persuade**, wheedle, cajole, talk into something, get round, prevail on, beguile, flatter, seduce, lure, entice, tempt, inveigle, woo, manoeuvre; informal sweet-talk, soft-soap, butter up, twist someone's arm; archaic blandish.

cobble verb
□ **cobble something together** *she cobbled together a rough draft*: **prepare roughly/hastily**, make roughly/hastily, put together roughly/hastily, scribble, improvise, devise, contrive, rig (up), patch together, jerry-build; informal throw together, whip up, fix, rustle up; Brit. informal knock up.

cock noun *a cock and two hens*: **rooster**, cockerel, male fowl, capon; literary chanticleer.
▶ verb **1** *he cocked his head towards the sound*: **tilt**, tip, angle, lean, slope, bank, slant, incline, pitch, dip, cant, bevel, camber, heel, careen, put at an angle.
2 *she cocked her little finger when she held a cup*: **bend**, flex, crook, angle, curve, kink.
3 *a greyhound cocked its leg against a tree*: **lift**, raise, lift up, hold up.
□ **cock and bull story** informal *I dismissed this as another cock and bull story*: **fairy story/tale**, made-up story, trumped-up story, fabrication, concoction, piece of fiction, fiction, falsification, falsity, lie, untruth, falsehood, fib, deception, barefaced lie; (little) white lie, half-truth, exaggeration, prevarication, departure from the truth; yarn, story, red herring, rumour, myth, flight of fancy, figment of the imagination; pretence, pretext, sham, ruse, wile, trickery, stratagem; informal tall story, tall tale, whopper; Brit. informal porky, pork pie, porky pie; humorous terminological inexactitude; vulgar slang bullshit; Austral./NZ vulgar slang bulldust.

cock-eyed adjective informal **1** *he knocked the top slightly cock-eyed*: **crooked**, awry, askew, lopsided, uneven, asymmetrical, to one side, off-centre, skewed, skew, misaligned; Scottish agley, squint, thrawn; Brit. informal skew-whiff, wonky, squiffy.
2 *you expect us to believe a cock-eyed story like that? | some wild, cock-eyed scheme*: **absurd**, preposterous, ridiculous, ludicrous, farcical, laughable, risible; idiotic, stupid, foolish, silly, inane, fanciful, imbecilic, insane, wild, hare-brained, impractical, impracticable, unworkable, unfeasible,

non-viable, impossible; unreasonable, irrational, illogical, nonsensical, pointless, senseless; outrageous, shocking, astonishing, monstrous, fantastic, incongruous, grotesque; unbelievable, incredible, unthinkable, implausible, improbable; informal half-baked, crazy, barmy, daft.

cocksure adjective *he made a change from the cocksure men she usually met*: **arrogant**, **conceited**, overconfident, overweening, cocky, smug, haughty, supercilious, disdainful, lofty, patronizing, proud, vain, vainglorious, self-important, swollen-headed, egotistical, presumptuous, lordly, pompous, blustering, boastful, brash, self-assertive, opinionated, bold, forward, insolent; informal high and mighty, throwing one's weight about/around, uppish; rare hubristic.
▷ANTONYMS modest, diffident.

cocky adjective *they appeared cocky even before they went one goal up*: **arrogant**, **conceited**, overconfident, overweening, cocksure, smug, haughty, supercilious, disdainful, lofty, patronizing, proud, vain, vainglorious, self-important, swollen-headed, egotistical, presumptuous, lordly, pompous, blustering, boastful, brash, self-assertive, opinionated, bold, forward, insolent; informal high and mighty, throwing one's weight about/around, uppish; rare hubristic.
▷ANTONYMS modest, diffident.

cocoon verb **1** *he cocooned her in a fluffy towel*: **wrap**, swathe, bundle up, swaddle, sheathe, muffle, pad, cloak, enfold, envelop, surround, encase, enclose, cover, fold, wind; literary lap.
▷ANTONYMS expose.
2 *this prig was cocooned in a wealthy upper class*: **protect**, keep safe, keep from harm, safeguard, shield, defend, shelter, screen, look after, take care of, care for, cushion, insulate, isolate, cloister.

coddle verb *don't coddle repeat offenders—some of them prefer jail*: **pamper**, cosset, mollycoddle, wait on someone hand and foot, cater to someone's every whim; spoil, indulge, overindulge, humour, pander to; spoon-feed, feather-bed, wrap in cotton wool; pet, baby, mother, nanny; archaic cocker.
▷ANTONYMS neglect, treat harshly, be strict with.

code noun **1** *a message in code*: **cipher**, secret language, secret writing, set of symbols, key, hieroglyphics; coded message, cryptogram; rare cryptograph.
2 *a strict social code among inmates*: **set of principles**, set of standards, set of customs; manners, ethics, morals; morality, convention, accepted behaviour, etiquette, protocol.
3 *the penal code*: **law**, laws, body of law, rules, regulations, constitution, system, charter, canon, jurisprudence.

> *Word links* **code**
>
> **cryptology** study of codes
> **cryptography** writing or cracking of codes
> **cryptographer** writer or cracker of codes
> **encipher**, **encode**, **encrypt** put into code
> **decipher**, **decrypt**, **crack** solve a code

codify verb *the bill codified these standards for the first time*: **systematize**, systemize, organize, arrange, order, marshal, set out, chart, structure, tabulate, catalogue, list, sort, dispose, index, classify, class, categorize, compile, group, range, file, log, grade, rate, assort.

coerce verb *he was coerced into giving evidence*: **pressure**, pressurize, bring pressure to bear on, use pressure on, put pressure on, constrain, lean on, press, push; force, compel, oblige, put under an obligation, browbeat, brainwash, bludgeon, bully, threaten, prevail on, work on, act on, influence, intimidate, dragoon, twist someone's arm, strong-arm; N. Amer. blackjack; informal bulldoze, railroad, squeeze, put the screws/squeeze on; Brit. informal bounce; N. Amer. informal hustle, fast-talk.
▷ANTONYMS persuade.

> *Choose the right word* **coerce, compel, force, oblige**
>
> See **compel**.

coercion noun *it wasn't slavery because no coercion was used*: **force**, compulsion, constraint, duress, oppression, enforcement, harassment, intimidation, threats, insistence, demand, arm-twisting, pressure, pressurization, influence.
▷ANTONYMS persuasion.

coffee noun N. Amer. joe, java.

coffer noun **1** *the small coffer which had held Herluin's treasury*: **strongbox**, money box, cash box, money chest, treasure chest, casket, trunk, box, safe, safety-deposit box, safe-deposit box, repository.
2 (**coffers**) *a huge donation to the Imperial coffers*: **fund**, funds, reserves, resources, money, finances, wealth, cash, wherewithal, capital, assets, purse, kitty, pool, bank, treasury, exchequer; N. Amer. fisc.

coffin noun **box**, sarcophagus; N. Amer. casket; humorous wooden overcoat; Archaeology cist.

cogency noun *the cogency of this argument*: **strength**, force, power, potency, weight, plausibility, effectiveness, efficacy, soundness, validity, foundation; impressiveness, eloquence, persuasiveness, credibility, influence, conclusiveness, unanswerability, authoritativeness, authority; **logic**, logicality, reasonableness, rationality, lucidity, coherence, good organization, orderliness, methodicalness, clarity, articulateness, consistency, relevance.
▷ANTONYMS weakness; illogicality; vagueness.

cogent adjective *a cogent argument*: **convincing**, compelling, strong, forceful, powerful, potent, weighty; **valid**, sound, well founded, plausible, effective, efficacious, telling; impressive, persuasive, irresistible, eloquent, credible, influential, conclusive, unanswerable, authoritative; **logical**, reasoned, well reasoned, rational, reasonable, lucid, coherent, well organized, systematic, orderly, methodical, clear, articulate, consistent, relevant.
▷ANTONYMS vague; unconvincing; muddled.

> *Choose the right word* **cogent, valid, sound**
>
> See **valid**.

cogitate verb *you were cogitating on some great matter*: **think (about)**, contemplate, consider, give thought to, give consideration to, mull over, meditate (on), muse (on), ponder (on/over), reflect (on), deliberate (about/on), ruminate (about/on/over), dwell on, brood (on/over), agonize (over), worry (about), chew over, puzzle (over), speculate about, weigh up, revolve, turn over in one's mind, review, study, be in a brown study; informal put on one's thinking cap; archaic pore on; rare cerebrate.

cogitation noun *Sorry, did I interrupt your cogitation?* **thought**, thinking, contemplation, consideration, mulling over, meditation, study, deliberation, pondering, reflection, rumination, musing, speculation, brooding, agonizing, worrying, puzzling; rare cerebration.

cognate adjective **1** *the large number of cognate words in English and German*: **related**, kindred, akin, with a common ancestor.
▷ANTONYMS unrelated.
2 *cognate subjects such as physics and chemistry*: **associated**, related, connected, allied, interconnected, linked, coupled, correlated; **similar**, like, alike, comparable, parallel, equivalent, corresponding, analogous, homologous.
▷ANTONYMS unconnected; dissimilar.

cognition noun *a theory of human cognition*: **perception**, discernment, awareness, apprehension, learning, understanding, comprehension, enlightenment, insight, intelligence, reason, reasoning, thinking, (conscious) thought.

cognizance noun formal *he brought the affair to the cognizance of the court*: **awareness**, notice, knowledge, consciousness, apprehension, perception, realization, recognition, appreciation.

cognizant adjective formal *everyone should be fully **cognizant of** what is happening*: **aware**, conscious, apprised, abreast; sensible of/to, alive to, sensitive to, alert to, familiar with, acquainted with, in the know about, au fait with, conversant with, au courant with, up to date (with), up with, well versed in, knowledgeable about, well informed about, no stranger to; informal well up on, genned up on, clued in on, wise to, hip to; archaic ware of.

cohabit verb *Mary is now **cohabiting with** Paul*: **live together**, live with, live (together) as husband/man and wife, sleep with, sleep together; informal shack up with; informal, dated live in sin, live over the brush.

cohere verb **1** *I wondered how this family had cohered in the past*: **stick together**, hold together, be united, bind, cling, fuse, form a whole.
▷ANTONYMS fall apart.
2 *this view does not cohere with some people's other beliefs*: **be consistent**, hang together.

coherence noun *this raises further questions on the coherence of state policy*: **consistency**, logicality, good sense, soundness, organization, orderliness, unity; clarity, articulacy; intelligibility, comprehensibility.
▷ANTONYMS incoherence.

coherent adjective *a coherent argument*: **logical**, reasoned, reasonable, well reasoned, rational, sound, cogent; consistent, well organized, systematic, orderly, methodical; clear, lucid, articulate, relevant, intelligible, comprehensible; informal joined-up.
▷ANTONYMS incoherent; muddled.

cohesion noun *rewarding individuals breaks the cohesion in the group*: **unity**, togetherness, solidarity, bond, sticking together, continuity, coherence, connection, linkage, interrelatedness.

cohort noun **1** *the Roman army was organized into centuries, cohorts, and legions*: **unit**, outfit, force; army, group, corps, division, brigade, battalion, regiment, squadron, company, commando, battery, troop, section, patrol, cadre, crew, detachment, contingent, column, squad, detail, band, legion.
2 *52% of the mothers in the 1946 cohort of births had two children*: **group**, grouping, category, categorization, grade, grading, classification, class, set, section, division, order, batch, list; age group, generation.

coil noun *Miles found himself in the water, tangled in coils of rope*: **loop**, twist, turn, curl, hoop, roll, ring, twirl, gyre, whorl, scroll, curlicue, convolution; spiral, helix, corkscrew; technical volute, volution.

▸ **verb** *he coiled a lock of her hair around his finger*: **wind**, loop, twist, curl, curve, bend, twine, entwine, snake; spiral, corkscrew, wreathe, meander; rare convolute.

coin noun **1** *a gold coin*: **piece**, bit.
2 *large amounts of coin*: **coins**, coinage, coin of the realm, (loose) change, small change, silver, copper, coppers, gold; formal specie.
▸ **verb 1** *guineas and half-guineas were coined*: **mint**, stamp, stamp out, strike, cast, punch, die, mould, forge, make, manufacture, produce.
2 *he coined the term 'desktop publishing'*: **invent**, create, make up, devise, conceive, originate, think up, dream up, formulate, fabricate.

> *Word links* **coin**
> **numismatic** relating to coins
> **numismatist** collector of coins

coincide verb **1** *the two events coincided*: **occur simultaneously**, happen together, happen at the same time, be concurrent, coexist, concur; clash, conflict.
2 *the interests of employers and employees do not always coincide | his version did not* **coincide with** *that of the other witnesses*: **tally**, correspond, agree, accord, concur, match, fit, be in agreement, be consistent, conform, equate, harmonize, be in tune, be compatible, dovetail, correlate; be the same as, parallel; informal square; N. Amer. informal jibe; archaic quadrate.
▷ANTONYMS differ.

coincidence noun **1** *the resemblances are too close to be mere coincidence*: **accident**, chance, serendipity, fate, a twist of fate, destiny, fortuity, fortune, providence, freak, hazard; a piece of good fortune, (a bit of) luck, (a bit of) good luck, a fluke, a happy chance; N. Amer. happenstance.
2 *the coincidence of rising inflation and unemployment*: **co-occurrence**, coexistence, conjunction, simultaneity, simultaneousness, contemporaneity, contemporaneousness, concomitance, synchronicity, synchrony; clash, conflict.
3 *a coincidence of interests*: **correspondence**, agreement, accord, concurrence, match, fit, consistency, conformity, harmony, compatibility, dovetailing, correlation, parallelism; similarity, likeness.

coincident adjective **1** *the rise of the novel was* **coincident with** *the decline of storytelling*: **concurrent**, coinciding, simultaneous, contemporaneous, concomitant, synchronous, coincidental, coexistent; at the same time (as).
2 *the pursuit of profits and the social interest are therefore coincident*: **in agreement**, in harmony, in accord, matching, consonant, consistent, compatible, reconcilable, congruent, in conformity, in step, in tune, in balance, in parallel; the same.
▷ANTONYMS incompatible.

coincidental adjective **1** *a coincidental resemblance*: **accidental**, chance, occurring by chance/accident, fortuitous, adventitious, fluky, casual, serendipitous, random, aleatory; unexpected, unforeseen, unanticipated, unforeseeable, unlooked-for; unintentional, unintended, inadvertent, involuntary, unplanned, unpremeditated, unthinking, unmeant.
▷ANTONYMS intentional, planned.
2 *the coincidental disappearance of some famous jewels and of a young American tourist*: **simultaneous**, concurrent, coincident, contemporaneous, concomitant, synchronous, coexistent; at the same time (as).

coitus noun formal See **sex**.

cold adjective **1** *a cold day*: **chilly**, cool, freezing, icy, snowy, icy-cold, glacial, wintry, crisp, frosty, frigid, bitter, bitterly cold, biting, piercing, numbing, sharp, raw, polar, arctic, Siberian; informal nippy, brass monkeys; Brit. informal parky; literary chill; rare hyperborean, boreal, hibernal, hiemal, gelid, brumal.
▷ANTONYMS hot.
2 *I'm very cold*: **chilly**, chilled, cool, freezing, frozen, frozen stiff, frozen/chilled to the bone/marrow, shivery, numbed, benumbed, suffering from hypothermia, hypothermic, suffering from exposure.
▷ANTONYMS hot.
3 *Rodrigo met with a cold and scornful reception*: **unfriendly**, cool, inhospitable, unwelcoming, unsympathetic, forbidding, stony, frigid, frosty, glacial, lukewarm, haughty, supercilious, disdainful, aloof, distant, remote, indifferent, reserved, withdrawn, uncommunicative, unresponsive, unfeeling, unemotional, dispassionate, passionless, wooden, impersonal, formal, stiff, austere; cold-blooded, cold-hearted, stony-hearted; informal stand-offish, offish; rare gelid.
▷ANTONYMS warm; friendly.
□ **get cold feet** *the groom also gets cold feet when he finds out what's been going on*: **hesitate**, falter, delay, drag one's feet, stall, think twice, change one's mind, waver, oscillate, fluctuate, vacillate, be undecided, be indecisive, be irresolute, see-saw, yo-yo; Brit. haver, hum and haw; informal sit on the fence, dilly-dally, shilly-shally, pussyfoot around, blow hot and cold.
□ **give someone the cold shoulder** *he was given the cold shoulder or treated like a ghost by certain of the dealers*: **snub**, ignore, slight, spurn, shun, disdain, look right through, look past, turn one's back on, cold-shoulder, freeze out, steer clear of; Brit. send to Coventry; informal give someone the brush-off, cut, cut dead, knock back, give someone the go-by; Brit. informal blank.
▷ANTONYMS acknowledge.

> *Word links* **cold**
> **cryo-** related prefix, as in *cryogenics, cryobiology*
> **cheimaphobia** fear of cold

cold-blooded adjective *a cold-blooded murderer*: **cruel**, savage, brutal, callous, barbaric, barbarous, sadistic, inhuman, pitiless, merciless, ruthless, unforgiving, unpitying, inhumane, unfeeling, uncaring, heartless; hard, severe, harsh, austere, cold, cold-hearted, unsympathetic, unemotional, unfriendly, uncharitable, hard-hearted, stony-hearted, with a heart of stone; informal hard-boiled, hard-nosed, thick-skinned.

cold-hearted adjective *Tony was unloved by his cold-hearted wife*: **unfeeling**, unloving, uncaring, unsympathetic, unemotional, unfriendly, uncharitable, unkind, insensitive, indifferent, detached; hard-hearted, stony-hearted, with a heart of stone, heartless, hard, harsh, austere, cold.
▷ANTONYMS warm-hearted.

collaborate verb **1** *India has collaborated with several nations on space projects*: **cooperate**, join (up), join forces, team up, get together, come together, band together, work together, work jointly, participate, unite, combine, merge, link, ally, associate, amalgamate, integrate, form an alliance, pool resources, club together.
2 *they were suspected of having collaborated with the enemy*: **fraternize**, conspire, collude, cooperate, consort, sympathize.
▷ANTONYMS resist.

collaboration noun **1** *he wrote on art and architecture in collaboration with John Betjeman*: **cooperation**, alliance, partnership, participation, combination, association, concert; teamwork, joint effort, working together, coopetition.
2 *Salengro had been accused of collaboration with the enemy*: **fraternizing**, fraternization, colluding, collusion, cooperating, cooperation, consorting, sympathizing, sympathy; conspiring.
▷ANTONYMS resistance.

collaborator noun **1** *his collaborator on the book*: **co-worker**, fellow worker, associate, colleague, partner, co-partner, confederate, ally, teammate; assistant, helper; Brit. informal oppo.
2 *he was a collaborator during the occupation*: **quisling**, fraternizer, collaborationist, colluder, (enemy) sympathizer, conspirator; traitor, fifth columnist, renegade, betrayer, turncoat, defector, informer, double agent.

collapse verb **1** *the roof collapsed*: **cave in**, fall in, subside, fall down, sag, slump, settle, give, give way, crumble, crumple, disintegrate, fall to pieces, come apart.
▷ANTONYMS hold up.
2 *he collapsed from loss of blood*: **faint**, pass out, black out, lose consciousness, fall unconscious, keel over; informal flake out, conk out, go out; literary swoon.
3 *she collapsed in tears*: **break down**, go to pieces, lose control, lose one's self-control, be overcome (with emotion), crumble, fall apart; informal crack up.
4 *the peace talks collapsed*: **break down**, **fail**, fall through, fold, founder, fall flat, miscarry, go wrong, come to nothing, come to grief, be frustrated, be unsuccessful, not succeed, disintegrate; come to a halt, end, terminate; informal flop, fizzle out.
▷ANTONYMS succeed.
▸ **noun 1** *the collapse of the roof*: **cave-in**, giving way, subsidence, crumbling, disintegration.
2 *she was reported to be 'poorly' after her collapse on stage yesterday*: **fainting fit**, blackout, fainting, faint, passing out, loss of consciousness; informal flaking out; literary swooning, swoon; Medicine syncope.
3 *the collapse of the peace talks*: **breakdown**, **failure**, disintegration, foundering, miscarriage, lack of success; halt, end, termination.
▷ANTONYMS outcome; success.
4 *he suffered a collapse from overwork*: **breakdown**, attack, seizure, prostration, nervous breakdown, nervous/mental collapse, nervous exhaustion, nervous tension, crisis, personal crisis, psychological trauma; informal crack-up.

collar noun **1** *a shirt collar*: **neckband**, choker; historical ruff, gorget, bertha, Vandyke; archaic rebato.
2 technical *a small collar can be fitted round the pump rod to limit the length of stroke*: **ring**, band, collet, sleeve, pipe, flange, rim, rib.
▸ **verb** informal **1** *the cricket star collared a thief who tried to nick his golf clubs*: **apprehend**, arrest, catch, capture, seize; take prisoner, take into custody, detain, put in jail, throw in jail, put behind bars, imprison, incarcerate; informal nab, nail, run in, pinch, bust, pick up, pull in, haul in, do, feel someone's collar; Brit. informal nick.
2 *an elderly chap collared me in the street*: **accost**, address, speak to, talk to, call to, shout to, hail, initiate a discussion with; approach, waylay, take aside, detain, stop, halt, grab, catch, confront, importune, solicit; informal buttonhole; Brit. informal nobble.

collate verb **1** *the police computer system is being used to collate information from across Britain*: **collect**, gather, accumulate, assemble; **combine**,

C

aggregate, put together; **arrange**, organize, order, put in order, sort, categorize, systematize, structure.
▷ANTONYMS separate.
2 *what follows is based mainly on collating these two sources*: **compare**, contrast, set side by side, juxtapose, weigh against, set against, balance, differentiate, discriminate.

collateral noun *she put up her house as collateral for the bank loan*: **security**, surety, guarantee, guaranty, pledge, bond, assurance, insurance, indemnity, indemnification, pawn, backing; bail, hostage; archaic gage, earnest.

colleague noun *one of her colleagues in the lab*: **fellow worker**, workmate, teammate, co-worker, associate, partner, co-partner, collaborator, ally, comrade, companion, confederate; French confrère; informal oppo; Austral./NZ informal offsider; archaic compeer; rare consociate.

collect verb **1** *he collected the picnic debris | dust and dirt collect so quickly*: **gather**, accumulate, assemble; amass, stockpile, pile up, heap up, rack up, run up, scrape together, store (up), hoard, save, cumulate, lay in/up, garner; mass, increase, multiply, accrue, snowball; Brit. tot up; informal stash (away).
▷ANTONYMS distribute; squander.
2 *a crowd soon collected*: **come together**, get together, gather, assemble, meet, muster, cluster, rally, congregate, convene, converge, flock together; rare foregather.
▷ANTONYMS disperse.
3 *I must collect the children from school*: **fetch**, go/come to get, go/come and get, call for, go/come for, meet.
▷ANTONYMS take, drop off.
4 *they are collecting money for charity*: **raise**, appeal for, ask for, ask people to give, solicit, secure, obtain, acquire, gather.
▷ANTONYMS distribute, give away.
5 *he paused for a moment to* **collect himself**: **recover**, regain one's composure, pull oneself together, take a hold of oneself, steady oneself; informal get a grip (on oneself), get one's act together, snap out of it.
6 *she returned to her room to collect her thoughts*: **muster**, summon (up), gather (together), get together, rally, call into action, marshal, mobilize, screw up.

collected adjective *when we found the lady she was very collected*: **calm**, cool, {cool, calm, and collected}, as cool as a cucumber, cool-headed, self-possessed, composed, controlled, self-controlled, poised; serene, tranquil, relaxed, unruffled, unperturbed, unflustered, undisturbed, unagitated, unmoved, unbothered, untroubled; equable, even-tempered, imperturbable, placid, quiet, sedate, unexcitable, impassive, dispassionate, unemotional, phlegmatic, stolid; informal unflappable, unfazed, together, laid-back; rare equanimous.
▷ANTONYMS excited; hysterical.

collection noun **1** *police found a collection of stolen items*: **hoard**, pile, heap, stack, gathering, stock, store, stockpile; accumulation, mass, build-up, reserve, supply, bank, pool, fund, mine, reservoir; conglomeration, cumulation, accrual, aggregation, accretion, agglomerate, agglomeration; rare amassment.
2 *a motley collection of shoppers, festival-goers, and trainspotters*: **group**, crowd, body, company, troupe, assembly, assemblage, gathering, throng; knot, cluster, huddle, multitude, bevy, party, number, band, horde, pack, drove, flock, swarm, stream, mob; informal gang, load, crew, gaggle.
3 *her collection of Victorian dolls*: **set**, series, array, assortment.
4 *a collection of short stories*: **anthology**, selection, compendium, treasury, compilation, miscellany, miscellanea, pot-pourri; collected works; archaic garland; rare analects, collectanea, ana, florilegium, spicilege.
5 *a collection for the poor*: **donations**, contributions, gifts, subscription(s), alms; informal whip-round.
6 *a church collection*: **offering**, offertory, tithe.

collective adjective *collective ownership of the means of production*: **common**, shared, joint, combined, mutual, communal, united, allied, cooperative, collaborative; aggregate, cumulative, undivided, pooled.
▷ANTONYMS individual; sectional.

college noun **1** *a college of technology*: **educational institution**, training establishment, centre of learning, seat of learning; school, academy, university, institute, seminary, conservatory, conservatoire; historical polytechnic.
2 *the College of Heralds*: **association**, society, club, group, band, circle, fellowship, body, guild, lodge, order, fraternity, confraternity, brotherhood, sisterhood, sorority, league, union, alliance, affiliation, institution, coterie, federation; rare sodality.

collide verb **1** *she collided with someone | two suburban trains collided*: **crash (into)**, come into collision (with), bang (into), slam (into), impact (with); hit, strike, run into, meet head-on, smash into, smack into, cannon into, plough into, bump into, crack into/against, knock into, dash against; N. Amer. informal barrel into.
2 *in his work, politics and metaphysics collide*: **conflict**, be in conflict, come into conflict, be in opposition, clash, differ, diverge, disagree, be at variance, be at odds, be incompatible.
▷ANTONYMS coalesce.

collision noun **1** *a collision on the road to Oxford*: **crash**, accident, smash, bump, knock, impact, hit, strike, clash; Brit. RTA (road traffic accident); N. Amer. wreck; informal smash-up, pile-up; Brit. informal prang, shunt.
2 *a collision between two mutually inconsistent ideas*: **conflict**, clash, opposition, disagreement, variance, incompatibility, contradiction.
▷ANTONYMS coalescence.

colloquial adjective *some students have a good grasp of colloquial language*: **informal**, conversational, everyday, casual, non-literary; natural, unofficial, unpretentious, familiar, chatty, friendly, idiomatic, slangy; vernacular, popular, demotic.
▷ANTONYMS literary; formal.

collude verb *corrupt border officials colluded with the importers of dubious goods*: **conspire**, connive, intrigue, be hand in glove, plot, participate in a conspiracy, collaborate, scheme; informal be in cahoots; rare machinate, cabal, complot.

collusion noun *there has been collusion between the security forces and paramilitary groups*: **conspiracy**, connivance, complicity, intrigue, plotting, secret understanding, collaboration, scheming.

colonist noun *the first European colonists of North America*: **settler**, colonizer, colonial, frontiersman, frontierswoman, pioneer; immigrant, newcomer; Brit. incomer; historical planter; N. Amer. historical homesteader, habitant, redemptioner, squatter.

colonize verb *the Germans colonized Tanganyika in 1885*: **settle (in)**, establish a colony in, people, populate, pioneer, open up, found; overrun, occupy, take over, seize, capture, take possession of, annex, subjugate.
▷ANTONYMS leave; grant independence to.

colonnade noun **row of columns**, peristyle; portico, arcade, loggia, covered walk, gallery, cloisters, stoa.

colony noun **1** *Belize is a former British colony*: **territory**, possession, holding, dependency, province, dominion, protectorate, satellite (state), settlement, outpost; historical tributary, fief.
2 *the entire British colony in New York*: **population**, community.
3 *an artists' colony*: **community**, association, commune, settlement, quarter, district, section, ghetto.

colossal adjective *a colossal building*: **huge**, massive, enormous, gigantic, very big, very large, great, giant, mammoth, vast, immense, tremendous, mighty, stupendous, monumental, epic, prodigious, mountainous, monstrous, titanic, towering, elephantine, king-sized, king-size, gargantuan, Herculean, Brobdingnagian; substantial, extensive, hefty, bulky, weighty, heavy, gross; informal mega, monster, whopping, whopping great, thumping, thumping great, humongous, jumbo, hulking, bumper, astronomical, astronomic; Brit. informal whacking, whacking great, ginormous.
▷ANTONYMS tiny.

Word toolkit

colossal	**immense**	**giant**
failure	pressure	step
waste	potential	leap
blunder	importance	screen
explosion	popularity	corporation
disappointment	relief	monster
mess	satisfaction	waves
tragedy	courage	oak

colour noun **1** *the lights flickered and changed colour*: **hue**, shade, tint, tone, tinge, cast, tincture.
2 *eight tubes of oil colour*: **paint**, pigment, colourant, coloration, dye, stain, tint, wash.
3 *add colour to her cheeks*: **redness**, pinkness, rosiness, reddening, ruddiness, blush, flush, high colour, glow, bloom.
▷ANTONYMS pallor.
4 *people of every colour, creed, and race*: **skin colour**, skin colouring, skin tone, complexion, colouring, pigmentation; race, ethnic group, stock.
5 *the anecdotes and examples were chosen to add colour to strictly academic material*: **vividness**, life, liveliness, vivacity, vitality, animation, excitement, interest, fascination, richness, zest, verve, spice, spiciness, bite, piquancy, sparkle, impact, vigour, vigorousness, force, forcefulness, point; informal oomph, pizzazz, zing, zip, zap, punch, kick; literary salt.
6 *woods were unjustifiably disafforested under colour of the Statute of 1327*: **the pretext**, the cloak, the mask, the pretence, the outward appearance, the guise, a false show, a show, a front, a facade, a semblance; on the excuse of.
7 **(colours)** *Lynn runs in the colours of the Oxford City club*: **strip**, **kit**, uniform, costume, livery, insignia, regalia; badge, ribbon, rosette, emblem.
8 **(colours)** *the regimental colours*: **flag**, standard, banner, pennant, pennon, streamer, ensign, banderole; Brit. pendant; Nautical **burgee**; in ancient Rome vexillum; rare gonfalon, guidon, labarum.
▶verb **1** *the wood was coloured with a penetrating dye*: **tint**, dye, tinge, shade, pigment, stain, colour-wash, colour in, paint.
2 *she* **coloured up** *with embarrassment*: **blush**, redden, go pink/red, turn red/crimson/scarlet, flush, crimson.

▷ANTONYMS pale.
3 *the experiences had coloured her whole existence*: **influence**, affect, slant, taint, pervert, warp, twist, skew, distort, bias, prejudice, poison.
4 *witnesses might colour evidence to make a story saleable*: **exaggerate**, overstate, overdraw, overdo, embroider, embellish, dramatize, enhance, varnish; **falsify**, give a false account of, misrepresent, misreport, disguise, fudge, garble, distort, manipulate, take/quote out of context, bend, put a spin on, massage, strain.

Word links **colour**

chromatic relating to colour
chromophobia fear of colour
colorimetry measurement of colour

colourful adjective **1** *a colourful array of fruit*: **brightly coloured**, bright-coloured, deep-coloured, brilliant, glowing, radiant, vivid, rich, vibrant; eye-catching, flamboyant, showy, gaudy, glaring, garish, flashy; multicoloured, multicolour, many-coloured, many-hued, rainbow, rainbow-like, varicoloured, variegated, harlequin, motley, prismatic, polychromatic, psychedelic; informal jazzy, (looking) like an explosion in a paint factory.
▷ANTONYMS colourless.
2 *he regaled her with a colourful account of that afternoon's meeting*: **vivid**, graphic, lively, animated, dramatic, striking, arresting, picturesque, interesting, stimulating, fascinating, scintillating, rich, evocative, detailed, highly coloured.
▷ANTONYMS colourless.

colourless adjective **1** *a colourless liquid*: **uncoloured**, white, bleached, faded, washed out; literary achromatic; technical achromic.
▷ANTONYMS coloured.
2 *colourless cheeks*: **pale**, pallid, wan, anaemic, bloodless, ashen, white, white as a ghost/sheet, grey, jaundiced, waxen, chalky, chalk-white, milky, pasty, pasty-faced, whey-faced, peaky, sickly, tired-looking, washed out, sallow, drained, drawn, sapped, ghostly, deathly, deathlike, bleached; rare etiolated.
▷ANTONYMS rosy.
3 *a colourless personality*: **uninteresting**, dull, boring, tedious, monotonous, dry, drab, dreary, wearisome; unexciting, bland, non-stimulating, unimaginative, uninspiring, uninspired, weak, insipid, lustreless, lacklustre, vapid, flat, stale, trite, vacuous, feeble, pallid, wishy-washy, limp, lame, tired, lifeless, torpid, unanimated, zestless, spiritless, sterile, anaemic, barren, tame, bloodless, antiseptic; middle-of-the-road, run-of-the-mill, commonplace, mediocre, nondescript, characterless, mundane, inoffensive, humdrum, prosaic.
▷ANTONYMS colourful.

column noun **1** *the arches were supported on massive columns*: **pillar**, post, pole, support, upright, vertical, baluster, pier, pile, piling, pilaster, stanchion, standard, prop, buttress; rod, shaft, leg, mast, tower, pylon; obelisk, monolith; technical newel, caryatid, telamon, herm.
2 *he writes a weekly column in a Sunday paper*: **article**, piece (of writing), item, story, report, account, write-up, feature, essay, composition, study, review, criticism, critique, notice, commentary, editorial, leader; Brit. informal crit.
3 *we walked in a column*: **line**, file, queue, procession, rank, row, string, chain, train, trail, progression, succession, cavalcade, parade, cortège, convoy; Brit. march past; informal crocodile.

columnist noun *a columnist for the Irish Times*: **writer**, feature writer, contributor, journalist, correspondent, newspaperman, newspaperwoman, newsman, newswoman; wordsmith, man/woman of letters, penman; humorist, critic, reviewer, commentator, chronicler; French littérateur; informal scribbler, scribe, pen-pusher, hack, hackette, journo, talking head; N. Amer. informal thumbsucker.

coma noun *the road crash left him in a coma*: **unconsciousness**, insensibility, stupor, oblivion, inertia; blackout, collapse, torpor, trance; Medicine persistent vegetative state, PVS; rare sopor.

comatose adjective **1** *comatose after the accident*: **unconscious**, in a coma, insensible, senseless, blacked out, passed out, insentient, insensate; rare soporose, soporous.
2 informal *a teenager lying comatose in the sun listening to a personal stereo*: **inert**, torpid, inactive, lethargic, sluggish, lifeless, listless, languid, lazy, idle, indolent, shiftless, slothful, heavy, stagnant, sleepy, drowsy, somnolent, languorous, apathetic, passive, hibernating, sleeping, dormant, supine.

comb verb **1** *she combed her hair*: **groom**, untangle, disentangle, smooth out, straighten, arrange, neaten, tidy, dress, rake; curry.
2 *the wool had been cleaned and combed*: **separate**, dress, card, tease, hackle, heckle, hatchel.
3 *the police combed the area for the murder weapon*: **search**, scour, look around in, explore, sweep, probe, hunt through, look through, scrabble about/around in, root about/around in, ferret (about/around) in, rummage about/around/round in, rummage in/through, forage through, fish about/around in, poke about/around in, dig in, grub about/around in, delve in, go through, sift through, rake, rifle through, ransack, turn over, go through with a fine-tooth comb; turn upside down, turn inside out, leave no stone unturned in; Brit. informal rootle around in; Austral./NZ informal fossick through; rare roust around in.

combat noun *3500 men were killed in combat*: **battle**, fighting, action, hostilities, conflict, armed conflict, war, warfare, bloodshed.
▸ verb *other cities have tried to combat the disease*: **fight**, battle against, do battle with, wage war against, take up arms against, strive against, contend with, tackle, attack, counter, oppose, resist, withstand, stand up to, face up to, make a stand against, put up a fight against, confront, defy; obstruct, impede, hinder, block, thwart, frustrate, inhibit, restrain; stop, halt, put an end to, prevent, check, stem, curb.
▷ANTONYMS give in to.

C

combatant noun **1** *he was involved in the war, but not as a combatant*: **fighter**, fighting man, fighting woman, soldier, serviceman, servicewoman, warrior, trooper.
▷ANTONYMS civilian.
2 *these are only some of the combatants in a new online war for your custom*: **contender**, antagonist, adversary, battler, opponent, contestant, competitor, player, challenger, disputant, rival.
▷ANTONYMS ally; non-participant.
▸ adjective *all the combatant armies went to war with machine guns*: **warring**, at war, opposing, contending, belligerent, combating, fighting, battling, conflicting, clashing.
▷ANTONYMS non-combatant.

combative adjective *Mosley's combative language and stormy oratory*: **pugnacious**, aggressive, antagonistic, quarrelsome, argumentative, contentious, hostile, truculent, threatening, belligerent, bellicose, militant, warlike, warmongering, hawkish, militaristic; informal spoiling for a fight; rare oppugnant.
▷ANTONYMS conciliatory.

combination noun **1** *an elegant combination of ancient and modern*: **amalgamation**, amalgam, merger, union, blend, mixture, mix, mingling, meld, fusion, fusing, compound, alloy, marriage, weave, coalescence, coalition, pooling, integration, conjunction, incorporation, synthesis, composite, composition, concoction; informal mash-up.
2 *the plaintiff acted in combination with his brother*: **cooperation**, collaboration, concert, synergy, association, union, alliance, partnership, coalition, league.
▷ANTONYMS conflict.

combine verb **1** *he attempts to combine comedy with more serious themes*: **amalgamate**, merge, unite, integrate, incorporate, fuse, blend, meld, mingle, coalesce, compound, alloy, homogenize, synthesize, consolidate, bind, bond, join, marry, put together, unify, pool, intermingle, mix, intermix, affiliate; literary commingle.
▷ANTONYMS separate.
2 *groups of teachers combined to tackle a variety of problems*: **cooperate**, collaborate, join forces, pool resources, get together, come together, join (together), band (together), club together, link (up), go into partnership, unite, team up, form an alliance, form an association, league, go into league, throw in one's lot; informal gang up.
▷ANTONYMS split up.

combustible adjective *they made small piles of combustible material to start the fire*: **inflammable**, flammable, incendiary, explosive; rare burnable, ignitable.
▷ANTONYMS incombustible.

combustion noun *the combustion of fossil fuels*: **burning**, firing, kindling, igniting, ignition.

come verb **1** *do come and listen*: **move nearer**, move closer, approach, advance, near, draw nigh, draw close/closer, draw near/nearer; proceed, make progress, make headway, forge.
▷ANTONYMS go away.
2 *they came last night*: **arrive**, get here/there, reach one's destination, make it, appear, put in an appearance, make an appearance, come on the scene, come up, approach, enter, present oneself, turn up, be along, come along, materialize; W. Indian reach; informal show up, show, roll in, roll up, blow in, show one's face.
▷ANTONYMS leave.
3 *they came to a stream*: **reach**, arrive at, meet, get to, get up to, get as far as, make, make it to, set foot on, gain, attain; come across, run across, run into, happen on, chance on, light on, come upon, stumble on, blunder on, find by chance; end up at, land up at, fetch up at; informal hit, wind up at, bump into; archaic run against.
4 *the dress **comes to** her ankles*: **extend**, stretch, continue, carry on, spread; reach, come as far as, not stop until.
▷ANTONYMS stop short of.
5 *she **comes from** Belgium*: **be from**, **be a native of**, have been born in, hail from, originate in, have one's roots in, be ... (by birth); live in, have one's home in, inhabit, be an inhabitant of, be settled in, reside in, be a resident of.
6 *the attacks came without warning*: **happen**, occur, take place, come about, transpire, fall, present itself, crop up, materialize, arise, arrive,

appear, surface, ensue, follow; literary come to pass, befall, betide; archaic hap; rare eventuate.
7 *the car does not come in red*: **be available**, be made, be produced, be for sale, be on offer.
8 informal **climax**, achieve orgasm, orgasm.
□ **come about** *the change came about in 1989*: **happen**, occur, take place, transpire, fall, present itself, crop up, materialize, arise, arrive, appear, surface, ensue, follow; literary come to pass, befall, betide; archaic hap; rare eventuate.
□ **come across 1** *they came across two of his friends | I came across some new evidence*: **meet/find by chance**, meet up with, run into, run across, come upon, chance on, stumble on, happen on, light on, hit on; discover, encounter, find, unearth, uncover, locate, bring to light; informal bump into, dig up. **2** *this emotion comes across in both books*: **be communicated**, be perceived, penetrate, get through, get across, be got across, be clear, be understood, be comprehended, register, be taken in, sink in, be grasped, strike home. **3** *she* ***came across as*** *cool and unemotional*: **seem**, appear, look, sound, give the impression of being, have the appearance/air of being, strike someone as, look as though one is, look to be; Brit. come over; N. Amer. come off. **4** informal *there was always a chance that she'd* ***come across with*** *some more information*: **hand over**, give, deliver, produce, part with, pay up; informal come up with, fork out, shell out, dish out, cough up; N. Amer. informal make with, ante up, pony up.
□ **come along 1** *the puppies are coming along nicely*: **progress**, make progress, develop, shape up, make headway; come on, turn out, take shape, go; improve, show improvement, get better, pick up, rally, recover, mend.
▷**ANTONYMS** deteriorate.
2 *That's our man, Watson! Come along!* **hurry**, hurry (it) up, be quick (about it), get a move on, come along, look lively, speed up, move faster; informal get moving, get cracking, step on it, step on the gas, move it, buck up, shake a leg, make it snappy; Brit. informal get one's skates on; Brit. informal, dated stir one's stumps; N. Amer. informal get a wiggle on; Austral./NZ informal rattle your dags; S. African informal put foot; dated make haste. ▷**ANTONYMS** dawdle.
□ **come apart** *if the straw is too short the bales come apart very easily*: **break up**, fall to bits/pieces, come to bits/pieces, disintegrate, splinter, come unstuck, crumble, separate, split, tear, collapse, dissolve.
□ **come back** *he came back from work that evening*: **return**, get back, arrive back, arrive home, come home, come again.
□ **come between** *nothing should come between brothers*: **alienate**, estrange, separate, divide, split up, break up, disunite, disaffect, set/pit against one another, cause disagreement between, sow dissension between, set at variance/odds.
▷**ANTONYMS** unite.
□ **come by** *good medical care was hard to come by*: **obtain**, acquire, gain, get, find, pick up, lay hold of, possess oneself of, come to have, procure, secure, get possession of; buy, purchase; informal land, get one's hands on, get one's mitts on, get hold of, grab, bag, score, swing, nab, collar, cop.
□ **come down** *the study comes down against kerbside collection*: **decide**, conclude, settle, reach a decision; choose, opt, plump.
□ **come down on** *the magistrate came down on him like a ton of bricks*. **rebuke**.
□ **come down to** *either he gives himself up or we arrest him; it comes down to the same thing*: **amount to**, add up to, constitute, be tantamount to, approximate to, boil down to, be equivalent to, comprise, count as.
□ **come down with** *many girls came down with minor ailments*: **become ill/sick with**, fall ill/sick with, be taken ill with, show symptoms of, become infected with, get, catch, develop, contract, take, sicken for, fall victim to, be struck down with, be stricken with; Brit. go down with; informal take ill with; N. Amer. informal take sick with.
▷**ANTONYMS** shake off.
□ **come forward** *a local trader came forward to pay the fines*: **volunteer**, step forward, offer one's services, make oneself available.
□ **come in** *a hen came in through the open door*: **enter**, gain admission, gain entrance, cross the threshold.
▷**ANTONYMS** go out.
□ **come in for** *he has come in for a lot of criticism*: **receive**, experience, sustain, undergo, meet with, encounter, face, go through, be subjected to, be the object of, bear the brunt of, suffer, have to put up with, have to bear, have to endure.
□ **come into** *then he came into money and set up his own business*: **inherit**, be/become heir to, be left, be willed, be bequeathed; Law be devised.
□ **come off 1** *when this fondue comes off it is a very fine dish indeed*: **succeed**, be successful, be a success, pan out, work, turn out well, work out, go as planned, produce the desired result, get results; informal make it, make the grade, pay off.
▷**ANTONYMS** fail.
2 *Anthony always came off worse in an argument*: **end up**, finish up.
□ **come on** *the marrows are coming on nicely*: **progress**, make progress, develop, shape up, make headway; come along, turn out, take shape; improve, show improvement.
□ **come out 1** *it came out that he'd been to Rome, too*: **become known**, become common knowledge, become apparent, come to light, emerge, transpire; get out, be discovered, be uncovered, be made public, be revealed, be divulged, leak out, be disclosed, be reported, be publicized, be released.
▷**ANTONYMS** be hushed up. **2** *lots of interesting books are coming out*: **be published**, be issued, be released, be brought out, be produced, be printed, appear, go on sale. **3** *the garden looks really nice in the summer when all the flowers come out*: **bloom**, come into bloom, flower, appear, open.
▷**ANTONYMS** wither. **4** *I expect it will come out all right*: **end**, finish, conclude, terminate, develop, result, work out, turn out; informal pan out; rare eventuate. **5** *if MPs don't come out voluntarily, they risk being outed by a tabloid newspaper*: **declare that one is homosexual**, come out of the closet.
6 Brit. dated *she came out in 1929*: **enter society**, be presented, debut, make one's debut in society.
□ **come out with** *she was puzzled that he should come out with this remark*: **utter**, say, speak, let out, blurt out, burst out with.
□ **come round 1** *he has just come round from anaesthetic*: **regain consciousness**, recover consciousness, come to, come to life, come to one's senses, recover, revive, awake, wake up. ▷**ANTONYMS** faint, go under.
2 *he argued at first but came round eventually | I* ***came round to*** *her point of view*: **be converted (to)**, be won over (by), agree (with), change one's mind, be persuaded (by), give way (to), yield (to), relent, concede, grant.
3 *the same combination of number and name only comes round every 260 days*: **occur**, take place, happen, come up, crop up, arise; **recur**, happen again, reoccur, occur again, be repeated, repeat (itself); come back (again), return; reappear, appear again. **4** *do come round for a drink*: **visit**, call (in/round), pay a call, pay a visit, look in, stop by, drop by/in/round/over, come over; informal pop in/round/over.
□ **come through** *his four shops came through the war intact*: **survive**, get through, ride out, weather, live through, pull through, outlast, outlive; **withstand**, stand up to, bear up against, stand, endure, rise above, surmount, overcome, resist; informal stick out.
□ **come to 1** *their bill came to £17.50*: **amount to**, add up to, run to, number, make, total, equal, be equal to, be equivalent to; Brit. tot up to.
2 *when I came to, I had a splitting headache*: **regain consciousness**, recover consciousness, come round, come to life, come to one's senses, recover, revive, awake, wake up.
▷**ANTONYMS** faint, go under.
□ **come up** *when the opportunity came up again we didn't hesitate*: **arise**, present itself, occur, happen, come about, transpire, emerge, surface, crop up, turn up, pop up.
□ **come up to 1** *she came up to his shoulder*: **reach**, come to, come up as far as, be as tall as, extend to, stretch to. **2** *Christmas never really came up to her expectations*: **measure up to**, match up to, live up to, reach, satisfy, fulfil, achieve, meet, equal, be equal to, be on a level with, compare with, admit of comparison, bear comparison with; be good enough, fit/fill the bill; informal hold a candle to, make the grade.
▷**ANTONYMS** exceed; fall short of.
□ **come up with** *I needed to come up with a solution*: **produce**, devise, propose, put forward, present, think up, submit, suggest, recommend, advocate, advance, move, introduce, bring forward, put on the table, put up, offer, proffer, tender, adduce, moot.

comeback noun **1** *he has made a determined comeback after his defeat in the world championship*: **resurgence**, recovery, return, rally, upturn, revival, rebound; Brit. fightback.
2 informal *some of my best comebacks go over people's heads*: **retort**, riposte, return, rejoinder, counter, retaliation, sally; answer, reply, response.

comedian noun **1** *one of Britain's best-loved comedians*: **comic**, funny man, funny woman, comedienne, comedy actor/actress, humorist, gagster, stand-up; N. Amer. tummler; French farceur.
2 *Dad was a comedian, but unaware of it*: **joker**, jester, wit, wag, comic, wisecracker, punner, jokester; prankster, clown, fool, buffoon; informal laugh, hoot, case, character, one; informal, dated card, caution, sketch, yell; Austral./NZ informal hard case.

comedienne noun See **comedian** (sense 1).

comedown noun informal **1** *Patrol duty? Bit of a comedown for a sergeant*: **loss of status**, loss of face; **downgrading**, mortification, humiliation, humbling, belittlement, lowering, demotion, reduction, degradation, disgrace.
2 *it's such a comedown after Christmas is over*: **anticlimax**, let-down, bathos, disappointment, disillusionment, deflation, decline, setback, reversal; informal washout.

comedy noun **1** *he excels in comedy | she has appeared in countless comedies*: **light entertainment**; **comic play/film**; farce, situation comedy, burlesque, pantomime, slapstick, satire, vaudeville, comic opera; informal sitcom.
▷**ANTONYMS** tragedy.
2 *advertising people see the comedy in their work*: **humour**, fun, funny side, comical aspect, funniness, ludicrousness, absurdity, absurdness, drollness, farce.
▷**ANTONYMS** gravity.

Word links **comedy**

Thalia the Muse of comedy

comely adjective *a comely young woman*: **attractive**, good-looking, nice-looking, beautiful, pretty, handsome, lovely, stunning, striking, arresting, gorgeous, prepossessing, winning, fetching, captivating, bewitching, beguiling, engaging, charming, charismatic, enchanting, appealing, delightful, irresistible; sexy, sexually attractive, sexual, seductive, alluring, tantalizing, ravishing, desirable, sultry, sensuous, sensual, erotic, arousing, luscious, lush, nubile; Scottish & N. English bonny; informal fanciable, beddable, tasty, hot, smashing, knockout, drop-dead gorgeous, out of this world, easy on the eye, come-hither, come-to-bed; Brit. informal fit; N. Amer. informal cute, foxy, bootylicious; Austral./NZ informal spunky; literary beauteous; dated taking, well favoured; archaic fair; rare sightly, pulchritudinous.
▷**ANTONYMS** ugly.

come-on noun informal *the come-on for investors is the potential licensing agreement with a major drug company*. See **inducement**.

comeuppance noun informal *in those films the villain always got his comeuppance*: **just deserts**, deserved fate, due, due reward, just punishment, retribution, requital; archaic recompense.

comfort noun **1** *they travel in comfort*: **ease**, freedom from hardship, repose, relaxation, serenity, tranquillity, contentment, content, well-being, cosiness, enjoyment; **luxury**, affluence, prosperity, prosperousness, wealth, opulence; plenty, sufficiency, welfare; bed of roses; rare easefulness.
▷**ANTONYMS** discomfort; hardship.
2 *a few words of comfort*: **consolation**, solace, condolence, sympathy, fellow feeling, commiseration; help, support, succour, relief, easement, alleviation; reassurance, cheer, gladdening.
▷**ANTONYMS** grief.
▶ **verb** *a friend tried to comfort her*: **console**, solace, bring comfort to, give solace to, condole with, give condolences to, commiserate with, give sympathy to, sympathize with; help, support, succour, ease; reassure, soothe, assuage, calm, relieve, cheer, hearten, gladden, uplift, give a lift to, encourage; informal buck up.
▷**ANTONYMS** distress; depress.

comfortable adjective **1** *a comfortable lifestyle*: **pleasant**, free from hardship, well off, well-to-do, affluent, luxurious, gracious, opulent, elegant.
▷**ANTONYMS** hard.
2 *a comfortable room*: **cosy**, snug, warm, pleasant, enjoyable, agreeable, congenial, plush, well furnished; sheltered, secure, safe, restful, homelike, homely; informal comfy.
▷**ANTONYMS** spartan.
3 *comfortable clothes*: **loose**, loose-fitting, casual, roomy, soft; informal comfy.
▷**ANTONYMS** uncomfortable, tight.
4 *a comfortable pace*: **leisurely**, unhurried, relaxed, unrushed, easy, easy-going, gentle, sedate, restful, effortless, undemanding, slow, plodding, lazy, dawdling, loitering, lingering; measured, steady; informal laid-back.
▷**ANTONYMS** frenetic.
5 *they appear very comfortable in each other's company*: **at ease**, at one's ease, relaxed, reassured, confident, secure, safe, serene, tranquil, unworried, contented, happy.
▷**ANTONYMS** vulnerable, threatened, unsettled; tense.

comforting adjective *Anne gave her a comforting hug*: **consoling**, consolatory, condoling, commiserative, sympathetic, understanding, compassionate, solicitous, gentle, tender, warm, protective, caring, loving; helpful, supportive, easing; reassuring, soothing, assuaging, calming, relieving, cheering, heartening, uplifting, encouraging.
▷**ANTONYMS** disquieting.

comfortless adjective **1** *life in his aunt's colourless, comfortless house was narrow and uninteresting*: **gloomy**, dreary, dull, dismal, bleak, drab, grim, sombre, dark, dim, dingy, funereal; miserable, wretched, joyless, cheerless, unhappy, depressing, disheartening, dispiriting, unwelcoming, uninviting, inhospitable; austere, severe, stark, bare, spartan, desolate; clinical, institutional, impersonal.
▷**ANTONYMS** bright, welcoming.
2 *he had left her comfortless*: **miserable**, broken-hearted, heartbroken, unhappy, sad, grief-stricken, grieving, sorrowful, sorrowing, mourning, anguished, distressed, desolate, devastated, despairing, inconsolable, disconsolate, downcast, down, downhearted, dejected, crestfallen, cheerless, depressed, melancholy, morose, gloomy, glum, mournful, doleful, dismal, forlorn, woeful, woebegone, abject, low-spirited, long-faced; informal blue, down in the mouth, down in the dumps; literary dolorous; archaic chap-fallen.
▷**ANTONYMS** buoyant.

comic adjective *the play is so inane as to be comic*: **humorous**, funny, droll, amusing, entertaining, diverting, absurd, ridiculous, comical, chucklesome, farcical, silly, slapstick, hilarious, uproarious, hysterical, hysterically funny, zany; witty, jocular, joking, facetious, waggish; informal priceless, side-splitting, rib-tickling, killing, killingly funny, screamingly funny, a scream, a hoot, a laugh, a barrel of laughs.
▷**ANTONYMS** serious.
▶ **noun** **1** *he told jokes in the style of a music hall comic*: **comedian**, comedienne, funny man, funny woman, comedy actor, comedy actress, humorist, wit, wag, quipster; joker, jester, prankster, clown; informal kidder, wisecracker; archaic buffoon.
2 *Tony was reading his comic*: **cartoon paper**, comic paper, funny magazine, comic book, graphic novel; informal funny.

comical adjective **1** *he could be comical while looking as serious as an owl*: **funny**, comic, humorous, droll, chucklesome, witty, waggish, facetious, light-hearted, jocular, hilarious, hysterically funny; amusing, diverting, entertaining; informal jokey, wacky, side-splitting, rib-tickling, killing, killingly funny, priceless, a scream, a hoot, a laugh; informal, dated a card, a caution; archaic sportive; rare jocose.
▷**ANTONYMS** sensible.
2 *don't they look comical in those suits?* **silly**, absurd, ridiculous, laughable, risible, droll, ludicrous, farcical, preposterous, foolish; bizarre, weird, strange, freakish, queer, odd, peculiar, curious, zany; informal wacky, freaky, crazy, off the wall; N. Amer. informal wacko; Brit. informal rum; rare derisible.
▷**ANTONYMS** normal.

coming adjective *they wanted to discredit the Government prior to the coming election*: **forthcoming**, imminent, impending, approaching, advancing, nearing, near; future, expected, anticipated; close, (close) at hand, in store, in the wind, in the air, in the offing, in the pipeline, on the horizon, on the way, on us, about to happen; informal on the cards.
▶ **noun** *primroses are associated with the coming of spring*: **approach**, advance, advent, arrival, nearing, looming, appearance, emergence, materialization, surfacing; birth, rise, start, onset.

command verb **1** *he commanded his men to retreat*: **order**, give orders to, give the order to, tell, direct, instruct, call on, enjoin, adjure, charge, require, prescribe; literary bid.
2 *he commanded a tank unit*: **be in charge of**, be in command of, have charge of, have control of, be the leader of, be the boss of, preside over, be in authority over, hold sway over; head, lead, rule, govern, control, direct, guide, manage, supervise, superintend, oversee; be in the driver's seat, be in the saddle, be at the helm, take the chair; informal head up, run the show, call the shots, call the tune.
3 *the clergy command great respect from the population*: **receive**, be given, get, gain, obtain, secure.
▶ **noun** **1** *the officers shouted their commands*: **order**, instruction, directive, direction, commandment, injunction, demand, stipulation, requirement, exhortation, bidding, request; decree, dictate, diktat, edict, ruling, resolution, pronouncement, ordinance, mandate, fiat, precept; literary behest; archaic hest; rare rescript.
2 *he had sixteen men under his command*: **authority**, control, charge, power, direction, dominion, domination, influence, sway, guidance; leadership, mastery, rule, government, management, supervision, superintendence, administration, jurisdiction.
3 *she had a brilliant **command of** English*: **knowledge**, mastery, grasp, grip, comprehension, understanding; ability in, fluency in.

commandeer verb *everything surrounding the base was commandeered by the army*: **seize**, take, take possession of, take away, requisition, appropriate, expropriate, sequestrate, sequester, confiscate, annex, take over, claim, lay claim to, pre-empt, secure; hijack, arrogate, arrogate to oneself, help oneself to, carry off, loot, grab; informal walk off with; Law distrain, attach, disseize; Scottish Law poind.

commander noun *he was commander of a special force combating drug trafficking*: **leader**, head, headman, boss, chief, director, manager, overseer, controller, master; commander-in-chief, C.-in-C., commanding officer, CO, officer, captain; informal boss man, skipper, number one, top dog, kingpin, bigwig, Mr Big, big cheese; Brit. informal gaffer, guv'nor; N. Amer. informal numero uno, sachem, big white chief, big wheel, head honcho, honcho, big kahuna, high muckamuck.

commanding adjective **1** *the world champion was in a commanding position*: **dominant**, dominating, controlling, superior, powerful, prominent, advantageous, favourable, preferable, more desirable, most desirable; rare prepotent, prepollent.
2 *his mother's voice was soft and commanding*: **authoritative**, masterful, assertive, confident, firm, emphatic, insistent, imperative, imposing, impressive; bossy, peremptory, autocratic, imperious, magisterial, lordly, high-handed, overbearing, domineering, dictatorial, dominating, bullish, forceful; informal pushy, not backward in coming forward; rare pushful.

commemorate verb *the event commemorated the courage of the villagers*: **celebrate**, pay tribute to, pay homage to, honour, salute, toast; **remember**, recognize, acknowledge, observe, mark, memorialize, immortalize, keep alive the memory of.

commemorative adjective *veterans of the battle will attend commemorative services*: **memorial**, remembrance, celebratory, celebrative; in remembrance of ..., in memory of ..., in honour of ....

commence verb formal *the headmaster commenced his tour of inspection | the meeting commenced at 10am*: **begin**, start, start off; get down to business, get the ball rolling, get going, get under way, get off the ground, make a start on, set about, go about, enter on, embark on, launch into, lead off, get down to, set in motion, ring up the curtain on, open, initiate, institute, inaugurate; go ahead; informal get cracking on, get stuck into, kick off, get the show on the road; Brit. informal get weaving (on).
▷**ANTONYMS** conclude.

C

C

commencement noun formal *students shall enrol at the commencement of the academic session*: **beginning**, start, starting point, opening, outset, onset, launch, initiation, inception, birth, dawn, origin; day one; informal kick-off.
▷ANTONYMS conclusion.

commend verb **1** *we should commend him for his remarkable altruism*: **praise**, compliment, congratulate, applaud, clap, cheer, toast, salute, admire, honour, glorify, extol, eulogize, sing the praises of, praise to the skies, heap praise on, go into raptures about, wax lyrical about, speak highly of, look on with favour, pay homage to, pay tribute to, take one's hat off to, pat on the back; N. Amer. informal ballyhoo; black English big someone up; dated cry someone up; archaic emblazon; rare laud, panegyrize.
▷ANTONYMS criticize.
2 *she's very hard-working—I commend her to you without reservation*: **recommend**, suggest, put forward, propose, advance; approve, endorse, advocate, vouch for, speak for, stand up for, champion, support, back; informal plug, push.
3 formal *I commend my students to your care*: **entrust**, trust, deliver, commit, hand over, give, give over, turn over, consign, assign.

commendable adjective *he tackled the tests with commendable zeal*: **admirable**, praiseworthy, laudable, estimable, meritorious, creditable, exemplary, exceptional, noteworthy, notable, honourable, worthy, deserving, respectable, sterling, fine, excellent; worthy of commendation, worthy of admiration; rare applaudable.
▷ANTONYMS reprehensible.

commendation noun **1** *he received letters of commendation from the chief constable*: **praise**, congratulation, appreciation, thanks; acclaim, acclamation, credit, recognition, regard, respect, esteem, admiration, adulation, approval, approbation, homage, tribute; eulogy, encomium, panegyric, paean; rare laudation, extolment, eulogium.
▷ANTONYMS criticism.
2 *he got a commendation for brave conduct*: **award**, accolade, prize, honour, honourable mention, mention, citation, recognition; pat on the back, round of applause.
▷ANTONYMS penalty.

commensurate adjective **1** *the clergy had privileges but they had commensurate duties*: **equivalent**, equal, corresponding, correspondent, comparable, proportionate, proportional; rare commensurable.
▷ANTONYMS disproportionate.
2 *your initial salary will be* ***commensurate with*** *your qualifications and experience*: **appropriate to**, in keeping with, in line with, consistent with, corresponding to, in accordance with, according to, relative to, in proportion with, proportionate to; dependent on, based on; rare commensurable with/to.

comment noun **1** *she was upset by their comments on her appearance*: **remark**, observation, statement, utterance, pronouncement, judgement, reflection, opinion, view, criticism.
2 *the story excited a great deal of comment*: **discussion**, debate, mention, consideration, interest.
3 *a comment had been inserted in the register for 1586*: **note**, notation, annotation, footnote, gloss, commentary, explanation, explication, interpretation, elucidation, exposition, exegesis; marginalia; rare scholium.
▸verb **1** *they* ***commented on*** *the quality of the water*: **remark on**, speak about, talk about, write about, discuss, mention, give a mention to, make mention of, make remarks about, make a comment on, express an opinion on, say something about, touch on, allude to.
2 *'It will soon be night,' he commented*: **remark**, observe, reflect, say, state, declare, announce, pronounce, assert, interpose, interject; come out with; rare opine.

commentary noun **1** *he spent the morning listening to the test match commentary*: **narration**, description, account, report, review, analysis.
2 *the second volume contains detailed textual commentary*: **explanation**, explication, elucidation, exegesis, examination, interpretation, analysis; **criticism**, critical analysis, critique, assessment, appraisal, opinion; notes, footnotes, comments, weblog, blog; rare scholia.

commentator noun **1** *he was a BBC television commentator for twenty-five years*: **narrator**, commenter, reporter, correspondent, journalist; announcer, presenter, anchor, anchorman, anchorwoman, broadcaster, newscaster, sportscaster; informal talking head.
2 *she was the ablest and most devastating political commentator*: **critic**, **analyst**, pundit, commenter, monitor, observer, blogger, judge, evaluator, interpreter, exponent, expounder; writer, author, speaker; rare scholiast; (**commentators**) the commentariat.

commerce noun *Hong Kong was a perfect harbour for eastern commerce*: **trade**, trading, buying and selling, business, bargaining, dealing, traffic, trafficking; (financial) transactions, dealings, negotiations; archaic merchandising.

commercial adjective **1** *the vessels were originally built for commercial purposes*: **trade**, trading, business, private enterprise, mercantile, merchant, sales; archaic merchandising.
2 *they help firms turn good ideas into commercial products*: **lucrative**, moneymaking, money-spinning, profitable, profit-making, for-profit, remunerative, financially rewarding, fruitful, gainful, productive; viable, cost-effective, economic, successful, commercially successful.
▷ANTONYMS loss-making.
3 *public opinion was inward-looking and brashly commercial*: **profit-orientated**, money-orientated, commercialized, materialistic, mercenary.
▷ANTONYMS non-profit-making.
▸noun *she appeared in a TV commercial for a brand of butter*: **advertisement**, promotion, display; informal ad, push, plug; Brit. informal advert.

commercialized adjective *the art world became increasingly commercialized*: **profit-orientated**, money-orientated, commercial, materialistic, mercenary.
▷ANTONYMS uncommercial.

commiserate verb *he* ***commiserated with*** *them for their sufferings*: **offer sympathy to**, be sympathetic to, express sympathy for, send condolences to, offer condolences to, condole with, sympathize with, empathize with, feel pity for, feel sorry for, feel for, be moved by, mourn for, sorrow for, grieve for; comfort, console, solace, give solace to; one's heart goes out to; archaic compassion, compassionate.

commiseration noun *the other actors offered him clumsy commiseration* | *our commiserations to those who didn't win*: **condolences**, sympathy, pity, comfort, solace, consolation; compassion, feeling, fellow feeling, understanding, consideration.

commission noun **1** *the customer is unlikely to know about the dealer's commission*: **percentage**, brokerage, share, portion, dividend, premium, fee, consideration, bonus, gratuity, tip, honorarium; informal cut, take, whack, rake-off, slice, slice of the cake, piece of the action; Brit. informal divvy; rare apportionment, quantum, moiety.
2 *he accepted the commission of building a house for the queen*: **task**, employment, job, work, piece of work, project, mission, assignment, undertaking, exercise, enterprise, endeavour; duty, charge, responsibility, burden; dated office.
3 *the items are made under royal commission*: **warrant**, licence, sanction, authority.
4 *their plan requires approval by an independent commission*: **committee**, board, board of commissioners, council, panel, directorate, advisory body, advisorate, convocation, delegation.
5 *they did not participate in the commission of any offence*: **perpetration**, committing, committal, execution, performance.
□ **in commission** *the company had thirty-six vessels in commission*: **in service**, in use, in employment, in action; working, functioning, functional, operative, going, running, up and running, in operation, in working order.
□ **out of commission** *five of the rescue vehicles were out of commission*: **not in service**, unavailable for use, not in use, out of action, unserviceable; not working, not functioning, not functional, inoperative, not in operation, not in working order, out of order; down; Brit. informal U/S.
▸verb **1** *he commissioned Van Dyck to paint his portrait*: **engage**, contract, charge, employ, hire, recruit, retain, appoint, enlist, co-opt, book, sign up; authorize, empower; Military detail.
2 *they decided to commission a sculpture of Molly Malone*: **order**, put in an order for, place an order for, contract for, pay for; authorize; rare bespeak.

commit verb **1** *he was on trial for a murder he had not committed*: **carry out**, do, perform, perpetrate, engage in, enact, execute, effect, accomplish; be responsible for, be to blame for, be guilty of; informal pull off; rare effectuate.
2 *she was committed to the care of the local authority*: **entrust**, trust, commend, consign, assign, deliver, give, give over, hand over, turn over, give up, relinquish.
3 *local business leaders committed themselves to community projects*: **pledge**, devote, apply, give, dedicate, bind, obligate.
4 *the judge committed him to prison for eight months*: **consign**, assign, send, deliver, confine.
5 *her husband had her committed after her eccentricity became dangerous*: **hospitalize**, **confine**, institutionalize, put away, lock away, lock up; certify.
▷ANTONYMS release.

commitment noun **1** *he resigned because of the pressure of other commitments*: **responsibility**, obligation, duty, tie, charge, liability, burden, pressure; undertaking, task, engagement, arrangement.
2 *her commitment to her students continued undiminished*: **dedication**, devotion, allegiance, loyalty, faithfulness, fidelity, bond, adherence, attentiveness.
3 *he made a commitment to carry on his father's work*: **vow**, promise, pledge, oath; covenant, contract, pact, deal, undertaking; decision, resolution, resolve; guarantee, assurance, affirmation.

committed adjective *they are committed Christians*: **devout**, devoted, loyal, dedicated, faithful, staunch, firm, steadfast, resolute, unwavering, sincere, wholehearted, keen, earnest, enthusiastic, zealous, passionate, ardent, fervent, active, sworn, pledged; dutiful, hard-working, diligent, studious, assiduous; French engagé; informal card-carrying, red-hot, true blue, mad keen, deep-dyed.
▷ANTONYMS apathetic.

commodious adjective *she was sitting in a commodious armchair*: **roomy**, capacious, spacious, ample, substantial, generous, sizeable, large, big, broad, wide, extensive; rare spacey.
▷ANTONYMS cramped.

commodity noun *improving productivity will lower the cost of a commodity*: **item**, material, type of produce, product, article, object, thing, artefact, piece of merchandise; import, export.

common adjective **1** *he gained a massive following among the common folk*: **ordinary**, normal, typical, average, unexceptional, run-of-the-mill, plain, simple.
2 *this booklet answers the most common questions asked | a very common art form*: **usual**, ordinary, customary, habitual, familiar, regular, frequent, repeated, recurrent, routine, everyday, daily, day-to-day, quotidian, standard, typical; conventional, stock, stereotyped, predictable, commonplace, mundane, run-of-the-mill; literary wonted.
▷ANTONYMS unusual.
3 *it is a common belief that elephants have long memories*: **widespread**, general, universal, popular, mainstream, prevalent, prevailing, rife, established, well established, conventional, traditional, traditionalist, orthodox, accepted; in circulation, in force, in vogue.
▷ANTONYMS rare.
4 *they work together for the common good*: **collective**, communal, community, public, popular, general; **shared**, joint, combined.
▷ANTONYMS private, individual.
5 *the fishermen's wives were far too common for my mother*: **uncouth**, vulgar, coarse, rough, unsavoury, boorish, rude, impolite, ill-mannered, unladylike, ungentlemanly, ill-bred, uncivilized, unsophisticated, unrefined, philistine, primitive, savage, brutish, oafish, gross; **lowly**, low, low-born, low-ranking, low-class, inferior, humble, ignoble, proletarian, plebeian; informal plebby, slobbish, cloddish, clodhopping; Brit. informal common as muck; archaic baseborn.
▷ANTONYMS refined; noble.
▶ **noun** Brit. informal *use a bit of common!* See **common sense**.

> *Word toolkit* **common**
>
> See **typical**.

commonly adverb *shift workers commonly complain of not being able to sleep*: **often**, frequently, regularly, repeatedly, recurrently, time and again, time and time again, over and over, all the time, routinely, habitually, customarily; N. Amer. oftentimes; informal lots; literary oft, oft-times.
▷ANTONYMS rarely.

commonplace adjective **1** *he had a tame and commonplace style of writing*: **ordinary**, run-of-the-mill, middle-of-the-road, mainstream, unremarkable, unexceptional, undistinguished, uninspired, unexciting, unmemorable, forgettable, indifferent, average, so-so, mediocre, pedestrian, prosaic, lacklustre, dull, bland, uninteresting, mundane, everyday, quotidian, humdrum, hackneyed, trite, banal, clichéd, predictable, overused, overdone, overworked, stale, worn out, time-worn, tired, unoriginal, derivative; Brit. common or garden; N. Amer. garden variety; informal nothing to write home about, nothing to get excited about, no great shakes, not so hot, not up to much, vanilla, plain vanilla, bog-standard, a dime a dozen, old hat, corny, played out; Brit. informal not much cop, ten a penny; N. Amer. informal ornery, bush-league, cornball, dime-store; Austral./NZ informal half-pie.
▷ANTONYMS outstanding; original.
2 *business trips abroad are now commonplace occurrences*: **common**, normal, usual, ordinary, familiar, routine, standard, everyday, day-to-day, daily, regular, frequent, habitual, conventional, typical, unexceptional, unremarkable.
▷ANTONYMS unusual.
▶ **noun 1** *early death was a commonplace in those days*: **everyday thing/event**; routine, nothing out of the ordinary.
2 *he had a great store of commonplaces which he adapted to any subject*: **platitude**, cliché, truism, hackneyed/trite/banal/overworked saying, stock phrase, old chestnut, banality, bromide.

common sense noun *he is quick to praise her professionalism and common sense*: **good sense**, sense, sensibleness, native wit, native intelligence, mother wit, wit, judgement, sound judgement, level-headedness, prudence, discernment, acumen, sharpness, sharp-wittedness, canniness, astuteness, shrewdness, judiciousness, wisdom, insight, intuition, intuitiveness, perceptiveness, perspicacity, vision, understanding, intelligence, reason, powers of reasoning; practicality, capability, initiative, resourcefulness, enterprise; informal horse sense, gumption, nous, savvy, know-how; Brit. informal common; N. Amer. informal smarts; rare sapience, arguteness.
▷ANTONYMS folly.

commotion noun *a commotion broke out in the street behind us*: **disturbance**, racket, uproar, tumult, ruckus, clamour, brouhaha, furore, hue and cry, palaver, fuss, stir, to-do, storm, maelstrom, melee; turmoil, disorder, confusion, chaos, mayhem, havoc, pandemonium, upheaval, unrest, fracas, riot, breach of the peace, disruption, agitation, excitement, hurly-burly, hubbub, disquiet, ferment, bother, folderol, bustle, hustle and bustle; Irish, N. Amer., & Austral. donnybrook; Indian tamasha; W. Indian bangarang; informal song and dance, pantomime, production, rumpus, ruction, ructions, ballyhoo, hoo-ha, hullabaloo, aggro, argy-bargy; Brit. informal carry-on, kerfuffle, row, stink, splash, hoopla; N. Amer. informal foofaraw; NZ informal bobsy-die; Law, dated affray; archaic broil.

communal adjective **1** *the bathrooms and the kitchen were communal*: **shared**, joint, common, general, public.
▷ANTONYMS private.
2 *the villagers farm on a communal basis*: **collective**, cooperative, community, communalist, united, combined, pooled, mass.
▷ANTONYMS individual.

commune noun (stress on the first syllable) *she was brought up in a commune in Vancouver*: **collective**, cooperative, co-op, community, communal settlement, kibbutz, fellowship.
▶ **verb** (stress on the second syllable) **1** *the purpose of praying is to commune with God*: **communicate**, speak, talk, converse, have a tête-à-tête, confer; be in touch, be in contact, interface.
2 *spare half an hour each day to* ***commune with*** *nature*: **empathize**, have a rapport, feel in close touch; feel at one, feel togetherness, identify, relate to, relate spiritually to, feel close to.

communicable adjective *they are concerned about the spread of communicable diseases*: **contagious**, **infectious**, transmittable, transmissible, transferable, conveyable, spreadable, spreading; informal catching; dated infective.

communicate verb **1** *he communicated the bad news to his boss*: **convey**, tell, impart, relay, transmit, pass on, hand on, transfer, make known, announce, report, recount, relate, set forth, present, divulge, disclose, mention; spread, disseminate, circulate, promulgate, proclaim, broadcast, make public; informal let on about.
▷ANTONYMS withhold from; keep secret.
2 *parents and teachers should communicate on a daily basis*: **liaise**, be in touch, be in contact, be in communication, make contact, have dealings, interface, commune, meet, meet up; talk, speak, converse, chat, have a conversation, have a chat, have a discussion; N. Amer. visit; informal have a confab, chew the fat, chew the rag, powwow; Brit. informal have a chinwag; N. Amer. informal shoot the breeze, shoot the bull.
3 *we have to learn how to communicate in an electronic environment*: **get one's ideas across**, get one's message across, make oneself understood, explain oneself, get through to someone, have one's say; be articulate, be fluent, be eloquent.
4 *the disease is communicated from one person to another*: **transmit**, transfer, spread, carry, pass on, hand on, convey.
5 *each bedroom* ***communicated with*** *a spacious bathroom*: **connect with**, be connected to, join up with, link up with, open on to, lead into, give access to.

communication noun **1** *meetings are used for the communication of research results*: **transmission**, imparting, conveying, reporting, presenting, passing on, handing on, relay, conveyance, divulgence, divulgation, disclosure; spreading, dissemination, promulgation, broadcasting, circulation, circulating.
2 *there had been no communication between them for years*: **contact**, dealings, relations, connection, association, communion, socializing, intercourse, social intercourse, social relations, interface, interchange, correspondence, dialogue, talk, conversation, discussion, speaking, talking, chatting, meeting, getting in touch; dated commerce; archaic traffic.
3 *there has been no official communication regarding an appeal*: **message**, statement, announcement, report, dispatch, communiqué, letter, bulletin, correspondence, news, word, information, intelligence, instruction; informal info, gen, low-down, dirt; literary tidings.

communications plural noun *the city has excellent road and rail communications*: **links**, connections, services, routes.

communicative adjective *she is always very pleasant and communicative*: **forthcoming**, expansive, informative, expressive, unreserved, uninhibited, vocal, outgoing, frank, open, candid; **talkative**, conversational, chatty, gossipy, loquacious, garrulous, voluble, verbose, effusive, gushing; informal mouthy, gabby, windy, gassy; rare multiloquent, multiloquous.
▷ANTONYMS uncommunicative.

communion noun **1** *we receive a strong sense of communion with others*: **affinity**, fellowship, kinship, friendship, fellow feeling, community, togetherness, closeness, sharing, harmony, understanding, rapport, connection, communication, association, empathy, sympathy, agreement, accord, concord, unity.
2 *he believed in Christ's presence among the faithful at Communion*: **Eucharist**, Holy Communion, Lord's Supper, Mass.

communiqué noun *the foreign ministry issued a communiqué*: **official communication**, press release, bulletin, message, missive, dispatch, statement, report, news flash, notification, announcement, declaration, proclamation, pronouncement; word, news, information; N. Amer. advisory; informal memo; literary tidings.

communism noun *the social and economic principles of communism*: **collectivism**, state ownership, socialism, radical socialism; Sovietism, Bolshevism, Marxism, neo-Marxism, Leninism, Marxism–Leninism, Trotskyism, Maoism.

C

communist noun & adjective *I was very left-wing but I was never a communist | a French communist writer*: **collectivist**, leftist, socialist, radical socialist; Soviet, Bolshevik, Bolshevist, Marxist, neo-Marxist, Leninist, Marxist–Leninist, Trotskyist, Trotskyite, Maoist; informal, derogatory Commie, Bolshie, red, lefty.

community noun **1** *we can work together for the good of the community*: **population**, populace, people, citizenry, public, general public, body politic, collective; society, nation, state, country, realm, commonwealth, homeland, fatherland, motherland; residents, inhabitants, citizens; humorous denizens, burghers.
2 *East Durham was very much a mining community*: **district**, region, zone, area, local area, locality, locale, neighbourhood; informal neck of the woods; Brit. informal manor; N. Amer. informal hood, nabe, turf.
3 *lesbians and gays are not one homogeneous community*: **group**, section, body, company, set, circle, clique, coterie, ring, band, faction; informal gang, bunch.
4 *the monastic community at Canterbury*: **brotherhood**, sisterhood, fraternity, confraternity, sorority, colony, institution, order, body, circle, association, society, league; rare sodality.
5 *they had a harmonious union based on a community of interests*: **similarity**, similar nature, likeness, sameness, comparability, correspondence, agreement, alignment, parallel, parallelism, closeness, affinity; archaic semblance.
▷ANTONYMS difference, incompatibility.
6 *the community of goods*: **joint ownership**, common ownership, shared possession; joint liability, joint participation.

commute verb **1** *they commute on a stuffy overcrowded train*: **travel to and from work**, travel to and fro, travel back and forth, come and go, shuttle.
2 *the death sentence was commuted to life imprisonment*: **reduce**, lessen, lighten, shorten, cut, scale down, limit, curtail, attenuate, mitigate, moderate, modify, adjust.
▷ANTONYMS increase; uphold.
3 *military service was often commuted for a money payment*: **exchange**, change, interchange, substitute, swap, trade, barter, switch; archaic truck.

commuter noun *railway engineering works caused widespread delays for commuters*: **daily traveller**, traveller, passenger; informal straphanger, suburbanite.

compact[1] (stress on the second syllable) adjective **1** *this type of knotting produces extremely compact rugs*: **dense**, packed close, close-packed, tightly packed, pressed together; thick, tight, firm, solid.
▷ANTONYMS loose.
2 *the computer is compact enough to fit in your lap*: **small**, little, petite, miniature, mini, small-scale, neat, economic of space; Scottish wee; informal teeny, teeny-weeny, teensy-weensy; Brit. informal dinky; N. Amer. little-bitty.
▷ANTONYMS large.
3 *her tale is compact and readable*: **concise**, succinct, condensed, compendious, crisp, terse, brief, pithy, epigrammatic, aphoristic, elliptical; to the point, short and sweet; informal snappy; rare lapidary.
▷ANTONYMS rambling.
▶ verb *the snow has been compacted by cars*: **compress**, condense, pack down, press down, tamp, tamp down, cram down, ram down, flatten.
▷ANTONYMS loosen.

compact[2] (stress on the first syllable) noun *they signed a compact with the United States*: **treaty**, pact, accord, agreement, contract, alliance, bargain, deal, settlement, covenant, indenture, concordat, protocol, entente; arrangement, understanding, pledge, promise, bond; rare engagement.

companion noun **1** *Harry and his companion settled down at a table*: **associate**, partner, escort, consort, colleague, workmate, co-worker, compatriot, confederate, ally; **friend**, intimate, confidant, confidante, comrade; French confrère; informal buddy, pal, chum, crony, cully, spar, sidekick; Brit. informal mate, oppo, china, mucker; NE English informal marrow, marrer, marra; N. Amer. informal amigo, compadre, paisan; N. Amer. & S. African informal homeboy, homegirl; S. African informal gabba; Austral./NZ informal offsider; archaic compeer; rare consociate.
2 *a lady's companion*: **attendant**, aide, helper, assistant, personal assistant, valet, equerry, squire, lady in waiting; chaperone, duenna, protector, protectress; carer, minder; informal sidekick.
3 *the CD is intended as a companion to their recent hit*: **complement**, counterpart, fellow, mate, twin, other half, match; **accompaniment**, supplement, addition, adjunct, appendage, accessory, auxiliary.
4 *The Cottage Gardener's Companion*: **handbook**, manual, guide, reference book, instruction book, ABC, primer; Latin vade mecum; informal bible; rare enchiridion.

companionable adjective *he was the most generous and companionable of men*: **friendly**, affable, cordial, genial, congenial, amiable, easy-going, approachable, sympathetic, well disposed, good-natured, neighbourly, hospitable, comradely, easy to get along with; sociable, convivial, outgoing, extrovert, extroverted, gregarious, company-loving, hail-fellow-well-met; informal chummy, pally; Brit. informal matey; N. Amer. informal buddy-buddy, clubby, regular.
▷ANTONYMS unfriendly.

companionship noun *she needed the companionship of like-minded young people*: **friendship**, fellowship, closeness, togetherness, amity, intimacy, rapport, camaraderie, comradeship, solidarity, mutual support, mutual affection, brotherhood, sisterhood; company, society, association, social intercourse, social contact, acquaintance; informal chumminess, palliness, clubbiness; Brit. informal mateyness.

company noun **1** *he works for the world's biggest oil company*: **firm**, business, corporation, house, establishment, agency, office, bureau, institution, organization, operation, concern, enterprise, venture, undertaking, practice; conglomerate, consortium, syndicate, group, chain, combine, multiple, multinational; informal outfit, set-up.
2 *I was greatly looking forward to the pleasure of his company*: **companionship**, presence, friendship, fellowship, closeness, amity, camaraderie, comradeship; society, association.
3 *I'm expecting company*: **guests**, a guest, visitors, a visitor, callers, a caller, people, someone; archaic visitants.
4 *he disentangled himself from the surrounding company of poets*: **group**, crowd, body, party, band, collection, assembly, assemblage, cluster, flock, herd, horde, troupe, swarm, stream, mob, throng, congregation, gathering, meeting, convention; informal bunch, gang, gaggle, posse, crew, pack; Brit. informal shower.
5 *he recognized the company of infantry as French*: **unit**, section, detachment, troop, corps, squad, squadron, platoon, battalion, division.
□ **keep someone company** *we had originally gotten him a dog to keep him company while we were away*: **accompany**, go with, go along with, travel with, tag along with, partner, escort, chaperone, attend, follow, conduct, lead, take, show, see, guide, steer, usher, pilot, convoy, help, assist, show someone the way; lead the way; Scottish chum; rare company, bear someone company, companion.

Word links **company**
corporate relating to a company

comparable adjective **1** *he had an income* ***comparable to*** *that of a king*: **similar**, close, near, approximate, akin, equivalent, corresponding, commensurate, proportional, proportionate, parallel, analogous, related; like, matching; bordering on, verging on, approaching; informal not a million miles away from; rare commensurable.
2 *nobody is* ***comparable with*** *the British hurdler*: **as good as**, equal to, in the same class as, in the same league as, of the same standard as, able to hold a candle to, on a par with, on a level with, on an equal footing with; the equal of, a match for.
▷ANTONYMS incomparable.

comparative adjective *they left the city for the comparative cool of the country*: **relative**, qualified, modified; in/by comparison.

compare verb **1** *we compared the data from our present and previous studies*: **contrast**, set side by side, juxtapose, collate, differentiate, weigh up, balance, weigh/balance/measure the differences between.
2 *James Dean was constantly being* ***compared to*** *Brando*: **liken**, equate, analogize; draw an analogy between, make an analogy between, mention in the same breath as, class with, bracket with, group with, put together with, set side by side with, regard as the same as, regard as identical to.
▷ANTONYMS contrast with.
3 *Chelsea porcelain was said to* ***compare with*** *Dresden's fine china*: **be (nearly) as good as**, be comparable to, bear comparison with, be the equal of, match up to, be on a par with, be in the same class as, be in the same league as, be on a level with, compete with, come up to, come near to, come close to, hold a candle to, be not unlike, be not dissimilar to, equal roughly; match, resemble, emulate, rival, approach, approximate, touch, nudge; informal be not a million miles from.
□ **beyond compare** *he was a hero beyond compare*: **without equal**, without match, without parallel, beyond comparison, second to none, in a class of one's own; peerless, matchless, unmatched, incomparable, inimitable, superlative, supreme, top, outstanding, consummate, unique, singular, rare, perfect; French par excellence.

comparison noun **1** *the table provides a comparison of our performance with last year's results*: **contrast**, juxtaposition, collation, differentiation; weighing up, balancing.
2 *there's no comparison between classical music and rap*: **resemblance**, likeness, similarity, similitude, correspondence, correlation, parallel, parity, symmetry, equivalence, comparability, analogy.
▷ANTONYMS difference.

compartment noun **1** *Benjamin examined the casket for a secret compartment*: **section**, part, partition, bay, recess, chamber, cavity, niche, nook, hollow; pocket, pouch, receptacle.
2 *they place magic, science, and religion into separate compartments*: **domain**, field, sphere, realm, area, department, sector, section, division, part; category, pigeonhole, bracket, class, group, set.

compartmentalize verb *we need to compartmentalize the issues we're working on*: **categorize**, pigeonhole, sectionalize, bracket, separate, distinguish, group; classify, characterize, stereotype, label, brand, tag, designate, grade, codify, sort, rank, rate.

compass noun *faith cannot be defined within the compass of human thought*: **scope**, range, extent, reach, span, breadth, width, orbit, ambit, stretch, limits, confines, parameters, extremities, bounds, boundary; area, field, sphere, zone, domain.

compassion noun *she gazed with compassion at the two dejected figures*: **pity**, sympathy, feeling, fellow feeling, empathy, understanding, care, concern, solicitude, solicitousness, sensitivity, tender-heartedness, soft-heartedness, warm-heartedness, warmth, love, brotherly love, tenderness, gentleness, mercy, mercifulness, leniency, lenience, tolerance, consideration, kindness, humanity, humaneness, kind-heartedness, charity, benevolence.
▷ANTONYMS indifference; heartlessness.

compassionate adjective *they showed a compassionate concern for the victims*: **pitying**, sympathetic, empathetic, understanding, caring, concerned, solicitous, sensitive, tender-hearted, soft-hearted, warm-hearted, warm, loving, tender, gentle, merciful, lenient, tolerant, considerate, thoughtful, kind, kindly, kind-hearted, humanitarian, humane, charitable, benevolent, good-natured, well disposed, big-hearted.
▷ANTONYMS indifferent; heartless.

compatibility noun *they felt the bond of true compatibility*: **like-mindedness**, similarity, agreement, affinity, closeness, fellow feeling, harmony, rapport, empathy, sympathy, friendship, camaraderie, togetherness, communion, concord.
▷ANTONYMS incompatibility.

compatible adjective **1** *the two young men were never compatible*: **well suited**, suited, well matched, like-minded, of the same mind, in agreement, in tune, in harmony, reconcilable; archaic accordant.
▷ANTONYMS incompatible.
2 *the bruising is compatible with his having had a fall*: **consistent**, reconcilable, consonant, congruous, congruent, fitting; in keeping, in accord, in tune, in step.
▷ANTONYMS inconsistent.

compatriot noun *Sampras defeated his compatriot Agassi in the final*: **fellow countryman**, fellow countrywoman, countryman, countrywoman, fellow citizen, fellow national.

compel verb **1** *the lords **compelled** the peasants **to** hand over their harvest*: **force**, coerce into, pressurize into, pressure, impel, drive, press, push, urge, prevail on; dragoon into, browbeat into, bully into, bludgeon into, intimidate into, terrorize into; **oblige**, require, put under an obligation, leave someone no option but to; make; informal bulldoze, railroad, steamroller, twist someone's arm, strong-arm, lean on, put the screws on; archaic constrain.
2 *they can compel compliance by issuing a directive*: **exact**, extort, demand, insist on, enforce, force, necessitate; archaic constrain.

Choose the right word **compel, force, coerce, oblige**

All these words refer to making someone do something that they would not otherwise choose to do. They are often used in the passive, underlining the sense that the person feels deprived of power or choice. All but *coerce* are used with an infinitive (e.g. *compelled to do something*), as in the examples given.

Someone who is **compelled** to do something is subjected to pressure that they feel unable to resist. Often, this pressure is applied by someone in authority and takes the form of the threat of penalties if the person fails to comply (*companies are compelled to comply with the regulations | the court had powers to compel witnesses to attend*). Adverse circumstances may also compel someone to do something (*he was compelled to retire on grounds of ill health*), or the pressure may be from one's own conscience (*I feel compelled to write this letter of complaint*).

Force is a more general term for using superior power to make someone do what one wants them to. The superior power may be that of uncontrollable circumstances (*the firm has been forced to make nineteen more workers redundant*) or that of someone physically stronger or better equipped (*the raider forced him to open the safe*). People may also *force* themselves to do something, steeling themselves for something necessary but unpleasant (*Lucy forced herself to sound calm*).

To **coerce** someone into doing something typically involves force or threats (*landlords might try to coerce their tenants into voting for them | they claimed that they had been coerced into making their televised confessions*). *Coercion* is nearly always applied by another person, not by circumstances or one's own conscience.

Typically, if someone is **obliged** to do something, they are legally or morally bound to do it rather than being forced or pressurized (*independent schools are not legally obliged to follow the National Curriculum | Stephen felt obliged to sit next to her*).

compelling adjective **1** *she gave a compelling and intensely dramatic performance*: **enthralling**, captivating, gripping, engrossing, riveting, spellbinding, entrancing, transfixing, mesmerizing, hypnotic, mesmeric, absorbing, fascinating, thrilling, irresistible, addictive; informal unputdownable.
▷ANTONYMS boring.
2 *he had no compelling arguments for changing the status quo*: **convincing**, persuasive, cogent, irresistible, forceful, powerful, potent, strong, weighty, plausible, credible, effective, efficacious, sound, valid, reasonable, reasoned, well reasoned, rational, well founded, telling, conclusive, irrefutable, unanswerable, authoritative, influential.
▷ANTONYMS weak.

C

compendious adjective *a compendious essay on Italian music*: **succinct**, pithy, short and to the point, short and sweet, potted, thumbnail, brief, crisp, compact, concise, condensed, shortened, contracted, compressed, abridged, abbreviated, summarized, summary, abstracted; in a nutshell, in a few well-chosen words; informal snappy; rare lapidary, epigrammatic, synoptic, aphoristic, gnomic.
▷ANTONYMS rambling; expanded.

compendium noun *a compendium of useful information about language*: **collection**, compilation, anthology, treasury, digest; summary, synopsis, precis, résumé, outline, summarization, round-up, summing-up; companion, handbook, manual; Latin vade mecum; rare conspectus, summa, epitome.

compensate verb **1** *you can never **compensate for** what you did to me*: **make amends**, make up, make restitution, make reparation, make recompense, recompense, atone, requite, pay; expiate, make good, put to rights, rectify, offset, square.
2 *terms were agreed to compensate him for his loss*: **recompense**, repay, pay back, reimburse, remunerate, recoup, requite, indemnify; settle up with, settle accounts with.
3 *he had sufficient flair to **compensate for** his faults*: **balance**, balance out, counterbalance, counteract, counterpoise, countervail, make up for, offset, cancel out, neutralize, nullify, even up, square up; rare equilibrize, negative, counterweigh.

compensation noun *they provide adequate compensation for any costs incurred*: **recompense**, repayment, payment, reimbursement, remuneration, requital, indemnification, indemnity, redress, satisfaction; damages, reparations; N. Amer. informal comp; archaic guerdon, meed; rare solatium.

compère noun *she was the compère of a recent Channel 4 series*: **host**, presenter, anchorman, anchorwoman, anchorperson, anchor, master of ceremonies, MC, link person, announcer; informal emcee, talking head.

compete verb **1** *young footballers are invited to **compete in** a five-a-side tournament*: **take part**, play, be a contestant, be a competitor, participate, be involved, get involved, engage; enter, go in for; informal throw one's hat in the ring, be in the running.
2 *they had to **compete with** other firms for the contract*: **contend**, vie, fight, battle, clash, tussle, grapple, wrestle, wrangle, jockey, wage war, cross swords, lock horns, go head to head; strive against, struggle against, pit oneself against; challenge, take on, try to beat; informal pitch oneself against.
3 *in this sort of form, no one can **compete with** him*: **rival**, challenge, keep up with, keep pace with, compare with, be the equal of, match up to, match, be on a par with, be in the same class as, be in the same league as, come near to, come close to, touch, approach, approximate, emulate; informal hold a candle to.

competence noun **1** *this area of research is beyond my technical competence*: **capability**, ability, competency, capacity, proficiency, accomplishment, adeptness, adroitness, knowledge, expertise, expertness, skill, skilfulness, prowess, mastery, resources, faculties, facilities, talent, bent, aptitude, artistry, virtuosity; informal savvy, know-how.
▷ANTONYMS incompetence.
2 *doubts arose over the competence of the system*: **adequacy**, appropriateness, suitability, fitness; effectiveness, efficacy, productiveness; value, worth, merit.
▷ANTONYMS inadequacy.
3 *these matters fall within the competence of the church courts*: **authority**, power, control, jurisdiction, ambit, scope, remit.

competent adjective **1** *he's an extremely competent carpenter*: **capable**, able, proficient, adept, adroit, accomplished, skilful, skilled, gifted, talented, masterly, virtuoso, expert, knowledgeable, qualified, trained; **efficient**, good, excellent, brilliant; informal great, mean, wicked, deadly, nifty, crack, ace, wizard, magic; N. Amer. informal crackerjack; vulgar slang shit-hot; archaic or humorous compleat; rare habile.
▷ANTONYMS incompetent.
2 *she spoke quite competent French*: **adequate**, acceptable, satisfactory, reasonable, fair, decent, good enough, sufficiently good, not bad, all right, average, tolerable, passable, moderate, middling; up to scratch, up to the mark, up to par; informal OK, okay, so-so, fair-to-middling, up to snuff.
▷ANTONYMS inadequate.
3 *the court determined that it was not competent to hear the case*: **fit**, fitted, equipped, suitable, suited, appropriate; qualified, empowered, authorized.
▷ANTONYMS unfit.

Choose the right word **competent, capable, efficient, able**

These words are all used to express approval of people who are good at what they do.

Someone described as **competent** has the necessary skill or knowledge to perform a particular task or fulfil a particular role (*a team of competent trainers | he has been pronounced competent to drive*). Alternatively, they may have the general skill and intelligence to cope with any task (*he is the most experienced and competent man around*). When applied to people engaged in an artistic activity, *competent* may convey mere technical proficiency, contrasted with brilliance or genius (*she was never more than a competent actress*).

Describing someone as **capable** conveys a sense of confidence that any task entrusted to them will be done reliably and well. The word suggests not only competence but also a practicality and organization which ensure that everything that is necessary will be done (*he left the management of their lives largely to his highly capable wife*). It is also used to refer to a specific quality or ability (*I've got players here capable of playing for England*).

An **efficient** person does whatever they have to do quickly and well and without wasting any effort (*he had a most efficient young secretary | teachers become more efficient at writing objectives the more they practise*).

Describing someone as **able** emphasizes the intellectual capacity or the talent that makes them good at what they do (*the department attracts able students from across the country*). Like *capable*, *able* can also refer to a more specific capacity (*if anything went wrong I wouldn't be able to cope*).

competition noun **1** *Stephanie came second in the competition*: **contest**, tournament, match, game, round, heat, fixture, event, meet, encounter; race; bout, fight, prizefight; quiz; trials, stakes.
2 *I'm just not interested in competition*: **rivalry**, competitiveness, vying, contesting, opposition, contention, conflict, feuding, battling, fighting, struggling, strife, war; informal keeping up with the Joneses.
3 *they upgraded their services to remain ahead of the competition*: **opposition**, opposing side, other side, other team, field, enemy, foe; challengers, opponents, rivals, opposers, adversaries, fellow contenders, fellow competitors; rare corrivals.

competitive adjective **1** *a very competitive player*: **ambitious**, competition-oriented, vying, combative, contentious, aggressive; insistent, driving, pushing, zealous, keen; informal pushy, go-ahead.
▷ANTONYMS apathetic.
2 *tourism is a highly sophisticated and competitive industry*: **ruthless**, merciless, aggressive, fierce; informal dog-eat-dog, cut-throat.
▷ANTONYMS gentlemanly.
3 *they produce quality merchandise at competitive prices*: **reasonable**, moderate, economical, keen; low, inexpensive, cheap, cheap and cheerful, budget, economy, bargain, sale, cut-rate, cut, reduced, marked down, discounted, discount, rock-bottom; informal bargain-basement.
▷ANTONYMS exorbitant; uncompetitive.

competitor noun **1** *there were more than forty competitors in the race*: **contestant**, contender, challenger, participant, candidate, entrant; runner, racer, player, athlete.
2 *we have to be more efficient than our European competitors*: **rival**, challenger, opponent, opposer, adversary, antagonist, combatant, enemy, foe; competition, opposition; rare corrival, vier.
▷ANTONYMS ally.

compilation noun *this is the best compilation of American folk tales*: **collection**, selection, anthology, treasury, compendium, album, corpus, miscellany, pot-pourri; miscellanea; archaic garland; rare ana, collectanea, analects, florilegium, spicilege.

compile verb *he compiled a dossier of patients with tropical diseases*: **assemble**, put together, make up, collate, compose, marshal, organize, arrange, sort out, systematize, systemize, anthologize; gather, collect, accumulate, amass.

complacency noun *success brings with it the danger of complacency*: **smugness**, self-satisfaction, self-approval, self-approbation, self-admiration, self-congratulation, self-regard; gloating, triumph, pride; satisfaction, contentment; carelessness, slackness, laxity, laxness, laziness; archaic self-content.
▷ANTONYMS dissatisfaction.

complacent adjective *no one in industry can afford to stand still and be complacent*: **smug**, self-satisfied, pleased with oneself, proud of oneself, self-approving, self-congratulatory, self-admiring, self-regarding; gloating, triumphant, proud; pleased, gratified, satisfied, content, contented; careless, slack, lax, lazy; informal like the cat that got the cream, I'm-all-right-Jack; N. Amer. informal wisenheimer; N. Amer. vulgar slang shit-eating.
▷ANTONYMS dissatisfied; humble.

Easily confused words **complacent or complaisant?**

See **complaisant**.

complain verb *the neighbours complained about his singing*: **protest**, grumble, moan, whine, bleat, carp, cavil, lodge a complaint, make a complaint, make a fuss; object to, speak out against, rail at, oppose, lament, bewail; criticize, find fault with, run down, inveigh against; informal whinge, kick up a fuss, kick up a stink, bellyache, beef, grouch, grouse, bitch, sound off, go on about, pick holes in; Brit. informal gripe, grizzle, chunter, create, be on at someone; N. English informal mither; N. Amer. informal kvetch; S. African informal chirp; Brit. dated crib, natter; archaic plain over.

complaint noun **1** *they lodged a complaint with the European Commission*: **protest**, protestation, objection, remonstrance, statement of dissatisfaction, grievance, charge, accusation, criticism; cavil, quibble, grumble, moan, whine; informal beef, gripe, grouse, grouch, whinge; Law, Brit. plaint.
2 *there appears to be little cause for complaint*: **protesting**, protestation, objection, exception, grievance, grumbling, carping, whining, moaning, muttering, murmuring; criticism, fault-finding, condemnation, disapproval, dissatisfaction, fulmination, outcry, fuss; informal beefing, bitching, whingeing, griping, grousing, grouching, bellyaching, nit-picking; N. English informal mithering.
3 *the patient has a kidney complaint*: **disorder**, disease, infection, affliction, illness, ailment, sickness, malady, malaise, infirmity, indisposition, weakness, condition, problem, upset; trouble; informal bug, virus; Brit. informal lurgy; Austral. informal wog.

complaisant adjective *he made drunken moves on complaisant chamber maids*: **willing**, assenting, acquiescent, agreeable, amenable, cooperative, accommodating, obliging, biddable, compliant, pliant, deferential, docile, obedient, conformable, tractable.
▷ANTONYMS unwilling.

Easily confused words **complaisant or complacent?**

Although **complaisant** and **complacent** both come from the Latin *complacere* 'to please', they do not mean the same thing. *Complaisant* means 'willing to please', and is often used to suggest that someone is too ready to do what someone else wants (*it would be impossible in future for the king to prolong the life of a complaisant parliament*). *Complacent*, the more common word, describes someone who is satisfied and confident, often inappropriately so (*we cannot afford to be complacent about what lies ahead | I was too complacent going into the competition*).

complement noun **1** *local ales provide the perfect complement to the food*: **accompaniment**, companion, addition, supplement, accessory, adjunct, trimming, finishing touch, final touch.
▷ANTONYMS contrast.
2 *the ship had a full complement of lifeboats*: **amount**, total, aggregate, contingent, company; capacity, allowance, quota.
▶ verb *this mouth-watering sauce complements the dessert beautifully*: **accompany**, go with, round off, set off, suit, harmonize with, be the perfect companion to, be the perfect addition to, add the finishing touch to, add the final touch to, add to, supplement, augment, enhance, complete.
▷ANTONYMS contrast.

Easily confused words **complement or compliment?**

Complement and **compliment** (together with their derivative adjectives **complementary** and **complimentary**) are frequently confused but have quite different meanings. As a verb, *complement* means 'add to (something) in a way that enhances, improves, or completes it' (*a classic blazer complements a look that's smart or casual*), while *compliment* means 'congratulate or praise (someone) for something' (*he complimented her on her appearance*). Both are ultimately derived from Latin *complere* 'to fill up, fulfil, or complete'; *compliment*, however, came into English via Italian *complimento* meaning 'a statement that fulfils the requirements of polite behaviour'.

complementary adjective *neutral tones allow the widest choice of complementary furnishings and decoration*: **harmonizing**, harmonious, complementing, supportive, supporting, reciprocal, interdependent, interrelated, compatible, corresponding, matching, twin; completing, finishing, perfecting; rare complemental.
▷ANTONYMS incompatible; contrasting.

complete adjective **1** *the complete interview will appear in next week's issue*: **entire**, whole, full, total, intact, uncut, unshortened, unabridged, comprehensive.
▷ANTONYMS incomplete.
2 *their research was complete*: **finished**, ended, concluded, completed, finalized, accomplished, achieved, fulfilled, discharged, settled, done; informal wrapped up, sewn up, polished off, sorted out; rare effectuated.
▷ANTONYMS unfinished.
3 *you're acting like a complete fool*: **absolute**, out-and-out, utter, total, real, outright, downright, thoroughgoing, through, positive, proper, veritable, prize, perfect, consummate, unqualified, unmitigated, sheer, rank; inveterate, congenital, dyed-in-the-wool, true blue; in every respect; N. Amer. full-bore; informal deep-dyed; Brit. informal right; Austral./NZ informal fair;

archaic arrant; rare right-down, apodictic.
▷ANTONYMS partial.
▶verb **1** *she advised him to complete his architectural training*: **finish**, end, conclude, bring to a conclusion, finalize, wind up, consummate, bring to fruition; crown, cap, set the seal on; informal wrap up, sew up, polish off, sort out.
▷ANTONYMS give up.
2 *the outfit was completed with a delicate veil*: **finish off**, round off, top off, make perfect, perfect, crown, cap, complement, add the finishing touch to, add the final touch to.
3 *entrants are required to complete an application form*: **fill in**, fill out, fill up, answer.

Word links **complete**

holo- related prefix, as in *holocaust, holophytic*

completely adverb *he had always been completely honest with her*: **totally**, entirely, wholly, thoroughly, fully, utterly, absolutely, perfectly, unreservedly, unconditionally, quite, altogether, downright; in every way, in every respect, in all respects, one hundred per cent, every inch, to the hilt, to the core, all the way; informal dead, deadly.
▷ANTONYMS partially.

completion noun *the money ran out before the scheme's completion*: **realization**, accomplishment, achievement, fulfilment, execution, consummation, finalization, resolution; **finish**, ending, conclusion, close, closing, cessation, termination; fruition, success; informal wind-up, winding up, sewing up, polishing off.

complex adjective **1** *a complex situation | criminal law is an extremely complex subject*: **complicated**, involved, intricate, convoluted, tangled, elaborate, serpentine, labyrinthine, tortuous, impenetrable, Byzantine, Daedalian, Gordian; difficult, hard, knotty, tricky, thorny, problematical; informal fiddly; rare involute, involuted.
▷ANTONYMS simple, straightforward.
2 *a complex structure*: **compound**, composite, compounded, multiplex.
▶noun **1** *a complex of mountain roads*: **network**, system, interconnected system/structure/scheme, nexus, web, tissue; combination, composite, synthesis, fusion, aggregation.
2 informal *there's no point having a complex about losing your hair*: **obsession**, phobia, fixation, preoccupation; neurosis; French idée fixe; informal hang-up, thing, bee in one's bonnet.

Word toolkit **complex**

See **intricate**.

complexion noun **1** *an attractive girl with a pale complexion*: **skin**, skin colour, skin colouring, skin tone, skin texture, pigmentation.
2 *this puts an entirely new complexion on things*: **perspective**, angle, slant, interpretation; aspect, appearance, light, look, countenance.
3 *successive governments of all complexions*: **type**, kind, sort; nature, character, disposition, description, cast, stamp, hue, ilk, kidney, grain, mould.

complexity noun *the complexities of family life | an issue of great complexity*: **complication**, problem, difficulty, twist, turn, convolution, entanglement; intricacy, complicatedness, involvement, convolutedness.
▷ANTONYMS simplicity.

compliance noun **1** *the company's* **compliance with** *international law*: **obedience to**, accordance with, observance of, observation of, adherence to, conformity to, respect for; archaic abidance by.
▷ANTONYMS violation, infringement.
2 *he had mistaken her lack of interest for compliance*: **acquiescence**, agreement, assent, consent, concession, concurrence, acceptance; complaisance, tractability, malleability, biddableness, pliability, docility, meekness, submissiveness, submission, passivity.
▷ANTONYMS defiance.

compliant adjective *her compliant husband*: **acquiescent**, amenable, biddable, tractable, complaisant, accommodating, cooperative, adaptable; **obedient**, docile, manageable, malleable, pliable, pliant, flexible, submissive, dutiful, tame, meek, yielding, easily handled, like putty in one's hands, controllable, unresisting, unassertive, passive, governable, persuadable, manipulable; informal, dated milky; rare persuasible.
▷ANTONYMS recalcitrant, bloody-minded.

Choose the right word **compliant, obedient, biddable, docile, dutiful**

See **obedient**.

complicate verb *involvement with Adam could only complicate her life*: **make (more) difficult**, make complex, make complicated, mix up; confuse, muddle, entangle, embroil; informal mess up, snarl up, screw up; archaic perplex, embarrass; rare ravel.
▷ANTONYMS simplify.

complicated adjective *the complicated election rules*: **complex**, intricate, involved, convoluted, tangled, elaborate, impenetrable, knotty, tricky, thorny, serpentine, labyrinthine, tortuous, cumbersome, Byzantine, Daedalian, Gordian; confused, confusing, bewildering, baffling, puzzling, perplexing, difficult to understand, above one's head; informal fiddly; rare involute, involuted.
▷ANTONYMS easy, simple, straightforward.

complication noun **1** *there is a complication concerning ownership of the site*: **difficulty**, problem, obstacle, hurdle, stumbling block, barrier, impediment; drawback, snag, catch, hitch; informal fly in the ointment, prob, headache, hiccup, facer; Brit. informal spanner in the works; N. Amer. informal monkey wrench in the works.
2 *the increasing complication of life in Western society*: **complexity**, complicatedness, difficulty, intricacy, convolution, convolutedness, elaboration; confusion, muddle.
▷ANTONYMS simplicity, straightforwardness.

complicity noun *they were accused of complicity in the attempt to overthrow the government*: **collusion**, involvement, collaboration, connivance, abetment; conspiracy; informal being in cahoots.
▷ANTONYMS ignorance.

compliment noun **1** *she blushed at the unexpected compliment*: **flattering remark**, tribute, accolade, commendation, bouquet, pat on the back, encomium; (**compliments**) praise, acclaim, acclamation, plaudits, admiration, approbation, homage, eulogy; flattery, blandishments, blarney, honeyed words; N. Amer. informal, dated trade last; rare laudation, eulogium.
▷ANTONYMS insult; criticism.
2 (**compliments**) *my compliments on your cooking*: **congratulations**, praise, commendations.
3 (**compliments**) *Lady Margaret sent her compliments to him*: **greetings**, good wishes, best wishes, regards, respects, salutations, felicitations; archaic remembrances; French, archaic devoirs.
▶verb *critics fell over themselves to compliment his performance*: **praise**, sing the praises of, heap praise on, pay tribute to, speak highly/well of, flatter, say nice things about, express admiration for, wax lyrical about, make much of, congratulate, commend, acclaim, pat on the back, take one's hat off to, throw bouquets at, applaud, salute, honour, eulogize, extol; N. Amer. informal ballyhoo; black English big someone/something up; dated cry someone/something up, crack someone/something up; archaic emblazon; rare laud, panegyrize, felicitate.
▷ANTONYMS criticize; condemn.

Easily confused words **compliment or complement?**

See **complement**.

complimentary adjective **1** *complimentary remarks*: **flattering**, **appreciative**, congratulatory, admiring, approving, commendatory, laudatory, highly favourable, glowing, eulogizing, adulatory; fulsome, honeyed, saccharine, sugary; informal rave; rare panegyrical, acclamatory, encomiastic, laudative.
▷ANTONYMS derogatory, scathing.
2 *complimentary tickets*: **free**, free of charge, gratis, for nothing; courtesy; informal on the house; N. Amer. informal comp.

comply verb *failure to* **comply with** *the regulations can result in a £2000 fine | Myra* **complied with** *his wishes*: **abide by**, act in accordance with, observe, obey, adhere to, conform to, follow, respect; **agree to**, assent to, consent to, concur with/in, fall in with, acquiesce in, go along with, yield to, submit to, bow to, defer to; satisfy, meet, fulfil, measure up to.
▷ANTONYMS ignore, disobey.

component noun *the components of electronic devices such as televisions and computers*: **part**, piece, bit, constituent, element, ingredient; unit, module, item; section, portion; rare integrant.
▶adjective *the water molecule's component elements*: **constituent**, integral; basic, essential, intrinsic; rare integrant.

comport verb rare
□ **comport oneself** *articulate students who comported themselves well in television interviews*: **conduct oneself**, acquit oneself; **behave**, act, perform; rare deport oneself.

compose verb **1** *the first poem composed by Shelley | she also composes music for television and films*: **write**, create, devise, make up, think up, frame, formulate, fashion, produce, originate, invent, contrive, concoct; pen, author, draft; literary rhyme, sing, verse; archaic indite.
2 *Vermeer probably used a camera obscura to help him compose his pictures*: **design**, arrange, plan, organize, work out, frame, balance, order, map out, construct, put together, shape, form, concoct.
3 *the National Congress is composed of ten senators*: **make up**, constitute, form, comprise.
□ **compose oneself calm down**, settle down, control oneself, regain/recover one's composure, pull oneself together, get control of oneself, collect oneself, steady oneself, keep one's head, simmer down; informal get a grip, keep one's cool, keep one's shirt on; N. Amer. informal decompress, stay loose.
▷ANTONYMS get worked up.

C

composed adjective *she seemed very composed as she went about her duties*: **calm**, collected, {cool, calm, and collected}, cool, as cool as a cucumber, cool-headed, controlled, self-controlled, serene, tranquil, relaxed, at ease, self-possessed, unruffled, unperturbed, unflustered, undisturbed, unmoved, unbothered, untroubled, unagitated; equable, even-tempered, level-headed, imperturbable; informal unflappable, unfazed, together, laid-back; rare equanimous.
▷ANTONYMS excited, overwrought.

composer noun **melodist**, symphonist, songwriter, singer-songwriter, songster, writer; informal tunesmith, songsmith.

composite adjective *a composite structure*: **compound**, complex; combined, blended, mixed, compounded, synthesized.
▸ noun *the English legal system is a composite of legislation and judicial precedent*: **amalgamation**, amalgam, combination, compound, fusion, synthesis, mixture, blend, meld, admixture, conglomeration; alloy; pastiche, patchwork, hybrid.

composition noun **1** *the composition of the new council*: **make-up**, constitution, configuration, structure, construction, conformation, formation, form, framework, fabric, anatomy, arrangement, organization, format, layout; informal set-up.
2 *Chopin's most romantic compositions | a literary composition*: **work of art**, work, creation, literary/musical/artistic work, opus, oeuvre, piece, arrangement; poem, novel, play, drama; symphony, concerto, opera; painting, drawing, picture.
3 *the composition of a poem*: **writing**, creation, devising, making up, thinking up, framing, formulation, production, fashioning, origination, invention, concoction, compilation.
4 *a school composition*: **essay**, paper, article, text, study, piece of writing; task; N. Amer. theme.
5 *the composition of the painting derives from Matteo's 'Madonna and Child'*: **arrangement**, disposition, layout, design, organization, construction; proportions, harmony, balance, symmetry.
6 *an adhesive composition*: **mixture**, compound, amalgam, blend, mix, admixture.

compost noun **fertilizer**, plant food, dressing, organic matter, vegetable waste, humus, peat.

composure noun *Juliet tried desperately to regain some composure*: **self-control**, self-possession, self-command, calmness, equanimity, equilibrium, calm, coolness, collectedness, serenity, tranquillity; aplomb, poise, presence of mind, sangfroid, self-assurance, assurance; imperturbability, placidity, placidness, impassiveness, impassivity, dispassion, phlegm, stolidity, unexcitability; informal cool, unflappability; rare countenance, ataraxy, ataraxia.
▷ANTONYMS agitation, nervousness, discomposure.

compound noun (stress on the first syllable) *a compound of two elements | a compound of energy and idealism*: **amalgam**, amalgamation, combination, composite, blend, mixture, mix, admixture, meld, fusion, synthesis, consolidation; alloy; hybrid; informal mash-up.
▸ adjective (stress on the first syllable) *a compound substance*: **composite**, complex; blended, fused, synthesized, compounded, combined.
▷ANTONYMS simple.
▸ verb (stress on the second syllable) **1** *a smell* ***compounded of*** *dust and mould*: **be composed of**, be made up of, be constituted of, be formed from.
2 *detergents consisting of liquid soaps compounded with disinfectant*: **mix**, **combine**, blend, put together, amalgamate, alloy, fuse, synthesize, coalesce, mingle, meld, intermingle; rare admix, commix, commingle.
3 *the prisoners' lack of contact with the outside world compounds their problems*: **aggravate**, **worsen**, make worse, add to, augment, exacerbate, intensify, heighten, increase, magnify; add insult to injury, rub salt in the wound, add fuel to the fire/flames; complicate.
▷ANTONYMS alleviate, improve.

comprehend verb **1** *Katie couldn't comprehend what he was saying*: **understand**, grasp, take in, see, apprehend, follow, make sense of, fathom, make out, puzzle out, get to the bottom of, penetrate; realize, perceive, discern, divine; unravel, decipher, interpret, piece together; informal work out, figure out, make head or tail of, get one's head around, wrap one's mind round, take on board, get a fix on, get the hang of, get the drift of, catch on to, latch on to, tumble to, crack, dig, get, see the light, get the picture; Brit. informal twig, suss out, suss; N. Amer. informal savvy.
2 formal *German parties comprehend as many political stances as do the British ones*: **comprise**, include, take in, encompass, embrace, involve, contain; cover.
▷ANTONYMS exclude.

comprehensible adjective *the information must be accurate and comprehensible*: **intelligible**, understandable, easy to understand, digestible, user-friendly, accessible; lucid, coherent, clear, crystal clear, transparent, plain, perspicuous, explicit, unambiguous, straightforward, self-explanatory, penetrable, fathomable, graspable.
▷ANTONYMS incomprehensible, opaque.

comprehension noun *matters which seemed beyond her comprehension*: **understanding**, ability to understand, grasp, grip, conception, apprehension, cognition, cognizance, ken, knowledge, awareness, perception, discernment; interpretation.
▷ANTONYMS ignorance, incomprehension.

comprehensive adjective *a comprehensive review of UK defence policy*: **inclusive**, all-inclusive, complete; **thorough**, full, extensive, all-embracing, overarching, umbrella, exhaustive, in-depth, encyclopedic, universal, catholic, eclectic; far-reaching, radical, sweeping, across the board, blanket, wholesale; broad, wide, wide-ranging, broad-ranging; widespread, nationwide, countrywide, coast-to-coast; detailed, compendious; informal wall-to-wall.
▷ANTONYMS partial, selective, limited.

compress verb **1** *the skirt can be folded and compressed into a relatively small bag*: **flatten**; **squeeze**, press, squash, crush, cram, jam, stuff, wedge; tamp, pack, wad, compact; constrict; informal scrunch, squidge; rare coarct, coarctate.
2 *Polly compressed her lips and sat down*: **purse**, press together, squeeze together, pinch, crimp; pucker.
3 *the material has been compressed into 17 pages*: **abridge**, shorten, cut, condense, abbreviate, contract, telescope; summarize, synopsize, precis, abstract, digest; truncate; rare epitomize.
▷ANTONYMS expand, pad out.

comprise verb **1** *the country comprises twenty states*: **consist of**, be made up of, be composed of, contain, take in, embrace, encompass, incorporate; include; involve, cover; formal comprehend.
2 *this breed comprises 50 per cent of the cattle population*: **make up**, constitute, form, compose; account for.

compromise noun **1** *eventually they reached a compromise*: **agreement**, **understanding**, settlement, terms, accommodation; deal, trade-off, bargain; halfway house, middle ground, middle course, happy medium, balance; Latin modus vivendi.
2 *the secret of a happy marriage is compromise*: **give and take**, concession, cooperation.
▷ANTONYMS intransigence.
▸ verb **1** *in the end we compromised*: **meet each other halfway**, find the middle ground, come to terms, come to an understanding, make a deal, make concessions, find a happy medium, strike a balance; give and take; informal split the difference.
2 *his actions could compromise his academic credibility*: **undermine**, weaken, be detrimental to, damage, injure, harm, do harm to; prejudice, be prejudicial to, jeopardize, endanger, imperil; bring into disrepute, reflect badly on, put in a bad light, discredit, dishonour, bring shame to, shame, embarrass.

compulsion noun **1** *he had been under no compulsion to go*: **obligation**, constraint, force, coercion, duress, pressure, pressurization, enforcement, oppression, intimidation; French force majeure.
2 *he felt an overwhelming compulsion to tell her the truth*: **urge**, impulse, need, necessity, desire, longing, motivation, drive; obsession, fixation, addiction; temptation, pull; US black English jones.

compulsive adjective **1** *a compulsive desire*: **irresistible**, uncontrollable, compelling, driving, overwhelming, overpowering, urgent, besetting; obsessive, neurotic.
2 *compulsive eating*: **obsessive**, obsessional, addictive, uncontrollable, out of control, ungovernable.
3 *a compulsive liar | compulsive drinkers*: **inveterate**, chronic, incorrigible, incurable, irredeemable, hardened, hopeless, persistent; obsessive, obsessional, addicted, habitual, dependent; informal pathological, hooked.
▷ANTONYMS occasional.
4 *it's compulsive viewing*: **fascinating**, compelling, gripping, riveting, engrossing, totally absorbing, enthralling, captivating, spellbinding, mesmerizing, mesmeric, entrancing; informal unputdownable.
▷ANTONYMS dull, tedious.

compulsory adjective *legislation which made the wearing of seat belts compulsory*: **obligatory**, mandatory, required, requisite, necessary, essential, statutory, prescribed; imperative, enforced, demanded, binding, forced, unavoidable, inescapable, incumbent, enforceable; contractual, stipulated, set; French de rigueur.
▷ANTONYMS optional, voluntary.

compunction noun *she had no compunction about deceiving them*: **scruples**, misgivings, qualms, worries, unease, uneasiness, hesitation, hesitancy, doubts, reluctance, reservations; **guilt**, feelings of guilt, guilty conscience, pangs/twinges of conscience, remorse, regret, contrition, contriteness, self-reproach, repentance, penitence.

compute verb *the hire charge is computed on a daily basis*: **calculate**, work out, reckon, figure, enumerate, determine, evaluate, assess, quantify, put a figure on; add up, add together, count up, tally, total, totalize; measure; Brit. tot up; rare cast.

computer noun

Word links **computer**

cyber- related prefix, as in *cybernetics, cybercafe*
cyberphobia fear of computers

comrade noun **companion**, friend; **colleague**, associate, partner, co-worker, fellow worker, workmate; fellow soldier; compatriot, confederate, ally; French confrère; informal pal, buddy, crony; Brit. informal mate, chum, oppo; archaic compeer; rare consociate.

comradeship noun **camaraderie**, friendship, companionship, fellowship, good fellowship, brotherliness, brotherhood, sisterhood, closeness, affinity, togetherness, solidarity, mutual support; team spirit; French esprit de corps.

con informal verb *she was jailed for conning her aunt out of £500,000.* See **swindle**.
▸ noun *a public relations con*: **swindle**, deception, trick, racket, bit of sharp practice, fraud; informal scam, con trick, sting, gyp, kite, diddle, rip-off, fiddle, swizzle, swizz; N. Amer. informal bunco, boondoggle, hustle, grift; Austral. informal rort.

concatenation noun *a concatenation of events which had finally led to the murder*: **series**, sequence, succession; **chain**, string, train, course, progression; nexus.

concave adjective **curved inwards**, hollow, hollowed out, scooped out, depressed, sunken; indented, recessed; rare incurved, incurvate.
▹ANTONYMS convex.

conceal verb **1** *a leather pouch was concealed under the folds of his kilt | a mass of clouds concealed the sun*: **hide**, keep out of sight, keep hidden, secrete, tuck away; screen, cover, obscure, block out, blot out, disguise, camouflage, mask, cloak, mantle, shroud; literary enshroud.
▹ANTONYMS reveal, expose.
2 *a cabinet minister with a reputation for concealing information | up to now, he'd always managed to conceal his true feelings*: **hide**, cover up, disguise, dissemble, mask, veil; **keep secret**, keep quiet about, keep dark, hush up, draw a veil over, sweep under the carpet, gloss over; suppress, repress, bottle up, bury; informal keep a/the lid on, keep under one's hat.
▹ANTONYMS show, disclose, confess.

concealed adjective *a concealed entrance | a concealed weapon*: **hidden**, not visible, secret, out of sight, unseen, invisible, screened, covered, disguised, camouflaged, obscured; inconspicuous, unnoticeable; private, privy; secreted, tucked away.

concealment noun **1** *the concealment of the weapons*: **hiding**, secretion.
2 *he darted forwards from the concealment of the bushes*: **cover**, shelter, protection, screen, hiding place; privacy, seclusion; secrecy.
3 *the deliberate concealment of material facts | the concealment of one's true opinions*: **keeping secret**, keeping hidden, hiding, hushing up, covering up, cover-up, suppression; disguise, camouflage; whitewash; Law, historical misprision.
▹ANTONYMS revelation, disclosure.

concede verb **1** *I had to concede that I'd overreacted*: **admit**, acknowledge, accept, allow, grant, recognize, own, confess; agree; informal take on board.
▹ANTONYMS deny.
2 *in 475, the emperor conceded the Auvergne to Euric*: **surrender**, yield, give up, relinquish, cede, hand over, turn over, part with, deliver up; forfeit, sacrifice.
▹ANTONYMS retain, gain.
□ **concede defeat capitulate**, give in, surrender, yield, give up the struggle, cave in, submit, raise/show the white flag, lay down one's arms; back down, climb down; informal throw in the towel, throw in the sponge.

conceit noun **1** *Polly's eyes widened at his extraordinary conceit*: **vanity**, narcissism, conceitedness, self-love, self-admiration, self-adulation, self-regard, egotism, egoism, egocentricity, egomania; **pride**, arrogance, hubris, boastfulness, cockiness, self-importance, immodesty; self-satisfaction, smugness, complacency; French amour propre; informal big-headedness, swollen-headedness, uppishness, uppitiness; literary vainglory.
▹ANTONYMS modesty, humility.
2 *the conceits of Shakespeare's early verse*: **image**, imagery, figurative expression, metaphor, simile, trope, figure of speech; **play on words**, pun, quip, witticism.
3 *the conceit of time travel*: **idea**, notion, fancy; archaic reverie.

conceited adjective *he's so conceited he'd never believe anyone would turn him down*: **vain**, narcissistic, pleased with oneself, self-loving, in love with oneself, self-admiring, self-regarding, self-centred, egotistic, egotistical, egoistic, egocentric, egomaniac; **proud**, arrogant, boastful, cocky, cocksure, full of oneself, above oneself, self-important, immodest, swaggering, strutting; self-satisfied, self-congratulatory, smug, complacent, supercilious, haughty, snobbish; informal big-headed, swollen-headed, too big for one's boots, puffed up, stuck-up, snooty, high and mighty, uppity, uppish, snotty, snot-nosed; Brit. informal toffee-nosed; N. Amer. informal chesty; literary vainglorious; rare peacockish; (**be conceited**) have an excessively high opinion of oneself, think too highly of oneself, think a lot of oneself, boast, brag, blow one's own trumpet; informal think one is the cat's whiskers/pyjamas, think one is God's gift (to women).
▹ANTONYMS modest, self-effacing.

Word toolkit

conceited	**smug**	**condescending**
jerk	look	tone
bastard	satisfaction	manner
pig	smirk	voice
idiot	superiority	remarks
jackass	confidence	message

conceivable adjective *the only conceivable reason for using nuclear weapons*: **imaginable**, possible; plausible, tenable, credible, believable, thinkable, feasible, creditable, admissible; understandable, comprehensible; informal mortal; rare cogitable.
▹ANTONYMS inconceivable.

conceive verb **1** *she was unable to conceive*: **get pregnant**, become pregnant, become impregnated, become inseminated, become fertilized.
2 *the project was conceived in 1977*: **think up**, think of, come up with, dream up, draw up, devise, form, formulate, design, frame, invent, coin, originate, create, develop, evolve; hatch, cook up, contrive.
3 *I could hardly conceive what it must be like in winter*: **imagine**, envisage, visualize, picture, picture in one's mind's eye, conjure up an image of, think, see, perceive, grasp, appreciate, apprehend; rare envision, ideate.

concentrate verb **1** *the government concentrated its efforts on resolving the financial crisis*: **focus**, direct, centre, centralize, bring to bear; home in on, zero in on.
▹ANTONYMS dissipate.
2 *Sabine tried to* **concentrate on** *the film*: **focus one's attention on**, focus on, pay attention to, keep one's mind on, apply oneself to, address oneself to, devote oneself to, get down to, put one's mind to; be absorbed in, be engrossed in, be immersed in; think about closely, consider closely, rack one's brains about/over, cudgel one's brains about/over; informal get stuck into.
▹ANTONYMS daydream, let one's mind wander.
3 *troops were concentrating on the western front*: **collect**, gather, congregate, draw together, converge, mass, cluster, rally; accumulate, amass; rare concentre.
▹ANTONYMS disperse.
4 *the liquid is filtered and concentrated*: **condense**, boil down, reduce, distil, thicken, compress; strengthen.
▹ANTONYMS dilute.
▸ noun *fruit and berry concentrates*: **distillation**, essence, extract; decoction, tincture, elixir, quintessence; rare decocture, apozem.

concentrated adjective **1** *a concentrated effort*: **strenuous**, concerted, intensive, intense, vigorous, assiduous; informal all-out.
▹ANTONYMS half-hearted.
2 *a concentrated solution*: **condensed**, distilled, reduced, evaporated, thick, thickened, dense; strong, undiluted.
▹ANTONYMS diluted.

concentration noun **1** *a task requiring great patience and total concentration*: **close attention**, close thought, attentiveness, application, industry, assiduousness, single-mindedness, absorption, engrossment.
▹ANTONYMS inattention, distraction.
2 *this concentration of effort on field work*: **focusing**, centring, centralization, direction.
3 *Islay is famous for its spectacular concentrations of barnacle geese*: **gathering**, cluster, mass, flock, congregation, assemblage, assembly, collection; accumulation, aggregation, agglomeration.

concept noun *the concept of society as an organic entity | the Freudian concept of the superego*: **idea**, notion, conception, abstraction, conceptualization; theory, hypothesis, postulation; belief, conviction, opinion, view, image, impression, picture.

Choose the right word **concept, idea, notion**

See **idea**.

conception noun **1** *preparations for pregnancy can begin before conception*: **inception of pregnancy**, conceiving, fertilization, impregnation, insemination; rare fecundation.
2 *the time between a product's conception and its launch*: **inception**, genesis, origination, creation, formation, formulation, invention; beginning, origin.
3 *the original conception involved a shopping complex run by local people*: **plan**, scheme, project, proposal, proposition, design, outline; intention, aim, idea.
4 *his conception of democracy*: **idea**, concept, notion, conceptualization, understanding, abstraction; theory, hypothesis, postulation; perception, image, impression, picture.
5 *the administration had no* **conception of** *women's problems*: **understanding**, ability to understand, ability to imagine, comprehension, appreciation, knowledge, grasp, apprehension; idea, inkling; informal clue about.

concern verb **1** *the report concerns events which took place immediately after the end of the war*: **be about**, deal with, cover, treat, have to do with; discuss, tell of, go into, examine, scrutinize, study, review, analyse; relate to, be connected with, pertain to, appertain to; archaic regard.
2 *that doesn't concern you, so it's best you don't know*: **affect**, be the business of, involve, be relevant to, apply to, pertain to, have a bearing on, bear on, impact on; be of importance to, be important to, interest, be of interest to.
3 *I'm too busy to* ***concern myself with*** *your affairs*: **involve oneself in**, interest oneself in, take an interest in, be interested/involved in, take a hand in, busy oneself with, occupy oneself with, devote one's time to, bother oneself with, notice, take notice of.
4 *the only thing that concerns me is that Tom might be upset*: **worry**, disturb, trouble, bother, perturb, unsettle, make anxious, distress, upset, agitate, cause disquiet to, disquiet.
▸ noun **1** *Katie's voice was full of concern*: **anxiety**, worry, disquiet, disquietude, apprehension, apprehensiveness, unease, uneasiness, perturbation, consternation, distress, agitation; N. Amer. archaic worriment.
▹ANTONYMS serenity, peace of mind.
2 *part of his attraction is his true concern for others*: **solicitude**, consideration, solicitousness, care, sympathy, thought, regard, caringness; archaic concernment.
▹ANTONYMS indifference.
3 *housing is the concern of the Housing Executive*: **responsibility**, **business**, affair, charge, duty, job, task, occupation; area of activity, area of interest, province, preserve, department, sphere; problem, worry, lookout; informal pigeon, baby, bag, funeral, headache, bailiwick.
4 *the question of how the mass media treats issues that* ***are of concern to*** *women*: **interest**, importance; be relevant to, have relevance for, have a bearing on, be applicable to.
5 *public awareness of Aboriginal concerns*: **affair**, issue, matter, question, consideration.
6 *a publishing concern*: **company**, business, firm, enterprise, venture, organization, operation, undertaking, industry, corporation, establishment, house, shop, office, bureau, agency, franchise, practice, partnership, consortium, cooperative, conglomerate, group, combine, syndicate; informal outfit, set-up.

concerned adjective **1** *her mother looked concerned*: **worried**, anxious, disturbed, perturbed, troubled, bothered, distressed, upset, disquieted, uneasy, ill at ease, apprehensive, agitated; rare unquiet.
▹ANTONYMS unconcerned.
2 *I'm gratified to find that you are so* ***concerned about*** *my welfare*: **solicitous**, caring; attentive to, considerate of.
3 *all concerned parties*: **interested**, involved, affected; connected, related, implicated.

concerning preposition *further revelations concerning his role in the affair*: **about**, regarding, on the subject of, relating to, relevant to, with regard to, as regards, to do with, with reference to, referring to, with respect to, respecting, as to, touching on, in the matter of, in connection with, re, apropos of; Scottish anent.

concert noun *a concert at the Albert Hall*: **musical performance**, musical entertainment, show, production, presentation; recital; prom, promenade concert; pop concert, rock concert; informal gig, jam session.
▫ **in concert** *we must take stronger action in concert with our European partners*: **together**, jointly, in combination, in collaboration, in cooperation, in league, shoulder to shoulder, side by side, cooperatively, concertedly; in unison.
▹ANTONYMS alone, independently.

concerted adjective **1** *you must make a concerted effort to curb this behaviour*: **strenuous**, vigorous, energetic, active, forceful, forcible, strong, intensive, intense, concentrated; informal all-out.
▹ANTONYMS half-hearted.
2 *there were calls for concerted action*: **joint**, united, jointly planned, coordinated, collaborative, collective, combined, cooperative, interactive, synergetic.
▹ANTONYMS separate, individual.

concession noun **1** *the government made several concessions over welfare cuts*: **compromise**, adjustment, modification; allowance, exception; point conceded, point lost, forfeit, something surrendered; informal sop.
2 *a concession of failure*: **admission**, acknowledgement, acceptance, recognition, confession.
▹ANTONYMS denial.
3 *the concession of territory*: **surrender**, yielding, giving up, ceding, relinquishment, sacrifice, handover; rare cession.
▹ANTONYMS retention, acquisition.
4 *tax concessions | there are concessions on all party bookings*: **reduction**, cut, discount, deduction, decrease; rebate; N. Amer. depletion allowance; informal tax break.
5 *the granting of new logging concessions*: **right**, privilege, favour; licence, permit, franchise, warrant, authorization.

conciliate verb **1** *concessions were made to conciliate the peasantry*: **appease**, placate, pacify, mollify, propitiate, assuage, calm down, soothe, humour, reconcile, disarm, win over, make peace with; Austral. square someone off; informal sweeten; rare disembitter.
▹ANTONYMS provoke.
2 *he sought to conciliate in the dispute*: **mediate**, act as a peacemaker, act as a mediator, arbitrate, make peace, restore harmony, reconcile differences, clear the air; pour oil on troubled waters.

conciliation noun *he held his hands up in a gesture of conciliation*: **appeasement**, pacification, peacemaking, placation, propitiation, mollification, reconciliation.
▹ANTONYMS provocation.

conciliator noun **peacemaker**, **mediator**, negotiator, go-between, middleman, intermediary, moderator, broker, honest broker, intervenor, interceder, intercessor, reconciler, pacifier, appeaser; dove.
▹ANTONYMS troublemaker.

conciliatory adjective *a conciliatory gesture*: **propitiatory**, placatory, appeasing, pacifying, pacific, mollifying, so as to pour oil on troubled waters, peacemaking, reconciliatory; rare pacificatory, propitiative, placative, irenic.
▹ANTONYMS antagonistic.

concise adjective *a concise account*: **succinct**, short, brief, to the point, pithy, incisive, short and sweet, crisp; abridged, condensed, compressed, abbreviated, compact, compendious, potted, thumbnail, in a nutshell; epigrammatic, aphoristic; **terse**, laconic, sparing; informal snappy; rare lapidary.
▹ANTONYMS lengthy, discursive, wordy.

> *Choose the right word* **concise, succinct**
>
> These words both refer to brevity in statements or pieces of writing. They are both mainly used approvingly: things described as *concise* or *succinct* are also described as *up-to-date*, *in-depth*, *clear*, *precise*, and *informative*. Compare the use of *brusque*, *abrupt*, *curt*, and *terse* (see **brusque**).
>
> **Concise** expresses approval of a statement that conveys information briefly. It suggests that by keeping the words used to a minimum, the speaker or writer has achieved clarity as well as brevity (*the instructions were clear and concise*). *Concise* can, however, be more neutral in tone (*the church committee may need a concise report every three or six months*). It is used mainly of written documents, such as *reports*, *instructions*, and *summaries*.
>
> **Succinct** language is pithy, made more forceful by its brevity, and is more often praiseworthy (*John McLeish considered this admirably succinct report*). Of the two words, *succinct* is the one more often used of speech or of shorter pieces of writing (*I told him my story in sharp, succinct phrases | each page is introduced by an imaginative, succinct heading*).

conclave noun *a conclave of American, European, and Japanese business leaders*: **(private) meeting**, gathering, assembly, conference, convention, convocation, council, session, summit, forgathering; informal parley, powwow, get-together.

conclude verb **1** *the meeting concluded at 9 o'clock*: **finish**, end, come to an end, draw to a close, wind up, be over, stop, terminate, close, cease; culminate.
▹ANTONYMS start, begin, commence.
2 *he concluded the press conference with another announcement about welfare reform*: **bring to an end**, bring to a close, finish, close, wind up, terminate, dissolve; round off; informal wrap up; dated put a period to.
▹ANTONYMS start, begin, open.
3 *an attempt to conclude a ceasefire*: **negotiate**, reach an agreement on, agree, come to terms on, reach terms on, broker, settle, seal, set the seal on, clinch, finalize, tie up, complete, shake hands on, close, bring about, arrange, effect, engineer, accomplish, establish, resolve, work out, pull off, bring off, thrash out, hammer out; informal sew up, swing, button up.
4 *from this letter, one can only conclude that he was a rather unpleasant man*: **come to the conclusion**, deduce, infer, draw the inference, gather, judge, decide; assume, presume, suppose, conjecture, surmise; N. Amer. figure; informal reckon; archaic collect.

conclusion noun **1** *the conclusion of the meeting | the conclusion of his speech*: **end**, ending, finish, close, closure, termination, wind-up, cessation; culmination, finale, denouement, coda; peroration, epilogue.
▹ANTONYMS beginning, start.
2 *the conclusion of a free-trade agreement*: **negotiation**, brokering, settlement, settling, clinching, completion, arranging, accomplishment, establishment, resolution.
3 *his original conclusions have been verified by later experiments*: **deduction**, inference, interpretation, reasoning; opinion, judgement, decision, diagnosis, verdict, determination; assumption, presumption, supposition, conjecture, surmise.
▫ **in conclusion finally**, lastly, in closing, to conclude, last but not least; **to sum up**, in short; rare in fine.

conclusive adjective **1** *conclusive proof*: **incontrovertible**, incontestable, irrefutable, unquestionable, undeniable, indisputable, unassailable, beyond dispute, beyond question, beyond doubt, beyond a shadow of a doubt, certain, decisive, convincing, clinching, definitive, definite, positive,

final, ultimate, categorical, demonstrative, unequivocal, unarguable, unanswerable, uncontroversial; airtight, watertight.
▷ANTONYMS inconclusive, unconvincing.
2 *a conclusive 5–0 win*: **emphatic**, resounding; informal thumping, thundering.
▷ANTONYMS narrow.

Word toolkit **conclusive**

See **final**.

concoct verb **1** *she began to concoct a dinner likely to appeal to him*: **prepare**, make, put together, assemble; cook; informal fix, rustle up; Brit. informal knock up.
2 *I wonder what story she has concocted to explain her presence*: **make up**, think up, dream up, fabricate, invent, contrive, manufacture, trump up; **devise**, create, form, formulate, fashion, forge; hatch, brew, plot, scheme; informal cook up.

concoction noun **1** *a concoction consisting of gin, vodka, and cherry brandy*: **mixture**, brew, preparation, creation; potion.
2 *a strange concoction of northern Mannerism and Italian Baroque*: **blend**, mixture, mix, combination, composite, compound; hybrid; informal mash-up.
3 *her story is an improbable concoction*: **fabrication**, piece of fiction, invention, falsification, contrivance; informal fairy story, fairy tale.

concomitant adjective *the rise of urbanism brought a concomitant risk of crime*: **attendant**, accompanying, associated, collateral, related, connected, linked; accessory, auxiliary; resultant, resulting, consequent.
▷ANTONYMS unrelated.

concord noun **1** *disputatious council meetings which occasionally ended in concord*: **agreement**, harmony, accord, consensus, concurrence, unity, unanimity, unison, oneness; rare concert.
▷ANTONYMS disagreement, discord.
2 *a concord was to be drawn up*: **treaty**, agreement, accord, concordat, entente, compact, pact, protocol, convention, settlement.

concourse noun *the station concourse*: **entrance**, foyer, lobby, hall; piazza, plaza.

concrete adjective **1** *concrete objects*: **solid**, material, real, physical, tangible, touchable, tactile, palpable, visible, existing.
▷ANTONYMS abstract, theoretical, imaginary.
2 *I haven't got any concrete proof | as yet nothing is concrete*: **definite**, specific, firm, positive, conclusive, definitive; fixed, decided, set in stone; factual, actual, real, genuine, substantial, material, tangible; Latin bona fide.
▷ANTONYMS vague.

concubine noun archaic **mistress**, paramour, kept woman; lover; informal fancy woman, bit on the side; archaic doxy, courtesan, leman; historical odalisque, hetaera, lorette.

concupiscence noun rare **sexual desire**, lust, lustfulness, sexual appetite, sexual longing, sexual passion, ardour, desire, passion; libido, sex drive, sexuality, biological urge; **lechery**, lecherousness, lasciviousness, lewdness, wantonness, carnality, licentiousness, salaciousness, prurience; informal horniness, raunchiness, the hots; Brit. informal randiness, the horn; rare salacity, nympholepsy.

concur verb **1** *there are many who would concur with this view*: **agree**, be in agreement, be in accord, be in accordance, accord, go along, fall in, be in harmony, be in sympathy; see eye to eye, be of the same mind, be of the same opinion.
▷ANTONYMS disagree.
2 *the two events concurred*: **coincide**, happen/occur together, happen/occur simultaneously, happen/occur at the same time, be simultaneous, be concurrent, synchronize, coexist; clash.

concurrent adjective **1** *Moore was sentenced to 17 concurrent life terms*: **simultaneous**, coincident, coinciding, contemporaneous, synchronous; parallel, side by side, coexisting, coexistent.
2 *concurrent lines*: **convergent**, converging, meeting, joining, uniting, intersecting.

concussion noun **1** *Mr Kirwan suffered concussion together with shoulder and chest injuries*: **temporary unconsciousness**, temporary loss of consciousness, bang on the head; Medicine mild cranial trauma.
2 *the ground shuddered with the concussion of the blast*: **force**, impact, shock; jarring, jolting, jolt, shaking.

condemn verb **1** *he condemned such players for dragging the name of football through the dirt*: **censure**, criticize, castigate, attack, denounce, deplore, decry, revile, inveigh against, blame, chastise, berate, upbraid, reprimand, rebuke, reprove, reprehend, take to task, find fault with, give someone/something a bad press; deprecate, disparage; informal slam, hammer, lay into, cane, blast; Brit. informal slate, slag off, have a go at; archaic slash, reprobate; rare excoriate, vituperate, arraign, objurgate, anathematize.
▷ANTONYMS praise, commend.
2 *the rebels had been condemned to death*: **sentence**, pass sentence on; convict, find guilty.
▷ANTONYMS acquit.
3 *the pool has been condemned as a health hazard*: **declare unfit**, declare unsafe; denounce, criticize.
4 *she could see in his eyes that her mistake had condemned her*: **incriminate**, prove to be guilty, prove one's guilt, implicate; archaic inculpate.
5 *the physical ailments that* ***condemned*** *him* ***to*** *a lonely childhood*: **doom**, destine, damn, foredoom, foreordain, mark someone out for; consign, assign; rare predoom.

condemnation noun *a comment which provoked widespread condemnation*: **censure**, criticism, castigation, stricture, denunciation, damnation, vilification, opprobrium; reproof, disapproval, disapprobation; informal flak, a bad press; rare reprobation, arraignment, excoriation, objurgation.
▷ANTONYMS praise, plaudits.

condemnatory adjective *a condemnatory press report*: **censorious**, critical, damning, damnatory, condemning, censuring, castigatory, fault-finding, denunciatory, vituperative, withering; reproving, reproachful, deprecatory, disapproving, unfavourable; rare reprobative, reprobatory.
▷ANTONYMS complimentary, approving.

condemned adjective **1** *a condemned building | condemned meat*: **unsafe**, dangerous, hazardous, perilous, precarious, insecure, treacherous; **dilapidated**, ramshackle, run down, broken-down, worn out, tumbledown, in (a state of) disrepair, in ruins, ruined, falling to pieces, falling apart; rickety, creaky, creaking, decrepit, deteriorating, crumbling, deteriorated; neglected, untended, unmaintained, gone to rack and ruin, gone to seed, on its last legs, the worse for wear; **unhealthy**, contaminated, unsound, infected, blighted, unwholesome, septic, rotten, bad.
▷ANTONYMS safe, in good repair, wholesome.
2 *condemned prisoners*: **damned**, doomed, lost, condemned to hell; sentenced, convicted, censured, faulted; literary accursed.

Word toolkit **condemned**

See **doomed**.

condensation noun **1** *the windows were misty with condensation*: **moisture**, water droplets, steam.
2 *the condensation of the vapour*: **precipitation**, liquefaction, deliquescence, liquidization; distillation.
3 *a readable condensation of the recent literature*: **abridgement**, **summary**, synopsis, precis, abstract, digest, encapsulation.
4 *the condensation of the report*: **shortening**, abridgement, abbreviation, cutting, summarization.

condense verb **1** *the moisture vapour in the air condenses into droplets of water*: **precipitate**, liquefy, become liquid, deliquesce, liquidize.
▷ANTONYMS vaporize, gasify.
2 *he condensed the three plays into a single three-hour drama*: **abridge**, **shorten**, cut, abbreviate, compress, compact, contract, telescope; summarize, synopsize, precis, abstract, digest, encapsulate; truncate, curtail; rare epitomize.
▷ANTONYMS lengthen, expand.

condensed adjective **1** *a condensed version of the book*: **abridged**, shortened, cut, cut-down, concise, contracted, compressed, abbreviated, reduced, truncated; summarized, summary, abstracted, precised, synoptic, synopsized, outline, thumbnail; informal potted, slimmed down.
2 *condensed soup | condensed milk*: **concentrated**, evaporated, thick, thickened, reduced; undiluted.
▷ANTONYMS diluted.

condescend verb **1** *take care not to* ***condescend to*** *your reader*: **patronize**, treat condescendingly, speak condescendingly to, speak haughtily to, talk down to, look down one's nose at, look down on, put down, be snobbish to.
▷ANTONYMS respect.
2 *a minor official condescended to see us*: **deign**, stoop, descend, lower oneself, humble oneself, demean oneself, debase oneself, vouchsafe, think fit, see fit, deem it worthy of oneself, consent; informal come down from one's high horse.

condescending adjective *she looked us up and down in a condescending manner*: **patronizing**, supercilious, superior, snobbish, snobby, scornful, disdainful, lofty, lordly, haughty, imperious; informal snooty, snotty, stuck-up; Brit. informal toffee-nosed.
▷ANTONYMS respectful.

Word toolkit **condescending**

See **conceited**.

condescension noun *with an air of great condescension he told me that he was 'prepared to give me a try-out'*: **superciliousness**, superiority, scorn, disdain, loftiness, airs, lordliness, haughtiness, imperiousness, snobbishness, snobbery; informal snootiness, snottiness; rare patronization.
▷ANTONYMS respect.

condition noun **1** *visually check the condition of your wiring*: **state**, shape, order; Brit. informal nick.

2 (**conditions**) *refugees were living in appalling conditions*: **circumstances**, surroundings; **environment**, situation, state of affairs, set-up, position, context, background, setting, ambience, atmosphere, climate, milieu, habitat, way of life; informal circs.
3 *he had the body of an athlete in tip-top condition*: **fitness**, physical fitness, health, state of health, form, shape, trim, fettle.
4 *a serious medical condition*: **disorder**, problem, defect, disease, illness, complaint, ailment, weakness, infirmity, malady, indisposition, malaise, sickness, affliction, infection, upset; informal bug, virus; Brit. informal lurgy.
5 *it is a condition of employment that employees should be paid through a bank*: **stipulation**, constraint, prerequisite, precondition, requirement, rule, term, specification, provision, proviso, qualification; necessity, essential, demand, restriction.
□ **out of condition** *maybe I can stop and rest my hopelessly out of condition body*: **unfit**, unhealthy, out of shape, in poor condition, in poor shape, flabby, debilitated, weak, infirm, decrepit.
▷ANTONYMS fit.
▸ **verb 1** *national choices are conditioned by the international political economy*: **constrain**, control, govern, determine, decide; exert influence on, affect, have an effect on, act on, work on, touch, have an impact on, impact on; change, alter, modify, transform, form, shape, guide, sway, bias.
2 *our minds are heavily conditioned by habit*: **train**, teach, educate, coach, tutor, guide, groom, drill, accustom, adapt, habituate, mould, inure.
3 *the boards will need to be conditioned with water*: **treat**, prepare, make ready, ready, prime, temper, process, acclimatize, acclimate, adapt, adjust, soften, season.
4 *some products contain vitamin E to condition your skin*: **improve**, make healthy, build up, nourish, tone, tone up, get something into shape.

conditional adjective **1** *the supporters' approval is* ***conditional on*** *success*: **subject to**, dependent on, depending on, contingent on, hingeing on, resting on, hanging on, based on, determined by, controlled by, tied to, bound up with.
▷ANTONYMS unconditional.
2 *he was only made a conditional offer of a university place*: **contingent**, dependent, qualified, with conditions (attached), with reservations, limited, restrictive, provisional; rare stipulatory, provisory.
▷ANTONYMS unconditional; absolute.

condolences plural noun *we offer our sincere condolences to his widow*: **sympathy**, commiseration(s), solace, comfort, consolation, fellow feeling, understanding, empathy, compassion, pity, solicitude, concern, support.

condom noun **contraceptive**, sheath; female condom; N. Amer. prophylactic; Brit. trademark Durex, Femidom; Brit. informal johnny, something for the weekend; N. Amer. informal rubber, safe, safety, skin; Brit. informal, dated French letter, Frenchy; dated protective.

condone verb *we cannot condone such dreadful behaviour*: **deliberately ignore**, not take into consideration, disregard, take no notice of, take no account of, accept, allow, make allowances for, let pass, turn a blind eye to, overlook, forget, wink at, blink at, connive at; forgive, pardon, excuse, let someone off with, let go, sink, bury; let bygones be bygones; informal let something ride.
▷ANTONYMS condemn; punish.

> *Choose the right word* **condone, forgive, pardon, excuse**
>
> See **forgive**.

conducive adjective *an environment which is* ***conducive to*** *learning*: **good for**, helpful to, instrumental in, calculated to produce, productive of, useful for; favourable, beneficial, valuable, advantageous, opportune, propitious, encouraging, promising, convenient; (**be conducive to**) contribute to, lead to, tend to promote, make for, facilitate, favour, aid, assist, help, benefit, encourage.
▷ANTONYMS unfavourable.

conduct noun (stress on the first syllable) **1** *townspeople regularly complained about students' conduct*: **behaviour**, way of behaving, performance, comportment, demeanour, bearing, deportment; actions, acts, activities, deeds, doings, handiwork, exploits, ways, habits, practices, manners.
2 *the conduct of the elections*: **management**, managing, running, direction, control, controlling, overseeing, supervision, regulation, leadership, masterminding, administration, organization, coordination, orchestration, handling, guidance, carrying out, carrying on; formal prosecution.
▸ **verb** (stress on the second syllable) **1** *the election was conducted according to new electoral law*: **manage**, direct, run, be in control of, control, oversee, supervise, be in charge of, preside over, regulate, mastermind, administer, organize, coordinate, orchestrate, handle, guide, govern, lead, carry out, carry on.
2 *Lucien was conducted through a maze of corridors*: **escort**, guide, lead, usher, pilot, accompany, show, show someone the way; shepherd, herd, drive, convoy; see, bring, take, help, assist.
3 *aluminium, being a metal, readily conducts heat*: **transmit**, convey, carry, transfer, pass on, hand on, communicate, impart, channel, bear, relay, dispatch, mediate; disseminate, spread, circulate, diffuse, radiate.
□ **conduct oneself** *I am proud of the way they conducted themselves*: **behave**, perform, act, acquit oneself, bear oneself, carry oneself; rare comport oneself, deport oneself.

conduit noun *spring water ran down a conduit into the brewery*: **channel**, duct, pipe, tube, gutter, groove, furrow, trough, trench, culvert, cut, sluice, spillway, race, flume, chute, ditch, drain.

confectionery noun **sweets**, bonbons; N. Amer. candy, sugar candy; informal sweeties; archaic sweetmeats.

confederacy noun *the Empire was a loosely organized confederacy of allies*: **federation**, confederation, alliance, league, association, coalition, combine, consortium, conglomerate, cooperative, partnership, syndicate, compact, band, group, circle, ring; bloc, axis; society, union, guild, fellowship; rare consociation, sodality.

confederate adjective *some local groups united to form confederate councils*: **federal**, confederated, federated, allied, in alliance, in league, cooperating, associated, united, combined, amalgamated.
▷ANTONYMS split.
▸ **noun** *he and a confederate shot the miller dead*: **associate**, partner, accomplice, abetter, accessory, helper, supporter, assistant, ally, collaborator, colleague; Brit. informal oppo; Austral./NZ informal offsider.

confederation noun *a confederation of trade unions*: **alliance**, league, confederacy, federation, association, coalition, combine, consortium, affiliation, conglomerate, cooperative, partnership, fellowship, syndicate, compact, band, group, circle, ring; society, union; rare consociation, sodality.

confer verb **1** *the Queen* ***conferred*** *an honorary knighthood* ***on*** *him*: **bestow on**, present with/to, grant to, award to, decorate with, honour with, give to, give out to, gift with, endow with, vest in, hand out to, extend to, vouchsafe to, accord to.
▷ANTONYMS withhold; remove.
2 *she broke off to confer with her colleagues*: **consult**, have discussions, discuss things, exchange views, talk, have a talk, speak, converse, communicate, have a chat, have a tête-à-tête; negotiate, have negotiations, have talks, parley, palaver; informal have a confab, chew the fat/rag, jaw, rap, powwow; formal confabulate.

conference noun **1** *an international conference on the environment*: **congress**, meeting, convention, seminar, colloquium, symposium, forum, convocation, summit, synod, conclave, consultation, awayday.
2 *he gathered them round the table for a conference*: **discussion**, consultation, exchange of views, debate, talk, conversation, dialogue, chat, tête-à-tête; negotiations, talks, parley, palaver; informal confab; formal confabulation.

confess verb **1** *he confessed that he had attacked the old man*: **admit**, acknowledge, reveal, make known, disclose, divulge, make public, avow, declare, blurt out, profess, own up to, tell all about, bring into the open, bring to light; informal blow the lid off; archaic discover.
▷ANTONYMS conceal; deny.
2 *they tried everything they could think of to make him confess*: **own up**, admit guilt, plead guilty, accept blame/responsibility, be completely honest, tell the truth, tell all, make a clean breast of it, unbosom oneself; informal come clean, fess up, spill the beans, let the cat out of the bag, get something off one's chest, let on; Brit. informal cough.
3 *I confess I don't know*: **acknowledge**, admit, concede, grant, allow, own, say, declare, affirm, accept, recognize, be aware of/that, realize, be conscious of/that.

confession noun *the interrogators soon got a confession out of him*: **admission**, owning up, acceptance of blame/responsibility, acknowledgement, profession, revelation, disclosure, divulgence, exposure, avowal, unbosoming.
▷ANTONYMS concealment; denial.

confidant, confidante noun *he was her confidant and business adviser*: **close friend**, bosom friend, best friend, close associate, companion, crony, intimate, familiar, second self; mentor, adviser, counsellor; Latin alter ego; Italian consigliere; informal chum, pal, buddy, main man; Brit. informal mate, oppo, mucker; rare fidus Achates.

confide verb **1** *he confided his fears to his mother*: **reveal**, disclose, divulge, leak, lay bare, make known, betray, impart, pass on, proclaim, announce, report, declare, intimate, uncover, unmask, expose, bring out into the open, unfold, vouchsafe, tell; confess, admit; let slip, let out, let drop, let fall, blurt out, babble, give away; informal blab, spill; archaic discover.
▷ANTONYMS keep from.
2 *I really need him to* ***confide in***: **open one's heart to**, unburden oneself to, unbosom oneself to, confess to, tell all to, tell one's all to, commune with.

confidence noun **1** *I have little confidence in these figures*: **trust**, belief, faith, credence, conviction; reliance, dependence.
▷ANTONYMS distrust, scepticism.
2 *she's brimming with confidence*: **self-assurance**, self-confidence, self-reliance, belief in oneself, faith in oneself, positiveness, assertiveness, self-possession, nerve, poise, aplomb, presence of mind, phlegm, level-headedness, cool-headedness, firmness, courage, boldness, mettle, fortitude.
▷ANTONYMS doubt; uncertainty.

3 *the girls exchanged confidences about their parents*: **secret**, private affair, confidential matter, confidentiality, intimacy.

confident adjective **1** *we are confident that business will improve*: **optimistic**, hopeful, sanguine; **sure**, certain, positive, convinced, in no doubt, unshakeable in one's belief, secure in one's belief, easy in one's mind, satisfied, assured, persuaded; (**be confident**) have no doubt, not question, hold the unwavering view.
2 *she was a confident, outgoing girl*: **self-assured**, assured, sure of oneself, self-confident, positive; assertive, self-assertive, self-possessed, believing in oneself, self-reliant, poised, filled with aplomb; cool, cool-headed, calm, collected, {cool, calm, and collected}, phlegmatic, level-headed, composed, nonchalant, unperturbed, imperturbable, unruffled, impassive, serene, tranquil, relaxed, at ease; informal unflappable, together, unfazed, laid-back; rare equanimous.

Word toolkit

confident	sanguine	optimistic
mood	expectation	outlook
smile	attitude	view
voice	temperament	forecast
tone	acceptance	prediction
manner	approach	assessment
assertion	response	estimate
stride	resignation	prognosis
swagger	conclusion	scenario

confidential adjective *anyone can have a confidential chat with adult education experts*: **private**, personal, intimate, privileged, quiet; secret, top secret, sensitive, classified, restricted, non-public, unofficial, off the record, not for publication, not for circulation, not to be made public, not to be disclosed, under wraps, unrevealed, undisclosed, unpublished; Latin sub rosa; informal hush-hush, mum; archaic privy.
▷ANTONYMS public, on the record.

confidentially adverb *he confidentially approached a number of very senior civil servants*: **privately**, in private, in confidence, between ourselves/themselves/yourselves, off the record, quietly, secretly, in secret, behind closed doors, in camera; Latin sub rosa; archaic privily.

configuration noun *the poor visibility is a result of the configuration of windows and pillars in the cockpit*: **arrangement**, layout, geography, design, organization, order, ordering, array, presentation, grouping, sorting, positioning, disposition, marshalling, ranging, alignment; shape, form, appearance, formation, structure, format; contours, lines, outline, silhouette, profile; cut, pattern, mould.

confine verb **1** *their cats are confined in the house*: **enclose**, incarcerate, imprison, intern, impound, hold captive, trap; shut in/up, keep, pen in/up, cage, lock in/up, coop (up), box up/in, immure, mew up; fence in, hedge in, hurdle, rail in, wall in/up; encircle, surround, ring, encompass, hem in, close in; N. Amer. corral; rare gird, compass.
▷ANTONYMS release.
2 *he **confined** his remarks **to** the job in hand*: **restrict**, limit; keep within the limits of, not allow to go beyond.

confined adjective *she had a fear of confined spaces*: **cramped**, constricted, restricted, limited, confining, small, narrow, compact, tight, pinched, squeezed, poky, uncomfortable, inadequate, meagre; archaic strait; rare incommodious, exiguous, incapacious.
▷ANTONYMS open; roomy.

confinement noun **1** *he was being held in solitary confinement*: **imprisonment**, internment, incarceration, custody, captivity, detention, restraint, arrest, house arrest; literary thraldom, thrall; archaic duress, durance.
▷ANTONYMS liberty.
2 *prolonged confinement of an animal is prohibited*: **penning**, caging, locking up, walling in/up, enclosure, encirclement, surrounding, encompassment; quarantine; N. Amer. corralling; rare immurement.
3 *she was admitted to hospital for her confinement*: **labour**, (expected) delivery, giving birth, birthing; birth, childbirth, nativity; technical parturition; archaic lying-in, accouchement, childbed, travail.

confines plural noun *recorded whale song was used to entice the whales out of the confines of Scapa Flow*: **limits**, outer limits, borders, boundaries, margins, extremities, edges, fringes, marches; periphery, perimeter, circumference, compass, precinct, pale.

confirm verb **1** *written records confirm the archaeological evidence*: **corroborate**, bear out, verify, show the truth of, prove, validate, authenticate, substantiate, give substance to, justify, vouch for, vindicate, give credence to, support, uphold, back up.
▷ANTONYMS contradict; repudiate.
2 *he confirmed that engineers would examine the road*: **affirm**, reaffirm, assert, reassert, give an assurance, assure someone, repeat, say again, state again, pledge, promise, guarantee.
▷ANTONYMS deny.
3 *his appointment as ambassador was confirmed by the President*: **ratify**, validate, sanction, endorse, formalize, certify, underwrite, authorize, warrant, accredit, approve, recognize, agree to, consent to, accept.
▷ANTONYMS revoke.

confirmation noun **1** *there was no independent confirmation of the reported deaths*: **corroboration**, verification, proof, testimony, endorsement, authentication, substantiation, justification, vindication, support, evidence.
2 *confirmation of your appointment is dependent upon satisfactory performance*: **ratification**, approval, authorization, validation, sanction, endorsement, formalization, certification, accreditation, recognition, acceptance; agreement to, consent to.

confirmed adjective *a confirmed bachelor*: **established**, long-established, long-standing, firm, committed, dyed-in-the-wool, through and through; seasoned, hardened, settled, set, fixed, rooted; staunch, loyal, faithful, devoted, dedicated, stalwart, steadfast; habitual, compulsive, obsessive, persistent, unapologetic, unashamed, incorrigible, irredeemable, unreformable, impenitent, inveterate, chronic, incurable; informal deep-dyed, card-carrying.

confiscate verb *the guards confiscated his camera*: **impound**, seize, commandeer, requisition, appropriate, expropriate, take possession of, sequester, sequestrate, take away, take over, take, annex; Law distrain, attach, disseize; Scottish Law poind.
▷ANTONYMS return.

confiscation noun *laws generally allow the confiscation of the proceeds of crime*: **seizure**, impounding, commandeering, requisition, requisitioning, appropriation, expropriation, sequestration, taking away, annexation; forfeiture; Law distraint, distrainment, attachment, disseizin; Scottish Law poind, poinding.
▷ANTONYMS return.

conflagration noun *the conflagration spread rapidly through the wooden buildings*: **fire**, blaze, flames, inferno, firestorm, holocaust.

conflict noun (stress on the first syllable) **1** *the industrial conflicts of the 1890s*: **dispute**, quarrel, squabble, disagreement, difference of opinion, dissension; discord, friction, strife, antagonism, antipathy, ill will, bad blood, hostility, falling-out, disputation, contention; clash, altercation, shouting match, exchange, war of words; tussle, fracas, affray, wrangle, tangle, passage of/at arms, battle royal, feud, schism.
▷ANTONYMS agreement.
2 *the Vietnam conflict*: **war**, armed conflict, action, military action, campaign, battle, fighting, fight, (armed) confrontation, (armed) clash, engagement, encounter, (armed) struggle, hostilities; warfare, warring, combat, strife; informal set-to, scrap; archaic rencounter.
▷ANTONYMS peace.
3 *there was a conflict between his business and domestic life*: **clash**, incompatibility, incongruity, lack of congruence, friction, opposition, mismatch, variance, difference, divergence, contradiction, inconsistency, discrepancy, divided loyalties.
▷ANTONYMS harmony.
▶ verb (stress on the second syllable) *parents' and children's interests sometimes conflict*: **clash**, be incompatible, be inconsistent, be incongruous, be in opposition, be at variance, vary, be at odds, be in conflict, come into conflict, differ, diverge, disagree, contrast, collide.

conflicting adjective *there are conflicting accounts of what occurred*: **contradictory**, incompatible, inconsistent, irreconcilable, incongruous, contrary, opposite, opposing, opposed, antithetical, clashing, discordant, differing, different, divergent, discrepant, varying, disagreeing, contrasting; at odds, in opposition, at variance; rare oppugnant.
▷ANTONYMS harmonious.

confluence noun *the confluence of the Rhine and the Mosel*: **convergence**, meeting, junction, joining, conflux, watersmeet; Indian sangam.

conform verb **1** *the kitchen does not **conform to** hygiene regulations | visitors have to **conform to** our rules*: **comply with**, abide by, obey, observe, follow, keep to, hold to, adhere to; satisfy, match up to, meet, fulfil, be in accordance with; stick to, stand by, act in accordance with, uphold, heed, pay attention to, agree to/with, consent to, accede to, accept, acquiesce in, go along with, fall in with, adapt to, accommodate to, adjust to, acknowledge, respect, defer to.
▷ANTONYMS flout.
2 *there are penalties for those who refuse to conform*: **follow convention**, be conventional, follow tradition, follow custom, fit in, adapt, adjust, follow the crowd, run with the pack, swim with the stream; comply, acquiesce, do what one is told, toe the line, obey the rules, comply with the rules, observe the rules, abide by the rules, adhere to the rules, act in accordance with the rules, follow the rules, keep to the rules, stick to the rules; submit, yield; informal play it by the book, play by the rules, keep in step, go with the flow.
▷ANTONYMS rebel.
3 *the goods must **conform to** their description*: **match**, fit, suit, answer, agree with, be like, be similar to, coincide with, correspond to, correlate to, be consistent with, be consonant with, be comparable with, measure up to, go with, tally with, square with, accord with, parallel, harmonize with.
▷ANTONYMS differ from.

C

conformist noun *he was too much of a conformist to wear anything but a suit at work*: **conventionalist**, **traditionalist**, orthodox person, conservative, bourgeois, (old) fogey, stickler, formalist, diehard, reactionary; crawler, truckler, kowtower, groveller, puppet, spaniel; informal stick-in-the-mud, stuffed shirt, yes-man.
▷ANTONYMS eccentric; rebel.

conformity noun **1** *conformity with the law*: **compliance with**, adherence to, accordance with, observance of, observation of, obedience to, acquiescence in, respect for, adaptation to, adjustment to, accommodation to; archaic abidance by.
▷ANTONYMS flouting.
2 *you cannot find more conformity than among young people*: **conventionality**, **traditionalism**, orthodoxy, fitting in, following the crowd, running with the pack, swimming with the stream; conservatism, formalism, reaction.
▷ANTONYMS eccentricity, rebellion.
3 *these changes are intended to ensure conformity between all schemes*: **similarity**, likeness, alikeness, resemblance, similitude; **correspondence**, correlation, matching, congruity, congruence, consonance, coincidence, compatibility, concurrence, agreement, harmony, accord, equivalence; comparability, comparableness, comparison, parallelism, mapping, parity, analogy, affinity, closeness, nearness; sameness, identity, identicalness, uniformity, symmetry; archaic semblance.
▷ANTONYMS dissimilarity.

confound verb **1** *the inflation figure confounded economic analysts*: **amaze**, astonish, dumbfound, stagger, surprise, startle, stun, stupefy, daze, nonplus; throw, shake, unnerve, disconcert, discompose, dismay, bewilder, set someone thinking, baffle, mystify, bemuse, perplex, puzzle, confuse; take someone's breath away, take by surprise, take aback, shake up, stop someone in their tracks, strike dumb, leave open-mouthed, leave aghast, catch off balance; N. Amer. informal buffalo; informal flabbergast, floor, knock for six, knock sideways, knock out, knock the stuffing out of someone, bowl over, blow someone's mind, blow away, flummox, discombobulate, faze, stump, beat, fox, make someone scratch their head, be all Greek to, fog; archaic wilder, gravel, maze, cause to be at a stand, distract, pose; rare obfuscate.
2 *the bad boy of country music has always confounded expectations*: **invalidate**, negate, contradict, counter, go against, discredit, give the lie to, drive a coach and horses through; quash, explode, demolish, shoot down, destroy; disprove, prove wrong, prove false, falsify; informal shoot full of holes, blow sky-high; rare controvert, confute, negative.

confront verb **1** *Jones confronted the alleged burglar*: **challenge**, square up to, oppose, resist, defy, beard, tackle, attack, assault; approach, face up to, face, meet, come face to face with, stand up to, brave, detain, accost, waylay, take aside, stop, halt; informal collar; Brit. informal nobble.
▷ANTONYMS avoid.
2 *the real problems that confront ordinary citizens*: **trouble**, bother, be in someone's way, burden, distress, cause trouble to, cause suffering to, face, beset, harass, worry, oppress, annoy, vex, irritate, exasperate, strain, stress, tax; torment, plague, blight, bedevil, rack, smite, curse, harrow; rare discommode.
3 *they've got to learn to confront their own problems*: **tackle**, get to grips with, apply oneself to, address oneself to, address, face, set about, go about, get to work at, busy oneself with, set one's hand to, grapple with, approach, take on, attend to, see to, throw oneself into, try to solve, try to deal with, try to cope with, learn to live with, try to sort out; deal with, take measures about, take care of, pursue, handle, manage; informal have a crack at, have a go at, have a shot at, get stuck into.
▷ANTONYMS avoid.
4 *she confronted him with the evidence she had unearthed*: **present**, bring face to face, face.
▷ANTONYMS spare.

confrontation noun *a peaceful protest turned into a violent confrontation with police*: **conflict**, clash, brush, fight, battle, contest, encounter, head-to-head, face-off, engagement, tangle, skirmish, collision, meeting, duel, incident, high noon; hostilities, fighting, warring; informal set-to, run-in, dust-up, shindig, shindy, showdown; archaic rencounter.

confuse verb **1** *there was no need to confuse students with too much controversy*: **bewilder**, baffle, mystify, bemuse, perplex, puzzle, confound, befog, nonplus, disconcert, throw, set someone thinking; informal flummox, discombobulate, faze, stump, beat, fox, make someone scratch their head, floor, fog; N. Amer. informal buffalo; archaic wilder, gravel, maze, cause to be at a stand, distract, pose; rare obfuscate.
▷ANTONYMS enlighten.
2 *the points made by the authors confuse rather than clarify the issue*: **complicate**, **muddle**, jumble, garble, make complex, make (more) difficult, blur, obscure, make unclear, cloud, obfuscate; archaic embroil.
▷ANTONYMS simplify.
3 *a lot of people **confuse** a stroke **with** a heart attack*: **mix up**, muddle up, confound; misinterpret as, mistake for, take for.
▷ANTONYMS distinguish.

confused adjective **1** *children could be confused about what was going on*: **bewildered**, bemused, puzzled, perplexed, baffled, stumped, mystified, stupefied, nonplussed, muddled, befuddled, fuddled, dumbfounded, at sea, at a loss, at sixes and sevens, thrown (off balance), taken aback, disoriented, disconcerted, discomposed, troubled, discomfited, unnerved, shaken, shaken up, dazed, stunned, astonished, astounded; informal flummoxed, bamboozled, discombobulated, clueless, fazed, floored, beaten; Canadian & Austral./NZ informal bushed; archaic wildered, mazed, distracted.
2 *her frail and confused elderly mother*: **demented**, bewildered, muddled, addled, befuddled, disoriented, disorientated, (all) at sea, unbalanced, unhinged, senile, with Alzheimer's disease.
▷ANTONYMS lucid.
3 *the first confused reports of the massacre*: **chaotic**, **muddled**, jumbled, unclear, untidy, disordered, disorderly, disarranged, out of order, disorganized, upset, topsy-turvy, at sixes and sevens; informal higgledy-piggledy.
▷ANTONYMS clear.
4 *a confused recollection*: **vague**, unclear, indistinct, imprecise, blurred, nebulous, hazy, woolly, foggy, shadowy, dim, imperfect, sketchy, obscure, remote.
▷ANTONYMS precise.
5 *the bones lay in a confused mass*: **disorderly**, disordered, disorganized, disarranged, in disarray, out of order, out of place, untidy, muddled, jumbled, in a jumble, in a mess, mixed up, chaotic, upset, haywire, upside-down, topsy-turvy, at sixes and sevens; informal higgledy-piggledy, every which way; Brit. informal shambolic, like a dog's dinner/breakfast.
▷ANTONYMS neat.

confusing adjective *the instructions are a little confusing*: **bewildering**, baffling, difficult (to understand), unclear, perplexing, puzzling, mystifying, mysterious, disconcerting; ambiguous, misleading, inconsistent, contradictory; unaccountable, inexplicable, impenetrable, unfathomable, above one's head, beyond one; complex, complicated, involved, intricate, convoluted, labyrinthine, Byzantine; archaic wildering.
▷ANTONYMS clear.

confusion noun **1** *there seems to be some confusion about which system does what*: **uncertainty**, lack of certainty, unsureness, indecision, hesitation, hesitancy, scepticism, doubt, ignorance; rare dubiety, incertitude.
▷ANTONYMS certainty.
2 *she looked about her in confusion*: **bewilderment**, bafflement, perplexity, puzzlement, mystification, stupefaction, disorientation, befuddlement, muddle; discomfiture, discomposure, shock, daze, devastation; wonder, wonderment, astonishment; informal bamboozlement, discombobulation; rare disconcertment, disconcertion.
3 *your personal life seems to have been thrown into utter confusion*: **disorder**, disarray, disorganization, disorderliness, untidiness, chaos, mayhem, bedlam, pandemonium, madness, havoc, turmoil, tumult, commotion, disruption, upheaval, furore, frenzy, uproar, babel, hurly-burly, maelstrom, muddle, mess, shambles; a mare's nest, anarchy, entropy; informal hullabaloo, all hell broken loose, a madhouse; N. Amer. informal a three-ring circus; rare disarrangement.
▷ANTONYMS order.
4 *a confusion of brown cardboard boxes*: **jumble**, muddle, mess, heap, tangle, entanglement, tumble, welter, litter, shambles.

confute verb formal *their assertion can certainly be confuted*. See **disprove**.

congeal verb *the blood had congealed around the cut*: **coagulate**, clot, cake, set, solidify, harden, thicken, stiffen, dry, gel, concentrate; archaic fix; rare inspissate.
▷ANTONYMS soften; liquefy.

congenial adjective **1** *I was working with a bunch of very congenial people*: **like-minded**, compatible, kindred, well suited, easy to get along with; **companionable**, sociable, sympathetic, comradely, convivial, neighbourly, hospitable, genial, personable, agreeable, friendly, pleasant, likeable, kindly, pleasing, amiable, nice, good-natured; French sympathique; Italian & Spanish simpatico.
▷ANTONYMS disagreeable, incompatible.
2 *Charles found himself in a fairly congenial environment*: **pleasant**, pleasing, to one's liking, agreeable, enjoyable, pleasurable, nice, appealing, engaging, satisfying, gratifying, fine, charming, delightful, relaxing, snug, welcome, welcoming, hospitable; suitable, suited, well suited, fit, appropriate, adapted, favourable.
▷ANTONYMS unpleasant.

congenital adjective **1** *multiple congenital defects*: **inborn**, inherited, hereditary, in the blood, in the family, innate, inbred, constitutional, built-in, inbuilt, ingrown, natural, native, original, inherent, unlearned, instinctual, deep-rooted, deep-seated; rare connate, connatural.
▷ANTONYMS acquired.
2 *he was a congenital liar*: **inveterate**, compulsive, persistent, chronic, regular, pathological, established, long-established, long-standing, hardened, confirmed, committed, seasoned, habitual, obsessive, obsessional; incurable, incorrigible, irredeemable, unreformable, hopeless; unashamed, shameless, unrepentant; dyed-in-the-wool, thoroughgoing, thorough, utter, complete.

congested adjective *more traffic will use the already congested road*: **crowded**, overcrowded, full, overfull, overflowing, full to overflowing/

bursting, crammed full, cram-full, thronged, packed, jammed, teeming, swarming, overloaded; obstructed, impeded, blocked (up), clogged, choked, plugged, stopped up; informal snarled up, gridlocked, jam-packed; Brit. informal like Piccadilly Circus.
▷ANTONYMS clear.

congestion noun *an attempt to relieve some of the congestion on the roads*: **crowding**, overcrowding; obstruction, blockage, stoppage, blocking, clogging, choking, plugging, stuffing; traffic jam, bottleneck; informal snarl-up, gridlock.
▷ANTONYMS flow.

conglomerate noun **1** *the conglomerate was broken up*: **corporation**, combine, group, grouping, consortium, partnership, joint concern, trust, merger, merged firms/companies/businesses; firm, company, business, multinational; Japanese zaibatsu.
2 *Austria–Hungary was a conglomerate of disparate peoples*: **mixture**, mix, combination, mingling, commingling, amalgamation, amalgam, union, conjunction, marriage, merging, compound, alloy, fusion, meld, composite, concoction, synthesis, homogenization; miscellany, jumble, hotchpotch; informal mash-up.
3 Geology *a rocky conglomerate*: **aggregate**, agglomerate.
▶ adjective *a conglomerate mass*: **aggregate**, agglomerate, amassed, gathered, clustered, combined.
▶ verb *the debris then conglomerated into planets*: **coalesce**, unite, join together, combine, merge, fuse, consolidate, amalgamate, integrate, mingle, meld, blend, intermingle, knit (together), link up, converge, come together; literary commingle.
▷ANTONYMS split up.

conglomeration noun *an extremely odd conglomeration of church buildings*: **collection**, **cluster**, assortment, mix, variety, medley, mixed bag, pot-pourri, miscellany, selection, combination; accumulation, mass, gathering, cumulation, package, aggregation, accretion, agglomerate, agglomeration; rare amassment.

congratulate verb **1** *she took the opportunity to congratulate Nicholas on his marriage*: **give someone one's good wishes**, wish someone good luck, wish someone joy, drink someone's health, toast, drink (a toast) to.
▷ANTONYMS curse.
2 *all three are to be congratulated for passing with flying colours*: **praise**, commend, applaud, salute, honour, eulogize, extol, acclaim, sing the praises of, heap praise on, pay tribute to, speak highly/well of, flatter, compliment, say nice things about, express admiration for, wax lyrical about, make much of, pat on the back, take one's hat off to, throw bouquets at; informal crack someone/something up; N. Amer. informal ballyhoo; black English big someone/something up; dated cry someone/something up; archaic emblazon; rare laud, panegyrize, felicitate.
▷ANTONYMS criticize.
□ **congratulate oneself** *he* ***congratulated himself on*** *his success*: **take pride in**, be/feel proud of, feel proud about, be proud of oneself for, flatter oneself on, preen oneself on, pat oneself on the back for, give oneself a pat on the back for; **find/take satisfaction in**, feel satisfaction at, take delight in, find/take pleasure in, glory in, bask in, delight in, exult in, plume oneself on; archaic pique oneself on/in.
▷ANTONYMS be ashamed of.

congratulations plural noun **1** *Lily and Stephen accepted Muriel's congratulations on their wedding*: **good wishes**, best wishes, greetings, compliments, felicitations.
2 *you all deserve congratulations for ensuring that the visit was such a success*: **praise**, commendation, applause, salutes, honour, acclaim, acclamation, tribute, cheers, ovation, accolade, plaudits, felicitations; approval, admiration, approbation, compliments, kudos, adulation, homage; a pat on the back, eulogy, encomium, panegyric, bouquets, laurels, testimonial; rare extolment, laudation, eulogium.
▷ANTONYMS blame.

congregate verb *some 4000 demonstrators had congregated at a border point*: **assemble**, gather, collect, come together, flock together, get together, convene, rally, rendezvous, muster, meet, amass, crowd, cluster, throng, group; rare foregather.
▷ANTONYMS disperse.

congregation noun **1** *he broke the news to the congregation in the church newsletter*: **parishioners**, parish, churchgoers, flock, fold, faithful, following, followers, adherents, believers, loyal members, fellowship, communicants, laity, brethren, brothers and sisters, souls.
2 *such congregations of birds may cause public harm | a large congregation of protesters gathered*: **gathering**, assembly, flock, swarm, bevy, herd, pack, group, body, crowd, mass, multitude, horde, host, mob; turnout, throng, company, rally, convocation, congress, council, conclave, synod, assemblage; informal get-together; historical conventicle.

congress noun **1** *an international congress of mathematicians*: **conference**, convention, seminar, colloquium, symposium, consultation, forum, meeting, assembly, gathering, congregation, rally, convocation, summit, synod, council, conclave; historical conventicle.
2 *elections for the new Congress were held on 8 November*: **legislature**, legislative assembly, parliament, convocation, diet, council, senate, chamber, chamber of deputies, house; upper house, lower house, upper chamber, lower chamber, second chamber.

congruence noun *he took care that there should be congruence of meaning and sound in his music*: **compatibility**, consistency, conformity, match, balance, consonance, rapport, parallelism, congruity; consilience; agreement, concord, accord, consensus, unanimity, harmony, unison, unity, concert.
▷ANTONYMS conflict.

conical adjective *a circular tower with a conical roof*: **cone-shaped**, tapered, tapering, pointed, funnel-shaped; informal pointy; technical infundibular, turbinate, conoid.

conjectural adjective *comments on inner-city areas are likely to be more conjectural*: **speculative**, suppositional, theoretical, hypothetical, putative, academic, notional, abstract; postulated, based on guesswork, inferred, suspected, presumed, assumed, presupposed, tentative; unproven, untested, unfounded, groundless, unsubstantiated; rare ideational, suppositious, suppositive, postulational.
▷ANTONYMS established.

conjecture noun *we find his conjectures implausible | some of the information is merely conjecture*: **guess**, speculation, surmise, fancy, notion, belief, suspicion, presumption, assumption, theory, hypothesis, postulation, supposition; inference, extrapolation, projection; approximation, estimate, rough calculation, rough idea; guesswork, guessing, surmising, imagining, theorizing; informal guesstimate, shot in the dark; N. Amer. informal **ballpark figure**.
▷ANTONYMS fact.
▶ verb *I conjectured that the game was about to end*: **guess**, speculate, surmise, infer, fancy, imagine, believe, think, suspect, presume, assume, hypothesize, take as a hypothesis, theorize, form/formulate a theory, suppose.
▷ANTONYMS know.

conjugal adjective *the conjugal bond*: **marital**, matrimonial, nuptial, marriage, married, wedded, connubial, bridal; Law spousal; literary hymeneal, epithalamic.

conjunction noun *the conjunction of low inflation and low unemployment came as a very pleasant surprise*: **co-occurrence**, concurrence, coincidence, coexistence, simultaneity, simultaneousness, contemporaneity, contemporaneousness, concomitance, synchronicity, synchrony; combination, juxtaposition.
□ **in conjunction** *he explained how they work in conjunction with the police to prevent crime in the area*: **together**, jointly, conjointly, in cooperation, cooperatively, in collaboration, in partnership, in combination, as one, in unison, in concert, concertedly, with one accord, in league, in alliance, in collusion, side by side, hand in hand, hand in glove, shoulder to shoulder, cheek by jowl; informal in cahoots.
▷ANTONYMS separately.

conjure verb **1** *he conjured another cigarette out of the air*: **make something appear**, produce, materialize, magic, summon, generate; whip up.
2 *the picture that his words* ***conjured up*** *left her breathless*: **bring to mind**, call to mind, put one in mind of, call up, evoke, summon up, recall, recreate; echo, allude to, suggest; rouse (up), stir (up), raise up, awaken.

conjuring noun *a demonstration of conjuring*: **magic**, illusion, sleight of hand, legerdemain, dexterity, deception, hocus-pocus; formal prestidigitation.

conjuror noun *the children were entertained by a local conjuror*: **magician**, illusionist; Brit. member of the Magic Circle; formal prestidigitator.

connect verb **1** *the electrodes were connected to a recording device*: **attach**, join, fasten, fix, affix, couple, link, bridge, secure, make fast, tie, tie up, bind, fetter, strap, rope, tether, truss, lash, hitch, moor, anchor, yoke, chain; stick, tape, adhere, glue, bond, cement, fuse, weld, solder; pin, peg, screw, bolt, rivet, batten, pinion, clamp, clip, hook (up); add, append, annex, subjoin; technical concatenate.
▷ANTONYMS disconnect.
2 *there are lots of customs* ***connected with*** *Twelfth Night*: **associate**, link, couple; identify, equate, bracket, compare; think of something together with, think of something in connection with; relate to, mention in the same breath as, set side by side with; draw a parallel with.
▷ANTONYMS dissociate.

connection noun **1** *he does not pursue the connection between commerce and art*: **link**, relationship, relation, relatedness, interrelation, interrelatedness, interconnection, interdependence, association, attachment, bond, tie, tie-in, correspondence, parallel, analogy; bearing, relevance.
2 *there's a poor connection in the plug*: **attachment**, joint, fastening, coupling.
3 *a politician with all the right connections*: **contact**, friend, acquaintance, ally, colleague, associate, sponsor; relation, relative, kindred, kin, kinsman, kinswoman.
□ **in connection with** *a man is being questioned in connection with the murder*: **regarding**, concerning, with reference to, referring to, with regard

C

C

to, with respect to, respecting, relating to, in relation to, on, touching on, dealing with, relevant to, with relevance to, in the context of, connected with, on the subject of, in the matter of, apropos, re; Scottish anent; Latin in re.

connivance noun *this infringement of the law had taken place with the connivance of officials*: **collusion**, complicity, collaboration, involvement, assistance, abetting; **tacit consent**; conspiracy, plotting, scheming, intrigue, machination, secret understanding; rare abetment, condonation.

connive verb **1** *wardens **connived at** offences in return for bribes*: **deliberately ignore**, overlook, not take into consideration, disregard, pass over, gloss over, take no notice of, take no account of, make allowances for, turn a blind eye to, close/shut one's eyes to, wink at, blink at, excuse, pardon, forgive, condone, let someone off with, let go, let pass; look the other way; informal let something ride.
▷ANTONYMS condemn; punish.
2 *the government had connived with security forces in permitting murder*: **conspire**, collude, be in collusion, collaborate, intrigue, be hand in glove, plot, participate in a conspiracy, scheme; informal be in cahoots; rare machinate, cabal, complot.

conniving adjective *a conniving little toady with an eye for the main chance*: **scheming**, plotting, colluding, cunning, crafty, calculating, devious, designing, wily, sly, tricky, artful, guileful, slippery, slick; **manipulative**, Machiavellian, unscrupulous, unprincipled, disingenuous; duplicitous, deceitful, underhand, treacherous; informal foxy; S. African informal slim; archaic subtle.

connoisseur noun *a connoisseur of fine wines*: **expert judge (of)**, authority (on), specialist (in); arbiter of taste, pundit, savant, one of the cognoscenti, aesthete; gourmet, epicure, gastronome; informal buff; N. Amer. informal maven.
▷ANTONYMS ignoramus.

connotation noun *the word 'discipline' has unhappy connotations of punishment and repression*: **overtone**, undertone, undercurrent, implication, hidden meaning, secondary meaning, nuance, flavour, feeling, aura, atmosphere, colouring, smack, hint, vein, echo, vibrations, association, intimation, suggestion, suspicion, insinuation; rare undermeaning, subcurrent.

connote verb *the British think that crying and showing emotion connote weakness*: **imply**, suggest, indicate, signify, have overtones of, have undertones of, hint at, give a feeling of, have an aura of, have an atmosphere of, give the impression of, smack of, be associated with, allude to.
▷ANTONYMS denote, mean.

conquer verb **1** *the Franks conquered the Visigoths in the South of France*: **defeat**, beat, vanquish, trounce, annihilate, triumph over, be victorious over, best, get the better of, worst, bring someone to their knees, overcome, overwhelm, overpower, overthrow, subdue, subjugate, put down, quell, quash, crush, repress, rout; informal lick, hammer, clobber, thrash, paste, pound, pulverize, demolish, destroy, drub, give someone a drubbing, cane, wipe the floor with, walk all over, give someone a hiding, take to the cleaners, blow someone out of the water, make mincemeat of, murder, massacre, slaughter, flatten, turn inside out, tank; Brit. informal stuff; N. Amer. informal blow out, cream, shellac, skunk, slam.
▷ANTONYMS lose to.
2 *Peru had been conquered by Spain*: **seize**, take possession of, take control of, take over, appropriate, subjugate, capture, occupy, invade, annex, overrun, win.
▷ANTONYMS liberate, lose.
3 *the first men to conquer Mount Everest*: **climb**, ascend, mount, scale, top, crest.
4 *the only way to conquer fear is to face it*: **overcome**, get the better of, control, get control of, master, gain mastery over, get a grip on, deal with, cope with, surmount, rise above, get over; curb, subdue, repress, quell, quash, defeat, vanquish, beat, triumph over, prevail over; informal lick.
▷ANTONYMS yield to.

conqueror noun *Robert Clive was known as the conqueror of Bengal*: **vanquisher**, defeater, subjugator; victor, winner, champion, hero, conquering hero, lord, master; Spanish conquistador.
▷ANTONYMS vanquished; loser.

conquest noun **1** *the conquest of the Aztecs by the Spanish*: **defeat**, beating, conquering, vanquishment, vanquishing, trouncing, annihilation, overpowering, overthrow, subduing, subjugation, rout, mastery, crushing; victory (over), triumph (over); informal hammering, clobbering, thrashing, drubbing, caning, murder, massacre.
▷ANTONYMS victory.
2 *Charlemagne's conquest of Italy*: **seizure**, seizing, takeover, acquisition, gain, appropriation, subjugation, subjection, capture, occupation, invasion, annexation, overrunning.
▷ANTONYMS surrender.
3 *the conquest of Everest*: **ascent**, climbing, scaling.
4 *he regarded her as someone he could display before his friends as his latest conquest*: **catch**, acquisition, captive, prize, slave; admirer, fan, worshipper; lover, love, boyfriend, girlfriend; informal fancy man, fancy woman, toy boy, sugar daddy; literary swain; archaic gallant, paramour, leman.

conscience noun *her conscience wouldn't allow her to keep silent any longer*: **sense of right and wrong**, sense of right, moral sense, still small voice, inner voice, voice within; morals, standards, values, principles, ethics, creed, beliefs; compunction, scruples, qualms.

conscience-stricken adjective *maybe he is conscience-stricken at having arranged their deaths*: **guilt-ridden**, troubled, disturbed, remorseful, ashamed, shamefaced, apologetic, sorry; chastened, contrite, guilty, full of regret, regretful, rueful, repentant, penitent, self-reproachful, abashed, sheepish; rare compunctious.
▷ANTONYMS untroubled, unrepentant.

conscientious adjective *a conscientious man, he took his duties very seriously*: **diligent**, industrious, punctilious, painstaking, sedulous, assiduous, dedicated, careful, meticulous, thorough, attentive, laborious, hard-working, ultra-careful, persevering, unflagging, searching, close, minute, accurate, correct, studious, rigorous, particular; religious, strict.
▷ANTONYMS casual.

conscious adjective **1** *the patient was barely conscious*: **aware**, **awake**, wide awake, compos mentis, alert, responsive, reactive, feeling, sentient.
▷ANTONYMS unconscious.
2 *he became **conscious of** people talking in the hall*: **aware of**, alive to, awake to, alert to, sensitive to, cognizant of, mindful of, sensible of; informal wise to, in the know about, hip to; archaic ware of; rare seized of, recognizant of, regardful of.
▷ANTONYMS unaware.
3 *he made a conscious effort to stop staring*: **deliberate**, intentional, intended, done on purpose, purposeful, purposive, willed, knowing, considered, studied, strategic; calculated, wilful, premeditated, planned, pre-planned, preconceived, volitional; aforethought; Law, dated prepense.

consciousness noun **1** *she failed to regain consciousness*: **awareness**, wakefulness, alertness, responsiveness, sentience.
▷ANTONYMS unconsciousness.
2 *her acute **consciousness of** Luke's presence*: **awareness of**, knowledge of the existence of, alertness to, sensitivity to, realization of, cognizance of, mindfulness of, perception of, apprehension of, recognition of.

conscript verb (stress on the second syllable) *they were conscripted into the army*: **call up**, enlist, recruit, mobilize, raise, muster; US draft; historical press, impress; archaic levy.
▶ noun (stress on the first syllable) *an army conscript*: **impressed man**, recruit; US draftee, enlisted man.
▷ANTONYMS volunteer.

consecrate verb **1** *the Bishop had consecrated two cathedrals in his time*: **sanctify**, bless, make holy, make sacred, hallow, set apart, dedicate to God; anoint, ordain, canonize, beatify, lay hands on; archaic frock.
▷ANTONYMS deconsecrate.
2 informal *the gun room was a male preserve, consecrated to sport*: **dedicate**, devote, give (over), set aside, set apart, assign, allot, allocate, reserve, commit, apply, consign, pledge, vow, offer, surrender, sacrifice.

consecutive adjective *shares prices fell for three consecutive days*: **successive**, succeeding, following, in succession, running, in a row, one after the other, back-to-back, continuous, solid, straight, uninterrupted, unbroken; informal on the trot.
▷ANTONYMS separate.

consensus noun **1** *there was consensus among most delegates*: **agreement**, harmony, concord, like-mindedness, concurrence, consent, common consent, accord, unison, unity, unanimity, oneness, solidarity, concert.
▷ANTONYMS disagreement.
2 *the consensus was that the Government should act now*: **general opinion/view**, majority opinion/view, common opinion/view.
▷ANTONYMS minority view.

consent noun *a change in the rules requires the consent of all members*: **agreement**, assent, concurrence, accord; permission, authorization, sanction, leave, clearance, acquiescence, acceptance, approval, seal of approval, stamp of approval, imprimatur, backing, endorsement, confirmation, support, favour, good wishes; informal go-ahead, thumbs up, green light, OK; formal approbation.
▷ANTONYMS dissent.
▶ verb *all the patients **consented to** surgery*: **agree to**, assent to, allow, give permission for, sanction, accept, approve, acquiesce in, go along with, accede to, concede to, yield to, give in to, submit to, comply with, abide by, concur with, conform to.
▷ANTONYMS dissent; forbid.

Choose the right word **consent, permission, authorization, leave**

See **permission**.

Choose the right word **consent, agree, assent, acquiesce**

See **agree**.

C

consequence noun **1** *inflation is a consequence of a rapid growth in the money supply*: **result**, upshot, outcome, out-turn, sequel, effect, reaction, repercussion, reverberations, ramification, end, end result, conclusion, termination, culmination, denouement, corollary, concomitant, aftermath, fruit(s), product, produce, by-product; Medicine sequelae; informal pay-off; dated issue; archaic success.
▷ANTONYMS cause.
2 *the past is of no consequence*: **importance**, import, significance, account, moment, momentousness, substance, note, mark, prominence, value, weightiness, weight, concern, interest, gravity, seriousness.

consequent adjective *this was the best we could do, and we hope that the consequent errors are not too great*: **resulting**, resultant, ensuing, consequential; following, subsequent, successive, sequential; attendant, accompanying, concomitant; collateral, associated, related, connected, linked.
▷ANTONYMS causal; unrelated.

consequential adjective **1** *the fire can be rapidly controlled and the consequential water and smoke damage reduced*: **resulting**, resultant, ensuing, consequent; following, subsequent, successive, sequential; attendant, accompanying, concomitant; collateral, associated, related, connected, linked.
▷ANTONYMS causal; unrelated.
2 *one of the President's more consequential initiatives*: **important**, significant, major, momentous, of moment, weighty, material, meaty, appreciable, memorable, far-reaching, serious; of consequence, of great import, of significance.
▷ANTONYMS insignificant, minor.

consequently adverb *many of the subjects available are not taught in school, and consequently may be unfamiliar*: **as a result**, as a consequence, in consequence, so, that being so, thus, therefore, accordingly, hence, for this/that reason, because of this/that, on this/that account; inevitably, necessarily; Latin ergo.

conservation noun *the conservation of tropical forests*: **preservation**, protection, safeguarding, safe keeping, keeping, guarding, saving, looking after; care, charge, custody, guardianship, husbandry, supervision; upkeep, keeping up, keeping going, keeping alive, maintenance, repair, restoration; ecology, environmentalism.

conservative adjective **1** *the conservative wing of the party*: **right-wing**, reactionary, traditionalist, unprogressive, establishmentarian, blimpish; fundamentalist; in the UK Tory; in the US Republican; informal true blue.
▷ANTONYMS socialist.
2 *they were held in check by the conservative trade-union movement*: **traditionalist**, traditional, conventional, orthodox, stable, old-fashioned, dyed-in-the-wool, unchanging, hidebound; cautious, prudent, careful, safe, timid, unadventurous, unenterprising, set in one's ways; moderate, middle-of-the-road, temperate; informal stick in the mud.
▷ANTONYMS radical.
3 *men should wear a dark conservative suit*: **conventional**, sober, quiet, modest, plain, unobtrusive, unostentatious, restrained, reserved, subdued, subtle, low-key, demure; informal square, straight.
▷ANTONYMS ostentatious.
4 *a conservative estimate*: **low**, cautious, understated, unexaggerated, moderate, reasonable.
▶ noun *liberals and conservatives are beginning to find common ground on one point*: **right-winger**, reactionary, rightist, diehard; in the UK Tory; in the US Republican.

conservatory noun **1** *keep plant cuttings in a frost-free conservatory*: **greenhouse**, glasshouse, hothouse; **summer house**, gazebo, pavilion, belvedere.
2 *he got a teaching job at the conservatory*: **conservatoire**, music school, drama school, academy/institute of music/drama.

conserve verb *a finite reserve of fossil fuel that should be conserved*: **preserve**, protect, maintain, save, safeguard, keep, take care of, care for, look after, sustain, keep intact, prolong, perpetuate; hoard, store up, stockpile, husband, use sparingly, reserve, nurse.
▷ANTONYMS squander, waste.
▶ noun *cherry conserve*: **jam**, preserve, jelly, spread, marmalade, confiture.

consider verb **1** *Isabel hesitated, considering her choices*: **think about**, contemplate, give thought to, reflect on, examine, appraise, review; study, mull over, ponder, deliberate over, cogitate about, chew over, meditate on/over, ruminate over, turn over in one's mind; assess, evaluate, compare, weigh up, judge, consider the pros and cons of, sum up; informal size up.
2 *I consider him irresponsible*: **regard as**, deem, hold to be, think, think of as, reckon, believe, judge, adjudge, rate, class as, account, count, gauge, look on as, view as, see as, take for, interpret as, suppose, find; esteem.
3 *embarrassed, he considered the ceiling*: **look at**, contemplate, observe, regard, survey, view, scrutinize, scan, examine, inspect; informal check out, have a gander at, have a squint at, get a load of; Brit. informal have a butcher's at, take a dekko at, take a shufti at, clock; N. Amer. informal eyeball.
4 *I hope the inquiry will consider all those issues*: **take into consideration**, take into account, take account of, make allowances for, respect, bear in mind, be mindful of, have regard to, reckon with, remember, mind, mark, heed, note, not forget, make provision for, take to heart, pay/have regard to, be guided by.
▷ANTONYMS ignore.

considerable adjective **1** *he escaped with a considerable amount of money*: **sizeable**, substantial, appreciable, significant; goodly, tolerable, fair, reasonable, tidy, hefty, handsome, comfortable, decent, worthwhile, worth having, worth taking into account; ample, plentiful, abundant, superabundant, great, large, lavish, profuse, generous; marked, noticeable; informal not to be sneezed at, OK; literary plenteous.
▷ANTONYMS paltry.
2 *he turned professional and met with considerable success*: **much**, a lot of, lots of, a great deal of, plenty of, a fair amount of, great.
▷ANTONYMS minor.
3 *he became a considerable gentleman cricketer*: **distinguished**, noteworthy, noted, important, significant, prominent, eminent, influential, illustrious; renowned, celebrated, acclaimed, highly rated, much touted, well thought of, well received, of repute, of high standing, of distinction.
▷ANTONYMS insignificant.

considerably adverb *alcoholic drinks vary considerably in strength*: **greatly**, much, very much, a great deal, a lot, lots, a fair amount; significantly, substantially, appreciably, markedly, noticeably, materially, signally; informal plenty, seriously.
▷ANTONYMS slightly.

considerate adjective *we were encouraged to be polite, modest, and considerate towards others*: **attentive**, thoughtful, concerned, solicitous, mindful, heedful, obliging, accommodating, helpful, cooperative, patient; kind, kindly, decent, unselfish, compassionate, sympathetic, caring, charitable, altruistic, generous; polite, sensitive, civil, tactful, diplomatic.
▷ANTONYMS inconsiderate.

consideration noun **1** *your case needs very careful consideration*: **thought**, deliberation, reflection, contemplation, cogitation, rumination, pondering, meditation, musing, mulling, examination, inspection, scrutiny, analysis, review, discussion; attention, heed, notice, regard.
2 *his health has to be the prime consideration*: **factor**, issue, point, concern, item, matter, element, detail, aspect, facet, feature, determinant.
3 *it's time for companies to show more consideration for their local communities*: **attentiveness**, considerateness, thoughtfulness, concern, care, solicitousness, solicitude, mindfulness; kindness, kindliness, understanding, respect, sensitivity, tact, discretion; unselfishness, compassion, sympathy, charity, generosity, benevolence, friendliness.
▷ANTONYMS disregard, thoughtlessness.
4 *perhaps, for a consideration, I might be able to arrange something*: **payment**, fee, premium, remuneration, compensation, recompense, emolument, perquisite; commission, percentage, share, portion, dividend; informal cut, take, whack, slice, slice of the cake, piece of the action.
□ **take into consideration** *the company must take into consideration a number of factors*: **consider**, give thought to, take into account, allow for, make allowances for, provide for, plan for, make plans for, foresee, anticipate, make provision for, make preparations for, prepare for, accommodate, make concessions for, arrange for, bargain for, reckon with.
▷ANTONYMS ignore.

considering preposition *considering his size he showed an astonishing turn of speed*: **bearing in mind**, taking into consideration, taking into account, making allowance(s) for, giving consideration to, keeping in mind, in view of, in the light of.
▷ANTONYMS apart from, ignoring.
▶ adverb informal *he'd been lucky, considering*: **all things considered**, considering everything, all in all, on the whole, taking everything into consideration/account, at the end of the day, when all's said and done.

consign verb **1** *he was **consigned to** a debtor's prison*: **send**, deliver, hand over, give over, turn over, sentence; **confine in**, imprison in, incarcerate in, lock up in, jail in, detain in, intern in, immure in; informal put away, put behind bars; Brit. informal bang up.
2 *the picture was consigned for sale at one of Sotheby's European offices*: **assign**, allocate, place, put, entrust, grant, remit, hand down, bequeath; archaic commend.
3 *the package was consigned by a company that flies products all over the world*: **send**, send off, dispatch, transmit, transfer, convey, post, mail, ship.
4 *I had a clear-out and consigned her picture to the bin*: **deposit**, commit, put away, banish, relegate.

consignment noun *a consignment of goods*: **delivery**, shipment, load, containerload, shipload, boatload, lorryload, truckload, cargo; batch, lot, haul, goods.

consist verb **1** *the exhibition **consists of** 180 drawings*: **be composed**, be made up, be formed; comprise, contain, include, incorporate, embody, involve, embrace.
2 *style **consists in** the choices that writers make in communicating their thoughts*: **exist**, subsist, inhere, be inherent, lie, reside, have its existence/being, be present, be contained; be expressed by, have as its main feature.

consistency noun **1** *the downward trend in consumption shows a remarkable degree of consistency*: **evenness**, steadiness, stability, constancy,

C

regularity, uniformity, equilibrium, unity, orderliness, lack of change, lack of deviation; dependability, reliability.
▷ANTONYMS inconsistency.
2 *you need a jug of rich cream of pouring consistency*: **thickness**, density, firmness, solidity, viscosity, cohesion, heaviness, degree of thickness, degree of density; **texture**.

consistent adjective 1 *there was consistent opinion-poll evidence that the ALP was likely to lose the next election*: **steady**, stable, constant, regular, even, uniform, orderly, unchanging, unvarying, unswerving, undeviating, unwavering, unfluctuating, homogeneous, true to type; dependable, reliable, unfailing, predictable.
▷ANTONYMS inconsistent, irregular.
2 *her injuries were* **consistent with** *an attack with a blunt instrument*: **compatible**, congruous, agreeing, accordant, consonant, in harmony, harmonious, in tune, in line, reconcilable, of a piece; corresponding to, conforming to.
▷ANTONYMS inconsistent, incompatible.

consolation noun *I murmured some words of consolation*: **comfort**, solace; sympathy, compassion, pity, commiseration, fellow feeling; relief, help, aid, support, moral support, cheer, encouragement, reassurance, fortification; soothing, easement, succour, assuagement, alleviation.

console[1] (stress on the second syllable) verb *his friends tried to console him, but he couldn't help thinking about the money*: **comfort**, solace, condole with, give condolences to; sympathize with, express sympathy to, show compassion to, pity, commiserate with, show fellow feeling to; help, aid, support, cheer (up), gladden, hearten, encourage, reassure, fortify; soothe, ease, succour, assuage, alleviate.
▷ANTONYMS distress, upset.

console[2] (stress on the first syllable) noun *he bent over the console, pushing buttons at random*: **control panel**, instrument panel, dashboard, keyboard, keypad; cabinet; informal dash.

consolidate verb 1 *we have been able to consolidate our position in the market*: **strengthen**, make stronger, make secure, secure, make stable, stabilize, reinforce, fortify, tighten, harden, stiffen, cement, enhance.
2 *you must consolidate the results of the audit into an action plan*: **combine**, unite, merge, integrate, amalgamate, fuse, blend, mingle, marry, synthesize, bring together; join, affiliate, federate, unify.

consonance noun *a constitution in consonance with the customs of the people*: **agreement**, concord, accord, accordance, harmony, unison, conformity; compatibility, congruity, congruence.

consonant adjective
□ **consonant with** *these findings are consonant with recent research*: **in agreement with**, agreeing with, consistent with, in accordance with, accordant with, consilient with, in harmony with, compatible with, congruous with, in tune with, reconcilable with.
▷ANTONYMS incompatible with.

consort noun (stress on the first syllable) *Queen Victoria and her consort, Prince Albert*: **partner**, companion, mate, helpmate, helpmeet; spouse, husband, wife.
▶ verb (stress on the second syllable) *my husband never consorted with other women*: **associate**, keep company, mix, mingle, go around, spend time, socialize, fraternize, have dealings, rub shoulders; N. Amer. rub elbows; informal hobnob, run around, hang around/round, hang out, knock about/around, pal around, chum around, be thick; Brit. informal hang about.

conspicuous adjective *lots of birds have highly conspicuous plumage | he showed conspicuous bravery*: **easily seen**, clear, visible, clearly visible, standing out, noticeable, observable, discernible, perceptible, perceivable, detectable; **obvious**, manifest, evident, apparent, marked, pronounced, prominent, outstanding, patent, crystal clear, as clear as crystal; vivid, striking, dramatic, eye-catching, flagrant, ostentatious, overt, blatant, as plain as a pikestaff, staring one in the face, writ large, as plain as day; distinct, recognizable, distinguishable, unmistakable, inescapable; informal as plain as the nose on one's face, standing/sticking out like a sore thumb, standing/sticking out a mile.
▷ANTONYMS inconspicuous.

conspiracy noun 1 *the company was involved in a conspiracy with bookmakers to manipulate starting prices*: **plot**, scheme, stratagem, plan, machination, cabal; deception, ploy, trick, ruse, dodge, subterfuge, sharp practice; informal frame-up, fit-up, racket, put-up job; rare complot, covin.
2 *he was due to stand trial for conspiracy to murder*: **plotting**, collusion, intrigue, connivance, machination, collaboration; treason.

conspirator noun *conspirators had planned to seize the state*: **conspirer**, **plotter**, schemer, intriguer, colluder, collaborator, conniver, machinator, confederate, cabalist; traitor.

conspire verb 1 *all six admitted conspiring to steal cars | they were accused of conspiring against the king*: **plot**, hatch a plot, form a conspiracy, scheme, plan, lay plans, intrigue, collude, connive, collaborate, consort, machinate, manoeuvre, be/work hand in glove; abet, be an accessory; informal be in cahoots; rare cabal.
2 *circumstances have conspired to make an immediate share issue an unattractive option*: **act together**, work together, combine, join, unite, ally, join forces, cooperate; informal gang up; rare coact.

constancy noun 1 *a familiar meditation on the theme of constancy and inconstancy between lovers*: **fidelity**, faithfulness, loyalty, trueness, commitment, dedication, devotion; dependability, reliability, trustworthiness.
▷ANTONYMS fickleness.
2 *there was no doubt about the determination and constancy of Henry VIII*: **steadfastness**, resolution, resoluteness, resolve, firmness, fixedness, steadiness; determination, perseverance, tenacity, doggedness, staunchness, dedication, commitment, application, staying power, obstinacy.
▷ANTONYMS indecision.
3 *this anecdote reminds us of a certain constancy of human motive*: **consistency**, permanence, persistence; durability, endurance; uniformity, invariableness, unchangingness, immutability, regularity, evenness, stability, steadiness, lack of change, lack of deviation.
▷ANTONYMS unpredictableness.

constant adjective 1 *the constant background noise of the city*: **continual**, continuous, persistent, sustained, abiding, round-the-clock; ceaseless, unceasing, perpetual, incessant, never-ending, everlasting, eternal, endless, unending, unabating, non-stop, perennial, unbroken, uninterrupted, unrelieved; interminable, unremitting, relentless, unrelenting, without respite; literary sempiternal.
▷ANTONYMS inconstant, fitful.
2 *the disc revolves at a constant speed*: **consistent**, regular, stable, steady, fixed, uniform, even, level, invariable, unvarying, unchanging, changeless, undeviating, unfluctuating, immutable.
▷ANTONYMS inconstant, variable.
3 *a constant friend*: **faithful**, loyal, devoted, true, fast, firm, unswerving, unwavering; steadfast, staunch, stalwart, dependable, trustworthy, trusty, reliable, dedicated, committed; bosom, boon.
▷ANTONYMS inconstant, fickle.
4 *there is a need for constant vigilance*: **steadfast**, steady, resolute, determined, persevering, tenacious, dogged, unwavering, unflagging, unshaken.
▶ noun *dread of cancer has been a constant during the last 100 years*: **unchanging factor**, unchanging state of affairs, unchanging situation, given.

> *Choose the right word* **constant, continual, continuous, ceaseless**
>
> See **continual**.

> *Choose the right word* **constant, faithful, loyal, true**
>
> See **faithful**.

constantly adverb *the English language is constantly in flux*: **always**, all the time, the entire time, continually, continuously, persistently, repeatedly, regularly; round the clock, without a break, night and day, day and night, {morning, noon, and night}; endlessly, non-stop, incessantly, unceasingly, ceaselessly, perpetually, eternally, perennially, forever; interminably, unremittingly, relentlessly, unrelentingly; Scottish aye; informal 24-7; literary sempiternally.
▷ANTONYMS occasionally, sometimes.

consternation noun *much to the consternation of his detractors, he emerged as a management guru*: **dismay**, perturbation, anxiety, distress, disquiet, disquietude, discomposure, angst, trepidation; surprise, amazement, astonishment, stupefaction; alarm, panic, hysteria, fear, fearfulness, fright, shock.
▷ANTONYMS satisfaction.

constituent adjective *they are independent but constituent parts of their universities*: **component**, integral; elemental, basic, essential, inherent; rare integrant.
▶ noun 1 *MPs have a duty to listen to the concerns of their constituents*: **voter**, elector, member of the electorate, member of a constituency.
2 *the harmful constituents of tobacco smoke*: **component**, component part, ingredient, element; part, piece, bit, integral part, unit, module, fragment, section, segment, portion; rare integrant.

constitute verb 1 *farmers constituted 10 per cent of the population*: **amount to**, add up to, account for, form, make up, compose, comprise, represent.
2 *an extract from a book used for the purpose of comment does not constitute a breach of copyright*: **be equivalent to**, be the equivalent of, be, embody, be tantamount to, be regarded as, act as, serve as.
3 *the superior courts were constituted in 1875*: **inaugurate**, initiate, establish, found, create, set up, put in place, start, begin, originate, form, organize, develop, shape; authorize, commission, charter, induct, invest, appoint, name, nominate, install, empower, ordain, decree.

constitution noun 1 *the constitution guarantees freedom of expression*: **charter**, social code, canon, body of law, system of laws/rules; bill of rights; laws, rules, regulations, fundamental principles; informal regs.

2 *the chemical constitution of the dye*: **composition**, make-up, structure, organization, construction, arrangement, configuration, framework, form, formation, anatomy, shape, design; informal set-up.
3 *a woman with the constitution of an ox*: **health**, **physique**, state of health, physical condition, physical strength, shape, fettle.

constitutional adjective 1 *the Amir's constitutional powers*: **legal**, lawful, legitimate, licit, authorized, permitted, permissible; sanctioned, ratified, codified, warranted, constituted, statutory, chartered, vested, official; in accordance with the constitution, within the law, by law.
▷ANTONYMS unconstitutional.
2 *a constitutional weakness*: **inherent**, inbred, intrinsic, innate, structural, fundamental, essential; congenital, organic, inborn, ingrained, deep-rooted, built-in.
▷ANTONYMS cosmetic.
▶ noun *she went out for a constitutional*: **walk**, stroll, saunter, turn, wander, amble, breather, airing, ramble, hike; promenade; N. Amer. paseo; Italian passegiata; informal mosey, tootle; Brit. informal pootle; rare perambulation.

constrain verb 1 *Ernie felt constrained to explain further*: **compel**, force, coerce, drive, impel, oblige, prevail on, require; press, push, pressure, pressurize, urge, bully, dragoon, browbeat; informal railroad, bulldoze, steamroller, hustle, twist someone's arm, strong-arm, lean on, put the screws on.
2 *prices were constrained by continuing state controls*: **restrict**, limit, curb, check, restrain, regulate, contain, hold back, keep down.
3 *only by acting on the systems which constrain them can women hope to free themselves*: **confine**, restrain, restrict, impede, hamstring, baulk, frustrate, stifle, hinder, hamper, check, retard, cramp, rein in; shut in, hem in, fence in, close in, coop up, chain, lock up, imprison, incarcerate, intern; literary trammel.

constrained adjective *he was acting in an oddly constrained manner*: **unnatural**, awkward, self-conscious, mannered, artificial, wooden, stilted, strained, forced, contrived, laboured; inhibited, repressed, uneasy, embarrassed, tongue-tied; restrained, reserved, reticent, guarded, distant, aloof, cold, cool, stand-offish.
▷ANTONYMS relaxed.

constraint noun 1 *the availability of water is the main constraint on food production*: **restriction**, limitation, curb, check, restraint, control, curtailment, damper, rein; hindrance, impediment, hampering, obstruction, handicap.
2 *on Saturday they would be able to get together, relax, and talk without constraint*: **inhibition**, uneasiness, embarrassment; restraint, reservedness, reticence, guardedness, formality, stand-offishness; self-consciousness, awkwardness, forcedness, unnaturalness, woodenness, stiltedness.
▷ANTONYMS openness.

constrict verb 1 *fat constricts the blood vessels | Caroline felt her throat constrict*: **narrow**, make/become narrower, tighten, compress, contract, make/become smaller, shrink, draw in; squeeze, choke, strangle, strangulate; archaic straiten.
▷ANTONYMS expand, dilate.
2 *scale build-up on shower heads constricts water flow*: **impede**, restrict, inhibit, obstruct, limit, interfere with, hinder, hamper, check, curb.
▷ANTONYMS assist.

constriction noun *there was a constriction in her throat*: **tightening**, narrowing, shrinking, squeezing; tightness, pressure, compression, contraction, cramp; obstruction, blockage, impediment, congestion; choking, strangulation; Medicine stricture, stenosis; archaic straitening.

construct verb 1 *the government has plans to construct a hydroelectric dam there*: **build**, erect, put up, set up, raise, establish, assemble, manufacture, fabricate, form, fashion, contrive, create, make.
▷ANTONYMS demolish.
2 *his work aimed to construct a science of public law entirely on empirical foundation*: **formulate**, form, put together; create, devise, design, invent, compose, concoct, contrive, work out, hatch; fashion, mould, model, shape, frame; forge, engineer, fabricate, manufacture, hammer out, thrash out.

construction noun 1 *the construction of a new airport*: **building**, erection, putting up, setting up, raising, establishment, assembly, manufacture, fabrication, forming, fashioning, contriving, creation, making.
2 *the central waterway was a spectacular construction*: **structure**, building, edifice, assembly, pile, framework.
3 *many candidates have little idea of the basics of sentence construction*: **composition**, formation, structure, organization.
4 *I might have known you'd put such a sordid construction on it all*: **interpretation**, reading, meaning, explanation, inference, explication, construal, analysis, version, understanding, view, impression; informal take.

constructive adjective *he described the talks as fruitful and constructive*: **positive**, **useful**, of use, helpful, encouraging; productive, practical, valuable, profitable, worthwhile, effective, beneficial, advantageous.
▷ANTONYMS destructive, negative.

construe verb *his actions could be construed as an admission of guilt*: **interpret**, understand, read, see, take, take to mean, parse, render, analyse, explain, elucidate, gloss, decode.

consul noun *the British consul in Israel*: **ambassador**, diplomat, chargé d'affaires, attaché, envoy, emissary, plenipotentiary, consul general; archaic legate.

consult verb 1 *if you consult a solicitor, making a will is a simple procedure*: **ask**, seek advice/information from, take counsel from, call on/upon/in, turn to, have recourse to; informal pick someone's brains.
2 *there is a growing pressure on managers to consult with employees*: **confer**, discuss, talk, talk things over, have a talk, exchange views, have discussions, converse, communicate, parley; deliberate, debate, negotiate; informal chew the fat, powwow, have a confab, talk turkey, palaver, put their heads together; formal confabulate.
3 *she consulted a large desk diary*: **refer to**, turn to, look something up in.
4 *she needed to consult her feelings before acting*: **consider**, take into consideration/account, have regard to, respect, have an eye to.

consultant noun 1 *an education and training consultant*: **adviser**, guide, counsellor; **expert**, specialist, authority, pundit; informal ace, whizz, wizard, hotshot; N. Amer. informal maven.
2 *he's a consultant at the Queen Elizabeth hospital*: **senior doctor**, specialist.

consultation noun 1 *the recommendations include increased consultation with local people*: **discussion**, dialogue, discourse, debate, negotiation, conference, deliberation.
2 *if it is a matter of urgency a consultation can be arranged quickly*: **meeting**, talk, discussion, interview, conference, audience, hearing, reception, forum; chat, tête-à-tête, parley, heart-to-heart, one-to-one, colloquy; appointment, session, engagement; informal powwow, confab; formal confabulation.

consume verb 1 *great plates of cakes were consumed with gusto | he had consumed nine pints of beer*: **eat**, eat up, devour, ingest, swallow, gobble, gobble up, wolf down, gorge oneself on, feast on; munch, snack on; **drink**, drink up, guzzle, gulp (down), swill, imbibe, take, sup, sip, lap; informal tuck into, scoff (down), put away, stuff down, polish off, dispose of, cram in, stuff one's face with, pig oneself on, graze on, down, neck, sink, kill, get one's laughing gear round; Brit. informal gollop, shift; N. Amer. informal scarf (down/up), snarf (down/up); formal manducate; rare ingurgitate.
2 *these factories consumed 600,000 tons of coal a day*: **use**, use up, utilize, expend; deplete, exhaust; waste, squander, go through, drain, dissipate, fritter away, swallow up.
3 *the fire consumed fifty houses in four hours*: **destroy**, demolish, lay waste, wipe out, annihilate, devastate; raze, gut, ravage, ruin, wreck.
4 *Carolyn was consumed with guilt*: **absorb**, preoccupy, engross; eat up, devour, obsess, grip, overwhelm, monopolize, enthral, dominate.

consumer noun *at the moment the consumer is not prepared to pay higher prices for organically farmed food*: **purchaser**, buyer, customer, shopper; user, end-user; client, patron; (**the consumer** or **consumers**) the public, the market, the clientele.

consuming adjective *his lifetime's consuming interest*: **absorbing**, compelling, preoccupying, engrossing, all-consuming, compulsive, besetting; devouring, obsessive, gripping, overwhelming, enthralling, dominating; intense, ardent, strong, powerful, burning, raging, fervid, profound, deep-seated.

consummate verb *they consummated the deal aboard his yacht*: **complete**, conclude, finish, accomplish, achieve; execute, carry out, discharge, perform, put into effect; put the finishing touch to, perfect, crown, cap, set the seal on; rare effectuate.
▶ adjective *he conducted his strategy with consummate skill*: **perfect**, **exemplary**, supreme, ultimate, faultless, quintessential; superb, superior, accomplished, expert, proficient, skilful, skilled, masterly, master, superlative, first-class; talented, gifted, polished, well versed, well trained, practised; complete, total, utter, absolute, pure, solid, sheer.

Word toolkit **consummate**

See **archetypal**.

consummation noun *the consummation of a takeover bid*: **completion**, accomplishment, achievement, attainment; execution, carrying out, discharge, performance; conclusion, realization, resolution, finalization, finishing, ending, fulfilment, effectuation, fruition, success; crowning, capping, perfecting, perfection.

consumption noun 1 *the fish were declared unfit for human consumption*: **eating**, devouring, ingestion, swallowing, gobbling (up); drinking, imbibing; formal manducation.
2 *the consumption of fossil fuels*: **using up**, use, utilization, expending, expenditure; depletion, exhaustion; waste, wasting, squander, squandering, draining, dissipation, dissipating.
3 archaic *his mother had died of consumption*: **tuberculosis**, pulmonary tuberculosis, TB, wasting disease, emaciation; archaic phthisis.

contact noun 1 *the disease can be transmitted through direct contact with rats*: **touch**, touching; proximity, exposure, contiguity, junction, union, tangency; association, connection, communication, intercourse, relations, dealings; archaic traffic.

2 *she was still in contact with her friends*: **communication**, connection, correspondence, touch, association.
3 *he had many contacts in Germany*: **connection**, acquaintance, associate, liaison, friend.
▸ **verb** *anyone with any information should contact the police*: **get in touch with**, communicate with, make contact with, approach, reach, notify, be in communication with; phone, call, ring up, speak to, talk to, write to; Brit. get on to; informal get hold of, drop a line to.

C

contagion noun *overcrowded and insanitary ships were a breeding ground for every kind of contagion*: **contamination**, infection, disease, illness, infirmity, pestilence, plague, blight; informal bug, virus.

contagious adjective *a contagious disease*: **infectious**, communicable, transmittable, transmissible, transferable, spreadable; informal catching; technical epidemic, pandemic, epizootic; dated infective.

contain verb 1 *government often contained men from both sides of the party divide*: **include**, comprise, take in, incorporate, involve, encompass, embrace, embody; consist of, be made up, be composed of.
2 *the boat contained four people*: **hold**, have room/space/seating/capacity for, carry, accommodate, seat.
3 *he must contain his hatred*: **restrain**, curb, rein in, suppress, repress, stifle, subdue, quell, limit, swallow, bottle up, keep under control, keep back, hold in, keep in check; control, master, gain control over, gain mastery over.

container noun *an airtight container*: **receptacle**, vessel, holder, repository, canister, drum, box, case.

contaminate verb *the water supply was contaminated with manure*: **pollute**, adulterate; make impure, defile, debase, corrupt, taint, infect, blight, foul, spoil, soil, mar, impair, stain, befoul; sully, tarnish; poison; radioactivate; formal vitiate.
▷ANTONYMS purify.

contemn verb archaic *would he contemn her for forwardness?* **despise**, scorn, treat with contempt, feel contempt for, look down on, disdain, slight, undervalue, disregard, deride, scoff/jeer at, mock, revile, spurn.
▷ANTONYMS value.

contemplate verb 1 *she contemplated her body in the mirror*: **look at**, view, regard, examine, inspect, observe, survey, study, scrutinize, scan, stare at, gaze at, eye, take a good look at; literary behold.
2 *she couldn't even contemplate the future*: **think about**, meditate on/over, consider, ponder, reflect on/about, mull over, muse on, dwell on, deliberate over, cogitate on/about, ruminate on/about, chew over, brood on/about, puzzle over, turn over in one's mind, weigh up.
3 *she contemplated walking out*: **consider**, think about, give thought to; have in mind/view, envisage, aim at, foresee, imagine, visualize; intend, propose, mean to, expect to.

contemplation noun 1 *the contemplation of beautiful objects*: **viewing**, regarding, examination, inspection, observation, survey, study, scrutiny, scanning, staring at, gazing at, eyeing.
2 *the monks sat in quiet contemplation*: **thought**, meditation, consideration, pondering, reflection, thinking, musing, rumination, deliberation, cogitation, reverie, concentration, introspection; informal brown study; formal cerebration.

contemplative adjective *a peaceful, contemplative mood*: **thoughtful**, pensive, reflective, meditative, musing, ruminative, introspective, brooding, intent, rapt, preoccupied, studious, deep/lost in thought; dreamy, daydreaming, with one's head in the clouds; informal in a brown study.
▷ANTONYMS active.

contemporary adjective 1 *contemporary writing says that the city's walls were formidable*: **contemporaneous**, concurrent, coeval, synchronous, synchronic, of the time, of the day, simultaneous; coexisting, coexistent; rare coetaneous.
2 *crime and violence in contemporary society*: **modern**, present-day, present, current, present-time, immediate, extant; up to date, up to the minute, fashionable, latest, recent, ultra-modern, newfangled, modish, voguish, in vogue; French à la mode; informal bang up to date, with it.
▷ANTONYMS old-fashioned, out of date.
▸ **noun** *the contemporaries of Chaucer*: **peer**, fellow; rare compeer, coeval.

> *Word toolkit* **contemporary**
>
> See **new**.

contempt noun 1 *she was showing little but contempt for him*: **scorn**, disdain, disrespect, deprecation, disparagement, denigration, opprobrium, odium, obloquy, scornfulness; derision, mockery, ridicule; disgust, loathing, detestation, abhorrence, hatred; archaic contumely.
▷ANTONYMS respect.
2 *he is guilty of contempt of court*: **disrespect**, disregard, slighting, neglect; Law contumacy.
▷ANTONYMS respect.

contemptible adjective *that jibe about Alison was mean and contemptible*: **despicable**, detestable, hateful, reprehensible, deplorable, loathsome, odious, revolting, execrable, unspeakable, heinous, shocking, offensive; disgraceful, shameful, ignominious, abject, low, mean, cowardly, unworthy, discreditable, pitiful, pitiable, petty, worthless, shabby, cheap, beyond contempt, beyond the pale, sordid, degenerate, base, vile, villainous; archaic scurvy.
▷ANTONYMS admirable.

contemptuous adjective *he spoke in a coldly contemptuous tone*: **scornful**, disdainful, disrespectful, insulting, insolent, full of contempt; derisory, derisive, mocking, sneering, jeering, scoffing, taunting, withering, scathing, snide; condescending, supercilious, arrogant, cavalier, high and mighty, imperious, proud, vain; informal sniffy, snotty, on one's high horse; archaic contumelious.
▷ANTONYMS respectful.

> *Word toolkit* **contemptuous**
>
> See **dismissive**.

contend verb 1 *none of the groups contending for power is strong enough yet*: **compete**, challenge, vie, contest; strive, struggle, tussle, grapple, wrestle, scuffle, squabble, skirmish, battle, combat, fight, war, wage war, join battle, cross swords, lock horns, go head to head; oppose, clash.
2 *the plaintiffs contended that their business plan was confidential*: **assert**, maintain, hold, claim, argue, profess, affirm, aver, avow, insist, state, declare, pronounce, allege, plead.
□ **contend with** *the peasants had to contend with lack of food and primitive living conditions*: **cope with**, face, grapple with, deal with, take on, pit oneself against; resist, withstand.

content[1] (stress on the second syllable) adjective *she seemed content with her lot in life*: **contented**, satisfied, pleased; gratified, fulfilled; happy, cheerful, cheery, glad, delighted; tranquil, unworried, untroubled, at ease, at peace, comfortable, serene, placid, complacent.
▷ANTONYMS discontented, dissatisfied.
▸ **verb** *her reply seemed to content him*: **soothe**, pacify, placate, appease, please, mollify, make happy, satisfy, still, quieten, silence.
□ **content oneself** *too confused to argue, she contented herself with a nod*: **be content**, be satisfied, satisfy oneself; be fulfilled, be gratified, be pleased, be happy, be glad.
▸ **noun** *she stood for a moment looking with content at her husband*. See **contentment**.

content[2] (stress on the first syllable) noun 1 *many restaurant meals are low in fibre content*: **amount**, **proportion**, quantity, bulk, total, quota; rare quantum.
2 *just as the novel's form is radical, so too is its content*: **subject matter**, subject, theme, burden, gist, argument, thesis, message, point, thrust, substance, matter, material, text, ideas.
▷ANTONYMS style.
3 (**contents**) *she went to examine the contents of the hamper*: **things inside**, content, load; informal guts, innards.
4 (**contents**) *the book's list of contents | he picked up the letter and scanned its contents*: **chapters**, sections, divisions; **subject matter**, subjects, themes, matter, substance, material, text; index; constituents, components, ingredients, elements, items.

contented adjective *he was contented with his job on the newspaper*. See **content**[1].

contention noun 1 *there were a number of points of contention between the Crown and Parliament*: **disagreement**, dispute, disputation, argument, variance; discord, hostility, conflict, friction, acrimony, enmity, strife, dissension, disharmony, quarrelling, feuding.
▷ANTONYMS agreement.
2 *her contention is that this event was the result of a conspiracy*: **argument**, claim, plea, submission, allegation; opinion, stand, position, view, belief, thesis, hypothesis, case, postulation; declaration, assertion, affirmation, pronouncement, announcement, statement.
□ **in contention** *he is in contention for a first-team place*: **in competition**, competing, contesting, contending, challenging, vying; striving, struggling, tussling, grappling, battling, fighting, warring.

contentious adjective 1 *the contentious issue of abortion*: **controversial**, disputable, debatable, disputed, contended, open to question/debate, moot, vexed; ambivalent, equivocal, unsure, uncertain, unresolved, undecided, unsettled, borderline; rare controvertible.
2 *a contentious debate*: **heated**, vehement, fierce, violent, intense, impassioned, committed.
3 *contentious people*. See **quarrelsome**.

contentment noun *he found contentment in living a basic life*: **contentedness**, content, satisfaction, fulfilment; happiness, pleasure, cheerfulness, gladness, gratification; ease, comfort, restfulness, well-being, peace, equanimity, serenity, tranquillity, placidity, placidness, repletion, complacency; archaic self-content.

contest noun (stress on the first syllable) 1 *a boxing contest*: **competition**, match, tournament, game, meet; event, trial, bout, heat, fixture, tie, race.
2 *a leadership contest*: **struggle**, conflict, confrontation, collision, clash,

battle, fight, combat, tussle, skirmish, duel, race.
▸ verb (stress on the second syllable) **1** *he made known his intention to contest the seat*: **compete for**, contend for, vie for, challenge for, fight for, fight over, battle for, struggle for, tussle for; try to win, try for, go for, throw one's hat in the ring.
2 *the elections were contested by fifteen parties*: **compete in**, contend in, fight in, battle in, enter, take part in, be a competitor in, participate in, put one's name down for, go in for.
3 *we contested the decision vigorously*: **oppose**, object to, challenge, dispute, take a stand against, resist, defy, strive/struggle against, take issue with; question, call into question, doubt; litigate.
▷ANTONYMS agree with.
4 *those conclusions which are not based on published research need to be contested*: **debate**, argue about, dispute, quarrel over.

contestant noun **competitor**, participant, player, contender, candidate, aspirant, entrant; rival, opponent, adversary, antagonist.

context noun **1** *the historical context out of which the novel arose*: **circumstances**, conditions, surroundings, factors, state of affairs; situation, environment, milieu, setting, background, backdrop, scene; climate, atmosphere, ambience, mood, feel.
2 *the quote taken out of context trivializes a dreadful crime*: **frame of reference**, contextual relationship; text, subject, theme, topic.

contiguous adjective *the contiguous states of New Mexico, Arizona, Texas, and California*: **adjacent**, neighbouring, adjoining, bordering, next-door; abutting, joining, connecting, meeting, touching, in contact, proximate; near, nearby, close; rare conterminous, vicinal.
▷ANTONYMS distant.

continent noun *the continent of Europe*: **mainland**.
▷ANTONYMS island.

contingency noun *a detailed contract which attempts to provide for all possible contingencies*: **eventuality**, (chance) event, incident, happening, occurrence, juncture, possibility, accident, chance, emergency; uncertainty; rare fortuity.

contingent adjective **1** *resolution of the conflict was* ***contingent on*** *the signing of a ceasefire*: **dependent**, conditional; subject to, based on, determined by, hingeing on, resting on, hanging on, controlled by.
2 *contingent events*: **chance**, accidental, fortuitous, possible, unforeseen, unforeseeable, unexpected, unpredicted, unpredictable, unanticipated, unlooked-for; random, haphazard.
▷ANTONYMS predictable.
▸ noun *a contingent of Japanese businessmen | a contingent of 2,000 marines*: **group**, party, body, band, set; deputation, delegation, mission; detachment, unit, division, squadron, section, company, corps, cohort; informal bunch, gang.

continual adjective **1** *the service has been disrupted by continual breakdowns*: **repeated**, **frequent**, recurrent, recurring, oft repeated, regular; constant, persistent, non-stop; informal more ... than one can shake a stick at.
▷ANTONYMS occasional, sporadic.
2 *his son was a continual source of delight to him | she was in continual pain*: **constant**, continuous, endless, unending, never-ending, perpetual, perennial, eternal, everlasting; **ceaseless**, incessant, unceasing, sustained, ongoing, uninterrupted, unbroken, round-the-clock, unremitting, unabating, relentless, unrelenting, unrelieved, chronic, interminable.
▷ANTONYMS temporary, momentary.

Choose the right word **continual, continuous, constant, ceaseless**

These words describe processes or situations which do not stop, but with different emphases.

Continual mainly describes an event that happens repeatedly, on successive occasions (*I regret that we hear continual criticisms of the committee*). However, it can also be used of a process or situation that never actually stops (*he was in continual pain*).

Continuous predominantly describes a non-stop process or situation (*fighting was continuous, both night and day*), but it can also refer to a series of occasions (*the bus service has been interrupted by continuous breakdowns*). It can also describe a physically unbroken object or line (*each farm was separated from its neighbour by a continuous stone wall*).

Constant describes not only something that does not stop (*a welcome relief from the constant travelling*), but also something that does not vary over time (*it is preferable to store samples at a controlled constant temperature*).

Ceaseless is a more literary word describing, typically, something bad that does not stop (*the fort had been subjected to ceaseless bombardment*).

All these words are used almost interchangeably when it is difficult or unnecessary to say whether something does, technically, happen repeatedly or without stopping at all, as with a *process*, *supply*, or *flow*, or with *change*, *need*, *improvement*, *growth*, or *use*.

continually adverb **1** *security measures are continually updated and improved*: **frequently**, regularly, repeatedly, recurrently, again and again, time and (time) again; constantly.
▷ANTONYMS occasionally, sporadically.
2 *patients were continually monitored*: **constantly**, continuously, round the clock, day and night, night and day, {morning, noon, and night}, without a break, non-stop; all the time, the entire time, always, forever, at every turn, incessantly, ceaselessly, endlessly, perpetually, eternally; N. Amer. informal 24–7.

continuance noun **1** *the continuance of the negotiations*: **continuation**, carrying on, prolongation, protraction; maintenance, preservation, keeping up, perpetuation.
2 *the trademarks shall be used only during the continuance of this agreement*: **duration**, period, term.

continuation noun **1** *the continuation of discussions | the continuation of old traditions*: **carrying on**, continuance, prolongation, protraction; maintenance, preservation, keeping up, perpetuation.
▷ANTONYMS end, cessation.
2 *he was avoiding any prospect of the continuation of the conversation begun that morning*: **resumption**, reopening, restart, renewal; formal recommencement.
3 *once a separate village, it is now a continuation of the suburbs*: **extension**, addition.

continue verb **1** *the government* ***continued with*** *its plans to reorganize the country's economy*: **carry on with**, go on with, keep on with, proceed with, pursue; **persist in/with**, press on with, persevere in/with, keep up, keep at, push on with, not stop, not give up, stay with; informal stick with/at, soldier on with, stick to one's guns.
▷ANTONYMS stop, discontinue, abandon.
2 *discussions continued throughout the year*: **go on**, carry on, extend, run on, drag on; keep up, hold, prevail, subsist.
▷ANTONYMS stop, cease.
3 *both are keen to continue their business relationship*: **maintain**, keep up, sustain, keep going, keep alive, preserve, prolong, extend, protract, perpetuate; retain.
▷ANTONYMS break off, suspend.
4 *their friendship continued for many years*: **last**, endure, go on, be prolonged, live on, survive; abide.
5 *they have indicated their willingness to continue in office*: **remain**, stay, carry on, keep going.
6 *we can continue our conversation after supper*: **resume**, pick up, take up, carry on with, return to, start/begin again; pick up the threads, pick up where one left off; formal recommence.
▷ANTONYMS end.

continuing adjective *a background of continuing civil war*: **ongoing**, continuous, sustained, persistent, steady, relentless, uninterrupted, unabating, unremitting, unrelieved, unrelenting, unceasing.
▷ANTONYMS sporadic.

continuity noun **1** *a breakdown in the continuity of care*: **continuousness**, uninterruptedness, flow, progression.
▷ANTONYMS discontinuity.
2 *the thematic continuity of the texts*: **interrelationship**, interrelatedness, intertextuality, interconnectedness, connection, linkage, cohesion, coherence; unity, whole, wholeness.

continuous adjective *for the past few days there had been continuous rain*: **continual**, uninterrupted, unbroken, constant, ceaseless, incessant, steady, sustained, solid, continuing, ongoing, unceasing, without a break, permanent, non-stop, round-the-clock, persistent, unremitting, relentless, unrelenting, unabating, unrelieved, without respite, endless, unending, never-ending, perpetual, without end, everlasting, eternal, interminable; consecutive, running; informal with no let-up; archaic without surcease.
▷ANTONYMS intermittent, sporadic.

Choose the right word **continuous, continual, constant, ceaseless**

See **continual**.

contort verb **1** *her face was contorted with terrible grief*: **twist**, screw up, distort; rare quirk.
2 *chunks of contorted metal*: **twist**, wrench/bend out of shape, misshape, warp, buckle, deform; N. Amer. pretzel.

contour noun *the perfect contours of her body*: **outline**, **shape**, form; lines, curves, figure; silhouette, profile; rare lineation.

contraband noun *the salt trade (and contraband in it) were very active in the town*: **smuggling**, illegal traffic, black marketeering, trafficking, bootlegging; the black market.
▸ adjective *contraband goods*: **smuggled**, black-market, bootleg, bootlegged, under the counter, illegal, illicit, unlawful; prohibited, banned, proscribed, forbidden, interdicted; informal hot.

contract noun (stress on the first syllable) *a legally binding contract*: **agreement**, commitment, arrangement, settlement, undertaking,

understanding, compact, covenant, pact, bond; deal, bargain; treaty, concordat, convention, entente; Commerce account; Law indenture; rare engagement.
▶ **verb** (stress on the second syllable) **1** *glass, like other substances, contracts as it cools | the market for such goods began to contract*: **shrink**, get smaller, become smaller; decrease, diminish, reduce, dwindle, decline, shrivel.
▷ANTONYMS expand; increase.
2 *her stomach muscles contracted | the exercises contract the knee muscles*: **tighten**, become/make tighter, tense, flex, constrict, draw in, become/make narrower, narrow.
▷ANTONYMS relax.
3 *Mrs Thornton contracted her brow*: **wrinkle**, knit, crease, corrugate; purse, pucker.
4 *the name 'Jacquenard' was soon contracted to 'Jack' in English*: **shorten**, abbreviate, cut, reduce, abridge, truncate.
▷ANTONYMS expand, lengthen.
5 *the company contracted to purchase 390 acres of forest*: **undertake**, pledge, promise, covenant, commit oneself, engage; agree, enter into an agreement, reach an agreement, make a deal, negotiate a deal.
6 *she contracted German measles*: **develop**, **catch**, get, pick up, come down with, become infected with, fall ill with, be taken ill with, be struck down with, be stricken with, succumb to; Brit. go down with; informal take ill with; N. Amer. informal take sick with.
7 *he contracted a debt of £3,300*: **incur**, become liable to pay, acquire, fall into; run up.
□ **contract out** *if you do not wish to be a member of the pension fund you must contract out*: **opt out**, leave, exclude oneself, withdraw, pull out, exit.
□ **contract something out** *local authorities will have to contract out waste management*: **subcontract**, outsource, farm out, assign to others.

contraction noun **1** *the contraction of industry*: **shrinking**, reduction in size, shrinkage; decline, decrease, diminution, dwindling.
▷ANTONYMS expansion, growth.
2 *neurons control the contraction of muscles | intestinal contractions*: **tightening**, tensing, flexing, constricting; spasm, convulsion, clench; Medicine myoclonus, hippus.
▷ANTONYMS relaxation.
3 *her contractions started just after midnight*: **labour pains**, labour; Braxton Hicks contractions; cramps; archaic travail.
4 *'goodbye' is a contraction of 'God be with you'*: **abbreviation**, short form, shortened form, elision; diminutive; technical crasis, syneresis.
▷ANTONYMS expansion.

contradict verb **1** *this statement was contradicted by the foreign minister*: **deny**, refute, rebut, dispute, counter; say the opposite of; formal gainsay; rare controvert, confute, negative.
▷ANTONYMS confirm, verify, agree with.
2 *nobody dared to contradict him*: **challenge**, **oppose**, argue against, go against, be at variance with; formal gainsay, impugn.
3 *this research contradicts computer models which predict a warmer, wetter world*: **conflict with**, be at odds with, be at variance with, disagree with, be inconsistent with, clash with, run counter to, give the lie to, belie; negate; informal fly in the face of, make a nonsense of, shoot full of holes, drive a coach and horses through.
▷ANTONYMS corroborate, support.

contradiction noun **1** *the profound contradiction between the economic and the social policies pursued by the government*: **conflict**, clash, disagreement, opposition, inconsistency, lack of congruence, incongruity, incongruousness, mismatch, variance; paradox, contradiction in terms; rare antinomy, aporia, antilogy.
▷ANTONYMS agreement.
2 *the second sentence appears to be a flat contradiction of the first*: **denial**, refutation, rebuttal, countering, counterstatement, opposite; negation; formal gainsaying; rare confutation.
▷ANTONYMS confirmation, reaffirmation.

contradictory adjective *the two attitudes are contradictory*: **opposed**, in opposition, opposite, antithetical, contrary, contrasting, conflicting, at variance, at odds, opposing, clashing, divergent, discrepant, different; **inconsistent**, incompatible, irreconcilable, incongruous; paradoxical; rare oppugnant, repugnant.
▷ANTONYMS consistent, compatible.

contraption noun *a newfangled contraption for making coffee*: **device**, **gadget**, apparatus, machine, appliance, mechanism, implement, utensil, invention, contrivance; Brit. Heath Robinson device; N. Amer. Rube Goldberg device; informal gizmo, widget, thingamajig, thingamabob, whatsit; Brit. informal doodah, doobry, gubbins; N. Amer. informal dingus, doodad, doojigger, doohickey; Austral. informal bitzer.

contrary adjective **1** (stress on the first syllable) *right-wing commentators expressed the contrary view*: **opposite**, opposing, opposed, contradictory, clashing, conflicting, antithetical, incompatible, irreconcilable; different, differing, contrasting, inconsistent, incongruous; reverse, counter; rare oppugnant, antipathic.
▷ANTONYMS compatible, same.
2 (stress on the second syllable) *'I don't know why you have to be so contrary,' she snapped*: **perverse**, awkward, difficult, uncooperative, unhelpful, obstructive, disobliging, unaccommodating, unreasonable, troublesome, tiresome, annoying, vexatious, disobedient, recalcitrant, refractory, wilful, headstrong, self-willed, capricious, wayward, cross-grained; stubborn, obstinate, obdurate, mulish, pig-headed, bull-headed, intractable; Scottish thrawn; informal cussed; Brit. informal bloody-minded, bolshie, stroppy; N. Amer. informal balky; archaic froward, contumacious; rare renitent, pervicacious, contrarious.
▷ANTONYMS accommodating, cooperative, obliging.
□ **contrary to** *the court ruled that the restrictions were contrary to the public interest*: **in conflict with**, against, at variance with, at odds with, in opposition to, not in accord with, counter to, conflicting with, incompatible with; rare repugnant.
▶ **noun** *in fact, the contrary is true*: **opposite**, reverse, converse, antithesis; technical contrariety.
□ **on the contrary** *there was no malice in her; on the contrary, she was very kind*: **conversely**, in contrast, quite/just the opposite, quite/just the reverse; rather, instead.

contrast noun (stress on the first syllable) **1** *the marked contrast between English and Scottish practice*: **difference**, dissimilarity, disparity, dissimilitude, distinction, contradistinction, divergence, variance, variation, differentiation; contradiction, incongruity, opposition, polarity; rare unlikeness.
▷ANTONYMS similarity, resemblance.
2 *vivacious and highly intelligent, Jane was a complete contrast to Sarah*: **opposite**, antithesis; foil, complement.
□ **by contrast 1** *by contrast, Anderson rejects this view*: **conversely**, in contrast, on the other hand; however. **2 by contrast with** *Crowe's ruddiness, Anthea looked pale*: **compared to/with**, next to, against, beside.
▶ **verb** (stress on the second syllable) **1** *this view **contrasts with** his earlier opinion*: **differ from**, be at variance with, be contrary to, conflict with, go against, be at odds with, be in opposition to, disagree with, clash with.
▷ANTONYMS resemble, echo.
2 *a dress of burnt sienna which **contrasted with** her pale gold hair*: **set off**, complement; clash with; informal scream at.
▷ANTONYMS match.
3 *people **contrasted** her **with** her sister*: **compare**, set side by side, juxtapose; measure against; distinguish from, differentiate from, draw a distinction between.
▷ANTONYMS liken.

contravene verb **1** *certain members of his administration had contravened the law*: **break**, breach, fail to comply with, fail to observe, violate, infringe, offend against, transgress against; defy, disobey, flout; Law infract.
▷ANTONYMS uphold, comply with.
2 *the Privy Council held that the prosecution contravened the rights of the individual*: **conflict with**, be in conflict with, be at odds with, be at variance with, be in opposition to, clash with, run counter to, be inconsistent with, be contrary to.

contravention noun *a **contravention of** EC regulations*: **breach**, violation, infringement, non-observance, breaking, transgression, neglect, dereliction; failure to observe, non-compliance with, departure from; Law infraction, delict.

contretemps noun **1** *her little contretemps with Terry*: **argument**, quarrel, squabble, altercation, clash, fight; **disagreement**, difference of opinion, dispute, dissension; informal tiff, set-to, run-in, spat; Brit. informal row, barney; Scottish informal rammy.
2 *there was one last contretemps before the end of the night*: **mishap**, misadventure, accident, mischance, unfortunate occurrence, awkward moment; problem, difficulty.

contribute verb **1** *the government contributed a million pounds to the fund*: **give**, donate, give/make a donation of, put up, come up with, subscribe, hand out, grant, bestow, present, gift, accord; provide, supply, furnish; informal chip in, pitch in, fork out, dish out, shell out, cough up; Brit. informal stump up; N. Amer. informal kick in, ante up, pony up.
2 *the colour scheme contributes a pervading sense of calm and peacefulness to the room*: **impart**, lend, add, give, confer.
3 *evidence suggests that a minimum wage would **contribute to** economic recovery*: **play a part in**, be instrumental in, be a factor in, be partly responsible for, have a hand in, be conducive to, make for, lead to, cause, give rise to; help, promote, advance, further, forward, oil the wheels of, open the door for, add to; formal conduce to.
▷ANTONYMS stand in the way of.

contribution noun **1** *the agency is financed mainly from voluntary contributions*: **donation**, gift, benefaction, offering, present, handout; subscription; grant, subsidy, allowance; bequest, endowment; historical alms; rare donative.
2 *local historians requested contributions for a forthcoming book on the area's history*: **article**, piece, story, item, chapter, paper, essay, a few paragraphs, a few words; (**contributions**) text, reading matter.
3 *her **contribution to** the discussion had been negligible*: **input into**, participation in, involvement in; informal one's pennyworth.

contributor noun **1** *one of the magazine's regular contributors*: **writer**, feature writer, columnist, correspondent, reporter, journalist, penman; critic, reviewer; freelancer, freelance; informal journo, pen-pusher, hack, hackette, scribbler.
2 *influential campaign contributors*: **donor**, benefactor, benefactress, giver, subscriber; supporter, backer, subsidizer, patron, sponsor; philanthropist; informal angel; rare benefactrice, benefactrix, philanthrope.

contrite adjective *he looked so contrite that she relented*: **remorseful**, repentant, penitent, regretful, full of regret, sorry, apologetic, self-reproachful, rueful, sheepish, hangdog; ashamed, chastened, shamefaced, conscience-stricken, guilt-ridden, in sackcloth and ashes; rare compunctious.
▷ANTONYMS unrepentant, defiant.

Word toolkit **contrite**

See **apologetic**.

contrition noun *his eyes were full of contrition*: **remorse**, remorsefulness, repentance, penitence, sorrow, sorrowfulness, regret, contriteness, ruefulness, pangs of conscience, prickings of conscience; shame, guilt, self-reproach, self-condemnation, compunction; archaic rue; rare sorriness.

contrivance noun **1** *a mechanical contrivance*: **device**, **gadget**, machine, appliance, contraption, apparatus, mechanism, implement, tool, labour-saving device, invention; informal gizmo, mod con, widget, thingamajig, thingamabob, whatsit; Brit. informal doodah, doobry, gubbins; N. Amer. informal dingus, doodad, doojigger, doohickey; Austral. informal bitzer.
2 *her matchmaking contrivances*: **scheme**, stratagem, tactic, manoeuvre, move, course/line of action, plan, ploy, gambit, device, wile; trick, ruse, plot, machination, subterfuge, artifice, expedient; Brit. informal wheeze; Austral. informal lurk; archaic shift, fetch.

contrive verb **1** *his opponents contrived a cabinet crisis | they contrived a plan*: **bring about**, engineer, cause to happen, manufacture, orchestrate, stage-manage, create; **devise**, concoct, construct, design, formulate, plan, work out, think up, dream up, come up with, fabricate, plot, hatch; informal wangle, set up, cook up; Law procure.
2 *Lomax **contrived to** bump into him as he left the house*: **manage**, find a way, engineer a way, arrange; succeed in; informal work it, swing it; archaic compass.

contrived adjective *David replied with contrived joviality | the ending of the novel is too contrived to be convincing*: **forced**, strained, studied, artificial, affected, put-on, pretended, false, feigned, manufactured, unnatural, non-spontaneous; laboured, overdone, elaborate; far-fetched; N. Amer. informal hokey; rare voulu.
▷ANTONYMS natural, spontaneous.

control noun **1** *the Dutch retained control over the western half of New Guinea | the whole operation is under the control of a production manager*: **jurisdiction**, sway, power, authority, command, dominance, domination, government, mastery, leadership, rule, reign, sovereignty, supremacy, ascendancy, predominance; charge, management, direction, guidance, supervision, superintendence, oversight; influence; rare prepotence, prepotency, prepollency.
2 *strict import controls*: **restraint**, **constraint**, limitation, restriction, check, curb, brake, rein; regulation.
3 *'How could you?' she yelled, her control slipping*: **self-control**, self-restraint, restraint, self-command, self-mastery, self-discipline; self-possession, composure, calmness, coolness; informal cool; rare countenance.
4 *the volume control | easy-to-use controls*: **switch**, **knob**, button, dial, handle, lever; (**controls**) console, instrument panel, dashboard; informal dash.
5 *mission control*: **headquarters**, HQ, base, centre of operations, command post.
6 *another Petri dish without the DNA solution was used as a control*: **standard of comparison**, benchmark, standard, check.
□ **out of control** *the world is increasingly out of control*: **uncontrollable**, unmanageable, ungovernable, wild, unruly, disorderly, recalcitrant, refractory, obstreperous, turbulent, intractable, incorrigible, disobedient, delinquent, insubordinate, defiant, non-compliant, undisciplined; Brit. informal stroppy, bolshie; archaic contumacious.
▷ANTONYMS under control, obedient, compliant.
▶verb **1** *one family had controlled the company since its formation | the entire country was strictly controlled by the government*: **be in charge of**, **run**, be in control of, manage, direct, administer, head, preside over, have authority over, supervise, superintend, oversee, guide, steer; command, rule, govern, lead, dominate, reign over, hold sway over, be at the helm, be the boss; informal head up, call the shots, call the tune, be in the driving seat, be in the saddle, run the show, pull the strings, rule the roost, hold the purse strings, have someone/something in the palm of one's hand, have someone eating out of one's hand; Brit. informal wear the trousers; N. Amer. have someone in one's hip pocket.
2 *she struggled to control her temper*: **restrain**, keep in check, curb, check, contain, hold back, bridle, rein in, keep a tight rein on, subdue, suppress, repress, master, damp down; informal keep a/the lid on.
3 *public spending was controlled*: **limit**, **restrict**, set/impose limits on, curb, cap, constrain; informal put the brakes on.
4 *the extractor fan is controlled by a thermostat | all these processes are controlled by genes*: **regulate**, modulate, adjust; affect, determine, govern.

controversial adjective *controversial issues such as abortion and hanging*: **contentious**, disputed, contended, at issue, moot, disputable, debatable, arguable, vexed, open to discussion/question, under discussion; tendentious; emotive, sensitive, delicate, difficult, awkward, problematic; rare controvertible.
▷ANTONYMS uncontroversial, anodyne.

controversy noun *he refused to be drawn into the political controversy | a major controversy in education*: **disagreement**, dispute, argument, debate, dissension, contention, disputation, altercation, wrangle, quarrel, squabble, war of words, storm; wrangling, quarrelling, squabbling, bickering; polemic; French cause célèbre; Brit. informal row; rare velitation.
▷ANTONYMS agreement, accord.

contumely noun archaic **abuse**, insults, slurs, aspersions, derision, invective, slander, defamation, denigration, disparagement, opprobrium, obloquy, vituperation, vilification; **insolence**, rudeness, impertinence, discourtesy; informal mud-slinging, bad-mouthing, bitchiness; archaic malapertness, billingsgate.
▷ANTONYMS compliments, flattery.

contusion noun See **bruise** (noun).

conundrum noun **1** *some of the conundrums facing policy-makers in the 1980s*: **problem**, difficult question, vexed question, difficulty, quandary, dilemma; puzzle, enigma, mystery; informal poser, facer, stumper, cruncher.
2 *Roderick enjoyed conundrums and crosswords*: **riddle**, puzzle, word game, anagram; informal brain-teaser, brain-twister.

convalesce verb *he went abroad to convalesce*: **recuperate**, get better, recover, get well, regain one's strength/health, get back on one's feet, get over something, get back to normal; be on the road to recovery, be on the mend, improve.
▷ANTONYMS deteriorate.

convalescence noun *a long period of convalescence*: **recuperation**, recovery, return to health, process of getting better, rehabilitation, improvement, mending, restoration.
▷ANTONYMS relapse.

convalescent adjective *you're still convalescent and you need to rest*: **recuperating**, recovering, getting better, on the road to recovery, improving, making progress; informal on the mend.

convene verb **1** *he had convened a secret meeting of military personnel*: **summon**, call, call together, order; hold; formal convoke.
2 *the committee convened for its final session*: **assemble**, gather, meet, get together, come together, congregate, collect, muster; rare foregather.
▷ANTONYMS disperse.

convenience noun **1** *the convenience of this arrangement pleased Paula*: **expedience**, expediency, advantageousness, advantage; favourableness, opportuneness, propitiousness, timeliness; suitability, appropriateness, fittingness.
▷ANTONYMS inconvenience.
2 *it combines the convenience of a portable with the power of a car phone*: **ease of use**, usability, usefulness, utility, serviceability, practicality, functionality; advantage, benefit.
▷ANTONYMS inconvenience; disadvantage.
3 *a shower and toilet were installed for the convenience of swimmers*: **benefit**, **use**, good, comfort, ease, enjoyment, satisfaction.
4 *the convenience of the nearby shopping centre*: **accessibility**, ease of access, handiness, nearness; rare propinquity.
▷ANTONYMS inaccessibility.
5 *the kitchen is bright and cheerful, with all the modern conveniences*: **appliance**, amenity, facility, device, labour-saving device, gadget, machine; informal gizmo, gimmick, mod con; formal appurtenance.
□ **at your convenience** *please telephone me at your convenience*: **at a convenient time**, at a time that suits you, when it suits you, at your leisure, in your own time, when you have a minute, when you can; in due course.
▷ANTONYMS immediately.

convenient adjective **1** *try to agree on a mutually convenient time*: **suitable**, appropriate, fitting, fit, suited, agreeable; opportune, timely, well timed, favourable, advantageous, expedient; archaic commodious, seasonable.
▷ANTONYMS inconvenient, awkward.
2 *pre-prepared food has become a tempting and convenient option in recent times*: **trouble-free**, labour-saving; useful, handy, practical, serviceable; user-oriented.
3 *a friendly, well-run hotel that's **convenient for** the beach*: **within easy reach of**, near (to), close to, well placed for, well situated for, handy for, just around the corner from, within walking distance of, at close quarters to, not far from; informal a stone's throw from, {a hop, skip, and a jump away from}, within spitting distance of.

Word toolkit **convenient**

See **nearby**.

C

convent noun **nunnery**; priory, abbey, religious house, religious community, cloister; rare coenobium, coenoby, beguinage.

convention noun **1** *social conventions | he was an upholder of convention and correct form*: **custom**, **usage**, practice, tradition, way, habit, norm; **rule**, code, canon, punctilio; accepted behaviour, conventionality, propriety, etiquette, protocol, formality, ceremonial; formal praxis; (**conventions**) mores; French moeurs.
2 *a convention signed by the six states bordering on the Black Sea*: **agreement**, accord, protocol, compact, pact; treaty, concordat, entente; understanding, arrangement; contract, bargain, deal.
3 *the annual convention of the Institute of Directors*: **conference**, meeting, congress, assembly, gathering, summit, council of delegates/representatives, symposium, forum, convocation, synod, conclave, diet, chapter; informal con, get-together; rare colloquium.

conventional adjective **1** *the conventional wisdom of the day*: **orthodox**, traditional, established, accepted, received, mainstream, prevailing, prevalent, accustomed, customary.
▷ANTONYMS unorthodox.
2 *a cross between a monorail and a conventional railway*: **normal**, standard, regular, ordinary, usual, traditional, typical, common; Brit. common or garden; N. Amer. garden variety.
3 *Karen was a very conventional woman*: **conservative**, traditional, traditionalist, conformist, bourgeois, old-fashioned, of the old school; formal, correct, proper, decorous, staid; small-town, suburban, parochial, narrow-minded; French bien pensant, comme il faut; historical Biedermeier; informal straight, square, strait-laced, stodgy, stuffy, stick-in-the-mud, fuddy-duddy.
▷ANTONYMS unconventional, radical, bohemian.
4 *an unexciting and rather conventional compilation*: **run-of-the-mill**, prosaic, pedestrian, commonplace, unimaginative, uninspired, uninspiring, unadventurous, unremarkable, unexceptional; **unoriginal**, derivative, formulaic, predictable, stock, hackneyed, clichéd, stereotypical, stereotyped, trite, platitudinous; informal old hat, plain vanilla, bog-standard; rare formulistic.
▷ANTONYMS original.

Word toolkit **conventional**
See **reactionary**.

converge verb **1** *Oxford Circus, a station where three lines converge*: **meet**, **intersect**, cross, come together, connect, link up, coincide; join, unite, merge.
▷ANTONYMS separate, diverge.
2 *the 90,000 soccer fans* ***converging on*** *Wembley*: **close in on**, bear down on, descend on; approach, draw near/nearer to, come close/closer to, move towards.
▷ANTONYMS leave, retreat from.

conversant adjective *the students are* ***conversant with*** *a wide range mathematical and computing skills*: **familiar with**, acquainted with, au fait with, at home with, no stranger to; **well versed in**, well informed about, well up on, knowledgeable about, informed about, abreast of, apprised of, up to date on, au courant with; experienced in, proficient in, practised in, skilled in; informal up to speed on, clued up on, genned up on, plugged into; formal cognizant of; dated perfect in.
▷ANTONYMS unfamiliar with; ignorant of.

conversation noun *he must have overheard her conversation with Victoria*: **discussion**, talk, chat, gossip, tête-à-tête, heart-to-heart, head-to-head, exchange, dialogue, parley, consultation, conference; Indian adda; NZ korero; informal confab, jaw, powwow, chit-chat, rap, gas; Brit. informal chinwag, natter, rabbit; Scottish & N. English informal crack; N. Amer. informal bull session, skull session, gabfest, schmooze; Austral./NZ informal yarn; formal confabulation; rare palaver, colloquy, converse.

conversational adjective **1** *a conversational tone | fluent, conversational English*: **informal**, chatty, casual, relaxed, friendly; colloquial, idiomatic.
▷ANTONYMS formal.
2 *like all dentists, he only became conversational when he had his patient at his mercy*: **talkative**, chatty, communicative, forthcoming, expansive, loquacious, garrulous, voluble.
▷ANTONYMS taciturn, uncommunicative.

converse[1] verb (stress on the second syllable) *they began to converse amicably*: **talk**, speak, chat, have a conversation, have a talk, have a discussion, discourse; confer, parley, consult with each other; chatter, gossip; informal chew the fat, chew the rag, gab, jaw, powwow, have a confab; Brit. informal natter, rabbit, witter, chunter; N. Amer. informal rap, shoot the breeze, shoot the bull; Austral./NZ informal mag; formal confabulate.

converse[2] (stress on the first syllable) noun *the converse is true*: **opposite**, reverse, obverse, inverse, contrary, antithesis; other side of the coin; Italian per contra; informal flip side.
▸ adjective *the converse attitude of many of those on the right of the party*: **opposite**, opposing, contrary, counter, antithetical; clashing, incompatible, in disagreement, disagreeing, conflicting, differing; reverse, obverse, inverse.

conversion noun **1** *the conversion of waste into energy*: **change**, changing, transformation, turning, altering, metamorphosis, transfiguration, transmutation, translation, sea change; humorous transmogrification.
2 *the conversion of the building*: **adaptation**, reconstruction, rebuilding, redevelopment, refashioning, redesign, restyling, revamping; renovation, rehabilitation; alteration, modification, customization.
3 *his religious conversion*: **spiritual rebirth**, regeneration, reformation; change of heart; rare proselytization.

convert verb (stress on the second syllable) **1** *plants convert the radiant energy of the sun into chemical energy*: **change**, turn, transform, metamorphose, transfigure, transmute, translate; humorous transmogrify; technical permute.
2 *the sofa* ***converts to*** *a bed*: **change into**, be able to be changed into, adapt to.
3 *we converted the derelict properties into a women's centre*: **adapt**, turn, rebuild, reconstruct, redevelop, remake, make over, refashion, redesign, restyle, revamp; renovate, rehabilitate; modify, alter, customize; N. Amer. bring up to code; informal do up, fix up; N. Amer. informal rehab.
4 *a novel which was later converted into a film script*: **adapt**, turn, rework, recast, reshape, refashion, remodel, remould; rehash.
5 *that's no way to convert sinners*: **proselytize**, evangelize, bring to God, redeem, save, reform, re-educate, cause someone to change their beliefs/mind, make someone see the light; persuade, convince, win over; N. Amer. proselyte.
6 *the formula for converting centigrade into Fahrenheit*: **change**, turn; exchange for, swap for; switch from.
▸ noun (stress on the first syllable) *Christian converts*: **proselyte**, neophyte, new believer; Christianity catechumen.

convertible adjective *assets that are readily convertible into cash*: **changeable**, able to be changed, exchangeable; adaptable, adjustable, modifiable.
▸ noun *a black Mercedes convertible*: **soft-top**, ragtop, targa; Brit. dated drophead.

convex adjective **curved outwards**, cambered; rounded, bulging, swelling, protuberant; curvilinear; gibbous; rare outcurved.
▷ANTONYMS concave.

convey verb **1** *a taxi service conveyed guests to Cerrig station | pipes were laid to convey water to the house*: **transport**, carry, bring, take, fetch, bear, move, ferry, shuttle, shift, transfer; send, forward, deliver, dispatch; channel, pipe, conduct.
2 *Mr Marr has conveyed the information to me*: **communicate**, pass on, make known, impart, relay, transmit, send, hand on; tell, relate, recount, announce, reveal, disclose, divulge.
3 *it's impossible to convey how lost I felt*: **express**, communicate, indicate, tell, say, put across/over, get across/over.
4 *he conveys an air of managerial competence*: **project**, exude, emit, emanate, send forth.
5 *a deed conveying property to a trustee*: **transfer**, give the right/title of, grant, cede, devolve, lease; bequeath, leave, will, pass on; N. Amer. deed; Law demise, devise.

conveyance noun **1** *the conveyance of agricultural produce from the Billingsgate area*: **transportation**, transport, carriage, carrying, transfer, transference, movement, delivery; haulage, portage, cartage, shipment, freightage.
2 formal *three-wheeled conveyances*: **vehicle**, means/method of transport; car, motor car, bus, coach, van, lorry, truck, carriage, bicycle, motorbike, motorcycle.
3 *the conveyance of meaning*: **communication**, imparting, transmission, passing on, conveying; expression.
4 *the conveyance of property*: **transfer**, transference, transferral, granting, ceding, devolution; bequest; Law demise; rare cession.

convict verb (stress on the second syllable) *her former boyfriend was* ***convicted of*** *assaulting her*: **declare/find/pronounce guilty**; sentence, give someone a sentence; Brit. informal send down for.
▷ANTONYMS acquit, clear.
▸ noun (stress on the first syllable) *two escaped convicts*: **prisoner**, inmate; criminal, offender, lawbreaker, felon; trusty; informal jailbird, con, (old) lag, lifer, crook; N. Amer. informal yardbird; S. African informal lighty; archaic transport.

conviction noun **1** *she will appeal against her conviction*: **declaration/pronouncement of guilt**, sentence, judgement.
▷ANTONYMS acquittal.
2 *his deeply held political and religious convictions*: **belief**, **opinion**, view, thought, persuasion, idea, position, stance; (article of) faith, credo, creed, tenet, dogma.
3 *she spoke with conviction*: **certainty**, certitude, assurance, confidence, sureness, positiveness; no shadow of a doubt.
▷ANTONYMS uncertainty, doubt.

convince verb **1** *Wilson convinced me that I was wrong*: **persuade**, satisfy, prove to, cause to feel certain; assure, reassure; put/set someone's mind at rest, dispel someone's doubts.

2 *eventually, I convinced her to marry me*: **induce**, prevail on, get, talk round, bring around, win over, sway; persuade, cajole, inveigle.

Choose the right word **convince, persuade, induce**

All these words refer to causing someone to do something that you wish them to do.

Convince refers primarily to getting someone to believe something by presenting them with arguments or evidence (*he managed to convince the police that his story was true*). The word can also mean 'persuade' (*she convinced my father to branch out on his own*), but this use is disapproved of by some people.

Persuade refers primarily to getting someone to do something through reasoning or argument, possibly against their better judgement or personal preference (*he persuaded Tom to accompany him | she was persuaded to return to work*). *Persuade* can also be used of causing someone to accept a belief, but *persuading* someone that something is the case may take considerable argument (*he persuaded her that nothing was going on | we need to be persuaded of the case*).

Induce is used only of getting someone to do something. It is a forceful word, suggesting a good deal of effort or sacrifice on the part of the inducer, and often the use of bribes or threats rather than argument (*we had to give the driver a huge tip to induce him to carry the luggage*).

convincing adjective **1** *this seemed to me to be a convincing argument*: **cogent**, **persuasive**, powerful, potent, strong, forceful, compelling, irresistible, telling, conclusive, incontrovertible, unanswerable, incontestable, unassailable; sound, well founded, plausible, credible, believable, carrying conviction, likely, probable; rare suasive, assuasive, verisimilar, colourable.
▷ANTONYMS unconvincing, improbable, far-fetched.
2 *a convincing 5–0 win*: **decisive**, conclusive, impressive, emphatic, resounding.
▷ANTONYMS narrow.

convivial adjective *he was always a convivial host | the convivial after-dinner atmosphere*: **friendly**, genial, affable, amiable, congenial, agreeable, good-humoured, cordial, warm, sociable, outgoing, gregarious, clubbable, companionable, hail-fellow-well-met; cheerful, jolly, jovial, merry, lively, enjoyable, festive; Scottish couthy; informal backslapping, chummy, pally; Brit. informal matey; N. Amer. clubby, buddy-buddy; rare conversable.
▷ANTONYMS unfriendly, unsociable.

conviviality noun **friendliness**, geniality, affability, amiability, congeniality, good humour, cordiality, warmth, warm-heartedness, good nature, sociability, gregariousness, clubbability, companionability; cheerfulness, cheeriness, good cheer, joviality, jollity, gaiety, liveliness, festivity; French bonhomie.
▷ANTONYMS unfriendliness.

convocation noun **assembly**, gathering, meeting, conference, convention, congress, rally, council, symposium, forum, conclave, congregation, synod, diet; in N. Amer. & NZ caucus; informal get-together; rare colloquium.

convoke verb formal *she sent messages convoking a council of ministers*: **convene**, summon, call together, call; order.

convoluted adjective *an extraordinarily convoluted narrative*: **complicated**, complex, involved, intricate, elaborate, impenetrable, serpentine, labyrinthine, tortuous, tangled, Byzantine, Daedalian, Gordian; confused, confusing, bewildering, baffling, puzzling, perplexing; informal fiddly, plotty; rare involute.
▷ANTONYMS simple, straightforward.

Word toolkit **convoluted**

See **intricate**.

convolution noun **1** *an elaborate tracery of convolutions and hatching*: **twist**, turn, coil, spiral, twirl, curl, helix, whorl, loop, curlicue, kink, sinuosity; technical volute, volution, gyrus.
2 *the convolutions of the plot*: **complexity**, intricacy, complication, twist, turn, entanglement, contortion; involvement, tortuousness, convolutedness; rare involution.

convoy noun *the convoy of vehicles left at 11.30 p.m.* **group**, fleet, cavalcade, motorcade, cortège, caravan, company, line, train, procession; Brit. informal crocodile.
▸ verb **1** *the 'Trumbull' was to convoy a provision ship to the San Domingo station*: **escort**, accompany, attend, flank; protect, guard, defend.
2 *Remington found himself convoying Miss Lawton through the hall*: **escort**, accompany, go with, attend, conduct, guide, shepherd, usher.

convulse verb *his whole body convulsed*: **shake uncontrollably/violently**, go into spasms, shudder, jerk, thrash about; suffer a fit.
□ **be convulsed with laughter laugh uproariously**, roar with laughter, hold one's sides, be doubled up with laughter; informal split one's sides, be rolling in the aisles, be in stitches, die laughing, laugh like a drain, bust a gut, break up; Brit. informal be creased up, fall about laughing.

convulsion noun **1** *she's started to have convulsions*: **fit**, seizure, paroxysm, spasm, attack, muscular contractions; throes; technical ictus.
2 (**convulsions**) *the audience collapsed in convulsions*: **fits of laughter**, paroxysms of laughter, gales of laughter, peals of laughter, uncontrollable laughter; informal hysterics, stitches.
3 *the political convulsions of the mid 20th century*: **upheaval**, eruption, turmoil, turbulence, disruption, agitation, disturbance, unrest, disorder, furore, upset, tumult, chaos; earthquake, cataclysm, storm; German Sturm und Drang.

convulsive adjective *convulsive movements*: **spasmodic**, jerky, paroxysmal, violent, uncontrollable.

cook verb **1** *I decided to cook a romantic dinner*: **prepare**, make, get, put together; bake; informal fix, knock up, rustle up.
2 informal *he was accused of cooking the books*: **falsify**, alter, doctor, tamper with, interfere with, massage, manipulate, rig, misrepresent; forge; Brit. informal fiddle.
3 informal *hey there, Rob, what's cooking?* **happen**, go on, occur, take place; N. Amer. informal go down.
□ **cook something up** *he'd already cooked up a little plan to entice Jessica to go with him*: **concoct**, devise, put together, create, contrive, fabricate, prepare, trump up, hatch, brew, plot, plan, scheme; invent, make up, think up, dream up.

cooking noun *authentic Italian cooking*: **cuisine**, cookery, baking; food.

Word links **cooking**

culinary relating to cooking

cool adjective **1** *a cool, cloudy day | a cool breeze*: **chilly**, cold; fresh, crisp, refreshing, invigorating, bracing, brisk; unheated, draughty; informal nippy; Brit. informal parky; literary chill.
▷ANTONYMS warm, hot.
2 *the proposal met with a cool response | David seemed distinctly cool*: **unenthusiastic**, lukewarm, tepid, indifferent, apathetic, half-hearted, negative; **unfriendly**, distant, remote, aloof, cold, chilly, frosty, unwelcoming, inhospitable, unresponsive, uninterested, unconcerned, offhand, detached, impersonal, dispassionate, undemonstrative, uncommunicative, unfeeling, unemotional, emotionless; informal stand-offish, off, offish, unenthused; rare Olympian, gelid.
▷ANTONYMS enthusiastic; friendly.
3 *no one could doubt his ability to keep cool in a crisis*: **calm**, {cool, calm, and collected}, composed, as cool as a cucumber, collected, cool-headed, level-headed, self-possessed, controlled, self-controlled, poised; serene, tranquil, relaxed, unruffled, unperturbed, unflustered, undisturbed, unagitated, unmoved, unbothered, untroubled; equable, even-tempered, imperturbable, placid, quiet, sedate, unexcitable, impassive, dispassionate, unemotional, phlegmatic, stolid; informal unflappable, unfazed, together, laid-back; rare equanimous.
▷ANTONYMS panic-stricken, agitated.
4 *a cool lack of morality*: **bold**, audacious, nerveless; **brazen**, shameless, unabashed.
5 informal *she thinks she's so cool*: **fashionable**, stylish, chic, up to the minute; sophisticated, cosmopolitan, elegant; French le dernier cri; informal **trendy**, funky, with it, hip, in, big, happening, now, groovy, sharp, swinging; N. Amer. informal kicky, tony, fly; black English down.
6 informal *it's a really cool song—I love it*. See **excellent**, **superb**.
▸ noun **1** *the cool of the evening*: **chill**, chilliness, coldness; coolness, freshness, crispness.
▷ANTONYMS warmth.
2 *Ken finally lost his cool and turned on her*: **self-control**, control, composure, self-command, self-possession, calmness, equanimity, equilibrium, calm, collectedness; aplomb, poise, sangfroid, presence of mind.
▸ verb **1** *cool the sauce in the fridge until you are ready to use it*: **chill**, refrigerate, make cold/colder.
▷ANTONYMS heat.
2 *allow the mixture to cool, stirring occasionally*: **get cold/colder**, cool down, lose heat.
3 *her reluctance to see him did nothing to cool his interest*: **lessen**, moderate, abate, diminish, reduce, dampen, pour cold water on; soothe, take the edge off, assuage, allay, mollify, temper, settle.
▷ANTONYMS inflame, arouse.
4 *Simpson's ardour had cooled*: **subside**, lessen, diminish, decrease, abate, moderate, die down, fade, dwindle, wane.
▷ANTONYMS intensify.
5 *after I'd cooled off, I realized I was being irrational*: **calm down**, recover/regain one's self-control, recover/regain one's composure, compose oneself, control oneself, pull oneself together, simmer down.
▷ANTONYMS lose one's temper.

coop noun *she released the hens from the coop*: **pen**, run, cage, hutch, enclosure, pound, lock-up; birdcage, aviary, mew; Scottish parrock.

C

▶ **verb**
□ **coop someone up** *he hates being cooped up at home all day*: **confine**, shut in, close in, shut up, mew up, keep, detain, trap; lock up, imprison, incarcerate, immure, intern, impound, hold captive, hold prisoner, put under lock and key; cage, cage in, pen in, fence in, rail in, wall in, hem in, enclose.
▷ANTONYMS set free.

cooperate verb **1** *police and social services cooperated in the operation*: **collaborate**, work together, work side by side, act together, act jointly, pull together, band together, come together, get together, join forces, team up, unite, combine, merge, amalgamate, pool resources, club together, make common cause, form an alliance; coordinate with each other, liaise with each other; conspire, connive, collude, be in collusion, work hand in glove; informal gang up; rare coact.
2 *they were more than happy to cooperate*: **be of assistance**, assist, help, lend a hand, be of service, give one's support, give one's backing, contribute, chip in, do one's bit, throw in one's lot; participate, take part, join in, get involved, go along; informal pitch in, play ball, tag along, get in on the act; Brit. informal muck in, get stuck in.

cooperation noun **1** *there has to be some cooperation between management and workers*: **collaboration**, working together, joint action, combined effort, teamwork, mutual support, partnership, coopetition, coordination, liaison, association, synergy, unity, concurrence, concord, accord, understanding, give and take, compromise; dealings, relations; rare coaction.
2 *thank you for your cooperation*: **assistance**, helpfulness, help, helping hand, aid, abettance, support, backing, contribution, participation; offices, good offices, services, ministrations.

cooperative adjective **1** *effective organizations depend on cooperative effort*: **collaborative**, collective, communal, combined, common, joint, shared, mutual, united, unified, allied, cross-party, pooled, mass, concerted, coordinated, interactive, unanimous, harmonious; rare coactive.
▷ANTONYMS individual.
2 *we have found the staff to be pleasant and cooperative*: **helpful**, eager to help, eager to please, glad to be of assistance, obliging, accommodating, indulgent; compliant, complaisant, willing, acquiescent, amenable, persuadable, biddable, tractable, pliable, pliant, adaptable, responsive; informal easy, game; rare persuasible, suasible.
▷ANTONYMS uncooperative.

coordinate verb **1** *the new leadership would coordinate all manufacturing efforts*: **harmonize**, correlate, interrelate, synchronize, bring together; fit together, mesh, dovetail; organize, arrange, order, systematize; rare concert.
2 *care workers coordinate at a local level*: **cooperate**, collaborate, work together, work side by side, act together, act jointly, pull together, band together, come together, get together, join forces, team up, unite, combine, merge, amalgamate, pool resources, club together, make common cause, form an alliance, liaise; conspire, connive, collude, work hand in glove; informal gang up; rare coact.
3 *she chose floral designs to* ***coordinate with*** *her decor*: **blend**, blend in, fit in, harmonize, go, go well, go together, be compatible, be in tune; **match**, suit, complement, set off.

cop[1] noun informal *the cop marched her to the station*. See **police officer**.

cop[2] verb
□ **cop out** informal *he tried to* ***cop out of*** *his responsibilities*: **avoid**, shirk, skip, dodge, sidestep, skirt round, bypass, steer clear of, evade, escape, run away from, shrink from, slide out of, back out of, pull out of, turn one's back on; informal duck, duck out of, wriggle out of, get out of; Brit. informal skive, skive off, funk; N. Amer. informal cut; Austral./NZ informal duck-shove; archaic decline, bilk.

cope verb *her elderly parents can no longer cope alone*: **manage**, survive, subsist, look after oneself, fend for oneself, shift for oneself, stand on one's own two feet, carry on, get through, get on, get along, get by, muddle through, muddle along, scrape by, bear up, make the grade, come through, hold one's own, keep one's end up, keep one's head above water, keep the wolf from the door, weather the storm; informal make out, hack it, paddle one's own canoe; informal rub along.
□ **cope with** *the agency helps people to cope with bereavement*: **deal with**, handle, manage, address, face, face up to, confront, tackle, sort out, take care of, take in hand, get to grips with, contend with, grapple with, wrestle with, struggle with, tussle with; put up with, get through, weather, endure, withstand, stand up to, bear, brave, accept, come to terms with; master, overcome, surmount, get over, get the better of, beat; informal stomach, swallow.

copious adjective *she listened to me and she took copious notes*: **abundant**, superabundant, plentiful, ample, profuse, full, extensive, considerable, substantial, generous, bumper, lavish, fulsome, liberal, bountiful, overflowing, abounding, teeming; in abundance; **many**, numerous, multiple, multifarious, multitudinous, manifold, countless, innumerable; informal a gogo, galore; S. African informal lank; literary bounteous, plenteous; myriad.
▷ANTONYMS sparse.

cop-out noun informal *they sometimes use their kids as a cop-out to retreat from commitment*: **excuse**, pretext, ostensible reason, pretence, front, cover, cover-up, subterfuge, fabrication, evasion, escape.

copper noun

> *Word links* **copper**
>
> **chalco-** related prefix, as in *chalcolithic*
> **cupric, cuprous** relating to copper
> **cupro-** related prefix, as in *cupro-nickel*

copse noun *tall firs form a copse at the back of the house*: **thicket**, grove, wood, coppice, stand, clump, brake; Brit. spinney; N. Amer. & Austral./NZ brush; archaic hurst, holt, boscage.

copulate verb formal *zebra finches copulate frequently | they believed that witches* ***copulated with*** *the devil*: **mate**, couple, breed; **have sex**, have sexual intercourse, make love, sleep together, go to bed; informal do it, do the business, go all the way, make whoopee, have one's way, bed, know someone in the biblical sense, tumble; Brit. informal bonk, get one's oats; N. Amer. informal boff, get it on; euphemistic be intimate; vulgar slang **fuck**, screw, bang, lay, get one's leg over, shaft, dick, frig, do, have, hump, poke, shtup, dip one's wick, ride, service, tup; Brit. vulgar slang have it away, have it off, shag, knob, get one's end away, knock someone off, give someone one, roger, grind, stuff; Scottish vulgar slang podger; N. Amer. vulgar slang ball, jump, jump someone's bones, bone, pork, diddle, nail; Austral./NZ vulgar slang root; formal fornicate with; archaic lie together, possess, swive, know.

copulation noun formal *the banned film contained a 15-second sequence of copulation*: **sexual intercourse**, sex, intercourse, lovemaking, making love, sexual relations, sexual/vaginal/anal penetration; mating, coupling, breeding; informal nooky; Brit. informal bonking, rumpy pumpy, a bit of the other, how's your father; S. African informal pata-pata; vulgar slang screwing, fucking; Brit. vulgar slang shagging; formal coitus, coition, fornication; archaic carnal knowledge, congress, commerce.

copy noun **1** *copies of his report had been sent to the tribunal*: **duplicate**, duplication, reprint, facsimile, photocopy, carbon copy, carbon, mimeograph, mimeo; transcript; informal dupe; trademark Xerox, photostat.
2 *a copy of a sketch by Leonardo da Vinci*: **replica**, reproduction, replication, print, imitation, likeness, lookalike, representation, mock-up, dummy; counterfeit, forgery, fake, sham, bootleg; informal pirate, phoney, knock-off, dupe.
3 *I checked my dad's original copy of the book*: **edition**, version, impression, imprint, issue; specimen, sample, example.
4 *it is an unfortunate truth that bad news makes good copy*: **material**; articles, stories, features.
▶ **verb 1** *each form had to be copied and sent to a different editor*: **duplicate**, photocopy, xerox, photostat, mimeograph, make a photocopy of, take a photocopy of, run off; transcribe, reproduce, replicate, clone.
2 *the portraits are copied from original paintings by Reynolds*: **reproduce**, replicate; forge, fake, falsify, counterfeit, bootleg.
3 *their sound was copied by a lot of jazz players*: **imitate**, mimic, ape, emulate, follow, echo, mirror, simulate, parrot, reproduce; plagiarize, poach, steal, 'borrow', infringe the copyright of; informal pirate, rip off, crib, lift; Brit. informal nick, pinch; archaic monkey.

coquettish adjective *she gave Dan a coquettish glance from beneath her eyelashes*: **flirtatious**, flirty, provocative, seductive, inviting, amorous, kittenish, coy, arch, teasing, playful, frisky, flighty, skittish, dallying, philandering; informal come-hither, vampish.

cord noun *her spectacles hung round her neck on a cord | a piece of thin cord*: **string**, thread, thong, lace, ribbon, strap, tape, tie, line, rope, cable, wire, ligature; twine, yarn, elastic, braid, cording, braiding; Falconry creance; rare fillis.

cordial adjective **1** *he would always receive a cordial welcome at their house*: **friendly**, warm, genial, affable, amiable, pleasant, fond, affectionate, warm-hearted, good-natured, gracious, hospitable, welcoming; sincere, earnest, wholehearted, heartfelt, hearty, enthusiastic, eager.
▷ANTONYMS unfriendly.
2 *I earned his cordial loathing*: **intense**, strong, acute, violent, fierce, keen, fervent, ardent, passionate; **heartfelt**, wholehearted, deep, deep-seated, deep-rooted, profound, overwhelming, overpowering; rare fervid, perfervid, passional.
▷ANTONYMS mild.
▶ **noun 1** *I often drank water with fruit cordial*: **squash**, crush, concentrate.
2 N. Amer. *ginger wine is a cordial drunk at Christmas time*: **liqueur**; alcoholic drink.

cordon noun *the crowds had broken through the police cordon*: **barrier**, line, column, row, file, ranks, chain, ring, circle; picket line; informal crocodile.
▶ **verb**
□ **cordon something off** *the city centre was cordoned off after a bomb threat*: **close off**, seal off, tape off, fence off, rope off, screen off, curtain off, shut off, partition off, separate off, isolate, segregate, quarantine; seal, close, shut, blockade; enclose, encircle, surround.

core noun **1** *they plan to harness the heat from the earth's core*: **centre**, interior, middle, nucleus, bosom; recesses, bowels, depths; informal innards; literary midst.
2 *this new paper goes to the core of the argument*: **heart**, nucleus, nub, hub,

kernel, marrow, meat; **essence**, quintessence, crux, gist, pith, substance, sum and substance, body, basis; bedrock, cornerstone, linchpin, mainspring, foundation, root, base, underpinning; fundamentals, essentials, basic principles, main ingredients; heart of the matter; informal nitty-gritty, brass tacks, nuts and bolts, ABC, basics.
▸ adjective *the core issue here is that of urban poverty*: **central**, key, basic, fundamental, elemental, principal, primary, main, chief, crucial, vital, essential; informal number-one.
▹ANTONYMS peripheral; minor.

cork noun *Kate pulled the cork from the bottle*: **stopper**, stop, plug, bung, peg, spigot, spile, seal; cap, top, lid, cover, covering; N. Amer. stopple.

Word links **cork**
suberose, suberous, subereous like cork

corn noun **1** *the mill was used for grinding corn*: **grain**, cereal, cereal crop.
2 *she opened a packet of baby corn*: **sweetcorn, maize**, corn on the cob, Indian corn; S. African mealie.

corner noun **1** *the cart lurched round the corner*: **bend**, curve, arc, kink, dog-leg, crook, deviation, turn, turning, junction, fork, intersection; angle, projection, apex, cusp; Brit. hairpin, hairpin bend.
2 *Benjamin hustled me away to a corner*: **nook**, cranny, niche, recess, bay, booth, alcove; inglenook, ingle, apse; crevice, cavity, hole, hollow, indentation; secret place, hideaway, hideout; informal hidey-hole.
3 *this corner of Italy is famed for its superb cooking*: **district**, region, area, section, quarter, part; informal neck of the woods.
4 *society and its rules had trapped him in a corner*: **predicament**, plight, tricky situation, ticklish situation, awkward situation, tight corner, tight spot, spot of trouble, bit of bother, difficulty, problem, puzzle, quandary, dilemma, muddle, mess, quagmire, mire, mare's nest, dire straits; with nowhere to turn; W. Indian comess; informal pickle, jam, stew, fix, hole, scrape, bind, fine kettle of fish, hot water, how-do-you-do.
□ **(just) around the corner 1** *my sister Gillian lives just around the corner*: **close by**, nearby, very near, near here, not far away, a short distance away, in the neighbourhood, close at hand, within walking distance, within reach, on the doorstep. **2** *better times are just around the corner*: **coming**, coming soon, coming up, approaching, close, imminent, forthcoming, brewing, in prospect, in the offing, in the wings, in the wind, on the way, on the horizon, nearly on us, close at hand, at hand; informal on the cards.
▸ verb **1** *the wolf had cornered his prey and was moving in for the kill*: **drive into a corner**, run to earth, run to ground, bring to bay, cut off, block off, trap, hem in, shut in, pen in, close in, enclose, surround; capture, catch, waylay, ambush; archaic ambuscade.
2 *crime syndicates have cornered the stolen car market*: **gain control of**, gain dominance of, take over, control, dominate, monopolize, capture; informal hog, sew up; archaic engross.

cornerstone noun *the theory of natural selection is a cornerstone of biological thought*: **foundation**, basis, keystone, mainspring, mainstay, linchpin, bedrock, fundament, base, key, fundamental principle, main ingredient, central component, centrepiece, core, heart, centre, focus, crux, prop, backbone, anchor.

corny adjective informal *the film is quite insubstantial and corny*: **banal**, trite, hackneyed, commonplace, clichéd, predictable, stereotyped, platitudinous, inane, fatuous, vapid, jejune, weak, feeble, tired, stale, overworked, overused, well worn; **mawkish**, sentimental, sickly, sickly-sweet, cloying, syrupy, sugary, saccharine, honeyed, oversweet, sickening, nauseating, choking; Brit. twee; informal old hat, out of the ark, played out, cheesy; mushy, slushy, sloppy, schmaltzy, cutesy, cute, gooey, drippy, treacly, icky, sick-making, toe-curling; Brit. informal soppy; N. Amer. informal cornball, dime-store, sappy, hokey; rare truistic, bromidic.
▹ANTONYMS original.

corollary noun *the corollary of increased car ownership has been a decline in public transport*: **consequence**, result, upshot, outcome, out-turn, effect, repercussion, reverberations, sequel, product, by-product, spin-off, conclusion, end, end result; accompaniment, concomitant, correlate; technical externality; Brit. knock-on effect.
▹ANTONYMS cause, origin.

coronation noun *they built a tower to celebrate Victoria's coronation*: **crowning**, enthronement, enthroning, accession to the throne, investiture, anointing, inauguration.

coronet noun *the queen put a coronet on the prince's head*: **crown**, diadem, tiara, circlet, chaplet, fillet, garland, wreath; literary coronal.

corporal adjective *corporal punishment* | *what seemed corporal melted, as breath into the wind*: **bodily**, fleshly, corporeal, carnal, mortal, earthly, worldly, physical, material, real, actual, tangible, substantial; rare somatic.
▹ANTONYMS spiritual.

corporate adjective *he emphasized the corporate responsibility of the congregation*: **collective**, shared, common, communal, joint, combined, united, allied, amalgamated, pooled, merged, concerted, collaborative, cooperative; company, business, house.
▹ANTONYMS individual.

corporation noun **1** *he was chairman of the corporation for three years*: **company**, firm, business, concern, operation, agency, office, bureau, house, guild, institution, organization, trust, partnership, federation, conglomerate, consortium, syndicate, group, chain, combine, multiple, multinational; informal outfit, set-up.
2 Brit. *the corporation refused two planning applications*: **council**, town council, municipal authority, civic authority; authorities.

corporeal adjective *they tried to bring Satan into corporeal existence*: **bodily**, fleshly, carnal, corporal, human, mortal, earthly; **physical**, material, actual, real, substantial, tangible, concrete.
▹ANTONYMS incorporeal.

corps noun *she belonged to the local Salvation Army corps* | *the press corps*: **unit**, division, detachment, section, company, troop, contingent, squad, squadron, regiment, garrison, battalion, brigade, platoon, force; **group**, body, band, team, party, troupe, gang, pack; in ancient Rome cohort; informal bunch, crew, gaggle, posse.

corpse noun *she found his corpse at the bottom of the stairs*: **dead body**, body, cadaver, carcass, skeleton; remains, relics; informal stiff; archaic corse.

Word links **corpse**
necro- related prefix, as in *necropolis*
necrophobia fear of corpses

corpulence noun *he had been called 'Bubbles' because of his corpulence*: **obesity**, fatness, plumpness, stoutness, chubbiness, chunkiness, paunchiness, portliness, roundness, rotundity, burliness, heaviness, fleshiness, meatiness; ample proportions, fat, weight, beer belly, paunch; informal tubbiness, pudginess, porkiness, beefiness, blubber; Brit. informal podginess, fubsiness; archaic embonpoint.

corpulent adjective *his corpulent figure seemed to fill the small pulpit*: **fat**, fattish, obese, overweight, plump, portly, stout, chubby, paunchy, beer-bellied, thickset, hefty, heavy, heavyset, burly, bulky, chunky, well padded, well covered, well upholstered, meaty, fleshy, rotund, round, well rounded, broad, broad in the beam, of ample proportions, big, large, gargantuan, elephantine; informal tubby, pudgy, beefy, porky, roly-poly, blubbery, poddy; Brit. informal podgy, fubsy; N. Amer. informal zaftig, corn-fed, lard-assed; Austral./NZ nuggety; technical pyknic; archaic squabby, pursy; rare abdominous.
▹ANTONYMS thin.

corpus noun *his work has no parallel in the whole corpus of Renaissance poetry*: **collection**, compilation, body, entity, whole, aggregation, mass.

corral N. Amer. noun *she was galloping a pony round the tiny corral*: **enclosure**, pen, fold, compound, pound, stockade, paddock; Scottish parrock; S. African kraal; in S. America potrero.
▸ verb *the sheep and goats were corralled at night*: **enclose**, confine, lock up, shut up, shut in, fence in, pen in, rail in, wall in, cage, cage in, coop up, mew in.

correct adjective **1** *the answer he gave was perfectly correct*: **right**, accurate, true, veracious, exact, precise, unerring, faithful, strict, faultless, flawless, errorless, error-free, perfect, word-perfect, scrupulous, meticulous; on the right track, along the right lines; informal OK, on the mark, on the beam, on the nail, on the button; Brit. informal spot on, bang on; N. Amer. informal on the money.
▹ANTONYMS incorrect, wrong.
2 *she wondered whether it was the correct thing to say*: **proper**, seemly, decorous, decent, respectable, right, suitable, fit, fitting, befitting, appropriate, apt; conventional, approved, accepted, standard, usual, customary, traditional, orthodox; French comme il faut; informal OK.
▹ANTONYMS improper.
▸ verb **1** *proofread your work and correct any mistakes you find*: **rectify**, put right, set right, right, amend, emend, remedy, redress, cure, square, make good, improve, better, ameliorate, repair, revise, alter, edit, rewrite, redraft, reword, rework; sort out, clear up, deal with; informal patch up, clean up, iron out.
2 *all homework should be corrected by your teacher*: **indicate errors in**, show mistakes in, point out faults in; mark, assess, evaluate, appraise.
3 *it is important that a vitamin deficiency is corrected by good diet*: **counteract**, offset, counterbalance, compensate for, make up for, neutralize.
4 *motorists can have their headlights corrected at a reduced price*: **adjust**, regulate, fix, set, set right, set to rights, standardize, normalize, calibrate, fine-tune, make good, put in working order, overhaul; informal jigger, tweak, twiddle, patch up, see to.
5 *'Courtesy if you please,' he corrected her*: **scold**, rebuke, chide, reprimand, reprove, admonish, lecture, berate, chastise, castigate.
▹ANTONYMS praise.

correction noun **1** *the detection and correction of errors is extremely difficult*: **rectifying**, rectification, righting, putting right, setting right, putting to rights, amendment, emendation, alteration, altering, adjustment, adjusting, modification, modifying, repair, remedy, resolution, revision, improvement, improving, amelioration, sorting out, clearing up; informal patching up, ironing out, tweaking; archaic reparation.

C

2 *he was sentenced to three days in the House of Correction*: **punishment**, reform, reformation, discipline; chastisement, castigation, admonition, reproof, reprimand.

corrective adjective **1** *he agreed to undergo corrective surgery*: **remedial**, therapeutic, restorative, curative, reparatory, reparative, rehabilitative, ameliorative.
2 *he was sentenced to four years in a corrective labour camp*: **correctional**, punitive, penal, disciplinary, disciplinarian, castigatory, reformatory; rare penitentiary, punitory, castigative.

correctly adverb **1** *the message had been sent and received correctly*: **accurately**, right, rightly, faithfully, unerringly, precisely, exactly, faultlessly, flawlessly, perfectly, without error, without flaws; Brit. informal spot on, bang on; N. Amer. informal on the money; dated aright.
▷ANTONYMS incorrectly.
2 *now let's be sensible and behave correctly*: **properly**, decorously, with decorum, decently, suitably, fittingly, appropriately, aptly; well, satisfactorily, in a satisfactory manner.
▷ANTONYMS inappropriately.

correlate verb **1** *inflammation will usually* ***correlate with*** *tissue damage*: **correspond**, agree, tally, match up, tie in, be consistent, be in agreement, be compatible, be consonant, be congruous, be in tune, be in harmony, harmonize, coordinate, dovetail; equate to, relate to, conform to; suit, fit, match, parallel; informal square; N. Amer. informal jibe; archaic quadrate.
▷ANTONYMS contrast.
2 *we can correlate trends in television news content and trends in public perceptions*: **connect**, analogize, associate, relate, compare, bring together, set side by side, show a connection between, show a relationship between, show an association between, show a correspondence between, draw an analogy between.

correlation noun *the correlation between smoking and lung cancer is well known*: **connection**, association, link, tie-in, tie-up, relation, relationship, interrelationship, interdependence, interconnection, interaction; correspondence, parallel, equivalence, reciprocity, mutuality, concurrence.

correspond verb **1** *this ideal model does not* ***correspond to*** *the facts*: **correlate with**, agree with, be in agreement with, be consistent with, be compatible with, be consonant with, be congruous with, be in tune with, be in harmony with, accord with, concur with, coincide with, tally with, match up with, tie in with, dovetail with; relate to, equate to, conform to; match, fit, suit, parallel; informal square; N. Amer. jibe with; archaic quadrate.
2 *the German rank of Feldwebel corresponded to the British rank of sergeant*: **be equivalent**, be analogous, be comparable, equate, be similar, be akin.
3 *in this diagram the nodes* ***correspond to*** *male members of a family*: **represent**, symbolize, stand for, signify, mean, denote, designate, indicate; literary betoken.
4 *he met Wordsworth in 1795 and* ***corresponded with*** *him thereafter* | *Debbie and I corresponded for years*: **exchange letters**, communicate, keep in touch, keep in contact; write to, write letters to; informal drop someone a line, drop someone a note.

correspondence noun **1** *there is some correspondence between the two variables*: **correlation**, similarity, resemblance, comparability, compatibility, agreement, consistency, congruity, conformity, uniformity, harmony, affinity, accordance, accord, concurrence, coincidence; association, relationship, connection, interaction.
2 *I caught up on some urgent correspondence*: **mail**, post, communication, written communication; letters, messages, missives.
3 *he kept up a ceaseless round of correspondence*: **letter writing**, writing, written communication.

correspondent noun **1** *I wrote to Jenny for a while but she wasn't much of a correspondent*: **letter-writer**, penfriend, pen pal; communicator.
2 *he joined a Sunday newspaper as a cricket correspondent*: **reporter**, journalist, columnist, writer, contributor, newspaperman, newspaperwoman, newsman, newswoman, commentator, chronicler; special correspondent, foreign correspondent; Brit. pressman; N. Amer. legman, wireman; Austral. roundsman; informal stringer, news hound, hack, hackette, journo; N. Amer. informal newsy.
▶ adjective *the price has been increased without any correspondent improvement in quality*: **corresponding**, equivalent, comparable, parallel, matching, related, similar, analogous, commensurate.

corresponding adjective *a change in money supply brings a corresponding change in expenditure*: **commensurate**, relative, proportional, proportionate, correspondent, comparable, equivalent, equal, consistent, parallel, correlated, analogous, complementary, matching; rare commensurable.

corridor noun *the bathroom is at the end of the corridor*: **passage**, passageway, aisle, gangway, hall, hallway, gallery, arcade, cloister.

corroborate verb *Thomas corroborated the boy's account of the attack*: **confirm**, verify, endorse, ratify, authenticate, validate, certify; support, back up, back, uphold, stand by, bear out, bear witness to, attest to, testify to, vouch for, give credence to, substantiate, sustain, bolster, reinforce, lend weight to.
▷ANTONYMS contradict.

corroboration noun *the paper shouldn't have run the story without corroboration*: **confirmation**, verification, attestation, affirmation, ratification, endorsement, accreditation, authentication, validation, certification, documentation, evidence, proof, substantiation; support, backing, bolstering, reinforcement, weight.

corrode verb **1** *iron objects corrode rapidly in damp conditions*: **rust**, become rusty, tarnish; deteriorate, waste away, disintegrate, crumble, fragment, be destroyed, perish, spoil.
2 *bleach at this strength may corrode the container*: **wear away**, wear down, eat away (at), gnaw away (at), bite into, burn into, burn through, erode, abrade, consume, dissolve; oxidize, oxidate; rust, tarnish, destroy, spoil.

corrosive adjective *the workers are exposed to corrosive chemicals*: **caustic**, corroding, eroding, erosive, abrasive, biting, mordant, burning, stinging; acid, alkali; destructive, damaging, harmful, harsh; rare consumptive.

corrugated adjective *the roof was made of corrugated iron*: **ridged**, fluted, channelled, furrowed, grooved, crimped, folded, crinkled, crinkly, puckered, creased, wrinkled, wrinkly, crumpled, rumpled; technical striate, striated.

corrupt adjective **1** *they alleged that the government was inefficient and corrupt*: **dishonest**, dishonourable, unscrupulous, unprincipled, amoral, untrustworthy, underhand, deceitful, double-dealing, disreputable, discreditable, shameful, scandalous; **corruptible**, bribable, buyable, venal, fraudulent, swindling, grafting, criminal, lawless, felonious, villainous, nefarious, iniquitous; Law malfeasant; informal crooked, shady, tricky, dirty, low-down, rascally, scoundrelly; Brit. informal bent, dodgy; archaic hollow-hearted.
▷ANTONYMS honest, law-abiding.
2 *the earth was corrupt in God's sight*: **sinful**, ungodly, unholy, irreligious, unrighteous, profane, blasphemous, impious, impure; **immoral**, depraved, degenerate, reprobate, vice-ridden, perverted, debauched, dissolute, dissipated, intemperate, decadent, profligate, wanton, abandoned, immodest, lustful, lascivious, lewd, lecherous, sordid; bad, wicked, evil, base, low; informal warped.
▷ANTONYMS moral.
3 *rural dialects were regarded as corrupt*: **impure**, adulterated, bastardized, alloyed, contaminated, debased, tainted, polluted, infected; deviant, distorted.
▷ANTONYMS pure.
▶ verb **1** *firms are corrupting politicians in the search for contracts*: **bribe**, suborn, buy, buy off, pay off; informal grease someone's palm, give someone a backhander, give someone a sweetener, keep someone sweet, get at, fix, square; Brit. informal nobble.
▷ANTONYMS purge.
2 *they argued that pornography did not corrupt its readers*: **pervert**, debauch, deprave, warp, subvert, make degenerate, lead astray, debase, degrade, defile, sully, infect, influence; archaic demoralize.
▷ANTONYMS purify.
3 *the apostolic writings had been corrupted by unknown persons*: **alter**, **falsify**, manipulate, tamper with, interfere with, tinker with, doctor, distort; adulterate, bastardize, dilute, contaminate, taint; informal fiddle with, cook; rare vitiate.

> *Word toolkit* **corrupt**
>
> See **illegal**.

corruption noun **1** *senior officials have been implicated in corruption*: **dishonesty**, dishonest dealings, unscrupulousness, deceit, deception, duplicity, double-dealing, fraud, fraudulence, misconduct, lawbreaking, crime, criminality, delinquency, wrongdoing, villainy; bribery, bribing, subornation, venality, graft, extortion, jobbery, profiteering; N. Amer. payola; informal crookedness, shadiness, sleaze, palm-greasing; Law malfeasance, misfeasance; archaic knavery; rare malversation.
▷ANTONYMS honesty.
2 *he is aware of his fall into corruption*: **sin**, sinfulness, ungodliness, unrighteousness, profanity, impiety, impurity; **immorality**, depravity, vice, iniquity, turpitude, degeneracy, perversion, pervertedness, debauchery, dissolution, dissoluteness, decadence, profligacy, wantonness, indecency, lasciviousness, lewdness, lechery; wickedness, evil, baseness, vileness.
▷ANTONYMS morality, purity.
3 *these figures have been subject to corruption*: **alteration**, **falsification**, doctoring, manipulation, manipulating, fudging, adulteration, debasement, degradation, abuse, subversion, misrepresentation, misapplication; rare vitiation.

corsair noun archaic *the ships had become game for the corsairs*: **pirate**, buccaneer, marauder, raider, plunderer, freebooter, privateer; archaic picaroon, filibuster, sea dog, sea rover, rover, reaver, scummer; rare marooner, sea thief, sea robber, sea wolf, sea rat, water rat.

corset noun *she wore a tight corset and bloomers*: **girdle**, panty girdle, foundation garment, foundation, support garment, corselette; Brit. roll-on; informal, dated waspie; Medicine truss; historical stays.

cortège noun **1** *the funeral cortège moved solemnly down the road*: **procession**, parade, cavalcade, motorcade, convoy, caravan, train, column,

file, line, trail, chain, rank, troop; Brit. march past; Brit. informal crocodile.
2 *the prince had an ever-present cortège*: **entourage**, retinue, train, suite, escort, court, company, attendant company; attendants, aides, associates, companions, followers, retainers.

cosmetic adjective **1** *some cosmetic products have been tested on animals*: **make-up**, beauty, beautifying.
2 *she spent large sums on cosmetic surgery*: **beautifying**, improving, non-medical; non-essential, inessential, not required, gratuitous, optional.
3 *alterations to the original building have been largely cosmetic*: **superficial**, surface, skin-deep, outward, exterior, external.
▷ANTONYMS fundamental; structural.
▶ noun (**cosmetics**) *their faces were heavily coated with cosmetics*: **make-up**, beauty products, beauty aids; informal warpaint, face paint, paint, slap; rare maquillage.

cosmic adjective **1** *social development forms part of the process of cosmic evolution*: **universal**, worldwide.
2 *the observatory surveyed cosmic X-ray sources*: **extraterrestrial**, in space, from space; heavenly, celestial, extramundane, other-worldly.
3 *the drama to be told was an epic of cosmic dimensions*: **vast**, huge, immense, enormous, massive, colossal, prodigious, immeasurable, incalculable, unfathomable, fathomless, measureless, infinite, limitless, boundless; informal mega, monster, whopping, whopping great, thumping, thumping great, humungous, jumbo, hulking, bumper, astronomical, astronomic; Brit. informal whacking, whacking great, ginormous.
▷ANTONYMS tiny.

cosmonaut noun **astronaut**, spaceman, spacewoman, space traveller, space pilot, space flyer, space cadet; N. Amer. informal jock.

cosmopolitan adjective **1** *the student body has a cosmopolitan character*: **international**, multiracial, worldwide, global, universal.
2 *he had a tolerant, cosmopolitan outlook on the world*: **worldly**, worldly-wise, well travelled, knowing, aware, mature, seasoned, experienced, unprovincial, cultivated, cultured, sophisticated, suave, urbane, polished, refined; liberal, broad-minded, unprejudiced; informal streetwise, cool.
▷ANTONYMS provincial; narrow; unsophisticated.

cosset verb *before her papa died she had been spoiled and cosseted*: **pamper**, indulge, overindulge, mollycoddle, coddle, baby, pet, mother, nanny, nursemaid, pander to, spoon-feed, feather-bed, spoil; wrap in cotton wool, wait on someone hand and foot, cater to someone's every whim, kill with kindness; archaic cocker.

cost noun **1** *there was a row over the cost of the equipment*: **price**, asking price, market price, selling price, fee, tariff, fare, toll, levy, charge, hire charge, rental; value, face value, valuation, quotation, rate, worth; informal, humorous damage.
2 *the human cost of centuries of conflict*: **penalty**, **sacrifice**, loss; expense, toll, price; suffering, harm, hurt, injury, damage, detriment, deprivation; disadvantage, downside, drawback, snag, undesirable consequences, adverse effects.
3 (**costs**) *the company is not making enough money to cover its costs*: **expenses**, outgoings, disbursements, overheads, running costs, operating costs, fixed costs; expenditure, spending, outlay, money spent, payments.
▶ verb **1** *the chair costs £186*: **be priced at**, sell for, be valued at, fetch, come to, amount to, be; informal set someone back, go for; Brit. informal knock someone back.
2 *the proposal has not yet been costed*: **value**, price, put a price on, put a value on, put a figure on, estimate the cost of, estimate the price of, evaluate.
3 *that act of heroism cost him his life*: **cause the loss of**, cause the sacrifice of, lead to the end of; destroy, result in harm to, result in damage to, harm, hurt, injure, damage.

costly adjective **1** *his work was published in small and costly editions*: **expensive**, dear, high-cost, high-priced, highly priced, overpriced, exorbitant, extortionate, immoderate, extravagant; lavish, rich, de luxe, choice, fine, exquisite; valuable, priceless, worth its weight in gold, worth a king's ransom; Brit. upmarket, over the odds; informal steep, pricey.
▷ANTONYMS cheap, inexpensive.
2 *in those weather conditions any mistakes could be costly*: **catastrophic**, ruinous, disastrous, calamitous, cataclysmic, devastating, crippling, crushing, fatal, lethal, damaging, harmful, injurious, deleterious, woeful, grievous, lamentable, dire, awful, terrible, unfortunate; literary direful.
▷ANTONYMS beneficial.

costume noun **1** *there's a prize for the best costume | the dancers wore Maltese national costume*: **outfit**, ensemble, suit; **dress**, clothing, attire, garb, uniform, livery, array, regalia; clothes, garments, robes; informal get-up, gear, togs, garms, duds, glad rags; Brit. informal clobber, kit, strip, rig-out; N. Amer. informal threads; formal apparel; literary raiment, habiliments; archaic vestments, vesture, habit.
2 Brit. *if you'd like a dip, we can lend you a costume*: **swimsuit**, bathing suit, bathing costume, swimming costume, bikini; pair of swimming trunks, pair of trunks; informal cossie, swimming togs; Austral./NZ informal bathers.

cosy adjective **1** *she lived in a cosy country cottage | I felt cosy and contented*: **snug**, comfortable, warm, restful, homelike, homey, homely, cheerful, welcoming, pleasant, agreeable; safe, sheltered, secure, at ease, mellow; N. Amer. down-home, homestyle; informal comfy, snug as a bug (in a rug).
▷ANTONYMS uncomfortable.
2 *she had a cosy chat with an old school friend*: **intimate**, relaxed, informal, friendly.

coterie noun *all prime ministers develop a small coterie of kindred spirits*: **clique**, set, circle, inner circle, crowd, in-crowd, gang, band, pack, crew, clan, club, fellowship, brotherhood, fraternity, sorority, sect, camp, community, league, alliance, faction, cabal, junta, caucus, syndicate, nucleus, cell; Austral./NZ push.

cottage noun *she had a cottage in Wales*: **small house**, house, bungalow, villa, lodge, chalet, cabin, shack, shanty; holiday home, holiday cottage, retreat; home, residence, place, abode; in Scotland **bothy**; in Russia **dacha**; in France **gîte**; Scottish **but and ben**; S. African **rondavel**; informal **pad**, **semi**; N. Amer. informal **crib**; Austral. informal **weekender**; literary **bower**; archaic **cot**.

couch noun *she seated herself on the couch*: **settee**, sofa, divan, chaise longue, chesterfield, love seat, settle, ottoman; Brit. put-you-up; N. Amer. day bed, davenport, studio couch, sectional; French canapé, tête-à-tête; rare squab.
▶ verb *his reply was couched in deferential terms*: **express**, phrase, word, frame, put, formulate, style, render, set forth, put across, convey, communicate, say, state, utter, voice.

cough noun *the child had a terrible cough*: **hack**, rasp, croak, wheeze, tickle in one's throat; informal bark, frog in one's throat; technical tussis.
▶ verb **1** *the room was heavy with cigarette smoke and she coughed*: **hack**, hawk, bark, clear one's throat, hem, croak, wheeze, gasp, choke, struggle for breath, fight for air.
2 Brit. informal *once he realized the information we had on him, he was ready to cough*: **confess**, talk, tell all, tell the truth, blab, open one's mouth, give the game away; informal come clean, let on, spill the beans, let the cat out of the bag, get something off one's chest; Brit. informal blow the gaff.
□ **cough up** informal *the tenants refused to cough up the rent | Richard had to cough up for the beer*: **pay**, pay up, pay out; come up with, hand over, part with, defray the cost of; foot the bill, settle up; informal fork out, shell out, dish out, lay out, come across with; Brit. informal stump up; N. Amer. informal make with, ante up, pony up.

> *Word links* **cough**
>
> **tussive** relating to coughing

council noun **1** *they won an election for their seats on the council*: **local authority**, local government, municipal authority, civic authority, legislative body, legislature, administration, executive, chamber, assembly, ministry, governing body, government, parliament, senate, congress, diet, cabinet; Brit. corporation.
2 *I took part in a project with the Schools Council*: **advisory body**, advisory group, board, board of directors, committee, commission, assembly, panel, trustees, delegates, delegation; synod, convocation, chapter; rare advisorate.
3 *the king had been sitting in council*: **conference**, conclave, assembly, convocation; meeting, gathering.

> *Easily confused words* **council or counsel?**
>
> Despite their similarity in pronunciation, **council** and **counsel** have different meanings. A *council* is a formally constituted body of people meeting for administrative or advisory purposes: *he was on the council of the League for Penal Reform. Counsel*, on the other hand, is a rather formal word for advice, as in *the wise counsel of his elder brother*. It can also be used as a verb, meaning 'advise, give advice': *older people counselled prudence*.

counsel noun **1** *he no longer came to me for counsel*: **advice**, guidance, direction, instruction, information, enlightenment; recommendations, suggestions, hints, tips, pointers, guidelines, ideas, opinions, views, facts, data; warning, admonition, caution.
2 *King Richard held counsel with the barons*: **conference**, consultation, discussion, deliberation, dialogue, conversation; talks, negotiations; formal confabulation.
3 *his counsel told the jury that the charges were false*: **barrister**, lawyer, counsellor, legal practitioner; N. Amer. attorney; N. Amer. & Irish counsellor-at-law; Scottish Law advocate; informal brief.
▶ verb *he counselled the team to withdraw from the deal*: **advise**, guide, direct, recommend, encourage, entreat, urge, warn, admonish, caution; give guidance to, give direction to, give one's opinion to, give one's suggestions to.

> *Easily confused words* **counsel or council?**
>
> See **council**.

counsellor noun *they talked through their problems with a trained counsellor | a debt counsellor*: **adviser**, consultant, guide, mentor, confidant, confidante; instructor, coach, teacher, tutor, guru, expert, specialist;

therapist, guidance counsellor, psychologist, psychiatrist, analyst, psychotherapist, mind doctor, head doctor, healer; informal shrink, trick cyclist, head shrinker.

count verb **1** *he was counting a stack of dollar bills*: **add up**, add together, find the sum of, sum up, reckon up, figure up, calculate, compute, enumerate, total, tally, add; Brit. tot up; dated cast up.
2 *you do need to be accurate in counting calories*: **keep a tally of**, keep a count of, keep a record of; count up, count off, enumerate, tell, work out.
3 *there were seventy people backstage, not counting the actors*: **include**, take into account, take account of, take into consideration, allow for, incorporate.
4 *I count it a privilege to be asked to become chairman*: **consider**, think, feel, regard, look on as, view as, see as, hold to be, judge, adjudge, rate as, deem to be, account, esteem.
5 *I was made to feel that, because I'm not married, my baby and I don't count*: **matter**, enter into consideration, be of consequence, be of account, be significant, signify, mean anything, mean a lot, amount to anything, rate, be important, be influential, carry weight, weigh, make an impression; informal cut any ice, have any clout.
□ **count on/upon 1** *he could usually be counted on to give lifts*: **rely on**, depend on, place reliance on, lean on, bank on, trust, be sure of, trust in, place one's trust in, have (every) confidence in, believe in, put one's faith in, pin one's faith on, swear by, take for granted, take on trust, take as read. **2** *they hadn't counted on Rangers' indomitable spirit*: **expect**, reckon on, anticipate, envisage, predict, foresee, forecast, foretell, think likely, contemplate the possibility of, allow for, be prepared for, bargain for, bargain on, bank on, plan on, calculate on; N. Amer. informal figure on; archaic apprehend.
□ **count someone/something in** *Marie nodded enthusiastically. 'Count me in!'*: **include**, involve, bring in, take in, admit, introduce, add, enter, incorporate; take into account, take account of, take note of, allow for; allow to participate, allow to take part, let someone in on something.
□ **count someone/something out** *I think you'd better count me out*: **exclude**, omit, leave out, rule out, except, reject, drop, eliminate, cut out, keep out; pass over, disregard, ignore.
▸ noun **1** *at the last count, the committee had 579 members*: **calculation**, enumeration, computation, reckoning, counting, telling, tally, tallying, totting up; poll, census, listing, register.
2 *tests showed she had a raised white blood cell count*: **amount**, number, tally, total, total number, sum total, grand total, full amount, aggregate, whole.
□ **out for the count** informal **unconscious**, comatose, knocked out, inert, insensible, senseless, insensate, insentient; anaesthetized, soundly asleep; informal out, out cold, zonked out, dead to the world, kayoed, KO'd; Brit. informal spark out; rare soporose, soporous.

countenance noun *he had a strikingly handsome and sensitive countenance*: **face**, features, physiognomy, profile; facial expression, expression, look, appearance, aspect, mien; informal mug, clock; Brit. informal mush, dial, phizog, phiz; Brit. rhyming slang boat race; Scottish & Irish informal coupon; N. Amer. informal puss, pan; literary visage, lineaments; archaic front.
▸ verb *they would not countenance any breach of fair play*: **tolerate**, permit, allow, admit of, approve (of), agree to, consent to, give one's blessing to, take kindly to, be in favour of, favour, hold with, go along with, put up with, endure, brook, stomach, swallow, bear; Scottish thole; informal stand for, stick, hack, give the go ahead to, give the green light to, give the thumbs up to, give the okay to; N. Amer. rare approbate.

counter[1] noun **1** *he left his groceries on the counter*: **worktop**, work surface, work table, table, bench, buffet, top, horizontal surface; checkout, bar, stand.
2 *the idea of the game is to collect the most counters*: **token**, chip, disc, jetton; piece, man, marker, wafer; N. Amer. check.

counter[2] verb *the workers countered accusations of dishonesty with claims of oppression*: **parry**, hit back at, answer, respond to, retort to, contradict, negate; ward off, fend off, stave off, deflect, rebuff, rebut, repel, repulse, hold at bay; combat, fight, attack, tackle, confront, stand up to, put up a fight against, oppose, resist, dispute, argue against; counteract; informal shoot full of holes, blow sky high; formal gainsay; rare controvert, confute, negative.
▷ANTONYMS support.
▸ adjective *after years of argument and counter argument there is no conclusive answer*: **opposing**, opposed, opposite, contrary, adverse, conflicting, contradictory, contrasting, obverse, different, differing.
▷ANTONYMS complementary.
▸ adverb *the policy would run* ***counter to*** *EC plans*: **against**, in opposition to, contrary to, at variance with, in defiance of, in contravention of, contrarily, contrariwise, conversely; against the tide, in the opposite direction, in the reverse direction, in the wrong direction.
▷ANTONYMS in accordance with.

counteract verb **1** *new measures were brought in to counteract counterfeiting*: **prevent**, thwart, frustrate, foil, impede, curb, restrain, forestall, hinder, hamper, baulk, oppose, act against, stall, check, resist, withstand, defeat, put a stop to, bring an end to; fend off, ward off, stave off, head off.
▷ANTONYMS encourage.
2 *studying foreign history counteracts tendencies to insularity*: **offset**, counterbalance, balance, balance out, cancel out, even out, counterpoise, countervail, compensate for, make up for, remedy; neutralize, nullify, annul, negate, invalidate; rare counterweigh, equilibrize, negative.
▷ANTONYMS enhance, exacerbate.

counterbalance verb *the risk of failure tends to be counterbalanced by high rewards*: **compensate for**, make up for, offset, balance, balance out, even out, equalize, neutralize, nullify, negate, undo, countervail, counterpoise, counteract; rare counterweigh, equilibrize, negative.

counterfeit adjective *they were charged with supplying counterfeit cassettes*: **fake**, faked, copied, forged, feigned, simulated, sham, spurious, bogus, imitation, substitute, dummy, ersatz; informal knock-off, pirate, pirated, phoney, pseud, pseudo; Brit. informal, dated cod.
▷ANTONYMS genuine.
▸ noun *the shopkeeper knew the notes to be counterfeits*: **fake**, forgery, copy, reproduction, replica, imitation, likeness, lookalike, mock-up, dummy, substitute, fraud, sham; informal phoney, pirate, knock-off, rip-off, put-on, dupe.
▷ANTONYMS original.
▸ verb *my signature is extremely hard to counterfeit*: **fake**, forge, copy, reproduce, replicate, imitate, simulate, feign, falsify, sham; informal pirate.

countermand verb *orders were being issued and then countermanded*: **revoke**, rescind, reverse, undo, repeal, retract, withdraw, take back, abrogate, abolish, quash, scrap, override, overturn, overrule, do away with, set aside, cancel, annul, invalidate, nullify, negate, veto, declare null and void; back-pedal on, backtrack on, do a U-turn on; Law disaffirm, discharge, avoid, vacate, vitiate; informal axe, ditch, dump, knock on the head; archaic recall; rare disannul.
▷ANTONYMS uphold.

counterpart noun *the president held talks with his Bangladeshi counterpart*: **equivalent**, opposite number, peer, equal, parallel, complement, match, twin, mate, fellow, brother, sister, analogue, correlative; copy, duplicate; rare compeer, coequal.

countless adjective *penicillin has relieved the suffering of countless patients*: **innumerable**, untold, legion, numberless, unnumbered, numerous, very many, manifold, multitudinous, multifarious; a great number of, incalculable numbers of, immeasurable numbers of, endless numbers of, infinite numbers of, a multitude of, a multiplicity of; more than one can count, too many to be counted; informal umpteen, no end of, loads of, stacks of, heaps of, masses of, oodles of, bags of, scads of, zillions of; N. Amer. informal a slew of, a bunch of, gazillions of, bazillions of; S. African informal lank; literary myriad, divers; rare innumerous, unnumberable.
▷ANTONYMS few.

countrified adjective *the countrified ambience was spoilt by the express trains*: **rural**, rustic, pastoral, bucolic, countryside, country; idyllic, unspoilt; literary Arcadian, sylvan; rare georgic, exurban.
▷ANTONYMS urban.

country noun **1** *he became the greatest ruler the country had known*: **state**, nation, sovereign state, kingdom, realm, territory, province, principality, palatinate, duchy, empire, commonwealth.
2 *I had a chance of representing my country*: **homeland**, native land, native soil, fatherland, motherland, mother country, country of origin, birthplace; the land of one's birth, the land of one's fathers, the old country, one's roots, one's home.
3 *they travelled through thickly forested country*: **terrain**, land, territory, parts; landscape, scenery, setting, surroundings, environment.
4 *the president made televised speeches to the country*: **people**, public, general public, population, populace, community, citizenry, nation, body politic, collective; inhabitants, residents, citizens, electors, voters, taxpayers, ratepayers, grass roots; Brit. informal Joe Public; rare indigenes.
5 *in 1700, ninety per cent of the population lived in* ***the country***: **countryside**, green belt, great outdoors; provinces, backwoods, wilds, wilderness, hinterland; a rural area, a rural district; farmland, agricultural land; Austral. outback, bush, back country, backblocks, booay; S. African backveld, platteland; informal sticks, back of beyond, middle of nowhere; N. Amer. informal boondocks, boonies, tall timbers; Austral. informal Woop Woop, beyond the black stump.
▷ANTONYMS city.
▸ adjective *she loved fresh air and country pursuits*: **rural**, countryside, outdoor, rustic, pastoral, bucolic; agrarian, agricultural, farming; literary sylvan, Arcadian; rare georgic, agrestic, exurban.
▷ANTONYMS urban.

countryman, countrywoman noun **1** *she was forced into a betrayal of her countrywoman*: **compatriot**, fellow citizen, fellow national, fellow countryman/countrywoman.
2 *the countryman takes a great interest in the weather*: **farmer**, farmhand, country dweller, country cousin, son/daughter of the soil; rustic, yokel, bumpkin, peasant, provincial; French paysan; Russian muzhik, kulak; Spanish campesino, paisano; Italian contadino, contadina; Egyptian fellah; Indian ryot; Irish informal culchie, bogman; N. Amer. informal hayseed, hick, hillbilly, rube,

schlub; Austral. informal bushy, ocker; archaic swain, hind, kern, carl, churl, cottier; rare bucolic.

countryside noun 1 *the hotel is set in acres of breathtaking countryside*: **landscape**, scenery, surroundings, setting, environment; terrain, land, country, parts.
2 (**the countryside**) *I was brought up in the countryside*: **a rural area**, a rural district, farmland, agricultural land, the country, the green belt, the great outdoors; the provinces, the backwoods, the wilds, the wilderness, the hinterland; Austral. the outback, the bush, the back country, the booay; S. African the backveld, the platteland; informal the sticks, the back of beyond, the middle of nowhere; N. Amer. informal the boondocks, the boonies, the tall timbers; Austral. informal Woop Woop, beyond the black stump.

county noun *the Northern counties of England*: **shire**, province, territory, administrative unit, sector, department, state; region, district, area, zone; archaic demesne.
▶ adjective Brit. *a county grande dame*: **landowning**, landed, upper-class, well born, high-born, noble-born, noble, aristocratic, patrician, titled, blue-blooded, born with a silver spoon in one's mouth; Brit. upmarket; informal upper-crust, top-drawer, {huntin', shootin', and fishin'}, tweedy, classy, posh; archaic gentle, of gentle birth.

coup noun 1 *the prime minister was deposed in a coup in 1995*: **seizure of power**, overthrow, takeover, ousting, deposition, regime change; bloodless coup, palace revolution; **rebellion**, revolt, insurrection, mutiny, revolution, insurgence, insurgency, rising, rioting, riot; French coup d'état, jacquerie; German putsch.
▷ANTONYMS election.
2 *securing Springsteen to open the new National Bowl was a coup for the owners*: **success**, triumph, feat, successful manoeuvre, stunt, accomplishment, achievement, attainment, stroke, master stroke, stroke of genius; scoop; French tour de force.

coup de grâce noun *he administered the coup de grâce with a knife*: **death blow**, finishing blow, killing, dispatch; kiss of death; informal KO, kayo.

coup d'état noun *the coup d'état which brought the general to power*: **seizure of power**, coup, overthrow, takeover, ousting, deposition, regime change; bloodless coup, palace revolution; **rebellion**, revolt, insurrection, mutiny, revolution, insurgence, insurgency, rising, rioting, riot; French jacquerie; German putsch.

couple noun 1 *the defenders feed a long pass to either of a couple of strikers*: **pair**, duo, twosome, set of two, match; doublets, twins; brace, span, yoke; two, two of a kind; rare duplet, dyad, duad, doubleton; archaic twain.
2 *a couple whose dream holiday plans have been ruined*: **husband and wife**, twosome; newly-weds, partners, lovers, cohabitees; informal item.
□ **a couple of** informal *a couple of drinks*: **a few**, two or three, a small number of; N. Amer. a couple.
▷ANTONYMS several.
▶ verb 1 *the use of weights **coupled with** longer exercise periods is very demanding*: **combine**, integrate, mix, incorporate, accompany, link, team, associate, connect, ally; add to, join to; formal conjoin.
▷ANTONYMS divorce.
2 *the vans could be coupled together to form a train*: **connect**, attach, join, fasten, fix, link, secure, tie, bind, strap, rope, tether, truss, lash, hitch, yoke, chain; stick, tape, glue, bond, cement, fuse, weld, solder; pin, peg, screw, bolt, rivet, clamp, clip, hook (up); add, append, annex, subjoin; technical concatenate.
▷ANTONYMS separate.

coupon noun 1 *the bumper membership pack includes money-off coupons*: **voucher**, token, ticket, document, certificate, carnet; chit, slip, stub, counterfoil, detachable portion, receipt, docket; Brit. informal chitty; N. Amer. informal ducat, comp.
2 *for further information, fill in the coupon below*: **form**, tear-off slip, entry form, application form.

courage noun *it takes courage to speak out against the tide of opinion*: **bravery**, braveness, courageousness, pluck, pluckiness, valour, fearlessness, intrepidity, intrepidness, nerve, daring, audacity, boldness; dauntlessness, doughtiness, stout-heartedness, hardihood, manfulness, heroism, gallantry; backbone, spine, spirit, spiritedness, mettle, determination, fortitude, resolve, resolution; informal guts, grit, spunk, gutsiness, gameness; Brit. informal bottle, ballsiness; N. Amer. informal moxie, cojones, sand; vulgar slang balls.
▷ANTONYMS cowardice; timidity.

courageous adjective *only the children were courageous enough to step out of hiding*: **brave**, plucky, fearless, valiant, valorous, intrepid, heroic, lionhearted, manful, bold, daring, daredevil, adventurous, audacious; undaunted, unflinching, unshrinking, unafraid, dauntless, indomitable, doughty, mettlesome, venturesome, stout-hearted, stout, spirited, gallant, stalwart, resolute, determined, death-or-glory; N. Amer. rock-ribbed; informal game, gutsy, spunky, ballsy, have-a-go; rare venturous.
▷ANTONYMS cowardly, timid.

courier noun 1 *the documents were sent by courier*: **messenger**, special messenger, dispatch rider, letter carrier, mail carrier, runner, bearer, message bearer, message carrier, delivery man, delivery woman, conveyor, envoy, emissary, harbinger, herald; historical pursuivant; archaic forerunner, legate, estafette.
2 *he worked as a courier on a package holiday to Majorca*: **representative**, guide, tour guide, travel guide, tour company representative; dragoman; N. Amer. tour director; informal (holiday) rep.

course noun 1 *the island was not very far off our course*: **route**, way, track, direction, tack, path, line, journey, itinerary, channel, trail, trajectory, flight path, bearing, heading, orbit, circuit, beat, round, run.
2 *a device which changed the course of history*: **progression**, development, progress, advance, advancement, evolution, unfolding, flow, movement, continuity, sequence, order, succession, rise, march, furtherance, forwarding, proceeding.
3 *what is the best course to adopt?* **plan (of action)**, course of action, method of working, MO, line of action, process, procedure, practice, approach, technique, style, manner, way, means, mode of behaviour, mode of conduct, methodology, system, policy, strategy, programme, formula, regimen; Latin modus operandi; rare praxis.
4 *the race is over ten laps of the course*: **track**, racetrack, racecourse, circuit, ground, stadium, speedway, velodrome, route, trail; in ancient Rome circus; rare cirque.
5 *the waiter served them their next course*: **dish**, menu item.
6 *work flowed in during the course of the day*: **duration**, passing, passage, lapse, period, term, span, spell, sweep.
7 *he's taking a course in art history*: **programme of study**, course of study, educational programme, set of lectures, curriculum, syllabus, schedule; classes, lectures, studies.
8 *a course of antibiotics*: **programme**, series, sequence, system, schedule, regimen.
9 *six courses of bricks were laid*: **layer**, thickness, stratum, seam, vein, band, bed.
□ **in due course** *I look forward to hearing from you in due course*: **at the appropriate time**, when the time is ripe, in time, in due time, in the fullness of time, in the course of time, at a later time, at a later date, at length, at a future time/date, at some point in the future, in the future, in time to come, as time goes on/by, by and by, one day, some day, sooner or later, in a while, after a bit, eventually.
□ **of course 1** *there are, of course, exceptions to the rule*: **naturally**, as might be expected, as you/one would expect, needless to say, not unexpectedly, certainly, to be sure, as was anticipated, as a matter of course; obviously, clearly, it goes without saying; informal natch. **2** *'Have you got a minute?' 'Of course.'*: **yes**, certainly, definitely, absolutely, by all means, with pleasure; informal sure thing.
□ **on course** *he remains on course for re-election in two years*: **on track**, on target, on schedule.
▶ verb 1 *she was aware of the blood coursing through her veins*: **flow**, pour, race, stream, run, rush, gush, pump, move, cascade, flood, surge, sweep, roll; Brit. informal sloosh.
2 *several hares are coursed each week on the estate*: **hunt**, chase, pursue, stalk, run down, run after, give chase to, follow, track, trail, shadow, hound, dog; informal tail.

court noun 1 *the court found him guilty*: **court of law**, law court, bench, bar, court of justice, judicature, tribunal, forum, chancery, assizes; courtroom; French palais de justice.
2 *a tennis court*: **playing area**, enclosure, field, ground, ring, rink, green, alley, stadium, track, arena; Brit. close; informal park.
3 *walking in the castle court*: **yard**, courtyard, quadrangle, square, close, enclosure, precinct, esplanade; in Spain plaza, patio; in Italy piazza; cloister, arcade; S. African lapa; informal quad.
4 *they often put on plays for the Queen's court*: **royal household**, establishment, retinue, entourage, train, suite, escort, company, attendant company, staff, personnel, cortège, following, bodyguard; aides, members of court, courtiers, companions, attendants, servants, retainers, associates, followers.
5 *she made her way to Queen Elizabeth's court in England*: **royal residence**, palace, castle, manor, hall; in France château; in Italy palazzo; in German-speaking countries schloss; in Spain alcazar; in Turkey, historical seraglio.
6 *statesmen came to pay court to the king*: **homage**, deference, obedience, suit, courtship, blandishments, respects, attention, addresses; (**pay court to**) **woo**, court, make up to, make advances to, pursue, seek the favour of; **grovel to**, creep to, crawl to, bow and scrape to, toady to, be obsequious to, be servile to, be sycophantic to, abase oneself to, demean oneself to, defer to, ingratiate oneself with, curry favour with, fawn on, flatter, dance attendance on, truckle to, submit to; informal suck up to, lick someone's boots, butter up; N. Amer. informal brown-nose; Austral./NZ informal smoodge to; vulgar slang kiss the arse of.
▶ verb 1 *Western politicians courted the leaders of the newly independent states*: **curry favour with**, make up to, play up to; ingratiate oneself with, cultivate, seek the favour of, try to win over, try to get on the good side of; **be obsequious towards**, grovel to, be servile towards, be sycophantic towards, kowtow to, pander to, abase oneself to, demean oneself to, bow and scrape to, prostrate oneself to, toady to, truckle to, dance attendance on, fawn on/over; informal suck up to, crawl to, creep to, be all over, lick

someone's boots, fall all over, rub up the right way, keep someone sweet, sweet-talk, soft-soap, butter up; N. Amer. brown-nose; vulgar slang lick/kiss someone's arse; archaic blandish.
2 *he was busily courting public attention*: **seek**, try to obtain, pursue, go after, strive for, go for, push towards, work towards, be intent on, aim at/for, have as a goal, have as an objective, aspire to; solicit, ask for.
3 *I knew I was courting disaster climbing without a rope*: **risk**, invite, attract, provoke, be likely to cause, bring on oneself; be likely to lead to.
4 dated *he's courting her sister*: **woo**, go out with, be involved with, be romantically linked with, pursue, run after, chase, seek the company of, make advances to, make up to, flirt with; informal see, go steady with, date, chat up, make (sheep's) eyes at, give the come-on to, be all over; Austral. informal track with, track square with; dated set one's cap at, pay addresses to, romance, pay suit to, pay court to, seek the hand of, make love to; archaic spark.
5 dated *we saw the film when we were courting*: **go out together**, go out, go with each other, keep company; informal date, go steady.

Word links **court**

forensic relating to law courts

courteous adjective *enquiries will be dealt with by our highly skilled, courteous staff*: **polite**, well mannered, civil, respectful, deferential, well behaved, well bred; gentlemanly, chivalrous, gallant; ladylike, genteel; cultivated, gracious, obliging, kind, considerate, pleasant, cordial, genial, affable, thoughtful, urbane, well brought up, well spoken; formal, proper, polished, refined, decorous, courtly, civilized, tactful, discreet, diplomatic; Brit. informal decent; dated mannerly.
▷ANTONYMS discourteous, rude.

Choose the right word **courteous, polite, civil**

See **polite**.

courtesan noun archaic *courtesans were invited into the palace to satisfy the Emperor's lust*. See **prostitute**.

courtesy noun **1** *customers deserve to be treated with courtesy*: **politeness**, courteousness, good manners, civility, respect, respectfulness, deference, chivalry, gallantry, gallantness, good breeding, gentility, graciousness, kindness, consideration, thought, thoughtfulness, cordiality, geniality, affability, urbanity, polish, refinement, courtliness, decorousness, tact, discretion, diplomacy; Brit. informal decency.
▷ANTONYMS discourtesy, rudeness.
2 *an outing by courtesy of the firm*: **benevolence**, kindness, generosity, indulgence, favour, consideration, consent, permission.

courtier noun *the Princess set up her own select circle of trusted courtiers*: **attendant**, retainer, companion, adviser, aide, henchman, follower; lady-in-waiting, lady of the bedchamber; cup-bearer, steward, train-bearer; lord, lady, noble, equerry, page, squire; historical liegeman.

courtly adjective *he gave a courtly bow*: **refined**, polished, cultivated, cultured, civilized, stylish, elegant, sophisticated, urbane, suave, debonair; **polite**, civil, courteous, gracious, well mannered, well bred, chivalrous, gallant, gentlemanly, ladylike, honourable, genteel, aristocratic, dignified, decorous, formal, ceremonious, stately, proper; informal couth; archaic gentle.
▷ANTONYMS uncouth.

courtship noun **1** *he married his wife after a whirlwind courtship*: **romance**, affair, love affair, going out, going steady, dating, engagement, keeping company.
2 *the supposed courtship of Harriet by Mr Elton*: **wooing**, courting, suit, pursuit, attentions, advances, blandishments; archaic addresses.

courtyard noun **yard**, court, quadrangle, square, close, enclosure, precinct; in Spain **plaza**, patio; in Italy **piazza**; cloister, arcade; S. African **lapa**; informal **quad**.

cove noun *the steps carved out of the cliff led down to a small sandy cove*: **bay**, inlet, indentation, fjord, natural harbour, anchorage; Scottish (sea) loch; Irish lough.

covenant noun *there is a landlord's covenant to repair the property*: **contract**, compact, treaty, pact, accord, deal, bargain, settlement, concordat, protocol, entente, agreement, arrangement, understanding, pledge, promise, bond, indenture, guarantee, warrant; undertaking, commitment.
▸ verb *the landlord covenants to repair the property*: **undertake**, give an undertaking, pledge, promise, agree, contract, vow, guarantee, warrant, commit oneself, bind oneself, give one's word, enter into an agreement, engage; archaic plight (oneself).

cover verb **1** *Jack covered the children with the blanket*: **put something on top of**, place something over, place under cover; protect, shield, shelter; envelop, enfold, engulf, enclose, tuck, cup, surround, house, sink, embed, bury, submerge, immerse.
▷ANTONYMS reveal.
2 *his car was covered in mud*: **cake**, coat, encrust, plaster, spread thickly, smother, daub, smear, bedaub, overspread; literary besmear.
3 *snow covered the fields*: **blanket**, overlay, overspread, carpet, overlie, extend over, layer, coat, film, submerge; literary mantle, pave.
4 *the scheme covers six local libraries*: **include**, involve, take in, deal with, contain, comprise, provide for, embrace, embody, incorporate, subsume, refer to, consider.
5 *the trial was covered by a range of newspapers*: **report**, write up, write about, describe, commentate on, tell of, write/give an account of, publish/broadcast details of, investigate, look into, enquire into.
6 *he turned on the radio to cover their conversation*: **mask**, disguise, obscure, hide, stop something being overheard, muffle, stifle, smother; camouflage, blot out, cloak, veil, shroud, swathe, secrete, envelop; literary enshroud.
7 *if the sergeant wants to know where you are, I'll cover for you*: **give an alibi to**, provide with an alibi, shield, protect; informal alibi.
▷ANTONYMS give away.
8 *they could train an extra secretary to* **cover for** *others who are on holiday or sick leave*: **stand in for**, fill in for, act as stand-in for, deputize for, act as deputy for, substitute for, act as substitute for, take over from, double for, be a substitute for; replace, relieve, take the place of, act in place of, do duty for, do a locum for, be a locum for, sit in for, understudy; hold the fort, step into the breach; informal sub for, fill someone's shoes/boots; N. Amer. informal pinch-hit for.
9 *can you make enough to cover your costs?* **offset**, **counterbalance**, balance, cancel out, make up for, pay back, pay, pay for, be enough for, fund, finance, make up, have enough money for, provide for.
10 *your home is covered against damage and loss*: **insure**, protect, secure, underwrite, provide insurance for, assure, indemnify.
11 *we covered ten miles each day*: **travel**, journey, go, do, put behind one, get under one's belt, travel over, pass over, journey over/across, traverse, cross, go across, make one's way across, range/tramp over.
□ **cover something up** *the government has repeatedly tried to cover up the army's role*: **conceal**, hide; keep secret, hush up, keep dark, draw a veil over, suppress, sweep under the carpet, gloss over; informal whitewash, keep a/the lid on.
▷ANTONYMS expose.
▸ noun **1** *a dust cover for the keyboard*: **sleeve**, **wrapping**, wrapper, covering, envelope, sheath, sheathing, housing, jacket, casing, cowling; awning, tarpaulin; lid, top, cap.
2 *a book cover*: **binding**, case; boards; jacket, dust jacket, dust cover, wrapper.
3 (**covers**) *she pulled the covers up over her head*: **bedclothes**, bedding, sheets, blankets, linen; duvet, quilt, eiderdown; bedspread, counterpane.
4 *a thick cover of snow*: **coating**, coat, covering, layer, carpet, blanket, overlay, topping, dusting, cloak, mantle, canopy, film, sheet, veneer, crust, surface, skim, skin, thickness, deposit, veil, pall, shroud.
5 *panicking onlookers ran for cover*: **shelter**, protection, refuge, hiding, concealment, housing, sanctuary; shield, defence, haven, hiding place.
6 *there is considerable game cover around the lake*: **undergrowth**, vegetation, shrubbery, greenery, ground cover, underwood, copsewood, brushwood, brush, scrub, underscrub; woodland, forest, jungle; bushes, plants; covert, thicket, copse, coppice; N. Amer. underbrush, underbush, shintangle; SE English **frith**; archaic **rone**; rare **herbage**, verdure.
7 *the company was a cover for an international swindle*: **front**, facade, smokescreen, screen, blind, deception, camouflage, disguise, mask, cloak, pretext, masquerade, feint.
8 Brit. *your policy already provides cover against damage by subsidence*: **insurance**, protection, security, assurance, indemnification, indemnity, compensation.
9 *the information you requested is being sent under separate cover*: **envelope**, wrapper, package; **wrapping**, packaging.

coverage noun *they praised the newspaper's coverage of sport*: **reporting**, reportage, description, treatment, handling, presentation; investigation, exploration, consideration, study, analysis, commentary; reports, accounts, articles, pieces, stories.

covering noun **1** *the canvas covering of the back of the wagon*: **awning**, tarpaulin, cowling, casing, housing; wrapping, wrapper, cover, envelope, sheath, sheathing, sleeve, jacket, lid, top, cap.
2 *a decent covering of snow on the slopes*: **layer**, **coating**, coat, cover, carpet, blanket, overlay, topping, dusting, cloak, mantle, canopy, film, sheet, veneer, crust, surface, skim, skin, thickness, deposit, veil, pall, shroud.
▸ adjective *a covering letter*: **accompanying**, associated; **explanatory**, expository, introductory, prefatory, descriptive.

coverlet noun *she pulled back the coverlet from the bed*: **bedspread**, bedcover, cover, throw, afghan; duvet, quilt; Brit. eiderdown; N. Amer. spread, comforter; dated counterpane.

covert adjective *a covert rescue mission at night*: **secret**, furtive, clandestine, surreptitious, stealthy, cloak-and-dagger, hole-and-corner, hole-in-the-corner, closet, behind-the-scenes, backstairs, back-alley, under-the-table, hugger-mugger, concealed, hidden, private; sly, sneaky, underhand; undercover, underground; informal hush-hush.
▷ANTONYMS overt; above board.

cover-up noun *the other officers charged were mostly implicated in the cover-up rather than the massacre itself*: **whitewash**, **concealment**,

deception, suppression, false front, facade, veneer, pretext; -gate, camouflage, disguise, mask.
▷ANTONYMS exposé.

covet verb *people still coveted things which didn't belong to them*: **desire**, be consumed with desire for, crave, have one's heart set on; **want**, wish for, long for, yearn for, dream of, aspire to, hanker for, hanker after, hunger after/for, thirst for, ache for, fancy, burn for, pant for.

covetous adjective *the covetous man will never have enough*: **grasping**, greedy, rapacious, insatiable, yearning, acquisitive, desirous, possessive, selfish; **jealous**, envious, green with envy, green, green-eyed; grudging, begrudging; N. Amer. informal grabby.
▷ANTONYMS satisfied.

covey noun *a covey of partridges | a covey of young ladies trooped through*: **group**, gang, troop, troupe, party, company, band, body, crowd, pack, army, herd, flock, bevy, drove, horde, galaxy, assemblage, gathering; knot, cluster; informal bunch, gaggle, posse, crew.

cow[1] noun

> *Word links* **cow**
>
> **bovine** relating to cows

cow[2] verb *has he cowed you all with his threats?* **intimidate**, daunt, browbeat, bully, badger, dragoon, bludgeon, tyrannize, overawe, awe, dismay, dishearten, unnerve, subdue, scare, terrorize, frighten, petrify; informal psych out, bulldoze, railroad.

coward noun *the cowards turned back as soon as it looked dangerous*: **weakling**, milksop, namby-pamby, mouse; informal chicken, scaredy-cat, fraidy-cat, yellow-belly, sissy, big baby; Brit. informal big girl's blouse; N. Amer. informal candy-ass, pussy; Austral./NZ informal dingo, sook; informal, dated funk; archaic poltroon, craven, recreant, caitiff.
▷ANTONYMS hero.

cowardice noun *he was charged with displaying cowardice in the face of the enemy*: **faint-heartedness**, spiritlessness, spinelessness, timidity, timorousness, fearfulness, pusillanimity, weakness, feebleness; informal gutlessness, wimpishness, wimpiness, sissiness; Brit. informal wetness; archaic poltroonery, recreancy, poor-spiritedness; rare cravenness.
▷ANTONYMS bravery, courage.

cowardly adjective *the cowardly little wretches were trying to keep out of his way*: **faint-hearted**, lily-livered, chicken-hearted, pigeon-hearted, spiritless, spineless, craven; **timid**, timorous, fearful, trembling, quaking, shrinking, cowering, afraid of one's own shadow, pusillanimous, weak, feeble, soft; informal yellow, chicken, weak-kneed, gutless, yellow-bellied, wimpish, wimpy, sissy, sissified; Brit. informal wet; N. Amer. informal candy-assed; N. Amer. vulgar slang chickenshit; archaic poltroon, recreant, poor-spirited.
▷ANTONYMS brave, courageous.

cowboy noun **1** *the cows were separated from the calves by a cowboy on horseback*: **cattleman**, cowhand, cowman, cowherd, herder, herdsman, drover, stockman, rancher; in Spanish-speaking America gaucho, llanero, ranchero, vaquero; N. Amer. informal cowpuncher, cowpoke, broncobuster; N. Amer. dated buckaroo; archaic herd.
2 informal *the builders we had were complete cowboys*: **cheat**, swindler, fraudster, trickster, charlatan, scoundrel, rogue, rascal, unscrupulous operator; **incompetent**, amateur, bungler, blunderer, bumbler; Brit. informal bodger.
▷ANTONYMS professional.

cower verb *I would cower in the corner and tremble*: **cringe**, shrink, crouch, recoil, flinch, pull back, back away, draw back, shudder, shiver, tremble, shake, quake, grovel, blench, blanch, quail.

coy adjective *she treated him to a coy smile of invitation*: **arch**, simpering, coquettish, flirtatious, kittenish, skittish; shy, modest, bashful, reticent, diffident, retiring, backward, self-effacing, shrinking, withdrawn, timid, demure.
▷ANTONYMS brazen.

coyness noun *she held the scarf across her face in practised coyness*: **archness**, simpering, coquettishness, flirtatiousness, kittenishness, skittishness; shyness, modesty, bashfulness, reticence, diffidence, self-effacement, timidity, demureness.
▷ANTONYMS brazenness.

cozen verb archaic *you'll not cozen me so*. See **trick**.

crabbed adjective **1** *her handwriting was crabbed and minuscule*: **cramped**, bad, shaky, scribbled, spidery, laboured, illegible, unreadable, indecipherable.
▷ANTONYMS bold; clear.
2 *a crabbed old man*. See **crabby**.

crabby adjective *she was regarded as crabby and reclusive*: **irritable**, fractious, fretful, cross, petulant, pettish, crabbed, crotchety, cantankerous, curmudgeonly, disagreeable, miserable, morose, peppery, on edge, edgy, impatient, complaining, querulous; bitter, moody, in a bad mood, grumpy, huffy, scratchy, out of sorts, out of temper, ill-tempered, bad-tempered, ill-natured, ill-humoured, peevish, sullen, surly, sulky, sour, churlish, touchy, testy, tetchy, snappish, waspish, prickly, crusty, bilious, liverish, dyspeptic, splenetic, choleric; informal snappy, chippy, grouchy, cranky, whingeing, whingy; Brit. informal narky, ratty, eggy, like a bear with a sore head; N. Amer. informal sorehead, soreheaded, peckish; Austral./NZ informal snaky; dated miffy.
▷ANTONYMS sweet-natured, easy-going, charming.

crack noun **1** *cracks spread from the bullet hole across the window*: **split**, fissure, crevice, break, fracture, rupture, breach, rift, cleft, slit, chink, gap, cranny, interstice; rare crazing.
2 *the crack of a rifle rang out*: **bang**, report, explosion, detonation, clap, pop, snap, crackle, knock, tap, clash, crash, smash, smack; informal wham, whump.
3 *he got a crack on the head*: **blow**, bang, hit, punch, knock, thump, rap, bump, thwack, smack, slap, welt, cuff, box; informal bash, whack, clobber, clout, clip, wallop, belt, tan, biff, bop, sock, lam, whomp; Brit. informal slosh; N. Amer. informal boff, bust, slug, whale; Austral./NZ informal dong; dated buffet.
4 informal *I fancy having a crack at winning a fourth title*: **attempt**, try, effort, endeavour, venture; informal go, shot, stab, whack, whirl; formal essay; archaic assay.
5 informal *it is easy to make cheap cracks about her hair and clothes*: **joke**, witticism, funny remark, witty remark, jest, quip, pun, sally, pleasantry, epigram, aphorism; repartee, banter; French bon mot; **jibe**, barb, jeer, sneer, taunt, insult, cutting remark, slight, affront, slur, insinuation; informal one-liner, gag, wisecrack, funny, dig.
▶verb **1** *take care not to crack the glass*: **split**, fracture, fissure, rupture, break, snap, cleave; rare craze.
2 *a gun cracked and the bullet fizzed overhead*: **go bang**, bang, pop, snap, crackle, crash, thud, thump, boom, ring out, clap; explode, detonate.
3 *she cracked him across the forehead*: **hit**, strike, beat, thump, hammer, knock, rap, pound, thud, punch, bump, thwack, smack, slap, slam, welt, cuff, pummel, buffet, box someone's ears; informal bash, whack, clobber, clout, clip, wallop, belt, tan, biff, bop, sock, lam, whomp; Brit. informal slosh; N. Amer. informal boff, bust, slug, whale; Austral./NZ informal dong.
4 *the witnesses cracked and the truth came out*: **break down**, give way, cave in, crumble, collapse, go to pieces, lose control, yield, succumb, founder; informal fall/come apart at the seams.
5 informal *the naval code proved harder to crack*: **solve**, find an/the answer to, find a/the solution to, resolve, work out, puzzle out, fathom, find the key to, decipher, decode, break, clear up, interpret, translate, straighten out, get to the bottom of, make head or tail of, unravel, disentangle, untangle, unfold, piece together, elucidate; informal figure out, suss out.
□ **crack down** *a nationwide drive to* ***crack down on*** *crime*: **get tough on**, take severe/stern measures against, clamp down on, come down heavily on; eliminate, abolish, eradicate, extinguish, quench, repress, stifle, suppress, put an end to, put a stop to, end, finish, get rid of, crush, put down, weed out, curb, nip in the bud, thwart, frustrate, scotch, squash, quash, quell, subdue, terminate, beat, overcome, defeat, rout, destroy, demolish, annihilate, wipe out, extirpate; limit, restrain, restrict, check, keep in check, control, keep under control; informal come down on like a ton of bricks, squelch, put the kibosh on, clobber.
□ **crack up** informal **1** *I feel I'm cracking up, always on the verge of tears*: **break down**, have a breakdown, lose control, be overcome, collapse, go to pieces, go out of one's mind, go mad, crumble, disintegrate; informal lose it, lose one's cool, fall/come apart at the seams, go crazy, freak out.
2 *she tried to keep a straight face but kept cracking up*: **burst out laughing**, dissolve into laughter, roar with laughter, shake with laughter, laugh uncontrollably, guffaw, be doubled up, split one's sides, hold one's sides; informal fall about, be in stitches, break up, crease up, be creased up, be rolling in the aisles, laugh like a drain.
▶adjective *he is a crack shot*. See **expert** (adjective).

crackdown noun *a crackdown on car crime*: **clampdown**, getting tough, severe/stern measures, repression, suppression, abolition, elimination, eradication, end, stop.

cracked adjective **1** *this cup is cracked*: **split**, broken, fissured, fractured, ruptured, splintered, cleft, slit; damaged, defective, flawed, imperfect; rare crazed.
2 informal *you're cracked!* See **mad**.

Word toolkit

cracked	fractured	shattered
mirror	skull	glass
lips	cheekbone	lives
voice	leg	dreams
sidewalk	pelvis	economy
plaster	rock	nerves

crackle verb *the fire crackled and spat sparks*: **sizzle**, frizzle, fizz, hiss, crack, snap, sputter; technical decrepitate; rare crepitate.

cradle noun **1** *the baby's cradle*: **crib**, bassinet, Moses basket, cot, carrycot.
2 *the cradle of democracy*: **birthplace**, fount, fountainhead, source, spring, fountain, origin, place of origin, breeding place, nursery, root, roots, seat, seed, germ; **beginning**, start, origination, genesis, birth, dawning,

C

dawn, emergence, inception, launch, creation, early stages, conception, inauguration, foundation, outset; Latin fons et origo; formal commencement; literary wellspring; rare radix.
3 *the lifeboat was displayed on a cradle*: **framework**, rack, holder, stand, base, support, mounting, mount, platform, prop, horse, rest, chock, plinth, bottom, trivet, bracket, frame, subframe, structure, substructure, chassis.
▸ **verb** *she cradled his head in her arms*: **hold**, support, prop up, rest, pillow, bolster, cushion, shelter, protect.

craft¹ **noun 1** *the old tailor was proud of his craft*: **skill**, skilfulness, facility, ability, capability, competence, art, technique, aptitude, talent, flair, gift, genius, cleverness, knack; artistry, mastery, dexterity, dexterousness, craftsmanship, workmanship, expertness, expertise, proficiency, adroitness, adeptness, deftness, ingenuity, virtuosity; informal know-how.
2 *the historian's craft*: **activity**, pursuit, occupation, work, line, line of work, profession, job, business, line of business, trade, employment, position, post, situation, career, métier, vocation, calling, skill, field, province, walk of life; Scottish way; informal racket, game; Austral. informal grip; archaic employ.
3 *he knew how to win by craft and diplomacy what he could not gain by force*: **cunning**, craftiness, guile, wiliness, artfulness, deviousness, slyness, trickery, trickiness; duplicity, dishonesty, cheating, deceitfulness, deceit, deception, sharp practice, chicanery, intrigue, scheming, strategy, subterfuge, evasion; wiles, ploys, schemes, stratagems, tactics, manoeuvres, tricks, ruses; informal foxiness, monkey business, funny business, hanky-panky, jiggery-pokery, every trick in the book.
▷**ANTONYMS** honesty; naivety.

craft² **noun** *the river was teeming with all sorts of craft*: **vessel**, ship, boat, watercraft, aircraft, machine, spacecraft, spaceship; Brit. informal, dated kite; literary keel, barque.

craftsman, craftswoman **noun** *the tiles are handmade by craftsmen*: **artisan**, craftsperson, tradesman, tradeswoman, tradesperson, mechanic, technician, operative, maker, smith, wright, journeyman; skilled worker, dedicated worker, meticulous worker, master, expert, artist; archaic artificer; rare handicraftsman, handicraftswoman.

craftsmanship **noun** *one of the finest examples of early twentieth-century Russian craftsmanship*: **workmanship**, artistry, craft, art, artisanship, handiwork, work; **skill**, skilfulness, technique, expertise, mastery.

crafty **adjective** *Mum knew them to be crafty rogues*: **cunning**, guileful, wily, artful, devious, sly, tricky, duplicitous, dishonest, underhand, cheating, deceitful, sharp, scheming, calculating, designing, evasive; shrewd, astute, canny; informal foxy; S. African informal slim; archaic subtle.
▷**ANTONYMS** honest; naive.

crag **noun** *the castle was set on a crag above the village*: **cliff**, bluff, ridge, precipice, rock face, overhang; height, peak, tor, pinnacle; promontory, headland; bank, slope, escarpment, scarp; rare eminence.

craggy **adjective 1** *the craggy cliffs*: **rocky**, rough, ragged, rugged, uneven, bumpy, stony, irregular, pitted, broken up, jagged, precipitous, cragged, rock-bound.
▷**ANTONYMS** smooth.
2 *his craggy, lined face*: **rugged**, rough-hewn, rough-textured, strong, manly, masculine; weather-beaten, weathered.
▷**ANTONYMS** delicate.

cram **verb 1** *the bookcases were crammed with dusty volumes*: **stuff**, pack, jam, fill, crowd, throng; overfill, fill up, fill to overflowing, stuff to the gills, fill to the brim, overcrowd, overload.
2 *they all crammed into the car*: **crowd**, crush, pack, jam, squash, wedge oneself, shove, push, jostle, throng, force one's way, thrust.
3 *he crammed the sandwiches into his mouth*: **force**, ram, thrust, plunge, push, pile, stick, jam, pack, compress, squeeze, wedge, press, tamp, pound, drive, hammer, bang; informal shove, stuff.
4 *most of the students are cramming for exams*: **study intensively**, revise; informal swot, mug up, bone up.

cramp **noun** *an attack of cramp*: **muscle/muscular spasm**, muscle/muscular contraction, pang, twinge; crick, kink, stitch, stiffness, pain, shooting pain, ache, convulsion, tic, twitch; Medicine clonus, hyperkinesis.
▸ **verb** *tighter rules will cramp economic growth*: **hinder**, impede, inhibit, hamper, constrain, hamstring, obstruct, block, thwart, slow, check, arrest, curb, bridle, shackle, encumber, retard, handicap, tie, interfere with; **restrict**, limit, confine, restrain, set/impose limits on, regulate, control, moderate, cut down on; informal stymie.

cramped **adjective 1** *the accommodation was cramped and the conditions primitive*: **restricted**, confined, constricted; small, tiny, narrow, compact, tight, poky, uncomfortable, minimal, sparse, inadequate; hemmed in, crowded, overfull, packed, jammed, congested; archaic strait; rare incommodious.
▷**ANTONYMS** spacious.
2 *he had very cramped handwriting*: **small**, **crabbed**, pinched, tightly packed, close, shaky, scribbled, laboured, illegible, unreadable, indecipherable.
▷**ANTONYMS** flowing; bold.

crane **noun** *the cargo was put aboard by crane*: **derrick**, winch, hoist, davit, windlass, tackle, block and tackle, lifting gear; Nautical sheer legs.

cranium **noun** **skull**, brain case; brain; head; informal brainpan.

crank¹ **verb** *you two crank the engine by hand*: **start**, turn (over), get going.
□ **crank something up** *they aim to crank up production capacity by the addition of a new factory*: **increase**, make larger, make bigger, make greater, add to, augment, build up, enlarge, expand, extend, raise, multiply, elevate, swell, inflate; magnify, intensify, amplify, heighten, escalate; worsen, make worse, exacerbate, aggravate, compound, reinforce; improve, make better, boost, ameliorate, enhance, upgrade; informal up, jack up, hike up, hike, bump up, step up.
▸ **noun** *even light pressure on the crank will turn the shaft*: **lever**, arm, bar, pedal.

crank² **noun** *I was treated like a crank by the so-called experts*: **eccentric**, oddity, odd fellow, unorthodox person, individualist, nonconformist, free spirit, bohemian, maverick, deviant, pervert, misfit, hippy, dropout; madman/madwoman, lunatic, psychotic; **fanatic**, fan, zealot, addict, enthusiast, devotee, aficionado; informal oddball, odd/queer fish, freak, character, weirdie, weirdo, crackpot, loony, nut, nutter, nutcase, head case, sicko, perv, fiend, maniac, buff, -head, a great one for; Brit. informal one-off, odd bod; Scottish informal radge; N. Amer. informal wacko, wack, screwball, kook, geek, jock; Austral./NZ informal dingbat; informal, dated case.

cranky **adjective 1** *a cranky diet*: **eccentric**, **bizarre**, weird, peculiar, odd, quirky, avant-garde, unconventional, strange, outlandish, ridiculous, ludicrous; mad, insane, crazy, absurd; informal wacky, screwy, nutty, nuts, crackpot, cracked, oddball, kinky, off the wall, way out, dippy, cuckoo; Brit. informal daft; N. Amer. informal kooky, wacko, left-field; Austral./NZ informal, dated dilly.
2 *the children were getting a bit tired and cranky*: **bad-tempered**, irritable, irascible, tetchy, testy, grumpy, grouchy, crotchety, in a (bad) mood, ill-tempered, ill-natured, ill-humoured, peevish; having got out of bed the wrong side, cross, as cross as two sticks, fractious, disagreeable, cantankerous, curmudgeonly, pettish, crabbed, crabby, waspish, prickly, peppery, touchy, scratchy, crusty, splenetic, shrewish, short-tempered, hot-tempered, quick-tempered, dyspeptic, choleric, bilious, liverish, cross-grained; informal snappish, snappy, chippy, on a short fuse, short-fused; Brit. informal shirty, stroppy, narky, ratty, eggy, like a bear with a sore head; N. Amer. informal ornery, peckish, soreheaded; Austral./NZ informal snaky; informal, dated waxy, miffy.

cranny **noun** *every little cranny was filled with drifted snow*: **chink**, crack, crevice, slit, split, fissure, rift, cleft, opening, gap, aperture, cavity, hole, hollow, niche, corner, recess, bay, booth, alcove, nook, interstice.

crash **verb 1** *the car **crashed into** a tree*: **smash into**, collide with, be in collision with, come into collision with, hit, strike, ram, smack into, slam into, bang into, cannon into, plough into, meet head-on, run into, drive into, bump into, knock into, crack into/against; dash against; N. Amer. impact.
2 *he has crashed his car again*: **smash**, wreck, bump; Brit. write off; Brit. informal prang; N. Amer. informal total.
3 *burning timbers crashed to the ground*: **fall**, plunge, hurtle, plummet, topple, tumble, overbalance, pitch.
4 *waves **crashed against** the shore*: **be hurled**, dash; **batter**, pound, pummel, lash, slam into.
5 *he crashed down the telephone receiver*: **slam**, bang, ram, smack.
6 *thunder crashed overhead*: **boom**, crack, roll, clap, explode, bang, blast, resound, reverberate, rumble, thunder, ring out, sound loudly, blare, echo, fill the air; clash, clang, clank, clatter, smash.
7 *he used up his fortune repaying creditors after his clothing company crashed*: **fail**, collapse, fold (up), go under, founder, be ruined, cave in; go bankrupt, become insolvent, cease trading, go into receivership, go into liquidation, be liquidated, be wound up, be closed (down), be shut (down); informal go broke, go bust, go bump, go to the wall, go belly up, come a cropper, flop.
8 informal *they crashed someone's party*: **gatecrash**, come uninvited to, sneak into, slip into, invade, butt in on, intrude on/into; informal horn in on.
▸ **noun 1** *there was a crash on the main road*: **accident**, collision, smash, bump, car crash, car accident, road accident, traffic accident, road traffic accident, RTA, multiple crash, multiple collision; rail accident, derailment; air accident, air crash; N. Amer. wreck; informal smash-up, pile-up, shunt; Brit. informal prang.
2 *I heard the crash when you knocked the statue over*: **bang**, smash, smack, crack, boom, bump, thud, thump, slam, clunk, clonk, clash, clang; report, explosion, detonation, shot; clangour, racket, din; informal wham, whump.
3 *the crash of the company meant that 150 jobs would go*: **failure**, collapse, foundering, ruin, ruination; **bankruptcy**, insolvency, cessation of trading, receivership, liquidation, winding up, closure, shutting.
▸ **adjective** *a crash course in diesel engine maintenance*: **intensive**, concentrated, telescoped, high-pressure, strenuous, vigorous, all-out, thorough, in-depth, all-absorbing, total-immersion, rapid, urgent.
▷**ANTONYMS** extensive.

crass **adjective 1** *the crass assumptions that men make about women*: **stupid**, insensitive, blundering, dense, thick, vacuous, mindless, witless, doltish, oafish, boorish, asinine, bovine, coarse, gross; informal pig-ignorant.
▷**ANTONYMS** intelligent.

2 *you committed an act of crass stupidity*: **gross**, utter, sheer, downright, total, out-and-out, outright, very great, complete, absolute, thorough, perfect, blatant, unmitigated, unqualified, glaring, undisguised, naked.

crate noun *the third crate contained the explosives*: **case**, packing case, chest, coffer, trunk, box, casket, strongbox, basket, hamper, pack, bin, drum, container, receptacle; technical lug.

crater noun *the crater has become a lake*: **hollow**, bowl, basin, pan, hole, cavity, pocket; shell hole; Geology caldera, maar, solfatara.

crave verb *he craved professional recognition*: **long for**, yearn for, hunger for, thirst for, dream of, aspire to, set one's heart on, have as one's aim, have as one's goal, seek, be bent on; desire, want, hope for, hanker after, wish for; sigh for, pant for, pine for; lust after, covet; informal have a yen for, itch for, be dying for; archaic be athirst for, be desirous of; rare desiderate, suspire for.

craven adjective *a craven surrender*. See **cowardly**.

craving noun *a craving for chocolate*: **longing**, yearning, hankering, hunger, hungering, thirst, pining, desire, want, wish, fancy, urge, need, appetite, greed, lust, ache, burning, addiction, aspiration, aim, goal; informal yen, itch; rare cacoethes.

crawl verb **1** *they crawled from under the table*: **creep**, go on all fours, move on hands and knees, inch, drag oneself along, pull oneself along, drag, trail, slither, slink, squirm, wriggle, writhe, scrabble, worm one's way, advance slowly/stealthily, sneak.
2 informal *let's stop trying to get women to support us by* ***crawling to*** *them*: **grovel to**, be obsequious towards, ingratiate oneself with, be servile towards, be sycophantic towards, kowtow to, pander to, abase oneself to, demean oneself to, bow and scrape to, prostrate oneself before, toady to, truckle to, dance attendance on, fawn on/over, curry favour with, cultivate, seek the favour of, try to win over, try to get on the good side of, make up to, play up to; informal suck up to, lick someone's boots, creep to, be all over, fall all over, rub up the right way, keep someone sweet, sweet-talk, soft-soap, butter up, twist someone's arm; N. Amer. brown-nose; vulgar slang lick/kiss someone's arse; archaic blandish.
3 *the place* ***was crawling with*** *soldiers*: **be full of**, overflow with, teem with, abound in/with, be packed with, be crowded with, be thronged with, be jammed with, be alive with, be overrun with, swarm with, be bristling with, be infested with, be thick with; informal be lousy with, be stuffed with, be jam-packed with, be chock-a-block with, be chock-full of; rare pullulate with.

craze noun *the latest fitness craze to sweep the country*: **fad**, vogue, trend, fashion, enthusiasm, passion, infatuation, love, obsession, mania, compulsion, fixation, fetish, weakness, fancy, taste, novelty, whim, fascination, preoccupation, rage; informal thing.

crazed adjective *he took off in pursuit of the crazed murderer*: **mad**, insane, out of one's mind, deranged, demented, certifiable, lunatic, wild, raving, distraught, berserk, manic, maniac, frenzied, hysterical, psychopathic; informal crazy, mental, off one's head, out of one's head, raving mad.
▷ANTONYMS sane.

> *Word toolkit* **crazed**
>
> See **psychotic**.

crazy adjective informal **1** *all the publicity nearly sent her crazy*: **mad**, insane, out of one's mind, deranged, demented, not in one's right mind, crazed, lunatic, non compos mentis, unbalanced, unhinged, unstable, disturbed, distracted, mad as a hatter, mad as a March hare, stark mad; informal mental, off one's head, out of one's head, off one's nut, nutty, nutty as a fruitcake, off one's rocker, not (quite) right in the head, round the bend, raving mad, stark staring/raving mad, bats, batty, bonkers, cuckoo, loopy, loony, bananas, loco, dippy, screwy, with a screw loose, touched, gaga, doolally, up the pole, not all there, off the wall, out to lunch, not right upstairs, away with the fairies; Brit. informal barmy, crackers, barking, barking mad, round the twist, off one's trolley, as daft as a brush, not the full shilling, one sandwich short of a picnic; N. Amer. informal buggy, nutsy, nutso, out of one's tree, meshuga, squirrelly, wacko, gonzo; Canadian & Austral./NZ informal bushed; NZ informal porangi.
▷ANTONYMS sane.
2 *children get all sorts of crazy ideas*: **absurd**, preposterous, ridiculous, ludicrous, farcical, laughable, risible; idiotic, stupid, foolish, foolhardy, unwise, imprudent, ill-conceived, silly, inane, puerile, infantile, fatuous, imbecilic, hare-brained, half-baked; unreasonable, irrational, illogical, nonsensical, pointless, senseless, impracticable, unworkable, unrealistic; outrageous, wild, shocking, astonishing, monstrous; unbelievable, incredible, unthinkable, implausible; peculiar, odd, strange, queer, weird, eccentric, bizarre, fantastic, incongruous, grotesque; informal barmy, daft, potty, cock-eyed.
▷ANTONYMS sensible.
3 *people in Barbados are just* ***crazy about*** *cricket*: **very enthusiastic**, passionate, fanatical, excited; very keen on, enamoured of, infatuated with, smitten with, devoted to, fond of; informal wild, mad, nutty, nuts, potty, gone on; informal, dated sweet on.
▷ANTONYMS apathetic, indifferent.

□ **like crazy** informal **1** *we are just working like crazy to make what we have efficient*: **energetically**, enthusiastically, madly, with a will, for all one is worth, passionately, intensely, ardently, fervently; informal like mad, hammer and tongs; Brit. informal, dated like billy-o. **2** *you were driving like crazy when something punctured one of the tyres*: **fast**, furiously, as fast as possible, hurriedly, quickly, rapidly, speedily, hastily; informal like mad, hammer and tongs, at warp speed.

creak verb *the floorboards creaked*: **squeak**, groan, grate; screech, squeal, grind, jar, rasp, rub, scrape; complain.

cream noun **1** *all sorts of creams for the skin*: **lotion**, ointment, rub, cosmetic, application, preparation, emollient, moisturizer, paste, gel, salve, unguent, embrocation, balm, liniment, pomade; archaic unction.
2 *the cream of the world's photographers*: **best**, finest, first class, top, choice, choicest, flower, prize, treasure, pearl, gem, jewel, the jewel in the crown, the crème de la crème; **elite**, elect, nonpareil; informal tops, pick of the bunch.
▷ANTONYMS dregs.
▶adjective *a cream dress*: **off-white**, whitish, cream-coloured, creamy, ivory, yellowish-white, pearly.
▶verb
□ **cream something off** *grammar schools creamed off the more academic pupils*: **pick and choose**; informal cherry-pick.

creamy adjective **1** *when mixed with water, the powder forms a creamy paste*: **smooth**, thick, whipped, velvety, of an even consistency, rich, buttery.
▷ANTONYMS lumpy; thin.
2 *the orchids had creamy flowers*: **off-white**, whitish, cream-coloured, cream, ivory, yellowish-white, pearly.

crease noun **1** *he always has trousers with creases*: **fold**, groove, ridge, furrow, line, ruck, pleat, tuck, corrugation; Brit. rare ruckle.
2 *she has creases at the corners of her eyes*: **wrinkle**, line, crinkle, pucker, laughter line; (**creases**) informal crow's feet.
▶verb **1** *if I lie on that, I'll crease my clothes*: **crumple**, wrinkle, crinkle, scrunch up, rumple, line, pucker, crimp, ruck up, gather, furrow; Brit. rare ruckle.
▷ANTONYMS press.
2 *his trousers were properly creased*: **press**, iron, put a crease in, fold; corrugate, pleat, tuck.
▷ANTONYMS crumple.

create verb **1** *the sculpture has been created out of Portland stone*: **generate**, produce, design, make, fabricate, fashion, manufacture, build, construct, erect, do, turn out; bring into being, originate, invent, initiate, engender, devise, frame, develop, shape, form, mould, forge, concoct, hatch; informal knock together, knock up, knock off.
▷ANTONYMS dismantle.
2 *regular socializing creates a good working team spirit*: **bring about**, result in, cause, be the cause of, give rise to, lead to, breed, generate, engender, produce, make, make for, prompt, promote, foster, sow the seeds of, contribute to, stir up, whip up, inspire; literary enkindle.
▷ANTONYMS destroy.
3 *the governments planned to create a free-trade zone*: **establish**, found, institute, constitute, inaugurate, launch, set up, put in place, start, lay the foundations of; form, organize, develop, build up; get something going, get something moving, get something working; informal kick something off.
4 *she was created a life peer in 1990*: **appoint**, make, install as, invest; name, nominate, designate.
5 *sometimes a child is created to replace the loss of another*: **conceive**, give birth to, bring into the world, bring into being, bring into existence, give life to, father, sire, spawn, produce; N. Amer. birth; informal drop; literary beget.

creation noun **1** *he embarked on the creation of an outstanding garden*: **design**, formation, forming, modelling, putting together, setting up, making, construction, constructing, fabrication, fabricating, fashioning, building, erection, erecting; production, generation, origination, devising, invention, initiation, inception, shaping, hatching.
▷ANTONYMS destruction.
2 *Aten was a universal god of all creation*: **the world**, the universe, the cosmos; the living world, the natural world, nature, life, living things.
3 *the Constitution allowed for the creation of a second vice-president*: **appointment**, installation, investing, investiture, inauguration; establishment, foundation, institution.
▷ANTONYMS removal.
4 *there is power associated with the creation and raising of children*: **conception**, bringing into the world, bringing into being, bringing into existence, fathering, siring, spawning, giving birth to; genesis, procreation; N. Amer. birthing; informal dropping; literary begetting.
5 *it was hard to distinguish between forgery and original creation*: **work**, work of art, achievement, production, opus, oeuvre, invention, handiwork, masterpiece, masterwork; Latin magnum opus; French chef-d'œuvre, pièce de résistance, tour de force; informal brainchild; rare opuscule.
6 *she wore a creation by designer Marianne Jessica*: **design**, dress, outfit; informal number.

C

C

Word links creation

-geny related suffix, as in *cosmogeny, ontogeny*

creative adjective *our pupils are encouraged to be creative | the creative manipulation of language*: **inventive**, imaginative, innovative, innovatory, innovational, experimental, original; artistic, expressive, inspired, visionary; productive, prolific, fertile; talented, gifted, resourceful, quick-witted, ingenious, clever, smart; unconventional, unorthodox, unusual, out of the ordinary; informal blue-sky.
▷ANTONYMS unimaginative, conservative.

creativity noun *challenging objectives motivate staff and encourage creativity*: **inventiveness**, imagination, imaginativeness, innovation, innovativeness, originality, individuality; artistry, expressiveness, inspiration, vision, creative power, creative talent, creative gift, creative skill, resourcefulness, ingenuity, enterprise.

creator noun **1** *the Sabbath is kept to honour the Creator*: **God**, the Lord, the Almighty, the Master of the Universe; one's Maker.
2 *he is the creator of several hit musicals*: **writer**, author, composer, designer, deviser, maker, inventor, producer, developer; originator, initiator, instigator, generator, engineer, architect, mastermind, prime mover, father, mother; literary begetter.

creature noun **1** *whales are the largest creatures living on earth*: **animal**, beast, brute; **living thing**, living entity, living soul, soul, mortal, being, life form, organism; informal critter.
2 *You're such a lazy creature!* **fellow**, individual, character, wretch, beggar, soul; person, personage, human being, human, man, woman, boy, girl; informal devil, bunny, cookie, customer, sort, type, thing; Brit. informal chap, bloke, geezer, bod, kid, brat; N. Amer. informal dude, hombre, guy, gal; informal, dated body, dog; Brit. informal, dated cove; vulgar slang bastard; Brit. vulgar slang sod, bugger; archaic wight.
3 *the village teacher was expected to be the creature of his employer*: **minion**, lackey, flunkey, hireling, subordinate, servant, retainer, vassal; puppet, pawn, tool, instrument, cat's paw, dupe; informal skivvy, stooge, sucker, yes-man; Brit. informal poodle, dogsbody; N. Amer. informal gofer.

credence noun **1** *psychoanalysis finds little credence among laymen*: **acceptance**, belief, faith, trust, confidence, reliance.
2 *the messenger gave credence to her tale*: **credibility**, credit, reliability, plausibility, believability.

credentials plural noun *the policemen went to check the driver's credentials*: **documents**, papers, identity papers, identification papers, bona fides; warrant, licence, permit, pass, ID, card, ID card, identity card, passport, proof of identity, proof of qualifications, certificate, diploma, voucher, documentation; references, testimonial, letter of introduction, letter of recommendation, missive, deed, title.

credibility noun **1** *the whole tale lacks credibility*: **plausibility**, believability, acceptability, tenability, probability, likelihood, authority, authoritativeness, impressiveness, cogency, weight, validity, soundness; truth, veracity, faithfulness, fidelity, authenticity, accuracy, factualness; rare veridicality; informal clout.
▷ANTONYMS implausibility.
2 *the party lacked the moral credibility to govern*: **trustworthiness**, reliability, dependability, integrity, character; reputation, standing, status, cachet, kudos, eminence, credit, acceptability.

credible adjective **1** *very few people found his story credible*: **believable**, plausible, able to hold water, within the bounds of possibility, reasonable, sound, compelling, persuasive; rare suasive, assuasive, verisimilar, colourable, cogitable.
▷ANTONYMS unbelievable.
2 *the existing lists did not form a credible basis for free and fair elections*: **acceptable**, trustworthy, reliable, dependable, sure, good, valid; feasible, viable, tenable, sustainable, maintainable.
▷ANTONYMS untrustworthy.

credit noun **1** *the writer got a very good press and a lot of credit*: **praise**, commendation, acclaim, approval, approbation, acknowledgement, recognition, kudos, glory, merit, regard, esteem, respect, admiration, adulation, veneration, tributes; thanks, gratitude, appreciation; informal bouquets, brownie points; rare laudation, extolment, eulogium.
2 *the speech did his credit no good in the House of Commons*: **reputation**, repute, character, image, name, good name, prestige, influence, standing, status, regard, esteem, estimation; **credibility**, acceptability; Indian izzat; informal clout; N. Amer. informal rep, rap; archaic honour, report; rare reputability.
3 *these men are a credit to their country*: **source of honour**, source of pride, feather in the cap, asset, proud boast, glory, flower, gem, treasure.
4 *his theory has been given very little credit*: **credence**, belief, faith, trust, reliance, confidence.
5 *the shop would be paid whether her credit was good or bad*: **financial standing**, financial status, solvency.
□ **on credit** *he purchased £300 worth of goods on credit*: **on hire purchase**, on (the) HP, by instalments, by deferred payment, on account; informal on tick, on the slate; Brit. informal on the never-never.
▶ **verb 1** *the wise will seldom credit all they hear*: **believe**, accept, give credence to, have confidence in, trust, have faith in, rely on, depend on, count on; informal go for, fall for, buy, swallow, {swallow something hook, line, and sinker}, take something as gospel.
▷ANTONYMS disbelieve.
2 *the success of the scheme can be **credited to** the team's frugality*: **ascribe**, attribute, assign, accredit, chalk up, put down, set down, impute; lay at the door of, connect with, associate with; informal stick something on.
3 *he **was credited with** inventing the lyre*: **be accredited with**, be recognized as, be given the credit for, be held responsible for.

creditable adjective *the team worked hard and produced a creditable performance*: **commendable**, praiseworthy, laudable, admirable, honourable, estimable, meritorious, exceptional, exemplary, noteworthy, notable, worthy, up to the mark, deserving, respectable, reputable, sterling; good, fine, excellent, outstanding, first-rate, first-class; worthy of commendation, worthy of admiration; informal A1, wicked, super, splendiferous, top-notch, fab, ace, tip-top; Brit. informal smashing, brill, champion, grand; N. Amer. informal bully; Austral./NZ informal beaut; Brit. informal top-hole; rare applaudable.
▷ANTONYMS deplorable.

credit crunch noun *when interest rates started rising, the ensuing credit crunch drove the economy into the deep recession of the early 1990s*: **credit squeeze**, economic decline, downturn, slump, slowdown, trough, recession, depression; stagnation, stagflation; hard times; informal bust.
▷ANTONYMS boom, upturn.

credulity noun *moneylenders prey upon their credulity and inexperience*: **gullibility**, gullibleness, credulousness, naivety, naiveness, blind faith, trustfulness, over-trustfulness, lack of suspicion, innocence, ingenuousness, unworldliness, lack of experience, lack of sophistication, guilelessness, greenness, callowness, childlikeness, simpleness, simplicity, ignorance.
▷ANTONYMS worldliness; suspicion.

credulous adjective *he sold 'miracle' cures to desperate and credulous clients*: **gullible**, naive, impressionable, trusting, over-trusting, over-trustful, exploitable, dupable, deceivable, easily deceived, easily taken in, easily led, unsuspicious, unwary, unguarded, unsceptical, uncritical, unquestioning; innocent, ingenuous, unworldly, inexperienced, unsophisticated, artless, guileless, green, as green as grass, callow, raw, immature, childlike, wide-eyed, simple, ignorant; informal wet behind the ears, born yesterday; rare incognizant, nescient.
▷ANTONYMS worldly; suspicious.

Choose the right word credulous, gullible

See **gullible**.

creed noun **1** *the godparents will swear that they believe in the creed*: **system of belief**, set of principles, statement of beliefs, profession of faith; doctrine, teaching, ideology, ethic, dogma, tenet, catechism, credo; beliefs, principles, canons, articles of faith, maxims, rules, laws.
2 *jobs should be available to all, irrespective of race or creed*: **faith**, religion, religious belief(s), religious persuasion, religious conviction, religious group, faith community, church; persuasion, affiliation, denomination, sect, body, following, communion, order, school, fraternity, brotherhood, sisterhood.

creek noun **1** Brit. *they're dredging for oysters in the creek*: **tidal inlet**, inlet, arm of the sea, estuary, bay, bight, fjord, gulf, sound; Scottish firth, frith; in Orkney & Shetland voe; technical ria; rare fleet, armlet.
2 N. Amer. & Austral./NZ **stream**, rivulet, brook, river, tributary, backwater.

creep verb **1** *he saw her creep under the bench*: **crawl**, move on all fours, move on hands and knees, pull oneself, inch, edge, slither, slide, squirm, wriggle, writhe, worm, worm one's way, insinuate oneself.
2 *Tim crept out of the house in his pyjamas*: **sneak**, steal, slip, slink, sidle, skulk, pad, prowl, tiptoe, pussyfoot, soft-shoe, tread warily, move stealthily, move furtively, move unnoticed, walk quietly.
3 informal *they're always **creeping to** the boss*: **grovel**, crawl, toady, fawn, cower, cringe, truckle, kowtow, bow and scrape, prostrate oneself; be servile towards, be sycophantic towards, dance attendance on, ingratiate oneself with, curry favour with; flatter, woo, pay court to, get round; informal suck up to, make up to, be all over, fall all over, lick someone's boots, butter up, rub up the right way, keep sweet, sweet-talk, soft-soap; N. Amer. informal brown-nose; archaic blandish.
▶ **noun 1** *he's just a little creep who's got his sights set on Bella's money*: **sycophant**, obsequious person, crawler, groveller, truckler, toady, fawner, flatterer, lickspittle, doormat, kowtower, spaniel, Uriah Heep; informal bootlicker, yes-man; N. Amer. informal suck-up, brown-nose, brown-noser; Brit. vulgar slang arse-licker, bum-sucker; N. Amer. vulgar slang ass-kisser, suckhole; archaic toad-eater.
2 informal *some creep had broken into his home*: **rogue**, villain, wretch, reprobate; informal beast, pig, swine, rat, bastard, louse, snake, snake in the grass, skunk, dog, weasel, lowlife, scumbag, heel, stinker, stinkpot, bad lot, son of a bitch, s.o.b., nasty piece of work; Brit. informal scrote;

Irish informal **spalpeen, sleeveen**; N. Amer. informal **rat fink, fink**; Austral. informal **dingo**; informal, dated **hound, bounder, blighter, rotter**; vulgar slang **shit**; dated **cad, scoundrel**; archaic **blackguard, dastard, vagabond, knave, varlet, cur, wastrel**.

creeper noun *the tree trunks were covered with creepers and fungi*: **climbing plant**, trailing plant; vine, trailer, climber, rambler.

creeps plural noun
□ **give someone the creeps** informal *his slow smile gave her the creeps*: **scare**, frighten, terrify, horrify, haunt; **repel**, repulse, revolt, disgust, sicken, nauseate, be repugnant to, be distasteful to, make shudder; make someone's flesh creep, make someone's skin crawl, make someone's blood run cold, make someone's gorge rise, turn someone's stomach; informal **freak someone out, give someone the heebie-jeebies, make someone want to throw up**.

creepy adjective informal *that house can be a pretty creepy place*: **frightening**, scaring, terrifying, hair-raising, spine-chilling, blood-curdling, chilling, petrifying, alarming, shocking, harrowing, horrifying, horrific, horrible, awful, nightmarish, macabre, ghostly; **disturbing**, eerie, sinister, weird, menacing, ominous, threatening; Scottish **eldritch**; informal **spooky, freaky, scary, hairy**.
▷ANTONYMS relaxing, pleasant.

crescent noun *the bay was a small pebbled crescent backed by smooth boulders*: **half-moon**, sickle-shape, semicircle; arc, curve, bow, arch, bend, crook; rare **demilune, lunula**.

crest noun **1** *the bird has a drooping black crest | he wears a gold helmet with a crest*: **comb**, plume, tuft, topknot, mane; aigrette, panache, tassel; technical **caruncle**.
2 *they reached the crest of the hill*: **summit**, peak, highest point, top, tip, pinnacle, brow, crown, head, cap, brink, apex, vertex, apogee, zenith; ridge, tor; French **aiguille, serac**.
▷ANTONYMS bottom.
3 *the plate bears the Duke of Wellington's crest*: **insignia**, regalia, badge, emblem, ensign, device, heraldic device, coat of arms, arms, armorial bearing, escutcheon, shield; Heraldry **bearing, charge**.

crestfallen adjective *he came back to his apartment empty-handed and crestfallen*: **downhearted**, downcast, despondent, disappointed, disconsolate, disheartened, discouraged, dispirited, dejected, depressed, desolate, heartbroken, broken-hearted, heavy-hearted, low-spirited, in the doldrums, sad, glum, gloomy, dismal, doleful, miserable, unhappy, woebegone, forlorn, long-faced, fed up; abashed, taken aback, dismayed, sheepish, hangdog, abject, defeated; informal **blue, choked, shattered, down in the mouth, down in the dumps**; Brit. informal **brassed off, cheesed off**; literary **dolorous**; archaic **chap-fallen**.
▷ANTONYMS cheerful.

crevasse noun *he rescued his climbing partner from a crevasse*: **chasm**, abyss, fissure, cleft, crack, split, breach, rift, gap, hole, opening, pit, cavity, crater.

crevice noun *the termites crawled into a crevice in the ground*: **crack**, fissure, cleft, chink, interstice, cranny, nook, vent, slot, slit, split, rift, gash, rent, fracture, rupture, breach, perforation; opening, gap, hole, aperture, orifice, pore, space, groove; Medicine **hiatus, foramen**; technical **scission**.

crew noun **1** *the captain was much loved by his officers and crew*: **sailors**, seamen, mariners, hands; ship's company, ship's complement.
2 *he resigned in front of a local television crew*: **team**, company, unit, party, working party, gang, shift, line-up, squad, force, corps, posse; workers, employees, staff.
3 informal *they're an odd crew, these money men*: **crowd**, lot, set, group, circle, band, gang, mob, pack, troop, swarm, herd, posse, company, collection; informal **bunch, gaggle, tribe**.

crib noun **1** *he made a simple crib for the baby*: **cot**, cradle, bassinet, Moses basket, carrycot.
2 *I must fill the oxen's cribs with hay*: **manger**, stall, trough, feeding trough, bin, box, rack, fodder rack, bunker; container, receptacle.
3 informal *an English crib of Caesar's Gallic Wars*: **translation**, key, guide.
4 informal *that's a crib from Walter's work*: **copy**, plagiarism, plagiarization, reproduction, replica, duplication, imitation; informal **pirate, rip-off, knock-off, dupe**.
5 N. Amer. informal *he took the girl back to his crib*: **house**, flat, apartment, penthouse, cottage, bungalow; living quarters, quarters, accommodation; home, residence, abode, place; Austral. **home unit**; informal **pad**; archaic **cot**.
▶ verb informal *she had cribbed the plot from a Shakespeare play*: **copy**, reproduce, duplicate, appropriate, plagiarize, poach, steal, 'borrow', bootleg; informal **pirate, rip off, lift**; Brit. informal **nick, pinch**; archaic **monkey**.

crick noun *he got a crick in the neck from keeping his head down*: **cramp**, spasm, muscle spasm, muscular contraction, rick, kink, twinge, pang, pain, shooting pain, ache; stiffness, discomfort, tenderness, soreness.
▶ verb *he cricked his neck during practice*: **strain**, sprain, pull, wrench, tear, twist, rick; injure, hurt, damage, impair.

crier noun *they heard the voice of a crier in the market place*: **announcer**, proclaimer, herald, town crier, messenger, bearer of tidings.

crime noun **1** *kidnapping is a very serious crime*: **offence**, unlawful act, illegal act, breach/violation/infraction of the law, misdemeanour, misdeed, wrong, felony, violation, transgression, fault, injury; Law **malfeasance, malefaction, tort**; archaic **trespass**.
2 *the reduced police presence has brought an increase in crime*: **lawbreaking**, delinquency, wrongdoing, transgression, misconduct, criminality, illegality, villainy, felony, corruption; informal **crookedness, shadiness, dodginess**; Law **malfeasance, malefaction**; archaic **knavery**; rare **malversation**.
3 *they condemned apartheid as a crime against humanity*: **immoral act**, sin, evil, evil action, wrong, wrongdoing, atrocity, abomination, enormity, disgrace, outrage, monstrosity, violation, abuse, injustice, affront.

> *Word links* **crime**
>
> **felonious** relating to crime
> **criminology** study of crime

criminal noun *she struck up a friendship with a convicted criminal*: **lawbreaker**, offender, villain, delinquent, malefactor, culprit, wrongdoer, transgressor, sinner; young offender, juvenile delinquent; felon, thief, robber, armed robber, burglar, housebreaker, shoplifter, mugger, rapist, fraudster, swindler, racketeer, gunman, gangster, outlaw, bandit, terrorist, bioterrorist, narcoterrorist, ecoterrorist, cyberterrorist, agroterrorist; in Japan **yakuza**; informal **crook, con, jailbird, (old) lag, lifer, baddy**; N. Amer. informal **yardbird, yegg**; Austral. informal **crim**; S. African informal **lighty**; W. Indian informal **tief**; Brit. rhyming slang **tea leaf**; informal, dated **cracksman**; Law **malfeasant, misfeasor, infractor**; archaic **miscreant, trespasser, trusty, transport**; rare **peculator, defalcator**.
▶ adjective **1** *they were found guilty of criminal conduct*: **unlawful**, illegal, illicit, illegitimate, lawbreaking, lawless, felonious, delinquent, culpable, villainous, nefarious, corrupt, fraudulent; indictable, punishable, actionable, unauthorized, unsanctioned, outlawed, banned, forbidden, interdicted, proscribed; wrong, bad, evil, wicked, iniquitous; informal **crooked, shady, dirty**; Brit. informal **bent, dodgy**; Law **malfeasant**.
▷ANTONYMS lawful.
2 informal *closing the railway would be criminal folly*: **deplorable**, preposterous, shameful, reprehensible, disgraceful, inexcusable, unforgivable, unpardonable, unacceptable; senseless, foolish, ridiculous, outrageous, monstrous, shocking, scandalous; wicked, sinful, immoral, iniquitous; rare **egregious**.
▷ANTONYMS commendable.

> *Word links* **criminal**
>
> **criminology** study of crime and criminals

crimp verb **1** *she crimped the edges of her two pies*: **flute**, pleat, corrugate, ruffle, furrow, groove, ridge, crease, wrinkle, crinkle, crumple, pucker, gather; pinch, press together, squeeze together; Brit. rare **ruckle**.
2 *her hair had been crimped by the tight ribbons*: **curl**, **crinkle**, kink, frizz, frizzle, coil, corkscrew, wave.

cringe verb **1** *I cringe in terror every time I have to face him*: **cower**, shrink, draw back, pull back, recoil, start, shy (away), wince, flinch, blench, blanch, dodge, duck, crouch, shudder, shake, tremble, quiver, quail, quake; get cold feet.
2 *it makes me cringe when I think how stupid I was*: **wince**, squirm, blush, flush, go red; feel embarrassed, feel ashamed, feel sheepish, feel mortified, wince with embarrassment.
3 *he was always **cringing to** the queen*: **kowtow**, bow and scrape, grovel, creep, crawl, toady, fawn, truckle, cower; be servile towards, be sycophantic towards, dance attendance on, ingratiate oneself with, curry favour with; flatter, woo, pay court to, get round; informal **suck up to, make up to, lick someone's boots, be all over, fall all over, sweet-talk, soft-soap**; N. Amer. **brown-nose**; archaic **blandish**.

crinkle verb *the skin around his eyes crinkled as he smiled*: **wrinkle**, crease, pucker, furrow, line, corrugate, crimp, crumple, rumple, ruck up, scrunch up; Brit. rare **ruckle**.
▶ noun *the film could be removed and replaced without crinkles*: **wrinkle**, crease, fold, pucker, gather, furrow, ridge, line, corrugation, groove, crumple, rumple.

crinkly adjective *the dress had dried all crinkly*: **wrinkled**, wrinkly, crinkled, crumpled, rumpled, creased, crimped, corrugated, fluted, gathered, puckered, furrowed, ridged, grooved, rippled, wavy, kinked, kinky.

cripple verb **1** *the car crash crippled a young woman for life*: **disable**, paralyse, immobilize, make lame, lame, incapacitate, debilitate, handicap; **maim**, impair, damage, injure, hamstring; rare **torpefy**.
2 *sugar producers have been crippled by plummeting prices*: **ruin**, destroy, wipe out, crush, break; impair, hamstring, hamper, impede, cramp, spoil, sabotage, scotch, scupper, bring to a standstill, paralyse, enfeeble, weaken, render powerless, put out of action, put out of business, bankrupt, make bankrupt, make insolvent, impoverish, reduce to penury, bring someone to their knees; informal **clean out, put the kibosh on, do for**; N. Amer. informal **rain on someone's parade**; archaic **bring to naught**; rare **vitiate, beggar, pauperize**.
▷ANTONYMS boost.

C

crippled adjective See **disabled**.

crisis noun **1** *events across the North Sea were building to a crisis*: **critical point**, decisive point, turning point, crossroads, critical period, crux, climax, climacteric, culmination, height, head, moment of truth, zero hour, point of no return, Rubicon; informal crunch.
2 *the country was in the grip of an economic crisis | the fisheries are in crisis*: **catastrophe**, calamity, cataclysm, emergency, disaster; predicament, plight, mess, dilemma, quandary, setback, reverse, reversal, upheaval, drama; **trouble**, dire straits, hard times, hardship, adversity, extremity, distress, difficulty; informal fix, pickle, jam, stew, scrape, bind, hole, sticky situation, hot water, hell, hell on earth, hassle, stress; Brit. informal spot of bother.

crisp adjective **1** *fry the bacon until it is brown and crisp*: **crunchy**, crispy, brittle, crumbly, breakable, shatterable, friable, frangible; rigid, hard; well cooked, well done.
▷ANTONYMS soft.
2 *the grass is looking crisp and healthy*: **firm**, fresh, unwilted, unwithered.
▷ANTONYMS limp.
3 *despite the sunshine it was quite a crisp day*: **brisk**, bracing, fresh, refreshing, invigorating, stimulating, energizing, exhilarating, rousing, fortifying, tonic; keen, raw, biting, cool, cold, chilly; informal pick-me-up, nippy; Brit. informal parky; literary chill.
▷ANTONYMS sultry.
4 *his message was disseminated in crisp language*: **terse**, succinct, concise, brief, short, short and sweet, tight, taut, incisive, pithy, epigrammatic, aphoristic, elliptical; laconic, sparing; precise, clear, clear-cut, explicit, unambiguous, straightforward; informal snappy; rare lapidary, compendious, synoptic, gnomic.
▷ANTONYMS rambling; ambiguous.
5 *she has a crisp and rather schoolmistressy manner*: **brusque**, brisk, vigorous, decisive, businesslike, no-nonsense, curt, blunt, short, sharp, snappy, snappish, abrupt, to the point, frank, plain-spoken, bald, brutal, indelicate, unceremonious, cavalier, offhand, gruff, rough, harsh, caustic, abrasive; pulling no punches, not mincing one's words, not beating about the bush, calling a spade a spade, speaking one's mind; informal upfront, straight from the shoulder.
6 *his new suit gave him a very crisp appearance*: **smart**, elegant, chic, spruce, dapper, neat, trim, clean-cut, well groomed; informal snappy, natty, sharp; N. Amer. informal spiffy; archaic trig.
▷ANTONYMS scruffy.

criterion noun *academic ability is not the sole criterion for allocating funds*: **basis**, point of reference, standard, norm, yardstick, benchmark, touchstone, test, formula, measure, gauge, scale, barometer, indicator, litmus test; specification, guide, guideline, guiding principle, principle, rule, law, canon, convention.

critic noun **1** *he was the foremost literary critic of the 1840s*: **commentator**, observer, monitor, pundit, expert, authority, arbiter, interpreter, exponent, expounder; writer, author, speaker; **reviewer**, appraiser, evaluator, analyst, judge; rare scholiast, exegete.
2 *he has fewer weaknesses than his critics have claimed*: **detractor**, censurer, attacker, fault-finder, carper, backbiter, caviller, reviler, vilifier, traducer, disparager, denigrator, deprecator, belittler; informal knocker, nit-picker; rare asperser.

critical adjective **1** *the safety committee produced a highly critical report*: **censorious**, condemnatory, condemning, castigatory, reproving, denunciatory, deprecatory, disparaging, disapproving, scathing, criticizing, fault-finding, judgemental, negative, unfavourable, unsympathetic; hypercritical, ultra-critical, overcritical, pedantic, pettifogging, cavilling, carping, quibbling, niggling; informal nit-picking, hair-splitting, pernickety, picky, griping, bitching, bellyaching, whingeing; rare reprobatory, reprobative.
▷ANTONYMS complimentary.
2 *there was critical agreement among Renaissance specialists*: **evaluative**, analytic, analytical, interpretative, expository, commentative, explanatory, explicative, elucidative.
3 *the hospital says her condition is critical*: **grave**, serious, dangerous, risky, perilous, hazardous, precarious, touch-and-go, in the balance, uncertain, desperate, dire, acute, very bad; life-and-death, life-threatening; informal chancy, dicey, hairy, iffy; Brit. informal dodgy; archaic or humorous parlous; Medicine peracute, profound; rare egregious.
▷ANTONYMS safe.
4 *the choice of materials is critical for product safety*: **crucial**, vital, essential, of the essence, all-important, important, of the utmost importance, of great consequence, high-priority, paramount, pre-eminent, fundamental, key, pivotal, deciding, decisive, climacteric, momentous; serious, urgent, pressing, compelling, exigent.
▷ANTONYMS unimportant.

criticism noun **1** *in football management you come to expect criticism*: **censure**, reproval, condemnation, denunciation, disapproval, disparagement, opprobrium, captiousness, fault-finding, carping, cavilling; chastisement, castigation, upbraiding, berating, abuse, vituperation, scolding, chiding; reproofs, remonstrances, broadsides, strictures, admonishments, recriminations, aspersions, slurs, smears; informal nit-picking, knocking, panning, slamming, flak, a bad press, brickbats, knocks, raps, bad notices; Brit. informal stick, verbal, slagging off, slating; archaic contumely; rare animadversion, objurgation, excoriation, reprobation, arraignment.
2 *the book was distributed to people for criticism*: **evaluation**, assessment, examination, appreciation, appraisal, analysis, judgement; **comment**, commentary, interpretation, explanation, explication, elucidation, annotation, notation; opinions, views, observations, pronouncements, remarks, notes; rare scholia.

criticize verb *they criticized the government's handling of the economy*: **find fault with**, censure, denounce, condemn, arraign, attack, lambaste, pillory, disapprove of, carp at, cavil at, rail against, inveigh against, cast aspersions on, pour scorn on, disparage, denigrate, deprecate, malign, vilify, besmirch, run down, give a bad press to; N. Amer. slur; informal knock, pan, slam, hammer, blast, bad-mouth, nit-pick about, throw brickbats at, give flak to, lay into, lace into, pull to pieces, pull apart, pick holes in, hit out at, maul, savage, roast, skewer, crucify; Brit. informal slag off, have a go at, give some stick to, monster, slate, rubbish; N. Amer. informal pummel, cut up, trash; Austral./NZ informal bag; dated rate; archaic slash, vituperate against, reprobate; rare animadvert on, objurgate, excoriate, asperse, derogate, reprehend.
▷ANTONYMS praise; approve of.

critique noun *he produced a critique of North American culture*: **analysis**, evaluation, assessment, appraisal, appreciation, review, write-up; criticism, critical essay, textual examination, commentary, study, treatise, discourse, exposition, disquisition, account, exegesis; Brit. informal crit; rare anatomization.

croak verb **1** *'You must excuse me,' croaked the old woman*: **rasp**, squawk, caw, crow, wheeze, gasp, choke, hack, hawk, bark, cough; speak hoarsely, speak huskily, speak throatily, speak harshly, speak thickly.
2 informal *the dog finally croaked in 1987*. See **die**.
▶noun *her voice emerged as a dry croak | the croak of a carrion crow*: **rasp**, wheeze, gasp, bark, hack, cough; caw, squawk, cackle, clack, cluck.

crock noun **1** *she took out bread and a crock of honey*: **earthenware pot**, pot, jar, urn, pitcher, jug, ewer; vessel, container, receptacle, repository; N. Amer. creamer; historical jorum; archaic reservatory.
2 (**crocks**) *I washed up the dirty crocks*: **crockery**, pots, dishes, plates, bowls, cups; dinner things, tea things; pottery, earthenware, stoneware.
3 informal *these days I'm a bit of an old crock*: **invalid**, infirm person, decrepit person, feeble person; **old person**, senior citizen, senior, pensioner, old-age pensioner, OAP; fogey, old fogey, dotard; informal crumbly, wrinkly, old stager, old timer, oldie, ancient; offensive geriatric.

crockery noun *the waitress dropped a tray of crockery*: **dishes**, pots, crocks, plates, bowls, cups, saucers; pottery, china, porcelain, earthenware, stoneware, tableware; dinner service, tea service; N. Amer. dinnerware; Irish delph.

crony noun informal *he spent the evening drinking with his cronies*. See **friend** (sense 1).

crook noun **1** informal *the crook got five years for swindling two families*: **criminal**, lawbreaker, offender, villain, delinquent, malefactor, culprit, wrongdoer, transgressor, sinner; young offender, juvenile delinquent; felon, thief, robber, armed robber, burglar, housebreaker, shoplifter, mugger, fraudster, confidence trickster, swindler, racketeer, gunman, gangster, outlaw, bandit, terrorist, rapist; in Japan yakuza; informal con, jailbird, (old) lag, lifer, baddy, shark, con man, con artist, hustler; N. Amer. informal yardbird, yegg; Austral. informal crim; S. African informal lighty; W. Indian informal tief; Brit. rhyming slang tea leaf; informal, dated cracksman; Law malfeasant, misfeasor, infractor; archaic miscreant, trespasser, trusty, transport; rare peculator, defalcator.
▷ANTONYMS law-abiding citizen.
2 *the leopard sat in the crook of a tree branch*: **bend**, curve, curvature, kink, bow, elbow, angle, fork, intersection; technical flexure.
▶verb *he crooked his finger and called over the waiter*: **cock**, flex, bend, curve, curl, angle, hook, bow.

crooked adjective **1** *the village was a maze of crooked streets*: **winding**, twisting, zigzag, meandering, deviating, sinuous, tortuous, serpentine, irregular; rare anfractuous.
▷ANTONYMS straight.
2 *the signpost was crooked*: **bent**, curved, twisted, contorted, warped, angled, bowed, hooked.
▷ANTONYMS straight.
3 *the poor boy has a crooked back*: **misshapen**, **deformed**, malformed, out of shape, distorted, contorted, wry, gnarled, disfigured; hunched, humped, bowed, curved; Scottish thrawn.
4 *the picture over the bed looked crooked*: **lopsided**, askew, awry, to one side, off-centre, uneven, unsymmetrical, asymmetrical, asymmetric, not straight, out of true, out of line, on one side, tilted, at an angle, angled, slanted, aslant, slanting, sloping, squint; Scottish agley, thrawn; informal cock-eyed; Brit. informal skew-whiff, wonky, squiffy.
5 informal *his business had almost certainly been crooked | a crooked cop*: **criminal**, illegal, unlawful, questionable, dubious, nefarious; **dishonest**, dishonourable, unscrupulous, unprincipled, amoral, untrustworthy, crafty, deceitful, shifty, underhand; corrupt, corruptible, buyable, venal, grafting,

swindling, fraudulent; informal shady, tricky; Brit. informal bent, dodgy; Law malfeasant.
▷ANTONYMS honest, law-abiding.

croon verb *he crooned a few bars | she rocked the baby and began to croon*: **sing softly**, hum, lilt, carol, warble, trill, quaver; rare troll.

crop noun **1** *some farmers lost their entire crop*: **harvest**, year's growth, yield, produce, vintage, gathering, reaping, gleaning, garnering; fruits.
2 *this month has brought a bumper crop of mail*: **batch**, lot, assortment, selection, collection, supply, intake.
3 *the fruit got wedged in the bird's crop*: **craw**, maw, gullet, throat; oesophagus, pharynx; informal, dated the red lane; archaic throttle, gorge, gula.
4 *the rider picked up his hat and crop*: **whip**, lash, scourge, cat, thong, switch, birch, cane, stick; riding crop, hunting crop.
▸ verb **1** *Sharon chose to crop her long brown hair*: **cut short**, cut, clip, trim, snip, shear, shave; pare, prune, fleece, lop, dock, remove, detach; cut off, hack off, chop off, take off; shorten, make shorter, cut shorter, cut into a bob; barber, tonsure.
2 *a flock of sheep were cropping the turf*: **graze on**, browse on, feed on, nibble (at), eat; pasture, ruminate.
3 *the hay was cropped several times this summer*: **harvest**, reap, mow; gather, collect, pick, pluck; gather in, take in, bring home; literary glean, garner, cull.
□ **crop up** *things kept cropping up to delay their work*: **happen**, occur, arise, arrive, turn up, spring up, pop up, surface, emerge, materialize, appear, come to light, present itself, make an appearance; informal show up; literary come to pass, befall; archaic hap.

> *Word links* **crop**
>
> **agronomy** science of crop production

cross noun **1** *his grave is marked by a bronze cross*: **crucifix**, rood.
2 *his wife's illness is a great cross to bear*: **burden**, trouble, worry, trial, tribulation, affliction, curse, bane, hardship; vicissitude, misfortune, adversity; millstone, albatross; misery, woe, pain, sorrow, suffering, torment; thorn in one's flesh, thorn in one's side; informal hassle, stress, headache; archaic cumber.
▷ANTONYMS blessing.
3 *the animal is a cross between a yak and a cow*: **hybrid**, hybridization, cross-breed, mixed breed, half-breed, half-blood, mixture, amalgam, blend, combination, composite, conglomerate; mongrel, cur.
▸ verb **1** *I warn you not to cross the moors at night*: **travel across**, go across, cut across, make one's way across, traverse, range over, tramp over, wander over; negotiate, navigate, cover.
2 *the lake was crossed by a fine stone bridge*: **span**, bridge, arch, ford; go across, extend across, stretch across, pass over, arch over, vault over.
3 *they reached the point where the two roads cross*: **intersect**, meet, join, connect, criss-cross, interweave, intertwine.
4 *if anybody crossed him he'd raise hell*: **oppose**, resist, defy, thwart, frustrate, foil, obstruct, impede, hinder, hamper, block, check, deny, contradict, argue with, quarrel with; stand up to, take a stand against, take issue with, put up a fight against, set one's face against, fly in the face of; formal gainsay; rare controvert.
▷ANTONYMS support.
5 *the breed was crossed with the similarly coloured Friesian*: **hybridize**, cross-breed, interbreed, cross-fertilize, cross-pollinate, intercross, mix, intermix, blend.
□ **cross something out** *he crossed out several sentences*: **delete**, strike out, strike through, ink out, score out, scratch out, block out, blank out, edit out, blue-pencil, cancel, eliminate, obliterate; technical dele.
▸ adjective *he was exhausted, but he never got cross*: **angry**, annoyed, irate, irritated, in a bad mood, peeved, vexed, upset, irked, piqued, out of humour, put out, displeased, galled, resentful; **irritable**, short-tempered, bad-tempered, hot-tempered, ill-humoured, surly, churlish, disagreeable, irascible, touchy, snappy, snappish, impatient, peevish, petulant, fractious, crotchety, grouchy, grumpy, querulous, cantankerous, testy, tetchy, crabby, captious, splenetic, choleric, dyspeptic, waspish; informal mad, hopping mad, wild, livid, as cross as two sticks, apoplectic, aerated, hot under the collar, riled, on the warpath, up in arms, foaming at the mouth, steamed up, in a lather, in a paddy, fit to be tied; Brit. informal shirty, stroppy, narky, ratty, eggy; N. English informal mardy; N. Amer. informal sore, steamed, bent out of shape, soreheaded, teed off, ticked off; Austral./NZ informal ropeable, snaky, crook; W. Indian informal vex; Brit. informal, dated in a bate, waxy; vulgar slang pissed off; N. Amer. vulgar slang pissed; literary ireful, wroth.
▷ANTONYMS pleased; good-humoured.

> *Word links* **cross**
>
> **cruci-** related prefix, as in *crucify, cruciform*

cross-examine verb *the victim did not wish to be cross-examined by the police*: **interrogate**, question, cross-question, quiz, catechize; interview, examine, probe, sound out, debrief; put questions to, ask questions of; informal grill, pump, give the third degree to, put through the third degree, put through the wringer, put through the mangle, put the screws on.

cross-grained adjective *old people as a group are neither sweet nor cross-grained*: **awkward**, difficult, uncooperative, perverse, contrary, unhelpful, obstructive, disobliging, unaccommodating, unreasonable, troublesome, tiresome, annoying, vexatious, disobedient, recalcitrant, refractory, wilful, headstrong, self-willed, capricious, wayward; stubborn, obstinate, obdurate, mulish, pig-headed, bull-headed, intractable; Scottish thrawn; informal cussed; Brit. informal bloody-minded, bolshie, stroppy; N. Amer. informal balky; archaic froward, contumacious; rare renitent, pervicacious, contrarious.
▷ANTONYMS easy-going.

crossing noun **1** *they came to a halt at a busy road crossing*: **junction**, crossroads, intersection, interchange; motorway junction, railway junction, level crossing.
2 *the driver failed to notice a child on the crossing*: **pedestrian crossing**, street crossing, pelican crossing, zebra crossing; informal the green man.
3 *the Mauretania held the Blue Riband for the fastest Atlantic crossing*: **traversal**, traverse, passage, voyage, journey; cruise, sail.

crosspatch noun informal *I'm sorry I've been an old crosspatch sometimes*: **shrew**, curmudgeon, discontent, complainer, grumbler, moaner, fault-finder, carper; **misery**, mope, dog in the manger, damper, dampener, spoilsport, pessimist, prophet of doom; N. Amer. crank; informal sourpuss, grouch, grump, virago, grouser, whinger, wet blanket, party-pooper, doom merchant; N. Amer. informal kvetch, sorehead; rare jade, melancholiac.

crossways, crosswise adverb *there was just about room to lie crossways in the bed*: **diagonally**, obliquely, transversely, aslant, cornerways, cornerwise, on the cross, on the slant, at an angle, on the bias; sideways, athwart; N. Amer. cater-cornered, cater-corner, kitty-corner.

crotch noun *she tipped her dinner over his crotch*: **groin**; lap.

crotchet noun *the natural crotchets of inveterate bachelors*: **whim**, whimsy, fancy, fad, vagary, notion, conceit, caprice, kink, twist, freak, fetish, passion, bent, foible, quirk, eccentricity, idiosyncrasy; French idée fixe; informal hang-up, thing; archaic megrim; rare singularity.

crotchety adjective *he was one of those crotchety old people who give ageing a bad name*. See **bad-tempered**.

crouch verb *Ian **crouched down** and peered under the wagon | we all crouched behind the wall*: **squat (down)**, duck (down), hunker down, bob down, hunch over; bend (down), stoop (down), bow (down), kneel (down), cower, cringe, shrink, huddle; N. Amer. informal scooch.

crow verb **1** *a cock crowed down in the village*: **squawk**, screech, hoot, cry, caw, croak.
2 *they all **crowed about** the jolly time they'd had*: **boast**, brag, trumpet, show off, bluster, swagger, swank, gloat, be smug, congratulate oneself, preen oneself, pride oneself, pat oneself on the back, sing one's own praises; glory in, exult in, triumph over, parade, flaunt; informal talk big, blow hard, rub it in, lay it on thick, shoot one's mouth off, blow one's own trumpet; Austral./NZ informal skite; literary vaunt, roister; archaic rodomontade, gasconade.
▸ noun

> *Word links* **crow**
>
> **murder** collective noun

crowd noun **1** *a crowd of people filled the town square*: **throng**, horde, mob, rabble, large number, mass, multitude, host, army, herd, flock, drove, swarm, sea, stream, troupe, pack, press, crush, flood, collection, company, gathering, assembly, assemblage, array, congregation, convention, concourse; informal gaggle; Brit. informal shower; archaic rout.
2 *she wanted to stand out from the crowd*: **majority**, multitude, common people, populace, general public, mob, masses, riff-raff, proletariat, rank and file, the commonality, the hoi polloi, the canaille, the great unwashed; informal the proles, the plebs.
3 *the theatrical crowd piled into Bernard's Bentley*: **set**, group, band, circle, company, fraternity, clique, coterie; camp, league, faction; informal lot, gang, bunch, pack, crew, posse, tribe; rare sodality, confraternity.
4 *every song received a warm response from the crowd*: **audience**, spectators, watchers, listeners, viewers, onlookers, patrons, house, gallery, stalls; turnout, attendance, gate; congregation; informal punters.
▸ verb **1** *they ignored the novelist and crowded around the poet*: **cluster**, gather, flock, swarm, throng, huddle, assemble, concentrate, congregate, come together, collect, amass, accumulate; rare foregather.
2 *the guests all crowded into the dining room*: **surge**, push one's way, shove, push, thrust forward, jostle, elbow, elbow one's way, shoulder, nudge, bulldoze; squeeze, pile, pack, jam, cram.
3 *the quayside was crowded with holidaymakers*: **throng**, pack, jam, cram, fill, overfill, congest, pervade, occupy all of.
4 *I felt as if he was crowding me*: **pressurize**, pressure, lean on, press, goad, prod, bulldoze, browbeat, brainwash, dragoon, strong-arm; harass, harry, hound, nag, badger, pester, torment, plague; informal hassle, railroad, put the screws on; Brit. informal bounce; N. Amer. informal hustle, fast-talk.

C

Word links crowd

demophobia, **ochlophobia** fear of crowds

crowded adjective *we took our places in the crowded cinema*: **packed**, congested, crushed, cramped, overcrowded, full, filled to capacity, full to bursting, overfull, overflowing, teeming, swarming, thronged, populous, overpopulated, overpeopled, busy; N. Amer. mobbed; informal stuffed, jam-packed, chock-a-block, chock-full, bursting at the seams, bulging at the seams, full to the gunwales, wall-to-wall; Austral./NZ informal chocker.

crown noun **1** *he placed the crown on the new monarch's head*: **coronet**, diadem, tiara, circlet, chaplet, fillet, wreath, garland, headband; literary coronal; in India, historical taj.
2 *she won the world indoor singles crown*: **title**, award, accolade, honour, distinction, glory, kudos; trophy, cup, medal, plate, shield, belt, prize; laurels, bays, palm, wreath, laurel wreath, victor's garland.
3 *his family were loyal servants of the Crown*: **monarch**, sovereign, king, queen, emperor, empress, tsar, tsarina, prince, princess, potentate, head of state, leader, chief, ruler, lord, overlord; **monarchy**, sovereignty, royalty; informal royals.
4 *she paused at the crown of the hill*: **top**, crest, summit, peak, pinnacle, tip, head, brow, cap, brink, highest point, zenith, apex, ridge; French aiguille, serac.
▷ANTONYMS bottom.
▸ verb **1** *David II was crowned at Scone in 1331*: **invest**, induct, install, instate, ordain, initiate, inaugurate, enthrone, swear in.
2 *a valuable teaching post at Harvard University crowned his career*: **round off**, top off, cap, be the culmination of, be the climax of, be a fitting climax to, add the finishing touch(es) to, perfect, consummate, complete, conclude.
3 *the steeple is crowned by a gilded weathercock*: **top**, cap, tip, head, surmount, overtop.
4 informal *someone crowned him with a poker*: **hit over the head**, hit on the head, hit, strike, buffet, bang, knock, thwack, slug, welt, cuff, punch, smash; concuss, stun; informal brain, skull, bop, clonk, clout, sock, biff, wallop, bash, plug, lam, deck, floor; Brit. informal clock, cosh, slosh, dot, stick one on someone; N. Amer. informal bean, conk, ding, boff, bust, whale; Austral./NZ informal dong, quilt; archaic smite, swinge.

crucial adjective **1** *a crucial debate on the Maastricht Treaty*: **pivotal**, critical, key, climacteric, decisive, deciding, determining, settling, testing, trying, searching; major, significant, influential, momentous, consequential, weighty, big, important, historic, epoch-making, far-reaching, life-and-death.
▷ANTONYMS minor.
2 *confidentiality is crucial in this case*: **very important**, of the utmost importance, of great consequence, of the essence, critical, high-priority, pre-eminent, paramount, all-important, essential, vital, vitally important, indispensable, mandatory, urgent, pressing, compelling, necessary, needed, required, requisite.
▷ANTONYMS unimportant.

Word toolkit crucial

See **vital**.

crucify verb **1** *the day on which Jesus was crucified*: **nail to a cross**, hang on a cross; **execute**, put to death, kill, martyr.
2 *she had been crucified by Hamish's departure*: **devastate**, crush, shatter, hurt deeply, wound, pain, distress, harrow, agonize, mortify, torment, torture; cause agony to, cause suffering to, cause pain to, inflict anguish on.
3 informal *modern teachers are being crucified for their methods*: **condemn**, criticize severely, attack, tear apart, tear to pieces, censure, denounce, arraign, lambaste, pillory, carp at, cavil at, rail against, inveigh against, cast aspersions on, pour scorn on, disparage, denigrate, deprecate, malign, revile, vilify, besmirch, run down, give a bad press to; N. Amer. slur; informal knock, pan, slam, hammer, blast, bad-mouth, nit-pick about, throw brickbats at, give flak to, lay into, lace into, pull to pieces, pull apart, pick holes in, hit out at, maul, savage, roast, skewer; Brit. informal slag off, have a go at, give some stick to, slate, rubbish, monster; N. Amer. informal pummel, cut up, trash; Austral./NZ informal bag; dated rate; archaic slash, vituperate against, reprobate; rare animadvert on/upon, objurgate, excoriate, asperse, derogate, reprehend.
▷ANTONYMS praise.
4 informal *he was crucified by Faldo in the 1990 championship*: **trounce**, defeat utterly, beat hollow, annihilate, drub, give a drubbing to, crush, rout; informal hammer, clobber, thrash, paste, pound, pulverize, slaughter, massacre, murder, flatten, demolish, destroy, wipe the floor with, take to the cleaners, make mincemeat of, turn inside out; Brit. informal stuff, marmalize; N. Amer. informal shellac, cream, skunk, blow out.

crude adjective **1** *they convert crude oil into petroleum*: **unrefined**, unpurified, unprocessed, untreated; unmilled, unworked, unpolished, coarse, unprepared; raw, natural, plain.
▷ANTONYMS refined.
2 *Prussian infantrymen lined the crude barricade*: **primitive**, simple, basic, rudimentary, rough, rough and ready, rough-hewn, make-do, makeshift, improvised, cobbled together, thrown together, homespun, unfinished, unpolished, unformed, undeveloped; dated rude.
▷ANTONYMS sophisticated.
3 *he was reprimanded for making crude jokes*: **vulgar**, rude, risqué, suggestive, racy, earthy, off colour, colourful, indecent, bawdy, obscene, offensive, lewd, salacious, licentious, ribald, Rabelaisian, boorish, coarse, uncouth, indelicate, crass, tasteless, sordid, smutty, dirty, filthy, pornographic, X-rated, scatological; profane, foul, foul-mouthed, blasphemous, abusive, scurrilous; informal naughty, blue, raunchy, sleazy, porno, porn, steamy, spicy, locker-room; Brit. informal fruity, saucy, near the knuckle, close to the bone; N. Amer. informal gamy; euphemistic adult.
▷ANTONYMS decent, inoffensive.

crudity noun **1** *we must allow for the crudity of these statistical methods*: **primitiveness**, simplicity, oversimplicity, roughness, inaccuracy; lack of refinement, lack of sophistication; dated rudeness.
▷ANTONYMS sophistication.
2 *she shrank from his crudity and teasing*: **vulgarity**, rudeness, suggestiveness, raciness, earthiness, bawdiness, blueness, smuttiness, smut, lewdness, salaciousness, licentiousness, ribaldry, seaminess, dirtiness, filthiness, dirt, filth, boorishness, coarseness, uncouthness, indecency, obscenity, indelicacy, indelicateness, crassness, tastelessness, offensiveness; informal naughtiness, raunchiness, sleaziness, steaminess, porn; Brit. informal fruitiness, sauciness; N. Amer. informal gaminess.
▷ANTONYMS decency.

cruel adjective **1** *the prisoner was a hard, cruel man | they think fox hunting a cruel practice*: **brutal**, savage, inhuman, barbaric, barbarous, brutish, bloodthirsty, murderous, homicidal, cut-throat, vicious, ferocious, fierce; wicked, evil, fiendish, devilish, diabolical, heinous, abominable, monstrous, atrocious, vile, hideous, ghastly, nasty, spiteful, mean; **callous**, sadistic, ruthless, merciless, unmerciful, pitiless, unsparing, unrelenting, remorseless, uncaring, unsympathetic, uncharitable, heartless, stony-hearted, hard-hearted, cold-hearted, cold-blooded, bloodless, unfeeling, unemotional, unkind, inhumane, severe, harsh, stern, inclement, flinty, draconian; Brit. informal beastly; archaic dastardly, sanguinary.
▷ANTONYMS compassionate, merciful.
2 *his mother's death was a cruel blow*: **harsh**, severe, grim, grievous, hard, tough, bitter, harrowing, heartbreaking, heart-rending, distressing, upsetting, traumatic, painful, agonizing, excruciating; rare distressful.
▷ANTONYMS mild.

cruelty noun **1** *he treated her with extreme cruelty*: **brutality**, savagery, savageness, inhumanity, barbarism, barbarousness, brutishness, bloodthirstiness, murderousness, viciousness, ferocity, ferociousness, fierceness; **callousness**, sadism, ruthlessness, relentlessness, mercilessness, pitilessness, remorselessness, lack of regard, lack of sympathy, lack of charity, heartlessness, cold-heartedness, cold-bloodedness, severity, harshness, inclemency; wickedness, badness, baseness, iniquity, blackness, black-heartedness, evil, fiendishness, devilishness, heinousness, nastiness, unkindness, abuse; rare ferity.
▷ANTONYMS compassion, mercy.
2 *the cruelty of a cold winter night*: **harshness**, severity, unkindness, relentlessness, grimness, hardness, toughness, bitterness, painfulness, wretchedness; torment, trauma, pain, distress, misery.
▷ANTONYMS mildness.

cruise noun *a cruise up the Thames | they sailed off on a luxury cruise*: **boat trip**; **sea trip**, sailing trip, sail, voyage, journey, passage.
▸ verb **1** *she cruised across the Atlantic*: **sail**, steam, voyage, journey; travel by boat, take a cruise, take a boat trip, take a sea trip, take a sailing trip, go sailing, go yachting, go boating.
2 *taxis cruised around the town centre*: **coast**, drift, meander, drive slowly, travel slowly, travel aimlessly; informal mosey, tootle; Brit. informal pootle, swan.

crumb noun *biscuit crumbs | there was only one crumb of comfort*: **fragment**, bit, morsel, particle, tiny piece, speck, scrap, shred, sliver, atom, grain, granule, trace, tinge, mite, iota, jot, whit, ounce, scintilla, vestige; French soupçon; Irish stim; informal smidgen, smidge, tad; archaic scantling, scruple.

crumble verb **1** *the building is crumbling away | his empire began to crumble around him*: **disintegrate**, fall down, fall to pieces, fall apart, collapse, break down/up, tumble down, fragment; decay, fall into decay, deteriorate, degenerate, go to rack and ruin, decompose, rot, rot away, come apart at the seams, moulder, perish, come to dust.
2 *she crumbled the dry earth into fine powdery dust*: **crush**, grind, break up, pulverize, pound, powder, granulate, fragment; technical triturate, comminute; archaic levigate, bray, powderize.

crumbly adjective **brittle**, breakable, friable, powdery, granular; short; crisp, crispy; rare pulverulent, brashy.
▷ANTONYMS solid.

crummy adjective informal *a crummy little flat in Stoke Newington*. See **second-rate**, **substandard**.

crumple verb **1** *she crumpled the note in her fist*: **crush**, scrunch up, screw up, squash, squeeze; Brit. scrumple.
▷ANTONYMS smooth out.
2 *his trousers were dirty and crumpled*: **crease**, wrinkle, crinkle, rumple, ruck up, tumble; Brit. rare ruckle.
▷ANTONYMS iron.
3 *her lower lip quivered and her face began to crumple*: **pucker**, screw up; fall, sag, look sad, look miserable.
4 *her resistance crumpled*: **collapse**, give way, cave in, go to pieces, break down, crumble, be overcome.
▷ANTONYMS hold out.

crunch verb **1** *Meryl crunched the biscuit with relish*: **munch**, chew noisily, chomp, champ, bite, gnaw, masticate; eat, devour, consume; rare chumble.
2 *the bomb had crunched the houses into rubble*: **crush**, pulverize, pound, grind, break, smash.
▶ noun informal *when the crunch comes, she'll be forced to choose*: **moment of truth**, critical point, crux, crisis, decision time, zero hour, point of no return; showdown.

crusade noun **1** *the medieval crusades*: **holy war**; military campaign.
2 *a crusade against crime | a crusade to improve education*: **campaign**, drive, push, move, movement, effort, struggle; battle, war, offensive.
▶ verb *you know how she likes **crusading for** the cause of the underdog*: **campaign**, fight, do battle, battle, take up arms, take up the cudgels, work, push, press, strive, struggle, agitate, lobby; champion, promote.

crusader noun **campaigner**, fighter, battler; champion, advocate, promoter, enthusiast; reformer.

crush verb **1** *essential oils in the leaves are released when the herbs are crushed or heated*: **squash**, squeeze, press, compress; pulp, mash, macerate, mangle; flatten, trample on, tread on; informal squidge, splat; N. Amer. informal smush.
2 *your dress will get crushed*: **crease**, crumple, rumple, wrinkle, crinkle, scrunch up, ruck up; Brit. scrumple up; Brit. rare ruckle.
▷ANTONYMS smooth out.
3 *crush the biscuits with a rolling pin | crushed stone*: **pulverize**, pound, grind, break up, smash, shatter, crumble, crunch, splinter; mill, pestle; technical triturate, comminute; archaic bray, levigate, powderize; rare kibble.
4 *he crushed her in his arms*: **hug**, squeeze, hold tight, clutch; embrace, enfold.
5 *the new regime ruthlessly crushed all popular uprisings*: **suppress**, put down, quell, quash, squash, stamp out, put an end to, put a stop to, overcome, overpower, defeat, extinguish, vanquish, triumph over, break, bring someone to their knees, repress, subdue.
6 *the England No 1 was crushed 15–7, 15–6, 15–6*: **defeat utterly**, beat hollow, win a resounding victory over, drub, rout, give someone a drubbing, overwhelm; informal hammer, clobber, thrash, paste, give someone a pasting, whip, pound, pulverize, demolish, destroy, wipe the floor with, take to the cleaners, make mincemeat of, annihilate, slaughter, murder, massacre, crucify, flatten, turn inside out, run rings around; Brit. informal stuff, marmalize; N. Amer. informal shellac, blow out, cream, skunk.
▷ANTONYMS lose, be defeated.
7 *Alan was crushed by her words*: **mortify**, humiliate, abash, chagrin, deflate, demoralize, flatten, squash; devastate, shatter; informal put down, shoot down in flames, take down a peg or two, cut down to size, put someone in their place, make someone eat humble pie, settle someone's hash, knock the stuffing out of; N. Amer. informal make someone eat crow.
▶ noun **1** *we were caught up in the crush of people*: **crowd**, throng, horde, swarm, sea, mass, pack, press, multitude, mob; huddle; jam, congestion; archaic rout.
2 informal *it was just a teenage crush*: **infatuation**, obsession, love, passion, passing fancy; informal pash, puppy love, calf love; rare mash.
3 *lemon crush*: **squash**, fruit juice, cordial, drink.

crust noun **1** *a loaf with a crisp brown crust*: **outer layer/part**, outside, exterior; heel, end, remnant.
2 informal *I'm just trying to earn an honest crust*: **living**, livelihood, means of subsistence, income, daily bread; informal bread and butter.
3 *the islands' food resources were buried under a crust of ice and snow*: **covering, layer**, coating, cover, coat, sheet, thickness, film, skin; topping, caking; encrustation, scab; rare concretion.

crusty adjective **1** *crusty French bread*: **crisp**, crispy, well baked, well done; crumbly, brittle, friable.
▷ANTONYMS soft, soggy.
2 *a crusty old man*: **irritable**, bad-tempered, irascible, grumpy, grouchy, crotchety, tetchy, testy, cantankerous, curmudgeonly, ill-tempered, ill-natured, ill-humoured, peevish, cross, fractious, disagreeable, pettish, crabbed, crabby, waspish, prickly, peppery, touchy, scratchy, splenetic, shrewish, short-tempered, quick-tempered, dyspeptic, choleric, bilious, liverish, cross-grained; argumentative, quarrelsome, captious; informal snappish, snappy, chippy, on a short fuse, short-fused; Brit. informal shirty, stroppy, narky, ratty, eggy, like a bear with a sore head; N. Amer. informal cranky, ornery, peckish, soreheaded; Austral./NZ informal snaky.
▷ANTONYMS good-natured, affable.

crux noun *the crux of the matter*: **nub**, heart, essence, most important point, central point, main point, essential part, core, centre, nucleus, kernel; informal the bottom line.

cry verb **1** *Mandy's face crumpled and she started to cry*: **weep**, shed tears, sob, wail, be in tears, cry one's eyes out, cry one's heart out, cry as if one's heart would break, bawl, howl, snivel, whimper, whine, squall, mewl, bleat; lament, grieve, mourn, keen; Scottish greet; informal boohoo, blub, blubber, turn on the waterworks; Brit. informal grizzle; literary pule, plain.
▷ANTONYMS laugh.
2 *'Wait!' he cried | the girl **cried out** in pain*: **call**, shout, exclaim, sing out, yell, shriek, scream, screech, bawl, bellow, roar, whoop; yowl, squeal, yelp, yawp; informal holler, yoo-hoo, cooee; rare ejaculate, vociferate, ululate.
▷ANTONYMS whisper.
□ **cry off** informal *he cried off at the last moment*: **back out**, pull out, cancel, withdraw, beg off, excuse oneself; change one's mind, go back on one's word, break one's promise; informal get cold feet, cop out, wimp out; N. Amer. informal crap out.
□ **cry out for** *the conduct chronicled in this report cries out for administrative action*: **require**, demand, need, necessitate, call for; want.
▶ noun **1** *Leonora had a good cry | the baby's cries*: **sob**, weep, crying fit, fit of crying; (**cries**) weeping, sobbing, wailing, bawling, howling, snivelling, whimpering.
▷ANTONYMS laugh, laughter.
2 *a cry of despair | his cries of pain*: **call**, shout, exclamation, yell, shriek, scream, screech, bawl, bellow, roar, whoop; howl, yowl, squeal, yelp, yawp; ejaculation, interjection; informal holler; rare vociferation, ululation.
3 *fund-raisers have issued a cry for help*: **appeal**, plea, entreaty, urgent request, cry from the heart; French cri de cœur.

crypt noun **tomb**, vault, mausoleum, burial chamber, sepulchre, catacomb, ossuary, undercroft; cellar, basement; Archaeology mastaba.

cryptic adjective *his cryptic comments taxed her powers of comprehension*: **enigmatic**, mysterious, hard to understand, confusing, mystifying, perplexing, puzzling, obscure, abstruse, arcane, oracular, Delphic, ambiguous, elliptical, oblique; informal as clear as mud.
▷ANTONYMS straightforward, clear.

crystallize verb **1** *different minerals crystallize at different temperatures*: **form crystals**, solidify, harden.
2 *the idea crystallized in her mind*: **become clear**, become definite, take shape, emerge, form, materialize; informal gel.

cub noun **1** *a lioness and her cubs*: **baby**; archaic whelp; (**cubs**) young, offspring.
2 *as a cub reporter, I was frequently sent out on the least desirable assignments*: **trainee**, apprentice, probationer, novice, tyro, new recruit, new boy, new girl, fledgling, learner, beginner; informal rookie, new kid (on the block), newie, newbie; N. Amer. informal greenhorn, probie, tenderfoot.
▷ANTONYMS veteran, old hand.

cubbyhole noun **1** *the glass-partitioned cubbyhole he called an office*: **small room**, booth, cubicle; den, snug; N. Amer. cubby.
2 *we went through every drawer and cubbyhole*: **compartment**, pigeonhole, niche; slot, recess.

cube noun hexahedron, cuboid, parallelepiped; block, brick, lump, chunk.

cuddle verb **1** *she sat on the bed, cuddling the baby*: **hug**, embrace, clasp, hold tight, hold in one's arms, fold in one's arms.
2 *the pair have been spotted kissing and cuddling*: **embrace**, hug, caress, pet, fondle; informal canoodle, smooch; informal, dated spoon, bill and coo.
3 *I **cuddled up to** him*: **snuggle**, nestle, curl, nuzzle, lie close; burrow against, huddle against; N. Amer. snug down.
▶ noun *come and give me a cuddle*: **hug**, embrace, bear hug.

cuddly adjective **huggable**, cuddlesome; plump, curvaceous, rounded, buxom, soft, warm; attractive, endearing, lovable; N. Amer. informal zaftig.

cudgel noun *a thick wooden cudgel*: **club**, bludgeon, stick, truncheon, baton, blackthorn, mace, bat; N. Amer. blackjack, billy, billy club, nightstick; in Ireland shillelagh; Indian lathi, danda; S. African kierie, knobkerrie; Brit. informal cosh, life preserver.
▶ verb *she was cudgelled to death*: **bludgeon**, club, beat, batter, bash; attack, assault; Brit. informal cosh.

cue noun *he looked at his watch and Sylvie knew it was a cue for her to leave*: **signal**, sign, indication, prompt, reminder, prompting; nod, word; hint, suggestion, intimation; N. Amer. informal high sign; Physiology zeitgeber.

cuff verb *Cullam grabbed him by the lapels and cuffed him on the head*: **hit**, strike, slap, smack, thump, thwack, beat, punch, swat, knock, rap, box someone's ears; Scottish & N. English skelp; informal clout, wallop, belt, whack, bash, clobber, bop, biff, sock, whop; Brit. informal slosh, dot; N. Amer. informal boff, slug; Austral./NZ informal dong, quilt; literary smite.
□ **off the cuff** informal **1** *an off-the-cuff remark*: **impromptu**, extempore, ad lib; unrehearsed, unscripted, unprepared, improvised, spontaneous, unplanned; offhand, casual; Latin ad libitum; rare extemporaneous. **2** *I spoke off the cuff*: **without preparation**, without rehearsal, impromptu, ad lib; spontaneously; Latin ad libitum; informal off the top of one's head, on the spur of the moment; rare extemporaneously.

cuisine noun **cooking**, cookery, fare, food; French haute cuisine, cordon bleu, nouvelle cuisine.

cul-de-sac noun **no through road**, blind alley, dead end.

cull verb **1** *anecdotes culled from Greek and Roman history*: **select**, choose, pick, take, obtain, get, glean.
2 *he sees culling deer as a necessity*: **slaughter**, kill, destroy; reduce the numbers of, thin out the population of.

C

culminate verb *nine days of processions and parades **culminating in** a dramatic fire-walking ceremony*: **come to a climax**, come to a crescendo, come to a head, reach a finale, peak, climax, reach a pinnacle; build up to, lead up to; come to an end with, end with, finish with, conclude with, close with, terminate with; informal wind up.
▷ANTONYMS start, begin; peter out.

culmination noun *the culmination of his career*: **climax**, pinnacle, peak, high point, highest point, height, high water mark, top, summit, crest, zenith, crowning moment, apotheosis; apex, apogee, vertex; finale, denouement; consummation, completion, finish, conclusion, close, termination; informal high noon.
▷ANTONYMS nadir.

culpability noun **guilt**, blame, fault, responsibility, accountability, liability, answerability; guiltiness, blameworthiness.
▷ANTONYMS innocence.

culpable adjective *I hold you personally culpable*: **to blame**, **guilty**, at fault, in the wrong, blameworthy, blameable, censurable, reproachable, reprovable, found wanting; responsible, answerable, liable, accountable.
▷ANTONYMS blameless, innocent.

culprit noun *the police are doing all they can to catch the culprit*: **guilty party**, offender, wrongdoer, person responsible; **criminal**, malefactor, lawbreaker, felon, delinquent, reprobate; evil-doer, transgressor, sinner; informal baddy, bad guy, wrong 'un, crook, crim; Law malfeasant, misfeasor, infractor; archaic miscreant.

cult noun **1** *a religious cult*: **sect**, religious group, denomination, religious order, church, faith, faith community, belief, persuasion, affiliation, movement; group, body, faction, clique.
2 *the cult of youth and beauty in Hollywood*: **obsession with**, fixation on, mania for, passion for; idolization of, admiration for, devotion to, worship of, veneration of, reverence for.
3 *the series has become a bit of a cult in the UK*: **craze**, fashion, fad, vogue; informal thing.

cultivate verb **1** *the peasants who cultivated the land became its owners*: **till**, plough, dig, turn, hoe; **farm**, work, prepare; fertilize, mulch.
2 *they were encouraged to cultivate basic food crops*: **grow**, raise, rear, bring on, tend; plant, sow.
3 *her father had cultivated Maud's friendship*: **try to acquire**, pursue, court; try to develop, work hard at, foster, nurture, encourage.
4 *it helps if you go out of your way to cultivate the local people*: **seek the friendship of**, seek the favour of, try to win over, try to get someone on one's side, try to get on someone's good side, woo, court, pay court to, rub up the right way, run after, make advances to, make up to, keep sweet, ingratiate oneself with, curry favour with; associate with, mix with, keep company with; informal get in someone's good books, butter up, suck up to; N. Amer. informal shine up to; vulgar slang brown-nose.
▷ANTONYMS ignore.
5 *he wants to cultivate his mind—to understand art and literature*: **improve**, better, refine, elevate, polish; educate, train, develop, enlighten, enrich, civilize, culture.

cultivated adjective *a remarkably cultivated man*: **cultured**, educated, well read, well informed; civilized, enlightened, discerning, discriminating, refined, polished; sophisticated, urbane, cosmopolitan; courteous, polite, well mannered, mannerly, gracious; informal couth.
▷ANTONYMS ignorant.

cultivation noun **1** *the cultivation of arable crops*: **growing**, raising, rearing, farming, culture; planting, sowing.
2 *the reclamation of land for cultivation*: **agriculture**, agronomy, horticulture, husbandry; tillage.
3 *the cultivation of the mind*: **improvement**, bettering; education, training, development.
4 *Minton could not disguise his underlying seriousness nor the depth of his cultivation*: **culture**, culturedness, intellectual/artistic awareness, education, erudition, learning, enlightenment, discrimination, good taste, taste, refinement.

cultural adjective **1** *cultural differences*: **ethnic**, racial, folk; societal, lifestyle.
2 *cultural achievements | cultural events*: **aesthetic**, artistic, intellectual; educational, civilizing, enlightening, edifying, enriching.

culture noun **1** *20th century popular culture*: **the arts**, the humanities; **intellectual achievement(s)**, intellectual activity; literature, music, painting, philosophy.
2 *a man of culture*: **intellectual/artistic awareness**, education, cultivation, enlightenment, discernment, discrimination, good taste, taste, refinement, polish; sophistication, urbanity, urbaneness; erudition, learning, letters; French belles-lettres.
3 *people from many different cultures | Afro-Caribbean culture*: **civilization**, society, way of life, lifestyle; customs, traditions, heritage, habits, ways, mores, values.
4 *the culture of crops*: **cultivation**, growing, farming; agriculture, husbandry, agronomy.

cultured adjective *a sensitive, cultured man*: **cultivated**, intellectually/artistically aware, artistic, enlightened, civilized, educated, well educated, well read, well informed, learned, knowledgeable, discerning, discriminating, with good taste, refined, polished; sophisticated, urbane; intellectual, highbrow, scholarly, erudite; informal arty.
▷ANTONYMS ignorant, unrefined, unsophisticated.

culvert noun **channel**, conduit, watercourse, trough; **drain**, gutter.

cumbersome adjective **1** *a cumbersome rubberized diving suit*: **unwieldy**, unmanageable, awkward, clumsy, ungainly, inconvenient, incommodious; **bulky**, large, heavy, hefty, weighty, burdensome; informal hulking, clunky; rare cumbrous, unhandy, lumbersome.
▷ANTONYMS manageable, convenient.
2 *cumbersome procedures*: **complicated**, complex, involved, inefficient, badly organized, wasteful, unwieldy, slow, slow-moving.
▷ANTONYMS straightforward, efficient.

cumulative adjective **increasing**, accumulative, accumulating, growing, progressive, accruing, snowballing, mounting; collective, aggregate, amassed; Brit. knock-on.

cunning adjective *he's been very cunning | a cunning scheme*: **crafty**, wily, artful, guileful, devious, sly, knowing, scheming, designing, tricky, slippery, slick, manipulative, Machiavellian, deceitful, deceptive, duplicitous; shrewd, astute, clever, canny, sharp, sharp-witted, skilful, ingenious, resourceful, inventive, imaginative, deft, adroit, dexterous; informal foxy, savvy, fiendish, sneaky; Brit. informal **fly**; Scottish & N. English informal pawky; S. African informal **slim**; archaic subtle; rare vulpine, carny.
▷ANTONYMS honest, guileless, naive.
▶ **noun** *you have to admire his political cunning*: **guile**, craftiness, wiliness, artfulness, deviousness, slyness, trickery, trickiness, duplicity, deceitfulness, deceit, chicanery; shrewdness, astuteness, cleverness, canniness, sharpness, ingenuity, resourcefulness, inventiveness, imagination, deftness, adroitness, dexterity, dexterousness; wiles, ploys, schemes, stratagems, tactics, manoeuvres, subterfuges, tricks, ruses; informal foxiness.
▷ANTONYMS guilelessness, naivety.

cup noun **1** *the winner was presented with a silver cup*: **trophy**, chalice; award, prize.
2 *a non-alcoholic fruit cup*: **punch**, drink, mixed drink.

cur noun **1** *a mangy cur*. See **mongrel** (noun).
2 informal *Neil was beginning to feel even more like a cur*. See **scoundrel**.

curable adjective *most skin cancers are curable*: **remediable**, treatable, medicable, operable, responsive to treatment.
▷ANTONYMS incurable.

curative adjective *the herb's curative properties*: **healing**, therapeutic, medicinal, remedial, curing, corrective; restorative, tonic, health-giving, healthful, sanative; rare febrifugal, vulnerary, analeptic, iatric.

curator noun **custodian**, keeper, conservator, guardian, caretaker, steward.

curb noun *a curb on public spending*: **restraint**, restriction, check, brake, rein, control, limitation, limit, constraint, stricture; deterrent, damper, suppressant, retardant; informal crackdown, clampdown; literary trammel.
▶ **verb** *he breathed deeply, trying to curb his temper | their failure to curb inflation*: **restrain**, hold back, keep back, hold in, repress, suppress, fight back, bite back, keep in check, check, control, keep under control, rein in, keep a tight rein on, contain, discipline, govern, bridle, tame, subdue, stifle, smother, swallow, choke back, muzzle, silence, muffle, strangle, gag; limit, put a limit on, keep within bounds, put the brakes on, slow down, retard, restrict, constrain, deter, impede, inhibit; freeze, peg; informal button up, keep a/the lid on; literary trammel.
▷ANTONYMS release.

curdle verb **clot**, coagulate, congeal, separate into curds/lumps, solidify, thicken, condense; turn, turn sour, sour, ferment.

cure verb **1** *Casey had been cured, but he needed to convalesce*: **heal**, restore to health, make well, make better, restore, rehabilitate, treat successfully; archaic cleanse.
2 *the belief that economic equality could cure all social ills*: **rectify**, remedy, put right, set right, right, set to rights, fix, mend, repair, heal, make better, ameliorate, alleviate, ease; solve, sort out, be the answer/solution to; eliminate, do away with, end, put an end to, remove, counteract, correct.
▷ANTONYMS exacerbate, aggravate.
3 *some farmers cured their own bacon*: **preserve**, smoke, salt, dry, kipper, pickle.
▶ **noun 1** *a cure for cancer*: **remedy**, curative, medicine, medication, medicament, restorative, corrective, antidote, antiserum; (course of) treatment, therapy, healing, alleviation; nostrum, panacea, cure-all;

archaic physic, specific.
2 *he was beyond cure*: **healing**, restoration to health.
3 *interest rate cuts are not the cure for the problem*: **solution**, answer, antidote, nostrum, panacea, cure-all, magic formula; informal quick fix, magic bullet.

cure-all noun **panacea**, universal cure, cure for all ills, universal remedy, sovereign remedy, heal-all, nostrum, elixir, wonder drug, perfect solution, magic formula, magic bullet; rare catholicon, diacatholicon, panpharmacon.

curio noun **trinket**, knick-knack, bibelot, ornament, bauble, gimcrack, gewgaw; antique, collector's item, object of virtu, rarity, curiosity; French objet, objet d'art; N. Amer. **kickshaw**; informal whatnot, dingle-dangle; Brit. informal doodah, doobry; N. Amer. informal tchotchke, tsatske; archaic folderol, furbelow, whim-wham, bijou, gaud, bygone.

curiosity noun **1** *his evasiveness roused my curiosity*: **inquisitiveness**, interest, spirit of enquiry; informal nosiness.
2 *the coins do have a certain curiosity value*: **peculiarity**, oddity, strangeness, oddness, idiosyncrasy, unusualness, novelty.
3 *the shop is a treasure trove of curiosities | geological curiosities*: **oddity**, curio, novelty, conversation piece, object of virtu, collector's item; rarity, wonder, marvel, phenomenon.

curious adjective **1** *she was obviously curious, but too polite to ask questions | the curious stares of her colleagues*: **inquisitive**, intrigued, interested, eager to know, dying to know, burning with curiosity, agog; quizzical, enquiring, searching, probing, querying, questioning, interrogative; perplexed, puzzled, baffled, mystified; informal nosy, nosy-parker, snoopy.
▷ANTONYMS uninterested.
2 *her curious behaviour intrigued him*: **strange**, odd, peculiar, funny, unusual, bizarre, weird, eccentric, queer, unexpected, unfamiliar, abnormal, out of the ordinary, atypical, anomalous, untypical, different, out of the way, surprising, incongruous, extraordinary, remarkable, puzzling, mystifying, mysterious, perplexing, baffling, unaccountable, inexplicable, irregular, singular, offbeat, unconventional, unorthodox, outlandish, aberrant, freak, freakish, deviant; uncanny, eerie, unnatural; Brit. out of the common; French outré; Scottish unco; informal off the wall, wacky; Brit. informal rum; N. Amer. informal wacko.
▷ANTONYMS ordinary.

> *Choose the right word* **curious, strange, odd, peculiar**
>
> See **strange**.

curl verb **1** *smoke curled up from his cigarette | the road curls round Sibton Park*: **spiral**, coil, wreathe, twirl, swirl, furl; **wind**, curve, bend, twist, twist and turn, loop, meander, snake, corkscrew, zigzag.
2 *Ruth curled her arms around his neck*: **wind**, twine, entwine, wrap.
3 *she washed and curled my hair*: **crimp**, wave, tong; **perm**.
4 *the rain had made his hair curl even more*: **go curly**, go frizzy, frizz out, frizzle, crinkle.
5 *they curled up together on the sofa*: **nestle**, snuggle, cuddle; huddle; N. Amer. snug down.
□ **make someone's hair curl** informal *I could tell you things about him that would make your hair curl*: **shock**, stun, horrify, appal, scandalize, make someone's blood run cold; informal make someone's hair stand on end.
▶ noun **1** *her blonde hair was a mass of tangled curls*: **ringlet**, corkscrew, coil, kink, wave; kiss-curl.
2 *a curl of smoke*: **spiral**, coil, wreath, twirl, swirl, furl, twist, corkscrew, curlicue, whorl, helix, gyre.

curly adjective *thick, curly hair*: **wavy**, curling, curled, crimped, permed, frizzy, frizzed, kinked, kinky, crinkly, fuzzy, corkscrew; wiry; rare ringletty, ringletted.
▷ANTONYMS straight.

curmudgeon noun **bad-tempered person**; N. Amer. crank; informal crosspatch, sourpuss, old trout; Brit. informal a bear with a sore head; N. Amer. informal kvetch, sorehead.

currency noun **1** *foreign currency*: **money**, legal tender, medium of exchange, cash, banknotes, notes, paper money, coins, coinage; N. Amer. bills; formal specie. See also **money**.
2 *since the war, the term has gained new currency*: **prevalence**, circulation, dissemination, publicity, exposure; acceptance, popularity, fashionableness, voguishness.

current adjective **1** *current events | current fashions*: **contemporary**, present-day, present, contemporaneous, ongoing; topical, in the news, live, alive, happening, burning; modern, latest, popular, fashionable, in fashion, in vogue, up to date, up to the minute; French de nos jours; informal trendy, now, in.
▷ANTONYMS past.
2 *the idea is still current in some quarters*: **prevalent**, prevailing, common, in general use, accepted, in circulation, circulating, going around, doing/making the rounds, popular, widespread, rife, about; talked of, on everyone's lips, bruited about.
▷ANTONYMS obsolete.
3 *a current driving licence*: **valid**, usable, up to date.
▷ANTONYMS old, out of date.
4 *the current prime minister*: **incumbent**, present, in office, in power; reigning.
▷ANTONYMS past; former.
▶ noun **1** *a current of air | ocean currents*: **steady flow**, stream, backdraught, slipstream; airstream, thermal, updraught, draught; undercurrent, undertow, tide.
2 *the current of human life*: **course**, progress, progression, flow, tide, movement.
3 *the current of opinion*: **trend**, drift, direction, tendency, swing, tenor.

> *Word links* **current**
>
> **galvanometer** instrument for measuring electric currents

curriculum noun **syllabus**, course of study/studies, programme of study/studies, educational programme, subjects, modules; timetable, schedule.

curse noun **1** *she'd put a curse on him*: **malediction**, the evil eye, imprecation, execration, voodoo, hoodoo; anathema, excommunication; N. Amer. hex; Irish cess; informal jinx; archaic malison, ban.
2 *those who seek to overcome the curse of racism*: **evil**, blight, scourge, plague, cancer, canker, poison.
3 *the curse of unemployment*: **affliction**, burden, cross to bear, bane, bitter pill, misfortune, misery, ordeal, trial, tribulation, torment, trouble, problem.
▷ANTONYMS blessing, advantage.
4 *I heard the sound of breaking glass and muffled curses*: **swear word**, expletive, oath, profanity, four-letter word, dirty word, obscenity, imprecation, blasphemy, vulgarism, vulgarity; swearing, bad/foul language, strong language; informal cuss, cuss word.
▶ verb **1** *it seemed as if the family had been cursed*: **put a curse on**, put the evil eye on, execrate, imprecate, hoodoo; anathematize, excommunicate, damn; N. Amer. hex; informal put a jinx on, jinx; rare accurse.
2 *Miss Lewis **was cursed with** self-consciousness and feelings of inadequacy*: **be afflicted with**, be troubled by, be plagued with, suffer from, be burdened with, be blighted with, be bedevilled by.
▷ANTONYMS be blessed with.
3 *drivers were cursing and sounding their horns*: **swear**, utter profanities, utter oaths, use bad/foul language, be foul-mouthed, blaspheme, be blasphemous, take the Lord's name in vain, swear like a trooper, damn; informal cuss, turn the air blue, eff and blind; archaic execrate.

cursed adjective *the cursed city of Anlec*: **under a curse**, damned, doomed, ill-fated, ill-starred, star-crossed; anathematized, excommunicated, excommunicate; Scottish fey; informal jinxed; literary accursed.

cursory adjective *a cursory inspection*: **perfunctory**, desultory, casual, superficial, token, uninterested, half-hearted, inattentive, unthinking, offhand, mechanical, automatic, routine; **hasty**, quick, hurried, rapid, brief, passing, fleeting, summary, sketchy, careless, slapdash.
▷ANTONYMS thorough, painstaking.

> *Word toolkit* **cursory**
>
> See **incomplete**.

curt adjective *'No,' was his curt reply*: **terse**, brusque, abrupt, clipped, blunt, short, monosyllabic, summary, snappy, snappish, sharp, crisp, tart; gruff, offhand, unceremonious, ungracious, rude, impolite, discourteous, uncivil; laconic, brief, succinct, compact, pithy, to the point, economical; informal snippy; Brit. rare dusty.
▷ANTONYMS polite, expansive.

> *Choose the right word* **curt, brusque, abrupt, terse**
>
> See **brusque**.

curtail verb *economic policies designed to curtail spending | his visit was curtailed*: **reduce**, cut, cut down, cut back, decrease, lessen, diminish, slim down, tighten up, retrench, pare down, trim, dock, lop, shrink; **shorten**, cut short, break off, truncate; restrict, put a restriction on, limit, put a limit on, curb, put the brakes on, rein in, rein back; informal chop.
▷ANTONYMS increase; lengthen.

> *Choose the right word* **curtail, shorten, abbreviate, abridge, truncate**
>
> See **shorten**.

curtailment noun *the curtailment of the government's public expenditure plans*: **reduction**, cut, cutback, decrease, lessening, diminution, retrenchment, shrinkage; shortening, truncation, guillotine; restriction, limitation.
▷ANTONYMS increase, expansion.

curtain noun **1** *Colin closed the window and drew the curtains*: **window hanging**, hanging, screen, blind; net curtain, cafe curtain, portière,

C

blackout; drop curtain, drop scene, tableau curtain, safety curtain; N. Amer. drape; in Muslim & Hindu societies purdah.
2 *the curtain of falling snow*: **screen**, cover, shield, cloak, veil, pall.
▸ **verb** *the bed was* ***curtained off*** *from the rest of the room | her unbound hair curtained her face*: **screen**, separate, isolate; **conceal**, hide, shield, mask, veil, shroud.

curtsy **verb** **bend the knee**, drop a curtsy, bob, genuflect.
▸ **noun** **bob**, genuflection; archaic courtesy, obeisance.

curvaceous **adjective** *a curvaceous young woman*: **shapely**, voluptuous, sexy, full-figured, rounded, buxom, full-bosomed, bosomy, Junoesque, Rubensesque, opulent; cuddly; informal curvy, well endowed, pneumatic, stacked, well upholstered, busty, chesty; archaic comely.
▷**ANTONYMS** skinny, boyish.

curve **noun** *the serpentine curves of the river*: **bend**, turn, loop, curl, twist, hook; arch, bow, half-moon; corner, dog-leg, oxbow; bulge, swell, curvature, camber; undulation, meander; Brit. hairpin bend, hairpin turn; technical flexure, trajectory, inflection; rare incurvation.
▸ **verb** *the road dipped steeply and then curved back on itself*: **bend**, turn, loop, wind, meander, undulate, snake, spiral, twist, coil, curl; arc, arch, bow; bulge, swell; technical inflect; rare incurve.

curved **adjective** **bent**, arched, bowed, crescent, curving, wavy, twisted, twisty, sinuous, serpentine, meandering, undulating, curvilinear, curvy; vaulted, rounded, concave, convex, domed, humped; hooked, aquiline; technical arcuate, falcate, falciform, circumflex, flexural; literary embowed; rare curviform.
▷**ANTONYMS** straight.

cushion **noun 1** *she leaned back against the cushions*: **pillow**, bolster, headrest; scatter cushion, floor cushion, beanbag, booster cushion, squab; hassock, kneeler, mat; historical pillion; rare zabuton.
2 *a cushion against fluctuations in demand*: **protection**, buffer, shield, defence, bulwark.
▸ **verb 1** *he stared out of the window, his chin cushioned on one hand*: **support**, cradle, prop (up), rest; pillow.
2 *George told me the news, trying hard to cushion the blow*: **soften**, lessen, diminish, decrease, mitigate, temper, allay, alleviate, reduce the effect of, take the edge off, dull, blunt, deaden, absorb, muffle, stifle.
▷**ANTONYMS** intensify, exacerbate.
3 *residents are cushioned from the outside world*: **protect**, shield, shelter, cocoon.
▷**ANTONYMS** expose.

cushy **adjective** informal *a cushy job*: **easy**, undemanding, untaxing; comfortable, secure; Brit. informal jammy.
▷**ANTONYMS** difficult, demanding.

custodian **noun** *the custodian of the archives | the acknowledged custodians of academic standards*: **curator**, keeper, conservator, guardian, overseer, superintendent; caretaker, steward, warden, warder, attendant; watchdog, protector, defender.

custody **noun 1** *the parent who has custody of the child | the property was placed in the custody of a trustee*: **care**, **guardianship**, charge, keeping, safe keeping, wardship, ward, responsibility, protection, guidance, tutelage; custodianship, trusteeship, trust, keep, possession, hands; supervision, superintendence, surveillance, control, aegis, auspices; Law escrow.
2 *he has been in custody for 12 months*: **imprisonment**, detention, confinement, incarceration, internment, captivity; remand; archaic duress, durance.

custom **noun 1** *he was unfamiliar with the local customs and culture*: **tradition**, practice, usage, observance, way, convention, procedure, ceremony, ritual, ordinance, form, formality, fashion, mode, manner; shibboleth, sacred cow, unwritten rule; mores, way of doing things; Scottish consuetude; formal praxis.
2 *it is our custom to visit the Lake District in October*: **habit**, **practice**, routine, way, wont; policy, rule; rare habitude.
3 Brit. *special offers to attract custom away from competitors*: **customers**, shoppers, buyers, purchasers, consumers; clientele; market share; Brit. informal punters; Law vendees; rare emptors.
4 Brit. *if you keep me waiting I will take my custom elsewhere*: **business**, patronage, trade, support.

customarily **adverb** *these discussions customarily take place in the early evening*: **usually**, traditionally, normally, as a rule, conventionally, generally, in the ordinary way, ordinarily, commonly; habitually, routinely.
▷**ANTONYMS** occasionally.

customary **adjective 1** *it is customary to mark such an occasion with a toast | customary social practices*: **usual**, traditional, normal, conventional; familiar, accepted, prevailing, routine, fixed, set, established, confirmed, everyday, ordinary, common, stock, well worn, time-honoured.
▷**ANTONYMS** unusual, exceptional, rare.
2 *she responded with her customary good sense*: **usual**, accustomed, habitual, wonted, regular.
▷**ANTONYMS** unusual, unaccustomed.

customer **noun 1** *businesses need to think up new ways of attracting customers*: **shopper**, consumer, buyer, purchaser; **patron**, client; regular, frequenter, habitué; (**customers**) clientele, patronage, business, trade; Brit. informal punter; Law vendee; rare emptor.
▷**ANTONYMS** seller.
2 informal *he's a tough customer—a man to be reckoned with*: **person**, individual, creature, fellow, man, woman; informal sort, type, fella, cookie, bunny, critter; Brit. informal bloke, chap, bod, geezer, gent; N. Amer. informal guy, gal, dame, dude, hombre; informal, dated dog; Brit. vulgar slang sod, bugger; archaic wight.

customs **plural noun** **import taxes**; duties, levies, dues, tolls, tariffs, imposts.

cut **verb 1** *the knife slipped and cut his finger*: **gash**, slash, lacerate, slit, pierce, penetrate, wound, injure; scratch, graze, nick, snick, notch, incise, score; lance.
2 *cut the red pepper into small pieces*: **chop**, cut up, slice, dice, cube, mince; carve; divide; N. Amer. hash.
3 *they cut the rope before he choked | he has cut his ties with the church*: **sever**, cleave, cut in two; literary rend; archaic sunder; rare dissever.
4 *she's had her hair cut | cut back the new growth to about half its length*: **trim**, snip, clip, crop, bob, barber, shear, shave; pare; prune, pollard, poll, lop, dock; mow.
5 *I went out into the garden to cut some flowers*: **pick**, pluck, gather; harvest, reap; literary garner, cull.
6 *she gazed at the lettering cut into the stonework*: **carve**, engrave, incise, etch, score; chisel, whittle.
7 *the government is likely to cut public expenditure | prices were cut by up to 15 per cent*: **reduce**, cut back/down on, decrease, lessen, retrench, diminish, trim, prune, slim down, ease up on; rationalize, downsize, slenderize, economize on; mark down, discount, lower; informal slash, axe.
▷**ANTONYMS** increase.
8 *the text has been substantially cut*: **shorten**, abridge, condense, abbreviate, truncate, pare down; edit; precis, summarize, synopsize; bowdlerize, expurgate; rare epitomize.
▷**ANTONYMS** lengthen, expand.
9 *you need to cut at least ten lines per page*: **delete**, remove, take out, edit out, excise, blue-pencil.
▷**ANTONYMS** add.
10 *oil supplies to the area had been cut*: **discontinue**, break off, suspend, interrupt; stop, end, put an end to.
▷**ANTONYMS** restore.
11 *he brought the car to a halt and cut the engine*: **turn off**, switch off, shut off, deactivate; informal kill.
▷**ANTONYMS** turn on.
12 *the point where the line cuts the vertical axis*: **cross**, intersect, bisect; meet, join; technical decussate.
▷**ANTONYMS** diverge.
13 dated *even Mrs Blenkinsop, the banker's wife, cut her at church*: **snub**, ignore, shun, give someone the cold shoulder, cold-shoulder, turn one's back on, cut dead, look right through, pretend not to see; rebuff, spurn, ostracize; Brit. send to Coventry; informal give someone the brush-off, freeze out, stiff-arm; N. Amer. informal give someone the bum's rush, give someone the brush; Austral. informal snout; informal, dated give someone the go-by.
14 *he realized the remark had cut her*: **hurt someone's feelings**, hurt, wound, upset, distress, make unhappy, grieve, pain, sting, cut to the quick.
15 *the demos which he cut for the recording company*: **record**, make a recording of, put on disc/tape, make a tape of, tape-record; informal lay down.
□ **be cut out** *I don't think I'm cut out for this sort of work*: **be suited**, be suitable, be right, be designed, be equipped; be qualified.
□ **cut across** *a movement which cut across class barriers*: **transcend**, go beyond, rise above.
□ **cut back** *some companies* ***cut back on*** *foreign investment | we're going to have to cut back*: **reduce**, cut, cut down, decrease, lessen, retrench, trim, prune, slim down, scale down; rationalize, downsize, economize on; pull/draw in one's horns, tighten one's belt; informal slash, axe.
□ **cut corners** *his staff complains that he is cutting corners to save money by putting ordinary cream cheese in the tiramisu*: skimp, economize; pinch pennies.
□ **cut someone/something down 1** *24 hectares of trees were cut down*: **fell**, chop down, hack down, saw down, hew. **2** *Barker had been cut down by a sniper's bullet*: **kill**, slaughter, dispatch; shoot down, mow down, gun down; cut someone off in their prime; informal take out, blow away, snuff out; literary slay.
□ **cut and dried** *there were agreements which needed to be cut and dried*: **definite**, decided, settled, explicit, specific, precise, unambiguous, clear-cut, unequivocal, black and white, hard and fast.
▷**ANTONYMS** vague.
□ **cut in** *'It's urgent,' Raoul cut in*: **interrupt**, butt in, break in, interject, interpose, chime in; Brit. informal chip in.
□ **cut something off 1** *they cut off his finger*: **sever**, chop off, hack off; amputate. **2** *Moscow threatened to cut off oil and gas supplies to Lithuania*: **discontinue**, break off, disconnect, interrupt, suspend; stop, end, bring to an end. ▷**ANTONYMS** restore. **3** *a community cut off from the mainland by*

the surging flood waters: **isolate**, separate, keep apart, keep away; seclude, closet, cloister, sequester.

□ **cut someone off** *Gabrielle's family cut her off without a penny*: **disinherit**, disown, repudiate, reject, have nothing more to do with, have done with, wash one's hands of.

□ **cut out** *both the lifeboat's engines cut out*: **stop working**, cease to function, stop, fail, give out; break down, malfunction; informal die, give up the ghost, conk out, go on the blink, go kaput; Brit. informal pack up.

□ **cut someone/something out 1** *I cut his photograph out of the paper | you need to cut out the diseased wood*: **remove**, take out, excise, extract; snip out, clip out. **2** *it's best to cut out alcohol altogether when you're pregnant*: **give up**, refrain from, abstain from, go without, stop drinking/eating; informal quit, leave off, pack in, lay off, knock off. **3** *his mother cut him out of her will*: **exclude**, leave out, omit, eliminate. ▷ANTONYMS include.

□ **cut and run** informal *only cowards cut and run*: **flee**, run, run away, run off, make a run for it, run for it, take flight, be gone, make off, take off, take to one's heels, make a break for it, bolt, beat a (hasty) retreat, make a quick exit, make one's getaway, escape, absent oneself, make oneself scarce, abscond, head for the hills, do a disappearing act; informal beat it, clear off, clear out, vamoose, skedaddle, split, leg it, show a clean pair of heels, turn tail, scram; Brit. informal do a runner, scarper, do a bunk; N. Amer. informal light out, bug out, cut out, peel out, take a powder, skidoo; Austral. informal go through, shoot through; vulgar slang bugger off; archaic fly.

□ **cut someone short** *Peter cut him short*: **interrupt**, cut off, butt in on, break in on.

□ **cut something short** *they decided to cut short their holiday*: **break off**, bring to a premature end, leave unfinished, shorten, truncate, curtail, terminate, end, stop, abort, bring to an untimely end.
▷ANTONYMS extend.

▶**noun 1** *blood ran from a cut on his jaw*: **gash**, slash, laceration, incision, slit, wound, injury; scratch, graze, nick, snick.
2 *a cut of beef*: **joint**, piece, section, bit.
3 informal *there wasn't much left after his agents took their cut*: **share**, portion, bit, quota, percentage; commission, dividend; informal whack, slice of the cake, rake-off, piece of the action.
4 *his hair was in need of a cut*: **haircut**, trim, clip, crop.
5 *a smart cut of the whip*: **blow**, slash, stroke; informal swipe.
6 *he followed this with the unkindest cut of all*: **insult**, slight, affront, slap in the face, jibe, barb, cutting remark, shaft; informal put-down, dig, brush-off.
7 *a 20 per cent pay cut | a cut in interest rates*: **reduction**, cutback, decrease, retrenchment, lessening, curtailment; N. Amer. rollback; informal slash.
▷ANTONYMS increase.
8 *fortunately the cut happened at night, and power was quickly restored*: **power cut**, loss of supply, interruption of supply, breakdown; blackout.
9 *the elegant cut of his dinner jacket*: **style**, design; tailoring, lines, fit.

□ **a cut above** informal *he considered himself to be a cut above the rest*: **superior to**, much better than; informal streets ahead of, way ahead of the field/pack.

Word links **cut**

-tomy, **-ectomy** related suffixes, as in *anatomy*, *appendectomy*

cutback noun *cutbacks in defence spending*: **reduction**, cut, decrease, retrenchment, trimming; economy, saving; N. Amer. rollback; informal slash.
▷ANTONYMS increase.

cute adjective *a picture of a cute kitten*: **endearing**, adorable, lovable, sweet, lovely, appealing, engaging, delightful, dear, darling, winning, winsome, charming, enchanting; attractive, pretty, as pretty as a picture; chocolate-box; Scottish & N. English bonny; informal cutesy, dinky, twee, pretty-pretty.
▷ANTONYMS unattractive, unappealing.

cut-throat noun dated *a band of robbers and cut-throats*: **murderer**, killer, assassin, butcher, liquidator, executioner; thug, bravo; informal hit man; N. Amer. informal button man; literary slayer; dated homicide.
▶**adjective 1** dated *cut-throat robbers*: **murderous**, homicidal, death-dealing, savage, brutal, violent, bloody, bloodthirsty, fierce, ferocious, vicious, barbarous, cruel.
2 *advertising is a cut-throat business*: **ruthless**, merciless, pitiless, unfeeling, relentless, aggressive; dog-eat-dog, fiercely competitive, intensely competitive.

C

cutting noun **1** *a newspaper cutting*: **clipping**, clip, snippet, extract, excerpt; article, piece, passage, column, paragraph.
2 *plant cuttings*: **scion**, slip; graft.
3 *fabric cuttings*: **piece**, bit, fragment, part; trimming.
▶**adjective 1** *a cutting remark*: **hurtful**, wounding, barbed, pointed, scathing, acerbic, mordant, trenchant, caustic, acid, abrasive, sarcastic, sardonic, snide, spiteful, malicious, mean, nasty, cruel, unkind, vicious, venomous, poisonous, vitriolic; N. Amer. acerb; informal bitchy, catty; Brit. informal sarky; N. Amer. informal snarky; rare acidulous, mordacious, squint-eyed.
▷ANTONYMS friendly, pleasant.
2 *cutting winter winds*: **icy**, bitterly cold, icy-cold, freezing, arctic, Siberian, glacial, bitter, chilling, chilly; **biting**, piercing, penetrating, raw, keen, sharp, stinging, harsh; literary chill; rare gelid.
▷ANTONYMS warm, balmy.

cut up adjective informal *he's pretty cut up about it*: **upset**, distressed, miserable, unhappy, sad, troubled, dismayed, saddened, grieved, hurt, devastated, traumatized; informal in a state, in a bad way.
▷ANTONYMS unaffected, phlegmatic.

cycle noun **1** *a myth embodying the cycle of birth, death, and rebirth*: **round**, rotation, revolution; circle, pattern, rhythm.
2 *the painting is one of a cycle of seven*: **series**, sequence, succession, run; set.
3 *cycles may be hired from the station*. See **bicycle**.

cyclical adjective *the cyclical fluctuations in demand*: **recurrent**, recurring, happening at regular intervals, regular, repeated, repetitive; **periodic**, seasonal, circular.

cyclone noun **hurricane**, typhoon, tropical storm, storm, tornado, windstorm, whirlwind, tempest; Austral./NZ informal willy-willy; N. Amer. informal twister.

cynic noun **sceptic**, doubter, doubting Thomas, scoffer; **pessimist**, prophet of doom, doom merchant, doom and gloom merchant, doomster, doomsayer, doom-monger, doomwatcher, Cassandra.
▷ANTONYMS idealist; optimist.

cynical adjective **sceptical**, doubtful, distrustful, suspicious, disbelieving, unbelieving, scoffing, doubting, incredulous; **pessimistic**, negative, hardbitten, hardened, hard, world-weary, disillusioned, disenchanted, jaundiced, sardonic, black, bleak; informal hard-boiled.
▷ANTONYMS optimistic; credulous.

cynicism noun **scepticism**, doubt, distrust, mistrust, doubtfulness, suspicion, disbelief, incredulity, unbelief, scoffing; **pessimism**, negative thinking, negativity, world-weariness, disillusion, disenchantment; rare dubiety, sardonicism.
▷ANTONYMS optimism.

cyst noun **growth**, abscess, boil, blister, bleb, wen, carbuncle; technical vesicle, vesication, hydatid, oocyst, saccule, steatoma.

dab verb *he dabbed his mouth with a napkin | she dabbed disinfectant on the cut*: **pat**, press, touch, blot, mop, swab, smudge; spread, daub, bedaub, apply, wipe, stroke, stipple.
▸ noun **1** *the screw can be held in place with a tiny dab of superglue*: **drop**, dash, spot, smear, dribble, trickle, splash, sprinkle, speck, taste, lick, trace, touch, hint, suggestion, soupçon, particle, bit, modicum; little; informal smidgen, tad.
2 *apply concealer with light dabs*: **pat**, press, touch, blot, mop, wipe, smudge, smear.

dabble verb **1** *they dabbled their feet in the rock pools*: **splash**, dip, paddle, wet, moisten, dampen, immerse, trail.
2 *he* ***dabbled in*** *politics*: **toy with**, dip into, scratch the surface of, flirt with, tinker with, potter about/around/round with, trifle with, play with, fiddle with, dally with, have a smattering of.

dabbler noun *he was a dabbler in psychology*: **amateur**, dilettante, non-professional, layman, layperson, tinkerer, potterer, trifler, dallier.
▷ANTONYMS expert, professional.

dab hand noun *he's a dab hand at rustling up a sandwich*. See **old hand**.

daemon noun **inspiring force**, genius, numen, demon; tutelary spirit, familiar spirit, attendant spirit; Latin genius loci.

daft adjective Brit. informal **1** *that's a daft idea*: **absurd**, preposterous, ridiculous, ludicrous, farcical, laughable, risible; idiotic, stupid, foolish, foolhardy, unwise, imprudent, ill-conceived, silly, inane, puerile, infantile, fatuous, imbecilic, hare-brained, half-baked; unreasonable, irrational, illogical, nonsensical, pointless, senseless, impracticable, unworkable, unrealistic; peculiar, odd, strange, queer, weird, eccentric, bizarre, fantastic, incongruous, grotesque; informal crazy, barmy, potty, cock-eyed.
▷ANTONYMS sensible.
2 *are you daft or something?* **simple-minded**, simple, stupid, idiotic, moronic, imbecilic, dull-witted, dull, dim-witted, slow-witted, slow, witless, half-witted, feeble-minded, dunce-like, cretinous, empty-headed, vacuous, vapid; deranged, unhinged, insane, mad; informal touched, thick, thick as two short planks, dim, dopey, dumb, dozy, birdbrained, pea-brained, pig-ignorant, bovine, slow on the uptake, soft in the head, brain-dead, boneheaded, lamebrained, chuckleheaded, dunderheaded, wooden-headed, fat-headed, muttonheaded, not all there, not quite right, crazy, mental, nuts, nutty, crackers, cracked, potty, barmy, batty, cuckoo, bonkers, dotty, dippy; Brit. informal not the full shilling; N. Amer. informal dumb-ass.
3 *she's* ***daft about*** *him*: **infatuated with**, enamoured of, obsessed by, smitten with, besotted by, doting on, very fond of; informal crazy, wild, mad, nutty, nuts, potty, gone on; informal, dated sweet on.

daily adjective *a daily event*: **occurring**/**done**/**produced every day**, everyday, day-to-day, quotidian; rare diurnal, circadian.
▸ adverb *the museum is open daily*: **every day**, seven days a week; once a day, day after day, day by day, per diem; rare diurnally.

dainty adjective **1** *a dainty china cup | her dainty body*: **delicate**, neat, refined, tasteful, fine, elegant, exquisite; graceful, petite, slight, slim, trim, pretty; Brit. informal dinky.
▷ANTONYMS unwieldy.
2 *a dainty morsel*: **tasty**, delicious, choice, palatable, luscious, mouth-watering, delectable, toothsome, succulent, juicy; appetizing, inviting, tempting; informal scrumptious, yummy, scrummy, finger-licking, moreish; literary ambrosial.
▷ANTONYMS tasteless; unpalatable.
3 *a dainty eater*: **fastidious**, fussy, hard to please, finicky, finical, faddish, squeamish; refined, particular, discriminating, discerning, critical, exacting, demanding, scrupulous, meticulous, careful, cautious; informal choosy, pernickety, picky; Brit. informal faddy; archaic nice.
▷ANTONYMS easy to please; undiscriminating.
▸ noun *home-made breads, jams, and dainties*: **delicacy**, tasty morsel, titbit, fancy, luxury, treat, nibble, savoury, appetizer, bonne bouche, confection, bonbon; N. Amer. tidbit; informal goody; archaic sweetmeat.

dais noun **platform**, stage, podium, rostrum, stand, grandstand, staging, apron, soapbox, stump; lectern, pulpit, box, dock; Indian mandapam; rare tribune.

dale noun **valley**, vale; hollow, hole, basin, gully, gorge, ravine; Brit. dene, combe, slade; N. English clough; Scottish glen, strath; literary dell, dingle.

dally verb **1** *there's no time to dally on the way to work*: **dawdle**, delay, loiter, linger, waste time, kill time, take one's time, while away time; lag, trail, straggle, fall behind; amble, plod, trudge, meander, drift; informal dilly-dally; archaic or literary tarry.
▷ANTONYMS hurry.
2 *he should stop dallying with film stars*: **trifle**, toy, play, amuse oneself, flirt, play fast and loose, tinker, philander, womanize, carry on; informal play around, mess about/around.

dam noun *the dam burst after torrential rain*: **barrage**, barrier, wall, embankment, levee, barricade, obstruction, hindrance, blockage.
▸ verb *the river was dammed to create a lake*: **block (up)**, obstruct, choke, clog (up), bung up, close; technical occlude.

damage noun **1** *did the thieves do any damage?* **harm**, injury, destruction, vandalization, vandalism; impairment, defilement, desecration, defacement, disfigurement, scarring, mutilation, vitiation, detriment; ruin, havoc, devastation; wear and tear, battering, friction, erosion, attrition, corrosion, abrasion, deterioration, degeneration; rare detrition.
2 informal *what's the damage?* **cost**, price, expense, charge, bill, account, total.
3 (**damages**) *she won £4,300 damages in the county court*: **compensation**, recompense, restitution, redress, reparation(s); repayment, reimbursement, remuneration, requital, indemnification, indemnity, satisfaction; N. Amer. informal comp; archaic guerdon, meed; rare solatium.
▸ verb *the parcel had been damaged by rough handl ing*: **harm**, do damage to, injure, mar, deface, mutilate, mangle, impair, blemish, disfigure, vandalize, blight, spoil, defile, desecrate; tamper with, sabotage, disrupt, play havoc with, vitiate; ruin, devastate, destroy, wreck, cripple; N. Amer. informal trash; rare disfeature.
▷ANTONYMS repair; improve.

damaging adjective *pesticides have had a damaging effect on a lot of wildlife*: **harmful**, detrimental, injurious, hurtful, inimical, dangerous, destructive, ruinous, calamitous, disastrous, deleterious, pernicious, ill, bad, evil, baleful, malign, corrupting, malignant, adverse, undesirable, prejudicial, unfavourable, unfortunate, counterproductive; unhealthy, unwholesome, poisonous, cancerous, noxious; literary malefic, maleficent; rare prejudicous.
▷ANTONYMS benign; beneficial.

damn verb **1** *if we did not believe in God, we would be damned*: **curse**, put a curse on, put the evil eye on, execrate, imprecate, hoodoo; anathematize, excommunicate; N. Amer. hex; informal put a jinx on, jinx; rare accurse.
▷ANTONYMS bless.

2 *we are certainly not going to damn a product just because it is non-traditional*: **condemn**, censure, criticize, attack, denounce, deplore, decry, revile, inveigh against; blame, chastise, castigate, berate, upbraid, reprimand, rebuke, reprove, reprehend, take to task, find fault with, give someone/something a bad press; deprecate, disparage; informal slam, hammer, lay into, cane, blast; Brit. informal slate, slag off, have a go at; archaic slash, reprobate; rare excoriate, vituperate, arraign, objurgate, anathematize.
▷ANTONYMS acclaim; praise.
▸ **noun** informal *your evidence isn't worth a damn | I don't care a damn*: **jot**, whit, iota, rap, scrap, bit; one bit, even a little bit, the smallest amount, the tiniest bit; informal hoot, two hoots, tinker's cuss/curse, brass farthing.

damnable adjective **1** *a damnable nuisance*: **unpleasant**, disagreeable, objectionable, offensive, execrable, horrible, horrid, ghastly, awful, nasty, dreadful, terrible; annoying, irritating, infuriating, maddening, exasperating; hateful, detestable, loathsome, foul, abominable, odious, obnoxious; informal beastly, pestilential; archaic scurvy.
▷ANTONYMS pleasant.
2 *we must keep this damnable magic from our shores*: **accursed**, cursed, under a curse, damned, diabolical, devilish, demonic, demoniac, fiendish, Mephistophelian, hellish, infernal, execrable, base, wicked, evil, sinful, iniquitous, heinous; rare anathematized.
▷ANTONYMS holy.

damnation noun *sins that risk eternal damnation*: **condemnation to hell**, eternal punishment, perdition, doom, hellfire; curse, execration, imprecation, excommunication, anathema, anathematization, malediction; N. Amer. hex; archaic malison.

damned adjective **1** *each of the damned souls was guarded by a demon*: **cursed**, accursed, doomed, lost, condemned to hell, execrated; anathematized, excommunicated; informal jinxed.
2 informal *this damned car won't start*: **blasted**, damn, flaming, precious, confounded, pestilential, rotten, wretched; Brit. informal blessed, flipping, blinking, blooming, bloody, bleeding, effing, chuffing; N. Amer. informal goddam; Austral./NZ informal plurry; Brit. informal, dated bally, ruddy, deuced; vulgar slang fucking, frigging; Brit. vulgar slang sodding; Irish vulgar slang fecking; dated cursed, accursed, damnable.

> *Word toolkit* **damned**
>
> See **doomed**.

damning adjective *in the face of such damning evidence Jakobs had little defence*: **incriminating**, condemnatory, condemning, damnatory; damaging, derogatory; conclusive, strong; rare implicatory.
▷ANTONYMS vindicatory; inconclusive.

damp adjective *her hair was still damp from the shower*: **moist**, moistened, wettish, dampened, dampish; humid, steamy, muggy, clammy, sweaty, sticky, dank, moisture-laden, wet, wetted, rainy, drizzly, showery, misty, foggy, vaporous, dewy.
▷ANTONYMS dry.
▸ **noun** *you could feel the damp in the air*: **moisture**, dampness, humidity, wetness, wet, water, liquid, condensation, steam, vapour, clamminess, mugginess, dankness, wateriness; rain, raininess, dew, drizzle, precipitation, spray; perspiration, sweat.
▷ANTONYMS dryness.
▸ **verb** *gradually sweat damped the edges of his hair | this did nothing to damp my enthusiasm*. See **dampen**.

> *Word links* **damp**
>
> **hygro-** related prefix, as in *hygrometer, hygroscopic*
> **hygrophobia** fear of damp

> *Word toolkit* **damp**
>
> See **wet**.

dampen verb **1** *the fine rain dampened her face*: **moisten**, damp, wet, dew, water, irrigate, humidify; literary bedew; rare sparge, humify, humect.
▷ANTONYMS dry; drench.
2 *nothing could dampen her enthusiasm*: **lessen**, decrease, diminish, reduce, lower, moderate, damp, damp down, put a damper on, throw cold water on, calm, cool, chill, dull, blunt, tone down, deaden, temper, discourage; **suppress**, extinguish, quench, stamp out, smother, stifle, muffle, blanket, mute, silence, quieten, overcome, curb, limit, check, still, restrain, inhibit, deter.
▷ANTONYMS heighten.

damper noun *this will put a damper on the liberal agenda for the next couple of years*: **curb**, check, restraint, restriction, limit, limitation, constraint, stricture, rein, brake, control, impediment, obstacle, hindrance; discouragement, depressant, depression, chill, pall, gloom, cloud.

dampness noun *dampness within the building encourages insects and fungi*: **moisture**, damp, humidity, wetness, wet, water, liquid, condensation, steam, vapour, clamminess, mugginess, dankness, wateriness; rain, raininess, dew, drizzle, precipitation, spray; perspiration, sweat.

damsel noun literary *a damsel in distress*. See **girl** (sense 2).

dance verb **1** *he danced with her at the party*: **trip**, sway, spin, whirl, twirl, pirouette, gyrate; informal bop, disco, rock, shake a leg, hoof it, cut a rug, trip the light fantastic; N. Amer. informal get down, step it; archaic foot it, tread a measure.
2 *a dozen sweet-faced little girls danced round me chanting*: **caper**, cavort, frisk, frolic, skip, prance, romp, gambol, jig, bound, leap, jump, spring, bob, hop, trip, bounce; rare rollick.
3 *she could see flames dancing in the fireplace*: **flicker**, sparkle, twinkle, shimmer, leap, ripple, dart, play, flick, flit, quiver, jiggle, joggle, oscillate.
▸ **noun** *they were going to a dance*: **ball**, discotheque; tea dance, dinner dance, masked ball, masquerade; N. Amer. prom, hoedown; French thé dansant; informal disco, hop, bop.

> *Word links* **dance**
>
> **Terpsichore** the Muse of dance

dancer noun French danseur, danseuse; informal bopper, hoofer; formal terpsichorean.

dandle verb *he dandled his two-year-old son on his knee*: **bounce**, jiggle, ride, dance, toss, pet, rock; hug, cradle, fondle, cuddle, caress.

dandy noun *I even smartened myself up, becoming something of a dandy*: **fop**, beau, man about town, bright young thing, glamour boy, rake; French boulevardier, petit-maître; informal swell, toff, dude, sharp dresser, snappy dresser, natty dresser, trendy, pretty boy; archaic blade, blood, buck, coxcomb, masher, peacock, popinjay, dapperling.
▸ **adjective** N. Amer. informal *our trip to Spain was dandy*. See **fine**[1].

danger noun **1** *there is an element of danger in the show*: **peril**, hazard, risk, jeopardy, endangerment, imperilment, insecurity; perilousness, riskiness, precariousness, uncertainty, instability.
▷ANTONYMS safety.
2 *such people are a danger to society*: **menace**, hazard, threat, risk, peril; source of apprehension, source of dread, source of fright, source of fear, source of terror.
3 *there is a serious danger of fire*: **possibility**, chance, risk, probability, likelihood, fear, prospect.

> *Choose the right word* **danger, peril, hazard, risk**
>
> **Danger** is the most general word for a possibility of suffering harm or injury (*they were in great danger*). It can also refer to a likely cause of harm or injury (*he is a danger to himself and others*) or, in the plural, to the quality of potentially causing harm (*the dangers of smoking*). *Danger* can have connotations of excitement (*the Prince has always enjoyed flirting with danger*).
>
> **Peril** is a more formal or literary word (*the self-government of this country is in peril | the immediate peril confronting the world in the early 1940s*), and is normally used in the plural when referring to a quality of something (*the perils of drink-driving*). *Peril* can refer to a possibility of harm that a person may knowingly undergo (*we ignore these warnings at our peril*).
>
> **Hazard** is principally used to describe an actual source of danger (*lead pipes are a serious hazard to health*), as well as the dangers inherent in something named (*cuts and grazes are a hazard of life*). It is used in the plural when referring to the dangerous quality of something (*increased official recognition of the hazards of asbestos*).
>
> **Risk** denotes a more predictable possibility of harm arising from an action or a situation, or from an action or object that increases the likelihood of harm (*ozone depletion may increase the risk of skin cancer | going on holiday without insurance is always a risk*). A *risk* may often be a danger that someone chooses to incur because it is outweighed by some other consideration (*you're taking a risk by meeting me*).

dangerous adjective **1** *a dangerous wild animal*: **menacing**, threatening, treacherous; **savage**, wild, vicious, murderous, desperate; rare minacious.
▷ANTONYMS harmless.
2 *overloading a power socket is dangerous*: **hazardous**, perilous, risky, high-risk, fraught with danger, unsafe, uncertain, unpredictable, precarious, insecure, exposed, vulnerable, touch-and-go, chancy, tricky, treacherous; breakneck, reckless, daredevil; Scottish unchancy; informal warm, dicey, sticky, hairy; Brit. informal dodgy; N. Amer. informal gnarly.
▷ANTONYMS safe.

dangle verb **1** *a long chain dangled from his belt*: **hang (down)**, droop, sag, swing, sway, wave, trail, stream; archaic depend.
2 *he dangled the speedboat's keys enticingly*: **wave**, swing, flap, jiggle, brandish, flourish, flaunt.
3 *the prince* **dangled** *money* **in front of** *the local chief*: **offer**, hold out; entice someone with, lure someone with, tempt someone with, tantalize someone with, seduce someone with.

d

dangling adjective *she had long, dangling earrings*: **hanging**, drooping, droopy, suspended, supported from above, pendulous, pendent, swinging, swaying, trailing, flowing, falling, tumbling; rare pensile.

Word toolkit **dangling**

See **sagging**.

dank adjective *he shivered as he entered the dank cellar*: **damp**, musty, chilly, clammy, wet, moist, unaired, moisture-laden, humid.
▷ANTONYMS dry.

dapper adjective *Pablo looked very dapper in his best clothes*: **smart**, spruce, trim, debonair, neat, tidy, neat and tidy, crisp, well dressed, besuited, well groomed, well turned out, smartly dressed, elegant, chic, dashing; French soigné; informal snazzy, snappy, natty, sharp, nifty; N. Amer. informal sassy, spiffy, fly, kicky; dated as if one had just stepped out of a bandbox; Brit. informal, dated swagger; archaic trig.
▷ANTONYMS scruffy.

dapple verb *fine rays of sunlight dappled the surface of a lake*: **dot**, spot, mark, fleck, streak, speck, speckle, bespeckle, mottle, stipple, marble.

dappled adjective *the dappled purple carpet of flowers*: **speckled**, blotched, blotchy, spotted, spotty, dotted, streaked, streaky, mottled, marbled, flecked, freckled, stippled, piebald, skewbald, pied, brindled, brindle, tabby, marled; patchy, variegated, multicoloured, particoloured; N. Amer. pinto; informal splotchy, splodgy; rare jaspé.

Word toolkit **dappled**

See **blotchy**.

dare verb **1** *nobody dared to say a word*: **be brave enough**, have the courage, pluck up courage, take the risk; **venture**, have the nerve, have the temerity, make so bold as, be so bold as, have the effrontery, have the audacity, presume, go so far as; risk doing, hazard doing, take the liberty of doing; informal stick one's neck out, go out on a limb; N. Amer. informal take a flyer; archaic make bold to.
2 *she dared him to go*: **challenge**, provoke, goad, taunt, defy, summon, invite, bid; throw down the gauntlet to.
▶noun *she didn't quite know why she accepted the dare*: **challenge**, provocation, goad, taunt; gauntlet, invitation, ultimatum, summons.

daredevil noun *spectators watched in horror as the nineteen-year-old daredevil smashed into the ground*: **madcap**, hothead, adventurer, exhibitionist, swashbuckler; **stuntman**; Brit. tearaway; informal show-off, showboat; dated desperado.
▷ANTONYMS coward.
▶adjective *a daredevil skydiver*: **daring**, bold, adventurous, madcap, hot-headed, audacious, courageous, brave, intrepid, fearless, death-or-glory, undaunted, dauntless, heedless; **reckless**, rash, hasty, impulsive, precipitous, impetuous, wild, desperate, foolhardy, incautious, imprudent, ill-advised, hare-brained; Brit. tearaway; informal harum-scarum, bull-in-a-china-shop.
▷ANTONYMS cowardly; cautious.

daring adjective *a lone torpedo-bomber attempted a daring attack on the battleship*: **bold**, audacious, adventurous, intrepid, venturesome, fearless, brave, unafraid, unshrinking, undaunted, dauntless, valiant, valorous, heroic, dashing; confident, enterprising; madcap, rash, reckless, heedless; informal gutsy, spunky, peppy, pushy; rare adventuresome, venturous.
▷ANTONYMS cowardly; cautious.
▶noun *this recording eclipses the others by its sheer daring*: **boldness**, audacity, temerity, audaciousness, fearlessness, intrepidity, bravery, courage, courageousness, valour, valorousness, heroism, pluck; **recklessness**, rashness, foolhardiness; adventurousness, enterprise, dynamism, spirit, mettle, confidence; informal nerve, guts, gutsiness, spunk, grit; Brit. informal bottle, ballsiness; N. Amer. informal moxie, cojones, sand; vulgar slang balls; rare venturousness, temerariousness.
▷ANTONYMS cowardice; caution.

Choose the right word **daring, bold, audacious**

See **bold**.

dark adjective **1** *a dark night*: **black**, pitch-black, pitch-dark, inky, jet-black, unlit, unlighted, unilluminated, ill-lit, poorly lit; starless, moonless, dim, dingy, gloomy, dusky, indistinct, shadowy, shady; leaden, overcast, sunless; literary crepuscular, tenebrous; rare Stygian, Cimmerian, Tartarean, caliginous.
▷ANTONYMS bright.
2 *keep it dark | a dark secret*: **mysterious**, **secret**, hidden, concealed, veiled, unrevealed, covert, clandestine; enigmatic, arcane, esoteric, obscure, abstruse, recondite, recherché, inscrutable, impenetrable, opaque, incomprehensible, cryptic.
3 *dark hair*: **brunette**, dark brown, auburn, tawny, copper-coloured, coppery, chestnut, chestnut-coloured, jet-black, sable, ebony; dark-haired.
▷ANTONYMS blonde.
4 *dark skin*: **swarthy**, sallow, olive, dusky, black, ebony; tanned, bronzed, suntanned, sunburned; dark-skinned.
▷ANTONYMS pale.
5 *the dark days of the war*: **tragic**, **disastrous**, calamitous, catastrophic, cataclysmic, ruinous, devastating; **dire**, ghastly, awful, unfortunate, dreadful, horrible, terrible, horrific, hideous, horrendous, frightful, atrocious, abominable, abhorrent, gruesome, grisly, monstrous, nightmarish, heinous, harrowing; wretched, woeful; literary direful.
▷ANTONYMS happy.
6 *my mind is full of dark thoughts*: **gloomy**, dismal, pessimistic, negative, defeatist, downbeat, gloom-ridden, cynical, bleak, grim, fatalistic, black, sombre, drab, dreary; **despairing**, despondent, depressed, dejected, demoralized, hopeless, cheerless, joyless, melancholy, glum, lugubrious, Eeyorish, grave, funereal, morose, mournful, doleful, suspicious, distrustful, doubting, alarmist.
▷ANTONYMS optimistic.
7 *Matthew flashed a dark look at her*: **moody**, brooding, sullen, dour, glum, morose, sulky, frowning, scowling, glowering, angry, forbidding, threatening, ominous.
▷ANTONYMS kindly.
8 *so many dark deeds had been committed | a dark secret*: **evil**, wicked, sinful, immoral, wrong, morally wrong, wrongful, bad, iniquitous; ungodly, unholy, irreligious, unrighteous, sacrilegious, profane, blasphemous, impious, godless, base, mean, vile; **shameful**, discreditable, unspeakable, foul, monstrous, shocking, outrageous, atrocious, abominable, reprehensible, hateful, detestable, despicable, odious, contemptible, horrible, heinous, execrable, diabolical, diabolic, fiendish, vicious, murderous, barbarous, black, rotten, perverted, reprobate, sordid, degenerate, depraved, dissolute, dishonourable, dishonest, unscrupulous, unprincipled; informal crooked, bent, warped, low-down, stinking, dirty, shady; Law malfeasant; rare dastardly, peccable, egregious, flagitious.
▷ANTONYMS good, virtuous.
▶noun **1** *he's afraid of the dark*: **darkness**, blackness, absence of light, gloom, gloominess, dimness, dullness, murk, murkiness, shadowiness, shadow, shade, shadiness, dusk, twilight, gloaming; rare tenebrosity.
▷ANTONYMS light.
2 *as dark fell, the street lights went on | she only went out after dark*: **night**, night-time, darkness, hours of darkness; **nightfall**, evening, twilight, sunset.
▷ANTONYMS day; dawn.
□ **in the dark** informal *we're being kept* ***in the dark about*** *what is happening*: **unaware of**, ignorant of, in ignorance of, oblivious to, uninformed about, unenlightened about, unacquainted with, unconversant with; rare nescient of.
▷ANTONYMS aware.

darken verb **1** *the sky darkened*: **grow dark/darker**, blacken, grow black/blacker, dim, grow dim, cloud over, lour.
▷ANTONYMS lighten.
2 *fixative can darken the colours in a picture*: **make dark/darker**, blacken, make black/blacker, make dim, shade, eclipse, fog, obscure.
3 *the misery that darkened his later life | his mood darkened*: **make/become gloomy**, make/become angry, make/become unhappy, make/become annoyed, make/become depressed, cast down, become cast down, deject, become dejected, weigh down, oppress, dampen the spirits of, make/become dispirited, make/become troubled, cast a pall over, blacken, look black, sadden; spoil, mar, detract from.

darkness noun **1** *lights shone in the darkness*: **dark**, blackness, absence of light, gloom, gloominess, dimness, dullness, murk, murkiness, shadowiness, shadow, shade, shadiness, dusk, twilight, gloaming; rare tenebrosity.
▷ANTONYMS light.
2 *the sun went down, and darkness fell*: **night**, night-time, dark, hours of darkness.
▷ANTONYMS day.
3 *the forces of darkness*: **evil**, wickedness, corruption, sin, sinfulness, iniquity, immorality, devilry, the Devil, hell.
▷ANTONYMS good.

Word links **darkness**

scotophobia fear of darkness

darling noun **1** *good night, darling*: **dear**, dearest, dear one, love, lover, sweetheart, beloved, sweet; informal honey, angel, pet, sweetie, sugar, babe, baby, doll, poppet, treasure; archaic sweeting.
2 *the darling of the media*: **favourite**, pet, apple of one's eye, celebrity, idol, hero, heroine; informal blue-eyed boy/girl; N. Amer. informal fair-haired boy/girl.
▶adjective **1** *his darling wife*: **dear**, dearest, precious, adored, loved, beloved, much loved, favourite, cherished, treasured, prized, esteemed, worshipped, idolized, lionized.
2 informal, dated *a darling little hat*. See **delightful**.

darn verb *Michael was darning his socks*: **mend**, repair, reinforce; sew up, stitch; cobble, botch, patch; informal vamp; archaic clout.
▸ noun *a sweater with darns in the elbows*: **patch**, repair, reinforcement, stitch, mend.

dart noun **1** *he was killed by a poisoned dart*: **small arrow**, flechette, bolt, shaft; missile, projectile; literary reed; historical quarrel.
2 *the cat made a dart for the door as he came in*: **dash**, rush, run, bolt, break, charge, race, sprint, bound, spring, leap, jump, lunge, pounce, dive, swoop, gallop, scurry, scamper, stampede, scramble, start, flight.
▸ verb **1** *Karl darted across the road*: **dash**, rush, tear, run, bolt, fly, flash, shoot, charge, race, sprint, bound, spring, leap, jump, lunge, dive, swoop, gallop, scurry, scamper, stampede, scramble, break, start; informal scoot.
2 *Tam darted a terrified glance over his shoulder*: **direct**, cast, throw, shoot, send, fling, toss, flash, bestow, give.

dash verb **1** *he dashed straight home to see his father*: **rush**, race, run, sprint, bolt, dart, gallop, career, charge, shoot, hurtle, hare, bound, fly, speed, streak, zoom, plunge, dive, whisk, scurry, scuttle, scamper, scramble; informal tear, belt, pelt, scoot, zap, zip, whip, step on it, get a move on, hotfoot it, leg it, go hell for leather, steam, put on some speed, go like a bat out of hell, burn rubber; Brit. informal bomb, go like the clappers, bucket, put one's foot down; Scottish informal wheech; N. Amer. informal boogie, hightail it, clip, barrel, get the lead out; informal, dated cut along; N. Amer. vulgar slang drag/tear/haul ass; literary fleet; archaic post, hie, haste.
▷ANTONYMS dawdle.
2 *he picked up the glass case and dashed it to the ground*: **hurl**, smash, crash, slam, throw, toss, fling, pitch, cast, lob, launch, flip, catapult, shy, aim, direct, project, propel, send, bowl; informal chuck, heave, sling, buzz, whang, bung; N. Amer. informal peg; Austral. informal hoy; NZ informal bish.
3 *the wind and rain* ***dashed against*** *the thick stone walls*: **be hurled**, crash, smash; batter, strike, beat, pound, pummel, lash, slam into.
4 *it was a 15-year-old newcomer who dashed her hopes for a third title*: **shatter**, destroy, wreck, ruin, crush, devastate, demolish, wreak havoc with, blast, blight, wipe out, overturn, torpedo, scotch, spoil, frustrate, thwart, baulk, check; burst someone's bubble; informal put the kibosh on, banjax, do for, blow a hole in, nix, put paid to, queer; Brit. informal scupper, dish; archaic bring to naught.
▷ANTONYMS raise.
□ **dash something off** *I dashed off a note to Dave*: **scribble**, write hurriedly, write untidily, write illegibly, scratch, scrawl, doodle, jot (down).
▸ noun **1** *they made a dash for the door*: **rush**, race, run, sprint, bolt, dart, leap, charge, plunge, dive, bound, break, scamper, scramble; stampede.
2 *the soup needs a dash of salt*: **small amount**, touch, sprinkle, pinch, taste, lick, spot, drop, dab, speck, smack, smattering, sprinkling, splash, dribble, trickle, grain, soupçon, trace, bit, modicum, little, suggestion, suspicion, hint, scintilla, tinge, tincture, whiff, whisper, overtone, undertone, nuance, colouring; informal smidgen, tad.
▷ANTONYMS lashings.
3 *he led the raids with such skill and dash*: **verve**, **style**, stylishness, flamboyance, gusto, zest, confidence, self-assurance, elan, flair, flourish, vigour, vivacity, vivaciousness, sparkle, brio, panache, éclat, exuberance, ebullience, enthusiasm, eagerness, vitality, dynamism, animation, liveliness, spirit, energy; informal pizzazz, pep, oomph, vim, zing, get-up-and-go.
▷ANTONYMS ineptitude; apathy.

dashing adjective **1** *she met and married a dashing test pilot*: **debonair**, jaunty, devil-may-care, breezy, raffish, sporty, stylish, dazzling, romantic, attractive, spirited, lively, buoyant, energetic, animated, exuberant, flamboyant, dynamic, gallant, bold, intrepid, daring, adventurous, venturesome, plucky, swashbuckling; informal peppy.
▷ANTONYMS boring, unadventurous.
2 *he was exceptionally dashing in his polo clothes | dashing suits for bridegrooms*: **stylish**, smart, elegant, chic, crisp, dapper, spruce, trim, debonair, well dressed, well groomed, well turned out, smartly dressed; tasteful, understated, attractive, flattering, fancy; **fashionable**, high-fashion, modish, voguish, in vogue, modern, up to date, up to the minute, ultra-modern, contemporary, designer; French à la mode, soigné; informal trendy, in, with it, bang up to date, now, hip, sharp, snappy, snazzy, classy, natty, nifty, dressy, swish; N. Amer. informal fly, spiffy, sassy, kicky, tony; dated as if one had just stepped out of a bandbox; Brit. informal, dated swagger; archaic trig.
▷ANTONYMS dowdy, unfashionable.

dastardly adjective archaic or humorous *a dastardly plan was hatched to kidnap him*. See **wicked** (sense 1).

data noun *there is a lack of data on the drug's effect on humans*: **facts**, figures, statistics, details, particulars, specifics, features; **information**, evidence, intelligence, material, background, input; proof, fuel, ammunition; statement, report, return, dossier, file, documentation, archive(s); informal info, gen, dope, low-down.

date noun **1** *the only dates he can remember are his birthday and 1066*: **day**, day of the month, occasion, year, anniversary, time.
2 *a later date than the 15th century is suggested for this bridge*: **age**, time, period, era, epoch, century, decade, year, stage.
3 *we have a lunch date*: **appointment**, meeting, engagement, rendezvous, assignation; commitment, fixture; literary tryst.
4 informal *have you got a date for tonight?* **partner**, escort, girlfriend, boyfriend, young lady, young man, woman friend, lady friend, man friend, man, boy, girl; informal steady, bird, fella.
□ **to date** *this is his best book to date*: **so far**, thus far, yet, as yet, up to now/then, till now/then, until now/then, as of now, up to the present (time), up to this/that point, hitherto; rare thitherto.
▷ANTONYMS since then; to come.
▸ verb **1** *this piece of sculpture can be dated very accurately*: **assign a date to**, establish/determine/ascertain the date of, put a date on/to, establish/determine/ascertain the age of.
2 *the present building* ***dates from*** *the early 16th century | this law* ***dates back to*** *the Middle Ages*: **was made in**, was built in, was created in, came into being in, bears the date of, originates in, comes from, belongs to, goes back to, has existed since.
3 *the very best films just don't date*: **become old-fashioned**, become outmoded, become obsolete, become dated, show its age.
4 informal *he's dating the girl next door*: **go out with**, take out, go around with, go with, be involved with, be romantically linked with, see, court, woo; informal go steady with; N. Amer. informal step out with; Austral. informal track square with.

Word links **date**

chronological relating to dates

dated adjective *the graphics are looking a little dated*: **old-fashioned**, out of fashion, out of date, outdated, outmoded, out of style, behind the times, last year's, superseded, archaic, obsolete, antiquated; unfashionable, unpopular, unstylish; bygone, old-fangled, crusty, olde worlde, prehistoric, antediluvian; French passé, démodé; informal old hat, out, square, out of the ark.
▷ANTONYMS modern, up to date.

daub verb *he daubed a rock with paint | they daubed blood on the walls*: **bedaub**, **smear**, plaster, bespatter, splash, stain, spatter, splatter, cake, cover thickly, smother, coat, deface; slap; literary besmear, befoul, besmirch, begrime.
▸ noun *these modernistic painters who just splash on daubs of paint*: **smear**, smudge, splash, blot, spot, patch, blotch, stain, mark; informal splodge.

daughter noun **female child**, girl; informal lass.

Word links **daughter**

filicide killing of one's daughter or son
filial relating to a daughter or son

daunt verb *it will take more than December sleet and gales to daunt the crews*: **intimidate**, abash, take aback, shake, ruffle, throw, demoralize, discourage; **deter**, put off, dishearten, dispirit, deject, sap, cow, overawe, awe, frighten, scare, alarm, unman, dismay, distress, disconcert, discompose, perturb, upset, discomfit, unsettle, unnerve, disquiet, subdue; throw off balance, put someone off their stroke, cause someone to lose their composure, confound, panic, stupefy, stun; informal rattle, faze, put into a flap, throw into a tizz, discombobulate, shake up, psych; Brit. informal put the wind up.
▷ANTONYMS encourage; hearten.

daunting adjective *the daunting task of raising five boys*: **intimidating**, formidable, disconcerting, unnerving, unsettling, dismaying; discouraging, disheartening, dispiriting, demoralizing; forbidding, ominous, awesome, frightening, fearsome; challenging, taxing, exacting.

Word toolkit **daunting**

See **formidable**.

dauntless adjective *an ambitious and dauntless woman, who truckled to no man*: **fearless**, determined, resolute, indomitable, intrepid, doughty, plucky, spirited, game, mettlesome, gritty, steely, confident, undaunted, undismayed, unalarmed, unflinching, unshrinking, unabashed, unfaltering, unflagging, bold, audacious, valiant, brave, stout-hearted, lionhearted, gallant, courageous, heroic, daring, daredevil; informal gutsy, spunky, ballsy, feisty.

dawdle verb **1** *holidaymakers were dawdling over breakfast*: **linger**, dally, take one's time, drag one's feet, be slow, waste time, kill time, fritter time away, idle; delay, procrastinate, stall, hang fire, mark time, potter about/around/round; informal dilly-dally, let the grass grow under one's feet; archaic or literary tarry.
▷ANTONYMS hurry.
2 *Ruth dawdled back through the wood*: **amble**, stroll, go/walk slowly, loiter (along), move at a snail's pace, not keep pace, hold back, lag behind, fall behind, trail behind; informal mosey, tootle; Brit. informal pootle, mooch, swan; N. Amer. informal putter.
▷ANTONYMS speed.

Choose the right word **dawdle, linger, loiter**

See **linger**.

dawn noun **1** *we got up at dawn*: **daybreak**, break of day, crack of dawn, sunrise, first light, daylight, first thing in the morning, early morning, cockcrow; N. Amer. sunup; literary dawning, peep of day, aurora, dayspring.
▷ANTONYMS dusk.
2 *the dawn of civilization*: **beginning**, start, birth, inception, conception, origination, genesis, emergence, advent, coming, appearance, debut, arrival, dawning, rise, starting point, origin, launch, institution, inauguration, opening, initiation, onset, outset, unfolding, development, infancy; day one; informal kick-off, the word go; formal commencement.
▷ANTONYMS end.
▶verb **1** *Thursday dawned crisp and sunny*: **begin**, open, break, arrive, emerge, grow light, lighten, brighten.
▷ANTONYMS end.
2 *a bright new future has dawned*: **begin**, start, come into being, be born, come into existence, appear, arrive, come forth, emerge, erupt, burst out; arise, rise, originate, break, unfold, develop, crop up, first see the light of day; formal commence.
▷ANTONYMS end.
3 *she became calmer as realization dawned | it* ***dawned on*** *him that he was not alone*: **occur to**, come to, come to mind, spring to mind, enter someone's mind/head, come into someone's head/mind, strike, hit, register with, enter someone's consciousness, flash across someone's mind, pass through someone's mind, cross someone's mind, suggest itself.

Word links **dawn**

eosophobia fear of dawn

day noun **1** *the festival lasts five days*: **twenty-four-hour period**, full day, twenty-four hours, working day; technical solar day, sidereal day.
2 *you could gamble at night and enjoy the beaches during the day*: **daytime**, daylight, daylight hours, hours of light, hours of sunlight, broad daylight, waking hours, the waking day.
▷ANTONYMS night.
3 *he was the leading architect of the day*: **period**, time, point in time, age, era, epoch, generation.
4 *in his day he exercised tremendous influence*: **heyday**, prime, hour, time, best days, best years, maturity; peak, pinnacle, height, zenith, ascendancy; youth, vigour, springtime, salad days, full flowering, bloom.
▷ANTONYMS decline, nadir.
□ **at the end of the day** Brit. informal *at the end of the day it is the judge's decision*: **ultimately**, eventually, in the end, in the long run, at length, finally, sooner or later, in time, in the fullness of time, after some time, in the final analysis, when all is said and done, one day, some day, sometime, at last, at long last; informal when push comes to shove.
□ **call it a day** informal *at five o'clock I decided to call it a day*: **admit defeat**, concede defeat, stop trying, give up, give in, surrender, capitulate, be beaten; despair, lose heart, abandon hope, give up hope; informal throw in the towel/sponge; Austral. informal drop one's bundle.
□ **day after day** *day after day, we learn of new allegations*: **repeatedly**, again and again, over and over (again), time and (time) again, frequently, often, many times, many a time, time after time, on many occasions, many times over; {year in, year out}, {week in, week out}, {day in, day out}, night and day, all the time; persistently, recurrently, constantly, continuously, without a break, ceaselessly, relentlessly, continually, regularly, habitually, unfailingly, always; N. Amer. oftentimes; Latin ad nauseam; informal 24-7; literary many a time and oft, oft, oft-times.
□ **day by day 1** *day by day they were being forced to retreat*: **gradually**, bit by bit, by degrees, by stages, inchmeal, inch by inch, little by little, step by step, slowly, slowly but surely, steadily, progressively. ▷ANTONYMS all at once. **2** *the sort of life they led day by day in their homes*: **daily**, every day, day after day, a day at a time; rare diurnally.
□ **day in, day out** *they mechanically pursue the same routine, day in, day out*: **repeatedly**, again and again, over and over (again), time and (time) again, frequently, often, many times, many a time, time after time, day after day, on many occasions, many times over; {year in, year out}, {week in, week out}, night and day, all the time; persistently, recurrently, constantly, continuously, without a break, ceaselessly, relentlessly, continually, regularly, habitually, unfailingly, always; N. Amer. oftentimes; Latin ad nauseam; informal 24-7; literary many a time and oft, oft, oft-times.

Word links **day**

diurnal relating to the day

daybreak noun *they rested for the night and journeyed on at daybreak*: **dawn**, break of day, crack of dawn, sunrise, daylight, first light, first thing in the morning, early morning, cockcrow; N. Amer. sunup; literary dawning, peep of day, aurora, dayspring.
▷ANTONYMS nightfall.

daydream noun **1** *she was lost in a daydream*: **reverie**, trance, fantasy, vision, fancy, hallucination, musing, brown study, imagining; inattention, inattentiveness, wool-gathering, preoccupation, brooding, obliviousness, engrossment, absorption, self-absorption, absent-mindedness, absence of mind, staring into space, abstraction, lack of concentration, lack of application; Scottish dwam; humorous blonde moment.
▷ANTONYMS concentration.
2 *the thought of living in a mews cottage had been one of her daydreams*: **dream**, pipe dream, fantasy, figment of the imagination, unrealizable dream, castle in the air, castle in Spain; wishful thinking; fond hopes, wishes; informal pie in the sky.
▶verb *stop daydreaming and pay attention*: **dream**, muse, be lost in thought, be in a brown study, stare into space, hallucinate; fantasize, indulge in fantasy, indulge in fancy, indulge in wool-gathering, be in cloud cuckoo land, be unrealistic, build castles in the air, build castles in Spain.
▷ANTONYMS concentrate, focus.

daydreamer noun *David was sacked from his very first job because he was a daydreamer*: **dreamer**, fantasist, fantasizer, romantic, romancer, wishful thinker, pipe-dreamer, castle-builder, Walter Mitty, idealist, impractical person, unrealistic person; visionary, theorizer, utopian, Don Quixote; rare fantast, reverist.

daylight noun **1** *do the test in daylight for maximum accuracy of colour matching*: **natural light**, sunlight, light of day.
▷ANTONYMS darkness.
2 *not many people go near it in daylight, never mind after dark*: **daytime**, daylight hours, day, hours of sunlight; broad daylight.
▷ANTONYMS night-time.
3 *police moved in at daylight to make arrests*: **dawn**, daybreak, break of day, crack of dawn, sunrise, first light, first thing in the morning, early morning, cockcrow; N. Amer. sunup; literary dawning, peep of day, aurora, dayspring.
▷ANTONYMS nightfall.
□ **see daylight 1** *Sam saw daylight. 'You think he might be your father?'*: **understand**, comprehend, realize, find out, see the light, work out what's going on, get the point; informal cotton on, catch on, tumble, latch on, get the picture, get the message, get the drift, get it, get wise, see what's what, savvy; Brit. informal twig. **2** *his project never saw daylight*: **be completed**, be accomplished, see (the) light of day; **be published**, be issued, come to public attention.

day-to-day adjective *day-to-day expenditure such as food, household goods, and petrol or bus fares*: **regular**, routine, habitual, everyday, daily, frequent, normal, standard, usual, familiar, typical.

daze verb **1** *he was dazed from being flung out of the car*: **stun**, stupefy, knock senseless, knock unconscious, knock out, lay out; informal knock for six, knock the stuffing out of.
2 *she was still dazed by the revelations of the past half hour*: **astound**, amaze, astonish, startle, take someone's breath away, dumbfound, stupefy, overwhelm, overcome, overpower, devastate, dismay, disconcert, stagger, shock, confound, bewilder, take aback, nonplus, shake up; informal flabbergast, knock for six, knock sideways, knock the stuffing out of, hit like a ton of bricks, bowl over, floor, blow away.
▶noun *he was walking around in a daze*: **stupor**, state of stupefaction, state of shock, trance-like state, haze, confused state, spin, whirl, muddle, jumble; confusion, bewilderment, distraction, numbness; Scottish dwam.

dazzle verb **1** *she was dazzled by the headlights*: **blind temporarily**, deprive of sight.
2 *I was dazzled by the beauty and breadth of the exhibition*: **overpower**, overcome, overwhelm, impress, bedazzle, strike, move, stir, affect, touch, sweep someone off their feet, awe, overawe, leave speechless, take someone's breath away, spellbind, hypnotize, fascinate, take aback, daze, stagger, floor, amaze, astonish; informal bowl over, blow away, knock out.
▶noun **1** *dazzle can be a problem to sensitive eyes*: **glare**, flare, blaze, brightness, brilliance, gleam, flash, shimmer, radiance, shine.
2 *he happily endured the dazzle of the limelight*: **sparkle**, glitter, showiness, flashiness, brilliance, glory; splendour, magnificence, glamour, attraction, lure, allure, draw, drawing power, fascination, captivation, appeal; informal razzle-dazzle, razzmatazz, pizzazz, pull.

dazzling adjective **1** *the sunlight was dazzling*: **extremely bright**, blinding, glaring, brilliant, gleaming, shining.
2 *they turned in yet another dazzling performance*: **impressive**, remarkable, extraordinary, outstanding, exceptional, staggering, incredible, amazing, astonishing, phenomenal, imposing, breathtaking, thrilling; **excellent**, wonderful, magnificent, splendid, marvellous, superb, very good, first-rate, first-class, awe-inspiring, superlative, matchless, peerless; informal mind-boggling, mind-blowing, out of this world, fabulous, fab, super, fantastic, tremendous, great, terrific, stellar, sensational, smashing, ace, A1, cool, awesome, magic, wicked, tip-top, top-notch, out of sight, way-out; Brit. informal brill; Austral./NZ informal bonzer; Brit. informal, dated capital, spiffing, topping, top-hole, wizard; literary wondrous.

deacon noun

> *Word links* **deacon**
>
> **diaconal** relating to a deacon

dead adjective **1** *my parents are dead*: **deceased**, expired, departed, gone, no more, passed on, passed away; late, lost, lamented; perished, fallen, slain, slaughtered, killed, murdered; lifeless, not breathing, having breathed one's last, defunct, extinct, inanimate, insentient, insensate, inert; informal (as) dead as a doornail, six feet under, pushing up daisies, under the sod; euphemistic with God, asleep, at peace; rare demised, exanimate.
▷**ANTONYMS** alive, living.
2 *there are patches of dead ground on both sides of the plain*: **barren**, lifeless, bare, empty, desolate, sterile; without life, without living things.
▷**ANTONYMS** fertile, lush.
3 *he is fluent in ancient Hebrew and other dead languages*: **obsolete**, extinct, defunct, discontinued, no longer in use, disused, fallen into disuse, lapsed, abandoned, discarded, superseded, vanished, forgotten; archaic, antiquated, fossilized, ancient, very old; literary of yore.
▷**ANTONYMS** current, modern.
4 *there was no dialling tone—the phone was dead*: **not working**, out of order, out of commission, inoperative, inactive, ineffective, in (a state of) disrepair, broken, broken-down, malfunctioning, defective; informal kaput, conked out, on the blink, bust, busted, gone phut, finished, done for, dud; Brit. informal knackered, duff; Brit. vulgar slang buggered.
▷**ANTONYMS** in working order.
5 *I gave him a dead leg*: **numb**, benumbed, deadened, desensitized, insensible, insensate, unfeeling; paralysed, crippled, incapacitated, immobilized, frozen, useless.
6 *his voice was dead and cold | she has dead eyes*: **emotionless**, unemotional, unfeeling, impassive, unresponsive, insensitive, indifferent, dispassionate, inexpressive, wooden, stony, cold, frigid, inert; deadpan, flat, toneless, hollow; blank, vacant, glazed, glassy.
▷**ANTONYMS** passionate.
7 *his old affection for Alison was not quite dead*: **extinguished**, quenched, quashed, quelled, suppressed, smothered, stifled; finished, terminated, over, gone, no more; a thing of the past, ancient history.
8 *this is such a dead town*: **uneventful**, uninteresting, unexciting, uninspiring, dull, boring, flat, quiet, sleepy, slow, stale, humdrum, tame, pedestrian, lacklustre, lifeless; tedious, tiresome, wearisome; backward, backwoods, behind the times; informal one-horse, dead-and-alive; N. Amer. informal dullsville.
▷**ANTONYMS** lively.
9 *there was dead silence in the room*: **complete**, absolute, total, entire, outright, utter, downright, out-and-out, thorough, unqualified, unmitigated.
▷**ANTONYMS** partial.
10 *Bill is a dead shot with a rifle or revolver*: **unerring**, unfailing, impeccable, sure, true, correct, accurate, exact, precise, direct; deadly, lethal; Brit. informal spot on, bang on.
▷**ANTONYMS** poor.
□ **dead end 1** *the alley was a dead end*: **no through road**, blind alley, cul-de-sac. **2** *his career has hit a dead end*: **impasse**, deadlock, stalemate, checkmate, stand-off; standstill, halt, stop, stoppage, full stop.
□ **dead loss** informal **1** *the competition was a dead loss*. See **failure** (sense 2). **2** *he was a dead loss as a cook*. See **failure** (sense 3).
□ **dead on one's feet** *I didn't stay long, as I was dead on my feet*. See **exhausted** (sense 1).
▸ **adverb 1** *he was dead serious in his accusations*: **completely**, absolutely, totally, utterly, deadly, perfectly, entirely, wholly, fully, quite, thoroughly, unreservedly; definitely, certainly, positively, unconditionally, categorically, unquestionably, no doubt, undoubtedly, without a doubt, without question, surely, unequivocally; exactly, precisely, decisively, conclusively, manifestly, in every way, in every respect, one hundred per cent, every inch, to the hilt.
▷**ANTONYMS** partially.
2 *red flares were seen dead ahead*: **directly**, exactly, precisely, immediately, right, straight, plumb, due, squarely; informal bang, slap bang, smack.
3 Brit. informal *the windows are dead easy to open*. See **very** (adverb).

deadbeat noun informal *there's no room for deadbeats in the navy*: **layabout**, loafer, lounger, idler, waster, wastrel, good-for-nothing, cadger, parasite, useless article; informal bum, scrounger, sponger, sponge, freeloader; Brit. informal skiver.

deaden verb **1** *surgeons used ether to deaden the pain*: **numb**, stifle, dull, blunt, suppress; **alleviate**, mitigate, moderate, weaken, diminish, reduce, decrease, lessen, palliate, abate, ease, soothe, relieve, assuage, subdue, take the edge off, get rid of, put an end to.
▷**ANTONYMS** intensify.
2 *the wood panelling deadened any noise from outside*: **muffle**, mute, smother, stifle, dull, damp, damp down, tone down, hush, silence, quieten, soften, cushion, blanket, buffer, absorb.
▷**ANTONYMS** amplify.
3 *laughing at the joke might deaden us to the moral issue*: **desensitize**, render insensitive, make insensitive, numb, benumb, anaesthetize; harden, toughen, harden someone's heart.
▷**ANTONYMS** sensitize.

deadline noun *they stipulated a deadline for the army's withdrawal*: **time limit**, limit, finishing date, finishing time, target date, target time, cut-off point.

deadlock noun **1** *the strike appeared to have reached a deadlock*: **stalemate**, **impasse**, checkmate, stand-off; standstill, halt, stop, stoppage, cessation, full stop, dead end.
2 *the game ended in a 1–1 deadlock*: **tie**, draw, dead heat.
3 *the deadlock can only be opened with a key*: **bolt**, lock, latch, catch, fastening, fastener; Scottish sneck, snib.

d

deadly adjective **1** *certain mixtures of drugs can be deadly | a deadly disease*: **fatal**, lethal, mortal, death-dealing, life-threatening; dangerous, destructive, injurious, harmful, pernicious, detrimental, deleterious, unhealthy; noxious, toxic, poisonous; terminal, incurable, untreatable, malignant; literary deathly, nocuous, mephitic; archaic baneful.
▷**ANTONYMS** harmless; beneficial.
2 *the two men rapidly became deadly enemies*: **mortal**, irreconcilable, implacable, remorseless, relentless, unrelenting, unappeasable, unforgiving, merciless, pitiless; **bitter**, hostile, antagonistic, murderous, fierce, grim, savage; informal at each other's throats.
3 *I noted their deadly seriousness*: **intense**, great, marked, extreme, excessive, immoderate, inordinate.
▷**ANTONYMS** mild.
4 *he was deadly pale and too weak to speak*: **deathly**, deathlike, ashen, ghostly, white, pallid, wan, pale, ghastly.
5 *his aim is deadly*: **unerring**, unfailing, impeccable, perfect, flawless, faultless, assured, sure, true, precise, accurate, correct, exact, direct, on target, on the mark; Brit. informal spot on, bang on; vulgar slang shit hot.
▷**ANTONYMS** poor, inaccurate.
6 informal *life in a small village can be deadly*. See **boring**.
▸ **adverb** *her voice was deadly calm*: **completely**, absolutely, totally, utterly, perfectly, entirely, wholly, fully, quite, dead, thoroughly; in every way, in every respect, in all respects, one hundred per cent, every inch, to the hilt, to the core.

deadpan adjective *he cracked jokes with a deadpan expression on his face*: **blank**, expressionless, unexpressive, inexpressive, impassive, inscrutable, poker-faced, straight-faced, dispassionate, unresponsive, stony, wooden, empty, vacant, glazed, fixed, lifeless.
▷**ANTONYMS** expressive; comical.

deaf adjective **1** *she is deaf and blind but fiercely independent*: **hard of hearing**, hearing-impaired, with impaired hearing, unhearing, stone deaf, deafened, profoundly deaf; informal deaf as a post.
2 *how could she be so **deaf to** their pleading?* **unmoved by**, untouched by, unaffected by, dispassionate about, indifferent to, heedless of, unresponsive to, unconcerned with, unmindful of, unaware of, unconscious of, oblivious to, insensible to, impervious to.
▷**ANTONYMS** heedful, attentive.

deafen verb *they were deafened by the explosion of a shell*: **make deaf**, make temporarily deaf, cause to be hard of hearing, deprive of hearing, impair someone's hearing, burst someone's eardrums.

deafening adjective *the guns started up with a deafening roar*: **very loud**, extremely noisy, ear-splitting, ear-piercing, ear-shattering; booming, thundering, thunderous, tumultuous, roaring, blaring, resounding, resonant, reverberating, reverberant, echoing, ringing, dinning, carrying; overpowering, overwhelming, almighty, mighty, tremendous.
▷**ANTONYMS** quiet.

deal noun *it may be some weeks before completion of the deal*: **agreement**, understanding, pact, compact, bargain, covenant, contract, treaty, protocol, concordat, entente, accord, arrangement, accommodation, compromise, settlement, negotiation; terms; transaction, sale; Commerce account; Law indenture; rare engagement.
□ **a great deal/a good deal** *the team have achieved a great deal | she is under a good deal of pressure*: **a lot**, a great amount, a large amount, a fair amount, much, plenty; informal lots, loads, heaps, bags, masses, piles, stacks, tons; Brit. informal a shedload; vulgar slang a shitload.
▷**ANTONYMS** very little.
▸ **verb 1** *they got advice on how to **deal with** difficult children*: **cope with**, handle, manage, attend to, see to, take care of, take charge of, take in hand, sort out, tackle, take on; control, master, influence, manipulate.
2 *the article **deals with** recent advances in chemistry*: **concern**, be about, be concerned with, concern itself with, have to do with, discuss, consider, cover, treat of, pertain to, appertain to; tackle, study, explore, investigate, examine, go into, review, analyse, weigh up; archaic regard.
3 *the security forces **deal firmly with** demonstrators*: **treat**, handle, serve, use; act towards, behave towards, conduct oneself towards.
4 *the company **deals in** high-tech goods*: **trade in**, buy and sell, be concerned with trading, be engaged in trading, do business in; sell, vend, purvey, supply, stock, offer, offer for sale, have for sale, peddle, market,

d

merchandise; traffic in, smuggle, run, rustle; informal push; Brit. informal flog.
5 *the cards were dealt for the last hand*: **distribute**, give out, share out, divide out, divide up, hand out, pass out, pass round, dole out, mete out, dispense, allocate, allot, assign, apportion, bestow; informal divvy up.
6 *the appeal court dealt a blow to government reforms*: **deliver**, administer, dispense, inflict, give, impose; direct, aim.

dealer noun **1** *he set up in business as an antique dealer*: **trader**, tradesman, tradesperson, merchant, salesman, saleswoman, salesperson, seller, buyer, buyer and seller, marketeer, merchandiser, distributor, supplier, vendor, shopkeeper, retailer, wholesaler, purveyor, marketer, trafficker; Brit. stockist; N. Amer. storekeeper; informal pusher, runner, fence; dated pedlar, chandler, hawker, shopman; archaic chapman.
2 *she is a dealer with a Japanese bank*: **stockbroker**, broker-dealer, broker, agent, negotiator; historical jobber.

dealing noun **1** *her husband took to drink and dishonest dealing*: **business methods**, business practices, business, commerce, trading, trafficking, marketing, merchandising, transactions, financial transactions; **behaviour**, conduct, actions, policy.
2 (**dealings**) *the government lacked diplomatic skill in its dealings with Washington*: **relations**, relationship, association, connections, contact, intercourse, interchange, communication, negotiations, bargaining, operations, transactions, proceedings; **trade**, trading, business, commerce, traffic, trafficking; informal truck, doings.

dean noun *student admission targets must be agreed with the dean*: **faculty head**, department head, head of faculty, head of department, college head, provost, university official; head, chief, director, leader, principal, president, governor.

dear adjective **1** *my dear sister was talking about you only today | he is a dear friend*: **beloved**, loved, much loved, darling, adored, cherished, precious; esteemed, respected, worshipped; close, intimate, confidential, bosom, boon, favourite, best.
▷ANTONYMS hated.
2 *her belongings were too dear to entrust to sea transport*: **precious**, treasured, valued, prized, cherished, special, favourite, favoured.
3 *your father was such a dear man*: **endearing**, adorable, lovable, appealing, engaging, charming, enchanting, captivating, winsome, winning, attractive, lovely, nice, pleasant, delightful, angelic, sweet, darling; N. Amer. cunning; Italian & Spanish simpatico; French sympathique; German sympatisch; dated taking.
▷ANTONYMS disagreeable.
4 *the dining car served rather dear meals*: **expensive**, costly, high-cost, high-priced, highly priced, overpriced, exorbitant, extortionate; immoderate, extravagant, lavish, valuable; Brit. upmarket, over the odds; informal pricey, steep, stiff.
▷ANTONYMS inexpensive.
□ **hold something/someone dear** *I may be about to lose all I hold dear | he has a lot of friends whom he holds very dear*: **cherish**, treasure, prize, value highly.
▶ noun **1** *there's no need to worry, my dear*: **darling**, dearest, love, beloved, loved one, sweetheart, sweet, precious, treasure; informal sweetie, sugar, honey, baby, babe, pet, sunshine, poppet; archaic sweeting.
2 *Philip's such a dear*: **lovable person**, adorable person, endearing person; darling, sweetheart, pet, angel, gem, treasure; informal star.
▶ adverb *they buy property cheaply and sell dear*: **at a high price**, at an excessive price, at an exorbitant price, at high cost, at great cost.

dearly adverb **1** *she dearly wanted to see her family | I love my son dearly*: **very much**, a great deal, greatly, deeply, profoundly, extremely; **fondly**, affectionately, devotedly, tenderly.
2 *our freedom has been bought dearly*: **at great cost**, at a high cost, at a high price, with great loss, with much loss, with much suffering, with much sacrifice.

dearth noun *there is a dearth of properly trained specialists*: **lack**, scarcity, scarceness, shortage, shortfall, want, deficiency, insufficiency, inadequacy, paucity, sparseness, meagreness, scantiness, rareness, infrequency, uncommonness, destitution, privation; famine, drought, poverty; absence, non-existence; rare exiguity, exiguousness.
▷ANTONYMS abundance; surfeit.

death noun **1** *she broke down when she learnt of her father's death*: **demise**, dying, end, passing, passing away, passing on, loss of life, expiry, expiration, departure from life, final exit, eternal rest; murder, killing, assassination, execution, dispatch, slaying, slaughter, massacre; informal snuffing, curtains, kicking the bucket; Law decease; rare quietus.
▷ANTONYMS life.
2 *their liberation was also the death of their dream*: **end**, finish, cessation, termination, extinction, extinguishing, collapse, ruin, ruination, destruction, extermination, eradication, annihilation, obliteration, extirpation.
▷ANTONYMS birth.
3 *Death gestured towards an open grave*: **the Grim Reaper**, the Dark Angel, the Angel of Death.
□ **put someone to death** *the rebels were captured and put to death*: **execute**, hang, send to the gibbet/gallows, behead, guillotine, decapitate, electrocute, send to the electric chair, send to the chair, shoot, put before a firing squad, send to the gas chamber, gas, crucify, stone, stone to death; **kill**, murder, assassinate, do to death, do away with, take the life of, eliminate, terminate, exterminate, destroy; informal string up, bump off, polish off, do in, knock off, top, wipe out, take out, croak, stiff, blow away; N. Amer. informal ice, rub out, waste, whack, scrag, smoke; literary slay.

Word links **death**
necr- related prefix, as in *necromancy*
-thanasia related suffix, as in *euthanasia*
necropolis ancient cemetery
thanatophobia fear of death
thanatology study of death

deathless adjective *the notion that animals have immaterial and deathless souls | his compositions are deathless*: **immortal**, undying, imperishable, inextinguishable, indestructible, unfading, enduring, everlasting, perpetual, eternal; timeless, ageless, memorable; rare sempiternal, perdurable.
▷ANTONYMS mortal; ephemeral.

deathly adjective **1** *the wounded soldiers had a deathly pallor*: **deathlike**, corpse-like, cadaverous, ghostly, ghostlike, ghastly, grim, haggard; ashen, chalky, chalk-white, white, pale, pallid, bloodless, colourless, wan, anaemic, pasty, sickly, drained, sapped; informal like death warmed up, peaky; rare etiolated.
2 literary *the eagle carried a snake in its deathly grasp*. See **deadly** (sense 1 of the adjective).

debacle, débâcle noun *the coup attempt resulted in an embarrassing debacle*: **fiasco**, failure, catastrophe, disaster, disintegration, mess, wreck, ruin; downfall, collapse, defeat, rout, overthrow, conquest, trouncing; informal foul-up, screw-up, hash, botch, washout; Brit. informal cock-up, pig's ear; N. Amer. informal snafu; vulgar slang fuck-up, balls-up.

debar verb **1** *women were no longer debarred from the club*: **exclude**, ban, bar, disqualify, disentitle, declare ineligible, preclude, rule out, shut out, lock out, keep out, reject, blackball; say no to, leave out in the cold, give the cold shoulder to, stand in the way of, refuse entrance to; N. Amer. disfellowship.
▷ANTONYMS admit.
2 *the unions were debarred from holding a strike ballot*: **prevent**, prohibit, proscribe, disallow, ban, interdict, block, stop, curb, restrict, restrain, obstruct, hinder; forbid to; Law enjoin, estop; archaic let.
▷ANTONYMS allow.

debase verb **1** *the code of chivalry has been debased and sentimentalized*: **degrade**, devalue, demean, lower the status of, reduce the status of, cheapen, prostitute, discredit, drag down, drag through the mud, tarnish, blacken, blemish; disgrace, dishonour, shame, bring shame to, humble, humiliate; damage, harm, undermine.
▷ANTONYMS enhance.
2 *copper hardens the coin without significantly debasing the silver*: **reduce in value**, reduce in quality; contaminate, adulterate, pollute, taint, defile, spoil, foul, sully, depreciate, corrupt, bastardize; dilute, alloy; rare vitiate.

debased adjective **1** *their moral downfall was the result of their debased amusements*: **immoral**, **debauched**, dissolute, abandoned, perverted, degenerate, profligate, degraded, wicked, sinful, vile, base, iniquitous, corrupt, corrupted, criminal, vicious, brutal, lewd, licentious, lascivious, lecherous, prurient, obscene, indecent, libertine.
▷ANTONYMS honourable.
2 *the myth lives on in a debased form*: **corrupt**, corrupted, bastardized, adulterated, diluted, polluted, tainted, sullied, spoiled, spoilt; rare vitiated.
▷ANTONYMS original; pure.

debatable adjective *the extent to which personality is inherited is debatable*: **arguable**, disputable, questionable, open to question, open to debate, subject to debate, controversial, contentious, doubtful, open to doubt, in doubt, dubious, uncertain, unsure, unclear, vague, borderline, inconclusive, moot, unsettled, unresolved, unconfirmed, undetermined, undecided, unknown, up in the air, not yet established; problematical, puzzling, perplexing, riddling; a controversial subject, a live issue, a moot point, a matter of opinion; informal iffy, on the back burner, on ice; rare controvertible, unestablished.
▷ANTONYMS indisputable.

debate noun *I would welcome a debate on the reforms | there is renewed debate about NATO's defence role*: **discussion**, exchange of views, discourse, parley; argument, dispute, wrangle, altercation, war of words; arguing, argumentation, wrangling, sparring, disputation, dissension, disagreement, controversy, contention, conflict, disharmony; negotiations, talks; dialogue, comment, interest; informal confab, powwow, rap session; rare velitation, contestation.
▶ verb **1** *MPs will debate the future of the railways*: **discuss**, confer about, talk over, talk through, talk about, exchange views on, exchange views about, thrash out, argue, argue about, argue the pros and cons of, dispute, wrangle

over, bandy words concerning, contend over, contest, controvert, moot; informal kick around/about, bat around/about; archaic altercate.
2 *he debated whether to telephone Charlotte*: **consider**, give some thought to, think over, think about, chew over, mull over, turn over in one's mind, weigh up, ponder, deliberate, reflect, contemplate, muse, meditate, cogitate; archaic pore on; rare cerebrate.

debauch verb *he had debauched sixteen schoolgirls*: **corrupt**, deprave, warp, pervert, subvert, lead astray, make degenerate, ruin; **seduce**, ravish, deflower, defile, sully, violate, abuse, brutalize; informal take someone's cherry; archaic demoralize; rare vitiate.

debauched adjective *our fleet is commanded by debauched young men*: **dissolute**, dissipated, degenerate, corrupt, depraved, louche, rakish, shameless, sinful, unprincipled, immoral, impure, unchaste, lascivious, lecherous, libertine, lewd, lustful, libidinous, licentious, promiscuous, loose, wanton, abandoned, unrestrained, fast, decadent, profligate, intemperate, sybaritic, voluptuary, pleasure-seeking, indulgent, self-indulgent; informal easy, swinging; archaic light; rare concupiscent.
▷ANTONYMS wholesome, clean-living.

debauchery noun *he was reviled for his playboy lifestyle and debauchery*: **dissipation**, dissoluteness, degeneracy, corruption, vice, turpitude, depravity, loucheness, rakishness, libertinism, immodesty, indecency, perversion, shamelessness, iniquity, wickedness, sinfulness, sinning, impropriety, lack of morals, lack of principles, immorality, impurity, unchastity, lasciviousness, salaciousness, lechery, lecherousness, lewdness, bawdiness, lust, lustfulness, libidinousness, licentiousness, promiscuity, wantonness, abandonment, abandon, profligacy, decadence, immoderateness, intemperance, lack of restraint, indulgence, self-indulgence, pleasure-seeking, hedonism, sybaritism; rare voluptuousness, concupiscence, lubricity, salacity.
▷ANTONYMS morality, clean living.

debilitate verb *she was severely debilitated by a stomach upset*: **weaken**, make weak, make feeble, enfeeble, enervate, devitalize, sap, drain, exhaust, weary, tire, fatigue, wear out, prostrate; undermine, impair, render infirm, indispose, incapacitate, disable, paralyse, immobilize, lay low, put out of action, confine to bed, confine to a wheelchair; informal knock out, do in, knacker, shatter; rare torpefy.
▷ANTONYMS strengthen, invigorate.

debilitating adjective *he was suffering the debilitating effects of flu*: **weakening**, enfeebling, enervating, enervative, devitalizing, draining, sapping, wearing, exhausting, tiring; impairing, crippling, paralysing.
▷ANTONYMS restorative.

debility noun *his chronic debility made it hard to do even the basic things*: **frailty**, weakness, feebleness, enfeeblement, enervation, devitalization, lack of energy, lack of vitality, lassitude, exhaustion, weariness, tiredness, overtiredness, fatigue, prostration; incapacity, impairment, indisposition, infirmity, illness, sickness, sickliness, decrepitude, malaise; informal weediness; Medicine asthenia.

debonair adjective *a debonair young man*: **suave**, urbane, sophisticated, cultured, self-possessed, self-assured, confident, charming, gracious, well mannered, civil, courteous, gallant, chivalrous, gentlemanly, refined, polished, well bred, genteel, dignified, courtly; well dressed, well groomed, well turned out, elegant, stylish, smart, dashing, dapper, spruce, trim, attractive; French soigné; informal smooth, swish, swanky, snappy, sharp, cool; N. Amer. informal spiffy, fly; dated mannerly; archaic trig, gentle.
▷ANTONYMS unsophisticated.

debrief verb *he was debriefed by an FBI agent*: **question**, quiz, interview, examine, cross-examine, interrogate, probe, sound out; put questions to, ask questions of; informal grill, pump, give the third degree to, put through the third degree, put through the wringer, put through the mangle, put the screws on.

debris noun *the irrigation channels were blocked with debris*: **detritus**, refuse, rubbish, waste, waste matter, discarded matter, litter, scrap, dross, chaff, flotsam and jetsam, lumber, rubble, wreckage, spoilage; remains, remnants, fragments, scraps, dregs, offscourings, odds and ends; slag; N. Amer. trash, garbage; Austral./NZ mullock; informal dreck, junk; Brit. informal grot, gash, odds and sods, gubbins; vulgar slang shit, crap; Archaeology debitage; rare draff, raffle, raff, cultch, orts.

debt noun **1** *the company was unable to pay its debts*: **bill**, account, tally, financial obligation, outstanding payment, amount due, money owing; dues, arrears, debits, charges; N. Amer. check; informal tab; archaic score.
2 *he wanted to acknowledge his debt to the author*: **indebtedness**, obligation, liability; gratitude, appreciation, thanks.
□ **in debt** *he was forever short of money and frequently in debt*: **owing money**, in arrears, behind with payments, late with payments, overdue with payments, overdrawn; insolvent, bankrupt, bankrupted, ruined, in the hands of the receivers; Brit. in liquidation; informal in the red, in Queer Street, on the rocks, gone to the wall, bust; Brit. informal, dated in Carey Street.
▷ANTONYMS in credit.
□ **in someone's debt** *after what Clive had done, Chris would be forever in his debt*: **indebted to**, beholden to, obliged to, duty-bound to, honour-bound to, obligated to, under an obligation to, owing someone a debt of gratitude, owing someone thanks; grateful, thankful, appreciative.

debtor noun *the summons gave the debtor fourteen days to pay*: **borrower**, mortgagor; bankrupt, bankrupt person, insolvent, defaulter.
▷ANTONYMS creditor.

debunk verb *he debunked the myth that savants rely on photographic memories*: **explode**, deflate, puncture, quash, knock the bottom out of, drive a coach and horses through, expose, show in its true light, discredit, disprove, contradict, controvert, confute, invalidate, negate, give the lie to, prove to be false, challenge, call into question; informal shoot full of holes, shoot down in flames, blow sky-high.
▷ANTONYMS confirm.

debut noun *the new car made its debut at the German Grand Prix*: **first appearance**, first showing, first performance, launch, launching, coming out, entrance, premiere, beginning, introduction, inception, inauguration; informal kick-off; formal commencement.
▷ANTONYMS swansong.

decadence noun *he attacked the decadence of modern society*: **dissipation**, dissoluteness, degeneracy, debauchery, corruption, depravity, loucheness, vice, sinfulness, perversion, moral decay, immorality, lack of morals, lack of principles, lack of restraint, lack of control, lack of self-control, immoderateness, intemperance, licentiousness, wantonness, self-indulgence, hedonism, epicureanism; rare sybaritism, voluptuousness.
▷ANTONYMS morality.

decadent adjective *he turned his back on decadent city life*: **dissolute**, dissipated, degenerate, corrupt, depraved, louche, rakish, shameless, sinful, unprincipled, immoral, licentious, wanton, abandoned, unrestrained, profligate, intemperate; sybaritic, voluptuary, epicurean, hedonistic, pleasure-seeking, indulgent, self-indulgent.
▷ANTONYMS moral.

decamp verb **1** *he sold their paintings and decamped with the proceeds*: **abscond**, make off, run off, run away, flee, bolt, take off, take flight, disappear, vanish, slip away, steal away, sneak away, beat a hasty retreat, escape, make a run for it, make one's getaway, leave, depart, make oneself scarce; informal split, scram, skedaddle, vamoose, skip, cut and run, make tracks, push off, shove off, clear off, hightail it, hotfoot it, show a clean pair of heels, do a bunk, do a runner, do a moonlight flit, do a disappearing act, head for the hills, fly the coop, take French leave, go AWOL; Brit. informal scarper; N. Amer. informal take a powder, go on the lam, light out, bug out, peel out, cut out; Brit. informal, dated hook it.
▷ANTONYMS return.
2 archaic *the armies of both chiefs had decamped*: **strike one's tents**, break camp, move on.
▷ANTONYMS encamp.

decant verb *the wine was decanted into a clean flask*: **pour out**, pour off, draw off, siphon off, drain, tap, tip, discharge, transfer.

decapitate verb *he was found guilty of high treason and decapitated*: **behead**, cut off the head of, guillotine, put on the block; archaic decollate.

decay verb **1** *the flesh of the corpses had decayed*: **decompose**, rot, putrefy, go bad, go off, spoil, fester, perish, deteriorate; degrade, break down, break up, moulder, shrivel, shrivel up, wither; technical mortify, necrotize, sphacelate; archaic corrupt.
2 *the inner cities in Britain continue to decay*: **deteriorate**, degenerate, decline, go downhill, slump, slip, slide, go to rack and ruin, go to seed, run to seed, worsen, crumble, disintegrate, fall to pieces, come apart at the seams, fall into disrepair, become dilapidated; fail, wane, ebb, dwindle, collapse; informal go to pot, go to the dogs, hit the skids, go down the tubes, go down the toilet; Austral./NZ informal go to the pack.
▷ANTONYMS improve.
▶ noun **1** *the fish showed no signs of decay*: **decomposition**, rotting, going bad, putrefaction, putrescence, putridity, festering, spoilage, perishing, withering, shrivelling; rot, mould, mildew, fungus; archaic corruption.
2 *consumption of sugar can lead to tooth decay*: **rot**, rotting, corrosion, corroding, decomposition; **caries**, cavities, holes; rare cariosity.
3 *they blame TV for the decay of American values*: **deterioration**, degeneration, debasement, degradation, decline, slipping, waning, ebb, shrinking, withering, weakening, atrophy, crumbling, disintegration, collapse, lapse, fall, failure; formal devolution; dated decadence.
▷ANTONYMS improvement.

> *Word links* **decay**
>
> **sapro-** related prefix, as in *saprophagous*

decayed adjective *she discovered his decayed body*: **decomposed**, decomposing, rotten, rotting, putrescent, putrid, bad, off, spoiled, spoilt, perished; mouldy, mouldering, mildewy, festering, fetid, stinking, smelly, rancid, rank; maggoty, worm-eaten, wormy, flyblown.

decaying adjective **1** *the decaying bodies of fish filled the pond*: **decomposing**, decomposed, rotting, rotten, putrescent, putrid, bad, off, spoiled, spoilt, perished; mouldy, mouldering, festering, fetid, stinking, smelly, rancid, rank; maggoty, worm-eaten, wormy, flyblown.

2 *Liverpool was a visibly decaying city*: **declining**, degenerating, dying, waning, crumbling, collapsing; run down, broken-down, tumbledown, ramshackle, shabby, battered, decrepit; in decline, on the decline, in ruins, in (a state of) disrepair, falling apart, falling to pieces; informal on its last legs, on the way out.

> *Word toolkit* **decaying**
>
> See **derelict**.

d

decease noun Law *her decease was imminent*. See **death** (sense 1).
▸ verb archaic *he deceased at his palace of Croydon*. See **die**.

deceased adjective *they removed the body of the deceased ambassador*: **dead**, expired, departed, gone, no more, passed on, passed away; late, lost, lamented; perished, fallen, slain, slaughtered, killed, murdered; lifeless, not breathing, having breathed one's last, defunct, extinct, inanimate, insentient, insensate, inert; informal (as) dead as a doornail, six feet under, pushing up daisies, under the sod; euphemistic with God, asleep, at peace; rare demised, exanimate.

deceit noun **1** *we are caught in an endless round of lies and deceit*: **deception**, deceitfulness, duplicity, double-dealing, fraud, fraudulence, cheating, trickery, duping, hoodwinking, chicanery, underhandedness, deviousness, slyness, cunning, craftiness, craft, wiliness, artfulness, guile, dissimulation, dissembling, bluff, bluffing, lying, pretence, artifice, treachery; informal crookedness, monkey business, funny business, hanky-panky, jiggery-pokery; N. Amer. informal monkeyshines; Irish informal codology; archaic management, knavery.
▹ANTONYMS honesty.
2 *their life is all a deceit*: **sham**, fraud, pretence, imposture, hoax, fake, misrepresentation, blind, wile, artifice, Trojan horse; trick, stratagem, device, ruse, scheme, dodge, manoeuvre, contrivance, machination, deception, subterfuge, cheat, swindle, confidence trick; informal con, con trick, set-up, game, scam, sting, gyp, leg-pull, flimflam; Brit. informal wheeze; N. Amer. informal bunco, grift; Austral. informal lurk, rort; S. African informal schlenter; Brit. informal, dated flanker; archaic shift, fetch, rig.

deceitful adjective **1** *he was surrounded by foolish and deceitful women*: **dishonest**, untruthful, lying, mendacious, insincere, false, deceiving, dissembling, disingenuous, untrustworthy, unscrupulous, unprincipled, two-faced, duplicitous, double-dealing, cheating, underhand, crafty, cunning, sly, guileful, scheming, calculating, conniving, designing, hypocritical, perfidious, treacherous, Machiavellian; informal sneaky, tricky, foxy, crooked, sharp, shady, shifty, slippery; Brit. informal bent; S. African informal slim; archaic subtle, hollow-hearted; rare false-hearted, double-faced, truthless, Punic.
▹ANTONYMS honest.
2 *they dismissed the allegations as deceitful*: **fraudulent**, counterfeit, fabricated, invented, concocted, made up, trumped up, untrue, hollow, false, sham, bogus, fake, illusory, spurious, specious, fallacious, deceptive, misleading, misguided, distorted; humorous economical with the truth.
▹ANTONYMS true.

deceive verb **1** *she had been deceived by a clever confidence trickster*: **swindle**, defraud, cheat, trick, hoodwink, hoax, dupe, take in, mislead, delude, fool, outwit, misguide, lead on, inveigle, seduce, ensnare, entrap, beguile, double-cross, gull; informal con, bamboozle, do, sting, gyp, diddle, fiddle, swizzle, rip off, shaft, bilk, rook, pull a fast one on, pull someone's leg, take for a ride, pull the wool over someone's eyes, throw dust in someone's eyes, put one over on, sell a pup to, take to the cleaners; N. Amer. informal sucker, snooker, stiff, euchre, bunco, hornswoggle; Austral. informal pull a swifty on; archaic cozen, sharp; rare mulct.
2 *he had deceived her with another woman*: **be unfaithful to**, be disloyal to, be untrue to, be inconstant to, cheat on, cheat, betray, break one's promise to, play someone false, fail, let down; informal two-time.

decelerate verb *there is a whine coming from the gearbox every time I decelerate*: **slow down**, slow up, slow, go slower, ease up, slack up, reduce speed, lessen one's speed, brake, put the brakes on, hit the brakes; Brit. informal slam on the anchors.
▹ANTONYMS accelerate.

decency noun **1** *TV companies need to maintain standards of taste and decency*: **propriety**, decorum, seemliness, good taste, respectability, dignity, correctness, good form, etiquette, appropriateness, fitness, suitability; morality, virtue, modesty, purity, delicacy, demureness, wholesomeness.
▹ANTONYMS indecency.
2 *he didn't have the decency to tell me he couldn't come*: **courtesy**, politeness, good manners, civility, respect, respectfulness; consideration, thought, thoughtfulness, tact, diplomacy.
▹ANTONYMS rudeness.

decent adjective **1** *they deserve a decent burial | after a decent interval, he married his late brother's fiancée*: **proper**, correct, appropriate, apt, apposite, fitting, fit, befitting, right, suitable, respectable, dignified, becoming, decorous, seemly, modest, nice, tasteful, in good taste, refined, genteel; conventional, accepted, approved, standard, traditional, orthodox; French comme il faut; informal pukka.
▹ANTONYMS indecent.
2 Brit. informal *he was a devoted husband and a very decent chap*: **honourable**, honest, trustworthy, dependable, worthy, respectable, upright, clean-living, incorrupt, virtuous, good, ethical, moral; obliging, helpful, accommodating, indulgent, unselfish, altruistic, generous, kind, kindly, thoughtful, considerate, courteous, civil, polite, well mannered, neighbourly, hospitable, pleasant, agreeable, amiable; informal squeaky clean; dated mannerly; rare regardful.
▹ANTONYMS disobliging; dishonest.
3 *she's trying to find a job with decent pay*: **satisfactory**, reasonable, fair, acceptable, adequate, sufficient, sufficiently good, good enough, ample, up to scratch, up to the mark, up to standard, up to par, competent, not bad, all right, average, tolerable, passable, suitable; informal OK, okay, up to snuff.
▹ANTONYMS unsatisfactory.

deception noun **1** *the court found that they had obtained money by deception*: **deceit**, deceitfulness, duplicity, double-dealing, fraud, fraudulence, cheating, trickery, duping, hoodwinking, chicanery, underhandedness, deviousness, slyness, cunning, craft, craftiness, wiliness, artfulness, guile, dissimulation, dissembling, bluff, bluffing, lying, pretence, artifice, treachery; informal crookedness, monkey business, funny business, hanky-panky, jiggery-pokery, kidology; N. Amer. informal monkeyshines; Irish informal codology; archaic management, knavery.
2 *she had proof that this was a deception*: **trick**, stratagem, device, ruse, scheme, dodge, manoeuvre, contrivance, machination, subterfuge, cheat, swindle, confidence trick; sham, fraud, pretence, imposture, hoax, fake, misrepresentation, blind, wile, artifice, Trojan horse; informal con, con trick, set-up, game, scam, sting, gyp, leg-pull, flimflam; Brit. informal wheeze; N. Amer. informal bunco, grift; Austral. informal lurk, rort; S. African informal schlenter; Brit. informal, dated flanker; archaic shift, fetch, rig.

deceptive adjective **1** *distances over water are very deceptive*: **misleading**, illusory, illusive, illusionary, ambiguous, deceiving, delusive, distorted, specious.
2 *deceptive practices account for at least half of the offences*: **deceitful**, duplicitous, fraudulent, counterfeit, sham, bogus, cheating, underhand, cunning, crafty, sly, guileful, scheming, perfidious, treacherous, Machiavellian, dissembling, disingenuous, untrustworthy, unscrupulous, unprincipled, dishonest, untruthful, lying, mendacious, insincere, false; informal crooked, sharp, shady, slippery, sneaky, tricky, foxy; Brit. informal bent; S. African informal slim; archaic subtle, hollow-hearted; rare false-hearted, double-faced, truthless, Punic.
▹ANTONYMS honest.

decide verb **1** *they took no time at all to decide | she decided to become a writer*: **resolve**, determine, make up one's mind, make a decision, come to a decision, reach a decision, come to a conclusion, reach a conclusion, settle on a plan of action; elect, choose, opt, plan, aim, commit oneself, have the intention, have in mind, set one's sights on.
▹ANTONYMS dither.
2 *further research is needed to decide a variety of questions*: **settle**, resolve, bring to a conclusion, determine, work out, answer, clinch, confirm; informal sort out, figure out.
3 *the court declined to decide the case*: **adjudicate**, arbitrate, adjudge, judge, umpire, referee; hear, try, examine; make a judgement on, pass judgement on, sit in judgement on, pronounce judgement on, pronounce on, give a verdict on, make a ruling on, rule on; informal ref.
□ **decide on** *we decided on a coffee*: **choose**, opt for, select, pick, pick out, go for, settle on, plump for/on, single out, take, fix on; Brit. pitch on.

> *Choose the right word* **decide, determine, resolve**
>
> All these words denote the settling of a question in one's mind as to one's future action.
>
> To **decide** is to make up one's mind, often after having to choose between competing possibilities (*I decided it was the moment for me to change my life | they have decided to go to Italy*).
>
> Decisively influencing something is the primary sense of **determine** (*the quality of the grapes is determined by their position in the vineyard*). Using *determine* to refer to someone's reaching a decision suggests that they have given careful consideration to the options and come to a firm conclusion (*she determined to tackle Stephen the next day*). This sense of an unwavering firmness of purpose is continued in the adjective *determined* (*I was determined to cash in on my success*).
>
> **Resolve** emphasizes the act of will involved in making a decision (*she must, she resolved, keep Robert firmly at a distance | I resolved to return and face the problem*).

decided adjective **1** *public officials have a decided advantage in the matter*: **distinct**, clear, clear-cut, marked, pronounced, obvious, striking, noticeable, unmistakable, patent, manifest, express, definite, certain, positive, absolute, emphatic, categorical, unambiguous, undeniable, unequivocal, indisputable, undisputed, unquestionable, assured, guaranteed; archaic sensible.

d

▷ANTONYMS possible.
2 *you could never talk him round—he was very decided*: **determined**, resolute, firm, strong-minded, strong-willed, dogged, purposeful, forceful, emphatic, dead set, unhesitating, unwavering, unswerving, unfaltering, unyielding, unbending, inflexible, unmalleable, unshakeable, unrelenting, obdurate, obstinate, stubborn, intransigent; N. Amer. rock-ribbed; rare indurate.
▷ANTONYMS indecisive.
3 *the future of the tribe is decided*: **settled**, established, resolved, determined, worked out, concluded, clinched, agreed, designated, allotted, chosen, ordained, prescribed, decreed; set, fixed, concrete, set in stone; informal sewn up, wrapped up.
▷ANTONYMS undecided.

decidedly adverb *they were decidedly hostile to one another*: **distinctly**, clearly, markedly, obviously, noticeably, unmistakably, patently, manifestly, expressly, emphatically, definitely, certainly, positively, absolutely, downright, undeniably, unquestionably, indisputably; extremely, exceedingly, exceptionally, uncommonly, unusually, singularly, particularly, especially; N. English right; Scottish unco; French très; informal terrifically, tremendously, desperately, devilishly, ultra, mucho, mega, majorly; Brit. informal jolly, ever so, dead, well, fair; N. Amer. informal real, mighty, awful, plumb, powerful; S. African informal lekker; informal, dated devilish, hellish; archaic exceeding, sore.

deciding adjective *the deciding factor may be the size of your budget*: **determining**, decisive, conclusive, final, settling, key, pivotal, crucial, critical, most influential, significant, major, chief, principal, prime, paramount.

decipher verb **1** *he was the only one who could decipher the code*: **decode**, decrypt, break, work out, solve, interpret, translate, construe, explain; make sense of, make head or tail of, get to the bottom of, unravel, find the key to, find the answer to, throw light on; informal crack, figure out; Brit. informal twig, suss, suss out.
▷ANTONYMS encode.
2 *the writing was rather wobbly and hard to decipher*: **make out**, discern, perceive, see, read, follow, fathom, penetrate, make sense of, interpret, understand, comprehend, apprehend, grasp; untangle, disentangle, sort out, piece together.

decision noun **1** *a number of factors led me to this decision*: **resolution**, conclusion, settlement, commitment, resolve, determination; choice, option, selection.
2 *they're delighted with the judge's decision*: **verdict**, finding, ruling, recommendation, judgement, pronouncement, adjudgement, adjudication, arbitration; sentence, decree, order, rule, injunction; findings, results; Law determination; N. Amer. resolve; rare arbitrament.
3 *his executive order had a ring of decision*: **decisiveness**, determination, resolution, resoluteness, resolve, firmness; strong-mindedness, single-mindedness, doggedness, strength of mind, strength of will, firmness of purpose, fixity of purpose, purpose, purposefulness.

decisive adjective **1** *Crane was a very decisive man*: **resolute**, firm, strong-minded, strong-willed, determined; dogged, purposeful, forceful, emphatic, dead set, unhesitating, unwavering, unswerving, unfaltering, unyielding, unbending, inflexible, unmalleable, unshakeable, unrelenting, obdurate, obstinate, stubborn, intransigent; N. Amer. rock-ribbed; rare indurate.
▷ANTONYMS indecisive.
2 *your qualifications are unlikely to be the decisive factor*: **deciding**, **conclusive**, determining, final, settling, key; pivotal, critical, crucial, momentous, significant, influential, important, major, chief, principal, prime, paramount.
▷ANTONYMS insignificant.

deck verb **1** *the cottage was decked with red, white, and blue bunting*: **decorate**, bedeck, adorn, ornament, trim, trick out, garnish, cover, hang, festoon, garland, swathe, wreathe; embellish, beautify, prettify, enhance, grace, set off; informal get up, do up, do out, tart up; literary bejewel, bedizen, caparison, furbelow.
2 *Ingrid was **decked out** in her Sunday best*: **dress up**, dress, clothe, attire, array, garb, robe, drape, accoutre, turn out, fit out, rig out, trick out, trick up, outfit, costume; informal doll up, get up, do up, tog up, tart up; archaic apparel, bedizen, caparison, invest, habit, trap out.

declaim verb **1** *he spoke like a preacher declaiming from the pulpit*: **make a speech**, give an address, give a talk, give a lecture, make an oration, deliver a sermon, give a sermon; speak, hold forth, orate, pronounce, preach, lecture, sermonize, moralize; informal sound off, mouth off, spiel, spout, speechify, preachify, jaw; rare perorate.
2 *they loved to hear him declaim poetry*: **recite**, say aloud, read aloud, read out loud, read out; quote, deliver, render; informal spout; rare bespout.
3 *he **declaimed against** the evils of society*: **speak out**, protest strongly, make a protest, make a stand, rail, inveigh, fulminate, rage, thunder; rant about, expostulate about, make a fuss about, express disapproval of; **condemn**, criticize, castigate, attack, decry, disparage; informal mouth off about, kick up a stink about, go on about; rare vociferate.

declamation noun *he delivered a passionate declamation*: **speech**, address, lecture, sermon, homily, discourse, delivery, oration, recitation, disquisition, monologue; harangue, tirade, diatribe, broadside, rant; informal spiel; N. Amer. informal stump speech; rare peroration, allocution, predication.

declamatory adjective *his speech-making was quiet and factual, very different from Clark's declamatory style*: **rhetorical**, oratorical, elaborate, ornate, bold, extravagant, flowery, florid, dramatic, theatrical, lofty, high-flown, high-sounding, bombastic, magniloquent, grandiloquent, overblown, overdone, overwrought, affected, orotund, inflated, overinflated, pompous, pretentious; informal highfalutin, purple; rare fustian, tumid, euphuistic, aureate, Ossianic.

declaration noun **1** *they issued a declaration at the close of the talks*: **announcement**, statement, communication, pronouncement, proclamation, memorandum, bulletin, communiqué, dispatch, report, edict, manifesto; N. Amer. advisory; in Spanish-speaking countries pronunciamento; Latin ipse dixit; informal memo; rare rescript.
2 *Parliament arranged the declaration of war*: **proclamation**, notification, announcement, revelation, disclosure, broadcasting, promulgation; archaic annunciation; rare asseveration.
3 *her words were taken as a declaration of faith*: **assertion**, profession, affirmation, acknowledgement, revelation, disclosure, manifestation, confirmation, proof, testimony, validation, certification, attestation; pledge, avowal, vow, oath, guarantee, protestation; rare asseveration, averment, maintenance.
▷ANTONYMS denial.

declare verb **1** *she loses no opportunity to declare her political principles*: **proclaim**, announce, make known, state, communicate, reveal, divulge, mention, talk about, raise, moot, air, bring into the open, voice, articulate, pronounce, express, vent, set forth, make public, publicize, disseminate, circulate, publish, broadcast, promulgate, trumpet, blazon; informal come out with, shout from the rooftops; literary noise abroad, blazon abroad; rare preconize.
2 *he declared that the defendants were guilty*: **assert**, maintain, state, aver, affirm, contend, argue, insist, hold, profess, move, claim, allege, avow, vow, swear, attest, testify, certify; informal make out; technical depose, represent; formal opine; archaic avouch; rare asseverate.
3 *his speech and bearing declared him a gentleman*: **show to be**, reveal as, confirm as, prove to be, validate as, certify to someone's being, attest to someone's being.

decline verb **1** *she declined all invitations | he offered me a cigarette but I declined*: **turn down**, **reject**, brush aside, refuse, rebuff, spurn, disdain, look down one's nose at, repulse, repudiate, dismiss, forgo, deny oneself, pass up, refuse to take advantage of, turn one's back on; abstain (from), say no to, shake one's head, send one's regrets; informal give the thumbs down (to), give the red light (to), give something a miss, give someone the brush-off; Brit. informal knock back; Austral. informal snout.
▷ANTONYMS accept.
2 *the number of small local traders has declined*: **decrease**, reduce, get smaller, grow smaller, lessen, get less, diminish, wane, dwindle, contract, shrink, fall off, taper off, tail off, peter out; drop, fall, go down, sink, slump, plummet, plunge; informal nosedive, take a nosedive, take a header, go into a tailspin, crash.
▷ANTONYMS increase.
3 *standards of craftsmanship steadily declined*: **deteriorate**, degenerate, decay, crumble, collapse, fail, fall, sink, slump, slip, slide, go downhill, worsen, get worse, go to rack and ruin, stagnate, atrophy, wither, weaken, fade, fade away, wane, ebb; be abandoned, be neglected, be disregarded, be forgotten; informal go to pot, go to the dogs, hit the skids, go down the toilet, go down the tubes; Austral./NZ informal go to the pack; rare retrograde.
▷ANTONYMS flourish.
▶ noun **1** *the company suffered a decline in profits*: **reduction**, decrease, downturn, downswing, lowering, devaluation, depreciation, lessening, diminishing, diminution, slackening, waning, dwindling, fading, ebb, falling off, abatement, drop, slump, plunge, tumble; informal nosedive, crash, let-up.
▷ANTONYMS increase.
2 *there is a link between pollution and forest decline*: **deterioration**, degeneration, degradation, shrinkage, shrinking, withering, atrophy, weakening, enfeeblement, fall, failure, death, decay, decaying; dated decadence; rare devolution.
□ **in decline** *the prosperity of the Mediterranean world was in decline*: **waning**, declining, on the decline, decaying, crumbling, collapsing, atrophying, failing, disappearing, dying, moribund, past its prime, obsolescent; informal on its last legs, on the way out.

Choose the right word **decline, refuse, reject, spurn**

See **refuse**[1].

decode verb *battle plans sent out on Germany's Enigma machine were quickly decoded*: **decipher**, decrypt, unravel, untangle, work out, sort out, piece together, solve, interpret, translate, construe, explain, understand, comprehend, apprehend, grasp; make sense of, get to the bottom of, find

d

the key to, find the answer to, throw light on; informal crack, figure out; Brit. informal twig, suss, suss out.

decompose verb 1 *the chemical prevents corpses from decomposing*: **decay**, rot, putrefy, go bad, go off, spoil, fester, perish, deteriorate, degrade, break down, break up, moulder; technical mortify, necrotize, sphacelate; archaic corrupt.
2 *some minerals decompose very rapidly*: **break up**, break apart, fall apart, fragment, disintegrate, crumble, dissolve; **break down**, decay.
3 *semantic markers decompose the meanings of words into more primitive elements*: **separate**, divide, break down, dissect, atomize, dissolve, resolve, reduce; rare fractionate.

decomposition noun 1 *the body is in an advanced state of decomposition*: **decay**, rotting, going bad, putrefaction, putrescence, putridity, festering, spoilage, perishing; archaic corruption.
2 *china clay is formed by the decomposition of granite*: **breaking up**, breaking apart, fragmenting, disintegration, crumbling, dissolution, dissolving; **breaking down**, decay, decaying.
3 *they presented a tree-like decomposition of a sentence into its parts*: **separation**, division, breakdown, break-up; **dissection**, atomization, dissolution, resolution, analysis, reduction; rare fractionation.

decontaminate verb **sanitize**, sterilize, disinfect, clean, cleanse, purify; fumigate; rare depurate.

decor noun *inside, the decor is elegant and traditional*: **decoration**, furnishing, furbishing, ornamentation; look, colour scheme.

decorate verb 1 *the door was decorated with a lion's head knocker*: **ornament**, adorn, trim, embellish, garnish, furnish, accessorize, enhance, grace, enrich; festoon, garland, trick out, bedeck, beautify, prettify; literary furbelow.
2 *a house painter called to decorate his home*: **paint**, **wallpaper**, paper, furbish, smarten up; renovate, refurbish, redecorate, retouch; informal do up, spruce up, do out, do over, fix up, tart up, give something a facelift, titivate.
3 *he was decorated for courage on the battlefields*: **give a medal to**, pin a medal on, honour, confer an award on; cite, mention in dispatches, reward.

decoration noun 1 *a vaulted ceiling with rich decoration*: **ornamentation**, adornment, trimming, embellishment, garnishing, gilding; beautification, prettification; enhancements, enrichments, frills, accessories, trimmings, finery, frippery.
2 *the carriages were built with simple but attractive internal decoration.* See **decor**.
3 *a Christmas tree decoration*: **ornament**, trinket, bauble, knick-knack, gimcrack, spangle, doodah, gewgaw, folderol, fandangle; trimming, tinsel.
4 *a decoration won on the field of battle*: **medal**, award, badge, star, ribbon, laurel, wreath, trophy, prize; colours, insignia; military slang fruit salad; Brit. informal gong.

decorative adjective *mirrors were used as decorative features*: **ornamental**, adorning, embellishing, garnishing, beautifying, prettifying, enhancing, non-functional; fancy, ornate, attractive, pretty, showy, for show, flashy.
▷ANTONYMS functional; plain.

decorous adjective *he always behaved towards her in a decorous way*: **proper**, seemly, decent, becoming, befitting, tasteful, in good taste; tactful, correct, appropriate, suitable, fitting, fit; polite, well mannered, well behaved, genteel, refined, polished, well bred, dignified, respectable, courtly, civilized; formal, reserved, modest, demure, sedate, staid, gentlemanly, ladylike; French comme il faut; dated mannerly; humorous couth.
▷ANTONYMS indecorous; unseemly; immodest.

decorum noun 1 *he had acted with the utmost decorum*: **propriety**, properness, seemliness, decency, decorousness, good taste, correctness, appropriateness; politeness, courtesy, good manners; refinement, breeding, deportment, dignity, respectability, modesty, demureness.
▷ANTONYMS impropriety.
2 *a breach of decorum*: **etiquette**, protocol, customary behaviour, good form, custom, convention, conformity, conventionality, usage, ritual; formalities, niceties, punctilios, politeness; French politesse; informal the thing to do.

decoy noun (stress on the first syllable) *we need a decoy to distract their attention*: **lure**, bait, red herring; enticement, inducement, temptation, attraction, allurement, draw, carrot, ensnarement, entrapment; snare, trap, pitfall, ambush.
▶verb (stress on the second syllable) *he was decoyed to the mainland by his enemies*: **lure**, entice, induce, inveigle, ensnare; tempt, seduce; entrap, snare, trap.

decrease verb (stress on the second syllable) 1 *pollution levels had been gradually decreasing*: **lessen**, grow/become less, grow/become smaller, reduce, drop, diminish, decline, dwindle, contract, shrink, fall off, die down; abate, subside, let up, tail off, ebb, wane, taper off, peter out, lighten; sink, slump, plummet, plunge.
▷ANTONYMS increase.
2 *you could exercise to decrease the amount of fat in your body*: **reduce**, lessen, make less/fewer, lower, cut down/back (on), cut, curtail, contract, diminish, narrow, pare down, slim down, tone down, temper, weaken, deplete, minimize; informal slash.
▶noun (stress on the first syllable) *a decrease in crime*: **reduction**, drop, lessening, lowering, decline, falling off; letting up, slackening, downturn, cut, cutback, curtailment, diminution, contraction, shrinkage, ebb, wane, de-escalation; dying down, abatement.
▷ANTONYMS increase.

decree noun 1 *an emergency presidential decree*: **order**, edict, command, commandment, mandate, proclamation, dictum, fiat, promulgation, precept; law, statute, act, bill, ordinance, regulation, rule, injunction, enactment, manifesto; in Tsarist Russia ukase; in Spanish-speaking countries pronunciamento; rare firman, decretal, irade, rescript.
2 *the council succeeded in obtaining a court decree against him*: **judgement**, verdict, adjudication, ruling, rule, resolution, arbitration, decision, conclusion; findings.
▶verb *the government decreed that a new national stadium should be built*: **order**, command, rule, dictate, lay down, prescribe, pronounce, proclaim, ordain; enact, adjudge, enjoin, direct, decide, determine.

decrepit adjective 1 *a decrepit old man*: **feeble**, enfeebled, infirm, weak, weakened, weakly, frail, debilitated, incapacitated, wasted, doddering, tottering, out of shape, in bad shape; **old**, elderly, aged, ancient, in one's dotage, long in the tooth, senile; superannuated, senescent; informal past it, over the hill, no spring chicken.
▷ANTONYMS strong, fit.
2 *a decrepit house*: **dilapidated**, rickety, run down, broken-down, tumbledown, ramshackle, worn out, derelict, in ruins, ruined, falling apart, falling to pieces, in (a state of) disrepair, creaky, creaking, gone to rack and ruin, on its last legs; battered, decayed, decaying, crumbling, deteriorated, deteriorating, antiquated, superannuated, the worse for wear.
▷ANTONYMS sound.

decrepitude noun 1 *over the years she fell into a state of decrepitude*: **feebleness**, enfeeblement, infirmity, weakness, frailty, debilitation, debility, sickliness, incapacitation, malaise; old age, agedness, elderliness, dotage, senility; superannuation, senescence.
▷ANTONYMS strength, fitness.
2 *the house had an air of decrepitude*: **dilapidation**, ricketiness, dereliction, ruin, disrepair, rack and ruin, decay, deterioration.
▷ANTONYMS soundness, good repair.

decry verb *she decried sexists' double standards*: **denounce**, condemn, criticize, censure, damn, attack, fulminate against, rail against, inveigh against, blame, carp at, cavil at, run down, pillory, rap, lambaste, deplore, disapprove of, vilify, execrate, revile; disparage, deprecate, discredit, derogate, cast aspersions on; informal slam, slate, blast, knock, snipe at, do a hatchet job on, hold forth against, come down on, pull to pieces, tear to shreds; formal excoriate, animadvert; rare asperse.
▷ANTONYMS praise; overrate.

dedicate verb 1 *she had dedicated her life to helping people and animals*: **devote**, commit, pledge, bind, obligate, give, give over, surrender, set aside, allot, allocate, consign, sacrifice.
2 *each book was dedicated to a noblewoman*: **inscribe**, address, name; assign, offer.
3 *the chapel was dedicated to the Virgin Mary*: **devote**, assign; bless, consecrate, sanctify, hallow, make holy, make sacred.

dedicated adjective 1 *a dedicated supporter | a dedicated musician*: **committed**, devoted, staunch, stalwart, firm, steadfast, resolute, unwavering, loyal, faithful, true, dyed-in-the-wool, through and through; wholehearted, single-minded, enthusiastic, eager, keen, earnest, zealous, ardent, passionate, fervent, fervid, fanatical; hard-working, dutiful, diligent, assiduous, studious; sworn, pledged; informal card-carrying, deep-dyed, as keen as mustard, mad keen.
▷ANTONYMS indifferent, apathetic.
2 *the data can be accessed by a dedicated machine or an ordinary personal computer*: **exclusive**, allocated, assigned, custom built, customized.

dedication noun 1 *success in sport requires tremendous dedication*: **commitment**, wholeheartedness, single-mindedness, enthusiasm, zeal, application, diligence, industry, assiduity, resolve, resoluteness, purposefulness, conscientiousness, perseverance, persistence, tenacity, doggedness, drive, staying power, backbone, sedulousness; hard work, effort, labour, striving.
▷ANTONYMS apathy, laziness.
2 *her superiors could not fault her dedication to the job*: **devotion**, devotedness, commitment, loyalty, faithfulness, adherence, allegiance, constancy, staunchness.
▷ANTONYMS indifference.
3 *the hardback edition contains a dedication to his wife*: **inscription**, address, message.
4 *the dedication of the church*: **blessing**, consecration, sanctification, hallowing, benediction.
▷ANTONYMS deconsecration.

deduce verb *from the observation of fossils, he deduced that the whole Earth had once been covered by water*: **conclude**, come to the conclusion, reason, work out, gather, infer, draw the inference; extrapolate, glean, divine, intuit, come to understand, understand, assume, presume, conjecture, surmise, reckon, dare say; N. Amer. figure; informal suss out.

deduct verb *any tax due will be deducted from the pension*: **subtract**, take away, take from, take off, withdraw, abstract, remove, debit, dock, discount; informal knock off, minus.
▷ANTONYMS add.

deduction noun **1** *the deduction of tax*: **subtraction**, taking away, taking off, withdrawal, abstraction, removal, debit, docking, discounting; informal knocking off.
▷ANTONYMS addition.
2 *NI contributions are worked out on gross pay, before all deductions*: **stoppage**, subtraction.
3 *she had been right in her deduction that he was in love with someone else*: **conclusion**, inference, supposition, hypothesis, thesis, assumption, presumption, suspicion, conviction, belief; reasoning; results, findings.

deed noun **1** *tales of knightly deeds*: **act**, action, activity; **feat**, exploit, performance, achievement, accomplishment, attainment, endeavour, effort; undertaking, enterprise.
2 *working-class unity must be established in deed and not only in words*: **fact**, reality, truth, actuality.
3 *mortgage deeds*: **legal document**, contract, legal agreement, indenture, instrument; title deed, deed of covenant.

deem verb *many of these campaigns have been deemed successful*: **regard as**, consider, judge, adjudge, hold to be, look on as, view as, see as, take to be, take for, class as, estimate as, count, rate, find, esteem, calculate to be, gauge, suppose, reckon, account, interpret as; think, believe to be, feel to be, imagine to be, conceive to be.

deep adjective **1** *a deep ravine*: **extending far down**; cavernous, yawning, gaping, huge, big, great, extensive, profound, unplumbed; bottomless, immeasurable, fathomless, unfathomable; rare chasmic.
▷ANTONYMS shallow.
2 *a deep shelf*: **extending far back/in**, extending a long way back, extensive.
▷ANTONYMS shallow.
3 *a puddle about two inches deep*: **in depth**, downwards, inwards, from top to bottom, from the surface, in vertical extent.
4 *I have a deep affection for you | he was viewed with deep suspicion*: **intense**, heartfelt, deeply felt, fervent, ardent, impassioned, wholehearted, deep-seated, deep-rooted, thorough, thoroughgoing, serious; sincere, honest, genuine, unfeigned; earnest, enthusiastic, keen, great; grave, abject.
▷ANTONYMS superficial, insincere.
5 *Laura drifted into a deep sleep*: **sound**, heavy, profound, intense.
6 *Helen was a deep thinker*: **clever**, intelligent, intellectual; **knowledgeable**, learned, wise, sagacious, sage, scholarly; discerning, penetrating, perspicacious, perceptive, percipient, insightful, keen, sharp, sharp-witted, quick-witted; **profound**, philosophical, complex, weighty, serious, difficult, abstruse, esoteric, recondite, impenetrable, unfathomable, mysterious, obscure.
▷ANTONYMS straightforward.
7 *he was deep in concentration*: **rapt**, absorbed, engrossed, preoccupied, immersed, steeped, lost, captivated, spellbound, riveted, gripped, enthralled, intent, engaged.
8 *a deep mystery*: **obscure**, mysterious, hidden, secret, unfathomable, fathomless, opaque, abstruse, recondite, esoteric, enigmatic, arcane, Delphic; puzzling, perplexing, baffling, mystifying, inexplicable; informal as clear as mud.
9 *his deep voice*: **low-pitched**, low, bass, full-toned, rich, powerful, resonant, rumbling, booming, resounding, sonorous.
▷ANTONYMS high.
10 *a deep reddish-brown colour*: **dark**; **intense**, vivid, rich, strong, brilliant, glowing, vibrant, bold, warm, flamboyant, eye-catching.
▷ANTONYMS light; thin.
▶ noun (**the deep**) **1** literary *the strange creatures of the deep*. See **sea** (sense 1 of the noun).
2 *in the deep of night*: **the middle**, the midst, the mid point, the central point; the depths, the thick, the dead, the heart, the kernel, the interior.
▶ adverb **1** *I dug deep*: **far down**, far in, deep down, way down, to a great depth.
2 *he brought them deep into thick woodland*: **far**, a long way, a great distance, a good way.

deepen verb **1** *the recession continues to deepen | his love for his wife had been deepened by the way she had stood by him*: **grow**, increase, intensify, strengthen, escalate, mushroom, snowball; add to, heighten, reinforce, enhance, boost, magnify, amplify, augment, enrich, promote, encourage; exacerbate, aggravate, inflame, worsen, make/become worse; informal hot up, step up.
2 *the archaeologists deepened and widened the hole*: **dig out**, make deeper, dig deeper, scoop out, scrape out, hollow out, excavate.

deeply adverb *she was deeply affected by the story*: **greatly**, enormously, extremely, very much, to a great extent/degree; strongly, powerfully, profoundly, intensely, keenly, sharply, acutely; thoroughly, completely, entirely; severely, awfully, terribly, painfully, desperately; informal well, seriously, majorly, jolly, oh-so; N. Amer. informal mighty, plumb.

deep-rooted adjective *a fear of deep-rooted taboos*: **deep-seated**, deep, profound, fundamental, basic; well established, established, settled, firm, ingrained, entrenched, unshakeable, irremovable, ineradicable, dyed-in-the-wool, inveterate, built-in, inbuilt, radical, secure; persistent, long-lasting, abiding, lingering.
▷ANTONYMS superficial, temporary.

deep-seated adjective *a deep-seated concern that values are in decline*. See **deep-rooted**.

deer noun

> *Word links* **deer**
>
> **cervine** relating to deer
> **stag** male
> **doe** female
> **herd, mob** collective noun

deface verb *a graffiti artist who defaced buildings and motorway bridges*: **vandalize**, disfigure, mar, spoil, ruin, deform, sully, tarnish, damage; injure, uglify, blight, blemish, impair; informal tag, trash.
▷ANTONYMS beautify.

de facto adverb *the republic has been de facto divided into two states*: **in practice**, in effect, in fact, in reality, really, actually, in actuality.
▷ANTONYMS in theory; de jure.
▶ adjective *they took de facto control of the land*: **actual**, existing, existent, real, effective.
▷ANTONYMS theoretical; de jure.

defamation noun *he sued the newspaper for defamation*: **libel**, **slander**, character assassination, defamation of character, calumny, vilification, traducement, obloquy, scandal, scandalmongering, malicious gossip, tittle-tattle, backbiting, aspersions, muckraking, abuse, malediction; disparagement, denigration, detraction, derogation, opprobrium, censure, criticism; smear, slur, lie, false report, smear campaign, rumour, insult; informal mud-slinging, slagging-off, knocking, bitching; N. Amer. informal bad-mouthing; archaic contumely.
▷ANTONYMS commendation.

defamatory adjective *there were defamatory statements in the book*: **libellous**, **slanderous**, defaming, calumnious, calumniatory, vilifying, traducing, scandalous, scandalmongering, malicious, vicious, backbiting, muckraking, abusive, maledictory, maledictive; disparaging, denigratory, detracting, derogatory, censorious, critical; insulting, slurring, injurious; informal mud-slinging, bitchy, catty; archaic contumelious.
▷ANTONYMS complimentary.

defame verb *he had been defamed by an article in a tabloid newspaper*: **libel**, **slander**, malign, cast aspersions on, smear, traduce, blacken the name/character of, give someone a bad name, defame someone's character, sully someone's reputation, run down, speak ill/evil of, back-bite, run a smear campaign against, calumniate, vilify, besmirch, tarnish, stigmatize, disparage, denigrate, discredit, decry, insult, lie about, tell lies about; informal do a hatchet job on, sling/fling/throw mud at, drag through the mud/mire; N. Amer. slur; Brit. informal slag off; N. Amer. informal bad-mouth; rare asperse, derogate, vilipend.

> *Choose the right word* **defame, malign, slander, libel, traduce**
>
> See **malign**.

default noun **1** *the recession has been accompanied by a rise in the incidence of defaults on loans*: **non-payment**, failure to pay, non-remittance; informal welshing, bilking; Brit. archaic levant.
▷ANTONYMS repayment.
2 *I became a TV presenter by default, rather than by design | in default of evidence*: **failure to act/appear**, inaction, omission, lapse, lack, exclusion, neglect, negligence, disregard; want, deficiency, delinquency, dereliction, absence, non-appearance.
▶ verb **1** *the dealer can repossess the goods if the customer defaults*: **fail to pay**, not pay, renege, fail to honour, back out, backtrack, backslide; break one's promise/word, go back on one's word; informal welsh, bilk.
▷ANTONYMS repay.
2 *when you start a fresh letter, the program will default to its own style*: **revert**; select automatically.

defaulter noun **1** *a mortgage defaulter*: **non-payer**, debt-dodger; tax-dodger; informal welsher, bilker; N. Amer. delinquent; Brit. archaic levanter.
2 Military *he was confined to the defaulters' room*: **minor offender**, wrongdoer, felon, delinquent, malefactor, culprit; archaic miscreant.

defeat verb **1** *the victorious army which defeated the Scots at Halidon Hill*: **beat**, conquer, win against, win a victory over, triumph over, prevail over, get the better of, best, worst, vanquish; rout, trounce, overcome, overpower, overthrow, overwhelm, crush, quash, bring someone to their

d

knees; quell, subjugate, subdue, repulse; informal lick, thrash, hammer, whip, wipe the floor with, walk all over, give someone a hiding, take to the cleaners, blow out of the water, run rings round/around, make mincemeat of, clobber, paste, pound, pulverize, crucify, murder, massacre, slaughter, demolish, drub, give someone a drubbing, cane, zap, flatten, turn inside out, tank; Brit. informal stuff, marmalize; N. Amer. informal blow out, cream, shellac, skunk, slam.
▷ANTONYMS lose to.
2 *budgets should not be so complex that they defeat their purpose*: **thwart**, block, frustrate, prevent, foil, baulk, ruin, put a stop to, scotch, obviate, forestall, debar, snooker, derail; obstruct, impede, hinder, hamper, deter, discomfit; informal put the kibosh on, nip in the bud, put paid to, put the stopper on, do for, stymie; Brit. informal scupper, put the mockers on, nobble.
▷ANTONYMS advance, assist.
3 *the motion was defeated*: **reject**, overthrow, throw out, dismiss, outvote, spurn, rebuff, turn down; informal give the thumbs down.
▷ANTONYMS pass.
4 *I managed to fit to the machine, but how to make it work defeats me*: **baffle**, puzzle, perplex, bewilder, mystify, bemuse, confuse, confound, frustrate, nonplus, throw; informal beat, flummox, discombobulate, faze, stump, fox, be all Greek to.
▶ **noun 1** *a crippling defeat for the government*: **loss**, beating, conquest, conquering, besting, worsting, vanquishing, vanquishment; rout, trouncing, overpowering, subjugation, subduing; **reverse**, debacle, downfall; informal thrashing, hiding, drubbing, licking, hammering, whipping, clobbering, pasting, pounding, pulverizing, massacre, slaughter, demolition, caning, flattening.
▷ANTONYMS victory.
2 *the defeat of his plans*: **failure**, downfall, breakdown, collapse, ruin, lack of success, discomfiture, rejection, frustration, foundering, misfiring, overthrow, abortion, miscarriage; undoing, reverse; disappointment, setback.
▷ANTONYMS success.

defeatist **adjective** *they were criticized for their defeatist attitude*: **pessimistic**, fatalistic, negative, resigned, cynical, discouraged, despondent, despairing, hopeless, bleak, gloomy, gloom-ridden, looking on the dark/black side.
▷ANTONYMS optimistic, positive.
▶ **noun pessimist**, fatalist, yielder, cynic, prophet of doom, doomwatcher; misery, killjoy, worrier, Job's comforter; informal quitter, doom and gloom merchant, doomster, wet blanket.
▷ANTONYMS optimist.

defecate **verb excrete**, pass/discharge/excrete faeces, have a bowel movement, have a BM, evacuate one's bowels, open one's bowels, void excrement, relieve oneself, go to the lavatory; informal do number two, do a pooh, do a whoopsie; vulgar slang crap, have a crap, shit, have a shit, dump, have a dump.

defecation **noun excretion**, passing/discharging/excreting faeces, evacuation of one's bowels, opening one's bowels, going to the lavatory; bowel movement, BM; informal number twos, poohing, whoopsies; vulgar slang crapping, crap, shitting, shit, dump.

defect[1] (stress on the first syllable) **noun** *a defect in the software*: **fault**, flaw, imperfection, deficiency, weakness, weak spot/point, inadequacy, shortcoming, limitation, failing, obstruction; snag, kink, deformity, blemish, taint, crack, break, tear, split, scratch, chip, fracture, spot; mistake, error; Computing bug, virus; informal glitch, gremlin.

defect[2] (stress on the second syllable) **verb** *their ruthlessness discouraged army officers from defecting | one MP* ***defected from*** *the party*: **desert**, go over to the enemy, change sides/loyalties/allegiances, turn traitor, rebel, renege, abscond, go AWOL, quit, escape; shift ground, break faith, be apostate, apostatize; abandon, renounce, repudiate, secede from, revolt against; informal rat on; archaic forsake; rare tergiversate.

defection **noun** *his defection to the United States*: **desertion**, absconding, decamping, flight; changing sides/allegiances, apostasy, recantation, secession; treason, betrayal, disloyalty, rebellion, mutiny, perfidy; rare tergiversation, recreancy.

defective **adjective 1** *a defective seat belt*: **faulty**, flawed, imperfect, shoddy, inoperative, not working, not functioning, non-functioning, malfunctioning, out of order, unsound; weak, deficient, incomplete; in disrepair, broken, cracked, torn, scratched, deformed, warped, buckled; informal gone wrong, on the blink; Brit. informal knackered, duff.
▷ANTONYMS working, perfect.
2 *these methods are defective in strength and durability*: **lacking**, wanting, deficient, inadequate, insufficient, short, low, scant.

defector **noun deserter**, turncoat, traitor, rebel, renegade, tergiversator, apostate, recreant, Judas, quisling; informal rat.

defence **noun 1** *the defence of fortresses against enemies*: **protection**, shielding, safeguarding, guarding; security, fortification, cover, shelter, screen, resistance, deterrent.
2 *the enemy's defences were sited all along the ridge*: **barricade**, fortification, bulwark, buttress, fortress, fastness, keep, rampart, outpost, bastion.
3 *he planned to speak in defence of his old chief*: **vindication**, justification, support, advocacy, approval, endorsement, promotion; apology, apologia, explanation, explication, excuse, extenuation, exoneration, palliation.
4 *they urged lower spending on defence*: **armaments**, weapons, weaponry, arms, military resources/measures; the military, the army, the navy, the air force; deterrence.
5 *the prisoner was unable to speak for pain, so his defence was never heard*: **rebuttal**, denial; **vindication**, explanation, mitigation, justification, rationalization, excuse, alibi, reason; plea, pleading; testimony, declaration, case.

defenceless **adjective 1** *it is a disgrace that these thugs terrorized defenceless animals*: **vulnerable**, **helpless**, powerless, impotent, weak, frail; susceptible, easily hurt/wounded/damaged; rare impuissant, resistless.
▷ANTONYMS well protected, resilient.
2 *scrapping the weapons would leave the country wholly defenceless*: **undefended**, unprotected, unguarded, unfortified, unshielded, unarmed, without arms, without defences; vulnerable, assailable, open to attack, wide open, open, exposed, endangered, in danger, in peril, in jeopardy, at risk, insecure; rare pregnable.
▷ANTONYMS well protected.

defend **verb 1** *a tower built to defend Ireland from Napoleon's threatened invasion | we will defend freedom of speech*: **protect**, guard, safeguard, keep from harm, preserve, secure, shield, shelter, screen; fortify, garrison, barricade; fight for, uphold, support, be on the side of, take up cudgels for; watch over, be the defender of.
▷ANTONYMS attack.
2 *he defended his policy of charging high interest rates*: **justify**, vindicate, argue/speak for, speak on behalf of, support, speak in support of, give an apologia for, make a case for, plead for, make excuses for, excuse, exonerate, palliate; explain, give reasons for, give the rationale behind.
▷ANTONYMS attack, criticize.
3 *the manager defended his players*: **support**, speak in support of, back, stand by, stick up for, stand up for, argue for, champion, endorse, uphold, come to the defence of, sustain, bolster; informal throw one's weight behind.
▷ANTONYMS criticize.

defendant **noun** *the defendant was charged with murder*: **accused**, prisoner at the bar; appellant, litigant, respondent; suspect, suspected person.
▷ANTONYMS plaintiff.

defender **noun 1** *the defenders of the rural environment*: **protector**, guard, guardian, preserver, bodyguard; custodian, watchdog, keeper, overseer, superintendent, caretaker, steward, trustee.
2 *a defender of colonialism*: **supporter**, upholder, backer, champion, advocate, endorser, sustainer, bolsterer, apologist, proponent, exponent, promoter, apostle, standard-bearer, torch-bearer, adherent, believer.
▷ANTONYMS attacker, critic.
3 *he burst between two defenders and cracked a shot at the bar*: **fullback**, back, sweeper; (**defenders**) back four.
▷ANTONYMS attacker, striker.

defensible **adjective 1** *this is a perfectly defensible attitude*: **justifiable**, arguable, tenable, defendable, maintainable, sustainable, supportable, plausible, well founded, sound, sensible, reasonable, rational, logical, able to hold water; acceptable, satisfactory, valid, legitimate, warrantable, permissible, excusable, pardonable, understandable, condonable, vindicable.
▷ANTONYMS indefensible, untenable.
2 *a defensible patch of territory*: **secure**, safe, fortified, protectable, able to be protected, holdable; invulnerable, impregnable, impenetrable, unattackable, unassailable.
▷ANTONYMS vulnerable.

defensive **adjective 1** *troops in defensive positions*: **defending**, **guarding**, safeguarding, protecting, protective, shielding, screening; wary, watchful; averting, withstanding, opposing.
▷ANTONYMS attacking.
2 *my innocent inquiry had provoked a defensive, almost hostile response*: **self-justifying**, oversensitive, thin-skinned, easily offended, prickly, paranoid, neurotic; informal uptight, twitchy; rare umbrageous.
▷ANTONYMS confident.

defer[1] **verb** *he deferred the final decision till a later meeting*: **postpone**, put off, adjourn, delay, hold over/off, put back, carry over; shelve, suspend, stay, hold in abeyance, prorogue, pigeonhole, mothball; N. Amer. put over, table, lay on the table, take a rain check on; N. Amer. Law continue; informal put on ice, put on the back burner, put in cold storage; rare remit, respite.

defer[2] **verb** *he readily* ***deferred to*** *his parents and to his eldest sister*: **yield**, submit, give way, give in, surrender, accede, bow, capitulate, acquiesce, knuckle under; comply with, agree with, respect, honour, truckle.
▷ANTONYMS stand up to, disobey.

deference **noun** *his writings show excessive deference to the gentry*: **respect**, respectfulness, regard, esteem; consideration, attentiveness, attention, thoughtfulness; courteousness, courtesy, politeness, civility, dutifulness, reverence, veneration, awe, homage; **submissiveness**, submission, obedience, yielding, surrender, accession, capitulation, acquiescence,

complaisance, obeisance.
▷**ANTONYMS** disrespect.

deferential adjective *a deferential batman*: **obsequious**, humble, respectful, considerate, attentive, thoughtful; courteous, polite, civil, dutiful, reverent, reverential, awed; obedient, submissive, subservient, fawning, toadying, yielding, acquiescent, complaisant, compliant, pliant, tractable, biddable, manageable, docile, slavish; dated mannerly; rare regardful, obeisant.
▷**ANTONYMS** arrogant; impolite.

Word toolkit **deferential**

See **humble**.

deferment noun *they allowed deferment of the repayments*: **postponement**, deferral, suspension, putting off/back, adjournment, delay, shelving, rescheduling, interruption, arrest, pause; respite, stay, moratorium, reprieve, grace; N. Amer. tabling; N. Amer. Law continuation; rare put-off.

defiance noun *he wasn't used to such outspoken defiance*: **resistance**, opposition, confrontation; non-compliance, disobedience, insubordination, dissent, recalcitrance, subversion, subversiveness; rebelliousness, mutinousness, provocation, daring, boldness, temerity, audacity, bravado, aggression; contempt, disregard, scorn, insolence, truculence, contumacy.
▷**ANTONYMS** submission, obedience.

defiant adjective *he is defiant in the face of critics*: **intransigent**, resistant, obstinate, uncooperative, non-compliant, recalcitrant, confrontational, challenging; aggressive, belligerent, pugnacious, bellicose, combative, ready for a fight, antagonistic, hostile; obstreperous, truculent, dissenting, argumentative, quarrelsome, contentious, disobedient, insubordinate, subversive, rebellious, mutinous; informal feisty, spoiling for a fight; Brit. informal stroppy, bolshie; N. Amer. informal scrappy; archaic or Law contumacious.
▷**ANTONYMS** apologetic; cooperative.

Word toolkit **defiant**

See **unruly**.

deficiency noun **1** *she has a vitamin deficiency in her diet*: **insufficiency**, lack, shortage, want, dearth, inadequacy, deficit, shortfall; scarcity, scarceness, scantiness, paucity, absence, undersupply, sparseness, deprivation, meagreness, shortness; rare exiguity, exiguousness.
▷**ANTONYMS** surplus.
2 *the team's big deficiency was in the front five*: **defect**, fault, flaw, imperfection, weakness, weak spot/point, inadequacy, shortcoming, limitation, failing.
▷**ANTONYMS** strength.

deficient adjective **1** *his diet is* ***deficient in*** *vitamin A*: **lacking**, wanting, defective, inadequate, insufficient, limited, poor, scant; short of/on, low on, with an insufficiency of, with too little/few ...; informal strapped for, pushed for.
▷**ANTONYMS** excessive.
2 *on all levels, this is deficient leadership*: **defective**, faulty, flawed, inadequate, imperfect, impaired, shoddy, scrappy, sketchy, weak, inferior, unsound, substandard, second-rate, poor, shabby, incomplete, leaving much to be desired; informal duff.
▷**ANTONYMS** perfect.

deficit noun *there was a large, continuing deficit in the federal budget*: **shortfall**, deficiency, shortage, undersupply, slippage; indebtedness, debt, arrears; minus amount, negative amount, loss.
▷**ANTONYMS** surplus, profit.

defile verb **1** *she was afraid that her very capacity for love had been defiled*: **spoil**, sully, mar, impair, debase, degrade; pollute, poison, corrupt, taint, tarnish, infect; foul, befoul, dirty, soil, stain; destroy, ruin.
▷**ANTONYMS** purify.
2 *the sacred bones had been defiled*: **desecrate**, profane, violate, treat sacrilegiously; make impure, contaminate, pollute, debase, degrade, dishonour, vitiate.
▷**ANTONYMS** sanctify.

defilement noun **1** *I cannot accept this town's continued defilement*: **degradation**, debasement, spoiling, sullying, impairment; pollution, poisoning, corruption, tainting, tarnishing.
▷**ANTONYMS** purification.
2 *any defilement disqualified priests from contact with holy things*: **desecration**, profanation, profanity, violation, sacrilege; impurity, contamination, pollution, debasement, degradation, dishonour, vitiation.
▷**ANTONYMS** sanctification.

definable adjective *Aunt Emily wasn't ill, at least she had no definable complaint*: **determinable**, ascertainable, known, definite, clear-cut, precise, exact, specific.
▷**ANTONYMS** indefinable.

define verb **1** *the dictionary defines it as a type of pasture*: **explain**, expound, interpret, elucidate, explicate, describe, clarify; give the meaning of, state precisely, spell out, put into words, express in words.
2 *the difficulty lay in defining the upper and lower limits of the middle class*: **determine**, establish, fix, specify, designate, decide, stipulate, settle, set out, mark out, mark off; **demarcate**, bound, delimit, delineate, circumscribe, set the boundaries/limits of.
3 *he could see the farm buildings defined against the fields beyond*: **outline**, delineate, silhouette; trace, pencil.

definite adjective **1** *I need a definite answer*: **explicit**, specific, express, precise, exact, defined, well defined, clear-cut; determined, fixed, established, confirmed, direct; concrete, hard, plain, outright.
▷**ANTONYMS** vague, indefinite.
2 *there is definite evidence of decreasing per capita incomes*: **certain**, sure, positive, absolute, conclusive, decisive, firm, concrete, final, unambiguous, unequivocal, unquestionable, unarguable, clear, manifest, obvious, patent, unmistakable, proven; black and white, hard and fast, as plain as the nose on your face, as plain as daylight; guaranteed, settled, decided, assured; informal cut and dried.
▷**ANTONYMS** uncertain, ambiguous.
3 *she had a definite dislike for Robert's wife*: **unmistakable**, irrefutable, unequivocal, unambiguous, certain, undisputed, decided, marked, distinct, unquestioned, not in question, not in doubt.
▷**ANTONYMS** vague, slight.
4 *some organizations occupy a definite geographical area*: **fixed**, marked, demarcated, delimited, stipulated, particular, circumscribed.
▷**ANTONYMS** indeterminate.

Choose the right word **definite, sure, certain, positive, convinced**

See **sure**.

definitely adverb *it was definitely a case of exploiting child labour*: **certainly**, surely, for sure, unquestionably, without/beyond doubt, without/beyond question, beyond any doubt, undoubtedly, indubitably, assuredly, positively, absolutely; undeniably, irrefutably, incontrovertibly, incontestably, unmistakably; plainly, clearly, obviously, patently, palpably, transparently, categorically, decidedly, unequivocally; easily, far and away, by a mile, without fail, there are no two ways about it, there's no denying it, needless to say; informal as sure as eggs is eggs.
▷**ANTONYMS** possibly.

definition noun **1** *there is no agreed definition of 'intelligence'*: **meaning**, denotation, sense; **interpretation**, explanation, elucidation, explication, description, clarification, exposition, expounding, illustration; deciphering, decoding; statement/outline of meaning.
2 *the definition of the picture can be aided by using computer graphics*: **clarity**, clearness, visibility, precision, sharpness, crispness, acuteness, distinctness; resolution, focus, contrast.
▷**ANTONYMS** blurriness, fuzziness.

definitive adjective **1** *a definitive decision*: **conclusive**, final, ultimate; **decisive**, unconditional, unqualified, absolute, categorical, positive, definite.
▷**ANTONYMS** provisional.
2 *the definitive guide to the movies*: **authoritative**, exhaustive, most reliable, most complete, most perfect, most scholarly, best, finest, consummate; classic, standard, recognized, accepted, approved, official, established.

deflate verb **1** *he deflated one of the tyres*: **let down**, empty the air out of, collapse, flatten, void; puncture.
▷**ANTONYMS** inflate; blow up.
2 *the balloon deflated*: **go down**, collapse, shrink, contract, flatten.
▷**ANTONYMS** inflate; expand.
3 *the news had deflated the old man*: **subdue**, humble, cow, humiliate, mortify, chasten, chagrin, dispirit, dismay, discourage, dishearten; squash, crush, flatten, bring down, bring low, take down a peg or two, take the wind out of someone's sails; informal cut down to size, knock the stuffing out of, put down.
▷**ANTONYMS** aggrandize.
4 *the budget deflated the economy*: **reduce**, slow down, make less active, diminish, lessen, lower; devalue, depreciate, depress.
▷**ANTONYMS** inflate.

deflect verb **1** *the bullet was deflected sideways | she was anxious to deflect attention from herself*: **turn aside/away**, divert, avert, sidetrack; distract, draw away; block, parry, stop, fend off, stave off.
2 *the ball deflected off the centre half*: **bounce**, glance, ricochet; turn aside/away, turn, alter course, change course/direction, diverge, deviate; veer, swerve, slew, drift, bend, swing, twist, curve.

deflection noun *the deflection of a missile away from its target*: **turning aside/away**, turning, diversion, drawing away; deviation, divergence, declination, aberration, turn, veer, swerve, slew, drift, straying, bend, swing, twist, curve; rare divarication, divagation.

deform verb *broad shoes that will not cramp or deform the toes*: **make misshapen**, distort the shape of, disfigure, bend out of shape, misshape, contort, buckle, twist, warp, damage, impair, maim, injure.

deformation noun *a deformation of the visual cortex*: **distortion**, malformation, misshaping, contortion, buckling, twisting, warping, bending, wrenching, misshaping; twist, warp, bend, buckle, curve.

deformed adjective *a deformed skeleton*: **misshapen**, distorted, malformed, contorted, out of shape; twisted, crooked, curved, warped, buckled, gnarled; crippled, maimed, injured, damaged, humpbacked, hunchbacked, disfigured; ugly, unsightly, grotesque, monstrous; marred, mutilated, mangled.

deformity noun *the frame can be used to correct bone deformities*: **malformation**, misshapenness, disproportion, distortion, crookedness; imperfection, abnormality, irregularity; ugliness, unsightliness, defacement, disfigurement; defect, flaw, blemish.

defraud verb *the men were alleged to have defrauded thousands of investors*: **swindle**, cheat, rob, deceive, dupe, hoodwink, double-cross, fool, trick; informal con, bamboozle, do, sting, diddle, fiddle, swizzle, rip off, shaft, bilk, rook, take for a ride, pull a fast one on, pull the wool over someone's eyes, put one over on, sell a pup to, take to the cleaners, gyp, gull, finagle, milk; N. Amer. informal sucker, snooker, stiff, euchre, bunco, hornswoggle; Austral. informal pull a swifty on; archaic cozen, sharp; rare mulct, do someone in the eye.

defray verb *the rest of the money was used to* ***defray the costs of*** *restoring the house*: **pay (for)**, cover, meet, square, settle, clear, discharge, liquidate; foot the bill for; N. Amer. informal pick up the tab/check for.

deft adjective *a deft piece of footwork | his deft handling of the situation*: **skilful**, adept, adroit, dexterous, agile, nimble, neat, nimble-fingered, handy, able, capable, skilled, proficient, accomplished, expert, experienced, practised, polished, efficient, slick, professional, masterful, masterly, impressive, finely judged, delicate; clever, shrewd, astute, canny, sharp, artful; informal nifty, nippy, mean, wicked, ace, wizard, crack; rare habile.
▷ANTONYMS clumsy, awkward, inept.

defunct adjective **1** *the now defunct local paper mill*: **disused**, no longer in use, unused, inoperative, non-functioning, unusable, obsolete; no longer in existence, discontinued; extinct, fossilized.
▷ANTONYMS working, extant.
2 *his defunct parents*: **dead**, deceased, expired, departed, gone; late; rare demised.
▷ANTONYMS alive, living.

defuse verb **1** *explosives specialists tried to defuse the grenade*: **deactivate**, disarm, disable, make safe.
▷ANTONYMS activate.
2 *a scheme that teaches officers how to defuse potentially explosive situations*: **reduce**, lessen, diminish, lighten, relieve, ease, alleviate, allay, moderate, mitigate, take the edge off; clear the air.
▷ANTONYMS heighten, intensify.

> *Easily confused words* **defuse or diffuse?**
>
> See **diffuse**.

defy verb **1** *61 rebel MPs defied the prime minister and voted against the bill | he had defied European and French laws*: **disobey**, refuse to obey, go against, rebel against, flout, fly in the face of, thumb one's nose at, disregard, ignore, set one's face against, kick against; break, violate, contravene, breach, infringe; informal cock a snook at; archaic set at naught.
▷ANTONYMS obey.
2 *about 150 settlers defied Sant'Anna's army of 5,000*: **resist**, withstand, take a stand against, hold out against, stand up to, confront, face, meet head-on, take on, square up to, beard, brave, outface.
▷ANTONYMS surrender.
3 *the logic of this defied her | his actions defy belief*: **elude**, escape, defeat; foil, frustrate, thwart, baffle.
4 *he glowered at her, defying her to mock him*: **challenge**, dare; throw down the gauntlet.

degeneracy noun *an attack on the sexual degeneracy and intellectual deterioration of the time*: **corruption**, corruptness, decadence, moral decay, dissipation, dissoluteness, dissolution, profligacy, depravity, perversion, pervertedness, vice, immorality, lack of morals, lack of principles, baseness, turpitude, wickedness, evil, sin, sinfulness, ungodliness; debauchery, lewdness, lechery, lecherousness, lasciviousness, licentiousness, libidinousness, promiscuity, wantonness, libertinism, intemperance.
▷ANTONYMS morality, purity.

degenerate adjective **1** *a degenerate form of High Renaissance classicism*: **debased**, degraded, corrupt, corrupted, vitiated, bastard, impure.
▷ANTONYMS pure.
2 *her degenerate brother*: **corrupt**, decadent, dissolute, dissipated, debauched, rakish, reprobate, profligate, depraved, perverted, despicable, base, vice-ridden, wicked, sinful, ungodly; immoral, unprincipled, amoral, dishonourable, disreputable, unsavoury, sordid, low, mean, ignoble; lewd, lecherous, lascivious, licentious, libidinous, loose, promiscuous, wanton, libertine, intemperate; informal pervy.
▷ANTONYMS moral.
▸ **noun** *a group of drunkards and degenerates*: **reprobate**, debauchee, rake, profligate, libertine, roué, loose-liver; pervert, deviant, deviate; informal perv; rare retrograde, dissolute.
▸ **verb 1** *certain areas of the city have degenerated into slums | their quality of life had degenerated*: **deteriorate**, decline, sink, slip, slide, worsen, get/grow worse, take a turn for the worse, lapse, fail, fall off, slump, go downhill, regress, retrogress; decay, rot, go to rack and ruin; informal go to pot, go to the dogs, hit the skids, go down the tubes, go down the toilet; Austral./NZ informal go to the pack; rare retrograde, devolve.
▷ANTONYMS improve.
2 *the muscles started to degenerate*: **waste away**, waste, atrophy, weaken, become debilitated.

degeneration noun *the social degeneration of the area*: **deterioration**, decline, decay, debasement, degradation, slide, sinking, descent, drop, regression, retrogression, lapse; atrophy; rare devolution.
▷ANTONYMS improvement.

degradation noun **1** *such poverty brings with it degradation, starvation, and the loss of human life*: **humiliation**, shame, loss of dignity, loss of self-respect, loss of pride, abasement, mortification, indignity, ignominy.
2 *the degradation of women*: **demeaning**, debasement, cheapening, devaluing, discrediting, dishonouring.
3 *the degradation of the tissues in rheumatoid arthritis*: **deterioration**, degeneration, atrophy, decay, wasting away; breakdown.

degrade verb **1** *many supposedly erotic pictures simply degrade women | British prisons should not degrade prisoners*: **demean**, debase, cheapen, devalue, prostitute, lower the status of, reduce, shame, humiliate, bring shame to, humble, mortify, abase, disgrace, dishonour; desensitize, dehumanize, brutalize.
▷ANTONYMS dignify, ennoble.
2 *the product, called a biopolymer, will not degrade until attacked by micro-organisms*: **break down**, deteriorate, degenerate, decay, atrophy.

degraded adjective **1** *you made me feel so degraded*: **humiliated**, demeaned, debased, cheapened, cheap, ashamed, abased; used.
▷ANTONYMS proud, dignified.
2 *he had revealed more of his degraded sensibilities than he realized*: **degenerate**, corrupt, corrupted, depraved, perverted, decadent, dissolute, dissipated, debauched, immoral, base, sordid.
▷ANTONYMS moral, pure.

degrading adjective *claiming benefit can be a degrading experience*: **humiliating**, demeaning, shaming, shameful, bringing shame, mortifying, abject, lowering, ignominious, undignified, inglorious, discrediting, wretched; menial; informal infra dig.
▷ANTONYMS ennobling.

degree noun **1** *those who have achieved a considerable degree of economic stability | the high degree of risk involved*: **level**, stage, point, rung, standard, grade, gradation, mark; amount, extent, measure, magnitude, intensity, strength; proportion, ratio.
2 archaic *persons of unequal degree*: **social class**, social status, rank, standing/position in society; dated station; archaic estate, condition.
□ **by degrees** *rivalries and prejudice were by degrees fading out*: **gradually**, little by little, bit by bit, inch by inch, by stages, step by step, day by day, slowly, slowly but surely; piecemeal; rare inchmeal, gradatim.
▷ANTONYMS suddenly, all at once.
□ **to a degree** *to a degree, it is possible to educate oneself*: **to some extent**, to a certain extent, up to a point, to a limited extent.

dehydrate verb **1** *alcohol and coffee dehydrate the skin*: **dry**, dry up, dry out, desiccate, make dry, dehumidify, remove the moisture from; parch, sear; technical effloresce; rare exsiccate.
▷ANTONYMS hydrate.
2 *amphibians' skins must be kept moist or they will dehydrate and die*: **dry up**, dry out, lose water, become dry; become thirsty.

deify verb **1** *she was deified by the early Romans as a fertility goddess*: **worship**, revere, venerate, reverence, hold sacred, pay homage to, extol, exalt, adore; immortalize; rare divinize.
2 *he was deified by his colleagues and the press*: **idolize**, apotheosize, lionize, hero-worship; idealize, glorify, aggrandize; informal put on a pedestal.
▷ANTONYMS demonize.

deign verb *I'm not going to hang around here waiting until you deign to come back to me*: **condescend**, stoop, lower oneself, descend, think fit, see fit, deem it worthy of oneself, consent, vouchsafe; demean oneself, humble oneself; informal come down from one's high horse.

deity noun **god**, **goddess**, divine being, celestial being, supreme being, divinity, immortal; creator, demiurge; godhead; daemon, numen; Hinduism avatar.

dejected adjective *he looked so dejected that Alice began to have second thoughts*: **downcast**, downhearted, despondent, disconsolate, dispirited, crestfallen, cast down, depressed, disappointed, disheartened, discouraged, demoralized, crushed, desolate, heartbroken, broken-hearted, heavy-hearted, low-spirited, in the doldrums, sad, unhappy, doleful, melancholy, miserable,

woebegone, forlorn, long-faced, fed up, wretched, glum, gloomy, dismal; shamefaced, hangdog; informal blue, choked, down, down in the mouth, down in the dumps; Brit. informal brassed off, cheesed off, looking as if one had lost a pound and found a penny; literary dolorous; archaic chap-fallen.
▷ANTONYMS cheerful, happy.

dejection noun *he wandered around in a state of utter dejection*: **despondency**, depression, downheartedness, dispiritedness, disconsolateness, disappointment, discouragement, desolation, despair, heavy-heartedness, unhappiness, sadness, sorrowfulness, sorrow, dolefulness, melancholy, misery, forlornness, wretchedness, glumness, gloom, gloominess, low spirits; informal the blues, the dumps; rare mopery.
▷ANTONYMS happiness.

de jure adverb & adjective **by right**, rightfully, legally, according to the law; rightful, legal.
▷ANTONYMS de facto.

delay verb **1** *a few guests were delayed by rush-hour traffic*: **detain**, hold up, make late, retard, keep (back), slow up, slow down, set back, bog down; hinder, hamper, impede, obstruct.
2 *time being of the essence, they delayed no longer*: **linger**, dally, take one's time, drag one's feet, be slow, hold back, lag/fall behind, dawdle, loiter, not keep pace, waste time; procrastinate, stall, play for time, buy time, hang fire, mark time, temporize, hesitate, dither, shilly-shally; stonewall, filibuster; informal dilly-dally, let the grass grow under one's feet; archaic or literary tarry.
▷ANTONYMS hurry.
3 *he may decide to delay the next cut in interest rates*: **postpone**, put off, defer, hold over, shelve, suspend, stay, hold in abeyance, pigeonhole; reschedule, adjourn; N. Amer. put over, table, lay on the table; N. Amer. Law continue; informal put on ice, put on the back burner, put in cold storage; rare remit, respite.
▷ANTONYMS advance, bring forward.
▸ noun **1** *drivers heading for the capital are certain to face lengthy delays | the delay between the exchange of contracts and completion*: **hold-up**, wait, waiting period, detainment; hindrance, impediment, obstruction, setback; interval, gap, interlude.
2 *the delay of his trial*: **postponement**, deferral, deferment, putting off, stay, respite; rescheduling, adjournment; N. Amer. Law continuation; rare put-off.
3 *I set off without delay*: **lingering**, dallying, dawdling, loitering; **procrastination**, stalling, hesitation, dithering, shilly-shallying; informal dilly-dallying; archaic or literary tarrying; rare cunctation.

delectable adjective **1** *a delectable meal*: **delicious**, mouth-watering, appetizing, flavoursome, flavourful, toothsome, inviting, very enjoyable, very palatable; succulent, luscious, rich, sweet; tasty, savoury, piquant; informal scrumptious, delish, scrummy, yummy, yum-yum; Brit. informal moreish; N. Amer. informal finger-licking, nummy; literary ambrosial; rare ambrosian, nectareous, nectarean, flavorous, sapid.
▷ANTONYMS inedible, unpalatable.
2 *the delectable Ms Davis*: **delightful**, lovely, adorable, captivating, charming, enchanting, winning, engaging, appealing, beguiling; **beautiful**, ravishing, gorgeous, stunning, pretty, extremely attractive, alluring, enticing, sexy, seductive, desirable, luscious; Scottish & N. English bonny; informal divine, heavenly, dreamy, sensational, knockout, drop-dead; Brit. informal tasty; N. Amer. informal babelicious, bodacious, bootylicious; archaic fair, comely; rare pulchritudinous.
▷ANTONYMS ugly, unattractive.

delectation noun *they had all manner of goodies for our delectation*: **enjoyment**, gratification, delight, pleasure, happiness, satisfaction, relish; entertainment, amusement, diversion; titillation.

delegate noun *delegates from the UN | trade union delegates*: **representative**, envoy, emissary, commissioner, agent, deputy, commissary; spokesperson, spokesman, spokeswoman; ambassador, plenipotentiary; messenger, go-between, proxy; Scottish depute; Roman Catholic Church nuncio; archaic legate.
▸ verb **1** *she must learn to delegate routine tasks to others*: **assign**, **entrust**, give, pass on, hand on/over, turn over, consign, devolve, depute, transfer.
2 *members of the Council delegated to negotiate with the Baltic States*: **authorize**, commission, depute, appoint, nominate, name, mandate, empower, charge, choose, select, designate, elect; Military detail.

delegation noun **1** *a delegation from the South African government*: **deputation**, delegacy, legation, (diplomatic) mission, commission; delegates, representatives, envoys, emissaries, deputies; contingent, group, party, body.
2 *the delegation of tasks to others*: **assignment**, entrusting, giving, committal, devolution, deputation, transference.

delete verb *the offending paragraph was deleted from the letter*: **remove**, cut out, take out, edit out, expunge, excise, eradicate, cancel; **cross out**, strike out, put a line through, blue-pencil, ink out, score out, scratch out, obliterate, white out; rub out, erase, efface, wipe out, blot out; Computing, informal kill; Printing dele; Brit. trademark Tippex out.
▷ANTONYMS add, insert.

deleterious adjective *these policies are having a deleterious effect on British industry*: **harmful**, damaging, detrimental, injurious, inimical, hurtful, bad, adverse, disadvantageous, unfavourable, unfortunate, undesirable; destructive, pernicious, ruinous.
▷ANTONYMS beneficial, advantageous.

deliberate adjective **1** *a deliberate attempt to provoke conflict*: **intentional**, calculated, conscious, done on purpose, intended, planned, meant, considered, studied, knowing, wilful, wanton, purposeful, purposive, premeditated, pre-planned, thought out in advance, prearranged, preconceived, predetermined; aforethought; voluntary, volitional; Law, dated prepense.
▷ANTONYMS accidental, unintentional.
2 *she took a couple of small, deliberate steps towards him*: **careful**, cautious, unhurried, measured, regular, even, steady; leisurely; laborious, ponderous.
▷ANTONYMS hasty.
3 *a careful and deliberate worker*: **methodical**, systematic, careful, painstaking, meticulous, thorough.
▷ANTONYMS careless.
▸ verb *there was a long painful silence while she* **deliberated on** *his words | they sat and deliberated what to do with him*: **think about**, think over, ponder, consider, contemplate, reflect on, muse on, meditate on, ruminate on, mull over, chew over, turn over in one's mind, give thought to, cogitate about; brood over, dwell on; put on one's thinking cap, be in a brown study; discuss, debate, weigh up; N. Amer. think on; archaic pore on; rare excogitate, cerebrate.

deliberately adverb **1** *he deliberately tried to hurt me*: **intentionally**, on purpose, purposely, by design, knowingly, wittingly, consciously, purposefully; premeditatedly, calculatedly, in cold blood, wilfully, wantonly; with malice aforethought.
▷ANTONYMS by mistake, accidentally.
2 *he rose and walked deliberately down the aisle*: **carefully**, unhurriedly, steadily, evenly, measuredly; cautiously, slowly, laboriously, ponderously.
▷ANTONYMS hastily.

deliberation noun **1** *after much deliberation, I decided to accept*: **thought**, thinking, consideration, reflection, contemplation, cogitation, pondering, weighing up, musing, meditation, rumination, brooding; discussion, debate, consultation, conferring; rare excogitation, cerebration.
2 *he replaced the glass on the table with deliberation*: **care**, carefulness, lack of haste, steadiness; caution, slowness, laboriousness, ponderousness.
▷ANTONYMS haste.

delicacy noun **1** *miniature pearls of exquisite delicacy | the fabric's delicacy*: **fineness**, exquisiteness, delicateness, intricacy, daintiness, airiness, elegance, gracefulness, grace; flimsiness, gauziness, floatiness, silkiness.
▷ANTONYMS crudeness, coarseness.
2 *the children's delicacy was apparently inherited from their mother*: **sickliness**, poor/ill health, valetudinarianism, frailty, frailness, fragility, feebleness, weakness, debility; infirmity.
▷ANTONYMS robustness.
3 *the delicacy of the situation*: **difficulty**, trickiness; **sensitivity**, sensitiveness, ticklishness, awkwardness, touchiness, controversiality.
4 *I have to treat this matter with the utmost delicacy*: **care**, sensitivity, tact, discretion, diplomacy, finesse, subtlety, consideration, considerateness, sensibility.
▷ANTONYMS clumsiness, ineptness, insensitivity.
5 *his delicacy of touch*: **deftness**, dexterousness, skill, skilfulness, adeptness, adroitness, expertise.
▷ANTONYMS clumsiness, ineptness.
6 *the delicacy of the mechanism*: **sensitivity**, precision, accuracy, exactness.
7 *the crabs are an Australian delicacy*: **choice food**, gourmet food, dainty, treat, luxury, titbit, bonne bouche; speciality; N. Amer. tidbit; archaic cate.

delicate adjective **1** *delicate embroidery | delicate fabrics*: **fine**, exquisite, intricate, dainty, airy, elegant, graceful; **flimsy**, gauzy, filmy, floaty, gossamer, diaphanous, chiffony, silky, wispy, thin, insubstantial, papery.
▷ANTONYMS crude; coarse.
2 *a delicate shade of blue*: **subtle**, soft, subdued, muted; **pastel**, pale, light.
▷ANTONYMS bold, vibrant; lurid.
3 *delicate bone-china cups*: **fragile**, breakable, easily broken/damaged, frail, frangible; eggshell.
▷ANTONYMS strong, durable.
4 *his wife is delicate*: **sickly**, in poor health, unhealthy, valetudinarian, frail, feeble, weak, weakly, debilitated; unwell, infirm, ailing, poorly; N. English informal nesh.
▷ANTONYMS healthy, strong, robust.
5 *a delicate issue*: **difficult**, tricky, sensitive, ticklish, awkward, problematic, problematical, touchy, prickly, controversial, emotive, embarrassing; informal sticky, dicey.
▷ANTONYMS uncontroversial.
6 *the matter required delicate handling*: **careful**, considerate, sensitive; **tactful**, diplomatic, discreet, gentle, kid-glove, softly-softly.
▷ANTONYMS inept, clumsy, insensitive.
7 *his delicate ball-playing skills*: **deft**, dexterous, skilled, skilful, expert,

finely judged, adept, adroit, neat, slick; informal nifty.
▷ANTONYMS clumsy, inept.
8 *Faustina's delicate palate*: **discriminating**, discerning; **fastidious**, fussy, finicky, dainty, hard to please; informal picky, choosy, pernickety, faddy, faddish.
9 *a delicate mechanism*: **sensitive**, precision, precise, accurate, exact.

delicious adjective 1 *a delicious meal*: **mouth-watering**, appetizing, tasty, flavoursome, flavourful, delectable, toothsome, inviting, very enjoyable, very palatable; succulent, luscious, rich, sweet; savoury, piquant; informal scrumptious, delish, scrummy, yummy, yum-yum; Brit. informal moreish; N. Amer. informal finger-licking, nummy; literary ambrosial; rare ambrosian, nectareous, nectarean, flavorous, sapid.
▷ANTONYMS inedible, unpalatable.
2 *a delicious languor was stealing over her*: **delightful**, exquisite, delectable, lovely, pleasurable, extremely pleasant/enjoyable; informal glorious, heavenly, divine.
▷ANTONYMS unpleasant, horrible.

d

delight verb 1 *her lack of reserve delighted him*: **please greatly**, charm, enchant, captivate, entrance, bewitch, thrill, excite, take someone's breath away; gladden, gratify, appeal to, do someone's heart good, entertain, amuse, divert; informal send, tickle, give someone a buzz, give someone a kick, tickle pink, bowl over.
▷ANTONYMS dismay, displease; disgust.
2 *Fabia* ***delighted in*** *his touch*: **take great pleasure**, find great pleasure, glory, revel, luxuriate, wallow; adore, love, relish, savour, enjoy greatly, lap up; informal get a kick out of, have a thing about, get a buzz out of, get a thrill out of, get a charge out of, get off on, dig; N. Amer. informal get a bang out of.
▷ANTONYMS dislike, loathe.
▶noun *she squealed with delight*: **pleasure**, happiness, joy, joyfulness, glee, gladness, gratification, relish, excitement, amusement; bliss, rapture, ecstasy, elation, euphoria; transports of delight; humorous delectation; rare jouissance.
▷ANTONYMS displeasure, pain.

delighted adjective *a delighted smile | we're delighted to have him back*: **very pleased**, glad, happy, joyful, thrilled, overjoyed, ecstatic, euphoric, elated, blissful, enraptured, on cloud nine/seven, walking on air, in seventh heaven, in transports of delight, jumping for joy, beside oneself with happiness, excited; enchanted, charmed, entertained, gratified, amused, diverted, like a child with a new toy; gleeful, triumphant, cock-a-hoop; French enchanté; informal over the moon, tickled pink, like a dog with two tails, as pleased as Punch, on top of the world, on a high, as happy as Larry, blissed out, sent; Brit. informal chuffed; N. English informal made up; N. Amer. informal as happy as a clam; Austral. informal wrapped.
▷ANTONYMS dismayed, disappointed.

delightful adjective 1 *a delightful evening*: **very pleasant**, lovely, greatly to one's liking, very agreeable, very pleasurable; enjoyable, congenial, amusing, entertaining, diverting, gratifying, satisfying; marvellous, wonderful, magnificent, splendid, magical, exciting, thrilling, sublime; informal great, super, fantastic, fabulous, fab, terrific, heavenly, divine, glorious, grand, magic, out of this world, cool; Brit. informal brilliant, brill, smashing; N. Amer. informal peachy, neat, ducky; Austral./NZ informal beaut, bonzer; Brit. informal, dated capital, wizard, corking, spiffing, ripping, cracking, top-hole, topping, champion, beezer; N. Amer. informal, dated swell; rare frabjous.
▷ANTONYMS unpleasant, disagreeable.
2 *the delightful Sally Drayton*: **charming**, enchanting, captivating, bewitching, entrancing, engaging, appealing, winning, fetching, sweet, endearing, cute; **lovely**, adorable, delectable, delicious, gorgeous, ravishing, beautiful, pretty, very attractive; Scottish & N. English bonny, couthy; informal dreamy, divine; Brit. informal tasty.
▷ANTONYMS unattractive, unappealing.

delimit verb *their responsibilities will be more strictly delimited*: **determine**, establish, set, fix, mark (out/off), demarcate, bound, define, delineate.

delineate verb 1 *the initial aims of the study as delineated by the deputy head*: **describe**, set forth, set out, present, outline, depict, portray, represent, characterize; map out, chart; define, detail, specify, identify, particularize; literary limn.
2 *a section on the map delineated in red marker pen*: **outline**, trace, draw the lines of, draw, sketch, block in, mark (out/off), delimit, mark the boundaries/limits of.

delineation noun *the accurate delineation of social problems in the area*: **portrayal**, description, presentation, depiction, representation, picture, portrait, account.

delinquency noun 1 *the social causes of teenage delinquency*: **crime**, wrongdoing, criminality, lawbreaking, lawlessness, misconduct, misbehaviour; misdemeanours, offences, misdeeds.
2 formal *he relayed this in such a manner as to imply grave delinquency on the host's part*: **negligence**, dereliction of duty, remissness, neglectfulness, irresponsibility.

delinquent adjective 1 *delinquent teenagers*: **lawless**, lawbreaking, criminal, offending; errant, badly behaved, troublesome, difficult, unmanageable, unruly, disobedient, uncontrollable, out of control.
▷ANTONYMS well behaved; conformist.
2 formal *delinquent parents need to face tougher penalties*: **negligent**, neglectful, remiss, careless of one's duty, irresponsible, lax, slack; N. Amer. derelict; rare disregardful, inadvertent, oscitant.
▷ANTONYMS dutiful.
▶noun *teenage delinquents*: **offender**, wrongdoer, malefactor, lawbreaker, culprit, criminal; hooligan, vandal, ruffian, hoodlum, lout; juvenile delinquent, young offender; informal juvie, tearaway; Brit. informal yob, yobbo, chav, hoodie; Austral./NZ informal hoon; archaic miscreant.

delirious adjective 1 *for much of the time she was delirious, but there were lucid intervals*: **incoherent**, raving, babbling, irrational, hysterical, wild, feverish, frenzied; **deranged**, demented, unhinged, mad, insane, crazed, out of one's mind.
▷ANTONYMS lucid, coherent.
2 *there was a great roar from the delirious crowd*: **ecstatic**, euphoric, elated, thrilled, overjoyed, beside oneself, walking on air, on cloud nine/seven, in seventh heaven, jumping for joy, in transports of delight, carried away, transported, rapturous, in raptures, exultant, jubilant, in a frenzy of delight, hysterical, wild with excitement, frenzied; informal blissed out, over the moon, on a high; N. Amer. informal wigged out; rare corybantic.
▷ANTONYMS disappointed, depressed.

delirium noun 1 *before she died she had fits of delirium*: **derangement**, dementia, dementedness, temporary madness/insanity; **incoherence**, raving, irrationality, hysteria, wildness, feverishness, frenzy, hallucination; rare calenture.
▷ANTONYMS lucidity, coherence.
2 *in the delirium of desire, she muttered his name over and over*: **ecstasy**, rapture, transports, wild emotion, passion, wildness, excitement, frenzy, feverishness, fever; euphoria, elation.

deliver verb 1 *the parcel was delivered to his house yesterday*: **bring**, take, take round, convey, carry, transport, distribute, drop-ship; send, dispatch, remit.
▷ANTONYMS collect.
2 *the money should have been* ***delivered up*** *to the official receiver*: **hand over**, turn over, transfer, make over, sign over; surrender, give up, yield, relinquish, cede, render up; consign, commit, entrust, trust, commend.
3 *he was delivered from his enemies*: **save**, rescue, set free, free, liberate, release, set at liberty, set loose, extricate, discharge, emancipate, redeem, ransom; literary disenthral; historical manumit.
4 *the President delivered a six-minute radio address | the court was due to deliver its verdict*: **utter**, give, make, read, recite, broadcast, give voice to, voice, speak, declaim; **pronounce**, announce, declare, proclaim, hand down, bring in, return, render, set forth.
5 *Paul delivered a two-handed blow to the back of his head*: **administer**, deal, inflict, give, direct, aim; informal land.
6 *as he delivered the first ball of his third over, he stumbled*: **bowl**, pitch, hurl, throw, cast, launch, lob; discharge, fire off; Brit. Sport flight.
7 *the trip delivered everything she had wanted*: **provide**, supply, furnish.
8 *we have taken significant action to* ***deliver on*** *our commitments*: **fulfil**, live up to, carry out, carry through, implement, make good; achieve; informal come up with, deliver the goods, come across.
9 *she returned to Madras to deliver her child*: **give birth to**, bear, be delivered of, have, bring into the world, bring forth; N. Amer. birth; informal drop; archaic be brought to bed of.

deliverance noun 1 *their deliverance from prison*: **liberation**, release, freeing, rescue, delivery, discharge, ransom, emancipation; salvation, redemption; historical manumission.
2 *the tone he adopted for such deliverances*: **utterance**, statement, announcement, pronouncement, declaration, proclamation; lecture, sermon, speech, oration, disquisition, peroration.

delivery noun 1 *the delivery of the goods*: **conveyance**, carriage, transportation, transporting, transport, distribution; dispatch, remittance; freightage, haulage, portage, shipment.
▷ANTONYMS collection.
2 *we are receiving several deliveries a day*: **consignment**, load, batch; shipment, container load, boatload, shipload, lorryload, truckload.
3 *practically all deliveries take place in hospital*: **birth**, childbirth; technical parturition; archaic confinement, accouchement.
4 *he reached 59 runs off only 42 deliveries*: **ball bowled**, throw, bowl, lob, pitch.
5 *her delivery was stilted*: **manner of speaking**, speech, pronunciation, enunciation, articulation, intonation, elocution; utterance, presentation, recitation, recital, performance, execution; French façon de parler.

delude verb *you're lying—why do you persist in trying to delude me?* **mislead**, deceive, fool, take in, trick, dupe, hoodwink, double-cross, gull, beguile, lead on; cheat, defraud, swindle; informal con, bamboozle, pull the wool over someone's eyes, pull a fast one on, lead up the garden path, take for a ride, put one over on; N. Amer. informal sucker, snooker, hornswoggle; Austral. informal pull a swifty on; literary cozen, illude.

deluge noun 1 *many homes were swept away by the deluge*: **flood**, flash flood, torrent; Brit. spate.

2 *yesterday's deluge had turned the pitch into a muddy swamp*: **downpour**, torrential rain, torrent of rain; thunderstorm, rainstorm, cloudburst.
▷ANTONYMS drizzle.
3 *a deluge of complaints*: **barrage**, volley; **flood**, torrent, avalanche, stream, storm, shower, cascade, spate, wave, rush, outpouring.
▷ANTONYMS trickle.
▶verb **1** *caravans were deluged by the heavy rains*: **flood**, inundate, engulf, submerge, swamp, drown.
2 *we have been deluged with calls for information*: **inundate**, overwhelm, overload, overrun, flood, swamp, snow under, engulf; shower, bombard.

delusion noun **1** *the male delusion that attractive young women are harbouring romantic thoughts about them*: **misapprehension**, mistaken impression, false impression, mistaken belief, misconception, misunderstanding, mistake, error, misinterpretation, misconstruction, misbelief; fallacy, illusion, figment of the imagination, fantasy, chimera; fool's paradise, self-deception.
2 *a web of delusion*: **deception**, misleading, deluding, fooling, tricking, trickery, duping.

delusive adjective *events showed that such hope was delusive*: **misleading**, deceptive; misconceived, mistaken, false, in error, illusory, chimerical, insubstantial; rare delusory, illusive.
▷ANTONYMS well founded, genuine.

de luxe adjective *a de luxe hotel*: **luxurious**, luxury, sumptuous, palatial, opulent, splendid, magnificent, lavish, grand, rich, superior, high-class, quality, exclusive, choice, select, elegant, well appointed, fancy; expensive, costly; Brit. upmarket; informal plush, plushy, posh, classy, ritzy, swanky, pricey, fancy-pants; Brit. informal swish; N. Amer. informal swank, loaded; rare palatian, Lucullan.
▷ANTONYMS basic, cheap, downmarket.

delve verb **1** *she delved in her pocket*: **rummage (about/around/round) in**, search (through), hunt through, scrabble about/around in, root about/around in, ferret (about/around) in, fish about/around in, poke about/around in, dig in, grub about/around in, go through, burrow in; rifle through, scour, ransack, turn upside down, turn inside out; Brit. informal rootle around in; Austral./NZ informal fossick through; rare roust around in.
2 *the society is determined to **delve deeper into** the matter*: **investigate**, conduct investigations into, make enquiries into, enquire into, probe, examine, explore, research, study, look into, go into; try to get to the bottom of.

demagogue noun **rabble-rouser**, political agitator, agitator, soapbox orator, firebrand; troublemaker, incendiary; informal tub-thumper.

demand noun **1** *his demands for electoral reform | I finally gave in to her demands*: **request**, call; command, order, dictate, ultimatum, stipulation; (**demands**) insistence, pressure, clamour, importunity, urging; Austral./NZ informal a big ask; archaic behest, hest.
2 *a job that fits in with the demands of a young family*: **requirement**, need, desire, wish, want; claim, imposition, exigency.
3 *the big **demand for** such toys*: **market**, call, appetite, desire; run on, rush on.
□ **in demand** *his work is much in demand by magazines who like such candid portraiture*: **sought-after**, desired, coveted, wanted, requested, required; marketable, desirable, popular, in vogue, fashionable, all the rage, at a premium, like gold dust; informal big, trendy, hot, to die for; Brit. informal, dated all the go.
▷ANTONYMS unpopular.
▶verb **1** *workers demanded wage increases*: **call for**, ask for, request, press for, push for, hold out for, clamour for, bay for; **insist on**, lay claim to, claim, requisition.
2 *Harvey **demanded that** I tell him the truth*: **order to**, command to, tell to, call on to, enjoin to, urge to; literary bid.
3 *'Where is she?' he demanded*: **ask**, enquire, question, interrogate; challenge.
4 *a complex activity demanding detailed knowledge*: **require**, need, necessitate, call for, take, involve, entail; cry out for, want.
5 *most of those who contacted us demanded complete anonymity*: **insist on**, stipulate, make a condition of, exact, impose; expect, look for.

demanding adjective **1** *a demanding task*: **difficult**, **challenging**, testing, taxing, exacting, tough, hard, onerous, burdensome, stressful, formidable; arduous, tiring, wearing, exhausting, wearying, wearisome, draining, uphill, rigorous, gruelling, back-breaking, Herculean, punishing; informal a tall order; Brit. informal knackering; archaic toilsome.
▷ANTONYMS easy, effortless.
2 *a demanding child | her demanding behaviour*: **nagging**, clamorous, importunate, insistent; possessive; trying, tiresome, hard to please; rare exigent.
▷ANTONYMS easy-going.

demarcate verb *plots of land demarcated by barbed wire*: **separate**, divide, mark (out/off), delimit, distinguish, differentiate, delineate; bound.

demarcation noun **1** *a clear demarcation of function between administrative and judicial business*: **separation**, distinction, differentiation, division; delimitation, marking off, definition.
2 *territorial demarcations*: **boundary**, border, borderline, frontier, bound, limit; dividing line, line, divide.

demean verb *his actions only served to demean him in the eyes of the public*: **discredit**, lower, lower someone's dignity, lower someone's status, degrade, debase, devalue, demote; **cheapen**, abase, humble, humiliate, disgrace, dishonour; (**demean oneself**) condescend, deign, stoop, descend.
▷ANTONYMS dignify, exalt.

demeaning adjective *a demeaning experience | demeaning work*: **degrading**, humiliating, shaming, shameful, bringing shame, mortifying, abject, lowering, ignominious, undignified, inglorious, discrediting; menial; informal infra dig.
▷ANTONYMS ennobling.

demeanour noun *his normally calm demeanour*: **manner**, air, attitude, appearance, look, aspect, mien, cast; **bearing**, carriage, way of carrying oneself; **behaviour**, conduct, way of behaving, comportment; Brit. deportment.

demented adjective *the ravings of a demented old man*: **mad**, insane, deranged, out of one's mind, not in one's right mind, crazed, lunatic, unbalanced, unhinged, unstable, disturbed, distracted, as mad as a hatter, as mad as a March hare, stark mad; Latin non compos mentis; informal crazy, mental, off one's head, out of one's head, off one's nut, nutty, nutty as a fruitcake, off one's rocker, not (quite) right in the head, round the bend, raving mad, stark staring/raving mad, bats, batty, bonkers, cuckoo, loopy, loony, bananas, loco, dippy, screwy, with a screw loose, touched, gaga, doolally, up the pole, not all there, out to lunch, off the wall, not right upstairs, away with the fairies; Brit. informal barmy, crackers, barking, barking mad, round the twist, off one's trolley, as daft as a brush, not the full shilling, one sandwich short of a picnic; N. Amer. informal buggy, nutsy, nutso, out of one's tree, meshuga, squirrelly, wacko, gonzo; Canadian & Austral./NZ informal bushed; NZ informal porangi.
▷ANTONYMS sane.

> *Word toolkit* **demented**
>
> See **psychotic.**

dementia noun **mental illness**, madness, insanity, derangement, lunacy; senile dementia, Alzheimer's disease, Alzheimer's; informal softening of the brain.
▷ANTONYMS sanity.

demise noun **1** *her tragic demise*: **death**, dying, passing, passing away, passing on, loss of life, expiry, expiration, end, departure from life, final exit; Law decease; rare quietus.
▷ANTONYMS birth.
2 *the demise of the Ottoman empire*: **end**, break-up, disintegration, fall, downfall, ruin; failure, collapse, foundering.
▷ANTONYMS start.

demobilize verb *the militia were demobilized*: **disband**, decommission, discharge; Brit. informal demob.
▷ANTONYMS conscript.

democracy noun **representative government**, elective government, constitutional government, popular government; self-government, government by the people, autonomy; republic, commonwealth.
▷ANTONYMS tyranny; dictatorship.

democratic adjective *a democratic government | democratic countries*: **elected**, representative, parliamentary, popular, of the people, populist; egalitarian, classless; self-governing, autonomous, republican.
▷ANTONYMS totalitarian, despotic.

demolish verb **1** *the explosion demolished a block of flats*: **knock down**, pull down, tear down, bring down, destroy, flatten, raze, raze to the ground, level, reduce to ruins, bulldoze, break up, topple; blow up, blow to bits/pieces, obliterate, annihilate, wipe off the face of the earth, wipe off the map; dismantle, disassemble; N. Amer. informal total; dated throw down; rare unbuild.
▷ANTONYMS build, construct.
2 *they have demolished her credibility*: **destroy**, ruin, wreck, put an end to, smash, crush, squelch, squash; refute, disprove, prove wrong, discredit, overturn, explode, give the lie to, drive a coach and horses through; informal shoot full of holes, blow sky-high, blow out of the water, do for.
▷ANTONYMS confirm, strengthen.
3 informal *Arsenal demolished Coventry City 3–0*. See **trounce** (sense 1).
4 informal *Brown was busy demolishing a sausage roll*. See **devour** (sense 1).

demolition noun **1** *the demolition of the building*: **destruction**, knocking down, pulling down, tearing down, flattening, razing, levelling, bulldozing, clearance; obliteration, annihilation.
▷ANTONYMS construction.
2 *the demolition of this theory*: **destruction**, wrecking; **refutation**, disproval, disproving.
▷ANTONYMS confirmation.
3 informal *New Zealand's demolition of England*: **defeat**, conquest,

d

vanquishing, trouncing, routing, rout; informal massacre, annihilation, slaughter, licking, thrashing, clobbering, hammering.

demon noun 1 *the demons from hell*: **devil**, fiend, evil spirit, fallen angel, cacodemon; incubus, succubus; hellhound; Arabian & Muslim mythology afreet; Hindu mythology rakshasa.
▷ANTONYMS angel.
2 *the man was a demon and he had hurt her to the depths of her being*: **monster**, ogre, fiend, devil, villain, brute, savage, beast, barbarian, animal.
▷ANTONYMS saint.
3 *Surrey's fast-bowling demon | a demon tennis player*: **genius**, wizard, expert, master, adept, virtuoso, maestro, past master, marvel, prodigy; star; German wunderkind; informal hotshot, wiz, whizz, whizz-kid, buff, old hand, pro, ace, something else, something to shout about, something to write home about; Brit. informal dab hand; N. Amer. informal maven, crackerjack; rare proficient.
▷ANTONYMS amateur.
4 *the demon of creativity*. See **daemon**.

Word links **demon**

demonology study of demons

demonic, demoniac, demoniacal adjective 1 *demonic powers*: **devilish**, diabolic, diabolical, fiendish, satanic, Mephistophelian, hellish, infernal, evil, wicked, ungodly, unholy; rare cacodemonic.
▷ANTONYMS angelic.
2 *the demonic intensity of his playing*: **wild**, **frenzied**, feverish, frenetic, hectic, frantic, furious, hysterical; **maniacal**, manic, like one possessed.

demonstrable adjective *there are demonstrable links between French and American art*: **verifiable**, provable, attestable, evincible; verified, proven, confirmed; obvious, clear, clear-cut, plain, evident, apparent, manifest, patent, conspicuous, prominent, transparent, striking, distinct, noticeable, perceptible, observable, unmistakable, undeniable, self-evident.
▷ANTONYMS unverifiable.

demonstrate verb 1 *his findings demonstrate that boys commit more offences than girls*: **show**, show beyond doubt, indicate, determine, establish, prove, validate, confirm, verify, corroborate, substantiate, constitute evidence, constitute proof.
2 *she was asked to demonstrate quilting to the Women's Institute*: **give a demonstration of**, show how something is done, show how something works; exhibit, display, show, illustrate, exemplify, give an idea of.
3 *his work demonstrated an analytical ability*: **reveal**, bespeak, indicate, signify, signal, denote, show, display, exhibit, express, manifest, evince, evidence, be evidence of, be an indication of, bear witness to, testify to; imply, intimate, give away; informal spell; literary betoken.
▷ANTONYMS hide.
4 *students demonstrated against the Government*: **protest**, rally, hold a rally, march, parade; sit in, stage a sit-in, picket, form a picket line, strike, go on strike, walk out; mutiny, rebel.

demonstration noun 1 *his book is a brilliant demonstration of this thesis*: **proof**, substantiation, confirmation, affirmation, corroboration, verification, validation; evidence, indication, witness, testament.
2 *there will be a talk on woodcarving followed by a demonstration*: **exhibition**, **presentation**, display, illustration, exposition, teach-in; informal demo, expo, taster.
3 *his paintings are a powerful demonstration of his talents*: **manifestation**, **indication**, revelation, sign, mark, token, embodiment, record; expression; rare evincement.
4 *he travelled to Paris to join an anti-racism demonstration*: **protest**, protest march, march, parade, rally, lobby, sit-in, sit-down, sleep-in, stoppage, strike, walkout, picket, picket line, blockade; Indian morcha, gherao, hartal; informal demo, get-together.

demonstrative adjective 1 *we were a very demonstrative family*: **expressive**, open, forthcoming, emotional, communicative, responsive, unreserved, unrestrained, effusive, expansive, gushing, non-reticent, affectionate, cuddly, loving, warm, friendly, approachable; informal touchy-feely, lovey-dovey.
▷ANTONYMS undemonstrative, reserved.
2 *these military successes are demonstrative of their skill*: **indicative**, indicatory, suggestive, illustrative, evincive, expository.
3 *he presented demonstrative evidence of his theorem*: **convincing**, definite, positive, telling, conclusive, certain, decisive, material, airtight, watertight; incontrovertible, incontestable, irrefutable, unquestionable, undeniable, indisputable, unassailable.
▷ANTONYMS inconclusive.

demoralize verb *they kept wages low, which demoralized the staff*: **dishearten**, dispirit, deject, cast down, depress, dismay, daunt, discourage, unman, unnerve, crush, sap, shake, throw, cow, subdue, undermine, devitalize, weaken, enfeeble, enervate; break someone's spirit, bring someone low; informal knock the stuffing out of, knock for six, knock sideways.
▷ANTONYMS encourage, hearten.

demoralized adjective *the king's demoralized army broke and fled*: **dispirited**, disheartened, downhearted, dejected, cast down, downcast, low, depressed, despairing; disconsolate, crestfallen, disappointed, dismayed, daunted, discouraged, unmanned, unnerved; crushed, humbled, cowed, subdued; sapped, drained, shaken, thrown, undermined, devitalized; informal fed up; Brit. informal brassed off, cheesed off; vulgar slang pissed off.

demote verb *she was demoted after a rift with her boss*: **downgrade**, relegate, declass, move down, lower in rank, reduce in rank, strip of rank, reduce to the ranks; depose, unseat, dethrone, displace, oust, drum out, remove from office; Military cashier, disrate; N. Amer. bust.
▷ANTONYMS promote.

demotic adjective *in trade journals he would adopt a more demotic style*: **popular**; **vernacular**, colloquial, idiomatic, vulgar, common; informal, everyday, non-literary, unofficial, slangy; rare enchorial.
▷ANTONYMS formal.

demur verb *Mr Steed demurred when the suggestion was put to him*: **raise objections**, object, take exception, take issue, protest, lodge a protest, cavil, dissent; raise doubts, express doubt, express reluctance, express reservations, express misgivings, be unwilling, be reluctant, baulk, hesitate, think twice, hang back, drag one's heels, refuse; informal be cagey, boggle, kick up a fuss, kick up a stink.
▶noun *they accepted the ruling without demur*: **objection**, protest, protestation, complaint, dispute, dissent, carping, cavilling, recalcitrance, opposition, resistance; reservation, hesitation, reluctance, unwillingness, disinclination, lack of enthusiasm; doubts, qualms, misgivings, second thoughts; a murmur, a peep, a word, a sound; informal niggling, griping, grousing, boggling; Law demurrers; rare demurral.

demure adjective *the painting shows a demure Victorian miss*: **modest**, unassuming, meek, mild, reserved, retiring, quiet, shy, bashful, diffident, reticent, timid, timorous, shrinking; coy; decorous, decent, seemly, ladylike, respectable, proper, virtuous, pure, innocent, maidenly, virginal, chaste; sober, sedate, staid, prim, prim and proper, priggish, prissy, prudish, goody-goody, strait-laced, puritanical, old-maidish; informal straight, starchy, uptight, square, butter-wouldn't-melt; archaic retired.
▷ANTONYMS brazen; shameless.

den noun 1 *the mink left its den*: **lair**, sett, earth, drey, lodge, burrow, hole, tunnel, cave, dugout, hollow, covert, shelter, hiding place, hideout; informal hidey-hole.
2 *the club was a notorious drinking den*: **haunt**, site, patch, hotbed, cradle, nest, pit, hole; place of crime, place of vice; informal joint, dive, dump.
3 *the poet was scribbling in his den*: **study**, studio, library; **sanctum**, retreat, sanctuary, hideaway, snuggery, snug, cubbyhole; N. Amer. **cubby**; informal hidey-hole; humorous sanctum sanctorum.

denial noun 1 *reports of a revolt met with a denial from field commanders*: **contradiction**, counterstatement, refutation, rebuttal, repudiation, disclaimer, retraction, abjuration; negation, dissent; Law disaffirmation; rare confutation, retractation.
▷ANTONYMS confirmation.
2 *the denial of insurance to people with certain medical conditions*: **refusal**, withholding, withdrawal; rejection, dismissal, rebuff, repulse, declination, veto, turndown; informal thumbs down, red light, knock-back.
▷ANTONYMS acceptance.
3 *the denial of all worldly values*: **renunciation**, renouncement, forsaking, eschewal, repudiation, disavowal, disowning, rejection, casting aside, casting off, abandonment, surrender, giving up, relinquishment; rare abjuration.
▷ANTONYMS embracing.

denigrate verb *it amused him to denigrate his guests*: **disparage**, belittle, diminish, deprecate, cast aspersions on, decry, criticize unfairly, attack, speak ill of, speak badly of, blacken the character of, blacken the name of, give someone a bad name, sully the reputation of, spread lies about, defame, slander, libel, calumniate, besmirch, run down, abuse, insult, slight, revile, malign, vilify; N. Amer. slur; informal bad-mouth, slate, do a hatchet job on, pull to pieces, pull apart, sling mud at, throw mud at, drag through the mud; Brit. informal rubbish, slag off, have a go at; rare asperse, derogate, vilipend, vituperate.
▷ANTONYMS extol.

denizen noun *the denizens of Bolton were hungry for answers*: **inhabitant**, resident, townsman, townswoman, native, local; occupier, occupant, dweller; informal, derogatory local yokel; historical burgher, burgess; rare habitant, residentiary, oppidan, indweller.

denominate verb *this baking process is technically denominated 'setting the sponge'*: **call**, name, term, designate, style, dub, label, entitle; christen, baptize; archaic clepe.

denomination noun 1 *in 1816 their religious leaders established a separate denomination*: **religious group**, **sect**, Church, cult, movement, faith community, body, persuasion, religious persuasion, communion, order, fraternity, brotherhood, sisterhood, school; faith, creed, belief, religious belief, religion; rare sodality.
2 *the banknotes come in a number of denominations*: **value**, unit, grade, size,

measure.
3 formal *they called the computer 'XT', a denomination that still stands today*: **name**, title, term, designation, epithet, label, tag, style, sobriquet, nickname, byname; informal handle, moniker; formal appellation, cognomen; rare agnomen, allonym, anonym, appellative.

denote verb **1** *the elaborate headdresses denoted accomplished warriors*: **designate**, **indicate**, be a sign of, be a mark of, signify, signal, symbolize, represent, stand for, mean; typify, characterize, distinguish, mark, identify; literary bespeak, betoken.
2 *he had an air about him that denoted an inner strength*: **suggest**, point to, be evidence of, smack of, conjure up, bring to mind, indicate, show, reveal, demonstrate, intimate, imply, connote, convey, give away, betray; informal spell; literary bespeak.

denouement, dénouement noun **1** *the film's denouement was unsatisfying and ambiguous*: **finale**, final scene, final act, last act, epilogue, coda, end, ending, finish, close; **culmination**, climax, conclusion, resolution, solution, clarification, unravelling; informal wind-up.
▷ANTONYMS beginning.
2 *the debate had an unexpected denouement*: **outcome**, upshot, consequence, result, end result, end, ending, termination, culmination, climax; informal pay-off; dated issue; archaic success.
▷ANTONYMS origin.

denounce verb **1** *the pope denounced abortion and the use of contraceptives*: **condemn**, criticize, attack, censure, castigate, decry, revile, vilify, besmirch, discredit, damn, reject, proscribe; find fault with, cast aspersions on, malign, pour scorn on, rail against, inveigh against, fulminate against, declaim against, give something a bad press, run something down; N. Amer. slur; informal bad-mouth, knock, pan, slam, hammer, blast, hit out at, lay into, lace into, pull to pieces, pull apart, savage, maul; Brit. informal slate, slag off, have a go at, give some stick to; archaic rate, slash, reprobate; rare vituperate, excoriate, arraign, objurgate, asperse, anathematize, animadvert on, denunciate.
▷ANTONYMS praise.
2 *he feared he would be denounced as a traitor*: **expose**, betray, inform against, inform on; incriminate, implicate, cite, name, accuse; informal do; archaic inculpate.

dense adjective **1** *she stumbled through a dense birch forest*: **close-packed**, closely packed, tightly packed, closely set, thick, packed, crowded, crammed, jammed together, compressed, compacted, compact, solid, tight; overgrown, jungle-like, jungly, impenetrable, impassable; archaic thickset.
▷ANTONYMS sparse.
2 *a fire can fill your home with dense smoke*: **thick**, heavy, opaque, soupy, murky, smoggy, impenetrable; concentrated, condensed, of high density.
▷ANTONYMS thin; light.
3 informal *they were dense enough to believe me*. See **stupid** (sense 1).

density noun *vitamin D deficiency causes a loss of bone density*: **solidity**, solidness, denseness, thickness, substance, bulk, weight, mass; compactness, tightness, hardness.

> *Word links* **density**
>
> **hydrometer** instrument for measuring density of liquids

dent noun **1** *her hat had a dent at the crown | I made a dent in his car*: **indentation**, dint, dimple, dip, depression, hollow, crater, pit, trough; rare concavity.
2 *lawyers' fees will make a nasty dent in their finances*: **reduction**, depletion, deduction, cut, hole.
▷ANTONYMS increase.
▶verb **1** *he grumbled that Jamie had dented his bike*: **make a dent in**, make an indentation in, dint, indent, mark.
2 *the experience did not dent her confidence*: **diminish**, reduce, lessen, shrink, weaken, erode, undermine, sap, shake, break, crush, cripple, destroy, damage, impair; informal put the kibosh on.
▷ANTONYMS increase.

denude verb *the island had been denuded of trees | the pines were denuded by a recent fire*: **divest**, strip, clear, deprive, bereave, rob; **lay bare**, make bare, bare, uncover, expose; deforest, defoliate; literary despoil.
▷ANTONYMS cover.

deny verb **1** *the report was denied by several witnesses*: **contradict**, repudiate, gainsay, declare untrue, dissent from, disagree with, challenge, contest, oppose; retract, take back, back-pedal; disprove, debunk, explode, discredit, refute, rebut, invalidate, negate, nullify, quash; informal shoot full of holes, shoot down (in flames); Law disaffirm; rare controvert, confute, negative.
▷ANTONYMS confirm.
2 *he found it difficult to deny the request*: **refuse**, turn down, reject, rebuff, repulse, decline, veto, dismiss; informal knock back, give the thumbs down to, give the red light to, give the brush-off to.
▷ANTONYMS accept.
3 *she was told that she must deny her father and mother*: **renounce**, turn one's back on, forswear, eschew, repudiate, disavow, disown, wash one's hands of, reject, discard, cast aside, cast off, abandon, surrender, give up, relinquish; archaic forsake; rare abjure, abnegate.
▷ANTONYMS embrace.

> *Easily confused words* **deny or refute?**
>
> See **refute**.

deodorant noun **1** *she uses an underarm deodorant*: **antiperspirant**, body spray, perfume, scent.
2 *in some cinemas they sprayed the auditorium with perfumed deodorant*: **air-freshener**, deodorizer, fumigant.

deodorize verb *the sewage waters were deodorized without chemicals*: **freshen**, sweeten, purify, disinfect, sanitize, sterilize; fumigate, aerate, air, ventilate; rare depollute.

depart verb **1** *James departed soon after lunch*: **leave**, go, go away, go off, take one's leave, take oneself off, withdraw, absent oneself, say one's goodbyes, quit, make an exit, exit, break camp, decamp, retreat, beat a retreat, retire; make off, clear out, make oneself scarce, run off, run away, flee, fly, bolt; set off, set out, start out, get going, get under way, be on one's way; informal make tracks, up sticks, pack one's bags, shove off, push off, clear off, take off, skedaddle, scram, split, scoot, flit; Brit. informal sling one's hook; N. Amer. informal vamoose, hightail it, cut out; formal repair, remove; literary betake oneself; rare abstract oneself.
▷ANTONYMS arrive.
2 *the budget announcement **departed from** the trend of recent years*: **deviate**, diverge, digress, drift, stray, slew, veer, swerve, turn away, turn aside, branch off, differ, vary, be different; be at variance with, run counter to, contrast with, contravene, contradict; rare divagate.

departed adjective *he saw the ghost of his departed wife*: **dead**, deceased, late, lost, lamented; gone, no more, passed away, passed on, perished, expired, extinct; informal (as) dead as a doornail; euphemistic with God, asleep, at peace; rare demised.
▷ANTONYMS living.

department noun **1** *Percy worked in the public health department*: **division**, section, sector, subsection, subdivision, unit, branch, arm, wing, segment, compartment; office, bureau, agency, ministry.
2 *the turnout was low in rural departments*: **district**, administrative district, canton, province, territory, state, county, shire, parish; region, area, zone, sector, division; archaic demesne.
3 *don't ask me about the food—that's Kay's department*: **domain**, territory, realm, province, preserve, jurisdiction, sphere, sphere of activity, area, area of interest, field, line, speciality, specialism; area of responsibility, responsibility, duty, function, business, affair, charge, task, occupation, job, concern; informal pigeon, baby, bag, thing, bailiwick, turf.

departure noun **1** *he thought of a ploy to delay her departure*: **leaving**, going, going away, going off, leave-taking, withdrawal, exit, egress, quitting, decamping, retreat, retirement, retiral; flight, fleeing, running away, desertion; setting off, setting out, starting out.
▷ANTONYMS arrival.
2 *a departure from normality*: **deviation**, divergence, digression, shift, variation, change.
3 *the film represents an exciting departure for feminist film-makers*: **change of direction**, change, difference of emphasis, innovation, novelty, rarity.

depend verb **1** *their career progression **depends on** getting a good reference*: **be contingent on**, be conditional on, be dependent on, turn on, pivot on, hinge on, hang on, rest on, be based on, rely on; be subject to, be controlled by, be determined by, be influenced by, be decided by, be resultant from, relate to.
2 *my employees and their families **depend on** me*: **rely on**, place reliance on, lean on, cling to, be supported by, be sustained by, be unable to manage without; count on, bank on, trust, trust in, put one's trust in, put one's faith in, have faith in, have (every) confidence in, believe in, swear by, be sure of, pin one's hope on.

dependable adjective *he was a solid and dependable person*: **reliable**, trustworthy, honourable, true, faithful, loyal, constant, unswerving, unwavering, unfailing, sure, steadfast, steady, stable, trusty; **sensible**, responsible, conscientious, competent; Brit. informal copper-bottomed.
▷ANTONYMS unreliable.

dependant noun *he wanted to provide for his dependants after his death*: **child**, minor; ward, charge, protégé; relative, family member; hanger-on, parasite; (**dependants**) offspring, progeny; archaic fosterling.

dependence noun **1** *she cast off her **dependence on** her brother*: **reliance on**, need for, seeking support from, leaning on, clinging to; trust in, faith in, confidence in, belief in.
2 *they help patients to cope with enforced dependence*: **helplessness**, weakness, defencelessness, vulnerability; subservience, subordination.
▷ANTONYMS independence.
3 *the figures show a rise in drug dependence*: **addiction**, dependency, over-reliance, reliance; craving, compulsion, fixation, obsession; abuse.

d

dependency noun **1** *he saw no problem in a wife's* ***dependency on*** *her husband*: **dependence**, reliance; need for, seeking support from, leaning on, clinging to.
2 *the automatic association of retirement with dependency*: **helplessness**, dependence, weakness, defencelessness, vulnerability; subservience, subordination, inferiority.
▷ANTONYMS independence.
3 *taking tranquillizers in large doses can lead to dependency*: **addiction**, dependence, over-reliance, reliance; craving, compulsion, fixation, obsession; abuse.
4 *the army invaded a British dependency*: **colony**, **protectorate**, province, dominion, outpost, satellite, satellite state; holding, possession; historical tributary, fief; archaic demesne.
5 *they work for a dependency of the parent firm*: **subsidiary**, subordinate company, peripheral unit, adjunct, appendage, offshoot, auxiliary, attachment, satellite, derivative; archaic tributary.

dependent adjective **1** *your placement will be* ***dependent on*** *the decision of a third party*: **conditional on**, contingent on, based on, depending on, resting on, hanging on, hingeing on; subject to, determined by, controlled by, influenced by, swayed by, resultant from.
2 *the army was still* ***dependent on*** *voluntary enlistment*: **reliant on**, relying on, counting on, leaning on; supported by, sustained by.
3 *these people are* ***dependent on*** *drugs*: **addicted to**, reliant on, over-reliant on, fixated on; given to using, given to abusing; informal hooked on.
4 *it's hard caring for someone who is ill and dependent*: **reliant**, needy; helpless, weak, feeble, incapable, debilitated; defenceless, vulnerable;
5 *the island is a United Kingdom dependent territory*: **subsidiary**, subject, subservient; satellite, ancillary; puppet; historical tributary.
▷ANTONYMS independent.

depict verb **1** *the painting depicts Christ and the Virgin Mary*: **portray**, represent, picture, illustrate, delineate, outline, reproduce, render; draw, paint, sketch, draft; literary limn.
2 *evolution is not the haphazard process depicted by Darwin's theory*: **describe**, detail, relate, narrate, recount, unfold; present, set forth, set out, outline, delineate, sketch, paint; represent, portray, characterize; record, chronicle.

depiction noun **1** *a mirror with a depiction of Aphrodite on the reverse*: **picture**, painting, portrait, drawing, sketch, study, illustration, portrayal, representation, image, likeness.
2 *he was criticized for his depiction of black women*: **portrayal**, representation, presentation, description, delineation, characterization.

deplete verb *clan warfare has severely depleted the food supply*: **exhaust**, use up, consume, expend, spend, drain, empty, sap, milk, suck dry, evacuate; reduce, decrease, diminish, lessen, lower, attenuate; slim down, pare down, cut back; informal bleed, slash.
▷ANTONYMS augment; increase.

depletion noun *they enquired into the depletion of fish stocks*: **exhaustion**, using up, use, consumption, expending, expenditure; draining, emptying, sapping, milking; reduction, decrease, dwindling, diminution, lessening, lowering, attenuation, impoverishment; informal bleeding.
▷ANTONYMS augmentation.

deplorable adjective **1** *the conduct of the workers is deplorable*: **disgraceful**, shameful, dishonourable, disreputable, discreditable, unworthy, shabby, inexcusable, unpardonable, unforgivable; reprehensible, despicable, abominable, base, sordid, vile, hateful, contemptible, loathsome, offensive, execrable, heinous, odious, revolting, unspeakable, beyond contempt, beyond the pale; rare egregious, flagitious.
▷ANTONYMS admirable.
2 *the back garden is in a deplorable state*: **lamentable**, regrettable, grievous, unfortunate, wretched, dire, atrocious, abysmal, very bad, awful, terrible, dreadful, diabolical; miserable, pitiable, pathetic, sorry, unhappy, sad, woeful; substandard, poor, inadequate, inferior, unsatisfactory, unacceptable; informal appalling, rotten, crummy, lousy, God-awful; Brit. informal chronic; dated frightful.
▷ANTONYMS excellent.

deplore verb **1** *we deplore all use of violence and provocation*: **abhor**, be shocked by, be offended by, be scandalized by, find unacceptable, be against, frown on; **disapprove of**, take a dim view of, look askance at, take exception to, detest, despise, execrate; **condemn**, denounce, decry, deprecate, censure, damn.
▷ANTONYMS admire.
2 *he deplored the lack of flair in the England squad*: **regret**, express regret about, lament, mourn, rue, bemoan, bewail, complain about, grieve over, express sorrow about, sorrow over, sigh over, cry over, weep over, shed tears over, beat one's breast about, wring one's hands over; archaic plain over.
▷ANTONYMS applaud.

deploy verb **1** *paramilitary forces were deployed at strategic locations*: **position**, station, post, place, install, locate, situate, site, establish; base, garrison; **distribute**, arrange, range, dispose, redistribute, spread out, extend, put into position; informal plant, park; rare posit.
▷ANTONYMS concentrate.
2 *the Empress deployed all her social skills*: **use**, utilize, employ, make use of, avail oneself of, turn to account, take advantage of, exploit; bring into service, bring into play, bring into action; have recourse to, call on, turn to, resort to.

deport verb **1** *they were fined and deported*: **expel**, banish, exile, transport, expatriate, extradite, repatriate; evict, oust, cast out, throw out, turn out, drive out, drum out; informal kick out, boot out, chuck out, give someone the boot, send packing, give someone their marching orders, throw someone out on their ear; Brit. informal turf out; N. Amer. informal give someone the bum's rush; dated out; in ancient Greece ostracize.
▷ANTONYMS admit.
2 rare *he has* ***deported himself*** *with great dignity*: **behave**, act, perform, conduct oneself, acquit oneself; bear oneself, carry oneself, hold oneself; rare comport oneself.

deportation noun *work visas he thought would spare them deportation*: **expulsion**, expelling, banishment, banishing, exile, exiling, transportation, transporting, extradition, extraditing, expatriation, expatriating, repatriation, repatriating; eviction, evicting, ejection, ejecting, ousting, throwing out, casting out, turning out, driving out, drumming out; informal kicking out, booting out; Brit. informal turfing out; dated outing; in ancient Greece ostracism.
▷ANTONYMS admission.

deportment noun **1** Brit. *poise is directly concerned with good deportment*: **gait**, **posture**, carriage, comportment, bearing, stance, way of standing, way of holding oneself, way of carrying oneself, way of bearing oneself; attitude, demeanour, mien, air, appearance, aspect, style, manner.
2 N. Amer. *she reprimanded him for unprofessional deportment*: **behaviour**, conduct, performance, way of behaving, way of acting, way of conducting oneself; etiquette, manners, ways, habits, practices; actions, acts, activities, exploits; informal capers.

depose verb **1** *the president was deposed by a right-wing junta*: **overthrow**, overturn, topple, bring down, remove from office, remove, unseat, dethrone, supplant, displace; dismiss, discharge, oust, drum out, throw out, force out, drive out, expel, eject; strip of rank, demote; Military cashier; informal sack, fire, axe, chuck out, boot out, get rid of, give someone the push, give someone the boot, give someone their marching orders, show someone the door; Brit. informal turf out.
2 Law *an independent witness deposed that he had seen the accused*: **swear**, testify, attest, undertake, assert, declare, profess, aver, submit, claim; swear on the Bible, swear under oath, state on oath, make a deposition, give an undertaking, solemnly promise; rare asseverate, represent.

deposit noun **1** *the floor was covered by a thick deposit of ash*: **accumulation**, sediment, sublimate; layer, covering, coating, dusting, blanket.
2 *they discovered a new copper deposit*: **seam**, vein, lode, layer, stratum, bed, accumulation.
3 *they made the booking and paid a deposit*: **down payment**, part payment, advance payment, prepayment, instalment, security, retainer, pledge, stake; front money, money up front.
▶verb **1** *she deposited a pile of school books on the table*: **put (down)**, place, lay (down), set (down), unload, rest, settle, sit; drop, let fall, throw down, fling down; informal dump, stick, park, plonk, pop, shove; Brit. informal bung; N. Amer. informal plunk; archaic unlade; rare posit.
▷ANTONYMS pick up.
2 *the silt was deposited by flood water*: **leave behind**, leave, set down, let settle, precipitate, dump; wash up, cast up.
3 *the gold had been deposited at the Bank of England*: **lodge**, bank, house, store, stow, put away, hoard, lay in; entrust, consign, commit; informal stash, squirrel away, salt away, put aside for a rainy day; rare reposit.

deposition noun **1** *a commissioner is to take depositions from witnesses*: **statement**, sworn statement, affidavit, attestation, affirmation, assertion; allegation, submission, declaration, pronouncement, profession; testimony, evidence; rare asseveration, averment, representation.
2 *the pebbles are formed by the deposition of calcium*: **depositing**, settling; accumulation, build-up; informal dumping; technical precipitation.
3 *the barons plotted the King's deposition*: **overthrow**, overturning, toppling, downfall, removal from office, removal, unseating, dethronement, supplanting, displacement, dismissal, discharge, ousting, drumming out, throwing out, forcing out, driving out, expulsion, expelling, ejection, ejecting; demotion; N. Amer. ouster; informal sacking, firing; Brit. informal turfing out; rare deposal.

depository noun *the burial chamber was used as a depository for a coin hoard*: **repository**, cache, store, storage place, storeroom, storehouse, warehouse, depot; vault, strongroom, safe, safe deposit, safety deposit, bank, treasure house, treasury; container, receptacle; in the Far East godown; informal lock-up; archaic garner.

depot noun **1** *the bus pulled into the depot*: **terminal**, terminus, station, garage; bus station, coach station, railway station, train station; headquarters, base.
2 *he was killed in an explosion at an arms depot*: **storehouse**, warehouse, store, storage place, storing place, repository, depository, cache; arsenal, magazine, armoury, ammunition dump, ordnance depot; archaic garner.

deprave verb *they have been depraved by pornography*: **corrupt**, lead astray, warp, subvert, pervert, debauch, debase, degrade, make degenerate, defile, sully, pollute, poison, contaminate, infect; archaic demoralize; rare vitiate.
▷ANTONYMS purify.

depraved adjective *a depraved father abused his two young daughters*: **corrupt**, corrupted, perverted, deviant, degenerate, debased, degraded, immoral, unprincipled, reprobate; **debauched**, dissolute, profligate, lewd, licentious, lascivious, lecherous, lustful, prurient, obscene, indecent, libertine, sordid; wicked, sinful, vile, base, iniquitous, nefarious, criminal, vicious, brutal; informal warped, twisted, pervy, sick, sicko.
▷ANTONYMS virtuous, moral.

depravity noun *she viewed her ex-husband as a monster of depravity*: **corruption**, corruptness, vice, perversion, pervertedness, deviance, degeneracy, degradation, immorality, shamelessness, debauchery, dissipation, dissoluteness, turpitude, loucheness, profligacy, licentiousness, lewdness, lasciviousness, salaciousness, lechery, lecherousness, prurience, obscenity, indecency, libertinism, sordidness; wickedness, sinfulness, vileness, baseness, iniquity, nefariousness, criminality, viciousness, brutality, brutishness; informal perviness; rare vitiation.
▷ANTONYMS morality.

deprecate verb **1** *the school deprecates the social mixing of older and younger boys*: **disapprove of**, deplore, abhor, find unacceptable, be against, frown on, take a dim view of, look askance at, take exception to, detest, despise, execrate; criticize, censure, condemn, denounce, protest against, inveigh against, rail against; informal knock, slam, hammer, cane, blast, bad-mouth, pull to pieces, pull apart, hit out at; Brit. informal slate, slag off, rubbish; archaic slash, vituperate against, reprobate; rare animadvert on, asperse, derogate.
▷ANTONYMS praise.
2 *he deprecates the value of children's television*: **belittle**, **disparage**, denigrate, run down, discredit, decry, cry down, play down, make little of, trivialize, underrate, undervalue, underestimate, diminish, depreciate, deflate; think little of, treat lightly, scoff at, sneer at, scorn, disdain; informal sell short, knock, pooh-pooh; archaic hold cheap; rare derogate, misprize, minify.
▷ANTONYMS emphasize; overrate.

> *Easily confused words* **deprecate or depreciate?**
>
> Although they are very similar in spelling and meaning, **deprecate** and **depreciate** are not identical. *Deprecate* means 'express disapproval of', as in *I deprecate his rather ungracious words*, while *depreciate* means 'disparage or belittle', as in *we should not depreciate the importance of art in education*.

deprecatory adjective **1** *he made deprecatory remarks about the opposition*: **disapproving**, censorious, censuring, critical, scathing, damning, damnatory, condemnatory, condemning, denunciatory; castigatory, reproachful, reproving, upbraiding, admonishing; informal slating, knocking; rare reprobative, reprobatory.
2 *Greene was deprecatory about his own writing*: **disparaging**, belittling, denigratory, derogatory, discrediting, diminishing, detracting, deflating, negative, unflattering, slighting; disdainful, derisive, snide, sneering, mocking, jibing.
3 *she gave a deprecatory smile at her mistake*: **apologetic**, regretful, full of regret, sorry, remorseful, contrite, penitent, repentant, rueful, appeasing; conscience-stricken, red-faced, shamefaced, sheepish, hangdog; rare propitiatory, compunctious.
▷ANTONYMS unrepentant.

depreciate verb **1** *these cars will depreciate heavily in the first year*: **decrease in value**, lose value, decline in price, drop in price, fall in price, cheapen, devalue.
▷ANTONYMS appreciate.
2 *the decision to depreciate land and property is good news for buyers*: **devalue**, cheapen, reduce, lower in value, lower in price, mark down, cut, discount; informal slash.
▷ANTONYMS raise.
3 *they depreciate the importance of art in education*: **belittle**, **disparage**, denigrate, decry, deprecate, make light of, treat lightly, discredit, underrate, undervalue, underestimate, deflate, detract from, diminish, minimize, trivialize, run down, traduce, defame; disdain, ridicule, deride, sneer at, scoff at, mock, scorn, pour scorn on; informal knock, slam, pan, bad-mouth, sell short, put down, pooh-pooh, look down one's nose at, do down, do a hatchet job on, take to pieces, pull apart, pick holes in, drag through the mud, have a go at, hit out at; Brit. informal rubbish, slate, slag off; dated cry down; archaic hold cheap; rare derogate, misprize, minify.
▷ANTONYMS appreciate.

> *Easily confused words* **depreciate or deprecate?**
>
> See **deprecate**.

depreciation noun *we are concerned about the depreciation of house prices*: **devaluation**, devaluing, decrease in value, lowering in value, reduction in value, cheapening, markdown, reduction, decline, downturn, downswing, drop, slump, plunge, tumble; informal nosedive, crash.
▷ANTONYMS rise.

depredation noun *few survived the depredation of the barbarian invasion*: **plundering**, plunder, looting, pillaging, robbing, robbery, raiding, ravaging, sacking, sack, ransacking, devastation, laying waste, wreckage, destruction, damage; ravages, raids, acts of destruction; literary despoiling, despoliation, rape, rapine, ravin; archaic spoliation, reaving.

depress verb **1** *the news from the doctor depressed him*: **make sad**, sadden, make unhappy, cast down, get down, make gloomy, make despondent, dispirit; dampen someone's spirits, break someone's spirit, dash someone's hopes, dishearten, demoralize, discourage, daunt, crush, shake, desolate, make desolate, weigh down, weigh heavily on, hang over, oppress; upset, distress, grieve, haunt, harrow, cause suffering to, break someone's heart, make someone's heart bleed, bring tears to someone's eyes; informal give someone the blues, make someone fed up, knock the stuffing out of, knock for six, knock sideways; archaic deject.
▷ANTONYMS cheer up.
2 *the government's economic policies depressed sales*: **slow down**, slow up, reduce, lower, weaken, sap, devitalize, impair, deflate; limit, check, curb, bridle, inhibit, restrict.
▷ANTONYMS encourage.
3 *the increase in EC imports will depress farm prices*: **reduce**, lower, cut, cheapen, put down, keep down, mark down, discount, deflate, depreciate, devalue, diminish, downgrade; informal slash, axe.
▷ANTONYMS raise.
4 *you have to depress each key in turn*: **push (down)**, press (down), exert pressure on, lower, hold down; thumb, tap; operate, activate, actuate.
▷ANTONYMS lift.

depressant noun *the drug is a stimulant rather than a depressant*: **sedative**, tranquillizer, calmative, sleeping pill, soporific, opiate, hypnotic; informal downer, trank, sleeper, dope; technical neuroleptic, stupefacient; literary nepenthes; dated bromide, sleeping draught.
▷ANTONYMS stimulant.

depressed adjective **1** *he turned to whisky because he felt lonely and depressed*: **sad**, saddened, unhappy, gloomy, glum, melancholy, miserable, sorrowful, dejected, disconsolate, downhearted, downcast, cast down, down, crestfallen, woebegone, despondent, dispirited, low, low in spirits, low-spirited, heavy-hearted, morose, dismal, desolate, weighed down, oppressed; tearful, upset, broken-hearted; disheartened, discouraged, daunted, pessimistic; informal blue, down in the dumps, down in the mouth, fed up, moody; literary dolorous, heartsick, heartsore; archaic chap-fallen.
▷ANTONYMS cheerful.
2 *there is a relationship between crime and a depressed economy*: **weak**, weakened, enervated, debilitated, devitalized, impaired; inactive, flat, quiet, slow, slow-moving, slack, sluggish, static, stagnant, dull.
▷ANTONYMS strong.
3 *he snapped up property at depressed prices*: **reduced**, lowered, cut, cheapened, cheap, devalued, marked down, discounted, discount; informal slashed.
▷ANTONYMS inflated.
4 *a depressed Lancashire cotton town*: **poverty-stricken**, poor, destitute, disadvantaged, deprived, needy, distressed; down at heel, run down, seedy, shabby; informal slummy.
▷ANTONYMS prosperous.
5 *a depressed fracture of the skull*: **sunken**, hollow, concave, indented, dented, pushed in, caved in, recessed, set back; rare incurved, incurvate.
▷ANTONYMS raised.

depressing adjective **1** *she wanted to get rid of her depressing thoughts*: **upsetting**, distressing, painful, heartbreaking, heart-rending, dispiriting, disheartening, discouraging, demoralizing; dismal, bleak, black, sombre, gloomy, grave, unhappy, melancholy, sad, saddening; wretched, doleful; daunting, disenchanting, unfavourable; informal morbid, blue; archaic dejecting; rare distressful, lachrymose.
2 *it was such a depressing room*: **gloomy**, bleak, dreary, grim, drab, sombre, dark, dingy, funereal, miserable, cheerless, joyless, comfortless, uninviting; literary drear.

depression noun **1** *she ate to ease her depression*: **melancholy**, misery, sadness, unhappiness, sorrow, woe, gloom, gloominess, dejection, downheartedness, despondency, dispiritedness, low spirits, heavy-heartedness, moroseness, discouragement, despair, desolation, dolefulness, moodiness, pessimism, hopelessness; the slough of despond; upset, tearfulness; informal the dumps, the doldrums, the blues, one's black dog, a low; N. Amer. informal the blahs, a funk, a blue funk; informal, dated the mopes; technical clinical depression, endogenous depression, reactive depression, post-natal depression, dysthymia, melancholia; literary dolour; archaic the megrims; rare mopery, disconsolateness, disconsolation.
▷ANTONYMS cheerfulness.
2 *the country was in the grip of an economic depression*: **recession**, slump, decline, downturn, slowdown, standstill; paralysis, inactivity, stagnation, credit crunch, credit squeeze; hard times, bad times; technical stagflation.
▷ANTONYMS boom.
3 *the car slid into a depression in the ground*: **hollow**, indentation, dent,

d

dint, cavity, concavity, dip, pit, hole, pothole, sink, sinkhole, excavation, trough, crater; valley, basin, bowl; Anatomy fossa, lacuna.
▷ANTONYMS protuberance.

deprivation noun **1** *the cause of the rioting was unemployment and deprivation*: **poverty**, impoverishment, penury, privation, hardship, destitution, need, neediness, want, distress, financial distress, indigence, pauperdom, beggary, ruin; reduced circumstances, straitened circumstances, hand-to-mouth existence; rare pauperism, pauperization, impecuniousness, impecuniosity.
▷ANTONYMS wealth.
2 *he was sentenced to one year's deprivation of political rights*: **dispossession**, withholding, withdrawal, removal, taking away, stripping, divestment, divestiture, wresting away, expropriation, seizure, confiscation, robbing, appropriation; denial, forfeiture, loss; absence, lack, unavailability, deficiency, dearth.
▷ANTONYMS possession.

deprive verb *she was* ***deprived of*** *her royal privileges*: **dispossess**, strip, divest, relieve, bereave; rob of, cheat out of, trick out of, do out of; deny, prevent from having, prevent from using; informal diddle out of.

deprived adjective *the most deprived sections of society*: **disadvantaged**, underprivileged, poverty-stricken, impoverished, poor, destitute, needy, in need, in want, badly off, unable to make ends meet, in reduced circumstances, unable to keep the wolf from the door; depressed, distressed, forlorn; Brit. on the bread line; formal penurious, impecunious; rare necessitous.
▷ANTONYMS fortunate; wealthy.

depth noun **1** *he wondered about the depth of the caves*: **deepness**, distance downwards, distance inwards, distance from the outside; drop, vertical drop, vertical extent, profundity.
▷ANTONYMS shallowness.
2 *Bill tested the depth of his knowledge*: **extent**, range, scope, breadth, width, extensiveness, comprehensiveness; compass, magnitude, scale, degree.
3 *they made remarks about the girls' lack of depth*: **profoundness**, profundity, deepness, wisdom, understanding, intelligence, sagacity, discernment, perceptiveness, penetration, perspicuity, insight, awareness, intuition, astuteness, acumen, shrewdness, acuity; learning, erudition, knowledgeability; rare sapience.
▷ANTONYMS shallowness.
4 *this book is a work of great depth*: **complexity**, intricacy, profoundness, profundity, gravity, seriousness, weight, importance, moment, solemnity.
▷ANTONYMS triviality.
5 *the vase has incredible depth of colour*: **intensity**, richness, deepness, darkness, vividness, strength, brilliance.
6 (**depths**) *they studied life in the depths of the sea*: **deepest part**, remotest area, bottom, floor, bed, abyss, back, pit; bowels.
▷ANTONYMS surface.
□ **in depth** *the student concentrates on one or two subjects in depth*: **thoroughly**, extensively, comprehensively, well, rigorously, exhaustively, completely, fully; meticulously, scrupulously, assiduously, painstakingly, methodically.
▷ANTONYMS superficially.

> *Word links* **depth**
>
> **bathymetry** measurement of depth of seas and lakes
> **bathophobia** fear of depth

deputation noun *the prime minister agreed to receive a suffrage deputation*: **delegation**, delegacy, legation, commission, committee, (diplomatic) mission; contingent, group, party, body, band, set; delegates, representatives, envoys, emissaries, legates; historical embassy; archaic embassage.

depute verb **1** *he was deputed to handle negotiations in Baldwin's absence*: **appoint**, designate, nominate, assign, commission, charge, choose, select, elect, co-opt; empower, authorize, mandate; Military detail.
2 *the judge deputed the examination of lesser cases to others*: **delegate**, transfer, turn over, hand over, hand on, pass on, consign, assign, entrust, give, devolve.

deputize verb *the assistant's task is to* ***deputize for*** *the account executive*: **stand in for**, sit in for, fill in for, cover for, substitute for, replace, take the place of, understudy, be a locum for, relieve, take over from; hold the fort, step into the breach; **act for**, act on behalf of, speak on behalf of, represent; informal sub for; N. Amer. informal pinch-hit for.

deputy noun *he handed over his duties to his deputy*: **second in command**, second, number two, subordinate, junior, auxiliary, adjutant, lieutenant, subaltern, assistant, personal assistant, PA, aide, helper, right-hand man, henchman, underling; substitute, stand-in, fill-in, relief, understudy, supply; representative, surrogate, proxy, delegate, agent, spokesperson, ambassador, legate; Scottish depute; Latin locum tenens; informal vice, man/girl Friday, sidekick, locum, temp.
▶ **adjective** *she brought in an old friend as deputy editor*: **assistant**; substitute, stand-in, acting, reserve, fill-in, caretaker, temporary, short-term, provisional, stopgap, surrogate, proxy, representative; Latin pro tempore, ad interim; informal second-string; N. Amer. informal pinch-hitting; rare expediential.

deranged adjective *five schoolchildren were shot by a deranged gunman*: **insane**, mad, of unsound mind, out of one's mind, not in one's right mind, disturbed, unbalanced, unhinged, unstable, crazed, demented, irrational, berserk, frenzied, maniac, lunatic, psychopathic, certifiable, raving, raving mad; Latin non compos mentis; informal touched, crazy, cracked, mental; Brit. informal barmy, barking, barking mad, round the twist.
▷ANTONYMS sane; rational.

derelict adjective **1** *a derelict old building*: **dilapidated**, ramshackle, run down, broken-down, worn out, tumbledown, in (a state of) disrepair, in ruins, ruined, falling to pieces, falling apart; rickety, creaky, creaking, decrepit, deteriorating, crumbling, deteriorated; neglected, untended, unmaintained, gone to rack and ruin, gone to seed, on its last legs, the worse for wear.
▷ANTONYMS in good repair.
2 *a vast, derelict airfield*: **disused**, abandoned, deserted, discarded, rejected, forsaken, cast off, relinquished, ownerless.
▷ANTONYMS in use.
3 N. Amer. *he was derelict in his duty to his country*: **negligent**, neglectful, remiss, lax, careless, sloppy, slipshod, slack, irresponsible, delinquent.
▷ANTONYMS dutiful, punctilious.
▶ **noun** *the community of derelicts who survive on the capital's streets*: **tramp**, vagrant, vagabond, down and out, homeless person, drifter, person of no fixed address/abode, knight of the road; beggar, mendicant; outcast, pariah, ne'er do well, good-for-nothing, wastrel; informal dosser, bag lady; N. Amer. informal hobo, bum; Austral./NZ informal derro.

Word toolkit

derelict	**disintegrating**	**decaying**
building	marriage	corpse
property	relationship	flesh
area	economy	leaves
mill	world	wood
housing	family	plants
farm	situation	logs
barn	infrastructure	fish
church	society	vegetation

dereliction noun **1** *more buildings were reclaimed from dereliction*: **dilapidation**, disrepair, decrepitude, deterioration, ruin, rack and ruin; **abandonment**, neglect, disuse, desertion, rejection, forsaking.
2 *he could have been shot for* ***dereliction of duty***: **negligence**, neglect, neglectfulness, delinquency, failure, non-performance; carelessness, remissness, lack of care, laxity, laxness, sloppiness, slackness, irresponsibility, oversight, omission; misconduct, unprofessionalism; informal slip-up.
▷ANTONYMS fulfilment.

deride verb *the decision was derided by environmentalists*: **ridicule**, mock, jeer at, scoff at, jibe at, make fun of, poke fun at, laugh at, hold up to ridicule, pillory; disdain, disparage, denigrate, pooh-pooh, dismiss, slight, detract from; sneer at, scorn, pour/heap scorn on, taunt, insult, torment; treat with contempt, vilify; lampoon, satirize; informal knock, take the mickey out of; Austral./NZ informal poke mullock at; vulgar slang take the piss out of; archaic contemn, flout at.
▷ANTONYMS respect, praise.

de rigueur adjective **1** *a straight brown bob and invisible make-up were de rigueur*: **fashionable**, in fashion, voguish, in vogue, modish, up to date, up to the minute, all the rage, trendsetting, latest; smart, chic, elegant, natty; informal trendy, with it, ritzy.
▷ANTONYMS unfashionable.
2 *an email address is considered de rigueur for business cards today*: **customary**, standard, conventional, normal, orthodox, usual, ubiquitous; compulsory; French comme il faut; informal done.

derision noun *my stories were greeted with disbelief and derision*: **mockery**, ridicule, jeering, jeers, sneers, scoffing, jibing, taunts; disdain, disparagement, denigration, disrespect, pooh-poohing; sneering, scorn, scornfulness, taunting, insults; contempt, vilification, obloquy; lampooning, satire; ragging, teasing, chaffing, raillery; archaic contumely.
▷ANTONYMS respect, praise.

> *Choose the right word* **derision, mockery, ridicule**
>
> See **mockery**.

derisive adjective *he gave a harsh, derisive laugh*: **mocking**, ridiculing, jeering, scoffing, jibing, pillorying, teasing, derisory, snide; disdainful, disparaging, denigratory, dismissive, slighting, detracting, contemptuous; sneering, scornful, taunting, insulting; caustic, scathing, sarcastic; satirical, lampooning; informal snidey; Brit. informal sarky; rare contumelious.
▷ANTONYMS respectful, praising.

Easily confused words **derisive or derisory?**

See **derisory**.

derisory adjective **1** *it was sold at auction for a derisory sum*: **inadequate**, insufficient, tiny, small, minimal, trifling, paltry, pitiful; miserly, miserable; negligible, token, nominal; **ridiculous**, laughable, ludicrous, risible, preposterous, absurd; insulting, contemptible, outrageous; informal measly, stingy, lousy, pathetic, piddling, piffling, mingy, poxy; N. Amer. informal nickel-and-dime.
2 *there were derisory calls from the crowd*. See **derisive**.

Easily confused words **derisory or derisive?**

Derisory and **derisive** are both derived from Latin *deridere* 'mock, scoff', but their meanings are connected with mockery in different ways. *Derisory* usually means 'ridiculously small or inadequate', as in *a derisory pay offer*. *Derisive*, on the other hand, means 'showing contempt', as in *he gave a derisive laugh*.

derivation noun **1** *the derivation of universal laws from empirical observation*: **deriving**, **induction**, deduction, deducing, inferring, inference, gathering, gleaning, drawing out, extraction, eliciting; rare eduction.
2 *the derivation of the word 'toff'*: **origin**, **etymology**; source, root, etymon, provenance; fountainhead, wellspring, origination, beginning, foundation, basis, cause; ancestry, descent, genealogy, development, evolution, extraction.

derivative adjective *her poetry was mannered and derivative*: **imitative**, unoriginal, uninventive, non-innovative, unimaginative, uninspired; copied, plagiarized, plagiaristic, second-hand, secondary, echoic; trite, hackneyed, clichéd, stale, tired, worn out, flat, rehashed, warmed-up, stock, banal; informal copycat, cribbed, old hat.
▷ANTONYMS original.
▶ noun **1** *laudanum is a derivative of opium*: **by-product**, spin-off, offshoot, subsidiary product.
2 *the word 'samurai' is a derivative of a verb meaning 'to serve'*: **derived word**, descendant.

derive verb **1** *he hated the work, only deriving consolation from his reading of poetry*: **obtain**, get, take, gain, acquire, procure, extract, attain, glean.
2 *'coffee' **derives from** the Turkish 'kahveh'*: **originate in**, have its origins in, have as a source, arise in; stem, descend, spring, be taken, be got.
▷ANTONYMS give rise to.
3 *his fortune **derives from** international property and finance*: **originate in**, have its origin in, be rooted in, be traceable to; stem, proceed, flow, pour, spring, emanate, issue, ensue, descend, come.

derogate verb **1** *his contribution has been underestimated and derogated by his critics*: **disparage**, denigrate, belittle, diminish, deprecate, downplay, detract from, deflate, decry, discredit, cast aspersions on, downgrade, slight, run down, criticize, defame, vilify, abuse, insult, attack, speak ill of, speak evil of, pour scorn on; informal bad-mouth, do a hatchet job on, take to pieces, pull apart, throw mud at, drag through the mud, slate, have a go at, hit out at, lay into, tear into, knock, slam, pan, bash, hammer, roast, skewer, bad-mouth, throw brickbats at; Brit. informal rubbish, slag off, monster; N. Amer. informal pummel, dump on; Austral./NZ informal bag; archaic contemn; rare vituperate, asperse, vilipend.
▷ANTONYMS praise.
2 *agreeing to swear such an oath would certainly have derogated the majesty of the king*: **detract from**, devalue, diminish; reduce, lessen, lower, depreciate, take away from; demean, cheapen, defame.
▷ANTONYMS improve, increase.
3 *there is no person who can make rules which override or **derogate from** an Act of Parliament*: **deviate**, diverge, depart, take away, digress, veer, swerve, drift, stray; differ, vary; change; conflict with, be incompatible with.

derogatory adjective *a derogatory remark*: **disparaging**, denigratory, belittling, diminishing, slighting, deprecatory, depreciatory, depreciative, detracting, deflating; disrespectful, demeaning, discrediting, dishonouring; critical, pejorative, negative, unfavourable, disapproving, uncomplimentary, unflattering, insulting; **offensive**, personal, abusive, vituperative, rude, spiteful, nasty, mean; hurtful, damaging, injurious; defamatory, slanderous, libellous, scurrilous, calumnious, calumniatory, vilifying, traducing; informal mud-slinging, bitchy, catty; archaic contumelious.
▷ANTONYMS complimentary, flattering.

Choose the right word **derogatory, offensive, insulting**

See **offensive**.

descend verb **1** *the plane started descending towards the runway*: **go down**, come down; drop, fall, sink, subside; dive, plummet, plunge, nosedive, pitch, tumble, slump.
▷ANTONYMS ascend, climb.
2 *she descended the stairs*: **climb down**, go down, come down, move down, pass down, walk down; shin down.
▷ANTONYMS ascend, climb.
3 *the road descends to a village situated on the shore*: **slope**, dip, slant, decline, go down, sink, fall away.
4 *she saw Leo **descend from** the local bus*: **alight**, disembark, get down; get off, dismount; detrain, deplane, debus; informal pile out.
▷ANTONYMS board.
5 *if they had right on their side they would not need to **descend to** such mean tricks*: **condescend**, **stoop**, lower oneself, abase oneself, humble oneself, demean oneself, debase oneself, deign; **resort**, be reduced, go as far as; informal come down from one's high horse.
6 *the army had descended into chaos*: **degenerate**, deteriorate, decline, sink, slide, fall, drop; go downhill, decay, worsen, get/grow worse, take a turn for the worse, go to rack and ruin; informal go to pot, go to the dogs, go to seed, hit the skids, go down the tubes, go down the toilet.
▷ANTONYMS improve.
7 *groups of visiting supporters **descended on** a local pub*: **come in force**, arrive in hordes, attack, assail, assault, storm, invade, pounce on, raid, swoop on, charge.
8 *he **is descended from** a Flemish family*: **be a descendant of**, originate from, issue from, spring from, have as an ancestor, derive from.
9 *his estates **descended to** his son*: **be handed down**, be passed down, pass by heredity, be transferred by inheritance; be inherited by.
▷ANTONYMS bequeath to.

descendant noun *a descendant of Charles Darwin*: **successor**, scion; offshoot, heir; (**descendants**) **offspring**, progeny, issue, family, lineage, line; archaic posterity, seed, fruit, fruit of someone's loins.
▷ANTONYMS ancestor.

descent noun **1** *the plane began its descent to Brussels*: **going down**, coming down; drop, fall, sinking, subsiding; dive, pitch, slump.
▷ANTONYMS ascent, climb.
2 *they started their descent of the mountain*: **downward climb**, descending.
▷ANTONYMS ascent, climb.
3 *a steep, badly eroded descent*: **slope**, incline, dip, drop, gradient, declivity, declination, slant, downslope, hill.
4 *he began his calamitous descent into alcoholism*: **degeneration**, degeneracy, deterioration, decline, sinking, slide, fall, drop, regression, retrogression, debasement, degradation, comedown.
5 *his mother was of Italian descent*: **ancestry**, parentage, ancestors, family; lineage, line, line of descent; extraction, origin, derivation, birth; genealogy, heredity, succession; stock, pedigree, blood, bloodline, strain; roots, origins, forefathers, antecedents; rare filiation, stirps.
6 *the descent of property can sometimes be traced over several generations through archives*: **inheritance**, passing down/on, succession.
7 *the sudden descent of the cavalry*: **attack**, assault, raid, onslaught, charge, thrust, push, drive, incursion, foray, sortie, sally, storming, assailing.

describe verb **1** *he described his experiences in a letter to his parents*: **report**, **narrate**, recount, relate, tell of, set out, chronicle; express, put into words, give a description/account of, give details of, detail, represent; evoke, conjure up; catalogue, give a rundown of, paint a word picture of, paint in words; explain, expound, elucidate, illustrate, discuss, comment on.
2 *a lawyer **described** him **as** a pathetic figure*: **designate**, pronounce, call, label, style, dub; characterize, classify, class, categorize, portray, depict, brand, hail, paint.
3 *the tip of the light pen described a circle*: **delineate**, mark out, outline, trace, draw, sketch.

description noun **1** *Darwin's description of the theory of sexual selection | the court demanded a written description of the missing animals*: **account**, explanation, elucidation, illustration, representation, interpretation; chronicle, report, narration, narrative, story, recounting, rendition, relation, commentary, version, portrayal, portrait, word picture, evocation; details.
2 *I object to your description of them as 'paper-shufflers'*: **designation**, styling, calling, labelling, naming, dubbing, pronouncement; **characterization**, classification, classing, categorization, branding; portrayal, depiction, hailing, painting.
3 *the roads were jammed with vehicles of every description*: **sort**, variety, kind, style, type, category, order, breed, species, class, designation, specification, genre, genus, brand, make, character, ilk, kidney, grain, stamp, mould; N. Amer. stripe.

descriptive adjective *his style uses colourful descriptive language*: **illustrative**, expressive, pictorial, depictive, graphic, picturesque, vivid, striking; explanatory, elucidatory, explicative, exegetic, expository; detailed, lively, circumstantial.

descry verb literary *she descried two figures*. See **discern**.

desecrate verb *invaders desecrated the temple*: **violate**, profane, treat sacrilegiously, treat with disrespect; pollute, contaminate, infect, befoul; defile, debase, degrade, dishonour, blaspheme against; vandalize, damage, destroy, deface.
▷ANTONYMS venerate; sanctify.

d

desecration noun *the desecration of the church*: **violation**, profanation, sacrilege; pollution, contamination, infection, befouling; defilement, debasement, degradation, degrading, dishonour, dishonouring, blasphemy; vandalism, damaging, destruction, defacement.
▷ANTONYMS veneration; sanctification.

desert[1] (stress on the second syllable) verb **1** *his wife had deserted him*: **abandon**, leave, give up, cast off, turn one's back on; throw over, betray, jilt, break (up) with; neglect, shun; leave high and dry, leave in the lurch, leave behind, strand, leave stranded, maroon; relinquish, renounce; informal walk/run out on, rat on, drop, dump, ditch; archaic forsake.
▷ANTONYMS stand by.
2 *his allies were quite capable of deserting the cause when it suited them*: **renounce**, renege on, repudiate, forswear, relinquish, wash one's hands of, have no more truck with, have done with, abjure, disavow; abandon, turn one's back on, betray; apostatize, recant; archaic forsake; rare disprofess.
3 *soldiers deserted in droves*: **abscond**, defect, run away, make off, decamp, flee, fly, bolt, turn tail, go absent without leave, take French leave, depart, quit, escape; informal go AWOL.
▷ANTONYMS stay.

desert[2] (stress on the first syllable) noun **1** *the desert of the Sinai peninsula*: **wasteland**, waste, wilderness, wilds, dust bowl, barren land.
2 *a cultural desert*: **uninteresting place/period**, unproductive place/period, wasteland.
▶ adjective **1** *animals have overgrazed the area, creating desert conditions*: **arid**, dry, moistureless, dried up, parched, scorched, burnt, hot, burning, torrid; barren, bare, stark; uncultivatable, infertile, non-fertile, unproductive, unfruitful, dehydrated, sterile.
▷ANTONYMS fertile.
2 *a desert island*: **uninhabited**, empty, solitary, lonely, desolate, bleak, dismal, waste; wild, uncultivated, untended, untilled.

deserted adjective **1** *a deserted wife*: **abandoned**, forsaken, cast off/aside, thrown over, betrayed, jilted; shunned, neglected; stranded, marooned; relinquished, renounced; forlorn, bereft; informal dumped, ditched, dropped.
2 *a deserted village*: **empty**, uninhabited, unoccupied, unpeopled, abandoned, evacuated, vacant, vacated; untenanted, tenantless, unfrequented, neglected; secluded, isolated, desolate, lonely, solitary, godforsaken, forlorn.
▷ANTONYMS crowded; populous.

deserter noun *a deserter from the Foreign Legion*: **absconder**, runaway, renegade, fugitive, truant, escapee; defector, turncoat, traitor, betrayer, apostate; informal rat.

desertion noun **1** *he petitioned for divorce on the grounds of his wife's desertion*: **abandonment**, leaving, forsaking; betrayal, neglect, shunning; stranding, jilting; relinquishment, renunciation.
2 *the desertion of the president's closest colleagues*: **defection**, reneging, betrayal; renunciation, repudiation, forswearing, relinquishment, abjuration; apostasy.
3 *soldiers were executed for desertion*: **absconding**, running away, decamping, flight, fleeing, flying, bolting, turning tail, truancy, going absent without leave, taking French leave, departure, escape, dereliction; defection, treason, betrayal, cowardice; informal going AWOL.

deserve verb *everyone involved with this book deserves the greatest praise*: **merit**, **earn**, warrant, rate, justify, be worthy of, be entitled to, have a right to, have a claim on, be qualified for, be good enough for.
▷ANTONYMS be unworthy of.

> *Choose the right word* **deserve, earn, merit**
>
> See **earn**.

deserved adjective *they clinched a deserved victory*: **well earned**, well deserved, earned, merited, warranted, justified, justifiable; rightful, due, right, just, fair, fitting, appropriate, suitable, proper, reasonable, apt; formal condign; archaic meet.
▷ANTONYMS undeserved.

deservedly adverb *a deservedly popular restaurant*: **justifiably**, **rightfully**, rightly, by rights, justly, fairly, appropriately, fittingly, suitably, aptly, according to one's due, duly; formal condignly.
▷ANTONYMS undeservedly.

deserving adjective **1** *the deserving poor*: **worthy**, meritorious, commendable, praiseworthy, laudable, excellent, fine, admirable, estimable, exemplary, creditable; respectable, decent, honourable, virtuous, righteous, upright, good.
▷ANTONYMS undeserving.
2 *a moral lapse **deserving of** punishment*: **meriting**, warranting, justifying, qualified for, suiting, suitable for, worthy.

desiccated adjective *desiccated coconut*: **dried**, dried up, dry, dehydrated, powdered.
▷ANTONYMS moist.

desideratum noun *integrity was a desideratum*: **requirement**, prerequisite, need, indispensable thing, desired thing, needed thing, essential, requisite, necessary; lack, want, missing thing; dream, ideal, hope, wish; Latin sine qua non.

design noun **1** *an architect submitted a design for the offices*: **plan**, blueprint, drawing, scale drawing, sketch, outline, map, plot, diagram, delineation, draft, depiction, representation, scheme, model, prototype, proposal.
2 *tableware with a sophisticated black and gold design*: **pattern**, motif, device; style, arrangement, composition, make-up, layout, constitution, configuration, organization, construction, shape, form, formation, figure.
3 *he was determined to carry out his design of reaching the top*: **intention**, aim, purpose, plan, intent, objective, object, goal, end, target, point, hope, desire, wish, dream, aspiration, ambition, idea.
□ **by design** *as much as by accident as by design, the group found themselves in a strong position*: **deliberately**, intentionally, on purpose, purposefully; knowingly, wittingly, consciously, premeditatedly, calculatedly.
▷ANTONYMS by accident, accidentally.
▶ verb **1** *this simple church was designed by John Hicks in 1869*: **plan**, draw plans of, draw, sketch, outline, map out, plot, block out, delineate, draft, depict.
2 *they designed a new kind of motor*: **invent**, originate, create, think up, come up with, devise, form, formulate, conceive; make, produce, develop, fashion, fabricate, forge, hatch, coin; informal dream up.
3 *this paper is designed to provoke discussion | a low-price laser printer designed for home use*: **intend**, aim; devise, contrive, purpose, plan; tailor, fashion, make fitting, adjust, adapt, fit, gear, equip; mean, destine, orient.

designate verb **1** *some organizations designate a press officer within the PR office*: **appoint**, nominate, depute, delegate; select, choose, pick, decide on, settle on; elect, name, identify, assign, allot, co-opt, ordain, induct; informal plump for.
2 *a few of the rivers are designated 'Sites of Special Scientific Interest'*: **classify**, class, pronounce, label, tag; name, call, entitle, term, christen, dub, style, brand; formal denominate.
3 *try designating the same time every week to catch up on paperwork*: **allot**, appoint, specify, define; **earmark**, set aside, devote, stipulate, state, particularize, pinpoint.

designation noun **1** *the designation of a leader*: **appointment**, nomination, selection, choice, choosing, picking, election, naming, identifying; co-opting, induction.
2 *one of its roles is the designation of nature reserves*: **classification**, classing, labelling, specification, definition, defining, earmarking, stipulation, particularization, pinpointing.
3 *he added to his existing titles the designation 'Generalissimo'*: **title**, denomination, honorific, label; name, epithet, tag, style, form of address; nickname, byname, sobriquet; rank, status, office, position; informal moniker, handle; formal cognomen, appellation.

designedly adverb *the atmosphere here is designedly old-fashioned*: **deliberately**, by design, on purpose, purposefully, intentionally; consciously, wilfully, intendedly.
▷ANTONYMS unintentionally.

designer noun **1** *he developed a reputation as a designer of farmhouses*: **creator**, deviser, producer, inventor, originator, planner, author, artificer, fabricator; maker, fashioner; architect, engineer, builder.
2 *she picked two young designers to make the wedding dress*: **couturier**, fashion designer, tailor, costumier, dressmaker.

designing adjective *Bob had fallen into the hands of this designing woman*: **scheming**, calculating, conniving, plotting, intriguing, conspiring; cunning, crafty, artful, wily, devious, guileful, canny, shrewd, astute, sharp, insidious, manipulative; treacherous, sly, underhand, deceitful, dishonest, Machiavellian, double-dealing, tricky; informal crooked, foxy.
▷ANTONYMS ingenuous.

desirability noun **1** *the desirability of the property*: **appeal**, attractiveness, allure; agreeableness, worth, eligibility, excellence.
▷ANTONYMS undesirability.
2 *the desirability of a more laissez-faire type of economy*: **advisability**, preferableness, advantage, expedience, benefit, merit, value, profit, profitability; rare advantageousness.
▷ANTONYMS undesirability, disadvantage.
3 *it was humiliating to have her desirability called into question*: **sexual attractiveness**, sexual attraction, attractiveness, beauty, handsomeness, good looks; charm, seductiveness, eroticism, fascination; informal sexiness.

desirable adjective **1** *hospitals are often sited in very desirable locations*: **attractive**, sought-after, in demand, popular, looked-for, longed-for, desired; eligible, appealing, agreeable, pleasant; valuable, good, excellent; covetable, enviable; informal to die for.
▷ANTONYMS undesirable.
2 *it is desirable that they should meet and get to know each other*: **advantageous**, advisable, wise, sensible, prudent, recommendable; helpful, useful, beneficial, worthwhile, profitable, preferable, expedient, in everyone's interests.
▷ANTONYMS disadvantageous.
3 *you're a very desirable woman*: **sexually attractive**, attractive, beautiful, pretty, handsome, appealing; seductive, alluring, enchanting, engaging,

erotic, fetching, fascinating, beguiling, captivating, bewitching, irresistible; informal sexy, beddable.
▷ANTONYMS unattractive, ugly.

desire noun 1 *I had a desire to see the world*: **wish**, want; fancy, inclination, aspiration, impulse, preference; **yearning**, longing, craving, hankering, pining, ache, hunger, thirst, itch, burning, need; eagerness, enthusiasm, determination; predilection, proclivity, predisposition; informal yen.
2 *he gazed at her, his eyes glittering with desire*: **lust**, lustfulness, sexual appetite, sexual attraction, passion, carnal passion, libido, sensuality, sexuality; lasciviousness, lechery, lecherousness, salaciousness, libidinousness, lewdness, licentiousness, prurience, wantonness, carnality; informal the hots, raunchiness, horniness; Brit. informal randiness; rare concupiscence.
▶ verb 1 *they earnestly desired peace*: **wish for**, **want**, long for, yearn for, crave, set one's heart on, hanker after/for, pine for/after, thirst for, itch for, be desperate for, be bent on, have a need for, covet, aspire to; have a fancy for, fancy, feel like, feel in need of; informal have a yen for, yen for, be dying for.
2 *she knew he wanted her as much as she desired him*: **be attracted to**, lust after, burn for, be captivated by, be infatuated by; informal fancy, lech after/over, have the hots for, have a crush on, be wild/mad about, go for.

desired adjective 1 *the cloth is then cut to the desired length*: **required**, necessary, proper, right, correct; appropriate, fitting, suitable, called for; preferred, chosen, selected, expected.
2 *the ruling party is able to manipulate the economy for the desired results on election day*: **wished for**, wanted; sought-after, longed for, yearned for, craved, pined for, needed, coveted.
▷ANTONYMS unwanted.

desirous adjective *he became restless and **desirous of** change*: **eager for**, desiring, wishing for, hoping for, anxious for, keen on/for, avid for, craving for, yearning for, itching for, longing for, thirsty for, hungry for, ravening for, greedy for; ambitious for, aspiring to; covetous, envious; informal dying for.
▷ANTONYMS averse to.

desist verb *we must **desist from** any industrial action that may disturb national unity*: **abstain**, refrain, forbear, hold back, keep; **stop**, cease, discontinue, suspend, give up, quit, break off, leave off, conclude, call a halt/stop to, forgo, drop, dispense with, eschew, have done with, wash one's hands of; informal lay off, give over, pack in, pack up; nautical slang belay.
▷ANTONYMS continue, persist in.

desk noun *he sat at his desk reading reports*: **table**, work surface, bureau, writing desk, writing table, roll-top desk, lectern; counter; Brit. davenport; French escritoire, secretaire.

desolate adjective 1 *the loch was bounded by desolate moorlands*: **barren**, bleak, stark, bare, dismal, grim; desert, waste, arid, sterile; wild, windswept, inhospitable, exposed.
▷ANTONYMS fertile.
2 *a desolate building on a lonely island*: **deserted**, uninhabited, unoccupied, depopulated, forsaken, godforsaken, abandoned, unpeopled, untenanted, evacuated; empty, vacated, vacant; unfrequented, unvisited, solitary, lonely, secluded, isolated, remote.
▷ANTONYMS populous.
3 *she is desolate because she had to disappoint you*: **miserable**, sad, unhappy, melancholy, gloomy, glum, despondent, comfortless, depressed, mournful, disconsolate; broken-hearted, heavy-hearted, grief-stricken; wretched, downcast, cast down, dejected, downhearted, dispirited, devastated, despairing, inconsolable, anguished, crushed, forlorn, crestfallen, upset, distressed, grieving, woebegone, bereft, in low spirits; informal blue, down, cut up.
▷ANTONYMS joyful.
▶ verb 1 *the droughts that desolated the dry plains*: **devastate**, ravage, ruin, make/leave desolate, leave in ruins, destroy, wreck, lay waste to, wreak havoc on; level, raze, demolish, wipe out, obliterate, annihilate, gut; depopulate, empty; rare depredate, spoliate.
2 *she was desolated by the sudden loss of her husband*: **dishearten**, dispirit, daunt, distress, depress, make sad/unhappy, sadden, cast down, deject, make miserable, make gloomy/despondent, weigh down, oppress; informal shatter, floor.
▷ANTONYMS cheer.

desolation noun 1 *the arid, stony desolation of the Gobi desert*: **barrenness**, bleakness, starkness, bareness, dismalness, grimness; aridity, sterility; wildness; isolation, solitude, solitariness, loneliness, remoteness.
▷ANTONYMS fertility.
2 *she was racked by a feeling of utter desolation*: **misery**, sadness, unhappiness, melancholy, gloom, gloominess, glumness, despondency, sorrow, comfortlessness, depression, grief, mournfulness, woe; broken-heartedness, heavy-heartedness, wretchedness, dejection, downheartedness, discouragement, devastation, despair, anguish, distress, low spirits.
▷ANTONYMS joy.

despair noun *many parents feel pain and despair about their teenage children*: **hopelessness**, desperation, distress, anguish, pain, unhappiness; dejection, depression, despondency, disconsolateness, gloom, melancholy, melancholia, misery, wretchedness; disheartenment, discouragement, resignedness, forlornness, defeatism, pessimism.
▷ANTONYMS hope; joy.
□ **be the despair of** *my handwriting was the despair of my teachers*: **be the bane of**, be the scourge of, be a burden on, be a trial to, be a thorn in the flesh/side of, be a bother to, be the ruin of, be the death of.
▶ verb *don't despair if you didn't win this time*: **lose hope**, give up hope, abandon hope, give up, lose heart, be discouraged, be despondent, be demoralized, resign oneself, throw in the towel/sponge, quit, surrender; be pessimistic, look on the black side; archaic despond.

despairing adjective *her mother gave me a despairing look*: **hopeless**, desperate, anguished, distressed, broken-hearted, heartbroken, grief-stricken, inconsolable, sorrowing, suicidal, in despair; dejected, depressed, despondent, disconsolate, gloomy, melancholy, miserable, wretched, desolate, forlorn; disheartened, discouraged, demoralized, devastated, downcast, resigned, defeatist, pessimistic; literary dolorous.
▷ANTONYMS cheerful, optimistic.

despatch verb & noun See **dispatch**.

desperado noun *a gun-toting desperado*: **bandit**, criminal, outlaw, renegade, marauder, raider, robber, lawbreaker, villain; thug, ruffian, tough, hooligan, cut-throat; gangster, pirate, swashbuckler, terrorist, gunman, hoodlum.

desperate adjective 1 *he gave me a desperate look*: **despairing**, hopeless; **anguished**, distressed, in despair, suicidal; miserable, wretched, desolate; forlorn, disheartened, discouraged, demoralized, devastated, downcast, resigned, defeatist, pessimistic; distraught, fraught, overcome, out of one's mind, at one's wits' end, beside oneself, at the end of one's tether; literary dolorous.
▷ANTONYMS cheerful; composed.
2 *a desperate attempt to escape*: **last-ditch**, last-chance, last-resort, last-minute, last-gasp, eleventh-hour, all-out, do-or-die, final; **frantic**, frenzied, wild, straining; futile, hopeless, doomed, lost.
3 *his finances were in a desperate state*: **grave**, serious, dangerous, risky, perilous, hazardous, precarious, critical, acute; **dire**, very bad, calamitous, appalling, awful, terrible, frightful, dreadful, outrageous, intolerable, deplorable, lamentable, sorry, poor; hopeless, irretrievable; informal lousy, chronic; archaic or humorous parlous.
4 *the church is in desperate need of repair*: **urgent**, pressing, compelling, crying; acute, critical, crucial, vital, drastic, serious, grave, dire, extreme, great; formal exigent.
5 *they were **desperate for** food | she is **desperate to** get back to work*: **in great need of**, urgently requiring, craving, in want of, lacking, wanting; **eager**, aching, longing, yearning, hungry, thirsty, thirsting, itching, crying out, desirous; informal dying.
6 *armed bands of desperate men | a desperate act*: **violent**, dangerous, lawless; reckless, rash, hasty, impetuous, foolhardy, incautious; death-or-glory, do-or-die, hazardous, risky.

desperately adverb 1 *he screamed desperately for help*: **in desperation**, in despair, despairingly, in anguish, in distress; miserably, wretchedly, hopelessly, desolately; forlornly, resignedly, defeatedly, pessimistically.
2 *many of them will become desperately ill*: **seriously**, gravely, severely, critically, acutely, dangerously, perilously, hazardously, precariously; very, extremely, awfully, terribly, tremendously, frightfully, dreadfully; hopelessly, irretrievably; informal chronically; archaic or humorous parlously.
▷ANTONYMS slightly.
3 *he desperately wanted to talk to me*: **urgently**, pressingly, intensely, with urgency, eagerly.

desperation noun 1 *he became a thief out of sheer desperation*: **hopelessness**, despair, distress; anguish, pain, agony, torment, torture, misery, wretchedness; disheartenment, discouragement, resignedness, forlornness, defeatism, pessimism.
2 *an act of desperation*: **recklessness**, rashness, impetuosity, foolhardiness, riskiness, audacity, boldness, wildness, imprudence, injudiciousness.

despicable adjective *these were particularly despicable crimes*: **contemptible**, loathsome, hateful, detestable, reprehensible, abhorrent, abominable, awful, heinous, beyond the pale; odious, execrable, repellent, repugnant, repulsive, revolting, disgusting, horrible, horrid, horrifying, obnoxious, nauseating, offensive, distasteful, beneath/below contempt; vile, base, low, mean, abject, shameful, degrading, ignominious, cheap, shabby, miserable, wretched, sorry, scurvy; infamous, villainous, ignoble, disreputable, discreditable, unworthy, unscrupulous, unprincipled, unsavoury; informal dirty, filthy, dirty rotten, rotten, low-down, no-good, beastly, lousy; archaic caitiff.
▷ANTONYMS admirable; noble.

despise verb *he despised weakness in any form*: **detest**, hate, loathe, abhor, abominate, execrate, regard with contempt, feel contempt for, shrink from, be repelled by, not be able to bear/stand/stomach, find intolerable, deplore, dislike; **scorn**, disdain, slight, look down on, pour/heap scorn on, deride, scoff at, jeer at, sneer at, mock, revile; spurn, shun; archaic contemn, disrelish.
▷ANTONYMS like, respect.

d

despite preposition *he was forced to step down as mayor despite his popularity with voters*: **in spite of**, notwithstanding, regardless of, in defiance of, without being affected by, in the face of, for all, even with, undeterred by.
▷ANTONYMS because of.

despoil verb literary **1** *a Cornish village that was despoiled by invaders*: **plunder**, pillage, rob, ravage, harry, maraud, ravish, rape, raid, ransack, loot, sack, rifle; devastate, lay waste, wreak havoc on, vandalize, destroy, ruin, wreck, raze, level, annihilate, gut; rare depredate; archaic reave.
2 *the robbers despoiled him of all he had*: **rob**, strip, deprive, dispossess, denude, divest, relieve, clean out; archaic reave.

despoliation noun *the despoliation of the countryside by the advance of civilization*: **devastation**, destruction, ruin, ruination, ravaging, vandalism, depredation, despoilment; plunder, plundering, looting, pillage, harrying, marauding, ransacking, raiding, ravishing, rape, raping, sacking; archaic reaving.

despondency noun *the mood became one of gloom and despondency*: **disheartenment**, discouragement, dispiritedness, downheartedness, low spirits, hopelessness, despair, wretchedness; melancholy, gloom, gloominess, glumness, melancholia, misery, depression, desolation, disappointment, dolefulness, dejection, sorrow, sadness, grief, distress, unhappiness; defeatism, pessimism; the doldrums; informal the blues, heartache.
▷ANTONYMS cheerfulness, hopefulness.

despondent adjective *they were tired and despondent*: **disheartened**, discouraged, dispirited, downhearted, low-spirited, in low spirits, hopeless, downcast, cast down, crestfallen, down, low, disconsolate, in despair, despairing, wretched, oppressed; melancholy, gloomy, glum, morose, Eeyorish, doleful, dismal, woebegone, miserable, depressed, dejected, distressed, sorrowful, sad; defeatist, pessimistic; informal blue, down in the mouth, down in the dumps, as sick as a parrot.
▷ANTONYMS hopeful; cheerful.

despot noun *we must not support such despots by arming them*: **tyrant**, dictator, absolute ruler, totalitarian, authoritarian, autocrat, oppressor, autarch, monocrat.
▷ANTONYMS democrat.

despotic adjective *a despotic regime*: **autocratic**, dictatorial, totalitarian, authoritarian, absolute, absolutist, arbitrary, unconstitutional, undemocratic, uncontrolled, unaccountable, summary; one-party, single-party, autarchic, monocratic; **tyrannical**, oppressive, tyrannous, repressive, harsh, ruthless, merciless, draconian, illiberal; domineering, imperious, arrogant, high-handed.
▷ANTONYMS democratic, accountable.

Choose the right word **despotic, autocratic, tyrannical**

See **autocratic**.

despotism noun **tyranny**, dictatorship, totalitarianism, authoritarianism, absolute rule, absolutism; oppression, repression, suppression; autocracy, monocracy, autarchy.
▷ANTONYMS democracy.

dessert noun **pudding**, sweet, sweet course/dish, second course, last course; Brit. informal afters, pud.

destabilize verb *the tsar's isolation helped to destabilize the regime*: **undermine**, weaken, impair, damage, subvert, sabotage, unsettle, upset, disrupt, wreck, ruin.
▷ANTONYMS strengthen, shore up.

destination noun *at around 1pm we arrived at our destination*: **journey's end**, end of the line, landing place, point of disembarkation; terminus, station, stop, stopping place, port of call; goal, target, objective, end, purpose.

destined adjective **1** *he seemed **destined for** a military career | he is **destined to** lead a troubled life*: **fated**, ordained, preordained, foreordained, predestined, predetermined, certain; sure, bound, assured, guaranteed, very likely; doomed, foredoomed, meant; written in the cards, in the wind/air.
2 *a consignment of computers **destined for** Pakistan*: **heading**, bound, en route, scheduled; directed to, routed to; **intended**, meant, designed, set; set apart, designated, appointed, allotted, booked, reserved.

destiny noun **1** *man is master of his own destiny*: **future**, fate, fortune, doom; lot, portion, due; nemesis; literary dole.
2 *the girl who found him that day was sent by destiny*: **fate**, providence; predestination; divine decree, God's will, kismet, the stars; luck, fortune, chance; Hinduism & Buddhism karma; Greek & Roman Mythology the Fates; Greek Mythology Moirai; Roman Mythology Parcae; Norse Mythology the Norns.

destitute adjective **1** *her parents died and she was left destitute*: **penniless**, impoverished, poverty-stricken, poor, impecunious, indigent, down and out, pauperized, without a penny to one's name, without two farthings/pennies to rub together; insolvent, ruined; needy, in need, in want, hard up, on the breadline, hard-pressed, in reduced/straitened circumstances, deprived, disadvantaged, distressed, badly off; beggarly, beggared; informal on one's uppers, up against it, broke, flat broke, strapped (for cash), without a brass farthing, without a bean, without a sou, as poor as a church mouse, on one's beam-ends; Brit. informal stony broke, skint, boracic (lint); N. Amer. informal stone broke, without a red cent, on skid row; formal penurious.
▷ANTONYMS rich.
2 *we were **destitute of** clothing*: **devoid**, bereft, deprived, in need; bankrupt, empty, drained, exhausted, depleted, bare, denuded; lacking, without, deficient in, wanting; informal sans.
▷ANTONYMS well provided with.

destitution noun *he died leaving a wife and child in destitution*: **dire poverty**, extreme poverty, poverty, impoverishment, insolvency, penury, pennilessness, impecuniousness, privation, indigence, ruin, ruination, pauperdom; hardship, neediness, need, want, reduced/straitened circumstances, dire straits, deprivation, disadvantage, distress, financial distress, difficulties; life on the breadline; beggary, mendicancy, vagrancy.
▷ANTONYMS wealth.

destroy verb **1** *their offices were completely destroyed by bombing*: **demolish**, knock down, pull down, tear down, level, raze (to the ground), fell, dismantle, break up, wreck, ruin, smash, shatter, crash, blast, blow up, blow to bits/pieces, dynamite, explode, bomb, torpedo.
▷ANTONYMS build; reconstruct.
2 *the increased traffic would destroy the adjoining conservation area*: **spoil**, ruin, wreck, disfigure, blight, mar, blemish, impair, flaw, deface, scar, injure, harm, devastate, damage, lay waste, ravage, wreak havoc on; literary waste; rare disfeature.
▷ANTONYMS preserve; restore.
3 *his illness destroyed his hopes of going to university*: **wreck**, ruin, spoil, disrupt, undo, upset, play havoc with, make a mess of, put an end to, end, bring to an end, put a stop to, terminate, prevent, frustrate, blight, crush, quell, quash, dash, scotch, shatter, vitiate, blast, devastate, demolish, sabotage, torpedo; upset someone's apple cart, cook someone's goose; informal mess up, muck up, screw up, louse up, foul up, make a hash of, do in, put paid to, put the lid on, put the kibosh on, do for, scupper, dish, stymie, queer, nix, banjax, blow a hole in; Brit. informal throw a spanner in the works of, muller; N. Amer. informal throw a monkey wrench in the works of; Austral. informal euchre, cruel; vulgar slang bugger up, fuck up, balls up; archaic bring to naught.
▷ANTONYMS raise.
4 *the horse broke its leg and had to be destroyed*: **kill**, kill off, put down, put to sleep, slaughter, terminate, exterminate.
5 *the brigade's mission was to destroy the enemy*: **annihilate**, wipe out, obliterate, wipe off the face of the earth, wipe off the map, eliminate, eradicate, liquidate, extinguish, finish off, erase, root out, extirpate; kill, slaughter, massacre, butcher, exterminate, decimate; informal take out, rub out, snuff out, zap; N. Amer. informal waste.
▷ANTONYMS spare.
6 *Rangers last night destroyed Leeds 4–0*: **defeat utterly**, beat hollow, win a resounding victory over, annihilate, vanquish, drub, trounce, rout, crush, give someone a drubbing, overwhelm; informal lick, thrash, hammer, clobber, paste, give someone a pasting, whip, pound, pulverize, demolish, wipe the floor with, take to the cleaners, make mincemeat of, slaughter, murder, massacre, crucify, flatten, turn inside out, run rings around; Brit. informal stuff, marmalize; N. Amer. informal shellac, blow out, cream, skunk.
▷ANTONYMS lose to.

destruction noun **1** *journalists reported considerable destruction within the town by allied bombers*: **demolition**, knocking down, pulling down, tearing down, levelling, razing (to the ground), felling, dismantling, breaking up, wrecking, ruination, smashing, shattering, blasting, blowing up, dynamiting, bombing, torpedoing.
2 *the continuing destruction of the countryside*: **spoliation**, devastation, spoiling, ruination, wrecking, blighting, marring, disfigurement, impairment, defacing, scarring, injury, harm, laying waste, desolation, ravaging; literary wasting.
3 *the destruction of BSE-infected cattle*: **killing**, killing off, putting down, putting to sleep, slaughter, slaughtering, extermination, termination.
4 *the careful and strategic destruction of the enemies' forces*: **annihilation**, wiping out, obliteration, elimination, eradication, liquidation, extinction, finishing off, rooting out, extirpation; killing, slaughter, slaughtering, massacre, massacring, butchery, butchering, extermination, decimation; informal taking out, rubbing out, snuffing out, zapping; N. Amer. informal wasting.

destructive adjective **1** *the most destructive war the world has seen*: **devastating**, ruinous, disastrous, catastrophic, calamitous, cataclysmic; pernicious, noxious, harmful, damaging, injurious, hurtful, wounding, violent, detrimental, deleterious, disadvantageous, ravaging, crippling, savage, fierce, brutal, dangerous, fatal, deadly, lethal, death-dealing.
▷ANTONYMS non-violent; creative.
2 *he takes a savage pleasure in destructive rather than constructive criticism*: **negative**, hostile, antagonistic; unhelpful, disobliging, obstructive, vexatious, vicious, unfriendly, discouraging.
▷ANTONYMS constructive.

desultory adjective *the Commission took only a desultory interest in humane slaughter methods*: **casual**, half-hearted, lukewarm, cursory, superficial, token, perfunctory, passing, incidental, sketchy, haphazard, random, aimless, rambling, erratic, unmethodical, unsystematic, automatic, unthinking, capricious, mechanical, offhand, chaotic, inconsistent, irregular, intermittent, occasional, sporadic, inconstant, fitful.
▷ANTONYMS keen; systematic; lasting.

detach verb **1** *he detached the front lamp from its bracket*: **unfasten**, disconnect, disengage, part, separate, uncouple, remove, loose, loosen, untie, unhitch, undo, unhook, unbutton, unzip, free, sever, pull off, cut off, clip off, hack off, chop off, prune off, nip off, tear off, break off, strip off, disunite; rare disjoin.
▷ANTONYMS attach.
2 *a policeman* ***detached himself from*** *the crowd*: **free**, separate, segregate; **move away**, walk away, move off, split off; leave, abandon.
▷ANTONYMS join.
3 *he has completely* ***detached himself from*** *the group whose principles he rejects*: **dissociate**, divorce, alienate, separate, segregate, isolate, cut off, delink; break away, become estranged, disaffiliate, defect; leave, quit, withdraw from, secede from, break with, part company with, sever connections with, break off relations with; reach a parting of the ways; Brit. informal bust up.
▷ANTONYMS associate; join.

detached adjective **1** *a detached collar*: **unfastened**, disconnected, disengaged, parted, separated, separate, uncoupled, removed, loosed, loosened, untied, unhitched, undone, unhooked, unbuttoned, unzipped, free, severed, cut off, hacked off, torn off, broken off.
▷ANTONYMS connected.
2 *she remained a detached observer of these events*: **dispassionate**, disinterested, indifferent, objective, uninvolved, aloof, outside, remote, distant, impersonal, open-minded, neutral, unbiased, unprejudiced, impartial, non-partisan, with no axe to grind, fair, fair-minded, just, equitable, even-handed, unselfish.
▷ANTONYMS biased; involved.
3 *a detached house*: **standing alone**, separate, unconnected, not attached.
▷ANTONYMS semi-detached; terraced.

detachment noun **1** *as an anthropologist you look on everything with detachment*: **objectivity**, **dispassion**, dispassionateness, disinterest, indifference, aloofness, remoteness, distance, open-mindedness, neutrality, lack of bias, lack of prejudice, impartiality, fairness, fair-mindedness, equitability, even-handedness, unselfishness.
▷ANTONYMS bias; involvement.
2 *a detachment of soldiers*: **unit**, detail, squad, troop, contingent, outfit, task force, crew, patrol, section, formation; squadron, flight, division, platoon, company, corps, regiment, brigade, battalion, force, garrison, legion.
3 *moisture coming through the plaster accounted for the detachment of the wallpaper*: **loosening**, disconnection, unfastening, disengagement, parting, separation, uncoupling, removal, loosing, untying, unhitching, undoing, unhooking, unbuttoning, unzipping, freeing, severing, pulling off, cutting off, hacking off, chopping off, pruning, breaking off, disuniting.
▷ANTONYMS attachment.

detail noun **1** *he had made a replica of the uniform, correct in every detail*: **particular**, feature, characteristic, respect, ingredient, attribute, item, specific, fact, piece of information, point, factor, element, circumstance, consideration, aspect, facet, side, part, unit, component, constituent, member, accessory.
▷ANTONYMS outline; overview.
2 *never mind—that's just a detail*: **unimportant point**, insignificant item, trivial fact, nicety, subtlety; **triviality**, technicality, minor detail, petty detail, mere detail, matter/thing of no importance, matter/thing of no consequence, trifle, fine point, incidental, non-essential, inessential, nothing; (**details**) trivia, minutiae.
▷ANTONYMS salient point.
3 *some clubs maintain their records with a considerable degree of detail*: **precision**, exactness, accuracy, rigour, strictness, thoroughness, carefulness, scrupulousness, meticulousness, particularity.
4 *the sergeant major was inspecting a guard detail*: **unit**, detachment, squad, troop, contingent, outfit, task force, crew, patrol, section, formation.
5 *I didn't often get the toilet detail*: **task**, job, duty, chore, charge, labour, piece of work, piece of business, assignment, function, commission, secondment, mission, engagement, occupation, undertaking, exercise, business, office, responsibility, errand.
□ **in detail** *this assumption will be examined in detail in Chapter 3*: **thoroughly**, in depth, exhaustively, from top to bottom, minutely, closely, point by point, item by item, blow by blow, meticulously, rigorously, scrupulously, assiduously, conscientiously, painstakingly, methodically, carefully, sedulously, completely, comprehensively, fully, to the fullest extent, intensively, extensively.
▸ verb **1** *the report details a series of objections to the plan*: **present**, describe, set out, set forth, draw up, delineate, frame; explain, expound, relate, give an account of, recount, narrate, recite, rehearse, catalogue, list, spell out, point out, itemize, enumerate, tabulate, particularize; **identify**, specify, define, state, declare, announce, cite, quote, instance, mention, name, designate, be specific about; rare individuate.
▷ANTONYMS outline.
2 *troops were detailed to prevent the feared rescue attempt*: **assign**, allocate, appoint, delegate, commission, ordain, charge, send, post, nominate, vote, elect, adopt, co-opt, select, choose.

detailed adjective *he was able to give the police a detailed description of his attacker*: **comprehensive**, full, complete, circumstantial, thorough, exhaustive, all-inclusive; elaborate, minute, intricate; explicit, specific, precise, exact, accurate, meticulous, painstaking; itemized, particularized, particular, blow-by-blow.
▷ANTONYMS general; brief.

detain verb **1** *they were detained for questioning*: **hold**, take into custody, put into custody, place in custody, remand in custody, hold in custody, keep in custody, take (in), seize, confine, imprison, lock up, put in jail, put behind bars, incarcerate, impound, intern, restrain, arrest, apprehend; informal pick up, run in, pull in, haul in, cop, bust, nab, nail, do, collar, feel someone's collar; Brit. informal nick, pinch.
▷ANTONYMS release.
2 *don't let me detain you*: **delay**, hold up, make late, retard, keep (back), slow up, slow down, set back, get bogged down; hinder, hamper, impede, obstruct.

detect verb **1** *because of the extractor fans, no one had detected the smell of diesel*: **notice**, become aware of, perceive, note, discern, make out, observe, spot, become conscious of, recognize, distinguish, mark, remark, identify, diagnose; catch, decry, sense, see, catch sight of, smell, scent, taste; Brit. informal clock; literary behold, descry, espy.
2 *the directors are responsible for preventing and detecting fraud*: **discover**, uncover, find, find out, turn up, unearth, dig up, dredge up, root out, hunt out, nose out, ferret out, expose, reveal, bring to light, bring into the open; come across, stumble on, chance on, hit on, encounter.
3 *police are still hoping to detect this crime*: **solve**, clear up, get to the bottom of, find the perpetrator of, find the person behind; informal figure out, crack.
4 *hackers can make huge sums of money before being detected*: **catch**, hunt down, find, expose, reveal, unmask, smoke out, ferret out, track down, apprehend, arrest; informal nail.

detection noun **1** *the detection of methane and ammonia in the atmosphere in the 1930s*: **observation**, noticing, noting, discernment, perception, spotting, awareness, recognition, distinguishing, identification, diagnosis; sensing, sight, smelling, tasting.
2 *the detection of insider dealing has increased*: **discovery**, uncovering, unearthing, rooting out, exposure, revelation.
3 *the detection rate for burglary in dwellings is now less than 20%*: **solving**, clear-up.
4 *somehow he managed to escape detection*: **capture**, identification, exposure, unmasking, tracking down, apprehension, arrest.

detective noun **investigator**, private detective, private investigator, operative; Brit. enquiry agent, CID officer, detective constable, DC, detective sergeant, DS, detective inspector, DI, detective chief inspector, DCI, detective superintendent, detective chief superintendent; informal private eye, PI, sleuth, sleuth-hound, jack, snoop, snooper; N. Amer. informal peeper, shamus, gumshoe; informal, dated dick, private dick, tec, bogey, hawkshaw, sherlock; N. Amer. dated Pinkerton.

detention noun *she was released after spending over a year in police detention*: **custody**, imprisonment, confinement, incarceration, internment, captivity, restraint, arrest, house arrest, remand, committal; quarantine; archaic duress, durance; rare detainment.

deter verb **1** *the high cost has deterred many from attending*: **put off**, discourage, dissuade, scare off; warn, caution; dishearten, demoralize, daunt, make worried/nervous/anxious, frighten, unnerve, intimidate.
▷ANTONYMS encourage.
2 *the presence of a caretaker deters crime*: **prevent**, stop, put a stop to, avert, nip in the bud, fend off, turn aside, stave off, ward off, head off, shut out, block, intercept, halt, arrest, check, stay, keep, hinder, impede, hamper, obstruct, baulk, foil, thwart, obviate, frustrate, forestall, counteract, inhibit, hold back, curb, restrain, preclude, pre-empt, save, help; archaic let.
▷ANTONYMS encourage.

> *Choose the right word* **deter, discourage, dissuade**
>
> See **discourage**.

detergent noun *use ordinary washing detergent*: **cleaner**, cleanser; washing powder, washing-up liquid; soap powder, soap flakes.
▸ adjective *staining that resists detergent action*: **cleaning**, cleansing; technical abstergent, surface-active.

deteriorate verb **1** *his condition has deteriorated in the intensive care unit*: **worsen**, get worse, decline, be in decline, degenerate, decay; collapse, fail, fall, drop, sink, slump, slip, slide, go downhill, go backwards, go to rack and ruin, stagnate, wane, ebb; informal go to pot, go to the dogs, hit the skids,

go down the toilet, go down the tubes; Austral./NZ informal go to the pack; rare retrograde.
▷ANTONYMS improve.
2 *many of these materials deteriorate badly if stored in damp conditions*: **decay**, degrade, degenerate, break down, decompose, rot, putrefy, go bad, go off, spoil, perish; wither, atrophy, weaken, fade, break up, disintegrate, become dilapidated, crumble, fall down, collapse, fall apart, fall to pieces; archaic corrupt.

deterioration noun 1 *a sharp deterioration in law and order*: **worsening**, decline, decay, collapse, failure, fall, drop, downturn, slump, slip, slide, stagnation, waning, ebb, retrogression.
▷ANTONYMS improvement.
2 *condensation in lofts can cause deterioration of the roof structure*: **decay**, degradation, degeneration, breakdown, decomposition, rot, putrefaction, spoliation, perishing; withering, atrophy, weakening, fading, break-up, disintegration, dilapidation, crumbling, collapse, falling down, falling apart, falling to pieces; archaic corruption.

d

determinate adjective *a determinate hierarchy of authority*: **fixed**, settled, specified, quantified, established, defined, explicit, known, determined, definitive, conclusive, express, precise, final, ultimate, absolute, categorical, positive, definite.
▷ANTONYMS indeterminate.

determination noun 1 *it took all her determination to stand her ground*: **resolution**, resolve, resoluteness; **will power**, strength of will, strength of character, single-mindedness, sense of purpose, firmness of purpose, fixity of purpose, purposefulness; intentness, decision, decidedness; steadfastness, staunchness, perseverance, persistence, indefatigability, tenacity, tenaciousness, staying power, strong-mindedness, backbone, the bulldog spirit, pertinacity, pertinaciousness; stubbornness, doggedness, obstinacy, obdurateness, obduracy, inflexibility; spiritedness, braveness, bravery, boldness, courage, courageousness, pluck, pluckiness, stout-heartedness; German sitzfleisch; informal guts, spunk, grit, stickability; N. Amer. informal stick-to-it-iveness; archaic intension; rare perseveration.
▷ANTONYMS weak-mindedness, pusillanimity.
2 *provision should be made for determination of the rent*: **setting**, fixing, specification, a decision about, settlement, designation, allotment, arrangement, choice, naming, nomination, appointment, establishment, authorization, prescription.
3 *the first determination of the speed of light*: **calculation**, discovery, ascertainment, establishment, fixing, deduction, divination, diagnosis, discernment, check, verification, confirmation.

determine verb 1 *it is this last pair of chromosomes which determines the sex of the embryo*: **control**, decide, regulate, direct, rule, dictate, govern, condition, form, shape; affect, have an effect on, influence, exert influence on, sway, act on, work on, mould, modify, alter, touch, have an impact on, impact on.
2 *he determined to sell up and go abroad*: **resolve**, decide, come to a decision, make a decision, reach a decision, make up one's mind, choose, elect, opt; formal purpose.
3 *the rent shall be determined by a qualified accountant*: **specify**, set, fix, decide on, come to a decision about, settle, assign, designate, allot, arrange, choose, name, appoint, establish, authorize, ordain, prescribe, decree.
4 *the first step is to determine the composition of the raw materials*: **find out**, discover, ascertain, learn, establish, fix, settle, decide, calculate, work out, make out, fathom (out), get/come to know, ferret out, deduce, divine, intuit, diagnose, discern, check, verify, confirm, make certain of, certify; informal figure out, get a fix on.
5 *I am not sure what determined her to write to me*: **prompt**, impel, induce, influence, sway, lead, move, cause, motivate, stimulate, prod, spur on, provoke, incite, dispose, incline, persuade, encourage, urge, inspire; make.

> *Choose the right word* **determine, decide, resolve**
>
> See **decide**.

determined adjective 1 *he was determined to have his way | she was absolutely* ***determined on*** *going*: **intent on**, bent on, set on, dead set on, insistent on, fixed on, resolved on/to, firm about, committed to, hell-bent on; single-minded about, obsessive about, obsessed with, fanatical about, fixated on.
2 *he sounds a very determined man*: **resolute**, full of determination, purposeful, purposive, resolved, decided, adamant, single-minded, firm, unswerving, unswervable, unwavering, undaunted, fixed, set, intent, insistent; steadfast, staunch, stalwart, earnest, manful, deliberate, unfaltering, unhesitating, unflinching, persevering, persistent, pertinacious, indefatigable, tenacious, bulldog, strong-minded, strong-willed, unshakeable, unshaken, steely, four-square, dedicated, committed; stubborn, dogged, obstinate, obdurate, inflexible, relentless, intransigent, implacable, unyielding, unbending, immovable, unrelenting; spirited, brave, bold, courageous, plucky, stout, stout-hearted, mettlesome, indomitable, strenuous, vigorous, gritty, stiff; N. Amer. rock-ribbed; informal gutsy, spunky; rare perseverant, indurate.
▷ANTONYMS irresolute; weak-willed, pusillanimous.

> *Word toolkit* **determined**
>
> See **staunch**[1].

determining adjective *the size of your house may be the determining factor*: **deciding**, decisive, conclusive, final, settling, definitive, key, pivotal, crucial, critical, most influential, significant, major, chief, principal, prime, paramount.

deterrent noun *complications of this nature are a deterrent to investors*: **disincentive**, discouragement, dissuasion, damper, brake, curb, check, restraint; obstacle, hindrance, impediment, obstruction, block, barrier, inhibition.
▷ANTONYMS incentive; encouragement.

detest verb *I do detest social climbers*: **abhor**, hate, loathe, despise, abominate, execrate, regard with disgust, feel disgust for, feel repugnance towards, feel distaste for, shrink from, recoil from, shudder at, be unable to bear, be unable to abide, feel hostility to, feel aversion to, feel animosity to, find intolerable, dislike, disdain, have an aversion to; archaic disrelish.
▷ANTONYMS love, admire.

detestable adjective *such behaviour is detestable and despicable*: **abhorrent**, detested, hateful, hated, loathsome, loathed, despicable, despised, abominable, abominated, execrable, execrated, repellent, repugnant, repulsive, revolting, disgusting, distasteful, horrible, horrid, horrifying, awful, heinous, reprehensible, obnoxious, odious, nauseating, offensive, contemptible.
▷ANTONYMS lovable, admirable.

detestation noun *their detestation of their ideological foes*: **hatred**, loathing, abhorrence, execration, revulsion, abomination, disgust, repugnance, horror, antipathy, odium, aversion, hostility, animosity, enmity, dislike, distaste, disdain, contempt; archaic disrelish; rare repellence, repellency.
▷ANTONYMS love.

dethrone verb *he had hoped to dethrone the king*: **depose**, oust, uncrown, topple, overthrow, bring down, unseat, remove from office, dislodge, discharge, displace, supplant, usurp, overturn, dismiss, eject; informal drum out; archaic unthrone.
▷ANTONYMS enthrone, crown.

detonate verb 1 *the depth charge detonated directly under the engine compartment*: **explode**, go off, be set off, blow up, burst apart, shatter, erupt; ignite; bang, blast, boom, go bang, go boom.
2 *they detonated the bomb by remote control*: **set off**, explode, discharge, let off, touch off, trigger; ignite, kindle, light, spark.

detonation noun *the detonation of the first atomic bomb*: **explosion**, discharge, blowing up, ignition, blast, burst, crack, bang, report.

detour noun *visiting Bagley meant a detour of only a mile or so*: **roundabout route**, indirect route, circuitous route, scenic route, tourist route, diversion, bypass, ring road, alternative route, digression, deviation, byway, bypath; Brit. relief road; Brit. informal rat run.
▷ANTONYMS direct route.

detract verb 1 *the few reservations I have expressed are not intended to* ***detract from*** *the book's excellence*: **belittle**, take away from, diminish, reduce, lessen, minimize, lower, make light of, play down, discount, soft-pedal, brush aside, gloss over, trivialize, decry, depreciate, denigrate, devalue, devaluate, deprecate; informal pooh-pooh; archaic hold cheap; rare derogate, misprize, minify.
▷ANTONYMS enhance.
2 *if too many patterns are used together, they will detract attention from each other*: **divert**, distract, turn away, turn aside, draw away, head off, deflect, avert, shift.
▷ANTONYMS attract.

detractor noun *detractors complained about the display's confused nature*: **critic**, disparager, denigrator, deprecator, belittler, attacker, censurer, fault-finder, carper, backbiter, caviller, reviler, vilifier, slanderer, libeller, calumniator, defamer, traducer; informal mud-slinger, knocker, nit-picker; rare asperser.

detriment noun *some light industry can generally be carried out in a residential area without detriment to its amenities*: **harm**, damage, injury, hurt, impairment, loss, prejudice, disadvantage, disservice, ill, wrong, mischief.
▷ANTONYMS benefit, good.

detrimental adjective *the erosion will have a detrimental effect on water quality*: **harmful**, damaging, injurious, hurtful, inimical, deleterious, dangerous, destructive, ruinous, calamitous, disastrous, pernicious, ill, bad, evil, baleful, malign, corrupting, malignant, adverse, undesirable, prejudicial, unfavourable, unfortunate, counterproductive; unhealthy, unwholesome, poisonous, cancerous, noxious, deadly, lethal, fatal; literary malefic, maleficent; rare prejudicious.
▷ANTONYMS benign; beneficial.

detritus noun *large areas of land are now littered with military detritus*: **debris**, waste, waste matter, discarded matter, refuse, rubbish, litter, scrap, flotsam and jetsam, lumber, rubble, wreckage; remains, remnants, fragments, scraps, spoilage, dregs, leavings, sweepings, dross, scum, chaff, offscourings, swill, slag; N. Amer. trash, garbage; Austral./NZ mullock; informal dreck, junk; Brit. informal grot, gash; vulgar slang shit, crap; Archaeology debitage; rare draff, raffle, raff, cultch, orts.

devalue verb *our culture devalues the reasons for getting married*: **belittle**, depreciate, disparage, denigrate, decry, deprecate, make light of, treat lightly, discredit, underrate, undervalue, underestimate, deflate, detract from, diminish, minimize, trivialize, run down, traduce, defame; informal knock, slam, pan, bad-mouth, sell short, put down, pooh-pooh, look down one's nose at, do down, do a hatchet job on, take to pieces, pull apart, pick holes in, drag through the mud, have a go at, hit out at; Brit. informal rubbish, slate, slag off; archaic cry down, hold cheap; rare derogate, misprize, minify.

devastate verb **1** *the city was devastated by a huge earthquake*: **destroy**, ruin, leave in ruins, wreck, lay waste, wreak havoc on, ravage, ransack, leave desolate, demolish, raze (to the ground), level, flatten, annihilate.
2 *he was devastated by the news*: **shatter**, shock, stun, daze, dumbfound, traumatize, crush, overwhelm, overcome, greatly upset, distress; informal knock for six, knock sideways, knock the stuffing out of.

devastating adjective **1** *a devastating cyclone struck Bangladesh in April*: **destructive**, ruinous, disastrous, catastrophic, calamitous, cataclysmic; pernicious, noxious, harmful, damaging, injurious, hurtful, wounding, violent, detrimental, deleterious, disadvantageous, ravaging, crippling, savage, fierce, brutal, dangerous, fatal, deadly, lethal, death-dealing.
2 *a bereavement can be a devastating blow*: **shattering**, shocking, traumatic, overwhelming, crushing, extremely upsetting, distressing, severe, savage, terrible, very great; informal gut-wrenching.
3 informal *he could look utterly devastating when he wanted to*: **gorgeous**, stunning, glamorous, dazzling, ravishing, striking, beautiful, lovely, captivating, bewitching, beguiling, engaging, charming, charismatic, enchanting, appealing, arresting, delightful, irresistible, desirable, luscious, sexy, sexually attractive, seductive, alluring; informal fanciable, beddable, tasty, hot, smashing, knockout, drop-dead gorgeous, out of this world, easy on the eye; Brit. informal fit; N. Amer. informal cute, foxy; Austral./NZ informal spunky; literary beauteous; archaic taking, well favoured, comely, fair; rare sightly, pulchritudinous.
4 informal *he presented devastating arguments against the plan*: **incisive**, highly effective, penetrating, cutting, mordant, trenchant; withering, blistering, searing, scathing, scorching, fierce, ferocious, savage, severe, stinging, biting, virulent, caustic, vitriolic, scornful, sharp, bitter, acid, harsh, unsparing; rare mordacious.

devastation noun **1** *the hurricane passed, leaving a trail of devastation in its wake*: **destruction**, ruin, desolation, depredation, waste, havoc, wreckage; ruins, ravages.
2 *the devastation of East Prussia by Russian troops in 1758*: **laying waste**, destruction, wrecking, ruination, despoliation, ransacking, ravaging; demolition, razing, levelling, flattening, annihilation; literary rape.
3 *the devastation you have caused the families of your victims*: **shock**, trauma, upheaval, distress, stress, strain, pain, anguish, suffering, upset, agony, misery, sorrow, grief, heartache, heartbreak, torture, traumatization.

develop verb **1** *France's space industry developed rapidly after 1973*: **grow**, evolve, mature, expand, enlarge, spread, advance, progress, prosper, succeed, thrive, get on well, flourish, blossom, bloom, burgeon, make headway, be successful; informal go great guns.
2 *a plan was developed to restore the company to profitability*: **initiate**, instigate, set in motion, put in place, institute, inaugurate, originate, invent, form, establish, fashion, generate; undertake, embark on.
3 *education allows people to develop their talents to the full*: **expand**, enlarge, add to, flesh out, supplement, reinforce, augment, extend, broaden, fill out, embellish, enhance, elaborate, amplify, refine, improve, polish, perfect.
4 *a row developed*: **come into being**, come about, start, begin, be born, come into existence, appear, arrive, come forth, emerge, erupt, burst out, arise, originate, break, unfold, crop up, follow, happen, result, ensue, break out; formal commence.
5 *he developed the disease at age 67*: **fall ill with**, be taken ill with, be struck down with, be stricken with, succumb to; contract, catch, get, pick up, come down with, become infected with; Brit. go down with; informal take ill with; N. Amer. informal take sick with.

development noun **1** *the next stage in the development of this form of transport*: **evolution**, growth, maturing, expansion, enlargement, spread, buildout, progress, success, blossoming, blooming, burgeoning, headway.
2 *the development of the idea of a nation*: **forming**, establishment, institution, initiation, instigation, inauguration, origination, invention, generation.
3 *have there been any developments?* **event**, turn of events, occurrence, happening, circumstance, incident, phenomenon, situation, issue, outcome, upshot.
4 *a housing development*: **estate**, complex, site, conglomeration.

deviant adjective *deviant behaviour*: **aberrant**, deviating, divergent, abnormal, atypical, untypical, non-typical, anomalous, digressive, irregular, non-standard; nonconformist, rogue, perverse, transgressing, wayward; strange, odd, peculiar, uncommon, unusual, freak, freakish, curious, bizarre, eccentric, idiosyncratic, unorthodox, exceptional, singular, unrepresentative; distorted, twisted, warped, perverted; informal bent, kinky, quirky.
▷ANTONYMS normal; orthodox.
▶ noun *lone parents are likely to be treated as deviants*: **nonconformist**, eccentric, maverick, individualist, exception, outsider, misfit, fish out of water, square peg in a round hole, round peg in a square hole; informal oddball, odd fish, weirdo, weirdie, freak; N. Amer. informal screwball, kook.

deviate verb *you must not* **deviate from** *the agreed route*: **diverge**, digress, drift, stray, slew, veer, swerve, turn away, turn aside, get sidetracked, branch off, differ, vary, change, depart, be different; be at variance with, run counter to, contrast with, contravene, contradict; rare divagate.

deviation noun *the slightest deviation from approved procedures could prove disastrous*: **divergence**, digression, turning aside, departure, deflection, difference, variation, variance, alteration, veering, straying, fluctuation, aberration, abnormality, irregularity, anomaly, inconsistency, discrepancy, variableness, oddness, freakishness; change, shift, veer, swerve, bend, drift.

device noun **1** *a device for measuring rapid pressure fluctuations*: **implement**, gadget, utensil, tool, appliance, piece of equipment, apparatus, piece of apparatus, piece of hardware, instrument, machine, mechanism, contrivance, contraption, invention, convenience, amenity, aid; informal gizmo, widget, mod con.
2 *he found an ingenious legal device to avoid facing prosecution*: **ploy**, plan, cunning plan, tactic, move, means, stratagem, scheme, plot, trick, ruse, gambit, manoeuvre, machination, intrigue, contrivance, expedient, dodge, artifice, subterfuge, game, wile; Brit. informal wheeze; archaic shift.
3 *their shields bear the device of the Blazing Sun*: **emblem**, symbol, logo, badge, stamp, trademark, crest, insignia, coat of arms, escutcheon, seal, mark, figure, design, rune, logotype, logogram, monogram, hallmark, tag, motto, token, motif, colophon, ideogram.

devil noun **1** *they perform the ritual of driving out the devils from their bodies*: **evil spirit**, demon, fiend, imp, bogie, ghost, spectre; informal spook; archaic bugbear; rare cacodemon.
2 *look what the cruel devil has done to me*: **brute**, beast, monster, savage, demon, fiend; villain, sadist, barbarian, terror, ogre; informal swine, bastard, pig; Scottish informal radge; vulgar slang shit.
3 informal *he is four and a naughty little devil*: **rascal**, rogue, imp, demon, fiend, monkey, wretch, scamp, mischief-maker, troublemaker, badly behaved child; informal mischief, monster, horror, holy terror; Brit. informal perisher; Irish informal spalpeen; N. English informal tyke, scally; N. Amer. informal varmint, hellion; archaic scapegrace, rapscallion, jackanapes.
4 informal *the poor devils looked as though they could do with some refreshment*: **wretch**, unfortunate, creature, soul, person, fellow; informal thing, beggar, bastard; Brit. vulgar slang sod, bugger.

> *Word links* **devil**
>
> **diabolical**, **diabolic** relating to the Devil

devilish adjective **1** *he gave a wide, devilish grin*: **diabolical**, diabolic, fiendish, satanic, demonic, demoniac, demoniacal, Mephistophelian; hellish, infernal, Hadean.
2 *what devilish torture had they dreamed up?* **wicked**, evil, accursed, sinful, iniquitous, nefarious, vile, foul, abominable, unspeakable, loathsome, monstrous, atrocious, heinous, hideous, odious, horrible, horrifying, shocking, appalling, dreadful, awful, terrible, ghastly, abhorrent, despicable, damnable, villainous, shameful, depraved, perverted, ungodly, dark, black, black-hearted, immoral, amoral; vicious, cruel, savage, brutish, bestial, barbaric, barbarous; rare cacodemonic, egregious, flagitious, facinorous.
3 *it turned out to be a devilish job*: **difficult**, tricky, ticklish, troublesome, thorny, awkward, problematic, problem, impossible, messy; informal a bitch of a, the (very) devil of a; archaic kittle.
▶ adverb informal, dated *a devilish clever plan*. See **extremely**.

devil-may-care adjective *those devil-may-care young pilots*: **reckless**, rash, incautious, heedless, unheeding, hasty, overhasty, precipitate, precipitous, impetuous, impulsive, daredevil, hot-headed; **irresponsible**, wild, foolhardy, headlong, over-adventurous, over-venturesome, audacious, death-or-glory, hare-brained, madcap, imprudent, unwise, unthinking; **nonchalant**, casual, airy, breezy, flippant, swaggering, insouciant, indifferent, happy-go-lucky, easy-going; unworried, untroubled, unconcerned; Brit. tearaway; informal harum-scarum; rare temerarious.
▷ANTONYMS solemn, serious.

devilment noun *we got up to all kinds of devilment*. See **devilry** (sense 2).

devilry, deviltry noun **1** *some devilry was afoot*: **wickedness**, evil, evil-doing, evilness, sin, sinfulness, iniquity, iniquitousness, vileness, foulness, baseness, badness, wrong, wrongdoing, dishonesty, unscrupulousness, roguery, villainy, rascality, delinquency, viciousness, devilishness, fiendishness, heinousness; informal crookedness, shadiness;

Law malfeasance; archaic knavery.
2 *a perverse sense of devilry urged her to lead him on*: **mischief**, naughtiness, badness, bad behaviour, misbehaviour, mischievousness, troublemaking, misconduct, misdemeanour, perversity, disobedience, pranks, impishness, tricks, larks, capers, nonsense, roguery, rascality, devilment, funny business; French diablerie; informal monkey tricks, monkey business, shenanigans, goings-on, hanky-panky; Brit. informal carry-on, carryings-on, jiggery-pokery.
3 *they dabbled in devilry*: **black magic**, sorcery, magic, witchcraft, wizardry, necromancy, enchantment, spell-working, incantation, the supernatural, occultism, the occult, the black arts, divination, malediction, voodoo, hoodoo, sympathetic magic, witching, witchery; charms, hexes, spells, jinxes; N. Amer. mojo, orenda; NZ makutu; S. African informal muti; rare sortilege, thaumaturgy, theurgy.

d

devious adjective **1** *he exposed the many devious ways in which governments bent the rules in their favour*: **underhand**, underhanded, deceitful, dishonest, dishonourable, disreputable, unethical, unprincipled, immoral, unscrupulous, fraudulent, cheating, dubious, dirty, unfair, treacherous, duplicitous, double-dealing, below the belt, two-timing, two-faced, unsporting, unsportsmanlike; crafty, cunning, calculating, artful, conniving, scheming, designing, sly, wily, guileful, tricky; sneaky, sneaking, furtive, secret, secretive, clandestine, surreptitious, covert, veiled, shrouded, cloak-and-dagger, hugger-mugger, hole-and-corner, hidden, back-alley, backstairs, under the table, conspiratorial; N. Amer. snide, snidey; informal crooked, shady, bent, low-down, murky, fishy; Brit. informal dodgy; Austral./NZ informal shonky; S. African informal slim.
▷ANTONYMS above board.
2 *the A832 is a devious route around the coastal fringes*: **circuitous**, roundabout, indirect, meandering, winding, serpentine, tortuous, rambling; rare anfractuous.
▷ANTONYMS direct.

devise verb *scientists have devised a method of recycling oil contaminated with PCBs*: **conceive**, think up, come up with, dream up, draw up, work out, form, formulate, concoct, design, frame, invent, coin, originate, compose, construct, fabricate, create, produce, put together, make up, develop, evolve; discover, hit on; hatch, cook up, contrive.

devitalize verb *her spirit had not been devitalized by the city*: **weaken**, make weak, make feeble, enfeeble, debilitate, enervate, sap, drain, tax, overtax, wash out, overtire, exhaust, weary, tire, tire out, fatigue, jade, wear out, prostrate, undermine, impair, render infirm, indispose, incapacitate, cripple, disable, paralyse, immobilize, lay low, put out of action; informal knock out, do in, knacker, shatter, whack, bush, frazzle, wear to a frazzle, poop, take it out of, fag out; rare torpefy.
▷ANTONYMS strengthen, reinforce.

devoid adjective *the moorland is **devoid of** interest except to grazing sheep*: **lacking**, without, free from/of, empty of, vacant of, void of, bare of, barren of, bereft of, drained of, denuded of, deprived of, depleted of, destitute of, bankrupt of; wanting, in need of; informal minus, sans.

devolution noun *the devolution of power to the regions*: **decentralization**, delegation, dispersal, distribution, transfer, surrender, relinquishment.
▷ANTONYMS centralization.

devolve verb *the move would devolve responsibility to local units*: **delegate**, pass (down/on), hand down/over/on, depute, transfer, transmit, commit, assign, consign, convey, entrust, turn over, make over, sign over, give, part with, let go of, leave, cede, surrender, relinquish, deliver; bestow, grant; offload, dump, get rid of, palm off, foist, fob off.
▷ANTONYMS centralize; retain.

devote verb *they need to devote considerable time to career planning*: **allocate**, assign, allot, commit, give, give over, afford, apportion, surrender, consign, sacrifice, pledge, dedicate, consecrate; set aside, earmark, reserve, designate, spare.

devoted adjective *a devoted follower*: **loyal**, faithful, true, true blue, staunch, steadfast, constant, committed, dedicated, devout; fond, loving, admiring, affectionate, caring, attentive, warm, ardent.
▷ANTONYMS disloyal; unfaithful; indifferent.

devotee noun **1** *a devotee of rock music*: **enthusiast**, fan, fanatic, addict, lover, aficionado, admirer; informal buff, freak, nut, fiend, maniac, a great one for; N. Amer. informal geek, jock; S. African informal fundi.
2 *devotees thronged the temple*: **follower**, adherent, supporter, upholder, defender, advocate, champion, disciple, votary, partisan, member, friend, stalwart, fanatic, zealot; believer, worshipper, attender; informal hanger-on, groupie; N. Amer. informal booster, cohort, rooter; rare janissary, sectary.

devotion noun **1** *Eleanor's devotion to her husband*: **loyalty**, faithfulness, fidelity, trueness, staunchness, steadfastness, constancy, commitment, adherence, allegiance, dedication, devoutness; fondness, love, admiration, affection, attentiveness, care, caring, warmness, closeness.
▷ANTONYMS disloyalty; indifference; hatred.
2 *the order's aim was to live a life of devotion*: **devoutness**, piety, religiousness, spirituality, godliness, holiness, sanctity, saintliness.
3 (**devotions**) *morning devotions*: **religious worship**, worship, religious observance; prayers, vespers, matins; prayer meeting, church service.

devotional adjective *the devotional paintings of the period*: **religious**, sacred, spiritual, divine, church, churchly, ecclesiastical.
▷ANTONYMS secular.

devour verb **1** *she watched him as he devoured his meal*: **eat hungrily**, eat quickly, eat greedily, eat heartily, eat up, swallow, gobble (up/down), guzzle (down), gulp (down), bolt (down), cram down, gorge oneself on, wolf (down), feast on, consume; informal scoff (down), pack away, demolish, dispose of, make short work of, polish off, shovel down, stuff one's face with, stuff oneself with, stuff (down), pig oneself on, pig out on, sink, put away, tuck away, get outside of, get one's laughing gear round; Brit. informal gollop, shift; N. Amer. informal scarf (down/up), snarf (down/up), inhale; rare ingurgitate.
2 *we watched in dismay as the flames devoured the old house*: **destroy**, consume, engulf, envelop, demolish, lay waste, wipe out, annihilate, devastate; raze, gut, ravage, ruin, wreck.
3 *he was devoured by remorse*: **afflict**, torture, plague, bedevil, trouble, harrow, rack; consume, swallow up, engulf, swamp, overcome, overwhelm.

devout adjective **1** *a devout Christian*: **pious**, religious, devoted, dedicated, reverent, God-fearing, believing, spiritual, prayerful, holy, godly, saintly, faithful, dutiful, righteous, churchgoing, orthodox.
▷ANTONYMS insincere; lapsed.
2 *a devout soccer fan*: **dedicated**, devoted, committed, loyal, faithful, staunch, genuine, firm, steadfast, resolute, unwavering, sincere, wholehearted, keen, earnest, enthusiastic, zealous, passionate, ardent, fervent, intense, vehement, active, sworn, pledged; French engagé; informal card-carrying, red-hot, true blue, mad keen, deep-dyed.
▷ANTONYMS apathetic.

> *Choose the right word* **devout, religious, pious**
>
> See **religious**.

dexterity noun **1** *the hand-decorating of china demanded great dexterity*: **deftness**, adeptness, adroitness, agility, nimbleness, handiness, ability, capability, talent, skilfulness, skill, proficiency, accomplishment, expertise, experience, efficiency, effortlessness, slickness, mastery, delicacy, knack, facility, artistry, sleight of hand, craft, finesse, felicity; informal niftiness, wizardry.
▷ANTONYMS clumsiness.
2 *his political dexterity*: **shrewdness**, astuteness, sharp-wittedness, sharpness, acuteness, acumen, acuity, intelligence; ingenuity, inventiveness, cleverness, smartness; sensitivity, alertness, wit, canniness, common sense, discernment, insight, understanding, penetration, perception, perceptiveness, perspicacity, perspicaciousness, discrimination, sagacity, sageness; cunning, artfulness, craftiness, wiliness, calculation, calculatedness; informal nous, horse sense, savvy; rare sapience, arguteness.
▷ANTONYMS stupidity; insensitivity.

dexterous adjective **1** *a dexterous flick of the wrist*: **deft**, adept, adroit, agile, nimble, neat, nimble-fingered, handy, able, capable, talented, skilful, skilled, proficient, accomplished, expert, experienced, practised, polished, efficient, effortless, slick, professional, masterful, masterly, impressive, finely judged, delicate; informal nifty, nippy, mean, wicked, ace, wizard, crack; rare habile.
▷ANTONYMS clumsy.
2 *Klein had achieved notoriety for his dexterous accounting abilities*: **shrewd**, ingenious, inventive, clever, intelligent, bright, brilliant, smart, sharp, sharp-witted, razor-sharp, acute, quick, quick-witted, astute, canny, intuitive, discerning, perceptive, perspicacious, insightful, incisive, sagacious, wise, judicious; cunning, artful, crafty, wily, calculating; informal on the ball, quick off the mark, quick on the uptake, brainy, streetwise, savvy; Brit. informal suss; N. Amer. informal heads-up; dated, informal long-headed; rare argute, sapient.
▷ANTONYMS stupid.

diabolic adjective *diabolic rituals had taken place*. See **diabolical** (sense 1).

diabolical adjective **1** *his diabolical skill*: **devilish**, fiendish, satanic, Mephistophelian, demonic, demoniacal, hellish, infernal, evil, wicked, ungodly, unholy; rare cacodemonic.
2 informal *the team manager was sacked after that diabolical performance*. See **poor** (sense 2).
3 informal *a diabolical liberty*: **very great**, extreme, excessive, undue, inordinate, immoderate, unconscionable, outrageous; uncalled for, unprovoked, intolerable, unacceptable, unreasonable, unjustifiable, unwarrantable, without justification, indefensible, inexcusable, unforgivable, unpardonable.

diadem noun *the queen wore a jewelled diadem*: **crown**, coronet, tiara, circlet, chaplet, headpiece, headband, fillet, wreath, garland; literary coronal; in India, historical taj.

diagnose verb *the neurologist diagnosed a possible brain haemorrhage*: **identify**, determine, distinguish, recognize, discover, spot, detect, pinpoint; pronounce, confirm, verify.

diagnosis noun **1** *the correct diagnosis of appendicitis depends on clinical acumen*: **identification**, recognition, discovery, detection, pinpointing, reading, determination; confirmation, verification.
2 *the experts could offer no diagnosis*: **opinion**, **prognosis**, judgement, verdict, pronouncement, conclusion, interpretation; solution, result.

diagonal adjective *he drew a diagonal line across the page*: **crossways**, crosswise, from corner to corner, slanting, slanted, aslant, slant, slantwise, sloping, oblique, inclined, inclining, tilted, tilting, angled, at an angle, cornerways, cornerwise; Scottish squint; N. Amer. cater-cornered, cater-corner, catty-cornered, kitty-cornered.

diagonally adverb *she cut the cake in half diagonally*: **obliquely**, at an angle, crossways, crosswise, on the cross, on the slant, slantwise, aslant, cornerwise, on the bias; N. Amer. cater-cornered, cater-corner, catty-cornered, kitty-cornered.

diagram noun *a diagram of the alimentary canal*: **drawing**, line drawing, illustration, picture; **schematic representation**, representation, scale drawing, technical drawing, plan, figure, sketch, draft, outline, delineation, exploded view, cutaway, layout; Computing graphic; rare schema.

diagrammatic adjective *the information is presented in diagrammatic form*: **graphic**, graphical, tabular, pictorial, delineative, illustrative, representational, representative, schematic.

dial verb *he grabbed the telephone and dialled 999 | she dialled her parents*: **telephone**, phone, phone up, call, call up; place a call to, make a call to, give someone a call, get on the phone to, get someone on the phone; Brit. ring, ring up, give someone a ring; informal buzz, give someone a buzz; Brit. informal give someone a bell, give someone a tinkle, get on the blower to; N. Amer. informal get someone on the horn.

dialect noun *Hilary found it hard to understand the moorland dialect*: **regional language**, local language, local tongue, local speech, local parlance, variety of language; **vernacular**, patois, non-standard language, idiom; regionalisms, localisms, provincialisms; informal lingo, local lingo, -ese, -speak; Linguistics acrolect, basilect, sociolect, idiolect.

dialectic noun *feminism has contributed a good deal to this dialectic*: **reasoning**, argumentation, contention, logic; **discussion**, debate, dialogue, logical argument; rare ratiocination.
▶ adjective *Japanese negotiation is different from the Western dialectic habit*: **rational**, rationalistic, logical, analytical; **disputatious**, dialectical, argumentative, contentious.

dialogue noun **1** *he studied dialogue among kindergarten children*: **conversation**, talk, communication, interchange, discourse, argument; chat, chatter, chit-chat, chitter-chatter, gossip; informal jawing, gassing, gabbing; Brit. informal nattering, chinwagging; formal confabulation; archaic converse; rare interlocution, duologue, colloquy.
2 *they called for a serious political dialogue*: **discussion**, exchange, debate, discourse, exchange of views, head-to-head, tête-à-tête, consultation, conference, parley, interview, question and answer session; talks, negotiations; informal powwow, rap session, confab; N. Amer. informal skull session, rap; formal confabulation.
3 *the actors learnt the dialogue by heart*: **script**, text, screenplay, speech; lines, words, parts, spoken parts.

diameter noun *the mill wheel is eight feet in diameter | the pipe has a diameter of 14mm*: **breadth**, width, depth, thickness; calibre, bore, gauge; size, extent.

diametrical, diametric adjective *they set themselves in diametrical opposition to their society*: **direct**, absolute, complete, exact, extreme.

diametrically adverb *their views are diametrically opposed*: **directly**, absolutely, completely, utterly.

diamond noun

> *Word links* **diamond**
>
> **diamantine** relating to diamonds

diaphanous adjective *she wore a diaphanous dress of pale gold*: **sheer**, fine, ultra-fine, delicate, light, lightweight, thin, insubstantial, floaty, flimsy, filmy, silken, chiffony, gossamer, gossamery, gossamer-thin, gossamer-like, gauzy, gauzelike, cobwebby, feathery; translucent, transparent, see-through; rare transpicuous, translucid.
▷ANTONYMS thick; opaque.

Word toolkit

diaphanous	transparent	translucent
gown	plastic	skin
veil	wall	paper
wings	crystals	powder
fabric	tape	resin

diarrhoea noun **loose motions**, looseness of the bowels; informal the skitters, the runs, the trots, gippy tummy, holiday tummy, Spanish tummy, Delhi belly, Montezuma's revenge, Aztec revenge, Aztec two-step; Brit. informal the squits; N. Amer. informal turista; Medicine dysentery, lientery; archaic the flux, lax.
▷ANTONYMS constipation.

diary noun **1** Brit. *that trip on the 4th should be pencilled into your diary*: **appointment book**, engagement book, organizer, personal organizer, calendar, agenda; schedule, timetable, programme; trademark Filofax.
2 *she kept a diary during the war*: **journal**, memoir, chronicle, log, logbook, weblog, blog, day-by-day account, daily record, history, annal, record, moblog; N. Amer. daybook.

diatribe noun *he launched into a diatribe against the Catholic Church*: **tirade**, harangue, verbal onslaught, verbal attack, stream of abuse, denunciation, broadside, fulmination, condemnation, criticism, stricture, reproof, reproval, reprimand, rebuke, admonishment, admonition; invective, upbraiding, vituperation, abuse, castigation; informal tongue-lashing, knocking, slamming, panning, bashing, blast, flak; Brit. informal slating; rare philippic, obloquy.

dicey adjective informal *refuelling at sea is a bit dicey in bad weather*: **risky**, uncertain, unpredictable, touch-and-go, precarious, unsafe, dangerous, perilous, high-risk, hazardous, fraught with danger; tricky, ticklish, delicate, difficult, awkward, thorny, problematical, problematic; Scottish unchancy; informal chancy, hairy, sticky, iffy; Brit. informal dodgy; N. Amer. informal gnarly; archaic or humorous parlous.
▷ANTONYMS safe; simple.

dichotomy noun *there is a great dichotomy between social theory and practice*: **division**, separation, divorce, split, gulf, chasm; **difference**, contrast, disjunction, polarity, lack of consistency, contradiction, antagonism, conflict; rare contrariety.

dicky adjective Brit. informal *he was rejected for military service because of his dicky heart*: **unsound**, unsteady, unreliable; **weak**, frail, infirm, unhealthy, ailing, poorly, sickly, sick; shaky, fluttery, fluttering, trembling; informal iffy; Brit. informal dodgy.
▷ANTONYMS robust.

dictate verb (stress on the second syllable) **1** *he sent for his secretary and dictated a letter*: **say aloud**, utter, speak, read out, read aloud, recite.
▷ANTONYMS write.
2 *the government's official position is dictated by the prime minister*: **prescribe**, **lay down**, impose, set down, set out; order, command, decree, ordain, direct, pronounce, enjoin, promulgate; **determine**, decide, influence, affect, choose, control, govern.
3 *my daughter is always* **dictating to** *her friends*: **give orders to**, order about/around, boss (about/around), impose one's will on, lord it over, bully, domineer, dominate, tyrannize, oppress, ride roughshod over, control, pressurize, browbeat; lay down the law, act the tin god; informal push around/about, bulldoze, walk all over; call the shots, throw one's weight about/around.
▶ noun (stress on the first syllable) **1** *he showed blind obedience to the dictates of his superior*: **order**, command, decree, edict, rule, ruling, ordinance, dictum, directive, direction, instruction, pronouncement, mandate, requirement, stipulation, injunction, ultimatum, demand, exhortation; (**dictates**) bidding, request, charge, promulgation; in Tsarist Russia ukase; in Spanish-speaking countries pronunciamento; informal say-so; literary behest; archaic hest; rare rescript.
2 *the dictates of fashion*: **principle**, guiding principle, code, canon, law, rule, regulation, precept, dictum, axiom, maxim.

dictator noun *the country was ruled by a right-wing dictator*: **autocrat**, monocrat, absolute ruler; **tyrant**, despot, oppressor, absolutist, totalitarian, authoritarian; informal supremo, Big Brother; rare autarch.

dictatorial adjective **1** *he wanted to retain dictatorial leadership*: **autocratic**, monocratic, undemocratic, totalitarian, authoritarian; **despotic**, tyrannical, tyrannous; **absolute**, unrestricted, unlimited, unaccountable, arbitrary, omnipotent, all-powerful, supreme; rare autarchic, autarchical.
▷ANTONYMS democratic.
2 *she became irritated by his dictatorial manner*: **tyrannical**, **domineering**, despotic, oppressive, draconian, iron-handed, iron-fisted, imperious, lordly, magisterial, officious, overweening, overbearing, bossy, repressive, peremptory, high-handed, authoritarian, autocratic, dogmatic, high and mighty; harsh, strict, severe, rigid, inflexible, unyielding; informal pushy, cocky; rare Neronian.
▷ANTONYMS liberal.

dictatorship noun **1** *the party was seeking to establish a dictatorship*: **totalitarian state**, autocracy, autarchy, monocracy; dystopia.
▷ANTONYMS democracy.
2 *an entire generation grew up in the shadow of dictatorship*: **absolute rule**, undemocratic rule, despotism, autocracy; **tyranny**, authoritarianism, totalitarianism, absolutism, Fascism; oppression, suppression, repression, subjugation, domination.
▷ANTONYMS democracy.

diction noun **1** *a dialogue coach was employed to improve the actors' diction*: **enunciation**, articulation, elocution, locution, pronunciation, speech, speech pattern, manner of speaking, intonation, inflection; delivery, utterance, speech-making, public speaking, declamation, oratory; fluency.

2 *he recognized the need for contemporary diction in poetry*: **phraseology**, phrasing, turn of phrase, choice of words, wording, language, parlance, usage, vocabulary, terminology, expression, idiom, style, locution; informal lingo; rare idiolect.

dictionary noun *half of the words in his text were not in the dictionary*: **lexicon**, wordbook, glossary, vocabulary list, vocabulary, word list, wordfinder.

Word links **dictionary**

lexicographic relating to dictionaries
lexicography writing of dictionaries
lexicographer writer of dictionaries

d

dictum noun **1** *he received the head's dictum with evident reluctance*: **pronouncement**, proclamation, direction, injunction, assertion, statement; **dictate**, command, commandment, mandate, order, decree, edict, fiat, promulgation, precept, requirement, stipulation, instruction; law, ordinance, rule, regulation; in Tsarist Russia ukase; in Spanish-speaking countries pronunciamento; rare rescript, firman, decretal, irade.
2 *'live well with all creatures' is an apt dictum for today*: **saying**, maxim, axiom, proverb, adage, aphorism, saw, precept, epigram, epigraph, motto, truism, platitude, commonplace; words of wisdom, pearls of wisdom; expression, phrase, formula, slogan, quotation, quote; rare apophthegm, gnome.

didactic adjective *the inmates preferred social rather than didactic activities*: **instructive**, instructional, educational, educative, informative, informational, doctrinal, preceptive, teaching, pedagogic, academic, scholastic, tuitional; edifying, improving, enlightening, illuminating, heuristic; pedantic, moralistic, homiletic; rare propaedeutic.

die verb **1** *he was eighteen when his mother died*: **pass away**, pass on, lose one's life, depart this life, expire, breathe one's last, draw one's last breath, meet one's end, meet one's death, lay down one's life, be no more, perish, be lost, go the way of the flesh, go the way of all flesh, go to glory, go to one's last resting place, go to meet one's maker, cross the great divide, cross the Styx; informal give up the ghost, kick the bucket, bite the dust, croak, conk out, buy it, turn up one's toes, cash in one's chips, go belly up, shuffle off this mortal coil, go the way of the dinosaurs; push up the daisies, be six feet under; Brit. informal snuff it, peg out, pop one's clogs, hop the twig/stick; N. Amer. informal bite the big one, buy the farm, check out, hand in one's dinner pail; Austral./NZ informal go bung; literary exit; archaic decease.
▷ANTONYMS live, survive.
2 *the last hope that there had been some mistake died*: **fade**, fall away, dwindle, melt away, dissolve, subside, decline, sink, lapse, ebb, wane, wilt, wither, evanesce, come to an end, end, vanish, disappear.
▷ANTONYMS exist.
3 informal *the car gave a stutter and the engine died*: **fail**, cut out, give out, stop, halt, break down, stop working, cease to function; peter out, fizzle out, run down, fade away, lose power; informal conk out, go kaput, give up the ghost, go phut; Brit. informal pack up.
▷ANTONYMS start.
4 informal *I'm going to* **die of** *boredom in this place*: **be overcome with**, be overwhelmed by, be overpowered by, collapse with, succumb to.
5 informal *she's just dying to meet you*: **be very eager**, be very keen, be desperate, long, yearn, burn, ache, itch; informal have a yen, yen.
▷ANTONYMS be reluctant.
□ **die away** *the sound of hoofbeats died away*: **fade (away)**, fall away, dwindle, melt away, subside, ebb, wane, come to an end.
□ **die down** *we sheltered until the wind had died down*: **abate**, subside, drop, drop off, drop away, fall away, lessen, ease (off), let up, decrease, diminish, moderate, decline, fade, dwindle, slacken, recede, tail off, peter out, taper off, wane, ebb, relent, become weaker, weaken, come to an end; archaic remit.
□ **die out** *the trout population could die out completely | the ceremony has died out in many areas*: **become extinct**, **vanish**, disappear, cease to be, cease to exist, be no more, perish, pass into oblivion; become less common, become rarer, dwindle, peter out.

diehard adjective *diehard traditionalists*: **hard-line**, hard-core, reactionary, ultra-conservative, conservative, traditionalist, unprogressive, dyed-in-the-wool, deep-dyed, long-standing, staunch, steadfast, intransigent, inflexible, immovable, unchanging, uncompromising, unyielding, indomitable, adamant, rigid, entrenched, set in one's ways; informal blimpish.
▶ **noun** *some of the diehards are refusing to reach an agreement*: **hardliner**, reactionary, ultra-conservative, conservative, traditionalist, intransigent, fanatic, zealot; informal stick-in-the-mud, blimp.
▷ANTONYMS modernizer.

diet¹ noun **1** *your health problems could be related to your diet*: **selection of food**, food and drink, food, foodstuffs, provisions, edibles, fare; menu, table, meals; nourishment, nutriment, sustenance; informal grub, nosh, eats, chow, scoff; formal comestibles, provender; archaic aliment, victuals, vittles, viands, commons.
2 *they aim to become slimmer by following a diet*: **dietary regime**, dietary regimen, dietary programme, restricted diet, crash diet; fast, period of fasting, abstinence.
▷ANTONYMS binge.
▶ **verb** *she had dieted for most of her life*: **follow a diet**, be on a diet, eat sparingly, eat selectively, abstain, fast; slim, lose weight, watch one's weight; N. Amer. reduce; informal weight-watch; N. Amer. informal slenderize.
▷ANTONYMS overindulge, binge.

diet² noun *the budget was passed by the diet's lower house*: **legislative assembly**, legislature, parliament, congress, senate, synod, council; assembly, committee, convocation, conclave.

differ verb **1** *child-rearing patterns differ across cultural groups*: **vary**, be different, be unlike, be dissimilar, be distinguishable, diverge.
▷ANTONYMS coincide.
2 *their beliefs* **differed from** *those of other religious parties*: **deviate from**, depart from, run counter to, contradict, contrast with, conflict with, be incompatible with, be at odds with, be in opposition to, go against.
▷ANTONYMS resemble.
3 *lawyers differ about the best interpretation of the legislation*: **disagree**, fail to agree, dissent, be at variance, be in dispute, be in opposition, take issue, conflict, clash, cross swords, lock horns, be at each other's throats; quarrel, argue, wrangle, quibble, squabble; informal fall out, scrap, argy-bargy, spat; archaic altercate.
▷ANTONYMS agree.

difference noun **1** *there is no difference between the two accounts*: **dissimilarity**, contrast, distinction, distinctness, differentiation; **variance**, variation, variability, divergence, deviation, polarity, gulf, breach, gap, split, disparity, imbalance, unevenness, incongruity, contradiction, contradistinction, nonconformity; rare unlikeness, contrariety, dissimilitude.
▷ANTONYMS similarity.
2 *the couple are patching up their differences*: **disagreement**, difference of opinion, misunderstanding, dispute, disputation, argument, debate, quarrel, wrangle, altercation, contretemps, clash, controversy, dissension; informal tiff, set-to, run-in, spat, ruction; Brit. informal row, barney, bit of argy-bargy.
3 *you pay a reduced amount and the bank makes up the difference*: **balance**, outstanding amount, remaining amount, remainder, rest, residue, excess, extra; technical residuum.

different adjective **1** *the plots of the two books are very different*: **dissimilar**, unalike, unlike, non-identical, contrasting, divergent, disparate, poles apart; incompatible, mismatched, inconsistent, opposed, at variance, at odds, clashing, conflicting, contradictory, contrary; informal like chalk and cheese; rare contrastive.
▷ANTONYMS similar.
2 *suddenly everything in her life was different*: **changed**, altered, modified, transformed, metamorphosed, other, new, unfamiliar, unknown, strange.
▷ANTONYMS the same.
3 *Gareth had tried fifteen different occupations*: **distinct**, separate, individual, discrete, non-identical, unrelated, unconnected, unassociated, independent; disparate.
▷ANTONYMS related, similar.
4 *the Bible was interpreted differently by different groups of reformers*: **various**, several, sundry, assorted, varied, varying, miscellaneous, diverse, diversified, manifold, multifarious; informal a mixed bag; literary divers.
5 *he wanted to try something different*: **unusual**, out of the ordinary, uncommon, unfamiliar, rare, unique, novel, new, fresh, original, unprecedented, unconventional, unorthodox, atypical, out of the way; special, singular, remarkable, noteworthy, exceptional, extraordinary, outrageous, outlandish, exotic; Brit. out of the common; informal way out, offbeat, off the wall.
▷ANTONYMS ordinary, conventional.

Word links **different**

allo- related prefix, as in *allopathy, allotrope*
hetero- related prefix, as in *heterogeneous, heterosexual*

differential adjective *differential treatment is accorded to working- and middle-class crime*: **distinctive**, different, dissimilar, contrasting, divergent, disparate, contrastive; distinguishing, discriminating, discriminatory.
▷ANTONYMS similar, the same.
▶ **noun** *the cost differential is rapidly diminishing*: **difference**, gap, gulf, divergence, disparity, discrepancy, imbalance, inequality, contrast, distinction.
▷ANTONYMS uniformity.

differentiate verb **1** *he is no longer able to* **differentiate between** *fantasy and reality | birds can differentiate colours*: **distinguish**, discriminate, make a distinction, draw a distinction, see a difference, discern a difference, tell the difference; discern, tell apart, recognize, identify, pick out, determine, contrast.
2 *they understand what differentiates their business from all other booksellers*: **make different**, distinguish, set apart, single out, separate, segregate, mark off, characterize, individualize, individuate.

3 *the cells differentiate into a wide variety of types*: **transform**, metamorphose, evolve, convert, change, become different, modify, alter, adapt.

differentiation noun *there is not enough differentiation between the two types of investment*: **distinction**, distinctness, disparity, polarity, contrast, difference, divergence, separation, demarcation, delimitation.
▷ANTONYMS association.

difficult adjective **1** *digging through the snow was becoming increasingly difficult*: **hard**, strenuous, arduous, laborious, heavy, tough, onerous, burdensome, demanding, punishing, gruelling, grinding, back-breaking, painful; exhausting, tiring, fatiguing, wearing, wearying, wearisome; informal hellish, killing; Brit. informal knackering; archaic toilsome; rare exigent.
▷ANTONYMS easy.
2 *she found maths very difficult*: **problematic**, hard, puzzling, baffling, perplexing, confusing, mystifying, mysterious; **complicated**, complex, involved, intricate, knotty, thorny, ticklish; obscure, abstract, abstruse, recondite, enigmatic, impenetrable, unfathomable, over one's head, above one's head, beyond one; informal fiddly, sticky, no picnic; N. Amer. informal gnarly; archaic wildering; rare involute, involuted.
▷ANTONYMS straightforward, simple.
3 *the office manager was a difficult man*: **troublesome**, tiresome, trying, exasperating, demanding, unmanageable, intractable, perverse, contrary, recalcitrant, obstreperous, refractory, fractious; **unaccommodating**, unhelpful, uncooperative, unamenable, unreasonable, disobliging, stubborn, obstinate, bull-headed, pig-headed; **hard to please**, hard to satisfy, fussy, particular, over-particular, fastidious, perfectionist, critical, hypercritical, finicky; Brit. awkward; Scottish thrawn; informal cussed; choosy, picky; Brit. informal bloody-minded, bolshie, stroppy; N. Amer. informal balky; archaic contumacious, froward; rare contrarious, finical.
▷ANTONYMS accommodating.
4 *you've come at a difficult time*: **inconvenient**, awkward, unfavourable, unfortunate, inappropriate, unsuitable, untimely, ill-timed, inopportune, inexpedient, disadvantageous; archaic unseasonable.
▷ANTONYMS convenient.
5 *the family have been through very difficult times*: **bad**, tough, grim, terrible, awful, dreadful, nightmarish, dark, black, hard, adverse, unpleasant, unwelcome, disagreeable, distressing, harrowing; straitened, hard-pressed; literary direful; archaic or humorous parlous.
▷ANTONYMS happy.

difficulty noun **1** *her note had been penned with obvious difficulty*: **strain**, struggling, awkwardness, trouble, toil, labour, laboriousness, strenuousness, arduousness; pains, problems, trials and tribulations; informal hassle, stress; literary dolour, travails.
▷ANTONYMS ease.
2 *the questions are arranged in order of difficulty*: **complexity**, complicatedness, intricacy, perplexity, knottiness, awkwardness; difficultness, trickiness, hardness; obscurity, abstruseness.
▷ANTONYMS simplicity.
3 *the cost of the journey was not an insurmountable difficulty*: **problem**, complication, disadvantage, snag, hitch, drawback, pitfall, handicap, impediment, hindrance, obstacle, hurdle, stumbling block, obstruction, barrier; informal fly in the ointment, prob, headache, hiccup, facer; Brit. informal spanner in the works; N. Amer. informal monkey wrench in the works; dated cumber; literary trammel.
4 *they felt unable to ask for help when they were in difficulty*: **trouble**, distress, crisis, hardship; **adversity**, extremity, need; hard times, dire straits; predicament, quandary, dilemma, plight; informal hot water, deep water, a fix, a jam, a spot, a scrape, a stew, a hole, a pickle.

diffidence noun *he regretted his diffidence and awkwardness in large groups*: **shyness**, bashfulness, unassertiveness, modesty, modestness, self-effacement, humility, humbleness, meekness, timidity, timidness, timorousness, reserve, reticence, introversion; **insecurity**, self-doubt, apprehension, uncertainty, hesitancy, nervousness, reluctance, restraint, inhibition, unease, uneasiness; self-consciousness, shame, embarrassment, sheepishness.
▷ANTONYMS confidence.

diffident adjective *underneath his diffident exterior there was a passionate temperament*: **shy**, bashful, modest, self-effacing, unassuming, unpresuming, humble, meek, unconfident, unassertive, timid, timorous, shrinking, reserved, withdrawn, introverted, inhibited; **insecure**, self-doubting, doubtful, wary, unsure, apprehensive, uncertain, hesitant, nervous, reluctant, fearful; self-conscious, ill at ease, ashamed, abashed, embarrassed, shamefaced, sheepish; Scottish mim; informal mousy.
▷ANTONYMS confident; conceited.

> *Choose the right word* **diffident, shy, bashful, timid**
>
> See **shy**[1].

diffuse verb *the light of the moon was diffused by cloud | such ideas were diffused widely in the 1970s*: **spread**, spread out, spread around, send out, scatter, disperse; disseminate, distribute, dispense, put about, circulate, communicate, impart, purvey, propagate, transmit, broadcast, promulgate; literary bruit abroad.
▷ANTONYMS concentrate; collect.
▸ adjective **1** *skylights give a diffuse illumination through the rooms*: **spread out**, diffused, scattered, dispersed, not concentrated.
▷ANTONYMS concentrated.
2 *Tania's narrative is rather diffuse*: **verbose**, wordy, prolix, long-winded, overlong, long-drawn-out, protracted, discursive, rambling, wandering, meandering, maundering, digressive, circuitous, roundabout, circumlocutory, periphrastic; loose, vague; informal windy, gassy; Brit. informal waffling; rare pleonastic, circumlocutionary, ambagious, logorrhoeic.
▷ANTONYMS succinct.

d

> *Easily confused words* **diffuse or defuse?**
>
> The verbs **diffuse** and **defuse** are quite different in meaning, though they are sometimes confused on account of their similarity in sound. *Diffuse* means 'scatter, spread widely' (*power is diffused and decentralized*). *Defuse*, on the other hand, means 'reduce the danger or tension in' (*the agreement was designed to defuse a dangerous rivalry*).

diffusion noun *he studies smoke diffusion in the atmosphere | the diffusion of Duchamp's thought and art*: **spreading**, scattering, dispersal, dispersing; dissemination, disseminating, distribution, distributing, circulation, circulating, putting about, propagation, transmission, broadcasting, broadcast, promulgation, issuance; archaic bruiting.

dig verb **1** *they dug my garden for me | he grabbed a shovel and began to dig*: **cultivate**, till, harrow, plough, turn over, work, break up, spade; delve, break up soil, break up earth, break up ground, move soil/earth.
2 *they tried to dig a tunnel under the house*: **excavate**, dig out, quarry, hollow out, scoop out, gouge out, cut, bore, tunnel, burrow, mine, channel.
3 *there were no cows to milk and no vegetables to dig*: **unearth**, dig up, pull up, grub up, root up, root out, bring to the surface, extract from the ground; harvest, gather, collect.
4 *Winnie dug her elbow into his ribs*: **poke**, prod, jab, stab, shove, ram, push, thrust, drive, nudge.
5 *they asked questions and dug into my past*: **delve**, **probe**, search, enquire, look; investigate, research, examine, scrutinize, check up on, vet; N. Amer. check out.
6 informal, dated *he's great and I dig talking with him*. See **like**[1] (sense 2).
7 informal, dated *this art is symbolic—do you dig me?* See **understand** (sense 1).
□ **dig something up 1** *the bodies were hastily dug up*: **exhume**, disinter, unearth, bring to the surface, bring out of the ground; rare disentomb, unbury. **2** *they dug up scandalous facts about top businessmen*: **uncover**, unearth, dredge up, root out, hunt out, ferret out, nose out, sniff out, track down, extricate, find (out), turn up, come across, discover, detect, reveal, bring to light, bring into the open, expose.
▸ noun **1** *Emma gave me a dig in the ribs*: **poke**, prod, jab, stab, shove, push, nudge, elbow.
2 informal *they're always making digs at one another*: **snide remark**, cutting remark, jibe, jeer, taunt, sneer, insult, barb, slur, slight, affront, insinuation; informal wisecrack, crack, put-down.

digest verb (stress on the second syllable) **1** *babies take longer to digest formula milk*: **break down**, dissolve, assimilate, absorb, take in, take up.
2 *they take ages to digest even simple facts*: **assimilate**, absorb, take in, understand, comprehend, grasp, master, learn, familiarize oneself with; consider, think about, contemplate, mull over, chew over, weigh up, reflect on, ponder, meditate on, study; informal get, get the hang of, pick up, get clued up about, get the point of.
3 *the source material needs to be digested*: **classify**, catalogue, tabulate, codify, arrange, order, dispose, systematize, methodize; **condense**, compress, compact, telescope, summarize, precis, abstract; rare epitomize.
▸ noun (stress on the first syllable) *a digest of current world news is published monthly*: **summary**, synopsis, abstract, precis, résumé, outline, sketch, (quick) rundown, round-up, abridgement, summation, review, compendium; N. Amer. wrap-up; archaic argument; rare epitome, summa, conspectus.

digestion noun *ineffective chewing prevents the proper digestion of food*: **breaking down**, maceration, dissolution; assimilation, absorption, taking in, taking up, ingestion; rare eupepsia.

digit noun **1** *we wanted to warm our frozen digits*: **finger**, thumb, toe; extremity.
2 *the door code has ten digits*: **numeral**, number, figure, integer; numerical symbol; rare cipher.

dignified adjective *the butler was dignified and courteous*: **stately**, noble, courtly, majestic, kingly; **distinguished**, proud, august, lofty, exalted, regal, lordly, imposing, impressive, grand; solemn, serious, grave, formal, proper, ceremonious, decorous, reserved, composed, sedate, staid; informal couth, just so, starchy.
▷ANTONYMS undignified.

dignify verb *they dignified their departure with a ceremony*: **distinguish**, add distinction to, add dignity to, honour, bestow honour on, grace, adorn, exalt, enhance, add lustre to, magnify, ennoble, glorify, elevate, make lofty, aggrandize, upgrade.

dignitary noun *there are many foreign dignitaries attending today's ceremony*: **grandee**, important person, VIP, very important person, notable, notability, worthy, personage, luminary, public figure, pillar of society, leading light, leader, panjandrum; famous person, distinguished person, eminent person, eminence, celebrity, celebutante, personality, name, big name, household name, star, superstar; informal heavyweight, bigwig, biggie, top brass, top dog, Mr Big, big gun, big shot, big noise, big fish, big cheese, big chief, supremo, somebody, someone, celeb, Lord Muck, Lady Muck; Brit. informal nob; N. Amer. informal big wheel, kahuna, big kahuna, big enchilada, top banana, macher, high muckamuck, high muckety-muck.
▷ANTONYMS nonentity.

d

dignity noun **1** *he is careful to uphold the dignity of the Crown*: **stateliness**, nobleness, nobility, majesty, regalness, regality, royalness, courtliness, augustness, loftiness, exaltedness, lordliness, impressiveness, grandeur, magnificence; ceremoniousness, formality, decorum, propriety, correctness, righteousness, respectability, worthiness, honourability, integrity; solemnity, gravity, gravitas, reserve, sobriety, sedateness, composure.
▷ANTONYMS informality.
2 *the prisoners were treated with little regard for human dignity*: **self-esteem**, self-worth, self-respect, pride, morale; decency, modesty, delicacy; feelings, sensibilities; French amour propre.
3 *Cnut promised dignities and favour to the noblemen*: **high rank**, high standing, high station, status, elevation, eminence, honour, glory, greatness, importance, prominence, prestige.
▷ANTONYMS dishonour; low rank.

digress verb *I have digressed a little from my original plan*: **deviate**, go off at a tangent, diverge, turn aside, turn away, depart, drift, stray, ramble, wander, meander, maunder; get off the subject, stray from the subject, stray from the point, deviate from the topic, get sidetracked, lose the thread; rare divagate.
▷ANTONYMS keep/stick to the point.

digression noun *her book is full of long digressions | Victorian novelists had a tendency toward verbosity and digression*: **deviation**, detour, diversion, departure, excursus; **aside**, incidental remark, footnote, parenthesis; deviation from the subject, straying from the topic, straying from the point, going off at a tangent, getting sidetracked, losing one's thread; divergence, straying, drifting, rambling, wandering, meandering, maundering; Latin obiter dictum; archaic excursion; rare apostrophe, divagation.

digs plural noun Brit. informal *he had just been thrown out of his digs*: **lodgings**, living quarters, quarters, rooms; accommodation, billet; lodging place, bedsit, flat, apartment, house, home; informal pad, place; formal abode, dwelling, dwelling place, residence, domicile, habitation.

dilapidated adjective *a terrace of dilapidated Edwardian houses*: **run down**, tumbledown, ramshackle, broken-down, in disrepair, shabby, battered, rickety, shaky, unsound, crumbling, in ruins, ruined, decayed, decaying, deteriorating, deteriorated, decrepit, worn out; neglected, uncared-for, untended, unmaintained, badly maintained; the worse for wear, falling to pieces, falling apart, gone to rack and ruin, gone to seed; informal shambly, slummy; N. Amer. informal shacky.
▷ANTONYMS smart; intact.

dilate verb **1** *she took a deep breath and her nostrils dilated*: **enlarge**, become larger, widen, become wider, expand, distend, swell.
▷ANTONYMS contract.
2 *he would dilate on any subject that took his fancy*: **expatiate**, expound, expand, enlarge, elaborate, speak at length, write at length, talk in detail.

dilatory adjective **1** *they were dilatory in providing the researchers with information*: **slow**, unhurried, tardy, unpunctual, lax, slack, sluggish, sluggardly, snail-like, tortoise-like, lazy, idle, indolent, slothful; N. Amer. informal lollygagging.
▷ANTONYMS fast; prompt.
2 *they resorted to dilatory procedural tactics*: **delaying**, stalling, temporizing, procrastinating, postponing, deferring, putting off, tabling, shelving; **time-wasting**, dallying, dilly-dallying, loitering, lingering, dawdling, tarrying; rare Fabian.

dilemma noun *a discussion with a colleague resolved her dilemma*: **quandary**, predicament, difficulty, problem, puzzle, conundrum, awkward situation, tricky situation, difficult situation, difficult choice, catch-22, vicious circle, plight, mess, muddle; trouble, perplexity, confusion, conflict, uncertainty, indecision; informal no-win situation, sticky situation, pickle, fix, spot, tight spot, tight corner, poser, facer; Brit. informal sticky wicket.
□ **on the horns of a dilemma between the devil and the deep blue sea**, between Scylla and Charybdis; informal in a no-win situation, between a rock and a hard place.

dilettante noun *there is no room for the dilettante in this business*: **dabbler**, potterer, tinkerer, trifler, dallier; **amateur**, non-professional, non-specialist, layman, layperson.
▷ANTONYMS professional.

diligence noun *they set about their assigned jobs with diligence*: **conscientiousness**, **assiduousness**, assiduity, industriousness, rigour, rigorousness, punctiliousness, meticulousness, carefulness, thoroughness, sedulousness, attentiveness, heedfulness, earnestness, intentness, studiousness; constancy, perseverance, persistence, tenacity, pertinacity, zeal, zealousness, dedication, commitment; tirelessness, indefatigability, doggedness; industry, hard work, application, effort, concentration, care, attention; archaic laboriousness, continuance; rare perseveration.
▷ANTONYMS laziness; carelessness.

diligent adjective *their drive to achieve makes them extremely diligent workers*: **industrious**, hard-working, assiduous; **conscientious**, particular, punctilious, meticulous, painstaking, rigorous, exacting, careful, thorough, sedulous, attentive, heedful, intent, earnest, studious; constant, persevering, persistent, tenacious, pertinacious, zealous, dedicated, committed, active, busy; unflagging, untiring, tireless, indefatigable, dogged, plodding, slogging; archaic laborious.
▷ANTONYMS lazy; casual.

> *Choose the right word* **diligent, hard-working, industrious**
>
> See **hard-working**.

dilly-dally verb informal *the board can't afford to dilly-dally over this issue*: **waste time**, dally, dawdle, loiter, linger, take one's time, delay, mark time, kill time, while away time, potter, trifle, temporize, stall, procrastinate, drag one's feet, play a waiting game; dither, hesitate, falter, vacillate, waver, fluctuate; Brit. haver, hum and haw; Scottish swither; informal shilly-shally, blow hot and cold, let the grass grow under one's feet, pussyfoot around; archaic or literary tarry.
▷ANTONYMS hurry.

dilute verb **1** *strong bleach can be diluted with water*: **make weaker**, weaken; **thin out**, thin, make thinner, water down, add water to; mix, doctor, lace, adulterate; informal cut.
▷ANTONYMS concentrate.
2 *I trust I have been able to dilute your misgivings*: **diminish**, reduce, decrease, lessen, attenuate, make weaker, weaken, mitigate, temper, quell, quieten, allay, assuage, alleviate, palliate, moderate, modify, tone down; rare lenify.
▷ANTONYMS intensify.
▸ **adjective** *the metal is etched with a dilute acid*: **weak**, diluted, thin, thinned out, watered down, watery; adulterated; informal cut.

diluted adjective *wash the brushes in diluted bleach*: **weak**, dilute, thin, thinned out, watered down, watery; adulterated.
▷ANTONYMS concentrated.

dim adjective **1** *the stage lighting was extremely dim*: **faint**, weak, feeble, soft, pale, dull, dingy, subdued, muted, flat, lustreless; informal wishy-washy.
▷ANTONYMS bright.
2 *it was a dim, grey day | he left her in a dim room*: **dark**, darkish, sombre, dingy, dismal, gloomy, dusky, murky; grey, overcast, leaden, cloudy, misty, foggy; badly lit, poorly lit, ill-lit, unlit, unilluminated; literary crepuscular, tenebrous; rare Stygian, Cimmerian, caliginous.
▷ANTONYMS bright.
3 *he glimpsed dim shapes through the foliage*: **indistinct**, ill-defined, unclear, vague, shadowy, imperceptible, nebulous, obscured, blurred, blurry, fuzzy, bleary; rare obfuscated.
▷ANTONYMS distinct.
4 *he had only dim memories of his late father*: **vague**, unclear, indistinct, imprecise, imperfect, confused, sketchy, hazy, blurred, shadowy, foggy, obscure, remote.
▷ANTONYMS clear.
5 informal *I expect you think I'm awfully dim*. See **stupid**.
6 *their prospects for the future looked fairly dim*: **gloomy**, sombre, unpromising, unfavourable, discouraging, disheartening, depressing, dispiriting.
▷ANTONYMS encouraging.
▸ **verb 1** *she insisted the lights be dimmed*: **turn down**, lower, dip; make dim, make faint, make less bright, make less intense, soften, subdue, mute; literary bedim.
▷ANTONYMS turn up.
2 *wait until the gas lamps dim*: **grow faint**, grow feeble, grow dim, fade, dull.
3 *the skies dimmed*: **grow dark**, darken, blacken, cloud over, become overcast, grow leaden, lour, become gloomy.
▷ANTONYMS brighten.
4 *my memories have not dimmed with the passage of time*: **fade**, become vague, become indistinct, grow dim, blur, become blurred, become shadowy, become confused; dull, numb, fail, disappear.
▷ANTONYMS sharpen.
5 *the fighting dimmed hopes of peace*: **diminish**, reduce, lessen, weaken, fade, make faint, undermine, impair.
▷ANTONYMS increase.

dimension noun **1** (usually **dimensions**) *the approximate dimensions of the master bedroom*: **proportions**, measurements, extent, size; length,

width, breadth, depth, area, volume, capacity; footage, acreage.
2 *we underestimated the dimension of the problem*: **size**, scale, extent, scope, range, measure, magnitude, largeness; greatness, importance, significance, value.
3 *water can add a new dimension to your garden*: **aspect**, feature, element, facet, side.

diminish verb **1** *the number of books published has not diminished*: **decrease**, decline, reduce, lessen, shrink, contract, grow smaller, fall off, drop off, slacken off; fall, drop, sink, slump, plummet, plunge; informal hit the floor, go through the floor, go downhill.
▷ANTONYMS increase.
2 *new legislation diminished the authority of the courts*: **reduce**, curtail, cut, cut down, cut back, prune, pare down, lessen, lower, decrease, shrink, contract, narrow, constrict, restrict, limit, curb, check, blunt; weaken, make weaker, erode, undermine, sap.
▷ANTONYMS increase.
3 *they returned to their homes as the fighting diminished*: **subside**, wane, abate, dwindle, fade, decline, slacken, moderate, ebb, recede, die away, die down, die out, peter out, tail off, cool off, let up, fizzle out, settle down, come to an end; archaic remit.
▷ANTONYMS flare up, get worse.
4 *she lost no opportunity to diminish him in her daughter's presence*: **belittle**, disparage, denigrate, deprecate, depreciate, devalue, demean, decry, cast aspersions on, speak ill of, speak badly of, run down, abuse, insult, revile, malign, vilify; N. Amer. slur; informal bad-mouth, pull to pieces, pull apart, sling mud at, do a hatchet job on; Brit. informal rubbish, slate, slag off, have a go at; rare asperse, derogate, vilipend, vituperate.
▷ANTONYMS boost.

diminution noun **1** *any diminution of freedom reduces the quality of life*: **curtailment**, curtailing, cutting back, cutback, cut, attenuation, reduction, lessening, lowering, decrease, contraction, constriction, restriction, limitation, limiting, curbing; weakening, undermining, sapping.
▷ANTONYMS increase, expansion.
2 *a gradual diminution in mental faculties*: **decline**, decrease, reduction, dwindling, shrinking, fading, failing, weakening, slackening, ebb, receding, wane, falling off; loss, erosion, depletion, impoverishment.
▷ANTONYMS increase, growth.

diminutive adjective *a diminutive breed of parrot*: **tiny**, small, little, petite, minute, miniature, mini, minuscule, microscopic, nanoscopic, small-scale, compact, pocket, toy, midget, undersized, short, stubby, elfin, dwarfish, dwarf, pygmy, bantam, homuncular, Lilliputian; Scottish wee; informal teeny, weeny, teeny-weeny, teensy-weensy, itty-bitty, itsy-bitsy, tiddly, dinky, baby, pint-sized, half-pint, sawn-off, knee-high to a grasshopper; Brit. informal titchy, ickle; N. Amer. informal little-bitty, vest-pocket.
▷ANTONYMS enormous.

dimple noun *she smiles, and two dimples appear in her cheeks*: **indentation**, concavity, depression, hollow, cleft, dent, dint, dip, pit.

dimwit noun informal *he's the biggest dimwit in the class*. See **fool**.

dim-witted adjective informal *a dim-witted muscleman*. See **stupid**.

din noun *he could not be heard above the din*: **uproar**, racket, loud noise, confused noise, commotion, cacophony, babel, hubbub, tumult, fracas, clangour, crash, clatter, clash; shouting, yelling, screaming, caterwauling, babble, babbling, clamour, outcry; brouhaha, fuss, disturbance, ado; pandemonium, bedlam, chaos, confusion; Scottish & N. English stramash; informal hullabaloo, rumpus, ruction; Brit. informal row; rare vociferation, ululation, charivari.
▷ANTONYMS silence; quiet.
▶verb **1** *since she was a child she had had the evils of drink **dinned into** her*: **instil**, drive, drum, hammer, drill, implant, ingrain, inculcate; teach over and over again, indoctrinate, brainwash.
2 *the sound dinning in my ears was the phone ringing*: **blare**, blast, clang, clatter, crash, clamour.

dine verb *they are dining at a downtown restaurant | they **dined on** lobster*: **have dinner**, have supper; eat, feed, feast, banquet; consume, take, partake of, devour; informal nosh, tuck into; Brit. informal **scoff**; dated sup, break bread.

dingle noun literary **valley**, dale, vale, hollow, gully; Brit. dene, combe, slade, nook; N. English **clough**; Scottish **glen**, strath; literary **dell**.

dingy adjective *a dingy bed-sitting room*: **gloomy**, drab, dark, dull, badly/poorly lit, dim; dismal, sombre, grim, dreary, cheerless; dirty, discoloured, grimy, soiled; faded, shabby, dowdy, worn, seedy, run down, tacky; literary tenebrous.
▷ANTONYMS bright; clean.

dinky adjective Brit. informal *a dinky toy rabbit*: **small**, little, petite, dainty, diminutive, mini, miniature; cute, neat, trim, dear, adorable; Scottish wee; informal teeny, teeny weeny, teensy-weensy; N. Amer. informal little-bitty.

dinner noun *a five-course dinner was served*: **evening meal**, supper, main meal, repast; lunch; feast, banquet, dinner party; Brit. tea; informal blowout, binge, feed; Brit. informal nosh-up, scoff, slap-up meal, spread, tuck-in; formal refection, collation.

> *Word links* **dinner**
>
> **prandial** relating to dinner

dint noun *the dints and holes were the work of arrows*: **dent**, indentation, depression, dip, dimple, cleft, hollow, crater, pit; notch, nick, chip, mark, cut, gouge, gash.
□ **by dint of** *our premier position is maintained by dint of sheer hard work*: **by means of**, by use of, by virtue of, on account of, as a result of, as a consequence of, owing to, by reason of, on grounds of, on the strength of, due to, thanks to, by, via.

d

diocese noun **bishopric**, see, parish.

dip verb **1** *he dipped a rag in the water*: **immerse**, submerge, plunge, duck, dunk, lower, sink; douse, soak, drench, souse, steep, saturate, bathe, rinse.
2 *the sun had dipped below the horizon*: **sink**, set, drop, go/drop down, fall, descend; fade, disappear, subside, vanish, be engulfed.
▷ANTONYMS rise.
3 *the news sent the stock dipping 5p to 663p*: **decrease**, fall, go down, drop, fall off, drop off, decline, diminish, dwindle, depreciate, deteriorate, slump, plummet, plunge; informal hit the floor.
▷ANTONYMS increase.
4 *the road dipped and we picked up speed*: **slope down**, slope, slant down, descend, go down, drop away, fall away, fall, sink, decline, be at an angle; droop, sag.
▷ANTONYMS rise.
5 *the flag was dipped*: **lower**, move downwards/down, let fall, let sink.
▷ANTONYMS raise.
6 *he dipped his headlights*: **dim**, **lower**, turn down, darken, make less intense.
▷ANTONYMS brighten, raise.
□ **dip into 1** *she dipped into her handbag*: **reach into**, put one's hand into. **2** *if an emergency arises, you might have to dip into your savings*: **draw on**, spend part of, touch, use, make use of, have recourse to, employ. **3** *it is an interesting book to dip into*: **browse through**, skim through, scan, look through, flick through, flip through, leaf through, riffle through, run through, glance at, peruse, read quickly, have a quick look at, run one's eye over, give something a/the once-over.
▶noun **1** *the pool is ideal for a relaxing dip*: **swim**, bathe, dive, plunge, splash, paddle.
2 *the best remedy is to give the fish a ten-minute dip in a salt bath*: **immersion**, plunge, ducking, dunking; sousing, dousing, soaking, drenching, steeping, saturation, bath, rinse, splash.
3 *the disposal of used sheep dip is tightly controlled*: **disinfectant**, parasiticide, germicide, bactericide, preservative; liquid preparation/mixture, solution.
4 *chicken satay with peanut dip*: **sauce**, dressing, relish, creamy mixture.
5 *there's a big hedge at the bottom of the dip*: **slope**, incline, decline, slant, descent, cant; **hollow**, concavity, depression, basin, indentation, dimple, trough.
6 *there was a dip in sales*: **decrease**, fall, drop, downturn, decline, falling off, dropping off, slump, reduction, lessening, diminution, lowering, slackening, ebb.
▷ANTONYMS increase.

diplomacy noun **1** *diplomacy has failed to win them independence*: **statesmanship**, statecraft; **negotiation(s)**, discussion(s), talks, consultation, conference, dialogue; international relations/politics, foreign affairs.
2 *she was uncertain of how to combine honesty and diplomacy in her answer*: **tact**, tactfulness, sensitivity, discretion, subtlety, finesse, delicacy; judiciousness, discernment, prudence, cleverness, skill; politeness, thoughtfulness, understanding, care; French savoir faire.
▷ANTONYMS tactlessness.

diplomat noun **1** *a British diplomat working in our consulate in Germany*: **ambassador**, envoy, emissary, consul, attaché, plenipotentiary, chargé d'affaires, official; archaic legate.
2 *'Gentlemen, please,' said Norman, ever the diplomat*: **tactful person**, conciliator, reconciler, peacemaker; mediator, negotiator, arbitrator, intermediary, moderator, go-between, middleman.

diplomatic adjective **1** *a month of hectic diplomatic activity*: **ambassadorial**, consular, foreign-policy, political; Brit. Foreign-Office.
2 *he tried his best to be diplomatic*: **tactful**, sensitive, subtle, delicate, discreet; judicious, discerning, prudent, politic, clever, skilful; polite, thoughtful, understanding, careful.
▷ANTONYMS indiscreet, tactless.

dire adjective **1** *the dire economic situation*: **terrible**, dreadful, appalling, frightful, awful, horrible, atrocious, grim, unspeakable, distressing, harrowing, alarming, shocking, outrageous; grave, serious, grievous, disastrous, ruinous, calamitous, catastrophic, cataclysmic, devastating, crippling; miserable, wretched, woeful; hopeless, irretrievable; informal lousy, chronic; literary direful; archaic or humorous parlous.
▷ANTONYMS good.

d

2 *he was in dire need of help*: **urgent**, desperate, pressing, crying, sore, grave, serious, extreme, acute, drastic; critical, crucial, vital.
▷ANTONYMS mild.
3 *dire warnings of fuel shortages*: **ominous**, portentous, gloomy, doom and gloom, sinister; grim, dreadful, dismal; unpropitious, inauspicious, unfavourable, pessimistic.
▷ANTONYMS encouraging.

direct adjective 1 *this was the most direct route*: **straight**, undeviating, unswerving, uncircuitous; shortest, quickest.
▷ANTONYMS indirect.
2 *he took a direct flight to Cyprus*: **non-stop**, unbroken, uninterrupted, straight through, through.
3 *he is very direct and honest*: **frank**, straightforward, honest, candid, open, sincere, straight, straight to the point, blunt, plain-spoken, outspoken, forthright, downright, uninhibited, unreserved, point blank, no-nonsense, matter-of-fact, bluff, undiplomatic, tactless; not afraid to call a spade a spade, not beating around the bush, speaking as one finds; explicit, clear, plain, unequivocal, unambiguous, unqualified, categorical; informal straight from the shoulder, upfront.
▷ANTONYMS evasive.
4 *he preferred to rely on direct contact with the leaders*: **face to face**, personal, unmediated, head-on, immediate, first-hand; French tête-à-tête; informal from the horse's mouth.
5 *a direct quotation*: **verbatim**, word for word, letter for letter, to the letter, faithful, undeviating, strict, exact, precise; unadulterated, unabridged, unvarnished, unembellished; accurate, correct.
▷ANTONYMS loose.
6 *Martin is his direct opposite*: **exact**, absolute, complete, diametrical, downright, thorough, extreme.
▶adverb *accommodation can be booked direct from the hotel*: **directly**, straight, in person, without an intermediary; French tête-à-tête.
▶verb 1 *the elders directed the affairs of the tribe*: **administer**, manage, run, control, govern, conduct, handle; be in charge of, be in control of, be in command of, be the boss of, lead, head, command, rule, preside over, exercise control over, be responsible for, be at the helm of; supervise, superintend, oversee, guide, regulate, orchestrate, coordinate, engineer, mastermind; informal run the show, call the shots, call the tune, pull the strings, be in the driving seat, be in the saddle.
2 *Jennifer was unsure if this comment was* ***directed at*** *her*: **aim**, point, level; **address to**, intend for, mean for, destine for; focus on, train on, turn on, fix on.
3 *most of these books are* ***directed at*** *teenage girls*: **target**, market; orient towards, pitch to/towards; design for, tailor to.
4 *a man in uniform directed them to the hall*: **give directions to**, show/point/indicate the way; guide, steer, lead; conduct, accompany, usher, escort, navigate, pilot.
5 *put all the documents in one package and direct it to me*: **address**, label, superscribe; post, send, mail, dispatch.
6 *the judge directed the jury to return a not guilty verdict*: **instruct**, tell, command, order, give orders to, charge, call on, require, dictate; adjure, enjoin; literary bid.

direction noun 1 *the village is over the moor in a northerly direction*: **way**, **route**, course, line, run, bearing, orientation.
2 *there's uncertainty over the political direction the newspaper might adopt*: **orientation**, inclination, leaning, tendency; bent, bias, preference, disposition; drift, aim, tack, attitude, tone, tenor, mood, feel, style, flavour, vein; current, trend.
3 *the department is under the direction of a senior executive*: **administration**, management, supervision, superintendence, government, regulation, orchestration; control, command, rule; conduct, handling, running, overseeing, masterminding; leadership, guidance.
4 *the ward sister gave explicit directions about nursing care*: **instruction**, command, order, bidding, charge, injunction, dictate, decree, edict, enjoinment, prescription, rule, regulation, requirement; guideline, recommendation, suggestion; (**directions**) guidance, information, briefing.

directive noun *an EC directive on drinking water*: **instruction**, direction, command, order, charge, injunction, enjoinment, prescription, demand; **rule**, ruling, regulation, law, dictate, decree, dictum, edict, notice, ordinance, mandate, fiat, diktat.

directly adverb 1 *the hijacker ordered the crew to fly directly to New York*: **straight**, right, in a straight line, as the crow flies, by a direct route, without deviation, in a beeline, by the shortest route.
2 *she'll be down here directly*: **immediately**, at once, instantly, right away, straight away, now, instantaneously, post-haste, without delay, without hesitation, forthwith; quickly, speedily, promptly; **soon**, as soon as possible, shortly, in a little while, in a second, in a moment, in a trice, in a flash, in (less than) no time, in no time at all, before you know it; informal pronto, double quick, p.d.q. (pretty damn quick), before you can say Jack Robinson, in a bit, in a jiffy, in two shakes (of a lamb's tail); Brit. informal in a tick, in two ticks, in a mo; archaic or informal anon.
3 *he'd never spoken directly to his lordship*: **face to face**, personally, in person, without an intermediary, at first hand, head on, direct, man to man; French tête-à-tête.
4 *they sat down directly opposite him*: **exactly**, immediately, precisely, right, squarely, just, dead; diametrically; informal bang.
5 *we didn't talk directly about sex*: **frankly**, bluntly, straightforwardly, openly, candidly, outspokenly, forthrightly, without beating around the bush, point-blank, matter-of-factly, without prevarication; explicitly, clearly, plainly, unequivocally, unambiguously, categorically; sincerely, truthfully.
▷ANTONYMS equivocally, euphemistically.
▶conjunction Brit. *directly he had finished praying he looked up*: **as soon as**, the moment, the instant, the second, once, when, immediately after.

director noun 1 *the director of a major British museum*: **administrator**, manager, chairman, chairwoman, chairperson, chair, head, chief, boss, principal, leader, governor, president, premier; managing director, MD, chief executive, CEO; superintendent, supervisor, controller, overseer, organizer; member of the board; informal kingpin, top dog, gaffer, bigwig, big cheese; N. Amer. informal honcho, head honcho, numero uno, Mister Big, big wheel.
2 *an Oscar-winning director*: **supervisor**, controller, regisseur, producer, auteur, choreographer.

directory noun *the London phone directory*: **index**, list, listing, register, catalogue, record, archive, inventory.

dirge noun *he wrote dirges for funerals*: **elegy**, lament, funeral song/chant, burial hymn, requiem, dead march; Irish & Scottish keen, coronach; rare threnody, threnode, monody.

dirt noun 1 *his face was streaked with dirt*: **grime**, dust, soot, smut; muck, mud, filth, mire, sludge, slime, ooze, dross, scum, pollution, waste; smudges, stains; informal crud, yuck, grot, gunge, grunge.
2 *the packed dirt of the road*: **earth**, soil, loam, clay, silt; turf, clod, sod; ground.
3 informal *a lawn covered in dog dirt*: **excrement**, excreta, droppings, faeces, dung, manure, ordure; muck, mess; informal poo; N. Amer. informal **poop**; vulgar slang crap, shit.
4 informal *they tried to dig up dirt on the President*: **scandal**, gossip, talk, revelations, rumour(s), tittle-tattle, tattle; slander, libel, calumny; smears; informal low-down, gen, dope; N. Amer. informal poop.
5 *we object to the dirt that television projects into homes*: **obscenity**, indecency, smut, smuttiness, filth, pornography, sordidness, coarseness, bawdiness, earthiness, suggestiveness, vulgarity, ribaldry, salaciousness, salacity, lewdness; informal sleaze, porn, sleaziness, naughtiness, raunchiness, steaminess, spiciness.

> *Word links* **dirt**
>
> **mysophobia** fear of dirt

dirty adjective 1 *a dirty sweatshirt | dirty water*: **soiled**, grimy, grubby, filthy, mucky, stained, unwashed, greasy, smeared, smeary, spotted, smudged, cloudy, muddy, dusty, sooty; unclean, sullied, impure, tarnished, polluted, contaminated, defiled, foul, unhygienic, insanitary, unsanitary; informal cruddy, yucky, icky; Brit. informal manky, gungy, grotty; literary befouled, besmirched, begrimed; rare feculent.
▷ANTONYMS clean.
2 *the deer was a dirty grey in colour*: **dull**, **cloudy**, muddy, dingy, dark, not clear, not pure, not bright.
▷ANTONYMS bright.
3 *a dirty joke*: **indecent**, obscene, rude, vulgar, smutty, coarse, crude, filthy, bawdy, suggestive, ribald, racy, salacious, risqué, prurient, offensive, lewd, lascivious, licentious, pornographic, explicit, X-rated; N. Amer. off colour; informal naughty, blue; euphemistic adult.
▷ANTONYMS clean.
4 *firms are resorting to dirty tricks to keep ahead of rivals | you dirty cheat!* **unfair**, dishonest, deceitful, unscrupulous, dishonourable, unsporting, ungentlemanly, below the belt, unethical, unprincipled, immoral; crooked, illegal, fraudulent; rotten, corrupt, double-dealing, treacherous, underhand, sly, crafty, cunning, wily, devious, Machiavellian, sneaky, guileful, conniving, designing, calculating; nasty, unpleasant, mean, base, low, vile, contemptible, despicable, cowardly, shameful, ignominious, sordid, beggarly, squalid; informal low-down; Brit. informal out of order, not cricket.
▷ANTONYMS honest; decent.
5 *she gave her brother a dirty look*: **malevolent**, smouldering, resentful, full of dislike/hate, hostile, black, dark, bitter; angry, indignant, annoyed, peeved, offended.
6 *dirty weather*: **unpleasant**, nasty, foul, inclement, rough, bad; stormy, squally, gusty, windy, blowy, rainy; misty, gloomy, murky, overcast, louring.
▷ANTONYMS fair.
7 *how dare you come here throwing around such dirty lies?* **scandalous**, defamatory, slanderous, libellous.
□ **do the dirty on** informal *his cook decided to do the dirty on him and not turn up for work*: **betray**, **cheat**, **double-cross**, defraud, trick, hoodwink,

mislead, deceive, swindle, break one's promise to, be disloyal to, be unfaithful to, break faith with, play false, fail, let down; informal two-time, stitch up, do the dirty on, sell down the river.

▸ **verb** *she didn't like him dirtying her nice clean towels*: **soil**, stain, muddy, blacken, mess up, spoil, tarnish, taint, make dirty; mark, spatter, bespatter, smudge, smear, daub, spot, splash, splatter; sully, pollute, foul, defile; literary befoul, besmirch, begrime.
▷ANTONYMS clean.

Word toolkit

dirty	**sordid**	**foul**
hands	affair	language
habit	details	smell
streets	past	breath
clothes	business	taste

disability noun *my disability makes getting into bed rather a slow process*: condition, disorder, affliction, ailment, complaint, illness, malady, disease; disablement, incapacity, infirmity; special needs; learning difficulties, learning disability; often offensive handicap, abnormality, defect, impairment.

Choose the right word **disability**

See **disabled**.

disable verb **1** *the gunfire could kill or disable the pilot*: **incapacitate**, impair, damage, put out of action, render/make powerless, weaken, enfeeble, debilitate, indispose, make unfit; immobilize, hamstring, paralyse, prostrate; rare torpefy.
2 *the bomb squad disabled the device*: **deactivate**, defuse, disarm, render inoperative, make ineffective, put out of action, make harmless.
▷ANTONYMS set, repair.
3 *after the Restoration he was disabled from holding public office*: **disqualify**, prevent, invalidate, declare incapable, rule out, preclude, debar, prohibit, disentitle; rare disenable.
▷ANTONYMS allow.

disabled adjective *they design computer aids for disabled people*: **having a disability**, wheelchair-using, paralysed; having a mental disability, learning-disabled, having learning difficulties, having special needs; often offensive handicapped, physically handicapped, physically impaired, crippled, lame; euphemistic physically challenged, differently abled; Medicine paraplegic, quadriplegic, tetraplegic, monoplegic, hemiplegic, paretic, paraparetic.
▷ANTONYMS able-bodied.

Choose the right word **disabled**

Disabled is the standard term for people who have physical or mental disabilities. In the past, it was acceptable to use terms such as **handicapped** or **crippled** but these may now cause offence and should be avoided. More recently, expressions such as **physically challenged** or **differently abled** have been coined as synonyms for *disabled* in a conscious attempt to eradicate any negative perception or stigma that may be felt to be attached to the older terms: these may be appropriate in certain situations but they are best avoided in formal writing. Similarly, **disability** should be used rather than words such as **handicap**, **incapacity**, or **impairment**.

disabuse verb *he had thought he was good enough to become a professional, and Dinah had disabused him*: **disillusion**, undeceive, correct, set right/straight, open the eyes of, enlighten, reveal the truth to, wake up, disenchant, shatter the illusions of, make sadder and wiser.

disadvantage noun **1** *price is probably the biggest disadvantage of rail travel*: **drawback**, snag, downside, stumbling block, catch, pitfall, fly in the ointment; weak spot/point, weakness, flaw, defect, fault; handicap, limitation, trouble, difficulty, problem, complication, liability, nuisance; hindrance, obstacle, impediment; informal minus, hiccup; Brit. informal spanner in the works; N. Amer. informal monkey wrench in the works.
▷ANTONYMS advantage, benefit.
2 *she could think of nothing to his disadvantage*: **detriment**, prejudice, disservice, harm, damage; loss, injury, hurt, mischief.
▷ANTONYMS advantage.
▸ **verb** *policies which unfairly disadvantage certain groups*: **treat unfavourably**, put at a disadvantage, treat harshly/unfairly, put in an unfavourable position, handicap, inflict a handicap on, do a disservice to, be unfair to, wrong.

disadvantaged adjective *a disadvantaged rural area*: **deprived**, **underprivileged**, depressed, in need, needy, in want, in distress; destitute, poor, poverty-stricken; discriminated against; Brit. on the bread line; rare necessitous.
▷ANTONYMS privileged.

disadvantageous adjective *a very disadvantageous position*: **unfavourable**, adverse, inauspicious, unpropitious, unfortunate, unlucky, bad; detrimental, prejudicial, deleterious, harmful, damaging, injurious, hurtful, destructive; inopportune, ill-timed, untimely, inexpedient.
▷ANTONYMS advantageous.

disaffected adjective *a plot by disaffected elements in the army*: **dissatisfied**, disgruntled, discontented, malcontent, restless, frustrated, fed up; alienated, estranged; disloyal, rebellious, insubordinate, mutinous, seditious, renegade, insurgent, insurrectionary, dissident, up in arms; hostile, antagonistic, unfriendly.
▷ANTONYMS contented, loyal.

disaffection noun *the government's oppressive policies heightened popular disaffection*: **dissatisfaction**, disgruntlement, discontent, restlessness, frustration; alienation, estrangement; disloyalty, rebellion, insubordination, mutiny, sedition, insurgence, insurrection, dissidence; hostility, antagonism, animosity, discord, dissension.
▷ANTONYMS contentment, loyalty.

disagree verb **1** *no one was willing to* ***disagree with*** *him*: **fail to agree**, be in dispute/contention, be at variance/odds, not see eye to eye, differ from, dissent from, diverge from; contradict, gainsay, challenge, oppose; argue, debate, quarrel, bicker, wrangle, squabble, spar, dispute, take issue, row, altercate, clash, be at loggerheads, cross swords, lock horns; informal fall out, have words, scrap; archaic disaccord.
▷ANTONYMS agree.
2 *they* ***disagreed with*** *American policy*: **disapprove of**, oppose, dissent from, think wrong, be against, demur about/against, not believe in, not support.
▷ANTONYMS agree.
3 *their accounts disagree on details*: **differ**, be dissimilar, be unlike, be different, vary; contradict each other, conflict, clash, contrast, diverge, not correspond, not accord, be discordant.
▷ANTONYMS agree.
4 *the North Sea crossing seemed to have* ***disagreed with*** *her*: **make ill**, make unwell, nauseate, sicken, upset, cause illness to, cause discomfort to, be injurious to, have an adverse effect on.

disagreeable adjective **1** *a disagreeable smell*: **unpleasant**, displeasing, nasty, horrible, dreadful, horrid, frightful, abominable, odious, offensive, obnoxious, objectionable, repugnant, repulsive, repellent, revolting, disgusting, foul, vile, nauseating, sickening, hateful, detestable, distasteful, unsavoury, unpalatable.
▷ANTONYMS pleasant.
2 *he was a very disagreeable character*: **bad-tempered**, ill-tempered, ill-natured, ill-humoured, curmudgeonly, cross, crabbed, irritable, grumpy, peevish, snappish, petulant, sulky, sullen, prickly; **unfriendly**, unpleasant, nasty, mean, mean-spirited; rude, surly, discourteous, impolite, brusque, abrupt, difficult, contrary, churlish, disobliging; cruel, vicious, spiteful; informal grouchy.
▷ANTONYMS likeable, pleasant.

disagreement noun **1** *at the conference there was disagreement over possible solutions*: **dissent**, lack of agreement, difference of opinion, dispute; variance, controversy, disaccord, discord, contention, divisions.
▷ANTONYMS consensus, agreement.
2 *a heated disagreement over politics*: **argument**, debate, quarrel, wrangle, squabble, altercation, dispute, disputation, war of words, contretemps, misunderstanding; discord, strife, conflict; bickering, sparring, contention, dissension, disharmony; informal falling-out, tiff, barney, set-to, shouting/slanging match, spat, ding-dong; Brit. informal row; Scottish informal rammy.
3 *there was disagreement between the results of the two assessments*: **difference**, dissimilarity, variation, variance, discrepancy, disparity, dissimilitude, unlikeness; incompatibility, incongruity, contradiction, conflict, clash, contrast; divergence, deviation, nonconformity.
▷ANTONYMS agreement, correspondence.

disallow verb *if the registration officer disallows your application he will let you know* | *Derby had two goals disallowed*: **reject**, refuse, dismiss, say no to; ban, bar, block, stop, debar, forbid, prohibit, blackball; cancel, declare null and void, invalidate, overrule, quash, overturn, countermand, reverse, throw out, set aside; veto, embargo, proscribe; informal give the thumbs down to, squash.
▷ANTONYMS allow.

disappear verb **1** *they disappeared through the gates of the house* | *most symptoms should disappear in six months*: **vanish**, pass from sight, cease to be visible, vanish from sight, recede from view, be lost to view/sight, fade, fade/melt away; withdraw, depart, retire, retreat; go, pass, ebb, wane, dissipate, be dispelled, dematerialize, evaporate; literary evanesce.
▷ANTONYMS appear; reappear.
2 *this way of life has disappeared*: **die out**, die, become extinct, cease to be/exist, be no more, come to an end, end, pass away, pass into oblivion, expire, perish, wither away, peter out, fizzle out, leave no trace.
▷ANTONYMS survive, live on.
3 *we had to change the locks after the keys disappeared*: **get lost**, go missing, be mislaid, be forgotten, be left behind; be stolen, be taken.

disappearance noun **1** *the sun's disappearance at night*: **vanishing**, fading, fading/melting away, passing from sight, receding from view;

d

d

withdrawal, departure, retirement, retreat; going, passing, exit; ebb, wane, dissipation, dematerialization, dissolution, evaporation; literary evanescence.
▷ANTONYMS appearance, reappearance.
2 *the disappearance of the last big predators from Western Europe*: **dying out**, dying, death, extinction, coming to an end, ending, passing away, passing into oblivion, expiry, vanishing, perishing, withering away, petering out, fizzling out.
3 *the disappearance of the money*: **loss**; **theft**, robbery, stealing, thieving, robbing, pilfering, pilferage, purloining.
▷ANTONYMS recovery.

disappoint verb 1 *he disappointed the home crowd by losing in the semi-finals*: **let down**, fail, dash the hopes of; dishearten, dispirit, discourage, upset, dismay, depress, sadden, dampen the spirits of, disenchant, disillusion, shatter the illusions of, dissatisfy, disgruntle, chagrin; fall short (of expectations).
▷ANTONYMS cheer; satisfy.
2 *his hopes were disappointed by the death of his patron*: **thwart**, frustrate, baulk, foil, dash, defeat, baffle, put a/the damper on, nip in the bud; hinder, obstruct, hamper, impede, interfere with; informal stymie, throw cold water on.
▷ANTONYMS fulfil.

disappointed adjective 1 *I was disappointed that my mother wasn't there*: **saddened**, upset, let down, disheartened, downhearted, cast down, downcast, depressed, dispirited, discouraged, despondent, dismayed, crestfallen, distressed, chagrined; disenchanted, disillusioned; displeased, discontented, dissatisfied, frustrated, disgruntled; informal choked, miffed, cut up; Brit. informal gutted, as sick as a parrot.
▷ANTONYMS pleased, satisfied.
2 *a bitter tale of disappointed hopes*: **thwarted**, frustrated, baulked, foiled, dashed, defeated, failed, baffled; informal stymied.
▷ANTONYMS fulfilled.

disappointing adjective 1 *the predominance of white, middle-class characters is disappointing*: **saddening**, disheartening, dispiriting, discouraging, upsetting, dismaying, depressing, distressing; disenchanting, disillusioning, dissatisfying; regrettable, unfortunate.
▷ANTONYMS encouraging, cheering.
2 *Derry made a disappointing start*: **unsatisfactory**, inadequate, insufficient, unworthy, substandard, not good enough; poor, inferior, deficient, second-rate, pathetic, lame, pitiful; anticlimactic; informal below par, not up to scratch, not up to snuff, sorry, not all it's cracked up to be; Brit. informal underwhelming, duff, ropy, rubbish.
▷ANTONYMS encouraging, satisfactory.

disappointment noun 1 *members expressed disappointment at the decision*: **sadness**, regret, dismay, sorrow; dispiritedness, despondency, heavy-heartedness, depression; distress, mortification, chagrin; disenchantment, disillusionment; displeasure, discontent, dissatisfaction, disgruntlement.
▷ANTONYMS satisfaction, happiness.
2 *he agreed that the recent defeats against Norway and the USA had been bitter disappointments*: **failure**, let-down, non-event, anticlimax; misfortune, setback, blow, reversal, stroke of bad luck, body blow, one in the eye; fiasco, disaster, catastrophe, mess, debacle; Brit. damp squib; informal flop, dud, washout, non-starter, lead balloon.
▷ANTONYMS success.
3 *the disappointment of the high hopes invested in reform*: **frustration**, thwarting, baulking, foiling, dashing, baffling; defeat, failure, lack of success.
▷ANTONYMS fulfilment.

disapprobation noun *she had braved her mother's disapprobation and slipped out to enjoy herself*. See **disapproval**.

disapproval noun *they expressed their strong disapproval of the law*: **disapprobation**, dislike; dissatisfaction, disfavour, displeasure, distaste, odium, objection, demurral, exception; dissent, disagreement; criticism, censure, condemnation, denunciation, opprobrium; blame, reproach, rebuke, reproof, remonstration; disparagement, deprecation; informal the thumbs down; rare animadversion.
▷ANTONYMS approval.

disapprove verb 1 *he disapproves of gamblers*: **have/express a poor opinion of**, dislike, be against, object to, find unacceptable, think wrong, take exception to, not believe in, not support, frown on, take a dim view of, look askance at; be dissatisfied with, be displeased with, be hostile towards; detest, deplore, despise, loathe; criticize, censure, blame, condemn, denounce, decry, reproach, rebuke, reprove, remonstrate against; disparage, deprecate; informal look down one's nose at, knock; rare animadvert.
▷ANTONYMS approve.
2 *the board disapproved the bank's plan*: **reject**, refuse, turn down, veto, disallow, set aside, throw out, dismiss, say 'no' to, rule against, rule out; informal give the thumbs down to.
▷ANTONYMS approve, accept.

disapproving adjective *he cast a disapproving glance at Bridget*: **reproachful**, reproving, full of reproof; **critical**, criticizing, censorious, condemnatory, condemning, denouncing, scathing, damning; disparaging, deprecatory, unfavourable, pejorative, derogatory; dissatisfied, displeased, hostile; informal knocking, slating.
▷ANTONYMS approving.

disarm verb 1 *the UN must disarm the country and arrest the warlords*: **deprive of arms**, take weapons from, render defenceless, make powerless; **demilitarize**, demobilize.
▷ANTONYMS arm, militarize.
2 *the militia had refused government demands to disarm*: **lay down arms/weapons**, demilitarize, turn over weapons, decommission arms/weapons, become unarmed; literary sheathe the sword, turn swords into ploughshares.
▷ANTONYMS arm.
3 *police disarmed a parcel bomb*: **defuse**, disable, deactivate, remove the fuse from, put out of action; make safe, make harmless.
▷ANTONYMS arm, set.
4 *the warmth in his voice disarmed her*: **win over**, charm, undermine someone's resistance, sweeten; persuade, convert; mollify, appease, placate, pacify, conciliate, humour, propitiate.
▷ANTONYMS antagonize.

disarmament noun *the public wanted peace and disarmament*: **demilitarization**, demobilization, deactivation of arms/weapons, decommissioning (of arms/weapons), laying down of arms/weapons; arms/weapons reduction, arms/weapons limitation, arms/weapons control, de-escalation.

disarming adjective *a disarming smile*: **winning**, charming, likeable, enchanting, beguiling; persuasive, irresistible; conciliatory, mollifying, placating, pacifying, propitiating.

disarrange verb *it's amazing how quickly my few possessions become disarranged*: **disorder**, bring/throw into disorder, put out of place, throw into disarray, make disorderly, disorganize, disturb, displace; make untidy, mess up, make a mess of; confuse, throw into confusion, jumble, mix up, muddle, turn upside-down, derange, scatter; dishevel, tousle, rumple; informal turn topsy-turvy, make a shambles of; N. Amer. informal muss up.
▷ANTONYMS arrange, tidy.

disarray noun 1 *the room was in disarray*: **disorder**, confusion, chaos; untidiness, dishevelment; mess, muddle, clutter, jumble, mix-up, tangle, hotchpotch, shambles.
▷ANTONYMS tidiness.
2 *the political disarray which followed the death of Offa*: **disorganization**, lack of order, discomposure, disunity; indiscipline, unruliness.
▷ANTONYMS orderliness.
▸ verb *her clothes were disarrayed*: **disarrange**, make untidy, bring/throw into disarray, bring/throw into disorder, disorganize, throw into a state of disorganization, turn upside-down, unsettle; dishevel, tousle, rumple.
▷ANTONYMS tidy, organize.

disassemble verb *the furniture was disassembled for transport*: **dismantle**, take apart, take to pieces, pull apart, pull to pieces, take/pull to bits, deconstruct, break up, strip down.
▷ANTONYMS assemble, put together.

disaster noun 1 *a railway disaster*: **catastrophe**, calamity, cataclysm, tragedy, act of God, holocaust; accident, mishap, misadventure, mischance; setback, reversal, reverse of fortune, contretemps, stroke of ill luck, problem, difficulty, heavy blow, shock, buffet; adversity, trouble, misfortune, ruin, ruination, tribulation, woe, distress; technical casualty; archaic bale; Scottish archaic mishanter.
▷ANTONYMS blessing.
2 *my personal life had been a disaster*: **failure**, fiasco, catastrophe, mess, debacle; Brit. damp squib; informal flop, dud, washout, dead loss, dead duck, non-starter, no-hoper.
▷ANTONYMS success.

disastrous adjective *a disastrous fire | a disastrous decision*: **catastrophic**, calamitous, cataclysmic, tragic; devastating, ravaging, ruinous, harmful, injurious, detrimental, adverse; dire, terrible, awful, shocking, appalling, dreadful, grievous, horrible, black, dark, bad; unfortunate, unlucky, ill-fated, ill-starred, inauspicious, unfavourable.
▷ANTONYMS fortunate, successful, beneficial.

disavow verb *the chairman publicly disavowed the press release*: **deny**, disclaim, disown, wash one's hands of; reject, repudiate; contradict, rebut, abjure, renounce, forswear, eschew.

disavowal noun *it's a complete disavowal of responsibility*: **denial**, disowning, disclaimer; rejection, repudiation, contradiction, rebuttal; renunciation, eschewal, casting off/aside, abandonment.

disband verb *the unit was scheduled to disband*: **break up**, disperse, demobilize, dissolve, scatter, separate, go separate ways, part company.
▷ANTONYMS assemble.

disbelief noun 1 *she stared at him in disbelief*: **incredulity**, incredulousness, lack of belief, lack of credence, lack of conviction, scepticism, doubt, doubtfulness, dubiety, dubiousness, questioning, cynicism, suspicion,

distrust, mistrust, wariness, chariness; bewilderment, bafflement, surprise, shock, stupefaction, confusion, perplexity.
▷ANTONYMS belief, credence.
2 *I'll burn in hell for disbelief*: **atheism**, unbelief, godlessness, ungodliness, impiety, irreligion, agnosticism, nihilism.
▷ANTONYMS faith.

disbelieve verb *he totally disbelieved her | he had come to* ***disbelieve in*** *his own assertions*: **not believe**, not credit, give no credence to, discredit, discount, doubt, distrust, mistrust, be suspicious of, have no confidence/faith in, be incredulous of, be unconvinced about; not accept, reject, repudiate, question, challenge, contradict; informal take with a pinch of salt.
▷ANTONYMS believe.

disbeliever noun *as a disbeliever I can still read the Bible for the beauty of its prose*: **unbeliever**, non-believer, atheist, irreligionist, nihilist; rationalist; sceptic, doubter, agnostic, doubting Thomas, questioner, challenger; cynic, scoffer; rare nullifidian.
▷ANTONYMS believer.

disbelieving adjective *he gave a disbelieving laugh*: **incredulous**, unbelieving, doubtful, dubious, unconvinced; distrustful, mistrustful, suspicious, lacking trust, cynical, sceptical.
▷ANTONYMS believing.

disburden verb *I decided to disburden myself of the task*: **relieve**, free, liberate, unburden, disencumber, discharge, ease, unload; excuse from, absolve from.
▷ANTONYMS burden.

disburse verb *the officers disbursed some £1.8 million on behalf of the fund*: **pay out**, lay out, spend, expend, dole out, hand out, part with, donate, give; informal fork out, shell out, dish out, lash out, cough up, splurge, blow; Brit. informal stump up; N. Amer. informal ante up, pony up.
▷ANTONYMS claim.

disbursement noun *the commission decided to delay the disbursement of funds*: **payment**, disbursal, paying out, laying out, spending, expending, expenditure, disposal, outlay, doling out, handing out, parting with, donation, giving.

disc, disk noun 1 *the sun was a huge scarlet disc*: **circle**, round, saucer, discus, ring.
2 *the module comes with a manual and software on disk*: **diskette**, floppy disk, floppy; hard disk; CD-ROM.
3 *this is one of the best of this conductor's discs*: **record**, album, LP, gramophone record, vinyl; **compact disc**, CD.

discard verb *his old suit had been discarded*: **dispose of**, throw away, throw out, get rid of, toss out; reject, jettison, scrap, dispense with, cast aside/off, repudiate, abandon, relinquish, drop, have done with, shed, slough off, shrug off, throw on the scrap heap; informal chuck (away/out), fling away, dump, ditch, axe, bin, junk, get shut of; Brit. informal get shot of; N. Amer. informal trash; archaic forsake.
▷ANTONYMS keep; acquire.

discern verb *in the dim light he could discern a handful of ghostly figures*: **perceive**, make out, pick out, detect, recognize, notice, observe, see, spot; identify, determine, distinguish, differentiate, discriminate, tell apart; become cognizant of, become aware of, become conscious of; literary descry, espy.
▷ANTONYMS overlook; miss.

discernible adjective *the figure was scarcely discernible in the pale moonlight*: **visible**, detectable, noticeable, perceptible, observable, perceivable, distinguishable, recognizable, identifiable; apparent, obvious, clear, manifest, conspicuous, patent, plain, evident, distinct, appreciable.
▷ANTONYMS imperceptible.

discerning adjective *we have some real treasures for the discerning collector*: **discriminating**, selective, judicious, tasteful, refined, cultivated, cultured, sophisticated, enlightened, sensitive, subtle, critical; perceptive, insightful, percipient, perspicacious, penetrating; astute, shrewd, ingenious, clever, intelligent, sharp, wise, erudite, aware, knowing, sagacious; rare sapient.
▷ANTONYMS undiscerning, indiscriminate.

discernment noun *each object in the room spoke of his taste and discernment*: **judgement**, taste, discrimination, refinement, cultivation, sophistication, enlightenment, sensitivity, subtlety; insight, perceptiveness, perception, perspicacity; astuteness, acumen, shrewdness, ingeniousness, cleverness, intelligence, sharpness, wisdom, erudition, awareness, sagacity; rare sapience.

discharge verb 1 *he was discharged from the RAF*: **dismiss**, remove, eject, expel, deprive of office, get rid of, throw out, oust; let go, give someone notice, lay off, make/declare redundant; Military cashier; informal sack, give someone the sack, fire, axe, send packing, give someone the boot, boot out, turf out, give someone their cards, give someone their marching orders, give someone the heave-ho, give someone the push, give someone the bullet, show someone the door.
▷ANTONYMS recruit, engage.
2 *he was discharged from prison*: **release**, liberate, free, set free, let go, let out, allow to leave, set/let/turn loose; acquit, clear, absolve, pardon, exonerate, reprieve, exculpate; deliver, spare, exempt; emancipate; informal let off (the hook); historical manumit.
▷ANTONYMS imprison.
3 *oil is routinely discharged from ships*: **send out**, **pour**, release, eject, emit, let out, void, issue, dispense, give off, exude, excrete, ooze, leak, gush, jet; Medicine extravasate; literary disembogue.
▷ANTONYMS absorb.
4 *he accidentally discharged a pistol*: **fire**, shoot, let off, set off, loose off, trigger, explode, detonate.
5 *there is an elevator for discharging grain from ships*: **unload**, offload, empty, unburden, disburden, remove, relieve; deliver, deposit, put off; rare unlade.
▷ANTONYMS load.
6 *the bank had failed to discharge its supervisory duties*: **carry out**, perform, conduct, do; complete, accomplish, achieve, fulfil, execute, implement, dispatch, bring off, bring about, effect; observe, abide by, stand by; rare effectuate.
7 *the executor must discharge the funeral expenses*: **pay**, pay off, pay in full, settle (up), clear, honour, meet, liquidate, satisfy, defray, make good; informal square.
▸ noun 1 *his discharge from the service*: **dismissal**, release, removal, ejection, ousting, expulsion, congé; Military cashiering; informal the sack, firing, axing, the axe, the boot, one's marching orders, the heave-ho, the push, the bullet.
▷ANTONYMS recruitment.
2 *she was given an absolute discharge by the magistrates*: **release**, liberation; **acquittal**, clearance, clearing; absolution, pardon, exoneration, reprieve, amnesty, exculpation; informal let-off, letting off; historical manumission.
▷ANTONYMS conviction.
3 *there was a discharge of diesel oil into the river*: **leak**, leaking, emission, release, exuding, oozing, excretion, ejection; emptying, voiding, voidance; literary disemboguing.
4 *symptoms include a watery discharge from the eyes*: **emission**, secretion, excretion, exudate, effusion; flow, ooze, seepage, suppuration; pus, matter.
5 *he killed eight birds with a single discharge of his gun*: **shot**, shooting, firing, discharging, explosion, detonation; blast, crack, bang, pop, report; burst, volley, salvo, fusillade, barrage; (**discharges**) gunfire.
6 *we have two hundred passengers and freight for discharge*: **unloading**, offloading, unburdening, disburdening, removal, removing, relieving; emptying; delivering, deposit; rare unlading.
▷ANTONYMS loading.
7 *the teachers appeared somewhat lax in the discharge of their duties*: **carrying out**, performance, performing, conduct, doing; completion, accomplishment, achievement, fulfilment, execution, implementation, dispatch, effectuation; observance.
8 *the residue of the estate after the discharge of all debts*: **payment**, repayment, paying (off), settlement, settling (up), clearance, clearing, honouring, meeting, liquidation, defraying, making good; informal squaring.

> *Word links* **discharge**
>
> **-rrhoea** related suffix, as in *diarrhoea, logorrhoea*

disciple noun 1 *the disciples of Jesus*: **apostle**; follower.
2 *a disciple of Rousseau*: **follower**, adherent, believer, admirer, devotee, acolyte, votary; pupil, student, protégé, learner; upholder, supporter, advocate, proponent, apologist; Hinduism chela, bhakta.
▷ANTONYMS critic, opponent.

disciplinarian noun **martinet**, hard taskmaster, authoritarian, stickler for discipline; tyrant, despot; N. Amer. ramrod; informal slave-driver.

discipline noun 1 *discipline in the camp was strict*: **control**, regulation, direction, order, authority, rule, strictness, a firm hand; routine, regimen; training, teaching, instruction, drill, drilling, exercise; use of punishment.
2 *it may take courage and discipline to do this, but it is worth the effort*: **self-control**, self-discipline, self-government, control, controlled behaviour, self-restraint; good behaviour, orderliness, obedience.
3 *sociology is a fairly new discipline*: **field (of study)**, branch of knowledge, course of study, subject, area; specialist subject, speciality, specialty.
▸ verb 1 *these families have different ways of disciplining their children | you must discipline yourself into adopting regular working methods*: **train**, drill, teach, school, coach, educate, regiment, indoctrinate; lay down the law to someone, bring into line.
2 *she had learned to discipline her emotions*: **control**, bring/keep under control, restrain, regulate, govern, keep in check, check, curb, keep a tight rein on, rein in, bridle, tame.
▷ANTONYMS give free rein to.
3 *a member of staff was to be disciplined by the management*: **punish**, penalize, take disciplinary action against, bring to book; **reprimand**, rebuke, reprove, chastise, castigate, upbraid, remonstrate with; informal dress down, give someone a dressing-down, rap over the knuckles, give someone a roasting, give someone a rocket, put on the mat; Brit. informal carpet, put on the carpet; archaic chasten.

disclaim verb **1** *the school disclaimed any responsibility for his death*: **deny**, refuse to accept, refuse to acknowledge, reject, wash one's hands of.
▷ANTONYMS acknowledge, accept.
2 Law *the earl disclaimed his title*: **renounce**, relinquish, resign, give up, abandon; repudiate, disown, cast off, discard, abjure, forswear, disavow; Law disaffirm.
▷ANTONYMS claim.

disclaimer noun **1** *the disclaimer of responsibility set out in the memorandum*: **denial**, refusal, rejection.
▷ANTONYMS acceptance, acknowledgement.
2 Law *a deed of disclaimer*: **renunciation**, relinquishment, resignation, abdication; repudiation, abjuration, disavowal, disaffirmation.

disclose verb **1** *the information is confidential and must not be disclosed to anyone*: **reveal**, make known, divulge, tell, impart, communicate, pass on, vouchsafe, unfold; release, make public, broadcast, publish, report, unveil, go public with; leak, betray, let slip, let drop, blurt out, give away; admit, confess; informal let on, blab, spill the beans about, spill, let the cat out of the bag about, blow the lid off, squeal about; Brit. informal blow the gaff; archaic discover, unbosom.
▷ANTONYMS conceal; hide.
2 *exploratory surgery disclosed an aneurysm*: **uncover**, expose to view, allow to be seen, reveal, show, exhibit, lay bare, bring to light; rare unclose.

disclosure noun **1** *she was acutely embarrassed by this unexpected disclosure*: **revelation**, surprising fact, divulgence, declaration, announcement, news, report; exposé, leak; admission, confession.
2 *the unauthorized disclosure of official information*: **publishing**, broadcasting; revelation, revealing, making known, communication, divulging, divulgence; release, uncovering, unveiling, exposure; leakage; Law discovery; rare divulgation.
▷ANTONYMS concealment.

discoloration noun *a brown discoloration on the skin*: **stain**, mark, patch, soiling, streak, spot, blotch, tarnishing; blemish, flaw, defect, disfigurement, bruise, contusion; birthmark; liver spot, age spot; informal splodge, splotch; technical ecchymosis, naevus.

discolour verb *smoke from the coal fire had discoloured the original paintwork*: **stain**, mark, soil, dirty, make dirty, streak, smear, spot, tarnish, sully, spoil, mar, disfigure, blemish; blacken, char; fade, bleach, wash out; rust, weather.

discoloured adjective *the shaft of the sword was twisted and discoloured*: **stained**, marked, spotted, dirty, soiled, tarnished, blackened; bleached, faded, yellowed; rusted, rusty, oxidized, weathered.
▷ANTONYMS shiny, clean.

discomfit verb *she kissed Sir John on the cheek, which discomfited him even more*: **embarrass**, make uncomfortable, make uneasy, abash, disconcert, nonplus, discompose, discomfort, take aback, unsettle, unnerve, put someone off their stroke, ruffle, confuse, fluster, agitate, disorientate, upset, disturb, perturb, distress; chagrin, mortify; informal faze, rattle, discombobulate, set someone back on their heels, make someone laugh on the other side of their face; N. Amer. informal make someone laugh out of the other side of their mouth.
▷ANTONYMS reassure.

discomfiture noun *Sweetman laughed at her obvious discomfiture*: **embarrassment**, unease, uneasiness, awkwardness, discomfort, discomposure, abashment, confusion, agitation, nervousness, flusteredness, disorientation, perturbation, distress; chagrin, mortification, shame, humiliation; informal discombobulation; rare disconcertment, disconcertion, nonplus.

discomfort noun **1** *he complained of increasing abdominal discomfort*: **pain**, aches and pains, soreness, tenderness, irritation, stiffness, malaise; ache, twinge, pang, throb, cramp, hurt; Brit. informal gyp.
2 *the discomforts of life at sea*: **inconvenience**, difficulty, bother, nuisance, vexation, drawback, disadvantage, trouble, problem, trial, tribulation; lack of comfort, unpleasantness, hardship, distress; informal hassle.
▷ANTONYMS comfort, luxury.
3 *Ruth flushed and Thomas noticed her discomfort*: **embarrassment**, discomfiture, unease, uneasiness, abashment, awkwardness, discomposure, confusion, agitation, nervousness, flusteredness, perturbation, distress, anxiety; chagrin, mortification, shame, humiliation; rare disconcertment, disconcertion.
▸ verb *his purpose was to discomfort the Prime Minister*: **discomfit**, make uneasy, make uncomfortable, embarrass, abash, disconcert, nonplus, discompose, take aback, unsettle, unnerve, put someone off their stroke, upset, ruffle, fluster, perturb, disturb; chagrin, mortify; informal rattle, discombobulate, faze, set someone back on their heels.
▷ANTONYMS reassure.

discomposure noun *she laughed to cover her discomposure*: **agitation**, discomfiture, discomfort, uneasiness, unease, confusion, disorientation, perturbation, distress, nervousness, flusteredness; anxiety, worry, consternation, disquiet, disquietude; embarrassment, abashment, chagrin, loss of face; informal discombobulation; rare disconcertment, disconcertion, inquietude.
▷ANTONYMS composure.

disconcert verb *the abrupt change of subject disconcerted her*: **unsettle**, nonplus, discomfit, throw/catch off balance, take aback, unnerve, disorient, perturb, disturb, perplex, confuse, bewilder, baffle, fluster, ruffle, shake, upset, agitate, worry, dismay, put out of countenance, discountenance, discompose; surprise, take by surprise, startle, stop someone in their tracks, put someone off (their stroke/stride), distract; embarrass, abash; informal throw, faze, make someone scratch their head, discombobulate, rattle, set someone back on their heels, psych out; archaic cause to be at a stand, gravel.
▷ANTONYMS reassure.

disconcerting adjective *it was disconcerting to be subjected to such intense scrutiny*: **unsettling**, unnerving, discomfiting, disturbing, perturbing, troubling, upsetting, worrying, alarming, embarrassing, awkward, bothersome, distracting; confusing, bewildering, perplexing; informal off-putting, anxious-making.
▷ANTONYMS reassuring.

disconnect verb **1** *the trucks will be disconnected from the train at various stopping places*: **detach**, disengage, uncouple, decouple, unhook, unhitch, unlink, undo, unfasten, unyoke, disarticulate; rare disjoin, disunite.
▷ANTONYMS attach, connect.
2 *take all the violence out of television drama and you disconnect it from reality*: **separate**, cut off, divorce, sever, isolate, divide, part, disengage, delink, dissociate, remove; rare dissever.
3 *by law, if your appliance is dangerous, the engineer has to disconnect it*: **deactivate**, shut off, turn off, switch off, unplug, de-energize, detach from a power supply.
▷ANTONYMS connect.
4 *the electricity board had disconnected the power supply*: **cut off**, stop.
▷ANTONYMS restore.
5 *her call was disconnected*: **terminate**, stop, discontinue, break off; **interrupt**, suspend.
▷ANTONYMS put through.

disconnected adjective **1** *I drove away feeling disconnected from the real world*: **detached**, separate, separated, divorced, cut off, isolated, dissociated, disengaged, removed, unconnected, unattached; apart.
2 *a disconnected narrative*: **disjointed**, **incoherent**, garbled, confused, jumbled, mixed up, unintelligible, rambling, wandering, disorganized, uncoordinated, ill-thought-out, illogical, irrational; haphazard, random.
▷ANTONYMS coherent.

disconsolate adjective *Giles was looking increasingly disconsolate*: **sad**, unhappy, doleful, woebegone, dejected, downcast, downhearted, despondent, dispirited, crestfallen, cast down, depressed, fed up, disappointed, disheartened, discouraged, demoralized, crushed, desolate, heartbroken, broken-hearted, inconsolable, heavy-hearted, low-spirited, forlorn, in the doldrums, melancholy, miserable, long-faced, wretched, glum, gloomy, dismal; informal blue, choked, down, down in the mouth, down in the dumps; Brit. informal brassed off, cheesed off, as sick as a parrot, looking as if one had lost a pound and found a penny; literary dolorous; archaic chap-fallen, heartsick, heartsore.
▷ANTONYMS cheerful, happy.

discontent noun *there were reports of growing discontent among the military*: **dissatisfaction**, disaffection, discontentment, discontentedness, disgruntlement, grievances, unhappiness, displeasure, bad feelings, resentment, envy; restlessness, unrest, uneasiness, unease, disquiet, fretfulness, frustration, impatience, irritation, chagrin, annoyance, pique; informal a chip on one's shoulder.
▷ANTONYMS contentment, satisfaction.

discontented adjective *his education only made him discontented with his lot in life*: **dissatisfied**, disgruntled, fed up, disaffected, discontent, malcontent, unhappy, aggrieved, displeased, resentful, envious; restless, impatient, querulous, fretful, complaining, frustrated, irritated, chagrined, annoyed, peeved, piqued; informal fed up to the (back) teeth, with a chip on one's shoulder, sick to death, sick and tired; Brit. informal browned off, cheesed off, brassed off, hacked off; N. Amer. informal teed off, ticked off; vulgar slang pissed off, peed off; N. Amer. vulgar slang pissed.
▷ANTONYMS contented, satisfied.

discontinue verb *the ferry service was discontinued | he discontinued his studies*: **stop**, end, terminate, bring to an end, put an end to, put a stop to, wind up, finish, bring to a halt, call a halt to, cancel, drop, dispense with, do away with, get rid of, abolish; suspend, interrupt, break off, phase out, withdraw; abandon, give up, cease, refrain from; informal cut, pull the plug on, axe, scrap, give something the chop, knock something on the head, leave off, pack in; N. Amer. informal quit; rare intermit.
▷ANTONYMS continue.

discontinued adjective *a discontinued product*: **no longer available**, no longer produced, no longer manufactured; obsolete, no longer in existence.
▷ANTONYMS new.

discontinuity noun *the discontinuity of policy frustrated industrialists and investors*: **disconnectedness**, disconnection, break, lack of unity, disruption, interruption, lack of coherence, disjointedness.
▷ANTONYMS continuity.

discontinuous adjective *a person with a discontinuous employment record*: **intermittent**, sporadic, broken, fitful, interrupted, on and off, disrupted, erratic, disconnected.
▷ANTONYMS continuous.

discord noun **1** *stress resulting from financial difficulties or family discord*: **strife**, conflict, friction, hostility; **disagreement**, lack of agreement, dissension, dispute, difference of opinion, discordance, disunity, division, incompatibility, variance; antagonism, antipathy, enmity, opposition, bad feeling, ill feeling, bad blood, argument, quarrelling, squabbling, bickering, wrangling, feuding, contention, clashing, falling-out, war, vendetta; archaic jar; rare disaccord.
▷ANTONYMS agreement, accord, harmony.
2 *the music faded in discord*: **dissonance**, discordance, lack of harmony, disharmony, cacophony, jarring, jangling.
▷ANTONYMS harmony.

discordant adjective **1** *the messages from Washington and London were discordant*: **in disagreement**, at variance, at odds, disagreeing, differing, divergent, discrepant, contradictory, contrary, in conflict, conflicting, opposite, opposed, opposing, clashing; incompatible, inconsistent, irreconcilable, inconsonant, incongruous; rare oppugnant.
▷ANTONYMS in agreement, harmonious, compatible.
2 *discordant sounds*: **inharmonious**, unharmonious, unmelodic, unmusical, tuneless, off-key, dissonant, harsh, jarring, grating, jangling, jangly, strident, shrill, screeching, screechy, cacophonous; sharp, flat; rare absonant, horrisonant.
▷ANTONYMS harmonious, dulcet.

discount noun (stress on the first syllable) *many rail commuters will get a discount on next year's season tickets*: **reduction**, deduction, markdown, price cut, cut, lower price, cut price, concession, concessionary price; rebate.
▸ verb (stress on the second syllable) **1** *I'd heard rumours, but discounted them*: **disregard**, pay no attention to, take no notice of, take no account of, pass over, overlook, dismiss, ignore, brush off, gloss over; disbelieve, give no credence to, reject, pooh-pooh; informal take with a pinch of salt.
▷ANTONYMS believe.
2 *top Paris hotels discounted 20 per cent off published room rates*: **deduct**, take off, rebate; informal knock off, slash.
▷ANTONYMS add.
3 *a recommended retail price of £82.95, but you'll find it discounted in many stores*: **reduce**, mark down, cut, lower, lessen; informal knock down.
▷ANTONYMS put up, increase.
4 *many titles are discounted by up to 40 per cent on the publishers' price*: **mark down**, reduce, put on sale.
▷ANTONYMS mark up.

discountenance verb **1** *Amanda was not discountenanced by the accusation*: **disconcert**, discomfit, unsettle, nonplus, throw/catch off balance, take aback, unnerve, disorient, perturb, disturb, perplex, confuse, bewilder, baffle, fluster, ruffle, shake, upset, agitate, worry, dismay, put out of countenance, discompose; put someone off their stroke/stride, distract; embarrass, abash; informal throw, faze, make someone scratch their head, discombobulate, rattle, set someone back on their heels, psych out; archaic cause to be at a stand, gravel.
2 *in some parts of the Puritan country, kissing was discountenanced at weddings*: **disapprove of**, frown on, take a dim view of, be against, not believe in, object to, find unacceptable, think wrong.

discourage verb **1** *we want to discourage children **from** smoking*: **deter**, dissuade, disincline, turn aside; put off, talk out of, scare off, warn off, advise against, urge against; rare dehort.
▷ANTONYMS encourage, persuade.
2 *Nicky was discouraged by his hostile tone*: **dishearten**, dispirit, demoralize, make despondent, make downhearted, cast down, depress, disappoint, dampen someone's hopes, dash someone's hopes, cause to lose heart; put off, unnerve, daunt, intimidate, cow, unman, crush; archaic deject.
▷ANTONYMS encourage, hearten.
3 *he looked the other way to discourage further conversation*: **prevent**, stop, put a stop to, avert, fend off, stave off, ward off; **inhibit**, hinder, check, curb, obstruct, suppress, put a damper on, throw cold water on.
▷ANTONYMS encourage.

Choose the right word **discourage, deter, dissuade**

Someone who lacks the authority to order another person not to do something may have to adopt other means of preventing them.

To **discourage** someone from doing something is to make them more reluctant to do or continue with it by undermining their confidence or optimism about their chances of success or about the desirability of what they are aiming to achieve (*her father discouraged her from going into the legal profession*). Circumstances, as well as a person, may have this effect (*their work experience has discouraged them from a career in engineering*), and the object of the verb can be an action rather than a person (*inflation discourages investment*). *Discourage* can also be used to express official disapproval that stops short of an actual order (*the Hospital discourages smoking*).

To **deter** someone from doing something involves creating, constituting, or pointing out a serious obstacle that will confront them if they go ahead with their plans (*high fees deter some patients from visiting a consultant*). The object of *deter* can also be an action (*the main aim of cruise missiles is to deter an attack*). The word is often associated with preventing crime and military aggression (*even an unwired alarm box is often sufficient to deter a burglar*), and this sense is continued in the noun *deterrent* (*NATO's nuclear deterrent*).

To **dissuade** someone is to use rational arguments that make them see the difficulty or undesirable nature of their proposed course of action (*we tried to dissuade Steven from marrying*). The object of *dissuade* is always a person (or body of people), not an action or event.

discouraged adjective *Doug must be feeling pretty discouraged*: **disheartened**, dispirited, demoralized, deflated, disappointed, let down, disconsolate, despondent, fed up, dejected, cast down, downcast, depressed, crestfallen, dismayed, low-spirited, gloomy, glum, pessimistic, unenthusiastic, having lost heart, lacking in enthusiasm, lacking in confidence, unconfident; put off, daunted, intimidated, cowed, crushed; informal down in the mouth, down in the dumps, unenthused, with cold feet; literary heartsick, heartsore; archaic chap-fallen.
▷ANTONYMS encouraged, optimistic.

discouragement noun **1** *his discouragement was partly caused by the failure to raise sufficient funds*: **dispiritedness**, downheartedness, dejection, depression, demoralization, disappointment, despondency, hopelessness, lack of enthusiasm, lack of confidence, pessimism, despair, gloom, gloominess, low spirits; informal cold feet.
▷ANTONYMS optimism.
2 *a discouragement to crime*: **deterrent**, disincentive; hindrance, obstacle, impediment, barrier, curb, check, damper, restraint, constraint, restriction; dissuasion; informal put-down; archaic damp.
▷ANTONYMS incentive, stimulus.

discouraging adjective *most news reports from the area are discouraging*: **depressing**, demoralizing, disheartening, dispiriting, disappointing, gloomy, off-putting; unfavourable, unpromising, not hopeful, not encouraging, unpropitious, inauspicious; archaic dejecting.
▷ANTONYMS encouraging, promising.

discourse noun (stress on the first syllable) **1** *a small group of women had chosen to prolong their discourse outside the door*: **discussion**, conversation, talk, dialogue, communication, conference, debate, consultation, verbal exchange; parley, powwow, chat; Indian adda; NZ korero; informal confab, chit-chat; formal confabulation; rare palaver, colloquy, converse, interlocution.
2 *a discourse on critical theory*: **essay**, treatise, dissertation, paper, study, critique, monograph, disquisition, tract; **lecture**, address, speech, oration, peroration; sermon, homily.
▸ verb (stress on the second syllable) **1** *she could discourse at great length on the history of Europe*: **hold forth**, expatiate, pontificate; talk, give a talk, give an address, give a speech, lecture, sermonize, preach, orate; write learnedly, write at length; informal spout, spiel, speechify, preachify, sound off; archaic perorate, lucubrate; rare dissertate.
2 *he spent an hour discoursing with his supporters*: **converse**, talk, speak, have a discussion, discuss matters, debate, confer, consult, parley, chat; informal have a confab, chew the fat, rap; formal confabulate.

discourteous adjective *it would be discourteous to ignore her*: **rude**, impolite, ill-mannered, bad-mannered, disrespectful, uncivil, unmannerly, unchivalrous, ungallant, ungentlemanly, unladylike, ill-bred, churlish, boorish, crass, ungracious, graceless, uncouth; insolent, impudent, cheeky, audacious, presumptuous; curt, brusque, blunt, offhand, unceremonious, short, sharp, uncomplimentary, offensive, insulting, derogatory, disparaging; informal ignorant; archaic malapert, contumelious; rare underbred, mannerless.
▷ANTONYMS polite, courteous.

discourtesy noun **rudeness**, impoliteness, ill manners, lack of manners, bad manners, ill-manneredness, lack of civility, incivility, disrespect, disrespectfulness, unmannerliness, ungentlemanly behaviour, ungraciousness, churlishness, boorishness, ill breeding, uncouthness, crassness; insolence, impudence, impertinence; curtness, brusqueness, abruptness.
▷ANTONYMS politeness, courtesy.

discover verb **1** *two guards discovered her hiding in the back of the minivan*: **find**, locate, come across, come upon, stumble on, chance on, light on, bring to light, uncover, unearth, turn up, track down; run down, run to earth, run to ground, smoke out.
▷ANTONYMS hide.
2 *I discovered that she had been lying | he was anxious to discover the truth*: **find out**, come to know, learn, realize, recognize, see, ascertain, work out, fathom out, detect, determine, spot, notice, perceive; dig up/out, ferret out, root out, nose out, dredge up; reveal, disclose; informal get wise to the fact, get wind of the fact, figure out, sniff out, rumble, tumble to; Brit. informal twig, suss out; N. Amer. informal dope out.
▷ANTONYMS conceal, hide.
3 *scientists have discovered a new way of dating fossil crustaceans*: **hit on**, come up with, invent, originate, devise, design, contrive, conceive of; pioneer, develop.

d

discoverer noun **1** *the annals of the famous European discoverers*: **explorer**, pioneer.
2 *the Bach flower remedies are named after their discoverer, Dr Edward Bach*: **originator**, inventor, creator, deviser, designer; pioneer, introducer.

discovery noun **1** *the discovery of the body*: **finding**, locating, location, uncovering, unearthing.
▷**ANTONYMS** concealment.
2 *the discovery that she was pregnant*: **finding out**, learning, realization, recognition, detection, determination; revelation, disclosure.
3 *the discovery of new drugs*: **invention**, origination, devising; pioneering, introduction.
4 *he failed to take out a patent on his discoveries*: **find**, finding; invention, breakthrough, innovation, advance, lucky strike.
5 *a voyage of discovery*: **exploration**, pioneering, research.

discredit verb **1** *I've been offered a lot of money for information which might discredit him*: **disgrace**, dishonour, bring into disrepute, damage someone's reputation, blacken someone's name, destroy someone's credibility, drag through the mud/mire, put/show in a bad light, reflect badly on, compromise, give someone a bad name, bring into disfavour; stigmatize, detract from, disparage, denigrate, devalue, diminish, demean, belittle; defame, slander, cast aspersions on, malign, vilify, calumniate, smear, tarnish, besmirch, soil; N. Amer. slur; informal do a hatchet job on; literary smirch, besmear.
▷**ANTONYMS** do credit to.
2 *that theory has since been discredited*: **disprove**, prove false, prove wrong, invalidate, explode, drive a coach and horses through, give the lie to, refute, reject, deny; challenge, dispute, raise doubts about, shake one's faith in; informal debunk, shoot full of holes, shoot down (in flames), blow sky-high, blow out of the water; rare controvert, confute, negative.
▷**ANTONYMS** prove, confirm.
▶ noun **1** *they committed crimes which brought discredit on the administration*: **dishonour**, disrepute, ill repute, loss of reputation, loss of respect, disgrace, shame, humiliation, ignominy, infamy, notoriety; censure, blame, reproach, odium, opprobrium; stigma, harm, damage, scandal; rare disesteem.
▷**ANTONYMS** honour, glory.
2 *the ships were a* ***discredit to*** *the country*: **disgrace**, source of disgrace, source of shame, reproach; bad reflection on, blot on the escutcheon of.
▷**ANTONYMS** credit.

discreditable adjective *his discreditable conduct*: **dishonourable**, **reprehensible**, shameful, deplorable, disgraceful, disreputable, blameworthy, culpable, wrong, bad, ignoble, shabby, objectionable, regrettable, unfortunate, indefensible, unjustifiable, unacceptable, unworthy, remiss; rare exceptionable.
▷**ANTONYMS** creditable, praiseworthy, good.

discreet adjective **1** *I'll make some discreet inquiries | we can rely on him to be discreet*: **careful**, circumspect, cautious, wary, chary, guarded, close-lipped, close-mouthed; **tactful**, diplomatic, considerate, politic, prudent, judicious, strategic, wise, sensible; delicate, kid-glove; informal softly-softly.
▷**ANTONYMS** indiscreet, rash.
2 *the discreet lighting*: **unobtrusive**, inconspicuous; **subtle**, low-key, understated, subdued, muted, soft, restrained, unostentatious, downbeat, low-profile.
▷**ANTONYMS** obtrusive.

Easily confused words **discreet or discrete?**

The words **discreet** and **discrete** sound the same, and both derive from Latin *discretus* 'separate'; but in English they have quite different meanings. *Discreet* means 'careful to avoid being noticed or giving offence' (*we made discreet inquiries*). *Discrete*, on the other hand, means 'separate, distinct' (*research tends to focus on discrete areas*).

discrepancy noun *the discrepancy between the two sets of figures*: **inconsistency**, **difference**, disparity, variance, variation, deviation, divergence, disagreement, dissimilarity, dissimilitude, mismatch, lack of similarity, contrariety, contradictoriness, disaccord, discordance, incongruity, lack of congruence, incompatibility, irreconcilability, conflict, opposition.
▷**ANTONYMS** similarity, correspondence.

discrete adjective *speech sounds are produced as a continuous signal rather than discrete units*: **separate**, distinct, individual, detached, unattached, disconnected, discontinuous, disjunct, disjoined.
▷**ANTONYMS** connected.

Easily confused words **discrete or discreet?**

See **discreet**.

discretion noun **1** *the negotiations have been carried out with the utmost discretion*: **circumspection**, care, carefulness, caution, wariness, chariness, guardedness; **tact**, tactfulness, diplomacy, delicacy, sensitivity, subtlety, consideration, prudence, judiciousness, judgement, discrimination, sense, good sense, common sense; kid gloves.
▷**ANTONYMS** indiscretion, rashness.
2 *honorary fellowships may be awarded at the discretion of the council*: **choice**, option, judgement, preference, disposition, volition; pleasure, liking, wish, will, inclination, desire.

discretionary adjective *a 12.5 per cent discretionary service charge*: **optional**, non-compulsory, voluntary, at one's discretion, up to the individual, non-mandatory, elective, open to choice; open, unrestricted; Law permissive; rare discretional.
▷**ANTONYMS** compulsory, obligatory.

discriminate verb **1** *at birth, a baby cannot* ***discriminate between*** *foreground and background in its visual field*: **differentiate**, distinguish, draw/recognize a distinction, tell the difference, discern a difference; separate, tell apart; separate the sheep from the goats, separate the wheat from the chaff.
2 *existing employment policies* ***discriminate against*** *women*: **be biased**, show prejudice, be prejudiced; treat differently, treat as inferior, treat unfairly, put at a disadvantage, disfavour, be intolerant towards; victimize.

discriminating adjective *a discriminating collector and patron of the arts*: **discerning**, perceptive, astute, shrewd, judicious, perspicacious, insightful; **selective**, with good taste, particular, fastidious, critical, keen, tasteful, refined, sensitive, cultivated, cultured, artistic, aesthetic; archaic nice; rare discriminative.
▷**ANTONYMS** indiscriminate.

discrimination noun **1** *victims of racial discrimination*: **prejudice**, bias, bigotry, intolerance, narrow-mindedness, unfairness, inequity, favouritism, one-sidedness, partisanship; sexism, chauvinism, racism, racialism, anti-Semitism, heterosexism, ageism, classism; positive discrimination, reverse discrimination, ableism; in S. Africa, historical apartheid.
▷**ANTONYMS** impartiality.
2 *the discrimination between right and wrong*: **differentiation**, distinction, telling the difference.
3 *those who could afford to buy showed little taste or discrimination*: **discernment**, judgement, perception, perceptiveness, perspicacity, acumen, astuteness, shrewdness, judiciousness, insight, subtlety; **selectivity**, (good) taste, fastidiousness, refinement, sensitivity, cultivation, culture, culturedness, connoisseurship, aestheticism.

discriminatory adjective *discriminatory employment practices*: **prejudicial**, biased, prejudiced, preferential, unfair, unjust, invidious, inequitable, weighted, one-sided, partisan; sexist, chauvinistic, chauvinist, racist, racialist, anti-Semitic, ageist, disablist, classist.
▷**ANTONYMS** impartial, fair.

discursive adjective **1** *dull, discursive prose*: **rambling**, digressive, meandering, wandering, maundering, diffuse, long, lengthy; circuitous, roundabout, circumlocutory, periphrastic; verbose, long-winded, prolix; informal wordy; Brit. informal waffly; rare pleonastic, logorrhoeic, ambagious.
▷**ANTONYMS** concise.
2 *an elegant piece of work combining sound judgement with an excellent discursive style*: **fluent**, flowing, fluid, eloquent, articulate, elegant, expansive.
▷**ANTONYMS** terse.

discuss verb **1** *I discussed the matter with my wife*: **talk over**, talk about, talk through, converse about, debate, confer about, put your heads together about, deliberate about, chew over, consider, exchange views on/about, weigh up, consider the pros and cons of, thrash out, argue, dispute; moot, air, ventilate; Brit. canvass; informal kick around/about, bat around/about.
2 *chapter three discusses this topic in more detail*: **examine**, explore, study, analyse, go into, scrutinize, review; **deal with**, treat, consider, concern itself with, write about, tackle.

discussion noun **1** *after a long discussion with her husband, she came to a decision*: **conversation**, talk, dialogue, discourse, conference, debate, exchange of views, consultation, deliberation; powwow, chat, tête-à-tête, heart-to-heart; seminar, symposium; talks, negotiations, parley; argument, dispute; Indian adda; NZ korero; informal confab, chit-chat, rap; N. Amer. informal skull session, bull session; formal confabulation; rare palaver, colloquy, converse, interlocution.
2 *the book's candid discussion of sexual matters*: **examination**, exploration, analysis, study, review, scrutiny; **treatment**, consideration.

disdain noun *she looked at him with open disdain*: **contempt**, scorn, scornfulness, contemptuousness, derision, disrespect; disparagement, condescension, superciliousness, hauteur, haughtiness, arrogance, lordliness, snobbishness, aloofness, indifference, dismissiveness; distaste, dislike, disgust; archaic despite, contumely.
▷**ANTONYMS** admiration, respect.
▶ verb **1** *she disdained such vulgar exhibitionism*: **scorn**, deride, pour scorn on, regard with contempt, show contempt for, be contemptuous about, sneer at, sniff at, curl one's lip at, pooh-pooh, look down on, belittle, undervalue, slight; despise; informal look down one's nose at, turn up one's nose at, thumb one's nose at; archaic contemn; rare misprize.

▷ANTONYMS respect, value.
2 *she pointedly disdained his invitation to sit down*: **spurn**, reject, refuse, rebuff, disregard, ignore, snub; decline, turn down, brush aside.
▷ANTONYMS accept.

disdainful adjective *she gave him a disdainful look*: **contemptuous**, scornful, full of contempt, derisive, sneering, withering, slighting, disparaging, disrespectful, condescending, patronizing, supercilious, haughty, superior, arrogant, proud, snobbish, lordly, aloof, indifferent, dismissive; mocking, jeering, insolent, insulting; informal high and mighty, hoity-toity, sniffy, snotty, on one's high horse, uppish; archaic contumelious.
▷ANTONYMS admiring, respectful.

disease noun **illness**, sickness, ill health; infection, ailment, malady, disorder, complaint, affliction, condition, indisposition, upset, problem, trouble, infirmity, disability, defect, abnormality; pestilence, plague, cancer, canker, blight; informal bug, virus; Brit. informal lurgy; Austral. informal wog; dated contagion.
▷ANTONYMS health.

Word links **disease**

patho- related prefix, as in *pathogenic*
noso- related prefix, as in *nosography*
-pathy related suffix, as in *neuropathy*
pathological relating to disease
epidemiology, **pathology**, **therapeutics** branches of medicine to do with diseases
pathophobia, **nosophobia** fear of disease

diseased adjective *the dogs were painfully thin and many were diseased | diseased organs*: **unhealthy**, **ill**, sick, unwell, ailing, infirm, sickly, unsound, unwholesome, infected, septic, contaminated, blighted, rotten, bad, abnormal; Austral. informal crook; archaic peccant.
▷ANTONYMS healthy, well.

disembark verb *we **disembarked from** the ferry at Dun Laoghaire*: **get off**, step off, leave; go ashore, debark, detrain; land, arrive; Brit. alight from; N. Amer. deplane; informal pile out.
▷ANTONYMS embark.

disembodied adjective *a disembodied spirit*: **bodiless**, incorporeal, spiritual, intangible, insubstantial, impalpable; ghostly, spectral, phantom, wraithlike; rare immaterial, discarnate, disincarnate, unbodied, phantasmal, phantasmic.

disembowel verb **eviscerate**, gut, draw, remove the innards from; rare embowel, disbowel, exenterate, gralloch, paunch.

disenchanted adjective *disenchanted with politics, he retired from the foreign service*: **disillusioned**, disappointed, let down, fed up, dissatisfied, discontented, disabused, undeceived, set straight; cynical, soured, jaundiced, sick, out of love, indifferent.

disenchantment noun **disillusionment**, disappointment, dissatisfaction, discontent, discontentedness, rude awakening; cynicism, disillusion.

disengage verb 1 *I disengaged his hand from mine*: **remove**, detach, disentangle, extricate, separate, release, loosen, loose, disconnect, unfasten, unclasp, uncouple, decouple, undo, unhook, unloose, unhitch, untie, unyoke, disentwine; free, set free, liberate; rare disjoin, disunite, disarticulate.
▷ANTONYMS attach, connect.
2 *his plan to **disengage from** conflict*: **withdraw**, leave, pull out of, move out of, quit, retreat from, retire from, delink from.
▷ANTONYMS enter.

disengagement noun 1 *his disengagement from the provisional government*: **withdrawal**, departure, retirement, retreat.
2 *the mechanism prevents accidental disengagement*: **disconnection**, detachment, separation, unfastening, uncoupling.
▷ANTONYMS attachment, connection.

disentangle verb 1 *Allen was on his knees disentangling a coil of rope*: **untangle**, unravel, remove the knots from, unknot, unsnarl, untwist, unwind, undo, untie, straighten out, smooth out; comb; card.
2 *he disentangled his fingers from her hair*: **extricate**, extract, free, remove, disengage, untwine, disentwine, release, liberate, loosen, unloose, detach, unfasten, unclasp, disconnect.

disfavour noun *the headmaster regarded her with disfavour*: **disapproval**, disapprobation, lack of favour; **dislike**, displeasure, distaste, dissatisfaction, low opinion, low esteem; archaic disesteem, disrelish.
▷ANTONYMS approval.
□ **fall into disfavour** *he fell into disfavour with the king*: **become unpopular**, become disliked, get on the wrong side of someone; informal be/get in someone's bad books, be/get in someone's black books, be in the doghouse; NZ informal be in the dogbox.
▷ANTONYMS be in favour.

disfigure verb *disused quarries remain to disfigure the landscape*: **mar**, spoil, deface, make ugly/unattractive, impair, scar, blemish, flaw; damage, injure, blight, mutilate, deform, maim, ruin; vandalize; rare uglify, disfeature.
▷ANTONYMS beautify, adorn, enhance.

disfigurement noun 1 *the disfigurement of Victorian and Edwardian buildings*: **defacement**, spoiling, scarring, mutilation, damage, damaging, vandalizing, ruin; rare uglification.
▷ANTONYMS beautification.
2 *a permanent facial disfigurement*: **blemish**, flaw, defect, imperfection, discoloration, blotch; scar, pockmark; deformity, malformation, misshapenness, misproportion, irregularity, abnormality, injury, wound; ugliness, unsightliness; technical stigma.

disgorge verb 1 *the combine disgorged a steady stream of grain*: **pour out**, discharge, eject, emit, expel, evacuate, empty, spit out, spew out, belch forth, spout; vomit, regurgitate, throw up; archaic regorge.
2 *any firm that infringes the rules will be required to disgorge its profits*: **surrender**, relinquish, hand over, give up, turn over, yield, cede, part with; renounce, resign, abandon.
▷ANTONYMS retain.

disgrace noun 1 *if he'd married her it would have brought disgrace on the family*: **dishonour**, **shame**, ignominy, discredit, degradation, disrepute, ill-repute, infamy, scandal, stigma, odium, opprobrium, obloquy, condemnation, vilification, contempt, disrespect, disapproval, disfavour, disapprobation; humiliation, embarrassment, loss of face; Austral. strife; rare disesteem, reprobation, derogation.
▷ANTONYMS honour, glory.
2 *the unemployment figures are a disgrace | the system is a **disgrace to** British justice*: **scandal**, outrage, source of shame; **discredit**, reproach, affront, insult; bad reflection on, stain on, blemish on, blot on, blot on the escutcheon of, black mark on; stigma, brand; black sheep; informal crime, sin; literary smirch on.
▷ANTONYMS credit.
□ **in disgrace** **out of favour**, unpopular, in bad odour; informal in someone's bad/black books, in the doghouse; NZ informal in the dogbox.
▷ANTONYMS in favour.
▶ verb 1 *you have disgraced the family name*: **bring shame on**, shame, dishonour, discredit, bring into disrepute, degrade, debase, defame, stigmatize, taint, sully, tarnish, besmirch, stain, blacken, drag through the mud/mire, give a bad name to, put in a bad light, reflect badly on; literary smirch, besmear; archaic spot.
▷ANTONYMS honour, do credit to.
2 *he has been publicly disgraced for offences of which he was not guilty*: **discredit**, dishonour, defame, disparage, stigmatize, reproach, censure, blame; **humiliate**, mortify, embarrass, cause to lose face, chasten, humble, demean, put someone in their place, take down a peg or two, cut down to size, show up; N. Amer. informal make someone eat crow.
▷ANTONYMS honour.

Choose the right word **disgrace, dishonour, shame, ignominy**

A person in **disgrace** has incurred general disapproval as a result of behaviour considered to be unacceptable (*Nixon had resigned in disgrace*). There is a suggestion of outrage and scandal. A person or thing can also be described as *a disgrace*, meaning that they deserve disapproval or condemnation (*you're an absolute disgrace | what went on at Westminster on Wednesday was a disgrace to Parliament*).

Dishonour is a less common word, perhaps because the notion of honour that it involves has itself become unfashionable. Typically it denotes a situation in which someone is considered to have behaved in a cowardly or dishonest way (*feelings which induce a man to prefer death to dishonour*).

Shame is frequently used in the same context as *guilt*, *embarrassment*, and *humiliation*. While a person who is in disgrace is disapproved of, someone who suffers shame feels intense distress as a result of this disapproval and their awareness of having done wrong (*she hung her head in shame*). *Shame* also describes a loss of respect in the eyes of other people (*the incident brought shame on his family*). A state of affairs seen as regrettable or unfortunate can be called *a shame* (*it is just a shame we don't treat our fellow human beings so well | what a shame Ellie won't be here to meet you*).

Ignominy is a literary word deriving from a Latin expression for the loss of one's 'good name'. It denotes great public humiliation (*he was not spared the ignominy of a public trial*).

disgraced adjective *the disgraced city financier*: **discredited**, shamed, humiliated, in disgrace, under a cloud, brought into disrepute.
▷ANTONYMS honoured, respected.

disgraceful adjective *she intended to tell him exactly what she thought of his disgraceful conduct*: **shameful**, shocking, scandalous, deplorable, despicable, contemptible, beyond contempt, beyond the pale, dishonourable, discreditable, reprehensible, objectionable, base, mean, low, blameworthy, unworthy, ignoble, shabby, inglorious, infamous, unprincipled, outrageous, abominable, atrocious, appalling, dreadful,

d

terrible, disgusting, shameless, vile, odious, monstrous, heinous, iniquitous, unspeakable, loathsome, sordid, bad, wicked, immoral, nefarious, indefensible, inexcusable, unforgivable, intolerable; embarrassing, humiliating, degrading; informal low-down, hateful, diabolical, criminal; archaic knavish, dastardly, scurvy; rare egregious, flagitious, exceptionable.
▷**ANTONYMS** admirable, honourable.

disgruntled adjective *he faced tough questioning from disgruntled shareholders*: **dissatisfied**, discontented, aggrieved, resentful, fed up, displeased, unhappy, disappointed, disaffected, malcontent; angry, irate, annoyed, cross, exasperated, indignant, vexed, irritated, piqued, irked, put out, out of temper; sulky, sullen, petulant, peevish, grumpy, churlish, testy; informal peeved, miffed, aggravated, hacked off, riled, peed off, hot under the collar, in a huff; Brit. informal cheesed off, browned off, narked, eggy; N. Amer. informal sore, teed off, ticked off; W. Indian informal vex; vulgar slang pissed off; N. Amer. vulgar slang pissed; archaic snuffy.
▷**ANTONYMS** pleased, contented.

disguise verb *she tried to disguise the bruises with make-up | Stephen's controlled voice disguised his true feelings*: **camouflage**, conceal, hide, cover up, make inconspicuous, mask, screen, shroud, veil, cloak; dissemble, dissimulate, gloss over, varnish over, paper over; put up a smokescreen, misrepresent, falsify, give a false picture of.
▷**ANTONYMS** reveal, expose.
□ **disguise oneself as** *Eleanor disguised herself as a man*: **dress oneself up as**, pass oneself of as, pretend to be, impersonate, pose as; rare personate.
▸ **noun 1** *his bizarre disguise drew stares from fellow shoppers*: **false appearance**, camouflage, concealment; outfit, costume; informal get-up.
2 *a counsellor hopes gradually to strip away the disguises and help partners to understand each other*: **facade**, front, false front, cover-up, masquerade, veneer, mask, veil; smokescreen, dissimulation, pretence, deception.

disguised adjective *a disguised police officer*: **in disguise**, camouflaged, incognito, under cover; unrecognizable; sailing under false colours.

disgust noun **1** *he reached into the bin with a look of disgust on his face*: **revulsion**, repugnance, aversion, distaste, abhorrence, loathing, detestation, odium, execration, horror; nausea; archaic disrelish; rare repellence, repellency.
▷**ANTONYMS** relish.
2 *the bowler hurled his cap to the ground in disgust*: **annoyance**, exasperation, anger, fury, outrage, indignation, contempt, disapproval, disapprobation, displeasure, dissatisfaction, disgruntlement, discontent, discontentment.
▸ **verb 1** *the hospital food disgusted me*: **revolt**, repel, repulse, sicken, nauseate, cause to feel nauseous, make shudder, turn someone's stomach, make someone's gorge rise; be repugnant to, be repulsive to, be distasteful to; informal turn off, make someone want to throw up; N. Amer. informal gross out.
▷**ANTONYMS** attract.
2 *he is disgusted by Clare's easy morals*: **outrage**, shock, horrify, appal, scandalize, offend, affront, dismay, displease, dissatisfy; annoy, anger, nauseate, sicken.
▷**ANTONYMS** please.

disgusting adjective **1** *Kirsty complained that the food was disgusting*: **revolting**, repellent, repulsive, sickening, nauseating, nauseous, stomach-churning, stomach-turning, off-putting, unpalatable, unappetizing, uninviting, unsavoury, distasteful, foul, nasty, obnoxious, odious; N. Amer. vomitous; informal yucky, icky, gross, sick-making, gut-churning; Brit. informal grotty; archaic disgustful.
▷**ANTONYMS** delicious.
2 *I find your racism absolutely disgusting*: **offensive**, **appalling**, outrageous, objectionable, displeasing, shocking, horrifying, scandalous, monstrous, unspeakable, shameless, shameful, vulgar, gross, vile, wicked, odious, heinous, abhorrent, loathsome, obnoxious, detestable, hateful, sickening, contemptible, despicable, deplorable, abominable, execrable; unforgivable, unpardonable, inexcusable, intolerable, insupportable, beyond the pale; informal horrid, ghastly, sick, God-awful; Brit. informal beastly; archaic disgustful, loathly, scurvy; rare egregious, exceptionable.
▷**ANTONYMS** charming; commendable.

dish noun **1** *place the ravioli on a dish and cover with sauce*: **bowl**, **plate**, soup plate, platter, salver; serving dish, oven dish; container, receptacle, vessel, repository; Scottish & N. English ashet; archaic trencher, charger, porringer; rare paten.
2 *she tried a new vegetarian dish*: **recipe**, item of food, course; special, dish of the day; food, fare; French plat du jour.
3 informal *she's quite a dish*: **beauty**, belle, goddess, Venus, siren, dream, vision, picture, sensation, joy to behold; informal stunner, knockout, looker, good-looker, cracker, smasher, peach, honey, lovely, eyeful, eye-catcher, sight for sore eyes.
▸ **verb**
□ **dish something out** *the waitress was dishing out free glasses of wine*: **distribute**, dispense, issue, disburse, hand out, give out, pass out, pass round; deal out, dole out, mete out, share out, allocate, allot, apportion.
▷**ANTONYMS** collect, reserve.
□ **dish something up 1** *Mrs Mackay dished up the porridge*: **serve (up)**, spoon out, ladle out, scoop out. **2** *they dish up remixes of their old hits*: **present**, offer, produce, prepare.

disharmony noun *they hope he will heal the racial disharmony in their city*: **discord**, **friction**, strife, conflict, hostility, acrimony, bad blood, bad feeling, enmity, dissension, disagreement; feuding, quarrelling; disunity, division, divisiveness; informal falling-out; rare disaccord, discordance.
▷**ANTONYMS** harmony.

dishearten verb *I thought the weather would dishearten him, but he kept going*: **discourage**, dispirit, demoralize, depress, dismay, daunt, deter, unman, unnerve, sap, shake, throw, crush, cast down, desolate, make dispirited, make dejected, make crestfallen, make downhearted, disappoint, sadden, weigh down, weigh heavily on, put a damper on, cow, subdue, undermine, enervate, weaken; informal give someone the blues, make someone fed up, knock the stuffing out of, knock for six, knock sideways; archaic deject.
▷**ANTONYMS** hearten, encourage.

disheartened adjective *the weather got worse and he felt cold and disheartened*: **downhearted**, dispirited, low-spirited, demoralized, despondent, depressed, disconsolate, dejected, dismayed, disappointed, daunted, discouraged, deterred, unmanned, unnerved, sapped, shaken, thrown, crushed, cast down, low, down, crestfallen, saddened, weighed down; informal blue, down in the mouth, down in the dumps.
▷**ANTONYMS** heartened.

dishevelled adjective *the young man's hair was long and dishevelled | a dishevelled old woman*: **untidy**, unkempt, scruffy, messy, in a mess, disordered, disarranged, rumpled, bedraggled; uncombed, ungroomed, tousled, tangled, tangly, knotted, knotty, matted, shaggy, straggly, windswept, windblown, wild; slovenly, sluttish, slatternly, blowsy, frowzy; informal ratty; N. Amer. informal mussed (up); archaic draggle-tailed.
▷**ANTONYMS** tidy; neat.

dishonest adjective *he is accused of dishonest business practices | a dishonest account of events*: **fraudulent**, corrupt, swindling, cheating, double-dealing; underhand, crafty, cunning, devious, designing, treacherous, perfidious, unfair, unjust, disreputable, rascally, roguish, dirty, unethical, immoral, dishonourable, unscrupulous, unprincipled, amoral; criminal, illegal, unlawful; **false**, untruthful, deceitful, deceiving, deceptive, lying, mendacious, untrustworthy; informal crooked, shady, tricky, sharp, shifty; Brit. informal bent, dodgy; Austral./NZ informal shonky; S. African informal slim; Law malfeasant; archaic knavish, subtle, hollow-hearted; rare false-hearted, double-faced, truthless.
▷**ANTONYMS** honest.

dishonesty noun *he lost money as a result of his solicitor's dishonesty*: **deceit**, deception, duplicity, lying, falseness, falsity, falsehood, untruthfulness; **fraud**, fraudulence, sharp practice, cheating, chicanery, craft, cunning, trickery, artifice, artfulness, wiliness, guile, double-dealing, underhandedness, subterfuge, skulduggery, treachery, perfidy, unfairness, unjustness, improbity, rascality, untrustworthiness, dishonour, unscrupulousness, corruption, criminality, lawlessness, lawbreaking, misconduct; informal crookedness, shadiness, foxiness, dirty tricks, kidology, shenanigans, monkey business, funny business, hanky-panky; Brit. informal jiggery-pokery; N. Amer. informal monkeyshines; Irish informal codology; Law malfeasance; archaic management, knavery, knavishness.
▷**ANTONYMS** probity.

dishonour noun *the incident brought dishonour upon the police profession*: **disgrace**, shame, discredit, humiliation, degradation, ignominy, scandal, infamy, disrepute, ill repute, loss of face, disfavour, ill favour, unpopularity, ill fame, notoriety, debasement, abasement, odium, opprobrium, obloquy; stigma; rare disesteem, reprobation, vitiation.
▷**ANTONYMS** honour.
▸ **verb** *you have betrayed our master and dishonoured the banner*: **disgrace**, bring dishonour to, bring discredit to, bring shame to, shame, embarrass, humiliate, discredit, degrade, debase, lower, cheapen, drag down, drag through the mud, blacken the name of, give a bad name to, show in a bad light; sully, stain, taint, smear, mar, blot, stigmatize.
▷**ANTONYMS** honour.

Choose the right word **dishonour, disgrace, shame, ignominy**

See **disgrace**.

dishonourable adjective *he is accused of dishonourable conduct*: **disgraceful**, shameful, shameless, shaming, disreputable, discreditable, degrading, debasing, ignominious, ignoble, blameworthy, contemptible, despicable, reprehensible, shabby, shoddy, sordid, sorry, base, low, improper, unseemly, unworthy; unprincipled, unscrupulous, corrupt, untrustworthy, treacherous, perfidious, traitorous, villainous; informal shady, crooked, low-down, dirty, rotten, rascally, scoundrelly; Brit. informal beastly; archaic scurvy, knavish.
▷**ANTONYMS** honourable.

disillusion verb *if they think we have a magic formula, don't disillusion them*: **disabuse**, undeceive, enlighten, set straight, open someone's eyes;

disenchant, shatter someone's illusions, disappoint, make sadder and wiser; informal throw cold water on.
▷ANTONYMS deceive, fool.
▶ noun *the future held almost certain disillusion*: **disenchantment**, disillusionment, disappointment, disaffection, dissatisfaction; a rude awakening.
▷ANTONYMS promise, enchantment.

disillusioned adjective *his experience at the club left him disillusioned*: **disenchanted**, disappointed, let down, cast down, downcast, discouraged; disabused, undeceived; cynical, sour, negative, world-weary.
▷ANTONYMS trusting, enthusiastic.

disincentive noun *high interest rates are a disincentive to investment*: **deterrent**, discouragement, dissuasion, damper, brake, curb, check, restraint, inhibition; obstacle, impediment, hindrance, obstruction, block, barrier.
▷ANTONYMS incentive.

disinclination noun *they show a disinclination to face up to these issues*: **reluctance**, unwillingness, lack of enthusiasm, indisposition, slowness, hesitancy, hesitance, diffidence; loathness, aversion, dislike, distaste; objection, demur, resistance, opposition, recalcitrance; archaic disrelish; rare nolition, sweerness.
▷ANTONYMS inclination, enthusiasm.

disinclined adjective *she was disinclined to abandon the old ways*: **reluctant**, unwilling, unenthusiastic, unprepared, indisposed, ill-disposed, not disposed, not in the mood, slow, hesitant, nervous, afraid; loath, averse, antipathetic, resistant, opposed, recalcitrant.
▷ANTONYMS inclined, willing.

disinfect verb *use bleach to disinfect your kitchen surfaces*: **sterilize**, sanitize, clean, cleanse, purify, decontaminate; fumigate; pasteurize; technical autoclave; rare deterge, depollute, depurate.
▷ANTONYMS infect, contaminate.

disinfectant noun *I swabbed the table with disinfectant*: **bactericide**, germicide, antiseptic, sterilizer, sanitizer, cleaning agent, cleansing agent, cleanser, decontaminant; fumigant.

disingenuous adjective *it would be disingenuous of us to pretend ignorance of our book's impact*: **dishonest**, deceitful, underhand, underhanded, duplicitous, double-dealing, two-faced, dissembling, insincere, false, lying, untruthful, mendacious; not candid, not frank, not entirely truthful; artful, cunning, crafty, wily, sly, sneaky, tricky, scheming, calculating, designing, devious, unscrupulous; informal shifty, foxy; humorous economical with the truth, terminologically inexact; archaic subtle, hollow-hearted; rare false-hearted, double-faced, truthless, unveracious.
▷ANTONYMS ingenuous, frank.

> *Easily confused words* **disingenuous or ingenuous?**
>
> See **ingenuous**.

disinherit verb *the Duke is seeking to disinherit his eldest son*: **cut someone out of one's will**, cut off, dispossess, impoverish; disown, repudiate, renounce, reject, oust, cast off, cast aside, wash one's hands of, have nothing more to do with, turn one's back on; informal cut off without a penny.

disintegrate verb **1** *the plane caught fire and disintegrated in the air | his empire quickly disintegrated*: **break up**, break apart, fall apart, fall to pieces, fall to bits, fragment, fracture, shatter, splinter; rupture, explode, blow up, blow apart, fly apart; crumble, dissolve, collapse, founder, fail, decline, go downhill, go to rack and ruin, degenerate, deteriorate; informal bust, be smashed to smithereens; rare shiver.
2 *some plastics will take over 400 years to disintegrate*: **break down**, decompose, decay, rot, moulder, perish, corrode, deteriorate.

> *Word links* **disintegrate**
>
> **-lysis** related suffix, as in *hydrolysis, autolysis*

disintegrating adjective *a corrupt and disintegrating culture*: **crumbling**, deteriorating, decaying, decomposing, derelict, decrepit.

> *Word toolkit* **disintegrating**
>
> See **derelict**.

disinter verb *his corpse was disinterred and reburied in another grave*: **exhume**, unearth, dig up, bring out of the ground, bring to the surface; rare disentomb, unbury, ungrave.

disinterest noun **1** *I do not pretend any scholarly disinterest with this book*: **impartiality**, neutrality, objectivity, detachment, disinterestedness, lack of bias, lack of prejudice; open-mindedness, fairness, fair-mindedness, equitability, equity, balance, even-handedness, unselfishness, selflessness.
▷ANTONYMS bias.
2 informal *he looked at us with complete disinterest*: **indifference**, lack of interest, lack of curiosity, lack of concern, lack of care, lack of enthusiasm, dispassionateness, dispassion, impassivity; boredom, apathy, nonchalance.
▷ANTONYMS interest.

disinterested adjective **1** *she is offering disinterested advice*: **unbiased**, unprejudiced, impartial, neutral, non-partisan, non-discriminatory, detached, uninvolved, objective, dispassionate, impersonal, clinical; open-minded, fair, just, equitable, balanced, even-handed, unselfish, selfless; free from discrimination, with no axe to grind, without fear or favour.
▷ANTONYMS biased.
2 informal *he looked at her with disinterested eyes*: **uninterested**, indifferent, incurious, unconcerned, unmoved, unresponsive, impassive, passive, detached, unfeeling, uncaring, unenthusiastic, lukewarm, bored, apathetic, blasé, nonchalant; informal couldn't-care-less.
▷ANTONYMS interested.

d

> *Easily confused words* **disinterested or uninterested?**
>
> **Disinterested** is frequently used as a synonym of **uninterested**, meaning 'having or showing no interest in something'. The traditional meaning of *disinterested*, however, is 'not biased; impartial', as in *bankers are under an obligation to give disinterested advice*. *Uninterested* is the preferred word used to mean 'having no interest', as in *he was totally uninterested in politics*.

disjointed adjective **1** *a disjointed series of impressions in her mind*: **unconnected**, disconnected, without unity, disunited, discontinuous, fragmented, fragmentary, disorganized, disordered, muddled, mixed up, jumbled, garbled, incoherent, confused, fitful, erratic, spasmodic, patchy, scrappy, bitty, piecemeal; rambling, wandering, aimless, directionless.
2 *the blast left him a twisted assembly of disjointed limbs*: **dislocated**, displaced, dismembered, disconnected, severed, separated, disarticulated, torn apart.

disk noun See **disc**.

dislike verb *I cannot defend a policy I candidly dislike*: **hate**, detest, loathe, abominate, abhor, despise, scorn, shun, execrate; **be averse to**, have an aversion to, hold in disfavour, have no liking for, disapprove of, object to, oppose, disagree with, take exception to, find distasteful, regard with distaste, regard with disgust, be unable to tolerate, find intolerable, be unable to bear, be unable to stand, be unable to abide, shrink from, shudder at, find repellent; informal be unable to stomach; rare antipathize, disrelish, disfavour.
▷ANTONYMS like.
▶ noun *she viewed the other woman with dislike*: **aversion**, distaste, disfavour, disapproval, disapprobation, disesteem, enmity, animosity, hostility, animus, antipathy, antagonism; hate, hatred, detestation, loathing, disgust, repugnance, revulsion, abhorrence, abomination, odium, disdain, contempt; rare disrelish, repellence, repellency.
▷ANTONYMS liking.

dislocate verb **1** *Georgina dislocated her hip*: **put out of joint**, put out of place, displace, disjoint, disconnect, disengage; informal put out; Medicine luxate, subluxate; dated slip; rare unjoint.
2 *trade was dislocated by a famine*: **disrupt**, disturb, throw into disorder, throw into disarray, throw into confusion, confuse, disorganize, disorder, disarrange, derange, turn upside-down; informal mess up.

dislodge verb *replace any stones you dislodge | economic sanctions failed to dislodge the dictator*: **remove**, move, shift, displace, knock out of place, knock out of position, knock over, upset; force out, drive out, oust, eject, get rid of, evict, unseat, depose, topple, overturn, bring down, bring low, bring about the downfall of; informal drum out, kick out, boot out; Brit. informal turf out.

disloyal adjective *many of her colleagues judged her disloyal*: **unfaithful**, faithless, false, false-hearted, untrue, inconstant, untrustworthy; treacherous, perfidious, traitorous, subversive, seditious, unpatriotic, two-faced, double-dealing, double-crossing, deceitful; dissident, renegade; adulterous; informal back-stabbing, two-timing; archaic recreant; rare hollow-hearted, double-faced, Punic, Janus-faced.
▷ANTONYMS loyal.

> *Word toolkit* **disloyal**
>
> See **unfaithful**.

disloyalty noun *they accused him of disloyalty and a lack of solidarity with other leaders*: **unfaithfulness**, infidelity, inconstancy, faithlessness, fickleness, unreliability, untrustworthiness, breach of trust, breach of faith, betrayal, falseness, false-heartedness, falsity; duplicity, double-dealing, treachery, perfidy, perfidiousness, treason, subversion, sedition, dissidence; adultery; informal back-stabbing, two-timing; rare hollow-heartedness, Punic faith, recreancy.
▷ANTONYMS loyalty.

dismal adjective **1** *he had a dismal look in his eyes*: **gloomy**, glum, mournful, melancholy, morose, doleful, woeful, woebegone, forlorn, abject, dejected, depressed, dispirited, downcast, crestfallen, despondent, disconsolate,

miserable, sad, unhappy, sorrowful, sorrowing, desolate, wretched, lugubrious; informal blue, fed up, down in the dumps, down in the mouth, as sick as a parrot; literary dolorous; archaic chap-fallen.
▷ANTONYMS cheerful.
2 *she led them into a dismal cavernous hall*: **dingy**, dim, dark, gloomy, sombre, dreary, drab, dull, desolate, bleak, cheerless, comfortless, depressing, grim, funereal, inhospitable, uninviting, unwelcoming.
▷ANTONYMS bright, cheerful.
3 informal *the team have produced a string of dismal performances*: **bad**, poor, dreadful, awful, terrible, pitiful, disgraceful, lamentable, deplorable; inferior, mediocre, unsatisfactory, inadequate, second-rate, third-rate, shoddy, inept, bungling; informal crummy, dire, diabolical, bum, rotten, pathetic, lousy, poxy; Brit. informal duff, rubbish, ropy, chronic, pants, a load of pants; vulgar slang crap, crappy, shitty; N. Amer. vulgar slang chickenshit; archaic direful; rare egregious.
▷ANTONYMS excellent.

Word toolkit

dismal	**dreary**	**bleak**
performance	existence	outlook
record	landscape	future
failure	weather	picture
year	lives	prospect
rating	months	period

dismantle verb *he began to dismantle the revolver | the old opera house was dismantled*: **take apart**, take to pieces, take to bits, pull apart, pull to pieces, deconstruct, disassemble, break up, strip (down); knock down, pull down, tear down, demolish, fell, destroy, flatten, level, raze (to the ground), bulldoze; rare unbuild.
▷ANTONYMS assemble, build.

dismay verb *he was dismayed by the change in his old friend*: **appal**, horrify, shock, shake, shake up; **disconcert**, take aback, confound, surprise, startle, alarm, frighten, scare, daunt, discomfit, unnerve, unman, unsettle, throw off balance, discompose, discountenance; **trouble**, bother, concern, perturb, disturb, upset, distress, sadden, dishearten, dispirit; informal rattle, spook, faze, psych, knock sideways, knock for six; archaic pother.
▷ANTONYMS encourage, please.
▶ noun *they greeted his decision with great dismay*: **alarm**, shock, surprise, consternation, concern, perturbation, disquiet, disquietude, discomposure, distress, upset, anxiety, trepidation, fear.
▷ANTONYMS pleasure, relief.

Choose the right word **dismay, appal, horrify**

These words all describe someone's reaction to bad news or adverse circumstances.

Something that **dismays** someone causes them concern and distress, ranging from the fairly mild (*Mark stopped, dismayed at finding himself breaking into rhyme*) to the intense (*she was dismayed to see that the damage was greater than she had expected*).

Appal suggests a response of extreme horror at something almost unbelievable (*we have waited 22 months for justice to be done and are appalled at the verdict*). In its adjectival form, *appalling*, it has a wide range of meaning (*guilty of appalling crimes against humanity | the appalling pile of rubbish strewn around the University campus*).

To **horrify** someone is to shock them deeply (*the surgeon was horrified by her injuries*) or cause them intense fear (*as Bernice watched, horrified, Bishop produced a large handgun*).

dismember verb *a stag carcass was in the process of being dismembered*: **disjoint**, joint, cut off the limbs of; pull apart, cut up, chop up, break up, dissect, divide, segment; mutilate, hack up, butcher, tear limb from limb; rare limb.

dismiss verb **1** *the president dismissed five of his ministers*: **give someone their notice**, throw out, get rid of, discharge; lay off, make redundant; oust, expel; informal **sack**, give someone the sack, fire, send packing, kick out, boot out, give someone the boot, give someone the elbow, give someone the (old) heave-ho, give someone their marching orders, give someone the push, give someone the bullet, show someone the door; Brit. informal give someone their cards, turf out; Military cashier.
▷ANTONYMS engage.
2 *the guards reported to HQ and were dismissed*: **send away**, let go, release, free; **disband**, disperse, dissolve, discharge, demobilize.
▷ANTONYMS form, assemble.
3 *he dismissed all morbid thoughts | they dismissed any suggestion of a rift*: **banish**, put away, set aside, lay aside, abandon, have done with, drop, disregard, brush off, shrug off, forget, think no more of, pay no heed to, put out of one's mind; **reject**, deny, repudiate, spurn, scoff at, sneer at; informal pooh-pooh.
▷ANTONYMS entertain.

dismissal noun **1** *the firm ultimately sanctions poor performance with dismissal*: **one's notice**, discharge; redundancy; expulsion, ousting; informal **the sack**, sacking, firing, laying off, the push, the boot, the axe, the elbow, the (old) heave-ho, one's marching orders; Brit. informal turfing out, one's cards, the chop; Military cashiering.
▷ANTONYMS recruitment.
2 *a condescending dismissal of ancient systems of thought*: **rejection**, repudiation, refusal, repulse, non-acceptance; snub, slight; informal pooh-poohing, brush-off, knock-back.
▷ANTONYMS acceptance.

dismissive adjective *she often talked of him in dismissive terms*: **contemptuous**, disdainful, scornful, sneering, snide, scathing, disparaging, negative, unenthusiastic, offhand, perfunctory; informal sniffy, snotty; rare dismissory.
▷ANTONYMS admiring; interested.

Word toolkit

dismissive	**contemptuous**	**snide**
attitude	look	remark
gesture	sneer	commentary
tone	disregard	innuendo
manner	smirk	sarcasm
shrug	glare	joke

dismount verb **1** *the postman slowed his bicycle and dismounted*: **alight**, get off, get down.
▷ANTONYMS mount.
2 *the horse had dismounted the trooper*: **unseat**, dislodge, throw, spill, upset, unhorse.

disobedience noun *he was scolded for his disobedience*: **insubordination**, unruliness, waywardness, indiscipline, bad behaviour, misbehaviour, misconduct, delinquency, disruptiveness, troublemaking, rebellion, defiance, mutiny, revolt, recalcitrance, lack of cooperation, non-compliance, wilfulness, intractability, awkwardness, perversity, perverseness, contrariness; naughtiness, mischievousness, mischief, roguery, impishness; informal carryings-on, acting-up; archaic or Law contumacy, infraction.
▷ANTONYMS obedience.

disobedient adjective *the slave masters punished anyone who became disobedient*: **insubordinate**, unruly, wayward, errant, badly behaved, disorderly, delinquent, disruptive, troublesome, rebellious, defiant, mutinous, recalcitrant, refractory, uncooperative, non-compliant, wilful, unbiddable, intractable, obstreperous, awkward, difficult, perverse, contrary; naughty, mischievous, impish, roguish, rascally; Brit. informal bolshie; archaic or Law contumacious.
▷ANTONYMS obedient.

disobey verb *the king severely chastised those who disobeyed his orders*: **defy**, go against, flout, contravene, infringe, overstep, transgress, violate, fail to comply with, resist, oppose, rebel against, fly in the face of; disregard, ignore, pay no heed to, fail to observe; informal cock a snook at; Law infract; archaic set at naught.
▷ANTONYMS obey.

disobliging adjective *we have such disobliging neighbours | a disobliging remark*: **unhelpful**, uncooperative, unaccommodating, unamenable, unyielding, inflexible, uncompromising, unreasonable, awkward, difficult, obstructive, contrary, perverse; discourteous, uncivil, unfriendly, unsympathetic.
▷ANTONYMS helpful; civil.

disorder noun **1** *he hates disorder in his house*: **untidiness**, disorderliness, mess, disarray, disorganization, chaos, confusion; clutter, jumble; a muddle, a mess, a shambles, a mare's nest; Brit. informal a dog's dinner, a dog's breakfast.
▷ANTONYMS order.
2 *4,000 people were arrested in incidents of public disorder*: **unrest**, disturbance, disruption, upheaval, tumult, turmoil, mayhem, pandemonium; violence, fighting; rioting, insurrection, rebellion, mutiny, lawlessness, anarchy; breach of the peace, riot, fracas, rumpus, brouhaha, melee, hubbub, furore, affray; informal hoo-ha, aggro, argy-bargy, snafu; N. Amer. informal wilding.
▷ANTONYMS order, peace.
3 *she nearly died of pneumonia and a blood disorder*: **disease**, infection, complaint, problem, condition, affliction, malady, sickness, illness, ailment, infirmity; defect, irregularity; informal bug, virus; Brit. informal lurgy.

disordered adjective **1** *Dorothy looked tired and her grey hair was disordered | a disordered pile of documents*: **untidy**, unkempt, messy, in a mess, disarranged, uncombed, unbrushed, ungroomed, tousled, tangled, tangly, knotted, knotty, matted, shaggy, straggly, windswept, windblown, wild; disorganized, chaotic, confused, jumbled, muddled, unsystematic, out of order, out of place; informal ratty; N. Amer. informal mussed (up), all over the place; Brit. informal shambolic; archaic draggle-tailed.

2 *a disordered digestive system*: **dysfunctional**, disturbed, unsettled, unbalanced, unstable, unsound, upset, poorly, sick, diseased; informal screwed up.

disorderly adjective **1** *a disorderly desk*: **untidy**, disorganized, messy, chaotic, cluttered, littered, jumbled, muddled, confused, unsystematic, irregular; out of order, out of place, in disarray, in a mess, in a jumble, in a muddle, upside-down, at sixes and sevens, haywire, haphazard; informal all over the place, like a bomb's hit it, higgledy-piggledy; Brit. informal shambolic.
▶ANTONYMS tidy.
2 *he was arrested for disorderly behaviour*: **unruly**, boisterous, rough, rowdy, wild, turbulent, tumultuous; disruptive, troublesome, antisocial, disobedient, undisciplined, lawless, unmanageable, uncontrollable, ungovernable, out of hand, out of control; obstreperous, refractory, rebellious, mutinous, insurrectionary, insurgent, seditious, anarchic, riotous, rioting.
▶ANTONYMS peaceful.

Word toolkit **disorderly**

See **messy**.

disorganized adjective **1** *a disorganized tool box*: **disorderly**, disordered, unorganized, mixed up, jumbled, muddled, untidy, messy, cluttered, chaotic, confused, topsy-turvy, haphazard, random; in disorder, in disarray, out of order, in a mess, in a muddle, in a shambles; informal all over the place, like a bomb's hit it, higgledy-piggledy; Brit. informal shambolic, all over the shop; N. Amer. informal all over the map, all over the lot; rare orderless.
▶ANTONYMS orderly.
2 *my boss decided that I was unproductive and disorganized*: **unmethodical**, unsystematic, undisciplined, unorganized, badly organized, unprepared, inefficient, ineffective, ineffectual, incapable; erratic, haphazard, indiscriminate, remiss, careless, slapdash, slipshod, slovenly, lax; informal sloppy, hit-or-miss; Brit. vulgar slang not capable of organizing a piss-up in a brewery.
▶ANTONYMS organized.

disorientated, disoriented adjective *when he emerged into the street he was completely disorientated*: **confused**, bewildered, perplexed, nonplussed, at a loss, (all) at sea, in a state of confusion, in a muddle; **lost**, adrift, astray, off-course, off-track, having lost one's bearings, going round in circles; informal all over the place, not knowing whether one is coming or going; archaic wildered, mazed.

disown verb *he has been disowned by his parents*: **reject**, cast off, cast aside, abandon, repudiate, renounce, deny; turn one's back on, wash one's hands of, have nothing more to do with, end relations with; disinherit, cut off (without a penny); informal ditch, drop, send packing; archaic forsake.
▶ANTONYMS acknowledge.

disparage verb *it has become fashionable to disparage Lawrence and his achievements*: **belittle**, denigrate, deprecate, depreciate, downgrade, play down, deflate, trivialize, minimize, make light of, treat lightly, undervalue, underrate, underestimate; disdain, dismiss, ridicule, deride, mock, scorn, pour scorn on, scoff at, sneer at, laugh at, laugh off; **run down**, defame, decry, discredit, slander, libel, malign, speak ill of, speak badly of, cast aspersions on, impugn, vilify, traduce, revile, criticize, condemn; N. Amer. slur; informal do down, do a hatchet job on, take to pieces, pull apart, pull to pieces, pick holes in, drag through the mud, hit out at, knock, slam, pan, bash, bad-mouth, pooh-pooh, look down one's nose at; Brit. informal rubbish, slate, slag off, have a go at; dated cry down; archaic hold cheap; rare misprize, minify, asperse, derogate, calumniate, vilipend, vituperate.
▶ANTONYMS praise; overrate.

disparaging adjective *people walked past him making disparaging comments*: **derogatory**, deprecating, deprecatory, denigratory, belittling, slighting, insulting, abusive; critical, scathing, negative, unfavourable, uncomplimentary, uncharitable, unsympathetic; contemptuous, scornful, snide, derisive, disdainful, sneering; informal bitchy, catty; archaic contumelious.
▶ANTONYMS complimentary.

disparate adjective *the document is made up from several disparate chunks*: **contrasting**, different, differing, dissimilar, unlike, unalike, poles apart; varying, various, diverse, diversified, heterogeneous, unrelated, unconnected, distinct, separate, divergent; literary divers, myriad; rare contrastive.
▶ANTONYMS homogeneous.

disparity noun *there was a disparity between the two sets of figures*: **discrepancy**, inconsistency, imbalance, inequality, incongruity, unevenness, disproportion; **variance**, variation, divergence, polarity, gap, gulf, breach; difference, dissimilarity, contrast, distinction, differential; rare unlikeness, dissimilitude, contrariety.
▶ANTONYMS parity, similarity.

dispassionate adjective **1** *she dealt with life's disasters in a dispassionate way*: **unemotional**, non-emotional, unsentimental, emotionless, impassive, nonchalant, cool, collected, calm, {cool, calm, and collected}, unruffled, unperturbed, composed, self-possessed, level-headed, self-controlled, temperate, sober, placid, equable, tranquil, serene, unexcitable, unflappable; clinical, cold, indifferent, unmoved, unfeeling, uncaring, unsympathetic; informal laid-back.
▶ANTONYMS emotional.
2 *a dispassionate analysis of the issues*: **objective**, detached, neutral, disinterested, uninvolved, impersonal, impartial, non-partisan, non-discriminatory, unbiased, unprejudiced, open-minded, fair, fair-minded, just, equitable, balanced, even-handed, unselfish; scientific, analytical, rational, logical, businesslike; free from discrimination, without fear or favour.
▶ANTONYMS biased.

dispatch, despatch verb **1** *the press releases have all been dispatched*: **send**, send off, post, mail, ship, freight; forward, transmit, consign, remit, convey.
2 *all serious business was dispatched in the morning*: **deal with**, finish, dispose of, conclude, settle, sort out, discharge, execute, perform; expedite, push through, accelerate, hasten, speed up, hurry on; informal make short work of.
3 *in such films the good guy must always dispatch a host of vicious villains*: **kill**, put to death, do to death, do away with, put an end to, finish off, take the life of, end the life of; slaughter, butcher, massacre, wipe out, mow down, shoot down, cut down, destroy, exterminate, eliminate, eradicate, annihilate; murder, assassinate, execute; informal bump off, knock off, polish off, do in, top, take out, snuff out, erase, croak, stiff, zap, blow away, blow someone's brains out, give someone the works; N. Amer. informal ice, off, rub out, waste, whack, smoke, scrag; N. Amer. euphemistic terminate with extreme prejudice; literary slay.
▶ **noun 1** *we have 125 cases of wine ready for dispatch*: **sending**, posting, mailing, shipping, transmittal, consignment.
2 *he carries out his duties with efficiency and dispatch*: **promptness**, speed, speediness, swiftness, rapidity, quickness, briskness, haste, hastiness, hurriedness, urgency; literary fleetness, celerity; rare expedition, expeditiousness, promptitude.
3 *she read out the latest dispatch from the front*: **communication**, communiqué, bulletin, release, report, account, announcement, statement, missive, letter, epistle, message, instruction; news, intelligence; informal memo, info, low-down, dope; literary tidings.
4 *the hound was used for the capture and dispatch of the wolf*: **killing**, slaughter, massacre, destruction, extermination, elimination, liquidation; murder, assassination, execution; literary slaying.

dispel verb *the sunshine did nothing to dispel her feelings of dejection*: **banish**, eliminate, dismiss, chase away, drive away, drive off, get rid of, dissipate, disperse, scatter, disseminate; relieve, allay, ease, calm, quell, check, put to rest.
▶ANTONYMS engender.

dispensable adjective *he regards all of his lieutenants as highly dispensable*: **expendable**, disposable, replaceable, inessential, unessential, non-essential; unnecessary, unneeded, needless, not required, redundant, superfluous, surplus to requirements, gratuitous, uncalled for.
▶ANTONYMS indispensable.

dispensation noun **1** *regulations control the dispensation of supplies*: **distribution**, provision, providing, supply, supplying, issue, issuing, passing round, passing out, giving out, handing out, dealing out, doling out, sharing out, dividing out, parcelling out; division, allocation, allotment, apportionment, assignment, bestowal, conferment, disbursement; informal dishing out.
2 *the dispensation of justice*: **administration**, administering, delivery, delivering, discharge, bestowal, dealing out, doling out, meting out; carrying out, execution, implementation, application, effectuation, operation, direction; imposition, enforcement.
3 *they were given dispensation from National Insurance contributions*: **exemption**, immunity, exception, exclusion, exoneration, freedom, release, relief, reprieve, remission, relaxation, absolution; impunity; informal a let-off.
4 *minorities have a special voice in the new constitutional dispensation*: **system**, order, scheme, plan, arrangement, organization.

dispense verb **1** *the servants are ready to dispense the drinks*: **distribute**, pass round, pass out, hand out, deal out, dole out, share out, divide out, parcel out, allocate, allot, apportion, assign, bestow, confer, supply, disburse; informal dish out.
▶ANTONYMS collect.
2 *the soldiers dispensed a form of summary justice*: **administer**, deliver, issue, discharge, deal, bestow, dole out, mete out; carry out, execute, implement, apply, operate, direct; inflict, impose, enforce, exact; rare effectuate.
▶ANTONYMS receive.
3 *the pharmacists dispense only licensed medicines*: **prepare**, make up, mix; **supply**, provide, sell.
4 *the pope nominated him as bishop, dispensing him from his impediment*: **exempt**, excuse, except, release, relieve, reprieve, absolve; grant someone a dispensation, grant someone an exemption; informal let off.
□ **dispense with 1** *I think we can dispense with the formalities*: **waive**,

omit, drop, leave out, forgo, give up, relinquish, renounce; ignore, disregard, pass over, brush aside; do away with, put a stop to, put an end to; informal cut out, give something a miss, knock something on the head.
▷ANTONYMS include.
2 *he was able to dispense with his crutches*: **get rid of**, throw away, throw out, cast aside, do away with, dispose of, discard, shed; manage without, do without, cope without; informal ditch, scrap, axe, junk, dump, chuck out, chuck away, get shut of; Brit. informal get shot of; N. Amer. informal trash.
▷ANTONYMS keep.

disperse verb **1** *the crowd began to disperse | police used tear gas to disperse the demonstrators*: **break up**, split up, disband, separate, scatter, leave, go their separate ways, go in different directions; dispel, drive away, drive off, chase away, put to flight, banish, get rid of; rare disunite.
▷ANTONYMS assemble.
2 *the blanket of fog finally dispersed*: **dissipate**, be dispelled, thin out, dissolve, melt away, fade away, vanish, disappear, clear, lift, rise.
3 *some plants rely on birds to disperse their seeds*: **scatter**, disseminate, distribute, spread, broadcast, diffuse, strew, sow, sprinkle, pepper; literary bestrew, besprinkle.
▷ANTONYMS gather.

> *Choose the right word* **disperse, dissipate, scatter**
>
> See **scatter**.

dispirit verb *the army was dispirited by the uncomfortable winter conditions*: **dishearten**, discourage, demoralize, cast down, make dejected, make downhearted, depress, dismay, disappoint, daunt, deter, unman, unnerve, crush, sap, shake, throw, cow, subdue, undermine; dampen someone's spirits, bring low; informal knock sideways, knock the stuffing out of, knock for six, give someone the blues; archaic deject.
▷ANTONYMS hearten.

dispirited adjective *she was tired and dispirited after her long journey*: **disheartened**, discouraged, demoralized, cast down, downcast, low, low-spirited, dejected, downhearted, depressed, disconsolate; crushed, shattered, sapped, shaken, thrown, cowed, subdued; informal blue, fed up; Brit. informal brassed off, cheesed off.

dispiriting adjective *the article gives a dispiriting view of the future*: **disheartening**, depressing, discouraging, disappointing, daunting, disenchanting, demoralizing; unfavourable, inauspicious, off-putting, pessimistic, hopeless, grim, dismal, gloomy, sombre, cheerless, black; informal morbid; archaic dejecting.

displace verb **1** *roof tiles are commonly displaced by gales*: **dislodge**, dislocate, upset, unsettle, move, shift, relocate, reposition; put out of place, move out of place, knock out of place, knock out of position, disarrange, derange, discompose, mess up, disorder, throw into disorder, throw into disarray; scatter, disperse.
▷ANTONYMS replace, put back; leave in place.
2 *they struggled to displace the ruling class*: **depose**, dislodge, unseat, dethrone, remove from office, remove, dismiss, eject, oust, expel, force out, throw out, drive out, drum out; overthrow, overturn, topple, bring down; informal sack, fire, boot out, give someone the boot, show someone the door; Brit. informal turf out; Military cashier; dated out.
▷ANTONYMS reinstate.
3 *fuel crops must not displace food crops*: **replace**, take the place of, take over from, supplant, oust, supersede, succeed, override; informal crowd out.

display noun **1** *a display of dolls and puppets | planned events include a motorcycle display*: **exhibition**, exposition, exhibit, array, arrangement, presentation, demonstration; **spectacle**, show, parade, pageant, extravaganza; informal expo, demo.
2 *every clansman was determined to outdo the Campbells in display*: **ostentation**, ostentatiousness, showiness, show, pomp, extravagance, ornateness, flamboyance, lavishness, resplendence, splendour, splendidness; informal swank, swankiness, pizzazz, razzle-dazzle, flashiness, glitz, glitziness, splashiness.
▷ANTONYMS modesty.
3 *any display of outrage or temperament was frowned upon*: **manifestation**, expression, show, showing, indication, evidence, betrayal, revelation, disclosure.
▷ANTONYMS concealment.
▶verb **1** *the Crown Jewels displayed are only copies*: **exhibit**, show, put on show, put on view, expose to view, present, unveil, set forth; arrange, dispose, array, lay out, set out.
2 *he uses the play to display his many theatrical talents*: **show off**, parade, flaunt, flourish, reveal; publicize, make public, make known, give publicity to, call attention to, draw attention to; informal flash, push, plug, hype, boost.
▷ANTONYMS hide.
3 *every so often she would display a vein of sharp humour*: **manifest**, show evidence of, evince, betray, give away, reveal, disclose; demonstrate, show.
▷ANTONYMS conceal.

displease verb *he was plainly displeased by Jenny's decision*: **annoy**, irritate, infuriate, incense, anger, irk, vex, provoke, pique, peeve, gall, nettle, exasperate, madden; **dissatisfy**, disgruntle, dismay, put out, affront, offend, insult, mortify, outrage, scandalize, disgust; bother, trouble, upset, perturb, disturb, discompose; informal aggravate, needle, bug, rile, rattle, miff, hack off; Brit. informal nark, wind up, get at; N. Amer. informal tee off, tick off, gravel; vulgar slang piss off.
▷ANTONYMS please.

displeasure noun *the scowl on his face indicated displeasure*: **annoyance**, irritation, crossness, infuriation, anger, vexation, wrath, pique, chagrin, rancour, resentment, indignation, exasperation; **dissatisfaction**, discontent, discontentment, discontentedness, disgruntlement, disfavour, disapproval, disapprobation, disgust, distaste, offence; perturbation, disturbance, discomposure, upset, dismay; informal aggravation; literary ire, choler.
▷ANTONYMS pleasure, satisfaction.

disposable adjective **1** *we ate off disposable plates*: **throwaway**, expendable, one-use, non-returnable, replaceable; paper, plastic; biodegradable, photodegradable.
2 *the family had little disposable income*: **available**, usable, accessible, obtainable, spendable.

disposal noun **1** *the ageing planes are earmarked for disposal*: **throwing away**, getting rid of, discarding, jettisoning, ejection, scrapping, destruction; informal dumping, ditching, chucking, chucking out, chucking away.
2 *we have twenty copies of this promotional album for disposal*: **distribution**, handing out, giving out, giving away, allotment, allocation, donation, transfer, transference, making over, conveyance, bestowal, bequest; sale.
3 *the disposal of the troops in two lines*: **arrangement**, arranging, ordering, positioning, placement, lining up, setting up, organization, disposition; marshalling, mustering, grouping, gathering; Military dressing.
4 *they may appeal against the decision of the Panel in the disposal of a case*: **settlement**, determination, deciding, conclusion.
□ **at someone's disposal** *Sir Henry placed £15,000 at the club's disposal*: **for use by**, in reserve for, in the hands of, in the possession of, within the reach of, within easy reach of, at someone's fingertips.

dispose verb **1** *the chief disposed his attendants in a circle*: **arrange**, order, place, put, position, orient, array, spread out, range, set up, form, organize, seat, stand; marshal, muster, gather, group, assemble; informal park, plant, pop, stick; rare posit.
2 *she hoped the trip might dispose her husband to be more charitable*: **incline**, encourage, persuade, predispose, make willing, make, move, prompt, lead, induce, inspire, tempt, motivate, actuate; bias, sway, influence, determine, direct.
□ **dispose of 1** *industrial waste was disposed of in official sites*: **throw away**, throw out, cast out, get rid of, do away with, discard, jettison, abandon, eject, unload; scrap, destroy; informal dump, ditch, chuck, chuck out, chuck away, junk, get shut of; Brit. informal get shot of; N. Amer. trash.
▷ANTONYMS retain. **2** *he had disposed of all his costumes, props, and scenery*: **part with**, **give away**, make over, hand over, deliver up, bestow, transfer; sell, auction; unload, palm off, fob off; informal get shut of, see the back of; Brit. informal get shot of. ▷ANTONYMS acquire; keep. **3** informal *she disposed of a fourth cake*. See **consume**. **4** informal *he robbed her and then disposed of her*. See **kill**. **5** *she disposed of her errand and went home*: **deal with**, discharge, execute, perform, do, sort out, settle, finish, conclude, end, dispatch.

disposed adjective **1** *for reasons of religious belief they are philanthropically disposed*: **inclined**, predisposed, minded.
2 *we are not disposed to argue with their recommendations*: **willing**, inclined, prepared, ready, minded, of a mind, in the mood; keen, eager; informal game.
3 *he was* **disposed to** *be cruel and self-centred*: **liable**, apt, inclined, likely, predisposed, given, prone, tending, subject; capable of, in danger of.

disposition noun **1** *the book is not recommended to readers of a nervous disposition*: **temperament**, nature, character, constitution, make-up, grain, humour, temper, mentality, turn of mind; informal kidney.
2 *he admired the Chief Justice because of his disposition to clemency*: **inclination**, tendency, proneness, propensity, proclivity, leaning, orientation, bias, bent, predilection.
▷ANTONYMS disinclination.
3 *the disposition and control of the armed forces*: **arrangement**, arranging, disposal, ordering, positioning, placement, lining up, setting up, organization, configuration; set-up, line-up, layout, array; marshalling, mustering, grouping, gathering; Military dressing.
4 Law *the court controls the disposition of the company's property*: **distribution**, disposal, allocation, transfer, transference, conveyance, making over, bestowal, bequest; sale, auction.
□ **at someone's disposition** *our wealth is at the disposition of the state*: **at the disposal of**, for use by, in reserve for, in the hands of, in the possession of, within the reach of, within easy reach of, at someone's fingertips.

dispossess verb **1** *the peasants have been dispossessed of their land*: **divest**, strip, rob, cheat out of, do out of, deprive, relieve, bereave; informal diddle out of; archaic reave.

2 *the rebels appear to have dispossessed the aristocrats*: **dislodge**, oust, eject, expel, drive out, evict, turn out, cast out, throw out, throw someone out on their ear, put out in the street, show someone the door; banish, exile; informal chuck out, kick out, boot out, heave out, bounce; Brit. informal turf out; N. Amer. informal give someone the bum's rush; dated out.

disproportionate adjective *the sentences are* ***disproportionate to*** *the offences they have committed | they obtained a disproportionate share of NHS resources*: **out of proportion to**, not in proportion to, not appropriate to, not commensurate with, relatively too large for, relatively too small for; **inordinate**, unreasonable, excessive, uncalled for, undue, unfair, unbalanced, uneven, unequal, irregular.
▷ANTONYMS proportional.

disprove verb *new forensic evidence disproved the allegations*: **refute**, prove false, show to be false, give the lie to, rebut, deny, falsify, debunk, negate, invalidate, contradict, confound, be at odds with, demolish, discredit; challenge, call into question; informal shoot full of holes, shoot down (in flames), blow sky-high, blow out of the water; formal confute, gainsay; rare controvert, negative.
▷ANTONYMS prove.

disputable adjective *some of these figures are disputable and some are out of date*: **debatable**, open to debate, open to discussion, arguable, contestable, moot, open to question, questionable, doubtful, dubious; controversial, contentious, disputed, contended, unconfirmed, unsettled, unsound; informal iffy; Brit. informal dodgy; rare controvertible.

disputation noun *we'll have no politics and no religious disputation in this house*: **debate**, discussion, dispute, argument, arguing, argumentation, altercation, wrangling, sparring, dissension, disagreement, disharmony, conflict, contention, controversy; polemics; rare contestation, velitation.

dispute noun 1 *the extent of the king's powers was the subject of constant dispute*: **debate**, discussion, discourse, disputation, argument, controversy, contention, disagreement, altercation, falling-out, quarrelling, variance, dissension, conflict, friction, strife, discord, antagonism; rare velitation, contestation.
▷ANTONYMS agreement.
2 *the police were called to resolve their dispute*: **quarrel**, argument, altercation, squabble, falling-out, shouting match, disagreement, difference of opinion, clash, wrangle, feud, fight, fracas, brawl; Irish, N. Amer., & Austral. donnybrook; informal tiff, spat, scrap, run-in; Brit. informal row, barney, slanging match, ding-dong, bust-up; Scottish informal rammy; N. Amer. informal rhubarb; archaic broil, miff.
▷ANTONYMS agreement.
▶ verb 1 *George visited him and disputed with him*: **debate**, discuss, exchange views; **quarrel**, argue, disagree, have a disagreement, have an altercation, clash, wrangle, bicker, squabble, bandy words, cross swords, lock horns; informal fall out, have words, argufy, scrap, have a tiff, have a spat; archaic altercate.
2 *there might be good reason to dispute his proposals*: **challenge**, contest, deny, doubt, question, call into question, impugn, quibble over, contradict, argue about, object to, oppose, disagree with, take issue with, protest against; formal gainsay; rare controvert.
▷ANTONYMS accept, agree with.

Choose the right word **dispute, quarrel, argue, wrangle, bicker**

See **quarrel**.

disqualified adjective *he admitted driving while disqualified*: **banned**, barred, disbarred, debarred; eliminated, precluded, disentitled; ineligible, unfit, unqualified; informal out of the running, ruled out, knocked out.
▷ANTONYMS allowed.

disqualify verb *he'd been disqualified from driving*: **ban**, bar, debar, prohibit, forbid, interdict, block; exclude, declare ineligible, rule out, preclude, disentitle; archaic unfit.
▷ANTONYMS allow.

disquiet noun *there has been grave disquiet about the state of the prisons*: **unease**, uneasiness, worry, anxiety, anxiousness, distress, concern; unrest, disquietude, inquietude; perturbation, consternation, upset, malaise; alarm, anguish, fear, fright, dread, panic, angst; nervousness, agitation, restlessness, fretfulness, jitteriness; foreboding, trepidation.
▷ANTONYMS calm.
▶ verb *I was so disquieted by the book that I finished it that evening*: **perturb**, agitate, upset, disturb, unnerve, unsettle, discompose, disconcert, ruffle, startle; make uneasy, worry, make anxious; trouble, bother, concern, distress, alarm, appal, frighten, panic, make fretful, make restless, vex.
▷ANTONYMS calm.

disquisition noun *his memoirs include disquisitions on film and football*: **essay**, dissertation, treatise, paper, discourse, tract, monograph, study, article; **discussion**, lecture, address, presentation, speech, talk, monologue; analysis, commentary, review, critique.

disregard verb *Annie disregarded the remark*: **ignore**, take no notice of, take no account of, pay no attention/heed to, refuse to acknowledge; discount, set aside, forget, overlook, dismiss; turn a blind eye to, turn a deaf ear to, shut one's eyes to, pass over, gloss over, brush off/aside, shrug off, look the other way; laugh off, make light of, thumb one's nose at, write off; Brit. informal blank.
▷ANTONYMS heed, pay attention to.
▶ noun *he drove with blithe disregard for the rules of the road*: **indifference**, non-observance; **inattention**, heedlessness, carelessness, neglect, lack of attention, lack of notice, lack of heed, negligence.
▷ANTONYMS heed, attention.

disrepair noun *a building in a state of disrepair*: **dilapidation**, decrepitude, shabbiness, ruin, ruination, rack and ruin, ricketiness; deterioration, decay, degeneration, collapse; abandonment, neglect, disuse.

disreputable adjective 1 *he fell into disreputable company*: **scandalous**, of bad reputation, infamous, notorious, louche; dishonourable, dishonest, villainous, rascally, ignominious, corrupt, unscrupulous, unprincipled, immoral, untrustworthy, discreditable; contemptible, reprehensible, despicable, disgraceful, shameful, shocking, outrageous; unworthy, base, low, mean; questionable, suspect, suspicious, dubious, unsavoury, slippery; seedy, sleazy, seamy, unwholesome; informal crooked, shady, shifty, fishy; Brit. informal dodgy.
▷ANTONYMS reputable, respectable.
2 *they looked so filthy and disreputable that a woman stopped to stare at them*: **scruffy**, shabby, slovenly, down at heel, seedy, untidy, unkempt, dishevelled, disordered, bedraggled, dilapidated, threadbare, tattered, sloppy.
▷ANTONYMS smart.

disrepute noun *Beth had shamed herself and brought the family name into disrepute*: **disgrace**, shame, dishonour, infamy, notoriety, ignominy, stigma, scandal, bad reputation, lack of respectability; degradation, humiliation, odium, opprobrium, obloquy; discredit, ill repute, disesteem, low esteem, loss of face; unpopularity, disfavour, ill favour.
▷ANTONYMS honour.

disrespect noun 1 *there is growing disrespect for authority*: **contempt**, lack of respect, scorn, disregard, disdain, opprobrium; derision, mockery, ridicule.
▷ANTONYMS respect, esteem.
2 *he said it on the spur of the moment, he meant no disrespect to anybody*: **discourtesy**, rudeness, impoliteness, incivility, unmannerliness, lack of respect, lack of civility, ungraciousness, irreverence, lack of consideration, ill/bad manners; insolence, impudence, impertinence, cheek, flippancy, churlishness; informal lip, nerve.
▷ANTONYMS respect, esteem.

disrespectful adjective *he was cheeky and disrespectful towards his parents*: **discourteous**, rude, impolite, uncivil, unmannerly, ill-mannered, bad-mannered, ungracious, irreverent, inconsiderate; insolent, impudent, impertinent, cheeky, flippant, insubordinate, churlish; contemptuous, disdainful, derisive, scornful, disparaging, insulting, abusive; informal fresh.
▷ANTONYMS respectful, polite.

disrobe verb *she began to disrobe*: **undress**, strip, strip naked, take off one's clothes, remove one's clothes, doff one's clothes, shed one's clothes, denude, uncover oneself; informal peel off; dated divest oneself of one's clothes.

disrupt verb 1 *a 24-hour strike disrupted public transport*: **throw into confusion**, throw into disorder, throw into disarray, cause confusion/turmoil in, play havoc with, derange, turn upside-down, make a mess of; **disturb**, disorder, disorganize, disarrange, interfere with, upset, unsettle, convulse; interrupt, suspend, discontinue; obstruct, impede, hamper; hold up, delay, retard, slow (down); Brit. informal throw a spanner in the works of; N. Amer. informal throw a monkey wrench in the works of.
2 *the explosion would disrupt the walls of the crater*: **distort**, damage, buckle, warp; break open/apart, shatter, split, sever, cleave, split asunder; literary rend; archaic sunder, rive.
▷ANTONYMS organize; arrange.

disruption noun *he was exasperated at this disruption of his plans*: **disturbance**, disordering, disarrangement, disarranging, interference, upset, upsetting, unsettling, confusion, confusing; disorderliness, disorganization, turmoil, disarray; interruption, suspension, discontinuation, stoppage; obstruction, impeding, hampering, spoiling, ruining, wrecking, undermining; holding up, delaying, delay, retardation.

disruptive adjective *a very disruptive child*: **troublemaking**, troublesome, unruly, rowdy, disorderly, undisciplined, riotous, wild, turbulent; unmanageable, uncontrollable, out of control/hand, unrestrained, obstreperous, truculent, fractious, divisive; badly behaved, misbehaving, errant, uncooperative, rebellious; disturbing, distracting, unsettling, upsetting, noisy, raucous; formal refractory.
▷ANTONYMS well behaved, manageable.

dissatisfaction noun *polls revealed widespread dissatisfaction with the new law*: **discontent**, discontentment, disappointment, disaffection, disquiet, unhappiness, malaise, disgruntlement, frustration, vexation,

d

d

annoyance, irritation, anger, exasperation, resentment; restlessness, restiveness; disapproval, disapprobation, disfavour, displeasure, grievance, disregard, disgust; regret, chagrin, dismay; German Weltschmerz.
▷ANTONYMS satisfaction.

dissatisfied adjective *the radical wing was dissatisfied with these policies | a dissatisfied customer*: **discontented**, malcontent, unsatisfied, disappointed, disaffected, disquieted, unhappy; disgruntled, aggrieved, frustrated, vexed, annoyed, irritated, angry, angered, exasperated, fed up, resentful; restless, restive, disapproving, displeased, unfulfilled, regretful; informal cheesed off, brassed off, browned off; vulgar slang pissed off.
▷ANTONYMS satisfied, contented.

dissatisfy verb *what is it about this wording that dissatisfies you?* **displease**, fail to satisfy, give cause for complaint, not be good enough; disappoint, let down; disquiet, disgruntle, aggrieve, frustrate, vex, annoy, irritate, put out, anger, exasperate.
▷ANTONYMS satisfy.

dissect verb **1** *the body was dissected in the infirmary*: **anatomize**, cut up, cut/lay open, dismember; vivisect.
2 *as the text of the gospels was dissected, some parts came to look earlier than others*: **analyse**, examine, study, inspect, scrutinize, probe, explore, pore over, investigate, sift, delve into, go over with a fine-tooth comb; break down, take apart, deconstruct.

dissection noun **1** *the dissection of corpses*: **cutting up**, cutting open, dismemberment; autopsy, post-mortem, necropsy, anatomy, vivisection, zootomy.
2 *a thorough dissection of the government's industrial policies*: **analysis**, examination, study, inspection, scrutiny, scrutinization, probe, probing, exploration, investigation, enquiry; evaluation, assessment, criticism; breakdown, deconstruction.

dissemble verb *she is an honest, sincere person who has no need to dissemble*: **dissimulate**, pretend, deceive, feign, act, masquerade, sham, fake, bluff, counterfeit, pose, posture, hide one's feelings, be dishonest, put on a false front, lie; cover up, conceal, disguise, hide, mask, veil, shroud.

dissembler noun *he was a born showman and dissembler*: **liar**, dissimulator, deceiver, deluder; humbug, bluffer, fraud, hoodwinker, impostor, actor, faker, hoaxer, charlatan, cheat, cheater.

disseminate verb *health authorities should foster good practice by disseminating information*: **spread**, circulate, distribute, disperse, diffuse, proclaim, promulgate, propagate, publicize, communicate, pass on, make known, put about; dissipate, scatter; broadcast, put on the air/airwaves, publish; herald, trumpet; literary bruit abroad/about.

dissemination noun *the collection and dissemination of information*: **spreading**, circulation, distribution, dispersal, diffusion; proclamation, promulgation, propagation, publicizing, communication, passing on, making known, putting about; dissipation, scattering; broadcasting, relaying, transmission, putting on the air/airwaves, publishing, publication.

dissension noun *there was dissension within the Cabinet over these policies*: **disagreement**, difference of opinion, dispute, dissent, variance, conflict, friction, strife, discord, discordance, discordancy, disunion, disaffection, rivalry, antagonism; argument, debate, controversy, disputation, contention, quarrelling, wrangling, bickering, squabbling, falling-out.
▷ANTONYMS agreement; harmony.

dissent verb *we do not dissent from the points that have been made*: **differ**, demur, diverge; **disagree with**, fail to agree with, express disagreement with, be at variance/odds with, argue with, take issue with; decline/refuse to support, not ratify, protest against, object to, dispute, challenge, quibble over; reject, repudiate, renounce, abjure.
▷ANTONYMS assent, agree, accept.
▸ noun *there were murmurs of dissent from the opposition benches*: **disagreement**, lack of agreement, difference of opinion, argument, dispute, demur; disapproval, objection, protest, opposition, defiance, insubordination; conflict, friction, strife; arguing, quarrelling, wrangling, bickering.
▷ANTONYMS agreement, acceptance.

dissenter noun **1** *there was a chorus of criticism from dissenters within the party*: **dissident**, dissentient, objector, protester, disputant; rebel, revolutionary, renegade, maverick, independent; apostate, heretic.
2 (**Dissenter**) *liberty of conscience for Dissenters*: **Nonconformist**, Protestant, freethinker, recusant; Puritan; Baptist, Methodist, Quaker, Calvinist, Lutheran; N. Amer. Mennonite; historical Anabaptist.

dissentient adjective *there were some dissentient voices*: **dissenting**, dissident, disagreeing, differing, discordant, contradicting, contrary, negative, anti-; opposing, opposed, objecting, protesting, complaining, rebellious, rebelling, revolutionary; **nonconformist**, non-compliant, unorthodox, recusant, heterodox, heretical; formal gainsaying.
▸ noun See **dissenter** (sense 1).

dissertation noun *a dissertation on the novels of the Brontë sisters*: **essay**, thesis, treatise, paper, study, composition, discourse, disquisition, tract, monograph; critique, exposition, criticism, appraisal, assessment, discussion.

disservice noun *not checking your headlines does your readers a disservice*: **unkindness**, bad turn, ill turn, disfavour, mischief; **injury**, harm, hurt, damage, offence; wrong, injustice; informal kick in the teeth.
▷ANTONYMS favour.

dissidence noun *the chairman was faced by dissidence within his own party*: **disagreement**, dissent, disaccord, discord, discontent, disapproval; **opposition**, resistance, protest, insurrection, rebellion, sedition.
▷ANTONYMS agreement, acceptance.

dissident noun *a dissident who had been jailed by the regime*: **dissenter**, objector, protester, disputant; freethinker, nonconformist, independent thinker; rebel, revolutionary, recusant, renegade; subversive, agitator, insurgent, insurrectionist, insurrectionary, mutineer; informal refusenik.
▷ANTONYMS conformist.
▸ adjective *a demonstration coordinated by dissident intellectuals and workers*: **dissentient**, dissenting, disagreeing; opposing, opposed, opposition, objecting, protesting, complaining; rebellious, rebelling, revolutionary, recusant; nonconformist, non-compliant.
▷ANTONYMS conforming.

dissimilar adjective *contact between dissimilar cultures*: **different**, differing, unlike, unalike, varying, variant, various, diverse, heterogeneous, disparate, unrelated, distinct, contrasting, contradictory, poles apart; divergent, mismatched, inconsistent; informal like chalk and cheese; literary divers, myriad; rare contrastive.
▷ANTONYMS similar.

> *Word toolkit* **dissimilar**
>
> See **divergent**.

dissimilarity noun *the enzymes' structural dissimilarity*: **difference(s)**, dissimilitude, variance, variation, diversity, heterogeneity, disparateness, disparity, distinctness, distinction, contrast, non-uniformity, incomparability, incongruity, polarity; divergence, deviation; unrelatedness, inconsistency, discrepancy; rare unlikeness.
▷ANTONYMS similarity.

dissimilitude noun *people are often drawn together by their very dissimilitude*. See **dissimilarity**.

dissimulate verb *now they have power, they no longer need to dissimulate*: **pretend**, deceive, feign, act, dissemble, masquerade, pose, posture, sham, fake, bluff, counterfeit, go through the motions, hide one's feelings, be dishonest, put on a false front, lie.

dissimulation noun *he was capable of great dissimulation and hypocrisy*: **pretence**, dissembling, misrepresentation, deceit, dishonesty, duplicity, lying, guile, subterfuge, feigning, falsification, shamming, faking, bluff, bluffing, counterfeiting, posturing, hypocrisy, double-dealing; concealment, concealing, masking, disguising, hiding, veiling, shrouding; Irish informal codology; informal kidology.

dissipate verb **1** *his anger had dissipated | the queue dissipated*: **disappear**, **vanish**, evaporate, dissolve, melt away, melt into thin air, be dispelled, dematerialize; disperse, scatter; drive away, dispel, banish; quell, allay, check; literary evanesce.
▷ANTONYMS grow, develop.
2 *he had dissipated his fortune*: **squander**, fritter (away), misspend, waste, throw away, make poor use of, be prodigal with; spend recklessly/freely, lavish, expend, spend like water, throw around like confetti; exhaust, drain, deplete, burn (up), use up, consume, run through, go through, lose; informal blow, splurge, pour/throw down the drain, spend money as if it grows on trees, spend money as if there were no tomorrow, spend money as if it were going out of style/fashion; Brit. informal blue; vulgar slang piss away.
▷ANTONYMS save.

> *Choose the right word* **dissipate, disperse, scatter**
>
> See **scatter**.

dissipated adjective *the new heir was a dissipated youth*: **dissolute**, **debauched**, decadent, intemperate, immoderate, profligate, abandoned, self-indulgent, wild, unrestrained; depraved, degenerate, corrupt, sinful, immoral, impure; rakish, louche; licentious, promiscuous, lecherous, libertine, wanton, lustful, libidinous, lewd, unchaste, loose; drunken.
▷ANTONYMS ascetic.

dissipation noun **1** *a day of drunken dissipation*: **debauchery**, decadence, dissoluteness, dissolution, intemperance, immoderation, excess, profligacy, abandonment, self-indulgence, wildness; depravity, degeneracy, corruption, sinfulness, immorality, vice, impurity; rakishness; licentiousness, promiscuity, lecherousness, lechery, libertinism, libertinage, wantonness, lustfulness, libidinousness, lewdness; drunkenness.
▷ANTONYMS asceticism, restraint.
2 *concern was expressed about the dissipation of the country's mineral wealth*: **squandering**, frittering (away), waste, misspending; expenditure, wild spending, draining, depletion, losing, loss.
▷ANTONYMS saving, preservation.

dissociate verb *the word 'spiritual' has become dissociated from religion*: **separate**, detach, disconnect, sever, cut off, divorce, set apart, segregate, distinguish; isolate, alienate.
▷ANTONYMS relate, connect.
□ **dissociate oneself from 1** *he dissociated himself from the Church of England*: **break away from**, break off relations with, end relations with, sever connections with; withdraw from, delink from, quit, leave, disaffiliate from, resign from, pull out of, drop out of, have nothing more to do with, part company with, defect, desert, secede from, take one's leave of, become estranged from.
▷ANTONYMS join.
2 *the French president dissociated himself from the statement*: **denounce**, disown, reject, condemn, disagree with, wash one's hands of, distance oneself from.
▷ANTONYMS endorse, support.

dissociation noun *there can be a dissociation of behaviour from consciousness*: **separation**, disconnection, detachment, severance, divorce, uncoupling, split, setting apart; segregation, distinction, division; isolation, alienation, distancing; literary sundering; rare disseverment.
▷ANTONYMS association, union.

dissolute adjective *a dissolute, disreputable rogue*: **dissipated**, debauched, decadent, intemperate, profligate, abandoned, self-indulgent, rakish, louche, licentious, promiscuous, lecherous, libertine, wanton, lustful, libidinous, lewd, unchaste, loose; wild, unrestrained, depraved, degenerate, corrupt, sinful, immoral, impure; drunken.
▷ANTONYMS ascetic.

dissolution noun **1** *the dissolution of parliament | he called for the dissolution of the secret police*: **cessation**, conclusion, end, ending, finish, termination, break-up, split-up, winding up/down, discontinuation, suspension; **disbandment**, disbanding, disestablishment, disunion, separation, dispersal, scattering; prorogation, recess.
2 technical *the dissolution of a polymer in a solvent*: **dissolving**, liquefaction, melting, deliquescence; breaking up, separation, resolution, decomposition, disintegration.
3 *the slow dissolution of the Ottoman empire*: **disintegration**, breaking up, fragmenting; decay, collapse, death, demise, extinction; destruction, ruin, overthrow.
4 *the corruption and dissolution of this moribund society*. See **dissipation** (sense 1).

dissolve verb **1** *heat the water until the sugar dissolves*: **go into solution**, become a solution, break down; liquefy, melt, deliquesce; disintegrate, diffuse; technical solvate.
▷ANTONYMS condense.
2 *his hopes dissolved*: **disappear**, vanish, melt away, evaporate, disperse, dissipate, disintegrate; dwindle, fade (away), fall away, subside, ebb, wane, peter out, fizzle out, crumble, decompose, wilt, wither; perish, die, be destroyed, cease to exist, come to an end, pass away, evanesce.
▷ANTONYMS appear.
3 *the crowd had dissolved*: **disperse**, disband, break up, split up, separate, scatter, go their separate ways, go in different directions, disjoin.
▷ANTONYMS join together.
4 *the National Assembly was dissolved after a coup*: **disband**, disestablish, dismiss; **bring to an end**, end, terminate, finish, cease, conclude, discontinue, break up, split up, close down, wind up/down, suspend; prorogue, adjourn; scrap, abolish, do away with, get rid of.
▷ANTONYMS establish.
5 *the marriage was dissolved in 1985*: **annul**, nullify, void; cancel, invalidate, overturn, repeal, rescind, revoke; divorce.
□ **dissolve into/in** *a timid child who was always the first to dissolve into tears*: **burst into**, break into, collapse into, break down into; be overcome with; informal crack up.

dissonance noun **1** *there is hardly any dissonance on this album*: **inharmoniousness**, discordance, unmelodiousness, atonality, cacophony; harshness, stridency, grating, jarring.
▷ANTONYMS harmony.
2 *there is dissonance between the form and content*: **incongruity**, disparity, discrepancy, disagreement, tension; difference, dissimilarity, variance, inconsistency; contradiction, clash.
▷ANTONYMS harmony; similarity.

dissonant adjective **1** *dissonant sounds*: **inharmonious**, disharmonious, discordant, unmelodious, atonal, tuneless, off-key, cacophonous; harsh, strident, grating, jarring.
▷ANTONYMS harmonious.
2 *Jackson employs both harmonious and dissonant colour choices*: **incongruous**, anomalous, irreconcilable, discrepant, disagreeing, clashing; disparate, different, dissimilar, inconsistent, incompatible, contradictory.
▷ANTONYMS harmonious, similar.

dissuade verb *I tried to* ***dissuade*** *him* ***from*** *telling that story*: **discourage**, deter, prevent, disincline, turn aside, divert, sidetrack; talk out of, persuade against, persuade not to, argue out of, put off, stop, scare off, warn off; advise against, urge against, advise/urge not to, caution against, expostulate against; rare dehort.
▷ANTONYMS persuade, encourage.

> *Choose the right word* **dissuade, discourage, deter**
>
> See **discourage**.

distance noun **1** *they measured the distance between Hartwell and Roade Station*: **interval**, space, span, gap, separation, interspace, stretch, extent; length, width, breadth, depth; range, reach.
2 *binocular vision gives us a perception of distance*: **remoteness**, farness; closeness.
3 *a mix of warmth and distance makes a good neighbour*: **aloofness**, remoteness, detachment, stand-offishness, unfriendliness, unapproachableness, haughtiness, hauteur, coolness, coldness, frigidity; reserve, reticence, restraint, stiffness, formality, unresponsiveness.
▷ANTONYMS friendliness.
□ **in the distance** *he could see them in the distance*: **far away**, far off, afar; yonder, just in view; on the horizon, in the background.
▷ANTONYMS close to.
▶ verb *he had distanced himself from her emotionally*: **withdraw**, detach, separate, dissociate, remove, isolate, put at a distance, keep at arm's length, set apart, place far off.
▷ANTONYMS draw closer.

> *Word links* **distance**
>
> **tele-** to or at a distance, as in *telephone, telekinesis*

distant adjective **1** *distant parts of the world*: **faraway**, far off, far; **remote**, out of the way, outlying, abroad, far-flung, obscure; isolated, cut off, off the beaten track.
▷ANTONYMS near.
2 *the distant past*: **long ago**, bygone; ancient, prehistoric, antediluvian, immemorial; literary olden, of yore.
▷ANTONYMS recent.
3 *the town lay half a mile distant*: **away**, off, apart, separated.
4 *a distant memory*: **vague**, faint, dim, faded, feeble; **indistinct**, obscure, unclear, uncertain, indefinite, indeterminate; confused, sketchy, hazy, rough.
▷ANTONYMS strong, intense.
5 *there is a distant family connection*: **remote**, indirect, slight.
▷ANTONYMS close.
6 *my father was always very distant with me*: **aloof**, reserved, remote, detached, unapproachable, stand-offish, keeping people at arm's length; withdrawn, restrained, reticent, taciturn, uncommunicative, undemonstrative, unforthcoming; cool, cold, frigid, chilly, icy, frosty; formal, stiff, stuffy, ceremonious, unresponsive, unfriendly, haughty, forbidding, austere.
▷ANTONYMS friendly.
7 *he had a distant look in his eyes*: **distracted**, **absent-minded**, absent, faraway, detached, distrait, vague.
▷ANTONYMS attentive.

> *Choose the right word* **distant, remote, faraway, far off**
>
> These words all describe something that is a long way away in space or time.
>
> **Distant** is the most general and neutral word for something that is a long way away (*fine views stretch to the distant mountains | the dim and distant past*).
>
> **Remote** suggests isolation and inaccessibility rather than just distance (*they went into hiding in a remote fishing village | areas remote from the coast*).
>
> **Faraway** may emphasize the difficulty of getting somewhere, but often it also suggests an exotic and romantic quality (*I dream of faraway exotic places*). It is always used before a noun in this sense.
>
> A **far-off** place or time is often very different from one with which it is tacitly compared (*an adventure story set in a far-off mystical land*).

distaste noun *she has shown a* ***distaste for*** *politics*: **dislike**, disfavour, disdain; **repugnance**, disgust, revulsion, contempt, antipathy, odium, hatred, loathing, detestation, execration, abomination, horror; disinclination towards, aversion to, disapproval of, disapprobation of, displeasure with, dissatisfaction with, discontent with; rare disrelish, repellence, repellency.
▷ANTONYMS liking.

distasteful adjective **1** *his behaviour has been distasteful*: **unpleasant**, disagreeable, displeasing, unpleasing, undesirable; off-putting, uninviting; objectionable, offensive, unsavoury, unpalatable, obnoxious, odious; disgusting, repellent, repulsive, revolting, repugnant, abhorrent, loathsome, detestable, obscene, foul, nasty, vile.
▷ANTONYMS agreeable.
2 *certain sea urchins make their eggs distasteful to predators*: **unpalatable**, unsavoury, unappetizing, inedible, disgusting, sickening, nauseating, nauseous, horrible, horrid.
▷ANTONYMS tasty.

d

distend verb *the pressure acts to distend blood vessels*: **swell**, bloat, bulge, puff out/up, blow up/out, expand, dilate, inflate, enlarge; rare tumefy, intumesce.
▷ANTONYMS shrink, contract.

distended adjective *a grossly distended belly*: **swollen**, bloated, tumescent, dilated, engorged, enlarged, inflated, stretched, blown up, pumped up/out; expanded, extended, ballooning, puffy, puffed up; bulbous, bulging, protuberant, prominent, sticking out; technical turgescent, ventricose; rare tumid.
▷ANTONYMS shrunken, deflated.

distil verb **1** *all the water used was distilled and deionized*: **purify**, refine, filter, treat, process; vaporize/evaporate and condense, sublime, sublimate; rare fractionate.
2 *oil distilled from marjoram*: **extract**, press out, squeeze out, express, draw out, take out.
3 *most Scotch whiskies are distilled from barley malt cured with peat*: **brew**, ferment, make.
4 *the solvent is distilled to leave the oil as a solid material*: **boil down**, reduce, concentrate, thicken, compress, condense; purify, refine, separate, rectify.
5 literary *she drew back from the dank breath that distilled out of the earth*: **emanate**, exude, drip, leak, trickle, dribble, flow.

distillation noun **1** *a way of making fresh water from seawater by distillation*: **distilling**, **purification**, refining, filtering, filtration, treatment, processing; sublimation; rare fractionation.
2 *the flowers were ready to gather for distillation*: **pressing**, squeezing; extraction, extracting, drawing out; concentration, condensation, reduction.

distinct adjective **1** *any employee would fall into one of two distinct categories*: **discrete**, **separate**, individual, different, unconnected, unassociated, detached; precise, specific, distinctive, dissimilar, unalike, contrasting, disparate, unique; Latin sui generis.
▷ANTONYMS indistinct; overlapping; approximate.
2 *the tail has distinct black tips*: **clear**, clear-cut, definite, well defined, sharp, marked, decided, unmistakable, easily distinguishable; recognizable, visible, perceptible, noticeable, obvious, plain, plain as day, evident, apparent, manifest, patent, palpable, unambiguous, unequivocal, pronounced, prominent, striking.
▷ANTONYMS indistinct; fuzzy; indefinite.

distinction noun **1** *the distinction between academic and vocational qualifications*: **difference**, contrast, dissimilarity, dissimilitude, divergence, variance, variation; division, separation, differentiation, contradistinction, discrimination, segregation, dividing line, gulf, gap, chasm.
▷ANTONYMS similarity.
2 *a painter of distinction*: **importance**, significance, note, consequence, account; **renown**, fame, celebrity, prominence, eminence, pre-eminence, repute, reputation, honour, prestige, status, high standing, illustriousness, name, mark, rank; merit, worth, greatness, excellence, glory, quality, superiority.
▷ANTONYMS mediocrity.
3 *he had served with distinction in the Great War*: **honour**, **credit**, excellence, merit.

distinctive adjective *each subculture developed a distinctive dress style*: **distinguishing**, characteristic, typical, individual, particular, peculiar, idiosyncratic, differentiating, unique, exclusive, special, especial; remarkable, unusual, singular, noteworthy, different, uncommon, extraordinary, original.
▷ANTONYMS common.

distinctly adverb **1** *there's something distinctly odd about him*: **decidedly**, markedly, definitely, emphatically; clearly, noticeably, obviously, plainly, evidently, unmistakably, manifestly, patently, palpably; blatantly, glaringly, conspicuously, pointedly; unquestionably, undeniably, indisputably; Brit. informal dead.
▷ANTONYMS vaguely, possibly.
2 *'No!' Laura said quite distinctly*: **clearly**, plainly, intelligibly, audibly, unambiguously, loud and clear, with clarity, precisely.
▷ANTONYMS indistinctly.

distinguish verb **1** *a food allergy may be difficult to distinguish from a viral infection*: **differentiate**, tell apart, discriminate, discern, determine, pick out; tell the difference between, decide between, make/draw a distinction between.
2 *he was able to distinguish the shapes of the trees in the dark*: **discern**, see, perceive, make out; observe, notice, spot, glimpse, catch sight of; detect, recognize, identify, pick out; formal apprehend; literary descry, espy.
3 *this is what distinguishes history from other disciplines*: **separate**, set apart, make distinctive, make different; **single out**, mark off, demarcate, delimit, delineate; characterize, individualize, individuate, identify, designate, categorize, classify.
□ **distinguish oneself** *he had distinguished himself during his university days*: **attain distinction**, be successful, bring fame/honour to oneself, become famous, dignify oneself, glorify oneself, excel oneself, win acclaim for oneself, ennoble oneself, become lionized, become immortalized, elevate oneself.

distinguishable adjective *chapels on this pattern were barely distinguishable from parish churches of the same period*: **discernible**, recognizable, identifiable, detectable; divisible, separable.
▷ANTONYMS indistinguishable.

distinguished adjective *a distinguished physicist*: **eminent**, famous, famed, renowned, prominent, well known; esteemed, respected, illustrious, august, venerable, honoured, acclaimed, celebrated, legendary, great; noted, notable, important, significant, influential.
▷ANTONYMS unknown; obscure.

distinguishing adjective *a distinguishing feature of British society*: **distinctive**, differentiating, discriminating, determining; individualistic, particular, peculiar, singular, idiosyncratic, unique, noteworthy, different, uncommon, extraordinary, original; characteristic, typical.
▷ANTONYMS unremarkable, common.

distort verb **1** *his face was distorted with anger*: **twist**, warp, contort, bend, buckle, deform, malform, misshape, disfigure; mangle, wrench, wring, wrest.
2 *he oversimplified and distorted the truth*: **misrepresent**, pervert, twist, falsify, misreport, misstate, prejudice, manipulate, garble, take/quote out of context; slant, bias, skew, colour, put a spin on, spin; tamper with, tinker with, doctor, alter, change.

distorted adjective **1** *a distorted face*: **twisted**, warped, contorted, bent, buckled, deformed, malformed, misshapen, disfigured, crooked, irregular, awry, wry, out of shape; mangled, wrenched, gnarled.
▷ANTONYMS straight.
2 *a distorted version of Freud's ideas*: **misrepresented**, perverted, twisted, falsified, misreported, misstated; **garbled**, inaccurate; biased, prejudiced, slanted, coloured, loaded, weighted; tampered with, tinkered with, doctored, altered, changed.
▷ANTONYMS accurate.

distortion noun **1** *strain on the muscles of the eye leading to a distortion in shape or structure*: **warp**, twist, contortion, bend, buckle, deformation, deformity, curve, curvature, malformation, disfigurement, crookedness; gnarl, knot.
2 *a gross distortion of the facts*: **misrepresentation**, perversion, twisting, falsification, misreporting, misstatement, manipulation; **garbling**, travesty; slant, bias, skew, colouring, prejudice, imbalance, spin; tampering, tinkering, doctoring, alteration, change.

distract verb *don't let me distract you from what you were saying | he was distracted by a ringing sound*: **divert**, deflect, sidetrack, turn aside/away, draw away; disturb, put off, cause to lose concentration.

distracted adjective *he glanced at me with a distracted smile*: **preoccupied**, diverted, inattentive, vague, absorbed, engrossed, abstracted, distrait, distant, absent, absent-minded, faraway; bemused, confused, bewildered, perplexed, puzzled, agitated, flustered, ruffled, disconcerted, discomposed, nonplussed, befuddled, mystified; troubled, pestered, harassed, worried, tormented; informal miles away, in a world of one's own, not with it, fazed, hassled, in a flap.
▷ANTONYMS attentive.

distracting adjective *some people find even the slightest noise distracting*: **disturbing**, unsettling, intrusive, disconcerting, bothersome, confusing; informal off-putting.

distraction noun **1** *he called these stories a distraction from the real issues*: **diversion**, interruption, disturbance, intrusion, interference, obstruction, hindrance.
2 *the frivolous distractions of student life*: **amusement**, entertainment, diversion, activity, pastime, recreation, interest, hobby, game, leisure pursuit, occupation, divertissement.
3 *he had been driven to distraction when his daughter would not settle down*: **frenzy**, hysteria, mental distress, madness, insanity, wildness, mania, derangement, delirium; bewilderment, befuddlement, perplexity, confusion, disturbance, agitation, perturbation, harassment; archaic crazedness.

distrait, distraite adjective *he was unusually distrait as he ate his breakfast*: **distracted**, preoccupied, absorbed, engrossed, abstracted, distant, faraway; **absent-minded**, absent, forgetful, vague, inattentive, oblivious, heedless, in a brown study, wool-gathering, with one's head in the clouds, in a world of one's own; informal scatterbrained, miles away.
▷ANTONYMS alert, concentrating.

distraught adjective *the poor child was distraught*: **worried**, **upset**, distressed, fraught, devastated, shattered; overcome, overwrought, beside oneself, out of one's mind, desperate, at one's wits' end; hysterical, frenzied, raving, deranged; informal in a state, worked up.

distress noun **1** *she was trying to conceal her distress*: **anguish**, suffering, pain, agony, ache, affliction, torment, torture, discomfort, heartache, heartbreak; misery, wretchedness, sorrow, grief, woe, sadness, unhappiness, desolation, despair; trouble, worry, anxiety, perturbation, uneasiness, disquiet, angst.
▷ANTONYMS happiness, comfort.
2 *a ship in distress*: **danger**, peril, difficulty, trouble, jeopardy, risk, hazard,

endangerment, imperilment; insecurity, instability, precariousness.
▷ANTONYMS safety.
3 *the poor were helped in their distress*: **hardship**, adversity, tribulation, misfortune, ill/bad luck, trouble, calamity; poverty, deprivation, privation, destitution, indigence, impoverishment, penury, need, want, lack, beggary, dire straits.
▷ANTONYMS prosperity, comfort.
▸verb 1 *he's been distressed by the trial*: **cause anguish to**, cause suffering to, pain, upset, make miserable, make wretched; grieve, sadden; trouble, worry, bother, arouse anxiety in, perturb, disturb, disquiet, agitate, vex, harrow, torment, torture, afflict, rack, curse, oppress, plague, dog; informal cut up.
▷ANTONYMS calm, soothe; please.
2 technical *the fireplaces were distressed*: **age**, season, condition, mellow, weather, simulate age in; damage, spoil, dent, scratch, chip, batter.
▷ANTONYMS restore.

distressing adjective *it was distressing to hear her talking like that*: **upsetting**, worrying, affecting, painful, traumatic, agonizing, harrowing, tormenting; sad, saddening, pitiful, heartbreaking, heart-rending, tragic, haunting; disturbing, unsettling, disquieting; shocking, alarming; informal gut-wrenching; rare distressful.
▷ANTONYMS comforting.

distribute verb 1 *his property was sold and the proceeds distributed among his creditors*: **give out**, deal out, hand out/round, issue, dispense, administer, pass round, dole out, dispose of; **allocate**, allot, apportion, assign, share out, divide out/up, measure out, mete out, parcel out, ration out; informal divvy up, dish out.
▷ANTONYMS collect.
2 *the newsletter is distributed free to all staff*: **circulate**, issue; hand out, deliver, convey, transmit.
3 *the cuckoo family is very large, with a hundred and thirty different species distributed worldwide*: **disperse**, diffuse, disseminate, scatter, spread, strew.

distribution noun 1 *the distribution of charity*: **giving out**, dealing out, handing out/round, issue, issuing, issuance, dispensation, administering, administration, passing round, doling out; allocation, allotment, apportioning, apportionment, assigning, assignment, sharing out, dividing up/out, division, measuring out, meting out, parcelling out, rationing out.
▷ANTONYMS collection.
2 *the geographical distribution of plants*: **dispersal**, diffusion, dissemination, scattering, spread; placement, position, location, disposition, arrangement, organization; grouping, classification, assortment.
3 *the towns were the centres of food distribution*: **supply**, supplying, delivery, transport, transportation, conveyance, dispatch, handling, mailing.
4 *this approach could involve studying the statistical distribution of the problem*: **frequency**, probability, prevalence, incidence, commonness, weighting.

district noun *the business district of Manila*: **neighbourhood**, area, region, place, locality, locale, community, quarter, sector, vicinity, zone, territory, block, part, spot, patch, domain; administrative division, ward, parish, constituency, department; informal neck of the woods; Brit. informal manor; N. Amer. informal turf.

distrust noun *the general distrust of authority amongst drug users*: **mistrust**, **suspicion**, wariness, chariness, lack of trust, lack of confidence, lack of faith; scepticism, doubt, doubtfulness, dubiety, cynicism; misgivings, questioning, qualms; disbelief, unbelief, incredulity, incredulousness, discredit; informal leeriness.
▷ANTONYMS trust.
▸verb *for some reason Aunt Louise distrusted him*: **mistrust**, be suspicious of, be wary/chary of, regard with suspicion, suspect, look askance at, have no confidence/faith in; be sceptical of, have doubts about, doubt, be unsure of/about, be unconvinced about, take with a pinch/grain of salt; have misgivings about, wonder about, question; disbelieve (in), not believe, discredit, discount, be incredulous of; informal be leery of, smell a rat.
▷ANTONYMS trust.

distrustful adjective *he was distrustful of local politicians*: **mistrustful**, **suspicious**, chary, apprehensive, lacking trust, lacking confidence, lacking faith; sceptical, unsure, doubtful, dubious, cynical; cautious, circumspect, careful, wary, uneasy; questioning, disbelieving, unbelieving, incredulous; informal leery, cagey.
▷ANTONYMS trusting.

disturb verb 1 *we need somewhere where we won't be disturbed while we have our chat*: **interrupt**, intrude on, butt in on, barge in on; **distract**, interfere with, disrupt, bother, trouble, pester, plague, harass, molest; informal horn in on, hassle.
2 *he does not want his books and papers disturbed*: **disarrange**, **muddle**, rearrange, disorganize, disorder, mix up, interfere with; confuse, throw into disorder/confusion, derange, get into a tangle; unsettle, convulse, turn upside down, make a mess of.
3 *the surface waters are constantly disturbed by winds*: **agitate**, churn up, stir up, whisk, beat, convulse, ruffle; literary roil.
4 *he wasn't disturbed by all the allegations*: **perturb**, trouble, concern, worry, upset; agitate, fluster, discomfit, disconcert, dismay, distress, discompose, unsettle, ruffle, stir up; alarm, frighten, startle, shake; confuse, bewilder, perplex, confound, daze, excite.
5 *his mother had told him not to disturb himself*: **inconvenience**, put out, put to trouble, discommode.

disturbance noun 1 *we oppose the new filling station because we are concerned about disturbance to local residents*: **disruption**, distraction, interference, bother, trouble, inconvenience, upset, annoyance, irritation; interruption, intrusion; harassment, molestation; informal hassle.
2 *the Tsar's policies gave rise to disturbances among the peasantry*: **riot**, fracas, affray, upheaval, brawl, street fight, melee, free-for-all; uproar, commotion, row, ruckus, furore, tumult, turmoil; W. Indian bangarang; informal ruction, hullabaloo, rumpus.
3 *the seal disappeared underwater, leaving ripples of disturbance*: **agitation**, churning (up), stirring (up), whisking, beating, convulsion, ruffling; literary roiling.
▷ANTONYMS stillness.
4 *poor educational performance is related to emotional disturbance*: **trouble**, perturbation, distress, concern, worry, upset; **agitation**, discomposure, discomfiture, dismay, fluster, alarm; **neurosis**, illness, sickness, disorder, complaint; bewilderment, perplexity; rare disconcertion, disconcertment.
▷ANTONYMS stability.

disturbed adjective 1 *he woke early after a disturbed sleep*: **disrupted**, interrupted, fitful, disconnected, discontinuous, intermittent, fragmentary, broken.
▷ANTONYMS undisturbed.
2 *a home for disturbed children*: **troubled**, distressed, unsettled, upset, distraught; unbalanced, unstable, disordered, dysfunctional, maladjusted, ill-adjusted; **neurotic**, emotionally confused, unhinged; informal screwed up, mixed up, messed up, hung up.
▷ANTONYMS well adjusted.

disturbing adjective *this is disturbing news*: **worrying**, perturbing, troubling, upsetting; distressing, agitating, discomfiting, disconcerting, disquieting, unsettling, off-putting, dismaying, discomposing; alarming, frightening, threatening, startling, devastating; informal gut-wrenching.

disunion noun *his rejection of disunion was consistent with his nationalism*: **breaking up**, dismantling, separation, dissolution, partition; splitting, parting, severance, schism.
▷ANTONYMS federation.

disunite verb *these nations are never to be disunited*: **break up**, separate, divide, split up, partition, segregate, part, dismantle; sever, disjoin, disperse; archaic sunder, rive.
▷ANTONYMS unite, unify.

disunity noun *there was disunity within the administration*: **disagreement**, dissent, dissension, argument, arguing, quarrelling, difference of opinion, feuding; conflict, strife, friction, discord, division, disharmony, acrimony, disaffection, disaccord, discordance.
▷ANTONYMS unity.

disuse noun *many of the mills fell into disuse*: **non-use**, non-employment, lack of use; **neglect**, abandonment, desertion; cessation, discontinuance, obsolescence; formal desuetude.
▷ANTONYMS use, employment.

disused adjective *a disused building*: **unused**, no longer in use, fallen into disuse, unemployed, idle; neglected, abandoned, deserted, vacated, evacuated, unoccupied, uninhabited, empty; discontinued, obsolete, defunct, superannuated, moribund.
▷ANTONYMS in use.

ditch noun *she rescued an animal from a ditch*: **trench**, trough, channel, dyke, drain, gutter, gully, moat, duct, watercourse, conduit; ha-ha; technical fosse; historical sap; rare fleet.
▸verb 1 *they started draining and ditching the coastal areas*: **dig a ditch in**, provide with ditches, trench, excavate, drain.
2 informal *she decided to ditch her old curtains | the plans were ditched following a public inquiry*: **throw out**, throw away, discard, get rid of, dispose of, do away with, shed; abandon, drop, shelve, scrap, jettison, throw on the scrap heap; informal dump, junk, scrub, axe, get shut of, chuck (away/out), pull the plug on, knock on the head; Brit. informal get shot of; N. Amer. informal trash.
▷ANTONYMS keep.
3 informal *she ditched her husband to marry the window cleaner*: **break up with**, jilt, cast aside, throw over, finish with; leave, desert, abandon, turn one's back on, leave high and dry, leave in the lurch; informal dump, drop, chuck, run out on, walk out on, give someone the elbow, give someone the heave-ho, leave someone holding the baby; Brit. informal give someone the push, give someone the big E; archaic forsake.

dither verb *they wasted several minutes while she dithered*: **hesitate**, falter, waver, teeter, vacillate, oscillate, fluctuate, change one's mind, be in two minds, be ambivalent, be indecisive, be unsure, be undecided; procrastinate, hang back, delay, stall, temporize, drag one's feet, dawdle, dally; Brit. hum and haw, haver; Scottish swither; informal shilly-shally, dilly-dally, blow hot and cold, pussyfoot around, sit on the fence.

diurnal adjective **1** *the patient's mood is determined by diurnal events*: **daily**, everyday, day-to-day, quotidian; occurring every day, occurring each day; technical circadian.
2 *flight demands good eyesight, so birds tend to be diurnal | a diurnal predator*: **active during the day**, non-nocturnal; daytime.

d

divan noun *Zoe curled up on a divan*: **day bed**, sofa bed; **settee**, sofa, couch; Brit. put-you-up; N. Amer. davenport, studio couch.

dive verb **1** *they strip off and dive into the clear water | the plane was diving towards the ground*: **plunge**, plummet, nosedive, descend, jump, fall, drop, swoop, pitch, bellyflop.
2 *the islanders dive for oysters*: **swim under water**, go under water, submerge, sink; snorkel, scuba dive.
3 *he opened fire, forcing them to dive for cover*: **leap**, jump, lunge, launch oneself, throw oneself, go headlong, bolt, dart, dash, rush, scurry; duck, dodge.
▸ noun **1** *he made daredevil dives into the pool*: **plunge**, plummet, nosedive, descent, jump, fall, drop, swoop, pitch, bellyflop; archaic plump.
2 *she made a sideways dive between a couple of stalls*: **lunge**, spring, jump, leap, bolt, dart, dash, dodge.
3 informal *John got into a fight in some dive*: **sleazy bar**, sleazy nightclub, drinking den; informal drinking joint, seedy joint, dump, hole.

diverge verb **1** *the two roads diverged*: **separate**, part, disunite, fork, branch off, divide, subdivide, split, go in different directions, go separate ways; technical bifurcate, divaricate, ramify.
▹ANTONYMS converge.
2 *there are inevitably areas where our views diverge*: **differ**, be different, be unlike, be dissimilar; disagree, be at variance, be at odds, be incompatible, come into conflict, conflict, clash.
▹ANTONYMS agree.
3 *suddenly he diverged from his text*: **deviate**, digress, depart, veer, swerve, turn away, turn aside, branch off, drift, stray; ramble, wander, meander, maunder; get sidetracked, stray from the point, get off the subject; rare divagate.

divergence noun **1** *the divergence of the human and great ape lineages*: **separation**, dividing, parting, forking, branching; fork, division; technical bifurcation.
2 *there is a marked political divergence between them*: **difference**, dissimilarity, variance, polarity, disparity, contrast; disagreement, discrepancy, incompatibility, mismatch, conflict, clash; rare unlikeness, dissimilitude.
▹ANTONYMS similarity.
3 *they record any divergence from standard behaviour*: **deviation**, digression, departure, shift, drift, drifting, straying, deflection, wandering, moving away; variation, change, alteration; rare divagation.

divergent adjective **1** *they adopted divergent approaches to almost every issue*: **differing**, varying, different, dissimilar, unlike, unalike, disparate, contrasting, contrastive, antithetical; opposed, disagreeing, conflicting, clashing, incompatible, contradictory; at odds, at variance, in opposition.
▹ANTONYMS similar.
2 *divergent statistical results*: **separating**, divagating, deviating, digressing, abnormal, aberrant.

Word toolkit

divergent	varying	dissimilar
views	degrees	materials
sequences	sizes	systems
opinions	levels	characters
paths	ages	elements
interests	lengths	triangles
goals	shades	species

divers adjective literary *he stood accused of divers abuses and misdemeanours*. See **several** (sense 1).

diverse adjective *the company has to manage data from diverse databases*: **various**, many and various, sundry, manifold, multiple; varied, varying, miscellaneous, assorted, mixed, diversified, divergent, variegated, heterogeneous; different, differing, distinct, unlike, dissimilar, distinctive, contrasting, conflicting; informal a mixed bag of; literary divers, myriad, legion; rare contrastive.
▹ANTONYMS similar, uniform.

Word toolkit

diverse	sundry	manifold
backgrounds	items	problems
population	expenses	sins
cultures	lists	forms
interests	knick-knacks	effects
needs	relatives	benefits

diversify verb **1** *farmers were forced to look for ways to diversify*: **branch out**, vary output, expand, enlarge operations, extend operations, spread one's wings, broaden one's horizons.
2 *the government launched a plan aimed at diversifying the economy*: **vary**, bring variety to, variegate, mix; modify, alter, change, transform; expand, enlarge, widen; rare permutate.

diversion noun **1** *the development requires the diversion of 19 rivers*: **re-routing**, redirection, turning aside, deflection, digression, deviation, divergence.
2 *there are traffic diversions along roads into Wales*: **detour**, deviation, alternative route, bypass.
3 *the bomb threats were intended to create a diversion*: **distraction**, disturbance, smokescreen.
4 *London is a city full of diversions | she was desperate for a little diversion*: **entertainment**, amusement, recreation, pastime, game, hobby; fun, relaxation, rest and relaxation, relief, play, pleasure, delight, merriment, enjoyment, beguilement; informal jollies, R and R; N. Amer. informal rec; dated sport; rare divertissement.

diversity noun *a diversity of abstract design styles | a land of astonishing geographical diversity*: **variety**, miscellany, assortment, mixture, mix, melange, range, array, medley, multiplicity; variation, variance, diverseness, diversification, variegation, heterogeneity, difference, unlikeness, dissimilarity, dissimilitude, distinctiveness, contrast.
▹ANTONYMS uniformity.

divert verb **1** *they planned to divert Siberia's rivers to desert areas*: **re-route**, redirect, change the course of, draw away, turn aside, head off, deflect, avert, transfer, channel.
2 *he diverted her from her studies*: **distract**, detract, sidetrack, lead away, draw away, be a distraction, put off, disturb someone's concentration.
▹ANTONYMS focus.
3 *only a richly variegated story can divert them*: **amuse**, entertain, distract, titillate, delight, give pleasure to, beguile, enchant, interest, fascinate, occupy, absorb, engross, rivet, grip, hold the attention of; informal tickle someone's fancy, tickle pink, bowl over, be a hit with; archaic recreate.
▹ANTONYMS bore.

diverting adjective *a diverting comedy about two New York kids*: **entertaining**, amusing, fun, enjoyable, pleasurable, pleasing, pleasant, agreeable, delightful, appealing, beguiling, captivating, engaging, interesting, fascinating, intriguing, absorbing, riveting, compelling; humorous, funny, chucklesome, witty, droll, comical, hilarious.
▹ANTONYMS boring.

divest verb **1** *he intends to* ***divest*** *you* ***of*** *all your power*: **deprive**, strip, dispossess, relieve; rob, cheat out of, trick out of, do out of; informal diddle out of; literary despoil; archaic reave.
2 dated *she* ***divested*** *him* ***of*** *his coat*: **strip**, relieve, denude; remove, take off, pull off, peel off, shed; unclothe, undress, disrobe; dated doff.

divide verb **1** *he divided his kingdom into four*: **split**, cut up, cleave, carve up, slice up, chop up, split up; dissect, bisect, halve, quarter; archaic sunder, rive; rare fractionate, disjoin.
▹ANTONYMS unify, join.
2 *a curtain divided her cabin from the galley*: **separate**, segregate, partition, detach, disconnect, screen off, section off, split off, demarcate, distinguish; sever, rend.
▹ANTONYMS unify, join.
3 *the stairs divide at the mezzanine*: **diverge**, separate, part, branch, branch off, fork, split, split in two, go in different directions, go separate ways; technical divaricate, bifurcate, furcate, ramify.
▹ANTONYMS converge.
4 *the time came to divide Aunt Bessie's property | Jack* ***divided up*** *the rest of the cash*: **share out**, allocate, allot, apportion, portion out, ration out, measure out, mete out, parcel out, deal out, dole out, hand out, distribute, dispense; split, carve up, slice up, break up; informal divvy up, dish out; rare admeasure.
5 *he aimed to divide and defeat his party's opponents*: **disunite**, drive apart, break up, split up; detach, divorce, separate, isolate, estrange, alienate, disaffect; set against one another, pit against one another, cause disagreement among, sow dissension among, drive a wedge between, set at variance, set at odds, come between; archaic sunder, tear asunder; rare dichotomize, factionalize, dissever.
▹ANTONYMS unite.
6 *biologists divide living things into three broad categories*: **classify**, sort,

sort out, categorize, order, group, pigeonhole, grade, rank; organize, arrange, dispose; separate, segregate, partition.
▷ANTONYMS combine.

▶ noun *the divide between the sacred and secular*: **breach**, gulf, gap, split, divergence, differentiation; borderline, boundary, dividing line.

dividend noun **1** *the shareholder receives a substantial annual dividend*: **share**, portion, percentage, premium, return, payback, gain, surplus, profit; informal cut, take, rake-off, divvy, whack, slice of the cake, piece of the action, pickings.
2 *the research will produce dividends for future heart patients*: **benefit**, advantage, gain, bonus, extra, added extra, plus, fringe benefit, additional benefit; informal perk; formal perquisite.
▷ANTONYMS disadvantage.

divination noun *she looked to divination for guidance when important decisions loomed*: **fortune telling**, divining, foretelling the future, forecasting the future, prophecy, prediction, soothsaying, augury; **clairvoyance**, second sight; magic, sorcery, witchcraft, spell-working; rare vaticination, sortilege, auspication, witchery.

> *Word links* **divination**
>
> **-mancy** related suffix, as in *necromancy*
> **mantic** relating to divination

divine[1] adjective **1** *Jesus is one person in both divine and human natures | he asked for divine guidance*: **godly**, godlike, angelic, seraphic, saintly, beatific; spiritual, heavenly, celestial, holy; rare empyrean, deiform, deific.
▷ANTONYMS mortal.
2 *he could not be persuaded to attend divine worship*: **religious**, holy, sacred, sanctified, consecrated, blessed, devotional, devoted to God, dedicated to God.
3 informal *don't you think he looks rather divine? | we ate the most divine food*: **lovely**, handsome, beautiful, good-looking, prepossessing, charming, delightful, appealing, engaging, winsome, ravishing, gorgeous, bewitching, beguiling; wonderful, glorious, marvellous, excellent, superlative, perfect; delicious, mouth-watering, delectable; Scottish & N. English bonny; informal heavenly, sublime, dreamy, sensational, knockout, stunning, super, great, tasty, fanciable, easy on the eye, a sight for sore eyes, as nice as pie; Brit. informal brilliant, brill, smashing; N. Amer. informal cute; Austral./NZ informal beaut; formal beauteous; dated taking; archaic comely, fair; rare sightly.
▷ANTONYMS mundane; dreadful.

▶ noun *puritan divines were concentrated on the salvation of the human soul*: **theologian**, clergyman, member of the clergy, churchman, churchwoman, cleric, ecclesiastic, man of the cloth, man of God, holy man, holy woman, preacher, priest; Scottish kirkman; informal reverend, Holy Joe, sky pilot; Austral. informal josser.

> *Word toolkit* **divine**
>
> See **heavenly**.

divine[2] verb **1** *Fergus had divined how afraid she was*: **guess**, surmise, conjecture, suspect, suppose, assume, presume, deduce, infer, work out, theorize, hypothesize; **discern**, intuit, perceive, recognize, see, realize, appreciate, understand, grasp, apprehend, comprehend; N. Amer. figure; informal figure out, latch on to, cotton on to, catch on to, tumble to, get, get the picture; Brit. informal twig, suss; N. Amer. informal savvy; rare cognize.
2 *they had divined through omens that this was an auspicious day*: **foretell**, predict, prophesy, forecast, foresee, prognosticate; forewarn, forebode; archaic previse, presage, foreshow, croak; Scottish archaic spae; rare vaticinate, auspicate.
3 *he divined water supplies for desert troops*: **dowse**, find by dowsing.

diviner noun *she asked a diviner about her son's prospects*: **fortune teller**, **clairvoyant**, crystal-gazer, visionary, psychic, seer, soothsayer, prognosticator, prophesier, prophet, prophetess, oracle, sibyl, sage, wise man, wise woman; Scottish spaewife, spaeman; rare oracler, vaticinator, haruspex.

divinity noun **1** *the divinity of Christ*: **divine nature**, divineness, godliness, deity, godhead, holiness, sanctity, sanctitude, sacredness, blessedness.
2 *they persuaded him to read mathematics, not divinity*: **theology**, religious studies, religion, scripture.
3 *the ancient religions worshipped a female divinity*: **deity**, god, goddess, mother goddess, divine being, celestial being, supreme being; creator, demiurge; godhead; daemon, numen, power; Hinduism avatar.

division noun **1** *they protested against the division of the island | a special kind of cell division*: **dividing**, dividing up, breaking up, break-up, cutting up, carving up, severance, splitting, dissection, bisection, cleaving; **partitioning**, separation, segregation, disconnection, detachment.
2 *she supervised the division of his estates*: **sharing out**, dividing up, parcelling out, allocation, allotment, apportionment, distribution, dispensation, disbursement; splitting up, carving up, slicing up; informal divvying up, dishing out.
▷ANTONYMS integration.
3 *the division between nomadic and urban cultures*: **dividing line**, divide, boundary, boundary line, borderline, border, partition, margin, demarcation line, line of demarcation, cut-off point.
4 *each of these classes is divided into nine divisions*: **section**, subsection, subdivision, part, portion, piece, bit, segment, slice, fragment, chunk, component, share; compartment, category, class, group, grouping, set, order, batch, family.
5 *an independent division of the Health and Safety Executive*: **department**, branch, arm, wing, sector, section, subsection, subdivision, subsidiary, detachment, office, bureau, offshoot, satellite, extension.
6 *the causes of social division were analysed*: **disunity**, disunion, conflict, discord, disagreement, dissension, disaffection, estrangement, alienation, isolation, detachment; variance, difference; difference of opinion, feud, breach, rupture, split, chasm; informal falling-out; rare scission.
▷ANTONYMS unity.

> *Word links* **division**
>
> **schizo-** related prefix, as in *schizocarp*

divisive adjective *they declared outrage at the divisive effects of government policy*: **alienating**, estranging, isolating, schismatic; discordant, disharmonious, inharmonious.
▷ANTONYMS unifying.

divorce noun **1** *his wife announced that she wanted a divorce | the church did not permit divorce*: **dissolution**, annulment, official separation, judicial separation, separation, disunion, break-up, split, split-up, severance, rupture, breach, parting; in Islamic law khula, talaq.
▷ANTONYMS marriage.
2 *there was a growing divorce between the church and people*: **separation**, division, severance, split, partition, disunity, disunion, distance, estrangement, alienation; variance, difference, schism, gulf, chasm.
▷ANTONYMS unity.

▶ verb **1** *she was a young child when her parents divorced | Rebecca divorced her husband*: **split up (with)**, end one's marriage (to), get a divorce (from), separate (from), part (from), split (from), break up (with), part company (with), dissolve one's marriage (to), annul one's marriage (to); repudiate; Brit. informal bust up (with).
▷ANTONYMS marry.
2 *what is learnt in school cannot be divorced from what happens outside*: **separate**, disconnect, divide, disunite, sever, disjoin, split, dissociate, detach, isolate, alienate, set apart, keep apart, cut off; archaic sunder; rare dissever.
▷ANTONYMS unite.

divulge verb *he refused to divulge Father O'Neill's whereabouts*: **disclose**, reveal, make known, tell, impart, communicate, pass on, publish, broadcast, proclaim, promulgate, declare; expose, uncover, make public, go public with, bring into the open, give away, let slip, let drop, blurt out, leak, confess, betray, admit, come out with; informal spill the beans about, let the cat out of the bag about, let on about, tell all about, blow the lid off, squeal about; Brit. informal blow the gaff on; archaic discover, unbosom.
▷ANTONYMS conceal.

dizzy adjective **1** *she loved spinning in circles and making herself dizzy*: **giddy**, light-headed, faint, weak, weak at the knees, unsteady, shaky, wobbly, off-balance; reeling, staggering, tottering, teetering; informal woozy, with legs like jelly, with rubbery legs; rare vertiginous.
2 *she was still dizzy from her long sleep*: **dazed**, confused, muddled, befuddled, bewildered, disoriented, disorientated, stupefied, groggy; informal woozy, muzzy, dopey, woolly, woolly-headed, not with it, discombobulated.
▷ANTONYMS clear-headed.
3 *the gondola cable car will take you to dizzy heights*: **giddy-making**, dizzy-making, causing dizziness, causing giddiness; rare vertiginous.
4 informal *she's not as dizzy as she sounds*: **silly**, foolish, giddy, light-headed, scatty, scatterbrained, feather-brained, hare-brained, empty-headed, vacuous, stupid, brainless; skittish, flighty, fickle, capricious, whimsical, inconstant; informal dippy, dopey, batty, dotty, nutty; N. Amer. informal ditzy.
▷ANTONYMS sensible; intelligent.

do verb **1** *she is expected to do most of the manual work*: **carry out**, undertake, discharge, execute, perpetrate, perform, accomplish, implement, achieve, complete, finish, conclude; bring about, engineer, effect, realize; informal pull off; rare effectuate.
2 *they are free to do as they please*: **act**, behave, conduct oneself, acquit oneself; rare comport oneself, deport oneself.
3 *if you can't get espresso, regular coffee will do*: **suffice**, be adequate, be satisfactory, be acceptable, be good enough, be of use, fill the bill, fit the bill, answer the purpose, serve the purpose, meet one's needs, pass muster; be enough, be sufficient; informal make the grade, cut the mustard, be up to snuff.
4 *the boys will do the dinner when they get home*: **prepare**, make, get ready, fix, produce, see to, arrange, organize, be responsible for, be in charge of, look after, take on.

5 *he noticed a portrait I had been doing | the company have done a small range of V-neck tops*: **paint**, draw, sketch; **make**, create, produce, turn out, fashion, design, fabricate, manufacture; informal knock up, knock together, knock off.
6 *each room was done in a different colour*: **decorate**, furnish, adorn, ornament, embellish; deck out, trick out, trim; informal do up; Brit. informal tart up.
7 *her maid would dress her and then do her hair*: **style**, arrange, adjust, groom, preen, primp, prink; brush, comb, wash, dry, cut; informal fix.
8 *I was doing a show to raise money for our local scouts*: **put on**, present, produce, give; perform in, act in, play in, take part in, participate in, be involved in, be engaged in.
9 *thanks—you've done me a favour*: **grant**, pay, render, afford, give, bestow.
10 *I'm doing the VAT on a multiple dispatch | show me how these equations should be done*: **work out**, figure out, calculate, add up; solve, resolve, puzzle out, decipher; Brit. tot up.
11 *she's doing archaeology at university*: **study**, read, learn, take a course in, take classes in, be taught.
12 *what does he do?* **do for a living**, work at, be employed as, earn a living as/at; what is ...'s job?.
13 *he was doing well at college*: **get on**, get along, progress, fare, make out, get by, manage, cope, survive; succeed, prosper.
14 *he was caught doing 80mph in a 50mph area*: **drive at**, travel at, go at, proceed at, move at.
15 *the cyclists do 30 to 40 miles per day*: **travel**, journey, go, cover, travel over, pass over, journey over, traverse, cross, range over, put behind one, get under one's belt, attain, achieve, log; informal chalk up, notch up.
16 informal *we're doing Scotland this summer*: **visit**, tour, sightsee in, look around/round, take in the sights of.
□ **do away with 1** *they want to do away with the old customs*: **abolish**, quash, get rid of, discard, remove, eliminate, discontinue, cancel, stop, end, terminate, put an end to, put a stop to, call a halt to, dispense with, drop, abandon, give up; informal bin, scrap, ditch, dump, axe, cut out, pack in, get shut of, pull the plug on, knock something on the head, give something the chop; Brit. informal get shot of. ▷ANTONYMS uphold.
2 *she tried to do away with her husband*: **kill**, put to death, do to death, put an end to, finish off, take the life of, end the life of, murder, assassinate, execute, slaughter, butcher, wipe out, mow down, shoot down, cut down; dispatch, liquidate, exterminate, eliminate, eradicate, destroy; informal do in, bump off, knock off, polish off, top, take out, snuff out, snuff, erase, croak, stiff, zap, blow away, blow someone's brains out, give someone the works; N. Amer. informal ice, off, rub out, waste, whack, scrag, smoke; N. Amer. euphemistic terminate with extreme prejudice; literary slay.
□ **do someone/something down** informal *he loves an opportunity to do down his colleagues*: **belittle**, disparage, denigrate, run down, deprecate, depreciate, cast aspersions on, discredit, vilify, defame, decry, criticize, abuse, insult, malign; N. Amer. slur; informal do a hatchet job on, take to pieces, take apart, pull apart, pick holes in, drag through the mud, have a go at, hit out at, knock, slam, pan, bash, bad-mouth, look down one's nose at; Brit. informal rubbish, slate, slag off; rare asperse, derogate, minify.
□ **do for someone** informal **1** *if we lose those values, we are done for*: **ruin**, destroy, reduce to nothing, spoil, mar, injure, blight, shatter, scotch, mess up; Brit. informal scupper; Austral. informal euchre; vulgar slang fuck up; archaic bring to naught. **2** *it was drink that did for him*: **kill**, cause the death of, take/end the life of, finish off; informal polish off, do in, knock off, take out; literary slay.
□ **do someone/something in** informal **1** *the poor devil's been done in*: **kill**, put to death, do to death, put an end to, finish off, take the life of, end the life of, murder, assassinate, execute, slaughter, butcher, wipe out, mow down, shoot down, cut down; dispatch, liquidate, exterminate, eliminate, eradicate, destroy; informal do away with, bump off, knock off, polish off, top, take out, snuff out, snuff, erase, croak, stiff, zap, blow away, blow someone's brains out, give someone the works; N. Amer. informal ice, off, rub out, waste, whack, scrag, smoke; N. Amer. euphemistic terminate with extreme prejudice; literary slay. **2** *the long walk home did me in*: **wear out**, tire out, exhaust, fatigue, weary, overtire, drain, prostrate, enervate, devitalize; informal fag out, shatter, whack, poop, take it out of. **3** *I did my back in and I can't work any more*: **injure**, hurt, damage, maim, cripple, disable, paralyse; Brit. informal knacker.
□ **do something out** Brit. informal *the basement is done out in limed oak*: **decorate**, furnish, adorn, ornament, embellish; deck out, trick out, trim; informal do up; Brit. informal tart up.
□ **do someone out of something** *he tried to do them out of their livestock profits*: **swindle out of**, cheat out of, trick out of, prevent from having, prevent from gaining, deprive of, dispossess of, rob of, strip of, relieve of; informal con out of, diddle out of.
□ **do someone over** informal *some men had been sent to do him over*: **beat up**, assault, attack, mug, batter, thrash, pummel, pound; informal knock about/around, work over, clobber, rough up, fill in, beat the living daylights out of, let someone have it; Brit. informal have a go at, duff someone up; N. Amer. informal beat up on.
□ **do something up 1** *she stopped to do her bootlace up*: **fasten**, tie, tie up, lace, knot, make a knot in, tie a bow in; make fast, secure, bind, tighten. ▷ANTONYMS undo. **2** informal *he's had his house done up*: **renovate**, refurbish, refit, restore, redecorate, decorate, revamp, make over, modernize, improve, spruce up, smarten up, brighten up, prettify, enhance; informal fix up, vamp up, give something a facelift; Brit. informal tart up, posh up; N. Amer. informal rehab.
□ **do without** *they were forced to do without certain bodily comforts*: **forgo**, dispense with, abstain from, refrain from, eschew, give up, renounce, forswear, swear off, keep off, keep away from, manage without; informal lay off, cut out, quit, give something a miss.
□ **have nothing to do with** *we have nothing to do with it and ignore it*: **steer clear of**, avoid, shun, evade, eschew, shy away from, fight shy of, recoil from, keep away from, keep one's distance from, give a wide berth to, leave alone; **snub**, give someone the cold shoulder, cold-shoulder, ignore, turn one's back on.
□ **have something to do with** *what does this have to do with me? | training has nothing to do with strength*: **relate to**, apply to, be relevant to, have relevance to, concern, refer to, have reference to, belong to, pertain to, be pertinent to, bear on, have a bearing on, appertain to, affect, involve, cover, touch; archaic regard.
▶**noun** Brit. informal *he invited us to this do in his mansion*: **party**, reception, gathering, celebration, function, affair, event, social event, social occasion, social function, social; French soirée; W. Indian jump-up; Jewish simcha; N. Amer. levee; informal bash, blowout, rave, shindig, shindy, shebang, junket; Brit. informal rave-up, thrash, knees-up, jolly, beanfeast, bunfight, beano; Austral./NZ informal shivoo, rage, jollo; S. African informal jol; informal, dated ding-dong.

docile adjective *Alex was of a docile nature and readily deferred to his parents*: **compliant**, obedient, pliant, dutiful, willing, passive, submissive, deferential, tame, meek, mild, lamblike, unassertive, unresisting, yielding, cooperative, amenable, accommodating, biddable, persuadable, ductile, manageable, controllable, tractable, malleable, manipulable, easily manipulated, easily handled, like putty in one's hands; informal, dated milky; rare persuasible.
▷ANTONYMS disobedient; wilful.

> *Choose the right word* **docile, obedient, biddable, compliant, dutiful**
>
> See **obedient**.

dock[1] noun *his boat was moored at the end of the dock*: **harbour**, marina, waterfront, port, anchorage; wharf, quay, pier, jetty, landing stage; dockyard, boatyard; archaic hithe; rare moorage, harbourage.
▶**verb** *the ship docked and began debarking troops*: **moor**, berth, land, beach, anchor, drop anchor, put in, tie up.
▷ANTONYMS put to sea.

dock[2] verb **1** *they enforce payment by docking money from the father's salary*: **deduct**, subtract, remove, debit, discount, take off, take away; informal knock off, minus.
▷ANTONYMS add.
2 *workers had their pay docked by three quarters*: **reduce**, cut, cut back, decrease, lessen, diminish.
▷ANTONYMS increase.
3 *the dog's tail is docked close to the body*: **cut off**, cut short, shorten, crop, lop, prune, truncate; remove, amputate, detach, disconnect, sever, hack off, chop off, take off; rare dissever.

docket Brit. noun *they write out an individual docket for every transaction*: **document**, chit, coupon, voucher, certificate, counterfoil, bill, receipt, sales slip, proof of purchase; label, tag, ticket, tab; documentation, paperwork; Brit. informal chitty; Law, dated acquittance.
▶**verb** *neatly docketed bundles*: **document**, record, register, log; label, tag, tab, mark, ticket.

doctor noun *Tim isn't well but he refuses to see a doctor*: **physician**, medical practitioner, medical man, medical woman, clinician, doctor of medicine, MD; Navy surgeon; informal doc, medic, medico, quack; archaic leech, sawbones.
▶**verb 1** informal *he doctored the horses' wounds with some strong-smelling salve*: **treat**, medicate, dose, soothe, cure, heal; tend, attend to, minister to, administer to, care for, take care of, nurse.
2 *he denied doctoring Stephen's drinks*: **adulterate**, contaminate, taint, tamper with, lace, mix, dilute, water down, thin out, weaken; informal spike, dope, cut, slip a Mickey Finn into; rare vitiate.
3 *the reports are bland and could have been doctored*: **falsify**, tamper with, tinker with, interfere with, manipulate, massage, rig, alter, change; forge, fake, trump up; fudge, pervert, distort; informal cook, juggle; Brit. informal fiddle (with).

> *Word links* **doctor**
>
> **iatro-** related prefix, as in *iatrogenic*

doctrinaire adjective *she is by no means a doctrinaire conservative*: **dogmatic**, rigid, inflexible, uncompromising, unyielding, holding fixed views, adamant, insistent, pontifical; authoritarian, domineering,

opinionated, intolerant, biased, prejudiced, fanatical, zealous, extreme.
▷ANTONYMS liberal; flexible.

doctrine noun *they rejected the doctrine of the Trinity*: **creed**, credo, dogma, belief, set of beliefs, code of belief, conviction, teaching; tenet, maxim, article of faith, canon; principle, precept, notion, idea, ideology, theory, thesis.

document noun *their solicitor drew up a document*: **official paper**, legal paper, paper, form, certificate, deed, charter, contract, legal agreement; record, report; Law instrument, indenture, acquittance; (**documents**) paperwork, documentation; informal treeware.
▸ verb *many aspects of school life have been documented*: **record**, register, report, log, chronicle, file, archive, catalogue, put on record, commit to paper, set down, take down, write down, set down in writing, set down in black and white, write about; detail, note, describe, cite, instance; tabulate, chart; rare diarize.

documentary adjective **1** *there is documentary evidence that a corn mill stood here in the 14th century*: **recorded**, documented, registered, written, chronicled, archived, archive, on record, in writing, on paper; tabulated, charted.
2 *the event will be the subject of a documentary film*: **factual**, non-fictional, real-life, true to life, fact-based.
▷ANTONYMS fictional.
▸ noun *the BBC showed a documentary about life in rural England*: **factual programme**, factual film; programme, film, report, presentation, broadcast, transmission.

dodder verb *the old couple doddered out of the hotel lounge*: **totter**, teeter, toddle, hobble, shuffle, shamble, falter, walk haltingly, walk with difficulty, move falteringly, stumble, stagger, sway, lurch, reel; wobble, shake, tremble, quiver; Scottish & N. English hirple; rare doddle.

doddering adjective *a doddering old man with an ear trumpet*: **tottering**, tottery, teetering, doddery, staggering, shuffling, shambling, faltering, shaking, shaky, unsteady, wobbly, wobbling, trembling, trembly, quivering; feeble, frail, weak, weakly, infirm, decrepit; aged, old, elderly, long in the tooth, in one's dotage, senile.
▷ANTONYMS sprightly.

doddery adjective *a doddery old lady*. See **doddering**.

dodge verb **1** *she dodged into a telephone booth*: **dart**, bolt, duck, dive, swerve, body-swerve, sidestep, veer, lunge, jump, leap, spring.
2 *he could easily dodge the two coppers in the car*: **elude**, evade, avoid, stay away from, steer clear of, escape, run away from, break away from, lose, leave behind, shake, shake off, fend off, keep at arm's length, give someone a wide berth, keep one's distance from; deceive, trick, cheat; N. Amer. end-run; informal ditch, give someone the slip.
3 *the Secretary of State may try to dodge the debate*: **avoid**, evade, shun, get out of, slide out of, back out of, steer clear of, sidestep, circumvent, skirt round, bypass, give something a miss, find a way out of; informal duck, wriggle out of, cop out of; Brit. informal funk, skive, skive off; N. Amer. informal cut; Austral./NZ informal duck-shove; archaic decline, bilk.
▷ANTONYMS face up to, tackle.
▸ noun **1** *he made a dodge to the right*: **dart**, bolt, duck, dive, swerve, jump, leap, spring.
2 *a clever dodge for covering up the car's real origins | a tax dodge*: **ruse**, ploy, scheme, tactic, stratagem, subterfuge, trick, hoax, wile, cheat, deception, blind, pretext, manoeuvre, device, machination, contrivance, artifice, expedient; swindle, fraud, loophole; informal scam, con, con trick, set-up, wangle; Brit. informal **wheeze**; N. Amer. informal **bunco**, **grift**; Austral. informal **lurk**, rort; Brit. informal, dated **flanker**; archaic **shift**.

dodgy adjective Brit. informal **1** *a dodgy second-hand car salesman*. See **dishonest**.
2 *the champagne was decidedly dodgy*: **second-rate**, third-rate, substandard, low-grade, low-quality, cheap; of low quality, of poor quality, not up to scratch, not up to par; awful, terrible, dreadful, woeful, dire, deplorable, unacceptable, unsatisfactory; Brit. cheap and nasty; N. Amer. cheapjack; informal cheapo, tenth-rate, not up to much; Brit. informal ropy, grotty, duff.

doer noun **1** *she is the doer of unspeakable deeds*: **performer**, perpetrator, executor, accomplisher, effectuator, operator, operative, agent, author.
2 *Daniel is a thinker more than a doer*: **worker**, organizer, activist, man of action, achiever, high achiever, succeeder, hustler, entrepreneur; informal mover and shaker, busy bee, eager beaver, live wire, go-getter, high-flyer, whizz kid, powerhouse, fireball, human dynamo, wheeler-dealer, success story.

doff verb dated *they doffed their coats*. See **take something off** (sense 2).

dog noun *she went for long walks with her dog*: **hound**, canine, mongrel, cur, tyke; **male dog**; bitch, pup, puppy, whelp; informal doggy, pooch, mutt; Austral. informal mong, bitzer.
□ **go to the dogs** informal *this country is definitely going to the dogs*: **deteriorate**, be in decline, degenerate, decay; collapse, slump, slip, slide, go downhill, go backwards, go to rack and ruin, stagnate, wane, ebb; informal go to pot, hit the skids, go down the toilet, go down the tubes; Austral./NZ informal go to the pack; rare retrograde.
▸ verb *they dogged him the length and breadth of the country | the scheme was dogged by bad weather*: **pursue**, follow, stalk, track, trail, shadow, hound; plague, beset, bedevil, assail, beleaguer, blight, trouble, torment, haunt; informal tail.

> *Word links* **dog**
>
> **canine** relating to dogs
> **dog** male
> **bitch** female
> **pup, puppy** young
> **pack** collective noun
> **cynophobia** fear of dogs

dogged adjective *he was a fine player and a dogged opening batsman*: **tenacious**, determined, resolute, resolved, purposeful, persistent, persevering, pertinacious, relentless, intent, dead set, single-minded, focused, dedicated, committed, undeviating, unshakeable, unflagging, indefatigable, untiring, never-tiring, tireless, unfailing, unfaltering, unwavering, unyielding, unbending, immovable, obdurate, strong-willed, firm, steadfast, steady, staunch, stout-hearted; archaic laborious; rare perseverant, indurate.
▷ANTONYMS hesitant; half-hearted.

dogma noun **1** *a dogma of the Sikh religion*: **teaching**, belief, conviction, tenet, principle, ethic, precept, maxim, article of faith, canon, law, rule; creed, credo, code of belief, set of beliefs, set of principles, doctrine, ideology, orthodoxy.
2 *they were urged to emancipate their minds from the fetters of dogma*: **blind faith**, unquestioning belief, certainty, invincible conviction, unchallengeable conviction, arrogant conviction.
▷ANTONYMS doubt; open-mindedness.

dogmatic adjective *he criticized the prime minister's strident, dogmatic style*: **opinionated**, **peremptory**, assertive, imperative, insistent, emphatic, adamant, doctrinaire, authoritarian, authoritative, domineering, imperious, high-handed, pontifical, arrogant, overbearing, dictatorial, uncompromising, unyielding, unbending, inflexible, rigid, entrenched, unquestionable, unchallengeable; intolerant, narrow-minded, small-minded.
▷ANTONYMS low-key, tentative; open-minded.

dogmatism noun *he avoided dogmatism and presented his subject as one open to debate*: **opinionatedness**, **peremptoriness**, assertiveness, imperativeness, doctrinairism, authoritarianism, imperiousness, high-handedness, arrogance, dictatorialness; inflexibility, rigidity, entrenchment, intolerance, narrow-mindedness, small-mindedness, bigotry.

dogsbody noun Brit. informal *she spent a year as a dogsbody in a Norwich theatre*: **drudge**, menial, menial worker, factotum, man of all work, maid of all work, servant, slave, galley slave, lackey, underling, minion; hewer of wood and drawer of water; informal gofer, running dog, runner, man/girl Friday; Brit. informal skivvy; N. Amer. informal peon; archaic scullion, servitor.

doing noun **1** *the doing of the act constitutes the offence*: **performance**, performing, carrying out, effecting, execution, implementation, implementing, bringing off, discharge, discharging, achievement, accomplishment, realization, completion, completing; informal pulling off; archaic acquittal; rare effectuation.
2 *he gave a brief account of his doings in Paris*: **exploit**, activity, act, action, undertaking, deed, feat, endeavour, work, venture, enterprise, achievement, accomplishment; (**doings**) performance, behaviour, conduct; handiwork; informal caper.
3 *it would take some doing to diffuse the situation*: **effort**, exertion, work, hard work, application, labour, toil, struggle, strain; pains; informal elbow grease; literary travail.
4 (**doings**) Brit. informal *he looked into the drawer where he kept the doings*: **thing**, whatever it is (called); informal **whatsit**, whatnot, doofer, thingummy, thingamajig, thingamabob, what's-its-name, what-d'you-call-it, oojamaflip, oojah, gizmo; Brit. informal doobry, doodah, gubbins; N. Amer. informal doodad, doohickey, doojigger, dingus, hootenanny.

doldrums plural noun *a fit of the winter doldrums*: **depression**, melancholy, gloom, gloominess, glumness, downheartedness, dejection, despondency, dispiritedness, heavy-heartedness, heartache, unhappiness, sadness, misery, woe, dismalness, despair, pessimism, hopelessness; inertia, apathy, listlessness, malaise, boredom, tedium, ennui; low spirits; informal blues; N. Amer. informal blahs.
▷ANTONYMS happiness.
□ **in the doldrums** *the property market is in the doldrums*: **inactive**, quiet, slow, slack, sluggish, subdued, stagnant, static, inert, flat, dull.
▷ANTONYMS busy, lively.

dole noun (**the dole**) Brit. informal *he was out of work and on the dole*: **unemployment benefit**, state benefit, government benefit, benefit, benefit payments, social security, social security payments, public assistance allowance, allowance, welfare, insurance money, grant; financial assistance; Scottish the buroo, the broo.

d

▶ verb
□ **dole something out** *Dad began to dole out the porridge*: **deal out**, share out, mete out, divide up, allocate, allot, apportion, assign, distribute, dispense, hand out, give out, pass out, pass round, issue, disburse; informal dish out, dish up, divvy up.

doleful adjective *she regarded him with doleful eyes*: **mournful**, woeful, sorrowful, sad, unhappy, depressed, dismal, gloomy, morose, melancholy, miserable, forlorn, wretched, woebegone, despondent, dejected, disconsolate, downcast, crestfallen, downhearted, heartbroken, heavy-hearted, despairing, desolate, grief-stricken; tearful, teary, lachrymose; informal blue, down, down in the mouth, down in the dumps, weepy; literary dolorous; archaic heartsick, heartsore.
▷ANTONYMS cheerful.

d

doll noun 1 *the child was sitting hugging a doll*: **puppet**, marionette, figure, figurine, model; **toy**, plaything; informal dolly.
2 informal *she was quite a doll, with good teeth and nice skin*: **beauty**, beautiful woman, attractive woman, belle, vision, Venus, goddess, beauty queen, English rose, picture; informal looker, good looker, stunner, lovely, knockout, bombshell, dish, cracker, smasher, peach, eyeful, sight for sore eyes, bit of alright.
▶ verb
□ **doll someone up** informal *she dolled herself up before he came round to dinner*: **dress up**, dress smartly, dress attractively; informal get up, do up, tog up, dress up to the nines, put on one's glad rags; Brit. informal tart up.
▷ANTONYMS dress down.

dollop noun informal *she had a little dollop of cream on her nose*: **blob**, glob, gobbet, lump, clump, ball, mound; Brit. informal gob, wodge.

dolorous adjective literary *a dolorous sigh*. See **doleful**.

dolour noun literary *the illness had long been a source of dolour to his brother*. See **sorrow**.

dolphin noun

Word links **dolphin**
school collective noun

dolt noun *he makes me feel like a dolt*: **fool**, nincompoop, clown, simpleton; informal idiot, ninny, dope, dimwit, chump, goon, dumbo, dummy, halfwit, nitwit, dum-dum, loon, jackass, cretin, imbecile, jerk, nerd, fathead, blockhead, numbskull, dunderhead, dunce, dipstick, bonehead, chucklehead, clod, goop, knucklehead, lamebrain, pea-brain, pudding-head, thickhead, wooden-head, pinhead, airhead, birdbrain, dumb-bell, donkey, stupe, noodle; Brit. informal nit, twit, numpty, clot, plonker, berk, prat, pillock, wally, git, wazzock, divvy, nerk, dork, twerp, charlie, mug, muppet; Scottish informal nyaff, balloon, sumph, gowk; Irish informal gobdaw; N. Amer. informal schmuck, bozo, boob, lamer, turkey, schlepper, chowderhead, dumbhead, goofball, goof, goofus, galoot, lummox, klutz, putz, schlemiel, sap, meatball, gink, cluck, clunk, ding-dong, dingbat, wiener, weeny, dip, simp, spud, coot, palooka, poop, squarehead, yo-yo, dingleberry; Austral./NZ informal drongo, dill, alec, galah, nong, bogan, poon, boofhead; S. African informal mompara; dated tomfool, muttonhead, noddy; archaic clodpole, loggerhead, spoony, mooncalf.

doltish adjective *the yokels are doltish but harmless*: **stupid**, idiotic, moronic, imbecilic, foolish, ignorant, simple, simple-minded, dense, brainless, mindless, dull-witted, dull, slow-witted, witless, half-witted, dunce-like, slow, cretinous, empty-headed, vacuous, vapid; gullible, naive; informal thick, thick as two short planks, dim, dopey, dumb, dozy, birdbrained, pea-brained, pig-ignorant, bovine, slow on the uptake, soft in the head, brain-dead, boneheaded, lamebrained, chuckleheaded, dunderheaded, wooden-headed, fat-headed, muttonheaded; Brit. informal daft, not the full shilling; N. Amer. informal dumb-ass.

domain noun 1 *they extended their domain by raiding neighbouring peoples | the garden was his domain*: **realm**, kingdom, empire, dominion, province, estate, territory, land, lands, dominions; state, country; **preserve**, zone, sphere, area, place; informal turf, spot, patch, stamping ground; Brit. informal manor.
2 *the report was very significant in the arts education domain*: **field**, area, arena, sphere, discipline, sector, section, region, province, world.

dome noun *the dome of St Paul's Cathedral*: **cupola**, vault, rotunda, arched roof, arched ceiling; mound, hemisphere.

domestic adjective 1 *her domestic commitments prevented her from returning to employment*: **family**, home, private; **household**, domiciliary.
▷ANTONYMS public.
2 *she was not at all domestic*: **housewifely**, domesticated, stay-at-home, home-loving, homely.
3 *I only treat small domestic animals*: **domesticated**, tame, pet, household, trained, not wild; Brit. house-trained; N. Amer. housebroken.
▷ANTONYMS wild.
4 *the domestic car manufacturing industry*: **national**, state, home, local, internal, interior, not foreign, not international.
▷ANTONYMS foreign, international.
5 *the flower garden housed domestic and exotic blooms*: **native**, indigenous, home-grown, home-bred, aboriginal; technical autochthonous.
▶ noun *all of the cleaning was undertaken by domestics*: **servant**, domestic servant, domestic worker, domestic help, hired help, home help, daily help, maid, housemaid, maid-of-all-work, cleaner, menial, housekeeper; Brit. dated charwoman, charlady, char; Brit. informal daily, daily woman, skivvy, Mrs Mop; archaic scullion.

domesticate verb 1 *the wild cat would have been troublesome for early man to domesticate*: **tame**, train, break in, gentle; master, subdue, subjugate, bring to heel; Brit. house-train.
2 *maize was first domesticated in Mexico*: **cultivate**, raise, rear; **naturalize**, establish, acclimatize, habituate, assimilate; N. Amer. acclimate.

domesticated adjective 1 *pollution harms wildlife and also domesticated animals*: **tame**, tamed, pet, domestic, broken-in; Brit. house-trained; N. Amer. housebroken.
▷ANTONYMS wild.
2 *the researchers are studying domesticated crops*: **naturalized**, acclimatized, habituated; cultivated.
▷ANTONYMS foreign; wild.
3 humorous *I like housework—I'm quite domesticated really*: **housewifely**, stay-at-home, home-loving, homely; Brit. informal house-trained; N. Amer. informal housebroken.

domicile formal noun *military service brings about frequent changes of domicile*: **residence**, **home**, house, address, residency, lodging, lodging place, accommodation, quarters, billet; informal pad; Brit. informal digs; formal dwelling, dwelling place, abode, habitation.
▶ verb (**be domiciled**) *born in the UK, he is now domiciled in Australia*: **settle**, establish oneself, live, make one's home, set up home, set up house, take up residence, put down roots, have one's domicile; go to live in, move to, emigrate to; N. Amer. set up housekeeping.

dominance noun *he is in a position of political dominance*: **supremacy**, superiority, ascendancy, pre-eminence, predominance, domination, dominion, mastery, power, authority, rule, command, control, sway, leverage, influence; literary puissance; rare predomination, paramountcy, prepotence, prepotency, prepollency.
▷ANTONYMS subservience, subjugation.

dominant adjective 1 *the dominant classes*: **presiding**, ruling, governing, controlling, commanding, ascendant, supreme, authoritative, most influential, most powerful, superior; rare prepotent, prepollent.
▷ANTONYMS subservient.
2 *he has a dominant personality*: **assertive**, self-assured, self-possessed, authoritative, forceful, domineering, commanding, controlling, bullish; informal feisty, not backward in coming forward, pushy; rare pushful.
▷ANTONYMS submissive.
3 *we will discuss the dominant issues in psychology*: **main**, principal, prime, premier, chief, cardinal, foremost, uppermost, leading, primary, predominant, most important, most prominent, paramount, pre-eminent, outstanding, prominent, prevailing; central, key, crucial, core, salient; informal number-one.
▷ANTONYMS secondary.

dominate verb 1 *the Romans dominated the parts of Britain that became England and Wales*: **control**, influence, exercise control over, be in control of, command, be in command of, be in charge of, rule, govern, direct, be the boss of, preside over, have ascendancy over, have mastery over, master, have the upper hand over; domineer, tyrannize, oppress, bully, intimidate, have the whip hand over, push around/about, boss (about/around), ride roughshod over, trample on, have under one's thumb; informal head up, call the shots, call the tune, be in the driver's seat, be in the saddle, be at the helm, rule the roost, lay down the law, walk all over; Brit. informal wear the trousers; N. Amer. informal have someone in one's hip pocket; literary sway.
2 *the Puritan work ethic still dominates*: **predominate**, prevail, reign, be prevalent, be paramount, be pre-eminent, be most important, be influential, be significant, be of consequence, be of account, count, matter, signify, carry weight, bulk large.
3 *the village is dominated by the railway viaduct*: **overlook**, command, tower above, tower over, stand over, project over, jut over, hang over, loom over, dwarf, overtop, overshadow, overhang; bestride, span, straddle, extend across.

domination noun *an evil empire bent on world domination*: **rule**, government, sovereignty, control, command, authority, power, dominion, dominance, mastery, supremacy, superiority, ascendancy, sway, influence; tyranny, intimidation, oppression, suppression, subjugation, dictatorship; the upper hand, the whip hand, the edge; rare paramountcy, prepotence, prepotency, prepollency.

domineer verb *all her life she was domineered by Granny*: **browbeat**, **bully**, intimidate, pressurize, menace, hector, boss (about/around), push around/about, order about/around, give orders to, lord it over, tyrannize, terrorize, persecute, oppress, dictate to, be overbearing, ride roughshod over, trample on, have under one's thumb, rule with an iron hand, rule with a rod of iron, use strong-arm tactics on, impose one's will on, bend to one's will, subjugate; informal bulldoze, walk all over, railroad, lean on, put the screws on, strong-arm, squeeze.

domineering adjective *he was brought up by a cold, domineering father*: **overbearing**, authoritarian, imperious, high-handed, high and mighty, autocratic, autarchic; officious, peremptory, bossy, arrogant, haughty, masterful, forceful, coercive, bullish, dictatorial, tyrannical, draconian, despotic, controlling, oppressive, subjugating, iron-fisted, iron-handed, strict, harsh, severe; informal throwing one's weight about; rare pushful.
▷ANTONYMS meek.

dominion noun **1** *France then decided to establish dominion over Laos and Cambodia*: **supremacy**, ascendancy, dominance, domination, superiority, predominance, pre-eminence, primacy, hegemony, authority, mastery, control, command, direction, power, sway, rule, government, jurisdiction, sovereignty, suzerainty, lordship, overlordship; leadership, influence; the upper hand, the whip hand, the edge, advantage, hold, grasp; archaic empire; rare predomination, paramountcy, prepotence, prepotency, prepollency.
2 *the country was a British dominion for over eighty years*: **dependency**, colony, protectorate, territory, province, outpost, satellite, satellite state; holding, possession; historical tributary, fief; archaic demesne; (**dominions**) realm, kingdom, empire, domain, country, nation, land.

don[1] noun *he had been a don at Oxford*: **university teacher**, (university) lecturer, fellow, professor, reader, lector, college tutor, academic, scholar; informal egghead; (**dons**) Brit. senior common room.

don[2] verb *he donned a heavy overcoat*: **put on**, get dressed in, dress (oneself) in, pull on, climb into, get into, fling on, throw on, slip into, slip on, change into, rig oneself out in, clothe oneself in, array oneself in, deck oneself out in, accoutre oneself in, put round one's shoulders, put on one's head; informal tog oneself up/out in, doll oneself up in, pour oneself into.
▷ANTONYMS take off.

donate verb *he donated his fee to charity*: **give**, give/make a donation of, make a gift of, contribute, make a contribution of, present, gift, subscribe, hand out, grant, bestow, pledge, put oneself down for, put up, come up with, accord; provide, supply, furnish; endow someone with, confer on someone; informal chip in, pitch in, fork out, dish out, shell out, cough up; Brit. informal stump up; N. Amer. informal kick in, ante up, pony up.
▷ANTONYMS keep; receive.

donation noun *his employer also made a donation to the fund*: **gift**, contribution, subscription, present, handout, grant, offering, gratuity, endowment; bestowal, giving; charity, benefaction, largesse; historical alms; rare donative.
▷ANTONYMS receipt.

done adjective **1** *a few days later the job was done*: **finished**, ended, concluded, terminated, complete, completed, finalized, accomplished, achieved, realized, fulfilled, perfected, consummated, discharged, settled, executed; informal wrapped up, sewn up, polished off, sorted out; rare effectuated.
▷ANTONYMS incomplete.
2 *is the meat done?* **cooked**, ready, cooked through, tender, crisp, browned.
▷ANTONYMS underdone; raw.
3 *those days are done*: **over**, at an end, finished, ended, concluded, terminated, no more, extinct, dead, run, gone, dead and gone, dead and buried, forgotten, over and done with, a thing of the past, in the past, ancient history.
▷ANTONYMS ongoing; to come.
4 informal *I can't do that—it's just not done*: **proper**, seemly, decorous, decent, respectable, right, correct, in order, suitable, fit, fitting, befitting, appropriate, apt; conventional, approved, accepted, acceptable, standard, usual, customary, traditional, orthodox; the done thing; French comme il faut; informal OK.
□ **be done with** *she was done with him*: **be/have finished with**, have done with, be through with, want no more to do with, have no further dealings with, turn one's back on, be no longer involved with/in, end relations with, give up, wash one's hands of, have no more truck with.
□ **done for** informal *if you're caught you will be done for*: **ruined**, finished, destroyed, broken, wrecked, undone, doomed, lost, defeated, beaten, foiled, frustrated, thwarted; informal toast, washed-up.
▷ANTONYMS safe; saved.
□ **done in** *you look done in*: **worn out**, exhausted, fatigued, tired, tired out, weary, wearied, strained, drained, worn, sapped, spent, washed out, on one's last legs; informal worn to a frazzle, done, all in, dog-tired, dead on one's feet, dead beat, fit to drop, played out, fagged out, shattered, bushed; Brit. informal knackered, whacked; N. Amer. informal pooped, tuckered out.
▷ANTONYMS fresh.
□ **have done with** *when I put something behind me I have done with it*: **be/have finished with**, be done with, be through with, want no more to do with, have no further dealings with, turn one's back on, be no longer involved with/in, end relations with, give up, wash one's hands of, have no more truck with.
▸ **exclamation** *'I'll lay three to one he's sane.' 'Done!'*: **agreed**, settled, all right, very well, that's a bargain, accepted, right; informal you're on, OK, okay, oke, okey-dokey, okey-doke; Brit. informal righto, righty-ho.

Don Juan noun *he was notorious as something of a Don Juan*: **womanizer**, philanderer, Casanova, Romeo, Lothario, flirt, ladies' man, playboy, seducer, rake, roué, libertine, debauchee, lecher; informal skirt-chaser, ladykiller, wolf, goat, lech; informal, dated gay dog.
▷ANTONYMS celibate.

donkey noun **1** *the cart was drawn by a donkey*: **ass**; jackass, jenny; mule, hinny; Spanish burro; Brit. informal moke, neddy; Scottish dated cuddy.
2 informal *you silly donkey!* See **fool**.
□ **donkey work** informal *he joked that he did most of the donkey work for the exhibition*: **work**, effort, endeavour, toil, labour, exertion, graft, the sweat of one's brow, drudgery; informal slog; Austral./NZ informal yakka.

Word links **donkey**

asinine relating to donkeys
jackass male
jennyass female

d

donnish adjective *you can never tell with these quiet, donnish types*: **scholarly**, studious, academic, scholastic, bookish, book-loving, intellectual, erudite, educated, learned, serious, earnest, thoughtful, cerebral, highbrow; pedantic; impractical, ivory-towerish; informal brainy, egghead; Brit. informal swotty; dated lettered; archaic clerkly.

donor noun *the cost has been met by a generous donor*: **giver**, contributor, benefactor, benefactress, subscriber, donator; supporter, backer, subsidizer, patron, sponsor; philanthropist; informal angel; rare benefactrice, benefactrix, philanthrope.
▷ANTONYMS recipient.

doom noun *John may have anticipated his impending doom*: **destruction**, downfall, grim/terrible fate, ruin, ruination, rack and ruin, catastrophe, disaster; extinction, annihilation, death, end, termination; rare quietus.
▸ **verb** *we were doomed to wait for ever | such attempts are usually doomed to failure*: **destine**, fate, predestine, ordain, preordain, foredoom, mean, foreordain, consign; condemn, sentence; (**doomed**) certain, sure, bound, guaranteed, assured, very likely.

doomed adjective *a doomed friendship*: **ill-fated**, ill-starred, ill-omened, star-crossed, under a curse, cursed, jinxed, foredoomed, hapless, damned, bedevilled, luckless, unlucky; Scottish fey.
▷ANTONYMS happy, lucky, promising.

Word toolkit

doomed	damned	condemned
romance	lies	man
voyage	fool	building
campaign	nuisance	murderer
mission	souls	property
planet	heretics	tunnel

door noun *she disappeared through a door*: **doorway**, portal, opening, hatch, entrance, entry, exit, egress.
□ **out of doors** *food tastes even better out of doors*: **outside**, outdoors, out, in/into the open air, alfresco, out of the house.

doorkeeper noun **doorman**, door attendant, commissionaire, gatekeeper; caretaker, janitor, custodian, concierge; Freemasonry tiler.

dope noun **1** informal *he was caught smuggling dope*: **drugs**, narcotics, addictive drugs, recreational drugs, illegal drugs; cannabis, heroin.
2 informal *what a dope she must have looked*. See **fool**.
3 informal *the government had plenty of dope on Mr Dixon*. See **information**.
▸ **verb 1** *the horse was doped before the race*: **drug**, administer drugs/opiates/narcotics to; tamper with, interfere with; disable, stupefy, sedate, befuddle, inebriate, intoxicate, narcotize, incapacitate, weaken; knock out, anaesthetize, give an anaesthetic to, make/render unconscious; Brit. informal nobble.
2 *they may have doped his drink at the club*: **add drugs to**, tamper with, adulterate, contaminate; informal lace, spike, slip a Mickey Finn into, doctor, cut.

dopey adjective informal *he became dopey and fell into a deep sleep*: **dazed**, confused, muddled, befuddled, bewildered, disoriented, disorientated, stupefied, groggy, dizzy; informal woozy, muzzy, woolly, woolly-headed, not with it, discombobulated.
▷ANTONYMS alert.

dormant adjective *the bacteria may lie dormant in the bird | a dormant company is entitled to exemption from auditing*: **asleep**, sleeping, slumbering, resting, reposing, drowsing, comatose, supine; **inactive**, passive, inert, latent, fallow, quiescent, inoperative, stagnant, sluggish, lethargic, torpid, motionless, immobile; Zoology aestivating.
▷ANTONYMS awake, active.

Word toolkit **dormant**

See **latent**.

d

dose noun **1** *a dose of cough mixture*: **amount**, quantity, measure, portion, dosage, drench, draught; overdose, lethal dose; informal hit.
2 *we all got a dose of diarrhoea*: **bout**, attack, outbreak, flare-up, fit, eruption, spell, burst.

dossier noun *I've built up a dossier on his drug and arms deals*: **file**, report, case history, case study, casebook; account, notes, document(s), documentation, data, information, evidence; annal(s), archive(s), chronicle(s), diary, journal, memoir, register, log, logbook; inventory, list, catalogue; rare muniments.

dot noun *the photograph is made up of tiny dots*: **spot**, speck, fleck, speckle, point, pinpoint, pinprick, mark, dab; bit, particle, atom, molecule, iota, jot, mote, mite; full stop, decimal point; rare macule, macula.
□ **on the dot** informal *at six o'clock on the dot | will they be here on the dot?* **precisely**, exactly, sharp, prompt, to the minute, on the nail; dead on, on the stroke of ...; **promptly**, punctually, on time; informal bang on, spot on; N. Amer. informal on the button, on the nose; Austral./NZ informal on the knocker.
▶ verb **1** *spots of rain began to dot his shirt*: **spot**, fleck, bespeckle, mark, dab, stipple, pock, freckle, sprinkle, dust; literary befleck, bestrew, besprinkle.
2 *North Africa was once dotted with freshwater lakes | restaurants are dotted around the site*: **scatter**, pepper, sprinkle, strew, litter; punctuate, stud, cover; spread, disperse, intersperse, distribute.

dotage noun *Uncle Henry was in his dotage*: **declining years**, winter/autumn of one's life; advanced years, old age, elderliness, agedness, oldness, senescence, senility, superannuation, decrepitude, second childhood; literary eld; rare caducity.
▷ANTONYMS childhood.

dote verb
□ **dote on** *she doted on the boy*: **adore**, love dearly, be devoted to, idolize, treasure, cherish, lavish affection on, worship, think very highly of, appreciate greatly, admire, hold dear, prize; indulge, spoil, pamper.
▷ANTONYMS hate; neglect.

doting adjective *all her doting admirers*: **adoring**, loving, amorous, besotted, infatuated, lovesick, passionate; affectionate, fond, devoted, solicitous, caring, tender, warm, warm-hearted; overindulgent, indulgent; informal lovey-dovey, touchy-feely.
▷ANTONYMS stony.

dotty adjective informal *it was enough to drive you dotty*. See **mad** (sense 1).

double adjective **1** *a double garage | double yellow lines*: **dual**, duplex, twin, binary, duplicate, matched, matching, paired, in pairs, complementary, coupled, twofold; Botany binate; rare binal.
▷ANTONYMS single.
2 *a double helping*: **twice the usual size**, doubled, twofold.
3 *he thought there was a double meaning in her words*: **ambiguous**, equivocal, dual, two-edged, ambivalent, open to debate, open to argument, arguable, debatable; Delphic, cryptic, enigmatic, gnomic, paradoxical, misleading; double-edged.
▷ANTONYMS unambiguous.
4 *he led a double life*: **deceitful**, double-dealing, two-faced, dual; hypocritical, back-stabbing, false, duplicitous, insincere, deceiving, dissembling, dishonest; disloyal, treacherous, perfidious, faithless; lying, untruthful, mendacious; rare Janus-faced.
▷ANTONYMS simple; honest.
□ **double Dutch** Brit. informal *to most readers these names are double Dutch*. See **gibberish**.
▶ adverb *we had to pay double*: **twice**, twice over, twice the amount, doubly.
▶ noun **1** *if it's not her, it's her double*: **lookalike**, twin, clone, duplicate, perfect likeness, exact likeness, replica, copy, facsimile, imitation, picture, image, living image, mirror image, counterpart, match, mate, fellow; German Doppelgänger; informal spitting image, dead ringer, ringer, (very) spit, dead spit, spit and image.
2 *she used a double for the stunts*: **stand-in**, body double, understudy, substitute.
□ **at the double** *Charlie disappeared across the parade ground at the double*: **very quickly**, as fast as one's legs can carry one, at a run, at a gallop, hotfoot, on the double, fast, swiftly, rapidly, briskly, speedily, at high speed, with all speed, at (full) speed, at the speed of light, at full tilt, express, post-haste, as fast as possible, with all possible haste, like a whirlwind, like an arrow from a bow, at breakneck speed, expeditiously, madly, with dispatch; informal double quick, in double quick time, p.d.q. (pretty damn quick), nippily, like (greased) lightning, at warp speed, hell for leather, like mad, like crazy, like blazes, like the wind, like a bomb, like nobody's business, like a scalded cat, like the deuce, a mile a minute, like a bat out of hell, at warp speed; Brit. informal like the clappers, at a rate of knots, like billy-o; N. Amer. informal lickety-split; literary apace.
▶ verb **1** *they offered to double his salary*: **multiply by two**, increase twofold, enlarge, magnify, repeat.
2 *the bottom sheet had been **doubled up** halfway down the bed*: **fold (back/up/down/over/under)**, turn back/up/down/over/under, tuck back/up/down/under, bend back/over, crease.
3 *the kitchen doubles as a dining room*: **function**, do, (also) serve; have/serve a dual purpose, have a dual role.
4 *the Customs officer was **doubling for** Immigration*: **stand in for**, fill in for, act as stand-in for, deputize for, act as deputy, substitute for, act as substitute for, take the place of, take over from, be a substitute for, cover for, replace, relieve, act in place of, do duty for, do a locum for, be a locum for, sit in for, understudy; hold the fort, step into the breach; informal sub for, fill someone's shoes/boots; N. Amer. informal pinch-hit for.

> *Word links* **double**
>
> **bi-** related prefix, as in *biped, bicameral*
> **di-** related prefix, as in *dihedral, dichromatic*
> **diplo-** related prefix, as in *diplodocus, diplococcus*
> **zygo-** related prefix, as in *zygodactyl, zygopteran*

double-cross verb *he was double-crossing his family behind their backs*: **betray**, **cheat**, defraud, trick, hoodwink, mislead, deceive, swindle, break one's promise to, be disloyal to, be unfaithful to, break faith with, play false, fail, let down; informal two-time, stitch up, do the dirty on, sell down the river.
▷ANTONYMS be loyal; play it straight.

double-dealing noun *one day his double-dealing would be discovered*: **duplicity**, treachery, betrayal, double-crossing, faithlessness, unfaithfulness, untrustworthiness, infidelity, bad faith, disloyalty, perfidy, perfidiousness, treason, breach of trust, fraud, fraudulence, underhandedness, cheating, dishonesty, deceit, deceitfulness, deception, falseness, stab in the back, back-stabbing, lying, mendacity, trickery, two-facedness; informal crookedness, two-timing; rare Punic faith.
▷ANTONYMS honesty, straightforwardness, trustworthiness.

double entendre noun *he was unable to resist a smutty double entendre*: **ambiguity**, double meaning, suggested meaning, suggestiveness, innuendo, play on words, wordplay, pun.

doubly adverb *we have to be doubly careful*: **twice as**, as ... again, in double measure, in two ways, for two; even more, especially, extra.

doubt noun **1** *there was some doubt as to the caller's identity*: **uncertainty**, lack of certainty, unsureness, indecision, hesitation, hesitancy, dubiousness, suspicion, confusion; question mark, queries, questions; rare dubiety, incertitude.
▷ANTONYMS certainty.
2 *a weak, indecisive leader racked by doubt*: **indecision**, hesitation, diffidence, uncertainty, insecurity, inhibition, unease, uneasiness, apprehension; hesitancy, wavering, vacillation, irresolution, lack of conviction, demurral.
▷ANTONYMS conviction, confidence.
3 *there is doubt about the motive behind this move*: **scepticism**, distrust, mistrust, lack of trust, doubtfulness, suspicion, cynicism, disbelief, incredulity, unbelief, misbelief, lack of confidence/conviction, uneasiness, apprehension, wariness, chariness, questioning; reservations, misgivings, suspicions, qualms; informal leeriness; rare dubiety.
▷ANTONYMS trust.
□ **in doubt 1** *the issue was never in doubt*: **doubtful**, uncertain, open to question, unsure, unconfirmed, unknown, unsettled, undecided, moot, unresolved, debatable, open to debate, in the balance, pending, in limbo, up in the air, confused, problematic, ambiguous; informal iffy. ▷ANTONYMS settled.
2 *if you are in doubt, ask for advice*: **irresolute**, hesitant, tentative, vacillating, dithering, wavering, teetering, fluctuating, faltering, ambivalent, divided; doubtful, unsure, uncertain, in two minds, shilly-shallying, undecided, indefinite, unresolved, undetermined; in a quandary/dilemma; informal sitting on the fence. ▷ANTONYMS sure, confident.
□ **no doubt** *it was all necessary, no doubt*: **doubtless**, undoubtedly, indubitably, doubtlessly, without (a) doubt, beyond (a) doubt, beyond the shadow of a doubt; unquestionably, beyond question, indisputably, undeniably, incontrovertibly, irrefutably; unequivocally, clearly, plainly, obviously, patently, positively, absolutely, certainly; decidedly, definitely, surely, assuredly, of course, indeed. ▷ANTONYMS possibly.
▶ verb **1** *they did not doubt my story*: **disbelieve**, distrust, mistrust, suspect, lack confidence in, have doubts about, be suspicious of, have suspicions about, have misgivings about, feel uneasy about, feel apprehensive about, call into question, cast doubt on, query, question, challenge, dispute, have reservations about; archaic misdoubt.
▷ANTONYMS trust.
2 *I doubt whether he will come*: **think something unlikely**, have (one's) doubts about, question, query, be dubious, lack conviction, have reservations about.
▷ANTONYMS be confident.
3 *stop doubting and believe more firmly!* **be undecided**, have doubts, be irresolute, be hesitant, be tentative, be ambivalent, be divided, be doubtful, be unsure, be uncertain, be in two minds, hesitate, shilly-shally, waver, falter, vacillate, dither, demur; informal sit on the fence.
▷ANTONYMS believe.

doubter noun *this is his chance to confound the doubters*: **sceptic**, doubting Thomas, non-believer, unbeliever, disbeliever, cynic, scoffer, questioner, challenger, nihilist, dissenter; irreligionist, atheist, agnostic, freethinker;

infidel, pagan, heathen; archaic paynim; rare Pyrrhonist, nullifidian.
▷ANTONYMS believer.

doubtful adjective 1 *at first I was doubtful about going*: **irresolute**, hesitant, tentative, vacillating, dithering, wavering, teetering, fluctuating, faltering, ambivalent, divided, in doubt, unsure, uncertain, in two minds, shilly-shallying, undecided, indefinite, unresolved, in a quandary/dilemma, undetermined; informal iffy, blowing hot and cold, sitting on the fence.
▷ANTONYMS confident, decisive.
2 *it is doubtful whether he will come*: **in doubt**, dubious, uncertain, open to question, questionable, unsure, unconfirmed, not definite, unknown, unsettled, undecided, unresolved, debatable, open to debate, moot, in the balance, pending, in limbo, up in the air; confused, problematic, ambiguous; informal iffy.
▷ANTONYMS certain.
3 *the whole trip is looking rather doubtful*: **unlikely**, improbable, not likely, dubious, unthinkable, implausible, impossible, far-fetched, inconceivable, unimaginable, remote, beyond the bounds of possibility.
▷ANTONYMS probable.
4 *they are doubtful of the methods used*: **distrustful**, mistrustful, suspicious, cautious, circumspect, careful, wary, uneasy, chary, apprehensive, lacking trust, lacking confidence, lacking faith; sceptical, unsure, ambivalent, dubious, cynical; questioning, disbelieving, unbelieving, incredulous; (**be doubtful**) have reservations, have misgivings; informal leery, cagey.
▷ANTONYMS trusting.
5 *this decision is of doubtful validity*: **questionable**, arguable, disputable, debatable, open to question, open to debate, subject to debate, controversial, contentious, open to doubt, in doubt, dubious, borderline; rare controvertible, unestablished; informal iffy; Brit. informal dodgy.
▷ANTONYMS sound.

doubtless adverb *Henry was doubtless glad of the opportunity*: **undoubtedly**, indubitably, doubtlessly, no doubt, without (a) doubt, beyond (a) doubt, beyond the shadow of a doubt; unquestionably, beyond question, indisputably, undeniably, incontrovertibly, irrefutably; unequivocally, clearly, plainly, obviously, patently, positively, absolutely, certainly, with certainty; decidedly, definitely, surely, assuredly, of course, indeed.
▷ANTONYMS possibly.

doughty adjective *a doughty fighter for democracy*: **fearless**, dauntless, determined, resolute, indomitable, intrepid, plucky, spirited, game, mettlesome, gritty, steely, confident, undaunted, undismayed, unalarmed, unflinching, unshrinking, unabashed, unfaltering, unflagging, bold, audacious, valiant, brave, stout-hearted, lionhearted, gallant, courageous, heroic, daring, daredevil; informal gutsy, spunky, ballsy, feisty.
▷ANTONYMS timid.

dour adjective *they were barely acknowledged by the dour receptionist*: **stern**, unsmiling, unfriendly, frowning, poker-faced, severe, forbidding, morose, sour, gruff, surly, uncommunicative, grim, gloomy, dismal, sullen, sombre, grave, sober, serious, solemn, austere, stony, unsympathetic, disapproving.
▷ANTONYMS cheerful; friendly.

douse, dowse verb 1 *a mob doused the thieves with petrol*: **drench**, soak, souse, saturate, drown, flood, inundate, deluge, wet, splash, slosh, hose down.
2 *a guard doused the flames with a fire extinguisher*: **extinguish**, put out, quench, stamp out, smother, beat out, dampen down; blow out, snuff out; Scottish dout.

dovetail verb 1 *the ends of the logs were cut and dovetailed*: **joint**, join, fit together, link, interlock, splice, mortise, tenon.
2 *this company will dovetail well with the division's existing activities*: **fit in**, go together, be consistent, agree, accord, concur, coincide, match, fit, be in agreement, conform, equate, harmonize, fall in, be in tune, correlate, correspond, tally; informal square; N. Amer. informal jibe; archaic quadrate.

dowdy adjective *she had serviceable but dowdy clothes*: **unfashionable**, frumpish, frumpy, drab, dull, old-fashioned, outmoded, out of style, not smart, inelegant, badly dressed, ill-dressed, shabby, scruffy, faded, untidy, dingy, frowzy; informal sad, tacky; Brit. informal mumsy; Austral./NZ informal daggy.
▷ANTONYMS fashionable.

down[1] adverb 1 *they went down in the lift*: **towards a lower position**, downwards, downstairs, towards the bottom, from top to bottom.
▷ANTONYMS up.
2 *they're down in the hall*: **in a lower position**, downstairs, at the bottom.
3 *she fell down*: **to the ground**, to the floor, over.
▶ preposition 1 *the lift plunged down the shaft*: **lower in/on**, to the bottom of.
▷ANTONYMS up.
2 *I walked down the street*: **along**, throughout the length of, to the other end of, from one end of ... to the other, through, across, by way of, via.
3 *we have done him many favours down the years*: **throughout**, through, during, in.
▶ adjective 1 *I'm feeling a bit down*: **depressed**, sad, saddened, unhappy, melancholy, miserable, wretched, sorrowful, gloomy, dejected, downhearted, disheartened, despondent, dispirited, low, in low spirits, low-spirited, heavy-hearted, glum, morose, dismal, downcast, cast down, tearful; informal blue, down in the dumps, down in the mouth, fed up.
▷ANTONYMS elated.
2 *the computer is down*: **not working**, not functioning, not functional, not in working order, not in operation, inoperative, malfunctioning, out of order, broken, broken-down, acting up, unserviceable, faulty, defective, in disrepair; **not in service**, unavailable for use, not in use, out of action, out of commission; informal conked out, bust, (gone) kaput, gone phut, on the blink, gone haywire, shot; Brit. informal knackered, jiggered, wonky; N. Amer. informal on the fritz, out of whack; Brit. vulgar slang buggered.
▷ANTONYMS working.
▶ verb informal 1 *he struck Slater on the face, downing him*: **knock down**, knock over, knock to the ground, throw to the ground, bring down, bring to the ground, fell, topple, prostrate, tackle, trip up; informal deck, floor, flatten.
2 *he downed his pint of beer*: **drink (up/down)**, gulp (down), guzzle, quaff, drain, imbibe, sup, slurp, suck, sip, swallow, finish off, polish off; informal sink, swig, swill (down), toss off, slug, knock back, put away, kill; N. Amer. informal scarf (down/up), snarf (down/up); rare ingurgitate.
▶ noun 1 (**downs**) *the ups and downs of running a business*: **setbacks**, upsets, reverses, reversals, reversals of fortune, downturns, mishaps, strokes of ill luck, strokes of bad luck, accidents, shocks, vicissitudes, crises, catastrophes, tragedies, calamities, trials, crosses, knocks, burdens, blows, buffets; informal glitches, (double) whammies, knock-backs; archaic foils.
▷ANTONYMS ups.
2 *he's having a bit of a down at the moment*: **fit of depression**, period of despondency; informal the blues, the dumps, one's black dog, a low; N. Amer. informal the blahs, a funk, a blue funk; informal, dated the mopes; literary dolour; archaic the megrims.
▷ANTONYMS high.
□ **have a down on** informal *poor Fairfax, I think they had a down on him*: **disapprove of**, be against, be prejudiced against, be set against, bear a grudge towards, show antagonism to, be hostile to, show/feel ill will towards; **persecute**, pick on, push around/about, lean on, bully, abuse, discriminate against, ill-treat, mistreat, maltreat, harass, hound, torment, terrorize, torture, punish unfairly; informal get at, have it in for, be down on, give someone a hard time, hassle, needle, get on someone's back, make things hot for someone.

down[2] noun *the young puffin stopped preening tufts of grey down from its feathers*: **soft feathers**, fluff, fuzz, floss, lint, bloom, fine hair, nap, pile.

down and out adjective *a novel about being down and out on the streets of London*: **destitute**, poverty-stricken, impoverished, indigent, penniless, insolvent, impecunious, ruined, pauperized, without a penny to one's name, without two farthings/pennies to rub together; needy, in need, in want, hard up, on the breadline, hard-pressed, in reduced/straitened circumstances, deprived, disadvantaged, distressed, badly off; beggarly, beggared; **homeless**, without a roof over one's head, on the streets, of no fixed abode/address, vagrant, sleeping rough, living rough; **unemployed**, jobless, out of a job, workless, redundant, laid off, idle, between jobs; informal on one's uppers, up against it, broke, flat broke, strapped (for cash), without a brass farthing, without a bean, without a sou, as poor as a church mouse, on one's beam-ends; Brit. informal stony broke, skint, boracic (lint), on the dole, signing on, 'resting'; N. Amer. informal stone broke, without a red cent, on skid row; Austral. informal on the wallaby track; formal penurious.
▷ANTONYMS wealthy, well heeled.
▶ noun (**down-and-out**) *he gave his packed lunch to a hungry down-and-out*: **poor person**, pauper, indigent, bankrupt, insolvent; beggar, mendicant; **homeless person**, vagrant, tramp, drifter, derelict, vagabond, person of no fixed address/abode, knight of the road, bird of passage, rolling stone; **unemployed person**, job-seeker; N. Amer. hobo; Austral. bagman, knockabout, overlander, sundowner, whaler; informal have-not, dosser, bag lady; N. Amer. informal bum, bindlestiff; Austral./NZ informal derro; S. African informal outie; (**down-and-outs**) the poor, the destitute, the needy, the homeless, the unemployed.

down at heel adjective 1 *the whole resort now looks down at heel*: **run down**, dilapidated, in disrepair, neglected, uncared-for, unmaintained, depressed; **seedy**, insalubrious, squalid, sleazy, slummy, seamy, sordid, dingy, mean, wretched; informal crummy, scruffy, scuzzy, grungy; Brit. informal grotty; N. Amer. informal shacky, skanky.
2 *a down-at-heel English journalist lived nearby*: **scruffy**, shabby, shabbily dressed, poorly dressed, shoddy, ragged, out at elbows, tattered, mangy, sorry, disreputable; **unkempt**, bedraggled, messy, dishevelled, ungroomed, ill-groomed, sleazy, seedy, slatternly, untidy, slovenly; **dirty**, squalid, filthy; informal tatty, the worse for wear, scuzzy, grungy, yucky; Brit. informal grotty; N. Amer. informal raggedy.
▷ANTONYMS smart, stylish.

downbeat adjective 1 *the overall mood is decidedly downbeat*: **pessimistic**, gloomy, negative, defeatist, gloom-ridden, cynical, bleak, fatalistic, dark, black, despairing, despondent, depressed, dejected, demoralized, hopeless, melancholy, glum, lugubrious, suspicious, distrustful, doubting, alarmist; informal given to looking on the black side.
▷ANTONYMS upbeat.
2 *the songs are full of downbeat joviality*: **relaxed**, easy-going, equable, free and easy, easy, at ease, casual, informal, nonchalant, insouciant,

d

understated, inconspicuous, low-key, subdued, discreet, muted, subtle, played down, toned down, unostentatious, blasé, cool; informal laid-back, unflappable, together.

downcast adjective *Morgan was understandably downcast following Scotland's defeat*: **despondent**, disheartened, discouraged, dispirited, downhearted, low-spirited, in low spirits, hopeless, cast down, crestfallen, down, low, disconsolate, in despair, despairing, wretched, oppressed; **sad**, melancholy, gloomy, glum, morose, doleful, dismal, woebegone, miserable, depressed, dejected, distressed, sorrowful; defeatist, pessimistic; informal blue, down in the mouth, down in the dumps, as sick as a parrot.
▷ANTONYMS elated.

d

downfall noun *the downfall of Napoleon III in 1870*: **undoing**, ruin, ruination, loss of power/prosperity/status; defeat, conquest, vanquishing, toppling, deposition, ousting, unseating, overthrow, nemesis, destruction, annihilation, elimination, end, collapse, fall, crash, failure, debasement, degradation, disgrace; Waterloo; rare labefaction.
▷ANTONYMS rise; salvation; survival.

downgrade verb **1** *there were plans to make six staff redundant and to downgrade three others*: **demote**, lower, lower in status, reduce/lower in rank, reduce in importance; relegate; N. Amer. informal bust; archaic degrade.
▷ANTONYMS upgrade, promote.
2 *I have no wish to downgrade their achievement*: **disparage**, denigrate, detract from, run down, decry, belittle, make light of, minimize, defame; N. Amer. informal bad-mouth.
▷ANTONYMS praise; talk up.

downhearted adjective *Stirling was obviously downhearted, but he did not show it*: **despondent**, disheartened, discouraged, dispirited, downcast, low-spirited, in low spirits, hopeless, cast down, crestfallen, down, low, disconsolate, in despair, despairing, wretched, oppressed; melancholy, gloomy, glum, morose, doleful, dismal, woebegone, miserable, depressed, dejected, distressed, sorrowful, sad; defeatist, pessimistic; informal blue, down in the mouth, down in the dumps, as sick as a parrot.
▷ANTONYMS elated.

downmarket adjective *the quality papers and the downmarket tabloids*: **cheap**, cheap and nasty, inferior, rubbishy; low-class, lowbrow, uncultured, unsophisticated, rough, poor, insalubrious, unfashionable, disreputable; informal tacky, dumbed down.
▷ANTONYMS upmarket, smart.

downpour noun *the drizzle was becoming a downpour*: **rainstorm**, cloudburst, torrent of rain, deluge; thunderstorm; torrential/pouring rain.

downright adjective **1** *smears, half-truths, and downright lies*: **complete**, total, absolute, utter, thorough, perfect, out-and-out, outright, thoroughgoing, all-out, sheer, positive, rank, pure, dyed-in-the-wool, deep-dyed, real, veritable, consummate, categorical, unmitigated, unqualified, unadulterated, unalloyed, unconditional, unequivocal; Brit. informal right, proper; archaic arrant.
▷ANTONYMS partial; anything but.
2 *a true downright character who did not care a damn for her*: **frank**, direct, straightforward, straight, straight to the point, blunt, plain-spoken, outspoken, forthright, uninhibited, unreserved, point blank, no-nonsense, matter-of-fact, bluff, undiplomatic, tactless; explicit, clear, plain, unequivocal, unambiguous, unqualified, categorical; honest, candid, open, sincere; not afraid to call a spade a spade, no beating around the bush, speaking as one finds; informal straight from the shoulder, upfront.
▷ANTONYMS devious.
▸ adverb *suppressing emotions is downright dangerous*: **thoroughly**, utterly, positively, simply, profoundly, really, absolutely, completely, totally, entirely, perfectly, properly, consummately, surpassingly, unconditionally, unreservedly, categorically, incontrovertibly, unquestionably, undeniably, in every respect, through and through, outright; informal plain, clean.
▷ANTONYMS slightly; not at all.

downside noun *the downside is that getting a patent costs big money*: **snag**, drawback, disadvantage, stumbling block, catch, pitfall, fly in the ointment; handicap, limitation, trouble, difficulty, problem, complication, liability, nuisance; hindrance, obstacle, impediment; weak spot/point, weakness, flaw, defect, fault; informal minus, flip side, hiccup; Brit. informal spanner in the works; N. Amer. informal monkey wrench in the works.
▷ANTONYMS benefit, advantage.

down-to-earth adjective *she seemed a good, down-to-earth type*: **practical**, sensible, realistic, matter-of-fact, responsible, full of common sense, reasonable, rational, logical, sound, balanced, sober, no-nonsense, pragmatic, level-headed, serious-minded, businesslike, commonsensical, hard-headed, sane, mundane, unromantic, unidealistic.
▷ANTONYMS idealistic; dreamy.

downtrodden adjective *they kept alive the spirit of a downtrodden nation during centuries of foreign occupation*: **oppressed**, subjugated, persecuted, subdued, repressed, tyrannized, ground down, crushed, enslaved, burdened, weighed down, exploited, disadvantaged, underprivileged, victimized, bullied, browbeaten, under the heel, powerless, helpless, prostrate; abused, misused, maltreated, ill-treated.

downward adjective *the downward flow of water*: **descending**, downhill, falling, sinking, going down, moving down, sliding, slipping, dipping, earthbound, earthward.
▷ANTONYMS upward.

> *Word links* **downward**
>
> **cata-** related prefix, as in *catastrophe, catadromous*

downy adjective *I stroked the downy hair on my tiny son's head*: **soft**, velvety, smooth, fleecy, fluffy, fuzzy, feathery, furry, woolly, silky, silken, satiny.
▷ANTONYMS rough; wiry.

dowry noun historical **marriage settlement**, (marriage) portion; Scottish & N. English tocher; archaic dot.

dowse verb See **douse**.

doze verb *he dozed but woke with a start*: **catnap**, nap, take a nap, take a siesta, sleep lightly, drowse, rest; informal snooze, have a snooze, snatch forty winks, get some shut-eye; Brit. informal kip, have a kip, get some kip, zizz, have a zizz, get some zizz; N. Amer. informal catch some Zs, catch a few Zs; literary slumber.
▷ANTONYMS be awake.
□ **doze off** *he dozed off in front of the fire*: **fall asleep**, go to sleep, drop off, get to sleep; informal nod off, go off, drift off, crash out, go out like a light, flake out, conk out; N. Amer. informal sack out, zone out.
▷ANTONYMS wake up; stay awake.
▸ noun *she had a short doze before work*: **catnap**, nap, siesta, light sleep, drowse, rest; informal snooze, forty winks; Brit. informal kip, zizz; literary slumber.

dozy adjective *the guard on night duty would be too dozy to spot anything*: **drowsy**, sleepy, half asleep, heavy-eyed, somnolent; **lethargic**, listless, lacking in energy, unenergetic, enervated, inactive, slow, torpid, languid, weary, tired, fatigued; lazy, idle, indolent, slothful, sluggardly; Medicine asthenic, neurasthenic; informal dopey, yawny; N. Amer. informal logy; archaic lymphatic.

drab adjective **1** *blocks of drab council flats*: **colourless**, grey, greyish, dull, dull-coloured, washed out, neutral, pale, muted, lacklustre, lustreless, muddy, watery; lightish brown, brownish, brownish-grey, mousy, dun-coloured; dingy, dreary, dismal, cheerless, gloomy, sombre, depressing.
▷ANTONYMS bright; cheerful.
2 *a drab suburban existence*: **uninteresting**, dull, boring, tedious, monotonous, dry, dreary, wearisome; unexciting, bland, non-stimulating, unimaginative, uninspiring, uninspired, insipid, lustreless, lacklustre, vapid, flat, stale, trite, vacuous, feeble, pallid, wishy-washy, colourless, limp, lame, tired, lifeless, zestless, spiritless, sterile, anaemic, barren, tame, bloodless, antiseptic; middle-of-the-road, run-of-the-mill, commonplace, mediocre, nondescript, characterless, mundane, unexceptional, unremarkable, humdrum, prosaic.
▷ANTONYMS interesting.

draconian adjective *collaborators suffered draconian reprisals*: **harsh**, severe, strict, extreme, drastic, stringent, tough, swingeing, cruel, brutal, oppressive, ruthless, relentless, summary, punitive, authoritarian, despotic, tyrannical, arbitrary, repressive, iron-fisted; rare suppressive.
▷ANTONYMS mild.

draft noun **1** *the draft of his speech*: **preliminary version**, rough sketch, outline, plan, blueprint, skeleton, abstract; main points, bones, bare bones.
▷ANTONYMS final version.
2 *a draft of the building to be erected*: **plan**, blueprint, design, diagram, drawing, scale drawing, outline, sketch, pattern, map, layout, representation.
3 *payment should be made by a banker's draft*: **cheque**, order, banker's order, money order, bill of exchange, postal order; technical negotiable instrument.

drag verb **1** *she dragged the heavy chair nearer to the bed*: **haul**, pull, draw, tug, heave, trail, trawl, tow; Irish streel; informal yank, lug; archaic hale.
2 *the day dragged for Anne*: **become tedious**, appear to pass slowly, go slowly, move slowly, creep along, limp along, crawl, hang heavy, go at a snail's pace, wear on, go on too long, go on and on.
□ **drag one's feet/heels** *Stop dragging your feet. We have to move.* **delay**, put off doing something, postpone action, defer action, procrastinate, be dilatory, use delaying tactics, stall, temporize, play for time, play a waiting game, dally, take one's time; informal dilly-dally, shilly-shally.
□ **drag on** *the war dragged on*: **persist**, continue, go on, carry on, extend, run on, be protracted, linger, endure, keep up, hold, prevail, subsist.
□ **drag something out** *that procedure was bound to drag out the negotiations*: **prolong**, protract, draw out, stretch out, spin out, string out, make something go on and on, extend, extend the duration of, lengthen, carry on, keep going, keep alive, continue; archaic wire-draw.
▸ noun **1** *the drag of the air brakes causes more rapid deceleration*: **pull**, tug, tow, heave, yank; resistance, braking, retardation.
2 informal *working nine to five can be a drag*: **bore**, tedious thing, tiresome thing, nuisance, bother, trouble, pest, annoyance, source of annoyance,

trial, vexation, thorn in one's flesh; tiresome person, tedious person; informal pain, pain in the neck, bind, headache, hassle; N. Amer. informal pain in the butt, nudnik; Austral./NZ informal nark; Brit. informal, dated blighter, blister, pill; Brit. vulgar slang pain in the arse.

dragoon noun historical *the dragoons charged our left flank*: **cavalryman**, mounted soldier, horse soldier, cavalier, knight, chevalier; carabineer, hussar, lancer, cuirassier, sabreur.
▸ verb *he dragooned his friends into amateur dramatics*: **coerce**, pressure, pressurize, bring pressure to bear on, use pressure on, put pressure on, constrain, lean on, press, push; force, compel, impel, oblige, put under an obligation, squeeze, hound, harass, nag, harry, badger, goad, drive, prod, pester, browbeat, brainwash, bludgeon, bully, threaten, tyrannize, prevail on, work on, act on, influence, intimidate, twist someone's arm, strong-arm; N. Amer. blackjack; informal bulldoze, railroad, put the screws/squeeze on; Brit. informal bounce; N. Amer. informal hustle, fast-talk.

drain verb 1 *there is a valve for draining the tank*: **empty (out)**, remove the contents of, void, clear (out), unload, evacuate.
▷ANTONYMS fill.
2 *then drain any surplus liquid*: **draw off**, extract, withdraw, remove, pump off, siphon off, milk, bleed, tap, void, filter, pour out, pour off, tip, discharge, transfer.
3 *the water drained away to the sea*: **flow**, pour, escape, leak, trickle, empty, well, ooze, seep, exude, drip, dribble, issue, filter, percolate, bleed, sweat, leach; stream, run, rush, gush, roll, cascade, flood, surge, sweep.
4 *jailing more people would just drain resources*: **use up**, exhaust, deplete, consume, expend, swallow up, absorb, get through, go through, run through, take up, occupy, empty, sap, strain, tax, bleed.
5 *he drained what was left in his glass*: **drink (up/down)**, gulp (down), guzzle, quaff, down, imbibe, sup, slurp, suck, sip, swallow, finish off, polish off; informal sink, swig, swill (down), toss off, slug, knock back, put away, kill, get one's laughing gear round; N. Amer. informal scarf (down/up), snarf (down/up); rare ingurgitate.
▸ noun 1 *a flash storm filled the drain with water*: **sewer**, channel, conduit, ditch, culvert, duct, pipe, tube, gutter, groove, furrow, trough, trench, cut, sluice, spillway, race, flume, chute.
2 *a significant drain on the camcorder's battery*: **strain**, demand, pressure, burden, load, imposition, tax; outflow, sapping, depletion.

dram noun *Menzies offered the man a dram from his flask*: **drink**, nip, tot, sip, thimbleful, mouthful, drop, finger, splash, little, spot, taste, small amount; Scottish informal scoosh; rare toothful.

drama noun 1 *a television drama*: **play**, show, piece, theatrical work, spectacle, dramatization; screenplay.
2 *he is studying drama*: **acting**, the theatre, the stage, the performing arts, dramatic art, dramatics, dramaturgy, stagecraft, theatricals, theatrics, the thespian art, show business; performing, performance, playing a role, appearing on stage; informal the boards, treading the boards, show biz; rare thespianism, histrionics.
3 *nothing could stop Granny when she wanted to create a drama*: **incident**, scene, spectacle, crisis; excitement, thrill, sensation, adventure, affair, business, occasion, circumstance; disturbance, row, commotion, turmoil, fracas; dramatics, theatrics, histrionics.

dramatic adjective 1 *dramatic art*: **theatrical**, stage, dramaturgical, thespian; show-business; informal showbiz; rare histrionic, theatric.
2 *a dramatic increase in speed*: **considerable**, substantial, sizeable, goodly, fair, reasonable, tidy, marked, pronounced; **noticeable**, measurable, perceptible, conspicuous, obvious, detectable, visible, appreciable; significant, striking, signal, notable, noteworthy, worthy of attention, remarkable, outstanding, extraordinary, exceptional, phenomenal; important, of importance, of consequence, consequential.
▷ANTONYMS insignificant.
3 *there were dramatic scenes in the capital's central square*: **exciting**, stirring, action-packed, sensational, spectacular, startling, unexpected, tense, suspenseful, rip-roaring, gripping, riveting, fascinating, thrilling, hair-raising, rousing, lively, animated, spirited, electrifying, impassioned, emotive, emotional, emotion-charged, moving, soul-stirring, powerful, heady; N. Amer. informal stem-winding; rare inspiriting, anthemic.
▷ANTONYMS boring.
4 *dramatic rocky headlands*: **striking**, eye-catching, impressive, imposing, spectacular, breathtaking, dazzling, vivid, amazing, astounding, astonishing, surprising, staggering, stunning, sensational, awesome, awe-inspiring, remarkable, notable, noteworthy, distinctive, graphic, extraordinary, outstanding, incredible, phenomenal, unusual, rare, uncommon, out of the ordinary.
▷ANTONYMS unimpressive.
5 *he flung out his arms in a dramatic gesture*: **exaggerated**, theatrical, ostentatious, actressy, stagy, showy, melodramatic, overacted, overdone, histrionic, affected, mannered, artificial, stilted, unreal, forced; informal hammy, ham, campy.
▷ANTONYMS natural, unaffected.

dramatist noun **playwright**, writer, tragedian; scriptwriter, screenwriter, scenarist; rare dramaturge, dramaturgist, comedist.

dramatize verb 1 *the novel was dramatized in six episodes for television*: **turn into a play/film**, adapt for the stage/screen, base a screenplay on, put into dramatic form, present as a play/film.
2 *the tabloids sought to dramatize an already dramatic event*: **exaggerate**, overdo, overstate, overemphasize, overplay, hyperbolize, overstress, magnify, amplify, inflate; sensationalize, embroider, colour, heighten, expand on, aggrandize, dress up, touch up, embellish, elaborate, gild; informal make a big thing out of, blow up (out of all proportion), lay it on thick, ham up.
▷ANTONYMS understate.

drape verb 1 *she draped a shawl round her shoulders*: **wrap**, arrange, wind, swathe, sling, hang, let fall in folds.
2 *the chair was draped with blankets*: **cover**, envelop, swathe, shroud, decorate, adorn, array, deck, bedeck, festoon, bundle up, muffle up, blanket, overlay, cloak, veil, wind, enfold, sheathe.
3 *the youth draped one leg over the arm of his chair*: **dangle**, hang, suspend, let fall, droop, drop, place loosely, lean.

drastic adjective *drastic measures were necessary*: **extreme**, serious, forceful, desperate, dire, radical, far-reaching, momentous, substantial; heavy, sharp, severe, harsh, rigorous, swingeing, punishing, excessive, oppressive, draconian.
▷ANTONYMS mild, moderate.

draught noun 1 *the draught made Robyn shiver*: **current of air**, rush of air, breath, whiff, waft, wind, breeze, gust, puff, blast, gale; informal blow; literary zephyr.
2 *he took another deep draught of his beer*: **gulp**, drink, swallow, mouthful; informal swig, swill, slug.

draw verb 1 *he drew the house in his notebook*: **sketch**, make a drawing (of), make a diagram (of), pencil; portray, depict, delineate, outline, draft, rough out, illustrate, render, represent, trace, map out, mark out, plot, chart, design; do drawings; literary limn.
2 *she drew her chair in to the table*: **pull**, haul, drag, tug, heave, trail, trawl, tow; Irish streel; informal yank, lug; archaic hale.
▷ANTONYMS push.
3 *the train drew into Victoria Station*: **move**, go, come, walk, proceed, progress, travel, continue, advance, get, make it, make one's way, pass, make a move, drive; crawl, creep, inch, roll, glide, cruise, drift, nose; sneak, steal, slip, slink, sidle; bear, press, blow, forge, sweep, lurch, be carried; back; budge, stir, shift, change position; rare locomote.
4 *the nurse drew the curtains*: **close**, shut, pull together, pull shut, pull to, draw to, lower; **open**, part, pull back, pull open, fling open, raise.
5 *he drew some fluid off the knee joint*: **drain**, extract, withdraw, remove, suck, pump, siphon, milk, bleed, tap, void, filter, pour, tip, discharge, transfer.
6 *he drew his gun and fired*: **pull out**, take out, bring out, draw out, produce, fish out, extract, withdraw; unsheathe.
▷ANTONYMS put away; put up.
7 *I **drew** £50 **out** of the bank*: **withdraw**, take out.
▷ANTONYMS deposit.
8 *while I draw breath*: **breathe in**, inhale, suck in, inspire, respire.
9 *she was drawing huge audiences | he drew the attention of millions of viewers*: **attract**, interest, win, capture, catch the eye of, catch, catch hold of, hold, grip, engage, allure, lure, entice, invite; absorb, occupy, rivet, engross, fascinate, mesmerize, hypnotize, spellbind, bewitch, captivate, entrance, enthral, enrapture.
10 *what conclusion can we draw?* **deduce**, infer, conclude, derive, gather, glean; formal educe.
□ **draw lots** See **lot**.
□ **draw on** *we can draw on centuries of experience*: **call on**, have recourse to, avail oneself of, turn to, look to, fall back on, rely on, make use of, exploit, use, employ, utilize, bring into play.
□ **draw something out 1** *he drew out a gun*. See **draw** (sense 6 of the verb).
2 *they always drew their parting out*: **prolong**, protract, drag out, stretch out, spin out, string out, make something go on and on, extend, extend the duration of, lengthen, carry on, keep going, keep alive, continue; archaic wire-draw.
□ **draw someone out** *show an interest in other people, draw them out with questions*: **get/persuade/encourage someone to talk**, put someone at their ease.
□ **draw up** *a car drew up beside us*: **stop**, pull up, come to a stop/halt, halt, come to a standstill, brake, park, arrive.
□ **draw something up 1** *the police drew up a list of five or six suspects*: **compose**, formulate, frame, write out, write down, put in writing, put down (on paper), draft, prepare, think up, devise, work out, map out, plan, conceive, create, invent, originate, coin, design. **2** *he drew up his forces in battle array*: **arrange**, marshal, muster, assemble, group, order, range, rank, line up, parade, place, dispose, position, put into position, set out, array, set forth.
▸ noun 1 *she won first prize in the Christmas draw*: **raffle**, lottery, sweepstake, sweep, tombola, ballot; Brit. trademark Instants; N. Amer. lotto, numbers game/pool/racket; Austral./NZ tote, pakapoo.
2 *the match ended in a draw*: **tie**, dead heat, stalemate.

3 *the draw of central London is considerable*: **attraction**, lure, allure, pull, appeal, glamour, allurement, enticement, temptation, bewitchment, enchantment, charm, seduction, persuasion, fascination, magnetism; informal come-on.

drawback noun *the major drawback to this method is that it can be very time-consuming*: **disadvantage**, snag, downside, stumbling block, catch, hitch, pitfall, fly in the ointment; weak spot/point, weakness, flaw, defect, imperfection, fault; handicap, limitation, trouble, difficulty, problem, complication, liability, nuisance; hindrance, obstacle, hurdle, impediment, obstruction, inconvenience, barrier, curb, check, discouragement, deterrent, damper; informal minus, hiccup; Brit. informal spanner in the works; N. Amer. informal monkey wrench in the works.
▷ANTONYMS benefit, advantage.

d

drawing noun *he did a pencil drawing of the house*: **sketch**, picture, illustration, representation, portrayal, delineation, depiction, composition, study, diagram, outline, design, plan; tracing.

Word links **drawing**

graphic relating to drawing

drawl verb *'Can't do that,' he drawled lazily*: **say slowly**, speak slowly; draw out one's vowels, drone.
▷ANTONYMS gabble.

drawn adjective *she looked pale and drawn*: **worn**, pinched, haggard, gaunt, drained, wan, hollow-cheeked; fatigued, tired, exhausted, sapped, spent; **tense**, stressed, strained, under pressure, overburdened, worried, anxious, harassed, fraught; informal hassled.

dread verb *I used to dread going home at night*: **fear**, be afraid of, worry about, be anxious about, have forebodings about, feel apprehensive about; be terrified by, cower at, tremble/shudder at, cringe from, shrink from, quail from, flinch from; informal have cold feet about, be in a blue funk about.
▷ANTONYMS look forward to.
▸ noun *she was filled with dread*: **fear**, fearfulness, apprehension, trepidation, anxiety, worry, concern, foreboding, disquiet, disquietude, unease, uneasiness, angst; fright, panic, alarm; terror, horror, trembling, shuddering, flinching; informal the jitters, a blue funk, the heebie-jeebies.
▷ANTONYMS confidence.
▸ adjective *a dread secret*: **awful**, feared, frightening, alarming, terrifying, frightful, terrible, horrible, dreadful, dire; dreaded, awesome.

dreadful adjective **1** *a dreadful accident*: **terrible**, frightful, horrible, grim, awful, dire; frightening, terrifying, horrifying, alarming; distressing, shocking, appalling, harrowing; ghastly, fearful, hideous, horrendous, monstrous, unspeakable, gruesome, tragic, calamitous, grievous, grisly; archaic terrific.
▷ANTONYMS mild.
2 *that dreadful woman | a dreadful brandy*: **unpleasant**, disagreeable, nasty; frightful, shocking, awful, abysmal, atrocious, disgraceful, deplorable, wretched, very bad, lamentable, repugnant, odious; poor, inadequate, inferior, unsatisfactory, distasteful; informal hopeless, pathetic, useless, woeful, crummy, rotten, sorry, third-rate, lousy, ropy, God-awful, poxy, not up to snuff, the pits, from hell; Brit. informal duff, chronic, rubbish, pants, a load of pants.
▷ANTONYMS pleasant, agreeable.
3 *you're a dreadful flirt*: **outrageous**, shocking; inordinate, immoderate, unrestrained; great, tremendous.

dreadfully adverb **1** *I'm dreadfully hungry*: **extremely**, very, really, frightfully, fearfully, exceedingly, immensely, terribly, exceptionally, uncommonly, remarkably, extraordinarily; decidedly, most, positively, particularly; N. English right; Scottish unco; N. Amer. quite; informal terrifically, tremendously, desperately, awfully, devilishly, ultra, too ... for words, mucho, mega, seriously, majorly, oh-so; Brit. informal jolly, ever so, dead, well, fair; N. Amer. informal real, mighty, awful, plumb, powerful; S. African informal lekker; informal, dated devilish, hellish; archaic exceeding, sore.
▷ANTONYMS slightly.
2 *she was missing James dreadfully*: **very much**, intensely, desperately, a great deal, a good deal, to a great extent, much, a lot, lots.
▷ANTONYMS slightly.
3 *the company has performed dreadfully*: **terribly**, awfully, very badly, atrociously, dismally, appallingly, abominably, execrably, poorly; informal abysmally, pitifully, crummily, diabolically, rottenly; rare egregiously.
▷ANTONYMS well.

dream noun **1** *I awoke from turbulent dreams*: **fantasy**, nightmare; vision, hallucination.
2 *Leonora went around in a dream the following week*: **daydream**, reverie, trance, daze, stupor, haze, hypnotic state, half-conscious state, state of unreality; Scottish dwam.
3 *he realized his childhood dream of running the estate*: **ambition**, aspiration, hope; goal, design, plan, aim, object, objective, grail, holy grail, target, intention, intent; desire, wish, notion, yearning; daydream, fantasy; illusion, delusion, pipe dream, chimera; (**dreams**) castles in the air, castles in Spain; informal pie in the sky.
4 *he's an absolute dream*: **delight**, joy, marvel, wonder, gem, treasure, pleasure; beauty, vision, vision of loveliness, pleasure to behold.
▸ verb **1** *she dreamed that she had been present at her own funeral*: **have a dream**, have dreams, have a nightmare, have nightmares.
2 *I **dreamed of** making the Olympic team*: **fantasize about**, daydream about; **wish for**, hope for, long for, yearn for, hunger for, hanker after, set one's heart on; aspire to, desire to, wish to; aim for, seek to, have as one's goal/aim, set one's sights on; literary thirst for/after.
3 *she's always dreaming—I think she lives in a world of her own*: **daydream**, be in a reverie, be in a trance, be lost in thought, be preoccupied, be abstracted, let one's thoughts wander, stare into space, indulge in wool-gathering, be in a brown study, be in cloud cuckoo land; muse, wonder.
4 *I wouldn't dream of being late for Aunt Louise*: **think**, consider, contemplate, conceive, entertain the thought of, visualize.
□ **dream something up** *I dreamed up some new excuse*: **think up**, invent, concoct, devise, hatch, contrive, create, fabricate, work out, come up with, conjure up; informal cook up, brew.
▸ adjective *he bought his Californian dream home for $3,000,000*: **ideal**, perfect, flawless, exemplary; fantasy.

Word links **dream**

oneiric relating to dreams
oneiromancy interpretation of dreams
oneirophobia fear of dreams

dreamer noun *you're just a bunch of naive dreamers*: **fantasist**, fantasizer, daydreamer; romantic, sentimentalist, romancer; **idealist**, impractical/unrealistic person, wishful thinker, pipe-dreamer, castle-builder, Utopian, Don Quixote, Walter Mitty; visionary; rare reverist; archaic fantast.
▷ANTONYMS realist.

dreamland noun **1** *I can't drift off to dreamland while she's pacing around the flat*: **sleep**, slumber, land of Nod.
2 *they must be living in dreamland if they thought their standards had risen to match those of Australia*: **the land of make-believe**, never-never land, fairyland, world of fantasy, cloud cuckoo land; paradise, (the Garden of) Eden, Utopia, heaven, seventh heaven, Shangri-La.
▷ANTONYMS the real world.

dreamlike adjective *the gardens have a special dreamlike quality*: **unreal**, unsubstantial, illusive, illusory, illusionary, imaginary, chimerical, ethereal, phantasmagorical, trance-like; surreal, psychedelic; nightmarish, Kafkaesque, ghostly, ghostlike; vague, dim, hazy, shadowy, misty, faint, indistinct, unclear.
▷ANTONYMS real, tangible.

dreamy adjective **1** *his eyes took on a dreamy expression*: **daydreaming**, dreaming; **pensive**, thoughtful, reflective, meditative, musing, ruminative, speculative, lost in thought; preoccupied, distracted, abstracted, rapt, inattentive, wool-gathering, vague, absorbed, distrait, absent-minded, with one's head in the clouds, in a world of one's own, far away, in a brown study; informal miles away.
▷ANTONYMS attentive, alert.
2 *Paul was impractical and dreamy*: **idealistic**, romantic, starry-eyed, impractical, unrealistic, Utopian, quixotic, out of touch with reality; **fanciful**, fantasizing, daydreaming, head-in-the-clouds; visionary, far-sighted, prophetic; Brit. informal airy-fairy.
▷ANTONYMS realistic, practical.
3 *a dreamy recollection*: **dreamlike**, vague, dim, hazy, shadowy, misty, faint, indistinct, unclear.
▷ANTONYMS clear, sharp.
4 *dreamy guitar pop*: **gentle**, tranquil, peaceful, relaxing, soothing, calming, lulling, romantic.
▷ANTONYMS harsh.
5 informal *I bet the prince was really dreamy*: **wonderful**, marvellous, terrific, fabulous, lovely, delightful; attractive, appealing; informal heavenly, divine, gorgeous.
▷ANTONYMS unpleasant, unattractive.

dreary adjective **1** *another dreary day at school*: **dull**, drab, uninteresting, flat, dry, banal, bland, insipid, colourless, lifeless, sterile, tedious, wearisome, boring, unexciting, unstimulating, uninspiring, desolate, vapid, jejune, bloodless, soul-destroying, as dry as dust; humdrum, routine, monotonous, uneventful, run-of-the-mill, prosaic, pedestrian, commonplace, everyday, unexceptional, unremarkable, quotidian, unvaried, repetitive, featureless, ho-hum.
▷ANTONYMS exciting.
2 *she shouldn't be thinking of dreary things like funerals*: **sad**, miserable, depressing, grim, gloomy, glum, sombre, grave, doleful, mournful, melancholic, joyless, cheerless, wretched.
▷ANTONYMS cheerful.
3 *it was a dark, dreary day*: **gloomy**, dismal, bleak, dull, dark, dingy, murky, overcast, depressing, sombre.
▷ANTONYMS bright.

Word toolkit **dreary**

See **dismal**.

dregs plural noun **1** *the dregs from a bottle of wine*: **sediment**, deposit, residue, remains, accumulation; slops, sludge; scum, debris, dross, detritus, refuse; lees, grounds, scourings; technical precipitate, sublimate, residuum, settlings, alluvium; literary draff; archaic grouts.
2 *the dregs of humanity*: **scum**, refuse; rabble, vermin; down-and-outs, good-for-nothings, outcasts, deadbeats, tramps, vagrants; the underclass, the untouchables, the lowest of the low, the great unwashed, the hoi polloi, the ragtag (and bobtail), the canaille; informal riff-raff, trash, dossers.

drench verb *rain was falling fast, drenching the countryside*: **soak**, saturate, wet through, wet thoroughly, permeate, drown, swamp, submerge, inundate, flood; douse, souse, swill down, sluice down, slosh; steep, bathe; rinse, wash.
▷ANTONYMS dry.

dress verb **1** *he dressed quickly and ran out of the house*: **put on clothes**, don clothes, slip into clothes, clothe oneself, get dressed.
▷ANTONYMS undress, strip.
2 *he was dressed in an expensive grey suit*: **clothe**, attire, garb, fit out, turn out, deck, deck out, trick out/up, costume, array, robe, accoutre; informal get up, doll up; literary bedizen; archaic apparel.
3 *they used to dress for dinner every day*: **wear formal clothes**, put on evening dress, dress up; change (one's clothes).
▷ANTONYMS dress informally, dress down.
4 *she'd enjoyed dressing the tree and singing carols*: **decorate**, adorn, ornament, trim, deck, bedeck, embellish, beautify, prettify, array, festoon, garland, rig, drape; garnish, furbish, enhance, grace, enrich; informal trick out, tart up; literary furbelow.
5 *they took him in and dressed his wounds*: **bandage**, cover, bind (up), wrap, swaddle, swathe, plaster, put a plaster on.
6 *she still had the chickens to dress*: **prepare**, get ready, make ready; clean.
7 *the field was dressed with unrotted farmyard manure*: **fertilize**, add fertilizer to, feed, enrich, manure, mulch, compost, top-dress.
8 *it takes two days to dress a pair of millstones*: **smooth**, polish, gloss, level, face.
9 *Patrick dressed Michelle's hair in a sculptured style*: **style**, groom, arrange, comb, brush, do, put in order, straighten, adjust, preen, primp; informal fix.
10 *the battalion dressed its ranks with precision*: **line up**, put in line, align, straighten, arrange, put into order, dispose, set out, get into rows/columns; fall in.
□ **dress down** *she was dressed down in a T shirt and torn jeans*: **dress informally**, dress casually, be untidy; informal slob around.
▷ANTONYMS dress up, dress smartly.
□ **dress someone down** informal *the president dressed down the media during the press conference*. See **reprimand** (verb).
□ **dress up 1** *Angela loved dressing up*: **dress smartly**, dress formally, wear evening dress; informal doll oneself up, dress to the nines, put on one's glad rags. ▷ANTONYMS dress casually, dress down.
2 *Hugh was dressed up as Santa Claus*: **disguise oneself**, dress; put on fancy dress, wear a costume, put on a disguise, wear disguise.
□ **dress something up** *tabloids make their money by dressing up the prejudices of their readers as informed opinion*: **present**, represent, portray, depict, characterize; embellish, enhance, touch up, embroider, gloss, adorn; ginger up; informal jazz up.
▶ noun **1** *she had on a long blue dress*: **frock**, gown, robe, shift.
2 *at ten o'clock Morton put on full evening dress*: **clothes**, clothing, garments, attire, costume, outfit, ensemble, garb, turnout; finery, regalia; informal gear, get-up, togs, duds, garms, glad rags, schmutter; Brit. informal clobber, kit, rig-out; N. Amer. informal threads; formal apparel, habiliment, raiment; archaic vestments.

Word links **dress**

sartorial relating to dress

dressing noun **1** *spoon the dressing over the salad*: **sauce**, relish, condiment, dip, flavouring.
2 *they put fresh dressings on her burns*: **bandage**, covering, plaster, gauze, lint, compress, ligature, swathe, poultice, salve; Medicine spica; trademark Elastoplast, Band-Aid.
3 *a dressing of farmyard manure*: **fertilizer**, mulch; manure, compost, dung, bonemeal, {blood, fish, and bone}, fishmeal, guano; humus, peat; top-dressing.

dressmaker noun **garment-maker**, seamstress, needlewoman, tailoress; tailor, outfitter, costumier, clothier; couturier, designer; dated modiste.

dressy adjective informal *nobody changes into anything dressy for dinner*: **smart**, formal, elaborate, ornate; stylish, elegant, dashing, sophisticated, chic, fashionable, modish; French à la mode; informal sharp, snappy, snazzy, natty, ritzy, classy, swish, trendy, with it.
▷ANTONYMS casual.

dribble verb **1** *the cat started to retch and dribble*: **drool**, slaver, slobber, salivate, drivel, water at the mouth; Scottish slabber.
2 *rainwater dribbled down her temples*: **trickle**, drip, fall in drops, drop, drizzle; leak, ooze, exude, seep.
▶ noun **1** *there was dribble down his chin*: **saliva**, spittle, spit, slaver, slobber, drool.
2 *there was a dribble of sweat on her forehead*: **trickle**, drip, driblet, small stream, drizzle; drop, dash, spot, smear, splash, speck, lick.

dried adjective *dried fruit*: **dehydrated**, desiccated, dry, dried up, moistureless.
▷ANTONYMS fresh.

d

drift verb **1** *his life raft drifted back over the horizon*: **be carried**, be carried (away/along), be borne, be wafted; float, bob, move slowly, go with the current, coast, meander.
2 *the guests drifted away from the centre of the room*: **wander**, wander aimlessly, roam, rove, meander, stray, coast; potter, dawdle, dally; Brit. informal mooch.
3 *don't allow your attention to drift*: **stray**, digress, depart, diverge, veer, swerve, deviate, get sidetracked; rare divagate.
4 *snow had drifted deep over the path*: **pile up**, bank up, heap up, accumulate, gather, form heaps/drifts, amass.
□ **drift off** informal *again, I felt myself drifting off*: **doze off**, drop off, fall asleep, go to sleep; informal nod off, go off, crash, crash out, flake out.
▶ noun **1** *there was a drift from the country to the urban areas*: **movement**, shift, flow, transfer, transferral, relocation, gravitation.
2 *the pilot had not noticed any appreciable drift*: **deviation**, digression, veering, straying.
3 *he caught the drift of her thoughts*: **gist**, essence, core, meaning, sense, thesis, substance, significance, signification; thrust, import, purport, tenor, vein, spirit; implication, intention, direction, course, tendency, trend.
4 *a drift of deep snow*: **pile**, heap, bank, mound, mass, accumulation, dune, ridge.

drifter noun **wanderer**, traveller, transient, roamer, tramp, vagabond, vagrant, person of no fixed abode; N. Amer. hobo; Austral./NZ informal derro.

drill noun **1** *a hydraulic drill*: **drilling tool**, boring tool, rotary tool, auger, (brace and) bit, gimlet, awl, bradawl.
2 *he used military discipline and drill to train the boys*: **training**, instruction, coaching, teaching, grounding; (physical) exercises, workout; discipline; informal square-bashing.
3 *Estelle seemed to know the drill*: **procedure**, routine, practice, pattern, regimen, programme, schedule, method, system, custom, order.
▶ verb **1** *drill the end of the piece of wood*: **bore a hole in**, make a hole in, cut a hole in, drill a hole in; **bore**, pierce, puncture, penetrate, perforate, sink.
▷ANTONYMS punch, gouge.
2 *a sergeant drilling new recruits*: **train**, instruct, coach, teach, ground, inculcate, discipline, exercise, make fit, rehearse, put someone through their paces.
3 *his mother had always* **drilled into** *him the need to pay for one's sins*: **instil**, hammer, drive, drum, din, bang, knock, implant, ingrain; teach, indoctrinate, inculcate, brainwash.

drink verb **1** *she drank her coffee*: **swallow**, gulp down, quaff, swill, guzzle, sup; imbibe, partake of, sip, consume, take; drain, toss off; informal swig, down, knock back, put away, neck, sink, kill, slug, inhale, wet one's whistle; N. Amer. informal scarf (down/up), snarf (down/up); rare ingurgitate.
2 *a churchgoing man who never drank*: **drink alcohol**, take alcohol, tipple, indulge; be a serious/heavy/hard drinker, be an alcoholic; carouse, go drinking; informal take a drop, hit the bottle, take to the bottle, booze, knock a few back, have a few, have one over the eight, tank up, get tanked up, drink like a fish, go on a binge/bender; Brit. informal bevvy; N. Amer. informal bend one's elbow, lush; archaic wassail, tope.
▷ANTONYMS be teetotal, be on the wagon.
3 *let's* **drink to** *the success of our venture*: **toast**, propose a toast to, wish success/luck/health to, salute.
□ **drink something in** *he drank in the details of the crime*: **absorb**, assimilate, digest, ingest, take in, be absorbed in, be immersed in, be rapt in, be lost in, be fascinated by, pay close attention to.
▶ noun **1** *he took another sip of his drink*: **beverage**, drinkable/potable liquid, liquid refreshment, thirst-quencher; dram, bracer, nightcap, nip, tot, spot; N. Amer. eye-opener; Scottish & Irish deoch an doris; Brit. informal cuppa, pint; rare potation, libation.
2 *he sought refuge in drink because of his loneliness*: **alcohol**, liquor, intoxicating liquor, alcoholic drink, strong drink, intoxicants; informal booze, hooch, the hard stuff, firewater, gut-rot, rotgut, moonshine, tipple, the demon drink, the bottle, juice, the sauce, grog, Dutch courage, John Barleycorn; Brit. informal wallop, bevvy.
3 *she took a drink of her wine*: **swallow**, gulp, sip, draught, swill; informal swig, slug.
4 *she asked if she could have a drink of orange juice*: **glass**, cup, mug.
5 (**the drink**) informal *he heaved the outboard motor into the drink*: **the sea**, the ocean, the water; informal the briny, Davy Jones's locker; literary the deep.

> *Word links* **drink**
>
> **potophobia** fear of drink

drinkable adjective *the well water is drinkable*: **fit to drink**, potable, palatable; pure, fresh, clean, safe, unpolluted, untainted, unadulterated, uncontaminated.
▷ANTONYMS undrinkable.

drinker noun *he was a notorious drinker and womanizer*: **drunkard**, drunk, inebriate, imbiber, tippler, sot, heavy drinker, hard drinker, serious drinker, problem drinker; alcoholic, dipsomaniac, chronic alcoholic, alcohol-abuser, alcohol addict, person with a drink problem; informal boozer, soak, lush, wino, alky, sponge, elbow-bender, barfly, tosspot; Austral./NZ informal hophead, metho; archaic toper; vulgar slang pisshead, piss artist.
▷ANTONYMS teetotaller.

d

drip verb **1** *there was a tap dripping in the kitchen*: **dribble**, drop, leak.
▷ANTONYMS gush.
2 *the sweat was dripping from his chin*: **drop**, dribble, trickle, drizzle, run, splash, sprinkle, plop, fall in drops; leak, ooze, seep, exude, be discharged, emanate, issue.
▸ noun **1** *a bucket to catch drips from the leak in the ceiling*: **drop**, dribble, bead, spot, trickle, splash, plop.
2 informal *I hope that drip from Oxford isn't still after you*: **weakling**, ninny, milksop, Milquetoast, namby-pamby, crybaby, pushover, softie, doormat, ineffective person; bore, tiresome person; informal **wimp**, weed, sissy, pansy, nebbish; Brit. informal wet, wally, big girl's blouse, chinless wonder; N. Amer. informal candy-ass, pantywaist, pussy, wuss.

drive verb **1** *you can't drive a car without a speedometer*: **operate**, pilot, steer, handle, manage; guide, direct, navigate.
2 *he drove to the police station*: **travel by car**, go by car, motor; informal travel on wheels, tool along, bowl along, spin.
▷ANTONYMS walk.
3 *I'll drive you to the airport*: **chauffeur**, run, give someone a lift, take, bring, ferry, transport, convey, carry.
4 *a two-litre engine drives the front wheels*: **power**, propel, move, push.
5 *he drove a nail into the sole of the boot*: **hammer**, screw, ram, bang, pound, sink, plunge, thrust, stab, propel, knock, send.
6 *I was allowed to drive cattle to market*: **impel**, urge, press, move, get going; **herd**, round-up, shepherd.
7 *a desperate mother driven to crime*: **force**, compel, constrain, impel, press, prompt, precipitate, catapult; oblige, coerce, make, pressure, goad, spur, prod.
8 *he drove himself and his staff extremely hard*: **work**, exert, push, tax; overwork, overtax, overburden.
□ **drive at** *I can see what you're driving at, but you're quite wrong*: **suggest**, imply, hint at, allude to, intimate, insinuate, indicate, have in mind; refer to, mean, intend; informal get at.
▸ noun **1** *a family out for a Sunday afternoon drive*: **excursion**, outing, trip, jaunt, tour, turn; ride, run, journey; Scottish hurl; informal spin, joyride.
2 *the house is approached by a long drive*: **driveway**, approach, access road; road, roadway, avenue.
3 *a low level of sexual drive*: **urge**, appetite, desire, need; impulse, instinct.
4 *she lacked the drive to start on a new career*: **motivation**, **ambition**, push, single-mindedness, will power, dedication, doggedness, tenacity, enterprise, initiative, enthusiasm, zeal, commitment, aggression, aggressiveness, forcefulness, spirit; energy, vigour, verve, vitality, liveliness, vim, pep; informal get-up-and-go, zip, pizzazz, punch.
▷ANTONYMS inertia.
5 *an anti-corruption drive*: **campaign**, crusade, movement, effort, push, surge, appeal.
6 Brit. *a whist drive*: **tournament**, competition, contest, event, match.

drivel noun *Walter was talking complete drivel*: **nonsense**, twaddle, claptrap, balderdash, gibberish, rubbish, mumbo-jumbo; informal rot, tommyrot, poppycock, phooey, hot air, eyewash, piffle, garbage, tripe, waffle, bosh, bull, bunk, blah, hogwash, baloney; Brit. informal cobblers, codswallop, cock, stuff and nonsense, tosh, double Dutch; N. Amer. informal flapdoodle, blathers, wack, bushwa, applesauce; informal, dated bunkum; vulgar slang crap, bullshit, bollocks, balls; Austral./NZ vulgar slang bulldust.
▷ANTONYMS sense.
▸ verb *you always **drivel on** like this*: **talk nonsense**, talk rubbish, babble, ramble, gibber, burble, blather, blether, prate, prattle, gabble, chatter, twitter, maunder; informal waffle, witter on, gab, talk through one's hat; vulgar slang bullshit.

driver noun **motorist**; chauffeur; pilot, operator, engineer.
▷ANTONYMS passenger.

drizzle noun **1** *they shivered in the cold drizzle*: **fine rain**, Scotch mist, sprinkle of rain, light shower, spray; N. English mizzle.
2 *top with a drizzle of sour cream*: **trickle**, dribble, drip, drop, droplet, stream, rivulet, runnel; topping, covering, sprinkle, sprinkling.
▸ verb **1** *it's beginning to drizzle*: **rain lightly**, shower, spot, spit; N. English mizzle; N. Amer. sprinkle.
2 *leave the jelly to cool and drizzle over the cream*: **trickle**, sprinkle, drip, dribble, pour, splash, spill.

droll adjective **1** *a droll comment*: **funny**, humorous, amusing, comic, comical, mirthful, chucklesome, hilarious, rollicking; clownish, farcical, zany, quirky, eccentric, preposterous; ridiculous, ludicrous, risible, laughable; jocular, light-hearted, facetious, waggish, witty, whimsical, wry, sportive, tongue-in-cheek; entertaining, diverting, engaging, sparkling; informal wacky, side-splitting, rib-tickling.
▷ANTONYMS serious.
2 *a droll little girl*: **quaint**, odd, strange, queer, eccentric, outlandish, bizarre, whimsical.

> *Word toolkit* **droll**
>
> See **witty**.

drone verb **1** *we heard a plane droning overhead*: **hum**, buzz, whirr, vibrate, murmur, rumble, purr, hiss, whisper, sigh.
2 *the president **droned on** about right and wrong*: **speak boringly**, speak monotonously, go on and on, talk interminably; intone, pontificate; informal spout, sound off, jaw, spiel, speechify, preachify.
▸ noun **1** *the drone of aircraft taking off*: **hum**, buzz, whirr, whirring, vibration, murmur, murmuring, purr, purring, hiss, hissing, whisper, whispering, sigh.
2 *students came to be regarded as drones supported by taxpayers' money*: **hanger-on**, parasite, leech, passenger; **idler**, loafer, layabout, lounger, good-for-nothing, do-nothing, sluggard, laggard; informal **lazybones**, scrounger, sponger, cadger, freeloader, bloodsucker, waster, skiver, slacker.

drool verb *his mouth was open and drooling*: **salivate**, dribble, slaver, slobber, drivel, water at the mouth; Scottish slabber.
▸ noun *a fine trickle of drool leaked from the corner of his mouth*: **saliva**, spit, spittle, dribble, slaver, slobber.

droop verb **1** *the horse had his tail drooping*: **hang down**, hang, dangle, bend, bow, stoop, sag, sink, slump, fall down, drop, flop, wilt, become limp, become flaccid, drape.
▷ANTONYMS be upright.
2 *Danny's eyelids were drooping*: **close**, shut, fall.
▷ANTONYMS open.
3 *he had to break some news to her that made her droop still more*: **be despondent**, lose heart, give up hope, become dispirited, become dejected, despond; flag, fade, languish, falter, weaken, wilt, go into a decline, waste away.
▷ANTONYMS cheer.
▸ noun *the lustreless droop of her hair*: **drooping**, sag, sagging, sinking, slump, slumping; bend, bow, bowing, stoop, stooping.

droopy adjective *a droopy moustache*: **hanging down**, drooping, hanging, dangling, falling, dropping, draped; bending, bent, bowed, bowing, stooping; sagging, sinking, slumping, flopping, wilting, becoming limp, becoming flaccid.
▷ANTONYMS upright.

> *Word toolkit* **droopy**
>
> See **sagging**.

drop verb **1** *Eric dropped a tea chest full of crockery*: **let fall**, let go (of), fail to hold, lose one's grip on; release, unhand, relinquish.
▷ANTONYMS hold on to; lift.
2 *stalactites are formed when water drops from a cave roof*: **drip**, fall in drops, fall, dribble, trickle, drizzle, flow, run, plop, leak.
3 *an aeroplane had dropped out of the sky*: **fall**, come/go down, descend, sink; plunge, plummet, dive, nosedive, tumble, pitch, slump.
▷ANTONYMS rise.
4 *she dropped to her knees*: **fall**, sink, collapse, descend, go down, slide, stumble, tumble.
▷ANTONYMS rise.
5 informal *I was dropping with exhaustion*: **collapse**, faint, pass out, black out, swoon, lose consciousness, fall unconscious, keel over, fall/sink down; informal flake out, conk out, go out.
6 *the track separated as it dropped from the ridge*: **slope downwards**, slope, slant downwards, descend, go down, decline, fall away, sink, dip.
▷ANTONYMS rise.
7 *they decided to drop the price | the exchange rate dropped*: **decrease**, lessen, make less, reduce, diminish, depreciate; fall, decline, become less, dwindle, sink, slump, slacken off, plunge, plummet.
▷ANTONYMS increase.
8 *pupils will be allowed to drop history or geography at 14*: **give up**, finish with, withdraw from, retire from, cancel; discontinue, end, stop, cease, halt, terminate; abandon, forgo, relinquish, dispense with, have done with, throw up; informal pack in, quit, cry off.
▷ANTONYMS take up; continue.

9 *he was dropped from the team*: **exclude**, discard, expel, oust, throw out, leave out, get rid of; dismiss, discharge, let go; informal boot out, kick out, chuck out, turf out.
▷ANTONYMS pick.
10 *he was determined to drop his more unsuitable friends*: **abandon**, desert, throw over; repudiate, renounce, disown, disclaim, disavow, turn one's back on, wash one's hands of; discard, reject, give up, cast off; neglect, shun; archaic forsake.
▷ANTONYMS keep, retain.
11 *he tried to look working-class and dropped his aitches | he dropped all reference to 'compensation'*: **omit**, leave out, leave off, eliminate, take out, miss out, delete, cut, erase; elide, contract, slur.
▷ANTONYMS pronounce.
12 *he* ***dropped*** *the tapes* ***off*** *| the taxi* ***dropped*** *her* ***off***: **deliver**, bring, take, convey, carry, transport; leave, put off, unload; allow to alight.
▷ANTONYMS pick up.
13 *drop the gun on the floor*: **put**, place, rest, deposit, set, set down, lay, leave, settle, shove, stick, position, station; informal pop, plonk.
▷ANTONYMS pick up.
14 *she dropped the names of her most prestigious clients*: **mention**, refer to, speak of, hint at; bring up, raise, broach, introduce; show off.
15 *the club has yet to drop a point in the second division*: **lose**, fail to win, concede, miss out on, give away, let slip.
▷ANTONYMS win.
□ **drop back/behind** *she dropped back unnoticed by the others*: **fall back/behind**, get left behind, lag behind, straggle, linger, dawdle, dally, hang back, loiter, bring/take up the rear; informal dilly-dally; archaic or literary tarry.
▷ANTONYMS go ahead, keep up.
□ **drop off 1** *trade between the two countries dropped off sharply*. See **drop** (sense 7 of the verb). **2** *insomnia can mean dropping off in the day*: **fall asleep**, go to sleep, get to sleep, doze (off), have a nap, catnap, drowse; informal nod off, go off, drift off, snooze, take forty winks, get some shut-eye, crash out, go out like a light, flake out, conk out; N. Amer. informal sack out, zone out.
▷ANTONYMS wake up.
□ **drop out** *he had* ***dropped out of*** *his studies*. See **drop** (sense 8 of the verb).
▶ **noun 1** *a drop of water*: **droplet**, blob, globule, bead, bubble, tear, dot, spheroid, oval; informal glob.
2 *it just needs a drop of oil*: **small amount**, little, bit, dash, spot, soupçon; dribble, driblet, sprinkle, trickle, splash, scintilla; lick, taste, dram, sip, trace, whiff, whisper, nuance, murmur, breath; pinch, dab, speck, grain, smattering, sprinkling; particle, modicum; informal smidgen, tad.
▷ANTONYMS large amount, great deal.
3 *an acid drop*: **sweet**, lozenge, pastille, piece of confectionery; chocolate, bonbon, fondant, toffee; N. Amer. candy.
4 *a small drop in profits*: **decrease**, reduction, decline, lowering, lessening, falling off, fall-off, downturn, slump; cut, cutback, curtailment, diminution; depreciation, devaluation.
▷ANTONYMS rise, increase.
5 *I walked over to the edge of the drop*: **cliff**, abyss, chasm, gorge, gully, precipice; slope, descent, incline, declivity, downslope, ramp.
6 (**the drop**) informal *they only just avoided the drop last season*: **relegation**, demotion, lowering, reduction, downgrading.
▷ANTONYMS promotion.
7 (**the drop**) *he walked around her like a hangman measuring her for the drop*: **hanging**, gibbeting; execution, capital punishment, death sentence/penalty; informal stringing up.

dropout noun *long hair was the trademark of the dropout*: **beatnik**, hippy, bohemian, nonconformist, free spirit, avant-gardist, rebel, misfit, outsider, loner, eccentric; idler, layabout, loafer, lounger, good-for-nothing; informal freak, oddball, deadbeat, waster, bum.

droppings plural noun *rat droppings*: **excrement**, excreta, faeces, stools, dung, ordure, manure; informal poo, doo-doo; vulgar slang shit, crap, turds.

dross noun *sometimes it's possible to find a little gem amongst the mass-produced dross*: **rubbish**, junk, debris, chaff, draff, detritus, flotsam and jetsam; N. Amer. trash, garbage; informal dreck; Brit. informal grot.

drought noun **dry spell**, dry period, lack of rain, shortage of water; Scottish drouth.

drove noun **1** *a drove of cattle*: **herd**, flock, pack, fold.
2 *they came down the street in droves*: **crowd**, swarm, horde, multitude, mob, throng, host, mass, army; collection, gathering, assembly, company; rabble, herd, crush, press, stream, sea.

drown verb **1** *he was shipwrecked, and very nearly drowned*: **suffocate in water**, inhale water; go under; go to a watery grave; informal go to Davy Jones's locker.
2 *when the ice melted, the valleys were drowned*: **flood**, submerge, immerse, inundate, deluge, swamp, engulf, drench, soak, cover, saturate.
▷ANTONYMS drain.
3 *his voice was drowned by the clatter of footsteps*: **make inaudible**, drown out, be louder than, overpower, overwhelm, overcome, override, engulf, swallow up, devour, bury; muffle, deaden, stifle, wipe out, extinguish, silence.
▷ANTONYMS augment.
4 *she had spent every waking hour working, trying to drown her private pain*: **suppress**, deaden, stifle, restrain, smother, bottle up, hold back, keep back, check, keep in check, curb, contain, bridle, put a lid on; extinguish, quash, quench, obliterate, wipe out, get rid of.

drowse verb *they were content to drowse in the sun*: **doze**, sleep (lightly), nap, take a nap, catnap, take a siesta, rest; informal snooze, have a snooze, snatch/get forty winks, get some shut-eye; Brit. informal kip, have a kip, get some kip; N. Amer. informal catch some Zs, catch a few Zs; literary slumber.
▷ANTONYMS be awake.
▶ **noun** *she had been alerted from her drowse*: **doze**, light sleep, nap, catnap, siesta, lie-down, rest; informal snooze, forty winks, shut-eye; Brit. informal kip, zizz; literary slumber.
▷ANTONYMS wakefulness.

drowsiness noun *these tablets often cause drowsiness*: **sleepiness**, somnolence, tiredness, fatigue, weariness, exhaustion; sluggishness, lethargy, listlessness, torpor, enervation, lifelessness, laziness, indolence, inertia, lassitude, apathy, debility; informal doziness, dopiness, grogginess.
▷ANTONYMS wakefulness; energy.

drowsy adjective **1** *the stove warmed the tent up and we became drowsy*: **sleepy**, half asleep, dozy, dozing, heavy, heavy-eyed, yawning, nodding, groggy, somnolent, ready for bed, hardly able to keep one's eyes open; tired, weary, fatigued, exhausted; lethargic, sluggish, torpid, lifeless, listless, languid, languorous, comatose, dazed, drugged; informal snoozy, dopey, yawny, dead beat, all in, done in, dog-tired; Brit. informal knackered; literary slumberous.
▷ANTONYMS wakeful, alert.
2 *a warm, drowsy afternoon*: **soporific**, sleep-inducing, sleepy, somniferous, narcotic, sedative, calmative, tranquillizing; lulling, soothing; dreamy; rare somnific.
▷ANTONYMS invigorating.

drubbing noun **1** *I decided to give her fancy man a good drubbing*: **beating**, thrashing, walloping, thumping, battering, pounding, pummelling, slapping, smacking, punching, bludgeoning, thwacking, cuffing, buffeting, mauling, pelting, lambasting; whipping, flogging, flaying, birching, cudgelling, clubbing; informal hammering, licking, clobbering, belting, bashing, pasting, whacking, slugging, tanning, biffing, bopping, hiding, beating-up, duffing-up, doing-over, working-over, kicking.
2 *Scotland's 3-0 drubbing by France*: **defeat**, beating, trouncing, rout, loss, vanquishing, crushing; informal licking, thrashing, clobbering.
▷ANTONYMS win.

drudge noun *her family reduced her to a household drudge*: **menial**, menial worker, slave, toiler, lackey; servant, labourer, hack, worker, maid/man of all work, houseboy, factotum, hewer of wood and drawer of water; informal skivvy, dogsbody, gofer, running dog, runner; N. Amer. peon; Brit. dated charwoman, charlady, char; archaic scullion, servitor.
▶ **verb** archaic *he was drudging in the fields as a day labourer*. See **toil** (sense 1 of the verb).

drudgery noun *the housewives were left alone with their drudgery*: **hard work**, menial work, donkey work, toil, toiling, labour, hard/sweated labour, chores, plodding; slavery; informal skivvying, grind, slog; Brit. informal graft; Austral./NZ informal (hard) yakka; archaic travail, moil.
▷ANTONYMS relaxation.

drug noun **1** *drugs prescribed by doctors can be extremely hazardous if misused*: **medicine**, medical drug, medication, medicament; remedy, cure, antidote; cure-all, panacea; nostrum; potion, elixir; informal magic bullet; archaic physic.
2 *she was obviously under the influence of drugs or booze*: **narcotic**, **stimulant**, hallucinogen, addictive drug, recreational drug, illegal drug, substance; informal dope, junk, gear, stuff, downer, upper; vulgar slang shit.
▶ **verb 1** *he was drugged and bundled into the boot of a car*: **anaesthetize**, give an anaesthetic to, narcotize, give drugs to, give narcotics to, give opiates to, poison; knock out, make/render unconscious, make/render insensible, stupefy, befuddle; informal dope.
2 *she had drugged his coffee*: **add drugs to**, tamper with, adulterate, contaminate, poison; informal dope, spike, lace, slip a Mickey Finn into, doctor.

> *Word links* **drug**
>
> **narco-** related prefix, as in *narcoterrorism*
> **pharmaco-** related prefix
> **pharmaceutical** relating to drugs
> **pharmacology** branch of medicine to do with drugs
> **pharmacophobia** fear of drugs
> Brit. **pharmacy**, **chemist's**, N. Amer. **drugstore** shop selling drugs
> Brit. **pharmacist**, **chemist**, N. Amer. **druggist** seller of drugs

drug addict noun See **addict**.

drugged adjective *he was obviously drunk or drugged when he wrote it*: **stupefied**, insensible, befuddled; delirious, hallucinating, narcotized; anaesthetized, knocked out, comatose; informal **stoned**, high, doped, dopey,

d

on a trip, tripping, spaced out, zonked, wasted, wrecked, high as a kite, off one's head, out of one's mind, flying, turned on, hyped up, freaked out, charged up; Brit. informal loved-up.
▷ANTONYMS sober.

drum noun **1** *the steady drum of raindrops*: **beat**, rhythm, patter, tap, chatter, pounding, thump, thumping, thud, thudding, rattle, rattling, pitter-patter, rat-a-tat, pit-a-pat, thrum, tattoo, vibration, throb, throbbing, pulsation; archaic bicker, clacket.
2 *a drum of radioactive waste*: **canister**, barrel, cylinder, tank, bin, can; container, receptacle, holder, vessel, repository.
▸verb **1** *she drummed her fingers on the desktop*: **tap**, beat, rap, knock, strike, thud, thump, hit; tattoo, thrum.
2 *an unwritten law which was* ***drummed into*** *us at school*: **instil**, drive, drive home, din, hammer, drill, drub, implant, ingrain, inculcate; teach over and over again, indoctrinate, brainwash.
□ **drum someone out** *he was* ***drummed out of*** *office*: **expel from**, dismiss from, discharge from, throw out of, oust from; drive out of, get rid of, thrust out of, push out of; exclude from, banish from; Military cashier; informal give someone the boot, boot out, kick out, give someone their marching orders, give someone the bullet, give someone the push, show someone the door, send packing.
□ **drum something up** *he was drumming up business for his new investment company*: **round up**, gather, collect; summon, obtain, get, attract; canvass, solicit, petition, bid for.

> *Word links* **drum**
>
> **drummer, timpanist, percussionist** player of drums

drunk adjective *they went to a pub and got drunk*: **intoxicated**, inebriated, drunken, befuddled, incapable, tipsy, the worse for drink, under the influence, maudlin; blind drunk, dead drunk, rolling drunk, roaring drunk, (as) drunk as a lord, (as) drunk as a skunk; sottish, tippling, toping, gin-soaked; informal tight, merry, the worse for wear, woozy, pie-eyed, two/three sheets to the wind, under the table, plastered, smashed, wrecked, sloshed, soused, well oiled, sozzled, blotto, blitzed, canned, stewed, pickled, tanked (up), soaked, bombed, hammered, blasted, off one's face, out of/off one's head, out of one's skull, wasted, wired, in one's cups, reeling, cock-eyed, zonked, guttered, fuddled, stinko, ratted; Brit. informal legless, steaming, bevvied, paralytic, Brahms and Liszt, half cut, out of it, having had a skinful, bladdered, trolleyed, well away, squiffy, tiddly, out of one's box, having had one over the eight, cut, steamed, mullered, slaughtered; Brit. vulgar slang pissed, as pissed as a newt/fart, rat-arsed, arseholed; Scottish informal fou; N. Amer. informal loaded, trashed, crock, juiced, sauced, squiffed, swacked, strung out, liquored up, out of one's gourd, in the bag, zoned; N. Amer. & Austral./NZ informal shickered, shot; Austral. informal full, as full as a goog, inked; S. African informal lekker; euphemistic tired and emotional; informal, dated stoned, lit up, as tight as a tick; Brit. informal, dated half seas over, pixilated; archaic sotted, besotted, foxed, screwed; rare crapulent, crapulous, inebriate, bibulous, ebrious, ebriose, ebriate.
▷ANTONYMS sober.
▸noun *a drunk lay slumped against a wall*: **drunkard**, inebriate, drinker, imbiber, tippler, sot; heavy drinker, hard drinker, serious drinker, problem drinker; alcoholic, dipsomaniac, chronic alcoholic, alcohol-abuser, alcohol addict, person with a drink problem; informal boozer, soak, lush, wino, alky, sponge, elbow-bender, barfly, tosspot; Austral./NZ informal hophead, metho; archaic toper; vulgar slang pisshead, piss artist.
▷ANTONYMS teetotaller.

drunken adjective **1** *a drunken driver*. See **drunk**.
2 *a drunken all-night party*: **debauched**, dissipated, riotous, carousing, revelling, roistering, uproarious, unruly, intemperate, unrestrained, uninhibited, abandoned; orgiastic, bacchanalian, Bacchic, wassailing, Dionysian, saturnalian; informal boozy.
▷ANTONYMS restrained.

drunkenness noun *he was prone to bouts of drunkenness*: **intoxication**, inebriation, insobriety, tipsiness; intemperance, overindulgence, debauchery; hard drinking, serious drinking, heavy drinking, alcoholism, alcohol abuse, dipsomania; rare inebriety, sottishness, crapulence, bibulousness.
▷ANTONYMS sobriety.

dry adjective **1** *the dry desert lay behind*: **arid**, parched, scorched, baked, burned, dried up/out, torrid, hot, sizzling, burning; waterless, moistureless, rainless; dehydrated, desiccated; thirsty; as dry as a bone, bone dry, as dry as dust; rare droughty, torrefied.
▷ANTONYMS wet.
2 *the crackle of dry leaves*: **parched**, dried, withered, shrivelled, wilted, wizened; crisp, crispy, brittle; dehydrated, desiccated, sun-baked; sapless, juiceless.
▷ANTONYMS fresh.
3 *the hamburgers were dry*: **hard**, hardened, dried out, stale, old, past its best, past its sell-by date, off.
▷ANTONYMS fresh; moist.
4 *the river is dry | a dry well*: **waterless**, dried out, empty.
5 *I brought a few beers in case you got dry*: **thirsty**, dehydrated, longing for a drink; informal parched, gasping.
6 *it was dry work*: **thirst-making**, thirst-provoking, thirsty, hot, strenuous, arduous, heavy, tiring, exhausting.
7 *a piece of dry toast*: **unbuttered**, plain, butterless.
8 *the story brings the dry facts to life*: **bare**, simple, basic, fundamental, stark, naked, bald, cold, hard, straightforward; unadorned, unembellished.
▷ANTONYMS embellished.
9 *a dry debate on science policy*: **dull**, uninteresting, boring, unexciting, tedious, tiresome, wearisome, dreary, monotonous, dry as dust, arid; unimaginative, sterile, flat, bland, insipid, lacklustre, stodgy, colourless, lifeless, prosaic, run-of-the-mill, humdrum, mundane, commonplace, workaday, quotidian, routine, vapid; stiff, leaden, wooden; informal deadly; Brit. informal samey; Scottish informal dreich.
▷ANTONYMS interesting, lively.
10 *he's got a dry sense of humour*: **wry**, subtle, low-key, laconic, sly, sharp; deadpan, straight-faced, poker-faced; ironic, sardonic, sarcastic, cynical, mordant, biting; satirical, mocking, scoffing, droll, waggish; Brit. informal sarky.
11 *he was nonplussed by this dry response to his cordial advance*: **unemotional**, indifferent, undemonstrative, impassive, cool, cold, clinical, passionless, emotionless; aloof, reserved, remote, distant, restrained, impersonal, formal, stiff, rigid, wooden, starchy.
▷ANTONYMS emotional, expressive.
12 *sorry, this is a dry state | she has been dry for almost a year*: **Prohibitionist**; **teetotal**, alcohol-free, non-drinking, abstinent; clean, sober; informal on the wagon, straight.
13 *dry white wine*: **crisp**, sharp, piquant, not sweet, tart, bitter.
▷ANTONYMS sweet.
14 Brit. *they deliberately selected dry candidates*: **monetarist**; **arch-conservative**, right-wing, reactionary; Economics supply-side; informal true-blue.
▷ANTONYMS wet; left-wing.
▸verb **1** *the hot sun had dried the ground again*: **make dry**, dry out/up, parch, scorch, sear, bake; dehydrate, desiccate, dehumidify.
▷ANTONYMS moisten.
2 *dry the leaves and break them into small pieces*: **dry up**, dehydrate, desiccate; wither, shrivel, wilt, wizen, mummify.
▷ANTONYMS moisten.
3 *I saw you drying your hair | he dried the dishes*: **dry off**, towel, rub; mop up, blot up, soak up, absorb, sop up, clean up; drain.
4 *she dried her eyes*: **wipe**, wipe tears from, rub, dab.
5 *there are various methods of drying meat*: **desiccate**, dehydrate, remove the moisture from; preserve, cure, smoke.
□ **dry out** *he has spent periods drying out in a clinic*: **give up drinking**, **give up alcohol**, become teetotal, overcome alcoholism, take the pledge; informal go on the wagon.
□ **dry up 1** informal *then he dried up, and Phil couldn't get another word out of him*: **stop speaking/talking**, fall silent, say no more, shut up; forget one's lines/words; informal belt up, put a sock in it. **2** *foreign investment may dry up*: **dwindle**, wane, disappear, fail, vanish, subside, peter out, fade (away), die away/out/off, taper off, trail away/off, ebb, melt away, evaporate, come to nothing, come to a halt/an end, run out, give out; become unproductive, grow barren/sterile, cease to yield. ▷ANTONYMS continue.
▸noun *on economic policy he is a dry*: **monetarist**; **arch-conservative**, right-winger, reactionary; Economics supply-sider.
▷ANTONYMS wet; left-winger.

> *Word links* **dry**
>
> **xero-** related prefix, as in *xeroderma, xerography*

dual adjective *a small flap fulfils a dual purpose as cupboard door and table*: **double**, twofold, binary; duplicate, duplex, twin, matched, matching, paired, in pairs, coupled; rare binate.
▷ANTONYMS single.

duality noun *there was a duality in her feelings towards Johnny*: **doubleness**, dualism, duplexity, ambivalence; dichotomy, polarity, separation, opposition, difference.

dub verb **1** *he was dubbed 'the world's sexiest man'*: **nickname**, call, name, give a name, label, christen, term, tag, entitle, style; **describe as**, designate, classify, class, categorize, characterize, denominate, nominate.
2 *this was followed by the dubbing of twenty four new knights*: **knight**, confer/bestow a knighthood on, invest with a knighthood.

dubiety noun rare *anxiety had been excited by the dubiety of his fate*. See **doubt** (senses 1 and 3 of the noun).

dubious adjective **1** *I was rather dubious about the whole idea*: **doubtful**, uncertain, unsure, in doubt, hesitant; undecided, unsettled, unconfirmed, undetermined, indefinite, unresolved, up in the air; wavering, vacillating, irresolute, in a quandary, in a dilemma, on the horns of a dilemma; sceptical, suspicious; informal iffy.
▷ANTONYMS certain, definite.

2 *a dubious businessman*: **suspicious**, suspect, under suspicion, untrustworthy, unreliable, undependable, questionable; informal shady, fishy, funny, not kosher; Brit. informal dodgy.
▷ANTONYMS trustworthy.
3 *she gave him a dubious reply*: **equivocal**, ambiguous, indeterminate, indefinite, unclear, vague, imprecise, hazy, puzzling, enigmatic, cryptic; open to question, debatable, questionable.
▷ANTONYMS decisive, clear, definite.

dubitable adjective rare *these beliefs are certainly dubitable*. See **debatable**.

duck[1] noun

> *Word links* **duck**
>
> **drake** male
> **duck** female
> **duckling** young

duck[2] verb **1** *the ball passed over the batsman as he ducked | he ducked behind the wall*: **bob down**, bend (down), bow down, stoop (down), crouch (down), squat (down), hunch down, hunker down, sit on one's haunches; cower, cringe, shrink, huddle; N. Amer. informal scooch.
▷ANTONYMS straighten up; stand.
2 *she was ducked in the river*: **dip**, dunk, plunge, immerse, submerge, lower, sink.
3 informal *he* ***ducked out of*** *history lessons | they cannot duck the issue much longer*: **shirk**, dodge, evade, avoid, steer clear of, run away from, elude, escape, find a way out of, back out of, pull out of, shun, eschew, miss; sidestep, bypass, skirt round, circumvent, give a wide berth to, find a way round, turn one's back on; informal cop out of, get out of, wriggle out of, worm one's way out of; Brit. informal skive, skive off, funk; N. Amer. informal cut; Austral./NZ informal duck-shove; archaic decline, bilk.
▷ANTONYMS take part in; face up to.

duct noun *the glands drain into a common duct | a ventilation duct*: **tube**, channel, passage, canal, vessel; conduit, culvert; pipe, pipeline, outlet, inlet, flue, shaft, vent, airway; Anatomy ductus, ductule, vas, trachea.

ductile adjective **1** *ductile metals are often used to make machinery*: **pliable**, pliant, flexible, supple, plastic, tensile, tractile; soft, malleable, workable, shapable, mouldable, bendable; informal bendy; rare fictile.
▷ANTONYMS brittle.
2 *the government found new ways to make the people ductile*: **docile**, obedient, submissive, subservient, meek, mild, lamblike, willing, accommodating, amenable, cooperative, complaisant, compliant, pliant, pliable, malleable, tractable, biddable, persuadable, manipulable, easily manipulated, easily controlled, controllable, easily handled, like putty in someone's hands; gullible; informal, dated milky; rare persuasible, suasible.
▷ANTONYMS intransigent.

dud informal noun *their new product turned out to be a complete dud*: **failure**, flop, let-down, disappointment; Brit. damp squib; informal washout, lemon, loser, no-hoper, non-starter, dead loss, dead duck, lead balloon; N. Amer. informal clinker.
▷ANTONYMS success.
▶ adjective **1** *a dud typewriter ribbon*: **defective**, faulty, unsound, inoperative, broken, broken-down, not working, not in working order, not functioning, malfunctioning, failed; informal bust, busted, kaput, on its last legs, conked out, done for; Brit. informal duff, knackered; Brit. vulgar slang buggered.
▷ANTONYMS in working order.
2 *he payed with a dud £50 note*: **counterfeit**, fraudulent, forged, fake, faked, false, bogus, spurious; bad, invalid, worthless; informal phoney.
▷ANTONYMS genuine.

dudgeon noun
□ **in high dudgeon** *Kirsty swept out of the room in high dudgeon*: **indignantly**, resentfully, angrily, furiously, wrathfully; in a temper, in indignation, in anger, with resentment, with displeasure, having taken offence, having taken umbrage; informal in a huff, in a lather, in a paddy, foaming at the mouth, fit to be tied, as cross as two sticks, seeing red; Brit. informal, dated in a bate, in a wax.

due adjective **1** *she reminded them that their fees were due*: **owing**, owed, to be paid, payable, payable now, payable immediately, receivable immediately; outstanding, overdue, unpaid, unsettled, undischarged; N. Amer. delinquent, past due.
▷ANTONYMS paid.
2 *the chancellor's Autumn statement is due today*: **expected**, required, awaited, anticipated, scheduled for.
3 *he was treated with the respect* ***due to*** *a great artist*: **deserved by**, merited by, earned by, warranted by; appropriate to, fit for, fitting for, suitable for, right for, proper to; archaic meet for.
▷ANTONYMS undeserved by.
4 *he drove without due care and attention*: **proper**, right and proper, correct, rightful, fitting, suitable, appropriate, apt, adequate, sufficient, enough, ample, satisfactory, requisite; formal condign; archaic meet.
▷ANTONYMS unsuitable.
□ **due to 1** *her death was due to an infection of the abdominal wall*: **attributable to**, caused by, ascribed to, ascribable to, assignable to, because of, put down to. **2** *the train was cancelled due to staff shortages*: **because of**, owing to, on account of, as a consequence of, as a result of, thanks to, by reason of, on grounds of, in view of.
▶ noun **1** *he attracts more criticism than is his due*: **rightful treatment**, fair treatment, deserved fate, just punishment; right, entitlement; rights, just deserts, deserts; informal comeuppance; archaic recompense.
2 (**dues**) *union members have already paid their dues*: **fee**, membership fee, subscription, charge, toll, levy; payment, contribution.
▶ adverb *he hiked due north and arrived back at his base*: **directly**, straight, exactly, precisely, without deviating, undeviatingly, dead, plumb, squarely.

d

duel noun **1** *the Baron was killed in a duel*: **affair of honour**, mano-a-mano, single combat; fight, battle, clash, encounter, confrontation, head-to-head; informal face-off, shoot-out; archaic field meeting, duello, judicial duel, rencounter, meeting, meeting for satisfaction of honour; rare monomachy.
2 *the snooker duel got under way in earnest*: **contest**, competition, match, game, event, fixture, meet; battle, fight, clash, encounter, engagement.
▶ verb *they duelled with swords*: **fight a duel**; fight, clash, battle, combat, contend; archaic go out.

duff adjective Brit. informal *he's made some really duff films*. See **bad**.

duffer noun informal *he's such a duffer—we shouldn't have hired him*: **bungler**, blunderer, incompetent, oaf, dunce, dolt, dunderhead, fool, idiot, booby, stupid person, moron, cretin, imbecile; informal chump, clot, clod, nitwit, dimwit, airhead, birdbrain, lamebrain, pea-brain, numbskull, thickhead, fathead, blockhead, bonehead, meathead, chucklehead, knucklehead, pinhead, wooden-head, dipstick, dumb-bell, dumbhead, dumbo, dum-dum, noodle, donkey, ass, nerd; Brit. informal berk, divvy, wally, numpty, wazzock, nit, mug, prat, twerp, twonk, pillock, muppet; Scottish informal balloon, galoot, cuddy, nyaff; N. Amer. informal doofus, goofball, goof, putz, bozo, boob, lamer, chowderhead, meatball, lummox, dummy, turkey, clunk, ding-a-ling, palooka; Austral./NZ informal galah, drongo, alec, dingbat.

dulcet adjective *the Grand Duchess Anna spoke in dulcet tones*: **sweet**, sweet-sounding, mellifluous, euphonious, soothing, mellow, honeyed, pleasant, agreeable; melodious, melodic, tuneful, musical, lilting, lyrical, harmonious, silvery, silver-toned, bell-like, golden; informal easy on the ear; rare mellifluent.
▷ANTONYMS harsh.

dull adjective **1** *he is the author of several dull novels*: **uninteresting**, boring, tedious, tiresome, wearisome, dry, dry as dust, flat, bland, characterless, featureless, colourless, monotonous, unexciting, uninspiring, unstimulating, lacking variety, lacking variation, lacking excitement, lacking interest, unimaginative, uneventful, lifeless, soulless, insipid; unoriginal, derivative, commonplace, prosaic, run-of-the-mill, humdrum, unremarkable, banal, lame, plodding, ponderous, pedestrian; informal dull as dishwater, deadly, no great shakes, not up to much; Scottish informal dreich; N. Amer. informal dullsville, ornery.
▷ANTONYMS interesting.
2 *it was a miserably dull Saturday morning*: **overcast**, cloudy, gloomy, dark, dim, dismal, dreary, bleak, sombre, grey, leaden, murky, sunless, louring; literary subfusc.
▷ANTONYMS sunny, bright.
3 *the window frames were painted in dull colours*: **drab**, dreary, sombre, dark, subdued, muted, toned down, lacklustre, lustreless, colourless, faded, washed out, muddy, watery, pale; literary subfusc.
▷ANTONYMS bright.
4 *he heard a dull sound outside his door*: **muffled**, muted, quiet, soft, softened, faint, indistinct; stifled, smothered, suppressed.
▷ANTONYMS loud; resonant.
5 *the edge of the chisel soon became dull*: **blunt**, blunted, not sharp, unkeen, unsharpened, dulled, edgeless, worn down.
▷ANTONYMS sharp.
6 *an otherwise dull stock market was enlivened by merger plans*: **slack**, sluggish, flat, slow, slow-moving, quiet, inactive, static, stagnant, depressed.
▷ANTONYMS brisk.
7 *the teacher was talking slowly to a rather dull child*: **unintelligent**, stupid, slow, dull-witted, slow-witted, witless, doltish, dunce-like, stolid, vacuous, empty-headed, brainless, mindless, foolish, half-witted, idiotic, moronic, imbecilic, cretinous, obtuse; informal dense, dim, dim-witted, thick, thick as two short planks, dumb, dopey, dozy, lamebrained, pig-ignorant, bovine, slow on the uptake, soft in the head, brain-dead, boneheaded, chuckleheaded, dunderheaded, wooden-headed, fat-headed, muttonheaded; Brit. informal daft, not the full shilling; N. Amer. vulgar slang dumb-ass.
▷ANTONYMS clever.
8 *her cold made her feel dull*: **sluggish**, lethargic, enervated, unenergetic, listless, languid, torpid, inactive, inert, slow, slow-moving, sleepy, somnolent, drowsy, weary, tired, fatigued, heavy, apathetic; informal dozy, dopey, yawny; N. Amer. informal logy; Medicine asthenic, neurasthenic; archaic lymphatic.
▷ANTONYMS lively.
▶ verb **1** *the pain was temporarily dulled by drugs*: **lessen**, decrease, diminish, reduce, dampen, depress, take the edge off, blunt, deaden, mute, soften, tone

d

down, allay, ease, soothe, assuage, alleviate, palliate, moderate, mitigate.
▷ANTONYMS intensify.
2 *sleep had dulled her mind*: **numb**, benumb, deaden, desensitize, render insensitive, stupefy, daze, stun; drug, sedate, tranquillize, narcotize; rare torpefy, obtund.
▷ANTONYMS enliven.
3 *the leaves are dulled by powdery mildew*: **fade**, pale, bleach, wash out, decolorize, decolour, dim, etiolate.
▷ANTONYMS enhance; brighten.
4 *the rain came in flurries, dulling the sky*: **darken**, blacken, dim, blur, veil, obscure, shadow, fog; literary bedim.
▷ANTONYMS brighten.
5 *the sombre atmosphere of that place dulled her spirit*: **dampen**, put a damper on, cast a pall over, cast down, lower, depress, crush, shake, sap, suppress, extinguish, smother, stifle.
▷ANTONYMS raise.

dullard noun *the MP was caricatured as a dupe and a dullard*: **idiot**, fool, stupid person, simpleton, ignoramus, oaf, dunce, dolt, moron, cretin, imbecile; informal duffer, nincompoop, booby, dope, chump, nitwit, dimwit, airhead, birdbrain, lamebrain, pea-brain, numbskull, thickhead, fathead, blockhead, bonehead, dunderhead, meathead, muttonhead, wooden-head, dipstick, dumb-bell, noodle, dumbo, dum-dum, ass, donkey, jerk; Brit. informal wally, berk, divvy, nit, mug, pillock, prat, wazzock, silly billy; N. Amer. informal doofus, goof, goofball, putz, bozo, boob, lamer, lummox, dummy, turkey; Austral./NZ informal galah, dingbat, drongo.

duly adverb 1 *the document was duly signed and authorized*: **properly**, correctly, in due manner, rightly, fittingly, fitly, aptly, appropriately, suitably.
▷ANTONYMS improperly.
2 *the footman duly arrived to collect Alice*: **at the proper time**, at the right time, in due time, on time, punctually.

dumb adjective 1 *he was born deaf and dumb | she stood dumb while he poured out a stream of abuse*: **mute**, unable to speak, without the power of speech; **speechless**, tongue-tied, wordless, silent, at a loss for words, voiceless, inarticulate, taciturn, uncommunicative, untalkative, tight-lipped, close-mouthed, saying nothing; informal mum; technical aphasic, aphonic.
2 informal *he is not as dumb as he wants people to believe*. See **stupid** (sense 1).

dumbfound verb *she was dumbfounded by Bruce's actions*: **astonish**, astound, amaze, stagger, surprise, startle, stun, confound, stupefy, daze, nonplus; throw, shake, unnerve, disconcert, discompose, bewilder; take someone's breath away, take by surprise, take aback, shake up, stop someone in their tracks, strike dumb, leave open-mouthed, leave aghast, catch off balance; informal flabbergast, floor, knock for six, knock sideways, knock out, knock the stuffing out of, bowl over, blow someone's mind, blow away.

dumbfounded adjective *when you told me I had won I was dumbfounded*: **astonished**, astounded, amazed, staggered, surprised, startled, stunned, confounded, nonplussed, stupefied, dazed, dumbstruck, open-mouthed, agape, speechless, at a loss for words, thunderstruck, goggle-eyed, wide-eyed; taken aback, thrown, shaken, unnerved, disconcerted, discomposed, bewildered; informal flabbergasted, floored, flummoxed, knocked for six, knocked sideways, knocked out, bowled over, blown away, unable to believe one's eyes/ears; Brit. informal gobsmacked.

dummy noun 1 *a shop-window dummy dressed in a military uniform*: **mannequin**, manikin, lifelike model, figure, lay figure.
2 *the book is just a dummy*: **mock-up**, imitation, likeness, lookalike, representation, substitute, sample, copy, replica, reproduction; counterfeit, sham, fake, forgery; informal dupe.
3 informal *if you still don't get it, you're a dummy*. See **idiot**.
▶ adjective *we were to mount a dummy attack on the airfield | a dummy bomb*: **simulated**, feigned, pretended, practice, trial, mock, make-believe; **fake**, artificial, false, bogus, sham, imitation, reproduction, replica; informal pretend, phoney.
▷ANTONYMS real.

dump noun 1 *it's time to take the rubbish to the dump*: **rubbish tip**, rubbish dump, refuse dump, rubbish heap, refuse heap, tip, dumping ground, dustheap, slag heap, midden, dunghill, dung heap; Brit. scrapyard; N. Amer. junkyard, nuisance grounds.
2 informal *the house is a dump, but the rent is cheap*: **hovel**, shack, slum, shanty, mess; informal hole, pigsty.
▶ verb 1 *he dumped a bag of groceries on the table*: **put down**, lay down, set down, deposit, place, put, unload; drop, let fall, throw down, fling down; informal stick, park, plonk, shove, pop; Brit. informal bung; N. Amer. informal plunk; archaic unlade; rare posit.
2 *they gained permission to dump asbestos at the site*: **dispose of**, get rid of, throw away, throw out, discard, scrap, bin, jettison, cast aside, cast out, fling out, toss out; informal ditch, junk, get shut of; Brit. informal get shot of; N. Amer. informal trash.
3 *pumps are used to dump effluent from the tanks*: **discharge**, empty out, pour out, tip out, unload, jettison, eject, spew out, throw out, force out.
4 informal *he dumped her and ran off with a richer woman*: **abandon**, desert, leave, leave in the lurch, leave high and dry, turn one's back on, jilt, break up with, finish with, cast aside, throw over; informal walk out on, run out on, rat on, drop, ditch, chuck, give someone the elbow, give someone the old heave-ho, leave someone holding the baby; Brit. informal give someone the push, give someone the big E; archaic forsake.

dumps plural noun
□ **down in the dumps** informal **unhappy**, sad, depressed, gloomy, glum, melancholy, melancholic, miserable, sorrowful, dejected, despondent, dispirited, disconsolate, downhearted, downcast, cast down, down, crestfallen, woebegone, low, low in spirits, low-spirited, heavy-hearted, morose, dismal, desolate, weighed down, oppressed; tearful, upset, broken-hearted; informal blue, down in the mouth, fed up, moody; literary dolorous, heartsick, heartsore; archaic chap-fallen.
▷ANTONYMS cheerful.

dumpy adjective *that skirt makes you look dumpy and middle-aged*: **short**, squat, stubby; **plump**, stout, chubby, chunky, portly, paunchy, corpulent, fat, bulky, broad, broad in the beam, well covered, well padded, well rounded; informal tubby, roly-poly, pudgy, porky; Brit. informal podgy, fubsy; N. Amer. informal zaftig; archaic pursy.
▷ANTONYMS tall; slender.

dun¹ adjective *the typical dun coat of a wild horse*: **greyish-brown**, brownish, dun-coloured, mud-coloured, mouse-coloured, mousy, muddy, khaki, umber.

dun² verb *he was constantly being dunned for the rent*: **importune**, solicit, petition, press, pressurize, plague, pester, nag, harass, hound, badger, beset; N. English mither; informal hassle, bug.

dunce noun *they all called him a dunce at school*: **fool**, idiot, stupid person, simpleton, halfwit, ignoramus, oaf, dolt, dullard, moron, imbecile, cretin; informal dummy, dumbo, dumb-bell, dum-dum, clot, thickhead, nitwit, dimwit, dope, duffer, booby, chump, numbskull, nincompoop, bonehead, blockhead, fathead, meathead, airhead, birdbrain, pea-brain, lamebrain, jerk, ninny, ass, donkey; Brit. informal wally, numpty, berk, twerp, twonk, divvy, nit, mug, pillock, wazzock, silly billy; N. Amer. informal doofus, goof, goofball, schmuck, putz, bozo, boob, lamer, lummox, turkey; Austral./NZ informal galah, drongo, dingbat.
▷ANTONYMS genius.

dune noun *high sand dunes fringe the beach*: **bank**, mound, hillock, hummock, rise, knoll, ridge, heap, drift, accumulation.

dung noun *they use cow dung as fertilizer*: **manure**, muck, animal excrement; faeces, droppings, ordure, cowpats; Indian gobar; N. Amer. informal cow chips, horse apples; vulgar slang shit, crap.

Word links **dung**

scatology study of fossilized dung
copraphagous dung-eating

dungeon noun *the king imprisoned him in the castle dungeon*: **underground cell**, underground prison, oubliette; cell, prison, jail, lock-up, black hole; archaic hole, thieves' hole, bocardo.

dupe verb *her daughters were duped by a handsome Lothario*: **deceive**, trick, hoodwink, hoax, swindle, defraud, cheat, double-cross, gull, mislead, take in, fool, delude, misguide, lead on, inveigle, seduce, ensnare, entrap, beguile; informal con, do, sting, gyp, rip off, diddle, swizzle, shaft, bilk, rook, bamboozle, finagle, pull the wool over someone's eyes, pull someone's leg, pull a fast one on, put one over on, sell a pup to, take to the cleaners; N. Amer. informal sucker, snooker, stiff, euchre, bunco, hornswoggle; Austral. informal pull a swifty on; archaic cozen, sharp; rare mulct.
▶ noun *you were an innocent dupe in Caroline's little game*: **victim**, gull, pawn, puppet, instrument; fool, simpleton, innocent; informal sucker, stooge, sitting duck, sitting target, soft touch, pushover, chump, muggins, charlie, fall guy; Brit. informal mug; N. Amer. informal pigeon, patsy, sap, schlemiel, mark; Austral./NZ informal dill; Brit. informal, dated juggins.
▷ANTONYMS swindler, con man.

duplicate noun *he made a duplicate of the invoice*: **copy**, carbon copy, carbon, photocopy, facsimile, mimeo, mimeograph, reprint; replica, reproduction, exact likeness, close likeness, twin, double, clone, match, mate, fellow, counterpart; informal dupe; trademark Xerox, photostat.
▷ANTONYMS original.
▶ adjective *she kept a duplicate copy of the parchment | duplicate keys*: **matching**, identical, twin, corresponding, equivalent; matched, paired, twofold, coupled.
▷ANTONYMS different.
▶ verb 1 *he urged readers to duplicate and circulate the newsletter*: **copy**, photocopy, photostat, xerox, mimeograph, make a photocopy of, take a photocopy of, make a carbon copy of, make a carbon of, make a facsimile of, reproduce, replicate, reprint, run off.
2 *a feat that will be difficult to duplicate*: **repeat**, do over again, do again, redo, perform again, replicate.

duplication noun *the new system will reduce the need for duplication of documents*: **copying**, duplicating, replicating, replication; photocopying, xeroxing, photostatting, reprinting.

duplicity noun *his conscience would not allow him to enter into duplicity*: **deceitfulness**, deceit, deception, deviousness, two-facedness, double-dealing, underhandedness, dishonesty, falseness, falsity, fraud, fraudulence, sharp practice, swindling, cheating, chicanery, trickery, craft, guile, artifice, subterfuge, skulduggery, treachery, unfairness, unjustness, perfidy, improbity; informal crookedness, shadiness, foxiness, dirty tricks, shenanigans, monkey business, funny business, hanky-panky; Brit. informal jiggery-pokery; N. Amer. informal monkeyshines; Irish informal codology; archaic knavery, knavishness, management.
▷ANTONYMS honesty.

durability noun *man-made fibres give the fabric extra durability*: **imperishability**, permanence, longevity, ability to last, lastingness, resilience, strength, sturdiness, toughness, robustness, soundness; rare durableness.
▷ANTONYMS fragility.

durable adjective **1** *they make highly durable carpets for hotels*: **long-lasting**, **hard-wearing**, heavy-duty, tough, resistant, strong, sturdy, stout, sound, substantial, imperishable, indestructible, made to last, well made, strongly made.
▷ANTONYMS flimsy, delicate.
2 *a durable peace can be established*: **lasting**, long-lasting, long-lived, long-term, enduring, persisting, persistent, abiding, continuing; constant, stable, secure, fast, firm, fixed, deep-rooted, permanent, unfading, undying, everlasting.
▷ANTONYMS short-lived.

duration noun *the student's fees will be paid for the duration of their course*: **full length**, length of time, time, time span, time scale, period, term, span, spell, stretch, fullness, length, extent, continuation, continuance, perpetuation, prolongation.

duress noun *their confessions were extracted under duress*: **coercion**, compulsion, force, pressure, pressurization, intimidation, threats, constraint, enforcement, exaction; informal arm-twisting.
▷ANTONYMS free will.

during preposition *the exhibit attracted 5,000 visitors during January*: **throughout**, through, in, in the course of, throughout the time of, for the time of, in the time of.

dusk noun *he arrived just before dusk | lighted windows shone through the dusk*: **twilight**, nightfall, sunset, sundown, evening, close of day; dark, darkness, semi-darkness, gathering darkness, gloom, gloominess, murk, murkiness, shades of evening; literary gloaming, eventide, eve, even, evenfall; rare tenebrosity, owl light, crepuscule.
▷ANTONYMS dawn; daylight.

dusky adjective *she looked out into the dusky countryside*: **shadowy**, dark, darkish, dim, gloomy, murky, shady, cloudy, misty, hazy, foggy; unlit, unlighted, unilluminated, sunless, moonless; literary crepuscular, tenebrous; rare Stygian, Cimmerian, Tartarean, caliginous.
▷ANTONYMS bright.

dust noun **1** *all of the furniture was covered in dust*: **fine powder**, fine particles; **dirt**, grime, filth, smut, soot.
2 *they rolled in the dust, fighting*: **earth**, soil, dirt, clay; ground, sod.
□ **bite the dust** informal **1** *they bit the dust with our harsh winter*: **die**, pass away/on, expire, decease, perish, depart this life, be no more, breathe one's last, draw one's last breath, meet one's end, meet one's death, meet one's Maker, give up the ghost, go to the great beyond, cross the great divide, shuffle off this mortal coil, go the way of the/all flesh, go to one's last resting place; informal kick the bucket, croak, conk out, buy it, turn up one's toes, cash in one's chips, go belly up; Brit. informal snuff it, peg out, pop one's clogs. **2** *he was devastated when the plans bit the dust*: **fail**, be unsuccessful, not succeed, lack success, fall through, fall flat, break down, abort, miscarry, be defeated, suffer defeat, be in vain, be frustrated, collapse, founder, misfire, backfire, not come up to scratch, meet with disaster, come to grief, come to nothing, come to naught, miss the mark, run aground, go astray; informal flop, fizzle out, come a cropper, bomb, blow up in someone's face, go down like a lead balloon.
□ **kick up a dust** informal **make a fuss**, kick up a fuss, cause a row, cause a commotion, cause a disturbance, cause uproar, cause a fracas, cause a rumpus, make a racket.
▶ verb **1** *she dusted her mantelpiece*: **wipe**, clean, buff, brush, sweep, mop.
2 *dust the cake with icing sugar*: **sprinkle**, scatter, powder, dredge, sift, spray, cover, spread, strew; dot, fleck, freckle, dab; literary befleck, bestrew, besprinkle.

> *Word links* **dust**
>
> **koniophobia** fear of dust

dust-up noun informal *they had a dust-up over money*. See **scrap**[2].

dusty adjective **1** *the shop was dark and dusty*: **dirty**, grimy, grubby, unclean, soiled, begrimed, befouled, mucky, sooty, stained, smudged, spotty; dust-covered, dust-filled, undusted; informal grungy, cruddy; Brit. informal manky, grotty, gungy; Austral./NZ informal scungy; literary besmirched.
▷ANTONYMS clean; dust-free.
2 *the walls are made of dusty brown sandstone*: **powdery**, crumbly, chalky, friable; granulated, granular, gritty, sandy.
3 *her eiderdown is a dusty pink*: **muted**, dull, flat, faded, pale, pastel, subtle, restrained; greyish, darkish, dirty.
▷ANTONYMS bright.
4 Brit. informal *I complained and they gave me a very dusty answer*: **curt**, abrupt, terse, brusque, blunt, short, clipped, snappy, snappish, sharp, crisp, tart, gruff, offhand, ungracious, rude, impolite, discourteous, bad-tempered; unhelpful, uncooperative, disobliging; informal snippy.
▷ANTONYMS expansive; helpful.

dutiful adjective *she helped out, as a dutiful daughter should*: **conscientious**, responsible, dedicated, devoted, faithful, loyal, attentive; **obedient**, compliant, pliant, docile, submissive, biddable, deferential, reverent, reverential, respectful, good, well disciplined, well trained; Brit. informal decent; rare regardful.
▷ANTONYMS remiss; disrespectful.

> *Choose the right word* **dutiful, obedient, biddable, docile, compliant**
>
> See **obedient**.

duty noun **1** *she was free of any binding love or duty*: **responsibility**, obligation, commitment, obedience, allegiance, loyalty, faithfulness, fidelity, respect, deference, reverence, homage; historical fealty.
2 *it was his duty to attend the king*: **job**, task, chore, assignment, commission, mission, function, charge, part, place, role, concern, requirement, responsibility, obligation; work, burden, onus; Brit. informal pigeon; dated office.
3 *the duty was raised on alcohol and tobacco*: **tax**, levy, tariff, excise, toll, fee, imposition, impost, exaction, tithe, payment, rate; customs, dues; rare mulct.
□ **off duty** *he helped at the hospital even when he was off duty*: **not working**, at leisure, on holiday, on leave, off, off work, free.
□ **on duty** *the night security man was on duty*: **working**, at work, busy, occupied, engaged; on call, on standby; informal on the job, tied up.

> *Choose the right word* **duty, task, job, chore**
>
> See **task**.

dwarf noun **1** offensive **small person**, short person, person of restricted growth; offensive midget, pygmy; rare manikin, homunculus, Lilliputian.
2 *the wizard captured the dwarf*: **gnome**, goblin, hobgoblin, troll, imp, elf, brownie, kelpie, leprechaun, fairy, pixie, sprite.
▷ANTONYMS giant.
▶ adjective *the driveway was flanked by dwarf conifers*: **miniature**, small, little, tiny, minute, toy, pocket, diminutive, baby, pygmy, stunted, undersized, undersize, small-scale, scaled-down; Scottish wee; N. Amer. vest-pocket; informal mini, teeny, teeny-weeny, teensy-weensy, itsy-bitsy, tiddly, pint-sized, half-pint, sawn-off, knee-high to a grasshopper; Brit. informal titchy, ickle; N. Amer. informal little-bitty.
▷ANTONYMS giant.
▶ verb **1** *either of the two blocks would dwarf any existing building in Ireland*: **dominate**, tower above, tower over, loom over, overlook, overshadow, overtop.
2 *her progress was dwarfed by the achievements of her sister*: **overshadow**, outshine, put in the shade, surpass, exceed, outclass, outstrip, outdo, top, cap, trump, transcend; shame, put to shame, diminish, minimize; archaic extinguish, outrival.

> *Choose the right word* **dwarf**
>
> The use of **dwarf** to mean 'an unusually small person' is normally considered to be offensive, as are **midget** or **pygmy**. However, no term has been established as a generally acceptable alternative: **person of restricted growth** has not gained wide currency. Words such as **homunculus** or **manikin** are sometimes found in literary or old-fashioned writing.

dwell verb formal *groups of gypsies still dwell in these amazing caves*: **reside**, live, have one's home, have one's residence, be settled, be housed, lodge, stay; informal hang out, hang one's hat, put up; formal abide, be domiciled, sojourn; archaic bide.
□ **dwell on** *she had no time to dwell on her disappointment*: **linger over**, mull over, muse on, brood about, brood over, think about, spend time thinking about, be preoccupied by, be obsessed by, eat one's heart out over; harp on about, discuss at length, expatiate on, elaborate on, expound on, keep talking about.

dwelling noun formal *she had been invited to his dwelling*: **residence**, place of residence, place of habitation, home, house, accommodation, lodging place, billet; lodgings, quarters, rooms; informal place, pad; Brit. informal digs; formal dwelling place, dwelling house, abode, domicile, habitation.

dwindle verb **1** *the porpoise population has dwindled*: **diminish**, decrease, reduce, get smaller, become smaller, grow smaller, become less, grow less, lessen, wane, contract, shrink, fall off, taper off, tail off, drop, fall, go down, sink, slump, plummet; disappear, vanish, die out; informal nosedive, take a nosedive.
▷ANTONYMS increase.
2 *her career dwindled over the years*: **decline**, degenerate, deteriorate, fail, ebb, wane, sink, slip, slide, go downhill, go to rack and ruin, decay, wither, fade, fade away; informal peter out, go to pot, go to the dogs, hit the skids, go down the toilet, go down the tubes; Austral./NZ informal go to the pack.
▷ANTONYMS flourish.

dye noun *the cloth had been soaked in blue dye*: **colourant**, colouring agent, colouring, colour, dyestuff, pigment, tint, stain, wash.
▸ verb *the gloves were dyed to match the dress*: **colour**, tint, pigment, stain, wash, colour-wash, tinge, shade.

dyed-in-the-wool adjective *she's a dyed-in-the-wool Conservative*: **inveterate**, confirmed, entrenched, established, long-established, long-standing, deep-rooted, diehard, complete, absolute, utter, thorough, thoroughgoing, out-and-out, true blue, through and through; firm, unshakeable, staunch, steadfast, committed, devoted, dedicated, loyal, faithful, unswerving, unwavering, unfaltering; unashamed, unapologetic, unrepentant, incurable, incorrigible; N. Amer. full-bore; informal deep-dyed, card-carrying, mad keen, keen as mustard; archaic arrant; rare right-down.

dying adjective **1** *he went to visit his dying aunt*: **terminally ill**, at death's door, on one's deathbed, in the jaws of death, on the point of death, near death, passing away, fading fast, sinking fast, expiring, moribund, breathing one's last, not long for this world; Latin in extremis; informal on one's last legs, with one foot in the grave, giving up the ghost.
2 *ballet is a dying art form*: **declining**, vanishing, fading, passing, ebbing, waning; in decline; informal on the way out, on its last legs.
▷ANTONYMS thriving.
3 *he strained to catch her dying words*: **final**, last, departing; deathbed.
▷ANTONYMS first.
▸ noun *there were no unhappy memories to taunt her in her dying*: **death**, demise, passing, passing away, passing on, expiry, expiration, departure from life, final exit, eternal rest; Law decease; rare quietus.

dynamic adjective *he was eclipsed by his more dynamic colleagues*: **energetic**, spirited, active, lively, zestful, vital, vigorous, strong, forceful, powerful, potent, positive, effective, effectual, high-powered, aggressive, driving, pushing, bold, enterprising; electric, magnetic, flamboyant, passionate, fiery; informal go-getting, zippy, peppy, sparky, high-octane, full of get-up-and-go, full of vim and vigour, full of beans, gutsy, spunky, ballsy, feisty, have-a-go, go-ahead; N. Amer. informal go-go.
▷ANTONYMS half-hearted; lethargic.

dynamism noun *there's real dynamism in his performance on the pitch*: **energy**, spirit, liveliness, zestfulness, vitality, vigour, vigorousness, strength, forcefulness, power, powerfulness, potency, positiveness, positivity, effectiveness, efficacy; aggression, aggressiveness, boldness, drive, push, ambition, enterprise; magnetism, flamboyance, passion, fire; informal go-getting, zip, pep, spark, get-up-and-go, vim and vigour, guts, balls, have-a-go attitude; N. Amer. informal feistiness.

dynasty noun *he was the fourth king of the Shang dynasty*: **bloodline**, line, ancestral line, lineage, house, family, ancestry, descent, extraction, succession, genealogy, family tree; regime, rule, reign, dominion, empire, sovereignty, ascendancy, government, authority, administration, jurisdiction.

dyspeptic adjective *a rather dyspeptic senator put the blame on his European counterpart*: **bad-tempered**, short-tempered, irritable, snappish, testy, tetchy, touchy, crabbed, crabby, crotchety, grouchy, cantankerous, peevish, cross, fractious, disagreeable, pettish, waspish, prickly, peppery, cross-grained; bilious, liverish; informal snappy, chippy, on a short fuse, short-fused; Brit. informal shirty, stroppy, narky, ratty, eggy, like a bear with a sore head; N. Amer. informal cranky, ornery, peckish, soreheaded; Austral./NZ informal snaky; informal, dated waxy, miffy.

each pronoun *there are five thousand books and each must be individually cleaned*: **every one**, each one, each and every one, one and all, all, the whole lot.
▸ determiner *he visited her each month*: **every**, each and every, every single.
▸ adverb *they contributed a tenner each*: **apiece**, per person, per capita, to each, for each, from each, individually, respectively; formal severally.

eager adjective **1** *small eager faces looked up and listened*: **keen**, enthusiastic, avid, fervent, ardent, zealous, passionate, motivated, wholehearted, dedicated, committed, earnest, diligent; informal bright-eyed and bushy-tailed, mad keen, (as) keen as mustard; rare fervid, perfervid, passional.
▷ANTONYMS apathetic.
2 *her friends were **eager for** news*: **anxious**, impatient, waiting with bated breath, longing, yearning, aching, wishing, hoping, hopeful, thirsty, hungry, greedy; desirous of, hankering after, intent on, bent on, set on; on the edge of one's seat, on pins and needles, on tenterhooks; informal hot, itching, gagging, dying.
▷ANTONYMS uninterested.

Choose the right word **eager, keen, enthusiastic, avid**

Someone who is **eager** wants to do or have something very much and feels excited pleasure at the prospect of it (*small eager faces looked up and listened* | *he seemed eager to talk to her*).

Keen also suggests intense interest and enjoyment, but without the connotations of bubbly anticipation. A *keen* person's interest in what they do results in commitment and concentration (*he is a keen rugby player*). *Keen* can also be used to indicate that someone is anxious to do something, typically because they think it will be advantageous (*Laughton is keen to add Davies to his squad*). To be *keen on* something can just mean to like or approve of it (*I'm not that keen on the food here*).

Someone who is **enthusiastic** about something shows great enjoyment of or approval for it (*make it clear that you are enthusiastic about the project*). An *enthusiastic* person does things with energy, gusto, and dedication (*an enthusiastic supporter of music from Africa*).

Avid derives from a Latin word meaning 'greedy, hungry'. Someone described as *avid* enjoys something so much that they can never have enough of it (*I am an avid reader of your magazine* | *she was avid for information about the murder inquiry*).

eagerness noun *they underestimated the eagerness of potential buyers*: **keenness**, enthusiasm, avidity, fervour, ardour, zest, zeal, passion, wholeheartedness, earnestness, commitment, dedication; impatience, desire, longing, yearning, wishing, thirst, hunger, greed, voracity, voraciousness, appetite, ambition; informal yen; rare appetency, fervency, ardency, passionateness.
▷ANTONYMS apathy, indifference.

eagle noun

Word links **eagle**

aquiline like an eagle
eaglet young
eyrie nest

ear noun **1** *Helen had an infection of the ear*: **organ of hearing**; Scottish & N. English or informal **lug**; informal **earhole**; Brit. informal **lughole, shell-like**.
2 *he had the ear of President Roosevelt*: **attention**, attentiveness, notice, heed, regard, consideration.
3 *he has an ear for a good song*: **appreciation**, discrimination, perception, musical taste.
□ **all ears** informal *if you have a suggestion I'm all ears*: **alert**, vigilant, wide awake, aware, watchful, attentive, observant, circumspect, wary, chary, heedful, canny; on one's guard, on one's toes, on the qui vive.
□ **play it by ear** *he had no special game plan and said he would play it by ear*: **improvise**, extemporize, ad lib; make it up as one goes along, take it as it comes, think on one's feet; Latin ad libitum; informal busk it, wing it.

Word links **ear**

aural, **auricular**, **otic** relating to the ear
auditory relating to hearing
binaural relating to both ears
audiology, **otology** branch of medicine concerning the ear
otolaryngology branch of medicine concerning the ears and throat
otorhinolaryngology branch of medicine concerning the ears, nose, and throat
otitis inflammation of the ear
otoplasty surgery to repair an ear

early adjective **1** *early copies of the book are now ready*: **advance**, forward, prior; initial, preliminary, first, primary; pilot, test, trial.
▷ANTONYMS late.
2 *an early death*: **untimely**, premature; too soon, too early, before time; archaic unseasonable.
3 *bronze was used widely by early man*: **primitive**, ancient, prehistoric, antediluvian, primeval, primordial; of long ago; literary of yore; rare primigenial, pristine.
▷ANTONYMS modern.
4 *he produced an early official statement*: **prompt**, timely, quick, speedy, rapid, fast, without delay, expeditious; archaic rathe.
▷ANTONYMS overdue.
▸ adverb **1** *Rachel has to get up early*: **early in the day**, in the early morning; at dawn, at daybreak, at cockcrow, with the lark.
▷ANTONYMS late.
2 *they hoped to leave school early*: **before the usual time**, before the appointed time; prematurely, too soon; ahead of time, ahead of schedule, in good time; literary betimes.

earmark verb *the cash had been **earmarked for** a big expansion of the firm*: **set aside**, lay aside, set apart, keep back, appropriate, reserve, keep; designate, assign, label, tag, mark; allocate to, allot to, devote to, pledge to, commit to, give over to; rare hypothecate.
▸ noun *he had all the earmarks of a big leaguer*: **characteristic**, attribute, feature, quality, essential quality, property, mark, trademark, hallmark; mannerism, way, tendency; literary lineament.

earn verb **1** *they earn £20,000 per year*: **be paid**, receive a salary of, take home, take home earnings of, gross; receive, get, make, obtain, draw, clear, collect, bring in; informal pocket, bank, rake in, pull in, haul in, net, bag.
▷ANTONYMS pay out.
2 *he has earned their trust over the years*: **deserve**, merit, warrant, justify,

be entitled to, be worthy of, be deserving of, have a right to; **gain**, win, attain, achieve, secure, establish, obtain, procure, get, acquire, come to have, find; informal clinch, bag, net, land.
▷ANTONYMS lose.

Choose the right word earn, deserve, merit

To **earn** something is to receive it as the appropriate result of what you have done (*his first foray into film earned him an Oscar nomination*).

Someone who **deserves** something ought to receive it for what they have done or by virtue of personal qualities, but they may not do so (*Middlesbrough deserved their win | he is a lovely man who deserves to be loved*).

Merit is a more formal term for deserving something (*the whole of the evidence merited consideration by a fresh jury*).

e

earnest adjective **1** *he had a reputation for being dreadfully earnest*: **serious**, serious-minded, solemn, grave, sober, humourless, staid, steady, intense; committed, dedicated, assiduous, keen, diligent, zealous, industrious, hard-working; studious, thoughtful, cerebral, deep, profound, bookish, donnish.
▷ANTONYMS frivolous; apathetic.
2 *they were engaged in earnest prayer*: **devout**, heartfelt, wholehearted, sincere, impassioned, deeply felt, from the heart, fervent, ardent, passionate, intense, burning, urgent; rare full-hearted, passional, perfervid, fervid.
▷ANTONYMS half-hearted.
▶ **noun**
▫ **in earnest 1** *we are in earnest about stopping burglaries*: **serious**, not joking, sincere, wholehearted, genuine; **committed**, firm, resolute, resolved, determined, insistent.
▷ANTONYMS joking.
2 *he started writing in earnest after the war*: **zealously**, purposefully, determinedly, resolutely, with enthusiasm, with dedication, with commitment; ardently, fervently, fervidly, passionately, wholeheartedly.
▷ANTONYMS half-heartedly.

earnestly adverb *he took my hand and looked at me earnestly*: **seriously**, solemnly, gravely, soberly, sincerely, intently, resolutely, firmly; **ardently**, fervently, warmly, keenly, eagerly, intensely, zealously.

earnings plural noun *they lived off his wife's earnings*: **income**, wages, salary, stipend, pay, take-home pay, gross pay, net pay; revenue, yield, profit, takings, proceeds, dividends, gain, return, remuneration, emolument; payment, fees, honoraria, fringe benefits; informal pickings, perks.

earth noun **1** *the moon moves in its orbit around the earth*: **world**, globe, planet, sphere, orb.
2 *he felt an infinitesimal trembling of the earth*: **land**, ground, dry land, solid ground, terra firma; floor.
3 *the blades ploughed gently into the soft earth*: **soil**, topsoil, loam, clay, silt, dirt, sod, clod, turf; ground, terrain.
4 *the fox ran back to its earth*: **den**, lair, sett, burrow, warren, tunnel, hole, cave; retreat, shelter, hideout, hideaway, hiding place; habitation; informal hidey-hole.

Word links earth

geo- related prefix
terrestrial, **telluric** relating to the earth
geography, **geology**, **geochemistry**, **geomorphology** study of the earth

earthenware noun *the Wedgwood potteries produced cream-coloured earthenware*: **pottery**, crockery, stoneware; china, porcelain; pots, crocks.

earthly adjective **1** *the mobile and metamorphosing earthly environment*: **terrestrial**, telluric, tellurian; rare terrene, subastral.
▷ANTONYMS extraterrestrial.
2 *they were seduced by the promise of earthly delights*: **worldly**, temporal, secular, mortal, human, mundane, material, non-spiritual, materialistic; carnal, fleshly, bodily, physical, corporal, corporeal, sensual; gross, base, sordid, vile, profane; rare somatic, sublunary, terrene.
▷ANTONYMS heavenly; spiritual.
3 informal *there can be no earthly explanation for his behaviour*: **feasible**, possible, likely, conceivable, imaginable, perceivable.

earthquake noun *many homes were destroyed in the earthquake*: **earth tremor**, tremor, convulsion, shock, foreshock, aftershock; informal quake, shake, trembler; technical microseism.

Word links earthquake

seismic relating to earthquakes
seismology study of earthquakes
seismograph instrument that measures earthquakes

earthy adjective **1** *the cellar had an earthy smell*: **soil-like**, dirt-like.
2 *preaching in the earthy Calvinistic tradition*: **down-to-earth**, unsophisticated, unrefined, homely, simple, plain, unpretentious, natural, uninhibited, rough, robust.
3 *she was shocked by Emma's earthy language*: **bawdy**, ribald, off colour, racy, rude, vulgar, lewd, crude, foul, coarse, uncouth, rough, dirty, filthy, smutty, unseemly, indelicate, indecent, indecorous, obscene; informal blue, raunchy, locker-room, X-rated; Brit. informal fruity, saucy, near the knuckle, close to the bone; N. Amer. informal gamy; euphemistic adult.
▷ANTONYMS decorous, proper, prim.

ease noun **1** *the 15-year old beat all the adult players with ease*: **effortlessness**, no difficulty, no trouble, no bother, facility, facileness, simplicity; deftness, adroitness, dexterity, proficiency, mastery.
▷ANTONYMS difficulty.
2 *friends recall his ease of manner with children*: **naturalness**, casualness, informality, unceremoniousness, lack of reserve, lack of constraint, relaxedness, amiability, affability; unconcern, composure, aplomb, nonchalance, insouciance.
▷ANTONYMS formality, stiffness.
3 *only in his sleep could he find any ease*: **peace**, peacefulness, calmness, tranquillity, composure, serenity, repose, restfulness, quiet, contentment, security, comfort.
▷ANTONYMS trouble, disturbance.
4 *a life of ease*: **affluence**, wealth, prosperity, prosperousness, luxury, opulence, plenty, sufficiency; **comfort**, cosiness, contentment, content, enjoyment, well-being, freedom from hardship, freedom from troubles; rare easefulness.
▷ANTONYMS hardship; poverty.
▫ **at ease/at one's ease** *when he woke he felt wonderfully at ease*: **relaxed**, calm, serene, tranquil, unworried, contented, content, happy; comfortable, secure, safe.
▷ANTONYMS tense; uncomfortable.
▶ **verb 1** *he hoped the alcohol would ease his pain*: **relieve**, alleviate, mitigate, assuage, allay, soothe, soften, palliate, ameliorate, mollify, moderate, tone down, blunt, dull, deaden, numb, take the edge off; lessen, reduce, lighten, diminish.
▷ANTONYMS aggravate.
2 *it was dawn before the rain **eased off***: **abate**, subside, die down, die away, die out, drop off, let up, slacken off, diminish, quieten, lessen, grow less, tail off, peter out, taper off, wane, ebb, relent, weaken, become weaker, come to an end; archaic remit.
▷ANTONYMS worsen.
3 *concentrating on work helped to ease her mind*: **calm**, quieten, pacify, soothe, comfort, bring comfort to, give solace to, solace, console; hearten, gladden, uplift, encourage.
4 *we want to ease our employees' adjustment to the new policy*: **facilitate**, make easy, make easier, expedite, speed up, assist, help, aid, advance, further, forward, smooth the way for, clear the way for, simplify.
▷ANTONYMS hinder.
5 *he eased out the champagne cork with his thumbs*: **guide**, manoeuvre, inch, edge, steer, slide, slip, squeeze.

easily adverb **1** *I overcame this problem quite easily in the end*: **effortlessly**, comfortably, simply, straightforwardly; with ease, without effort, with no trouble, with no bother, without difficulty, without a hitch, smoothly; skilfully, deftly, nimbly, smartly, very well; informal no sweat.
▷ANTONYMS laboriously.
2 *he's easily the best military brain in the country*: **undoubtedly**, doubtlessly, without doubt, without question, indubitably, indisputably, undeniably, definitely, certainly, assuredly, positively, absolutely, clearly, obviously, patently, simply, surely, by far, far and away, by a mile, beyond the shadow of a doubt; informal as sure as eggs is eggs.

east noun (**the East**) **the Orient**.
▷ANTONYMS the West.
▶ **adjective** *the cathedral's east face | a biting east wind*: **eastern**, easterly, eastwardly, oriental.
▷ANTONYMS west.
▶ **adverb** *traffic wishing to go east on the North Circular*: **to the east**, eastward, eastwards, eastwardly.
▷ANTONYMS west.

easy adjective **1** *Wilf's task was very easy*: **uncomplicated**, not difficult, undemanding, unexacting, unchallenging, effortless, painless, trouble-free, facile, simple, straightforward, elementary, idiot-proof, plain sailing; informal easy-peasy, easy as pie, as easy as falling off a log, as easy as ABC, a piece of cake, child's play, kids' stuff, a cinch, no sweat, a doddle, a breeze, a pushover, money for old rope, money for jam; N. Amer. informal duck soup, a snap; Austral./NZ informal a bludge; S. African informal a piece of old tackle; Brit. vulgar slang a piece of piss; dated a snip.
▷ANTONYMS difficult.
2 *some parents have easy babies and amenable children*: **docile**, manageable, amenable, biddable, tractable, compliant, pliant, yielding, acquiescent, accommodating, obliging, cooperative, easy-going, flexible.
▷ANTONYMS difficult; demanding.
3 *the thug thought he had picked an easy target*: **vulnerable**, susceptible,

exploitable, defenceless, naive, gullible, trusting, credulous, impressionable.
▷ANTONYMS streetwise.
4 *Vic's easy manner made everyone feel at home*: **natural**, casual, informal, unceremonious, unreserved, uninhibited, unconstrained, unforced, unaffected, free and easy, easy-going, familiar, amiable, affable, genial, congenial, agreeable, good-humoured; carefree, nonchalant, unconcerned, composed, insouciant, urbane, suave; informal laid-back, unflappable, together.
▷ANTONYMS formal.
5 *they are hoping for an easy life*: **calm**, tranquil, serene, quiet, peaceful, trouble-free, untroubled, undisturbed, unworried, contented, relaxed, comfortable, secure, safe; informal cushy.
▷ANTONYMS uneasy.
6 *the walkers set off at an easy pace*: **leisurely**, leisured, unhurried, unrushed, comfortable, unexacting, undemanding, easy-going, gentle, sedate, moderate, steady, regular, even; informal laid-back.
▷ANTONYMS demanding.
7 informal *she had a reputation at school for being easy*: **promiscuous**, sexually indiscriminate, free with one's favours, of easy virtue, unchaste, loose, wanton, abandoned, licentious, dissolute, dissipated, debauched; informal swinging, sluttish, whorish, tarty, slaggy; N. Amer. informal roundheeled; W. Indian informal slack; archaic light; rare concupiscent, riggish.
▷ANTONYMS chaste.
□ **take it easy** *the doctor was still advising me to take it easy.* See **relax** (sense 1).

easy-going adjective *Fred was easy-going and a pleasure to work with*: **relaxed**, even-tempered, equable, placid, mellow, mild, happy-go-lucky, serene, blithe, carefree, free and easy, nonchalant, insouciant, unruffled, unworried, untroubled, imperturbable, unexcitable; amiable, considerate, undemanding, forbearing, patient, tolerant, lenient, liberal, broad-minded, open-minded, understanding, generous, indulgent; good-natured, good-humoured, pleasant, agreeable, cordial; informal laid-back, together, unflappable, unfazed.
▷ANTONYMS tense; intolerant.

eat verb **1** *we ate a hearty breakfast and then set off*: **consume**, devour, ingest, partake of, gobble (up/down), gulp (down), bolt (down), wolf (down), cram down, finish (off); swallow, chew, munch, chomp, champ; informal guzzle, nosh, put away, pack away, tuck into, tuck away, scoff (down), demolish, dispose of, make short work of, polish off, shovel down, get stuck into, stuff one's face with, stuff down, pig out on, sink, get outside of, get one's laughing gear round; Brit. informal gollop, shift; N. Amer. informal scarf (down/up), snarf (down/up), inhale; rare ingurgitate.
▷ANTONYMS starve; fast.
2 *we ate at a local restaurant*: **have a meal**, partake of food, take food, consume food, feed; breakfast, lunch, dine, have breakfast, have lunch, have dinner, have supper; feast, banquet; informal snack, graze, nosh; dated sup, break bread.
3 *acidic water can* **eat away at** *concrete pipes*: **erode**, corrode, abrade, wear away (at), wear down, wear through, gnaw away (at), bite into, burn into, burn through, consume, dissolve, disintegrate, crumble, waste away, rot, decay; damage, destroy, spoil.
□ **eat one's heart out** See **heart**.
□ **eat up** *he ate up all the French fries*. See **eat** (sense 1).

> *Word links* **eat**
>
> **-phagous** related suffix, as in *anthropophagous*
> **-vorous** related suffix, as in *carnivorous*

eatable adjective *the soufflé's not perfect, but it is eatable*: **edible**, palatable, digestible; fit to eat, fit for consumption, fit to be consumed; rare comestible.
▷ANTONYMS inedible.

eats plural noun informal *we had to pay for our own booze and eats*. See **food** (sense 1).

eavesdrop verb *we tried to* **eavesdrop on** *his telephone conversation*: **listen in**, spy, intrude; monitor, tap, wiretap, record, overhear; informal snoop, bug; Austral./NZ informal stickybeak.

ebb verb **1** *the tide ebbed in the afternoon*: **recede**, **go out**, retreat, flow back, draw back, fall back, fall away, abate, subside; rare retrocede.
▷ANTONYMS come in.
2 *his courage began to ebb*: **diminish**, dwindle, wane, fade away, melt away, peter out, decline, die away, die down, die out, flag, let up, lessen, decrease, weaken, dissolve, disappear, come to an end; deteriorate, decay, degenerate; archaic remit.
▷ANTONYMS increase, intensify.
▸ noun **1** *the rocks were revealed by the ebb of the tide*: **receding**, going out, flowing back, retreat, retreating, drawing back, abating, subsiding; rare retrocession.
2 *they welcomed the ebb of the fighting*: **abatement**, subsiding, easing, waning, dwindling, petering out, dying away, dying down, dying out, fading away, de-escalation, decrease, decline, diminution, diminishing, lessening.
▷ANTONYMS intensification.

ebony adjective *he stared at her with his ebony eyes*: **black**, jet-black, pitch-black, coal-black, ink-black, black as night, black as pitch, sable, inky, sooty, raven, dark; literary ebon.
▷ANTONYMS ivory.

ebullience noun *the director's ebullience is a fantastic morale booster for the cast*: **exuberance**, buoyancy, cheerfulness, joy, joyfulness, gladness, cheeriness, merriment, jollity, sunniness, breeziness, jauntiness, light-heartedness, high spirits, high-spiritedness, exhilaration, elation, euphoria, jubilation, animation, sparkle, effervescence, vivacity, enthusiasm, zest, irrepressibility, perkiness; informal bubbliness, chirpiness, bounciness, pep, zing, zip, fizz; archaic good cheer.
▷ANTONYMS depression.

ebullient adjective *the superb weather put him in an ebullient mood*: **exuberant**, buoyant, cheerful, joyful, cheery, merry, sunny, breezy, jaunty, light-hearted, in high spirits, high-spirited, exhilarated, elated, euphoric, jubilant, animated, sparkling, effervescent, vivacious, enthusiastic, irrepressible; informal bubbly, bouncy, peppy, zingy, upbeat, chipper, chirpy, smiley, sparky, full of beans; N. Amer. informal peart; literary gladsome, blithe, blithesome; dated gay; archaic as merry as a grig, of good cheer.
▷ANTONYMS depressed.

eccentric adjective *they were worried by his eccentric behaviour*: **unconventional**, uncommon, abnormal, irregular, aberrant, anomalous, odd, queer, strange, peculiar, weird, bizarre, outlandish, freakish, extraordinary; **idiosyncratic**, quirky, singular, nonconformist, capricious, whimsical; French outré, avant garde; informal way out, far out, offbeat, dotty, nutty, screwy, freaky, oddball, wacky, cranky, off the wall, madcap, zany; Brit. informal rum; N. Amer. informal kooky, wacko, bizarro, in left field.
▷ANTONYMS ordinary; conventional.
▸ noun *like all princes he was something of an eccentric*: **oddity**, odd fellow, unorthodox person, character, individualist, individual, free spirit, misfit; informal oddball, queer fish, weirdo, weirdie, freak, nut, nutter, nutcase, case, head case, crank, crackpot, loony, loon; Brit. informal one-off, odd bod; N. Amer. informal wacko, wack, screwball, kook; Austral./NZ informal dingbat.

Word toolkit

eccentric	quirky	bizarre
millionaire	comedy	twist
inventor	humour	coincidence
loner	mannerism	ritual
recluse	charm	antics
aristocrat	lyric	spectacle
genius	sensibility	juxtaposition
uncle	melody	incident
spinster	styling	behaviour

eccentricity noun *a charming example of English eccentricity*: **unconventionality**, unorthodoxy, singularity, oddness, queerness, strangeness, weirdness, bizarreness, quirkiness, freakishness, extraordinariness; peculiarity, irregularity, abnormality, anomaly, foible, idiosyncrasy, caprice, whimsy, quirk; informal nuttiness, dottiness, screwiness, freakiness, wackiness, crankiness, zaniness; N. Amer. informal kookiness.
▷ANTONYMS conventionality.

ecclesiastic noun *the consecration could only be performed by a high ecclesiastic*: **clergyman**, clergywoman, priest, churchman, churchwoman, man/woman of the cloth, man/woman of God, cleric, minister, preacher, chaplain, father; divine, theologian; bishop, pastor, vicar, rector, parson, (assistant) curate, deacon, deaconess; Scottish kirkman; French abbé, curé; N. Amer. dominie; informal reverend, padre, Holy Joe, sky pilot; Austral. informal josser; informal, derogatory Bible-basher, God-botherer.
▸ adjective See **ecclesiastical**.

ecclesiastical adjective *his ecclesiastical duties*: **priestly**, ministerial, clerical, ecclesiastic, prelatic, canonical, parsonical, pastoral; **church**, churchly, religious, spiritual, non-secular, non-temporal, holy, divine; informal churchy; rare sacerdotal.

echelon noun *he reached the upper echelons of government*: **level**, rank, grade, step, rung, tier, stratum, plane, position, order, division, sector.

echo noun **1** *the hills sent back a faint echo of my shout*: **reverberation**, reverberating, reflection, resounding, ringing, repetition, repeat, reiteration, answer.
2 *the scene she described was an echo of the one Lisa had always imagined*: **duplicate**, copy, replica, facsimile, reproduction, imitation, exact/close likeness, mirror image, twin, double, clone, match, mate, fellow, counterpart, parallel; informal lookalike, spitting image, ringer, dead ringer.
3 *was there even the slightest echo of the love they had known?* **trace**, vestige, remains, remnant, relic, survival, ghost, memory, evocation, recollection,

remembrance, reminiscence, reminder, souvenir, sign, mark, indication, token, suggestion, hint, evidence, clue, allusion, intimation; overtones, reminiscences.

▶ verb 1 *his laughter echoed round the room*: **reverberate**, re-echo, resonate, resound, reflect, ring, pulsate, vibrate, be repeated.

2 *Bill echoed Rex's words in a sarcastic sing-song*: **repeat**, say again, restate, reiterate, copy, imitate, parrot, parody, mimic; reproduce, iterate, recite, quote, rehearse, recapitulate, regurgitate; informal recap, trot out; rare reprise, ingeminate.

éclat noun *he finished his recital with great éclat*: **style**, stylishness, flamboyance, confidence, self-assurance, elan, dash, flair, flourish, vigour, vivacity, vivaciousness, gusto, verve, zest, sparkle, brio, panache, exuberance, ebullience, enthusiasm, eagerness, vitality, dynamism, animation, liveliness, spirit, energy; informal pizzazz, pep, oomph, vim, zing, get-up-and-go.

▷ANTONYMS lethargy.

e

eclectic adjective 1 *they played an eclectic mix of party music*: **wide-ranging**, wide, broad, broad-ranging, broad-based, extensive, comprehensive, encyclopedic, general, universal, varied, diverse, diversified, catholic, liberal, all-embracing, non-exclusive, inclusive, indiscriminate, many-sided, multifaceted, multifarious, heterogeneous, miscellaneous, assorted.

▷ANTONYMS narrow.

2 *an eclectic approach to teaching the curriculum*: **selective**, selecting, choosing, picking and choosing; discriminating, discerning, critical.

▷ANTONYMS dogmatic.

eclipse noun 1 *the eclipse of the sun*: **blotting out**, blocking, covering, obscuring, hiding, concealing, veiling, shrouding, darkening; Astronomy occultation.

2 *the eclipse of the empire*: **decline**, fall, failure, decay, deterioration, degeneration, weakening, ebb, waning, withering, descent, sinking, slide, tumble, regression, lapse, collapse, comedown, crash.

▷ANTONYMS rise.

3 *the eclipse of his rival*: **outshining**, overshadowing, surpassing, excelling, outclassing, outstripping, outdistancing, outdoing, transcending, dwarfing, upstaging, shaming.

▶ verb 1 *the last piece of the sun was eclipsed by the moon*: **blot out**, block, cover, obscure, veil, shroud, hide, conceal, obliterate, darken, dim; shade, cast a shadow over; Astronomy occult.

2 *the use of procaine was eclipsed by the discovery of cortisone*: **outshine**, overshadow, put in the shade, surpass, exceed, excel, be superior to, outclass, outstrip, outdistance, outdo, top, cap, trump, transcend, tower above/over, dwarf, upstage, shame, put to shame; informal be head and shoulders above, be a cut above; archaic extinguish, outrival.

economic adjective 1 *the government's commitment to economic reform*: **financial**, monetary, pecuniary, budgetary, fiscal, commercial, trade, mercantile.

2 *many organizations must become larger if they are to remain economic*: **profitable**, profit-making, moneymaking, money-spinning, lucrative, remunerative, financially rewarding, fruitful, gainful, productive; **solvent**, viable, cost-effective, successful, commercial, commercially successful.

▷ANTONYMS unprofitable.

3 *rugs or matting are a practical and economic alternative to fitted carpets*: **cost-effective**, effective, efficient, worthwhile, valuable, advantageous, cheap, inexpensive, low-cost, low-price, low-budget, budget, economy, reasonable, reasonably priced, cut-price.

▷ANTONYMS extravagant.

Easily confused words **economic or economical?**

These two words are related to different senses of *economy* and hence have different meanings. **Economic** means 'relating to a country's wealth and resources' (*the government's economic policy*), 'justifiable in terms of profitability' (*if prices remained high, it could become economic to develop cobalt deposits in other parts of the world*), or 'requiring fewer resources' (*this type of construction provided an economic solution to the problem*). **Economical**, on the other hand, relates to *economy* in the sense 'careful managing of resources' and means 'costing little to run' (*a safe and economical heating system*) or 'taking care not to be extravagant' (*he was economical in all areas of life*).

economical adjective 1 *it is a very economical little car*: **cheap**, inexpensive, low-cost, low-price, low-budget, budget, economy, reasonable, reasonably priced, cut-price, cut-rate, discount, discounted, bargain, bargain-basement.

▷ANTONYMS expensive.

2 *my friend is a very economical shopper with a keen eye for a bargain*: **thrifty**, careful (with money), provident, prudent, canny, sensible, frugal, sparing, scrimping, economizing, abstemious; N. Amer. forehanded.

▷ANTONYMS spendthrift.

economize verb *they economized by growing their own vegetables*: **save (money)**, cut expenditure, cut costs; **cut back**, make cutbacks, make cuts, retrench, husband one's resources, budget, be (more) economical, make economies, be thrifty, be sparing, be frugal, buy (more) cheaply, use less, reduce/decrease wastage, scrimp, scrimp and save, scrimp and scrape, cut corners, tighten one's belt, draw in one's horns, count the/your pennies, watch the/your pennies; N. Amer. pinch the/your pennies; black English rake and scrape.

▷ANTONYMS spend, be extravagant.

economy noun 1 *the nation's economy*: **wealth**, (financial) resources; **financial system**, financial state, financial management.

2 *Mrs Beeton attempted to combine good living with economy*: **thrift**, **providence**, prudence, thriftiness, canniness, carefulness, care, good management, good husbandry, careful budgeting, economizing, saving, scrimping and saving, scrimping, restraint, frugality, abstemiousness; meanness, penny-pinching, miserliness, niggardliness, parsimony; N. Amer. forehandedness; informal stinginess; rare sparingness, frugalness.

▷ANTONYMS extravagance.

ecstasy noun *the ecstasy of loving him*: **rapture**, bliss, elation, euphoria, cloud nine, seventh heaven, transports, rhapsodies; joy, joyousness, jubilation, exultation, heaven, paradise, delight; informal the top of the world.

▷ANTONYMS misery.

ecstatic adjective *she was sometimes ecstatic with love*: **enraptured**, elated, transported, in transports, in raptures, euphoric; rapturous, joyful, joyous, overjoyed, blissful, beatific; on cloud nine, in seventh heaven, delirious (with happiness), beside oneself with joy/happiness, jumping for joy, rhapsodic, ravished, enchanted, enthusiastic, delighted, thrilled, jubilant, exultant, happy; informal over the moon, on top of the world, blissed out; orgasmic; Austral. informal wrapped.

▷ANTONYMS miserable.

ecumenical adjective *an ecumenical church service*: **non-denominational**, non-sectarian, universal, catholic, all-embracing, all-inclusive.

▷ANTONYMS denominational.

eddy noun *the river was smooth apart from the small eddies at the edge*: **swirl**, whirlpool, vortex, maelstrom; countercurrent, counterflow; N. Amer. informal suckhole; literary Charybdis.

▶ verb *cold air eddied around her*: **swirl**, whirl, spiral, wind, churn, swish, circulate, revolve, spin, twist; flow, ripple, stream, surge, seethe, billow, foam, froth, boil, ferment.

edge noun 1 *the edge of the lake*: **border**, boundary, extremity, fringe; margin, side, lip, rim, brim, brink, verge; perimeter, circumference, periphery, contour, outline; limit, limits, outer limit, bound, bounds; literary marge, bourn, skirt.

▷ANTONYMS middle.

2 *'What do you mean?' I asked, with an edge in my voice*: **sharpness**, severity, bite, sting, pointedness, asperity, pungency, mordancy, acerbity, acidity, tartness, trenchancy; **sarcasm**, acrimony, malice, spite, venom; rare causticity, mordacity.

▷ANTONYMS kindness.

3 *they have an edge over their rivals*: **advantage**, lead, head, head start, trump card, the whip hand; **superiority**, the upper hand, dominance, ascendancy, supremacy, primacy, precedence, power, mastery, control, sway, authority; N. Amer. informal the catbird seat; Austral./NZ informal the box seat.

▷ANTONYMS disadvantage.

□ **on edge** *she felt on edge and wanted to get moving*: **tense**, **nervous**, edgy, highly strung, anxious, apprehensive, uneasy, ill at ease, unsettled, unstable; excitable, twitchy, jumpy, keyed up, fidgety, restive, skittish, neurotic, brittle, hysterical; sensitive, insecure; **irritable**, touchy, tetchy, testy, crotchety, irascible, peevish, querulous, bad-tempered, short-tempered, hot-tempered, quick-tempered, temperamental, snappy, captious, crabbed, prickly; Brit. nervy; informal uptight, wired.

▷ANTONYMS calm.

□ **take the edge off** *it took the edge off the pain*: **allay**, assuage, alleviate, ease, relieve, reduce, diminish, decrease, lessen, soothe, soften, dull, cushion, mollify, moderate, calm, lull, temper, mitigate, palliate, blunt, deaden, abate, tone down; rare lenify.

▶ verb 1 *the tall poplars that edged the orchard*: **border**, fringe, rim, verge, skirt, be alongside; **surround**, enclose, encircle, circle, encompass, bound, line, flank.

2 *a white party frock edged with lace*: **trim**, pipe, band, decorate, finish; border, fringe; bind, hem.

3 *he edged closer to the fire | he* **edged his way** *carefully out along the branch*: **creep**, inch (one's way), worm (one's way), work (one's way), pick one's way, nose (one's way), ease (oneself), ease (one's way), advance slowly; advance stealthily, sidle, steal, slink.

edgy adjective *she felt edgy, dreading tomorrow*: **tense**, **nervous**, on edge, highly strung, anxious, apprehensive, uneasy, ill at ease, unsettled, unstable; excitable, twitchy, jumpy, keyed up, fidgety, restive, skittish, neurotic, brittle, hysterical; sensitive, insecure; **irritable**, touchy, tetchy, testy, crotchety, irascible, peevish, querulous, bad-tempered, short-tempered, hot-tempered, quick-tempered, temperamental, snappy, captious, crabbed, prickly; Brit. nervy; informal uptight, wired.

▷ANTONYMS calm.

edible adjective *are these edible mushrooms?* **safe to eat**, fit to eat, fit to be eaten, fit for human consumption, wholesome, good to eat, consumable, digestible, palatable, comestible.
▷ANTONYMS inedible.

edict noun *oil exploration is prohibited by government edict*: **decree**, order, command, commandment, mandate, proclamation, pronouncement, dictum, dictate, fiat, promulgation, precept; law, statute, act, enactment, bill, ordinance, regulation, rule, ruling, injunction, manifesto; in Tsarist Russia ukase; in Spanish-speaking countries pronunciamento; rare firman, decretal, irade, rescript.

edification noun formal *museum administrators are tempted to place profit above edification*: **education**, instruction, tuition, teaching, schooling, tutoring, coaching, training, tutelage, guidance; **enlightenment**, cultivation, development, information, inculcation, indoctrination, improvement, bettering, uplifting, elevation.

edifice noun formal **building**, structure, construction, erection, pile, complex, assembly; property, development, premises, establishment, place.

edify verb formal *no doubt Hamish will edify us on the subject*: **educate**, instruct, teach, school, tutor, coach, train, guide; **enlighten**, inform, cultivate, develop, inculcate, indoctrinate, improve, better, uplift, elevate.

edit verb **1** *she has expertly edited the text to avoid anything that would jar in an English context*: **correct**, **check**, copy-edit; **improve**, revise, emend, polish, modify, adapt, rewrite, reword, rework, redraft, rephrase; assemble, prepare for publication; shorten, condense, cut, abridge; approve, censor; informal clean up, iron out; rare redact.
2 *this volume of essays and interviews was edited by a consultant psychotherapist*: **select**, choose, assemble, organize, put together, arrange, rearrange.
3 *he edited The Times for many years*: **be the editor of**, control the content of, control, direct, run, manage, be in charge of, be responsible for, be at the helm of, be chief of, head, lead, supervise, superintend, oversee, preside over, be the boss of; informal head up.

edition noun *the early editions of tomorrow's papers*: **issue**, number, volume; printing, impression, publication; version, recension, redaction, revision.

educate verb *they decided to educate Edward at home*: **teach**, school, tutor, instruct, coach, train, upskill, drill, prime, prepare, guide, inform, enlighten, edify, cultivate, develop, inculcate, indoctrinate, improve, better, uplift, elevate.

educated adjective *an educated workforce learns how to exploit new technology*: **informed**, literate, schooled, tutored, well informed, well read, learned, knowledgeable, intellectually aware, enlightened, discerning, discriminating; intellectual, academic, erudite, scholarly, studious, bookish, highbrow, literary, cultivated, cultured, refined; informal cerebral; dated lettered.
▷ANTONYMS uneducated.

education noun **1** *the education of children with special needs*: **teaching**, schooling, tuition, tutoring, instruction, coaching, training, tutelage, drilling, preparation, guidance, indoctrination, inculcation, enlightenment, edification, cultivation, development, improvement, bettering.
2 *a young woman of some education*: **learning**, knowledge, literacy, schooling, scholarship, enlightenment, cultivation, culture, refinement; archaic letters.
▷ANTONYMS ignorance.

> *Word links* **education**
>
> **pedagogy** profession or theory of education
> **pedagogic** relating to education

educational adjective **1** *an educational establishment*: **academic**, scholastic, school, for study, learning, teaching, pedagogic, tuitional, instructional.
2 *it was a very educational experience*: **instructive**, instructional, educative, informative, informational, illuminating, pedagogic, doctrinal, preceptive, enlightening, edifying, improving, didactic, heuristic; pedantic, moralistic, homiletic; rare propaedeutic.

educative adjective *the educative value of broadcasting*: **educational**, instructive, instructional, informative, informational, illuminating, pedagogic, doctrinal, preceptive, enlightening, edifying, improving, didactic, heuristic; pedantic, moralistic, homiletic; rare propaedeutic.

educator noun **teacher**, tutor, instructor, pedagogue, schoolteacher, schoolmaster, schoolmistress, master, mistress; educationalist, educationist; supply teacher; coach, trainer; lecturer, professor, don, fellow, reader, academic; guide, mentor, guru, counsellor; Scottish dominie; Indian pandit; N. Amer. informal schoolmarm; Brit. informal beak; Austral./NZ informal chalkie, schoolie; archaic doctor, schoolman, usher; rare preceptor.
▷ANTONYMS pupil.

eel noun

> *Word links* **eel**
>
> **elver** young
> **anguilliform** eel-shaped

eerie adjective *an eerie silence descended over the house*: **uncanny**, sinister, ghostly, spectral, unnatural, unearthly, preternatural, supernatural, otherworldly, unreal, mysterious, strange, abnormal, odd, curious, queer, weird, bizarre, freakish; **frightening**, spine-chilling, hair-raising, blood-curdling, scaring, terrifying, petrifying, chilling; Scottish eldritch; informal creepy, scary, spooky, freaky; Brit. informal rum.
▷ANTONYMS normal, reassuring.

efface verb **1** *the young ladies have made an impression on my mind which will not easily be effaced*. See **erase** (sense 1).
2 *he retired to the largest chair and attempted to efface himself*: **make oneself inconspicuous**, keep out of sight, keep oneself to oneself, keep quiet, keep out of the public eye, avoid publicity, keep out of the limelight, lie low, keep a low profile, regard/treat oneself as unimportant, be modest/diffident/retiring, withdraw.
▷ANTONYMS make one's presence felt.

effect noun **1** *the effect of these changes is hard to assess*: **result**, consequence, upshot, outcome, out-turn, sequel, reaction, repercussions, reverberations, ramifications; end result, conclusion, termination, culmination, denouement, corollary, concomitant, aftermath, fruit(s), product, by-product; Medicine sequelae; informal pay-off; dated issue; archaic success.
▷ANTONYMS cause.
2 *the effect of this drug can be long-lasting*: **impact**, action, effectiveness, efficacy, efficaciousness, influence; power, potency, strength, usefulness, success.
3 *with effect from tomorrow*: **force**, operation, enforcement, implementation, execution, action, effectiveness; validity, lawfulness, legality, legitimacy, authenticity, legal acceptability.
4 *he said 'See you later', or words to that effect*: **sense**, meaning, theme, drift, thread, import, purport, intent, intention, burden, thrust, tenor, significance, message; gist, essence, substance, spirit; mood, character, vein, flavour; archaic strain.
5 (**effects**) *they went through the dead man's effects*: **belongings**, possessions, personal possessions, personal effects, goods, worldly goods, chattels, goods and chattels, accoutrements, appurtenances; property, paraphernalia; luggage, baggage; informal gear, tackle, kit, things, stuff, junk, rubbish, bits and pieces, bits and bobs; Brit. informal clobber, gubbins; vulgar slang shit, crap.
□ **have an effect on** *their behaviors have an effect on others*: **affect**, influence, exert influence on, act on, work on, condition, touch, have an impact on, impact on, take hold of, attack, infect, strike, strike at, hit; change, alter, modify, transform, form, shape, control, govern, determine, decide, guide, sway, bias.
□ **in effect** *the battle had, in effect, already been won*: **really**, in reality, in truth, in fact, in actual fact, effectively, essentially, in essence, virtually, practically, in practical terms, for all practical purposes, to all intents and purposes, in all but name, all but, as good as, more or less, as near as dammit, almost, nearly, well nigh, nigh on, just about; S. African plus-minus; informal pretty much, pretty nearly, pretty well.
□ **be in effect** *is this law yet in effect?* **be in force**, be in operation, act, stand, apply, be applied, run, be/remain valid, be current, function, be efficacious, hold good, be the case, be the order of the day, obtain, hold, be the case, be prevalent, prevail, pertain, be established.
□ **put something into effect** *the plans have not yet been put into effect*: **implement**, apply, put into action, put into practice, execute, enact, carry out, carry through, perform, administer; fulfil, discharge, accomplish, bring about, achieve, realize, contrive, effect; enforce, impose; rare effectuate.
□ **take effect 1** *these measures will take effect on 23rd November*: **come into force**, come into operation, come into being, begin, become operative, become valid, become law, apply, be applied.
▷ANTONYMS lapse.
2 *the drug started to take effect*: **work**, act, be effective, produce results, have the desired effect, be efficacious.
▷ANTONYMS wear off.
□ **to no effect 1** *his efforts were all to no effect*: **ineffective**, ineffectual, inefficacious, vain, in vain, futile, to no avail, unavailing, useless, unsuccessful, non-successful, nugatory, failed, fruitless, unproductive, profitless, unprofitable, pointless, to no purpose, abortive, inadequate; archaic for nought, bootless; rare Sisyphean.
▷ANTONYMS effective, successful.
2 *they can bluster to their hearts' content to no effect*: **in vain**, unsuccessfully, vainly, without success, to no avail, to no purpose, ineffectually, with no result, fruitlessly, profitlessly, unproductively.
▷ANTONYMS successfully.
▶ verb *the government effected a good many changes*: **achieve**, accomplish, carry out, succeed in, realize, attain, manage, bring off, carry off, carry

through, execute, conduct, fix, engineer, perform, do, perpetrate, discharge, fulfil, complete, finish, consummate, conclude; **cause**, bring about, cause to happen/occur, initiate, put in place, create, produce, make, give rise to; provoke, call forth, occasion, bring to pass; generate, originate, engender, precipitate, actuate, wreak, kindle; rare effectuate.

Easily confused words **effect or affect?**

See **affect²**.

e

effective adjective **1** *there is no effective treatment for this condition*: **successful**, effectual, efficacious, productive, constructive, fruitful, functional, potent, powerful; worthwhile, helpful, of help, of assistance, beneficial, advantageous, valuable, useful, of use.
▷ANTONYMS ineffective; incompetent; weak.
2 *a more effective argument can be constructed in support of the opposite point of view*: **convincing**, compelling, strong, forceful, forcible, powerful, potent, weighty, plausible, efficacious, sound, valid, well founded, telling; impressive, persuasive, irresistible, credible, influential, conclusive, unanswerable, authoritative; **logical**, reasoned, reasonable, well reasoned, rational, lucid, coherent, cogent, eloquent, clear, articulate.
▷ANTONYMS weak.
3 *the new law will become effective three months from now*: **operative**, in force, in effect, in operation, valid, official, signed and sealed; lawful, legal, licit, legitimate, legally binding, binding; Law effectual.
▷ANTONYMS invalid.
4 *the region did not come under effective Dutch control until 1904*: **virtual**, practical, essential, operative, actual, implied, implicit, unacknowledged, tacit.
▷ANTONYMS theoretical.
□ **be effective** *no one doubts that these measures will be effective*: **succeed**, be successful, work, work out, turn out well, go as planned, have the desired result, get results, be efficacious; **have an effect**, take effect, be efficacious, function, act, have results, take hold; informal come off, pay off, do the trick, do the business; N. Amer. informal turn the trick.
▷ANTONYMS fail; have no effect.

Easily confused words **effective or efficient?**

Both these words express approval of the way in which someone or something works; but their meanings are different. **Effective** describes something which successfully produces an intended result, without reference to morality, economy of effort, or efficient use of resources (*the drug is more effective in treating ulcers than its predecessors | the trap was hideously unpleasant and equally hideously effective*). **Efficient**, on the other hand, applies to someone or something able to produce results with the minimum expense or effort, as a result of good organization or good design and making the best use of available resources (*staff offer efficient and unobtrusive service*).

effectiveness noun *pupils' progress is a far better measure of a school's effectiveness*: **success**, successfulness, efficacy, productiveness, fruitfulness, potency, power; benefit, advantage, value, virtue, use, usefulness; rare effectuality, constructiveness.
▷ANTONYMS ineffectiveness.

effectual adjective **1** *effectual political action*: **effective**, successful, efficacious, productive, constructive, fruitful, potent, powerful; worthwhile, helpful, of help, of assistance, beneficial, advantageous, valuable, useful, of use.
▷ANTONYMS ineffectual.
2 Law *an effectual document*: **valid**, authentic, legally acceptable, proper, bona fide, genuine, official, signed and sealed; lawful, legal, licit, legitimate, (legally) binding, contractual; in force, in effect, effective.

effeminate adjective *as his manicured fingers played with the gold medallion around his neck, he looked very effeminate*: **womanish**, unmanly, effete, foppish, affected, niminy-piminy, mincing, posturing; informal campy, queeny; informal, derogatory poncey, limp-wristed, pansyish, faggy.
▷ANTONYMS manly.

effervesce verb **1** *heat the mixture until it effervesces*. See **fizz** (sense 1 of the verb).
2 *managers are supposed to effervesce with praise and encouragement*. See **sparkle** (sense 2 of the verb).

effervescence noun **1** *sparkling wines of uniform effervescence and taste*. See **fizz** (sense 1 of the noun).
2 *the youngsters' cheeky effervescence*. See **vivacity**.

effervescent adjective **1** *an effervescent drink*. See **fizzy**.
2 *thousands of effervescent young people*. See **vivacious**.

effete adjective **1** *effete trendies from art colleges*: **affected**, over-refined, ineffectual, artificial, studied, pretentious, precious, chichi, flowery, mannered; informal twee, la-di-da, pseud; Brit. informal poncey, toffee-nosed; rare alembicated.
▷ANTONYMS unpretentious.
2 *I distrusted the effete young man*: **effeminate**, unmasculine, unmanly; womanish, girlish, feminine; **weak**, soft, timid, timorous, fearful, cowardly, lily-livered, limp-wristed, spineless, craven, milksoppish, pusillanimous, chicken-hearted, weak-kneed; informal sissy, wimpish, wimpy, pansy-like.
▷ANTONYMS manly.
3 *the whole fabric of society is becoming effete*: **weakened**, enfeebled, enervated, worn out, exhausted, finished, burnt out, played out, drained, spent, powerless.
▷ANTONYMS powerful.

efficacious adjective *a change in diet may be as efficacious as treatment with steroids*. See **effective**.

efficacy noun *information on the safety and efficacy of drugs*. See **effectiveness**.

efficiency noun **1** *there was a need to reform local government to bring greater efficiency*: **organization**, order, orderliness, planning, regulation, logicality, coherence, productivity, effectiveness, cost-effectiveness.
▷ANTONYMS inefficiency.
2 *I must compliment you all on your efficiency and your bravery*: **competence**, capability, ability, proficiency, adeptness, deftness, expertise, professionalism, skilfulness, skill, effectiveness, productivity, organization.
▷ANTONYMS incompetence.

efficient adjective **1** *efficient managerial techniques*: **well organized**, methodical, systematic, structured, well planned, logical, coherent, well regulated, well run, well ordered, orderly, businesslike, systematized, streamlined, productive, effective, labour-saving, cost-effective.
▷ANTONYMS inefficient; disorganized.
2 *a most efficient young secretary*: **competent**, capable, able, proficient, adept, deft, expert, professional, skilful, skilled, effective, productive, organized, workmanlike, businesslike; French rangé.
▷ANTONYMS inefficient; incompetent.

Easily confused words **efficient or effective?**

See **effective**.

Choose the right word **efficient, competent, capable, able**

See **competent**.

effigy noun *they venerate an effigy of the saint*: **statue**, statuette, carving, sculpture, graven image, model, dummy, figure, figurine, guy; likeness, representation, image; bust, head.

effluent noun *the effluent from papermaking contains many contaminants*: **(liquid) waste**, sewage, effluvium, outflow, discharge, emission; pollutant, pollution.

effort noun **1** *they made an effort to reach a settlement*: **attempt**, try, endeavour; informal crack, go, shot, stab, bash, whack; formal essay; archaic assay.
2 *Guy's score of 68 was a fine effort*: **achievement**, accomplishment, performance, attainment, result, feat, deed, exploit, undertaking, enterprise; work, handiwork, creation, production, opus; **triumph**, success, positive result, coup, master stroke, stroke of genius.
3 *it requires little effort to operate the handle*: **exertion**, force, power, energy, work, muscle, application, labour, the sweat of one's brow, striving, endeavour, toil, struggle, slog, strain, stress, trouble, bother; informal sweat, elbow grease; Brit. informal graft; Austral./NZ informal (hard) yakka; archaic travail, moil.
□ **make an effort** *more than four in ten adults have made an effort to cut their carb intake*: **try**, attempt, endeavour, strive, seek, exert oneself, do one's best, labour, work, toil, struggle, apply oneself; undertake, aim, set out, take it on oneself; informal have a go/shot/crack/stab/bash; Austral./NZ informal give it a burl, give it a fly; formal essay; archaic assay.
□ **make every effort** *the directors of almost all the parks are making every effort to draw in visitors with new attractions*: **try hard**, strive, aim, aspire, venture, undertake, seek, make an effort, spare no effort, exert oneself, do one's best, do all one can, do one's utmost, attempt, give one's all, labour, work, toil, strain, struggle, apply oneself; informal bend/fall/lean over backwards, go all out, give it one's best shot, pull out all the stops, bust a gut, do one's damnedest, go for broke, knock oneself out, break one's neck, move heaven and earth.
□ **spare no effort** See **make every effort** above.
□ **with effort** *'It's bad, sir', he said, controlling his voice with effort*: **with difficulty**, with/after a struggle, painfully, arduously, laboriously, hard.
▷ANTONYMS easily.

effortless adjective **1** *the trade was perceived as an effortless way to attract much-needed foreign currency*. See **easy** (sense 1).
2 *Alexei rose to his feet in a single effortless movement*. See **fluid** (sense 4 of the adjective).

effrontery noun *I am amazed at the effrontery with which the previous speaker lauds himself*: **impudence**, impertinence, cheek, insolence, cheekiness, audacity, temerity, brazenness, forwardness, front,

presumption, nerve, gall, pertness, boldness, shamelessness, impoliteness, disrespect, bad manners, unmannerliness, overfamiliarity; answering back, talking back; informal brass, brass neck, neck, face, lip, mouth, cockiness; Brit. informal sauce; Scottish informal snash; N. Amer. informal sass, sassiness, nerviness, chutzpah, back talk; informal, dated hide; Brit. informal, dated crust, backchat; rare malapertness, contumely, procacity, assumption.
▷ANTONYMS timidity.
□ **have the effrontery** *one councillor had the effrontery to suggest that 80,000 objectors were an insufficient number of people to be taken into consideration*: **dare**, make so bold as, be so bold as, presume, have the temerity, have the audacity, have the nerve, be brave enough, have the courage, go so far as; take the liberty of.

effusion noun **1** *a massive effusion of poisonous gas from a volcanic lake*: **outflow**, outpouring, outflowing, outrush, rush, current, flood, deluge, emission, discharge, issue; spurt, surge, jet, fountain, cascade, spout, stream, torrent, gush, outburst, flow, flux, welling, leakage, escape, voidance, drain, drainage, outflux, emanation, effluence, exudation; technical efflux.
2 (usually **effusions**) *newspaper reporters' flamboyant effusions*: **outburst**, outpouring, gush, stream of words, flow of speech; utterance, wordiness, speech, address, talk, words, writing(s); informal spiel, verbiage.

effusive adjective *a barrage of effusive compliments*: **gushing**, gushy, unrestrained, unreserved, extravagant, fulsome, demonstrative, lavish, enthusiastic, rhapsodic, lyrical, exuberant, ebullient; expansive, wordy, verbose, long-winded, profuse; informal over the top, OTT, all over someone.
▷ANTONYMS restrained.

egg noun **ovum**, gamete, germ cell, zygote; informal nit; Austral. informal goog; (**eggs**) clutch, roe, spawn, seed, flyblow.
□ **bad egg** informal *he assured my parents that I'm not a bad egg*. See **scoundrel**.
▸ verb
□ **egg someone on** *'Teach him a lesson', shouted the boys, egging their friend on*: **urge**, goad, incite, provoke, prick, sting, propel, push, drive, prod, prompt, induce, impel, spur on, cheer on; encourage, exhort, stimulate, motivate, galvanize, act as a stimulus to, act as an incentive to, inspire, stir; N. Amer. informal root on, light a fire under; rare incentivize.

Word links **egg**

oval, **ovate**, **ovoid** egg-shaped
oology study or collecting of birds' eggs

egghead noun informal *in spite of her love of reading Eva denies being an egghead*. See **genius** (sense 3).

ego noun *he needed a boost to his ego*: **self-esteem**, self-importance, self-worth, self-respect, self-conceit, self-image, self-confidence; French amour propre.

egocentric adjective *most children are unshakeably egocentric up to the age of seven*. See **egotistic**.

egotism, egoism noun *in his arrogance and egotism, he underestimated Gill*: **self-centredness**, egocentricity, egomania, self-interest, selfishness, self-seeking, self-serving, self-regard, self-absorption, self-obsession, self-love, narcissism, self-admiration, self-adulation, vanity, conceit, conceitedness, self-conceit, pride, self-esteem, self-importance; **boastfulness**, boasting, bragging, blowing one's own trumpet; French amour propre; informal looking after number one; rare braggadocio.
▷ANTONYMS altruism; modesty.

egotist, egoist noun *boxing is a sport that breeds egotists and exhibitionists*: **self-seeker**, egocentric, egomaniac, self-admirer, narcissist; **boaster**, brag, bragger, braggart, show-off; informal blowhard, swank, big-head; N. Amer. informal showboat; Austral./NZ informal skite; Brit. informal, dated swankpot.
▷ANTONYMS altruist.

egotistic, egoistic adjective *an egotistic lifestyle is a very bad sign indeed*: **self-centred**, selfish, egocentric, egomaniacal, self-interested, self-seeking, self-regarding, self-absorbed, self-obsessed, self-loving, narcissistic, vain, conceited, proud, self-important; **boastful**, bragging.
▷ANTONYMS altruistic; modest.

egregious adjective *an egregious error of judgement*. See **appalling**.

egress noun **1** *the egress from the gallery was blocked*. See **exit** (sense 1 of the noun).
2 *a means of egress for the crowds*. See **exit** (sense 3 of the noun).

eight cardinal number **octet**, eightsome, octuplets; Poetry octrain, octameter; Music octuplet, octave; technical octad; rare ogdoad, octarchy.

Word links **eight**

octo-, **octa-** related prefixes
octagon plane figure with eight sides
octahedron solid figure with eight faces
octuple consisting of eight parts or things
ontonary relating to eight
octennial relating to eight years

ejaculate verb **1** **emit semen**; climax, have an orgasm, orgasm; informal come, shoot one's load.
2 *the sperm is ejaculated*: **emit**, eject, discharge, release, expel, excrete, disgorge, exude, spout, shoot out, squirt out, spew out, spurt out.
3 *'What?' he ejaculated*: **exclaim**, cry out, call out, yell, sing out, utter suddenly, blurt out; burst out with, come out with.

ejaculation noun **1** *the ejaculation of fluid*: **emission**, ejection, discharge, release, expulsion, exudation, excretion, disgorgement.
2 *he suffers from premature ejaculation*: **emission of semen**; climax, orgasm; night emission; informal coming, wet dream.
3 *the usual chorus of ejaculations of welcome*: **exclamation**, interjection, cry, call, shout, yell, utterance.

eject verb **1** *the volcano ejected ash at a phenomenal rate*: **emit**, spew out, pour out, discharge, give off, give out, send out, belch, vent; exude, excrete, expel, cast out, release, disgorge, spout, vomit, throw up, spit out, cough up; rare disembogue.
▷ANTONYMS take in.
2 *the pilot had time to eject*: **bail out**, escape, leave the aircraft, get out, parachute to safety.
3 *his opponents were ejected from the hall*: **expel**, throw out, turn out, put out, cast out, remove, oust; put out in the street, evict, dispossess, banish, deport, exile; informal chuck out, kick out, turf out, boot out, heave out, bounce.
▷ANTONYMS admit.
4 *he was swiftly ejected from his first job*: **dismiss**, remove, discharge, oust, expel, deprive of office, get rid of, throw out, turn out, fling out, force out, drive out; let someone go, give notice to, lay off, make/declare redundant; Military cashier; informal sack, give the sack to, fire, axe, send packing, give someone the boot, boot out, chuck out, kick out, give someone their marching orders, give someone the push, give someone the (old) heave-ho, throw someone out on their ear, give someone the bullet, show someone the door; Brit. informal give someone their cards, give someone the chop, turf out; N. Amer. informal give someone the bum's rush.
▷ANTONYMS appoint.

ejection noun **1** *the ejection of an electron from an atom*: **emission**, discharge, expulsion, release, exudation, excretion, elimination, disgorgement.
▷ANTONYMS absorption.
2 *fans were angry at their ejection from the ground*: **expulsion**, throwing out, removal, ousting; eviction, dispossession, banishment, deportation, exile.
▷ANTONYMS admission.
3 *the crowd called for his ejection from office*: **dismissal**, removal, discharge, ousting, expulsion, lay-off, redundancy, notice; Military cashiering; informal sacking, the sack, firing, axing, the boot, the push, the (old) heave-ho, the bullet; Brit. informal turfing out, one's cards, the chop; N. Amer. informal the bum's rush.
▷ANTONYMS appointment.

eke verb
□ **eke something out 1** *she eked out a living as a washerwoman*: **scrape**, scratch, scrimp; **survive**, live, stay alive, exist, support oneself, cope, manage, fare, get along, get by, get through, make (both) ends meet, keep body and soul together; informal keep the wolf from the door, keep one's head above water, make out. **2** *people would eke out their supplies through the winter*: **economize on**, skimp on, be (more) economical with, make economies with, scrimp and scrape, save; **be thrifty with**, be frugal with, be sparing with, cut back on, make cutbacks in, budget, husband; informal go easy on. ▷ANTONYMS squander. **3** *the emergency rations need to be eked out with other food to maintain health*: **augment**, add to, increase, supplement; enlarge, expand, amplify, make bigger, pad out, fill out, bulk out, stretch out.

elaborate adjective **1** *an elaborate political system*: **complicated**, detailed, intricate, complex, involved, tortuous, convoluted, serpentine, tangled, knotty, confusing, bewildering, baffling; painstaking, careful; inextricable, entangled, impenetrable, Byzantine, Daedalian, Gordian; rare involute, involuted.
▷ANTONYMS simple.
2 *an elaborate plasterwork ceiling*: **ornate**, decorated, embellished, adorned, ornamented, fancy, over-elaborate, fussy, busy, ostentatious, extravagant, showy, baroque, rococo, florid, wedding-cake, gingerbread; informal flash, flashy.
▷ANTONYMS plain.
▸ verb *both sides refused to* **elaborate on** *their reasons*: **expand on**, enlarge on, add to, flesh out, add flesh to, put flesh on the bones of, add detail to, expatiate on; supplement, reinforce, augment, extend, broaden, develop, fill out, embellish, enhance, amplify, refine, improve.

elan, élan noun *they performed with uncommon elan*: **flair**, stylishness, smartness, elegance, grace, gracefulness, poise, polish, suaveness, sophistication, urbanity, chic, finesse, panache, flourish, taste; **vigour**,

e

energy, pep, dynamism, forcefulness, force, strength, determination, motivation, push, vehemence, fanaticism, go, vitality, vivacity, buoyancy, liveliness, animation, sprightliness, zest, sparkle, effervescence, fizz, verve, spirit, spiritedness, ebullience, life, dash, brio; **enthusiasm**, eagerness, keenness, passion, zeal, fervour, relish, gusto, feeling, ardour, fire, fieriness, drive; French esprit; informal class, pizzazz, ritziness, zing, zip, vim, punch, get-up-and-go, oomph, feistiness.
▷ANTONYMS clumsiness.

elapse verb *a month elapsed before the appeal hearing began*: **pass**, go by/past, proceed, progress, advance, wear on, march on, slip by/away/past, roll by/past, glide by/past, slide by/past, steal by/past, tick by/past; fly by/past; creep by/past, crawl by/past.

elastic adjective **1** *the elastic waist fits most people*: **stretchy**, elasticated, stretchable, springy, flexible, pliant, pliable, supple, yielding, rubbery, plastic, rebounding, recoiling, resilient, bouncy; rare tensible.
▷ANTONYMS rigid.
2 *this option is probably the most elastic way of working*: **adaptable**, flexible, adjustable, pliant, compliant, accommodating, malleable, variable, fluid, versatile, conformable; informal easy.

elasticity noun **1** *the skin's natural elasticity*: **stretchiness**, flexibility, pliancy, suppleness, rubberiness, plasticity, resilience, springiness; informal give.
▷ANTONYMS rigidity.
2 *there may be elasticity in a government with a very narrow majority*: **adaptability**, flexibility, adjustability, fluidity, accommodation, versatility, variability, malleability, conformability.
▷ANTONYMS dogmatism.

elated adjective *she was elated at having pocketed some £400,000*: **thrilled**, exhilarated, happy, delighted, overjoyed, joyous, gleeful, excited, animated, jubilant, beside oneself with happiness, exultant, ecstatic, euphoric, rapturous, in raptures, enraptured, rapt; walking on air, on cloud nine/seven, in seventh heaven, jumping for joy, in transports of delight, transported, carried away, in a frenzy of delight, delirious (with happiness), hysterical, wild with excitement, frenzied; informal blissed out, over the moon, on a high; N. Amer. informal wigged out; rare corybantic.
▷ANTONYMS miserable.

elation noun *we shared the general mood of elation at the success*: **happiness**, exhilaration, joy, joyousness, delight, glee; excitement, animation, jubilation, exultation, ecstasy, euphoria, bliss, rapture, rhapsody, rhapsodies, transport(s), cloud nine, heaven, paradise, seventh heaven; informal the top of the world.
▷ANTONYMS misery.

elbow noun **1** *leaning on one's elbow*: **arm joint**, bend of the arm.
2 *you need to fit a 15mm elbow to the end of the pipe*: **bend**, joint, curve, corner, (right) angle, crook; technical flexure.
□ **elbow grease** informal *homemade cleaners may require more elbow grease than commercial spray-and-wipe products*: **hard work**, work, labour, toil, exertion, effort, slog, drudgery; industry; informal grind, sweat, donkey work, spadework; Brit. informal graft, fag; Austral./NZ informal yakka; archaic travail, moil.
□ **give someone the elbow** informal *200 staff have been given the elbow today*: **dismiss**, axe, give someone notice, make redundant, throw out, get rid of, lay off, let go, discharge; informal **sack**, fire, kick out, boot out, give someone the sack, give someone the boot, give someone the bullet, give someone the (old) heave-ho, give someone the push, give someone their marching orders, show someone the door; Brit. informal give someone their cards.
▸ verb *she elbowed him out of the way | he elbowed his way through the crowd*: **push (one's way)**, shove (one's way), force (one's way), shoulder (one's way), jostle (one's way), nudge, muscle, bulldoze, bludgeon one's way.

elbow room noun *the province wants a little more elbow room within the federation*: **room to manoeuvre**, room, space, breathing space, scope, freedom, play, free rein, licence, latitude, leeway, margin, clearance; German Lebensraum.

elder adjective *he has an elder brother*: **older**, senior, first, firstborn, more grown up, big.
▷ANTONYMS younger; little.
▸ noun **1** *he longed for the approval of his elders*: **senior**, old/older person.
2 *the church elders*: **leader**, senior figure, official, patriarch, father, guiding light, guru.

elderly adjective *she has an elderly mother in a nursing home*: **aged**, old, mature, older, senior, ancient, venerable; advanced in years, getting on, ageing; in one's dotage, long in the tooth, as old as the hills; grey, grey-haired, grey-bearded, grizzled, hoary; past one's prime, not as young as one was, not as young as one used to be; decrepit, doddering, doddery, not long for this world, senile, superannuated; septuagenarian, octogenarian, nonagenarian, centenarian; informal past it, over the hill, no spring chicken; formal senescent; rare longevous.
▷ANTONYMS young.
▸ noun (**the elderly**) *purpose-built accommodation for the elderly*: **old people**, older people, elderly people, elders, geriatrics, senior citizens, (old-age) pensioners, OAPs, retired people; N. Amer. seniors, retirees, golden agers; informal (golden) oldies, wrinklies; N. Amer. informal oldsters, woopies.
▷ANTONYMS the young.

eldest adjective *my eldest son*: **oldest**, first, firstborn, most grown up, big, biggest.
▷ANTONYMS youngest, littlest.

elect verb *they have just elected a new president*: **vote (for)**, **vote in**, choose (by ballot), cast one's vote for; pick, select, return, appoint, put in, put in power, opt for, decide on, settle on, fix on, plump for.
▷ANTONYMS vote out.
▸ adjective *the president elect*: **future**, -to-be, soon-to-be, designate, chosen, elected, coming, next, appointed, presumptive.
▸ noun (**the elect**) *those who are numbered among the elect*: **the chosen**, the elite, the select, the favoured; the crème de la crème.

election noun **1** *he was defeated in the 1992 election*: **ballot**, vote, poll, referendum, plebiscite, general election, local election, popular vote, straw vote/poll, show of hands.
2 *the election of a new leader*: **voting (in)**, choosing, picking, selection, choice, appointment.
▷ANTONYMS voting out.

> *Word links* **election**
>
> **psephology** study of elections

electioneer verb *he accused the opposition of electioneering by raising the issue*: **campaign**, canvass, go on the hustings, doorstep; Brit. informal go out on the knocker.

elector noun *each elector has one vote*: **voter**, member of the electorate, enfranchised person, constituent, member of a constituency, selector.

electric adjective **1** *electric power*: **generated by electricity**, galvanic, voltaic.
2 *an electric kettle*: **electric-powered**, powered by electricity, electrically operated, electrically powered, mains-operated, battery-operated, electrically charged.
3 *the atmosphere was electric*: **tense**, charged, electrifying; **exciting**, dramatic, exhilarating, intoxicating, dynamic, thrilling, stimulating, galvanizing, invigorating, animating, energizing, rousing, stirring, heady, moving, jolting, shocking, startling, knife-edge, explosive, volatile, cliffhanging; informal buzzy.
▷ANTONYMS lifeless.

electricity noun **power**, electric power, energy, current, static, power supply; Brit. mains; Canadian hydro; Brit. informal leccy; historical galvanism.

> *Word links* **electricity**
>
> **electrophobia** fear of electricity

electrify verb **1 convert to electricity**, wire up, install electric wiring in.
2 *both lecturers have for several years electrified students at Columbia University*: **excite**, thrill, stimulate, arouse, rouse, inspire, stir (up), exhilarate, intoxicate, galvanize, move, motivate, fire (with enthusiasm), fire someone's imagination, invigorate, animate, get someone going; startle, jolt, shock; N. Amer. light a fire under; informal give someone a buzz, give someone a kick; N. Amer. informal give someone a charge.
▷ANTONYMS bore.

elegance noun **1** *the elegance of their suave escorts*: **style**, stylishness, grace, gracefulness, smoothness; taste, tastefulness, discernment, refinement, sophistication, dignity, distinction, propriety, poise, finesse; fashion, culture, beauty; charm, polish, suaveness, urbanity, panache, flair, dash; luxury, sumptuousness, opulence, grandeur, plushness, exquisiteness; informal swankiness.
▷ANTONYMS inelegance, gaucheness.
2 *they liked the elegance of the idea*: **neatness**, simplicity; **ingenuity**, cleverness, deftness, intelligence, inventiveness.
▷ANTONYMS messiness.

elegant adjective **1** *she was dressed in an elegant black outfit*: **stylish**, graceful, tasteful, discerning, refined, sophisticated, dignified, cultivated, distinguished, classic, smart, fashionable, modish, decorous, beautiful, artistic, aesthetic, lovely; charming, polished, suave, urbane, cultured, dashing, debonair; luxurious, sumptuous, opulent, grand, plush, high-class, exquisite; informal swanky.
▷ANTONYMS inelegant, gauche.
2 *an elegant solution*: **neat**, simple, effective; **ingenious**, clever, deft, intelligent, inventive.
▷ANTONYMS messy.

> *Word toolkit* **elegant**
>
> See **gracious**.

elegiac adjective *a movingly elegiac piece for small orchestra*: **mournful**, melancholic, melancholy, plaintive, sorrowful, sad, lamenting, doleful; funereal, dirgelike; touching, moving, poignant; literary dolorous; rare threnodic, threnodial.
▷ANTONYMS cheerful.

elegy noun *I wrote an elegy for my father*: **funeral poem/song**, burial hymn, lament, dirge, plaint, requiem, keening; Irish & Scottish keen, coronach; rare threnody, threnode.

element noun **1** *village shops are an essential element of the local community*: **component**, constituent, part, section, portion, piece, segment, bit; factor, feature, facet, ingredient, strand, detail, point; member, unit, module, item; essential; rare integrand.
2 *there is an element of truth in this stereotype*: **trace**, touch, hint, smattering, suspicion, soupçon.
3 (**elements**) *it is assumed that the reader is familiar with the elements of thermodynamics*: **basics**, essentials, principles, first principles; foundations, fundamentals, rudiments; informal nuts and bolts, ABC.
4 *Graham was in his element building a fire and cooking the steaks*: **natural environment**, favoured environment, familiar territory, territory, habitat, medium, milieu, sphere, field, domain, realm, circle, resort, haunt.
5 (**the elements**) *having come prepared with an umbrella, I braved the elements*: **the weather**, the climate, meteorological conditions, atmospheric conditions/forces; the wind, the rain, storms.

elemental adjective **1** *the elemental principles of accountancy*: **basic**, primary, principal, fundamental, essential, elementary, radical, root, underlying; rudimentary, primitive, primordial.
2 *a thunderstorm is the inevitable outcome of battling elemental forces*: **natural**, atmospheric, meteorological, environmental.

elementary adjective **1** *an elementary astronomy course | the elementary principles of accountancy*: **basic**, rudimentary, fundamental, basal; primary, preparatory, introductory, initiatory, early; essential, radical, underlying; rare rudimental.
▷ANTONYMS advanced.
2 *playing the blues really is elementary*: **easy**, simple, straightforward, uncomplicated, undemanding, unexacting, effortless, painless, uninvolved, child's play, plain sailing; rudimentary, facile, simplistic; informal as easy as falling off a log, as easy as pie, as easy as ABC, a piece of cake, easy-peasy, no sweat, kids' stuff.
▷ANTONYMS difficult, complicated.

elephantine adjective *a ring of elephantine boulders*: **enormous**, huge, great, massive, giant, immense, tremendous, colossal, mammoth, gargantuan, vast, prodigious, gigantic, monumental, stupendous, titanic, monstrous, very big, very large; bulky, heavy, weighty; ponderous, lumbering, clumsy, laborious; informal jumbo, hulking, whopping, whopping great, thumping, thumping great, humongous, monster, almighty, dirty great, socking great; Brit. informal whacking, whacking great, ginormous.
▷ANTONYMS small.

elevate verb **1** *we have to rely on a breeze to elevate the kite*: **raise**, lift (up), raise up/aloft, buoy up, upraise, bear aloft; hoist, hike up, haul up, heft up, boost.
▷ANTONYMS lower.
2 *in the 1920s he was elevated to Secretary of State*: **promote**, give promotion, upgrade, improve the position/status of, give a higher rank, advance, move up, raise, give advancement, prefer; ennoble, exalt, aggrandize, dignify; informal kick upstairs, move up the ladder.
▷ANTONYMS demote.

elevated adjective **1** *an elevated motorway*: **raised**, upraised, uplifted, lifted up, high up, aloft, aerial, overhead, hoisted.
2 *he told the story with the elevated language of an old Roman*: **lofty**, exalted, high, grand, fine, sublime; inflated, pompous, bombastic, orotund; rare fustian.
▷ANTONYMS lowly, base.
3 *the parish gentry were conscious of their elevated status*: **dignified**, grand, lofty, noble, eminent, exalted, revered, august, great, high, higher, high/higher up, superior; magnificent, sublime, inflated.
▷ANTONYMS humble.

elevation noun **1** *his elevation to the peerage*: **promotion**, upgrading, advancement, advance, preferment, aggrandizement, move up, step up; ennoblement; informal step up the ladder, kick upstairs, leg-up.
▷ANTONYMS demotion.
2 *as the road gains elevation, the maples begin to appear*: **altitude**, height, distance above the sea/ground; loftiness.
3 *most early plantation development was at the higher elevations*: **height**, hill, mound, mountain, mount, eminence, rise; high ground, raised ground, rising ground; formal acclivity.
▷ANTONYMS depth.
4 *houses with plastered elevations and tiled roofs*: **side**, face, facade, aspect.
5 *elevation of thought*: **grandeur**, greatness, nobility, magnificence, loftiness, majesty, grandioseness, sublimity.

elf noun *birthmarks were thought to be bruises left by elves*: **pixie**, fairy, sprite, imp, brownie; dwarf, gnome, goblin, hobgoblin; leprechaun, puck, troll; Irish Sidhe; rare nix, nixie.

elfin adjective *her short hair accentuated her elfin face*: **elflike**, elfish, elvish, pixie-like; puckish, impish, playful, mischievous; **dainty**, delicate, small, petite, slight, little, tiny, diminutive.

elicit verb *the police claimed that his fingerprints had been found in order to elicit admissions from him*: **obtain**, bring out, draw out, extract, evoke, bring about, bring forth, induce, excite, give rise to, call forth, prompt, generate, engender, spark off, trigger, kindle; extort, exact, wrest, derive, provoke, wring, screw, squeeze; informal worm out.

eligible adjective **1** *she had paid sufficient contributions to be eligible to receive unemployment benefit*: **entitled**, permitted, allowed, qualified; **acceptable**, suitable, appropriate, fit, fitting, worthy, competent.
▷ANTONYMS ineligible.
2 *an eligible bachelor*: **desirable**; **available**, single, unmarried, unattached, unwed.

eliminate verb **1** *the cause of the disease has been eliminated*: **remove**, get rid of, abolish, put an end to, do away with, banish; end, stop, terminate, eradicate, destroy, annihilate, stamp out, obliterate, wipe out, extinguish, quash, finish off; informal give something the chop, knock something on the head.
2 *he was eliminated from the title race*: **knock out**, beat, get rid of; rule out, disqualify.

elite noun *the party attracted the elite of London society*: **best**, pick, cream, flower, nonpareil, elect; aristocracy, nobility, gentry, upper class, privileged class, first class, establishment; high society, jet set, beautiful people; Indian bhadralok; French beau monde, haut monde, crème de la crème; N. Amer. informal four hundred.
▷ANTONYMS dregs.

elixir noun **1** *an elixir guaranteed to induce love*: **potion**, concoction, brew, philtre, decoction; medicine, tincture, tonic; literary draught; archaic potation.
2 *a cough elixir*: **mixture**, solution, potion, tincture; extract, essence, concentrate, distillate, distillation.

elliptical adjective **1** *an elliptical orbit*: **oval**, egg-shaped, elliptic, ovate, ovoid, oviform, ellipsoidal; technical obovate.
2 *the elliptical phraseology of the law*: **terse**, concise, succinct, compact, economic, brief, laconic, sparing, pithy, curt, clipped; abstruse, cryptic, ambiguous, obscure, incomprehensible, unfathomable, oblique, recondite, Delphic.
▷ANTONYMS clear, direct.

elocution noun *she had lessons in singing and elocution*: **pronunciation**, enunciation, articulation, diction, speech, voice production, intonation, voicing, vocalization, modulation; phrasing, delivery, utterance, fluency; public speaking, oratory, speech-making, declamation.

elongate verb **1** *the door had been elongated so that the wheelchair could go in*: **lengthen**, stretch out, make longer, extend, broaden, widen, enlarge.
▷ANTONYMS shorten.
2 *he elongated and emphasized the word*: **prolong**, protract, draw out, string out, drag out, continue, sustain.
▷ANTONYMS shorten.

elope verb *perhaps they'll elope to Gretna Green*: **run away to marry**, run off/away together, slip away, sneak off, steal away; run off/away with a lover.

eloquence noun **1** *he was known for the eloquence of his sermons*: **oratory**, rhetoric, grandiloquence, magniloquence; expressiveness, articulacy, articulateness, fluency, facility, persuasiveness; diction, enunciation, locution; command of language, power of speech; informal gift of the gab, way with words, blarney.
▷ANTONYMS inarticulacy.
2 *the quality and eloquence of the string playing*: **expressiveness**, sensitivity, meaningfulness, significance, suggestiveness.

eloquent adjective **1** *an eloquent and well-informed speech*: **persuasive**, expressive, articulate, fluent; strong, forceful, powerful, potent; well spoken, silver-tongued, smooth-tongued, well expressed, graceful, lucid, vivid, effective, graphic; glib.
▷ANTONYMS inarticulate.
2 *her dark eloquent eyes lifted up*: **expressive**, sensitive, meaningful, suggestive, revealing, telling, significant, indicative.

elsewhere adverb *the negatives are stored in one place, and the prints are stored elsewhere*: **somewhere else**, in/at/to another place, in/at/to a different place; not here, not present, absent, away, abroad, not at home, gone, out, hence.
▷ANTONYMS here, in the same place.

elucidate verb *collections of letters can elucidate what was uppermost in an artist's mind*: **explain**, make clear, make plain, illuminate, throw/shed light on, clarify; comment on, interpret, explicate, expound on, gloss, annotate, spell out; clear up, sort out, resolve, straighten up/out, unravel, untangle.
▷ANTONYMS confuse, obscure.

e

elucidation noun *his elucidation of the finer points of horse racing is excellent*: **explanation**, clarification, illumination; commentary, interpretation, explication, gloss, annotation, account, report, setting out, exegesis; comment, exposition.

elude verb *the murderer managed to elude the police for several weeks*: **evade**, avoid, get away from, dodge, flee, escape (from), run (away) from; lose, duck, shake off, give the slip to, slip away from, throw off the scent; informal slip through someone's fingers, slip through the net; archaic circumvent, bilk.
▷ANTONYMS be caught by.

elusive adjective **1** *he tried to reach her by telephone, but she continued to be elusive*: **difficult to catch/find**, difficult to track down; evasive, slippery, shifty; informal always on the move, cagey.
2 *the notion of meaning is exceedingly elusive and complex*: **subtle**, indistinct, indefinite, ambiguous, indefinable, intangible, impalpable, unanalysable, fugitive, deceptive, baffling.
▷ANTONYMS clear.
3 *as usual she gave an elusive answer*: **ambiguous**, baffling, puzzling, misleading, evasive, equivocal, deceptive; rare elusory.

Elysian adjective *an Elysian vision*: **heavenly**, paradisal, paradisiacal, celestial, empyrean, superlunary, divine.
▷ANTONYMS hellish; mundane.

Elysium noun Greek Mythology *a chariot ready to convey the human soul to Elysium*: **heaven**, paradise, the Elysian fields, empyrean, Arcadia, Arcady, Shangri-La; eternity, kingdom come, the next life, the afterlife, the next world, the hereafter; bliss; Scandinavian Mythology Valhalla; Classical Mythology the islands of the blessed; Arthurian Legend Avalon.

emaciated adjective *the captives were sick and emaciated men*: **thin**, skeletal, bony, wasted, thin as a rake; scrawny, skinny, scraggy, skin and bones, raw-boned, angular, stick-like, size-zero; starved, underfed, undernourished, underweight, half-starved; cadaverous, shrivelled, shrunken, withered; gaunt, haggard, drawn, pinched, wizened, attenuated, atrophied; informal anorexic, looking like a bag of bones; archaic phthisical.
▷ANTONYMS fat.

emaciation noun *animal rescue workers took away goats suffering from emaciation*: **thinness**, boniness, scrawniness, skinniness, scragginess; **starvation**, underfeeding, undernourishment; cadaverousness, shrunkenness, gauntness, haggardness, attenuation, atrophy; informal anorexia; archaic phthisis.
▷ANTONYMS obesity.

emanate verb **1** *policy statements which emanate from government departments*: **emerge**, flow, pour, proceed, issue, ensue, come out, come forth, spread out, come; be uttered, be emitted, be transmitted; arise, originate, stem, derive, spring, start.
2 *the delicious aura of perfume which the women emanated*: **exude**, give off, give out, send out, send forth, pour out, throw out, spread, discharge, disgorge, emit, exhale, radiate; literary distil.

emanation noun **1** *we can look at what is on the page as an emanation of its time and place*: **product**, consequence, result, fruit; corollary, concomitant, by-product, side effect.
2 *the risk of radon gas emanation*: **discharge**, emission, radiation, diffusion, effusion, exhalation, exudation, outflow, outpouring, flow, secretion, leak; effluent, effluvium; technical efflux.

emancipate verb *the serfs privately owned by members of the nobility were emancipated*: **free**, liberate, set free, release, let loose/out, set loose/free, discharge; unchain, unfetter, unshackle, untie, unyoke, uncage, unbridle; give rights to, free from restriction/restraint; historical manumit; rare disenthral.
▷ANTONYMS enslave.

emancipated adjective *an emancipated woman of the twenty-first century*: **liberated**, independent, unconstrained, unrepressed, uninhibited, free and easy, free.

emancipation noun *the emancipation of the serfs*: **freeing**, liberation, liberating, setting free, release, releasing, letting loose/out, setting loose/free, discharge; unchaining, unfettering, unshackling, untying, unyoking, uncaging, unbridling; freedom, liberty; historical manumission; rare disenthralment.
▷ANTONYMS enslavement, slavery.

emasculate verb **1** *the Parliament Act of 1911 which emasculated the House of Lords*: **weaken**, make feeble/feebler, debilitate, enfeeble, enervate, dilute, erode, undermine, impoverish, cripple, reduce the powers of; remove the sting from, pull the teeth of; informal water down.
▷ANTONYMS strengthen.
2 *young cocks should be emasculated at three months old*: **castrate**, neuter, geld, cut, desex, asexualize, sterilize, remove the testicles of; unman; N. Amer. & Austral. alter; informal doctor, fix; rare evirate, caponize, eunuchize.

embalm verb **1** *the Egyptians used citrus juices for embalming their dead*: **preserve**, mummify, lay out, anoint.
2 *the poem ought to embalm his memory*: **conserve**, preserve, immortalize, enshrine; cherish, treasure, store, consecrate.

embankment noun *a steep grassy embankment*: **bank**, mound, ridge, earthwork, causeway, barrier, levee, dam, dyke; slope, verge.

embargo noun *an embargo on oil sales*: **ban**, bar, prohibition, stoppage, interdict, proscription, veto, moratorium; restriction, restraint, blockage, check, barrier, impediment, obstruction, hindrance; boycott.
▸ verb *arms sales were embargoed*: **ban**, bar, prohibit, stop, interdict, debar, proscribe, outlaw, make illegal; restrict, restrain, block, check, impede, obstruct, hinder; boycott, blacklist, ostracize.
▷ANTONYMS allow.

embark verb **1** *he stood on the pier to watch me embark*: **board ship**, go on board, go aboard, climb aboard, step aboard, take ship; take off; informal hop on, jump on.
▷ANTONYMS disembark; land.
2 *he was about to* **embark on** *a career in the family's department store chain*: **begin**, start, commence, undertake, set about, enter on, go into, take up; venture into, launch into, plunge into, turn one's hand to, engage in, settle down to; institute, initiate, tackle; informal have a go/crack/shot at.

embarrass verb *he was embarrassed by a front-page story which alleged that he had had an affair*: **shame**, humiliate, make ashamed, demean, abash; mortify, horrify, appal, crush; make uncomfortable, make awkward, make self-conscious, make uneasy; upset, disconcert, discomfit, discompose, confuse, fluster, agitate, nonplus, discountenance, distress, chagrin; discredit, dishonour; informal show up, faze, rattle, discombobulate.

embarrassed adjective *she felt embarrassed at having been so frank before a servant*: **awkward**, **self-conscious**, uneasy, uncomfortable, unsettled, sheepish, red-faced, blushing, shy; shamed, ashamed, shamefaced, humiliated, humbled, demeaned, abashed; mortified, horrified, appalled, crushed; upset, disconcerted, discomfited, discomposed, confused, flustered, agitated, nonplussed, discountenanced, distressed, chastened, chagrined; discredited, dishonoured; informal with egg on one's face, wishing the earth would swallow one up.
▷ANTONYMS unabashed.

embarrassing adjective **1** *he was frightened of making an embarrassing mistake*: **shaming**, shameful, humiliating, mortifying, demeaning, degrading, ignominious; upsetting, disconcerting, discomfiting, discomposing, confusing, flustering, agitating, discountenancing, distressing; discreditable, dishonouring, disgraceful; informal blush-making.
2 *there may be some embarrassing questions at the shareholders' meeting*: **awkward**, uncomfortable, difficult, tricky, delicate, sensitive, problematic, troublesome, thorny, knotty, vexatious, ticklish; compromising, humiliating; informal sticky, dicey, hairy, cringeworthy, cringe-making; Brit. informal dodgy.

embarrassment noun **1** *Louise's heightened colour betrayed her embarrassment*: **awkwardness**, **self-consciousness**, unease, uneasiness, discomfort, discomfiture, edginess; shame, humiliation, mortification, ignominy; sheepishness, shyness, bashfulness; discomposure, flusteredness, perturbation, confusion, agitation, distress, chagrin.
▷ANTONYMS confidence.
2 *his current financial embarrassment*: **difficulty**, predicament, plight, problem, mess, entanglement, imbroglio; dilemma, quandary; informal bind, jam, pickle, fix, scrape.
3 *an embarrassment of riches*: **surplus**, excess, overabundance, superabundance, profusion, glut, surfeit, superfluity, more than enough, too many, too much, enough and to spare; avalanche, deluge, flood, abundance, plethora.
▷ANTONYMS dearth.

embassy noun **1** *the Italian embassy*: **consulate**, legation, ministry.
2 historical *Charles sent an embassy to the Lombards*: **envoy**, representative, legate, delegate, emissary; **delegation**, deputation, delegacy, legation, (diplomatic) mission; archaic embassage.

embed, imbed verb *the plaque was embedded in a wall at the rear of the house*: **implant**, plant, set, fix, lodge, root, insert, place; sink, submerge, immerse; drive in, hammer in, ram in.

embellish verb **1** *weapons were often embellished with precious metal*: **decorate**, adorn, ornament, dress, dress up, furnish; beautify, enhance, enrich, grace; trim, garnish, gild, varnish; brighten up, ginger up; deck, bedeck, festoon, emblazon, bespangle; informal do up, do out, jazz up; Brit. informal tart up; literary bejewel, bedizen, caparison, furbelow, befrill.
2 *the legend was embellished further by a visiting American academic*: **elaborate**, embroider, colour, expand on, exaggerate, dress up, touch up, gild.
▷ANTONYMS simplify.

embellishment noun **1** *the embellishments in medieval manuscripts*: **decoration**, ornamentation, adornment; beautification, enhancement, trimming, trim, garnishing, gilding, frill, enrichment; varnishing, embroidery; decorating, embellishing, bedecking, festooning, emblazoning.
2 *stripped of her embellishments, the core of hard facts was disappointingly*

small: **elaboration**, addition, exaggeration; digression, deviation.

ember noun *the fire's dying embers*: **glowing coal**, live coal; cinder; (**embers**) ashes, residue, clinker, charcoal.

embezzle verb *he was charged with embezzling more than £5,000 from a country club*: **misappropriate**, steal, rob, thieve, pilfer, appropriate, abstract, defraud someone of, siphon off, pocket, take, take for oneself, help oneself to, line one's pockets/purse with; put one's hand in the till, dip into the public purse, commit white-collar crime, commit fraud; informal rip off, filch, swipe, lift, skim, snaffle; Brit. informal pinch, nick, half-inch, whip, nobble; formal peculate, defalcate, purloin.

embezzlement noun *the embezzlement of public funds*: **misappropriation**, theft, stealing, robbing, robbery, thieving, pilfering, pilferage, appropriation, abstraction, swindling; white-collar crime, fraud, larceny, misuse of funds; informal ripping off, filching, swiping, lifting, skimming, snaffling, monkey business; Brit. informal pinching, nicking, half-inching, whipping, nobbling; formal peculation, defalcation, purloining.

embitter verb *Hugh was embittered by William's failure to keep his word*: **make bitter**, make resentful, sour, anger, poison, envenom, make rancorous, jaundice, antagonize, vex, frustrate, alienate; disillusion, disaffect, dissatisfy, discourage; N. Amer. rankle.

emblazon verb 1 *each shirt was emblazoned with the company name*: **adorn**, decorate, ornament, embellish, illuminate; colour, paint.
2 *a flag with a hammer and sickle emblazoned on it*: **display**, depict, exhibit, show, present.

emblem noun *the white rose was the emblem of the Yorkist side*: **symbol**, representation, token, image, figure, mark, sign; **crest**, badge, device, insignia, stamp, seal, design, heraldic device, coat of arms, shield; logo, trademark.

emblematic, emblematical adjective 1 *the experience of these writers was seen as emblematic of the social mobility of post-war writers*: **symbolic**, representative, demonstrative, suggestive, symptomatic, indicative, typical, characteristic.
2 *emblematic works of art*: **allegorical**, symbolic, symbolizing, metaphorical, parabolic, evocative, figurative.
▷ANTONYMS representational, realistic.

embodiment noun *she was the living embodiment of '80s values*: **personification**, incarnation, incorporation, realization, manifestation, expression, representation, actualization, concretization, symbol, symbolization; paradigm, epitome, paragon, soul, model; type, typification, essence, quintessence, exemplification, example, exemplar, ideal, idea, textbook example; formal reification.

embody verb 1 *he embodies what everybody takes to be typical of the skinhead movement*: **personify**, incorporate, give human form/shape to, realize, manifest, express, concretize, symbolize, represent, epitomize, stand for, encapsulate, typify, exemplify; formal reify; rare incarnate, image.
2 *the proposals were eventually embodied in legislation*: **incorporate**, include, contain, take in, consolidate, encompass, assimilate, integrate, concentrate; organize, systematize; combine, bring together, gather together, collect.

embolden verb *emboldened by the brandy, he walked over to her table*: **give courage**, make brave/braver, encourage, hearten, strengthen, fortify, stiffen the resolve of, lift the morale of; rouse, stir, stimulate, cheer, rally, give confidence, brace; fire, inflame, animate, motivate, invigorate, vitalize; informal buck up; rare inspirit.
▷ANTONYMS dishearten, discourage.

embrace verb 1 *he ran to meet Jacob and embraced him*: **hug**, take/hold in one's arms, hold, cuddle, clasp to one's bosom, clasp, squeeze, clutch, seize, grab; nuzzle, caress; enfold, enclasp, encircle, enclose, envelop, entwine oneself around; informal canoodle, smooch; literary embosom.
2 *many women are turning their backs on careers and embracing family life*: **welcome**, accept, receive enthusiastically/wholeheartedly, take up, take to one's heart, welcome/receive with open arms, adopt; support, be in favour of, back, champion; formal espouse.
▷ANTONYMS reject.
3 *the faculty embraces a wide range of departments*: **include**, take in, cover, involve, take into account, contain, comprise, incorporate, encompass, encapsulate, embody, subsume, comprehend.
▷ANTONYMS exclude.
▶ noun *they were locked in an embrace*: **hug**, cuddle, squeeze, clasp, hold, clutch, clinch, nuzzle, caress; bear hug; informal necking session.

embrocation noun *a rub with embrocation*: **ointment**, lotion, cream, rub, salve, emollient, preparation, application, liniment, balm, poultice, unguent.

embroider verb 1 *the cushion was embroidered with a pattern of golden keys*: **decorate**, adorn, ornament, embellish; **sew**, stitch.
2 *she embroidered her stories with colourful detail*: **elaborate**, embellish, colour, enlarge on, exaggerate; add detail to, go into detail about, flesh out, add flesh to; touch up, dress up, gild, ginger up; informal jazz up.
▷ANTONYMS simplify.

embroidery noun 1 *my mother decided I should learn embroidery*: **needlework**, needlepoint, needlecraft, sewing, cross stitch, tatting, crochet, crewel work; tapestry, sampler.
2 *fanciful embroidery of the facts*: **elaboration**, embellishment, adornment, ornamentation, colouring, enhancement; exaggeration, overstatement, hyperbole; touching up, dressing up, gilding, varnishing, gingering up; informal jazzing up.
▷ANTONYMS simplification.

embroil verb *she became embroiled in a dispute between the two women*: **involve**, entangle, ensnare, enmesh, catch up, mix up, bog down, mire.

embryo noun 1 *the development of the embryo in the uterus*: **fetus**, fertilized egg, unborn child/baby.
2 *the building is used as the embryo of a university for the island*: **rudimentary version**, germ, nucleus, seed, root, source; rudiments, basics; beginning, start, basis, mainspring.

> *Word links* **embryo**
> **embryology** branch of medicine concerning embryos

embryonic adjective 1 *an embryonic chick*: **fetal**, unborn, unhatched.
▷ANTONYMS mature.
2 *an embryonic pro-democracy movement*: **rudimentary**, undeveloped, unformed, immature, incomplete, incipient, inchoate, just beginning; fledgling, budding, beginning, potential, nascent, emerging, developing; early, primary, elementary, germinal.
▷ANTONYMS mature, developed.

emend verb *the journalistic practice of emending quotations in the areas of grammar and syntax*: **correct**, rectify, repair, fix; improve, enhance, polish, refine, clarify; edit, alter, rewrite, revise, copy-edit, subedit, amend, change, modify; redraft, recast, rephrase, reword, rework; expurgate, censor, bowdlerize; rare redact.

emendation noun *different editors applied rival principles of textual emendation*: **correction**, rectification; improvement, improving, enhancement, enhancing, polishing, refinement, refining, clarification; editing, alteration, rewriting, revision, copy-editing, subediting, amendment, modification; redrafting, recasting, rephrasing, rewording, reworking; expurgation, censorship, censoring, bowdlerization; rare redaction.

emerge verb 1 *a policeman emerged from the alley*: **come out**, appear, come into view, become visible, make an appearance; turn up, spring up, come up, surface, crop up, pop up; materialize, manifest oneself, arise, proceed, issue, come forth, emanate.
▷ANTONYMS disappear.
2 *the results were collected and several unexpected facts emerged*: **become known**, become apparent, become evident, be revealed, come to light, come out, transpire, come to the fore, enter the picture, unfold, turn out, prove to be the case; become common knowledge, get around.

emergence noun 1 *we are witnessing the emergence of a new generation of managers*: **appearance**, arrival, coming; turning up, springing up, surfacing, cropping up, popping up; advent, inception, dawn, birth, origination, start; development, rise, blossoming, blooming; materializing, materialization, arising, issue, emanation.
▷ANTONYMS disappearance.
2 *the emergence of the facts*: **disclosure**, becoming known, coming to light, exposure, unfolding, publication, publicizing, publishing, broadcasting.

emergency noun *your quick response in an emergency could be a lifesaver*: **crisis**, urgent situation, extremity, exigency; accident, disaster, catastrophe, calamity; difficulty, plight, predicament, tight spot, tight corner, mess; quandary, dilemma; unforeseen circumstances, dire/desperate straits, danger; informal scrape, jam, fix, pickle, spot, hole, hot water, crunch, panic stations.
▶ adjective 1 *an emergency meeting*: **urgent**, crisis; impromptu, extraordinary.
2 *an emergency exit*: **alternative**, substitute, replacement, spare, extra, standby, auxiliary, reserve, backup, fill-in, fallback, in reserve.
▷ANTONYMS main, primary.

emergent adjective *their methods suited the needs of the emergent recording industry*: **emerging**, beginning, coming out, arising, dawning; developing, budding, burgeoning, embryonic, infant, fledgling, nascent, incipient; rising, promising, potential, up-and-coming.
▷ANTONYMS declining; mature.

emigrate verb **move abroad**, move overseas, leave one's country, migrate; relocate, resettle, start a new life; defect.
▷ANTONYMS immigrate.

emigration noun *the major financial reason for emigration was higher salaries*: **moving abroad**, moving overseas, expatriation, departure, withdrawal, migration, evacuation; exodus, diaspora; relocation, resettling; defection.
▷ANTONYMS immigration.

e

eminence noun **1** *his eminence as a scientist is well known*: **illustriousness**, distinction, renown, pre-eminence, notability, greatness, calibre, prestige, importance, reputation, repute, note; fame, celebrity, prominence; stature, standing, rank, station.
2 *her first-class mind made her an eminence in the British establishment*: **important person**, influential person, distinguished person, dignitary, luminary, worthy, grandee, notable, notability, personage, leading light, VIP; informal somebody, someone, bigwig, big shot, big noise, big gun, big cheese, nob, lady muck, heavyweight; N. Amer. informal big wheel, big kahuna, top banana, big enchilada.
3 formal *the hotel dominated Scarborough from its eminence above the sea*: **elevation**, rise, rising/raised ground, height, hill, bank, mound.

eminent adjective **1** *an eminent man of letters*: **illustrious**, distinguished, renowned, esteemed, pre-eminent, notable, noteworthy, great, prestigious, important, significant, influential, outstanding, noted, of note; famous, celebrated, prominent, well known, lionized, acclaimed; superior, of high standing, high-ranking, exalted, revered, elevated, august, grand, lofty, venerable, foremost, leading, paramount, legendary; informal big-time, big/major league.
▷ANTONYMS unimportant; unknown.
2 *the eminent reasonableness of their wage claims*: **obvious**, clear, conspicuous, marked, singular, signal, outstanding; total, complete, utter, absolute, thorough, perfect, downright, sheer.

eminently adverb *this car is eminently suitable for town driving*: **very**, most, greatly, highly, exceedingly, extremely, particularly, positively, exceptionally, supremely, remarkably, uniquely; **obviously**, clearly, conspicuously, markedly, singularly, signally, outstandingly, strikingly, notably, prominently, surpassingly; totally, completely, utterly, absolutely, thoroughly, perfectly, downright; French par excellence.

emissary noun *he sent an emissary to Constantinople for bilateral talks*: **envoy**, ambassador, diplomat, delegate, attaché, legate, consul, plenipotentiary, minister; agent, representative, deputy, factor, proxy, surrogate, liaison, messenger, courier, herald; informal go-between; Roman Catholic Church nuncio.

emission noun *targets for reducing carbon dioxide emissions*: **discharge**, release, outpouring, outflow, outrush, leak, excretion, secretion, ejection; emanation, radiation, exhalation, exudation, exuding, venting, effusion, ejaculation, disgorgement, issuance, issue; oozing, leaking.

emit verb **1** *hydrocarbons are emitted from vehicle exhausts*: **discharge**, release, give out/off, pour out, send forth, throw out, void, effuse, vent, give vent to, issue; leak, ooze, shed, excrete, disgorge, secrete, eject; spout, belch, spew out; emanate, radiate, exhale, ejaculate, exude; rare eruct.
▷ANTONYMS absorb.
2 *suddenly he emitted a loud cry*: **utter**, voice, let out, produce, give vent to, issue, come out with, pronounce, express; declare, articulate, vocalize.

emollient adjective **1** *a rich emollient shampoo*: **moisturizing**, palliative, balsamic; soothing, softening; technical humectant.
▷ANTONYMS irritating.
2 *he gave a confidently emollient response*: **conciliatory**, conciliating, appeasing, soothing, calming, pacifying, assuaging, placating, mollifying, relaxing, propitiatory.
▷ANTONYMS aggravating.
▸ noun *always moisturize exposed skin with an effective emollient*: **moisturizer**, cream, oil, ointment, rub, lotion, salve, unguent, balsam; technical humectant; dated pomade.
▷ANTONYMS irritant.

emolument noun formal *the emoluments of the director*: **payment**, fee, charge, consideration; salary, pay, wage(s), earnings, allowance, stipend, honorarium; income, revenue, return, profit, gain, proceeds; reward, compensation, premium, recompense; informal perks, pickings; formal perquisites.

emotion noun **1** *she was good at hiding her emotions*: **feeling**, sentiment, sensation; reaction, response.
2 *overcome by emotion, she turned away*: **passion**, intensity, warmth, ardour, fervour, vehemence, fire, fieriness, excitement, spirit, soul.
▷ANTONYMS coldness, indifference.
3 *we are not basing our views on emotion, but on pure business considerations*: **instinct**, intuition, gut feeling, inclination; sentiment, sentimentality, the heart; tenderness, softness, soft-heartedness, tender-heartedness.
▷ANTONYMS intellect.

emotional adjective **1** *their emotional needs are often ignored*: **spiritual**, inner, psychic, psychological, of the heart.
▷ANTONYMS material.
2 *an emotional young man*: **passionate**, feeling, hot-blooded, warm, ardent, fervent, excitable, temperamental, melodramatic, tempestuous, overcharged, responsive; demonstrative, tender, loving, sentimental, sensitive.
▷ANTONYMS apathetic, cold.
3 *he paid an emotional tribute to his wife*: **poignant**, moving, touching, affecting, powerful, stirring, emotive, heart-rending, heartbreaking, heart-warming, soul-stirring, uplifting, impassioned, dramatic; harrowing, tragic, haunting, pathetic; sentimental, over-sentimental, mawkish, cloying, sugary, syrupy, saccharine, lachrymose; informal tear-jerking, soppy, mushy, schmaltzy, weepy, cutesy, lovey-dovey, gooey, drippy; N. Amer. informal cornball, sappy, hokey, three-hankie.
▷ANTONYMS dry, unfeeling, emotionless.
4 *an emotional issue*: **emotive**, sensitive, delicate, difficult, problematic; controversial, contentious, subjective.

emotionless adjective *a flat, emotionless voice*: **unemotional**, unfeeling, dispassionate, passionless; unexpressive, cool, cold, cold-blooded, impassive; reserved, controlled, restrained, self-controlled, {cool, calm, and collected}, indifferent, detached, remote, aloof; toneless, flat, dead, expressionless, bland, blank, wooden, stony, deadpan, hollow, vacant, undemonstrative, imperturbable, frigid, phlegmatic, glacial.
▷ANTONYMS emotional.

emotive adjective *fox-hunting is another emotive issue*: **inflammatory**, controversial, contentious, emotional; sensitive, delicate, difficult, problematic, touchy, awkward.

empathize verb *counsellors need to be able to* **empathize with** *people*: **identify**, be in tune, have a rapport, feel togetherness, feel at one, commune, sympathize, be in sympathy; be on the same wavelength as, talk the same language as; understand, relate to, feel for, have insight into; informal put oneself in the shoes of.

emperor noun *the Emperor of Austria*: **ruler**, sovereign, king, monarch, potentate, lord, overlord; formerly, in certain Muslim countries **khan**; Russian, historical **tsar**; German, historical **kaiser**; Japanese, historical **mikado**; in ancient Rome imperator; rare ethnarch, autarch.

> *Word links* **emperor**
>
> **imperial** relating to an emperor

emphasis noun **1** *the curriculum for 16-year-olds gave more emphasis to reading and writing*: **prominence**, importance, significance; stress, weight, attention, priority, urgency, force, forcibleness, insistence, underlining, underscoring, intensity; import, power, moment, mark, pre-eminence.
2 *the emphasis is on the word 'little'*: **stress**, accent, accentuation, weight, force, prominence; beat; Prosody ictus.

emphasize verb **1** *the prime minister emphasized his commitment to reform*: **bring/call/draw attention to**, focus attention on, highlight, point up, spotlight, foreground, play up, make a point of; stress, weight, put/lay stress on, give an emphasis to, give prominence to, bring to the fore; dwell on, harp on, insist on, belabour; accent, accentuate, underline, intensify, strengthen, heighten, deepen, italicize, underscore, prioritize; informal press home, rub it in.
▷ANTONYMS understate, play down.
2 *'It's only a bachelor pad' I said, emphasizing the word 'bachelor'*: **stress**, put the stress/accent/force on, accent, accentuate, weight.

emphatic adjective **1** *he was emphatic that athletes would not be paid to take part | an emphatic denial*: **vehement**, firm, wholehearted, forceful, forcible, energetic, vigorous, ardent, assertive, insistent; certain, direct, definite, out-and-out, one hundred per cent; decided, determined, earnest; categorical, unqualified, unconditional, unequivocal, unambiguous, absolute, explicit, downright, outright, clear.
▷ANTONYMS hesitant, tentative.
2 *an emphatic victory*: **conclusive**, decisive, marked, pronounced, decided, unmistakable, positive, definite, strong, powerful, striking, distinctive; resounding, telling, momentous; informal thumping, thundering.
▷ANTONYMS narrow.

empire noun **1** *the Ottoman Empire*: **kingdom**, realm, domain, territory, province; commonwealth, federation, confederation; power, world power, superpower; jurisdiction; Latin res publica.
2 *a worldwide shipping empire*: **organization**, corporation, multinational, conglomerate, consortium, company, business, firm, operation, institution, establishment, body.

> *Word links* **empire**
>
> **imperial** relating to an empire

empirical adjective *many of these predictions have received empirical confirmation*: **observed**, seen, factual, actual, real, verifiable, first-hand; **experimental**, experiential; practical, pragmatic, hands-on, applied; technical heuristic; rare empiric.
▷ANTONYMS theoretical.

employ verb **1** *Mary bought a Daimler and employed a chauffeur*: **hire**, engage, recruit, take on, take into employment, secure the services of, sign up, sign, put on the payroll, enrol, appoint, commission, enlist; retain, have in employment, have on the payroll; indenture, apprentice; informal take on board.
▷ANTONYMS dismiss.

2 *Sam was employed in carving a stone figure*: **occupy**, engage, involve, keep busy, tie up; absorb, engross, immerse.

3 *the reactors employ carbon dioxide gas as a coolant | the team employed subtle psychological tactics*: **use**, utilize, make use of, avail oneself of, put into service; implement, apply, exercise, practise, put into practice, exert, bring into play, bring into action, bring to bear; draw on, resort to, turn to, have recourse to, take advantage of.

employed adjective *employed married women tend to delay their childbearing*: **working**, in work, in employment, with a job, holding down a job, with a career; professional, career; earning, waged, in gainful employment, earning one's living, breadwinning.
▷ANTONYMS unemployed.

employee noun *the firm supports employees who show ambition*: **worker**, member of staff, member of the workforce; blue-collar worker, white-collar worker, workman, labourer, artisan, hand, hired hand, hired man, hired person, hired help, hireling; wage-earner, breadwinner; (**employees**) personnel, staff, workforce.

employer noun **1** *his employer gave him a glowing reference*: **boss**, manager, manageress, patron, proprietor, director, managing director, chief executive, principal, president, head man, head woman; informal boss man, skipper; Brit. informal gaffer, governor, guv'nor; N. Amer. informal padrone, sachem.

2 *the largest private sector employer in Sheffield*: **firm**, company, business, organization, manufacturer.

employment noun **1** *Christine found employment as a clerk*: **job**, post, position, situation, occupation, profession, trade, livelihood, career, business, line, line of work, calling, vocation, craft, pursuit; **work**, labour, service; French métier; informal racket, game; archaic employ.

2 *they forbid the employment of children under ten years old*: **hiring**, hire, engagement, engaging, taking on, signing up, enrolment, enrolling, commissioning, enlisting; apprenticing.

3 *the employment of nuclear weapons*: **use**, utilization, implementation, application, exercise; putting into operation.

emporium noun *he was working at a boot and shoe emporium*: **shop**, store, boutique, outlet, retail outlet, reseller; department store, chain store, supermarket, hypermarket, superstore, megastore; establishment; informal shed; N. Amer. informal big box.

empower verb **1** *the act empowered Henry to punish heretics*: **authorize**, license, entitle, permit, allow, sanction, warrant, commission, delegate, certify, accredit, qualify; give someone the authority, give someone permission; enable, equip, give the power to, give the means to; informal give the go-ahead to, give the green light to, OK, give the OK to, give the thumbs up to.
▷ANTONYMS forbid.

2 *movements to empower the poor*: **emancipate**, unyoke, unfetter, unshackle, unchain, set free, give freedom to; historical enfranchise.
▷ANTONYMS enslave.

empress noun *the Empress of Austria*: **ruler**, sovereign, monarch, potentate; Russian, historical tsarina; rare imperatrix, autarch, ethnarch.

emptiness noun **1** *the peaceful emptiness of her mother's sitting room*: **vacantness**, bareness, blankness, clearness, barrenness, desolation; lack of contents, lack of adornment; rare voidness.
▷ANTONYMS crowdedness; fullness.

2 *the emptiness of his boasting*: **meaninglessness**, hollowness, idleness, ineffectiveness, ineffectuality, uselessness, futility, worthlessness, fruitlessness, insubstantiality.
▷ANTONYMS meaningfulness.

3 *she was suffering from a sense of utter emptiness*: **futility**, purposelessness, pointlessness, aimlessness, meaninglessness, worthlessness, valuelessness, hollowness, barrenness, senselessness, banality, triviality, insignificance, unimportance; archaic bootlessness.
▷ANTONYMS worth.

4 *Sarah had filled an emptiness in his life*: **void**, vacuum, vacuity, empty space, blank space, gap, vacancy, hiatus, hole, hollow, cavity, chasm, abyss, gulf.

5 *she was shocked by the emptiness in his eyes*: **blankness**, expressionlessness, vacancy, vacantness, vacuousness, glaze, fixedness, woodenness, stoniness, impassivity, emotionlessness, unresponsiveness, inscrutability; lack of life, lack of animation.
▷ANTONYMS expressiveness.

empty adjective **1** *an empty house*: **vacant**, unoccupied, uninhabited, untenanted, clear, free, bare, desolate, deserted, abandoned.
▷ANTONYMS full.

2 *the aspirin bottle was empty*: **containing nothing**, without contents, unfilled, not filled, void, emptied.
▷ANTONYMS full.

3 *my teacher did not issue empty threats*: **meaningless**, aimless, worthless, useless, idle, vain, insubstantial, ineffective, ineffectual.
▷ANTONYMS meaningful.

4 *without her my life is empty*: **futile**, pointless, purposeless, motiveless, worthless, meaningless, valueless, of no value, useless, of no use, senseless, hollow, barren, unsatisfactory, unimportant, insignificant, inconsequential, trivial, trifling, nugatory.
▷ANTONYMS worthwhile.

5 *his face was grey and his eyes were empty*: **blank**, expressionless, vacant, deadpan, wooden, stony, impassive, inanimate, vacuous, absent, glazed, fixed, lifeless, emotionless, unresponsive, inscrutable.
▷ANTONYMS expressive.

▶verb **1** *he was emptying the dishwasher*: **unload**, unpack, unburden, disburden, clear, make vacant, vacate, evacuate, void; rare unlade.
▷ANTONYMS fill; load.

2 *the wine had been secretly opened and emptied*: **drain**, discharge, draw off, extract, withdraw, remove, siphon off, pump out, pour out, tap, milk, bleed; **deplete**, exhaust, use up, sap, consume.

empty-headed adjective *certain types of men treat me like some empty-headed bimbo*: **stupid**, unintelligent, idiotic, foolish, silly, brainless, half-witted, witless, vacuous, vapid, hare-brained, feather-brained, birdbrained, pea-brained, scatterbrained, scatty, giddy, skittish, flighty, frivolous, thoughtless; informal dumb, dense, dim, airheaded, brain-dead, dippy, dizzy, dopey, dozy, batty, dotty, screwy, soft in the head, slow on the uptake; Brit. informal daft, not the full shilling; N. Amer. informal ditzy, dumb-ass.
▷ANTONYMS intelligent.

empyrean literary adjective *the empyrean regions*. See **heavenly** (sense 2).
▶noun (**the empyrean**) See **heaven** (sense 3).

emulate verb *they tried to emulate Lucy's glowing performance*: **imitate**, copy, reproduce, mimic, mirror, echo, follow, model oneself on, take as a model, take as an example; **match**, equal, parallel, be the equal of, be on a par with, be in the same league as, come near to, come close to, approximate; compete with, contend with, rival, vie with, surpass; informal take a leaf out of someone's book.

enable verb **1** *the act enabled ordinary citizens to operate radio stations*: **authorize**, sanction, warrant, license, qualify, allow, permit, entitle, empower, accredit, legalize, validate; commission, delegate; informal OK, give the OK to, give the green light to, give the thumbs up to.
▷ANTONYMS forbid.

2 *these scholarships have enabled graduates to pursue diverse studies*: **allow**, permit, let, give the means to, give the resources to, equip, prepare, facilitate, capacitate, fit.
▷ANTONYMS prevent.

enact verb **1** *the government enacted an environmental protection bill*: **make law**, pass, approve, ratify, validate, sanction, authorize, accept, give the seal of approval to; order, decree, ordain, legislate, legalize, rule; impose, lay down, implement, bring into effect, bring to bear, put into practice; informal give the go-ahead to, give the green light to, give the thumbs up to, OK, give the OK to.
▷ANTONYMS repeal.

2 *members of the church are to enact a nativity play*: **act out**, act, perform, play, appear in, stage, mount, put on, present, do; represent.

enactment noun **1** *the enactment of a bill of rights*: **passing**, making law, ratification, ratifying, validation, validating, sanction, sanctioning, approval, approving, endorsement, adoption; decreeing, ordaining, legislating; application, appliance, implementation.
▷ANTONYMS repeal.

2 *parliamentary enactments covering food safety*: **bill**, act, law, by-law, order, decree, resolution, ruling, rule, regulation, statute, edict, measure, motion, command, commandment, pronouncement, proclamation, dictate, dictum, diktat, fiat; (**enactments**) legislation; N. Amer. ordinance.

3 *the enactment of the play | a classic enactment of the character*: **acting**, playing, performing, performance, staging, appearance; portrayal, depiction, representation, personification; formal personation.

enamoured adjective *she was secretly* ***enamoured of*** *the prince*: **in love with**, infatuated with, besotted with, smitten with, captivated by, charmed by, enchanted by, fascinated by, bewitched by, beguiled by, enthralled by, entranced by, enraptured by, keen on, taken with, head over heels for, under the spell of, consumed with desire for; informal mad about, crazy about, wild about, nuts about, potty about, dotty about, bowled over by, hot for, gone on, hooked on, stuck on, struck on, sweet on, soft on, hung up on, carrying a torch for; Brit. informal daft about; literary ensorcelled by.
▷ANTONYMS indifferent to.

encampment noun *they planned an attack on the enemy's encampment*: **camp**, military camp, bivouac, cantonment, barracks, base, station, post; campsite, camping ground; tents; S. African historical laager.

encapsulate verb **1** *their conclusions are encapsulated in one brief sentence*: **summarize**, sum up, give a summary of, precis, abridge, digest, abbreviate, condense, compress, compact, contract, telescope; capture, express, record, sketch, give the gist of, give the main points of, put in a nutshell; rare epitomize, capsulize.

2 *the adult worms are encapsulated in a cyst*: **enclose**, encase, contain, confine, envelop, enfold, sheath, cocoon, surround.

enchant verb *the play continued to enchant all who watched it*: **captivate**, charm, delight, dazzle, enrapture, entrance, enthral, beguile, bewitch,

spellbind, ensnare, fascinate, hypnotize, mesmerize; divert, absorb, engross, rivet, grip, transfix; informal tickle someone pink, bowl someone over, get under someone's skin; rare rapture.
▷ANTONYMS repel; bore.

enchanter noun *they have been trapped by an evil enchanter*: **wizard**, witch, sorcerer, warlock, magician, necromancer, spellbinder, magus, conjuror; hypnotist, mesmerist; witch doctor, medicine man, shaman, voodooist, occultist; Irish pishogue; N. Amer. & W. Indian conjure man/woman; rare thaumaturge, thaumaturgist, theurgist, spell-caster, mage, magian. See also **enchantress**.

enchanting adjective *Erica smiled an enchanting smile*: **captivating**, charming, delightful, attractive, appealing, engaging, winning, dazzling, bewitching, beguiling, alluring, tantalizing, seductive, ravishing, disarming, irresistible, spellbinding, entrancing, enthralling, fetching, dreamy; Scottish & N. English bonny; dated taking.
▷ANTONYMS repulsive.

e

Word toolkit

enchanting	irresistible	appealing
story	force	option
music	urge	idea
voice	temptation	prospect
place	charm	alternative
evening	impulse	quality
experience	attraction	design
performance	smile	candidate

enchantment noun **1** *the horses had been turned to wood by enchantment*: **magic**, witchcraft, sorcery, wizardry, necromancy, conjuration; hypnotism, mesmerism; occultism, voodoo, the black arts; charms, spells, incantations; N. Amer. mojo; rare spell-working, sortilege, thaumaturgy, theurgy.
2 *to look through one of these shop windows is instant enchantment | the enchantment of the garden by moonlight*: **captivation**, entrancement, bewitchment, fascination, attraction, temptation, seduction, allure, enticement; **delight**, charm, beauty, attractiveness, appeal, irresistibility, magnetism, pull, draw, lure.
▷ANTONYMS repulsion.
3 *being with him was sheer enchantment*: **bliss**, ecstasy, heaven, rapture, joy.
▷ANTONYMS misery.

enchantress noun *she was under the spell of an enchantress*: **witch**, sorceress, magician, fairy, fairy godmother; N. Amer. hex, conjure woman; Greek Mythology Circe, siren; rare spell-caster, thaumaturge, thaumaturgist, Wiccan, pythoness. See also **enchanter**.

encircle verb *medieval walls encircle the town*: **surround**, enclose, circle, ring, encompass, circumscribe, border, bound, edge, skirt, fringe, form a ring around, form a barrier round; close in, shut in, fence in, wall in, hem in, lock in, cut off, confine; literary gird, girdle, engird.

enclose verb **1** *tall trees enclosed the garden | he bought new fences to enclose his sheep*: **surround**, circle, ring, encompass, encircle, circumscribe, border, bound, edge, skirt, fringe, hem, line, flank; **confine**, close in, shut in, fence in, wall in, hedge in, hem in, lock in, lock up, cut off; literary gird, girdle, engird.
2 *please enclose a stamped addressed envelope with your order*: **include**, insert, put in, enfold; send.

Word links **enclose**

claustrophobia fear of enclosed spaces

enclosure noun **1** *they drove the donkeys into the enclosure*: **paddock**, fold, pen, compound, stockade, ring, yard, pound; sty, coop, cage; Scottish parrock; N. Amer. corral; S. African kraal; in S. America potrero; rare circumvallation.
2 *she watched the race from the royal enclosure*: **area**, special area, assigned area, compound, arena; box, compartment.
3 *her cheque arrived and the only other enclosure was a compliments slip*: **insertion**, inclusion, addition; thing enclosed.

encomium noun *the poet produced an appropriate encomium after the king's death*: **eulogy**, speech of praise, panegyric, paean, accolade, tribute, testimonial, compliment; praise, acclaim, acclamation, homage, extolment; rare laudation, eulogium.

encompass verb **1** *the ancient monument is encompassed by Hunsbury Country Park*: **surround**, enclose, ring, encircle, circumscribe, skirt, bound, border, fringe; close in, shut in, fence in, wall in, hedge in, hem in, confine; literary gird, girdle, engird; rare compass, environ.
2 *the debates encompassed a vast range of subjects*: **cover**, embrace, include, incorporate, take in, contain, comprise, involve, deal with; formal comprehend.

encore noun *the audience roared approval and demanded an encore*: **repeat performance**, extra performance, additional performance, replay, repeat, repetition; curtain call.

encounter verb **1** *I encountered a girl I used to know*: **meet**, meet by chance, run into, run across, come across, come upon, stumble across, stumble on, chance on, happen on; informal bump into; archaic run against.
2 *the guides will help if you encounter any problems*: **experience**, come into contact with, run into, come across, come up against, face, be faced with, confront, be forced to contend with.
3 *the soldiers encountered a large crowd of demonstrators*: **confront**, accost, oppose, meet head-on; clash with, come into conflict with, engage with, struggle with, contend with, fight, do battle with, skirmish with.
▶noun **1** *I told them of my encounter with the priest*: **meeting**, chance meeting, brush, rendezvous; contact.
2 *the monument is thought to commemorate a Viking encounter*: **battle**, fight, clash, conflict, confrontation, engagement, skirmish, brush; informal run-in, set-to, dust-up, scrap; archaic rencounter.

encourage verb **1** *the players were encouraged by the crowd's response*: **hearten**, cheer, buoy up, uplift, inspire, motivate, egg on, spur on, stir, stir up, whip up, fire up, stimulate, animate, invigorate, vitalize, revitalize, embolden, fortify, rally, incite; lift the spirits of, raise the morale of, stiffen the resolve of; informal buck up, pep up, give a shot in the arm to; N. Amer. informal light a fire under; rare inspirit, spirit someone up, fillip, incentivize.
▷ANTONYMS discourage.
2 *he would never encourage Joan to leave her husband*: **persuade**, coax, urge, press, push, pressure, pressurize, exhort, spur, prod, goad, egg on, prompt, influence, sway; informal put the heat on, put the screws on, twist someone's arm.
▷ANTONYMS dissuade.
3 *the Government was keen to encourage local businesses*: **support**, back, endorse, champion, advocate, recommend, promote, further, advance, forward, foster, strengthen, enrich; help, assist, aid, abet, boost, fuel, favour.
▷ANTONYMS hinder.

encouragement noun **1** *she needed a bit of encouragement*: **heartening**, cheering, cheering up, buoying up, pepping up, uplifting, inspiration, rallying, motivation, incitement, stimulation, animation, invigoration, invigorating, emboldening, fortification; morale-boosting; informal bucking up, a shot in the arm; rare spiriting up, inspiriting.
▷ANTONYMS discouragement.
2 *they required no encouragement to get back to work*: **persuasion**, coaxing, urging, pushing, pressure, pressurization, exhortation, prodding, egging on, prompting; spur, goad, inducement, incentive, bait, lure, motive; informal arm-twisting, carrot, kick up the backside.
▷ANTONYMS dissuasion.
3 *the encouragement of foreign investment*: **supporting**, support, backing, endorsement, championship, championing, sponsoring, advocacy, promotion, furtherance, furthering, advance, advancing, forwarding, fostering, strengthening, nurture, cultivation; help, assistance, boosting, fuelling, favouring; N. Amer. informal boosterism.
▷ANTONYMS hindering.

encouraging adjective **1** *the Scottish team made an encouraging start*: **promising**, hopeful, auspicious, propitious, favourable, bright, rosy, cheerful, full of promise; heartening, reassuring, stimulating, inspiring, uplifting, cheering, comforting, welcome, pleasing, gratifying.
▷ANTONYMS discouraging.
2 *my parents were very encouraging*: **supportive**, reassuring, affirmative, sympathetic, sensitive, understanding, helpful; positive, responsive, enthusiastic, appreciative.
▷ANTONYMS unsupportive.

encroach verb *she didn't want to* ***encroach on*** *his privacy*: **intrude**, trespass, impinge, butt in, barge in, cut in, obtrude, impose oneself; invade, infiltrate, interrupt, infringe, violate, interfere with, disturb, disrupt; tread on someone's toes, step on someone's toes; informal gatecrash, horn in on, muscle in on, invade someone's space; archaic entrench on.

encroachment noun *I resisted even the slightest* ***encroachment on*** *my territory*: **intrusion into**, trespass on, invasion of, infiltration of, incursion into, obtrusion into, overrunning of, usurping of, appropriation of; infringement of, impingement on, impinging on.

encumber verb **1** *her movements were encumbered by her heavy skirts*: **hamper**, hinder, obstruct, impede, check, cramp, inhibit, restrict, limit, constrain, restrain, bog down, retard, slow, slow down, stall, delay; inconvenience, disadvantage, handicap.
▷ANTONYMS aid, facilitate.
2 *they are heavily encumbered with debt*: **burden**, load, weigh down, saddle; tax, overtax, stress, strain, overwhelm, overload, overburden; Brit. informal lumber; literary trammel.

encumbrance noun **1** *he found the equipment a great encumbrance*: **hindrance**, obstruction, obstacle, impediment, restraint, constraint, handicap, inconvenience, nuisance, disadvantage, drawback; archaic cumber.
▷ANTONYMS help; asset.

2 *I am twenty-nine and without encumbrances of any kind*: **responsibility**, obligation, liability; imposition, burden, weight, load, tax, stress, strain, pressure, trouble, worry; millstone, albatross, cross to bear; literary trammel; archaic cumber.

encyclopedic adjective *he has an encyclopedic knowledge of food*: **comprehensive**, complete, thorough, thoroughgoing, full, exhaustive, in-depth, wide-ranging, broad-ranging, broad-based, all-inclusive, all-embracing, all-encompassing, universal, vast, compendious; across the board; informal wall-to-wall.

end noun **1** *Laura's house was at the end of the row*: **extremity**, furthermost part, limit, margin, edge, border, boundary, periphery; point, tip, tail end; N. Amer. tag end.
▷**ANTONYMS** beginning; middle.
2 *I never plan the end of the novel I'm writing*: **conclusion**, termination, ending, finish, close, resolution, climax, finale, culmination, denouement; epilogue, coda, peroration; informal wind-up.
▷**ANTONYMS** beginning, start.
3 *he jabbed a cigarette end into the ashtray*: **butt**, stub, stump, remnant, fragment, vestige; (**ends**) leftovers, remains, remainder; informal fag end, dog end.
4 *to her, wealth is a means and not an end in itself*: **aim**, goal, purpose, objective, object, grail, holy grail, target, mission; intention, intent, design, motive; aspiration, wish, desire, ambition; French raison d'être.
5 *the commercial end of the music business*: **aspect**, side, section, area, field, part, share, portion, segment, province.
6 *he knew that his end might come at any time*: **death**, dying, demise, passing, passing on, passing away, expiration, expiry; doom, extinction, annihilation, extermination, destruction; downfall, ruin, ruination, Waterloo; informal curtains, croaking, snuffing; Law decease; rare quietus.
▷**ANTONYMS** birth.
□ **make ends meet** *even with no children to support, she couldn't make ends meet*: **manage**, cope, get by, survive, exist, subsist, muddle through/along, scrape by/along/through, get along, make do, barely/scarcely have enough to live on, keep the wolf from the door, keep one's head above water, scrimp, scrape a living; informal make out.
□ **put an end to something 1** *early marriage and early widowhood put an end to her dreams*: **destroy**, kill, bring to an end, be the end of, end, extinguish, dash, quell, quash, ruin, wreck, shatter, smash, crush, scotch; stop, block, frustrate, thwart, put a stop to, prevent, defeat, derail; informal put paid to, do for, put the lid on, put the kibosh on, stymie, queer; Brit. informal scupper, dish. **2** *it took over a hundred years to put an end to child labour*. See **abolish**.
▶ verb **1** *the show ended with a wedding scene*: **finish**, conclude, terminate, come to an end, draw to a close, close, stop, cease; culminate, climax, build up to, lead up to, reach a finale, come to a head; informal wind up.
▷**ANTONYMS** begin, start.
2 *she attempted to end the relationship*: **break off**, call off, bring to an end, put an end to, call a halt to, halt, stop, drop, finish, terminate, discontinue, dissolve, cancel, annul; informal nip something in the bud, wind something up, knock something on the head, give something the chop, pull the plug on, axe, scrap, pack in, get shut of; Brit. informal get shot of; archaic sunder.
▷**ANTONYMS** begin.
3 *the young artist chose to end his life*: **destroy**, put an end to, extinguish, snuff out, do away with, wipe out, take.
□ **end up** *instead of going to Alaska, he ended up in Africa*: **finish up**, land up, arrive, find oneself, turn up, come, go, appear; informal wind up, fetch up, show up, roll up, blow in.

endanger verb *river pollution is likely to endanger fish*: **imperil**, jeopardize, risk, put at risk, put in danger, expose to danger, put in jeopardy, leave vulnerable, put someone's life on the line; **threaten**, pose a threat to, be a danger to, be detrimental to, damage, injure, harm, do harm to; archaic peril.

Choose the right word **endanger, imperil, jeopardize, risk**

Endanger is the most general term for putting someone or something in a position where they might be harmed (*the company admitted endangering workers by failing to maintain safety standards*). The past participle *endangered* is used particularly of plants and animals that are threatened with extinction (*sea turtles are an endangered species*).

Imperil is a more literary word, used to emphasize the serious nature of a danger (*troops moved from their positions on the Somme to bolster their imperilled comrades at Verdun*).

Jeopardize is generally used with an abstract object which is likely to be adversely affected by a certain course of action (*a devaluation of the dollar would jeopardize New York's position as a financial centre*).

Risk is most often used of consciously exposing someone or something to harm, generally oneself or one's possessions, as the price of something regarded as more important (*a father risked his life to save his children from a fire*).

endearing adjective *hedgehogs are endearing creatures*: **lovable**, adorable, cute, sweet, dear, delightful, lovely, charming, appealing, attractive, engaging, winning, captivating, enchanting, beguiling, winsome; Scottish & N. English bonny; dated taking.

endearment noun **1** (usually **endearments**) *between kisses she murmured endearments*: **sweet nothings**, sweet words, sweet talk, affectionate talk, soft words; term of affection, term of endearment, pet name, affectionate name; rare hypocoristic, hypocorism.
2 *he spoke to her formally and without endearment*: **affection**, fondness, tenderness, feeling, sentiment, warmth, love, liking, care, regard, attachment.

endeavour verb *the company* **endeavoured to** *expand its activities*: **try**, attempt, venture, undertake, aspire, aim, seek, set out; strive, struggle, labour, toil, work hard, try hard, exert oneself, apply oneself, do one's best, do one's utmost, give one's all, be at pains; work at, try one's hand at; informal slog away, give something a whirl, have a go at, have a shot at, have a stab at, give something one's best shot, do one's damnedest, go all out, bend over backwards, break one's neck, bust a gut, move heaven and earth; formal essay.
▶ noun **1** *an endeavour to build a more buoyant economy*: **attempt**, try, bid, effort, trial, venture; informal go, crack, shot, stab, bash, whack, whirl.
2 *after several days of endeavour he completed the task*: **striving**, struggling, labouring, struggle, labour, hard work, hard slog, effort, exertion, application, industry; pains; informal sweat, {blood, sweat, and tears}, elbow grease; Brit. informal graft; Austral./NZ informal (hard) yakka; archaic travail, moil.
3 *what you are proposing is an extremely unwise endeavour*: **undertaking**, enterprise, venture, pursuit, exercise, activity, exploit, deed, act, action, move; scheme, plan, project; informal caper.

ending noun *the story has a happy ending | the ending of the Cold War*: **end**, finish, close, closing, conclusion, resolution, summing-up, denouement, finale, final scene, last act; cessation, stopping, termination, discontinuation, breaking off; informal wind-up, winding up.
▷**ANTONYMS** beginning.

endless adjective **1** *she was a caring woman with endless energy*: **unlimited**, limitless, infinite, inexhaustible, boundless, unbounded, untold, immeasurable, measureless, incalculable, inestimable; abundant, abounding, great; **ceaseless**, unceasing, unending, without end, everlasting, constant, continuous, continual, interminable, unfading, unfailing, perpetual, eternal, enduring, lasting, round-the-clock; informal loads of, stacks of, heaps of, masses of, oodles of, bags of.
▷**ANTONYMS** limited; transient.
2 *as children we played endless games*: **countless**, innumerable, untold, legion, numberless, unnumbered, numerous, very many, manifold, multitudinous, multifarious; a great number of, countless numbers of, infinite numbers of, a multitude of, a multiplicity of, more than one can count, too many to be counted; informal umpteen, no end of, loads of, stacks of, heaps of, masses of, oodles of, scads of, zillions of; N. Amer. informal gazillions of, bazillions of; literary myriad, divers; rare innumerous, unnumberable.
▷**ANTONYMS** few.
3 *the tobacco moves through the machine on an endless belt*: **continuous**, unbroken, uninterrupted, never-ending, without end, non-stop.

endorse verb **1** *they fully endorse a general trade agreement*: **support**, back, approve (of), be in agreement with, favour; recommend, advocate, champion; subscribe to, uphold, affirm, confirm, authorize, authenticate, ratify, sanction, warrant; informal throw one's weight behind, stick up for.
▷**ANTONYMS** oppose.
2 *the cheque should be endorsed and sent to the third party*: **countersign**, sign on the back, initial, autograph, put one's mark on, inscribe, superscribe; witness, validate; archaic underwrite, side-sign; rare chirographate.

endorsement noun **1** *the proposal received their overwhelming endorsement*: **support**, backing, approval, seal of approval, agreement, acceptance, recommendation, advocacy, championship, patronage; affirmation, confirmation, authorization, authentication, ratification, sanction, warrant, validation, licence; rubber stamp; informal the nod, the thumbs up, the OK.
▷**ANTONYMS** opposition.
2 *several cheques required endorsement*: **countersigning**, signing on the back, autographing, initialling, inscribing, superscribing; witnessing, validation; archaic underwriting, side-signing.

endow verb **1** *Henry II endowed a hospital for poor pilgrims*: **finance**, fund, pay for, donate money for, give money towards, provide capital for, subsidize, support financially; bequeath money for, leave money for, settle money on; establish, set up, institute, put in place, initiate, start, create, bring into being; informal fork out for, shell out for, cough up for, chip in for, pitch in for; Brit. informal stump up for; N. Amer. informal ante up for, kick in for, pony up for.
2 *nature endowed the human race with intelligence*: **provide**, supply, furnish, equip, invest, give, present, favour, bless, grace, award, gift, confer, bestow, enrich, arm; literary endue.

e

endowment noun **1** *the endowment of a chair of botany*: **funding**, financing, subsidizing; donation of money for, provision of capital for, bequest of money for; establishment, establishing, foundation, institution, setting up, inauguration.
2 *a generous endowment from the will of the late professor*: **bequest**, bequeathal, legacy, inheritance; **gift**, present, benefaction, bestowal, grant, award, donation, contribution, subsidy, settlement, provision; Law devise, hereditament; historical alms; rare donative.
3 *his taste and inquiring mind were natural endowments*: **quality**, characteristic, feature, attribute, facility, faculty, ability, talent, gift, strength, aptitude, capability, capacity.

endurable adjective *his confinement had gradually become endurable*: **bearable**, tolerable, supportable, manageable, sufferable, sustainable; rare brookable.
▷ANTONYMS unbearable.

endurance noun **1** *she had pushed him beyond the limit of his endurance*: **toleration**, **bearing**, tolerance, sufferance, fortitude, forbearance, patience, acceptance, resignation, stoicism.
2 *the race is a test of endurance*: **stamina**, **staying power**, fortitude, perseverance, persistence, tenacity, pertinacity, doggedness, indefatigability, tirelessness, resoluteness, resolution, determination; informal stickability, guts, grit, spunk; Brit. informal bottle.
3 *Edward III had a vested interest in the endurance of Balliol's rule*: **continuance**, continuity, continuation, lasting power, durability, permanence, longevity; constancy, stability, changelessness, immutability; rare lastingness, everlastingness.

endure verb **1** *he had to endure a great deal of suffering*: **undergo**, go through, live through, experience, meet, encounter; cope with, deal with, face, face up to, handle, suffer, tolerate, put up with, brave, bear, withstand, sustain, weather; become reconciled to, reconcile oneself to, become resigned to, get used to, become accustomed to, learn to live with, make the best of; Scottish thole.
2 *she would not endure a marriage that was a travesty*: **tolerate**, **bear**, put up with, go along with, suffer, submit to, countenance, accept, give one's blessing to, brook, support, take; informal stick, hack, stand for, stomach, swallow, abide, hold with, be doing with; Brit. informal wear.
3 *our love will endure forever*: **last**, live, live on, go on, hold on, abide, continue, persist, remain, stay, survive; literary bide, tarry.
▷ANTONYMS fade.

enduring adjective *an enduring commitment to democracy and human rights*: **lasting**, long-lasting, durable, continuing, remaining, persisting, prevailing, abiding, eternal, perennial, permanent, unending, everlasting; constant, stable, steady, steadfast, fixed, firm, unwavering, unfaltering, unchanging, changeless, long-standing, long-established, long-running, long-term; rare perdurable, sempiternal.
▷ANTONYMS short-lived.

enemy noun *he aimed the gun at his enemy*: **foe**, adversary, opponent, rival, antagonist, combatant, challenger, competitor, opposer, hostile party; (**the enemy**) the opposition, the competition, the other side, the opposing side; rare corrival, vier.
▷ANTONYMS friend, ally.

energetic adjective **1** *a skinny, energetic young man*: **active**, lively, dynamic, zestful, spirited, animated, vital, vibrant, sparkling, bouncy, bubbly, perky, bright and breezy, frisky, sprightly, tireless, indefatigable, enthusiastic, zealous, fiery, passionate; informal peppy, zippy, sparky, full of get-up-and-go, full of vim and vigour, full of beans, full of the joys of spring, bright-eyed and bushy-tailed; N. Amer. informal go-go, peart.
▷ANTONYMS inactive, lethargic.
2 *energetic exercises*: **vigorous**, strenuous, brisk, lively; rigorous, hard, arduous, demanding, taxing, tough.
▷ANTONYMS gentle.
3 *an energetic advertising campaign*: **forceful**, aggressive, vigorous, high-powered, all-out, determined, zealous, fiery, impassioned, emphatic, bold, pushing, driving, effective, effectual, powerful, potent; intense, intensive, hard-hitting, pulling no punches; informal pushy, punchy, gutsy, in-your-face, go-ahead, high-octane, feisty.
▷ANTONYMS half-hearted.

energize verb **1** *people are energized by his ideas*: **enliven**, liven up, animate, vitalize, invigorate, perk up, excite, electrify, dynamize, stimulate, stir up, fire up, rouse, motivate, move, move to action, drive, spur on, encourage, embolden, galvanize; informal pep up, buck up, give a shot in the arm to; rare activate, inspirit.
▷ANTONYMS demotivate.
2 *a bell sounds when the distress frequency is energized*: **activate**, trigger, trigger off, trip, operate, actuate, switch on, turn on, start, start up, get going, set going; power, supply power to, supply energy to.
▷ANTONYMS deactivate.

energy noun **1** *she set out feeling full of energy*: **vitality**, vigour, life, liveliness, animation, vivacity, spirit, spiritedness, fire, passion, ardour, zeal, verve, enthusiasm, zest, vibrancy, spark, sparkle, effervescence, exuberance, buoyancy, perkiness, sprightliness; strength, stamina, forcefulness, power, might, potency, dynamism, drive, push; informal zip, zing, pep, pizzazz, punch, bounce, fizz, oomph, go, get-up-and-go, vim and vigour; N. Amer. informal feistiness.
2 *the panels turn solar energy into electricity*: **power**.

enervate verb *the scorching sun enervated her*: **exhaust**, tire, fatigue, weary, wear out, devitalize, drain, sap, weaken, make weak, make feeble, enfeeble, debilitate, incapacitate, indispose, prostrate, immobilize, lay low, put out of action; informal knock out, do in, take it out of one, shatter, poop, frazzle, wear to a frazzle, fag out; Brit. informal knacker; rare torpefy.
▷ANTONYMS invigorate.

enervation noun *his enervation is due to his lingering illness*: **fatigue**, exhaustion, tiredness, overtiredness, weariness, lassitude, lack of energy, lack of vitality, devitalization, weakness, feebleness, impotence, enfeebled state, debilitation, incapacitation, indisposition, prostration, immobility; informal weediness; Medicine asthenia.

enfeeble verb *the animal was enfeebled by lack of nutrition*: **weaken**, make weak, make feeble, debilitate, incapacitate, indispose, prostrate, immobilize, lay low, disable, handicap, cripple, paralyse; drain, sap, exhaust, tire, fatigue, devitalize; informal knock out, do in, shatter; Brit. informal knacker; rare torpefy.
▷ANTONYMS strengthen.

enfold verb **1** *the summit was enfolded in white cloud*: **envelop**, engulf, sheathe, swathe, swaddle, cocoon, shroud, veil, cloak, drape, cover, conceal, mask; surround, encircle, circle, enclose, encase; literary enshroud, mantle, pall, pave, lap; rare obnubilate.
2 *he enfolded her in his arms*: **clasp**, hold, fold, wrap, squeeze, clutch, take, gather; embrace, hug, cuddle, cradle; literary embosom; archaic strain.

enforce verb **1** *the sheriff enforced the law and judged local disputes*: **impose**, apply, carry out, administer, implement, bring to bear, discharge, fulfil, execute, prosecute; rare effectuate.
2 *they cannot enforce cooperation between the parties*: **force**, compel, exact, extort, demand, insist on, require, necessitate; archaic constrain.

enforced adjective *an enforced break from work*: **compulsory**, obligatory, mandatory, involuntary, forced, exacted, coerced, imposed, demanded, required, requisite, stipulated, contractual, binding, necessitated, necessary, unavoidable, inescapable, obliged, impelled, constrained, dictated, ordained, prescribed; French de rigueur.
▷ANTONYMS voluntary.

enforcement noun **1** *they were responsible for the enforcement of the law*: **imposition**, implementation, application, carrying out, administration, administering, discharge, fulfilment, execution, prosecution, pursuance; rare effectuation.
2 *the enforcement of school attendance*: **forcing**, compelling, exacting, exactment, extorting, extortion, demanding, requiring; archaic constraint.

enfranchise verb **1** *women over thirty were enfranchised in 1918*: **give voting rights to**, give the vote to, give suffrage to, grant suffrage to, grant franchise to.
▷ANTONYMS disenfranchise.
2 historical *he is said to have enfranchised his slaves*: **emancipate**, liberate, free, set free, release, empower; unchain, unyoke, unfetter, unshackle; naturalize, grant citizenship to, confer citizenship on; historical manumit; rare affranchise, disenthral, citizenize.
▷ANTONYMS enslave.

engage verb **1** *the tasks must engage the children's interest*: **capture**, catch, arrest, grab, seize, draw, attract, gain, win, captivate, hold, grip, engross, absorb, occupy.
▷ANTONYMS lose.
2 *he engaged a nursemaid to look after them*: **employ**, hire, recruit, take on, take into employment, secure the services of, put on the payroll, enrol, appoint, commission, enlist; retain, have in employment, have on the payroll; informal take on board.
▷ANTONYMS dismiss.
3 *he engaged to pay them £10,000*: **contract**, promise, agree, pledge, vow, covenant, commit oneself, bind oneself, undertake, enter into an agreement, reach an agreement, negotiate a deal.
4 *they like to **engage in** active sports* | *in 1793 he wrote a famous letter to King George III refusing to **engage in** trade*: **participate in**, take part in, join in, become involved in, go in for, partake in/of, occupy oneself with, throw oneself into; share in, play a part in, play a role in, be a participant in, be associated with, have a hand in, be a party to, enter into, undertake, embark on, set about, launch into.
5 *they were sent to engage enemy aircraft*: **do battle with**, fight with, enter into combat with, wage war on, wage war against, take up arms against, attack, mount an attack on, take on, set upon, clash with, skirmish with, grapple with, wrest with; encounter, meet; informal scrap with.
6 *he engaged the gears with a crash*: **interlock**, interconnect, mesh, intermesh, fit together, join together, join, unite, connect, yoke, mate, couple.
▷ANTONYMS disengage.

engaged adjective **1** *the phone lines are constantly engaged*: **busy**, unavailable, occupied; in use, active; informal tied up; (**be engaged**) have a prior engagement.
▷ANTONYMS free; unoccupied.
2 *many engaged couples had to postpone their weddings*: **betrothed**, affianced, promised in marriage; attached, involved; informal spoken for; archaic plighted, espoused.
▷ANTONYMS unattached.

Choose the right word **engaged, busy, occupied, active**

See **busy**.

engagement noun **1** *they broke off their engagement*: **betrothal**, betrothment, marriage contract; French fiançailles; archaic plighting of one's troth, espousal, affiance, affiancing, handfast; rare sponsalia, subarrhation.
2 *he had a business engagement that morning*: **appointment**, arrangement, commitment, meeting, interview, consultation, session; date, assignation, rendezvous; literary tryst.
3 *some 80,000 workers were on more than a three-year engagement*: **contract**, agreement, bond, pact, compact, covenant, pledge, promise, obligation, stipulation.
4 *Britain's continued engagement in open trading*: **participation**, participating, taking part, sharing, partaking, involvement, association.
5 *his engagement as a curate*: **employment**, appointment, work, job, post, situation; hiring, hire, enrolment, enrolling, enlisting; apprenticing.
6 *all of his men were killed in an engagement at sea*: **battle**, fight, clash, confrontation, encounter, conflict, struggle, skirmish, affray, attack, assault, offensive; warfare, action, combat; hostilities; informal dogfight, shoot-out, scrap.

engaging adjective *she had such an engaging smile*: **charming**, appealing, attractive, pretty, delightful, lovely, pleasing, pleasant, agreeable, likeable, lovable, sweet, winning, winsome, fetching, dazzling, arresting, captivating, enchanting, bewitching, alluring, irresistible, dreamy, heavenly, divine, gorgeous; Scottish & N. English bonny; Brit. informal smashing; dated taking; archaic comely, fair.
▷ANTONYMS unappealing.

engender verb *his works engendered considerable controversy*: **cause**, be the cause of, give rise to, bring about, lead to, result in, produce, create, generate, arouse, rouse, provoke, incite, kindle, trigger, spark off, touch off, stir up, whip up, induce, inspire, instigate, foment, effect, occasion, promote, foster; literary beget, enkindle; rare effectuate.

engine noun **1** *a car engine*: **motor**, mechanism, machine, power source, drive.
2 *industrialization was the main engine of change*: **cause**, agent, instrument, driver, originator, initiator, generator.
3 *siege towers and other engines of war*: **device**, contraption, gadget, apparatus, machine, appliance, mechanism, implement, instrument, tool, utensil, aid, invention, contrivance; machinery, means.

engineer noun **1** *the structural engineer's drawings*: **designer**, planner, builder, architect, producer, fabricator, developer, creator; inventor, originator, deviser, contriver, mastermind.
2 *the ship's engineer rarely came up to the bridge*: **engineering officer**, controller, handler, driver; **operator**, mechanic, machinist, technician, fitter; Military artificer; informal mech.
▸ verb *he engineered the overthrow of the Conservative majority*: **bring about**, cause, arrange, pull off, bring off, fix, set up, plot, scheme, contrive, plan, put together, devise, manoeuvre, manipulate, negotiate, organize, orchestrate, choreograph, mobilize, mount, stage, put on, mastermind, originate, manage, stage-manage, coordinate, control, superintend, direct, conduct, handle, concoct; informal wangle; rare concert.

England noun Brit. informal Blighty; Austral./NZ informal Old Dart; literary Albion.

Word links **England**

Anglo- related prefix
Anglomania mania for English things
Anglophobia hatred or fear of English people and things

engrain verb See **ingrain**.

engrained adjective See **ingrained**.

engrave verb **1** *the stone was engraved with his name*: **carve**, inscribe, cut (in), incise, chisel, chase, score, etch, imprint, impress, print, mark.
2 *the picture she had just seen was engraved in her mind*: **fix**, set, imprint, stamp, brand, impress, embed, etch, ingrain, lodge, register, record.

engraving noun **1** *an engraving of a Georgian coffee house*: **etching**, print, impression, block, plate, dry point, cut, woodcut, linocut, vignette.
2 *he was skilled at drawing and engraving*: **etching**, inscribing, inscription, cutting, incising, incision, chiselling, chasing, scoring, notching, imprinting, impressing.

engross verb **1** *the notes on the staves totally engrossed him*: **preoccupy**, absorb, engage; rivet, grip, hold, interest, catch, captivate, enthral, charm, spellbind, bewitch, fascinate, entrance, beguile, intrigue, arrest, immerse, involve, envelop, engulf, fixate, hypnotize, mesmerize.
▷ANTONYMS bore.
2 Law *the solicitors will submit a draft conveyance and engross the same after approval*: **copy**, reproduce, type (out); print out the final version of, rewrite/reproduce in larger/final form.

engrossed adjective *he was **engrossed in** his book*: **absorbed**, involved, immersed, caught up, rapt, interested; preoccupied by, engaged in/with, riveted by, gripped by, intent on, captivated by, beguiled by, intrigued by, fixated by, hypnotized by, mesmerized by.
▷ANTONYMS inattentive.

engrossing adjective *a taut, engrossing thriller*: **absorbing**, involving, engaging, riveting, gripping, captivating, compelling, compulsive, irresistible, arresting, interesting, fascinating, intriguing, enthralling, spellbinding, entrancing, bewitching, beguiling, hypnotic, mesmeric; informal unputdownable.

engulf verb *their new home was engulfed by stinking brown flood water*: **inundate**, flood, deluge, immerse, swamp, wash out, swallow up, submerge; bury, envelop, snow under, overtake, overwhelm, overrun.

enhance verb *his dramatic appearance enhanced his reputation*: **increase**, add to, intensify, magnify, amplify, inflate, strengthen, build up, supplement, augment, boost, upgrade, raise, lift, escalate, elevate, exalt, aggrandize, swell; **improve**, enrich, complement, heighten, deepen, stress, reinforce, underline, emphasize; informal jack up, hike.
▷ANTONYMS diminish; mar.

enhancement noun *the enhancement of the school's reputation*: **improvement**, intensification, magnification, amplification, increase, strengthening, inflation, augmenting, augmentation; boost, rise, increment, lift; escalation, elevation, exaltation, aggrandizement, swelling, heightening, emphasis, stress, reinforcement, enrichment; informal jacking up, hike.
▷ANTONYMS diminution.

enigma noun *how it works is a complete enigma to me*: **mystery**, puzzle, riddle, conundrum, paradox, problem, unsolved problem, question, question mark, quandary, a closed book; informal poser, teaser, brain-teaser, stumper.

enigmatic adjective *she smiled that enigmatic smile again*: **mysterious**, puzzling, hard to understand, mystifying, inexplicable, baffling, perplexing, bewildering, confusing, impenetrable, inscrutable, incomprehensible, unexplainable, unfathomable, indecipherable, Delphic, oracular; ambiguous, equivocal, paradoxical, sibylline, unaccountable, insoluble, obscure, elliptical, oblique; arcane, abstruse, recondite, secret, esoteric, occult, cryptic; informal as clear as mud.
▷ANTONYMS straightforward.

enjoin verb **1** *the Code enjoined members to trade fairly and responsibly*: **urge**, encourage, try to persuade, adjure, admonish, press, prompt, prod, goad, egg on, spur, push, pressure, put pressure on, use pressure on, pressurize, lean on; **instruct**, order, command, direct, give the order to, give the command to, tell, require, call on, demand, charge, warn; entreat, exhort, implore, appeal to, beg, beseech, plead with, nag; informal put the heat on, put the screws on, twist someone's arm, railroad into, bulldoze into; literary bid.
2 Law *the company was **enjoined from** making any further assertions*: **prohibit**, ban, bar, prevent, inhibit, interdict; forbid to; Law restrain.
▷ANTONYMS compel.

enjoy verb **1** *he enjoys playing the piano*: **like**, love, be fond of, be entertained by, be amused by, be pleased by, find/take pleasure in, be keen on, delight in, appreciate, rejoice in, relish, revel in, adore, lap up, savour, luxuriate in, bask in, wallow in, glory in; informal fancy, get a kick out of, get a thrill out of, get a buzz out of, go a bundle on.
▷ANTONYMS dislike; hate.
2 *they enjoyed considerable legal protection*: **benefit from**, have the benefit of, reap the benefits of, have the advantage, have the use of, have available, avail oneself of, be blessed with, be favoured with, be endowed with, be born with, be possessed of; have, possess, own, boast; archaic participate of.
▷ANTONYMS lack.
□ **enjoy oneself** *she travels purely to enjoy herself*: **have fun**, have a good time, enjoy life, be happy, live, live life to the full, have the time of one's life; party, make merry, celebrate, revel, roister; informal have a ball, have a whale of a time, groove, make whoopee, whoop it up, let one's hair down.
▷ANTONYMS be miserable.

enjoyable adjective *a most enjoyable film*: **entertaining**, amusing, delightful, nice, to one's liking, pleasant, congenial, lovely, fine, good, great, agreeable, pleasurable, delicious, delectable, diverting, satisfying, gratifying; marvellous, wonderful, magnificent, splendid, magical, exciting, thrilling, sublime; informal super, fantastic, fabulous, fab, terrific, glorious, grand, magic, out of this world, cool; Brit. informal brilliant, brill, smashing; N. Amer. informal peachy, neat, ducky; Austral./NZ informal beaut, bonzer;

Brit. informal, dated capital, wizard, corking, spiffing, ripping, cracking, top-hole, topping, champion, beezer; N. Amer. informal, dated swell; rare frabjous.
▷ANTONYMS disagreeable.

enjoyment noun **1** *he has brought enjoyment and happiness to millions | Rupert devoured his sandwich with enjoyment*: **pleasure**, entertainment, amusement, diversion, recreation, relaxation; comfort, relief, delight, happiness, merriment, gladness, joy, fun, gaiety, jollity, satisfaction, gratification; liking, zeal, relish, gusto; N. Amer. informal rec; humorous delectation; dated sport; rare beguilement.
▷ANTONYMS displeasure.
2 *the enjoyment of one's rights*: **benefit**, advantage, use, possession, ownership, blessing, favour, exercise, endowment, availability.
▷ANTONYMS lack.

e

enlarge verb **1** *they've enlarged their house | the pressure causes the eyeball to enlarge*: **make/become bigger**, make/become larger, make/become greater, increase in size, grow, expand; extend, amplify, augment, top up, build up, add to, supplement; magnify, intensify, multiply; stretch, swell, distend, bloat, bulge, dilate, snowball, mushroom, blow up, puff up, fatten, fill out, balloon; widen, make/become wider, broaden, make/become broader, lengthen, elongate, make/become longer, deepen, make/become deeper, thicken, make/become thicker; informal jumboize; literary wax; rare tumefy, intumesce, protuberate.
▷ANTONYMS dwindle, reduce.
2 *he didn't choose to* **enlarge on** *his remark*: **elaborate on**, expand on, add to, build on, flesh out, add flesh to, put flesh on the bones of, add detail to, expatiate on; supplement, reinforce, augment, extend, broaden, develop, fill out, embellish, embroider, enhance, amplify, refine, improve, polish, perfect.

enlargement noun **1** *the modernization and enlargement of the factory*: **expansion**, growth, increase in size, extension, amplification, augmentation, topping up, building up, addition, supplementing; magnification, intensification, multiplication; stretching, swelling, distension, dilatation, blowing up, puffing up, fattening, filling out, ballooning; widening, broadening, lengthening, elongation, deepening, thickening; literary waxing; rare tumefaction, intumescence.
▷ANTONYMS reduction; diminution.
2 *a photographic enlargement*: **blow-up**, magnification, large print; Brit. enprint.
▷ANTONYMS reduction.

enlighten verb **1** *will you kindly enlighten me as to what this is?* **inform**, make aware, notify, tell, advise, let know, illuminate, open someone's eyes, apprise; explain the situation to, explain the circumstances to, describe the state of affairs to, brief, update, give details to, give information to, bring up to date; informal clue in, fill in, put wise, tip off, put in the picture, bring up to speed.
▷ANTONYMS keep in the dark.
2 *museums were built to enlighten the people*: **civilize**, bring civilization to, bring culture to; sophisticate, socialize, humanize; improve, better; edify, educate, instruct, teach, tutor, indoctrinate; rare acculturate.
▷ANTONYMS stultify.

enlightened adjective *without an informed and free press there cannot be an enlightened people*: **informed**, aware, educated, knowledgeable, learned, wise, literate, intellectual, tutored, illuminated, apprised; civilized, refined, cultured, cultivated, sophisticated, advanced, developed, liberal, open-minded, broad-minded.
▷ANTONYMS ignorant; benighted.

enlightenment noun *the reader will be hoping for enlightenment from the text*: **understanding**, insight, education, learning, knowledge, awareness, information, erudition, wisdom, instruction, teaching; illumination, light, edification, awakening; culture, refinement, cultivation, civilization, sophistication, advancement, development, liberalism, open-mindedness, broad-mindedness.
▷ANTONYMS ignorance; benightedness.

enlist verb **1** *he had* **enlisted in** *the Royal Engineers*: **join up**; join, enrol in, sign up for, volunteer for; Brit. archaic take the King's shilling.
▷ANTONYMS leave.
2 *he was enlisted in the army*: **recruit**, call up, enrol, sign up; mobilize, raise, muster, rally, hire, employ, take on, engage, conscript; N. Amer. draft, induct; historical press, press-gang; archaic levy, list.
▷ANTONYMS discharge.
3 *he has enlisted the help of a friend*: **obtain**, engage, win, get, procure, secure.
▷ANTONYMS spurn.

enliven verb **1** *several attractive illustrations enliven the text*: **brighten up**, make more interesting, make more exciting, liven up, put some spirit into, add colour to, wake up, give a lift/boost to, ginger up; improve, enhance, season, leaven, add spice to, spice up, revitalize, vitalize; informal perk up, jazz up, pep up.
▷ANTONYMS detract from.
2 *her visit had clearly enlivened my mother*: **cheer up**, brighten up, liven up, raise someone's spirits, uplift, gladden, ginger up, buoy up, make lively, waken/wake up; hearten, stimulate, galvanize, fire, light a fire under, boost, rejuvenate, animate, give life to, vivify, vitalize, exhilarate, invigorate, restore, revive, rouse, refresh; informal perk up, buck up, pep up.
▷ANTONYMS subdue.

en masse adverb French *the Cabinet immediately resigned en masse*: **(all) together**, as a group, in a body, as one, as a whole, in a mass, wholesale; simultaneously, all at once, at the same time, at one and the same time, at the same instant, at the same moment, contemporaneously; in unison, in concert, in chorus; French en bloc, ensemble; rare synchronously.
▷ANTONYMS singly.

enmesh verb *the party became increasingly enmeshed in the parliamentary system*: **entangle**, ensnare, snare, trap, entrap, ensnarl, embroil, involve, catch up, mix up, bog down, mire; rare trammel.

enmity noun *a world free from enmity between nations and races*: **hostility**, animosity, antagonism, friction, antipathy, animus, opposition, dissension, rivalry, feud, conflict, discord, contention; acrimony, bitterness, rancour, resentment, aversion, dislike, ill feeling, bad feeling, ill will, bad blood, hatred, hate, loathing, detestation, abhorrence, odium; malice, spite, spitefulness, venom, malevolence, malignity; grudges, grievances; Brit. informal needle.
▷ANTONYMS friendship; goodwill.

ennoble verb **1** *he was ennobled by the Emperor in 1875*: **elevate to the nobility/peerage**, raise to the nobility/peerage, make/create someone a noble; Brit. send to the House of Lords; informal kick upstairs; archaic nobilitate.
2 *choreography tended to ennoble rustic figures*: **dignify**, honour, bestow honour on, exalt, elevate, raise, enhance, add distinction to, add dignity to, distinguish, add lustre to; magnify, glorify, lionize, make lofty, aggrandize, upgrade.
▷ANTONYMS demean, disennoble.

ennui noun French *an ennui bred of long familiarity*: **boredom**, tedium, listlessness, lethargy, lassitude, languor, restlessness, weariness, sluggishness, enervation; **malaise**, dissatisfaction, unhappiness, uneasiness, unease, melancholy, depression, despondency, dejection, disquiet; German Weltschmerz.
▷ANTONYMS animation; contentment.

enormity noun **1** *they were aware of the enormity of the task*: **immensity**, vastness, massiveness, hugeness; size, extent, magnitude, expanse, greatness, largeness, bigness; rare enormousness.
▷ANTONYMS triviality, smallness.
2 *there must be a severe penalty for the enormity of what you have done*: **wickedness**, evilness, vileness, baseness, blackness, depravity; outrageousness, monstrousness, hideousness, dreadfulness, heinousness, awfulness, nastiness, horror, atrocity; villainy, cruelty, inhumanity, mercilessness, brutality, brutalism, bestiality, barbarism, barbarousness, savagery, viciousness; rare nefariousness.
▷ANTONYMS goodness.
3 *the enormities of the regime*: **outrage**, horror, evil, villainy, atrocity, barbarity, act of brutality, act of savagery, act of wickedness, act of cruelty, abomination, monstrosity, obscenity, iniquity; violation, crime, transgression, wrong, wrongdoing, offence, injury, affront, disgrace, scandal, injustice, abuse; Law malfeasance, tort.

enormous adjective *enormous waves batter the archipelago's western shores*: **huge**, vast, extensive, expansive, broad, wide; boundless, immeasurable, limitless, infinite, gigantic, very big, very large, great, giant, massive, colossal, mammoth, immense, tremendous, mighty, stupendous, monumental, epic, prodigious, mountainous, monstrous, titanic, towering, elephantine, king-sized, king-size, gargantuan, Herculean, Brobdingnagian, substantial; hefty, bulky, weighty, heavy, gross; informal mega, monster, whopping, whopping great, thumping, thumping great, humongous, jumbo, hulking, bumper, astronomical, astronomic; Brit. informal whacking, whacking great, ginormous.
▷ANTONYMS tiny.

enormously adverb **1** *an enormously important factor*: **very**, extremely, exceedingly, exceptionally, especially, tremendously, immensely, vastly, hugely; extraordinarily, extra, excessively, overly, over, abundantly, inordinately, singularly, significantly, distinctly, outstandingly, uncommonly, unusually, decidedly, particularly, eminently, supremely, highly, remarkably, really, truly, mightily, thoroughly; all that, to a great extent, most, so, too; Scottish unco; French très; N. English right; informal terrifically, awfully, terribly, devilishly, madly, majorly, seriously, desperately, mega, ultra, oh-so, too-too, stinking, mucho, damn, damned, too ... for words; informal, dated devilish, hellish, frightfully; Brit. informal ever so, well, dead, bloody, dirty, jolly, fair; N. Amer. informal real, mighty, powerful, awful, plumb, darned, way, bitching; S. African informal lekker; archaic exceeding, sore.
▷ANTONYMS moderately.
2 *prices vary enormously*: **considerably**, greatly, much, very much, a great deal, a lot, lots, a fair amount; significantly, substantially, appreciably, markedly, noticeably, materially, signally; informal plenty, seriously.
▷ANTONYMS slightly; not at all.

enough determiner *have we enough food?* **sufficient**, adequate, ample, abundant, as much ... as necessary, the necessary; informal plenty of.
▷ANTONYMS insufficient.
▸ pronoun *there's enough for everyone*: **sufficient**, plenty (of), a sufficient amount (of), an adequate amount (of), as much as necessary; a sufficiency, an adequacy, an ample supply, a satisfactory amount, a passable amount, a tolerable amount, an acceptable amount, an abundance, an amplitude; full measure.
▷ANTONYMS insufficient.
▸ adverb *in large enough numbers*: **sufficiently**, adequately, amply, satisfactorily, passably, tolerably, reasonably, fairly.
▷ANTONYMS insufficiently.

en passant adverb French *the report mentions, en passant, certain features of the Danish system*: **in passing**, incidentally, by the way, parenthetically, while on the subject, apropos.

enquire, inquire verb **1** *I enquired about part-time training courses*: **ask**, make enquiries, ask questions, pose a question, request information; want to know, look to someone for answers.
2 *the commission is to* ***enquire into*** *alleged illegal payments*: **conduct an enquiry**, make enquiries, probe, look; **investigate**, research, examine, explore, scan, sift, delve, dig, search, scrutinize, study, inspect, survey, analyse, consider, appraise; subject to an examination; informal check out, suss out, snoop.

enquiring, inquiring adjective *youngsters with enquiring minds*: **inquisitive**, curious, interested, questioning, probing, investigative, analytical, analytic, exploring, searching, scrutinizing; burning with curiosity, dying to know.

enquiry, inquiry noun **1** *telephone enquiries*: **question**, query.
2 *there is to be an enquiry into alleged security leaks*: **investigation**, examination, exploration, probe, search, scrutiny, scrutinization, study, inspection; inquest, hearing.

enrage verb *the scheme is bound to enrage farmers*: **anger**, incense, infuriate, madden, inflame, incite, antagonize, provoke, rub up the wrong way, ruffle someone's feathers, exasperate; informal hack off, drive mad/crazy, drive up the wall, make someone see red, make someone's blood boil, make someone's hackles rise, get someone's back up, get someone's dander up, get someone's goat, get under someone's skin, get up someone's nose, rattle someone's cage; Brit. informal wind up, get on someone's wick, nark; N. Amer. informal burn up, tee off, tick off, gravel; vulgar slang piss off; Brit. vulgar slang get on someone's tits; rare empurple.
▷ANTONYMS placate; please.

enraged adjective *an enraged mob screamed abuse and hurled missiles*: **very angry**, irate, furious, infuriated, angered, in a temper, incensed, raging, incandescent, fuming, ranting, raving, seething, frenzied, in a frenzy, beside oneself, outraged, in high dudgeon; hostile, antagonistic, black, dark; informal mad, hopping mad, wild, livid, as cross as two sticks, boiling, apoplectic, aerated, hot under the collar, on the warpath, up in arms, with all guns blazing, foaming at the mouth, steamed up, in a lather, in a paddy, in a filthy temper, fit to be tied; Brit. informal shirty, stroppy; N. Amer. informal sore, bent out of shape, soreheaded, teed off, ticked off; Austral./NZ informal ropeable, snaky, crook; W. Indian informal vex; Brit. informal, dated in a bate, waxy; vulgar slang pissed off; N. Amer. vulgar slang pissed; literary wrathful, ireful, wroth.
▷ANTONYMS calm, good-humoured.

enrapture verb *all of us in the theatre were enraptured by the music*: **delight**, give great pleasure to, give joy to, please greatly, charm, enchant, captivate, enthral, entrance, bewitch, beguile, transport, ravish, thrill, excite, exhilarate, intoxicate, take someone's breath away; gladden, gratify, appeal to, do one's heart good, entertain, amuse, divert; informal give someone a buzz, give someone a kick, tickle someone pink, bowl someone over, turn someone on, send; N. Amer. informal give someone a charge.
▷ANTONYMS repel.

enrich verb **1** *the fine arts can certainly enrich our society*: **enhance**, make richer, improve, add to, augment, supplement, complement, boost, upgrade, reinforce; raise, lift, refine, polish, heighten, deepen, elevate, aggrandize, intensify, exalt.
▷ANTONYMS spoil, devalue.
2 *many convenience foods are enriched with minerals and vitamins*: **make more nutritious**, improve, vitaminize.
3 *ants enrich, drain, and air the soil*: **fertilize**, add fertilizer to, make more fertile, improve; compost, dung, manure, mulch, dress.
▷ANTONYMS impoverish.

enrol verb **1** *they both* ***enrolled for*** *the course*: **register**, sign on, sign up, apply, volunteer, put one's name down, matriculate; go in for, enter, join, become a member of, take up.
▷ANTONYMS leave.
2 *280 new members were enrolled this year*: **accept**, admit, take on, register, sign on, sign up, matriculate, recruit, engage.
▷ANTONYMS expel; reject.

en route adverb French *he was en route from Paris to Bordeaux*: **on the way**, in transit, on the journey, during the journey, during transport, along/on the road, on the move, in motion; coming, going, proceeding, journeying, travelling.

ensconce verb *Agnes* ***ensconced herself*** *in their bedroom*: **settle**, install, establish, park, shut, plant, lodge, position, seat, entrench, shelter, screen; nestle, curl up, snuggle up; informal dig in.

ensemble noun **1** *the ensemble includes two flutes*: **group**, band, orchestra, combo; company, troupe, cast, chorus, corps, circle, association; duo, trio, quartet, quintet, sextet, septet, octet, nonet.
2 *the buildings in the square present a charming provincial ensemble*: **whole**, whole thing, entity, unit, unity, body, piece, object, discrete item; collection, set, combination, package, accumulation, conglomeration, sum, total, totality, entirety, assemblage, aggregate, composite; informal whole caboodle.
3 *she wore a pink and black ensemble*: **outfit**, costume, suit, coordinates, matching separates, set of clothes; informal get-up, rig-out.

e

enshrine verb *the following rights should be enshrined in the treaty*: **set down**, set out, spell out, express, lay down, set in stone, embody, realize, manifest, incorporate, represent, contain, include, preserve, treasure, immortalize, cherish.

enshroud verb literary *grey clouds enshrouded the city*. See **envelop**.

ensign noun *the ship flew a British ensign*: **flag**, standard, colour(s), jack, banner, pennant, pennon, streamer, banderole; Brit. pendant; Nautical burgee; in ancient Rome vexillum; rare gonfalon, guidon, labarum.

enslave verb *there were few natives left to enslave*: **sell into slavery**, condemn to slavery, take away someone's human rights, disenfranchise, condemn to servitude; subject to forced labour; **subjugate**, suppress, tyrannize, oppress, dominate, exploit, persecute; rare enthral, bind, yoke.
▷ANTONYMS liberate; emancipate.

enslavement noun *the enslavement of Africans continued for most of the nineteenth century*: **subjugation**, disenfranchisement, suppression, tyranny, subjection, oppression, domination, exploitation, persecution; **slavery**, servitude, bondage, forced labour; bonds, chains, fetters, shackles, restraints, yoke; Biology dulosis; literary thraldom, thrall; historical serfdom, vassalage, helotage, helotry, helotism; archaic enthralment, duress.
▷ANTONYMS liberation; emancipation.

ensnare verb *the larvae construct pits to ensnare their prey*: **capture**, catch, seize, trap, entrap, snare, entangle, enmesh, net, bag, ambush, ensnarl; rare springe.
▷ANTONYMS release.

ensue verb *a fierce argument* ***ensued from*** *his remark*: **result**, follow, develop, stem, spring, arise, derive, evolve, proceed, emerge, emanate, issue, flow; occur, happen, take place, surface, crop up, spring up, present itself, come next, come about, transpire, supervene; be caused by, be brought about by, be produced by, originate in, accompany, be attended by, be consequent on, come after; Philosophy supervene on; literary come to pass, befall, betide; archaic hap; rare eventuate.

ensure verb **1** *ensure that the surface to be painted is completely clean | we will ensure equal opportunities for all*: **make sure**, make certain, see to it; secure, guarantee, warrant, certify, set the seal on, clinch; confirm, check, verify, corroborate, establish; informal sew up.
2 *the project has been set up to ensure the future of small woodlands*: **safeguard**, protect, guard, shield, shelter, fortify, make invulnerable; **assure**, secure, make safe, watch over, look after, take care of.

> *Easily confused words* **ensure or insure?**
>
> In both British and American English the primary meaning of **insure** is the commercial one of providing financial compensation for loss or damage. **Ensure** is not used at all in this sense; it means 'take care, and take action if necessary, to make certain that something is the case' (*the client must ensure that accurate records are kept*).

entail verb *this proposal will entail additional expenditure*: **necessitate**, make necessary, require, need, demand, call for; presuppose, assume, warrant, be grounds for; involve, mean, imply; cause, bring about, produce, result in, end in, culminate in, finish in, terminate in, lead to, give rise to, occasion, engender, generate, prompt, effect, evoke, elicit, precipitate, trigger, spark off, provoke.

entangle verb **1** *all four bodies were entangled in a heap*: **intertwine**, entwine, tangle, intertwist, twist, ravel, snarl, knot, coil, mat, jumble, muddle.
▷ANTONYMS disentangle.
2 *the thread entangles the insect and brings it down*: **catch**, capture, trap, snare, ensnare, entrap, enmesh, ensnarl.
▷ANTONYMS disentangle; release.
3 *he felt no call to entangle himself in the political questions of his day*: **involve**, implicate, embroil, mix up, catch up, bog down, mire.
▷ANTONYMS steer clear of.

entanglement noun **1** *he would not contemplate foreign entanglements whose outcome was unpredictable*: **involvement**, complication, mix-up,

adventure, undertaking.
2 *his entanglements with the opposite sex*: **affair**, relationship, love affair, romance, fling, flirtation, dalliance, liaison, involvement, attachment, affair of the heart, intrigue; relations; French affaire, affaire de/du cœur, amour; informal hanky-panky; Brit. informal carry-on.

entente noun *the Foreign Office was reluctant to upset the entente with France*: **understanding**, agreement, arrangement, entente cordiale, covenant, settlement; deal, alliance, treaty, pact, accord, compact, concordat, protocol, convention.

enter verb **1** *police entered the house | knock and enter*: **go in/into**, come in/into, get in/into, set foot in, cross the threshold of, pass into, move into, gain access to, be admitted to, make/effect an entrance into, break into, burst into, irrupt into, intrude into, invade, infiltrate.
▷ANTONYMS leave.
2 *a bullet entered his chest*: **penetrate**, pierce, puncture, perforate, make a hole in, make a wound in; impale, stick, spike, stab, spear, skewer, run through, transfix; rare transpierce.
▷ANTONYMS leave.
3 *America entered the war | she rarely entered into the conversation*: **join (in)**, get involved in, go in for, throw oneself into, engage in, embark on, venture into/on, launch into, plunge into, undertake, take up; **participate in**, take part in, share in, play a part in, play a role in, be a participant in, partake in, contribute to, be associated with, associate oneself with, have a hand in, have something to do with, be (a) party to; cooperate in, help with, assist with, lend a hand with; informal get in on the act, pitch in with.
▷ANTONYMS leave.
4 *the planning entered a new phase*: **begin**, start, move into, go into, enter on; informal kick off; formal commence.
▷ANTONYMS finish.
5 *both boys entered the Army at eighteen*: **join**, become a member of, enrol in/for, enlist in, volunteer for, sign up for, take up, become connected/associated with, commit oneself to.
▷ANTONYMS leave.
6 *Mum entered a national cookery competition*: **go in for**, put one's name down for, register for, enrol for, sign on/up for, become a competitor in, become a contestant in, obtain/gain entrance to; compete in, take part in, participate in, be a competitor in, be a contestant in, play in; informal throw one's hat in the ring, be in the running.
▷ANTONYMS scratch.
7 *the cashier entered the details in a ledger*: **record**, write down, set down, put in writing, put down, take down, note, make a note of, jot down, put down on paper, commit to paper; **document**, put on record, minute, register, chronicle, file, put on file, chart, docket, log; list, catalogue, make an inventory of; rare diarize.
▷ANTONYMS erase.
8 Law *he entered a plea of guilty*: **submit**, register, lodge, put on record, record, table, file, put forward, place, advance, lay, present, press, prefer, tender, offer, proffer.
▷ANTONYMS withdraw.

enterprise noun **1** *approaching such an aggressive and powerful creature is a dangerous enterprise*: **undertaking**, endeavour, venture, pursuit, exercise, activity, operation, exploit, mission, deed, act, action, move, measure, task, business, affair, proceeding; scheme, plan, plan of action, programme, campaign; project, proposal, proposition, suggestion, idea, conception; informal caper; Brit. informal wheeze.
2 *the school showed enterprise in its attempt to attract pupils*: **initiative**, resourcefulness, resource, imagination, imaginativeness, ingenuity, inventiveness, originality, creativity; quick-wittedness, cleverness, native wit, talent, ability, capability; spirit, spiritedness, enthusiasm, dynamism, leadership, drive, zest, dash, ambition, ambitiousness, energy, verve, vigour, vitality; boldness, daring, spirit of adventure, audacity, courage, intrepidity; informal gumption, get-up-and-go, go, push, oomph, pizzazz, pep, zip, vim.
▷ANTONYMS unimaginativeness; fecklessness.
3 *a fan club should be a service rather than a profit-making enterprise*: **business**, company, firm, (commercial) undertaking, venture, organization, operation, concern, industry, corporation, establishment, house, shop, office, bureau, agency, franchise, practice, partnership, consortium, cooperative, conglomerate, group, combine, syndicate; informal outfit, set-up.

enterprising adjective *an enterprising farmer is now charging visitors £1 each to park in her field*: **resourceful**, imaginative, ingenious, inventive, original, creative; quick-witted, clever, bright, sharp, talented, gifted, able, capable; spirited, enthusiastic, dynamic, ambitious, energetic, entrepreneurial, vigorous; bold, daring, audacious, courageous, intrepid, adventurous; informal go-ahead.
▷ANTONYMS unimaginative; feckless.

entertain verb **1** *he wrote his first stories to entertain his children*: **amuse**, divert, distract, delight, please, charm, cheer, beguile, interest, fascinate, enthral, engage, involve, occupy, absorb, immerse, engross, preoccupy, hold the attention of.
▷ANTONYMS bore.
2 *he often entertains foreign visitors at home*: **receive**, play host/hostess to, show hospitality to, invite to a meal/party, invite (round/over), ask (round/over), have (round/over), give someone a meal, throw a party for; dine, wine and dine, feast, cater for, serve, feed, treat, welcome, host, fête.
3 *I expect you entertain a lot*: **receive guests**, have guests, play host/hostess, provide hospitality, have people round/over, have company, hold/throw a party, keep open house, have a dinner/lunch party.
4 *would you entertain the possibility of undertaking such a venture again?* **consider**, give consideration to, take into consideration, think about, contemplate, give thought to, bear in mind; countenance, tolerate, brook, suffer, agree to, approve of, support.
▷ANTONYMS reject.
5 *he entertained the suspicion that he was being swindled*: **harbour**, nurture, foster, nurse, cherish, hold, have, bear, hold (on to), possess, cling to, retain, maintain, brood over, hide, conceal.
▷ANTONYMS eschew.

entertainer noun *one of Hollywood's highest-paid entertainers*: **performer**, artiste, artist; rare executant.

entertaining adjective *she found him a charming and entertaining companion | a very entertaining play*: **delightful**, **enjoyable**, diverting, amusing, pleasurable, pleasing, pleasant, agreeable, nice, to one's liking, congenial, charming, appealing, beguiling, enchanting, captivating, engaging, interesting, fascinating, intriguing, absorbing, riveting, compelling; humorous, funny, chucklesome, witty, droll, comical, hilarious; informal fun.
▷ANTONYMS boring; uninteresting.

entertainment noun **1** *he read the books purely for entertainment*: **amusement**, pleasure, leisure, relaxation, fun, enjoyment, interest, occupation, refreshment, restoration, distraction, diversion, divertissement, play; informal R and R, jollies; Brit. informal beer and skittles; N. Amer. informal rec; dated sport; archaic disport.
2 *a theatre company is to present an entertainment for the Emperor*: **show**, performance, presentation, production, staging, spectacle, extravaganza.

enthral verb *last night he enthralled fans from six to sixty*: **captivate**, charm, enchant, bewitch, fascinate, beguile, entrance, enrapture, delight, attract, allure, lure; win, ensnare, dazzle, absorb, engross, rivet, grip, transfix, root someone to the spot, transport, carry away, hypnotize, mesmerize, intrigue, spellbind, hold spellbound; informal get under someone's skin.
▷ANTONYMS bore; repel.

enthralling adjective *wildlife programmes on television are enthralling viewing*: **fascinating**, entrancing, enchanting, bewitching, captivating, charming, beguiling, enrapturing; **delightful**, attractive, alluring, winning, dazzling, absorbing, engrossing, memorable, compelling, riveting, readable, gripping, exciting, transfixing, transporting, hypnotic, mesmerizing, intriguing, spellbinding; informal unputdownable.
▷ANTONYMS boring, dull.

enthuse verb **1** *I immediately **enthused about** the idea*: **rave**, be enthusiastic, gush, wax lyrical, bubble over, effervesce, be effusive, rhapsodize, go into raptures; praise to the skies, heap praise on, make much of, throw bouquets at, eulogize, extol, acclaim; informal go wild/mad/crazy, get all worked up, go over the top; N. Amer. informal ballyhoo; black English big someone/something up; dated cry someone/something up; rare laud, panegyrize.
2 *He is a brilliant producer. He enthuses people*: **motivate**, inspire, stimulate, encourage, spur (on), galvanize, arouse, rouse, excite, stir (up), fire, fire with enthusiasm, make enthusiastic, fire the imagination of; rare inspirit, incentivize.

enthusiasm noun **1** *Watkins worked quickly and with enthusiasm*: **eagerness**, keenness, ardour, fervour, warmth, passion, zeal, zealousness, zest, gusto, brio, pep, go, sap, liveliness, vivacity, vivaciousness, energy, verve, vigour, dynamism, vehemence, fire, excitement, exuberance, ebullience, spirit, avidity, avidness; wholeheartedness, commitment, willingness, readiness, devotion, devotedness, fanaticism, earnestness; informal oomph, zing, zip, zap, vim, get-up-and-go; rare fervency, ardency, passionateness.
▷ANTONYMS apathy.
2 *they can put their skills and enthusiasms to good use*: **interest**, passion, obsession, fad, craze, mania, rage; inclination, preference, penchant, predilection, fancy, impulse; pastime, hobby, recreation, (leisure) pursuit, leisure activity, entertainment; informal bug, thing.

enthusiast noun *a good present for a railway enthusiast*: **fan**, fanatic, devotee, aficionado, addict, lover, admirer, supporter, follower; **expert**, wizard, connoisseur, authority, pundit, cognoscente, one of the cognoscenti, savant; informal buff, freak, nut, fiend, maniac, ham, a great one for; N. Amer. informal maven, geek, jock, nerd; S. African informal fundi.

enthusiastic adjective *an enthusiastic supporter of Scottish rugby*: **eager**, keen, avid, ardent, fervent, warm, passionate, zealous, lively, vivacious, energetic, vigorous, dynamic, vehement, fiery, excited, exuberant, ebullient, spirited, hearty, wholehearted, committed, willing, ready, devoted, fanatical, earnest.
▷ANTONYMS apathetic.

> *Choose the right word* **enthusiastic, eager, keen, avid**
>
> See **eager**.

entice verb *the show should entice a new audience into the theatre*: **tempt**, allure, lure, attract, dangle a carrot in front of; appeal to, invite, persuade, convince, inveigle, induce, beguile, cajole, wheedle, coax, woo; seduce, lead astray, lead on, decoy; informal sweet-talk, smooth-talk.

> *Choose the right word* **entice, lure, tempt**
>
> See **tempt**.

enticement noun *the enticement of power*: **lure**, temptation, allure, attraction, desirability, bait, draw, pull, call, appeal; glamour, allurement, bewitchment, enchantment, charm, seduction, persuasion, fascination, captivation, magnetism; informal come-on.

enticing adjective *we caught enticing glimpses of tables laden with food*: **tempting**, alluring, attractive, appealing, fetching, inviting, glamorous, captivating, seductive; enchanting, beguiling, charming, fascinating, intriguing, tantalizing, magnetic; irresistible; informal, dated come-hither.

entire adjective **1** *I have devoted my entire adult life to the pursuit of my ideals*: **whole**, complete, total, full; continuous, unbroken, uninterrupted, undivided.
▷ANTONYMS partial.
2 *the arch of one of the gates is entire*: **intact**, unbroken, undamaged, unharmed, unimpaired, unflawed, unscathed, unspoilt, unmutilated, unblemished, unmarked, perfect, inviolate, in one piece; sound, solid.
▷ANTONYMS broken, partial.
3 *an ideological system with which he is in entire agreement*: **absolute**, total, utter, out-and-out, thorough, thoroughgoing, wholehearted; unqualified, unreserved, unmitigated, unmodified, unmixed, unalloyed, unrestricted, perfect, outright, pure, sheer.
▷ANTONYMS partial, qualified.

> *Word links* **entire**
>
> **pan-** related prefix, as in *pan-African, panacea*

entirely adverb **1** *his solution was entirely out of the question*: **absolutely**, completely, totally, fully, wholly; altogether, utterly, quite, in every respect, in every way, in all respects, {lock, stock, and barrel}; unreservedly, without reservation, without exception, thoroughly, perfectly, downright, one hundred per cent, every inch; to the hilt, to the core, all the way; informal bang, dead.
▷ANTONYMS partially, slightly.
2 *the gift was entirely for charitable purposes*: **solely**, only, exclusively, purely, merely, simply, just, alone.
▷ANTONYMS partially.

entirety noun *in the 1920s, cheap production constituted almost the entirety of British film-making*: **whole**, sum, total, aggregate, totality, gross, sum total, grand total.
▷ANTONYMS part.
□ **in its entirety** *the scheme was approved in its entirety*: **completely**, entirely, totally, fully, wholly; in every respect, in every way, in all respects, {lock, stock, and barrel}, one hundred per cent, from beginning to end, alpha and omega, all the way, every inch, to the hilt, to the core.
▷ANTONYMS in part.

entitle verb **1** *this pass entitles you to free entrance to the museum*: **qualify**, make eligible, authorize, sanction, allow, permit, grant, grant/give the right, give permission; enable, empower, accredit; enfranchise, capacitate.
2 *the concluding chapter was entitled 'Comedy and Tragedy'*: **title**, name, call, give the title of, label, term, designate, dub; baptize, christen; rare denominate.

entitlement noun **1** *their entitlement to social-security benefits*: **right**, prerogative, claim, title, licence; permission, dispensation, privilege, liberty.
2 *your annual holiday entitlement*: **allowance**, allocation, allotment, quota, ration, grant, limit.

entity noun **1** *a single biological entity*: **being**, body, creature, individual, organism, life form; person; object, article, thing, piece of matter, real thing; substance, quantity, existence; Philosophy ens.
2 *the subsidiary company is a distinct entity*: **organization**, institution, establishment, body, operation; structure, system, unit, whole; informal set-up, outfit.
3 *the distinction between entity and nonentity*: **existence**, being; life, living, animation, animateness, vital force; substance, essence, reality, actuality; essential nature, quintessence; Philosophy quiddity, esse.
▷ANTONYMS nonentity, non-existence.

entomb verb *mummified bodies were entombed in the pyramids*: **inter**, place in a tomb, lay to rest, bury, consign to the grave; informal place six feet under, plant; literary inhume, sepulchre.

entombment noun *the ritual entombment of the pharaoh*: **interment**, laying to rest, burial, burying, consignment to the grave, committal, inhumation; funeral, obsequies; rare exequies.

entourage noun *the king's entourage*: **retinue**, escort, company, cortège, train, suite, court, staff, bodyguard; attendants, companions, followers, retainers, members of court, camp followers, associates, hangers-on; informal groupies.

entrails plural noun *the embalmers removed the entrails*: **intestines**, internal organs, bowels, guts, vital organs, viscera; offal; informal insides, innards; Brit. archaic numbles.

entrance[1] (stress on the first syllable) noun **1** *the main entrance to the site*: **entry**, way in, means of entry/access, ingress, access, approach; door, doorway, portal, gate, gateway; opening, mouth; drive, driveway, passageway, gangway; entrance hall, foyer, lobby, porch, concourse, threshold; N. Amer. entryway.
▷ANTONYMS exit.
2 *they were interrupted by the entrance of Mrs Little*: **appearance**, arrival, entry, ingress, coming, coming/going in, materialization, approach, introduction.
▷ANTONYMS departure, exit.
3 *he was refused entrance until somebody arrived who could vouch for him*: **admission**, admittance, entry, access, ingress, entrée, permission to enter, right of entry, the opportunity to enter.

entrance[2] (stress on the second syllable) verb **1** *I was entranced by the bird's beauty*: **enchant**, bewitch, beguile, enrapture, captivate, capture, mesmerize, hypnotize, spellbind, hold spellbound, send into transports/raptures; enthral, grip, engage, rivet, engross, absorb, fascinate, carry away; stun, overpower, take someone's breath away; charm, delight; thrill, excite, electrify; informal bowl over, knock out; literary ravish.
▷ANTONYMS bore.
2 literary *Orpheus entranced the wild beasts*: **cast a spell on**, put a spell on, put under a spell, put in a trance, bewitch, witch, hex, spellbind, hypnotize, mesmerize; literary trance.

entrant noun **1** *the majority of our entrants are school-leavers from the United Kingdom*: **new member**, new arrival, beginner, newcomer, fresher, freshman, recruit, new boy/girl; novice, trainee, apprentice, probationer, tyro, initiate, neophyte; N. Amer. tenderfoot, hire; informal rookie, greenhorn, new kid, newbie, cub.
▷ANTONYMS veteran.
2 *the prize will be awarded to the entrant who wins the tiebreak*: **competitor**, contestant, contender, challenger, participant, player, candidate, applicant.

entrap verb **1** *discarded fishing lines can entrap wildlife*: **trap**, snare, ensnare, entangle, enmesh; catch, capture, net, bag, hook, land.
▷ANTONYMS release.
2 *his client had been entrapped by an undercover police officer*: **entice**, lure, tempt, inveigle; bait, decoy, lay a trap for, trap; lead on, seduce; **trick**, deceive, dupe, gull, hoodwink, delude; informal **set up**, frame; Brit. informal fit up.

entreat verb *my lord, I entreat you to believe what you find in this letter*: **implore**, beseech, beg, plead with, supplicate, pray, ask, request; bid, enjoin, appeal to, call on, petition, solicit; exhort, urge, importune; dated crave; rare impetrate, obtest, obsecrate.

entreaty noun *he ignored her entreaties*: **plea**, appeal, request, petition, cry from the heart; suit, application, claim; beseeching, pleading, begging, solicitation, importuning, supplication; bidding, exhortation, urge, demand, enjoinment; prayer; French cri de cœur; rare impetration, obtestation, obsecration, imploration.

entrée noun **1** *there is a choice of half a dozen entrées on the menu*: **main course**, main dish, main meal.
▷ANTONYMS starter; dessert.
2 *university dramatic societies were an excellent entrée into the acting profession*: **means of entry**, entrance, entry, ingress, opportunity to enter; route, path, avenue, way, key, passport; access, admission, admittance, acceptance, right of entry.

entrench, intrench verb *this country is entrenched in a litigation mentality*: **establish**, settle, ensconce, lodge, set, root, install, plant, embed, anchor, seat, station; informal dig in.
▷ANTONYMS dislodge.

entrenched, intrenched adjective *officials tended to cling to entrenched attitudes*: **ingrained**, established, well established, long-established; confirmed, fixed, set firm, firm; deep-seated, deep-rooted, rooted, deep-set; unshakeable, irremovable, indelible, ineradicable, inveterate, immutable, inexorable, dyed-in-the-wool.
▷ANTONYMS superficial.

entre nous adverb French *entre nous, the old man's a bit of a case*: **between ourselves**, between us, between you and me, in (strict) confidence, confidentially, in private, privately, off the record; informal between you and me and the bedpost/gatepost/wall; Latin sub rosa; archaic under the rose.

e

entrepreneur noun *an entrepreneur who had set up his own firms*: **businessman, businesswoman**, business person, business executive, enterpriser, speculator, tycoon, magnate; dealer, trader, buyer and seller, merchant; commercial intermediary, intermediary, middleman, promoter, impresario; informal **wheeler-dealer**, mogul, big shot, bigwig, whizz-kid, mover and shaker, go-getter, high-flyer, hustler.

entrust verb **1** *he was entrusted with the task of liaising with fellow intellectuals*: **give responsibility for**, charge, invest, endow; burden, encumber, saddle, tax.
2 *there are a great many powers* **entrusted to** *the Home Secretary*: **assign**, confer on, bestow on, vest in, consign; delegate, depute, devolve; put into the hands of, give into the charge/care/custody of, turn over, hand over, give, grant, vouchsafe.
3 *she was afraid to entrust the children to the hospital*: **hand over**, give custody of, make over, turn over, commit, assign, consign, deliver; formal commend.

entry noun **1** *my moment of entry was masked by smoke*: **appearance**, arrival, entrance, ingress, coming, coming/going in, approach, introduction, materialization.
▷**ANTONYMS** departure.
2 *the entry to a block of flats*: **entrance**, way in, means of entry/access, ingress, access, approach; door, doorway, portal, gate, gateway; drive, driveway, passageway, gangway; entrance hall, foyer, lobby, porch, concourse, threshold; N. Amer. entryway.
▷**ANTONYMS** exit.
3 *he was refused entry to the meeting*: **admission**, admittance, entrance, access, ingress, entrée, permission to enter, right of entry, the opportunity to enter.
4 *the entries in the cash book*: **item**, record, statement, note, listing, jotting; memo, memorandum; account, description.
5 *pull-down menus make data entry a snap*: **recording**, noting, filing, registering, archiving, logging, taking down, setting down, documenting, documentation, capture.
6 *the judges had the difficult task of choosing a winner from the 340 entries*: **contestant**, competitor, contender, challenger, entrant, participant, player, candidate, applicant; **submission**, attempt, try, effort, turn; entry form, application; informal go.

entwine verb *her hair was entwined with ropes of pearls*: **wind round**, twist round, coil round, wrap round, weave, intertwine, interlink, interlace, interweave, interthread, criss-cross, entangle, tangle; twine, link, lace, braid, plait, knit, wreathe; literary pleach.
▷**ANTONYMS** unravel, disentangle.

enumerate verb **1** *he enumerated four objectives for the company*: **list**, itemize, catalogue, set out, set forth, give; cite, name, mention, specify, identify, spell out, detail, particularize; summarize, recount, recite, rehearse, recapitulate, quote, relate; run through, reel off, rattle off, tick/check off.
2 *research projects have attempted to enumerate hospital readmission rates*: **calculate**, compute, count, add up, sum up, tally, total, number, put a figure on, quantify; reckon, figure up, work out; Brit. tot up; archaic tell.

enunciate verb **1** *she enunciated each word slowly and carefully*: **pronounce**, articulate; say, speak, utter, express, voice, vocalize, sound, mouth; informal get one's tongue round; rare enounce.
2 *in the speech I enunciated a belief which I still hold to*: **express**, utter, state, give voice/expression to, put into words, give utterance to, declare, profess, set forth, assert, affirm; put forward, raise, table, air, ventilate; propound, proclaim, promulgate, publish, broadcast, preach; informal come out with.

envelop verb *the gases of the atmosphere that envelop the Earth*: **surround**, cover, enfold, enwrap, blanket, swathe, swaddle, wrap (up), engulf, encircle, encompass, cocoon, sheathe, encase, enclose; cloak, conceal, hide, obscure, cover (up), screen, shield, mask, veil, shroud; literary mantle, enshroud; rare obnubilate.

envelope noun *she tore open the envelope*: **wrapper**, wrapping, wrap, sleeve, cover, covering; casing, case.

envenom verb **1** *the arrows are envenomed with asp drool*: **poison**, add poison to, spike, lace, contaminate.
2 *incidents like this can envenom international relations*: **embitter**, make bitter, sour, poison, make rancorous, jaundice, colour, taint; anger, aggravate, antagonize.
▷**ANTONYMS** sweeten.

enviable adjective *this hotel has an enviable position on the main square*: **desirable, attractive**, sought-after, desired, admirable, fortunate, lucky, favoured, blessed, worth having, excellent; covetable, exciting envy, tempting; informal to die for.
▷**ANTONYMS** unenviable.

envious adjective *she felt envious of her friend's beauty*: **jealous**, covetous, desirous; grudging, begrudging, resentful; jaundiced, bitter, malicious, spiteful; green with envy, green, green-eyed; formal emulous.
▷**ANTONYMS** generous.

Word toolkit

envious	**jealous**	**grudging**
glance	rage	respect
eyes	boyfriend/girlfriend	admiration
friends	lover	acknowledgment
thoughts	type	praise
colleague	glare	recognition

environ verb *at home I am environed by pets*: **surround**, encircle, enclose, ring, envelop; blanket, swathe, swaddle, wrap, cloak.

environment noun **1** *birds and mammals from a wide range of environments*: **habitat**, territory, domain, home, abode; surroundings, conditions, environs, circumstances.
2 *potential hazards in the hospital environment are numerous*: **situation**, **setting**, milieu, medium, background, backdrop, scene, scenario, location, locale, context, framework; sphere, world, realm; preserve, province; ambience, atmosphere, climate, mood, air, aura.
3 (**the environment**) *the impact of pesticides on the environment*: **the natural world**, nature, the living world, the world, the earth, the ecosystem, the biosphere, Mother Nature, Gaia; wildlife, flora and fauna, the countryside, the landscape.

Word links **environment**

ecology study of the environment
ecocide destruction of the environment

environmentalist noun *environmentalists are pressing for a ban on logging*: **conservationist**, preservationist, ecologist, green, nature-lover, eco-activist; informal, derogatory econut, ecofreak, tree hugger.

environs plural noun *the environs of London*: **surroundings**, surrounding area, vicinity; locality, neighbourhood, district, region; outskirts, suburbs, suburbia, precincts, borders, periphery, purlieus; N. Amer. vicinage.

envisage verb **1** *it was envisaged that such hospitals would be opened in all the principal towns*: **foresee**, predict, forecast, foretell, anticipate, expect, think likely, envision; **intend**, propose, mean.
2 *I cannot envisage what the circumstances will be in twenty years time*: **imagine**, contemplate, visualize, envision, picture, see in one's mind's eye; conceive of, think of, understand, grasp, appreciate, apprehend; rare ideate.

envision verb *we now have the chance to build the world envisioned by the founders of the UN*: **visualize, imagine**, envisage, picture, see in one's mind's eye, conjure up an image of; intend, propose, mean; conceive of, think of, see; rare ideate.

envoy noun **1** *he served as an envoy to France*: **ambassador**, emissary, diplomat, legate, consul, attaché, chargé d'affaires, plenipotentiary; Roman Catholic Church nuncio.
2 *a visit by the president's personal envoy*: **representative**, delegate, deputy, agent, intermediary, mediator, negotiator, proxy, surrogate, liaison, broker, accredited messenger, courier, spokesperson, spokesman, spokeswoman, mouthpiece, stand-in; informal go-between; archaic factor.

envy noun **1** *Carla felt a sharp pang of envy*: **jealousy**, enviousness, covetousness, desire; resentment, resentfulness, bitterness, discontent, spite; the green-eyed monster.
▷**ANTONYMS** generosity.
2 *France has a film industry that is the envy of Europe*: **object/source of envy; best**, finest, pride, top, cream, pick, choice, elite, prize, jewel, jewel in the crown, flower, paragon, leading light, glory, the crème de la crème.
▷**ANTONYMS** shame; dregs.
▸ **verb 1** *I admired and envied her*: **be envious of**, be jealous of; begrudge, grudge, be resentful of.
▷**ANTONYMS** be glad for.
2 *most girls would have envied her lifestyle*: **covet**, be covetous of; desire, aspire to, wish for, want, long for, yearn for, hanker after/for, be consumed with desire for, crave, have one's heart set on; informal have the hots for.

ephemeral adjective *fashions are ephemeral*: **transitory**, transient, fleeting, passing, short-lived, momentary, brief, short, cursory, temporary, impermanent, short-term; fading, evanescent, fugitive, fly-by-night; literary fugacious.
▷**ANTONYMS** long-lived, permanent.

Word links **ephemeral**

ephemerist collector of ephemeral things

Choose the right word **ephemeral, transient, transitory, fleeting**

See **transient**.

epic noun **1** *the epics of Homer*: **heroic poem**, long poem, long story; **saga**, legend, romance, lay, history, chronicle, myth, fable, folk tale, folk story.
2 *a big Hollywood epic*: **epic film**, long film; informal **blockbuster**.
▶ **adjective 1** *a traditional epic poem*: **heroic**, **long**, grand, monumental, vast, Homeric, Miltonian; lofty, grandiloquent, high-flown, high-sounding, extravagant, bombastic.
▷ANTONYMS understated.
2 *their epic journey through the mountains*: **ambitious**, heroic, grand, arduous, extraordinary, Herculean; very long, very great, very large, huge, monumental.

epicene adjective **1** *the epicene shape resolved into that of a cloaked female*: **sexless**, asexual, neuter, unsexed; bisexual, androgynous, hermaphrodite; technical monoclinous, gynandrous, gynandromorphic, parthenogenetic; rare androgyne.
2 *he gave an epicene titter*: **effeminate**, womanish, unmanly, unmasculine, girlish; effete, weak, namby-pamby; informal sissy, girly, camp, limp-wristed, nancy, pansified, queeny.
▷ANTONYMS masculine, macho.

epicure noun *as an epicure, he is entranced by their new range of speciality foods*: **gourmet**, gastronome, gourmand, connoisseur; glutton, sensualist, hedonist; French bon viveur, bon vivant; informal foodie.

epicurean noun *a generous, life-loving epicurean*: **hedonist**, sensualist, pleasure seeker, pleasure lover, sybarite, voluptuary; epicure, gourmet, gastronome, connoisseur, gourmand, glutton; French bon viveur, bon vivant.
▷ANTONYMS puritan.
▶ **adjective 1** *their careers have been undone by epicurean excess*: **hedonistic**, sensualist, pleasure-seeking, self-indulgent, indulgent, libertine, sybaritic, voluptuary, lotus-eating; dissolute, decadent, louche, licentious, sinful, shameless, depraved; wanton, abandoned, unrestrained, profligate, extravagant, intemperate, immoderate; sensual, carnal; Dionysiac, Bacchanalian, saturnalian; gluttonous, gourmandizing, greedy.
▷ANTONYMS puritanical.
2 *an epicurean feast*: **gourmet**, gastronomic.

epidemic noun **1** *an epidemic of typhoid*: **outbreak**, plague, scourge, infestation; widespread illness/disease; Medicine pandemic, epizootic; formal recrudescence, boutade.
2 *he's a victim of the county's joyriding epidemic*: **spate**, rash, wave, explosion, eruption, outbreak, outburst, flare-up, craze; flood, torrent, burst, blaze, flurry; upsurge, upswing, upturn, increase, growth, rise, mushrooming; rare ebullition, boutade.
▶ **adjective** *the obsession with the motor car is now epidemic*: **rife**, rampant, widespread, wide-ranging, extensive, sweeping, penetrating, pervading; global, universal, inescapable, ubiquitous; prevalent, predominant; Medicine endemic, pandemic, epizootic.
▷ANTONYMS limited, local.

epigram noun **1** *a witty epigram*: **quip**, witticism, gem, play on words, jest, pun, sally, nice turn of phrase; French bon mot, double entendre, jeu d'esprit; informal one-liner, gag, crack, wisecrack; rare paronomasia, equivoque.
2 *a collection of ancient epigrams*: **proverb**, saying, maxim, adage, axiom, aphorism, saw, gnome, dictum, precept, epigraph, motto, catchphrase; cliché, truism, commonplace; words of wisdom, pearls of wisdom; informal (old) chestnut; rare apophthegm.

epigrammatic adjective *her short, epigrammatic verses*: **concise**, succinct, terse, pithy, aphoristic, compact, condensed, compressed, short, brief; laconic, sparing, clipped, elliptical; tight, crisp, incisive, pointed, to the point, short and sweet; witty, clever, amusing, quick-witted, piquant, ingenious; sharp, trenchant, well tuned, finely honed, in well-chosen words; informal snappy; rare lapidary, compendious, synoptic, gnomic, apophthegmatic.
▷ANTONYMS expansive, rambling.

epilogue noun *the body of the book is summarized in the epilogue*: **afterword**, postscript, PS, coda, codicil, appendix, tailpiece, supplement, addendum, postlude, rider, back matter; conclusion, concluding speech, denouement, swan song, peroration; rare postlude.
▷ANTONYMS prologue.

episode noun **1** *the most hair-raising episode of his career*: **incident**, event, occurrence, happening, occasion, interlude, chapter, experience, adventure, exploit; matter, affair, business, circumstance, set of circumstances, thing; ordeal, trial.
2 *the final episode of the series*: **instalment**, section, chapter, scene, act, passage; part, division, portion, subsection, segment, component; programme, show.
3 *an episode of childhood illness*: **period**, spell, bout, fit, attack, interval, phase; informal dose.

episodic adjective **1** *episodic wheezing*: **intermittent**, irregular, sporadic, periodic, fitful, spasmodic, occasional; uneven, scattered, patchy, on and off, on again and off again, in fits and starts.
▷ANTONYMS continuous.
2 *the film is an episodic account of how a group of people had been affected by the war*: **in episodes**, in instalments, in sections, in parts.

epistle noun formal **letter**, missive, communication, written message, written communication, dispatch, report, bulletin, note, line; correspondence, news, information, intelligence, word; Roman Catholic Church encyclical.

epitaph noun *an epitaph on a tombstone*: **elegy**, commemoration, obituary, funeral oration; **inscription**, engraving, etching, legend.

epithet noun **1** *these works earned him the epithet 'the Spanish Heretic'*: **sobriquet**, nickname, byname, title, name, label, tag; **description**, descriptive word/expression/phrase, designation, denomination, characterization, identification; informal moniker, handle; formal appellation, cognomen, anonym.
2 *he felt the urge to hurl epithets in his face*: **obscenity**, expletive, swear word, term of abuse, oath, curse, four-letter word, exclamation; informal dirty word; N. Amer. informal cuss word.

e

epitome noun **1** *he was the epitome of conservative respectability*: **personification**, embodiment, incarnation, paragon; essence, quintessence, archetype, paradigm, typification, type; exemplar, definitive example, prototype; representation, model, soul, example, byword, classic example/case; acme, ultimate, zenith, height; rare avatar.
2 *an epitome of a larger work*: **summary**, abstract, synopsis, precis, résumé, outline, digest, recapitulation, summation, compendium, potted version; abridgement, abbreviation, condensation; N. Amer. wrap-up; archaic argument, summa; rare conspectus.
▷ANTONYMS complete version, full text.

epitomize verb **1** *the railway station epitomizes the spirit of the nineteenth century*: **embody**, give form/shape to, incorporate; typify, exemplify, represent, be representative of, encapsulate, manifest, symbolize, stand for, illustrate, sum up; personify; formal reify; rare incarnate.
2 rare *for the benefit of our readers, we will epitomize the pamphlet*. See **summarize**.

epoch noun *the Tudor epoch*: **era**, age, period, time, aeon, span; stage, point in history; date.

equable adjective **1** *he was in a remarkably equable mood*: **even-tempered**, calm, composed, collected, self-possessed, cool, {cool, calm, and collected}, relaxed, easy-going, at ease, as cool as a cucumber; nonchalant, insouciant, blithe, mellow, mild; serene, tranquil, placid, steady, stable, quiet, level-headed; imperturbable, unexcitable, unruffled, unperturbed, unflustered, undisturbed, unagitated, untroubled, well balanced; informal unflappable, unfazed, together, laid-back; rare equanimous.
▷ANTONYMS temperamental, excitable.
2 *the island enjoys an equable climate*: **stable**, constant, steady, even, uniform, regular, unvarying, consistent, unchanging, changeless; moderate, temperate, non-extreme, fair.
▷ANTONYMS uneven, extreme.

equal adjective **1** *two lines of equal length*: **identical**, uniform, alike, like, the same, one and the same, equivalent, indistinguishable; matching, twin; comparable, similar, corresponding, correspondent, commensurate.
▷ANTONYMS unequal, different.
2 *fares were* **equal to** *a fortnight's wages for a skilled craftsman*: **equivalent**, identical, amounting; proportionate, tantamount; the same as, commensurate with, on a par with.
▷ANTONYMS unequal; more than; less than.
3 *the right to equal treatment before the law*: **unbiased**, impartial, non-partisan, fair, fair-minded, just, even-handed, equitable; unprejudiced, unbigoted, non-discriminatory, free from discrimination, egalitarian; neutral, objective, disinterested, without fear or favour.
▷ANTONYMS unequal; discriminatory.
4 *a fair and equal contest*: **evenly matched**, evenly balanced, even, balanced, level, evenly proportioned, well matched, on a par, on an equal footing; informal fifty-fifty, level pegging, neck and neck.
▷ANTONYMS uneven, unequal.
□ **equal to** *Patricia was equal to the task*: **capable of**, fit for, up to, good/strong enough for, adequate for, sufficient for, ready for; suitable for, suited to, appropriate for; informal up to scratch, having what it takes.
▶ **noun** *they did not treat him as their equal*: **equivalent**, **peer**, fellow, coequal, like; mate, twin, alter ego, counterpart, match, parallel; rare compeer.
▷ANTONYMS superior; inferior.
▶ **verb 1** *thirty six divided by two equals eighteen*: **be equal to**, be equivalent to, be the same as, correspond to; come to, amount to, make, total, add up to; Brit. tot up to.
2 *he equalled the world record*: **match**, reach, parallel, come up to, be level with, measure up to, achieve.
3 *the fable equals that of any other poet*: **be as good as**, be equal/even/level with, be a match for, match, measure up to, come up to, equate with, be in the same league as, be in the same category as, be tantamount to; rival, compete with, contend with, vie with.
▷ANTONYMS lose to; beat.

Word links **equal**

iso- related prefix, as in *isobar, isochronous*

e

equality noun **1** *the union's efforts to promote equality for women*: **fairness**, justness, equitability, impartiality, even-handedness, egalitarianism, equal rights, equal opportunities, non-discrimination; justice, freedom, emancipation; rare coequality.
▷ANTONYMS inequality.
2 *equality between the demand for, and supply of, money*: **parity**, sameness, identicalness, identity, equalness; likeness, alikeness, similarity, comparability, resemblance; uniformity, evenness, levelness, balance, equilibrium, correspondence, consistency, agreement, concord, congruence, parallelism, symmetry; rare coequality.
▷ANTONYMS difference.

equalize verb **1** *attempts to equalize men and women's earnings*: **make equal**, make even, even out/up/off, make level, level (up/off), make uniform, make the same, make consistent, regularize, standardize, bring into line, balance, square, match.
2 *Northampton equalized ten minutes into the second half*: **level the score**, even up the score, draw.

equanimity noun *she was able to confront the daily crises with equanimity*: **composure**, calmness, calm, level-headedness, self-possession, self-control, even-temperedness, coolness, cool-headedness, presence of mind; serenity, placidity, tranquillity, phlegm, impassivity, imperturbability, unexcitability, equilibrium; poise, self-assurance, assurance, self-confidence, aplomb, sangfroid, nerve; informal cool, unflappability; rare ataraxy.
▷ANTONYMS anxiety.

equate verb **1** *his single-mindedness led him to* ***equate*** *criticism* ***with*** *treachery*: **regard as the same as**, regard as identical to; **identify**, liken to, compare; bracket, class, associate, connect, pair, link, relate, ally, think of together, set side by side.
2 *the rent* ***equates to*** *£24 per square foot*: **correspond**, be equivalent, amount; equal, be the same as.
3 *the price moved to equate supply and demand*: **equalize**, balance, even out/up/off, level up/off, square, tally, match; make equal, make even, make level, make equivalent, make identical, make the same, make uniform.

equation noun **1** *a boy was solving a quadratic equation*: **mathematical problem**, sum, calculation, question; equality.
2 *the equation of success with material rewards*: **equating**, equalization, identification, association, connection, likening, matching; equivalence, likeness, identity, correspondence, agreement, comparison, balance, balancing.
3 (**the equation**) *other factors also came into the equation*: **the situation**, the problem, the case, the question, the quandary, the predicament.

equatorial adjective *the equatorial regions*: **tropical**, hot, torrid, sweltering; humid, sultry, steamy, sticky, oppressive; jungle-like.
▷ANTONYMS polar; temperate.

equestrian adjective *an equestrian statue*: **on horseback**, mounted, riding, in the saddle.
▸ noun *a network of tracks for equestrians*: **horseman**, **horsewoman**, rider, horse rider, jockey; cavalryman, trooper; archaic hussar, cavalier.

equilibrium noun **1** *the equilibrium of the economy*: **balance**, symmetry, equipoise, parity, equality, evenness; stability, steadiness; archaic counterpoise, equipollence.
▷ANTONYMS imbalance.
2 *he was hardly ever shaken from his equilibrium by the excesses of criminals*: **composure**, calmness, calm, equanimity, collectedness, sangfroid, coolness; steadiness, stability, level-headedness, cool-headedness, imperturbability, poise, presence of mind; self-possession, self-control, self-command; impassiveness, impassivity, unexcitability, placidity, placidness, tranquillity, serenity; informal cool, unflappability; rare ataraxy, ataraxia.
▷ANTONYMS agitation, nervousness.

equip verb **1** *each was equipped with a flare gun*: **provide**, furnish, supply, issue, fit out, kit out, rig out, deck out, stock, provision, arm; array, attire, dress, outfit, accoutre; informal fix up.
2 *the course will equip graduates for careers in software development*: **prepare**, qualify, suit, endow; enable, facilitate.

equipment noun *the museum has a collection of early sound-recording equipment*: **apparatus**, paraphernalia, articles, appliances, impedimenta; tools, utensils, implements, instruments, hardware, gadgets, gadgetry; stuff, things; kit, rig, tackle, outfit; resources, amenities, supplies; furniture, furnishings, fittings; odds and ends, bits and pieces, bits and bobs; trappings, appurtenances, accoutrements, regalia; Military materiel, baggage; informal gear, box of tricks; Brit. informal clobber, gubbins, odds and sods; archaic equipage.

equipoise noun **1** *this wine represents a marvellous equipoise of power and elegance*: **equilibrium**, balance, evenness, symmetry, parity, equality, equity; stability, steadiness, poise; archaic counterpoise, equipollence.
▷ANTONYMS imbalance.
2 *capital flow acts as an equipoise to international imbalances in savings*: **counterweight**, counterbalance, counterpoise, balance; ballast, stabilizer, makeweight; compensation, recompense; archaic countercheck.

equitable adjective *Parliament is to distribute the burden of tax in an equitable way*: **fair**, just; impartial, even-handed, fair-minded, unbiased, unprejudiced, non-discriminatory, unbigoted, egalitarian, with no axe to grind, without fear or favour; honest, right, rightful, proper, decent, good, honourable, upright, scrupulous, conscientious, above board; reasonable, sensible; disinterested, objective, neutral, uncoloured, dispassionate, non-partisan, balanced, open-minded; informal fair and square, upfront, on the level; N. Amer. informal on the up and up.
▷ANTONYMS inequitable, unfair.

Word toolkit

equitable	**unbiased**	**neutral**
distribution	opinion	position
share	reporting	zone
treatment	source	ground
solution	data	country
compensation	jury	territory
terms	expert	party

equity noun **1** *the equity of Finnish society*: **fairness**, fair-mindedness, justness, justice, equitableness, fair play; impartiality, even-handedness, lack of discrimination/bias/prejudice/bigotry, egalitarianism; honesty, integrity, rightness, rightfulness, rectitude, uprightness, righteousness, properness, decency, goodness, honourableness, scrupulousness, conscientiousness; reasonableness, sensibleness; disinterest, disinterestedness, neutrality, objectivity, balance, open-mindedness.
▷ANTONYMS inequity, imbalance.
2 *the builder owns 25% of the equity in the property*: **value**, worth, valuation; ownership, rights, proprietorship, right of possession.

equivalence noun *equivalence of birth and death rates is rare in human populations*: **equality**, equalness, sameness, identicalness, identity, interchangeability, indistinguishability, uniformity, agreement; similarity, likeness, resemblance, comparability, correspondence, commensurateness, parallelism, closeness, nearness, affinity; rare coequality.

equivalent adjective *a sound quality* ***equivalent to*** *that of CDs | you must have a degree or equivalent qualification*: **equal**, identical; similar, parallel, analogous, comparable, corresponding, correspondent, interchangeable; like, commensurate with, the same as, synonymous with, much the same as; amounting, tantamount, approximate, near, close; of a kind, of a piece; rare coequal.
▷ANTONYMS different; dissimilar.
▸ noun *the campaign was backed by Denmark's equivalent of the Daily Mirror*: **counterpart**, parallel, alternative, match, complement, analogue, double, twin, opposite number; equal, peer, rival; answer; rare coequal.

Word toolkit **equivalent**

See **identical**.

equivocal adjective *an equivocal statement*: **ambiguous**, indefinite, non-committal, vague, indeterminate, imprecise, inexact, indistinct, inexplicit, blurry, hazy, foggy, nebulous, borderline; obscure, unclear, cryptic, enigmatic, puzzling, perplexing, gnomic, Delphic; ambivalent, uncertain, unsure, indecisive, inconclusive, doubtful; roundabout, oblique, circumlocutory, circuitous, periphrastic; misleading, evasive, elusive, duplicitous, equivocating, prevaricating; contradictory, confusing, two-edged, double-edged, paradoxical, confused, muddled.
▷ANTONYMS unequivocal; definite.

equivocate verb *the government have equivocated too often in the past*: **prevaricate**, be evasive, be non-committal, be vague, be ambiguous, evade/dodge the issue, beat about the bush, hedge, hedge one's bets, fudge the issue; fence, parry questions; vacillate, shilly-shally, cavil, waver, quibble; temporize, hesitate, stall (for time), shuffle about; Brit. hum and haw; informal pussyfoot around, waffle, flannel, sit on the fence, duck the issue/question; archaic palter; rare tergiversate.

equivocation noun *these attacks must be condemned without equivocation*: **prevarication**, vagueness, qualification, ambiguity, uncertainty, ambivalence, indecision, doubt; beating about the bush, evasion, dodging, hedging, fudging, doublespeak; fencing, parrying; vacillation, shilly-shallying, cavilling, wavering, quibbling, quibble; temporizing, hesitation, stalling (for time), shuffling; Brit. humming and hawing; informal pussyfooting (around), waffle, waffling, flannel, weasel words; archaic paltering; rare tergiversation.
▷ANTONYMS directness.

era noun *the Napoleonic era*: **epoch**, age, period, time, aeon, span; generation; stage, point in history, date; times, days, years.

eradicate verb *make sure that the lice have all been eradicated*: **get rid of**, eliminate, do away with, remove, suppress; **exterminate**, destroy, annihilate, extirpate, obliterate, kill, wipe out, liquidate, decimate, finish off; abolish, stamp out, extinguish, quash, wipe off the face of the earth, wipe off the map; erase, efface, excise, expunge; root out, uproot, weed out; informal zap; rare deracinate.

eradication noun *the eradication of smallpox*: **elimination**, removal, suppression; **extermination**, destruction, annihilation, extirpation, obliteration, killing, liquidation, decimation, wiping out, extinction; abolition, extinguishing, quashing; erasure, effacement, excision, expunction, expunging, blotting out, rubbing out; rare deracination.

erasable adjective *erasable ink*: **removable**, eradicable, washable, deletable, non-permanent.
▷ANTONYMS permanent.

erase verb **1** *they erased his name from all street signs and monuments*: **delete**, rub out, wipe out/off; cross out, strike out, score out, blot out, blank out, scratch out, scrape off, cancel, put a line through; efface, expunge, excise, remove, obliterate, eliminate, remove all traces of; censor, blue-pencil, bowdlerize; technical dele.
2 *the old national differences in styles of play are being gradually erased by the globalization of football*: **destroy**, wipe out, obliterate, eradicate, abolish, stamp out, quash, do away with, get rid of, remove, dissolve.

erasure noun *the erasure of files from the hard disk*: **deletion**, rubbing out, wiping out/off; crossing out, striking out, scoring out, blotting out, blanking out, scratching out, cancelling, cancellation; effacement, expunction, expunging, excision, removal, obliteration, elimination; censorship, censoring, bowdlerization; rare erasement.

erect adjective **1** *she held her body erect*: **upright**, bolt upright, straight, vertical, perpendicular, plumb, standing up; Heraldry rampant.
▷ANTONYMS bent; flaccid.
2 *an erect penis*: **engorged**, enlarged, swollen, tumescent; hard, rigid, stiff, firm.
▷ANTONYMS limp.
3 *the hairs stood erect around his neck*: **bristling**, standing up (on end), upright.
▷ANTONYMS flat.
▸verb **1** *the bridge was erected as a temporary measure*: **build**, construct, put up; assemble, put together, fabricate, form, manufacture.
▷ANTONYMS demolish.
2 *it took three minutes to erect the inner tent*: **assemble**, put up, set up, set upright, fit together, put together, piece together; pitch, position, fix in position, place, locate.
▷ANTONYMS dismantle.
3 *someone had erected a red flag*: **put up**, raise, elevate, mount.
▷ANTONYMS lower.
4 *the party that erected the welfare state*: **establish**, form, set up, put in place, found, institute, initiate, formulate, devise, create, organize, frame.
▷ANTONYMS break up.

erection noun **1** *the erection of a house*: **construction**, building, putting up; assembly, putting together, fitting together, fabrication, forming, manufacture, production; raising, elevation.
▷ANTONYMS demolition.
2 *the cafe was a bleak concrete erection*: **building**, structure, edifice, construction, pile.
3 *men who cannot get an erection*: **phallus**, erect penis; **tumescence**, tumidity, turgescence, hardness, rigidity, stiffness, firmness; vulgar slang hard-on, stiffy, boner, ramrod; Brit. vulgar slang horn.

eremite noun **hermit**, recluse, solitary, ascetic, coenobite; historical anchorite, anchoress, stylite; rare solitudinarian.

ergo adverb Latin *I'm a writer, ergo I write*: **therefore**, consequently, so, as a result, as a consequence, hence, thus, accordingly, for that reason, this/that being so, this/that being the case, on this/that account; formal whence, wherefore, thence.

erode verb *the soil has been eroded by the rainwater | a world whose moral base has been eroded*: **wear away/down**, abrade, scrape away, grind down, crumble, dissolve, weather; eat (away at), gnaw (away at), chip away at, corrode, consume, devour; waste away, rot, decay; undermine, weaken, sap, disintegrate, deteriorate, destroy, spoil.

erosion noun *the erosion of the cliffs | the erosion of democratic freedoms*: **wearing away**, abrasion, scraping away, grinding down, crumbling, wear and tear, weathering, dissolving, dissolution; eating away, gnawing away, chipping away, corrosion, corroding, attrition; wasting away, rotting, decay; undermining, weakening, sapping, deterioration, disintegration, destruction, spoiling; rare detrition.

erotic adjective *erotic literature*: **sexually arousing**, sexually exciting, sexually stimulating; **titillating**, salacious, prurient, lubricious, suggestive; pornographic, sexually explicit, lewd, smutty, hard-core, soft-core, dirty, off colour, indecent, improper, filthy, vulgar, crude; libidinous, lustful, lascivious, lecherous, licentious; sexual, sexy, sensual, carnal, venereal, amatory; seductive, alluring, tantalizing, desirable, aphrodisiac; racy, risqué, ribald, naughty, bawdy, earthy, spicy, Rabelaisian; erogenous, erotogenic; informal blue, X-rated, steamy, raunchy, randy, horny; euphemistic adult; formal concupiscent; rare venereous, anacreontic.

err verb **1** *the Court of Appeal ruled that the judge had erred in not allowing new evidence*: **make a mistake**, **be wrong**, be in error, be mistaken, mistake, make a blunder, blunder, be incorrect, be inaccurate, misjudge, miscalculate, get things/something/it wrong, bark up the wrong tree, get the wrong end of the stick, be wide of the mark; informal slip up, screw up, blow it, foul up, goof, boob, fluff something, make a hash of something, put one's foot in it, make a boo-boo, make a bloomer, drop a brick; vulgar slang fuck something up, bugger something up.
▷ANTONYMS be right.
2 *she struck their fingers with a ruler when they erred*: **misbehave**, **do wrong**, go wrong, behave badly, misconduct oneself, be bad, be naughty, get up to mischief, get up to no good, act up, act badly, give someone trouble, cause someone trouble; sin, go astray, transgress, trespass, fall from grace, lapse, degenerate; clown about/around, fool about/around, act the clown, act the fool, act the goat, act foolishly, forget oneself; informal mess about/around; Brit. informal muck about/around, play up.

errand noun *he ran errands for local shopkeepers*: **task**, job, chore, assignment; collection, delivery, shopping; trip, run, journey; mission, expedition; operation, undertaking, commission, business; Scottish message.

errant adjective **1** *financial penalties were imposed on errant local authorities*: **offending**, guilty, culpable, misbehaving, delinquent, lawless, lawbreaking, criminal, transgressing, aberrant, deviant, erring, sinning; mischievous, badly behaved, troublesome, difficult, unmanageable, unruly, disobedient, uncontrollable, out of control.
▷ANTONYMS innocent; well behaved.
2 archaic *a knight errant*: **travelling**, wandering, itinerant, journeying, rambling, roaming, roving, drifting, floating, wayfaring, voyaging, touring; peripatetic, unsettled, rootless, restless, on the move, on the go, on the wing; nomadic, vagabond, vagrant, migrant, migratory, migrating, transient, displaced; globetrotting, jet-setting.
▷ANTONYMS sedentary.

erratic adjective *can you explain his swings of mood, his erratic behaviour?* **unpredictable**, inconsistent, changeable, variable, inconstant, uncertain, irregular, unstable, turbulent, unsteady, unsettled, unreliable, undependable, changing, ever-changing, volatile, varying, shifting, fluctuating, fluid, mutable, protean, fitful, wavering, full of ups and downs; mercurial, capricious, whimsical, fickle, flighty, giddy, impulsive, wayward, temperamental, highly strung, excitable, moody; informal blowing hot and cold; technical labile; rare fluctuant, changeful.
▷ANTONYMS predictable; consistent.

erring adjective *the court case resulted in a heavy fine for the erring skipper*: **offending**, guilty, culpable, misbehaving, delinquent, lawless, lawbreaking, criminal, transgressing, aberrant, deviant, errant, sinning.
▷ANTONYMS innocent, well behaved.

erroneous adjective *the report was based on an erroneous assumption*: **wrong**, incorrect, mistaken, in error, inaccurate, not accurate, inexact, not exact, imprecise, invalid, untrue, false, fallacious, wide of the mark, off target; misleading, illogical, unsound, specious, unfounded, without foundation, faulty, flawed, spurious; informal off beam, bogus, phoney, out, way out, full of holes, dicey, iffy; Brit. informal dodgy; archaic abroad.
▷ANTONYMS right; correct.

error noun *the common error of calling schizophrenia a split personality*: **mistake**, fallacy, misconception, delusion; inaccuracy, miscalculation, misreckoning; blunder, fault, flaw, oversight; misprint, literal, erratum, misinterpretation, misreading; informal slip-up, bloomer, boob, boo-boo, howler, boner.
□ **in error** *£86 million of tax was collected in error*: **wrongly**, by mistake, mistakenly, incorrectly, inappropriately, misguidedly; **accidentally**, by accident, inadvertently, unintentionally, unwittingly, unknowingly, unconsciously, by chance.
▷ANTONYMS correctly; intentionally.

ersatz adjective *ersatz coffee*: **artificial**, substitute, imitation, synthetic, fake, false, faux, mock, simulated; pseudo, sham, bogus, spurious, counterfeit, forged, pretended, so-called, plastic; manufactured, man-made, unnatural, fabricated; replica, reproduction, facsimile; **inferior**, low-quality, poor-quality, low-grade, shoddy, substandard, unsatisfactory, adulterated; informal phoney.
▷ANTONYMS genuine.

erstwhile adjective *written in memory of the composer's erstwhile teacher*: **former**, old, past, one-time, sometime, ex-, late, then; previous, prior, foregoing; formal quondam; archaic whilom.
▷ANTONYMS present; future.

erudite adjective *he was so erudite that only men who were his equals in scholarship could understand him | erudite editions of minor classical writers*: **learned**, scholarly, well educated, knowledgeable, well read, widely read, well versed, well informed, lettered, cultured, cultivated, civilized, intellectual; intelligent, clever, academic, literary, bookish, highbrow, studious, sage, wise, sagacious, discerning, donnish, cerebral,

enlightened, illuminated, sophisticated, pedantic; esoteric, obscure, recondite; informal brainy; rare sapient.
▷ANTONYMS ignorant; ill-educated.

erudition noun *a man of immense talent and massive erudition*: **learning**, scholarship, knowledge, education, culture, intellect, academic attainment, attainments, acquirements, enlightenment, illumination, edification, book learning, insight, information, understanding, sageness, wisdom, sophistication, training; letters.
▷ANTONYMS ignorance.

erupt verb **1** *the volcano erupted*: **emit lava**, belch lava, become active, flare up, eject/vent material, explode.
▷ANTONYMS lie dormant.
2 *lava was erupted close to the summit*: **emit**, discharge, eject, expel, spew out, belch (out), pour (out), disgorge, give off/out; gush, spout, spurt, stream, flow, issue.
3 *fighting erupted in the streets*: **break out**, flare up, blow up, boil over, start suddenly; ensue, arise, happen.
▷ANTONYMS die down.
4 *a boil had erupted on her temple*: **appear**, break out, flare up, come to a head, burst forth, make an appearance, pop up, emerge, become visible.
▷ANTONYMS heal.

e

eruption noun **1** *a volcanic eruption*: **discharge**, venting, ejection, emission, explosion.
2 *a sudden eruption of street violence*: **outbreak**, flare-up, upsurge, outburst, epidemic, breakout, sudden appearance, start, rash, wave, spate, flood, explosion, burst, blaze, flurry; rare recrudescence, ebullition, boutade.
3 *a skin eruption*: **rash**, outbreak, inflammation.

escalate verb **1** *in three years' time prices will have escalated*: **increase rapidly**, soar, rocket, shoot up, mount, surge, spiral, grow rapidly, rise rapidly, climb, go up; informal be jacked up, go through the ceiling, go through the roof, skyrocket, balloon.
▷ANTONYMS plunge.
2 *the dispute escalated into a sit-in*: **grow**, develop, mushroom, increase, be increased, be stepped up, build up, heighten, strengthen, intensify, accelerate, be extended, be enlarged, be magnified, be amplified.
▷ANTONYMS shrink.

escalation noun **1** *an escalation in oil prices*: **rapid increase**, rise, hike, advance, growth, leap, upsurge, upturn, upswing, climb, jump, spiralling.
▷ANTONYMS plunge.
2 *a drastic escalation of the conflict*: **intensification**, aggravation, exacerbation, compounding, increase, enlargement, magnification, mushrooming, amplification, augmentation; expansion, stepping-up, build-up, buildout, heightening, widening, worsening; deterioration.
▷ANTONYMS relaxation.

escapade noun *he is a paragliding fanatic famous for his flying escapades*: **exploit**, stunt, caper, skylarking, mischief, romp, antic(s), fling, spree, prank, jape, game, trick; adventure, venture, mission; deed, feat, trial, experience, incident, occurrence, event, happening, episode, affair; informal lark, scrape, fooling around, shenanigans; rare frolic.

escape verb **1** *he had escaped from prison*: **get away**, get out, run away, run off, break out, break free, get free, break loose, make a break for it, bolt, clear out, flee, fly, take flight, make off, take off, decamp, abscond, take to one's heels, make a/one's escape, make good one's escape, make a/one's getaway, beat a (hasty) retreat, show a clean pair of heels, run for it, make a run for it; disappear, vanish, slip away, steal away, sneak away; get out of someone's clutches; informal bust, do a bunk, do a moonlight flit, cut and run, skedaddle, skip, head for the hills, do a disappearing/vanishing act, fly the coop, take French leave, scarper, vamoose, hightail it, leg it; Brit. informal do a runner, hook it; N. Amer. informal take a powder, go on the lam.
▷ANTONYMS be captured; be imprisoned.
2 *he escaped his pursuers*: **get away from**, escape from, elude, avoid, dodge, leave behind, shake off, fend off, keep at arm's length, keep out of someone's way, steer clear of, give someone a wide berth; informal give someone the slip; archaic bilk.
▷ANTONYMS be caught by.
3 *all three drivers escaped injury | I came in here to escape the washing-up*: **avoid**, evade, dodge, elude, miss, cheat, trick, sidestep, circumvent, skirt, keep out of the way of, bypass, shun, steer clear of, shirk; informal duck.
▷ANTONYMS suffer.
4 *a lethal gas escaped from a pesticide factory*: **leak (out)**, spill (out), seep (out), ooze (out), exude, discharge, emanate, issue, flow (out), pour (out), gush (out), drip, drain, bleed; stream, spurt, spout, squirt, spew, jet.
▶noun **1** *he had been at large since his escape from prison*: **getaway**, breakout, bolt for freedom, running away, flight, bolting, absconding, decamping, fleeing, flit; disappearance, vanishing act; informal, dated springing.
▷ANTONYMS capture; imprisonment.
2 *a narrow escape from death*: **avoidance of**, evasion of, dodging of, eluding of, circumvention of; informal ducking of; rare elusion of.
3 *a gas escape*: **leak**, leakage, spill, seepage, drip, dribble, discharge, emanation, issue, flow, outflow, outpouring, gush; stream, spurt, spout, squirt, jet; technical efflux.
4 *boarding school seemed to me an escape from boredom*: **distraction**, diversion, interruption.

escapee noun **runaway**, escaper, jailbreaker, fugitive, absconder, truant, deserter, defector; refugee, displaced person, DP, asylum seeker; archaic runagate.

escapism noun *musicals always do well in a recession because people want escapism*: **fantasy**, fantasizing, dreaming, daydreaming, daydreams, reverie, romance, illusion(s), fancy, imagination, flight(s) of fancy, pipe dreams, castles in the air, castles in Spain, wishful thinking, wool-gathering; informal pie in the sky.
▷ANTONYMS realism.

eschew verb *he firmly eschewed political involvement*: **abstain from**, refrain from, give up, forgo, forswear, shun, renounce, swear off, abjure, steer clear of, have nothing to do with, give a wide berth to, fight shy of, relinquish, reject, dispense with, disavow, abandon, deny, gainsay, disclaim, repudiate, renege on, spurn, abnegate, abdicate, wash one's hands of, drop; informal kick, jack in, pack in; Law disaffirm; archaic forsake.
▷ANTONYMS indulge in.

escort noun (stress on the first syllable) **1** *they were given a police escort*: **guard**, bodyguard, protector, safeguard, defender, minder, custodian; attendant, guide, chaperone, retainer, aide, assistant, personal assistant, right-hand man, right-hand woman, lady in waiting, 'aunt', duenna, equerry, squire; entourage, retinue, suite, train, cortège, attendant company, caravan; protection, defence, convoy.
2 *she didn't like going to clubs by herself and Graham was a great escort*: **companion**, partner, beau, attendant; informal date.
3 *we offer a wide selection of young, good-looking, fun escorts*: **paid companion**, hostess; male escort, gigolo; in Japan geisha (girl); in China sing-song girl; archaic courtesan.
▶verb (stress on the second syllable) **1** *Father Barnes was escorted home by police officers*: **conduct**, accompany, guide, convoy, lead, usher, shepherd, take, direct, steer; guard, protect, safeguard, defend.
2 *he escorted her in to dinner*: **accompany**, partner, take, bring, come with, go with, take out, go out with.

esoteric adjective *the question is dominated by esoteric debate*: **abstruse**, obscure, arcane, recherché, rarefied, recondite, abstract, difficult, hard, puzzling, perplexing, enigmatic, inscrutable, cryptic, Delphic; complex, complicated, involved, over/above one's head, incomprehensible, opaque, unfathomable, impenetrable, mysterious, occult, little known, hidden, secret, private, mystic, magical, cabbalistic; rare involuted.
▷ANTONYMS simple; familiar.

especial adjective **1** *especial care is required*: **exceptional**, particular, special, extra special, extraordinary, outstanding, superior, unusual, marked, singular, signal; out of the ordinary, uncommon, rare, unwonted, notable, noteworthy, surprising, remarkable, striking, unique.
▷ANTONYMS standard.
2 *her own especial brand of charm*: **distinctive**, individual, special, particular, distinct, peculiar, personal, own, unique, singular, exclusive, specific, private.
▷ANTONYMS common, general.

especially adverb **1** *work continued to pour in, especially from South Africa*: **mainly**, mostly, chiefly, principally, for the most part, in the main, on the whole, largely, by and large, to a large extent, to a great degree, predominantly, above all, first and foremost, basically, substantially, overall, in general, particularly, in particular, primarily, generally, usually, typically, commonly, as a rule.
2 *a committee formed especially for the purpose*: **expressly**, specially, specifically, exclusively, just, particularly, uniquely, precisely, explicitly, purposefully, on purpose; with someone/something in mind.
3 *especially talented*: **exceptionally**, particularly, specially, very, extremely, singularly, peculiarly, distinctly, unusually, extraordinarily, extra, uncommonly, uniquely, remarkably, strikingly, outstandingly, amazingly, incredibly, awfully, terribly, really, unwontedly, notably, markedly, decidedly, surprisingly, conspicuously, signally; N. English powerful, right; informal seriously, majorly, mucho; Brit. informal jolly, dead, well; informal, dated devilish, frightfully.

espionage noun *the shadowy world of espionage*: **spying**, undercover work, cloak-and-dagger activities, surveillance, reconnaissance, intelligence, eavesdropping, infiltration, counter-espionage, counter-intelligence; in Japan ninjutsu; informal bugging, wiretapping, recon.

espousal noun *they began to retreat from their espousal of populist causes*: **adoption**, embracing, taking up, taking to, taking to one's heart, enthusiastic/wholehearted reception, acceptance, welcome; **support**, backing, championship, help, assistance, aid, siding with, favouring, preferring, abetting, aiding and abetting, encouragement; defence; sponsorship, vouching for, promotion, furtherance, endorsement, advocacy, sanctioning, approval.
▷ANTONYMS rejection; opposition.

espouse verb *the government espoused the concept of sustainable economic development*: **adopt**, embrace, take up, take to, take to one's heart,

receive enthusiastically/wholeheartedly, accept, welcome; **support**, back, champion, give help to, help, assist, aid, be on the side of, side with, be in favour of, favour, prefer, abet, aid and abet, encourage; vote for, ally oneself with, stand behind, fall in with, stand up for, defend, take someone's part, take up the cudgels for; sponsor, vouch for, promote, further, endorse, advocate, sanction, approve of, give one's blessing to, smile on; informal stick up for, throw one's weight behind.
▷ANTONYMS reject; oppose.

espy verb literary *he espied a niche up in the rocks*. See **discern**.

essay noun (stress on the first syllable) **1** *he wrote an essay on overpopulation*: **article**, piece of writing, composition, study, paper, dissertation, assignment, thesis, discourse, treatise, text, tract, disquisition, monograph; leader, commentary, critique, criticism, exposition, appraisal, assessment, discussion; N. Amer. theme; informal piece.
2 formal *the device was Alexander Graham Bell's first essay in telecommunications*: **attempt**, effort, endeavour, try, venture, trial, experiment, undertaking; informal crack, go, shot, stab, bash, whack.
▸ **verb** (stress on the second syllable) formal *many essayed to travel that way*: **attempt**, make an attempt at, try, strive, aim, venture, endeavour, seek, set out, do one's best, do all one can, do one's utmost, make an effort, make every effort, spare no effort, give one's all, take it on oneself; have a go at, undertake, embark on, try one's hand at, try out, take on; informal give it a whirl, give it one's best shot, go all out, pull out all the stops, bend over backwards, knock oneself out, bust a gut, break one's neck, move heaven and earth, have a crack at, have a shot at, have a stab at.

essence noun **1** *uncertainty is part of the very essence of economic activity*: **quintessence**, soul, spirit, ethos, nature, life, lifeblood, core, heart, centre, crux, nub, nucleus, kernel, marrow, meat, pith, gist, substance, principle, central part, fundamental quality, basic quality, essential part, intrinsic nature, sum and substance, reality, actuality; Philosophy quiddity, esse; informal nitty-gritty.
2 *essence of ginger*: **extract**, concentrate, concentration, quintessence, distillate, elixir, abstraction, decoction, juice, tincture, solution, suspension, dilution; scent, perfume.
□ **in essence** *for them society was in essence a collection of discrete individuals*: **basically**, fundamentally, elementally, essentially, at bottom, at heart, primarily, principally, chiefly, firstly, predominantly, substantially, in substance, materially; above all, first of all, most of all, first and foremost; effectively, in effect, virtually, to all intents and purposes, intrinsically, inherently; French au fond; informal at the end of the day, when all is said and done, when you get right down to it.
□ **of the essence** *approval can take months when speed is not of the essence*: **vital**, essential, indispensable, crucial, key, necessary, needed, required, called for, requisite, important, all-important, vitally important, of the utmost importance, of great consequence, critical, life-and-death, imperative, mandatory, compulsory, obligatory, urgent, pressing, burning, compelling, acute, paramount, pre-eminent, high-priority, significant, consequential.
▷ANTONYMS inessential.

essential adjective **1** *it is essential to remove all the old plaster*: **crucial**, necessary, key, vital, indispensable, needed, required, called for, requisite, important, all-important, vitally important, of the utmost importance, of great consequence, of the essence, critical, life-and-death, imperative, mandatory, compulsory, obligatory, compelling, urgent, pressing, burning, acute, paramount, pre-eminent, high-priority, significant, consequential.
▷ANTONYMS inessential, unimportant, optional.
2 *the essential simplicity of his style*: **basic**, inherent, fundamental, quintessential, intrinsic, underlying, characteristic, innate, rudimentary, primary, principal, cardinal, chief, elementary, elemental; central, pivotal, critical, key, focal, salient, staple, vital, necessary, indispensable, foundational, ingrained.
▷ANTONYMS secondary.
3 *he is the essential English gentleman*: **ideal**, absolute, complete, perfect, quintessential.
▸ **noun 1** *the gift of the gab was an essential for an up-and-coming broadcaster*: **necessity**, necessary/essential item, prerequisite, requisite, requirement, need; condition, precondition, specification, stipulation; qualification; Latin desideratum, sine qua non; informal must.
▷ANTONYMS inessential.
2 (**essentials**) *they were taught the essentials of the job in three days*: **fundamentals**, basics, rudiments, principles, first principles, foundations, preliminaries, groundwork; essence, basis, core, kernel, nub, marrow, meat, crux, bedrock; facts, hard facts, practicalities, realities; Latin sine qua non; informal nitty-gritty, brass tacks, nuts and bolts, ABC.
▷ANTONYMS minutiae.

> *Choose the right word* **essential, necessary, requisite, indispensable**
>
> See **necessary**.

> *Choose the right word* **essential, inherent, intrinsic, innate**
>
> See **inherent**.

establish verb **1** *the company is hoping to establish an office in Moscow*: **set up**, start, begin, get going, put in place, initiate, institute, form, found, create, bring into being, inaugurate, organize, lay the foundations of, build, construct, install, plant.
▷ANTONYMS disband; demolish.
2 *there was sufficient evidence to establish his guilt*: **prove**, demonstrate, show, show to be true, show beyond doubt, indicate, signify, signal, display, exhibit, manifest, denote, attest to, evidence, determine, validate, confirm, verify, certify, ratify, corroborate, substantiate, evince, bespeak, constitute evidence of, constitute proof of.
▷ANTONYMS disprove.

established adjective **1** *this approach flies in the face of established practice*: **accepted**, traditional, orthodox, habitual, confirmed, entrenched, set, fixed, official, settled, dyed-in-the-wool, inveterate; **usual**, customary, common, normal, general, prevailing, accustomed, familiar, wonted, popular, expected, routine, regular, typical, conventional, mainstream, standard, stock.
▷ANTONYMS unfamiliar.
2 *he is an established composer of international repute*: **well known**, recognized, acclaimed, esteemed, acknowledged; respected, respectable, famous, prominent, noted, renowned.
▷ANTONYMS unknown.

establishment noun **1** *the establishment of a democratic constitution*: **setting up**, start, getting going, initiation, institution, formation, founding, foundation, inception, creation, inauguration, organization, building, construction, installation.
▷ANTONYMS disbandment; demolition.
2 *her house was turned into a dressmaking establishment*: **business**, place of business, premises, firm, company, concern, enterprise, venture, organization, operation, undertaking, industry; factory, plant, house, shop, store, emporium, office, bureau, agency, franchise, practice, partnership, consortium, cooperative, corporation, conglomerate, group, combine, syndicate; informal outfit, set-up.
3 *graduates of higher educational establishments*: **institution**, place, premises, foundation, institute.
4 (**the Establishment**) *an irreverent comedy series that dared to poke fun at the Establishment*: **the powers that be**, the authorities, the system, the ruling class, the regime, bureaucracy, officialdom; the status quo, the prevailing political/social order; informal Big Brother; archaic the regimen.

estate noun **1** *she had a house on the Balmoral estate*: **property**, grounds, garden(s), park, parkland, land(s), piece of land, tract, landholding, manor, domain, territory; archaic demesne.
2 *a housing estate*: **area**, site, development, complex, piece of land, land, region, tract.
3 *a large coffee estate*: **plantation**, farm, holding; forest, vineyard; N. Amer. ranch; in Spanish-speaking countries hacienda; in the W. Indies pen; in E. Africa shamba; in the Indian subcontinent tope.
4 *he left an estate worth £610,000*: **assets**, capital, wealth, riches, holdings, fortune, property, worth, resources, effects, possessions, belongings, things, goods, worldly goods, stuff, chattels, valuables; legacy, bequest; Law personalty, goods and chattels; informal gear; S. African informal trek.
5 archaic *the estate of matrimony*: **state**, condition, situation, position, circumstance, lot, fate.

estate agent noun **property agent**; Brit. house agent; N. Amer. realtor, real estate agent.

estate car noun N. Amer. station wagon; Brit. informal estate; N. Amer. informal wagon; Brit. dated shooting brake, traveller.
▷ANTONYMS saloon; hatchback.

esteem noun *she was held in high esteem by colleagues*: **respect**, **admiration**, (high) regard, (high/good) opinion, estimation, acclaim, approbation, approval, appreciation, favour, popularity, recognition, veneration, awe, reverence, deference, honour, praise, adulation, extolment, homage; rare laudation.
▷ANTONYMS disrespect.
▸ **verb 1** *contemporary Japanese ceramics are highly esteemed*: **respect**, **admire**, value, regard, hold in (high) regard, think (highly) of, acclaim, approve of, appreciate, like, prize, treasure, favour, recognize, venerate, hold in awe, look up to, revere, reverence, honour, praise, adulate, extol, pay homage to.
▷ANTONYMS disparage.
2 formal *I would esteem it a favour if you could speak to him*: **consider**, regard as, deem, hold to be, think, think of as, reckon, count, account, believe, judge, adjudge, rate, class as, gauge, look on as, view as, see as, interpret as.

estimate verb **1** *the first thing to do is to estimate the cost*: **roughly calculate**, approximate, make an estimate of, guess, evaluate, judge, gauge, reckon, rate, appraise, form an opinion of, form an impression of, get the

measure of, determine, weigh up; informal size up, guesstimate.
2 *we* ***estimate*** *the carpet* ***to be*** *worth about £50,000*: **consider**, believe, guess, reckon, deem, hold, judge, adjudge, surmise, rate, gauge, take, suppose; regard as being, view as being, see as being, class as being, think of as being, look on as being; be of the opinion, conjecture; formal opine.
▶ **noun 1** *an estimate of the repair cost*: **rough calculation**, approximation, estimation, educated/informed guess, rough guess; approximate price/cost/value, estimated price/cost/value; costing, quotation, pricing, valuation, evaluation, assessment, appraisal; informal guesstimate.
2 *his estimate of Paul's integrity dropped a few notches*: **evaluation**, estimation, judgement, gauging, rating, appraisal, opinion, view, analysis.

estimation noun **1** *the Treasury first makes an estimation of economic growth*: **estimate**, rough calculation, approximation, educated/informed guess, rough guess, evaluation, assessment, appraisal; informal guesstimate.
2 *his hard bargaining raised him even higher in Chapman's estimation*: **assessment**, evaluation, judgement, gauging, rating, appraisal, esteem, opinion, view, analysis.

e

estrange verb *she realized that she had estranged her favourite uncle*: **alienate**, antagonize, disaffect, make hostile/unfriendly, destroy the affections of, turn away, drive away, distance, put at a distance; sever connections between, set against, set at variance, set at odds with, make hostile to, drive a wedge between, cause antagonism between, sow dissension between.
▷ANTONYMS attract, unite.

estrangement noun *there had been a definite estrangement between her and her daughter-in-law*: **alienation**, turning away, antagonism, antipathy, disaffection, hostility, unfriendliness, embitteredness, isolation, variance, difference; parting, separation, division, divorce, disunity, distance, break-up, split, breach, severance, schism.
▷ANTONYMS unity; reconciliation.

estuary noun **(river) mouth**, firth; delta; archaic embouchure, debouchure, debouchment, discharge, disemboguement; Scottish archaic beal, inver, water mouth.

et cetera, etcetera adverb *you need wellingtons, raincoats, umbrella, et cetera*: **and so on**, and so forth, and so on and so forth, and the rest, and/or the like, and/or suchlike, and/or more of the same, and/or similar things, et cetera et cetera, and others, among others, et al., etc.; informal and what have you, and whatnot.

etch verb **1** *the metal is etched with a dilute acid*: **corrode**, bite into, eat into/away, burn into.
2 *a Pictish stone etched with mysterious designs*: **engrave**, carve, inscribe, cut (in), incise, chisel, chase, score, notch, imprint, impress, stamp, print, mark.

etching noun *the gallery contains drawings, etchings, and watercolours*: **engraving**, print, impression, block, plate, dry point, cut, woodcut, linocut, vignette.

eternal adjective **1** *the hope of eternal happiness*: **everlasting**, never-ending, endless, without end, perpetual, undying, immortal, deathless, indestructible, imperishable, immutable, abiding, permanent, enduring, infinite, boundless, timeless; rare sempiternal, perdurable.
▷ANTONYMS transient.
2 *the price of freedom is eternal vigilance*: **constant**, continual, continuous, perpetual, persistent, sustained, unremitting, relentless, unrelenting, unrelieved, uninterrupted, unbroken, unabating, interminable, never-ending, non-stop, round-the-clock, incessant, endless, ceaseless.
▷ANTONYMS intermittent.

eternally adverb **1** *I shall be eternally grateful*: **forever**, permanently, for always, for good, for good and all, perpetually, (for) evermore, for ever and ever, for all (future) time, until/to the end of time, world without end, endlessly, timelessly, for eternity, in perpetuity, everlastingly, enduringly; Scottish aye; N. Amer. forevermore; informal for keeps, until hell freezes over, until doomsday, until the cows come home; archaic for aye; rare immortally, deathlessly, imperishably, abidingly, sempiternally, perdurably.
▷ANTONYMS temporarily.
2 *he was eternally squabbling with the referee*: **constantly**, continually, continuously, always, all the time, the entire time, persistently, repeatedly, regularly; round-the-clock, without a break, night and day, day and night, {morning, noon, and night}; endlessly, non-stop, incessantly, unceasingly, ceaselessly, perpetually, perennially, forever; interminably, unremittingly, relentlessly, unrelentingly; informal 24-7.
▷ANTONYMS never.

eternity noun **1** *his reply will ring in my ears for eternity*: **ever**, all time, perpetuity.
2 *eventually we shall all be in eternity*: **the afterlife**, everlasting life, life after death, the life to come, the life hereafter, the hereafter, the world hereafter, the afterworld, the next world, the beyond; heaven, paradise, nirvana, immortality.
▷ANTONYMS limbo; hell.
3 informal *I waited* ***an eternity*** *for a bus*: **a long time**, an age, ages (and ages), a time, a lifetime; hours, days, months, years, aeons, hours/days/months on end, a month of Sundays, the duration; (seemingly) forever; Brit. informal yonks, donkey's years.
▷ANTONYMS instant.

ethereal adjective **1** *melodic phrases of ethereal beauty*: **delicate**, exquisite, dainty, elegant, graceful, beautiful, lovely; fragile, airy, gossamer, gossamery, light, fine, diaphanous, thin, tenuous, subtle, insubstantial, shadowy.
▷ANTONYMS tangible, substantial.
2 *theologians may discuss abstract and ethereal ideas*: **celestial**, heavenly, spiritual, unearthly, other-worldly, paradisical, Elysian, sublime, divine, holy; rare empyrean, superlunary.
▷ANTONYMS earthly.

ethical adjective **1** *there is an ethical dilemma to be faced*: **moral**; social, behavioural; having to do with right and wrong.
2 *an ethical investment policy*: **morally correct**, right-minded, right-thinking, principled, irreproachable, unimpeachable, blameless, guiltless; righteous, upright, upstanding, high-minded, virtuous, good, moral; exemplary, clean, law-abiding, lawful; just, honest, honourable, unbribable, incorruptible; scrupulous, reputable, decent, respectable, noble, lofty, elevated, worthy, trustworthy, meritorious, praiseworthy, commendable, admirable, laudable; pure, pure as the driven snow, whiter than white, sinless, saintly, saintlike, godly, angelic; Christianity immaculate, impeccable; informal squeaky clean.
▷ANTONYMS unethical.

ethics plural noun *the ethics of journalism*: **moral code**, morals, morality, moral stand, moral principles, moral values, rights and wrongs, principles, ideals, creed, credo, ethos, rules of conduct, standards (of behaviour), virtues, dictates of conscience.

ethnic adjective *a wide spectrum of ethnic groups*: **racial**, race-related, ethnological, genetic, inherited; cultural, national, tribal, ancestral, traditional, folk; rare autochthonous.

ethos noun *the governing body has responsibility for the ethos of the school*: **spirit**, character, atmosphere, climate, prevailing tendency, mood, feeling, temper, tenor, flavour, essence, quintessence; **animating principle**, dominating characteristic, motivating force, disposition, rationale, code, morality, moral code, attitudes, beliefs, principles, standards, ethics.

etiquette noun *the club's brochure includes advice on etiquette*: **protocol**, polite behaviour, good manners, manners, acceptable behaviour, accepted behaviour, proper behaviour, code of behaviour, rules of conduct/behaviour, decorum, form, good form; courtesy, politeness, civility, propriety, formalities, niceties, punctilios; custom, customary behaviour, convention, conformity, conventionality; French politesse; informal the thing to do.

etymology noun **derivation**, word history, development, origin, source.

eulogize verb *the police eulogized the positive effect of speed cameras*: **praise enthusiastically**, go into raptures about/over, wax lyrical about, sing the praises of, praise to the skies, heap praise on, rhapsodize about/over, rave about/over, enthuse about/over, gush about/over, throw bouquets at, express delight over, acclaim, extol; informal go wild about, be mad about, go on about; N. Amer. informal ballyhoo; black English big someone/something up; dated cry someone/something up; rare laud, panegyrize.
▷ANTONYMS criticize.

eulogy noun *his lifelong collaborator delivered a graveside eulogy*: **accolade**, speech of praise, panegyric, paean, encomium, tribute, testimonial, compliment, commendation; praise, acclaim, acclamation, raving, homage, plaudits, bouquets; rare extolment, laudation, eulogium.
▷ANTONYMS attack.

euphemism noun *'professional foul' is just a euphemism for cheating*: **polite term**, substitute, mild alternative, indirect term, understatement, underplaying, softening, politeness, genteelism, coy term.
▷ANTONYMS dysphemism, calling a spade a spade.

euphemistic adjective *euphemistic expressions for sacking someone, such as 'letting them go'*: **polite**, substitute, mild, understated, softened, indirect, neutral, evasive, diplomatic, coded, newspeak, vague, inoffensive, genteel.
▷ANTONYMS dysphemistic.

euphonious adjective *the great woodrush's euphonious scientific name, Luzula sylvatica*: **pleasant-sounding**, sweet-sounding, mellow, mellifluous, dulcet, sweet, honeyed, lyrical, silvery, silver-toned, golden, bell-like, rhythmical, lilting, pleasant, agreeable, soothing; harmonious, melodious, melodic, tuneful, musical, symphonious; informal easy on the ear; rare mellifluent, canorous.
▷ANTONYMS cacophonous.

euphoria noun *they were swept up in the euphoria of victory*: **elation**, happiness, joy, joyousness, delight, glee, excitement, exhilaration, animation, jubilation, exultation; ecstasy, bliss, rapture, rhapsody, rhapsodies, intoxication, transport(s), cloud nine, heaven, paradise, seventh heaven; informal the top of the world.
▷ANTONYMS misery; depression.

euphoric adjective *the liberators received a euphoric welcome*: **elated**, happy, joyful, joyous, delighted, gleeful, excited, exhilarated, animated,

jubilant, exultant, ecstatic, blissful, enraptured, rapturous, rhapsodic, in rhapsodies, intoxicated, transported, on cloud nine, in heaven, in paradise, in seventh heaven; informal on top of the world, over the moon, on a high.
▷ANTONYMS miserable.

euthanasia noun **mercy killing**, assisted suicide, physician-assisted suicide; merciful release, happy release; rare quietus.

evacuate verb **1** *200 residents were evacuated while an unexploded bomb was made safe*: **remove**, clear, move out, shift, take away, turn out, expel, evict.
2 *people evacuated the bombed town*: **leave**, vacate, abandon, desert, move out of, get out of, exit from, quit, withdraw from, go away from, be gone from, retreat from, retire from, decamp from, disappear from, take oneself off from, flee, depart from, escape from, pull out of; archaic forsake.
▷ANTONYMS return to.
3 *police cordoned off and evacuated the area*: **clear**, ask/force people to leave, make people leave, make people get out, empty, depopulate; rare unpeople.
4 *patients had difficulty evacuating their bowels*: **empty (out)**, void, open, move, purge, drain; defecate.
5 *he suddenly doubled over to evacuate the contents of his stomach*: **expel**, eject, discharge, excrete, pass, eliminate, void, empty (out), drain; rare egest.
▷ANTONYMS retain.

evacuation noun **1** *the evacuation of civilians*: **removal**, clearance, shifting, expulsion, eviction, deportation.
2 *the evacuation of military bases*: **clearance**, emptying, depopulation; abandonment, quitting, vacation, desertion, leaving, forsaking; departure from, withdrawal from, retreat from, pull-out from, disappearance from, exodus from, flight from; rare unpeopling.
3 *terror and stress can cause involuntary evacuation of the bowels*: **emptying (out)**, voidance, voiding, opening, purging, drainage; (bowel) movement, defecation, urination, vomiting.
4 *the evacuation of waste products from the body*: **expulsion**, ejection, discharge, excretion, passing, elimination, voidance, voiding, emptying (out), purging, emptying, draining; rare egestion.
▷ANTONYMS retention.
5 *dysenteric evacuations frequently contain blood*: **bowel movement/motion**, stools, excrement, excreta, faeces, bodily waste, droppings, dung; urine, vomit; rare feculence, egesta.

evade verb **1** *they split up to evade the border guards*: **elude**, avoid, dodge, escape (from), stay away from, steer clear of, run away from, break away from, lose, leave behind, shake, shake off, keep at arm's length, keep out of someone's way, give someone a wide berth, sidestep, keep one's distance from; deceive, trick, cheat; N. Amer. end-run; informal ditch, give someone the slip; archaic bilk.
▷ANTONYMS confront; run into.
2 *he evaded the question*: **avoid**, not give a straight answer to, dodge, sidestep, bypass, hedge, fence, fend off, parry, skirt round, fudge, quibble about, be equivocal about, be evasive about; get out of, find a way round; not pay; informal duck, cop out of.
▷ANTONYMS face.

evaluate verb *it is important to evaluate the results of surgery*: **assess**, assess the worth of, put a value/price on; judge, gauge, rate, estimate, appraise, form an opinion of, check something out, form an impression of, make up one's mind about, get the measure of, weigh up, analyse; informal size up.

evaluation noun *proper evaluation of results is crucial*: **assessment**, appraisal, judgement, gauging, rating, estimation, ranking, weighing up, summing up, consideration, assay, analysis, opinion; informal sizing up.

evanescent adjective **1** *they were operating on an evanescent budget*: **vanishing**, fading, evaporating, melting away, disappearing, diminishing, dwindling, shrinking, fugitive; rare fugacious.
▷ANTONYMS unlimited.
2 *this has only an evanescent effect on the rate of inflation*: **ephemeral**, fleeting, short-lived, short-term, passing, transitory, transient, fugitive, momentary, temporary, brief, here today and gone tomorrow; rare fugacious.
▷ANTONYMS permanent.

evangelical adjective **1** *evangelical Christianity*: **scriptural**, biblical, Bible-believing, fundamentalist, orthodox.
2 *an evangelical preacher*: **evangelistic**, evangelizing, missionary, crusading, propagandist, propagandizing, converting, proselytizing, televangelical; informal Bible-bashing, Bible-thumping, Bible-punching.

evangelist noun *people flocked to hear evangelists preach*: **preacher**, missionary, gospeller, proselytizer, converter, crusader, propagandist, campaigner, televangelist.

evangelistic adjective *the evangelistic work of Billy Graham*: **missionary**, preaching, evangelical, evangelizing, revivalist, crusading, propagandist, campaigning, converting, proselytizing, televangelical.

evangelize verb *some small groups have been evangelized by Protestant missionaries*: **convert**, proselytize, bring to God/Christ/Jesus, bring into the fold, redeem, save, make someone change their beliefs/mind, make someone see the light, spread the gospel/faith/word (to), preach (to), seek/make converts (among), act as a missionary; crusade, campaign; win over, recruit; N. Amer. proselyte.

evaporate verb **1** *most of the water soon evaporated*: **vaporize**, become vapour, volatilize.
▷ANTONYMS condense.
2 *a stream of hot air is used to evaporate the water*: **dry up**, vaporize.
▷ANTONYMS condense.
3 *rock salt is mined, then washed and evaporated before being left to crystallize*: **dry out**, remove moisture from, dehydrate, desiccate, dehumidify.
▷ANTONYMS wet.
4 *the feeling has evaporated*: **end**, come to an end, cease to exist/be, pass away, pass, die out, be no more, fizzle out, peter out, wear off; vanish, fade, disappear, melt away, dissolve, disperse; rare evanesce.
▷ANTONYMS materialize.

evasion noun **1** *her quick-witted evasion of an assassination attempt*: **avoidance**, dodging, eluding, elusion, sidestepping, bypassing, circumvention, shunning, shirking; getting out of, finding a way round; informal ducking, the go-by; archaic bilking.
▷ANTONYMS confrontation.
2 *she grew tired of all the evasion*: **prevarication**, evasiveness, beating about the bush, hedging, fencing, shilly-shallying, shuffling, dodging the issue, dodging, sidestepping the issue, sidestepping, pussyfooting, equivocation, vagueness, quibbling, cavilling, temporization, stalling, stalling for time; Brit. humming and hawing; informal ducking, ducking the issue; rare tergiversation.
▷ANTONYMS directness.

evasive adjective **1** *they picked the missile up on the radar and had to take evasive action*: **avoiding**, dodging, escaping, eluding, sidestepping.
▷ANTONYMS direct.
2 *she was undeterred by evasive replies*: **prevaricating**, elusive, ambiguous, equivocal, equivocating, indefinite, non-committal, vague, indeterminate, imprecise, inexact, indistinct, inexplicit; cryptic, enigmatic, obscure, unclear, puzzling, perplexing, gnomic, Delphic; roundabout, indirect, oblique, circumlocutory, circuitous, periphrastic; informal cagey.
▷ANTONYMS frank.

eve noun **1** *on the eve of the election*: **day before**, evening before, night before; period before, the run-up to.
▷ANTONYMS day after.
2 literary *a summer eve*: **evening**, night, late afternoon, end of day, close of day; twilight, dusk, nightfall, sunset, sundown; literary even, eventide, evenfall, gloaming.
▷ANTONYMS morning.

even adjective **1** *it is easier to print on an even surface*: **flat**, smooth, uniform, featureless, unbroken, undamaged, unwrinkled; level, levelled, plane, flush, true; informal (as) flat as a pancake; technical planar; rare homaloidal.
▷ANTONYMS uneven, bumpy.
2 *electric fan ovens have a more even temperature than gas*: **uniform**, constant, steady, stable, consistent, changeless, unvarying, unchanging, unwavering, unfluctuating, unaltering, regular.
▷ANTONYMS variable, irregular.
3 *all participants are given an even chance*: **equal**, the same, much the same, identical, like, alike, similar, to the same degree, comparable, commensurate, corresponding, parallel, on a par, on an equal footing, evenly matched; informal even-steven(s).
▷ANTONYMS unequal.
4 *he played a perfect ball to keep the score even*: **level**, drawn, tied, all square, balanced, on a par, on an equal footing; neck and neck, nip and tuck, with nothing to choose between them; Brit. level pegging; informal even-steven(s).
▷ANTONYMS unequal, uneven.
5 *the child was of an even disposition*: **even-tempered**, well balanced, stable, equable, placid, serene, calm, composed, poised, tranquil, cool, {cool, calm, and collected}, cool-headed, relaxed, easy, imperturbable, unexcitable, unruffled, unflustered, unagitated, unworried, untroubled, unbothered; informal together, laid-back, unflappable, unfazed; rare equanimous.
▷ANTONYMS moody; excitable.
□ **get even** *he has been wronged and he has sworn to get even*: **have one's revenge**, take one's revenge, be revenged, revenge oneself, avenge oneself, take vengeance, even the score, settle accounts, settle the score, hit back, give as good as one gets, return tit for tat, return like for like, pay someone back, repay someone, reciprocate, retaliate, take reprisals, exact retribution, demand an eye for an eye and a tooth for a tooth; give someone their just deserts, let someone see how it feels; informal get back at someone, get one's own back, give someone a taste of their own medicine, give someone their comeuppance, fix someone, sort someone out, settle someone's hash, cook someone's goose.
▶ verb **1** *the canal bottom was evened out*: **flatten**, make flat, make level, level,

e

level off, level out, smooth, smooth out, smooth off, make flush, plane, make uniform, make regular.
2 *the union wants to* ***even up*** *the differences in wages*: **equalize**, make equal, make even, make level, level up, make the same, balance, square; make uniform, make comparable, standardize, regularize; rare equilibrize.
▸ **adverb 1** *the weather became even colder*: **still**, yet, more so, all the more, all the greater, to a greater extent.
2 *even the best hitters missed the ball*: **surprisingly**, unexpectedly, paradoxically, though it may seem strange, believe it or not, as it happens.
3 *she is too afraid, even ashamed, to ask for help*: **indeed**, you could say, possibly, more precisely, veritably, in truth, actually, or rather, nay.
4 *she couldn't even afford the essentials*: **so much as**, hardly, barely, scarcely.
□ **even as** *we laugh even as we empathize with his discomfort*: **while**, whilst, as, at the (same) time that, just as, at the very time that, at the very moment that, exactly when, during the time that.
□ **even so** *I feel better, but the doubts persist even so*: **nevertheless**, nonetheless, all the same, just the same, anyway, anyhow, still, yet, however, notwithstanding, despite that, in spite of that, for all that, be that as it may, in any event, at any rate; informal still and all; archaic withal, natheless, howbeit.

e

even-handed adjective *teachers must have an even-handed approach towards both sexes*: **fair**, just, equitable, impartial, unbiased, unprejudiced, non-partisan, non-discriminatory; disinterested, dispassionate, detached, uninvolved, objective, neutral, impersonal, fair-minded, open-minded, with no axe to grind.
▷ANTONYMS unfair; biased.

evening noun **1** *he came over to see me one evening*: **night**, late afternoon, end of day, close of day; twilight, dusk, nightfall, sunset, sundown; literary eve, even, eventide, evenfall, gloaming.
▷ANTONYMS morning.
2 *the evening of her life*: **latter part**, last part, latter stage, close, end, later years, declining years; autumn.
▷ANTONYMS springtime.

Word links **evening**

vespertine relating to evening

event noun **1** *the school trip was an annual event*: **occurrence**, happening, proceeding, episode, incident, affair, circumstance, occasion, business, matter, experience, eventuality, phenomenon; function, gathering, get-together, jamboree; informal bash, do, jolly, shindig, shindy.
2 *the British team lost the event*: **competition**, contest, tournament, round, heat, game, match, fixture, meet, meeting, encounter; race, bout, fight; play-off, replay, rematch; Canadian & Scottish playdown; N. Amer. split; informal, dated mill; archaic tourney.
□ **in any event/at all events** *he is going to prison in any event, guilty plea or not*: **regardless**, regardless of what happens, whatever happens, come what may, no matter what, at any rate, in any case, anyhow, anyway, even so, still, nevertheless, nonetheless; informal still and all; N. Amer. informal anyways; archaic howbeit, natheless.
□ **in the event** *in the event, they squabbled and the plan fell through*: **as it turned out**, as it happened, in the end; as the outcome, as a result, as a consequence, as an effect.

even-tempered adjective *Russell was a gentle and even-tempered man*: **serene**, calm, composed, poised, tranquil, relaxed, easy-going, mild, mellow, unworried, untroubled, unbothered, unruffled, unflustered, unexcitable, imperturbable, placid, equable, stable, well balanced, level-headed; informal unflappable, together, laid-back, unfazed; rare equanimous.
▷ANTONYMS excitable, unstable.

eventful adjective *it had been a long and eventful day*: **busy**, event-filled, action-packed, full, lively, active, hectic, strenuous; **momentous**, significant, noteworthy, notable, remarkable, outstanding, important, crucial, critical, historic, consequential, fateful, decisive.
▷ANTONYMS dull, uneventful.

eventual adjective *the eventual outcome of the competition*: **final**, ultimate, concluding, closing, endmost, end, terminal; resulting, ensuing, consequent, subsequent.

eventuality noun *it is impossible to anticipate every eventuality*: **event**, incident, occurrence, happening, development, phenomenon, thing, situation, circumstance, case, contingency, chance, likelihood, possibility, probability; **outcome**, result, upshot; rare fortuity.

eventually adverb *eventually we arrived at a small town* | *the offender will be allowed out eventually*: **in the end**, in due course, by and by, in time, after some time, after a period of time, after a long time, after a bit, finally, at last, at long last; **ultimately**, in the long run, in the fullness of time, at some point in the future, at a future date, at the end of the day, one day, one of these fine days, some day, sometime, in time to come, sooner or later, when all is said and done.
▷ANTONYMS immediately; never.

eventuate verb rare **1** *you never know what might eventuate*: **happen**, occur, take place, chance to happen, arise, emerge, come about, transpire, materialize, appear, surface, crop up, spring up, present itself; **ensue**, follow, result, develop, supervene, be the result, be the consequence; N. Amer. informal go down; literary come to pass, befall, betide, bechance; archaic hap, arrive.
2 *the fight* ***eventuated in*** *the death of Mr Gonzales*: **result in**, end in, have as a result, have as a consequence, lead to, give rise to, bring about, cause.

ever adverb **1** *it's the best thing I've ever done*: **at any time**, at any point, on any occasion, under any circumstances, on any account; up till now, until now.
2 *ever the optimist, he was intent on winning*: **always**, forever, at all times, eternally, until the end of time; informal until the twelfth of never, until the cows come home, until hell freezes over, until doomsday.
▷ANTONYMS never.
3 *the statistics show an ever increasing rate of crime*: **continually**, constantly, always, at all times, endlessly, perpetually, incessantly, unceasingly, unremittingly, repeatedly, recurrently.
4 *will she ever learn?* **at all**, in any way, on earth.
□ **ever so** Brit. informal *she's ever so happy*. See **extremely**.

everlasting adjective **1** *gold is the symbol of everlasting love*: **eternal**, never-ending, endless, without end, perpetual, undying, immortal, deathless, indestructible, immutable, abiding, enduring, infinite, boundless, timeless; rare sempiternal, perdurable.
▷ANTONYMS transient.
2 *they got tired of my everlasting complaints*: **constant**, continual, continuous, persistent, sustained, unremitting, relentless, unrelenting, unrelieved, uninterrupted, unbroken, unabating, endless, interminable, never-ending, non-stop, round-the-clock, incessant, ceaseless.
▷ANTONYMS occasional.

evermore adverb *we pray that we may evermore dwell in Him*: **always**, forever, for ever and ever, ever, for always, for all time, until the end of time, eternally, in perpetuity; endlessly, without end, ceaselessly, unceasingly, constantly; ever after, henceforth; Brit. for evermore, forever more; N. Amer. forevermore; Latin in perpetuum, ad infinitum; informal until the cows come home, until the twelfth of never, until hell freezes over; formal hereafter; archaic for aye.

every determiner **1** *he exercised his hounds every day*: **each**, each and every, every single.
2 *the firm will make every effort to satisfy its clients*: **all possible**, all probable, the utmost, as much as possible, as great as possible.
▷ANTONYMS no.

everybody pronoun *everybody complains about taxes these days*: **everyone**, every person, each person, each one, each and every one, all, one and all, all and sundry, the whole world, the world at large, the public, the general public, people everywhere; informal {every Tom, Dick, and Harry}, every man jack, every mother's son.

everyday adjective **1** *the everyday demands of a baby*: **daily**, day-to-day, quotidian; rare diurnal, circadian.
2 *everyday drugs like aspirin*: **commonplace**, ordinary, common, usual, regular, familiar, conventional, run-of-the-mill, typical, standard, stock, plain, workaday; household, domestic, family; unexceptional, unremarkable; Brit. common or garden; N. Amer. garden variety; informal bog-standard, a dime a dozen.
▷ANTONYMS unusual.

everyone pronoun *she didn't want everyone to know her business*: **everybody**, every person, each person, each one, each and every one, all, one and all, all and sundry, the whole world, the world at large, the public, the general public, people everywhere; informal {every Tom, Dick, and Harry}, every man jack, every mother's son.

everything pronoun *the guards searched through everything*: **each item**, each thing, every article, every single thing, the lot, the whole lot, the entirety, the total, the aggregate; all; informal the whole (kit and) caboodle, the whole shooting match, the whole shebang, everything but the kitchen sink; Brit. informal the full monty; N. Amer. informal the whole ball of wax, the whole nine yards.
▷ANTONYMS nothing.

Word links **everything**

panphobia, panophobia, pantophobia fear of everything

everywhere adverb *he searched everywhere for his horse*: **all over**, all around, in all places, in every place, in every spot, in every part, in every nook and cranny, in each place, far and wide, near and far, high and low, here and there, {here, there, and everywhere}, throughout the land, the world over, worldwide; widely, extensively, exhaustively, thoroughly; informal all over the place; Brit. informal all over the shop; N. Amer. informal all over the map.
▷ANTONYMS nowhere.

evict verb *the police moved in and evicted the squatters*: **expel**, eject, oust, remove, dislodge, turn out, put out, force out, throw out, throw out on the streets, throw out on one's ear, drum out, drive out; dispossess, expropriate; informal chuck out, kick out, boot out, heave out, bounce, give someone the (old) heave-ho, throw someone out on their ear, show someone the door; Brit. informal turf out; N. Amer. informal give someone the bum's rush; dated out.
▷**ANTONYMS** admit.

eviction noun *the eviction of workers from company houses*: **expulsion**, ejection, ousting, throwing out, drumming out, driving out, banishing, banishment, removal, dislodgement, displacement, clearance; dispossession, expropriation; informal booting out, chucking out, kicking out, bouncing; Brit. informal turfing out; humorous defenestration; Law ouster; dated outing.
▷**ANTONYMS** admission.

evidence noun **1** *they found* ***evidence of*** *his participation in the burglary*: **proof**, confirmation, verification, substantiation, corroboration, affirmation, authentication, attestation, documentation; support for, backing for, reinforcement for, grounds for.
2 *the court refused to accept Mr Scott's evidence*: **testimony**, statement, sworn statement, attestation, declaration, avowal, plea, submission, claim, contention, charge, allegation; Law deposition, representation, affidavit; rare asseveration, averment.
3 *the room showed evidence of a struggle*: **signs**, indications, pointers, marks, traces, suggestions, hints; manifestation.
□ **in evidence** *team spirit was much in evidence*: **noticeable**, conspicuous, obvious, perceptible, perceivable, visible, on view, on display, easily seen, easily noticed, plain to see; palpable, tangible, unmistakable, undisguised, unconcealed, prominent, striking, glaring, writ large; informal as plain as the nose on your face, as plain as a pikestaff, standing/sticking out like a sore thumb, standing/sticking out a mile, right under one's nose, staring someone in the face, written all over someone; archaic sensible.
▸ verb *the rise of racism is evidenced by the increase in racial attacks*: **indicate**, show, reveal, be evidence of, display, exhibit, manifest, denote, evince, signify; testify to, attest to, verify, confirm, prove, substantiate, endorse, back up, support, bear out, give credence to.
▷**ANTONYMS** disprove.

evident adjective *he regarded her with evident interest*: **obvious**, apparent, noticeable, conspicuous, perceptible, perceivable, visible, observable, discernible, transparent, clear, crystal clear, clear-cut, writ large, plain, manifest, patent, palpable, tangible, distinct, pronounced, marked, striking, glaring, blatant; unmistakable, indisputable, undoubted, incontrovertible, incontestable; informal as plain as the nose on your face, as plain as a pikestaff, standing/sticking out like a sore thumb, standing/sticking out a mile, written all over someone, as clear as day; archaic sensible.
▷**ANTONYMS** unnoticeable.

evidently adverb **1** *he was evidently dismayed by what he saw*: **obviously**, clearly, plainly, perceptibly, visibly, discernibly, transparently, manifestly, patently, palpably, distinctly, markedly, blatantly; unmistakably, indisputably, undeniably, undoubtedly, incontrovertibly, without question, without doubt; informal as sure as eggs is eggs.
2 *evidently, she believed herself to be unobserved*: **seemingly**, apparently, so it seems, as far as one can tell, from all appearances, on the face of it, to all intents and purposes, on the surface, outwardly, ostensibly; it seems (that), it would seem (that), it appears (that), it would appear (that); rare ostensively.

evil adjective **1** *an evil deed | the most evil man he had ever met*: **wicked**, bad, wrong, morally wrong, wrongful, immoral, sinful, ungodly, unholy, foul, vile, base, ignoble, dishonourable, corrupt, iniquitous, depraved, degenerate, villainous, nefarious, sinister, vicious, malicious, malevolent, demonic, devilish, diabolic, diabolical, fiendish, dark, black-hearted; monstrous, shocking, despicable, atrocious, heinous, odious, contemptible, horrible, execrable; informal low-down, stinking, dirty, shady, warped, bent, crooked; archaic dastardly, black; rare egregious, flagitious, peccable.
▷**ANTONYMS** good, virtuous.
2 *the evil influence of society | an evil spirit*: **harmful**, hurtful, injurious, detrimental, deleterious, inimical, bad, mischievous, pernicious, malignant, malign, baleful, venomous, noxious, poisonous; corrupting, subversive; calamitous, disastrous, destructive, ruinous; literary malefic, maleficent; rare prejudicious.
▷**ANTONYMS** good, beneficial.
3 *his army suffered in the evil weather*: **unpleasant**, disagreeable, nasty, horrible, foul, filthy, vile; inclement, wet, rainy, stormy, squally, blustery, cold, freezing, foggy.
▷**ANTONYMS** pleasant; fine.
4 *she helped those who had fallen on evil times*: **unlucky**, unfortunate, unfavourable, adverse, unhappy, disastrous, catastrophic, ruinous, calamitous, unpropitious, inauspicious, dire, woeful.
▸ noun **1** *I sense the evil in our midst*: **wickedness**, bad, badness, wrong, wrongdoing, sin, sinfulness, ungodliness, immorality, vice, iniquity, turpitude, degeneracy, vileness, baseness, perversion, corruption, depravity, villainy, nefariousness, atrocity, malevolence, devilishness; informal shadiness, crookedness; rare peccability, peccancy.
▷**ANTONYMS** goodness.
2 *nothing but evil would come out of such a meeting*: **harm**, pain, hurt, misery, sorrow, suffering, trauma, trouble, disaster, detriment, destruction, loss, misfortune, catastrophe, calamity, affliction, woe, ruin, hardship; ills.
▷**ANTONYMS** benefit.
3 *the evils of war*: **abomination**, atrocity, obscenity, outrage, enormity, crime, monstrosity, barbarity, barbarism; torment, curse, bane.
▷**ANTONYMS** blessing.

evil-doer noun *they exacted vengeance on the evil-doers*: **wrongdoer**, transgressor, criminal, delinquent, offender, villain, malefactor, reprobate, scoundrel, rogue, sinner, sinful person, wicked person, evil person, bad person; informal baddy, bad guy, crook, crim, wrong 'un, ne'er-do-well, nasty piece of work, ratbag, scumbag, bad egg; Law malfeasant, misfeasor, infractor; archaic miscreant, knave, blackguard, varlet, trespasser.

e

evil-doing noun *a fiend bent on evil-doing*: **wrongdoing**, wrong, badness, bad, evil, sin, sinfulness, immorality, iniquity, turpitude, vileness, baseness, corruption, depravity, villainy, nefariousness, atrocity, malevolence, devilishness; informal shadiness, crookedness; Law malfeasance; archaic knavery, trespassing; rare peccability, peccancy.

evince verb *his letters evince the excitement he felt*: **reveal**, show, make clear, make plain, make obvious, make manifest, manifest, indicate, display, exhibit, demonstrate, be evidence of, evidence, attest to, testify to, bear witness to; convey, communicate, proclaim, impart, bespeak; disclose, divulge, betray, give away, expose, lay bare.
▷**ANTONYMS** conceal.

eviscerate verb *the goat had been skinned and eviscerated*: **disembowel**, gut, remove the innards from, draw, dress; rare embowel, disbowel, exenterate, gralloch, paunch.

evocative adjective *dark interiors are highly* ***evocative of*** *past centuries | evocative lyrics*: **reminiscent**, suggestive, redolent; resonant with; **expressive**, vivid, graphic, powerful, haunting, moving, poignant; rare remindful of.

evoke verb *the poems evoke a sense of desolate emptiness*: **bring to mind**, call to mind, put one in mind of, call up, conjure up, summon up, summon, invoke, give rise to, bring forth, elicit, induce, kindle, stimulate, stir up, awaken, arouse, excite, raise, suggest; recall, echo, reproduce, encapsulate, capture, express; formal educe.

evolution noun **1** *the evolution of the Internet as an advertising medium*: **development**, advancement, growth, rise, progress, progression, expansion, extension, unfolding; transformation, adaptation, modification, revision, reworking, reconstruction, recasting, change; humorous transmogrification; rare evolvement.
2 *early ecologists were not interested in evolution*: **Darwinism**, natural selection.

evolve verb **1** *the economies of all four nations evolved in different ways*: **develop**, progress, make progress, advance, move forward, make headway, mature, grow, open out, unfold, unroll, expand, enlarge, spread, extend; alter, change, transform, adapt, metamorphose, differentiate; humorous transmogrify.
2 Chemistry *on reacting the two acids, a gas is evolved*: **emit**, yield, give off, discharge, release, produce.

exacerbate verb *political changes have exacerbated the conflict*: **aggravate**, make worse, worsen, inflame, compound; intensify, increase, heighten, magnify, add to, amplify, augment; make matters worse, compound the problem; informal add fuel to the fire/flames, fan the flames, rub salt in the wounds, add insult to injury.
▷**ANTONYMS** calm; reduce.

Easily confused words **exacerbate or exasperate?**

See **exasperate**.

exact adjective **1** *write an exact description of everything you see*: **precise**, accurate, correct, faithful, close, true, veracious, literal, strict, unerring, faultless, errorless, error-free, perfect, impeccable; explicit, detailed, minute, meticulous, thorough, blow-by-blow; informal on the nail, on the mark, on the beam, on the button; Brit. informal spot on, bang on; N. Amer. informal on the money.
▷**ANTONYMS** inexact, inaccurate.
2 *he didn't approve of sloppiness and liked to be exact*: **careful**, meticulous, painstaking, precise, punctilious, conscientious, rigorous, scrupulous, exacting; methodical, systematic, well organized, ordered, orderly, controlled.
▷**ANTONYMS** careless.
▸ verb **1** *she exacted high standards of cleanliness from them*: **demand**, require, insist on, command, call for, impose, request, ask for, expect, look for; extract, compel, force, wring, wrest, squeeze, obtain; archaic constrain.

2 *they exacted a terrible vengeance on the helpless tribe*: **inflict**, impose, deliver, administer, issue, apply.

> *Choose the right word* **exact, accurate, precise**
>
> See **accurate**.

exacting adjective 1 *he set himself an exacting training routine*: **demanding**, hard, tough, stringent, testing, challenging, difficult, onerous, arduous, laborious, tiring, taxing, gruelling, punishing, back-breaking, burdensome, Herculean; archaic toilsome; rare exigent.
▷ANTONYMS easy.
2 *a highly efficient but exacting boss*: **strict**, stern, firm, demanding, rigorous, tough, hard, harsh, rigid, inflexible, uncompromising, unyielding, unbending, unsparing, imperious; hard to please; Austral./NZ informal solid.
▷ANTONYMS easy-going.

> *Word toolkit* **exacting**
>
> See **finicky**.

exactly adverb 1 *the room's exactly as I expected it to be*: **precisely**, entirely, absolutely, completely, totally, just, quite, in every way, in every respect, one hundred per cent, every inch, to the hilt; informal on the nail, bang on, spot on, to a T; N. Amer. informal on the money.
▷ANTONYMS not at all.
2 *mention your source and write the quotation out exactly*: **accurately**, precisely, correctly, without error, without flaws, without mistakes, unerringly, faultlessly, perfectly; **verbatim**, word for word, letter for letter, to the letter, literally, closely, faithfully, in every detail, with strict attention to detail; rare veridically.
▷ANTONYMS inaccurately, inexactly.
□ **not exactly** *I'm not exactly a spring chicken any more*: **by no means**, not by any means, not, not at all, in no way, certainly not; not really.
▸ exclamation *'You mean she escaped?' 'Exactly.'*: **precisely**, yes, right, that's right, just so, quite so, quite, indeed, absolutely, truly, certainly, definitely, assuredly, undoubtedly, indubitably, without a doubt; informal you bet, you got it, I'll say.

exactness, exactitude noun *in this job, detail and exactness are essential*: **precision**, accuracy, accurateness, correctness, veracity, faithfulness, fidelity, closeness; care, carefulness, meticulousness, scrupulousness, punctiliousness, conscientiousness, rigour, rigorousness, thoroughness, strictness; rare veridicality, scrupulosity.
▷ANTONYMS inaccuracy; negligence.

exaggerate verb *the conflict was exaggerated by the media | they often exaggerate for dramatic effect*: **overstate**, overemphasize, overstress, overestimate, overvalue, magnify, amplify, aggrandize, inflate; embellish, embroider, colour, elaborate, over-elaborate, oversell, overdraw, overplay, dramatize; hyperbolize, add colour, stretch the truth; Brit. overpitch; informal pile it on, lay it on thick, lay it on with a trowel/shovel, make a mountain out of a molehill, blow something out of all proportion, make a drama out of a crisis, make a big thing of; Brit. informal shoot a line; archaic draw the longbow.
▷ANTONYMS play down; understate.

exaggerated adjective *I gave her an exaggerated account of my exploits*: **overstated**, overemphasized, inflated, magnified, amplified, aggrandized, excessive, hyperbolic, over-elaborate, overdone, overplayed, overdramatized, theatrical, dramatic, highly coloured, extravagant, melodramatic, sensational, sensationalist, sensationalistic; informal over the top, OTT, tall.
▷ANTONYMS understated.

exaggeration noun *the debate is characterized by confusion and exaggeration*: **overstatement**, overemphasis, magnification, amplification, aggrandizement, overplaying, dramatization, overdramatization, enhancement, elaboration, over-elaboration, embellishment, over-embellishment, embroidery, hyperbole, overkill, gilding the lily; informal purple prose, puffery.

exalt verb 1 *they exalted their hero*: **glorify**, extol, praise, acclaim, pay homage to, pay tribute to, revere, reverence, venerate, worship, hero-worship, lionize, idolize, deify, esteem, hold in high regard, hold in high esteem, hold in awe, look up to; informal put on a pedestal; rare laud, magnify.
▷ANTONYMS disparage; despise.
2 *this power exalts the peasant above his brethren*: **elevate**, promote, raise, advance, boost, upgrade, ennoble, dignify, aggrandize; improve the status of, improve the standing of, give someone a higher rank.
▷ANTONYMS lower.
3 *the works of Milton and Wordsworth exalted me*: **uplift**, elevate, inspire, excite, stimulate, animate, enliven, exhilarate, elate, delight, transport.
▷ANTONYMS depress.

exaltation noun 1 *her heart was full of exaltation*: **elation**, exultation, joy, joyfulness, joyousness, rapture, ecstasy, bliss, happiness, delight, gladness, glee, exuberance, exhilaration, excitement; transports.
▷ANTONYMS sadness.
2 *their exaltation of Shakespeare*: **praise**, praising, extolment, acclamation, glory, glorification, glorifying, reverence, revering, veneration, venerating, worship, worshipping, hero-worship, hero-worshipping, adoration, idolization, idolizing, lionization, lionizing, deification, deifying; homage, tribute, high regard, high esteem; rare laudation, lauding, magnification, magnifying.
▷ANTONYMS disparagement.
3 *the resurrection and exaltation of Christ*: **elevation**, raising, rise, promotion, advancement, upgrading, ennoblement, aggrandizement.
▷ANTONYMS lowering.

exalted adjective 1 *he is no longer fit to retain his exalted office*: **high**, high-ranking, elevated, prominent, superior, lofty, grand, noble, dignified, eminent, prestigious, august, illustrious, distinguished, esteemed, venerable; influential, important, powerful.
▷ANTONYMS low.
2 *their hearts were stirred by his exalted aims*: **noble**, lofty, high-minded, elevated, intellectual, ideal, sublime; inflated, pretentious.
▷ANTONYMS base.
3 *she felt tired but spiritually exalted*: **elated**, exultant, jubilant, joyful, joyous, triumphant, rapturous, rhapsodic, ecstatic, blissful, transported, delighted, happy, gleeful, exuberant, exhilarated; informal high, up.
▷ANTONYMS depressed, low.

exam noun *she prepared for her biology exam*: **test**, examination, paper, question paper, oral, practical, assessment; set of questions, set of exercises; Brit. viva, viva voce; N. Amer. quiz.

examination noun 1 *the artefacts were spread on a table for examination*: **scrutiny**, inspection, perusal, study, scanning, vetting, investigation, exploration, consideration, analysis, appraisal, evaluation.
2 *employees are required to undergo a medical examination*: **inspection**, check, check-up, assessment, review, appraisal; exploration, probe, test, scan; informal going-over, once-over, overhaul.
3 *there was an examination at the end of the course*: **test**, exam, paper, question paper, oral, practical, assessment; set of questions, set of exercises; Brit. viva, viva voce; N. Amer. quiz.
4 Law *the examination of witnesses in open court*: **questioning**, **interrogation**, cross-questioning, cross-examination, inquisition; the third degree; informal pumping, grilling.

> *Word links* **examination**
>
> **-scopy** related suffix, as in *microscopy, endoscopy*

examine verb 1 *fraud squad officers wanted to examine the bank records*: **inspect**, survey, scrutinize, look at, look into, enquire into, study, investigate, scan, sift, delve into, dig into, explore, probe, check out, consider, appraise, weigh, weigh up, analyse, review, vet; subject to an examination.
2 *students were examined after nine months' instruction*: **test**, quiz, question, set an examination for; assess, appraise.
3 *they must name in advance all the witnesses to be examined*: **interrogate**, put questions to, ask questions of, quiz, question, cross-examine, cross-question; catechize, give the third degree to, probe, sound out; informal grill, pump, put through the wringer, put through the mangle.

examiner noun *a university examiner | the accounts are checked by an independent examiner*: **tester**, questioner, interviewer, assessor, marker, inspector; auditor, analyst, appraiser, reviewer; arbiter, adjudicator, judge, scrutineer, scrutinizer; rare examinant, scrutinator.

example noun 1 *a fine example of a 16th-century longhouse*: **specimen**, sample, exemplar, exemplification, instance, case, representative case, typical case, case in point, illustration.
2 *we ought to follow their example*: **precedent**, lead, guide, model, pattern, blueprint, template, paradigm, exemplar, ideal, standard; parallel case; role model.
3 *he was found guilty as an example to would-be burglars*: **warning**, caution, lesson, deterrent, admonition; sign, signal message, moral.
□ **for example** *their teeth resemble those of many mammals, for example, bears*: **for instance**, e.g., to give an example, to give an instance, by way of illustration, as an illustration, to illustrate, such as, as, like; in particular, namely, viz.

exasperate verb *Smith's erratic behaviour exasperated him*: **infuriate**, incense, anger, annoy, irritate, madden, enrage, send into a rage, inflame, antagonize, provoke, irk, vex, gall, pique, try someone's patience, get on someone's nerves, make someone's blood boil, make someone's hackles rise, make someone see red, get someone's back up, rub up the wrong way, ruffle someone's feathers, drive to distraction; informal aggravate, drive mad, drive crazy, bug, needle, rile, miff, hack off, get to, get at, get up someone's nose, get under someone's skin, put someone's nose out of joint, get someone's goat, give someone the hump, rattle someone's cage, get someone's dander up; Brit. informal nark, wind up, get on someone's wick;

N. Amer. informal tee off, tick off, burn up, rankle, ride, gravel; rare exacerbate, hump, rasp.
▷ANTONYMS please, delight.

Easily confused words **exasperate or exacerbate?**

These words may be confused on account of their similar sound; but their meanings are different. **Exasperate** means 'irritate intensely' (*his colleague's erratic behaviour exasperated him*). **Exacerbate**, on the other hand, means 'make (an existing problem) worse' (*anaemia may be exacerbated by some medicines*). Someone's late arrival may *exasperate* his colleagues, and this in turn may *exacerbate* the tension between them.

exasperating adjective *he has such exasperating habits*: **infuriating**, annoying, irritating, maddening, antagonizing, provoking, irking, irksome, vexing, vexatious, galling, trying, troublesome, bothersome, displeasing; informal aggravating, cussed, pesky, confounded, infernal, plaguy, pestilent.
▷ANTONYMS pleasing, delightful.

exasperation noun *she provoked exasperation among her colleagues*: **irritation**, annoyance, chagrin, vexation, anger, fury, rage, wrath, spleen, ill humour, crossness, tetchiness, testiness, pique, indignation, resentment, disgruntlement, disgust, discontent, displeasure; informal aggravation, crabbiness; Brit. informal stroppiness; literary ire, choler, bile.
▷ANTONYMS pleasure, delight.

excavate verb **1** *the animal has excavated a narrow tunnel*: **dig**, dig out, hollow out, scoop out, gouge, cut out, bore, burrow, tunnel, sink; quarry, mine.
2 *numerous artefacts have been excavated*: **unearth**, dig up, bring out of the ground, bring to the surface, uncover, reveal; disinter, exhume; rare unbury.

excavation noun **1** *the excavation of a medieval grave*: **unearthing**, digging up, uncovering, revealing; disinterment, exhumation.
2 *the excavation of an extra moat*: **digging**, digging out, hollowing out, scooping out, gouging, boring, channelling, sinking; quarrying, mining.
3 *a number of agricultural implements were found in the excavations*: **hole**, hollow, cavity, pit, crater, cutting, trench, trough; **archaeological site**.

exceed verb **1** *the total cost will exceed £400*: **be more than**, be greater than, be over, run over, go over, go beyond, overshoot, overreach, pass, top.
▷ANTONYMS fall short of.
2 *Brazil far exceeds America in available fertile land*: **surpass**, outdo, outstrip, outshine, outclass, transcend, top, cap, beat, be greater than, be superior to, be better than, go one better than, better, pass, eclipse, overshadow, put in the shade, put to shame; informal best, leave standing, be head and shoulders above, be a cut above; archaic extinguish, outrival, outvie.

exceeding archaic adjective *she spoke warmly of his exceeding kindness*. See **great** (sense 2).
▸ adverb *the Lord has been exceeding gracious*. See **extremely**.

exceedingly adverb *an exceedingly comfortable home*: **extremely**, exceptionally, especially, tremendously, immensely, supremely, very, really, truly, most, distinctly, decidedly; Scottish unco; French très; N. English right; informal terribly, awfully, devilishly, majorly, seriously, mega, ultra, oh-so, damn, damned; Brit. informal ever so, well, dead, jolly; N. Amer. informal real, mighty, awful, darned; archaic exceeding.

Word links **exceedingly**

ultra- related prefix, as in *ultra-modern, ultramicroscopic*

excel verb **1** *he excelled at football*: **shine**, be very good, be excellent, be brilliant, be outstanding, be skilful, be talented, be proficient, be expert, be pre-eminent, reign supreme, wear the crown, stand out, be the best, be unrivalled, be unparalleled, be unequalled, be without equal, be second to none, be unsurpassed; rare be unexampled.
2 *she excelled him in her command of the language*: **surpass**, outdo, outshine, outclass, outstrip, beat, beat hollow, top, cap, transcend, be better than, be superior to, go one better than, better, pass, eclipse, overshadow, put in the shade, put to shame; informal best, leave standing, be head and shoulders above, be a cut above; archaic extinguish, outrival, outvie.

Choose the right word **excel, surpass, outdo**

All these words denote superiority or pre-eminence.

Excel is most often used without a direct object, emphasizing someone's outstanding ability (*he excelled at maths and won a scholarship to Cambridge | it was not enough to excel in the swimming and running*). The most common transitive use is to *excel oneself*, which is to do better than one has ever done before (*Miss Lodsworth, who organized the flower rota, had excelled herself*). It is comparatively rare to *excel someone else*.

Surpass literally means 'go beyond'. It indicates that someone has passed a previous limit, proving themselves greater or better (*he won five races and surpassed the all-time record*). It is also quite common to *surpass someone* (*he was never surpassed by recent comedians*); its reflexive use, to *surpass oneself*, has the same sense as *excel oneself* (*he surpassed himself once more in the 1991 Ryder Cup*).

Outdo indicates that someone is more successful or goes to greater lengths than their competitors (*they tried to outdo each other in generosity | she could not hope to outdo the big contractors*). The note of competition with others is strongest in this word (*everybody was trying to outdo each other with stories of how exciting their holidays had been | not to be outdone, Pentos also produced its own fully-illustrated catalogue*). It is unusual to *outdo oneself*.

excellence noun *the children's hospital is a centre of medical excellence*: **distinction**, quality, high quality, superiority, brilliance, greatness, merit, calibre, eminence, pre-eminence, supremacy, peerlessness, transcendence, value, worth; skill, talent, genius, virtuosity, accomplishment, expertness, mastery, prowess, ability; rare supereminence.
▷ANTONYMS inferiority, mediocrity.

excellent adjective *the wine was good and the meal excellent*: **very good**, superb, outstanding, magnificent, of high quality, of the highest quality, of the highest standard, exceptional, marvellous, wonderful, sublime, perfect, eminent, pre-eminent, matchless, peerless, supreme, first-rate, first-class, superior, superlative, splendid, admirable, worthy, sterling, fine; informal A1, ace, great, terrific, tremendous, fantastic, fab, top-notch, tip-top, class, awesome, magic, wicked, cool, out of this world, too good to be true, mind-blowing; Brit. informal brilliant, brill, smashing, champion, bosting; Austral. informal beaut, bonzer; Brit. informal, dated spiffing, ripping, topping, top-hole, wizard, capital; N. Amer. informal, dated swell; vulgar slang shit hot; rare applaudable.
▷ANTONYMS poor, inferior.

except preposition *the shop is open every day except Monday | there was no sound* ***except for*** *the rain*: **excluding**, not including, excepting, omitting, leaving out, not counting, but, besides, barring, bar, other than, exclusive of, saving, save, apart from, aside from; with the exception of, with the omission of, with the exclusion of; informal outside of; archaic forbye.
▷ANTONYMS including.
▸ verb *you're all crooks, present company excepted*: **exclude**, omit, leave out, rule out, count out, disregard, pass over, bar.
▷ANTONYMS include.

exception noun *an unexpected outcome was more the rule than the exception*: **anomaly**, irregularity, deviation, special case, departure, inconsistency, quirk, peculiarity, abnormality, oddity; misfit; informal freak.
□ **take exception** *they* ***took exception to*** *the story we printed*: **object**, raise an objection, express objections; be offended by, take offence at, take umbrage at, resent, demur at, disagree with, cavil at, argue against, protest against, lodge a protest against, take a stand against, oppose, complain about; informal kick up a fuss about, kick up a stink about, beef about, gripe about.
▷ANTONYMS approve of.
□ **with the exception of** *everyone shook their heads with the exception of Alice*: **except**, except for, excepting, excluding, not including, omitting, leaving out, not counting, but, besides, barring, bar, other than, exclusive of, saving, save, apart from, aside from; with the omission of, with the exclusion of; informal outside of; archaic forbye.
▷ANTONYMS including.

exceptionable adjective rare *this passage is the most exceptionable in the whole poem*. See **objectionable**.

exceptional adjective **1** *meteorologists described the drought as exceptional*: **unusual**, uncommon, abnormal, atypical, extraordinary, out of the ordinary, out of the way, rare, singular, unprecedented, unexpected, surprising; strange, odd, queer, bizarre, freakish, anomalous, peculiar, inconsistent, deviant, divergent, aberrant, unheard of; Brit. out of the common; informal weird, way out, freaky, something else; dated seldom; rare unexampled.
▷ANTONYMS usual, normal.
2 *we were taught by men of quite exceptional ability*: **outstanding**, extraordinary, remarkable, unusually good, special, especial, excellent, phenomenal, prodigious; unequalled, unparalleled, unrivalled, unsurpassed, unsurpassable, unexcelled, peerless, matchless, second to none, in a league of their own, first-rate, first-class, of the first order, of the first water; informal A1, top-notch, tip-top, stellar.
▷ANTONYMS average.

Word toolkit

exceptional	unique	remarkable
circumstances	opportunity	achievement
case	features	recovery
quality	combination	career
service	perspective	transformation
value	insight	similarity

e

exceptionally adverb **1** *that winter was exceptionally cold*: **unusually**, uncommonly, abnormally, atypically, extraordinarily, unexpectedly, surprisingly; strangely, oddly, freakishly; informal weirdly, freakily.
2 *she had an exceptionally acute mind*: **outstandingly**, extraordinarily, remarkably, exceedingly, especially, specially, phenomenally, prodigiously.

excerpt noun *he read an excerpt from his book*: **extract**, part, section, piece, portion, fragment, snippet, clip, bit, selection, reading; citation, quotation, quote, line, paragraph, passage, scene, verse, stanza, canto; N. Amer. cite; rare pericope.

excess noun **1** *an excess of calcium in the bloodstream*: **surplus**, surfeit, overabundance, superabundance, superfluity, oversufficiency, profusion, plethora, glut; too much, more than enough, enough and to spare; informal more ... than one can shake a stick at; rare nimiety.
▷ANTONYMS dearth; lack.
2 *we eat more than we need, so the excess is turned into fat*: **remainder**, rest, residue, remaining quantity, overflow, overspill; leftovers, remnants, leavings; surplus, extra, difference; technical residuum.
3 *he lived a life of excess*: **overindulgence**, intemperance, intemperateness, immoderation, profligacy, lack of restraint, prodigality, lavishness, excessiveness, extravagance, decadence, self-indulgence, self-gratification, debauchery, dissipation, dissolution, dissoluteness.
▷ANTONYMS moderation, restraint.
□ **in excess of** *the book sold in excess of 10,000 copies*: **more than**, over, above, over and above, upwards of, beyond.
▷ANTONYMS fewer than, less than.
▸ adjective *cleansing gets rid of excess skin oils*: **surplus**, superfluous, spare, redundant, unwanted, unneeded, unused, excessive, leftover; extra, additional, reserve.

excessive adjective **1** *his excessive alcohol consumption*: **immoderate**, intemperate, imprudent, overindulgent, unrestrained, unrestricted, uncontrolled, uncurbed, unbridled, lavish, extravagant; superfluous, superabundant.
2 *the cost is excessive*: **exorbitant**, extortionate, unreasonable, outrageous, undue, uncalled for, extreme, inordinate, unwarranted, unnecessary, needless, disproportionate, too much; informal over the top, OTT, a bit much.

excessively adverb *her father had excessively high standards | he drank excessively*: **inordinately**, unduly, unnecessarily, unreasonably, absurdly, ridiculously, overly, to too great a degree, extra, very, extremely, exceedingly, exceptionally, unusually, impossibly, illogically, irrationally; **immoderately**, intemperately, too much, overmuch, without restraint, without control, without reserve; informal too-too.

Word links **excessively**
hyper- related prefix, as in *hypercritical, hyperventilate*

exchange noun **1** *they aim to promote the open exchange of ideas*: **interchange**, trade, trading, trade-off, swapping, barter, giving and taking, traffic, trafficking, bandying, reciprocity; archaic truck.
2 *he became a broker on the exchange*: **stock exchange**, money market, bourse.
3 *they had a brief and acrimonious exchange*: **conversation**, dialogue, chat, talk, word, discussion, meeting, conference; debate, argument, altercation, war of words; Brit. informal confab, row, barney, slanging match; formal confabulation; rare colloquy.
▸ verb *we exchanged shirts*: **trade**, swap, switch, barter, change, interchange; reciprocate; archaic truck.
□ **exchange blows** *they exchanged blows with men from a nearby village*: **fight**, brawl, grapple, scuffle, tussle, box, come to blows, engage in fisticuffs; hit each other; informal scrap, have a set-to, have a ding-dong; Brit. informal have a punch-up; Scottish informal swedge; N. Amer. informal rough-house; Austral./NZ informal stoush, go the knuckle.
□ **exchange words** *the two exchanged words and a fight ensued*: **argue**, disagree, quarrel, squabble, clash, have an argument, have a disagreement, have a quarrel, have a squabble; Brit. informal have a slanging match.

excise[1] (stress on the first syllable) noun *measures to generate further revenue included higher excise*: **duty**, tax, levy, tariff, toll, tithe; customs, customs duties; rare mulct.

excise[2] (stress on the second syllable) verb **1** *the tumours were excised immediately*: **cut out**, cut off, cut away, snip out, take out, extract, remove, eradicate, extirpate; technical resect.
▷ANTONYMS replace; insert.
2 *all unnecessary detail should be excised*: **delete**, cross out, cross through, strike out, score out, scratch out, cancel, put a line through, blue-pencil, ink out, edit out, blank out; erase, efface, take out, remove, cut out, cut, expunge, eliminate; expurgate, bowdlerize; informal axe, scrub, scrap, give something the chop; Computing, informal kill; Printing dele.
▷ANTONYMS add.

excitable adjective *the horses were very excitable*: **temperamental**, mercurial, volatile, emotional, sensitive, highly strung, easily upset, easily agitated, easily frightened, unstable, nervous, tense, brittle, edgy, jumpy, twitchy, skittish, unsettled, uneasy, neurotic; tempestuous, hot-tempered, quick-tempered, hot-headed, passionate, fiery, irascible, testy, moody, touchy, snappy; informal uptight, wired, blowing hot and cold.
▷ANTONYMS placid.

excite verb **1** *the prospect of a holiday excited me*: **thrill**, exhilarate, animate, enliven, rouse, stir, move, stimulate, galvanize, electrify, fire the imagination of, fire the enthusiasm of; delight, enrapture, intoxicate; informal send, tickle, tickle someone pink, buck up, pep up, ginger up, give someone a buzz, give someone a kick, get someone going; N. Amer. informal light a fire under, give someone a charge; rare inspirit.
▷ANTONYMS bore, depress.
2 *she wore a chiffon nightgown to excite him*: **arouse**, arouse sexually, make someone feel sexually excited, stimulate, titillate, inflame; please, attract, entice; informal turn someone on, give someone a thrill, get someone going, float someone's boat, do it for someone, light someone's fire, tickle someone's fancy.
▷ANTONYMS turn off.
3 *his clothes excited envy and admiration*: **provoke**, stir up, elicit, rouse, arouse, stimulate, kindle, trigger (off), touch off, spark off, awaken, incite, instigate, foment, bring out, cause, bring about; literary enkindle.

excited adjective **1** *Louise felt excited and proud of her achievement*: **thrilled**, exhilarated, elevated, animated, enlivened, electrified, stirred, moved; delighted, exuberant, enraptured, intoxicated, feverish, enthusiastic, eager; informal high, high as a kite, fired up, tickled, tickled pink, full of beans, bright-eyed and bushy-tailed, peppy, sparky.
▷ANTONYMS indifferent; depressed.
2 **aroused**, sexually aroused, stimulated, titillated, inflamed, impassioned; attracted; informal turned on, on fire, hot, horny, sexed up; Brit. informal randy; N. Amer. informal squirrelly; rare concupiscent.
▷ANTONYMS turned off.

excitement noun **1** *the excitement of seeing a leopard in the wild*: **thrill**, thrilling sensation, exciting sensation, adventure, treat; pleasure, delight, joy; informal kick, buzz, high; N. Amer. informal charge.
2 *he saw the excitement in her eyes*: **exhilaration**, elation, animation, enthusiasm, eagerness, anticipation, feverishness, fever, delirium, agitation, emotion, fire, fieriness, intensity, zeal, zest; informal pep, vim, zing, spark.
▷ANTONYMS boredom, indifference.
3 **arousal**, sexual arousal, passion, fire, glow; stimulation, titillation, attraction; informal turning on.

exciting adjective **1** *I think your stories are really exciting*: **thrilling**, exhilarating, stirring, rousing, stimulating, intoxicating, electrifying, invigorating, moving, inspiring; gripping, compelling, sensational, powerful, dramatic, shocking, startling, hair-raising, explosive, knife-edge, cliffhanging; informal mind-blowing; N. Amer. informal stem-winding.
▷ANTONYMS boring.
2 *the intimacy had been both frightening and exciting*: **arousing**, sexually arousing, stimulating, sexually stimulating, titillating, tantalizing, provocative, erotic, sexual, sexy; informal raunchy, steamy.
▷ANTONYMS off-putting.

exclaim verb *'Well, I never!' she exclaimed*: **cry out**, cry, declare, come out with, burst out with, blurt out, utter suddenly; call, call out, shout, sing out, yell, shriek, scream, screech, roar, bellow; rare ejaculate, vociferate, ululate.
▷ANTONYMS mutter, whisper.

exclamation noun *an exclamation of amazement*: **cry**, call, shout, yell, shriek, roar, bellow, interjection, sudden utterance; expletive; rare ejaculation.

exclude verb **1** *women had been excluded from many scientific societies | she was trying to exclude David from the conversation*: **keep out**, deny access to, shut out, debar, disbar, bar, ban, prohibit, put an embargo on, embargo; reject, blackball, ostracize, banish; cut out, freeze out; Brit. send to Coventry.
▷ANTONYMS accept, admit.
2 *clauses designed to exclude any possibility of judicial review*: **eliminate**, rule out, factor out; preclude, prevent the occurrence of; formal except.
▷ANTONYMS allow for.
3 *the price excludes postage and packing*: **be exclusive of**, not include, not be inclusive of.
▷ANTONYMS include.
4 *I was surprised to see that he excluded his own name from the list*: **leave out**, omit, miss out, fail to include.
▷ANTONYMS include.

exclusion noun **1** *the exclusion of women from the society*: **barring**, keeping out, debarment, debarring, disbarring, banning, ban, prohibition, embargo; rejection, ostracism, banishment.
▷ANTONYMS acceptance, admission.
2 *the exclusion of other factors*: **elimination**, ruling out, factoring out; precluding.
▷ANTONYMS inclusion.
3 *the exclusion of pupils from the school*: **expulsion**, removal, ejection,

throwing out; suspension.
▷ANTONYMS admission.

exclusive adjective **1** *one of Britain's most exclusive clubs*: **select**, chic, high-class, elite, fashionable, stylish, elegant, choice, special, premier, grade A; expensive; restrictive, restricted, limited, private, closed, cliquish, cliquey, clannish, snobbish; Brit. upmarket; N. Amer. high-toned; informal posh, ritzy, classy, upper-crust, top-drawer, top-people's; Brit. informal swish; N. Amer. informal swank, tony; rare discriminative.
▷ANTONYMS open.
2 *his exclusive concern with himself*: **complete**, full, entire, whole, total, absolute; to the exclusion of everything else.
▷ANTONYMS partial.
3 *I have reserved a room for your exclusive use*: **sole**, undivided, unshared, unique, only, individual, personal, private, single, especial; dedicated.
4 *prices are* ***exclusive of*** *VAT and delivery*: **not including**, excluding, leaving out, omitting, excepting, with the omission/exception of, except for, not counting, leaving aside, barring.
▷ANTONYMS inclusive of.
5 *mutually exclusive alternatives*: **incompatible**, irreconcilable.
▶noun *the magazine's six-page exclusive*: **scoop**, exposé, revelation, special, inside story; coup.

excoriate verb **1** technical *the surrounding skin had been excoriated*: **abrade**, rub away, rub off, rub raw, scrape, scratch, chafe, damage; strip away, peel away, skin; technical decorticate.
2 rare *he was excoriated in the press for covering up the truth*. See **criticize**.

excrement noun **faeces**, excreta, stools, droppings; waste matter, ordure, dung, manure, mess, muck; sewage, black water; informal poo, doo-doo, doings; Brit. informal cack, whoopsies, jobbies; N. Amer. informal poop; vulgar slang shit, crap, turds; archaic night soil, sullage; rare egesta.

> *Word links* **excrement**
> **copro-, scato-** related prefixes
> **scatology** medical study of excrement
> **scatologcal** obsessed with excrement and excretion
> **coprophobia** fear of excrement
> **coprophagous** excrement-eating

excrescence noun **1** *a large excrescence on his leg*: **growth**, lump, swelling, protuberance, protrusion, knob, nodule, outgrowth; wart, boil, pustule, carbuncle, tumour.
2 *the new buildings around the cathedral were an excrescence*: **eyesore**, blot on the landscape, monstrosity, disfigurement; informal sight.

excrete verb *the process by which waste products are excreted from the body*: **expel**, pass, void, discharge, eject, evacuate, eliminate; exude, emit; defecate, urinate; rare egest.
▷ANTONYMS absorb, ingest.

excruciating adjective *an excruciating pain in her head*: **agonizing**, extremely painful, severe, acute, intense, extreme, savage, violent, racking, searing, piercing, stabbing, raging, harrowing, tormenting, grievous; dreadful, awful, terrible, unbearable, unendurable, more than one can bear, more than flesh and blood can bear; informal splitting, thumping, pounding, killing; literary exquisite.
▷ANTONYMS slight, mild.

excursion noun *an excursion to Blackpool*: **trip**, outing, jaunt, expedition, journey, tour; day trip, day out, drive, run, ride; informal junket, spin, hop; Scottish informal hurl.

excusable adjective *an excusable mistake under the circumstances*: **forgivable**, pardonable, defensible, justifiable, condonable, understandable, explainable; venial.
▷ANTONYMS inexcusable, unforgivable.

excuse verb **1** *eventually she excused him, as she always did*: **forgive**, pardon, absolve, exonerate, acquit; make allowances for; informal let someone off (the hook); rare exculpate.
▷ANTONYMS punish, blame.
2 *such conduct can never be excused*: **justify**, defend, make excuses for, make a case for, explain (away), rationalize, condone, vindicate, warrant; mitigate, palliate; apologize for; forgive, overlook, disregard, ignore, pass over, turn a blind eye to, turn a deaf ear to, wink at, blink at, indulge, tolerate, sanction; rare extenuate.
▷ANTONYMS condemn.
3 *she has been* ***excused from*** *her duties for now*: **let off**, release, relieve, exempt, spare, absolve, free, liberate; rare dispense.
▷ANTONYMS hold to.
▶noun **1** *that's no excuse for stealing*: **justification**, defence, reason, explanation, mitigating circumstances, mitigation, extenuation, palliation, vindication; grounds, cause, basis, call; argument, apology, apologia, plea.
2 *he needed an excuse to get away from his family*: **pretext**, ostensible reason, pretence, front, cover-up, fabrication, evasion; informal story, alibi, line, cop-out; Brit. informal get-out.
3 informal *that pathetic* ***excuse for*** *a man!* **travesty of**, apology for, poor specimen of, pitiful example of, mockery of; pale shadow of, poor imitation of.

> *Choose the right word* **excuse, forgive, pardon, condone**
> See **forgive**.

execrable adjective *an execrable piece of work*: **appalling**, awful, dreadful, terrible, frightful, atrocious, very bad, lamentable; disgusting, deplorable, disgraceful, reprehensible, shameful, abominable, abhorrent, loathsome, odious, heinous, hateful, detestable, despicable, foul, vile, scandalous, contemptible, repugnant, repellent, revolting, unspeakable, wretched; informal abysmal, diabolical, shocking, rotten, woeful, lousy, dire, the pits, God-awful, tenth-rate; Brit. informal chronic, pants, a load of pants; vulgar slang crap, shit; rare egregious.
▷ANTONYMS good, admirable.

execrate verb *the men were execrated as dangerous and corrupt*: **revile**, denounce, decry, condemn, vilify; **detest**, loathe, hate, abhor, abominate, despise, regard with disgust, feel disgust for, feel aversion/revulsion to; rare excoriate, anathematize, vilipend.
▷ANTONYMS praise; adore.

execute verb **1** *he was convicted of treason and executed*: **put to death**, carry out a sentence of death on, kill; hang, send to the gibbet, behead, guillotine, decapitate, electrocute, shoot, put before a firing squad, send to the gas chamber, garrotte, crucify, stone to death; lynch; N. Amer. send to the electric chair, send to the chair; informal string up; N. Amer. informal fry; in Turkey, historical bowstring.
2 *the corporation executed a series of financial deals*: **carry out**, accomplish, perform, implement, effect, bring off, bring about, achieve, carry off, carry through, complete, enact, enforce, put into effect, put into practice, do, discharge, prosecute, engineer, administer, attain, realize, fulfil; perpetrate; informal pull off, swing, cut; archaic acquit oneself of; rare effectuate.
3 *a variety act which is cleverly conceived and fairly well executed*: **perform**, present, render; stage, put on.

execution noun **1** *the execution of the plan*: **implementation**, carrying out, accomplishment, performance, effecting, bringing off, bringing about, achievement, carrying off, carrying through, completion, enactment, enforcement, discharge, prosecution, engineering, attainment, realization, fulfilment; perpetration.
2 *the execution of the play*: **performance**, presentation, rendition, rendering, staging; delivery, technique, style.
3 *thousands were sentenced to execution or imprisonment*: **capital punishment**, the death penalty, being put to death, killing; the gibbet, the gallows, the noose, the rope, the scaffold, the guillotine, the firing squad; N. Amer. the (electric) chair; informal the drop; N. Amer. informal necktie party; historical noyade.

executioner noun **hangman**, official killer; firing squad; historical headsman, Jack Ketch.

executive adjective *a district assembly with executive powers*: **administrative**, decision-making, directorial, directing, controlling, managerial; law-making, regulating; professional, white-collar.
▶noun **1** *a top-level meeting of executives at the investment bank*: **chief**, head, principal, senior official, senior manager, senior administrator; director, managing director, MD, CEO, chief executive officer, president, chairman, chairwoman, controller; Brit. director general; informal boss, boss man, top dog, bigwig, big wheel, big Daddy, big Chief, exec, suit; Brit. informal guv'nor; N. Amer. informal numero uno, Mister Big, (head) honcho, big kahuna, big white chief, sachem, padrone; derogatory fat cat.
2 *the executive has increased in number*: **administration**, leadership, management, directorate, directors; government, legislative body; informal top brass.

exegesis noun *the exegesis of ancient texts*: **interpretation**, explanation, exposition, explication, elucidation, clarification; gloss, annotation.

exemplar noun *he was regarded as an exemplar of rationality and decorum*: **epitome**, perfect example, shining example, model, paragon, ideal, type, exemplification, definitive example, textbook example, embodiment, essence, quintessence; paradigm, archetype, prototype, pattern, blueprint, standard, criterion, benchmark, yardstick; byword; rare avatar.

exemplary adjective **1** *her exemplary behaviour*: **perfect**, ideal, model, faultless, without fault, copybook, flawless, impeccable, consummate; excellent, outstanding, exceptional, admirable, fine, very good, commendable, laudable, praiseworthy, meritorious, honourable, estimable, above/beyond reproach, blameless, irreproachable, unimpeachable; rare applaudable.
▷ANTONYMS deplorable, unworthy.
2 *exemplary jail sentences*: **serving as a deterrent**, example-setting, lesson-teaching; **cautionary**, warning, admonitory; rare monitory.
3 *her works are exemplary of certain feminist arguments*: **typical**, characteristic, representative, illustrative; archetypal, paradigmatic; rare epitomic.
▷ANTONYMS unrepresentative, atypical.

e

Word toolkit **exemplary**

See **archetypal**.

exemplify verb **1** *a case study of a police operation which exemplifies current trends*: **typify**, epitomize, be a typical example of, serve as a typical example of, represent, be representative of, symbolize; personify, embody, be the embodiment of; demonstrate, show.
2 *he exemplified his point with an anecdote*: **illustrate**, give an example of, give an instance of, demonstrate, instance; rare instantiate.

exempt adjective *these patients are* ***exempt from*** *all charges*: **free from**, not liable to, not subject to; exempted, spared, excepted, excused, absolved, released, discharged; immune.
▷ANTONYMS liable to, subject to.
▶ verb *he had been* ***exempted from*** *military service*: **excuse**, free, release, exclude, give/grant immunity, spare; let off, relieve of, make an exception of/for; liberate, absolve, discharge; informal let off the hook; N. Amer. informal grandfather; rare dispense.

exemption noun *exemption from the payment of road tax*: **immunity**, exception, dispensation, indemnity, exclusion, freedom, release, relief, absolution, exoneration; special treatment, privilege, favouritism; impunity; informal let-off; rare derogation.
▷ANTONYMS liability.

exercise noun **1** *exercise improves your heart and lung power*: **physical activity**, movement, exertion, effort, work; a workout, working-out, training, drilling; gymnastics, sports, games, PE (physical education), PT (physical training), aerobics, step aerobics, jogging, running, circuit training, aquarobics, callisthenics, isometrics, eurhythmics, keep-fit, dancercise, bodybuilding; informal physical jerks; informal, dated one's daily dozen; trademark Boxercise.
2 *translation exercises from and into French*: **task**, piece of work, problem, assignment, piece of school work, piece of homework; Music étude.
3 *the exercise of professional skill*: **use**, utilization, employment; **practice**, putting into practice, application, operation, exertion, performance, implementation, discharge, accomplishment.
4 **(exercises)** *military exercises*: **manoeuvres**, operations; war games, field day.
▶ verb **1** *she still exercised every day*: **work out**, do exercises, keep fit, train, drill, engage in physical activity; informal pump iron.
2 *he must learn to exercise patience*: **use**, employ, make use of, utilize, avail oneself of, put to use; **practise**, apply, bring to bear, bring into play, implement, exert, wield.
3 *the problem continued to exercise him*: **worry**, trouble, concern, make anxious, bother, disturb, perturb, perplex, puzzle, distress, occupy someone's thoughts, preoccupy, prey on someone's mind, gnaw at, lie heavy on, burden, make uneasy, agitate; informal bug, make someone scratch their head, do someone's head in; archaic pother.

exert verb **1** *he exerted considerable emotional pressure on me*: **bring to bear**, apply, bring into play, exercise, employ, use, make use of, utilize, deploy; wield; expend, spend.
2 *he had been* ***exerting himself*** *to make a good impression on her*: **make an effort**, try hard, strive, endeavour, apply oneself, do one's best, do all one can, do one's utmost, give one's all, make every effort, spare no effort, be at pains, put oneself out; struggle, labour, toil, strain, push oneself, drive oneself, work hard, work like a Trojan; rack/cudgel one's brains; informal give it one's best shot, go all out, pull out all the stops, bend/lean over backwards, put one's back into it, knock oneself out, do one's damnedest, move heaven and earth, beaver away, slog away, keep one's nose to the grindstone, work one's socks off, break sweat; N. Amer. informal do one's darnedest/durnedest, bust one's chops; Austral. informal go for the doctor.

exertion noun **1** *she was panting with the exertion*: **effort**, strain, struggle, toil, endeavour, hard work, labour, industry, {blood, sweat, and tears}; pains, assiduity, assiduousness; exercise, activity; informal elbow grease, sweat; Brit. informal graft; Austral./NZ informal yakka; literary travail, moil.
2 *the exertion of pressure*: **use**, application, appliance, bringing to bear, exercise, employment, utilization; expenditure.

exhalation noun **1** *a long exhalation of relief*: **breath**, breathing out; sigh; technical expiration.
▷ANTONYMS inhalation.
2 *the exhalation of gases | noxious exhalations*: **emission**, giving off, emanation, discharge; fume, vapour, effluvium, effluent; rare exsufflation.

exhale verb **1** *he exhaled a cloud of cigarette smoke*: **breathe out**, blow out, puff out; technical expire.
▷ANTONYMS inhale.
2 *the jungle exhaled mists of early morning*: **give off**, emanate, send forth, emit, discharge; rare exsufflate.

exhaust verb **1** *the effort had exhausted him*: **tire out**, wear out, overtire, overtax, fatigue, weary, tire, drain, run someone into the ground, run someone ragged, enervate, sap, debilitate, prostrate, enfeeble; wear oneself to a shadow; informal do in, take it out of one, wipe out, fag out, knock out, shatter, wear oneself to a frazzle, frazzle, nearly kill; Brit. informal knacker; N. Amer. informal poop, tucker out; Austral./NZ & Irish informal root.
▷ANTONYMS invigorate, refresh.
2 *the country has exhausted its treasury reserves*: **use up**, run through, go through, consume, finish, deplete, expend, spend, dissipate, waste, squander, fritter away; empty, milk, drain, suck dry, impoverish; informal blow, bleed.
▷ANTONYMS replenish, restock.
3 *I think we've exhausted the subject*: **say all there is to say about**, leave nothing left to say about, do to death; treat thoroughly, develop completely, expound in great detail about, study in great detail, research completely, leave no stone left unturned, go over with a fine-tooth comb.
▷ANTONYMS touch on.

exhausted adjective **1** *I must go to bed—I'm exhausted*: **tired out**, worn out, weary, dog-tired, bone-tired, bone-weary, ready to drop, on one's last legs, asleep on one's feet, drained, fatigued, enervated, debilitated, spent; jet-lagged; out of breath, breathless, panting, puffing, puffed, puffed out, puffing and blowing, gasping (for breath); informal done in, all in, dead on one's feet, beat, dead beat, shattered, bushed, fagged out, knocked out, wiped out, running on empty, zonked out, worn to a frazzle, frazzled, bushwhacked; Brit. informal knackered, whacked (out), shagged out, jiggered; Scottish informal wabbit; N. Amer. informal pooped, tuckered out, fried, whipped; Austral./NZ informal stonkered; Brit. vulgar slang buggered; Austral./NZ vulgar slang rooted; archaic toilworn; rare fordone.
▷ANTONYMS fresh as a daisy, raring to go.
2 *the treasury's exhausted reserves*: **used up**, at an end, consumed, finished, spent, depleted; empty, drained, impoverished, bankrupt.
▷ANTONYMS replenished, restocked.

exhausting adjective *a long and exhausting journey*: **tiring**, wearying, taxing, fatiguing, wearing, enervating, draining, sapping, debilitating; arduous, strenuous, uphill, onerous, punishing, demanding, exacting, burdensome, gruelling, back-breaking, crushing, crippling; informal killing, murderous, hellish; Brit. informal knackering; rare exigent.
▷ANTONYMS invigorating, refreshing.

exhaustion noun **1** *sheer exhaustion forced Paul to give up*: **extreme tiredness**, overtiredness, fatigue, weariness, lack of energy, enervation, debilitation, debility, faintness, prostration, enfeeblement, lassitude; jet lag; Medicine inanition, asthenia.
▷ANTONYMS vigour.
2 *the rapid exhaustion of fossil fuel reserves*: **consumption**, depletion, using up, expenditure; draining, emptying, sapping.
▷ANTONYMS replenishment.

exhaustive adjective *an exhaustive study of the subject*: **comprehensive**, all-inclusive, complete, full, full-scale, all-embracing, all-encompassing, encyclopedic, thorough, in-depth, thoroughgoing, extensive, intensive, all-out, profound, far-reaching, sweeping, umbrella; definitive; detailed, minute, meticulous, painstaking, careful; informal wall-to-wall.
▷ANTONYMS perfunctory, incomplete.

exhibit verb **1** *a selection of the paintings were exhibited at Sotheby's*: **put on display**, put on show, display, show, show to the public, put on public view, present, unveil, model, parade, showcase; set out, lay out, array, arrange; hang.
2 *Luke had begun to exhibit signs of jealousy*: **show**, reveal, display, manifest, evince, betray, give away, disclose; express, indicate, demonstrate, present, make clear, make plain, evidence; parade, flaunt.
▷ANTONYMS conceal, hide.
▶ noun **1** *it is now an exhibit at the British Museum*: **object on display**, item, piece.
2 N. Amer. *people flocked to the exhibit*. See **exhibition**.

exhibition noun **1** *an exhibition of French sculpture*: **(public) display**, show, showing, presentation, demonstration, showcase, mounting, spectacle; retrospective, biennale; exposition, Expo, fair, trade fair, world fair; N. Amer. exhibit; informal demo.
2 *a false but convincing exhibition of concern*: **display**, show, demonstration, manifestation, expression, indication; revelation, betrayal, disclosure; parade.

exhibitionist noun **show-off**, posturer, poser, self-publicist; extrovert; N. Amer. informal showboat; Austral./NZ informal lair; rare attitudinizer.
▷ANTONYMS shrinking violet.

exhilarate verb *he was exhilarated by the boat's speed*: **thrill**, excite, intoxicate; **elate**, make someone's spirits soar, make very happy, give someone great pleasure, delight, gladden, brighten, cheer up, enliven, animate, invigorate, energize, lift, stimulate, raise someone's spirits, revitalize, refresh; informal give someone a kick, give someone a thrill, give someone a buzz, turn someone on; N. Amer. informal give someone a charge; rare inspirit.
▷ANTONYMS depress.

exhilarating adjective *an exhilarating experience*: **thrilling**, exciting, intoxicating, heady, stimulating, invigorating, electrifying, energizing, uplifting, enlivening, revitalizing, vitalizing, stirring, breathtaking;

refreshing, bracing; informal mind-blowing.
▷ANTONYMS boring, depressing.

Word toolkit **exhilarating**

See **bracing**.

exhilaration noun *a feeling of exhilaration swept through her*: **elation**, euphoria, exultation, exaltation, joy, happiness, delight, joyousness, jubilation, rapture, ecstasy, bliss, rhapsody; excitement, intoxication, invigoration, ebullience, high spirits, glee, gleefulness, gaiety, animation, revitalization.
▷ANTONYMS dejection, depression.

exhort verb *he exhorted delegates to fight corruption and bureaucracy*: **urge**, encourage, call on, enjoin, adjure, charge, try to persuade, press, pressure, put pressure on, use pressure on, pressurize, lean on, push; egg on, spur, incite, goad; bid, appeal to, entreat, implore, beseech; advise, counsel, admonish, warn.
▷ANTONYMS discourage.

exhortation noun **1** *no amount of exhortation had any effect*: **urging**, encouragement, persuasion, pressure, pressurization, pushing, insistence; incitement, goading, egging on; beseeching; admonishment, warning; rare paraenesis.
▷ANTONYMS discouragement.
2 *the government's exhortations to the electorate*: **enjoinder**, call, charge, injunction; **entreaty**, appeal; admonition, warning, sermon, lecture, harangue; rare obtestation, protreptic.

exhume verb *four years later his body was exhumed*: **disinter**, dig up, unearth, bring out of the ground; rare disentomb, unbury, ungrave.
▷ANTONYMS bury.

exigency noun rare **1** *the exigencies of the continuing war*: **need**, demand, requirement, want; necessity, essential, requisite.
2 *financial exigency dictated that the government adopt a peace policy*: **urgency**, emergency, extremity, crisis, difficulty, pressure.

exiguous adjective rare *the exiguous post-war sugar ration*. See **meagre** (sense 1).

exile noun **1** *his exile from the land of his birth*: **banishment**, expulsion, expatriation, deportation, eviction; uprooting, separation; extradition; historical transportation; in ancient Greece ostracism.
▷ANTONYMS return.
2 *political exiles*: **émigré**, expatriate; displaced person, refugee, deportee; outcast, pariah; informal DP, expat.
▸ verb *a corrupt dictator who had been exiled from his country*: **expel**, **banish**, expatriate, deport, ban, bar; drive out, throw out, cast out, eject, oust, outlaw; uproot, separate; extradite; Christianity excommunicate; historical transport, displace; in ancient Greece ostracize.

exist verb **1** *animals which existed at some time in the distant past*: **live**, be alive, be living, have life, breathe, draw breath; be, have being, have existence, be extant.
2 *the liberal climate that existed during his presidency*: **prevail**, **occur**, be found, be met with, be in existence; remain, obtain, continue, last, endure; be the case.
3 *she had to exist on an average income of £50 a week*: **survive**, subsist, live, stay alive, support oneself, eke out a living, eke out an existence; manage, make do, keep going, struggle along, scrape by, keep one's head above water, make ends meet; informal get by, keep the wolf from the door.

existence noun **1** *a crisis that threatened the industry's continued existence*: **actuality**, **being**, existing, reality, fact; survival, continuance, continuation, subsistence, living; Philosophy quiddity, esse.
▷ANTONYMS non-existence.
2 *her drab suburban existence*: **way of life**, way of living, manner of living, life, lifestyle, circumstances, situation.
□ **in existence 1** *scientists believe there are several million unidentified species in existence*: **alive**, existing, extant, existent.
▷ANTONYMS extinct.
2 *the only copy of the book still in existence*: **surviving**, remaining, undestroyed, lasting, continuing, enduring; about, around, in circulation.
▷ANTONYMS destroyed, lost.

existent adjective *species that are no longer existent*: **in existence**, alive, existing, living, extant, surviving, remaining, undestroyed, enduring, lasting; around, about in circulation; prevailing, current.
▷ANTONYMS non-existent.

exit noun **1** *the fire exit*: **way out**, door, egress, passage out, escape route; doorway, gate, gateway, portal; outlet, vent.
▷ANTONYMS entrance.
2 *take the second exit on the left*: **turning**, turn-off, turn, side road; N. Amer. turnout.
3 *his sudden exit from America*: **departure**, leaving, withdrawal, retirement, going, decamping, retreat, pull-out, evacuation; leave-taking, farewell, adieu; flight, exodus, escape; informal quitting.
▷ANTONYMS arrival.
▸ verb *the doorway through which the doctor had just exited*: **leave**, go (out), depart, take one's leave, make one's departure, make an exit; withdraw, retreat, retire; informal quit.
▷ANTONYMS enter.

exodus noun *a mass exodus of refugees from the stricken city*: **mass departure**, withdrawal, evacuation, leaving, exit; migration, emigration, hegira, diaspora; flight, escape, retreat, fleeing; S. African informal chicken run.
▷ANTONYMS arrival.

exonerate verb **1** *the inquiry exonerated Lewis and his company*: **absolve**, clear, acquit, declare innocent, find innocent, pronounce not guilty, discharge; vindicate; rare exculpate.
▷ANTONYMS charge, convict.
2 *Pope Clement V exonerated the king from his oath to the barons*: **release**, discharge, relieve, free, liberate; excuse, exempt, except; informal let off; rare dispense.
▷ANTONYMS hold to.

exoneration noun **1** *despite his exoneration, he resigned*: **vindication**, freeing from blame, absolution, acquittal, discharge; rare exculpation.
▷ANTONYMS conviction, blaming.
2 *we should not seek exoneration from the consequences of our acts*: **immunity**, exemption, indemnity, dispensation; release, freedom; informal let-off; rare derogation.
▷ANTONYMS liability.

exorbitant adjective *the fees charged by the consultants were exorbitant*: **extortionate**, excessively high, extremely high, excessive, sky-high, prohibitive, outrageous, unreasonable, preposterous, inordinate, immoderate, inflated, monstrous, unwarranted, unconscionable, huge, enormous, disproportionate; punitive, ruinous; expensive, extravagant; Brit. over the odds; informal criminal, steep, stiff, over the top, OTT, costing an arm and a leg, costing a bomb, costing the earth, daylight robbery, a rip-off.
▷ANTONYMS reasonable, competitive.

exorcism noun **1** *the exorcism of evil spirits*: **driving out**, casting out, expulsion; rare insufflation.
2 *returning to the scene of the crime would be a kind of exorcism for them both*: **catharsis**, cleansing, purification, purgation, release, deliverance; rare lustration.

exorcize verb **1** *an attempt to exorcize a spirit*: **drive out**, cast out, expel.
2 *Jesuit priests were called in to exorcize the house of the demon*: **rid**, deliver, free, purify, cleanse, purge; rare lustrate.

exotic adjective **1** *exotic birds*: **foreign**, non-native, tropical; alien, imported, introduced, non-naturalized, unnaturalized.
▷ANTONYMS native.
2 *exotic places*: **foreign**, faraway, far off, far-flung, unfamiliar; distant, remote.
▷ANTONYMS familiar, nearby.
3 *Linda's exotic appearance*: **striking**, colourful, eye-catching; **unusual**, unconventional, out of the ordinary, extravagant, remarkable, sensational, astonishing, strange, outlandish, bizarre, fantastic, peculiar, weird, outrageous, curious, different, unfamiliar; Bohemian, alternative, avant-garde, foreign-looking; attractive, glamorous, romantic, fascinating; Brit. out of the common; informal offbeat, off the wall.
▷ANTONYMS unremarkable, conventional.
4 *exotic dancers*: **erotic**, sexy, provocative, go-go, striptease, titillating, risqué; informal raunchy.

Word toolkit **exotic**

See **unfamiliar**.

expand verb **1** *metals expand when heated*: **increase in size**, become larger, enlarge; swell, become distended, dilate, inflate, balloon, puff out/up; lengthen, stretch; thicken, fatten, fill out; rare intumesce, tumefy.
▷ANTONYMS shrink, contract, condense.
2 *the company is expanding | an excellent opportunity for him to expand his business*: **grow**, become/make larger, become/make bigger, increase in size/scope; extend, augment, broaden, widen, develop, diversify, multiply, add to, build up, scale up; branch out, broaden one's horizons, extend one's operations; spread, proliferate, mushroom.
▷ANTONYMS shrink, scale down.
3 *the young leaves began to expand*: **open out**, unfold, unfurl, spread out, unroll.
4 *the minister **expanded on** the government's proposals*: **elaborate on**, enlarge on, add detail to, go into detail about, flesh out, put flesh on the bones of, develop, supplement, amplify, expatiate on; embellish, embroider, pad out, fill out.
▷ANTONYMS touch on.
5 *she was made to feel witty and entertained—she expanded and flourished*: **relax**, unbend, become relaxed, grow friendlier, become less reserved, become more sociable; informal loosen up; N. Amer. informal hang loose.
▷ANTONYMS tense up, clam up.

e

expanse noun *this wide expanse of grass and heather*: **area**, stretch, sweep, tract, swathe, plain, field, belt, region; sea, carpet, blanket, sheet; breadth, range, spread, reach, space, extent, vastness.
▷ANTONYMS confined space, enclosure.

expansion noun **1** *the expansion and contraction of blood vessels*: **enlargement**, increase in size, swelling, distension, dilation; lengthening, elongation, stretching, thickening; Medicine dilatation.
▷ANTONYMS contraction.
2 *the expansion of the company*: **growth**, increase in size, enlargement, extension, augmentation, development, evolution; diversification, build-up, buildout, scaling up, aggrandizement; spread, proliferation, mushrooming, multiplication; rare evolvement.
▷ANTONYMS reduction in size.
3 *the book is an expansion of a lecture given last year*: **elaboration**, enlargement, amplification, development; embellishment.
▷ANTONYMS summary, abridgement.

e

expansive adjective **1** *fine views of the expansive moorland*: **extensive**, sweeping, rolling; spacious.
2 *chapters which are expansive in their historical coverage*: **wide-ranging**, extensive, broad, wide, all-embracing, comprehensive, thorough, inclusive.
▷ANTONYMS limited, restricted.
3 *after a glass or two of wine, Cara became engagingly expansive*: **communicative**, forthcoming, sociable, friendly, outgoing, unreserved, uninhibited, open, affable, amiable, genial, chatty, talkative, conversational, garrulous, loquacious, voluble, effusive, demonstrative, extrovert, extroverted; discursive.
▷ANTONYMS uncommunicative, reserved, taciturn.

expatiate verb *she* ***expatiated on*** *the subject at some length*: **hold forth about**, speak/write at length about, pontificate about, discourse on, expound, go into detail about, go on about, dwell on; expand on, enlarge on, elaborate on, amplify, embellish; informal spout about, sound off about; rare perorate on, dilate on, dissertate on.

expatriate noun *the level of salary paid to expatriates working overseas*: **emigrant**, non-native, émigré, migrant, economic migrant, guest worker; displaced person, refugee, exile; German Gastarbeiter; informal expat, DP.
▷ANTONYMS national.
▶ adjective *expatriate workers*: **emigrant**, living abroad, working abroad, non-native, émigré; displaced, refugee, exiled; informal expat.
▷ANTONYMS native, indigenous.
▶ verb **1** *he never visited Europe—still less was he tempted to* ***expatriate himself***: **settle abroad**, live abroad, relocate abroad.
2 *he was expatriated for the term of his natural life*: **exile**, deport, banish, expel; historical displace, transport.
▷ANTONYMS repatriate.

expect verb **1** *I expect she'll be late*: **suppose**, presume, think it likely, think, believe, imagine, assume, conjecture, surmise, calculate, judge; trust; informal guess, reckon; N. Amer. informal figure.
2 *I'm expecting a letter from him | a 10 per cent rise in profits was expected*: **anticipate**, await, look for, hope for, watch for, look forward to, look ahead to, have in prospect; contemplate, bargain for/on, bank on, be prepared for, plan for; predict, forecast, foresee, prophesy, envisage, envision.
3 *we expect total discretion and loyalty*: **require**, ask for, call for, look for, wish, want, hope for; count on, rely on; insist on, demand.

> *Choose the right word* **expect, anticipate, foresee**
>
> See **anticipate**.

expectancy noun **1** *an atmosphere of feverish expectancy*: **anticipation**, expectation, eagerness, hope, hopefulness; excitement, suspense.
2 *a life expectancy of 77.6 years*: **likelihood**, probability, outlook, prospect.

expectant adjective **1** *hundreds of expectant fans*: **eager**, **excited**, agog, waiting with bated breath, breathless, waiting, anticipatory, hopeful; in suspense, on tenterhooks, on the edge of one's seat, keyed up, on pins and needles, anxious.
▷ANTONYMS uninterested.
2 *an expectant mother*: **pregnant**, having a baby, having a child, carrying a child; French enceinte; informal expecting, in the family way, expecting a happy event, eating for two, preggers, preggy, with a bun in the oven, with one in the oven; Brit. informal up the duff, in the club, in the pudding club, up the spout, up the stick; N. Amer. informal knocked up; Austral. informal preggo, clucky; informal, dated in trouble, in pod; technical gravid, parturient; archaic with child, heavy/big with child, in a delicate condition, in an interesting condition, childing, on the way; rare impregnate.

expectation noun **1** *her expectations were unrealistic*: **supposition**, assumption, belief, presupposition, presumption, conjecture, surmise, reckoning, calculation, prediction, forecast, projection; assurance, confidence, trust.
2 *his body grew tense with expectation*: **anticipation**, expectancy, eagerness, hope, hopefulness; excitement, suspense.
3 archaic *a young man of expensive habits and no expectations*: **prospects**, prospects of inheritance, hopes, outlook, lookout.

expecting adjective informal *his wife's expecting again*: **pregnant**, expecting a baby, having a baby, having a child, carrying a child; French enceinte; informal in the family way, expecting a happy event, eating for two, preggers, preggy, with a bun in the oven, with one in the oven; Brit. informal in the club, in the pudding club, up the duff, up the spout, up the stick; N. Amer. informal knocked up; Austral. informal preggo, clucky; informal, dated in trouble, in pod; technical gravid, parturient; archaic with child, heavy/big with child, in a delicate condition, in an interesting condition, childing, on the way; rare impregnate.

expediency, expedience noun *he has abandoned his principles for the sake of political expediency*: **convenience**, **advantage**, advantageousness, usefulness, utility, benefit, profitability, profit, gain, gainfulness, effectiveness; practicality, pragmatism; prudence, judiciousness, desirability, suitability, advisability, appropriateness, aptness, fitness, timeliness, opportunism, propitiousness.
▷ANTONYMS disadvantage.

expedient adjective *a politically expedient strategy*: **convenient**, **advantageous**, in one's own interests, to one's own advantage, useful, of use, of service, beneficial, of benefit, profitable, gainful, effective, helpful; practical, pragmatic, strategic, tactical; politic, prudent, wise, judicious, sensible, desirable, suitable, advisable, appropriate, apt, fit, timely, opportune, propitious.
▷ANTONYMS inexpedient, ill-advised.
▶ noun *a temporary expedient adopted for the purpose of settling the financial crisis*: **measure**, means, method, stratagem, scheme, plan, course of action, move, tactic, manoeuvre, recourse, resource, device, tool, contrivance, ploy, plot, machination, trick, ruse, artifice, invention; stopgap; informal dodge; Austral. informal lurk; archaic shift, fetch.

expedite verb *the court has the power to expedite the decree absolute*: **speed up**, accelerate, hurry, hasten, step up, quicken, precipitate, rush; advance, facilitate, ease, make easier, further, promote, aid, push through, push, give a push to, press, urge on, forward, boost, give a boost to, stimulate, spur on, help along, oil the wheels for, smooth the way for, clear a path for; finish/accomplish/achieve quickly, dispatch; informal dash off, make short work of.
▷ANTONYMS delay; hinder.

expedition noun **1** *Captain Scott's expedition to the South Pole*: **journey**, voyage, tour, odyssey; undertaking, enterprise, mission, project, quest, operation, commission, assignment, exploit; exploration, safari, trek, hike, survey; archaic peregrination.
2 informal *a shopping expedition*: **trip**, excursion, outing, journey, jaunt, run; informal junket, hop.
3 *Gould was the only member of the expedition satisfied with its outcome*: **group**, team, party, company, crew, band, troop, squad, crowd.
4 formal *he was told to use all expedition possible*: **speed**, haste, hastiness, hurriedness, promptness, speediness, swiftness, quickness, rapidity, briskness, promptitude, velocity; alacrity, urgency, readiness, dispatch; rare expeditiousness; literary fleetness, celerity.

expeditious adjective *the expeditious processing of his application*: **speedy**, swift, quick, rapid, fast; prompt, punctual, immediate, instant, sudden; high-speed, fast-track, whistle-stop, lightning, meteoric, whirlwind; brisk, nimble; efficient, diligent; hasty, summary, abrupt; literary fleet, rathe.
▷ANTONYMS slow.

expel verb **1** *the opposition leader was expelled from her party*: **throw out**, bar, ban, debar, drum out, thrust out, push out, turn out, oust, remove, get rid of; reject, dismiss; blackball, blacklist; Military cashier; informal chuck out, sling out, fling out, kick/boot out, heave out, send packing; Brit. informal turf out; N. Amer. informal give someone the bum's rush; dated out.
▷ANTONYMS admit; welcome.
2 *he was released and expelled from the country*: **banish**, exile, deport, evict, expatriate, dismiss, displace; oust, drive out, throw out, cast out, purge, proscribe, outlaw; in ancient Greece ostracize.
3 *Dolly expelled a hiss*: **let out**, discharge, eject, force out, issue, send forth; excrete, evacuate, ejaculate, belch, disgorge, eliminate, void, spew out, spit out, vomit.

expend verb **1** *they had already expended $75,000 in legal costs*: **spend**, pay out, lay out, disburse, dole out, get through, go through; lavish, squander, waste, fritter (away), dissipate, spend like water, throw around like confetti; informal fork out, shell out, dish out, cough up, blow, splurge, pour/throw down the drain, spend money as if it grows on trees, spend money as if there were no tomorrow, spend money as if it were going out of style/fashion; Brit. informal splash out, stump up, blue; N. Amer. informal ante up, pony up.
▷ANTONYMS save, conserve.
2 *pushing heavy crates expends a lot of energy*: **use up**, use, utilize, make use of, consume, eat up, deplete, drain, sap; exhaust, empty, get through, go through, finish off.
▷ANTONYMS conserve.

expendable adjective **1** *he was tossed out of work when an accountant decided he was expendable*: **dispensable**, able to be sacrificed, replaceable;

non-essential, inessential, not essential, unimportant, unnecessary, unneeded, not required; superfluous, extraneous; disposable.
▷ANTONYMS indispensable; important.
2 *an expendable satellite launcher*: **disposable**, throwaway, one use, single-use, replaceable.

expenditure noun 1 *the expenditure of funds*: **spending**, paying out, outlay, disbursement, doling out; lavishing, squandering, waste, wasting, frittering (away), dissipation, dissipating.
▷ANTONYMS saving; conservation.
2 *the government is anxious to reduce public expenditure*: **outgoings**, costs, payments, expenses, overheads, dues, money spent; spending, outlay.
▷ANTONYMS income.

expense noun 1 *Nigel resented the expense of entertaining*: **cost**, price; charge, outlay, fee, tariff, toll, levy, payment, amount, rate, figure; informal, humorous damage.
2 *most regular expenses can be paid by standing order*: **outgoing**, payment, outlay, disbursement, expenditure, charge, bill, overhead; (**expenses**) incidentals.
3 *the imposition of stringent pollution controls will come at the expense of jobs*: **sacrifice**, cost, loss.

expensive adjective *an expensive restaurant*: **costly**, dear, high-priced, high-cost, exorbitant, extortionate, overpriced; immoderate, extravagant, lavish; valuable, precious, priceless, worth its weight in gold, worth a king's ransom; Brit. over the odds; informal steep, pricey, sky-high, costing an arm and a leg, costing the earth, costing a bomb, daylight robbery.
▷ANTONYMS cheap; economical.

experience noun 1 *salary will be commensurate with qualifications and experience*: **skill, practical knowledge**, practice; training, learning, education, grounding, knowledge, understanding, wisdom, professionalism; background, record, history, past; maturity, worldliness, sophistication, suaveness; French savoir faire; informal know-how.
2 *an enjoyable experience*: **incident**, occurrence, event, happening, affair, episode, encounter; adventure, exploit, escapade; circumstance, case; test, trial, ordeal.
3 *David gained his first* ***experience of*** *business with his father and brothers*: **involvement in**, participation in; **contact with**, acquaintance with, exposure to; observation of, awareness of; familiarity with, conversance with, understanding of, impression of, insight into.
▶ verb *policemen can experience harassment and distress*: **undergo**, encounter, meet, have experience of, come into contact with, run into, come across, come up against, face, be faced with, confront, be forced to contend with; feel, know, become familiar with; live/go through, sustain, suffer, endure, tolerate; participate in, taste, try.

> *Word links*
>
> **empirical** based on experience rather than theory or logic

experienced adjective 1 *an experienced pilot*: **knowledgeable**, skilful, skilled, expert, accomplished, adept, adroit, master, consummate, professional; proficient, trained, competent, capable, qualified, well trained, well versed; seasoned, with experience, practised, mature, veteran, long-serving, time-served, hardened, battle-scarred; informal crack, ace, mean, wizard.
▷ANTONYMS inexperienced, novice.
2 *she was naive, but deluded herself that she was experienced*: **worldly wise**, sophisticated, suave, urbane, polished, refined, mature, cultivated, cultured, knowing, initiated; worldly, well travelled, unprovincial; informal having been around, streetwise.
▷ANTONYMS naive.

experiment noun 1 *she carried out experiments in the breeding of silkworms*: **test**, investigation, trial, enquiry, demonstration; examination, observation; assessment, evaluation, appraisal, inspection, analysis, scrutiny, study, probe; trial run, try-out, pilot study, dummy run, dry run.
2 *these results have been established by experiment*: **research**, experimentation, observation, trial and error, analysis, testing.
▷ANTONYMS theory.
▶ verb *in 1809 he experimented with a glider capable of lifting a man*: **conduct experiments**, carry out trials/tests, conduct research; test, trial, put to the test, do tests on, try out, carry out trials on, assess, appraise, evaluate; investigate, examine, explore, observe, verify.

> *Word links* **experiment**
>
> **empirical** relating to experiment

experimental adjective 1 *interactive computing was still at an experimental stage*: **exploratory**, investigational, probing, fact-finding, trial and error; trial, test, pilot; speculative, conjectural, hypothetical, tentative; preliminary, probationary, prototype, under review, under the microscope, on the drawing board, empirical, observational; untested, untried.
▷ANTONYMS finished; theoretical.
2 *he started making music that was far more experimental*: **innovative**, innovatory, new, original, inventive, radical, avant-garde, alternative, fringe; unfamiliar, unorthodox, unconventional, eccentric, offbeat, bohemian; N. Amer. left-field; informal go-ahead, way-out.
▷ANTONYMS stale, hackneyed.

expert noun *he is an expert in kendo*: **specialist**, authority, pundit, oracle; adept, maestro, virtuoso, master, past master, professional, genius, wizard; connoisseur, aficionado, one of the cognoscenti, cognoscente, doyen, savant; informal ace, buff, pro, whizz, hotshot, old hand; Brit. informal dab hand; N. Amer. informal maven, crackerjack; rare proficient.
▷ANTONYMS inexpert, amateur.
▶ adjective *an expert chess player*: **skilful**, skilled, adept, accomplished, talented, fine; master, masterly, brilliant, virtuoso, bravura, magnificent, marvellous, wonderful, outstanding, great, exceptional, superlative, formidable, excellent, dazzling, first-class, first-rate, elite, superb; proficient, good, able, apt, capable, competent, clever; experienced, practised, qualified, knowledgeable, well versed; specialist, professional; deft, dexterous, adroit; French au fait; informal wizard, ace, stellar, class, crack, top-notch, out of this world, mean, A1, demon; vulgar slang shit hot.
▷ANTONYMS inexpert, incompetent.

expertise noun *GPs will require a high level of expertise in psychiatry*: **skill**, skilfulness, expertness, prowess, proficiency, competence; knowledge, command, mastery, virtuosity; ability, aptitude, facility, knack, capability, gift; deftness, dexterity, adroitness; calibre, professionalism; informal know-how.
▷ANTONYMS incompetence.

expiate verb *an attempt to expiate his sins*: **atone for**, make amends for, make up for, do penance for, pay for, redress, redeem, offset, square, make good, make redress for, make reparation for, make recompense for, make restitution for, purge.

expiation noun *a great drama of revenge and expiation*: **atonement**, redemption, redress, reparation, restitution, recompense, requital, purgation, penance; amends.

expire verb 1 *my contract expires at the end of the season*: **run out**, become invalid, become void, be no longer valid, lapse, cease, become obsolete; **end**, finish, stop, come to an end, conclude, terminate, be over, be at an end.
▷ANTONYMS begin.
2 *a plaque marks the spot where he expired*: **die**, pass away/on, decease, perish, depart this life, be no more, breathe one's last, draw one's last breath, meet one's end, meet one's death, meet one's Maker, give up the ghost, go to the great beyond, cross the great divide, shuffle off this mortal coil, go the way of the/all flesh, go to one's last resting place; informal kick the bucket, bite the dust, croak, conk out, buy it, turn up one's toes, cash in one's chips, go belly up; Brit. informal snuff it, peg out, pop one's clogs.
3 technical *afterwards the breath is expired*: **breathe out**, exhale, puff out, blow out, expel, emit.
▷ANTONYMS inhale, inspire.

expiry noun 1 *the expiry of the lease*: **lapse**, expiration, invalidity.
2 *the expiry of his term of office*: **end**, finish, termination, conclusion, discontinuation, cessation.
▷ANTONYMS beginning.
3 archaic *the sad expiry of their friend*: **death**, demise, passing (away/on), dying; Law decease; rare quietus.
▷ANTONYMS birth.

explain verb 1 *a technician explained the procedure*: **describe**, give an explanation of, make clear/plain/intelligible, spell out, put into words, express in words; elucidate, expound, explicate, delineate; clarify, unfold, throw light on, clear up, simplify; gloss, interpret, decipher, decode, translate; demonstrate, show, teach, illustrate; unravel, untangle, resolve, solve; informal get across, get over.
▷ANTONYMS obscure.
2 *there was nothing in his file to explain his new-found wealth*: **account for**, give an explanation for, give a reason for; justify, give a justification for, give an excuse/alibi/apologia for, make excuses for, explain away, rationalize, give a rationale for; defend, vindicate, legitimize, mitigate; rare extenuate.

explanation noun 1 *an explanation of the ideas contained in the essay*: **clarification**, simplification; description, report, version, statement; elucidation, exposition, expounding, explication, delineation; gloss, interpretation, deciphering, decoding, translation, commentary, exegesis; demonstration, illustration; resolution, solution; informal the why and wherefore.
2 *I suppose I owe you an explanation about Louise*: **account**, reason; justification, excuse, alibi, apologia, rationalization, rationale; defence, vindication, mitigation; rare extenuation.

explanatory adjective *an explanatory leaflet*: **explaining**, descriptive, describing, illustrative, illuminative, elucidative, elucidatory, explicative, evaluative, interpretive, expository, revelatory, by way of explanation; prefatory; rare exegetic, hermeneutic.

e

expletive noun **1** *she let out an expletive and slammed the phone down*: **swear word**, oath, curse, obscenity, profanity, epithet, imprecation, four-letter word, exclamation; (**expletives**) bad language, foul language, strong language, swearing; informal dirty word; N. Amer. informal cuss word, cuss.
2 technical *expletives are employed for the sake of the metre, not the sense*: **filler**, fill-in, stopgap, meaningless word/phrase, redundant word/phrase, superfluous word/phrase, unnecessary word/phrase.

explicable adjective *the success of the revolution is explicable in terms of the weakness of the king*: **explainable**, interpretable, definable; understandable, comprehensible, accountable, intelligible; rare exponible.
▷ANTONYMS inexplicable.

explicate verb *scholars who have been devoted to explicating these stories*: **explain**, explain in detail, make explicit, clarify, make plain/clear, spell out; interpret, elucidate, expound, comment on, develop, work out; illuminate, throw light on, unfold, untangle, clear up, put into plain English; criticize, appraise.
▷ANTONYMS obscure.

explicit adjective **1** *Cara's instructions had been quite explicit*: **clear**, direct, plain, obvious, straightforward, clear-cut, crystal clear, clearly expressed, easily understandable, blunt; **precise**, exact, definite, distinct, express, emphatic, absolute, specific, positive, unequivocal, unambiguous, unmistakable, overt, manifest; detailed, minute, comprehensive, exhaustive, categorical.
▷ANTONYMS vague.
2 *sexually explicit material*: **uncensored**, unrestrained, unreserved, unrestricted, uninhibited, graphic; open, candid, frank, forthright, direct, plain-spoken, outspoken, point-blank, straight from the shoulder; full-frontal, no holds barred.
▷ANTONYMS suggestive, implicit.

explode verb **1** *a bomb exploded at the university*: **blow up**, detonate, blow, burst (apart), fly apart, fly into pieces, shatter, go off, erupt; bang, crack, boom; informal go bang; literary fulminate.
2 *the first British atomic device was exploded in the Monte Bello islands*: **detonate**, set off, let off, discharge, touch off, trigger (off), fire off, let fly.
▷ANTONYMS disarm.
3 *he exploded in a torrent of foul language*: **lose one's temper**, give vent to one's feelings, blow up, rage, rant and rave, storm, bluster, get angry, become enraged, go into a rage, go berserk; informal fly off the handle, hit the roof, go through the roof, go up the wall, blow one's cool/top, blow a fuse/gasket, flip one's lid, freak out, go wild, go bananas, see red, go off the deep end, lose one's rag, go ape, burst a blood vessel; Brit. informal go spare, go crackers, do one's nut, get one's knickers in a twist, throw a wobbly; N. Amer. informal blow one's lid/stack.
4 *the city's exploding pet population*: **increase suddenly**, increase rapidly, increase dramatically, mushroom, snowball, escalate, multiply, burgeon, rocket, shoot up, accelerate, heighten.
5 *this report explodes the myth that men are the bed-hopping rogues*: **disprove**, refute, deny, rebut, invalidate, gainsay, negate, repudiate, discredit, debunk, belie, give the lie to, expose, deflate, puncture, quash, contradict, ridicule; blow up, blow sky-high, knock the bottom out of, drive a coach and horses through, cut down to size, pick holes in; informal shoot full of holes, shoot down (in flames), blow out of the water; rare controvert, confute, negative.
▷ANTONYMS confirm.

exploit verb (stress on the second syllable) **1** *platinum was originally exploited by the Indians of Colombia and Ecuador*: **utilize**, **make use of**, put to use, use, use to good advantage, turn/put to good use, make the most of, capitalize on, benefit from, turn to account, draw on; profit from/by, make capital out of; informal cash in on, milk.
2 *a ruling class which exploited workers*: **take advantage of**, make use of, abuse, impose on, prey on, play on, misuse, ill-treat, bleed, suck dry, squeeze, wring, enslave, treat unfairly, withhold rights from; manipulate, cheat, swindle, fleece, victimize, live off the backs of; informal walk (all) over, take for a ride, put one over on, cash in on, rip off.
▷ANTONYMS treat fairly.
▸ noun (stress on the first syllable) *his exploits brought him fame and notoriety*: **feat**, deed, act, adventure, stunt, escapade, manoeuvre, enterprise, undertaking, move; achievement, accomplishment, attainment, triumph; (**exploits**) handiwork; informal lark, caper.

exploitation noun **1** *the exploitation of mineral resources*: **utilization**, utilizing, use, making use of, putting to use, making the most of, capitalization on; informal cashing in on, milking.
2 *the* ***exploitation of*** *the poor by the wealthy*: **taking advantage**, making use, abuse of, misuse, ill-treatment, unfair treatment, bleeding dry, sucking dry, squeezing, wringing; manipulation, cheating, swindling, fleecing, victimization; enslavement, slavery, oppression; imposing on, preying on, playing on.

exploration noun **1** *the exploration of space*: **investigation**, study, survey, research, search, inspection, probe, examination, enquiry, scrutiny, observation; consideration, analysis, review, anatomy.
2 *a base for explorations into the mountains*: **expedition**, trip, tour, journey, voyage, odyssey, safari, trek, hike; (**explorations**) travels; archaic peregrination.

exploratory adjective *an oil company has started exploratory drilling in the region*: **investigative**, investigational, explorative, probing, fact-finding, analytic, searching; experimental, trial, test, pilot, preliminary, provisional, tentative.

explore verb **1** *they wanted to explore the possibility of achieving a longer-term solution*: **investigate**, look into/over, enquire into, consider, check out; examine, research, survey, scrutinize, scan, study, review, probe, dissect, take stock of, go into, go over with a fine-tooth comb.
2 *an opportunity to explore the stunning scenery all around them*: **travel over**, tour, traverse, range over; survey, take a look at, inspect, investigate, scout, reconnoitre, search, prospect; informal recce, give something a/the once-over, give something a look-see, give something a going-over.

explorer noun **traveller**, discoverer, voyager, rambler, globetrotter, rover; tourer, surveyor, scout, reconnoitrer, prospector; **adventurer**, pioneer; informal gallivanter.

explosion noun **1** *Edward was in the car when he heard the explosion*: **detonation**, discharge, eruption, blowing up, ignition; **bang**, blast, boom, rumble, crash, crack, report, thunder, roll, clap, pop; informal wham, whump; literary fulmination.
2 *an explosion of anger*: **outburst**, flare-up, blow-up, outbreak, eruption, storm, rush, spate, surge, rash, wave, access, effusion; fit, paroxysm, spasm, attack, spell; informal paddy; rare ebullition, boutade.
3 *the explosion of human populations in the last hundred years*: **sudden increase**, rapid increase, dramatic increase, mushrooming, snowballing, escalation, multiplication, burgeoning, rocketing, shooting up.

explosive adjective **1** *the danger of explosive gases*: **volatile**, inflammable, flammable, combustible, incendiary, eruptive, unstable.
2 *Marco's explosive temper*: **fiery**, stormy, violent, volatile, volcanic, angry, fierce, impassioned, passionate, intense, vehement, tempestuous, turbulent, touchy, irritable, irascible, hot-headed, short-tempered, quick-tempered.
3 *he had been able to defuse an explosive situation*: **tense**, charged, highly charged, overwrought; critical, serious, dangerous, perilous, hazardous, knife-edge, touch-and-go; sensitive, delicate, unstable, volatile, inflammable, volcanic, ugly, nasty; informal iffy, dicey.
4 *pressure on the land was increased by explosive population growth*: **sudden**, dramatic, rapid, abrupt, meteoric; mushrooming, snowballing, escalating, rocketing, accelerating.
▸ noun *stocks of explosives*: **bomb**, incendiary device, incendiary, device.

exponent noun **1** *an exponent of free-trade policies*: **advocate**, supporter, proponent, upholder, backer, defender, champion; promoter, propagandist, spokesperson, spokesman, spokeswoman, speaker; campaigner, fighter, battler, crusader, missionary, evangelist, pioneer, apostle; enthusiast, apologist, arguer, expounder.
▷ANTONYMS critic; opponent.
2 *a female karate exponent*: **practitioner**, performer, player; interpreter, presenter; rare executant.

export verb **1** *most hard currency comes from exporting raw materials*: **sell overseas/abroad**, market overseas/abroad, send overseas/abroad, trade internationally, transport.
▷ANTONYMS import.
2 *he is trying to export his gastronomic ideas to America*: **transmit**, spread, disseminate, circulate, communicate, pass on, put about, convey; literary bruit about/abroad.

expose verb **1** *the gold covering was flaking away, exposing the white plaster*: **reveal**, uncover, lay bare, bare, leave unprotected.
▷ANTONYMS cover.
2 *he was* ***exposed to*** *asbestos at his workplace*: **make vulnerable**, make subject, subject, lay open; **put at risk of**, put in jeopardy of, leave unprotected from; endanger by, imperil by, jeopardize by.
▷ANTONYMS protect from.
3 *the colony had been* ***exposed to*** *new liberal ideas*: **introduce**; **bring into contact with**, present with, make familiar/conversant/acquainted with, familiarize with, acquaint with, make aware of.
▷ANTONYMS keep away from, keep free of.
4 *he has been exposed as a liar and a traitor*: **uncover**, reveal, show, display, exhibit, disclose, manifest, unveil, unmask; discover, bring to light, bring into the open, make known, unearth, let out, divulge, make obvious; denounce, condemn; detect, find out, catch out, smoke out; betray, give away; informal spill the beans on, blow the whistle on, pull the plug on.
□ **expose oneself** *police are hunting a man who exposed himself to a young woman*: informal flash.

exposé noun *a TV exposé on chart hyping*: **revelation**, disclosure, exposure, uncovering, divulgence; **report**, feature, piece, column; scandal; informal scoop.
▷ANTONYMS cover-up.

exposed adjective *the farm is on an exposed hillside*: **unprotected**, open, wide open, without shelter/protection, unsheltered, open to the elements/

weather; barren, bare, windswept; vulnerable, defenceless, undefended, unshielded, susceptible; rare pregnable.
▷ANTONYMS sheltered, protected.

exposition noun **1** *a lucid exposition of educational theories*: **explanation**, description, elucidation, explication, interpretation, illustration; account, commentary, study, article, essay, thesis, paper, treatise, dissertation, disquisition; critique, criticism, appraisal, assessment, discussion, discourse; formal exegesis.
2 *the exposition will feature exhibits by 165 companies*: **exhibition**, fair, trade fair, display, show, presentation, demonstration; N. Amer. exhibit; informal expo, demo.

expository adjective *the film suffers from too obviously expository dialogue*: **explanatory**, descriptive, describing, elucidatory, elucidative, explicatory, explicative, interpretative, illustrative, illuminating; rare exegetic, hermeneutic.

expostulate verb *one of the prisoners expostulated with him*: **remonstrate**, disagree, argue, take issue, reason, express disagreement; make a protest to, protest to, raise objections to, object to, complain to.

exposure noun **1** *the exposure of the lizard's vivid blue tongue alarms the attacker*: **revealing**, revelation, uncovering, presentation; baring, laying bare, stripping, denudation.
2 *injuries resulting from exposure to harmful chemicals*: **subjection**, submission, vulnerability, laying open.
▷ANTONYMS protection from.
3 *the only survivor was suffering from exposure*: **frostbite**, cold, hypothermia.
4 ***exposure to** great literature*: **introduction**, presentation; **experience of**, contact with, familiarity with, conversance/conversancy with, acquaintance with, awareness of, insight into.
5 *the exposure of a banking scandal*: **uncovering**, revelation, showing, display, exhibition, disclosure, manifestation, unveiling, unmasking; discovery, unearthing, rooting out, divulgence; denunciation, condemnation; detection, betrayal; exposé, publication, publishing.
6 *we're getting a lot of exposure for our new act*: **publicity**, publicizing, advertising, advertisement; public attention, public notice, public interest, the public eye, media interest/attention, the limelight; dissemination, broadcasting, airing; informal hype.
7 *the exposure is perfect—a gentle slope to the south-west*: **outlook**, aspect, view, frontage, direction; position, setting, location.

expound verb **1** *he expounded his theories on the cultural state of the nation*: **present**, put forward, set forth, proffer, offer, advance, propose, propound, frame, give an account of, recount; **explain**, give an explanation of, detail, spell out, describe, discuss, explicate, delineate, elucidate.
2 *a detailed treatise expounding Paul's teachings*: **explain**, interpret, explicate, elucidate; comment on, give a commentary on, annotate, gloss, illustrate.
□ **expound on** *he expounded on the virtues of books and learning*: **elaborate on**, expand on, expatiate on, dwell on, harp on, discuss at length.

express[1] verb **1** *community leaders expressed anger over the result of the referendum*: **communicate**, convey, indicate, show, demonstrate, reveal, intimate, manifest, make manifest, exhibit, evidence, put across/over, get across/over; **articulate**, put into words, utter, voice, give voice to, give expression to, enunciate, pronounce, verbalize, word, phrase, render, frame, couch; state, assert, proclaim, profess, air, make public, give vent to, vent; say, tell, speak, mouth, point out; denote, illustrate, symbolize, signify, embody; rare evince, asseverate.
2 *the grapes are trodden until all the juice is expressed*: **squeeze out**, press out, wring out, force out, extract, expel.
□ **express oneself** *he had difficulty expressing himself*: **communicate one's thoughts/opinions/views**, put thoughts into words, speak one's mind, say one's piece, say what's on one's mind.

express[2] adjective *an express bus*: **rapid**, swift, fast, quick, speedy, high-speed, brisk, flying, prompt, expeditious; non-stop, direct, uninterrupted, undeviating, unswerving, uncircuitous; informal nippy.
▷ANTONYMS slow; indirect.
▸ noun *we travelled on an overnight express*: **express train**, fast train, direct train.

express[3] adjective **1** *the letter made express reference to the confidential nature of the information*: **explicit**, clear, direct, plain, distinct, unambiguous, unequivocal, unmistakable, obvious; specific, precise, clear-cut, crystal clear, straightforward, certain, categorical, positive, conclusive, pointed; well defined, exact, manifest, outright, emphatic.
▷ANTONYMS vague; implied.
2 *they bought the land with the express purpose of giving it to the trust*: **sole**, specific, particular, special, especial, singular, exclusive, specified, fixed, purposeful.

expression noun **1** *the government refused to allow the free expression of opposition views*: **utterance**, uttering, voicing, pronouncement, declaration, articulation, verbalization, statement, proclamation, assertion, announcement, setting forth, venting, mouthing; dissemination, broadcast, circulation, communication, spreading, promulgation, publicizing, publication; rare asseveration.
2 *he raised his eyebrows in an expression of sympathy*: **indication**, intimation, demonstration, show, exhibition, manifestation, token; conveyance, communication, illustration, revelation, disclosure, embodiment.
3 *Blanche invariably wore an expression of harassed fatigue*: **look**, **appearance**, air, manner, bearing, countenance, guise, cast, aspect, impression; formal mien.
4 *the old expression 'curiosity killed the cat'*: **idiom**, phrase, idiomatic expression, set phrase; proverb, saying, adage, maxim, axiom, aphorism, saw, motto, platitude, cliché, quotation, quote, formula; term, word; informal old chestnut; formal locution.
5 *the height of poetic expression*: **diction**, style, choice of words, turn of phrase, wording, phrasing, phraseology, language; delivery, execution; speech, intonation.
6 *these pieces are very different from one another, both in choice of instruments and expression*: **emotion**, feeling, passion, intensity, poignancy; **style**, intonation, tone, nuance; artistry, depth, spirit, imagination; vividness, ardour, power, force.
7 *essential oils obtained by distillation or expression*: **squeezing**, pressing, wringing, forcing out, extraction, extracting.

expressionless adjective **1** *his face was expressionless, giving nothing away*: **inscrutable**, unreadable, deadpan, poker-faced; blank, empty, vacant, emotionless, unemotional, unexpressive, inexpressive; glazed, fixed, lifeless, stony, wooden, impassive, inanimate, unresponsive.
▷ANTONYMS expressive.
2 *he spoke in a flat, expressionless tone*: **dull**, dry, toneless, monotonous, drab, boring, tedious, flat, static, wooden, unmodulated, unvarying, undemonstrative, devoid of feeling/emotion; apathetic, unimpassioned, uninspiring, weak.
▷ANTONYMS interesting, lively.

expressive adjective **1** *he gave an expressive shrug*: **eloquent**, meaningful, telling, revealing, demonstrative, suggestive.
▷ANTONYMS expressionless.
2 *a haunted and expressive song*: **emotional**, full of emotion/feeling, indicating emotion/feeling, passionate, intense, deeply felt, poignant, moving, stirring, striking, evocative, artistic; vivid, graphic, descriptive, ardent, powerful, charged, imaginative, inspired, visionary.
▷ANTONYMS inexpressive; unemotional.
3 *his diction is very expressive of his Englishness*: **indicative**, demonstrative, demonstrating, showing, suggesting, revealing, underlining.

expressly adverb **1** *he was expressly forbidden to discuss the matter*: **explicitly**, clearly, directly, plainly, distinctly, unambiguously, unequivocally, unmistakably, obviously, absolutely; precisely, specifically, straightforwardly, certainly, categorically, positively, conclusively, pointedly, markedly, exactly, manifestly, patently, emphatically.
2 *a machine expressly built for spraying paint*: **solely**, specifically, particularly, specially, especially, singularly, exclusively, purposefully, just, only, explicitly, with something/someone in mind.

expropriate verb *legislation to expropriate land from absentee landlords*: **seize**, take away, take over, take, appropriate, take possession of, requisition, commandeer, claim, make claim to, assume, acquire, sequestrate, wrest; impound, confiscate; misappropriate, usurp, arrogate, hijack; Law distrain, disseize, attach; Scottish Law poind.

expulsion noun **1** *they faced expulsion from the party*: **removal**, debarment, dismissal, exclusion, discharge, ejection, rejection, blackballing, blacklisting; suspension; banishment, exile, deportation, eviction, expatriation, repatriation, purging, displacement, transportation; informal sacking, drumming out, the bounce.
▷ANTONYMS admission.
2 *the expulsion of bodily wastes*: **discharge**, ejection, excretion, voiding, voidance, evacuation, ejaculation, disgorgement, elimination, emptying out, passing, draining.

expunge verb *that moment can never be expunged from his memory*: **erase**, remove, delete, rub out, wipe out, efface; cross out, strike out, blot out, blank out; cancel, annul, destroy, obliterate, eradicate, extinguish, eliminate, abolish, annihilate, extirpate.

expurgate verb *a book which had been expurgated for use in schools*: **censor**, bowdlerize, blue-pencil, cut, edit; clean up, purge, purify, sanitize, make acceptable, make palatable, make presentable, water down, emasculate.

exquisite adjective **1** *a piece of exquisite antique glass*: **beautiful**, lovely, elegant, graceful; magnificent, superb, superlative, excellent, wonderful, well-crafted, well-made, well-executed, perfect; delicate, fragile, dainty, subtle; intricate, tasteful, fine, choice.
▷ANTONYMS crude.
2 *the garden was tended with exquisite taste*: **discriminating**, discerning, sensitive, selective, fastidious; refined, cultivated, cultured, educated, appreciative; impeccable, polished, consummate.

3 *an exquisite agony*: **intense**, acute, keen, piercing, sharp, severe, racking, excruciating, agonizing, harrowing, torturous, tormenting, searing; unbearable, insufferable, unendurable, more than one can bear, more than flesh and blood can stand.
▸ noun *even among these snappy dressers, he was an exquisite*: **dandy**, fop, beau, man about town, bright young thing, glamour boy, rake; dilettante, aesthete; informal swell, dude, sharp dresser, snappy dresser, natty dresser; archaic blade, blood.

extant adjective *only one copy of Cavendish's book is extant*: **still existing**, in existence, surviving, remaining, abiding, enduring, undestroyed, present, existent; living, alive.
▷ANTONYMS no longer existing, non-existent, dead.

extemporary, extemporaneous adjective *a member of the audience made notes of his extemporaneous address*: **extempore**, impromptu, spontaneous, unscripted, ad lib, on-the-spot; improvised, improvisatory, unrehearsed, unplanned, unprepared, unarranged, unpremeditated; makeshift, thrown together, cobbled together; informal off-the-cuff, spur-of-the-moment, off the top of one's head.
▷ANTONYMS rehearsed, planned.

extempore adjective *an extempore speech*: **impromptu**, spontaneous, unscripted, ad lib; on-the-spot, extemporary, extemporaneous; improvised, improvisatory, unrehearsed, unplanned, unprepared, unarranged, unpremeditated; makeshift, thrown together, cobbled together, rough and ready; Latin ad libitum; informal off-the-cuff, spur-of-the-moment, off the top of one's head.
▷ANTONYMS rehearsed, planned.
▸ adverb *he was speaking extempore*: **spontaneously**, extemporaneously, ad lib; on the spot, unpremeditatedly, without preparation, without rehearsal, without planning; Latin ad libitum; informal off the cuff, on the spur of the moment, off the top of one's head, just like that, at the drop of a hat.
▷ANTONYMS from notes, with preparation.

extemporize verb *in modern jazz players extemporize in a very free manner*: **improvise**, ad lib, play it by ear, think on one's feet, throw/cobble something together, make it up as one goes along, take it as it comes; informal busk it, wing it, do something off the cuff, do something off the top of one's head, do something on the spur of the moment.

extend verb 1 *in 1712 he attempted to extend his dominions*: **expand**, enlarge, increase, make larger, make bigger, make greater; lengthen, widen, broaden; stretch, stretch out, draw out, elongate.
▷ANTONYMS reduce, shrink.
2 *the garden extends down to the road*: **continue**, carry on, run on, last, stretch (out), spread, range, reach, lead; unroll, unfurl.
3 *we have continued to extend our range of services*: **widen**, expand, broaden; augment, supplement, increase, add to, enhance, amplify, develop, top up, build up, diversify.
▷ANTONYMS narrow.
4 *a bill to extend the life of parliament*: **prolong**, lengthen, increase, continue, run on, keep going, perpetuate, sustain; stretch out, protract, spin out, string out, drag out; postpone, defer, delay, put back, put off.
▷ANTONYMS shorten.
5 *lie flat on the floor with your arms and legs extended*: **stretch out**, spread out, reach out, straighten out, open out; unroll, unfurl.
6 *he extended a hand in greeting*: **hold out**, put out, stick out, hold forth, put forth, reach out; offer, give, outstretch, proffer.
7 *the society wishes to extend their sincere thanks to Mr Bayes*: **offer**, proffer, hold out, advance; give, grant, bestow, accord, present, confer, impart.
□ **extend to** *her tolerance did not always extend to her staff*: **include**, go/extend as far as, take in, incorporate, encompass, comprise, comprehend, subsume, be applicable to.

extended adjective 1 *an extended legal battle*: **prolonged**, protracted, long-lasting, long-drawn-out, drawn out, spun out, dragged out, strung out; extensive, lengthy, long; lengthened, increased, stretched out; elongated, enlarged, widened.
▷ANTONYMS shortened; short.
2 *an extended family*: inclusive, comprehensive, expanded, enlarged, widened, broad, far-reaching.
▷ANTONYMS immediate; nuclear.

extension noun 1 *they plan an extension at the hospital to create a new outpatients' department*: **addition**, add-on, adjunct, addendum, augmentation, supplement, appendage, appendix; annexe, wing, supplementary building; N. Amer. ell.
2 *scientific method has led to a marvellous extension of knowledge*: **expansion**, increase, enlargement; widening, broadening, deepening, diversification, heightening; augmentation, enhancement, amplification; development, growth, continuation; elongation, lengthening, stretching, drawing out.
▷ANTONYMS shrinking, contraction.
3 *an extension of opening hours*: **prolongation**, lengthening, increase, protraction, continuation, perpetuation.
▷ANTONYMS shortening.
4 *I need an extension for my assessed essay*: **postponement**, deferral, delay; longer period, more/extra time, increased time, additional time.

extensive adjective 1 *a mansion with extensive grounds*: **large**, large-scale, sizeable, substantial, considerable, ample, great, huge, vast, immense, boundless, immeasurable; spacious, capacious, commodious, voluminous, roomy; broad, expansive, sweeping.
▷ANTONYMS small.
2 *his extensive knowledge of antiques made the shop popular*: **comprehensive**, thorough, complete, exhaustive, profound, boundless; broad, wide, vast, wide-ranging, all-inclusive, all-embracing, all-encompassing, sweeping, wholesale, catholic, universal, across the board.
▷ANTONYMS small; limited.

extent noun 1 *the garden was about two acres in extent*: **area**, size, expanse, length, stretch, range, scope, compass; proportions, dimensions.
2 *she kept the full extent of her father's illness from her cousin*: **degree**, scale, level, magnitude, scope, extensiveness, amount, size; coverage, breadth, width, reach, range, compass, comprehensiveness, thoroughness, completeness, all-inclusiveness.

extenuate verb rare *I've no wish to extenuate his transgressions*. See **excuse** (sense 2 of the verb).

extenuating adjective *there were extenuating circumstances*: **mitigating**, excusing, exonerative, palliating, palliative, justifying, justificatory, vindicating, exculpatory; moderating, qualifying, softening, tempering, diminishing, lessening.
▷ANTONYMS aggravating.

exterior adjective *the exterior walls are bare brick*: **outer**, outside, outermost, outward, external, surface, superficial, extrinsic, visible.
▷ANTONYMS interior.
▸ noun *the exterior of the building*: **outside**, outside surface, outer surface, external surface, outward appearance, outward aspect, externals, facade, front; shell, skin, covering, coating, finish.
▷ANTONYMS interior.

> *Word links* **exterior**
>
> **ecto-** related prefix, as in *ectoderm*
> **exo-** related prefix, as in *exoskeleton*
> **extra-** related prefix, as in *extraterritorial*

exterminate verb *the invaders intended simply to exterminate any natives they found*: **kill**, put to death, do to death, do away with, put an end to, finish off, take the life of, end the life of, get rid of, dispatch; slaughter, butcher, massacre, wipe out, mow down, shoot down, cut down, put to the sword, send to the gas chambers, ethnically cleanse, destroy, eliminate, eradicate, annihilate, extirpate; murder, assassinate, execute; informal bump off, knock off, polish off, do in, top, take out, snuff out, erase, croak, stiff, zap, blow away, blow someone's brains out, give someone the works; N. Amer. informal ice, off, rub out, waste, whack, smoke, scrag; N. Amer. euphemistic terminate with extreme prejudice; literary slay.

extermination noun *such feuds could be settled only by the extermination of an entire family*: **killing**, murder, assassination, putting to death, doing to death, execution, dispatch, slaughter, massacre, genocide; taking of someone's life, homicide, manslaughter, liquidation, elimination, destruction, eradication, annihilation, wiping out, extinction; literary slaying.

external adjective 1 *an external wall*: **outer**, outside, outermost, outward, exterior, surface, superficial; visible, extrinsic, extraneous.
▷ANTONYMS internal.
2 *the exam scripts then have to be sent to an external examiner*: **outside**, non-resident, visiting, from elsewhere, extramural, independent, consultant, consulting, advisory.
▷ANTONYMS local; resident; in-house.

> *Word links* **external**
>
> **ecto-** related prefix, as in *ectoderm*
> **exo-** related prefix, as in *exoskeleton*
> **extra-** related prefix, as in *extraterritorial*

extinct adjective 1 *an extinct species*: **vanished**, lost, died out, dead, defunct, no longer existing, no longer extant, wiped out, destroyed, exterminated, gone.
▷ANTONYMS extant; living.
2 *an extinct volcano*: **inactive**, old, former, no longer active.
▷ANTONYMS active; dormant.

extinction noun *the sudden extinction of the mammoths*: **dying out**, disappearance, vanishing, death; extermination, destruction, elimination, eradication, annihilation.

extinguish verb 1 *the fire had to be extinguished*: **douse**, put out, quench, stamp out, smother, beat out, dampen down; blow out, snuff out; Scottish dout.
▷ANTONYMS light.
2 *the Liberal majority was extinguished by 1910*: **destroy**, **end**, finish off, put an end to, put a stop to, bring to an end, terminate, remove, annihilate, wipe out, wipe off the face of the earth, wipe off the map, erase, eliminate, eradicate, obliterate, liquidate, expunge, abolish, exterminate, kill,

extirpate, obscure, suppress, disrupt, undo, upset; informal take out, rub out, snuff out.
▷ANTONYMS start up.

extirpate verb *the use of every legal measure to extirpate this horrible evil from the land*: **weed out**, destroy, eradicate, stamp out, root out, eliminate, suppress, crush, put down, put an end to, put a stop to, do away with, get rid of, wipe out, abolish, extinguish, quash, squash.
▷ANTONYMS found; support.

extol verb *nutritionists have long extolled the virtues of rice*: **praise enthusiastically**, go into raptures about/over, wax lyrical about, sing the praises of, praise to the skies, heap praise on, eulogize, rhapsodize over, rave about, enthuse about/over, gush about/over, throw bouquets at, express delight over, acclaim; informal go wild about, be mad about, go on about; N. Amer. informal ballyhoo; black English big someone/something up; dated cry someone/something up; rare laud, panegyrize.
▷ANTONYMS criticize.

extort verb *he was convicted of extorting money from local residents*: **force**, obtain by force, obtain by threat(s), blackmail someone for, extract, exact, coerce, wring, wrest, screw, squeeze, milk, worm something out of someone; N. Amer. & Austral. informal put the bite on someone for; archaic rack.

extortion noun *he was arrested on a charge of extortion*: **demanding money with menaces**, exaction, extraction, blackmail; N. Amer. shakedown.

extortionate adjective **1** *extortionate prices*: **exorbitant**, excessively high, excessive, sky-high, outrageous, preposterous, immoderate, unreasonable, inordinate, prohibitive, ruinous, punitive, inflated, more than one can afford; Brit. over the odds; informal criminal, steep, stiff, over the top, OTT.
▷ANTONYMS reasonable.
2 *an unreasonable and extortionate clause in the contract*: **grasping**, bloodsucking, avaricious, greedy, rapacious, predatory, usurious, exacting, harsh, severe, rigorous, hard, oppressive; informal money-grubbing; N. Amer. informal grabby.

extortionist noun *he was once a big-time kidnapper and extortionist*: **racketeer**, extortioner, extorter, profiteer, exploiter, blackmailer, black marketeer; in Japan yakuza; informal bloodsucker; Austral. informal urger; dated rack-renter.

extra adjective *a potential source of extra income*: **additional**, more, added, supplementary, supplemental, further, auxiliary, ancillary, subsidiary, secondary, attendant, accessory; other, another, new, fresh.
▷ANTONYMS normal.
▸ adverb **1** *we have to work extra hard tonight*: **exceptionally**, particularly, specially, especially, very, extremely, singularly, peculiarly, distinctly; **unusually**, extraordinarily, uncommonly, uniquely, remarkably, strikingly, outstandingly, amazingly, incredibly, awfully, terribly, really, unwontedly, notably, markedly, decidedly, surprisingly, conspicuously, signally; informal seriously, majorly, mucho; Brit. informal jolly, dead, well; informal, dated devilish, frightfully; N. English powerful, right.
2 *postage has to be charged extra*: **in addition**, additionally, as well, also, too, besides, over and above that, on top (of that), further, into the bargain, to boot; then, again, furthermore; archaic withal, forbye.
▷ANTONYMS included.
▸ noun **1** *an optional extra*: **addition**, supplement, adjunct, addendum, add-on, bonus, accompaniment, complement, companion, additive, extension, appendage, accessory, attachment, retrofit; Computing peripheral.
▷ANTONYMS standard item; necessity, essential.
2 *a film extra*: **walk-on**, supernumerary, spear carrier; walk-on part, minor role, non-speaking role, bit part.

extract verb (stress on the second syllable) **1** *he switched off the recorder and extracted the cassette*: **take out**, draw out, bring out, pull out, remove, withdraw, pluck out, fish out, prize out, extricate; wrench out, tear out, uproot, unsheathe; produce; free, release; rare deracinate.
▷ANTONYMS insert.
2 *the Crown was adept at extracting money from its subjects*: **wrest**, exact, wring, screw, squeeze, milk, force, coerce, obtain by force, obtain by threat(s), extort, blackmail someone for, worm something out of someone; N. Amer. & Austral. informal put the bite on someone for; archaic rack.
3 *the roots are crushed to extract the sugary juice*: **squeeze out**, express, separate, press out, obtain, distil.
▷ANTONYMS add.
4 *the table is extracted from the report*: **excerpt**, select, choose, reproduce, repeat, copy, quote, cite, cull, take, abstract.
▷ANTONYMS insert.
5 *the following ideas are extracted from a variety of theories*: **derive**, develop, evolve, deduce, infer, conclude, gather, elicit, obtain, get, take, gain, acquire, procure, attain, glean; formal educe.
▸ noun (stress on the first syllable) **1** *an extract from his article*: **excerpt**, passage, abstract, citation, selection, quotation, cutting, clipping, snippet, fragment, piece; (**excerpts**) rare analects.
2 *an extract of the ginseng root*: **decoction**, distillation, distillate, abstraction, concentrate, essence, juice, solution, tincture, elixir, quintessence; rare decocture, apozem.

extraction noun **1** *the extraction of gall bladder stones*: **removal**, taking out, drawing out, pulling out, extrication, wrenching out, tearing out, uprooting, withdrawal, unsheathing; production; freeing, release; rare deracination.
▷ANTONYMS insertion.
2 *the extraction of rights has been a constant struggle*: **exaction**, exacting, wresting, coercion, extortion.
▷ANTONYMS relinquishment.
3 *the extraction of grape juice*: **squeezing**, expressing, separation, pressing, obtaining, distillation.
4 *a man of Irish extraction*: **descent**, ancestry, parentage, ancestors, family; lineage, line, line of descent; race, origin, derivation, birth; genealogy, heredity, succession; stock, pedigree, blood, bloodline, strain; roots, origins, forefathers, antecedents; rare filiation, stirps.

extradite verb **1** *the Russian government announced that it would extradite him to Germany*: **deport**, hand over, send back, send home, repatriate, expel, banish.
2 *the British government attempted to extradite suspects from Belgium and the Netherlands*: **have someone deported**, request the extradition of, have someone handed over, have someone sent back, have someone sent home, bring back.

extradition noun *they are in Pentonville Prison, fighting extradition to Hong Kong on fraud charges*: **deportation**, handover, repatriation, expulsion, banishment.

extraneous adjective **1** *do not allow extraneous considerations to influence your judgement*: **irrelevant**, immaterial, beside the point, not to the point, neither here nor there, nothing to do with it, not pertinent, not germane, not to the purpose, off the subject, unrelated, unconnected, inapposite, inappropriate, inapplicable, inconsequential, incidental, pointless, out of place, wide of the mark, peripheral, tangential.
▷ANTONYMS material.
2 *extraneous influences came to bear*: **external**, outside, exterior, extrinsic, outward, adventitious, alien, foreign.
▷ANTONYMS intrinsic.

extraordinary adjective **1** *an extraordinary coincidence*: **remarkable**, exceptional, amazing, astonishing, astounding, marvellous, wonderful, sensational, stunning, incredible, unbelievable, miraculous, phenomenal, prodigious, spectacular; **striking**, outstanding, momentous, impressive, singular, signal, pre-eminent, memorable, unforgettable, never to be forgotten, unique, arresting, eye-catching, conspicuous, noteworthy, notable, great; out of the ordinary, unusual, uncommon, rare, surprising, curious, strange, odd, peculiar, uncanny; Scottish unco; informal fantastic, terrific, tremendous, stupendous, awesome, out of this world, unreal; literary wondrous.
▷ANTONYMS ordinary.
2 *moving with extraordinary speed*: **very great**, considerable, tremendous, huge, enormous, immense, colossal, massive, prodigious, stupendous, monumental, mammoth, vast, gigantic, giant, mighty, epic, monstrous, substantial; informal astronomical, almighty.
▷ANTONYMS negligible.

extravagance noun **1** *the sumptuous sofa had been bought in a fit of extravagance*: **profligacy**, lack of thrift, unthriftiness, thriftlessness, improvidence, wastefulness, waste, overspending, prodigality, squandering, lavishness; immoderation, excess, recklessness, lack of restraint, irresponsibility; spendthrift behaviour, free-spending ways.
▷ANTONYMS thrift.
2 *the costliest brands are an extravagance*: **luxury**, indulgence, self-indulgence, comfort, treat, extra, non-essential, frill, refinement.
▷ANTONYMS necessity.
3 *the extravagance of the decor*: **ornateness**, elaborateness, decoration, embellishment, adornment, ornamentation, showiness; overstatement, ostentation, exaggeration, over-elaborateness.
▷ANTONYMS plainness.
4 *the extravagance of his compliments*: **excessiveness**, exaggeration, exaggeratedness, unreservedness, outrageousness, immoderation; preposterousness, absurdity, irrationality, recklessness, wildness; excess, overkill, lack of restraint/reserve.

extravagant adjective **1** *he siphoned off money to fund his extravagant lifestyle*: **spendthrift**, profligate, unthrifty, thriftless, improvident, wasteful, free-spending, prodigal, squandering, lavish; immoderate, excessive, imprudent, reckless, irresponsible.
▷ANTONYMS thrifty.
2 *extravagant gifts like computer games*: **expensive**, costly, dear, high-priced, high-cost, exorbitant, extortionate, overpriced; immoderate, lavish; valuable, precious, priceless, worth its weight in gold, worth a king's ransom; Brit. over the odds; informal pricey, costing an arm and a leg, costing the earth, costing a bomb, daylight robbery.
▷ANTONYMS cheap.
3 *extravagant prices*: **exorbitant**, extortionate, excessive, high, unreasonable, outrageous, undue, uncalled for, extreme, inordinate, unwarranted, unnecessary, needless, disproportionate, too much;

informal sky-high, over the top, OTT, a bit much, fancy-pants.
▷ANTONYMS reasonable, low.
4 *he was touched by the extravagant praise heaped on him*: **excessive**, immoderate, exaggerated, gushing, gushy, unrestrained, unreserved, effusive, fulsome; outrageous, preposterous, absurd, irrational, reckless, wild; informal steep, over the top, OTT.
▷ANTONYMS moderate.
5 *mirror frames which are decorated in an extravagant style*: **ornate**, elaborate, decorated, embellished, adorned, ornamented, fancy; over-elaborate, fussy, busy, ostentatious, exaggerated, overstated, showy, baroque, rococo, florid, wedding-cake, gingerbread; informal flash, flashy.
▷ANTONYMS plain.

extravaganza noun *a live extravaganza featuring a host of stars*: **spectacular**, display, spectacle, exhibition, performance, presentation, show, pageant.

e

extreme adjective 1 *they were in extreme danger*: **utmost**, uttermost, very great, greatest, greatest possible, maximum, maximal, highest, ultimate, supreme, paramount, great, acute, major, intense, enormous, severe, high, superlative, exceptional, extraordinary.
▷ANTONYMS slight.
2 *such an appalling situation calls for extreme measures*: **drastic**, serious, forceful, desperate, dire, radical, far-reaching, momentous, consequential, substantial; unrelenting, unbending, unyielding, remorseless, uncompromising, unmitigated; heavy, sharp, severe, austere, stern, harsh, tough, strict, rigorous, swingeing, punishing, punitive, excessive, oppressive, draconian, ferocious.
▷ANTONYMS mild.
3 *a person of extreme views*: **radical**, **extremist**, immoderate, exaggerated, intemperate, outrageous, unreasonable; fanatical, diehard, overzealous, revolutionary, rebel, rebellious, subversive, militant, combative; informal over the top, OTT.
▷ANTONYMS moderate.
4 *extreme sports*: **dangerous**, hazardous, risky, high-risk; reckless, foolhardy, daredevil, breakneck, daring, adventurous.
▷ANTONYMS safe; tame.
5 *the extreme tip of a narrow peninsula*: **furthest**, farthest, furthermost, farthermost, furthest/farthest away, very, utmost, outermost, most distant, aftermost, endmost, ultimate, final, last, terminal, remotest; rare outmost.
▷ANTONYMS near.
▶ noun 1 *the two extremes of standardized and non-standardized interviews*: **opposite**, antithesis, (other) side of the coin, (opposite) pole, contrary, (exclusive) alternative; opposing pair; rare antipode.
▷ANTONYMS medium.
2 *this attitude is taken to its extreme in the following quote*: **limit**, extremity, highest/greatest degree, maximum, height, high, low; ceiling, top, zenith, pinnacle, peak, apex, climax, ultimate, optimum, acme, epitome.
▷ANTONYMS minimum.
□ **in the extreme** *David was generous in the extreme*. See **extremely**.

> *Word links* **extreme**
>
> **ultra-** related prefix, as in *ultra-cautious*

extremely adverb *we are all extremely worried*: **very**, exceedingly, exceptionally, especially, extraordinarily, to a fault, in the extreme, extra, tremendously, immensely, vastly, hugely, abundantly, intensely, acutely, singularly, significantly, distinctly, outstandingly, uncommonly, unusually, decidedly, particularly, eminently, supremely, highly, remarkably, really, truly, mightily, thoroughly; all that, to a great extent, most, so; Scottish unco; French très; N. English right; informal terrifically, awfully, fearfully, terribly, devilishly, majorly, seriously, mega, ultra, oh-so, stinking, mucho, damn, damned; informal, dated devilish, hellish, frightfully; Brit. informal ever so, well, bloody, dead, dirty, jolly, fair; N. Amer. informal real, mighty, powerful, awful, plumb, darned, way, bitching; S. African informal lekker; archaic exceeding.
▷ANTONYMS moderately; slightly; by no means.

extremism noun *the dangers of political extremism*: **fanaticism**, radicalism, zealotry, zeal, fundamentalism, dogmatism, bigotry, militancy, activism; sectarianism, chauvinism, partisanship.
▷ANTONYMS moderation.

extremist noun *with little to gain from moderation, the extremists rule the day*: **fanatic**, **radical**, zealot, fundamentalist, hardliner, dogmatist, bigot, diehard, militant, activist; sectarian, chauvinist, partisan; informal ultra, maniac, crank.
▷ANTONYMS moderate.

extremity noun 1 *the eastern extremity of the county*: **limit**, end, edge, side, farthest point, boundary, border, frontier, boundary line, bound, bounding line, partition line, demarcation line, end point, cut-off point, termination; perimeter, circumference, outside, outline, confine, periphery, outskirts, margin, brink, rim, lip, fringe, verge, threshold, compass; literary bourn, marge, skirt; rare ambit.
▷ANTONYMS middle.
2 (**extremities**) *she began to regain some feeling in her extremities*: **hands and feet**, fingers and toes, limbs.
3 *the extremity of the violence concerns us greatly*: **intensity**, high degree, magnitude, acuteness, ferocity, vehemence, fierceness, violence, severity, seriousness, strength, power, powerfulness, potency, vigour, force, forcefulness, gravity, graveness, severeness, grievousness.
4 *he has promised that in extremity he will send for her*: **dire straits**, trouble, difficulty, hard times, hardship, adversity, misfortune, distress; **crisis**, emergency, disaster, catastrophe, calamity, cataclysm; predicament, plight, mess, dilemma; setback, reverse, reversal; destitution, indigence, exigency; informal fix, pickle, jam, spot, bind, stew, scrape, hole, sticky situation, hot water, deep water, hell, hell on earth; Brit. informal spot of bother.

extricate verb *Deborah managed to extricate herself from the melee*: **extract**, free, release, disentangle, get out, remove, withdraw, let loose, loosen, unloose, detach, disengage, disencumber, untwine, disentwine, unfasten, unclasp, disconnect; liberate, rescue, save, deliver; informal get someone/oneself off the hook.
▷ANTONYMS entangle; involve.

extrinsic adjective *the animal population is influenced by extrinsic factors like food supply and predation*: **external**, extraneous, exterior, outside, outward, alien, foreign, adventitious, superficial, surface.
▷ANTONYMS intrinsic.

extrovert noun *like most extroverts he was a good dancer*: **outgoing person**, sociable person, life and soul of the party, socializer, mixer, mingler, social butterfly, socialite.
▷ANTONYMS introvert.
▶ adjective *his extrovert personality made him the ideal host*: **outgoing**, hail-fellow-well-met, extroverted, sociable, gregarious, socializing, social, genial, cordial, affable, friendly, people-oriented, lively, exuberant, uninhibited, unreserved, demonstrative.
▷ANTONYMS introverted.

extrude verb *lava that has been extruded under water*: **force out**, thrust out, squeeze out, express, press out, eject, expel, release, give off, emit, void, exude, excrete.
▷ANTONYMS suck in.

exuberance noun 1 *the wild exuberance of the dance*: **ebullience**, buoyancy, cheerfulness, sunniness, breeziness, jauntiness, light-heartedness, high spirits, exhilaration, excitement, elation, exultation, euphoria, joy, joyfulness, cheeriness, gaiety, jubilation, sparkle, effervescence, vivacity, enthusiasm, irrepressibility, energy, animation, life, liveliness, vigour, zest; informal bubble, bounce, pep, zing, chirpiness; N. Amer. informal peartness; literary gladsomeness, blitheness, blithesomeness; archaic good cheer.
▷ANTONYMS gloom.
2 *the exuberance of the bougainvillea flowers*: **luxuriance**, lushness, richness, abundance, superabundance, profusion, proliferation, copiousness, riotousness, vigour; denseness, thickness; jungle; rare plentifulness, prolificness, rankness, rampancy.
▷ANTONYMS meagreness.

exuberant adjective 1 *exuberant groups of guests were dancing on the terrace*: **ebullient**, buoyant, cheerful, sunny, breezy, jaunty, light-hearted, in high spirits, high-spirited, exhilarated, excited, elated, exultant, euphoric, joyful, cheery, merry, jubilant, sparkling, effervescent, vivacious, enthusiastic, irrepressible, energetic, animated, full of life, lively, vigorous, zestful; informal bubbly, bouncy, peppy, zingy, upbeat, chipper, chirpy, smiley, sparky, full of beans; N. Amer. informal peart; dated gay; literary gladsome, blithe, blithesome; archaic as merry as a grig, of good cheer.
▷ANTONYMS gloomy.
2 *an exuberant coating of mosses*: **luxuriant**, lush, rich, abundant, abounding, superabundant, profuse, copious, plentiful, riotous, prolific, teeming, flourishing, thriving, vigorous; dense, thick, rank, rampant, overgrown, jungle-like; verdant, green; informal jungly.
▷ANTONYMS meagre, stunted.
3 *she flung her arms wide apart in exuberant welcome*: **effusive**, lavish, extravagant, fulsome, expansive, gushing, gushy, demonstrative, exaggerated, unreserved, unrestrained, unlimited, wholehearted, generous; excessive, superfluous, prodigal; informal over the top, OTT.
▷ANTONYMS restrained.

exude verb 1 *milkweed exudes a milky sap*: **give off/out**, discharge, release, send out, send forth, emit, issue, emanate; ooze, weep, leak, leach, secrete, excrete; Medicine extravasate.
▷ANTONYMS absorb, take up.
2 *slime exudes from the fungus*: **ooze**, seep, trickle, issue, filter, percolate, escape, discharge, flow, well, drip, dribble, leak, leach, drain, bleed, sweat; Medicine extravasate; rare filtrate, transude, exudate.
3 *a charismatic character who exuded self-confidence*: **emanate**, radiate, ooze, give out, give forth, send out, issue, emit; display, show, exhibit, manifest, demonstrate, transmit, breathe, embody, be a/the picture of.

exult verb 1 *her opponents exulted when she left*: **rejoice**, be joyful, be happy, be pleased, be glad, be delighted, be elated, be ecstatic, be euphoric,

be overjoyed, be as pleased as Punch, be cock-a-hoop, be jubilant, be rapturous, be in raptures, be transported, be beside oneself with joy, be delirious, be thrilled, jump for joy, be on cloud nine, be walking/treading on air, be in seventh heaven, glory, triumph, be triumphant; celebrate, cheer, revel, make merry; informal be over the moon, be on top of the world, be blissed out, whoop it up; Austral. informal be wrapped; rare joy, jubilate.
▷ANTONYMS sorrow.
2 *he exulted in the triumph of the new order*: **rejoice at/in**, take delight in, find/take pleasure in, find/take satisfaction in, feel satisfaction at, find joy in, enjoy, appreciate, revel in, glory in, bask in, delight in, relish, savour, luxuriate in, wallow in; **be/feel proud of**, feel proud about, be proud of oneself for, congratulate oneself on, flatter oneself on, preen oneself on, pat oneself on the back for, give oneself a pat on the back for; **crow about**, feel self-satisfied about, vaunt, boast about, brag about, gloat over; archaic pique oneself on/in.
▷ANTONYMS sorrow.

exultant adjective *the exultant winners waved to the crowd*: **jubilant**, thrilled, triumphant, delighted, exhilarated, happy, overjoyed, joyous, joyful, gleeful, cock-a-hoop, excited, animated, exulting, rejoicing, beside oneself with happiness, ecstatic, euphoric, elated, rapturous, in raptures, enraptured, rapt, walking on air, on cloud nine/seven, in seventh heaven, jumping for joy, in transports of delight, transported, carried away, in a frenzy of delight, delirious (with happiness), hysterical, wild with excitement, frenzied; **crowing**, gloating, boastful, swaggering; informal blissed out, over the moon, on a high; N. Amer. informal wigged out; rare corybantic.
▷ANTONYMS sorrowing, gloomy.

exultation noun *to have won the first prize filled me with exultation*: **jubilation**, rejoicing, happiness, pleasure, joy, gladness, delight, glee, elation, cheer, euphoria, exhilaration, delirium, ecstasy, rapture, transports (of delight), exuberance, glory, triumph; celebration, revelry, merrymaking, festivity, feasting; **crowing**, gloating, boasting.
▷ANTONYMS gloom, depression.

eye noun **1** *he rubbed his eyes wearily*: **organ of sight**, eyeball; informal peeper; literary orb; archaic or humorous optic; rare globe.
2 (**eyes**) *his sharp eyes had missed nothing*: **eyesight**, vision, sight, power of sight, faculty of sight, ability to see, power of seeing, powers of observation, observation, perception, visual perception.
3 *shoppers with an eye for a bargain*: **appreciation**, awareness, alertness, perception, discernment, discrimination, taste, judgement, recognition, consciousness, knowledge, understanding, comprehension, cognizance, feeling, sensitivity, instinct, intuition, nose.
4 *her nervous movement did not escape his watchful eye*: **watch**, observance, lookout, gaze, stare, regard; observation, surveillance, vigilance, view, notice, contemplation, examination, inspection, study, scrutiny.
5 (also **eyes**) *to desert was despicable in their eyes | the picture quality is, to my eye, excellent*: **opinion**, thinking, way of thinking, mind, view, viewpoint, point of view, attitude, stance, stand, standpoint, position, perspective, belief, contention, conviction, judgement, assessment, analysis, evaluation, gauging, rating, appraisal, estimation, estimate.
6 *the eye of a needle*: **hole**, opening, aperture, eyelet, gap, slit, slot, crevice, chink, crack, perforation, interstice.
7 *the eye of the storm*: **centre**, middle, nucleus, heart, core, hub, pivot, kernel, bosom, interior, depths, thick.
▷ANTONYMS edge.
□ **an eye for an eye (and a tooth for a tooth)** *an eye for an eye simply escalates violence*. See **revenge** (sense 1 of the noun).
□ **clap/lay/set eyes on** informal *I have never clapped eyes on him before*: **see**, observe, notice, spot, sight, have sight of, spy, catch sight of, glimpse, catch/get a glimpse of, make out, discern, perceive, pick out, detect; literary behold, espy, descry.
□ **see eye to eye** *we don't always see eye to eye about things*: **agree**, concur, be in agreement, be of the same mind/opinion, be in accord, be in sympathy, sympathize, be united, think as one; be on the same wavelength, get on, get along, feel a rapport.
▷ANTONYMS disagree.
□ **up to one's eyes** *not now, I'm afraid, I'm up to my eyes this morning*: **very busy**, fully occupied; overwhelmed, inundated, overloaded, overburdened, overworked, overtaxed, under pressure, hard-pressed, harassed, rushed/run off one's feet, with one's back to the wall; informal pushed, up against it, up to here.
▶verb **1** *he eyed the stranger suspiciously*: **look at**, see, observe, view, gaze at, gaze upon, stare at, scan, regard, contemplate, survey, inspect, examine, scrutinize, study, consider, glance at, take a glance at; **watch**, keep an eye on, keep under observation, keep watch on, keep under scrutiny, keep under surveillance, monitor, watch like a hawk, keep a weather eye on; spy on; informal have/take a gander at, have a squint at, get a load of, give someone/something a once-over, check out, gawp at, size up, keep a beady eye on, keep tabs on, keep a tab on; Brit. informal have/take a butcher's at, have/take a dekko at, have/take a shufti at, clock; N. Amer. informal eyeball; literary behold; rare twig, surveil.
▷ANTONYMS ignore.
2 *sometimes he would eye young women in the street*: **ogle**, leer at, stare at, gaze at, make eyes at, make sheep's eyes at; informal eye up, give someone the glad eye, give someone a/the once-over, lech after/over, undress with one's eyes, give someone the come-on; Brit. informal gawp at, gawk at; Austral./NZ informal perv on.

Word links **eye**

ocular, **ophthalmic**, **optic** relating to the eye
ophthalmitis inflammation of the eye
ophthalmology branch of medicine concerning the eye
ophthalmometry measurement of the eye

eyebrow noun **brow**; informal monobrow.

eye-catching adjective *each pot is decorated with eye-catching designs*: **striking**, arresting, conspicuous, noticeable, dramatic, impressive, imposing, spectacular, breathtaking, dazzling, amazing, astounding, astonishing, surprising, staggering, stunning, sensational, awesome, awe-inspiring, engaging, remarkable, notable, noteworthy, distinctive, extraordinary, outstanding, incredible, phenomenal, unusual, rare, uncommon, out of the ordinary.
▷ANTONYMS inconspicuous; unexceptional.

eyeful noun informal **1** *did you get an eyeful of that?* **look at**, peep at, peek at, glimpse of, view of, stare at, gaze at, gape at, ogle at, glance at; examination of, inspection of, scan of, survey of, study of; sight of; informal gander at, load of, squint at; Brit. informal dekko at, shufti at, butcher's at; Austral./NZ informal geek at, squiz at.
2 *even now, in middle age, she was still quite an eyeful*: **beautiful sight**, vision, joy to behold, picture, dream, sensation, beauty, dazzler; belle, beauty queen, goddess, Venus; informal stunner, looker, knockout, sight for sore eyes, bombshell, dish, cracker, smasher, lovely, good-looker, peach, honey, eye-catcher, bit of all right; Brit. informal, dated bobby-dazzler.
▷ANTONYMS eyesore.

eyelash noun **lash**; technical cilium.

Word links **eyelash**

ciliary relating to eyelashes

eyelid noun **lid**; technical palpebra, nictitating membrane.

Word links **eyelash**

palpebral, **ciliary** relating to the eyelids
blepharitis inflammation of the eyelid
blepharoplasty surgery to repair eyelids

eyesight noun *he has poor eyesight*: **sight**, vision, power of sight, faculty of sight, ability to see, power of seeing, powers of observation, observation, perception, visual perception.

Word links **eyesight**

optometry measurement of eyesight

eyesore noun *the rubbish tip is an eyesore*: **ugly sight**, blot (on the landscape), mess, scar, blight, disfigurement, blemish, defacement, defect, monstrosity, horror, carbuncle, excrescence, atrocity, disgrace, ugliness; informal sight, fright.
▷ANTONYMS vision.

eyewitness noun *eyewitnesses stated that one plane crashed in the harbour*: **observer**, onlooker, witness, looker-on, bystander, spectator, watcher, viewer, passer-by; informal rubberneck; literary beholder.

fable noun **1** *the fable of the sick lion and the wary fox*: **moral tale**, parable, apologue, allegory, bestiary.
2 *the fables of ancient Greece*: **myth**, legend, saga, epic, folk tale, folk story, traditional story, tale, story, fairy tale, narrative, romance; folklore, lore, mythology, fantasy, oral history, tradition, folk tradition, old wives' tales; technical mythos, mythus; informal yarn.
3 *it's a fable that I have a taste for fancy restaurants*. See **lie**[1] (noun).

fabled adjective **1** *a fabled god-giant of Irish myth*: **legendary**, mythical, mythic, mythological, fabulous, folkloric, fairy-tale, heroic, traditional; fictitious, imaginary, imagined, made up, unreal, hypothetical, fantastic, proverbial, apocryphal; allegorical, symbolic, parabolic.
▷ANTONYMS real, historical.
2 *the fabled high quality of French cabinetmaking*: **celebrated**, renowned, famed, famous, well known, (rightly) prized, much publicized, noted, notable, distinguished, acclaimed, illustrious, pre-eminent, prominent, great, esteemed, prestigious, well thought of, of note, of consequence, of repute, of high standing.
▷ANTONYMS unknown; unsung; derided.

fabric noun **1** *they weave silks into the finest fabric*: **cloth**, material, textile, stuff, tissue, web.
2 *the fabric of the building has deteriorated*: **structure**, framework, frame, form, make-up, constitution, composition, construction, organization, infrastructure, foundations, mechanisms, anatomy, essence.

> *Word links* **fabric**
>
> **clothier**, **draper** seller of fabrics

fabricate verb **1** *he was found to have fabricated research data*: **forge**, falsify, fake, counterfeit, make up, invent.
2 *he is guilty of fabricating a pack of lies*: **concoct**, make up, contrive, think up, dream up, invent, manufacture, trump up; informal cook up.
3 *you will have to fabricate an exhaust system*: **make**, create, manufacture, produce; construct, build, assemble, put together, cobble together, form, fashion, contrive, model, shape, forge; erect, put up, set up, raise, elevate.
▷ANTONYMS destroy, dismantle.

fabrication noun **1** *the story was a complete fabrication*: **invention**, concoction, piece of fiction, fiction, falsification, falsity, lie, untruth, falsehood, fib, deception, made-up story, trumped-up story, fairy story/tale, cock and bull story, barefaced lie; (little) white lie, half-truth, exaggeration, prevarication, departure from the truth; yarn, story, red herring, rumour, myth, flight of fancy, figment of the imagination; pretence, pretext, sham, ruse, wile, trickery, stratagem; informal tall story, tall tale, whopper; Brit. informal porky, pork pie, porky pie; humorous terminological inexactitude; vulgar slang bullshit; Austral./NZ vulgar slang bulldust.
2 *the lintels are galvanized after fabrication*: **manufacture**, making, creation, production; construction, building, assembly, putting together, forming, fashioning, contriving, modelling, shaping, forging; erection, putting up, setting up, raising, elevation.

fabulous adjective **1** *they are paid fabulous salaries*: **tremendous**, stupendous, prodigious, phenomenal; extraordinary, remarkable, exceptional; astounding, amazing, astonishing, fantastic, breathtaking, overwhelming, staggering, unthinkable, inconceivable, unimaginable, incredible, unbelievable, unheard of, unthought of, unspeakable, unutterable, untold, ineffable, implausible, improbable, unlikely, impossible, undreamed of, beyond one's wildest dreams, beyond the realm of reason; informal mind-boggling, mind-blowing.
▷ANTONYMS ordinary; tiny.
2 informal *we had a fabulous time*: **excellent**, marvellous, superb, very good, first-rate, first-class, wonderful, outstanding, exceptional, magnificent, splendid, superlative, matchless, peerless; informal great, super, terrific, tremendous, smashing, fantastic, sensational, stellar, ace, fab, A1, cool, awesome, magic, wicked, tip-top, top-notch, out of sight, out of this world, way-out, capital; Brit. informal brill; Austral./NZ informal bonzer; Brit. informal, dated spiffing, topping, top-hole, wizard; humorous super-duper.
▷ANTONYMS bad; boring.
3 *a fabulous horse-like beast with a female human head*: **mythical**, legendary, mythic, mythological, fabled, folkloric, fairy-tale, heroic, traditional; fictitious, imaginary, imagined, made up, unreal, hypothetical, fantastic, proverbial, apocryphal; allegorical, symbolic, symbolical.

facade, façade noun **1** *the house has a half-timbered facade*: **front**, frontage, face, aspect, elevation, exterior, outside.
2 *a facade of laughing bonhomie*: **show**, front, appearance, false display, pretence, simulation, affectation, semblance, illusion, posture, pose, sham, fake, act, masquerade, charade, guise, mask, cloak, veil, veneer.

face noun **1** *she has a beautiful face*: **countenance**, physiognomy, profile, features; informal mug, kisser, clock; Brit. informal mush, dial, phizog, phiz; Brit. rhyming slang boat race; Scottish & Irish informal coupon; N. Amer. informal puss, pan; literary visage, lineaments; archaic front.
2 *her face grew sad again*: **expression**, facial expression, look, appearance, air, manner, bearing, countenance, guise, cast, aspect, impression; formal mien.
3 *he made a face at the sourness of the drink*: **grimace**, scowl, wry face, wince, frown, glower, smirk, pout, moue.
4 *a cube has six faces*: **side**, aspect, flank, vertical, surface, plane, facet, wall, elevation; front, frontage, facade; slope.
5 *the face of a watch*: **dial**, display.
6 *a number of dramatic events changed the face of the industry*: **(outward) appearance**, aspect, air, nature, image.
7 *he put on a brave face for his audience*: **front**, show, display, act, appearance, false front, facade, exterior, guise, mask, masquerade, pretence, charade, pose, illusion, smokescreen, veneer, camouflage.
8 *criticism, if it is to be constructive, should never cause the recipient to lose face*: **respect**, honour, esteem, regard, admiration, approbation, acclaim, approval, favour, appreciation, popularity, estimation, veneration, awe, reverence, deference, recognition, prestige, standing, status, dignity, glory, kudos, cachet, image; self-respect, self-esteem, self-image.
9 informal *they had the face to upbraid others*: **effrontery**, audacity, nerve, gall, brazenness, brashness, shamelessness; defiance, boldness, temerity, impudence, impertinence, insolence, presumption, presumptuousness, forwardness, cheek, cheekiness; impoliteness, unmannerliness, bad manners, rudeness; informal brass, brass neck, neck, cockiness; Brit. informal sauce; Scottish informal snash; N. Amer. informal sass, sassiness, chutzpah; informal, dated hide; Brit. informal, dated crust.
□ **face to face** *the two men stood face to face*: **facing (each other)**, confronting (each other), opposite (each other), across from each other, opposing (each other); informal eyeball to eyeball (with).
□ **fly in the face of** *this flies in the face of the facts*: **go against**, flout, defy,

disobey, refuse to obey, rebel against, thumb one's nose at, disregard, ignore, set one's face against, kick against; break, violate, contravene, breach, infringe; informal cock a snook at; archaic set at naught.
▷ANTONYMS obey.
□ **on the face of it** *on the face of it, the government's decision is the height of folly*: **ostensibly**, to the casual eye, at face value, to all appearances, from appearances, to go/judge by appearances, to all intents and purposes, at first glance, on the surface, superficially; **apparently**, seemingly, evidently, outwardly, it seems (that), it would seem (that), it appears (that), it would appear (that), as far as one knows, as far as one can see/tell, by all accounts, so it seems; so the story goes, so I'm told, so it appears/seems, so it would appear/seem; allegedly, supposedly, reputedly.
▸ **verb 1** *the hotel faces the sea*: **look out on**, front on to, look towards, be facing, have/afford/command a view of, look over/across, open out over, look on to, overlook, give on to, give over, be opposite (to).
▷ANTONYMS back on to.
2 *you'll just have to face facts | we should be strong enough to* **face up to** *the situation*: **accept**, come to accept, become reconciled to, reconcile oneself to, reach an acceptance (of), get used to, become accustomed to, adjust to, accommodate oneself to, acclimatize oneself to; learn to live with, cope with, deal with, come to terms with, get to grips with, become resigned to, make the best of; confront, meet head-on.
▷ANTONYMS dodge.
3 *he is likely to face a humiliating rejection*: **be confronted by**, be faced with, encounter, experience, come into contact with, run into, come across, meet, come up against, be forced to contend with.
4 *those are the problems that face our police force*: **beset**, worry, distress, cause trouble to, trouble, bother, confront, burden; harass, oppress, vex, irritate, exasperate, strain, stress, tax; torment, plague, blight, bedevil, rack, smite, curse, harrow; rare discommode.
5 *though unprepared for such a challenge, he faced it boldly*: **brave**, face up to, encounter, meet, meet head-on, confront, dare, defy, oppose, resist, withstand.
▷ANTONYMS succumb to.
6 (usually **be faced with**) *a low, curving wall faced with flint*: **cover**, clad, veneer, skin, overlay, surface, dress, pave, put a facing on, laminate, inlay, plate, coat, line.
□ **face down** *he faced down his harshest critic*: **stand up to**, outface, cow, overawe, intimidate, browbeat, confront, beard, outstare, stare out/down, defy.

facelift noun **1** *she's planning to have a facelift when she gets older*: **cosmetic surgery**, plastic surgery; technical rhytidectomy.
2 informal *the theatre is reopening after a £200,000 facelift*: **renovation**, redecoration, refurbishment, revamp, revamping, makeover, rehabilitation, reconditioning, overhauling, modernization, restoration, repair, redevelopment, rebuilding, reconstruction, remodelling, updating, improvement; gentrification, upgrading; refit.

facet noun **1** *a larger number of small facets preserves the size of the gem*: **surface**, face, side, plane, angle, slant.
2 *she'd also seen other facets of his character*: **aspect**, feature, side, dimension, particular, characteristic, detail, point, ingredient, strand, factor; component, constituent, element, part, section, portion, piece, bit; angle, slant, sense, respect, regard, way, viewpoint, standpoint.

facetious adjective *no facetious remarks, please*: **flippant**, flip, glib, frivolous, tongue-in-cheek, waggish, whimsical, joking, jokey, jesting, jocular, playful, roguish, impish, teasing, arch, mischievous, puckish; in fun, in jest, witty, amusing, funny, droll, comic, comical, chucklesome, light-hearted, high-spirited, bantering; archaic frolicsome, sportive; rare jocose.
▷ANTONYMS serious.

facile adjective **1** *that's too facile an explanation*: **simplistic**, superficial, oversimple, oversimplified, schematic, black and white; shallow, pat, glib, slick, jejune, naive; N. Amer. informal dime-store, bubblegum.
▷ANTONYMS thorough, profound.
2 *he achieved a facile six-lengths victory*. See **easy** (sense 1).

facilitate verb *working in pairs appears to facilitate learning*: **make easy/easier**, ease, make possible, make smooth/smoother, smooth, smooth the path of, smooth the way for, clear the way for, open the door for; enable, assist, help, help along, aid, oil, oil the wheels of, lubricate, expedite, speed up, accelerate, forward, advance, promote, further, encourage; simplify.
▷ANTONYMS impede.

facility noun **1** (**facilities**) *many shopping centres include car-parking facilities*: **provision**, space, means, potential, prerequisite, equipment.
2 *the camera has a zoom facility*: **possibility**, opportunity, feature.
3 *there is a wealth of local facilities*: **amenity**, resource, service, advantage, convenience, benefit.
4 *a medical facility deep in the jungle*: **establishment**, centre, installation, place, depot, station, location, premises, site, post, base, camp; informal joint, outfit, set-up.
5 *his facility for drawing*: **aptitude**, **talent**, gift, flair, bent, skill, knack, finesse, genius; ability, proficiency, competence, capability, potential, capacity, faculty; expertise, expertness, adeptness, prowess, mastery, artistry; propensity, inclination, natural ability, suitability, fitness; head, mind, brain; informal know-how.
6 *I was turning out poetry with facility*: **ease**, effortlessness, no difficulty, no trouble, no bother, facileness, simplicity; deftness, adroitness, dexterity, proficiency, mastery.

facing noun **1** *a tartan smoking jacket with green velvet facings*: **covering**, trimming, lining, interfacing, reinforcement, backing.
2 *the bricks were used as a facing on a concrete core*: **cladding**, veneer, skin, protective/decorative layer, surface, facade, front, fronting, false front, coating, covering, dressing, overlay, revetment, paving, lamination, inlay, plating; N. Amer. siding.

facsimile noun **1** *a facsimile of the manuscript*: **copy**, reproduction, duplicate, photocopy, mimeograph, mimeo, replica, likeness, carbon, carbon copy, print, reprint, offprint, image; fax, telefax; clone; N. Amer. telecopy; Printing autotype; trademark Xerox, photostat.
▷ANTONYMS original.
2 *somewhere out there a facsimile of Jenny roamed*: **double**, lookalike, twin, clone, duplicate, perfect likeness, exact likeness, echo, replica, copy, imitation, picture, image, living image, mirror-image; German Doppelgänger; informal spitting image, dead ringer, ringer, (very) spit, dead spit, spit and image.

fact noun **1** *it is a fact that the water supply is seriously polluted*: **reality**, actuality, certainty, factuality, certitude; truth, naked truth, verity, gospel.
▷ANTONYMS lie; fiction.
2 *every fact in the report was double-checked*: **detail**, piece of information, particular, item, specific, element, point, factor, feature, characteristic, respect, ingredient, attribute, circumstance, consideration, aspect, facet; (**facts**) information, itemized information, whole story; informal info, gen, low-down, score, dope.
3 *he was charged with being an accessory after the fact*: **event**, happening, occurrence, incident, act, deed.
□ **in fact** *he said that he was going home, but in fact he went to the pub*: **actually**, in actuality, in actual fact, really, in reality, in point of fact, as a matter of fact, in truth, if truth be told, to tell the truth, the truth is/was; dated indeed, truly; archaic in sooth, verily; rare in the concrete.

faction noun **1** *he was supported by a faction of the Liberal Party*: **clique**, coterie, caucus, cabal, bloc, camp, group, grouping, side, sector, section, wing, arm, branch, division, contingent, set, ring, lobby; ginger group, pressure group, splinter group, fringe movement, minority group.
2 *the council was increasingly split by faction*: **infighting**, dissension, dissent, dispute, discord, strife, contention, conflict, friction, argument, difference of opinion, disagreement, controversy, quarrelling, wrangling, bickering, squabbling, disputation, falling-out, debate, division, divisiveness, clashing, disharmony, disunity, variance, rupture, tumult, turbulence, upheaval, dissidence, rebellion, insurrection, sedition, mutiny, schism.
▷ANTONYMS harmony.

factious adjective *he had transformed a fragmented, factious resistance movement into a monolithic one*: **divided**, split, sectarian, schismatic, dissenting, contentious, discordant, conflicting, argumentative, disagreeing, disputatious, quarrelling, quarrelsome, clashing, warring, at variance, at loggerheads, at odds, disharmonious, tumultuous, turbulent, dissident, rebellious, insurrectionary, seditious, mutinous.
▷ANTONYMS harmonious.

factitious adjective *the outcry was, to a certain extent, factitious*. See **bogus**.

factor noun **1** *this had been a key factor in his decision to withdraw*: **element**, part, component, ingredient, strand, constituent, point, detail, item, feature, facet, aspect, characteristic, consideration, influence, circumstance, thing, determinant.
2 Scottish *he worked as a factor in Perthshire*: **agent**, representative, deputy, middleman, intermediary, go-between; **estate manager**, land agent, land steward, reeve.

factory noun **works**, plant, manufacturing complex/facility, yard, mill, industrial unit; workshop, shop; shop floor; archaic manufactory.

factotum noun *in former times he might have been a nobleman's factotum*: **odd-job man**, (general) handyman, general employee, man of all work, maid of all work, jack of all trades, personal assistant; Brit. PA; Austral. knockabout; informal (Mr) Fixit, man/girl Friday.

factual adjective *a factual account of events*: **truthful**, true, accurate, authentic, historical, genuine, fact-based, realistic, real; true-to-life, lifelike, telling it like it is, as it really happened, correct, circumstantial, sure, veritable, exact, precise, honest, fair, faithful, literal, matter-of-fact, verbatim, word for word, unbiased, objective, unprejudiced, unvarnished, unadorned, unadulterated, unexaggerated; rare verisimilar, veristic, veridical.
▷ANTONYMS fictitious.

faculty noun **1** *the faculty of speech*: **power**, capability, capacity, facility, potential, potentiality, propensity, wherewithal, means, preparedness; (**faculties**) senses, wits, reason, intelligence.

2 *he had a quite unusual faculty for unearthing contributors*: **ability**, proficiency, competence, capability, potential, capacity, facility, readiness; **aptitude**, talent, gift, flair, bent, skill, knack, finesse, genius; expertise, expertness, adeptness, adroitness, dexterity, prowess, mastery, artistry, accomplishment; propensity, inclination, natural ability, suitability, fitness; head, mind, brain; informal know-how.
3 *the arts faculty*: **department**, school, division, section.
4 *the vicar introduced certain ornaments without the necessary faculty to do so*: **authorization**, authority, power, right, permission, consent, leave, sanction, licence, dispensation, assent, acquiescence, agreement, approval, seal of approval, approbation, endorsement, imprimatur, clearance; informal the go-ahead, the thumbs up, the OK, the green light, say-so; rare permit.

fad noun *there is a general fad for see-through products*: **craze**, vogue, trend, fashion, mode, enthusiasm, passion, infatuation, love, obsession, mania, rage, compulsion, fixation, fetish, weakness, fancy, taste, novelty, whim, fascination, preoccupation; informal thing, latest.

f

faddy adjective Brit. informal *offering a varied diet can be difficult when a child is faddy*: **fussy**, finicky, difficult/hard to please, over-particular, faddish, over-fastidious, dainty, exacting, demanding, selective; informal choosy, picky, pernickety; N. Amer. informal persnickety; archaic nice, overnice; rare finical.

fade verb **1** *the paintwork has faded and peeled*: **become pale**, grow pale, pale, become bleached, become washed out, lose colour, decolour, decolorize, discolour; dull, dim, grow dull, grow dim, lose lustre.
▷ANTONYMS brighten.
2 *sunlight had faded the picture*: **bleach**, wash out, make pale, decolour, decolorize, blanch, whiten; dull, discolour, dim, etiolate.
▷ANTONYMS enhance; brighten.
3 *remove the flower heads as they fade*: **wither**, wilt, droop, shrivel, decay, die, perish; technical become marcescent; rare etiolate.
4 *the afternoon light began to fade | the noise **faded away***: **dim**, grow dim, grow faint, grow feeble, fail, dwindle, grow less, die away, wane, disappear, vanish, decline, dissolve, peter out, melt away, evanesce.
▷ANTONYMS increase.
5 *the industry was **fading away***: **decline**, die out, diminish, deteriorate, degenerate, decay, crumble, collapse, fail, fall, sink, slump, slip, slide, go downhill, go to rack and ruin; informal go to pot, go to the dogs, go down the toilet, go down the tubes, hit the skids; Austral./NZ informal go to the pack; rare retrograde.
▷ANTONYMS thrive.

faeces plural noun **excrement**, bodily waste, waste matter, ordure, dung, manure, scat; excreta, stools, droppings; dirt, filth, muck, mess; informal poo, doo-doo, doings, turds; Brit. informal cack, whoopsies, jobbies; N. Amer. informal poop; vulgar slang crap, shit; archaic night soil; rare egesta, feculence.

Word links **faeces**

scato-, **copro-** related prefixes
scatology medical study of faeces
coprophobia fear of faeces
scatophagous, **coprophagous** faeces-eating

fag[1] Brit. informal **noun** *it's too much of a fag to drive all the way there and back*: **chore**, slog, grind, drudgery, exertion, trouble, bother, pain, hardship, bore; informal sweat.

fag[2] noun Brit. informal *he had a fag clamped between his teeth.* See **cigarette**.

fagged adjective *I'm off to bed now—I'm absolutely **fagged out***: **exhausted**, tired, tired out, worn out, fatigued, weary, wearied, drained, sapped, spent, washed out, on one's last legs; informal done in, all in, dog tired, dead beat, dead on one's feet, fit to drop, shattered, bushed, frazzled, worn to a frazzle; Brit. informal knackered; N. Amer. informal tuckered, pooped.

fail verb **1** *they could not explain why the enterprise had failed*: **be unsuccessful**, not succeed, lack success, fall through, fall flat, break down, abort, miscarry, be defeated, suffer defeat, be in vain, be frustrated, collapse, founder, misfire, backfire, not come up to scratch, meet with disaster, come to grief, come to nothing, come to naught, miss the mark, run aground, go astray; informal flop, fizzle out, come a cropper, bite the dust, bomb, blow up in someone's face, go down like a lead balloon.
▷ANTONYMS succeed.
2 *he failed all his examinations*: **be unsuccessful in**, not pass; be found wanting, be found deficient, not make the grade, not pass muster, not come up to scratch, be rejected; informal flunk.
▷ANTONYMS pass.
3 *he felt that his friends had failed him*: **let down**, disappoint, break one's promise to, dash someone's hopes, fall short of someone's expectations; neglect, desert, abandon; betray, be disloyal to, be unfaithful to, break faith with, play someone false; informal do the dirty on; N. Amer. informal bail on; archaic forsake.
▷ANTONYMS support.
4 *the crops failed*: **be deficient**, be wanting, be lacking, fall short, be insufficient, be inadequate; not come to ripeness, wither.
▷ANTONYMS thrive.
5 *they went to bed when the daylight failed*: **fade**, grow less, grow dim, dim, die away, dwindle, wane, disappear, vanish, peter out, dissolve.
6 *the ventilation system failed*: **break down**, break, stop working, cease to function, cut out, stop, stall, crash, give out; malfunction, act up, go wrong, develop a fault, be faulty, be defective; informal conk out, go kaput, go phut, give up the ghost, go on the blink, be on the blink; Brit. informal pack up, play up.
▷ANTONYMS work, be in working order.
7 *Ceri's health was failing*: **deteriorate**, degenerate, decline, go into decline, fade, diminish, dwindle, wane, ebb, sink, collapse, decay.
▷ANTONYMS improve.
8 *there are 900 businesses failing a week*: **collapse**, crash, go under, go bankrupt, become insolvent, go into receivership, be in the hands of the receivers, go into liquidation, cease trading, cease production, be closed, be shut down, close down, be wound up; informal fold, flop, go bust, go broke, go bump, go to the wall, go belly up.
▷ANTONYMS thrive.
▶ noun
□ **without fail** *she went to Mass every Sunday without fail*: **without exception**, unfailingly, constantly, regularly, invariably, dependably, conscientiously, reliably, faithfully, predictably, punctually, religiously, whatever happened, always; informal like clockwork.

failing noun *Jeanne accepted him despite his failings*: **fault**, shortcoming, weakness, weak point, weak spot, imperfection, defect, flaw, blemish, frailty, infirmity, foible, quirk, idiosyncrasy, vice; deficiency, inadequacy, limitation.
▷ANTONYMS strength.
▶ preposition *failing further financial assistance, you should declare yourself bankrupt*: **in the absence of**, in default of, lacking, wanting, notwithstanding.

failure noun **1** *the failure of the assassination attempt*: **lack of success**, non-success, non-fulfilment, abortion, miscarriage, defeat, frustration, collapse, foundering, misfiring, coming to nothing, falling through; informal fizzling out.
▷ANTONYMS success.
2 *every one of his schemes had been a failure*: **fiasco**, debacle, catastrophe, disaster, blunder, vain attempt, abortion, defeat; Brit. damp squib; informal flop, botch, hash, foul-up, screw-up, washout, let-down, dead loss, dead duck, lead balloon, lemon; Brit. informal cock-up, pig's ear; N. Amer. informal snafu, clinker; vulgar slang fuck-up, balls-up.
▷ANTONYMS success.
3 *I was regarded by everyone as a failure*: **loser**, born loser, incompetent, nonachiever, underachiever, ne'er-do-well, disappointment, write-off; no one, nobody; informal no-hoper, flop, dud, non-starter, washout, dead loss, lemon.
▷ANTONYMS success.
4 *he felt guilty for what seemed like a failure in duty*: **negligence**, remissness, non-observance, non-performance, dereliction; omission, neglect, oversight.
5 *any crop failure could affect a farming business*: **inadequacy**, insufficiency, deficiency, lack, dearth, scarcity, shortfall.
6 *he was puzzled by the failure of the camera*: **breaking down**, breakdown, non-function, cutting out, seizing up; **malfunction**, faultiness; crash; informal conking out; Brit. informal playing up.
7 *the failure of several state-owned companies*: **collapse**, crash, going under, bankruptcy, insolvency, liquidation, close-down, closure, closing, shutting down, winding up, termination; decline, failing, foundering, sinking, ruin, ruination; informal folding, flop.
▷ANTONYMS success.

Word links **failure**

kakorrhaphiaphobia fear of failure

faint adjective **1** *her skirt had a faint mark or two*: **indistinct**, vague, unclear, indefinite, ill-defined, obscure, imperceptible, hardly noticeable, hardly detectable, unobtrusive; pale, light, faded, bleached.
▷ANTONYMS clear.
2 *the baby gave a faint cry*: **quiet**, muted, muffled, stifled, subdued; **feeble**, weak, thin, whispered, murmured, indistinct, scarcely audible, scarcely perceptible, hard to hear, hard to make out, vague; low, soft, gentle.
▷ANTONYMS loud.
3 *the faint possibility of his returning*: **slight**, slender, slim, small, tiny, minimal, negligible, remote, distant, vague, unlikely, improbable, doubtful, dubious, far-fetched; poor, outside; informal minuscule; rare exiguous.
▷ANTONYMS great.
4 *only faint praise was offered to the management team*: **unenthusiastic**, half-hearted, weak, feeble, low-key; informal wishy-washy.
▷ANTONYMS strong.
5 *I suddenly felt hot and faint*: **dizzy**, giddy, light-headed, muzzy, weak, weak at the knees, unsteady, shaky, wobbly, off-balance, reeling;

informal woozy, woolly, woolly-headed, dopey, trembly, all of a quiver; rare vertiginous.

▶ **verb** *he was so pale she thought he would faint*: **pass out**, lose consciousness, fall unconscious, black out, collapse; informal flake out, keel over, conk out, zonk out, drop, go out, go out like a light; literary swoon.

▶ **noun** *she collapsed to the floor in a dead faint*: **blackout**, fainting fit, loss of consciousness, collapse; coma; literary swoon; Medicine syncope.

faint-hearted adjective *the more faint-hearted tenants left after the raid*: **timid**, timorous, nervous, easily scared, easily frightened, scared, fearful, afraid, trembling, quaking, cowering, daunted; **cowardly**, craven, spiritless, spineless, pusillanimous, weak, weak-willed, unmanly, lily-livered, pigeon-hearted, weak-kneed, weakling; Brit. nervy; Scottish feart; informal soft, jumpy, jittery, chicken, chicken-hearted, chicken-livered, yellow, yellow-bellied, gutless, sissy, wimpy, wimpish; Brit. informal wet; N. Amer. informal spooked, candy-assed; N. Amer. vulgar slang chickenshit; archaic recreant, poor-spirited; archaic, informal funky.
▷ANTONYMS bold; brave.

faintly adverb **1** *Maria called his name faintly*: **indistinctly**, softly, gently, weakly, feebly; in a whisper, in a murmur, in a low voice, in subdued tones.
▷ANTONYMS brightly; loudly.
2 *the newcomer looked faintly bewildered*: **slightly**, vaguely, somewhat, quite, fairly, rather, a little, a bit, a little bit, a touch, a shade; to some extent, to a certain extent, to some degree; informal sort of, kind of, kinda, ish.
▷ANTONYMS extremely.

fair[1] adjective **1** *the courts were generally regarded as fair*: **just**, equitable, fair-minded, open-minded, honest, upright, honourable, trustworthy; impartial, unbiased, unprejudiced, non-partisan, non-discriminatory, objective, neutral, even-handed, dispassionate, disinterested, detached; above board, lawful, legal, legitimate, proper, good; informal legit, kosher, pukka, on the level, square; N. Amer. informal on the up and up.
▷ANTONYMS unfair.
2 *I am hoping for fair weather for next week's trip*: **fine**, dry, bright, clear, sunny, sunshiny, sunlit, cloudless, without a cloud in the sky; warm, balmy, summery, clement, benign, agreeable, pleasant, good.
▷ANTONYMS inclement.
3 *their voyage was helped by fair winds and calm seas*: **favourable**, advantageous, helpful, benign, beneficial; opportune, timely; on one's side, in one's favour.
▷ANTONYMS unfavourable.
4 *she had fair curling hair*: **blond(e)**, yellow, yellowish, golden, flaxen, light, light brown, light-coloured, strawberry blonde, tow-coloured, platinum, ash blonde, bleached, bleached-blonde, sun-bleached, peroxide, bottle-blonde; fair-haired, light-haired, golden-haired, flaxen-haired, tow-headed.
▷ANTONYMS dark; brunette.
5 *Belinda's skin was very fair*: **pale**, light, light-coloured, white, cream-coloured, creamy, peaches and cream.
▷ANTONYMS dark.
6 archaic *he won the fair maiden's heart*. See **beautiful**.
7 *scoring twenty points was a fair achievement*: **reasonable**, passable, tolerable, satisfactory, acceptable, respectable, decent, all right, good enough, goodish, pretty good, not bad, moderate, average, middling, ample, adequate, sufficient; informal OK, okay, so-so, fair-to-middling.
□ **fair and square** *I won the race fair and square*: **honestly**, fairly, without cheating, without foul play, by the book, according to the rules, in accordance with the rules; lawfully, legally, licitly, legitimately; informal on the level; N. Amer. informal on the up and up.
□ **fair play** *she had a clear sense of fair play*: **justice**, justness, fair-mindedness, equity, equitableness, even-handedness, impartiality, lack of prejudice, open-mindedness.

fair[2] noun **1** *an English country fair*: **fête**, gala, festival, carnival, funfair.
2 *a local antiques fair*: **market**, bazaar, mart, exchange, sale; open-air market, indoor market, flea market; archaic emporium.
3 *Manchester is to host a new British art fair*: **exhibition**, display, show, showing, presentation, demonstration, exposition, spectacle, extravaganza; N. Amer. exhibit; informal expo, demo.

fairly adverb **1** *all pupils were treated fairly*: **justly**, equitably, impartially, without bias, without prejudice, without fear or favour, with an open mind, open-mindedly, even-handedly, objectively, neutrally, disinterestedly; properly, lawfully, legally, legitimately, licitly, by the book, in accordance with the rules, according to the rules; equally, the same; informal fairly and squarely.
▷ANTONYMS unfairly.
2 *the pipes are in fairly good condition*: **reasonably**, passably, tolerably, satisfactorily, sufficiently, adequately, moderately, quite, rather, somewhat, relatively, comparatively; informal pretty, kind of, sort of, kinda, ish.
▷ANTONYMS insufficiently; extremely.
3 *he fairly hauled her along the street*: **positively**, really, veritably, simply, actually, absolutely, decidedly; practically, almost, nearly, all but, to all intents and purposes; informal plain, plumb.

fair-minded adjective *he was respected as a fair-minded chief*: **fair**, just, even-handed, equitable, egalitarian, impartial, non-partisan, non-discriminatory, unbiased, unprejudiced, open-minded, objective, dispassionate, unselfish, with no axe to grind; honest, honourable, trustworthy, upright, decent; informal on the level; N. Amer. informal on the up and up.

fairy noun *all of the children believed in fairies*: **sprite**, pixie, elf, imp, brownie, puck; dwarf, gnome, goblin, hobgoblin, troll; Scottish Folklore kelpie; Irish Folklore leprechaun, pishogue, Sidhe; S. African Folklore tokoloshe; Persian Mythology peri; literary faerie, fay; rare nix, nixie, hob, elfin.

fairy tale, fairy story noun **1** *the film was inspired by a fairy tale*: **folk tale**, folk story, traditional story, myth, legend, romance, fantasy, fable, fiction; informal yarn.
2 informal *she accused him of telling fairy tales*: **lie**, white lie, fib, half-truth, untruth, falsity, falsehood, story, tall story, tall tale, made-up story, trumped-up story, fabrication, invention, piece of fiction, falsification; informal whopper, cock and bull story, angler's tale; Brit. informal porky, porky pie, pork pie; humorous terminological inexactitude.

faith noun **1** *he completely justified his boss's faith in him*: **trust**, belief, confidence, conviction, credence, reliance, dependence; optimism, hopefulness, hope, expectation.
▷ANTONYMS mistrust.
2 *she gave her life for her faith*: **religion**, church, sect, denomination, persuasion, religious persuasion, religious belief, belief, code of belief, ideology, creed, teaching, dogma, doctrine.
□ **break faith with be disloyal to**, be unfaithful to, be untrue to, betray, play someone false, break one's promise to, fail, let down, disappoint; double-cross, deceive, cheat, stab in the back, be a Judas to, give away; informal do the dirty on, stitch up, rat on, sell down the river.
□ **keep faith with be loyal to**, be faithful to, be true to, stand by, stick by, keep one's promise to, make good one's promise to.

faithful adjective **1** *she stayed faithful all her married life | his faithful assistant*: **loyal**, constant, true, devoted, true-blue, true-hearted, unswerving, unwavering, staunch, steadfast, dedicated, committed; trusted, trusty, trustworthy, dependable, reliable, obedient, dutiful.
▷ANTONYMS unfaithful.
2 *a faithful copy of a famous painting*: **accurate**, precise, exact, errorless, error-free, unerring, without error, faultless, true, close, strict; realistic, authentic, convincing; informal on the button, on the mark, on the beam, on the nail; Brit. informal spot on, bang on; N. Amer. informal on the money; rare verisimilar.
▷ANTONYMS inaccurate.

▶ **noun** (**the faithful**) *he read the sacred scriptures to the faithful*: **believers**, communicants; adherents, followers, loyal followers, loyal members; congregation, brethren, flock.

> *Choose the right word* **faithful, loyal, constant, true**
>
> All these words are used to describe an unwavering commitment to someone or something.
>
> Someone who is **faithful** shows unchanging affection or support for a person or cause, often in the face of difficulty or some temptation to desert. It can refer to marital fidelity (*he has been faithful to his wife for 42 years*) or religious faith (*faithful Jews were required to make the pilgrimage to Jerusalem three times a year*) and is used informally of inanimate objects regarded as absolutely reliable (*he drove his faithful Toyota overland from Saudi Arabia*).
>
> **Loyal** typically refers to allegiance to a superior or employer (*he proved to be a loyal subject of the king | a loyal workforce*) or support for a business or other organization (*we look forward to providing our loyal customers with a first-class service*). A *loyal friend* will show unwavering support, particularly in standing by one in the face of criticism or hostility from others.
>
> **Constant** is a rather literary term for unchanging and utterly reliable fidelity (*they are constant and dependable, consistently dispensing happiness*).
>
> **True** has a rather archaic ring when used to convey fidelity (*she is as true to me as the day is long*), since the sense tends to merge with the sense 'real' (*a true friend*). It is also used in the phrase *true to* (*true to his word, he schooled her in horsemanship*).

faithfulness noun **1** *she never doubted her husband's faithfulness*: **fidelity**, loyalty, constancy, devotion, trueness, true-heartedness, dedication, commitment, allegiance, adherence; dependability, reliability, trustworthiness, staunchness, steadfastness; historical fealty.
▷ANTONYMS unfaithfulness.
2 *the faithfulness of the description*: **accuracy**, precision, exactness, closeness, strictness, fairness, justness, factuality, truth, truthfulness, veracity, authenticity, reliability, dependability; rare veridicality.
▷ANTONYMS inaccuracy.

faithless adjective **1** *she left her faithless lover*: **unfaithful**, disloyal, inconstant, false, false-hearted, untrue, adulterous, traitorous, treacherous, perfidious, fickle, flighty, untrustworthy, unreliable, undependable,

f

deceitful, deceiving, two-faced, double-dealing, double-crossing; informal cheating, two-timing, back-stabbing; rare double-faced, Janus-faced.
▷ANTONYMS faithful.
2 *the natives were ungodly and faithless*: **unbelieving**, non-believing, irreligious, without religious faith, disbelieving, doubting, sceptical, agnostic, atheistic; pagan, heathen; rare nullifidian.

fake noun **1** *one of the sculptures was found to be a fake*: **forgery**, counterfeit, copy, sham, fraud, hoax, imitation, mock-up, dummy, reproduction, lookalike, likeness; informal phoney, pirate, knock-off, rip-off, dupe.
2 *that doctor is a fake*: **charlatan**, quack, mountebank, sham, fraud, humbug, impostor, pretender, masquerader, hoodwinker, hoaxer, cheat, cheater, deceiver, dissembler, trickster, confidence trickster, fraudster; informal phoney, con man, con artist; dated confidence man.
▶ **adjective 1** *he gave his wife fake banknotes*: **counterfeit**, forged, fraudulent, sham, imitation, false, bogus, spurious, pseudo; worthless, invalid; informal phoney, dud.
▷ANTONYMS genuine.
2 *they adorn themselves with fake diamonds*: **imitation**, artificial, synthetic, simulated, reproduction, replica, ersatz, plastic, man-made, dummy, false, mock, sham, bogus, so-called; informal pretend, phoney, pseudo.
▷ANTONYMS genuine.
3 *she adopted a fake accent*: **feigned**, faked, put-on, assumed, improvised, invented, affected, pseudo, insincere, unconvincing, artificial, imitation, mock, sham; informal phoney, pseud, pretend; Brit. informal cod.
▷ANTONYMS authentic.
▶ **verb 1** *her death certificate was faked*: **forge**, counterfeit, falsify, sham, feign, mock up, copy, reproduce, replicate; doctor, alter, tamper with, tinker with; informal pirate; Brit. informal fiddle (with).
2 *he faked a yawn*: **feign**, pretend, simulate, sham, put on, make-believe, affect; give the appearance of, make a show of, make a pretence of, go through the motions of.

fall verb **1** *bombers screamed above and bombs began to fall*: **drop**, drop down, plummet, descend, come down, go down, plunge, sink, dive, nosedive, tumble, pitch; cascade; technical gravitate.
▷ANTONYMS rise.
2 *he lost his balance and fell*: **topple over**, tumble over, keel over, fall down, fall over, go head over heels, go end over end, fall headlong, go headlong, collapse, fall in a heap, take a spill, pitch forward; trip, trip over, stumble, stagger, slip, slide; informal come a cropper, go for six; dated measure one's length.
▷ANTONYMS get up.
3 *little by little, the river began to fall*: **subside**, recede, ebb, fall back, flow back, fall away, go down, get lower, sink; abate, settle; rare retrocede.
▷ANTONYMS rise; flood.
4 *inflation is expected to fall*: **decrease**, decline, diminish, fall off, drop off, go down, grow less, lessen, dwindle; plummet, plunge, slump, sink; depreciate, decrease in value, lose value, decline in price, cheapen, devalue; informal hit the floor, go through the floor, nosedive, take a nosedive, take a header, go into a tailspin, crash.
▷ANTONYMS rise, increase.
5 *the Mogul empire fell several centuries later*: **decline**, deteriorate, degenerate, go downhill, go to rack and ruin; die, decay, atrophy, wither, fade, fail; informal go to the dogs, go to pot, hit the skids, go down the toilet, go down the tubes; Austral./NZ informal go to the pack; rare retrograde.
▷ANTONYMS flourish.
6 *a monument to those who fell in the Civil War*: **die**, be killed, be slain, be a casualty, be a fatality, be lost, lose one's life, perish, drop dead, meet one's end, meet one's death; informal bite the dust, croak, buy it; Brit. informal snuff it, peg out; N. Amer. informal bite the big one; archaic decease.
7 *the town fell to the barbarians*: **surrender**, yield, submit, give in, give up, give way, capitulate, succumb; be overthrown by, be taken by, be defeated by, be conquered by, be overcome by, be overwhelmed by, lose one's position to, pass into the hands of, fall victim to.
▷ANTONYMS resist.
8 *Easter falls on 23rd April*: **occur**, take place, happen, come about, come to pass.
9 *he waited for night to fall*: **come**, arrive, appear, occur, arise, materialize.
10 *my grandmother fell ill*: **become**, come/get to be, grow, get, turn.
11 *more of the domestic tasks may* **fall to him**: **be the responsibility of**, be the duty of, be borne by, be one's job, be one's task; come someone's way.
□ **fall about laughing** *I didn't know whether to get angry or fall about laughing*: **guffaw**, chuckle, chortle, cackle, howl, roar, ha-ha, fall about, roar/hoot with laughter, shake with laughter, be convulsed with laughter, dissolve into laughter, split one's sides, be doubled up; informal be in stitches, die laughing, be rolling in the aisles, laugh like a drain, bust a gut, break up, be creased up, crease up, crack up.
□ **fall apart 1** *my boots fell apart*: **fall to pieces**, come to pieces, fall to bits, come to bits, come apart (at the seams); **disintegrate**, fragment, break up, break apart, crumble, dissolve, degenerate, decay, moulder, perish; go downhill, go to rack and ruin; informal bust. ▷ANTONYMS remain intact.
2 *I was gentle with him when he fell apart*: **break down**, have a breakdown, go to pieces, fall to pieces, lose control, lose one's self-control, crumble; informal crack up, freak, freak out.
□ **fall asleep** *Claire tried not to fall asleep*: **doze off**, drop off, go to sleep; informal nod off, go off, drift off, crash, crash out, flake out, conk out, go out like a light; N. Amer. informal sack out, zone out.
▷ANTONYMS stay awake; wake up.
□ **fall away** *the ground fell away abruptly*: **slope down**, slope, slant down, go down, incline downwards, tilt downwards, drop away, drop, descend, dip, sink, plunge; rare decline.
▷ANTONYMS rise.
□ **fall back** *the force of her blow caused him to fall back*: **retreat**, withdraw, back off, draw back, pull back, pull away, move away, retire, pull out; turn tail, flee, take flight, beat a (hasty) retreat.
▷ANTONYMS advance.
□ **fall back on** *you can always fall back on the support of relatives*: **resort to**, turn to, look to, call on, call into play, call into action, call into service, press into service, have recourse to, make use of, use, employ; rely on, depend on, lean on.
□ **fall behind 1** *she walked so fast that the others soon fell behind*: **lag**, lag behind, trail, trail behind, be left behind, fall back, drop back, not keep up, lose one's place, not keep pace, bring up the rear; straggle, dally, dawdle, hang back, drag one's feet, take one's time. ▷ANTONYMS overtake. **2** *customers fell behind on their payments*: **get into debt**, get into arrears, default, be in the red, be late, be overdue; not keep up with. ▷ANTONYMS be up to date.
□ **fall down 1** *I spin round and round till I fall down*: **fall over**, fall, topple over, tumble down, keel over, collapse, fall in a heap, trip, take a spill, stumble, stagger; informal come a cropper, go for six; dated measure one's length. **2** *the federation fell down in some areas*: **fail**, be unsuccessful, not succeed, lack success, not make the grade, not come up to expectations, fall short, fall flat, disappoint; miss the mark, run aground, go astray, suffer defeat; informal come a cropper, flop.
▷ANTONYMS come through, succeed.
□ **fall for 1** *she fell for a younger man*: **fall in love with**, become infatuated with, lose one's heart to, take a liking to, take a fancy to, be smitten by, be attracted to, desire; informal fancy, be turned on by, have the hots for.
2 *Jenkins is far too astute to fall for that trick*: **be deceived by**, be duped by, be fooled by, be taken in by, accept, believe, trust, be convinced by, have confidence in; informal go for, buy, swallow, {swallow something hook, line, and sinker}, take something as gospel.
□ **fall in 1** *the roof of our house fell in*: **collapse**, cave in, come down about one's ears, crash in, fall down; subside, sag, slump, sink inwards; give way, crumple, crumble, disintegrate, fall to pieces.
▷ANTONYMS hold up.
2 *he ordered his troops to fall in*: **get in formation**, get in line, line up, take one's position, get in order, get into rows/columns; Military dress; Brit. informal form a crocodile.
▷ANTONYMS fall out.
□ **fall into place 1** *it was at this point that everything began to fall into place*: **become clear**, come home to one, make sense, dawn, register, get through, sink in; informal click. **2** *almost miraculously, the pieces fell into place*: **take shape**, come together, take form, become definite.
□ **fall in with 1** *he fell in with a bad crowd*: **get involved with**, take up with, join up with, go around with, string along with, become friendly with, make friends with, strike up a friendship with, start seeing, make the acquaintance of; informal hang out with, hang about with, knock about/around with. **2** *he refused to fall in with their demands*: **comply with**, go along with, support, back, give one's backing to, cooperate with, act in accordance with, obey, yield to, submit to, bow to, defer to, adhere to, conform to; agree to, agree with, accept, assent to, concur with.
▷ANTONYMS disobey.
□ **fall off** *the amount of container shipping has fallen off*: **decrease**, decline, diminish, drop off, go down, go downhill, grow less, lessen, dwindle, plummet, plunge, slump, sink; informal hit the floor, go through the floor, nosedive, take a nosedive, take a header, go into a tailspin, crash.
▷ANTONYMS increase.
□ **fall on 1** *the army fell on the besiegers*: **attack**, assail, assault, make an assault on, fly at, let fly at, launch oneself at, set about, set upon, pounce upon, ambush, surprise, accost, rush, storm, charge; informal jump, lay into, lace into, tear into, sail into, pitch into, get stuck into, let someone have it, beat someone up; Brit. informal have a go at; N. Amer. informal light into.
2 *the cost should not fall on the students*: **be borne by**, be carried by, be the responsibility of, be paid by.
□ **fall out 1** *let's not fall out over silly things*: **quarrel**, argue, row, fight, have a row, have a fight, squabble, bicker, have words, disagree, differ, have a difference of opinion, have a disagreement, be at odds, clash, wrangle, get into conflict, get into a dispute, cross swords, lock horns, be at loggerheads, be at each other's throats; informal scrap, argufy, go at it hammer and tongs, argy-bargy; archaic altercate, chop logic; Scottish archaic threap. ▷ANTONYMS make up.
2 *the soldier fell out without permission*: **move out of formation**, move out of line, get out of line, get out of formation; stand at ease. ▷ANTONYMS fall in.
3 *it fell out that we lost*: **happen**, occur, come about, take place, turn out, chance, arise, befall, result.

□ **fall short** *the results fall short of what was expected*: **fail to meet**, fail to reach, fail to live up to; **be deficient**, be inadequate, be insufficient, be wanting, be lacking, disappoint, fail, fail to live up to one's expectations; informal not come up to scratch.
▷**ANTONYMS** measure up (to).

□ **fall through** *unfortunately the deal fell through*: **fail**, be unsuccessful, come to nothing, come to naught, fail to happen, miscarry, abort, go awry, be frustrated, collapse, founder, come to grief; come to a halt, grind to a halt, end, terminate; informal fizzle out, flop, fold, come a cropper, blow up in someone's face, go down like a lead balloon.
▷**ANTONYMS** succeed.

□ **fall to** dated *you must take off your coats and fall to.* See **start** (sense 4 of the verb).

▶**noun 1** *he had an accidental fall*: **tumble**, trip, spill, topple, stumble, slip; collapse; informal nosedive, header, cropper.
2 *September's reports showed a fall in sales*: **decline**, fall-off, drop, dropping off, decrease, cut, lessening, lowering, dip, diminishing, dwindling, reduction, plummet, plunge, slump, deterioration, downswing; informal nosedive, crash, let-up.
▷**ANTONYMS** increase.
3 *the fall of the Roman Empire*: **downfall**, ruin, ruination, collapse, failure, decline, deterioration, degeneration, destruction, overthrow, demise.
▷**ANTONYMS** rise.
4 *the fall of the city to the enemy*: **surrender**, surrendering, capitulation, yielding, giving in, submission, acquiescence, succumbing, resignation, laying down of arms; defeat.
5 *there is a fall of some fifty feet down to the ocean*: **descent**, declivity, slope, downward slope, downward slant, incline; N. Amer. downgrade.
▷**ANTONYMS** ascent.
6 Christianity *the Fall of Man*: **sin**, sinning, wrongdoing, transgression, error, yielding to temptation, offence, lapse, fall from grace, backsliding; original sin.
7 (**falls**) *they went on rafting trips below the falls*: **waterfall**, cascade, cataract, chute, torrent; rapids, white water; N. English force; Scottish archaic linn.

fallacious adjective *the fallacious assumption underlying this reasoning*: **erroneous**, **false**, untrue, wrong, incorrect, faulty, flawed, inaccurate, inexact, imprecise, mistaken, misinformed, misguided, misleading, deceptive, delusive, delusory, illusory, sophistic, specious, fictitious, spurious, fabricated, distorted, made up, trumped up; baseless, groundless, unfounded, foundationless, unsubstantiated, unproven, unsupported, uncorroborated, ill-founded, without basis, without foundation; informal bogus, phoney, iffy, dicey, full of holes, (way) off beam; Brit. informal dodgy.
▷**ANTONYMS** true, correct.

fallacy noun *the fallacy that we all work from nine to five*: **misconception**, mistaken belief, misbelief, delusion, false notion, mistaken impression, misapprehension, misjudgement, miscalculation, misinterpretation, misconstruction, error, mistake, untruth, inconsistency, illusion, myth, fantasy, deceit, deception, sophism; sophistry, casuistry, faulty reasoning, unsound argument.

fallen adjective **1** *he attended a mass for his fallen comrades*: **dead**, killed, murdered, slain, slaughtered, perished, expired, deceased; lost, late, lamented, departed, gone; rare demised.
▷**ANTONYMS** surviving.
2 dated *they encouraged the moral reform of fallen women.* See **promiscuous** (sense 1).

fallible adjective *all human beings are fallible*: **error-prone**, erring, errant, liable to err, prone to err, open to error; imperfect, flawed, frail, weak.
▷**ANTONYMS** infallible.

fallow adjective **1** *fallow farmland*: **uncultivated**, unploughed, untilled, unplanted, unsown, unseeded, unused, undeveloped, dormant, resting, empty, bare, virgin; neglected, untended, unmaintained, unmanaged.
▷**ANTONYMS** cultivated.
2 *trading is set to emerge from a fallow period*: **inactive**, dormant, quiet, slack, slow, slow-moving, flat, idle, inert, static, stagnant, depressed; barren, unproductive, unfruitful.
▷**ANTONYMS** busy.

false adjective **1** *he gave a false account of his movements*: **incorrect**, untrue, wrong, erroneous, fallacious, faulty, flawed, distorted, inaccurate, inexact, imprecise, invalid, unfounded; untruthful, fictitious, concocted, fabricated, invented, made up, trumped up, unreal, counterfeit, forged, fraudulent, spurious, misleading, deceptive.
▷**ANTONYMS** correct; truthful.
2 *Briggs proved himself a false friend*: **faithless**, unfaithful, disloyal, untrue, inconstant, false-hearted, treacherous, traitorous, perfidious, two-faced, double-dealing, double-crossing, deceitful, deceiving, deceptive, dishonourable, dishonest, duplicitous, hypocritical, untrustworthy, unreliable; untruthful, lying, mendacious; informal cheating, two-timing, back-stabbing; rare hollow-hearted, double-faced, Janus-faced.
▷**ANTONYMS** faithful.
3 *she would never wear false pearls*: **fake**, artificial, imitation, synthetic, simulated, reproduction, replica, ersatz, faux, plastic, man-made, dummy, mock, sham, bogus, so-called; counterfeit, feigned, forged; informal phoney, pretend, pseudo.
▷**ANTONYMS** genuine.

falsehood noun **1** *this is an exaggeration if not a downright falsehood*: **lie**, fib, untruth, false statement, falsification, fabrication, invention, piece of fiction, fiction, story, yarn, made-up story, trumped-up story, cock and bull story, flight of fancy, figment of the imagination; barefaced lie, (little) white lie, half truth, departure from the truth, red herring; informal tall story, tall tale, fairy story, fairy tale, whopper; Brit. informal porky, porky pie, pork pie; humorous terminological inexactitude.
▷**ANTONYMS** truth.
2 *no one has accused me of falsehood before*: **lying**, mendacity, untruthfulness, fibbing, fabrication, invention, perjury, perfidy, perfidiousness, lack of veracity, telling stories, misrepresentation, prevarication, equivocation; deceit, deception, deceitfulness, pretence, artifice, falseness, two-facedness, double-dealing, double-crossing, dissimulation, treachery; Irish informal codology; informal kidology.
▷**ANTONYMS** truthfulness, honesty.

falsetto noun *he sang in a piercing falsetto*: **high voice**, high-pitched voice, high-pitched tone, shrill tone, piercing tone, ear-piercing tone.

falsification noun *the illegal falsification of records*: **forgery**, counterfeiting, fabrication, invention, alteration, changing, doctoring, distortion, manipulation, manipulating, tampering, fudging, adulteration, debasement, perversion, corruption, misrepresentation, misapplication; rare vitiation.

falsify verb **1** *she falsified the accounts*: **forge**, fake, counterfeit, fabricate, invent, alter, change, doctor, tamper with, fudge, manipulate, massage, adulterate, pervert, corrupt, debase, misrepresent, misreport, distort, warp, embellish, embroider, colour, put a spin on; rare vitiate.
2 *the theory is falsified by the evidence*: **disprove**, show to be false, prove unsound, refute, rebut, deny, debunk, negate, invalidate, contradict, confound, be at odds with, demolish, discredit; informal shoot full of holes, shoot down (in flames), blow sky-high, blow out of the water; formal confute, gainsay; rare controvert, negative.

falsity noun *he was compelled to reveal the falsity of his assertions*: **untruthfulness**, untruth, fallaciousness, falseness, falsehood, fictitiousness, fiction, inaccuracy, inexactness, hollowness; mendacity, fabrication, dishonesty, deceitfulness, deceit, hypocrisy; rare unveracity.

falter verb **1** *when war seemed imminent the government faltered*: **hesitate**, delay, drag one's feet, stall, think twice, get cold feet, change one's mind, waver, oscillate, fluctuate, vacillate, be undecided, be indecisive, be irresolute, see-saw, yo-yo; Brit. haver, hum and haw; informal sit on the fence, dilly-dally, shilly-shally, pussyfoot around, blow hot and cold; rare tergiversate.
2 *she faltered over his name*: **stammer**, stutter, stumble, speak haltingly, hesitate, pause, halt, splutter, flounder, blunder, fumble.

fame noun *she is a designer of international fame*: **renown**, celebrity, stardom, popularity, notability, note, distinction, prominence, esteem, importance, account, consequence, greatness, eminence, pre-eminence, glory, honour, illustriousness, prestige, stature, standing, reputation, repute; notoriety, infamy; rare supereminence.
▷**ANTONYMS** obscurity; disgrace.

famed adjective *he is famed for his grace and artistry*: **famous**, celebrated, well known, prominent, noted, notable, renowned, distinguished, esteemed, respected, acclaimed, honoured, exalted, remarkable, legendary, lionized, much publicized; notorious, infamous.

familiar adjective **1** *I see a lot of familiar faces | a familiar task*: **well known**, known, recognized, accustomed; common, everyday, day-to-day, ordinary, commonplace, frequent, habitual, usual, customary, repeated, routine, standard, stock, mundane, run-of-the-mill, conventional; household, domestic; Brit. common or garden; N. Amer. garden variety; informal bog-standard; literary wonted.
▷**ANTONYMS** unfamiliar.
2 *she was an old and familiar friend*: **close**, intimate, dear, near, confidential, bosom; friendly, neighbourly, sociable, amicable, easy; informal pally, chummy, matey, buddy-buddy, palsy-walsy, thick, thick as thieves.
3 *he enjoyed the familiar atmosphere in their house*: **informal**, non-formal, casual, relaxed, comfortable, easy, free, free and easy, at ease, at home, friendly, unceremonious, unrestrained, unconstrained, unreserved, open, natural, simple, unpretentious.
▷**ANTONYMS** formal.
4 *they object to him* **being familiar with** *the staff*: **overfamiliar**, unduly familiar, over-free, presumptuous, disrespectful, forward, bold, impudent, impertinent, intrusive; making passes at, chatting up, making advances towards; informal pushy.
▷**ANTONYMS** formal.
□ **familiar with** *are you familiar with the subject?* **acquainted with**, conversant with, versed in, informed about, knowledgeable about, well

informed about, instructed in, skilled in, proficient in; at home with, no stranger to, au fait with, au courant with, apprised of, abreast of, up to date with, in touch with; informal well up on, in the know about, genned up on, clued in on, clued up on, plugged into; Brit. informal switched on to; archaic ware of.
▷ANTONYMS unfamiliar with.

familiarity noun **1** *he wants to gain greater* ***familiarity with*** *European politics*: **acquaintance with**, acquaintanceship with, awareness of, experience of, insight into, conversancy with, conversance with; knowledge of, understanding of, comprehension of, cognizance of, grasp of, mastery of, skill with, skill in, proficiency in, expertise in.
2 *the reassuring familiarity of his parents' home*: **ordinariness**, customariness, normality, conventionality.
3 *they feel comfortable with you because of your familiarity*: **informality**, casualness, ease, comfortableness, friendliness, lack of ceremony, lack of restraint, lack of reserve, naturalness, simplicity.
4 *she was affronted by his familiarity*: **overfamiliarity**, presumption, presumptuousness, forwardness, boldness, audacity, cheek, impudence, impertinence, intrusiveness, disrespect, disrespectfulness; liberties; informal sauce, cockiness; archaic assumption.
5 *our familiarity allows us to give each other nicknames*: **closeness**, intimacy, attachment, affinity, friendliness, friendship, amity; informal chumminess, palliness; Brit. informal mateyness.

familiarize verb **1** *I aim to* ***familiarize*** *pupils* ***with*** *the creation and use of a database*: **make conversant**, make familiar, acquaint, get up to date, keep up to date; accustom to, habituate to, instruct in, coach in, train in, teach in, educate in, school in, prime in, indoctrinate in, initiate into, introduce to; informal gen up on, clue in on, clue up on, put in the picture about, put wise to, keep up to speed with, give the gen about, give the low-down on, give a rundown of, fill in on.
2 *the exercises help to familiarize the terms used*: **make known**, make better known, make familiar, bring to notice, bring to public attention.

family noun **1** *growing up in the bosom of one's family*: household, ménage; nuclear family; informal brood.
2 *I wanted to meet his family*: **relatives**, relations, blood relations, family members, kin, next of kin, kinsfolk, kinsmen, kinswomen, kindred, one's (own) flesh and blood, connections; extended family; clan, tribe; informal folks, nearest and dearest; dated people.
3 *a prospective husband must come from the right kind of family*: **ancestry**, parentage, birth, pedigree, genealogy, background, family tree, descent, lineage, line, line of descent, bloodline, blood, extraction, derivation, race, strain, stock, breed; dynasty, house; forebears, forefathers, antecedents, progenitors, roots, origins; rare filiation, stirps.
4 *she is married with a family*: **children**, little ones, youngsters; offspring, progeny, descendants, scions, heirs; brood; informal kids, kiddies, kiddiewinks, tots, sprogs, quiverful; Law issue.
5 *a member of the weaver bird family*: **taxonomic group**, group, order, class, subclass, genus, species; stock, strain, line; technical taxon, phylum.

family tree noun *I traced my own family tree*: **ancestry**, genealogy, descent, lineage, line, line of descent, bloodline, blood, parentage, pedigree, background, extraction, derivation, race, strain, stock, breed; family, dynasty, house; forebears, forefathers, antecedents, roots, origins; rare filiation, stirps.

famine noun **1** *the nation is threatened by famine*: **scarcity of food**, food shortages; deprivation, want.
▷ANTONYMS plenty.
2 *the cotton famine of the 1860s*: **shortage**, scarcity, lack, dearth, want, deficiency, insufficiency, shortfall, undersupply, scantiness, rareness, paucity, poverty, drought, unavailability; rare exiguity, exiguousness.

famished adjective *the troops were exhausted and famished*: **very hungry**, **ravenous**, starving, starving to death, starved, dying of hunger, faint from lack of food, deprived of food, empty; undernourished, malnourished, half-starved, unfed; informal peckish; rare sharp-set, esurient.
▷ANTONYMS well fed; full up.

famous adjective *a famous pop star*: **well known**, celebrated, prominent, famed, popular, having made a name for oneself; **renowned**, noted, notable, eminent, pre-eminent, leading, distinguished, esteemed, respected, venerable, august, of high standing, of distinction, of repute; illustrious, acclaimed, honoured, exalted, great, glorious, remarkable, signal, legendary, lionized, much publicized; notorious, infamous.
▷ANTONYMS unknown; obscure.

Choose the right word **famous, well known, celebrated, renowned**

Someone or something **famous** is known by large numbers of people and typically much admired (*Turner's famous painting 'Rain, Steam, and Speed'*). A *famous landmark*, however, may be widely recognized but little admired.

Well known conveys the idea of being recognized by a large number of people but generally without the glamorous connotations of *famous* (*many well-known companies built ships*). Someone may be *well known* without being admired, although the adjective itself (unlike *notorious*) does not carry any bad connotations.

Celebrated suggests that someone or something is highly thought of (*a portrait of a celebrated actress | one of Rodin's most celebrated works*). Something *celebrated* is not necessarily also famous—*the celebrated book 'Pedagogy of the Oppressed'* is highly regarded but is not known by a large group of people.

Renowned means widely known and, in almost all cases, admired, and is a slightly more formal word than *famous* (*the nation and its people were renowned for fair play | many internationally renowned chefs*). It is typically applied to a person, and when not directly to a person, then it often relates to something for which a person is professionally responsible and deserves credit (*Burgundy is renowned for its beef, poultry and wine*).

fan[1] noun *his living room had a couple of ceiling fans*: **air-cooler**, air conditioner, ventilator, blower, aerator; Indian punkah.
▸verb **1** *she lifted a hand to fan her hot cheeks*: **cool**, **air**, aerate, blow, ventilate; freshen, refresh.
2 *the article fanned the public's fear of nuclear radiation*: **intensify**, increase, agitate, inflame, exacerbate; stimulate, stir up, work up, whip up, incite, fuel, animate; ignite, kindle, trigger, spark, instigate, arouse, excite, provoke, foment.
3 *the police squad* ***fanned out*** *with their weapons at the ready*: **spread**, open, branch, stretch; outspread, unfurl, unfold.
□ **fan the flames of** *instead of being a calming force you fanned the flames of hostility*: **stir up**, whip up, encourage, incite, stoke up, fuel, kindle, ignite, inflame, stimulate, instigate, provoke, excite, arouse, awaken, waken, inspire, trigger, spark off, ferment, foment; literary enkindle.

fan[2] noun *a fan of classical violin music | an Arsenal fan*: **enthusiast**, devotee, admirer, lover, addict; **supporter**, follower, disciple, adherent, backer, zealot, champion, votary; expert, connoisseur, aficionado; informal buff, fiend, freak, bug, nut, maniac, groupie, junkie; N. Amer. informal jock.

fanatic noun **1** *a religious fanatic*: **zealot**, extremist, militant, dogmatist, devotee, sectarian, bigot, chauvinist, partisan, radical, diehard, ultra, activist, apologist, adherent; visionary; informal maniac, crank, freak.
▷ANTONYMS moderate.
2 informal *a keep-fit fanatic*: **enthusiast**, fan, devotee, lover, addict; informal nut, maniac, fiend, freak, junkie, bug, crank, buff, ...head, a great one for; N. Amer. informal geek, jock.

fanatical adjective **1** *they are fanatical about their faith*: **zealous**, **extremist**, extreme, militant, dogmatic, sectarian, bigoted, rabid, maniacal, radical, diehard, activist; prejudiced, chauvinistic, intolerant, narrow-minded, single-minded, partisan, blinkered, illiberal, inflexible, uncompromising.
▷ANTONYMS moderate; open-minded.
2 informal *the band gained a fanatical following*: **enthusiastic**, eager, keen, fervent, ardent, fervid, passionate, devoted, dedicated; over-enthusiastic, obsessive, obsessed, infatuated, fixated, compulsive, immoderate, frenzied, frenetic; informal wild, gung-ho, nuts, potty, dotty, crazy, hooked.
▷ANTONYMS indifferent.

Word toolkit **fanatical**

See **zealous**.

fanaticism noun **1** *a study of fanaticism during the French Revolution*: **zealotry**, zeal, extremism, militancy, sectarianism, fundamentalism, bigotry, dogmatism, chauvinism, radicalism, immoderation.
▷ANTONYMS moderation.
2 informal *his love of James Dean verged on fanaticism*: **obsessiveness**, over-enthusiasm, addiction, fixation, madness, monomania, immoderation, passion, infatuation; enthusiasm, dedication, devotion, single-mindedness; informal fandom; rare fervency, ardency, passionateness.
▷ANTONYMS indifference.

fancier noun *a keen pigeon fancier*: **enthusiast**, devotee, hobbyist, lover, addict, fan, fanatic; expert, connoisseur, aficionado; breeder; informal buff, fiend, freak, bug, nut, maniac, junkie.

fanciful adjective **1** *Maria is a fanciful girl*: **imaginative**, inventive; **whimsical**, impractical, capricious, flighty, dreamy, daydreaming, quixotic, chimerical, head in the clouds, out of touch with reality, in a world of one's own; archaic visionary.
▷ANTONYMS down-to-earth.
2 *some of these stories were pretty fanciful*: **fantastic**, extravagant, far-fetched, romantic, unbelievable, ridiculous, absurd, preposterous; **imaginary**, fancied, unreal, illusory, made-up, make-believe; mythical, fabulous, legendary, fairy tale; informal far out, tall, crackpot, cock and bull, hard to swallow/take.
▷ANTONYMS literal.
3 *the fanciful cornices and turrets of an imperial palace*: **ornate**, exotic, imaginative, creative, fancy; curious, odd, bizarre, strange, eccentric, unusual, original; extravagant, fantastic, grotesque, gothic, baroque.
▷ANTONYMS practical.

fancy verb 1 Brit. informal *I fancied a change of scene*: **wish for**, want, desire; long for, yearn for, crave, have a yearning/craving for, hanker after, hunger for, thirst for, sigh for, pine for, dream of, covet; informal have a yen for, itch for; archaic be desirous of; rare desiderate.
2 *she'd fancied him for ages*: **be attracted to**, find attractive, be captivated by, be infatuated with, be taken with, desire; lust after, burn for; informal have taken a shine to, have a crush on, have the hots for, be wild/mad/crazy about, have a thing about, have a pash on, have a soft spot for, be soft on, have eyes for, carry a torch for, go for, lech after/over.
3 *I fancied that I could see lights to the south*: **think**, imagine, guess, believe, have an idea, suppose; gather, surmise, suspect, conjecture, be of the opinion, be of the view, be under the impression, think it likely/conceivable; informal reckon.
□ **fancy oneself** *a couple of lads who fancy themselves*: **have a high opinion of oneself**, be confident of one's abilities; informal think one is the cat's whiskers/pyjamas, think one is God's gift (to women); Brit. informal reckon oneself.
▷ANTONYMS be modest.
▶ adjective *he is too hard up to buy fancy clothes*: **elaborate**, ornate, ornamented, ornamental, decorated, decorative, adorned, embellished, intricate, baroque, rococo, fussy, busy; **ostentatious**, showy, flamboyant, gaudy; luxurious, sumptuous, lavish, extravagant, expensive, de luxe, select, superior, high-class, quality, prime; informal flash, flashy, fancy-pants, jazzy, ritzy, glitzy, snazzy, posh, classy, over the top, OTT; Brit. informal swish.
▷ANTONYMS plain, unobtrusive.
▶ noun 1 *he was able to indulge his fancy to own a farm*: **desire**, urge, wish, want; inclination, bent; **whim**, impulse, caprice, notion, whimsy, eccentricity, peculiarity, quirk, kink; preference, fondness, liking, partiality, predilection, predisposition, taste, relish, love, humour, penchant; yearning, longing, hankering, craving, pining, ache, hunger, thirst, need; informal yen, itch.
2 *they appeal to our wildest fancy rather than our judgement*: **imagination**, imaginative faculty/power, creativity, creative faculty/power, conception, fancifulness, inventiveness, invention, originality, ingenuity, cleverness, wit, artistry; images, mental images, visualizations.
▷ANTONYMS intellect.
3 *they had a vague fancy that it was cruel to leave the dolls in the dark*: **idea**, notion, thought, supposition, opinion, belief, impression, image, understanding, conceptualization; feeling, suspicion, sneaking suspicion, hunch, inkling, intimation; illusion, fantasy, dream.
□ **take a fancy to** *Joe met this lovely young girl who took a fancy to him*. See **fancy** (sense 2 of the verb).

fanfare noun 1 *a fanfare announced the arrival of the duchess*: **peal of trumpets**, flourish, fanfaronade, trumpet call, trumpet blare; archaic trump, tucket.
2 *the laying of the foundation stone was greeted with great fanfare*: **fuss**, commotion, stir, show, showiness, display, ostentation, flashiness, publicity, sensationalism, pageantry, splendour, hubbub, brouhaha; informal ballyhoo, hullabaloo, hype, to-do, pizzazz, razzle-dazzle, glitz, ritziness.

fantasize verb *I fantasized about London and what I'd do when I lived there*: **daydream**, dream, muse, indulge in fantasy, indulge in fancy, make-believe, play-act, pretend, imagine, give free rein to one's imagination, build castles in the air, build castles in Spain, live in a dream world, indulge in wool-gathering.

fantastic adjective 1 *it's a fantastic notion, but it would explain everything*: **fanciful**, extravagant, extraordinary, irrational, wild, mad, absurd, far-fetched, nonsensical, incredible, unbelievable, unthinkable, implausible, improbable, unlikely, doubtful, dubious; strange, peculiar, odd, queer, weird, eccentric, insane, whimsical, capricious; imaginary, visionary, romantic, unreal, illusory, make-believe; informal crazy, barmy, potty, daft, cock-eyed, oddball, off the wall.
▷ANTONYMS rational.
2 *a memory of fantastic accuracy*: **tremendous**, remarkable, great, terrific, enormous, huge, striking, impressive, outstanding, phenomenal, monumental, overwhelming.
3 *the mountains assumed weird and fantastic shapes*: **strange**, weird, bizarre, outlandish, queer, peculiar, eccentric, grotesque, freakish, surreal, exotic; whimsical, fanciful, quaint, imaginative, elaborate, ornate, intricate, rococo, baroque, phantasmagoric, Kafkaesque.
▷ANTONYMS ordinary, unremarkable.
4 informal *a fantastic new car*: **marvellous**, wonderful, sensational, magnificent, outstanding, superb, superlative, excellent, very good, first-rate, first-class, dazzling, out of this world, breathtaking; informal great, terrific, tremendous, smashing, fabulous, fab, mega, super, stellar, ace, magic, A1, cracking, cool, wicked, awesome, way-out, def; Brit. informal brilliant, brill, bosting; Austral./NZ informal bonzer; Brit. informal, dated spiffing, topping, tip-top, top-notch, capital.
▷ANTONYMS ordinary, poor.

fantasy noun 1 *the movie is ambitious in its mix of fantasy and realism*: **imagination**, creativity, fancy, invention, originality, vision, speculation, make-believe, daydreaming, reverie.
▷ANTONYMS truth, realism.
2 *his fantasy about appearing on television*: **dream**, daydream, pipe dream, flight of fancy, fanciful notion, wish, wishful thinking; fond hope, chimera, delusion, illusion, figment of the imagination, castle in the air, castle in Spain; informal pie in the sky, cloud cuckoo land.
3 *fantasy was considered a subset of science fiction for a long time*: **myth**, legend, fable, fairy tale, romance; science fiction, sci-fi, horror; sword and sorcery; escapism.
▷ANTONYMS realism.

far adverb 1 *not far from the palace a fine garden was built*: **a long way**, a great distance, a good way, afar.
▷ANTONYMS near.
2 *the liveliness of the production far outweighs any flaws*: **much**, very much, considerably, markedly, immeasurably, decidedly, greatly, significantly, substantially, appreciably, noticeably, materially, signally; to a great extent/degree, by much, by a great amount, by a great deal, by a long way, by far, by a mile, easily.
▷ANTONYMS slightly.
□ **by far** *this would be by far the best solution*: **by a great amount**, by a good deal, by a long way/chalk/shot, by a mile, far and away; undoubtedly, doubtlessly, without doubt, without question, decidedly, markedly, positively, absolutely, easily, immeasurably; significantly, substantially, appreciably, noticeably, materially, beyond the shadow of a doubt, much; informal as sure as eggs is eggs.
□ **far and away** *they were far and away the most powerful union*. See **by far**.
□ **far and near** *guests had travelled from far and near to be there*. See **everywhere**.
□ **far and wide** *he was known far and wide*. See **everywhere**.
□ **far from** *staff were far from happy with the outcome*: **not**, not at all, nowhere near, a long way from, the opposite of.
□ **go far** *she was a girl who would go far*: **be successful**, succeed, prosper, flourish, thrive, get on, get on in the world, make good, make one's way in the world, make headway/progress, gain advancement, climb the ladder of success, rise in the world, set the world on fire; Brit. set the Thames on fire; informal make a name for oneself, make one's mark, go places, make it, make the grade, cut it, get somewhere, do all right for oneself, arrive, find a place in the sun, be someone.
▷ANTONYMS fail.
□ **go too far** *they locked him up because he went too far*: **go over the top**, go to extremes, go overboard, not know when to stop.
□ **so far** 1 *nobody had taken any notice of me so far*: **until now**, up till/to now, up to this point, as yet, thus far, hitherto, up to the present, until/till the present, to date, by this time; rare heretofore, thitherto. 2 *his liberalism only extends so far*: **to a certain extent**, to a limited extent, up to a point, to a degree, to some extent, within reason, within limits.
▶ adjective 1 *he'd travelled to far places in the war*: **distant**, faraway, far off; remote, out of the way, far flung, far removed, outlying, obscure, isolated, cut-off, inaccessible, off the beaten track, in the back of beyond, godforsaken.
▷ANTONYMS near; neighbouring.
2 *a building on the far side of the campus*: **further**, more distant; opposite.
▷ANTONYMS near.

faraway adjective 1 *flying to exotic faraway places*: **distant**, far off, far; remote, out of the way, far flung, far removed, outlying, obscure, isolated, secluded, cut off, off the beaten track, in the back of beyond, in the middle of nowhere.
▷ANTONYMS nearby; neighbouring.
2 *Noreen had that faraway look in her eyes*: **dreamy**, daydreaming, abstracted, absent-minded, distracted, preoccupied, absorbed, engrossed, vague, lost in thought, somewhere else, not there, not with us, in a world of one's own, with one's head in the clouds; informal miles away.
▷ANTONYMS alert.

> *Choose the right word* **faraway, far off, distant, remote**
>
> See **distant**.

farce noun 1 *at one or two points the stories approach bedroom farce*: **slapstick comedy**, broad comedy, slapstick, burlesque, vaudeville, travesty, buffoonery; skit, squib; rare pasquinade.
▷ANTONYMS tragedy.
2 *he denounced the trial as a farce*: **absurdity**, mockery, travesty, sham, pretence, masquerade, charade, piece of futility, joke, waste of time, laughing stock; apology, excuse, poor substitute; informal shambles.

farcical adjective 1 *he considered the whole idea farcical*: **ridiculous**, preposterous, ludicrous, absurd, laughable, risible, nonsensical; futile, senseless, pointless, useless, vain, in vain, to no avail, ineffectual; silly, foolish, idiotic, stupid, imbecilic, asinine, hare-brained; informal crazy, barmy, daft.
2 *the farcical goings-on in a witty comedy of manners*: **madcap**, zany, slapstick, comic, comical, clownish, light-hearted, humorous, amusing, chucklesome, droll, witty, entertaining; hilarious, uproarious, hysterical,

hysterically funny; informal wacky, side-splitting, rib-tickling, killing, priceless.

fare noun **1** *we can't afford the air fare*: **ticket price**, transport cost, price, cost, charge, fee, payment, toll, tariff, levy.
2 *when they eat at home they prefer simple fare*: **food**, meals, board, sustenance, nourishment, nutriment, foodstuffs, refreshments, eatables, provisions, daily bread; cooking, cuisine; menu, diet, table; Scottish vivers; informal grub, nosh, eats, chow; Brit. informal scoff, scran; formal comestibles, provender; archaic vittles, commons, victuals, viands, aliment.
▸ verb *they went to see how their old friend was faring*: **get on**, proceed, get along, progress, make out, do, manage, muddle through/along, cope, survive; succeed, prosper.

farewell exclamation *farewell, Patrick!* **goodbye**, so long, adieu; Austral./NZ hooray; S. African check you; French au revoir; Italian ciao; German auf Wiedersehen; Spanish adios; Japanese sayonara; Latin vale; informal bye, bye-bye, cheerio, see you, see you later, cheers, toodle-oo, toodle-pip; Brit. informal ta-ta; N. Amer. informal later, laters.
▸ noun *an emotional farewell*: **valediction**, **goodbye**, adieu; leave-taking, parting, departure, departing, going away; send-off.

f

far-fetched adjective *the storyline was too far-fetched*: **improbable**, unlikely, implausible, scarcely credible, difficult to believe, dubious, doubtful, unconvincing, incredible, unbelievable, unthinkable, beyond the bounds of possibility; **contrived**, strained, laboured, forced, elaborate, overdone; fanciful, unrealistic, ridiculous, absurd, preposterous; informal hard to swallow/take, fishy; N. Amer. informal hokey.
▷ANTONYMS credible, likely.

farm noun *a farm of 100 acres*: **smallholding**, holding, farmstead, steading, grange, plantation, estate; farmland, land, acreage, acres; vineyard; Scottish croft; N. Amer. ranch; Austral./NZ station; in the W. Indies pen; in East Africa shamba; in the Indian subcontinent tope.
▸ verb **1** *his dad farmed near Marlborough*: **be a farmer**, practise farming, cultivate/till/work the land, till the soil, rear livestock, do agricultural work.
2 *the marshes are being drained in order to farm the land*: **cultivate**, bring under cultivation, till, work, plough, dig, plant.
3 *the family has been farming cranberries for generations*: **grow**, cultivate, raise, plant, tend, bring on, harvest; breed, rear, keep.
□ **farm someone out** *he had farmed the child out*: **have fostered**, have cared for, send to a childminder, put in care.
□ **farm something out** *the job of building the models was farmed out to the Shawcraft firm*: **contract out**, outsource, assign to others, subcontract, delegate.

farmer noun **agriculturalist**, agronomist, smallholder, grazier, farmhand, countryman, son/daughter of the soil; Scottish crofter; N. Amer. rancher; Austral./NZ informal cocky; archaic yeoman, husbandman.

farming noun **agriculture**, cultivation, tilling, tillage, husbandry, land management, farm management; agriscience, agronomy; breeding, keeping, raising, rearing, tending; culture, planting, sowing; rare geoponics.
▷ANTONYMS industry.

> *Word links* **farming**
>
> **agrarian** relating to agriculture
> **agri-** related prefix, as in *agribusiness*
> **agro-** related prefix, as in *agrochemical*

far out adjective informal *some club owners thought our music was too far out*: **unconventional**, unorthodox, unusual, nonconformist, individual, individualistic, idiosyncratic, quirky, out of the ordinary; weird, bizarre, outlandish, freakish; avant-garde, innovative, groundbreaking, radical, bohemian, extreme, esoteric; French outré; informal way out, offbeat, left-field, oddball, wacky, off the wall.
▷ANTONYMS conventional.

farrago noun *academics exposed the whole business as a farrago of fantasies and errors*. See **jumble** (sense 1 of the noun).

far-reaching adjective *a far-reaching change in the law*: **extensive**, wide-ranging, radical, profound, comprehensive, widespread, all-embracing, overarching, across the board, sweeping, blanket, wholesale; important, significant, major, of great import, of significance, ambitious, momentous, of moment, weighty, consequential, of consequence.
▷ANTONYMS limited, insignificant.

far-sighted adjective *his far-sighted management brought great prosperity*: **prudent**, prescient, foresighted, discerning, judicious, shrewd, percipient, provident, forearmed, politic, canny; cautious, careful, watchful; wise, sagacious, visionary.
▷ANTONYMS short-sighted, short-termist.

farther adverb & adjective See **further**.

farthest adjective & adverb See **furthest**.

fascinate verb *he was fascinated by Laura's stories*: **engross**, captivate, absorb, interest, enchant, beguile, bewitch, enthral, enrapture, entrance, hold spellbound, transfix, rivet, mesmerize, hypnotize, spellbind, occupy, engage, compel; allure, lure, tempt, entice, draw, tantalize; charm, attract, intrigue, delight, divert, entertain, amuse.
▷ANTONYMS bore; repel.

fascinating adjective *a fascinating story*: **engrossing**, captivating, absorbing, interesting, enchanting, beguiling, bewitching, enthralling, enrapturing, entrancing, spellbinding, transfixing, riveting, mesmerizing, hypnotizing, engaging, compelling, compulsive, gripping, thrilling; alluring, tempting, enticing, irresistible, tantalizing, seductive; charming, attractive, intriguing, delightful, diverting, entertaining, amusing; informal unputdownable.
▷ANTONYMS boring; dull.

fascination noun *crime and criminals are topics of endless fascination*: **interest**, preoccupation, passion, obsession, compulsion, captivation, enchantment; allure, lure, allurement; charm, attraction, intrigue, attractiveness, appeal, magnetism, pull, draw.
▷ANTONYMS boredom.

fascism noun **authoritarianism**, totalitarianism, dictatorship, despotism, autocracy, absolute rule, Nazism, rightism, militarism; nationalism, xenophobia, racism, anti-Semitism, chauvinism, jingoism, isolationism; neo-fascism, neo-Nazism; corporativism, corporatism; German, historical Hitlerism; Spanish, historical Francoism, Falangism.
▷ANTONYMS democracy; liberalism.

fascist noun *he was branded a fascist and an anti-Semite*: **authoritarian**, totalitarian, autocrat, Nazi, extreme/far right-winger, rightist, blackshirt, militarist; nationalist, xenophobe, racist, anti-Semite, chauvinist, jingoist, isolationist; neo-fascist, neo-Nazi; corporativist, corporatist; Brit. historical Mosleyite; German, historical Hitlerite; Spanish, historical Francoist, Falangist.
▷ANTONYMS democrat; liberal.
▸ adjective *the fascist regimes in Europe*: **authoritarian**, totalitarian, dictatorial, despotic, draconian, autocratic, Nazi, undemocratic, illiberal, extreme/far right-wing, rightist, militarist; nationalist, nationalistic, xenophobic, racist, anti-Semitic, chauvinist, jingoistic, isolationist; neo-fascist, neo-Nazi; corporativist, corporatist; Brit. historical Mosleyite; German, historical Hitlerite; Spanish, historical Francoist, Falangist.
▷ANTONYMS democratic; liberal.

fashion noun **1** *the fashion for figure-hugging clothes*: **vogue**, trend, craze, rage, mania, mode, fad, fancy, passing fancy; current/latest style, latest thing, latest taste; style, look; general tendency, convention, custom, practice, usage; informal thing.
2 *she was always interested in fashion*: **clothes**, the clothes industry, clothes design, couture; glamour; informal the rag trade.
3 *a Victorian lady of fashion*: **fashionable society**, high society, society, social elite, the beautiful people, the beau monde, the A-list; informal the jet set.
4 *it needs to be run in a sensible and organized fashion*: **manner**, way, style, method, mode; system, approach.
5 *they built a boat of some fashion*: **type**, kind, sort, make, design, description.
□ **after a fashion** *the arrangement worked after a fashion*: **to a certain extent**, in a way, in a rough way, somehow or other, somehow, in an approximate manner, in a manner of speaking, in its way; informal ish.
□ **in fashion** *the Sixties look is in fashion again*: **fashionable**, in vogue, up to date, up to the minute, all the rage, bang up to date; smart, chic, elegant; French de rigueur, à la mode; informal trendy, with it, cool, in, the in thing, hot, big, hip, happening, now, sharp, groovy, mod, swinging; N. Amer. kicking, tony, fly; Brit. informal, dated all the go.
▷ANTONYMS out of fashion.
□ **out of fashion** *such gallantry is out of fashion*: **unfashionable**, out of style, no longer fashionable, old-fashioned, out of date, outdated, dated, outmoded, behind the times, last year's, superseded; unstylish, unpopular; French passé, démodé; informal old hat, out, square, out of the ark, old school.
▷ANTONYMS in fashion.
▸ verb *the head section was fashioned from a separate sheet of lead*: **construct**, build, manufacture, make, create, fabricate, contrive; cast, frame, shape, form, mould, sculpt; forge, hew, carve, whittle, hammer, chisel.

fashionable adjective *a fashionable wine bar*: **in fashion**, in vogue, voguish, popular, (bang) up to date, up to the minute, modern, all the rage, modish, trendsetting; stylish, smart, chic, glamorous, elegant, classy, high-class, high-toned; French à la mode, de rigueur; informal trendy, with it, cool, in, the in thing, hot, big, massive, hip, happening, now, sharp, groovy, mod, swinging, snazzy; N. Amer. informal kicking, tony, fly; Brit. informal, dated all the go.
▷ANTONYMS unfashionable; old-fashioned.

fast[1] adjective **1** *a fast sports car | the game is played at a fast pace*: **speedy**, quick, swift, rapid; brisk, nimble, sprightly, lively; fast-moving, high-speed, turbo, sporty, accelerated, express, flying; whirlwind, blistering, breakneck, pell-mell, meteoric, smart; hasty, hurried; unhesitating, expeditious; fleet-footed; informal nippy, zippy, spanking, scorching, blinding, supersonic; Brit. informal cracking; literary fleet; rare tantivy, alacritous, volant.
▷ANTONYMS slow.

2 *his hand slammed against the door, holding it fast*: **secure**, secured, fastened, tight, firmly fixed; stuck, jammed, immovable, unbudgeable, stiff; closed, shut, to.
▷ANTONYMS loose.
3 *the dyes are boiled with yarn to produce a fast colour*: **indelible**, lasting, permanent, stable.
▷ANTONYMS temporary.
4 *they remained fast friends*: **loyal**, devoted, faithful, firm, steadfast, staunch, true, boon, bosom, inseparable; constant, lasting, unchanging, unwavering, enduring, unswerving; informal as thick as thieves.
5 *a fast woman*: **promiscuous**, licentious, dissolute, impure, unchaste, wanton, abandoned, of easy virtue; informal easy; N. Amer. informal roundheeled; W. Indian informal slack; derogatory sluttish, whorish, tarty, slaggy; dated loose; archaic light.
▷ANTONYMS chaste.
6 *the fast life she led in London*: **wild**, dissipated, dissolute, debauched, intemperate, immoderate, louche, rakish, decadent, unrestrained, reckless, profligate, self-indulgent, shameless, sinful, immoral, extravagant; informal swinging.
▷ANTONYMS sedate.
□ **fast and furious** *the fun was fast and furious*: **frantic**, wild, frenetic, hectic, fraught, feverish, fevered, mad, crazed, manic, hyperactive, energetic, intense, turbulent, tumultuous.
□ **make fast** *the craft is made fast to the shore*: **attach**, fasten, secure, fix, affix, join, connect, couple, link, tie, tie up, bind, fetter, strap, rope, tether, truss, lash, hitch, moor, anchor, yoke, chain.
▸ **adverb 1** *she drove fast towards the gates*: **quickly**, rapidly, swiftly, speedily, briskly, at speed, at full speed, at full tilt; energetically; hastily, with all haste, in haste, hurriedly, in a hurry, post-haste, pell-mell; without delay, expeditiously, with dispatch, like a shot, like a flash, in a flash, in the blink of an eye, in a wink, in a trice, in no time (at all), on the double, at the speed of light, like an arrow from a bow; informal double quick, in double quick time, p.d.q. (pretty damn quick), nippily, like (greased) lightning, at warp speed, hell for leather, like mad, like crazy, like the wind, like a bomb, like nobody's business, like a scalded cat, like the deuce, a mile a minute, like a bat out of hell, at warp speed; Brit. informal like the clappers, at a rate of knots, like billy-o; N. Amer. informal lickety-split; literary apace.
▷ANTONYMS slowly.
2 *his wheels were stuck fast*: **securely**, tightly, immovably, fixedly, firmly.
3 *Richard's fast asleep*: **deeply**, sound, completely.
4 *she lived fast and dangerously*: **wildly**, dissolutely, intemperately, immoderately, rakishly, recklessly, self-indulgently, extravagantly.

> *Word links* **fast**
>
> **tachy-** related prefix, as in *tachycardia, tachygraphy*

fast² **verb** *the ministry instructed people to fast, pray, and read scripture*: **abstain from food**, refrain from eating, deny oneself food, go without food, go hungry, eat nothing, starve oneself; go on hunger strike.
▷ANTONYMS eat; indulge oneself.
▸ **noun** *a five-day fast*: **period of fasting**, period of abstinence; hunger strike; diet.
▷ANTONYMS feast.

fasten **verb 1** *he fastened the door behind him*: **bolt**, lock, secure, make secure, make fast, chain, seal.
▷ANTONYMS unfasten, unlock.
2 *they fastened splints to his leg*: **attach**, fix, affix, clip, pin, tack; stick, bond.
▷ANTONYMS unfasten, remove.
3 *the belt was fastened with an enormous silver buckle*: **buckle**, join, do up, connect, couple, close, unite, link; lace (up), knot; button (up); zip (up).
▷ANTONYMS unfasten, open.
4 *he fastened his horse to a sapling on the bank of the river*: **tie**, tie up, bind, tether, truss, fetter, lash, hitch, anchor, strap, rope.
▷ANTONYMS unfasten, untie.
5 *the dress fastens at the front with ten small buttons*: **become closed**, close, do up; button (up), zip (up).
▷ANTONYMS unfasten, undo.
6 *his gaze **fastened on** me*: **focus**, fix, be riveted, concentrate, zero in, zoom in, be brought to bear; direct at, aim at, point at.
7 *blame had been **fastened on** some unknown nutter*: **ascribe to**, attribute to, assign to, chalk up to, impute to; lay on, pin on, lay at the door of.
8 *the critics **fastened upon** two sections of the report*: **single out**, concentrate on, focus on, select, pick out, fix on, seize on.

fastidious **adjective** *he was fastidious about personal hygiene*: **scrupulous**, punctilious, painstaking, meticulous, assiduous, sedulous, perfectionist, fussy, finicky, dainty, over-particular; critical, overcritical, hypercritical, hard/difficult/impossible to please; pedantic, precise, exact, hair-splitting, exacting, demanding; informal pernickety, nit-picking, choosy, picky; N. Amer. informal persnickety; archaic nice, overnice.
▷ANTONYMS easy-going; sloppy.

> *Word toolkit* **fastidious**
>
> See **finicky**.

fat **adjective 1** *a fat man walked in*: **plump**, stout, overweight, heavy, large, solid, chubby, portly, rotund, flabby, paunchy, pot-bellied, beer-bellied, dumpy, meaty, broad in the beam, of ample proportions, Falstaffian; buxom; obese, corpulent, bloated, gross, gargantuan, elephantine; fleshy; informal tubby, roly-poly, beefy, porky, blubbery, poddy, chunky, well padded, well covered, well upholstered; Brit. informal podgy, fubsy; N. Amer. informal lard-assed; Scottish literary sonsy; rare pursy, abdominous.
▷ANTONYMS thin, skinny.
2 *fat bacon*: **fatty**, greasy, oily, oleaginous, unctuous; formal pinguid, adipose, sebaceous.
▷ANTONYMS lean.
3 *those fat books you're always reading*: **thick**, big, chunky, substantial, extended, long.
▷ANTONYMS thin.
4 informal *a fat salary*: **large**, substantial, considerable, sizeable; generous, handsome, ample, excellent, good, competitive.
▷ANTONYMS small.
5 informal *fat chance she had of influencing Guy*: **very little**, not much, minimal, hardly any.
▷ANTONYMS good.
▸ **noun 1** *whales insulate themselves with layers of fat*: **fatty tissue**, fat cells, blubber, adipose tissue.
2 *he was tall and running to fat*: **fatness**, **plumpness**, stoutness, heaviness, chubbiness, tubbiness, portliness, rotundity, podginess, flabbiness, bulk, excessive weight; obesity, corpulence, grossness; paunch, pot belly, beer belly, beer gut; informal flab, blubber, beef.
▷ANTONYMS thinness.
3 *fried bread in sizzling fat*: **cooking oil**, animal fat, vegetable fat, grease; lard, suet, butter, margarine.

> *Word links* **fat**
>
> **lipoid** relating to fat
> **lipo-** related prefix, as in *liposuction, lipoprotein*

fatal **adjective 1** *a fatal disease*: **deadly**, lethal, mortal, causing death, death dealing, killing; final, terminal, incurable, untreatable, inoperable, malignant; tragic; literary deathly; archaic baneful.
▷ANTONYMS harmless; superficial.
2 *don't make the fatal mistake of assuming others think as you do*: **disastrous**, devastating, ruinous, catastrophic, calamitous, cataclysmic, destructive, grievous, dire, crippling, crushing, injurious, harmful, costly; literary direful.
▷ANTONYMS harmless; beneficial.

fatalism **noun** *he experienced a sense of fatalism that kept his fear at bay*: **passive acceptance**, resignation, acceptance, acceptance of the inevitable, stoicism; defeatism, pessimism, negativism, negative thinking, gloominess, doom and gloom, gloom; predeterminism, predestinarianism, necessitarianism, fate, fatedness.

fatality **noun 1** *there were hundreds of fatalities from radiation contamination*: **death**, casualty, mortality, victim, loss, dead person; (**fatalities**) dead.
2 *the programme is a recipe for increased fatalities on our roads*: **fatal accident**, tragedy, disaster, catastrophe, calamity.

fate **noun 1** *I was ready for whatever fate had in store for me*: **destiny**, providence, God's will, nemesis, kismet, astral influence, the stars, what is written in the stars, one's lot in life; predestination, predetermination; chance, luck, serendipity, fortuity, fortune, hazard, Lady Luck, Dame Fortune; Hinduism & Buddhism karma; archaic dole, cup, heritage.
2 *I didn't want to put my fate in someone else's hands*: **future**, destiny, outcome, issue, upshot, end, lot, due; archaic doom, dole.
3 *the authorities warned that a similar fate would befall other convicted killers*: **death**, demise, end, destruction, doom; ruin, downfall, undoing, finish, disaster, catastrophe; retribution, sentence.
4 (**the Fates**) *the Fates might decide that it was his time to die*: **the weird sisters**; Roman Mythology the Parcae; Greek Mythology the Moirai; Scandinavian Mythology the Norns.
▸ **verb** (**be fated**) *his daughter was fated to face the same problem*: **be predestined**, be preordained, be foreordained, be destined, be meant, be doomed, be foredoomed, be cursed, be damned; be sure, be certain, be bound, be guaranteed; be inevitable, be inescapable, be ineluctable.

fateful **adjective 1** *that fateful day when she met him*: **decisive**, determining, critical, crucial, pivotal; momentous, important, of great importance, all-important, key, significant, far-reaching; historic, weighty, consequential, of great consequence, epoch-making, portentous, apocalyptic; informal earth-shattering, world-shattering, earth-shaking, world-shaking.
▷ANTONYMS trivial, unimportant.

f

2 *the fateful defeat of 1402*: **disastrous**, ruinous, calamitous, cataclysmic, devastating, destructive, tragic, awful, terrible, harmful, fatal, deadly.

father noun **1** *he went home to see his mother and father*: **male parent**, begetter, patriarch, paterfamilias; birth/biological father; adoptive father, foster father, stepfather; informal dad, daddy, pop, poppa, pa, old boy, old man; Brit. informal, dated pater.
▷ANTONYMS child.
2 (usually **fathers**) literary *let me be free to follow the religion of my fathers*: **ancestor**, forefather, forebear, progenitor, predecessor, antecedent, forerunner, precursor; rare primogenitor.
▷ANTONYMS descendant.
3 *he was the father of democracy*: **originator**, initiator, founder, founding father, inventor, creator, maker, author, prime mover, instigator, architect, engineer, designer, deviser, planner, contriver, mastermind; literary begetter.
4 *the city fathers*: **leader**, elder, senior figure, patriarch, senator, guiding light, official.
5 (**Father**) *our heavenly Father*: **God**, Lord, Lord God, Deity.
6 (usually **Father**) *the Father joined the other priests*: **priest**, pastor, parson, clergyman, father confessor, churchman, man of the cloth, man of God, cleric, minister, preacher; in French-speaking countries abbé, curé; informal reverend, padre.
▸verb **1** *he fathered six children*: **be the father of**, sire, engender, generate, bring into being, bring into the world, give life to, spawn; procreate, reproduce, breed; literary beget.
2 *he fathered a strand of applied economics*: **establish**, institute, originate, initiate, put in place, invent, found, create, generate, conceive.

Word links **father**
paternal relating to a father
patri- related prefix, as in *patriarch, patrilineal*
patricide killing of one's father

fatherland noun *they were considered to be traitors to the fatherland*: **native land**, native country, homeland, home, mother country, motherland, native soil, native heath, land of one's birth, land of one's fathers, the old country.

fatherly adjective *his son needs some fatherly advice*: **paternal**, fatherlike, avuncular; protective, supportive, encouraging, vigilant; kindly, kind, warm, affectionate, tender, caring, compassionate, benevolent, sympathetic, understanding, indulgent; patriarchal.
▷ANTONYMS hostile.

fathom verb **1** *Charlie tried to fathom the expression on his friend's face*: **understand**, comprehend, work out, fathom out, make sense of, grasp, catch, follow, perceive, make out, penetrate, divine, search out, ferret out, puzzle out, take in, assimilate, absorb, get to the bottom of; interpret, decipher, decode, disentangle, untangle, unravel, piece together; informal make head or tail of, take on board, get a fix on, get/catch the drift of, tumble to, crack, dig, get, get the picture, get the message, see what's what; Brit. informal twig, suss (out); N. Amer. informal savvy; rare cognize.
2 *an attempt to fathom the ocean*: **measure the depth of**, sound, plumb, probe; gauge, estimate.

fathomless adjective **1** *her serene, fathomless eyes*: **enigmatic**, mysterious, impenetrable, incomprehensible, unfathomable, opaque, profound, deep.
2 *a fathomless well*: **bottomless**, unfathomable, unfathomed, unsounded, immeasurable, endless, infinite, measureless; very deep, unplumbed, profound, yawning, cavernous, gaping; literary abysmal; rare chasmic.
▷ANTONYMS shallow.

fatigue noun **1** *his face was grey with fatigue*: **tiredness**, weariness, exhaustion, overtiredness; drowsiness, somnolence; lethargy, sluggishness, lassitude, debility, enervation, listlessness, prostration, lack of energy, lack of vitality.
▷ANTONYMS energy, vigour.
2 (**fatigues**) Military *right, Private, it's kitchen fatigues for you*: **menial work**, drudgery, chores, donkey work; informal dirty work, skivvying.
3 (**fatigues**) Military *a conscript dressed in battle fatigues*: **khakis**, camouflage clothing/gear; informal camo clothing/gear.
▸verb *the troops were fatigued by nine days of marching*: **tire**, tire out, exhaust, wear out, drain, make weary, weary, wash out, tax, overtax, overtire, jade, make sleepy; prostrate, enervate; informal knock out, take it out of, do in, fag out, whack, poop, shatter, bush, frazzle, wear to a frazzle; Brit. informal knacker; Brit. vulgar slang shag out.
▷ANTONYMS invigorate, refresh.

Word links **fatigue**
kopophobia fear of fatigue

fatness noun *his fatness was the result of good living*: **plumpness**, stoutness, heaviness, largeness, chubbiness, portliness, rotundity, flabbiness, paunchiness, dumpiness, meatiness; obesity, corpulence, bloatedness, grossness; fleshiness; excessive weight, bulk; paunch, pot belly, beer belly, beer gut; informal tubbiness, beefiness, porkiness, chunkiness, podginess.
▷ANTONYMS thinness.

fatten verb **1** *a farm where livestock are fattened*: **make fat/fatter**, feed up, feed, build up; overfeed, bloat.
2 *we're sending her home to her parents to* ***fatten up***: **put on weight**, gain weight, get heavier, grow fat/fatter, get fat, flesh out, fill out; thicken, widen, broaden, expand, spread out.
▷ANTONYMS lose weight.

fatty adjective *fatty foods*: **greasy**, oily, fat, oleaginous, unctuous; formal pinguid, adipose, sebaceous.
▷ANTONYMS lean.

fatuous adjective *she was irritated by a fatuous question*: **silly**, foolish, stupid, inane, nonsensical, childish, puerile, infantile, idiotic, brainless, mindless, vacuous, imbecilic, asinine, witless, empty-headed, hare-brained; pointless, senseless; ridiculous, ludicrous, absurd, preposterous, laughable, risible; informal daft, moronic, cretinous, dumb, gormless.
▷ANTONYMS intelligent, sensible.

fault noun **1** *he has his faults, but he's a good man*: **defect**, failing, imperfection, flaw, blemish, shortcoming, weakness, weak point, weak spot, frailty, foible, vice, limitation, lack, deficiency, Achilles heel, chink in one's armour.
▷ANTONYMS merit, strength.
2 *engineers have still not located the fault*: **defect**, flaw, imperfection, snag; error, mistake, inaccuracy, oversight, blunder, gaffe, slip; Computing bug; informal glitch, gremlin, slip-up, boob, boo-boo, clanger, howler, foul-up, snarl-up; Brit. informal cock-up.
3 *it was my fault for being late*: **responsibility**, liability, culpability, blameworthiness, guilt; accountability, answerability; informal rap.
4 *don't blame one child for another's faults*: **misdeed**, wrongdoing, offence, misdemeanour, misconduct, sin, vice, lapse, indiscretion, peccadillo, transgression, trespass.
□ **at fault** *police say the driver was not at fault*: **to blame**, blameworthy, blameable, censurable, reproachable; culpable, accountable, answerable; responsible, guilty, in the wrong, offending, erring, errant.
▷ANTONYMS innocent.
□ **find fault with** *someone who enjoys finding fault with everything and putting people down*. See **fault** (verb).
□ **to a fault** *Barry's generous to a fault*: **excessively**, unduly, immoderately, overly, in the extreme, out of all proportion, overmuch, needlessly; informal over the top, OTT.
▸verb *you couldn't fault any of the players*: **find fault with**, find lacking; criticize, attack, censure, condemn, impugn, reproach, reprove, run down, take to task, haul over the coals; complain about, quibble about, carp about, moan about, grouse about, grouch about, whine about, arraign; informal knock, slam, hammer, lay into, gripe about, beef about, bellyache about, bitch about, whinge about, nit-pick over, pick holes in, sound off about; Brit. informal slag off, have a go at, give some stick to, slate, rubbish.

fault-finding noun *the manager tries to get results by fault-finding and nagging*: **criticism**, captiousness, cavilling, quibbling, niggling, pedantry, hair-splitting; complaining, grumbling, carping, moaning, whining, bleating; informal nit-picking, griping, grousing, grouching, bellyaching; archaic overnice.
▷ANTONYMS praise.
▸adjective *a fault-finding spectator*: **critical**, **censorious**, carping, captious, cavilling, quibbling, niggling; overcritical, hypercritical, pedantic, over-precise, over-exact, over-rigorous, over-strict, hair-splitting, hard/difficult/impossible to please, pettifogging; informal nit-picking, pernickety.

faultless adjective **1** *he replied in faultless English*: **perfect**, flawless, without fault, error-free, without blemish, unblemished, impeccable, accurate, precise, exact, correct, unerring; exemplary, model, ideal, copybook, scrupulous, meticulous, just so; Brit. informal spot on, bang on, on the mark, on the nail, on the button.
▷ANTONYMS flawed, faulty.
2 *the wife of the prisoner was faultless*: **guiltless**, without guilt, innocent, blameless, above reproach, irreproachable, sinless, pure, unsullied.
▷ANTONYMS guilty.

faulty adjective **1** *a faulty electric blanket*: **malfunctioning**, broken, damaged, defective, not working, not functioning, in disrepair, out of order, out of commission, inoperative, unsound, unusable, useless; informal on the blink, on its last legs, kaput, bust, busted, conked out, acting/playing up, gone haywire, gone phut, done for, wonky, dud; Brit. informal knackered, duff; informal on the fritz.
▷ANTONYMS working, functioning.
2 *her logic is faulty*: **defective**, flawed, unsound, distorted, inaccurate, incorrect, erroneous, imprecise, fallacious, wrong; impaired, weak, invalid.
▷ANTONYMS sound.

Word links **faulty**

dys- related prefix, as in *dysfunction, dysphasia*

faux pas noun *I committed a faux pas which they never let me forget*: **gaffe**, blunder, mistake; indiscretion, impropriety, breach/lapse of etiquette, solecism, gaucherie, peccadillo; informal boob, boo-boo, slip-up, clanger, howler, boner; N. Amer. informal blooper; Brit. informal, dated bloomer.

favour noun **1** *will you do me a favour?* **good turn**, service, kind act, good deed, act of kindness, kindness, courtesy, indulgence; benefit, boon.
▷ANTONYMS disservice.
2 *she looked on him with favour*: **approval**, approbation, commendation, esteem, goodwill, kindness, benevolence, friendliness.
▷ANTONYMS disfavour; disapproval.
3 *they accused you of showing favour to one of the players*: **favouritism**, bias, partiality, unfair preference, prejudice, partisanship, one-sidedness.
4 *serve the king well and you shall receive his favour*: **patronage**, backing, support, aid, assistance, championship, aegis; auspices.
5 archaic *I am your lady and you shall wear my favours*: **ribbon**, rosette, badge; token, token of affection, token of esteem; keepsake, souvenir, memento; archaic remembrancer.
□ **in favour** *the firm remains in favour with investors*: **popular**, well liked, liked, favoured, well received, approved, admired, accepted, welcome, sought-after, in demand, desired, wanted.
□ **in favour of** *two thirds of them were in favour of a strike*: **on the side of**, pro, for, all for, giving support to, giving backing to, right behind, encouraging of, approving of, sympathetic to.
▷ANTONYMS against.
□ **out of favour** *a company that is out of favour with the stock market*: **in disgrace**, unpopular, in bad odour; informal in someone's bad/black books, in the doghouse; NZ informal in the dogbox.
▷ANTONYMS in favour.
▸ verb **1** *the party favours reform of the electoral system*: **advocate**, recommend, advise, subscribe to, approve of, look on with favour, be in favour of, support, back, champion; campaign for, stand up for, argue for, press for, lobby for, urge, promote, espouse, endorse, sanction, vouch for; informal plug, push.
▷ANTONYMS oppose.
2 *Robyn favours loose dark clothes*: **prefer**, go in for, go for, choose, opt for, select, pick, plump for, single out, incline towards, lean towards, be partial to, like; informal fancy.
▷ANTONYMS dislike.
3 *he was angry that his father always favoured George*: **show favouritism towards**, have a bias towards, treat with partiality, have as a favourite, think more highly of, hold in higher regard; indulge, pamper, spoil.
4 *the conditions favoured the other team*: **benefit**, be to the advantage of, be advantageous to, oblige, help, assist, aid, lend a hand to, advance, abet, succour, serve, be of service to, do someone a favour, meet the needs of.
▷ANTONYMS hinder.
5 *he favoured Lucy with a smile*: **oblige**, accommodate, gratify, satisfy, humour, indulge, pander to, put oneself out for; honour.
6 informal *Travis favours our father in colouring*. See **resemble**.

favourable adjective **1** *a favourable assessment of his ability*: **approving**, commendatory, commending, praising, complimentary, flattering, glowing, appreciative, enthusiastic; good, pleasing, agreeable, successful, positive; informal rave.
▷ANTONYMS unfavourable; critical.
2 *the birds nest where conditions are favourable*: **advantageous**, beneficial, of benefit, in one's favour, on one's side, helpful, good, right, conducive, convenient, suitable, fit, fitting, appropriate; **propitious**, auspicious, hopeful, promising, fair, encouraging.
▷ANTONYMS disadvantageous.
3 *he hoped for a favourable reply to his request*: **positive**, affirmative, assenting, agreeing, concurring, approving, in the affirmative; encouraging, reassuring, supportive, in one's favour.
▷ANTONYMS negative.

favourably adverb *they were desperate to be judged favourably by their superiors*: **positively**, approvingly, well, sympathetically, agreeably, enthusiastically, appreciatively, admiringly.
▷ANTONYMS unfavourably.

favoured adjective *he is the president's favoured candidate for prime minister*: **preferred**, favourite, recommended, chosen, choice, selected, most-liked, ideal, particular, special, pet; informal blue-eyed.

favourite adjective *Laura was his favourite aunt*: **best-loved**, most-liked, favoured, dearest, treasured, pet, special, closest to one's heart; preferred, chosen, choice, ideal; of choice.
▷ANTONYMS least-liked.
▸ noun **1** *Brutus was always Caesar's favourite*: **first choice**, choice, pick, preference, pet, beloved, darling; idol, hero, god, goddess, gem, jewel, jewel in the crown; informal blue-eyed boy, golden boy, teacher's pet, the apple of one's eye; N. Amer. informal fair-haired boy.
▷ANTONYMS bête noire.
2 *the favourite fell at the very first fence*: **expected winner**, probable winner, front runner.
▷ANTONYMS underdog.

favouritism noun *we want one rule for everyone and no favouritism*: **partiality**, partisanship, unfair preference, preferential treatment, special treatment, preference, favour, one-sidedness, prejudice, bias, inequality, unfairness, inequity, discrimination, positive discrimination, reverse discrimination; nepotism, keeping it in the family, looking after one's own; Brit. jobs for the boys.

fawn[1] adjective *a thick fawn carpet*: **beige**, yellowish-brown, pale brown, buff, sand, sandy, oatmeal, wheaten, biscuit, café au lait, camel, kasha, ecru, taupe, stone, stone-coloured, greige, greyish-brown, mushroom, putty; neutral, natural, naturelle.

fawn[2] verb *congressmen **fawn over** him whenever he comes to town* | *the most important men in town will come to **fawn on** me*: **be obsequious to**, be sycophantic to, be servile to, curry favour with, pay court to, play up to, crawl to, creep to, ingratiate oneself with, dance attendance on, fall over oneself for, kowtow to, toady to, truckle to, bow and scrape before, grovel before, cringe before, abase oneself before; **flatter**, praise, sing the praises of, praise to the skies, praise to excess, eulogize; informal sweet-talk, soft-soap, suck up to, make up to, smarm around, be all over, fall all over, butter up, lick someone's boots, rub up the right way, lay it on thick, lay it on with a trowel; Austral./NZ informal smoodge to; vulgar slang kiss someone's arse.

fawning adjective *a circle of fawning civil servants*: **obsequious**, servile, sycophantic, flattering, ingratiating, unctuous, oleaginous, oily, toadyish, slavish, bowing and scraping, grovelling, abject, crawling, creeping, cringing, prostrate, over-deferential, Uriah Heepish; informal bootlicking, smarmy, slimy, sucky, soapy; N. Amer. informal brown-nosing; Brit. vulgar slang arse-kissing, bum-sucking; N. Amer. vulgar slang kiss-ass, ass-kissing, suckholing; rare saponaceous.

fear noun **1** *she felt fear at entering the house*: **terror**, fright, fearfulness, horror, alarm, panic, agitation, trepidation, dread, consternation, dismay, distress; **anxiety**, worry, angst, unease, uneasiness, apprehension, apprehensiveness, nervousness, nerves, timidity, disquiet, disquietude, discomposure, unrest, perturbation, foreboding, misgiving, doubt, suspicion; informal the creeps, the willies, the heebie-jeebies, the shakes, the collywobbles, jitteriness, twitchiness, butterflies (in the stomach); Brit. informal funk, blue funk, the (screaming) abdabs; Austral. rhyming slang the Joe Blakes; N. Amer. archaic worriment; rare inquietude.
▷ANTONYMS calmness; confidence.
2 *she sought help to overcome her fears*: **phobia**, aversion, antipathy, dread, bugbear, bogey, nightmare, horror, terror; anxiety, neurosis, complex, mania; abnormal fear, irrational fear, obsessive fear; French bête noire; informal hang-up.
3 archaic *the fear of God*: **awe**, wonder, wonderment, amazement; reverence, veneration, respect; **dread**.
▷ANTONYMS indifference.
4 *there's no fear of me leaving you alone*: **likelihood**, likeliness, prospect, possibility, chance, odds, probability, expectation, conceivability, feasibility, plausibility; risk, danger.
▸ verb **1** *she feared her husband*: **be afraid of**, be fearful of, be scared of, be apprehensive of, dread, live in fear of, go in terror of, be terrified of, be terrified by, cower before, tremble before, cringe from, shrink from, flinch from; be anxious about, worry about, panic about, feel consternation about, have forebodings about, feel apprehensive about; Brit. informal be in a blue funk about.
2 *he fears heights and open spaces*: **have a phobia about**, have a horror of, have a dread of, shudder at, take fright at.
3 *he **feared to** let them know he was awake*: **be too afraid**, be too scared, be too apprehensive, hesitate; dare not; informal have cold feet about.
4 *they all **feared for** his health*: **worry about**, feel anxious/concerned about, have anxieties about, have qualms about, feel disquiet for, be solicitous for.
5 archaic *all who fear the Lord*: **stand in awe of**, regard with awe, revere, reverence, venerate, respect; **dread**, be intimidated by.
6 *I fear that you may be right*: **suspect**, have a (sneaking) suspicion, have a (sneaking) feeling, feel, be inclined to think, be afraid, have a foreboding, have a hunch, think it likely, be of the opinion, suppose, reckon.

Word links **fear**

-phobia suffix meaning 'fear of something', as in *claustrophobia*
phobophobia fear of fear

fearful adjective **1** *they are fearful of being overheard by the enemy*: **afraid**, frightened, scared, scared stiff, scared to death, terrified, petrified; alarmed, panicky, nervous, tense, apprehensive, uneasy, hesitant, disquieted, worried, worried sick, anxious; Brit. nervy; informal jittery, jumpy, in a (blue) funk; Brit. informal strung up; dialect frit; archaic afeared, affrighted.
2 *the guards were ill trained and fearful*: **nervous**, trembling, quaking, quivering, shrinking, cowering, cowed, daunted; **timid**, timorous, diffident,

f

faint-hearted, cowardly, pusillanimous; Brit. nervy; informal jittery, jumpy, twitchy, keyed up, yellow, chicken, in a cold sweat, a bundle of nerves, like a cat on a hot tin roof, frightened of one's own shadow; Brit. informal having kittens, like a cat on hot bricks, windy; N. Amer. informal spooked, spooky, antsy; dated overstrung, unquiet.
3 *there has been a fearful accident*: **terrible**, dreadful, awful, appalling, frightful, ghastly, horrific, horrible, horrifying, horrendous, very bad, terribly bad, shocking, atrocious, abominable, hideous, monstrous, dire, grim, unspeakable, gruesome, grievous, lamentable, distressing, harrowing, alarming.
▷ANTONYMS minor.
4 informal *he was in a fearful hurry*: **very great**, great, extreme, real, dreadful; informal terrible, impossible; Brit. informal right, proper.

fearfully adverb **1** *she opened the door fearfully*: **apprehensively**, uneasily, nervously, timidly, timorously, diffidently, hesitantly; with apprehension/trepidation, with bated breath, with one's heart in one's mouth.
2 informal *Stephanie looked fearfully glamorous*: **extremely**, exceedingly, exceptionally, remarkably, uncommonly, extraordinarily, incredibly, most, very, really, immensely, thoroughly, positively, decidedly, downright; Scottish unco; N. Amer. quite; informal tremendously, awfully, terribly, frightfully, dreadfully, terrifically, desperately, seriously, devilishly, hugely, fantastically, madly, ultra, too ... for words, mucho, mega, majorly, oh-so; Brit. informal jolly, ever so, dead, well, fair, right; N. Amer. informal real, mighty, awful, plumb, powerful, way; S. African informal lekker; informal, dated devilish, hellish, frightfully; archaic exceeding.

f

fearless adjective *the most fearless man I've ever seen in battle*: **bold**, brave, courageous, intrepid, valiant, valorous, gallant, plucky, lionhearted, stout-hearted, heroic, daring, dynamic, spirited, mettlesome, confident, audacious, indomitable, doughty; unafraid, undaunted, unflinching, unshrinking, unblenching, unabashed; informal game, gutsy, spunky, ballsy, go-ahead, have-a-go, feisty; rare venturous.
▷ANTONYMS timid; cowardly.

fearsome adjective *the crocodile's teeth are a fearsome sight*: **frightening**, horrifying, terrifying, menacing, chilling, spine-chilling, hair-raising, alarming, startling, unnerving, daunting, formidable, forbidding, dismaying, disquieting, disturbing, harrowing; appalling, dreadful, monstrous, horrendous; awe-inspiring, awesome, impressive, imposing, tremendous; informal scary, hairy.

> *Word toolkit* **fearsome**
>
> See **formidable**.

feasibility noun *they will consider the feasibility of an aid programme*: **practicability**, practicality, workability, workableness, viability, achievability, attainability, reasonableness, sensibleness; usefulness, suitability, expedience, helpfulness, constructiveness, use, utility, value; possibility, likelihood, likeliness, chance, conceivability; informal doability.
▷ANTONYMS impracticability.

feasible adjective *there is only one feasible solution*: **practicable**, practical, workable, achievable, attainable, realizable, viable, realistic, sensible, reasonable, within reason, within the bounds of possibility; useful, suitable, expedient, helpful, constructive; possible, likely, conceivable, imaginable; informal doable, earthly; rare accomplishable.
▷ANTONYMS impractical; impossible.

feast noun **1** *the occasion was celebrated with a great feast*: **banquet**, celebration meal, lavish dinner, sumptuous repast, large meal, formal meal, formal dinner; treat, entertainment, jollification; revels, festivities; informal blowout, feed, junket, spread, binge, bash, do; Brit. informal nosh-up, beanfeast, bunfight, beano, scoff, slap-up meal, tuck-in.
▷ANTONYMS snack; fast.
2 *the feast of St Stephen*: **festival**, religious festival, feast day, saint's day, holy day, holiday, fête, festivity, celebration.
3 *the decorations are a feast for the eyes*: **treat**, delight, joy, pleasure, gratification.
▶verb **1** *they **feasted on** lobster and beef*: **gorge on**, dine on, eat one's fill of, indulge in, overindulge in; eat, devour, consume, partake of; banquet; informal binge on, stuff one's face with, stuff oneself with, stuff down, shovel down, wolf down, pig oneself on, pig out on, make a pig of oneself on, cram in, tuck into, put away, pack away, make short work of, get outside of, get one's laughing gear round; Brit. informal gollop, shift; N. Amer. informal snarf; rare gourmandize.
2 *they feasted the deputation*: **hold a banquet for**, throw a feast for, wine and dine, ply with food and drink, give someone a meal, feed, cater for; entertain lavishly, regale, treat, fête, throw a party for, play host to.

feat noun *the mounting of the expedition was a remarkable feat*: **achievement**, accomplishment, attainment, coup, master stroke, triumph; **undertaking**, enterprise, venture, operation, exercise, endeavour, effort, performance; deed, act, action, manoeuvre, move, exploit, stunt; (**feats**) doings; informal caper.

feather noun *the bird preened its feathers*: **plume**, quill; (**feathers**) **plumage**, feathering, down, eider (down), hackles, crest, tuft, topknot, pinion; technical covert, remex, rectrix, plumule, semi-plume; vibrissae; archaic flag.

> *Word links* **feather**
>
> **pteronophobia** fear of feathers

feathery adjective **1** *the feathery grey bodies of the geese*: **feathered**, plumed, plumy; downy, fluffy, fuzzy, fleecy; technical plumose, plumate.
▷ANTONYMS bald.
2 *she wore a feathery nightdress*: **flimsy**, delicate, diaphanous, fine, thin, sheer, gossamer, gossamer-like, gossamer-thin, gossamery, gauzelike, gauzy, wispy, floaty, insubstantial, unsubstantial, ethereal, incorporeal, vaporous, airy; light, lightweight, feather-like, light as a feather.

feature noun **1** *a typical feature of French music*: **characteristic**, attribute, quality, property, trait, mark, hallmark, trademark; aspect, facet, side, point, detail, factor, ingredient, component, constituent, element, theme; peculiarity, idiosyncrasy, quirk, oddity.
2 (**features**) *his eyes swept over her delicate features*: **face**, countenance, physiognomy, profile; informal mug, kisser, clock; Brit. informal mush, phiz, phizog, dial; Brit. rhyming slang boat race; Scottish & Irish informal coupon; N. Amer. informal puss, pan; literary visage, lineaments; archaic front.
3 *she made a feature of her garden sculptures*: **centrepiece**, **special attraction**, attraction, highlight, focal point, focus, focus of attention, centre of interest, draw, crowd-pleaser, cynosure; selling point; informal crowd-puller.
4 *the journal contains a series of short features*: **article**, piece, item, report, story, column, review, commentary, criticism, analysis, write-up, exposé; N. Amer. theme.
▶verb **1** *Radio Ulster intends to feature a week of live concerts*: **present**, promote, make a feature of, give prominence to, focus attention on, call attention to, spotlight, highlight, accent.
2 *she is to feature in a major advertising campaign*: **star**, appear, participate, play a part, have a place, have prominence.

febrile adjective *the patient was febrile and had abdominal pain*: **feverish**, fevered, hot, burning, burning up, fiery, flushed, sweating, in a cold sweat; shivering; delirious; informal with a temperature; rare pyretic.

feckless adjective *a feckless lot of layabouts*: **useless**, worthless, incompetent, inefficient, inept, good-for-nothing, ne'er-do-well; lazy, idle, slothful, indolent, shiftless, spiritless, apathetic, aimless, unambitious, unenterprising; informal no-good, no-account, lousy.

fecund adjective *a lush and fecund garden*. See **fertile** (sense 1).

federal adjective *an assembly consisting of delegations from the federal states*: **confederate**, federated, federative; **combined**, allied, united, amalgamated, integrated, linked, associated, cooperating, in alliance, in league, in partnership, banded together.

federate verb *the organizations will be federated at national level*: **confederate**, **combine**, ally, unite, unify, merge, amalgamate, integrate, fuse, marry, link, join, join up, align, associate, band together, team up.

federation noun *a world federation of Protestant denominations*: **confederation**, confederacy, federacy, league; **combination**, combine, alliance, coalition, union, syndicate, guild, consortium, partnership, co-partnership, cooperative, association, amalgamation, entente, alignment; German Bund; rare consociation, sodality.

fed up adjective *he looked tired, fed up, and exhausted*: **exasperated**, irritated, annoyed, exasperated, irked, put out, peeved, piqued, disgruntled; discontented, discouraged, disheartened, depressed; bored, weary, tired; informal hacked off, cheesed off, brassed off, narked; vulgar slang pissed off.
▷ANTONYMS contented, satisfied, happy, cheerful.

fee noun *he delivered the parcels for a very modest fee*: **payment**, emolument, wage, salary, allowance, stipend, handout; **price**, cost, charge, tariff, toll, rate, amount, sum, figure, percentage, commission, consideration, honorarium; (**fees**) remuneration, dues, earnings, pay.

feeble adjective **1** *he was very old and feeble*: **weak**, weakly, weakened, puny, wasted, frail, infirm, delicate, sickly, ailing, unwell, poorly, failing, helpless, powerless, impotent, enfeebled, enervated, debilitated, incapacitated, effete; decrepit, doddering, doddery, tottering, tottery, shaky, trembling, trembly; Scottish shilpit; rare etiolated.
▷ANTONYMS strong.
2 *this is a transparently feeble argument*: **ineffective**, ineffectual, unsuccessful, inadequate, unconvincing, implausible, unsatisfactory, poor, weak, inept, tame, paltry, shallow, thin, flimsy, insubstantial; futile, useless, profitless, fruitless.
▷ANTONYMS effective.
3 *he's too feeble to stand up to his boss*: **cowardly**, craven, faint-hearted, spineless, spiritless, lily-livered, chicken-livered, pigeon-hearted; timid, timorous, fearful, unassertive, soft, weak, ineffective, ineffectual,

inefficient, incompetent, inadequate, indecisive; informal wishy-washy, wimpy, sissy, sissified, gutless, weak-kneed, yellow, yellow-bellied, chicken; Brit. informal wet; N. Amer. informal candy-assed; N. Amer. vulgar slang chickenshit; archaic poor-spirited.
▷**ANTONYMS** brave; forceful.
4 *the lamp shed a feeble light*: **faint**, dim, weak, pale, soft, subdued, muted, indistinct, unclear, vague; informal wishy-washy.
▷**ANTONYMS** strong.

Word toolkit feeble

See **weak**.

feeble-minded adjective *don't be so feeble-minded*: **stupid**, idiotic, moronic, imbecilic, foolish, half-baked, half-witted, dim-witted, witless, dunce-like, doltish, cretinous, empty-headed, vacuous, vapid; informal daft, dumb, dim, dopey, dozy, birdbrained, pea-brained, fat-headed, lamebrained, chuckleheaded, dunderheaded, wooden-headed, muttonheaded, boneheaded, crazy, mental, nuts, nutty, crackers, cracked, potty, barmy, batty, cuckoo, bonkers, dotty, dippy; N. Amer. informal dumb-ass.
▷**ANTONYMS** clever.

feed verb **1** *I have a large family to feed*: **give food to**, provide food for, provide for, cater for, prepare food for, cook for, make a meal for, wine and dine; nourish, sustain; suckle, breastfeed, bottle-feed; dated victual.
2 *the baby spends all day sleeping and feeding*: **eat**, take nourishment, partake of food, consume food, devour food, have a meal; informal snack, graze; Brit. informal nosh; dated sup.
3 *there are too many cows feeding in a small area*: **graze**, browse, crop, pasture, ruminate; eat.
4 *the birds* **feed on** *a varied diet of fish*: **live on**, live off, exist on, subsist on, rely for nourishment on, depend on, thrive on; eat, consume, take in, have as food.
5 *we all have ways of feeding our self-esteem*: **strengthen**, fortify, support, bolster, reinforce, boost, augment, supplement, add to, add fuel to, fuel, encourage, gratify, minister to.
▷**ANTONYMS** undermine.
6 *she fed secrets to the Russians*: **supply**, provide, give, deliver, present, furnish, issue, impart, sell.
▸ **noun 1** *he provides feed for his goats and sheep*: **fodder**, food, foodstuff, forage, pasturage, herbage, silage; formal comestibles, provender.
2 informal *the hikers had decided to halt for their feed*: **meal**, lunch, dinner, supper, repast; feast, banquet; Brit. tea; informal spread, blowout, binge; Brit. informal nosh, nosh-up, scoff, tuck-in; formal refection, collation.

feel verb **1** *she encourages her customers to feel the fabrics*: **touch**, stroke, caress, fondle, finger, thumb, handle, manipulate, fiddle with, play with, toy with, maul; put one's hand on, lay a finger on; informal paw.
2 *she felt a steady breeze on her back*: **perceive**, sense, detect, discern, make out, notice, observe, identify; be sensible of, have a sensation of, be aware of, be conscious of.
3 *the patient does not feel pain during the procedure*: **experience**, undergo, go through, bear, endure, suffer, be forced to contend with; know, have.
4 *he began to feel his way towards the door*: **grope**, fumble, scrabble, pick, poke, explore.
5 *feel the temperature of the water*: **test**, try, try out, assess.
6 *he feels that he should go to the meeting*: **believe**, think, consider it right, consider, fancy, be of the opinion, hold, maintain, judge, deem; suspect, suppose, assume, presume, conclude, come to the conclusion that; N. Amer. figure; informal reckon.
▷**ANTONYMS** doubt.
7 *I feel that he is only biding his time*: **sense**, have a feeling, get the impression, feel in one's bones, have a hunch, have a funny feeling, just know, intuit.
8 *the air feels damp*: **seem**, appear, strike one as.
□ **feel for** *the press persecuted John and I felt for him*: **sympathize with**, be sorry for, pity, feel pity for, feel sympathy for, feel compassion for, empathize with, identify with, be moved by, weep for, grieve for, sorrow for; commiserate with, condole with; archaic compassion.
□ **feel like** *I feel like an ice cream*: **want**, would like, wish for, desire, fancy, feel in need of, feel the need for, long for, crave, hanker after, pine for, thirst for, be desperate for, be bent on; informal have a yen for, yen for, be dying for.
▸ **noun 1** *in murky water the divers work by feel*: **touch**, sense of touch, tactile sense, tactility, feeling, feeling one's way, contact; texture.
2 *he liked the feel of the paper*: **texture**, surface, finish, grain, nap; weight, thickness, consistency; quality, character.
3 *lighting can radically alter the feel of a room*: **atmosphere**, ambience, aura, mood, feeling, air, impression, climate, character, overtone, undertone, tenor, spirit, quality, flavour, colour; informal vibrations, vibes, vibe; rare subcurrent.
4 *he has a real feel for the language*: **aptitude**, knack, flair, bent, talent, gift, art, trick, faculty, ability, propensity, inclination; head, mind, brain; informal know-how.

feeler noun **1** *the fish has two feelers at the front of the head*: **antenna**, tentacle, horn; whisker, hair, barb; tactile organ, sensory organ; technical palp, palpus, pedipalp, antennule, tactor.
2 (usually **feelers**) *the prime minister put out feelers to members of other parties*: **tentative enquiry**, tentative proposal, tentative suggestion; advance, approach, overture, appeal; probe, trial balloon; French ballon d'essai.

feeling noun **1** *it's important to assess the fabric by feeling*: **touch**, feel, sense of touch, tactile sense, tactility, contact, using one's hands.
2 *she was overcome by a feeling of nausea*: **sensation**, sense; awareness, consciousness, perception, impression.
3 *I had a feeling that I would win*: **suspicion**, sneaking suspicion, notion, inkling, hunch, fancy, apprehension, presentiment, premonition, foreboding; idea, vague idea, impression; informal gut feeling, feeling in one's bones, funny feeling, sixth sense.
4 *he was amazed at the strength of her feeling*: **love**, care, affection, fondness, tenderness, warmth, warmness, emotion, sentiment; passion, ardour, desire, lust, infatuation; adulation, adoration, reverence, devotion.
5 *the government is out of touch with public feeling*: **sentiment**, emotion, emotional state; **opinion**, attitude, belief; ideas, views.
6 *Emma felt a rush of feeling for the poor child*: **compassion**, sympathy, empathy, fellow feeling, understanding, care, concern, solicitude, solicitousness, tender-heartedness, tenderness, love, brotherly love; pity, sorrow, commiseration, condolences.
7 (**feelings**) *he hadn't meant to hurt her feelings*: **sensibilities**, sensitivities, self-esteem, ego, pride; emotions, passions, sentiments.
8 *my feeling is that his claim is true*: **opinion**, belief, view, impression, intuition, instinct, hunch, estimation, guess, theory, hypothesis, thought, way of thinking, point of view.
9 *a feeling of peace prevailed in the quiet street*: **atmosphere**, ambience, aura, air, feel, mood, impression, climate, character, overtone, undertone, tenor, spirit, quality, flavour, colour; informal vibrations, vibes, vibe; rare subcurrent.
10 *he has a remarkable feeling for language*: **aptitude**, knack, flair, bent, talent, gift, skill, art, trick, faculty, ability, propensity, inclination; head, mind, brain; informal know-how.
▸ **adjective** *he considers himself to be a feeling man*: **sensitive**, warm, warm-hearted, tender, tender-hearted, caring, soft-hearted, sympathetic, compassionate, understanding, empathetic, responsive, receptive, intuitive, thoughtful; emotional, demonstrative, passionate, fiery; archaic sensible.

feign verb **1** *she lay still and feigned sleep*: **simulate**, fake, sham, affect, give the appearance of, make a show of, make a pretence of, play at, go through the motions of; informal put on.
2 *he's not really ill, he's only feigning*: **pretend**, put it on, fake, sham, bluff, pose, posture, masquerade, make believe, act, play-act, go through the motions, put on a false display; malinger; informal kid; Brit. informal mess.

feigned adjective *he accepted the invitation with feigned enthusiasm*: **pretended**, simulated, assumed, affected, artificial, insincere, put-on, fake, faked, false, sham; apparent, ostensible, seeming, surface, avowed, professed; informal pretend, pseudo, phoney; Brit. informal cod.
▷**ANTONYMS** sincere.

feint noun *the attack on the main gate was merely a feint*: **bluff**, blind, ruse, deception, subterfuge, hoax, trick, ploy, device, wile, sham, pretence, artifice, cover, smokescreen, distraction, expedient, contrivance, machination; informal dodge, put-on, put-up job, red herring.

felicitations plural noun *I extend my felicitations to you on the occasion of your marriage*. See **congratulations** (sense 1).

felicitous adjective **1** *his nickname was particularly felicitous*: **apt**, well chosen, well expressed, well put, choice, fitting, suitable, appropriate, apposite, pertinent, germane, to the point, relevant, congruous, apropos; informal spot on.
▷**ANTONYMS** inappropriate.
2 *the view is the room's only felicitous feature*: **fortunate**, advantageous, good, favourable, lucky, happy, pleasing, encouraging.
▷**ANTONYMS** unfortunate.

felicity noun **1** *a scene of domestic felicity*: **happiness**, joy, joyfulness, joyousness, rapture, bliss, euphoria, delight, cheer, cheerfulness, gaiety; contentedness, satisfaction, pleasure, fulfilment; transports.
▷**ANTONYMS** unhappiness.
2 *David expressed his feelings with his customary felicity*: **eloquence**, aptness, appropriateness, suitability, suitableness, applicability, fitness, relevance, pertinence, correctness, rightness.
▷**ANTONYMS** inappropriateness.

feline adjective *she moved with feline grace*: **catlike**, leonine; graceful, sleek, sinuous, slinky, sensual; stealthy.
▸ **noun** *she gave a silly name to her pet feline*: **cat**, domestic cat, wild cat, alley cat, kitten; tabby, tomcat, tom, queen, mouser; informal puss, pussy, pussy cat; Brit. informal moggie, mog; archaic grimalkin.

fell[1] verb **1** *all the dead sycamores had to be felled*: **cut down**, chop down, hack down, saw down, knock down, hew, demolish, tear down, bring down, raze, level, clear.
2 *she felled him with one punch | he was felled by a sniper's bullet*: **knock down**, knock over, knock to the ground, bowl over, strike down, bring down, bring to the ground, topple, ground, prostrate, catch off balance; knock out, knock unconscious; kill, cut down, mow down, pick off, shoot down, gun down, blast; informal deck, floor, flatten, down, knock for six, knock into the middle of next week, lay out, KO.

fell[2] adjective
□ **at/in one fell swoop** *she solved all her problems in one fell swoop*: **all at once**, together, at the same time, in one go, with one move, outright.

fellow noun **1** informal *he's a decent sort of fellow*: **man**, boy; person, individual, soul; informal guy, lad, fella, codger, sort, character, customer, punter, devil, bunny, bastard; Brit. informal chap, bloke, gent, geezer, bod; Scottish & Irish informal bodach; N. Amer. informal dude, hombre; Austral./NZ informal digger; S. African informal ou, oke; Indian informal admi; informal, dated body, dog; Brit. informal, dated cove; Scottish archaic carl.
2 informal *she longed to be like ordinary girls and have a fellow*: **boyfriend**, lover; informal fella.
3 *he exchanged relieved glances with his fellows*: **companion**, friend, crony, comrade, partner, associate, co-worker, colleague; informal chum, pal, buddy; Brit. informal mate, oppo.
4 *some peasants were wealthier than their fellows*: **peer**, equal, contemporary, brother; French confrère; archaic compeer; rare coeval, coequal.
5 *the fellow to the absent key lay on the table*: **counterpart**, mate, partner, match, twin, brother, double; copy, duplicate.
□ **fellow feeling** *she felt a rush of fellow feeling for the unfortunate woman*: **sympathy**, **empathy**, feeling, compassion, care, concern, solicitude, solicitousness, warmth, tenderness, brotherly love; pity, sorrow, commiseration, condolences; affinity, rapport, harmony, understanding, fellowship, closeness, togetherness, connection, communion; rare caritas.

fellowship noun **1** *a community bound together in fellowship*: **companionship**, companionability, sociability, comradeship, fraternization, camaraderie, friendship, mutual support, mutual respect, mutual liking; amiability, amity, affability, geniality, kindliness, cordiality, intimacy; social intercourse, social contact, association, closeness, togetherness, solidarity; informal chumminess, palliness, clubbiness; Brit. informal mateyness.
2 *a new member of the church fellowship*: **association**, society, club, league, union, guild, lodge, affiliation, alliance, order, fraternity, brotherhood, sorority; band, group, circle, ring, clan, set, coterie; rare consociation, sodality.

female adjective *typical female attributes*: **feminine**, womanly, womanlike, ladylike; she-, to do with women; pretty, graceful, delicate, gentle; archaic feminal.
▷ANTONYMS male.
▸ noun *the author was a female*. See **woman**.

feminine adjective **1** *a very feminine young woman*: **womanly**, womanlike, ladylike, girlish, female; soft, delicate, gentle, tender, graceful, refined, modest; informal girly; archaic feminal.
▷ANTONYMS masculine.
2 *his friends thought him slightly feminine*: **effeminate**, womanish, unmanly, unmasculine, effete, weak, soft, milksoppish; informal sissy, sissyish, wimpy, wimpish, limp-wristed, pansy-like, queeny.
▷ANTONYMS manly; butch.

femininity noun *she had always delighted in her femininity*: **womanliness**, feminineness, womanhood, womanly qualities, feminine qualities.
▷ANTONYMS masculinity.

feminism noun *she was a great pioneer of feminism*: **the women's movement**, the feminist movement, women's liberation, female emancipation, women's rights; post-feminism, womanism; informal women's lib.

femme fatale noun *a femme fatale who plays men off against each other*. See **seductress**.

fen noun *they opposed the drainage of the fen*: **marsh**, marshland, salt marsh, fenland, wetland, bog, peat bog, bogland, swamp, swampland; Scottish & N. English moss, carr; Irish corcass; N. Amer. bayou, moor, pocosin, salina; archaic marish.

fence noun **1** *she crept through a gap in the fence*: **barrier**, paling, railing, rail, bar, hurdle, enclosure; wall, hedge, hedgerow, windbreak, groyne, partition; barricade, stockade, palisade, rampart, protection, defence; rare circumvallation.
2 informal *he was an accomplished fence, dealing mainly in jewellery*: **receiver of stolen goods**, dealer in stolen goods; receiver, dealer, trafficker; informal pusher.
□ **(sitting) on the fence** informal *they were on the fence about the whole issue*: **undecided**, uncommitted, uncertain, unsure, vacillating, wavering, dithering, hesitant, tentative, doubtful, irresolute, ambivalent, torn, in two minds, in a dilemma, on the horns of a dilemma, in a quandary; abstaining; neutral, impartial, non-aligned, non-partisan, unbiased, open-minded; Brit. humming and hawing; informal iffy, blowing hot and cold.
▸ verb **1** *they intend to* ***fence off*** *many acres of wild land*: **enclose**, surround, circumscribe, encircle, circle, encompass, bound, form a barrier around, form a ring round; divide up, section off, separate off, partition off, cut off, cordon off, close off, isolate, segregate, seal, close; literary gird, girdle, engird; rare compass.
2 *he needed more wire to* ***fence in*** *his chickens*: **confine**, pen in, coop up, rail in, box in, wall in, hedge in, hem in, close in, shut in, shut up, mew up, immure, lock in, shut off, separate off, cut off; intern, impound, hold captive, keep under lock and key; enclose, surround; secure, protect, defend; N. Amer. corral.
3 *the man fenced but Jim persisted with his questions*: **be evasive**, be vague, be ambiguous, be non-committal, equivocate, prevaricate, stall, vacillate, quibble, hedge, beat about the bush, dodge the issue, sidestep the issue, parry questions, fudge the issue, mince one's words; informal pussyfoot around, duck the question, duck the issue, waffle, flannel, shilly-shally; rare palter, tergiversate.
4 informal *these fellows fenced for a band of grave robbers*: **receive stolen goods**, deal in stolen goods.

fend verb *they were unable to* ***fend off*** *a Viking invasion | Mary tried to* ***fend off*** *his questions*: **ward off**, head off, stave off, hold off, keep off, repel, repulse, resist, forestall, pre-empt, fight off, defend oneself against, guard against, discourage, prevent, stop, put a stop to, block, intercept, halt, arrest, check, curb, hold back, baulk, foil, thwart, keep at bay, keep at arm's length; parry, turn aside, divert, deflect, avert; skirt round, dodge, duck, escape, evade.
▷ANTONYMS encourage.
□ **fend for oneself** *how could any mother leave a child to fend for itself?* **take care of oneself**, look after oneself, provide for oneself, shift for oneself, manage by oneself, get by alone, get by without help, cope alone, cope unaided, stand on one's own two feet, hold one's own, make it on one's own; informal paddle one's own canoe.

feral adjective **1** *a pack of feral dogs*: **wild**, untamed, undomesticated, untrained, unused to humans; unbroken, not broken in; Brit. not house-trained; N. Amer. not housebroken.
▷ANTONYMS tame; pet.
2 *he gave a feral snarl*: **fierce**, ferocious, vicious, savage, aggressive, tigerish, wolfish, predatory, menacing, threatening, bloodthirsty.

ferment verb (stress on the second syllable) **1** *the beer continues to ferment in the cask*: **undergo fermentation**, brew; **effervesce**, fizz, foam, froth, bubble, seethe, boil; rise.
2 *the mixture is fermented by the addition of yeast*: **brew**; **subject to fermentation**, cause to ferment, cause to effervesce.
3 *the brutalizing environment that ferments prison disorder*: **cause**, bring on, bring about, give rise to, lead to, result in, generate, engender, spawn, instigate, prompt, provoke, incite, excite, arouse, stir up, whip up, foment, kindle, trigger off, spark off, touch off; literary beget, enkindle; rare effectuate.
▸ noun (stress on the first syllable) *a ferment of revolutionary upheaval*: **fever**, furore, frenzy, tumult, storm, flurry, bustle, hubbub, brouhaha, stir, fuss, stew, ruckus, clamour; **turmoil**, upheaval, unrest, disquiet, uproar, agitation, turbulence, hurly-burly, excitement, disruption, confusion, disorder, chaos, mayhem; informal hoo-ha, to-do, rumpus; Brit. informal kerfuffle, carry-on, aggro, argy-bargy, hoopla; archaic moil, coil.

Word links **ferment**

zymology science of fermentation

fern noun (**ferns**) **bracken**; archaic brake.

Word links **fern**

pteridology study of ferns

ferocious adjective **1** *bears are ferocious animals*: **fierce**, savage, wild, feral, untamed; predatory, rapacious, ravening, aggressive, dangerous.
▷ANTONYMS tame; gentle.
2 *a ferocious attack on a policeman*: **brutal**, brutish, vicious, violent, bloody, barbarous, barbaric, savage, sadistic, ruthless, remorseless, cruel, pitiless, merciless, heartless, bloodthirsty, murderous, tigerish, wolfish; wicked, inhuman, monstrous, abominable, fiendish, hellish, diabolical; Brit. informal beastly; literary fell; archaic sanguinary.
▷ANTONYMS gentle.
3 *the ferocious midday sun | a ferocious headache*: **intense**, extreme, strong, powerful, fierce, burning, searing; severe, acute, unbearable, insufferable, hellish, diabolical.
▷ANTONYMS mild.

ferocity noun *detectives were shocked by the ferocity of the attack*: **savagery**, brutality, brutishness, barbarity, fierceness, violence, aggression, bloodthirstiness, murderousness; ruthlessness, cruelty, pitilessness,

mercilessness, heartlessness, inhumanity, sadism; intensity, severity, extremity, force, strength; rare ferity.
▷ANTONYMS gentleness.

ferret verb **1** *she ferreted in her handbag*: **rummage**, search about, scrabble around, feel around, grope around, forage around, fish about/around, poke about/around, scratch about/around, delve, dig, hunt; search through, hunt through, rifle through, sift through, go through, scour, ransack, explore; Brit. informal rootle around; Austral./NZ informal fossick through; rare roust around.
2 *our headmistress was good at **ferreting out** misdemeanors*: **unearth**, uncover, discover, detect, search out, elicit, bring to light, bring into the open, reveal, get at, run to earth, track down, turn up, dig up, dig out, root out, hunt out, fish out, nose out, sniff out; informal get wind of, get wise to, rumble; rare uncloak.

Word links **ferret**

jack male
jill female
kit young
busyness collective noun

ferry noun *I took the ferry from Dover to Calais*: **passenger boat**, passenger ship, ferry boat, packet boat, packet, shuttle; car ferry, train ferry, drive-on ferry, roll-on/roll-off ferry; ship, boat, vessel; S. African pont; in Venice traghetto.
▸ verb **1** *the ship will ferry passengers to and from the Continent*: **transport**, convey, carry, bear, ship, run, chauffeur, take, bring, shuttle.
2 *the boat ferried hourly across the river*: **go back and forth**, shuttle, come and go, run.

fertile adjective **1** *the soil is moist and fertile*: **fecund**, fruitful, productive, high-yielding, prolific, proliferating, propagative, generative; rich, lush; rare fructuous.
▷ANTONYMS infertile.
2 *even couples who are fertile may adopt a child*: **able to conceive**, able to have children, fecund, potent, generative, reproductive.
▷ANTONYMS barren.
3 *he has a particularly fertile brain*: **imaginative**, inventive, innovative, innovational, creative, visionary, original, ingenious, resourceful, constructive; productive, prolific.
▷ANTONYMS unimaginative.

fertility noun **1** *he uses compost to maintain the fertility of his land*: **fecundity**, fruitfulness, productiveness, prolificacy, propagativeness, generativeness; richness, lushness.
2 *happiness has an effect on one's fertility*: **ability to conceive**, ability to have children, virility, fecundity, potency, reproductiveness.

fertilization noun *the sex of the embryo is determined at fertilization*: **conception**, impregnation, insemination, implantation, inception of pregnancy; pollination, propagation; rare fecundation.

fertilize verb **1** *the field is ploughed up and fertilized*: **add fertilizer to**, enrich with fertilizer, feed, mulch, compost, manure, dung, dress, top-dress; make more fertile; rare fecundate, fructify.
2 *the eggs were fertilized during the breeding season*: **impregnate**, inseminate; rare fecundate.
3 *these orchids are fertilized by insects*: **pollinate**, cross-pollinate, cross-fertilize, make fruitful; rare fecundate, fructify.

fertilizer noun *farmers rely on fertilizer to expand output*: **plant food**, dressing.

fervent adjective *Annie uttered a fervent prayer | a fervent rugby supporter*: **impassioned**, passionate, intense, vehement, ardent, sincere, feeling, profound, deep-seated, heartfelt, deeply felt, emotional, animated, spirited; enthusiastic, zealous, fanatical, wholehearted, avid, eager, earnest, keen, committed, dedicated, devout; informal mad keen, card-carrying, true blue; Brit. informal keen as mustard; rare fervid, perfervid, passional.
▷ANTONYMS apathetic.

Word toolkit **fervent**

See **zealous**.

fervid adjective rare *fervid protestations of love*. See **fervent**.

fervour noun *he preached and laboured with tremendous fervour*: **passion**, ardour, intensity, zeal, vehemence, vehemency, emotion, warmth, sincerity, earnestness, avidness, avidity, eagerness, keenness, enthusiasm, excitement, animation, vigour, energy, fire, fieriness, heat, spirit, zest, appetite, hunger, urgency; dedication, devoutness, assiduity, commitment, committedness; rare fervency, ardency, passionateness.
▷ANTONYMS apathy.

fester verb **1** *the deep wound in his neck festered*: **suppurate**, become septic, form pus, secrete pus, discharge, run, weep, ooze; come to a head; technical maturate, be purulent; rare rankle, apostemate.
2 *rubbish festered in the crowded streets*: **rot**, moulder, decay, decompose, putrefy, go bad, go off, perish, spoil, deteriorate, disintegrate, degrade, break down, break up; technical mortify, necrotize; archaic corrupt.
3 *we must not allow our resentment to fester*: **rankle**, chafe, gnaw (at one's mind), eat away at one's mind, ferment, brew, smoulder; cause bitterness, cause resentment, cause vexation, cause annoyance.

festival noun **1** *we took part in the town's autumn festival*: **fête**, fair, gala day, gala, carnival, fiesta, jamboree, pageant; celebrations, festivities; arts festival, festival of music and drama, musical festival, festival of music, science festival; Welsh eisteddfod.
2 *forty days' fasting precede the festival*: **holy day**, feast day, saint's day, holiday; anniversary, commemoration, day of observance; rite, ritual, ceremony.

festive adjective *everyone was in a festive mood despite the recession*: **jolly**, merry, joyous, joyful, happy, jovial, light-hearted, cheerful, cheery, jubilant, convivial, good-time, high-spirited, gleeful, mirthful, uproarious, rollicking, backslapping, hilarious; celebratory, holiday, carnival; Christmassy; informal chirpy; dated gay; archaic festal, frolicsome, sportive.
▷ANTONYMS miserable.

festivity noun **1** (**festivities**) *food plays an important part in the festivities*: **celebration**, festival, festive event, festive occasion, entertainment, party, jamboree; merrymaking, feasting, revelry, carousal, carousing, jollification; revels, fun and games, frolics, celebrations, festive proceedings; informal bash, shindig, shindy; Brit. informal rave-up, thrash, knees-up, jolly, beanfeast, bunfight, beano.
2 *the festivity of the Last Night of the Proms*: **jollity**, jolliness, merriment, gaiety, cheerfulness, cheeriness, cheer, joyfulness, euphoria, jubilance, conviviality, gleefulness, glee, high spirits, jocularity, revelry; dated sport; archaic sportiveness.

festoon noun *the streets are hung with festoons of paper flowers*: **garland**, chain, lei, swathe, swag, wreath, chaplet, loop.
▸ verb *the room was festooned with streamers*: **decorate**, adorn, ornament, trim, dress up, array, deck (out), hang, loop, thread, cover, drape, swathe, garland, wreathe, bedeck, beribbon, bespangle; informal do up, do out, get up, tart up, trick out; literary bedizen, furbelow, caparison, befrill, bejewel.

fetch verb **1** *he went to fetch a doctor from the village*: **get**, go and get, go for, call for, summon, pick up, collect, bring, carry, deliver, convey, ferry, transport; escort, conduct, lead, usher in.
2 *the land could fetch a million pounds*: **sell for**, bring in, raise, realize, yield, make, earn, command, cost, be priced at, come to, amount to; informal go for, set one back, pull in, rake in; Brit. informal knock someone back.
□ **fetch up** informal *the boat somehow fetched up on a remote Pacific island*: **end up**, finish up, turn up, arrive, appear, pop up, materialize, find itself; land, beach, wash up; informal wind up, pitch up, show up.

fetching adjective *she looked rather fetching in her nurse's uniform*: **attractive**, appealing, adorable, sweet, winsome, pretty, lovely, delightful, charming, prepossessing, captivating, enchanting; sexy, alluring, seductive, ravishing, desirable, irresistible; Scottish & N. English bonny; informal divine, heavenly, smashing, tasty, hot, fanciable, easy on the eye; Brit. informal fit; N. Amer. informal cute, foxy; dated taking; archaic comely, fair.

fête noun Brit. *the village fête was held on the green*: **gala**, gala day, garden party, bazaar, fair, feast, festival, fiesta, jubilee, pageant, carnival, funfair; fund-raiser, charity event; Dutch & N. Amer. kermis.

fetid, foetid adjective *the air was heavy and fetid*: **stinking**, smelly, foul-smelling, evil-smelling, malodorous, stinking to high heaven, reeking, pungent, acrid, high, rank, foul, unpleasant, nasty, noxious; W. Indian fresh; informal stinky, reeky; Brit. informal niffing, niffy, pongy, whiffy, humming; N. Amer. informal funky; literary noisome, mephitic; rare miasmic, miasmal, olid.
▷ANTONYMS fragrant.

fetish noun **1** *he developed a rubber fetish*: **fixation**, sexual fixation, obsession, compulsion, mania; weakness, fancy, taste, fascination, craze, fad; French idée fixe; informal thing, hang-up.
2 *he worshipped an African fetish*: **juju**, talisman, charm, amulet; totem, icon, idol, image, effigy, doll, statue, figure, figurine; archaic periapt.

fetter verb **1** *the captive was branded and fettered*: **shackle**, manacle, handcuff, clap in irons, put in chains, chain (up), bind, tie (up), tether, rope, hobble; secure, restrain; informal cuff; rare enfetter, gyve.
2 *these obligations do not fetter the company's powers*: **restrict**, restrain, constrain, confine, limit; hinder, hamper, impede, obstruct, handicap, hamstring, encumber, inhibit, check, curb, tie down; tie someone's hands, cramp someone's style; literary trammel.

fetters plural noun *the prisoner lay bound with fetters of iron*: **shackles**, manacles, handcuffs, irons, leg irons, chains, bonds; tethers, ropes, restraints; informal cuffs, bracelets; archaic trammels, gyves, darbies, bilboes.

fettle noun *his best players were in fine fettle*: **shape**, trim, fitness, physical fitness, health, state of health; **condition**, form, repair, state of repair, state, order, working order, way; informal kilter; Brit. informal nick.

f

fetus, foetus noun *antibodies are passed via the placenta to the fetus*: **embryo**, fertilized egg, unborn baby, unborn child.

> *Word links* **fetus**
>
> **feticide** killing of a fetus

feud noun *a region riven by tribal feuds*: **vendetta**, conflict, war; rivalry, hostility, enmity, strife, discord, bad blood, animosity, antagonism, grudge, estrangement, schism; quarrel, argument, bickering, falling-out; archaic broil.
▸ verb *he feuded with management and teammates*: **quarrel**, fight, argue, bicker, squabble, dispute, clash, differ, be at odds, be at daggers drawn; wage war, take up arms; informal scrap, fall out, go at it hammer and tongs, fight like cat and dog.

fever noun **1** *he subsequently developed fever*: **feverishness**, high temperature, febricity, febrility; shivering; delirium; Medicine pyrexia; informal temperature, temp; rare calenture.
2 *Terry was in a fever of excitement*: **ferment**, frenzy, furore, ecstasy, rapture, hubbub, hurly-burly.
3 *World Cup football fever*: **excitement**, frenzy, agitation, turmoil, restlessness, unrest, passion.

> *Word links* **fever**
>
> **febrile** relating to fever
> **febriphobia** fear of fever
> **febrifuge** medicine for fever

fevered adjective **1** *Fernando soothed her fevered brow*: **feverish**, febrile, hot, burning, sweating; rare pyretic.
2 *a lunatic with a fevered imagination*: **excited**, agitated, energetic, frenzied, overwrought, frantic, worked up, fervid.

feverish adjective **1** *she's really sick and feverish*: **febrile**, fevered, with a high temperature, hot, burning, sweating; shivering; delirious; informal with a temperature; rare pyretic.
2 *he was thrown into a state of feverish excitement*: **frenzied**, frenetic, hectic, agitated, excited, restless, nervous, worked up, overwrought, frantic, furious, distracted, hysterical, wild, manic, maniacal, like one possessed; uncontrolled, unrestrained; informal in a tizzy.
▷ANTONYMS calm.

few determiner *police are revealing few details about the victim*: **not many**, hardly any, scarcely any; a small number of, a small amount of, a small quantity of, one or two, a handful of, a sprinkling of; little; informal a couple of.
▷ANTONYMS many.
▸ adjective *though the car parks are few, they are strategically placed*: **scarce**, scant, scanty, meagre, insufficient, negligible, in short supply; thin on the ground, scattered, seldom met with, few and far between, infrequent, uncommon, rare, sporadic.
▷ANTONYMS many, plentiful.
▸ pronoun
□ **a few** *to a few, overcoming their fear of flying becomes a challenge*: **a small number**, a handful, a sprinkling, one or two, a couple, two or three; not many, hardly any.
▷ANTONYMS a lot.

> *Word links* **few**
>
> **oligo-** related prefix, as in *oligarch, oligosaccharide*

fiancée, fiancé noun *he went back to the valley to marry his fiancée*: **betrothed**, wife-to-be, husband-to-be, bride-to-be, future wife/husband, prospective wife/husband, prospective spouse; informal, dated intended.

fiasco noun *the whole thing was a total fiasco*: **failure**, disaster, catastrophe, debacle, shambles, farce, mess, wreck, ruin, ruination, blunder, botch, abortion; informal flop, washout, dud, hash, lead balloon, foul-up, screw-up; Brit. informal pig's ear, cock-up; N. Amer. informal snafu; Austral./NZ informal fizzer; vulgar slang fuck-up, balls-up.
▷ANTONYMS success.

fiat noun *a political union was imposed through imperial fiat*. See **decree** (sense 1 of the noun).

fib noun *you're telling a fib*: **lie**, untruth, falsehood, made-up story, trumped-up story, invention, fabrication, deception, piece of fiction, fiction, falsification, fairy story/tale, cock and bull story; (little) white lie, half-truth, exaggeration, departure from the truth; informal tall story, tall tale, whopper; Brit. rhyming slang pork pie, porky pie, porky; humorous terminological inexactitude.
▷ANTONYMS truth, fact.
▸ verb *she had bunked off school, fibbing about a sore throat*: **lie**, tell a fib, tell a lie, invent a story, make up a story, dissemble, dissimulate, pretend, depart from the truth; exaggerate, stretch the truth; pull the wool over someone's eyes, pull someone's leg; informal lie through one's teeth, con, kid; humorous be economical with the truth, tell a terminological inexactitude; vulgar slang bullshit.
▷ANTONYMS tell the truth.

fibre noun **1** *fibres from the murderer's jumper were found on the victim's body*: **thread**, strand, tendril, filament; technical fibril.
2 *designer clothing in natural fibres*: **material**, substance, cloth, fabric, stuff.
3 *a man with no fibre*. See **moral fibre**.
4 *a lack of fibre in his diet*: **roughage**, bulk, fibrous material.

fickle adjective *today's fickle fans demand instant success*: **capricious**, changeable, variable, volatile, mercurial, vacillating, fitful, irregular; inconstant, disloyal, undependable, unstable, unsteady, unfaithful, faithless; irresolute, flighty, giddy, skittish, erratic, impulsive; unpredictable, random; informal blowing hot and cold; technical **labile**; literary mutable.
▷ANTONYMS constant; stable.

> *Choose the right word* **fickle, inconstant, changeable, capricious**
>
> See **inconstant.**

fickleness noun *the fickleness of public taste*: **capriciousness**, changeability, variability, volatility, vacillation, fitfulness, irregularity, tendency to blow hot and cold; disloyalty, undependability, inconstancy, instability, unsteadiness, infidelity, unfaithfulness, faithlessness; irresolution, flightiness, giddiness, skittishness, impulsiveness; unpredictability, unpredictableness, randomness; technical lability; literary mutability.
▷ANTONYMS constancy, stability.

fiction noun **1** *the traditions of British fiction*: **novels**, stories, creative writing, imaginative writing, works of the imagination, prose literature, narration, story telling; romance, fable.
▷ANTONYMS non-fiction.
2 *the president dismissed the allegation as absolute fiction*: **fabrication**, invention, lies, fibs, concoction, untruth, falsehood, fantasy, fancy, illusion, sham, nonsense; vulgar slang bullshit; Austral./NZ vulgar slang **bulldust**.
▷ANTONYMS fact; truth.

fictional adjective *a fictional character*: **fictitious**, **invented**, imaginary, imagined, made up, make-believe, unreal, fabricated, concocted, devised, mythical, storybook, the product of someone's imagination.
▷ANTONYMS real; actual.

fictitious adjective **1** *police said the name was fictitious*: **false**, fake, counterfeit, fabricated, sham; untrue, bogus, spurious, assumed, affected, adopted, feigned, invented, made up, concocted, improvised; informal pretend, phoney; Brit. informal, dated cod.
▷ANTONYMS genuine.
2 *a fictitious character*: **fictional**, imaginary, imagined, invented, made up, make-believe, unreal, non-existent, mythical, storybook, apocryphal; fabricated, concocted, devised; the product of someone's imagination, a figment of someone's imagination.
▷ANTONYMS factual.

fiddle informal noun **1** *their feet moved in time with the fiddle*: **violin**, viola, cello, double bass; historical kit.
2 *the men were involved in a major VAT fiddle*: **fraud**, swindle, fix, wangle, confidence trick, ruse, wile, piece of deception, bit of sharp practice; informal racket, con trick, flimflam, sting.
▸ verb **1** *he **fiddled with** a beer mat*: **fidget**, play, toy, twiddle, fuss, fool about/around, trifle; finger, thumb, handle, feel, touch; waste time, act aimlessly; informal mess about/around, paw.
2 *he **fiddled with** some dials and buttons*: **tinker**, play about/around, tamper, meddle, interfere, monkey; adjust.
3 *the government is trying to fiddle the figures*: **falsify**, manipulate, massage, rig, distort, pervert, misrepresent, juggle, doctor, alter, tamper with, interfere with; informal cook, fix, diddle, finagle, flimflam, cook the books.

fiddling adjective *fiddling little details*: **trivial**, petty, trifling, insignificant, unimportant, inconsequential, inconsiderable, negligible, paltry, footling, minor, small, slight, incidental, of little/no account; informal piddling, piffling, penny-ante; Brit. informal twopenny-halfpenny; N. Amer. informal nickel-and-dime, picayune; N. Amer. vulgar slang chickenshit.
▷ANTONYMS important; large.

fidelity noun **1** *she was never tempted to stray from fidelity to her husband*: **faithfulness**, loyalty, constancy; devotedness, devotion, commitment, adherence; true-heartedness, trustworthiness, trustiness, honesty, dependability, reliability; monogamy; archaic troth.
▷ANTONYMS disloyalty; infidelity.
2 *fidelity to your king*: **loyalty**, allegiance, obedience, constancy, fealty, homage; staunchness, fastness.
3 *the fidelity of the reproduction*: **accuracy**, exactness, exactitude, precision, preciseness, correctness, scrupulousness; strictness, closeness, faithfulness, correspondence, literalness, conformity; realism, verisimilitude, veracity,

authenticity, naturalism.
▷ANTONYMS inaccuracy.

fidget verb **1** *the audience had begun to fidget | she fidgeted with her scarf*: **move restlessly**, wriggle, squirm, twitch, jiggle, writhe, twist, shuffle, be jittery, be anxious, be agitated; play, fuss, toy, twiddle, fool about/around, trifle; informal fiddle, mess about/around, have ants in one's pants.
▷ANTONYMS sit still, be at ease.
2 *she seemed to fidget him*: **make uneasy**, worry, agitate, bother, upset, ruffle.
▶noun **1** *he disturbed other people with convulsive fidgets*: **twitch**, wriggle, squirm, jiggle, shuffle, tic, spasm, shudder.
2 *what a fidget you are!* **restless person**, bundle of nerves; informal cat on hot bricks, cat on a hot tin roof.
3 (**the fidgets**) *that woman gives me the fidgets*: **restlessness**, nervousness, fidgetiness, unease, uneasiness; informal the jitters, twitchiness.

fidgety adjective *I get a bit fidgety around females*: **restless**, restive, on edge, uneasy, nervous, keyed up, anxious, agitated, discomposed; jumpy, shaky, quivering; Brit. nervy; informal jittery, like a cat on hot bricks, twitchy.
▷ANTONYMS calm; still.

field noun **1** *a large ploughed field*: **meadow**, pasture, paddock, green, pen, grassland, pastureland, sward; park; N. Amer. corral; Irish & Canadian bawn; literary glebe, lea, mead, greensward.
2 *a football field*: **pitch**, ground, sports field, playing field, recreation ground, arena; stadium; Brit. informal park.
3 *a pioneer in the field of biotechnology*: **area**, **sphere**, area of activity, discipline, province, department, domain, sector, line, branch, subject, speciality, specialty, specialization, specialism; French métier, forte; informal scene, bailiwick, pigeon.
4 *you can't see events out of your field of vision*: **scope**, range, sweep, reach, extent, purview; limits, confines, parameters, bounds, horizons.
5 *her superb technique means she is head and shoulders ahead of the field*: **competitors**, entrants, competition, runners; applicants, candidates, possibles, possibilities, hopefuls.
▶verb **1** *she could field a ball with the best of the boys*: **catch**, stop, retrieve; **return**, throw back.
2 *they should have been kicked out of the competition for fielding an ineligible player*: **put in the team**, send out, play, put up.
3 *they can field an army of about one million*: **deploy**, position, post, station, range, dispose.
4 *he fielded a battery of awkward questions*: **deal with**, handle, cope with, answer, reply to, respond to, react to; parry, deflect, turn aside, evade, sidestep, avoid, dodge, answer evasively, fend off; informal duck.
▶adjective **1** *he has field experience in educational research*: **practical**, hands-on, applied, actual, active, experiential, empirical, in the field, non-theoretical; rare empiric.
▷ANTONYMS theoretical.
2 *field artillery*: **mobile**, portable, transportable, movable, manoeuvrable, light, lightweight; rare portative.
▷ANTONYMS heavy.

fiend noun **1** *a fiend had taken possession of him*: **demon**, devil, evil spirit, imp, bogie; incubus, succubus; hellhound; informal spook; rare cacodemon.
2 *a fiend bent on global evil-doing*: **brute**, beast, villain, barbarian, monster, ogre, sadist, evil-doer; informal baddy, swine; archaic blackguard.
3 informal *a drug fiend*: **addict**, abuser, user; informal junkie, ...head/freak.
4 informal *I'm a fiend for Mexican food*: **enthusiast**, fanatic, maniac, addict; devotee, fan, lover, follower; aficionado, connoisseur, appreciator; informal buff, freak, nut, ham, sucker, great one.

fiendish adjective **1** *a fiendish torturer*: **wicked**, cruel, vicious, evil, nefarious, unspeakable; brutal, brutish, savage, barbaric, barbarous, beastly, inhuman, murderous, bloodthirsty, ferocious; ruthless, heartless, pitiless, merciless, black-hearted, unfeeling; malevolent, malicious, villainous, malignant, devilish, diabolical, hellish, demonic, satanic, Mephistophelian, ungodly; odious, base; archaic or humorous dastardly.
2 *a fiendish plot*: **cunning**, clever, ingenious, artful, crafty, canny, wily, guileful, devious, scheming, shrewd, astute, sharp, sharp-witted, imaginative; informal foxy, savvy, sneaky, cute; Scottish & N. English informal pawky; S. African informal slim; rare vulpine, carny.
3 *a fiendish puzzle*: **difficult**, complex, complicated, intricate, involved, knotty, thorny, ticklish, abstruse, impenetrable, unfathomable; challenging, puzzling, baffling, perplexing, bemusing; frustrating.

fierce adjective **1** *a fierce black mastiff*: **ferocious**, savage, vicious; wild, feral, untamed, undomesticated; aggressive, bloodthirsty, dangerous; cruel, brutal, murderous; menacing, threatening, terrible, grim.
▷ANTONYMS gentle; tame.
2 *they are facing fierce competition from American firms*: **aggressive**, cut-throat, competitive; keen, intense, strong, relentless.
▷ANTONYMS mild.
3 *a fierce, murderous jealousy lanced through Meredith*: **intense**, powerful, vehement, passionate, impassioned, fervent, fervid, fiery, flaming, ardent, uncontrolled, immoderate, intemperate, inordinate.
▷ANTONYMS mild.
4 *a fierce wind coming in off the sea*: **powerful**, strong, violent, forceful, bitter; stormy, blustery, gusty, boisterous, tempestuous, raging, furious, turbulent, tumultuous, cyclonic, typhonic; destructive, devastating.
▷ANTONYMS gentle.
5 *a fierce pain shot between his eyes*: **severe**, extreme, intense, acute, grave, very bad, awful, dreadful, grievous; excruciating, agonizing, torturous, tormenting, piercing, penetrating, harrowing.
▷ANTONYMS mild.

fiery adjective **1** *the fiery breath of dragons*: **burning**, blazing, flaming, raging; on fire, ablaze, afire, lighted, lit; incandescent, red-hot, scorching.
2 *she had blushed a fiery red*: **bright**, brilliant, vivid, vibrant, intense, deep, rich, strong, bold.
3 *her fiery spirit*: **passionate**, impassioned, ardent, fervent, fervid, lively, zealous, spirited; uncontrollable, ungovernable; quick-tempered, ill-tempered, bad-tempered, volatile, explosive, angry, heated, aggressive, determined, resolute.
▷ANTONYMS bland, indifferent.

fiesta noun *a five-day fiesta*: **festival**, carnival, holiday, celebration, party.

fight verb **1** *he saw two men fighting*: **brawl**, come to blows, exchange blows, attack/assault each other, hit/punch each other; box; struggle, grapple, wrestle, scrimmage; do battle, engage in conflict, contend; spar, joust, tilt, cross swords, lock horns, lock antlers; informal scrap, have a dust-up, have a set-to; Brit. informal have a punch-up; Scottish informal swedge; N. Amer. informal rough-house; Austral./NZ informal stoush, go the knuckle.
2 *Edward went to fight in the First World War*: **battle**, do battle, give battle, wage war, go to war, make war, take up arms; attack, mount an attack; combat, engage, meet, clash, skirmish; be a soldier, fight for Queen/King and country; crusade.
3 *a war fought for freedom*: **engage in**, wage, conduct, prosecute, carry on, pursue, undertake, practise, proceed with, go on with.
4 *she and her sister are always fighting*: **quarrel**, argue, row, bicker, squabble, have a row/fight, wrangle, dispute, be at odds, disagree, fail to agree, differ, be at variance, have words, bandy words, be at each other's throfats, be at loggerheads; battle, feud; informal fall out, scrap, go at it hammer and tongs, fight like cat and dog, argufy; archaic altercate, chop logic; Scottish archaic threap.
5 *the firemen fought the blaze*: **try to extinguish**, try to put out.
6 *textile workers fought against further wage reductions*: **campaign**, strive, battle, struggle, contend, grapple, war, crusade, agitate; speak, lobby; work, push, press.
7 *party leaders warned that they would fight the decision*: **oppose**, contest, contend with, confront, challenge, combat, dispute, object to, quarrel with, argue against/with; withstand, resist, defy, fly in the face of; strive/struggle against, take a stand against, put up a fight against, stand up and be countecatd against, take issue with, question; rare controvert.
▷ANTONYMS accept, support.
8 *Donaldson fought the urge to put his tongue out*: **repress**, restrain, suppress, stifle, smother, hold back, keep back, fight back, keep in check, check, curb, contain, control, keep under control, rein in, silence, muffle, bottle up, choke back, swallow, strangle, gag; informal button up, keep the lid on, cork up.
▷ANTONYMS give in to.
□ **fight back 1** *use your pent-up anger to fight back*: **retaliate**, counterattack, strike back, hit back, reply, respond, react, reciprocate, return fire, give tit for tat, give as good as one gets, return the compliment, defend oneself, put up a fight, return like for like, get back at someone, give someone a dose/taste of their own medicine; formal requite something; archaic serve someone out, give someone a Roland for an Oliver.
▷ANTONYMS turn the other cheek.
2 *she had to fight back tears of frustration*: **repress**, restrain, suppress, stifle, smother, hold back, keep back, keep in check, check, curb, contain, control, keep under control, rein in, silence, muffle, bottle up, choke back, swallow, strangle, gag; informal button up, keep the lid on, cork up.
▷ANTONYMS give in to, let out.
□ **fight for** *a militant who fought for the rights of all workers*: **champion**, promote, advocate, plead for, defend, protect, uphold, support, back, espouse, stand up for, campaign for, lobby for, battle for, crusade for, take up the cudgels for.
□ **fight like cat and dog** (or **like cats and dogs**) informal *we are both extremely volatile and have always fought like cat and dog*. See **fight** (sense 4 of the verb).
□ **fight someone/something off** *he fought off a bull terrier that attacked his dog*: **repel**, repulse, beat off, stave off, ward off, hold off, fend off, keep/hold at bay, drive away/back, force back, beat back, push back, resist.
□ **fight shy of** *some people fight shy of taking out a personal loan*: **flinch from**, demur from, recoil from, hang back from; have scruples about, scruple about, have misgivings about, have qualms about, be averse to, be chary of, not be in favour of, be against, be opposed to, be diffident about, be bashful about, be shy about, be coy about; be loath to, scruple to, be reluctant to, be unwilling to, be disinclined to, not be in the mood to, be indisposed to, be slow to, be hesitant to, be afraid to, hesitate to, hate to, not like to, not have the heart to, drag one's feet/heels over, waver

about, vacillate about, think twice about, baulk at, quail at, mind doing something; informal be cagey about, boggle at; archaic disrelish.

▶ noun 1 *he'd got into a fight outside a club*: **brawl**, fracas, melee, row, rumpus, confrontation, skirmish, sparring match, exchange, struggle, tussle, scuffle, altercation, wrangle, scrum, clash, disturbance; fisticuffs, rough and tumble; Irish, N. Amer., & Austral. donnybrook; informal scrap, dust-up, set-to, shindy, shindig, free-for-all; Brit. informal punch-up, bust-up, ruck, bit of argy-bargy, barney; Scottish informal rammy, swedge, square go; N. Amer. informal rough house, brannigan; Austral./NZ informal stoush; Law, dated affray; rare broil, bagarre.
2 *a heavyweight championship fight*: **boxing match**, bout, match, meeting, fixture, game, encounter.
3 *Britain might have given up her fight against Germany*: **battle**, engagement, clash, conflict, contest, encounter; skirmish, scuffle, tussle, struggle, brush, exchange; war, campaign, crusade, warfare, combat, action, hostilities.
4 *I just had a fight with my girlfriend*: **argument**, quarrel, squabble, row, wrangle, disagreement, difference of opinion, falling-out, contretemps, tangle, altercation, fracas; dispute, disputation, contention; feud; informal tiff, set-to, shindig, shindy, stand-up, run-in, spat, scrap, ruction; Brit. informal slanging match, barney, bunfight, ding-dong, bust-up, ruck.
5 *their fight for control of the company*: **struggle**, battle, campaign, endeavour, drive, push, effort, movement, move.
6 *she had no fight left in her*: **will to resist**, power to resist, resistance, morale, spirit, courage, pluck, pluckiness, gameness, will to win, strength, backbone, spine, mettle, stout-heartedness, determination, firmness of purpose, resolution, resolve, resoluteness, confidence; **aggression**, aggressiveness, belligerence, militancy, boldness, audacity, forcefulness; informal guts, grit, spunk; Brit. informal bottle; N. Amer. informal sand, moxie.

fightback noun Brit. *Hibs mounted a spirited fightback*: **counterattack**, counteroffensive; rally, recovery, recuperation, resurgence, revival, rebound; informal comeback.

fighter noun 1 *a guerrilla fighter*: **soldier**, fighting man, fighting woman, warrior, combatant, serviceman, servicewoman, trooper; in the US GI, enlisted man; Brit. informal squaddie; archaic man-at-arms.
2 *the bout ends when a fighter is knocked to the ground*: **boxer**, pugilist, prizefighter; wrestler, grappler; contestant, contender, competitor; informal champ, bruiser, scrapper, pug.
3 *he was shot down by enemy fighters*: **warplane**, armed aircraft.

fighting adjective *Hugh was a fighting man*: **violent**, combative, aggressive, pugnacious, truculent, belligerent, bellicose, disputatious, antagonistic, argumentative, hawkish.
▷ANTONYMS peaceful.
▶ noun *more than 200 were injured in the fighting*: **violence**, hostilities, conflict, combat; warfare, war, battles, skirmishing, affray, rioting; bloodshed, slaughter, slaying, killing, carnage, butchery, massacre, murder, bloodletting; informal action.
▷ANTONYMS peace.
□ **fighting fit** *I should be fighting fit at the start of next season*. See **fit**[1] (sense 4 of the adjective).

figment noun *all this nonsense about ghosts is just a* ***figment of her imagination***: **invention**, production, creation, concoction, fabrication; hallucination, illusion, delusion, mirage, apparition, chimera, fancy, fiction, fable, falsehood, imagining, vision.

figurative adjective *a figurative expression*: **metaphorical**, non-literal, symbolic, allegorical, representative, emblematic; imaginative, fanciful, poetic, ornate, literary, flowery, florid; rare tropical, parabolic.
▷ANTONYMS literal.

figure noun 1 *the production figure is down 27 per cent*: **statistic**, number, integer, quantity, amount, level, total, sum; (**figures**) data, information, particulars.
2 *the second figure was a nine*: **digit**, numeral, numerical symbol, character; rare cipher.
3 *he can't put a figure on how much this is going to cost*: **price**, cost, amount, quantity, value, valuation, quotation, quote, rate; total, sum, aggregate; informal, humorous damage.
4 (**figures**) *I'm good at figures*: **arithmetic**, mathematics, sums, calculations, reckoning, computation, numbers, statistics, counting; Brit. informal maths; N. Amer. informal math.
5 *her petite, curvaceous figure*: **physique**, build, frame, body, proportions, torso, shape, form, stature; informal vital statistics, chassis, bod.
6 *a dark figure emerged from the shadows*: **silhouette**, outline, shape, form, profile, shadow.
7 *a figure of authority*: **person**, personage, individual, man, woman, character, personality, presence; representative, embodiment, personification, epitome, symbol, representation, exemplification, exemplar.
8 *the show features life-size figures*: **human representation**, image of a person, effigy; likeness.
9 *the figure that is formed when a smaller square is cut out of a large square*: **shape**, pattern, design, motif, device, depiction.
10 *this structure is shown in figure 4*: **diagram**, illustration, drawing, picture, plate, graphic, sketch, chart, plan, map.
▶ verb 1 *an awesome beast who figured in Egyptian legend*: **feature**, appear, be featured/mentioned, be referred to; participate, play a part, play a role, be conspicuous, have prominence, have a place; star.
2 *a way to figure the values*: **calculate**, work out, total, sum, reckon, compute, enumerate, determine, evaluate, quantify, assess, count, add up, put a figure on, tally, totalize, gauge; Brit. tot up; rare cast.
3 N. Amer. informal *I figured that I didn't have much of a chance*: **suppose**, think, believe, fancy, consider, expect, take it, suspect, have a sneaking suspicion, sense; assume, dare say, conclude, take it as read, presume, be of the opinion, trust; deduce, infer, gather, glean, divine; N. Amer. guess.
4 N. Amer. informal *'Rosemary's away.' 'That figures.'*: **make sense**, be understandable, seem reasonable, stand to reason, be to be expected, be logical, follow, add up, stand up, hold up; ring true, be convincing; be likely/probable, go without saying.
□ **figure on** N. Amer. informal *I figured on starting the day with a good breakfast*: **plan on**, calculate on, count on, rely on, bank on, bargain on, depend on, pin one's hopes on; anticipate, expect to, take for granted, take as read.
□ **figure something out** informal *he tried to figure out how to switch on the lamp*: **work out**, make out, fathom, reason, puzzle out, decipher, solve, ascertain, make sense of, think out, think through, get to the bottom of, find an answer/solution to, unravel, untangle; understand, comprehend, see, grasp, get the hang of, get the drift of; calculate, compute, reckon, assess; informal make head or tail of, twig, crack; Brit. informal suss out.

figurehead noun 1 *the president was just a figurehead*: **titular head**, nominal leader, leader in name only, front man, cipher, token, mouthpiece, puppet, instrument, man of straw.
2 *the figurehead on the Cutty Sark*: **carving**, bust, sculpture, image, statue.

filament noun *a network of lace-like filaments*: **fibre**, thread, strand, tendril; string, wire, cable, cord; technical fibril, cilium.

filch verb informal *she had filched a bottle of claret*. See **steal** (sense 1 of the verb).

file[1] noun 1 *he opened the file and began to read*: **folder**, portfolio, binder, box, document case; filing cabinet.
2 *we maintain files on all the major companies*: **dossier**, document, record, report, case history, case study; (**files**) data, information, particulars, case notes, documentation, annals, archives.
3 *when saving a file the summary information menu may be displayed*: **batch of data**, document, text; program.
▶ verb 1 *make sure that this material is filed in such a way that it is easy to find*: **categorize**, classify, organize, put in place, put in order, order, arrange, catalogue, tabulate, index, pigeonhole; put on record, record, enter, store, log, archive.
2 *Debbie has filed for divorce*: **apply**, put in, register, sign up, ask.
3 *two women have filed a civil suit against him*: **bring**, press, lodge, place, lay, prefer, put forward, present, submit.

file[2] noun *a file of boys in football kit making their way along the path*: **line**, column, row, string, chain, queue, procession, train, convoy, caravan; Brit. informal crocodile.
▶ verb *we filed out into the car park*: **walk in a line**, proceed in a line, march, parade, troop, pass in formation.

file[3] verb *when I have nothing else to do I file my nails*: **smooth**, buff, rub, rub down, polish, burnish, furbish; shape, refine; scrape, abrade, rasp, sandpaper.

filial adjective *a display of filial affection*: **dutiful**, devoted, loyal, faithful, compliant, respectful, dedicated, affectionate, loving; **befitting a son or daughter**, familial.

filibuster noun *many hours in committee characterized by filibuster and slow progress*: **delaying tactics**, stonewalling, procrastination, obstruction, delaying, blocking, hold-up; informal speechifying, speechification.
▶ verb *it is an abuse of the house for the opposition to filibuster*: **waste time**, stall, play for time, stonewall, procrastinate, buy time, employ delaying tactics; obstruct, delay, block; speak/talk at length, speak/talk on and on; informal speechify.

filigree noun *a bench decorated with gold filigree*: **wirework**, fretwork, fret, latticework, lattice, grillwork, scrollwork, lacework, lace, tracery.

fill verb 1 *he filled a bowl with breakfast cereal | his eyes filled*: **make/become full**, fill up, fill to the brim, fill to overflowing, top up, charge, load (up), pack.
▷ANTONYMS empty.
2 *guests filled the parlour*: **crowd**, throng, pack (into), jam, occupy all of, press into, squeeze into, cram (into); overcrowd, congest, overfill.
3 *he began filling his shelves with a selection of beers*: **stock**, pack, load; supply, furnish, provide, replenish, restock, refill.
4 *fill all the holes with a wood-repair compound*: **block up**, bung up, stop (up), plug, seal, caulk, close, clog (up), choke, obstruct, occlude, dam up.
▷ANTONYMS unblock, open.
5 *the perfume filled the room*: **pervade**, spread throughout/through, permeate, suffuse, be diffused through, diffuse through, imbue, penetrate,

pass through, infuse, perfuse, extend throughout, be disseminated through, flow through, run through, saturate, impregnate.
6 *he was going to fill a government post*: **occupy**, hold, take up, be in, have; informal hold down.
7 *we filled a big order for a Yorkshire company*: **carry out**, complete, fulfil, execute, perform, implement, discharge, bring about; rare effectuate.
□ **fill in** *I'm going to fill in for Jim on the project*: **substitute**, deputize, stand in, cover, provide cover, take over, act, act as deputy, act as stand-in, sit in, act as understudy, understudy, be a proxy, act as locum tenens; take the place of; informal sub, fill someone's shoes/boots, step into someone's shoes/boots; N. Amer. informal pinch-hit.
□ **fill someone in** *Iain filled me in on the essential details*: **inform of**, advise of, tell about, notify of, acquaint with, apprise of, brief on, enlighten about, update with, bring up to date about, make conversant with, report to about; informal put wise about, put in the picture about, clue in about, bring up to speed on, tip off about.
□ **fill something in** Brit. *he filled in all the forms*: **complete**, answer, fill up; N. Amer. fill out.
□ **fill out** *she had filled out a little since Sarah had last seen her*: **grow fatter**, become plumper, become rounder, flesh out, put on weight, gain weight, get heavier.
□ **fill something out 1** *this account needs to be filled out by detailed evidence from local studies*: **expand**, enlarge, add to, round out, elaborate, add substance/detail to, flesh out, add flesh to, put flesh on the bones of; supplement, reinforce, extend, broaden, develop, amplify. **2** N. Amer. *he filled out the requisite forms*. See **fill something in**.
▶ **noun**
□ **one's fill** *I've eaten my fill*: **enough**, sufficient, plenty, ample, as much as necessary, all one wants, a sufficiency, an abundance, as much as one can take, more than enough.

filling noun *filling for cushions and mattresses*: **stuffing**, padding, wadding, filler, quilting, cushioning, lining, packing.
▶ **adjective** *a cheap but filling meal*: **substantial**, hearty, ample, abundant, solid, nutritious, nourishing, satisfying, square; heavy, stodgy, starchy, leaden.

fillip noun *they are reducing their lending rates to give a fillip to the housing market*: **stimulus**, stimulation, stimulant, boost, encouragement, incitement, incentive, impetus, inducement, motivation; tonic, uplift, lift, reviver, spur, goad, prod, push, prompt, aid, help; informal shot in the arm, pick-me-up.
▷**ANTONYMS** curb.

film noun **1** *there was a film of sweat on his face*: **layer**, coat, coating, covering, cover, surface, sheet, patina, blanket, dusting, skin, overlay, screen, mask, wash, glaze, varnish, veneer, veil.
2 *Emma was watching a film*: **movie**, picture, feature, feature film; programme, broadcast, transmission; N. Amer. motion picture; dated moving picture; informal flick, pic, vid; dated, informal talkie.
3 *she would like to work in film*: **cinema**, movies, the pictures.
▶ **verb 1** *he immediately filmed the next scene*: **record on film**, shoot, record, take pictures of, make a film of, capture on film, video, photograph.
2 *the book was filmed in 1983*: **adapt for film**, make into a film.
3 *his eyes had filmed over*: **cloud**, mist, fog, haze; become blurred, blur, dull; archaic blear.

Word links **film**
cinematographic relating to film

film star noun *a Hollywood film star*: **actor**, **actress**, film actor/actress, leading man, leading woman, leading lady, lead, principal, performer, starlet; **celebrity**, celebutante, star, famous actor/actress, personality, household name, superstar; N. Amer. movie star; informal celeb; dated matinee idol; Brit. informal luvvie.

filmy adjective *a filmy black blouse*: **diaphanous**, transparent, see-through, translucent, sheer, gauzelike, gauzy, gossamer, gossamery, cobwebby, shimmering; delicate, fine, ultra-fine, light, thin, airy, floaty, wispy, silky; fragile, flimsy, unsubstantial, insubstantial.
▷**ANTONYMS** thick, coarse, opaque.

filter noun *pass the water through a carbon filter*: **strainer**, sifter; sieve, riddle, colander; gauze, netting.
▶ **verb 1** *the farmers filter the water*: **sieve**, strain, sift, filtrate, riddle; clarify, purify, clear, clean, make pure, refine, treat, process, decontaminate.
2 *the rain had succeeded in filtering through her jacket*: **seep**, percolate, leak, trickle, ooze, dribble, bleed, flow; drain, well, exude, escape, leach.

filth noun **1** *he grew up among the filth of the coal mines and steel mills*: **dirt**, muck, grime, mud, mire, sludge, slime, ooze, foul matter; excrement, excreta, dung, manure, ordure, sewage; rubbish, refuse, garbage, trash, dross, scum; pollution, contamination, defilement, decay, putrefaction, putrescence; squalor, squalidness, sordidness, shabbiness, sleaziness, filthiness, uncleanness, foulness, nastiness; informal crud, grot, gunge, grunge, yuck.
2 *I felt sick to my stomach after reading that filth*: **pornography**, pornographic literature/films/videos, dirty books, smut, vice; obscenity, indecency, corruption, lewdness, rudeness, vulgarity, coarseness, crudeness, grossness, vileness, nastiness, immorality; informal porn, hard porn, soft porn, porno, raunchiness.

filthy adjective **1** *the room was filthy*: **dirty**, mucky, grimy, muddy, murky, slimy, unclean; foul, squalid, sordid, shabby, sleazy, nasty, soiled, sullied, scummy; polluted, contaminated, unhygienic, unsanitary; rotten, defiled, decaying, putrid, putrefied, smelly, fetid, faecal; informal cruddy, grungy, yucky; Brit. informal grotty; literary befouled, besmirched, begrimed; rare feculent.
▷**ANTONYMS** clean.
2 *his face was filthy*: **unwashed**, unclean, dirty, grimy, dirt-encrusted, smeared, smeary, grubby, muddy, mucky, black, blackened, begrimed, stained, unkempt.
▷**ANTONYMS** clean, scrubbed.
3 *she told filthy jokes*: **obscene**, indecent, dirty, smutty, rude, improper, corrupt, coarse, bawdy, unrefined, indelicate, vulgar, lewd, racy, raw, off colour, earthy, ribald, risqué, licentious, 'adult'; vile, depraved, foul, impure, offensive, prurient, salacious, pornographic, explicit, foul-mouthed; informal blue, raunchy, near the knuckle/bone, nudge-nudge, porn, porno, X-rated.
▷**ANTONYMS** clean, polite.
4 *you filthy brute!* **despicable**, contemptible, nasty, low, base, mean, vile, disgusting, unpleasant, obnoxious, wretched, shabby, sordid; informal dirty, dirty rotten, low-down, no-good, beastly, lousy.
5 *he was in a filthy mood*: **bad**, foul, unpleasant, bad-tempered, ill-tempered, irritable, grumpy, grouchy, cantankerous, curmudgeonly, aggressive, cross, fractious, peevish, short-tempered, hot-tempered, quick-tempered; informal snappish, snappy, chippy, on a short fuse, short-fused; Brit. informal shirty, stroppy, narky, ratty; N. Amer. informal cranky, ornery, peckish, soreheaded; informal, dated waxy, miffy.
▷**ANTONYMS** good.
▶ **adverb** *he wants to be filthy rich*: **very**, extremely, tremendously, immensely, vastly, hugely, remarkably; disgustingly, excessively, exceedingly, abominably, revoltingly; informal stinking, terrifically, awfully, terribly, madly, seriously, mega, ultra, damn, damned, too ... for words.

Word toolkit

filthy	grubby	grimy
water	little hands	windows
habit	paws	floors
streets	mitts	mirror
animals	fingernails	pots and pans
conditions	children	dishes

final adjective **1** *their final year of study*: **last**, closing, concluding, finishing, end, ending, terminating, terminal, culminating, ultimate, eventual, endmost.
▷**ANTONYMS** first, initial.
2 *the experts' decisions are final*: **irrevocable**, unalterable, absolute, conclusive, irrefutable, incontrovertible, indisputable, unappealable, unchallengeable, binding; decisive, definitive, definite, settled, determinate, ultimate.
▷**ANTONYMS** provisional.
▶ **noun** *the FA Cup final*: **decider**, final game/match.
▷**ANTONYMS** qualifier.

Word toolkit

final	irrevocable	conclusive
decision	damage	evidence
score	undertaking	proof
analysis	divorce	results
word	loss	data
version	changes	argument
outcome	step	research

finale noun *the work ends with an elaborate finale*: **climax**, culmination; end, ending, finish, close, conclusion, termination, resolution; denouement, last act, final scene, final curtain, epilogue, coda, peroration; informal wind-up.
▷**ANTONYMS** beginning.

finality noun *'No,' she said with finality*: **conclusiveness**, decisiveness, decision, definiteness, definitiveness, absoluteness, completeness; irrevocability, irrefutability, incontrovertibility, unalterableness; certainty, certitude, sureness, fixedness.
▷**ANTONYMS** indecision.

finalize verb *the two countries had yet to finalize a peace treaty*: **conclude**, complete, bring to a conclusion, clinch, settle, establish, work out, resolve, decide, secure, tie up, wrap up, put the finishing touches to, set the seal on, seal, confirm; negotiate, broker, reach (an) agreement on, agree on, come to terms on, reach terms on, shake hands on; informal sew up, wind up, polish off, put the icing on the cake, thrash out, hammer out.

finally adverb **1** *she finally got her man to the altar*: **eventually**, ultimately, in the end, by and by, at length, after a long time, after some time; at last, at long last, in the long run, when all was said and done, in the fullness of time; Brit. informal at the end of the day.
▷ANTONYMS immediately.
2 *finally, wrap the ribbon round the edge of the board*: **lastly**, last, in conclusion, to conclude, in closing, to end, last but not least.
▷ANTONYMS firstly, initially.
3 *this should finally dispel the belief that the auditors are clients of the company*: **conclusively**, irrevocably, decisively, definitively, definitely, absolutely, for ever, for good, for all time, once and for all, permanently.
▷ANTONYMS temporarily.

finance noun **1** *the job taught him a great deal about finance*: **financial affairs**, **money matters**, pecuniary matters, fiscal matters, economics, money management, commerce, business, investment, banking, accounting.
2 *companies seeking short-term finance*: **funds**, assets, money, capital, resources, cash, wealth, reserves, wherewithal, revenue, income, stock; funding, backing, subsidy, sponsorship; (**finances**) financial condition/state, cash flow, budget.
▶ verb *the project was financed by grants*: **fund**, pay for, back, capitalize, provide capital/security for, endow, subsidize, invest in; underwrite, guarantee, furnish credit for, sponsor, act as guarantor of, support; informal foot the bill for, pick up the tab for; N. Amer. bankroll.

Word links **finance**
fiscal relating to finance

financial adjective *a major financial institution*: **monetary**, money, economic, pecuniary, banking, commercial, business, investment, accounting, fiscal, budgetary.

financier noun *a corporate financier*: **investor**, speculator, banker, capitalist, industrialist, tycoon, magnate, business person, businessman, businesswoman, stockbroker; informal money man.

find verb **1** *I found a book on dreams in the library*: **locate**, spot, pinpoint, unearth, obtain, detect, put one's finger on; search out, nose out, track down, dig up, hunt out, root out, sniff out, smell out; **come across**, chance on, light on, happen on, stumble on, hit on, encounter, run across, run into, come upon; informal bump into; literary espy, descry.
2 *he claims to have found a cure for rabies*: **discover**, think of, invent, come up with, hit on, turn up, bring to light, uncover, unearth, ferret out.
3 *the police found her purse*: **retrieve**, recover, get back, regain, repossess, recoup, recuperate, reclaim.
▷ANTONYMS lose.
4 *I hope you find peace*: **obtain**, acquire, get, procure, come by, secure, gain, earn, achieve, attain, lay hold of, come to have, win; informal bag, wangle, swing, land, get one's hands/mitts on, get hold of.
5 *I found the courage to speak*: **summon (up)**, gather, muster (up), screw up, command, call up, rally.
6 (**be found**) *caffeine is found in coffee and tea*: **be present**, occur, exist, be met with, be existent, appear, show itself, manifest itself, be; rare obtain.
7 *you'll find that many lively towns are but a short drive away*: **discover**, become aware, realize, observe, notice, note, perceive, learn, detect.
8 *I respect their decision, but I find it strange*: **consider**, think, believe to be, hold to be, feel to be, look on as, view as, see as, take to be, take for, judge, deem, gauge, rate, regard as, reckon, suppose, account, interpret as, esteem.
9 *he was found guilty of driving without due care and attention*: **judge**, adjudge, adjudicate, deem, rule, hold, consider, count, rate, reckon, see as; declare, determine, pronounce.
10 *she knew the barb had found its mark*: **arrive at**, reach, attain, gain, achieve, hit, strike.
□ **find one's feet** *a new arrival trying to find his feet at a big club*: **adapt**, become accustomed, adjust, get used, become acclimatized, orient oneself, habituate oneself, assimilate.
□ **find something out** *I found out that my husband was having an affair | he found out the truth*: **discover**, become aware, learn, detect, discern, perceive, observe, notice, note, get/come to know, work out, deduce, fathom out, realize; bring to light, reveal, expose, unearth, disclose, lay bare, unmask, ferret out, dig out/up; establish, determine, make certain of, pin down, grasp; informal figure out, get a fix on, latch on to, cotton on to, catch on to, tumble to, rumble, get the picture, get the message, get the drift, get wise; Brit. informal twig, suss; N. Amer. informal savvy; rare cognize.
▶ noun **1** *this exciting find dates from the second century*: **discovery**, acquisition, asset; unearthing, uncovering.
2 *this table is a real find for anyone who's short of space*: **good buy**, bargain; godsend, boon, windfall.

finding noun **1** *the finding of the leak*: **discovery**, location, locating, detection, detecting, uncovering, unearthing.
2 (often **findings**) *he appealed against the tribunal's findings*: **conclusion**, result; **decision**, verdict, pronouncement, judgement, ruling, rule, decree, order, recommendation, resolution; Law determination; N. Amer. resolve.

fine[1] adjective **1** *fine wines | a fine collection of furniture*: **excellent**, first-class, first-rate, great, exceptional, outstanding, admirable, quality, superior, splendid, magnificent, beautiful, exquisite, choice, select, prime, supreme, superb, wonderful, sublime, superlative, very good, of high quality, of a high standard, second to none, top, rare; informal A1, top-notch, splendiferous, stellar; N. Amer. informal dandy; Brit. informal, dated top-hole.
▷ANTONYMS poor.
2 *he proposed marriage to a fine lady*: **worthy**, admirable, praiseworthy, laudable, estimable, upright, upstanding, respectable, seemly, ladylike, gentlemanly; attractive, good-looking, handsome, lovely, pretty, striking, stunning, delightful, well favoured; Scottish & N. English bonny; archaic comely, fair.
3 *the advertising initiative is fine, but it's not enough on its own*: **all right**, acceptable, suitable, good, good enough, agreeable, fair, passable, satisfactory, adequate, reasonable, up to scratch, up to the mark, up to standard, up to par, average, tolerable; informal OK, tickety-boo.
▷ANTONYMS unsatisfactory.
4 *I feel fine*: **in good health**, well, healthy, all right, fit, fighting fit, as fit as a fiddle, as fit as a flea, robust, strong, vigorous, blooming, thriving, in good shape, in good condition, in fine fettle; informal OK, in the pink, up to snuff.
▷ANTONYMS ill.
5 *it was a fine day*: **fair**, dry, bright, clear, sunny, sunshiny, cloudless, unclouded, without a cloud in the sky, warm, balmy, summery, clement, agreeable, pleasant, nice, benign.
▷ANTONYMS inclement.
6 *a fine old eighteenth-century house*: **impressive**, imposing, dignified, striking, splendid, grand, majestic, magnificent, august, lofty, stately.
7 *she went out to show off her fine clothes*: **elegant**, stylish, graceful, expensive, smart, chic, fashionable, modish, high fashion; fancy, luxurious, sumptuous, lavish, opulent, grand, plush, exquisite; informal flashy, flash, snazzy, snappy, swanky, ritzy, sharp.
8 *he has a fine mind*: **keen**, **quick**, alert, acute, sharp, bright, brilliant, astute, clever, intelligent, perspicacious, finely honed, penetrating.
▷ANTONYMS slow.
9 *a fine china tea service*: **delicate**, fragile, frail, breakable, dainty, insubstantial; formal frangible.
▷ANTONYMS coarse.
10 *her fine golden hair*: **thin**, light, delicate, wispy, floaty, flyaway, feathery.
▷ANTONYMS thick.
11 *she sharpened her pencil to a fine point*: **sharp**, keen, acute, sharpened, honed, razor-sharp, razor-like, whetted; narrow, slender, slim, thin.
▷ANTONYMS blunt, thick.
12 *the fine material of her nightdress*: **sheer**, light, lightweight, thin, flimsy, ultra-fine, insubstantial; diaphanous, filmy, chiffony, gossamer, gossamery, wispy, silky, gauzelike, gauzy, cobwebby, shimmering, transparent, translucent, see-through, airy, ethereal.
▷ANTONYMS coarse, thick.
13 *a fine gold chain*: **pure**, sterling, solid, refined, unadulterated, unalloyed, unmixed, unblended, unpolluted, uncontaminated, one hundred per cent, flawless, perfect.
▷ANTONYMS plated, alloyed.
14 *a beach of fine sand*: **fine-grained**, powdery, dusty, chalky, floury, powdered, ground, granulated, crushed, pulverized; technical comminuted, triturated; archaic pulverulent, levigated.
▷ANTONYMS coarse.
15 *for fine detailed work you could use a smaller brush*: **intricate**, delicate, detailed, minute, elaborate, ornate, dainty, meticulous, painstaking.
16 *there is a fine distinction between the two*: **subtle**, fine-drawn, ultra-fine, precise, minute, nice, narrow, tenuous; hair-splitting, elusive, abstruse, overnice.
17 *you have no respect for people's finer feelings*: **elevated**, lofty, exalted, high, grand, sublime; **refined**, cultivated, cultured, civilized, distinguished, sophisticated.
▷ANTONYMS base.
18 *there's no better gift you could choose to show your fine taste*: **discerning**, discriminating, tasteful, refined, sensitive, cultivated, cultured, fastidious, particular, critical, intelligent, stylish; rare discriminative.
▷ANTONYMS vulgar.
▶ adverb informal *you're doing fine*: **well**, all right, not badly, satisfactorily, in a satisfactory manner/way, adequately, nicely, tolerably, suitably, aptly, appropriately; informal OK, good.
▷ANTONYMS badly.

fine[2] noun *if convicted they face heavy fines*: **financial penalty**, punishment, forfeit, forfeiture, sanction, punitive action, penalty, fee, charge, penance; (**fines**) damages; formal mulct; Brit. historical amercement.
▶ verb *they were fined for breaking environmental laws*: **penalize**, punish by fining, impose a fine on, exact a penalty from, charge; informal sting; formal mulct; Brit. historical amerce.

finery noun *she was in all her bridal finery*: **regalia**, elaborate/best clothes, garb, best, Sunday best; splendour, showiness, gaudiness, trumpery, frippery, adornment, trappings, decorations; informal glad rags, best gear, best bib and tucker, clobber; formal apparel; rare fallalery.
▷ANTONYMS rags.

finesse noun **1** *the comedy is performed with masterly finesse*: **skill**, subtlety, expertise, flair, knack, panache, dash, flourish, elan, polish, adroitness, skilfulness, adeptness, artistry, art, artfulness, virtuosity, mastery, genius; informal know-how.
2 *these decisions call for a little delicacy and a modicum of finesse*: **tact**, tactfulness, discretion, diplomacy, delicacy, sensitivity, discernment, perceptiveness, prudence, judgement, consideration; refinement, grace, elegance, sophistication, wisdom, worldly wisdom; French savoir faire.
3 *he won by a clever finesse*: **winning move**, trick, stratagem, ruse, manoeuvre, scheme, artifice, machination, bluff, wile; informal dodge.
▶ **verb** *he could hardly finesse his way out of a serious downturn*: **bluff**, manoeuvre, cheat, evade, trick, feign.

finger noun **1** *he wagged his finger at her*: **digit**; thumb, index finger, forefinger, first finger, middle finger, ring finger, little finger; N. Amer. pinkie.
2 *a dark finger of land*: **strip**, rectangle, sliver, streak, pencil.
□ **all fingers and thumbs** Brit. informal See **thumb** (noun).
▶ **verb 1** *she fingered her brooch uneasily*: **touch**, feel, handle, manipulate, stroke, rub, caress, fondle, toy with, play (about/around) with, fiddle with, twiddle with, maul, meddle with, manhandle, pull, grab; put one's hands on, lay a finger on; informal paw, mess.
2 N. Amer. informal *any seasoned thriller addict will immediately finger the culprit*: **identify**, recognize, single out, pick out, spot, choose, select, point out; inform on, denounce; informal point the finger at, grass on, rat on, squeal on, tell tales about, tell on, blow the whistle on, spill the beans about, sell down the river, snitch on, peach.

Word links **finger**

digital relating to fingers

finicky adjective *these intellectuals with their fancy words and finicky manners*: **fussy**, fastidious, punctilious, over-particular, hard to please, overcritical, difficult, awkward, exacting, demanding, perfectionist; informal picky, choosy, pernickety; N. Amer. informal persnickety; archaic nice.

Word toolkit

finicky	fastidious	exacting
eater	attention	standards
customer	detail	task
appetite	art	specifications
tastes	care	schedule
child	grooming	process

finish verb **1** *Mrs Porter had just finished the task*: **complete**, end, conclude, close, bring to a conclusion, bring to an end, bring to a close, consummate, finalize, bring to fruition; crown, cap, set the seal on, round off, put the finishing touches to; stop, cease, terminate; accomplish, execute, discharge, carry out, deal with, do, get done, fulfil; informal wind up, wrap up, sew up, polish off, knock off.
▷ANTONYMS start; leave unfinished.
2 *Hitch finished his dinner and got up*: **consume**, eat, devour, drink, finish off, polish off, gulp (down), guzzle, quaff; use, use up, exhaust, empty, deplete, drain, expend, dispatch, dispose of, get through, go through, run through; informal down.
▷ANTONYMS start; leave unfinished.
3 *when the programme has finished it displays the 'Press any key' message*: **end**, come to an end, stop, conclude, come to a conclusion/end/close, cease, terminate; informal wind up.
▷ANTONYMS start, begin.
4 *some items were finished in a black lacquer*: **varnish**, lacquer, veneer, coat, stain, wax, shellac, enamel, put a finish on, glaze, give a shine to, gloss, polish, burnish, smooth off.
5 *she went to Switzerland to finish her education*: **perfect**, polish, refine, put the final/finishing touches to, crown.
□ **finish someone/something off 1** *the executioners finished them off with bayonets*: **kill**, cause the death of, take/end the life of, destroy, execute, annihilate, exterminate, liquidate, put an end to, do away with, dispose of, get rid of, eradicate, deliver the coup de grâce to; informal wipe out, do in, bump off, polish off, knock off, top, take out, croak, stiff, blow away; N. Amer. informal ice, off, rub out, waste, whack. **2** *financial difficulties finished off the business*: **overpower**, overwhelm, overcome, defeat, get the better of, best, worst, rout, conquer, bring down; informal drive to the wall.
▶ **noun 1** *a party to celebrate the finish of filming*: **end**, ending, completion, conclusion, close, closing, cessation, finalization, termination; final part, final stage, final act, finale, denouement, last stages; accomplishment, execution, fulfilment, realization, achievement, consummation, resolution, fruition; informal winding up, wind-up, sewing up, polishing off.
▷ANTONYMS start; beginning.
2 *it was a real gallop to the finish*: **finishing line**, finishing post, tape, end point.
3 *this furniture has a mellow antiquated paint finish*: **veneer**, lacquer, lamination, coating, covering, coat; **surface**, texture, grain; glaze, lustre, gloss, polish, shine, patina.

finished adjective **1** *he looked approvingly at the finished job*: **completed**, concluded, consummated, finalized, terminated, over and done with, over, in the past, at an end; accomplished, executed, discharged, done with, done, fulfilled, settled; achieved, attained, realized; informal wound up, wrapped up, sewn up, polished off, knocked off; rare effectuated.
▷ANTONYMS unfinished, incomplete.
2 *a finished performance*: **accomplished**, polished, flawless, faultless, perfect; expert, proficient, masterly, impeccable, classic, virtuoso, consummate, skilful, skilled, dexterous, adroit, professional, talented, gifted, elegant, graceful.
▷ANTONYMS crude.
3 *he was old and almost finished*: **ruined**, doomed, lost, bankrupt, wrecked, broken, defeated, beaten, thwarted; at an end, gone, gone to the wall, over with; informal washed up, over the hill, past it, played out, through, toast.

finite adjective *there is a finite amount of water in the system*: **limited**, not infinite, subject to limitations, restricted; definable, defined, determinate, fixed; bounded, terminable; delimited, demarcated.
▷ANTONYMS infinite.

fire noun **1** *a fire broke out in the kitchen*: **blaze**, conflagration, inferno, holocaust, firestorm; flames, burning, combustion.
2 *he turned on the electric fire*: **heater**, radiator, convector.
3 *he lacked fire and animation*: **dynamism**, energy, vigour, animation, vitality, vibrancy, exuberance, ebullience, zest, elan; passion, ardour, impetuosity, intensity, zeal, spirit, life, liveliness, verve, vivacity, vivaciousness; sparkle, scintillation, dash; enthusiasm, eagerness, gusto; fervour, fervency, force, potency, vehemence; inspiration, imagination, creativity, inventiveness, flair; informal pep, vim, zing, go, get-up-and-go, oomph, pizzazz.
4 *rapid machine-gun fire*: **gunfire**, firing, sniping, flak, bombardment; fusillade, volley, barrage, salvo, cannonade.
5 *journalists would be better off directing their fire at the prime minister*: **criticism**, censure, condemnation, castigation, denunciation, opprobrium, admonishments, vituperation, scolding, chiding; disapproval, hostility, antagonism, animosity, ill will, enmity; informal flak, brickbats, knocks, raps.
□ **catch fire** *the driver got out before the car caught fire*: **ignite**, catch light, burst into flames, go up in flames, begin to burn.
□ **on fire 1** *the restaurant was on fire*: **burning**, ablaze, blazing, aflame, in flames, flaming, raging, fiery; alight, lit, lighted, ignited; literary afire. **2** *she was on fire with passion*: **ardent**, passionate, fervent, intense, excited, aflutter; eager, enthusiastic.
▶ **verb 1** *howitzers that fired shells in a high arc*: **launch**, shoot, discharge, eject, hurl, throw, send flying, let fly with, loose off, shy, send; N. Amer. informal pop.
2 *someone fired a gun at me*: **shoot**, discharge, let off, trigger, set off, blast; let fly with.
3 informal *he was fired for serious misconduct*: **dismiss**, discharge, give someone their notice, make redundant, lay off, let go, throw out, get rid of, oust, depose; Military cashier; informal sack, give the sack to, axe, kick out, boot out, give someone the boot, give someone the bullet, give someone the (old) heave-ho, give someone the elbow, give someone the push, give someone their marching orders, show someone the door; Brit. informal give someone their cards.
4 *the engine fired and she put her foot down*: **ignite**, start, catch, get started, get going.
5 archaic *I fired the straw*: **light**, ignite, kindle, set fire to, set on fire, set alight, set ablaze, put a match to, touch off, spark off, incinerate; informal torch; literary enkindle, inflame.
▷ANTONYMS put out.
6 *she fired my imagination with her tales of warfare and terror*: **stimulate**, stir up, excite, enliven, awaken, arouse, rouse, draw/call forth, bring out, engender, evoke, inflame, put/breathe life into, animate; inspire, motivate, quicken, incite, drive, impel, spur on, galvanize, electrify, trigger, impassion.
▷ANTONYMS deaden.
□ **fire up 1** *the entrepreneurial spirit that fired him up seventeen years ago*: **activate**, motivate, stimulate, actuate, move, drive, rouse, stir, stir up, arouse, energize, animate, fire; prompt, incite, spark off, influence, impel, spur on, urge, goad. **2** *derby games invariably fire up the supporters*: **stir up**, rouse, excite, galvanize, electrify, stimulate, inspire, move, fire the enthusiasm of, fire the imagination of, get going, whip up, inflame, agitate, goad, provoke, spur on, urge, encourage, animate, incite, egg on; N. Amer. light a fire under; rare inspirit.

Word links **fire**

pyro- related prefix, as in *pyroclastic*
pyrophobia fear of fire
pyromania obsession with fire

firearm noun **gun**, weapon; informal shooter, cannon; N. Amer. informal heater, piece, gat, rod, roscoe, shooting iron.

Word links **firearm**

gunsmith seller of firearms

firebrand noun *a political firebrand*: **radical**, revolutionary; **troublemaker**, agitator, rabble-rouser, demagogue, soapbox orator, incendiary, subversive; informal tub-thumper.

f

fireproof adjective *he wore fireproof overalls*: **non-flammable**, non-inflammable, incombustible, unburnable, fire resistant, flame resistant, flame retardant, heatproof.
▷ANTONYMS flammable, inflammable.

fireworks plural noun **1** *many people watch fireworks at organized displays*: **pyrotechnics**, explosions, illuminations; French feu d'artifice.
2 *there have been times when his stubbornness has produced some fireworks*: **uproar**, trouble, mayhem, fuss; tantrums, hysterics, paroxysms; rage, fit, outburst, frenzy, row.

firm[1] adjective **1** *the ground is fairly firm*: **hard**, solid, unyielding, resistant; solidified, hardened; compacted, compressed, condensed, dense, close-grained; stiff, rigid, inflexible, inelastic; congealed, frozen, set, gelled; stony, steely; literary adamantine.
▷ANTONYMS soft, yielding.
2 *no building can stand without firm foundations*: **secure**, secured, stable, steady, strong, sturdy, fixed, fast, set, taut, established, tight; immovable, irremovable, unshakeable; stationary, motionless; anchored, moored, rooted, embedded; riveted, braced, cemented, nailed, tied.
▷ANTONYMS unstable.
3 *a firm handshake*: **strong**, vigorous, sturdy, robust, forceful.
▷ANTONYMS limp.
4 *I was very firm about what I wanted to do | he was a firm supporter of the National Democratic Party*: **resolute**, determined, decided, resolved, steadfast; adamant, assertive, emphatic, insistent, single-minded, in earnest, whole-hearted; unfaltering, unwavering, unflinching, unswerving, unyielding, unbending, inflexible, obdurate, obstinate, stubborn, intransigent; implacable, relentless, unrelenting, hard-line, strict, unmalleable; strong-willed, dominant, domineering; committed, dyed-in-the-wool, through-and-through, seasoned, hardened.
▷ANTONYMS irresolute.
5 *she became a firm friend of the couple*: **close**, good, boon, intimate, confidential, inseparable, dear, special, fast, valued, treasured, cherished; **constant**, enduring, abiding, devoted, loving, faithful, durable, reliable, deep-rooted, long-standing, long-lasting, steady, steadfast, stable, staunch.
▷ANTONYMS distant.
6 *she had no firm plans for the next day*: **definite**, fixed, settled, decided, established, confirmed, agreed, exact, clear-cut, concrete, hard and fast; unalterable, unchangeable, irreversible, writ in stone.
▷ANTONYMS indefinite.

firm[2] noun *a law firm*: **company**, business, concern, enterprise, venture, undertaking, house, establishment, organization, corporation, conglomerate, franchise, cooperative, office, bureau, service, agency, practice, partnership, consortium, syndicate; informal outfit, set-up, shop.

firmament noun (**the firmament**) literary **the sky**, heaven, the blue, the wide blue yonder, the azure, the heavens, the skies; literary the vault (of heaven), the celestial sphere, the empyrean, the welkin.

first adjective **1** *the first chapter of Genesis*: **earliest**, initial, opening, introductory, original.
▷ANTONYMS last, closing.
2 *the management decided to start from first principles*: **fundamental**, basic, rudimentary, primary, beginning, elemental, underlying, basal, foundation; key, cardinal, central, chief, vital, essential.
▷ANTONYMS developed.
3 *his first priority would be law and order*: **foremost**, principal, highest, greatest, paramount, top, topmost, utmost, uppermost, prime, chief, leading, main, major; pre-eminent, overriding, outstanding, supreme, premier, predominant, prevailing, most important, of greatest importance, of prime importance; vital, key, essential, crucial, central, core, focal, pivotal, dominant; ruling, head; informal number-one.
▷ANTONYMS last.
4 *he is hoping to win the £3,000 first prize*: **top**, best, prime, premier, superlative; winner's, winning, champion.
▶ adverb **1** *they went back to the room they had first entered*: **at first**, to begin with, at the beginning/start, first of all, at the outset, initially.
2 *she would eat first, she decided*: **before anything else**, first and foremost, firstly, in the first place; without further ado, now.
▷ANTONYMS last.
3 *she longed to go abroad, but not at this man's expense—she'd die first!* **in preference**, more willingly, sooner, rather.
▶ noun **1** *from the first, surrealism was theatrical*: **the beginning**, the very beginning, the start, the outset, the commencement; informal the word go, square one, the off.
▷ANTONYMS the end.
2 informal *we travelled by air, a first for both of us*: **novelty**, new experience, first experience, first occurrence, unusual event; informal a turn-up for the books.

Word links **first**

proto-: *prototype, protohuman*, **ur-:** *urtext* related prefixes

first-class adjective *a first-class hotel*: **superior**, first-rate, high-quality, top-quality, top, top-tier, quality, high-grade, five-star, fine; prime, premier, premium, grade A, best, finest, select, of the first water; exclusive, elite, special; excellent, exceptional, exemplary, superlative, superb; French par excellence; informal tip-top, A1, top-notch, stellar, plum.
▷ANTONYMS poor.

first-hand adjective *they have first-hand experience of bringing up children*: **direct**, immediate, personal, unmediated, hands-on, experiential, empirical, from the original source.
▷ANTONYMS vicarious, indirect.
▶ adverb *an event she witnessed first-hand*: **directly**, immediately, personally, at first hand, from the original source, with one's own eyes/ears.
▷ANTONYMS vicariously, indirectly.

first name noun *my first name's Gordon*: **forename**, Christian name, given name, baptismal name.
▷ANTONYMS surname.

first-rate adjective *they have done a first-rate job*: **top quality**, high quality, top grade, first class, second to none, top, five star, premier, premium, fine, grade A; superlative, excellent, superb, outstanding, exceptional, exemplary, marvellous, magnificent, admirable, very good, splendid; matchless, peerless, unparalleled; informal tip-top, top-notch, ace, A1, super, crack, great, terrific, tremendous, smashing, fantastic, stellar, sensational, fabulous, fab, out of this world, capital; Brit. informal brill, bosting; Brit. informal, dated spiffing, topping, top-hole, wizard.

fiscal adjective *the government's fiscal policies*: **tax**, budgetary, revenue; financial, economic, monetary, money, pecuniary, capital.

fish verb **1** *some people were fishing in the lake*: **go fishing**, angle, cast, trawl.
2 *she opened her handbag and fished for her purse*: **search**, delve, look, hunt, cast about/around/round; grope, ferret (about/around), root about/around, rummage (about/around/round), scrabble, fumble; seek, look high and low.
3 *I'm not fishing for compliments*: **try to get**, seek to obtain, solicit; make a bid, angle, aim, cast about/around/round, hope, look; informal be after.
□ **fish something out** *they fished him out of the water*: **pull out**, haul out, take out, bring out; remove, extricate, extract, retrieve; rescue from, save from.

Word links **fish**

ichthyo-, pisci- related prefixes
fry young fish
school, run collective noun
ichthyology study of fish
pisciculture, mariculture fish farming
piscivorous fish-eating
ichthyophobia fear of fish

fisherman noun **angler**; informal rod; archaic fisher; rare piscator, piscatorian.

fishing noun *they went to sea for a day's fishing*: **angling**, trawling, catching fish.

Word links **fishing**

halieutic relating to fishing

fishy adjective **1** *a fishy smell*: **fishlike**, piscine, of fish.
2 *she had round fishy eyes*: **expressionless**, inexpressive, vacant, deadpan; dull, lacklustre, wooden, glassy, glassy-eyed.
3 informal *there was something fishy about the whole set-up*: **suspicious**, questionable, dubious, doubtful, suspect; odd, queer, peculiar, strange, not quite right; mysterious, murky, dark, shifty, disreputable, underhand; informal funny, shady, crooked, bent, not kosher, off; Brit. informal dodgy; Austral./NZ informal shonky.
▷ANTONYMS honest, open.

fission noun *the fission of uranium atoms*: **splitting**, parting, division, dividing, cleaving, rupture, breaking, severance, separation, disjuncture; technical scission.
▷ANTONYMS fusion.

fissure noun *fissures in the ocean floor*: **opening**, crevice, crack, cleft, cranny, chink, slit, groove, gap, hole, breach, aperture, vent, interstice; crevasse, chasm, ravine, crater; break, fracture, fault, rift, rupture, split, rent, gash; technical scission, grike.

fist noun **clenched hand**; informal duke, meat hook, paw, mitt; Brit. informal bunch of fives; Scottish & N. English nieve.

fit[1] adjective **1** *the house is fit for human habitation | he is a fit subject for such a book*: **suitable**, good enough; relevant, pertinent, apt, appropriate, suited, apposite, apropos, -worthy; fitting, befitting, proper, due, seemly, decorous, decent, right, correct; French comme il faut; archaic meet.
▷ANTONYMS unfit, inappropriate.
2 *do you think you're fit to look after a child?* **competent**, **able**, capable; adequate, good enough, satisfactory, proficient; ready, prepared, qualified, trained, equipped, eligible, worthy; informal up to scratch.
▷ANTONYMS unfit, incapable.
3 informal *you look fit to commit murder!* **ready**, prepared, on the point of, set, all set, in a fit state, primed, disposed, likely, about; informal up for, geared up, psyched up.
4 *he looked tanned and fit*: **healthy**, well, in good health; **in good shape**, in shape, in good trim, in trim, in good condition, in tip-top condition, in fine fettle, fighting fit, as fit as a fiddle, as fit as a flea, as strong as an ox; strong, robust, hale and hearty, sturdy, hardy, stalwart, lusty, vigorous, sound; athletic, muscular, strapping, tough, powerful, rugged; informal right as rain, husky.
▷ANTONYMS unfit, unwell.
□ **fit to be tied** informal *I was fit to be tied, I was so mad*: **livid**, furious, angry, infuriated, irate, fuming, raging, seething, incensed, enraged, angered, beside oneself, wrathful, ireful, maddened, cross, annoyed, irritated, exasperated, indignant; informal mad, boiling, wild, hot under the collar, foaming at the mouth, steamed up.
▶ verb **1** *my overcoat should fit you | a gown that did not fit*: **be the right/correct size (for)**, be big/small enough (for), be the right shape (for); informal fit like a glove.
▷ANTONYMS be too big/small (for).
2 *it makes sense to have your carpet fitted professionally*: **lay**, put in place/position, position, place, fix, insert; arrange, adjust, shape.
3 *some cameras are fitted with a backlight button*: **equip**, provide, supply, fit out, rig out, furnish, outfit, endow.
4 *concrete slabs were fitted together | I could not see how to fit the various pieces of evidence together*: **join**, connect, put together, piece together, attach, unite, link, splice, fuse, weld.
5 *a sentence that fits his crimes*: **be appropriate to**, suit, correspond to; agree with, tally with, go with, be in agreement with, accord with, correlate to, be congruous with, be congruent with, concur with, dovetail with, conform to, be consonant with, match.
6 *an MSc fits the student for a professional career*: **qualify**, prepare, make ready, make suitable, prime, condition, train, coach, groom, tailor.
□ **fit in** *he made the effort to fit in with the locals*: **conform**, be in harmony, belong, blend in; accord, agree, concur, be in line; be assimilated into; match, square with; informal click.
□ **fit someone/something out/up** *the carriage was fitted out with everything they would need*: **equip**, provide, supply, furnish, kit out, rig out, outfit, accoutre, array, stock.
□ **fit someone up** Brit. informal *the security forces are trying to fit me up*: **falsely incriminate**, entrap, fabricate charges/evidence against; informal **frame**, set up.
▶ noun *the degree of fit between a school's philosophy and its classroom practice*: **correlation**, correspondence, agreement, consistency, equivalence, match, similarity, resemblance, comparability, compatibility, affinity, concurrence.

fit[2] noun **1** *an epileptic fit*: **convulsion**, spasm, paroxysm, seizure, attack; (**fits**) throes; Medicine ictus.
2 *a fit of the giggles | she had a coughing fit*: **outbreak**, outburst, burst, attack, bout, spell, eruption, explosion, flare-up, blow-up; rare access.
3 *my mother would have a fit if she heard that*: **tantrum**, fit of temper, outburst of anger, outburst of rage, frenzy, fury; informal paddy, state, stress; N. Amer. informal blowout, hissy fit; rare ebullition, boutade.
4 *she went walking when the fit took her*: **mood**, whim, fancy, impulse, caprice, urge, notion, whimsy; desire, wish, inclination, bent.
□ **in/by fits and starts** *he spoke in fits and starts*: **spasmodically**, intermittently, sporadically, erratically, irregularly, interruptedly, fitfully, haphazardly, on and off, off and on, now and then, now and again.
▷ANTONYMS steadily, regularly.

fitful adjective *I drifted off into a brief and fitful sleep*: **intermittent**, sporadic, spasmodic, broken, disturbed, disrupted, patchy, irregular; variable, uneven, unsettled, disconnected, unsteady, on and off, off and on; restless, sleepless, wakeful, insomniac, tossing and turning.
▷ANTONYMS constant.

fitfully adverb *I slept fitfully that night*: **intermittently**, sporadically, spasmodically, irregularly, patchily, discontinuously, erratically, in/by fits and starts, in snatches; variably, unevenly, disconnectedly, unsteadily, on and off, off and on.

fitness noun **1** *polo requires tremendous fitness*: **health**, strength, robustness, sturdiness, hardiness, vigour, lustiness, stalwartness; athleticism, toughness, ruggedness, physical fitness, muscularity, tone; **good health**, good condition, good shape, well-being; state of health, condition, shape, trim, fettle; informal huskiness; Brit. informal nick.
▷ANTONYMS unfitness.
2 *he was called before medical boards to assess his fitness for active service*: **suitability**, capability, competence, competency, proficiency, ability, aptitude; readiness, preparedness, qualification, eligibility, worthiness, appropriateness; adequacy.
▷ANTONYMS unfitness, unsuitability.

fitted adjective **1** *a fitted sheet*: **shaped**, contoured, fitting tightly/well; N. Amer. contour.
2 *a fitted wardrobe*: **built-in**, integral, integrated, incorporated; fixed, permanent.
3 *I don't think he was fitted for the job*: **suited**, well suited, right, suitable, ideal; equipped, fit, appropriate; informal cut out.
▷ANTONYMS unsuited.

fitting noun **1** *the centre light fitting*: **attachment**, connection, installation; part, piece, component, accessory.
2 (**fittings**) *a manufacturer of bathroom fittings*: **furnishings**, furniture, units, fixtures, fitments, equipment, appointments, accoutrements, appurtenances.
3 *the fitting of catalytic converters to vehicles*: **installation**, installing, install, putting in, fixing, placing, situating.
▶ adjective *his story provides a fitting conclusion for this book*: **apt**, **appropriate**, suitable, apposite; fit, proper, due, right, seemly, correct, becoming; convenient, expedient, opportune, felicitous, timely; French comme il faut; archaic meet.
▷ANTONYMS unsuitable.

> *Choose the right word* **fitting, appropriate, suitable, proper**
>
> See **appropriate**.

five cardinal number **quintet**, quintuplets; Poetry pentameter, cinquain; technical pentad; archaic quintain; rare quintuple, fivesome.

> *Word links* **five**
>
> **quin-**, **quinque-**, **penta-** related prefixes
> **quinary** relating to five
> **pentagon** five-sided figure
> **quinquennial** relating to five years
> **quincentenary** five-hundredth anniversary

fix verb **1** *twenty-five signs were fixed to lamp posts*: **fasten**, attach, affix, secure; make fast, join, connect, couple, link; install, implant, plant, embed, anchor; stick, glue, bond, cement; pin, nail, screw, bolt, clamp, clip; bind, tie, lash; establish, position, station, situate.
▷ANTONYMS remove.
2 *the words have remained fixed in my memory*: **stick**, lodge, implant, embed, anchor.
3 *Ben nodded, his eyes fixed on the ground*: **focus**, direct, level, point, rivet, train, turn; converge, zero in.
4 *modern television techniques of fixing human attention*: **attract**, draw; **hold**, grip, engage, captivate, absorb, rivet.
▷ANTONYMS lose.
5 *he fixed my washing machine*: **repair**, mend, patch up, put right, put to rights, set right, get working, make as good as new, see to; restore, restore to working order, remedy, rectify, put back together; overhaul, service, renovate, recondition, rehabilitate, rebuild, reconstruct, refit, adjust; N. English fettle.
▷ANTONYMS break, damage.
6 *James fixed it for his parents to watch the show from the wings*: **arrange**, organize, contrive, sort out, see to, see about; manage, engineer, orchestrate, find a way; informal swing, wangle, pull strings.
7 informal *Laura was fixing her hair*: **neaten**, arrange, put in order, adjust; style, groom, comb, brush, preen, primp, dress; informal do.
8 *Chris will fix supper*: **prepare**, cook, make, make ready, put together, get; informal rustle up, knock up.
9 *the committee will fix a date for a special meeting*: **decide on**, select, choose, resolve on; determine, arrive at, settle, set, finalize, arrange, prearrange, establish, allot, prescribe; designate, define, name, ordain, appoint, specify, stipulate.
10 *chemicals must be used to fix the dye*: **make permanent**, make fast, set.
11 informal *the fight was fixed*: **rig**, arrange fraudulently, prearrange/

predetermine the result of; tamper with, manipulate, manoeuvre, twist, influence; informal fiddle, set up.
12 informal *don't tell anybody what I said, or I'll fix you!* **revenge oneself on**, get one's revenge on, be revenged on, avenge oneself on, wreak vengeance on, take retribution on, get even with, give someone their just deserts, hit back at, get back at, settle the/a score with, settle accounts with, take reprisals against, punish, deal with; informal get one's own back on, pay someone back/out, give someone their comeuppance, sort someone out, settle someone's hash, cook someone's goose.
13 informal *two junkies looking for a place where they could fix*: **inject drugs**, take drugs; informal shoot up, mainline, get one's fix.
14 *the cat has been taken to the vet to be fixed*: **castrate**, neuter, geld, cut, emasculate; **spay**; desex, sterilize; N. Amer. & Austral. alter; informal doctor; rare evirate, caponize, eunuchize.
□ **fix someone up** *we need to get Dolly fixed up with a job*: **provide**, supply, furnish, accommodate, equip, endow.
□ **fix something up** *he fixed up a holiday in St Tropez*: **organize**, arrange, make arrangements for, plan, fix, sort out, see to, put together, see about; mastermind, choreograph, orchestrate.

f

▸ **noun** informal **1** *they got themselves into a bit of a fix*: **predicament**, plight, difficulty, difficult situation, awkward situation, spot of trouble, bit of bother, corner, ticklish/tricky situation, tight spot; muddle, mess, mare's nest; quandary, dilemma; dire straits; informal pickle, jam, hole, spot, scrape, bind, pinch, sticky situation, hot water, the soup.
2 *he needed his fix*: **dose**; informal hit, rush.
3 *I don't believe that there is a quick fix for the coal industry*: **solution**, answer, resolution, way out; remedy, antidote, cure, nostrum, panacea; informal magic bullet.
4 *the quiz was a complete fix*: **fraud**, swindle, pretence, hoax, trick, charade, sham; informal set-up, scam, con trick, fiddle, sting.

fixated adjective *she has for some time been **fixated on** photography*: **obsessed with**, preoccupied with/by, obsessive about, single-minded about, possessed by, gripped by, in the grip of; engrossed in, immersed in, taken up with, wrapped up in; devoted to, dedicated to; enthusiastic about, fanatical about; infatuated with, besotted with; focused, keen, hell-bent; informal hung up on, hooked on, gone on, wild on, nuts about, potty about, dotty about, crazy about.
▹ANTONYMS uninterested.

fixation noun *the modern **fixation on** fitness*: **obsession with**, preoccupation with, mania for; monomania, fetish, addiction, complex, neurosis, compulsion; French idée fixe; informal hang-up, thing, yen, rage, bug, craze, fad, bee in one's bonnet.

fixed adjective **1** *there are fixed ropes on the rock face*: **fastened**, secure, fast, firm, stable; rooted, riveted, moored, anchored, permanent.
▹ANTONYMS temporary.
2 *a contract for a fixed period of time*: **predetermined**, set, established, allotted, settled, prearranged, arranged, specified, decided, agreed, determined, confirmed, prescribed, decreed; definite, defined, explicit, express, precise, exact; not subject to change, inflexible, unalterable, unchangeable, irreversible, rigid, hard and fast, writ in stone.
▹ANTONYMS flexible.
3 *he stood watching with a fixed grin*: **insincere**, false, fake, vacuous; **emotionless**, lifeless, motionless.
▹ANTONYMS sincere.

fixture noun **1** *the hotel retains many of the original fixtures and fittings*: **fixed appliance**, attachment, installation, unit.
▹ANTONYMS movable.
2 Brit. *their first fixture of the season*: **match**, **race**, game, competition, contest, meet, meeting, encounter, sporting event.

fizz verb **1** *the mixture fizzed like mad*: **effervesce**, sparkle, bubble, froth, foam, seethe; literary roil, spume.
2 *all the screens were fizzing*: **crackle**, sputter, buzz, hiss, fizzle, crack.
▸ **noun 1** *this process puts the fizz in champagne*: **effervescence**, sparkle, fizziness, bubbles, bubbliness, gassiness, carbonation, aeration; froth, foam, lather, suds, head.
2 informal *they all had another glass of fizz*: **sparkling wine**, champagne; informal bubbly, champers, sparkler.
3 informal *their set is a little lacking in fizz*: **ebullience**, exuberance, liveliness, life, vivacity, animation, vigour, brio, energy, verve, dash, spirit, sparkle, enthusiasm, buoyancy, jauntiness, zest; informal pizzazz, pep, zing, zip, go, get-up-and-go, oomph.
4 *the fizz of the static*: **crackle**, crackling, buzz, buzzing, hiss, hissing, sizzle, sizzling, crack, sputter, white noise; Brit. informal zizz; literary bombination, susurration, susurrus; rare sibilation.

fizzle verb *the loudspeaker fizzled again*: **crackle**, sputter, buzz, hiss, crack; rare sibilate, crepitate.
□ **fizzle out** *their romance will just fizzle out*: **peter out**, die off, blow over, ease off, cool off, let up; tail off, taper off, trail away/off, wither away, grind to a halt; ebb, wane, wilt; come to nothing, fall through, come to grief; informal flop, fold; archaic remit.
▹ANTONYMS flourish.
▸ **noun 1** *the electric fizzle of the waves*: **hiss**, hissing, buzz, buzzing, crackle, crackling, sputter, sputtering, crack, cracking, white noise; Brit. informal zizz; literary bombination, susurration, susurrus; rare sibilation.
2 informal *we'll look ridiculous if the whole thing turns out to be a fizzle*: **failure**, fiasco, debacle, catastrophe, disaster, blunder; Brit. damp squib; informal flop, washout, let-down, botch, hash, foul-up, screw-up, dead loss, dead duck, lead balloon, lemon; Brit. informal cock-up, pig's ear; N. Amer. informal snafu, clinker; vulgar slang fuck-up, balls-up.
▹ANTONYMS success.

fizzy adjective *a fizzy drink*: **effervescent**, sparkling, carbonated, gassy, aerated, bubbly, bubbling, frothy, foaming; French mousseux, pétillant; Italian spumante, frizzante; German Schaum-, Perl-.
▹ANTONYMS still, flat.

flab noun informal *fight the flab with aerobic dance*: **fat**, fatty tissue, excessive weight, fatness, plumpness, bulk, fleshiness, flesh; paunch, pot belly, beer belly, beer gut; informal beef.

flabbergast verb informal *we were flabbergasted when we found out*: **astonish**, astound, amaze, surprise, startle, shock, take aback, take by surprise; dumbfound, strike dumb, render speechless, stun, stagger, stop someone in their tracks, take someone's breath away, confound, daze, overcome, overwhelm, nonplus, stupefy, disconcert, unsettle, bewilder; informal bowl over, knock for six, knock sideways, knock the stuffing out of, floor; Brit. informal gobsmack.

flabbiness noun informal *there was a little flabbiness in her lower belly*: **fat**, fatness, fleshiness, plumpness, chubbiness, portliness, rotundity, meatiness, obesity, corpulence, bloatedness, grossness; **softness**, looseness, flaccidity, slack, laxity, droopiness, sag, limpness; informal flab, blubber, tubbiness, beefiness, porkiness.
▹ANTONYMS leanness; firmness.

flabby adjective **1** *his flabby stomach*: **soft**, loose, flaccid, unfirm, yielding, slack, lax, out of tone, drooping, droopy, sagging, saggy, pendulous, limp.
▹ANTONYMS firm, taut.
2 *she was a flabby woman*: **fat**, fleshy, overweight, plump, chubby, portly, rotund, meaty, broad in the beam, of ample proportions, obese, corpulent, bloated, gross; informal blubbery, out of shape, tubby, roly-poly, beefy, porky, well padded, well covered, well upholstered; N. Amer. informal lard-assed.
▹ANTONYMS thin, lean.

flaccid adjective **1** *your muscles are sagging, they're flaccid*: **soft**, loose, flabby, unfirm, yielding, slack, lax, out of tone, toneless; drooping, droopy, sagging, saggy, pendulous, limp, floppy, wilting.
▹ANTONYMS firm, taut.
2 *his play seemed flaccid and lifeless*: **lacklustre**, ineffective, ineffectual, lifeless, listless, muted, spiritless, lustreless, uninspiring, apathetic, unanimated, tame; worthless, futile, fruitless.
▹ANTONYMS spirited.

flag[1] noun *the Irish flag*: **banner**, standard, ensign, pennant, pennon, banderole, streamer, jack; bunting; colours; symbol, emblem, representation, figure, image; Brit. pendant; Nautical burgee; in ancient Rome vexillum; rare gonfalon, guidon, labarum.
▸ **verb** *spelling checkers can flag words that are not in a dictionary*: **indicate**, identify, pick out, point out; mark, mark out, label, tab, tag, tick.
□ **flag someone/something down** *she flagged down a police car*: **hail**, wave down, signal to stop, gesture to stop, motion to stop, make a sign to; stop, halt, summon.

Word links **flag**

vexillary relating to flags
vexillology study of flags

flag[2] noun *the stone flags beneath his feet*. See **flagstone**.

flag[3] verb **1** *they were flagging as the finish came into sight*: **tire**, become fatigued, grow tired/weary, weaken, grow weak, lose (one's) strength/energy, falter, languish, wilt, droop, sag.
▹ANTONYMS revive.
2 *one's mental energy flags in the afternoon*: **fade**, fail, decline, deteriorate, wane, ebb, diminish, decrease, lessen, abate, dwindle, erode, recede, sink, slump, taper off; wither, melt away, peter out, die away, die down, die out, die off; informal go downhill.
▹ANTONYMS increase.

flagellate verb *he was constantly flagellating pupils*: **flog**, whip, beat, scourge, lash, birch, switch, tan, strap, belt, cane, thrash, leather, flail, flay, welt, horsewhip, tan/whip someone's hide, give someone a hiding, strike, hit, spank; informal beat the living daylights out of.

flagellation noun *the use of flagellation for discipline and pleasure*: **flogging**, whipping, beating, scourging, lashing, birching, switching, tanning, strapping, belting, caning, thrashing, flailing, flaying, welting, horsewhipping, spanking; sadomasochism (S & M, SM), algolagnia.

flagon noun *a flagon of mead*: **jug**, vessel, container, bottle, carafe, flask, decanter, mug, tankard, ewer, pitcher, crock, demijohn; dated seidel.

flagrant adjective *a flagrant disregard for human rights*: **blatant**, glaring, obvious, overt, evident, conspicuous; naked, barefaced, shameless, brazen, audacious, brass-necked; undisguised, unconcealed, patent, transparent, manifest, palpable; out and out, utter, complete; outrageous, scandalous, shocking, disgraceful, reprehensible, dreadful, terrible; gross, enormous, heinous, atrocious, monstrous, wicked, iniquitous, villainous; archaic arrant.
▷ANTONYMS unobtrusive; slight.

flagstone noun **paving slab**, paving stone, stone block, slab, flag, sett.

flail verb **1** *he fell headlong, his arms flailing*: **wave**, swing, thrash about, flap about, beat about, windmill, move erratically.
2 *I was flailing about in the water*: **flounder**, struggle, thrash, thresh, squirm, wriggle, writhe, twist, splash, stumble, blunder, fumble, wiggle, twitch.
3 *he flailed their shoulders with his cane*: **thrash**, beat, strike, batter, drub, flog, whip, lash, scourge, flay, flagellate, strap, switch, tan, cane, tan/whip someone's hide, give someone a hiding, beat the living daylights out of, clout, welt, belabour; informal wallop, whack, lam, give someone a (good) hiding, larrup.

flair noun **1** *an activist with a flair for publicity*: **aptitude**, talent, gift, knack, instinct, natural ability, ability, capability, capacity, faculty, facility, skill, bent, feel, genius.
▷ANTONYMS inability.
2 *she dressed with flair*: **style**, stylishness, panache, verve, dash, elan, finesse, poise, elegance, sparkle, brio; inventiveness, creativity; taste, good taste, discernment, discrimination; informal class, pizzazz.

flak noun *he has come in for a lot of flak from the press*: **criticism**, censure, disapproval, disapprobation, hostility, complaints; castigation, condemnation, denunciation; opprobrium, obloquy, calumny, calumniation, execration, excoriation, vilification, abuse, revilement, lambasting; informal brickbats, knocking, panning, slamming, tongue-lashing, a bad press; Brit. informal stick, verbal, slagging off.

flake[1] noun *flakes of pastry | soap flakes*: **sliver**, wafer, shaving, paring, peeling; chip, shard, scale, crumb, grain, speck, spillikin; fragment, scrap, shred, bit, particle; Scottish skelf; technical spall, lamina.
▶ verb *the paint on the door was flaking*: **peel off**, peel, chip, scale off, blister, come off, come off in layers; technical desquamate, exfoliate.

flake[2] verb
□ **flake out** informal *he flaked out on my bed*: **fall asleep**, go to sleep, drop off; collapse, drop, keel over; faint, pass out, lose consciousness, black out; informal conk out, go out, go out like a light, nod off; N. Amer. informal sack out, zone out; literary swoon.

flaky adjective *the door was covered with flaky green paint*: **flaking**, peeling, cracking, scaly, blistering; scabrous; technical desquamative, exfoliative, furfuraceous.

flamboyant adjective **1** *she was famed for her flamboyant personality*: **ostentatious**, exuberant, confident, lively, buoyant, animated, energetic, vibrant, vivacious, extravagant, theatrical, showy, swashbuckling, dashing, rakish; informal over the top (OTT), fancy-pants.
▷ANTONYMS modest, restrained.
2 *a flamboyant cravat*: **colourful**, brilliantly coloured, brightly coloured, bright, rich, vibrant, vivid; exciting, dazzling, eye-catching, bold, splendid, resplendent, glamorous; showy, gaudy, garish, lurid, loud, flashy, brash, ostentatious; informal jazzy; dated gay.
▷ANTONYMS dull, restrained.
3 *a flamboyant architectural style*: **elaborate**, ornate, fancy; baroque, rococo, arabesque.
▷ANTONYMS simple.

flame noun **1** (**flames**) *they could see flames shooting up into the air*: **fire**, blaze, conflagration, inferno, holocaust, firestorm.
2 (**flames**) *the flames of her anger*: **passion**, passionateness, warmth, ardour, fervour, fervency, fire, intensity, keenness; excitement, eagerness, enthusiasm.
3 informal *an old flame*: **sweetheart**, boyfriend, girlfriend, lover, love, partner, beloved, beau, darling, escort, suitor; Italian inamorato, inamorata; informal steady.
□ **in flames** *two ships are in flames*: **on fire**, burning, alight, flaming, blazing, raging, fiery, lit, lighted, ignited; literary afire.
▷ANTONYMS extinguished.
▶ verb **1** *logs crackled and flamed*: **burn**, blaze, be ablaze, be alight, be on fire, be in flames, be aflame; burst into flame, catch fire.
2 *pour the whisky over the lobster and flame it*: **ignite**, light, set light to, set fire to, set on fire, set alight, kindle, inflame, burn, touch off; informal set/put a match to.
▷ANTONYMS extinguish.
3 *the log flamed orange and pink behind the trees*: **glow**, shine, flash, beam, glare, sparkle.
4 *Erica's cheeks flamed*: **become red**, go red, blush, flush, redden, grow pink/crimson/scarlet, colour, glow, be suffused with colour.

flameproof adjective *flameproof gloves*: **non-flammable**, non-inflammable, flame-resistant, fire-resistant, flame-retardant, incombustible, uninflammable, unburnable.
▷ANTONYMS flammable.

flaming adjective **1** *a flaming bonfire*: **blazing**, ablaze, burning, on fire, afire, in flames, aflame; ignited, lit, lighted; fiery, red-hot, raging, flaring; glowing, flickering, smouldering.
▷ANTONYMS extinguished.
2 *she had green eyes and flaming hair*: **bright**, brilliant, vivid, flamboyant; **red**, reddish-orange, scarlet, crimson, ginger.
▷ANTONYMS dull.
3 *we had a flaming row*: **furious**, violent, vehement, frenzied, angry, incensed, passionate, raging.
▷ANTONYMS mild.
4 *a girl in a flaming temper*: **furious**, enraged, fuming, seething, incensed, infuriated, mad, angry, raging, wrathful, irate; informal livid, wild; Brit. informal, dated waxy.
▷ANTONYMS placid.
5 informal *where's that flaming ambulance?* **wretched**, unspeakable, rotten, hellish, cursed, accursed; informal **damned**, damnable, blasted, blessed, precious, confounded, infernal; Brit. informal flipping, blinking, blooming, bleeding, effing, chuffing; Brit. informal, dated bally, ruddy, deuced.

f

flammable adjective *hazardous commodities such as flammable liquids*: **inflammable**, burnable, combustible, incendiary, unstable; rare ignitable, deflagrable.
▷ANTONYMS non-flammable.

flank noun **1** *he touched the horse's flanks*: **side**, haunch, loin, quarter, thigh.
2 *the southern flank of the Eighth Army*: **side**, wing; face, aspect, facet.
▶ verb *the garden is flanked by two great rivers*: **edge**, bound, line, border, fringe, skirt, be situated along; surround, circle, ring, circumscribe.

flannel noun **1** Brit. *she dabbed her face with a cold flannel*: **facecloth**, cloth; N. Amer. washcloth, washrag; Austral. washer.
2 Brit. informal *don't accept any flannel from salespeople*: **smooth talk**, flattery, blarney, blandishments, honeyed words; prevarication, hedging, equivocation, evasion, doubletalk, doublespeak; nonsense, rubbish; informal **spiel**, soft soap, sweet talk, buttering up, weasel words, baloney, rot, waffle, hot air, poppycock, tripe, bosh, bunk; Irish informal codology; Austral./NZ informal guyver, smoodging.
▷ANTONYMS straight-talking.
▶ verb Brit. informal *she can tell if you're flannelling*: **use flattery**, talk blarney, flatter, pull the wool over someone's eyes; prevaricate, hedge, equivocate, be evasive, vacillate, blather, evade/dodge the issue, stall; Brit. hum and haw; informal waffle, shilly-shally, soft-soap, sweet-talk, butter someone up, pussyfoot around; N. Amer. informal fast-talk; rare tergiversate.

flap verb **1** *the mallards flapped their wings angrily*: **beat**, flutter, move up and down, agitate, wave, wag, waggle, shake, swing, twitch; thresh, thrash, flail; vibrate, quiver, tremble, oscillate.
2 *his shirt tails flapped in the breeze*: **flutter**, swing, sway, ripple, undulate, stir, shake, quiver, shiver, tremble, fly, blow.
3 informal *it was a deliberate ploy to make us flap*: **panic**, go into a panic, become flustered, be agitated, fuss; informal press the panic button, be in a state, be in a tizzy, be in a dither, be in a twitter.
▶ noun **1** *large pockets with buttoned flaps*: **fold**, overhang, overlap, covering; lappet, lap, tab.
2 *the surviving bird made a few final despairing flaps*: **flutter**, fluttering, beat, beating, waving, shaking, flailing.
3 *I'm in a frightful flap about leaving*: **panic**, fluster, state of panic/agitation; informal state, dither, twitter, blue funk, stew, tizz, tizzy, tiz-woz; N. Amer. informal twit.
4 informal *she created a flap when she came out with her controversial statement*: **fuss**, agitation, commotion, stir, hubbub, excitement, tumult, ado, storm, uproar, flurry; controversy, to-do, palaver, brouhaha, furore; informal ballyhoo, hoopla, hoo-ha, song and dance; Brit. informal carry-on, kerfuffle.

flare noun **1** *the flare of the match lit up his face*: **blaze**, flash, dazzle, glare, burst; unsteady flame, flicker, glimmer, shimmer, gleam.
2 *a helicopter spotted a flare set off by the crew*: **distress signal**, **rocket**, Very light, beacon, light, flashlight, signal.
3 *Kelly felt a flare of anger within her*: **burst**, rush, attack, eruption, explosion, bout, spasm; rare access.
4 *a skirt with a flare*: **widening**, spread.
▶ verb **1** *a match flared as he lit a cigarette*: **blaze**, flash, flare up, flame, burn unsteadily, burn violently, burn up; gleam, glow, glisten, sparkle, glitter, flicker, glimmer, scintillate.
2 *her nostrils flared*: **spread**, broaden, widen, get wider, expand, splay; dilate.
□ **flare up 1** *the wooden houses flared up like matchsticks*: **burn**, blaze, be ablaze, be alight, be on fire, be in flames, flame, be aflame; blaze up, burn up, go up, go up in flames; literary be afire; archaic be ardent. **2** *the injury flared up again at the end of the year*: **recur**, reoccur, reappear; **break out**, burst out, start suddenly, burst forth, erupt. **3** *I flared up at him right off*: **lose one's temper**, lose control, become enraged, go into a rage, fly into a temper/passion, boil over, boil over with rage, fire up, go berserk, throw a

tantrum, explode; informal blow one's top, fly off the handle, lose one's cool, get mad, go crazy, go wild, go bananas, hit the roof, go through the roof, go up the wall, see red, go off the deep end, blow a fuse/gasket, lose one's rag, go ape, burst a blood vessel, flip, flip one's lid, foam at the mouth, get all steamed up, get worked up, have a fit; Brit. informal go spare, go crackers, do one's nut, get one's knickers in a twist, throw a wobbly; N. Amer. informal flip one's wig, blow one's lid/stack, have a cow, go postal, have a conniption fit; vulgar slang go apeshit.
▷ANTONYMS keep one's temper, remain calm.

flash verb **1** *a torch flashed*: **light up**, shine, flare, blaze, glare, beam, gleam, glint, sparkle, spark, burn, fluoresce; **blink**, wink, flicker, shimmer, twinkle, glimmer, glisten, scintillate; literary glister, coruscate, fulgurate, effulge.
2 *the computer flashed the result on the scoreboard*: **display**, show, present, set forth, unveil.
3 informal *he was flashing all this money about in the pub*: **show off**, flaunt, flourish, display, exhibit, parade, brag about, exult in.
4 informal *he opened his coat and flashed at me*: **expose oneself**, show/display/reveal one's genitals, commit indecent exposure.
5 *racing cars flashed past*: **zoom**, streak, tear, shoot, dash, dart, fly, whistle, hurtle, rush, hurry, bolt, race, bound, speed, career, charge, hare, whizz, whoosh, buzz; informal scoot, skedaddle, belt, zap, zip, scorch; Brit. informal bomb, bucket, burn rubber, go like the clappers; N. Amer. informal barrel, lay rubber.
▸ **noun 1** *a flash of light*: **flare**, blaze, burst, glare, pulse, blast; gleam, glint, sparkle, flicker, shimmer, twinkle, glimmer; beam, shaft, ray, streak, bar, finger, stream.
2 *a basic uniform with no flashes*: **emblem**, insignia, badge, marking; patch, bright patch, streak, stripe, bar, chevron.
3 *a sudden flash of inspiration*: **burst**, outbreak, outburst, wave, rush, surge, stab, flush, blaze; sudden show, brief display/exhibition.
□ **in/like a flash** *it was all over in a flash*: **instantly**, suddenly, abruptly, immediately, instantaneously, all of a sudden; quickly, rapidly, swiftly, speedily, without delay; in an instant, in a moment, in a (split) second, in a minute, in a trice, like a shot, straight away, in a wink, in the blink of an eye, in the twinkling of an eye, in two shakes (of a lamb's tail), before you know it, on the double, at the speed of light, like an arrow from a bow; informal in a jiffy, before you can say Jack Robinson, double quick, in double quick time, p.d.q. (pretty damn quick), like (greased) lightning, at warp speed.
▷ANTONYMS eventually, slowly.
▸ **adjective** informal *a flash sports car*. See **flashy**.

flashy adjective *a flashy car*: **ostentatious**, showy, bold, flamboyant, conspicuous, obtrusive, extravagant, expensive, pretentious; vulgar, tasteless, in bad/poor taste, tawdry, brash, lurid, garish, loud, gaudy, crude, trashy; informal snazzy, nifty, fancy, swanky, flash, jazzy, glitzy, ritzy, tacky, fancy-pants, naff, kitsch, Brummagem; N. Amer. informal bling-bling.
▷ANTONYMS understated, tasteful.

flask noun *a flask of whisky*: **bottle**, container, vessel; hip flask, vacuum flask; trademark Thermos.

flat[1] adjective **1** *a flat surface*: **level**, horizontal, levelled; smooth, even, uniform, consistent, featureless, flush, plumb, regular, unvarying, continuous, unbroken, plane.
▷ANTONYMS vertical; bumpy.
2 *the sea was flat*: **calm**, still, tranquil, pacific, undisturbed, without waves, like a millpond; glassy, motionless, waveless, unagitated; literary stilly.
▷ANTONYMS choppy.
3 *a flat wooden box*: **shallow**, not deep, wide.
▷ANTONYMS deep.
4 *she put on some flat sandals*: **low**, low-heeled, heelless, without heels.
▷ANTONYMS high-heeled.
5 *his voice was flat and without expression*: **monotonous**, toneless, droning, boring, dull, tedious, uninteresting, unexciting, soporific; bland, vapid, vacant, insipid, prosaic, dreary, colourless, featureless, jejune; emotionless, unfeeling, unexcited, unexpressive, expressionless, lifeless, spiritless, lacklustre, dead; informal deadly.
▷ANTONYMS exciting; emotional.
6 *he felt flat, used-up, weary*: **depressed**, dejected, dispirited, despondent, downhearted, disheartened, discouraged, low, low-spirited, down, gloomy, glum, unhappy, blue, desolate, weighed down, oppressed; without energy, enervated, sapped, weary, tired out, worn out, exhausted, devitalized, drained; informal down in the mouth, down in the dumps.
▷ANTONYMS cheerful, full of beans.
7 *the market was flat*: **slow**, inactive, sluggish, slow-moving, slack, quiet, not busy, depressed, stagnant, static, dead, unproductive.
▷ANTONYMS busy.
8 *flat champagne*: **still**, dead, no longer effervescent.
▷ANTONYMS sparkling.
9 Brit. *a flat battery*: **expired**, dead, finished, used up, run out; informal kaput, dud; Brit. informal duff.
▷ANTONYMS fresh; working.
10 *a flat tyre*: **deflated**, punctured, burst, collapsed, blown out, ruptured, pierced, empty of air, decompressed, depressurized.
▷ANTONYMS inflated.
11 *I charge a flat £30 fee*: **fixed**, set, regular, established, unchanging, unvarying, invariable, unfluctuating, consistent, constant, uniform, straight, hard and fast.
12 *a flat denial of any impropriety*: **outright**, direct, point blank, out and out, downright, absolute, definite, positive, straight, stark, all out; plain, explicit; firm, resolute, adamant, assertive, emphatic, insistent, final, conclusive; complete, utter, categorical, unconditional, sheer, thorough, thoroughgoing; unqualified, unmodified, unequivocal, unquestionable, unrestricted, unmitigated.
▸ **adverb 1** *I lay down flat on the floor*: **stretched out**, outstretched, spreadeagled, prone, reclining, sprawling, supine, prostrate, recumbent; on one's back, on one's stomach/front, (flat) on one's face; rare procumbent.
2 informal *I thought you'd turn me down flat*: **outright**, directly, absolutely; plainly, explicitly; firmly, resolutely, adamantly, assertively, emphatically, insistently, finally, conclusively; completely, utterly, categorically, unconditionally, thoroughly, definitely; unequivocally, unquestionably.
□ **fall flat** *I just felt a lot of the jokes fell flat*: **fail**, be unsuccessful, not succeed, lack success, fall through, break down, abort, miscarry, be defeated, suffer defeat, be in vain, be frustrated, collapse, founder, misfire, backfire, not come up to scratch, meet with disaster, come to grief, come to nothing, come to naught, miss the mark, run aground, go astray.
□ **flat out** *I'd been working flat out*: **hard**, as hard as possible, for all one's worth, vigorously, with a vengeance, to the utmost, to the full, to the limit, all out; **at full speed**, as fast as possible, post-haste, at full tilt, at breakneck speed, full steam ahead; informal hell for leather, hammer and tongs, like crazy, like mad, like a bat out of hell, at a lick, like the wind, like a bomb, like greased lightning; Brit. informal like billy-o, like the clappers, at a rate of knots.
▷ANTONYMS moderately.

flat[2] noun *a two-bedroom flat*: **apartment**, set of rooms, penthouse, home, residence, accommodation; rooms, living quarters, quarters; Austral. home unit; informal pad, digs; N. Amer. informal crib.

flatten verb **1** *Tom flattened the crumpled paper | my stomach has flattened*: **make/become flat**, make/become even, make/become smooth, smooth (out/off), level (out/off), even out; iron, steamroller.
▷ANTONYMS roughen, make uneven.
2 *he had trampled around and flattened the grass*: **compress**, press down, crush, squash, compact; trample, tread, tramp, wear.
3 *tornadoes can flatten buildings in seconds*: **demolish**, raze, raze to the ground, level, tear down, knock down, destroy, wipe out, topple, wreck, reduce to ruins, devastate, annihilate, pulverize, obliterate, ravage, smash, wipe off the face of the earth, wipe off the map; N. Amer. informal total; rare unbuild.
4 informal *Flynn flattened him with a single punch*: **knock down**, knock over, knock to the ground, knock off one's feet, fell, topple, prostrate; informal lay out, floor, deck, knock for six, knock into the middle of next week.
5 *I flattened a drunken heckler with a couple of speedy put-downs*: **humiliate, crush**, quash, squash, deflate, subdue, humble, cow, chasten, bring down/low, take down a peg or two, mortify; informal put down, floor, cut down to size, put someone in their place, settle someone's hash.

flatter verb **1** *it amused him to flirt with her and flatter her*: **compliment**, praise, commend, admire, express admiration for, pay tribute to, say nice things about; pay court to, pay blandishments to, fawn on, wax lyrical about, make much of; cajole, humour, flannel, blarney; informal sweet-talk, soft-soap, butter up, lay it on thick, lay it on with a trowel, play up to, suck up to, crawl to, creep to, be all over, fall all over; archaic blandish; rare laud, panegyrize.
▷ANTONYMS insult.
2 *I was flattered to be asked to join them*: **honour**, gratify, please, give pleasure to, make someone pleased/glad, delight, gladden; informal tickle pink.
▷ANTONYMS offend.
3 *a hairstyle that flattered her small features*: **suit**, become, set off, show to advantage, enhance, look good on, look right on, be appropriate to, go well with, embellish, ornament, grace, befit; informal do something for.
▷ANTONYMS clash with.

flatterer noun *the prince is surrounded by flatterers*: **sycophant**, groveller, fawner, lackey, obsequious person, kowtower, time server; informal crawler, creep, toady, bootlicker, yes man, lickspittle, doormat, truckler; N. Amer. informal suck-up, brown-nose; Brit. vulgar slang arse-licker, arse-kisser; formal encomiast; archaic toad-eater.
▷ANTONYMS critic.

flattering adjective **1** *these are very flattering remarks*: **complimentary**, praising, favourable, commending, admiring, applauding, appreciative; honeyed, sugary, cajoling, flannelling, blarneying, silver-tongued, honey-tongued; fawning, obsequious, ingratiating, servile, sycophantic, unctuous, oleaginous, oily; informal sweet-talking, soft-soaping, crawling, creeping, bootlicking, smarmy; rare encomiastic, encomiastical.
▷ANTONYMS unflattering, insulting.
2 *Mr Crosbie said it was very flattering to be nominated*: **pleasing**, gratifying, honouring, gladdening.
▷ANTONYMS offensive.

3 *she had worn her most flattering dress*: **becoming**, enhancing, appropriate, embellishing, ornamenting, gracing, befitting.
▷ANTONYMS unflattering, unbecoming.

flattery noun *the old man sounded mollified by the flattery*: **praise**, adulation, compliments, blandishments, admiration, honeyed words, pats on the back; fawning, simpering, puffery, blarney, cajolery, wheedling; informal sweet talk, soft soap, spiel, buttering up, cosying up, toadying, currying favour, weasel words; Brit. informal flannel; Brit. vulgar slang arse-kissing, arse-licking; N. Amer. vulgar slang brown-nosing, ass-kissing, ass-licking; rare laudation.
▷ANTONYMS criticism.

flatulence noun **1** *medications that help with flatulence*: **intestinal gas**, wind, gas; informal farting; formal flatus, borborygmus.
2 *the flatulence of his latest recordings*: **pomposity**, pompousness, pretension, pretentiousness, posing, posturing, grandiosity, grandness, grandiloquence, bombast, turgidity, hot air.

flaunt verb *he hated the way the rich flaunted their possessions*: **show off**, display ostentatiously, draw attention to, make a (great) show of, put on show, put on display, parade, exhibit; flourish, brandish, wave, dangle; exult in, brag about, crow about, vaunt; informal flash.
▷ANTONYMS be modest about, hide.

> *Easily confused words* **flaunt or flout?**
>
> It is a common error to use **flaunt** as though it meant the same as **flout**. *Flaunt* means 'display ostentatiously', as in *tourists flaunting their wealth*. *Flout*, on the other hand, means 'defy or disobey (a rule)', as in *timber companies are continuing to flout environmental laws*. Saying that someone *flaunts the rules* is an error due to similarity in sound and to the element of ostentation involved in *flouting* a regulation.

flavour noun **1** *the slightly sweet flavour of prosciutto*: **taste**, savour, tang, relish, palate; rare sapor.
2 *salami can give extra flavour to spaghetti sauces*: **flavouring**, seasoning, tastiness, tang, tanginess, interest, relish, bite, piquancy, pungency, savour, smack, spice, spiciness, sharpness, zest, raciness, edge; informal zing, zip, punch.
▷ANTONYMS blandness.
3 *the tournament had a strong international flavour*: **character**, quality, feel, feeling, ambience, atmosphere, aura, air, mood, aspect, tone, tenor, complexion, style, stamp, property; element, vein, strand, streak; spirit, essence, soul, nature, heart; informal vibe.
4 *this excerpt will give a flavour of the report*: **impression**, indication, suggestion, hint, taste, nuance.
□ **flavour of the month** informal *he's flavour of the month in Tinseltown*: **all the rage**, the latest thing, the fashion, the trend, in vogue, in (great) demand; a flash in the pan, a one-hit wonder; informal hot, in, cool; Brit. informal, dated all the go.
▸ verb *many cuisines use spices to flavour their foods*: **add flavour to**, add flavouring to, season, spice (up), add seasoning/herbs/spices to, add piquancy to, ginger up, enrich, enliven, liven up; informal spike, pep up.

flavouring noun **1** *this cheese is often combined with other cheeses or flavourings*: **seasoning**, spice, herb, additive, added flavour; condiment, dressing, relish, sauce, dip.
2 *vanilla flavouring*: **essence**, extract, tincture, concentrate, concentration, distillate.

flaw noun *the type of reactor used at Chernobyl had a design flaw | he had two small flaws in his character*: **defect**, blemish, fault, imperfection, deficiency, weakness, weak spot/point, inadequacy, shortcoming, limitation, failing, foible; shortfall, insufficiency, lack, want, omission; snag, kink, deformity, taint, crack, fissure, break, tear, split, scratch, chip, fracture, spot; mistake, error; Computing bug, virus; informal glitch, gremlin.
▷ANTONYMS strength.

> *Choose the right word* **flaw, blemish, imperfection**
>
> See **blemish**.

flawed adjective **1** *a flawed mirror blurred the Hubble telescope's vision*: **faulty**, defective, imperfect, shoddy; broken, cracked, torn, scratched, deformed, distorted, warped, buckled; malfunctioning, inoperative, not working, not functioning, non-functioning, out of order, in disrepair, unsound; weak, deficient, incomplete; informal gone wrong, on the blink; Brit. informal duff, knackered.
▷ANTONYMS flawless.
2 *the Commission's findings were fundamentally flawed*: **unsound**, defective, faulty, distorted, inaccurate, incorrect, erroneous, imprecise, fallacious, wrong; impaired, weak, invalid.
▷ANTONYMS sound.

flawless adjective *her smooth, flawless skin*: **perfect**, without blemish, unblemished, unmarked, unimpaired; whole, intact, sound, unbroken, undamaged, as sound as a bell, mint, as good as new, pristine; stainless, spotless, pure, impeccable, immaculate, consummate, superb, superlative, masterly, accurate, correct, faultless, without fault, error-free, unerring; exemplary, model, ideal, copybook, just so; Brit. informal tip-top, A1.
▷ANTONYMS flawed.

> *Word toolkit* **flawless**
>
> See **impeccable**.

flay verb **1** *one shoulder had been flayed to reveal the muscles*: **skin**, strip the skin off; technical excoriate.
2 *he flayed the government for not moving fast enough on economic reform*: **criticize**, attack, berate, censure, condemn, denounce, denigrate, revile, castigate, pillory, belabour, lambaste, savage, tear/pull to pieces, find fault with, run down, abuse; informal knock, slam, pan, bash, take apart, crucify, hammer, lay into, roast, skewer, bad-mouth; Brit. informal slate, rubbish, slag off, monster; N. Amer. informal pummel, cut up; Austral./NZ informal bag; rare excoriate.

f

flea bite noun *the proposed energy tax amounted to little more than a flea bite*: **very small sum**, pittance, trifle, trifling sum, drop in the ocean, insignificant sum, derisory sum, paltry sum; small change, pence; next to nothing, hardly anything; informal peanuts, chicken feed, piddling amount, shoestring; N. Amer. informal chump change; S. African informal tickey; archaic driblet.
▷ANTONYMS fortune.

fleck noun *a dusty grey colour interspersed with flecks of pale blue*: **spot**, mark, patch, dot, speck, speckle, freckle, smudge, smear, streak, stain, blotch, blot, splash, dab, daub; technical petechia; informal splotch, splosh, splodge; rare macule, macula.
▸ verb *the deer's red flanks were flecked with white*: **spot**, mark, stain, dot, speckle, bespeckle, freckle, stipple, stud, bestud, blotch, mottle, smudge, streak, splash, spatter, bespatter, scatter, sprinkle; dirty, soil; informal splotch, splosh, splodge; Scottish & Irish informal slabber; literary besmirch, smirch.

fledgling noun *the bird had been ringed as a fledgling*: **chick**, baby bird, nestling.
▸ adjective *fledgling industries in the developing world*: **emerging**, emergent, arising, sunrise, dawning, beginning; developing, in the making, budding, rising, burgeoning, growing, embryonic, infant, nascent, incipient; promising, potential, up-and-coming.
▷ANTONYMS declining; mature.

flee verb **1** *she fled to her room and hid*: **run**, run away, run off, make a run for it, run for it, take flight, be gone, make off, take off, take to one's heels, make a break for it, bolt, beat a (hasty) retreat, make a quick exit, make one's getaway, escape, absent oneself, make oneself scarce, abscond, head for the hills, do a disappearing act; informal beat it, clear off, clear out, vamoose, skedaddle, split, cut and run, leg it, show a clean pair of heels, turn tail, scram; Brit. informal do a runner, scarper, do a bunk; N. Amer. informal light out, bug out, cut out, peel out, take a powder, skidoo; Austral. informal go through, shoot through; vulgar slang bugger off; archaic fly.
2 *they fled the country*: **run away from**, leave hastily/abruptly, fly, escape from; informal skip.

fleece noun *a sheep's fleece*: **wool**, coat, hair, fur, pelt.
▸ verb informal *the traders are notorious for fleecing tourists*. See **cheat** (sense 1 of the verb).

fleecy adjective *a fleecy tracksuit*: **fluffy**, woolly, downy, fuzzy, feathery, furry, velvety, shaggy; soft, smooth, silky, silken, satiny, cushiony; technical floccose, lanate, pilose; rare lanose.
▷ANTONYMS coarse.

fleet[1] noun *the fleet set sail*: **navy**, naval force, (naval) task force, armada, flotilla, squadron, convoy, column.

fleet[2] adjective literary *the horse was strong but fleet, built for speed*. See **nimble** (sense 1), **fast[1]** (sense 1 of the adjective).

fleeting adjective *we only had a fleeting glimpse of the sun*: **brief**, transient, short-lived, short, momentary, sudden, cursory, transitory, ephemeral, fugitive, evanescent, fading, vanishing, flying, fly-by-night, passing, flitting, here today and gone tomorrow, temporary, impermanent, short-term, rapid, quick, swift, rushed; literary fugacious.
▷ANTONYMS lasting.

> *Choose the right word* **fleeting, transient, transitory, ephemeral**
>
> See **transient**.

flesh noun **1** *you're as thin as a rake—you need a sight more flesh on your bones*: **muscle**, tissue, muscle tissue, meat, brawn; informal beef.
2 *the villagers used to eat turtle eggs and flesh*: **meat**.
3 *Mrs Barnet carried too much flesh on her small frame*: **fat**, weight, obesity, corpulence; Anatomy adipose tissue; informal blubber, flab.

4 *cut the melon in half and scoop out the flesh*: **pulp**, soft part, fleshy part, marrow, meat.
5 (**the flesh**) *a fierce inner struggle against the pleasures of the flesh*: **the body**, the human body, human nature, man's physical nature, physicality, corporeality, carnality, animality; sensuality, sensualism, sexuality.
□ **one's (own) flesh and blood** *the child was after all their own flesh and blood*: **family**, relative(s), relation(s), blood relation(s), family member(s), kin, next of kin, kinsfolk, kinsman, kinsmen, kinswoman, kinswomen, kindred, connection(s); informal folks, nearest and dearest; dated people.
□ **in the flesh** *he seems just as charming in the flesh as on television*: **in person**, before one's eyes, in front of one, before one's very eyes, in one's presence; in real life, in actual life, live; physically, bodily, in bodily/human form, incarnate.
▷ANTONYMS on screen.
□ **put flesh on the bones of** *Parliament will soon put flesh on the bones of the principle by drafting a law*. See **flesh something out**.
▶ verb
□ **flesh out** *the once lean physique had fleshed out*: **put on weight**, gain weight, get heavier, grow fat/fatter, fatten up, get fat, fill out; thicken, widen, broaden, expand, spread out.
▷ANTONYMS slim.
□ **flesh something out** *the shadow chancellor tried to flesh out his party's economic philosophy*: **expand (on)**, elaborate on, add to, build on, add flesh to, put flesh on (the bones of), add detail to, expatiate on, supplement, reinforce, augment, extend, broaden, develop, fill out, enlarge on, embellish, embroider, enhance, amplify, refine, improve, polish, perfect.
▷ANTONYMS condense.

> *Word links* **flesh**
>
> **carn-** related prefix, as in *carnivore, carnosaur*
> **carnivorous** flesh-eating
> **sarc-** related prefix, as in *sarcoma, sarcophagus*
> **selaphobia** fear of flesh

fleshly adjective **1** *he urged the audience to abstain from fleshly lusts*: **carnal**, sexual, sensual, erotic, lustful, lascivious, libidinous, lecherous, licentious, lewd, prurient, salacious, coarse, physical, animal, bestial, gross, lubricious, venereal.
▷ANTONYMS spiritual; noble.
2 *those film stars were fleshly analogues of the American cars of the time*: **physical**, bodily, corporeal, corporal, mortal; material, concrete, earthly, worldly, mundane, of this world, real, actual, tangible, substantial; rare somatic.

fleshy adjective *Rufus had curiously sharp features for so fleshy a man*: **plump**, chubby, portly, fat, fattish, obese, overweight, stout, corpulent, paunchy, beer-bellied, thickset, hefty, heavy, heavyset, burly, bulky, chunky, well padded, well covered, well upholstered, meaty, rotund, round, well rounded, of ample proportions, big, large; informal tubby, pudgy, beefy, porky, roly-poly, blubbery, poddy; Brit. informal podgy, fubsy; N. Amer. informal zaftig, corn-fed, lard-assed; Austral./NZ nuggety; technical pyknic; rare squabby, pursy, abdominous.
▷ANTONYMS thin.

flex[1] verb **1** *he would flex his knees and then spring up*: **bend**, curve, crook, hook, cock, angle, kink, buckle, double up.
▷ANTONYMS straighten.
2 *Rachel stood up and flexed her cramped muscles*: **tighten**, tauten, make taut, tense (up), tension, contract, stiffen, brace, knot.
▷ANTONYMS relax.

flex[2] noun Brit. *an electric flex*: **cable**, wire, lead, extension; N. Amer. cord.

flexibility noun **1** *the boat's very short timbers are designed to give flexibility*: **pliability**, suppleness, pliancy, malleability, mouldability, stretchability, workability, limberness, ductility, plasticity; elasticity, stretch, stretchiness, whippiness, springiness, spring, resilience, give, bounce, bounciness; informal bendiness; rare flexility, tensility.
▷ANTONYMS rigidity.
2 *he likes the flexibility of his endowment loan*: **adaptability**, adjustability, open-endedness, openness, openness to change, changeability, freedom, latitude, mobility, variability, fluidity, versatility.
▷ANTONYMS inflexibility.
3 *the panel will normally show some flexibility over this deadline*: **willingness to compromise**, accommodation, adaptability, amenability, cooperation, tolerance, forgivingness.
▷ANTONYMS intransigence.

flexible adjective **1** *the shoe is comfortable and flexible*: **pliable**, supple, easily bent, bendable, pliant, malleable, mouldable, stretchable, workable, limber, ductile, tensile, plastic; **elastic**, whippy, springy, resilient; informal bendy; rare flexile.
▷ANTONYMS rigid.
2 *job sharing and other flexible arrangements*: **adaptable**, adjustable, open-ended, open, open to change, changeable, variable, fluid, versatile.
▷ANTONYMS inflexible.
3 *they have accepted the need to be flexible towards tenants*: **accommodating**, adaptable, amenable, biddable, willing to compromise, cooperative, tolerant, forgiving, long-suffering, easy-going.
▷ANTONYMS intransigent.

flick noun *a flick of the wrist*: **jerk**, snap, flip, stroke, brush, sweep, swipe, whisk, dab, jab, click, touch.
▶ verb **1** *he flicked the switch on his intercom*: **click**, snap, flip, jerk; pull, tug, tweak; informal yank.
2 *the horse flicked its tail*: **swish**, twitch, wave, wag, waggle, shake, whip, twirl, swing, brandish.
□ **flick through** *Christina flicked through her diary*: **thumb (through)**, leaf through, flip through, run through, skim through, scan, look through, riffle through, browse through, dip into, glance at/through, peruse, read quickly, have a quick look at, run one's eye over, give something a/the once-over.
▷ANTONYMS pore over.

flicker verb **1** *the gas lamp flickered in the wind*: **glimmer**, glint, gleam, flare, shine, dance, gutter; **twinkle**, sparkle, blink, wink, flash, scintillate, glisten, shimmer, glitter; literary glister; rare coruscate, fulgurate, effulge.
▷ANTONYMS burn steadily.
2 *his eyelids flickered in his sleep*: **flutter**, quiver, vibrate, tremble, wobble, shiver, shudder, spasm, jerk, twitch, bat, flap, wink, blink, open and shut; technical nictitate, nictate.

flight noun **1** *the machine was modelled on the flight of a bird*: **flying**, soaring, gliding.
2 *the history of flight*: **aviation**, flying, air transport, aerial navigation, aeronautics.
3 *did you have a good flight?* **plane trip**, trip by air, air trip, journey by air, air journey.
4 *Newton's theories allow us to predict the flight of a cricket ball*: **trajectory**, track, flight path, orbit, glide path, approach.
5 *a noisy flight of birds went over*: **flock**, flying group; skein, bevy, covey; swarm, cloud, knot, cluster.
6 *chroniclers recorded his flight from England after Cnut's death*: **escape**, getaway, fleeing, running away, absconding, retreat, departure, hasty departure, exit, exodus, decamping, disappearance, vanishing.
7 *she ran up a **flight of stairs***: **staircase**, set of steps/stairs.
□ **put someone to flight** *the Scots were put to flight with heavy casualties*: **chase away**, chase off, drive back/away, drive off, drive out, send away, scare off, scatter, scatter to the four winds, disperse, stampede, rout; Brit. see off; informal send packing.
□ **take flight** *many took flight at the air-raid warning*: **flee**, run, run away, run off, make a run for it, run for it, be gone, make off, take off, take to one's heels, make a break for it, bolt, beat a (hasty) retreat, make a quick exit, make one's getaway, escape, absent oneself, make oneself scarce, abscond, head for the hills, do a disappearing act; informal beat it, clear off, clear out, vamoose, skedaddle, split, cut and run, leg it, show a clean pair of heels, turn tail, scram; Brit. informal do a runner, scarper, do a bunk; N. Amer. informal light out, bug out, cut out, peel out, take a powder, skidoo; Austral. informal go through, shoot through; vulgar slang bugger off; archaic fly.
▷ANTONYMS remain.

flighty adjective *you may be seen as too flighty for such responsibility*: **fickle**, erratic, changeable, inconstant, irresolute, mercurial, skittish, whimsical, capricious, volatile, unsteady, unstable, unbalanced, impulsive; **irresponsible**, flippant, giddy, silly, frivolous, light-minded, feather-brained, scatterbrained, scatty, reckless, wild, careless, thoughtless, heedless, carefree, insouciant; informal dippy, dopey, batty, dotty, nutty; N. Amer. informal ditzy.
▷ANTONYMS steady; responsible.

flimsy adjective **1** *a succession of great waves had carried away all the flimsy wooden buildings*: **insubstantial**, slight, light, fragile, breakable, frail, shaky, unstable, wobbly, tottery, rickety, ramshackle, makeshift; **jerry-built**, badly built, thrown together, cheap, shoddy, gimcrack.
▷ANTONYMS sturdy.
2 *the flimsy material of her dress*: **thin**, light, lightweight, fine, ultra-fine, diaphanous, sheer, delicate, insubstantial, floaty, filmy, silken, chiffony, gossamer, gossamer-thin, gossamer-like, gossamery, gauzy, gauzelike, cobwebby, feathery; translucent, transparent, see-through; rare transpicuous, translucid.
▷ANTONYMS thick.
3 *this is very flimsy evidence on which to base any such assessment*: **weak**, feeble, poor, inadequate, insufficient, thin, unsubstantial, unconvincing, implausible, unsatisfactory, paltry, trifling, trivial, shallow.
▷ANTONYMS sound.

flinch verb **1** *Curtis flinched as the passenger window imploded*: **wince**, start, shy (away), recoil, shrink, pull back, back away, shy away, draw back, withdraw, blench, cringe, squirm, quiver, shudder, shiver, tremble, quake, shake, quail, cower, waver, falter, hesitate, get cold feet, blanch.
▷ANTONYMS stand firm.
2 *he has never **flinched from** the job in hand*: **shrink**, recoil, shy away, turn away, swerve, hang back, demur; dodge, evade, avoid, duck, baulk at, jib at, quail at, fight shy of; informal boggle at.

fling verb *he flung the axe into the river*: **throw**, toss, sling, hurl, cast, pitch, lob, bowl, launch, flip, shy, send, propel, project, aim, direct, catapult, fire, send flying, let fly with; informal chuck, heave, bung, buzz, whang; N. Amer. informal peg; Austral. informal hoy; NZ informal bish.
▸ noun **1** *it was his birthday, so he decided he was entitled to a fling*: **good time**, binge, spree, bit of fun, bit of amusement, night on the town; fun and games, enjoyment, entertainment, recreation, revelry, skylarking, larks.
2 *Eva's husband left her when she had her fling with Androulis*: **affair**, love affair, relationship, romance, flirtation, dalliance, liaison, entanglement, romantic entanglement, involvement, attachment, affair of the heart, intrigue; relations; French affaire, affaire de/du cœur, amour; informal hanky-panky; Brit. informal carry-on.

flip verb **1** *he saw a car* ***flip over*** *and land upside down | their upturned catamaran had been flipped by a huge wave*: **overturn**, turn over, tip over, roll over, upturn, capsize, turn topsy-turvy; keel over, topple over, turn turtle; throw over, overthrow, upend, invert, knock over; Nautical pitchpole; informal roll; archaic overset.
2 *he flipped the key through the air to McGowan*: **throw**, flick, toss, fling, sling, pitch, cast, spin, twist, hurl, shy, lob, propel, launch, project, send, dash, bowl; informal chuck, bung.
3 *I flipped the transmitter switch*: **flick**, click, snap, jerk, pull, tug, tweak; informal yank.
□ **flip side 1** *anger is often considered the flip side of depression*: **other side**, reverse side, back, rear, underside, wrong side, B-side, verso. **2** *after suffering injury Phil discovered the flip side of a footballer's life*: **downside**, drawbacks, disadvantages, pitfalls.
□ **flip through** *he flipped through his address book*: **thumb (through)**, leaf through, flick through, run through, skim through, scan, look through, riffle through, browse through, dip into, glance at/through, peruse, read quickly, have a quick look at, run one's eye over, give something a/the once-over.
▷ANTONYMS pore over.

flippancy noun *as someone bereaved through the disease, I was upset by the flippancy with which you dealt with it*: **frivolousness**, levity, superficiality, shallowness, glibness, thoughtlessness, carefreeness, irresponsibility, insouciance, offhandedness; **disrespect**, irreverence, facetiousness, cheek, cheekiness, pertness, overfamiliarity; Brit. informal sauciness; N. Amer. informal sassiness.
▷ANTONYMS seriousness; respect.

flippant adjective *a flippant remark*: **frivolous**, superficial, shallow, glib, thoughtless, carefree, irresponsible, insouciant, offhand; **disrespectful**, irreverent, facetious, cheeky, pert, overfamiliar, impudent, impertinent; informal flip; Brit. informal saucy; N. Amer. informal sassy.
▷ANTONYMS serious; respectful.

flirt verb **1** *she's always* ***flirting with*** *the boys*: **trifle with**, toy with, tease, lead on, philander with, dally with, make romantic advances to, court, woo, vamp; informal pull, chat up, make eyes at, make sheep's eyes at, give the come-on to, come on to, be all over; dated set one's cap at.
2 *those conservatives who* ***flirted with*** *fascism*: **dabble in**, toy with, trifle with, amuse oneself with, play with, entertain the idea/possibility of, consider, give thought to, potter about/around/round with, tinker with, dip into, scratch the surface of.
3 *the Prince has always enjoyed* ***flirting with*** *danger*: **dice with**, court, risk, not be afraid of, treat frivolously, make light of.
▸ noun *Anna was quite a flirt in those days*: **tease**, trifler, philanderer, coquette, heartbreaker; informal puss, ladies' man; vulgar slang cock-teaser, prick-teaser; archaic fizgig, gallant.

flirtation noun *she always engaged in a bit of mild flirtation at parties*: **coquetry**, teasing, trifling, toying, dalliance, philandering, romantic advances; informal chat-up, come-on.

flirtatious adjective *he observed Doreen's blatantly flirtatious manner towards the men*: **coquettish**, flirty, provocative, seductive, inviting, amorous, kittenish, coy, arch, teasing, playful, frisky, flighty, skittish, dallying, philandering; informal come-hither, vampish.

flit verb *butterflies flitted among the tall grasses*: **dart**, dance, skip, play, dash, trip, flick, skim, flutter, bob, bounce, spring, scoot, hop, gambol, caper, cavort, prance, frisk, scamper; informal beetle.

float verb **1** *oil floats on water*: **stay afloat**, stay on the surface, be buoyant, be buoyed up.
▷ANTONYMS sink.
2 *the huge craft floated above the surface of the planet*: **hover**, levitate, be suspended, hang, defy gravity.
3 *a dark cloud floated across the moon*: **drift**, glide, sail, slip, slide, waft, flow, stream, move, travel, be carried.
▷ANTONYMS rush.
4 *the Chancellor floated the idea of offering dual citizenship*: **suggest**, put forward, come up with, submit, raise, moot, propose, advance, offer, proffer, posit, present, table, test the popularity of; informal run something up the flagpole (to see who salutes).
▷ANTONYMS withdraw.
5 *the company was floated on the Stock Exchange*: **launch**, get going, get off the ground, offer, sell, introduce, establish, set up, institute, promote.
▷ANTONYMS wind up; buy back.

floating adjective **1** *a floating piece of seaweed*: **buoyant**, buoyed up, non-submerged, on the surface, above water, afloat, drifting.
▷ANTONYMS sunken.
2 *floating gas balloons*: **hovering**, levitating, suspended, hanging, defying gravity.
▷ANTONYMS grounded.
3 *floating voters*: **uncommitted**, undecided, in two minds, torn, split, uncertain, unsure, wavering, vacillating, indecisive, in a quandary, in a dilemma, in doubt; **non-partisan**, non-aligned, unaffiliated, unattached, neutral, impartial, independent, undeclared; informal iffy, blowing hot and cold, sitting on the fence.
▷ANTONYMS committed.
4 *a floating population*: **unsettled**, not settled, not fixed, transient, temporary, variable, fluctuating; migrant, wandering, nomadic, moving, on the move, migratory, travelling, drifting, roving, roaming, itinerant, gypsy, vagrant, vagabond.
▷ANTONYMS settled.
5 *a floating currency exchange rate*: **variable**, changeable, changing, fluid, fluctuating, free, not fixed; informal up and down.
▷ANTONYMS fixed.

flock noun **1** *a flock of sheep*: **herd**, drove, fold.
2 *a flock of birds*: **group**, flight, congregation.
3 (**flocks**) *flocks of people*: **crowd**, throng, horde, mob, rabble, large number, mass, multitude, host, army, pack, swarm, sea, stream, troupe, press, crush, flood, collection, company, gathering, assembly, assemblage; informal gaggle; Brit. informal shower; archaic rout.
▸ verb **1** *people flocked around him asking for autographs*: **gather**, collect, congregate, assemble, come together, get together, converge, convene, rally, rendezvous, muster, meet, mass, amass, crowd, throng, cluster, herd, group, bunch, swarm, huddle, mill; rare foregather.
2 *collectors flocked to the tiny village*: **stream**, go in large numbers, swarm, surge, seethe, spill, crowd, herd, troop.

flog verb **1** *the Romans used to flog their victims*: **whip**, **scourge**, flagellate, lash, birch, switch, tan, strap, belt, cane, thrash, beat, leather, tan/whip someone's hide, give someone a hiding, beat the living daylights out of.
2 *they were* ***flogging themselves*** *to finish the project on schedule*: **try one's hardest**, try as hard as one can, do one's best, do one's utmost, do all one can, give one's all, make every effort; strive, struggle, strain, drive, push, apply oneself, exert oneself, work hard, endeavour, try; informal do one's damnedest, bend over backwards, go all out, kill oneself, pull out all the stops, bust a gut, move heaven and earth, give it one's best shot; Austral./NZ informal go for the doctor.
3 Brit. informal *insurance brokers flogging life policies*. See **sell** (sense 2).

flood noun **1** *several villages were cut off by the flood*: **inundation**, swamping, deluge; torrent, overflow, flash flood, freshet; downpour, cloudburst; Brit. spate.
2 *she came home in a flood of tears*: **outpouring**, torrent, rush, stream, gush, surge, cascade, flow.
3 *a flood of complaints*: **succession**, series, string, chain; barrage, volley, battery; avalanche, torrent, stream, tide, spate, storm, shower, cascade, wave, rush, outpouring.
▷ANTONYMS trickle.
▸ verb **1** *the dam burst, flooding a small town*: **inundate**, swamp, deluge, immerse, submerge, drown, engulf.
2 *the major river in the area has already flooded*: **overflow**, burst its banks, brim over, run over; rare overbrim, disembogue.
3 *imports were allowed to flood the domestic market*: **glut**, swamp, saturate, oversupply, overfill, overload, overwhelm.
4 *congratulatory messages flooded in*: **pour**, stream, surge, swarm, pile, crowd, throng.
▷ANTONYMS trickle.

Word links **flood**

diluvial relating to floods
antlophobia fear of floods

floor noun **1** *he put the parcel down on the floor*: **ground**, flooring.
2 *they live on the second floor*: **storey**, level, tier, deck; piano nobile, mezzanine, entresol.
▸ verb **1** informal *he threw a punch which floored the other man*: **knock down**, knock over, bring down, fell, prostrate; catch off balance; informal lay out.
2 *that question had always floored him*: **baffle**, defeat, perplex, puzzle, nonplus, mystify, confound, bewilder, bemuse, dumbfound, confuse, discomfit, disconcert, throw; informal beat, flummox, discombobulate, faze, stump, fox, fog, make someone scratch their head, be all Greek to; N. Amer. informal buffalo; archaic wilder, gravel, maze, cause to be at a stand, pose; rare obfuscate.

flop verb **1** *he flopped into a chair*: **collapse**, slump, crumple, subside, sink, drop, fall, tumble.

2 *his blonde hair flopped over his eyes*: **hang (down)**, drop, hang loosely/limply, dangle, droop, sag, flap, loll.
3 informal *the play flopped*: **be unsuccessful**, fail, not work, fall flat, founder, misfire, backfire, be a disappointment, do badly, lose money, be a disaster, meet with disaster, come to grief, miss the mark, run aground; informal bomb, bellyflop, fold, go to the wall, come a cropper, go down like a lead balloon, bite the dust, blow up in someone's face; N. Amer. informal tank.
▷ANTONYMS be successful.
▶ **noun** informal *the play was a flop*: **failure**, disaster, debacle, catastrophe, loser; Brit. damp squib; informal flopperoo, washout, also-ran, bellyflop, dud, dog, lemon, lead balloon, no-hoper, no-go, non-starter; N. Amer. clinker.
▷ANTONYMS success.

floppy adjective *the bloodhound's floppy ears*: **limp**, flaccid, slack, flabby, relaxed; drooping, droopy, sagging, saggy, hanging, dangling, pendulous; loose, flowing.
▷ANTONYMS erect; stiff.

f

floral adjective **1** *a floral arrangement*: **flower**, (made) of flowers.
2 *a floral dress*: **flower-patterned**, flower-pattern, flower-covered, flowery; rare florid.

florid adjective **1** *a florid complexion*: **ruddy**, red, red-faced, reddish, rosy, rosy-cheeked, pink, pinkish, roseate, rubicund; healthy-looking, glowing, fresh; flushed, blushing, high-coloured, blowsy; archaic sanguine; rare erubescent, rubescent.
▷ANTONYMS pale.
2 *the florid plasterwork of the ceilings*: **ornate**, fancy, very elaborate, over-elaborate, embellished, curlicued, extravagant, flamboyant, baroque, rococo, fussy, busy, ostentatious, showy, wedding-cake, gingerbread.
▷ANTONYMS plain.
3 *endearments in florid English*: **flowery**, flamboyant, high-flown, high-sounding, magniloquent, grandiloquent, ornate, fancy, baroque, orotund, rhetorical, oratorical, bombastic, laboured, strained, overwrought, elaborate, over-elaborate, overblown, overdone, convoluted, turgid, inflated; informal highfalutin, purple; rare tumid, pleonastic, euphuistic, aureate, Ossianic, fustian, hyperventilated.
▷ANTONYMS plain.

flotsam noun **1** *we were still finding interesting pieces of flotsam on the beach*: **wreckage**, lost cargo, floating remains.
2 *the room was cleared of boxes and other flotsam*: **rubbish**, debris, detritus, waste, waste matter, discarded matter, dross, refuse, remains, scrap, lumber, odds and ends; N. Amer. trash, garbage; Austral./NZ **mullock**; informal dreck, junk; Brit. informal grot, gash; vulgar slang shit, crap; Archaeology debitage; rare draff, raffle, raff, cultch, orts.

flounce[1] verb *she rose from the table in a fury and flounced out*: **storm**, stride angrily, sweep, stomp, stamp, march, strut, stalk.
▷ANTONYMS slink.

flounce[2] noun *a black suit with a little white flounce at the neckline*: **frill**, ruffle, ruff, peplum, jabot, furbelow, ruche, ruching, gather, tuck, fringe; archaic purfle.

flounder verb **1** *the dragoons were floundering in the boggy ground*: **struggle**, thrash, thresh, flail, toss and turn, twist and turn, pitch, splash, stagger, stumble, falter, lurch, blunder, fumble, grope, squirm, writhe.
▷ANTONYMS make good progress.
2 *you may find yourself floundering as you try to answer a question you have not really understood*: **struggle mentally**, be out of one's depth, be in the dark, have difficulty, be confounded, be confused, be dumbfounded; informal scratch one's head, be flummoxed, be clueless, be foxed, be fazed, be floored, be beaten.
3 *more firms are floundering*: **struggle financially**, be in dire straits, face financial ruin, be in difficulties, face bankruptcy/insolvency.
▷ANTONYMS prosper.

flourish verb **1** *rainforests flourish because of the heat and the rain*: **grow**, **thrive**, prosper, grow/do well, develop, burgeon, increase, multiply, proliferate; spring up, shoot up, bloom, blossom, bear fruit, burst forth, run riot; put on a spurt, boom, mushroom.
▷ANTONYMS die; wither.
2 *the arts flourished in this period*: **thrive**, prosper, bloom, be in good shape, be in good health, be well, be strong, be vigorous, be in its heyday; **progress**, make progress, advance, make headway, develop, improve, become better, mature; evolve, make strides, move forward (in leaps and bounds), move ahead, get ahead, expand; informal be in the pink, go places, go great guns, get somewhere.
▷ANTONYMS decline.
3 *he flourished the sword at them in a mocking salute*: **brandish**, wave, shake, wield, raise, hold aloft; swing, twirl, wag, swish, flap; display, exhibit, flaunt, vaunt, parade, show off.

> *Choose the right word* **flourish, thrive, prosper**
>
> All three words denote a healthy or successful state.
>
> **Flourish** and **thrive** both mean 'grow healthily' or 'be successful, active, or widespread', and are used especially of plants, but also of people (either physically or emotionally), animals, businesses, activities, and abstract things such as ideas and movements (*only algae will thrive in such an environment | Macedonian religious and cultural life continued to flourish under the Byzantines*). Both are often found in their adjectival forms, *flourishing* and *thriving*, which predominantly have a financial sense (*he joined his father's thriving business*).
>
> **Thrive** is also used with *on* in a sense tending towards 'enjoy' (*the kind of plants that thrive on heat and dust | he is the kind of person who thrives on arguments*).
>
> **Prosper** is used of people and groups of people and refers mainly to material or financial success (*the company has grown and prospered*). Although the adjective *prosperous* is an everyday word, *to prosper* can have a slightly archaic ring.

flourishing adjective *a flourishing economy*: **thriving**, prosperous, prospering, booming, burgeoning, successful, strong, vigorous, buoyant; productive, profitable, fruitful, lucrative; growing, developing, progressing, improving, expanding, mushrooming, snowballing, ballooning; informal going strong.
▷ANTONYMS moribund.

flout verb *retailers have been flouting the law by selling tobacco to under-16s*: **defy**, refuse to obey, go against, rebel against, scorn, disdain, show contempt for, fly in the face of, thumb one's nose at, make a fool of, poke fun at; disobey, break, violate, fail to comply with, fail to observe, contravene, infringe, breach, commit a breach of, transgress against; ignore, disregard, set one's face against, kick against; informal cock a snook at; Law infract; archaic set at naught.
▷ANTONYMS observe.

> *Easily confused words* **flout or flaunt?**
>
> See **flaunt**.

flow verb **1** *the water flowed down the channel she had dug*: **run**, move, go along, course, pass, proceed, glide, slide, drift, circulate, trickle, dribble, drizzle, spill, gurgle, babble, ripple; stream, swirl, surge, sweep, gush, cascade, pour, roll, rush, whirl, well, spurt, spout, squirt, spew, jet; leak, seep, ooze, percolate, drip.
2 *many questions flow from today's announcement*: **result**, proceed, arise, follow, ensue, derive, stem, accrue; originate, emanate, spring, emerge; be caused by, be brought about by, be produced by, originate in.
▶ **noun** *the pump produces a good flow of water*: **movement**, motion, course, passage, current, flux, drift, circulation; **stream**, swirl, surge, sweep, gush, roll, rush, welling, spate, tide, spurt, squirt, jet, outpouring, outflow; trickle, leak, seepage, ooze, percolation, drip.

> *Word links* **flow**
>
> **rheo-** related prefix, as in *rheostat, rheology*
> **-rrhoea** related suffix, as in *diarrhoea, logorrhoea*
> **-rrhagia** related suffix, as in *menorrhagia*

flower noun **1** *the shrub produces blue flowers in early summer*: **bloom**, blossom, floweret, floret.
2 *a man in the flower of his strength*: **prime**, peak, pinnacle, zenith, acme, height, ascendancy, climax, culmination, crowning point, perfection, heyday, springtime, bloom, flowering, salad days.
3 *the flower of the nation's youth*: **best**, finest, top, pick, choice, choicest, prime, cream, prize, treasure, pearl, gem, jewel, the jewel in the crown, the crème de la crème, first class, elite, elect; informal the tops.
▷ANTONYMS dregs.

> *Word links* **flower**
>
> **floral** relating to flowers
> **flor-** related prefix, as in *floriated*
> **antho-** related prefix, as in *anthophilous*
> **anthophobia** fear of flowers
> **florist** seller of flowers

flowery adjective **1** *flowery patterns*: **floral**, flower-covered, flower-patterned.
2 *his flowery language made no impression*: **florid**, flamboyant, high-flown, high-sounding, magniloquent, grandiloquent, ornate, fancy, baroque, orotund, rhetorical, oratorical, bombastic, laboured, strained, overwrought, elaborate, over-elaborate, overblown, overdone, convoluted, turgid, inflated; informal highfalutin, purple; rare tumid, pleonastic, euphuistic, aureate, Ossianic, fustian, hyperventilated.
▷ANTONYMS plain.

flowing adjective **1** *she pushed back her long flowing hair*: **loose**, hanging loose/free, unconfined; limp, flaccid, floppy.
▷ANTONYMS stiff; curly.
2 *the new model will have soft, flowing lines and no hard edges*: **sleek**, streamlined, trim, aerodynamic, smooth, clean, uncluttered, unfussy; elegant, graceful; technical faired.
▷ANTONYMS jagged.

3 *he writes in an easy, flowing style*: **fluent**, fluid, free-flowing, effortless, easy, natural, smooth, unbroken, uninterrupted, continuous, graceful, elegant.
▷ANTONYMS stilted; halting.

fluctuate verb **1** *the size of harvest fluctuates from year to year*: **vary**, differ, shift, change, alter, waver, swing, oscillate, alternate, rise and fall, go up and down, see-saw, yo-yo, be unstable, be unsteady.
▷ANTONYMS be steady.
2 *she fluctuates between wanting to go and being afraid of going*: **vacillate**, hesitate, waver, falter, veer, swing, sway, oscillate, alternate, teeter, totter, hover, see-saw, yo-yo, go from one extreme to the other, vary, change one's mind, be in two minds, be ambivalent, be indecisive, be unsure, be undecided; Brit. hum and haw, haver; Scottish swither; informal shilly-shally, dilly-dally, blow hot and cold, pussyfoot around, sit on the fence, wobble.

fluctuation noun *a natural fluctuation in the earth's temperature*: **variation**, shift, change, alteration, swing, movement, oscillation, undulation, alternation, rise and fall, rising and falling, see-sawing, yo-yoing, instability, unsteadiness.
▷ANTONYMS stability.

flue noun **duct**, tube, passage, channel, canal, conduit, shaft, air passage, airway, vent, well; funnel, chimney, chimney stack, smokestack; pipe, pipeline, outlet, inlet.

fluency noun **1** *a job that calls for verbal fluency*: **eloquence**, articulacy, articulateness, expressiveness, communicativeness, coherence, cogency, intelligibility, comprehensibility, lucidity, vividness, persuasiveness, glibness, volubility.
▷ANTONYMS inarticulacy.
2 *fluency in Japanese will be a major asset*: **articulacy**, facility, ability to speak or write ... easily and accurately; command of.
3 *his walk had a feline kind of fluency to it*: **fluidity**, flow, smoothness, effortlessness, ease, naturalness; grace, gracefulness, elegance; regularity, rhythm, rhythmicity; rare flowingness.
▷ANTONYMS jerkiness.

fluent adjective **1** *a fluent introductory speech*: **articulate**, eloquent, expressive, communicative, coherent, cogent, illuminating; vivid, silver-tongued, persuasive, glib, voluble.
▷ANTONYMS inarticulate.
2 *he soon became fluent in Welsh*: **articulate**, able to speak or write ... easily and accurately; (**be fluent in**) have a (good) command of.
3 *he has a very fluent running style*: **free-flowing**, smooth, effortless, easy, natural, fluid, unbroken, uninterrupted, continuous; graceful, elegant; regular, rhythmic.
▷ANTONYMS jerky.

fluff noun **1** *there was fluff all over my coat*: **fuzz**, lint, dust; N. Amer. dustballs, dust bunnies; Scottish ooze.
2 *on his head was a fluff of pale downy hair*: **down**, soft/fine hair, soft fur, soft feathers, downiness, fuzz, floss, nap, pile.
3 informal *commentary should be free of fluffs such as mispronounced words or hesitations*: **mistake**, error, gaffe, blunder, fault, slip, slip of the tongue, solecism, indiscretion, oversight, inaccuracy, botch; French faux pas; Latin lapsus linguae, lapsus calami; informal slip-up, clanger, boner, boo-boo, howler; Brit. informal boob; N. Amer. informal goof, blooper, bloop; Brit. informal, dated bloomer, floater.
▶ verb **1** informal *the out-takes show him hopelessly fluffing his lines*: **bungle**, deliver badly, muddle up, make a mess of; forget; informal mess up, foul up, screw up, cock up.
▷ANTONYMS get right.
2 informal *he fluffed his tee shot on the fourteenth hole*: **bungle**, fumble, miss; informal mess up, make a mess of, make a hash of, hash, muff, foozle, butcher, make a botch of, foul up, bitch up, screw up, blow, louse up; Brit. informal make a muck of, make a pig's ear of, cock up, make a Horlicks of; N. Amer. informal flub, goof up, bobble; vulgar slang fuck up, bugger up, balls up, bollix up.
▷ANTONYMS succeed in, make a good job of.

fluffy adjective *a fluffy toy rabbit*: **fleecy**, woolly, fuzzy, shaggy, hairy, feathery, downy, furry, velvety, cushiony; soft; rare floccose, flocculent, lanate, lanose.
▷ANTONYMS rough.

fluid noun *he designed instruments to measure the flow of fluids*: **flowing substance**; liquid, watery substance, moisture, solution, juice, sap; gas, gaseous substance, vapour.
▷ANTONYMS solid.
▶ adjective **1** *in fluid magmas, these gas bubbles can expand freely*: **flowing**, able to flow easily; liquid, liquefied, melted, molten, uncongealed, running; gaseous, gassy; technical fluxional.
▷ANTONYMS solid.
2 *at this stage his plans were still fluid*: **adaptable**, flexible, adjustable, open-ended, open, open to change, changeable, not fixed, not settled, variable, versatile.
▷ANTONYMS firm.
3 *take advantage of our fluid state to let us know what you think the magazine should look like*: **fluctuating**, changeable, subject/likely to change, unsteady, (ever-)shifting, mobile, inconstant; **unstable**, unsettled, turbulent, volatile, mercurial, protean, kaleidoscopic, knife-edge, explosive.
▷ANTONYMS static.
4 *he stood up in one fluid movement*: **free-flowing**, flowing, fluent, smooth, effortless, easy, natural, unbroken, uninterrupted, continuous; graceful, elegant; regular, rhythmic.
▷ANTONYMS jerky.

Choose the right word **fluid, liquid**

See **liquid**.

fluke noun *by a fluke I had a cancellation*: **chance**, coincidence, accident, a twist of fate; **piece/stroke of luck**, piece/stroke of good luck, piece/stroke of good fortune, lucky stroke, happy/lucky chance, lucky break.

fluky adjective *we didn't deserve to win—our goals were a bit fluky*: **lucky**, fortunate, providential, timely, opportune, serendipitous, expedient, heaven-sent, auspicious, propitious, felicitous, convenient, apt; chance, fortuitous, accidental; unexpected, unanticipated, unforeseen, unlooked-for, coincidental, haphazard, inadvertent, random, unintended; Brit. informal jammy.
▷ANTONYMS planned.

flummox verb *Linear B script had flummoxed generations of academics*: **baffle**, bewilder, mystify, bemuse, perplex, puzzle, confuse, confound, nonplus, disconcert, throw, throw off balance, disorientate, take aback, set thinking; informal bamboozle, discombobulate, faze, stump, beat, fox, make someone scratch their head, be all Greek to, make someone's head spin, floor, fog; N. Amer. informal buffalo; archaic wilder, gravel, maze, cause to be at a stand, distract, pose; rare obfuscate.

flummoxed adjective *I was flummoxed until I remembered something*: **baffled**, bewildered, mystified, bemused, perplexed, puzzled, confused, confounded, nonplussed, disconcerted, thrown, thrown off balance, at sea, at a loss, disorientated, taken aback; informal bamboozled, discombobulated, fazed, stumped, beat, foxed, floored; Canadian & Austral./NZ informal bushed; archaic wildered, distracted, mazed.

flunkey noun **1** *a flunkey brought us a bottle of champagne*: **liveried manservant**, liveried servant, lackey, steward, butler, footman, valet, retainer, attendant, factotum, houseboy, page.
2 *government flunkeys searched his offices*: **minion**, lackey, hireling, subordinate, underling, servant, retainer, vassal; puppet, spaniel, pawn, tool, creature, instrument, cat's paw; informal skivvy, stooge, sucker, yes-man; Brit. informal poodle, dogsbody; N. Amer. informal gopher.

flurried adjective *I was so flurried that I broke the cork*: **agitated**, flustered, ruffled, in a panic, worked up, beside oneself, overwrought, perturbed, frantic; informal in a flap, in a state, in a twitter, in a fluster, in a dither, all of a dither, all of a lather, in a tizz/tizzy, in a tiz-woz; Brit. informal in a (flat) spin, having kittens; N. Amer. informal in a twit.
▷ANTONYMS calm.

flurry noun **1** *he opened the door and a flurry of snow blew in*: **swirl**, whirl, eddy, billow, shower, gust, rush, burst, gale, squall, storm.
2 *there was a renewed flurry of activity outside*: **burst**, outbreak, spurt, fit, spell, bout, rash, blaze, eruption; informal spot.
3 *his account of the deliberations caused a **flurry of excitement** in the press*: **fluster**, fuss, bustle, whirl, stir, ferment, hubbub, commotion, hustle, tumult; agitation, disturbance, furore, perturbation, state of anxiety, panic; informal to-do, flap; archaic pother.
4 *there was a flurry of imports*: **spate**, wave, flood, deluge, torrent, stream, tide, avalanche, storm, shower, cascade; series, succession, string; barrage, volley, battery; outbreak, rash, explosion, run, rush.
▷ANTONYMS dearth; trickle.
▶ verb *gusts of snow flurried through the door*: **swirl**, whirl, eddy, billow, gust, blast, blow, rush, wind, churn, swish, spin, twist, spurt, surge, seethe, stream, flow, puff, squall, squirt, boil.

flush[1] verb **1** *he kissed her cheek and she flushed in embarrassment*: **blush**, redden, turn/go pink, turn/go red, turn/go crimson, turn/go scarlet, colour (up), change colour, crimson, tint, burn up; archaic mantle.
▷ANTONYMS pale.
2 *fruit helps to flush toxins from the body*: **rinse (out)**, wash (out/down), sluice, swill, cleanse, clean, hose (down), swab; Brit. informal sloosh (down).
3 *one of the beaters was flushing birds from their hiding places*: **drive**, send up, chase, force, dislodge, expel, frighten, scare.
▶ noun **1** *a flush crept over her face*: **blush**, reddening, high colour, colour, rosiness, pinkness, ruddiness, bloom.
▷ANTONYMS paleness.
2 *in the first flush of manhood*: **bloom**, glow, freshness, radiance, vigour, rush.

flush[2] adjective informal **1** *the company was flush with cash*: **well supplied with**, replete with, overflowing with, bursting with, brimful with,

f

brimming with, loaded with, overloaded with, abounding in, well provided with, well stocked with, rich in, abundant in, rife with; crammed with, crowded with, packed with, jammed with, stuffed with, teeming with, swarming with, thick with, solid with, charged with, fraught with; informal jam-packed with, chock-a-block with, chock-full of, awash with; Austral./NZ informal chocker with.
▷ANTONYMS bereft of; low on.
2 *the years when cash was flush*: **plentiful**, **abundant**, copious, ample, profuse, superabundant, infinite, inexhaustible, opulent, prolific, teeming, in abundance; informal a gogo, galore; S. African informal lank; literary bounteous, plenteous.
▷ANTONYMS lacking; low.

flushed adjective **1** *the children's happy, flushed faces*: **red**, pink, ruddy, glowing, reddish, pinkish, florid, high-coloured, healthy-looking, aglow, burning, flaming, feverish, rubicund, roseate, rosy; blushing, red-faced, blowsy, embarrassed, shamefaced; archaic sanguine; rare erubescent, rubescent.
▷ANTONYMS pale.
2 *flushed with success, he was now getting into his stride*: **elated**, thrilled, exhilarated, happy, delighted, overjoyed, joyous, gleeful, excited, animated, jubilant, exultant, ecstatic, euphoric, rapturous, in raptures, enraptured, intoxicated, beside oneself, transported, carried away, impassioned, in a frenzy, delirious, hysterical, wild, frenzied; informal blissed out, over the moon, high, on a high; N. Amer. informal wigged out; rare corybantic.
▷ANTONYMS dismayed.

fluster verb *what could have flustered the normally imperturbable Robert?* **unsettle**, make nervous, unnerve, agitate, ruffle, upset, bother, put on edge, discompose, disquiet, disturb, worry, alarm, panic, perturb, disconcert, confuse, throw off balance, confound, nonplus; informal hassle, rattle, faze, discombobulate, put into a flap, throw into a tizz; Brit. informal send into a spin.
▷ANTONYMS calm.
▶ noun *his appearance put the household into quite a fluster*: **state of agitation**, state of anxiety, nervous state, flutter, panic, frenzy, fever, fret, upset, turmoil, commotion; informal dither, flap, tizz, tizzy, tiz-woz, twitter, state, sweat, stew; N. Amer. informal twit.
▷ANTONYMS state of calm.

fluted adjective *the roof is supported by fluted columns*: **grooved**, channelled, furrowed, ribbed, corrugated, ridged.
▷ANTONYMS smooth; plain.

flutter verb **1** *a couple of butterflies fluttered around the garden*: **flit**, hover, flitter, dance.
2 *a small white tern was fluttering its wings*: **flap**, move up and down, beat, quiver, agitate, vibrate, twitch, shake, wag, waggle, swing, oscillate, thresh, thrash, flail.
3 *she fluttered her eyelashes*: **flicker**, bat.
4 *flags fluttered from every mast*: **flap**, wave, ripple, undulate, stir, shake, quiver, shiver, tremble; fly, blow.
5 *her heart fluttered when she found that his eyes were still on her*: **beat weakly/irregularly**, palpitate, miss/skip a beat, quiver, go pit-a-pat; Medicine exhibit arrhythmia; rare quop.
▶ noun **1** *the flutter of the birds' wings*: **agitation**, beating, flapping, quivering, vibrating, twitching, shaking, wagging, oscillation, threshing, thrashing, flailing.
2 *a flutter of dark eyelashes*: **flicker**, bat.
3 *the flutter of the flags in the breeze*: **flapping**, waving, rippling.
4 *a flutter of nervousness started up inside her*: **tremor**, wave, rush, surge, flash, stab, flush, tremble, quiver, shake, shaking, shakiness, shiver, frisson, chill, thrill, tingle, vibration, quaver, quake, shudder, palpitation, pulsation, throb, oscillation, fluctuation, waver, ripple, flicker.
5 *she was in a flutter at the unexpected news*: **fluster**, flurry, bustle, panic, state of panic/agitation; informal state, dither, twitter, blue funk, stew, tizz, tizzy, tiz-woz; N. Amer. informal twit.
6 Brit. informal *he enjoys a flutter on the horses*: **bet**, wager, gamble; Brit. informal punt.

flux noun **1** *the flux of water vapour along the tube*: **flow**, movement, motion, transfer, course, passage, current, drift, circulation, trickle, stream, swirl, surge, sweep, gush, roll, rush, welling, spate, tide.
2 *prices are in a state of flux*: **continuous change**, changeability, changeableness, variability, inconstancy, fluidity, instability, unsteadiness, unpredictability, irregularity, fitfulness, unreliability, fickleness; fluctuation, variation, shift, alteration, swing, movement, oscillation, alternation, rise and fall, rising and falling, see-sawing, yo-yoing.
▷ANTONYMS stability.

fly[1] verb **1** *a bird flew overhead*: **travel through the air**, wing its way, wing, glide, soar, wheel; flutter, flit; hover, hang; take wing, take to the air, mount.
2 *they flew to Paris*: **travel/go by air**, travel/go by plane, jet.
3 *military planes flew in food supplies*: **transport by air/plane**, airlift, lift, jet.
4 *he would pretend not to know how to fly the plane*: **pilot**, operate, control, manoeuvre, steer, guide, direct, navigate.
5 *the ship was flying a quarantine flag*: **display**, show, exhibit; have hoisted, have run up.
6 *the British flag flew proudly from the roof*: **flutter**, flap, wave, blow, waft, float, stream.
7 *doesn't time fly when you're having fun?* **go quickly**, fly by/past, pass swiftly, slip past, rush past.
8 *the runners flew by*: **race**, hurry, hasten, flash, dash, dart, rush, shoot, speed, hurtle, streak, really move, spank along, whirl, whizz, go like lightning, go hell for leather, whoosh, buzz, zoom, swoop, blast, charge; stampede, gallop, chase, career, bustle, sweep, hare, wing, scurry, scud, scutter; informal belt, scoot, scorch, tear, zap, zip, whip (along), get cracking, get a move on, step on it, burn rubber, go like a bat out of hell; Brit. informal bomb, bucket, shift, put one's foot down; N. Amer. informal clip, boogie, hightail, barrel, lay rubber; N. Amer. vulgar slang drag/tear/haul ass; literary fleet; archaic post, hie.
9 archaic *the beaten army had to fly*. See **flee** (sense 1).
10 dated *he was forced to fly the country*. See **flee** (sense 2).
□ **fly at** *Robbie flew at him, fists clenched*: **attack**, assault, make an assault on, launch an attack on, pounce on, set upon, set about, launch oneself at, weigh into, let fly at, turn on, round on, lash out at, hit out at, strike out at, beset, belabour, fall on, accost, mug, charge, rush, storm; informal lay into, tear into, lace into, sail into, pitch into, get stuck into, wade into, let someone have it, beat up, jump; Brit. informal have a go at; N. Amer. informal light into.
□ **fly off the handle** informal *touch on anything emotional and Andrew flies off the handle*: **lose one's temper**, become very angry, fly into a rage, explode, blow up, erupt, lose control, go berserk, breathe fire, begin to rant and rave, flare up, boil over; informal go mad, go crazy, go wild, go bananas, have a fit, see red, blow one's top, blow a fuse, blow a gasket, do one's nut, hit the roof, go through the roof, go up the wall, go off the deep end, lose one's cool, go ape, flip, flip one's lid, lose one's rag, lose it, freak out, be fit to be tied, be foaming at the mouth, burst a blood vessel, get one's dander up, go non-linear; Brit. informal go spare, go crackers, throw a wobbly, get one's knickers in a twist; N. Amer. informal flip one's wig; Austral./NZ informal go crook; vulgar slang go apeshit.
□ **let fly** See **let**.

fly[2] noun
□ **fly in the ointment** informal *the only fly in the ointment was Adrian*: **snag**, hitch, catch, drawback, difficulty, problem, weakness, defect, pitfall, complication; obstacle, hurdle, barrier, stumbling block, bar, hindrance, impediment, handicap, disadvantage, restriction, limitation; informal hiccup, facer; Brit. informal spanner in the works; N. Amer. informal monkey wrench in the works.
□ **fly on the wall** *I would love to be a fly on the wall at some of those meetings*: **observer**, spectator, onlooker, watcher, looker-on, viewer, witness, eyewitness.

fly[3] adjective Brit. informal *she's fly enough not to get done out of it*. See **shrewd**.

fly-by-night adjective *sometimes these fly-by-night contractors take off without paying us at all*: **unreliable**, undependable, irresponsible, untrustworthy; **dishonest**, deceitful, not to be trusted, dubious, double-dealing, treacherous, traitorous, two-faced, unfaithful, duplicitous, dishonourable, unprincipled, unscrupulous, corrupt, underhand; informal iffy, shady, shifty, slippery, crooked; Brit. informal dodgy, bent; Austral./NZ informal shonky.
▷ANTONYMS reputable.

flyer, flier noun **1** *we have increased the privileges and awards for our most frequent flyers*: **air traveller**, air passenger, airline customer.
2 *the memorial was for flyers killed in a raid*: **aviator**, airman/airwoman, pilot, co-pilot, aeronaut, wingman; N. Amer. informal jock.
3 *he was handing out flyers promoting a new sandwich bar*: **handbill**, bill, handout, leaflet, circular, bulletin, pamphlet, brochure, advertisement, announcement, poster, public notice; Brit. fly-poster; N. Amer. & Austral. dodger; French affiche; informal ad; Brit. informal advert.

flying adjective **1** *a flying beetle*: **airborne**, in the air, in flight; fluttering, flitting, flapping, hovering, floating, gliding, wind-borne, soaring, winging, wheeling; winged; rare volitant.
2 *a flying visit*: **brief**, short, whistle-stop, lightning, fleeting, hasty, rushed, hurried, quick, cursory, perfunctory; momentary; informal quickie; rare fugacious.
▷ANTONYMS long.

foal noun **young horse/donkey/pony/mule**; colt, filly.

foam noun *the white foam on the huge breaking waves*: **froth**, spume, surf, spindrift, spray; fizz, effervescence, bubbles, head; lather, suds.
▶ verb *the water churned and foamed*: **froth**, froth up, cream, bubble, fizz, effervesce, spume, lather, ferment, rise, boil, seethe, simmer.

foamy adjective *leave the yeast mixture until it is foamy*: **frothy**, foaming, spumy, bubbly, aerated, bubbling; sudsy; whipped, whisked; rare spumous, spumescent.

fob verb
□ **fob someone off** *I wasn't going to be fobbed off with excuses*: **put off**, stall, give someone the runaround, deceive; placate, appease; deter, discourage, daunt, scare off, intimidate, unnerve.
□ **fob something off on** *he fobbed off the chairmanship on Clifford*: **impose**, palm off, unload, dump, get rid of, foist, offload, inflict, thrust; saddle someone with something, land someone with something, lumber someone with something, burden someone with something.

focus noun **1** *schools are a focus of community life*: **centre**, focal point, central point, centre of attention, hub, pivot, nucleus, heart, cornerstone, linchpin, kingpin, bedrock, basis, anchor, backbone, cynosure.
2 *the focus of this criticism is on helping people find solutions*: **emphasis**, accent, priority, attention, concentration.
3 *the main focus of this chapter is elected local government*: **subject**, theme, concern, subject matter, topic, issue, question, text, thesis, content, point, motif, thread; substance, essence, gist, matter.
4 *the resulting light beams are brought to a focus at the eyepiece*: **focal point**, point of convergence.
□ **in focus** *colour snaps will do as long as they are in focus*: **sharp**, crisp, distinct, clear-cut, clear, well defined, well focused.
▷**ANTONYMS** out of focus.
□ **out of focus** *why are some of the shots out of focus?* **blurred**, unfocused, indistinct, blurry, fuzzy, hazy, misty, cloudy, foggy, fogged, shadowy, smoky, faint; unclear, vague, indefinite, obscure, lacking definition, ill-defined, nebulous; woolly, muzzy, bleary; archaic blear.
▷**ANTONYMS** in focus.
▸ verb **1** *he focused his binoculars on the distant tower*: **bring into focus**, bring to a focus; aim, point, turn.
2 *the investigation will **focus on** areas of social need*: **concentrate**, fix, centre, pivot, zero in, zoom in; address itself to, pay attention to, pinpoint, spotlight, revolve around, have as its starting point.

foe noun *these horsemen were a well-armed foe*: **enemy**, adversary, opponent, rival, antagonist, combatant, challenger, competitor, opposer, hostile party; (**the foe**) the opposition, the competition, the other side, the opposing side; rare corrival, vier.
▷**ANTONYMS** friend.

fog noun **1** *he lost his way in the fog*: **mist**, mistiness, fogginess, haar, smog, murk, murkiness, haze, haziness, gloom, gloominess; N. English (sea) fret; informal pea-souper; literary brume, fume.
2 *I was in such a fog that I couldn't write my name*: **daze**, stupor, trance, haze, muddle; state of bewilderment, state of confusion, state of disorientation.
▸ verb **1** *the windscreen **fogged up** | his breath fogged the glass*: **steam up**, mist over, cloud over, film over, become misty, become blurred, become covered in condensation; make hazy, make cloudy, obscure, shade, veil; literary befog, becloud.
▷**ANTONYMS** clear.
2 *his brain was fogged with sleep*: **muddle**, daze, stupefy, fuddle, befuddle, bewilder, confuse, perplex, baffle, obscure; literary bedim, becloud; rare obfuscate.

> *Word links* **fog**
> **homichlophobia** fear of fog

foggy adjective **1** *the weather was wet and foggy*: **misty**, smoggy, hazy, overcast, murky, gloomy, grey, dark, dim, dingy, dull; smoky, steamy; informal soupy; Brit. informal fuggy.
▷**ANTONYMS** clear.
2 *the foggy recesses of her mind*: **muddled**, fuddled, befuddled, confused, bewildered, dazed, stupefied, numb, numbed, benumbed, groggy, fuzzy, bleary; dark, dim, hazy, shadowy, cloudy, clouded, blurred, obscure, remote, vague, indistinct, unclear; informal dopey, woolly, muzzy, woozy, out of it; archaic blear.
▷**ANTONYMS** clear.

foible noun *we have to tolerate each other's little foibles*: **weakness**, weak point, weak spot, failing, shortcoming, flaw, imperfection, blemish, fault, defect, frailty, infirmity, inadequacy, limitation; quirk, kink, idiosyncrasy, eccentricity, peculiarity, abnormality; Achilles heel, chink in one's armour; informal hang-up.
▷**ANTONYMS** strength.

foil[1] verb *his attempts to escape were constantly foiled*: **thwart**, frustrate, counter, oppose, baulk, disappoint, impede, obstruct, hamper, hinder, snooker, cripple, scotch, derail, smash, dash; stop, check, block, prevent, defeat, nip in the bud; informal mess up, screw up, do for, put paid to, stymie, cook someone's goose; Brit. informal scupper, nobble, queer, put the mockers on; Austral./NZ & Irish vulgar slang root; archaic traverse.
▷**ANTONYMS** assist.

foil[2] noun *the black gown was the perfect foil for her colouring*: **contrast**, background, setting, relief, antithesis; **complement**.

foist verb **1** *poor-quality lagers are being **foisted on** unsuspecting drinkers*: **impose**, force, thrust, offload, unload, dump, palm off, fob off; shift on to; pass off, get rid of; (**foist something on to someone**) saddle someone with, land someone with, burden someone with, lumber someone with.
2 *he attempted to foist a new minister into the conference*: **sneak**, insinuate, interpolate, insert, introduce, squeeze, edge; informal stick.

fold[1] verb **1** *I helped him fold his sheets*: **double**, double over, double up, crease, turn under, turn up, turn over, bend, overlap; tuck, gather, pleat, crimp, bunch.
2 *fold the cream into the chocolate mixture*: **mix**, blend, stir gently; envelop, introduce, spoon.
3 *he folded her in his arms*: **enfold**, wrap, wrap up, envelop; take, gather, clasp, squeeze, clutch; embrace, hug, cuddle, cradle; literary embosom; archaic strain.
4 *the firm finally folded in the mid '70s*: **fail**, collapse, crash, founder, be ruined, cave in; **go bankrupt**, become insolvent, cease trading, go into receivership, go into liquidation, be liquidated, be wound up, be closed (down), be shut (down); informal go bust, go broke, go bump, go under, go to the wall, go belly up, come a cropper, flop.
▸ noun *the curtain falls in soft folds*: **pleat**, gather, ruffle, bunch, turn, folded portion, double thickness, overlap, layer; crease, knife-edge; wrinkle, crinkle, pucker, furrow.

fold[2] noun **1** *the sheep were pushing into the fold*: **enclosure**, pen, paddock, pound, compound, ring, stall; sty, coop; Scottish parrock; N. Amer. corral; S. African kraal; in S. America potrero.
2 *he urged them to return to the Roman Catholic fold*: **community**, company, group, body, mass, throng, congregation, assembly; Church, church membership, brethren, parishioners, churchgoers; informal flock.

folder noun *he tucked the notes into a folder*: **file**, binder, ring binder, portfolio, document case; envelope, sleeve, jacket, wrapper, wallet.

foliage noun *a garden full of green and gold foliage*: **leaves**, leafage, greenery, vegetation; rare herbage, verdure.

folk noun **1** *he doesn't work the same hours as ordinary folk | the folk of East Anglia*: **people**, humans, persons, individuals, (living) souls, mortals; citizenry, inhabitants, residents, populace, population, public, {men, women, and children}; informal peeps; rare denizens.
2 (**folks**) informal *my folks came from the north*: **relatives**, relations, blood relations, family, family members, kinsfolk, kinsmen, kinswomen, kin, kindred, next of kin, flesh and blood; informal nearest and dearest; dated people.

folklore noun *he studied the local customs and folklore*: **mythology**, lore, oral history, tradition, folk tradition; **legends**, fables, myths, folk tales, folk stories, old wives' tales; technical mythus, mythos.

follow verb **1** *I'll go with you and we'll let the others follow*: **come behind**, come after, go behind, go after, walk behind, tread on the heels of.
▷**ANTONYMS** lead.
2 *he was expected to follow his father in the business*: **take the place of**, replace, succeed, take over from, supersede, supplant; informal step into someone's shoes, fill someone's shoes/boots.
3 *loads of people used to **follow** the band **around***: **accompany**, go along with, go around with, travel with, escort, attend, trail around with; informal tag along with, string along with.
▷**ANTONYMS** lead.
4 *the KGB man followed her everywhere*: **shadow**, trail, pursue, chase, stalk, hunt, track, dog, hound, course; give chase to, be hot on someone's heels; informal tail.
5 *always follow the manufacturer's guidelines*: **act in accordance with**, abide by, adhere to, stick to, keep to, comply with, conform to, obey, observe, heed, pay attention to, note, have regard to, mind, bear in mind, take to heart, be guided by, accept, yield to, defer to, respect.
▷**ANTONYMS** flout.
6 *a new way of life **followed from** contact with Europeans*: **result**, arise, develop, ensue, emanate, issue, proceed, spring, flow, originate, stem; be a consequence of, be caused by, be brought about by, be produced by, be a result of, come after.
▷**ANTONYMS** lead to.
7 *he said something complicated and I couldn't follow it*: **understand**, comprehend, apprehend, take in, grasp, fathom, appreciate, keep up with, see; informal make head or tail of, latch on to, catch on to, tumble to, get, get the hang of, figure out, get one's head around, get one's mind around, take on board, get the picture, get the drift, get the message, see the light; Brit. informal suss out; N. Amer. informal savvy; rare cognize.
▷**ANTONYMS** misunderstand.
8 *Rembrandt's last pupil followed the style of his master*: **imitate**, copy, mimic, ape, reproduce, mirror, echo; **emulate**, take as a pattern, take as an example, take as a model, adopt the style of, style oneself on, model oneself on; informal take a leaf out of someone's book.
9 *he follows Manchester United*: **be a fan of**, be a supporter of, support, be a follower of, be an admirer of, be a devotee of, be devoted to; be interested in, cultivate an interest in.
▷**ANTONYMS** dislike.
□ **follow something through** *they lack the resources to follow the project through*: **complete**, bring to completion, bring to a finish, continue to the

end, see something through; continue with, carry on with, keep on with, keep going with, stay with; informal stick something out.
▷ANTONYMS abandon.
□ **follow something up** *I've had one of my hunches and I'm going to follow it up*: **investigate**, research, find out about, look into, dig into, delve into, make enquiries into, enquire about, ask questions about, pursue, chase up; informal check out; N. Amer. informal scope out.

follower noun **1** *the president summoned his closest followers*: **acolyte**, assistant, attendant, satellite, companion, retainer, henchman, minion, lackey, toady, servant, page, squire; informal hanger-on, camp follower, sidekick; archaic liegeman, pursuivant.
▷ANTONYMS leader.
2 *the picture was painted by a follower of Caravaggio*: **imitator**, emulator, copier, copyist, mimic, ape; pupil, tutee, trainee, disciple; informal copycat.
3 *a follower of Christ*: **disciple**, apostle, supporter, defender, champion; believer, worshipper, votary.
▷ANTONYMS opponent.
4 *she's a follower of the Rolling Stones*: **fan**, enthusiast, admirer, devotee, lover, supporter, adherent; informal groupie, camp follower, hanger-on; N. Amer. informal rooter, booster.

following noun *the Jacobite cause retained a substantial following*: **body of support**, backing, patronage; public, audience, circle, coterie; retinue, train; supporters, backers, admirers, fans, adherents, devotees, advocates, patrons; informal groupies.
▸ adjective **1** *he sent a reply the following day*: **next**, ensuing, succeeding, subsequent, successive; archaic after.
▷ANTONYMS preceding.
2 *candidates must satisfy the following criteria*: **upcoming**, about to be mentioned, about to be specified, further on, below, underneath, at the end; formal hereunder, hereinafter.
▷ANTONYMS aforementioned.

folly noun *he cursed himself for his folly*: **foolishness**, foolhardiness, stupidity, idiocy, imbecility, silliness, inanity, lunacy, madness, rashness, recklessness, imprudence, injudiciousness, lack of caution, lack of foresight, lack of sense, irrationality, illogicality, irresponsibility, thoughtlessness, indiscretion; informal craziness; Brit. informal daftness.
▷ANTONYMS wisdom; good sense.

foment verb *they were accused of fomenting civil unrest*: **instigate**, incite, provoke, agitate, excite, stir up, whip up, arouse, inspire, encourage, urge, actuate, initiate, generate, cause, prompt, start, bring about, kindle, spark off, trigger off, touch off, fan the flames of; rare enkindle, effectuate.

fond adjective **1** *she was* ***fond of*** *dancing | I'm very* ***fond of*** *Chris*: **keen on**, partial to, addicted to, enthusiastic about, passionate about; attached to, attracted to, enamoured of, in love with, with a soft spot for; informal into, hooked on, gone on, wild about, nuts about, potty about, dotty about, crazy about, sweet on, struck on.
▷ANTONYMS indifferent to.
2 *his fond father plied him with cakes*: **adoring**, devoted, doting, loving, caring, affectionate, warm, tender, kind, attentive, solicitous; indulgent, overindulgent, overfond.
▷ANTONYMS unfeeling.
3 *fond hopes of success*: **unrealistic**, **naive**, foolish, foolishly optimistic, over-optimistic, deluded, delusory, absurd, empty, vain; rare Panglossian.
▷ANTONYMS realistic.

fondle verb *he fondled the Labrador's ears*: **caress**, stroke, pat, pet, pull, finger, touch, tickle, twiddle, play with, massage, knead; maul, molest; informal paw, grope, feel up, touch up, cop a feel of.

fondness noun **1** *they look at each other with such fondness*: **affection**, love, liking, warmth, tenderness, kindness, devotion, care, endearment, feeling, sentiment, attachment, closeness, friendliness, familiarity, intimacy; regard, respect, admiration, adoration, worship, reverence.
▷ANTONYMS hatred.
2 *he has a fondness for spicy food*: **liking**, love, taste, partiality, preference, keenness, inclination, penchant, predilection, fancy, relish, passion, proclivity, appetite; weakness, soft spot, susceptibility, addiction; informal thing, yen; rare appetency.
▷ANTONYMS dislike.

food noun **1** *he went three days without food*: **nourishment**, sustenance, nutriment, subsistence, fare, bread, daily bread; cooking, baking, cuisine; **foodstuffs**, edibles, refreshments, meals, provisions, rations, stores, supplies; solids; Scottish vivers; informal eats, eatables, nosh, grub, chow, nibbles; Brit. informal scoff, tuck; N. Amer. informal chuck; archaic victuals, vittles, viands, commons, meat; rare comestibles, provender, aliment, commissariat, viaticum.
2 *food for the cattle and horses*: **fodder**, feed, forage, herbage, pasturage, silage; rare comestibles, provender.
□ **food for thought mental stimulation**, mental nourishment, something to think about, something to be seriously considered.

Word links **food**

alimentary, **culinary** relating to food
-trophic related suffix, as in *oligotrophic, mycotrophic*
cibophobia, **sitophobia** fear of food

foodie noun informal *he is an avid foodie and successful restaurateur*. See **epicure**.

fool noun **1** *you've acted like a complete fool*: **idiot**, ass, halfwit, nincompoop, blockhead, buffoon, dunce, dolt, ignoramus, cretin, imbecile, dullard, moron, simpleton, clod; informal dope, ninny, chump, dimwit, goon, dumbo, dummy, dum-dum, dumb-bell, loon, jackass, bonehead, fathead, numbskull, dunderhead, chucklehead, knucklehead, muttonhead, pudding-head, thickhead, wooden-head, airhead, pinhead, lamebrain, pea-brain, birdbrain, zombie, jerk, nerd, dipstick, donkey, noodle; Brit. informal nit, nitwit, numpty, twit, clot, goat, plonker, berk, prat, pillock, wally, git, wazzock, divvy, nerk, dork, twerp, charlie, mug, muppet; Scottish informal nyaff, balloon, sumph, gowk; Irish informal gobdaw; N. Amer. informal schmuck, bozo, boob, lamer, turkey, schlepper, chowderhead, dumbhead, goofball, goof, goofus, galoot, lummox, klutz, putz, schlemiel, sap, meatball, gink, cluck, clunk, ding-dong, dingbat, wiener, weeny, dip, simp, spud, coot, palooka, poop, squarehead, yo-yo, dingleberry; Austral./NZ informal drongo, dill, alec, galah, nong, bogan, poon, boofhead; S. African informal mompara; archaic tomfool, noddy, clodpole, loggerhead, spoony, mooncalf.
2 *she always makes a fool of him*: **laughing stock**, dupe, butt, gull, pushover, easy mark, tool, cat's paw; informal stooge, sucker, mug, fall guy; N. Amer. informal sap.
3 historical *the fool in King James's court*: **jester**, court jester, clown, buffoon, comic, joker, jokester, zany, merry andrew; wearer of the motley, harlequin, Pierrot, Punchinello, Pantaloon.
▸ verb **1** *he found he'd been fooled by a schoolboy*: **deceive**, trick, play a trick on, hoax, dupe, take in, mislead, delude, hoodwink, bluff, beguile, gull, make a fool of, outwit; swindle, defraud, cheat, double-cross; informal con, bamboozle, pull a fast one on, pull someone's leg, take for a ride, pull the wool over someone's eyes, throw dust in someone's eyes, put one over on, have on, diddle, fiddle, swizzle, rip off, do, sting, gyp, shaft; Brit. informal sell a pup to; N. Amer. informal sucker, snooker, stiff, euchre, bunco, hornswoggle; Austral. informal pull a swifty on; rare cozen, sharp, mulct.
2 *she screamed but they thought she was fooling*: **pretend**, make believe, feign, put on an act, act, sham, fake, counterfeit; tease, joke, jest, play tricks, clown about/around, play the fool; informal kid, mess about/around; Brit. informal wind someone up, have someone on, muck someone about/around.
3 *she* ***fooled around*** *with a bunch of keys while she spoke*: **fiddle**, play (about/around), toy, trifle, meddle, tamper, interfere, monkey about/around; informal mess about/around; Brit. informal muck about/around.
4 informal *my husband's been* ***fooling around*** *behind my back*: **philander**, womanize, flirt, have an affair, commit adultery; informal play around, mess about/around, carry on, play the field, play away, sleep around, swing; vulgar slang screw around; rare coquet.

foolery noun *we had to endure his foolery all afternoon*: **clowning**, fooling, tomfoolery, hoaxing, mischief, buffoonery, silliness, silly behaviour, skylarking, horseplay; antics, capers, practical jokes, pranks; foolishness, stupidity, idiocy; informal larking around, larks, shenanigans; Brit. informal monkey tricks; N. Amer. informal didoes; archaic harlequinade.

foolhardy adjective *he'd been stupid and foolhardy*: **reckless**, rash, incautious, careless, heedless, unheeding, thoughtless, unwise, imprudent, irresponsible, injudicious, impulsive, hot-headed, impetuous, daredevil, devil-may-care, death-or-glory, madcap, hare-brained, precipitate, precipitous, desperate, hasty, overhasty, over-adventurous, over-venturesome; literary temerarious.
▷ANTONYMS wise.

Choose the right word **foolhardy, rash, reckless**

See **rash²**.

foolish adjective *her desperation led her to do something foolish*: **stupid**, silly, idiotic, half-witted, witless, brainless, mindless, thoughtless, imprudent, incautious, irresponsible, injudicious, indiscreet, unwise, unintelligent, unreasonable; ill-advised, ill-considered, impolitic, rash, reckless, foolhardy, lunatic; absurd, senseless, pointless, nonsensical, inane, fatuous, ridiculous, laughable, risible, derisible; informal dumb, dim, dim-witted, dopey, gormless, damfool, half-baked, hare-brained, crackbrained, pea-brained, wooden-headed, thickheaded, nutty, mad, crazy, dotty, batty, dippy, cuckoo, screwy, wacky; Brit. informal barmy, daft; Scottish & N. English informal glaikit; N. Amer. informal dumb-ass, chowderheaded; W. Indian informal dotish.
▷ANTONYMS sensible; wise.

Word toolkit

foolish	silly	vacuous
mistake	hat	rhetoric
child	superstition	expression
grin	joke	celebrity
decision	game	statement
idea	story	existence
behaviour	song	TV show

foolishly adverb *he'd be very cross with me if I acted foolishly*: **stupidly**, idiotically, ineptly, inanely, senselessly, unwisely, ill-advisedly, incautiously, indiscreetly, short-sightedly; without thinking, without forethought; fatuously, absurdly; informal crazily; Brit. informal barmily.

foolishness noun *I regretted my foolishness over the matter*: **folly**, foolhardiness, stupidity, idiocy, imbecility, silliness, inanity, lunacy, madness, rashness, recklessness, imprudence, injudiciousness, lack of caution/foresight/sense, irrationality, illogicality, irresponsibility, thoughtlessness, indiscretion; informal craziness; Brit. informal daftness.
▷ANTONYMS wisdom; sense.

foolproof adjective *we need a foolproof security system*: **infallible**, never failing, unfailing, unerring, dependable, reliable, trustworthy, certain, sure, guaranteed, safe, sound, effective, efficacious, tried and tested; watertight, airtight, flawless, perfect; informal sure-fire.
▷ANTONYMS flawed.

foot noun **1** *he trod on someone's foot*: informal tootsie, trotter; (**feet**) rhyming slang plates of meat; N. Amer. informal dogs.
2 *a four-footed animal*: **paw**, forepaw, hind paw, hoof, trotter, pad; technical tarsus, ungula; rare slot, dewclaw.
3 *she lived at the foot of the hill*: **bottom**, base, toe, edge, end, lowest part, lowest point, lower limits; foundation.
▶ verb
□ **foot the bill** informal *ministers expected the taxpayer to foot the bill*: **pay**, pay up, pay out, pay the bill, settle up; bail someone out; informal pick up the tab, cough up, fork out, shell out, come across, chip in; Brit. informal stump up; N. Amer. informal ante up, pony up, pick up the check.

Word links **foot**

ped-: *pedal, pedometer* related prefix
-pod(e): *gastropod, megapode* related suffix
chiropody medical treatment of the feet

footing noun **1** *Jenny lost her footing and plunged into the river*: **foothold**, toehold, hold, grip, anchorage, purchase, secure position, firm contact, support; steadiness, stability, balance, equilibrium.
2 *the business was put on a solid financial footing*: **basis**, base, foundation, underpinning, support, cornerstone.
3 *female clerks should be on an equal footing with male clerks*: **standing**, status, state, station, position, rank, grade; condition, arrangement, basis, foundation; relationship, relations, terms.

footling adjective *she insisted on some footling changes to the text*: **trivial**, trifling, petty, insignificant, unimportant, minor, silly, pointless, immaterial, irrelevant, inessential, non-essential, time-wasting, fiddling, hair-splitting, paltry, nugatory, worthless; of little account, not worth bothering about, not worth mentioning; informal piddling, piffling, penny-ante; Brit. informal twopenny-halfpenny; N. Amer. informal nickel-and-dime, small-bore, picayune.
▷ANTONYMS important; major.

footnote noun *the journal has discreet and informative footnotes*: **note**, marginal note, annotation, comment, gloss; aside, incidental remark, digression, parenthesis; (**footnotes**) notation, marginalia, commentary; rare scholium.

footprint noun *the walkway was covered with footprints*: **footmark**, footstep, track, print, mark, spoor, trace, impression.

footslog verb *they footslogged around two villages*: **trudge**, traipse, slog, hike, trek, tramp, plod, troop, walk, march, pace, stride; toil, labour, drag oneself; Brit. informal yomp, trog; N. Amer. informal schlep.
▶ noun *the eighteen-mile footslog raised £600 for charity*: **hike**, trek, slog, traipse, trudge, tramp, walk, march, route march, long haul; Brit. informal yomp; N. Amer. informal schlep.

footstep noun **1** *her footsteps echoed down the bare corridor*: **footfall**, step, stride, tread, pace, stomp, stamp.
2 *they left their footsteps in the sand*: **footprint**, footmark, track, print, mark, spoor, trace, impression.

fop noun *a flamboyant bunch of young fops*: **dandy**, beau, poseur, glamour boy, man about town, bright young thing, rake; French boulevardier, petit-maître; informal swell, toff, snappy dresser, sharp dresser, natty dresser, trendy, pretty boy; archaic coxcomb, popinjay, peacock, buck.

foppish adjective *the clothes were less foppish than his usual attire*: **dandyish**, dandified, dapper, dressy, spruce; affected, dainty, preening, vain; **effeminate**, effete, girly, niminy-piminy, mincing, posturing; informal la-di-da, natty, sissy, camp, campy, queeny; informal, derogatory poncey, pansyish.

forage verb *villagers were forced to forage for food*: **hunt**, hunt around, search, look about/around/round, cast about/around/round, rummage (about/around/round), ferret (about/around), root about/around, scratch about/around, nose around/about/round, scour, look high and low; seek, look, explore; informal scrounge around; Brit. informal rootle around.
▶ noun **1** *there was little forage for the horses*: **fodder**, feed, food, foodstuff, herbage, pasturage; silage, hay, straw; formal comestibles, provender.
2 *a nightly forage for food*: **scavenge**, hunt, search, look, exploration, quest, scout, probe.

foray noun *the garrison made a foray against Richard's camp*: **raid**, attack, assault, incursion, swoop, strike, charge, sortie, sally, rush, onrush, push, thrust, onslaught, offensive, bombardment; act of aggression, act of war, blitz, campaign; archaic onset.

forbear verb *the boy forebore from touching anything*: **refrain**, abstain, desist, keep, restrain oneself, stop oneself, hold back, withhold; resist the temptation to, steer clear of, give a wide berth to, fight shy of; eschew, avoid, shun, decline to; cease, give up, break off; informal lay off, leave off, swear off; Brit. informal give over, jack in; nautical slang belay.
▷ANTONYMS persist in.

forbearance noun *her unfailing courtesy and forbearance under provocation*: **tolerance**, toleration, patience, resignation, endurance, fortitude, stoicism, long-sufferingness, leniency, lenity, clemency, indulgence; **restraint**, self-restraint, self-control, moderation, temperance, mildness.

forbearing adjective *he was tactful and forbearing when I got angry*: **patient**, tolerant, easy-going, forgiving, merciful, understanding, accommodating, indulgent, kind; uncomplaining, long-suffering, resigned, stoical, stoic; **restrained**, self-restrained, self-controlled, moderate, mild, easy, calm; informal unflappable, cool; rare longanimous.
▷ANTONYMS impatient, intolerant.

forbid verb *the act forbade discrimination on the grounds of sex*: **prohibit**, ban, outlaw, make illegal, veto, proscribe, disallow, preclude, exclude, rule out, bar, debar, block, stop, put a stop to, put an end to, declare taboo; informal give the red light to, give the thumbs down to, put the kibosh on; N. Amer. interdict; Law enjoin, restrain.
▷ANTONYMS permit.

Choose the right word **forbid, ban, prohibit**

These words refer to the issuing of orders by people in a position of authority, to prevent something from happening or to exclude someone from somewhere.

To **forbid** is to order someone not to do something or to say that something may not be done, typically in matters of custom, religion, or personal conduct (*her father forbade her to see Philip again* | *the code of business ethics forbids bribery*).

To **ban** something is to make an official order, often a law or rule, abolishing an existing practice or item (*the government pledged itself to ban hunting*). It can be followed by *from* and either an activity (*he was banned from driving for a year*) or a place (*a proposal to ban tankers from Venice*).

To **prohibit** something is usually done by means of a law or regulation (*legislation prohibiting late abortions* | *vehicles will be prohibited from entering High Row*). *Prohibit* can also mean 'make impossible' (*severe physical problems prohibited these children from entering regular school*).

forbidden adjective *smoking is now forbidden in certain areas*: **prohibited**, banned, debarred, vetoed, proscribed, ruled out, not allowed, disallowed, taboo, impermissible, not acceptable, unauthorized, unsanctioned; outlawed, illegal, unlawful, illicit, illegitimate, criminal; N. Amer. interdicted; German verboten; Islam haram; NZ tapu; informal no go, not on, out; rare non licet.
▷ANTONYMS permitted; legal.

forbidding adjective **1** *he had a rather forbidding manner*: **hostile**, unwelcoming, unfriendly, unsympathetic, unapproachable, harsh, grim, stern, hard, tough, cool, cold, chilly, frosty; disagreeable, nasty, mean, abhorrent, repellent; informal off-putting.
▷ANTONYMS friendly.
2 *the dark castle looked forbidding*: **threatening**, ominous, menacing, sinister, brooding, daunting, fearsome, frightening, chilling, disturbing, disquieting; hostile, unwelcoming, uninviting, unfriendly; foreboding, unpromising, inauspicious, evil-looking, suggestive of evil; informal spooky, scary, creepy; archaic direful, bodeful.
▷ANTONYMS inviting.

force noun **1** *Eddie delivered a blow with all his force*: **strength**, power, energy, might, potency, vigour, muscle, stamina, effort, exertion, impact, pressure, weight, impetus; informal punch.
▷ANTONYMS weakness.

f

2 *they used force to achieve their aims*: **coercion**, compulsion, constraint, duress, oppression, enforcement, harassment, intimidation, threats, pressure, pressurization, influence; **violence**; French force majeure; informal arm-twisting.
3 *they couldn't deny the force of the argument*: **cogency**, weight, effectiveness, efficacy, efficaciousness, soundness, validity, strength, might, power, significance, influence, authority, impressiveness, eloquence, persuasiveness, credibility, conclusiveness; logic, logicality, foundation, reasonableness, coherence; informal bite, punch.
▷ANTONYMS weakness.
4 *he gave a performance of staggering expressive force*: **intensity**, feeling, passion, vigour, vigorousness, vehemence, drive, fierceness; vividness, impact; informal pizzazz, oomph, zing, zip, zap, punch.
▷ANTONYMS shallowness.
5 *they see male lust as a corrupting force*: **agency**, power, influence, instrument, vehicle, means, cause, effect.
6 *the government sent in a peacekeeping force*: **body**, body of people, group, outfit, party, team; **corps**, detachment, unit, squad, squadron, company, battalion, division, patrol, regiment, army; in ancient Rome cohort; informal bunch.
□ **in force 1** *the state of emergency remained in force*: **effective**, in operation, operative, operational, in action, valid, on the statute book, current, live, active; binding; informal up and running. **2** *her fans were out in force*: **in great numbers**, in great quantities, in hordes, in full strength.
▸ **verb 1** *the raiders forced him to open the safe*: **compel**, coerce, make, constrain, oblige, impel, drive, necessitate, pressurize, pressure, press, push; exert force on, use force on, urge by force, use duress on, bring pressure to bear on, press-gang, browbeat, steamroller, bully, dragoon, bludgeon, terrorize, menace; informal put the squeeze on, put the bite on, put the screws on, tighten the screws on, lean on, twist someone's arm, use strong-arm tactics on, strong-arm, railroad, bulldoze.
2 *the doors had to be forced*: **break open**, force open, burst open, prise open, kick in, knock down, blast; crack.
3 *water was forced through a hole in the pipe*: **propel**, push, thrust, shove, drive, press, pump, expel.
4 *they forced a confession out of the kids*: **extract**, elicit, exact, extort, wrest, wring, wrench, drag, screw, squeeze, milk; informal bleed.
□ **force out** *seventeen people were forced out of their homes*: **evict**, expel, eject, oust, remove, dislodge, turn out, put out, throw out, throw out on the streets, throw out on one's ear, drum out, drive out; informal chuck out, kick out, boot out, heave out, throw someone out on their ear.

> *Choose the right word* **force, compel, coerce, oblige**
>
> See **compel**.

forced adjective **1** *a programme of forced industrialization*: **enforced**, compulsory, obligatory, mandatory, involuntary, exacted, coerced, imposed, demanded, compelled, required, requisite, stipulated, dictated, ordained, prescribed; necessitated, unavoidable, inescapable; French de rigueur.
▷ANTONYMS voluntary.
2 *her vivacity seemed a little bit forced*: **strained**, laboured, unnatural, artificial, false, feigned, simulated, contrived, stilted, wooden, stiff, studied, mannered, self-conscious, overdone, overworked, affected, unconvincing, insincere, hollow; informal phoney, pretend, pseudo, put on.
▷ANTONYMS natural.

forceful adjective **1** *she had a forceful personality*: **dynamic**, energetic, assertive, authoritative, vigorous, powerful, potent, strong, strong-willed, pushing, driving, determined, insistent, commanding, bullish, dominant, domineering; bold, confident, self-confident, self-assured, self-possessed, audacious, enterprising, competitive, go-ahead, zealous; informal pushy, bossy, in-your-face, not backward in coming forward, feisty.
▷ANTONYMS weak; submissive.
2 *the board was persuaded by his forceful arguments*: **cogent**, convincing, compelling, strong, powerful, potent, weighty, plausible, effective, efficacious, sound, valid, well founded, telling; impressive, persuasive, irresistible, eloquent, credible, influential, conclusive, unanswerable, authoritative; **logical**, reasoned, reasonable, rational, lucid, coherent.
▷ANTONYMS weak; unconvincing.

forcible adjective **1** *they checked the doors for signs of forcible entry*: **forced**, violent; by force, using force, with force.
2 *there was no attempt at forcible conversion*: **compulsory**, forced, enforced, obligatory, mandatory, involuntary, imposed, exacted, coerced, demanded, compelled, required, stipulated, dictated, ordained, prescribed; unavoidable, inescapable.
3 *a forcible demonstration of his changed attitude*: **forceful**, cogent, convincing, compelling, strong, powerful, potent, weighty, plausible, effective, efficacious, valid, telling; impressive, persuasive, eloquent, credible, influential, conclusive, unanswerable.

forcibly adverb **1** *he was thrown out of the club forcibly*: **by force**, against one's will, under protest, compulsorily, under compulsion, under coercion, of necessity; with force, with violence, violently, roughly, unceremoniously, willy-nilly; bodily.
2 *they made their point forcibly*: **forcefully**, vigorously, powerfully, potently, dynamically, energetically, assertively, heartily, eagerly, zealously, strenuously, aggressively; **cogently**, effectively, persuasively, convincingly, authoritatively, tellingly, movingly, impressively.

ford noun *a ford across the Tweed*: **crossing place**, crossing, causeway; shallow place; S. African drift.
▸ **verb** *if I could find the river, I could ford it somehow*: **cross**, traverse; wade across, walk across, drive across, travel across, make it across, make one's way across.

forebear noun *she speaks the language of her forebears*: **ancestor**, forefather, predecessor, progenitor, father, grandfather, parent, grandparent; antecedent, forerunner, precursor; rare primogenitor.
▷ANTONYMS descendant.

forebode verb literary *this lull foreboded some new assault upon him*: **presage**, augur, portend, prognosticate, foreshadow, foreshow, foretell, forecast, predict, prophesy, forewarn, warn of, be a warning of, herald, be an omen of, be a harbinger of; signify, mean, indicate, add up to, point to, announce, promise; informal spell; literary foretoken, betoken, harbinger; rare prefigure.

foreboding noun **1** *she was seized with a feeling of foreboding*: **apprehension**, apprehensiveness, anxiety, perturbation, trepidation, disquiet, disquietude, unease, uneasiness, misgiving, suspicion, worry, fear, fearfulness, dread, alarm; informal butterflies (in the stomach), the willies, the heebie-jeebies, the jitters, jitteriness, twitchiness; rare inquietude.
▷ANTONYMS calm.
2 *in the end their forebodings proved justified*: **premonition**, presentiment, intuition, feeling, vague feeling, suspicion, inkling, hunch; warning, omen, portent, sign, token; prediction, augury, prophecy, presage, prognostication, forecast; informal gut feeling, feeling in one's bones, funny feeling, sixth sense.

forecast verb *they forecast that shares in the company will start trading at a profit soon*: **predict**, prophesy, prognosticate, augur, divine, foretell, foresee, forewarn; guess, hazard a guess, conjecture, speculate, estimate, calculate, reckon, expect; Scottish archaic spae; rare presage, previse, vaticinate, auspicate.
▸ **noun** *a gloomy forecast of the impact of global warming*: **prediction**, prophecy, forewarning, prognostication, augury, divination, prognosis, projection, calculation; guess, estimate, conjecture, speculation; warning, signal, sign, token; informal guesstimate; literary foretoken; rare prognostic, vaticination, auspication.

forefather noun *they gave up the wicked customs of their forefathers*: **forebear**, ancestor, predecessor, progenitor, father, grandfather, parent, grandparent; antecedent, forerunner, precursor; rare primogenitor.
▷ANTONYMS descendant.

forefront noun *a cabinet post thrust him to the forefront of British politics*: **vanguard**, van, spearhead, head, lead, fore, front, front line, cutting edge, foreground, foremost/leading position, position of prominence.
▷ANTONYMS rear, background.

forego verb See **forgo**.

foregoing adjective *despite the foregoing criticisms, we welcome the changes*: **preceding**, aforesaid, aforementioned, previously mentioned, earlier, above, above-stated; antecedent, previous, prior; rare anterior, prevenient, precedent, precursive, supra.
▷ANTONYMS following.

foregone adjective literary *the ghosts of foregone dreams*: **past**, former, earlier, previous, prior, bygone, old, of old, ancient, long-ago; forgotten; literary of yore; rare forepassed.
□ **a foregone conclusion** *they accepted an interest rate rise as a foregone conclusion*: **certainty**, predictable result, predictable outcome, inevitability, matter of course; informal sure thing, cert, dead cert.
▷ANTONYMS possibility.

foreground noun **1** *she repainted the figures in the foreground*: **front**, fore, forefront, forepart, foremost part, nearest part, closest part.
2 *he was in the foreground of the political drama*: **forefront**, vanguard, van, spearhead, head, lead, fore, front, front line, cutting edge, foremost position, leading position, position of prominence.

forehead noun *she brushed a lock of hair from her forehead*: **brow**, temple; Zoology frons.

> *Word links* **forehead**
>
> **frontal** relating to the forehead

foreign adjective **1** *foreign branches of UK banks*: **overseas**, distant, remote, far off, far flung, external, outside; alien, non-native, adventitious.
▷ANTONYMS domestic.
2 *the concept is very foreign to us Westerners*: **unfamiliar**, unknown, unheard of, strange, alien, exotic, outlandish, odd, peculiar, curious,

bizarre, weird, queer, funny; novel, new.
▷ANTONYMS familiar.
3 formal *this matter is altogether **foreign to** the affair in hand*: **irrelevant**, not pertinent, inappropriate, inapposite, extraneous, unrelated, unconnected; outside, distant from, remote from, disconnected from, different from; rare extrinsic.
▷ANTONYMS relevant.

foreigner noun *the country was ruled by a foreigner*: **alien**, non-native, immigrant, settler, newcomer, stranger, outsider; visitor, tourist; Brit. incomer; N. English offcomer; SE Asian gweilo.

Word links **foreigner**
xenophobia fear of foreigners

foreman, forewoman noun *the foreman was left in charge of the printing works*: **supervisor**, overseer, superintendent, manager, manageress, boss, team leader, line manager, controller; foreperson; Brit. chargehand, captain, ganger; Scottish grieve; S. African induna; in the Indian subcontinent maistry; informal chief, head honcho, governor, super; Brit. informal gaffer, guv'nor; N. Amer. informal ramrod, straw boss; Austral. informal pannikin boss; Mining overman.

foremost adjective *one of the foremost Spanish Renaissance artists*: **leading**, principal, premier, prime, elite, top, top-tier, top-level, first-rate, greatest, best, supreme, pre-eminent, major, most important, most prominent, most influential, most skilled, most illustrious, outstanding, notable, noteworthy, of note; first, primary, main, paramount, chief, key, central; N. Amer. ranking; informal number-one, top-notch.
▷ANTONYMS minor.

foreordained adjective *the outcome of the matter was foreordained*: **predetermined**, **preordained**, ordained, predestined, destined, fated; rare predestinated.

forerunner noun 1 *archosaurs were the forerunners of dinosaurs*: **predecessor**, precursor, antecedent, ancestor, forebear; prototype; rare primogenitor.
▷ANTONYMS descendant.
2 *the pain was feared as a forerunner of something worse*: **herald**, harbinger, usher, advance guard; precursor, prelude; sign, signal, warning, token, portent, omen, augury.

foresee verb *Harry foresaw further problems for them*: **anticipate**, predict, forecast, expect, envisage, envision, see, think likely; foretell, prophesy, divine, prognosticate, augur; literary foreknow, forebode; Scottish archaic spae; rare vaticinate, auspicate.

Choose the right word **foresee, anticipate, expect**
See **anticipate**.

foreshadow verb *the city's decline was foreshadowed by earlier events*: **augur**, presage, portend, prognosticate, foreshow, foretell, indicate, suggest, signal, herald, forewarn, warn of, promise, point to, anticipate; literary forebode, foretoken, betoken, harbinger; rare prefigure.

foresight noun *a little foresight might have saved them a lot of money*: **forethought**, anticipation, planning, forward planning, provision, prescience, circumspection, watchfulness, attentiveness, vigilance, prudence, care, caution, precaution, readiness, preparedness; **far-sightedness**, discernment, presence of mind, judiciousness, discrimination, perspicacity, vision, awareness, penetration; N. Amer. forehandedness.
▷ANTONYMS hindsight.

forest noun *they came to a clearing in the forest*: **wood(s)**, woodland, trees, tree plantation, plantation; jungle; archaic greenwood, holt.

Word links **forest**
sylvan relating to forests

forestall verb *they will resign to forestall a vote of no confidence*: **pre-empt**, get in before, get ahead of, steal a march on, anticipate, second-guess, nip in the bud, thwart, frustrate, foil, stave off, ward off, fend off, avert, preclude, obviate, prevent, intercept, check, block, hinder, impede, obstruct; informal beat someone to it, beat someone to the draw/punch.

forestry noun **forest management**, forest planting, forest cultivation, tree growing, forestation, afforestation, agroforestry; woodcraft, woodsmanship; technical arboriculture, silviculture, dendrology.

foretaste noun *the opening parade gives a foretaste of the spectacle to come*: **sample**, taster, taste, preview, trailer, appetizer, tester, specimen, example; indication, suggestion, hint, whiff; warning, forewarning, advance warning, omen; informal tip-off, try-out.

foretell verb 1 *it all happened as she had foretold*: **predict**, forecast, foresee, anticipate, envisage, envision, see, prophesy, prognosticate, augur, divine; warn, forewarn; archaic foreshow, croak; Scottish archaic spae; rare vaticinate, auspicate.
2 *the shootings foretold more terrible violence*: **augur**, presage, portend, foreshadow, indicate, signal, point to, add up to, be an omen of, be a warning of, be a harbinger of; literary forebode, foretoken, betoken, harbinger; rare prefigure.

forethought noun *forethought is needed before you embark on such a project*: **anticipation**, planning, forward planning, provision, precaution, prescience, circumspection, prudence, care, caution; foresight, far-sightedness, discernment, presence of mind, judiciousness, perspicacity, vision, awareness, penetration; N. Amer. forehandedness.

foretoken verb literary *a shiver in the night air foretokens December*. See **signal**[1] (sense 3 of the verb).

forever adverb 1 *their love would last forever*: **for always**, evermore, for ever and ever, for good, for good and all, for all time, until the end of time, eternally, undyingly, perpetually, in perpetuity; Brit. for evermore; N. Amer. forevermore; informal for keeps, until the cows come home, until hell freezes over, until the twelfth of never, until doomsday, until kingdom come; archaic for aye.
2 *he was forever banging into things*: **continually**, continuously, constantly, perpetually, incessantly, endlessly, persistently, repeatedly, regularly; always, all the time, the entire time, non-stop, day and night, {morning, noon, and night}; Scottish aye; informal 24-7.
▷ANTONYMS occasionally; never.

forewarn verb *he had been **forewarned of** a coup plot*: **warn**, prewarn, warn in advance, give advance warning, give fair warning, give notice, advise, apprise, inform; put on one's guard about, alert about, caution about; informal tip off about, put wise to, put in the picture about, clue in about; Brit. informal tip someone the wink about; rare premonish.
▷ANTONYMS take by surprise.

forewarning noun *when dogs howled at night it was a forewarning of death*: **harbinger**, omen, augury, sign, signal, herald, indication, presage, portent, promise, prediction, forecast, premonition; warning, advance warning, prior warning; informal tip-off; literary foretoken.

foreword noun *he wrote the foreword to one of her books*: **preface**, introduction, prologue, preamble, opening remarks, opening statement, preliminary matter, front matter, forward matter; informal intro, prelims; rare prolegomenon, proem, prooemium, exordium, prolusion.

forfeit verb *they had to forfeit benefits for the period of the strike*: **surrender**, relinquish, hand over, deliver up, part with, yield, sacrifice, give up, renounce, be stripped of/deprived of, lose; informal pass up, lose out on.
▷ANTONYMS retain.
▶noun *if they fail to obey they are liable to a forfeit*: **penalty**, financial penalty, fine, fee, charge, sanction, punitive action, penance; damages; confiscation, loss, relinquishment, forfeiture; Law sequestration; English Law, historical amercement; rare mulct.

forfeiture noun *non-compliance may lead to forfeiture of the lease*: **confiscation**, sequestration, loss, losing, denial; relinquishment, giving up, surrender, surrendering, sacrifice, sacrificing, yielding, ceding; historical attainder.

forge[1] verb 1 *the smith forged swords and knives*: **hammer out**, beat into shape, found, cast, mould, model; **fashion**, form, shape, make, manufacture, produce, turn out; informal knock together, knock up, knock off.
2 *they forged a partnership with city government*: **build**, build up, construct, form, create, establish, set up, put together.
3 *it took great skill to forge the signature*: **fake**, falsify, counterfeit, copy fraudulently, copy, imitate, reproduce, replicate, simulate; informal pirate.

forge[2] verb *he forged through the busy side streets*: **advance steadily**, advance gradually, press on, push on, soldier on, march on, push forward, move forward, move along, proceed, progress, make progress/headway.
□ **forge ahead** *Jack's horse forged ahead and took the lead*: **advance rapidly**, progress quickly, make swift progress, increase speed, put a spurt on.

forged adjective *he was charged with passing forged banknotes*: **fake**, faked, false, counterfeit, imitation, reproduction, replica, copied; sham, bogus, dummy, ersatz, invalid; informal phoney, dud, pretend, crooked.
▷ANTONYMS genuine.

forger noun *the painting was the work of a forger*: **counterfeiter**, falsifier, faker, copyist, imitator; archaic coiner.

forgery noun 1 *the defendant was found guilty of forgery*: **counterfeiting**, fraudulent copying, fraudulent imitation; falsification, faking, fabrication; archaic coining.
2 *the painting was discovered to be a forgery*: **fake**, counterfeit, sham, fraud, imitation, dummy, mock-up, reproduction, replica, copy, print, lookalike, likeness; informal phoney, pirate, bootleg, knock-off, rip-off, dupe.

forget verb 1 *he forgot where he had parked his car*: **fail to remember**, fail to recall, fail to think of, let slip.
▷ANTONYMS remember.

f

2 *how could you forget your notes?* **leave behind**, omit to take, overlook, lose track of, mislay, misplace, lose.
3 *I forgot to close the door*: **neglect**, fail, omit, not remember; archaic pretermit.
4 *the rich world would love to forget Africa*: **stop thinking about**, think no more of, cease to think of, cease to remember, put out of one's mind, shut out, blank out, pay no heed to, not worry about, ignore, overlook, never mind, take no notice of, banish from one's thoughts, put away, get over, set aside, lay aside, pass over, abandon, have done with, drop, disregard, brush off, shrug off.
□ **forget oneself** *I'm sorry about that—I forgot myself*: **act improperly**, misbehave, do wrong, go wrong, behave badly, be misbehaved, misconduct oneself, be bad, be naughty, get up to mischief, get up to no good, act up, give/cause someone trouble; sin, go astray, transgress, trespass, fall from grace, lapse, degenerate; Brit. informal muck about, play up.

forgetful adjective **1** *those forgetful members who have not renewed their membership*: **absent-minded**, apt to forget, amnesic, amnesiac, vague, abstracted; informal scatterbrained, with a mind/memory like a sieve.
▷ANTONYMS reliable.
2 *she was forgetful of the time*: **heedless**, neglectful, careless, unmindful, disregardful; inattentive to, negligent about, oblivious to, lax about, indifferent to, remiss in/about.
▷ANTONYMS heedful.

forgetfulness noun **1** *loss of function of some brain cells can result in forgetfulness*: **absent-mindedness**, amnesia, poor memory, a lapse of memory, vagueness, abstraction.
▷ANTONYMS a good memory; reliability.
2 *a forgetfulness of duty*: **neglect**, negligence, heedlessness, carelessness, disregard; inattention to, obliviousness to, indifference to; rare unmindfulness.
▷ANTONYMS heed.

forgivable adjective *I reckon the odd lapse is forgivable*: **pardonable**, excusable, condonable, understandable, tolerable, permissible, allowable, justifiable; all right, within accepted bounds; minor, petty, slight, unimportant, insignificant, trivial, venial, not serious.
▷ANTONYMS unforgivable.

forgive verb **1** *she would not forgive him for deceiving her*: **pardon**, excuse, exonerate, absolve, acquit, let off, grant an amnesty to, amnesty; make allowances for, stop feeling resentful towards, feel no resentment towards, stop feeling malice towards, feel no malice towards, harbour no grudge against, bury the hatchet with; let bygones be bygones; informal let someone off the hook, go easy on; rare exculpate.
▷ANTONYMS blame; convict; resent.
2 *you must forgive his rude conduct*: **excuse**, overlook, disregard, ignore, pass over, make allowances for, allow; **condone**, let go, let pass, sanction, turn a blind eye to, turn a deaf ear to, wink at, connive at, blink at, indulge, tolerate; rare extenuate.
▷ANTONYMS punish.

Choose the right word **forgive, pardon, excuse, condone**

Forgive is the standard word used when someone to whom a wrong has been done makes a deliberate decision to put aside the feelings of anger and blame occasioned by that wrong (*he forgave the bomber who killed his daughter* | *she could never forgive her friend's betrayal*). It is also used informally in the sense of 'excuse', especially in the passive, to indicate that an error is understandable (*you could be forgiven for thinking that our basic foods haven't changed for years*).

Pardon is used mainly to refer to the official remission of a punishment to which an offender has been sentenced (*the President pardoned nine prisoners with heavy sentences*). When used as a synonym for *forgive*, it has a rather old-fashioned or mannered tone (*you have pardoned all their wrongs*).

A circumstance that **excuses** an action provides reasons for seeing it as less blameworthy than it would otherwise be (*nothing can excuse a teacher who fails to draw attention to these facts* | *his friend's betrayal could be excused as a simple error of judgement*). *Excuse* implies that wrongdoing is merely being overlooked, rather than that the wrongdoer is absolved.

Condone is a more critical term than the other three and is used only of relatively serious misdemeanours. It suggests that someone who does not condemn behaviour that is morally wrong is in turn wrong to be so forgiving, so is often used in the negative. The object is always an action, not a person (*union leaders cannot condone the use of violence*).

forgiveness noun *we beg your forgiveness for keeping you waiting*: **pardon**, absolution, exoneration, remission, dispensation, indulgence, understanding, tolerance, purgation, clemency, mercy, pity, lenience, leniency, quarter; reprieve, discharge, amnesty, delivery, acquittal, clearing, pardoning, condoning, condonation, vindication, exculpation; informal let-off, letting off; archaic shrift, shriving.
▷ANTONYMS mercilessness; punishment.

forgiving adjective *Oliver Cromwell was not renowned for his forgiving nature*: **merciful**, lenient, compassionate, pitying, magnanimous, humane, clement, mild, soft-hearted, forbearing, tolerant, easy-going, indulgent, accommodating, understanding, placable.
▷ANTONYMS merciless; vindictive.

forgo, forego verb *no one else on the team was prepared to forgo his lunch hour*: **do without**, go without, give up, waive, renounce, surrender, disavow, relinquish, part with, drop, sacrifice, forswear, abjure, swear off, steer clear of, abandon, cede, yield, abstain from, refrain from, eschew, cut out; decline, refuse, repudiate, spurn.
▷ANTONYMS keep.

forgotten adjective *Vivaldi's operas are largely forgotten*: **unremembered**, out of mind, gone clean out of someone's mind, past recollection, beyond/past recall, consigned to oblivion, obliterated, blotted out, buried, left behind, bygone, past, gone, lost, irrecoverable, irretrievable; neglected, overlooked, ignored, disregarded, unappreciated, unrecognized, of no interest.
▷ANTONYMS remembered.

fork verb *where the road forks, bear left*: **branch**, split, divide, subdivide, separate, part, diverge, go in different directions, go separate ways, bifurcate, split in two; branch off; technical furcate, divaricate, ramify.
□ **fork out** informal *to enjoy those benefits, you will have to fork out twelve pounds a month* | *he resents having to fork out for these freeloaders*: **pay**, pay up, pay out; come up with, hand over, part with, defray the cost of; foot the bill, settle up; informal cough up, shell out, dish out, lay out, come across with; Brit. informal stump up; N. Amer. informal make with, ante up, pony up.

forked adjective *the red kite has a forked tail*: **branching**, branched, diverging, Y-shaped, V-shaped, pronged, divided, split, separated; technical bifurcate, divaricate.
▷ANTONYMS straight.

forlorn adjective **1** *she looked so forlorn that Maggie's heart lurched*: **unhappy**, sad, miserable, sorrowful, dejected, despondent, disconsolate, wretched, abject, morose, regretful, broken-hearted, heartbroken, down, downcast, dispirited, downhearted, heavy-hearted, crestfallen, depressed, melancholy, blue, gloomy, glum, mournful, despairing, doleful, woebegone, woeful, tearful, long-faced, joyless, cheerless, out of sorts; pitiful, pitiable, heart-rending, piteous, pathetic, uncared-for; informal down in the mouth, down in the dumps, fed up; rare lachrymose.
▷ANTONYMS happy.
2 *Brooke End signal box was left to stand forlorn*: **desolate**, deserted, abandoned, forsaken, forgotten, neglected.
3 *his voice rose in a forlorn attempt to drown the racket*: **hopeless**, with no chance of success, beyond hope; useless, futile, pointless, purposeless, vain, unavailing, nugatory; unsuccessful, failed; archaic bootless.

Word toolkit **forlorn**

See **melancholy**.

form noun **1** *the general form of the landscape was well established before the glaciations*: **shape**, configuration, formation, conformation, structure, construction, arrangement, disposition, appearance, outward form/appearance, exterior; contours, lines, outline, silhouette, profile; design, format; cut, pattern, mould.
2 *the human form*: **body**, shape, figure, silhouette, proportions, stature, build, frame, physique, anatomy; informal vital statistics, chassis, bod.
3 *as a dramatist he was a perfectionist about the form of his work*: **structure**, arrangement, construction, framework, format, layout, design, organization, system, planning, order, orderliness, symmetry, proportion.
▷ANTONYMS content.
4 *many of these diseases take the form of persistent infections*: **manifestation**, appearance, embodiment, incarnation, semblance, shape, guise, character, description, expression.
5 *sponsorship is a form of advertising*: **kind**, sort, type, order, class, classification, category, variety, genre, brand, style; species, genus, family, generation, breed, strain, denomination; technical phylum.
6 *put the mixture into a form*: **mould**, cast, shape, matrix, die, pattern.
7 *Are fish knives passé? What is the correct form?* **etiquette**, social practice, custom, usage, use, habit, wont, protocol, procedure, rules, convention, tradition, fashion, style, routine, ritual, pattern, regimen, policy, method, system, way, rule, formula, set formula; Latin modus operandi; formal praxis.
8 *they handed her a form to fill in*: **questionnaire**, document, coupon, tear-off slip, sheet of paper, paper; application (form), entry form, report, return, record.
9 *what form is your daughter in?* **class**, year, school group, tutor group, set, stream, band; N. Amer. grade.
10 *he has been working hard to get into top form for the Olympics*: **fitness**, physical fitness, condition, fettle, shape, trim, health, state of health; Brit. informal nick.
11 Brit. informal *he must have form—I'd swear he's been in prison*: **a criminal record**, a police record, previous convictions, a history of crime; informal previous.
12 Brit. *people sat on forms by wooden tables*: **bench**, long seat, pew, settle, stall.

□ **good form** *it is not good form to leave visitors on their own*: **good manners**, manners, polite behaviour, correct behaviour, acceptable conduct, convention, etiquette, protocol; informal the done thing.
▷ANTONYMS bad form.

▶ **verb 1** *the urns were formed from unbaked clay*: **make**, fashion, shape, model, mould, forge, found, cast, sculpt, hew, carve; construct, build, manufacture, fabricate, assemble, put together; create, produce, concoct, devise, contrive, frame.
2 *he formed a plan to write about the period*: **formulate**, devise, conceive, work out, think up, prepare, make ready, get ready, work up, lay, draw up, put together, produce, fashion, concoct, construct, frame, forge, hatch, develop, organize; informal dream up.
3 *they plan to form a new company*: **set up**, devise, establish, found, launch, float, create, bring into being, put in place, organize, institute, start, begin, get going, initiate, bring about, inaugurate, lay the foundations of.
▷ANTONYMS abolish; dissolve.
4 *a mist was forming in the valley*: **materialize**, come into being/existence, crystallize, emerge, spring up, develop; **take shape**, appear, loom, show up, become visible, come into view, present itself, reveal itself, show itself.
▷ANTONYMS disappear.
5 *the horse may form bad habits which are destructive to itself*: **acquire**, develop, get, pick up, contract, grow into, slip into, get into.
▷ANTONYMS avoid; get out of.
6 *his men formed themselves into an arrowhead*: **arrange**, draw up, line up, assemble, organize, sort, order, range, array, dispose, marshal, deploy, gather, group, place, position, rank, grade.
7 *they assume that the parts of society form an integrated whole*: **comprise**, make, make up, constitute, compose, add up to, account for, represent.
8 *the city formed a natural meeting point for traders and adventurers*: **constitute**, serve as, act as, function as, perform the function of, do duty for, make, embody, compose, comprise.
9 *natural objects are most important in forming the mind of the child*: **develop**, mould, shape, train, teach, instruct, educate, school, tutor, coach, groom, drill, discipline, prime, prepare, guide, direct, inform, verse, enlighten, inculcate, indoctrinate, edify, cultivate, improve, better, uplift, elevate.

> *Word links* **form**
>
> **morpho-** related prefix, as in *morphology, morphometry*
> **-morph** related suffix, as in *polymorph, ectomorph*

formal adjective **1** *a formal dinner*: **ceremonial**, ceremonious, ritualistic, ritual, conventional, traditional, orthodox, prescribed, fixed, set; stately, courtly, solemn, dignified; elaborate, ornate, dressy.
▷ANTONYMS informal.
2 *he has a very formal manner*: **aloof**, reserved, remote, detached, unapproachable, stand-offish, keeping people at arm's length; stiff, prim, stuffy, staid, ceremonious, correct, proper, decorous, conventional, precise, exact, punctilious, unbending, inflexible, strait-laced; unresponsive, unfriendly, unsympathetic, haughty, forbidding, austere; withdrawn, restrained, reticent, taciturn, uncommunicative, undemonstrative, unforthcoming; unsocial, antisocial.
▷ANTONYMS informal; casual.
3 *in the US 'autumn' is a formal alternative to 'fall'*: **literary**, scholarly, learned, intellectual, erudite, bookish, highbrow, academic, cultivated.
▷ANTONYMS informal; colloquial.
4 *a formal garden*: **symmetrical**, regular, orderly, arranged, methodical, systematic, in straight lines, regimented.
▷ANTONYMS informal.
5 *formal permission is required to demolish a listed building*: **official**, legal, authorized, approved, validated, certified, endorsed, documented, sanctioned, licensed, recognized, authoritative, accepted, verified, legitimate, lawful, valid, bona fide, proper, prescribed, pro forma.
▷ANTONYMS informal; unofficial.
6 *she had had no formal education*: **conventional**, mainstream, rigid; school, institutional.
▷ANTONYMS informal.

formality noun **1** *he disliked the formality of the occasion*: **ceremony**, ceremoniousness, ritual, conventionality, red tape, protocol, decorum; stateliness, courtliness, solemnity, etiquette.
▷ANTONYMS informality.
2 *the book tells of Pétain's formality as a colonel*: **aloofness**, reserve, remoteness, detachment, unapproachability, stand-offishness; stiffness, primness, stuffiness, staidness, correctness, decorum, punctiliousness, inflexibility; reticence, taciturnity; antisocial nature.
▷ANTONYMS informality.
3 (**formalities**) *when you apply for a loan, we keep the formalities to a minimum*: **official procedure**, rule, regulation, convention, ritual, custom, matter of form, formal gesture; bureaucracy, red tape, paperwork, form, punctilio, protocol.
4 *the medical examination is just **a formality***: **routine**, routine practice, normal procedure.
▷ANTONYMS exceptional measure.
5 *politicians were confident that Cabinet approval would be a formality*: **matter of course**, foregone conclusion, inevitability, certainty; informal sure thing.
▷ANTONYMS possibility; unlikely possibility.

format noun *the journal has been well received in its new format*: **design**, style, presentation, appearance, look; form, shape, size; arrangement, plan, scheme, composition, make-up, configuration, structure, set-up.

formation noun **1** *they are trying to date the formation of the island's sand ridges*: **emergence**, coming into being, genesis, development, evolution, origination, shaping, generation.
▷ANTONYMS destruction; disappearance.
2 *the formation of a new government*: **establishment**, setting up, start, getting going, initiation, institution, founding, foundation, inception, creation, inauguration, organization, building, construction, installation, planting.
▷ANTONYMS dissolution.
3 *the aircraft were flying in tight formation*: **configuration**, arrangement, pattern, array, alignment, positioning, disposition, order, ordering, organization, design, marshalling, grouping, layout, format.

formative adjective **1** *schooling is not the only significant element in a child's formative years*: **developmental**, developing, growing, mouldable, malleable, impressionable, susceptible.
2 *the early Fabians had a formative influence on the social history of the United Kingdom*: **determining**, controlling, influential, guiding, decisive, forming, shaping, moulding, determinative.

former adjective **1** *the former Bishop of London*: **one-time**, erstwhile, sometime, late; **previous**, foregoing, preceding, old, earlier, prior, precursory, antecedent, ex-, past, last; French ci-devant; rare quondam, whilom, anterior, precedent.
▷ANTONYMS future; next.
2 *in former times*: **earlier**, old, past, bygone, long-ago, forgotten, immemorial, remote; ancient, primeval, primordial, prehistoric, antediluvian; gone by, long ago, long departed, long gone, long past, of old; literary of yore, olden, foregone; rare primigenial, pristine.
▷ANTONYMS present; future.
3 *those who take the former view*: **first-mentioned**, first.
▷ANTONYMS latter.

formerly adverb *he was formerly the head of a large comprehensive school*: **previously**, earlier, earlier on, before, until now/then, hitherto, née, once, once upon a time, at one time, at an earlier time, in the past, in days gone by, back in the day, in years gone by, in times gone by, in bygone days, in times past, in former times, in earlier times, time was when; back, ago; formal heretofore.

formidable adjective **1** *every man wore a formidable curved dagger*: **intimidating**, forbidding, redoubtable, daunting, alarming, frightening, terrifying, petrifying, horrifying, chilling, disturbing, disquieting, dreadful, brooding, awesome, fearsome, ominous, foreboding, sinister, menacing, threatening, dangerous; informal spooky, scary, creepy; archaic direful, bodeful.
▷ANTONYMS pleasant-looking; comforting.
2 *they face a formidable task*: **onerous**, arduous, taxing, difficult, hard, heavy, laborious, burdensome, strenuous, vigorous, back-breaking, stiff, uphill, relentless, Herculean, monumental, colossal; demanding, trying, tough, challenging, exacting, overwhelming; exhausting, wearying, fatiguing, tiring, punishing, gruelling, grinding; informal killing, no picnic; Brit. informal knackering; rare toilsome, exigent.
▷ANTONYMS easy.
3 *a formidable opponent*: **capable**, able, proficient, adept, adroit, accomplished; **impressive**, strong, powerful, mighty, terrific, tremendous, great, redoubtable, indomitable, invincible; seasoned, skilful, skilled, gifted, talented, masterly, virtuoso, expert, knowledgeable, qualified, trained; efficient, good, excellent, brilliant, outstanding, first-class, first-rate; informal mean, wicked, deadly, nifty, crack, ace, stellar, wizard, magic; N. Amer. informal crackerjack; vulgar slang shit-hot; archaic or humorous compleat; rare habile.
▷ANTONYMS weak.

Word toolkit

formidable	fearsome	daunting
opponent	creature	task
competitor	battle	challenge
barrier	beast	prospect
partnership	temper	odds
adversary	warrior	proposition
candidate	attack	mission
threat	claws	circumstances
intellect	predator	schedule
talent	teeth	responsibility

f

formless adjective *the tremor turned several houses into a formless heap of rubble*: **shapeless**, amorphous, unformed, unshaped; nebulous, vague, hazy, misty, shadowy, ill-defined, indistinct, obscure, blurred, blurry, indefinite, indeterminate; structureless, unstructured, ill-organized.
▷ANTONYMS shaped; definite.

formula noun **1** *a legal formula*: **form of words**, set expression, phrase, saying, aphorism; code, set of words, set of symbols; rare formulary.
2 *the four foreign ministers failed to agree on a formula*: **recipe**, prescription, blueprint, plan, method, procedure, technique, system; rules, principles, precepts; modus operandi, mechanism, convention, ritual.
3 *a formula for removing grease from clothing*: **preparation**, concoction, mixture, compound, creation, substance; cream, lotion, liquid, solution, potion, application, paste.

formulate verb **1** *the miners formulated a plan to keep the mines open*: **draw up**, put together, work out, map out, plan, prepare, get ready, compose, produce, construct, make, develop, contrive, hatch, devise, think up, conceive, create, frame, lay, invent, originate, coin, design; write out, write down, put in writing, put down (on paper), draft.
2 *there is a problem with the way you have formulated this question*: **express**, articulate, put into words, utter, state, say, verbalize, word, phrase, render, frame, couch, voice, give voice to, give form to, give expression to; convey, communicate, put across/over, get across/over; specify, define, particularize, itemize, detail, indicate, designate, systematize.

f

fornication noun formal *the punishment for fornication was flogging*: **extramarital sex**, extramarital relations, adultery, infidelity, unfaithfulness, cuckoldry; affair, liaison, sexual intercourse, sex, intercourse, sexual relations, coupling; informal hanky-panky, a bit on the side, bonking, rumpy pumpy, a bit of the other, how's your father; S. African informal pata-pata; archaic carnal knowledge, congress, commerce.

forsake verb **1** archaic *she forsook her child, giving him up for adoption | he forsook his wife*: **abandon**, desert, leave, quit, depart from, leave behind, leave high and dry, turn one's back on, cast aside, give up, reject, disown; break (up) with, jilt, strand, leave stranded, leave flat, leave in the lurch, throw over, cast aside/off, betray; informal run/walk out on, rat on, drop, dump, ditch, chuck; N. Amer. informal give someone the air.
▷ANTONYMS stay with; return to.
2 *it was never expected that voters would forsake their loyalties*: **renounce**, give up, relinquish, dispense with, forgo, desist from, forswear, disclaim, disown, disavow, discard, set aside, wash one's hands of, turn one's back on, repudiate, have done with; withdraw, drop, do away with, jettison; betray, renege on; informal ditch, scrap, scrub, axe, junk.
▷ANTONYMS keep.

forsaken adjective **1** *when the bride failed to appear the forsaken groom fled to the men's room*: **abandoned**, deserted, jilted, stranded, discarded, shunned, renounced, betrayed, rejected, disowned; informal dropped, dumped, ditched.
2 *what brought those poor unfortunates to this forsaken place?* **desolate**, bleak, godforsaken, remote, isolated, sequestered, lonely, solitary, deserted, derelict, dreary, forlorn, uninviting, cheerless, depressing, sad.

forswear verb *we are formally forswearing the use of chemical weapons*: **renounce**, swear off, forgo, abjure, reject, relinquish, abstain from, refrain from, shun, avoid, eschew, do without, go without, steer clear of, give a wide berth to, have nothing to do with, decline, refuse, repudiate, spurn; **give up**, dispense with, stop, cease, finish, discontinue, break off, drop, cut out; informal kick, quit, jack in.
▷ANTONYMS adhere to; persist with.

fort noun **fortress**, castle, citadel, blockhouse, burg, keep, tower, donjon, turret; stronghold, redoubt, fortification, bastion; fastness; in Spain alcazar; rare hold, fortalice.
□ **hold the fort** *I'll hold the fort until you get back*: **stand in**, fill in, act as stand-in, deputize, act as deputy, substitute, act as substitute, take over, be a substitute; take someone's place, act in someone's place, do duty, do a locum, be a locum, sit in, understudy; step into the breach; informal fill someone's shoes/boots; N. Amer. informal pinch-hit.

forte noun *acting had always been her forte*: **strength**, strong point, speciality, long suit, strong suit, talent, special ability, skill, bent, gift, claim to fame, department; French métier, pièce de résistance; informal bag, thing, cup of tea.
▷ANTONYMS weakness.

forth adverb **1** *smoke billowed forth when the air was still*: **out**, outside, away, off, ahead, forward, away from home, abroad; into view, into the open, out of hiding; into existence.
2 *from that day forth*: **onward**, onwards, on, forward, forwards; for ever, into eternity; until now.

forthcoming adjective **1** *forthcoming events*: **imminent**, impending, coming, approaching, advancing, nearing, near; future, expected, anticipated, prospective; close, (close) at hand, in store, in the wind, in the air, in the offing, in the pipeline, on the horizon, on the way, on us, about to happen; informal on the cards.
▷ANTONYMS past; current.
2 *no reply was forthcoming*: **available**, made available, ready, at hand, accessible, obtainable, at someone's disposal, on offer; obtained, given, vouchsafed to someone; informal up for grabs, on tap.
▷ANTONYMS unavailable.
3 *most viewers voiced no opinions, but some were more forthcoming*: **communicative**, expansive, informative, expressive, unreserved, uninhibited, outgoing, frank, open, candid; **talkative**, conversational, chatty, gossipy, loquacious, garrulous, voluble, verbose, effusive, gushing; informal mouthy, gabby, windy, gassy; rare multiloquent, multiloquous.
▷ANTONYMS uncommunicative.

forthright adjective *he was forthright in speaking out against human rights abuses*: **frank**, direct, straightforward, honest, candid, open, sincere, straight, straight to the point, blunt, plain-spoken, outspoken, downright, uninhibited, unreserved, point blank, no-nonsense, matter-of-fact, bluff, undiplomatic, tactless; not afraid to call a spade a spade, not beating around the bush, speaking as one finds; explicit, clear, plain, unequivocal, unambiguous, unqualified, categorical; informal straight from the shoulder, upfront.
▷ANTONYMS secretive; dishonest.

Choose the right word **forthright, blunt, candid, frank, outspoken**

See **candid**.

forthwith adverb *the government insisted that all the hostages be released forthwith*: **immediately**, at once, instantly, directly, right away, straight away, now, this/that (very) minute, this/that instant, then and there, there and then, here and now, in/like a flash, instantaneously, by return, post-haste, without delay, without further/more ado, without hesitation, unhesitatingly; quickly, as quickly as possible, fast, speedily, with all speed, promptly, as soon as possible, a.s.a.p., expeditiously; N. Amer. momentarily, in short order; French tout de suite; informal straight off, toot sweet, pronto, double quick, p.d.q. (pretty damn quick), in double quick time, at warp speed; Indian informal ekdam; archaic straightway, instanter, forthright.
▷ANTONYMS sometime.

fortification noun **1** *to demolish enemy fortifications, heavy guns had been developed*: **rampart**, defensive wall, defences, bulwark, palisade, stockade, redoubt, earthwork, outwork, bastion, parapet, battlement, blockhouse, barricade, buttress, stronghold; rare fieldwork, ravelin, fortalice.
2 *forced labour was used in the fortification of ports and harbours*: **strengthening**, reinforcement, consolidation, shoring up, bracing, boosting, buttressing, toughening; informal beefing up.
3 *the fortification of Madeira with brandy began in the mid-eighteenth century*: **strengthening**, reinforcement, bolstering, stiffening, supplementing, augmenting; informal beefing up.
▷ANTONYMS adulteration.

fortify verb **1** *the knights fortified their citadel as a defence against raids*: **build defences round**, strengthen with defensive works, secure, protect, surround; rare embattle, rampart, mound.
2 *such a timber enclosure may have been fortified by a masonry wall*: **strengthen**, reinforce, toughen, consolidate, bolster, shore up, brace, buttress, stiffen, support, hold up.
▷ANTONYMS weaken.
3 *he fortified himself with a large tot of rum*: **invigorate**, strengthen, energize, enliven, liven up, animate, vitalize, rejuvenate, restore, revive, refresh; galvanize, dynamize, fire up, rouse, motivate, boost, perk up, stimulate, inspire, pick up, embolden, give courage to, encourage, cheer, hearten, buoy up, reassure, make confident, brace, sustain; informal pep up, buck up, give a shot in the arm to; rare activate, inspirit.
▷ANTONYMS sedate; subdue.
4 *fortified wine*: **add spirits/alcohol to**, strengthen.
▷ANTONYMS dilute.
5 *breakfast cereals are fortified with vitamins*: **add vitamins/minerals to**, boost, improve; informal beef up.

fortitude noun *he accepted his increasing illness with fortitude*: **courage**, bravery, strength of mind, strength of character, moral strength, toughness of spirit, firmness of purpose, strong-mindedness, resilience, backbone, spine, mettle, spirit, nerve, pluck, pluckiness, doughtiness, fearlessness, valour, intrepidity, stout-heartedness, endurance; stoicism, steadfastness, patience, long-suffering, forbearance, tenacity, pertinacity, perseverance, resolve, resolution, resoluteness, determination; informal guts, grit, spunk.
▷ANTONYMS faint-heartedness.

fortress noun **fort**, castle, citadel, blockhouse, burg, keep, tower, donjon, turret, bunker; stronghold, redoubt, fortification, bastion; fastness; in Spain alcazar; rare hold, fortalice.

fortuitous adjective **1** *his success depended on entirely fortuitous events*: **chance**, unexpected, unanticipated, unpredictable, unforeseen, unlooked-for, serendipitous, casual, incidental, coincidental, haphazard, random, accidental, inadvertent, unintentional, unintended, unplanned, unpremeditated.
▷ANTONYMS predictable.

2 *United were saved by a fortuitous penalty*: **lucky**, fortunate, providential, advantageous, timely, opportune, serendipitous, expedient, heaven-sent, auspicious, propitious, felicitous, convenient, apt; informal fluky; Brit. informal jammy.

fortunate adjective **1** *he was fortunate that the punishment was so slight*: **lucky**, favoured, blessed, blessed with good luck, in luck, born with a silver spoon in one's mouth, born under a lucky star, having a charmed life, charmed, happy; informal sitting pretty; Brit. informal jammy.
▷ANTONYMS unfortunate.
2 *in a fortunate position*: **favourable**, advantageous, providential, auspicious, welcome, heaven-sent, beneficial, propitious, fortuitous, promising, encouraging, fruitful, opportune, happy, felicitous, profitable, gainful, rewarding, helpful, useful, valuable, timely, well timed, convenient, expedient; archaic seasonable.
▷ANTONYMS unfavourable.
3 *we have to raise money in more fortunate areas like Oxfordshire*: **wealthy**, rich, affluent, opulent, prosperous, well off, moneyed, well-to-do, well heeled, comfortable; favoured, privileged, advantaged, socially advantaged, enviable; successful, flourishing.
▷ANTONYMS underprivileged.

fortunately adverb *fortunately, the church was in very sound structural order*: **luckily**, happily, providentially, opportunely, by good luck, by good fortune, as luck would have it, propitiously; mercifully, thankfully; thank goodness, thank God, thank heavens, thank the stars.

fortune noun **1** *some malicious act of fortune keeps them separate | fortune smiled on them*: **chance**, accident, coincidence, serendipity, twist of fate, destiny, fortuity, providence, freak, hazard; **fate**, Lady Luck, Dame Fortune; N. Amer. happenstance.
2 *the company has enjoyed two drastic changes of fortune over the past twenty years*: **luck**, fate, destiny, predestination, the stars, fortuity, serendipity, karma, kismet, lot, what is written in the stars.
3 (**fortunes**) *there should be an upswing in Sheffield's fortunes*: **circumstances**, state of affairs, condition, financial/material position, financial/material situation, financial/material status; resources, means, finances, income; plight, predicament; station in life, lot, lifestyle; future, prospects.
4 *he made his fortune in wholesale grocery*: **wealth**, riches, substance, property, assets, resources, means, possessions, treasure, estate; affluence, prosperity.
5 (**a fortune**) informal *this place costs a fortune to run*: **a huge amount**, a small fortune, a king's ransom, a vast sum, a large sum of money, a lot, millions, billions; informal a packet, a mint, a bundle, a pile, a wad, a pretty penny, an arm and a leg, a tidy sum, a killing; Brit. informal a bomb, loadsamoney, shedloads; N. Amer. informal big bucks, big money, gazillions; Austral. informal big bickies.

fortune teller noun **clairvoyant**, crystal-gazer, psychic, prophet, forecaster of the future, seer, oracle, soothsayer, prognosticator, prophesier, augur, diviner, sibyl; medium, spiritualist; telepathist, telepath, mind-reader; palmist, palm-reader, chiromancer; astrologer; Scottish spaewife, spaeman; rare haruspex, vaticinator, oracler, chirosophist, spiritist, palmister.

forum noun **1** *forums were held for staff to air grievances and make suggestions*: **meeting**, assembly, gathering, conference, seminar, convention, colloquy, convocation, congress, rally, council, symposium, conclave, congregation, synod, diet; in N. Amer. & NZ **caucus**; informal get-together; rare colloquium.
2 *the UN could provide a valuable forum for discussions*: **setting**, place, scene, context, stage, framework, backdrop; medium, means, agency, channel, avenue, vehicle, mechanism, apparatus, auspices.
3 *every Roman town of any size had a forum and a temple*: **public meeting place**, public square, marketplace; in Greece agora.

forward adverb **1** *the traffic moved slowly forward*: **ahead**, forwards, onwards, onward, on, further.
2 *police asked witnesses to come forward*: **towards the front**, frontwards, out, forth, into view, into the open, into public notice, into prominence.
3 *from that day forward*: **onward**, onwards, on, forth, forwards; for ever, into eternity; until now.
▶ adjective **1** *in a forward direction*: **moving forwards**, moving ahead, onward, advancing, progressing, progressive.
▷ANTONYMS backward.
2 *the fortress served as the Austrian army's forward base against the Russians*: **front**, advance, foremost, head, leading, frontal.
▷ANTONYMS rear.
3 *forward planning*: **future**, forward-looking, for the future, prospective.
4 *the girls seemed very forward to a middle-class boy like him*: **bold**, **brazen**, brazen-faced, barefaced, brash, shameless, immodest, audacious, daring, presumptuous, presuming, assuming, familiar, overfamiliar; irreverent, over-assertive, overconfident, overweening, aggressive, thrusting, pert, impudent, impertinent, cheeky, insolent, unabashed; informal brass-necked, cocky, fresh.
▷ANTONYMS shy.
5 *I never saw the trees so forward as they are this year*: **advanced**, well advanced, early, premature; precocious.
▷ANTONYMS late.
▶ verb **1** *my mother forwarded me your letter the day she received it*: **send on**, post on, redirect, readdress, pass on.
2 *the goods were forwarded by sea*: **send**, dispatch, transmit, carry, convey, deliver, remit, post, mail, ship, freight.
3 *my five months in England were used to forward my plans*: **advance**, further, hasten, hurry along, expedite, accelerate, speed up, step up, aid, assist, help, foster, encourage, contribute to, promote, favour, support, back, give backing to, facilitate.

forward-looking adjective *meanwhile, the forward-looking countries of Europe forged ahead*: **progressive**, enlightened, go-ahead, dynamic, pushing, bold, modern, enterprising, ambitious, pioneering, progressivist, positive, reforming, radical, liberal; informal go-getting.
▷ANTONYMS backward-looking.

forwardness noun *Constance was so appalled at his forwardness that she burst out, 'Don't be cheeky!'*: **boldness**, brashness, brazenness, barefacedness, shamelessness, immodesty, audacity, effrontery, daring, presumption, familiarity, overfamiliarity, irreverence, over-assertiveness, overconfidence, overweening nature; aggressiveness, aggression, pertness, impudence, impertinence, cheek, insolence; informal neck, brass neck, face, cockiness, freshness.
▷ANTONYMS shyness.

forwards adverb See **forward**.
▷ANTONYMS backwards.

fossil noun *fossils of eels have been found in rocks a hundred million years old*: **petrified remains**, petrified impression, cast, impression, mould, remnant, relic; Geology reliquiae.

Word links **fossil**

palaeontology, **palaeobiology** study of fossil animals and plants
palaeobotany study of fossil plants

fossilized adjective **1** *the fossilized remains of extinct animals*: **petrified**, ossified; rare lapidified.
2 *a traditional pattern of etiquette was the fossilized norm in the royal court*: **archaic**, antiquated, antediluvian, old-fashioned, quaint, outdated, outmoded, behind the times, anachronistic, stuck in time; informal prehistoric.

foster verb **1** *a ruler known for fostering the arts*: **encourage**, promote, further, stimulate, advance, forward, cultivate, nurture, strengthen, enrich, help, aid, abet, assist, contribute to, support, endorse, champion, speak for, proselytize, sponsor, espouse, uphold, back, boost, give backing to, facilitate.
▷ANTONYMS neglect; suppress; destroy.
2 *they have fostered a succession of children*: **bring up**, rear, raise, care for, take care of, look after, nurture, provide for; mother, parent.

foul adjective **1** *the skunk produces a foul stench*: **disgusting**, revolting, repellent, repulsive, repugnant, abhorrent, loathsome, offensive, detestable, awful, dreadful, horrible, terrible, horrendous, hideous, appalling, atrocious, vile, abominable, frightful, sickening, nauseating, nauseous, stomach-churning, stomach-turning, off-putting, uninviting, unpalatable, unappetizing, unsavoury, distasteful, nasty, obnoxious, objectionable, odious; noxious, evil-smelling, foul-smelling, smelly, stinking, high, rank, rancid, fetid, malodorous; N. Amer. vomitous; informal ghastly, horrid, gruesome, God-awful, gross, diabolical, putrid, yucky, icky, grotty, sick-making, gut-churning; Brit. informal beastly, whiffy, pongy, niffy; N. Amer. informal lousy, skanky, funky; Austral. informal on the nose; literary noisome, mephitic; archaic disgustful, loathly; rare miasmic, miasmal, olid.
▷ANTONYMS fragrant.
2 *get your foul clothes out of my bedroom*: **dirty**, filthy, mucky, grimy, grubby, stained, dirt-encrusted, muddy, muddied, unclean, unwashed; squalid, sordid, shabby, sleazy, nasty, soiled, sullied, scummy; rotten, defiled, decaying, putrid, putrefied, smelly, fetid; informal cruddy, yucky, icky; Brit. informal manky, gungy, grotty; literary befouled, besmirched, begrimed; rare feculent.
3 *she's been foul to poor Adam*: **unkind**, unfriendly, disagreeable, inconsiderate, uncharitable, rude, churlish, spiteful, malicious, mean, mean-spirited, ill-tempered, ill-natured, ill-humoured, bad-tempered, hostile, vicious, malevolent, evil-minded, surly, obnoxious, poisonous, venomous, vindictive, malign, malignant, cantankerous, hateful, hurtful, cruel, wounding, abusive; informal bitchy, catty; vulgar slang shitty.
▷ANTONYMS kind.
4 *foul weather*: **inclement**, unpleasant, disagreeable, dirty, nasty, rough, bad; stormy, squally, gusty, windy, blustery, blowy, wild, rainy, wet; foggy, misty, gloomy, murky, overcast, louring.
▷ANTONYMS fair.
5 *foul drinking water was blamed for the outbreak*: **contaminated**, polluted,

adulterated, infected, tainted, defiled, impure, filthy, dirty, unclean; rare feculent.
▷ANTONYMS clean.
6 *the foul fiend | these foul deeds cannot be ignored.* See **evil** (sense 1 of the adjective).
7 *she had been subjected to abuse and foul language*: **vulgar**, obscene, profane, blasphemous, gross, coarse, crude, filthy, dirty, indecent, indelicate, suggestive, smutty, off colour, low, lewd, ribald, salacious, scatological, offensive, abusive; informal blue.
▷ANTONYMS mild.
8 *he was booked for a foul tackle in the 67th minute*: **unfair**, against the rules, illegal, unsporting, unsportsmanlike, below the belt, dirty, dishonourable, dishonest, underhand, unscrupulous, unjust, unprincipled, immoral, crooked, fraudulent; informal shady.
▷ANTONYMS fair.
▶**verb 1** *every stream was being fouled with chemical waste*: **dirty**, soil, stain, blacken, muddy, begrime, splash, spatter, smear, befoul, besmirch, blight, defile, make filthy, infect, pollute, contaminate, poison, taint, adulterate, sully; literary besmear.
2 *the vessel had fouled her nets*: **tangle up**, entangle, snarl, catch, entwine, enmesh, twist, tangle.
3 *the rivers have been fouled by silt*: **clog**, choke, block, jam, obstruct, congest, bung up, dam (up), plug, silt up, stop up, seal, fill up, close; informal gunge up; technical occlude, obturate.

Word toolkit **foul**

See **dirty**.

foul-mouthed adjective *a drunken, foul-mouthed yob | foul-mouthed racist abuse*: **vulgar**, crude, coarse; **obscene**, rude, smutty, dirty, filthy, indecent, indelicate, offensive, distasteful, obnoxious, risqué, suggestive, racy, earthy, off colour, colourful, ribald, Rabelaisian, bawdy, lewd, salacious, vile, depraved, sordid, X-rated, scatological; profane, foul, blasphemous, abusive, scurrilous; informal blue.

foul play noun *he died of a head wound, but foul play is not suspected*: **criminal activity**, crime, a criminal offence, villainy, murder, criminal violence, criminality; informal dirty deeds.

found verb **1** *he founded his company in 1989*: **establish**, set up, start, begin, get going, initiate, institute, put in place, form, create, bring into being, launch, float, originate, develop, inaugurate, constitute, endow.
▷ANTONYMS dissolve; liquidate.
2 *they abandoned Attica and founded a new city*: **build**, construct, erect, put up, elevate; plan, lay plans for; start to build, lay the foundations of.
▷ANTONYMS abandon; demolish.
3 *the British parliamentary system **is founded** on debate and opposition*: **base**, build, construct, establish; ground in, root in; rest, hinge, depend.

foundation noun **1** (often **foundations**) *the weight of the roof is transmitted through the walls down to the foundations*: **footing**, foot, base, substructure, understructure, underpinning; bottom, bedrock, substratum.
2 *keeping records is the foundation of any personnel system*: **basis**, starting point, base, point of departure, beginning, premise; fundamental point/principle, principal constituent, main ingredient; principles, fundamentals, rudiments; cornerstone, core, heart, thrust, essence, kernel, nub, underpinning, groundwork.
3 *there was no foundation for the claim*: **justification**, grounds, defence, reason, cause, mitigating circumstances, mitigation, extenuation, explanation, occasion, basis, motive, motivation, excuse, call, pretext, provocation.
4 *soon after the foundation of the company*: **founding**, establishing, setting up, starting, initiation, institution, forming, creation, launch, flotation, origination, development, inauguration, constitution, endowment.
▷ANTONYMS dissolution; liquidation.
5 *in his will he set up an educational foundation*: **endowed institution**, institution, charitable body, funding agency, source of funds.

founder[1], foundress noun *Thomas Bodley, the founder of Oxford's Bodleian Library*: **originator**, creator, initiator, institutor, instigator, organizer, father, founding father, prime mover, architect, engineer, designer, deviser, developer, pioneer, author, planner, framer, inventor, mastermind, maker, producer, builder, constructor; literary begetter; rare establisher.

founder[2] verb **1** *the ship foundered on a voyage to Holland*: **sink**, go to the bottom, go down, be lost at sea, submerge, capsize, run aground, be swamped; informal go to Davy Jones's locker.
2 *the scheme foundered due to lack of organizational backing*: **fail**, be unsuccessful, not succeed, lack success, fall through, fall flat, break down, abort, miscarry, be defeated, suffer defeat, be in vain, be frustrated, collapse, misfire, backfire, not come up to scratch, meet with disaster, come to grief, come to nothing, come to naught, miss the mark, run aground, go wrong, go awry, go astray; informal flop, fizzle out, come a cropper, bite the dust, blow up in someone's face, go down like a lead balloon.
▷ANTONYMS succeed.
3 *some of their horses foundered in the river bed*: **stumble**, trip, trip up, lose one's balance, lose/miss one's footing, slip, pitch, stagger, lurch, totter, fall, fall down, fall over, fall headlong, tumble, topple, sprawl, go lame, collapse.

foundling noun *the foster family was seen as the best place for foundlings*: **abandoned infant**, waif, stray, orphan, outcast; French enfant trouvé; archaic wastrel.

fountain noun **1** *a fountain sprayed cool water into the air*: **jet**, spray, spout, spurt, well, fount, cascade.
2 *the head porter needs to be a fountain of knowledge*: **source**, fount, fountainhead, well head, wellspring, well; reservoir, fund, mass, mine, repository; informal walking encyclopedia.

four cardinal number **quartet**, foursome, tetralogy, quadruplets; Poetry quatrain, tetrastich; Music quadruplet; technical quaternion, tetrad; rare quaternary, quadrumvirate.

Word links **four**

quadr- related prefix, as in *quadraphonic*
tetra- related prefix, as in *tetralogy*
quaternary relating to four
quadrilateral four-sided plane figure
tetrahedron four-sided solid figure
quadrennial relating to four years

four-square adjective *a four-square and formidable hero.* See **resolute**.

fowl noun **poultry**; domestic fowl.

fox noun literary Reynard.

Word links **fox**

vulpine relating to foxes
fox male
vixen female
cub young
skulk collective noun
earth, hole, burrow home

foxy adjective **1** informal *Alexis was a clever, foxy woman.* See **cunning** (adjective).
2 informal *a photo of a foxy girl in a bikini.* See **sexy** (sense 1).

foyer noun *I'll meet you in the hotel foyer*: **entrance hall**, hall, hallway, entrance, entry, porch, portico, reception area, atrium, concourse, lobby, vestibule, anteroom, antechamber, outer room, waiting room; N. Amer. entryway.

fracas noun *two officers were kicked and punched in a fracas earlier this week*: **disturbance**, quarrel, scuffle, brawl, affray, tussle, melee, free-for-all, fight, clash, skirmish, brouhaha, riot, uproar, commotion; **argument**, altercation, angry exchange, war of words, shouting match, tiff, dispute, disagreement, row, wrangle, squabble, rumpus; Scottish stooshie; Irish, N. Amer., & Austral. donnybrook; W. Indian bangarang; informal falling-out, set-to, run-in, shindig, shindy, dust-up, punch-up, scrap, spat, ruckus, argy-bargy, ruction, fisticuffs; Brit. informal barney, bunfight, ding-dong, bust-up, ruck, slanging match; Scottish informal rammy; N. Amer. informal rhubarb; archaic broil, miff.

fraction noun **1** *a fraction of the population*: **part**, subdivision, division, portion, segment, section, sector; proportion, percentage, ratio; share, ration, allotment, apportionment, helping, slice, lot, measure, quota, allocation; bit, piece; element, constituent, unit, module, ingredient; informal cut, whack.
▷ANTONYMS whole.
2 *these are only a fraction of the collection*: **tiny part**, small part, fragment, snippet, snatch, smattering, selection.
3 *he moved a fraction closer to her*: **tiny amount**, little, bit, touch, hint, soupçon, trifle, mite, scrap, dash, spot, modicum, shade, jot; informal smidgen, smidge, tad.

fractious adjective **1** *they fight and squabble like fractious children*: **grumpy**, grouchy, crotchety, in a (bad) mood, cantankerous, bad-tempered, ill-tempered, ill-natured, ill-humoured, peevish, having got out of bed the wrong side, cross, as cross as two sticks, disagreeable, pettish; **irritable**, irascible, tetchy, testy, curmudgeonly; crabbed, crabby, waspish, prickly, peppery, touchy, scratchy, crusty, splenetic, shrewish, short-tempered, hot-tempered, quick-tempered, dyspeptic, choleric, bilious, liverish, cross-grained; informal snappish, snappy, chippy, on a short fuse, short-fused; Brit. informal shirty, stroppy, narky, ratty, eggy, like a bear with a sore head; N. Amer. informal cranky, ornery, peckish, soreheaded; Austral./NZ informal snaky; informal, dated waxy, miffy.
▷ANTONYMS contented; affable.
2 *the National Olympic Committee has to hold its fractious members together*: **wayward**, unruly, uncontrollable, unmanageable, out of hand, obstreperous, difficult, headstrong, refractory, recalcitrant, intractable; disobedient, insubordinate, disruptive, disorderly, undisciplined, troublemaking, rebellious, mutinous, anarchic; defiant, stubborn, obstinate, contrary, wilful; archaic contumacious.
▷ANTONYMS dutiful.

fracture noun **1** *fracture will probably occur at the stress point*: **breaking**, breakage, cracking, cleavage, rupture, shattering, fragmentation, splintering, splitting, separation, bursting, disintegration.
2 *she sustained two fractures to her leg*: **break**, breakage, crack, split.
3 *crystals grow in the pores of the rock, causing tiny fractures*: **crack**, split, fissure, crevice, break, rupture, breach, rift, cleft, slit, chink, gap, cranny, interstice, opening, aperture, rent; crazing.
▶ verb *she had fallen and fractured her skull | second-hand glass may fracture under pressure*: **break**, snap, crack, cleave, rupture, shatter, smash, smash to smithereens, fragment, splinter, split, separate, burst, blow out; sever, divide, tear, rend; disintegrate, fall to bits, fall to pieces; informal bust; rare shiver.

fractured adjective *he's laid up with a fractured collarbone*: **broken**, cracked, splintered, shattered, ruptured.

Word toolkit **fractured**
See **cracked**.

fragile adjective **1** *she was anxious about her fragile porcelain*: **breakable**, easily broken, brittle, frangible, smashable, splintery, flimsy, weak, frail, insubstantial, delicate, dainty, fine; eggshell.
▷ANTONYMS robust.
2 *moves were made to consolidate the fragile ceasefire*: **tenuous**, easily broken, easily destroyed, easily threatened, vulnerable, perilous, flimsy, shaky, rocky, risky, unreliable, suspect, nebulous, unsound, insecure; informal iffy, dicey; Brit. informal dodgy.
▷ANTONYMS sound; durable.
3 *she is still very fragile after her ordeal*: **weak**, delicate, frail, debilitated, tottery, shaky, trembly, ill, unwell, ailing, poorly, sickly, infirm, feeble, enfeebled, unsound; Brit. informal dicky.
▷ANTONYMS strong.

fragility noun **1** *they were worried by the fragility of the bridge*: **frailty**, flimsiness, weakness, delicacy, daintiness, fineness, brittleness; rare frangibility.
▷ANTONYMS robustness.
2 *this is a movie about the fragility of relationships*: **tenuousness**, vulnerability, flimsiness, shakiness, rockiness, riskiness, unreliability, nebulosity, unsoundness, insecurity; informal iffiness; Brit. informal dodginess.

fragment noun (stress on the first syllable) **1** *more than 5000 meteorite fragments*: **piece**, bit, particle, speck; chip, shard, sliver, splinter; shaving, paring, snippet, scrap, offcut, flake, shred, tatter, wisp, morsel, shiver, spillikin; (**fragments**) smithereens; Scottish skelf; technical spall.
2 *I overheard a fragment of conversation*: **snatch**, snippet, scrap, bit, smattering, extract, excerpt; part, section, chapter, movement.
▶ verb (stress on the second syllable) *frequent explosions caused the chalk to fragment | the dangers of fragmenting the health service*: **break up**, break, break into pieces, crack open/apart, shatter, splinter, fracture, burst apart, explode, blow apart, implode; disintegrate, come to pieces, fall to pieces, fall apart, collapse, break down, tumble down; smash, smash to smithereens; informal bust; technical spall; rare shiver.

fragmentary adjective *fragmentary evidence*: **incomplete**, fragmental, fragmented, disconnected, disjointed, broken, discontinuous, piecemeal, in pieces; incoherent, inconsistent, scrappy, bitty, sketchy, uneven, patchy, deficient, untidy, unsystematic, jumbled, inconclusive.
▷ANTONYMS extensive; complete.

fragrance noun **1** *sweet williams add fragrance to a herbaceous border*: **sweet smell**, scent, perfume, bouquet, aroma, odour, redolence, nose, balm, balminess.
▷ANTONYMS stench.
2 *a bottle of fragrance*: **perfume**, scent, eau de toilette, toilet water; eau de cologne, cologne; aftershave; informal scoosh.

fragrant adjective *fragrant herbs play a great part in aromatherapy*: **sweet-scented**, sweet-smelling, scented, perfumed, aromatic, sweet; literary redolent; rare fragranced, aromatized, perfumy.
▷ANTONYMS smelly.

frail adjective **1** *her elderly parents had become frail*: **infirm**, weak, weakened, feeble, enfeebled, debilitated, incapacitated, crippled, wasted; delicate, slight, slender, puny; ill, ailing, unwell, sickly, poorly, in poor health; decrepit, doddering, tottering, shaky; informal weedy.
▷ANTONYMS strong; fit.
2 *some houses are frail structures of cardboard and plywood*: **fragile**, breakable, easily broken, easily damaged, delicate, flimsy, insubstantial; unsteady, unstable, rickety, ramshackle; informal teetery, jerry-built; Brit. informal wonky, dicky, dodgy; rare frangible.
▷ANTONYMS robust.
3 *the workers were frail creatures enslaved by the machines*: **weak**, easily led/tempted, susceptible, impressionable, malleable, vulnerable, defenceless, impotent; fallible, errant, erring, flawed, imperfect; rare resistless.
▷ANTONYMS strong.

Word toolkit **frail**
See **weak**.

frailty noun **1** *I hated my elders for their frailty*: **infirmity**, infirmness, weakness, weakliness, feebleness, enfeeblement, debility, incapacity, impairment, indisposition; fragility, delicacy, slightness, puniness; illness, sickness, sickliness, ill health; decrepitude, dodderiness, shakiness; informal weediness.
▷ANTONYMS strength; healthiness.
2 *human beings are full of frailties*: **weakness**, susceptibility, impressionability, vulnerability, fallibility; foible, weak point, flaw, blemish, imperfection, defect, failing, fault, shortcoming, deficiency, inadequacy, limitation; informal hang-up, chink in one's armour.
▷ANTONYMS strength.

frame noun **1** *the plane is based on a wooden frame*: **framework**, structure, substructure, skeleton, chassis, shell, casing, body, bodywork; support, scaffolding, foundation.
2 *his clothes clung to his tall, slender frame*: **body**, figure, form, shape, physique, build, size, proportions; skeleton, bones, framework, structure; informal bod, chassis.
3 *the photograph hung in a polished frame*: **setting**, mount, mounting, surround, fixture, support, stand.
4 *an appropriate frame through which to explore dramatic situations*: **structure**, framework, context; scheme, system, plan, order, form, fabric, constitution, organization.
□ **frame of mind** *she was in a relaxed and receptive frame of mind*: **mood**, state of mind, emotional state, humour, temper, spirit, vein, attitude, perspective, condition, persuasion.
▶ verb **1** *the picture was painted and framed by a local artist*: **mount**, set in a frame; surround, enclose, encase.
2 *the legislators who frame the regulations*: **formulate**, draw up, plan, draft, map out, sketch out, work out, shape, compose, put together, arrange, form, devise, create, establish, conceive, think up, hatch, originate, orchestrate, engineer, organize, coordinate; informal dream up, cook up.
3 informal *he didn't kill those blokes—he was framed*: **falsely incriminate**, fabricate charges against, fabricate evidence against, entrap; informal fit up, set up.

frame-up noun informal *he was allegedly the victim of a police frame-up*: **conspiracy**, plot, scheme, collusion; trick, trap, deception, entrapment; false charge, trumped-up charge; informal put-up job, fit-up, set-up.

framework noun **1** *the mannequins were made of plastic on a metal framework*: **frame**, **substructure**, structure, skeleton, chassis, shell, body, bodywork; support, scaffolding, foundation.
2 *the changing framework of society*: **structure**, shape, fabric, frame, order, scheme, system, organization, construction, configuration, composition, constitution, architecture, anatomy; informal set-up, make-up.

France noun

Word links **France**
Franco-, **Gallo-** related prefixes
Francophobia, **Gallophobia** hatred or fear of French people and things
Francophile lover of French people and things

franchise noun **1** *the working class had to struggle for the franchise*: **suffrage**, the vote, the right to vote, voting rights, enfranchisement; a voice, one's say.
▷ANTONYMS disenfranchisement.
2 *the company lost its TV franchise*: **warrant**, charter, licence, permit, authorization, permission, sanction; concession, privilege, prerogative; seal of approval.

frank[1] adjective **1** *he is disarmingly frank about his attitudes*: **candid**, direct, forthright, plain, plain-spoken, straight, straightforward, straight from the shoulder, explicit, unequivocal, unambiguous, unvarnished, bald, to the point, no-nonsense, matter-of-fact; open, honest, truthful, sincere, guileless, artless; outspoken, bluff, blunt, brutal, unsparing, not afraid to call a spade a spade; informal upfront, warts and all, on the level; N. Amer. informal on the up and up; archaic round, free-spoken.
▷ANTONYMS secretive; dishonest.
2 *she looked at Sam with frank admiration*: **open**, undisguised, unconcealed, naked, unmistakable, clear, obvious, transparent, patent, manifest, evident, noticeable, visible, perceptible, palpable; blatant, barefaced, flagrant, glaring, bold, stark.
▷ANTONYMS hidden.

Choose the right word **frank, candid, outspoken, forthright, blunt**
See **candid**.

frank² verb *he franked the letter and sent it off*: **stamp**, postmark, imprint, print, mark.
▶ noun *an envelope with a first class frank*: **stamp**, postmark, imprint, mark, official mark.

frankly adverb **1** *frankly, I'm not very interested*: **to be frank**, to be honest, to tell you the truth, to be truthful, in all honesty, in all sincerity, as it happens. **2** *he stated the case quite frankly*: **candidly**, directly, straightforwardly, straight from the shoulder, forthrightly, openly, honestly, truthfully, without dissembling, without beating about the bush, without mincing one's words, without prevarication, point-blank, matter-of-factly, unequivocally, unambiguously, categorically, plainly, explicitly, clearly; bluntly, baldly, starkly, outspokenly, with no holds barred.
▷ANTONYMS evasively.

frantic adjective *her mother is frantic about her safety | a frantic attempt to break free*: **panic-stricken**, panic-struck, panicky, beside oneself, at one's wits' end, berserk, distraught, overwrought, worked up, agitated, distressed; **frenzied**, wild, frenetic, fraught, fevered, feverish, hysterical, mad, crazed, out of control, uncontrolled, unhinged, out of one's mind, maniacal, demented, desperate; informal in a state, in a tizzy/tizz, wound up, het up, in a flap, in a cold sweat, tearing one's hair out; Brit. informal having kittens, in a flat spin.
▷ANTONYMS calm.

f

fraternity noun **1** *the meeting engendered a spirit of fraternity*: **brotherhood**, fellowship, kinship, friendship, companionship, support, mutual support, solidarity, community, union, togetherness; sisterhood. **2** *the dedicated enthusiasts among the teaching fraternity*: **profession**, body of workers; band, group, set, circle. **3** N. Amer. *we belonged to the same college fraternity*: **society**, club, association, guild, lodge, union, organization, alliance, brotherhood; group, set, circle, clique, coterie, clan; sorority, sisterhood; rare sodality, confraternity.

fraternize verb *she forbade her musicians to fraternize with the dancers*: **associate**, mix, mingle, consort, socialize, go around, keep company, rub shoulders; N. Amer. rub elbows; informal hang around/round, hang out, run around, knock about/around, hobnob, pal up, pal around, chum around, be thick with; Brit. informal hang about.

fraud noun **1** *his business partner was arrested for fraud*: **fraudulence**, sharp practice, cheating, swindling, trickery, artifice, deceit, deception, double-dealing, duplicity, treachery, chicanery, skulduggery, imposture, embezzlement; informal monkey business, funny business, crookedness, hanky-panky, shenanigans, flimflam; Brit. informal jiggery-pokery; N. Amer. informal monkeyshines; archaic management, knavery. **2** *they were accomplices in a fraud*: **deception**, trick, cheat, hoax, subterfuge, stratagem, wile, ruse, artifice, swindle, racket; informal scam, con, con trick, rip-off, leg-pull, sting, gyp, kite, diddle, fiddle, swizzle; N. Amer. informal bunco, boondoggle, hustle, grift; Austral. informal rort. **3** *they exposed him as a fraud*: **impostor**, fake, sham, pretender, hoodwinker, masquerader, charlatan, quack, mountebank; **swindler**, fraudster, racketeer, cheat, cheater, double-dealer, trickster, confidence trickster; informal phoney, con man, con artist; dated confidence man. **4** *the report is a fraud*: **sham**, hoax, imitation, copy, dummy, mock-up; **fake**, forgery, counterfeit; informal phoney, dupe.

fraudulent adjective *he was convicted of fraudulent share dealing*: **dishonest**, cheating, swindling, corrupt, criminal, illegal, unlawful, illicit; deceitful, double-dealing, duplicitous, dishonourable, unscrupulous, unfair, unjust, unethical, unprincipled; informal crooked, sharp, shady, tricky, shifty, dirty; Brit. informal bent, dodgy; Austral./NZ informal shonky.
▷ANTONYMS honest, above board.

> *Word toolkit* **fraudulent**
>
> See **illegal**.

fraught adjective **1** *their world is* **fraught with** *danger*: **full of**, filled with, swarming with, rife with, thick with, bristling with, charged with, loaded with, brimful of, brimming with; attended by, accompanied by. **2** *she scanned the platform with a fraught expression*: **anxious**, worried, upset, distraught, overwrought, agitated, distressed, distracted, desperate, frantic, panic-stricken, panic-struck, panicky; beside oneself, at one's wits' end, at the end of one's tether, out of one's mind; informal stressed, hassled, wound up, worked up, in a state, in a flap, in a cold sweat, tearing one's hair out; Brit. informal having kittens, in a flat spin.
▷ANTONYMS calm.

fray¹ verb **1** *cheap fabric soon frays*: **unravel**, wear, wear thin, wear out, wear away, wear through, become worn, become threadbare, become tattered, become ragged, go into holes, go through. **2** *despite the situation, remarkably few nerves were frayed*: **strain**, tax, overtax, irritate, put on edge, make edgy, make tense.

fray² noun *the swordsman launched himself into the fray*: **battle**, engagement, conflict, armed conflict, fight, clash, skirmish, altercation, tussle, struggle, scuffle, melee, brawl, riot, commotion, disturbance; contest, competition; informal scrap, dust-up, set-to, free-for-all; Brit. informal punch-up, bust-up, ruck; Scottish informal rammy, swedge; Law, dated affray.

frayed adjective **1** *the shirt had frayed cuffs*: **unravelling**, unravelled, worn, well worn, threadbare, tattered, ragged, holey, moth-eaten, shabby; torn, ripped, split; worn out, worn through, worn thin, in holes, in tatters, falling to pieces, the worse for wear; informal tatty, ratty; N. Amer. informal raggedy. **2** *his frayed nerves couldn't take much more*: **strained**, taxed, overtaxed, irritated, edgy, tense, stressed, fraught.

freak noun **1** *the mouse was a genetically engineered freak*: **aberration**, abnormality, irregularity, oddity, monster, monstrosity, malformation, mutant; freak of nature. **2** *they were dismissed as a bunch of freaks*: **oddity**, eccentric, eccentric person, peculiar person, strange person, unorthodox person, individualist, free spirit, maverick, misfit; crank, lunatic; informal queer fish, oddball, weirdo, weirdie, nutcase, nut, nutter; Brit. informal odd bod; N. Amer. informal wacko, screwball, kook; informal, dated case. **3** *the accident was a complete freak*: **fluke**, anomaly, aberration, rogue, rarity, quirk, oddity, unusual occurrence, peculiar turn of events, twist of fate; chance, coincidence, hazard, accident, mistake. **4** informal *he's a radio ham and an electronics freak*. See **fan²**.
▶ adjective *the flood was caused by a freak storm*: **unusual**, anomalous, atypical, untypical, unrepresentative, abnormal, aberrant, irregular, fluky, exceptional, unparalleled, unaccountable, bizarre, queer, peculiar, odd, freakish; unpredictable, unforeseeable, unexpected, unanticipated, surprise, surprising; rare, singular, isolated.
▷ANTONYMS normal.
▶ verb informal *he* **freaked out** *and started smashing the place up*: **go crazy**, go mad, go out of one's mind, go to pieces, crack, snap, lose control, lose one's self-control, lose control of the situation, act wildly; panic, get worked up, get hysterical; informal lose it, crack up, lose one's cool, go bananas, blow one's top, fly off the handle; Brit. informal go crackers, throw a wobbly; N. Amer. informal blow one's stack.
▷ANTONYMS calm down.

freakish adjective *his behaviour had been so freakish*. See **freaky**.

freaky adjective informal *the freaky characters in his films*: **strange**, peculiar, odd, bizarre, queer, curious, funny, eccentric, outlandish, offbeat; unusual, abnormal, atypical, untypical, anomalous, out of the ordinary, out of the way, extraordinary, irregular, deviant, aberrant, freakish; surreal, eerie, unnatural, perverse; unexpected, surprising; French outré; Scottish unco; informal screwy, way out, wacky, oddball, fishy, creepy, spooky; Brit. informal rum; N. Amer. informal wacko, bizarro.

free adjective **1** *elementary education should be free*: **without charge**, free of charge, for nothing, complimentary, gratis, gratuitous, at no cost; informal for free, on the house.
▷ANTONYMS paid for; expensive.
2 *she was* **free of** *any pressures*: **unencumbered by**, unaffected by, clear of, without, devoid of, lacking in; exempt from, not liable to, safe from, immune to, relieved of, released from, excused of, exempted from; rid of; informal sans, minus.
▷ANTONYMS encumbered by.
3 *he will be free at the weekend*: **unoccupied**, not at work, not working, not busy, not tied up, between appointments, off duty, off work, off, on holiday, on leave; idle, at leisure, with time on one's hands, with time to spare; available, contactable.
▷ANTONYMS occupied; unavailable.
4 *he found a free seat on the bus*: **vacant**, empty, available, spare, unoccupied, untaken, unfilled, unused, not in use; uninhabited, tenantless; informal up for grabs.
▷ANTONYMS occupied, engaged, taken.
5 *a citizen of a proud free nation*: **independent**, self-governing, self-governed, self-ruling, self-legislating, self-determining, self-directing, non-aligned, sovereign, autonomous, autarkic, democratic, emancipated, enfranchised; self-sufficient; historical manumitted.
▷ANTONYMS dependent.
6 *a known child killer is still free*: **on the loose**, at liberty, at large; loose, unconfined, unbound, untied, unchained, untethered, unshackled, unfettered, unrestrained, unsecured.
▷ANTONYMS captive.
7 *people are* **free to** *choose where they wish to live*: **able to**, in a position to, capable of; **allowed**, permitted, unrestricted.
▷ANTONYMS unable.
8 *the free flow of water between adjoining tanks*: **unobstructed**, unimpeded, unrestricted, unhampered, unlimited, clear, open, unblocked.
▷ANTONYMS obstructed.
9 *she caught the free end of the rope*: **unattached**, unfastened, unsecured, unhitched, untied, uncoupled, not fixed, detached, loose.
▷ANTONYMS attached.
10 *she was always free with her money*: **generous**, lavish, liberal, open-handed, unstinting, giving, munificent, bountiful, bounteous, charitable, extravagant, prodigal.
▷ANTONYMS mean.

11 *he was known for his free and hearty manner*: **easy-going**, free and easy, tolerant, liberal, permissive, indulgent, relaxed, casual, informal, unceremonious, unforced, natural, open, frank, spontaneous, uninhibited, artless, ingenuous; good-humoured, affable, friendly; informal laid-back, unflappable.
▷ANTONYMS strained; formal.
12 *the children were rather too free with us*: **impudent**, impertinent, disrespectful; familiar, overfamiliar, over-free, presumptuous, forward, bold, assertive; informal cheeky, cocky, pushy.
▷ANTONYMS polite.
□ **free and easy** *the restaurant has a free and easy atmosphere*: **easy-going**, relaxed, casual, informal, unceremonious, unforced, natural, open, spontaneous, uninhibited, friendly; breezy, airy, jaunty, carefree; informal laid-back, upbeat.
▷ANTONYMS formal.
□ **a free hand** *he was allowed a free hand in appointing new staff*: **free rein**, freedom, licence, latitude, leeway, scope, flexibility; liberty, independence; French carte blanche.
□ **free spirit** *you're too much of a free spirit for him*: **individualist**, individual, nonconformist, unorthodox person, unconventional person, original, eccentric, bohemian, maverick, rare bird, rarity; lone wolf, outsider; Latin rara avis.
□ **make free with** *he was unhappy about her making free with his belongings*: **help oneself to**, take, take possession of, take over, hijack, appropriate, 'borrow', steal; use without asking, treat without respect; informal walk off with; Brit. informal nick, pinch.
▸ **verb 1** *the government freed all political prisoners*: **release**, liberate, discharge, emancipate, set free, let go, set at liberty, set loose, let loose, turn loose, deliver; untie, unchain, unfetter, unshackle, unmanacle, uncage, unleash; spare, pardon, reprieve, clear; informal let off, let off the hook; literary disenthral; historical manumit.
▷ANTONYMS confine, lock up.
2 *earthquake victims had to be freed by firefighters*: **extricate**, extract, disentangle, disentwine, disengage, disencumber, loosen, release, remove, get out, pull out, pull free, get loose, get free; **rescue**, set free.
▷ANTONYMS trap.
3 *they wish to be* ***freed from*** *all legal ties*: **exempt**, make exempt, except, excuse, absolve; relieve of, absolve of, unburden of, disburden of; strip of; rare dispense from.

freebooter **noun** *the islands offered sanctuary to freebooters*. See **pirate** (sense 1 of the noun).

freedom **noun 1** *the prisoners made a desperate bid for freedom*: **liberty**, liberation, release, emancipation, deliverance, delivery, discharge, non-confinement, extrication; amnesty, pardoning; historical manumission; rare disenthralment.
▷ANTONYMS captivity.
2 *a national revolution was the only path to freedom*: **independence**, self-government, self-determination, self-legislation, self rule, home rule, sovereignty, autonomy, autarky, democracy; self-sufficiency, individualism, separation, non-alignment; emancipation, enfranchisement; historical manumission.
▷ANTONYMS dependence.
3 *they want freedom from local political accountability*: **exemption**, immunity, dispensation, exception, exclusion, release, relief, reprieve, absolution, exoneration; impunity; informal letting off, a let-off; rare derogation.
▷ANTONYMS liability.
4 *the law interfered with their* ***freedom of*** *expression*: **right to**, entitlement to; privilege, prerogative, due.
5 *patients have more freedom to choose who treats them*: **scope**, latitude, leeway, margin, flexibility, facility, space, breathing space, room, elbow room; licence, leave, free rein, a free hand; leisure; French carte blanche.
▷ANTONYMS restriction.
6 *I admire her freedom of manner*: **naturalness**, openness, lack of reserve/inhibition, casualness, informality, lack of ceremony, spontaneity, ingenuousness.
7 *he treats her with too much freedom*: **impudence**; familiarity, overfamiliarity, presumption, forwardness; informal cheek.

> *Word links* **freedom**
>
> **eleutherophobia** fear of freedom

> *Choose the right word* **freedom, liberty, independence**
>
> See **liberty**.

free-for-all **noun** *prompt action by staff prevented a violent free-for-all*: **brawl**, fight, scuffle, tussle, struggle, battle, confrontation, clash, altercation, fray, fracas, melee, rumpus, riot, commotion, disturbance; breach of the peace; Scottish rammy, swedge; Irish, N. Amer., & Austral. donnybrook; informal dust-up, scrap, set-to, shindy, shindig; Brit. informal punch-up, bust-up, ruck, barney; N. Amer. informal brannigan; Austral./NZ informal stoush; Law, dated affray; rare broil, bagarre.

freely **adverb 1** *he felt a reluctance to talk freely*: **openly**, candidly, frankly, plainly, matter-of-factly, straightforwardly, directly, explicitly, bluntly, outspokenly, unreservedly, without constraint, without inhibition; truthfully, honestly, without beating about the bush, without mincing one's words, without prevarication.
▷ANTONYMS evasively.
2 *these workers gave their time and labour freely*: **voluntarily**, willingly, readily; of one's own volition, of one's own accord, of one's own free will, without being asked, without being forced, without reluctance.
▷ANTONYMS under duress.

freethinker **noun** **nonconformist**, individualist, independent, maverick, dissenter, heretic; **libertine**, agnostic, atheist, non-believer, unbeliever, disbeliever, sceptic, doubter, doubting Thomas, apostate, humanist; pagan, heathen, infidel; archaic paynim, renegade; rare nullifidian.
▷ANTONYMS conformist; believer.

freewheel **verb** *she freewheeled downhill on her bicycle*: **coast**, cruise, drift, glide, sail, skim, float.
▷ANTONYMS pedal.

free will **noun** *they take for granted their blessed right to free will*: **volition**, independence, self-determination, self-sufficiency, autonomy, spontaneity; freedom, liberty.
□ **of one's own free will** *she left of her own free will*: **voluntarily**, willingly, readily, freely, spontaneously, without reluctance, without being forced, without being asked, without being encouraged; of one's own accord, of one's own volition, of one's own choosing, by one's own preference.
▷ANTONYMS under duress.

freeze **verb 1** *it was so cold that the river Thames froze*: **turn into ice**, ice over, ice up, solidify, harden; archaic glaciate.
▷ANTONYMS thaw, melt.
2 *they freeze the fish as soon as they catch them*: **deep-freeze**, quick-freeze, freeze-dry, put in the freezer, pack in ice, put on ice, ice; store at a low temperature, chill, cool, refrigerate; preserve.
▷ANTONYMS thaw; warm up.
3 *the campers stifled in summer and froze in winter*: **feel very cold**, go numb with cold, turn blue with cold, shiver, shiver with cold, get chilled, get chilled to the bone/marrow; informal feel Jack Frost's fingers.
▷ANTONYMS overheat.
4 *when under attack the animals freeze*: **stop dead**, stop in one's tracks, stop, stand (stock) still, go rigid, become motionless, become paralysed.
▷ANTONYMS run away.
5 *the prices of basic foodstuffs were frozen*: **fix**, suspend, hold, peg, set; limit, restrict, curb, check, cap, confine, control, regulate; hold/keep down.
▷ANTONYMS change.
□ **freeze someone out** informal *she was frozen out by her husband's relatives*: **exclude**, leave out, shut out, cut out, neglect, ignore, ostracize, reject, disown, spurn, slight, snub, shun, cut, cut dead, turn one's back on, cold-shoulder, give someone the cold shoulder, leave out in the cold; Brit. send to Coventry; informal knock back, brush off, give someone the brush-off, stiff-arm, hand someone the frozen mitt; Brit. informal blank; N. Amer. informal give someone the brush; Austral. informal snout; informal, dated give someone the go-by; Christianity excommunicate.
▷ANTONYMS include; welcome.
▸ **noun 1** *only three race meetings have escaped the big freeze*: **cold snap**, spell of cold weather, freeze-up, frost.
▷ANTONYMS heatwave.
2 *a two-year wage freeze*: **fix**, suspension, hold.

> *Word links* **freeze**
>
> **cryo-** related prefix, as in *cryonic, cryolite*

freezing **adjective 1** *a freezing wind blew across the moor*: **bitterly cold**, cold, chill, chilling, frosty, frozen, glacial, wintry, sub-zero; raw, biting, piercing, penetrating, cutting, stinging, numbing; arctic, polar, Siberian; rare gelid, brumal, rimy, algid, circumpolar.
▷ANTONYMS balmy.
2 *come inside—you must be freezing*: **frozen**, extremely cold, painfully cold, numb with cold, very chilly, chilled through, chilled to the bone/marrow, frozen to the core, frozen stiff, shivery, shivering; frostbitten; informal frozen to death.
▷ANTONYMS hot.

freight **noun 1** *the Panama Canal has lost importance because of air freight*: **transportation**, transport, conveyance, freightage, carriage, carrying, portage, haulage, distribution, delivery; traffic.
2 *the freight is unloaded here*: **cargo**, load, haul, consignment, delivery, shipment; merchandise, goods; rare lading, freightage.
▸ **verb** *the goods were freighted to Kansas City*: **transport**, transport in bulk, convey, carry, ship, drive; send, send off, dispatch.

f

f

frenetic adjective *the frenetic bustle of the metropolis*: **frantic**, wild, frenzied, hectic, fraught, feverish, fevered, mad, manic, hyperactive, energetic, intense, fast and furious, turbulent, tumultuous, confused, confusing; exciting, excited.
▷ANTONYMS calm.

frenzied adjective *the workrooms were a hive of frenzied activity*: **frantic**, wild, frenetic, hectic, fraught, feverish, fevered, mad, crazed, manic, hyperactive, energetic, intense, furious, fast and furious, turbulent, tumultuous, confused, confusing; panic-stricken, panic-struck, panicky, hysterical, desperate.
▷ANTONYMS calm.

frenzy noun **1** *the crowd worked themselves into a state of frenzy*: **hysteria**, madness, mania, insanity, derangement, dementedness, delirium, feverishness, fever, wildness, distraction, agitation, turmoil, tumult; wild excitement, euphoria, elation, ecstasy; informal craziness; rare deliration.
2 *he contorted his face in a frenzy of anger*: **fit**, seizure, paroxysm, spasm, bout, outburst; ferment, fever, storm.

frequency noun *the frequency of errors*: **rate of occurrence**, commonness, frequentness, prevalence, incidence, amount; rate of repetition, recurrence, repetition, persistence, regularity; Statistics distribution.

frequent adjective (stress on the first syllable) **1** *he has frequent bouts of chest infection*: **recurrent**, recurring, repeated, persistent, periodic, perennial, chronic, continuing, occurring often, continual, constant, incessant, non-stop, endless; many, very many, a great many, numerous, countless, quite a few, quite a lot of, lots of, several; informal eternal, loads of, masses of, heaps of, dozens of, hundreds of, thousands of, millions of, more ... than one can shake a stick at.
▷ANTONYMS infrequent; few.
2 *she's a frequent business traveller*: **habitual**, customary, regular, common, everyday, daily, routine; continual, constant, incessant; literary wonted.
▷ANTONYMS infrequent; rare.
▶verb (stress on the second syllable) *he frequented the most chic supper clubs*: **visit**, visit often, be a regular visitor to, be a regular client of, go to regularly, go to repeatedly, attend, attend frequently; haunt, patronize, spend time in, spend all of one's time in, loiter in, linger in; informal hang out at, hang around at, show up often at.

frequenter noun *he was known as a* ***frequenter of*** *public houses*: **regular visitor to**, regular customer of, regular client of, regular patron of, regular of, habitué of, familiar face at, haunter of; Brit. informal regular punter at.

frequently adverb *he frequently attended church*: **regularly**, often, very often, all the time, habitually, customarily, routinely, usually, normally, commonly; again and again, time and again, over and over again, repeatedly, recurrently, continually, constantly; many times, many a time, lots of times, on several occasions; N. Amer. oftentimes; literary oft, oft-times.

fresh adjective **1** *salads made with fresh, wholesome ingredients*: **newly harvested**, garden-fresh, not stale, crisp, firm, unwilted, unfaded; raw, natural, unprocessed, unpreserved, undried, uncured, unsmoked, without additives, without preservatives.
▷ANTONYMS stale; processed.
2 *she drew on a fresh sheet of paper*: **clean**, blank, empty, bare, clear, plain, white; unused, new, pristine, unmarked, unfilled, untouched.
▷ANTONYMS used.
3 *a fresh approach to studying*: **new**, brand new, recent, latest, up to date, modern, modernistic, ultra-modern, newfangled; **original**, novel, different, innovative, unusual, uncommon, unwonted, out of the ordinary, unconventional, unorthodox, offbeat, radical, revolutionary; Brit. out of the common.
▷ANTONYMS old, well-worn.
4 *the general knew fresh forces were coming*: **additional**, further, extra, added, supplementary, supplemental, auxiliary; more, other, new.
5 *a row of fresh recruits*: **young**, youthful, juvenile, adolescent, boyish, girlish, new, newly arrived; **inexperienced**, untrained, unqualified, untried, raw, callow, green, immature, artless, ingenuous, naive; informal wet behind the ears.
▷ANTONYMS experienced.
6 *I must be fresh for work in the morning*: **refreshed**, rested, restored, revived, like a new person; fresh as a daisy, energetic, vigorous, invigorated, full of vim and vigour, vital, lively, vibrant, spry, sprightly, bright, alert, bouncing, perky; informal full of beans, raring to go, bright-eyed and bushy-tailed, chirpy, chipper.
▷ANTONYMS tired.
7 *she had the fresh complexion of a true Celt*: **healthy**, healthy-looking, clear, bright, youthful, youthful-looking, wholesome, blooming, glowing, unblemished; fair, rosy, rosy-cheeked, pink, pinkish, reddish, ruddy, flushed, blushing.
▷ANTONYMS unhealthy.
8 *the morning was clear and fresh*: **cool**, crisp, refreshing, invigorating, tonic; pure, clean, clear, unpolluted, uncontaminated, untainted.
9 *a fresh wind had sprung up from the east*: **chilly**, cool, cold, brisk, bracing, invigorating; bleak, wintry, snowy, frosty, icy, ice-cold, icy-cold, glacial, polar, arctic, raw, bitter, bitterly cold, biting; informal nippy; Brit. informal parky; literary chill; rare gelid, brumal.
▷ANTONYMS warm, sultry.
10 informal *that young man has been getting a little too fresh*: **impudent**, impertinent, insolent, presumptuous, audacious, forward, cheeky, irreverent, discourteous, disrespectful, insubordinate, rude, crude, brazen, brazen-faced, brash, shameless, pert, defiant, bold, (as) bold as brass, outrageous, shocking, out of line; informal brass-necked, cocky, lippy, mouthy, flip; Brit. informal saucy, smart-arsed; N. Amer. informal sassy, nervy, smart-assed; rare malapert, contumelious, tossy, mannerless.
▷ANTONYMS polite.

freshen verb **1** *the water chilled his face and freshened him*: **refresh**, revitalize, restore, revive, reinvigorate, reanimate, wake up, rouse, enliven, liven up, energize, stimulate, brace, fortify, invigorate; informal buck up, pep up, blow away the cobwebs; rare inspirit.
▷ANTONYMS tire.
2 *he opened a window to freshen the room*: **ventilate**, air, aerate, fan, oxygenate, deodorize, purify, cleanse; refresh, cool; rare depollute.
3 *she went to* ***freshen up*** *before dinner*: **have a wash**, wash oneself, bathe, shower; tidy oneself (up), spruce oneself up, smarten up, groom oneself, preen oneself, primp oneself, prink oneself; N. Amer. wash up; informal titivate oneself, do oneself up, doll oneself up; Brit. informal tart oneself up; literary lave; formal or humorous perform one's ablutions; archaic plume oneself, trig oneself, make one's toilet.
4 N. Amer. *the waitress freshened their coffee*: **refill**, top up, fill up, replenish, recharge, reload, resupply; Scottish plenish.
▷ANTONYMS empty.
5 *it was getting dark and the wind had freshened*: **become stronger**, strengthen; **become colder**, become more bracing, cool, cool off.

freshman, freshwoman noun *a freshman at Miami University*: **first-year student**, undergraduate; newcomer, new recruit, starter, probationer, fledgling; beginner, learner, novice; N. Amer. tenderfoot; informal undergrad; Brit. informal fresher; N. Amer. informal greenhorn, rookie, frosh.

fret verb **1** *the workers fretted about being displaced by machines*: **worry**, be anxious, feel uneasy, be distressed, be upset, upset oneself, concern oneself, feel unhappy; agonize, anguish, sorrow, sigh, pine, brood, mope; fuss, make a fuss, complain, grumble, whine, eat one's heart out; informal stew, feel peeved.
2 *his absence began to fret her*: **trouble**, bother, concern, perturb, disturb, disquiet, disconcert, make anxious, cause anxiety, distress, upset, torment, alarm, panic, cause to panic, agitate; informal rattle, eat away at; archaic pother.
▷ANTONYMS comfort.

fretful adjective *the heat was making the child fretful*: **distressed**, upset, miserable, unsettled, uneasy, ill at ease, uncomfortable, agitated, distraught, overwrought, wrought up, worked up, tense, stressed, restive, fidgety; **irritable**, cross, crabbed, fractious, peevish, petulant, out of sorts, bad-tempered, ill-natured, edgy, irascible, grumpy, crotchety, touchy, captious, testy, tetchy; querulous, complaining, grumbling, whining; N. Amer. cranky; informal het up, uptight, twitchy, rattled, crabby; dated overstrung, unquiet.

friable adjective *the soil was dark and friable*: **crumbly**, easily crumbled, powdery, dusty, chalky, soft; dry, crisp, brittle; rare pulverulent, levigated, brashy.

friar noun **monk**, brother, male member of a religious order, religious, contemplative; prior, abbot; Dominican, Black Friar, Carmelite, White Friar, Franciscan, Friar Minor, Grey Friar, Minorite, Augustinian, Augustine, Austin Friar, Crutched Friar, Capuchin, Servite; historical mendicant; rare coenobite, cloisterer, religioner, religieux.

friction noun **1** *the friction of the rope on the winding sheave*: **abrasion**, abrading, rubbing, chafing, grating, rasping, scraping, excoriation, grinding, gnawing, eating away, wearing away/down; resistance, drag, adhesion, traction, grip, purchase; rare attrition, fretting, detrition.
2 *there was considerable friction between father and son*: **discord**, disharmony, disunity, strife, conflict, disagreement, dissension, dissent, opposition, variance, clashing, contention, dispute, disputation, arguing, argument, quarrelling, bickering, squabbling, wrangling, fighting, feuding, rivalry; hostility, animosity, antipathy, enmity, antagonism, resentment, acrimony, bitterness, bad feeling, ill feeling, ill will, bad blood; grudges, grievances; informal falling-out; rare jar, disaccord, discordance.
▷ANTONYMS harmony.

Word links **friction**

tribo- related prefix, as in *triboelectricity*
tribology study of friction

friend noun **1** *she went to stay with her friend in the next town*: **companion**, boon companion, bosom friend, best friend, close friend, intimate, confidante, confidant, familiar, soul mate, alter ego, second self, shadow, playmate, playfellow, classmate, schoolmate, workmate, ally, comrade,

associate; sister, brother; informal pal, bosom pal, buddy, bosom buddy, chum, spar, sidekick, cully, crony, main man; Brit. informal mate, oppo, china, mucker, butty; N. English informal marrow, marrer, marra; N. Amer. informal amigo, compadre, paisan, homie; N. Amer. & S. African informal homeboy, homegirl; S. African informal gabba; Austral./NZ informal offsider; archaic compeer; rare fidus Achates.
▷ANTONYMS enemy.
2 *a meeting of the friends of the Royal Botanic Garden*: **patron**, backer, supporter, benefactor, benefactress, sponsor; well-wisher, defender, champion; informal angel; rare benefactrice, benefactrix, Maecenas.
▷ANTONYMS opponent.

friendless adjective *she cared for those who were poor and friendless*: **alone**, all alone, by oneself, solitary, with no ties, unattached, single, lone, isolated; without friends, companionless, unbefriended, unpopular, unwanted, unloved, uncared-for, abandoned, deserted, rejected, forsaken, outcast, shunned, spurned; lonely, with no one to turn to, forlorn, desolate; N. Amer. lonesome.
▷ANTONYMS popular.

friendliness noun *she appreciated her host's friendliness*: **affability**, amiability, geniality, congeniality, cordiality, good nature, good humour, warmth, affection, affectionateness, demonstrativeness, conviviality, joviality, companionability, companionableness, sociability, gregariousness, clubbability, comradeship, neighbourliness, hospitableness, approachability, accessibility, easy-going manner, communicativeness, openness, lack of reservation, lack of inhibition, good-naturedness, kindness, kindliness, sympathy, amenability, benevolence; French bonhomie; informal chumminess, palliness, clubbiness; Brit. informal mateyness, decency.
▷ANTONYMS unfriendliness.

friendly adjective **1** *she is a naturally friendly child*: **affectionate**, **affable**, amiable, genial, congenial, cordial, warm, demonstrative, convivial, companionable, company-loving, sociable, gregarious, outgoing, clubbable, comradely, neighbourly, hospitable, approachable, easy to get along with, accessible, communicative, open, unreserved, easy-going, good-natured, kindly, benign, amenable, agreeable, obliging, sympathetic, well disposed, benevolent; Scottish couthy; informal chummy, pally, clubby; Brit. informal matey, decent; N. Amer. informal buddy-buddy; rare conversable.
▷ANTONYMS unfriendly.
2 *she drew him into friendly conversation*: **amicable**, congenial, cordial, pleasant, good-natured, easy, casual, informal, unceremonious, comradely, confidential, close, intimate, familiar; peaceable, peaceful, conciliatory, harmonious, non-hostile.
▷ANTONYMS hostile.
3 *a friendly wind swept the boat to the shore*: **favourable**, advantageous, beneficial, benevolent, helpful, well disposed, good; lucky, providential.
▷ANTONYMS unfavourable.

friendship noun *their friendship was based on mutual liking and respect*: **relationship**, friendly relationship, close relationship, attachment, mutual attachment, alliance, association, close association, bond, tie, link, union; **amity**, camaraderie, friendliness, comradeship, companionship, fellowship, fellow feeling, closeness, affinity, rapport, understanding, harmony, unity; intimacy, mutual affection; cordial relations.
▷ANTONYMS enmity.

fright noun **1** *Amanda was paralysed with fright*: **fear**, fearfulness, terror, horror, alarm, panic, dread, trepidation, uneasiness, nervousness, apprehension, apprehensiveness, consternation, dismay, perturbation, disquiet, discomposure; informal jitteriness, twitchiness.
2 *the experience gave everyone a bit of a fright*: **scare**, shock, surprise, turn, jolt, start; the shivers, the shakes; informal the jitters, the heebie-jeebies, the willies, the creeps, the collywobbles, a cold sweat; Brit. informal the (screaming) abdabs, butterflies (in one's stomach).
3 informal *she didn't want to look a fright on her wedding day*: **ugly sight**, horrible sight, grotesque sight, eyesore, monstrosity, horror, frightful spectacle; informal mess, sight, state, blot on the landscape.
▷ANTONYMS beauty.

frighten verb *she was frightened by the strange sounds outside*: **scare**, startle, alarm, terrify, petrify, shock, chill, appal, agitate, panic, throw into panic, fluster, ruffle, shake, disturb, disconcert, unnerve, unman, intimidate, terrorize, cow, daunt, dismay; fill someone with fear, strike terror into, put the fear of God into, chill someone's blood, chill someone to the bone, chill someone to the marrow, make someone's blood run cold, freeze someone's blood, make someone's flesh crawl, give someone goose pimples; informal scare the living daylights out of, scare stiff, scare someone out of their wits, scare witless, scare someone (half) to death, scare the pants off, rattle, spook, make someone's hair stand on end, throw into a blue funk, make someone jump out of their skin; Brit. informal put the wind up, give someone the heebie-jeebies, make someone's hair curl; Irish informal scare the bejesus out of; vulgar slang scare shitless; archaic affright.
▷ANTONYMS reassure, comfort.

> *Choose the right word* **frighten, scare, startle**
>
> These three words can all describe the generation of fear.
>
> **Frighten** is the most general word (*he only meant to frighten his victim, not to kill him*). The fear may be of immediate harm (typically physical) or of longer-term misfortune or suffering (*I was uncertain what would happen and frightened about the future*).
>
> **Scare** is a less formal word, especially when applied to fear of something other than an immediate physical threat. Saying that someone is *scared* may imply that they lack courage or strength of character (*I was scared of meeting people*).
>
> **Startle** denotes a sudden, momentary feeling of fear on being surprised by something (*a sudden sound in the doorway startled her*).

frightening adjective *she had many vivid and frightening dreams*: **terrifying**, horrifying, alarming, startling, shocking, chilling, spine-chilling, hair-raising, blood-curdling, appalling, disturbing, disconcerting, unnerving, intimidating, daunting, dismaying, upsetting, harrowing, traumatic; eerie, sinister, fearsome, dreadful, horrible, awful, nightmarish, monstrous, grim, gruesome, macabre, menacing; Scottish eldritch; informal scary, spooky, creepy, hairy.
▷ANTONYMS comforting.

frightful adjective **1** *he had some frightful wounds*: **horrible**, gruesome, grisly, ghastly, hideous, grim, revolting, repulsive, disgusting, horrendous, grievous, dreadful, terrible, nasty, dire, unspeakable; alarming, shocking, terrifying, harrowing, appalling, daunting, unnerving, fearful, fearsome; informal horrid, beastly; archaic or humorous parlous.
▷ANTONYMS mild.
2 informal *the children were making a frightful racket*: **awful**, very bad, terrible, dreadful, appalling, ghastly, nasty, abominable; unpleasant, disagreeable, lamentable, deplorable, insufferable, unbearable, annoying, irritating; informal beastly, God-awful.
▷ANTONYMS pleasant.

frigid adjective **1** *the frigid climate of the north*: **very cold**, bitterly cold, bitter, freezing, frozen, frosty, icy, icy-cold, ice-cold, chilly, wintry, bleak, sub-zero, arctic, Siberian, polar, glacial; informal nippy; Brit. informal parky; literary chill; rare Hyperborean, hibernal, boreal, hiemal, gelid, algid, brumal, rimy.
▷ANTONYMS hot; tropical.
2 *she addressed him with frigid politeness*: **stiff**, formal, stony, steely, flinty, wooden, impersonal, indifferent, unresponsive, unemotional, unfeeling, unsmiling, unenthusiastic, austere, distant, aloof, remote, reserved, unapproachable; frosty, cold, icy, cool, lukewarm, forbidding, unfriendly, unwelcoming, hostile; informal offish, stand-offish.
▷ANTONYMS friendly.
3 *he said that his wife was frigid*: **sexually unresponsive**, unresponsive, undemonstrative, unaffectionate, cold, cold-blooded, cold-hearted, passionless, unfeeling, unemotional, unloving, uncaring.
▷ANTONYMS passionate.

frill noun **1** *a full skirt with a wide frill*: **ruffle**, flounce, ruff, furbelow, jabot, peplum, flute, ruche, ruching, gather, tuck, fringe; archaic purfle.
2 (**frills**) *a comfortable flat with no frills*: **ostentation**, ornamentation, decoration, embellishment, fanciness, fuss, chichi, garnishing, garnishment, gilding, excess; trimmings, affectations, extras, additions, non-essentials, luxuries, extravagances, superfluities; informal jazz, jazziness, flashiness, fandangle; rare folderols, fallalery.

frilly adjective *she wore a mob cap and frilly apron*: **ruffled**, flounced, frilled, crimped, gathered, pleated, ruched, tucked, trimmed, lacy, frothy; fancy, ornate.

fringe noun **1** *he lived on the city's northern fringe*: **perimeter**, periphery, border, borderline, margin, rim, outer edge, edge, extremity, limit; outer limits, limits, borders, bounds, outskirts, marches; literary marge, bourn, skirt; rare ambit.
▷ANTONYMS middle.
2 *the curtains are blue with a honey-coloured fringe*: **edging**, edge, border, hem, trimming, frill, flounce, ruffle; tassels; archaic purfle.
▶ adjective *he played small parts in fringe theatre*: **unconventional**, unorthodox, offbeat, alternative, avant-garde, experimental, innovative, innovatory, radical, extreme; peripheral, unofficial; N. Amer. left-field, off Broadway; informal way out.
▷ANTONYMS mainstream.
▶ verb **1** *she fringed the edges of the cloak with black velvet*: **trim**, hem, edge, border, rim, bind, braid; tassel; decorate, adorn, ornament, embellish, finish; archaic purfle; rare befringe, befrill.
2 *the lake is fringed by a belt of trees*: **border**, edge, bound, skirt, line, hem, flank, verge, surround, enclose, encircle, circle, encompass, ring, circumscribe; literary gird, girdle, engird; rare compass, environ.

fringe benefit noun *they were attracted to the deal by the fringe benefits*: **added extra**, additional benefit, privilege, benefit, advantage, bonus, dividend, extra, plus, premium, consideration, reward; N. Amer. lagniappe; informal perk, freebie, plus, plus point; formal perquisite; rare appanage.

f

frippery noun **1** *a functional building with not a hint of frippery*: **ostentation**, showiness, embellishment, ornamentation, ornament, adornment, decoration, trimming, garnishing, garnishment, gilding, beautification, prettification, gingerbread; finery, luxury; informal flashiness, glitz, glitziness, bells and whistles; archaic trumpery.
2 (usually **fripperies**) *one of those shops that sells charming fripperies*: **trinket**, bauble, knick-knack, gewgaw, gimcrack, bibelot, furbelow, ornament, novelty, curiosity, gimmick, trifle, bagatelle; informal whatnot; Brit. informal doodah, doobry; archaic folderol, fallalery, whim-wham, kickshaw, bijou, gaud.

frisk verb **1** *the spaniels frisked around my ankles*: **frolic**, gambol, cavort, caper, cut capers, sport, scamper, skip, dance, romp, trip, prance, leap, spring, hop, jump, bounce, bob; rare curvet, rollick, capriole.
2 *he raised his arms to allow the officer to frisk him*: **search**, body-search, check, inspect, examine; informal give someone the once-over; N. Amer. informal shake down.

frisky adjective *the donkey was quite frisky and pranced around the field*: **lively**, bouncy, bubbly, perky, active, energetic, animated, zestful, full of vim and vigour; playful, full of fun, coltish, skittish, spirited, high-spirited, in high spirits, exuberant; informal high, frolicky, full of beans, full of get-up-and-go, sparky, zippy, peppy, bright-eyed and bushy-tailed; archaic frolicsome, gamesome, sportive, frolic, wanton; rare ludic.

fritter verb *he **frittered away** the money his father left him*: **squander**, waste, misuse, misspend, spend unwisely, throw away, dissipate, make poor use of; overspend, spend like water, throw around like confetti, be prodigal with, be wastefully extravagant with, run through, get through, lose, let money slip through one's fingers; informal blow, splurge, pour/chuck something down the drain, spend money as if it grew on trees, spend money as if there were no tomorrow, spend money as if it were going out of style; Brit. informal, dated blue; vulgar slang piss away.
▷ANTONYMS save; spend wisely.

frivolity noun *he avoided the realities of life by resorting to frivolity*: **light-heartedness**, levity, joking, jocularity, gaiety, fun, frivolousness, silliness, foolishness, zaniness, giddiness, flightiness, skittishness; flippancy, facetiousness, inanity, superficiality, shallowness, vacuity, empty-headedness; informal dizziness, dippiness; Brit. informal daftness; N. Amer. informal ditziness.
▷ANTONYMS seriousness.

frivolous adjective **1** *all of the girls were indolent and frivolous*: **giddy**, silly, foolish, facetious, zany, light-hearted, merry, superficial, shallow, lacking seriousness, non-serious, light-minded, whimsical, skittish, flighty, irresponsible, thoughtless, lacking in sense, feather-brained, empty-headed, pea-brained, birdbrained, vacuous, vapid; informal dizzy, dippy, dopey, batty, dotty, nutty; N. Amer. informal ditzy.
▷ANTONYMS sensible, serious.
2 *they never indulged in frivolous remarks*: **flippant**, glib, waggish, joking, jokey, light-hearted, facetious, fatuous, inane, shallow, superficial, senseless, thoughtless, ill-considered, non-serious; informal flip; Brit. informal daft; archaic frolicsome, sportive, jocose.
▷ANTONYMS serious.
3 *her face was thickly painted and her clothes were frivolous*: **impractical**, frothy, flimsy, insubstantial.
▷ANTONYMS practical.
4 *new rules to stop frivolous lawsuits*: **time-wasting**, trivial, trifling, minor, petty, lightweight, insignificant, unimportant, worthless, valueless, pointless, paltry, niggling, peripheral.
▷ANTONYMS important.

frizzle[1] verb *a hamburger frizzled in the frying pan*: **sizzle**, crackle, fizz, hiss, spit, sputter, crack, snap; fry, cook; technical decrepitate; rare crepitate.

frizzle[2] verb *their hair was powdered and frizzled*: **curl**, coil, crimp, crinkle, kink, wave, frizz.
▷ANTONYMS straighten.

frizzy adjective *she had frizzy blonde hair*: **curly**, curled, corkscrew, crimped, crinkled, crinkly, kinked, kinky, waved, frizzed, corrugated; permed; rare ringletty, ringletted.
▷ANTONYMS straight.

frock noun *she looked demure in a cream silk frock*: **dress**, gown, robe, shift; garment, costume.

frog noun

> *Word links* **frog**
>
> **tadpole** young
> **batrachian**, **anuran** relating to frogs

frolic verb *the children frolicked on the sand*: **frisk**, gambol, cavort, caper, cut capers, sport, scamper, skip, dance, romp, trip, prance, leap, spring, hop, jump, bounce, bob; rare curvet, rollick, capriole.
▶ noun *the youngsters enjoyed their frolic*: **antic**, caper, game, romp, stunt, escapade, exploit, revel, spree, sport, fling; prank, jape; giggle, laugh; (**frolics**) fun (and games), merrymaking, amusement; informal lark, skylark.

frolicsome adjective archaic *he met a group of frolicsome girls*. See **playful** (sense 1).

front noun **1** *a little deck at the front of the boat*: **forepart**, fore, foremost part, anterior, forefront, nose, head; bow, prow; foreground, nearest part, closest part; informal sharp end; rare fore-end.
▷ANTONYMS rear, back.
2 *the car swerved and crashed into a shop front*: **frontage**, face, facing, facade; window.
3 *the battlefield surgeons who work at the front*: **front line**, vanguard, van, first line, firing line, battlefield, battleground, field of battle, combat zone; trenches; historical lists.
4 *she pushed her way to the front of the queue*: **head**, beginning, start, top, lead; forefront.
▷ANTONYMS back.
5 *she kept up a brave front for most of the week*: **appearance**, look, expression, face, manner, air, countenance, demeanour, bearing, posture, pose, mien, aspect, exterior, veneer, (outward) show, false display, act, pretence, affectation.
6 *he kept a shop as a front for dealing in stolen goods*: **cover**, cover-up, pretext, false front, blind, disguise, facade, mask, cloak, screen, smokescreen, camouflage.
7 informal *he's got a bit of talent and a lot of front*: **self-confidence**, boldness, forwardness, audacity, audaciousness, temerity, brazenness, presumption, presumptuousness; rashness, daring; informal cockiness, pushiness, nerve, face, neck, brass neck; archaic assumption.
▷ANTONYMS shyness.
□ **in front** *she could hardly see the runners in front*: **ahead**, to the fore, at the fore, at the head, up ahead, in the vanguard, in the van, in the lead, leading, coming first; at the head of the queue; informal up front.
▷ANTONYMS behind.
□ **in front of 1** *he stepped out in front of me*: **ahead of**, before, preceding.
▷ANTONYMS behind. **2** *she sat in front of the mirror*: **facing**, before. **3** *I won't embarrass him in front of his new friends*: **in the presence of**, before, before the very eyes of, in the sight of, under the nose of.
□ **up front** *they didn't have the cash to pay me up front*: **in advance**, beforehand, ahead of time, in readiness.
▶ adjective **1** *she was in the front garden*: **at the front**, foremost.
▷ANTONYMS back.
2 *the front runners headed towards the finish*: **leading**, lead, first, foremost; in first place.
▷ANTONYMS last.
▶ verb *the houses **fronted on** a reservoir*: **overlook**, look on to, look out on, look out over, look towards, face (towards), lie opposite (to); have a view of, command a view of.
▷ANTONYMS back on to.

frontier noun *the lakes sit astride the US–Canadian frontier*: **border**, boundary, partition, borderline, dividing line, bounding line, demarcation line; perimeter, limit, edge, rim; marches, bounds.

> *Choose the right word* **frontier, border, boundary**
>
> See **border**.

frost noun **1** *the hedges and trees were covered with frost*: **ice crystals**, ice, rime, rime ice, verglas; rime frost, white frost, black frost, hoar frost, ground frost; informal Jack Frost; archaic hoar.
2 *there had been a frost overnight*: **cold snap**, period of cold weather; hoar frost, ground frost; informal freeze, freeze-up.
▷ANTONYMS heatwave.
3 *there was frost in his tone*: **coldness**, coolness, frostiness, ice, iciness, glaciality, frigidity; hostility, unfriendliness, stiffness, stand-offishness.
▷ANTONYMS friendliness.

frosty adjective **1** *a frosty autumn morning*: **freezing**, frigid, glacial, arctic, wintry, bitter, bitterly cold, cold, ice-cold, icy-cold, cool, chilly, crisp, bleak; frozen, rimy, icy; informal nippy; Brit. informal parky; literary frore, chill; rare gelid, brumal.
2 *Mary fixed a frosty gaze on him*: **unfriendly**, unsympathetic, inhospitable, unwelcoming, forbidding, hostile, disdainful, haughty, stony, stern, hard, fierce; icy, glacial, frigid, cold, cool.

froth noun **1** *the froth on top of stout*: **foam**, lather, head, suds; bubbles, frothiness, fizz, effervescence; scum; literary spume.
2 *the froth of party politics*: **trivia**, trifles, irrelevancies, nonsense, rubbish, trash, pap; Brit. candyfloss; informal drivel, twaddle, hot air, gas.
▷ANTONYMS nitty-gritty.
▶ verb *the beer frothed up*: **bubble**, fizz, foam, cream, lather; effervesce, aerate; churn, seethe; literary roil, spume.

frothy adjective **1** *the beer was sharp and frothy*: **foaming**, foamy, bubbling, bubbly, fizzy, sparkling, effervescent, gassy, carbonated, aerated; creamy, yeasty, sudsy; literary spumy, spumous.
▷ANTONYMS flat, still.

2 *a frothy pink evening dress*: **frilly**, flouncy, insubstantial.
▷ANTONYMS plain.
3 *a frothy love song*: **insubstantial**, light, lightweight, lacking substance, superficial, shallow, slight, empty; trivial, trifling, frivolous, petty, paltry, insignificant, worthless, of no account, of no merit, of no value.
▷ANTONYMS deep.

frown verb *the old lady frowned at him*: **scowl**, glower, glare, lour, look sullen, make a face, look daggers; give someone black looks; knit/furrow one's brows; informal give someone dirty looks.
▷ANTONYMS smile.
□ **frown on** *drink-driving was frowned on by the interviewees*: **disapprove of**, view with dislike/disfavour, show/indicate disapproval of, dislike, discourage, look askance at, not take kindly to, not think much of, take a dim view of, find unacceptable, be against, take exception to, object to, think wrong, discountenance, have a low opinion of.
▷ANTONYMS smile on, approve of.
▸ noun *I put the phone down with a frown*: **scowl**, glower, glare, black look, dirty look; knitted brows, furrowed brows.
▷ANTONYMS smile.

frowsty adjective Brit. *a frowsty room*: **stuffy**, musty, airless, unventilated, fusty, close, muggy, stifling, suffocating, oppressive; stale, stagnant, smelly; N. Amer. funky; rare mucid.
▷ANTONYMS airy, ventilated.

frowzy adjective 1 *a frowzy old biddy*: **scruffy**, unkempt, untidy, sloppy, messy, dishevelled, slovenly, slatternly, bedraggled, down at heel, ill-dressed, badly dressed, dowdy; N. Amer. informal raggedy.
▷ANTONYMS tidy.
2 *the frowzy room above the saloon*: **dingy**, gloomy, dull, drab, dark, badly/poorly lit, dim; **stuffy**, close, musty, stale, stagnant, stifling, suffocating, unfresh; shabby, seedy, run down, tacky; Brit. frowsty, fuggy.

frozen adjective 1 *the frozen ground*: **ice-cold**, ice-covered, icy, ice-bound, frosted; hard, solid, hard as iron; literary rimy.
2 *frozen fish*: **chilled**, iced, preserved.
3 *the frozen countryside*: **bitterly cold**, wintry, frosty, icy, glacial, frigid, arctic, sub-zero, Siberian, polar, raw, extreme; rare gelid, algid.
4 *his hands were frozen*: **freezing**, very cold, chilled, chilled to the bone/marrow/core, numb with cold, numb, numbed, frozen stiff; shivering; informal frozen to death.
▷ANTONYMS boiling.

frugal adjective 1 *she lives a frugal life*: **thrifty**, sparing, economical, saving; careful, cautious, prudent, provident, unwasteful, sensible, canny; abstemious, abstinent, austere, self-denying, ascetic, non-indulgent, self-disciplined, spartan, puritanical, nunlike, monastic, monkish; miserly, parsimonious, niggardly, scrimping, cheese-paring, penny-pinching, close-fisted, ungenerous, grasping; N. Amer. forehanded; informal tight-fisted, tight, mingy, stingy; N. Amer. informal cheap.
▷ANTONYMS extravagant.
2 *the boys finished their frugal breakfast*: **meagre**, scanty, scant, paltry, skimpy, insufficient; plain, simple, moderate, temperate, austere, ascetic, spartan, restrained; inexpensive, cheap, economical.
▷ANTONYMS lavish.

frugality noun *he was known for his frugality and modesty*: **thriftiness**, carefulness, scrimping and saving, conservation, good management; caution, prudence, providence, canniness; abstemiousness, abstinence, austerity, asceticism, self-discipline, restraint, moderation, puritanism, monasticism, monkishness; miserliness, meanness, parsimoniousness, niggardliness, close-fistedness; informal tight-fistedness, tightness, stinginess; rare sparingness.
▷ANTONYMS extravagance.

fruit noun (also **fruits**) *the fruit of victory | the fruits of their labours*: **reward**, benefit, advantages; product, produce, profit, return, yield, legacy, issue, deserts; outcome, upshot, result, results, consequences, effect, effects.
▸ verb *the strawberries should fruit in May*: **produce fruit**, bear fruit.

Word links **fruit**

fruct-, **frug-**, **carp-**, **pom-** related prefixes, as in *fructification*
carpology study of fruit and seeds
fruiterer, Brit. **greengrocer**, Brit. dated **costermonger** seller of fruit
pomiculture, **orcharding**, **citriculture** fruit-growing
pomology science of fruit-growing
frugivorous fruit-eating

fruitful adjective 1 *a fruitful tree*: **fruit-bearing**, fructiferous, fruiting; **fertile**, fecund, high-yielding, lush, abundant, profuse, prolific, bounteous; generative, progenitive; rare fructuous.
▷ANTONYMS infertile.
2 *the two days of talks had been fruitful*: **productive**, constructive, useful, of use, worthwhile, helpful, of help, of assistance, beneficial, valuable, rewarding, profitable, advantageous, gainful, successful, effective, effectual, well spent.
▷ANTONYMS fruitless, futile.

fruition noun *scientific projects need a great deal of time to come to fruition*: **fulfilment**, realization, actualization, materialization; achievement, attainment, accomplishment, resolution; success, completion, consummation, conclusion, close, finish, perfection; maturity, maturation, ripening, ripeness; effecting, implementation, execution, performance; informal winding up, sewing up, polishing off; rare effectuation, reification.
▷ANTONYMS inception.

fruitless adjective *the search proved fruitless*: **futile**, vain, in vain, to no avail, to no effect, idle; pointless, useless, worthless, needless, wasted, hollow; ineffectual, ineffective, inefficacious; unproductive, unrewarding, profitless, unsuccessful, unavailing, barren, for naught; abortive; archaic bootless.
▷ANTONYMS fruitful, productive.

Choose the right word **fruitless, futile, vain, pointless**

See **futile**.

fruity adjective 1 *fruity jam*: **tasting of fruit**, containing fruit.
2 *he had a wonderfully fruity voice*: **resonant**, deep, rich, full, full-toned, full-bodied; mellow, smooth; clear, strong, vibrant, loud, booming.
▷ANTONYMS thin.
3 Brit. informal *a fruity story*: **smutty**, bawdy, naughty, spicy, earthy, broad, wicked; racy, risqué, juicy, ribald, Rabelaisian, raw; indecent, improper, dirty, rude, indelicate, vulgar, coarse, lewd, sordid, off colour, filthy, profane, obscene, scatological, offensive; sexy, suggestive, titillating, salacious, prurient; N. Amer. gamy; euphemistic **adult**; informal blue, near the knuckle, nudge-nudge, raunchy, locker-room; Brit. informal saucy.
▷ANTONYMS clean.

frumpy adjective *her mother's frumpy clothes*: **dowdy**, frumpish, unfashionable, old-fashioned; drab, dull, shabby, scruffy; Brit. informal mumsy; Austral./NZ informal daggy.
▷ANTONYMS fashionable.

frustrate verb 1 *the settlers' attempts at agriculture were frustrated by the climate*: **thwart**, defeat, foil, block, stop, put a stop to, counter, spoil, check, baulk, circumvent, disappoint, forestall, bar, dash, scotch, quash, crush, derail, nip in the bud, baffle, nullify, snooker; obstruct, impede, hamper, hinder, stifle, fetter, hamstring, cripple, put a brake on, stand in the way of, spike someone's guns; informal stymie, foul up, screw up, put the kibosh on, put the lid on, banjax, do for; Brit. informal scupper.
▷ANTONYMS help, facilitate.
2 *the objections of his colleagues clearly frustrated him*: **exasperate**, infuriate, annoy, anger, madden, vex, irritate, irk, embitter, sour, get someone's back up, try someone's patience; **discourage**, dishearten, dispirit, depress, dissatisfy, make discontented; informal aggravate, drive mad, drive crazy, bug, miff, hack off, get to, get under someone's skin, give someone the hump; Brit. informal wind up, get on someone's wick, nark.
▷ANTONYMS please.

frustration noun 1 *he clenched his fists in frustration*: **exasperation**, annoyance, anger, vexation, irritation, bitterness, resentment; disappointment, discouragement, disheartenment, dispiritedness, depression, dissatisfaction, discontentment, discontent; informal aggravation.
▷ANTONYMS satisfaction.
2 *the repeated frustration of his attempts to introduce changes*: **thwarting**, defeat, foiling, blocking, stopping, countering, spoiling, checking, baulking, circumvention, forestalling, dashing, scotching, quashing, crushing; disappointment, derailment, baffling, snookering; obstruction, hampering, hindering, stifling, crippling; failure, collapse, foundering, lack of success, non-success; Brit. informal scuppering.
▷ANTONYMS success; promotion.

fuddled adjective *she forced her weary fuddled brain to work*: **stupefied**, addled, befuddled, confused, muddled, bewildered, dumbfounded, dazed, stunned, dizzy, muzzy, groggy, foggy, fuzzy, vague, disorientated, disoriented, all at sea, mixed up, at a loss, at sixes and sevens; informal dopey, woozy, woolly-minded, discombobulated, fazed, not with it.
▷ANTONYMS clear, sharp.

fuddy-duddy noun informal *he called me an old fuddy-duddy*: **fogy**, conservative, traditionalist, conformist; museum piece, fossil, dinosaur, troglodyte; informal stick-in-the-mud, square, stuffed shirt, back number, dodo; N. Amer. informal sobersides.

fudge noun 1 *she helped herself to a square of fudge*: **chewy sweet**, toffee.
2 *the latest proposals are a fudge*: **compromise**, **cover-up**, halfway house; equivocation, spin, casuistry, sophistry, speciousness; informal cop-out.
▷ANTONYMS straightforwardness.
▸ verb 1 *I am sure a no-nonsense chap like you will not fudge the issue*: **evade**, dodge, skirt, avoid, duck, shift ground about; hedge, prevaricate, vacillate, be non-committal, shuffle, parry questions, stall, shilly-shally, beat about the bush, mince (one's) words; Brit. hum and haw; informal waffle, cop out, flannel, sit on the fence; rare tergiversate.
▷ANTONYMS be forthright about.

f

2 *the government has been fudging figures*: **falsify**, fake, distort, manipulate, misrepresent, misreport, bend, spin, put a spin on, massage, tamper with, tinker with, interfere with, change, doctor, juggle; embellish, embroider, warp, colour; informal cook, fiddle with.

fuel noun **1** *one aircraft ran out of fuel and had to ditch*: **power source**, combustible, propellant; petrol, diesel oil; N. Amer. gasoline, gas.
2 *she got up to add more fuel to the fire*: **firewood**, wood, kindling, logs; coal, coke, anthracite; charcoal; oil, paraffin, kerosene; heat source.
3 *we all need fuel to keep our bodies going*: **nourishment**, sustenance, nutriment, nutrition, food, fodder.
4 *his antics added fuel to the Republican cause*: **encouragement**, incentive, ammunition, incitement, stimulus; provocation, goading.
▶ verb **1** *power stations fuelled by low-grade coal*: **power**, charge, fire, stoke up, supply with fuel.
2 *pictures of the two of them together fuelled rumours*: **stimulate**, boost, encourage, intensify, fortify, support, nurture; incite, inflame, exacerbate, animate, vitalize, fan, feed, whip up; provoke, goad.
▷ANTONYMS dampen.

f

fug noun Brit. informal *the fug of the bar*: **stuffiness**, fustiness, frowstiness, staleness, stuffy atmosphere.
▷ANTONYMS airiness.

fuggy adjective *a fuggy little room*: **stuffy**, smoky, close, muggy, stale, fusty, unventilated, airless, suffocating, stifling, oppressive; heavy.
▷ANTONYMS airy.

fugitive noun *he is a hunted fugitive*: **escapee**, escaper, runaway, deserter, refugee, renegade, absconder; archaic runagate.
▶ adjective **1** *a fugitive criminal*: **escaped**, escaping, runaway, fleeing, deserting; on the loose, at large, wanted; informal AWOL, on the run; N. Amer. informal on the lam.
2 *ours is a fugitive life*: **fleeting**, transient, transitory, ephemeral, evanescent, flitting, flying, fading, momentary, short-lived, short, brief, passing, impermanent, fly-by-night, here today and gone tomorrow; literary fugacious.
▷ANTONYMS permanent, long-lasting.

fulfil verb **1** *I knew I could fulfil my ambition to be a millionaire before I was thirty*: **succeed in**, attain, realize, consummate, satisfy, manage, bring off, bring about, carry off, carry out, carry through, bring to fruition, deliver; informal pull something off, clinch.
▷ANTONYMS fail in.
2 *some officials were dismissed because they could not fulfil their duties*: **carry out**, accomplish, achieve, execute, perform, discharge, implement, effect, effectuate, conduct; complete, bring to completion, finish, conclude, perfect; honour, be true to, keep faith with, make good, observe.
▷ANTONYMS neglect.
3 *they fulfilled the criteria for entry into the programme*: **comply with**, satisfy, conform to, fill, answer, meet, obey, adhere to, respond to.
▷ANTONYMS fail.

fulfilled adjective *I am confident in this role, and feel fulfilled*: **satisfied**, content, contented, happy, pleased, gratified, comfortable, serene, placid, untroubled, at ease, at peace.
▷ANTONYMS unfulfilled, discontented.

full adjective **1** *her glass was full*: **filled**, filled up, filled to capacity, filled to the brim, brimming, brimful, topped up; overflowing, running over.
▷ANTONYMS empty.
2 *the bus was quite full*: **crowded**, packed, crammed, cramped, congested, crushed, solid (with people), full of people, full to capacity, full to bursting, overfull, teeming, swarming, overcrowded, thronged; N. Amer. mobbed; informal jam-packed, wall-to-wall, stuffed, chock-a-block, chock-full, bursting at the seams, bulging at the seams, packed to the gunwales.
▷ANTONYMS empty.
3 *all the seats were full*: **occupied**, taken, in use, engaged, unavailable.
▷ANTONYMS empty.
4 *the shelves are full*: **well stocked**, well supplied, filled, loaded, packed, burdened, stuffed, crammed, stacked.
▷ANTONYMS empty.
5 *he was too full to protest when the waiter took his plate away*: **replete**, satisfied, well fed, sated, satiated, full up, full to bursting, having had enough; gorged, glutted, cloyed; informal stuffed; archaic satiate, surfeited.
▷ANTONYMS hungry.
6 *he was full of mirth*: **abounding in**, bursting with, brimming with, rich in, possessed by; informal awash with.
▷ANTONYMS free of.
7 *she'd had a full life*: **eventful**, interesting, exciting, lively, action-packed, noteworthy; busy, strenuous, hectic, frantic, energetic, active.
▷ANTONYMS uneventful, limited.
8 *we can provide a full list of sailing clubs*: **comprehensive**, thorough, exhaustive, all-inclusive, all-encompassing, all-embracing, in depth; complete, entire, whole, unabridged, uncut; extensive, long.
▷ANTONYMS incomplete, selective.
9 *the prospectus contains full details of the degree courses offered*: **abundant**, plentiful, ample, copious, profuse, rich, lavish, liberal; detailed, in detail, specific, precise, exact, accurate, minute, particular; sufficient, satisfying; broad-ranging, complete.
▷ANTONYMS partial; vague.
10 *a fire engine driven at full speed*: **maximum**, top, greatest, highest.
▷ANTONYMS low.
11 *she had a full figure*: **well rounded**, rounded, round, plump, buxom, shapely, ample, curvaceous, voluptuous, womanly, Junoesque, Rubensesque; informal busty, chesty, curvy, well upholstered, well endowed; N. Amer. informal zaftig.
▷ANTONYMS thin.
12 *the dress had a full skirt*: **loose-fitting**, loose, baggy, easy-fitting, generously cut, roomy, voluminous, capacious, billowing.
▷ANTONYMS tight.
13 *this song relies on his full and husky voice*: **resonant**, rich, sonorous, deep, full-bodied, vibrant, fruity, clear, loud, strong.
▷ANTONYMS thin.
14 *the full flavour of a Bordeaux*: **rich**, intense, deep, heavy, vivid, strong, vibrant, bold, warm.
▷ANTONYMS thin, watery.
▶ adverb **1** *she looked full into his face*: **directly**, right, straight, squarely, square, just, dead, point-blank; informal smack (bang), bang, slap, plumb.
▷ANTONYMS indirectly.
2 *he knows full well that four out of five investments will be lost*: **very**, perfectly, quite, extremely, entirely; informal darn, damn, damned; Brit. informal jolly, bloody; N. Amer. informal darned; archaic or N. English right.
□ **full out** *he was working full out to supply the demand*: **to the maximum**, flat out; at full speed, at maximum speed, as fast as possible, with maximum power, at full tilt, at full pelt, at breakneck speed; informal hell for leather, hammer and tongs, like crazy, like mad, like a bat out of hell; Brit. informal like the clappers, like billy-o.
▶ noun
□ **in full** *my letter was published in full*: **in its entirety**, in total, without omission/abridgement, unabridged, uncut, fully; Latin in toto.
▷ANTONYMS in part, partially.
□ **to the full** *do your best to live life to the full*: **fully**, thoroughly, completely, to the utmost, to capacity, to the limit, to the maximum, for all one's worth, with a vengeance, with all the stops out.

full-blooded adjective *a full-blooded price war*: **all out**, complete, total, uncompromising, committed, out and out, thorough, thoroughgoing, vigorous, strenuous, intense; unrestrained, uncontrolled, unbridled, hard-hitting, pulling no punches.
▷ANTONYMS half-hearted.

full-blown adjective *this problem could flare up into a full-blown crisis*: **fully developed**, full-scale, full-blooded, fully fledged, complete, total, thorough, entire, full, advanced.
▷ANTONYMS partial.

full-bodied adjective *a full-bodied claret*: **full-flavoured**, flavourful, flavoursome, full of flavour, rich, intense, fruity, deep, heavy, strong, robust, bold, warm, mellow, redolent, well-matured.
▷ANTONYMS tasteless.

full-grown adjective *a full-grown woman*: **adult**, mature, grown-up, of age, having reached one's majority; fully grown, fully developed, fully fledged, in full bloom, ripe, in one's prime.
▷ANTONYMS infant; immature.

fullness noun **1** *the honesty and fullness of the information they provide*: **completeness**, comprehensiveness, thoroughness, exhaustiveness, all-inclusiveness, extensiveness, length, depth.
▷ANTONYMS incompleteness.
2 *the fullness of her body*: **roundedness**, roundness, plumpness, buxomness, shapeliness, ampleness, curvaceousness, voluptuousness, womanliness; informal bustiness, chestiness, curviness.
▷ANTONYMS thinness.
3 *the recording has a fullness and warmth*: **resonance**, richness, depth, vibrancy, fruitiness, clarity, intensity, loudness, strength.
▷ANTONYMS weakness, thinness.
□ **in the fullness of time** *I hoped my ploy would get results in the fullness of time*: **in due course**, when the time is ripe, eventually, in time, in time to come, at a later date, one day, some day, sooner or later, in a while, after a while, after a bit, ultimately, finally, in the end; Brit. informal at the end of the day.
▷ANTONYMS immediately; never.

full-scale adjective **1** *a full-scale model*: **full-size**, unreduced, actual size.
▷ANTONYMS scale, scaled down.
2 *a full-scale public inquiry*: **thorough**, comprehensive, extensive, exhaustive, complete, all-encompassing, all-inclusive, all-embracing, thoroughgoing, wide-ranging, sweeping, major, in-depth, profound, far-reaching.
▷ANTONYMS partial.

fully adverb **1** *the panel are fully aware of the law*: **completely**, entirely, wholly, totally, thoroughly, quite, utterly, perfectly, altogether, exhaustively, extensively, intimately, in all respects, in every respect,

without reservation, without exception, {lock, stock, and barrel}, from first to last, to the hilt.
▷ANTONYMS partially.
2 *fully two minutes must have passed*: **at least**, without exaggeration, easily, quite; informal without a word of a lie.
▷ANTONYMS nearly.
□ **fully fledged** *he never gave up on the dream of becoming a fully fledged artist*: **mature**, adult, grown-up, grown, fully grown, full-grown, fully developed.

fully fledged adjective *her ambition to become a fully fledged teacher*: **trained**, qualified, proficient; experienced, time-served; mature, fully developed, full grown, full scale, full blown.
▷ANTONYMS novice.

fulminate verb **1** *ministers and preachers* ***fulminated against*** *the new curriculum*: **protest**, rail, rage, rant, thunder, storm, declaim, inveigh, speak out, make/take a stand; denounce, decry, condemn, criticize, censure, disparage, attack, execrate, arraign; informal mouth off about, kick up a fuss/stink about, go on about; rare animadvert, excoriate, vociferate about, vituperate.
2 literary *thunder fulminated around the house*: **explode**, flash, crack, detonate, blow up, go off; rumble.

fulmination noun **1** *the fulminations of media moralists*: **protest**, objection, complaint, rant; denunciation, condemnation, criticism, censure, disparagement, attack, broadside; (**fulminations**) decrying, railing, invective, tirade, diatribe, harangue, philippic, obloquy, execration, arraignment; informal brickbat, tongue-lashing, bashing, blast; Brit. informal slating; formal excoriation, vociferation, vituperation.
2 literary *the echo of the previous fulminations faded away*: **explosion**, flash, crack, crash, bang, report, detonation, eruption, blowing up; rumbling.

fulsome adjective *he paid fulsome tribute to his secretary*: **enthusiastic**, ample, profuse, extensive, generous, liberal, lavish, glowing, gushing, gushy; **excessive**, extravagant, overdone, immoderate, inordinate, over-appreciative; fawning, ingratiating; adulatory, laudatory, acclamatory, eulogistic, rapturous, flattering, complimentary, effusive, cloying, unctuous, saccharine, sugary, honeyed; informal over the top, OTT, buttery; formal encomiastic.

fumble verb **1** *he fumbled for his keys*: **grope**, feel about, search blindly, scrabble around, muddle around; fish, delve, cast about/around/round for; archaic grabble for.
2 *he fumbled about in the dark but could not find her*: **stumble**, blunder, flounder, lumber, bumble, stagger, totter, lurch, move clumsily, move awkwardly; feel one's way, grope one's way.
3 *the keeper fumbled the ball*: **fail to catch**, miss, drop, mishandle, handle awkwardly; misfield.
4 *he had fumbled the initiative*: **botch**, bungle, mismanage, mishandle, spoil; blunder, make a mistake; informal make a mess of, make a hash of, fluff, muff, screw up, foul up, blow, louse up; Brit. informal make a pig's ear of, make a muck of, cock up; N. Amer. informal flub.
▶ **noun 1** *a fumble from the goalkeeper*: **slip**, miss, drop, mishandling; misfielding; mistake, error, gaffe, fault, botch; informal slip-up, clanger, boob, boo-boo, howler, foul-up; Brit. informal cock-up.
2 informal *a kiss and a fumble*: **fondle**, grope, caress, hug, embrace, cuddle; informal feel-up.

fume verb **1** *a liquid which fumes in moist air*: **emit smoke**, emit gas, smoke; archaic reek.
2 *I am absolutely fuming that our young people are missing out again*: **be furious**, be enraged, be angry, seethe, smoulder, simmer, boil, be livid, be incensed, bristle, be beside oneself, spit, chafe; rage, rant and rave, lose one's temper, lose control, explode, flare up, go berserk, bluster; informal be up in arms, be hot under the collar, be at boiling point, be all steamed up, get steamed up, get worked up, fly off the handle, foam at the mouth, raise the roof, flip one's lid, blow one's top, hit the roof, go up the wall, blow a fuse, see red; Brit. informal spit feathers.
▶ **noun** (**fumes**) **1** *a fire giving off toxic fumes*: **smoke**, vapour, gas, exhalation, exhaust, effluvium, pollution; archaic miasma.
2 *her perfume overpowered the tobacco fumes*: **smell**, stink, reek, stench, odour; Brit. informal pong, niff, whiff, hum; Scottish informal guff; N. Amer. informal funk; rare fetor, malodour, mephitis.

fumigate verb *we got sulphur candles to fumigate the house*: **disinfect**, purify, sterilize, sanitize, sanitate, decontaminate, cleanse, clean out; smoke out; rare depollute, depurate, deterge.

fun noun **1** *I joined in with the fun*: **pleasure**, entertainment, enjoyment, amusement, excitement, gratification; jollification, merrymaking; leisure, relaxation, relief, respite, rest, refreshment; recreation, diversion, distraction; good time, great time; informal R and R (rest and recreation), living it up, junketing, a ball, whoopee, beer and skittles.
▷ANTONYMS boredom.
2 *he plays the role with an infectious sense of fun*: **merriment**, cheerfulness, cheeriness, cheer, joy, jollity, joviality, jocularity, high spirits, gaiety, mirth, mirthfulness, laughter, hilarity, glee, gladness, light-heartedness, levity; vivacity, liveliness, exuberance, ebullience, buoyancy, perkiness, zest, sunniness, brightness, enthusiasm, vibrancy, vividness, vitality, energy, vigour, vim; dated sport.
▷ANTONYMS misery.
3 *he became a figure of fun in the music press*: **ridicule**, derision, mockery, laughter, scorn, scoffing, contempt; joking, jokes, jesting, jeering, sneering, jibing, teasing, taunting, ragging, lampooning.
▷ANTONYMS respect.
□ **fun and games** **cavorting**, clowning about/around, fooling around, horseplay, play, playfulness, tomfoolery, buffoonery, mischief; revels, frolics, revelry, larks, antics, high jinks; informal skylarking.
□ **in fun** *the teasing was all in fun*: **playful**, in jest, joking, jokey, as a joke, tongue in cheek, light-hearted, high-spirited, unserious, facetious, flippant, flip, glib, frivolous, for a laugh; to tease, teasing, bantering, whimsical; archaic frolicsome, sportive; rare jocose.
▷ANTONYMS in earnest, serious.
□ **make fun of** *he was making fun of her*. See **make**.
▶ **adjective** informal **1** *a fun evening out*: **enjoyable**, amusing, diverting, pleasurable, pleasing, agreeable, interesting.
▷ANTONYMS boring.
2 *a smart, fun girl*: **entertaining**, lively, amusing, fun-loving, witty, convivial, clubbable.
▷ANTONYMS serious.

function noun **1** *the main function of the machine*: **purpose**, task, use, role; reason, basis, justification.
2 *the committee's function is to arrange social activities*: **responsibility**, duty, concern, province, aim, activity, assignment, obligation, charge; task, chore, job, role, errand, mission, detail, undertaking, commission; capacity, post, situation, office, occupation, employment, business, operation; French raison d'être; informal thing, bag, line of country, pigeon.
3 *casualties are a function of war*: **consequence**, result, outcome, ramification, corollary, concomitant; dated issue.
▷ANTONYMS cause.
4 *he was obliged to attend political functions*: **social event**, party, occasion, social occasion, affair, gathering, reception, soirée, celebration, jamboree, gala; N. Amer. levee; informal do, bash, shindig, shindy, blowout; Brit. informal rave-up, thrash, knees-up, jolly, beanfeast, bunfight, beano, lig.
▶ **verb 1** *if we unplug a TV set, it ceases to function*: **work**, go, run, be in working/running order, operate, perform, be in action, be operative.
▷ANTONYMS malfunction.
2 *the museum intends to* ***function as*** *an educational and study centre*: **serve**, act, operate, perform, work, behave; have/do the job of, play the role of, act the part of, perform the function of, do duty as, constitute, form.

functional adjective **1** *an ugly functional concrete building*: **practical**, useful, utilitarian, utility, workaday, serviceable; minimalist, plain, simple, basic; severe, spartan, ascetic, bare, modest, unadorned, undecorated, unornamented, unembellished, unostentatious, uncluttered, unfussy, without frills; impersonal, characterless, soulless, colourless, institutional, antiseptic, clinical; informal no frills.
▷ANTONYMS ornate; impractical.
2 *the air vent needs clearing to keep it fully functional*: **working**, in working order, functioning, effective, usable, in service, in use; going, running, operative, operating, in operation, in commission, in action; informal up and running.
▷ANTONYMS out of order, malfunctioning.

functionary noun *a Whitehall functionary*: **official**, office-bearer, office-holder, public servant, civil servant, bureaucrat, administrator, apparatchik; Brit. jack-in-office.

fund noun **1** *an emergency fund*: **collection**, kitty, reserve, pool, purse; endowment, foundation, trust, charity, grant; investment, capital; savings, nest egg; informal stash.
2 (**funds**) *I was very short of funds*: **money**, cash, hard cash, ready money; wealth, means, assets, resources, savings, capital, reserves, the wherewithal; informal dough, bread, loot, dosh, green, the ready, folding money; Brit. informal lolly, spondulicks.
3 *his fund of stories seems inexhaustible*: **stock**, store, supply, accumulation, mass, collection, cumulation, bank, pool; mine, reservoir, storehouse, treasury, treasure house, hoard, repository.
▶ **verb** *the agency was funded by the Treasury*: **finance**, pay for, back, capitalize, sponsor, provide finance/capital for, put up the money for, subsidize, underwrite, endow, support, be a patron of, float, maintain; informal foot the bill for, pick up the tab for; N. Amer. informal bankroll, stake.

fundamental adjective *a fundamental political principle*: **basic**, foundational, rudimentary, elemental, elementary, underlying, basal, radical, root; primary, cardinal, initial, original, prime, first, primitive, primordial; principal, chief, capital, key, central; structural, organic, constitutional, inherent, intrinsic, ingrained; vital, essential, important, indispensable, necessary, crucial, pivotal, critical.
▷ANTONYMS secondary, unimportant.

f

Choose the right word **fundamental, basic**

See **basic**.

fundamentally adverb **1** *they were of fundamentally different temperaments*: **basically**, elementally, radically; structurally, organically, constitutionally, inherently, intrinsically, materially; vitally, essentially; crucially, centrally, critically.
▷ANTONYMS superficially.
2 *she was, fundamentally, a good person*: **essentially**, in essence, basically, at heart, at bottom, deep down, principally, predominantly, above all, first of all, most of all, first and foremost, on the whole, by and large, substantially; French au fond; informal at the end of the day, when all is said and done, when you get right down to it.
▷ANTONYMS ostensibly.

fundamentals plural noun *he taught me the fundamentals of the job*: **basics**, essentials, rudiments, foundations, basic principles, first principles, preliminaries; crux, essence, core, nucleus, heart, base, bedrock, groundwork, crux of the matter, heart of the matter; Latin sine qua non; informal nuts and bolts, nitty-gritty, brass tacks, ABC.
▷ANTONYMS advanced principles.

funeral noun **1** *he'd attended a funeral*: **burial**, burying, interment, entombment, committal, inhumation, laying to rest, consignment to the grave; cremation; funeral rites, obsequies, last offices; wake, vigil; rare sepulture, exequies.
▷ANTONYMS exhumation.
2 informal *remember, it was you who asked—it's your funeral*: **responsibility**, problem, worry, concern, business, affair; informal headache; Brit. informal lookout, pigeon.

funereal adjective **1** *the funereal atmosphere of the place*: **solemn**, sombre, grave, serious; gloomy, dismal, doleful, dreary, sad, cheerless, joyless, bleak, melancholy, miserable, morose, sorrowful, morbid, maudlin, dark, depressing, woeful, lugubrious, sepulchral; literary dolorous; rare exequial, funebrial.
▷ANTONYMS cheerful, lively.
2 *funereal colours*: **dark**, black, drab.

fungus noun **mushroom**, toadstool; mould, mildew, rust, fungal disease, rot, decay; technical mycelium, saprophyte.

Word links **fungus**

myco-, fungi- related prefixes
mycology science of fungi
fungivorous fungus-eating
fungicide chemical that destroys fungus

funk informal noun **1** Brit. *he put us all into a funk*: **panic**, state of fear, fluster; informal cold sweat, flap, state, tizzy, tizz, tiz-woz, dither, stew; Brit. informal blue funk; N. Amer. informal twit.
2 N. Amer. *he was in a deep funk because his wife had left him*: **depression**; informal the dumps, the doldrums, low; N. Amer. informal blue funk.
▶ verb Brit. *I'm certain he funked it*: **avoid**, evade, dodge, escape from, run away from, baulk at, flinch from; informal chicken out of, duck, wriggle out of, cop out of, get out of.

funnel noun **1** *fluid was being poured through the funnel*: **tube**, pipe, channel, conduit.
2 *smoke was pouring from the funnel*: **chimney**, flue, vent, shaft; Scottish & N. English lum.
▶ verb *some of the money was funnelled through secret bank accounts*: **channel**, guide, feed, direct, convey, move, pass; pour, filter, siphon.
▷ANTONYMS scatter, splurge.

funny adjective **1** *a book with many funny episodes*: **amusing**, humorous, comic, comical, droll, laughable, chucklesome; hilarious, hysterical, riotous, uproarious; witty, quick-witted, waggish, facetious, jolly, jocular, light-hearted; entertaining, diverting, sparkling, scintillating; silly, absurd, ridiculous, ludicrous, risible, farcical, preposterous, slapstick; informal side-splitting, rib-tickling, laugh-a-minute, wacky, zany, off the wall, daft, killing, a scream, rich, priceless.
▷ANTONYMS serious; tragic.
2 *a funny coincidence*: **strange**, **peculiar**, odd, queer, weird, bizarre, curious, freakish, freak, quirky; mysterious, mystifying, puzzling, perplexing; unusual, uncommon, anomalous, irregular, abnormal, exceptional, singular, rare, unique, out of the ordinary, extraordinary, outlandish; Brit. out of the common; Scottish unco; Brit. informal, dated rum.
▷ANTONYMS obvious, straightforward.
3 *make sure there are no funny characters hanging around outside*: **suspicious**, suspect, dubious, untrustworthy, questionable; informal shady, fishy, not kosher; Brit. informal dodgy; Austral./NZ shonky.
▷ANTONYMS trustworthy.

fur noun *a layer of fur*: **hair**, wool; coat, mane, fleece, pelt; technical pelage; archaic fell.

Word links **fur**

doraphobia fear of fur

furbish verb *the kitchen was furbished with every kind of modern gadget*: **supply**, furnish, provide, equip, kit out, rig out, fit, appoint.

furious adjective **1** *he was furious when he learned about it*: **enraged**, raging, infuriated, very angry, inflamed, incandescent, fuming, boiling, seething, incensed, irate, frenzied, in a frenzy, raving mad, mad, maddened, ranting, raving, wrathful, in a temper, beside oneself; in high dudgeon, indignant, outraged; informal livid, hot under the collar, hopping mad, wild, as cross as two sticks, apoplectic, riled, aerated, on the warpath, up in arms, foaming at the mouth, steamed up, in a lather, in a paddy, fit to be tied, up the wall; N. Amer. informal sore, bent out of shape, soreheaded; Austral./NZ informal ropeable, snaky, crook; W. Indian informal vex; Brit. informal, dated in a bate; literary ireful, wroth.
▷ANTONYMS calm, placid.
2 *a furious argument*: **fierce**, wild, violent; intense, vehement, unrestrained; heated, hot, passionate, fiery, 'lively'; tumultuous, turbulent, tempestuous, stormy, boisterous; blustery, gusty, gusting, windy, squally, rough, raging, howling, roaring, foul, filthy, dirty, nasty.
▷ANTONYMS mild, calm.

furnish verb **1** *the bedrooms are elegantly furnished*: **provide with furniture**, fit out, rig out, kit out, appoint, outfit, embellish, enhance.
2 *grooms furnished us with horses for our journey*: **supply**, equip, provide, provision, issue, kit out, fix up, grant, present; give, offer, make available, serve, confer, afford, purvey, bestow, endow.
▷ANTONYMS divest.

furniture noun **furnishings**, house fittings, fittings, fitments, movables, fixtures, appointments, appliances, effects, chattels, amenities, units, equipment, paraphernalia; informal stuff, things.

furore noun *the letter caused a furore in Britain*: **commotion**, uproar, outcry, disturbance, hubbub, hurly-burly, fuss, upset, tumult, brouhaha, palaver, to-do, pother, turmoil, tempest, agitation, pandemonium, confusion; stir, excitement; scandal, sensation; informal song and dance, hoo-ha, hullabaloo, ballyhoo, hoopla, rumpus, flap, tizz, tizzy, tizz-woz, stink, performance, pantomime, scene; Brit. informal carry-on, kerfuffle; N. Amer. informal snafu.

furrow noun **1** *regular furrows in a ploughed fields*: **groove**, trench, rut, trough, ditch, channel, seam, gutter, gouge, hollow, fissure, gash, track.
2 *the furrows on either side of her mouth*: **wrinkle**, line, crease, crinkle, crow's foot, cleft, indentation, corrugation; scar; technical sulcus.
▶ verb *his brow furrowed*: **wrinkle**, crease, line, crinkle, pucker, crumple, screw up, scrunch up, corrugate.
▷ANTONYMS smooth.

furry adjective *a small furry animal*: **covered with fur**, hairy, long-haired, downy, fleecy, soft, fluffy, fuzzy, woolly.

further adverb **1** *Orkney is further from the mainland than the Western Isles*: **at a greater distance**, more distant, farther.
▷ANTONYMS closer.
2 *nothing could be **further from** the truth*: **more unlike**, less like; farther.
▷ANTONYMS closer.
3 *this theme will be developed further in Chapter 6*: **additionally**, more, to a greater extent.
4 *further, firms' employment practices may be discriminatory when they appear not to be*: **furthermore**, moreover, what's more, also, additionally, in addition, besides, as well, too, to boot, on top of that, over and above that, into the bargain, by the same token; archaic withal, forbye.
▶ adjective **1** *the further side of the field*: **more distant**, more remote, remoter, more advanced, more extreme, further away/off, farther; far, other, opposite.
▷ANTONYMS nearer; near.
2 *the further reaches of the valley*: **remote**, distant, far away/off/removed.
▷ANTONYMS near.
3 *for further information please contact the Visitors' Office*: **additional**, more, extra, supplementary, supplemental, other; new, fresh.
▶ verb *he decided to further his career in politics*: **promote**, advance, forward, develop, stimulate; facilitate, aid, assist, help, help along, lend a hand to, abet; expedite, hasten, speed up, accelerate, step up, spur on, oil the wheels of, push, give a push to, boost, encourage, cultivate, nurture, succour; back, contribute to, foster, champion.
▷ANTONYMS impede.

furtherance noun *he was acting in the furtherance of his business interests*: **promotion**, furthering, advancement, forwarding, improvement, development, betterment, stimulation; facilitating, aiding, assisting, helping, abetting; expediting, hastening, speeding up, acceleration, pushing, boosting, encouragement, cultivation, nurturing, succouring, backing, fostering, championing, endorsement, patronage.
▷ANTONYMS hindrance.

furthermore adverb *This program is simple to use. Furthermore, it can be used as a powerful document transmission system*: **moreover**, further, what's more, also, additionally, in addition, besides, as well, too, to boot, on top of that, over and above that, into the bargain, by the same token; archaic withal, forbye.

furthest adjective *the furthest limits of the universe*: **most distant**, most remote, remotest, furthest/farthest away, farthest, furthermost, farthermost; outlying, outer, outermost, extreme, uttermost, ultimate, very; rare outmost.
▷ANTONYMS nearest.

furtive adjective *they cast furtive glances at one another*: **secretive**, secret, surreptitious; sly, sneaky, wily, underhand, under the table; clandestine, hidden, covert, cloaked, conspiratorial, underground, cloak and dagger, hole and corner, hugger-mugger; stealthy, sneaking, skulking, slinking; sidelong, sideways, oblique, indirect; informal hush-hush, shifty.
▷ANTONYMS open; above board.

fury noun **1** *she exploded with fury*: **rage**, anger, wrath, passion, outrage, spleen, temper, savagery, frenzy, madness; crossness, indignation, umbrage, annoyance, exasperation; literary ire, choler, bile.
▷ANTONYMS good humour; calmness.
2 *the fury of the storm*: **fierceness**, ferocity, violence, turbulence, tempestuousness, savagery; severity, intensity, vehemence, force, forcefulness, power, potency, strength; rare ferity.
▷ANTONYMS mildness.
3 *she turned on Mother like a fury*: **virago**, hellcat, termagant, spitfire, vixen, shrew, hag, harridan, dragon, gorgon, ogress, harpy, tartar, fishwife; **(Furies)** Greek Mythology Eumenides.

fuse verb **1** *they found a wider audience by fusing rap with rock*: **combine**, amalgamate, put together, blend, merge, meld, mingle, intermix, intermingle, synthesize; coalesce, compound, alloy, agglutinate; unite, marry; rare admix, commingle, commix, interflow.
▷ANTONYMS separate.
2 *when fired in a kiln the film of metal fuses on to the pot*: **bond**, stick, join, attach, bind, integrate, weld, solder; **melt**, smelt, dissolve, liquefy.
▷ANTONYMS disconnect.
3 Brit. *a light had fused*: **short-circuit**, burn out, stop working, trip, break; informal go, blow.
▸ **noun** *a plug fitted with a fuse*: **circuit-breaker**, trip switch, residual current device.

fusillade noun *a fusillade of missiles*: **salvo**, volley, barrage, bombardment, cannonade, battery, burst, blast, hail, shower, rain, stream, broadside, blitz, discharge.

fusion noun **1** *the fetus originates from the fusion of two sex cells*: **blend**, blending, combination, amalgamation, joining, bonding, binding, merging, melding, mingling, integration, intermixture, intermingling, synthesis; coalescence, compounding, agglutination; uniting, marrying, alliance, unification; rare commingling, commixture, interflow.
▷ANTONYMS separation.
2 *the fusion of resin and glass fibre in the moulding process*: **melting**, smelting, dissolving, dissolution, liquefaction.

fuss noun **1** *there was all that fuss over his marriage breaking up*: **ado**, excitement, agitation, uproar, to-do, stir, commotion, confusion, disturbance, tumult, hubbub, rigmarole, folderol, brouhaha, furore, storm in a teacup, much ado about nothing; upset, worry, bother, row; fluster, flurry, bustle; informal palaver, hoo-ha, ballyhoo, flap, tizzy, stew, song and dance, performance, pantomime; Brit. informal carry-on, kerfuffle; N. Amer. informal fuss and feathers; literary pother.
2 *she liked to cook with a minimum of fuss*: **bother**, trouble, inconvenience, effort, exertion, labour; informal hassle.
▷ANTONYMS convenience.
3 *children make a fuss when limits are set down*: **protest**, complaint, objection; grumble, whine; tantrum, outburst, hysterics; commotion, trouble; informal grouse, gripe.
▸ **verb 1** *he has a tendency to fuss over detail*: **worry**, fret, be agitated, be worried, take pains, make a big thing out of; make a mountain out of a molehill; informal get worked up, be in a flap, flap, be in a tizzy, be in a stew, make a meal of, make a (big) thing of.
▷ANTONYMS get into perspective.
2 *he fussed about like an old hen*: **bustle**, dash, rush, scurry, charge, fly; tear around, buzz around, run round in circles.
3 Brit. *oh for heaven's sake, don't fuss me*: **pester**, disturb, harass; irritate, annoy, vex, bother, nag; informal hassle.

fusspot noun informal **fussy person**, worrier, perfectionist, stickler, grumbler; informal nit-picker, old woman; N. Amer. informal fussbudget.

fussy adjective **1** *she's very fussy about the wine she drinks*: **finicky**, particular, over-particular, fastidious, discriminating, selective, dainty, punctilious; hard to please, difficult, exacting, demanding; faddish, faddy; informal pernickety, choosy, picky, nit-picking, old womanish, old maidish; N. Amer. informal persnickety; archaic nice, overnice; rare finical.
▷ANTONYMS easy to please, indiscriminate.
2 *a fussy, frilly bridal gown*: **over-elaborate**, over-embellished, over-decorated, over-ornate, overdone, overworked, busy, cluttered, laboured, strained, florid; ornate, fancy.
▷ANTONYMS understated.

fusty adjective **1** *a fusty drawing room*: **stuffy**, musty, stale, stagnant, airless, unventilated, close, suffocating, oppressive, mouldering; damp, mildewed, mildewy; Brit. frowsty.
▷ANTONYMS airy, ventilated.
2 *a fusty conservative*: **old-fashioned**, out of date, outdated, behind the times, antediluvian, backward-looking, past it; crusty, fogeyish; informal square, out of the ark, creaky, mouldy.
▷ANTONYMS modern, up-to-date.

futile adjective *I wore my cape in a futile attempt to keep dry*: **fruitless**, vain, pointless; **useless**, worthless, ineffectual, ineffective, inefficacious, to no effect, of no use, in vain, to no avail, unavailing; unsuccessful, failed, thwarted; unproductive, barren, unprofitable, abortive; impotent, hollow, empty, forlorn, idle, sterile, nugatory, valueless; hopeless, doomed, lost; Austral./NZ informal no good to gundy; archaic bootless.
▷ANTONYMS useful; fruitful.

Choose the right word **futile, fruitless, vain, pointless**

These words all describe unsuccessful undertakings, but some refer to the prospects of success, some to the outcome, and some can refer to either.

A **futile** undertaking has no chance of success, which may or may not be recognized by the person embarking on it (*it would be futile to argue | the Bank of England threw away £10 billion in a futile attempt to prop up sterling*).

Fruitless is most commonly used to describe an undertaking that turns out unsuccessfully (*an aerial search of the area proved fruitless, and the men were presumed dead | talks collapsed after months of fruitless negotiation*).

Vain is a more literary word, which can refer either to the prospects of success (*I pulled the blankets over my head in a vain attempt to shut out the ugly visions*) or the result, usually in the phrase *in vain* (*after I had waited in vain for six months, I lost hope*).

Pointless describes something that serves no useful purpose (*pointless committee meetings*), so is used to convey the lack of any prospect of success, which should be obvious to the person contemplating the action (*I knew it would be pointless expecting him to change his mind*).

futility noun *he could see the futility of his actions*: **fruitlessness**, vanity, pointlessness; **uselessness**, worthlessness, ineffectuality, ineffectiveness, inefficacy; failure, unproductiveness, barrenness, unprofitability, abortiveness; impotence, hollowness, emptiness, meaningless, forlornness, hopelessness, sterility, valuelessness; archaic bootlessness.
▷ANTONYMS usefulness, fruitfulness.

future noun **1** *Mike's plans for* ***the future***: **time to come**, time ahead; what lay/lies ahead, coming times; the fullness of time; formal hereafter.
▷ANTONYMS past.
2 *she knew that her future lay in acting*: **destiny**, fate, fortune, doom; prospects, expectations, chances, likely success/advancement/improvement.
□ **in future** *I modified the program so that in future it would keep accessible records*: **from now on**, after this, in the future, from this day forth/forward, from this day/time on, hence, henceforward, subsequently, in time to come; formal hereafter, hereinafter.
▸ **adjective 1** *customers guarantee repayment at a future date*: **later**, following, ensuing, succeeding, subsequent, upcoming, to come, coming.
▷ANTONYMS past.
2 *it was here that he met his future wife*: **destined**, **intended**, planned, to be, prospective, expected, anticipated.

fuzz[1] noun **1** *his face is covered with white fuzz*: **hair**, **fluff**, fur, down, floss, fine hair.
2 *there was plenty of fuzz from the guitars*: **distortion**, buzz, hiss, fizz, buzzing, hissing, fizzing, white noise.

fuzz[2] noun informal *the fuzz came in with a warrant*. See **police**.

fuzzy adjective **1** *I stroked the baby's fuzzy head*: **downy**, down-covered, frizzy, woolly, velvety, silky, silken, satiny, linty, napped, soft; technical floccose, lanate.
2 *a fuzzy picture*: **blurry**, blurred, indistinct; unclear, bleary, misty, distorted, out of focus, unfocused, lacking definition, low resolution, nebulous; **ill-defined**, indefinite, vague, hazy, imprecise, inexact, loose, woolly.
▷ANTONYMS clear, sharp.
3 *my mind was so fuzzy*: **confused**, muddled, addled, fuddled, befuddled, groggy, disoriented, disorientated, mixed up, fazed, perplexed, dizzy, stupefied, benumbed; foggy, misty, shadowy, blurred.
▷ANTONYMS clear.

gab informal **verb** *they were all gabbing away like crazy*. See **chat** (verb).
▶ **noun** *their meetings turn into marathons of gab*. See **chatter** (noun).
□ **the gift of the gab** *you'd make a good lawyer—you've got the gift of the gab*: **eloquence**, fluency, clarity of speech, expressiveness, articulateness, articulacy, good command of the language; persuasiveness; informal a way with words, blarney.
▷**ANTONYMS** inarticulacy.

gabble **verb** *the hysterical child just gabbled at me*: **jabber**, babble, prattle, rattle, blabber, gibber, cackle, blab, drivel, twitter, splutter; talk rapidly, talk incoherently, talk unintelligibly; Brit. informal waffle, chunter, witter.
▶ **noun** *the boozy gabble of the crowd*: **jabbering**, babbling, chattering, gibbering, babble, chatter, rambling; gibberish, drivel, twaddle, nonsense; informal flannel, blah, mumbo-jumbo; Brit. informal waffle, waffling, chuntering, double Dutch.

gabby **adjective** informal *we are an incurably gabby lot*. See **talkative**.

gad **verb** *she looked worn out and must have been **gadding about** too much*: **gallivant**, jaunt around, flit around, run around, travel around, roam (around); wander, rove, ramble, traipse, meander, stray.

gadabout **noun** *she was an inveterate gadabout*: **gallivanter**, pleasure-seeker; **wanderer**, rover, rambler, drifter, bird of passage; traveller, journeyer, explorer, globetrotter.

gadget **noun** *the kitchen had every kind of modern gadget*: **appliance**, apparatus, instrument, implement, tool, utensil, contrivance, contraption, machine, mechanism, device, labour-saving device, convenience, invention, thing; Heath Robinson device; N. Amer. Rube Goldberg device; informal widget, gismo, thingummy, gimmick, mod con; Brit. informal doobry, doodah.

gaffe **noun** *I made some real gaffes at work*: **blunder**, mistake, error, slip; indiscretion, impropriety, breach of etiquette, miscalculation, gaucherie, solecism; French faux pas; Latin lapsus linguae, lapsus calami; informal slip-up, howler, boo-boo, boner, botch, fluff; Brit. informal boob, bloomer, clanger; N. Amer. informal blooper, bloop, goof; Brit. informal, dated floater; vulgar slang fuck-up.

gaffer **noun 1** Brit. informal *being the gaffer's gone to her head*: **boss**, manager, manageress, foreman, forewoman, overseer, controller, supervisor, superintendent; Brit. ganger; informal bossman, number one, kingpin, top dog, bigwig, big cheese, Mr Big, skipper; Brit. informal governor, guv'nor; N. Amer. informal honcho, head honcho, numero uno, padrone, sachem, big wheel, big kahuna, big white chief, high muckamuck.
2 informal *old gaffers tottering past on sticks*: **old man**, elderly man, senior citizen, pensioner, OAP, grandfather; Scottish & Irish bodach; informal old bloke, old boy, old guy, old codger, old geezer, old-timer, greybeard, grandad, wrinkly; Brit. informal buffer, josser; N. Amer. informal old coot; archaic grandsire, ancient; rare senex.

gag[1] **verb 1** *a dirty rag was used to gag her mouth*: **stop up**, block, plug, clog, stifle, smother, muffle; put a gag on, silence, hush, quiet.
2 *the press is gagged by more and more complex rules*: **silence**, muzzle, mute, muffle, stifle, smother, strangle, subdue, suppress, repress; censor, curb, check, restrain, fetter, shackle, restrict, limit.
▷**ANTONYMS** encourage; give a voice to.
3 *the stench grew worse, making her gag*: **retch**, heave, dry-heave, convulse, almost vomit, feel nauseous; choke, gasp, struggle for breath, fight for air; informal keck.
▶ **noun** *his scream was muffled by the gag*: **muzzle**, tie, restraint.

gag[2] **noun** informal *even the worst of gags will amuse someone somewhere*: **joke**, jest, witticism, quip, pun, play on words, double entendre, funny remark, witty remark; flash of wit, rejoinder, sally; French bon mot; informal crack, wisecrack, one-liner, funny, comeback.

gaiety **noun 1** *there was unusual gaiety in her manner*: **cheerfulness**, cheer, light-heartedness, merriment, glee, gladness, happiness, joy, joyfulness, joyousness, delight, pleasure, high spirits, good spirits, good humour, jollity, jolliness, hilarity, mirth, joviality, exuberance, elation, exultation, euphoria, jubilation; liveliness, vivacity, animation, effervescence, levity, buoyancy, sprightliness, zest, zestfulness; French joie de vivre; informal chirpiness, bounce, pep, zing; literary gladsomeness, blitheness, blithesomeness; rare gayness.
▷**ANTONYMS** misery.
2 *the hotel restaurant was a scene of gaiety*: **merrymaking**, festivity, fun, fun and games, frolics, revels, revelry, jollification, celebration, rejoicing, pleasure; informal living it up, larking about; dated sport.

gaily **adverb 1** *she skipped gaily along the path*: **merrily**, cheerfully, cheerily, happily, joyfully, joyously, light-heartedly, blithely, jauntily, gleefully, with pleasure.
▷**ANTONYMS** miserably.
2 *a harbour full of gaily painted boats*: **brightly**, brilliantly, colourfully, flamboyantly.
▷**ANTONYMS** sombrely.
3 *pedestrians skipped gaily into the fast-moving traffic*: **heedlessly**, unthinkingly, thoughtlessly, without thinking, without care, without consideration; **casually**, nonchalantly, airily, breezily, lightly, uncaringly.
▷**ANTONYMS** anxiously.

gain **verb 1** *he gained an entrance scholarship to the college*: **obtain**, get, acquire, come by, procure, secure, attain, achieve, earn, win, capture, clinch, pick up, carry off, reap, gather; receive, be given, be awarded, come away with; informal land, net, bag, pot, scoop, wangle, swing, score, nab, collar, cop, hook, get one's hands on, get one's mitts on, get hold of, walk away with, walk off with.
▷**ANTONYMS** lose.
2 *the workers gain high salaries*: **earn**, bring in, make, get, get paid, pocket, clear, gross, net, realize; informal rake in, haul in, bag.
3 *they stood to **gain from** the deal*: **profit**, make money, reap financial reward, reap benefits, benefit; do well out of, make capital out of; informal make a killing, milk, cash in on.
▷**ANTONYMS** lose.
4 *all four patients recovered and gained weight*: **increase in**, put on, add on, build up; acquire more of something.
▷**ANTONYMS** lose.
5 *we were in the lead but the others were **gaining on** us*: **catch up with**, catch up on, catch someone up, catch, narrow the gap between, get nearer to, draw nearer to, close in on, creep up on, come up to, approach, near.
6 *it took a while to gain the high ridge*: **reach**, arrive at, get to, come to, get as far as, make, make it to, attain, set foot on; end up at, land up at, fetch up at; informal hit, wind up at.
□ **gain ground** *the trend is gaining ground rapidly*: **make headway**, make progress, make strides, progress, advance, proceed, move, get on, get ahead, come on, come along; informal be getting there.
▷**ANTONYMS** retrogress; stagnate.
□ **gain time** *the government was using the negotiations to gain time*: **play for time**, stall, procrastinate, delay, use delaying tactics, temporize, hold

back, hang back, hang fire, dally, drag one's feet, use dilatory tactics; informal put something on the back burner.
▶ **noun 1** *his gain from the deal was negligible*: **profit**, earnings, income, advantage, benefit, reward, emolument, yield, return, winnings, receipts, proceeds, dividend, interest, percentage, takings; informal pickings, cut, take, rake-off, divvy, whack, slice of the cake; Brit. informal bunce.
▷ANTONYMS loss.
2 *the effect of overeating is weight gain*: **increase**, augmentation, addition, rise, increment, accretion, accumulation.
▷ANTONYMS decrease.
3 *he made the biggest gain in the last leg of the race*: **advance**, advancement, progress, forward movement, headway, improvement, step forward.

gainful adjective *they see no prospect of finding gainful employment*: **profitable**, paid, well paid, remunerative, lucrative, moneymaking, financially rewarding; rewarding, fruitful, worthwhile, useful, productive, constructive, beneficial, advantageous, valuable; rare fructuous.

gainsay verb formal *it was difficult to gainsay his claim*: **deny**, dispute, disagree with, argue with, dissent from, contradict, repudiate, declare untrue, challenge, oppose, contest, counter, fly in the face of; disprove, debunk, explode, discredit, refute, rebut, brush aside; informal shoot full of holes, shoot down (in flames); Law disaffirm; rare controvert, confute.
▷ANTONYMS confirm.

gait noun *he had the gait of a professional soldier*: **walk**, step, stride, pace, tread, manner of walking, way of walking; bearing, carriage, comportment, way of holding oneself, way of carrying oneself; Brit. deportment.

gala noun *the village is holding its annual summer gala*: **fête**, gala day, fair, feast, festival, carnival, pageant, jubilee, jamboree, party, garden party, celebration; festivities; fund-raiser, charity event, charity show; Dutch & N. Amer. kermis.
▶ **adjective** *his concerts have been gala occasions for some years*: **festive**, celebratory, merry, joyous, joyful; diverting, entertaining, enjoyable, spectacular, showy; dated gay.

galaxy noun **1** *he focused his telescope on the galaxy*: **star system**, solar system, constellation, cluster, nebula; spiral galaxy, Seyfert galaxy; stars, heavens.
2 *a galaxy of the rock world's biggest stars*: **brilliant gathering**, dazzling assemblage, illustrious group; host, multitude, array, mass, bevy, horde, company, army, flock, group.

gale noun **1** *the church spire was blown down during a gale*: **storm**, tempest, squall, hurricane, tornado, cyclone, typhoon, whirlwind; strong wind, high wind; N. Amer. windstorm; informal burster, buster; literary flaw.
2 *she collapsed in gales of laughter*: **outburst**, burst, eruption, explosion, effusion, attack, fit, paroxysm; peal, howl, hoot, shriek, scream, shout, roar.

gall[1] noun **1** *Melanie had the gall to ask Nick for money*: **impudence**, insolence, impertinence, cheek, cheekiness, nerve, audacity, brazenness, effrontery, temerity, presumption, presumptuousness, brashness, shamelessness, pertness, boldness; bad manners, rudeness, impoliteness; informal brass neck, brass, neck, face, chutzpah, cockiness; Brit. informal sauce, sauciness; Scottish informal snash; N. Amer. informal sass, sassiness, nerviness; informal, dated hide; Brit. informal, dated crust; rare malapertness, procacity, assumption.
2 *scholarly gall was poured forth upon this work*: **acrimony**, resentment, rancour, sourness, acerbity, asperity; bitterness, bile, spleen, malice, spite, spitefulness, malignity, venom, vitriol, poison, malevolence, virulence, nastiness, animosity, antipathy, hostility, enmity, bad blood, ill feeling, ill will, animus; literary choler.

gall[2] noun **1** *this was a gall that she frequently had to endure*: **irritation**, irritant, annoyance, vexation, pest, nuisance, provocation, bother, torment, plague, source of vexation, source of irritation, source of annoyance, thorn in one's side/flesh; informal aggravation, peeve, pain, pain in one's neck, bind, bore, headache, hassle; Scottish informal nyaff, skelf; N. Amer. informal pain in the butt, nudnik, burr under someone's saddle; Austral./NZ informal nark.
2 *a bay horse with a gall on its side*: **sore**, ulcer, ulceration, canker; abrasion, scrape, scratch, graze, chafe.
▶ **verb 1** *it galled him to have to sit impotently in silence*: **irritate**, annoy, vex, make angry, make cross, anger, exasperate, irk, pique, put out, displease, get/put someone's back up, antagonize, get on someone's nerves, rub up the wrong way, ruffle, ruffle someone's feathers, make someone's hackles rise, raise someone's hackles; infuriate, madden, drive to distraction, goad, provoke; informal aggravate, peeve, hassle, miff, rile, nettle, needle, get, get to, bug, hack off, get under someone's skin, get in someone's hair, get up someone's nose, put someone's nose out of joint, get someone's goat, rattle someone's cage, get someone's dander up, drive mad/crazy, drive round the bend/twist, drive up the wall, make someone see red; Brit. informal wind up, nark, get across, get on someone's wick, give someone the hump; N. Amer. informal tee off, tick off, burn up, rankle, ride, gravel; informal, dated give someone the pip; rare exacerbate, hump, rasp.
2 *the straps galled their shoulders*: **chafe**, abrade, rub (against), rub painfully, rub raw, scrape, graze, skin, scratch, rasp, bark, fret; rare excoriate.

gallant adjective **1** *a gallant band of British officers*: **brave**, courageous, valiant, valorous, bold, plucky, daring, fearless, intrepid, heroic, lionhearted, stout-hearted, doughty, mettlesome, great-spirited; honourable, noble, manly, manful, macho, dashing, daredevil, death-or-glory, undaunted, unflinching, unshrinking, unafraid, dauntless, indomitable; informal gutsy, spunky, ballsy, have-a-go; rare venturous.
▷ANTONYMS cowardly.
2 *he made a gallant remark to a self-conscious girl*: **chivalrous**, gentlemanly, courtly, courteous, respectful, polite, attentive, gracious, considerate, thoughtful, obliging; dated mannerly; archaic gentle.
▷ANTONYMS discourteous, rude.
▶ **noun** archaic **1** *a young gallant resplendent in red and white silks*: **fine gentleman**, man about town, man of fashion, dandy, fop, beau, cavalier, swashbuckler; playboy, man of the world, ladies' man; informal swell, toff, ladykiller; archaic gay dog, rip, dude, blade, blood, coxcomb.
2 *she was delighted to see her amorous gallant*: **suitor**, wooer, admirer, worshipper; beau, sweetheart, lover, love, beloved, boyfriend, young man, man friend, escort, partner; informal fancy man, flame, fella; literary swain; archaic paramour.

gallantry noun **1** *he received medals for gallantry*: **bravery**, braveness, courage, courageousness, valour, pluck, pluckiness, nerve, daring, boldness, fearlessness, dauntlessness, intrepidity, intrepidness, manliness, heroism, doughtiness, stout-heartedness, backbone, spine, spirit, spiritedness, mettle, determination, fortitude; informal guts, grit, spunk, gutsiness, gameness; Brit. informal bottle, ballsiness; N. Amer. informal moxie, cojones, sand; vulgar slang balls.
▷ANTONYMS cowardice.
2 *she acknowledged his selfless gallantry*: **chivalry**, chivalrousness, gentlemanliness, courtliness, graciousness, respectfulness, respect, courtesy, courteousness, politeness, good manners, mannerliness, attentiveness, consideration, considerateness, thoughtfulness.
▷ANTONYMS rudeness.

gallery noun **1** *his paintings were bought by a London gallery*: **exhibition room**, display room, art gallery, museum.
2 *they sat up in the gallery*: **balcony**, circle, upper circle; informal gods.
3 *a long gallery with doors along each side*: **passage**, passageway, corridor, hall, hallway, walkway, arcade.

galling adjective *his display of hypocrisy was extremely galling*: **annoying**, irritating, vexing, vexatious, infuriating, maddening, irksome, provoking, exasperating, trying, tiresome, troublesome, bothersome, displeasing, disagreeable; informal aggravating.
▷ANTONYMS pleasing.

gallivant verb *he goes gallivanting about looking for excitement*: **gad**, flit, jaunt, run, roam, wander, travel, range, rove, ramble, traipse, stray.

gallop verb *the horse galloped away*: **race**, **canter**, run, rush, dash, tear, sprint, bolt, fly, shoot, dart, hurry, hasten, speed, streak, hurtle, career, hare, scamper, scurry, scud, go like lighting, go like the wind; lope, prance, frisk; informal zoom, pelt, scoot, hotfoot it, leg it, belt, zip, whip, go like a bat out of hell; Brit. informal bomb.
▷ANTONYMS amble.

gallows plural noun **1** *the felon had been hanged on the gallows*: **gibbet**, scaffold; archaic gallow-tree, Gregorian tree, derrick, three-legged mare, nubbing cheat, nub; archaic, informal leafless tree, triple tree, Tyburn tree.
2 (**the gallows**) *they were condemned to the gallows*: **hanging**, being hanged, the noose, the rope, the gibbet, the scaffold; the death penalty, execution, being executed; informal the drop, being strung up.

galore adjective *the shop contained fine furniture and paintings galore*: **aplenty**, in abundance, in profusion, in great quantity, in large numbers, by the dozen; to spare; everywhere, all over (the place); informal a gogo, by the truckload, by the shedload.
▷ANTONYMS in short supply.

galvanize verb *the letter managed to galvanize him into action*: **jolt**, shock, startle, impel, stir, spur, prod, urge, motivate, stimulate, electrify, excite, rouse, arouse, awaken, invigorate, fire, fuel, animate, vitalize, energize, exhilarate, thrill, dynamize, inspire; get someone going; informal light a fire under, give someone a shot in the arm, give someone a kick; rare inspirit, incentivize.
▷ANTONYMS demotivate.

gambit noun *the most ambitious financial gambit in history*: **stratagem**, machination, scheme, plan, tactic, manoeuvre, move, course of action, line of action, device, operation; ruse, trick, ploy, artifice; Brit. informal wheeze, wangle.

gamble verb **1** *I go to the races when I want to gamble*: **bet**, wager, place a bet, lay a bet, stake money on something, back the horses, try one's luck on the horses; informal play the ponies; Brit. informal punt, chance one's arm, have a flutter; rare game.
2 *we gambled today and we were fortunate to get away with it*: **take a chance**, take a risk, take a leap in the dark, leave things to chance, speculate, venture, buy a pig in a poke; N. Amer. take a flyer; informal stick one's neck out, go out on a limb; Brit. informal chance one's arm.

3 *he gambled on finding someone to give him a lift*: **act in the hope of**, trust in, take a chance on, bank on.
▶ noun 1 *his grandfather enjoyed a gamble*: **bet**, wager, speculation; game of chance; Brit. informal flutter, punt.
2 *I took a gamble and it paid off*: **risk**, chance, hazard, speculation, venture, random shot, leap in the dark; pig in a poke, pot luck, blind bargain; lottery.

gambler noun *he was a daring and fortunate gambler*: **backer**, staker, speculator, risk-taker, better; N. Amer. **bettor**; informal plunger; Brit. informal **punter**; N. Amer. informal high roller, piker; Austral./NZ informal spieler, dasher.

gambol verb *the foal gambolled beside its mother*: **frolic**, frisk, cavort, caper, skip, dance, romp, prance, leap, hop, jump, spring, bound, bounce; play; dated sport; rare rollick, curvet, capriole.

game noun 1 *the children invented a new game*: **pastime**, diversion, entertainment, amusement, distraction, divertissement, recreation, sport, activity, leisure activity; frolic, romp, source of fun.
2 *he broke his leg two weeks before the big game*: **match**, contest, tournament, meeting, sports meeting, meet, event, athletic event, fixture, tie, cup tie, test match, final, cup final, play-off; Canadian & Scottish playdown; N. Amer. split; archaic tourney.
3 *we were only playing a game on him*: **practical joke**, **prank**, jest, trick, hoax; informal lark.
4 *I spoiled his little game*: **scheme**, plot, ploy, stratagem, strategy, gambit, cunning plan, master plan, grand design, crafty designs, tactics; trick, artifice, device, manoeuvre, wile, dodge, ruse, machination, contrivance, subterfuge; informal con, set-up, scam; Brit. informal wheeze; archaic shift.
5 *he spent his time shooting game in the parks*: **wild animals**, wild fowl, big game; quarry, prey.
□ **on the game** Brit. informal *she says she's an 'escort', but actually she's on the game*: **working as a prostitute**, involved in prostitution, whoring, prostituting oneself, selling oneself, selling one's body, walking the streets, on the streets, practising the oldest profession, working in the sex industry; a prostitute, a whore, a call girl.
▶ adjective 1 *they weren't game enough to join in*: **brave**, courageous, valiant, plucky, bold, intrepid, stout-hearted, lionhearted, unafraid, daring, dashing, spirited, mettlesome; fearless, dauntless, undaunted, unblenching, unflinching; informal gutsy, spunky, ballsy; rare venturous.
▷ANTONYMS timid.
2 *I need a bit of help—are you game?* **willing**, favourably inclined, prepared, disposed, in the mood, of a mind, desirous, eager, keen, interested, enthusiastic, ready.
▷ANTONYMS unwilling.
▶ verb rare *they were drinking and gaming all evening*: **gamble**, bet, place bets, lay bets, wager, stake money; Brit. informal have a flutter, punt.

gamin, gamine noun dated *a crowd of gamins playing in the gutter*. See **urchin**.

gamut noun *the complete gamut of human emotion*: **range**, spectrum, span, sweep, compass, scope, area, breadth, width, reach, extent, catalogue, scale, sequence, series; variety.

gang noun 1 *a gang of teenagers*: **band**, group, crowd, pack, horde, throng, mob, herd, swarm, multitude, mass, body, troop, drove, cluster; company, gathering, assemblage, assembly; informal posse, bunch, gaggle, load.
2 informal *John was one of our gang*: **circle**, social circle, social set, group of friends, clique, in-crowd, coterie, lot, ring, clan, club, league, faction, cabal; fraternity, sorority, brotherhood, sisterhood; informal crew, posse; rare sodality, confraternity.
3 *a work gang hammering cobbles into the highway*: **squad**, team, troop, shift, detachment, posse, troupe; working party.
▶ verb
□ **gang up** *they all ganged up to put me down*: **conspire**, cooperate, work together, act together, combine, join up, join forces, team up, club together, get together, unite, ally; rare coact.

gangling, gangly adjective *a gangling teenager in jeans*: **lanky**, rangy, wiry, stringy, bony, angular, skinny, skin-and-bones, spindly, spindling, scrawny, thin, spare, gaunt, skeletal, size-zero; loosely built, loosely jointed; awkward, uncoordinated, ungainly, gawky, inelegant, graceless, ungraceful; informal like a bag of bones; dated spindle-shanked.
▷ANTONYMS squat.

gangster noun *they were held up at gunpoint by gangsters*: **hoodlum**, racketeer, bandit, robber, ruffian, thug, tough, desperado, outlaw, villain, lawbreaker, criminal; gunman, murderer, assassin, terrorist; gang member, member of a criminal gang, member of the Mafia, Mafioso; in Japan yakuza; informal mobster, crook, hit man, hatchet man, heavy; N. Amer. informal hood; literary brigand.

gaol noun Brit. dated See **jail**.

gaoler noun Brit. dated See **jailer**.

gap noun 1 *she peered through a gap in the shutters*: **opening**, aperture, space, breach, chink, slit, slot, vent, crack, crevice, cranny, cavity, hole, orifice, interstice, perforation, break, fracture, rift, rent, fissure, cleft, divide, discontinuity; technical scission, grike.
2 *a gap between meetings*: **pause**, intermission, interval, interlude, delay, break, breathing space, breather, respite, hiatus; N. Amer. recess.
3 *there appears to be a gap in our records*: **omission**, blank, blank space, empty space, lacuna, hiatus, void, vacuity.
4 *the gap between the rich and the poor*: **chasm**, gulf, rift, polarity, split, separation, breach; contrast, difference, disparity, divergence, variation, variance, imbalance, unevenness.

gape verb 1 *she gaped at him in astonishment*: **stare**, stare open-mouthed, stare in wonder, gawk, goggle, gaze, ogle, look fixedly, look vacantly; informal rubberneck; Brit. informal gawp.
2 *he wore a leather jerkin which gaped at every seam*: **open wide**, open up, yawn; part, crack, split.

gaping adjective *the volcano collapsed to form a gaping crater*: **cavernous**, yawning, wide, broad; vast, huge, enormous, immense, extensive.

garage noun 1 *he let them park in his garage*: **car port**, lock-up.
2 *she called at the garage for petrol*: **petrol station**, service station; Austral. informal servo.
3 *a new bus garage was to be built*: **depot**, terminus, terminal, base, headquarters; bus station, coach station.

garb noun *he was dressed in the garb of a Catholic priest*: **clothes**, clothing, garments, attire, dress, costume, outfit, wear, uniform, turnout, array; livery, regalia, trappings, finery; informal gear, get-up, togs, garms, rig-out, duds, glad rags; Brit. informal clobber; N. Amer. informal threads; formal apparel; literary raiment, habiliment, habit, vestments.
▶ verb *both men were garbed in black*: **dress**, clothe, attire, fit out, turn out, deck (out), trick out/up, kit out, costume, array, robe, accoutre, cover; informal get up, doll up; Brit. informal tart up; rare bedizen, apparel.

garbage noun 1 *the garbage is taken to landfill sites*: **rubbish**, refuse, domestic refuse, waste, waste material, debris, detritus, litter, junk, scrap, discarded matter; filth, swill, muck, dross; scraps, scourings, leftovers, remains, slops; N. Amer. trash; Austral./NZ mullock; informal drek, dreck; Brit. informal grot, gash; Archaeology debitage; rare draff, raffle, raff, cultch, orts.
2 *most of what they write will be garbage*. See **nonsense** (sense 1).

garble verb *the message was garbled in transmission*: **mix up**, muddle, jumble, confuse, blur, slur, obscure, distort, twist, twist around, warp, misstate, misquote, misreport, misrepresent, mistranslate, misinterpret, misconstrue; tamper with, tinker with, change, alter, doctor, falsify, pervert, corrupt, adulterate; rare misarticulate, misrender.

garden noun *she longed for a house with a garden*: **piece of land**, plot; lawn; park, estate, grounds; N. Amer. yard; archaic garth.
□ **garden variety** N. Amer. *he is just your harmless garden variety attention-seeking buffoon*. See **commonplace** (sense 1 of the adjective).
□ **lead someone up the garden path** informal **deceive**, mislead, lead on, delude, hoodwink, dupe, trick, ensnare, entrap, tempt, entice, allure, lure, beguile, tantalize, tease, frustrate, flirt with, inveigle, seduce, take in, fool, pull the wool over someone's eyes, gull; informal string along, take for a ride, put one over on.

> *Word links* **garden**
>
> **horticultural** relating to gardens

gargantuan adjective *a gargantuan wedding cake*: **enormous**, extremely big, extremely large, massive, huge, colossal, vast, immense, tremendous, gigantic, giant, monstrous, towering, mammoth, prodigious, elephantine, mountainous, mighty, monumental, epic, king-size, king-sized, titanic, Herculean, Brobdingnagian, substantial, hefty, weighty, bulky; informal whopping, whopping great, thumping, thumping great, humongous, mega, monster, jumbo, hulking, bumper; Brit. informal whacking, whacking great, ginormous.
▷ANTONYMS tiny.

garish adjective *they wore silly hats in garish colours*: **gaudy**, lurid, loud, over-bright, harsh, glaring, violent, flashy, showy, glittering, brassy, brash; tasteless, in bad taste, vulgar, distasteful, unattractive, nauseating, bilious, sickly; informal flash, tacky.
▷ANTONYMS drab; tasteful.

garland noun *she wore a garland of flowers*: **festoon**, lei, wreath, chain, loop, ring, circle, swathe, swag; coronet, crown, coronal, chaplet, fillet, headband.
▶ verb *the gardens were garlanded with coloured lights*: **festoon**, wreathe, swathe, hang, loop, thread, drape, cover; adorn, ornament, embellish, decorate, deck, trim, dress, array, bedeck, bespangle; informal do up, do out, get up, trick out; literary bedizen, furbelow, caparison.

garlic noun

> *Word links* **garlic**
>
> **alliaceous** relating to garlic

garment noun *she wore a shapeless black garment*: **item of clothing**, article of clothing, item of dress; costume, outfit, habit, robe, shift; cover, covering; (**garments**) clothes, clothing, dress, garb, attire; informal get-up, rig-out, gear, togs, rags, duds, garms.

garner verb *Edward garnered ideas and experience from his travels*: **gather**, collect, accumulate, amass, assemble; store, lay up, lay by, put away, stow away, hoard, stockpile, reserve, save, preserve; informal stash away.

garnish verb *garnish the dish with chopped parsley*: **decorate**, adorn, trim, dress, ornament, embellish, enhance, grace, beautify, prettify, brighten up, set off, add the finishing touch to; informal jazz up.
▶ noun *a cucumber garnish for the lobster salad*: **decoration**, adornment, trim, trimming, ornament, ornamentation, embellishment, enhancement, beautification, finishing touch; rare garniture.

garret noun *the innkeeper gave them a bed in the garret*: **attic**, loft, roof space, cock loft; mansard, loft conversion, attic room; informal, dated sky parlour.

garrison noun **1** *the rebels attacked the English garrison in their barracks*: **armed force**, force, military detachment, military unit, unit, platoon, brigade, regiment, squadron, battalion, company, legion, corps; troops, militia, soldiers.
2 *the bombardment left gaping holes in the garrison*: **fortress**, fort, fortification, stronghold, blockhouse, citadel, camp, encampment, cantonment, command post, base, station; barracks, billet, quarters; rare casern.
▶ verb **1** *French infantry garrisoned the town*: **defend**, guard, protect, preserve, fortify, barricade, shield, secure; man, occupy, supply with troops.
2 *the troops are garrisoned in various regions*: **station**, post, put on duty, assign, billet, deploy, install; base, site, place, position, locate, situate.

garrulity noun *they were irritated by his ungovernable garrulity*: **talkativeness**, garrulousness, loquacity, loquaciousness, volubility, verbosity, verboseness, long-windedness, wordiness, chattiness, effusiveness, profuseness, communicativeness, expansiveness; informal mouthiness, gabbiness, windiness, gassiness, yakking, big mouth, gift of the gab; Brit. informal wittering; rare logorrhoea, multiloquence.
▷ANTONYMS taciturnity.

garrulous adjective **1** *a garrulous old man who chattered like a magpie*: **talkative**, loquacious, voluble, verbose, long-winded, chatty, chattery, chattering, gossipy, gossiping, babbling, blathering, prattling, prating, jabbering, gushing, effusive, expansive, forthcoming, conversational, communicative; informal mouthy, gabby, gassy, windy, yacking, big-mouthed, with the gift of the gab, having kissed the Blarney Stone; Brit. informal wittering, able to talk the hind legs off a donkey; rare multiloquent, multiloquous.
▷ANTONYMS taciturn; reticent.
2 *his garrulous and unreliable reminiscences*: **long-winded**, wordy, verbose, prolix, lengthy, prolonged; rambling, wandering, maundering, meandering, digressive, diffuse, discursive, periphrastic; gossipy, chatty; informal windy, gassy.
▷ANTONYMS concise.

Word toolkit **garrulous**

See **talkative**.

gash noun *there was blood running from a gash on his forehead*: **laceration**, cut, slash, tear, gouge, puncture, score, incision, slit, split, rip, rent, nick, cleft; scratch, scrape, graze, abrasion; wound, injury, lesion, contusion; Medicine trauma, traumatism.
▶ verb *Frank gashed his hand on some broken glass*: **lacerate**, cut (open), slash, tear (apart), gouge, puncture, incise, score, slit, split, rend, nick, snick, notch, cleave; scratch, scrape, graze, abrade; wound, injure, hurt, damage, maim.

gasp verb *the ice cold water made him gasp*: **pant**, puff, puff and pant, blow, heave, wheeze, breathe hard, breathe heavily, catch one's breath, draw in one's breath, gulp, choke, fight for breath, struggle for air.
▶ noun *a gasp of pain*: **pant**, puff, blow, breath, inhalation, inspiration, drawing in of breath, choke, gulp (of air); exclamation, ejaculation.

gastric adjective *he suffers from excessive gastric acid*: **stomach**, **intestinal**, enteric, duodenal, coeliac, abdominal, ventral; technical gastrocolic; rare stomachic, stomachical.

gate noun **1** *the horse vaulted over the gate*: **barrier**, wicket, wicket gate, lychgate, five-barred gate, turnstile; Brit. kissing gate; Scottish port; in China moon gate; in ancient Egypt pylon.
2 *a small girl came out of the gate*: **gateway**, doorway, entrance, exit, egress, opening; door, portal; N. Amer. entryway.

gather verb **1** *we gathered in the hotel lobby*: **congregate**, convene, assemble, meet, collect, come/get together, muster, rally, converge; cluster together, crowd, mass, flock together; rare foregather.
▷ANTONYMS scatter.
2 *he gathered a coterie of followers | he paused to gather his thoughts*: **summon**, summon up, call together, bring together, assemble, convene, rally, round up; collect, muster, marshal, organize; formal convoke.
▷ANTONYMS disperse.
3 *badgers gather bedding throughout the year*: **collect**, get together, put together, accumulate, amass, assemble, garner; store, stockpile, heap up, pile up, stack up, hoard, put by, put away, lay by, lay in, set aside; informal stash away, squirrel away.
4 *the people gather fruits, berries, and roots*: **harvest**, collect, reap, pick, pluck, garner, crop, glean.
5 *the show soon gathered a fanatical following*: **attract**, draw, pull, pull in, collect, pick up, whip up, raise.
6 *I gather he's a keen footballer*: **understand**, be given to understand, believe, be led to believe, think, conclude, come to the conclusion, deduce, infer, draw the inference, assume, surmise, fancy; take it, hear, hear tell, be informed, notice, see, learn, discover.
7 *he gathered her to his chest*: **clasp**, clutch, take, pull, embrace, enfold, hold, hug, cuddle, squeeze; literary embosom; archaic strain.
8 *his tunic was gathered at the waist*: **pleat**, shirr, pucker, tuck, fold, corrugate, ruffle, crimp, crease, scrunch up.

gathering noun **1** *she rose to address the gathering*: **assembly**, meeting, meet, convention, rally, turnout, congress, convocation, conclave, council, synod, symposium, forum, muster; assemblage, collection, company, congregation, audience, crowd, throng, mass, multitude, group, party, band, knot, flock, mob, horde, pack; informal get-together; formal concourse; historical conventicle.
2 *the gathering of data for a future book*: **collecting**, collection, garnering, amassing, accumulation, accrual, cumulation, assembly, assembling; stockpiling, hoarding, building up, build-up; rare amassment.

gauche adjective *she grew from a gauche teenager into a poised young woman*: **awkward**, gawky, inelegant, graceless, ungraceful, ungainly, bumbling, maladroit, inept; socially awkward, socially inept, lacking in social grace(s), unpolished, unsophisticated, uncultured, uncultivated, unrefined, raw, inexperienced, uneducated, unworldly.
▷ANTONYMS elegant; sophisticated.

gaudy adjective *he wears cheap, gaudy clothes*: **garish**, lurid, loud, over-bright, glaring, harsh, violent, flashy, showy, glittering, brassy, ostentatious; tasteless, in bad taste, vulgar, distasteful, unattractive, nauseating, bilious, sickly; informal flash, tacky; N. Amer. informal bling-bling.
▷ANTONYMS drab; tasteful.

gauge noun **1** *she checked the temperature gauge*: **measuring instrument**, measuring device, meter, measure; indicator, dial, scale, index, display.
2 *exports are an important gauge of economic activity*: **measure**, indicator, barometer, basis, standard, point of reference, guide, guideline, touchstone, yardstick, benchmark, criterion, example, model, pattern, formula, exemplar, sample, test, litmus test.
3 *the railway has a track gauge of two feet*: **size**, measure, extent, degree, scope, capacity, magnitude; width, breadth, area, thickness, span, depth, height; bore, calibre, diameter.
▶ verb **1** *astronomers can gauge the star's intrinsic brightness*: **measure**, calculate, compute, work out, determine, ascertain; count, weigh, quantify, put a figure on.
2 *it is difficult to gauge how effective the ban was*: **assess**, evaluate, appraise, analyse, weigh up, get the measure of, judge, adjudge, rate, reckon, determine, estimate, guess; form an opinion of, form an impression of, make up one's mind about; informal guesstimate, size up.

gaunt adjective **1** *a gaunt, greying man with thick spectacles*: **haggard**, drawn, cadaverous, skeletal, emaciated, skin-and-bones, skinny, spindly, thin, over-thin, size-zero, spare, bony, angular, lank, lean, raw-boned, pinched, hollow-cheeked, hollow-eyed, lantern-jawed, scrawny, scraggy, shrivelled, wasted, withered, raddled; as thin as a rake, as thin as a reed, without an ounce of fat; informal looking like death warmed up, looking like a bag of bones; dated spindle-shanked; archaic starveling.
▷ANTONYMS plump.
2 *the gaunt ruin of Pendragon Castle*: **bleak**, stark, barren, bare, drab, desolate, dreary, dismal, gloomy, sombre, forlorn, grim, stern, harsh, forbidding, uninviting, unwelcoming, cheerless.
▷ANTONYMS cheerful.

Word toolkit **gaunt**

See **thin**.

gauzy adjective *she wore a loose gauzy nightdress*: **translucent**, transparent, sheer, see-through, gauzelike, fine, ultra-fine, delicate, flimsy, filmy, gossamer, gossamer-like, diaphanous, chiffony, wispy, thin, light, airy, insubstantial; Brit. floaty.
▷ANTONYMS thick; coarse.

gawk verb *he gawked unashamedly at the beautiful girl*: **gape**, goggle, gaze, ogle, stare, stare stupidly, stare open-mouthed, stare in wonder, look fixedly, look vacantly; informal rubberneck; Brit. informal gawp.

gawky adjective *she had been a thin, gawky adolescent*: **awkward**, ungainly, inelegant, graceless, ungraceful, gauche, maladroit, inept, bumbling,

blundering, lumbering; socially awkward, socially unsure, unpolished, unsophisticated, uncultured, uncultivated, unworldly; nervous, shy, bashful; Brit. nervy.
▷ANTONYMS graceful; adroit.

gay adjective **1** *an organization for gay youngsters*: **homosexual**, lesbian, sapphic, lesbigay, GLBT (gay, lesbian, bisexual, or transgendered); rare homophile, Uranian; informal pink, lavender, camp, lezzy, les, lesbo, butch, dykey; informal, derogatory queer, limp-wristed, that way, swinging the other way, homo; Brit. informal, derogatory bent, poofy; N. Amer. informal, derogatory fruity.
▷ANTONYMS heterosexual, straight.
2 dated *her children all looked chubby and gay*: **cheerful**, cheery, merry, jolly, light-hearted, mirthful, jovial, glad, happy, bright, in good spirits, in high spirits, joyful, elated, exuberant, animated, lively, sprightly, vivacious, buoyant, bouncy, bubbly, perky, effervescent, playful, frolicsome; informal chirpy, on top of the world, as happy as a sandboy; N. Amer. informal as happy as a clam.
▷ANTONYMS gloomy.
3 dated *they were having a gay old time*: **jolly**, merry, convivial, hilarious, amusing, uproarious, rollicking, entertaining, enjoyable; festive.
▷ANTONYMS dull.
4 dated *the windows sported gay checked curtains*: **bright**, brightly coloured, vivid, brilliant, rich, vibrant; richly coloured, many-coloured, multicoloured; flamboyant, gaudy.
▷ANTONYMS drab.
▶noun *in Denmark gays can marry in church*: **homosexual**, lesbian, gay person, lesbigay; rare invert, homophile, Uranian; informal queen, friend of Dorothy, dyke, les, lesbo, lezzie, butch, femme; informal, derogatory queer, homo, pansy, nancy, bumboy, nelly; Brit. informal, derogatory poof, poofter, ponce, jessie, woofter, shirtlifter, bender; N. Amer. informal, derogatory cupcake, swish, twinkie; Austral. informal wonk; S. African informal, derogatory moffie; W. Indian informal, derogatory batty boy, batty man.
▷ANTONYMS heterosexual, straight.

> *Choose the right word* **gay**
>
> **Gay** meaning 'homosexual' became established in the 1960s as the term preferred by homosexual men. It is now the standard accepted term throughout the English-speaking world. As a result, the centuries-old other senses of **gay** meaning either 'carefree' or 'bright and showy' have more or less dropped out of natural use. The word **gay** cannot be readily used today in these older senses without double entendre, despite attempts to keep them alive. **Gay** in its modern sense typically refers to men (**lesbian** being the standard term for homosexual women) but in some contexts it can be used of both men and women.

gaze verb *he gazed at the photograph*: **stare**, look fixedly, look vacantly, look, take a good look, gape, goggle, peer, leer; ogle, eye, contemplate, survey, scan, study; informal gawk at, rubberneck at, give something the once-over, get a load of, check out; Brit. informal gawp at; N. Amer. informal eyeball; literary behold.
▶noun *she raised her head and met his piercing gaze*: **stare**, fixed look, intent look, gape, eye; regard, watch, observance, inspection, scrutiny.

gazebo noun *a little gazebo in front of the house*: **summer house**, pavilion, belvedere; arbour, bower; shelter, hut, shed; archaic,(in Turkey & Iran) kiosk.

gazette noun *she put a notice in the local gazette*: **newspaper**, paper, tabloid, broadsheet, journal, periodical, weekly, organ, news-sheet, newsletter, bulletin; digest, review; informal rag, scandal sheet; N. Amer. informal tab; Indian informal eveninger; dated extra.

gear noun **1** *he dropped out of the race with damaged gears*: **gearwheel**, toothed wheel, cog, cogwheel.
2 *my bike has five gears*: **gear ratio**, speed.
3 *the steering gear of a boat*: **mechanism**, gears, machinery, works.
4 informal *he stowed the fishing gear in the aft locker*: **equipment**, apparatus, paraphernalia, articles, appliances, impedimenta; tools, utensils, implements, instruments, hardware, gadgets, gadgetry; stuff, things; kit, rig, tackle, outfit; resources, amenities, supplies; furniture, furnishings, fittings; odds and ends, bits and pieces, bits and bobs; trappings, appurtenances, accoutrements, regalia; Military materiel, baggage; informal box of tricks; Brit. informal clobber, gubbins, odds and sods; archaic equipage.
5 informal *I'll go back to my hotel and pick up my gear*: **belongings**, possessions, effects, personal effects, property, baggage, chattels, movables, paraphernalia, appurtenances, impedimenta, miscellaneous articles, odds and ends, bits and pieces, bits and bobs, trappings, accessories; informal things, stuff, kit, junk, rubbish, dunnage, traps; Brit. informal clobber, gubbins, odds and sods.
6 informal *the best designer gear*: **clothes**, clothing, garments, articles of clothing/dress, attire, garb; dress, wear, wardrobe; outfit, costume, turnout; finery; informal togs, duds, garms, get-up, glad rags; Brit. informal clobber, kit, rig-out; N. Amer. informal threads; formal apparel; literary raiment, habiliments, habit; archaic vestments.**verb**
□ **gear up** *we are all gearing up for the start of a new season*: **prepare**, make preparations, make provisions, get everything ready, make ready, take the necessary steps, do the necessary.
□ **gear oneself up** *the band are gearing themselves up for a massive party*: **get ready**, prepare, make preparations, arrange things, make provision, get everything set, take the necessary steps, do the necessary, lay the groundwork, do the spadework, gird up one's loins, kit oneself out, rig oneself out, arm oneself; informal psych oneself up.

gel, jell verb **1** *the meat and broth are put into moulds to gel*: **set**, stiffen, solidify, thicken, harden; cake, congeal, coagulate, clot; rare gelatinize.
▷ANTONYMS melt; liquefy.
2 *they got the team they wanted and things started to gel*: **take shape**, come together, fall into place, happen, take form, form, emerge, crystallize, materialize, become definite.
▷ANTONYMS fall apart.

gelatinous adjective *the grain is cooked until it becomes gelatinous*: **jelly-like**, glutinous, ropy, gummy, sticky, gluey, slimy, thick, viscous; technical mucilaginous, colloidal, viscid; informal gooey, gunky, gloopy, cloggy, icky; N. Amer. informal gloppy; rare viscoid.
▷ANTONYMS runny.

geld verb *it is best to geld a colt before he is one year old*: **castrate**, neuter, cut, desex, remove the testicles of; N. Amer. & Austral. alter; informal doctor, fix; rare caponize, emasculate, eunuchize, evirate.

gelid adjective *the gelid green spikes of the glacier*: **frozen**, freezing, icy, ice-cold, arctic, glacial, polar, frosty, wintry, snowy, bitterly cold, sub-zero, chilly, Siberian, hyperborean, hyperboreal; rare algid.
▷ANTONYMS hot.

gem noun **1** *diamonds, rubies, and other gems*: **jewel**, precious stone, semi-precious stone, stone, solitaire, brilliant, baguette, cabochon; archaic bijou.
2 *the gem of the collection is the tyrannosaurus skeleton*: **best**, finest, pride, prize, treasure, glory, wonder, flower, pearl, jewel, the jewel in the crown, masterpiece, chef-d'œuvre, leading light, pick, choice, paragon, prime, cream, the crème de la crème, elite, elect; outstanding example, shining example, perfect example of its kind, model, epitome, archetype, ideal, exemplar, nonpareil, paradigm, embodiment, personification, quintessence, standard, prototype, apotheosis, acme; informal one in a million, the bee's knees, something else, the tops.
▷ANTONYMS dregs.

genealogy noun *a lengthy genealogy of the kings of France*: **pedigree**, ancestry, descent, lineage, line, line of descent, family tree, extraction, derivation, origin, heritage, parentage, paternity, birth, family, dynasty, house, race, strain, stock, breed, blood, bloodline, history, background, roots; rare stirps, filiation, stemma.

general adjective **1** *they are moderately priced and suitable for general use*: **widespread**, common, extensive, universal, wide, popular, public, mainstream, prevalent, prevailing, rife, established, well established, conventional, traditional, traditionalist, orthodox, accepted; in circulation, in force, in vogue.
▷ANTONYMS restricted.
2 *a general pay increase*: **comprehensive**, overall, across the board, blanket, umbrella, mass, total, complete, wholesale, sweeping, panoramic, broad, broad-ranging, extended, inclusive, all-inclusive, all-round, generic, outright, encyclopedic, indiscriminate, catholic; universal, global, worldwide, international, nationwide, countrywide, coast-to-coast, company-wide.
▷ANTONYMS localized.
3 *a general store | general knowledge*: **miscellaneous**, mixed, assorted, variegated, diversified, composite, heterogeneous.
▷ANTONYMS specialist.
4 *it is the general practice for players to receive all the prize money*: **usual**, customary, habitual, traditional, normal, conventional, typical, standard, regular; familiar, accepted, prevailing, routine, run-of-the-mill, fixed, set, established, confirmed, everyday, ordinary, common, stock, well worn, time-honoured; popular, favourite.
▷ANTONYMS exceptional.
5 *most guidebooks give only a general description of the island*: **broad**, imprecise, inexact, rough, sweeping, overall, loose, basic, approximate, non-specific, unspecific, vague, hazy, fuzzy, woolly, ill-defined, indefinite, unfocused; N. Amer. informal ballpark; rare undetailed.
▷ANTONYMS detailed.
□ **in general 1** *he was in general an excellent friend*: **generally**, **normally**, as a (general) rule, in the general run of things, by and large, more often than not, almost always, in the main, mainly, mostly, for the most part, in most cases, most of the time, predominantly, on the whole; usually, habitually, customarily, standardly, routinely, regularly, typically, ordinarily, commonly, conventionally, traditionally, historically.
▷ANTONYMS occasionally. **2** *we want the public in general to understand the public health issues*: **as a whole**, as a body, generally, at large, in the main.
▷ANTONYMS in particular, specifically.

generality noun **1** *the debate has moved from generalities to specifics*: **generalization**, general statement, general principle, general truth, non-specific statement, loose/vague statement, indefinite statement, sweeping

statement, abstraction, extrapolation.
▷ANTONYMS specific.
2 *there were exceptions to the generality of this principle*: **universality**, comprehensiveness, all-inclusiveness, extensiveness, broadness, catholicity.
3 *the generality of people are kind*: **majority**, larger part/number, greater part/number, best/better part, main part; bulk, mass, weight, (main) body, preponderance, predominance, lion's share; most, almost all, more than half.
▷ANTONYMS minority.

generally adverb **1** *the summers were generally fairly good*: **normally, in general**, as a (general) rule, in the general run of things, by and large, more often than not, almost always, in the main, mainly, mostly, for the most part, in most cases, most of the time, predominantly, on the whole; usually, habitually, customarily, standardly, routinely, regularly, typically, ordinarily, commonly, conventionally, traditionally, historically.
▷ANTONYMS occasionally.
2 *France was moving generally to the left*: **overall**, in general terms, in a general sense, generally speaking, altogether, all in all, broadly, on average, principally, basically, substantially, effectively.
3 *it is too early to say whether the method will be generally accepted*: **widely**, commonly, extensively, comprehensively, universally, popularly.
▷ANTONYMS sporadically.

generate verb **1** *the move should generate extra business*: **cause**, give rise to, lead to, result in, bring about, bring into being, create, make, produce, initiate, engender, spawn, sow the seeds of, occasion, effect, originate, bring to pass, bring on, precipitate, prompt, provoke, kindle, trigger, spark off, touch off, stir up, whip up, induce, inspire, promote, foster, conjure; literary beget, enkindle; rare effectuate.
▷ANTONYMS destroy.
2 *many factors determine which male is most likely to generate offspring*: **procreate**, breed, father, sire, engender, spawn, create, produce, give life to, give birth to, bring into being, bring into the world, bring forth, have; reproduce, propagate; literary beget.

generation noun **1** *people of the same generation*: **age**, age group, peer group, cohort, stage of life.
2 (**generations**) *generations ago*: **ages**, an age, years, aeons, an aeon, a long time, an eternity; Brit. informal donkey's years, yonks.
3 *the next generation of computers*: **crop**, batch, wave, type, range.
4 *creativity is the generation of novel ideas*: **creation**, causing, causation, making, engendering, spawning, production, initiation, origination, inception, occasioning, prompting, kindling, triggering, inspiration.
▷ANTONYMS destruction.
5 *the male role in human generation*: **procreation**, reproduction, propagation, breeding, fathering, siring, engendering, spawning, creation; literary begetting.

generic adjective **1** *'assault' is used as a generic term for the separate offences of assault and battery*: **general**, common, collective, non-specific, inclusive, all-inclusive, all-encompassing, broad, comprehensive, blanket, umbrella, sweeping, universal.
▷ANTONYMS specific.
2 *generic drugs are generally cheaper than branded drugs*: **unbranded**, untrademarked, non-proprietary.
▷ANTONYMS branded.

generosity noun **1** *the generosity of our host*: **liberality**, lavishness, magnanimity, magnanimousness, munificence, open-handedness, free-handedness, bounty, unselfishness, indulgence, prodigality, princeliness; literary bounteousness; rare benignancy, liberalness.
▷ANTONYMS meanness.
2 *with her generosity of spirit, she always forgave me*: **magnanimity**, kindness, kindliness, benevolence, beneficence, altruism, charity, philanthropism, nobility, nobleness, loftiness, high-mindedness, big-heartedness, honourableness, honour, goodness, unselfishness, self-sacrifice, lack of prejudice, disinterest.
3 *diners certainly cannot complain about the generosity of portions*: **abundance**, plentifulness, copiousness, amplitude, profuseness, richness, lavishness, liberality, munificence, largeness, superabundance, infinity, inexhaustibility, opulence; literary bounteousness, plenteousness.

generous adjective **1** *generous with money*: **liberal**, lavish, magnanimous, munificent, giving, open-handed, free-handed, bountiful, unselfish, ungrudging, unstinting, unsparing, free, indulgent, prodigal, princely; literary bounteous, plenteous; rare eleemosynary, benignant.
▷ANTONYMS mean; selfish.
2 *he was generous in spirit, often refusing to hurt an opponent in trouble*: **magnanimous**, kind, kindly, benevolent, beneficent, altruistic, charitable, philanthropic, noble, lofty, high-minded, big-hearted, honourable, good, unselfish, self-sacrificing, unprejudiced, disinterested.
▷ANTONYMS mean.
3 *you will need a generous amount of fabric*: **lavish**, plentiful, copious, ample, liberal, munificent, bountiful, large, huge, great, abundant, profuse, rich, bumper, flush, overflowing, superabundant, infinite, inexhaustible, opulent, prolific, teeming; in plenty, in abundance; informal a gogo, galore; S. African informal **lank**; literary bounteous, plenteous.
▷ANTONYMS meagre.

Word toolkit

generous	unselfish	benevolent
support	player	dictator
offer	service	creator
donation	devotion	fund
gift	commitment	society
terms	love	force
portion	efforts	patriarch
benefactor	courage	organization

genesis noun **1** *the hatred had its genesis in something darker*: **origin**, source, root, beginning, commencement, start, outset.
2 *the influence of a childhood trauma on the subsequent genesis of neurosis*: **formation**, emergence, development, evolution, coming into being, inception, origination, birth, creation, shaping, formulation, invention, engendering, generation, propagation.

genial adjective *Fred is genial and well liked*: **friendly**, affable, cordial, congenial, amiable, warm, easy-going, approachable, sympathetic, well disposed, good-natured, good-humoured, cheerful, cheery, neighbourly, hospitable, companionable, comradely, bluff, easy to get along with; sociable, convivial, outgoing, extrovert, extroverted, gregarious, company-loving, hail-fellow-well-met; informal chummy, pally; Brit. informal matey; N. Amer. informal buddy-buddy, clubby, regular.
▷ANTONYMS unfriendly; morose.

geniality noun *his geniality made him the centre of a circle of faithful friends*: **friendliness**, affability, cordiality, congeniality, amiability, warmth, easy-going nature, approachability, sympathetic nature, good nature, good humour, cheerfulness, cheeriness, neighbourliness, hospitality, companionableness, bluffness; sociability, conviviality, gregariousness; informal chumminess, palliness; Brit. informal mateyness.
▷ANTONYMS unfriendliness.

genitals plural noun **private parts**, genitalia, sexual organs, reproductive organs, pudenda, nether regions, crotch, groin; informal privates, bits, naughty bits, dangly bits.

genius noun **1** *the world had already heard of Hawking's genius*: **brilliance**, great intelligence, great intellect, great ability, cleverness, brains, erudition, wisdom, sagacity, fine mind, wit, artistry, flair, creative power, precocity, precociousness.
▷ANTONYMS stupidity.
2 *that woman has a genius for organization*: **talent**, gift, flair, aptitude, facility, knack, technique, touch, bent, ability, expertise, capacity, power, faculty; endowment, strength, strong point, forte, brilliance; dexterity, adroitness, skill, cleverness, virtuosity, artistry.
3 *the boy is an absolute genius*: **brilliant person**, mental giant, mastermind, Einstein, intellectual, intellect, brain, highbrow, expert, master, artist, polymath; prodigy, gifted child; French idiot savant; informal egghead, brains, bright spark, whizz, wizard, walking encyclopedia; Brit. informal brainbox, clever clogs, boffin; N. Amer. informal brainiac, rocket scientist, maven.
▷ANTONYMS dunce.

genocide noun *the killing of native Americans was the biggest genocide in world history*: **racial killing**, massacre, wholesale slaughter, mass slaughter, wholesale killing, indiscriminate killing; mass murder, mass homicide, mass destruction, annihilation, extermination, elimination, liquidation, eradication, decimation, butchery, bloodbath, bloodletting; pogrom, ethnic cleansing, holocaust, Shoah; literary slaying; rare battue, hecatomb.

genre noun *a whole new genre of novels*: **category**, class, classification, categorization, group, grouping, bracket, head, heading, list, listing, set; type, sort, kind, variety, species, breed, style, brand, make, model, family, school, stamp, cast, ilk, kidney; division, section, department, compartment.

genteel adjective *an extremely genteel couple who have fallen on hard times*: **refined**, respectable, polished, decorous, proper, polite, correct, seemly, well mannered, well bred, cultivated, cultured, sophisticated, courteous, ladylike, gentlemanly, civil, elegant, stylish, urbane, civilized, courtly, dignified, gracious, punctilious; affected; Brit. informal posh; dated mannerly.
▷ANTONYMS uncouth.

gentility noun **1** *her grandmother's pretensions to gentility*: **social superiority**, respectability, refinement, pre-eminence, pride of place, distinction, ascendancy; Brit. informal poshness.
▷ANTONYMS vulgarity.
2 *an aura of elegance and gentility*: **respectability**, refinement, polish, decorousness, correctness, seemliness, politeness, good manners, culture, breeding, cultivation, sophistication, courtesy, ladylikeness, gentlemanliness, civility, elegance, style, stylishness, urbanity, civilization,

courtliness, dignity, grace, graciousness, punctiliousness; affectedness, affectation, ostentation, ostentatiousness; dated mannerliness.

gentle adjective **1** *he was powerful, though his manner was gentle*: **kind**, kindly, tender, benign, humane, lenient, merciful, forgiving, forbearing, sympathetic, considerate, understanding, clement, compassionate, benevolent, kind-hearted, tender-hearted, good-natured, sweet-tempered, loving; **mild**, soft, quiet, shy, demure, modest, humble, retiring, unassuming, still, tranquil, peaceful, peaceable, pacific, placid, serene, reposeful, reverent, meek, docile, lamblike, dovelike.
▷ANTONYMS unkind; brutal.
2 *a gentle breeze*: **light**, soft, zephyr-like, moderate, pleasant.
▷ANTONYMS strong.
3 *a gentle slope*: **gradual**, slight, easy, imperceptible.
▷ANTONYMS steep.
4 archaic *a woman of gentle birth*. See **aristocratic** (sense 1).

gentlemanly adjective *the girls declined his gentlemanly offer to allow them to go first*: **chivalrous**, gallant, honourable, noble, courtly, courteous, civil, respectful, polite, well mannered, well bred, well behaved, attentive, gracious; considerate, thoughtful, obliging, accommodating; cultivated, cultured, civilized, polished, refined, suave, urbane; dated mannerly; archaic gentle.
▷ANTONYMS rude; unbecoming.

g

gentleness noun *Jack treated these outbursts with firmness as well as gentleness*: **kindness**, kindliness, tenderness, benignity, humaneness, humanity; leniency, mercy, clemency, forgiveness, forbearance; sympathy, considerateness, consideration, understanding, compassion, benevolence, kind-heartedness, tender-heartedness, good nature, love; **mildness**, softness, quietness, shyness, demureness, modesty, humility, stillness, tranquillity, peacefulness, peaceableness, placidness, serenity, repose, reverence, meekness, docility.
▷ANTONYMS unkindness; brutality.

gentry noun (**the gentry**) **the upper classes**, **the upper middle class**, the privileged classes, the wealthy, the elite, high society, the establishment, the haut monde, the county set, the smart set; Indian **bhadralok**; informal the upper crust, the jet set, the beautiful people, the crème de la crème, the top drawer; Brit. informal nobs, toffs; informal, dated swells.

genuine adjective **1** *is that a genuine Picasso?* **authentic**, real, actual, original, pukka, bona fide, true, veritable, unfeigned, unadulterated, unalloyed; sterling; attested, undisputed, rightful, legitimate, lawful, legal, valid, sound; German echt; informal the real McCoy, the genuine article, the real thing, your actual, kosher, honest-to-goodness; Austral./NZ informal dinkum; rare simon-pure.
▷ANTONYMS bogus.
2 *she's a very genuine person*: **sincere**, honest, truthful, unhypocritical, meaning what one says, straightforward, direct, frank, candid, open; artless, natural, unaffected, guileless, ingenuous; informal straight, upfront, on the level; N. Amer. informal on the up and up; Austral./NZ informal dinkum.
▷ANTONYMS fake; bogus; insincere.

> *Choose the right word* **genuine, sincere, unfeigned, unaffected**
>
> See **sincere**.

genus noun **1** Biology *the largest genus of plants with fleshy fruits*: **group**, subdivision, subfamily.
2 *he had created a new genus of music*: **type**, sort, kind, genre, style, variety, category, class; species, breed, brand, make, model, family, stamp, cast, ilk, kidney; division, subdivision, section, department, compartment.

germ noun **1** *the powerful cleansing action kills germs as well*: **microbe**, micro-organism, bacillus, bacterium, virus; informal bug.
2 *a fertilized germ*: **embryo**, bud, nucleus, seed, spore, egg, ovum; technical ovule.
3 *he had the germ of a brilliant idea*: **start**, beginning(s), commencement, starting point, genesis, inception, seed, embryo, bud, root, rudiment, origin, source, fountain, potential (for); **core**, nucleus, heart, kernel, nub, essence; Latin fons et origo; literary fountainhead, wellspring, fount.

> *Word links* **germ**
>
> **germicide** substance that destroys germs

germane adjective *those factors are not germane to the present discussion*: **relevant**, pertinent, applicable, apposite, material; apropos, to the point, to the purpose, admissible; appropriate, apt, fitting, suitable, suited, proper, felicitous; connected, related, linked, akin, allied, analogous; Latin ad rem; rare appurtenant.
▷ANTONYMS irrelevant.

Germany noun

> *Word links* **Germany**
>
> **Germano-, Teuto-** related prefixes
> **Germanic, Teutonic** relating to Germany
> **Germanophobia, Teutophobia** fear of German people and things

germinate verb **1** *the grain is allowed to germinate*: **sprout**, put forth shoots, shoot, shoot up, bud, put forth buds, form/develop buds; develop, grow, spring up, swell; rare burgeon, vegetate, pullulate.
2 *the idea of a songwriting partnership began to germinate in his mind*: **develop**, take root, grow, spring up, arise, emerge, evolve, mature, expand, enlarge, spread, advance, progress.

gestation noun **1** *tree shrews give birth after a gestation of thirty days*: **pregnancy**, development, incubation, maturation, ripening; rare gravidity, parturiency.
2 *the law underwent a long period of gestation*: **development**, origination, drafting, formation, evolution, emergence, coming into being, materializing.

gesticulate verb *they were gesticulating wildly and pointing at the tyres*: **gesture**, make gestures, signal, make signals, sign, motion, wave.

gesticulation noun *the rudder had stuck, hence the pilot's gesticulation towards the tail!* **gesturing**, gesture, hand movement, signalling, signals, signing, signs, motioning, waving, wave, indication; body language.

gesture noun **1** *he threw out both hands in a gesture of surrender*: **signal**, signalling, sign, signing, motion, motioning, wave, indication, gesticulation.
2 *they burned the flag as a symbolic gesture*: **action**, deed, act, move.
▶verb *he gestured to her to remain where she was*: **signal**, make a gesture, make a sign, give a sign, sign, motion, wave, indicate, gesticulate.

get verb **1** *I got the impression he didn't like me | where did you get that hat?* **acquire**, **obtain**, come by, come to have, come into possession of, receive, gain, earn, win, come into, come in for, take possession of, take receipt of, be given; buy, purchase, procure, possess oneself of, secure; gather, collect, pick up, appropriate, amass, build up, hook, net, land; achieve, attain; informal get one's hands on, get one's mitts on, get hold of, grab, bag, score, swing, nab, collar, cop.
▷ANTONYMS give.
2 *I was glad to get your letter*: **receive**, be sent, be in receipt of, accept delivery of, be given.
▷ANTONYMS send.
3 *your tea's getting cold*: **become**, grow, turn, go, come to be, get to be; literary wax.
4 *I'll get the children from school*: **fetch**, collect, go for, call for, pick up, bring, carry, deliver, convey, ferry, transport; escort, conduct, lead, usher.
▷ANTONYMS take; leave.
5 *the chairman gets £650,000 a year*: **earn**, be paid, receive a salary of, take home, take home earnings of, bring in, make, receive, collect, clear, gross; informal pocket, bank, rake in, pull in, haul in, net, bag.
6 *have the police got their man?* **apprehend**, catch, arrest, capture, seize, take; take prisoner, take captive, take into custody, detain, put in jail, throw in jail, put behind bars, imprison, incarcerate; informal collar, grab, nab, nail, run in, pinch, bust, pick up, pull in, haul in, do, feel someone's collar; Brit. informal nick.
7 *I got a taxi in the end*: **travel by/on/in**, journey by/on/in; take, catch, use, make use of, utilize.
8 *one winter she got flu*: **succumb to**, develop, go/come down with, sicken for, fall victim to, be struck down with, be stricken with, be afflicted by/with, be smitten by/with; become infected with/by, catch, contract, become ill/sick with, fall ill/sick with, be taken ill with, show symptoms of; Brit. go down with; informal take ill with; N. Amer. informal take sick with.
9 *I got a sharp pain in my right arm*: **experience**, suffer, be afflicted with, undergo, sustain, feel, have.
10 *I could get him on the radio and ask*: **contact**, get in touch with, communicate with, make contact with, reach, be in communication with; phone, call, ring up, radio, speak to, talk to; Brit. get on to; informal get hold of.
11 *I didn't get what he said*: **hear**, recognize, discern, distinguish, make out, pick out, perceive, follow, keep up with, take in.
12 *sorry, I don't get the joke*: **understand**, comprehend, grasp, see, take in, fathom, follow, puzzle out, work out, perceive, apprehend, get to the bottom of, unravel, decipher; informal get the drift of, catch on to, latch on to, make head or tail of, figure out, get the picture, get the message; Brit. informal twig, suss out, suss.
13 *we got there early*: **arrive**, reach, come, make it, turn up, appear, put in an appearance, make an appearance, come on the scene, come up, approach, enter, present oneself, be along, come along, materialize; informal show up, show, roll in, roll up, blow in, show one's face.
14 *we got her to go*: **persuade**, induce, prevail on, influence, talk round; wheedle into, talk into, cajole into, inveigle into; win over, bring around, sway.
15 *I'd like to get to meet him sometime*: **contrive**, arrange, find a way, engineer a way, manage; succeed in, organize; informal work it, fix it;

archaic compass.
16 *I'll get supper if you wash up afterwards*: **prepare**, get ready, cook, make, put together, assemble, muster, dish up, concoct; informal fix, rustle up; Brit. informal knock up.
17 informal *I'll get him for that*: **take revenge on**, be revenged on, exact/wreak revenge on, get one's revenge on, avenge oneself on, take vengeance on, get even with, settle a/the score with, pay back, pay out, retaliate on/against, get back at, take reprisals against, exact retribution on, give someone their just deserts, give someone a dose/taste of their own medicine; give/return like for like, give tit for tat, take an eye for an eye (and a tooth for a tooth); informal give someone their comeuppance; Brit. informal get one's own back on.
18 *He scratched his head. 'You've got me there.'*: **baffle**, nonplus, perplex, puzzle, bewilder, mystify, bemuse, confuse, confound, disconcert, throw, set someone thinking; informal flummox, discombobulate, faze, stump, beat, fox, make someone scratch their head, floor, fog; archaic wilder, gravel, maze, cause to be at a stand, pose.
19 *what gets me is how neurotic she is*: **annoy**, irritate, exasperate, anger, irk, vex, inflame, put out, nettle, needle, provoke, incense, infuriate, madden, rub up the wrong way, try someone's patience, make someone's blood boil, ruffle someone's feathers, make someone's hackles rise, get someone's hackles up, rattle someone's cage; informal aggravate, peeve, miff, rile, get to, hack off, get someone's back up, get on someone's nerves, get up someone's nose, get under someone's skin, get someone's goat, give someone the hump, get someone's dander up, get in someone's hair, be a thorn in someone's flesh, drive mad, drive crazy, drive nuts, make someone see red; Brit. informal wind up, nark, get across, get someone's wick; N. Amer. informal tee off, tick off, eat, burn up; vulgar slang piss off; Brit. vulgar slang get on someone's tits.
□ **get about** *he has to rely on a wheelchair to get about*: **move about**, move around, travel.
□ **get something across** *a photo will help to get the message across*: **communicate**, get over, put over, impart, convey, transmit, make understood, make clear, express.
□ **get ahead** *people with ideas and the desire to get ahead*: **prosper**, flourish, thrive, do well, get on well; succeed, be successful, make it, do all right for oneself, progress, make progress, make headway, advance, get on in the world, rise in the world, go up in the world, fly high, make one's mark, make good, become rich, strike gold/oil, be in clover; informal go places, get somewhere, go great guns, make the big time.
□ **get along 1** *does he get along with his family?* **be friendly**, be on friendly terms, be in harmony, be compatible, get on, feel a rapport; agree, see eye to eye, concur, be in agreement, be in accord, be in sympathy; be of the same mind/opinion (as); informal hit it off, be on the same wavelength (as). **2** *he was getting along well at school*: **fare**, manage, progress, advance, get on, do, cope, survive, muddle through/along; succeed, prosper, flourish; informal get by, make out.
□ **get around 1** *she certainly gets around*: **travel**, circulate, socialize, make the rounds. **2** See **get round**.
□ **get at 1** *it's difficult to get at the timbers once you have insulated*: **access**, gain access to, get to, reach, touch. **2** *he had been got at by government officials*: **corrupt**, suborn, influence, bribe, buy off, pay off; informal give someone a backhander, give someone a sweetener, grease someone's palm, fix, square; Brit. informal nobble. **3** informal *what are you getting at?* **imply**, suggest, intimate, insinuate, hint, mean, intend, lead up to, drive at, allude to. **4** Brit. informal *I don't like being got at*: **criticize**, pick on, find fault with, carp at, nag; **bully**, victimize, attack, tyrannize, torment, persecute, punish repeatedly and unfairly, discriminate against; informal have it in for, have a down on, be down on; Brit. informal be on at.
□ **get away** *the prisoners got away*: **escape**, run away, run off, get out, break out, break/get free, break loose, make a break for it, bolt, flee, fly, take flight, make off, take off, decamp, abscond, take to one's heels, make a/one's escape, make good one's escape, make a/one's getaway, beat a hasty retreat, show a clean pair of heels, run for it, make a run for it; disappear, vanish, slip away, steal away, sneak away; get out of someone's clutches; informal do a bunk, do a moonlight flit, cut and run, skedaddle, skip, head for the hills, do a disappearing/vanishing act, fly the coop, take French leave, scarper, vamoose, hightail it, leg it; Brit. informal do a runner, hook it; N. Amer. informal take a powder, go on the lam.
□ **get away with** *it's not our policy to let kidnappers get away with their crimes*: **escape blame for**, escape punishment for.
□ **get back** *they should get back at dawn*: **return**, come home, come back, arrive home, arrive back, come again.
▷ANTONYMS set out.
□ **get something back** *she got her gloves back from the lost property office*: **retrieve**, regain (possession of), win back, recover, take back, recoup, reclaim, repossess, recapture, retake, redeem; find (again), track down, trace; claw back; Law replevin, replevy.
▷ANTONYMS lose.
□ **get back at** *she made the story up to get back at the teacher for punishing her*: **take revenge on**, be revenged on, exact/wreak revenge on, get one's revenge on, avenge oneself on, take vengeance on, get even with, settle a/the score with, pay back, pay out, retaliate on/against, take reprisals against, exact retribution on, let someone see how it feels, give someone their just deserts, give someone a dose/taste of their own medicine, give as good as one gets; give/return like for like, give tit for tat, take an eye for an eye (and a tooth for a tooth); informal get, give someone their comeuppance; Brit. informal get one's own back on.
▷ANTONYMS forgive.
□ **get back to** *please get back to me and let me know how things work out*: **come back to**; answer, reply to, respond to, give a response to.
□ **get by** *he had just enough money to get by*: **manage**, cope, survive, exist, subsist, muddle through/along, scrape by/along/through, make ends meet, get on, get along, make do, barely/scarcely have enough to live on, keep the wolf from the door, keep one's head above water, scrimp, scrape a living; informal make out.
□ **get someone down** *sometimes I can laugh it off but inside it gets me down*: **depress**, make sad, sadden, make unhappy, cast down, make gloomy, make despondent, dispirit; dampen/break someone's spirit, dash someone's hopes, dishearten, demoralize, discourage, daunt, crush, shake, desolate, weigh down, weigh heavily on, hang over, oppress; upset, distress, grieve, haunt, harrow, cause suffering to, break someone's heart, make one's heart bleed, bring tears to one's eyes; informal give someone the blues, make someone fed up, knock the stuffing out of, knock for six, knock sideways.
▷ANTONYMS cheer someone up.
□ **get down to** *he once again got down to work*: **begin**, start, make a start on, go about, set about, set to, get to work on, get going on, embark on, tackle, attack, address oneself to, buckle down to, undertake; formal commence.
□ **get off 1** *Sally got off the bus outside her house*: **alight (from)**, step off, climb off, dismount (from), get down (from), descend (from), disembark (from), leave, exit; formal deplane (from), detrain (from), debus.
▷ANTONYMS get on. **2** informal *he was charged with fraud but got off*: **escape punishment**, **be acquitted**, be absolved, be cleared, be exonerated, be exculpated, be declared/found innocent, be vindicated.
□ **get on 1** *we got on the train at Kinshasa*: **board**, enter, go on board, go aboard, step aboard, climb on, mount, ascend, embark, catch; informal hop on, jump on; formal emplane, entrain, embus. ▷ANTONYMS get off.
2 *how are you getting on?* **fare**, manage, progress, advance, get along, do, cope, survive, muddle through/along; succeed, prosper, flourish; informal get by, make out.
3 *he just got on with his job*: **continue**, proceed, go ahead, carry on, go on, keep on, press on, push on, press ahead, persist, persevere; keep at; informal stick with/at, soldier on with. ▷ANTONYMS give up.
4 *my father and I don't get on*: **be friendly**, be on friendly terms, be in harmony, be compatible, get along, feel a rapport; agree, see eye to eye, concur, be in agreement, be in accord, be in sympathy, sympathize, be united, be as one man, accord; be of the same mind/opinion (as); informal hit it off, be on the same wavelength (as).
□ **get out 1** *several prisoners had got out*: **escape**, break out, break free, get free, break loose, make a break for it, bolt, clear out, run away, run off, get away, flee, fly, take flight, make off, take off, decamp, abscond, take to one's heels, make a/one's escape, make good one's escape, make a/one's getaway, beat a hasty retreat, show a clean pair of heels, run for it, make a run for it; disappear, vanish, slip away, steal away, sneak away; get out of someone's clutches; informal bust, do a bunk, do a moonlight flit, cut and run, skedaddle, skip, head for the hills, do a disappearing/vanishing act, fly the coop, take French leave, scarper, vamoose, hightail it, leg it; Brit. informal do a runner, hook it; N. Amer. informal take a powder, go on the lam. **2** *the news has got out*: **become known**, become common knowledge, become apparent, come to light, emerge, transpire, materialize, prove to be the case; come out, be discovered, be uncovered, be made public, be revealed, be divulged, be disclosed, be reported, be publicized, be released, leak out; literary be noised about/abroad.
□ **get out of** *he tried to get out of paying the survivors any compensation*: **evade**, dodge, shirk, slide out of, avoid, escape, sidestep; informal duck, duck out of, wriggle out of, cop out of; Brit. informal skive off, funk; N. Amer. informal cut; Austral./NZ informal duck-shove; archaic decline.
▷ANTONYMS agree to.
□ **get over 1** *I have only just got over flu*: **recover from**, recuperate from, get better after, pull through, shrug off, survive, come round from.
▷ANTONYMS sicken for. **2** *to get over this problem the architect angled the exit into the piazza slightly*. See **get round** (sense 2).
□ **get something over** *that should get the point over to the manufacturers*: **communicate**, get across, put over, impart, convey, transmit, make understood, make clear, express.
□ **get round 1** *he got round his mother and she bought it for him*: **cajole**, persuade, wheedle, coax, manoeuvre, prevail on, win someone over, bring someone round, sway, beguile, blarney, flatter, seduce, lure, entice, charm, tempt, inveigle, induce, influence, woo; talk into; informal sweet-talk, soft-soap, butter up, twist someone's arm; archaic blandish. **2** *we can get round these difficulties*: **overcome**, surmount, prevail over, triumph over, get the better of, master; get over, circumvent, find an/the answer to, find a/the solution to; sort out, take care of, resolve, solve, crack; deal with, cope with; informal lick.
□ **get through 1** *I managed to get through the audition and land the job*: **pass**, be successful in, succeed in, gain a pass in, come through, meet the

g

requirements of, pass muster in; informal come up to scratch in, come up to snuff in, sail through, scrape through. ▷ANTONYMS fail. **2** *how did we get through a pack of twelve so fast?* **consume**, go through, use, exhaust, deplete, expend, spend, waste, fritter away, squander, dissipate. **3** *I never really got the chance to* ***get through to*** *her*: **communicate with**, get one's message across to, explain oneself to. **4** *I think the message got through*: **register**, make an impression, sink in, fall into place, penetrate, have an effect, dawn, strike home, be understood.

□ **get to** informal *what really got to me was the lack of respect*: **irritate**, annoy, anger, vex, irk, nettle, pique, exasperate, infuriate, get on someone's nerves, rub up the wrong way, get/put someone's back up, ruffle someone's feathers, try someone's patience; **goad**, provoke, bait, taunt, pester, harass, prick, prod, sting; informal aggravate, rile, niggle, hassle, bug, miff, peeve, get under someone's skin, get up someone's nose, hack off; Brit. informal wind up, get at, nark, get across; N. Amer. informal ride; vulgar slang piss off; rare exacerbate, hump, rasp.

□ **get together 1** *your job is to get together the best bunch of writers you can find*: **collect**, gather, assemble, bring together, call together, rally, muster, marshal, line up, congregate, convene, amass, scrape together; formal convoke.

▷ANTONYMS disperse. **2** *we must get together soon*: **meet**, meet up, have a meeting, rendezvous, see each other, socialize.

□ **get up** *Rose used to get up very early*: **get out of bed**, rise, stir, rouse oneself, bestir oneself, get going; informal surface, show signs of life; formal arise.

▷ANTONYMS go to bed.

□ **get someone up** informal *he was got up in his finery*. See **dress** (sense 2 of the verb).

getaway noun *guards spotted the gunman as he tried to make his getaway*: **escape**, breakout, break, bolt for freedom, running away, flight, bolting, absconding, decamping, fleeing, flit; disappearance, vanishing act; rare abscondment, decampment.

get-together noun *we're having a get-together after work*: **party**, gathering, meeting, social occasion/event/gathering/meeting; informal do, bash; Brit. informal rave-up, thrash, knees-up, jolly, beanfeast, bunfight, beano.

get-up noun informal *I adore your get-up—such an amusing hat*: **outfit**, clothes, costume, ensemble, suit, clothing, dress, attire, garments, garb, turnout, rig, uniform, livery, array, regalia, robes, finery; informal gear, togs, garms, duds, glad rags; Brit. informal clobber, kit, strip, rig-out; N. Amer. informal threads; formal apparel; literary raiment, habiliments; archaic vestments, vesture, habit.

get-up-and-go noun informal *alas, I don't have the get-up-and-go to find the money to make a film*: **drive**, initiative, enterprise, enthusiasm, eagerness, ambition, motivation, push, go, dynamism, energy, gusto, vigour, vitality, verve, fire, fervour; single-mindedness, will power, dedication, doggedness, tenacity, zeal, commitment, forcefulness, spirit; informal gumption, oomph, vim, pep, zing, zip, pizzazz, punch.

▷ANTONYMS lethargy.

ghastly adjective **1** *he is implicated in several ghastly stabbings*: **terrible**, frightful, horrible, grim, awful, dire; frightening, terrifying, horrifying, alarming; distressing, shocking, appalling, harrowing; dreadful, fearful, hideous, horrendous, monstrous, unspeakable, gruesome, tragic, calamitous, grievous, grisly.

▷ANTONYMS pleasant.

2 *it's hard to escape the ghastly visitor centres*: **unpleasant**, objectionable, offensive, disagreeable, distasteful, displeasing, unacceptable, off-putting, undesirable, obnoxious; **nasty**, disgusting, awful, terrible, dreadful, frightful, foul, repulsive, repellent, repugnant, revolting, abhorrent, loathsome, hateful, odious, detestable, reprehensible, deplorable, appalling, insufferable, intolerable, despicable, contemptible, beyond the pale, vile, obscene, unsavoury, unpalatable, sickening, nauseating, nauseous, noxious; informal horrible, horrid, sick-making; Brit. informal beastly; archaic disgustful, loathly; rare exceptionable, rebarbative.

▷ANTONYMS charming.

3 *the patient feels ghastly on getting out of bed*: **ill**, unwell, washed out, peaky; sick, queasy, nauseous, nauseated, green about the gills; Brit. off, off colour, poorly; informal rough, lousy, rotten, terrible, awful, horrible, dreadful, crummy; Brit. informal grotty, ropy; Scottish informal wabbit, peely-wally; Austral./NZ informal crook; dated queer, seedy; rare peaked, peakish.

▷ANTONYMS fine.

4 *a ghastly mistake*: **serious**, severe, grave, very bad, grievous, dreadful, terrible, awful, frightful, dire; unforgivable, inexcusable, indefensible, reprehensible, disgraceful, shameful; archaic or humorous parlous.

▷ANTONYMS trivial; excusable.

5 *her face had a ghastly pallor*: **pale**, white, pallid, pasty, pasty-faced, wan, colourless, anaemic, bloodless, washed out, peaky, peakish, ashen, ashen-faced, ashy, chalky, chalk-white, grey, whitish, white-faced, whey-faced, waxen, waxy, blanched, drained, pinched, green, sickly, sallow, as white as a sheet, as white as a ghost, deathly pale, cadaverous, corpse-like, ghostlike, spectral; informal like death warmed up; Scottish informal peely-wally; rare livid, etiolated, lymphatic.

▷ANTONYMS healthy.

ghost noun **1** *it is said that his ghost still haunts the crypt*: **spectre**, phantom, wraith, spirit, soul, shadow, presence; vision, apparition, hallucination; Scottish & Irish **bodach**; German **Doppelgänger**; W. Indian **duppy**; informal **spook**; literary phantasm, shade, revenant, visitant, wight; rare eidolon, manes, lemures.

2 *she gave the ghost of a smile*: **trace**, hint, suggestion, impression, faint appearance, touch, suspicion, tinge, modicum, dash, soupçon; **glimmer**, semblance, shadow, breath, whiff, undertone, whisper.

> *Word links* **ghost**
>
> **phasmophobia** fear of ghosts

ghostly adjective *a ghostly figure appeared at the end of the tunnel*: **ghostlike**, **spectral**, phantom, wraithlike, phantasmal, phantasmic, unearthly, unnatural, supernatural, other-worldly, insubstantial, illusory, unreal, shadowy, eerie, weird, uncanny, mysterious, magical, mystic, strange, abnormal, freakish; frightening, spine-chilling, hair-raising, blood-curdling, scaring, terrifying, petrifying, chilling, sinister; Scottish eldritch; informal creepy, scary, spooky, freaky; Brit. informal rum.

ghoulish adjective **1** *the torchlight gave his face a ghoulish appearance*: **macabre**, grisly, gruesome, grotesque, ghastly, morbid.

2 *he had a ghoulish hobby of collecting 'In Memoriam' notices*: **unhealthy**, perverted, death-obsessed, morbid, black; horrible, unwholesome, revolting; informal sick.

giant noun **colossus**, man mountain, behemoth, Brobdingnagian, mammoth, leviathan, monster, monstrosity, ogre; informal jumbo.

▷ANTONYMS dwarf.

▶adjective *a dredger resembling a giant vacuum cleaner*: **huge**, colossal, massive, enormous, gigantic, very big, very large, great, mammoth, vast, immense, tremendous, mighty, stupendous, monumental, epic, prodigious, mountainous, monstrous, titanic, towering, elephantine, king-sized, king-size, gargantuan, Herculean, Brobdingnagian; substantial, extensive, hefty, bulky, weighty, heavy, gross; informal mega, monster, whopping, whopping great, thumping, thumping great, humongous, jumbo, hulking, bumper, astronomical, astronomic; Brit. informal whacking, whacking great, ginormous.

▷ANTONYMS miniature.

> *Word toolkit* **giant**
>
> See **colossal**.

gibber verb *what are you gibbering about?* **prattle**, rattle on, chatter, babble, ramble, drivel, jabber, patter, gabble, bumble, burble, twitter, flannel, go on, run on, mutter, mumble, maunder, prate, bleat, cackle; Scottish & Irish slabber; informal gab, yak, yap, yackety-yak, yabber, yatter, natter, yammer, blabber, jibber-jabber, blather, blether, blither, jaw, gas, shoot one's mouth off; Brit. informal witter, rabbit, chunter, waffle; N. Amer. informal run off at the mouth; Austral./NZ informal mag; archaic clack, twaddle, twattle.

gibberish noun *he just stared at her as if she was talking gibberish*: **nonsense**, rubbish, balderdash, blather, blether; informal drivel, gobbledegook, mumbo-jumbo, rot, tripe, hogwash, baloney, bilge, bosh, bull, bunk, guff, eyewash, piffle, twaddle, poppycock, phooey, hooey, malarkey, dribble; Brit. informal cobblers, codswallop, tosh, cack, cock, stuff and nonsense, double Dutch; Scottish & N. English informal havers; N. Amer. informal garbage, flapdoodle, blathers, wack, bushwa, applesauce; informal, dated bunkum, tommyrot, cod, gammon, toffee; vulgar slang shit, bullshit, horseshit, crap, bollocks, balls; Austral./NZ vulgar slang bulldust.

▷ANTONYMS sense.

gibe noun & verb See **jibe**.

giddiness noun *I nearly fell down with giddiness*: **dizziness**, light-headedness, loss of balance/equilibrium, spinning/swimming of the head; faintness, weakness at the knees, unsteadiness, shakiness, wobbliness; Scottish mirligoes, dwalm; informal wooziness, legs like jelly, rubbery legs; technical megrim, sturdy, scotoma; archaic turnsick; rare vertiginousness.

▷ANTONYMS steadiness.

giddy adjective **1** *she felt giddy with the sickly heat*: **dizzy**, light-headed, faint, weak, weak at the knees, unsteady, shaky, wobbly, off balance; reeling, staggering, tottering, teetering; informal woozy, with legs like jelly, with rubbery legs; rare vertiginous.

▷ANTONYMS steady.

2 *she was so young and giddy that she had no understanding of the problem*: **flighty**, silly, frivolous, skittish, irresponsible, flippant, whimsical, capricious, light-minded, feather-brained, scatterbrained, scatty; careless, thoughtless, heedless, carefree, insouciant; informal dippy, dopey, batty, dotty, nutty; N. Amer. informal ditzy.

▷ANTONYMS sensible.

gift noun **1** *he made the hospital a gift of £2 million*: **present**, donation, offering, contribution, handout, presentation, bestowal, largesse, alms, charity, bonus, award, premium, bounty, boon, favour, bequest, legacy,

inheritance, settlement, subsidy, grant, endowment, benefaction; tip, gratuity, baksheesh; giving; French pourboire; informal freebie, perk, prezzie, sweetener; formal perquisite; archaic conferment.
2 *he had a unique gift for melody*: **talent**, flair, aptitude, facility, knack, technique, touch, bent, ability, expertise, capacity, capability, power, faculty; endowment, strength, strong point, forte, genius, brilliance; dexterity, adroitness, skill, cleverness, virtuosity, artistry.
▸ **verb** *he has gifted a new composition to the BBC Symphony Orchestra*: **present**, give, bestow, confer, donate, contribute, endow, award, accord, grant; pledge, vouchsafe, furnish, bequeath, hand over, turn over, make over, leave, will.

gifted **adjective** *she was already a gifted artist*: **talented**, skilful, skilled, accomplished, expert, consummate, master(ly), first-rate, polished, adroit, dexterous, able, competent, capable, apt, deft, adept, proficient; **intelligent**, clever, bright, brilliant, quick, sharp, perceptive; precocious, advanced for one's age, old beyond one's years, forward, ahead of one's peers, mature; informal crack, top-notch, top-drawer, top-hole, ace, wizard.
▷ANTONYMS inept, stupid.

gigantic **adjective** *the college is a gigantic Victorian building*: **huge**, enormous, vast, extensive, expansive, broad, wide; very big/large, great, giant, massive, colossal, mammoth, immense, tremendous, mighty, stupendous, monumental; boundless, immeasurable, limitless, infinite; epic, prodigious, mountainous, monstrous, titanic, towering, elephantine, king-sized, king-size, gargantuan, Herculean, Brobdingnagian, substantial; informal mega, monster, whopping, whopping great, thumping, thumping great, humongous, jumbo, hulking, bumper, astronomical, astronomic; Brit. informal whacking, whacking great, ginormous.
▷ANTONYMS tiny.

giggle **verb** *Rory couldn't help but giggle at the ridiculous picture*: **titter**, snigger, snicker, tee-hee, give a half-suppressed laugh, chuckle, chortle; smirk, sneer, simper.
▸ **noun** *she suppressed a giggle with difficulty*: **titter**, snigger, snicker, tee-hee, half-suppressed laugh, chuckle, chortle; smirk, sneer, simper.

gigolo **noun** *their wives frivolously whittled away the family money on a succession of gigolos*: **playboy**, beau, admirer; **(male) dancing partner**, (male) escort, (male) companion; informal fancy man; Brit. informal toy boy.

gild **verb 1** (usually **gilded**) *the steeple was crowned by a gilded weathercock*: **cover with gold**, paint gold, lacquer gold, inlay with gold.
2 *there was no need to gild the truth*: **elaborate**, embellish, embroider, sugar-coat, window-dress, camouflage, disguise, dress up, touch up, ginger up, colour, exaggerate, enlarge on, expand on; informal jazz up.

gimcrack **adjective** *they lived in gimcrack villas you'd be afraid to sneeze in*: **shoddy**, jerry-built, badly built, flimsy, insubstantial, rickety, ramshackle, thrown together, makeshift, inferior, poor-quality, second-rate, third-rate, low-grade, cheap, cheapjack, tawdry, rubbishy, kitschy, trashy, crude, tinny; informal tacky, tatty, junky; Brit. informal ropy, duff, rubbish, grotty.
▷ANTONYMS sound, solid.

gimmick **noun** *a quality newspaper shouldn't have to resort to gimmicks like bingo*: **publicity device**, stunt, contrivance, eye-catching novelty, scheme, trick, dodge, ploy, stratagem; loss-leader; informal shtick.

gingerly **adverb** *he stepped gingerly on to the ice*: **cautiously**, carefully, with caution, with care, circumspectly, delicately, warily, charily, guardedly, prudently, judiciously, on one's guard, on the alert, on the lookout, on the qui vive, suspiciously, attentively, heedfully, watchfully, vigilantly, observantly, alertly, cannily; hesitantly, timidly, timorously.
▷ANTONYMS carelessly; recklessly.

gird **verb** literary **1** *Sir Hector girded on his sword*: **fasten**, belt, bind, tie.
2 *the island was girded by treacherous rocks*: **surround**, enclose, encircle, circle, ring, encompass, circumscribe, border, bound, edge, skirt, fringe, form a ring around, form a barrier round; close in, shut in, fence in, wall in, hem in, pen up/in, lock in, cut off, confine; literary girdle, engird, compass.
3 *the Persians girded themselves for an attack*: **prepare**, get ready, make ready, gear up, nerve, steel, galvanize, brace, strengthen, fortify, bolster, buttress; informal psych oneself up.

girdle **noun 1** *round his waist was a diamond-studded girdle*: **belt**, sash, strap, cummerbund, waistband, band, girth, cord, fillet; Japanese obi; rare baldric, cincture, ceinture, cestus, cingulum, zone.
2 *her stockings were held up by her girdle*: **corset**, corselet, foundation garment, panty girdle; Medicine truss.
▸ **verb** literary *a formal garden girdled the house*: **surround**, enclose, encircle, circle, ring, encompass, circumscribe, border, bound, edge, skirt, fringe, form a ring around, form a barrier round; close in, shut in, fence in, wall in, hem in, pen up/in, lock in, cut off, confine; literary gird, engird, compass.

girl **noun 1** *a five-year-old girl*: **female child**; daughter; schoolgirl; Scottish & N. English lass, bairn; informal kid, kiddie, kiddiewink, nipper, tot, tiny tot; derogatory brat, chit.
2 *a tall dark girl got off the train*: **young woman**, young lady, miss; Scottish lass, lassie; Irish colleen; French Mademoiselle; Italian signorina; Spanish señorita; German Fräulein; informal chick, girlie, filly; Brit. informal bird, bint, popsy; N. Amer. informal gal, broad, dame, jane, babe; derogatory informal tart, piece, bit, mare, baggage; Austral./NZ informal sheila; black English bitch, sister; Brit. informal, dated Judy; N. Amer. dated frail; literary maid, maiden, damsel, demoiselle; archaic wench, petticoat.
3 *his girl eloped with an accountant*: **girlfriend**, sweetheart, woman, partner, lover, significant other, fiancée; Italian inamorata; informal steady, WAGs (wives and girlfriends); Irish informal mot; Brit. informal bird; N. Amer. informal squeeze, patootie; Austral. informal dona; Indian informal bibi; dated lady, lady friend, lady love, young lady, betrothed; archaic leman.

> *Choose the right word* **girl, woman, lady**
>
> See **woman**.

girlfriend **noun** *Richard's split up with his girlfriend*: **sweetheart**, woman, girl, partner, significant other, lover, fiancée; Italian inamorata; informal steady, date, WAGs (wives and girlfriends); Brit. informal bird; Irish informal mot; N. Amer. informal squeeze, patootie; Austral. informal dona; Indian informal bibi; dated lady, lady friend, lady love, young lady, betrothed; archaic leman.

girlish **adjective** *her girlish giggles*: **youthful**, childlike, childish, immature; feminine; coquettish, flirtatious, kittenish; informal girly, flirty.

girth **noun 1** *a tree that was 150 feet in height and 10 feet in girth*: **circumference**, width, perimeter; size, bulk, measure.
2 *he tied the towel around his girth*: **stomach**, midriff, middle, abdomen, belly, gut; informal tummy, tum.
3 *a horse's girth*: N. Amer. cinch.

gist **noun** *the gist of his speech*: **essence**, substance, quintessence, main idea/theme, central idea/theme, nub, core, heart, heart of the matter, nucleus, kernel, pith, marrow, meat, burden, crux, important point; thrust, direction, drift, sense, meaning, significance, import; informal nitty-gritty.

give **verb 1** *he had given them nearly two thousand pounds*: **present with**, provide with, supply with, furnish with, gift with; hand, let someone have; offer, proffer; award, grant, bestow, accord, confer; donate, contribute, put up; hand over, turn over, make over, leave, will, bequeath, pledge, vouchsafe; lend, slip; informal fork out, shell out, lay out, cough up; Brit. informal stump up; N. Amer. informal ante up, pony up.
▷ANTONYMS receive, accept, take; withhold.
2 *can I give him a message?* **convey**, pass on, impart, communicate, transmit, transfer; send, deliver, relay, purvey; tell.
3 *a baby given into their care*: **entrust**, commit, put into someone's hands, consign, assign, render; formal commend.
4 *he gave his life for his country*: **sacrifice**, give up, relinquish; devote, dedicate, set aside.
5 *he decided to give her time to think things over*: **allow**, permit, let have, grant, accord; offer.
6 *this leaflet gives our opening times*: **show**, display, set out, set forth, indicate, detail, give details of, list.
7 *the animals became docile and gave no further trouble*: **cause**, be a source of, make, create, occasion.
8 *some salamis are wrapped in garlic which gives additional flavour*: **produce**, yield, afford, result in; **impart**, lend.
9 *he gave a drinks party to celebrate*: **organize**, arrange, lay on, provide, be responsible for; **throw**, host, hold, have.
10 *Dominic gave a small bow*: **perform**, execute, carry out; make, do.
11 *she gave a warning shout*: **utter**, let out, emit; produce, make.
12 *he gave Harry a beating*: **administer**, deliver, deal; inflict, impose.
13 *the door gave after the fifth push*: **give way**, cave in, collapse, break, fall apart, come apart; bend, buckle, sink.
□ **give someone/something away 1** *his face gave little away*: **reveal**, disclose, divulge, let slip, leak, let out; give the game away. **2** *Luke would never forgive her if she gave him away*: **betray**, inform on; English Law turn Queen's/King's evidence; informal split on, blow the whistle on, rat on, peach on, stitch up, do the dirty on, sell down the river, squeal on, squeak on; Brit. informal grass on, shop, sneak on; N. Amer. informal rat out, drop a/the dime on, finger, job; Austral./NZ informal dob on, pimp on, pool, shelf, put someone's pot on, point the bone at.
□ **give in** *in the end, he was forced to give in*: **capitulate**, admit/concede defeat, give up, surrender, yield, submit, climb down, back down, give way, defer, acquiesce, relent, succumb, comply; informal throw in the towel/sponge.
▷ANTONYMS hold out.
□ **give something off/out** *a small fire burned, giving off more smoke than heat*: **emit**, produce, send out, send forth, pour out, throw out; discharge, release, exude, exhale, vent; rare exsufflate.
□ **give out 1** *his strength was giving out*: **run out**, be used up, be consumed, be exhausted, be depleted, come to an end, fail, flag; dry up. **2** *he gave out that he would hold a meeting*: **announce**, declare, state, make known, notify, give notice, communicate, broadcast, report, publish; disclose, reveal, divulge, let it be known.
□ **give something out** *thousands of leaflets were given out*: **distribute**, issue, hand out, pass round, dole out, dispense; mete out; allocate, allot, apportion, assign, share out, parcel out; disseminate; informal dish out.
▷ANTONYMS collect.

g

g

□ **give rise to** *usually this principle would not give rise to any problems*: **produce**, bring about, cause, occasion, generate, engender, lead to, result in, effect, induce, initiate, start, set off; contribute to, make for, be conducive to, foster, promote; provoke, precipitate, breed, spark off, trigger; literary beget.
□ **give up** *he isn't the kind of man to give up easily*: **admit defeat**, concede defeat, stop trying, call it a day, give in, surrender, capitulate, be beaten; despair, lose heart, abandon hope, give up hope; informal throw in the towel/sponge; Austral. informal drop one's bundle.
□ **give something up** *I'm determined to give up smoking | she gave up her job*: **stop**, cease, discontinue, desist from, swear off, forbear from, abstain from, cut out, renounce, forswear, forgo, abandon, have done with; resign from, stand down from; informal quit, kick, leave off, knock off, pack in, lay off, jack in, chuck, ditch.
▷ANTONYMS take up; continue.
▸ **noun** informal *the jacket has a major drawback—there isn't enough give under the arms*: **elasticity**, flexibility, stretch, stretchiness; slack, play.

give and take noun *there has to be some give and take on both sides*: **compromise**, concession; cooperation, reciprocity, teamwork, interplay; adaptability, flexibility.
▷ANTONYMS intransigence.

given adjective **1** *a given number of years*: **specified**, stated, designated, set, particular, specific, named, identified, delineated, prescribed; agreed, appointed, decided, prearranged, predetermined.
▷ANTONYMS unspecified.
2 *she was given to having temper tantrums*: **prone**, liable, inclined, disposed, predisposed, apt, likely; (**given to**) in the habit of.
▸ **preposition** *given the complexity of the issues involved, a summary of the discussion is difficult*: **considering**, taking into consideration, taking into account, in view of, bearing in mind, giving consideration to, keeping in mind, in the light of; making allowances for; assuming.
▸ **noun** *in this theory, aggression is taken as a given which must find some outlet*: **established fact**, reality, certainty; French donnée.

giver noun **donor**, contributor, donator, benefactor, benefactress, provider; supporter, backer, subsidizer, patron, sponsor, subscriber; philanthropist, well-wisher, helper; informal angel, fairy godmother; rare benefactrice, benefactrix, philanthrope.
▷ANTONYMS recipient.

glacial adjective **1** *glacial conditions*: **freezing**, bitterly cold, icy, ice-cold, sub-zero, frozen, wintry; arctic, polar, Siberian; bitter, biting, piercing, raw, cutting; literary chill, frore; rare gelid, brumal, rimy, algid.
▷ANTONYMS tropical, hot.
2 *Polly's tone was glacial*: **unfriendly**, frosty, icy, wintry, cold, chilly, frigid, hostile, unwelcoming; rare gelid.
▷ANTONYMS friendly, warm.

glad adjective **1** *I'm really glad you're coming with me*: **pleased**, **happy**, delighted, as pleased as Punch, well pleased, thrilled, overjoyed, cock-a-hoop, elated, like a dog with two tails, like a child with a new toy, gleeful; satisfied, contented, gratified, grateful, thankful; French enchanté; informal tickled pink, over the moon, as happy as Larry; Brit. informal **chuffed**; N. English informal made up; N. Amer. informal as happy as a clam; Austral. informal wrapped; humorous gruntled.
▷ANTONYMS dismayed; annoyed.
2 *I'd be glad to help*: **more than willing**, eager, happy, pleased, delighted; ready, prepared, nothing loath; informal game.
▷ANTONYMS unwilling, reluctant.
3 *glad tidings*: **pleasing**, welcome, happy, joyful, delightful, cheering, heart-warming, heartening, gratifying; literary gladsome.
▷ANTONYMS unwelcome, distressing.
□ **glad rags** informal *it's time to put your glad rags on*: **best clothes**, finery, Sunday best; informal best bib and tucker.

gladden verb *it gladdened him to see her again*: **delight**, please, make happy, make someone feel good, give someone pleasure, exhilarate, elate; **raise someone's spirits**, cheer, cheer up, hearten, do someone's heart good, warm the cockles of someone's heart, brighten up, buoy up, give someone a lift, uplift; gratify; informal give someone a buzz, give someone a kick, tickle someone pink, buck up; archaic glad.
▷ANTONYMS sadden, depress.

gladly adverb *I would gladly have given him the money*: **with pleasure**, happily, cheerfully; **willingly**, readily, eagerly, freely, without hesitation, without reluctance, with good grace, ungrudgingly; archaic fain, lief.
▷ANTONYMS reluctantly, unwillingly.

glamorous adjective **1** *a glamorous woman*: **alluring**, beautiful, attractive, elegant, chic, smart, well dressed, stylish, fashionable; charming, charismatic, fascinating, intriguing, beguiling, appealing, lovely, bewitching, enchanting, entrancing, irresistible, seductive, tantalizing; informal classy, glitzy, ritzy, glam.
▷ANTONYMS plain, drab, dowdy.
2 *a glamorous lifestyle*: **exciting**, stimulating, thrilling, fascinating, high profile, dazzling, glittering, glossy, tinselled; cosmopolitan, colourful, exotic; informal ritzy, glitzy, sexy, fast-lane, jet-setting.
▷ANTONYMS dull, boring.

glamour noun **1** *she had undeniable glamour*: **beauty**, **allure**, attractiveness, elegance, chic, style; charisma, charm, fascination, magnetism, seductiveness, desirability; rare witchery.
2 *the glamour of working in show business*: **allure**, attraction, attractiveness, fascination, charm, enchantment, captivation, magic, romance, mystique, exoticism, spell; excitement, thrill, glitter, brilliance, the bright lights, the high life; informal glitz, pizzazz, glam.

glance verb **1** *Rachel glanced at him nervously*: **take a quick look**, look quickly, look briefly, peek, peep; glimpse, catch a glimpse of; Scottish keek; informal sneak a look, take a gander; Brit. informal take a dekko, have a shufti, take a butcher's; Austral./NZ informal **squiz**; archaic glance one's eye.
▷ANTONYMS gaze, scrutinize.
2 *I glanced through the report*: **read quickly**, scan, have a quick look, run one's eye over; skim, leaf, flick, flip, thumb, browse; dip into; informal give something a/the once-over.
▷ANTONYMS study, pore over.
3 *a bullet glanced off the ice*: **ricochet**, rebound, be deflected; fly, bounce; graze, clip, make contact with; Billiards & Pool cannon, carom; rare resile.
4 *the bright sunlight glanced off her copper hair*: **reflect**, **flash**, gleam, glint, glitter, glisten, glimmer, shimmer, flicker, sparkle, twinkle; rare coruscate.
▸ **noun 1** *he took a quick glance at his watch*: **peek**, peep, brief look, quick look; glimpse; Scottish keek; French coup d'œil; informal gander; Brit. informal dekko, shufti, butcher's; Austral./NZ informal **squiz**, geek.
2 literary *a glance of light*: **flash**, gleam, glitter, glint, glimmer, shimmer, flicker, sparkle, twinkle.
□ **at first glance** *at first glance, nothing much seemed to have changed*: **on the face of it**, on the surface, at first sight, to the casual eye, to all appearances, to go/judge by appearances; apparently, seemingly, outwardly, superficially, it seems (that), it would seem (that), it appears (that), it would appear (that), as far as one can see/tell, by all accounts, so it seems, to all intents and purposes.

gland noun

> *Word links* **gland**
>
> **glandular** relating to glands
> **adeno-** related prefix, as in *adenoids, adenocarcinoma*

glare verb **1** *she glared at him, her eyes flashing*: **stare angrily**, scowl, glower, look daggers, frown, lour, give someone a black look, look threateningly/menacingly; informal give someone a dirty look; archaic glout; Scottish archaic glunch.
▷ANTONYMS smile.
2 *the sun glared out of a clear blue sky*: **blaze**, be dazzling, be blinding, shine brightly, flare, flame, beam.
▸ **noun 1** *she gave Harley a cold glare*: **angry stare**, scowl, glower, frown, black look, threatening/menacing look; informal dirty look.
▷ANTONYMS smile.
2 *the harsh glare of the arc lights*: **strong light**, dazzling light, blaze, dazzle, shine, beam, flare; radiance, brilliance, luminescence, fluorescence.

glaring adjective **1** *the glaring lights*: **dazzling**, blinding, blazing, strong, extremely bright, harsh; fluorescent.
▷ANTONYMS dim, soft.
2 *a glaring omission*: **obvious**, conspicuous, plain to see, unmistakable, obtrusive, striking, flagrant, blatant, staring someone in the face, as plain as a pikestaff, as plain as day, inescapable, unmissable, outrageous, gross; overt, patent, transparent, manifest, visible, apparent, unconcealed, undisguised; informal as plain as the nose on one's face, standing/sticking out like a sore thumb, standing/sticking out a mile, right under one's nose; rare egregious.
▷ANTONYMS inconspicuous, minor.

glass noun **1** *we sell china and glass*: **glassware**, crystal, crystalware; rare vitrics.
2 Brit. *she put it on and looked at herself in the glass*: **mirror**, looking glass.

> *Word links* **glass**
>
> **vitreous** relating to glass
> **nerophobia** fear of glass
> **glazier** glass-fitter

glasses plural noun *a pair of thick-lensed glasses*: **spectacles**; N. Amer. eyeglasses; informal specs.

glasshouse noun See **greenhouse**.

glassy adjective **1** *the glassy surface of the lake*: **smooth**, mirror-like, glass-like, gleaming, shining, shiny, sheeny, glossy, polished; slippery, slick, icy, ice-covered; clear, crystal clear, transparent, translucent, limpid, pellucid; calm, still, flat, unruffled, even, waveless, like a millpond; informal slippy; technical vitreous, hyaloid.

▷ANTONYMS rough; murky.
2 *a glassy stare*: **expressionless**, glazed, blank, empty, vacant, fixed, unmoving, motionless, emotionless, fishy, impassive, lifeless, wooden, dull, vacuous; deadpan.
▷ANTONYMS expressive.

glaze verb 1 *the newly made pots are glazed when they are completely dry*: **varnish**, enamel, lacquer, japan, shellac, paint, coat; gloss, make shiny.
2 *choux pastry glazed with caramel sauce*: **cover**, coat; ice, frost.
3 *his eyes glazed over*: **become glassy**, grow expressionless, go blank, be motionless; mist over, film over.
▶ noun 1 *a pottery jar with a rich blue glaze*: **varnish**, enamel, lacquer, finish, coating; lustre, shine, gloss.
2 *brush the cake with an apricot glaze*: **coating**, topping; icing, frosting.

gleam verb *the new brass nameplate gleamed in the moonlight*: **shine**, glimmer, glint, catch the light, glitter, shimmer, glow, sparkle, twinkle, flicker, blink, wink, glisten, flash, flare, beam, fluoresce; reflect light; literary glister; rare coruscate, scintillate, fulgurate, effulge, luminesce, incandesce, phosphoresce.
▶ noun 1 *a gleam of light*: **glimmer**, glint, shimmer, glow, twinkle, sparkle, flicker, blink, spark, flash, flare; beam, ray, shaft, finger, pencil.
2 *the gleam of polished brass*: **shine**, lustre, gloss, sheen; glint, glitter, glimmer, sparkle, brightness, brilliance, radiance, glow, luminescence, luminosity, phosphorescence, incandescence; literary glister; rare lambency, scintillation, effulgence, refulgence, fulguration, coruscation.
3 *a gleam of hope appeared in Ray's eyes*: **glimmer**, glimmering, flicker, ray, spark, trace, suggestion, hint, faint sign, scintilla.

glean verb *the information is gleaned from press cuttings*: **obtain**, get, take, draw, derive, extract, cull, garner, gather, reap; select, choose, pick; learn, find out.

glee noun *Agnes clapped her hands together with glee*: **delight**, pleasure, happiness, joy, joyfulness, gladness, elation, euphoria, exhilaration, cheerfulness, amusement, mirth, mirthfulness, merriment, joviality, jollity, jocularity; excitement, animation, gaiety, high spirits, exuberance, verve, liveliness, triumph, jubilation, relish, satisfaction, gratification; German Schadenfreude; humorous delectation; rare joyousness, jouissance.
▷ANTONYMS gloom, disappointment.

gleeful adjective *a gleeful chuckle*: **delighted**, pleased, joyful, happy, glad, amused, mirthful, cheerful, overjoyed, elated, euphoric, exhilarated; merry, gay, high-spirited, in high spirits, jolly, jovial, exuberant; cock-a-hoop, jubilant; informal over the moon; literary joyous.
▷ANTONYMS gloomy.

glib adjective *the glib phrases rolled off his tongue | a glib PR official*: **slick**, pat, neat, plausible, silky, smooth-talking, fast-talking; **smooth**, urbane, smooth-tongued, silver-tongued, smooth-spoken; **fluent**, voluble, loquacious, having kissed the Blarney Stone; disingenuous, insincere, facile, shallow, superficial, simplistic, oversimplified, easy, ready, flippant; informal flip, sweet-talking, with the gift of the gab.
▷ANTONYMS sincere, thoughtful; inarticulate.

Choose the right word **glib, slick, smooth, urbane**

These words, with varying degrees of disapproval, describe extreme ease and confidence in speech or manner.

To be **glib** is always bad. The word most commonly describes utterances that are too easy, fluent, and inadequate to deal with the complexity of an issue, or are too readily produced to be sincere (*they should be on their guard against accepting glib answers*).

Slick is used of a person or their actions or utterances; it indicates expertise and the assurance that that brings, but it usually implies that this is at the expense of content (*a slick public relations campaign*) or of honesty and altruism (*slick financiers and face-grinding industrialists*).

Someone described as **smooth** is regarded as possibly insincere or too charming to be trusted (*he was too smooth, and his charm a little too insincere, to be a real gentleman*).

Urbane is the most positive term. It is used of a person, action, or utterance and indicates a polished and relaxed ease and charm (*his urbane discourse is both enlivening and instructive*). *Urbane* is almost always used to describe men and not women.

glide verb 1 *two gondolas glided past*: **slide**, move smoothly, slip, sail, float, drift, flow; coast, freewheel, roll; skim, skate, glissade.
▷ANTONYMS hurtle.
2 *seagulls gliding gracefully over the waves*: **soar**, wheel, plane; fly.
3 *Toby glided out of the back door*: **slip**, move lightly/quietly, steal, slink.
▷ANTONYMS stamp.

glimmer verb *moonlight glimmered on the lawn*: **gleam**, shine, glint, flicker, shimmer, glisten, glow, twinkle, sparkle, glitter, catch the light, blink, wink, flash; literary glister; rare scintillate, coruscate, fulgurate, effulge, luminesce, incandesce, phosphoresce.
▶ noun 1 *a faint glimmer of light*: **gleam**, glint, flicker, shimmer, glow, twinkle, sparkle, blink, flash, ray.
2 *a glimmer of hope*: **gleam**, glimmering, flicker, ray, trace, faint sign, scintilla, suggestion, hint.

glimpse noun *a fleeting glimpse of her face*: **brief look**, quick look; glance, peek, peep; sight, sighting; French coup d'œil.
▶ verb *he glimpsed a figure standing in the shade*: **catch sight of**, catch/get a glimpse of, see briefly, get a sight of, notice, discern, spot, spy, sight, note, pick out, make out; Brit. informal clock; literary espy, descry.

glint verb *the diamond ring glinted in the sunlight*: **shine**, gleam, catch the light, glitter, sparkle, twinkle, blink, wink, glimmer, shimmer, glow, flicker, glisten, flash; reflect light; literary glister; rare coruscate, scintillate, fulgurate, effulge, luminesce, incandesce, phosphoresce.
▶ noun *the glint of the silverware*: **glitter**, gleam, sparkle, twinkle, blink, wink, glimmer, flash.

glisten verb *the sea glistened in the early morning light*: **shine**, sparkle, twinkle, glint, glitter, catch the light, glimmer, shimmer, glow, flicker, blink, wink, flash; literary glister; rare coruscate, scintillate, fulgurate, effulge, luminesce, incandesce, phosphoresce.

glitter verb *silver and crystal glittered in the candlelight*: **shine**, sparkle, twinkle, glint, gleam, shimmer, glimmer, flicker, blink, wink, catch the light, flash, spangle; literary glister; rare scintillate, coruscate, fulgurate, effulge, luminesce, incandesce, phosphoresce.
▶ noun 1 *the glitter of sunlight on the water*: **sparkle**, twinkle, glint, gleam, shimmer, glimmer, flicker, blink, flash; brightness, brilliance, light, luminescence, phosphorescence, luminosity; rare lambency, scintillation, coruscation, fulguration, effulgence.
2 *the glitter of show business*: **glamour**, excitement, thrills, attractions, appeal; showiness, dazzle, tinsel; informal razzle-dazzle, razzmatazz, glitz, glitziness, ritziness, pizzazz, flashiness.

gloat verb *she gloated over his recent humiliation | I hadn't time to gloat over my good fortune*: **delight in**, relish, take great pleasure in, enjoy greatly, revel in, rejoice in, glory in, exult in, triumph over, crow over; boast about, brag about, feel self-satisfied about, be smug about, congratulate oneself on, preen oneself about, pat oneself on the back about; rub one's hands together; informal rub it in; archaic pique oneself on.

global adjective 1 *the global economy*: **worldwide**, international, world, intercontinental; universal.
▷ANTONYMS national, local.
2 *a global view of the problem*: **comprehensive**, overall, general, all-inclusive, all-encompassing, encyclopedic, universal, exhaustive, blanket; **broad**, wide-ranging, far-reaching, extensive, sweeping.
▷ANTONYMS partial, restricted.

globe noun 1 *a city full of tourists from every corner of the globe*: **world**, earth, universe, planet; literary orb.
2 *the sun is a globe, not the flat disc it appears to be*: **sphere**, orb, ball, spheroid, round; globule; rare spherule.

globular adjective *the plant's globular pinkish-green blooms*: **spherical**, round, globe-shaped, ball-shaped, orb-shaped, rounded, bulbous, bulb-shaped; rare spheroid, spheroidal, spheric, globate, globose, globoid, orbicular, orbiculate.

globule noun *globules of sweat*: **droplet**, drop, dewdrop, bead, tear, ball, bubble, pearl, particle; informal blob, glob; technical prill.

gloom noun 1 *Sharpe peered into the gloom*: **darkness**, semi-darkness, dark, gloominess, dimness, blackness, murkiness, murk, shadows, shade, shadiness, obscurity; dusk, twilight, gloaming; rare tenebrosity.
▷ANTONYMS light.
2 *his gloom deepened*: **despondency**, depression, dejection, downheartedness, dispiritedness, heavy-heartedness, melancholy, melancholia, unhappiness, sadness, glumness, gloominess, low spirits, dolefulness, misery, sorrow, sorrowfulness, forlornness, woefulness, woe, wretchedness, lugubriousness, moroseness, mirthlessness, cheerlessness; despair, pessimism, hopelessness, the slough of despond, negativity; German Weltschmerz; informal the blues, the dumps; N. Amer. informal the blahs; rare mopery.
▷ANTONYMS happiness.

gloomy adjective 1 *a gloomy room filled with mahogany furniture*: **dark**, ill-lit, poorly lit, shadowy, sunless, dim, sombre, dingy, frowzy, drab, dismal, dreary, murky, depressing, unwelcoming, uninviting, cheerless, joyless, comfortless, funereal; grey, leaden, overcast, cloudy; literary crepuscular, tenebrous; rare Stygian, Tartarean, caliginous, subfusc.
▷ANTONYMS bright, sunny, well lit.
2 *Joanna looked gloomy | his gloomy expression*: **despondent**, downcast, downhearted, dejected, disconsolate, dispirited, crestfallen, cast down, depressed, disappointed, disheartened, discouraged, demoralized, desolate, heavy-hearted, in low spirits, low-spirited, sad, unhappy, glum, full of gloom, doleful, melancholy, miserable, woebegone, mournful, sorrowful, forlorn, long-faced, fed up, in the doldrums, subdued, wretched, lugubrious, Eeyorish, morose, sepulchral, saturnine, dour, mirthless, woeful; informal blue, down, down in the mouth, down in the dumps;

Brit. informal brassed off, cheesed off, looking as if one had lost a pound and found a penny; literary dolorous; archaic chap-fallen, adust.
▷ANTONYMS happy, cheerful.
3 *gloomy forecasts about the economy*: **pessimistic**, depressing, downbeat, looking on the black side, disheartening, disappointing, dispiriting, unpromising, unfavourable, bleak, bad, dark, black, sombre, melancholy, saddening, distressing, grim, cheerless, comfortless, hopeless.
▷ANTONYMS optimistic, upbeat.

glorify verb 1 *their prime purpose is to glorify God*: **give praise to**, praise, extol, exalt, laud, worship, revere, reverence, venerate, pay homage/tribute to, honour, adore, thank, give thanks to, bless; archaic magnify.
2 *a poem written to glorify the memory of those men killed in the war | a football video glorifying violence*: **ennoble**, exalt, elevate, lift up, add dignity to, dignify, add lustre to, add distinction to, enhance, increase, augment, promote, boost; praise, sing/sound the praises of, celebrate, honour, extol, laud, eulogize, hymn, lionize, acclaim, applaud, hail; glamorize, aggrandize, idealize, romanticize, put on a pedestal, enshrine, apotheosize, canonize, immortalize; black English big up; dated cry up; rare emblazon, panegyrize, heroize.
▷ANTONYMS dishonour, vilify.

g

glorious adjective 1 *a glorious victory*: **illustrious**, celebrated, famous, famed, renowned, acclaimed, distinguished, honoured, eminent, excellent, outstanding, great, magnificent, splendid, impressive, noble, supreme, sublime, triumphant; immortal, unforgettable.
▷ANTONYMS undistinguished.
2 *glorious views of the Cotswolds*: **wonderful**, marvellous, magnificent, superb, sublime, spectacular, lovely, excellent, fine, delightful, enjoyable, pleasurable; informal super, great, smashing, amazing, stunning, fantastic, terrific, tremendous, incredible, sensational, stellar, heavenly, divine, gorgeous, dreamy, grand, fabulous, fab, fabby, fantabulous, awesome, magic, ace, out of this world; Brit. informal brilliant, brill, bosting; N. Amer. informal peachy, dandy, jim-dandy, neat; Austral./NZ informal beaut, bonzer; Brit. informal, dated capital, champion, wizard, corking, ripping, spiffing, top-hole, topping, beezer; N. Amer. informal, dated swell, keen; literary wondrous, beauteous; archaic goodly; rare frabjous, splendacious, splendiferous, splendorous.
▷ANTONYMS horrid, miserable.

glory noun 1 *a sport that has won him glory abroad*: **renown**, fame, prestige, honour, distinction, kudos, eminence, pre-eminence, acclaim, acclamation, celebrity, praise, accolades, laurels, recognition, note, notability, credit, repute, reputation, name, illustriousness, lustre; informal bouquets; rare laudation.
▷ANTONYMS shame; obscurity.
2 *glory be to God in the highest*: **praise**, worship, glorification, adoration, veneration, honour, reverence, exaltation, extolment, homage, tribute, thanksgiving, thanks, blessing; rare laudation, magnification.
3 *a late 17th century house restored to its former glory*: **magnificence**, splendour, resplendence, grandeur, majesty, greatness, impressiveness, gloriousness, nobility, pomp, stateliness, sumptuousness, opulence, beauty, elegance, brilliance, gorgeousness, splendidness.
▷ANTONYMS lowliness, modesty.
4 *the glories of Vermont*: **wonder**, beauty, delight, wonderful thing, glorious thing, marvel, phenomenon; sight, spectacle.
▸ verb *individuals who **gloried in** their independence*: **take great pleasure in**, exult in, rejoice in, delight in, revel in; relish, savour, greatly enjoy; take great pride in, preen oneself on, congratulate oneself on, be proud of; boast about, crow about, gloat about; informal get a kick out of, get a thrill out of; archaic plume oneself on, pique oneself on.
▷ANTONYMS feel ashamed of.

gloss[1] noun 1 *the healthy gloss of her jet-black hair*: **shine**, sheen, lustre, gleam, patina, shininess, glossiness, brightness, brilliance, shimmer, sparkle; polish, burnish, glaze, varnish.
▷ANTONYMS dullness.
2 *beneath the gloss of success was a tragic private life*: **facade**, veneer, surface, front, show, camouflage, disguise, mask, semblance, smokescreen, outward appearance, false appearance; window dressing, attractive appearance.
▸ verb 1 *she licked her lips in order to gloss them*: **make glossy**, shine, give a shine to; glaze, polish, burnish.
2 *the company has tried to **gloss over** the seriousness of the situation*: **conceal**, cover up, hide, camouflage, disguise, mask, veil, draw a veil over, whitewash; explain away; evade, avoid, shrug off, brush aside, play down, downplay, minimize, understate, make light of, soft-pedal, de-emphasize; informal brush something under the carpet; rare gloze over.
▷ANTONYMS disclose; exaggerate.

gloss[2] noun *glosses are provided in the right-hand margin*: **explanation**, interpretation, exegesis, explication, elucidation; annotation, note, marginal note, footnote, commentary, comment, critique; translation, paraphrase; rare scholium.
▸ verb *difficult words are glossed in a footnote*: **explain**, give an explanation of, interpret, explicate, elucidate; annotate, add notes/footnotes to, add a commentary to, comment on; translate, paraphrase, construe; rare footnote, margin, marginalize.

glossy adjective 1 *the glossy wooden floor*: **shiny**, shining, gleaming, lustrous, bright, brilliant, sparkling, shimmering, glistening, sleek, silky, silken, satiny, sheeny, smooth, glassy; polished, burnished, glazed, waxed, japanned, shellacked, lacquered; rare nitid, patinated.
▷ANTONYMS dull, lustreless; matt.
2 *a glossy fashion magazine*: **expensive**, high-quality, well produced; stylish, fashionable, glamorous, sophisticated; attractive, artistic; Brit. upmarket; coffee-table; informal classy, ritzy, glitzy, arty.
▷ANTONYMS cheap, downmarket.

Word toolkit

glossy	lustrous	satiny
paper	hair	dress
brochure	gold	fabric
photos	metal	finish
lips	fur	sheets
leaves	wool	skin

glove noun **mitten**, mitt, gauntlet; Computing dataglove.

glow verb 1 *lights glowed from the windows of the high-street shops*: **shine**, radiate, shed a glow; gleam, glimmer, flicker, flare; rare incandesce, phosphoresce, luminesce.
2 *the remains of a fire glowed in the hearth*: **radiate heat**, burn without flames, smoulder.
3 *her cheeks began to glow with embarrassment*: **flush**, blush, redden, go red, colour, colour up, go pink, crimson, go scarlet, be suffused with colour; burn, radiate heat; archaic mantle.
▷ANTONYMS pale.
4 *she glowed with pride*: **radiate**, tingle, thrill; beam.
▸ noun 1 *the golden glow of the fire*: **radiance**, light, brightness, luminosity, shine, gleam, glimmer, incandescence, phosphorescence, luminescence; richness, vividness, brilliance; warmth, heat; rare lambency, lucency, irradiance.
2 *a delicate glow spread over her face*: **flush**, blush, rosiness, pinkness, redness, crimson, scarlet, reddening, ruddiness, high colour; bloom, radiance; warmth.
▷ANTONYMS pallor.
3 *she felt a warm glow deep inside her*: **happiness**, contentment, pleasure, satisfaction, gratification, gladness.

glower verb *she glowered at him suspiciously*: **scowl**, glare, stare angrily, look daggers, frown, lour, give a someone black look, pull a face; informal give someone a dirty look; archaic glout; Scottish archaic glunch.
▷ANTONYMS smile, grin.
▸ noun *the icy glower on her father's face*: **scowl**, glare, angry stare, frown, black look; informal dirty look.

glowing adjective 1 *glowing street lights | the glowing coals*: **bright**, shining, radiant, glimmering, flickering, twinkling, incandescent, candescent, luminous, luminescent, phosphorescent; lit up, lighted, illuminated, ablaze; aglow, smouldering; literary lambent, lucent, rutilant, ardent, fervent, fervid.
2 *his glowing cheeks*: **rosy**, pink, red, reddish, rose-red, flushed, blushing; healthy-looking, fresh, radiant, blooming, ruddy, high-coloured, florid; hot, burning; archaic sanguine; rare erubescent, rubescent, rubicund.
▷ANTONYMS pale.
3 *the glowing colours of the textiles*: **vivid**, vibrant, bright, brilliant, colourful, rich, intense, strong, radiant, warm, flaming.
▷ANTONYMS dull.
4 *a glowing report*: **highly complimentary**, highly favourable, enthusiastic, full of praise, commendatory, praising, admiring, lionizing, ecstatic, rapturous, rhapsodic, eulogistic, laudatory, acclamatory, adulatory; fulsome; informal rave; rare encomiastical, panegyrical, laudative.
▷ANTONYMS critical; unenthusiastic.

glue noun *a tube of glue*: **adhesive**, fixative, gum, paste, cement; epoxy, epoxy resin, sealant, size, glair; N. Amer. mucilage; N. Amer. informal stickum.
▸ verb 1 *strips of plywood were glued together*: **stick**, gum, paste; affix, fix, cement, epoxy; rare agglutinate, conglutinate.
2 (**be glued to**) informal *her eyes were glued to the television screen*: **be riveted to/by**, be gripped by, be hypnotized by, be mesmerized by; be fixed on, be fastened on, be pinned to, be locked on.

glum adjective *Kenneth looked glum and resentful*: **gloomy**, downcast, downhearted, dejected, disconsolate, dispirited, despondent, crestfallen, cast down, depressed, disappointed, disheartened, discouraged, demoralized, desolate, heavy-hearted, in low spirits, low-spirited, sad, unhappy, doleful, melancholy, miserable, woebegone, mournful, forlorn, long-faced, fed up, in the doldrums, wretched, lugubrious, morose, sepulchral, saturnine, dour, mirthless; informal blue, down, down in the mouth, down in the dumps; Brit. informal brassed off, cheesed off, looking as if one had lost a pound and found a penny; literary dolorous; archaic

chap-fallen, adust.
▷ANTONYMS cheerful, merry.

glut noun *there is a glut of cars on the market*: **surplus**, excess, surfeit, superfluity, overabundance, superabundance, oversupply, mountain; too many, too much, more than enough, plethora; informal more ... than one can shake a stick at; rare nimiety.
▷ANTONYMS dearth, scarcity.
▶ verb *the factories for recycling paper are glutted*: **cram full**, fill to excess, overfill, overload, oversupply, saturate, supersaturate, flood, inundate, deluge, swamp; choke, clog; informal stuff.

glutinous adjective *a glutinous liquid*: **sticky**, viscous, tacky, glue-like, gluey, gummy, treacly; mucilaginous, mucous; cohesive, adhesive; Brit. claggy; informal gooey, gloopy, cloggy; N. Amer. informal gloppy; rare viscid, viscoid.
▷ANTONYMS dry.

glutton noun **gourmand**, gourmandizer, overeater, gorger, big eater; informal pig, greedy pig, hog, gannet, greedy guts, gutbucket, human dustbin, gobbler, guzzler; N. Amer. informal chowhound; rare trencherman.

gluttonous adjective **greedy**, gourmandizing, voracious, insatiable, wolfish; informal piggish, piggy, hoggish, gannet-like, with eyes bigger than one's stomach; rare edacious, esurient, gourmand, ventripotent.
▷ANTONYMS moderate, abstemious.

gluttony noun **greed**, greediness, overeating, gourmandism, gourmandizing, gluttonousness, voraciousness, voracity, wolfishness, insatiability; informal piggishness, hoggishness, gutsiness; technical polyphagia, hyperphagia; rare edaciousness, edacity, gulosity, esurience.
▷ANTONYMS moderation, abstinence.

gnarled adjective **1** *the gnarled trunk of an old crab-apple tree*: **knobbly**, knotty, knotted, gnarly, lumpy, bumpy, nodular, rough; twisted, bent, crooked, distorted, contorted; rare knurled, nodulous, nodose.
2 *his gnarled hands*: **twisted**, bent, arthritic, misshapen; knotty, rough, leathery, weather-beaten, weathered, wrinkled, wizened; Scottish thrawn; archaic wry.

gnash verb *she wailed and gnashed her teeth*: **grind**, strike together, grate, rasp, grit; archaic gristbite.

gnaw verb **1** *the dog **gnawed at** a large piece of bone*: **chew**, bite, nibble, munch, crunch, champ, chomp, masticate; worry, tear; rare manducate, chumble.
2 *pressures which are **gnawing away** the industry's independence*: **erode**, wear away, wear down, eat away (at), chip away (at), bite into, corrode, consume, devour; rare fret.
3 *the doubts continued to **gnaw at** her*: **prey on someone's mind**, nag, plague, torment, torture, trouble, distress, worry, haunt, oppress, weigh heavily on someone's mind, be a weight on someone's mind, burden, hang over, harry, bother, exercise, fret; niggle, rankle with; fester.

gnawing adjective *a gnawing pain in her abdomen | his gnawing doubts*: **persistent**, nagging, niggling, lingering, constant, continual, unrelenting, unabating; worrying worrisome, troubling, disturbing.

go verb **1** *she went forwards, step by step | he's gone into town*: **move**, proceed, make one's way, advance, progress, pass, walk, wend one's way; travel, journey; repair, remove, retire; literary betake oneself.
2 *the road goes to London*: **extend**, continue, carry on, stretch, reach; lead.
3 *the money raised will go to charity*: **be given**, be donated, be assigned, be allotted, be granted, be presented, be awarded; be applied, be devoted; be handed (over), be turned over, be made over, be ceded.
4 *it's time to go*: **leave**, depart, take one's leave, take oneself off, go away, go off, withdraw, absent oneself, say one's goodbyes, quit, make an exit, exit; set off, set out, start out, get going, get under way, be on one's way; decamp, retreat, beat a retreat, retire, make off, clear out, make oneself scarce, slope off, run off, run away, flee; Brit. make a move; informal make tracks, shove off, push off, clear off, beat it, take off, skedaddle, scram, split, scoot, up sticks, pack one's bags; Brit. informal sling one's hook; N. Amer. informal vamoose, hightail it, cut out; rare abstract oneself.
▷ANTONYMS arrive, come.
5 *three years **went past***: **pass**, pass by, elapse, slip by/past, roll by/past, tick away; wear on, march on; fly by/past.
6 *a golden age that has now gone for good*: **come to an end**, cease to exist, disappear, vanish, be no more, be over, run its course, fade away, melt away, evaporate; blow over; finish, end, stop, cease, terminate; rare evanish.
▷ANTONYMS return.
7 *25 of their 80 staff have gone*: **be dismissed**, be given (one's) notice, be made redundant, be laid off, be let go; informal get the sack, be sacked, be fired, be given the boot, be given the push, get one's marching orders, be booted out, be axed, get the axe/chop; Brit. informal be given one's cards.
8 *her purse had gone*: **be stolen**, be taken; **go missing**, disappear, be lost, be mislaid.
9 *after a few weeks, all our money had gone*: **be used up**, be spent, be finished, be at an end, be exhausted, be consumed, be drained, be depleted.
10 *I'd like to see my grandchildren before I go*: **die**, pass away, pass on, expire, depart this life, be no more, breathe one's last, draw one's last breath, meet one's end, meet one's death, meet one's Maker, give up the ghost, go to the great beyond, cross the great divide, shuffle off this mortal coil, perish, go the way of the/all flesh, go to one's last resting place; informal kick the bucket, bite the dust, croak, conk out, buy it, turn up one's toes, cash in one's chips, go belly up; Brit. informal snuff it, peg out, pop one's clogs.
11 *there was no warning at all before the bridge went*: **collapse**, give way, fall down, cave in, fall in, crumble, disintegrate, break, fall to pieces.
12 *his hair had gone grey*: **become**, get, turn, grow, come to be; literary wax.
13 *he heard the bell go*: **make a sound**, make a noise, sound, reverberate, sound out, resound; ring, chime, peal, toll, ding, clang.
14 *everything went well*: **turn out**, work out, fare, progress, develop, come out; result, end, end up; informal pan out; rare eventuate.
15 *the carpet and curtains don't really go*: **match**, go together, be harmonious, harmonize, blend, suit each other, be suited, complement each other, be complementary, coordinate with each other, be compatible.
16 *my car won't go*: **function**, work, be in working order, run, operate, be operative, perform.
17 *where does the cutlery go?* **be kept**, belong, have a place, be found, be located; be situated, lie, stand.
18 *this all goes to prove my point*: **contribute**, help, serve; incline, tend.
□ **get going 1** *it's been wonderful seeing you again, but I think it's time we got going.* See **go** (sense 4 of the verb). **2** *the campaign got going in 1983*: **start**, begin, get under way, go ahead; informal kick off; formal commence.
□ **get someone going** *his letter to the editor really got me going*: **stir up**, rouse, arouse, excite, galvanize, electrify, stimulate, inspire, move, fire up, fire the enthusiasm of, fire the imagination of, whip up, inflame, agitate, goad, provoke, spur on, urge, encourage, animate, incite.
□ **get something going** *we got the car going again after much trying*: **operate**, switch on, turn on, start, start off, start up, set going, trigger off, trigger, trip, set in motion, activate, actuate, initiate, initialize, energize, animate.
□ **go about** *Ruth went about her tasks enthusiastically*: **set about**, begin, embark on, make a start on, start, address oneself to, get down to, get to work on, get going on, undertake; approach, tackle, attack; informal get cracking on/with; formal commence.
□ **go along with** *he seemed happy enough to go along with your plans*: **agree to/with**, fall in with, comply with, concur with, cooperate with, acquiesce in, assent to, follow; submit to, bow to, yield to, defer to.
□ **go away** *just go away and leave me in peace*: **leave**, go, depart, get going, get out, be off with you, shoo; informal scram, be on your way, run along, beat it, skedaddle, split, vamoose, scat, get lost, push off, buzz off, shove off, clear off, go (and) jump in the lake; Brit. informal hop it, bog off, naff off, on your bike, get along, sling your hook; N. Amer. informal bug off, light out, haul off, haul ass, take a powder, hit the trail, take a hike; Austral. informal nick off; Austral./NZ informal rack off; S. African informal voetsak, hamba; vulgar slang bugger off, piss off, fuck off; Brit. vulgar slang sod off; literary begone, avaunt.
▷ANTONYMS return.
□ **go back on** *she went back on her promise*: **renege on**, break, fail to honour, default on, backtrack on, back out of, repudiate, retract; go back on one's word, break one's word, break one's promise, do an about-face; informal cop out (of), rat on.
▷ANTONYMS keep, honour.
□ **go by** *we have to go by the referee's decision*: **obey**, abide by, comply with, observe, keep to, conform to, follow, be guided by, heed, take as a guide; defer to, respect.
▷ANTONYMS flout.
□ **go down 1** *the ship went down in a storm*: **sink**, be submerged, founder, go under. **2** *interest rates are going down*: **decrease**, get lower, fall, drop, be reduced, decline; plummet, plunge, slump. ▷ANTONYMS rise.
3 informal *they went down 2–1 in the first leg*: **lose**, **be beaten**, be defeated, suffer defeat, be vanquished, collapse, come to grief. ▷ANTONYMS win.
4 *his name will go down in history*: **be remembered**, be recorded, be commemorated, be immortalized.
□ **go down well** *the production went down well with the audience*: **be successful**, be a success, achieve success, triumph, make an impression, have an impact, get an enthusiastic reception; informal be a hit, be a winner, be a sell-out, go down a storm, score.
□ **go down with** Brit. *she's gone down with flu*: **fall ill with**, get, develop, contract, pick up, succumb to, fall victim to, be struck down with, become infected with; informal take ill with; N. Amer. informal take sick with.
□ **go far** *you're a smart girl—you'll go far*: **be successful**, succeed, be a success, do well (for oneself), do all right for oneself, make progress, achieve a great deal, get on, get somewhere, get on in the world, get ahead, advance oneself, make good, set the world on fire; informal make a name for oneself, make it, make one's mark, find a place in the sun.
□ **go for 1** *I went for the grilled tuna*: **choose**, pick, opt for, select, plump for, take, settle on, decide on. ▷ANTONYMS reject.
2 *he lost his temper and went for her*: **attack**, assault, hit, strike, give someone a beating, beat up, assail, launch oneself at, set upon, spring at/on, rush at, let fly at, tear into, lash out at; informal lay into, rough up, let someone have it, beat the living daylights out of; Brit. informal have a go at, duff up; N. Amer. informal beat up on, light into. **3** *Philip's seeing Sarah—he goes for older women*: **be attracted to**, find attractive, like, fancy; prefer, favour,

choose, be drawn to, gravitate towards; informal have a thing about.
▷ANTONYMS dislike.
□ **go in for** *we don't normally go in for this sort of thing*: **take part in**, participate in, be a participant in, engage in, get involved in, join in, enter into, occupy oneself with, play a part in, be a party to, undertake; practise, pursue; take up, espouse, adopt, embrace.
□ **go into** *you'll need to go into the subject in greater detail*: **investigate**, examine, enquire into, look into, research, study, probe, explore, delve into, try to get to the bottom of; discuss, consider, review, analyse, weigh up.
□ **go off 1** *the bomb went off at 9.20*: **explode**, detonate, blow up, burst, erupt; informal go bang. **2** Brit. *the milk's gone off*: **go bad**, go stale, go sour, turn, spoil, go rancid; decompose, go mouldy, be rotten; be past its sell-by date.
□ **go on 1** *the lecture went on for three hours*: **last**, continue, carry on, run on, proceed; endure, persist, stay, remain; take. **2** *she went on about how much she loved the sea*: **talk at length**, ramble, rattle on, talk on and on, carry on talking, chatter, prattle, prate, gabble, maunder, blether, blather, twitter; informal gab, yak, yackety-yak, yabber, yatter, shoot one's mouth off; Brit. informal witter, rabbit, natter, waffle, chunter; N. Amer. informal run off at the mouth. **3** *I'm not sure what went on that night*: **happen**, take place, occur, transpire; N. Amer. informal go down; literary come to pass, betide, chance; rare eventuate, hap.

g

□ **go out 1** *the lights went out | the fire had gone out*: **be turned off**, be extinguished; stop burning, die out, be doused, be quenched. **2** *he's been going out with her for about two months*: **see**, take out, be someone's boyfriend/girlfriend, be romantically involved with, go around with, keep company; informal **date**, go steady with, go with; Austral. informal track square with; Brit. informal, dated walk out with; N. Amer. informal, dated step out with; dated court, woo.
□ **go over 1** *I need to go over the figures*: **examine**, study, scrutinize, inspect, read over, look at/over, scan, run over, check; analyse, consider, appraise, weigh up, review; informal give something the once-over. **2** *we spent the time going over our lines*: **rehearse**, practise, read/run through.
□ **go round 1** *the wheels were still going round*: **spin**, revolve, turn, rotate, whirl. **2** *there's a nasty rumour going round*: **be spread**, be passed round, be circulated, be put about, be in circulation, circulate, pass round, be disseminated, be broadcast.
□ **go through 1** *no one can imagine what she and the children have gone through*: **undergo**, experience, face, suffer, be subjected to, live through, endure, brave, bear, tolerate, stand, withstand, put up with, brook, cope with, weather, come in for, receive, sustain; Scottish thole. **2** *he went through hundreds of pounds of his mother's money*: **spend**, use up, run through, get through, expend, consume, exhaust, deplete; waste, fritter away, squander. **3** *he went through Susie's bag*: **search**, look through, hunt through, rummage in/through, rifle through, dig into, ferret (about/around) in, root about/around in, turn inside out; check; informal frisk, inspect; Austral./NZ informal fossick through. **4** *it took me three hours to go through the report*: **examine**, study, scrutinize, inspect, read over, look at/over, scan, run over, check; analyse, consider, appraise, weigh up, review. **5** *the deal has finally gone through*: **be completed**, be concluded, be brought to a conclusion, be carried through, be brought off, be pulled off; be approved, be signed, be rubber-stamped.
□ **go under** *over 1,000 businesses went under in the last three months*: **go bankrupt**, cease trading, go into receivership, go into liquidation, become insolvent, be liquidated, be wound up, be closed (down), be shut (down); fail; informal go broke, go to the wall, go belly up, fold.
□ **go without 1** *I decided to go without breakfast*: **abstain from**, forgo, refrain from, do without, deny oneself; give up, cut out, swear off. **2** *she tried to make sure the children did not go without*: **lack for something**, go short, go hungry, be in need, be deprived, be in want, suffer deprivation.
▶**noun 1** *his second go*: **attempt**, try, effort, bid, endeavour; informal shot, stab, crack, bash, whirl, whack; formal essay; archaic assay.
2 *he still has plenty of go in him*: **energy**, vigour, vitality, life, liveliness, animation, vivacity, spirit, spiritedness, verve, enthusiasm, zest, vibrancy, spark, sparkle, effervescence, exuberance, brio, buoyancy, perkiness, sprightliness; stamina, dynamism, drive, push, determination; informal zip, zing, pep, pizzazz, punch, bounce, fizz, oomph, get-up-and-go, vim and vigour; N. Amer. informal feistiness.
□ **have a go at** Brit. informal *his dad had had a real go at him*: **attack**, censure, criticize, denounce, condemn, arraign, find fault with, lambaste, pillory, disapprove of, carp at, cavil at, rail against, inveigh against, cast aspersions on, pour scorn on, disparage, denigrate, deprecate, malign, vilify, besmirch, run down, give a bad press to; N. Amer. slur; informal knock, pan, slam, hammer, blast, bad-mouth, nit-pick about, throw brickbats at, give flak to, lay into, lace into, pull to pieces, pull apart, pick holes in, hit out at, maul, savage, roast, skewer, crucify; Brit. informal slag off, give some stick to, slate, monster, rubbish; N. Amer. informal pummel, cut up, trash; Austral./NZ informal bag; dated rate; archaic slash, vituperate against, reprobate; rare animadvert on, objurgate, excoriate, asperse, derogate, reprehend.
□ **on the go** informal *she hardly has time to watch TV because she's always on the go*: **busy**, occupied, employed, hard at work, wrapped up; rushed off one's feet (with), hard-pressed; at work (on), on the job, absorbed in, engrossed in, immersed in, preoccupied with; active, lively, industrious, bustling, energetic, tireless; informal busy as a bee, hard at it; Brit. informal on the hop.

goad noun **1** *he applied his goad energetically to the cattle's hindquarters*: **prod**, spiked stick, spike, staff, crook, pole, rod; Indian **ankus**; archaic prick.
2 *the offer of economic help acted as a goad to political change*: **stimulus**, **incentive**, encouragement, stimulant, stimulation, inducement, fillip, impetus, impulse, spur, prod, prompt; incitement; motive, motivation; informal kick in the pants, kick up the backside, shot in the arm.
▶**verb** *the government was finally goaded into action*: **provoke**, spur, prick, sting, prod, egg on, hound, badger, incite, rouse, stir, move, stimulate, motivate, excite, inflame, work/fire up, impel, pressure, pressurize, dragoon, prompt, induce, encourage, urge, inspire.

go-ahead informal **noun** *officials have given **the go-ahead** for the scheme*: **permission**, consent, leave, licence, dispensation, warrant, clearance; authorization, assent, acquiescence, agreement, approval, seal of approval, approbation, endorsement, sanction, blessing, imprimatur, acceptance, rubber stamp, accreditation; authority, right, power, mandate; informal the thumbs up, the OK, the green light, the nod, someone's say-so; rare permit, nihil obstat.
▷ANTONYMS refusal.
▶**adjective** *this technology is now standard in go-ahead companies*: **enterprising**, resourceful, imaginative, ingenious, inventive, original, creative, innovative; progressive, pioneering, modern, liberal, advanced, forward-looking, forward-thinking, enlightened; spirited, enthusiastic, ambitious, energetic, entrepreneurial, vigorous, vital, high-powered; bold, daring, audacious, courageous, intrepid, adventurous; rising, up-and-coming, new, dynamic, avant-garde; informal go-getting.
▷ANTONYMS conservative; unambitious.

goal noun *our long-term goal is a nuclear-free world*: **aim**, objective, object, grail, holy grail, end, target, design, desire, desired result, intention, intent, plan, purpose, idea, point, object of the exercise; ambition, aspiration, wish, dream, hope; resolve; French raison d'être.

goat noun **1** *a herd of goats*: billy goat, billy, nanny goat, nanny, kid.
2 Brit. informal *he was in the mood for playing the silly goat*. See **fool**.
3 informal *Sally, just you be careful of that old goat*: **lecher**, lecherous man, lascivious man, libertine, womanizer, seducer, adulterer, pervert, debauchee, rake, roué, profligate, wanton, loose-liver, sensualist, sybarite, voluptuary, Don Juan, Casanova, Lothario, Romeo; informal lech, dirty old man, DOM, wolf, ladykiller; dated rip; formal fornicator.

Word links **goat**

caprine relating to goats
billy goat male
nanny goat female
kid young
flock, **herd**, **trip** collective noun

gobble verb *he paused only to gobble down his lunch*: **eat greedily/hungrily**, guzzle, bolt, gulp, swallow hurriedly, devour, wolf, cram, gorge (oneself) on, gorge oneself; informal tuck into, put/pack away, demolish, polish off, scoff (down), down, stuff (down), murder, shovel down, stuff one's face (with), pig oneself (on), nosh; Brit. informal gollop, shift; N. Amer. informal scarf (down/up), snarf (down/up); rare gluttonize, gourmandize, ingurgitate.
▷ANTONYMS nibble.

gobbledegook noun informal *the authority wrote him a letter full of legal gobbledegook*: **jargon**, unintelligible language, obscure language; **gibberish**, claptrap, nonsense, rubbish, balderdash, blather, blether, argle-bargle; informal mumbo-jumbo, drivel, rot, tripe, hogwash, baloney, bilge, bosh, bull, bunk, guff, eyewash, piffle, twaddle, poppycock, phooey, hooey, malarkey, dribble; Brit. informal cobblers, codswallop, cock, stuff and nonsense, double Dutch, tosh, cack; Scottish & N. English informal havers; N. Amer. informal garbage, flapdoodle, blathers, wack, bushwa, applesauce; informal, dated bunkum, tommyrot, cod, gammon, toffee; vulgar slang shit, bullshit, horseshit, crap, bollocks, balls; Austral./NZ vulgar slang bulldust.

go-between noun *an American firm acted as go-between in the transaction*: **intermediary**, middleman, agent, representative, broker, dealer, factor, liaison, liaison officer, link, linkman, linkwoman, linkperson, messenger, contact, contact man/woman/person; negotiator, honest broker, interceder, intercessor, mediator; medium.

goblet noun **wine glass**, chalice; glass, beaker, tumbler, cup; archaic stoup; Scottish archaic tass; (**goblets**) N. Amer. stemware.

goblin noun **hobgoblin**, gnome, dwarf, troll, imp, elf, sprite, brownie, fairy, pixie; Scottish **kelpie**; Irish **leprechaun**, **pooka**; archaic **bugbear**, **hob**.

god noun **1** *sacrifices were made to appease the gods*: **deity**, goddess, divine being, celestial being, supreme being, divinity, immortal; creator, demiurge; godhead; daemon, numen; Hinduism avatar.
2 *wooden gods*: **idol**, graven image, icon, golden calf, totem, talisman, fetish, mascot, juju.

Word links **god**

divine relating to gods
theology study of God
theophobia fear of God

godforsaken adjective *I realize that you are bored in this godforsaken town*: **wretched**, miserable, dreary, dismal, depressing, grim, cheerless, bleak, desolate, joyless, gloomy, uninviting, discouraging, disheartening, unpromising, hopeless, dire; **deserted**, abandoned, unfrequented, unvisited, neglected, solitary, lonely, isolated, forlorn, remote, in the back of beyond, backward; Brit. informal grotty; literary drear.
▷ANTONYMS charming; bustling.

godless adjective **1** *a godless society*: **atheistic**, unbelieving, non-believing, agnostic, sceptical, heretical, faithless, irreligious, ungodly, unholy, impious, profane; infidel, barbarian, barbarous, heathen, heathenish, idolatrous, pagan; satanic, devilish, fiendish, demonic, diabolical, infernal; rare nullifidian.
▷ANTONYMS religious.
2 *godless pleasures*: **immoral**, **wicked**, sinful, wrong, morally wrong, wrongful, evil, bad, iniquitous, corrupt, irreligious, unrighteous, sacrilegious, profane, blasphemous, impious, irreverent, criminal, nefarious, depraved, degenerate, reprobate, vice-ridden, debauched, dissolute, perverted, dissipated, intemperate, decadent, unprincipled, erring, fallen, impure, sullied, tainted; rare peccable.
▷ANTONYMS virtuous.

godlike adjective *the Titans were godlike giants who created order from chaos*: **divine**, godly, angelic, seraphic, transcendent, superhuman; spiritual, heavenly, celestial, sacred, holy, saintly, beatific, blessed; rare empyrean, deiform, deific.
▷ANTONYMS mortal.

godly adjective *the Puritans' verbal assaults on their less godly neighbours*: **religious**, devout, pious, reverent, faithful, devoted, committed, believing, God-fearing, dutiful, saintly, holy, prayerful, churchgoing, practising.
▷ANTONYMS irreligious.

godsend noun *hire purchase was a godsend to thousands of people*: **boon**, blessing, bonus, good thing, benefit, help, aid, advantage, gain, asset, privilege, luxury; windfall, bonanza, stroke of luck, piece of good fortune; informal perk, plus, plus point, pro; formal perquisite; literary benison.
▷ANTONYMS scourge.

goggle verb *they goggled at the well-stocked liquor stores*: **stare**, gape, stare open-mouthed, stare in wonder/amazement, gawk, gaze, ogle, look fixedly, look vacantly; informal rubberneck; Brit. informal gawp.
▷ANTONYMS glance; ignore.

going-over noun informal **1** *he is subjected to a comprehensive going-over in two biographies*: **examination**, inspection, exploration, investigation, probe, check, check-up; assessment, review, discussion, study, analysis, appraisal, critique; treatment, consideration, coverage, handling; informal once-over.
2 *the flat needs a going-over before you have visitors*: **clean**, wipe, sponge, mop, swab, flush, scrub, hose-down, swill, lather, soap; informal vacuum, once-over.
3 *the thugs gave him a good going-over*: **beating**, thrashing, thumping, pounding, pummelling, drubbing, slapping, smacking, hammering, hitting, striking, punching, knocking, thwacking, cuffing, buffeting, battering, boxing, mauling, pelting, lambasting; assault, attack; flaying, whipping, horsewhipping, lashing, cudgelling, clubbing, birching; corporal punishment, chastisement; N. Amer. bullwhipping; informal beating-up, duffing-up, doing-over, belting, bashing, pasting, walloping, whacking, clobbering, slugging, tanning, biffing, bopping, hiding.

goings-on plural noun *all those disturbing goings-on in soap operas*: **events**, happenings, affairs, business; behaviour, conduct; mischief, misbehaviour, misconduct, funny business, chicanery, dishonesty, deception, deceit, trickery, intrigue, skulduggery, subterfuge, machinations; informal monkey business, hanky-panky, shenanigans, carryings-on, carry-on, fooling around, playing around; Brit. informal jiggery-pokery, monkey tricks; N. Amer. informal monkeyshines; archaic knavery.

gold noun *Holland won the gold*: **gold medal**, first prize.
□ **like gold dust** *good salespeople are like gold dust*: **scarce**, **in great demand**, at a premium, hard to come by, in short supply, thin on the ground, few and far between, not to be had, rare, rare/scarce as hen's teeth; informal not to be had for love or money.

Word links **gold**

auric, **aurous** relating to gold
aur-, **chrys-** related prefixes
auriferous containing gold
aurophobia, **chrysophobia** fear of gold

golden adjective **1** *her beautiful golden hair*: **gold-coloured**, blonde, yellow, yellowish, fair, flaxen, tow-coloured; bright, gleaming, resplendent, brilliant, shining; rare aureate.
▷ANTONYMS brunette, dark.
2 *it was a golden time indeed*: **successful**, prosperous, flourishing, thriving; favourable, propitious, auspicious, providential, encouraging, lucky, fortunate; happy, joyful, delightful, glorious, precious, treasured.
▷ANTONYMS unsuccessful; unhappy.
3 *it will be a golden opportunity for us*: **excellent**, fine, superb, splendid, tremendous, special, unique, favourable, opportune, exciting, promising, bright, brilliant, rosy, full of promise, optimistic, hopeful, advantageous, profitable, valuable, fortunate, providential, auspicious, propitious.
4 *the golden girl of British tennis*: **gifted**, talented, skilful, skilled, accomplished, brilliant, expert, consummate; **popular**, admired, attractive, favourite, favoured, cherished, beloved, pet, acclaimed, applauded, praised, lauded; informal blue-eyed, crack, top-notch, ace, wizard.

gone adjective **1** *I wasn't gone long*: **away**, absent, off, out, not present, non-attending, truant; missing, lacking, unavailable; Latin in absentia; informal AWOL.
▷ANTONYMS present.
2 *those days are gone*: **past**, gone by, over, over and done with, no more, done, dead and buried, finished, completed, ended, forgotten, extinct.
▷ANTONYMS extant, here.
3 *the milk's all gone*: **used up**, consumed, exhausted, finished, spent, depleted, drained, at an end.
4 *an aunt of mine, long since gone*: **dead**, deceased, expired, departed, no more, passed on, passed away; late, lost, lamented; perished, fallen, slain, slaughtered, killed, murdered; lifeless, having breathed one's last, defunct, extinct; informal (as) dead as a doornail, six feet under, pushing up daisies, under the sod; euphemistic with God, asleep, at peace; rare demised, exanimate.
▷ANTONYMS alive.

good adjective **1** *there is always a market for a good product*: **fine**, of high quality, of a high standard, quality, superior; **satisfactory**, acceptable, adequate, in order, up to scratch, up to the mark, up to standard, up to par, competent, not bad, all right; **excellent**, superb, outstanding, magnificent, of the highest quality, of the highest standard, exceptional, marvellous, wonderful, first-rate, first-class, superlative, splendid, admirable, worthy, sterling; informal great, OK, hunky-dory, A1, ace, terrific, tremendous, smashing, fantastic, fab, top-notch, tip-top, class, awesome, magic, wicked; Brit. informal brilliant, brill, bosting; Austral. informal beaut, bonzer; Brit. informal, dated spiffing, ripping, cracking, topping, top-hole, wizard, capital, champion; N. Amer. informal, dated swell.
▷ANTONYMS bad.
2 *he is basically a good person*: **virtuous**, righteous, moral, morally correct, ethical, upright, upstanding, high-minded, right-minded, right-thinking, principled, exemplary, clean, law-abiding, lawful, irreproachable, blameless, guiltless, unimpeachable, just, honest, honourable, unbribable, incorruptible; scrupulous, reputable, decent, respectable, noble, lofty, elevated, worthy, trustworthy, meritorious, praiseworthy, commendable, admirable, laudable; pure, pure as the driven snow, whiter than white, sinless, saintly, saintlike, godly, angelic; informal squeaky clean.
▷ANTONYMS wicked.
3 *the children are good with most of their teachers*: **well behaved**, **obedient**, dutiful, well mannered, well brought up, polite, civil, courteous, respectful, deferential, manageable, compliant, acquiescent, tractable, malleable.
▷ANTONYMS naughty.
4 *it was a good thing to do*: **right**, correct, proper, decorous, seemly; appropriate, fitting, apt, suitable; convenient, expedient, favourable, auspicious, propitious, opportune, felicitous, timely, well judged, well timed; archaic meet, seasonable.
5 *she's a good driver | that was good work*: **capable**, able, proficient, adept, adroit, accomplished, seasoned, skilful, skilled, gifted, talented, masterly, virtuoso, expert, knowledgeable, qualified, trained; informal great, mean, wicked, deadly, nifty, crack, ace, wizard, magic; N. Amer. informal crackerjack; vulgar slang shit-hot.
6 *he's been a good friend to me*: **reliable**, dependable, trustworthy, true, tried and true, faithful, devoted, steady, steadfast, staunch, unswerving, unwavering, constant, loyal, trusty, dutiful, dedicated, committed, unfailing.
7 *the dogs look in good condition*: **healthy**, fine, sound, tip-top, hale, hale and hearty, hearty, lusty, fit, robust, sturdy, strong, vigorous.
▷ANTONYMS poor; ill; diseased.
8 *that was a good party*: **enjoyable**, pleasant, agreeable, pleasing, pleasurable, delightful, great, nice, lovely, amusing, diverting, jolly, merry, lively, festive, cheerful, convivial, congenial, sociable; informal super, fantastic, fabulous, fab, terrific, glorious, grand, magic, out of this world, cool; Brit. informal brilliant, brill, smashing; N. Amer. informal peachy, neat, ducky; Austral./NZ informal beaut, bonzer; Brit. informal, dated capital, wizard, corking, spiffing, ripping, top-hole, topping, champion, beezer; N. Amer. informal, dated swell; rare frabjous.
▷ANTONYMS terrible.
9 *it was good of you to come*: **kind**, kindly, kind-hearted, good-hearted,

g

g

friendly, obliging, generous, charitable, magnanimous, gracious, sympathetic, benevolent, benign, altruistic, unselfish, selfless.
▷ANTONYMS unkind.
10 *tomorrow would be a good time to call*: **convenient**, suitable, appropriate, fitting, fit, suited, agreeable; **opportune**, timely, well timed, favourable, advantageous, expedient, felicitous, propitious, auspicious, happy, providential; archaic commodious, seasonable.
▷ANTONYMS inconvenient.
11 *milk is good for you*: **wholesome**, health-giving, healthful, healthy, nourishing, nutritious, nutritional, strengthening, beneficial, salubrious, salutary.
▷ANTONYMS bad.
12 *are these eggs still good?* **edible**, safe to eat, fit to eat, fit to be eaten, fit for human consumption; fresh, wholesome, consumable, comestible.
▷ANTONYMS bad.
13 *the restaurant provided good food*: **delicious**, mouth-watering, appetizing, tasty, flavoursome, flavourful, delectable, toothsome, inviting, enjoyable, palatable; succulent, luscious, rich, sweet; savoury, piquant; informal scrumptious, delish, scrummy, yummy, yum-yum; Brit. informal moreish; N. Amer. informal finger-licking, nummy; literary ambrosial; rare ambrosian, nectareous, nectarean, flavorous, sapid.
▷ANTONYMS bad.
14 *give me one good reason why I should go*: **valid**, genuine, authentic, legitimate, sound, bona fide; **convincing**, persuasive, forceful, striking, telling, potent, powerful, strong, cogent, compelling; trenchant, weighty, important, meaningful, influential.
▷ANTONYMS bad.
15 *we had to wait a good hour*: **whole**, full, entire, complete, solid, not less than, at least.
16 *a good number of them lost their lives*: **considerable**, sizeable, substantial, appreciable, significant; goodly, tolerable, fair, reasonable, tidy, hefty; ample, plentiful, abundant, superabundant, great, large, lavish, profuse, generous; marked, noticeable; informal not to be sneezed at, OK; literary plenteous.
▷ANTONYMS small.
17 *this is something you would only tell a good friend*: **close**, intimate, dear, bosom; close-knit, inseparable, attached, loving, devoted, faithful, constant; special, best, fast, firm, valued, treasured, cherished.
▷ANTONYMS distant.
18 *don't you go getting your good clothes grubby*: **best**, finest, newest, nice, nicest, smart, smartest, special, party, Sunday, formal; informal dressy.
▷ANTONYMS casual; scruffy.
19 *good weather*: **fine**, fair, dry; bright, clear, sunny, sunshiny, cloudless, unclouded, without a cloud in the sky; calm, windless, tranquil; warm, mild, balmy, summery, clement; agreeable, pleasant, nice, benign.
□ **in good part** *luckily the police* **took** *the joke* **in good part**: **good-naturedly**, good-humouredly, without offence, amicably, favourably, with forbearance, patiently, tolerantly, indulgently, cheerfully, well; not be offended by, not take offence at, not be upset by, not be bothered by, not disapprove of, not resent, not mind, take kindly to.
□ **make good** *the working-class boy who made good*: **succeed**, achieve success, be successful, be a success, do well, get ahead, reach the top, become famous, achieve recognition, distinguish oneself, set the world on fire; prosper, flourish, thrive, advance; Brit. set the Thames on fire; informal make it, make the grade, cut it, crack it, make a name for oneself, make one's mark, get somewhere, arrive, do all right for oneself, bring home the bacon, find a place in the sun.
▷ANTONYMS fail.
□ **make something good 1** *he promised to make good any damage*: **repair**, mend, fix, patch up, put right, set right, put to rights, see to; restore, remedy, rectify, put back into its original condition, make as good as new; rebuild, reconstruct, remodel, refit, refurbish, recondition; N. English fettle. **2** *they made good their escape*: **effect**, conduct, perform, implement, execute, carry out, perpetrate; **achieve**, accomplish, succeed in, realize, attain, manage, engineer, bring about, bring off, carry off, carry through; rare effectuate. **3** *they hope he will make good his promise of payment*: **fulfil**, carry out, carry through, implement, execute, effect, discharge, perform, honour, redeem; keep, observe, abide by, comply with, obey, respect, conform to, stick to, act in accordance with, act according to, have regard to, heed, follow, pay attention to, defer to, take notice of, be bound by, keep faith with, live up to, stand by, adhere to.
▶ **noun 1** *complex issues of good and evil*: **virtue**, **righteousness**, virtuousness, goodness, morality, ethicalness, uprightness, upstandingness, integrity, principle, dignity, rectitude, rightness; honesty, truth, truthfulness, honour, incorruptibility, probity, propriety, worthiness, worth, merit; irreproachableness, blamelessness, purity, pureness, lack of corruption, justice, justness, fairness.
▷ANTONYMS wickedness.
2 *don't worry, it's all for your good*: **benefit**, advantage, profit, gain, interest, welfare, well-being, enjoyment, satisfaction, comfort, ease, convenience; help, aid, assistance, use, usefulness, avail, service, behalf.
▷ANTONYMS disadvantage.
□ **for good** *those bad old days are gone for good*: **forever**, permanently, for always, for good and all, perpetually, eternally, (for) evermore, for ever and ever, for all (future) time, until/to the end of time, world without end, endlessly, timelessly, for eternity, in perpetuity, everlastingly, enduringly, never to return; Scottish aye; N. Amer. forevermore; informal for keeps, until hell freezes over, until doomsday, until the cows come home; archaic for aye; rare immortally, deathlessly, imperishably, abidingly, sempiternally, perdurably.
▷ANTONYMS temporarily.
▶ **exclamation** *good, that's settled*: **fine**, very well, all right, right, right then, right you are, yes, agreed; informal okay, OK, oke, okey-dokey, okey-doke, wilco, roger; Brit. informal righto, righty-ho; Indian informal acha.

goodbye **exclamation** *goodbye, safe journey!* **farewell**, adieu; Austral./NZ hooray; S. African check you; French au revoir; Italian ciao; German auf Wiedersehen; Spanish adios; Japanese sayonara; Latin vale; informal bye, bye-bye, so long, see you, see you later, catch you later; Brit. informal cheers, cheerio, ta-ta; N. English informal ta-ra; N. Amer. informal later, laters; informal, dated toodle-oo, toodle-pip, pip pip.
▷ANTONYMS hello.

good-for-nothing **adjective** *a good-for-nothing layabout*: **useless**, worthless, incompetent, inefficient, inept, ne'er-do-well; lazy, idle, slothful, indolent, shiftless, spiritless, apathetic, aimless, unambitious, unenterprising; informal no-good, no-account, lousy.
▷ANTONYMS worthy.
▶ **noun** *he considered the workers lazy good-for-nothings*: **ne'er-do-well**, layabout, do-nothing, idler, loafer, slob, lounger, sluggard, laggard, slugabed, malingerer, shirker; informal skiver, waster, slacker, lazybones, lead-swinger, couch potato; Brit. informal scrimshanker; archaic wastrel; French, archaic fainéant.

good-humoured **adjective** *he was too good-humoured to be offended*: **genial**, friendly, affable, cordial, congenial, amiable, warm, easy-going, approachable, sympathetic, well disposed, good-natured, cheerful, cheery, neighbourly, hospitable, companionable, comradely, bluff, easy to get along with; sociable, convivial, outgoing, extrovert, extroverted, gregarious, company-loving, hail-fellow-well-met; informal chummy, pally; Brit. informal matey; N. Amer. informal buddy-buddy, clubby, regular.
▷ANTONYMS grumpy.

good-looking **adjective** *she was still good-looking without her make-up*: **attractive**, nice-looking, beautiful, pretty, as pretty as a picture, handsome, lovely, stunning, striking, arresting, gorgeous, prepossessing, winning, fetching, captivating, bewitching, beguiling, engaging, charming, charismatic, enchanting, appealing, delightful, irresistible; sexy, sexually attractive, sexual, seductive, alluring, tantalizing, ravishing, desirable, sultry, sensuous, sensual, erotic, arousing, luscious, lush, nubile; Scottish & N. English bonny; informal fanciable, beddable, tasty, hot, smashing, knockout, drop-dead gorgeous, out of this world, easy on the eye, come-hither, come-to-bed; Brit. informal fit; N. Amer. informal cute, foxy, bootylicious; Austral./NZ informal spunky; literary beauteous; dated taking, well favoured; archaic comely, fair; rare sightly, pulchritudinous.
▷ANTONYMS ugly.

goodly **adjective** *£1500 is a goodly sum*: **fairly large**, sizeable, substantial, considerable, not inconsiderable, respectable, significant, largish, biggish, decent, decent-sized, generous, handsome; Scottish & N. English bonny; informal tidy, not to be sneezed at, serious.
▷ANTONYMS paltry.

good-natured **adjective** *the crowd was rowdy but good-natured*: **warm-hearted**, friendly, amiable; neighbourly, benevolent, well disposed, favourably disposed, kind, kindly, kind-hearted, generous, magnanimous, unselfish, considerate, thoughtful, obliging, helpful, supportive, charitable; understanding, sympathetic, lenient, tolerant, easy-going, patient, accommodating; Brit. informal decent.
▷ANTONYMS malicious.

goodness **noun 1** *he was a dangerous criminal, but he had some goodness in him*: **virtue**, virtuousness, good, righteousness, morality, ethicalness, uprightness, upstandingness, integrity, principle, dignity, rectitude, rightness; honesty, truth, truthfulness, honourableness, honourability, honour, incorruptibility, probity, propriety, decency, respectability, nobility, nobility of soul/spirit, nobleness, worthiness, worth, merit, trustworthiness, meritoriousness, irreproachableness, blamelessness, purity, pureness, lack of corruption; justice, justness, fairness, equity, equitableness, impartiality, lawfulness, legality.
▷ANTONYMS wickedness.
2 *his goodness towards us*: **kindness**, kindliness, kind-heartedness, warm-heartedness, tender-heartedness, humaneness, humanity, mildness, benevolence, benignity, tenderness, warmth, motherliness, fatherliness, affection, lovingness, love, goodwill; sympathy, compassion, care, concern, understanding, tolerance, patience, indulgence, generosity, charity, charitableness, leniency, clemency, forbearance, magnanimity; helpfulness, considerateness, thoughtfulness, consideration, niceness, courtesy, politeness, decency, graciousness, neighbourliness, pleasantness, public-spiritedness, friendliness, geniality, congeniality, amiability, cordiality.
▷ANTONYMS meanness.

3 *slow cooking can help to retain the goodness of the food*: **nutritional value**, nutrition, nutrients, wholesomeness, nourishment; rare nutriment.

goods plural noun **1** *the manufacturer then dispatches the goods to a wholesaler*: **merchandise**, wares, stock, commodities, line, lot, produce, products, articles; imports, exports; rare vendibles.
2 *they had to dispose of the dead man's goods*: **property**, possessions, personal possessions, personal effects, effects, worldly goods, chattels, goods and chattels, valuables, accoutrements, appurtenances, paraphernalia, trappings; informal things, stuff, junk, gear, kit, rubbish, bits and pieces, bits and bobs; Brit. informal clobber, gubbins; vulgar slang shit, crap.
3 Brit. *most goods went by train*: **freight**, cargo; load, haul, consignment, delivery, shipment; archaic lading; rare freightage.

good-tempered adjective *he remained good-tempered in spite of being in such demand*: **equable**, even-tempered, imperturbable, unexcitable; unruffled, unperturbed, unflustered, undisturbed, unagitated, untroubled, well balanced; easy-going, calm, relaxed, composed, collected, self-possessed, cool, {cool, calm, and collected}, at ease, as cool as a cucumber; nonchalant, insouciant, blithe, mellow, mild; serene, tranquil, placid, steady, stable, quiet, level-headed; informal unflappable, unfazed, together, laid-back; rare equanimous.
▷ANTONYMS excitable.

goodwill noun *the UN is dependent on the goodwill of its most powerful members*: **benevolence**, compassion, kind-heartedness, big-heartedness, goodness, kindness, kindliness, consideration, charity; cooperation, collaboration, friendliness, thoughtfulness, decency, amity, sympathy, understanding, amenability, neighbourliness, mutual support.
▷ANTONYMS hostility.

goody-goody adjective informal *the goody-goody prefects will probably tell the headmistress*: **self-righteous**, sanctimonious, pious; **prim and proper**, prim, proper, strait-laced, prudish, priggish, puritanical, moralistic, prissy, mimsy, niminy-piminy, shockable, Victorian, old-maidish, schoolmistressy, schoolmarmish, governessy; informal starchy, square, fuddy-duddy, stick-in-the-mud; rare Grundyish, Pecksniffian.

gooey adjective informal **1** *he wiped off the gooey mess with towels*. See **sticky** (sense 2).
2 *Mrs McSpadden got all gooey over young Kenneth*. See **sentimental** (sense 2).

goose noun

Word links **goose**

gander male
goose female
gosling young
gaggle (on land), **skein/team/wedge (in flight)** collective noun
anserine relating to geese

gore[1] noun *the film's gratuitous gore*: **blood**, bloodiness; bloodshed, slaughter, carnage, butchery; rare cruor, grume.

gore[2] verb *he was gored in the leg by the bull*: **pierce**, stab, stick, impale, puncture, penetrate, spear, spit, horn.

gorge noun *here the river rushes through a gorge*: **ravine**, canyon, gully, pass, defile, couloir, deep narrow valley; chasm, abyss, gulf; S. English chine, bunny; N. English clough, gill, thrutch; Scottish cleuch, heugh; N. Amer. gulch, coulee, flume; American Spanish arroyo, barranca, quebrada; Indian nullah, khud; S. African sloot, kloof, donga; rare khor.
▸ verb **1** *they gorged themselves on Cornish cream teas*: **stuff**, cram, fill; glut, satiate, sate, surfeit, overindulge, overfill, overeat; informal pig.
2 *huge carrion birds* **gorged on** *the flesh*: **eat greedily/hungrily**, guzzle, gobble, bolt, gulp (down), swallow hurriedly, devour, wolf, cram; informal tuck into, put/pack away, demolish, polish off, scoff (down), down, stuff (down), murder, shovel down, stuff one's face (with), nosh; Brit. informal gollop, shift; N. Amer. informal scarf (down/up), snarf (down/up), inhale; rare raven, gluttonize, gourmandize, ingurgitate.
▷ANTONYMS nibble.

gorgeous adjective **1** *a simply gorgeous man*: **good-looking**, attractive, nice-looking, handsome, lovely, beautiful, pretty, as pretty as a picture, stunning, striking, arresting, prepossessing, winning, fetching, captivating, bewitching, beguiling, engaging, charming, charismatic, enchanting, appealing, delightful, irresistible; sexy, sexually attractive, sexual, seductive, alluring, tantalizing, ravishing, desirable, sultry, sensuous, sensual, erotic, arousing, luscious, lush, nubile; Scottish & N. English bonny; informal fanciable, beddable, tasty, studly, hot, smashing, knockout, out of this world, easy on the eye, come-hither, come-to-bed; Brit. informal fit; N. Amer. informal cute, foxy, bootylicious; Austral./NZ informal spunky; literary beauteous; dated taking, well favoured; archaic comely, fair; rare sightly, pulchritudinous.
▷ANTONYMS ugly.
2 *a little restaurant with gorgeous views across the valley*: **spectacular**, splendid, superb, wonderful, grand, impressive, awe-inspiring, awesome, astounding, astonishing, amazing, stunning, breathtaking, stupendous, incredible; informal sensational, out of this world, fabulous, fantastic; literary wondrous.
▷ANTONYMS uninteresting.
3 *gorgeous uniforms of scarlet and gold*: **resplendent**, magnificent, stately, imposing, sumptuous, luxurious, elegant, opulent, dazzling, brilliant, glittering.
▷ANTONYMS drab.
4 informal *gorgeous weather*: **excellent**, marvellous, superb, very good, first-rate, first-class, wonderful, delightful, outstanding, exceptional, magnificent, splendid, superlative, matchless, peerless; informal great, glorious, terrific, tremendous, smashing, fantastic, sensational, fabulous, ace, fab, A1, cool, awesome, magic, wicked, tip-top, top-notch, out of sight, out of this world, way-out, capital; Brit. informal brilliant, brill; Austral./NZ informal bonzer; Brit. informal, dated spiffing, topping, top-hole, wizard.
▷ANTONYMS terrible.

gorilla noun

Word links **gorilla**

silverback mature male mountain gorilla
band collective noun

gory adjective **1** *the ritual slaughter is a gory ceremony*: **grisly**, gruesome, violent, bloodthirsty, bloody, brutal, savage; ghastly, frightful, horrid, horrifying, fearful, hideous, macabre, spine-chilling, horrible, horrendous, grim, awful, dire, dreadful, terrible, horrific; disgusting, repulsive, repugnant, revolting, repellent, sickening, distressing, shocking, appalling, abominable, loathsome, abhorrent, odious, monstrous, unspeakable; informal blood-and-thunder, blood-and-guts, sick, sick-making, gut-churning, gross; archaic sanguinary, disgustful, loathly.
▷ANTONYMS charming; uplifting.
2 *gory pieces of human skin and bone*: **bloody**, bloodstained, bloodsoaked, blood-spattered.

gospel noun **1** (**the gospel**) *the Gospel was spread informally by missionaries*: **Christian teaching**, Christ's teaching, the life of Christ, the word of God, the good news, Christian doctrine, the New Testament, the writings of the evangelists.
2 *one should not treat any historical document as gospel*: **the truth**, the whole truth, the naked truth, gospel truth, God's truth, the honest truth; fact, actual fact, what actually/really happened, reality, actuality, factuality, the case, so, verity, a certainty.
▷ANTONYMS a lie.
3 *the Dalai Lama's gospel of non-violence*: **doctrine**, dogma, teaching, principle, ethic, creed, credo, theory, thesis, ideology, idea, ideal, position; belief, tenet, canon, conviction, persuasion, opinion.

gossamer noun *her dress swirled like gossamer*: **cobweb**, spider's web; silk, silky substance, Japanese silk, gauze, tissue, chiffon; thistledown, down, feather.
▸ adjective *beautiful ladies in gossamer veils*: **ultra-fine**, fine, diaphanous, gauzy, gauzelike, gossamer-thin, gossamer-like, gossamery, delicate, filmy, floaty, chiffony, cobwebby, feathery, silky, silken, wispy, thin, light, lightweight, insubstantial, papery, flimsy, frail; translucent, transparent, see-through, sheer; rare transpicuous, translucid.
▷ANTONYMS heavy; opaque.

gossip noun **1** *tell me all the gossip about the new tenants*: **tittle-tattle**, tattle, rumour(s), whispers, stories, tales, canards, titbits; idle talk, scandal, hearsay; malicious gossip, whispering campaign, smear campaign; French bavardage, on dit; German Kaffeeklatsch; W. Indian labrish, shu-shu; informal dirt, buzz, mud-slinging; Brit. informal goss; N. Amer. informal scuttlebutt; S. African informal skinder; rare bruit.
▷ANTONYMS facts, the truth.
2 *they then adjourn to the pub for a glass and a gossip*: **chat**, talk, conversation, chatter, heart-to-heart, tête-à-tête, powwow, blether, blather; conference, discussion, dialogue, exchange; Indian adda; informal chit-chat, jaw, gas, confab, goss; Brit. informal natter, chinwag, rabbit; Scottish & N. English informal crack; N. Amer. informal rap, bull session, gabfest; Austral./NZ informal mag, yarn; rare confabulation, colloquy.
3 *Myra is a dear, but she's also a gossip*: **scandalmonger**, gossipmonger, tattler, tittle-tattler, busybody, muckraker; informal bad-mouth, bad-mouther; rare quidnunc, calumniator.
▸ verb **1** *she had gossiped about his wife's illness*: **spread rumours**, spread gossip, circulate rumours, spread stories, tittle-tattle, tattle, talk, whisper, tell tales, muckrake; informal dish the dirt; S. African informal skinder; literary bruit something abroad/about.
2 *people sat around gossiping as they drank*: **chat**, talk, converse, speak to each other, discuss things, have a talk, have a chat, have a tête-à-tête, have a conversation, engage in conversation; informal gas, have a confab, chew the fat/rag, jaw, rap, yak, yap; Brit. informal natter, have a chinwag, chinwag; N. Amer. informal shoot the breeze, shoot the bull, visit; Austral./NZ informal mag; formal confabulate.

gouge verb *a tunnel had been gouged out of the mountain*: **scoop out**, burrow (out), hollow out, excavate; cut (out), hack (out), chisel (out), dig (out), scrape (out), claw (out), scratch (out); literary delve.

gourmand noun *gourmands who care more for quantity than quality*: **glutton**, gourmandizer, overeater, big/good eater, (good) trencherman, (good) trencherwoman; informal pig, greedy pig, hog, gannet, greedy guts, gutbucket, human dustbin, gobbler, guzzler; N. Amer. informal chowhound.

gourmet noun *even the most demanding gourmets adore the restaurants on Lake Como*: **gastronome**, epicure, epicurean; connoisseur; French bon vivant, bon viveur; informal foodie.

govern verb **1** *the Conservative Party governed the province for the next five years*: **rule**, preside over, be in power over, reign over, control, exercise control over, have control of, be in control of, be in charge of, command, hold sway over, lead, be the leader of, dominate, run, head, direct, administer, order, manage, regulate, guide, conduct, oversee, supervise, superintend, be at the helm of, steer, pilot; informal be in the driving seat; literary sway.
2 *the rules governing social behaviour*: **determine**, decide, control, regulate, direct, rule, dictate, condition, form, shape; affect, have an effect on, influence, exert influence on, be a factor in, sway, act on, work on, mould, modify, alter, touch, have an impact on, impact on.
3 *Maria made a fresh effort to govern her feelings*: **control**, restrain, keep in check, check, curb, hold back, keep back, bridle, rein in, keep a tight rein on, subdue, constrain, contain.

g

governess noun **tutor**, instructress, duenna; French Mademoiselle; archaic tutoress, tutress, tutrice, tutrix.

government noun **1** *the government has announced defence cuts of a billion pounds*: **administration**, executive, regime, authority, powers that be, directorate, council, leadership, management; cabinet, ministry; rule, term of office, incumbency; informal top brass.
2 *the executive council was to assist him in the government of the country*: **rule**, running, direction, administration, leadership, leading, control, regulation, guidance, guiding, management, conduct, supervision, superintendence, steering.

governor noun *the governor of the province | a prison governor*: **administrator**, ruler, chief, leader, principal, head; premier, president, viceroy, chancellor; manager, director, chairman, chairwoman, chairperson, chair, superintendent, supervisor, commissioner, controller, master, warden, overseer, organizer; member of the board; informal boss.

Word links **governor**

gubernatorial relating to a governor

gown noun **dress**, frock, shift, robe; garment, costume.

grab verb **1** *Doreen grabbed his arm, swinging him round*: **seize**, grasp, snatch, seize hold of, grab hold of, take hold of, catch hold of, lay hold of, lay (one's) hands on, get one's hands on, take a grip of, fasten round, grapple, grip, clasp, clutch; catch at, take, pluck; informal collar.
▷ANTONYMS release.
2 informal *Clint Eastwood grabbed a fistful of awards last night*: **obtain**, acquire, come by, carry off, come to have, get, receive, gain, earn, win, come into, come in for, take possession of, take receipt of, be given; buy, purchase, procure, possess oneself of, secure, snap up; gather, collect, pick up, appropriate, amass, build up, hook, net, land; achieve, attain; informal get/lay one's hands on, get one's mitts on, get hold of, bag, score, swing, nab, collar, pull down, cop; Brit. informal blag.
▶ noun *she made a* ***grab for*** *his gun*: **lunge for**, attempt to grab.
□ **up for grabs** informal *dozens of prizes are up for grabs*: **available**, obtainable, to be had, there for the taking; up for sale, on the market, waiting to be bought; untaken, unengaged; informal yours for the asking, on tap, gettable.

grace noun **1** *she has the natural grace of a ballerina*: **elegance**, stylishness, poise, finesse, charm; gracefulness, dexterity, adroitness; deftness, fluidity of movement, fluency, flow, suppleness, smoothness, ease, effortlessness, naturalness, neatness, precision, agility, nimbleness, light-footedness; informal poetry in motion; rare flowingness, lightsomeness.
▷ANTONYMS stiffness, inelegance.
2 *he at least had the grace to look sheepish*: **courtesy**, courteousness, politeness, manners, good manners, mannerliness, civility, decorum, decency, propriety, breeding, respect, respectfulness; consideration, thought, thoughtfulness, tact, tactfulness, diplomacy, etiquette.
▷ANTONYMS effrontery.
3 *Americans found it hard to see another president fall from grace*: **favour**, approval, approbation, acceptance, commendation, esteem, regard, respect, preferment, liking, support, goodwill.
▷ANTONYMS disfavour.
4 *he was granted a house by grace of the king*: **favour**, good will, generosity, kindness, benefaction, beneficence, indulgence.
5 *they have been given five days' grace to decide*: **deferment**, deferral, postponement, suspension, putting off/back, adjournment, delay, shelving, rescheduling, interruption, arrest, pause; respite, stay, moratorium, reprieve; N. Amer. tabling; N. Amer. Law continuation; rare put-off.
6 *say grace*: **prayer of thanks**, thanksgiving, blessing, benediction.
□ **with good grace** *we accept the decision with good grace*: **willingly**, without hesitation, unhesitatingly, gladly, happily, cheerfully, with pleasure, without reluctance, ungrudgingly, voluntarily; eagerly, promptly, quickly.
▶ verb **1** *the occasion was graced by the presence of Lady Thomson*: **dignify**, distinguish, add distinction to, add dignity to, honour, bestow honour on, favour, enhance, add lustre to, magnify, ennoble, glorify, elevate, make lofty, aggrandize, upgrade.
2 *the dolphin fresco may originally have graced the floor of an upper chamber*: **adorn**, embellish, decorate, furnish, ornament, add ornament to, enhance; beautify, prettify, enrich, bedeck, deck (out), garnish, emblazon, gild, set off; informal get up, do up, do out; literary bejewel, bedizen, caparison, furbelow.

graceful adjective **1** *her simple, graceful clothes have won legions of devotees*: **elegant**, stylish, tasteful, refined, sophisticated, dignified, distinguished, discerning, with good taste, poised; fashionable, cultured, cultivated, beautiful, attractive, appealing, lovely, comely; charming, polished, suave, urbane, dashing; luxurious, sumptuous, opulent, grand, plush, exquisite; informal swanky.
▷ANTONYMS inelegant.
2 *graceful dancers*: **fluid**, fluent, flowing, supple, smooth, easy, effortless, natural, elegant, stylish, neat, precise, agile, nimble, light-footed, deft, dexterous, adroit.
▷ANTONYMS stiff; ungainly.

graceless adjective *a loud, graceless teenager*: **gauche**, maladroit, inept, socially awkward, socially inept, socially unsure, lacking in social graces, unpolished, unsophisticated, uncultured, uncultivated, unrefined; **clumsy**, awkward, ungainly, ungraceful, inelegant, uncoordinated, gawky, gangling, bumbling, blundering, lumbering; tactless, thoughtless, inconsiderate; inexperienced, raw, uneducated, unworldly; nervous, shy, bashful; Brit. nervy; informal cack-handed, ham-fisted, ham-handed, butterfingered.
▷ANTONYMS graceful; sophisticated.

gracious adjective **1** *she was ever the gracious hostess*: **courteous**, polite, civil, chivalrous, well mannered, decorous, gentlemanly, ladylike, civilized, tactful, diplomatic; **kind**, kindly, kind-hearted, warm-hearted, benevolent, considerate, thoughtful, obliging, accommodating, charitable, indulgent, magnanimous, beneficent, benign; **friendly**, pleasant, amiable, affable, cordial, hospitable; informal couth; Brit. informal decent; dated mannerly.
▷ANTONYMS ungracious.
2 *tree-lined avenues with gracious colonial buildings*: **elegant**, stylish, tasteful, graceful, comfortable, luxurious, sumptuous, opulent, grand, plush, high-class, exquisite, smart, sophisticated, fashionable, modish, chic; informal swanky.
▷ANTONYMS homely.
3 *God's gracious intervention*: **merciful**, forgiving, compassionate, kind, kindly, lenient, clement, pitying, forbearing, humane, mild, soft-hearted, tender-hearted, sympathetic; patient, humanitarian, liberal, easy-going, permissive, tolerant, indulgent, generous, magnanimous, beneficent, benign, benignant, benevolent.
▷ANTONYMS cruel.

Word toolkit

gracious	elegant	stylish
host/hostess	style	clothes
smile	simplicity	shoes
hospitality	design	production
manners	dining	leather
gesture	dress	apartment
winner	room	decor
concession	home	sunglasses
reception	hotel	furniture

gradation noun **1** *within the woodpecker family there is a gradation of drilling ability*: **range**, scale, gamut, spectrum, sweep, compass, span; progression, sequence, succession, series; variety; hierarchy, ladder, ranking, pecking order.
2 *each of the bands has a number of gradations within it*: **level**, rank, position, standing, status, station, degree, grade, stage, standard, echelon, rung, point, mark, step, notch; class, stratum, group, grouping, set, classification.

grade noun **1** *hotels within the same grade*: **category**, class, classification, grouping, group, set, section, bracket, division, type, brand.
2 *they appointed him to the lowest grade*: **rank**, level, echelon, standing, station, position, placing, class, status, order; stage, step, rung, rung on the ladder, notch, stratum, tier; degree of proficiency, degree of quality, degree of merit.
3 N. Amer. *they got the best grades in the school*: **mark**, score, grading, assessment, evaluation, appraisal.
4 N. Amer. *a kid in the fifth grade*: **class**, form, study group, school group, set, stream, band; year.

5 N. Amer. *roads on steep grades*: **slope**, gradient, incline, acclivity, declivity, tilt, angle; hill, rise, bank, ramp.

□ **make the grade** informal *he lacked the experience to make the grade*: **come up to standard**, come up to scratch, qualify, pass, pass muster, measure up, measure up to expectation; succeed, be successful, come through, come through with flying colours, win through, get through; informal be up to snuff, cut it, cut the mustard, crack it.

▷ANTONYMS fail.

▶ **verb 1** *the weights were graded in the box by size*: **classify**, class, categorize, bracket, sort, group, order, arrange, type, pigeonhole, brand, size; rank, evaluate, rate, value, range, graduate, calibrate.

2 N. Amer. *children should be told how they have been graded*: **assess**, mark, score, judge, evaluate, appraise.

3 *all these categories grade into one another*: **pass**, shade, change, merge, blend, transmute, turn.

gradient **noun 1** *the road was on a steep gradient*: **slope**, incline, hill, rise, rising ground, bank, ramp, acclivity; drop, descent, declivity; N. Amer. grade.

2 *the gradient of the line*: **steepness**, angle, slant, slope, inclination, leaning.

gradual **adjective 1** *the gradual transition from military to civilian rule*: **slow**, moderate, measured, unhurried, restrained, cautious, circumspect, unspectacular; piecemeal, step by step, little by little, bit by bit; progressive, successive, continuous, systematic; regular, steady, even, consistent, uniform; informal softly-softly.

▷ANTONYMS sudden; abrupt.

2 *a gradual slope*: **gentle**, not steep, moderate, slight, easy, subtle, imperceptible.

▷ANTONYMS steep.

gradually **adverb** *you can begin to introduce new ideas gradually*: **slowly**, moderately, unhurriedly, cautiously, gently, gingerly, circumspectly, unspectacularly; piecemeal, step by step, little by little, bit by bit, inch by inch, piece by piece, drop by drop, by degrees; progressively, successively, continuously, systematically, slowly but surely; regularly, steadily, evenly, constantly, consistently, uniformly, at a regular pace; rare inchmeal, gradatim.

▷ANTONYMS suddenly, abruptly.

graduate **noun** *we need to recruit more graduates*: **degree-holder**, person with a degree; Bachelor of Arts, BA, Bachelor of Science, BSc, Master of Arts, MA, Master of Science, MSc, doctor, PhD, DPhil.

▶ **verb 1** *he wants to be a teacher when he graduates*: **qualify**, pass one's exams, pass, be certified, be licensed; take an academic degree, receive/get one's degree, become a graduate, complete one's studies.

2 *she wants to graduate to serious emotional drama*: **progress**, advance, move up, go up, proceed, develop; gain promotion, be promoted.

▷ANTONYMS regress; be demoted.

3 *a proposal to graduate income tax*: **arrange in a series**, arrange in order, order, group, classify, class, categorize, rank, grade, range.

4 *the thermometer was graduated in Fahrenheit*: **calibrate**, mark off, measure off/out, divide into degrees, grade.

graft[1] **noun 1** *such grafts may die from lack of water*: **scion**, cutting, shoot, offshoot, bud, slip, new growth, sprout, sprig.

2 *she had a skin graft*: **transplant**, implant, implantation.

▶ **verb 1** *they graft on a bud higher up the stem*: **affix**, slip, join, insert, splice; rare engraft.

2 *a technique in which living tissue is grafted on to the patient's cornea*: **transplant**, implant, transfer.

3 *a Victorian mansion grafted on to a seventeenth-century farmhouse*: **fasten**, attach, add, fix, join, insert.

graft[2] Brit. informal **noun** *he earned success through hard graft*: **work**, effort, endeavour, toil, labour, exertion, the sweat of one's brow, drudgery, donkey work; perseverance, persistence; informal slog; Austral./NZ informal yakka.

▶ **verb** *the players are not frightened to graft for each other*: **work hard**, exert oneself, toil, labour, hammer away, grind away, sweat; plod away, slave away, work like a Trojan, work like a dog, keep one's nose to the grindstone; persevere, persist, keep at it, stick with it; informal slog away, plug away, beaver away, put one's back into something, work one's socks off, work one's guts out, sweat blood, kill oneself; Brit. informal get one's head down; Brit. vulgar slang work one's balls/arse/nuts off; N. Amer. vulgar slang work one's ass/butt off; archaic drudge, travail, moil.

graft[3] **noun** *the new president has started a campaign against graft*: **corruption**, bribery, bribing, dishonesty, deceit, fraud, fraudulence, subornation, unlawful practices, illegal means, underhand means; N. Amer. payola; informal palm-greasing, back-scratching, hush money, kickback, crookedness, shadiness, shady business, dirty tricks, dirty dealings, wheeling and dealing, sharp practices.

▷ANTONYMS honesty.

grain **noun 1** *it's uneconomical for local farmers to grow grain*: **cereal**, cereal crops.

2 *a grain of corn*: **kernel**, seed, grist, fruit.

3 *grains of sand*: **granule**, particle, speck, spot, mote, mite, dot; bit, piece; scrap, crumb, fragment, flake, morsel, iota, molecule, atom.

4 *there was a grain of truth in what he said*: **trace**, hint, suggestion, suspicion, tinge, shadow; **small amount**, bit, little bit, soupçon; spark, scintilla, ounce, modicum, iota, jot, whit, scrap, shred, spot, drop, pinch; Irish stim; informal smidgen, smidge, tad; archaic scantling, scruple.

5 *the grain of the timber | a kind of leather with a fine grain*: **texture**, intertexture, surface, finish, feel; **weave**, nap, fibre, fabric, pattern.

grammar **noun syntax**, rules of language, morphology, semantics; linguistics, phonology; technical langue.

grammatical **adjective 1** *the grammatical structure of a sentence*: **syntactic**, morphological, semantic; linguistic, phonological.

2 *the report should be written in short grammatical sentences*: **well formed**, correct, idiomatic, acceptable, allowable.

▷ANTONYMS ungrammatical, solecistic.

grand **adjective 1** *a grand hotel*: **magnificent**, imposing, impressive, awe-inspiring, splendid, resplendent, superb, striking, monumental, majestic, glorious; palatial, stately, large; luxurious, sumptuous, lavish, opulent, princely, fit for a king; Brit. upmarket; N. Amer. upscale; informal fancy, posh, plush, classy, swanky; Brit. informal swish.

▷ANTONYMS inferior, unimpressive.

2 *rousing speeches and grand schemes*: **ostentatious**, grandiose, showy, extravagant, lordly, imperious; ambitious, bold, epic, big.

3 *a grand old lady*: **august**, distinguished, illustrious, eminent, esteemed, great, elevated, exalted, honoured, venerable, dignified, refined, respectable; pre-eminent, prominent, leading, notable, renowned, highly regarded, celebrated, well thought of, of distinction, famous; aristocratic, noble, regal, upper-class, blue-blooded, high-born, well born, patrician, elite; informal posh, upper-crust, upmarket, top-drawer.

▷ANTONYMS humble, ordinary.

4 *we raised a grand total of £2,000*: **complete**, comprehensive, total, all-inclusive, inclusive, exhaustive, final.

▷ANTONYMS partial.

5 *the grand staircase*: **main**, principal, foremost, major, central, prime; biggest, largest.

▷ANTONYMS minor, secondary.

6 informal *you're doing a grand job*: **excellent**, very good, marvellous, splendid, first-class, first-rate, wonderful, brilliant, outstanding, sterling, of the first water, fine, admirable, commendable, creditable; informal superb, terrific, great, super, top-notch, A1, fab, ace, tip-top, out of this world, wicked; Brit. informal smashing, brill, top-hole, champion, magic, bosting; N. Amer. informal bully; Austral./NZ informal beaut; Brit. informal, dated top-hole, wizard; rare applaudable.

▷ANTONYMS poor.

▶ **noun** informal *a cheque for ten grand*: **thousand pounds/dollars**; informal thou, K; N. Amer. informal G, gee.

grandeur **noun** *the grandeur of formal royal occasions*: **splendour**, magnificence, impressiveness, glory, gloriousness, resplendence, splendidness, superbness, majesty, greatness; stateliness, pomp, pomp and circumstance, ceremony, ceremonial, ceremoniousness.

grandfather **noun 1** *his grandfather was a mathematician*: informal grandad, grandpa, grandpop; N. Amer. informal gramps, grand daddy.

2 *he was the grandfather of modern liberalism*: **founder**, inventor, originator, creator, initiator, instigator, father, founding father, pioneer, framer, mastermind; literary begetter; rare establisher.

3 *our Victorian grandfathers*: **forefather**, forebear, ancestor, progenitor, antecedent.

▶ **verb** N. Amer. informal *smokers who worked here before the ban have been grandfathered*: **exempt**, excuse, make an exception of/for, give/grant immunity to, let off, release, exclude, exonerate; informal let off the hook.

grandiloquent **adjective** *their grandiloquent phrases failed to convince me*: **pompous**, bombastic, magniloquent, pretentious, ostentatious, high-flown, high-sounding, rhetorical, orotund, fustian, florid, flowery; laboured, strained, overwrought, overblown, overdone; wordy, periphrastic; epic, Homeric, Miltonian; informal highfalutin, purple; rare tumid, pleonastic, euphuistic, aureate, hyperventilated.

▷ANTONYMS unpretentious; concise.

grandiose **adjective 1** *the grandiose town hall*: **magnificent**, impressive, grand, imposing, awe-inspiring, splendid, resplendent, superb, striking, monumental, majestic, glorious, elaborate; palatial, stately, large; luxurious, lavish, opulent; informal plush, classy, swanky, flashy, flash.

▷ANTONYMS unimpressive, humble.

2 *a grandiose plan of urban renewal*: **ambitious**, bold, epic, big; overambitious, ostentatious, showy, extravagant, high-flown, high-sounding, flamboyant; informal over the top, OTT.

▷ANTONYMS modest, humble.

grandmother **noun** *my grandmother's ill*: informal grandma, granny; in Russia babushka; N. Amer. Jewish bubbie; S. African ouma; Brit. informal gran, nana, nan; N. Amer. informal gramma.

grant **verb 1** *he granted them leave of absence*: **allow**, accord, permit, afford, concede, vouchsafe.

▷ANTONYMS refuse.

2 *the programme granted them £20 million*: **bestow on**, confer on, give, impart to, present with; award to, present to, donate to, contribute to, provide with, endow with, hand out to; furnish with, supply with; allocate to, allot to, assign to.

3 *I grant that the difference is not absolute*: **admit**, accept, concede, yield, cede, allow, appreciate, recognize, acknowledge, confess; agree, concur, go along with.

▷ANTONYMS deny.

□ **take something for granted** *they took it for granted that we knew what we were doing*: **assume**, presume, suppose, take it, take as read, take it as given, presuppose, conjecture, surmise, conclude, come to the conclusion, deduce, infer, draw the inference, reckon, reason, guess, imagine, think, fancy, suspect, expect, accept, believe, be of the opinion, understand, be given to understand, gather, glean; N. Amer. figure; formal opine; archaic ween.

▶ **noun** *he has received a grant for equipment from the council*: **endowment**, subvention, award, donation, bursary, contribution, allowance, subsidy, handout, allocation, allotment, gift, present; scholarship, sponsorship; stipend; formal benefaction.

granular adjective *plant food in a new granular form*: **powder**, powdered, powdery, grainy, granulated, gritty, sandy; technical comminuted.

g

granulate verb *all that's left to do is to granulate the tea leaves to make instant tea*: **powder**, crush, crumble, pulverize, grind, pound, mince, shred, grate, mash, smash, fragment; technical triturate, comminute; archaic levigate, bray, powderize.

granule noun *minute granules of gold*: **grain**, particle, fragment, bit, sliver; scrap, crumb, morsel, mite, mote, speck, spot, dot, molecule, atom, iota, jot, whit; informal smidgen, smidge.

grape noun **1** *a bunch of grapes*: **berry**, vine fruit.

2 informal *a glass of the grape*: **wine**; informal vino, plonk.

> *Word links* **grape**
>
> **viticulture**, **viniculture** farming of grapes

graph noun *use graphs to analyse your data*: **chart**, diagram, grid; histogram, bar chart, pie chart, scatter diagram, nomogram, nomograph.

▶ **verb** *we can calculate and graph new prices*: **plot**, trace, draw up, delineate.

graphic adjective **1** *writing is a graphic representation of language*: **visual**, **symbolic**, pictorial, depictive, illustrative, diagrammatic, drawn, written, in writing, delineative.

2 *a graphic account of the horrors of war*: **vivid**, explicit, expressive, detailed, uninhibited, striking, forceful, powerful, punchy; lively, colourful, highly coloured, rich; lurid, shocking, startling; cogent, clear, lucid; realistic, descriptive, illustrative, pictorial, well defined, well delineated, well drawn, well expressed, photographic; telling, effective.

▷ANTONYMS vague; softened.

▶ **noun** Computing *this printer's good enough for churning out letters, and the odd graphic*: **picture**, illustration, image; icon, logo; diagram, graph, chart.

Word toolkit

graphic	**picturesque**	**vivid**
image	village	memory
detail	town	colour
violence	setting	description
depiction	view	account
representation	landscape	imagination
scene	spot	dream
portrayal	location	reminder
footage	harbour	example

graphic novel noun **comic**, comic book, cartoon; Japanese manga.

grapple verb **1** *he threw himself forward and grappled with him*: **wrestle**, struggle, tussle; brawl, fight, scuffle, clash, combat, battle; close, engage.

2 *he launched into the crowd to grapple his unfortunate prey*: **seize**, grab, lay hold of, take hold of, grip, hold, grasp, clasp, clench, catch hold of, catch, lay one's hands on, get one's hands on.

▷ANTONYMS let go of, release.

3 *a writer grappling with the problems of exile*: **tackle**, confront, address oneself to, face, attend to, attack, get down to; deal with, cope with, get/come to grips with; concentrate on, focus on, apply oneself to, devote oneself to; informal get stuck into, get cracking on, get weaving on, have a crack at, have a go at, have a shot at, have a stab at.

▷ANTONYMS avoid.

grasp verb **1** *she grasped his hands*: **grip**, clutch, clasp, hold, clench, lay hold of; catch, seize, grab, snatch, latch on to, catch at, grapple, get one's hands on.

▷ANTONYMS release.

2 *after the lectures she made sure everybody had grasped the important points*: **understand**, comprehend, follow, take in, realize, perceive, see, apprehend, assimilate, absorb, make sense of, master, get to the bottom of, penetrate; informal get, catch on to, figure out, get one's head around, get a fix on, take on board, get the picture, get the drift, make head or tail of; Brit. informal twig, suss (out).

3 *Henry grasped the opportunity*: **take advantage of**, act on; seize, grasp with both hands, grab (at), leap at, snatch, jump at, pounce on.

▷ANTONYMS miss, overlook.

▶ **noun 1** *his grasp on her hand was fierce*: **grip**, hold; clutch, clasp, clench.

2 *he broke free from his domineering mother's grasp*: **control**, power, clutches, command, mastery, domination, dominion, rule, tyranny, evil embrace.

3 *a mighty prize lay within their grasp*: **reach**, scope, capacity, power, limits, range, compass.

4 *your grasp of history impresses me*: **understanding**, comprehension, perception, apprehension, awareness, grip, conception, realization, knowledge, cognizance, ken; mastery, command; insight, familiarity.

grasping adjective *a grasping corporate executive*: **avaricious**, acquisitive, greedy, rapacious, grabbing, usurious, covetous, venal; mercenary, materialistic, money-orientated; mean, miserly, parsimonious, niggardly, scrimping, penny-pinching, cheese-paring, hoarding, selfish, possessive, close; N. Amer. forehanded; informal tight-fisted, tight, stingy, money-grubbing, money-grabbing, on the make; N. Amer. informal cheap, grabby; Austral./NZ informal hungry; vulgar slang tight-arsed.

▷ANTONYMS generous, altruistic.

grass noun **1** *he sat down on the grass*: **turf**, greenery, green, sod; lawn, field, pasture, meadow, grassland, grasslands; blades of grass; S. African **veld**; literary sward, mead, lea.

2 informal *they spent their afternoons smoking grass*. See **cannabis**.

3 Brit. informal *few pubs were without a grass or an undercover policeman*: **informer**, mole, stool pigeon; informal snitch, snout, stoolie, whistle-blower, snake in the grass, supergrass, rat, scab, nose; Brit. informal **nark**; N. Amer. informal fink.

▶ **verb 1** *the hill is completely grassed*: **cover with grass**, grass over, turf, lay grass on.

2 Brit. informal *he was suspected of* ***grassing on*** *the airport robbers*: **inform**, tell; give away, betray, denounce, sell out, be a Judas to; informal split, blow the whistle, rat, peach, squeal, squeak, do the dirty, grass up, tell tales about, spill the beans about, stitch up, sell down the river; Brit. informal **sneak**, shop; N. Amer. informal drop a/the dime, finger, rat out, job; Austral./NZ informal dob, pimp, pool, shelf, put someone's pot on, point the bone at; N. Irish & Scottish informal tout; archaic delate.

▷ANTONYMS keep quiet about; protect.

> *Word links* **grass**
>
> **graminaceous** relating to grass
> **agrostology** study of grasses
> **graminivorous** grass-eating

grate verb **1** *she started to grate the cheese*: **shred**, rub into pieces, pulverize, mince, grind, granulate, crush, crumble, mash, smash, fragment, macerate; technical triturate.

2 *he gripped her so hard that her bones grated together*: **rasp**, scrape, jar, scratch, grind, rub, drag, grit; squeak, screech, creak.

3 *the jingly tune grates slightly*: **irritate**, set someone's teeth on edge, jar; irk, exasperate, annoy, vex, nettle, peeve, rankle, anger, rub up the wrong way, chafe, fret, eat away at; informal get on someone's nerves, get under someone's skin, rile, aggravate, get someone's goat.

grateful adjective *I was most grateful for your hospitality*: **thankful**, filled with gratitude, appreciative; indebted, obliged, obligated, under obligation, in your debt, beholden.

▷ANTONYMS ungrateful.

> *Choose the right word* **grateful, thankful, appreciative**
>
> These words indicate various forms of awareness of having been fortunate or well treated.
>
> Someone who is **grateful** realizes that someone else has helped them or treated them kindly, and has warm feelings towards that person (*we're most grateful for your help* | *her whole family is grateful to the surgeons who saved her*). *Grateful*, in fact, suggests more of an impulse to thank someone than *thankful* does. It is also used in polite requests such as *I would be grateful if you could let me know*.
>
> **Thankful** is typically more concerned with a person's attitude to their good fortune than with their feelings towards anyone responsible for it. It suggests that someone is relieved or pleased about a situation or turn of events, often one for which no particular person can be identified as responsible (*she was thankful that she felt so much better* | *I have a lot to be thankful for*).
>
> The main use of **appreciative** is to say that someone recognizes the merits or appeal of something and expresses that recognition in actions or words (*they were the most appreciative audience we'd played to*). If what is appreciated is a kindness or service, *appreciative* is used with *of* and often also implies gratitude (*the team are very appreciative of your support*).

gratification noun *ours is the civilization of instant gratification*: **satisfaction**, fulfilment, indulgence, relief, quenching, slaking, satiation, appeasement, assuagement; **pleasure**, enjoyment, thrill, relish; informal kicks.

gratify verb **1** *it gratified him to be seen in her company*: **please**, gladden, give pleasure to, make happy, make content, delight, make someone feel good, satisfy, warm the cockles of the heart, thrill; informal tickle someone pink, give someone a buzz/kick, buck someone up.
▷ANTONYMS displease.
2 *he was gratifying his strange desires*: **satisfy**, fulfil, indulge, relieve, humour, comply with, pander to, cater to, give in to, quench, slake, satiate, pacify, appease, assuage, provide for, feed, accommodate.
▷ANTONYMS frustrate.

grating[1] adjective **1** *pushing his chair from the table with a grating noise*: **scraping**, scratching, grinding, rasping, creaking, jarring, abrasive.
2 *her high grating voice*: **harsh**, raucous, strident, piercing, shrill, ear-piercing, screeching, squawking, squawky, squeaky, sharp; discordant, dissonant, cacophonous; brassy, blaring; hoarse, croaky, rough, gravelly.
▷ANTONYMS pleasing, harmonious.
3 *it's written in grating pseudo-teenspeak language*: **irritating**, annoying, infuriating, rankling, vexatious, irksome, galling, exasperating, maddening, displeasing; **jarring**, discordant, inharmonious, out of place, unsuitable, inappropriate, ill suited; tiresome, troublesome, niggling, disagreeable, unpleasant, offensive; informal aggravating.
▷ANTONYMS pleasing; appropriate.

grating[2] noun *a strong iron grating*: **framework**, grid, grate, network, grille, grillwork, lattice, trellis, criss-cross, matrix; mesh, gauze, netting, net, web, webbing, tracery, interlacing, reticulation, reticulum; technical plexus, graticule, decussation.

gratis adverb *a monthly programme was issued gratis to dancers*: **free of charge**, free, without charge, for nothing, at no cost, without payment, without paying, freely, gratuitously; informal on the house, for free.
▷ANTONYMS for a fee.

gratitude noun *Maureen ought to show gratitude for the money*: **gratefulness**, thankfulness, thanks, appreciation, recognition, acknowledgement, credit, regard, respect; sense of obligation, indebtedness.
▷ANTONYMS ingratitude.

gratuitous adjective **1** *student demonstrations developed an edge of gratuitous violence*: **unjustified**, without reason, uncalled for, unwarranted, unprovoked, undue; indefensible, unjustifiable; needless, unnecessary, superfluous, redundant, avoidable, inessential, non-essential, unmerited, groundless, ungrounded, causeless, without cause; senseless, careless, wanton, indiscriminate, unreasoning, brutish; excessive, immoderate, disproportionate, inordinate; unfounded, baseless, inappropriate; French de trop.
▷ANTONYMS justifiable, necessary.
2 *the worker is not there to offer gratuitous advice*: **free**, gratis, complimentary, voluntary, volunteer, unpaid, unrewarded, unsalaried, free of charge, without charge, for nothing, at no cost, without payment; Law pro bono (publico); informal for free, on the house; Brit. informal buckshee.
▷ANTONYMS paid, professional.

gratuity noun formal *under no circumstances was any officer to receive a gratuity*: **tip**, gift, present, donation, reward, handout, recompense, boon, baksheesh; fringe benefit, bonus, extra payment, little extra, bit extra; (**gratuities**) largesse, benefaction; French pourboire, douceur; informal perk; formal perquisite; rare guerdon, lagniappe.

grave[1] noun *a cross marks the grave*: **burying place**, tomb, sepulchre, vault, burial chamber, burial pit, mausoleum, crypt, catacomb; last home, last resting place; historical tumulus, barrow; rare undercroft.

grave[2] adjective **1** *a grave matter*: **serious**, important, all-important, profound, significant, momentous, weighty, of great consequence; vital, crucial, critical, acute; urgent, pressing, exigent; pivotal, precarious, touch-and-go, life-and-death, in the balance; dire, terrible, awful, dreadful, alarming, drastic, sore; perilous, hazardous, dangerous, threatening, menacing, risky; informal dicey, hairy, iffy, chancy; Brit. informal dodgy; rare egregious.
▷ANTONYMS trivial.
2 *Jackie looked grave*: **solemn**, earnest, serious, sombre, sober, severe; unsmiling, long-faced, stone-faced, grim-faced, grim, gloomy; preoccupied, thoughtful, dignified, staid, dour, aloof, forbidding.
▷ANTONYMS carefree, cheerful.

gravel noun *his boots crunched on the gravel*: **shingle**, grit, pebbles, stones.

gravelly adjective **1** *a gravelly beach*: **shingly**, pebbly, gritty, containing gravel.
2 *his gravelly voice answered immediately*: **husky**, gruff, throaty, deep, croaking, raspy, rasping, grating, harsh, low, rough, rough-sounding, thick, guttural.

gravestone noun **headstone**, tombstone, stone, monument, memorial, plaque, tablet.

graveyard noun **cemetery**, burial ground, churchyard, memorial park, necropolis, burial place, burying place, garden of remembrance; Scottish kirkyard; informal boneyard; historical potter's field, charnel house, urnfield; archaic God's acre.

gravitas noun *a man of gravitas*: **dignity**, seriousness, solemnity, gravity, loftiness, grandeur, decorum, sobriety, sedateness.
▷ANTONYMS frivolity.

gravitate verb *he naturally **gravitated towards** Paris*: **move**, head, be pulled, drift; tend, have a tendency, lean, incline, veer; be drawn to, be attracted to.

gravity noun **1** *gravity attracts objects towards each other*: **attraction**, attracting force, downward force, pull, weight, heaviness.
2 *I hope they realize the gravity of the situation*: **seriousness**, importance, profundity, significance, momentousness, moment, weightiness, weight, consequence, magnitude; criticalness, acuteness, cruciality; urgency, exigence; direness, terribleness, awfulness, dreadfulness; precariousness, perilousness, peril, hazard, danger, threat, menace, risk; informal hairiness, iffiness, chanciness; Brit. informal dodginess; formal egregiousness.
▷ANTONYMS triviality.
3 *she was baffled by the gravity of his demeanour*: **solemnity**, seriousness, sombreness, sobriety, soberness, severity; unsmilingness, stone-facedness, long-facedness, grim-facedness, grimness, humourlessness, gloominess; preoccupation, thoughtfulness, dignity, staidness, dourness, aloofness.
▷ANTONYMS cheerfulness, levity.

graze[1] verb *a group of deer grazed*: **feed**, eat, crop, browse, ruminate, pasture, nibble, take nourishment.

graze[2] verb **1** *he grazed his knuckles on the corner of the fuse box*: **scrape**, abrade, skin, scratch, chafe, bark, scuff, rasp, break the skin of, cut, nick, snick; Medicine excoriate.
2 *his shot grazed the far post*: **touch**, touch lightly, brush, brush against, rub lightly, shave, skim, kiss, caress, sweep, scrape, glance off, clip.
▶ noun *cuts and grazes on the skin*: **scratch**, scrape, abrasion, cut, injury, sore; Medicine trauma, traumatism.

grease noun **1** *axle grease*: **lubricant**, lubrication, unguent; informal lube.
2 *the kitchen was filmed with grease*: **fat**, oil, cooking oil, animal fat; lard, suet, butter, margarine, dripping.
3 *his hair was smothered with grease*: **oil**, ointment, lotion, cream; trademark Brylcreem.
▶ verb *grease a shallow baking dish*: **lubricate**, oil, smear with grease/oil, make slippery, make smooth, make oily.

greasy adjective **1** *a greasy fish supper*: **fatty**, oily, fat, swimming in oil/fat, buttery, oleaginous; technical adipose, sebaceous, pinguid, unctuous.
▷ANTONYMS lean; crisp.
2 *a man with greasy grey hair*: **oily**, shiny, glossy.
▷ANTONYMS dry.
3 *the game had made the pitch very greasy*: **slippery**, slick, slimy, slithery, oily, glassy, smooth; informal slippy, skiddy.
▷ANTONYMS dry.
4 *that greasy little coward*: **ingratiating**, fawning, grovelling, sycophantic, toadying, obsequious, cringing, flattering, effusive, gushing, gushy, abject, truckling, self-effacing, Uriah Heepish; unctuous, oily, smooth-tongued, smooth, glib, suave, slick, reptilian; informal slimy, smarmy, bootlicking, all over someone, soapy, sucky.

great adjective **1** *academics waited with great interest for the book*: **considerable**, substantial, pronounced, sizeable, significant, appreciable, serious, exceptional, inordinate, extraordinary, special.
▷ANTONYMS little.
2 *a great expanse of water*: **large**, big, extensive, expansive, broad, wide, sizeable, ample, spacious; vast, immense, huge, enormous, gigantic, massive, colossal, mammoth, monstrous, prodigious, tremendous, stupendous, unlimited, boundless; informal humongous, whopping, whopping great, thumping, thumping great, dirty great; Brit. informal whacking, whacking great, ginormous.
▷ANTONYMS small.
3 *a great big house*: **very**, extremely, exceedingly, exceptionally, especially, tremendously, immensely, extraordinarily, remarkably, really, truly; informal dirty.
4 *you great fool!* **absolute**, total, utter, out-and-out, downright, thorough, complete; perfect, pure, positive, prize, decided, arrant, sheer, rank, unmitigated, unqualified, unadulterated, unalloyed, consummate, veritable, egregious; informal thundering; Brit. informal right, proper.
5 *the great writers of the Romantic age*: **prominent**, eminent, pre-eminent, important, distinguished, august, illustrious, noble; celebrated, noted, notable, noteworthy, famous, famed, honoured, esteemed, revered, renowned, acclaimed, admired, well known; **leading**, top, high, high-ranking, chief, major, main, principal, central; gifted, talented; outstanding, foremost, remarkable, exceptional, highly rated, first-rate, incomparable, superlative, unsurpassed, unexcelled, matchless, peerless, star, arch-; N. Amer. informal major league.
▷ANTONYMS minor.

6 *a great power with a formidable navy*: **powerful**, dominant, influential, strong, potent, formidable, redoubtable; leading, important, illustrious, top rank, of the first rank, first rate; foremost, major, main, chief, principal, capital, paramount, primary.
▷ANTONYMS minor.
7 *the great castle of Montellana-Coronil*: **magnificent**, imposing, impressive, awe-inspiring, grand, splendid, majestic, monumental, glorious, sumptuous, resplendent, lavish, beautiful.
▷ANTONYMS modest.
8 *he's a great sportsman*: **expert**, skilful, skilled, adept, adroit, accomplished, talented, fine, able, masterly, master, brilliant, virtuoso, magnificent, marvellous, outstanding, first class, first rate, elite, superb, proficient, very good; informal crack, ace, wizard, A1, class, hot, top-notch, stellar, out of this world, mean, demon; vulgar slang shit hot.
▷ANTONYMS poor.
9 *I'm not really a great follower of fashion*: **enthusiastic**, eager, keen, zealous, devoted, ardent, fervent, fanatical, passionate, dedicated, diligent, assiduous, intent, habitual, active, vehement, hearty, wholehearted, committed, warm.
▷ANTONYMS unenthusiastic.
10 *he's having a great time*: **enjoyable**, amusing, delightful, lovely; pleasant, congenial, diverting; exciting, thrilling; **excellent**, marvellous, wonderful, superb, first-class, first-rate, admirable, fine, splendid, very good, good; informal terrific, tremendous, smashing, fantastic, fabulous, fab, super, glorious, grand, magic, out of this world, cool; Brit. informal brilliant, brill, champion, bosting; Austral./NZ informal bonzer, beaut; Brit. informal, dated capital, wizard, corking, spiffing, ripping, cracking, top-hole, topping, champion, beezer; N. Amer. informal, dated swell.
▷ANTONYMS bad.
11 *the great thing is to regret nothing*: **important**, essential, crucial, critical, pivotal, vital, salient, significant, big; chief, main, principal, major, most important, uppermost, primary, prime, cardinal, central, key, supreme, paramount, overriding; momentous, weighty, dominant, consequential; informal number one.
▷ANTONYMS inessential.

greatly adverb *a frantic training programme greatly increases the risk of injury*: **very much**, much, by a considerable amount, considerably, to a great extent, substantially, appreciably, significantly, markedly, sizeably, seriously, materially, signally, profoundly, to a great extent/degree; enormously, vastly, immensely, tremendously, hugely, mightily, abundantly, extremely, exceedingly, remarkably; informal plenty, majorly, well, to the nth degree.
▷ANTONYMS slightly; not at all.

greatness noun 1 *a woman destined for greatness*: **eminence**, distinction, pre-eminence, illustriousness, lustre, repute, reputation, status, standing, high standing; **importance**, significance, value, merit, worth; celebrity, noteworthiness, fame, prominence, renown.
▷ANTONYMS insignificance, obscurity.
2 *Wilde's greatness as a writer*: **brilliance**, genius, prowess, talent, expertise, expertness, mastery, artistry, virtuosity, flair, skill, skilfulness, finesse, panache, power, adeptness, proficiency; calibre, distinction.
▷ANTONYMS mediocrity.
3 *a city fallen from greatness*: **grandeur**, grandness, magnificence, impressiveness, splendour, gloriousness, glory, majesty, loftiness.

greed, greediness noun 1 *wasting resources in order to satisfy human greed*: **avarice**, acquisitiveness, covetousness, rapacity, graspingness, cupidity, avidity, possessiveness, materialism; mercenariness, predatoriness; informal money-grubbing, money-grabbing; N. Amer. informal grabbiness; rare Mammonism, pleonexia.
▷ANTONYMS generosity.
2 *her mouth began to water with unashamed greed*: **gluttony**, hunger, ravenousness, voraciousness, voracity, insatiability; gourmandizing, gourmandism; intemperance, overeating, self-indulgence; informal swinishness, piggishness, hoggishness, gutsiness; rare edacity, esurience.
▷ANTONYMS temperance, asceticism.
3 *he appealed to their greed for power*: **desire**, urge, need, appetite, hunger, craving, longing, yearning, hankering, hungering, thirst, pining; avidity, eagerness, enthusiasm, impatience; informal yen, itch.
▷ANTONYMS indifference.

greedy adjective 1 *a greedy eater*: **gluttonous**, ravenous, ravening, voracious, gourmandizing, gourmand, intemperate, self-indulgent, insatiable, insatiate, wolfish, gannet-like; informal piggish, piggy, swinish, hoggish, gutsy; rare esurient, edacious; (**be greedy**) have eyes bigger than one's stomach; black English have a/the big eye.
▷ANTONYMS temperate, ascetic.
2 *a greedy millionaire*: **avaricious**, acquisitive, covetous, rapacious, grasping, venal, cupidinous, materialistic, mercenary, predatory, usurious, possessive; grabbing, hoarding, Scrooge-like; informal money-grubbing, money-grabbing; N. Amer. informal grabby; rare pleonectic, Mammonish, Mammonistic.
▷ANTONYMS generous, altruistic.
3 *she is **greedy for** a title*: **eager**, avid, hungry, craving, longing, yearning, hankering, thirsty, pining, enthusiastic, impatient, anxious; desirous of; informal dying, itching, hot, gagging.
▷ANTONYMS indifferent.

green adjective 1 *a green scarf*: **greenish**, viridescent; olive green, pea green, emerald green, lime green, bottle green, Lincoln green, sea green, sage green, acid green, eau de Nil, aquamarine, aqua; literary virescent, glaucous.
2 *a pleasant green island*: **verdant**, grassy, grass-covered, leafy, verdurous; rural, pastoral.
▷ANTONYMS barren.
3 (usually **Green**) *he has become preoccupied with Green issues*: **environmentalist**, ecologist, conservationist, preservationist.
4 *a green alternative to diesel cars*: **environmentally friendly**, environmentally/ecologically sound, non-polluting, ozone-friendly.
▷ANTONYMS environmentally unfriendly.
5 *green bananas*: **unripe**, not ripe, immature.
6 *green timber*: **unseasoned**, not aged, unfinished; pliable, supple.
▷ANTONYMS dry.
7 *finely sliced green bacon*: **raw**, fresh, unsmoked, uncured.
▷ANTONYMS cured.
8 *the new lieutenant was very green*: **inexperienced**, unversed, callow, immature; new, raw, unseasoned, untried; inexpert, untrained, unqualified, ignorant; simple, unsophisticated, unpolished; **naive**, innocent, ingenuous, credulous, gullible, unworldly; informal wet behind the ears, born yesterday.
▷ANTONYMS experienced.
9 *his still green recollection of that memorable night*: **vivid**, fresh, flourishing; remembered, unforgotten.
▷ANTONYMS dim.
10 *his aunt was still flourishing in a green old age*: **vigorous**, strong, sturdy, sound, healthy, flourishing.
▷ANTONYMS weak.
11 *he went green, and I thought he was going to be sick*: **pale**, wan, pallid, ashen, ashen-faced, pasty, pasty-faced, grey, whitish, washed out, whey-faced, waxen, waxy, blanched, drained, pinched, sallow; **sickly**, nauseous, ill, sick, unhealthy.
▷ANTONYMS ruddy.
▶noun 1 *that lovely canopy of green over Stratford Road*: **foliage**, greenery, plants, leaves, leafage, vegetation; rare herbage, verdure, frondescence.
2 *a small village green*: **lawn**, common, grassy area, sward, grass; archaic greensward, mead, lea.
3 (**greens**) *they had roast beef, potatoes, and greens for lunch*: **vegetables**, leaf vegetables; informal veg, veggies.
4 (usually **Green**) *Greens are against multinationals*: **environmentalist**, conservationist, preservationist, nature-lover, eco-activist; informal, derogatory econut, ecofreak, tree hugger.

> *Word links* **green**
>
> **chloro-** related prefix, as in *chlorophyll, chlorine*

greenery noun *the hotel is surrounded by lush greenery*: **foliage**, vegetation, plants, green, leaves, leafage, undergrowth, plant life, flora; rare herbage, verdure, frondescence.

greenhorn noun N. Amer. informal *as a greenhorn he was bound to make a few mistakes*: **novice**, beginner, starter, tyro, neophyte, new recruit, raw recruit, fledgling, new boy/girl, novitiate; trainee, learner, student, pupil, mentee, probationer; N. Amer. tenderfoot; informal rookie, new kid (on the block), newie, newbie; N. Amer. informal punk.
▷ANTONYMS veteran.

greenhouse noun **hothouse**, glasshouse, conservatory.

green light noun *he was given **the green light** to implement his proposals*: **authorization**, permission, approval, assent, consent, sanction; leave, clearance, warranty, agreement, imprimatur, one's blessing, the seal/stamp of approval, the rubber stamp; authority, licence, dispensation, empowerment, freedom, liberty; informal the OK, the go-ahead, the thumbs up, the say-so, the nod; rare permit, nihil obstat.
▷ANTONYMS the red light; refusal.
□ **give the green light to** *transport bosses gave the green light to major road safety improvements*: **authorize**, give permission for, permit, sanction, allow, agree to, approve, give one's consent/assent to, consent to, assent to, accede to, countenance; license, legalize, make legal, legitimize, legitimatize; ratify, endorse, validate, accredit, warrant; informal give the go-ahead for, give the OK to, OK, give the thumbs up to; N. Amer. informal green-light; N. Amer. rare approbate.
▷ANTONYMS forbid, veto.

greet verb 1 *she greeted Hank cheerily*: **say hello to**, address, salute, hail, halloo; nod to, wave to, raise one's hat to, tip one's hat to, acknowledge the presence of.
▷ANTONYMS ignore.
2 *I greeted him at the door with a martini*: **welcome**, meet, receive; show in, usher in, admit, accept, let in.
3 *the decision was greeted with a chorus of outrage*: **receive**, acknowledge, respond to, react to, take; hear, listen to.

greeting noun **1** *he shouted a greeting*: **hello**, salute, salutation, address, welcome, hailing; nod, wave, acknowledgement.
▷ANTONYMS farewell.
2 (**greetings**) *they passed on birthday greetings*: **best wishes**, good wishes, regards, kind/kindest regards, congratulations, compliments, respects, felicitations; archaic one's devoirs, remembrances.

gregarious adjective **1** *he was fun-loving and gregarious*: **sociable**, social, company-loving, companionable, convivial, clubbable; outgoing, friendly, affable, amiable, genial, congenial, cordial, hospitable, neighbourly, welcoming, warm, pleasant, comradely, hail-fellow-well-met; Scottish couthy; informal chummy, pally; Brit. informal matey, decent; N. Amer. informal clubby, buddy-buddy; rare conversable.
▷ANTONYMS unsociable; reserved.
2 *these fish are small and gregarious*: **social**, organized, living in shoals/flocks/herds.

grey adjective **1** *a grey suit*: greyish, silvery; silver-grey, pearl-grey, pearly, gunmetal grey, slate-grey, smoke-grey, smoky, sooty.
2 *his thinning grey hair*: **white**, silver, hoary.
3 *a grey old man*: **grey-haired**, hoary, grizzled; **elderly**, old, aged, senior, ancient, venerable; in one's dotage, long in the tooth, as old as the hills; past one's prime, not as young as one was, not as young as one used to be; decrepit, doddering, doddery, not long for this world; informal past it, over the hill, no spring chicken; formal senescent.
▷ANTONYMS young.
4 *it was a dim, grey day*: **cloudy**, overcast, dull, dim, dark, sunless; gloomy, dreary, dismal, sombre, drab, bleak, cheerless, depressing, glum; misty, foggy, murky.
▷ANTONYMS bright, sunny.
5 *her face looked grey*: **ashen**, wan, pale, pasty, pallid, colourless, sallow, leaden, bloodless, anaemic, white, waxen, chalky; sickly, peaked, drained, sapped, washed-out, drawn, deathly, deathlike, ghostly; informal peaky.
▷ANTONYMS ruddy.
6 *if you drive the idiosyncrasies out of football, what is left can be grey indeed*: **characterless**, colourless, nondescript, unremarkable, faceless; lifeless, soulless, passionless, spiritless, insipid, jejune, flat, bland, dry, stale; dull, uninteresting, unimaginative, boring, tedious, monotonous; neutral, anonymous, wishy-washy.
▷ANTONYMS colourful, lively.
7 *a grey area*: **ambiguous**, doubtful, unclear, uncertain, indistinct, indefinite, indeterminate, open to question, debatable; mixed, neither one thing nor the other, neither fish nor fowl.
▷ANTONYMS black and white, certain.
8 *grey importing is not illegal*: **unofficial**, informal, irregular, back-door.
□ **grey matter** informal *the team had enough grey matter to finish ahead of others*: **intelligence**, intellect, intellectual capacity, mental capacity, brains, brainpower, cleverness, wit, wits, powers of reasoning, reasoning, wisdom, sagacity, acumen, discernment, shrewdness, judgement, understanding, common sense, sense; informal nous, savvy, braininess, upper storey.
▸ verb *health bills rose as the population greyed*: **age**, get old, grow old, mature.

grid noun **1** *the castings were placed on to a metal grid*: **grating**, mesh, gauze, grille, grillwork, lattice, framework, network, criss-cross.
2 *the grid of streets*: **matrix**, network, reticulation, reticulum; technical plexus, decussation, graticule.

grief noun **1** *Amanda's grief for her father*: **sorrow**, misery, sadness, anguish, pain, distress, agony, torment, affliction, suffering, heartache, heartbreak, broken-heartedness, heaviness of heart, woe, desolation, despondency, dejection, despair, angst, mortification; **mourning**, mournfulness, bereavement, lamentation, lament; remorse, regret, pining; informal blues; literary dolour, dole.
▷ANTONYMS joy.
2 informal *the police gave me loads of grief*: **trouble**, annoyance, bother, irritation, vexation, harassment, nuisance; informal aggravation, aggro, hassle, headache.
□ **come to grief** *the scheme came to grief because of the opposition of the Cabinet Secretary*: **fail**, meet with failure, meet with disaster, miscarry, go wrong, go awry, fall through, fall flat, be frustrated, break down, collapse, founder, fold, come to nothing, come to naught; informal come unstuck, come a cropper, flop, fizzle out, go phut, go down like a lead balloon, bomb, go to the wall, bite the dust; Brit. informal go pear-shaped; N. Amer. informal tank.
▷ANTONYMS succeed.

grief-stricken adjective *a grief-stricken widow*: **sorrowful**, overcome with sorrow, heavy with grief, sorrowing, miserable, sad, anguished, pained, distressed, tormented, suffering, heartbroken, broken-hearted, heartsick, woeful, doleful, desolate, despondent, dejected, despairing, devastated, upset, inconsolable, dismal, angst-ridden, mortified, wretched, crushed; **mourning**, grieving, mournful, bereaved, lamenting; remorseful, regretful, pining; informal cut up; Brit. informal gutted; literary dolorous.
▷ANTONYMS joyful.

grievance noun **1** *civil disorder could be the result of a real or imagined grievance*: **injustice**, unjust act, wrong, injury, ill, offence, disservice, unfairness, evil, outrage, atrocity, damage; affront, insult, indignity.
2 *the phone line lets callers air grievances about public services*: **complaint**, criticism, objection, protestation, charge, protest, grumble, moan, cavil, quibble, problem; grudge, ill feeling, hard feeling, bad feeling, resentment, bitterness, rancour, pique, umbrage; informal grouse, gripe, whinge, grouch, niggle, beef, bone to pick, chip on one's shoulder; N. Amer. informal crow to pluck; literary plaint.
▷ANTONYMS commendation.

grieve verb **1** *she continued to grieve for Mary*: **mourn**, lament, be mournful, be sorrowful, sorrow, be sad, be miserable; cry, sob, weep, shed tears, keen, weep and wail, beat one's breast; suffer, ache, be in anguish, be distressed, be in distress, eat one's heart out.
▷ANTONYMS be happy, rejoice.
2 *Alexander was grieved to lose such a good friend*: **hurt**, wound, pain, harrow, sting, gall; **sadden**, upset, distress, devastate, cause suffering to, crush, break someone's heart, make someone's heart bleed, hit someone hard.
▷ANTONYMS please.

grievous adjective **1** *no money can compensate her for her grievous injuries*: **serious**, severe, grave, bad, critical, dreadful, terrible, awful; painful, agonizing, hurtful, afflicting, wounding, damaging, injurious; sharp, acute; Medicine peracute.
▷ANTONYMS slight, trivial.
2 *that is most grievous news*: **disastrous**, calamitous; crushing, distressing, traumatic, harrowing; sorrowful, mournful, sad.
▷ANTONYMS good.
3 *a grievous sin*: **heinous**, grave, deplorable, shocking, appalling, atrocious, gross, dire, outrageous, dreadful, egregious, iniquitous, nefarious, shameful, lamentable; flagrant, glaring; rare flagitious.
▷ANTONYMS trivial, venial.

grim adjective **1** *she took in his grim expression*: **stern**, forbidding, uninviting, unapproachable, aloof, distant; formidable, strict, dour, harsh; steely, flinty, stony; fierce, ferocious, threatening, menacing; cross, churlish, crabbed, surly, sour, ill-tempered, unsmiling; cruel, ruthless, merciless.
▷ANTONYMS amiable, pleasant.
2 *she was caught between a rock and a hard place, she realized with grim humour*: **black**, dark, mirthless, bleak, cynical, fatalistic.
▷ANTONYMS light-hearted.
3 *the asylum holds some grim secrets*: **dreadful**, dire, ghastly, horrible, horrendous, horrid, terrible, awful, appalling, frightful, shocking, unspeakable, atrocious, harrowing; grisly, gruesome, hideous, disgusting, revolting, gory, macabre, morbid; depressing, distressing, upsetting, worrying, unpleasant, disagreeable.
4 *a grim little hovel*: **bleak**, dreary, dismal, dingy, wretched, miserable, disheartening, depressing, cheerless, comfortless, joyless, gloomy, sombre, uninviting, drab; informal God-awful.
5 *two beasts locked in grim combat*: **merciless**, cruel, ruthless, pitiless, savage, vicious, brutal, harsh, severe.
6 *there was grim determination in every line of her face*: **resolute**, determined, firm, decided, steadfast, dead set; obstinate, stubborn, obdurate; unyielding, uncompromising, unbending, unwavering, unfaltering, unshakeable, intractable, adamant, inflexible; unrelenting, relentless, dogged, tenacious, inexorable, persistent, strong-willed.
▷ANTONYMS irresolute.

grimace noun *his mouth twisted into a grimace*: **scowl**, frown, sneer, pout, moue, wince, distorted expression; face, wry face.
▷ANTONYMS smile.
▸ verb *Nina grimaced at Joe*: **scowl**, frown, sneer, pout, wince, glower, lour; make a face, make faces, pull a face; Brit. gurn.
▷ANTONYMS smile.

grime noun *her skirt was smeared with grime*: **dirt**, smut, soot, dust, mud, filth, mire, sludge, dross, pollution; informal muck, gunge, yuck, crud, goo; Brit. informal grot.
▸ verb *concrete grimed by diesel exhaust*: **begrime**, blacken, dirty, make grimy, make dirty, make sooty, stain, soil, befoul, defile; literary besmirch.
▷ANTONYMS clean.

grimy adjective *reporters in grimy anoraks*: **dirty**, grimed, begrimed, grubby, soiled, stained, smeared, filthy, uncleaned, messy; dirt-encrusted, smutty, sooty, dusty, muddy, muddied, mud-caked, polluted; informal mucky, yucky, cruddy; Brit. informal manky, grotty, gungy; Austral./NZ scungy; literary besmirched, besmeared.
▷ANTONYMS clean.

Word toolkit **grimy**

See **filthy**.

grin verb *Guy grinned merrily at her*: **smile**, smile broadly, beam, grin from ear to ear, smile from ear to ear, grin like a Cheshire cat, smirk; informal be all smiles.
▷ANTONYMS frown; scowl.

□ **grin and bear it** *we just had to grin and bear it*: **put up with it**, stick it out, keep at it, keep going, stay with it, see it through, see it through to the end; persevere, persist, carry on, struggle on; informal hang in there, soldier on, tough it out, peg away, plug away, bash on.
▷ANTONYMS give up.
▸ **noun** *a silly grin*: **smile**, broad smile, smirk.
▷ANTONYMS frown; scowl.

grind verb **1** *grind the praline into a fine powder*: **crush**, pound, pulverize, mill, powder, granulate, grate, mince, shred, crumble, pestle, mash, smash, press, fragment, kibble; technical triturate, comminute; archaic levigate, bray.
2 *a knife being ground on a wheel*: **sharpen**, whet, make sharp/sharper, hone, file, strop; smooth, polish, sand, sandpaper.
3 *one tectonic plate grinds against another*: **rub**, grate, scrape, rasp.
4 *Mitch ground his teeth in fury*: **gnash**, grit.
5 *a car grinding up the other side of the hill*: **move laboriously**, strain, struggle, drag oneself, fight one's way, labour; chug; N. Amer. informal putter.
□ **grind someone down** *I've never let male colleagues grind me down*: **oppress**, persecute, tyrannize, suppress; afflict, maltreat, ill-treat, scourge; torture, torment, molest, harass, harry.
□ **grind on** *the meeting ground on*: **drag on**, go on and on, plod on, pass slowly, move slowly, creep along, limp along, crawl, hang heavy, go at a snail's pace, wear on, go on too long; **continue**, carry on, go on, keep on, keep going, proceed.
▷ANTONYMS race by, fly.
□ **grind something out** *a hack grinding out newspaper copy*: **produce**, generate, crank out, turn out; informal churn out, trot out, bang out.
▸ **noun** *teaching could be a grind*: **chore**, slog, travail; **drudgery**, toil, hard work, donkey work, labour, slavery, exertion; informal fag, sweat.

grip verb **1** *she gripped the edge of the table*: **grasp**, clutch, hold, clasp, grasp/take/lay hold of, latch on to, grab, seize, clench, cling to, catch, catch at, get one's hands on, pluck; squeeze, press; archaic gripe.
▷ANTONYMS release; hold lightly.
2 *Harry was gripped by a sneezing fit*: **afflict**, affect, take over, beset, rack, torment, convulse.
3 *we were gripped by the drama*: **engross**, enthral, entrance, absorb, rivet, spellbind, hold spellbound, bewitch, fascinate, hold, catch, compel, mesmerize, arrest, ensnare, enrapture; interest, intrigue, engage, distract, divert, entertain, amuse.
▷ANTONYMS repel; bore.
▸ **noun 1** *she never released her grip on the handrail*: **grasp**, hold, clutch, clasp, clench; archaic gripe.
2 *the car's back wheels lost all grip on the slick surface*: **traction**, purchase, friction, adhesion, resistance.
3 *he was in the grip of an obsession he was powerless to resist*: **control**, power, mastery, hold, stranglehold, clutches, domination, dominion, command, influence, possession; rule, tyranny, evil embrace.
4 *he took Moran's hand in a firm grip*: **handshake**, hand grip, hand clasp.
5 *he was having difficulty getting a* **grip on** *what she was saying*: **understanding of**, comprehension of, perception of, awareness of, grasp of, apprehension of, conception of, realization of, knowledge of, cognizance of, ken of, mastery of, command of; insight into, familiarity with.
6 *she watched him pack his grip*: **travelling bag**, bag, holdall, overnight bag, overnighter, flight bag, kitbag, Gladstone bag, valise, portmanteau.
7 *he was offered a job as a grip at the studio*: **stagehand**, theatrical assistant.
□ **come/get to grips with** *it's time the council got to grips with this problem*: **deal with**, cope with, handle, grasp, grasp the nettle of; tackle, undertake, take on, grapple with, contend with, close with; face, face up to, meet head on, confront, encounter; take the bit between one's teeth.
▷ANTONYMS avoid.

gripe informal verb *he was griping about the boss*. See **complain**.
▸ **noun** *my only gripe is that the game is a little too easy*. See **complaint** (sense 1).

gripping adjective *a gripping thriller*: **engrossing**, enthralling, entrancing, absorbing, riveting, captivating, spellbinding, bewitching, fascinating, compulsive, addictive, compelling, mesmerizing, arresting; thrilling, exciting, action-packed, dramatic, stimulating; interesting, engaging, distracting, diverting, entertaining, amusing; informal unputdownable.
▷ANTONYMS boring.

grisly adjective *the grisly details of human sacrifices*: **gruesome**, ghastly, frightful, horrid, horrifying, fearful, hideous, macabre, spine-chilling, horrible, horrendous, grim, awful, dire, dreadful, terrible, horrific; disgusting, repulsive, repugnant, revolting, repellent, sickening, distressing, shocking, appalling, abominable, loathsome, abhorrent, odious, monstrous, unspeakable; informal sick, sick-making, gut-churning, gross; archaic disgustful, loathly.
▷ANTONYMS pleasant; attractive.

gristly adjective *a gristly piece of meat*: **stringy**, **sinewy**, fibrous, ropy; tough, leathery, leather-like, chewy; technical coriaceous.
▷ANTONYMS tender.

grit noun **1** *the grit from the paths got into her sandals*: **gravel**, pebbles, stones, shingle, sand, dust, dirt.
2 informal *I'm very impressed by your grit*: **courage**, courageousness, bravery, pluck, mettle, mettlesomeness, backbone, spirit, strength of character, strength of will, moral fibre, steel, nerve, gameness, valour, fortitude, toughness, hardiness, resolve, determination, resolution; stamina, doggedness, tenacity, perseverance, endurance; informal gumption, guts, spunk; Brit. informal bottle; vulgar slang balls.
▸ **verb** *Gina gritted her teeth to keep her temper under control*: **clench**, clamp together, press together, shut tightly; grate, grind, gnash, scrape, rasp.

gritty adjective **1** *she filled the pots with gritty soil*: **sandy**, grainy, granular, gravelly, pebbly, stony; powdery, dusty.
2 *his many gritty displays as an all-round cricketer*: **courageous**, brave, plucky, mettlesome, stout-hearted, lionhearted, valiant, bold, spirited, intrepid, game, hardy, tough, steely, determined, resolute, purposeful; dogged, tenacious, enduring, unfaltering, unswerving, unyielding, unflinching; informal gutsy, spunky, ballsy, feisty; rare perseverant.

grizzle verb Brit. informal *the baby grizzled when she went away*: **cry**, cry fretfully, weep, whimper, whine, whinge, mewl, moan, bleat, snivel, sob, wail, howl, bawl; Scottish greet; informal boohoo, blubber, blub, turn on the waterworks.

grizzled adjective *he tugged at his grizzled beard*: **grey**, greying, greyish, silver, silvery, snowy, snowy-white, white, whitish, grizzly, hoary, hoar, salt-and-pepper; grey-haired, grey-headed; rare griseous, canescent.

groan verb **1** *Ashley groaned and put a hand to her stomach*: **moan**, murmur, whine, whimper, mewl, bleat, sigh; wail, howl, sob, cry, call out.
2 *she gets home and groans about the working day*: **complain**, grumble, moan, mutter, lament, protest, object, make a fuss, find fault; informal grouse, gripe, niggle, beef, bellyache, bitch, whinge.
3 *the car juddered and groaned alarmingly*: **creak**, grate, grind, jar; squeak, screech, squeal.
▸ **noun 1** *he uttered a groan of anguish*: **moan**, murmur, whine, whimper, mewl, bleat, sigh; wail, howl, sob, cry, lamentation.
2 *she listens with sincerity to all their moans and groans*: **complaint**, grumble, objection, protest, protestation, grievance, moan, mutter, muttering, carping; informal grouse, grouch, gripe, beef, beefing, bellyaching, bitching, whinge, whingeing.
3 *we could hear the groan of the elevator*: **creaking**, creak, grating, grinding, jarring; squeak, screech, squeal, squealing.

groggy adjective *she is still feeling groggy from the anaesthetic*: **dazed**, muzzy, stupefied, in a stupor, befuddled, fuddled, muddled, confused, bewildered, disoriented, disorientated, vague, benumbed, numb, stunned, dizzy, punch-drunk, shaky, staggering, reeling, unsteady, wobbly, weak, faint; informal dopey, woozy, woolly, woolly-headed, discombobulated, not with it.

groin noun *she kicked her attacker in the groin*: **crotch**, crutch, genitals; lap.

Word links **groin**
inguinal relating to the groin

groom verb **1** *her hair was groomed to a silken sheen*: **brush**, comb, smooth, do, dress, arrange, adjust, put in order, tidy, make tidy, spruce up, smarten up, preen, primp, freshen up; informal fix.
2 *she groomed her dark bay pony*: **curry**, brush, comb, rub, rub down.
3 *the youngsters were being groomed for stardom*: **prepare**, prime, make ready, ready, condition, tailor; coach, train, instruct, tutor, drill, teach, educate, school.
▸ **noun 1** *he tossed his horse's reins to a groom*: **stable hand**, stableman, stable lad, stable boy, stable girl; historical equerry.
2 *she walked out of the chapel with her groom*: **bridegroom**, new husband, husband-to-be; newly-married man, newly-wed.

groove noun **1** *water had worn a groove in the surface of the rock*: **furrow**, channel, trench, trough, canal, gouge, hollow, indentation, rut, gutter, cutting, cut, score, fissure, seam; technical rabbet, rebate.
2 *the company had become stuck in a groove*: **rut**, routine, boring routine, habit, dead end, humdrum existence, same old round, grind, daily grind, treadmill.

grope verb **1** *Ruth groped for her sunglasses*: **fumble**, scrabble, fish, ferret (about/around), rummage (about/around/round), root about/around, feel, cast about/around/round, search, hunt, look; Brit. informal rootle around; rare grabble, roust around.
2 informal *he was accused of groping his secretaries*: **fondle**, touch; **molest**, interfere with, assault, sexually assault, abuse, sexually abuse; informal paw, maul, feel up, touch up, goose.

gross adjective **1** *I feel gross and even my legs feel flabby*: **obese**, corpulent, overweight, fat, big, large, outsize, outsized, massive, immense, huge, colossal, fleshy, flabby, portly, bloated, bulky, lumpish; informal hulking, porky, pudgy, tubby, blubbery, roly-poly; Brit. informal podgy, fubsy; N. Amer. vulgar slang lard-assed; rare pursy, abdominous.
▷ANTONYMS slender.
2 *they used gross insults to intimidate her*: **vulgar**, coarse, crude, obscene, rude, ribald, lewd, bawdy, dirty, filthy, earthy, smutty, risqué, indecent,

indelicate, improper, impure, unseemly, offensive, pornographic; informal sleazy, porno, porn, raunchy, naughty, blue, steamy, spicy, locker-room; Brit. informal fruity, saucy, near the knuckle, close to the bone; N. Amer. informal gamy; euphemistic adult; rare concupiscent.
▷ANTONYMS pure.
3 *don't go throwing yourself at men of gross natures*: **boorish**, loutish, oafish, thuggish, brutish, bearish, Neanderthal, philistine, coarse, uncouth, unsavoury, crass, vulgar, common, unrefined, unsophisticated, uncultured, uncultivated, undiscriminating, tasteless, insensitive, unfeeling, imperceptive, callous; informal cloddish, slobbish, plebby, clodhopping; Brit. informal yobbish; Austral./NZ informal ocker.
▷ANTONYMS refined.
4 informal *I threw up—it was gross*: **disgusting**, repellent, repulsive, abhorrent, loathsome, detestable, sickening, nauseating, nauseous, stomach-churning, stomach-turning, off-putting, unpalatable, unappetizing, uninviting, unsavoury, distasteful, foul, nasty, obnoxious, odious; N. Amer. vomitous; informal yucky, icky, sick-making, gut-churning; Brit. informal grotty; archaic disgustful.
▷ANTONYMS lovely.
5 *the report is a gross distortion of the truth*: **flagrant**, blatant, glaring, obvious, overt, evident, conspicuous; naked, barefaced, shameless, brazen, audacious, brass-necked; undisguised, unconcealed, patent, transparent, manifest, palpable; out and out, utter, complete; outrageous, scandalous, shocking, disgraceful, reprehensible, dreadful, terrible; enormous, heinous, atrocious, monstrous, wicked, iniquitous, villainous; archaic arrant.
▷ANTONYMS minor.
6 *tax is deducted from their gross income*: **total**, whole, entire, complete, full, overall, comprehensive, aggregate; before deductions, before tax.
▷ANTONYMS net.
▶ **verb** *he grosses over a million dollars a month*: **earn**, make, bring in, take, get, receive, fetch, draw, collect; informal rake in, pull in, haul in, bag.
□ **gross out** N. Amer. informal *luckily he wasn't one to get grossed out by blood*: **disgust**, revolt, repel, repulse, sicken, nauseate, cause to feel nauseous, make shudder, turn someone's stomach, make someone's gorge rise; be repugnant to, be repulsive to, be distasteful to; informal turn off, make someone want to throw up.

grotesque adjective **1** *a grotesque creature with a flattened body and a squashed head*: **malformed**, deformed, misshapen, misproportioned, distorted, twisted, gnarled, mangled, mutilated; ugly, unsightly, monstrous, hideous; **freakish**, unnatural, abnormal, bizarre, outlandish, strange, odd, peculiar; fantastic, fanciful, whimsical; informal weird, freaky; Brit. informal rum.
▷ANTONYMS ordinary, normal.
2 *stories of grotesque mismanagement and wasting of money*: **outrageous**, monstrous, shocking, astonishing, preposterous, ridiculous, ludicrous, farcical, unbelievable, unthinkable, incredible; informal crazy.

grotto noun *a grotto had been hollowed out of the mountain*: **cave**, cavern, cavity, hollow, recess, alcove; tunnel, pothole, underground chamber.

grouch noun *he's an ill-mannered grouch*: **grumbler**, complainer, moaner, discontent, malcontent, fault-finder, carper; grumpy person, miserable person, moper, pessimist, prophet of doom; informal grump, sourpuss, crosspatch, bear with a sore head, grouser, whinger, wet blanket, party-pooper, doom merchant; Brit. informal griper, misery; N. Amer. informal sorehead, kvetcher.
▶ **verb** *there's not a lot to grouch about*: **grumble**, complain, grouse, moan, whine, bleat, carp, cavil, grieve, sigh; informal whinge, beef, bellyache, bitch, sound off, kick up a fuss, kick up a stink; Brit. informal gripe, grizzle, chunter, create; N. Amer. informal kvetch; S. African informal chirp.

grouchy adjective **grumpy**, cross, irritable, bad-tempered, crotchety, crabby, crabbed, cantankerous, curmudgeonly, moody, miserable, morose, sullen, surly, churlish; touchy, testy, tetchy, huffy, snappish, waspish, prickly; informal snappy, cranky; Brit. informal narky, ratty, eggy, like a bear with a sore head, whingy; N. Amer. informal soreheaded, sorehead, peckish; Austral./NZ snaky; dated miffy.
▷ANTONYMS easy-going.

ground noun **1** *she stumbled and then collapsed on the ground*: **floor**, earth, terra firma; flooring; informal deck.
2 *their feet sank into the soggy ground*: **earth**, soil, topsoil, dirt, clay, loam, turf, clod, mould, sod, dust; land, terrain.
3 *the team won at their home ground*: **stadium**, pitch, field, arena, park; track, course, racetrack, racecourse, ring, rink; N. Amer. bowl.
4 (**grounds**) *a balcony overlooking the embassy grounds*: **estate**, gardens, lawns, park, parkland, land, acres, property, surroundings, domain, holding, territory; archaic demesne.
5 (**grounds**) *his actions constituted grounds for dismissal*: **reason**, cause, basis, base, foundation, justification, rationale, argument, premise, occasion, factor, excuse, pretext, motive, motivation, inducement.
6 (**grounds**) *there were coffee grounds in the bottom of the cup*: **sediment**, precipitate, settlings, dregs, lees, deposit, residue, sludge; rare grouts.
□ **get off the ground** *prefab housing never quite got off the ground*: **get going**, get under way, begin, start, start off, go ahead; informal kick off; formal commence.
□ **get something off the ground** *he thanked the hardworking committee who successfully got the project off the ground*: **set in motion**, get under way, get going, start, begin, activate, institute, initiate, launch, get in operation, get working/functioning; formal commence.
□ **go to ground** *he went to ground when we asked for elaboration*: **hide**, hide out, hide oneself, conceal oneself, secrete oneself, shelter, take cover, lie low, go to earth, go underground; informal hole up; Brit. informal lie doggo.
▷ANTONYMS come out into the open.
□ **stand one's ground** *he looked so sad but I had to stand my ground*: **stand firm**, be firm, make a stand, be resolute, insist, be determined, show determination, hold on, hold out, be emphatic, not take no for an answer, brook no refusal; informal stick to one's guns.
▷ANTONYMS give up.
▶ **verb 1** *a bitter wind blew and the bombers were grounded*: **prevent from flying**, keep on the ground.
2 *the boat grounded on a mud bank*: **run aground**, become stranded, run ashore, beach, become beached, land, be high and dry.
▷ANTONYMS float; put to sea.
3 *this assertion was grounded on results of several studies*: **base**, found, establish, set, settle, root, build, construct, form.
4 *her governess **grounded** her **in** Latin and Greek*: **instruct**, coach, tutor, educate, school, train, upskill, drill, prime, prepare; teach, familiarize with, acquaint with, make conversant with, inform about; informal give the gen about, give the low-down on, gen up on, clue up on, clue in on, fill in on, put in the picture about.

groundless adjective *she dismissed their fears as groundless*: **baseless**, without basis, without foundation, foundationless, ill-founded, unfounded, unsupported, uncorroborated, unproven, not backed up, empty, idle, vain, chimerical, imaginary, illusory, false, unsubstantiated, unwarranted, unjustified, unjustifiable, uncalled for, unprovoked, without cause, without reason, without justification, unreasonable, irrational, illogical, unsound, unreliable, questionable, misguided, spurious, specious, fallacious, erroneous.

groundwork noun *I had to do the groundwork for a revolutionary new project*: **preliminary work**, preliminaries, preparations, preparatory measures, basic work, spadework, legwork, hard work, donkey work, hack work; planning, arrangements, organization, homework; basics, rudiments, essentials, fundamentals, underpinning, footing, foundation, cornerstone; informal nitty-gritty, nuts and bolts, brass tacks.

group noun **1** *she sorted the coins into groups*: **category**, class, classification, grouping, set, lot, batch, bracket, type, sort, kind, variety, family, species, genus, breed, style; grade, grading, rank, status.
2 *a group of passengers awaited their plane*: **crowd**, band, company, party, body, gathering, congregation, assembly, collection, cluster, flock, pack, troop, gang, batch; informal bunch.
3 *a coup attempt was mounted by a group within the parliament*: **faction**, division, section, clique, coterie, circle, set, ring, camp, bloc, caucus, cabal, junta, fringe movement, splinter group, minority group.
4 *the women's group meets in the early afternoon*: **association**, club, society, league, guild, circle, union, consortium, cooperative, partnership, syndicate; rare consociation.
5 *a small group of islands*: **cluster**, knot, collection, mass, clump, bunch.
▶ **verb 1** *patients were grouped according to their symptoms*: **categorize**, classify, class, sort, bracket, pigeonhole, grade, rate, rank; designate, label, tag, brand; file, catalogue, list, tabulate, index, assign.
2 *she grouped the flowers beautifully in a small alcove*: **assemble**, collect, gather together, mass, amass, cluster, clump, bunch; arrange, organize, marshal, range, line up, dispose.
3 *the two parties **grouped together** for negotiating purposes*: **unite**, join up, join together, team up, join forces, pool resources, club together, get together, come together, gather; collaborate, work together, pull together, cooperate; link, ally, associate, fraternize, form an alliance, affiliate, federate; amalgamate, combine, merge, integrate, consolidate.
▷ANTONYMS split up.

grouse verb *she **groused about** having to sit next to Kim*: **grumble**, complain, moan, groan, protest, whine, bleat, carp, cavil, lodge a complaint, make a complaint, make a fuss; object to, speak out against, rail at, oppose, lament, bewail, grieve over, sorrow about, sorrow for, sigh over; informal bellyache, beef, bitch, grouch, whinge, kick up a fuss, kick up a stink, sound off, go on; Brit. informal gripe, grizzle, chunter, create; N. Amer. informal kvetch; S. African informal chirp; Brit. dated crib, natter; archaic plain over.
▶ **noun** *our biggest grouse was about the noise*: **grumble**, complaint, moan, groan, whine, grievance, objection, protest, protestation, cavil, quibble; informal beef, gripe, bellyache, whinge, grouch; Law, Brit. plaint.

Word links **grouse**

cock male
hen female
cheeper young
pack, covey collective noun

g

g

grove noun *a villa sited in an olive grove*: **copse**, wood, thicket, coppice, group of trees; orchard, plantation; Brit. spinney; archaic hurst, holt.

grovel verb **1** *George grovelled at his feet*: **crawl**, creep, cringe, crouch, prostrate oneself, kneel, fall on one's knees; throw oneself at someone's feet.
2 *they dislike leaders who* ***grovel to*** *foreign patrons*: **behave obsequiously**, be obsequious, be servile, be sycophantic, fawn, kowtow, bow and scrape, toady, truckle, abase oneself, humble oneself, prostrate oneself; curry favour with, flatter, court, woo, dance attendance on, make up to, play up to, ingratiate oneself with; informal crawl, creep, suck up, butter up, be all over, fall all over, lick someone's boots, rub up the right way; archaic blandish.

grow verb **1** *the baby is growing and looking healthy | the food mountains continue to grow*: **get bigger**, get taller, get larger, increase in size, increase in weight, fill out, fatten; heighten, lengthen, enlarge, extend, expand, stretch, spread, widen; swell, increase, multiply, snowball, mushroom, balloon, augment, build up, mount up, pile up.
▷ANTONYMS shrink.
2 *grass and flowers grew among the rocks*: **sprout**, shoot up, spring up, develop, bud, burst forth, germinate, bloom; emerge, arise, spread; flourish, thrive, run riot; rare pullulate, vegetate, burgeon.
▷ANTONYMS fail.
3 *he grew beautiful flowers in his garden*: **cultivate**, produce, propagate, raise, rear, bring on, nurture, tend; farm, plant, sow.
4 *the family businesses grew over the years*: **expand**, improve, advance, develop, progress, make progress, make headway; **flourish**, thrive, burgeon, prosper, succeed, be successful, get on well, boom; informal go great guns, rocket, skyrocket.
▷ANTONYMS decline; fail.
5 *the fable grew from an ancient Indian source*: **originate**, stem, spring, arise, have its origin, emerge, issue, spread, extend; develop, evolve.
6 *after an hour of waiting Leonora grew bored*: **become**, come to be, get to be, get, turn, start to feel.

growl verb **1** *the black dog growled at him*: **snarl**, bark, yap, bay.
2 *'Get out of my pub,' growled Jim*: **say roughly**, say brusquely, say nastily, say angrily, say abruptly, bark, snap, snarl, fling, hurl; round on someone; informal jump down someone's throat.

grown-up noun *she wanted to be treated like a grown-up*: **adult**, grown person, grown-up person, mature person; woman, grown woman, mature woman, man, grown man, mature man, lady, gentleman.
▷ANTONYMS child.
▸ adjective *Christine has two grown-up daughters and seven grandchildren*: **adult**, mature, of age, having reached one's majority; fully grown, full-grown, fully developed, fully fledged.
▷ANTONYMS infant, juvenile.

growth noun **1** *many countries have rapid population growth*: **increase**, expansion, augmentation, proliferation, multiplication, enlargement, amplification, mushrooming, snowballing, rise, escalation, build-up; development, evolution.
▷ANTONYMS decrease.
2 *the hormone stimulates the growth of the pancreas*: **growing**, extension, widening, thickening, broadening, heightening, swelling, magnification, ballooning.
▷ANTONYMS shrinking.
3 *harsh weather stunts the growth of plants*: **development**, maturation, growing, germination, shooting up, springing up, sprouting; blooming, flourishing, thriving; rare vegetation, burgeoning, pullulation.
▷ANTONYMS withering.
4 *the marked growth of local enterprises*: **expansion**, development, progress, advance, advancement, headway, improvement, furtherance, extension, spread, buildout, escalation; rise, success, thriving, flourishing, blooming; boom, upturn, upswing.
▷ANTONYMS decline; failure.
5 *he went to hospital to have a growth removed*: **tumour**, cancerous growth, malignant growth, malignancy, cancer; lump, outgrowth, swelling, protuberance, protrusion, knob, nodule; cyst, polyp; technical process, bulla; rare excrescence, intumescence, tumescence, tumefaction.

> *Word links* **growth**
>
> **-plasia** suffix related to growth, as in *dysplasia, achondroplasia*
> **onco-** prefix related to growths, as in *oncogenic*
> **-oma** suffix related to growths, as in *carcinoma, melanoma*
> **oncology** branch of medicine concerned with growths

grub noun **1** *the grub becomes a fully grown beetle*: **larva**, maggot; caterpillar.
2 informal *we had third helpings of delicious pub grub*. See **food**.
▸ verb **1** *kids like* ***grubbing around in*** *the dirt*: **dig**, excavate, burrow, tunnel; poke about/around, scratch about/around, rake through, sift through, explore, probe; literary delve.
2 *they* ***grub up*** *the old trees and replace them*: **dig up**, unearth, disinter, uproot, root out, root up, pull up, pull out, tear out, take out of the ground; literary deracinate.
▷ANTONYMS plant.
3 *he began* ***grubbing about in*** *the waste-paper basket*: **search**, hunt, delve, dig, rummage, scrabble, scour, probe, ferret (about/around), root, rifle, fish, poke; go through, turn upside down, turn inside out; Brit. informal rootle; Austral./NZ informal fossick through; rare roust.
4 *she achieved financial independence without having to grub for it*: **slave**, toil, labour, grind, plod, sweat, struggle, strive, overwork oneself, work very hard, work one's fingers to the bone, work like a Trojan/dog, keep one's nose to the grindstone; informal slog away, plug away, peg away, kill oneself, put one's back into it, sweat blood, knock oneself out; Brit. informal graft, fag; archaic drudge, travail, moil.
▷ANTONYMS take it easy.

grubby adjective *grubby net curtains*: **dirty**, grimy, filthy, unwashed, stained, soiled, smeared, spotted, muddy, dusty, sooty; messy, scruffy, shabby, untidy, unkempt, slovenly, slatternly, sordid, squalid; unhygienic, unsanitary, insanitary; informal mucky, cruddy, yucky, icky; Brit. informal manky, grotty, gungy; literary befouled, besmirched, besmeared, begrimed; rare feculent.
▷ANTONYMS clean.

> *Word toolkit* **grubby**
>
> See **filthy**.

grudge noun *the attack was carried out by someone with a grudge*: **grievance**; resentment, bitterness, rancour, pique, umbrage, displeasure, dissatisfaction, disgruntlement, bad feelings, hard feelings, ill feelings, ill will, venom, hate, hatred, dislike, aversion, animosity, antipathy, antagonism, enmity, animus; informal a chip on one's shoulder.
▸ verb **1** *he grudged the time that the meetings involved*: **begrudge**, resent, feel aggrieved/bitter about, be annoyed about, be angry about, be displeased about, be resentful of, mind, object to, take exception to, regret; give unwillingly, give reluctantly, give resentfully, give stintingly.
2 *I do not grudge you your success*: **envy**, begrudge, resent, mind; be jealous of, be envious of, be resentful of.

grudging adjective *she offered a grudging apology*: **reluctant**, unwilling, disinclined, forced, half-hearted, unenthusiastic, hesitant; begrudging, resentful, envious, jealous, sullen, sulky, sour, bitter.
▷ANTONYMS eager.

> *Word toolkit* **grudging**
>
> See **envious**.

gruelling adjective *he undertook a gruelling three-mile run*: **exhausting**, tiring, fatiguing, wearying, enervating, taxing, draining, sapping, debilitating; demanding, exacting, trying, difficult, hard, arduous, laborious, back-breaking, strenuous, harsh, severe, stiff, punishing, crushing, crippling, grinding, brutal, relentless, unsparing; informal killing, murderous, hellish; Brit. informal knackering; rare exigent.

gruesome adjective *the gruesome evidence of a recent massacre*: **grisly**, ghastly, frightful, horrid, horrifying, fearful, hideous, macabre, spine-chilling, horrible, horrendous, grim, awful, dire, dreadful, terrible, horrific; disgusting, repulsive, repugnant, revolting, repellent, sickening, distressing, shocking, appalling, abominable, loathsome, abhorrent, odious, monstrous, unspeakable; informal sick, sick-making, gut-churning, gross; archaic disgustful, loathly.
▷ANTONYMS pleasant.

gruff adjective **1** *a gruff reply | his gruff exterior hid a sensitive nature*: **abrupt**, brusque, curt, short, blunt, bluff, no-nonsense; laconic, taciturn; surly, churlish, grumpy, crotchety, crabby, crabbed, cross, bad-tempered, short-tempered, ill-natured, crusty, tetchy, bearish, sullen, sour, uncivil, rude, unmannerly, impolite, discourteous, ungracious, unceremonious, offhand; informal grouchy, off, offish.
▷ANTONYMS friendly; courteous.
2 *a gruff male voice bade them enter*: **rough**, hoarse, harsh, guttural, throaty, husky, croaking, rasping, raspy, gravelly, growly, growling; low, thick.
▷ANTONYMS soft, mellow.

grumble verb **1** *the players* ***grumble about*** *the referee*: **complain**, moan, groan, whine, mutter, grouse, bleat, carp, cavil, protest; object to, speak out against, find fault with; informal bellyache, beef, bitch, grouch, whinge, sound off, go on, pick holes in; Brit. informal gripe, grizzle, chunter, create; N. English informal mither; N. Amer. informal kvetch; S. African informal chirp; Brit. dated crib, natter; archaic plain over.
2 *my stomach was starting to grumble audibly*: **rumble**, gurgle, murmur, growl, roar.
▸ noun **1** *he listens to his customers' grumbles*: **complaint**, moan, groan, whine, muttering, grievance, objection, protest, protestation, cavil, quibble, criticism, charge, accusation; informal grouse, grouch, whinge, beef,

beefing, bellyaching, bitching, grouching, whingeing; Brit. informal gripe; Law, Brit. plaint.
2 *the grumble of his stomach*: **rumble**, gurgle, murmur, growl, roar.

grumpy adjective *she can be grumpy first thing in the morning*: **bad-tempered**, ill-tempered, short-tempered, crotchety, crabby, crabbed, tetchy, testy, waspish, prickly, peppery, touchy, irritable, irascible, crusty, cantankerous, curmudgeonly, bearish, surly, churlish, ill-natured, ill-humoured, peevish, cross, as cross as two sticks, fractious, disagreeable, pettish; having got out of bed on the wrong side; informal grouchy, snappy, snappish, chippy, on a short fuse, short-fused; Brit. informal shirty, stroppy, narky, ratty, eggy, like a bear with a sore head; N. Amer. informal cranky, ornery, soreheaded; Austral./NZ informal snaky; informal, dated miffy, waxy.
▷ANTONYMS good-humoured.

guarantee noun **1** *all repairs have a one-year guarantee*: **warranty**, warrant, contract, covenant, bond, assurance, promise.
2 *they gave their guarantee that the hospital would stay open*: **promise**, assurance, word, word of honour, pledge, vow, oath, bond, commitment.
3 *banks usually demand a personal guarantee for loans*: **collateral**, security, surety, guaranty, assurance, insurance, indemnity, indemnification; archaic gage, earnest.
4 *I will not venture to be your guarantee*: **guarantor**, warrantor, underwriter, voucher, sponsor, supporter, backer; Law bondsman.
▶ verb **1** *they have to guarantee the loan with their own personal assets*: **underwrite**, sponsor, support, back, insure, indemnify, vouch for, put up collateral for, give earnest money for, provide surety for, provide (financial) security for; informal be ready to pick up the tab for; N. Amer. informal bankroll.
2 *can you guarantee that he wasn't involved?* **promise**, swear, swear to the fact, pledge, vow, undertake, give one's word, give an assurance, give assurances, give an undertaking, give a pledge, swear an oath, take an oath, cross one's heart (and hope to die); archaic plight.

guarantor noun *a guarantor of the company's debts*: **warrantor**, guarantee, underwriter, voucher, sponsor, supporter, backer; Law bondsman.

guard verb **1** *the infantry guarded the barricaded bridge*: **protect**, stand guard over, watch over, look after, keep an eye on, take care of, cover, patrol, police, defend, shield, safeguard, preserve, save, keep safe, secure, screen, shelter; fortify, garrison, barricade; man, occupy.
2 *the prisoners were guarded by armed men*: **keep under surveillance**, keep under guard, keep watch over, mind, supervise, restrain, control.
3 *the forest wardens have to* ***guard against*** *poachers*: **beware of**, keep watch for, be alert to, take care for, keep an eye out for, be on the alert for, be on the qui vive for, be on the lookout for; informal keep one's eyes peeled/skinned for.
▶ noun **1** *they were caught by border guards*: **sentry**, sentinel, security guard, nightwatchman; protector, defender, guardian, custodian, keeper; scout, lookout, watch; garrison; informal bouncer; archaic watchman.
2 *she slipped easily past her prison guard*: **jailer**, warder, wardress, warden, prison officer, keeper, incarcerator, captor, sentry; informal screw; Law detainer; archaic turnkey.
3 *he let his guard slip and they escaped*: **vigilance**, vigil, watch, close watch, monitoring, policing, surveillance, sentry duty; watchfulness, caution, heed, attention, care, wariness.
4 *all machines must be fitted with a guard*: **safety guard**, safety device, protective device, shield, bulwark, screen, fence, fender, bumper, buffer, cushion, pad.
□ **off (one's) guard** *he was caught off guard when the man charged towards him*: **unprepared**, unready, inattentive, unwary, unwatchful, with one's defences down, by surprise, cold, unsuspecting; informal napping, asleep on the job, asleep at the wheel, on the hop.
▷ANTONYMS prepared.
□ **on one's guard** *police are urging horse owners to be on their guard*: **vigilant**, alert, on the alert, wary, watchful, cautious, careful, heedful, chary, circumspect, on the lookout, on the qui vive, on one's toes, prepared, ready, wideawake, attentive, observant, keeping one's eyes peeled; informal all ears, beady-eyed, on the ball, not missing a trick, keeping a weather eye on things, cagey, leery; rare regardful, Argus-eyed.
▷ANTONYMS inattentive.

guarded adjective **1** *his colleagues showed guarded enthusiasm for the proposal*: **cautious**, careful, circumspect, wary, chary, reluctant, non-committal, reticent, restrained, reserved, controlled, moderate, discreet, unrevealing, vague, diplomatic, prudent, politic, tactful; with reservations; informal cagey, leery.
▷ANTONYMS revealing; obvious.
2 *more guerrillas could be rounded up for the attack on the heavily guarded bridge*: **secured**, secure, protected, shielded, manned, policed, defended, under guard, under surveillance.

> *Word toolkit* **guarded**
>
> See **protected**.

guardian noun *an indefatigable guardian of public morality*: **protector**, defender, preserver, champion, custodian, warden, guard, keeper; conservator, curator, caretaker, steward, trustee, supervisor.

> *Word links* **guardian**
>
> **tutelary** relating to a guardian

guerrilla noun *there was fierce fighting between guerrillas and government troops*: **freedom fighter**, underground fighter, irregular soldier, irregular, resistance fighter, member of the resistance, partisan; rebel, radical, revolutionary, revolutionist; terrorist.

guess verb **1** *she was asked to guess the weight of the animal*: **estimate**, calculate, approximate, make a guess at, make an estimate of; **hypothesize**, postulate, predict, speculate, conjecture, surmise, reckon, fathom; evaluate, judge, gauge, determine, rate, appraise, weigh up, form an opinion of; informal guesstimate, size up.
2 informal *I guess I owe you an apology*: **suppose**, think, believe, imagine, expect, assume, presume, judge, consider, feel, suspect, dare say, fancy, divine, deem, conjecture, surmise, conclude, hazard a guess, be of the opinion, be given to understand; N. Amer. figure; informal reckon.
▶ noun *my guess is that he is a receiver of stolen cars*: **hypothesis**, theory, prediction, postulation, conjecture; conclusion, belief, opinion, surmise, estimate, reckoning, judgement, supposition, assumption, speculation, notion, suspicion, impression, feeling; informal guesstimate.

guesswork noun *their estimates were based largely on guesswork*: **guessing**, conjecture, surmise, supposition, assumption, presumption, suspicion, speculation, hypothesizing, theorizing, prediction, expectation; approximations, rough calculations; feelings, hunches; informal guesstimates; N. Amer. informal ballpark figures.

guest noun **1** *he took dinner with his guests*: **visitor**, caller; company; archaic visitant.
▷ANTONYMS host.
2 *the hotel allowed two towels per guest*: **patron**, client, person staying; **boarder**, lodger, resident, tenant, paying guest, PG; N. Amer. roomer.
▷ANTONYMS landlady, landlord.

guest house noun *she spent three nights in a Blackpool guest house*: **boarding house**, bed and breakfast, B&B, hotel, motel; inn, hostelry.

guffaw verb *he guffawed at his own punchline*: **laugh heartily**, laugh loudly, roar with laughter, hoot with laughter, laugh uncontrollably; roar, bellow, cackle, howl; informal laugh like a drain.
▶ noun *his joke brought a great guffaw from the youth*: **hearty laugh**, loud laugh, roar of laughter, hoot of laughter, shriek of laughter, peal of laughter, belly laugh.

guidance noun **1** *she looked to her instructor for guidance*: **advice**, counsel, direction, instruction, teaching, counselling, enlightenment, intelligence, information; recommendations, suggestions, tips, hints, pointers, guidelines, ideas, facts, data; informal info, gen, dope, the low-down, the inside story.
2 *we are working under the guidance of a strong chairman*: **direction**, control, leadership, management, supervision, superintendence, government, regulation, orchestration, charge, rule, command; handling, conduct, running, overseeing.

guide noun **1** *this man will be your guide in the jungle*: **escort**, attendant, conductor, courier, pilot, usher, chaperone; rare cicerone, convoy.
2 *the abbot is their inspiration and their guide*: **adviser**, mentor, counsellor, guidance counsellor; confidant, tutor, teacher, guru, consultant; therapist; informal main man.
3 *the techniques outlined are meant as a guide*: **model**, pattern, blueprint, template, archetype, prototype, sample, example, exemplar; standard, touchstone, measure, benchmark, yardstick, gauge, norm, paradigm, ideal, precedent, guiding principle.
4 *she studied a pocket guide of Washington*: **guidebook**, tourist guide, travel guide, Baedeker, travelogue, directory, handbook, manual, ABC, A to Z; Latin vade mecum; rare enchiridion.
▶ verb **1** *could you guide me back to the house?* **lead**, lead the way, conduct, show, show someone the way, usher, shepherd, direct, steer, pilot, escort, accompany, attend; see, take, help, assist.
▷ANTONYMS follow.
2 *the chairman must guide the meeting*: **direct**, steer, control, manage, command, lead, conduct, run, be in charge of, take charge of, take control of, have control of, govern, rule, preside over, superintend, supervise, oversee; handle, regulate, manipulate, manoeuvre.
3 *they guide adolescents through their critical years*: **advise**, counsel, give advice to, give counsel to, give counselling to, direct, give direction to, make recommendations to, make suggestions to, give someone tips, give someone hints, give someone pointers, inform, give information to; illuminate, educate, instruct, teach, give instruction to, be responsible for the education of.

guidebook noun *they followed the tour in the museum guidebook*: **guide**, travel guide, tourist guide, Baedeker, travelogue; visitor's guide, companion, handbook, directory, manual, ABC, A to Z; reference book; Latin vade mecum; informal bible; rare enchiridion, promptuary.

guideline noun *the planning authorities have fairly strict guidelines*: **recommendation**, instruction, direction, suggestion, advice; regulation, rule, requirement, specification, prescription, precept, principle, guiding principle; standard, criterion, measure, gauge, yardstick, benchmark, touchstone; procedure, parameter, constraint, limit.

guild noun *a member of the Women's Cooperative Guild*: **association**, society, union, league, alliance, coalition, federation, consortium, syndicate, combine, trust, organization, company, cooperative, partnership, fellowship, club, order, lodge, sisterhood, sorority, brotherhood, fraternity; rare consociation, sodality.

guile noun *they penetrated the city's defences by guile*: **cunning**, craftiness, craft, artfulness, art, artifice, wiliness, slyness, deviousness, shrewdness, canniness, ingenuity; wiles, ploys, schemes, stratagems, manoeuvres, subterfuges, tricks, ruses; deception, deceit, duplicity, underhandedness, double-dealing, trickiness, sharp practice, treachery, chicanery, fraud, skulduggery; informal foxiness; archaic knavery, knavishness, management.
▷ANTONYMS honesty; candour.

g

guileless adjective *Paulette's questioning had the guileless innocence of a child*: **artless**, ingenuous, open, honest, sincere, genuine, naive, natural, simple, childlike, innocent, unsophisticated, unworldly, unsuspicious, trustful, trusting; honourable, truthful, frank, candid, straightforward, forthright, unaffected, unpretentious; N. Amer. on the up and up.
▷ANTONYMS scheming.

guilt noun **1** *the new evidence made them doubt his guilt*: **culpability**, guiltiness, blameworthiness, wrongdoing, wrong, wrongfulness, criminality, unlawfulness, misconduct, delinquency, sin, sinfulness, iniquity; responsibility, accountability, liability, answerability.
▷ANTONYMS innocence.
2 *eat your food and enjoy it without guilt*: **self-reproach**, self-accusation, self-condemnation, feelings of guilt, guiltiness, a guilty conscience, a bad conscience, pangs of conscience; **remorse**, remorsefulness, regret, contrition, contriteness, repentance, penitence, compunction; shame, disgrace, dishonour; archaic rue.
▷ANTONYMS shamelessness.

guiltless adjective *I am entirely guiltless in this matter*: **innocent**, blameless, free from guilt, free from blame, not to blame, without fault, above reproach, beyond criticism, above suspicion, in the clear, uncensurable, unimpeachable, irreproachable, faultless, sinless, spotless, stainless, immaculate, unsullied, uncorrupted, undefiled, untainted, unblemished, untarnished, impeccable; informal squeaky clean, whiter than white, as pure as the driven snow.
▷ANTONYMS guilty.

> *Choose the right word* **guiltless, blameless, innocent**
>
> See **innocent**.

guilty adjective **1** *he was found guilty of a criminal offence*: **culpable**, to blame, blameworthy, blameable, at fault, in the wrong, responsible, answerable, accountable, liable; censurable, reproachable, condemnable, reprehensible, erring, errant, delinquent, offending, sinful, felonious, iniquitous, criminal, convicted; archaic peccant.
▷ANTONYMS innocent.
2 *he felt guilty at deceiving his family*: **ashamed**, guilt-ridden, conscience-stricken, remorseful, sorry, regretful, contrite, repentant, penitent, rueful, abashed, shamefaced, sheepish, hangdog; mortified, discomfited, distressed, uncomfortable; in sackcloth and ashes; informal with one's tail between one's legs; rare compunctious.
▷ANTONYMS unrepentant.

guise noun **1** *the god appeared in the guise of a swan*: **likeness**, external appearance, appearance, semblance, form, outward form, shape, image, aspect; disguise, false colours; costume, clothes, outfit, dress.
2 *the king sent forces into Flanders under the guise of a crusade*: **pretence**, false show, false front, false display, show, front, facade, illusion, cover, blind, screen, smokescreen, masquerade, posture, pose, act, charade; informal put-on, put-up job.

gulf noun **1** *our ship sailed east into the gulf*: **inlet**, creek, bight, fjord, estuary, sound, arm of the sea; bay, cove; Scottish firth, frith; in Orkney & Shetland voe; technical ria; rare fleet, armlet.
2 *the ice gave way and a gulf widened slowly*: **opening**, gap, fissure, cleft, split, rift, crevasse, hole, pit, cavity, chasm, abyss, void; ravine, gorge, canyon, gully.
3 *there is a growing gulf between the rich and the poor*: **divergence**, contrast, polarity, divide, division, separation, difference, wide area of difference; **schism**, breach, rift, split, severance, rupture, divorce; chasm, abyss, gap; rare scission.

gull verb *she knew she wouldn't be able to gull him*. See **deceive** (sense 1).
▶ noun *she is unaware of being the gull of John's plot*. See **victim** (sense 2).

gullet noun **oesophagus**, throat, pharynx; crop, craw, maw; informal, dated the red lane; archaic weasand, throttle, gorge, gula.

> *Word links* **gullet**
>
> **oesophageal** relating to the gullet

gullible adjective *the swindler preyed upon gullible old women*: **credulous**, over-trusting, over-trustful, trustful, easily deceived/led, easily taken in, exploitable, dupable, deceivable, impressionable, unsuspecting, unsuspicious, unwary, unguarded, unsceptical, ingenuous, naive, innocent, simple, inexperienced, unworldly, green, as green as grass, childlike, ignorant; foolish, silly; informal wet behind the ears, born yesterday.
▷ANTONYMS cynical; suspicious.

> *Choose the right word* **gullible, credulous**
>
> A **gullible** person is easy to deceive because they are too ready to believe or trust someone (*professional manipulators intent on pulling the wool over the eyes of a gullible public*). They are particularly likely to believe something that would be to their advantage or that they want to be true. *Gullible* carries a note of scornful pity at someone's foolish failure to examine the evidence critically.
>
> **Credulous** also describes people who are too ready to believe or accept what they are told (*the very incomprehensibility of the modern world has made us even more credulous*), but, unlike *gullible*, *credulous* does not necessarily imply that anyone is deliberately trying to take advantage of an easily-fooled person.

gully noun **1** *the climber plunged 300 feet down an icy gully*: **ravine**, canyon, gorge, pass, defile, couloir, deep narrow valley; gulf, chasm, abyss; S. English chine, bunny; N. English clough, gill, thrutch; Scottish cleuch, heugh; N. Amer. gulch, coulee, flume; S. African sloot, kloof, donga.
2 *the water runs from the drainpipe into a gully*: **channel**, conduit, trench, ditch, drain, culvert, cut, flume, gutter, furrow, groove, depression.

gulp verb **1** *Belinda gulped her juice*: **swallow**, quaff, swill down, down; drain one's glass; informal swig, slug down, knock back, toss off.
▷ANTONYMS sip.
2 *the spaniels **gulped down** what was left on the plates*: **gobble**, guzzle, bolt, wolf, cram, stuff; devour, gorge (oneself) on, eat greedily, eat hungrily; informal tuck into, put away, pack away, demolish, polish off, stuff one's face with, pig oneself on, murder, shovel down; Brit. informal scoff, shift.
▷ANTONYMS pick at.
3 *Jenny **gulped back** her tears*: **choke back**, fight back, hold back, hold in, keep back, restrain, suppress, stifle, smother, strangle, muffle, quench, curb, check, withhold, contain, bottle up.
▷ANTONYMS let out.
▶ noun *he took a gulp of the cold beer*: **mouthful**, swallow, draught; informal swig.
▷ANTONYMS sip.

gum[1] noun *the photographs were stuck down with gum*: **glue**, adhesive, fixative, paste, cement, resin, epoxy resin, superglue; N. Amer. mucilage; N. Amer. informal stickum.
▶ verb *the receipts were gummed into a special book*: **stick**, glue, paste, cement; fix, affix, attach, fasten, post.
□ **gum something up 1** *check the valves to make sure that they don't get gummed up*: **clog (up)**, choke (up), stop up, dam up, plug, congest, jam, obstruct, occlude, close; informal bung up, gunge up. **2** *perfectionism tends to gum up the works*: **obstruct**, impede, hinder, interfere with, bring to a halt.

gum[2] noun Anatomy

> *Word links* **gum**
>
> **gingival** relating to the gums
> **gingivitis** inflammation of the gums

gummy adjective *conifers exude a gummy substance*: **sticky**, tacky, gluey, adhesive, resinous, viscous, viscid, glutinous, mucilaginous; Brit. claggy; Scottish & N. English clarty; informal gooey, gloopy, cloggy, gungy, icky; N. Amer. informal gloppy; rare viscoid.

gumption noun informal *she had the gumption to go and make a better life for herself*: **initiative**, resourcefulness, enterprise, imagination, imaginativeness, ingenuity, inventiveness; cleverness, astuteness, shrewdness, acumen, discernment, understanding, reason, wisdom, sagacity, sense, common sense, wit, mother wit, native wit, native ability, practicality; spirit, forcefulness, backbone, pluck, mettle, nerve, courage; informal get-up-and-go, grit, spunk, oomph, nous, savvy, horse sense; Brit. informal loaf, common; N. Amer. informal smarts.
▷ANTONYMS stupidity.

gun noun **firearm**, weapon; informal shooter, cannon; N. Amer. informal piece, heater, gat, rod, roscoe, shooting iron.
□ **go great guns** informal *her fashion business is going great guns*: **prosper**, do well, get on well, go well, fare well; **thrive**, flourish, flower, bloom,

burgeon, blossom; boom, expand, spread, pick up, improve, come on; succeed, be successful, make it, do all right for oneself, get ahead, progress, make progress, make headway, advance, get on in the world, go up in the world, arrive, fly high, make one's mark, make good, become rich, strike gold/oil, be in clover; informal go places, make the big time, be in the pink, be fine and dandy; archaic make good speed.verb

□ **gun down** *they were gunned down in a senseless act of violence*: **shoot**, shoot down, mow down, hit, wound, injure, cut down, bring down; put a bullet in, pick off, bag, fell, kill; execute, put before a firing squad; informal pot, blast, pump full of lead, plug, zap; literary slay.

gunfire noun *they heard the distant sounds of gunfire*: **gunshots**, shots, shooting, firing, sniping; artillery fire, strafing, shelling, bombardment.

gunman noun *the gunman broke into the bank through the roof*: **armed robber**, hold-up man, bandit, gangster, terrorist, gunfighter; sniper, assassin, murderer, killer, liquidator; informal stick-up man, hit man, gun, hired gun, contract man, hatchet man, trigger man, gunslinger, mobster; N. Amer. informal shootist, hood, button man.

gurgle verb **1** *the creek splashes and gurgles in a series of pools*: **babble**, burble, tinkle, bubble, ripple, murmur, purl, lap, trickle, splash; literary plash.
2 *the baby gurgled and smiled at Ruth*: **burble**, babble, chuckle, giggle, laugh, crow.
▸ noun **1** *there was silence except for the gurgle of a small brook*: **babble**, babbling, tinkle, bubbling, ripple, rippling, trickling, murmur, murmuring, purling, splashing; literary plashing.
2 *Catherine gave a gurgle of laughter*: **chuckle**, chortle, burble, giggle; crow.

guru noun **1** *his guru instructed him to set off on a pilgrimage*: **spiritual teacher**, teacher, tutor, sage, counsellor, mentor, guiding light, spiritual leader, leader, master; Indian acharya, pandit; Hinduism swami, Maharishi; Buddhism Roshi; Judaism rabbi, rav, rebbe.
▷ANTONYMS disciple.
2 *a natural childbirth guru*: **expert**, authority, leading light, professional, master, pundit; informal buff, whizz, boffin.
▷ANTONYMS amateur.

gush verb **1** *the white waters gushed through the weir*: **surge**, burst, spout, spurt, jet, stream, rush, pour, spill, well out, cascade, flood; flow, run, issue, emanate; Brit. informal sloosh; rare disembogue.
2 *they were gushing about her dress for the dance*: **enthuse**, over-enthuse, be enthusiastic, be effusive, effuse; **rave**, rhapsodize, go into raptures, wax lyrical, effervesce, bubble over; get carried away, make too much of, overstate the case, praise to the skies; informal go mad, go crazy, go wild, get all worked up, go over the top; N. Amer. informal ballyhoo; black English big something up; dated cry something up.
▸ noun *the pipe sent forth a gush of water*: **surge**, stream, spurt, jet, spout, outpouring, outflow, burst, rush, cascade, flood, torrent, sweep; technical flux, efflux.

gushing, gushy adjective *the gushing praise of the critics*: **effusive**, over-effusive, enthusiastic, over-enthusiastic, unrestrained, unreserved, extravagant, fulsome, lavish, rhapsodic, lyrical, exuberant, ebullient, expansive; informal over the top, OTT, hyped up, laid on with a trowel.
▷ANTONYMS restrained.

gust noun **1** *a sudden gust of wind*: **flurry**, blast, puff, blow, rush, squall.
2 *a great gust of delighted laughter came from downstairs*: **outburst**, burst, outbreak, gale, effusion, eruption, explosion, storm, surge, peal, howl, hoot, shriek, roar; fit, paroxysm.
▸ verb *the wind gusted around chimneys*: **bluster**, flurry, blow, blast, roar.

gusto noun *he was attacking his breakfast with some gusto*: **enthusiasm**, relish, appetite, enjoyment, delight, glee, pleasure, satisfaction, gratification, appreciation, liking, fondness; zest, zeal, fervour, verve, keenness, avidity; humorous delectation.
▷ANTONYMS apathy; distaste.

> *Choose the right word* **gusto, zest, verve**
>
> See **zest**.

gusty adjective *a gusty autumnal night*: **blustery**, breezy, windy, squally, gusting, blustering; stormy, tempestuous, wild, turbulent, violent; informal blowy.
▷ANTONYMS calm.

gut noun **1** (also **guts**) *he had an ache in his gut*: **stomach**, belly, abdomen; intestines, bowels, colon; informal tummy, tum, insides, innards, breadbasket; Austral. informal bingy; Medicine solar plexus.
2 (**guts**) *they threw away the fish heads and guts*: **intestines**, entrails; **vital organs**, bodily organs, vital parts, viscera; offal; informal insides, innards; Brit. archaic numbles.
3 (**guts**) informal *Nicola had the guts to say exactly what she felt*: **courage**, courageousness, bravery, valour, backbone, nerve, fortitude, pluck, pluckiness, mettle, mettlesomeness, spirit, boldness, audacity, daring, fearlessness, hardiness, toughness, forcefulness, determination, resolve, resolution; informal grit, gumption, spunk, gutsiness, gameness; Brit. informal bottle, ballsiness; N. Amer. informal moxie, cojones, sand; vulgar slang balls.
▷ANTONYMS cowardice.
▸ adjective informal *she had a gut feeling that something was not right*: **instinctive**, instinctual, intuitive, impulsive, natural, basic, emotional, heartfelt, deep-seated; knee-jerk, automatic, involuntary, spontaneous, unthinking.
▸ verb **1** *the pilchards had to be gutted and salted*: **disembowel**, eviscerate, draw, dress, clean, remove the innards from, remove the guts from; rare embowel, disbowel, exenterate, gralloch, paunch.
2 *the entire church was gutted by fire*: **devastate**, destroy, demolish, wipe out, lay waste to, ravage, consume, ruin, leave in ruins, wreck, raze, level, flatten; literary despoil.

> *Word links* **gut**
>
> **visceral**, **enteric** relating to the gut
> **enter-** related prefix, as in *enteritis, enterovirus*

gutless adjective informal *he's too gutless to stand up to them*. See **cowardly**.

gutsy adjective informal *he is a gutsy and popular player*: **courageous**, brave, mettlesome, plucky, bold, valiant, valorous, intrepid, heroic, lionhearted, daring, fearless, daredevil, adventurous, audacious, undaunted, unflinching, unshrinking, unafraid, dauntless, indomitable, doughty, venturesome, stout-hearted, spirited; determined, resolute, forceful, death-or-glory; N. Amer. rock-ribbed; informal spunky, game, ballsy, have-a-go; rare venturous.
▷ANTONYMS gutless.

gutter noun *a tide of rainwater swept into the gutter*: **drain**, sluice, sluiceway, culvert, spillway, flume, sewer; channel, conduit, pipe, duct, chute; trough, trench, ditch, furrow, cut.

guttersnipe noun *the child was a penniless guttersnipe*: **urchin**, street urchin, ragamuffin, waif, stray, outcast, orphan; informal scarecrow; dated gamin; archaic mudlark, scapegrace, street Arab, wastrel, tatterdemalion.

guttural adjective *he heard guttural shouts in a foreign language*: **throaty**, husky, gruff, gravelly, growly, growling, croaky, croaking, harsh, harsh-sounding, rough, rasping, raspy, grating, jarring; deep, low, thick.

guy noun **1** informal *he's quite a handsome guy*: **man**, fellow, gentleman; lad, youth, boy; individual, person, soul; informal fella, geezer, gent, character, customer, creature, sort, type; Brit. informal chap, bloke, bod; N. Amer. informal dude, hombre; Austral./NZ informal digger, bastard; S. African informal ou, oom, oke; Indian informal admi; Brit. informal, dated cove; Brit. vulgar slang sod, bugger; archaic wight; Scottish archaic carl.
2 Brit. *the kids asked passing workers for pennies for the guy*: **effigy of Guy Fawkes**; effigy, figure, representation, likeness, image, model, dummy.
▸ verb *he didn't realize I was guying the whole idea*. See **ridicule** (verb).

guzzle verb *he guzzled all that was on the table*: **gobble (up)**, gulp, bolt, wolf, devour, eat greedily, eat hungrily, cram oneself with, stuff oneself with, gourmandize on; informal tuck into, put away, pack away, demolish, polish off, stuff one's face with, pig oneself on, murder, shovel down; Brit. informal scoff, shift.

gypsy, gipsy noun **Romany**, Rom, chal, chai, gitano, gitana, tzigane, Zingaro, Zigeuner, zingana, didicoi; traveller, New Age traveller, New Ager; nomad, migrant, rover, roamer, wanderer, wayfarer; Bedouin, Bohemian; informal, derogatory gyppo, gippy; derogatory transient, vagrant, vagabond, tinker.

gyrate verb *flashing lights gyrate above the dance floor*: **rotate**, revolve, move in circles, go round in circles, circle, spiral, wheel round, turn round, whirl, pirouette, twirl, swirl, spin, swivel.

gyration noun *the gyration of the Earth on its own axis*: **rotation**, revolution, turning, circling, convolution, spinning, swivelling; wheeling, whirling, pirouetting, twirling, swirling; rare circumrotation.

habit noun **1** *sensible eating habits*: **practice**, custom, pattern, routine, style, convention, policy, wont, way, manner, mode, norm, tradition, matter of course, rule, usage; tendency, propensity, inclination, bent, proclivity, proneness, disposition, predisposition.
2 *his habit of pulling his ear as he made a point he thought important*: **mannerism**, quirk, characteristic gesture, characteristic, foible, trick; trait, tendency, idiosyncrasy, peculiarity, singularity, oddity, eccentricity, way, feature, custom, practice.
3 *the scientific **habit of mind** helps us to deal intelligently with problems*: **disposition**, temperament, character, nature, make-up, constitution, frame of mind, bent.
4 *they financed their drug habit through prostitution*: **addiction**, dependence, dependency, craving, fixation, compulsion, obsession, weakness; informal monkey; N. Amer. informal jones.
5 *a monk's habit*: **garment**, outfit, robe, costume, uniform, attire, dress, garb, clothes, clothing, garments; informal get-up, rig-out, gear, togs, clobber, rags; formal apparel.
□ **in the habit of** *they were in the habit of phoning each other regularly*: **accustomed to**, used to, given to, habituated to, addicted to, no stranger to, not new to; wont to, inclined to.
▷ANTONYMS unaccustomed to.

habitable adjective *contractors worked around the clock to make the building habitable*: **fit to live in**, inhabitable, fit to occupy, in good repair, usable, liveable in, suitable for residential use; formal tenantable.
▷ANTONYMS uninhabitable.

habitat noun *a record of new plants in their native habitat*: **natural environment**, natural element, natural territory, natural surroundings, natural terrain, home, domain, haunt; formal habitation, abode.
▷ANTONYMS unnatural surroundings.

habitation noun **1** *the house is fit for human habitation*: **occupancy**, occupation, residence, residency, living in, housing, billeting, quartering, tenure; formal dwelling; rare inhabitancy, habitancy, inhabitance, domiciliation.
2 formal *we walked for an hour without passing a single habitation*: **house**, home, seat, lodging, lodging place, a roof over one's head, billet, quarters, living quarters, rooms, accommodation, housing; informal pad, digs, diggings; formal residence, place of residence, dwelling, dwelling place, abode, domicile.

habit-forming adjective *habit-forming drugs*: **addictive**, causing addiction, causing dependency; compelling, compulsive; Brit. informal moreish.
▷ANTONYMS non-addictive.

habitual adjective **1** *father's habitual complaints and strictures*: **constant**, persistent, continual, continuous, perpetual, non-stop, recurrent, repeated, frequent; interminable, incessant, ceaseless, endless, relentless, unrelenting, never-ending, unremitting, sustained, unabating; informal eternal.
▷ANTONYMS infrequent.
2 *habitual drinkers*: **inveterate**, confirmed, addicted, compulsive, obsessive, incorrigible, hardened, ingrained, dyed-in-the-wool, chronic, by habit, regular; informal pathological, hooked.
▷ANTONYMS occasional.
3 *the commuters assembled in their habitual positions along the platform*: **customary**, accustomed, regular, usual, normal, set, fixed, established, routine, common, ordinary, familiar, traditional, typical, general, characteristic, standard, time-honoured; literary wonted.
▷ANTONYMS unaccustomed.

> *Word toolkit* **habitual**
>
> See **incorrigible**.

habituate verb *school had **habituated** him **to** shabbiness and discomfort*: **accustom**, make used, adapt, adjust, attune, acclimatize, acculturate, inure, harden; make familiar with, familiarize with; season; condition, teach, train, school, educate, discipline, break in; N. Amer. acclimate.

habitué noun *a habitué of the West End*: **frequent visitor**, regular visitor, regular customer, regular patron, regular client, familiar face, regular, patron, frequenter, haunter.
▷ANTONYMS passing trade; tourist.

hack[1] verb **1** *Stuart hacked the padlock off* | *they had to hack their way through the jungle*: **cut**, chop, hew, lop, saw; slash.
2 *he was wheezing and hacking*: **cough**, bark, rasp, wheeze.
□ **hack it** informal *Adam moved out because he couldn't hack it*: **cope**, manage, get on, get along, get by, carry on, muddle through, muddle along, come through, stand on one's own two feet, weather the storm; stand it, tolerate it, bear it, endure it, put up with it; Scottish thole it; informal make out, handle it, abide it, stick it; Brit. informal rub along, be doing with it.
□ **hack someone off** informal *it hacks him off when he misses a putt*.
See **annoy**.
▶ noun *a smoker's hack*: **cough**, bark, rasp, wheeze.

hack[2] noun **1** *he briefed the media's industry hacks before the party conference*: **journalist**, reporter, correspondent, newspaperman, newspaperwoman, newsman, newswoman, writer, feature writer, contributor, columnist, Grub Street writer; Brit. pressman; N. Amer. legman, wireman; Austral. roundsman; informal news hound, journo, scribbler, scribe, hackette, stringer; N. Amer. informal newsy; archaic penny-a-liner.
2 *a hard-working, clerical hack*: **drudge**, menial, menial worker, factotum, toiler, plodder, doormat, hewer of wood and drawer of water; servant, lackey, labourer, slave; informal dogsbody, skivvy, running dog, runner; N. Amer. peon, gofer; archaic scullion, servitor.
3 *the average riding-school hack*: **nag**, inferior horse, tired-out horse, worn-out horse, Rosinante; informal bag of bones, crock; N. Amer. informal plug, crowbait; Austral./NZ informal moke; Brit. informal, dated screw; archaic jade, rip, keffel.
4 N. Amer. *they hailed an empty hack*: **taxi**, cab, taxi cab, minicab, hackney cab; Brit. formal hackney carriage; historical fiacre.

hackle noun
□ **make someone's hackles rise** *his impatient reply made her hackles rise*: **annoy**, irritate, exasperate, anger, irk, vex, put out, nettle, provoke, incense, gall, rile, infuriate, antagonize, get on someone's nerves, rub up the wrong way, make someone's blood boil, ruffle someone's feathers, ruffle, try someone's patience; offend, pique, peeve, rankle with; informal aggravate, needle, make someone see red, hack off, get someone's back up, get someone's goat, get under someone's skin, get up someone's nose, get in someone's hair, get someone's dander up, bug, get, miff; Brit. informal wind up, get at, nark, get across, get on someone's wick; N. Amer. informal tee off, tick off, burn up, rankle, ride, gravel; informal, dated give someone the pip; vulgar slang piss off; rare exacerbate, hump, rasp.
▷ANTONYMS appease.

hackneyed adjective *hackneyed old sayings*: **overused**, overworked, overdone, worn out, time-worn, platitudinous, vapid, stale, tired, threadbare; **trite**, banal, hack, clichéd, hoary, commonplace, common, ordinary, stock, conventional, stereotyped, predictable; unimaginative, unoriginal, derivative, uninspired, prosaic, dull, boring, pedestrian, run-of-the-mill, routine, humdrum; informal old hat, corny, played out; N. Amer. informal cornball, dime-store; rare truistic, bromidic.
▷ANTONYMS original, fresh.

> *Choose the right word* **hackneyed, trite, stale**
>
> See **trite**.

Hades noun *the fires of Hades*: **hell**, the underworld, the land/abode of the dead, the infernal regions, the netherworld, the nether regions, the abyss; eternal damnation, eternal punishment, perdition; Biblical Gehenna, Tophet, Abaddon; Judaism Sheol; Greek Mythology Tartarus, Acheron; Roman Mythology Avernus; Scandinavian Mythology Niflheim; Brit. the other place; literary the pit, the shades; archaic the lower world.
▷ANTONYMS heaven.

haft noun *my fingers gripped the haft of the knife*: **handle**, shaft, shank, hilt, butt, stock, grip, handgrip, helve.
▷ANTONYMS blade, head.

hag noun *the old hag lifted her skinny hand*: **crone**, old woman, witch, gorgon; informal cow, old cow, old bag, old bat.

haggard adjective *he looked terrible, all grey and haggard*: **careworn**, tired, drained, drawn, raddled; unwell, unhealthy, sickly, spent, sapped, washed out, rundown, exhausted; gaunt, grim, pinched, peaked, peaky, hollow-cheeked, hollow-eyed; pale, wan, grey, ashen, pallid, pasty-faced, sallow; thin, emaciated, wasted, cadaverous, ghastly, ghostlike, deathlike.
▷ANTONYMS fresh, healthy.

haggle verb *tourists haggled over exotic handicrafts*: **barter**, bargain, negotiate, discuss terms, quibble, wrangle; beat someone down, drive a hard bargain; deal, wheel and deal, trade, traffic; N. Amer. dicker; formal treat; archaic chaffer, palter.

hag-ridden adjective *she was hag-ridden by her misgivings*: **tormented**, troubled, anguished, agonized, distressed, tortured, harrowed, racked with suffering, angst-ridden, ground down, worn out, despairing.
▷ANTONYMS untroubled.

hail[1] verb **1** *a friend hailed him from the upper deck*: **greet**, salute, address, halloo, speak to, call out to, shout to, say hello to, initiate a discussion with, talk to; nod to, wave to, smile at, signal to, lift one's hat to, acknowledge; accost, approach, waylay, stop, catch; informal collar, buttonhole; Brit. informal nobble.
▷ANTONYMS say goodbye to.
2 *he hailed a cab*: **flag down**, wave down, signal to stop, gesture to stop, make a sign to; call to, shout to; summon, accost.
3 *the critics hailed the new film as a masterpiece*: **acclaim**, praise, applaud, commend, rave about, extol, eulogize, vaunt, hymn, lionize, express approval of, express admiration for, pay tribute to, speak highly of, sing the praises of, make much of; **glorify**, cheer, salute, exalt, honour, hurrah, hurray, toast, welcome, pay homage to; N. Amer. informal ballyhoo; black English big up; dated cry up; archaic emblazon; rare laud, panegyrize.
▷ANTONYMS criticize, condemn.
4 *the band's twenty-six members all* ***hail from*** *Wales*: **come from**, be from, be a native of, have been born in, originate in, have one's roots in; be ... (by birth); live in, have one's home in, inhabit, be an inhabitant of, be settled in, reside in, be a resident of.
▸noun *a hearty hail greeted me*: **greeting**, hello, hallo, halloo, call, cry, shout, salutation; acknowledgement, welcome, salute.
▷ANTONYMS farewell.

hail[2] noun **1** *frequent heavy showers of rain and hail*: **frozen rain**, hailstones, sleet, precipitation; hailstorm, hail shower.
2 *a hail of bullets*: **barrage**, volley, shower, deluge, torrent, burst, stream, storm, flood, spate, rain, tide, avalanche, blaze, onslaught; bombardment, cannonade, battery, blast, broadside, salvo.
▸verb *tons of dust* ***hailed down on*** *us*: **beat**, shower, rain, fall, pour, drop; pelt, pepper, batter, bombard, volley, assail.

hail-fellow-well-met adjective *he was a hail-fellow-well-met type of guy*: **convivial**, sociable, outgoing, gregarious, companionable, friendly, genial, affable, amiable, congenial, agreeable, good-humoured, extrovert, extroverted, uninhibited; Scottish couthy; informal backslapping, chummy, pally, clubbable, clubby, buddy-buddy; Brit. informal matey; rare conversable.
▷ANTONYMS unsociable.

hair noun **1** *thick black curly hair*: **head of hair**, shock of hair, mop of hair, mane; locks, tresses, curls; wig, toupee, hairpiece, switch; informal rug, thatch; Brit. informal barnet; rare postiche.
2 *your hair looks lovely*: **hairstyle**, haircut, cut, style, coiffure; informal hairdo, do, coif.
3 *muscular dogs with wide heads and short, blue-grey hair*: **fur**, wool; coat, fleece, pelt, hide, skin; mane; archaic fell.
□ **a hair's breadth** *the American bison was saved from extinction by a hair's breadth*: **the narrowest of margins**, a narrow margin, the skin of one's teeth, a split second, a fraction, a nose; informal a whisker.
▷ANTONYMS a wide margin.
□ **get in someone's hair** informal *she got in my hair until I couldn't bear it another day*: **annoy**, irritate, gall, irk, pique, needle, nettle, bother, vex, provoke, displease, offend, affront, upset, anger, exasperate, disgruntle, ruffle, put someone's back up, get on someone's nerves, make someone's hackles rise, raise someone's hackles; informal peeve, aggravate, miff, get, get to, bug, nark, wind up, get under someone's skin, get up someone's nose, hack off, get someone's goat, ruffle someone's feathers, get on someone's wick, give someone the hump, rub up the wrong way, get across someone; N. Amer. informal tick off, rankle, ride, gravel; vulgar slang piss off; Brit. vulgar slang get on someone's tits; rare exacerbate, hump, rasp.
▷ANTONYMS appease.
□ **let one's hair down** informal *visitors young and old let their hair down and enjoyed the entertainment*: **have a good time**, have a great time, enjoy oneself, have fun, make merry, have the time of one's life, let oneself go, have a fling; informal have a ball, whoop it up, make whoopee, paint the town red, live it up, have a whale of a time, let it all hang out; Brit. informal push the boat out, have a rave-up; N. Amer. informal hang loose, chill out; S. African jol.
□ **make someone's hair stand on end** *the dossier on him would make your hair stand on end*: **horrify**, shock, appal, scandalize, dismay, stun; make someone's blood run cold, freeze someone's blood; informal make someone's hair curl; Brit. informal put the wind up someone.
▷ANTONYMS reassure.
□ **not turn a hair** *if I was told I'd been sacked, I wouldn't turn a hair*: **remain calm**, keep calm, keep cool, remain composed, remain unruffled, appear unaffected, maintain one's equilibrium, keep control of oneself, not show emotion, not lose one's head, bite one's lip, keep a stiff upper lip; informal keep one's cool, not bat an eyelid; Brit. informal keep one's hair on.
▷ANTONYMS panic.
□ **split hairs** *a pompous professor who uses language to equivocate and split hairs*: **quibble**, raise trivial objections, find fault, cavil, carp, niggle, argue over nothing; informal nit-pick; archaic pettifog.

> *Word links* **hair**
>
> **capillaceous** relating to hair
> **tricho-** related prefix, as in *trichology*
> **trichophobia** fear of hair

hairdo noun informal **hairstyle**, haircut, cut, style, hair, coiffure; informal do, coif.

hairdresser noun **hairstylist**, stylist, barber; French coiffeur, coiffeuse, friseur; informal crimper; rare tonsor, tonsorialist.

hairless adjective **bald**, bald-headed; shaven, shaved, shorn, clean-shaven, smooth-shaven, beardless, smooth, smooth-faced, depilated; Scottish & Irish baldy; technical glabrous, glabrate; archaic tonsured, bald-pated.
▷ANTONYMS hairy.

hairpiece noun **wig**, toupee, false hair, extension, torsade, switch; informal rug; rare merkin, postiche.

hair-raising adjective *I thought ski jumping was hair-raising, but rafting beats it*: **terrifying**, frightening, petrifying, alarming, chilling, horrifying, shocking, scaring, spine-chilling, blood-curdling, appalling, dreadful, fearsome, nightmarish; eerie, sinister, weird, ghostly, unearthly; Scottish eldritch; informal hairy, spooky, scary, creepy, spine-tingling.
▷ANTONYMS relaxing, pleasant.

hair-splitting adjective *legal experts have a particularly hair-splitting mentality*: **quibbling**, fault-finding, niggling, cavilling, carping, captious, critical, criticizing, disapproving, censorious, judgemental, overcritical, hypercritical, pedantic, punctilious, pettifogging; informal **nit-picking**, pernickety, picky; N. Amer. informal persnickety; archaic nice, overnice.

hairstyle noun *she had a smart black dress and a sophisticated hairstyle*: **haircut**, cut, style, hair, coiffure; informal hairdo, do, coif.

hairy adjective **1** *the shirt was unbuttoned, revealing a hairy chest | a rather hairy young man*: **hirsute**, **shaggy**, bushy, hair-covered, long-haired; woolly, furry, fleecy, fuzzy; bearded, unshaven, unshorn, bewhiskered, stubbly, bristly; technical pilose, pileous, pappose; rare crinite, crinigerous.
▷ANTONYMS hairless; short-haired.
2 informal *it got very hairy when we ran into some troops guarding the border*: **risky**, unsafe, dangerous, perilous, hazardous, high-risk, touch-and-go, fraught with danger; tricky, ticklish, difficult, awkward, uncertain, unpredictable, precarious; Scottish unchancy; informal chancy, dicey, sticky, iffy; Brit. informal dodgy; N. Amer. informal gnarly; archaic or humorous parlous.
▷ANTONYMS safe.

halcyon adjective **1** *hot, halcyon days of sunshine*: **serene**, calm, pleasant, balmy, tranquil, peaceful, temperate, mild, quiet, gentle, placid, still, windless, stormless.
▷ANTONYMS stormy.

2 *the halcyon days of the 1960s*: **happy**, carefree, blissful, golden, joyful, joyous, contented, idyllic, palmy; flourishing, thriving, prosperous, successful.
▷ANTONYMS troubled.

hale adjective *only just sixty, very hale and hearty*: **healthy**, well, fit, fighting fit, in good health, bursting with health, in excellent shape, in fine fettle, fit as a fiddle, fit as a flea, in tip-top condition; flourishing, blooming, strong, robust, vigorous, hardy, sturdy, hearty, lusty, able-bodied; informal in the pink, right as rain, full of vim, up to snuff.
▷ANTONYMS unwell.

half noun *half a bar of chocolate*: **fifty per cent of**, bisection of.
▷ANTONYMS all.
□ **by halves** *he operated on a grand scale and never did anything by halves*: **incompletely**, imperfectly, inadequately, insufficiently, partially, scrappily, skimpily, to a limited extent/degree.
▷ANTONYMS thoroughly.
□ **too ... by half** *Rosemary is too clever by half*: **unduly**, overly, excessively, exceedingly, inordinately, disproportionately, far too, to too great an extent/degree, by an excessive amount; enormously, considerably, uncommonly, very, ultra-; informal too-too.
▶ **adjective** *he ate a half grapefruit for breakfast*: **halved**, divided in two, part, partial; bisected, in two equal parts/portions.
▷ANTONYMS whole.
▶ **adverb 1** *the chicken is half cooked*: **partially**, partly, incompletely, inadequately, insufficiently, slightly, barely, in part, part, to a limited extent/degree, in some measure; not totally, not wholly, not entirely, not fully.
▷ANTONYMS completely.
2 *I am half inclined to believe you*: **to a certain extent/degree**, to a limited extent/degree, to some extent/degree, (up) to a point, in part, partly, in some measure; almost, nearly, very nearly, just about, all but; informal ish.
▷ANTONYMS fully.
□ **not half** informal **1** *that doesn't half make you feel old!* **really**, certainly, definitely, decidedly, assuredly, surely, very much, to a great extent, to a considerable extent, for sure, indeed; undeniably, undoubtedly, indubitably, irrefutably, incontrovertibly, incontestably, unequivocally.
2 *the players are not half bad*: **not at all**, not a bit, not in any way, by no means, absolutely not, most certainly not, not for a moment, not nearly, not the slightest bit, to no extent.

> *Word links* **half**
>
> **demi-**, **hemi-**, **semi-**, related prefixes, as in *demi-pension, hemisphere, semicircle*

half-baked adjective **1** *half-baked moral theories*: **not thought through**, not fully developed, undeveloped, unformed, hare-brained; poorly planned, unplanned, ill-conceived, ill-judged; impractical, unrealistic, unworkable, injudicious, ridiculous; informal crazy, crackpot, cock-eyed.
▷ANTONYMS sensible, well reasoned.
2 *her half-baked young nephew*: **foolish**, stupid, silly, idiotic, doltish, asinine, simple-minded, feeble-minded, empty-headed, hare-brained, feather-brained, feather-headed, brainless, senseless, witless, unintelligent, ignorant; inexperienced, immature, callow, green, credulous; informal crazy, dim, dopey, dumb, thick, damfool, half-witted, dim-witted, birdbrained, lamebrained, dunderheaded, wet behind the ears, as thick as two short planks; Brit. informal gormless, daft, divvy, dozy; Scottish & N. English informal glaikit; N. Amer. informal dumb-ass, chowderheaded; S. African informal dof; W. Indian informal dotish.
▷ANTONYMS sensible.

half-hearted adjective *the plan received a half-hearted welcome*: **unenthusiastic**, lukewarm, cool, apathetic, perfunctory, cursory, superficial, desultory, feeble, faint, weak, tepid; indifferent, unconcerned, listless, lacklustre, dispassionate, uninterested, unemotional, languid, passive; rare Laodicean.
▷ANTONYMS enthusiastic.

halfway adjective *the halfway point*: **midway**, middle, mid, central, centre, intermediate, equidistant between two points; mean, median, average; technical medial, mesial; rare intermedial.
▶ **adverb 1** *he stopped halfway down the passage*: **midway**, at the mid point, in the middle, in the centre; to the middle, to the mid point; part of the way, at some point, part-way.
2 *he seemed halfway friendly*: **to some extent/degree**, to a certain extent/degree, in some measure, rather, relatively, comparatively, moderately, cautiously, somewhat, (up) to a point; in part, partly, part, just about, almost, nearly; informal ish.
□ **meet someone halfway** *I was willing to meet him halfway*: **reach a compromise**, find the middle ground, come to terms, come to an understanding, reach an agreement, make a deal, make concessions, find a happy medium, strike a balance; give and take; informal split the difference, go fifty-fifty.

halfwit noun informal See **fool**.

half-witted adjective informal See **stupid**.

hall noun **1** *hang your coat in the hall*: **entrance hall**, hallway, entry, entrance, lobby, foyer, vestibule, reception area, atrium, concourse; passageway, passage, corridor; N. Amer. entryway.
2 *the building is used as a village hall*: **assembly hall**, assembly room, meeting room, large public room, chamber; conference hall, lecture room, theatre, concert hall, auditorium, dance hall, church hall, village hall, town hall, guildhall.

hallmark noun **1** *the hallmark on silver*: **assay mark**, official mark, authentication mark, stamp of authenticity, stamp of authentication.
2 *the tiny bubbles are the hallmark of fine champagnes*: **distinctive feature**, mark, sign, indicator, indication, sure sign, telltale sign; feature, characteristic, trait, attribute, property, quality; trademark, earmark, stamp, badge, symbol.

halloo verb *they hallooed and shouted as they passed*: **call out**, shout, cry out, yell, bawl, bellow, scream, shriek, screech, roar, whoop; **call hello to**, hail, greet; informal holler, yoo-hoo, cooee.

hallowed adjective *water was sprayed over the hallowed ground*: **holy**, sacred, consecrated, sanctified, blessed, blest; revered, reverenced, venerated, honoured, sacrosanct, worshipped, divine, inviolable.
▷ANTONYMS cursed.

> *Word toolkit* **hallowed**
>
> See **holy**.

hallucinate verb *the drug was making me hallucinate*: **have hallucinations**, imagine things, see things, see visions, be delirious, have delirium tremens, fantasize, daydream, dream; informal have a trip, trip, see pink elephants, have daymares.

hallucination noun *a hallucination caused by trauma*: **delusion**, illusion, figment of the imagination, vision, apparition, mirage, chimera, fantasy, dream, daydream; (**hallucinations**) delirium, phantasmagoria; informal trip, pink elephants; literary phantasm.

halo noun **ring of light**, nimbus, aureole, aureola, glory, crown of light, corona, disc, radiance, aura; technical halation; rare gloriole.

halt verb **1** *Len halted and turned round*: **stop**, come to a halt, come to a stop, come to a standstill, come to rest, pull up, draw up, stand still, draw to a stand.
▷ANTONYMS start; go.
2 *the restoration work has temporarily halted*: **cease**, stop, finish, discontinue, terminate, conclude, come to an end, come to a halt, come to a stop, draw to a close, come to a standstill, be over, be abandoned; pause, be broken off, be suspended.
▷ANTONYMS start; continue.
3 *a further strike has halted production*: **terminate**, end, stop, cease, finish, suspend, bring to a stop, bring to a close, bring to an end, put an end to, put a stop to, break off, wind up; arrest, impede, check, curb, stem, staunch, block, stall, hold back; informal pull the plug on, put the kibosh on.
▷ANTONYMS start; continue.
▶ **noun 1** *the car drew to a halt*: **stop**, standstill.
2 *a halt in production*: **cessation**, termination, stoppage, stopping, close, end, discontinuation, discontinuance; break, pause, interval, interruption, interlude, intermission, suspension, rest, respite, hiatus, breathing space, time out; informal breather.
▷ANTONYMS start; continuation.

halter noun **harness**, head collar, bridle; N. Amer. headstall; technical chase-halter.

halting adjective **1** *a rather halting conversation | he spoke to us in halting English*: **hesitant**, disjointed, faltering, hesitating, stumbling, stammering, stuttering; **broken**, non-fluent, imperfect, laboured.
▷ANTONYMS fluent.
2 *his halting gait*: **unsteady**, awkward, uneven, faltering, stumbling, limping, hobbling.
▷ANTONYMS steady, adroit, nimble.

halve verb **1** *halve the tomatoes and scoop out the pips*: **cut in half**, divide into two equal parts, divide in two, split in two, sever in two, divide equally, share equally, bisect.
2 *interest rates have halved*: **reduce by fifty per cent**, decrease by fifty per cent, lessen by fifty per cent.

halves plural noun
□ **by halves** See **half**.

ham-fisted adjective *his ham-fisted handling of the situation*: **clumsy**, bungling, incompetent, amateurish, inept, unskilful, inexpert, maladroit, gauche, awkward, inefficient, bumbling, useless, unhandy; informal cack-handed, butterfingered, ham-handed; Brit. informal all thumbs, all fingers and thumbs.
▷ANTONYMS expert.

hammer noun *they work the stone with hammer and chisel*: **mallet**, beetle, gavel.
▶ **verb 1** *the alloy is hammered into a circular shape*: **beat**, forge, shape, form, mould, fashion, make.
2 *Sally **hammered** at the door*: **batter**, pummel, beat, bang, pound; strike, hit, knock on, thump on; cudgel, bludgeon, club, pelt, assail, thwack; informal bash, wallop, clobber, whack.
3 *they have been **hammering away at** their non-smoking campaign*: **work hard**, labour, slog away, plod away, grind away, slave away, work like a Trojan, work like a dog, keep one's nose to the grindstone; persist with, persevere with, keep on with, press on with, not cease from; informal stick at, peg away at, beaver away at, plug away at, work one's socks off on, sweat blood for, soldier on with, kill oneself with; Brit. informal graft away at; rare drudge away at.
▷**ANTONYMS** give up on; abandon.
4 *anti-racism had been **hammered into** her*: **drum**, instil, inculcate, knock, drive, din; drive home to, impress upon, teach repeatedly to, reiterate to; ingrain.
5 informal *he got hammered for an honest mistake*: **criticize**, censure, attack, condemn, castigate, chastise, lambaste, pillory, reprimand, rebuke, admonish, remonstrate with, take to task, haul over the coals, berate, reproach, reprove; informal knock, slam, lay into, roast, cane, blast, bawl out, dress down; Brit. informal carpet, slate, slag off, monster, rollick; N. Amer. informal chew out, ream out, pummel, cut up; Austral./NZ informal bag; rare excoriate, objurgate, reprehend.
▷**ANTONYMS** praise.
6 informal *we have hammered them twice this season*: **trounce**, defeat, beat, beat hollow, worst, best, overwhelm, rout, annihilate, bring someone to their knees; informal thrash, clobber, lick, demolish, slaughter, murder, paste, pound, drub, give someone a drubbing, wipe the floor with, take to the cleaners, run rings round, walk all over, make mincemeat of, turn something inside out; Brit. informal stuff, marmalize; N. Amer. informal shellac, cream, skunk, blow out.
▷**ANTONYMS** lose to.
□ **hammer something out** *the area chairmen hammered out a national plan*: **thrash out**, work out, agree on, sort out, decide on, bring about, effect, produce, broker, negotiate, reach an agreement on, come to terms about, come to a decision on, come to a satisfactory conclusion on, form a resolution about.
▷**ANTONYMS** fail to agree about.

hamper[1] noun *a picnic hamper*: **basket**, pannier, wickerwork basket; box, container, holder.

hamper[2] verb *an attempt to hamper the investigations*: **hinder**, obstruct, impede, inhibit, retard, baulk, thwart, foil, curb, delay, set back, slow down, hold back, hold up, interfere with; restrict, restrain, constrain, block, check, curtail, frustrate, cramp, bridle, handicap, cripple, hamstring, shackle, fetter, encumber; informal stymie; Brit. informal throw a spanner in the works of; N. Amer. informal bork, throw a monkey wrench in the works of; rare cumber, trammel.
▷**ANTONYMS** help.

> *Choose the right word* **hamper, hinder, impede, obstruct**
>
> See **hinder**.

hamstring verb **1** *the enemy was trying to hamstring his horse*: **cripple**, lame, hock, disable, handicap, injure.
2 *we were hamstrung by a total lack of knowledge*: **handicap**, constrain, restrict, cripple, shackle, fetter, encumber, block, frustrate, cramp, bridle; hamper, hinder, obstruct, impede, inhibit, retard, baulk, thwart, foil, curb, delay, set back, slow down, hold back, hold up; restrain, check, curtail; informal stymie; N. Amer. informal bork; literary trammel; rare cumber.
▷**ANTONYMS** help.

hand noun **1** *big, strong hands*: **fist**, palm; informal paw, mitt, duke, hook, meat hook; Scottish & N. English nieve; technical manus, metacarpus.
▷**ANTONYMS** foot.
2 *the clock's second hand*: **pointer**, indicator, needle, arrow, marker, index.
3 (**hands**) *the concentration of wealth in the hands of the entrepreneurial class*: **control**, power, charge, authority; command, responsibility, guardianship, management, care, supervision, jurisdiction; possession, keeping, custody, clutches, grasp; disposal; informal say-so; literary thrall.
4 *come and give me **a hand** with the tidying up*: **help**, a helping hand, assistance, aid, support, succour, relief; a good turn, a favour, a kindness; rare abettance.
▷**ANTONYMS** hindrance.
5 informal *his fans gave him a **big hand***: **round of applause**, clap, handclap, ovation, standing ovation; applause, handclapping, praise, acclaim.
▷**ANTONYMS** booing; catcalls.
6 *the document was written in his own hand*: **handwriting**, writing, script, longhand, letters, pen; penmanship, calligraphy, chirography.
7 *a factory hand*: **worker**, factory worker, manual worker, unskilled worker, blue-collar worker, workman, workwoman, workperson, working man, labourer, operative, hired hand, hireling, roustabout, employee, artisan; farmhand, farm worker, field hand; crewman, sailor, deckhand; Spanish-American **peon**; Austral./NZ rouseabout; Indian mazdoor, khalasi; archaic mechanical.
□ **at hand 1** *you need to keep the manual **close at hand***: **readily available**, available, handy, to hand, near at hand, within reach, accessible, ready, close, close by, near, nearby, at the ready, at one's fingertips, at one's disposal, convenient; informal get-at-able, on tap.
▷**ANTONYMS** far away.
2 *the time for starting the campaign is at hand*: **imminent**, close at hand, approaching, forthcoming, coming, coming soon, about to happen, nearly on us, just around the corner, on the horizon; impending.
▷**ANTONYMS** a long time away.
□ **by hand** *each chocolate is decorated by hand*: **manually**, with one's hands, using one's hands, not by machine, not mechanically, freehand.
▷**ANTONYMS** by machine.
□ **from hand to mouth** *they live from hand to mouth—from one benefit day to the next*: **precariously**, from day to day, not knowing where one's next meal is coming from, uncertainly, insecurely, in poverty, meagrely; improvidently; Brit. on the breadline.
▷**ANTONYMS** securely; without financial worries.
□ **get/lay one's hands on** informal *I haven't got my hands on a copy yet* | *thieves break into parked vehicles and steal anything they can lay their hands on*: **obtain**, acquire, come by, secure, procure, come into possession of, pick up, be given; gain, derive, earn, achieve, attain, win, draw, reap; buy, purchase; informal get/lay hold of, get one's mitts on, grab, bag, land, net; Brit. informal blag; S. African informal schlenter.
□ **hand in glove** *they were working hand in glove with our enemies*: **in close collaboration**, in close association, in close cooperation, very closely, closely together, in partnership, in league, in collusion; informal in cahoots.
□ **hand in hand 1** *two small children were walking hand in hand*: **holding hands**, clasping hands, with hands clasped, with hands joined; arm in arm.
2 *poverty goes hand in hand with war*: **in close association**, closely together, together, in partnership, closely, conjointly, concurrently, side by side, in concert.
□ **hands down** *we won hands down*: **easily**, effortlessly, with ease, with no trouble, with very little trouble, without effort, with very little effort; informal by a mile, no sweat.
▷**ANTONYMS** with difficulty.
□ **have a hand in something** *the girls had a hand in writing the lyrics*: **play a part in**, contribute to, be a factor in, be (partly) responsible for.
□ **in hand 1** *the task in hand*: **being dealt with**, receiving attention, being attended to, under way; under control. **2** *we have money in hand to cover next month's expenses*: **available for use**, ready, available, put by; spare, in reserve.
□ **old hand** *whether you are a novice gardener or an old hand*: **expert**, past master, virtuoso, master, wizard, genius, artist, adept, professional, doyen, veteran, maestro, connoisseur, authority, grandmaster, master hand, skilled person; informal ace, buff, pro, star, whizz, hotshot; Brit. informal dab hand; N. Amer. informal maven, crackerjack.
□ **on hand** *police and volunteers were on hand to keep things running smoothly*: **ready**, at the ready, available, accessible, handy, at one's fingertips; **prepared**, primed, on standby, standing by, on stand-to, on call, on full alert; informal on tap.
□ **out of hand** *the situation was getting out of hand*: **out of control**, uncontrollable, unmanageable, ungovernable, unruly, disorderly, rowdy, wild, boisterous, difficult, disruptive, ill-disciplined, undisciplined, refractory, recalcitrant, intractable, impossible, obstreperous, fractious, wayward, incorrigible; informal stroppy; archaic contumacious.
▷**ANTONYMS** manageable, controllable.
□ **take someone/something in hand** *their parents are incapable of taking their children in hand* | *matters have to be taken in hand*: **deal with**, handle, manage, cope with, tackle, take care of, take charge of, attend to, give one's attention to, see to, sort out.
□ **to hand** *the bullies pelted us with anything that was to hand*: **readily available**, available, handy, near at hand, within reach, accessible, ready, close, close by, near, nearby, at the ready, at one's fingertips, at one's disposal, convenient; informal get-at-able.
□ **try one's hand** *I would like to **try my hand at** bonsai*: **make an attempt at**, have a shot at; attempt, try, try out, give something a try; informal have a go at, have a crack at, have a stab at, have a bash at, give something a whirl; formal essay; archaic assay.
▶ **verb 1** *he handed each man a glass*: **pass**, give, reach, let someone have, throw, toss; pass to, hand over to, deliver to, present to, transfer to, convey to; informal chuck, bung.
▷**ANTONYMS** take away from.
2 *he handed him into a carriage*: **assist**, help, aid, give someone a hand, give someone a helping hand, give someone assistance; guide, convey, conduct, lead.
□ **hand something down** *the family jewellery is handed down from generation to generation*: **pass on**, pass down; **bequeath**, will, leave, leave in one's will, make over, endow, gift, transfer, give, transmit; Law demise, devise.

□ **hand something on** *the drugs were handed on to a dealer*: **give**, pass, hand, transfer, grant, cede, surrender, relinquish; part with, let go of; bequeath, will, leave.
▷ANTONYMS receive.
□ **hand something out** *the attendant handed out prayer books*: **distribute**, hand round, give out, give round, pass out, pass round, share out, dole out, dish out, deal out, mete out, issue, circulate, dispense; allocate, allot, apportion, disburse, disseminate.
▷ANTONYMS collect in.
□ **hand something over** *it is suggested that he might hand over power to his son*: **yield**, give, give up, pass, grant, entrust, surrender, relinquish, cede, turn over, deliver up, forfeit, sacrifice; confer on, bestow on.
▷ANTONYMS keep.

Word links **hand**
manual relating to the hands
chiro- related prefix, as in *chirography, chiropody*

handbag noun **bag**, shoulder bag, clutch bag, evening bag, pochette; flight bag, travelling bag, handgrip, overnighter; French **minaudière**, pompadour; Brit. holdall; N. Amer. purse, pocketbook; rare reticule, caba, keister, Dorothy bag, peggy bag, purse-bag, vanity bag.

h

handbill noun **notice**, advertisement, flyer, leaflet, circular, handout, bulletin, pamphlet, brochure; N. Amer. & Austral. dodger; informal ad, junk mail; Brit. informal advert.

handbook noun **manual**, instructions, instruction booklet, instruction manual, reference manual, ABC, A to Z, almanac, companion, directory, compendium; **guide**, guidebook, travel guide, tourist guide, Baedeker; Latin vade mecum; rare enchiridion, promptuary, desk-book.

handcuff verb *they handcuffed the prisoner to a warder*: **manacle**, fetter, shackle; restrain, secure, put handcuffs on, put someone in irons, clap someone in irons, put someone in chains; informal cuff; rare enfetter, gyve.
▷ANTONYMS free.

handcuffs plural noun **manacles**, fetters, shackles, irons, bonds, restraints; informal cuffs, bracelets, darbies; rare gyves, wristlets, snips, stringers.

handful noun **1** *we've received only **a handful of** letters*: **a small number**, a small amount, a small quantity, a sprinkling, a smattering, a scattering, a trickle; a few, one or two, several, some, not many.
▷ANTONYMS a lot.
2 informal *the child is a real handful*: **nuisance**, problem, bother, irritant, source of annoyance, thorn in someone's flesh, thorn in someone's side, bugbear; informal pest, headache, pain, pain in the neck, pain in the backside, blister; Scottish informal nyaff, skelf; N. Amer. informal pain in the butt, nudnik, burr under/in someone's saddle; Austral./NZ informal nark; Brit. vulgar slang pain in the arse.
▷ANTONYMS blessing.

handgun noun **pistol**, revolver, gun, side arm, automatic pistol, six-shooter, thirty-eight, derringer, Browning automatic; N. Amer. informal piece, shooting iron, Saturday night special, rod, roscoe; trademark Colt, Webley, Luger.

handicap noun **1** *he was born with a significant visual handicap*. See **disability**.
2 *this legislation is a handicap to the competitiveness of the industry*: **impediment**, hindrance, obstacle, barrier, bar, encumbrance; **disadvantage**, drawback, stumbling block, difficulty, shortcoming, obstruction, limitation, constraint, straitjacket, restriction, check, block, curb; ball and chain, albatross, millstone round someone's neck; literary trammel.
▷ANTONYMS benefit; advantage.
▶verb *delivery of services has been handicapped by inadequate investment*: **hamper**, impede, hinder, impair, disadvantage, put at a disadvantage, hamstring, curtail; **restrict**, check, obstruct, block, curb, bridle, hold back, constrain, limit, encumber; informal stymie; N. Amer. informal bork; literary trammel.
▷ANTONYMS help.

handicapped adjective See **disabled**.

handicraft noun *handicraft and sewing workshops*: **craft**, handiwork, craftwork; craftsmanship, workmanship, artisanship, art, skill.

handiwork noun *the dressmakers stood back to survey their handiwork*: **creation**, product, work, achievement, design, doing, action, result; **handicraft**, craft, craftwork.

handkerchief noun **pocket handkerchief**; tissue, paper handkerchief; trademark Kleenex; Scottish & N. English napkin; French mouchoir; Indian corah, Malabar, pullicate; informal **hanky**, nose rag, snot rag; informal, dated nose-wiper, sneezer, wipe, wiper; literary **kerchief**; archaic clout, muckender, monteith, fogle, foulard, stook, Barcelona.

handle verb **1** *bladed tools can cause serious injury if they are not handled and stored with care*: **hold**, pick up, grasp, grip, lift; **feel**, touch, finger, thumb, toy with, play with; informal paw.
2 *she handled the car well on the wet roads*: **control**, drive, steer, operate, manoeuvre, manipulate.
3 *she handled the job formidably*: **deal with**, manage, cope with, tackle, take care of, take charge of, contend with, attend to, give one's attention to, see to, sort out, apply oneself to, take something in hand, control.
▷ANTONYMS neglect.
4 *the paper handled the race story with constraint*: **treat**, examine, tackle, explore, go into, report, review, discuss, discourse on.
5 *the advertising company that is handling the account*: **administer**, manage, control, conduct, direct, guide, supervise, oversee, be in charge of, take care of, look after.
6 *some dealers handle antiquities that lack honest pedigrees*: **trade in**, deal in, do business in, buy, sell, supply, stock, carry, peddle, traffic in, purvey, hawk, tout, market; informal push; Brit. informal flog.
▶noun *the handle of the knife*: **haft**, shank, stock, shaft, grip, handgrip, hilt, helve, butt; knob.
▷ANTONYMS head; blade.

hand-me-down adjective *a faded hand-me-down dress*: **second-hand**, used, nearly new, handed-down, passed-on, cast-off, worn, old, pre-owned; Brit. informal reach-me-down.
▷ANTONYMS new.

handout noun **1** (**handouts**) *she existed on handouts as her husband couldn't work*: **charity**, aid, benefit, financial support, gifts of money, gifts of food, subsidies, payments, donations; Brit. informal dole; historical alms.
▷ANTONYMS earned income.
2 *a plastic carrier containing a selection of freebies and handouts*: **free sample**, free gift, contribution, offering, present; informal freebie, perk, prezzie, sweetener; archaic perquisite.
▷ANTONYMS purchase.
3 *there are a number of handouts to read before the next session*: **leaflet**, pamphlet, brochure, bulletin; advertising leaflet, handbill, flyer, notice, circular, mailshot; literature, printed matter.

hand-picked adjective *the lecture was attended by a hand-picked audience*: **specially chosen**, specially selected, invited, screened, vetted; choice, elite, select.
▷ANTONYMS random.

handsome adjective **1** *a handsome, dark-haired young man*: **good-looking**, nice-looking, attractive, personable, striking, stunning, fine, well-proportioned, well-formed; informal hunky, dishy, gorgeous, drop-dead gorgeous, tasty, fanciable, knockout; Brit. informal fit; N. Amer. informal cute; Austral./NZ informal spunky; rare sightly.
▷ANTONYMS ugly.
2 *a handsome woman of 30*: **striking**, imposing, prepossessing, elegant, stately, dignified, statuesque, good-looking, nice-looking, attractive, personable.
▷ANTONYMS plain.
3 *the pub was running at a handsome profit | a handsome present*: **substantial**, considerable, sizeable, large, big, ample, abundant, bumper, plentiful; generous, lavish, liberal, bountiful, princely; Scottish & N. English bonny; informal tidy, whopping, whopping great, thumping, thumping great, kingly, not to be sneezed at; Brit. informal whacking, whacking great, ginormous; literary plenteous, bounteous.
▷ANTONYMS meagre.

handwriting noun *clear and legible handwriting*: **writing**, **script**, hand, longhand, letters, pen; penmanship, calligraphy, chirography; informal scrawl, scribble.

Word links **handwriting**
graphology study of handwriting

handy adjective **1** *a handy reference tool*: **useful**, convenient, practical, easy-to-use, well-designed, user-friendly, user-oriented, helpful, functional, serviceable, utilitarian; informal neat, nifty.
▷ANTONYMS inconvenient.
2 *it has eight pockets to keep everything you need handy*: **readily available**, available, at hand, to hand, near at hand, within reach, accessible, ready, close, close by, near, nearby, at the ready, at one's fingertips, at one's disposal, convenient; informal get-at-able, on tap.
3 *he's handy with a needle*: **skilful**, skilled, dexterous, deft, nimble-fingered, adroit, practical, able, adept, proficient, capable; masterly, gifted, talented, expert; clever with one's hands, good with one's hands; informal nifty, wizard, ace; N. Amer. informal crackerjack; vulgar slang shit-hot; rare habile.
▷ANTONYMS inept.

handyman noun **odd-job man**, odd-jobber, factotum, jack of all trades, man of all work; DIY expert, DIYer; Austral. knockabout, rouseabout, loppy; French bricoleur; informal Mr Fixit.

hang verb **1** *lanterns hung from the ridgepole of the tent*: **be suspended**, hang down, be pendent, dangle, swing, sway; archaic depend.
▷ANTONYMS rise.

2 *it's best to hang your pictures at eye level*: **put up**, fix, attach, affix, fasten, post, display, suspend, stick up, pin up, tack up, nail up, put on a hook.
▷ANTONYMS take down.
3 *size the wall before you hang the wallpaper*: **paste up**, glue on, stick up, fasten on, fix on, attach.
▷ANTONYMS peel off.
4 *the room was hung with banners and streamers*: **decorate**, adorn, drape, festoon, deck out, trick out, bedeck, array, furnish, garland, swathe, cover, ornament; informal get up, do up, do out, tart up; literary bedizen, caparison, furbelow.
5 *they hanged the prisoners at a triple gallows*: **execute by hanging**, hang by the neck, send to the gallows, send to the gibbet, send to the scaffold, gibbet, put to death; lynch; informal string up.
6 *pollutants hang in the air over the motorway*: **hover**, float, drift, linger, remain static, be suspended, be poised.
▷ANTONYMS be dispersed.
□ **hang about/around/round** informal **1** *they spent most of their time hanging around restaurants or bars*: **loiter in**, linger in, wait around in, spend time in, loaf (around/about) in, lounge (around/about) in; waste time, kill time, mark time, while away the/one's time, dally; kick one's heels, cool one's heels, twiddle one's thumbs; frequent, be a regular visitor to, be a regular client of, haunt; informal hang out in. **2** *hang about, see what it says here?* **wait**, hold on, wait a minute; informal hang on, hold your horses. **3** *he was hanging around with a fellow called Mick*: **associate**, mix, go around, keep company, spend time, mingle, socialize, fraternize, consort, rub shoulders; N. Amer. rub elbows; informal hang out, run around, knock about/around, be thick, hobnob. ▷ANTONYMS have nothing to do with.
□ **hang back** *she hung back, scared to face the old woman*: **stay back**, hold back, stay in the background, shrink back, shy away, be reluctant to come forward, hesitate, demur, recoil, turn away.
□ **hang fire** *we should hang fire for things to cool off*: **delay**, hang back, hold back, hold on, stall, stop, pause, cease, halt, discontinue, procrastinate, vacillate, adopt Fabian tactics; informal hang about, hang around, sit tight, hold one's horses.
□ **hang on 1** *he* ***hung on to*** *the back of her coat*: **hold on to**, hold fast to, grip, clutch, grasp, hold tightly, cling to, cling on to; literary cleave to. ▷ANTONYMS let go of. **2** *the whole credibility of electoral reform hangs on this decision*: **depend on**, be dependent on, turn on, hinge on, rest on, be based on, be conditional on, be contingent upon, be determined by, be decided by, be conditioned by, revolve around. **3** *she hung on his every word*: **listen closely to**, attend closely to, pay close attention to, be very attentive to, concentrate hard on, pay heed to, lend an ear to, give ear to, be rapt by; informal be all ears for; archaic hearken to. ▷ANTONYMS pay no attention to. **4** *I will hang on until there are other people who can take the campaign forward*: **persevere**, **hold out**, hold on, go on, carry on, keep on, keep going, keep at it, not give up; **continue**, persist, remain, stay the course, stay with it, struggle on, plod on, plough on; informal soldier on, plug away, peg away, stick at it, stick it out, hang in there, bash on. ▷ANTONYMS give up. **5** informal *hang on, let me think for a moment*: **wait**, wait a minute, hold on, stop; hold the line; informal hold your horses, sit tight; Brit. informal hang about.
□ **hang out** informal *he spent a lot of time hanging out with other musicians*: **associate**, mix, go around, keep company, spend time, mingle, socialize, fraternize, consort, rub shoulders; N. Amer. rub elbows; informal hang around, run around, knock about/around, be thick, hobnob; Brit. informal hang about.
□ **hang something out** *you can hang out the washing in the laundry room*: **peg out**, peg up, stick up, pin up, drape, fix, fasten.
□ **hang over 1** *two girls hung over the rail of the ferry*: **lean over**, bend over, bend downwards, bend forwards, lean forwards, droop forwards, bow over. **2** *the threat of budget cuts* ***is hanging over us***: **be imminent**, threaten, approach, be close, be impending, impend, loom, draw near, be in prospect, be on the horizon, be just around the corner.
▶ **noun**
□ **get the hang of** informal *I never got the hang of roller skating*: **get the knack of**, master, learn, acquire the technique of, acquire the skill of, learn the art of, become proficient in, become expert in, manage, catch on to, pick up; **understand**, grasp, comprehend.

hangdog adjective *the hangdog look of a condemned man*: **shamefaced**, ashamed, guilty-looking, sheepish, abashed, abject, cowed, cringing, downcast, crestfallen, woebegone, disconsolate, embarrassed, uncomfortable; browbeaten, defeated, intimidated, wretched.
▷ANTONYMS confident, frank.

hanger-on noun **follower**, flunkey, toady, camp follower, sycophant, fawner, parasite, leech; henchman, minion, lackey, vassal, dependant, retainer, acolyte, underling; N. Amer. cohort; informal groupie, sponger, freeloader, passenger, sidekick; Brit. informal ligger; archaic liegeman, pursuivant.
▷ANTONYMS leader.

hanging noun *silk wall hangings*: **drape**, curtain, drop, drop cloth, drop curtain, drop scene, tableau curtain, frontal, dossal; drapery; informal tab.
▶ **adjective** *hanging fronds of honeysuckle*: **pendent**, suspended, supported from above, dangling, swinging, swaying, trailing, flowing, falling, tumbling; pendulous, drooping, droopy, sagging, flaccid; rare pensile.

hang-out noun *this place was a favourite student hang-out*: **haunt**, stamping ground, favourite spot, meeting place, territory, domain, purlieu, resort; den, nook, nest, refuge, retreat, hideout; informal hidey-hole; Brit. informal local, patch, manor.

hangover noun **headache**; informal the morning after the night before, head; literary crapulence, crapulousness; S. African babalaas; N. Amer. informal, dated katzenjammer.

hang-up noun *people with hang-ups about their age*: **neurosis**, preoccupation, fixation, obsession, phobia, mania; inhibition, mental block, psychological block, block, difficulty; French idée fixe; informal complex, thing, bee in one's bonnet.

hank noun *hanks of pale green yarn | a hank of hair*: **coil**, skein, length, roll, bunch, clump, loop, twist, piece; shock, lock, ringlet, curl.

hanker verb *she still hankered to go back | they hankered for the bright lights of the capital*: **yearn**, long, have a longing, have a hankering, crave, desire, wish, want, hunger, thirst, lust, ache, be aching, itch, be itching, burn, be burning, pant, want badly, be eager, be desperate, be hungry, be greedy, be thirsty, be consumed with a/the desire, be eating one's heart out; fancy, pine for, have one's heart set on; informal be dying, have a yen; archaic be desirous, be athirst; rare suspire.
▷ANTONYMS be averse.

> *Choose the right word* **hanker, yearn, long, pine**
>
> See **yearn**.

hankering noun *a hankering for the sea*: **longing**, yearning, craving, desire, wish, need, hunger, thirst, urge, ache, itch, lust, burning, pining, appetite, passion, fancy; informal yen; rare appetency, appetence.
▷ANTONYMS aversion.

hanky-panky noun informal *the public takes a dim view of hanky-panky among public officials*: **goings-on**, funny business, mischief, misbehaviour, misconduct, chicanery, dishonesty, deception, deceit, trickery, intrigue, skulduggery, subterfuge, machinations; **extramarital sex**, infidelity, unfaithfulness, adultery, liaison, affair, fling; informal monkey business, shenanigans, carryings-on, carry-on, fooling around, playing around; Brit. informal jiggery-pokery, monkey tricks; N. Amer. informal monkeyshines; formal fornication; archaic knavery.
▷ANTONYMS good behaviour; fidelity.

haphazard adjective *things were strewn around in a haphazard fashion*: **random**, unplanned, unsystematic, unmethodical, disorganized, disorderly, irregular, indiscriminate, chaotic, hit-and-miss, arbitrary, orderless, aimless, undirected, careless, casual, slapdash, slipshod; chance, accidental; informal higgledy-piggledy.
▷ANTONYMS methodical; systematic.

hapless adjective *the hapless victims of exploitation*: **unfortunate**, unlucky, luckless, out of luck, ill-starred, ill-fated, jinxed, cursed, doomed; unhappy, forlorn, wretched, miserable, woebegone; informal down on one's luck; literary star-crossed.
▷ANTONYMS lucky.

> *Choose the right word* **hapless, unfortunate, unlucky, ill-starred**
>
> See **unfortunate**.

happen verb **1** *she could not explain how the accident happened | this is what happens when the mechanism goes wrong*: **occur**, take place, come about, come off, come into being; **ensue**, result, transpire, materialize, arise, be, crop up, come up, fall out, pan out, turn out, follow, develop, emerge, surface, present itself, supervene; N. Amer. informal go down; literary come to pass, betide, chance; rare eventuate, hap.
2 *I wonder what* ***happened to*** *Susie?* **become of**, be the fate of, be the lot of, overtake, be visited on; literary befall, betide.
3 *they happened to be in London when the news was received*: **chance**, have the good/bad/ill fortune, have the good/bad/ill luck, be someone's fortune/misfortune.
4 *he* ***happened on*** *a linnet's nest*: **discover unexpectedly**, find unexpectedly, find by chance, chance on, stumble on, hit on, light on, come on, come across, run across, blunder on, unearth, uncover, locate, bring to light; meet by chance, run into, encounter; informal bump into, dig up; archaic run against.

happening noun *he was a witness to these bizarre happenings*: **occurrence**, event, incident, scene, affair, circumstance, phenomenon, episode, adventure, experience, occasion, action, activity, development, eventuality, accident, case, business, thing.
▶ **adjective** informal *nightclubs for the young are the happening thing*: **fashionable**, modern, popular, new, latest, up to date, up to the minute, in

fashion, in vogue; French de rigueur, le dernier cri; informal **trendy**, funky, hot, cool, with it, hip, in, big, now, groovy, sharp, swinging; N. Amer. informal kicky, tony, fly; black English down.
▷ANTONYMS old-fashioned.

happily adverb **1** *the children played happily on the sand for hours*: **contentedly**, merrily, delightedly, joyfully, gaily, cheerfully, cheerily, agreeably, blithely, light-heartedly, gleefully, blissfully, with pleasure, to one's heart's content; literary joyously.
▷ANTONYMS miserably.
2 *I will happily leave my car behind*: **willingly**, gladly, readily, freely, cheerfully, ungrudgingly, unhesitatingly, with pleasure, with all one's heart and soul; archaic lief, fain.
▷ANTONYMS unwillingly.
3 *happily, we are living in enlightened times*: **fortunately**, luckily, thankfully, mercifully, opportunely, providentially, felicitously, by chance, by good luck, by good fortune, as luck would have it; thank goodness, thank God, thank heavens, thank the stars.
▷ANTONYMS unfortunately.

happiness noun *her eyes shone with happiness*: **contentment**, pleasure, contentedness, satisfaction, cheerfulness, cheeriness, merriment, merriness, gaiety, joy, joyfulness, joyousness, joviality, jollity, jolliness, glee, blitheness, carefreeness, gladness, delight, good spirits, high spirits, light-heartedness, good cheer, well-being, enjoyment, felicity; exuberance, exhilaration, elation, ecstasy, delirium, jubilation, rapture, bliss, blissfulness, euphoria, beatitude, transports of delight; heaven, paradise, seventh heaven, cloud nine; humorous delectation; rare jouissance.
▷ANTONYMS unhappiness.

h

happy adjective **1** *Melissa came in looking happy and excited*: **contented**, content, cheerful, cheery, merry, joyful, jovial, jolly, joking, jocular, gleeful, carefree, untroubled, delighted, smiling, beaming, grinning, glowing, satisfied, gratified, buoyant, radiant, sunny, blithe, joyous, beatific, blessed; cock-a-hoop, in good spirits, in high spirits, in a good mood, light-hearted, good-humoured; thrilled, exuberant, elated, exhilarated, ecstatic, blissful, euphoric, overjoyed, exultant, rapturous, rapt, enraptured, in seventh heaven, on cloud nine, over the moon, walking on air, beside oneself with joy, jumping for joy; informal chirpy, on top of the world, as happy as a sandboy, tickled pink, tickled to death, like a dog with two tails, as pleased as Punch, on a high, blissed out, sent; Brit. informal chuffed, as happy as Larry; N. English informal made up; N. Amer. informal as happy as a clam; Austral. informal wrapped; dated gay; rare blithesome, jocose, jocund.
▷ANTONYMS sad.
2 *we will be happy to advise you*: **willing**, **glad**, ready, pleased, delighted, contented; disposed, inclined; informal game.
▷ANTONYMS unwilling.
3 *by a happy coincidence the date was Richard's birthday | a happy choice of venue*: **fortunate**, lucky, favourable, advantageous, opportune, timely, well-timed, convenient, propitious, felicitous, auspicious, beneficial, helpful; **appropriate**, apt, fitting, fit, good, right, apposite, proper, seemly, befitting.
▷ANTONYMS unfortunate.

happy-go-lucky adjective *their casual, happy-go-lucky manner*: **easy-going**, carefree, casual, free and easy, devil-may-care, blithe, nonchalant, insouciant, blasé, unconcerned, untroubled, unworried, light-hearted; heedless, reckless, irresponsible, improvident; informal slap-happy, laid-back.
▷ANTONYMS anxious; serious.

harangue noun *father began a harangue about my monstrous behaviour*: **tirade**, lecture, diatribe, homily, polemic, rant, fulmination, broadside, verbal attack, verbal onslaught, invective; criticism, berating, censure, admonition, reproval, admonishment; exhortation, declamation, oration, peroration, speech, talk, address; informal sermon, tongue-lashing, spiel, pep talk; rare philippic, obloquy.
▷ANTONYMS panegyric.
▸verb *the union leaders harangued the workers over loudspeakers*: **deliver a tirade to**, rant at, lecture, hold forth to, preach to, pontificate to, sermonize to, spout to, declaim to, give a lecture to; berate, castigate, criticize, attack, lambaste, censure, pillory, upbraid; informal earbash, speechify to, preachify to, sound off to, spiel to.

harass verb **1** *children always harass their mother*: **pester**, badger, hound, harry, plague, torment, bedevil, persecute, bother, annoy, exasperate, worry, disturb, trouble, agitate, provoke, vex; stress, stress out, nag, keep on at, chivvy; tease, bait, molest; informal hassle, bug, give someone a hard time, drive someone up the wall, drive someone round the bend; Brit. informal drive someone round the twist; N. English informal mither; N. Amer. informal devil, ride.
▷ANTONYMS leave in peace.
2 *they were sent to harass the enemy flanks and rear*: **harry**, attack repeatedly, raid, press hard, beleaguer, set upon, assail, maraud, ravage, oppress.

harassed adjective *the programme of activities is a godsend for harassed parents*: **stressed**, strained, frayed, harried, stressed out, worn out, hard-pressed, careworn, worried, troubled, vexed, beleaguered, agitated, fretting, distraught; under stress, under pressure, at the end of one's tether, with one's back to the wall, with one's back up against the wall; N. Amer. at the end of one's rope; informal hassled.
▷ANTONYMS carefree.

harassment noun *he knows how to make a noise and claim police harassment*: **persecution**, harrying, pestering, badgering, intimidation, bother, annoyance, aggravation, irritation, pressure, pressurization, force, coercion, molestation; informal hassle; rare bedevilment.
▷ANTONYMS cooperation; assistance.

harbinger noun *witch hazels are the harbingers of spring*: **herald**, sign, indicator, indication, signal, prelude, portent, omen, augury, forewarning, presage, announcer; forerunner, precursor, messenger, usher; French avant-courier; literary foretoken.

harbour noun **1** *the boat was tied up in the harbour*: **port**, dock, haven, marina, dockyard, boatyard, mooring, anchorage, roads, waterfront; jetty, quay, pier, slipway, wharf, landing stage; rare harbourage, moorage, roadstead, hithe.
2 *I am looking for a kind man who is a safe harbour for me*: **refuge**, haven, safe haven, shelter, sanctuary, retreat, asylum, place of safety, place of security, port in a storm, oasis, sanctum.
▸verb **1** *he was suspected of harbouring an escaped prisoner*: **shelter**, conceal, hide, shield, protect, give asylum to, give sanctuary to, give shelter to, provide a refuge for; accommodate, lodge, put up, take in, billet, house.
▷ANTONYMS hand over.
2 *he had never harboured any hostile feelings against them*: **bear**, nurse, nurture, cherish, entertain, foster, feel secretly, hold on to, cling to, possess, maintain, retain.

hard adjective **1** *the ground was as hard as a rock*: **firm**, solid, dense, rigid, stiff, resistant, unbreakable, inflexible, unpliable, impenetrable, unyielding, solidified, hardened, compact, compacted, steely, tough, strong, stony, rock-like, flinty, close-packed, compressed, as hard as iron, as hard as stone; frozen; rare adamantine, unmalleable, renitent.
▷ANTONYMS soft.
2 *it was hard physical work*: **arduous**, strenuous, tiring, fatiguing, exhausting, wearying, back-breaking, gruelling, heavy, laborious; difficult, taxing, exacting, testing, challenging, demanding, punishing, tough, formidable, onerous, rigorous, uphill, Herculean; informal murderous, killing, hellish; Brit. informal knackering; rare toilsome, exigent.
▷ANTONYMS easy.
3 *hard workers*: **diligent**, hard-working, industrious, sedulous, assiduous, conscientious, energetic, keen, enthusiastic, zealous, earnest, persevering, persistent, unflagging, untiring, indefatigable; studious.
▷ANTONYMS lazy.
4 *we have a hard problem to solve*: **difficult**, puzzling, perplexing, baffling, bewildering, mystifying, knotty, thorny, ticklish, problematic, enigmatic, complicated, complex, intricate, involved, tangled, insoluble, unfathomable, impenetrable, incomprehensible, unanswerable; informal spiny, mind-bending; N. Amer. informal gnarly; rare insolvable, wildering.
▷ANTONYMS simple.
5 *times are hard and jobs are scarce*: **harsh**, **grim**, difficult, bad, bleak, dire, tough, austere, unpleasant, disagreeable, uncomfortable, intolerable, unendurable, unbearable, insupportable; straitened, spartan, dark, severe, distressing, painful, awful.
▷ANTONYMS comfortable; luxurious.
6 *he can be such a hard taskmaster*: **strict**, harsh, firm, severe, stern, tough, rigorous, demanding, exacting, unkind, unfriendly, unsympathetic, cold, heartless, hard-hearted, cold-hearted, unfeeling, intransigent, unbending, uncompromising, inflexible, intolerant, implacable, stubborn, obdurate, unyielding, unrelenting, unsparing, lacking compassion, grim, ruthless, merciless, oppressive, tyrannical, pitiless, callous, cruel, vicious, unjust, unfair; standing no nonsense, ruling with a rod of iron; informal hard-boiled; Austral./NZ informal solid.
▷ANTONYMS easy-going; kind.
7 *a hard winter*: **bitterly cold**, cold, bitter, harsh, severe, extreme, bleak, freezing, icy, icy-cold, arctic, polar, Siberian, glacial.
▷ANTONYMS mild.
8 *a hard blow to the head*: **forceful**, heavy, strong, sharp, smart, violent, powerful, vigorous, mighty, hefty, tremendous.
▷ANTONYMS light.
9 *hard facts about the underclass are maddeningly elusive*: **reliable**, definite, true, actual, confirmed, undeniable, indisputable, unquestionable, verifiable; plain, cold, bare, bold, harsh, unvarnished, unembellished.
▷ANTONYMS unverified.
10 *they do not touch hard liquor*: **alcoholic**, strong, intoxicating, inebriating, stiff, potent, spirituous, vinous, intoxicant.
▷ANTONYMS non-alcoholic; low-alcohol.
11 *hard drugs*: **addictive**, habit-forming, causing dependency; strong, harmful, narcotic.
▷ANTONYMS soft.
□ **hard and fast** *there are no hard-and-fast rules about this*: **definite**, fixed, set, strict, rigid, binding, stringent, rigorous, clear-cut, cast-iron, established, inflexible, immutable, unalterable, invariable,

unvarying, unchangeable, unchanging, incontestable, incontrovertible, uncompromising.
▷ANTONYMS flexible.
□ **hard feelings** *I had no hard feelings about being fired*: **resentment**, animosity, ill feeling, ill feelings, ill will, bitterness, bad blood, resentfulness, rancour, malice, acrimony, antagonism, antipathy, animus, friction, anger, hostility, hate, hatred.
▷ANTONYMS goodwill.
▶ adverb **1** *George pushed her hard away from him*: **forcefully**, forcibly, fiercely, roughly, powerfully, strongly, strenuously, heavily, sharply, vigorously, intensely, energetically, with all one's might, with might and main, with vigour, with force, with great effort.
▷ANTONYMS gently.
2 *they work hard at school*: **diligently**, industriously, assiduously, conscientiously, sedulously, busily, intensely, enthusiastically, energetically, earnestly, persistently, doggedly, steadily, indefatigably, untiringly, all out, with application, with perseverance; informal like mad, like crazy, like billy-o.
▷ANTONYMS lackadaisically.
3 *this prosperity has been hard won*: **with difficulty**, with effort, after a struggle, painfully, arduously, laboriously.
▷ANTONYMS easily.
4 *her death hit him hard*: **severely**, badly, intensely, harshly, acutely, deeply, keenly, seriously, profoundly, violently, forcefully, grievously, gravely.
▷ANTONYMS slightly.
5 *it was raining hard*: **heavily**, strongly, intensely, in torrents, in sheets, cats and dogs; steadily; Brit. informal buckets, bucketloads, stair rods; N. Amer. informal pitchforks.
▷ANTONYMS lightly.
6 *my mother looked hard at me*: **closely**, attentively, intently, critically, carefully, keenly, searchingly, earnestly, sharply, scrutinizingly.
▷ANTONYMS casually.
□ **hard by** *a little shop, hard by the St Paul Hotel*: **close to**, right by, close by, beside, near, near to, nearby, not far from, a short distance from, a step away from, a stone's throw from, on the doorstep of, in the vicinity of, in the neighbourhood of, round the corner from, within easy reach of, adjacent to; informal within spitting distance of, within sniffing distance of, {a hop, skip, and a jump away from}.
▷ANTONYMS far from.
□ **hard on/upon** *his banishment followed hard on the quarrel*: **soon after**, hard on the heels of, quickly after, promptly after, shortly after, immediately after, directly after, straight after, right after, a short time after, without delay after.
▷ANTONYMS long after.
□ **hard up** informal *I'm too hard up to buy fancy clothes*: **poor**, short of money, short of cash, impoverished, impecunious, in financial difficulties, financially embarrassed, financially distressed, in reduced circumstances, in straitened circumstances, unable to make ends meet; penniless, moneyless, destitute, poverty-stricken, bankrupt, in the red, without a sou, without means of support; informal broke, stony broke, flat broke, bust, on one's beam-ends; Brit. informal skint, cleaned out, strapped for cash, on one's uppers, not having two pennies/farthings to rub together, in Queer Street, without a shot in one's locker, without a brass farthing; N. Amer. informal stone broke, without a red cent.
▷ANTONYMS rich.

> *Word links* **hard**
>
> **sclero-** related prefix, as in *sclerosis, scleroderma*

hardbitten adjective *a hardbitten war reporter*: **hardened**, tough, cynical, hard-headed, callous, as hard as nails, unsentimental, lacking sentiment, world-weary, case-hardened, toughened by experience; informal hard-nosed, hard-boiled, as tough as old boots; rare indurate, indurated.
▷ANTONYMS sentimental.

hard-boiled adjective informal *a hard-boiled undercover agent*: **cynical**, tough, hardened, hardbitten, hard-headed, callous, as hard as nails, unsentimental, lacking sentiment, world-weary, case-hardened, toughened by experience; informal hard-nosed, as tough as old boots; rare indurate, indurated.
▷ANTONYMS sentimental.

hard-core adjective *a hard-core following*: **diehard**, staunch, dedicated, committed, steadfast, hard-line, dyed-in-the-wool, long-standing; extreme, entrenched, radical, intransigent, uncompromising, rigid; informal deep-dyed.
▷ANTONYMS moderate.

harden verb **1** *this glue will harden in four hours*: **solidify**, set, become hard, become solid, congeal, clot, coagulate, stiffen, thicken, cake, freeze, bake, crystallize; strengthen, reinforce; technical anneal, vulcanize, ossify, petrify; rare indurate, inspissate, gelatinize.
▷ANTONYMS liquefy.
2 *their suffering had hardened them*: **toughen**, desensitize, inure, make insensitive, make tough, make unfeeling, case-harden, harden someone's heart; deaden, numb, benumb, anaesthetize; brutalize, make callous; rare indurate.
▷ANTONYMS soften.

hardened adjective **1** *he was hardened to the violence he had seen and inflicted*: **inured**, desensitized, deadened, accustomed, habituated, acclimatized, used; coarsened; rare indurate.
▷ANTONYMS unaccustomed.
2 *a hardened criminal*: **inveterate**, seasoned, habitual, chronic, compulsive, confirmed, accustomed, dyed-in-the-wool; through and through; incorrigible, incurable, irredeemable, impenitent, unreformable, unregenerate, reprobate, obdurate, shameless.
▷ANTONYMS infrequent.
3 *the silos are hardened against air attack*: **strengthened**, fortified, reinforced, toughened, thickened; literary girded; rare embastioned.
▷ANTONYMS unfortified.

> *Word toolkit* **hardened**
>
> See **incorrigible**.

hard-headed adjective *a hard-headed businessman*: **unsentimental**, practical, pragmatic, businesslike, realistic, sensible, rational, tough, clear-thinking, cool-headed, hardbitten, down-to-earth, matter-of-fact, no-nonsense, with one's/both feet on the ground; shrewd, astute, sharp, sharp-witted; informal hard-nosed, hard-boiled.
▷ANTONYMS idealistic.

hard-hearted adjective *only the most hard-hearted man would not have offered comfort*: **unfeeling**, heartless, cold, hard, unsympathetic, uncaring, unloving, unconcerned, indifferent, intolerant, unmoved, unkind, uncharitable, unemotional, stony, cold-hearted, cold-blooded, lacking compassion, mean-spirited, without sentiment, stony-hearted, with a heart of stone, hard as nails; cruel, brutal, callous, savage, inhuman, merciless, pitiless.
▷ANTONYMS compassionate.

hard-hitting adjective *the campaign against speeding included a hard-hitting television advertisement*: **uncompromising**, blunt, forthright, frank, honest, direct, tough; critical, condemnatory, unsparing, strongly worded, straight-talking, all out, pulling no punches, no holds barred, not mincing one's words, not beating about the bush; informal upfront, straight from the shoulder.
▷ANTONYMS mild.

hardihood noun dated *the soldiers showed great hardihood and endurance*. See **bravery**.

hardiness noun *this breed is renowned for its hardiness*: **robustness**, healthiness, strength, toughness, vigour, ruggedness, sturdiness, resilience, stamina, good health.
▷ANTONYMS frailty.

hard-line adjective *a hard-line nationalist*: **uncompromising**, strict, diehard, extreme, tough, inflexible, immoderate, intransigent, intractable, unyielding, undeviating, unwavering, single-minded, not giving an inch; rare indurate.
▷ANTONYMS moderate.

hardly adverb **1** *we hardly know each other | Dad had hardly got a word out before she cut him off*: **scarcely**, barely, only just, not much, faintly, narrowly, slightly, rarely, little; by a very small margin, by the narrowest of margins, by the skin of one's teeth, by a hair's breadth, by a nose; almost not, not quite; informal by a whisker.
▷ANTONYMS fully.
2 *she could hardly sit up straight*: **only with difficulty**, barely, scarcely, only with effort, only just, almost not; Brit. informal at a push.
▷ANTONYMS easily.

hardness noun **1** *the hardness of the ground*: **firmness**, solidity, stiffness, rigidity, denseness, inflexibility, inelasticity, resistance.
▷ANTONYMS softness.
2 *there was a core of calculating hardness to this man*: **hard-heartedness**, heartlessness, cold-heartedness, lack of compassion, lack of feeling, lack of sentiment, callousness, unkindness, flintiness, steeliness; harshness, severity, strictness, sternness, toughness.
▷ANTONYMS compassion, kindness.

hard-nosed adjective informal *hard-nosed businessmen*: **tough-minded**, unsentimental, down-to-earth, no-nonsense, hard-headed, hardbitten, pragmatic, clear-thinking, realistic, practical, rational, shrewd, astute, businesslike; informal hard-boiled.
▷ANTONYMS sentimental.

hard-pressed adjective **1** *the hard-pressed French infantry*: **under attack**, closely pursued, hotly pursued, harried, hounded.
2 *organizations that are hard-pressed financially*: **in difficulties**, under pressure, under stress, troubled, beleaguered, harassed, with one's back

to the wall, with one's back up against the wall, in a tight corner, in a tight spot, between a rock and a hard place; busy, overburdened, overworked, overloaded, overtaxed, rushed off one's feet; N. Amer. at the end of one's rope; informal pushed, up against it.
▷ANTONYMS untroubled.

hardship noun *the world depression caused severe hardship*: **privation**, deprivation, destitution, poverty, austerity, penury, want, need, neediness, beggary, impecuniousness, impecuniosity, financial distress; misfortune, distress, suffering, affliction, trouble, pain, misery, wretchedness, tribulation, adversity, disaster, ruin, ruination, calamity; trials, trials and tribulations, dire straits; informal hassle; literary travails.
▷ANTONYMS prosperity; ease.

hardware noun *tanks and other military hardware*: **equipment**, apparatus, gear, paraphernalia, tackle, kit, machinery; tools, articles, implements, instruments, appliances, gadgets; informal stuff, things; Brit. informal clobber, gubbins; rare equipage.

hard-wearing adjective *a hard-wearing fabric*: **durable**, strong, tough, resilient, lasting, solid, stout, rugged, long-lasting, made to last, well made, wear-resistant, heavy-duty, strongly made; rare infrangible.
▷ANTONYMS delicate; flimsy.

hard-working adjective *loyal and hard-working employees*: **diligent**, industrious, conscientious, assiduous, sedulous, painstaking, persevering, unflagging, untiring, tireless, indefatigable, studious; energetic, keen, enthusiastic, zealous, busy, with one's shoulder to the wheel, with one's nose to the grindstone; archaic laborious.
▷ANTONYMS lazy.

Choose the right word **hard-working, diligent, industrious**

Hard-working is the most general term but is typically applied to people in paid work (*you can search for an honest, hard-working mechanic in your area*).

Diligent describes a careful, conscientious person (such as a *pupil*, *teacher*, *parent*, or *student*) or their actions (such as *research*, *enquiries*, *practice*, or a *search*). A *diligent* person typically works hard from a sense of duty or dedication (*she had been diligent about her piano lessons | skilled and diligent nursing staff*).

industrious conveys an impression of worthiness (*she wanted energetic, industrious people around her*), being commonly used alongside *energetic*, *loyal*, *sober*, or *obedient*.

hardy adjective *a couple of hardy outdoor types | hardy trees and shrubs*: **robust**, healthy, fit, strong, sturdy, tough, rugged, hearty, lusty, vigorous, hale and hearty, fit as a fiddle, fighting fit, in fine fettle, in good health, in good condition; Brit. in rude health; dated stalwart.
▷ANTONYMS delicate; tender.

hare noun

Word links **hare**

buck male
doe female
leveret young
form home
down, mute, husk collective noun
leporine relating to hares

hare-brained adjective **1** *a hare-brained scheme*: **ill-judged**, rash, foolish, foolhardy, reckless, madcap, wild, silly, stupid, ridiculous, preposterous, absurd, idiotic, asinine, imprudent, impracticable, unworkable, unrealistic, unconsidered, half-baked, ill-thought-out, ill-advised, ill-conceived; informal daft, crackpot, crackbrained, cock-eyed, crazy, barmy.
▷ANTONYMS sensible.
2 *a hare-brained young girl*: **foolish**, silly, idiotic, unintelligent, empty-headed, scatterbrained, feather-brained, birdbrained, pea-brained, brainless, giddy; informal dippy, dizzy, dopey, dotty, airheaded.
▷ANTONYMS intelligent.

harem noun **women's quarters**; in Muslim societies, formerly **seraglio**; in India & Persia **zenana**; in ancient Greece & Rome **gynaeceum**; rare **haremlik**, **serai**.

hark verb literary *hark, I hear a warning note*. See **listen**.
□ **hark back** *these newest styles* ***hark back to*** *the seventies*: **recall**, call to mind, look back to, turn back to, cause one to remember, cause one to recollect, cause one to think back to.

harlequin noun **jester**, joker, merry andrew, droll; rare zany.
▸ adjective *a harlequin pattern*: **varicoloured**, variegated, colourful, particoloured, multicoloured, multicolour, many-coloured, many-hued, rainbow, jazzy, kaleidoscopic, psychedelic, polychromatic, chequered; informal (looking) like an explosion in a paint factory; rare motley.
▷ANTONYMS plain.

harlot noun archaic **prostitute**, whore, call girl, sex worker, white slave; promiscuous woman, slut, hussy; euphemistic model, escort, masseuse; French fille de joie, demi-mondaine, grande horizontale; Spanish puta; informal tart, pro, tail, brass nail, tom, woman on the game, working girl, member of the oldest profession, floozie, moll; Brit. informal scrubber, slag, slapper; N. Amer. informal hooker, tramp, hustler, roundheel; black English ho; dated streetwalker, woman of the streets, woman of the night, scarlet woman, loose woman, fallen woman, woman of easy virtue, cocotte, wanton; archaic strumpet, courtesan, trollop, woman of ill repute, lady of pleasure, Cyprian, doxy, drab, quean, trull, wench.

harm noun **1** *the voltage is not sufficient to cause harm*: **injury**, hurt, pain, suffering, distress, anguish, trauma, torment, grief; **damage**, impairment, destruction, loss, ruin, defacement, defilement, mischief.
▷ANTONYMS benefit.
2 *I can't see any harm in it*: **evil**, badness, wrong, mischief, wrongdoing, immorality, ill, wickedness, vice, iniquity, sin, sinfulness, nefariousness.
▷ANTONYMS good.
▸ verb *he's never harmed anybody in his life | this could harm his World Cup prospects*: **injure**, hurt, wound, maltreat, mistreat, misuse, ill-treat, ill-use, abuse, molest, inflict pain on, inflict suffering on, handle/treat roughly, do violence to, lay a finger on; **damage**, spoil, mar, destroy, do mischief to, impair, deface, defile, blemish, tarnish, taint.
▷ANTONYMS benefit; improve.

harmful adjective *the harmful effects of cigarette smoking | a harmful influence*: **damaging**, injurious, detrimental, dangerous, deleterious, unfavourable, negative, disadvantageous, unhealthy, unwholesome, hurtful, baleful, wounding, destructive; noxious, hazardous, poisonous, toxic, deadly, lethal; bad, evil, malign, malignant, malevolent, corrupting, subversive, pernicious; rare baneful, maleficent, malefic.
▷ANTONYMS beneficial; harmless.

harmless adjective **1** *a harmless substance*: **safe**, innocuous, benign, gentle, mild, wholesome, non-dangerous, non-toxic, non-poisonous, non-irritant, non-addictive; rare innoxious.
▷ANTONYMS dangerous; harmful.
2 *he seems harmless enough*: **inoffensive**, innocuous, unobjectionable, unexceptionable, unoffending, tame, gentle.
▷ANTONYMS objectionable.

Word toolkit

harmless	benign	non-toxic
fun	neglect	paint
drug	lesion	cleaning products
bacteria	tumour	compound
flirting	disease	ingredients
creature	growth	concentration
prank	dictatorship	chemicals

harmonious adjective **1** *harmonious music*: **tuneful**, melodious, melodic, sweet-sounding, pleasant-sounding, sweet-toned, mellifluous, dulcet, lyrical; **euphonious**, euphonic, harmonic, harmonizing, polyphonic, consonant; informal easy on the ear; rare symphonious, canorous, mellifluent.
▷ANTONYMS discordant.
2 *a harmonious relationship between business and customer*: **friendly**, amicable, cordial, amiable, agreeable, congenial, easy, peaceful, peaceable, cooperative, good-natured; fraternal, compatible, sympathetic, united, attuned, in harmony, in rapport, in tune, in accord, of one mind, seeing eye to eye, free from disagreement.
▷ANTONYMS hostile.
3 *the decor is a harmonious blend of traditional and modern*: **congruous**, coordinated, matching, balanced, proportional, in proportion, compatible, well matched, well proportioned, well balanced.
▷ANTONYMS incongruous.

harmonize verb **1** *the colours harmonize well*: **coordinate**, **go together**, match, fit together, blend, mix, balance, tone in; be compatible, be harmonious, be congruous, be consonant, be well coordinated, suit each other, set each other off.
▷ANTONYMS clash.
2 *the need to harmonize tax laws across Europe*: **coordinate**, systematize, correlate, match, integrate, synchronize, homogenize, bring together, make consistent, bring in line (with), bring in tune (with), tie in; rare concert.
3 *he tried to harmonize relations between the quarrelling factions*: **reconcile**, make harmonious, restore harmony to, make peaceful, patch up, repair, smooth out.

harmony noun **1** *the quartet owes its air of tranquillity largely to the subtle harmony*: **euphony**, polyphony, consonance; tunefulness, melodiousness, mellifluousness, mellifluence.
▷ANTONYMS dissonance.
2 *the simplicity of the individual parts focused attention on the harmony of the whole structure*: **balance**, symmetry, congruity, consonance, coordination, blending, correspondence, compatibility.
▷ANTONYMS incongruity.
3 *the villagers live together in harmony | man and machine in perfect*

harmony: **concord**, accord, agreement, peace, peacefulness, amity, amicability, friendship, fellowship, comradeship, solidarity, cooperation, understanding, consensus, unity, sympathy, rapport, goodwill, like-mindedness; unison, union, concert, oneness, synthesis, concurrence.
▷ANTONYMS disagreement.

harness noun *a horse's harness*: **tack**, tackle, equipment, trappings, straps, yoke; informal gear; archaic equipage.
□ **in harness** *it was good to be back in harness again*: **at work**, working, employed, in an occupation, in action, active, busy.
▷ANTONYMS unemployed.
▶verb **1** *Dad harnessed a horse and put it between the shafts*: **hitch up**, put something in harness, saddle, yoke, couple.
▷ANTONYMS unhitch.
2 *attempts to harness solar energy | organizations that try to harness the creativity of their workforce*: **control**, exploit, utilize, use, make use of, put to use, render useful, make productive, turn to good account; channel, mobilize, employ, apply, capitalize on.
▷ANTONYMS underuse.

harp verb *guys who are constantly **harping on about** the war*: **keep on about**, go on about, persist in talking about, keep talking about, labour the point about, dwell on, expatiate on, elaborate on, expound on, make an issue of, discuss something at length; complain repeatedly about, nag someone about, badger someone about; informal witter on about, rabbit on about, hassle someone about.

Word links **harp**
harpist, **harper** harp player

harpoon noun **spear**, trident, arrow, dart, barb; rare gaff, leister.

harridan noun **shrew**, **virago**, harpy, termagant, vixen, nag, hag, crone, dragon, ogress; fishwife, hellcat, she-devil, fury, gorgon, martinet, tartar, spitfire; informal old bag, old bat, old trout, old cow, bitch, battleaxe, witch; rare scold, Xanthippe.

harried adjective *it was full of harried women with crying children*: **harassed**, hard-pressed, beleaguered, agitated, flustered, bothered, troubled, distressed, vexed, beset, hag-ridden, hounded, plagued, tormented; informal hassled, up against it.
▷ANTONYMS untroubled.

harrow verb *to read those words harrowed her very soul*: **distress**, trouble, afflict, grieve, torment, torture, crucify, rack, sear, pain, wound, mortify, cause agony to, cause suffering to; informal cut up.
▷ANTONYMS calm; comfort.

harrowing adjective *harrowing pictures of starving children | a harrowing experience*: **distressing**, traumatic, upsetting, heartbreaking, heart-rending, shocking, disturbing, painful, affecting, haunting, appalling, tragic, horrifying; informal gut-wrenching; rare distressful.
▷ANTONYMS heartening.

harry verb **1** *after the battle, they harried the retreating enemy*: **attack**, assail, assault, maraud, ravage, devastate, wreak havoc on; plunder, rob, sack, ransack, raid, pillage, lay waste to; literary despoil; rare depredate, reave, spoliate.
2 *the government is being mercilessly harried by a new lobby*: **harass**, hound, pressurize, bring pressure to bear on, put pressure on, lean on, keep on at, go on at, chivvy, bedevil, torment, pester, bother, disturb, worry, annoy, badger, nag, plague, persecute, molest; informal hassle, bug, give someone a hard time, drive someone round the bend, drive someone up the wall, be in someone's hair, get on someone's back, breathe down someone's neck; Brit. informal drive someone round the twist.
▷ANTONYMS leave in peace.

harsh adjective **1** *his shrill, harsh voice*: **grating**, jarring, grinding, rasping, raspy, strident, raucous, brassy, jangling, metallic, ear-piercing, discordant, dissonant, disagreeable, unharmonious, cacophonous, unmelodious; screeching, shrill, tinny, squeaky, squawking; rough, coarse, guttural, hoarse, gruff, croaky, croaking, growly, growling; rare stridulant.
▷ANTONYMS soft; dulcet.
2 *drenched in a harsh white neon light | harsh colours*: **glaring**, bright, dazzling, brilliant; loud, flashy, garish, gaudy, lurid, bold, showy, crude, vulgar.
▷ANTONYMS subdued.
3 *during his harsh rule, thousands were exiled*: **cruel**, severe, savage, barbarous, despotic, dictatorial, tyrannical, tyrannous, ruthless, merciless, pitiless, relentless, unrelenting, hard, strict, intolerant, illiberal; hard-hearted, heartless, unkind, inhuman, inhumane, unfeeling, unsympathetic, unmerciful, unpitying; rare suppressive.
▷ANTONYMS enlightened; kind.
4 *politicians are taking harsh measures to clear the homeless from the streets*: **severe**, stringent, firm, austere, punitive, draconian, stiff, cruel, brutal, hard, stern, rigid, rigorous, grim, uncompromising, inflexible.
▷ANTONYMS lenient.
5 *harsh words are exchanged when tempers get frayed*: **rude**, discourteous, uncivil, impolite, unfriendly, sharp, acerbic, bitter, abusive, unkind, disparaging; abrupt, brusque, blunt, curt, gruff, short, surly, ungracious, disrespectful, ill-mannered, bad-mannered, offhand.
▷ANTONYMS friendly.
6 *the harsh conditions of the refugee camps*: **austere**, grim, spartan, hard, rough, severe, comfortless, inhospitable, stark; bleak, desolate, barren, bitter, wild.
▷ANTONYMS comfortable.
7 *a harsh winter*: **hard**, severe, cold, bitter, bitterly cold, bleak, freezing, icy, icy-cold, arctic, polar, Siberian, glacial, extreme, nasty.
▷ANTONYMS balmy.
8 *harsh cleaners scratch stains away*: **abrasive**, strong, caustic; coarse, rough, bristly, hairy, scratchy.
▷ANTONYMS mild; smooth.

harum-scarum adjective informal *he was a harum-scarum young fellow*: **reckless**, impetuous, impulsive, imprudent, rash, wild, daredevil, madcap, precipitous, precipitate, frivolous, hot-headed, hare-brained, giddy, foolhardy, thoughtless, incautious, careless, heedless, hasty, overhasty; informal devil-may-care, scatty, dotty, dippy; Brit. informal divvy; rare temerarious.
▷ANTONYMS cautious.

harvest noun **1** *the women and girls helped with the harvest*: **gathering in of the crops**, harvesting, harvest time, harvest home; **reaping**, picking, collecting; rare garnering, ingathering, gleaning, culling.
2 *a poor harvest*: **yield**, crop, vintage, year's growth; fruits, produce.
3 *in terms of science, Apollo yielded a meagre harvest*: **return**, result, fruits; product, effect, consequence, output.
▶verb **1** *once he's harvested the wheat crop, there are still the beans*: **gather in**, gather, bring in, take in; reap, pick, collect; rare garner, ingather, glean, cull.
2 *he harvested a hat-trick of honours*: **acquire**, obtain, gain, get, procure, secure, earn; accumulate, amass, gather, collect; informal land, net, bag, scoop, cop.

hash¹ noun *I used a whole hash of excuses*: **mixture**, assortment, variety, array, mixed bag, mix, miscellany, random collection, motley collection, selection, medley, melange, mishmash, hotchpotch, hodgepodge, ragbag, pot-pourri, jumble, farrago, patchwork; informal mash-up; rare gallimaufry, omnium gatherum, olio, olla podrida, salmagundi, macédoine, motley.
□ **make a hash of** informal *he made a hash of a simple penalty*: **make a mess of**, bungle, botch, fluff, fumble, butcher, mess up; mismanage, mishandle, misdirect, misgovern, misconduct, mar, spoil, ruin, wreck; informal muff, muck up, foul up, screw up, louse up, bitch up, blow, foozle; Brit. informal make a muck of, make a pig's ear of, make a Horlicks of, cock up; N. Amer. informal flub, goof up, bobble; vulgar slang balls up, bugger up, fuck up.
▷ANTONYMS manage successfully.

hash² noun informal See **cannabis**.

hassle informal noun **1** *parking in the city centre is a hassle | the hassle of child care*: **inconvenience**, bother, nuisance, problem, struggle, difficulty, annoyance, irritation, thorn in one's flesh/side, bane of one's life; trials and tribulations, fuss, trouble; informal aggravation, aggro, stress, headache, pain, pain in the neck/backside; N. Amer. informal pain in the butt; Brit. vulgar slang pain in the arse.
2 N. Amer. *you'd better not get into a hassle with that guy*: **disagreement**, quarrel, argument, dispute, altercation, squabble, wrangle, shouting match, difference of opinion, contretemps, falling-out, war of words; fight, tussle, struggle, fracas, free-for-all, brawl; Irish, N. Amer., & Austral. donnybrook; informal tiff, set-to, run-in, spat, scrap, dust-up; Brit. informal row, barney, slanging match, ding-dong, bust-up, bit of argy-bargy, ruck; Scottish informal rammy; N. Amer. informal rhubarb; archaic broil, miff; Scottish archaic threap, collieshangie.
▷ANTONYMS agreement.
▶verb *they were hassling him to pay up*: **harass**, pester, nag, go on at, keep on at, keep after, badger, hound, harry, harp on at, chivvy, trouble, bother, worry, torment, annoy, plague, bedevil, persecute; informal bug, give someone a hard time, get in someone's hair, get on someone's case, get on someone's back, breathe down someone's neck; N. English mither; N. Amer. informal devil, ride; Austral./NZ informal heavy; rare discommode.
▷ANTONYMS leave in peace.

hassled adjective informal *he was hassled and rushed off his feet*: **harassed**, stressed, stressed out, harried, frayed, hard-pressed, agitated, flustered, beleaguered, hounded, plagued, bothered, troubled, distressed, beset, hag-ridden, tormented; under stress, under pressure, at the end of one's tether, with one's back up against the wall; N. Amer. at the end of one's rope; informal up against it, in a state, hot and bothered.
▷ANTONYMS calm, relaxed.

haste noun *working with feverish haste*: **speed**, hastiness, hurry, hurriedness, swiftness, rapidity, rapidness, quickness, promptness, briskness, immediateness; impetuosity, precipitateness, rush, rushing; literary celerity, fleetness; rare expedition, expeditiousness, promptitude.
▷ANTONYMS slowness, delay.
□ **in haste quickly**, rapidly, fast, speedily, with alacrity, with urgency, in a rush, in a hurry, with dispatch.
□ **make haste** *I made haste down the stairs.* See **hasten** (sense 1).

h

hasten verb **1** *we hastened back to Paris*: **hurry**, go fast, go quickly, make haste, hurtle, dash, dart, race, rush, fly, flash, shoot, streak, bolt, bound, blast, charge, chase, career, hurry up, speed up, scurry, scramble, scamper, scuttle, sprint, run, gallop, go like lightning, go hell for leather; Brit. scutter; informal whizz, whoosh, vroom, tear, scoot, hare, pelt, zip, whip, zoom, belt, beetle, buzz, get a move on, step on it, hotfoot it, leg it, burn rubber, go like a bat out of hell; Brit. informal bomb, bucket, shift, put one's foot down, go like the clappers; Scottish informal wheech; N. Amer. informal hightail, barrel, boogie, clip, lay rubber, get the lead out; N. Amer. vulgar slang drag/tear/haul ass; informal, dated cut along; archaic post, hie, fleet.
▷ANTONYMS dawdle; crawl.
2 *stress chemicals can hasten ageing*: **speed up**, make faster, accelerate, quicken, precipitate, expedite, advance, hurry on, step up, push forward, urge on, spur on; facilitate, aid, assist, help, boost; informal crank up, gee up.
▷ANTONYMS delay; slow down.

hastily adverb **1** *Meg retreated hastily as the blades began to rotate*: **quickly**, hurriedly, in a hurry, fast, swiftly, rapidly, speedily, briskly, expeditiously, without delay, post-haste, at high speed, at full speed, with all speed, at full tilt, at the speed of light, as fast as possible, with all possible haste, like a whirlwind, like an arrow from a bow, at breakneck speed, as fast as one's legs can carry one, at a run, at a gallop, hotfoot, on the double; cursorily, perfunctorily, briefly, fleetingly, sketchily, superficially; informal double quick, in double quick time, p.d.q. (pretty damn quick), nippily, like (greased) lightning, hell for leather, like mad, like crazy, like blazes, like the wind, like a bomb, like nobody's business, like a scalded cat, like the deuce, a mile a minute, like a bat out of hell, at warp speed; Brit. informal at a rate of knots, like the clappers, like billy-o; N. Amer. informal lickety-split; literary apace.
▷ANTONYMS slowly.
2 *an agreement was hastily drawn up*: **hurriedly**, speedily, quickly, in a hurry; impetuously, impulsively, recklessly, precipitately, precipitously, rashly, incautiously, imprudently, on the spur of the moment, prematurely.
▷ANTONYMS carefully, deliberately.

hasty adjective **1** *Fran took several hasty steps backwards*: **quick**, hurried, fast, swift, rapid, speedy, brisk, hurrying, expeditious; cursory, perfunctory, brief, short, fleeting, passing, flying, transitory; literary fleet, rathe.
▷ANTONYMS slow.
2 *hasty decisions*: **rash**, impetuous, impulsive, reckless, precipitate, precipitous, incautious, imprudent, spur-of-the-moment, premature, ill-considered, unconsidered, unthinking, ill-advised, ill-judged, injudicious; rare temerarious.
▷ANTONYMS considered.

hat noun Brit. informal titfer.
□ **keep something under one's hat** informal *at the moment it's all a bit hush-hush, so keep it under your hat*: **conceal**, hide, cover up, disguise, dissemble, mask, veil; **keep secret**, keep quiet about, keep dark, hush up, draw a veil over, sweep under the carpet, gloss over; suppress, repress, bottle up, bury; informal keep a/the lid on.
▷ANTONYMS show, disclose, confess.
□ **old hat** *something that is exceedingly popular today is usually old hat by tomorrow*: **out of date**, outdated, dated, old-fashioned, out, out of fashion, outmoded, unfashionable, last year's, frumpish, frumpy, out of style, outworn, old, old-time, old-world, behind the times, archaic, obsolescent, obsolete, ancient, antiquated, superannuated, defunct; medieval, prehistoric, antediluvian, old-fogeyish, old-fangled, conservative, backward-looking, quaint, anachronistic, crusted, feudal, fusty, moth-eaten, olde worlde; French passé, démodé, vieux jeu; informal square, not with it, out of the ark, creaky, mouldy; N. Amer. informal horse-and-buggy, clunky, rinky-dink, mossy; archaic square-toed.
▷ANTONYMS modern, up to date, fashionable.
□ **take one's hat off to** *he was truly magnificent and I take my hat off to him*: **praise**, pay tribute to, sing the praises of, speak highly of, express admiration of, commend, acclaim, applaud, salute, honour, show appreciation of, appreciate, recognize, acknowledge, give recognition to, show gratitude to, be grateful for, pay homage to, extol; rare laud.

> *Word links* **hat**
>
> **hatter** seller of hats
> **milliner** seller of women's hats

hatch verb **1** *the duck hatched a clutch of eggs*: **incubate**, brood, sit on, cover; bring forth.
2 *the little plot that you and Sylvia* **hatched up** *last night*: **devise**, conceive, contrive, concoct, brew, invent, plan, design, formulate; think up, make up, dream up, trump up, put together; informal cook up.

hatchet noun axe, cleaver, mattock, tomahawk; Brit. chopper.
□ **do a hatchet job on** informal *I didn't want to do a hatchet job on a man when he was down*: **savage**, attack, lambaste, condemn, criticize severely, flay, shoot down, pillory, revile; informal jump on, tear to pieces, take to pieces, take/pull apart, lay into, pitch into, hammer, slam, bash, crucify, give something a battering, roast, skewer, throw brickbats at, knock; Brit. informal slate, rubbish, slag off; N. Amer. informal bad-mouth, pummel; Austral./NZ informal trash, bag, monster, give someone bondi; archaic excoriate, slash.
▷ANTONYMS praise, commend, applaud.

hate verb **1** *the boys hate each other*: **loathe**, detest, dislike greatly, abhor, abominate, despise, execrate, feel aversion towards, feel revulsion towards, feel hostile towards, be repelled by, be revolted by, regard with disgust, not be able to bear/stand, be unable to stomach, find intolerable, shudder at, recoil from, shrink from; informal hate someone's guts; rare disrelish.
▷ANTONYMS love; like.
2 *I hate to bother you*: **be sorry**, be reluctant, be loath, be unwilling, be disinclined; regret, dislike, not like, hesitate.
▶ noun **1** *feelings of hate and revenge*: **loathing**, hatred, detestation, dislike, distaste, abhorrence, abomination, execration, resentment, aversion, hostility, ill will, ill feeling, bad feeling; enmity, animosity, antagonism, antipathy, bitterness, animus, revulsion, disgust, contempt, repugnance, odium, rancour; rare disrelish.
▷ANTONYMS love; liking.
2 *Richard's* **pet hate** *is filling in his tax returns*: **bugbear**, bane, bogey, bugaboo, pet aversion, thorn in one's flesh/side, bane of one's life; French bête noire.
▷ANTONYMS favourite thing.

hateful adjective *that hateful arrogant old woman*: **detestable**, horrible, horrid, unpleasant, awful, nasty, disagreeable, despicable, objectionable, insufferable, revolting, rotten, loathsome, abhorrent, abominable, damnable, execrable, odious, repugnant, repellent, repulsive, disgusting, distasteful, obnoxious, offensive, foul, vile, heinous; informal ghastly; Brit. informal beastly, God-awful, yucky; vulgar slang shitty; archaic loathly, disgustful.
▷ANTONYMS delightful; lovable.

hatred noun *full of hatred and bitterness*: **loathing**, hate, detestation, dislike, distaste, abhorrence, abomination, execration, resentment, aversion, hostility, ill will, ill feeling, bad feeling; enmity, animosity, antagonism, antipathy, bitterness, animus, revulsion, disgust, contempt, repugnance, odium, rancour; rare disrelish.
▷ANTONYMS love; liking.

> *Word links* **hatred**
>
> **mis-** related prefix, as in *misogyny, misanthrope*

haughtiness noun **arrogance**, pride, conceit, hubris, self-importance, egotism, sense of superiority, pomposity, high-handedness, swagger, boasting, bumptiousness, bluster, condescension, disdain, contempt, imperiousness; vanity, immodesty; loftiness, lordliness, snobbishness, snobbery, superciliousness, smugness; pretension, pretentiousness, affectation; scorn, mocking, sneering, scoffing; informal snootiness, uppitiness, big-headedness.
▷ANTONYMS modesty.

haughty adjective *his bearing was both haughty and disdainful*: **proud**, vain, arrogant, conceited, snobbish, stuck-up, pompous, self-important, superior, egotistical, supercilious, condescending, lofty, patronizing, smug, scornful, contemptuous, disdainful, overweening, overbearing, imperious, lordly, cavalier, high-handed, full of oneself, above oneself; informal snooty, sniffy, hoity-toity, uppity, uppish, cocky, big-headed, swollen-headed, puffed up, high and mighty, la-di-da, fancy-pants, on one's high horse, too big for one's boots; Brit. informal toffee-nosed; N. Amer. informal chesty; informal, dated too big for one's breeches; literary vainglorious.
▷ANTONYMS modest; humble.

haul verb **1** *she hauled the laden basket up the slope*: **drag**, pull, tug, heave, hump, trail, draw, tow, manhandle; informal lug; N. Amer. informal schlep; archaic hale.
▷ANTONYMS push.
2 *a contract to haul coal over a five-year period*: **transport**, convey, cart, carry, ship, ferry, move, shift, take.
□ **haul someone over the coals** *he can expect to be hauled over the coals for criticizing his club*. See **reprimand** (verb).
▶ noun *the thieves were forced to abandon their haul*: **booty**, loot, plunder; spoils, stolen goods, gains, ill-gotten gains; informal swag, the goods, hot goods, boodle.

haunches plural noun **rump**, rear, rear end, backside, seat; buttocks, thighs, hips, hindquarters; Brit. **bottom**; French derrière; German Sitzfleisch; informal behind, sit-upon, stern, BTM, tochus; Brit. informal bum, botty, prat, jacksie; Scottish informal bahookie; N. Amer. informal butt, fanny, tush, tushie, tail, duff, buns, booty, caboose, heinie, patootie, keister, tuchis, bazoo, bippy; W. Indian informal batty; humorous fundament, posterior; black English rass, rusty dusty; Brit. vulgar slang arse; N. Amer. vulgar slang ass; technical nates; archaic breech.

haunt verb **1** *a ghost haunts this eighteenth-century house*: **appear in**, materialize in; visit; informal spook.
2 *he haunts street markets*: **frequent**, spend time in, patronize, visit regularly, be a regular visitor to, be a regular client of, loiter in, linger in; informal hang around/round/out in; Brit. informal hang about in.

3 *the sight haunted me for years*: **torment**, obsess, oppress, disturb, trouble, worry, plague, burden, beset, beleaguer, bedevil, besiege, torture; prey on, weigh on, gnaw at, nag at, weigh heavily on, lie heavy on; prey on one's mind, weigh heavily on one's mind, be a weight on one's mind; informal bug.
▶ **noun** *a favourite haunt of artists of the time*: **hang-out**, stamping ground, meeting place, territory, domain, purlieu, resort, den, retreat, favourite spot; informal hidey-hole; Brit. informal local, patch, manor.

haunted **adjective** **1** *a haunted house*: **possessed**, cursed, jinxed; ghostly, eerie, unearthly, other-worldly; informal spooky.
2 *haunted eyes stared at her*: **tormented**, anguished, troubled, plagued, bedevilled, beleaguered, oppressed, obsessed, tortured, preoccupied, worried, disturbed.
▷**ANTONYMS** untroubled.

haunting **adjective** *the sweet haunting sound of pan pipes*: **evocative**, affecting, moving, touching, emotive, expressive, powerful, stirring, atmospheric, soul-stirring; **poignant**, nostalgic, wistful, plaintive; memorable, unforgettable, indelible, not/never to be forgotten.
▷**ANTONYMS** unaffecting; unmemorable.

hauteur **noun** *his natural coolness and aristocratic hauteur*: **haughtiness**, superciliousness, loftiness, arrogance, pride, conceit, snobbery, snobbishness, superiority, self-importance, disdain, disdainfulness, condescension, contempt, scorn; airs, airs and graces; informal snootiness, uppitiness, uppishness, la-di-da; Brit. informal side.

have **verb** **1** *he had a new car and a boat*: **possess**, own, be in possession of, be the owner of, be the (proud) possessor of, have in one's possession, have to one's name, count among one's possessions, be blessed with, boast, enjoy; keep, maintain, retain, hold, use, utilize, occupy.
▷**ANTONYMS** be bereft of.
2 *the flat has five rooms*: **comprise**, consist of, contain, include, incorporate, be composed of, be made up of, be formed of; embrace, embody, encompass, take in; formal comprehend.
3 *they had beans on toast | we had three cups of tea*: **eat**, consume, devour, partake of; **drink**, empty, drain, quaff; informal demolish, dispose of, put away, get outside of, scoff (down), pack away, tuck away; imbibe, sink, knock back; Brit. informal shift, bevvy; N. Amer. informal scarf (down/up), snarf (down/up), inhale; rare ingurgitate, bib.
4 *she had a letter from Mark*: **receive**, get, be given, be sent, obtain, acquire, procure, come by, take receipt of.
▷**ANTONYMS** send; give.
5 *we've decided to have a party*: **organize**, arrange, hold, give, host, throw, provide, put on, lay on, set up, fix up, make arrangements for, make preparations for, pencil in, prepare for, plan for.
▷**ANTONYMS** cancel.
6 *she's going to have a baby*: **give birth to**, bear, produce, be delivered of, bring into the world; informal drop; archaic be brought to bed of, bring forth, beget.
7 *we are having guests for dinner*: **entertain**, be host to, cater for, receive; invite round, invite over, ask round, ask over, show hospitality to, invite to a meal, invite to a party, wine and dine; **accommodate**, put up, take in, give a bed to.
▷**ANTONYMS** visit.
8 *the driver had trouble finding the restaurant*: **experience**, encounter, undergo, face, meet, find, go through, run into, come across, be subjected to, have experience of, be faced with.
9 *I have a headache*: **be suffering from**, be afflicted by, be affected by, be troubled with, be a sufferer from; informal be a martyr to.
10 *I went to a few parties and had a good time*: **experience**, enjoy, taste.
11 *many pilots have doubts about the safety of the new computer system*: **harbour**, feel, entertain, foster, nurse, cherish, nurture, bear, sustain, maintain, keep in one's mind.
12 *he had little patience with technological gadgetry*: **manifest**, show, display, exhibit, demonstrate, express, evince.
13 *he had his bodyguards throw Chris out*: **cause to**, **make**, ask to, request to, get to, tell to, require to, persuade to, induce to, prevail upon someone to; order to, command to, direct to, enjoin to, oblige to, force to, compel to, coerce to.
14 *I can't have you insulting Tom like that*: **tolerate**, endure, bear, support, accept, put up with, go along with, take, countenance, brook; permit to, allow to; informal stand, abide, stick, stomach, hold with; Brit. informal be doing with.
15 *I **have to** get up at 6.30 tomorrow morning*: **must**, have got to, be obliged to, be required to, be compelled to, be forced to, be bound to, be duty-bound to, be under an obligation to.
16 informal *I realized I'd been had*: **trick**, fool, deceive, cheat, dupe, take in, outwit, double-cross, hoodwink, swindle; informal do, con, diddle, bilk, rip off, shaft, pull a fast one on, put one over on, take to the cleaners; N. Amer. informal sucker, snooker, stiff.
□ **have done with** *the drug scene is behind me—I have done with it*: **be finished with**, have finished with, be done with, be through with, want no more to do with, be no longer involved with/in, have given up, have no further dealings with, have turned one's back on, have washed one's hands of, have no more truck with.
▷**ANTONYMS** get into.
□ **have had it** informal **1** *in private they admit that they've had it*: **have no chance**, have no hope, have failed, be finished, be out, be defeated, have lost, have no chance of success, have come to nothing; informal have flopped, have bitten the dust, have come a cropper. ▷**ANTONYMS** succeed.
2 *if you ever let this information get out to the public, you've had it*: **be in trouble**, be going to be punished, be going to suffer the consequences, be going to pay the price, be in for a scolding, be going to answer for something; informal be for it, be for the high jump, be in hot water, be in deep water, be in (deep) shtook, be going to take the rap, be going to catch it.
□ **have it away/off (with)** Brit. vulgar slang *Steph had it off with Tony while he was going out with Lani*: **have sexual intercourse (with)**, have sex (with), **make love (to)**, sleep with/together, go to bed with/together; mate (with); seduce, rape, ravish; informal do it, do the business, go all the way, make whoopee, have one's way with, bed, know in the biblical sense, tumble; Brit. informal bonk, get one's oats; N. Amer. informal boff, get it on (with); euphemistic be intimate (with); vulgar slang fuck, screw, bang, lay, get one's leg over, shaft, dick, frig, do, have, hump, poke, shtup, dip one's wick, ride, service, tup; Brit. vulgar slang shag, knob, get one's end away, knock someone off, give someone one, roger, grind, stuff; Scottish vulgar slang podger; N. Amer. vulgar slang ball, jump, jump someone's bones, bone, pork, diddle, nail; Austral./NZ vulgar slang root; formal copulate (with); archaic fornicate (with), possess, lie with/together, couple (with), swive, know.
□ **have (got) it in for** informal *he's had it in for me since I started seeing Gwen*: **be hostile to**, show/feel ill will towards, show antagonism to, bear a grudge towards, be against, be set against, be prejudiced against, disapprove of; **persecute**, pick on, push around/about, lean on, bully, abuse, discriminate against, ill-treat, mistreat, maltreat, harass, hound, torment, terrorize, torture, punish unfairly; informal have a down on, be down on, give someone a hard time, hassle, needle, get on someone's back, make things hot for someone.
□ **have (got) nothing on** informal *I am not worried—they've got nothing on me*: **have no evidence against**, know nothing bad about, know nothing damning about, have no incriminating information about.
□ **have someone on** Brit. informal *that's just too neat—you're having me on*: **play a trick on**, play a joke on, joke with, trick, tease, rag, pull someone's leg, fool about/around; informal kid, rib, take the mickey out of, make a monkey out of, take for a ride, lead up the garden path; Brit. informal wind up; N. Amer. informal put on, pull someone's chain; Brit. vulgar slang take the piss out of; dated make sport of.
□ **have (got) something on** **1** *she had a blue dress on*: **be wearing**, be dressed in, be clothed in, be garbed in, be attired in, be turned out in, be decked out in, be tricked out in, be robed in; archaic be apparelled in. **2** Brit. *I have got a lot on at the moment*: **be committed to**, have arranged, have planned, have organized, have fixed up, have on the agenda, have made arrangements for.
□ **let someone have it** informal **1** *as soon as you see the enemy, let them have it!* **attack**, assault, beat, beat up, batter, thrash, pound, pummel, assail, set upon, fall upon, set about, strike at, let fly at, tear into, lash out at; informal jump, paste, do over, work over, knock about/around, rough up, lay into, lace into, sail into, pitch into, get stuck into, beat the living daylights out of; Brit. informal have a go at, duff someone up; N. Amer. informal beat up on, light into. **2** *she let me have it, in a stream of obscenities*: **scold**, rebuke, reprimand, reproach, reprove, admonish, remonstrate with, chastise, chide, upbraid, berate, take to task, pull up, castigate, lambaste, read someone the Riot Act, give someone a piece of one's mind, go on at, haul over the coals, criticize, censure; informal tell off, give someone a talking-to, give someone a telling-off, dress down, give someone a dressing-down, give someone an earful, give someone a roasting, give someone a rocket, give someone a rollicking, rap, rap over the knuckles, slap someone's wrist, send someone away with a flea in their ear, bawl out, give someone hell, come down on, blow up, pitch into, lay into, lace into, give someone a caning, put on the mat, slap down, blast, rag, keelhaul; Brit. informal tick off, have a go at, carpet, monster, give someone a mouthful, tear someone off a strip, give someone what for, give someone some stick, wig, give someone a wigging, give someone a row, row; N. Amer. informal chew out, ream out, take to the woodshed; Brit. vulgar slang bollock, give someone a bollocking; N. Amer. vulgar slang chew someone's ass, ream someone's ass; dated call down, rate, give someone a rating, trim; rare reprehend, objurgate.

haven **noun** **1** *they stopped off in small harbours and havens*: **anchorage**, harbour, port, mooring, roads; cove, inlet, bay, fjord; rare harbourage, moorage, roadstead, hithe.
2 *a safe haven in times of trouble*: **refuge**, retreat, shelter, sanctuary, asylum, place of safety, place of security, port in a storm, harbour, oasis, sanctum.

haversack **noun** **knapsack**, rucksack, backpack, pack, kitbag.

havoc **noun** **1** *the hurricane ripped through Florida causing havoc*: **devastation**, destruction, damage, desolation, depredation, despoliation, ruination, ruin, disaster, ravagement, waste, catastrophe.
2 *hyperactive children create havoc wherever they go*: **disorder**, chaos,

disruption, mayhem, bedlam, pandemonium, turmoil, tumult, confusion, uproar; commotion, upheaval, furore, shambles; informal hullabaloo, a madhouse; N. Amer. informal a three-ring circus.
▷ANTONYMS peace.

hawk verb *street traders were hawking costume jewellery*: **peddle**, sell, tout, vend, trade in, deal in, traffic in, push, offer for sale, sell from door to door; Brit. informal flog.

Word links **hawk**

chick, eyas young hawk
cast collective noun

hawker noun dated **trader**, seller, dealer, purveyor, vendor, tout, barrow boy, door-to-door salesman, travelling salesman; W. Indian higgler; informal pusher; dated pedlar; archaic chapman, packman; rare huckster, crier, colporteur.

hawk-eyed adjective *a hawk-eyed policeman saved the lives of dozens of shoppers*: **vigilant**, observant, alert, sharp-eyed, keen-eyed, gimlet-eyed, eagle-eyed, lynx-eyed, with one's eyes open, on the alert, on the lookout, with one's eyes opened/skinned/peeled; informal beady-eyed, not missing a trick, on the ball, leery; rare regardful, Argus-eyed.
▷ANTONYMS inattentive.

h

hay noun forage, dried grass, pasturage, herbage, silage, fodder, straw.
□ **make hay while the sun shines** **make the most of an opportunity**, exploit an opportunity, take advantage of an opportunity, capitalize on an advantage, strike while the iron is hot, seize the day; Latin carpe diem.

haywire adjective informal *a bug that makes computers go haywire*: **out of control**, out of order, erratic, faulty, not functioning properly; **chaotic**, confused, crazy, wild, disorganized, disordered, topsy-turvy; informal on the blink, shambolic; Brit. informal up the spout, wonky.
▷ANTONYMS in order; under control.

hazard noun **1** *the hazards of high-energy radiation*: **danger**, risk, peril, threat, menace; difficulty, problem, pitfall; jeopardy, perilousness, endangerment, imperilment.
2 *we can form no calculation concerning the laws of hazard*: **chance**, probability, fortuity, luck, fate, destiny, fortune, providence, serendipity, accident; N. Amer. happenstance.
▶verb **1** *he hazarded a guess*: **venture**, put forward, proffer, advance, volunteer; conjecture, speculate, surmise; formal opine.
2 *the cargo business is too risky to hazard money on*: **risk**, put at risk, jeopardize, chance, gamble, stake, bet, take a chance with; **endanger**, imperil, expose to danger, put in jeopardy.
▷ANTONYMS keep safe.

Choose the right word **hazard, danger, peril, risk**

See **danger**.

hazardous adjective **1** *we work in hazardous conditions*: **dangerous**, risky, unsafe, perilous, precarious, insecure, tricky, unpredictable, uncertain, high-risk, touch-and-go, fraught with danger; informal dicey, hairy, sticky, iffy; Brit. informal dodgy; N. Amer. informal gnarly; archaic or humorous parlous.
▷ANTONYMS safe; secure.
2 *a hazardous venture*: **chancy**, uncertain, undependable, unpredictable, precarious, speculative.
▷ANTONYMS certain.

haze noun **1** *there was a thick haze on this October morning*: **mist**, fog, cloud, smog; cloudiness, mistiness, fogginess, smokiness, vapour, steam.
2 *the evening passed in a haze of euphoria*: **blur**, daze, confusion, vagueness, muddle, befuddlement; obscurity, dimness, indistinctness.

hazy adjective **1** *it was a beautiful day but quite hazy*: **misty**, foggy, cloudy, clouded, smoggy, murky, overcast.
▷ANTONYMS bright, sunny.
2 *hazy memories*: **vague**, indistinct, unclear, faint, dim, indefinite, ill-defined, nebulous, shadowy, blurred, fuzzy, muzzy, woolly, confused, muddled.
▷ANTONYMS clear.

head noun **1** *she was hurt when her head hit the ground*: **skull**, cranium, crown; informal **nut**, noodle, noddle, nob, noggin, dome; Brit. informal bonce, napper; Scottish & N. English informal poll; informal, dated bean, conk; archaic pate, Costard, crumpet.
2 *this new job meant he had to use his head*: **brain**, brains, brainpower, intellect, intelligence, intellectual capacity, mental capacity, powers of reasoning; wit, wits, wisdom, mind, sense, reasoning, rationality, mentality, understanding, common sense; informal nous, grey matter, savvy, brainbox, brain cells, upper storey; Brit. informal loaf; N. Amer. informal smarts; S. African informal kop.
3 *she had a good head for business*: **aptitude**, faculty, flair, talent, gift, capacity, ability, knack, bent; mind, brain.
4 *the head of the Dutch Catholic Church*: **leader**, chief, boss, controller, master, supervisor, governor, superintendent, foreman, forewoman, headman; commander, commanding officer, captain; director, managing director, chief executive, manager; principal, head teacher, headmaster, headmistress; president, premier, prime minister, ruler; chair, chairman, chairwoman, chairperson; N. Amer. chief executive officer, CEO; informal boss man, kingpin, top dog, big cheese, bigwig, Mr Big, skipper; Brit. informal gaffer, guv'nor; N. Amer. informal numero uno, head honcho, padrone, sachem, big white chief, big kahuna, big wheel, high muckamuck.
▷ANTONYMS subordinate.
5 *at the head of the queue*: **front**, beginning, start, fore, forefront, top, leading position, foremost position.
▷ANTONYMS back, bottom.
6 *the head of the River Thames*: **source**, origin, well head, headspring, headwater, headwaters; S. African eye; literary wellspring, fount, fountain.
▷ANTONYMS mouth.
7 *beer with a creamy head*: **froth**, foam, bubbles, spume, fizz, effervescence, lather, suds.
8 Nautical *they were cleaning out the heads*. See **toilet**.
□ **at the head of** *his years at the head of the company*: **in charge of**, in control of, in command of, at the top of, at the helm of, at the controls of, as leader of, in the driving seat of, at the wheel of, responsible for, accountable for, liable for; **managing**, running, administering, directing, supervising, overseeing, controlling, commanding, leading, heading up, looking after, taking care of.
□ **be head and shoulders above** informal *he was always head and shoulders above the rest but he was very modest*: **outclass**, surpass, be superior to, be better than, outshine, overshadow, eclipse, dwarf, put in the shade, upstage, transcend; top, cap, trump, trounce, beat, defeat, better, put to shame, exceed, leave behind, outrank; informal be a cut above, run rings round, leave standing, walk away from; archaic outrival, outvie.
□ **come to a head** *the violence came to a head with the deaths of six youths*: **reach a crisis**, come to a climax, reach a critical point, reach a turning point, reach a crossroads; informal come to the crunch.
□ **go to someone's head 1** *the wine has gone to my head*: **intoxicate**, inebriate, befuddle, make someone intoxicated, make someone drunk, make someone dizzy, make someone's head spin; informal make someone woozy. **2** *her victory went to her head*: **make someone conceited**, make someone arrogant, turn someone's head, make someone full of themselves, puff someone up.
□ **keep one's head** *he takes chances but keeps his head*: **keep/stay calm**, keep/stay cool, remain unruffled, keep control of oneself, keep one's self-control, maintain one's equilibrium, maintain one's composure; informal keep one's cool, keep one's shirt on.
▷ANTONYMS lose control of oneself.
□ **lose one's head** *I lost my head and started a big fuss*: **lose control of oneself**, lose one's composure, lose one's self-control, lose one's equilibrium, lose control of the situation, go to pieces, fall to pieces; panic, go mad, get flustered, get confused, get angry, get excited, get hysterical; informal lose one's cool, freak out, crack up; Brit. informal go into a (flat) spin, throw a wobbly.
▷ANTONYMS keep control of oneself.
▶adjective *the head waiter*: **chief**, principal, leading, main, first, front, prime, premier, foremost, top, topmost, highest, supreme, pre-eminent, high-ranking, top-ranking, most important; N. Amer. ranking; informal top-notch.
▷ANTONYMS subordinate.
▶verb **1** *the St George's Day procession was headed by the mayor*: **be at the front of**, lead, be the leader of, be at the head of; be first, go first, lead the way.
▷ANTONYMS be at the back of, bring up the rear of.
2 *an organizational unit headed by a line manager | he will* **head up** *the new communications division*: **be in charge of**, be at the head of, be in command of, command, be in control of, control, lead, be the leader of, run, manage, direct, administer, supervise, superintend, oversee, preside over, rule, govern, captain, be the boss of, be at the helm of.
▷ANTONYMS be subordinate.
3 *he was* **heading for** *the exit*: **move towards**, go towards, make for, aim for, make one's way towards, go in the direction of, direct one's steps towards, be bound for, steer for, make a beeline for; set out in the direction of, set out for, start out for.
▷ANTONYMS move away from.
□ **head someone/something off 1** *he ran up the road to head off approaching cars*: **intercept**, divert, deflect, redirect, re-route, turn aside, draw away, turn away, cut off. **2** *they headed off a row by ordering further study of both plans*: **forestall**, avert, ward off, fend off, stave off, hold off, nip in the bud, keep at bay; prevent, avoid, stop, check, thwart.
▷ANTONYMS precipitate.
□ **head something up** See **head** (sense 2 of the verb).

Word links **head**

cephalo- related prefix, as in *cephalopod*
cephalometry measurement of the head

headache noun **1** *I've got a splitting headache*: **sore head**, migraine; neuralgia; informal head; rare cephalalgy, hemicrania.
2 informal *their disruptive behaviour was a headache for Mr Jones*: **nuisance**, trouble, problem, bother, bugbear, hassle, pain, pest, worry, inconvenience, vexation, irritant, source of irritation, source of annoyance, bane of one's life, thorn in one's flesh; informal aggravation, bind, pain in the neck/backside; N. Amer. informal pain in the butt; Austral./NZ informal nark; Brit. vulgar slang pain in the arse.
▷ANTONYMS blessing.

head case noun informal **madman/madwoman**, maniac, lunatic; informal loony, nut, nutcase, nutter, fruitcake, basket case, headbanger, schizo, crank, crackpot, oddball, weirdo, weirdie, sicko; Brit. informal odd bod; Scottish informal radge; N. Amer. informal screwball, crazy, kook, geek, nutso, meshuggener, wacko, wack; N. Amer. & Austral./NZ informal dingbat; informal, dated case.

head first adjective & adverb **1** *she dived head first into the water*: **head foremost**, headlong, on one's head; diving.
▷ANTONYMS feet first.
2 *don't plunge head first into a new relationship*: **without thinking**, without forethought, precipitately, precipitously, impetuously, rashly, recklessly, carelessly, heedlessly, hastily, in haste, head over heels, headlong.
▷ANTONYMS cautiously.

heading noun **1** *chapter headings*: **title**, caption, legend, subtitle, subheading, wording, rubric, inscription, name, headline, banner headline.
2 *this topic falls under four main headings*: **category**, division, classification, class, categorization, head, section, group, grouping, subject, topic, branch, department.

headland noun **cape**, promontory, point, head, foreland, peninsula, ness, spit, tongue, horn, bill, bluff; Scottish mull.

headlong adverb **1** *he fell headlong into the tent*: **head foremost**, head first, on one's head; diving.
▷ANTONYMS feet first.
2 *those who rush headlong to join in the latest craze*: **without thinking**, without forethought, precipitately, precipitously, impetuously, rashly, recklessly, carelessly, heedlessly, hastily, in haste, head first, head over heels.
▷ANTONYMS cautiously.
▶ **adjective** *a headlong dash through the house*: **breakneck**, whirlwind; reckless, precipitate, precipitous, rash, impetuous, hasty, careless, heedless.
▷ANTONYMS cautious.

> *Choose the right word* **headlong, impetuous, impulsive, precipitate**
>
> See **impetuous**.

headman noun **chief**, chieftain, leader, ruler, head, overlord, master, commander, suzerain, seigneur, lord, liege, liege lord, potentate; among American Indians sachem.
▷ANTONYMS underling.

head-on adjective **1** *a head-on collision*: **direct**, involving the front of a vehicle, front-to-front.
2 *the advantage of this proposal is that it avoids a head-on confrontation*: **direct**, face to face, personal; informal eyeball to eyeball.

headquarters plural noun **head office**, main office, HQ, base, nerve centre, mission control; general headquarters, GHQ, command post, depot, centre of operations.

headstone noun **gravestone**, tombstone, stone, monument, memorial, plaque, tablet.

headstrong adjective *she has been rather headstrong and argumentative*: **wilful**, self-willed, strong-willed, contrary, perverse, wayward, unruly, refractory, ungovernable, unyielding, stubborn, obstinate, obdurate; reckless, heedless, rash, capricious, impulsive, wild.
▷ANTONYMS tractable.

> *Choose the right word* **headstrong, wilful, obstinate, stubborn**
>
> See **obstinate**.

head teacher noun **headmaster**, **headmistress**, head, principal, director, master, mistress; dean, rector, warden, chancellor, vice-chancellor, president, provost, governor; N. Amer. informal prexy, prex.

headway noun
□ **make headway** *they appear to be making headway in bringing the rebels under control*: **make progress**, make strides, gain ground, progress, advance, proceed, move, get on, get ahead, come on, come along, shape up, take shape, move forward in leaps and bounds; informal be getting there.
▷ANTONYMS retrogress; stagnate.

heady adjective **1** *several bottles of heady local wine*: **potent**, intoxicating, inebriating, strong, alcoholic, spirituous, vinous, intoxicant.
▷ANTONYMS non-alcoholic.
2 *she felt heady with excitement*: **exhilarated**, thrilled, elated, excited, euphoric, ecstatic, enraptured, overwhelmed, overjoyed, overpowered, in seventh heaven, on cloud nine; informal over the moon, on top of the world, on a high.
▷ANTONYMS bored.
3 *the heady days of my youth*: **exhilarating**, exciting, thrilling, stimulating, invigorating, galvanizing, electrifying, rousing, arousing; informal mind-blowing.
▷ANTONYMS boring.

heal verb **1** *his concern is to heal sick people*: **make better**, make well, cure, treat successfully, restore to health, get someone back on their feet, put someone on the road to recovery; make good, mend, remedy, restore.
▷ANTONYMS make worse.
2 *he would have to wait until his knee had healed*: **get better**, get well, be cured, become healthy, recover, mend, be on the mend, improve, show improvement, be restored.
▷ANTONYMS get worse.
3 *time will eventually heal the pain of grief*: **alleviate**, assuage, palliate, relieve, ameliorate, ease, help, soften, lessen, mitigate, attenuate, allay, salve.
▷ANTONYMS aggravate.
4 *we've been trying to heal the rift between them*: **put right**, set right, put to rights, repair, remedy, resolve, correct, settle, make good, patch up, soothe, conciliate, reconcile, harmonize.
▷ANTONYMS worsen.

healing adjective *this flower is said to have healing properties*: **curative**, therapeutic, medicinal, remedial, curing, corrective, reparative; restorative, tonic, health-giving, healthful, beneficial, salubrious; rare sanative, analeptic, iatric.
▷ANTONYMS harmful.

> *Word links* **healing**
>
> **iatro-** related prefix, as in *iatrogenic*, *iatrochemistry*

health noun **1** *he was restored to health*: **good physical condition**, healthiness, fitness, physical fitness, well-being, haleness, good trim, good shape, fine fettle, good kilter; robustness, strength, vigour, soundness, salubrity.
▷ANTONYMS illness.
2 *bad health forced him to retire*: **state of health**, physical state, physical health, physical shape, condition, constitution, form.

> *Word links* **health**
>
> **salubrious** health-giving
> **sanitary** relating to health

healthful adjective *garlic was considered very healthful in winter*: **good for one**, good for one's health, healthy, health-giving, beneficial, salubrious, salutary; wholesome, nourishing, nutritious.
▷ANTONYMS unhealthy.

healthy adjective **1** *feeling fit and healthy*: **in good physical condition**, in good health, well, all right, fine, fit, physically fit, in good trim, in good shape, in fine fettle, in good kilter, in top form, aerobicized, in tip-top condition; flourishing, blooming, thriving, hardy, hale, hearty, robust, strong, vigorous, hale and hearty, fighting fit, fit as a fiddle, fit as a flea, bursting with health, the picture of health; Brit. in rude health; informal OK, in the pink, right as rain, up to snuff.
▷ANTONYMS ill.
2 *a healthy balanced diet*: **good for one**, good for one's health, health-giving, healthful, wholesome, nutritious, nourishing, beneficial, salubrious, salutary.
▷ANTONYMS unwholesome.
3 *the island has a healthy climate*: **beneficial**, health-giving, healthful, salubrious, salutary; invigorating, bracing, refreshing, tonic, stimulating; hygienic, clean, sanitary.
▷ANTONYMS unhealthy.

heap noun **1** *a disordered heap of boxes*: **pile**, stack, mass, mound, mountain, quantity, load, lot, bundle, jumble; collection, accumulation, gathering; assemblage, store, stock, supply, stockpile, hoard, aggregation, agglomeration, accrual, conglomeration; Scottish, Irish, & N. English rickle; Scottish bing; rare amassment.
2 *we have heaps of room* | *a heap of troubles*: **a lot**, **lots**, a large amount, a fair amount, much, a good/great deal, a deal, a great quantity, quantities, an abundance, a wealth, a profusion, plenty, masses; **many**, a great many, a large number, a considerable number, a huge number, numerous, scores, hundreds, thousands, millions, billions; informal a load, loads, loadsa, a pile, piles, oodles, stacks, scads, reams, wads, pots, oceans, a mountain, mountains, miles, tons, zillions, gazillions, bazillions, more ... than one

can shake a stick at; Brit. informal a shedload, lashings; N. Amer. informal gobs; Austral./NZ informal a swag; vulgar slang a shitload.
▷ANTONYMS a little, not much; a few, not many.
▶ **verb** *she heaped logs on the fire*: **pile up**, pile, stack up, stack, make a pile of, make a stack of, make a mound of; assemble, accumulate, collect, amass; store, store up, stock up, stockpile, hoard.
□ **heap something on/upon** *they heaped praise on her*: **shower on**, lavish on, load on; **bestow on**, confer on, give, grant, vouchsafe, assign to, award to, favour with, furnish with.

hear verb **1** *behind her she could hear men's voices*: **perceive**, catch, get, make out, take in, apprehend, discern; overhear; listen to, attend to, give ear to.
2 *they heard that I had moved*: **be informed**, be told, find out, discover, learn, gather, glean, ascertain, get word, be made aware, be given to understand, hear tell, get wind, pick up.
▷ANTONYMS be unaware.
3 *an all-woman jury heard the case*: **try**, judge, sit in judgement on; adjudicate (on), adjudge, pass judgement on, give a ruling on.

hearing noun **1** *people who have very acute hearing*: **ability to hear**, faculty of hearing, sense of hearing, aural faculty, auditory perception.
2 *she had moved out of hearing*: **earshot**, hearing distance, hearing range, carrying range, range of one's voice, auditory range, sound, range.
3 *I think I had a fair hearing*: **chance to speak**, opportunity to be heard, opportunity to express one's point of view, opportunity to put one's case, chance to put one's side of the story; interview, audience.
4 *he gave evidence at the hearing*: **trial**, court case, enquiry, inquest, tribunal, legal proceedings; investigation, review, examination, inquisition.

Word links **hearing**

auditory, audial, aural, acoustic relating to hearing
audio- related prefix
audiology branch of medicine to do with hearing
audiometry measurement of hearing

hearsay noun *a story based only on hearsay*: **rumour**, gossip, tittle-tattle, tattle, idle chatter, idle talk, mere talk, report; stories, tales, titbits; French bavardage, on dit; German Kaffeeklatsch; W. Indian labrish, shu-shu; informal buzz, the grapevine; Brit. informal goss; N. Amer. informal scuttlebutt; Austral./NZ informal furphy; S. African informal skinder; rare bruit.
▷ANTONYMS confirmed facts.

heart noun **1** *his heart had stopped beating*: informal ticker.
2 *he poured out his heart to me | she captured my heart*: **emotions**, feelings, sentiments, soul, mind, bosom, breast; **love**, affection, passion; sympathy, pity, concern, compassion.
3 *he has no heart*: **compassion**, sympathy, humanity, feeling(s), fellow feeling, concern for others, brotherly love, tender feelings, tenderness, empathy, understanding; kindness, kindliness, goodwill, benevolence, humanitarianism.
4 *they may lose heart as the work mounts up*: **enthusiasm**, keenness, eagerness, spirit, determination, resolution, resolve, purpose, courage, backbone, spine, nerve, stomach, will, will power, fortitude, bravery, stout-heartedness; informal guts, spunk, grit; Brit. informal bottle; vulgar slang balls.
5 *right in the heart of the city*: **centre**, central part, middle, hub, core, nucleus, kernel, eye, bosom, navel.
▷ANTONYMS edge.
6 *the heart of the matter*: **essence**, quintessence, crux, core, nub, root, gist, meat, marrow, pith, substance, sum and substance, essential part, intrinsic nature, kernel, nucleus; informal nitty-gritty.
▷ANTONYMS peripherals.
□ **after one's own heart** *he looked like a man after my own heart*: **like-minded**, of the same mind, similar to oneself, kindred, compatible, congenial, sharing one's tastes; **to one's liking**, of the kind that one likes, attractive to one, desirable, attractive, appealing, pleasing; informal on the same wavelength.
▷ANTONYMS dissimilar; unappealing.
□ **at heart** *he's a good lad at heart*: **basically**, fundamentally, essentially, at bottom, deep down, in essence, intrinsically, innately; **really**, actually, truly, in fact, in truth; French au fond; informal when you get right down to it.
▷ANTONYMS superficially.
□ **by heart** *I know the poem by heart*: **from memory**, off pat, by rote, off by heart, word for word, verbatim, parrot-fashion, word-perfect.
□ **do one's heart good** *it did the rector's heart good to see so many at church*: **give one pleasure**, make one happy, cheer, cheer one up, delight, please, gladden, hearten, gratify, satisfy, make one feel good, raise one's spirits, give one a lift, bring joy to; informal give one a buzz, tickle one pink, buck one up.
▷ANTONYMS sadden.
□ **eat one's heart out** *I stayed in London, eating my heart out for you*: **pine**, long, ache, brood, mope, fret, sigh, sorrow, suffer, bleed, yearn, agonize, weep and wail, regret someone's loss/absence; grieve, mourn, lament, shed tears; be filled with envy; informal die; literary repine.
□ **from the (bottom of one's) heart** *I have told the truth from the bottom of my heart | she spoke from the heart*: **sincerely**, with all one's heart, earnestly, fervently, passionately, truly, truthfully, genuinely, devoutly, heartily, heart and soul, with all sincerity.
□ **give/lose one's heart to** *he lost his heart to a French girl*: **fall in love with**, fall for, become infatuated with, be smitten by; informal fall head over heels for, be swept off one's feet by, develop a crush on.
□ **have a change of heart** *you can have your money back if you have a change of heart*: **change one's mind**, change one's tune, have second thoughts, have a rethink, think again, think differently, think twice; informal get cold feet.
□ **have a heart** *have a heart—this is my last chance*: **be compassionate**, be kind, be merciful, be lenient, be sympathetic, be considerate, take pity, have mercy.
□ **heart and soul** *they had committed themselves heart and soul to the project*: **wholeheartedly**, enthusiastically, eagerly, zealously, unreservedly, absolutely, thoroughly, completely, entirely, fully, totally, utterly, body and soul, to the hilt, with open arms, one hundred per cent, all the way.
□ **in one's heart of hearts** *deep down, in my heart of hearts, I still feel the same*: **inwardly**, inside, internally, within, deep down (inside), deep within, at heart, in one's mind, to oneself; privately, secretly, confidentially.
□ **set one's heart on** *she had set her heart on going to college*. See **set**[1].
□ **take heart** *Mary took heart from the encouragement handed out*: **be encouraged**, be heartened, be comforted, derive comfort, derive satisfaction; cheer up, brighten up, perk up, liven up, become livelier, revive; informal buck up.
▷ANTONYMS lose heart.
□ **with one's heart in one's mouth** *she watched with her heart in her mouth as the plane lost height*: **in alarm**, in fear, fearfully, with apprehension, apprehensively, on edge, in a state of agitation, in a state of nerves, in fear and trembling, with trepidation, in suspense, in a cold sweat, with bated breath, on tenterhooks, with one's stomach in knots; informal with butterflies in one's stomach, in a state, in a stew, all of a dither, in a sweat; Brit. informal having kittens; N. Amer. informal in a twit; Brit. vulgar slang shitting bricks, bricking oneself; dated overstrung.

Word links **heart**

cardiac relating to the heart
cardio- related prefix
cardiology branch of medicine to do with the heart
carditis inflammation of the heart
coronary relating to the arteries of the heart
cardiophobia fear of heart disease

heartache noun **anguish**, grief, suffering, distress, unhappiness, misery, sorrow, sadness, heartbreak, pain, hurt, agony, angst, wretchedness, despondency, despair, woe, desolation, torment, torture; anxiety, worry; literary dolour.
▷ANTONYMS happiness.

heartbreak noun *an unforgettable tale of joy and heartbreak*: **distress**, grief, suffering, unhappiness, misery, sorrow, sadness, anguish, trauma, heartache, pain, hurt, agony, angst, wretchedness, bitterness, despondency, despair, woe, dejection, devastation, desolation, torment, torture; literary dolour.
▷ANTONYMS happiness.

heartbreaking adjective *it would be heartbreaking to see it all collapse*: **distressing**, upsetting, disturbing, heart-rending, sad, tragic, painful, saddening, traumatic, agonizing, desolating, harrowing, excruciating; pitiful, piteous, poignant, plaintive, affecting, moving, tear-jerking; rare distressful.
▷ANTONYMS comforting.

heartbroken adjective *I was heartbroken at his death*: **anguished**, devastated, broken-hearted, heavy-hearted, suffering, grieving, grief-stricken, grieved, inconsolable, crushed, shattered, desolate, despairing; upset, distressed, miserable, sorrowful, sad, dejected, dispirited, disheartened, downcast, disconsolate, crestfallen, disappointed, despondent, in low spirits; informal choked, down in the mouth, down in the dumps, cut up; Brit. informal gutted; literary dolorous, heartsick; archaic chap-fallen.
▷ANTONYMS delighted.

heartburn noun **indigestion**, dyspepsia, acidity, hyperacidity; technical pyrosis.

hearten verb *their success greatly heartened him*: **cheer up**, cheer, raise someone's spirits, encourage, comfort, reassure, console, boost, buoy up, perk up, ginger up; invigorate, revitalize, energize, animate, rouse, revivify, exhilarate, uplift, elate; informal buck up, pep up, give a shot in the arm to; rare inspirit.
▷ANTONYMS dishearten.

heartfelt adjective *our heartfelt thanks*: **sincere**, genuine, unfeigned, deeply felt, from the heart; earnest, profound, deep, wholehearted, ardent,

fervent, passionate, enthusiastic, eager, kindly, warm, cordial; honest, bona fide; rare full-hearted.
▷ANTONYMS insincere.

heartily adverb **1** *this development is something that we should heartily welcome*: **wholeheartedly**, sincerely, genuinely, unfeignedly, warmly, cordially, deeply, profoundly, from the bottom of one's heart, from the heart, with all one's heart, heart and soul; **eagerly**, enthusiastically, with eagerness, with enthusiasm, zealously, energetically, earnestly, vigorously, ardently, resolutely.
▷ANTONYMS with reservations; half-heartedly.
2 *they were heartily sick of the whole subject*: **very**, very much, completely, entirely, totally, absolutely, extremely, thoroughly, fully, decidedly, really, exceedingly, immensely, uncommonly, extraordinarily, most, downright, one hundred per cent; Scottish unco; N. Amer. quite; French très; informal right, too ... for words, seriously, majorly; Brit. informal jolly, ever so, dead, well, fair; N. Amer. informal real, mighty, plumb, powerful, way; S. African informal lekker; informal, dated devilish; archaic exceeding.

heartless adjective *heartless thieves stole the pushchair of a two-year-old boy*: **unfeeling**, unsympathetic, unkind, uncaring, unloving, unmoved, unconcerned, insensitive, inconsiderate, hard-hearted, stony-hearted, cold-hearted, cold-blooded, with a heart of stone, lacking compassion, mean-spirited, without sentiment, hard as nails; cold, hard, harsh, stern, callous, cruel, brutal, merciless, pitiless, ruthless, inhuman.
▷ANTONYMS compassionate.

heart-rending adjective *a heart-rending cry of torment*: **distressing**, upsetting, disturbing, heartbreaking, sad, tragic, painful, saddening, traumatic, agonizing, desolate, harrowing, excruciating; pitiful, piteous, poignant, plaintive, affecting, moving, tear-jerking; rare distressful.
▷ANTONYMS comforting.

heartsick adjective literary *weary and heartsick, she forced herself to search through the remains of the village.* See **dejected**.

heart-throb noun informal **idol**, pin-up, popular figure, darling, star, superstar, hero, heroine; informal dreamboat.

heart-to-heart adjective *a heart-to-heart chat*: **intimate**, candid, frank, open, unreserved, personal, honest, truthful, sincere, man-to-man, woman-to-woman.
▷ANTONYMS guarded.
▶ **noun** *they had a long heart-to-heart in the garden*: **private conversation**, private word, cosy chat, tête-à-tête, one-on-one, one-to-one, head-to-head, conversation, chat, talk, word; informal confab, chit-chat, chinwag; Brit. informal natter.

heart-warming adjective *the sympathy in his voice was heart-warming*: **touching**, moving, affecting, heartening, stirring, rewarding, uplifting, pleasing, cheering, gladdening, encouraging, gratifying, satisfying, warming, soul-stirring; literary gladsome.
▷ANTONYMS distressing.

hearty adjective **1** *a hearty and boisterous character*: **exuberant**, cheerful, jovial, ebullient, backslapping, unreserved, uninhibited, effusive, lively, loud, animated, vivacious, energetic, spirited, dynamic, enthusiastic, eager; warm, cordial, friendly, affable, amiable, warm-hearted, good natured.
▷ANTONYMS introverted.
2 *he expressed his hearty agreement | hearty congratulations*: **wholehearted**, heartfelt, sincere, genuine, real, true, unfeigned, from the heart, complete, total, absolute, thorough; **earnest**, fervent, ardent, enthusiastic, warm, cordial.
▷ANTONYMS half-hearted.
3 *a formidably hearty spinster of fifty-five*: **robust**, healthy, hardy, hale, hale and hearty, fit, flourishing, blooming, spirited, fighting fit, fit as a fiddle, fit as a flea, bursting with health; **active**, energetic, vigorous, sturdy, strong, sound; Brit. in rude health; informal full of vim; dated stalwart.
▷ANTONYMS frail.
4 *they end each day with a hearty meal*: **substantial**, ample, sizeable, filling, large, abundant, generous, square, solid; **wholesome**, nutritious, nourishing, healthy, health-giving, good for one's health.
▷ANTONYMS light; unhealthy.

heat noun **1** *it is sensitive to both heat and cold*: **hotness**, warmth, warmness, high temperature; fever, feverishness; rare calefaction.
▷ANTONYMS cold.
2 *the oppressive heat was making both men sweat*: **hot weather**, hotness, warm weather, warmth, warmness, sultriness, closeness, mugginess, humidity, swelter; heatwave, hot spell; literary dog days; rare torridness, torridity.
▷ANTONYMS cold weather.
3 *conciliation services are designed to take the heat out of disputes*: **passion**, intensity of feeling, ardour, fervour, vehemence, warmth, intensity, animation, earnestness, eagerness, enthusiasm, excitement, agitation; anger, fury, violence; rare fervency, ardency, passionateness.
▷ANTONYMS apathy.
▶ **verb 1** *the room faces north and is difficult to heat | the food was heated on a portable stove*: **warm**, warm up, heat up, make hot, make warm, raise something's temperature; reheat, cook, boil, bake, roast, toast, stew, fry, grill; informal hot, hot up.
▷ANTONYMS cool.
2 *the pipes expand as they **heat up***: **become hot**, become warm, grow hot, grow warm, become hotter, become warmer, get hotter, get warmer, increase in temperature, rise in temperature; informal hot up.
▷ANTONYMS cool down.
3 *he seemed to calm down as quickly as he had **heated up***: **become impassioned**, become excited, become animated, grow passionate, grow vehement; get angry, become enraged, get annoyed.
▷ANTONYMS calm down.

Word links **heat**

thermal, **caloric** relating to heat
therm-, **calor-** related prefixes, as in *thermionic, calorific*
thermophobia fear of heat

heated adjective **1** *a heated swimming pool | heated milk*: **made warm**, made hot, warmed up; reheated; hot, piping hot.
▷ANTONYMS cooled.
2 *she had a heated argument with an official*: **vehement**, passionate, impassioned, animated, spirited, 'lively', intense, fiery; **angry**, bitter, furious, fierce, violent, frenzied, raging, stormy, tempestuous; rare fervid, perfervid, passional, full-hearted.
▷ANTONYMS half-hearted.
3 *Robert grew heated as he spoke of the risks*: **excited**, roused, animated, inflamed, worked up, wound up, keyed up; angry, furious, enraged; informal het up, in a state, uptight.
▷ANTONYMS calm.

heater noun **warmer**, radiator, convector, fire, brazier; electric heater, gas heater, convector heater, fan heater, storage heater, water heater, geyser, immersion heater, block heater; Austral./NZ chip heater.
▷ANTONYMS cooler.

heath noun **moor**, heathland, moorland, scrub, scrubs, common land, open country, upland.

heathen noun **1** *he said non-believers were wicked heathens*: **pagan**, infidel, idolater, idolatress; **unbeliever**, non-believer, disbeliever, atheist, agnostic, sceptic, heretic; rare paynim, nullifidian.
▷ANTONYMS Christian; believer.
2 *heathens who spoil the flavour of good whisky with ice*: **philistine**, boor, oaf, ignoramus, lout, yahoo, vulgarian, plebeian; **barbarian**, savage, beast, brute; informal, derogatory pleb, peasant; Brit. informal oik; Austral./NZ informal hoon.
▷ANTONYMS civilized person.
▶ **adjective** *it is a heathen practice to worship idols*: **pagan**, infidel, idolatrous, heathenish; **unbelieving**, non-believing, atheistic, agnostic, heretical, faithless, godless, irreligious, ungodly, unholy; **barbarian**, barbarous, savage, uncivilized, uncultured, unenlightened, primitive, ignorant, philistine, brutish, barbaric; rare nullifidian.
▷ANTONYMS Christian; civilized.

heave verb **1** *she heaved the sofa back into place*: **haul**, pull, lug, manhandle, drag, draw, tug; lift, raise, hoist, heft; informal hump, yank; rare upheave.
▷ANTONYMS push.
2 informal *she heaved half a brick at him*: **throw**, fling, cast, toss, hurl, lob, pitch, send, dash, let fly; informal bung, chuck, sling; N. Amer. informal peg; Austral. informal hoy; NZ informal bish.
3 *he heaved a euphoric sigh of relief*: **let out**, breathe, give, sigh, gasp, emit, utter.
4 *the sea heaved up and down beneath her*: **rise and fall**, roll, swell, surge, churn, boil, seethe, swirl, billow.
5 *she crawled to the rail and heaved into the sea*: **vomit**, retch, gag, bring up, cough up; Brit. be sick; N. Amer. get sick; informal throw up, puke, chunder, chuck up, hurl, spew, do the technicolor yawn, keck; Brit. informal honk, sick up; Scottish informal boke; N. Amer. informal spit up, barf, upchuck, toss one's cookies.

heaven noun **1** *those who practised good deeds would receive the reward of a place in heaven*: **paradise**, nirvana, the kingdom of heaven, the promised land, the heavenly kingdom, the City of God, the celestial city, the abode of God, the abode of the saints, the abode of the angels, Zion, Abraham's bosom, the empyrean; the beyond, the hereafter, the next world, the next life, the afterworld, the afterlife; among American Indians happy hunting ground; Christianity the New Jerusalem; Hinduism Swarga; Classical Mythology Elysium, the Elysian Fields, the Islands of the Blessed; Scandinavian Mythology Valhalla; Arthurian Legend Avalon.
▷ANTONYMS hell, purgatory.
2 *lying by the pool with a good book is my idea of heaven*: **ecstasy**, bliss, rapture, contentment, happiness, delight, joy, felicity, supreme happiness, supreme joy, perfect contentment, seventh heaven, cloud nine; paradise, Eden, Utopia, nirvana, Shangri-La, idyll; literary Arcadia, Arcady.
▷ANTONYMS misery; hell on earth.
3 (usually **the heavens**) *Galileo used a telescope to observe the heavens*:

the sky, the skies, the upper atmosphere, the stratosphere; literary the firmament, the vault of heaven, the blue, the (wide) blue yonder, the welkin, the ether, the empyrean, the azure, the upper regions, the sphere, the celestial sphere.

□ **in seventh heaven ecstatic**, euphoric, thrilled, elated, delighted, overjoyed, on cloud nine/seven, walking/treading on air, jubilant, rapturous, beside oneself with joy, jumping for joy, exultant, transported, delirious, enraptured, blissful, in raptures, like a child with a new toy; informal over the moon, on top of the world, on a high, tickled pink, as pleased as Punch, cock-a-hoop, as happy as a sandboy; Brit. informal as happy as Larry; N. English informal made up; N. Amer. informal as happy as a clam; Austral. informal wrapped.

□ **move heaven and earth** informal *if he had truly loved her he would have moved heaven and earth to get her back*: **try one's hardest**, try as hard as one can, do one's best, do one's utmost, do all one can, give one's all, make every effort, spare no effort, put oneself out; strive, struggle, exert oneself, work hard, endeavour, try; informal bend over backwards, do one's damnedest, go all out, pull out all the stops, bust a gut, break one's neck, kill oneself; N. Amer. informal do one's darnedest/durnedest; Austral./NZ informal go for the doctor.

Word links **heaven**

celestial, **empyrean** relating to heaven
uranophobia fear of heaven

heavenly adjective **1** *they saw visions of angels and heavenly choirs*: **divine**, holy, celestial, godlike, godly, angelic, seraphic, cherubic, blessed, blest, beatific, immortal; literary empyrean, empyreal; rare paradisical, paradisaical, deiform, deific.
▷ANTONYMS mortal; infernal.
2 *heavenly constellations*: **celestial**, cosmic, stellar; planetary; extraterrestrial, extramundane, unearthly, other-worldly; literary empyrean, empyreal; rare superterrestrial.
▷ANTONYMS terrestrial, earthly.
3 informal *it was a heavenly morning for a ride | a combination of heavenly blues and yellows*: **delightful**, wonderful, marvellous, glorious, perfect, excellent, ideal, superb, sublime, idyllic, first-class, first-rate; blissful, pleasurable, enjoyable, gratifying, rapturous; **exquisite**, beautiful, lovely, gorgeous, sensational, enchanting, entrancing, ravishing, alluring; informal divine, super, great, fantastic, fabulous, smashing, terrific, wicked, out of this world; Brit. informal brilliant, brill, bosting.
▷ANTONYMS dreadful; ugly.

Word toolkit

heavenly	divine	angelic
host	intervention	face
kingdom	right	voice
reward	inspiration	smile
light	law	wings
experience	retribution	child
gates	guidance	souls

heaven-sent adjective *she was so afraid of losing this heaven-sent opportunity*: **auspicious**, providential, propitious, felicitous, opportune, golden, favourable, advantageous, serendipitous, lucky, happy, good, right, fortunate, timely, well timed.
▷ANTONYMS inopportune.

heavily adverb **1** *Dad walked heavily towards the door*: **laboriously**, slowly, ponderously, steadily, deliberately, woodenly, stiffly, with heavy steps, with leaden steps; with difficulty, painfully, awkwardly, clumsily; gloomily, dejectedly, sluggishly, dully.
▷ANTONYMS easily, quickly.
2 *our troops were heavily defeated*: **decisively**, utterly, completely, thoroughly, totally, conclusively, roundly, soundly, absolutely.
▷ANTONYMS narrowly.
3 *he started drinking heavily*: **excessively**, to excess, immoderately, copiously, inordinately, intemperately, a great deal, too much, very much, overmuch, to a great extent, to too great an extent, without restraint, without control.
▷ANTONYMS moderately.
4 *the area is heavily planted with pine trees*: **densely**, closely, thickly, compactly.
▷ANTONYMS lightly.
5 *I became heavily involved in politics*: **deeply**, extremely, very, greatly, exceedingly, enormously, terribly, tremendously, awfully, profoundly; informal seriously; majorly; Brit. informal jolly, ever so.
▷ANTONYMS to a limited extent.

heavy adjective **1** *the pan was too heavy for me to carry*: **weighty**, hefty, big, large, substantial, massive, ponderous; solid, dense, leaden; burdensome; informal hulking, weighing a ton.
▷ANTONYMS light.
2 *he was a heavy man of about sixty*: **overweight**, large, bulky, stout, stocky, portly, plump, paunchy, fleshy, fat, obese, corpulent, of ample build, ample, well upholstered, well padded, broad in the beam, Falstaffian; informal hulking, tubby, beefy, porky, pudgy, blubbery, poddy; Brit. informal podgy; archaic pursy.
▷ANTONYMS thin.
3 *a heavy blow to the head*: **forceful**, hard, strong, violent, powerful, vigorous, mighty, hefty, tremendous, sharp, smart, severe, grievous.
▷ANTONYMS gentle.
4 *a gardener comes in to do the heavy work for me*: **arduous**, hard, physical, laborious, demanding, difficult, exacting, strenuous, tough, onerous, back-breaking, tiring, fatiguing, exhausting, wearying, gruelling; informal murderous, killing, hellish; Brit. informal knackering; rare toilsome, exigent.
▷ANTONYMS easy.
5 *a heavy burden of responsibility*: **onerous**, burdensome, demanding, challenging, difficult, formidable, weighty, worrisome, wearisome, stressful, trying, crushing, exacting, oppressive; rare toilsome, exigent.
▷ANTONYMS undemanding.
6 *the helicopter ran into heavy fog*: **dense**, thick, opaque, soupy, murky, smoggy, impenetrable.
▷ANTONYMS light, wispy.
7 *a heavy thundery sky*: **overcast**, cloudy, clouded, clouded over, overclouded, sunless, grey, dull, gloomy, murky, dark, darkened, black, stormy, leaden, louring, promising rain; literary tenebrous.
▷ANTONYMS sunny, bright.
8 *we had heavy overnight rain*: **torrential**, relentless, copious, intense, teeming, excessive, strong, severe.
▷ANTONYMS light.
9 *the summer weather is very heavy here*: **humid**, sultry, muggy, close, sticky, clammy, steamy, oppressive, airless, like a Turkish bath, like a sauna.
▷ANTONYMS fresh; arid.
10 *this tool is ideal for breaking up heavy soil*: **clayey**, clay, viscous, viscid, muddy, sticky, glutinous, gluey, difficult, wet; Brit. claggy; Scottish & N. English clarty; informal gooey, gloopy, cloggy; N. Amer. informal gloppy.
▷ANTONYMS friable; dry.
11 *heavy losses | a heavy fine*: **sizeable**, substantial, hefty, colossal, big, considerable; stiff; informal tidy, whopping (great), steep, astronomical; Brit. informal whacking (great).
▷ANTONYMS small.
12 *the boat encountered very heavy seas*: **tempestuous**, turbulent, wild, violent, rough, stormy, storm-tossed, choppy, squally.
▷ANTONYMS calm.
13 *the battalion was involved in heavy fighting*: **intense**, intensive, fierce, vigorous, concentrated, relentless, all-out, severe, serious, excessive, considerable, immoderate.
▷ANTONYMS half-hearted.
14 *he is a heavy drinker*: **immoderate**, intemperate, overindulgent, unrestrained, uncontrolled, excessive.
▷ANTONYMS moderate.
15 *you shouldn't eat a heavy meal after 6 pm*: **substantial**, filling, hearty, large, big, ample, sizeable, generous, square, solid.
▷ANTONYMS light.
16 *the Japanese diet is* **heavy on** *soybeans and vegetables*: **abounding in**, abundant in, lavish with, generous with, liberal with, profuse with, extravagant with, free with, unstinting with, using a lot of; overabundant in, using too much of, overusing.
▷ANTONYMS light on.
17 *he felt heavy and very tired*: **lethargic**, listless, sluggish, torpid, languid, apathetic, lacking in energy.
▷ANTONYMS energetic; animated.
18 *I left him with a heavy heart*: **sad**, sorrowful, melancholy, gloomy, downcast, downhearted, heartbroken, disheartened, dejected, disconsolate, demoralized, discouraged, despondent, depressed, crestfallen, crushed, disappointed, desolate, grief-stricken, grieving; informal blue, down, down in the mouth, down in the dumps; literary dolorous; archaic heartsick, heartsore.
▷ANTONYMS cheerful.
19 *these poems are dull and heavy | the editors of the heavy dailies*: **tedious**, difficult, dull, dry, serious, over-serious, heavy-going, dreary, boring, turgid, uninteresting, wearisome, dry as dust; informal deadly.
▷ANTONYMS readable.
20 *branches heavy with blossoms*: **laden**, loaded, covered, filled, groaning, bursting, teeming, abounding, weighed down, weighted down.
21 *we had a heavy crop of good quality fruit*: **bountiful**, plentiful, abundant, large, bumper, handsome, lavish, rich, copious, considerable, sizeable, profuse; informal whopping, thumping; Brit. informal whacking; literary plenteous, bounteous.
▷ANTONYMS meagre.
22 *he had a big moustache and heavy features*: **coarse**, rough, rough-hewn, ungraceful, unrefined, inelegant; rugged, craggy.
▷ANTONYMS delicate.

heavy-handed adjective **1** *they tend to be heavy-handed with the equipment*: **clumsy**, awkward, maladroit, unhandy, inept, unskilful,

inexpert, graceless, ungraceful; informal ham-handed, ham-fisted, cack-handed; Brit. informal all thumbs, all fingers and thumbs.
▷ANTONYMS dexterous.
2 *heavy-handed policing*: **insensitive**, oppressive, overbearing, high-handed, harsh, hard, stern, severe, tyrannical, despotic, autocratic, ruthless, merciless; tactless, undiplomatic, thoughtless, inconsiderate, inept.
▷ANTONYMS sensitive.

heavy-hearted adjective **melancholy**, sad, sorrowful, melancholic, mournful, lugubrious, gloomy, pensive; depressed, desolate, despondent, dejected, down, downhearted, downcast, crestfallen, disconsolate, glum, sunk in gloom, miserable, wretched, dismal, dispirited, discouraged, low, in low spirits, in the doldrums, blue, morose, funereal, woeful, woebegone, doleful, wistful, unhappy, joyless, low-spirited, sombre; informal down in the dumps, down in the mouth, blue; literary dolorous; archaic heartsick, heartsore, chap-fallen.
▷ANTONYMS cheerful.

heckle verb *he was booed and heckled when he tried to address the demonstrators*: **jeer**, taunt, jibe at, shout down, shout at, boo, hiss, disrupt, interrupt, harass; shout catcalls at; Brit. & Austral./NZ barrack; informal give someone a hard time.
▷ANTONYMS cheer.

hectic adjective *a hectic business schedule | a hectic street market*: **frantic**, frenetic, frenzied, feverish, manic, restless, very busy, very active, fast and furious; lively, brisk, bustling, buzzing, vibrant, crowded.
▷ANTONYMS leisurely; quiet.

hector verb *he hectored the witness into incoherence*: **bully**, intimidate, browbeat, cow, badger, chivvy, harass, torment, plague; coerce, pressurize, strong-arm, threaten, menace, ride roughshod over, use strong-arm tactics on, dragoon; informal bulldoze, railroad, steamroller; N. Amer. informal bullyrag.

hedge noun **1** *houses concealed behind high hedges*: **hedgerow**, row of bushes, fence; windbreak, barrier, barricade, boundary; Brit. quickset.
2 *he sees the new fund as an excellent hedge against a fall in sterling*: **safeguard**, protection, shield, screen, guard, buffer, cushion; cover, insurance, security, provision, insurance cover.
3 *his analysis is full of hedges like 'probably' and 'perhaps'*: **equivocation**, evasion, fudge, quibble, qualification, qualifying expression; temporizing, uncertainty, prevarication, vagueness.
▷ANTONYMS absolute, certainty.
▶verb **1** *the fields were hedged with hawthorn*: **surround**, enclose, encircle, circle, ring, border, edge, bound; literary gird, girdle, engird.
2 *she was hedged in by her imperfect education*: **confine**, restrict, limit, hinder, obstruct, impede, constrain, trap; hem in, shut in, close, keep within bounds.
3 *he hedged at every new question*: **prevaricate**, equivocate, vacillate, quibble, hesitate, stall, evade the issue, dodge the issue, fudge the issue, sidestep the issue, be non-committal, be evasive, be indecisive, be vague, hedge one's bets, beat about the bush, parry questions, pussyfoot around, mince one's words, shilly-shally; Brit. hum and haw; informal sit on the fence, duck the question; Brit. informal waffle, flannel; rare tergiversate.
▷ANTONYMS come to the point.
4 *the company hedged its investment position on the futures market*: **safeguard**, protect, shield, guard, cushion, cover, insure, take out insurance, take out insurance cover.
▷ANTONYMS expose to risk.

hedgehog noun

Word links **hedgehog**

erinaceous relating to hedgehogs

hedonism noun **self-indulgence**, indulgence, pursuit of pleasure, pleasure-seeking, lotus-eating, epicureanism, epicurism, self-gratification; lack of self-restraint, intemperance, intemperateness, immoderation, overindulgence, excess, extravagance; luxury, the high life, high living; sensualism, voluptuousness; Italian la dolce vita; rare sybaritism.
▷ANTONYMS self-restraint.

hedonist noun **sybarite**, sensualist, voluptuary, pleasure seeker, pleasure lover; libertine, playboy, debauchee, loose-liver; epicure, gastronome, gourmand; French bon viveur, bon vivant.
▷ANTONYMS ascetic.

hedonistic adjective **self-indulgent**, indulgent, pleasure-seeking, pleasure-loving, sybaritic, lotus-eating, epicurean; luxurious, unrestrained, intemperate, immoderate, overindulgent, excessive, extravagant; sensual, voluptuous, decadent.
▷ANTONYMS ascetic.

heed verb *he should have heeded the warnings*: **pay attention to**, take notice of, take note of, pay heed to, be heedful of, attend to, listen to, notice, note, pay regard to, bear in mind, be mindful of, mind, mark, consider, take into account, take into consideration, be guided by, follow, obey, keep, keep to, adhere to, abide by, observe, take to heart, give ear to, be alert to; be cautious of, watch out for.
▷ANTONYMS disregard.
▶noun *if he heard, he paid no heed*: **attention**, notice, note, regard, heedfulness, attentiveness, consideration, thought, care.

heedful adjective *on every side they cast a heedful eye*: **attentive**, careful, mindful, cautious, prudent, circumspect, alert, aware, wary, chary, observant, watchful, vigilant, taking notice, paying attention, on guard, on the alert, on one's toes, on the qui vive; rare regardful.
▷ANTONYMS heedless; inattentive.

heedless adjective *someone had stayed behind, **heedless of** the warnings*: **unmindful of**, taking no notice of, paying no heed to, careless of, disregardful of, regardless of, unheeding of, neglectful of, unconscious of, oblivious to, inattentive to, blind to, deaf to; incautious, imprudent, rash, reckless, foolhardy, blithe, precipitate, unthinking, thoughtless, improvident, unwary, unobservant, unwatchful.
▷ANTONYMS heedful; attentive.

Choose the right word **heedless, careless, thoughtless**

See **careless**.

heel[1] noun **1** *shoes with low heels*: **wedge**, wedge heel, stiletto, stiletto heel, platform heel, spike heel, Cuban heel, kitten heel, Louis heel, stacked heel.
2 *there was the heel of a loaf in the cupboard*: **tail end**, crust, end, remnant, remainder, remains, stump, butt, vestige.
□ **bring someone/something to heel** *organized crime and corruption have not yet been brought to heel*: **subjugate**, conquer, vanquish, defeat, crush, quell, quash, gain mastery over, gain ascendancy over, gain control of, bring under the yoke, bring someone to their knees, overcome, overpower; tame, break; informal lick, clobber, hammer, wipe the floor with, walk all over.
□ **take to one's heels** *he shouted a warning and took to his heels*: **run away**, run off, make a run for it, run for it, take flight, make off, take off, make a break for it, bolt, flee, beat a (hasty) retreat, make a quick exit, make one's getaway, escape, head for the hills; informal beat it, clear off, clear out, vamoose, skedaddle, split, cut and run, leg it, hightail it, hotfoot it, show a clean pair of heels, turn tail, scram, hook it, fly the coop, skip off, do a fade; Brit. informal do a runner, scarper, do a bunk; N. Amer. informal light out, bug out, cut out, peel out, take a powder, skidoo; Austral. informal go through, shoot through; archaic fly, levant.
▷ANTONYMS stay put.

heel[2] verb *the ship was beginning to heel to starboard*: **lean over**, list, cant, careen, tilt, tip, incline, slant, slope, keel over, be at an angle.

heft verb *Donald hefted a stone jar of whisky into position*: **lift**, lift up, raise, raise up, heave, hoist, haul, manhandle; carry, cart, lug, tote; informal hump, yank; rare upheave.
▷ANTONYMS put down.

hefty adjective **1** *a hefty young man*: **burly**, heavy, sturdy, strapping, bulky, brawny, husky, strong, muscular, large, big, massive, weighty, solid, well built, solidly built, powerfully built; portly, stout; informal hulking, hunky, beefy; literary stalwart, thewy.
▷ANTONYMS slight, gaunt.
2 *he aimed a hefty kick at the door*: **powerful**, violent, hard, forceful, heavy, vigorous, mighty, thunderous.
▷ANTONYMS feeble.
3 *the horses hauled hefty loads of timber and metal*: **heavy**, weighty, bulky, leaden, big, large, substantial, massive, ponderous; unwieldy, cumbersome, burdensome, awkward; informal hulking, weighing a ton.
▷ANTONYMS light.
4 *they face a hefty fine*: **substantial**, sizeable, considerable, stiff, high-cost, extortionate, inflated, large, huge, excessive, colossal; Brit. over the odds; informal steep, astronomical, whopping, thumping; Brit. informal whacking, whacking great.
▷ANTONYMS small, paltry.

hegemony noun *Germany was united under Prussian hegemony after 1871*: **leadership**, dominance, dominion, supremacy, ascendancy, predominance, primacy, authority, mastery, control, power, sway, rule, sovereignty; rare predomination, paramountcy, prepotence, prepotency, prepollency.
▷ANTONYMS self-government.

height noun **1** *we measured the height of the wall | three metres in height*: **highness**, tallness, loftiness, distance upwards, extent upwards, vertical measurement, elevation, stature, altitude, distance above the ground; vertical distance above sea level.
2 *his eyes swept around the mountain heights*: **summit**, top, peak, crest, crown, tip, cap, pinnacle, apex, vertex, brow, ridge, highest point, hilltop, mountain top; French aiguille, serac.
▷ANTONYMS base.
3 *they were at the height of their fame*: **high point**, highest point, crowning moment, culminating point, peak, acme, apotheosis, zenith, apogee, pinnacle, climax, culmination, consummation, high water mark.
▷ANTONYMS nadir, low point.

4 *it would be the height of bad manners not to attend the wedding*: **epitome**, acme, zenith, quintessence, limit, very limit, culmination, ultimate, utmost; Latin ne plus ultra.
5 (**heights**) *he is terrified of heights*: **high places**, sheer drops, steep inclines, high ground, steep ground; precipices, cliffs.

> *Word links* **height**
>
> **acro-**, **hypso-**, **alti-** related prefixes
> **altimetry**, **hypsometry** measurement of height
> **acrophobia** fear of heights

heighten verb **1** *raising the floor level meant the roof had to be heightened*: **make higher**, raise, lift, lift up, elevate, upraise.
▷ANTONYMS lower.
2 *the pleasure was heightened by the sense of guilt that accompanied it*: **intensify**, increase, enhance, make greater, add to, raise, augment, boost, strengthen, sharpen, deepen, magnify, amplify, reinforce; aggravate, make worse, worsen, exacerbate, inflame, compound.
▷ANTONYMS reduce.

heinous adjective *child abuse is considered a most heinous offence*: **odious**, wicked, evil, atrocious, monstrous, disgraceful, abominable, detestable, contemptible, reprehensible, despicable, horrible, horrific, horrifying, terrible, awful, abhorrent, loathsome, outrageous, shocking, shameful, hateful, hideous, unspeakable, unpardonable, unforgivable, inexcusable, execrable, ghastly, iniquitous, villainous, nefarious, beneath contempt, beyond the pale; rare egregious, flagitious.
▷ANTONYMS admirable.

heir, heiress noun *his eldest son and heir*: **successor**, next in line, inheritor, heir apparent, heir presumptive, heir-at-law, descendant, beneficiary, legatee, scion; Law devisee, grantee, parcener, coparcener; Scottish Law heritor.
▷ANTONYMS predecessor.

> *Word links* **heir**
>
> **hereditary** relating to an heir

helix noun **spiral**, coil, curl, corkscrew, twist, twirl, loop, gyre, whorl, scroll, curlicue, convolution; technical volute, volution.

hell noun **1** *they feared they would be consumed by flames in hell*: **the netherworld**, the land/abode of the dead, the infernal regions, the Inferno, the nether regions, the abyss; the abode of the damned, eternal damnation, eternal punishment, perdition; hellfire, fire and brimstone; Biblical Gehenna, Tophet, Abaddon; Judaism Sheol; Greek Mythology Hades, Tartarus, Acheron; Roman Mythology Avernus; Scandinavian Mythology Niflheim; literary the pit, the shades; archaic the lower world.
▷ANTONYMS heaven.
2 *he made her life hell*: **a misery**, purgatory, hell on earth, torture, agony, a torment, a nightmare, an ordeal, a trauma; suffering, affliction, anguish, wretchedness, woe, tribulation, trials and tribulations.
▷ANTONYMS paradise.
□ **get hell** informal *later he got hell from his father*: **be severely reprimanded**, be upbraided, be scolded, get a scolding, be admonished, be castigated, be rebuked, be chastised, be censured, be criticized severely, be taken to task, get into trouble, be hauled over the coals; informal catch it, get what for, be told off, get into hot/deep water, get into shtook, get a dressing-down, get an earful, get a roasting, get a rocket, get a rollicking, get a rap over the knuckles, get a slap on the wrist.
▷ANTONYMS be praised, be commended.
□ **give someone hell** informal **1** *when the truth came out I gave him hell*: **reprimand severely**, rebuke, admonish, chastise, chide, upbraid, reprove, reproach, scold, remonstrate with, berate, take to task, pull up, castigate, lambaste, read someone the Riot Act, give someone a piece of one's mind, haul over the coals, lecture, criticize, censure; informal tell off, give someone a talking-to, give someone a telling-off, dress down, give someone a dressing-down, give someone an earful, give someone a roasting, give someone a rocket, give someone a rollicking, rap, rap over the knuckles, slap someone's wrist, send someone away with a flea in their ear, let someone have it, bawl out, come down hard on, blow up, pitch into, lay into, lace into, give someone a caning, blast, rag, keelhaul; Brit. informal tick off, have a go at, carpet, give someone a mouthful, tear someone off a strip, give someone what for, give someone some stick, wig, give someone a wigging; N. Amer. informal chew out, ream out; Austral. informal monster; Brit. vulgar slang bollock, give someone a bollocking; N. Amer. vulgar slang chew someone's ass, ream someone's ass; dated call down, rate, give someone a rating, trim; rare reprehend, objurgate. ▷ANTONYMS praise, commend.
2 *she gave me hell when I was her junior*: **harass**, hound, plague, badger, harry, pester, bother, worry, annoy, trouble, bully, intimidate, pick on, bait, molest, bedevil, victimize, terrorize; N. Amer. devil; informal hassle, give someone a hard time, get on someone's back, make it/things hot for someone; Austral. informal heavy. ▷ANTONYMS leave in peace.
□ **hell for leather** *the cars went hurtling down the lane, hell for leather*: **as fast as possible**, as quickly as possible, very fast, very quickly, very rapidly, very speedily, very swiftly, hurriedly, at full speed, at the double, at full tilt, at full pelt, headlong, hotfoot, post-haste, pell-mell, helter-skelter, at the speed of light, at breakneck speed, like an arrow from a bow; informal like a bat out of hell, at a lick, like the wind, like greased lightning, at warp speed, like a bomb, like mad, like crazy, like blazes; Brit. informal like the clappers, at a rate of knots, like billy-o; N. Amer. informal **lickety-split**; literary apace, hurry-scurry.
▷ANTONYMS at moderate speed.
□ **raise hell** informal **1** *they were hollering and raising hell*: **cause a disturbance**, cause a commotion, be loud and noisy, run riot, run wild, behave wildly, go on the rampage, get out of control; have a (wild) party, party, carouse, revel; informal raise the roof, raise Cain. ▷ANTONYMS keep the peace.
2 *he raised hell with real estate developers and polluters*: **remonstrate**, expostulate, be very angry, be furious, be enraged, argue, protest loudly to, object noisily to, complain vociferously to; informal kick up a fuss, kick up a stink.

> *Word links* **hell**
>
> **infernal** relating to hell
> **hadephobia**, **stygiophobia** fear of hell

hell-bent adjective *why are you hell-bent on leaving?* **intent**, bent, determined, set, dead set, insistent, fixed, resolved, settled; firm about, single-minded about, inflexible about, obsessive about, fanatical about, fixated on.
▷ANTONYMS half-hearted.

hellish adjective **1** *the hellish face of Death*: **infernal**, Hadean; **devilish**, diabolical, diabolic, fiendish, satanic, demonic, demoniac, demoniacal, Mephistophelian, ungodly, evil, wicked; Greek Mythology Stygian; rare cacodemonic.
▷ANTONYMS godly, angelic.
2 informal *it had been a hellish week*. See **ghastly**.
▶ **adverb** informal, dated *it's hellish hard work*. See **extremely**.

helm noun *the second mate took the helm*: **tiller**, wheel; steering gear, rudder.
□ **at the helm** *they are family-run empires whose founders remain at the helm*: **in charge**, in command, in control, responsible, at the top, in authority, in the seat of authority, at the wheel, in the driving seat, in the saddle; **managing**, running, administering, directing, supervising, overseeing, controlling, commanding, leading, heading up; informal holding the reins, running the show, pulling the strings, calling the shots.

help verb **1** *they helped her with domestic chores | can you help me please?* **assist**, aid, help out, lend a hand to, lend a helping hand to, give assistance to, come to the aid of, succour, aid and abet; be of service to, be of use to, be useful to; **do someone a favour**, do someone a service, do someone a good turn, bail/bale someone out, come to someone's rescue, give someone a leg up; cooperate with, do one's bit for, rally round, pitch in, chip in; informal get someone out of a tight spot, save someone's bacon, save someone's skin; Brit. informal muck in with, get stuck in with.
▷ANTONYMS hinder.
2 *using this affinity card helps cancer research*: **support**, **contribute to**, give money to, give a donation to; promote, boost, give a boost to, back, give backing to, forward, encourage, further the interests of; N. Amer. informal bankroll.
▷ANTONYMS impede.
3 *sore throats can be helped by gargles*: **relieve**, soothe, ameliorate, alleviate, make better, ease, improve, assuage, palliate, lessen, mitigate; **remedy**, cure, heal, restore.
▷ANTONYMS worsen, aggravate.
4 *can I help you?* **serve**, be of assistance to, be of help to, be of service to, give help to.
□ **cannot help** *he could not help laughing*: **be unable to stop**, be unable to prevent oneself from, be unable to refrain from, be unable to keep from, be unable to forbear from, be unable to break the habit of.
□ **help oneself to** *he helped himself to the wages she had brought home*: **steal**, take, appropriate, take possession of, 'borrow', 'liberate', pocket, purloin, commandeer, make free with, use without asking; informal swipe, nab, filch, snaffle, blag, walk off with, run off with; Brit. informal nick, pinch, whip, knock off; N. Amer. informal heist, glom; W. Indian informal tief.
▶ **noun 1** *I asked for help from my neighbours | this could be of help to you*: **assistance**, aid, a helping hand, support, succour, advice, guidance; **benefit**, use, advantage, service, comfort, avail; cooperation, collaboration, backing, encouragement; informal a shot in the arm.
▷ANTONYMS hindrance.
2 *he sought help for his eczema*: **relief**, amelioration, alleviation, easing, improvement, assuagement, mitigation, healing; **a remedy**, a cure, a balm, a salve, a restorative, a corrective.
▷ANTONYMS irritant.
3 *they treated the help like dirt*: **domestic worker**, domestic help,

domestic servant, cleaner, cleaning woman, cleaning lady, home help, maid, housemaid, housekeeper, servant, hired help, helper, assistant, employee, worker; Brit. informal daily, daily woman, skivvy, Mrs Mop; Brit. dated charwoman, charlady, char; archaic scullion, abigail.

Choose the right word **help, aid, assist, support**

Help is the most general term for acting in such a way as to make it easier for someone else to do something or, more generally, to make their life more comfortable (*she helped him to find a job | helping the poor*). When followed by an infinitive, as in the first example above, *to* can be omitted (*we can help give these youngsters a better start in life*).

Aid is used in more formal contexts, and typically in the case of help in the achievement of something (*these posters aid employees in the identification of pests*). It is often used with impersonal or abstract subjects and objects (*some additions have been made to the text to aid understanding*), and as *aided* in constructions such as *computer-aided design*.

Assist is also a more formal term for *help* (*a charge of murder was brought against him for assisting a woman to commit suicide | two approaches might assist in tackling the problem*), and it can be used specifically to indicate that someone plays a subordinate part in a joint action (*a subcommittee should be appointed to assist the chairman*).

To **support** someone or something is to show one's approval or agreement and, where necessary, to give practical, especially financial, assistance (*we want to support all efforts for peace | they supported many local charities*). Often the suggestion is that the help provided is important or essential for something's survival or success (*he could not have earned enough to support his family*). *Support* is also used of giving emotional help and comfort (*his wife has supported him through many difficult periods*).

helper noun *there was no shortage of helpers to relieve us during breaks*: **assistant**, co-worker, fellow worker, workmate, teammate, helpmate, helpmeet, associate, aider, aide, colleague, supporter, partner, collaborator, abetter; **subordinate**, deputy, auxiliary, second, second in command, number two, right-hand man, right-hand woman, attendant, junior, acolyte; accessory, accomplice, henchman; informal sidekick.

helpful adjective **1** *the staff are friendly and helpful*: **obliging**, eager to help, eager to please, friendly, pleasant, kind, accommodating, considerate, thoughtful, supportive, cooperative, sympathetic, caring, hospitable, neighbourly, charitable, benevolent, beneficent.
▷ANTONYMS unobliging, unsympathetic.
2 *we find it very helpful to receive comments*: **useful**, of use, of service, of benefit, beneficial, valuable, profitable, fruitful, advantageous, worthwhile, productive, constructive, practical; informative, instructive.
▷ANTONYMS useless.
3 *we recommend this helpful new power tool*: **handy**, useful, convenient, practical, easy-to-use, well-designed, user-friendly, user-oriented, functional, serviceable, utilitarian; informal neat, nifty.
▷ANTONYMS inconvenient.

helping noun *there will be enough for six to eight helpings*: **portion**, serving, piece, slice, share, spoonful, plate, plateful, bowlful, ration, allocation; informal dollop.

helpless adjective *the cubs are born blind and helpless*: **dependent**, **incapable**, powerless, impotent, weak, weakly, feeble; **defenceless**, unprotected, vulnerable, exposed, easily hurt, easily destroyed, open to attack.
▷ANTONYMS independent, capable of looking after oneself.

helpmate noun **1** *a crowing rooster was the helpmate of the goddess of the sun*: **companion**, partner, associate, assistant, helper, helpmeet, attendant, escort; supporter, friend.
2 *she couldn't survive on her own and happily submitted to the role of helpmate once again*: **spouse**, partner, consort, mate, husband, wife; informal other half, better half.

helter-skelter adverb *the children ran helter-skelter down the valley*: **headlong**, pell-mell, hotfoot, post-haste, hastily, in a hurry, hurriedly, as fast as possible, as quickly as possible, at full speed, at full pelt, at full tilt, hell for leather, recklessly, precipitately, impetuously, impulsively, carelessly, heedlessly, wildly; informal like a bat out of hell, at a lick, like the wind, like greased lightning, like a bomb, like mad, like crazy, like blazes; Brit. informal like the clappers, at a rate of knots, like billy-o; N. Amer. informal lickety-split; literary apace, hurry-scurry.
▷ANTONYMS at moderate speed.
▶ adjective *the village was a helter-skelter collection of dwellings*: **disordered**, disorderly, chaotic, muddled, jumbled, untidy, haphazard, disorganized, unorganized, disarranged, topsy-turvy; in a mess, in a muddle, in a shambles, at sixes and sevens, out of order; informal higgledy-piggledy, all over the place; Brit. informal shambolic, all over the shop; N. Amer. informal all over the map, all over the lot; rare orderless.
▷ANTONYMS orderly.

hem noun *she let down the hem of her dress*: **edge**, edging, border, trim, trimming; fringe, frill, flounce, valance.
▶ verb *Nanna taught me to hem skirts*: **edge**, put a hem on, border, trim, bind, fringe.
□ **hem someone/something in 1** *the bay was hemmed in by pine trees*: **surround**, border, edge, encircle, circle, ring, enclose, skirt, flank, fringe, encompass; literary gird, girdle, engird. **2** *he was hemmed in by the furniture | we were hemmed in by the rules*: **restrict**, confine, trap, close in, shut in, hedge in, fence in, pen in, box in, keep within bounds, immure; constrain, restrain, limit, circumscribe, curb, check; N. Amer. corral; rare compass.

he-man noun informal **muscleman**, strongman, macho, macho man, iron man, Hercules, Atlas, Samson, Tarzan; informal **hunk**, tough guy, beefcake, stud, bruiser; N. Amer. informal studmuffin.
▷ANTONYMS wimp.

hence adverb *many vehicle journeys (and hence a lot of pollution) would be saved*: **in consequence**, consequently, as a consequence, for this reason, therefore, thus, so, accordingly, as a result, because of that, that being so, that being the case, on that account; Latin ergo.

henceforth adverb *henceforth the director will be solely responsible for the whole establishment*: **from now on**, as of now, after this, in future, in the future, hence, henceforward, subsequently, from this day on, from this time on, from this day forth, from this day forward; formal hereafter, hereinafter.

henchman noun *the local dictator arrived with a group of henchmen*: **follower**, supporter, assistant, aide, helper, adjutant, right-hand man; subordinate, underling, minion, lackey, flunkey, toady, stooge, acolyte, satellite, shadow; bodyguard, minder, protector; informal sidekick, crony, heavy, man/girl Friday.
▷ANTONYMS leader.

h

henpecked adjective *he was a henpecked husband at the end of his tether*: **browbeaten**, downtrodden, bullied, dominated, nagged, subjugated, oppressed, repressed, intimidated, ground down, without a mind of one's own, tied to someone's apron strings, under someone's heel; meek, timid, docile, cringing, cowering, abject; informal under someone's thumb, led by the nose, treated like dirt.
▷ANTONYMS domineering.

herald noun **1** *a herald announced the armistice*: **messenger**, courier, bearer of tidings; proclaimer, announcer, crier, town crier.
2 *they considered the first primroses as the herald of spring*: **harbinger**, sign, indicator, indication, signal, prelude, portent, omen, augury, forewarning, presage, announcer; forerunner, precursor, messenger, usher; French avant-courier; literary foretoken.
▶ verb **1** *screams and shouts heralded their approach*: **proclaim**, announce, broadcast, publicize, declare, trumpet, make public, make known, blazon; advertise, promote, beat the drum about.
2 *the speech heralded a change in policy*: **signal**, indicate, announce, point to, spell, presage, augur, portend, promise, prefigure, foreshadow, foretell, usher in, show in, pave the way for, open the way for, be a harbinger of, be a forerunner, be a precursor of; precede, come before; rare forebode, foretoken, betoken, harbinger.

Herculean adjective **1** *a Herculean task*: **arduous**, gruelling, laborious, back-breaking, onerous, strenuous, difficult, formidable, burdensome, hard, tough, huge, heavy, massive, uphill, Sisyphean; demanding, exhausting, taxing, exacting, wearying, wearisome, fatiguing; informal killing; Brit. informal knackering; archaic toilsome.
▷ANTONYMS easy.
2 *he was a man of Herculean build*: **strong**, muscular, muscly, powerful, sturdy, robust, solid, well built, powerfully built, solidly built, strapping, brawny, burly, broad-shouldered, as strong as an ox, as strong as a horse, as strong as a lion; informal hunky, beefy, hulking; literary stalwart, thewy, stark.
▷ANTONYMS puny.

herd noun **1** *large farms with big dairy herds*: **flock**, drove, pack, group, collection, fold.
2 *we ran into a herd of movie actors*: **crowd**, group, bunch, horde, mass, mob, host, pack, multitude, throng, swarm, army, company, press.
3 (**the herd**) *they consider themselves above the herd*: **the common people**, the masses, the public, the people, the rank and file, the populace, the multitude, the crowd, the commonality, the commonalty, the third estate, the plebeians; derogatory the hoi polloi, the mob, the proletariat, the common herd, the rabble, the riff-raff, the canaille, the ragtag (and bobtail), the great unwashed, the proles, the plebs, the peasants.
▷ANTONYMS the elite.
▶ verb **1** *he and the boys herded the sheep into the pen*: **drive**, round up, shepherd, gather, collect, assemble, guide.
2 *we all herded into a storage room*: **crowd**, pack, flock; cluster, huddle, group, gather.
3 *they live by herding reindeer*: **look after**, take care of, keep, tend, watch, watch over, mind, guard.
▷ANTONYMS neglect.

herdsman, herdswoman noun **stockman**, herder, drover, shepherd, cattleman, cowherd, cowhand, cowman, cowboy, rancher; N. Amer. sheepman;

in Spanish-speaking America gaucho, llanero, ranchero, vaquero; N. Amer. informal cowpuncher, cowpoke, broncobuster; N. Amer. dated buckaroo; archaic herd.

here adverb **1** *they have lived here most of their lives*: **at/in this place**, at/in this spot, at/in this location.
2 *I am here now*: **present**, in attendance, attending, at hand, available.
▷ANTONYMS absent.
3 *come here tomorrow morning*: **to this place**, to this spot, to this location, to here, over here, near, nearer, close, closer; literary hither.
4 *here is your opportunity*: **now**, at this moment, at this point, at this point in time, at this time, at this juncture, at this stage.
□ **here and now** *I wanted to be popular here and now*. See **now** (sense 1).
□ **here and there 1** *a landscape of ferns with clumps of heather here and there*: **in various places**, in different places, hither and thither, at random.
2 *they darted here and there, adjusting and correcting*: **from place to place**, around, about, to and fro, hither and thither, back and forth, in all directions, from pillar to post.

hereafter adverb formal *nothing I say hereafter is intended to relate to the second decision*: **from now on**, after this, as of now, from this day on, from this time on, from this moment forth, from this day forth, from this day forward, subsequently, in future, in the future, hence, henceforth, henceforward; formal hereinafter.
▸ noun (**the hereafter**) *suffering is part of our preparation for the hereafter*: **life after death**, the afterlife, the life to come, the afterworld, the next world, the beyond; immortality, eternity, heaven, paradise.

h

hereditary adjective **1** *in the past, the aristocracy had a hereditary right to elect the king*: **inherited**, obtained by inheritance; bequeathed, willed, handed-down, passed-down, passed-on, transferred, transmitted; ancestral, family, familial; rare lineal.
2 *cystic fibrosis is our most common fatal hereditary disease*: **genetic**, genetical, congenital, inborn, inherent, inherited, inbred, innate, in the family, in the blood, in the genes.

heredity noun *the relative influence of heredity and environment*: **congenital characteristics**, congenital traits, genetics, genetic make-up, genes; ancestry, descent, extraction, parentage.

heresy noun *Huss was burned for heresy*: **dissension**, dissent, dissidence, blasphemy, nonconformity, unorthodoxy, heterodoxy, apostasy, freethinking, schism, faction; scepticism, agnosticism, atheism, non-belief, unbelief, idolatry, paganism, separatism, sectarianism, revisionism; rare tergiversation, recreancy, recusancy.
▷ANTONYMS orthodoxy.

heretic noun *he was condemned as a heretic and executed at the stake*: **dissident**, dissenter, nonconformist, unorthodox thinker, heterodox thinker, apostate, freethinker, iconoclast, schismatic, renegade; sceptic, agnostic, atheist, non-believer, unbeliever, idolater, idolatress, pagan, heathen; separatist, sectarian, revisionist; rare tergiversator, recreant, recusant, nullifidian; archaic paynim.
▷ANTONYMS conformist; believer.

heretical adjective *he was punished for his heretical views*: **dissident**, dissenting, nonconformist, unorthodox, heterodox, apostate, freethinking, iconoclastic, schismatic, renegade; sceptical, agnostic, atheistical, non-believing, unbelieving, idolatrous, pagan, heathen, impious; separatist, sectarian, revisionist; rare recreant, recusant, nullifidian; archaic paynim.
▷ANTONYMS orthodox.

heritage noun **1** *they had stolen his heritage*: **inheritance**, birthright, patrimony; legacy, bequest, endowment, estate, bequeathal; Law devise, hereditament.
2 *Europe's varied cultural heritage*: **tradition**, history, background, culture, customs, past.
3 *he felt the pull of his Greek heritage*: **ancestry**, lineage, descent, extraction, parentage, roots, background, heredity, pedigree.

hermaphrodite noun **epicene**; technical bisexual, gynandromorph; rare androgyne.
▸ adjective *hermaphrodite creatures in classical sculpture*: **androgynous**, hermaphroditic, epicene; technical bisexual, monoclinous, gynandrous, gynandromorphic.

hermetic adjective *a hermetic seal that ensures perfect waterproofing*: **airtight**, tight, sealed, shut; watertight, waterproof.

hermit noun **recluse**, solitary, loner, ascetic; rare anchorite, anchoress, eremite, stylite, pillarist, pillar hermit, pillar saint, solitudinarian.

> *Word links* **hermit**
>
> **eremitic** relating to a hermit

hermitage noun **retreat**, refuge, haven, sanctuary, sanctum, asylum, hideaway, hideout, hiding place, shelter; Latin sanctum sanctorum; informal hidey-hole.

hero noun **1** *his father was a war hero*: **brave man**, champion, man of courage, great man, man of the hour, conquering hero, victor, winner, conqueror, lionheart, warrior, paladin, knight; French chevalier.
▷ANTONYMS coward; loser.
2 *a football hero*: **star**, idol, superstar, megastar, celebrity, celebutante, luminary, lion; ideal, ideal man, paragon, exemplar, shining example, perfect example; favourite, darling; knight in shining armour, knight on a white charger; French beau idéal; informal celeb.
3 *the hero of the film is a young pianist*: **male protagonist**, principal male character; principal male role, lead actor, lead, leading man, leading role, male lead, star role, starring role, star part, male star.
▷ANTONYMS villain.

heroic adjective **1** *a national flag can motivate citizens to heroic deeds* | *heroic rescuers*: **brave**, courageous, valiant, valorous, intrepid, bold, daring, audacious, superhuman, Herculean, fearless, doughty, undaunted, dauntless, unafraid, plucky, indomitable, stout-hearted, lionhearted, mettlesome, venturesome, gallant, stalwart, chivalrous, noble; N. Amer. rock-ribbed; informal gutsy, spunky, ballsy, feisty; rare venturous.
▷ANTONYMS cowardly; fearful.
2 *a heroic achievement*: **prodigious**, grand, enormous, huge, massive, titanic, colossal, monumental, stupendous; epic, Homeric; informal mega.
▷ANTONYMS modest.

heroine noun **1** *Nicky was a heroine—she saved my baby from being snatched*: **brave woman**, hero, woman of courage, great woman, woman of the hour; victor, winner, conqueror.
▷ANTONYMS coward; loser.
2 *the literary heroine of Moscow*: **star**, idol, superstar, megastar, celebrity, celebutante, luminary, lion; ideal, ideal woman, paragon, exemplar, shining example, perfect example, favourite, darling; informal celeb.
3 *the film's heroine takes a feminist stand*: **female protagonist**, principal female character; principal female role, lead actress, lead, leading lady, leading role, female lead, star role, starring role, star part, female star, prima donna, diva.
▷ANTONYMS villain.

heroism noun *many of the women distinguished themselves by great acts of heroism*: **bravery**, braveness, courage, courageousness, valour, valiance, intrepidity, intrepidness, boldness, daring, audacity, audaciousness, fearlessness, doughtiness, dauntlessness, pluck, indomitability, stout-heartedness, lionheartedness; backbone, spine, spirit, fortitude, mettle, gallantry, chivalry; informal guts, grit, spunk, gutsiness; Brit. informal bottle, ballsiness; N. Amer. informal moxie, cojones, sand; vulgar slang balls.
▷ANTONYMS cowardliness; fearfulness.

hero-worship noun *the hero-worship of the fans gathered at the airport*: **idolization**, adulation, admiration, idealization, awe, high esteem, high regard, putting on a pedestal; worship, adoration, glorification, exaltation, veneration, reverence; rare magnification.
▷ANTONYMS disparagement, lack of respect.

herself pronoun
□ **by herself** See **by oneself** at **by**.

hesitancy noun **1** *they gave the impression of hesitancy and doubt*: **uncertainty**, hesitation, hesitance, unsureness, doubt, doubtfulness, dubiousness, irresolution, irresoluteness, indecision, indecisiveness, equivocation, vacillation, wavering, scepticism, nervousness, second thoughts; **dithering**, stalling, shilly-shallying, temporizing, temporization, pausing, delay, hanging back, waiting; Brit. havering, humming and hawing; Scottish swithering; informal dilly-dallying, blowing hot and cold; rare dubiety, incertitude, cunctation.
▷ANTONYMS certainty, resolution.
2 *there was a little hesitancy in her voice*: **reluctance**, unwillingness, disinclination, unease, uneasiness, ambivalence, demurral, compunction; misgivings, qualms, scruples, reservations.
▷ANTONYMS willingness.

hesitant adjective **1** *clients are hesitant about buying*: **uncertain**, undecided, unsure, doubtful, in doubt, dubious, tentative, half-hearted, ambivalent, sceptical, reluctant, nervous, having misgivings, having qualms, hanging back, stalling, delaying; **irresolute**, hesitating, indecisive, dithering, vacillating, wavering, oscillating, shilly-shallying, in two minds, in a quandary, in a dilemma, on the horns of a dilemma; Brit. havering, humming and hawing; informal iffy, dilly-dallying, blowing hot and cold; rare cunctatory.
▷ANTONYMS certain; decisive.
2 *she was timid and hesitant*: **lacking confidence**, diffident, timid, shy, bashful, insecure, self-effacing; stammering, stuttering, stumbling, faltering.
▷ANTONYMS confident.

> *Word toolkit* **hesitant**
>
> See **unwilling**.

hesitate verb **1** *she hesitated, unsure of what to say*: **pause**, delay, hang back, wait, shilly-shally, dither, stall, temporize, be in two minds, be in a quandary, be in a dilemma, be on the horns of a dilemma; **be uncertain**,

be hesitant, be unsure, be doubtful, be indecisive, equivocate, vacillate, oscillate, waver, have second thoughts; Brit. haver, hum and haw; Scottish swither; informal dilly-dally, blow hot and cold.
▷ANTONYMS be resolute, be certain.
2 *please do not hesitate to contact me*: **be reluctant**, be unwilling, be disinclined, scruple; have misgivings about, have qualms about, be ambivalent about, feel uneasy about, shrink from, demur from, hang back from, think twice about, be diffident about, baulk at, boggle at.
▷ANTONYMS be willing.

hesitation noun 1 *she answered without hesitation*: **pausing**, delay, hanging back, waiting, shilly-shallying, dithering, stalling, temporizing, temporization; **uncertainty**, hesitancy, hesitance, unsureness, doubt, doubtfulness, dubiousness, irresolution, irresoluteness, indecision, indecisiveness, equivocation, vacillation, oscillation, wavering, scepticism, nervousness, second thoughts; Brit. havering, humming and hawing; Scottish swithering; informal dilly-dallying, blowing hot and cold; rare dubiety, incertitude, cunctation.
▷ANTONYMS resolution, certainty.
2 *I have no hesitation in recommending him*: **reluctance**, misgivings, qualms, scruples, reservations, compunction, unwillingness, disinclination, ambivalence, unease, uneasiness, demurral.
▷ANTONYMS willingness.

heterodox adjective *public expression of such heterodox views is impossible*: **unorthodox**, heretical, dissenting, dissident, blasphemous, nonconformist, apostate, freethinking, iconoclastic, schismatic, rebellious, renegade, separatist, sectarian, revisionist; sceptical, agnostic, atheistical, non-believing, unbelieving, idolatrous, pagan, heathen, impious; archaic paynim; rare recreant, recusant, nullifidian.
▷ANTONYMS orthodox.

heterogeneous adjective *a large and heterogeneous collection*: **diverse**, diversified, varied, varying, miscellaneous, assorted, mixed, sundry, contrasting, disparate, different, differing, divergent, unrelated, variegated, wide-ranging; motley; literary divers, myriad, legion; rare contrastive.
▷ANTONYMS homogeneous.

heterosexual adjective informal **straight**, hetero, het.
▷ANTONYMS homosexual, gay.

hew verb 1 *master carpenters would hew the logs with an axe*: **chop**, hack, chop down, hack down, cut down, saw down, fell, lop, axe, cleave.
2 *steps had been hewn into the rock wall*: **cut**, carve, shape, fashion, form, chip, hammer, chisel, sculpt, sculpture, model, whittle, rough-hew.

heyday noun *the paper has lost millions of readers since its heyday in 1964*: **prime**, peak, height, high point, high spot, peak of perfection, pinnacle, acme, zenith, day, time, bloom, flowering, culmination, crowning point; prime of life, best days, best years, salad days.
▷ANTONYMS low point.

hiatus noun 1 *there has been a hiatus in space exploration following the Viking missions*: **pause**, break, interval, interruption, suspension, intermission, interlude, gap, lacuna, lull, rest, respite, breathing space, time out; N. Amer. recess; informal breather, let-up; archaic surcease.
2 Medicine *the diaphragmatic hiatus was larger than necessary*: **opening**, aperture, cavity, hole, gap, cleft, breach, fissure; Medicine foramen.

hibernate verb *some species hibernate in tree roosts*: **lie dormant**, lie torpid, sleep, winter, overwinter, hole up.

hidden adjective 1 *they watched the action through a hidden camera*: **concealed**, secret, not visible, invisible, unseen, not on view, out of sight, covered, camouflaged, disguised, masked, shrouded, veiled, unrevealed.
▷ANTONYMS visible.
2 *what is the hidden meaning behind his words?* **unknown**, not obvious, unclear, concealed, obscure, indistinct, indefinite, vague, unfathomable, inexplicable; **cryptic**, mysterious, secret, covert, abstruse, arcane, recondite, ulterior, deep, subliminal, coded, under wraps.
▷ANTONYMS obvious, clear.

> *Word links* **hidden**
>
> **crypto-** related prefix, as in *cryptogram*, *cryptozoology*

hide[1] verb 1 *he hid the money in the house*: **conceal**, secrete, put in a hiding place, put out of sight, camouflage; lock up, bury, store away, stow away, cache; informal stash.
▷ANTONYMS flaunt, expose.
2 *they eluded the police by hiding in an air vent*: **conceal oneself**, secrete oneself, hide out, take cover, keep hidden, find a hiding place, keep out of sight; go into hiding, lie low, go to ground, go to earth, go underground, lurk; informal hole up; Brit. informal lie doggo.
▷ANTONYMS remain visible.
3 *clouds rolled up and hid the moon*: **obscure**, block out, blot out, obstruct, cloud, shroud, veil, blanket, envelop, darken, eclipse; literary enshroud.
▷ANTONYMS reveal.
4 *Herbert could hardly hide his dislike*: **keep secret**, keep unknown, conceal, cover up, keep dark, keep quiet about, hush up, bottle up, suppress, repress, withhold; **disguise**, mask, camouflage, veil, dissemble; informal keep mum about, keep under one's hat, keep a/the lid on.
▷ANTONYMS disclose.

hide[2] noun *the hide should be tanned as soon as possible*: **skin**, pelt, coat, fur, fleece; **leather**; archaic fell.

hideaway noun *a mass of shrubs creates a secluded hideaway*: **retreat**, refuge, hiding place, hideout, den, shelter, sanctuary, sanctum, hermitage, cache, bolt-hole, lair, nest, nook; Latin sanctum sanctorum; informal hidey-hole.

hidebound adjective *the hidebound traditionalists refused to accept the changes*: **conservative**, reactionary, conventional, orthodox, fundamentalist, diehard, hard-line, dyed-in-the-wool, ultra-conservative, fixed in one's views, set in one's opinions, set in one's ways; narrow-minded, narrow, petty-minded, small-minded, intolerant, intractable, uncompromising, rigid, prejudiced, bigoted, strait-laced; Brit. blimpish.
▷ANTONYMS liberal, broad-minded.

hideous adjective 1 *his smile made him look more hideous than ever*: **ugly**, unsightly, repulsive, repellent, revolting, gruesome, disgusting, grotesque, monstrous, grim, ghastly, macabre, misshapen, misproportioned, reptilian; informal weird, freaky, as ugly as sin; Brit. informal like the back end of a bus.
▷ANTONYMS beautiful.
2 *hideous cases of torture continue to be reported*: **horrific**, terrible, appalling, awful, dreadful, frightful, fearful, horrible, horrendous, horrifying, shocking, sickening, gruesome, ghastly, very bad, terribly bad, unspeakable, outrageous, abhorrent, monstrous, heinous, abominable, foul, vile, odious, loathsome, contemptible, execrable, indescribable; informal God-awful; Brit. informal beastly; rare egregious.
▷ANTONYMS pleasant.

hideout noun *the kidnappers did not want their hideout discovered*: **hiding place**, hideaway, retreat, refuge, shelter, bolt-hole, foxhole, lair, safe house, sanctuary, sanctum, hermitage; Latin sanctum sanctorum; informal hidey-hole.

hiding[1] noun informal *they took off after him, caught him, and gave him a hiding*: **beating**, battering, thrashing, thumping, pounding, pummelling, drubbing, slapping, smacking, spanking, hammering, cuffing, thwacking, mauling, pelting; flogging, flaying, whipping, caning, lashing, cudgelling, clubbing, birching; informal licking, belting, bashing, pasting, lathering, larruping, walloping, whacking, clobbering, tanning, biffing, bopping, horsewhipping; N. Amer. informal whaling.

hiding[2] noun
□ **in hiding** *the fugitive priest was in hiding*: **hidden**, concealed, lying low, gone to ground, gone to earth, gone underground, in a safe house; in seclusion, in retreat; Brit. informal lying doggo.

hiding place noun *they passed within inches of my hiding place*: **hideaway**, hideout, retreat, refuge, den, shelter, sanctuary, bolt-hole, foxhole, lair, safe house, asylum, sanctum, hermitage, oasis, haven, harbour, place of safety; informal hidey-hole.

hie verb archaic *they heard voices and hied away*. See **hurry** (sense 1 of the verb).

hierarchy noun *the initiative was with those lower down in the hierarchy*: **pecking order**, ranking, grading, ladder, social order, social stratum, social scale, class system.

hieroglyphic noun (**hieroglyphics**) 1 *his exploits were recorded in hieroglyphics on a stone monument*: **symbols**, signs, ciphers, code; **cryptograms**, cryptographs, runes.
2 *tattered notebooks filled with illegible hieroglyphics*: **scribble**, scrawl, illegible writing, squiggles, jottings, writing, shorthand.
▶ adjective 1 *the piece is inlaid with hieroglyphic brass ornamentation*: **symbolic**, stylized, figurative, emblematic.
2 *he wrote the prescription in hieroglyphic handwriting*: **illegible**, indecipherable, unreadable, scribbled, scrawled, squiggly.

higgledy-piggledy informal adjective *a higgledy-piggledy mountain of newspapers*: **disordered**, disorderly, untidy, disorganized, messy, chaotic, jumbled, muddled, confused, unsystematic, irregular, cluttered, littered; out of order, out of place, in disarray, in a mess, in a jumble, in a muddle, upside-down, at sixes and sevens, haywire, haphazard; informal all over the place, like a bomb's hit it; Brit. informal shambolic, all over the shop; N. Amer. informal all over the map, all over the lot; rare orderless.
▷ANTONYMS tidy, ordered.
▶ adverb *the cars were parked higgledy-piggledy*: **in disorder**, in a muddle, in a jumble, in disarray, in a disorganized manner, untidily, haphazardly, indiscriminately, in a mess, in confusion, in a heap, anyhow, any old how, pell-mell, topsy-turvy; informal all over the place, every which way; Brit. informal all over the shop; N. Amer. informal all over the map, all over the lot.
▷ANTONYMS tidily, in an orderly fashion.

high adjective 1 *the top of a high mountain*: **tall**, lofty, towering, soaring, elevated, giant, big; multi-storey, high-rise, sky-scraping.
▷ANTONYMS short.

2 *he is in a high position in the government*: **high-ranking**, high-level, leading, top, top-level, prominent, eminent, pre-eminent, foremost, senior, influential, distinguished, powerful, important, elevated, notable, principal, prime, premier, chief, main, upper, ruling, exalted, illustrious; N. Amer. ranking; informal top-notch.
▷ANTONYMS low-ranking, lowly.
3 *you should hold on to your high principles*: **high-minded**, noble-minded, lofty, moral, ethical, honourable, admirable, upright, principled, honest, virtuous, righteous.
▷ANTONYMS amoral.
4 *shop around to avoid high prices*: **inflated**, excessive, unreasonable, overpriced, sky-high, unduly expensive, dear, costly, top, exorbitant, extortionate, outrageous, prohibitive; Brit. over the odds; informal steep, stiff, pricey, over the top, OTT, criminal.
▷ANTONYMS reasonable.
5 *I have always insisted upon high standards*: **excellent**, outstanding, exemplary, exceptional, admirable, fine, great, good, very good, first-class, first-rate, superior, superlative, superb, commendable, laudable, praiseworthy, meritorious, blameless, faultless, flawless, impeccable, irreproachable, unimpeachable, perfect, unequalled, unparalleled; informal tip-top, A1, top-notch; rare applaudable.
▷ANTONYMS poor, deplorable.
6 *it was freezing cold with high winds*: **strong**, powerful, violent, intense, extreme, forceful, sharp, stiff; blustery, gusty, stormy, squally, tempestuous, turbulent; rare boisterous.
▷ANTONYMS light; calm.
7 *he lived the high life among the London glitterati*: **luxurious**, lavish, extravagant, rich, grand, sybaritic, hedonistic, opulent; prodigal, overindulgent, intemperate, immoderate; Brit. upmarket; N. Amer. upscale; informal fancy, classy, swanky.
▷ANTONYMS abstemious.
8 *I have a high opinion of your talents*: **favourable**, good, positive, approving, admiring, complimentary, commendatory, appreciative, flattering, glowing, adulatory, approbatory, rapturous, full of praise; rare panegyrical, acclamatory, laudative, encomiastical.
▷ANTONYMS unfavourable.
9 *the voices rose to hit a high note*: **high-pitched**, high-frequency, soprano, treble, falsetto, shrill, acute, sharp, piping, piercing, penetrating.
▷ANTONYMS low-pitched, deep.
10 informal *some of them were already high on alcohol and Ecstasy*: **intoxicated**, inebriated, on drugs, drugged, stupefied, befuddled, delirious, hallucinating; informal on a high, stoned, turned on, on a trip, tripping, hyped up, freaked out, spaced out, zonked, wasted, wrecked, high as a kite, off one's head, out of one's mind, flying, charged up.
▷ANTONYMS sober.
11 *the partridges were pretty high*: **gamy**, smelly, strong-smelling; stinking, reeking, rank, malodorous, going bad, going off, off, rotting, spoiled, tainted; Brit. informal pongy, niffy, whiffy; N. Amer. informal funky; literary noisome, miasmic.
▷ANTONYMS fresh; aromatic.
□ **high and dry** *your family would be left high and dry by the death of the breadwinner*: **destitute**, bereft, helpless, without help, without assistance, without resources, in the lurch, in difficulties, forsaken, abandoned, stranded, marooned.
▷ANTONYMS well provided for.
□ **high and mighty** informal *her family were high and mighty and gave themselves airs*: **self-important**, condescending, patronizing, disdainful, supercilious, superior, snobbish, snobby, haughty, arrogant, proud, conceited, above oneself, egotistic, egotistical, imperious, overweening, overbearing; informal stuck-up, snooty, snotty, hoity-toity, la-di-da, uppity, uppish, too big for one's boots; Brit. informal posh, toffee-nosed.
▷ANTONYMS unassuming, modest.
□ **in high dudgeon** See **dudgeon**.
▶noun *commodity prices were actually at a rare high*: **high level**, high point, record level, peak, record, high water mark; top, pinnacle, zenith, apex, acme, apogee, apotheosis, culmination, climax, height, summit.
▷ANTONYMS low.
□ **on a high** informal *he was on a high following his team's triumph*: **ecstatic**, euphoric, delirious, elated, thrilled, overjoyed, beside oneself, walking on air, on cloud nine/seven, in seventh heaven, jumping for joy, in transports of delight, carried away, transported, rapturous, in raptures, exultant, jubilant, in a frenzy of delight; excited, overexcited, hysterical, wild with excitement, frenzied; informal blissed out, over the moon, on top of the world; N. Amer. informal wigged out; Austral./NZ informal wrapped; rare corybantic.
▷ANTONYMS depressed.
▶adverb *a jet was flying high overhead*: **at great height**, high up, far up, way up, at altitude; in the air, in the sky, on high, aloft, overhead, above one's head, over one's head.
▷ANTONYMS low.
□ **high and low** *we searched for her high and low*: **everywhere**, all over, all around, in all places, in every place, far and wide, far and near, {here, there, and everywhere}, extensively, exhaustively, thoroughly, widely, broadly, in every nook and cranny; informal all over the place, every which way; Brit. informal all over the shop; N. Amer. informal all over the map.
▷ANTONYMS in a cursory way.

Word links **high**
acrophobia, **hypsophobia** fear of high places **batophobia** fear of high buildings

high-born adjective *a high-born Portuguese family*: **noble**, aristocratic, of noble birth, noble-born, well born, titled, patrician, blue-blooded, upper-class; Brit. county; informal posh, upper-crust, top-drawer; archaic gentle, of gentle birth.
▷ANTONYMS plebeian, working-class.

highbrow adjective *innovatory art had a small, mostly highbrow following*: **intellectual**, scholarly, bookish, cultured, cultivated, academic, educated, studious, serious, donnish, bluestocking, well read, widely read, well informed, sophisticated, erudite, learned; informal brainy, egghead; archaic lettered, clerkly.
▷ANTONYMS lowbrow, unsophisticated.
▶noun *highbrows who squirm when they hear popular music*: **intellectual**, scholar, academic, bluestocking, bookish person, man/woman of letters, don, thinker, pedant; informal egghead, brain, bookworm; Brit. informal brainbox, boffin; N. Amer. informal brainiac, rocket scientist, Brahmin.
▷ANTONYMS lowbrow, philistine.

high-class adjective *a high-class boarding school*: **superior**, upper-class, first-rate, high-quality, top-quality, high-grade, excellent, select, elite, exclusive, choice, premier, top, top-flight, grade A; luxurious, de luxe, elegant, fancy; Brit. upmarket; N. Amer. high-toned; informal tip-top, top-notch, top-drawer, A1, stellar, super, super-duper, classy, posh; Brit. informal, dated top-hole; Austral./NZ informal bonzer; Brit. informal, dated spiffing, topping.
▷ANTONYMS low-class, ordinary.

higher-up noun informal *he gave staff a vacation without getting approval from higher-ups*: **superior**, senior, supervisor, controller, overseer, administrator, manager, boss, chief, superintendent; informal bossman, skipper; Brit. informal gaffer, guv'nor; N. Amer. informal honcho.
▷ANTONYMS subordinate.

highfalutin adjective informal *the report was cloaked in highfalutin language*: **pretentious**, affected, high-sounding, high-flown, lofty, grandiose, magniloquent grandiloquent, ornate, florid, flowery, overblown, overdone, overwrought, verbose, inflated, rhetorical, oratorical, turgid; **pompous**, bombastic, declamatory, sonorous, portentous, pedantic, boastful, boasting, bragging; informal windy, purple, la-di-da, fancy-pants, hoity-toity; Brit. informal poncey, posh; rare fustian, euphuistic, orotund, tumid.
▷ANTONYMS unpretentious.

high-flown adjective *his novels seem high-flown and absurd*: **grand-sounding**, high-sounding, extravagant, exaggerated, elaborate, flowery, florid, ornate, overblown, overdone, overwrought, grandiloquent, magniloquent, grandiose, lofty, rhetorical, oratorical, verbose, inflated, affected, pretentious, turgid, bombastic, declamatory; informal windy, purple, highfalutin, la-di-da; rare fustian, euphuistic, orotund, tumid.
▷ANTONYMS plain.

high-handed adjective *people are becoming disenchanted with his high-handed approach*: **imperious**, arbitrary, peremptory, arrogant, haughty, domineering, bossy, overbearing, overweening, heavy-handed, high and mighty, lordly, inflexible, rigid; **autocratic**, authoritarian, dictatorial, oppressive, repressive, despotic, tyrannical; informal pushy, cocky; rare pushful.
▷ANTONYMS liberal.

high jinks plural noun *they get up to all kinds of high jinks on their trips away*: **antics**, **pranks**, larks, escapades, stunts, practical jokes, tricks, romps, frolics; **fun**, fun and games, skylarking, mischief, horseplay, silliness, foolish behaviour, tomfoolery, foolery, clowning, buffoonery; informal shenanigans, capers; Brit. informal monkey tricks, monkey business; N. Amer. informal didoes; archaic harlequinades.

highland noun *Peru's Andean highland*: **uplands**, highlands, mountains, hills, heights, moors, hilly country, mountainous region; plateau, upland, tableland, mesa, elevated plain, ridge; Brit. wolds.
▷ANTONYMS lowland.

highlight noun 1 *he views that season as the highlight of his career*: **high point**, high spot, best part, climax, culmination, peak, pinnacle, height, top, acme, zenith, apex, summit, apogee, apotheosis, crowning moment, high water mark, most memorable part, most outstanding feature; Latin ne plus ultra.
▷ANTONYMS lowest point, nadir.
2 *the highlight of the lunch will be a speech by the minister*: **main feature**, focal point, focus, focus of attention, centre of interest, most interesting part, cynosure.
▶verb *this has highlighted a number of shortcomings in the technical arrangements*: **call attention to**, focus attention on, focus on, spotlight, foreground, underline, underscore, feature, point up, play up, show up,

bring out, accentuate, accent, give prominence to, bring to the fore, zero in on, bring home to one, stress, emphasize, place emphasis on, give emphasis to.
▷ANTONYMS play down.

highly adverb **1** *a highly dangerous substance*: **very**, most, really, thoroughly, extremely, exceedingly, particularly, tremendously, hugely, greatly, decidedly, distinctly, exceptionally, immensely, eminently, supremely, inordinately, singularly, extraordinarily, vastly, overly; very much, to a great extent; Scottish unco; French très; N. English right; informal terrifically, awfully, terribly, devilishly, madly, majorly, seriously, desperately, mega, ultra, oh-so, too-too, stinking, mucho, damn, damned, too ... for words; informal, dated devilish, hellish, frightfully; Brit. informal ever so, well, bloody, dead, dirty, jolly, fair; N. Amer. informal real, mighty, powerful, awful, plumb, darned, way, bitching; S. African informal lekker; archaic exceeding, sore.
▷ANTONYMS slightly.
2 *he was highly regarded by his colleagues*: **favourably**, well, warmly, appreciatively, admiringly, approvingly, positively, glowingly, enthusiastically, with praise, with admiration, with approbation.
▷ANTONYMS unfavourably, disparagingly.

highly strung adjective *a young artist with a highly strung temperament*: **nervous**, excitable, temperamental, sensitive, unstable, brittle, easily upset, easily agitated, on edge, edgy, jumpy, keyed up, irritable, fidgety, restive, restless, anxious, overanxious, tense, taut, stressed, overwrought, neurotic; Brit. nervy; informal uptight, twitchy, wired, wound up, het up; Brit. informal strung up; Austral./NZ informal toey; dated overstrung.
▷ANTONYMS easy-going.

high-minded adjective *high-minded civil libertarians*: **high-principled**, principled, honourable, moral, upright, upstanding, right-minded, right-thinking, noble-minded, good, honest, decent, ethical, righteous, virtuous, worthy, idealistic.
▷ANTONYMS unprincipled.

high-mindedness noun *he had a reputation for honour and high-mindedness*: **integrity**, **principle**, honour, honourableness, morals, morality, uprightness, right-mindedness, noble-mindedness, decency, goodness, honesty, righteousness, rectitude, probity, virtue, nobility, scrupulousness, incorruptibility.
▷ANTONYMS dishonourableness.

high-pitched adjective *his voice was high-pitched*: **high**, high-frequency, soprano, treble, falsetto, shrill, acute, sharp, piping, piercing, penetrating.
▷ANTONYMS low-pitched, deep.

high-powered adjective *the women described themselves as high-powered careerists*: **dynamic**, energetic, ambitious, go-ahead, assertive, fast-track, effective, enterprising, vigorous, forceful, aggressive, pushy, pushing, driving; informal go-getting, full of get-up-and-go, high-octane; N. Amer. informal go-go.
▷ANTONYMS unambitious.

high-pressure adjective *unscrupulous salesmen using high-pressure tactics*: **forceful**, insistent, persistent, persuasive, pressurizing, pushy, pushing, intensive, high-powered, importunate, aggressive, bludgeoning, coercive, compelling, thrusting, not taking no for an answer; rare pushful.
▷ANTONYMS laid-back.

high-priced adjective *there is a growing market for high-priced wines*: **expensive**, costly, high-cost, dear, overpriced, exorbitant, extortionate, immoderate, extravagant; Brit. upmarket, over the odds; informal pricey, steep, stiff, costing an arm and a leg, costing the earth, costing a bomb.
▷ANTONYMS inexpensive.

high-sounding adjective *they clouded the issues with high-sounding words*: **grand-sounding**, grandiloquent, magniloquent, high-flown, extravagant, exaggerated, elaborate, flowery, florid, ornate, overblown, overdone, overwrought, grandiose, lofty, rhetorical, oratorical; verbose, inflated, affected, pretentious, turgid, bombastic, declamatory; informal windy, purple, highfalutin, la-di-da; rare fustian, euphuistic, orotund, tumid.
▷ANTONYMS plain.

high-speed adjective *a modern high-speed train operates between the major cities*: **fast**, fast-moving, quick, rapid, speedy, swift, breakneck, lightning, whistle-stop, brisk, prompt, expeditious; turbo, sporty; express, non-stop, direct, uninterrupted; informal nippy, zippy, souped-up, supersonic; rare fleet, tantivy, alacritous, volant.
▷ANTONYMS slow; indirect.

high-spirited adjective *he is just an ordinary, high-spirited little boy*: **lively**, spirited, full of life, full of fun, fun-loving, animated, vibrant, vital, zestful, dynamic, active, energetic, vigorous, boisterous, bouncy, bubbly, sparkling, vivacious, effervescent, buoyant, cheerful, joyful, exuberant, ebullient, jaunty, irrepressible; informal chirpy, peppy, sparky, bright-eyed and bushy-tailed, bright and breezy, full of beans, full of vim and vigour; N. Amer. informal peart; archaic frolicsome.
▷ANTONYMS lifeless, apathetic.

high spirits plural noun *they were young, strong, and bursting with high spirits*: **liveliness**, vitality, spirit, spiritedness, animation, zest, dynamism, energy, vigour, boisterousness, bounciness, sparkle, vivacity, buoyancy, cheerfulness, good cheer, good humour, joy, joyfulness, exuberance, ebullience, verve; French joie de vivre; informal go, pep, oomph, pizzazz, zing, zip, fizz.
▷ANTONYMS lifelessness, apathy.
□ **in high spirits** *the team were in high spirits following their victory*: **ebullient**, buoyant, cheerful, sunny, breezy, jaunty, light-hearted, high-spirited, exhilarated, excited, elated, exultant, euphoric, joyful, cheery, merry, jubilant, sparkling, effervescent, vivacious, enthusiastic, irrepressible, energetic, animated, full of life, lively, vigorous, zestful; informal bubbly, bouncy, peppy, zingy, upbeat, chipper, chirpy, smiley, sparky, full of beans; N. Amer. informal peart; dated gay; literary gladsome, blithe, blithesome; archaic as merry as a grig, of good cheer.
▷ANTONYMS gloomy.

highwayman noun historical **bandit**, brigand, robber, outlaw, ruffian, desperado, plunderer, marauder, raider, ravager, pillager, freebooter, criminal, thug, gangster; Spanish bandolero, ladrone; Indian dacoit; informal, dated knight of the road, footpad, land-pirate, tobyman; archaic reaver, snaphance, thief errant; Scottish archaic mosstrooper.

hijack verb *three armed men hijacked a white van*: **commandeer**, seize, take over, take possession of, skyjack; appropriate, expropriate, confiscate; informal snatch.

hike noun *a 21-mile hike on the North Yorkshire Moors*: **walk**, trek, tramp, trudge, traipse, slog, footslog, plod, march, journey on foot; ramble, wander, stroll; Brit. informal yomp; archaic peregrination, perambulation.
▷ANTONYMS drive.
□ **take a hike** N. Amer. informal *he essentially told them to take a hike*: **go away**, get out, leave; be off with you!, shoo!, make yourself scarce!, on your way!; informal beat it, push off, clear off, clear out, shove off, scram, scoot, skedaddle, buzz off; Brit. informal hop it, sling your hook; Austral./NZ informal rack off; N. Amer. informal bug off; S. African informal voetsak, hamba; vulgar slang piss off, bugger off; archaic begone.
▶ verb *they hiked across the moors for miles*: **walk**, go on foot, trek, tramp, trudge, traipse, slog, footslog, plod, march; ramble, wander, stroll; informal hoof it, leg it, take Shanks's pony; Brit. informal yomp, trog; rare peregrinate, perambulate.
▷ANTONYMS drive.
□ **hike something up 1** *Roy hiked up his trousers to reveal his socks*: **hitch up**, pull up, jerk up, lift, raise, hoist; informal yank up. ▷ANTONYMS pull down.
2 *the government hiked up the price of milk by 40 per cent*: **increase**, raise, up, put up, mark up, push up, make higher, inflate; informal jack up, bump up; dated advance.
▷ANTONYMS lower.

hilarious adjective **1** *she told hilarious stories about her friends*: **very funny**, extremely amusing, hysterically funny, hysterical, uproarious, riotous, farcical, side-splitting, rib-tickling, too funny for words; humorous, entertaining, comic, chucklesome; informal priceless, a scream, a hoot; dated killing, killingly funny.
▷ANTONYMS sad.
2 *we had a really hilarious evening*: **amusing**, entertaining, animated, high-spirited, lively, funny, witty, droll, merry, jolly, jovial, jocular, mirthful, cheerful, vivacious, sparkling, uproarious, boisterous, noisy, rowdy; informal wacky.
▷ANTONYMS serious.

hilarity noun *his incredulous expression was the cause of much hilarity*: **amusement**, mirth, laughter, merriment, light-heartedness, levity, fun, humour, jocularity, jollity, joviality, gaiety, delight, glee, comedy, frivolity, exuberance, boisterousness, high spirits; dated sport.
▷ANTONYMS seriousness.

hill noun **1** *he lived in a big house at the top of the hill*: **high ground**, rising ground, prominence, eminence, elevation, rise, hillock, mound, mount, knoll, hummock, tor, tump, fell, pike, mesa; bank, ridge, hogback, saddleback, whaleback; **(hills) heights**, downs, downland, foothills; Geology drumlin, inselberg, monadnock; Brit. wold; Scottish & Irish drum; Scottish brae; N. Amer. or technical butte; S. African koppie, berg; in N. Africa & the Middle East jebel; archaic holt.
▷ANTONYMS plain.
2 *they were climbing a steep hill in low gear*: **slope**, rise, drop, incline, gradient, elevation, acclivity, declivity, ascent, descent, eminence, hillside, hillock, sloping ground, rising ground.
▷ANTONYMS flat ground.
3 *a hill of rubbish*: **heap**, pile, stack, mass, mound, mountain, quantity, load; Scottish, Irish, & N. English rickle; Scottish bing; rare amassment.
□ **over the hill** informal *it was generally believed that over 30 was over the hill in tennis*: **past one's prime**, not as young as one was, not as young as one used to be; in one's dotage, long in the tooth, as old as the hills; elderly, old, aged, senior, ancient, venerable; decrepit, doddering, doddery, not long for this world; informal past it, no spring chicken; formal senescent.

hillock noun **mound**, small hill, prominence, eminence, elevation, rise, knoll, hummock, hump, tump, dune, barrow, tumulus; bank, ridge; N. English howe; N. Amer. knob; S. African koppie; archaic knap, monticle.

h

hilt noun **handle**, haft, handgrip, grip, shaft, shank, stock, helve.
▷ANTONYMS head, blade.
□ **to the hilt** *we will support our leaders to the hilt*: **completely**, fully, wholly, totally, entirely, utterly, unreservedly, unconditionally, in every respect, in all respects, one hundred per cent, every inch, to the full, to the maximum extent, all the way, body and soul, heart and soul.
▷ANTONYMS partially, to a limited extent.

himself pronoun
□ **by himself** See **by oneself** at **by**.

hind adjective *the horse shied and stood up on its hind legs*: **back**, rear, hinder, hindmost, posterior; technical dorsal, caudal, posticous.
▷ANTONYMS fore, front.

hinder verb *technical difficulties have hindered our progress*: **hamper**, be a hindrance to, obstruct, impede, inhibit, retard, baulk, thwart, foil, baffle, curb, delay, arrest, interfere with, set back, slow down, hold back, hold up, forestall, stop, halt; restrict, restrain, constrain, block, check, curtail, frustrate, cramp, handicap, cripple, hamstring, shackle, fetter, encumber; informal stymie; Brit. informal throw a spanner in the works of, throw a spoke in the wheel of; N. Amer. informal bork, throw a monkey wrench in the works of; rare cumber, trammel.
▷ANTONYMS help; facilitate.

Choose the right word **hinder, hamper, impede, obstruct**

All these words apply to making progress slower or more difficult.

Hinder refers generally to the creation of difficulties or delays that hold people back from doing something or prevent processes from proceeding smoothly (*ministers were suspected of deliberately hindering the progress of the bill*).

Hamper is typically used of physical burdens that weigh someone down or make their movement awkward (*he was laden with parcels and further hampered by an enormous umbrella*), and, by extension, it is applied to problems and handicaps that interfere with effective action (*they were hampered by shortage of funds*). It rarely refers to a deliberate action or has a person as its subject.

Impede refers to slowing something down or getting in the way (*rivers impeded north–south communications | in what ways did economic factors impede progress?*).

Obstruct is used primarily of a physical object that literally blocks the way (*the horse charged between the trees which obstructed its path*). Its use is extended to the typically deliberate creation of non-physical obstacles, making something difficult though usually not impossible (*he was charged with obstructing the police investigation*), and is often used in legal or criminal contexts.

hindmost adjective *you should all follow the stroke of the hindmost oar in the boat*: **furthest back**, last, rear, rearmost, end, endmost, final, tail, aftermost, nearest the rear, at the end, furthest behind.
▷ANTONYMS first, leading.

hindrance noun *the bad weather was a major hindrance to the relief effort*: **impediment**, obstacle, barrier, bar, obstruction, handicap, block, check, curb, brake, hurdle, restraint, restriction, limitation, encumbrance, deterrent, complication, delay, interruption, stoppage; drawback, setback, difficulty, inconvenience, snag, catch, hitch, stumbling block; informal fly in the ointment, hiccup, facer; Brit. informal spanner in the works; N. Amer. informal monkey wrench in the works; literary trammel, cumber.
▷ANTONYMS help; advantage.

hinge verb *the future of the industry could* **hinge on** *the outcome of next month's election*: **depend**, hang, rest, turn, pivot, centre, be based, be contingent, be dependent, be conditional; be subject to, be determined by, be decided by, revolve around.

hint noun **1** *he had given no hint that he was going to leave*: **clue**, inkling, suggestion, indication, indicator, sign, signal, pointer, intimation, insinuation, innuendo, mention, allusion, whisper, a word to the wise.
2 *handy hints about what to buy*: **tip**, suggestion, piece of advice, word of advice, pointer, clue, cue, guideline, recommendation; advice, help; informal how-to, wrinkle.
3 *the wine had a fresh flavour, with a hint of mint*: **trace**, touch, suspicion, suggestion, dash, soupçon, tinge, modicum, breath, whiff, taste, scent, whisper, undertone; informal smidgen, sniff, tad.
▷ANTONYMS lashings.
▶ verb *he has hinted that his ambitions lie in Hollywood | what are you hinting at?* **imply**, insinuate, intimate, suggest, indicate, signal, whisper, give a clue, give an inkling, let it be known, allude to the fact, make a reference to the fact, refer to the fact, give someone to understand, give someone to believe; **allude to**, refer to, drive at, mean; informal get at.

Choose the right word **hint, suggestion, innuendo, insinuation**

A **hint** is a message that one person conveys to another without stating it explicitly, often because it is a request or involves something that they are embarrassed to say directly. It may be conveyed verbally or through someone's behaviour (*the girl dropped increasingly blatant hints about her affair | she picked up her book, but Sandra did not take the hint*). *Hint* can also refer to an explicit piece of practical advice or information given (*handy hints for home buyers*) or a trace of something (*smoked gammon with a hint of chilli*).

A **suggestion** is an idea put forward for consideration without any implication of indirectness or concealment (*he shrugged off suggestions that he was planning to quit politics*). This sense tends to merge with that of a 'piece of advice' (*Louise made her suggestion that Nora leave the girl behind*).

Innuendo is an indirect way of conveying an idea through the undertones and implications of what is said. The message conveyed typically has a sexual content or is to someone's discredit (*walk away, unless you are in the mood to parry age-old male posturings and sexual innuendo | innuendos about his sources of finance*).

Insinuation is the most consistently negative of these words. Whereas *innuendo* may sometimes refer to an exploitation of implicit meanings that is intended simply to amuse, an *insinuation* is always meant to hurt or distress someone by implying (but not directly stating) something to their discredit (*she faced insinuations about the immorality of her private life*).

hinterland noun *early settlers were driven from the coastal areas into the hinterland*: **the back of beyond**, the middle of nowhere, the backwoods, the wilds, the bush, remote areas, a backwater; Austral./NZ the outback, the back country, the backblocks, the booay; S. African the backveld, the platteland; informal the sticks; N. Amer. informal the boondocks, the boonies, the tall timbers; Austral./NZ informal Woop Woop, beyond the black stump.
▷ANTONYMS civilization.

hip adjective informal *it's becoming hip to be environmentally conscious*. See **fashionable**.

hippy noun **flower child**, bohemian, dropout, free spirit, nonconformist, unconventional person; (**hippies**) flower people.

hips plural noun **pelvis**, hindquarters, haunches, thighs, loins, buttocks, posterior, rear.

Word links **hips**

sciatic relating to the hips

hire verb **1** *we hired a car and drove to Wales*: **rent**, lease, charter, pay for the use of; dated engage.
▷ANTONYMS buy.
2 *management hired and fired labour in line with demand*: **employ**, engage, recruit, appoint, take on, sign on, sign up, enrol, commission, enlist, take into employment, secure the services of, put on the payroll.
▷ANTONYMS dismiss.
▶ noun *the agreed rate for the hire of the machine*: **rent**, rental, hiring, lease, leasing, charter; dated engagement, engaging.
▷ANTONYMS purchase.

hire purchase noun *these schemes are a flexible form of hire purchase*: **instalment plan**, instalment-payment plan, HP, credit, finance, instalments, deferred payment, easy terms; N. Amer. instalment buying; Brit. informal the never-never.

hirsute adjective *the rest of his body was similarly hirsute*: **hairy**, shaggy, bushy, hair-covered, long-haired, woolly, furry, fleecy, fuzzy; bearded, unshaven, unshorn, bewhiskered, stubbly, bristly; technical pilose, pileous, pappose, hispid; rare crinite, crinigerous.
▷ANTONYMS hairless; short-haired.

hiss verb **1** *the escaping gas was now hissing*: **fizz**, fizzle, whistle, wheeze, buzz, shrill; rare sibilate.
2 *the audience hissed loudly at the mention of his name*: **jeer**, catcall, utter catcalls, whistle, shout disapproval; scoff, taunt, hoot, jibe, deride; informal blow raspberries.
▷ANTONYMS cheer.
▶ noun **1** *the hiss of the escaping steam*: **fizz**, fizzing, whistle, hissing, sibilance, wheeze, wheezing, buzz, buzzing; rare sibilation.
2 *the speaker received hisses and boos*: **jeer**, catcall, whistle, shout of derision, raspberry; (**hisses**) abuse, scoffing, taunting, derision; Brit. informal the bird.
▷ANTONYMS cheer.

historian noun **chronicler**, annalist, archivist, recorder, biographer, historiographer, palaeographer, antiquarian, chronologist.

historic adjective *we are standing on a historic site | historic events*: **famous**, famed, important, significant, notable, celebrated, renowned, momentous, consequential, outstanding, extraordinary, memorable, unforgettable, remarkable, landmark, groundbreaking, epoch-making, red-letter, of importance, of significance, of consequence, earth-shaking, earth-shattering.
▷ANTONYMS insignificant.

historical adjective **1** *the historical background to such studies*: **documented**, recorded, chronicled, attested, factual, verified, confirmed,

archival, authentic, actual, true.
▷ANTONYMS legendary.
2 *famous historical figures*: **past**, bygone, ancient, old, former, prior, from the past; literary of yore.
▷ANTONYMS contemporary.

history noun **1** *this is a wonderful opportunity to use my interest in history*: **the past**, former times, historical events, days of old, the old days, the good old days, time gone by, bygone days, yesterday, antiquity; literary days of yore, the olden days, yesteryear; archaic the eld.
▷ANTONYMS the future.
2 *I was reading a history of the Civil War*: **chronicle**, archive, record, report, narrative, story, account, study, tale, saga; memoir, biography, autobiography; public records, annals.
3 *Kirsty calmly related the details of her history*: **background**, past, family background, life story, antecedents; experiences, adventures, fortunes.

Word links **history**

Clio the Muse of history

histrionic adjective *a histrionic outburst*: **melodramatic**, theatrical, affected, dramatic, exaggerated, actressy, stagy, showy, artificial, overacted, overdone, unnatural, mannered, stilted, unreal; informal hammy, ham, camp.
▷ANTONYMS unaffected.

histrionics plural noun **dramatics**, drama, theatrics, theatricality, tantrums; **affectation**, staginess, artificiality, unnaturalness.

hit verb **1** *the woman hit her child for stealing sweets*: **strike**, slap, smack, cuff, punch, beat, thrash, thump, batter, belabour, drub, hook, pound, smash, slam, welt, pummel, hammer, bang, knock, swat, whip, flog, cane, sucker-punch, rain blows on, give someone a (good) beating/drubbing, box someone's ears; informal whack, wallop, bash, biff, bop, clout, clip, clobber, sock, swipe, crown, lick, beat the living daylights out of, give someone a (good) hiding, belt, tan, lay one on, lay into, pitch into, lace into, let someone have it, knock into the middle of next week, lam, whomp, deck, floor; Brit. informal stick one on, dot, slosh, twat; N. Amer. informal slug, boff, bust, whale; Austral./NZ informal dong, quilt, king-hit; literary smite, swinge; dated baste, buffet, birch.
2 *a car hit the barrier*: **crash into**, run into, bang into, smash into, smack into, knock into, bump into, cannon into, plough into, collide with, meet head-on; N. Amer. impact; N. Amer. informal barrel into.
3 *the banking sector has been hit by the recession | the tragedy has hit her hard*: **affect badly**, devastate, damage, harm, hurt, ruin, leave a mark on, have a negative effect on, have a negative impact on, do harm to, impinge on; **upset**, shatter, crush, shock, overwhelm, traumatize, touch, make suffer; informal knock back, knock for six, knock sideways, knock the stuffing out of.
▷ANTONYMS have no effect on.
4 informal *capital spending this year is likely to hit £1,800 million*: **reach**, attain, touch, arrive at, get to, rise to, climb to; achieve, accomplish, gain, secure.
▷ANTONYMS fall to.
5 *I was a mile away when it hit me that I had forgotten to get the information I needed*: **occur to**, strike, dawn on, come to; enter one's head, enter one's mind, cross one's mind, come to mind, spring to mind, flash across one's mind, come into one's consciousness.
□ **hit back** *prison officers* ***hit back at*** *the critical report*: **retaliate against**, respond to, reply to, react to, strike back at, counter, defend oneself against; rare controvert.
▷ANTONYMS turn the other cheek.
□ **hit home** *she could see that her remark had hit home*: **have the intended effect**, make the intended impression, strike home, hit the mark, be registered, be understood, be comprehended, get through, sink in.
▷ANTONYMS have no effect.
□ **hit it off** informal *they make an unlikely pair, but they've always hit it off*: **get on well**, get on, get along, be on good terms, be friends, be friendly, be compatible, relate well to each other, feel a rapport, see eye to eye, take to each other, warm to each other, find things in common; informal click, get on like a house on fire, be on the same wavelength.
▷ANTONYMS rub someone up the wrong way.
□ **hit on/upon** *she hit on a novel idea for fund-raising*: **discover**, come up with, think of, conceive of, dream up, work out, invent, create, originate, develop, devise, design, pioneer, uncover, contrive, realize; stumble on, chance on, light on, come upon, blunder on, arrive at; informal put one's finger on.
□ **hit out at** *he hit out at the government's lack of action*: **criticize**, attack, denounce, lash out at, rant at, inveigh against, rail against, fulminate against, run down, find fault with; condemn, censure, harangue, berate, upbraid, castigate, vilify, malign, assail, lambaste; informal knock, slam, hammer, blast, lay into, pitch into, lace into, bawl out, bad-mouth, tear someone off a strip, give someone hell, give someone a roasting; Brit. informal slate, slag off, monster, have a go at, rubbish; N. Amer. informal pummel, cut up; Austral./NZ informal bag; dated rate, reprobate; rare vituperate, excoriate, arraign, objurgate, asperse, anathematize, animadvert on, denunciate.
▷ANTONYMS praise.
▶ noun **1** *he took a few minutes to recover after a hit from behind | few structures can withstand a hit from a speeding car*: **blow**, thump, punch, knock, bang, thwack, box, cuff, slap, smack, spank, tap, crack, stroke, welt; impact, collision, bump, crash; informal whack, wallop, bash, belt, biff, clout, sock, swipe, clip, clobber; Brit. informal slosh; N. Amer. informal boff, bust, slug, whale; Austral./NZ dong; dated buffet.
2 *he could not resist a hit at his friend's religiosity*: **jibe**, taunt, jeer, sneer, barb, cutting remark, barbed remark, attack, insult; informal dig, put-down, crack, wisecrack.
▷ANTONYMS compliment.
3 *he was the director of many big hits*: **success**, box-office success, sell-out, winner, triumph, sensation; best-seller; French tour de force; informal knockout, crowd-puller, smash, smash hit, smasher, cracker, wow, biggie.
▷ANTONYMS failure, flop.

hitch verb **1** *she hitched the blanket around her*: **pull**, jerk, hike, lift, raise; informal yank.
2 *Thomas hitched the pony to his cart*: **harness**, yoke, couple, fasten, connect, attach, tie, tether, bind.
▷ANTONYMS unhitch.
3 informal *they hitched there and back*: **hitch-hike**; informal thumb a lift, hitch a lift.
▶ noun *everything went without a hitch*: **problem**, difficulty, snag, setback, catch, hindrance, obstacle, obstruction, complication, impediment, barrier, stumbling block, block, trouble; **hold-up**, interruption, delay, check, stoppage; informal headache, glitch, hiccup; Brit. informal spanner in the works; N. Amer. informal monkey wrench in the works.
□ **get hitched** informal *she got hitched last August to Rob, her boyfriend of two years*: **marry**, get married, wed, become man and wife, plight/pledge one's troth; informal tie the knot, walk down the aisle, take the plunge, get spliced, get yoked, say 'I do'; archaic become espoused.

hither adverb literary *a change of fortune summoned me hither*. See **here** (sense 3).

hitherto adverb *hitherto a part of French West Africa, Benin achieved independence in 1960*: **previously**, formerly, earlier, so far, thus far, before, beforehand, to date, as yet; until now, until then, up until now, up until then, till now, till then, up to now, up to then; rare heretofore.

hit-or-miss adjective *her work can be rather hit-or-miss*: **haphazard**, disorganized, undisciplined, erratic, unmethodical, uneven, careless, slapdash, slipshod, casual, offhand, remiss, cursory, lackadaisical, perfunctory, random, aimless, undirected, indiscriminate, trial-and-error; informal sloppy, all over the place, slap-happy; Brit. informal all over the shop.
▷ANTONYMS meticulous, systematic.

hoard noun *they found a secret hoard of paintings and porcelain*: **cache**, stockpile, stock, store, collection, supply, reserve, reservoir, fund, accumulation, heap, pile, mass, aggregation, conglomeration, treasure house, treasure trove; informal stash; rare amassment.
▶ verb *many of the boat people had hoarded rations*: **store**, store up, stock up on, stockpile, put aside, put by, put away, lay by, lay in, lay up, set aside, stow away, buy up, cache, amass, heap up, pile up, stack up; **collect**, save, gather, garner, accumulate, husband, squirrel away, put to one side, put away for a rainy day; informal stash away, salt away.
▷ANTONYMS squander.

Easily confused words **hoard or horde?**

These words are quite distinct in meaning despite their identical pronunciation. A **hoard** is a secret stock or store of something, as in *a hoard of treasure*. **Horde**, on the other hand, is a disparaging word for a large group of people, as in *hordes of fans descended on the stage*.

hoarder noun **collector**, saver, gatherer, accumulator, magpie, squirrel.

hoar frost noun **frost**, ground frost, rime, rime frost, verglas; informal Jack Frost; archaic hoar.

hoarse adjective *their voices were hoarse from shouting*: **rough**, harsh, croaky, croaking, throaty, gruff, husky, guttural, gravelly, growly, cracked, grating, rasping, raucous; rare stridulant.
▷ANTONYMS mellow; soft.

hoary adjective **1** *majestic old oaks and hoary willows*: **greyish-white**, grey, white, silver, silvery; frost-covered, frosty, rimy.
2 *he began to think of himself as a hoary ancient*: **elderly**, aged, old, getting on, ancient, venerable, long in the tooth, of an advanced age, advanced in years; grey-haired, white-haired, silvery-haired, grizzled, grizzly; informal past it, over the hill; rare longevous, senescent.
▷ANTONYMS young.
3 *the hoary old adage often used by Fleet Street editors*: **trite**, hackneyed, clichéd, banal, platitudinous, vapid, ordinary, commonplace, common, stock, conventional, stereotyped, predictable, overused, overdone, overworked, stale, worn out, time-worn, tired, threadbare, hack,

h

unimaginative, unoriginal, derivative, uninspired, prosaic, routine, pedestrian, run-of-the-mill; informal old hat, corny, played out; N. Amer. informal cornball, dime-store; rare truistic, bromidic.
▷ANTONYMS original.

hoax noun *they recognized the plan as a hoax*: **practical joke**, joke, jest, prank, trick, jape; **ruse**, deception, fraud, imposture, cheat, swindle, bluff, humbug, confidence trick; informal con, spoof, scam, fast one, put-on.
▶ verb *on April 1st the radio station hoaxed its listeners*: **play a practical joke on**, play a joke on, play a jest on, play a prank on, trick, fool; **deceive**, hoodwink, delude, dupe, take in, lead on, cheat, bluff, gull, humbug; informal con, kid, have on, pull a fast one on, put one over on, take for a ride, lead someone up the garden path, pull the wool over someone's eyes; informal, dated gammon; N. Amer. informal sucker, snooker, hornswoggle; Austral. informal pull a swifty on; vulgar slang bullshit; archaic cozen.

hoaxer noun **practical joker**, joker, prankster, trickster; fraudster, impostor, hoodwinker, swindler, cheat, confidence trickster; informal spoofer, con man; N. Amer. informal bunco artist; Austral. informal illywhacker.

hobble verb *he was hobbling around on crutches*: **limp**, walk with a limp, walk with difficulty, move unsteadily, walk unevenly, walk lamely, walk haltingly; shuffle, shamble, falter, totter, dodder, stagger, stumble, reel, lurch; Scottish hirple.
▷ANTONYMS stride.

h

hobby noun *her hobbies are reading and gardening*: **pastime**, leisure activity, leisure pursuit, leisure interest, amateur interest, sideline, diversion, avocation, divertissement, enthusiasm; recreation, relaxation, entertainment, amusement; informal thing.
▷ANTONYMS work, job.

hobgoblin noun **imp**, sprite, goblin, elf, brownie, pixie, leprechaun, gnome, dwarf; bogey, bogeyman, troll, evil spirit; Scottish kelpie; rare hob, nix, nixie, elfin.

hobnob verb informal *he was hobnobbing with the great and good*. See **mix** (sense 2 of the verb).

hocus-pocus noun **1** *he is a master of legal hocus-pocus*: **jargon**, unintelligible language, obscure language, mumbo-jumbo, argle-bargle, gibberish, balderdash, claptrap, nonsense, rubbish, twaddle; informal gobbledegook, double Dutch, hokum, bull, rot, garbage, tripe; N. Amer. informal flapdoodle; informal, dated bunkum.
2 *the hocus-pocus was just for the show*: **magic words**, magic formula, mumbo-jumbo, abracadabra, incantation, chant, invocation, charm.

hodgepodge noun See **hotchpotch**.

hog noun **pig**, sow, swine, porker, piglet, boar; children's word piggy; rare grunter, baconer.
▶ verb informal *he never hogged the limelight*: **monopolize**, keep to oneself, dominate, take over, corner, control; N. Amer. informal bogart.
▷ANTONYMS share.

hogwash noun informal *some of the statements in the article are undiluted hogwash*. See **nonsense**.

hoi polloi noun (**the hoi polloi**) *royalty are reluctant to let the hoi polloi into their homes*: **the masses**, the common people, the populace, the public, the people, the multitude, the rank and file, the lower orders, the crowd, the commonalty, the commonality, the commons, the third estate, the plebeians; derogatory the mob, the proletariat, the common herd, the herd, the rabble, the riff-raff, the canaille, the great unwashed, the many, the ragtag (and bobtail), the plebs, the proles, the peasants.
▷ANTONYMS the elite, the aristocracy.

hoist verb *as we travelled north we hoisted a large mainsail*: **raise**, raise up, lift, lift up, haul up, heave up, jack up, hike up, winch up, pull up, upraise, uplift, elevate, erect; rare upheave.
▷ANTONYMS lower.
▶ noun *mechanical lifts or hoists for firefighting purposes*: **lifting gear**, crane, winch, tackle, block and tackle, pulley, windlass, davit, derrick.

hoity-toity adjective informal *he's too hoity-toity to make friends with his fellow cadets*. See **haughty**.

hold verb **1** *she was holding a brown leather suitcase*: **clasp**, hold on to, clutch, grasp, grip, clench, cling to, have in one's hand; **carry**, bear; literary cleave to.
▷ANTONYMS release, let go of.
2 *I wanted to hold her in my arms*: **embrace**, hug, clasp, cradle, fold, enfold, envelop, squeeze, hold tight, hold in one's arms; literary embosom.
3 *candidates must hold a clean driving licence*: **possess**, have, own, bear, carry, be the owner of, have in one's possession, be in possession of, have to one's name.
4 *I reached up to the nearest branch which seemed likely to hold my weight*: **support**, bear, carry, take, hold up, keep up, sustain, prop up, bolster up, shore up, buttress, brace.
5 *the police were holding him on a murder charge*: **detain**, hold in custody, imprison, lock up, shut up, put behind bars, put in prison, put in jail, incarcerate, keep under lock and key, confine, impound, immure, intern, constrain, keep under constraint; informal put away, put inside.
▷ANTONYMS let go.
6 *their minimal costumes are a way of holding an audience's attention*: **maintain**, keep, keep up, keep alive, occupy, engross, absorb, interest, captivate, fascinate, enthral, rivet, monopolize; engage, catch, capture, grip, arrest.
▷ANTONYMS lose.
7 *he held a senior post in the Foreign Office*: **occupy**, have, be in, fill; informal hold down.
8 *the tank held twenty-four gallons | the church is big enough to hold 400 people*: **have a capacity of**, take, have room for, have space for, contain, comprise; **accommodate**, fit, seat, have seats for.
9 *they hold that all literature is empty of meaning | the Court of Appeal held that there was no evidence to support the judge's assessment*: **believe**, think, consider, take the view, feel, maintain, swear, deem, be of the opinion, subscribe to the opinion; **adjudge**, judge, rule, decide; N. Amer. **figure**; informal reckon; formal esteem, opine.
10 *let's hope the good weather holds for the rest of the week*: **continue**, carry on, go on, hold on, hold out, keep up, keep going, last, persist, endure, stay, remain, remain unchanged.
▷ANTONYMS end.
11 *I'll have that coffee now, if the offer still holds*: **remain available**, remain valid, remain in force, hold good, stand, apply, remain, exist, operate, obtain, be the case, be in force, be in operation, be in effect.
▷ANTONYMS be no longer valid.
12 *the president held a meeting with party leaders*: **convene**, call, assemble, summon; **conduct**, have, organize, run, preside over, officiate at; formal convoke.
▷ANTONYMS disband.
□ **hold back** *he held back, remembering the mistake he had made before*: **hesitate**, pause, stop oneself, restrain oneself, desist, forbear, discontinue, withhold from doing something, refrain from doing something.
▷ANTONYMS carry on.
□ **hold someone back** *my lack of experience held me back a bit*: **hinder**, hamper, inhibit, impede, obstruct, check, curb, block, thwart, baulk, hamstring, restrain, frustrate, retard, delay, prevent from making progress, stand in someone's way; informal stymie; N. Amer. informal bork; literary trammel.
▷ANTONYMS help, facilitate.
□ **hold something back 1** *Jane struggled to hold back the tears*: **suppress**, keep back, hold in, bite back, fight back, choke back, stifle, smother, subdue, rein in, repress, restrain, check, curb, control, keep in check, keep under control, keep a tight rein on; informal keep the lid on, button up, cork up. ▷ANTONYMS release.
2 *you're not holding anything back from me, are you?* **withhold**, hide, conceal, keep back, keep secret, keep hidden, keep silent about, keep quiet about, hush up, refuse to disclose, suppress; informal sit on, keep under one's hat. ▷ANTONYMS disclose.
□ **hold someone/something dear** *fidelity is something most of us hold dear*: **cherish**, treasure, prize, appreciate, value highly, rate highly, care very much for/about, place a high value on, attach great importance to, set great store by; informal put on a pedestal.
▷ANTONYMS think little of.
□ **hold someone down** *the people are held down by a repressive military regime*: **oppress**, repress, suppress, subdue, tyrannize, dominate, subjugate, keep down, keep under, keep in subjection, keep in submission.
□ **hold something down 1** *he is determined to hold down inflation*: **keep down**, keep low, keep at a low level, peg down, freeze, fix. **2** informal *holding down two jobs was proving tiring for him*: **occupy**, hold, have, be in, fill.
□ **hold forth** *he was holding forth about the qualities of good wine*: **speak at length**, talk at length, speak, talk, go on, sound off; **declaim**, discourse, spout, expatiate, pontificate, orate, preach, sermonize; lecture, harangue, fulminate; informal spiel, speechify, preachify, drone on; rare perorate.
□ **hold something in** *she tried to stop laughing, but it was too much to hold in*. See **hold something back** (sense 1).
□ **hold off 1** *fortunately, the rain held off until the evening*: **be delayed**, keep off, stay away, not begin, not occur, not happen, not arrive.
▷ANTONYMS start.
2 *if I was in their shoes, I'd hold off for a couple of days*: **wait**, hold back, pause, delay, hang back, hang fire, take no action, bide one's time, play a waiting game; postpone, defer, refrain from, put something off, keep from doing something, avoid doing something; informal hold one's horses, sit tight. ▷ANTONYMS proceed.
□ **hold something off** *he held off a late challenge by Vose to win by thirteen seconds*: **resist**, repel, repulse, rebuff, parry, deflect, keep off, fend off, stave off, ward off, keep at bay.
▷ANTONYMS submit to, be overpowered by.
□ **hold on 1** *hold on a minute, I'll be right back!* **wait**, wait a minute, just a moment, just a second, stay here, stay put, remain here; hold the line; informal hang on, hang around, stick around, sit tight, hold your horses; Brit. informal hang about; archaic or literary tarry. **2** *if only they could hold on a little longer*: **keep going**, keep on, survive, last, continue, persevere, struggle on, carry on, go on, hang on, hold out, not give up, see it through, stay the course; informal soldier on, stick at it, stick it out, hang in there.
▷ANTONYMS give up.

□ **hold on to 1** *he held on to the back of a chair*: **clutch**, hold, hang on to, clasp, grasp, grip, cling to; literary cleave to. ▷ANTONYMS release, let go of.
2 *the industry is trying to hold on to experienced staff*: **retain**, keep, hang on to, keep possession of, retain possession of, retain use of, retain ownership of, not sell, not give away, keep for oneself. ▷ANTONYMS lose.
□ **hold one's own** See **own**.
□ **hold out 1** *British troops **held out against** constant attacks*: **resist**, withstand, hold off, fight off, fend off, keep off, keep at bay, stand up to, square up to, fight against, bear up against, stand fast against, stand firm against, hold the line against. ▷ANTONYMS yield to.
2 *we can stay here as long as our supplies hold out*: **last**, remain, be extant, continue. ▷ANTONYMS run out.
□ **hold something out** *Celia held out her hand*: **extend**, proffer, offer, present, outstretch, reach out, stretch out, put out, hold forth; literary outreach.
▷ANTONYMS withdraw.
□ **hold something over** *the usual family gathering was held over until late January*: **postpone**, put off, put back, delay, defer, adjourn, suspend, shelve, hold in abeyance; N. Amer. put over, table, take a rain check on; informal put on ice, put on the back burner, put in cold storage, mothball; rare remit, respite.
▷ANTONYMS bring forward.
□ **hold the fort** See **fort**.
□ **hold up** *their views still seem to hold up extremely well*: **be convincing**, be logical, hold, hold water, bear examination, survive investigation, be verifiable, be provable.
▷ANTONYMS be unconvincing.
□ **hold something up 1** *they held up the trophy for all to see*: **display**, hold aloft, exhibit, show, show off, put on show, present, flourish, flaunt, brandish; informal flash. ▷ANTONYMS keep out of sight.
2 *concrete pillars hold up the elevated section of the motorway*: **support**, hold, bear, carry, take, sustain, keep up, prop up, bolster up, shore up, buttress.
3 *our return flight was held up for seven hours*: **delay**, detain, make late, set back, keep back, retard, slow down, slow up. ▷ANTONYMS speed up.
4 *a lack of cash has held up progress*: **obstruct**, **impede**, hinder, hamper, inhibit, baulk, thwart, curb, hamstring, frustrate, foil, baffle, be a hindrance to, interfere with, put a brake on, stop; informal stymie; Brit. informal throw a spanner in the works of, put a spoke in the wheel of; N. Amer. informal bork, throw a monkey wrench in the works of. ▷ANTONYMS facilitate.
5 *a masked raider held up the post office*: **rob**, commit armed robbery on, make an armed raid on; waylay, mug; informal stick up.
□ **hold water** See **water**.
□ **hold with** *I don't hold with fighting or violence*: **approve of**, agree with, be in favour of, go along with, endorse, accept, countenance, support, give support to, subscribe to, give one's blessing to, take kindly to; informal stand for, give the thumbs up to, give the okay to; Brit. informal be doing with; N. Amer. rare approbate.
▷ANTONYMS disapprove of.
▶ **noun 1** *the little girl kept a firm hold on my hand | he lost his hold and fell*: **grip**, grasp, clasp, clutch; **purchase**, foothold, footing, toehold.
2 *he discovered that Tom had some kind of hold over his father*: **influence**, power, control, dominance, pull, sway, mastery, authority, leverage; informal clout.
3 *military forces tightened their hold on the capital*: **control**, grip, power, stranglehold, dominion, authority, ascendancy.
□ **get hold of** informal **1** *if you can't get hold of ripe tomatoes, add some tomato purée*: **obtain**, acquire, get, find, come by, pick up, procure, get possession of; buy, purchase; informal get one's hands on, lay one's hands on, get one's mitts on. **2** *I'll try and get hold of Mark*: **contact**, get in touch with, communicate with, make contact with, approach, reach, notify, be in communication with; phone, call, speak to, talk to, write to; Brit. ring (up), get on to; informal drop a line to.
□ **put something on hold** *the proposed rematch has been put on hold*: **postpone**, put off, put back, hold off, defer, delay, adjourn, shelve, suspend, hold in abeyance; N. Amer. put over, take a rain check on; informal put on ice, put on the back burner, put in cold storage, mothball; rare remit, respite.
▷ANTONYMS bring forward.

holder noun **1** *a large knife in a leather holder*: **container**, receptacle, case, casing, cover, covering, housing, sheath; stand, rest, support, base, rack.
2 *a British passport holder | the holder of the office of commander-in-chief*: **bearer**, owner, possessor, keeper, proprietor; **incumbent**, occupant, custodian.

holdings plural noun *they have UK gilts and holdings in offshore funds*: **possessions**, belongings, valuables; **stock**, property, capital, estate; **assets**, funds, resources, savings, investments, securities, equities, bonds, stocks and shares, reserves.

hold-up noun **1** *I ran into a hold-up and nearly didn't get here*: **delay**, setback, hitch, snag, difficulty, problem, trouble, wait, waiting period, stoppage; **traffic jam**, jam, bottleneck, tailback, gridlock, congestion; informal snarl-up, glitch, hiccup.
2 *there has been another bank hold-up*: **robbery**, raid, armed robbery, armed raid, theft, burglary, mugging; informal stick-up, snatch; N. Amer. informal heist.

hole noun **1** *there was a hole in the roof where the tiles had fallen away*: **opening**, aperture, gap, space, orifice, slot, vent, outlet, chink, breach; **break**, crack, leak, rift, rupture; puncture, perforation, cut, incision, split, gash, rent, slit, cleft, crevice, fissure; spyhole, peephole, keyhole; Medicine foramen; archaic loophole.
2 *they were digging a hole in the ground*: **pit**, ditch, trench, cavity, crater, depression, hollow; well, borehole, excavation, shaft, mineshaft, dugout; cave, cavern, pothole, chamber, gorge, chasm, canyon, ravine.
3 *they dug the badger out of his hole*: **burrow**, lair, den, covert, earth, sett, drey, retreat, shelter, cave.
4 *the captives were thrown into a black hole*: **dungeon**, cell, underground cell, oubliette, prison.
5 *a recent article highlighted some holes in their argument*: **flaw**, fault, defect, weakness, weak point, shortcoming, inconsistency, discrepancy, loophole, error, mistake, fallacy.
6 informal *I was living in a real hole*: **hovel**, slum, shack, mess; informal dump, dive, pigsty, tip, joint.
▷ANTONYMS palace.
7 informal *they have been known to embezzle their clients' money when they are in a hole*. See **predicament**.
□ **pick holes in** informal *it's really not too difficult to pick holes in the plan*: **find fault with**, criticize, attack, condemn; disparage, denigrate, deride, belittle, run down, complain about, quibble about, carp about, cavil at, scoff at, moan about, grouse about, grouch about, grumble about, whine about; informal knock, bad-mouth, do down, gripe about, beef about, bellyache about, bitch about, whinge about, nit-pick over, sound off about, pull to pieces; Brit. informal slag off, have a go at, rubbish.
▷ANTONYMS praise.
▶ **verb** *a fuel tank was holed by the attack and a fire started*: **puncture**, make a hole in, perforate, pierce, penetrate, rupture, spike, stab, split, slit, rent, lacerate, gash, gore.
□ **hole up 1** *it was getting time for the bears to hole up*: **hibernate**, lie dormant, winter, overwinter, lie torpid, go to sleep. **2** informal *the snipers holed up in a nearby farmhouse*: **hide**, hide out, hide oneself, conceal oneself, secrete oneself, shelter, take cover, lie low, go to ground, go to earth, go underground; Brit. informal lie doggo.
▷ANTONYMS come out into the open.

hole-and-corner adjective *they expressed regret at the hole-and-corner tactics being used*: **secret**, secretive, in secret, private, clandestine; **underhand**, surreptitious, covert, furtive, devious, stealthy, sneaky, backstairs, closet, undercover, hugger-mugger, cloak-and-dagger, behind-the-scenes, under-the-table, under-the-counter; informal hush-hush.
▷ANTONYMS open, above board.

holiday noun **1** *she took a 10-day holiday*: **vacation**, break, rest, period of leave, day off, week off, month off, recess, school holiday, half-term; **time off**, time out, leave, leave of absence, furlough, sabbatical; trip, tour, journey, expedition, voyage; informal hols, vac; formal sojourn.
▷ANTONYMS working time; term time.
2 *in Antigua the twenty-fourth of May is a holiday*: **public holiday**, bank holiday, festival, festival day, feast day, gala day, carnival day, fête, fiesta, festivity, celebration, anniversary, jubilee; saint's day, holy day, religious festival, day of observance.
▷ANTONYMS working day.

> *Choose the right word* **holiday, vacation, leave, break**
>
> **Holiday** denotes a period when someone does not have to work. It can refer to: a day when most businesses are closed by law or custom (*10 June is a public holiday*), a period of time allowed off work (*staff are entitled to 24 working days' holiday per year*), time in between school terms (*the school summer holidays*), or a leisure trip away from home (*a driving holiday in France*).
>
> **Vacation** is used for the period between two law or university terms (*many students found jobs in the long vacation*), and is in addition the American term for a trip away from home (*your dream vacation in Mexico*).
>
> **Leave** is time off duty in the armed forces (*Joe was home on leave*) or a formal term for time off work for a variety of reasons (*sick leave | annual leave*).
>
> A **break** means any sort of pause, a short period of rest from work (*he wanted to talk to her during the coffee break*), or a shorter-than-average leisure trip away from home (*a weekend countryside break*).

holier-than-thou adjective *they had quite a critical, holier-than-thou approach*: **sanctimonious**, self-righteous, complacent, smug, self-satisfied, priggish, pious, pietistic, Pharisaic; Scottish unco guid; informal goody-goody, preachy; rare religiose.
▷ANTONYMS humble, meek.

holiness noun *a life of holiness and total devotion to God*: **sanctity**, divinity, godliness, saintliness, sanctitude, sacredness, faith, devotion, devoutness,

h

divineness, blessedness, spirituality, religiousness, piety, piousness, righteousness, goodness, perfection, virtue, virtuousness, purity, sinlessness.
▷ANTONYMS wickedness.

holler informal verb *he hollers when he wants feeding*: **shout**, yell, cry, cry out, call, call out, roar, howl, bellow, bawl, bark, shriek, scream, screech, bay, wail, whoop, boom, thunder, raise one's voice, call at the top of one's voice; rare vociferate.
▷ANTONYMS whisper.
▶ noun *the audience responded with whoops and hollers*: **shout**, cry, yell, roar, howl, bellow, bawl, shriek, scream, screech, bay, wail, whoop; rare vociferation.
▷ANTONYMS whisper.

hollow adjective **1** *each fibre has a hollow core*: **empty**, not solid, void, unfilled, vacant, hollowed out.
▷ANTONYMS solid.
2 *her cheeks were hollow and her face bony*: **sunken**, deep-set, concave, depressed, dented, indented, caved in; rare incurvate.
3 *'Goodbye,' he said in a hollow voice*: **dull**, low, flat, toneless, expressionless; muffled, muted; deep, rumbling, echoing, sepulchral.
4 *the result was a hollow victory*: **meaningless**, empty, valueless, worthless, useless, pyrrhic, futile, of no use, of no value, of no avail, fruitless, profitless, pointless, unavailing; archaic bootless.
▷ANTONYMS worthwhile.
5 *the women believed it was nothing but a hollow promise*: **insincere**, hypocritical, feigned, pretended, artificial, false, dissembling, dissimulating, deceitful, sham, cynical, counterfeit, spurious, untrue, unsound, flimsy, two-faced, double-dealing; informal phoney, pretend.
▷ANTONYMS sincere.
□ **beat someone hollow** *he was a mere boy, but he beat them hollow*: **trounce**, defeat utterly, beat, annihilate, drub, give a drubbing to, crush, rout, worst, overwhelm, outclass; informal hammer, clobber, thrash, lick, best, paste, pound, pulverize, crucify, slaughter, massacre, murder, flatten, demolish, destroy, walk over, wipe the floor with, take to the cleaners, make mincemeat of, turn inside out; Brit. informal stuff, marmalize; N. Amer. informal shellac, cream, skunk, blow out.
▷ANTONYMS lose to.
▶ noun **1** *a hollow at the base of a large tree*: **hole**, pit, cavity, crater, trough, cave, cavern; **depression**, indentation, concavity, dent, dint, dip, dimple, dish, basin, niche, nook, cranny, recess.
2 *a village nestled in a hollow in the Cotswolds*: **valley**, vale, dale; Brit. dene, combe, slade; N. English clough; Scottish glen, strath; literary dell, dingle.
▶ verb *a tunnel* ***hollowed out*** *in a mountain range*: **gouge out**, scoop out, dig out, cut out, excavate, channel.

holocaust noun *apocalyptic thoughts have surfaced due to the spectre of a nuclear holocaust*: **cataclysm**, disaster, catastrophe, destruction, devastation, demolition, annihilation, ravaging; inferno, fire, conflagration; massacre, slaughter, mass murder, carnage, butchery, extermination, liquidation, genocide, ethnic cleansing.

holy adjective **1** *people from all over the Muslim world visit the tombs of the holy men*: **saintly**, godly, saintlike, pious, pietistic, religious, devout, God-fearing, spiritual, canonized, beatified, ordained, deified; righteous, good, virtuous, moral, sinless, pure, perfect.
▷ANTONYMS sinful, irreligious.
2 *it is forbidden to say the name of this holy place aloud*: **sacred**, consecrated, hallowed, sanctified, venerated, revered, reverenced, divine, religious, blessed, blest, dedicated.
▷ANTONYMS unsanctified, cursed.

Word toolkit

holy	hallowed	sacred
city	halls	vow
grail	ground	relic
water	turf	music
book	portals	ritual
scriptures	corridors	cow
war	institution	text

homage noun *he intended his book as an act of homage*: **respect**, recognition, admiration, esteem, adulation, acclaim, acclamation, commendation, honour, reverence, worship; **tribute**, acknowledgement, eulogy, accolade, panegyric, paean, encomium, salute; rare laudation.
▷ANTONYMS criticism.
□ **pay homage to** *they paid homage to the local boy who became president*: **honour**, acclaim, applaud, praise, commend, extol, salute, celebrate, commemorate, glorify, laud, magnify, pay tribute to, sing the praises of, give recognition to, speak highly of, take one's hat off to.
▷ANTONYMS criticize.

home noun **1** *the floods forced people to flee their homes*: **place of residence**, accommodation, property, a roof over one's head; quarters, lodgings, rooms; address, location, place; informal pad; Brit. informal digs; formal residence, domicile, abode, dwelling, dwelling place, habitation.
2 *there is a growing demand for new homes*: **house**, flat, apartment, bungalow, cottage, terraced house, semi-detached house, detached house; informal semi.
3 *I spent long stretches of time far from my home*: **native land**, homeland, home town, birthplace, roots, fatherland, motherland, mother country, country of origin, land of one's fathers, the old country.
4 *a private home for the elderly*: **institution**, residential home, nursing home, old people's home, retirement home, convalescent home, rest home, children's home; hospice, shelter, refuge, retreat, asylum, hostel.
5 *Piedmont is the home of Italy's finest red wines*: **domain**, realm, place of origin, source, cradle, fount, fountainhead.
6 *Montana is home to a surprising number of rare animals*: **natural habitat**, natural environment, natural territory, habitat, home ground, stamping ground, haunt.
□ **at home 1** *I told him I'd be at home most of the day*: **in**, in one's house, present, available, indoors, inside, here. ▷ANTONYMS out.
2 *Milan was one of the big cities where she felt very much at home*: **at ease**, comfortable, relaxed, content, confident, at peace, in one's element.
▷ANTONYMS ill at ease.
3 *he was not particularly* ***at home with*** *mathematics*: **confident with**, conversant with, proficient in, competent at, used to, familiar with, au fait with, au courant with, skilled in, experienced in, well versed in; informal well up on. ▷ANTONYMS unused to.
4 *she took to her room and was not* ***at home to*** *friends*: **entertaining**, receiving, playing host to, showing hospitality to.
□ **bring something home to someone** *Art's illness brought home to them the gravity of the situation*: **make someone realize**, make someone understand, make someone aware of, make someone conscious of, make something clear to someone, drive home, press home, impress upon someone, draw attention to, focus attention on, point up, underline, highlight, spotlight, foreground, emphasize, stress.
□ **hit home** See **hit**.
□ **nothing to write home about** informal *his looks were nothing to write home about*: **unexceptional**, mediocre, ordinary, common, commonplace, indifferent, average, middle-of-the-road, run-of-the-mill, middling, medium, moderate, everyday, workaday, tolerable, passable, adequate, fair, nothing out of the ordinary; informal OK, so-so, bog-standard, fair-to-middling, (plain) vanilla, no great shakes, not so hot, not up to much; Brit. informal common or garden; N. Amer. informal ornery; NZ informal half-pie.
▷ANTONYMS exceptional.
▶ adjective **1** *we need to stimulate demand within the UK home market*: **domestic**, internal, local, national, interior, native.
▷ANTONYMS foreign, international.
2 *a sale of home produce*: **home-made**, home-grown, locally produced, family, local.
▶ verb
□ **home in on** *a teaching style which homes in on what is of central importance for each pupil*: **focus on**, focus attention on, concentrate on, zero in on, centre on, fix on, aim at, highlight, spotlight, underline, pinpoint; informal zoom in on.

Word links **home**

oikophobia fear of home

homeland noun *he left his homeland to settle in London*: **native land**, native country, country of origin, home, fatherland, motherland, mother country, land of one's fathers, the old country.

homeless adjective *the plight of young homeless people*: **without a roof over one's head**, on the streets, vagrant, sleeping rough, living rough; destitute, down and out, derelict, itinerant; Brit. informal dossing; formal of no fixed abode.
▶ noun (**the homeless**) *charities for the homeless*: **homeless people**, vagrants, down-and-outs, tramps, beggars, vagabonds, itinerants, transients, migrants, derelicts, drifters, beachcombers; N. Amer. hobos; Austral. bagmen, knockabouts, overlanders, sundowners, whalers; informal bag ladies; Brit. informal dossers; N. Amer. informal bums, bindlestiffs; Austral./NZ informal derros; S. African informal outies; formal people of no fixed abode.

homely adjective **1** *a modern hotel with a homely atmosphere*: **cosy**, homelike, homey, comfortable, snug, welcoming, friendly, congenial, hospitable, informal, relaxed, intimate, warm, pleasant, cheerful; N. Amer. down-home, homestyle; informal comfy.
▷ANTONYMS uncomfortable, formal.
2 *he interested himself in the homely pursuit of keeping chickens*: **unsophisticated**, everyday, ordinary, domestic, plain, simple, modest, natural, down-to-earth, homespun, folksy, unrefined, unpretentious, unaffected, unassuming.
▷ANTONYMS sophisticated.
3 N. Amer. *the girl is clumsy, homely, and desperate for a date*: **unattractive**, plain, plain-featured, plain-looking, plain as a pikestaff, ordinary-looking,

unprepossessing, unlovely, ill-favoured, ugly; informal not much to look at, short on looks; Brit. informal no oil painting; Austral./NZ informal drack.
▷ANTONYMS attractive.

Homeric adjective *some of us exert a Homeric effort*: **epic**, large-scale, grand, monumental, vast, heroic, impressive, imposing.

homespun adjective *he was a source of homespun rural philosophy*: **unsophisticated**, unpolished, unrefined, plain, simple, rustic, folksy, artless, modest, natural; coarse, rough, rude, crude, rudimentary.
▷ANTONYMS sophisticated.

homey adjective **1** *the house is homey yet elegant*: **cosy**, homelike, homely, comfortable, snug, welcoming, friendly, congenial, hospitable, informal, relaxed, intimate, warm, pleasant, cheerful; N. Amer. down-home, homestyle; informal comfy.
▷ANTONYMS uncomfortable, formal.
2 *an idealized vision of traditional peasant life as simple and homey*: **unsophisticated**, homely, unrefined, unpretentious, ordinary, plain, simple, modest, down-to-earth, homespun.
▷ANTONYMS sophisticated.

homicidal adjective *he had homicidal tendencies*: **murderous**, violent, brutal, savage, ferocious, fierce, vicious, bloody, bloodthirsty, barbarous, barbaric, cruel; mortal, deadly, lethal, death-dealing; dated cut-throat; archaic sanguinary, fell.
▷ANTONYMS peaceable.

homicide noun **1** *he was charged with homicide*. See **murder**.
2 dated *a convicted homicide*. See **murderer**.

homily noun *she delivered her homily about the need for patience*: **sermon**, lecture, discourse, address, lesson, talk, speech, oration, declamation; preaching, teaching; informal spiel; rare peroration, allocution, postil.

homogeneity noun *the cultural homogeneity of Europe*: **uniformity**, homogeneousness, similarity, similar nature, similitude, likeness, alikeness, sameness, identicalness, consistency, resemblance, comparability, correspondence; rare analogousness.
▷ANTONYMS variety, difference.

homogeneous adjective **1** *the elderly are far from a homogeneous group*: **uniform**, identical, unvaried, unvarying, consistent, similar, undistinguishable; alike, all alike, of the same kind, much the same, all the same, the same, all one, all of a piece; informal much of a muchness.
▷ANTONYMS heterogeneous.
2 *you must consider cost efficiency to compete with homogeneous products*: **similar**, comparable, equivalent, like, analogous, corresponding, correspondent, parallel, matching, kindred, related, correlative, congruent, cognate.
▷ANTONYMS different; dissimilar.

homogenize verb *they wanted to wipe out the differences between towns and villages—to homogenize society*: **make uniform**, make similar, unite, integrate, fuse, merge, blend, meld, coalesce, amalgamate, synthesize, combine, join together; literary commingle; archaic commix.
▷ANTONYMS diversify.

homogenous adjective See **homogeneous**.

homologous adjective *the cell has two sets of homologous chromosomes*: **similar**, comparable, equivalent, like, analogous, corresponding, correspondent, parallel, matching, kindred, related, correlative, congruent, cognate.
▷ANTONYMS different, dissimilar.

homosexual adjective **gay**, lesbian, sapphic, lesbigay, GLBT (gay, lesbian, bisexual, or transgendered); rare homophile, Uranian; informal pink, lavender, camp, lezzy, les, lesbo, butch, dykey; informal, derogatory queer, limp-wristed, that way, swinging the other way, homo; Brit. informal, derogatory bent, poofy; N. Amer. informal, derogatory fruity.
▷ANTONYMS heterosexual, straight.
▶ **noun gay**, lesbian, gay person, lesbigay; rare invert, homophile, Uranian; informal queen, friend of Dorothy, dyke, les, lesbo, lezzie, butch, femme; informal, derogatory queer, homo, pansy, nancy, bumboy, nelly; Brit. informal, derogatory poof, poofter, ponce, jessie, woofter, shirtlifter, bender; N. Amer. informal, derogatory cupcake, swish, twinkie; Austral. informal wonk; S. African informal, derogatory moffie; W. Indian informal, derogatory batty boy, batty man.
▷ANTONYMS heterosexual, straight.

Word links **homosexual**

homophobia fear of homosexuals

hone verb *he was carefully honing the curved blade*: **sharpen**, make sharper, make sharp, whet, strop, grind, file, put an edge on; rare edge, acuminate.
▷ANTONYMS blunt.

honest adjective **1** *I did the only right and honest thing | he is an honest man*: **morally correct**, upright, honourable, moral, ethical, principled, righteous, right-minded, respectable; **virtuous**, good, worthy, decent, law-abiding, high-minded, upstanding, just, fair, incorruptible, truthful, true, veracious, trustworthy, trusty, reliable, conscientious, scrupulous, reputable, dependable, loyal, faithful; informal on the level, honest-to-goodness.
▷ANTONYMS dishonest.
2 *I haven't been totally honest with you*: **truthful**, sincere, candid, frank, direct, open, forthright, straight, straightforward, genuine, blunt, plain-spoken, plain-speaking, matter-of-fact, outspoken, as straight as a die, straight from the shoulder; informal upfront; archaic free-spoken.
▷ANTONYMS insincere.
3 *he'd made an honest mistake*: **genuine**, real, authentic, actual, true; legitimate, above board, fair and square; Latin bona fide; informal legit, kosher, on the level, honest-to-goodness.
▷ANTONYMS intentional.
4 *they had given their honest opinion*: **objective**, impartial, unbiased, balanced, unprejudiced, disinterested, even-handed, fair, just, equitable.
▷ANTONYMS biased.

honestly adverb **1** *he'd come by the money honestly*: **fairly**, lawfully, legally, legitimately, honourably, decently, ethically, morally, by fair means, by just means, without corruption, in good faith, by the book, in accordance with the rules; informal on the level.
▷ANTONYMS dishonestly.
2 *we honestly believe this is the best investment you will ever make*: **frankly**, candidly, sincerely, genuinely, truthfully, truly, wholeheartedly, freely, openly, plainly, straight out, straight from the shoulder; informal straight up.
3 *quite honestly, I'm not very interested in men*: **truthfully**, really, truly, actually, to be honest, to tell you the truth, to be frank, speaking truthfully, speaking frankly, in all honesty, in all sincerity, in plain language, in plain English; without pretence, without dissembling; informal Scout's honour; dated honest Injun.

honesty noun **1** *a character reference should provide evidence of honesty*: **moral correctness**, uprightness, honourableness, honour, integrity, morals, morality, ethics, principle, (high) principles, nobility, righteousness, rectitude, right-mindedness, upstandingness; **virtue**, goodness, probity, worthiness, high-mindedness, justness, fairness, incorruptibility, truthfulness, truth, veracity, trustworthiness, reliability, conscientiousness, scrupulousness, reputability, dependability, loyalty, faithfulness, fidelity.
▷ANTONYMS dishonesty.
2 *they spoke with convincing honesty about their fears*: **truthfulness**, truth, sincerity, candour, frankness, directness, forthrightness, openness, straightforwardness, plainness, genuineness, bluntness, outspokenness.
▷ANTONYMS insincerity.

honey noun

Word links **honey**

apiculture honey production
melliferous yielding or producing honey
mellivorous honey-eating

honeyed adjective *he wooed her with honeyed words*: **sweet**, sweet-sounding, saccharine, sugary, pleasant, agreeable, flattering, adulatory, unctuous; dulcet, soothing, soft, mellow, lyrical, mellifluous.
▷ANTONYMS harsh.

honorarium noun **fee**, payment, consideration, allowance; remuneration, pay, expenses, compensation, recompense, reward; formal emolument.

honorary adjective **1** *he received an honorary doctorate from Harvard University*: **titular**, nominal, in name only, in title only, unofficial, token, so-called; Latin honoris causa, ex officio.
2 *she took office as honorary treasurer*: **unpaid**, unsalaried, without pay, without payment, for nothing; voluntary, volunteer, unrewarded; Law pro bono (publico).
▷ANTONYMS paid.

honour noun **1** *the general's record shows that he was a man of honour*: **integrity**, honourableness, honesty, uprightness, ethics, morals, morality, principle, (high) principles, righteousness, rectitude, nobility, high-mindedness, right-mindedness, noble-mindedness; **virtue**, goodness, decency, probity, scrupulousness, worthiness, worth, fairness, justness, justice, truthfulness, trustworthiness, reliability, dependability, faithfulness, fidelity.
▷ANTONYMS dishonour.
2 *he earned the honour of having the archive named after him | a mark of honour*: **distinction**, privilege, glory, tribute, kudos, cachet, prestige, fame, renown, merit, credit, importance, illustriousness, notability; **respect**, esteem, approbation.
▷ANTONYMS disgrace.
3 *our national honour is at stake*: **reputation**, good name, name, character, repute, prestige, image, kudos, cachet, standing, stature, status; Indian izzat.
4 *he was welcomed with honour by the king*: **acclaim**, acclamation, commendation, applause, accolades, tributes, compliments,

congratulations, salutes, plaudits, bouquets, paeans, homage, praise, glory, eulogy, adoration, reverence, veneration, adulation, exaltation, glorification; rare extolment, laudation, eulogium.
▷ANTONYMS contempt.
5 *Mrs Young had the honour of being received by the Queen*: **privilege**, pleasure, pride, satisfaction, joy, compliment, favour, source of pleasure, source of pride.
▷ANTONYMS shame.
6 *the highest military honours*: **accolade**, award, reward, prize, decoration, distinction, order, title, medal, ribbon, star, laurel, laurel wreath, bay, palm; Military, informal fruit salad; Brit. informal gong.
7 *she died defending her honour*: **chastity**, virginity, virtue, maidenhood, maidenhead, purity, innocence, modesty; informal cherry; Theology immaculateness.
▸**verb 1** *we should love and honour our parents*: **hold in great respect**, hold in high esteem, have a high regard for, esteem, respect, admire, defer to, look up to, think highly of; appreciate, value, prize, cherish; reverence, revere, venerate, worship; informal put on a pedestal.
▷ANTONYMS dishonour.
2 *talented writers were honoured at a special ceremony*: **applaud**, acclaim, praise, salute, recognize, celebrate, commemorate, commend, glorify, hail, lionize, exalt, fête, eulogize, give credit to, pay homage to, pay tribute to, show appreciation of, give accolades to, sing the praises of, sing paeans to; archaic magnify; rare laud, panegyrize, emblazon.
▷ANTONYMS disgrace, criticize.
3 *make sure the franchisees honour the terms of the contract*: **fulfil**, observe, keep, discharge, implement, perform, execute, effect, obey, heed, follow, carry out, carry through, keep to, abide by, adhere to, comply with, conform to, act in accordance with, be true to, be faithful to, live up to; rare effectuate.
▷ANTONYMS disobey.
4 *the bank informed him that the cheque would not be honoured*: **cash**, **accept**, take, clear, pass, encash, convert into cash, convert into money.
▷ANTONYMS bounce.

honourable adjective **1** *he took the honourable course and resigned | a decent and honourable man*: **morally correct**, honest, moral, ethical, principled, righteous, right-minded, full of integrity; decent, respected, respectable, venerable, virtuous, good, upstanding, upright, worthy, noble, high-principled, fair, just, truthful, trustworthy, trusty, law-abiding, incorruptible, reliable, reputable, dependable, faithful.
▷ANTONYMS dishonourable, crooked.
2 *a long and honourable career*: **illustrious**, distinguished, eminent, great, admirable, glorious, prestigious, noble, notable, creditable, renowned, esteemed.
▷ANTONYMS deplorable.

hood noun **head covering**, cowl, snood, scarf, head scarf.

hoodlum noun **1** *a bunch of hoodlums just looking for trouble*: **hooligan**, thug, lout, delinquent, tearaway, vandal, ruffian, rowdy; Austral./NZ larrikin; informal tough, rough, bruiser, roughneck; Brit. informal yob, yobbo, bovver boy, lager lout, chav, hoodie; Scottish & N. English informal keelie, ned; Austral./NZ informal roughie, hoon.
2 *Pesci plays a hoodlum for whom killing is a pleasure*: **gangster**, gang member, mobster, criminal, gunman, thug, racketeer, ruffian, member of a criminal gang, member of the Mafia, Mafioso, Yardie; in Japan yakuza; informal hit man, hatchet man, heavy, gorilla; N. Amer. informal hood, goon.

hoodoo noun *she's working some hoodoo on us*: **witchcraft**, magic, black magic, sorcery, wizardry, devilry, voodoo, necromancy; N. Amer. mojo; NZ makutu; S. African muti; rare witchery, demonry, thaumaturgy, theurgy.

hoodwink verb *he kept on the lookout for the young man who had hoodwinked him*: **deceive**, trick, dupe, outwit, fool, delude, cheat, take in, bluff, hoax, mislead, misguide, lead on, defraud, double-cross, swindle, gull, finagle, get the better of; informal con, bamboozle, do, have, sting, gyp, diddle, fiddle, swizzle, shaft, bilk, rook, rip off, lead up the garden path, pull a fast one on, put one over on, take for a ride, pull the wool over someone's eyes, throw dust in someone's eyes, sell a pup to, take to the cleaners; N. Amer. informal sucker, snooker, stiff, euchre, bunco, hornswoggle, make a sucker of; Austral. informal pull a swifty on; archaic cozen, sharp, befool; rare mulct.

hoof noun *there was a clatter of hoofs as a rider came up to us*: **foot**, trotter, cloven hoof; technical ungula, cloot.

> *Word links* **hoof**
>
> **ungual** relating to hooves

hook noun **1** *she hung her jacket on the hook*: **peg**, holder.
2 *the back of the dress fastens with a hook and eye*: **fastener**, fastening, catch, clasp, hasp, clip, pin, buckle, hook and eye; Archaeology fibula.
3 *I had a fish on the end of my hook*: **fish hook**, barb, snare, trap.
4 *he used a hook to clear the undergrowth*: **billhook**, scythe, sickle.
5 *a perfectly timed right hook to the chin*: **punch**, blow, hit, box, cuff, thump, smack, crack, knock, thwack; Scottish & N. English skelp; informal belt, bop, biff, sock, clout, whack, wallop, plug, slug, whop; Brit. informal slosh, dot; N. Amer. informal boff; Austral./NZ informal dong.
□ **by hook or by crook** *the government intends, by hook or by crook, to hold on to the land*: **by any means**, by any means whatsoever, somehow, somehow or other, no matter how, in one way or another, by fair means or foul.
□ **hook, line, and sinker** *he fell hook, line, and sinker for this year's April Fool joke*: **completely**, totally, utterly, entirely, absolutely, thoroughly, wholly, through and through, one hundred per cent, {lock, stock, and barrel}.
▷ANTONYMS to a limited extent.
□ **off the hook** informal *I lied to get him off the hook*: **out of trouble**, free, in the clear, under no obligation; **acquitted**, cleared, reprieved, exonerated, absolved, vindicated, found not guilty; informal let off.
▸**verb 1** *they hooked baskets onto the ladder rungs*: **attach**, fix, hitch, fasten, secure, clasp; archaic hasp, grapple.
▷ANTONYMS unhitch.
2 *he hooked his thumbs in his belt*: **curl**, bend, crook, loop, angle, curve.
3 *he hooked a 24 lb pike*: **catch**, take, land, net, bag, snare, ensnare, trap, entrap.
▷ANTONYMS release.

hookah noun **pipe**, water pipe, hubble-bubble, chillum, narghile, kalian.

hooked adjective **1** *he had a hooked nose*: **curved**, hook-shaped, hook-like, aquiline, bent, bowed, angular; technical falcate, falciform, uncinate.
▷ANTONYMS straight.
2 informal *they are **hooked on** cocaine*: **addicted to**, dependent on, with a ... habit; informal using; US black slang have a jones for.
▷ANTONYMS clean.
3 informal *he has been **hooked on** crosswords since his teens*: **very keen on**, very enthusiastic about, devoted to, addicted to, obsessed with, fixated on, fanatical about; informal mad about, crazy about, gone on, wild about, nuts about, potty about, dotty about, a sucker for; N. Amer. informal nutso over; Austral./NZ informal shook on.
▷ANTONYMS indifferent.

hooligan noun *the violence was caused by football hooligans*: **hoodlum**, thug, lout, delinquent, tearaway, vandal, ruffian, rowdy, troublemaker; Austral./NZ larrikin; informal tough, rough, bruiser, roughneck; Brit. informal yob, yobbo, bovver boy, lager lout, chav, hoodie; Scottish & N. English informal keelie, ned; Austral./NZ informal roughie, hoon.

hoop noun **ring**, band, circle, circlet, loop, wheel, round, girdle; technical annulus.

hoot noun **1** *she heard the hoot of an owl*: **cry**, call, screech, tu-whit tu-whoo.
2 *the hoot of a horn was followed by the roar of an engine*: **blast**, blare, sound, beep, honk, toot.
3 *there were hoots of derision*: **shout**, yell, cry, howl, scream, shriek, whoop, whistle; **boo**, hiss, jeer, mock, taunt, catcall; informal raspberry.
▷ANTONYMS cheer.
4 informal *your mum's a real hoot—I always have a giggle with her*: **amusing person**, character, clown, somebody very funny; **amusing situation**, piece of fun, something very funny; informal scream, laugh, card, case, one, riot, giggle, lark, barrel of laughs; informal, dated caution.
□ **give a hoot** informal *I don't give a hoot about what anyone else thinks*: **care**, be concerned, mind, be bothered, be interested; informal give a damn, give a rap, give a hang, give a tinker's curse/damn, give a monkey's, lose sleep, get worked up.
▷ANTONYMS be unconcerned.
▸**verb 1** *in the stillness of the night an owl hooted*: **cry**, call, utter a hoot, screech, tu-whit tu-whoo.
2 *a car horn hooted, frightening her*: **sound**, blare, blast, beep, honk, toot, make a loud sound.
3 *the delegates hooted in disgust*: **shout**, yell, cry, howl, scream, shriek, whoop, whistle; **boo**, hiss, jeer, mock, taunt, catcall; informal blow raspberries.
▷ANTONYMS cheer.

hop verb **1** *he hopped along beside her*: **jump**, bound, spring, bounce, skip, jig, trip, flit, leap, prance, caper, dance, frolic, gambol.
2 informal *she hopped over the Atlantic for a bit for shopping*: **go**, dash, rush; informal **pop**, whip; Brit. informal nip.
▸**noun 1** *put the rabbit on the floor to have a hop around*: **jump**, bound, bounce, prance, leap, spring, skip, gambol.
2 informal *it's just a short hop here by taxi*: **journey**, distance, ride, drive, run, trip, jaunt; flight, plane trip; informal spin.
3 informal *what about coming to the hop on Saturday*: **dance**, social, party, jamboree, gathering, function, disco; informal bash, bop, shindig, shindy, do; Brit. informal rave-up, knees-up, beanfeast, beano, bunfight.
□ **on the hop** Brit. informal **1** *he was caught on the hop*: **unprepared**, unready, off guard, unawares, by surprise, with one's defences down; informal napping, asleep at the wheel; Brit. informal with one's trousers down;

N. Amer. informal with one's pants down. ▷ANTONYMS prepared.
2 *we were always kept on the hop*: **busy**, occupied, employed, working, at work, rushed off one's feet, hard-pressed, on the job; informal busy as a bee, on the go. ▷ANTONYMS idle.

hope noun **1** *I had high hopes of making the Olympic team*: **aspiration**, desire, wish, expectation, ambition, aim, plan, dream, daydream, pipe dream; longing, yearning, craving, hankering.
2 *most of us begin married life filled with hope*: **hopefulness**, optimism, expectation, expectancy; confidence, faith, trust, belief, conviction, assurance.
3 *he does see some hope for the future*: **optimism**, grounds for hope, promise, light at the end of the tunnel.
▷ANTONYMS pessimism.
▸ verb **1** *he's **hoping for** an offer of compensation*: **expect**, anticipate, look for, wait for, be hopeful of, pin one's hopes on, want; wish for, dream of, hope against hope for.
▷ANTONYMS despair of.
2 *we're hoping to address all these issues*: **aim**, intend, be looking, have the/every intention, have in mind, plan, aspire.

hopeful adjective **1** *he remained hopeful that something could be worked out*: **optimistic**, full of hope, confident, positive, buoyant, sanguine, bullish, cheerful, assured, expectant, anticipative, disposed to look on the bright side; informal upbeat.
▷ANTONYMS pessimistic.
2 *there are some hopeful signs of recovery in the US market*: **promising**, encouraging, heartening, reassuring, auspicious, favourable, optimistic, propitious, gladdening, cheering, bright, rosy, full of promise, full of hope.
▷ANTONYMS discouraging.

hopefully adverb **1** *he rode on hopefully*: **optimistically**, with hope, full of hope, confidently, expectantly, with anticipation, with assurance, buoyantly, sanguinely, bullishly.
▷ANTONYMS pessimistically.
2 *hopefully it should be finished by next year*: **all being well**, it is to be hoped that, if all goes well, if everything turns out all right, God willing, most likely, with luck, probably, conceivably, feasibly; informal touch wood, fingers crossed.

hopeless adjective **1** *Jess looked at him in mute hopeless appeal*: **despairing**, without hope, in despair, desperate, dejected, downhearted, despondent, demoralized, disconsolate, downcast, wretched, woebegone, forlorn, negative, pessimistic, defeatist, resigned.
▷ANTONYMS optimistic.
2 *she gave up on him as a hopeless case*: **irremediable**, beyond hope, lost, beyond remedy, beyond repair, beyond recovery, irreparable, irreversible, incorrigible, despaired of; **past cure**, incurable, grave, fatal, deadly.
▷ANTONYMS remediable; curable.
3 *although the situation was hopeless, they sent in more troops*: **impossible**, beyond hope, with no chance of success, useless, no-win, futile, unworkable, impracticable, forlorn, pointless, vain; archaic bootless, parlous.
▷ANTONYMS hopeful.
4 *Joseph was hopeless at school*: **very bad**, very poor, awful, terrible, dreadful, appalling, frightful, atrocious, inferior, incompetent, inadequate, ineffective; informal pathetic, useless, lousy, rotten, a dead loss, abysmal, dire; Brit. informal **duff**, rubbish, a load of pants, unable to do something for toffee, unable to do something to save one's life.
▷ANTONYMS accomplished.

hopelessly adverb **1** *she began to cry hopelessly*: **despairingly**, without hope, in despair, in anguish, in distress, desperately, dejectedly, downheartedly, despondently, disconsolately, wretchedly, miserably, forlornly, resignedly, pessimistically.
▷ANTONYMS optimistically.
2 *she was hopelessly confused and lost*: **utterly**, completely, irretrievably, impossibly; extremely, very, desperately, totally, awfully, terribly, tremendously, frightfully, dreadfully; informal chronically.
▷ANTONYMS slightly.

horde noun *a horde of paparazzi burst into the office*: **crowd**, large group, mob, pack, gang, troop, army, swarm, mass; throng, multitude, host, drove, band, flock, gathering, assemblage, press; informal crew, tribe, load; archaic rout.

> *Easily confused words* **horde or hoard?**
>
> See **hoard**.

horizon noun **1** *the sun rose above the horizon*: **skyline**, range of vision, field of view, vista, view.
2 *she wanted to leave home and broaden her horizons*: **range of experience**, **outlook**, perspective, scope, perception, compass, sphere, ambit, orbit, purview.
□ **on the horizon** *trouble could be on the horizon*: **imminent**, impending, close, near, approaching, coming, forthcoming, in prospect, at hand, on the way, about to happen, upon us, in the offing, in the pipeline, in the air, in the wind, in the wings, just around the corner; brewing, looming, threatening, menacing; informal on the cards.

horizontal adjective **1** *draw a horizontal line near the top of the wall*: **parallel**, level, even, straight, plane, flush.
▷ANTONYMS vertical.
2 *she was stretched horizontal on a sun lounger*: **flat**, supine, prone, prostrate, lying down.
▷ANTONYMS upright.

horn noun

> *Word links* **horn**
>
> **corneous** like horn

horny adjective informal *she was making him very horny*. See **excited** (sense 2).

horrendous adjective *she suffered horrendous injuries | a horrendous sight*. See **horrible**.

horrible adjective **1** *there was a horrible murder here earlier this year*: **dreadful**, **horrifying**, horrific, horrendous, frightful, fearful, awful, terrible, shocking, appalling, hideous, grim, grisly, ghastly, harrowing, gruesome, heinous, vile, nightmarish, macabre, unspeakable, hair-raising, spine-chilling; loathsome, monstrous, abhorrent, detestable, hateful, execrable, abominable, atrocious, sickening, nauseating.
2 *the tea tasted horrible | a horrible little man*: **nasty**, disagreeable, unpleasant, horrid, awful, dreadful, terrible, appalling, horrendous, disgusting, foul, revolting, repulsive, repellent, ghastly; obnoxious, hateful, odious, objectionable, offensive, insufferable, vile, loathsome, abhorrent; informal frightful, lousy, God-awful, hellish; Brit. informal beastly, grotty, bitchy, catty; N. Amer. informal **hellacious**; archaic disgustful, loathly; rare rebarbative.
▷ANTONYMS pleasant; agreeable.

horrid adjective **1** *horrid apparitions*. See **horrible** (sense 1).
2 *the teachers at school were horrid*. See **horrible** (sense 2).

horrific adjective *he lay in a coma following a horrific car crash*: **dreadful**, horrendous, horrifying, horrible, frightful, awful, terrible, fearful, shocking, appalling, atrocious, hideous, grim, grisly, ghastly, harrowing, gruesome, unspeakable, monstrous, nightmarish, sickening, nauseating.

horrify verb **1** *she loved to horrify us with tales of ghastly happenings*: **frighten**, scare, terrify, petrify, alarm, panic, terrorize, scare stiff, scare/frighten to death, fill with fear, scare someone out of their wits, scare/frighten the living daylights out of, throw into a panic, make someone's hair stand on end, make someone's blood run cold; informal scare the pants off, make someone's hair curl; Brit. informal throw into a blue funk, put the wind up; Irish informal scare the bejesus out of; N. Amer. informal spook; vulgar slang scare shitless, scare the shit out of; archaic affright.
2 *Lucien was horrified by her remarks, but said nothing*: **shock**, appal, outrage, scandalize, offend, dismay, throw off balance; disgust, revolt, repel, nauseate, sicken; informal rattle, faze, knock sideways, knock for six; archaic pother.
▷ANTONYMS please.

> *Choose the right word* **horrify, appal, dismay**
>
> See **dismay**.

horror noun **1** *children screamed in horror*: **terror**, fear, fear and trembling, fearfulness, fright, alarm, panic, dread, trepidation.
▷ANTONYMS delight.
2 *to her horror she found that a thief had stolen the machine*: **dismay**, consternation, perturbation, alarm, distress; disgust, outrage, shock.
▷ANTONYMS satisfaction.
3 *photographs showed the horror of the tragedy*: **awfulness**, frightfulness, cruelty, savagery, gruesomeness, ghastliness, hideousness; atrocity, outrage, crime, barbarity.
4 informal *that little horror Zach was around*: **rascal**, devil, imp, monkey, scamp; informal terror, holy terror, scallywag; Brit. informal **perisher**; N. English informal tyke, scallion; N. Amer. informal varmint, hellion; archaic scapegrace, rapscallion.
□ **have a horror of** *Laura had a horror of pubs*: **hate**, detest, loathe, greatly dislike, have a strong aversion to, abhor, abominate, be unable to bear/stand.
▷ANTONYMS love.

horror-struck, horror-stricken adjective *horror-struck, she stared at him with frightened eyes*: **horrified**, terrified, petrified, frightened, afraid, fearful, scared, panic-stricken, terror-struck, scared/frightened to death, scared stiff, scared witless, scared out of one's wits; shocked, stunned, stupefied, awestruck, aghast, appalled; vulgar slang scared shitless, shit-scared.
▷ANTONYMS delighted; relaxed.

h

horse noun **mount**, charger, yearling; cob, draught horse, carthorse, packhorse, racehorse; pony, foal, colt, stallion, gelding, mare, filly; nag, hack; N. Amer. bronco; Austral./NZ moke, yarraman; archaic steed, jade; children's word gee-gee.
▶ verb
□ **horse around/about** informal *they were talking silly and horsing around*: **fool around/about**, play the fool, act foolishly, act the clown, act the fool, play about/around, clown about/around, monkey about/around, play tricks, indulge in horseplay, engage in high jinks; informal mess about/around, lark (about/around); Brit. informal muck about/around; N. Amer. informal cut up; Brit. vulgar slang piss about/around, arse about/around, bugger about/around; dated play the giddy goat.
▷ANTONYMS be serious.

Word links **horse**

equine, **hippic** relating to horses
hippo- related prefix, as in *hippodrome, hippopotamus*
stallion male
gelding castrated male
mare female
foal young
colt young male
filly young female
drove, **string**, **stud**, **team** collective noun
equestrian relating to riding horses
hippophobia fear of horses
horse-coper Brit. archaic seller of horses

horseman, horsewoman noun **rider**, equestrian, horse rider, jockey; cavalryman, horse soldier, trooper, dragoon, knight; archaic hussar, cavalier.

horseplay noun *this ridiculous horseplay has gone far enough*: **fooling around**, foolish behaviour, clowning, fooling, tomfoolery, buffoonery; pranks, practical jokes, antics, larks, capers, high jinks; rough and tumble, romping, skylarking; informal shenanigans, monkey business; Brit. informal monkey tricks; N. Amer. informal didoes.

horse sense noun informal *she has the horse sense to keep Dan from those wild schemes*: **common sense**, good sense, sense, sensibleness, native wit, native intelligence, mother wit, wit, judgement, sound judgement, level-headedness, prudence, discernment, acumen, sharpness, sharp-wittedness, canniness, astuteness, shrewdness, judiciousness, wisdom, insight, intuition, intuitiveness, perceptiveness, perspicacity, vision, understanding, intelligence; informal nous, gumption, savvy, know-how, the sense one was born with; Brit. informal common; N. Amer. informal smarts; rare sapience, arguteness.
▷ANTONYMS stupidity.

hortatory adjective *the hortatory moralism of many contemporary churchmen*: **exhortatory**, exhortative, exhorting, moralistic, homilectic, didactic, pedagogic; informal preachy.

horticulture noun **gardening**, floriculture, arboriculture, agriculture, cultivation, cultivation of plants, garden management.

hosanna noun *their hosannas rose up to the heavens*: **shout of praise**, alleluia, hurrah, hurray, cheer, paean, glorification; archaic huzza; rare laudation.

hose noun **1** *a thirty-foot garden hose*: **pipe**, piping, tube, tubing, conduit, channel, line, duct, outlet, pipeline, siphon.
2 *her hose had been laddered*. See **hosiery**.

hosiery noun **stockings**, tights, stay-ups, nylons; hose; **socks**, knee socks, ankle socks; N. Amer. pantyhose.

hospitable adjective *two friendly, hospitable brothers run the hotel*: **welcoming**, friendly, congenial, genial, sociable, convivial, cordial, gracious, amicable, well disposed, amenable, helpful, obliging, accommodating, neighbourly, warm, warm-hearted, kind, kindly, kind-hearted, generous, liberal, bountiful, open-handed.
▷ANTONYMS inhospitable; unfriendly.

hospital noun **medical institution**, medical centre, health centre, clinic, infirmary, sanatorium, nursing home, convalescent home, hospice; Brit. cottage hospital; Austral./NZ base hospital; Military field hospital; archaic lazaretto.

hospitality noun **1** *Scotland is renowned for its hospitality*: **friendliness**, hospitableness, welcome, warm reception, helpfulness, neighbourliness, warmth, warm-heartedness, kindness, kind-heartedness, congeniality, geniality, sociability, conviviality, cordiality, amicability, amenability, generosity, liberality, bountifulness, open-handedness.
▷ANTONYMS unfriendliness.
2 *the inn's hospitality includes a selection of real ales, bar menu, and live music on Thursday nights*: **entertainment**, catering, food, accommodation.

host[1] noun **1** *the host greeted the new guests*: **party-giver**, entertainer, hostess.
▷ANTONYMS guest.
2 *he was the host of a half-hour TV series*: **presenter**, compère, master of ceremonies, MC, anchor, anchorman, anchorwoman, announcer, link person; informal emcee.
▶ verb **1** *the Queen hosted a dinner for 600 guests*: **give**, throw, have, hold, provide, put on, lay on, arrange, organize.
▷ANTONYMS be a guest at.
2 *the show is hosted by Angus Deayton*: **present**, introduce, compère, front, anchor, announce, be the presenter of; informal emcee.

host[2] noun **1** *a host of memories rushed into her mind*: **multitude**, myriad, lot, large number, great quantity, score, abundance, wealth, flood, profusion, array; informal load, heap, mass, pile, ton; Brit. informal shedload; Austral./NZ informal swag.
▷ANTONYMS small number.
2 *she joined a host of other stars at the London fashion show*: **crowd**, throng, pack, band, flock, herd, drove, swarm, troop, horde, mob, army, legion, crush, press; collection, assembly, assemblage, gathering; archaic rout.
▷ANTONYMS small group.

hostage noun *the hijackers released all the hostages*: **captive**, prisoner, detainee, internee; pawn, security, surety, pledge.

hostel noun **cheap hotel**, youth hostel, YMCA, YWCA, bed and breakfast, B&B, boarding house, guest house, pension; hall of residence, dormitory.

hostile adjective **1** *he wrote a ferociously hostile attack*: **antagonistic**, aggressive, confrontational, belligerent, bellicose, pugnacious, militant, truculent, combative, warlike; **unfriendly**, unkind, bitter, unsympathetic, malevolent, malicious, vicious, spiteful, rancorous, venomous, biting, wrathful, angry; literary malefic, maleficent.
▷ANTONYMS friendly; mild.
2 *he painted a grim picture of hardship in hostile climatic conditions*: **unfavourable**, adverse, bad, harsh, grim, hard, tough, inhospitable, forbidding, uncomfortable, unwelcoming.
▷ANTONYMS favourable.
3 *people are very* ***hostile to*** *the idea*: **opposed**, averse, antagonistic, ill-disposed, unsympathetic, antipathetic, inimical; opposing, against, dead set against, at odds with; informal anti, down on.
▷ANTONYMS in favour of.

hostility noun **1** *the boy glared at her with hostility*: **antagonism**, **unfriendliness**, bitterness, malevolence, malice, unkindness, spite, spitefulness, rancour, rancorousness, venom, wrath, anger, hatred; aggression, aggressiveness, belligerence, bellicosity, pugnaciousness, militancy, truculence, warlikeness.
▷ANTONYMS friendliness.
2 *there is a great amount of hostility to the present regime*: **opposition**, antagonism, animosity, antipathy, animus, ill will, ill feeling, bad feeling, resentment, aversion, enmity, inimicalness.
▷ANTONYMS approval.
3 (**hostilities**) *he called for an immediate cessation of hostilities*: **fighting**, conflict, armed conflict, combat, warfare, war, bloodshed, violence, action, military action, battles, strife.
▷ANTONYMS peace.

hot adjective **1** *they provided plenty of good hot food*: **heated**, piping, piping hot, sizzling, steaming, roasting, boiling, boiling hot, searing, scorching, scalding, red-hot.
▷ANTONYMS cold.
2 *it was a beautiful hot day*: **very warm**, balmy, summery, tropical, boiling, boiling hot, blazing hot, baking, scorching, roasting, searing, flaming, parching, blistering, oven-like; sweltering, torrid, sultry, humid, muggy, close, airless, oppressive, stifling.
▷ANTONYMS chilly.
3 *she felt hot and her throat was parched*: **feverish**, fevered, febrile, burning, flushed; informal with a temperature; rare pyretic.
4 *a very hot dish cooked with green chilli*: **spicy**, spiced, peppery, piquant, highly seasoned, sharp, fiery, strong, pungent, aromatic.
▷ANTONYMS mild.
5 *hot rage surged through him again*: **angry**, indignant, furious, fiery, seething, raging, boiling, fuming; wrathful, enraged, infuriated, inflamed.
▷ANTONYMS calm.
6 *it remains the subject of hot debate*: **animated**, heated, fierce, 'lively', intense, passionate, impassioned, spirited, ardent, fervent, feverish; **furious**, violent, ferocious, acrimonious, stormy, tempestuous, savage; rare fervid, passional.
▷ANTONYMS dispassionate.
7 *he found the competition too hot*: **fierce**, intense, keen, competitive, cut-throat, dog-eat-dog, ruthless, aggressive, strong, powerful.
▷ANTONYMS weak.
8 informal *the romance was the hottest story in Fleet Street*: **new**, fresh, recent, late, up to date, up to the minute; brand new, just out, just released, just issued, hot off the press; informal bang up to date.
▷ANTONYMS old.

9 informal *this band is seriously hot*: **popular**, in demand, sought-after, in favour, well liked, well loved; **fashionable**, in fashion, in vogue, all the rage; informal big, in, now, hip, trendy, cool; Brit. informal, dated all the go.
▷ANTONYMS unpopular, out of fashion.
10 informal *Tony is hot on local history*: **knowledgeable about**, well informed about, au fait with, up on, well versed in, au courant with; skilled at, expert at, enthusiastic about, keen on; informal clued up about, genned up about.
▷ANTONYMS ill-informed; apathetic.
11 informal *computer hardware is the most saleable category of hot goods*: **stolen**, illegally obtained, under the counter, illegal, illicit, unlawful, smuggled, bootleg, contraband; Brit. informal dodgy.
▷ANTONYMS lawful.
□ **blow hot and cold** informal *he had been stringing her along, blowing hot and cold*: **vacillate**, keep changing one's mind, dither, shilly-shally, oscillate, waver, be indecisive, be irresolute, be undecided, be uncertain, be unsure, hesitate; Brit. haver, hum and haw; Scottish swither; informal dilly-dally.
▷ANTONYMS be decisive.
□ **hot on the heels of** *critique followed hot on the heels of this pioneering work*: **close behind**, soon after, shortly after, directly after, right after, straight after, immediately after, hard on the heels of, following closely.
▷ANTONYMS far behind.
□ **hot under the collar** informal *Nick got really hot under the collar about the issue*: **angry**, **annoyed**, furious, irate, infuriated, incensed, enraged, cross, in a temper, irritated, put out, fed up, aggrieved; informal aggravated, peeved, miffed, mad, riled, hacked off, peed off; Brit. informal cheesed off, brassed off, narked, ratty, shirty; N. Amer. informal teed off, ticked off, sore, bent out of shape; Austral./NZ informal snaky, crook; vulgar slang pissed off; literary ireful.
▷ANTONYMS pleased.
□ **make it/things hot for someone** informal *make it hot for her and she'll soon go away*: **harass**, hound, plague, badger, harry, pester, bother, bully, intimidate, pick on, persecute, victimize, terrorize; N. Amer. devil; informal hassle, give someone hell, give someone a hard time, get on someone's back; Austral. informal heavy.
▷ANTONYMS leave in peace.

hot air noun informal *they dismissed the theory as a load of hot air*. See **nonsense** (sense 1).

hotbed noun *the country was a hotbed of revolt and dissension*: **breeding ground**, nursery, cradle, nest, den, seedbed, forcing house.

hot-blooded adjective *hot-blooded young lovers*: **passionate**, impassioned, amorous, amatory, sensual, sexy, ardent; **lustful**, libidinous, lecherous, sex-hungry; informal horny, randy, raunchy; rare concupiscent, lickerish.
▷ANTONYMS cold, frigid.

hotchpotch, hodgepodge noun *it was a rambling hotchpotch of roof lines and gables*: **mixture**, mix, mixed bag, assortment, assemblage, collection, selection, jumble, ragbag, miscellany, medley, patchwork, pot-pourri; melange, mess, mishmash, confusion, clutter, farrago; informal mash-up; rare gallimaufry, olio, olla podrida, salmagundi.

hotel noun **inn**; motel, boarding house, guest house, lodge, bed and breakfast, B&B, hostel; aparthotel, boatel; French pension, auberge; Spanish parador, posada; Portuguese pousada; Italian pensione; German Gasthaus.

hotfoot adverb *he rushed hotfoot to the planning office to object*: **hastily**, hurriedly, speedily, quickly, fast, rapidly, swiftly, without delay, in haste, at top speed, at full tilt, as fast as possible; headlong, post-haste, pell-mell, helter-skelter; informal at a lick, like the wind, like greased lightning, at warp speed, like a bomb, like mad, like crazy, like blazes; Brit. informal like the clappers, at a rate of knots, like billy-o; N. Amer. informal lickety-split; literary apace, hurry-scurry.
▷ANTONYMS at moderate speed.
▸ verb
□ **hotfoot it** informal *we hotfooted it after him*: **hurry**, dash, run, race, sprint, bolt, dart, gallop, career, charge, shoot, hurtle, hare, bound, fly, speed, zoom, streak, make haste, hasten; informal tear, belt, pelt, scoot, zap, zip, whip, leg it, steam, go like a bat out of hell, burn rubber; Brit. informal bomb, bucket; Scottish informal wheech; N. Amer. informal boogie, hightail it, clip, barrel; N. Amer. vulgar slang drag/tear/haul ass; archaic post, hie, haste.
▷ANTONYMS dawdle.

hothead noun *a few hotheads urged their comrades to break the police roadblocks*: **madcap**, daredevil; Brit. tearaway; informal loony, nut, nutter; N. Amer. informal screwball; dated desperado, hotspur.

hot-headed adjective *a number of hot-headed youths caused the bother*: **impetuous**, impulsive, headstrong, reckless, rash, irresponsible, foolhardy, madcap, wild, excitable, volatile, precipitate, overhasty, unruly, fiery, hot-tempered, quick-tempered; informal harum-scarum, crazy, crackpot; archaic hasty.
▷ANTONYMS cool-headed.

hothouse noun **greenhouse**, glasshouse, conservatory, orangery, vinery, alpine house, winter garden; summer house, gazebo, pavilion, belvedere.
▸ adjective *the school's isolated location has encouraged a hothouse atmosphere*: **intense**, oppressive, stifling; oversheltered, overprotected, pampered, coddled, shielded.

hotly adverb **1** *the rumours were hotly denied*: **vehemently**, vigorously, strenuously, fiercely, passionately, heatedly, with a vengeance; angrily, indignantly, furiously, in anger, with indignation.
▷ANTONYMS calmly.
2 *he rushed out, hotly pursued by Boris*: **closely**, swiftly, quickly, hotfoot, without delay; eagerly, enthusiastically, energetically.

hot-tempered adjective *he is arrogant, hot-tempered, and capable of violence*: **irascible**, quick-tempered, short-tempered, irritable, fiery, impatient, huffy, brusque, ill-tempered, bad-tempered, ill-natured, ill-humoured, touchy, volatile, testy, tetchy, fractious, snarling, waspish, prickly, crusty, peppery, bilious, liverish, dyspeptic, splenetic, choleric; informal snappish, snappy, chippy, on a short fuse; Brit. informal narky, ratty, eggy, like a bear with a sore head; N. Amer. informal peckish, soreheaded; Austral./NZ informal snaky; informal, dated miffy.
▷ANTONYMS easy-going.

hound noun **dog**, hunting dog, canine, mongrel, cur; informal doggy, pooch, mutt; Austral. informal mong, bitzer.
▸ verb **1** *she was hounded by the Italian press*: **harass**, persecute, harry, pester, bother, trouble, annoy, badger, torment, bedevil, keep after; nag, bully, browbeat, chivvy, keep on at, go on at; informal hassle, bug, give someone a hard time; N. Amer. informal devil, ride; Austral. informal heavy.
▷ANTONYMS leave in peace.
2 *his opponents used the allegations to hound him out of office*: **force**, drive, pressure, pressurize, propel, push, urge, coerce, impel, dragoon, strong-arm; informal bulldoze, railroad; Brit. informal bounce; N. Amer. informal hustle.
3 *he led the race from start to finish but was hounded all the way by Phillips*: **pursue**, chase, follow, shadow, give chase to, follow on the heels of, be hot on someone's heels; hunt, hunt down, stalk, track, trail; informal tail.

> *Word links* **hound**
>
> **pack**, **cry** collective noun

house noun **1** *the new estate comprises 200 houses*: **home**, place of residence, homestead, lodging place, a roof over one's head; formal habitation, residence, dwelling, dwelling place, abode, domicile.
2 *make yourself scarce before you wake the whole house*: **household**, family, family circle, ménage, clan, tribe; informal brood.
3 *the power and prestige of the house of Stewart*: **clan**, kindred, family, tribe, race, strain; dynasty, line, lineage, ancestry, ancestors, bloodline, descent, family tree.
4 *the publishing and printing house grew to become self-financing*: **firm**, business, company, corporation, enterprise, establishment, institution, concern, organization, operation; informal outfit, set-up.
5 *the sixty-member National Council, the country's upper house*: **legislative assembly**, legislative body, chamber, council, parliament, diet, congress, senate.
6 *the house burst into applause*: **audience**, crowd, those present, listeners, spectators, viewers, gathering, assembly, assemblage, congregation; gallery, stalls; informal punters.
7 *the house offers a wide variety of real ales*: **inn**, bar, tavern, hostelry, taproom; restaurant, hotel, eating house; Brit. pub, public house; informal eatery, boozer; historical alehouse, taphouse, beerhouse; N. Amer. historical saloon.
□ **on the house** informal *our first rounds always came on the house*: **free**, free of charge, without payment, without charge, at no cost, for nothing, gratis; courtesy, complimentary; informal for free; N. Amer. informal comp.
▷ANTONYMS paid for.
▸ verb **1** *they converted a disused cinema to house twelve employees*: **accommodate**, provide accommodation for, provide with accommodation, give accommodation to, make space for, make room for, give someone a roof over their head, provide a roof over someone's head, provide with a place to work, harbour; lodge, quarter, board, billet, take in, provide shelter for, shelter; sleep, put up, give a bed to, provide with a place to sleep.
▷ANTONYMS evict.
2 *the rear panel houses the selector switch*: **contain**, hold, store, cover; protect, enclose, encase, sheathe, keep safe.
▷ANTONYMS expose.

household noun *the whole household was asleep*: **family**, house, family circle, ménage, clan, tribe; informal brood.
▸ adjective *they had all kinds of household goods on offer*: **domestic**, family, workaday, ordinary, everyday, usual, common, run-of-the-mill; Brit. common or garden.
▷ANTONYMS exotic.

householder noun **homeowner**, owner, occupant, resident, head of the household; tenant, leaseholder; proprietor, landlady, landlord, freeholder; Brit. occupier, owner-occupier; formal dweller.

housekeeping noun *she did as much of the cooking and housekeeping as she could*: **household management**, domestic work, domestic duties, homemaking, the running of the home; home economics, domestic science; rare housecraft, housewifery.

houseman noun Brit. **junior doctor**, house doctor, newly qualified doctor, medical officer, MO; Brit. house officer; N. Amer. intern, resident.

house-trained adjective Brit. *the cat is not completely house-trained yet*: **domesticated**, trained; N. Amer. housebroken.

housing noun **1** *they invest in housing and other ventures*: **homes**, houses, places of residence, buildings; accommodation, living quarters; formal dwellings, dwelling places, habitations, abodes, domiciles.
2 *the large spheres provide protective housing for the radio antennae*: **casing**, covering, case, cover, encasement, container, enclosure, holder, sheath, jacket, shell, capsule; technical integument.

hovel noun *people were living in rat-infested hovels*: **shack**, slum, shanty, hut, shed, cabin; informal dump, hole; Scottish bothy.

hover verb **1** *army helicopters hovered overhead*: **be suspended**, be poised, hang, float, levitate, drift, fly, flutter.
2 *she hovered anxiously in the background*: **linger**, loiter, wait about, stay nearby; informal hang around, stick around; Brit. informal hang about.

h

however adverb **1** *people tend to put on weight in middle age—however, gaining weight is not inevitable*: **but**, **nevertheless**, nonetheless, still, yet, though, although, even so, (but) for all that, (but) despite that, (but) in spite of that; anyway, anyhow, be that as it may, having said that, notwithstanding; informal still and all; archaic howbeit, withal, natheless.
2 *however you look at it, you can't criticize that*: **in whatever way**, regardless of how, no matter how.

howl noun **1** *at midnight she heard the howl of a wolf*: **baying**, bay, howling, crying, cry, yowl, yowling, bark, barking, yelp, yelping.
2 *he let out a howl of anguish*: **wail**, cry, yell, yelp, yowl, bawl, bellow, roar, shout, shriek, scream, screech, caterwaul; informal holler; rare ululation.
▸ verb **1** *they heard dogs howling in the distance*: **bay**, cry, yowl, bark, yelp.
2 *a baby started to howl*: **wail**, cry, yell, yelp, yowl, bawl, bellow, roar, shout, shriek, scream, screech, caterwaul; informal holler; rare ululate.
3 *the audience howled and whooped with laughter*: **laugh**, guffaw, roar, laugh loudly, roar with laughter, dissolve into laughter, be creased up, be doubled up, split one's sides; informal fall about, crack up, be in stitches, be rolling in the aisles, laugh fit to bust.

howler noun informal *the occasional schoolboy howler would amuse the examiners*: **mistake**, error, blunder, fault, gaffe, slip, slip of the pen; Latin lapsus calami; informal slip-up, boo-boo, boner, botch, fluff; Brit. informal boob, bloomer, clanger; N. Amer. informal blooper, bloop, goof; vulgar slang fuck-up; technical malapropism, solecism.

hub noun **1** *the spokes radiate from the hub of the wheel*: **pivot**, axis, fulcrum, centre, centre point.
2 *the kitchen was the hub of family life*: **centre**, centre of activity, core, heart, focus, focal point, middle, nucleus, kernel, nerve centre.
▷ANTONYMS periphery.

hubbub noun **1** *his wife's voice could be heard above the hubbub*: **noise**, loud noise, din, racket, commotion, clamour, ruckus, cacophony, babel; informal rumpus; Brit. informal row; rare vociferation.
2 *she fought through the hubbub*: **confusion**, chaos, pandemonium, bedlam, mayhem, uproar, disorder, turmoil, tumult, fracas, hurly-burly, havoc, brouhaha; Scottish & N. English stramash; W. Indian bangarang; informal hullabaloo.
▷ANTONYMS calm.

hubris noun *the self-assuring hubris among economists was shaken in the late 1960s*: **arrogance**, conceit, conceitedness, haughtiness, pride, vanity, self-importance, self-conceit, pomposity, superciliousness, feeling of superiority; French hauteur; informal uppitiness, big-headedness.
▷ANTONYMS modesty.

huckster noun rare **trader**, dealer, seller, purveyor, vendor, barrow boy, salesman, door-to-door salesman; W. Indian higgler; informal pusher; dated pedlar, hawker; archaic chapman, packman; rare crier, colporteur.

huddle verb **1** *they huddled together for warmth*: **crowd**, gather, throng, flock, herd, pile, bunch, cluster, collect, group, congregate; press, pack, squeeze, cram, jam; rare foregather.
▷ANTONYMS disperse.
2 *he huddled beneath the sheets*: **curl up**, snuggle, cuddle, nestle, hunch up; N. Amer. snug down.
▷ANTONYMS stretch out.
▸ noun **1** *a huddle of passengers gathered round the information desk*: **crowd**, gathering, throng, flock, herd, swarm, press, pack; cluster, bunch, knot, band, collection, circle, small group, assemblage; informal gaggle.
2 *a huddle of barns and outbuildings*: **collection**, group, cluster, number, mass, selection, array; jumble, confusion, muddle, heap, tangle, mess.
3 informal *each team went into a huddle and then wrote down its answer*: **consultation**, discussion, debate, talk, parley, meeting, conference; informal confab, powwow; rare confabulation.

hue noun **1** *seaweeds are found in a variety of hues*: **colour**, tone, shade, tint, tinge, cast, tincture.
2 *men of all political hues submerged their feuds*: **complexion**, type, kind, sort, cast, light, stamp, nuance, aspect, character, nature.

hue and cry noun *her relatives raised a hue and cry after the accident*: **commotion**, outcry, uproar, fuss, clamour, racket, storm, ado, stir, furore, ruckus, ballyhoo, brouhaha, palaver, pother; informal hoo-ha, hullabaloo, to-do, flap, song and dance, rumpus, splash; Brit. informal kerfuffle, carry-on, row, stink; NZ informal bobsy-die.

huff noun *she walked off in a huff*: **bad mood**, sulk, fit of bad humour, fit of pique, pet, temper, tantrum, rage, fury, passion; informal grump, snit; Brit. informal strop, paddy; N. Amer. informal blowout, hissy fit; Brit. informal, dated bate, wax; archaic paddywhack, miff.
▷ANTONYMS good mood.

huffy adjective *he was huffy with me for ages*: **irritable**, irritated, annoyed, cross, grumpy, huffish, bad-tempered, crotchety, crabby, crabbed, cantankerous, curmudgeonly, moody, petulant, miserable, morose, sullen, surly, churlish; touchy, testy, tetchy, crusty, snappish, waspish, prickly; informal snappy, cranky; Brit. informal narky, narked, miffed, ratty, eggy, shirty, like a bear with a sore head, whingy; N. Amer. informal soreheaded, peckish; Austral./NZ snaky; vulgar slang pissed off; dated miffy.
▷ANTONYMS cheerful, friendly.

hug verb **1** *people kissed and hugged each other*: **embrace**, cuddle, squeeze, clasp, clutch, cling to, hold someone close, hold someone tight, take someone in one's arms, enfold someone in one's arms, clasp/press someone to one's bosom; literary embosom.
2 *I headed north, hugging the coastline all the way*: **keep close to**, stay near to, follow closely, follow the course of.
▷ANTONYMS keep away from.
3 *we hugged the comforting thought that we were safe from foreign foes*: **cling to**, hold on to, cherish, harbour, nurture, nurse, foster, retain, maintain, keep in one's mind.
▷ANTONYMS abandon.
▸ noun *there were hugs and tears as they were reunited*: **embrace**, cuddle, squeeze, bear hug, hold, clasp, clutch, clinch, caress.

huge adjective *a huge amount of raw materials come from abroad* | *a huge slab of rock*: **enormous**, vast, immense, very large, very big, great, massive, colossal, prodigious, gigantic, gargantuan, mammoth, monumental, tremendous, stupendous; **giant**, towering, hefty, bulky, weighty, heavy, gross, monstrous, elephantine, mountainous, titanic; epic, Herculean, Brobdingnagian; princely, generous, handsome; informal jumbo, mega, monster, whopping, whopping great, thumping, thumping great, humongous, hulking, bumper, almighty, astronomical, astronomic; Brit. informal whacking, whacking great, ginormous.
▷ANTONYMS insignificant; tiny.

hugely adverb *they are fighting a hugely expensive legal battle*: **very**, most, really, thoroughly, extremely, exceedingly, particularly, tremendously, highly, greatly, decidedly, distinctly, exceptionally, immensely, eminently, supremely, inordinately, singularly, extraordinarily, vastly, overly; very much, to a great extent; Scottish unco; French très; N. English right; informal terrifically, awfully, terribly, devilishly, madly, majorly, seriously, desperately, mega, ultra, oh-so, too-too, stinking, mucho, damn, damned, too ... for words; informal, dated devilish, hellish, frightfully; Brit. informal ever so, well, bloody, dead, dirty, jolly, fair; N. Amer. informal real, mighty, powerful, awful, plumb, darned, way, bitching; S. African informal lekker; archaic exceeding, sore.
▷ANTONYMS slightly.

hugger-mugger adjective **1** *a spirit of careless frivolity where all was hugger-mugger*: **disorderly**, confused, disorganized, chaotic, muddled, haphazard, in a mess, in a shambles, in disarray, topsy-turvy, at sixes and sevens; informal higgledy-piggledy; Brit. informal shambolic.
▷ANTONYMS orderly.
2 *no more hugger-mugger dealings for me!* **clandestine**, secret, covert, furtive, cloak-and-dagger, hole-in-the-corner, behind-the-scenes, under-the-table, sneaky, sly, underhand; undercover, underground; informal hush-hush.
▷ANTONYMS above board.

hulk noun **1** *the rusting hulks of ships*: **wreck**, shipwreck, ruin, shell, skeleton, hull, frame, framework, derelict.
2 *a great clumsy hulk of a man*: **oaf**; informal clodhopper, ape, gorilla; N. Amer. informal lummox, klutz; N. Amer. & Scottish informal galoot; archaic lubber, clodpole.

hulking adjective informal *a hulking man stood aside as I entered*. See **big** (sense 2).

hull[1] noun *the wooden hull of the ship*: **framework**, body, frame, skeleton, shell, structure, basic structure; exterior.

hull[2] noun **shell**, husk, pod, case, casing, covering, seed case; rind, skin, peel; N. Amer. shuck; technical pericarp, capsule, legume; rare integument.

▸ **verb** *a beak which the bird uses effectively in hulling seeds*: **shell**, husk, peel, pare, skin; N. Amer. shuck; technical decorticate.

hullabaloo noun informal *there was a terrific hullabaloo over the by-election*: **fuss**, commotion, uproar, hubbub, outcry, furore, ruckus, ado, palaver, brouhaha, hue and cry; pandemonium, mayhem, tumult, turmoil, hurly-burly; roar, racket, din, noise, clamour, bedlam, babel; informal rumpus, ruction, hoo-ha, to-do, song and dance; Brit. informal kerfuffle, carry-on, row.

hum verb **1** *the engine was humming and ready to go*: **purr**, whirr, throb, vibrate, murmur, buzz, thrum, drone; literary susurrate, bombinate.
2 *humming a tune*: **sing**, croon, murmur, drone.
3 *the repair shops are humming as the tradesmen set about their various tasks*: **be busy**, be active, be lively, buzz, bustle, be bustling, be a hive of activity, throb, vibrate, pulsate, pulse.
▷ANTONYMS be quiet.
4 Brit. informal *when the wind drops this stuff really hums*: **smell**, stink, stink to high heaven, reek, have a bad smell, be malodorous; Brit. informal pong.
□ **hum and haw** Brit. *they waste a lot of time humming and hawing before going into action*: **be indecisive**, hesitate, dither, vacillate, procrastinate, equivocate, prevaricate, waver, falter, fluctuate; Brit. haver; Scottish swither; informal shilly-shally, dilly-dally, blow hot and cold, pussyfoot around; archaic or literary tarry.
▷ANTONYMS be decisive.
▸ **noun** *a low hum of conversation*: **murmur**, murmuring, drone, droning, vibration, purr, purring, buzz, buzzing, whirr, whirring, throb, throbbing, thrum, thrumming; literary susurration, susurrus, bombination.

human adjective **1** *the survival of the human race*: **anthropoid**.
▷ANTONYMS animal.
2 *they're only human and therefore mistakes do occur | accidents due to human frailty*: **mortal**, flesh and blood; **fallible**, weak, frail, imperfect, vulnerable, susceptible, erring, error-prone; physical, bodily, fleshly, carnal, corporal.
▷ANTONYMS infallible.
3 *the human side of politics is getting stronger*: **compassionate**, humane, kind, kindly, kind-hearted, considerate, understanding, sympathetic, tolerant; approachable, accessible.
▷ANTONYMS inhuman.
▸ **noun** *the complex link between humans and animals*: **person**, human being, personage, mortal, member of the human race; man, woman, child; individual, living soul, soul, being; earthling; Latin Homo sapiens; informal, dated body; archaic wight.
▷ANTONYMS animal; alien.

Word links **human**

anthropo- related prefix
anthropology study of humankind
anthropometry measurement of the human body
anthropophagous, cannibalistic eating of other humans

humane adjective *regulations ensuring the humane treatment of animals*: **compassionate**, kind, kindly, kind-hearted, considerate, understanding, sympathetic, tolerant, civilized, good, good-natured, gentle; lenient, forbearing, forgiving, merciful, mild, tender, clement, benign, humanitarian, benevolent, charitable, generous, magnanimous; approachable, accessible; rare benignant.
▷ANTONYMS cruel; inhumane.

Word toolkit

humane	lenient	solicitous
treatment	punishment	hospitality
prison	scoring	husband/wife
trap	laws	suitor
death	judge	service

humanitarian adjective **1** *they sought his release on humanitarian grounds | a humanitarian act*: **compassionate**, humane; unselfish, altruistic, generous, magnanimous, benevolent, civilized, merciful, kind, good, sympathetic; rare benignant.
▷ANTONYMS selfish.
2 *a humanitarian organization*: **charitable**, philanthropic, public-spirited, socially concerned, doing good works, welfare.
▷ANTONYMS for profit.
▸ **noun philanthropist**, altruist, benefactor, social reformer, do-gooder, good Samaritan; historical almsgiver; rare philanthrope, Maecenas.
▷ANTONYMS self-seeker.

humanities plural noun **liberal arts**, arts, literature; classics, classical studies, classical languages, classical literature; Latin literae humaniores.

humanity noun **1** *humanity evolved from the higher apes*: **humankind**, the human race, the human species, mankind, man, people, mortals; Latin Homo sapiens.
▷ANTONYMS the animal kingdom.
2 *the humanity of Christ*: **human nature**, humanness, mortality, flesh and blood.
3 *he praised them for their standards of humanity, care, and dignity*: **compassion**, brotherly love, fellow feeling, humaneness, kindness, kind-heartedness, consideration, understanding, sympathy, tolerance, goodness, good-heartedness, gentleness, leniency, mercy, mercifulness, pity, tenderness, benevolence, charity, generosity, magnanimity.
▷ANTONYMS cruelty; inhumanity.

humanize verb *schools should try to humanize their pupils*: **civilize**, improve, better; educate, enlighten, edify, instruct, sophisticate, socialize, refine, polish; informal rub the rough edges off.

humankind noun **the human race**, the human species, humanity, mankind, man, people, mortals; Latin Homo sapiens.
▷ANTONYMS the animal kingdom.

humble adjective **1** *her bearing was very humble and apologetic*: **meek**, deferential, respectful, submissive, self-effacing, unassertive, unpresuming; **modest**, unassuming, self-deprecating, free from vanity, hiding one's light under a bushel; obsequious, sycophantic, servile; Scottish mim; archaic resistless.
▷ANTONYMS proud, overbearing.
2 *she came from a humble, unprivileged background*: **low-ranking**, low, lowly, lower-class, plebeian, proletarian, working-class, undistinguished, poor, mean, ignoble, of low birth, low-born, of low rank; common, commonplace, ordinary, simple, inferior, unimportant, unremarkable, insignificant, inconsequential; informal plebby; archaic baseborn.
▷ANTONYMS noble.
3 *welcome to my humble abode*: **unpretentious**, modest, unostentatious, plain, simple, ordinary.
▷ANTONYMS grand.
▸ **verb 1** *I knew he had humbled himself to ask for my help*: **humiliate**, abase, demean, belittle, lower, degrade, debase, bring down, bring low; mortify, shame, put to shame, abash, subdue, chasten, make someone eat humble pie, take down a peg or two; informal put down, cut down to size, settle someone's hash; N. Amer. informal make someone eat crow.
2 *Wales were humbled at Cardiff Arms Park by Romania*: **defeat**, beat, beat hollow, crush, trounce, conquer, vanquish, rout, smash, overwhelm, get the better of, give a drubbing to, bring someone to their knees; informal lick, clobber, hammer, slaughter, murder, massacre, crucify, wipe the floor with, walk all over; N. Amer. informal shellac, blow out, cream, skunk.
▷ANTONYMS be victorious over.

Word toolkit

humble	meek	deferential
opinion	voice	tone
servant	acceptance	treatment
apologies	husband/wife	standard
request	little mouse	society
heart	whimper	habits

humbug noun **1** *to dress it all up as a 'green' tax is sheer humbug*: **hypocrisy**, hypocritical talk/behaviour, sanctimoniousness, posturing, cant, empty talk; insincerity, dishonesty, falseness, falsity, sham, deceit, deception, deceptiveness, imposture, pretence; fraud, trickery, cheating; informal phoneyness, con, kidology; Irish informal codology; rare Tartufferie.
2 *you are a coward as well as a humbug*: **hypocrite**, hypocritical person, plaster saint, whited sepulchre; charlatan, impostor, fraud, cheat, deceiver, dissembler, fake, sham; informal con man, con artist, phoney; rare Tartuffe.
▸ **verb** *poor Dave is easily humbugged*: **deceive**, trick, delude, mislead, fool, hoodwink, dupe, hoax, take in, beguile, bamboozle, gull, cheat; informal con, kid, put one over on, have on, pull the wool over someone's eyes; vulgar slang bullshit; archaic cozen.

humdrum adjective *humdrum routine work*: **mundane**, dull, dreary, boring, tedious, monotonous, banal, ho-hum, tiresome, wearisome, prosaic, unexciting, uninteresting, uneventful, unvarying, unvaried, unremarkable, repetitive, repetitious, routine, ordinary, everyday, day-to-day, quotidian, run-of-the-mill, commonplace, common, workaday, usual, pedestrian, customary, regular, normal; N. Amer. garden variety; informal typical, vanilla, plain vanilla; Brit. informal common or garden; rare banausic.
▷ANTONYMS remarkable; exciting.

humid adjective *a hot and humid day*: **muggy**, close, sultry, sticky, steamy, oppressive, airless, stifling, suffocating, stuffy, clammy, soupy, heavy, fuggy, like a Turkish bath, like a sauna; damp, dank, moist, wet, misty.
▷ANTONYMS fresh; arid.

humidity noun *a climate of warm temperatures and high humidity*: **mugginess**, humidness, closeness, sultriness, stickiness, steaminess, airlessness, stuffiness, clamminess; dampness, damp, dankness, moisture,

moistness, wetness, mistiness.
▷ANTONYMS freshness; aridity.

Word links humidity

hygrometry, psychrometry measurement of humidity

humiliate verb *you'll humiliate me in front of the whole school*: **embarrass**, mortify, humble, show up, shame, make ashamed, put to shame; disgrace, discomfit, chasten, subdue, abash, abase, debase, demean, degrade, deflate, crush, quash, squash, bring down, bring low, cause to feel small, cause to lose face, make someone eat humble pie, take down a peg or two; informal put down, cut down to size, settle someone's hash; N. Amer. informal make someone eat crow.
▷ANTONYMS aggrandize.

humiliating adjective *a humiliating election defeat*: **embarrassing**, mortifying, humbling, ignominious, inglorious, shaming, shameful; discreditable, undignified, discomfiting, chastening, debasing, demeaning, degrading, deflating, crushing, quashing, squashing, bringing down, bringing low; informal blush-making; rare humiliatory.
▷ANTONYMS glorious.

humiliation noun *only a few go through the humiliation of having the bailiffs at the door*: **embarrassment**, mortification, shame, indignity, ignominy, disgrace, dishonour, discomfiture, degradation, discredit, obloquy, opprobrium, loss of pride, loss of face; affront, insult, rebuff, snub, put-down, blow to one's pride, slap in the face, smack in the face, kick in the teeth; informal brush-off; rare disesteem, reprobation, vitiation.
▷ANTONYMS honour.

h

humility noun *he needs the humility to accept that their way may be better*: **modesty**, humbleness, modestness, meekness, lack of pride, lack of vanity, diffidence, unassertiveness.
▷ANTONYMS pride.

hummock noun **hillock**, hump, mound, knoll, tump, prominence, eminence, elevation, rise, dune, barrow, tumulus; N. Amer. knob; S. African koppie; archaic knap, monticle.

humorist noun **comic writer**, writer of comedy, wit, wag; funny man, funny woman, comic, comedian, comedienne, joker, jokester, clown, jester; cartoonist, caricaturist; informal card, laugh, scream, hoot, riot, barrel of laughs; informal, dated caution.

humorous adjective *the novel is a humorous account of a developing relationship*: **amusing**, funny, entertaining, comic, comical, chucklesome, diverting, witty, jocular, light-hearted, tongue-in-cheek, wry, waggish, whimsical, playful; hilarious, uproarious, riotous, zany, facetious, farcical, absurd, droll; informal priceless, wacky, side-splitting, rib-tickling, a scream, a hoot, a laugh, a barrel of laughs; informal, dated killing; rare jocose.
▷ANTONYMS serious; boring.

humour noun **1** *the humour of the situation is central to the film*: **comical aspect**, comic side, funny side, comedy, funniness, hilarity, jocularity; absurdity, absurdness, ludicrousness, drollness, facetiousness; satire, irony.
▷ANTONYMS seriousness.
2 *the familiar stories are spiced up with humour*: **jokes**, joking, jests, jesting, quips, witticisms, witty remarks, funny remarks, puns; **wit**, wittiness, comedy, jocularity, waggishness, drollery, repartee, badinage, banter, raillery; French doubles entendres, bons mots; informal gags, wisecracks, cracks, one-liners.
3 *his good humour was infectious*: **mood**, temper, disposition, temperament, frame of mind, state of mind; spirits.
▶verb *she was always humouring him to prevent trouble*: **indulge**, pander to, yield to, bow to, cater to, give way to, give in to, go along with, comply with, adapt to, accommodate; **pamper**, spoil, overindulge, cosset, coddle, mollycoddle, mollify, soothe, placate, gratify, satisfy.
▷ANTONYMS stand up to.

humourless adjective *she was thought of as a hard-working, humourless academic*: **serious**, serious-minded, solemn, earnest, sober, sombre, grave, stern, grim, dour, morose, unsmiling, stony-faced; **gloomy**, glum, depressed, sad, melancholy, dismal, doleful, mournful, dejected, despondent, joyless, cheerless, lugubrious, in low spirits, with a long face; boring, tedious, dull, dry, heavy-going.
▷ANTONYMS light-hearted; jovial.

hump noun *his back rose into a kind of hump at the base of the spine*: **protuberance**, lump, bump, knob, protrusion, prominence, projection, bulge, swelling, hunch, nodule, node, mass, growth, outgrowth, excrescence; rare tumescence, tumefaction, intumescence.
□ **give someone the hump** informal See **annoy**.
□ **over the hump** *now we have reached this point we are over the hump*: **over the worst part**, over the worst of it, out of the woods, on the road to recovery, on the up and up, on the way up, getting better, making progress, in the clear.
▷ANTONYMS in difficulties.

▶verb **1** *he turned and humped his body to avoid a rope*: **arch**, curve, hunch, bend, bow, curl, crook.
▷ANTONYMS straighten.
2 informal *he continued to hump cases up and down the hotel corridor*: **carry**, lug, heave, lift, shoulder, hoist, heft, tote; informal schlep; Scottish informal humph; rare upheave.

humped adjective *he had a grotesquely humped back*: **arched**, bent, bowed, curved, rounded, hunched; humpbacked, hunchbacked; technical kyphotic; literary embowed, crookbacked; rare curviform.
▷ANTONYMS straight.

hunch verb **1** *he thrust his hands in his pockets, hunching his shoulders*: **arch**, curve, hump, bend, bow, curl, crook.
▷ANTONYMS straighten.
2 *I **hunched up** as small as I could*: **crouch**, huddle up, curl up, hunker down, bend, stoop, squat; N. Amer. informal scooch.
▷ANTONYMS stretch out.
▶noun **1** *he had a hunch on his back*: **protuberance**, hump, lump, bump, knob, protrusion, prominence, projection, bulge, swelling, nodule, node, mass, growth, outgrowth, excrescence; rare tumescence, tumefaction, intumescence.
2 *my hunch is that these may not be the end of the changes*: **feeling**, guess, suspicion, sneaking suspicion, impression, inkling, idea, notion, fancy, presentiment, premonition, intuition; informal gut feeling, feeling in one's bones, funny feeling, sixth sense.

hundred cardinal number **century**; informal ton.

Word links hundred

centi-, hecto- related prefixes, as in *centipede, hectogram*
centenary, centennial relating to a hundred

hunger noun **1** *she was faint with hunger*: **lack of food**, need for food, hungriness, ravenousness, emptiness; starvation, famine, malnutrition, malnourishment, undernourishment; rare famishment, inanition.
2 *there is a global hunger for news*: **desire**, craving, longing, yearning, pining, hankering, thirst, appetite, lust, ache, want, need; informal itch, yen; rare appetence, appetency.
▷ANTONYMS aversion.
▶verb
□ **hunger after/for** *all actors hunger for such a role*: **desire**, crave, have a craving for; long for, yearn for, have a yearning for, pine for, ache for, thirst for, have an appetite for, hanker after, lust after, want, need; informal have a yen for, itch for, be dying for, be gagging for; archaic be athirst for, be desirous of.
▷ANTONYMS have an aversion to.

hungry adjective **1** *I was feeling ravenously hungry*: **ravenous**, empty, hollow, faint from hunger; starving, starved, famished, dying from hunger, deprived of food, half-starved, malnourished, undernourished, underfed; informal peckish, able to eat a horse, with one's stomach thinking one's throat's cut; rare sharp-set, esurient.
▷ANTONYMS full; well fed.
2 *the new team are **hungry for** success*: **eager**, keen, avid, longing, yearning, pining, aching, greedy, thirsting, with an appetite; craving, desiring, desirous of, covetous of, hankering after, lusting after, in need of, in want of; informal itching, dying, gagging, hot, with a yen; archaic athirst.
▷ANTONYMS averse to; indifferent to.

hunk noun **1** *the soup was served with a hunk of bread*: **chunk**, large piece, slab, wedge, block, lump, mass, square, gobbet, dollop, portion; Scottish dod; Brit. informal wodge; N. Amer. informal gob; rare nub.
2 informal *the calendar gives you a different hunk each month*: **muscleman**, strongman, macho, macho man, iron man, Hercules, Atlas, Samson, Tarzan; informal tough guy, he-man, beefcake, stud, bruiser; N. Amer. informal studmuffin.
▷ANTONYMS wimp.

hunt verb **1** *in the autumn they hunted deer*: **chase**, give chase to, pursue, stalk, course, hunt down, run down; track, trail, follow, shadow, hound, dog; informal tail.
2 *police are **hunting for** her attacker*: **search**, look, look high and low, scour around; seek, try to find; cast about/around/round, rummage (about/around/round), root about/around, fish about/around, forage about/around, ferret (about/around); Brit. informal rootle about/around.
▶noun **1** *they enjoyed the thrill of the hunt*: **chase**, pursuit, stalking, course, coursing; tracking, trailing, shadowing; informal tailing.
2 *police have stepped up the hunt for the killer*: **search**, look, quest; seeking, rummaging, foraging, ferreting (about/around).

hunted adjective *his eyes had a hunted look*: **harassed**, persecuted, harried, hounded, besieged, beleaguered, troubled, stressed, tormented; careworn, haggard, downtrodden, browbeaten, distraught, desperate; informal hassled, up against it.
▷ANTONYMS carefree.

hunter noun **huntsman**, **huntswoman**, stalker, trapper, woodsman; nimrod, Orion; predator; French **chasseur**; Indian **shikari**; rare **venator**, **venerer**.

hunting noun **blood sports**, field sports, stalking, trapping, coursing, fox-hunting, the chase; poaching; Indian **shikar**; archaic **venery**.

hurdle noun **1** *he hit a hurdle and cut his leg badly*: **fence**, jump, barrier, barricade, bar, railing, rail, wall, hedge, hedgerow.
2 *this was the final hurdle to overcome in the college's bid for university status*: **obstacle**, difficulty, problem, barrier, bar, snag, stumbling block, impediment, obstruction, complication, handicap, hindrance; informal **hiccup**, **headache**, **fly in the ointment**; Brit. informal **spanner in the works**; N. Amer. informal **monkey wrench in the works**.

hurl verb *rioters hurled a brick through the windscreen of a car*: **throw**, toss, fling, pitch, cast, lob, launch, flip, catapult, shy, dash, send, bowl, aim, direct, project, propel, fire, let fly; informal **chuck**, **heave**, **sling**, **buzz**, **whang**, **bung**; N. Amer. informal **peg**; Austral. informal **hoy**; NZ informal **bish**.
▷ANTONYMS catch, hold.

hurly-burly noun *they wanted to escape from the hurly-burly of city life*: **bustle**, hustle, commotion, hubbub, confusion, chaos, disorder, fuss, turmoil, uproar, tumult, turbulence, pandemonium, mayhem, bedlam, furore, brouhaha; upheaval, unrest, disruption, trouble, agitation; informal **hoo-ha**, **hullabaloo**, **ballyhoo**, **rumpus**; Brit. informal **kerfuffle**.
▷ANTONYMS calm, order.

hurricane noun **cyclone**, typhoon, tornado, storm, tropical storm, tempest, windstorm, gale, squall, whirlwind; N. Amer. informal **twister**; Austral./NZ informal **willy-willy**.

hurried adjective **1** *he left in long, hurried strides | hurried glances*: **quick**, fast, swift, rapid, speedy, brisk, hasty, hurrying, expeditious, breakneck; cursory, perfunctory, brief, short, fleeting, passing, flying, superficial; literary **fleet**, **rathe**.
▷ANTONYMS slow, leisurely.
2 *a hurried decision*: **hasty**, rushed, speedy, quick; **rash**, impetuous, impulsive, reckless, precipitate, precipitous, incautious, imprudent, spur-of-the-moment, premature; rare **temerarious**.
▷ANTONYMS considered.

hurriedly adverb *she got up and dressed hurriedly*: **hastily**, speedily, quickly, fast, rapidly, swiftly, briskly, expeditiously, without delay, in haste, in a hurry, at a run, at a gallop, at top speed, at full tilt, at the double, as fast as possible; headlong, hotfoot, post-haste, pell-mell, helter-skelter; informal **at a lick**, **like the wind**, **like greased lightning**, **like a bomb**, **at warp speed**, **like mad**, **like crazy**, **like blazes**, **double quick**, **in double quick time**; Brit. informal **like the clappers**, **at a rate of knots**, **like billy-o**; N. Amer. informal **lickety-split**; literary **apace**, **hurry-scurry**.
▷ANTONYMS slowly; at moderate speed.

hurry verb **1** *you'd better hurry or you'll be late*: **be quick**, hurry up, move quickly, go fast, hasten, make haste, speed, speed up, lose no time, press on, push on, run, dash, rush, hurtle, dart, race, fly, flash, shoot, streak, bolt, bound, blast, charge, chase, career, scurry, scramble, scamper, scuttle, sprint, gallop, go hell for leather, go like lightning; Brit. **scutter**; informal **whizz**, **whoosh**, **vroom**, **tear**, **scoot**, **hare**, **pelt**, **zip**, **whip**, **zoom**, **belt**, **beetle**, **buzz**, **get a move on**, **step on it**, **get cracking**, **get moving**, **shake a leg**, **go like a bat out of hell**, **hotfoot it**, **leg it**, **burn rubber**; Brit. informal **bomb**, **bucket**, **shift**, **put one's foot down**, **get one's skates on**, **go like the clappers**, **stir one's stumps**; Scottish informal **wheech**; N. Amer. informal **hightail**, **barrel**, **boogie**, **clip**, **lay rubber**, **get the lead out**, **get a wiggle on**; S. African informal **put foot**; N. Amer. vulgar slang **drag/tear/haul ass**; informal, dated **cut along**; archaic **post**, **hie**, **fleet**.
▷ANTONYMS move slowly; dawdle.
2 *she hurried him across the landing*: **hustle**, hasten, push (on), urge (on), drive on, spur on, goad, prod; informal **gee up**.
▷ANTONYMS slow down; delay.
▸ noun *in all the hurry, we forgot the picnic*: **haste**, flurry, bustle, confusion, commotion, hubbub, hustle, urgency, agitation, turmoil; **rush**, race, scramble, scurry; speed, swiftness, rapidity, quickness; literary **fleetness**, **celerity**; archaic **hurry scurry**, **pother**.
▷ANTONYMS calmness.

hurt verb **1** *my back hurts*: **be painful**, be sore, be tender, cause pain, cause discomfort, ache, smart, sting, burn, tingle, throb; informal **be killing**, **be playing up**.
▷ANTONYMS be healed.
2 *Dad had hurt his leg*: **injure**, wound, damage, disable, incapacitate, impair, maim, mutilate, cause injury to, cause pain to; bruise, cut, gash, graze, scrape, scratch, lacerate; abuse, torture, maltreat, ill-treat, molest.
▷ANTONYMS heal.
3 *his cruel words hurt her deeply*: **distress**, pain, wound, offend, sting, upset, sadden, devastate, mortify, grieve, aggrieve, be hurtful to, hurt someone's feelings, cause sorrow, cause suffering, cause anguish, make unhappy, give offence to, cut to the quick.
▷ANTONYMS please; comfort.
4 *high interest rates are hurting the local economy*: **harm**, damage, do harm to, be detrimental to, weaken, spoil, mar, blemish, blight, impair, impede, jeopardize, undermine, ruin, wreck, sabotage, cripple; informal **foul up**.
▷ANTONYMS benefit, improve.
▸ noun **1** *rolling properly into a fall minimizes hurt | he rubbed the hurt on his chin*: **harm**, injury, wounding, pain, suffering, discomfort, soreness, aching, smarting, stinging, throbbing, pangs; bruise, graze, scrape, cut, gash, scratch, laceration.
2 *she loved him, in spite of all the hurt he had caused her*: **distress**, pain, suffering, grief, misery, anguish, torment, trauma, woe, upset, sadness, sorrow, wretchedness; harm, damage, injury, trouble, misfortune, affliction, wrong, detriment, disadvantage; informal **mischief**.
▷ANTONYMS joy.
▸ adjective **1** *the doctor looked at my hurt hand*: **injured**, wounded, bruised, grazed, scratched, cut, gashed, lacerated, sore, painful, aching, burning, smarting, throbbing.
▷ANTONYMS healed.
2 *Anne's hurt expression spoke volumes*: **pained**, distressed, aggrieved, displeased, disgruntled, anguished, resentful, offended, piqued, upset, sad, saddened, sorrowful, grief-stricken; informal **miffed**, **peeved**, **narked**, **browned off**, **hacked off**; Brit. informal **cheesed off**; N. Amer. informal **sore**; vulgar slang **pissed off**.
▷ANTONYMS pleased.

hurtful adjective **1** *hurtful words*: **upsetting**, distressing, wounding, painful; **unkind**, cruel, nasty, mean, malicious, spiteful, snide, acerbic, cutting, biting, barbed, vicious, offensive; informal **catty**, **bitchy**; Brit. informal **sarky**; N. Amer. informal **snarky**; rare **acidulous**, **mordacious**.
▷ANTONYMS pleasant; comforting.
2 *such a move would be hurtful to the interests of women*: **detrimental**, harmful, damaging, injurious, disadvantageous, unfavourable, prejudicial, baleful, deleterious, destructive, disastrous, pernicious, ruinous, inimical; literary **malefic**, **maleficent**; rare **baneful**, **prejudicious**.
▷ANTONYMS beneficial.

hurtle verb *a runaway car hurtled towards them*: **speed**, rush, race, chase, bolt, bowl, dash, career, careen, cannon, sweep, whizz, buzz, zoom, flash, blast, charge, shoot, streak, run, gallop, stampede, hare, fly, wing, scurry, scud, go like the wind; informal **belt**, **pelt**, **tear**, **scoot**, **tool**, **zap**, **zip**, **whip**, **burn rubber**, **go like a bat out of hell**; Brit. informal **bomb**, **bucket**, **shift**, **go like the clappers**; N. Amer. informal **clip**, **boogie**, **hightail**, **barrel**; archaic **post**, **hie**.
▷ANTONYMS go slowly.

husband noun **spouse**, partner, mate, consort, man; groom, bridegroom; informal **hubby**, **old man**, **one's better half**; Brit. informal **other half**; humorous **lord and master**; archaic **helpmate**, **helpmeet**.
▸ verb *reserves of oil and gas should be husbanded*: **use economically**, use sparingly, economize on, be frugal with, manage thriftily; **conserve**, preserve, save, safeguard, save for a rainy day, put aside, put by, lay in, reserve, store, stockpile, hoard.
▷ANTONYMS squander, waste.

husbandry noun **1** *farmers have no money to invest in new methods of husbandry*: **farm management**, farming, agriculture, land management, agronomy, agronomics, agribusiness, cultivation, tillage; animal husbandry.
2 *they have gained some reward from the careful husbandry of their slender resources*: **conservation**, careful management, good housekeeping, economy, thrift, thriftiness, frugality; saving, budgeting; rare **sparingness**.
▷ANTONYMS wastefulness.

hush verb **1** *he placed a finger before pursed lips to hush her*: **silence**, quieten, quieten down, shush; gag, muzzle; informal **shut up**.
2 *the lights dimmed and everyone hushed*: **fall silent**, become silent, stop talking, quieten, quieten down; informal **pipe down**, **shut up**.
▷ANTONYMS become noisy.
3 *she tried to hush their fears*: **calm**, allay, assuage, still, quieten, soften, ease, soothe, lessen, reduce, moderate.
▷ANTONYMS aggravate.
4 *management took steps to **hush up** the dangers*: **keep secret**, conceal, hide, suppress, cover up, keep dark, keep quiet about, not divulge, stifle, squash, whitewash, smother, obscure, veil, sweep under the carpet; informal **sit on**, **keep under one's hat**.
▷ANTONYMS disclose.
▸ exclamation *Hush! Someone will hear you*: **be quiet**, keep quiet, quieten down, be silent, stop talking, hold your tongue; informal **shut up**, **shut your face**, **shut your mouth**, **shut your trap**, **button your lip**, **pipe down**, **cut the cackle**, **put a sock in it**, **give it a rest**, **not another word**; Brit. informal **shut your gob**, **wrap it up**, **wrap up**; N. Amer. informal **save it**.
▷ANTONYMS speak up.
▸ noun *a hush descended over the crowd*: **silence**, quiet, quietness, quietude, soundlessness, noiselessness; stillness, still, peacefulness, peace, calmness, calm, tranquillity.
▷ANTONYMS noise.

hush-hush adjective informal *this is meant to be hush-hush*. See **secret** (sense 1 of the adjective).

h

husk noun **shell**, hull, pod, case, casing, covering, seed case; rind, skin, peel; (**husks**) chaff, bran; N. Amer. shuck; technical pericarp, capsule, legume; rare integument.

husky adjective **1** *his voice deepened to a husky growl*: **throaty**, gruff, deep, gravelly, hoarse, coarse, croaking, croaky, rough, rough-sounding, thick, guttural, harsh, rasping, raspy.
▷ANTONYMS shrill; soft.
2 *Paddy looked a husky guy*: **strong**, muscular, muscly, muscle-bound, brawny, hefty, burly, chunky, strapping, thickset, solid, powerful, heavy, robust, rugged, sturdy, Herculean, big and strong, broad-shouldered, well built, powerfully built, solidly built; informal beefy, hunky, hulking; dated stalwart; literary thewy, stark.
▷ANTONYMS puny.

hussy noun **minx**, madam, coquette, tease, seductress, Lolita, Jezebel; trollop, slut, loose woman; informal floozie, tart, puss; Brit. informal scrubber, slapper, slag; N. Amer. informal tramp, vamp; archaic baggage, hoyden, fizgig, jade, quean, wanton, strumpet.

hustle verb **1** *they were hissed and hustled as they went*: **jostle**, push, push roughly, bump, knock, shove, nudge, elbow, shoulder; crowd, mob.
2 *I was hustled away to a cold cell*: **manhandle**, push, shove, thrust, frogmarch, bulldoze; rush, hurry, hasten, whisk, sweep; informal bundle.
3 informal *don't be hustled into anything unless you really want to do it*: **coerce**, force, compel, pressure, pressurize, badger, pester, hound, harass, nag, harry, urge, goad, prod, spur; browbeat, bludgeon, bulldoze, steamroller, dragoon, prevail on, strong-arm; informal railroad; Brit. informal bounce; N. Amer. informal fast-talk.
▸ noun *we were tired of the hustle and bustle of city life*: **activity**, bustle, hustle and bustle, hurly-burly, commotion, tumult, hubbub, brouhaha, busyness, action, liveliness, animation, movement, life, excitement, agitation, fuss, flurry, stir, whirl; informal toing and froing, comings and goings, rumpus, ballyhoo, hoo-ha, hullabaloo, to-do; archaic hurry scurry, pother.
▷ANTONYMS peace.

hut noun **shack**, shanty, cabin, log cabin, shelter, shed, lean-to, den, hovel; Scottish bothy, shieling, shiel; N. Amer. cabana; Canadian tilt; S. African hok; Austral. gunyah, mia-mia, humpy; NZ whare; American Indian hogan, wickiup; in Brazil favela; N. Amer. archaic shebang.

hybrid noun *this is a hybrid between a brown and albino mouse*: **cross**, cross-breed, mixed-breed; mixture, blend, meld, amalgam, amalgamation, combination, composite, compound, conglomerate, fusion, synthesis; informal mash-up.
▸ adjective *hybrid varieties of rose*: **composite**, cross-bred, interbred; mixed, compound, combined, blended, mongrel, impure;
▷ANTONYMS pure-bred.

hybridize verb *a few gardeners hybridize their roses*: **cross-breed**, cross, interbreed, mix, intermix, blend, combine, amalgamate; cross-fertilize, cross-pollinate.

hygiene noun *poor standards of food hygiene*: **cleanliness**, personal hygiene, personal cleanliness, purity, sterility, disinfection, sanitation, sanitariness; public health, environmental health, sanitary measures.
▷ANTONYMS uncleanliness.

hygienic adjective *this will leave the whole kitchen clean and hygienic*: **sanitary**, clean, germ-free, dirt-free, disinfected, sterilized, sterile, antiseptic, aseptic, uninfected, unpolluted, uncontaminated, salubrious, healthy, pure, wholesome; informal squeaky clean, as clean as a whistle.
▷ANTONYMS dirty; insanitary.

hymn noun **religious song**, **anthem**, song of praise, canticle, chorale, psalm, carol, chant; antiphon, introit, doxology, spiritual, paean, plainsong; rare lay, miserere.

> *Word links* **hymn**
>
> **Erato** the Muse of hymns and lyric poetry

hype informal noun *she relied on hype and headlines to stoke up interest in her music*: **publicity**, advertising, promotion, marketing, puff, puffery, propaganda, exposure; boost, push, fanfare, build-up; informal plug, plugging, razzmatazz, ballyhoo.
▸ verb *this was another stunt to hype a new product*: **publicize**, advertise, promote, push, boost, merchandise, give publicity to, give a puff to, puff, puff up, build up, talk up, beat/bang the drum for; informal plug.
▷ANTONYMS play down.

hyperbole noun *the media hyperbole which accompanied their European Championship match*: **exaggeration**, overstatement, magnification, amplification, embroidery, embellishment, overplaying, excess, overkill; informal purple prose, puffery.
▷ANTONYMS understatement.

hypercritical adjective *he was a sarcastic, hypercritical man*: **carping**, captious, overcritical, fault-finding, hair-splitting, cavilling, niggling, quibbling, pedantic, pettifogging, fussy, finicky, over-censorious, over-exacting, over-rigorous, over-particular, over-strict; informal **picky**, nit-picking, pernickety; N. Amer. informal persnickety; archaic nice, overnice.
▷ANTONYMS easy-going; uncritical.

hypnosis noun **mesmerism**, hypnotism, hypnotic suggestion, auto-suggestion.

hypnotic adjective *her voice had a hypnotic quality*: **mesmerizing**, mesmeric, spellbinding, entrancing, bewitching, fascinating, irresistible, compelling; **soporific**, sleep-inducing, sleep-producing, somnolent, somniferous, sedative, numbing; Medicine stupefacient, stupefactive; rare somnific.
▷ANTONYMS invigorating.

hypnotism noun **mesmerism**, hypnosis, hypnotic suggestion, auto-suggestion.

hypnotize verb **1** *a witness had been hypnotized to enhance his memory*: **mesmerize**, send into a trance, put under, put out, put to sleep.
2 *they were hypnotized by the dancers*: **fascinate**, entrance, beguile, spellbind, hold spellbound, enthral, transfix, be unable to take one's eyes off, captivate, bewitch, enrapture, grip, rivet, absorb, magnetize; informal bowl over, knock out.
▷ANTONYMS bore.

hypochondria noun **imagined ill health**, **valetudinarianism**, anxiety about one's health, preoccupation with one's health, health obsession; neurosis; rare hypochondriasis, hypochondriacism.

hypochondriac noun *she was a hypochondriac who could not manage without her pills*: **valetudinarian**, valetudinary, neurotic; French malade imaginaire; archaic melancholico; rare hypochondriast.
▸ adjective *her tiresome hypochondriac husband*: **valetudinarian**, valetudinary, malingering, neurotic, health-obsessed, obsessed with one's health, preoccupied with ill health, anxious about one's health; rare hypochondriacal, hypochondric.

hypocrisy noun *plain speaking was important to him—he hated hypocrisy*: **sanctimoniousness**, sanctimony, pietism, piousness, affected piety, affected superiority, false virtue, cant, humbug, pretence, posturing, speciousness, empty talk; insincerity, falseness, falsity, deceptiveness, deceit, deceitfulness, deception, dishonesty, dissembling, dissimulation, duplicity, imposture, two-facedness, double-dealing; informal phoneyness; rare Pharisaism, Tartufferie.
▷ANTONYMS honesty; sincerity.

hypocrite noun *he condemned her as superficial and a hypocrite*: **sanctimonious person**, pietist, whited sepulchre, plaster saint, humbug, pretender, deceiver, dissembler, impostor; informal phoney, Holy Willie; Brit. informal creeping Jesus; N. Amer. informal bluenose; rare Pharisee, Tartuffe, Pecksniff, canter.

hypocritical adjective *a hypocritical morality regarding sexual behaviour*: **sanctimonious**, pious, pietistic, self-righteous, holier-than-thou, superior, insincere, specious, feigned, pretended, hollow, false; deceitful, deceptive, dishonest, untruthful, lying, dissembling, duplicitous, two-faced, double-dealing, untrustworthy; informal phoney, pretend; rare Pharisaic, Pharisaical, Tartuffian, Janus-faced, canting.
▷ANTONYMS sincere.

hypodermic noun **needle**, syringe; informal hype, spike.

hypothesis noun *his 'steady state' hypothesis of the origin of the universe*: **theory**, theorem, thesis, conjecture, supposition, speculation, postulation, postulate, proposition, premise, surmise, assumption, presumption, presupposition; notion, concept, idea, contention, opinion, view, belief.

hypothetical adjective *a hypothetical case | the hypothetical tenth planet*: **theoretical**, **speculative**, conjectured, imagined, notional, suppositional; supposed, assumed, presumed, putative; made up, unreal; academic.
▷ANTONYMS real, actual.

hysteria noun *his voice had an edge of hysteria*: **frenzy**, wildness, feverishness, irrationality; **hysterics**, loss of control; panic, panic attack, alarm, outburst/fit of agitation, loss of reason, fit of madness, neurosis, delirium, derangement, mania, distress, mental distress; Brit. informal the screaming abdabs/habdabs.
▷ANTONYMS calmness, self-possession.

hysterical adjective **1** *Janet became hysterical and began screaming | hysterical laughter*: **overwrought**, emotional, uncontrolled, uncontrollable, out of control, unrestrained, unrestrainable, frenzied, in a frenzy, frantic, wild, feverish; beside oneself, driven to distraction, in a panic, agitated, neurotic; mad, crazed, berserk, maniac, maniacal, manic, delirious, unhinged, deranged, out of one's mind, out of one's wits, raving; informal in a state.
▷ANTONYMS calm, self-possessed.
2 informal *her attempts to teach them to dance were hysterical*: **hilarious**, uproarious, very funny, very amusing, comical, comic, farcical; informal hysterically funny, side-splitting, rib-tickling, killing, killingly funny,

screamingly funny, a scream, a hoot, a laugh, a barrel of laughs, a laugh a minute.
▷ANTONYMS serious.

hysterics plural noun informal **1** *she was throwing a fit of screaming hysterics*: **hysteria**, wildness, feverishness, irrationality, frenzy, loss of control, loss of reason; neurosis, delirium, derangement, mania, distress, mental distress; Brit. informal the screaming abdabs/habdabs.
▷ANTONYMS calmness, self-possession.
2 *this started them both giggling and they fled upstairs in hysterics*: **fits of laughter**, gales of laughter, peals of laughter, uncontrollable laughter, convulsions, fits, guffawing, howling; informal stitches, hooting; rare cachinnation.

ice noun **1** *the lake was covered with ice*: **frozen water**; icicle, iceberg, glacier; black ice, glaze, verglas, frost, rime.
2 *assorted ices*: **ice cream**; sorbet, water ice; N. Amer. sherbet.
3 *the ice in her voice had no effect on him*: **coldness**, coolness, frost, frostiness, iciness, chilliness, glaciality, frigidity, lack of warmth; hostility, unfriendliness, stiffness, distance, stand-offishness, aloofness.
□ **on ice** informal *Govan's transfer to the City team was still on ice last night*: **in abeyance**, pending, ongoing, (up) in the air, (still) open, hanging fire, in the balance; in suspension, in a state of suspension, suspended, put to one side, in a state of uncertainty, in limbo, betwixt and between; deferred, postponed, put off; awaiting attention, awaiting decision, awaiting action, unattended to, outstanding, unfinished, incomplete; unresolved, undetermined, undecided, unsettled, unconcluded, uncertain; informal on the back burner, in cold storage.
▷**ANTONYMS** in hand.
□ **with ice** *would you like your Scotch with ice?* informal **on the rocks**.
▶**verb 1** *the lake has iced over*: **freeze**, freeze over, turn into ice, harden, solidify; archaic glaciate.
▷**ANTONYMS** thaw.
2 (usually **iced**) *a refreshingly iced lemonade*: **cool**, chill, make cold, refrigerate, add ice to.
▷**ANTONYMS** hot.
3 *she had iced the cake and written 'Good Luck' on it*: **cover with icing**, glaze; N. Amer. frost, spread frosting over.

> *Word links* **ice**
>
> **gelid**, **glacial** relating to ice
> **cryophobia** fear of ice

ice-cold adjective *the ice-cold waters of the fjord*: **icy**, freezing, bitterly cold, glacial, sub-zero, frozen, wintry; arctic, polar, Siberian; bitter, biting, piercing, raw, cutting, chilly; refreshing, bracing, invigorating; literary chill, frore; rare gelid, brumal, rimy, algid.
▷**ANTONYMS** hot, warm.

icing noun *a big cake with white icing*: **glaze**, sugar paste; royal icing, butter icing, glacé icing, fondant icing; N. Amer. frosting.

icon noun *an icon of the Madonna hangs on the wall*: **image**, idol, portrait, likeness, representation, symbol, figure, statue, model.

iconoclast noun *she is an iconoclast, called to shatter the myth of restaurants she feels are too popular*: **critic**, sceptic, questioner; heretic, nonconformist, dissident, dissenter, dissentient; malcontent, rebel, subversive, renegade, mutineer; maverick; original, innovator.

iconoclastic adjective *a fresh, even an iconoclastic, influence could work wonders*: **critical**, sceptical, questioning; heretical, irreverent, nonconformist, dissident, dissenting, dissentient; malcontent, rebellious, subversive, renegade, mutinous; maverick, original, innovative, groundbreaking.
▷**ANTONYMS** conformist.

icy adjective **1** *icy roads*: **frozen**, frozen over, iced over, ice-bound, ice-covered, iced up, frosty, frosted, glassy, like a sheet of glass, slippery; informal slippy; literary rimy.
2 *an icy wind*: **freezing**, frigid, chill, chilly, chilling, frosty, biting, bitter, raw, arctic, glacial, Siberian, polar, gelid.
▷**ANTONYMS** hot, warm.
3 *'What did you say?' said an icy voice*: **unfriendly**, unwelcoming, inhospitable, hostile, forbidding; cold, cool, chilly, frigid, frosty, glacial, wintry; stiff, aloof, distant, unsympathetic, disdainful, haughty, stony, stern, hard, fierce; rare gelid.
▷**ANTONYMS** friendly.

idea noun **1** *the idea of death scares her*: **concept**, notion, conception, conceptualization, thought, image, mental picture, visualization, abstraction, perception; hypothesis, postulation.
2 *our idea is to open a new shop*: **plan**, design, scheme, project, proposal, proposition, suggestion, recommendation, aim, intention, objective, object, purpose, end, goal, target.
3 *Elizabeth had other ideas on the subject*: **thought**, theory, view, viewpoint, opinion, feeling, outlook, belief, judgement, conclusion.
4 *you had an idea that it might happen?* **sense**, feeling, suspicion, fancy, inkling, hunch, understanding, theory, hypothesis, thesis, interpretation, assumption, presumption, supposition, surmise, postulation, conclusion, deduction, inference, notion, impression.
5 *the idea of the letter was to get patients to protest*: **purpose**, point, aim, object, objective, goal, intention, end, end in view, design, reason, use, utility, sense, motive; value, advantage.
6 *could you give me some idea of the cost?* **estimate**, estimation, guess, approximation, conjecture, rough calculation, rough idea, surmise; guesswork; informal guesstimate; N. Amer. informal a ballpark figure.

> *Choose the right word* **idea, concept, notion**
>
> **Idea** has the widest range of these words, with uses dividing roughly into ways of understanding something and plans or intentions. An *idea* may be a belief or opinion, in particular someone's impression of what something is like (*most people form their idea of reality from experience*). This often merges into feelings about what something ideally should be (*a cookery course wasn't her idea of fun*). An idea can also be a thought or suggestion about something that should be done, typically one arrived at as a possible solution to a problem, and this sense extends to that of a plan, hope, or intention (*it might be a good idea to get more rest | the idea is to reduce costs*).
>
> A **concept** is an understanding of what something is, usually quite a broad subject; it is more fully and consciously worked out than an *idea* (*his theories rest on his concept of consciousness | modern concepts of democracy*).
>
> **Notion** may refer either to beliefs about matters of fact or to ideas and wishes about things to do (*the notion that public bodies should be representative*). A *notion* is generally vaguer or more tentatively held than an *idea*, and there may be a suggestion, not present in the other two words, that the beliefs in question are mistaken or absurd (*the misguided notion that the policy would remove the problem of homelessness | he rejects any notion of de-skilling*).

ideal adjective **1** *it was ideal flying weather*: **perfect**, best possible, consummate, supreme, absolute, complete, copybook, flawless, faultless, without fault, exemplary, classic, archetypal, model, ultimate, quintessential.
▷**ANTONYMS** bad.
2 *a unified European culture remained as an ideal concept that inspired future kings and emperors*: **abstract**, **theoretical**, conceptual, notional, intellectual, metaphysical, philosophical, academic; hypothetical, speculative, conjectural, conjectured, suppositional, putative; rare

suppositious, suppositive, ideational.
▷ANTONYMS concrete.
3 *the film-makers portray an ideal world*: **unattainable**, unachievable, impracticable, unworkable, unfeasible; **unreal**, fictitious, hypothetical, theoretical, ivory-towered, imaginary, idealized, Utopian, romantic, quixotic, visionary, fanciful, fairy-tale.
▷ANTONYMS attainable; real.
▶ **noun 1** *she endeavoured to be what she imagined was his ideal*: **perfection**, paragon, epitome, ne plus ultra, beau idéal, nonpareil, crème de la crème, the last word, the ultimate, a dream; informal one in a million, the tops, the best/greatest thing since sliced bread, the bee's knees; archaic a nonsuch.
2 *an ideal to aim at*: **model**, pattern, exemplar, example, paradigm, archetype, prototype, criterion, yardstick.
3 *the service of others is the highest ideal*: **principle**, standard, rule of living, moral value, belief, conviction, persuasion; (**ideals**) morals, morality, ethics, code of behaviour, code of honour, ideology, creed; integrity, uprightness, high-mindedness, righteousness, virtue, probity, rectitude, sense of honour, honour, decency, conscience, sense of duty, scruples.

idealism noun *the Liberal Party had about it the idealism of youth*: **Utopianism**, wishful thinking, romanticism, fantasizing, quixotism, daydreaming, impracticability.
▷ANTONYMS realism; cynicism; defeatism.

idealist noun *he came to power with the reputation of a left-wing idealist*: **Utopian**, visionary, wishful thinker, pipe-dreamer, fantasist, fantasizer, romantic, romanticist, romancer, castle-builder, Walter Mitty, Don Quixote, dreamer, daydreamer, impractical person, unrealistic person; rare fantast, reverist.
▷ANTONYMS realist; cynic; defeatist.

idealistic adjective *their creed appeals to the idealistic young*: **Utopian**, visionary, romantic, quixotic, dreamy, unrealistic, impractical, castle-building.
▷ANTONYMS realistic; cynical; defeatist.

> *Word toolkit* **idealistic**
>
> See **quixotic**.

idealize verb *they tend to idealize the post-war years*: **romanticize**, romance, be unrealistic about, look at something through rose-tinted/rose-coloured spectacles, paint a rosy picture of, glamorize; idolize, apotheosize, deify.

ideally adverb *ideally, everyone should have enough to live on*: **in a perfect world**, in a Utopia; preferably, if possible, for preference, by preference, from choice, by choice, as a matter of choice, much rather, rather; all things being equal, theoretically, hypothetically, in theory, in principle, on paper; French en principe.
▷ANTONYMS in practice, in reality.

idée fixe noun French *his other idée fixe was his belief in the existence of a ninth planet*: **obsession**, fixation, ruling/consuming passion, passion, mania, compulsion, preoccupation, enthusiasm, infatuation, addiction, fetish, craze, hobby horse; phobia, complex, neurosis; informal bee in one's bonnet, hang-up, thing, bug.

identical adjective **1** *a contingent of businessmen wearing identical lapel badges*: **similar**, alike, (exactly) the same, indistinguishable, uniform, twin, interchangeable, undifferentiated, homogeneous, of a piece, cut from the same cloth; corresponding, correspondent, commensurate, equivalent, matching, like, parallel, analogous, comparable, cognate, equal; informal like (two) peas in a pod, much of a muchness, (like) Tweedledum and Tweedledee.
▷ANTONYMS different, unlike.
2 *try again, using **the identical** technique*: **the same**, the very same, one and the same, the selfsame, the very; **aforementioned**, previously mentioned, aforesaid, aforenamed, previously described, above, above-stated; foregoing, preceding, precedent, earlier, previous.
▷ANTONYMS different.

Word toolkit

identical	same	equivalent
twins	time	amounts
results	place	levels
sequences	page	units
copies	sex	value
circumstances	day	doses
DNA	team	rates

identifiable adjective *there are no easily identifiable features on the shoreline*: **distinguishable**, recognizable, known, noticeable, perceptible, discernible, appreciable, detectable, observable, perceivable, visible, notable, measurable; **distinct**, marked, conspicuous, unmistakable, clear, apparent, evident; archaic sensible.
▷ANTONYMS unrecognizable; inconspicuous.

identification noun **1** *the identification of the suspect by the victim carries great weight*: **recognition**, singling out, picking out, spotting, pointing out, pinpointing, naming, placing; discerning, distinguishing, discovery, finding, location; N. Amer. informal fingering.
2 *early identification of problems was important*: **determining**, establishment, ascertainment, finding out, discovery, fixing, settling, diagnosis, divination, discerning, distinguishing; verification, confirmation.
3 *may I see your identification?* **ID**, papers, identity papers, identification papers, bona fides, documents, credentials; ID card, identity card, pass, badge, warrant, licence, permit, passport, proof of identity; proof of qualifications, certificate, diploma, references, testimonial, letter of introduction, letter of recommendation.
4 *the identification of Nonconformity with Victorian values*: **association**, link, linkage, connection, tie, bracketing, relatedness, interrelation, interconnection, interdependence.
5 *his identification with the music is evident from the opening bars*: **empathy**, rapport, fellow feeling, togetherness, unity, bond of sympathy, sympathetic cord, sympathy, understanding; informal good vibes.

identify verb **1** *she identified her attacker in a police line-up*: **recognize**, single out, pick out, spot, point out, pinpoint, pin down, put one's finger on, put a name to, name, place, know, know again, know by sight, discern, distinguish, discover, find, locate; remember, recall, recollect, call to mind; informal put the finger on; N. Amer. informal finger.
2 *I was able to identify four problem areas*: **determine**, establish, ascertain, find out, discover, learn, fix, settle, decide, make out, ferret out, diagnose, deduce, divine, intuit, discern, distinguish; verify, confirm, make certain of, certify; informal figure out, get a fix on.
3 *tobacco sponsorship is aimed at a market that **identifies** sport **with** glamour*: **associate**, link, connect, couple, relate, bracket, think of together; think of in connection with, draw a parallel with, mention in the same breath as, set side by side with.
▷ANTONYMS distinguish.
4 *children usually **identify with** the hero*: **empathize**, be in tune, have a rapport, feel togetherness, feel at one, commune, sympathize, be in sympathy; be on the same wavelength as, speak/talk the same language as; understand, relate to, feel for, have insight into; informal put oneself in the shoes of.
5 *it is tempting to **identify** him **with** an Athenian painter of the same name*: **equate with**, identify someone as, consider someone/something to be, regard as being the same as, regard as being identical to.

identity noun **1** *they eventually discovered the identity of the owner*: **name**; specification.
2 *she was afraid of losing her identity if she became his wife*: **individuality**, self, selfhood, ego, personality, character, originality, distinctiveness, distinction, singularity, peculiarity, uniqueness, differentness.
3 *a case of mistaken identity*: **identification**, recognition, naming, singling out, picking out, pinpointing, placing; discerning, distinguishing; N. Amer. informal fingering.
4 *management need to secure an identity of interests with shareholders*: **identicalness**, sameness, selfsameness, oneness, congruity, congruence, indistinguishability, interchangeability; likeness, alikeness, uniformity, similarity, closeness, accordance, alignment, parallelism, symmetry.
▷ANTONYMS mismatch.

ideology noun *the party has to jettison outdated ideology*: **beliefs**, ideas, ideals, principles, doctrine, creed, credo, teaching, dogma, theory, thesis, tenets, canon(s); conviction(s), persuasion, opinions, position, ethics, morals.

idiocy noun *to reduce funding by a further 20% would seem to be the height of idiocy | the idiocies of mankind*: **stupidity**, folly, foolishness, foolhardiness, madness, insanity, lunacy, silliness, brainlessness, thoughtlessness, senselessness, lack of sense, indiscretion, irresponsibility, injudiciousness, imprudence, rashness, recklessness, ineptitude, inaneness, inanity, irrationality, illogicality, absurdity, nonsense, ludicrousness, ridiculousness, fatuousness, fatuity, asininity, pointlessness, meaninglessness, futility, fruitlessness; informal craziness; Brit. informal daftness.
▷ANTONYMS sense.

idiom noun **1** *'Far out,' she replied, using a rather dated idiom*: **expression**, idiomatic expression, turn of phrase, set phrase, fixed expression, phrase; formal locution.
2 *the poet's idiom is elegantly terse*: **language**, mode of expression, style of speech, speech, talk, -speak, way/manner of speaking, usage, phraseology, phrasing, choice of words, vocabulary, parlance, tongue, vernacular, jargon, patter, argot, patois, cant; French façon de parler; informal lingo; formal locution.

idiomatic adjective *the texts have been translated from Italian into idiomatic English*: **natural**, native-speaker, grammatical, correct; vernacular, colloquial, everyday, conversational.
▷ANTONYMS unidiomatic.

idiosyncrasy noun *his idiosyncrasies included the recycling of cigar butts | sleep patterns show a high degree of idiosyncrasy*: **peculiarity**, individual/

personal trait, oddity, eccentricity, mannerism, quirk, whim, whimsy, fancy, fad, vagary, notion, conceit, caprice, kink, twist, freak, fetish, passion, bent, foible, crotchet, habit, characteristic, speciality, quality, feature; individuality; unconventionality, unorthodoxy; archaic megrim; rare singularity.

idiosyncratic adjective *each researcher had his or her own idiosyncratic interest | some might think this a rather idiosyncratic approach*: **distinctive**, **individual**, characteristic, distinct, distinguishing, peculiar, individualistic, different, typical, special, specific, representative, unique, personal, private, essential; **eccentric**, unconventional, uncommon, abnormal, irregular, aberrant, anomalous, odd, quirky, queer, strange, weird, bizarre, outlandish, freakish, extraordinary; rare singular.

idiot noun informal *that idiot was driving far too fast*: **fool**, ass, halfwit, nincompoop, blockhead, dunce, dolt, ignoramus, cretin, imbecile, dullard, moron, simpleton, clod; informal dope, ninny, chump, dimwit, goon, dumbo, dummy, dum-dum, dumb-bell, loon, dork, jackass, bonehead, fathead, numbskull, dunderhead, chucklehead, knucklehead, muttonhead, pudding-head, thickhead, wooden-head, airhead, pinhead, lamebrain, pea-brain, birdbrain, zombie, jerk, nerd, dipstick, donkey, noodle; Brit. informal nit, nitwit, twit, numpty, clot, plonker, berk, prat, pillock, wally, git, wazzock, divvy, nerk, twerp, twonk, charlie, mug, muppet; Scottish informal nyaff, balloon, sumph, gowk; Irish informal gobdaw; N. Amer. informal schmuck, bozo, boob, lamer, turkey, schlepper, chowderhead, dumbhead, goofball, goof, goofus, galoot, lummox, klutz, putz, schlemiel, sap, gink, cluck, clunk, ding-dong, dingbat, wiener, weeny, dip, simp, spud, coot, palooka, poop, squarehead, yo-yo, dingleberry; Austral./NZ informal drongo, dill, alec, galah, nong, bogan, poon, boofhead; S. African informal mompara; archaic tomfool, noddy, clodpole, loggerhead, spoony, mooncalf.
▷ANTONYMS genius.

idiotic adjective *I'm trying to stop Suzanne making an idiotic mistake*: **stupid**, silly, foolish, half-witted, witless, brainless, mindless, thoughtless, imprudent, incautious, irresponsible, injudicious, indiscreet, unwise, unintelligent, unreasonable; ill-advised, ill-considered, impolitic, rash, reckless, foolhardy; absurd, senseless, pointless, nonsensical, inane, fatuous, ridiculous, laughable, risible, derisible; informal dumb, dim, dim-witted, dopey, gormless, damfool, half-baked, hare-brained, crackbrained, pea-brained, wooden-headed, thickheaded, nutty, mad, crazy, dotty, batty, dippy, cuckoo, screwy, wacky; Brit. informal barmy, daft; Scottish & N. English informal glaikit; N. Amer. informal dumb-ass, chowderheaded; W. Indian informal dotish.
▷ANTONYMS sensible.

idle adjective **1** *an idle fellow*: **lazy**, indolent, slothful, work-shy, shiftless, loafing, inactive, inert, sluggish, lethargic, languorous, listless, torpid; remiss, negligent, slack, lax, lackadaisical, impassive, good-for-nothing, do-nothing; leisurely; informal bone idle; French, archaic fainéant; rare otiose.
▷ANTONYMS industrious.
2 *'I was getting bored with being idle,' she told her new employer*: **unemployed**, jobless, out of work, out of a job, redundant, between jobs, workless, unwaged, unoccupied; Brit. informal on the dole, signing on, 'resting'; Austral./NZ informal on the wallaby track.
▷ANTONYMS employed.
3 *instead of leaving the machine idle, I sold it*: **not in use**, out of use, not operating, not working, inactive, out of action, inoperative, non-functioning, out of service, unused, unoccupied, unemployed; disused, no longer in use, fallen into disuse, mothballed.
▷ANTONYMS working.
4 *they filled their idle hours with endless gossiping sessions*: **unoccupied**, spare, empty, vacant, unfilled, available.
▷ANTONYMS busy; full.
5 *he didn't indulge in idle remarks or mere social chit-chat*: **frivolous**, trivial, trifling, minor, petty, foolish, lightweight, shallow, superficial, insignificant, unimportant, worthless, valueless, pointless, paltry, niggling, peripheral, without depth, inane, fatuous, senseless, meaningless, purposeless, unnecessary, time-wasting.
▷ANTONYMS serious; meaningful.
6 *she was not a woman to make idle threats*: **empty**, meaningless, aimless, pointless, worthless, useless, vain, in vain, insubstantial, futile, ineffective, ineffectual; groundless, without grounds, baseless, without/lacking foundation.
▷ANTONYMS serious.
▶ verb **1** *Lily idled on the window seat: she hated Sundays*: **do nothing**, be inactive, vegetate, sit back, take it easy, rest on one's oars, mark time, kick one's heels, twiddle one's thumbs, kill time, languish, laze (around/about), lounge (around/about), loll (around/about), loaf (around/about), slouch (around/about); go to seed, degenerate, moulder, stagnate; informal hang around, veg out; Brit. informal hang about, mooch about/around, slummock; N. Amer. informal bum around, bat around/about, lollygag, lay on one's oars.
2 *the men **idled** their time **away** on street corners*: **fritter**, while, laze, loiter; **pass**, spend, use, employ, use up, occupy, take up, fill up, fill in, fill, beguile, expend, devote, waste, dissipate, kill.
3 *Robert idled along the pavement*: **saunter**, stroll, dawdle, drift, potter, amble, go/walk slowly, loiter, maunder, wander, straggle; informal mosey, tootle; Brit. informal pootle, mooch, swan; N. Amer. informal putter.
4 *he slowed the car at a junction, letting the engine idle*: **tick over**, run slowly in neutral.

> *Word links* **idle**
>
> **thassophobia** fear of being idle

> *Choose the right word* **idle, lazy, indolent**
>
> See **lazy**.

idleness noun **1** *he was birched for his idleness at school*: **laziness**, indolence, slothfulness, sloth, shiftlessness, inertia, sluggishness, lethargy, languor, torpidity, torpor; remissness, negligence, slackness, laxity; French, archaic fainéance; rare otiosity, hebetude.
▷ANTONYMS industry.
2 *we suffered a period of enforced idleness*: **inactivity**, inaction, unemployment, rest, repose.
▷ANTONYMS activity.

idler noun *you were not brought into this world to be an idler—you'll have to set your mind to something*: **loafer**, layabout, good-for-nothing, ne'er-do-well, do-nothing, lounger, shirker, sluggard, laggard, slugabed, malingerer; informal skiver, waster, slacker, cyberslacker, slowcoach, slob, lazybones; N. Amer. informal slowpoke; archaic wastrel; French, archaic fainéant.
▷ANTONYMS workaholic; swot.

idol noun **1** *an idol in a shrine*: **icon**, god, image, likeness, fetish, totem, statue, figure, figurine, doll, carving; graven image, false god, effigy, golden calf.
2 *the pop world's latest idol*: **hero**, **heroine**, star, superstar, icon, celebrity, celebutante; favourite, darling, beloved, pet, apple of one's eye; informal pin-up, heart throb, blue-eyed boy/girl, golden boy/girl; N. Amer. informal fair-haired boy/girl.

idolatrous adjective **1** *idolatrous religions*: **idol-worshipping**, icon-worshipping, fetishistic; pagan, heathen, heretical, infidel, sacrilegious.
2 *America's idolatrous worship of the auto*: **idolizing**, fetishistic; adulatory, adoring, reverential, glorifying, uncritical, lionizing; worshipping, worshipful, hero-worshipping.
▷ANTONYMS vilifying.

idolatry noun **1** *Jeremiah preached against idolatry*: **idol worship**, idolatrism, fetishism, iconolatry, icon worship; paganism, heathenism, heresy, sacrilege, ungodliness.
2 *our idolatry of art*: **idolization**, idolizing, fetishization, worship, worshipping, adulation, adoration, adoring, reverence, glorification, lionizing, lionization, love, admiration, loving, admiring, hero-worshipping.
▷ANTONYMS vilification.

idolize verb *he idolized professional wrestlers*: **hero-worship**, worship, revere, venerate, deify, lionize, adulate, adore, stand in awe of, reverence, look up to, admire, exalt, love, dote upon; informal put on a pedestal.
▷ANTONYMS vilify.

idyll noun **1** *he looked back on this time as an idyll | they lived in an idyll unspoilt by machines*: **perfect time**, ideal time, wonderful time, moment of bliss, honeymoon; **paradise**, heaven, heaven on earth, Garden of Eden, Shangri-La, fairyland, Utopia; literary Arcadia, Arcady, Erewhon.
▷ANTONYMS hell on earth.
2 *the poem began as a two-part idyll*: **pastoral**, eclogue, georgic, rural poem.

idyllic adjective *their idyllic times together | the idyllic English countryside*: **perfect**, ideal, idealized, wonderful, blissful, halcyon, happy; heavenly, paradisal, Utopian, Elysian; peaceful, picturesque, pastoral, rural, rustic, bucolic, unspoilt; literary Arcadian, sylvan.
▷ANTONYMS hellish.

if conjunction **1** *if the weather is fine, we can walk to the village*: **on condition that**, provided (that), providing (that), presuming (that), supposing (that), assuming (that), on the assumption that, allowing (that), as long as, given that, with the provision/proviso that, with/on the understanding that, if and only if, contingent on, in the event that, allowing that.
▷ANTONYMS unless.
2 *if I go out she gets nasty*: **whenever**, every time.
3 *I wonder if he noticed*: **whether**, whether or not.
4 *a useful, if unintended innovation*: **although**, albeit, but, even though, even if, despite being, in spite of being, yet, whilst.
▶ noun *there is of course one if in all this*: **uncertainty**, doubt, lack of certainty, hesitation, vagueness; **condition**, stipulation, provision, proviso, constraint, prerequisite, precondition, requirement, specification, restriction, supposition, modification.

iffy adjective informal **1** *the windscreen's a bit iffy, but it's a good car*: **substandard**, second-rate, low-grade, low-quality, of low quality, of poor

quality; **doubtful**, dubious, questionable; informal not up to much; Brit. informal dodgy, ropy, not much cop.
▷ANTONYMS perfect.
2 *that date is a bit iffy*: **tentative**, undecided, unsettled, unsure, unreliable, unresolved, in doubt, in the balance; informal up in the air.
▷ANTONYMS settled.

ignite verb **1** *he got to safety moments before the petrol ignited*: **catch fire**, catch, burst into flames, be set off, erupt, explode; burn up, burn, flame up; rare kindle.
▷ANTONYMS go out.
2 *he lit a cigarette which ignited the petrol fumes*: **light**, set fire to, set on fire, set alight, set burning, fire, kindle, inflame, touch off; informal set/put a match to.
▷ANTONYMS extinguish.
3 *the campaign failed to ignite voter interest*: **arouse**, kindle, trigger, spark, instigate, excite, provoke, foment; agitate, stimulate, stir up, work up, whip up, incite, fuel, animate.
▷ANTONYMS dampen.

ignoble adjective *the war is being fought over an ignoble cause*: **dishonourable**, unworthy, base, shameful, contemptible, despicable, shabby, abject, low, sordid, degraded, corrupt, mean, wrong; improper, unprincipled, unchivalrous, uncharitable, discreditable, blameworthy, reprehensible.
▷ANTONYMS noble.

ignominious adjective **1** *the leader's ignominious defeat*: **humiliating**, undignified, embarrassing, mortifying, shameful, disgraceful, dishonourable, discreditable, ignoble, inglorious, abject, sorry, wretched, miserable, pitiful; rare humiliatory.
▷ANTONYMS glorious.
2 *the regime's most ignominious crimes*: **heinous**, infamous, scandalous, disgraceful, shameful, contemptible, despicable, shabby, wicked, vile, villainous, base, low, ignoble, wretched.
▷ANTONYMS admirable.

ignominy noun *the ignominy of a public trial*: **shame**, humiliation, embarrassment, mortification; disgrace, dishonour, stigma, disrepute, discredit, degradation, abasement, opprobrium, obloquy, scandal, infamy, indignity, ignobility, loss of face.
▷ANTONYMS honour.

Choose the right word **ignominy, shame, disgrace, dishonour**

See **disgrace**.

ignoramus noun *he was a foul-mouthed ignoramus*. See **fool**.

ignorance noun **1** *his ignorance of economics*: **incomprehension**, unawareness, unconsciousness, inexperience, innocence; unfamiliarity with, lack of enlightenment about, lack of knowledge about, lack of information about; informal cluelessness; literary nescience.
▷ANTONYMS knowledge, education.
2 *their attitudes are based on ignorance and fear*: **lack of knowledge**, lack of education; unenlightenment, benightedness; lack of intelligence, unintelligence, stupidity, foolishness, idiocy, denseness, brainlessness, mindlessness, slow-wittedness; informal thickness, dimness, dumbness, dopiness, doziness.
▷ANTONYMS knowledge, education.

ignorant adjective **1** *an ignorant country girl*: **uneducated**, unknowledgeable, untaught, unschooled, untutored, untrained, illiterate, unlettered, unlearned, unread, uninformed, unenlightened, unscholarly, unqualified, benighted, backward; inexperienced, unworldly, unsophisticated; unintelligent, stupid, simple, empty-headed, mindless; informal pig-ignorant, thick, airheaded, (as) thick as two short planks, dense, dumb, dim, dopey, wet behind the ears, slow on the uptake, dead from the neck up, a brick short of a load, two sandwiches short of a picnic; Brit. informal dozy, divvy, daft, not the full shilling; Scottish & N. English informal glaikit; N. Amer. informal chowderheaded, dumb-ass; W. Indian informal dotish; S. African informal dof; rare hebete.
▷ANTONYMS educated, knowledgeable.
2 *middle-class women were **ignorant of** working-class life*: **without knowledge**, unaware, unconscious, insensible; unfamiliar with, unacquainted with, unconversant with, inexperienced in, uninitiated in, blind to, oblivious to, naive about, innocent about, green about, a stranger to; uninformed about, unenlightened about, unschooled in; informal in the dark about, clueless about, not knowing the first thing about, not having the faintest about; literary nescient, strange to.
▷ANTONYMS knowledgeable about.
3 informal *she could be very ignorant, and he had no intention of getting in an argument*: **rude**, impolite, ill-mannered, bad-mannered, unmannerly, ungracious, discourteous, insensitive, uncivil, ill-humoured, surly, sullen; boorish, oafish, loutish, crude, coarse, vulgar, gross.
▷ANTONYMS polite.

Word toolkit

ignorant	illiterate	uninformed
masses	peasants	readers
fool	adults	investors
comments	villagers	voters
bigot	parents	decision
bliss	children	consumers

ignore verb **1** *he ignored the customers and began counting money*: **disregard**, take no notice of, pay no attention to, pay no heed to, pass over, shut one's eyes to, be oblivious to, turn a blind eye to, turn a deaf ear to, brush aside, shrug off, push aside, never mind; look the other way.
▷ANTONYMS pay attention to.
2 *he was ignored by the countess*: **snub**, slight, spurn, shun, disdain, look right through, look past, turn one's back on, give someone the cold shoulder, cold-shoulder, freeze out, steer clear of; Brit. send to Coventry; informal give someone the brush-off, cut, cut dead, knock back, give someone the go-by; Brit. informal blank.
▷ANTONYMS acknowledge.
3 *doctors ignored her husband's instructions*: **set aside**, pay no attention to, take no account of, veto; break, contravene, fail to comply with, fail to observe, disobey, breach, defy, flout, fly in the face of; omit, leave out, bypass, overlook, neglect, disregard, exclude; informal skip.
▷ANTONYMS obey.

ilk noun *Mrs Taylor and her ilk talk utter tripe*: **type**, sort, class, category, group, set, bracket, genre, kidney, grain, species, race, strain, vintage, make, model, brand, stamp, variety, family.

ill adjective **1** *Mama was seriously ill* | *she had begun to feel rather ill*: **unwell**, sick, not (very) well, ailing, poorly, sickly, peaky, afflicted, indisposed, infirm, liverish; out of sorts, not oneself, not in good shape, not up to par, under/below par, bad, in a bad way; bedridden, invalided, on the sick list, valetudinarian; queasy, nauseous, nauseated; weak, feeble, frail; diseased, infected; Brit. off colour; informal under the weather, not up to snuff, laid up, dicky, funny, peculiar, iffy, crummy, lousy, rough, groggy, green about the gills, at death's door, like death warmed up; Brit. informal ropy, grotty; Scottish informal wabbit; Austral./NZ informal crook; dated queer, seedy.
▷ANTONYMS well, healthy.
2 *the ill effects of tobacco smoke*: **harmful**, damaging, detrimental, deleterious, adverse, injurious, hurtful, destructive, pernicious, inimical, dangerous, ruinous, calamitous, disastrous, malign, malignant; unhealthy, unwholesome, poisonous, noxious, cancerous; literary malefic, maleficent, nocuous, baneful.
▷ANTONYMS good, beneficial.
3 *the ill feeling between him and the Woodvilles*: **hostile**, antagonistic, acrimonious, inimical, antipathetic, poisonous; belligerent, bellicose, aggressive, pugnacious, truculent, contentious; unfriendly, unkind, unsympathetic, harsh, cruel; rancorous, resentful, spiteful, malicious, vindictive, vitriolic, malevolent, bitter, mean, nasty; informal bitchy, catty.
▷ANTONYMS friendly, warm.
4 *a bird of ill omen*: **unlucky**, adverse, unfavourable, unfortunate, unpropitious, inauspicious, unpromising, infelicitous, bad, gloomy; threatening, menacing, ominous, sinister, disturbing, dire, evil, baleful, forbidding, portentous; archaic direful; rare minatory, minacious.
▷ANTONYMS auspicious.
5 *the ill manners of her spouse*: **rude**, discourteous, unmannerly, impolite; bad, objectionable, unpleasant, disagreeable; impertinent, insolent, impudent, audacious, uncivil, disrespectful, churlish, crass, ungracious, graceless, boorish; informal ignorant.
▷ANTONYMS good, polite.
6 *the ill management of their finances*: **bad**, poor, unsatisfactory, incompetent, unacceptable, inadequate, deficient, defective, faulty, unskilful, inexpert, amateurish.
▷ANTONYMS good, competent.
□ **ill at ease** *he looked ill at ease in morning dress*: **awkward**, uneasy, uncomfortable, self-conscious, out of place, unnatural, inhibited, gauche, strained; embarrassed, shy, bashful, blushing, retiring, shrinking; unsure, uncertain, unsettled, hesitant, faltering; restless, restive, fidgety, unrelaxed, disquieted, disturbed, discomfited, troubled, worried, anxious, on edge, edgy, nervous, tense, on tenterhooks; apprehensive, distrustful; Brit. nervy; informal fazed, discombobulated, twitchy, on pins and needles, jittery; N. Amer. informal antsy; rare unquiet.
▷ANTONYMS at ease, comfortable.
▸ **adverb 1** *it ill became the king to behave as a vassal*: **poorly**, badly, imperfectly; wrongly, unsuccessfully.
▷ANTONYMS well.
2 *the look on her face boded ill for anyone who crossed her path*: **unfavourably**, adversely, badly, unhappily, inauspiciously.
▷ANTONYMS well, auspiciously.
3 *he can ill afford the loss of income*: **barely**, scarcely, hardly, just, only just, just possibly, narrowly; with difficulty, only with effort; Brit. informal at a push.

▷ANTONYMS easily.
4 *if things go ill, it's all over*: **badly**, adversely, unsuccessfully, unfavourably; unfortunately, unluckily, hard, inauspiciously.
▷ANTONYMS well, according to plan.
5 *we are ill prepared for floods*: **inadequately**, unsatisfactorily, insufficiently, imperfectly, deficiently, defectively, poorly, badly, negligently.
▷ANTONYMS well, satisfactorily.
□ **speak ill of** *nobody wants to speak ill of the dead*: **denigrate**, disparage, cast aspersions on, criticize, be critical of, speak badly of, speak of with disfavour, be unkind about, be malicious about, be spiteful towards, blacken the name of, blacken the character of, besmirch, run down, insult, abuse, attack, slight, revile, malign, vilify; N. Amer. slur; informal bad-mouth, slate, bitch about, do a hatchet job on, pull to pieces, sling mud at, throw mud at, drag (someone's name) through the mud; Brit. informal rubbish, slag off, have a go at, have a pop at; rare asperse, derogate, vilipend, vituperate.
▷ANTONYMS compliment, extol.
▶noun **1** (**ills**) *the government had failed to cure many of society's ills*: **problems**, troubles, difficulties, misfortunes, strains, trials, tribulations, trials and tribulations, worries, anxieties, concerns; pain, suffering, hardship, misery, woe, affliction, distress, disquiet, malaise; informal headaches, probs, hassles; archaic travails.
2 *he wished them no ill*: **harm**, hurt, injury, damage, mischief, pain, trouble, unpleasantness, misfortune, grievance, suffering, distress, anguish, trauma, grief.
3 (**ills**) *the body's ills*: **illnesses**, ill/poor health; ailments, disorders, complaints, afflictions, sicknesses, diseases, maladies, infirmities, indispositions; infections, contagions.

ill-advised adjective *an ill-advised business venture*: **unwise**, injudicious, misguided, imprudent, impolitic, incautious, ill-considered, ill-judged, ill-conceived, ill-thought-out, badly planned, inexpedient; foolhardy, hare-brained, rash, hasty, overhasty, short-sighted, thoughtless, unthinking, careless, reckless; foolish, silly, asinine, wrong-headed; informal crazy, crackpot, crackbrained, cock-eyed; Brit. informal daft.
▷ANTONYMS wise, judicious.

Choose the right word **ill-advised, unwise, imprudent, injudicious**

See **unwise**.

ill-assorted adjective *an ill-assorted travelling party*: **mismatched**, ill-matched, incongruous, unsuited, incompatible, inharmonious, discordant, clashing, discrepant; dissimilar, unlike, unalike, varying, varied, at variance, disparate, divergent, diverse, contrasting, distinct.
▷ANTONYMS well matched, similar.

ill-bred adjective *she was unlikely to be amused by ill-bred behaviour*: **ill-mannered**, bad-mannered, rude, unmannerly, impolite, discourteous, uncivil; boorish, churlish, loutish, vulgar, common, coarse, crass, gross, uncouth, crude, unpolished, uncivilized, ungentlemanly, unladylike, unsophisticated, unrefined, ungallant, indelicate, indecorous, unseemly; informal yobbish, ignorant, plebby, cloddish; Brit. informal common as muck.
▷ANTONYMS well bred, genteel.

ill-considered adjective *the government can force through this ill-considered legislation*: **rash**, unconsidered, ill-advised, ill-judged, injudicious, imprudent, unwise, hasty, overhasty; misjudged, ill-conceived, badly thought out, not thought through, unthought-out, unguarded, wild, hare-brained; literary temerarious.
▷ANTONYMS judicious.

ill-defined adjective *the boundary between the two manors was rather ill-defined*: **vague**, indistinct, unclear, imprecise, inexplicit; blurry, blurred, fuzzy, hazy, woolly, nebulous, shadowy, dim.
▷ANTONYMS well defined, sharp.

ill-disposed adjective *the court may be ill-disposed to foreign companies*: **hostile**, antagonistic, unfriendly, unsympathetic, antipathetic, inimical, unfavourable; opposing, opposed, averse, contrary, at odds; informal anti, down on.
▷ANTONYMS well disposed, friendly.

illegal adjective **1** *gangs operating illegal gambling*: **unlawful**, illicit, illegitimate, criminal, lawbreaking, actionable, felonious; unlicensed, unauthorized, unsanctioned, unwarranted, unofficial; outlawed, banned, forbidden, barred, prohibited, interdicted, proscribed, not allowed, not permitted; contraband, black-market, under the counter, bootleg; Law malfeasant; German verboten; informal crooked, shady; Brit. informal bent, dodgy; rare non licet.
▷ANTONYMS legal; lawful.
2 *illegal play will be penalized by surrendering possession of the ball*: **foul**, against the rules; unfair, unsporting, unsportsmanlike, below the belt, dirty, dishonourable, dishonest, underhand, cheating.
▷ANTONYMS legal; legitimate.

Word toolkit

illegal	fraudulent	corrupt
drugs	claims	officials
dumping	transaction	government
weapons	documents	politician
substances	accounting	system
gambling	conveyance	regime
entry	election	society
parking	charges	judge

illegible adjective *an illegible signature*: **unreadable**, indecipherable, unintelligible, hard to read; scrawled, scribbled, squiggly, crabbed, hieroglyphic, obscure; informal clear as mud.
▷ANTONYMS legible; clear.

illegitimate adjective **1** *illegitimate share trading*: **illegal**, unlawful, illicit, criminal, lawbreaking, actionable, felonious; unlicensed, unauthorized, unsanctioned, unwarranted, unofficial; banned, forbidden, barred, prohibited, outlawed, interdicted, proscribed, not allowed, not permitted, against the rules; contraband, black-market, under the counter, bootleg; fraudulent, corrupt, dishonest, dishonourable; German verboten; Law malfeasant; informal crooked, shady; Brit. informal bent, dodgy.
▷ANTONYMS legitimate, lawful.
2 *an illegitimate child*: **born out of wedlock**, born of unmarried parents; love; dated born on the wrong side of the blanket, unfathered; archaic bastard, natural, misbegotten, baseborn, spurious, nameless; rare adulterine.
▷ANTONYMS legitimate.
3 *it is quite illegitimate to treat such a person as a swindler*: **incorrect**, illogical, invalid, unsound, spurious, wrongly inferred, wrongly deduced.
▷ANTONYMS legitimate, correct.

ill-fated adjective *an ill-fated rebellion*: **doomed**, blighted, condemned, damned, cursed, ill-starred, ill-omened, jinxed; unlucky, luckless, unfortunate, hapless, unhappy; literary star-crossed.

ill-favoured adjective *an ill-favoured old woman*: **unattractive**, plain, unappealing, ugly, ugly looking, hideous, unsightly, unlovely, plain as a pikestaff; N. Amer. homely; informal not much to look at, short on looks; Brit. informal no oil painting; Austral./NZ informal drack.
▷ANTONYMS attractive.

ill-founded adjective *your faith in his expertise was ill-founded*: **baseless**, groundless, without foundation, foundationless, without basis, unjustified, unsupported; unsubstantiated, unproven, unverified, uncorroborated, unconfirmed, unauthenticated, not backed up by evidence, speculative, conjectural; unsound, unreliable, questionable, misinformed, misguided, spurious, trumped-up.
▷ANTONYMS well-founded.

ill humour noun *the downward tilt to her mouth betrayed her ill humour*: **bad mood**, bad temper, ill temper, irritability, irascibility, cantankerousness, peevishness, petulance, pettishness, pique, fit of pique, querulousness, crabbiness, testiness, tetchiness, fractiousness, snappishness, waspishness, touchiness, moodiness, sullenness, sulkiness, surliness, resentment, rancour, spleen, dyspepsia, biliousness, sourness, annoyance, anger, crossness.
▷ANTONYMS good humour.

ill-humoured adjective *an ill-humoured little man*: **bad-tempered**, ill-tempered, short-tempered, hot-tempered, quick-tempered, in a (bad) mood, cross, as cross as two sticks; irritable, irascible, tetchy, testy, crotchety, touchy, thin-skinned, scratchy, cantankerous, curmudgeonly, peevish, fractious, waspish, prickly, peppery, pettish, shrewish; grumpy, grouchy, crabbed, crabby, disagreeable, volatile, splenetic, dyspeptic, choleric, bilious, liverish, cross-grained; informal snappish, snappy, chippy, on a short fuse, short-fused; Brit. informal shirty, stroppy, narky, ratty, eggy, like a bear with a sore head; N. Amer. informal cranky, ornery, peckish, soreheaded; Austral./NZ informal snaky; informal, dated waxy, miffy.
▷ANTONYMS good-humoured, amiable.

illiberal adjective *the government moved towards more illiberal policies*: **intolerant**, narrow-minded, unenlightened, puritanical, fundamentalist; reactionary, conservative, hidebound; undemocratic, authoritarian, strict, repressive, totalitarian, despotic, tyrannical, draconian, oppressive, fascist.
▷ANTONYMS liberal.

illicit adjective **1** *illicit drugs*: **illegal**, unlawful, illegitimate; outlawed, banned, forbidden, prohibited, interdicted, proscribed, not allowed, not permitted; criminal, lawbreaking, actionable, felonious; unlicensed, unauthorized, unsanctioned, unwarranted, unofficial; contraband, black-market, under the counter, bootleg; Law malfeasant; German verboten; rare non licet.
▷ANTONYMS licit, legal.
2 *an illicit love affair*: **taboo**, forbidden, ruled out, impermissible, not acceptable, unacceptable, against the rules; secret, clandestine, furtive, sly; German verboten; Islam haram; NZ tapu.
▷ANTONYMS above board.

illimitable adjective *the great illimitable space we were in*: **limitless**, unlimited, without limits, unbounded; endless, unending, never-ending, without end, infinite, immeasurable, inestimable.
▷ANTONYMS limited.

illiteracy noun **1** *the ineffective educational system meant that illiteracy was widespread*: **illiterateness**, inability to read or write.
▷ANTONYMS literacy.
2 *his economic illiteracy*: **ignorance**, unawareness, inexperience, unenlightenment, benightedness, lack of knowledge, lack of education; informal cluelessness; literary nescience.

illiterate adjective **1** *he was no illiterate peasant*: **unable to read or write**, unlettered, analphabetic, functionally illiterate.
▷ANTONYMS literate.
2 *a politically illiterate youth*: **ignorant**, unknowledgeable, uneducated, untaught, unschooled, untutored, untrained, uninstructed, uninformed, unlearned, unread, unenlightened, benighted, backward; literary nescient.
▷ANTONYMS literate; knowledgeable.

Word toolkit **illiterate**

See **ignorant**.

ill-judged adjective *she flinched at his ill-judged choice of words*: **ill-considered**, ill-thought-out, ill-conceived; unwise, imprudent, incautious, injudicious, misguided, ill-advised, impolitic, inexpedient; foolhardy, foolish, rash, hasty, overhasty, short-sighted, thoughtless, unthinking, careless, reckless, spur of the moment.
▷ANTONYMS judicious, well thought out.

ill-mannered adjective *ill-mannered children*: **bad-mannered**, rude, unmannerly, mannerless, impolite, discourteous, uncivil, abusive, disagreeable; insolent, impertinent, impudent, cheeky, audacious, presumptuous, disrespectful; badly behaved, ill-behaved, boorish, loutish, oafish, uncouth, uncivilized, ill-bred, coarse, gross; informal ignorant.
▷ANTONYMS well mannered, polite.

ill-natured adjective *a disagreeable, ill-natured girl*: **mean**, nasty, spiteful, malicious, disagreeable, bitter, poisonous, venomous; ill-tempered, bad-tempered, ill-humoured, moody, irritable, irascible, surly, sullen, peevish, petulant, cross, fractious, crabbed, crabby, tetchy, testy, grouchy, waspish; perverse, disobliging.
▷ANTONYMS good-natured.

illness noun *he was making a steady recovery from his recent illness*: **sickness**, disease, ailment, disorder, complaint, malady, affliction, attack, infection, contagion, disability, indisposition; ill health, poor health, infirmity, valetudinarianism; informal bug, virus; Brit. informal lurgy; Austral. informal wog.
▷ANTONYMS good health.

Word links **illness**

noso- related prefix, as in *nosography*
-pathy related suffix, as in *neuropathy*
nosophobia fear of illness

illogical adjective *he drew a strange and illogical conclusion*: **irrational**, unreasonable, unsound, unreasoned, unfounded, groundless, unjustifiable, unjustified; incorrect, erroneous, wrong, invalid, spurious, faulty, flawed, fallacious, unscientific, inconsistent, unproved; specious, sophistic, casuistic; absurd, preposterous, untenable, implausible, impossible, beyond belief, beyond the bounds of possibility; senseless, meaningless, nonsensical, insane, ridiculous, idiotic, stupid, foolish, silly, inane, imbecilic; informal crazy, off beam, way out, full of holes; Brit. informal daft, barmy.
▷ANTONYMS logical.

ill-starred adjective *some people have lost everything because they invested in that ill-starred venture*: **ill-fated**, doomed, blighted, ill-omened, foredoomed, infelicitous; unlucky, unfortunate, hapless, luckless, bedevilled, damned; inauspicious, unpropitious, unpromising, ominous; informal jinxed; literary star-crossed.
▷ANTONYMS destined for success; blessed.

Choose the right word **ill-starred, unfortunate, unlucky, hapless**

See **unfortunate**.

ill temper noun *her ill temper was caused by an argument with her boyfriend*: **bad mood**, annoyance, irritation, vexation, exasperation, indignation, huff, moodiness, pet, pique, fit of pique, displeasure; anger, crossness, fury, rage, outrage, bad temper, tantrum; irritability, irascibility, peevishness, tetchiness, testiness, dyspepsia, spleen; informal grump; Brit. informal paddy, strop; N. Amer. informal blowout, hissy fit; Brit. informal, dated bate, wax.
▷ANTONYMS good mood; calmness.

ill-tempered adjective *an ill-tempered woman*: **bad-tempered**, short-tempered, hot-tempered, quick-tempered, ill-humoured, moody; in a (bad) mood, cross, as cross as two sticks, annoyed; irritable, irascible, tetchy, testy, crotchety, touchy, crusty, thin-skinned, scratchy, cantankerous, curmudgeonly, peevish, fractious, waspish, shrewish, prickly, peppery, sharp, pettish; grumpy, grouchy, crabbed, crabby, disagreeable, volatile, splenetic, dyspeptic, choleric, bilious, liverish, cross-grained; informal snappish, snappy, chippy, on a short fuse, short-fused; Brit. informal shirty, stroppy, narky, ratty, eggy, like a bear with a sore head; N. Amer. informal cranky, ornery, peckish, soreheaded; Austral./NZ informal snaky; informal, dated waxy, miffy.
▷ANTONYMS good-tempered, amiable.

ill-timed adjective *their ill-timed foray into overseas property markets*: **untimely**, mistimed, badly timed; premature, early, hasty; inopportune, inconvenient, awkward, unwelcome; inappropriate, unsuitable, inapt; disadvantageous, unfavourable, unfortunate, inept.
▷ANTONYMS opportune; timely.

ill-treat verb *her mother had ill-treated her when she was young*: **abuse**, mistreat, maltreat, treat badly, ill-use, misuse, victimize; manhandle, handle roughly, mishandle, maul, molest; harm, injure, damage; informal knock about/around.
▷ANTONYMS pamper.

ill-treatment noun *he died from medical neglect and ill-treatment*: **abuse**, mistreatment, maltreatment, bad treatment, ill use, ill usage, misuse, victimization; manhandling, rough treatment, mishandling.
▷ANTONYMS pampering.

illuminate verb **1** *the bundle of clothes was illuminated by the officer's torch*: **light**, light up, throw light on, cast light upon, brighten, make brighter, shine on, flood with light, floodlight, irradiate; literary illumine.
▷ANTONYMS darken.
2 *the manuscripts are illuminated in brilliant inks*: **decorate**, illustrate, embellish, adorn, ornament, enhance, emblazon, highlight.
3 *documents often illuminate people's thought processes*: **clarify**, elucidate, explain, reveal, make clear, shed light on, cast light on, give insight into, clear up; make explicit, spell out, explicate, expound, rationalize.
▷ANTONYMS conceal; confuse.

illuminating adjective *an illuminating account of the writer's style*: **informative**, enlightening, revealing, explanatory, instructive, instructional, helpful, educational, educative, edifying, rewarding, enriching.

illumination noun **1** *the flickering illumination of the match | a floodlamp provided additional illumination*: **light**, lighting, radiance, gleam, glitter, brilliance, glow, glare, dazzle, flash, shimmer; shining, gleaming, glowing; irradiation, luminescence, incandescence, fluorescence, phosphorescence; rare illumining, irradiance, lucency, lambency, effulgence, refulgence, coruscation, fulguration.
▷ANTONYMS darkness.
2 *the illumination of a medieval manuscript*: **decoration**, illustration, embellishment, adornment, ornamentation.
3 *these books form the most sustained analysis and illumination of the subject*: **clarification**, elucidation, explanation, revelation, explication, exposition, exegesis, rationalization.
4 *there were moments of real illumination*: **enlightenment**, insight, revelation, discovery; understanding, awareness; explanation, instruction; learning, education, information, knowledge, edification.
▷ANTONYMS ignorance.

illusion noun **1** *I was under no illusion about the difficulty of my job | he had destroyed her illusions*: **delusion**, misapprehension, misconception, deception, false impression, mistaken impression; fantasy, dream, chimera, fool's paradise, self-deception, castles in the air, castles in Spain; fallacy, error, misjudgement, fancy.
2 *the lighting helps to increase the illusion of depth*: **appearance**, impression, imitation, semblance, pretence, sham; false appearance, deceptive appearance, deception, misperception; rare simulacrum.
▷ANTONYMS reality.
3 *the magical illusion is created using mirrors, lights, and paint*: **mirage**, hallucination, apparition, phantasm, phantom, vision, spectre, fantasy, figment of the imagination, will-o'-the-wisp, trick of the light; Latin ignis fatuus.
4 *he is keen to dispel any impression that his illusions are achieved using TV trickery*: **magic trick**, conjuring trick, trick, deception; (**illusions**) magic, conjuring, sleight of hand, legerdemain, trickery.

illusory adjective *the comfort these theories give is illusory*: **delusory**, delusional, delusive; illusionary, imagined, imaginary, fancied, non-existent, unreal, hallucinatory; sham, hollow, deceptive, deceiving, false, fallacious, fake, bogus, mistaken, erroneous, misleading, misguided, untrue, specious, fanciful, notional, chimerical; rare illusive, Barmecide.
▷ANTONYMS real, genuine.

illustrate verb **1** *the etchings and photographs that illustrate the book are gruesome*: **decorate**, adorn, ornament, embellish, accompany; add pictures/drawings/sketches to, provide artwork for.

2 *the complex interplay of such pressures can be illustrated through a brief example*: **explain**, elucidate, clarify, make clear, make plain, demonstrate, point up, show, bring home, emphasize, interpret; describe, sum up, summarize, gloss; informal get across, get over.
3 *he possessed a quicksilver wit, as illustrated by his remark to Lucy*: **exemplify**, show, demonstrate, display, instance, encapsulate, represent; rare instantiate.

illustrated adjective *an illustrated weekly magazine*: **with illustrations**, with pictures, with drawings, with sketches, pictorial; decorated, adorned, ornamented, embellished.

illustration noun **1** *the illustrations in children's books*: **picture**, drawing, sketch, figure, graphic; plate, print, engraving, etching, cut, woodcut, linocut, photogravure, duotone, half-tone.
▷ANTONYMS text.
2 *the way in which tax relief is obtained can best be described by way of illustration*: **exemplification**, demonstration, showing, instancing; example, typical case, representative case, case in point, instance, specimen, sample, exemplar, analogy.
3 *students interested in a career in illustration*: **artwork**, design, graphic design; ornamentation, decoration, embellishment, adornment.

illustrative adjective *historians provide illustrative details and examples*: **exemplifying**, explanatory, explaining, elucidatory, elucidative, explicative, expository, interpretative, illuminative, exegetic; rare evincive.

illustrious adjective *an illustrious general*: **eminent**, distinguished, acclaimed, noted, notable, noteworthy, prominent, pre-eminent, foremost, leading, paramount, prestigious, important, significant, influential, lionized; renowned, famous, famed, well known, celebrated; esteemed, honoured, respected, exalted, venerable, august, highly regarded, well thought of, of distinction, of repute, of high standing; splendid, brilliant, remarkable, outstanding, great, noble, glorious, grand, lofty.
▷ANTONYMS unknown, obscure.

ill will noun *he didn't bear his wife any ill will*: **animosity**, hostility, enmity, acrimony, animus, hatred, hate, loathing, detestation, antipathy; ill feeling, bad blood, antagonism, unfriendliness, unkindness, aversion, dislike; spite, spitefulness, rancour, resentment, hard feelings, bitterness, venom, poison, bile, vitriol, malice, malevolence, odium; archaic disrelish.
▷ANTONYMS goodwill.

image noun **1** *an image of the Madonna*: **likeness**, resemblance; **depiction**, portrayal, representation; statue, statuette, sculpture, bust, effigy, figure, figurine, doll, carving; painting, picture, portrait, drawing, sketch.
2 *Voyager 2 sent back images of the planet Neptune*: **picture**, facsimile, photograph, snapshot, photo; optical representation, reproduction.
3 *he contemplated his image in the mirrors*: **reflection**, mirror image, likeness; echo.
4 *the world has an image of this country as democratic*: **conception**, impression, idea, concept, perception, notion; mental picture, mental representation, conceptualization, vision, fancy, thought.
5 *his poetry is constructed around biblical images*: **simile**, **metaphor**, metonymy; figure of speech, trope, figurative expression, turn of phrase, rhetorical device, conceit; word painting, word picture.
6 *everyone expects him to live up to his heart-throb image*: **public perception**, public conception, public impression, persona, profile, face, identity, front, facade, mask, guise, role, part; portrayal, depiction.
7 *Ma says I'm the image of my grandfather*: **double**, living image, replica, lookalike, clone, copy, reproduction, twin, duplicate, exact likeness, facsimile, counterpart, mirror image; German Doppelgänger; informal very spit, dead spit, spitting image, chip off the old block, ringer, dead ringer; archaic similitude.
8 *a graven image*: **idol**, icon, fetish, false god, golden calf, totem, talisman.
▶ verb *she imaged imposing castles and cathedrals*: **envisage**, envision, imagine, conceive of, picture, dream up, see in one's mind's eye.

> *Word links* **image**
>
> **icono-** related prefix
> **iconography**, **iconology** study of images

imaginable adjective *the most severe weather conditions imaginable*: **thinkable**, conceivable, supposable, believable, credible, creditable, comprehensible; possible, plausible, feasible, tenable, within the bounds/realms of possibility, under the sun; rare cogitable.
▷ANTONYMS unimaginable, inconceivable.

imaginary adjective *the imaginary world of the novel*: **unreal**, non-existent, fictional, fictitious, pretend, make-believe, mythical, mythological, legendary, storybook, fanciful, fantastic; made-up, dreamed-up, invented, concocted, fabricated, fancied, the product of someone's imagination; illusory, illusive, figmental, hallucinatory, phantasmal, phantasmic, a figment of someone's imagination; dreamy, dreamlike, shadowy, unsubstantial, chimerical, ethereal; virtual, notional, hypothetical, theoretical; assumed, supposed, suppositious; archaic visionary.
▷ANTONYMS real, actual.

imagination noun **1** *he had a very vivid imagination*: **imaginative faculty**, creative power, fancy; informal mind's eye.
2 *the government needs imagination in dealing with these problems*: **creativity**, imaginativeness, creativeness; vision, inspiration, insight, inventiveness, invention, resourcefulness, initiative, ingenuity, enterprise; originality, innovation, innovativeness; individuality, unorthodoxy, nonconformity; cleverness, wit, quick-wittedness, genius, flair, panache; artistry, artistic power.
3 *every once in a while an album captures the public's imagination*: **interest**, fascination, attention, passion, curiosity, preoccupation.

imaginative adjective *a strong, imaginative storyline | an imaginative solution*: **creative**, visionary, inspired, insightful, inventive, resourceful, ingenious, enterprising; original, innovative, innovatory, individual, unorthodox, unconventional, nonconformist, unusual, out of the ordinary; fanciful, whimsical; informal blue-sky.
▷ANTONYMS unimaginative; pedestrian.

imagine verb **1** *one can imagine the cloud-capped towers of the castle*: **visualize**, envisage, envision, picture, form a picture of, see in the mind's eye, conjure up, conceptualize; dream about, fantasize about; dream up, think up, conceive, think of; plan, project, scheme.
2 *I imagine he was at home with his wife*: **assume**, presume, expect, take it, take it for granted, take it as read, take it as given, presuppose; suppose, think it likely, dare say, think, surmise, conjecture, believe, be of the opinion that, fancy, feel, be of the view, be under the impression; N. Amer. figure; informal guess, reckon; formal opine; archaic ween.
▷ANTONYMS doubt.

imbalance noun *the political imbalance between North and South*: **disparity**, variance, unevenness, polarity, contrast, variation, disproportion, lopsidedness, lack of proportion, lack of harmony, lack of relation; gulf, breach, split, gap.
▷ANTONYMS balance, parity.

imbecile informal noun *I'd have to be an imbecile to do such a thing*: **fool**, idiot, cretin, moron, dolt, halfwit, ass, dunce, dullard, simpleton, nincompoop, blockhead, ignoramus, clod; informal dope, thickhead, ninny, chump, dimwit, dummy, dum-dum, dumb-bell, jackass, bonehead, fathead, numbskull, dunderhead, airhead, pinhead, lamebrain, pea-brain, birdbrain, dipstick, donkey, noodle; Brit. informal nit, nitwit, twit, numpty, clot, muppet, plonker, berk, prat, pillock, wally, wazzock, divvy; N. Amer. informal bozo, turkey, goofus.
▷ANTONYMS genius.
▶ adjective *try not to make imbecile remarks*: **stupid**, foolish, idiotic, silly, doltish, half-witted, witless, dull, brainless, mindless, unintelligent, unwise; senseless, absurd, crazy, mad, fatuous, inane, asinine, ridiculous; informal dense, dumb, thickheaded, dim, dim-witted, dopey, gormless, half-baked, hare-brained, crackbrained, pea-brained, nutty, dotty, batty, dippy, cuckoo, screwy, wacky; Brit. informal barmy, daft.
▷ANTONYMS intelligent.

imbed verb See **embed**.

imbibe verb **1** *he was flushed from the Scotch he'd imbibed*: **drink**, consume, sup, sip, quaff, swallow, down, guzzle, gulp (down), swill, lap, slurp; informal swig, knock back, sink; Brit. informal neck.
2 *he had imbibed too liberally*: **drink alcohol**, drink, take strong drink, indulge, tipple, swill; informal booze, hit the bottle, take to the bottle, knock a few back, wet one's whistle; Brit. informal bevvy; N. Amer. informal bend one's elbow; archaic wassail, tope.
3 *he has spent a lifetime imbibing his local club's history*: **assimilate**, absorb, soak up, take in, digest, ingest, drink in, learn, acquire, grasp, gain, pick up, familiarize oneself with.

imbroglio noun *a man caught up in a political imbroglio*: **complicated situation**, complication, complexity, problem, difficulty, predicament, plight, trouble, entanglement, confusion, muddle, mess, quandary, dilemma; informal bind, jam, pickle, fix, scrape, corner, tight corner, hole, sticky situation, mare's nest, hot water, deep water.

imbue verb *a society imbued with a sense of fairness*: **permeate**, saturate, diffuse, suffuse, pervade; impregnate, inject, inculcate, instil, ingrain, inspire, inform; fill, charge, load.

imitate verb **1** *it was quite acceptable for artists to imitate other artists*: **emulate**, copy, take as a model, model oneself on, take as a pattern, pattern oneself on/after, follow the example of, take as an example, take as a role model, take after, follow, follow in someone's steps/footsteps; echo, parrot; follow suit, take a leaf out of someone's book; informal rip off.
2 *he was a splendid mimic, and loved to imitate Winston Churchill*: **mimic**, do an impression of, impersonate, ape; parody, caricature, burlesque, travesty, mock; masquerade as, pose as, pass oneself off as; informal take off, send up, spoof, do; N. Amer. informal make like; archaic monkey; rare personate.
3 *the tombs imitated houses*: **resemble**, look like, be like, simulate; match, echo, mirror; bring to mind, remind one of.

imitation noun **1** *she wore an imitation of a sailor's hat*: **copy**, simulation, reproduction, replica; counterfeit, forgery, fake.
2 *learning by imitation*: **emulation**, copying, following, echoing, parroting.
3 *he did a perfect imitation of Francis*: **impersonation**, impression, parody,

mockery, caricature, burlesque, travesty, lampoon, pastiche; mimicry, mimicking, imitating, aping, mocking; informal send-up, take-off, spoof.
▶ adjective *imitation ivory | imitation Louis Quinze furniture*: **artificial**, synthetic, simulated, man-made, manufactured, ersatz, substitute; reproduction, replica, repro, facsimile, model; mock, sham, fake, counterfeit, bogus, spurious; informal pseudo, phoney, dummy; Brit. informal cod.
▷ANTONYMS real, genuine.

imitative adjective **1** *the fear that young people would be provoked into imitative crime by television*: **similar**, like; **mimicking**, mimetic, mimic, parrot-like; informal **copycat**.
2 *I found the film empty and imitative*: **derivative**, unoriginal, uninventive, non-innovative, unimaginative, uninspired, plagiarized, plagiaristic, copied, second-hand, rehashed, warmed-up; clichéd, hackneyed, stale, trite, tired, worn out, flat, banal, stock; informal cribbed, old hat.
▷ANTONYMS original.
3 *words which are imitative, like 'peewit'*: **onomatopoeic**, echoic.

imitator noun **1** *the show's success has sparked off many imitators*: **copier**, copyist, emulator, follower, mimic, plagiarist, ape, parrot, echo; informal copycat; rare epigone.
2 *an Elvis imitator*: **impersonator**, impressionist, mimicker; parodist, caricaturist, lampooner, lampoonist.

immaculate adjective **1** *an immaculate white shirt*: **clean**, spotless, pristine, unsoiled, unstained, unsullied, speckless, ultra-clean; whiter than white, snowy-white, lily-white; shining, shiny, gleaming; neat, tidy, neat and tidy, spick and span, neat as a new pin; informal squeaky clean, as clean as a whistle.
▷ANTONYMS dirty, grubby.
2 *a guitar in immaculate condition*: **perfect**, pristine, mint, as good as new; flawless, faultless, without blemish, unblemished, unimpaired, unspoilt, undamaged, unmarred; excellent, impeccable, prime, peak; informal tip-top, A1.
▷ANTONYMS bad; damaged.
3 *that wouldn't look good on his otherwise immaculate record*: **unblemished**, spotless, pure, impeccable, unsullied, undefiled, untarnished, stainless; innocent, virtuous, incorrupt, guiltless, sinless; informal squeaky clean, as pure as the driven snow.
▷ANTONYMS blameworthy.

immanent adjective **1** *the material insecurity immanent in the forced commodification of labour*: **inherent**, intrinsic, innate, built-in, latent, essential, fundamental, basic, ingrained, natural.
2 *God is immanent in His creation*: **pervasive**, pervading, permeating; omnipresent, ubiquitous, present everywhere; rare permeative, suffusive, permeant.
▷ANTONYMS transcendent.

immaterial adjective **1** *the difference in our ages was immaterial*: **irrelevant**, unimportant, inconsequential, insignificant, of no matter/moment, of little account, beside the point, not to the point, neither here nor there, inapposite, not pertinent, not germane; trivial, trifling, petty, superficial; peripheral, tangential, extraneous.
▷ANTONYMS important, significant.
2 *he believed in the immortality of an immaterial soul*: **intangible**, incorporeal, not material, bodiless, unembodied, disembodied, impalpable, ethereal, unsubstantial, insubstantial, airy, aerial; spiritual, ghostly, spectral, wraithlike, transcendental, unearthly, supernatural; rare discarnate, disincarnate, unbodied, phantasmal, phantasmic.
▷ANTONYMS physical, tangible.

immature adjective **1** *white Stilton is a very young, immature Stilton*: **unripe**, not ripe, not mature, not matured, unmellowed; undeveloped, unformed, imperfect, unfinished, incomplete; crude, raw, green.
▷ANTONYMS ripe, mature.
2 *she is an extremely shy and immature girl*: **childish**, babyish, infantile, juvenile, puerile, jejune, callow, green, inexperienced, unsophisticated, unworldly, naive, ingenuous; informal wet behind the ears, born yesterday.
▷ANTONYMS mature.

> *Word toolkit* **immature**
>
> See **youthful**.

immaturity noun **1** *the immaturity of the fruit | the immaturity of the technology*: **unripeness**, greenness, sourness; newness, rawness, crudeness, crudity, imperfection, incompleteness, lack of completion, lack of development.
2 *they were shocked by such immaturity in a grown man*: **childishness**, babyishness, infantilism, juvenility, puerility, lack of experience, inexperience, unworldliness, naivety, ingenuousness.

immeasurable adjective *he dreamed of possessing immeasurable riches*: **incalculable**, inestimable, innumerable, unfathomable, fathomless, indeterminable, measureless, untold; limitless, boundless, unbounded, unlimited, illimitable, infinite, endless, never-ending, interminable, inexhaustible, bottomless; vast, immense, great, abundant; informal no end of; literary myriad; rare innumerous, unnumberable.
▷ANTONYMS few.

immediate adjective **1** *the UN resolution called for immediate action*: **instant**, instantaneous, on-the-spot, prompt, swift, speedy, rapid, quick, expeditious; sudden, hurried, hasty, precipitate, abrupt; lightning, whirlwind, overnight; informal snappy, p.d.q. (pretty damn quick); literary fleet, rathe; rare alacritous.
▷ANTONYMS delayed; gradual.
2 *there are no immediate plans to launch the product*: **current**, present, existing, existent, actual, extant; urgent, pressing; archaic instant.
▷ANTONYMS past; future.
3 *the immediate past is of more importance than a remoter period*: **recent**, not long past, just gone; occurring recently.
▷ANTONYMS remote.
4 *they have strong ties with their immediate neighbours*: **nearest**, near, close, closest, next-door; adjacent, adjoining, abutting, contiguous, proximate.
▷ANTONYMS distant.
5 *the coroner identified the immediate cause of death*: **direct**, primary.
▷ANTONYMS indirect.

immediately adverb **1** *it was necessary to make a decision immediately*: **straight away**, at once, right away, right now, instantly, now, directly, promptly, forthwith, this/that (very) minute, this/that instant, there and then, here and now, in a flash, without delay, without hesitation, without further ado, post-haste; quickly, as fast as possible, fast, speedily, with all speed, as soon as possible, a.s.a.p.; French tout de suite; informal before you can say Jack Robinson, pronto, double quick, in double quick time, p.d.q. (pretty damn quick), toot sweet; Indian informal ekdam; archaic straightway, instanter, forthright.
2 *I sat immediately behind him*: **directly**, right, exactly, precisely, squarely, just, dead; close, closely, at close quarters; informal slap bang; N. Amer. informal smack dab.

immemorial adjective *an immemorial custom*: **ancient**, old, very old, age-old, antediluvian, timeless, dateless, archaic, long-standing, long-lived, time-worn, time-honoured; ancestral, traditional, atavistic; of yore, rooted in the past.
▷ANTONYMS recent.

immense adjective *an immense brick church dominates the town*: **huge**, vast, massive, enormous, gigantic, colossal, great, very large, very big, extensive, expansive, monumental, towering, mountainous, tremendous, prodigious, substantial; giant, elephantine, monstrous, mammoth, titanic, Brobdingnagian, king-size, king-sized; informal mega, monster, whopping, whopping great, thumping, thumping great, humongous, jumbo, hulking; Brit. informal whacking, whacking great, ginormous.
▷ANTONYMS tiny.

> *Word toolkit* **immense**
>
> See **colossal**.

immensely adverb *it was an immensely difficult decision*: **extremely**, very, exceedingly, exceptionally, especially, extraordinarily, tremendously, vastly, hugely, abundantly, intensely, acutely, singularly, significantly, distinctly, outstandingly, uncommonly, unusually, decidedly, particularly, eminently, supremely, highly, remarkably, really, truly, mightily, thoroughly, to a fault, in the extreme, extra; all that, to a great extent, most, so; Scottish unco; French très; N. English right; informal terrifically, awfully, fearfully, terribly, devilishly, majorly, seriously, mega, ultra, oh-so, stinking, mucho, damn, damned; informal, dated devilish, hellish, frightfully; Brit. informal ever so, well, bloody, dead, dirty, jolly, fair; N. Amer. informal real, mighty, powerful, awful, plumb, darned, way, bitching; S. African informal lekker; archaic exceeding.
▷ANTONYMS slightly; by no means.

immerse verb **1** *litmus paper turns red on being immersed in acid*: **submerge**, plunge, dip, dunk, duck, sink; douse, souse, soak, drench, imbue, saturate, cover, rinse, wet.
2 *the new Christian would be immersed in the river*: **baptize**, christen; purify; informal, dated dip; rare lustrate.
3 *Elliot was immersed in his work*: **absorb**, engross, occupy, engage, involve, engulf, bury; busy, employ, distract, divert, preoccupy; informal lose oneself in, get lost in.

immigrant noun *the country traditionally welcomes immigrants*: **newcomer**, settler, incomer, new arrival, migrant, emigrant; non-native, foreigner, alien, outsider, stranger; naturalized citizen, expatriate; informal expat.

imminent adjective *there was speculation that a ceasefire was imminent*: **impending**, at hand, close, near, approaching, fast approaching, coming, forthcoming, on the way, about to happen, upon us, in store, in the offing, in the pipeline, on the horizon, in the air, in the wind, brewing, looming, looming large; threatening, menacing; expected, anticipated; informal on the cards.
▷ANTONYMS remote.

immobile adjective *she sat immobile for a long time*: **motionless**, unmoving, without moving, still, stock-still, static, stationary, at rest, at a standstill, dormant; rooted to the spot, fixed to the spot, rigid, frozen, stiff, riveted, transfixed, like a statue, as if turned to stone, not moving a muscle, immobilized.
▷ANTONYMS moving.

immobilize verb *the officer wanted to immobilize their vehicle*: **put out of action**, disable, prevent from moving/working, make inoperative, render inactive, inactivate, deactivate, paralyse, cripple; bring to a standstill, bring to a halt, halt, stop; clamp, wheel-clamp; rare disenable.

immoderate adjective *they were concerned about his immoderate drinking*: **excessive**, heavy, intemperate, unrestrained, unrestricted, uncontrolled, unlimited, unbridled, uncurbed, self-indulgent, overindulgent, imprudent, reckless, wild; undue, inordinate, unreasonable, unjustified, unwarranted, uncalled for, outrageous, egregious; extravagant, lavish, prodigal, profligate, wanton, dissipative.
▷ANTONYMS moderate.

immoderation noun *he paid a high price for his immoderation*: **excess**, excessiveness, intemperance, intemperateness, lack of restraint, lack of self-control, self-gratification, self-indulgence, overindulgence, lavishness, extravagance, decadence, profligacy, wantonness, dissipation, dissoluteness, dissolution.
▷ANTONYMS moderation.

immodest adjective *her clothes and manner were most immodest*: **indecorous**, improper, indecent, indelicate, indiscreet, immoral; forward, bold, brazen, impudent, unblushing, unchaste, unvirtuous, shameless, loose, wanton; informal fresh, cheeky, naughty, saucy.

i

immolate verb *in the old days, the priests used to immolate their sacrifices at the shrine*: **sacrifice**, offer up, offer as a sacrifice, kill as a sacrifice; kill, slaughter, burn.

immoral adjective *they deplored immoral behaviour among the upper classes*: **unethical**, bad, morally wrong, wrongful, wicked, evil, unprincipled, unscrupulous, dishonourable, dishonest, unconscionable, iniquitous, disreputable, fraudulent, corrupt, depraved, vile, villainous, nefarious, base, unfair, underhand, devious; sinful, impure, unchaste, unvirtuous, shameless, degenerate, debauched, abandoned, dissolute, reprobate, perverted, indecent, lewd, licentious, wanton, bawdy, lustful, promiscuous, whorish; informal shady, low-down; Brit. informal dodgy, crooked, not cricket; archaic miscreant.
▷ANTONYMS moral, ethical; chaste.

> *Easily confused words* **immoral or amoral?**
>
> See **amoral**.

immorality noun *he believed his father had been punished by God for his immorality*: **wickedness**, immoral behaviour, badness, evil, vileness, iniquity, corruption, dishonesty, dishonourableness; sinfulness, sin, impurity, unchastity, depravity, vice, turpitude, degeneracy, debauchery, dissolution, perversion, indecency, lewdness, licentiousness, lustfulness, wantonness, promiscuity, shamelessness; informal shadiness; Brit. informal crookedness.
▷ANTONYMS morality; chastity.

immortal adjective **1** *they believe that their souls are immortal*: **undying**, never dying, deathless, eternal, ever living, everlasting, never-ending, endless, perpetual, lasting, enduring, constant, abiding; imperishable, indestructible, inextinguishable, unfading, immutable, indissoluble; rare sempiternal, perdurable.
▷ANTONYMS mortal.
2 *the immortal children's classic 'The Wind in the Willows'*: **timeless**, perennial, evergreen, classic, traditional, ageless, time-honoured, abiding, enduring, unforgettable, memorable, remembered; **famous**, famed, renowned, legendary, great, eminent, outstanding, acclaimed, celebrated, commemorated, honoured.
▷ANTONYMS forgettable; obscure.
▶noun **1** *the many Greek temples of the immortals*: **god**, **goddess**, deity, divine being, immortal being, celestial being, supreme being, divinity; Olympian.
▷ANTONYMS mortal.
2 *he will always be one of the immortals of soccer*: **great**, hero, Olympian; genius, celebrity.

immortality noun **1** *eating the fruit gave the gods immortality*: **eternal life**, everlasting life, deathlessness, everlastingness, endlessness, perpetuity; indestructibility, imperishability.
2 *occasionally a guide book has achieved immortality*: **timelessness**, legendary status; lasting fame/renown/repute/glory; durability, permanence.

immortalize verb *the battle was immortalized in prose by Pushkin*: **commemorate**, memorialize, keep alive the memory of, eternalize, perpetuate, preserve, enshrine; celebrate, pay tribute to, pay homage to, honour, salute, exalt, laud, glorify; literary eternize.

immovable adjective **1** *it's best to lock your bike to something immovable*: **fixed**, secure, stable, rooted, riveted, moored, anchored, braced, set firm, set fast, fast, firm; stuck, jammed, stiff, unbudgeable.
▷ANTONYMS mobile.
2 *she shook him but he sat immovable*: **motionless**, unmoving, stationary, still, stock-still, at a standstill, not moving a muscle, rooted to the spot, dead still, statue-like; transfixed, paralysed, frozen.
▷ANTONYMS moving.
3 *she was so immovable in her loyalties*: **steadfast**, unwavering, unswerving, resolute, determined, adamant, firm, unshakeable, unfailing, dogged, tenacious, stubborn, obdurate, inflexible, unyielding, unbending, uncompromising, unrelenting, inexorable, iron-willed, strong-willed, steely, dead set; N. Amer. rock-ribbed; informal stiff-necked; rare indurate.
▷ANTONYMS fickle; unsure.

immune adjective *they are **immune to** hepatitis B | our business is **immune to** the economic conditions*: **resistant**, not subject, not liable, unsusceptible, not vulnerable, not open, not exposed; protected from, safe from, secure against, not in danger of, exempt from, clear of, free from, unaffected by, proof against; freed from, absolved from, released from, excused from, relieved of, spared from, excepted from, exempted from; informal let off.
▷ANTONYMS susceptible.

immunity noun **1** *the children have an **immunity to** malaria*: **resistance to**, resilience to, non-susceptibility to, lack of susceptibility to, protection from, ability to fight off, ability to withstand, ability to counteract, defences against; immunization against, inoculation against.
▷ANTONYMS susceptibility to.
2 *the rebels were given **immunity from** prosecution*: **exemption**, exception, freedom, release, impunity, dispensation, exoneration; non-liability for; informal a let-off; rare derogation.
3 *he could not be sued since he possessed diplomatic immunity*: **indemnity**, privilege, prerogative, special treatment, right, liberty, licence, permission; asylum; legal exemption, impunity, protection, freedom; French carte blanche; Law, historical droit.

> *Word links* **immunity**
>
> **immunology** branch of medicine to do with immunity

immunize verb *he **immunized** the children **against** measles*: **vaccinate**, inoculate, inject; protect from, shield from, safeguard from; informal give someone a jab, give someone a shot.

immure verb *the monks were immured in Newgate jail*: **confine**, intern, shut up, lock up, incarcerate, imprison, jail, put away, put behind bars, put under lock and key, hold captive, hold prisoner; coop up, mew up, fence in, wall in, close in; detain, keep, hold, trap.

immutable adjective *a precise and immutable set of rules*: **unchangeable**, fixed, set, rigid, inflexible, unyielding, unbending, permanent, entrenched, established, well-established, unshakeable, irremovable, indelible, ineradicable; **unchanging**, unchanged, changeless, unvarying, unvaried, undeviating, static, constant, lasting, abiding, enduring, persistent, perpetual.
▷ANTONYMS variable.

imp noun **1** *imps are thought to sprout from Satan*: **demon**, little devil, devil, fiend; hobgoblin, goblin, elf, sprite, puck; archaic bugbear; rare cacodemon.
2 *the child's a cheeky young imp*: **rascal**, scamp, monkey, fiend, demon, devil, mischief-maker, troublemaker, prankster, rogue, wretch, brat, urchin, whippersnapper, tearaway; minx, chit; informal monster, horror, mischief, holy terror; Brit. informal perisher; Irish informal spalpeen; N. English informal tyke, scally; N. Amer. informal hellion, varmint; archaic scapegrace, jackanapes, rapscallion, rip.

impact noun (stress on the first syllable) **1** *car parts were spread by the impact over a wide region*: **collision**, crash, smash, clash, bump, bang, knock, jolt, thump, whack, thwack, slam, smack; contact.
2 *no car can withstand the impact of a train*: **force**, full force, shock, brunt, impetus, pressure, weight.
3 *the job losses will have a major impact | the impact of agriculture on wildlife*: **effect**, influence, impression; results, consequences, repercussions, ramifications, reverberations; informal pay-off.
▶verb (stress on the second syllable) **1** N. Amer. *a comet impacted the earth sixty million years ago*: **crash into**, smash into, collide with, be in collision with, hit, strike, ram, smack into, slam into, bang into, cannon into, plough into, meet head-on, dash against.
2 *high interest rates have **impacted on** retail spending*: **affect**, influence, have an effect, have an influence, exert influence, make an impression, act, work; strike, hit, touch, change, alter, modify, transform, shape, control, govern, determine, decide, sway, bias.

impair verb *even one drink can impair driving performance*: **damage**, harm, diminish, reduce, weaken, lessen, decrease, blunt, impede, hinder, mar, spoil, disable; undermine, compromise, threaten; informal foul up, put the kibosh on; rare vitiate.
▷ANTONYMS improve, enhance.

impale verb *his head was impaled on a pike for all to see*: **stick**, skewer, spear, spike, pin, transfix; pierce, stab, run through, bayonet, harpoon, lance; gore, disembowel; puncture, perforate; rare transpierce.

impalpable adjective *a glimpse of an idea that remained as impalpable as a dream*: **intangible**, insubstantial, incorporeal, unable to be touched, imperceptible to the touch; **indefinable**, elusive, hard to define/describe, undescribable; rare immaterial, unbodied, discarnate.
▷ANTONYMS palpable.

impart verb **1** *she had news that she couldn't wait to impart*: **communicate**, pass on, convey, transmit, relay, relate, recount, set forth, present, tell, make known, make public, go public with, report, announce, proclaim, spread, disseminate, circulate, promulgate, broadcast; disclose, reveal, divulge, bring into the open; informal let on about, tell all about, blab, spill; archaic discover, unbosom.
▷ANTONYMS keep to oneself.
2 *the brush imparts a good sheen to the dog's coat*: **give**, bestow, confer, grant, lend, accord, afford, provide, supply, offer, yield, contribute.
▷ANTONYMS remove.

impartial adjective *the referee is obliged to be impartial*: **unbiased**, unprejudiced, neutral, non-partisan, non-discriminatory, disinterested, uninvolved, uncommitted, detached, dispassionate, objective, open-minded, equitable, even-handed, fair, fair-minded, just; without favouritism, free from discrimination, with no axe to grind, without fear or favour; informal on the fence.
▷ANTONYMS biased, partisan.

impassable adjective *many roads were impassable after the flood*: **blocked**, closed, obstructed, impenetrable; pathless, trackless; unnavigable, untraversable, unpassable.

impasse noun *the negotiations seemed to have reached an impasse*: **deadlock**, dead end, stalemate, checkmate, stand-off; standstill, halt, stop, stoppage, full stop.

impassioned adjective *she made an impassioned plea for the return of her abducted child*: **emotional**, heartfelt, wholehearted, from the heart, earnest, sincere, fervent, ardent, vehement, intense, burning, urgent, passionate, feverish, frantic, emotive, zealous; rare fervid, perfervid, passional, full-hearted.
▷ANTONYMS half-hearted.

impassive adjective *she smiled at him, but his features remained impassive*: **expressionless**, unexpressive, inexpressive, inscrutable, blank, deadpan, poker-faced, straight-faced, dispassionate; stony, wooden, unresponsive; empty, vacant, glazed, fixed, lifeless.
▷ANTONYMS expressive.

impatience noun **1** *he was shifting in his seat with impatience*: **restlessness**, restiveness, frustration, agitation, nervousness, edginess, jitteriness, excitability; **eagerness**, keenness, avidity, hunger, greed, longing, yearning.
2 *she crumpled up the pages in a burst of impatience*: **irritability**, testiness, tetchiness, snappiness, irascibility, querulousness, peevishness, intolerance, disgruntlement, frustration, exasperation, annoyance, pique, discontent, dissatisfaction, displeasure; abruptness, brusqueness, shortness, curtness; informal aggravation.

impatient adjective **1** *the hours ticked by and Melissa grew impatient*: **restless**, restive, agitated, nervous, anxious, ill at ease, fretful, edgy, jumpy, jittery, worked up, keyed up; Brit. nervy; informal twitchy, uptight.
▷ANTONYMS calm; indifferent.
2 *they are impatient to get back home*: **anxious**, **eager**, keen, avid, desirous, yearning, longing, aching; informal itching, dying, raring, gagging, straining at the leash.
▷ANTONYMS reluctant.
3 *he dismissed them with an impatient gesture*: **irritated**, annoyed, angry, testy, tetchy, snappy, cross, crabby, moody, grumpy, querulous, fretful, peevish, peeved, piqued, discontented, displeased, disgruntled; intolerant, short-tempered, quick-tempered; abrupt, curt, brusque, terse, short; informal aggravated, grouchy; Brit. informal narked, narky, ratty, eggy, shirty.
▷ANTONYMS pleased.

impeach verb **1** N. Amer. *congressional moves to impeach the president*: **indict**, charge, accuse, bring a charge against, bring a case against, lay charges against, prefer charges against, arraign, take to court, put on trial, bring to trial, prosecute; informal have the law on.
▷ANTONYMS acquit.
2 *the headlines did much to impeach their clean image*: **challenge**, question, call into question, cast doubt on, raise doubts about.
▷ANTONYMS confirm.

impeccable adjective *a youth of impeccable character*: **flawless**, faultless, unblemished, spotless, stainless, untarnished, perfect, exemplary, ideal, model; **virtuous**, pure, moral, sinless, upright, irreproachable, unimpeachable, blameless, guiltless, above suspicion, beyond reproach, beyond criticism, incorrupt, uncorrupted; informal squeaky clean, whiter than white, lily-white, as pure as the driven snow.
▷ANTONYMS imperfect; sinful.

Word toolkit

impeccable	flawless	pristine
timing	skin	wilderness
taste	execution	beaches
credentials	technique	environment
manners	game	nature
character	beauty	forest
integrity	diamond	lakes
style	craftsmanship	landscape

impecunious adjective *she came from a respectable but impecunious family*: **penniless**, penurious, in penury, poor, impoverished, indigent, insolvent, moneyless, hard up, poverty-stricken, needy, in need, in want, destitute; poor as a church mouse, without a sou, in straitened circumstances, on one's beam ends, unable to make ends meet; Brit. on the breadline, without a penny (to one's name); informal broke, flat broke, strapped for cash, cleaned out, strapped, on one's uppers, without two pennies/brass farthings to rub together; Brit. informal skint, boracic, stony broke, in Queer Street; N. Amer. informal stone broke; rare pauperized, beggared.
▷ANTONYMS wealthy.

impede verb *the programme has been impeded by several problems*: **hinder**, obstruct, hamper, handicap, hold back, hold up, delay, interfere with, disrupt, retard, slow, slow down, brake, put a brake on, restrain, fetter, shackle, hamstring, cramp, cripple; block, check, bar, curb, stop, thwart, frustrate, baulk, foil, derail, stand in the way of; informal stymie, foul up, screw up; Brit. informal scupper, throw a spanner in the works of; N. Amer. informal bork, throw a monkey wrench in the works of; rare cumber.
▷ANTONYMS facilitate.

Choose the right word **impede, obstruct, hinder, hamper**

See **hinder**.

impediment noun **1** *the country's debt was a serious impediment to economic improvement*: **hindrance**, obstruction, obstacle, barrier, bar, handicap, block, check, curb, brake, restraint, restriction, limitation, encumbrance, deterrent; drawback, setback, difficulty, snag, catch, hitch, stumbling block; informal fly in the ointment, hiccup, facer; Brit. informal spanner in the works; N. Amer. informal monkey wrench in the works; rare cumber.
▷ANTONYMS benefit.
2 *she spoke with an impediment*: **speech defect**, speech impediment, stammer, stutter, lisp; hesitancy, faltering.

impedimenta plural noun *all the tedious impedimenta of a teacher's working life*: **paraphernalia**, trappings, equipment, accoutrements, appurtenances, accessories, bits and pieces, bits and bobs, odds and ends, things, tackle, effects, possessions, belongings, goods, movables; baggage, luggage; informal stuff, gear, traps, junk, rubbish; Brit. informal clobber, gubbins, odds and sods; archaic equipage.

impel verb **1** *her sense of duty impelled her to keep up appearances*: **force**, compel, constrain, oblige, necessitate, require, demand, make, urge, exhort, press, apply pressure, pressure, pressurize, drive, push, spur, prod, goad, incite, prompt, persuade, inspire.
2 *vital energies impel him in unforeseen directions*: **propel**, drive, drive forwards, move forwards, move, actuate, set in motion, get going, get moving.

impending adjective *she had a strange feeling of impending danger*: **imminent**, at hand, close, close at hand, near, nearing, approaching, coming, forthcoming, upcoming, to come, on the way, about to happen, upon us, in store, in the offing, in the pipeline, on the horizon, in the air, in the wind, brewing, looming, looming large, threatening, menacing; informal on the cards.

impenetrable adjective **1** *the ships had impenetrable armoured plating*: **impervious**, impermeable, solid, dense, thick, hard, unyielding, unbreakable, indestructible, puncture-proof, unpierceable, resistant; invulnerable, impregnable, inviolable, unattackable, unassailable; waterproof, closed, sealed, hermetically sealed, tight; secure, safe.
▷ANTONYMS permeable; vulnerable.
2 *a dark, impenetrable forest*: **impassable**, unpassable, inaccessible, unnavigable, untraversable, pathless, trackless, untrodden; dense, thick, overgrown, jungly, jungle-like; archaic thickset.
▷ANTONYMS accessible; sparse.
3 *an impenetrable clique*: **exclusive**, closed, secretive, secret, private; restrictive, restricted, limited; rare discriminative.
▷ANTONYMS open.
4 *these statistics can seem impenetrable and tedious*: **incomprehensible**, impossible to understand, unfathomable, fathomless, inexplicable, unintelligible, unclear, baffling, bewildering, puzzling, perplexing, confusing, abstruse, obscure, opaque, recondite, inscrutable, mysterious,

cryptic, Delphic; complex, complicated, difficult, hard; archaic wildering; rare insolvable.
▷ANTONYMS clear.

impenitent adjective *I am quite impenitent at having encouraged her rebellion*: **unrepentant**, unrepenting, without regret/remorse, uncontrite, remorseless, unremorseful, shameless, unashamed, unblushing, unapologetic, unabashed, brazen, conscienceless.
▷ANTONYMS penitent.

imperative adjective **1** *it is imperative that you find him*: **vitally important**, of vital importance, all-important, vital, crucial, critical, essential, of the essence, a matter of life and death, of great consequence, necessary, indispensable, exigent, pressing, urgent; required, compulsory, mandatory, obligatory.
▷ANTONYMS unimportant; optional.
2 *the imperative note in her voice was unmistakable*: **peremptory**, commanding, imperious, authoritative, masterful, lordly, magisterial, autocratic, dictatorial, domineering, overbearing, assertive, firm, insistent, bossy, high-handed, overweening.
▷ANTONYMS submissive.

imperceptible adjective *the change was slow and imperceptible*: **unnoticeable**, undetectable, indistinguishable, indiscernible, unapparent, inappreciable, invisible, inaudible, impalpable, unobtrusive, impossible to detect; slight, small, subtle, faint, fine, inconsequential, negligible, tiny, minute, minuscule, microscopic, nanoscopic, infinitesimal; indistinct, unclear, obscure, vague, indefinite, shadowy, hard to make out.
▷ANTONYMS obvious, noticeable.

i

imperfect adjective **1** *the goods were returned as imperfect*: **faulty**, flawed, defective, shoddy, unsound, unsaleable, unfit, inferior, second-rate, below par, below standard, substandard; damaged, impaired, blemished, broken, cracked, torn, scratched, deformed, warped, shabby; inoperative, malfunctioning, not functioning, not working, out of order, in a state of disrepair; informal not up to snuff, not up to scratch, tenth-rate, crummy, lousy; Brit. informal duff, ropy, rubbish, not much cop.
▷ANTONYMS perfect.
2 *the manuscript was published in imperfect form in 1888 and fully in 1947*: **incomplete**, abridged, not whole, not entire, partial, unfinished, half-done; deficient, lacking, wanting, unpolished, unrefined, patchy, rough, crude.
▷ANTONYMS complete.
3 *she spoke imperfect Arabic*: **broken**, disjointed, faltering, halting, hesitant, rudimentary, limited, non-fluent, deficient.
▷ANTONYMS perfect, fluent.

imperfection noun **1** *the glass is free from bubbles and other imperfections*: **defect**, fault, flaw, deformity, discoloration, disfigurement; crack, break, scratch, chip, dent, pit, notch, nick; blemish, stain, spot, mark, streak.
2 *he was aware of his own imperfections*: **flaw**, fault, failing, deficiency, weakness, weak point, weak spot, shortcoming, fallibility, frailty, infirmity, foible, inadequacy, limitation; Achilles heel, chink in one's armour; informal hang-up.
▷ANTONYMS strength.
3 *nature is full of imperfection*: **flaws**, faults, faultiness, irregularity, abnormality, distortion, deformity, malformation, misshapenness; ugliness, disfigurement.
▷ANTONYMS perfection.
4 *the imperfection of the fossil record*: **incompleteness**, patchiness, partialness, deficiency; roughness, crudeness.
▷ANTONYMS completeness.

> *Word links* **imperfection**
>
> **atelophobia** fear of imperfection

> *Choose the right word* **imperfection, blemish, flaw**
>
> See **blemish**.

imperial adjective **1** *the symbol figured on the imperial banners*: **royal**, regal, monarchal, monarchial, monarchical, sovereign, kingly, queenly, princely, majestic; rare imperatorial.
2 *her imperial bearing*: **majestic**, grand, dignified, proud, stately, noble, aristocratic, regal; magnificent, great, distinguished, imposing, impressive, august, lofty.
3 *our customers thought we were imperial and uninterested in them*: **imperious**, high-handed, commanding, peremptory, dictatorial, domineering, bossy, arrogant, overweening, overbearing, authoritarian, tyrannical, authoritative, lordly, officious.

imperil verb *a radiation leak would imperil life and health over a wide area*: **endanger**, jeopardize, risk, put at risk, put in danger, expose to danger, put in jeopardy, expose, leave vulnerable, put someone's life on the line; threaten, pose a threat to, be a danger to, be detrimental to, damage, injure, harm, do harm to; archaic peril.

> *Choose the right word* **imperil, endanger, jeopardize, risk**
>
> See **endanger**.

imperious adjective *he spoke to her in a very imperious manner*: **peremptory**, high-handed, commanding, imperial, overbearing, overweening, domineering, authoritarian, dictatorial, authoritative, lordly, officious, assertive, dominating, bullish, forceful, bossy, arrogant; informal pushy, high and mighty, throwing one's weight around; rare pushful.
▷ANTONYMS meek.

imperishable adjective *the fruits of his inspired labours are imperishable*: **enduring**, everlasting, undying, deathless, immortal, timeless, ageless, perennial, lasting, long-lasting; indestructible, inextinguishable, ineradicable, unfading, undiminished, permanent, never-ending, never dying, without end; rare sempiternal, perdurable.

impermanent adjective *life has value precisely because it is impermanent*: **temporary**, non-permanent, not permanent, transient, transitory, passing, fleeting, momentary, ephemeral, fugitive, fading; short-lived, short-term, short, brief, here today and gone tomorrow; literary evanescent, fugacious.
▷ANTONYMS permanent.

impermeable adjective *the product is packaged in impermeable containers*: **watertight**, waterproof, damp-proof, water-resistant, water-repellent, airtight, tight, sealed, hermetically sealed, closed; impenetrable, impregnable, inviolable, resistant; rare imperviable.
▷ANTONYMS permeable.

impersonal adjective **1** *the hand of fate is brutal but impersonal*: **neutral**, unbiased, non-partisan, non-discriminatory, unprejudiced, unswayed, objective, detached, disinterested, dispassionate, free from discrimination, without favouritism, with no axe to grind, without fear or favour; fair, just, equitable, balanced, even-handed.
▷ANTONYMS biased.
2 *even his children found him strangely impersonal*: **aloof**, distant, remote, reserved, withdrawn, unemotional, unfeeling, unsentimental, dispassionate, passionless, cold, cool, frigid, unresponsive, indifferent, unconcerned; **formal**, stiff, rigid, wooden, starchy, stilted, restrained, self-controlled, matter-of-fact, businesslike, clinical; informal stand-offish; rare gelid.
▷ANTONYMS warm; emotional.

impersonate verb *she tried to impersonate her boss*: **imitate**, mimic, do an impression of, ape; parody, caricature, burlesque, travesty, mock, satirize, lampoon; masquerade as, pose as, pass oneself off as, profess to be, purport to be, represent oneself as; informal take off, do, spoof, send up; N. Amer. informal make like; archaic monkey; rare personate.

impersonation noun *he did an impersonation of Fred Astaire*: **impression**, imitation; parody, caricature, mockery, burlesque, travesty, lampoon, pastiche; informal take-off, send-up, spoof; rare personation.

impertinence noun *they gasped at the impertinence of the suggestion*: **rudeness**, insolence, impoliteness, unmannerliness, bad manners, lack of civility, discourtesy, discourteousness, disrespectfulness, incivility; **impudence**, cheek, cheekiness, audacity, temerity, effrontery, nerve, gall, boldness, brazenness, brashness, shamelessness, presumptuousness, presumption, forwardness; informal brass, brass neck, neck, face, front, cockiness; Brit. informal sauce; Scottish informal snash; N. Amer. informal sass, sassiness, nerviness, chutzpah; informal, dated hide, crust; archaic malapertness; rare procacity, assumption.
▷ANTONYMS politeness.

impertinent adjective **1** *she asked a lot of impertinent questions*: **rude**, insolent, impolite, unmannerly, ill-mannered, bad-mannered, uncivil, discourteous, disrespectful; **impudent**, cheeky, audacious, bold, brazen, brash, shameless, presumptuous, forward, pert; tactless, undiplomatic, unsubtle, personal; informal brass-necked, fresh, flip; Brit. informal saucy; N. Amer. informal sassy, nervy; archaic malapert, contumelious; rare mannerless.
▷ANTONYMS polite.
2 formal *talk of 'rhetoric' is impertinent to this process*: **irrelevant**, inapplicable, inapposite, inappropriate, immaterial, unrelated, unconnected, not germane; beside the point, out of place, nothing to do with it, neither here nor there.
▷ANTONYMS relevant, pertinent.

imperturbable adjective *my father was a solid, imperturbable man*: **self-possessed**, composed, collected, calm, {cool, calm, and collected}, as cool as a cucumber, cool-headed, self-controlled, poised, tranquil, serene, relaxed, easy-going, unexcitable, even-tempered, placid, sedate, phlegmatic; unperturbed, unflustered, untroubled, unbothered, unruffled, undismayed, unagitated, undisturbed, unmoved, nonchalant, at ease; informal unflappable, unfazed, together, laid-back; rare equanimous.
▷ANTONYMS edgy; excitable.

impervious adjective **1** *he seemed* ***impervious to*** *the chill wind | she is* ***impervious to*** *his suggestions*: **unaffected by**, untouched by, immune to, invulnerable to, insusceptible to, not susceptible to, proof against,

unreceptive to, closed to, resistant to, indifferent to, heedless of, unresponsive to, oblivious to, unmoved by, deaf to.
▷ANTONYMS receptive to, susceptible to.
2 *an impervious damp-proof course*: **impermeable**, impenetrable, impregnable, waterproof, watertight, water-resistant, water-repellent; sealed, hermetically sealed; rare imperviable.
▷ANTONYMS permeable.

impetuous adjective **1** *she might live to regret this impetuous decision*: **impulsive**, rash, hasty, overhasty, reckless, heedless, foolhardy, incautious, imprudent, injudicious, ill-conceived, ill-considered, unplanned, unreasoned, unthought-out, unthinking; spontaneous, impromptu, spur-of-the-moment, precipitate, precipitous, headlong, hurried, rushed.
▷ANTONYMS cautious, considered.
2 *an impetuous flow of water*: **torrential**, powerful, forceful, vigorous, violent, raging, rampant, relentless, unrestrained, uncontrolled, unbridled; rapid, fast, fast-flowing, rushing.
▷ANTONYMS sluggish, weak.

Choose the right word **impetuous, impulsive, precipitate, headlong**

These words all refer to haste and lack of forethought.

Impetuous and **impulsive** are very similar in meaning, applying to people, their characters, or their actions, but *impetuous* emphasizes the irresponsibility involved (*I was a bit impetuous offering him the job just like that | she might live to regret this impetuous decision*), while to be *impulsive* can be endearing (*an act of impulsive generosity | they married as young, impulsive teenagers*).

Precipitate is used of actions, not people; a *precipitate* act is typically undesirable and lacks proper planning or consideration of its possible effect (*the danger of inappropriate and precipitate intervention which fails to protect the child*).

When used as an adjective, **headlong** applies only to actions, not to people. It describes actions which, after their initial impetus, are not guided by any plan and quickly get out of control (*our headlong rush to develop and industrialize the world*). As an adverb, *headlong* can also apply to people in this sense (*I'm going to enjoy each day while it lasts, instead of dashing headlong into the future*).

impetus noun **1** *the flywheel lost all its impetus*: **momentum**, propulsion, impulsion, impelling force, motive force, driving force, drive, thrust, continuing motion; energy, force, power, push, steam, strength.
2 *new products were introduced to give the sales force fresh impetus*: **motivation**, stimulus, incitement, incentive, inducement, inspiration, encouragement, boost; urging, pressing, goading, spurring, prodding; informal a shot in the arm.

impiety noun **1** *a world of impiety and immorality*: **godlessness**, ungodliness, unholiness, irreligion, sinfulness, sin, vice, immorality, unrighteousness, sacrilege, profaneness, irreverence, disrespect; apostasy, atheism, agnosticism, paganism, heathenism, non-belief, disbelief, unbelief, scepticism, doubt.
▷ANTONYMS piety; faith.
2 *one impiety will cost me my eternity in paradise*: **sin**, transgression, wrongdoing, evil-doing, wrong, misdeed, misdemeanour, bad deed, act of wickedness, immoral act, fall from grace; profanity, blasphemy.
▷ANTONYMS good deed.

impinge verb **1** *these issues* ***impinge on*** *all of us*: **affect**, have an effect on, have a bearing on, touch, influence, exert influence on, make an impression on, make an impact on, leave a mark on.
2 *the proposed fencing would* ***impinge on*** *a public bridleway*: **encroach on**, intrude on, infringe, invade, trespass on, obtrude into, make inroads into, cut through, interfere with; violate; informal muscle in on; archaic entrench on.
3 technical *electrically charged particles* ***impinge on*** *the lunar surface*: **strike**, hit, dash against, collide with.

impious adjective *the church was shamefully plundered by impious villains*: **godless**, ungodly, unholy, irreligious, sinful, immoral, unrighteous, sacrilegious, profane, blasphemous, irreverent, disrespectful; apostate, atheistic, agnostic, pagan, heathen, faithless, non-believing, unbelieving, disbelieving, doubting; rare nullifidian.
▷ANTONYMS pious.

impish adjective **1** *he takes an impish delight in shocking the press*: **mischievous**, naughty, wicked, devilish, rascally, roguish, prankish, playful, waggish; mischief-making, full of mischief, troublemaking; archaic sportive.
2 *she has an engaging impish grin*: **elfin**, elflike, elfish, elvish, pixieish, pixie-like, puckish; mischievous, roguish, arch.

implacable adjective *he was their most implacable critic*: **unappeasable**, unpacifiable, unplacatable, unmollifiable, unforgiving, unsparing, grudge-holding; **inexorable**, intransigent, adamant, determined, unshakeable, unswerving, unwavering, inflexible, unyielding, unbending, uncompromising, unrelenting, relentless, ruthless, remorseless, merciless, pitiless, heartless, cruel, hard, harsh, stern, steely, tough.

implant verb (stress on the second syllable) **1** *the collagen is implanted under the skin*: **insert**, embed, bury, lodge, place, put in place, install, introduce; graft, engraft.
▷ANTONYMS extract.
2 *he implanted the idea in my mind*: **instil**, inculcate, insinuate, introduce, inject, plant, sow, sow the seeds of, infuse, impress, imprint, root, lodge.
▶ noun (stress on the first syllable) *the hormone encourages the bone and the implant to bond*: **transplant**, graft, implantation, insert.

implausible adjective *they despaired of his adherence to implausible theories*: **unlikely**, not likely, improbable, questionable, doubtful, debatable; hard to believe, unconvincing, far-fetched, unrealistic, incredible, unbelievable, unimaginable, inconceivable, fantastic, fanciful, ridiculous, absurd, preposterous; informal hard to swallow, cock and bull, tall.
▷ANTONYMS plausible, convincing.

Word toolkit **implausible**

See **impossible**.

implement noun *garden implements*: **tool**, utensil, instrument, device, apparatus, contrivance, gadget, contraption, appliance, machine, labour-saving device; informal gizmo.
▶ verb *the cost of implementing the new law*: **execute**, apply, put into effect/action, put into practice, carry out, carry through, perform, enact, administer; fulfil, discharge, accomplish, bring about, achieve, realize, contrive, effect; enforce, impose; rare effectuate.

implementation noun *I became responsible for the implementation of the plan*: **execution**, application, carrying out, carrying through, performance, enactment, administration; fulfilment, fulfilling, discharge, accomplishment, achievement, realization, contrivance, prosecution, effecting; enforcement, imposition; rare effectuation.

implicate verb **1** *he had been implicated in a financial scandal*: **incriminate**, compromise; involve, connect, embroil, enmesh, ensnare; expose; archaic inculpate.
▷ANTONYMS absolve.
2 *viruses are known to be* ***implicated in*** *the development of certain cancers*: **involve in**, concern with, associate with, connect with, tie up with.
3 *when one asks a question one implicates that one desires an answer*. See **imply**.

implication noun **1** *he was smarting at their implication that he didn't believe in what he was doing*: **suggestion**, inference, insinuation, innuendo, hint, intimation, imputation, indication; connotation, overtone, undertone, hidden meaning, secondary meaning.
▷ANTONYMS explicit statement.
2 *there was a meeting to discuss the implications of the ban*: **consequence**, result, ramification, repercussion, reverberation, effect.
3 *at the first whiff of implication in a murder case he'd probably burn everything*: **incrimination**, involvement, connection, entanglement, association; archaic inculpation.

implicit adjective **1** *the implicit assumptions of much sociological writing on women*: **implied**, indirect, inferred, understood, hinted, suggested, deducible; unspoken, unexpressed, undeclared, unstated, unsaid, tacit, unacknowledged, silent, taken for granted, taken as read, assumed.
▷ANTONYMS explicit, direct.
2 *there are a number of assumptions implicit in the way the questions are asked*: **inherent**, latent, underlying, inbuilt, incorporated; fundamental.
▷ANTONYMS explicit, direct.
3 *an implicit trust in human nature*: **absolute**, complete, entire, total, wholehearted, perfect, sheer, utter; unqualified, unconditional, unreserved, unadulterated, unalloyed, undiluted, positive; unshaken, unshakeable, unhesitating, unquestioning, firm, steadfast, constant.
▷ANTONYMS limited.

Choose the right word **implicit, tacit, unspoken**

These words all describe ideas that can be understood despite not being directly expressed.

A meaning or message that is **implicit** is not stated openly but can be worked out by reasoning from what has been said (*the speech contained an implicit condemnation of nuclear weapons*). Similarly, an *implicit* attitude or belief can be inferred from the behaviour that it prompts (*we must examine assumptions implicit in the way the questions are asked*).

Tacit, from the Latin for 'silent', is typically used to describe situations involving agreement or cooperation in which the underlying attitude, though not expressed directly, is nevertheless understood and accepted by the parties involved (*the government depended on a tacit agreement with other parties | tacit support for the rebels*).

Unspoken basically means that something is not said aloud (*'It was Father's,' she said to his unspoken question*), and depending on context it can have opposite implications. Something may be unspoken because it is to be kept secret (*unspoken resentment*), or it may describe a message that is made very clear and is possibly all the more effective for not being explicit (*there was always an element of unspoken threat*).

implicitly adverb *he trusted Sarah implicitly*: **completely**, absolutely, totally, wholeheartedly, utterly, unconditionally, unreservedly, without reservation, without reserve, without qualification, one hundred per cent; informal all the way.

implied adjective *there was implied criticism of the king's choice of commanders*: **implicit**, indirect, hinted, suggested, insinuated, deducible, inferred, understood; oblique, unspoken, unexpressed, undeclared, unstated, unsaid, tacit, unacknowledged, not spelt out, silent, taken for granted, taken as read, assumed.
▷ANTONYMS explicit, direct.

implore verb *his mother implored him to continue studying*: **plead with**, beg, entreat, beseech, appeal to, pray, ask, request, solicit, supplicate, importune, call on; exhort, urge, enjoin, press, push, petition, encourage, bid; rare obtest, obsecrate, impetrate.

imply verb **1** *she seemed to be implying that he was mad*: **insinuate**, suggest, hint, intimate, implicate, say indirectly, indicate, give someone to understand, give someone to believe, convey the impression, signal; informal make out.
2 *the forecast traffic increase implied more roads and more air pollution*: **involve**, entail; mean, point to, signify, indicate, signal; necessitate, require.

i

Easily confused words **imply or infer?**

See **infer**.

impolite adjective *it would have been impolite to leave in the middle of the band's set*: **rude**, bad-mannered, ill-mannered, unmannerly, discourteous, uncivil, disrespectful, inconsiderate, boorish, churlish, ill-bred, ungentlemanly, unladylike, ungracious, ungallant; insolent, impudent, impertinent, cheeky, pert, audacious, brassy, offensive, insulting, derogatory; loutish, rough, crude, unrefined, indelicate, indecorous, brash, vulgar; informal ignorant, fresh, lippy; archaic malapert, contumelious; rare underbred, mannerless.
▷ANTONYMS polite.

impolitic adjective *it would be impolitic not to make amends with this man*: **imprudent**, unwise, injudicious, incautious, irresponsible; ill-judged, ill-advised, misguided, ill-considered, careless, rash, reckless, foolhardy, foolish, short-sighted; undiplomatic, indiscreet, indelicate, tactless.
▷ANTONYMS prudent, wise.

import verb (stress on the second syllable) *the UK imports 95 per cent of its charcoal*: **buy from abroad**, bring from abroad, bring in, buy in, ship in, source from abroad.
▷ANTONYMS export.
▸noun (stress on the first syllable) **1** *a tax levied on imports*: **imported commodity**, foreign commodity, non-domestic commodity.
▷ANTONYMS export.
2 *a ban on the import of foreign books*: **importation**, importing, introduction, bringing in, bringing from abroad, buying from abroad, sourcing from abroad, shipping in.
▷ANTONYMS export.
3 *a matter of great import*: **importance**, significance, consequence, moment, momentousness, magnitude, substance, weight, weightiness, note, noteworthiness, gravity, seriousness.
▷ANTONYMS insignificance.
4 *Seb suddenly realized the full import of her words*: **meaning**, sense, essence, gist, drift, purport, message, thrust, substance, sum and substance, implication, signification, point, burden, tenor, spirit; pith, core, nub; informal nitty-gritty.

importance noun **1** *the signing of the treaty was an event of immense importance*: **significance**, momentousness, import, consequence, note, noteworthiness, substance, value; seriousness, graveness, gravity, weightiness, urgency.
▷ANTONYMS unimportance, insignificance.
2 *she had a fine sense of her own importance*: **power**, influence, authority, sway, weight, dominance; prominence, eminence, pre-eminence, notability, worth, account; prestige, high rank, status, standing, stature, superiority, mark, fame, renown, greatness, grandness; informal clout, pull.
▷ANTONYMS unimportance, insignificance.

important adjective **1** *an important meeting*: **significant**, consequential, momentous, of great moment, of import, of great import, of great consequence, far-reaching, major; critical, crucial, vital, pivotal, decisive, urgent, epoch-making, historic, seminal; serious, grave, substantial, weighty, signal, material.
▷ANTONYMS unimportant, trivial.
2 *the important thing is that you do well in your A levels*: **main**, chief, principal, key, major, salient, prime, dominant, foremost, supreme, predominant, paramount, overriding, cardinal, crucial, vital, indispensable, critical, essential, significant, urgent; central, fundamental, basic; informal number-one.
▷ANTONYMS unimportant, inessential.
3 *the school was important to the community*: **of value**, valuable, valued, useful, of use, beneficial, necessary, essential, indispensable, vital, of the essence; **of concern**, of interest, relevant, pertinent, material, germane.
▷ANTONYMS unimportant, irrelevant.
4 *he was an important man*: **powerful**, influential, of influence, well-connected, high-ranking, high-level, top-level, controlling, dominant, formidable; prominent, eminent, pre-eminent, notable, noteworthy, of note; distinguished, esteemed, respected, prestigious, celebrated, famous, great, grand; leading, foremost, outstanding; informal big, big time, major league, big league.
▷ANTONYMS unimportant, insignificant.

importunate adjective *an importunate beggar*: **persistent**, insistent, tenacious, persevering, dogged, unremitting, unrelenting, tireless, indefatigable; stubborn, intransigent, obstinate, obdurate; pressing, urgent, demanding, entreating, nagging, exacting, clamorous, clamant; aggressive, high-pressure; informal pushy; formal exigent, pertinacious, suppliant.

importune verb **1** *he importuned her for some spare change*: **beg**, beseech, entreat, implore, plead with, appeal to, apply to, call on, supplicate, solicit, petition, enjoin; **harass**, pester, beset, press, dun, badger, bother, torment, plague, hound, nag, harry, go on at, harp on at; N. English **mither**; informal hassle, bug; rare obsecrate.
2 *they arrested me for importuning*: **solicit**, make sexual advances, offer one's services as a prostitute; accost, approach; informal proposition; N. Amer. informal hustle.

impose verb **1** *he imposed his ideas on the art director*: **foist**, force, thrust, inflict, obtrude, press, urge; informal saddle someone with, land someone with, lumber someone with.
2 *new taxes will be imposed on all non-renewable forms of energy*: **levy**, charge, exact, apply, enforce; set, establish, fix, put, lay, institute, introduce; decree, ordain, enact, promulgate, bring into effect, bring to bear; informal clap, slap.
3 *how dare you* ***impose on*** *me like this!* **take advantage of**, abuse, exploit, take liberties with, misuse, ill-treat, treat unfairly, manipulate; bother, trouble, disturb, inconvenience, put out, put to trouble, take for granted; be a burden on, prey on; informal walk all over.
□ **impose oneself** *he struggled to* ***impose himself on*** *a fractious party*: **force oneself**, foist oneself, thrust oneself; intrude, break in, obtrude, interlope, trespass, impinge, butt in, barge in; control, gain control of, take charge of; informal gatecrash, crash, horn in, muscle in, call the shots, call the tune, be in the driving seat, be in the saddle, run the show, pull the strings, rule the roost.

imposing adjective *an imposing mansion | his imposing physical presence*: **impressive**, striking, arresting, eye-catching, dramatic, spectacular, staggering, stunning, awesome, awe-inspiring, remarkable, formidable; splendid, grand, majestic, august, lofty, stately, dignified, resplendent.
▷ANTONYMS unimposing, modest.

imposition noun **1** *the imposition of an alien culture on the indigenous inhabitants*: **imposing**, foisting, forcing, inflicting, obtruding, pressing.
2 *the imposition of VAT on domestic fuel*: **levying**, charging, exacting, application, applying, enforcement, enforcing; setting, establishment, fixing, laying, introduction, institution; decreeing, ordainment, enactment, promulgation; informal slapping, clapping.
3 *it would be no imposition, I assure you*: **burden**, load, onus, encumbrance, strain, demand, pressure, charge, bother, worry; informal hassle.
4 *the government began levying special impositions*: **tax**, levy, duty, charge, tariff, toll, excise, tithe, fee, impost, exaction, payment; rare mulct.

impossible adjective **1** *gale force winds made fishing impossible*: **not possible**, beyond the bounds of possibility, out of the question, not worth considering; unfeasible, impractical, impracticable, non-viable, unworkable, beyond one; unthinkable, unimaginable, inconceivable; paradoxical, illogical, irrational; informal undoable.
▷ANTONYMS possible; easy.
2 *six months ago his ambition had seemed an impossible dream*: **unattainable**, unachievable, unobtainable, hopeless, impractical, implausible, far-fetched, impracticable, unworkable; forlorn, vain; incredible, unbelievable, absurd, ludicrous, ridiculous, laughable, risible, preposterous, outlandish, outrageous; wild, hare-brained.
▷ANTONYMS possible, attainable.
3 *a ban on buses would have made life impossible for many residents*: **unbearable**, intolerable, unendurable, unsustainable; informal no-win.
▷ANTONYMS bearable, tolerable.
4 informal *your mother is the most impossible woman in the world*: **unmanageable**, intractable, recalcitrant, wayward, objectionable, difficult, demanding, awkward, perverse, ungovernable; intolerable, unbearable, unendurable; exasperating, maddening, infuriating.
▷ANTONYMS manageable, easy to please.

Word toolkit

impossible	unattainable	implausible
task	goal	scenario
odds	dream	claim
feat	standard	explanation
mission	beauty	story
demands	perfection	ending
question	woman	theory
choice	level	excuses

impostor, imposter noun **impersonator**, masquerader, pretender, deceiver, hoaxer; fake, fraud, sham, humbug; charlatan, quack, mountebank; trickster, fraudster, swindler, hoodwinker, bluffer, deluder, duper, cheat, cheater, defrauder, exploiter, rogue, wolf in sheep's clothing; informal phoney, con man, con artist, flimflammer, flimflam man; dated confidence man/woman.

imposture noun *by the time the imposture had been discovered the real prince had fled*: **misrepresentation**, pretence, deceit, deception, duping, cheating, trickery, artifice, subterfuge; hoax, trick, ruse, dodge, blind, wile; fraudulence, fraud, swindling; charlatanry, quackery; informal con, con trick, scam, sting, flimflam, kidology; Brit. informal wheeze; Irish informal codology.

impotent adjective **1** *the legal sanctions are regarded as impotent*: **powerless**, ineffective, ineffectual, inadequate, weak, useless, worthless, vain, futile, unavailing, unsuccessful, profitless, fruitless; literary impuissant.
▷ANTONYMS powerful, effective.
2 *there are powerful natural forces which man is impotent to control*: **unable**, incapable, helpless, powerless, incompetent, unfit, unfitted.
▷ANTONYMS able.
3 *an impotent opposition party*: **weak**, powerless, ineffective, lame, feeble, effete; informal past it.
▷ANTONYMS strong, effective.

impound verb **1** *officials began impounding documents yesterday*: **confiscate**, appropriate, take possession of, seize, commandeer, expropriate, requisition, sequester, sequestrate, take; Law distrain, disseize, attach; Scottish Law poind.
2 *the cattle were rounded up and impounded*: **pen in**, shut up/in, fence in, coop up, hem in, box in, hedge in, rail in; cage, enclose, confine; N. Amer. corral.
3 *the poor unfortunates impounded in the prison*: **lock up**, incarcerate, imprison, confine, intern, immure, hold captive, hold prisoner, put under lock and key; informal put behind bars.

impoverish verb **1** *a widow who had been impoverished by inflation*: **make poor**, make penniless, reduce to penury, reduce to destitution, bring to ruin, bring someone to their knees, bankrupt, ruin, make insolvent; wipe out, clean out, break, cripple; rare pauperize, beggar.
▷ANTONYMS make wealthy.
2 *the trees were considered to be impoverishing the soil*: **weaken**, sap, exhaust, drain, empty, diminish, deplete, enervate, suck dry; informal bleed.
▷ANTONYMS strengthen, enrich.

impoverished adjective **1** *an impoverished peasant farmer*: **poor**, poverty-stricken, penniless, penurious, destitute, indigent, impecunious, needy, pauperized, in distressed/reduced/straitened circumstances, in want, in need, down and out, on the breadline; bankrupt, ruined, insolvent, wiped out, cleaned out, broken, crippled, without a penny to one's name; informal broke, flat broke, stony broke, on one's uppers, strapped (for cash), on one's beam ends, bust, hard up, without two pennies/farthings to rub together, without a bean, without a sou, as poor as a church mouse, on skid row; Brit. informal skint, without a shot in one's locker; Brit. rhyming slang boracic (lint); N. Amer. informal stone broke, without a red cent; rare beggared.
▷ANTONYMS rich, wealthy.
2 *the soil is impoverished*: **weakened**, exhausted, drained, sapped, diminished, depleted, enervated, sucked dry, used up, spent, played out; barren, unproductive, unfertile, arid, uncultivatable.
▷ANTONYMS rich, fertile.

impracticable adjective *my colleagues thought it an impracticable plan*: **unworkable**, non-viable, impossible to carry out, unfeasible, inoperable, out of the question, not worth considering, unachievable, unattainable, unrealizable; impractical; informal undoable.
▷ANTONYMS workable, feasible.

Easily confused words **impracticable or impractical?**

See **impractical**.

impractical adjective **1** *an impractical suggestion*: **unrealistic**, unworkable, unfeasible, non-viable, impracticable; ill-considered, ill-thought-out, illogical, unreasonable, far-fetched, impossible, silly, foolish, absurd, wild; informal cock-eyed, crackpot, crazy, half-baked.
▷ANTONYMS practical, sensible.
2 *she wore impractical white ankle boots*: **unsuitable**, not sensible, inappropriate, unserviceable.
▷ANTONYMS practical, sensible.
3 *an unworldly and impractical scholar*: **unrealistic**, idealistic, head-in-the-clouds, out of touch with reality, romantic, dreamy, fanciful, starry-eyed, visionary, quixotic; informal airy-fairy.
▷ANTONYMS practical, down to earth.

Easily confused words **impractical or impracticable?**

Although similar in spelling, these words have distinct meanings. **Impractical** means 'not sensible or realistic', and applies either to things that are not designed to be useful in everyday situations or to an outlook that does not take the realities of life into account (*Paul was impractical and dreamy | you're wearing rather impractical clothes*). **Impracticable**, on the other hand, describes an idea or plan that is impossible to put into action (*the small population made it impracticable to provide separate schools for boys and girls*). An *impractical dreamer* might well be preoccupied with *impracticable projects*.

imprecation noun formal **1** *he cursed himself with the most dreadful imprecations*: **curse**, malediction, anathema; N. Amer. hex; Irish cess; archaic execration, malison, ban.
▷ANTONYMS bless.
2 *he abused her with a stream of imprecations*: **swear word**, curse, expletive, oath, profanity, four-letter word, obscenity, epithet, dirty word; (**imprecations**) swearing, cursing, blaspheming, blasphemy, sacrilege, bad language, foul language, strong language, colourful language; N. Amer. cuss word; archaic execration.

imprecise adjective **1** *this is a rather imprecise definition*: **vague**, loose, indefinite, inexplicit, indistinct, non-specific, unspecific, broad, general, sweeping; hazy, fuzzy, blurred, unfocused, woolly, nebulous; confused, ambiguous, equivocal, uncertain, non-committal.
▷ANTONYMS precise, narrow.
2 *an imprecise estimate*: **inexact**, approximate, estimated, rough; inaccurate, incorrect, wrong, erroneous, wide of the mark, off target, out; N. Amer. informal ballpark.
▷ANTONYMS precise, exact.

impregnable adjective **1** *such a castle must have been impregnable*: **invulnerable**, impenetrable, unattackable, unassailable, inviolable, secure, strong, stout, safe, well fortified, well defended; invincible, unconquerable, unbeatable, indestructible.
▷ANTONYMS vulnerable.
2 *an impregnable parliamentary majority*: **unassailable**, unbeatable, undefeatable, unshakeable, invincible, indomitable, unconquerable, unstoppable, invulnerable.
▷ANTONYMS vulnerable.
3 *as a working theory, this is impregnable*: **irrefutable**, incontrovertible, undeniable, indisputable, incontestable, unquestionable, unassailable, beyond question, beyond doubt, indubitable; flawless, faultless, watertight, airtight, foolproof, without loopholes.
▷ANTONYMS flawed.

Word toolkit **impregnable**

See **indomitable**.

impregnate verb **1** *a pad impregnated with natural oils*: **infuse**, soak, steep, saturate, drench; permeate, suffuse, imbue, pervade, fill, load, charge.
2 *he was obliged to marry the woman he had impregnated*: **make pregnant**, get pregnant, inseminate, fertilize; informal put in the family way; Brit. informal get up the duff, put in the club, get up the spout, get up the stick; N. Amer. informal knock up; informal, dated get into trouble; archaic fecundate, get with child.

impresario noun *a theatrical impresario*: **organizer**, manager, producer, stage manager; promotor, publicist, showman; controller, arranger, fixer; financier, moneyman; director, conductor, maestro.

impress verb **1** *Hazel had impressed him mightily*: **make an impression on**, have an impact on, influence, affect, leave a mark on, move, stir, rouse, excite, inspire, galvanize; dazzle, overcome, overwhelm, overpower, awe, overawe, take someone's breath away, take someone aback, amaze, astonish; (**be impressed**) feel admiration, feel respect; informal grab, stick in someone's mind.
▷ANTONYMS disappoint.
2 *goldsmiths impressed his likeness on medallions*: **imprint**, print, stamp, mark, engrave, emboss, punch, etch, carve, inscribe, cut, chisel.
3 *you must* ***impress upon*** *her that she has to come to school*: **emphasize to**, stress to, bring home to, establish in someone's mind, fix deeply in someone's mind, instil in, inculcate in, drum into, knock into, drive into, din into, ingrain in, leave in no doubt.

impression noun **1** *he got the impression that she was hiding something*: **feeling**, sense, fancy, suspicion, sneaking suspicion, inkling, intuition,

hunch, apprehension; notion, idea, thought, belief, opinion, conviction; informal funny feeling, gut feeling, feeling in one's bones, sixth sense.
2 *she had formed a favourable impression of him*: **opinion**, view, conception, image, picture, perception, judgement, verdict, estimation.
3 *school made a profound impression on me*: **impact**, effect, influence.
4 *the cap had left a circular impression on his hair*: **indentation**, dent, hollow, concavity, depression, dip, mark, outline, stamp, stamping, imprint.
5 *he did a good impression of their science teacher*: **impersonation**, imitation, mimicry; parody, caricature, burlesque, travesty, mockery, lampoon, pastiche; informal take-off, send-up, spoof; rare personation.
6 *an artist's impression of the finished gardens*: **representation**, portrayal, depiction, rendition, rendering, interpretation, picture, drawing.
7 *a revised impression of the 1981 edition*: **print run**, printing, imprinting, imprint, reprint, issue, edition, version, publication.

impressionable adjective *an impressionable adolescent girl*: **easily influenced**, easily led, suggestible, susceptible, receptive, persuadable, pliable, malleable, pliant, mouldable; vulnerable, exploitable, ingenuous, trusting, naive, credulous, gullible.
▷ANTONYMS unimpressionable.

impressive adjective **1** *the hall is an impressive building*: **magnificent**, majestic, imposing, splendid, spectacular, grand, august, awe-inspiring, stirring, stunning, breathtaking; stately, monumental, palatial, noble, dignified.
▷ANTONYMS unimpressive, ordinary.
2 *they played some impressive football*: **admirable**, accomplished, expert, skilled, skilful, masterly, consummate; excellent, formidable, outstanding, first-class, first-rate, fine; informal great, mean, nifty, cracking, crack, stellar, ace, wizard; N. Amer. informal crackerjack.
▷ANTONYMS unimpressive, mediocre.

imprint verb (stress on the second syllable) **1** *patterns can be imprinted in the clay*: **stamp**, print, impress, mark, engrave, emboss.
2 *he knew he'd always have this ghastly image imprinted on his mind*: **fix**, establish, stick, lodge, implant, embed; stamp, impress, etch, engrave, print.
▶ **noun** (stress on the first syllable) **1** *her feet left imprints on the floor*: **impression**, print, mark, indentation.
2 *colonialism has left its imprint*: **impact**, lasting effect, influence, impression.

imprison verb *she was imprisoned for sedition*: **incarcerate**, put in prison, send to prison, jail, lock up, take into custody, put under lock and key, put away, intern, confine, detain, hold prisoner, hold captive, hold, put into detention, put in chains, put in irons, clap in irons; Brit. detain at Her Majesty's pleasure; informal send down, put behind bars, put inside; Brit. informal bang someone up; rare immure.
▷ANTONYMS free, release.

imprisoned adjective *an imprisoned dissident*: **incarcerated**, in prison, in jail, jailed, locked up, in custody, under lock and key, interned, confined, detained, held prisoner, captive, held captive, in chains, in irons, clapped in irons; Brit. detained at Her Majesty's pleasure; informal sent down, behind bars, doing time, inside, away; Brit. informal doing porridge, doing bird, banged up; rare immured.
▷ANTONYMS free.

imprisonment noun *he was sentenced to two months' imprisonment*: **incarceration**, internment, confinement, detention, custody, captivity; penal servitude, hard labour; informal time; Brit. informal porridge, bird, chokey; archaic durance, duress.
▷ANTONYMS freedom.

improbability noun *his belief in the improbability of war in Europe*: **unlikelihood**, implausibility; doubtfulness, uncertainty, dubiousness; unthinkability, inconceivability, incredibility.
▷ANTONYMS probability, certainty.

improbable adjective **1** *it seemed improbable that the hot weather should continue much longer*: **unlikely**, not likely, doubtful, dubious, debatable, questionable, uncertain; difficult to believe, implausible, far-fetched, fanciful; unthinkable, inconceivable, unimaginable, incredible.
▷ANTONYMS probable, certain.
2 *the impression created by some advertisers is an improbable exaggeration*: **inauthentic**, unconvincing, unbelievable, incredible, ridiculous, absurd, preposterous; contrived, laboured, strained, forced; informal hard to swallow.
▷ANTONYMS believable, realistic.

impromptu adjective *he gave an impromptu lecture*: **unrehearsed**, unprepared, unscripted, extempore, extemporized, improvised, improvisational, improvisatory, improvisatorial, spontaneous, unstudied, unpremeditated, unarranged, unplanned, on the spot, snap, ad lib; ad hoc, thrown together, cobbled together, rough and ready; Latin ad libitum; informal off-the-cuff, spur-of-the-moment; rare extemporaneous.
▷ANTONYMS prepared, rehearsed.
▶ **adverb** *they played the song impromptu*: **extempore**, spontaneously, without preparation, without rehearsal, on the spur of the moment, offhand, ad lib; Latin ad libitum; informal off the cuff, off the top of one's head; rare extemporaneously.

improper adjective **1** *it was improper for policemen to accept gifts*: **inappropriate**, unacceptable, unsuitable, unprofessional, irregular, illegitimate, against the rules; unethical, corrupt, immoral, dishonest, dishonourable, unscrupulous; informal crooked, not cricket.
▷ANTONYMS acceptable, proper.
2 *it would have been thought improper for two young ladies to drive a young man home*: **unseemly**, indecorous, unbecoming, unfitting, out of keeping, unladylike, ungentlemanly, indiscreet, indelicate, impolite, undignified; indecent, unwholesome, immodest, immoral; outrageous, scandalous, shocking, offensive, distasteful; forward, bold, brazen, shameless; informal fresh, cheeky.
▷ANTONYMS proper.
3 *he recited an extremely improper poem*: **indecent**, risqué, off colour, indelicate, suggestive, naughty, ribald, earthy, Rabelaisian, smutty, dirty, filthy, vulgar, crude, rude, obscene, lewd, pornographic; informal blue, raunchy, steamy, near the knuckle/bone, nudge-nudge; Brit. informal fruity, saucy.
▷ANTONYMS decent.

impropriety noun **1** *he was outraged at any suggestion of impropriety*: **wrongdoing**, misconduct, dishonesty, corruption, unscrupulousness, illegitimacy, unprofessionalism, irregularity; inappropriateness; unseemliness, indecorousness, indiscretion, indelicacy, injudiciousness, indecency, immorality, unwholesomeness, immodesty, indecorum, bad taste, impoliteness.
▷ANTONYMS propriety.
2 *the director was jailed for a list of fiscal improprieties*: **transgression**, misdemeanour, offence, misdeed, improper act, sin, crime, felony; indiscretion, mistake, slip, error, blunder, lapse, peccadillo; archaic trespass.

improve verb **1** *staff looked for ways to improve the service*: **make better**, better, ameliorate, upgrade, refine, enhance, boost, build on, help, raise, revamp, brush up, polish up, perk up, tweak; informal give a facelift to; rare meliorate.
▷ANTONYMS worsen, impair.
2 *communications improved during the 18th century*: **get better**, become better, advance, progress, develop; make headway, come along, make progress, take steps forward, pick up, rally, perk up, make strides; informal look up.
▷ANTONYMS worsen, deteriorate.
3 *the dose is not repeated for as long as the patient continues to improve*: **recover**, get better, get well, recuperate, convalesce, gain strength, rally, revive, strengthen, regain one's strength/health, get back on one's feet, get over something; be on the road to recovery, be on the mend; informal turn the corner, take a turn for the better, take on a new lease of life; Brit. informal be on the up and up.
▷ANTONYMS deteriorate, become ill.
4 *resources are needed to improve the offer*: **increase**, make larger, make bigger, raise, put up, add to, augment, supplement, top up, enlarge; informal up, jack up, hike up, bump up, crank up, step up.
▷ANTONYMS decrease.
□ **improve on** *I cannot improve on his comments*: **surpass**, better, do better than, outdo, exceed, beat, top, trump, cap, outstrip, overshadow, go one better than.

improvement noun *an improvement in the quality of Britain's rivers | many areas in the design could do with improvement*: **advance**, development, upgrade, change for the better, refinement, enhancement, furtherance, advancement, forwarding; boost, augmentation, raising; correction, rectification, rectifying, upgrading, amelioration; rally, recovery, upswing, breakthrough.
▷ANTONYMS deterioration.

improvident adjective *a feckless and improvident lifestyle*: **spendthrift**, thriftless, unthrifty, wasteful, prodigal, profligate, extravagant, squandering, uneconomical, free-spending, lavish, immoderate, excessive; shiftless, feckless; imprudent, irresponsible, incautious, careless, reckless, rash, impetuous, hasty, thoughtless.
▷ANTONYMS thrifty; cautious.

improvisation noun *some of the best things in the film came out of improvisation*: **extemporization**, ad-libbing, spontaneity, lack of premeditation; rare autoschediasm.

improvise verb **1** *she was improvising in front of the cameras*: **extemporize**, ad lib, speak impromptu, make it up as one goes along, think on one's feet, take it as it comes; informal speak off the cuff, speak off the top of one's head, play it by ear, busk it, wing it.
2 *she improvised a sandpit for the children to play in*: **contrive**, devise, throw together, cobble together, concoct, rig, jury-rig, put together; Brit. informal knock up; informal whip up, fix up, rustle up.

improvised adjective **1** *an improvised short speech*: **impromptu**, improvisational, improvisatory, unrehearsed, unprepared, unscripted, extempore, extemporized, spontaneous, unstudied, unpremeditated, unarranged, unplanned, on the spot, ad lib; Latin ad libitum; informal off-the-cuff, spur of the moment; rare improvisatorial.
▷ANTONYMS prepared, rehearsed.

2 *an improvised shelter*: **makeshift**, thrown together, cobbled together, devised, rigged, jury-rigged, rough and ready, make-do, emergency, stopgap, temporary, short-term, pro tem; Latin ad hoc, pro tempore, ad interim.

imprudent adjective *the banks were imprudent in making the loans*: **unwise**, injudicious, incautious, unwary; ill-considered, ill-judged, ill-conceived, impolitic, misguided, ill-advised; thoughtless, unthinking, improvident, irresponsible, short-sighted, foolish, careless, hasty, overhasty, rash, reckless, heedless, foolhardy.
▷**ANTONYMS** prudent, sensible.

> *Choose the right word* **imprudent, unwise, injudicious, ill-advised**
>
> See **unwise**.

impudence noun **impertinence**, insolence, effrontery, cheek, audacity, temerity, brazenness, shamelessness, immodesty, pertness; presumption, presumptuousness, disrespect, insubordination, irreverence, flippancy, bumptiousness, brashness, boldness; rudeness, impoliteness, ill manners, bad manners, unmannerliness, discourteousness, gall, ill breeding; informal freshness, cockiness, brass neck, sauce, sauciness, lip, mouth, face, nerve; N. Amer. informal sassiness, chutzpah, nerviness.

impudent adjective *these impudent youngsters*: **impertinent**, insolent, cheeky, audacious, brazen, shameless, immodest, pert; presumptuous, forward, disrespectful, insubordinate, irreverent, flippant, bumptious, brash, bold, bold as brass; rude, impolite, ill-mannered, bad-mannered, unmannerly, discourteous, insulting, ill-bred; informal fresh, cocky, brass-necked, saucy, lippy, mouthy, flip; N. Amer. informal sassy, nervy; archaic malapert, contumelious.
▷**ANTONYMS** polite, respectful.

impugn verb *he had impugned the Prime Minister's honour*: **call into question**, challenge, question, dispute, query, take issue with, impeach.
▷**ANTONYMS** support.

impulse noun **1** *she had an impulse to run and hide somewhere*: **urge**, instinct, drive, compulsion, need, itch; whim, caprice, desire, fancy, notion.
2 *he was a man of impulse*: **spontaneity**, impetuosity, wildness, recklessness, irresponsibility, rashness.
▷**ANTONYMS** premeditation, carefulness.
3 *passions provide the main impulse of poetry and music*: **inspiration**, stimulation, stimulus, incitement, motivation, encouragement, fillip, spur, prod, catalyst.
4 *neurons conduct impulses from the spinal cord to the muscles*: **pulse**, current, wave; **signal**, message, brainwave, communication.
□ **on (an) impulse** *Valerie and I married on impulse*: **impulsively**, spontaneously, on the spur of the moment, without forethought, without planning, without thinking twice, without premeditation, unpremeditatedly.
▷**ANTONYMS** with forethought.

impulsive adjective **1** *he had an impulsive nature*: **impetuous**, spontaneous, hasty, passionate, emotional, uninhibited, unrepressed, abandoned; rash, reckless, foolhardy, madcap, devil-may-care, daredevil, hot-headed, wild, daring, adventurous.
▷**ANTONYMS** cautious.
2 *his impulsive decision to leave his job and join the army*: **impromptu**, snap, spontaneous, unpremeditated, spur-of-the-moment, extemporaneous; impetuous, precipitate, hasty, headlong, rash, reckless, incautious, imprudent, injudicious; sudden, quick, ill-considered, ill-thought-out, unplanned, thoughtless, unthinking.
▷**ANTONYMS** premeditated.

> *Choose the right word* **impulsive, impetuous, precipitate, headlong**
>
> See **impetuous**.

impunity noun *the impunity enjoyed by military officers implicated in civilian killings*: **immunity**, indemnity, exemption from punishment, freedom from punishment, exemption, non-liability, licence; amnesty, dispensation, pardon, reprieve, stay of execution, exoneration; privilege, special treatment, favouritism; French carte blanche.
▷**ANTONYMS** liability, responsibility.
□ **with impunity** *criminals who appear to flout the law with impunity*: **unpunished**, with no ill consequences, with no ill effects, without being punished, without punishment; scot-free.

impure adjective **1** *a small amount of impure gold*: **adulterated**, mixed, combined, blended, alloyed; debased, degraded, defiled; technical admixed.
▷**ANTONYMS** pure.
2 *the water was impure*: **contaminated**, polluted, tainted, infected, sullied, defiled, unwholesome, poisoned; dirty, filthy, unclean, foul; unhygienic, unsanitary, insanitary; literary befouled; rare feculent.
▷**ANTONYMS** pure, clean.
3 *they cleared their minds of any impure notions*: **immoral**, corrupt, sinful, wrongful, wicked, dishonourable; depraved, degenerate, debauched, dissolute; **unchaste**, lustful, lecherous, lewd, lascivious, prurient, obscene, dirty, indecent, unclean, wanton, ribald, risqué, smutty, improper, crude, vulgar, coarse, gross, pornographic; rare concupiscent.
▷**ANTONYMS** pure, chaste.

impurity noun **1** *the brittleness of cast iron resulted from its impurity*: **adulteration**, debasement, degradation.
▷**ANTONYMS** purity.
2 *the impurity of the air breathed by pitmen*: **contamination**, pollution; dirtiness, filthiness, uncleanliness, foulness, unwholesomeness; rare feculence.
▷**ANTONYMS** purity, cleanliness.
3 *all the impurities are left in the beer*: **contaminant**, adulterant, pollutant, foreign body; dross, dirt, filth, grime, scum; (**impurities**) bits, foreign matter.
4 *a struggle to rid the soul of sin and impurity*: **immorality**, corruption, sin, sinfulness, vice, wickedness, dishonour; depravity, degeneracy, debauchery, dissolution; **unchastity**, lustfulness, lechery, lecherousness, lewdness, lasciviousness, prurience, obscenity, dirtiness, indecency, wantonness, ribaldry, smut, smuttiness, impropriety, crudity, crudeness, vulgarity, coarseness, grossness; rare concupiscence.
▷**ANTONYMS** purity, chastity.

impute verb *he imputes selfish views to me*: **attribute**, ascribe, assign, credit, accredit, chalk up; connect with, associate with, lay on, lay at the door of; informal pin on, stick on.

in preposition **1** *she was hiding in a wardrobe*: **inside**, within, in the middle of, within the bounds/confines of; surrounded by, enclosed by.
▷**ANTONYMS** outside.
2 *he was covered in mud*: **with**, by.
3 *he put a fruit gum in his mouth*: **into**, inside, into the interior of.
4 *they met in 1921*: **during**, in the course of, in the time of, over.
5 *I'll see you in half an hour*: **after**, at the end of, following, subsequent to; within, in less than, in under, in no more than, before a ... is up.
6 *the tax is charged at ten pence in the pound*: **to**, per, every, each.
□ **in for** *she is in for a huge pay rise*: **due for**, in line for, likely to receive; expecting, about to receive, about to experience; up for, ready for.
□ **in for it** *we're in for it now!* **in trouble**, about to be punished, about to suffer the consequences, about to pay the price, in for a scolding; informal for it, for the high jump, in hot water, in deep water, in (deep) shtook, about to take the rap, about to catch it.
□ **in on** *now you're in on my secret*: **privy to**, aware of, acquainted with, informed about/of, advised of, apprised of, mindful of, sensible of; informal wise to, clued in on, up on, in the know about, hip to, in the loop; archaic ware of.
▶ adverb **1** *his mum walked in*: **inside**, indoors, into the interior, into the room/house/building, within.
▷**ANTONYMS** out.
2 *the tide's in*: **high**, at its highest level, rising.
▷**ANTONYMS** out, low.
▶ adjective **1** *we knocked at the door but there was no one in*: **present**, home, at home; **inside**, indoors, in the house/room.
▷**ANTONYMS** out.
2 informal *back when beards were in*: **fashionable**, in fashion, in vogue, voguish, stylish, in style, popular, (bang) up to date, up to the minute, modern, modish, trendsetting, chic; French à la mode, de rigueur; informal trendy, all the rage, with it, cool, the in thing, hot, hip, happening, now, swinging; Brit. informal, dated all the go.
▷**ANTONYMS** unfashionable, out.
3 *I was in with all the right people*: **in favour**, popular, friendly, friends; favoured by, liked by, approved of by, admired by, accepted by; informal in someone's good books.
▷**ANTONYMS** unpopular.
▶ noun
□ **ins and outs** *our instructors will teach novices the ins and outs of the sport*: **details**, particulars, facts, features, points, characteristics, traits, nuts and bolts, particularities; intricacies, peculiarities, idiosyncrasies; informal nitty gritty, ABC, A to Z.

inability noun **lack of ability**, incapability, incapacity, powerlessness, impotence, helplessness; incompetence, ineptitude, inaptitude, unfitness, ineffectiveness, uselessness, inefficacy; Medicine insufficiency.
▷**ANTONYMS** ability.

inaccessible adjective **1** *an inaccessible woodland site*: **unreachable**, out of reach, beyond reach; cut-off, isolated, remote, in the middle of nowhere, in the back of beyond, out of the way, off the map, lonely, godforsaken; secluded, sequestered; informal unget-at-able; archaic unapproachable.
▷**ANTONYMS** accessible.
2 *the radio station was accused of being elitist and inaccessible*: **esoteric**, obscure, abstruse, recondite, recherché, arcane, rarefied; cerebral, intellectual; elitist, exclusive, pretentious, snobby, snobbish.

inaccuracy noun **1** *the inaccuracy of recent opinion polls*: **incorrectness**, inexactness, inexactitude, imprecision, erroneousness, mistakenness,

fallaciousness, faultiness.
▷ANTONYMS accuracy, correctness.
2 *the article contained a number of inaccuracies*: **error**, mistake, miscalculation, fallacy, slip, oversight, fault, blunder, gaffe, defect, flaw; erratum, typographical error, slip of the pen, printer's error, literal, corrigendum; slip of the tongue; Latin lapsus calami, lapsus linguae; informal slip-up, foul-up, clanger, howler, boob, boo-boo, typo; N. Amer. informal blooper, goof; Brit. informal, dated bloomer.

inaccurate adjective *the maps were notoriously inaccurate*: **inexact**, imprecise, incorrect, wrong, erroneous, faulty, imperfect, flawed, defective, unsound, unreliable; out, adrift, wide of the mark, off target; fallacious, false, mistaken, untrue, not true, not right; falsified, distorted, garbled; informal off beam, full of holes.
▷ANTONYMS accurate.

inaction noun *wildlife is threatened by government inaction*: **inactivity**, passivity, non-intervention; neglect, negligence, disregard, apathy; inertia, indolence, laziness, idleness, sloth, slothfulness, sluggishness, lethargy, torpor.
▷ANTONYMS action.

inactivate verb *coffee tends to inactivate homeopathic remedies*: **disable**, deactivate, render inactive, make inoperative, prevent from working, halt, stop, immobilize; informal scupper.
▷ANTONYMS activate.

inactive adjective 1 *over the next few days I was horribly inactive*: **idle**, indolent, lazy, lifeless, slothful, lethargic, inert, slow, sluggish, stagnant, dozy, unenergetic, listless, languishing, vegetating, torpid; immobile.
▷ANTONYMS active.
2 *the device remains inactive while the computer is started up*: **inoperative**, non-functioning, idle, turned off, dormant; not working, out of service, unused, out of use, not in use, unoccupied, unemployed, inert, dead.
▷ANTONYMS active, in use.

> *Word toolkit* **inactive**
>
> See **inert**.

inactivity noun 1 *don't suddenly take up violent exercise after years of inactivity*: **idleness**, indolence, laziness, lifelessness, slothfulness, shiftlessness, lethargy, inertia, slowness, sluggishness, stagnancy, doziness, listlessness; immobility; Italian dolce far niente.
▷ANTONYMS activity.
2 *people are frustrated with government inactivity*: **inaction**, passivity, non-intervention, laissez-faire; neglect, negligence, disregard, apathy.
▷ANTONYMS activity, action.

inadequacy noun 1 *the inadequacy of available resources*: **insufficiency**, deficiency, scantness, scarcity, scarceness, sparseness, dearth, paucity, poverty, shortage, want, lack, undersupply; paltriness, meagreness, niggardliness; sketchiness, incompleteness, limitedness, restrictedness; rare exiguity, exiguousness.
▷ANTONYMS abundance, surplus.
2 *her feelings of personal inadequacy*: **incompetence**, incapability, unfitness, ineffectiveness, ineffectuality, inefficiency, inefficacy, inexpertness, lack of skill, lack of proficiency, ineptness, uselessness, hopelessness, impotence, powerlessness; amateurishness, inferiority, unsatisfactoriness, substandardness.
▷ANTONYMS competence.
3 *the inadequacies of the present system*: **shortcoming**, defect, fault, failing, weakness, weak point, limitation, flaw, imperfection, Achilles heel; loophole.
▷ANTONYMS strong point.

inadequate adjective 1 *inadequate water supplies | inadequate wages*: **insufficient**, not enough, deficient, poor, scant, scanty, scarce, sparse, too little, too few, short, in short supply; paltry, meagre, niggardly; skimpy, sketchy, incomplete, restricted, limited; informal measly, pathetic, piddling; rare exiguous.
▷ANTONYMS adequate, sufficient.
2 *inadequate staff*: **incompetent**, incapable, unsatisfactory, not good enough, no good, found wanting, not up to scratch, lacking, leaving much to be desired, unfit, ineffective, ineffectual, inefficient, unskilful, inexpert, inept, unproficient, amateurish, substandard, poor, bad, hopeless, useless, inferior; impotent, powerless; informal not up to snuff, lousy; Brit. informal duff, not much cop, no great shakes; vulgar slang half-arsed.
▷ANTONYMS competent.

inadmissible adjective *inadmissible evidence*: **not allowable**, invalid, not acceptable, unacceptable, unallowable, impermissible, disallowed, forbidden, prohibited, precluded; inappropriate, inapplicable, inapposite, irrelevant, immaterial, impertinent, not germane, beside the point.
▷ANTONYMS admissible.

inadvertent adjective *an inadvertent omission*: **unintentional**, unintended, accidental, unpremeditated, unplanned, unmeant, innocent, uncalculated, unconscious, unthinking, unwitting, involuntary; chance, coincidental; careless, thoughtless.
▷ANTONYMS deliberate, intentional.

inadvertently adverb *his name had been inadvertently omitted from the list*: **accidentally**, by accident, unintentionally, unwittingly; unawares, without noticing, in all innocence; by mistake, mistakenly.
▷ANTONYMS deliberately.

inadvisable adjective *an economically inadvisable move*: **unwise**, ill-advised, imprudent, ill-judged, ill-considered, injudicious, impolitic, inexpedient, foolish, incautious, misguided, misconceived, wrong-headed, silly, thoughtless, foolhardy.
▷ANTONYMS shrewd, wise.

inalienable adjective *the inalienable rights of every citizen*: **inviolable**, absolute, sacrosanct, unchallengeable, unassailable; **untransferable**, non-transferable, non-negotiable; inherent; Law imprescriptible, indefeasible.

inane adjective *an inane remark*: **silly**, foolish, stupid, fatuous, idiotic, absurd, ridiculous, ludicrous, laughable, risible, imbecilic, moronic, cretinous, unintelligent, witless, asinine, pointless, senseless, frivolous, nonsensical, brainless, mindless, thoughtless, vacuous, vapid, empty-headed; childish, puerile, infantile, jejune; informal daft, dumb, dim, half-baked, gormless, damfool; Brit. informal divvy; Scottish & N. English informal glaikit; N. Amer. informal dumb-ass; S. African informal dof.
▷ANTONYMS intelligent, sensible.

inanimate adjective *inanimate objects*: **lifeless**, insentient, insensate, without life, inert, motionless; inorganic, non-organic, mineral; dead, defunct, extinct; rare exanimate, abiotic.
▷ANTONYMS living.

inapplicable adjective *inapplicable moral criteria*: **irrelevant**, immaterial, not germane, not pertinent, unrelated, unconnected, extraneous, beside the point, nothing to do with it; inadmissible; inappropriate, inapposite, inapt; rare impertinent.
▷ANTONYMS relevant, applicable.

inapposite adjective *a singularly inapposite remark*: **inappropriate**, unsuitable, inapt, out of place, infelicitous, misplaced, misguided, ill-considered, ill-judged, ill-advised; irrelevant, immaterial, not germane, not pertinent, inapplicable; rare impertinent.
▷ANTONYMS appropriate.

inappreciable adjective *an inappreciable difference*: **imperceptible**, barely perceptible, minute, tiny, minuscule, slight, small, infinitesimal, microscopic, nanoscopic; **insignificant**, inconsequential, unimportant, immaterial, negligible, petty, trivial, trifling, minor, paltry, of no account, not worth mentioning, not worth bothering about; informal piddling, piffling; rare exiguous.
▷ANTONYMS considerable; significant.

inappropriate adjective *inappropriate behaviour | inappropriate clothes for the office*: **unsuitable**, unfitting, ill-suited, unseemly, unbecoming, unprofessional, unfit, unbefitting, indecorous, improper, lacking in propriety, ungentlemanly, unladylike; **incongruous**, out of place, out of keeping, wrong, amiss, inapposite, inapt; inexpedient, inadvisable, injudicious, ill-advised, ill-judged, ill-considered, infelicitous, unfortunate, regrettable, misguided, misplaced, ill-timed, untimely, inopportune, undue, untoward, tactless, tasteless, in poor/bad taste, undesirable; informal out of order; rare malapropos.
▷ANTONYMS appropriate, suitable.

inapt adjective *an inapt remark*. See **inappropriate**.

inarticulate adjective 1 *an inarticulate young man*: **tongue-tied**, lost for words, at a loss for words, unable to express oneself, unable to get a word out, poorly spoken; mute, dumb, speechless; rare mumchance.
▷ANTONYMS articulate, silver-tongued.
2 *an inarticulate reply*: **unintelligible**, incomprehensible, incoherent, unclear, indistinct, mumbled, muttered, muffled; hesitant, faltering, hesitating, halting, stumbling, stuttering, stammering; confused, garbled, muddled, rambling, disjointed, jumbled.
▷ANTONYMS articulate, fluent.
3 *I was filled with inarticulate rage*: **unspoken**, silent, unexpressed, wordless, unvoiced, unsaid, unuttered, unvocalized; voiceless, soundless.
▷ANTONYMS vocal.

inattention noun 1 *a moment of inattention which could have cost lives*: **lack of concentration**, distraction, inattentiveness, preoccupation, absent-mindedness, daydreaming, dreaminess, reverie, wool-gathering, abstraction, staring into space, obliviousness; brown study.
▷ANTONYMS attention, concentration.
2 *his inattention to duty*: **negligence**, neglect, neglectfulness, disregard, slackness, remissness, laxness; forgetfulness, carelessness, thoughtlessness, heedlessness; indifference, unconcern, inconsideration; rare oscitation.
▷ANTONYMS care.

inattentive adjective 1 *an inattentive pupil*: **not concentrating**, distracted, lacking concentration, preoccupied, absent-minded, daydreaming, dreamy, dreaming, wool-gathering, lost in thought, off in a world of one's own, in a brown study, with one's head in the clouds, abstracted, distrait, oblivious,

not with us, unheeding; informal miles away.
▷ANTONYMS attentive, alert.
2 *I was disappointed by the food and the inattentive service*: **negligent**, neglectful, remiss, slack, sloppy, slapdash, lackadaisical, lax; forgetful, careless, thoughtless, heedless, unthinking; indifferent, unconcerned, inconsiderate.
▷ANTONYMS attentive.

inaudible adjective *Michelle's response was inaudible*: **unheard**, not heard, out of earshot; hard to hear, hard to make out, indistinct, imperceptible, faint, muted, soft, low, muffled, stifled, whispered, muttered, murmured, mumbled.
▷ANTONYMS audible.

inaugural adjective *the inaugural meeting of the Geographical Society*: **first**, initial, introductory, initiatory, launching; **opening**, maiden; dedicatory.
▷ANTONYMS final; closing.

inaugurate verb 1 *he inaugurated a new policy of trade and exploration*: **initiate**, begin, start, institute, launch, start off, set in motion, get going, get under way, get off the ground, establish, originate, put in place, lay the foundations of, lay the first stone of, lay the cornerstone of, bring up the curtain on; bring in, usher in; informal kick off; formal commence.
▷ANTONYMS end, wind up.
2 *the new President will be inaugurated in January*: **admit to office**, install, instate, induct, swear in; invest, ordain; crown, enthrone.
3 *the museum was inaugurated on September 12*: **open**, open officially, declare open; dedicate, consecrate; unveil, take the wraps off; rare hansel.
▷ANTONYMS close.

inauguration noun 1 *the inauguration of an independent prosecution service*: **initiation**, institution, setting up, launch, establishment, foundation, founding, origination, formation; beginning, start, inception; formal commencement.
▷ANTONYMS demise, winding up.
2 *the President's inauguration*: **installation**, instatement, induction, swearing in; investiture; coronation, enthronement, crowning.
3 *the inauguration of the Modern Art Museum*: **opening**; dedication, consecration; unveiling.
▷ANTONYMS closure.

inauspicious adjective *an inauspicious start to the season*: **unpromising**, unpropitious, unfavourable, adverse, unfortunate, infelicitous, unhappy, ill-omened, ominous, ill-fated, ill-starred, untoward, untimely, inopportune, disadvantageous; discouraging, disheartening, gloomy, bleak, black, bad; Scottish unchancy.
▷ANTONYMS promising, auspicious.

inborn adjective *a child's inborn linguistic ability*: **innate**, congenital, existing from birth; inherent, inherited, hereditary, in the family, in one's genes, bred in the bone, inbred; natural, native, constitutional, deep-seated, deep-rooted, ingrained, in one's blood, inbuilt, instinctive, instinctual, unlearned; rare connate, connatural.
▷ANTONYMS acquired, learned.

inbred adjective *his inbred courtesy*. See **inborn**.

inbuilt adjective 1 *a personal computer with an inbuilt CD-ROM drive*: **built-in**, integral, incorporated.
▷ANTONYMS add-on.
2 *our inbuilt survival instinct*: **inherent**, intrinsic, innate, ingrained, congenital, natural, native; basic, fundamental, essential, deep-rooted; rare connatural, connate.

incalculable adjective *archaeological treasures of incalculable value*: **inestimable**, indeterminable, untold, immeasurable, uncountable, incomputable, not to be reckoned; infinite, endless, without end, limitless, measureless, boundless, fathomless, bottomless; enormous, immense, huge, vast, innumerable, countless, without number, numberless, multitudinous; rare innumerous, unnumberable, unnumbered, unsummed.
▷ANTONYMS limited.

incandescent adjective 1 *incandescent fragments of lava*: **white-hot**, intensely hot, red-hot, burning, fiery, on fire, blazing, ablaze, aflame; glowing, aglow, radiant, bright, brilliant, dazzling, shining, luminous, gleaming; literary fervid, fervent, ardent, rutilant, lucent, candescent.
2 *the minister was said to be incandescent*: **furious**, enraged, raging, very angry, incensed, seething, infuriated, fuming, boiling, inflamed, irate, wrathful, in a temper, beside oneself; in high dudgeon, indignant, outraged; informal livid, hot under the collar, up in arms, foaming at the mouth, mad, hopping mad, wild, as cross as two sticks, apoplectic, riled, aerated, on the warpath, steamed up, in a lather, in a paddy, fit to be tied, up the wall; N. Amer. informal bent out of shape, soreheaded; Austral./NZ informal ropeable, snaky, crook; W. Indian informal vex; Brit. informal, dated in a bate; literary ireful, wroth.
▷ANTONYMS calm.

incantation noun 1 *he muttered some weird incantations*: **chant**, invocation, conjuration, magic spell, magic formula, rune; abracadabra, open sesame; N. Amer. hex, mojo; NZ makutu.
2 *the ritual incantation of such words*: **chanting**, intonation, recitation.

incapable adjective 1 *a manager must train staff without making them feel stupid or incapable*: **incompetent**, inept, lacking ability, no good, inadequate, not good enough, leaving much to be desired, inexpert, unproficient, unskilful, ineffective, ineffectual, inefficacious, feeble, unfit, unfitted, unqualified, inferior; unequal to the task; informal not up to scratch, out of one's depth, not up to it, not up to snuff, useless, hopeless, pathetic, a dead loss, cack-handed, ham-fisted; Brit. informal not much cop; Brit. vulgar slang not knowing one's arse from one's elbow, half-arsed, not capable of organizing a piss-up in a brewery.
▷ANTONYMS capable, competent.
2 *he was judged to be mentally incapable*: **incapacitated**, helpless, powerless, impotent.
3 *she was* ***incapable of*** *fending for herself*: **unable to**, not capable of, lacking the ability to, not equipped to, lacking the experience to.
▷ANTONYMS capable of, able to.
4 *a problem which is* ***incapable of*** *solution*: **not open to**, not admitting of, not susceptible to, resistant to, impervious to.
▷ANTONYMS capable of, open to.

incapacitated adjective *Richard was temporarily incapacitated*: **disabled**, debilitated, indisposed, unfit; **immobilized**, paralysed, out of action, out of commission; French hors de combat; informal laid up.
▷ANTONYMS fit.

incapacity noun 1 *evidence of his mental incapacity*: **disability**, incapability, inability, debility, impairment, indisposition, unfitness; powerlessness, impotence, helplessness, weakness; incompetence, inadequacy, ineffectiveness, ineffectuality, inefficiency.
▷ANTONYMS ability, capability.
2 *legal incapacity*: **disqualification**, lack of entitlement, lack of legal right.
▷ANTONYMS qualification.

incarcerate verb 1 *he was incarcerated for expressing counter-revolutionary opinions*: **imprison**, put in prison, send to prison, jail, lock up, take into custody, put under lock and key, put away, intern, confine, detain, hold, put into detention, immure, put in chains, clap in irons, hold prisoner, hold captive; Brit. detain at Her Majesty's pleasure; informal send down, put behind bars, put inside; Brit. informal bang someone up.
▷ANTONYMS free, release.
2 *the long evening incarcerated below decks had given her a headache*: **confine**, shut away, shut up, coop up; immure, cage.

incarceration noun *throughout his years of incarceration, he was allowed out of his cell for one hour a day*: **imprisonment**, internment, confinement, detention, custody, captivity, restraint; penal servitude, hard labour; informal time; Brit. informal porridge, chokey; archaic durance, duress.
▷ANTONYMS freedom.

incarnate adjective *she looked at me as though I were the devil incarnate*: **in human form**, in the flesh, in physical form, in bodily form, made flesh, made manifest; corporeal, physical, fleshly, embodied.

incarnation noun 1 *Beethoven was seen as the incarnation of artistic genius*: **embodiment**, personification, exemplification, type, epitome; manifestation, bodily form, representation in the flesh; rare avatar.
2 *they believed they had been together in a previous incarnation*: **lifetime**, life, existence.

incautious adjective *his anger made him incautious*: **rash**, unwise, careless, heedless, thoughtless, reckless, unthinking, imprudent, misguided, ill-advised, ill-judged, injudicious, impolitic, unguarded, foolhardy, foolish; unwary, unwatchful, off-guard, inattentive, unobservant; informal asleep on the job, asleep at the wheel, leading with one's chin.
▷ANTONYMS cautious, circumspect.

incendiary adjective 1 *an incendiary bomb*: **combustible**, flammable, inflammable, fire-producing, fire-raising.
2 *her incendiary speech provoked more rioting*: **inflammatory**, rabble-rousing, provocative, seditious, subversive, revolutionary, insurrectionary, insurrectionist; arousing, stirring; contentious, controversial.
▷ANTONYMS conciliatory.
▶ noun 1 *an aircraft loaded with incendiaries*: **explosive**, bomb, incendiary device.
2 *incendiaries set the village on fire*: **arsonist**, fire-bomber, fire-setter; pyromaniac; Brit. fire-raiser; informal firebug, pyro; N. Amer. informal torch.
3 *a political incendiary*: **agitator**, demagogue, rabble-rouser, firebrand, troublemaker, revolutionary, revolutionist, insurgent, subversive, instigator, inciter, soapbox orator; French agent provocateur; informal tub-thumper, stirrer.

incense[1] verb (stress on the second syllable) *the glint of amusement in his eyes incensed her*: **enrage**, infuriate, anger, madden, send into a rage, outrage, inflame, exasperate, antagonize, provoke, irritate greatly, rile, gall; informal make someone see red, make someone's blood boil, make someone's hackles rise, get someone's back up, hack off, dri ve mad/crazy, drive up the wall, get someone's dander up, get someone's goat, get up someone's nose, rattle someone's cage; Brit. informal wind up, get on someone's wick, nark; N. Amer. informal burn up, tick off, gravel; vulgar slang piss off; Brit. vulgar slang get on someone's tits; rare empurple.
▷ANTONYMS placate; please.

incense² noun (stress on the first syllable) *Corbett caught a whiff of incense*: **perfume**, fragrance, scent; aroma, bouquet, redolence, balm.

incensed adjective *Leonora glared back at him, incensed*: **enraged**, very angry, irate, furious, infuriated, angered, in a temper, raging, incandescent, fuming, seething, beside oneself, outraged, in high dudgeon; informal mad, hopping mad, wild, livid, as cross as two sticks, boiling, apoplectic, aerated, hot under the collar, on the warpath, up in arms, with all guns blazing, foaming at the mouth, steamed up, in a lather, in a paddy, in a filthy temper, fit to be tied; Brit. informal shirty, stroppy; N. Amer. informal sore, bent out of shape, soreheaded, ticked off; Austral./NZ informal ropeable, snaky, crook; W. Indian informal vex; Brit. informal, dated in a bate, waxy; vulgar slang pissed off; N. Amer. vulgar slang pissed; literary wrathful, ireful, wroth.
▷ANTONYMS calm.

incentive noun *tax laws which give factories a financial incentive to reduce pollution*: **inducement**, motivation, motive, reason, stimulus, stimulant, spur, impetus, encouragement, impulse; incitement, goad, provocation; attraction, lure, bait; informal carrot, sweetener, come-on; rare premium, douceur.
▷ANTONYMS deterrent, disincentive.

inception noun *the inception of the EEC in 1958*: **establishment**, institution, foundation, founding, formation, initiation, setting up, origination, constitution, inauguration, opening; **beginning**, start, starting point, outset; birth, dawn, genesis, origin, rise; debut, day one; informal kick-off; formal commencement.
▷ANTONYMS end.

incessant adjective *incessant rain fell for several days*: **ceaseless**, unceasing, constant, continual, unabating, interminable, endless, unending, never-ending, everlasting, eternal, perpetual, continuous, non-stop, uninterrupted, unbroken, ongoing, unremitting, persistent, relentless, unrelenting, unrelieved, sustained, unflagging, unwearying, untiring; recurrent.
▷ANTONYMS intermittent, occasional.

incessantly adverb *she talked about him incessantly*: **constantly**, continually, all the time, non-stop, without stopping, without a break, interminably, unremittingly, round the clock, ceaselessly, endlessly, without cessation, unceasingly, perpetually; informal 24-7.
▷ANTONYMS occasionally.

incidence noun *an increased incidence of heart disease in women in their thirties*: **occurrence**, prevalence, commonness; **rate**, frequency; amount, degree, quantity, extent.

incident noun **1** *his memories of incidents from his youth*: **event**, occurrence, occasion, episode, experience, happening, proceeding, eventuality, affair, business; adventure, exploit, escapade, deed, feat; matter, circumstance, fact, development.
2 *police are now investigating the incident*: **disturbance**, fracas, melee, commotion, rumpus, scene; fight, skirmish, clash, brawl, free-for-all, encounter, conflict, confrontation, altercation, contretemps; Irish, N. Amer., & Austral. donnybrook; W. Indian bangarang; informal ruction, ruckus, argy-bargy; Law, dated affray.
3 *the journey was not without incident*: **excitement**, adventure, exciting experiences, drama; danger, peril, dangerous/perilous experiences.

incidental adjective **1** *incidental details*: **less important**, of less importance, secondary, subsidiary, subordinate, ancillary, auxiliary; **minor**, peripheral, background, by-the-way, by-the-by, non-essential, inessential, unimportant, insignificant, inconsequential, unnecessary, trivial, trifling, negligible, petty, tangential, extrinsic, extraneous, dispensable, expendable.
▷ANTONYMS crucial; essential.
2 *the implications of this incidental discovery*: **chance**, by chance, accidental, by accident, random, casual, fortuitous, serendipitous, adventitious, coincidental, unlooked-for; rare fluky; rare aleatory.
▷ANTONYMS deliberate.
3 *the risks necessarily* ***incidental to*** *a fireman's job*: **connected with**, related to, associated with, accompanying, attending, attendant on, concomitant to.
▸ noun (**incidentals**) *an allowance to cover meals, taxis, and other incidentals*: **extras**, contingencies, odds and ends; expenses.

incidentally adverb **1** *incidentally, I haven't had a reply from Hartley yet*: **by the way**, by the by(e), in passing, en passant, speaking of which, while on the subject; parenthetically; informal BTW, as it happens.
2 *the infection was discovered incidentally at post-mortem examination*: **by chance**, by accident, accidentally, fortuitously, by a fluke, as luck would have it, by a twist of fate; coincidentally, by coincidence; N. Amer. by happenstance.

incinerate verb *household waste should be incinerated to generate electricity*: **burn**, burn up, reduce to ashes, consume by fire, carbonize; cremate.

incipient adjective *a system to detect incipient problems early*: **developing**, impending, growing, emerging, emergent, dawning; just beginning, starting, inceptive, initial; nascent, embryonic, fledgling, in its infancy, germinal; rudimentary, inchoate; rare embryonal.
▷ANTONYMS full-blown.

incise verb **1** *the abdomen of each rat was incised*: **cut**, cut into, make an incision in, slit, slit open, lance; gash, slash.
2 *an inscription incised in Roman letters*: **engrave**, etch, carve, cut, chisel, inscribe, score, chase, notch; archaic scotch.

incision noun **1** *a surgical incision*: **cut**, opening, slit.
2 *the incisions were made on the underside of the jar*: **notch**, nick, snick, scratch, scarification; gash, slash; archaic scotch.

incisive adjective *an incisive political commentator*: **penetrating**, acute, sharp, sharp-witted, razor-sharp, keen, rapier-like, astute, shrewd, trenchant, piercing, perceptive, insightful, percipient, perspicacious, discerning, analytical, intelligent, canny, clever, smart, quick; concise, succinct, pithy, to the point, crisp, clear; informal punchy, on the ball; N. Amer. informal heads-up; rare argute, sapient.
▷ANTONYMS rambling, vague.

incite verb **1** *Rico was arrested for inciting racial hatred*: **stir up**, whip up, work up, encourage, fan the flames of, stoke up, fuel, kindle, ignite, inflame, stimulate, instigate, provoke, excite, arouse, awaken, waken, inspire, trigger, spark off, ferment, foment, agitate for/against; cause, generate, bring about; literary enkindle.
▷ANTONYMS suppress.
2 *she had incited him to commit murder*: **egg on**, encourage, urge, goad, provoke, spur on, drive on, stimulate, push, prod, prompt, induce, impel, motivate, make, influence; arouse, rouse, excite, inflame, stir up, sting, prick; informal put up to; N. Amer. informal root on; Law procure.
▷ANTONYMS dissuade, deter.

incitement noun *this amounted to an incitement to commit murder*: **egging on**, urging, goading, spurring on, motivation, persuasion, inducement; **instigation**, encouragement, stirring up, whipping up, stoking up, kindling, fuelling, stimulation, provocation, arousing, rousing, **fomentation**; literary enkindling.
▷ANTONYMS suppression, discouragement.

incivility noun *lateness, absenteeism, and incivility on the part of staff will not be tolerated*: **rudeness**, discourtesy, discourteousness, impoliteness, lack of politeness; **bad manners**, ill-manneredness, lack of manners, unmannerliness, disrespect, disrespectfulness, boorishness, uncouthness, lack of refinement, ungraciousness, lack of social grace, ungentlemanly behaviour, unladylike behaviour; insolence, impertinence, impudence.
▷ANTONYMS politeness, good manners.

inclement adjective *the work was delayed by the inclement weather*: **cold**, chilly, bitter, bleak, raw, wintry, freezing, snowy, icy; **wet**, rainy, drizzly, damp; stormy, blustery, wild, rough, squally, tempestuous, windy; unpleasant, bad, foul, nasty, filthy, severe, extreme, harsh, adverse.
▷ANTONYMS fine, mild, sunny.

inclination noun **1** *his political inclinations often got him into trouble | she showed no inclination to leave*: **tendency**, propensity, proclivity, leaning; predisposition, disposition, predilection, weakness, proneness; desire, wish, readiness, impulse; bent; archaic list, humour; rare velleity.
▷ANTONYMS aversion, disinclination.
2 *she had no inclination for housework*: **liking**, penchant, partiality, preference, appetite, fancy, fondness, affection, love; interest, affinity; stomach, taste; informal yen; rare appetency.
▷ANTONYMS dislike.
3 *an inclination of his head*: **bowing**, bow, bending, nod, nodding, lowering, dip.
4 *an inclination in excess of 90 degrees*: **gradient**, incline, slope, pitch, ramp, bank, ascent, rise; acclivity, descent, declivity; slant, lift, tilt; cant, camber, bevel; angle.

incline verb (stress on the second syllable) **1** *his prejudice inclines him to overlook obvious facts*: **predispose**, lead, make, make of a mind to, dispose, bias, prejudice; prompt, induce, influence, sway; persuade, convince.
2 *I* ***incline to*** *the opposite view*: **prefer**, have a preference for, favour, be favourably disposed to, go for, have a penchant for, have a liking for; tend, lean, swing, veer, gravitate, be drawn, be attracted; N. Amer. trend.
3 *he inclined his head*: **bend**, bow, nod, bob, lower, dip.
▷ANTONYMS raise, lift.
4 *the columns incline several degrees away from the vertical*: **lean**, tilt, angle, tip, slope, slant, bend, curve, bank, cant, bevel; list, heel; deviate.
▸ noun (stress on the first syllable) *a steep incline*: **slope**, gradient, pitch, ramp, bank, ascent, rise, acclivity, upslope, dip, descent, declivity, downslope; hill; N. Amer. grade, downgrade, upgrade.

inclined adjective **1** *I'm inclined to believe her*: **disposed**, minded, of a mind, willing, ready, prepared; predisposed.
▷ANTONYMS disinclined.
2 *she's inclined to gossip with complete strangers*: **liable**, likely, prone, disposed, given, apt, wont, with a tendency; in the habit of.
▷ANTONYMS unlikely.

include verb **1** *extra-curricular activities include sports, drama, music, and chess*: **incorporate**, comprise, encompass, cover, embrace, involve, take in, number, contain; consist of, be made up of, be composed of; formal comprehend.

▷ANTONYMS exclude, omit.
2 *don't forget to include the cost of tyres and bodywork repairs*: **allow for**, count, take into account, take into consideration.
▷ANTONYMS exclude, leave out.
3 *include your name, address, and telephone number*: **add**, insert, put in, append, enter, build in.
▷ANTONYMS leave out.

including preposition *a wide range of sports facilities, including squash, tennis, and badminton*: **which include(s)**, inclusive of, counting; as well as, plus, together with.
▷ANTONYMS excluding.

inclusion noun *material suitable for inclusion in the programme*: **incorporation**, addition, insertion, introduction; involvement, taking in, encompassing.
▷ANTONYMS exclusion, omission.

inclusive adjective 1 *the company quoted an inclusive price | an inclusive definition*: **all-in**, all-inclusive, with everything included, comprehensive, in toto; overall, full, all-round, across the board, umbrella, blanket, catch-all, all-encompassing, all-embracing, without exception.
▷ANTONYMS exclusive.
2 *prices are **inclusive of** VAT*: **including**, incorporating, taking in, counting, taking account of; comprising, covering, embracing.
▷ANTONYMS excluding.

incognito adjective & adverb *he travelled incognito*: **under an assumed name**, under a false name, with one's identity concealed, in disguise, disguised, under cover, in plain clothes, camouflaged; unrecognized, unidentified; secretly, covertly, anonymously; informal incog.

incognizant adjective rare *she was incognizant of his presence*. See **unaware**.

incoherent adjective 1 *a long and incoherent speech*: **unclear**, confused, muddled, unintelligible, incomprehensible, hard to follow, disjointed, disconnected, unconnected, disordered, mixed up, garbled, jumbled, scrambled; rambling, wandering, discursive, disorganized, uncoordinated, illogical; inarticulate, mumbled, muttered, stuttered, stammered, slurred; rare inchoate.
▷ANTONYMS coherent, lucid, intelligible.
2 *Melanie was incoherent and shivering violently*: **delirious**, raving, babbling, hysterical, irrational.
▷ANTONYMS lucid.

incombustible adjective **non-flammable**, non-combustible, not inflammable, unburnable; fireproof, fire resistant, fire retardant; flameproof, flame resistant, flame retardant; heatproof, ovenproof; informal non-flam; rare asbestine.
▷ANTONYMS flammable, inflammable.

income noun *each spouse is responsible for paying tax on their own income*: **earnings**, salary, pay, remuneration, wages, stipend, emolument; **revenue**, receipts, takings, profits, gains, proceeds, turnover, yield, dividend, incomings, money received; means; N. Amer. take.
▷ANTONYMS expenditure, outgoings.

incoming adjective 1 *the incoming train*: **arriving**, entering; **approaching**, coming, coming in.
▷ANTONYMS outgoing.
2 *the incoming president*: **succeeding**, new, next, future, soon to take office; elect, to-be, designate, elected.
▷ANTONYMS outgoing.
▶ noun (**incomings**) *keep an account of your incomings and outgoings*. See **income**.

incommensurate adjective *the penalty is **incommensurate with** his crime*: **out of proportion to**, not in proportion to, disproportionate to, relatively too large/small for, not appropriate for; out of keeping with, at odds with; insufficient, inadequate; excessive, inordinate, unreasonable, uncalled for, undue, unfair.
▷ANTONYMS proportional.

incommunicable adjective *his incommunicable grief*: **indescribable**, inexpressible, unutterable, unspeakable, undefinable, ineffable, beyond words, beyond description; overwhelming, intense, profound.

incomparable adjective *the incomparable beauty of Venice*: **without equal**, beyond compare, unparalleled, matchless, peerless, without peer, unmatched, without match, without parallel, beyond comparison, second to none, in a class of its own, unequalled, unrivalled, inimitable, nonpareil; transcendent, superlative, surpassing, unsurpassed, unsurpassable, supreme, top, outstanding, consummate, unique, singular, rare, perfect; French par excellence, hors concours; informal one-in-a-million; rare unexampled.
▷ANTONYMS ordinary, commonplace.

incomparably adverb *this beach is incomparably superior to the others on the island*: **far and away**, by far, infinitely, immeasurably, beyond compare, beyond comparison, easily; inimitably, unbeatably, supremely, superlatively, transcendently, uniquely.
▷ANTONYMS slightly.

incompatible adjective 1 *she and McBride are totally incompatible*: **unsuited**, mismatched, ill-matched, poles apart, worlds apart, like day and night; ill-assorted; Brit. like chalk and cheese.
▷ANTONYMS well matched, suited.
2 *incompatible economic objectives*: **irreconcilable**, conflicting, opposed, opposite, contradictory, antagonistic, antipathetic; clashing, inharmonious, discordant; mutually exclusive.
▷ANTONYMS compatible; complementary.
3 *his theory was **incompatible with** that of his predecessor*: **inconsistent with**, at odds with, out of keeping with, different to, differing from, divergent from, at variance with, incongruous with, inconsonant with, contrary to, in conflict with, in opposition to, diametrically opposed to, counter to, not in accord with, irreconcilable with, not able to be reconciled with, alien to; rare repugnant to, oppugnant to.
▷ANTONYMS consistent.

incompetence noun *allegations of professional incompetence*: **ineptitude**, ineptness, inability, lack of ability, incapability, incapacity, lack of skill, lack of proficiency, amateurishness, inexpertness, clumsiness, ineffectiveness, inadequacy, deficiency, inefficiency, ineffectuality, ineffectualness, insufficiency; informal cack-handedness, ham-fistedness, uselessness, hopelessness.
▷ANTONYMS competence, prowess.

incompetent adjective *he lost his job due to his incompetent performance*: **inept**, unskilful, unskilled, inexpert, amateurish, unprofessional, lacking ability, bungling, blundering, clumsy, unproficient, inadequate, substandard, inferior, ineffective, deficient, inefficient, ineffectual, no good, not good enough, wanting, lacking, leaving much to be desired; incapable, unfitted, unfit, unsuitable, unqualified; informal useless, pathetic, cack-handed, ham-fisted, not up to it, a dead loss, not up to scratch, not up to snuff; Brit. informal unable to do something for toffee, unable to do something to save one's life, not much cop; vulgar slang half-arsed, not knowing one's arse from one's elbow, not capable of organizing a piss-up in a brewery.
▷ANTONYMS competent, skilful.

incomplete adjective 1 *the monument was still incomplete ten years after his death*: **unfinished**, uncompleted, not finished, not completed, half-finished, half-done, half-completed, partially finished, partially complete, partial, not concluded; unaccomplished, undone, unexecuted, unperformed.
▷ANTONYMS complete, finished.
2 *inaccurate or incomplete information*: **deficient**, insufficient, imperfect, defective, partial, patchy, sketchy, fragmentary, fragmented, scrappy, bitty; lacking, wanting, not entire, not whole, not total, abridged, shortened; qualified, restricted.
▷ANTONYMS full.

Word toolkit

incomplete	cursory	vague
information	glance	notion
picture	examination	memory
knowledge	reading	promises
work	inspection	reference
sentence	investigation	answers

incomprehensible adjective 1 *April muttered something incomprehensible*: **unintelligible**, indecipherable; incoherent, inarticulate.
▷ANTONYMS intelligible, comprehensible.
2 *legalistic and largely incomprehensible documents*: **unintelligible**, impossible to understand, impenetrable, unclear, too difficult/hard to understand, beyond comprehension, beyond one, beyond one's grasp, unfathomable, unaccountable, inexplicable, inscrutable, baffling, bewildering, mystifying, puzzling, confusing, perplexing, abstruse, obscure, opaque, esoteric, recondite, arcane, mysterious, Delphic; complicated, complex, involved, intricate; informal over one's head, all Greek to someone; Brit. informal double Dutch; archaic wildering.
▷ANTONYMS intelligible, understandable, clear.

inconceivable adjective *it seemed inconceivable that the president had been unaware of what was going on*: **beyond belief**, unbelievable, extremely difficult to believe, scarcely credible, incredible, unthinkable, unimaginable, extremely unlikely, not in the least likely, extremely implausible, extremely doubtful; impossible, beyond the bounds of possibility, out of the question, preposterous, ridiculous, ludicrous, absurd, incomprehensible; informal hard to swallow, mind-boggling.
▷ANTONYMS likely.

inconclusive adjective *their findings were inconclusive*: **indecisive**, proving nothing, resolving nothing, leaving matters open; indefinite, indeterminate, undetermined, unresolved, unproved, unsettled, still open to question, still open to doubt, debatable, unconfirmed, not yet established; moot; vague, ambiguous; informal up in the air, left hanging.
▷ANTONYMS conclusive, open-and-shut.

i

incongruity noun *the incongruity of his fleshy face and skinny body disturbed her*: **inappropriateness**, incongruousness, unsuitability, lack of harmony, discordance, inharmoniousness, dissonance, incompatibility, inconsistency, difference, disparity, discrepancy, irreconcilability; strangeness, oddity, absurdity, bizarreness, extraneousness; rare disconsonance.
▷ANTONYMS appropriateness.

incongruous adjective **1** *the women looked incongruous in their smart hats and fur coats*: **out of place**, out of keeping, inappropriate, unsuitable, unsuited, not in harmony; discordant, dissonant, conflicting, clashing, jarring, wrong, at odds, in opposition, contrary, contradictory, irreconcilable; strange, odd, absurd, bizarre, off-key, extraneous; informal like a fish out of water, sticking/standing out a mile; rare disconsonant.
▷ANTONYMS appropriate.
2 *an incongruous collection of objects*: **ill-matched**, ill-assorted, mismatched, unharmonious, inconsistent, incompatible, different, dissimilar, contrasting, disparate, discrepant.
▷ANTONYMS harmonious.

inconsequential adjective *inconsequential scraps of information*: **insignificant**, unimportant, of little/no importance, of little/no consequence, of little/no account, of no moment, neither here nor there, incidental, inessential, non-essential, immaterial, irrelevant; negligible, inappreciable, inconsiderable, slight, minor, trivial, trifling, petty, paltry, nugatory, not worth mentioning, not worth bothering about, not worth speaking of, insubstantial, silly, lightweight; informal piddling, fiddling, piffling; N. Amer. informal small-bore, picayune.
▷ANTONYMS significant, important.

Word toolkit

inconsequential	petty	paltry
matter	crime	sum
details	jealousy	salary
piece	rules	attendance
role	insult	meal
event	complaint	gain

inconsiderable adjective *a not inconsiderable amount of money*: **insignificant**, negligible, trifling, small, tiny, little, minuscule, nominal, token, petty, slight, niggling, minor, inappreciable, insubstantial, not worth mentioning, not worth bothering about, inconsequential; paltry, derisory, pitiful, niggardly, beggarly; informal piffling, piddling, fiddling, pathetic, measly, mingy; Brit. informal poxy; N. Amer. informal nickel-and-dime, small-bore; rare exiguous.
▷ANTONYMS considerable, large.

inconsiderate adjective *his inconsiderate behaviour hurt her dreadfully*: **thoughtless**, unthinking, insensitive, selfish, self-centred, self-seeking, unsympathetic, uncaring, unthoughtful, unconcerned, heedless, unmindful, unkind, uncharitable, ungracious, impolite, discourteous, rude, disrespectful; tactless, undiplomatic, indiscreet, indelicate; callous, heartless, unfair; informal ignorant.
▷ANTONYMS considerate, thoughtful.

inconsistency noun **1** *he earned a reputation for political inconsistency*: **unpredictability**, inconstancy, lack of consistency, changeableness, variability, instability, irregularity, unevenness, unsteadiness; self-contradiction, self-contradictoriness, contradiction, contrariety; capriciousness, fickleness, unreliability, undependability, flightiness, volatility; rare erraticism.
▷ANTONYMS consistency.
2 *the inconsistency between his expressed attitudes and his actual behaviour*: **incompatibility**, conflict, difference, dissimilarity, lack of similarity, disagreement, lack of accord, opposition, clash, irreconcilability, lack of congruence, incongruity, lack of harmony, mismatch, discordance, disparity, discrepancy; rare disconsonance, inconsonance, repugnancy, oppugnancy.
▷ANTONYMS consistency, harmony.

inconsistent adjective **1** *his behaviour was inconsistent and irrational*: **erratic**, changeable, unpredictable, variable, varying, changing, inconstant, unstable, irregular, fluctuating, unsteady, unsettled, uneven; self-contradictory, contradictory, paradoxical; capricious, fickle, flighty, whimsical, unreliable, undependable, mercurial, volatile, ever-changing, protean, chameleon-like, chameleonic; informal blowing hot and cold, up and down; technical labile; rare changeful, fluctuant.
▷ANTONYMS consistent, predictable.
2 *this finding is **inconsistent with** the conclusions of previous surveys*: **incompatible with**, conflicting with, in conflict with, at odds with, at variance with, differing from, different to, in disagreement with, disagreeing with, not in accord with, contrary to, in opposition to, opposed to, irreconcilable with, not in keeping with, out of keeping with, out of place with, out of step with, not in harmony with, incongruous with, discordant with, discrepant with; antithetical to, diametrically opposed to; rare disconsonant with, inconsonant with, repugnant to, oppugnant to.
▷ANTONYMS consistent.

inconsolable adjective *normally stoic in the face of adversity, Tom was inconsolable*: **heartbroken**, broken-hearted, unable to be comforted, unable to be consoled, grief-stricken, prostrate with grief, beside oneself with grief, devastated, wretched, sick at heart, desolate, despairing, distraught, comfortless; miserable, unhappy, sad; literary heartsick, dolorous.

inconspicuous adjective *Isabel tried to remain as inconspicuous as possible | an inconspicuous building*: **unobtrusive**, unnoticeable, unremarkable, unspectacular, unostentatious, unimposing, undistinguished, unexceptional, modest, unassuming, discreet, hidden, concealed; ordinary, plain, run-of-the-mill, insignificant, characterless, forgettable, unmemorable; in the background, unnoticed, unseen, behind the scenes, out of the public eye, out of the spotlight, backstage, out of the limelight, low-profile, low-key; quiet, retiring.
▷ANTONYMS conspicuous, noticeable; high-profile.

inconstant adjective **1** *the exact dimensions are not easily measured since they are inconstant*: **variable**, varying, changeable, changing, irregular, shifting, fluctuating, inconsistent, not constant, unsettled, unfixed, mutable, unstable, unsteady; technical labile; rare changeful, fluctuant, variational.
▷ANTONYMS constant, consistent.
2 *an inconstant lover*: **fickle**, faithless, unfaithful, false, false-hearted, wayward, undependable, unreliable, untrustworthy, changeable, capricious, volatile, mercurial, flighty, chameleon-like, unpredictable, erratic, unstable; informal blowing hot and cold, cheating, two-timing.
▷ANTONYMS faithful, dependable.

Choose the right word **inconstant, changeable, capricious, fickle**

These words all indicate that someone or something is liable to change and cannot be relied upon.

Inconstant is a rather literary word suggesting that changes are not only sudden and frequent but also inexplicable. It is applied particularly to someone who is not faithful in love (*a widely held belief that women were by nature inconstant*).

Changeable is a more common word for people and things liable to frequent variation (*she experienced changeable moods and panic attacks | conflicting and changeable political objectives*) and is often used of the weather (*outlook for tomorrow: changeable with rain at times*).

Capricious emphasizes the fact that someone's changes of mind and behaviour spring from irrational and unpredictable whims, making them totally unreliable (*it was hopeless to try and argue with her capricious husband*). A *capricious* person is irresponsible and inconsiderate, possibly to the point of cruelty (*a capricious and often brutal administration*).

Fickle, deriving from an Old English word meaning 'deceitful', is a disapproving description of someone who changes their views or allegiances very rapidly or readily (*the fickle Viennese public had once flocked to hear Mozart*). A *fickle lover* is shallow and transfers their affections repeatedly from one person to another (*men are so fickle, always on the lookout for someone new*).

incontestable adjective *finally, we had incontestable proof of their guilt*: **incontrovertible**, indisputable, undeniable, irrefutable, unassailable, beyond dispute, unquestionable, beyond question, indubitable, not in doubt, beyond doubt, beyond a shadow of a doubt; compelling, convincing, clinching, airtight, watertight, unarguable, undebatable, unanswerable, emphatic, categorical; unequivocal, unambiguous, unmistakable, clear, clear-cut, certain, sure, definite, definitive, proven, demonstrable, self-evident, positive, decisive, conclusive, final, ultimate; rare inarguable, irrefragable, apodictic.
▷ANTONYMS questionable.

incontinent adjective *their incontinent hysteria*: **unrestrained**, uncontrolled, lacking self-restraint, unbridled, unchecked, ungoverned, uncurbed, unsuppressed, unfettered, untrammelled; uncontrollable, ungovernable.
▷ANTONYMS restrained.

incontrovertible adjective *their judgement is based on the evidence of incontrovertible facts*: **indisputable**, incontestable, undeniable, irrefutable, unassailable, beyond dispute, unquestionable, beyond question, indubitable, not in doubt, beyond doubt, beyond a shadow of a doubt, unarguable, inarguable, undebatable, unanswerable; unequivocal, unambiguous, unmistakable, certain, sure, definite, definitive, proven, positive, decisive, conclusive, final, ultimate; clear, clear-cut, straightforward, plain, as plain as a pikestaff, transparent, obvious, manifest, evident, self-evident, staring one in the face, patent, demonstrative, demonstrable, observable, palpable; uncontroversial, accepted, acknowledged; marked, pronounced, express, emphatic, categorical, compelling, convincing, clinching, airtight, watertight; rare irrefragable, apodictic.
▷ANTONYMS questionable.

inconvenience noun **1** *we apologize for any inconvenience caused*: **trouble**, bother, problems, disruption, nuisance value, disadvantage,

difficulty, embarrassment, disturbance, vexation, harassment, worry, anxiety, distress, concern, disquiet, unease, irritation, annoyance, stress, agitation, unpleasantness; informal aggravation, hassle.
▷ANTONYMS help.
2 *his early arrival was clearly an inconvenience to his hosts*: **nuisance**, trouble, bother, source of disruption/vexation/irritation/annoyance, vexation, worry, trial, tribulation, bind, pest, bore, plague, irritant, thorn in someone's flesh, cross to bear, the bane of someone's life, burden, hindrance, problem; informal headache, pain, pain in the neck, pain in the backside, drag, aggravation, hassle; N. Amer. informal pain in the butt, burr under/in someone's saddle; Austral./NZ informal nark; Brit. informal, dated blister; vulgar slang pain in the arse.
▷ANTONYMS convenience.
▸ **verb** *the general public was not greatly inconvenienced by the demonstration*: **trouble**, bother, put out, put someone to trouble, be a problem to, disrupt, be a nuisance to, disadvantage, cause someone difficulty, impose on, burden, harass, plague, beset, embarrass, disturb; vex, worry, annoy, upset, irritate; informal hassle; Austral./NZ informal heavy; rare discommode.
▷ANTONYMS help.

inconvenient adjective *visitors often park their cars in inconvenient places*: **awkward**, difficult, unsuitable, inappropriate, troublesome, bothersome, problematic, disruptive; inopportune, untimely, ill-timed, unfavourable, inexpedient, unfortunate, disadvantageous; tiresome, irritating, vexing, annoying, worrisome, distressing, embarrassing; informal aggravating; archaic unseasonable.
▷ANTONYMS convenient.

incorporate verb **1** *part of Ukraine was incorporated into Moldavian territory*: **absorb**, include, subsume, assimilate, integrate, take in, swallow up, engulf, consolidate.
▷ANTONYMS separate.
2 *the most expensive model incorporates some advanced features*: **embody**, include, comprise, contain, embrace, build in, encompass.
3 *a small amount of salt is uniformly incorporated with the butter*: **blend**, mix, mingle, combine, put together, merge, fuse, unite, unify, join, bring together, amalgamate, integrate; fold in, stir, whisk; meld, marry, mesh, compound, alloy, coalesce, homogenize, emulsify, intermingle, intermix; informal blunge; rare commingle, commix.

incorporeal adjective *millions believe in a supreme but incorporeal being*: **intangible**, impalpable, non-material, non-physical; bodiless, unembodied, disembodied; ethereal, unsubstantial, insubstantial, airy, aerial; spiritual, ghostly, spectral, phantom, wraithlike, transcendental, unearthly, supernatural; unreal, imaginary, illusory, chimerical, hallucinatory; rare immaterial, discarnate, disincarnate, unbodied, phantasmal, phantasmic.
▷ANTONYMS tangible.

incorrect adjective **1** *an incorrect answer*: **wrong**, **mistaken**, in error, erroneous, inaccurate, not accurate, inexact, not exact, imprecise, invalid, untrue, false, fallacious, wide of the mark, off target; misleading, illogical, unsound, unfounded, without foundation, faulty, flawed; informal off beam, out, way out, full of holes, iffy; archaic abroad.
▷ANTONYMS correct.
2 *most food contamination is caused by incorrect storage at home | incorrect behaviour*: **inappropriate**, wrong, unsuitable, inapt, inapposite, undesirable; **ill-advised**, ill-considered, ill-judged, impolitic, injudicious, infelicitous, unacceptable, beyond the pale, unwarranted, unfitting, out of keeping, improper, unseemly, unbecoming, indecorous, lacking in propriety; informal out of order.

incorrigible adjective *she's an incorrigible flirt*: **inveterate**, habitual, confirmed, hardened; incurable, unreformable, irreformable, irredeemable, intractable, hopeless, beyond hope/redemption; chronic, diehard, deep-dyed, dyed-in-the-wool, long-standing, addicted, hard-core; impenitent, uncontrite, unrepentant, unapologetic, unashamed; informal impossible.
▷ANTONYMS occasional; repentant.

Word toolkit

incorrigible	hardened	habitual
optimist	criminal	offender
flirt	cynic	drunkenness
womanizer	soldier	smoker
spendthrift	warrior	liar
gossip	terrorist	snoring

incorruptibility noun *he claimed that his Ministers enjoyed an untarnished reputation for incorruptibility*: **honesty**, honour, trustworthiness, scrupulousness, conscientiousness, correctness, rectitude, probity, integrity, uprightness, high-mindedness, righteousness, right-mindedness, virtue, nobility, respectability, decency.
▷ANTONYMS venality.

incorruptible adjective **1** *a conscientious and incorruptible detective*: **unbribable**, honest, trustworthy, scrupulous, conscientious, principled, high-principled, proper, correct, honourable, upright, straight, upstanding, high-minded, righteous, right-minded, moral, ethical, good, virtuous, just, noble, respectable, decent.
▷ANTONYMS venal.
2 *as it was incorruptible, gold was considered special*: **imperishable**, indestructible, non-biodegradable, not decaying, non-corroding, indissoluble, durable, made to last, enduring, everlasting, eternal; rare perdurable.
▷ANTONYMS perishable.

increase verb (stress on the second syllable) **1** *gas demand is likely to increase*: **grow**, get bigger, get larger, become greater, enlarge, expand, swell; rise, climb, escalate, soar, surge, rocket, shoot up, spiral; improve, intensify, strengthen; heighten, lengthen, extend, stretch, spread, widen; multiply, snowball, mushroom, proliferate, balloon, build up, mount up, pile up, accrue, accumulate; literary wax.
▷ANTONYMS decrease.
2 *higher expectations will increase user demand*: **add to**, make larger, make bigger, make greater, augment, supplement, top up, build up, enlarge, expand, extend, raise, multiply, elevate, swell, inflate; magnify, intensify, strengthen, amplify, heighten, escalate; improve, make better, boost, ameliorate, enhance, enrich, upgrade; worsen, make worse, exacerbate, aggravate, inflame, compound, reinforce; informal up, jack up, hike up, hike, bump up, crank up, step up.
▷ANTONYMS reduce.
▸ **noun** (stress on the first syllable) *the increase in size | an increase in demand*: **growth**, rise, enlargement, expansion, extension, multiplication, elevation, swelling, inflation; increment, addition, augmentation; magnification, intensification, strengthening, amplification, stepping up, step up, heightening; climb, escalation, surge, upsurge, upswing, spiral; improvement, boost, amelioration, enhancement, upgrade, upturn; worsening, exacerbation, aggravation; development, advance, boom, spurt, snowballing, mushrooming; informal hike.
▷ANTONYMS decrease, reduction.

increasingly adverb *the regime became increasingly draconian*: **more and more**, progressively, to an increasing extent, steadily more, continuously more, gradually more; rare growingly.
▷ANTONYMS less and less.

incredible adjective **1** *to be honest, I find his story incredible*: **unbelievable**, beyond belief, hard to believe, scarcely credible, unconvincing, far-fetched, strained, laboured, implausible, improbable, highly unlikely, not in the least likely, questionable, dubious, doubtful, inconceivable, unthinkable, unimaginable, impossible, astonishing, astounding, breathtaking, staggering, absurd, preposterous, phenomenal, extraordinary; unheard of, fictitious, mythical, fanciful, fantastic, unrealistic; feeble, weak, unsound, thin, transparent, poor, tame, paltry, lame, trifling, shallow, inadequate, unsatisfactory, ineffectual, half-baked, pathetic; informal hard to swallow/take, tall, cock and bull.
▷ANTONYMS believable; likely.
2 *an incredible feat of engineering*: **magnificent**, wonderful, marvellous, spectacular, remarkable, phenomenal, prodigious, miraculous, sublime; **breathtaking**, dazzling, amazing, stunning, astounding, astonishing, awe-inspiring, staggering, extraordinary, unbelievable; formidable, imposing, impressive, supreme, great, awesome, superhuman; Scottish unco; informal fantastic, terrific, tremendous, stupendous, mind-boggling, mind-blowing, out of this world, unreal; literary wondrous; archaic awful.
▷ANTONYMS unspectacular.

incredulity noun *reports of UFO sightings were met with incredulity*: **disbelief**, incredulousness, lack of belief, unbelief, lack of credence, doubt, doubtfulness, dubiety, dubiousness, lack of conviction; distrust, mistrust, suspicion, questioning, lack of trust, cynicism, scepticism, wariness, chariness.
▷ANTONYMS credulity; belief.

incredulous adjective *he was frankly incredulous when told the cost*: **disbelieving**, unbelieving, doubtful, dubious, unconvinced; distrustful, distrusting, mistrustful, mistrusting, suspicious, questioning, lacking trust, cynical, sceptical, wary, chary.
▷ANTONYMS credulous.

increment noun *an annual salary increment*: **increase**, addition, gain, augmentation, step up, supplement, addendum, adjunct, accretion, accrual; enlargement, enhancement, boost, advance; informal hike.
▷ANTONYMS reduction.

incriminate verb *Drury persuaded one witness to incriminate Cooper*: **implicate**, involve; blame, accuse, denounce, inform against, blacken the name of; entrap; informal frame, set up, point the finger at, stick/pin the blame on, grass on, rat on; Brit. informal fit up; archaic inculpate.
▷ANTONYMS absolve, clear.

inculcate verb **1** *parents try to **inculcate** a sense of responsibility **in** their children*: **instil**, implant, fix, ingrain, infuse, impress, imprint, introduce; engender, produce, generate, induce, inspire, promote, foster; hammer into, drum into, drive into, drill into, din into.
2 *he tries to inculcate students with a sense of the beauty and joy of the subject*: **imbue**, infuse, inspire, instil; brainwash, indoctrinate; teach.

inculpate verb archaic See **incriminate**.

incumbent adjective **1** *it is incumbent on the government to give a clear lead*: **binding**, obligatory, mandatory, necessary, compulsory, required, requisite, essential, imperative.
▷ANTONYMS optional.
2 *the incumbent President had been defeated*: **current**, existing, present, in office, in power; reigning.
▷ANTONYMS past; future.
▶ noun *the first incumbent of the post was appointed in 1961*: **holder**, bearer, occupant; office-holder, office-bearer, officer, functionary, official.

incur verb *the company incurred a loss of two million pounds | kicking one's opponent incurs a 25-point penalty*: **suffer**, sustain, experience, bring upon oneself, expose oneself to, lay oneself open to; run up, collect; attract, invite, provoke, earn, arouse, induce, cause, give rise to, bring on, be liable/subject to, meet with, draw.
▷ANTONYMS avoid.

incurable adjective **1** *an incurable illness*: **untreatable**, inoperable, irremediable, beyond cure; terminal, fatal, deadly, mortal; chronic, persistent, long-standing, constantly recurring, long-term; rare immedicable.
▷ANTONYMS curable.
2 *an incurable romantic*: **inveterate**, dyed-in-the-wool, confirmed, entrenched, established, long-established, long-standing, deep-rooted, diehard, complete, absolute, utter, thorough, thoroughgoing, out-and-out, true blue, through and through; firm, unshakeable, staunch, steadfast, committed, devoted, dedicated, loyal, faithful, unswerving, unwavering, unfaltering; unashamed, unapologetic, unrepentant, incorrigible, hopeless, beyond hope; N. Amer. full-bore; informal deep-dyed, card-carrying, mad keen, keen as mustard; archaic arrant; rare right-down.

incursion noun *the first Ottoman **incursion into** Europe*: **attack on**, assault on, raid on, invasion of, storming of, overrunning of, foray into, blitz on, sortie into, sally against/into, advance on/into, push into, thrust into, descent on; intrusion into, trespass on, infiltration of, obtrusion into, appropriation of.
▷ANTONYMS retreat.

indebted adjective *I shall always be indebted to them for their help*: **beholden**, under an obligation, obliged, obligated, bound, duty-bound, honour-bound, grateful, thankful, filled with gratitude, appreciative; in someone's debt, owing someone a debt of gratitude.

indecency noun *a man was up in court this week on a charge of indecency*: **indecent behaviour**, gross indecency, pornography; **obscenity**, rudeness, coarseness, dirtiness, smuttiness, vulgarity, grossness, crudity, crudeness, bawdiness, lewdness, raciness, salaciousness, wickedness, impropriety, indelicacy, unseemliness, impurity, ribaldry, lasciviousness, licentiousness; prurience, profanity, foulness, vileness.

indecent adjective **1** *he was fined for importing indecent material*: **obscene**, dirty, filthy, rude, coarse, vulgar, gross, crude, bawdy, lewd, racy, risqué, salacious, wicked, improper, indelicate, unseemly, impure, smutty, spicy, raw, off colour, ribald, Rabelaisian, lascivious, licentious; pornographic, offensive, prurient, sordid, scatological, low, profane, foul, vile; informal blue, naughty, near the knuckle/bone, nudge-nudge, porn, porno, X-rated, raunchy, skin; Brit. informal fruity, saucy; euphemistic adult.
▷ANTONYMS decent, proper.
2 *most of her clothes are rather indecent*: **revealing**, short, brief, skimpy, scanty, insubstantial, low-cut, flimsy, thin, see-through; erotic, arousing, sexy, suggestive, titillating.
▷ANTONYMS modest.
3 *the company took her pass and desk away from her with indecent haste*: **unseemly**, improper, indecorous, unceremonious, indiscreet, indelicate, demeaning, unbecoming, ungentlemanly, unladylike, unworthy, unfitting, unbefitting, degrading, debasing, cheapening, belittling, lowering, shaming, shameful, humiliating, mortifying, dishonourable, ignominious, undignified, discreditable, ignoble, inglorious, scandalous, disgraceful, outrageous; untoward, unsuitable, inappropriate; in bad taste, tasteless, unacceptable, offensive, crass.

indecipherable adjective *the taxi driver scribbled something indecipherable upon the back of a cigarette packet*: **illegible**, unreadable, hard to read, indistinguishable, indiscernible, unclear, indistinct; scribbled, scrawled, hieroglyphic, squiggly, shaky, small, cramped, crabbed, pinched, bad; unintelligible, unfathomable, impenetrable, enigmatic, puzzling, mystifying, inexplicable, baffling, bewildering.
▷ANTONYMS legible.

indecision noun *she was rooted to the spot, torn by indecision*: **indecisiveness**, irresolution, irresoluteness, lack of resolution, hesitancy, hesitation, tentativeness; ambivalence, doubt, doubtfulness, unsureness, uncertainty; vacillation, equivocation, oscillation, wavering, teetering, fluctuation, faltering, second thoughts; delay, hanging back, waiting, shilly-shallying, dithering, stalling, temporizing, temporization; Brit. havering, humming and hawing; Scottish swithering; informal dilly-dallying, blowing hot and cold, sitting on the fence; rare dubiety, incertitude, cunctation.
▷ANTONYMS decision, decisiveness.

indecisive adjective **1** *these experimental results are indecisive*: **inconclusive**, proving nothing, settling nothing, open, indeterminate, undecided, unsettled, borderline, indefinite, unclear, ambiguous, contradictory, ambivalent, conflicting, confusing, two-edged, double-edged, paradoxical; informal up in the air.
▷ANTONYMS decisive.
2 *he came across as a weak, indecisive leader*: **irresolute**, hesitant, tentative, weak; vacillating, equivocating, dithering, wavering, teetering, fluctuating, faltering, shilly-shallying; ambivalent, divided, in two minds, in a dilemma, in a quandary, torn; doubtful, unsure, uncertain; undecided, uncommitted, unresolved, undetermined; informal iffy, blowing hot and cold, sitting on the fence.
▷ANTONYMS decisive.

indecorous adjective *kissing in public is considered indecorous in many countries*: **improper**, unseemly, unbecoming, undignified, immodest, indecent, indelicate, indiscreet, immoral, shameless, loose, wanton, unvirtuous; inappropriate, incorrect, wrong, unsuitable, inapt, inapposite, undesirable, unfitting, out of keeping, unacceptable, impolite, discourteous, in bad taste, ill-bred, ill-mannered, beyond the pale.
▷ANTONYMS decorous.

indecorum noun *it would have been the height of indecorum to send one's daughter unchaperoned to a ball*: **impropriety**, unseemliness, unbecomingness, indignity, immodesty, indecency, indelicacy, indiscretion, immorality, shamelessness; inappropriateness, incorrectness, unsuitability, inaptness, inappositeness, undesirability, unacceptability, impoliteness, discourtesy, bad taste, ill breeding, bad manners; rare improperness.
▷ANTONYMS decorum.

indeed adverb **1** *there was, indeed, quite a furore*: **as expected**, to be sure, in fact, in point of fact, as a matter of fact, in truth, truly, actually, really, in reality, as it happens/happened, certainly, surely, for sure, undeniably, veritably, nay, if truth be told, you could say; archaic in sooth, verily.
2 *'Are you well?' 'Indeed!' | indeed I did*: **yes, certainly**, assuredly, emphatically, absolutely, exactly, precisely, of course, definitely, quite, positively, naturally, without (a) doubt, without question, unquestionably, undoubtedly, doubtlessly, indubitably; by all means; informal you bet, you got it, I'll say.
3 *Ian's future with us looked rosy indeed*: **very**, extremely, exceedingly, exceptionally, especially, extraordinarily, to a fault, in the extreme, extra, tremendously, immensely, singularly, significantly, distinctly, outstandingly, uncommonly, unusually, decidedly, particularly, eminently, supremely, highly, remarkably, really, truly, mightily, thoroughly; all that, to a great extent, most, so; Scottish unco; French très; N. English right; informal terrifically, awfully, fearfully, terribly, devilishly, majorly, seriously, mega, ultra, oh-so, mucho, damn, damned; informal, dated devilish, hellish, frightfully; Brit. informal ever so, well, bloody, dead, jolly, fair; N. Amer. informal real, mighty, powerful, awful, plumb, darned, way, bitching; S. African informal lekker; archaic exceeding.
▷ANTONYMS moderately, slightly; by no means.

indefatigable adjective *he is one of those indefatigable researchers who won't take no for an answer*: **tireless**, untiring, never-tiring, unwearied, unwearying, unflagging; energetic, dynamic, enthusiastic; unrelenting, relentless, unremitting, unswerving, unfaltering, unshakeable, indomitable; persistent, tenacious, determined, dogged, single-minded, assiduous, industrious.
▷ANTONYMS idle; feeble.

indefensible adjective **1** *indefensible cruelty*: **inexcusable**, unjustifiable, unjustified, unpardonable, unforgivable, inexpiable; uncalled for, unprovoked, gratuitous, without justification, without cause, without reason, unreasonable, unnecessary; regrettable, unacceptable, unworthy, remiss, blameworthy, culpable, reprehensible, censurable, unwarrantable; excessive, immoderate, unconscionable, outrageous.
▷ANTONYMS justifiable, excusable.
2 *an indefensible system of dual justice*: **untenable**, insupportable, unsustainable, unwarrantable, unwarranted, unjustifiable, unjustified, unadmissible, unsound, ill-founded, unfounded, groundless, baseless, flimsy, weak, shaky, flawed, faulty, defective, invalid, specious, arbitrary, implausible, absurd, illogical, irrational, preposterous, senseless, unacceptable.
▷ANTONYMS tenable.
3 *an indefensible island*: **undefendable**, defenceless, undefended, unfortified, unguarded, unprotected, unshielded, unarmed, without arms, without weapons, without defences; vulnerable, exposed, assailable, open to attack, wide open, open, endangered, in danger, in peril, in jeopardy, at risk, insecure; rare pregnable.
▷ANTONYMS defensible; well protected.

indefinable adjective *the curious, indefinable quality which sets his sculptures apart*: **hard to define**, hard to describe, indescribable, inexpressible, nameless; vague, obscure; indefinite, unanalysable, intangible, impalpable, incorporeal, elusive, fugitive.
▷ANTONYMS definable.

indefinite adjective **1** *an indefinite period*: **unknown, indeterminate,** unspecified, unlimited, unrestricted, undecided, undetermined, undefined, unfixed, unsettled, unresolved, uncertain; limitless, infinite, endless, immeasurable.
▷ANTONYMS fixed, limited.
2 *a word with an indefinite meaning*: **vague,** ill-defined, unclear, loose, general, imprecise, inexact, nebulous, blurred, fuzzy, hazy, confused, obscure, ambiguous, equivocal, doubtful, dubious.
▷ANTONYMS clear.

indefinitely adverb **1** *the trial has been postponed indefinitely*: **for an unspecified time/period,** for an unlimited time/period, without a fixed limit; Law sine die.
2 *the state of affairs could continue indefinitely*: **forever,** for always, for good, for good and all, evermore, for ever and ever, for all time, until the end of time, eternally, undyingly, permanently, perpetually, in perpetuity; Brit. for evermore; N. Amer. forevermore; informal for keeps, until the cows come home, until hell freezes over, until the twelfth of never, until doomsday, until kingdom come; archaic for aye.
▷ANTONYMS temporarily.

indelible adjective *indelible ink | the story made an indelible impression on me*: **ineradicable,** inerasable, ineffaceable, unexpungeable, indestructible, permanent, lasting, persisting, enduring, stubborn, ingrained, unfading, imperishable; unforgettable, haunting, memorable, not/never to be forgotten.
▷ANTONYMS erasable.

indelicacy noun *the magazine printed the photographs with manifest indelicacy for commercial ends*: **impropriety,** unseemliness, unbecomingness, indignity, immodesty, indecency, obscenity, indecorum, indiscretion, immorality, shamelessness; insensitivity, tactlessness; undesirability, unacceptability, impoliteness, discourtesy, bad taste, ill breeding, bad manners.
▷ANTONYMS delicacy; propriety.

indelicate adjective **1** *forgive me if I am indelicate in asking*: **insensitive,** tactless, undiplomatic, impolitic, indiscreet.
▷ANTONYMS tactful.
2 *an indelicate sense of humour*: **vulgar,** coarse, rude, gross, crude, bawdy, racy, risqué, ribald, Rabelaisian, earthy, indecent, improper, indecorous, unseemly, unrefined, off colour, obscene, dirty, filthy, impure, smutty, lewd, salacious, raw, lascivious, licentious; informal blue, naughty, near the knuckle/bone, nudge-nudge, raunchy; Brit. informal fruity, saucy.
▷ANTONYMS clean; polite.

indemnify verb **1** *he should be indemnified for his losses in the war*: **reimburse,** compensate, recompense, repay, pay back, remunerate, recoup, requite, make restitution/amends to; settle up with, settle accounts with.
2 *the author is required to indemnify the publishers against any such loss*: **insure,** assure, guarantee, protect, secure, make secure, give security to, warrant; agree to pay.

indemnity noun **1** *an outgoing partner should insist on indemnity against future liabilities of the firm*: **insurance,** assurance, protection, security, indemnification, surety, endorsement, guarantee, warranty, safeguard.
2 *those charged with political offences were granted indemnity from prosecution*: **immunity,** exemption, exception, dispensation, exclusion, freedom, release, relief, absolution, exoneration; special treatment, privilege, favouritism; impunity; informal a let-off; rare derogation.
3 *the public purse would be saved the burden of paying indemnity*: **reimbursement,** compensation, recompense, repayment, restitution, payment, remuneration, requital, redress, reparation(s), damages; N. Amer. informal comp; archaic guerdon, meed; rare solatium.

indent verb (stress on the second syllable) **1** *the first line of a paragraph is indented by using the tab key*: **move to the right,** move further from the margin, start in from the margin.
2 *the many lochs that indent the isle of Mull*: **notch,** nick, make an indentation in, make notches/nicks in, scallop, serrate, pink, cut, mark, score, incise, carve, engrave, scratch, gash, slit, snick, gouge, groove, furrow, dent.
3 *you'll have to* **indent for** *a new uniform*: **order,** put in an order for, requisition, apply for, put in for, request, put in a request for, ask for, claim, put in a claim for, call for, demand.
▶ **noun** (stress on the first syllable) Brit. *he cancelled the indent for silk scarves*: **order,** requisition, purchase order, request, call, application; claim, demand, summons.

indentation noun *there was a slight indentation in his chin | indentations in the coastline*: **hollow,** depression, dent, dint, cavity, concavity, dip, pit, trough, crater; dimple; cleft, slot, snick, notch; nick, mark, cut, gouge, gash; recess, alcove, niche, bay; inlet, cove, creek, fjord, firth, ria; Anatomy fossa, lacuna.

indenture noun *the indenture allowed for moneys to be returned in certain circumstances*: **contract,** agreement, covenant, compact, bond, pledge, promise, warrant, undertaking, commitment, settlement, arrangement, understanding; lease, guarantee, warranty; certificate, deed, document, instrument; rare engagement.

independence noun **1** *the struggle for American independence*: **self-government,** self-rule, home rule, self-legislation, self-determination, sovereignty, autonomy, non-alignment, freedom, liberty; rare autarky.
▷ANTONYMS dependence; subservience.
2 *one disadvantage of marriage is the individual's lack of independence*: **self-sufficiency,** self-reliance, self-support, self-sustenance, self-standing.
▷ANTONYMS dependence.
3 *you must be able to rely on an adviser's independence*: **impartiality,** neutrality, disinterest, disinterestedness, uninvolvement, detachment, dispassionateness, lack of bias, lack of prejudice, objectivity, open-mindedness, even-handedness, fairness, fair-mindedness, justice; rare equitableness.
▷ANTONYMS partiality.
4 *there is a tendency for select committees to show some greater independence of spirit*: **individualism,** unconventionality, unorthodoxy; freedom, liberation, boldness, unconstraint, lack of constraint/restraint; indiscipline, unruliness, wilfulness, contrariness.
▷ANTONYMS constraint; orthodoxy.

> *Choose the right word* **independence, liberty, freedom**
>
> See **liberty.**

independent adjective **1** *an independent country*: **self-governing,** self-legislating, self-determining, sovereign, autonomous, autonomic, autarkic, free, non-aligned.
▷ANTONYMS dependent; subservient.
2 *the auditing of a company's accounts is done by independent accountants*: **unconnected,** unrelated, unassociated, dissociated, unattached, separate.
▷ANTONYMS connected.
3 *the Institute will quickly become a fully independent unit*: **separate,** discrete, different, distinct, free-standing, self-contained, complete.
▷ANTONYMS subordinate.
4 *an independent school*: **private,** public, non-state-controlled, non-state-run, non-public, private-sector, private-enterprise, fee-paying, commercial; privatized, denationalized.
▷ANTONYMS private; state-run.
5 *one has to be very careful about offering money to proud and independent old folk*: **self-sufficient,** self-supporting, self-sustaining, self-reliant, self-standing, able to stand on one's own two feet; self-contained, self-made; informal living on one's hump.
▷ANTONYMS dependent.
6 *an independent financial adviser*: **impartial,** unbiased, unprejudiced, neutral, disinterested, uninvolved, uncommitted, detached, dispassionate, objective, open-minded, equitable, non-partisan, even-handed, fair, fair-minded, just; without favouritism, free from discrimination, non-discriminatory, with no axe to grind, without fear or favour; informal on the fence.
▷ANTONYMS biased; tied.
7 *entrepreneurs are independent spirits*: **freethinking,** individualistic, unconventional, maverick; free, liberated, bold, unconstrained, unrestrained, unfettered, untrammelled, unhampered; undisciplined, wild, wilful, headstrong, contrary.
▷ANTONYMS constrained; orthodox.

independently adverb *he prefers to work independently | we'll get there independently and then meet up*: **alone,** all alone, on one's own, in a solitary state, separately, singly, solitarily, unaccompanied, solo; unaided, unassisted, without help, without assistance, by one's own efforts, under one's own steam, single-handed(ly), off one's own bat, on one's own initiative, autonomously, as one's own boss; informal by one's lonesome; Brit. informal on one's tod, on one's lonesome, on one's jack, on one's Jack Jones; formal severally.
▷ANTONYMS accompanied; jointly; assisted.

indescribable adjective *the indescribable thrill of the chase*: **inexpressible,** undefinable, beyond words/description, beggaring description, nameless, incommunicable, ineffable, unutterable, unspeakable; intense, extreme, acute, strong, powerful, profound; incredible, extraordinary, remarkable, prodigious; indefinite, unanalysable, intangible, impalpable, elusive, fugitive.

indestructible adjective *indestructible plastic containers | the indestructible spirit of man*: **unbreakable,** shatterproof, non-breakable; toughened, sturdy, stout, hard-wearing, heavy-duty, resistant, durable, lasting, made to last; enduring, everlasting, perennial, deathless, undying, immortal, endless, inextinguishable, imperishable, ineradicable, long-lasting; literary adamantine; rare infrangible.
▷ANTONYMS fragile; ephemeral.

indeterminate adjective **1** *a woman of indeterminate age*: **undetermined,** undefined, unspecified, unfixed, unsettled, indefinite, unknown, uncounted, uncertain, unpredictable.
▷ANTONYMS known.
2 *indeterminate background noise*: **vague,** indefinite, unspecific, unclear, obscure, nebulous, indistinct, some kind of; ambiguous, ambivalent,

equivocal; amorphous, shapeless, formless, unformed, unshaped, structureless, unstructured; inexact, imprecise, inexplicit, ill-defined; hazy, faint, shadowy, dim; rare nebulose.
▷ANTONYMS definite, clear.

index noun **1** *the book has a very complete index*: **register**, list, listing, inventory, directory, guide, key, catalogue, table of contents.
2 *literature is an index to the condition of civilization*: **guide**, clue, hint, indication, indicator, lead, sign, signal, mark, token, evidence, symptom, implication, intimation, suggestion.
3 *the index jumped up the dial*: **pointer**, indicator, needle, hand, finger, marker.

indicate verb **1** *sales indicate a growing market for such art | the scowl on his face indicated his displeasure*: **demonstrate**, show, point to, be a sign of, be evidence of, evidence, testify to, bear witness to, be a symptom of, be symptomatic of, denote, connote, mark, signal, signify, suggest, imply; manifest, reveal, betray, evince, display, reflect, represent; literary bespeak, betoken.
2 *the Prime Minister indicated that the government would take no further action*: **state**, declare, make (it) known, announce, communicate, mention, say, reveal, divulge, disclose, register, record, put it on record; admit; informal come out with.
3 *please indicate your choice of prize*: **designate**, specify, stipulate; show.
4 *he indicated the room to me*: **point to**, point out, gesture towards.

indicated adjective *these remedies can be of great value, even when surgery is indicated*: **advisable**, desirable, recommended, suggested, desired, preferable, best, sensible, wise, commonsensical, prudent; appropriate, suitable; helpful, useful, effective, advantageous, beneficial, valuable, profitable, gainful, in someone's (best) interests; **necessary**, needed, required, called for, essential.

indication noun **1** *pain may be an indication of injury*: **sign**, indicator, symptom, mark, manifestation, signal, demonstration, evidence, attestation, proof; omen, augury, portent, warning, forewarning, pointer, guide, hint, clue.
2 *her face was turned away as an indication of her contempt*: **expression**, demonstration, show, exhibition, display, manifestation, revelation, disclosure, register, record; declaration, communication, intimation.

indicative adjective *the President's visit was indicative of improving diplomatic relations*: **symptomatic**, expressive, suggestive, evocative, typical, characteristic, representative, symbolic, emblematic; archaic indicatory.

indicator noun **1** *these tests are a reliable indicator of performance*: **measure**, gauge, barometer, index, mark, sign, signal; guide to; standard, touchstone, yardstick, benchmark, criterion, point of reference, guideline, test, litmus test.
2 *the depth indicator is calibrated in metres*: **meter**, measuring instrument, measuring device, measure, gauge, dial, display, scale, index.
3 *a red position indicator points at flap settings*: **pointer**, needle, hand, arrow, marker, index.

indict verb *he was* ***indicted for murder***: **charge with**, accuse of, arraign for, take to court for, put on trial for, bring to trial for, prosecute for; summons, cite, make accusations about, lay charges against, file charges against, prefer charges against; N. Amer. impeach for.
▷ANTONYMS acquit.

indictment noun *the indictment named only one defendant*: **charge**, accusation, arraignment, citation, summons; allegation, imputation; Brit. plaint; N. Amer. impeachment; N. Amer. informal beef; archaic inculpation.
▷ANTONYMS acquittal.

indifference noun **1** *he has a total* ***indifference to*** *public opinion*: **lack of concern about**, unconcern about, apathy about/towards, nonchalance about, lack of interest in, disregard for, obliviousness to, uninvolvement in/with; heedlessness of, mindlessness of, carelessness of, dismissiveness of; boredom with, weariness of, unresponsiveness to, lack of enthusiasm about; impassiveness, impassivity, dispassionateness, aloofness, insouciance, detachment, distance, coldness, coolness, unresponsiveness, passionlessness, emotionlessness, lack of feeling, lack of sympathy, callousness; rare poco-curantism.
▷ANTONYMS heed; care.
2 *the indifference of the team's midfield players*: **mediocrity**, ordinariness, commonplaceness, lack of inspiration, passableness, adequacy; **inferiority**, lack of distinction, amateurism.
▷ANTONYMS brilliance.

indifferent adjective **1** *Government cannot be* ***indifferent to*** *the long-term success of business*: **unconcerned about**, apathetic about/towards, uncaring about, casual about, nonchalant about, offhand about, uninterested in, uninvolved in/with; heedless of, mindless of, careless of, regardless of, oblivious to; reckless about, cavalier about, frivolous about, dismissive of; unimpressed by, bored by, weary of, unmoved by, unresponsive to, lukewarm about, unenthusiastic about, phlegmatic about; impassive, dispassionate, aloof, insouciant, detached, distant, cold, cool, unresponsive, passionless, unemotional, emotionless, unmoved, unfeeling, unsympathetic, callous; rare poco-curante.
▷ANTONYMS heedful; caring.
2 *both players played indifferent shots*: **mediocre**, ordinary, commonplace, average, middle-of-the-road, middling, medium, moderate, everyday, workaday, tolerable, passable, adequate, fair; **inferior**, second-rate, uninspired, undistinguished, unexceptional, unexciting, unremarkable, run-of-the-mill, not very good, pedestrian, prosaic, lacklustre, forgettable, amateur, amateurish; informal OK, so-so, bog-standard, fair-to-middling, (plain) vanilla, nothing to write home about, no great shakes, not so hot, not up to much; NZ informal half-pie.
▷ANTONYMS brilliant.

indigence noun *he did valuable work towards the relief of indigence*: **poverty**, penury, impoverishment, impecuniousness, impecuniosity, destitution, pennilessness, privation, hand-to-mouth existence, pauperism; insolvency, bankruptcy, ruin, ruination; need, neediness, want, reduced/straitened/narrow circumstances, dire straits, deprivation, disadvantage, hardship, distress, financial distress, difficulties; beggary, mendicancy, vagrancy; rare pauperdom.
▷ANTONYMS wealth.

indigenous adjective *indigenous peoples are being slowly wiped out as prospectors invade their lands*: **native**, aboriginal, local; original, earliest, first, initial; ancient, primitive, primeval, primordial; rare autochthonous, autochthonic.
▷ANTONYMS expatriate; migrant; adventitious.

> *Word toolkit* **indigenous**
>
> See **original**.

indigent adjective *the first state pensions were given to indigent people over seventy*: **poor**, impecunious, destitute, penniless, impoverished, poverty-stricken, down and out, pauperized, without a penny to one's name, without two farthings/pennies to rub together; insolvent, ruined; needy, in need, in want, hard up, on the breadline, hard-pressed, in reduced/straitened circumstances, deprived, disadvantaged, distressed, badly off; beggarly, beggared; informal on one's uppers, up against it, broke, flat broke, strapped (for cash), without a brass farthing, without a bean, without a sou, as poor as a church mouse, on one's beam-ends; Brit. informal stony broke, skint, boracic (lint); N. Amer. informal stone broke, without a red cent, on skid row; formal penurious.
▷ANTONYMS rich.

indigestion noun *crisps give me indigestion*: **dyspepsia**, hyperacidity, acidity, heartburn, (a) stomach ache, (an) upset stomach, (a) stomach upset, a gastric upset; informal (a) bellyache, (a) tummy ache, collywobbles; technical pyrosis.

indignant adjective *he was indignant at the way he was being treated*: **aggrieved**, resentful, affronted, disgruntled, discontented, dissatisfied, angry, distressed, unhappy, disturbed, hurt, pained, upset, offended, piqued, in high dudgeon, riled, nettled, vexed, irked, irritated, annoyed, put out, chagrined; informal peeved, miffed, aggravated, in a huff; Brit. informal cheesed off, browned off; N. Amer. informal sore, steamed; vulgar slang pissed off; N. Amer. vulgar slang pissed.
▷ANTONYMS content.

indignation noun *she was filled with indignation at having been blamed so unjustly*: **resentment**, umbrage, affront, disgruntlement, anger, distress, unhappiness, discontent, dissatisfaction, displeasure, hurt, pain, upset, offence, pique, spleen, crossness, exasperation, vexation, irritation, annoyance, chagrin; informal aggravation; literary ire.
▷ANTONYMS contentment.

indignity noun *Annie has suffered the indignity of being dumped by her husband*: **shame**, humiliation, loss of self-respect, loss of pride, embarrassment, mortification, abasement, degradation; disgrace, dishonour, stigma, disrepute, discredit, opprobrium, scandal, infamy, ignobility, loss of face; affront, insult, abuse, mistreatment, injury, offence, injustice, outrage, slight, snub, contempt, disrespect, discourtesy; informal slap in the face, kick in the teeth; rare obloquy.
▷ANTONYMS honour; glory.

indirect adjective **1** *motherhood has an indirect effect on pay*: **incidental**, accidental, unintended, secondary, subordinate, ancillary, collateral, concomitant, accompanying, contingent, resulting, resultant, consequential, derived, derivative.
▷ANTONYMS direct.
2 *the indirect route is usually less congested*: **roundabout**, circuitous, deviant, divergent, wandering, meandering, serpentine, winding, curving, tortuous, zigzag; rare anfractuous.
▷ANTONYMS direct.
3 *an indirect attack on the Archbishop*: **oblique**, inexplicit, roundabout, circuitous; implicit, implied, allusive.

indirectly adverb **1** *the losses suffered by Lloyd's members indirectly affect us all*: **incidentally**, accidentally, secondarily, concomitantly, contingently, consequentially.
▷ANTONYMS directly.
2 *I heard of the damage indirectly*: **second-hand**, at second hand, in a

roundabout way, from others; informal on the grapevine, on the bush/jungle telegraph.
3 *both writers refer, if only indirectly, to a wealth of other art*: **obliquely**, by implication, by hinting, allusively.

indiscernible adjective **1** *the transition from brush to pen is indiscernible*: **unnoticeable**, imperceptible, invisible, undetectable, indistinguishable, unapparent, inappreciable, barely perceptible, impalpable, unobtrusive, impossible to detect, hidden; tiny, minute, minuscule, microscopic, nanoscopic, infinitesimal, negligible, inconsequential, slight, subtle, faint, fine.
▷ANTONYMS discernible.
2 *an indiscernible shape among the shadows | his words were indiscernible in the din*: **indistinct**, unclear, fuzzy, obscure, vague, indefinite, nebulous, amorphous, shadowy, dim, hard to make out; unintelligible, incomprehensible, hard to understand, inaudible; archaic blear.
▷ANTONYMS distinct.

indiscreet adjective **1** *I wouldn't be so indiscreet as to reveal my source | an indiscreet remark*: **imprudent**, impolitic, unwise, injudicious, incautious, irresponsible; ill-judged, ill-advised, misguided; ill-considered, careless, rash, unwary, hasty, reckless, precipitate, impulsive, foolhardy, foolish, short-sighted; undiplomatic, indelicate, tactless, insensitive; inexpedient, untimely, infelicitous.
▷ANTONYMS discreet.
2 *he looked long into her eyes—remarkably indiscreet behaviour with his wife present*: **immodest**, indecorous, improper, indecent, indelicate, unseemly; forward, bold, brazen, impudent, unblushing, shameless; informal fresh, cheeky, naughty, saucy.
▷ANTONYMS decorous.

indiscretion noun **1** *they were obsessed with the need for secrecy and the dangers of indiscretion*: **imprudence**, injudiciousness, lack of caution, incaution, irresponsibility; carelessness, rashness, unwariness, haste, recklessness, precipitateness, impulsiveness, foolhardiness, foolishness, folly, poor judgement, short-sightedness; indelicacy, tactlessness, lack of diplomacy, insensitivity.
▷ANTONYMS discretion.
2 *he admitted his past indiscretions to investigators*: **blunder**, lapse, gaffe, mistake, error, breach of etiquette, slip, miscalculation, impropriety; misdemeanour, transgression, peccadillo, offence, misdeed, crime, felony, sin; (**indiscretions**) wrongdoing, misconduct, mischief, mischievousness, wickedness, misbehaviour, bad behaviour; French faux pas; informal slip-up; archaic trespass.

indiscriminate adjective *the indiscriminate bombing of cities | the furnishings were an indiscriminate mess*: **non-selective**, unselective, undiscriminating, uncritical, aimless, hit-or-miss, haphazard, random, unsystematic, unmethodical; wholesale, general, sweeping, blanket; broad-based, wide, catholic, eclectic, varied, miscellaneous, heterogeneous, motley, confused, chaotic; thoughtless, unthinking, unconsidered, casual, careless; rare promiscuous.
▷ANTONYMS selective, discriminating; systematic.

indiscriminately adverb *his armies slaughtered men, women, and children indiscriminately*: **randomly**, at random, unsystematically, aimlessly, unmethodically, without method, haphazardly, blindly, uncritically, undiscriminatingly, non-selectively, injudiciously; chaotically, erratically, casually, desultorily, arbitrarily; carelessly, unthinkingly, thoughtlessly, mindlessly; wholesale, without exception, across the board; rare undiscerningly, unselectively, promiscuously.
▷ANTONYMS selectively; systematically.

indispensable adjective *education is indispensable for the preservation of democracy*: **essential**, crucial, necessary, key, vital, needed, required, called for, requisite, important, all-important, vitally important, of the utmost importance, of great consequence, of the essence, critical, life-and-death, imperative, mandatory, compulsory, obligatory, compelling, urgent, pressing, burning, acute, paramount, pre-eminent, high-priority, significant, consequential.
▷ANTONYMS dispensable, superfluous, non-essential.

> *Choose the right word* **indispensable, necessary, requisite, essential**
>
> See **necessary**.

indisposed adjective **1** *the billed soloist was indisposed*: **ill**, unwell, sick, on the sick list, infirm, poorly, ailing, not (very) well, not oneself, not in good shape, out of sorts, not up to par, under/below par; in bed, bedridden, confined to bed, laid up, out of commission, out of action; Brit. off, off colour; French hors de combat; informal under the weather.
▷ANTONYMS well.
2 *she was indisposed to criticize the same fault in others*: **reluctant**, unwilling, disinclined, loath, unprepared, not ready, not disposed, not keen, not minded, not in the mood; slow, hesitant, afraid; averse, antipathetic, resistant, opposed; nervous about, not in favour of, unenthusiastic about.
▷ANTONYMS willing.

indisposition noun **1** *due to an indisposition, Herr Gesner will not be able to continue his performance*: **illness**, ailment, disorder, sickness, affliction, malady, infirmity, malaise, disease, infection, upset; condition, complaint, problem, trouble; ill health; informal bug, virus; Brit. informal lurgy; Austral. informal wog.
2 *an utter indisposition to do anything whatever*: **reluctance**, unwillingness, disinclination, unpreparedness; slowness, hesitation, hesitancy; aversion, resistance, opposition; nervousness about, antipathy towards, dislike of, distaste for, lack of enthusiasm for.
▷ANTONYMS willingness.

indisputable adjective *the facts are indisputable*: **incontrovertible**, incontestable, undeniable, irrefutable, unassailable, beyond dispute, unquestionable, beyond question, indubitable, not in doubt, beyond doubt, beyond a shadow of a doubt, unarguable, inarguable, undebatable, unanswerable; unequivocal, unambiguous, unmistakable, certain, sure, definite, definitive, proven, positive, decisive, conclusive, final, ultimate; clear, clear-cut, straightforward, plain, as plain as a pikestaff, transparent, obvious, manifest, evident, self-evident, staring one in the face, patent, demonstrative, demonstrable, observable, palpable; uncontroversial, accepted, acknowledged; marked, pronounced, express, emphatic, categorical, compelling, convincing, clinching, airtight, watertight; rare irrefragable, apodictic.
▷ANTONYMS questionable.

indistinct adjective **1** *the distant shoreline behind them was indistinct*: **blurred**, out of focus, fuzzy, hazy, misty, foggy, cloudy, shadowy, smoky, dim, nebulous; unclear, obscure, vague, faint, indefinite, indistinguishable, barely perceptible, undefined, lacking definition, hard to see, hard to make out; archaic blear; rare obfuscated, nebulose.
▷ANTONYMS distinct; clear.
2 *the last two digits of the number are indistinct*: **indecipherable**, illegible, barely legible, unreadable, unintelligible, unfathomable, hard to read, hard to make out; undefined, ill-defined, lacking definition, formless, indeterminate; pale, faded, smudged; informal as clear as mud.
▷ANTONYMS legible.
3 *indistinct sounds emerged from the building*: **muffled**, muted, dull, low, quiet, soft, faint, weak, feeble, inaudible, scarcely audible, scarcely perceptible, hard to hear, hard to make out; muttered, mumbled, stifled, strangled, smothered, suppressed.
▷ANTONYMS loud; clear.

indistinguishable adjective **1** *the two girls were indistinguishable*: **identical**, almost identical, the same, alike, very similar; cut from the same cloth, two of a kind, difficult to tell apart; informal as like as two peas in a pod, like Tweedledum and Tweedledee.
▷ANTONYMS dissimilar; easy to tell apart.
2 *in choral music the words are frequently indistinguishable*: **unintelligible**, incomprehensible, hard to understand, hard to make out, indistinct, unclear, indefinite; inappreciable, indiscernible, imperceptible, inaudible.
▷ANTONYMS clear, distinguishable.

individual adjective **1** *exhibitions devoted to individual artists*: **single**, separate, discrete, independent; sole, lone, solitary, isolated.
2 *he had his own individual style of music*: **characteristic**, distinctive, distinct, typical, particular, peculiar, personal, personalized, special; rare especial.
▷ANTONYMS collective.
3 *he has a chic and highly individual apartment*: **original**, unique, exclusive, singular, idiosyncratic, different, unusual, novel, unorthodox, atypical, out of the ordinary.
▷ANTONYMS ordinary.
▶noun **1** *Peter was a rather stuffy individual*: **person**, human being, human, being, mortal, soul, creature, thing; man, gentleman, boy, woman, lady, girl; figure, personage; informal character, type, sort, beggar, cookie, customer, guy, devil, bunny, bastard; Brit. informal bod, geezer, gent, punter; informal, dated body, dog; Brit. informal, dated cove; Brit. vulgar slang sod, bugger; archaic wight.
2 *she enjoyed the freedom of being an individual*: **individualist**, free spirit, nonconformist, original, eccentric, character, bohemian, maverick, rare bird, rarity; loner, lone wolf, outsider; Latin rara avis; Brit. informal one-off, oner.

individualism noun *collectivism is a more powerful force for productivity than individualism*: **independence**, self-direction, self-reliance, freethinking, free thought, originality; unconventionality, eccentricity; libertarianism.

individualist noun *he was regarded as not merely an individualist but something of a crank*: **free spirit**, individual, nonconformist, unorthodox person, unconventional person, original, eccentric, bohemian, maverick, rare bird, rarity; lone wolf, outsider; Latin rara avis; Brit. informal one-off, loner.
▷ANTONYMS conformist.

individualistic adjective *he took an individualistic approach to his subject*: **unconventional**, unorthodox, uncommon, atypical, singular, unique, original, nonconformist, independent, freethinking, liberated, unconstrained, unfettered, untrammelled, pioneering, groundbreaking; eccentric, bohemian, maverick, strange, odd, peculiar, idiosyncratic.

i

individuality noun *we are motivated by the need to assert our individuality*: **uniqueness**, originality, singularity, particularity, peculiarity, distinctiveness, distinction, differentness, separateness; personality, character, identity, self.

individually adverb *a panel will look at all of the applications individually*: **one at a time**, one by one, singly, separately, independently, discretely, apart; Latin seriatim; formal severally.
▷ANTONYMS together.

indoctrinate verb *they use alien dogmas to indoctrinate the masses*: **brainwash**, propagandize, proselytize, inculcate, re-educate, persuade, convince, condition, discipline, mould; instruct, teach, school, drill, ground.

indolence noun *my failure is probably due to my own indolence*: **laziness**, idleness, slothfulness, sloth, shiftlessness, inactivity, inaction, inertia, lifelessness, sluggishness, lethargy, languor, languidness, torpor, torpidity, slowness, dullness; remissness, negligence, slackness, laxity; rare otiosity, hebetude.
▷ANTONYMS industriousness; energy.

indolent adjective *the pub is full of indolent young men*: **lazy**, idle, slothful, loafing, work-shy, shiftless, apathetic, lackadaisical, inactive, inert, lifeless, sluggish, lethargic, listless, languid, torpid, slow, slow-moving, dull, plodding; slack, lax, remiss, negligent, good-for-nothing; informal bone idle; French, archaic fainéant; rare otiose.
▷ANTONYMS industrious; energetic.

Choose the right word **indolent, lazy, idle**

See **lazy**.

indomitable adjective *these indomitable warriors have never been subjugated by an invading force*: **invincible**, unconquerable, unbeatable, unassailable, impregnable, invulnerable, unsurpassable, unshakeable; indefatigable, unyielding, unbending, stalwart, stout-hearted, lionhearted, strong-willed, strong-minded, staunch, resolute, firm, steadfast, determined, intransigent, inflexible, adamant; unflinching, courageous, brave, valiant, heroic, intrepid, fearless, plucky, mettlesome, gritty, steely.
▷ANTONYMS submissive; weak.

Word toolkit

indomitable	unassailable	impregnable
spirit	lead	fortress
courage	position	barrier
enemy	truth	wall
strength	record	defense
presence	authority	vault
determination	logic	stronghold
faith	reputation	castle

indubitable adjective *he furnished indubitable evidence of his identity*: **unquestionable**, undoubtable, indisputable, unarguable, inarguable, undebatable, incontestable, undeniable, irrefutable, incontrovertible, unmistakable, unequivocal, certain, sure, positive, definite, absolute, conclusive, emphatic, categorical, compelling, watertight, clear, clear-cut; beyond doubt, beyond the shadow of a doubt, beyond dispute, beyond question, not in question, not in doubt; rare irrefragable, apodictic.
▷ANTONYMS doubtful.

induce verb **1** *the pickets induced many workers to stay away*: **persuade**, convince, prevail upon, get, make, prompt, move, inspire, instigate, influence, exert influence on, press, urge, incite, encourage, impel, actuate, motivate; coax into, wheedle into, cajole into, talk into, prod into; Law procure; informal twist someone's arm.
▷ANTONYMS dissuade.
2 *these activities induce a feeling of social togetherness*: **bring about**, bring on, cause, be the cause of, produce, effect, create, give rise to, generate, originate, instigate, engender, occasion, set in motion, develop, lead to, result in, have as a consequence, have as a result, trigger off, spark off, whip up, stir up, kindle, arouse, rouse, foster, promote, encourage; literary beget, enkindle; rare effectuate.
▷ANTONYMS prevent.

Choose the right word **induce, convince, persuade**

See **convince**.

inducement noun *shopkeepers began offering free gifts as an inducement to trade*: **incentive**, attraction, encouragement, temptation, incitement, stimulation, stimulus, bait, lure, pull, draw, spur, goad, impetus, motive, motivation, provocation; bribe, reward; informal carrot, come-on, sweetener, perk; rare douceur.
▷ANTONYMS deterrent.

induct verb **1** *eighteen new junior ministers were* ***inducted into*** *the government*: **admit to**, allow into, introduce to, initiate into, install in, instate in, swear into; appoint to; be engaged by, be taken on by.
▷ANTONYMS bar from.
2 *my master* ***inducted*** *me* ***into*** *the skills of magic*: **introduce to**, acquaint with, familiarize with, make familiar with, make conversant with, make aware of, inform of, give information about; ground in, instruct in, teach in, educate in, school in; informal fill in on, gen up on, clue up on, clue in on, put in the picture about.

indulge verb **1** *Sally indulged her passion for long walks*: **satisfy**, gratify, fulfil, satiate, quench, appease, feed, accommodate; go along with, yield to, give in to, give way to, pander to, cater to, comply with.
▷ANTONYMS frustrate.
2 *she* ***indulged in*** *a fit of sulks*: **wallow in**, give oneself up to, give way to, yield to, abandon oneself to, give rein to, give free rein to; luxuriate in, revel in, lose oneself in.
▷ANTONYMS stifle.
3 *she did not like her children to be indulged*: **pamper**, spoil, overindulge, coddle, mollycoddle, cosset, nanny, nursemaid, mother, baby, pet, spoon-feed, feather-bed, wrap in cotton wool; pander to, humour, wait on someone hand and foot, cater to someone's every whim, kill someone with kindness; archaic cocker.
□ **indulge oneself** *a man should indulge himself now and then*: **treat oneself**, give oneself a treat, luxuriate in something, give oneself up to pleasure; splash out; informal have a spree, go to town, splurge.
▷ANTONYMS deny oneself.

indulgence noun **1** *he squandered his money on the indulgence of all his desires*: **satisfaction**, satisfying, gratification, gratifying, fulfilment, fulfilling, satiation, appeasement, assuagement, quenching, slaking; accommodation.
▷ANTONYMS denial.
2 *he took exercise as an antidote to excess indulgence*: **self-gratification**, self-indulgence, overindulgence, intemperance, immoderation, immoderateness, dissipation, dissolution, dissoluteness, debauchery, excess, excessiveness, lack of restraint, prodigality, extravagance, decadence, pleasure-seeking, wantonness, lack of self-control; rare sybaritism.
▷ANTONYMS moderation.
3 *they viewed holidays abroad as an indulgence*: **extravagance**, luxury, treat, comfort, non-essential, extra, frill.
▷ANTONYMS necessity.
4 *her indulgence left him spoilt*: **pampering**, coddling, mollycoddling, cosseting, babying, mothering, nannying; spoiling, humouring, catering to someone's every whim; partiality.
5 *his parents view his lapses with indulgence*: **tolerance**, forbearance, humanity, compassion, kindness, understanding, sympathy, liberalness, liberality, forgiveness, leniency, lenience, clemency, mercy, mercifulness.
▷ANTONYMS severity.

indulgent adjective *she had a very indulgent father*: **permissive**, easy-going, broad-minded, liberal, tolerant, forgiving, forbearing, lenient, merciful, clement, mild, humane, kind, kindly, soft-hearted, caring, compassionate, understanding, sympathetic; fond, doting, pampering, mollycoddling, cosseting, soft; compliant, obliging, accommodating.
▷ANTONYMS strict; intolerant.

industrial adjective **1** *the industrial areas of the city*: **manufacturing**, factory; **commercial**, business, trade.
2 Brit. *their colleagues voted for industrial action*: **strike**, protest.

industrialist noun **manufacturer**, producer, factory owner, factory boss; captain of industry, big businessman, top executive, magnate, tycoon, capitalist, financier, investor; informal, derogatory fat cat.

industrious adjective *he was honest, sober, and industrious*: **hard-working**, diligent, assiduous, sedulous, conscientious, steady, painstaking, persistent, persevering, pertinacious, unflagging, untiring, tireless, indefatigable, studious; busy, busy as a bee, active, bustling, energetic, on the go, vigorous, determined, dynamic, zealous, productive; with one's shoulder to the wheel, with one's nose to the grindstone; archaic laborious.
▷ANTONYMS indolent.

Choose the right word **industrious, diligent, hard-working**

See **hard-working**.

industry noun **1** *the decline of British industry*: **manufacturing**, production, fabrication, construction.
2 *the publishing industry*: **business**, trade, field, line, line of work, line of business, commercial enterprise, service; profession, occupation, craft; informal racket.
3 *the kitchen was a hive of industry*: **hard work**, industriousness, diligence, assiduity, application, sedulousness, sedulity, conscientiousness, steadiness, tirelessness, persistence, pertinacity, perseverance, dedication, determination, rigour, rigorousness; **activity**, busyness, energy, vigour, effort, labour, dynamism, zeal, productiveness; archaic laboriousness, continuance; rare perseveration.
▷ANTONYMS indolence.

inebriated adjective *they helped to put the inebriated man to bed*: **drunk**, intoxicated, inebriate, drunken, tipsy, the worse for drink, under the influence; blind drunk, dead drunk, rolling drunk, roaring drunk, as drunk as a lord, as drunk as a skunk; sottish, gin-soaked; informal tight, merry, the worse for wear, pie-eyed, three sheets to the wind, plastered, smashed, hammered, sloshed, soused, sozzled, well oiled, paralytic, wrecked, wasted, blotto, stewed, pickled, tanked up, soaked, blasted, ratted, off one's face, out of one's head, out of one's skull; Brit. informal legless, bevvied, Brahms and Liszt, half cut, out of it, bladdered, trolleyed, mullered, slaughtered, well away, squiffy, tiddly, out of one's box; Scottish informal fou; N. Amer. informal loaded, trashed, out of one's gourd; Brit. vulgar slang pissed, rat-arsed, arseholed; informal, dated in one's cups, lit up; euphemistic tired and emotional; archaic sotted, foxed, screwed; rare crapulent, crapulous, bibulous, ebriate.
▷ANTONYMS sober.

inebriation noun *he's in a state of extreme inebriation*: **intoxication**, drunkenness, insobriety, tipsiness; informal tightness; rare crapulence.
▷ANTONYMS sobriety.

inedible adjective *they were served with inedible fruit*: **uneatable**, indigestible, unconsumable, unpalatable, unwholesome, unsavoury; stale, not fit to eat, rotten, off, bad, putrid, rancid.
▷ANTONYMS edible.

ineffable adjective **1** *the ineffable natural beauty of the Everglades*: **inexpressible**, indescribable, beyond words, beyond description, beggaring description; undefinable, unutterable, untold, unheard of, unthought of, unimaginable; overwhelming, marvellous, wonderful, breathtaking, staggering, astounding, amazing, astonishing, fantastic, fabulous.
2 *the ineffable name of God*: **unutterable**, not to be uttered, not to be spoken, not to be said, unmentionable; taboo, forbidden, off limits, out of bounds; informal no go.

ineffective adjective **1** *they made an ineffective attempt to resolve the issue*: **unsuccessful**, non-successful, unproductive, fruitless, profitless, unprofitable, abortive, failed, futile, purposeless, worthless, useless, ineffectual, inefficient, inefficacious, inadequate, vain, unavailing, to no effect; idle, feeble, weak, inept, lame; archaic bootless; rare unfructuous, inutile.
▷ANTONYMS effective.
2 *he was a weak and ineffective president*: **ineffectual**, inefficient, inefficacious, unsuccessful, powerless, impotent, inadequate, incompetent, incapable, unfit, inept, lame, feeble, weak, poor; informal useless, hopeless.
▷ANTONYMS effective.

ineffectual adjective **1** *the state was under the control of ineffectual rulers*: **inefficient**, ineffective, inefficacious, unsuccessful, powerless, impotent, inadequate, inept, incompetent, incapable, unfit, lame, feeble, weak, poor; informal useless, hopeless, rotten, lousy, no good.
2 *she made an ineffectual effort to escape*: **ineffective**, unproductive, unsuccessful, non-successful, profitless, fruitless, futile, failed, abortive, vain, unavailing, useless, worthless, inadequate, inefficient, inefficacious, lame, inept, bungled, bungling; archaic bootless; rare unfructuous, inutile.

inefficacious adjective *the old way of doing things was suddenly inefficacious*. See **ineffective**.

inefficient adjective **1** *my boss thinks I'm inefficient*: **ineffective**, ineffectual, inefficacious, incompetent, inept, incapable, unfit, unsuitable, unskilled, unskilful, inexpert, amateurish; disorganized, badly organized, unprepared, undisciplined, negligent, lax, slipshod, sloppy, slack, remiss, careless; informal lousy, useless; Brit. vulgar slang not capable of organizing a piss-up in a brewery.
▷ANTONYMS efficient.
2 *a series of elaborate and inefficient processes*: **uneconomical**, wasteful, purposeless, unproductive, time-wasting, slow, slow-moving, awkward, unwieldy, cumbersome, badly arranged, deficient, disorganized, unsystematic.
▷ANTONYMS efficient.

inelegant adjective **1** *Amanda gave an inelegant bellow of laughter*: **unrefined**, uncouth, unsophisticated, unpolished, uncultured, uncultivated, gauche; crude, ill-bred, coarse, vulgar, rude, impolite, unmannerly.
▷ANTONYMS refined; polite.
2 *she danced in a stiff and inelegant way*: **ungraceful**, graceless, ungainly, uncoordinated, gawky, gangling, awkward, clumsy, lumbering, blundering; inept, unskilful, inexpert; informal with two left feet, like a bull in a china shop.
▷ANTONYMS elegant.

ineligible adjective *students are ineligible for housing benefit*: **unqualified**, ruled out, disqualified, legally disqualified, disentitled; Law incompetent.
▷ANTONYMS eligible.

inept adjective *my attempts at baking were inept but I fumbled on*: **incompetent**, unskilful, unskilled, inexpert, amateurish, crude, rough; clumsy, awkward, maladroit, unhandy, heavy-handed, bungling, blundering, bumbling, botched; unproductive, unsuccessful, ineffectual, inadequate, inferior, substandard, wanting, lacking, not up to scratch; informal cack-handed, ham-fisted, ham-handed, butterfingered; Brit. informal all thumbs, all fingers and thumbs; N. Amer. informal klutzy.
▷ANTONYMS competent.

inequality noun *a society without social inequality*: **imbalance**, inequity, unevenness, disproportion, inconsistency, variation, variability; divergence, polarity, disparity, discrepancy, dissimilarity, difference, contrast, distinction, differential; bias, prejudice, discrimination, unfairness, unfair treatment.
▷ANTONYMS equality; uniformity.

inequitable adjective *a crude and inequitable process for setting salary rates*: **unfair**, unjust, discriminatory, preferential, one-sided, unequal, uneven, unbalanced, loaded, weighted, slanted, non-objective, biased, partisan, partial, prejudiced.
▷ANTONYMS fair; impartial.

inequity noun *we wish to emphasize the inequity of the present law*: **unfairness**, injustice, unjustness, one-sidedness, partisanship, partiality, favouritism, bias, prejudice, discrimination.

inert adjective **1** *she lay inert in her bed*: **unmoving**, motionless, immobile, still, stock-still, stationary, static, dormant, sleeping; unconscious, out cold, comatose, lifeless, inanimate, insensible, senseless, insensate, insentient; inactive, idle, indolent, slack, lazy, loafing, slothful, dull, sluggish, lethargic, stagnant, languid, listless, torpid; unconcerned, apathetic, indifferent; informal dead to the world; French, archaic fainéant; rare soporose, soporous, otiose.
▷ANTONYMS moving; active.
2 *the inert gases in meteorites*: **chemically inactive**.

Word toolkit

inert	motionless	inactive
gas	body	duty
element	form	lifestyle
particle	water	members
placebo	traffic	children

inertia noun *he showed signs of lapsing into inertia*: **inactivity**, inaction, inactiveness, inertness, passivity, apathy, accidie, malaise, stagnation, dullness, enervation, sluggishness, lethargy, languor, languidness, listlessness, torpor, torpidity, idleness, indolence, laziness, sloth, slothfulness; motionlessness, immobility, lifelessness; French, archaic fainéance; rare stasis, otiosity, hebetude.
▷ANTONYMS activity; energy.

inescapable adjective *they concluded that political reform was inescapable*: **unavoidable**, inevitable, ineluctable, inexorable, assured, sure, certain, bound to happen, sure to happen, preordained, predestined, predetermined; necessary, required, compulsory, mandatory; rare ineludible.
▷ANTONYMS avoidable.

inessential adjective *he cut out the inessential details*: **unnecessary**, not necessary, not essential, non-essential, not needed, not required, unwanted, uncalled-for, needless, redundant, superfluous, excessive, excess, surplus, dispensable, expendable, optional, ornamental, cosmetic; unimportant, minor, secondary, peripheral; rare supererogatory.
▷ANTONYMS essential.

inestimable adjective *he believes the diet brings inestimable benefits*: **immeasurable**, incalculable, innumerable, unfathomable, fathomless, indeterminable, measureless, untold; limitless, boundless, unbounded, unlimited, illimitable, infinite, endless, never-ending, interminable, inexhaustible, bottomless; vast, immense, great, abundant; informal no end of; literary myriad; rare innumerous, unnumberable.
▷ANTONYMS few.

inevitable adjective *his resignation was inevitable*: **unavoidable**, inescapable, bound to happen, sure to happen, inexorable, assured, certain, for sure, sure, fated, predestined, predetermined, preordained, ineluctable; necessary, compulsory, required, obligatory, mandatory, prescribed; rare ineludible.
▷ANTONYMS avoidable; uncertain.

inevitably adverb *the poor crop will inevitably affect the price of the wine*: **naturally**, automatically, as a matter of course, necessarily, of necessity, by force of circumstance, inescapably, unavoidably, ineluctably, certainly, surely, definitely, incontrovertibly, undoubtedly; as a result, as a consequence, consequently, accordingly; Latin nolens volens; informal like it or not; formal perforce.

inexact adjective *his description of the procedure is inexact*: **imprecise**, not accurate, not exact, approximate, rough, crude, general, vague, hazy, woolly; incorrect, erroneous, wrong, false, fallacious, wide of the mark, off target, off, out, wanting, lacking; N. Amer. informal ballpark.
▷ANTONYMS exact.

inexcusable adjective *Geoffrey's behaviour was inexcusable*: **indefensible**, unjustifiable, unjustified, unwarrantable, unwarranted, unpardonable, unforgivable, inexpiable; blameworthy, censurable, reprehensible,

deplorable, unconscionable, outrageous, disgraceful, regrettable, unacceptable, unreasonable, unworthy; uncalled-for, unprovoked, gratuitous, without cause, without reason, without justification.
▷ANTONYMS excusable.

inexhaustible adjective **1** *her patience seemed inexhaustible*: **unlimited**, limitless, illimitable, without limit, infinite, unbounded, boundless, endless, never-ending, unending, without end, unfailing, everlasting, bottomless, measureless, immeasurable, incalculable, inestimable, untold; copious, abundant.
▷ANTONYMS limited.
2 *the dancers were inexhaustible*: **tireless**, indefatigable, untiring, unwearying, weariless, unfaltering, unfailing, unflagging, unwavering, unremitting, persevering, persistent, dogged.
▷ANTONYMS weary; lacking stamina.

inexorable adjective **1** *the inexorable advance of science*: **relentless**, unstoppable, unavoidable, inescapable, inevitable, irrevocable; persistent, continuous, non-stop, steady, unabating, interminable, incessant, unceasing, unending, unremitting, unrelenting.
2 *fifty debtors were detained by inexorable creditors*: **intransigent**, unbending, unyielding, inflexible, unswerving, unwavering, adamant, obdurate, determined, immovable, unshakeable, implacable, unappeasable, unpacifiable, unplacatable, unmollifiable, unforgiving, unsparing, uncompromising; strict, severe, iron-handed, stringent, harsh, hard, tough, exacting, rigorous, draconian, cruel, ruthless, relentless, unrelenting, pitiless, merciless, remorseless; rare indurate.

inexpedient adjective *it was inexpedient to antagonize these people*: **unadvisable**, injudicious, unwise, impolitic, imprudent, incautious, irresponsible, thoughtless, careless, foolhardy, foolish, silly, wrong-headed, short-sighted; ill-advised, ill-judged, ill-considered; undiplomatic, tactless, indiscreet, inappropriate; disadvantageous, detrimental, prejudicial, harmful, damaging.
▷ANTONYMS advisable; wise.

inexpensive adjective *a retail chain specializing in inexpensive furniture*: **cheap**, low-priced, low-price, low-cost, economical, economic, competitive, affordable, reasonable, reasonably priced, moderately priced, keenly priced, budget, economy, cheap and cheerful, bargain, cut-rate, cut-price, half-price, sale-price, sale, reduced, on special offer, marked down, discounted, discount, rock-bottom, giveaway; informal bargain-basement, slashed, going for a song, dirt cheap.
▷ANTONYMS expensive.

inexperience noun *his mistakes will be put down to youthful inexperience*: **ignorance**, unawareness, unenlightenment, lack of knowledge, lack of education; unworldliness, naivety, naiveness, innocence, rawness, freshness, greenness, immaturity; informal cluelessness; literary nescience.

inexperienced adjective *the new secretary was enthusiastic but inexperienced*: **inexpert**, unpractised, lacking experience, untrained, untutored, unschooled, unqualified, unskilled, amateur, uninitiated; uninformed, ignorant, unacquainted, unversed, unfledged, untried, unseasoned; naive, unsophisticated, callow, immature, fresh, green, raw; informal wet behind the ears, wide-eyed, out of one's depth, born yesterday.
▷ANTONYMS experienced.

inexpert adjective *the crane was manoeuvred by inexpert operators*: **unskilled**, unskilful, amateur, amateurish, unprofessional, untrained, unpractised, unqualified, inexperienced; inept, incompetent, maladroit, clumsy, awkward, bungling, bumbling, blundering, heavy-handed, unhandy; informal cack-handed, ham-fisted, ham-handed, butterfingered; Brit. informal all fingers and thumbs, all thumbs.
▷ANTONYMS expert.

inexplicable adjective *she had had an inexplicable change of heart*: **unaccountable**, unexplainable, incomprehensible, unfathomable, impenetrable, insoluble, unsolvable, baffling, puzzling, perplexing, mystifying, bewildering, mysterious, strange, weird, abstruse, enigmatic; beyond comprehension, beyond understanding; archaic wildering; rare insolvable.
▷ANTONYMS understandable.

inexpressible adjective *he felt inexpressible gratitude towards her*: **indescribable**, undefinable, unutterable, unspeakable, incommunicable, ineffable; beyond words, beyond description, beggaring description; unimaginable, inconceivable, unthinkable, untold, overwhelming, intense, profound.

inexpressive adjective *their faces were utterly inexpressive*: **expressionless**, unexpressive, impassive, inscrutable, unreadable, emotionless, blank, bland, vacant, empty, glazed, fixed, lifeless, inanimate, deadpan, wooden, stony; poker-faced, straight-faced.
▷ANTONYMS expressive.

inextinguishable adjective *he's known for his inextinguishable good humour*: **irrepressible**, unquenchable, imperishable, indestructible, undying, unfading, unfailing, unceasing, ceaseless, enduring, lasting, everlasting, eternal, persistent, incessant.

inextricable adjective **1** *the past and the present are inextricable*: **inseparable**, impossible to separate, indivisible, entangled, tangled, ravelled, mixed up, confused.
2 *an inextricable situation*: **inescapable**, impossible to escape from, unavoidable.

infallible adjective **1** *she had an infallible sense of timing*: **unerring**, error-free, unfailing, faultless, flawless, impeccable, perfect, true, uncanny, precise, accurate, meticulous, scrupulous; Brit. informal spot on; N. Amer. informal on the money.
2 *infallible cures for a variety of ailments*: **unfailing**, never failing, always effective, guaranteed, dependable, trustworthy, reliable, sure, certain, safe, sound, tried and tested, foolproof, effective, efficacious; informal sure-fire.

infamous adjective **1** *a portrait of an infamous mass murderer*: **notorious**, disreputable, ill-famed, of ill-repute; legendary, fabled, well-known.
▷ANTONYMS reputable.
2 *they disqualified the doctor for infamous misconduct*: **abominable**, outrageous, shocking, shameful, disgraceful, dishonourable, discreditable, unworthy, unprincipled, unscrupulous; monstrous, atrocious, appalling, dreadful, terrible, heinous, detestable, disgusting, loathsome, hateful, wicked, vile, base, unspeakable, unforgivable, iniquitous, criminal, odious, nefarious, scandalous; informal dirty, filthy, low-down; Brit. informal beastly; formal egregious, flagitious, exceptionable.
▷ANTONYMS honourable.

infamy noun **1** *these acts brought him fame and infamy*: **notoriety**, disrepute, disreputableness, ill repute, ill fame, loss of reputation, disgrace, discredit, shame, dishonour, ignominy, scandal, censure, blame, disapprobation, condemnation, contempt; humiliation, loss of face; rare disesteem.
▷ANTONYMS honour; anonymity.
2 *she was to be suitably punished for her infamy*: **wickedness**, evil, baseness, sordidness, vileness, iniquity, iniquitousness, depravity, degeneracy, turpitude, immorality, unscrupulousness, corruption, dissolution; sin, wrong, offence, violation, abuse, indignity.
▷ANTONYMS virtue.

infancy noun **1** *her two daughters died in infancy*: **babyhood**, early childhood; one's early years, one's early days.
▷ANTONYMS old age.
2 *the infancy of radio broadcasting*: **beginnings**, very beginnings, early days, early stages, seeds, roots; start, launch, debut, rise, emergence, outset, onset, dawn, dawning, birth, cradle, inception, conception, genesis; formal commencement.
▷ANTONYMS end.

infant noun *she picked up the fretful infant*: **baby**, newborn, young child, little child, little one; Scottish & N. English bairn, wean; informal tot, tiny tot, tiny, sprog; literary babe, babe in arms; technical neonate.
▶ adjective *the protection of infant industries*: **developing**, emergent, emerging, dawning, embryonic, nascent, new, fledgling, budding, burgeoning, growing, up-and-coming.

infantile adjective *he refused to play their infantile games*: **childish**, babyish, immature, puerile, juvenile, adolescent; silly, foolish, inane, fatuous, jejune.
▷ANTONYMS mature.

infantry noun *casualties were high among the infantry*: **infantrymen**, foot soldiers, foot guards; the ranks, the rank and file, cannon fodder; in the US GIs; Brit. informal Tommies; military slang infanteers, grunts; US informal, dated dogfaces, doughboys; historical footmen.

infatuated adjective *Sarah seemed to be* ***infatuated with*** *John*: **besotted**, in love, head over heels in love, hopelessly in love, obsessed, taken; passionate about, consumed with desire for, (greatly) enamoured of, very attracted to, devoted to, charmed by, captivated by, enchanted by, beguiled by, bewitched by, fascinated by, enraptured by, under the spell of, hypnotized by; informal smitten with, sweet on, keen on, gone on, mad about, wild about, crazy about, nuts about, potty about, stuck on, hung up on, turned on by, swept off one's feet by, bowled over by, carrying a torch for.

infatuation noun *he was aware of his brother's* ***infatuation with*** *Joan | an* ***infatuation with*** *motorcycles*: **passion for**, love for, adoration of, desire for, fondness for, feeling for, regard for, devotion to, penchant for, preoccupation with, obsession with, fixation with, craze for, mania for, addiction to; fancy, passing fancy; informal crush on, thing about, hang-up about; pash, puppy love, calf love; rare mash.
▷ANTONYMS indifference to.

infect verb **1** *people with HIV can infect their partners*: **pass infection to**, transmit infection to, spread disease to, contaminate; cause infection in, cause disease in.
2 *the nitrates were infecting more and more river systems*: **contaminate**, pollute, make impure, taint, foul, dirty, blight, spoil, mar, impair, damage, ruin; poison, radioactivate; rare vitiate.
▷ANTONYMS purify; disinfect.
3 *his high spirits often infect all those present*: **affect**, have an effect on, influence, have an impact on, impact on, touch, take hold of; excite, inspire, stimulate, animate.

infection noun **1** *she was treated for a kidney infection*: **disease**, virus, contagion; disorder, condition, affliction, problem, complaint, illness,

ailment, sickness, infirmity, indisposition; informal bug; Brit. informal lurgy.
2 *an attempt to reduce the infection in his head wounds*: **contamination**, poison; **septicity**, septicaemia, ulceration, suppuration, inflammation; germs, bacteria, microbes; technical sepsis.

infectious adjective **1** *the control of infectious disease by vaccination*: **contagious**, communicable, transmittable, transmissible, transferable, conveyable, spreadable, spreading; informal catching; technical epidemic, pandemic, epizootic; dated infective.
2 *infectious body fluids*: **contaminating**, germ-laden, polluting, pestilential, virulent; poisonous, toxic, noxious.
3 *her laughter is infectious*: **irresistible**, compelling; **contagious**, catching, spreading, communicable.

infelicitous adjective *his infelicitous use of certain phrases*: **unfortunate**, regrettable, unsuitable, inappropriate, inapposite, inapt, inadvisable, injudicious, untimely, inopportune; imprudent, incautious, indiscreet, indelicate, tactless, insensitive.
▷**ANTONYMS** felicitous; appropriate.

infelicity noun *I bear full responsibility for any infelicities in the text*: **mistake**, error, blunder, slip, lapse, solecism, misusage, impropriety.

infer verb *the judge inferred that the deceased was murdered*: **deduce**, reason, work out, conclude, come to the conclusion, draw the inference, conjecture, surmise, theorize, hypothesize; gather, understand, presume, assume, take it, come to understand, glean, extrapolate, reckon; read between the lines; N. Amer. figure; Brit. informal suss, suss out; archaic collect.

Easily confused words **infer or imply?**

Infer is often used as though it meant the same as **imply**, but the two are in fact quite distinct. To *infer* something is to work it out from a statement or other evidence that suggests or entails it but does not make it explicit (*if he gives no explanation of his action the court may infer that he had no good reason*). To *imply* something, on the other hand, is to allow it to be understood from what one says without making it explicit (*you implied that I was free to go*). *Infer* and *imply* can describe the same event of someone's deducing an unspoken message from a statement, but *infer* looks at it from the viewpoint of the person who does the interpreting, while *imply* looks at it from the viewpoint of the one conveying the message.

inference noun *the doctor's inference appears legitimate*: **deduction**, conclusion, reasoning, conjecture, speculation, surmise, thesis, theorizing, hypothesizing, presumption, assumption, supposition, reckoning, extrapolation, reading between the lines; guesswork, guessing; informal guesstimate; rare ratiocination.

inferior adjective **1** *they are regarded as inferior by other staff*: **lower in status**, lesser, second-class, second-fiddle, minor, subservient, lowly, humble, menial, not very important, not so important, below someone, beneath someone, under someone's heel; lower-ranking, lower in rank, subordinate, junior, secondary, subsidiary, ancillary.
▷**ANTONYMS** superior; senior.
2 *I had to put up with inferior accommodation*: **second-rate**, substandard, low-quality, low-grade, downmarket, indifferent, mediocre, unsatisfactory, shoddy, shabby, deficient, flawed, imperfect, unsound; poor, bad, awful, dreadful, disagreeable, deplorable, wretched, leaving much to be desired; informal grotty, crummy, dire, rotten, lousy, poxy, third-rate, God-awful, not up to much, not up to snuff, the pits; Brit. informal duff, rubbish, ropy, pants, a load of pants.
▷**ANTONYMS** first-rate, high quality.
▸ noun *how dare she treat him as an inferior?* **subordinate**, junior, underling, minion, menial.
▷**ANTONYMS** superior.

inferiority noun **1** *he was overcoming his feelings of inferiority*: **lowliness**, inferior status, inferior position, secondary status, secondary position, subordination, subservience, subjection, servitude.
▷**ANTONYMS** superiority.
2 *the inferiority of the goods they sold*: **shoddiness**, second-rateness, substandardness, unfitness, unsatisfactoriness, poorness, cheapness, mediocrity, indifference; imperfection, faultiness, deficiency; Brit. informal grottiness.

infernal adjective **1** *the infernal regions*: **of hell**, **hellish**, lower, nether, subterranean, underworld; Hadean, Plutonic, Plutonian, Stygian, Styxian, Tartarean, Acherontic, Avernal; rare chthonic, helly.
2 informal *you're an infernal nuisance*: **damned**, damn, damnable, wretched, accursed, rotten, horrible; annoying, irritating, infuriating, exasperating; informal flaming, blasted, blessed, dratted, cussed, pesky, pestiferous, pestilential, aggravating; Brit. informal blinking, bloody, bleeding, blooming, flipping, effing, chuffing; Austral./NZ informal plurry; Brit. informal, dated bally, ruddy, deuced, dashed, cursed; vulgar slang frigging, fucking.

infertile adjective **1** *their land has infertile, stony soil*: **barren**, non-fertile, unfruitful, unproductive, non-productive, uncultivatable, lifeless, sterile, impoverished, arid; rare unfructuous.
▷**ANTONYMS** fertile.
2 *she was infertile as a result of the illness*: **sterile**, barren; childless; Medicine infecund.
▷**ANTONYMS** fertile.

infest verb *a plague of field mice infested the housing estate*: **overrun**, spread through, take over, overspread, swarm over, crawl over, run riot over; invade, penetrate, infiltrate, pervade, permeate, inundate, overwhelm; beset, pester, plague.

infested adjective *her house is infested with cockroaches*: **overrun**, swarming, teeming, crawling, bristling, alive, ridden, infiltrated, permeated; plagued, beset; rare vermined.

infidel noun *a holy war against the infidels*: **unbeliever**, disbeliever, non-believer, heathen, pagan, idolater, idolatress, heretic, agnostic, atheist, nihilist, apostate, freethinker, libertine, dissenter, nonconformist; archaic paynim; rare nullifidian.

infidelity noun *her husband never knew of her infidelity*: **unfaithfulness**, adultery, unchastity, cuckoldry, extramarital relations, extramarital sex; faithlessness, disloyalty, falseness, breach of trust, treachery, double-dealing, duplicity, deceit, perfidy, perfidiousness; affair, liaison, intrigue, amour; informal fooling around, playing around, playing the field, cheating, two-timing, hanky-panky, a bit on the side; formal fornication.
▷**ANTONYMS** fidelity, faithfulness.

infiltrate verb **1** *he sought to infiltrate the smuggling operation*: **penetrate**, invade, intrude on, insinuate oneself into, worm one's way into, sneak into, slip into, creep into, impinge on, trespass on, butt into; informal gatecrash, muscle in on.
2 *mineral solutions infiltrate the rocks*: **permeate**, penetrate, pervade, filter through, percolate through, spread through, seep into, seep through, soak into, flow into, pass into, get into, enter.

infiltrator noun *the constant vigilance needed to outwit enemy infiltrators*: **spy**, agent, secret agent, undercover agent, operative, plant, intruder, interloper, subversive, informant, informer, mole, entrist, entryist; informal gatecrasher; N. Amer. informal spook; archaic intelligencer.

infinite adjective **1** *the universe is spatially infinite*: **boundless**, unbounded, unlimited, limitless, without limit, without end, never-ending, interminable; measureless, immeasurable, fathomless, unfathomed, bottomless; extensive, vast.
▷**ANTONYMS** limited.
2 *an infinite number of small birds*: **countless**, uncountable, inestimable, indeterminable, innumerable, numberless, immeasurable, incalculable, untold, very many; great, vast, enormous, immense, prodigious, multitudinous; rare innumerous, unnumberable.
▷**ANTONYMS** limited; small.
3 *she bathed the wound with infinite care*: **very great**, immense, supreme, absolute, total, real; endless, unending, unlimited; informal no end of.
▷**ANTONYMS** very little.

infinitesimal adjective *a tiny fish with infinitesimal white scales*: **minute**, tiny, minuscule, extremely small, very small; microscopic, nanoscopic, barely perceptible, imperceptible, inappreciable, indiscernible, invisible to the naked eye; Scottish wee; informal teeny, teeny-weeny, teensy-weensy, eensy-weensy, itsy-bitsy, itty-bitty, tiddly; Brit. informal titchy; N. Amer. informal little-bitty.
▷**ANTONYMS** huge.

infinity noun **1** *she stared out into the infinity of space*: **endlessness**, infinitude, infiniteness, boundlessness, limitlessness, unlimitedness, extensiveness, vastness, immensity; infinite distance.
2 *an infinity of different molecules*: **infinite number**, unlimited number, very great number, abundance, profusion, host, multitude, mass, wealth; informal heap, stack, ton; Brit. informal shedload.
▷**ANTONYMS** limited number.

Word links **infinity**

apeirophobia fear of infinity

infirm adjective *she looks after elderly and infirm people*: **frail**, weak, feeble, enfeebled, weakly, debilitated, decrepit, bedridden; ill, unwell, sick, sickly, poorly, indisposed, in poor/declining health, failing, ailing; doddering, doddery, tottering, wobbly, unsteady, unstable.
▷**ANTONYMS** strong, healthy.

infirmity noun **1** *they excused themselves on grounds of age and infirmity*: **frailty**, weakness, feebleness, enfeeblement, delicacy, fragility, debility, debilitation, decrepitude, disability, impairment; illness, sickness, indisposition, poor health, declining health; lameness, dodderiness, shakiness, unsteadiness, instability.
▷**ANTONYMS** strength, good health.
2 *the infirmities of old age*: **ailment**, malady, illness, disease, disorder, sickness, affliction, complaint, upset, condition, indisposition.
3 *he struggled throughout his life with his own infirmity of will*: **weakness**, hesitation, uncertainty, inconstancy; indecision, irresolution, irresoluteness, vacillation, fluctuation.
▷**ANTONYMS** strength, certainty.

inflame verb **1** *the play's impact inflames anti-Semitism*: **incite**, arouse, rouse, provoke, animate, stir up, work up, whip up, kindle, fire, ignite, touch off, foment, actuate, inspire; stimulate, agitate, spur on.
▷ANTONYMS dampen, calm.
2 *he made comments that inflamed what was already a sensitive situation*: **aggravate**, exacerbate, intensify, worsen, make worse, compound; add fuel to the flames, fan the flames, rub salt in the wound.
▷ANTONYMS soothe.
3 *his opinions so inflamed his rival that they came to blows*: **enrage**, incense, anger, infuriate, exasperate, madden, send into a rage, provoke, antagonize, rile, gall; informal make someone see red, make someone's blood boil, drive mad/crazy; rare empurple.
▷ANTONYMS placate.

inflamed adjective **1** *they treated her inflamed skin*: **swollen**, puffed up; **red**, reddened, raw, hot, burning, itchy, itching, chafing, smarting, stinging, angry, angry-looking; sore, painful, tender, sensitive; infected, festered, septic.
2 *her face was inflamed with rage*: **red**, flushed, high-coloured, burning, flaming, florid.

inflammable adjective *inflammable gases*: **flammable**, combustible, incendiary, explosive; unstable, volatile; rare burnable, ignitable, deflagrable.
▷ANTONYMS incombustible, fireproof, non-flammable.

inflammation noun *inflammation of the gums*: **swelling**, puffiness; redness, rawness, hotness, heat, burning, smarting, stinging; soreness, pain, painfulness, tenderness, sensitivity; infection, festering, eruption, suppuration, septicity.

inflammatory adjective **1** *an inflammatory lung condition*: **causing inflammation**, causing swelling; irritant; technical erythrogenic.
2 *a play containing inflammatory material*: **provocative**, provoking, inflaming, incendiary, inciting, agitating, stirring, rousing, instigative, fomenting; like a red rag to a bull; rabble-rousing, demagogic, hate-mongering, seditious, mutinous, revolutionary, rebellious, insurgent, anarchic; fiery, passionate, emotional, emotive; controversial, contentious.
▷ANTONYMS uncontroversial.

inflate verb **1** *we started to inflate the balloons | the mattress inflated*: **blow up**, **fill with air**, aerate, fill up, puff up, puff out, pump up; dilate, distend, swell.
▷ANTONYMS deflate.
2 *one effect of the demand for second homes was to inflate prices*: **increase**, raise, put up, boost, escalate, step up; informal hike up, jack up, bump up.
▷ANTONYMS decrease, depress.
3 *numbers have been greatly inflated by the local press*: **exaggerate**, magnify, pump up, overplay, overstate, dramatize, elaborate, enhance, embellish, touch up, blow up, blow up out of all proportion; increase, extend, amplify, augment, expand, intensify, swell; stretch the truth; informal make a big thing out of.
▷ANTONYMS play down, understate.

inflated adjective **1** *an inflated balloon*: **blown up**, aerated, filled, puffed up, puffed out, pumped up; dilated, distended, stretched, expanded, engorged, enlarged, swollen.
▷ANTONYMS deflated.
2 *consumers pay inflated food prices*: **increased**, raised, boosted; **high**, excessive, sky-high, unreasonable, unwarranted, disproportionate, prohibitive, outrageous, overinflated, exorbitant, extortionate; Brit. over the odds; informal over the top, OTT, steep.
▷ANTONYMS reduced, low.
3 *he had an inflated opinion of his worth*: **exaggerated**, magnified, aggrandized, unwarranted, immoderate, pumped up, overblown, overstated, overplayed.
▷ANTONYMS low, humble.
4 *inflated language*: **high-flown**, extravagant, exaggerated, elaborate, flowery, florid, ornate, overblown, overdone, overwrought, grandiloquent, magniloquent, grandiose, lofty, rhetorical, oratorical, verbose, affected, pretentious, turgid, bombastic, declamatory; informal windy, purple, highfalutin, la-di-da; rare fustian, euphuistic, orotund, tumid.
▷ANTONYMS plain, simple.

inflection noun **1** *these distinctions are often encoded in verbal inflections*: **conjugation**, declension; form, ending, case.
2 *his voice was completely without inflection*: **stress**, cadence, rhythm, accentuation, intonation, emphasis, modulation, metre, measure, rise and fall, swing, lilt, beat, change of pitch, change of tone, change of timbre.
3 technical *a point of inflection*: **curving**, curvature, bending, turning; curve, bend, turn, bow, crook, angle, arc, arch.

inflexible adjective **1** *the committee's inflexible attitude*: **stubborn**, obstinate, obdurate, intractable, intransigent, unbending, immovable, inexorable, unadaptable, unaccommodating; hidebound, set in one's ways, blinkered, single-minded, pig-headed, mulish; uncompromising, dogged, adamant, firm, resolute, diehard, steely, iron-willed, dyed-in-the-wool; formal refractory.
▷ANTONYMS flexible, accommodating.
2 *a landlady with inflexible house rules*: **unalterable**, unchangeable, unvarying, unwavering, unshakeable, entrenched; firm, fixed, set, established, hard and fast, uncompromising; stringent, rigorous, strict, severe, inexorable, immutable.
▷ANTONYMS flexible.
3 *an inflexible metal plate*: **rigid**, stiff, non-flexible, unyielding, unbending, unbendable, taut, hard, firm, inelastic; rare impliable, unmalleable.
▷ANTONYMS flexible, pliable.

inflict verb **1** *I came close to **inflicting** a serious injury **on** Frank*: **administer to**, deal out to, mete out to, serve out to, deliver to, apply to; lay, impose, exact, wreak; cause to, give to.
2 *I had no desire to inflict an alcoholic parent on my children*: **impose**, force, press, thrust, foist; saddle someone with, land someone with, lumber someone with, burden someone with.

infliction noun *there is no need for the infliction of pain on a horse*: **inflicting**, administering, administration, dealing out, meting out, serving out, delivering, application, applying; exaction, imposition, wreaking, perpetration.

influence noun **1** *the influence of parents on their children*: **effect**, impact; control, sway, hold, power, authority, ascendancy, mastery, domination, supremacy, leadership; guidance, direction, pressure.
2 *she has been denounced as a bad **influence on** young girls*: **example to/for**, exemplar for, role model for, model for, guide for, inspiration to.
3 *he had used his political influence in the firm's interests*: **power**, authority, sway, leverage, weight, standing, prestige, stature, rank, ranking, position, social position, station, connections, contacts; informal clout, pull, muscle, teeth; N. Amer. informal drag.
▶verb **1** *bosses can influence the careers of subordinates*: **affect**, have an effect on, exert influence on; determine, guide, control, form, shape, govern, decide, regulate; change, alter, modify, transform, impact on.
2 *an attempt to influence the jury*: **sway**, bias, affect, prejudice, colour, predispose, suborn; bring pressure to bear on, pressurize, coerce, lean on; informal pull strings with, twist someone's arm; Brit. informal nobble.
3 *some voters were influenced to change their allegiances*: **persuade**, convince, talk round, talk into, win over, bring round, sway, coax, induce, inveigle, impel, incite, entice, tempt, lure, cajole, manipulate, prompt; coerce, dragoon, intimidate, browbeat, brainwash.

influential adjective **1** *the most influential political organization on the continent*: **powerful**, authoritative, dominant, controlling, strong; **important**, prominent, predominant, leading, prestigious, distinguished, noteworthy.
▷ANTONYMS unimportant, insignificant.
2 *her school had been very influential in shaping her enthusiasm for physics*: **significant**, important, crucial, pivotal; instrumental, guiding, persuasive, inspiring.
▷ANTONYMS insignificant.

influx noun **1** *we have a large influx of tourists in the summer*: **inundation**, inrush, rush, stream, flood, incursion, ingress; invasion, intrusion.
2 *the lakes are fed by influxes of meltwater*: **inflow**, inrush, flood, inundation.

inform verb **1** *she informed him that she was ready to leave | we'll keep you informed of any new developments*: **tell**, let someone know, notify, apprise, advise, announce to, impart to, communicate to; brief, prime, enlighten, send word to, keep posted; informal put in the picture, fill in, clue in/up, give the low-down to.
2 *he **informed on** two well-known villains*: **denounce**, give away, betray, incriminate, inculpate, report, tell the authorities/police about; double-cross, sell out, stab in the back, be a Judas to, give someone a Judas kiss; English Law turn Queen's/King's evidence; informal rat, squeal, squeak, blab, split, tell, tell tales about, blow the whistle, spill the beans, put the finger on, sell down the river, nark, snitch, peach, stitch up, do the dirty on; Brit. informal grass, shop, sneak; Scottish informal clype; N. Amer. informal rat out, drop a/the dime on, finger, job; Austral./NZ informal dob, pimp, pool, shelf, put someone's pot on, point the bone at; rare delate.
3 *half of the articles were informed by feminism*: **suffuse**, pervade, permeate, infuse, imbue, saturate; illuminate, animate; characterize, typify.

informal adjective **1** *an informal discussion*: **casual**, relaxed, easy-going, natural, unceremonious, unofficial, non-formal, unstudied, unaffected; open, friendly, intimate; simple, unpretentious, easy; informal unstuffy, unbuttoned, chummy, pally, matey.
▷ANTONYMS formal, official.
2 *an informal speech style*: **colloquial**, vernacular, idiomatic, demotic, non-standard, popular, dialectal, non-literary; simple, natural, familiar, everyday, unofficial, unpretentious; informal slangy, chatty, folksy.
▷ANTONYMS formal, literary.
3 *the guys wore very informal clothes*: **casual**, relaxed, comfortable, everyday, sloppy, leisure; French sportif; informal comfy, laid-back, sporty.
▷ANTONYMS formal, smart.
4 *an informal job sector has developed*: **unofficial**, irregular, grey, black, back-door, illegal, illicit.

informality noun *the informality of the occasion | his genial informality*: **lack of ceremony**, casualness, unceremoniousness, non-formality,

unpretentiousness; homeliness, cosiness; **ease**, ease of manner, naturalness, relaxedness, approachability, accessibility.
▷ANTONYMS formality.

information noun *for further information write to the address below*: **details**, particulars, facts, figures, statistics, data; knowledge, intelligence; instruction, advice, guidance, direction, counsel, enlightenment; news, notice, word; material, documentation, documents; informal info, gen, the low-down, the dope, the inside story, the latest, bumf.

informative adjective *an informative booklet*: **instructive**, instructional, illuminating, enlightening, revealing, explanatory, telling, communicative, factual; educational, educative, edifying, didactic, improving; chatty, gossipy; informal newsy.

informed adjective *an informed society*: **knowledgeable**, enlightened, illuminated, literate, well informed, well educated, educated, schooled, instructed; sophisticated, cultured; well briefed, well versed, abreast of the facts, primed, up to date, up to speed, in the picture, in the know; French au courant, au fait; informal clued up, genned up, filled in, plugged in; Brit. informal switched-on, sussed; US black English down.
▷ANTONYMS ill-informed, ignorant.

informer noun *the police had a good network of informers*: **informant**; betrayer, traitor, Judas, collaborator, double-crosser, fifth columnist, double agent, spy, infiltrator, plant, turncoat; N. Amer. tattletale; informal rat, squealer, stool pigeon, stoolie, telltale, taleteller, whistle-blower, snake in the grass, canary, snitch, peacher; Brit. informal grass, supergrass, nark, snout, nose; Scottish informal clype; Scottish & N. Irish informal tout; N. Amer. informal fink; Austral./NZ informal fizgig, pimp, shelf; archaic intelligencer, beagle.

infraction noun *an infraction of the rules*: **infringement**, contravention, breach, violation, transgression, breaking; neglect, dereliction, non-observance, failure to observe, non-compliance; Law delict, contumacy.

infrequent adjective *his infrequent trips abroad*: **rare**, uncommon, unusual, exceptional, few and far between, few, like gold dust, as scarce as hens' teeth; unaccustomed, unwonted; isolated, scarce, thin on the ground, scattered; sporadic, irregular, intermittent, fitful; Brit. out of the common; N. Amer. sometime; informal once in a blue moon; dated seldom.
▷ANTONYMS frequent, common.

infringe verb **1** *the takeover bid infringed EU competition rules*: **contravene**, violate, transgress, break, breach, commit a breach of, disobey, defy, flout, fly in the face of, ride roughshod over, kick against; fail to comply with, fail to observe, disregard, take no notice of, ignore, neglect; go beyond, overstep, exceed; Law infract; informal cock a snook at.
▷ANTONYMS obey, comply with.
2 *such widespread surveillance could infringe personal liberties*: **undermine**, erode, diminish, weaken, impair, damage, compromise; limit, curb, check, place a limit on, encroach on, interfere with, disturb, disrupt.
▷ANTONYMS preserve, strengthen.
3 *he shall be restrained from ever infringing your territory*: **trespass on**, encroach on, impinge on, intrude on, enter, invade; barge in on, burst in on; archaic entrench on.

infringement noun **1** *an infringement of the law*: **contravention**, violation, transgression, breach, breaking, non-observance, non-compliance, neglect, dereliction, failure to observe; Law infraction, delict.
▷ANTONYMS compliance.
2 *an infringement of his liberty*: **undermining**, erosion, weakening, compromise; limitation, curb, check, encroachment, disruption, disturbance.
▷ANTONYMS preservation, strengthening.

infuriate verb *his arrogance was beginning to infuriate her*: **enrage**, incense, anger, madden, inflame, send into a rage, make someone's blood boil, stir up, fire up; **exasperate**, antagonize, provoke, rile, make one's hackles rise, annoy, irritate, nettle, gall, get on someone's nerves, rub up the wrong way, ruffle someone's feathers, try someone's patience, irk, vex, pique; N. Amer. rankle, ride; informal aggravate, make one see red, get someone's back up, get someone's dander up, get someone's goat, peeve, needle, get under someone's skin, get up someone's nose, hack off; Brit. informal wind up, get at, nark, get across, get on someone's wick, brown off, cheese off; N. Amer. informal bug, tick off, gravel; vulgar slang piss off.
▷ANTONYMS please; soothe.

infuriating adjective *his infuriating know-it-all attitude*: **exasperating**, maddening, provoking, annoying, irritating, irksome, vexing, vexatious, trying, tiresome, bothersome; informal aggravating, pesky, cussed, confounded, infernal, pestiferous, plaguy, pestilent.

infuse verb **1** *she was infused with a sense of exhilaration*: **fill**, pervade, permeate, suffuse, charge, saturate, imbue, inspire, inundate.
2 *his arrival infused new life and energy into the group*: **instil**, breathe, inject, impart, inculcate, introduce, implant, add.
3 *infuse the dried leaves in boiling water*: **steep**, brew, stew, soak, immerse, marinate, souse; Brit. informal mash.

ingenious adjective *an ingenious engineer | an ingenious solution*: **inventive**, creative, imaginative, original, innovative, resourceful, enterprising, insightful, inspired, perceptive, intuitive; clever, intelligent, bright, smart, brilliant, masterly, talented, gifted, skilful, capable; sharp, astute, sharp-witted, razor-sharp, quick, quick-witted, shrewd; elaborate, sophisticated, trailblazing, pioneering; informal on the ball, thinking outside the box.
▷ANTONYMS unimaginative.

ingenuity noun *considerable ingenuity must be employed in writing software*: **inventiveness**, creativity, imagination, originality, innovation, resourcefulness, enterprise, insight, inspiration, perceptiveness, perception, intuition, flair, finesse, artistry, genius; cleverness, intelligence, brilliance, mastery, talent, skill; sharpness, astuteness, acumen, acuity, sharp-wittedness, quick-wittedness, quickness, shrewdness; sophistication; informal thinking outside the box.

ingenuous adjective *he looked at her with wide, ingenuous eyes*: **naive**, innocent, simple, childlike, trusting, trustful, over-trusting, unwary, unsuspicious, unguarded, unsceptical, uncritical, unworldly, wide-eyed, inexperienced, green; open, sincere, honest, frank, candid, undeceitful; direct, forthright, artless, guileless, genuine, unaffected, unstudied, unsophisticated.
▷ANTONYMS disingenuous; artful.

Easily confused words **ingenuous or disingenuous?**

Although **ingenuous** is sometimes used as though it meant **disingenuous**, the words are almost opposite in meaning. *Ingenuous* means 'innocent, unsuspecting, and straightforward' (*his love for her was plain on his ingenuous face*). *Disingenuous*, on the other hand, means 'dishonest and devious', often suggesting that someone is concealing something (*the Minister's argument is disingenuous*). The confusion may be due partly to the similarity between *ingenuous* and *ingenious*, the idea being that concealment and insincerity call for clever planning.

Choose the right word **ingenuous, naive, artless**

See **naive**.

inglorious adjective *an inglorious retreat*: **shameful**, dishonourable, ignominious, discreditable, disgraceful, humiliating, mortifying, demeaning, shaming, ignoble, abject, unheroic, undignified, wretched, shabby; scandalous, shocking.
▷ANTONYMS glorious.

ingrain, engrain verb *societal norms were ingrained in his mind*: **entrench**, establish, fix, inculcate, instil, implant, root; drive home, hammer home, drill into, drive into, din into.

ingrained, engrained adjective **1** *his ingrained attitudes towards women*: **entrenched**, established, fixed, implanted, deep-rooted, rooted, deep-seated, settled, firm, unshakeable, ineradicable, driven in; inveterate, dyed-in-the-wool, abiding, enduring, stubborn, unfading; inbred, instinctive, intrinsic, gut.
▷ANTONYMS transient.
2 *the ingrained dirt on the flaking paintwork*: **ground-in**, fixed, infixed, planted, implanted, embedded; permanent, indelible, ineradicable, ineffaceable, inexpungible.
▷ANTONYMS superficial.

ingratiate verb
□ **ingratiate oneself** *he was determined to ingratiate himself with Stephen*: **curry favour with**, find the favour of, cultivate, win over, get on the good side of, get in someone's good books; toady to, crawl to, grovel to, fawn over, be obsequious towards, kowtow to, bow and scrape to, play up to, truckle to, pander to, be a yes man/woman to, be a sycophant to, flatter, court, dance attendance on; informal keep someone sweet, suck up to, rub up the right way, lick someone's boots.

ingratiating adjective *he sidled up to her with an ingratiating smile*: **sycophantic**, toadying, fawning, crawling, creeping, unctuous, obsequious, servile, submissive, Uriah Heepish; flattering, insincere; smooth, smooth-talking, smooth-tongued, honey-tongued, silver-tongued, slick, slippery; cloying, nauseating, sickening, greasy, oily, saccharine; wheedling, cajoling; informal smarmy, slimy, creepy, sucky, bootlicking; N. Amer. informal brown-nosing.

ingratitude noun *Harry was fuming at her ingratitude*: **ungratefulness**, thanklessness, unthankfulness, lack of gratitude, lack of appreciation, non-recognition.
▷ANTONYMS gratitude.

ingredient noun *investment is an essential ingredient of corporate success*: **constituent**, component, component part, element; part, piece, integral part, bit, section, strand, portion, unit, item, feature, aspect, attribute; (**ingredients**) contents, makings; rare integrant.

ingress noun **1** *two large doors offered ingress to the station*: **entry**, entrance, access, means of entry, admittance, admission; way in, approach, means of approach; right of entry.
▷ANTONYMS egress, exit.
2 *the joints are sealed against the ingress of water*: **seepage**, leakage, inundation, inrush, intrusion, incursion, entry, entrance.

inhabit verb *some thirty or forty huts, inhabited by 200 or 300 people*: **live in**, occupy; settle in, settle, people, populate, colonize, make one's home in, set up home in; dwell in, reside in, tenant, lodge in, have one's home in, be an inhabitant of, be established in, be ensconced in; formal be domiciled in, abide in.

inhabitable adjective *an inhabitable apartment*: **habitable**, fit to live in, fit to occupy, usable, liveable-in, suitable for residential use; formal tenantable.
▷ANTONYMS uninhabitable.

inhabitant noun *the inhabitants of the village*: **resident**, occupant, occupier, dweller, settler; local, native; (**inhabitants**) population, populace, people, public, community, citizenry, folk, townsfolk, townspeople; humorous denizen, burgher; rare residentiary, habitant, oppidan, indweller.

inhale verb *he inhaled smoke deeply*: **breathe in**, draw in, suck in, sniff in, gasp, gulp, inspire, drink in; rare inbreathe.
▷ANTONYMS exhale, expire.

inharmonious adjective **1** *inharmonious sounds*: **unmelodious**, unharmonious, unmusical, tuneless, discordant, dissonant, off-key; harsh, grating, jarring, jangling, cacophonous, screeching, raucous, strident; rare horrisonant, absonant.
▷ANTONYMS harmonious, musical.
2 *the inharmonious modern building on the south of the square*: **out of place**, unsuitable, inappropriate, ill suited, clashing, conflicting, incompatible, mismatched, ill-matched, contradictory, irreconcilable, jarring, discordant.
▷ANTONYMS harmonious, fitting.
3 *a family whose relationships are inharmonious*: **antagonistic**, quarrelsome, argumentative, disputatious, captious, cantankerous, confrontational, belligerent, bellicose, combative.
▷ANTONYMS harmonious, congenial.

inherent adjective *his belief in the inherent goodness of man*: **intrinsic**, innate, immanent, built-in, inborn, ingrained, deep-rooted; essential, fundamental, basic, implicit, structural, characteristic, organic; inseparable, permanent, indelible, ineradicable, ineffaceable, inexpungible; natural, instinctive, instinctual, congenital, native; rare connate, connatural.
▷ANTONYMS acquired; alien.

> *Choose the right word* **inherent, intrinsic, essential, innate**
>
> These words are all applied to qualities or features that are a central element in something's or someone's nature.
>
> **Inherent** is typically used to qualify words having negative connotations (*any form of mountaineering has its inherent dangers* | *the anti-male sexism inherent in some areas of child care*). It tends to be used as a warning, indicating the undesirable features or consequences of something.
>
> **Intrinsic** is a more general term for an element regarded as central to something's nature. A feature or quality described as *intrinsic* is typically either neutral or good (*access to the arts is intrinsic to a high quality of life*). *Intrinsic* is often used to emphasize that something possesses a quality in its own right, not through external or incidental factors (*the analysis is worthwhile because of its intrinsic interest*).
>
> An **essential** feature of someone or something is one that is so important to their nature that without it they would not be the same person or thing (*ensuring that others have their turn is an essential feature of citizenship* | *human expertise is essential to any organization*). Something may therefore be defined or summarized by reference to an *essential* element (*his essential point is that those who hold information hold power*). *Essential* may be used to suggest that a characteristic is in fact fundamental to someone, even if more superficial characteristics conceal or contradict it (*a belief in the essential goodness of human nature*).
>
> An **innate** characteristic is literally one with which someone is born, contrasted with one that is acquired at some later stage in life (*everything speaks of innate good taste* | *students with innate ability*). *Innate* is also used in a weakened sense of 'great' or 'deep-seated' (*he had an innate respect for a fellow professional sportsman*).

inherit verb **1** *she inherited her uncle's farm*: **become heir to**, fall heir to, come into/by, be bequeathed, be left, be willed; Law be devised.
2 *his older brother inherited the title*: **succeed to**, accede to, assume, take over, come into; be elevated to, have conferred on one.

inheritance noun **1** *he came into a comfortable inheritance*: **legacy**, bequest, endowment, birthright, estate, heritage, bestowal, bequeathal, benefaction, provision, patrimony; Law devise, hereditament.
2 *his inheritance of the title*: **succession to**, accession to, assumption of, taking over of, elevation to.

> *Word links* **inheritance**
>
> **hereditary** relating to inheritance

inheritor noun **heir**, **heiress**, legatee, recipient, receiver; successor, next in line; Law devisee, grantee, parcener, coparcener, cestui que trust; Scottish Law heritor.

inhibit verb **1** *the obstacles which inhibit change*: **impede**, hinder, hamper, hold back, discourage, interfere with, obstruct, put a brake on, slow, slow down, retard; curb, check, suppress, repress, restrict, restrain, constrain, bridle, rein in, shackle, fetter, cramp, baulk, frustrate, arrest, stifle, smother, prevent, block, thwart, foil, quash, stop, halt, put an end/stop to, nip in the bud.
▷ANTONYMS assist, encourage.
2 *no one need feel inhibited from taking part*: **prevent**, disallow, exclude, forbid, prohibit, preclude, ban, bar, debar, interdict, proscribe.
▷ANTONYMS allow.

inhibited adjective *older people are sometimes inhibited about discussing the past*: **shy**, reticent, self-conscious, reserved, diffident, bashful, coy, embarrassed, uneasy, wary, reluctant, uncomfortable, hesitant, apprehensive, nervous, insecure; unconfident, unassertive, timid, timorous, subdued, withdrawn, tongue-tied; repressed, constrained, restrained, undemonstrative; informal uptight, hung up.
▷ANTONYMS uninhibited; extrovert.

inhibition noun **1** (usually **inhibitions**) *not everyone managed to overcome their inhibitions*: **shyness**, reticence, self-consciousness, reserve, diffidence, bashfulness, coyness, embarrassment, unease, wariness, reluctance, discomfort, hesitance, hesitancy, apprehension, nerves, nervousness, insecurity; lack of confidence, unassertiveness, timidity, timorousness; repression, restraint, constraint, reservation, mental block, psychological block; informal hang-up.
2 *the inhibition of news publishing by libel laws*: **hindrance**, hampering, holding back, discouragement, obstruction, impediment, retardation; curbing, checking, suppression, repression, restriction, restraint, constraint, bridling, shackling, fettering, cramping, baulking, frustration, arrest, stifling, smothering, prevention, blocking, thwarting, foiling, quashing, stopping, halting, putting an end/stop to, nipping in the bud; curb, check, bar, barrier, straitjacket.
▷ANTONYMS encouragement, promotion.

inhospitable adjective **1** *the inhospitable landscape*: **uninviting**, unwelcoming; bleak, lonely, empty, forbidding, cheerless, hostile, harsh, inimical; uninhabitable, barren, bare, sterile, desolate, austere, severe, stark, spartan.
2 *forgive me if I seem inhospitable, but I'm very busy*: **unwelcoming**, unfriendly, unsociable, unsocial, antisocial, unneighbourly, uncongenial, cool, cold, chilly, frosty, glacial, aloof, stand-offish, haughty, disdainful, distant, remote, indifferent, offhand; uncivil, discourteous, ungracious; ungenerous, unkind, unsympathetic, ill-disposed; hostile, inimical, xenophobic.
▷ANTONYMS hospitable, welcoming.

inhuman adjective **1** *the inhuman treatment meted out to political prisoners*: **cruel**, harsh, inhumane, brutal, callous, sadistic, severe, savage, vicious, barbaric, barbarous; bestial, monstrous, fiendish, diabolical, evil, wicked, heinous; merciless, ruthless, pitiless, unpitying, remorseless, cold-blooded, heartless, hard-hearted, stone-hearted, with a heart of stone, unforgiving; unkind, unkindly, inconsiderate, unsympathetic, unfeeling, uncaring; informal hard-boiled, hard-nosed; Brit. informal, dated beastly; archaic dastardly, sanguinary; rare egregious, flagitious.
▷ANTONYMS humane, compassionate.
2 *the macabre, inhuman vampires of old films*: **non-human**, non-mortal, monstrous, devilish, demonic, demoniac, ghostly; subhuman, animal; strange, odd, bizarre, unearthly.
▷ANTONYMS human.

inhumane adjective *torture and inhumane treatment are banned in this country*: **cruel**, harsh, brutal, callous, sadistic, severe, savage, vicious, barbaric, barbarous; bestial, monstrous, inhuman, fiendish, diabolical, evil, wicked, heinous; merciless, ruthless, pitiless, unpitying, remorseless, cold-blooded, heartless, hard-hearted, stone-hearted, with a heart of stone, unforgiving; unkind, unkindly, inconsiderate, unsympathetic, unfeeling, uncaring; informal hard-boiled, hard-nosed; Brit. informal, dated beastly; archaic dastardly, sanguinary; rare egregious, flagitious.
▷ANTONYMS humane, compassionate.

inhumanity noun *the vicious inhumanity of the apartheid system*: **cruelty**, harshness, brutality, callousness, sadism, severity, savagery, viciousness, barbarity, barbarism; bestiality, monstrousness, fiendishness, evil, evilness, wickedness, heinousness; mercilessness, ruthlessness, pitilessness, remorselessness, cold-bloodedness, heartlessness, hard-heartedness, stone-heartedness, unforgivingness; unkindness, unkindliness, inconsiderateness, uncaringness, lack of compassion, lack of feeling, lack of sympathy; Brit. informal, dated beastliness; archaic dastardliness; rare egregiousness, flagitiousness.
▷ANTONYMS humanity, compassion.

inhumation noun **1** *cremation took over from inhumation as the dominant burial rite*: **burial**, burying, interment, committal, entombment, laying to rest, consignment to the grave; rare sepulture, exequies.
▷ANTONYMS exhumation.
2 *the burial chamber contained two inhumations*: **corpse**, body, dead body, cadaver, carcass, skeleton; remains, relics; archaic corse.

inhume verb literary *no hand his bones shall gather or inhume*. See **bury** (sense 1).

inimical adjective **1** *party politics are inimical to genuine democracy*: **harmful**, injurious, detrimental, deleterious, pernicious, damaging, hurtful, dangerous, destructive, ruinous, calamitous; antagonistic, contrary, antipathetic, unfavourable, adverse, opposed, hostile, at odds, not conducive, prejudicial; literary malefic, maleficent.
▷ANTONYMS helpful, advantageous.
2 *he fixed her with an inimical gaze*: **hostile**, unfriendly, antagonistic, ill-disposed, unkind, unsympathetic, malevolent, malign; inhospitable, unwelcoming, cold, icy, frosty, glacial.
▷ANTONYMS friendly, warm.

inimitable adjective *in his own inimitable style he provides sound advice*: **unique**, distinctive, individual, special, idiosyncratic, quirky, exclusive, rare; incomparable, unparalleled, unrivalled, matchless, unmatched, peerless, unequalled, unsurpassed, unsurpassable, superlative, supreme, without equal, without match, beyond compare, beyond comparison, second to none, in a class of one's own; model, faultless, perfect, consummate, ideal, unexampled, nonpareil.

iniquitous adjective **1** *we protest against this iniquitous decision*: **wicked**, sinful, evil, immoral, improper; villainous, criminal, heinous, nefarious; vile, foul, base, odious, abominable, execrable, atrocious, dreadful, egregious, malicious; outrageous, monstrous, obscene, intolerable, shocking, scandalous, reprehensible; unjust, unfair; Law malfeasant; humorous dastardly; archaic facinorous.
▷ANTONYMS good.
2 *his iniquitous uncle*: **dishonourable**, unprincipled; wicked, evil, criminal, lawless; degenerate, corrupt, reprobate, immoral, dissolute; devilish, diabolical, fiendish; informal crooked; archaic blackguardly.
▷ANTONYMS virtuous.

iniquity noun **1** *the iniquity of his conduct*: **wickedness**, sinfulness, immorality, impropriety, vice, evil, sin; villainy, criminality, crime, heinousness, nefariousness, knavery; vileness, foulness, baseness, odiousness, atrociousness, dreadfulness, egregiousness; outrageousness, outrage, monstrousness, obscenity, reprehensibility; ungodliness, godlessness, impiety, devilry.
▷ANTONYMS goodness, virtue.
2 *I will forgive their iniquity*: **sin**, crime, transgression, wrongdoing, wrong, offence, injury, vice, violation, atrocity, outrage.
▷ANTONYMS virtue.

initial adjective *we are at the initial stages*: **beginning**, opening, commencing, starting, inceptive, embryonic, fledgling; first, early, earliest, prime, primary; preliminary, elementary, foundational, preparatory, rudimentary; introductory, inaugural, incipient, inchoate; pilot, test, trial.
▷ANTONYMS final.
▶ noun *the initials stand for the State Earnings Related Pension*: **initial letter**, beginning letter; (**initials**) **abbreviation**, acronym, initialism.
▶ verb **1** *he initialled the three warrants*: **put one's initials on**, sign, countersign, autograph, endorse, put one's mark on, inscribe, superscribe, witness; archaic underwrite.
2 *Greece and the United States initialled a new agreement*: **ratify**, accept, approve, agree to, consent to, authorize, validate, recognize.
▷ANTONYMS reject, repeal.

initially adverb *initially, Steve cleared tables and washed up*: **at first**, at the start, at the outset, in/at the beginning, to begin with, to start with, originally, in the early stages, in the first instance.
▷ANTONYMS finally, in the end.

initiate verb **1** *the government has initiated an extensive programme*: **begin**, start off, commence, take action on, usher in; **institute**, inaugurate, put in place, launch, open, instigate, bring about, get under way, set in motion, trigger off, actuate; establish, set up, lay the foundations of, lay the first stone of, lay the cornerstone of, sow the seeds of, start the ball rolling; originate, pioneer; informal get cracking on, get going on, kick off.
▷ANTONYMS complete, finish.
2 *he had been newly initiated into a cult*: **introduce**, admit, let, induct, install, instate, incorporate, ordain, invest, enlist, enrol, recruit, sign up, swear in; convert.
▷ANTONYMS expel.
3 *they were* **initiated into** *the mysteries of mathematics*: **teach about**, instruct in, coach in, tutor in, school in, train in, drill in, prime in, ground in, familiarize with, acquaint with, make conversant with, make aware of; indoctrinate, inculcate; informal break someone in, show someone the ropes.
▶ noun *an initiate in the cult of an Egyptian god*: **novice**, starter, beginner, newcomer; learner, student, pupil, trainee, apprentice, probationer; new boy, new girl, new recruit, raw recruit, recruit, tyro, neophyte; member; Christianity postulant, novitiate; informal rookie, new kid (on the block), newie, newbie; N. Amer. informal greenhorn.

initiation noun **1** *the initiation of a programme to privatize state monopolies*: **beginning**, starting, commencement; institution, inauguration, launch, opening, instigation, actuation, origination, devising, inception; establishment, setting up; informal kick-off.
▷ANTONYMS completion, finish.
2 *a rite of initiation into the tribe*: **induction**, introduction, admission, admittance, installation, incorporation, ordination, investiture, investment, enlistment, enrolment, recruitment; baptism.
▷ANTONYMS expulsion.

initiative noun **1** *interviewers are looking for enthusiasm and initiative*: **enterprise**, inventiveness, resourcefulness, capability; imagination, imaginativeness, ingenuity, originality, creativity; drive, dynamism, ambition, ambitiousness, motivation, spirit, verve, dash, energy, vitality, vigour, leadership, vision; informal get-up-and-go, zing, push, pep, zip, punch, pizzazz.
▷ANTONYMS unimaginativeness.
2 *he had lost the initiative*: **advantage**, upper hand, edge, lead, whip hand, trump card; first step, first move, first blow, opening move, opening gambit, gambit; beginning, start, commencement.
3 *a recent initiative on recycling*: **plan**, scheme, strategy, stratagem, measure, technique, proposal, step, action, act, manoeuvre, gambit; approach, tack, tactic; French démarche.

inject verb **1** *the doctor was about to inject a dose of codeine*: **administer**, introduce; administer a drug to; inoculate, vaccinate; drug-users' slang shoot, shoot up, mainline, fix (up), pop.
2 *a pump which injects air into the compartment*: **insert**, introduce, place, push, force, drive, shoot, feed.
3 *he injected new life and enthusiasm into the department*: **introduce**, instil, bring in, infuse, imbue, inculcate, breathe.

injection noun **1** *an anti-tetanus injection*: **inoculation**, vaccination, vaccine, immunization, booster, dose; informal jab, shot, hype; drug-users' slang fix, hit, pop.
2 *the injection of adrenalin into the circulation*: **administration**, introduction.
3 *the injection of a note of enthusiasm can alter the whole tenor of a meeting*: **introduction**, instilling, infusion, imbuing, inculcation.

injudicious adjective *he will probably pay dearly for his injudicious comments*: **imprudent**, unwise, inadvisable, ill-advised, misguided; ill-considered, ill-judged, incautious, hasty, rash, spur-of-the-moment, unguarded, foolish, foolhardy, hare-brained, hot-headed; indiscreet, tactless, inappropriate, unsuitable, wrong, wrong-headed; impolitic, inexpedient, undesirable; informal dumb.
▷ANTONYMS judicious, prudent.

> *Choose the right word* **injudicious, unwise, imprudent, ill-advised**
>
> See **unwise**.

injunction noun *a High Court injunction to prevent Sunday trading*: **order**, ruling, direction, directive, command, instruction, demand; decree, edict, prescription, dictum, dictate, fiat, mandate, ordainment, enjoinment, exhortation, admonition, precept, ultimatum; in Tsarist Russia ukase; rare monition, firman, decretal, irade.

injure verb **1** *she was injured in a road accident | he injured his foot*: **hurt**, wound, harm, damage, disable; maim, mutilate, deform, mangle, crush, shatter, smash, break, do mischief to; Brit. informal knacker; archaic scathe.
▷ANTONYMS heal.
2 *she worried that her son would injure his health by overstudy*: **harm**, damage, impair, undermine, diminish, impede, weaken, enfeeble; have a bad effect on, have a negative effect on, do harm to; rare vitiate.
3 *a libel calculated to injure the company's reputation*: **damage**, mar, spoil, ruin, blight, blemish, besmirch, tarnish, blacken.
4 *I have injured no one save myself by my folly*: **wrong**, do an injury to, do an injustice to, offend against, be detrimental to; abuse, maltreat, mistreat, ill-treat, treat badly, ill-use; informal do the dirty on.

injured adjective **1** *an injured player | his injured arm*: **hurt**, wounded, harmed, sore, damaged, bruised, on the sick list, disabled; maimed, mutilated, deformed, mangled, crushed, shattered, smashed, broken, fractured; Brit. informal knackered, gammy; Austral./NZ informal crook; dated game.
▷ANTONYMS healthy, fit.
2 *they were required to render compensation to the injured party*: **wronged**, offended, abused, maltreated, mistreated, ill-treated, ill-used, harmed; defamed, vilified, maligned, insulted, dishonoured, impugned, denigrated.
▷ANTONYMS offending.
3 *'No doubt you would' she replied in an injured tone*: **upset**, hurt, wounded, reproachful, offended, piqued, pained, aggrieved; unhappy, cut to the quick, put out, disgruntled, displeased.

injurious adjective *food which is injurious to health*: **harmful**, damaging, deleterious, detrimental, hurtful, dangerous; disadvantageous, unfavourable, undesirable, adverse, inimical, unhealthy, unwholesome, destructive, pernicious, malignant; literary malefic, maleficent.
▷ANTONYMS favourable.

injury noun **1** *he was taken to hospital with minor injuries*: **wound**, bruise, cut, gash, tear, rent, slash, gouge, scratch, graze, laceration, abrasion, contusion, lesion, sore; technical trauma.
2 *they are reasonably safe from personal injury*: **harm**, hurt, wounding, damage, pain, suffering, impairment, affliction, disablement, incapacity,

disability; disfigurement.
3 *compensation for injury to feelings*: **offence**, abuse; wrong, wrongdoing, injustice, disservice, grievance; affront, insult, slight, snub, indignity, slap in the face, outrage.

> *Word links* **injury**
>
> **traumatophobia** fear of injury

injustice noun **1** *he was protesting at the injustice of the world*: **unfairness**, unjustness, inequity, corruption; cruelty, brutality, tyranny, despotism, repression, suppression, exploitation; bias, prejudice, bigotry, favouritism, partiality, one-sidedness, discrimination, partisanship, intolerance.
▷ANTONYMS justice.
2 *his sacking was an injustice*: **wrong**, injury, offence, unjust act, evil, villainy, crime, sin, iniquity, misdeed, outrage, atrocity, scandal, disgrace, monstrosity, affront, grievance.

inkling noun *I had an inkling of what was going on | they had no inkling of his intentions*: **idea**, vague idea, notion, glimmering; sense, impression, suggestion, indication, whisper, suspicion, sneaking suspicion, fancy, hunch; knowledge, slight knowledge; hint, clue, intimation, sign, pointer, insinuation, innuendo; Brit. informal the foggiest idea, the foggiest, the faintest idea, the faintest.

inky adjective *the inky darkness of the tunnel*: **black**, jet-black, jet, pitch-black, pitch-dark, pitch, black as pitch, coal-black, black as night, sable, ebony, dark; literary Stygian, Cimmerian;

i

inlaid adjective *a plaque inlaid with mother of pearl | an inlaid mahogany sideboard*: **inset**, set, enchased, ornamented, decorated, studded, lined, panelled, tiled; tessellated, mosaic, intarsia, marquetry, parquetry; rare damascened, empaestic.

inland adjective **1** *we enjoyed exploring the inland areas*: **interior**, non-coastal, central, inshore, internal, upcountry.
▷ANTONYMS coastal.
2 *inland trade*: **domestic**, internal, home, local.
▷ANTONYMS international, foreign.
▶ adverb *the goods were carried inland by barges*: **towards the interior**, away from the coast.

inlet noun **1** **arm of the sea**, cove, bay, bight, creek, estuary, fjord, sound; in Orkney & Shetland voe; Scottish **firth**, **sea loch**; technical ria; rare **fleet**, armlet.
2 *a fresh air inlet*: **vent**, flue, shaft, conduit, duct, channel, pipe, pipeline, passage, tube.
▷ANTONYMS outlet.

inmate noun **1** *the inmates of the hospital*: **patient**, inpatient, hospital case; convalescent; resident, inhabitant, occupant.
2 *the prison's 1,300 inmates*: **prisoner**, convict, captive, detainee, internee; informal jailbird, con; Brit. informal lag; N. Amer. informal **yardbird**.

inmost adjective See **innermost**.

inn noun **tavern**, bar, hostelry, taproom; hotel, guest house; Brit. pub, public house; Scottish **howff**; Canadian **beer parlour**; informal **watering hole**; historical alehouse, pot-house, taphouse, beerhouse.

innards plural noun informal *he scales the fish and removes the innards*: **entrails**, internal organs, vital organs, viscera, intestines, bowels, guts; informal insides; Brit. archaic **numbles**.

innate adjective *people differ in terms of their innate abilities*: **inborn**, natural, inbred, congenital, inherent, intrinsic, instinctive, intuitive, spontaneous, unlearned, untaught; hereditary, inherited, in the blood, in the family; quintessential, organic, essential, basic, fundamental, constitutional, built-in, inbuilt, ingrown, deep-rooted, deep-seated; rare connate, connatural.
▷ANTONYMS acquired.

> *Choose the right word* **innate, inherent, intrinsic, essential**
>
> See **inherent**.

inner adjective **1** *she lives in inner London*: **central**, innermost, mid, middle, interior, nuclear; the centre of, the middle of, the heart of.
▷ANTONYMS outer.
2 *the major went to close the inner gates*: **internal**, interior, inside, inmost, innermost, intramural.
▷ANTONYMS external, outer.
3 *the inner circle of the Imperial court*: **privileged**, restricted, exclusive, secret, private, confidential, intimate.
▷ANTONYMS outer.
4 *a reinterpretation of the inner meaning of the Christian faith*: **unapparent**, veiled, obscure, esoteric, hidden, secret, unrevealed; deep, profound, underlying.
▷ANTONYMS apparent.
5 *the uniqueness of an individual's inner life*: **mental**, intellectual, psychological, psychic, spiritual, emotional; of the mind, of the heart; rare psychical, mindly.

innermost, inmost adjective **1** *the innermost shrine of the Temple*: **central**, middle, internal, interior; furthest in, deepest within.
2 *she was ashamed to reveal her innermost feelings*: **deepest**, deep, deep-seated, profound, inward, underlying, intimate, private, personal, secret, hidden, veiled, masked, concealed, unexpressed, unrevealed, unapparent; true, real, honest; informal bottled up.

innkeeper noun archaic **landlord**, **landlady**, hotelier, hotel owner, hotel keeper, proprietor, manager, manageress, host; publican, pub owner, licensee, barman, barmaid, barperson, barkeeper, restaurateur; archaic alewife.

innocence noun **1** *the accused protested his innocence*: **guiltlessness**, blamelessness, freedom from guilt, freedom from blame, irreproachability, clean hands.
▷ANTONYMS guilt.
2 *they questioned the innocence of our motives*: **harmlessness**, innocuousness, lack of malice, inoffensiveness.
3 *the youthfulness and innocence of his bride*: **virginity**, chastity, chasteness, purity, lack of sin, sinlessness, impeccability, spotlessness; virtue, virtuousness, integrity, honour, righteousness, morality, decency, wholesomeness; Christianity **immaculateness**.
4 *he had taken advantage of Isabel's innocence*: **naivety**, naiveness, ingenuousness, credulity, credulousness, trustfulness, inexperience, gullibility, simpleness, simplicity, unworldliness, lack of experience, lack of sophistication, guilelessness, greenness, childlikeness.
▷ANTONYMS experience.

innocent adjective **1** *the police realized he was entirely innocent*: **guiltless**, guilt-free, not guilty, blameless, not to blame, in the clear, unimpeachable, irreproachable, above suspicion, beyond criticism, without fault, faultless; honourable, honest, upright, upstanding, law-abiding, incorrupt; informal squeaky clean.
▷ANTONYMS guilty.
2 *the game was nothing but innocent fun*: **harmless**, innocuous, safe, non-injurious, unobjectionable, inoffensive, playful.
3 *they pick on nice innocent girls*: **virtuous**, pure, sinless, free of sin, moral, decent, righteous, upright, wholesome, demure, modest, chaste, virginal, virgin, impeccable, pristine, spotless, stainless, unblemished, unsullied, incorrupt, uncorrupted, uncontaminated, undefiled; informal squeaky clean, whiter than white, as pure as the driven snow; Christianity **immaculate**.
▷ANTONYMS sinful.
4 *she is genuinely **innocent of** guile*: **free from**, without, lacking (in), empty of, clear of, unacquainted with, ignorant of, unaware of, unfamiliar with, untouched by; rare **nescient of**.
5 *he took advantage of innocent foreigners*: **naive**, ingenuous, trusting, trustful, over-trusting, credulous, unsuspicious, unsuspecting, unwary, unguarded, unsceptical, impressionable, gullible, easily deceived, easily taken in, easily led; inexperienced, unworldly, unsophisticated, green, wide-eyed; simple, artless, guileless, childlike, frank, open; informal wet behind the ears, born yesterday, as green as grass.
▷ANTONYMS worldly.
6 *innocent tumours made up of blood vessels*: **benign**, non-cancerous, non-malignant, non-dangerous, harmless, not life-threatening; curable, remediable, treatable; technical **benignant**.
▷ANTONYMS malignant.
▶ noun *I was an innocent let loose in a strange land*: **unworldly person**, naive person; child; novice, greenhorn; French ingénue; literary babe in arms, babe.

> *Choose the right word* **innocent, blameless, guiltless**
>
> **Innocent** is the most general word for someone who has not done wrong. It can be used, both generally and as a legal term, to declare someone not responsible for a particular wrongful act (*fabricating evidence against men whom they know to be innocent*). More generally, it indicates that someone has no malicious intentions or is not corrupt. It is often used to suggest the unfairness of harm done to people who have not harmed anyone themselves (*the innocent victims of the conflict*).
>
> **Blameless** is a more unusual word, which typically refers to a general way of life that does not lay someone open to reproach of any kind (*they have all three led blameless lives*).
>
> **Guiltless** is also not a very common word, It can indicate an absence of actual guilt (*Isabelle was guiltless: I was to blame for everything*) or an absence of any guilty feeling (*lavish menus for those who enjoy guiltless eating*).

innocuous adjective **1** *an innocuous fungus that grows on trees*: **harmless**, safe, non-dangerous, non-poisonous, non-toxic, non-irritant, non-injurious, innocent; edible, eatable, wholesome; rare innoxious.
▷ANTONYMS harmful.
2 *an innocuous young man | an innocuous comment*: **inoffensive**, unobjectionable, unexceptionable, unoffending, harmless, mild, peaceful, gentle, tame, insipid; anodyne, bland, unremarkable, commonplace, run-of-the-mill.
▷ANTONYMS obnoxious.

innovation noun *they favoured the traditional approach and resisted innovation*: **change**, alteration, revolution, upheaval, transformation, metamorphosis, reorganization, restructuring, rearrangement, recasting, remodelling, renovation, restyling, variation; **new measures**, new methods, new devices, novelty, newness, unconventionality, modernization, modernism; a break with tradition, a shift of emphasis, a departure, a change of direction; informal a shake up; N. Amer. informal a shakedown; humorous transmogrification.

innovative adjective *the store's products are innovative and effective*: **original**, innovatory, innovational, new, novel, fresh, unconventional, unorthodox, unusual, unfamiliar, unprecedented, avant-garde, experimental, inventive, ingenious; advanced, modern, modernistic, ultra-modern, state-of-the-art, futuristic, pioneering, groundbreaking, trailblazing, revolutionary, radical, newfangled; rare new-fashioned, neoteric.

innovator noun *the 19th century's prolific scientific innovators*: **pioneer**, developer, groundbreaker, trailblazer, pathfinder, front runner, spearhead, prime mover; modernizer, reformer, reformist, progressive, progressivist; experimenter, inventor, creator.

innuendo noun *he became the butt for their smutty innuendoes*: **insinuation**, implication, hint, suggestion, intimation, overtone, undertone, whisper, allusion, nuance, reference, imputation, aspersion, slur.

Choose the right word **innuendo, hint, suggestion, insinuation**

See **hint**.

innumerable adjective *she served on innumerable committees*: **countless**, numerous, very many, manifold, multitudinous, multifarious, untold, incalculable, numberless, unnumbered, beyond number; a great number of, incalculable numbers of, endless numbers of, a multitude of, a multiplicity of, a raft of, more than one can count, too many to be counted; informal umpteen, masses of, oodles of, no end of, loads of, stacks of, heaps of, bags of, zillions of; N. Amer. informal a slew of, a whole bunch of, gazillions of, bazillions of; S. African informal lank; literary myriad, legion, divers; rare innumerous, unnumberable.
▷ANTONYMS few.

inoculate verb *he **inoculated** his patients **against** smallpox*: **immunize**, vaccinate, inject; protect from, shield from, safeguard from; informal give someone a jab, give someone a shot.

inoculation noun **immunization**, vaccination, vaccine, injection, booster; informal jab, shot.

Word links **inoculation**

trypanophobia, **vaccinophobia** fear of inoculation

inoffensive adjective *the victim was an inoffensive law-abiding citizen*: **harmless**, innocuous, unobjectionable, unexceptionable, unoffending, non-aggressive, non-violent, non-combative; mild, peaceful, peaceable, gentle, tame, innocent; unremarkable.

inoperable adjective **1** *an inoperable brain tumour*: **untreatable**, incurable, beyond cure, beyond surgery, irremediable; malignant; terminal, fatal, deadly, lethal, mortal; rare immedicable.
▷ANTONYMS operable, curable.
2 *the airfield was bombed and left inoperable*: **unusable**, out of action, out of order, out of service, not in service, not operative, not in operation, not working, non-active, unable to be used.
3 *the unions say the agreement is now inoperable*: **impractical**, unworkable, unfeasible, unrealistic, non-viable, impracticable, unserviceable, unsuitable, inappropriate, inconvenient.
▷ANTONYMS workable.

inoperative adjective **1** *the ventilating fan is inoperative*: **not working**, not in working order, not functioning, broken, broken-down, out of order, out of service, out of commission, acting up, unserviceable, faulty, defective, non-functional, in disrepair; down; informal conked out, bust, (gone) kaput, gone phut, on the blink, gone haywire, shot; Brit. informal knackered, jiggered, wonky; N. Amer. informal on the fritz, out of whack; Brit. vulgar slang buggered.
▷ANTONYMS operative, working.
2 *their actions rendered the contract inoperative*: **void**, null and void, nullified, ineffective, invalid, cancelled, revoked, rescinded, terminated, discontinued, not binding, not in force, non-viable; worthless, useless, valueless, vain, pointless, nugatory, futile, unproductive, abortive.
▷ANTONYMS valid.

inopportune adjective *she turned up at the most inopportune moment*: **inconvenient**, untimely, ill-timed, badly timed, mistimed, inappropriate, unsuitable, inapt, ill-chosen, infelicitous, unfavourable, unfortunate, unpropitious, inauspicious, inexpedient, disadvantageous; awkward, difficult, troublesome, bothersome, problematic, disruptive, disturbing; archaic unseasonable.
▷ANTONYMS opportune, convenient.

inordinate adjective *the job had taken an inordinate amount of time*: **excessive**, undue, unreasonable, unjustifiable, unwarrantable, disproportionate, out of all proportion, unconscionable, unwarranted, unnecessary, needless, uncalled for, exorbitant, extreme, outrageous, preposterous; immoderate, overabundant, superfluous, extravagant, unrestrained, unrestricted, unlimited; informal over the top, OTT.
▷ANTONYMS moderate; limited.

inorganic adjective *the spontaneous generation of life from inorganic matter*: **inanimate**, not living, lifeless, dead, defunct, extinct, inert; not natural, not organic, mineral, man-made.
▷ANTONYMS organic.

input noun *the program has an error resulting from invalid input*: **data**, details, material, resources; facts, figures, information, statistics, particulars, specifics; informal info.
▸ verb *you must input data into a named database file*: **feed in**, put in, load, insert; key in, type in; code, capture, process, store.

inquest noun *they held an inquest into the death of her daughter*: **enquiry**, investigation, inquisition, probe, review, study, survey, analysis, examination, exploration, scrutinization; hearing, case.

inquire verb See **enquire**.

inquiring adjective See **enquiring**.

inquiry noun See **enquiry**.

inquisition noun *she sat down opposite him and started on her inquisition*: **interrogation**, questioning, quizzing, cross-examination, cross-questioning, catechism; investigation, enquiry, inquest, fact-finding; informal grilling, pumping, giving someone the third degree; Law examination.

inquisitive adjective *their inquisitive neighbours had gathered at the gate*: **curious**, intrigued, interested, burning with curiosity, agog; over-curious, over-interested, prying, spying, scrutinizing, eavesdropping, intrusive, interfering, busybody, meddling, meddlesome; enquiring, questioning, probing; informal nosy, nosy-parker, snooping, snoopy; rare busy.
▷ANTONYMS uninterested.

insalubrious adjective *he moved from one insalubrious dwelling to another*: **seedy**, unsavoury, sordid, seamy, sleazy, unpleasant, dingy, mean, wretched, dismal; **slummy**, slum-like, squalid, shabby, ramshackle, tumbledown, run down, down at heel, dilapidated, neglected, uncared-for, unmaintained, crumbling, decaying, gone to rack and ruin; informal scruffy, scuzzy, crummy, grungy, shambly; Brit. informal grotty; N. Amer. informal shacky, skanky.
▷ANTONYMS salubrious; smart.

insane adjective **1** *she was examined by three doctors and declared insane*: **mentally ill**, severely mentally disordered, of unsound mind, certifiable, psychotic, schizophrenic; mad, mad as a hatter, mad as a March hare, deranged, demented, out of one's mind, out of one's head, not in one's right mind, sick in the head, unhinged, unbalanced, unstable, disturbed, crazed, crazy, hysterical; Latin non compos mentis; informal raving mad, stark staring/raving mad, away with the fairies, not all there, bonkers, cracked, batty, bats, cuckoo, loony, loopy, nuts, nutty, nutty as a fruitcake, screwy, bananas, off one's rocker, off one's head, off one's chump, off one's nut, off the wall, round the bend; Brit. informal crackers, barmy, barking, barking mad, off one's trolley, round the twist, as daft as a brush, not the full shilling; N. Amer. informal buggy, nutsy, nutso, out of one's tree, wacko, squirrelly; Canadian & Austral./NZ informal bushed; NZ informal porangi.
▷ANTONYMS sane.
2 *he made an insane suggestion*: **extremely foolish**, idiotic, stupid, silly, senseless, nonsensical, pointless, absurd, ridiculous, ludicrous, farcical, laughable, preposterous, weird, bizarre, fatuous, inane, imbecilic, moronic, asinine, mindless, hare-brained, half-baked, ill-conceived; impracticable, untenable, implausible, unreasonable, irrational, illogical, unrealistic, unthinkable; informal potty, crazy, mad, off beam, way out, full of holes, cock-eyed; Brit. informal daft, barmy.
▷ANTONYMS sensible.
3 *the fly's buzzing had been driving me insane*: **mad**, crazy; angry, annoyed, irritated, cross, vexed, exasperated, incensed, enraged; informal aggravated, hot under the collar, foaming at the mouth; Brit. informal spare, crackers.
▷ANTONYMS calm.

insanitary adjective *disease spreads quickly in crowded and insanitary conditions*: **unhygienic**, unsanitary, dirty, filthy, unclean, impure, contaminated, polluted, foul, feculent, infected, infested, germ-ridden, disease-ridden, unhealthy, insalubrious, unwholesome, deleterious, detrimental, harmful; informal germy.
▷ANTONYMS sanitary, hygienic.

insanity noun **1** *insanity runs in her family*: **mental illness**, mental disorder, mental derangement, madness, insaneness, dementia, dementedness, lunacy, instability, unsoundness of mind, loss of reason; delirium, hysteria, mania, psychosis; informal craziness; archaic crazedness; rare deliration.
▷ANTONYMS sanity.
2 *it would be pure insanity to take this loan*: **folly**, foolishness, foolhardiness, idiocy, stupidity, imbecility, asininity, lunacy, madness,

silliness, senselessness, brainlessness, thoughtlessness, irrationality, illogicality, absurdity, ludicrousness, ridiculousness; informal craziness; Brit. informal daftness.
▷ANTONYMS sense.

> *Word links* **insanity**
>
> **lyssophobia, maniphobia** fear of insanity

insatiable adjective *Steve had an insatiable appetite for apple pudding*: **unquenchable**, unappeasable, uncontrollable, voracious, prodigious, gluttonous, greedy, hungry, ravenous, ravening, wolfish, avid, eager, keen; never satisfied, unable to be satisfied; informal piggish, piggy, hoggish, swinish, gutsy; Brit. informal gannet-like; rare insatiate, edacious, esurient.

inscribe verb **1** *his name was now inscribed above the door*: **carve**, **write**, engrave, etch, cut, chisel, chase, score, incise; imprint, stamp, impress, mark, brand; archaic scotch.
2 *the book was personally inscribed to him by the author*: **dedicate**, address, name, sign.

inscription noun **1** *she read the inscription on the marble sarcophagus*: **engraving**, **wording**, writing, lettering, legend, epitaph, epigraph, etching, carving; words.
2 *the book had an inscription in green ink*: **dedication**, address, message; signature, autograph.

inscrutable adjective **1** *her inscrutable face gave nothing away*: **enigmatic**, unreadable, impenetrable, mysterious, impossible to interpret, cryptic; unexpressive, inexpressive, emotionless, unemotional, expressionless, impassive, blank, vacant, deadpan, dispassionate; informal poker-faced.
▷ANTONYMS expressive.
2 *the ways of the gods are inscrutable*: **mysterious**, inexplicable, unexplainable, incomprehensible, beyond comprehension, beyond understanding, impossible to understand, unintelligible, impenetrable, unfathomable, fathomless, opaque, puzzling, perplexing, baffling, bewildering, confusing, abstruse, arcane, obscure; literary sibylline; archaic wildering.
▷ANTONYMS transparent.

insect noun

> *Word links* **insect**
>
> **entomo-** related prefix
> **entomology** study of insects
> **flight, swarm** collective noun
> **insectivorous, entomophagous** insect-eating
> **entomophobia** fear of insects
> **insecticide** substance that kills insects

insecure adjective **1** *a gauche, rather insecure young man*: **unconfident**, lacking confidence, lacking self-confidence, not self-assured, diffident, self-effacing, self-conscious, unforthcoming, uncertain, unsure, doubtful, self-doubting, hesitant, unassertive, retiring, shrinking, shy, timid, timorous, meek, passive, inhibited, introverted; anxious, fearful, apprehensive, worried, ill at ease; informal mousy.
▷ANTONYMS confident.
2 *burglars can gain access through insecure doors and windows*: **unguarded**, unprotected, ill-protected, vulnerable, defenceless, undefended, unshielded, exposed, assailable, open to attack, in danger; unlocked, unbolted, unfastened, unsecured; rare pregnable.
▷ANTONYMS secure.
3 *an insecure footbridge*: **unstable**, unsecured, loose, rickety, rocky, wobbly, shaky, unsteady, precarious; unsubstantial, weak, flimsy, frail, fragile, spindly, decrepit, unsound, unsafe; informal jerry-built, teetery; Brit. informal wonky, dicky, dodgy.
▷ANTONYMS secure, stable.

insecurity noun **1** *he tried to conceal his insecurity*: **lack of confidence**, lack of self-confidence, self-doubt, diffidence, unassertiveness, humility, humbleness, meekness, timidity, timidness, timorousness, uncertainty, nervousness, hesitancy, inhibition, self-consciousness; anxiety, apprehension, worry, unease, uneasiness.
2 *we were conscious of the insecurity of our situation*: **vulnerability**, defencelessness, unguardedness, lack of protection, perilousness, peril, danger, riskiness; instability, fragility, frailty, shakiness, rockiness, unsteadiness, unreliability, tenuousness; informal chanciness, iffiness; Brit. informal dodginess.

insensate adjective *the patient was permanently insensate*. See **insensible** (sense 1).

insensible adjective **1** *I found her insensible on the floor*: **unconscious**, insensate, senseless, insentient, comatose, knocked out, passed out, blacked out, inert, stupefied, stunned; numb, benumbed, numbed, lacking feeling, lacking sensation; informal out, out cold, out for the count, out of it, zonked (out), dead to the world; Brit. informal spark out; rare soporose, soporous.
▷ANTONYMS conscious; responsive.
2 *they were not* ***insensible of*** *the problem* | *he was* ***insensible to*** *the risks*: **unaware of**, ignorant of, without knowledge of, unconscious of, unmindful of, mindless of, oblivious to; indifferent to, impervious to, deaf to, blind to, careless of, unmoved by, untouched by, unaffected by, unresponsive to; informal in the dark about; rare insensitive of, negligent of.
▷ANTONYMS aware; heedful.
3 *he filled even the most insensible person with terror*: **insensitive**, dispassionate, cool, passionless, emotionless, unfeeling, unconcerned, detached, indifferent, aloof, hard, hardened, hard-hearted, stony-hearted, as hard as nails, with a heart of stone, tough, cruel, callous; informal hard-boiled; rare marble-hearted.
▷ANTONYMS caring, sensitive.
4 *the almost insensible result of the various improvements*: **imperceptible**, unnoticeable, undetectable, indistinguishable, indiscernible, unapparent, inappreciable, invisible, inaudible, impalpable, unobtrusive, impossible to detect; slight, small, subtle, faint, fine, inconsequential, negligible, tiny, minute, minuscule, microscopic, nanoscopic, infinitesimal.

insensitive adjective **1** *their leader is an insensitive bully*: **heartless**, unfeeling, inconsiderate, thoughtless, thick-skinned, hard-hearted, stony-hearted, cold-hearted, cold-blooded, with a heart of stone, as hard as nails, lacking compassion, compassionless, uncaring, unconcerned, unsympathetic, unkind, callous, hard, harsh, cruel, merciless, pitiless, unpitying, uncharitable, inhuman.
▷ANTONYMS sensitive; compassionate.
2 *he was* ***insensitive to*** *his son's feelings*: **impervious to**, oblivious to, unaware of, unappreciative of, unresponsive to, indifferent to, unaffected by, unmoved by, untouched by, immune to; informal in the dark about; rare incognizant of, nescient of.

insentient adjective *insentient beings*: **inanimate**, lifeless, inorganic, inert; insensate, lacking physical sensation; unconscious, comatose, anaesthetized, desensitized, numb; stupefied, knocked out, passed out, blacked out; informal dead to the world, out, out cold, out for the count, out of it; Brit. informal spark out.

inseparable adjective **1** *the three girls were inseparable friends*: **devoted**, bosom, close, fast, firm, good, best, intimate, confidential, boon, constant, loyal, faithful; informal as thick as thieves.
2 *their moral and religious laws are inseparable*: **indivisible**, indissoluble, inextricable, entangled, ravelled, mixed up, impossible to separate; the same, one and the same.

insert verb (stress on the second syllable) **1** *he inserted a tape in the recorder*: **put**, place, press, push, thrust, slide, slip, load, fit, position, slot, lodge, install; drive, wedge, work, tuck; informal pop, stick, shove, bung, jam.
▷ANTONYMS take out, extract.
2 *John has inserted a clause to that effect into the contract*: **enter**, put, introduce, incorporate, interpolate, interpose, interject, inset, infix, build.
▷ANTONYMS remove.
▸**noun** (stress on the first syllable) *the local newspaper carried an insert*: **enclosure**, insertion, inset, inlay, addition, supplement; circular, advertisement, notice, slip, pamphlet, leaflet; informal ad.

insertion noun **1** *the insertion of a catheter into the portal vein*: **introduction**, introducing, putting, placing, installing, fitting, positioning, lodging, sliding.
2 *the fair was advertised on special newspaper insertions*. See **insert** (noun).

inside noun (stress on the second syllable) **1** *my breath misted up the inside of my visor* | *the inside of a volcano*: **interior**, inner part, inner side, inner surface; centre, core, middle, heart, nucleus.
▷ANTONYMS outside, exterior.
2 (**insides**) informal *my insides are out of order*: **stomach**, gut, bowels, intestines; internal organs, viscera, entrails; informal belly, tummy, guts, bread basket.
▸**adjective** (stress on the first syllable) **1** *he took an envelope from his inside pocket*: **inner**, interior, internal, inmost, innermost; on the inside.
▷ANTONYMS outer.
2 *the directors used inside information to their own advantage*: **confidential**, classified, restricted, reserved, privileged, private, internal, secret, top secret, exclusive, off the record, not for publication; informal hush-hush; archaic privy.
▷ANTONYMS public.
▸**adverb** (stress on the second syllable) **1** *the old woman ushered me inside*: **indoors**, within, in; into the interior, into the house, into the building, into the room.
▷ANTONYMS outside.
2 *don't let them know how you feel inside*: **inwardly**, within, secretly, privately, deep down, at heart, in one's heart, in one's mind, emotionally, intuitively, instinctively.
▷ANTONYMS outwardly.
3 informal *if I commit another offence I'll be back inside*: **in prison**, in jail, in custody, under lock and key; locked up, imprisoned, incarcerated; informal behind bars, doing time; Brit. informal doing porridge, doing bird, banged up.

Word links **inside**

intra- related prefix, as in *intravenous, intraday*

insider noun *a Home Office insider leaked the information*: **member**, staff member, member of staff, worker, employee, representative; participant; person in the know; informal one of the in-crowd.
▷ANTONYMS outsider.

insidious adjective *the insidious erosion of rights and liberties*: **stealthy**, subtle, surreptitious, sneaking, cunning, crafty, Machiavellian, artful, guileful, sly, wily, tricky, slick, deceitful, deceptive, dishonest, underhand, backhanded, indirect; informal sneaky.
▷ANTONYMS straightforward.

insight noun **1** *your knowledge and insight have been invaluable to us*: **intuition**, perception, awareness, discernment, understanding, comprehension, apprehension, appreciation, cognizance, penetration, acumen, astuteness, perspicacity, perspicaciousness, sagacity, sageness, discrimination, judgement, shrewdness, sharpness, sharp-wittedness, acuity, acuteness, flair, breadth of view, vision, far-sightedness, prescience, imagination; informal nous, horse sense, savvy; rare sapience, arguteness.
2 *the book provides a rare* **insight into** *the complexities of government*: **understanding of**, appreciation of, revelation about, illumination of; introduction to, experience of, description of; informal eye-opener.

insightful adjective *he gives an insightful analysis of the text*: **intuitive**, perceptive, discerning, penetrating, penetrative, astute, percipient, perspicacious, sagacious, wise, judicious, shrewd, sharp, sharp-witted, razor-sharp, keen, incisive, acute, imaginative, appreciative, intelligent, thoughtful, sensitive, deep, profound; visionary, far-sighted, prescient; informal savvy; rare sapient, argute.

insignia noun *his tunic bore the insignia of the Légion d'Honneur*: **badge**, crest, emblem, symbol, sign, device, mark, seal, colours; decoration, medal, medallion, pin, ribbon, star, award; military slang fruit salad; Brit. informal gong.

insignificant adjective *too many articles are devoted to insignificant details*: **unimportant**, of minor importance, of no importance, of little importance, of little import, trivial, trifling, footling, negligible, inconsequential, of little consequence, of no consequence, of no account, of no moment, inconsiderable, not worth mentioning, not worth speaking of, nugatory, meagre, paltry, scanty, petty, insubstantial, unsubstantial, flimsy, frivolous, pointless, worthless, irrelevant, immaterial, peripheral, extraneous, non-essential; informal piddling; N. Amer. informal dinky.
▷ANTONYMS significant.

insincere adjective *an insincere smile | insincere political rhetoric*: **false**, fake, hollow, artificial, feigned, pretended, put-on, exaggerated, overdone, lacking sincerity, not candid, not frank; **disingenuous**, dissembling, dissimulating, devious, hypocritical, cynical, deceitful, deceptive, duplicitous, dishonest, underhand, double-dealing, faithless, disloyal, treacherous, two-faced, lying, untruthful, mendacious, evasive, shifty, slippery; informal phoney, pretend, pseud.
▷ANTONYMS sincere.

insinuate verb **1** *he insinuated that she lied*: **imply**, suggest, hint, intimate, whisper, indicate, convey the impression, give a clue, give an inkling, allude to the fact, make reference to the fact, let it be known, give someone to understand, give someone to believe; informal make out, tip someone the wink.
2 *he insinuated his right hand under her arm*: **slide**, slip, manoeuvre, insert, edge, work, move into position.
□ **insinuate oneself into** *he was insinuating himself into their family*: **worm one's way into**, work one's way into, ingratiate oneself with, curry favour with; foist oneself on, introduce oneself into, squeeze oneself into, edge one's way into; infiltrate, invade, sneak into, intrude on, impinge on; informal get in with, muscle in on.

insinuation noun *he winced at the insinuation that he was past it*: **implication**, inference, suggestion, hint, intimation, imputation, innuendo, reference, allusion, indication, undertone, overtone; aspersion, slur, allegation.

Choose the right word **insinuation, hint, suggestion, innuendo**

See **hint**.

insipid adjective **1** *they drank endless mugs of insipid coffee*: **tasteless**, flavourless, unflavoured, savourless, bland, weak, thin, watery, watered-down, unappetizing, unpalatable; informal wishy-washy; Scottish, dated wersh.
▷ANTONYMS tasty.
2 *a rather insipid little boy*: **uninteresting**, boring, vapid, dull, spiritless, zestless, bloodless, lifeless, characterless, lacking personality, lacking charisma, anaemic, wishy-washy, pathetic; ordinary, commonplace, middle-of-the-road, run-of-the mill, not amounting to much.
▷ANTONYMS interesting.
3 *many artists continued to churn out insipid works*: **unimaginative**, uninspired, uninspiring, characterless, flat, bland, vapid, uninteresting, unexciting, lacklustre, lustreless, dull, prosaic, boring, monotonous, tedious, wearisome, dry, dry as dust, jejune, humdrum, run-of-the-mill, commonplace, pedestrian, trite, banal, tired, hackneyed, stale, lame, tame, poor, inadequate, half-hearted, bloodless, sterile, anaemic, barren; Brit. informal common or garden.
▷ANTONYMS imaginative; interesting.

Word toolkit

insipid	tedious	uneventful
performance	process	day
lyrics	work	life
display	task	vacation
dialogue	exercise	childhood
music	reading	summer
commentary	negotiations	conclusion

insist verb **1** *if they won't see you, be prepared to insist*: **stand firm**, be firm, stand one's ground, make a stand, stand up for oneself, be resolute, be determined, show determination, hold on, hold out, be emphatic, not take no for an answer, brook no refusal; persevere, persist, not give up, keep on at someone; informal stick to one's guns, stick it out, hang in there.
▷ANTONYMS give up.
2 *Tom insisted that the fees be paid within thirty days*: **demand**, command, require, dictate; importune, entreat, urge, exhort.
3 *he insisted that he knew nothing about the plot*: **maintain**, assert, hold, contend, argue, protest, claim, aver, avow, vow, swear, state, declare, announce, pronounce, proclaim, propound, be emphatic, emphasize, stress, repeat, reiterate; archaic avouch; rare asseverate, represent.

insistence noun **1** *she sat beside Julia at Anne's insistence*: **demand**, bidding, command, dictate, instruction, requirement, request, entreaty, urging, exhortation, importuning; informal say-so, arm-twisting; literary behest, hest.
2 *there was too much vehemence in his insistence that he loved her*: **assertion**, declaration, contention, statement, claim, proclamation, announcement, pronouncement, assurance, attestation, affirmation, avowal, averment, profession, swearing, emphasis, stress; rare maintenance, asseveration.

insistent adjective **1** *Tony's insistent questioning | she was very insistent that I call her*: **persistent**, determined, adamant, importunate, tenacious, unyielding, obstinate, dogged, unrelenting, unfaltering, unwavering, inexorable; demanding, urgent, pressing; emphatic, determined, firm, assertive, decided, resolute, resolved; informal pushy; rare pushful, exigent.
2 *the insistent buzzing of the bees*: **incessant**, constant, unremitting, iterative, repeated, repetitive; clamorous, vociferous, loud, noisy, obtrusive, intrusive.

insobriety noun *he had a tendency to insobriety*: **drunkenness**, intoxication, inebriation, tipsiness; intemperance, overindulgence, debauchery; hard drinking, serious drinking, heavy drinking, alcoholism, alcohol abuse, dipsomania; rare inebriety, sottishness, bibulousness, crapulence.
▷ANTONYMS sobriety.

insolence noun *I will not stand for your insolence!* **impertinence**, impudence, cheek, cheekiness, bad manners, ill-manneredness, unmannerliness, rudeness, impoliteness, incivility, lack of civility, discourtesy, discourteousness, disrespect, insubordination, contempt; audacity, boldness, brazenness, brashness, pertness, forwardness, effrontery, gall, presumptuousness, presumption; insults, abuse, offensiveness; informal brass, brass neck, neck, face, front, cockiness, freshness, backchat, bad-mouthing; Brit. informal sauce; Scottish informal snash; N. Amer. informal chutzpah, sass, sassiness, nerviness; informal, dated hide, crust; archaic contumely, malapertness.
▷ANTONYMS politeness.

insolent adjective *the girl had been continually insolent*: **impertinent**, impudent, cheeky, ill-mannered, bad mannered, unmannerly, rude, impolite, uncivil, lacking civility, discourteous, disrespectful, insubordinate, contemptuous, presumptuous; audacious, bold, brazen, brash, pert, forward; insulting, abusive, offensive; informal fresh, flip, cocky, lippy; Brit. informal saucy; N. Amer. informal sassy, nervy; archaic contumelious, malapert; rare mannerless.
▷ANTONYMS polite.

insoluble adjective **1** *we must face the fact that some problems are insoluble*: **unsolvable**, insolvable, unable to be solved, without a solution, unanswerable, unresolvable; unfathomable, impenetrable, unexplainable, inscrutable; baffling, puzzling, perplexing, enigmatic, obscure, mystifying, mysterious, inexplicable.
2 *these minerals are relatively insoluble*: **not soluble**, indissoluble, incapable of dissolving.

insolvency noun *the firm is on the brink of insolvency*: **bankruptcy**, liquidation, failure, collapse, ruin, financial ruin, ruination; pennilessness,

penury, impecuniousness, beggary; Brit. administration, receivership; informal folding; rare pauperdom.
▷ANTONYMS solvency.

insolvent adjective *the bank was declared insolvent*: **bankrupt**, unable to pay one's debts, ruined, collapsed, defaulting, liquidated, wiped out; penniless, impoverished, penurious, impecunious, without a sou; Brit. in the hands of the receivers, in receivership, in administration, without a penny (to one's name); informal bust, broke, flat broke, belly-up, gone under, gone to the wall, on the rocks, in the red, hard up, strapped for cash; Brit. informal skint, in Queer Street, stony broke, cleaned out, without two pennies to rub together; Brit. informal, dated in Carey Street; rare pauperized, beggared.
▷ANTONYMS solvent.

insomnia noun *Anna was suffering from anxiety and insomnia*: **sleeplessness**, wakefulness, restlessness; inability to sleep; archaic watchfulness.

insouciance noun *his anxieties increased, despite Jen's insouciance*: **nonchalance**, unconcern, lack of concern, indifference, heedlessness, relaxedness, calm, calmness, equanimity, coolness, composure, casualness, ease, easy-going attitude, airiness, carefreeness, frivolousness, carelessness; informal cool.
▷ANTONYMS anxiety, concern.

insouciant adjective *he had an insouciant attitude to their money problems*: **nonchalant**, untroubled, unworried, unruffled, unconcerned, lacking concern, indifferent, blasé, heedless, relaxed, calm, equable, equanimous, serene, composed, casual, easy, easy-going, airy, breezy, carefree, free and easy, free from care, free from worry, happy-go-lucky, light-hearted, frivolous, unserious; informal cool, laid back, upbeat.
▷ANTONYMS anxious, concerned.

inspect verb *the safety equipment is inspected by officials each year*: **examine**, check (over), scrutinize, vet, investigate, test, monitor, survey, study, go over, look over, look at, take a look at, pore over, view, scan, observe, explore, probe, subject to an examination, subject to an inspection, go over with a fine-tooth comb; assess, appraise, review; informal check out, give something the once-over, give something a going-over, give something a look-see.

inspection noun *he ordered an inspection of all aircraft | all reactors require regular inspection*: **examination**, check, check-up, survey, scrutiny, look-over, probe, exploration, perusal, view, scan, observation, investigation, assessment, appraisal, review, evaluation; examining, checking, surveying, vetting, investigating, assessing, appraising, consideration; informal once-over, going-over, look-see, overhaul.

inspector noun *the machinery was not acceptable to the factory inspector*: **examiner**, checker, scrutinizer, scrutineer, investigator, surveyor, assessor, appraiser, reviewer, analyst; observer, overseer, supervisor, monitor, watchdog, ombudsman; auditor; rare examinant, scrutinator.

inspiration noun **1** *her idea proved a real inspiration to others*: **stimulus**, stimulation, motivation, motivating force, fillip, encouragement, influence, muse, goad, spur, lift, boost, incentive, incitement, impulse, catalyst; example, model, guiding light; informal shot in the arm; rare afflatus.
2 *these writings lack inspiration*: **creativity**, inventiveness, innovation, innovativeness, ingenuity, imagination, imaginativeness, originality, individuality; artistry, expressiveness, creative power, creative talent, creative skill, genius, insight, vision, wit, finesse, flair, brilliance, sophistication.
3 *Emily racked her brain and had a sudden inspiration*: **bright idea**, brilliant idea, timely thought, revelation; informal brainwave; N. Amer. informal brainstorm.
4 *she experiences pain on deep inspiration*: **inhalation**, breathing in, drawing in of breath; respiration, breathing.

inspire verb **1** *the landscape inspired Hardy to write this fine poem*: **stimulate**, motivate, cause, incline, persuade, encourage, influence, rouse, move, stir, spur (on), goad, energize, galvanize, incite, impel; animate, fire the imagination of, fire with enthusiasm; rare inspirit, incentivize, fillip.
2 *the film inspired a musical on the London stage*: **give rise to**, lead to, result in, bring about, cause, be the cause of, prompt, produce, spawn, engender; be the inspiration for; literary beget.
3 *Charles inspired awe in those who worked with him*: **arouse**, awaken, prompt, cause, induce, ignite, trigger, kindle, produce, generate, bring out, bring about, give rise to, sow the seeds of; literary enkindle.
▷ANTONYMS extinguish.

inspired adjective *an inspired performance | she is an inspired gardener*: **outstanding**, wonderful, marvellous, excellent, magnificent, fine, exceptional, formidable, first-class, first-rate, virtuoso, supreme, superlative, dazzling, exciting, thrilling, enthralling, memorable; gifted, talented, creative, imaginative, inventive, innovative, innovatory, innovational, ingenious, original, resourceful, enterprising; informal tremendous, superb, super, smashing, ace, A1, mean, wicked, awesome, magic, out of this world; Brit. informal brilliant, brill.
▷ANTONYMS mediocre, poor.

inspiring adjective *he was an inspiring example to his pupils*: **inspirational**, encouraging, heartening, uplifting, stirring, rousing, stimulating, electrifying, exhilarating, exciting; moving, affecting, memorable, striking, impressive, influential; rare stimulative.
▷ANTONYMS uninspiring; dull.

instability noun **1** *the instability of political life*: **unreliability**, uncertainty, unpredictability, unpredictableness, precariousness, unsteadiness, insecurity, vulnerability, perilousness, riskiness; impermanence, temporariness, transience, inconstancy, changeability, variability; fluidity, fluctuation, rise and fall, rising and falling; informal chanciness, iffiness; Brit. informal dodginess; literary mutability.
▷ANTONYMS stability.
2 *her emotional instability*: **changeableness**, variability, capriciousness, volatility, flightiness, fitfulness, vacillation, oscillation, unpredictability, unpredictableness; moodiness, a tendency to blow hot and cold; unsoundness, frailty, infirmity, weakness, irregularity, abnormality; rare erraticism.
▷ANTONYMS stability.
3 *the instability of the building's foundations*: **unsteadiness**, unsoundness, shakiness, ricketiness, wobbliness, frailty, fragility, flimsiness, insubstantiality.
▷ANTONYMS stability; soundness.

install verb **1** *a colour photocopier was installed in the office*: **put**, position, place, put in place, set in place, fix, fit, locate, situate, station, site, lodge, establish; insert; informal plonk, park.
▷ANTONYMS remove.
2 *the National Congress installed a new president*: **swear in**, induct, instate, inaugurate, invest, institute, introduce, appoint, admit to office, take on; ordain, consecrate, anoint; enthrone, crown.
▷ANTONYMS remove.
3 *Katie* ***installed herself*** *behind the table*: **ensconce**, establish, position, settle, seat, lodge, plant, plump; sit, sit down, take a seat, take a chair, perch; informal plonk, park; Brit. informal take a pew.

installation noun **1** *the installation of a central heating system*: **installing**, install, fitting, putting in, putting in place; insertion; attachment.
2 *the installation of the new chancellor*: **swearing in**, induction, instatement, inauguration, investiture, appointment; ordination, consecration; enthronement, crowning, coronation.
3 *the computer installation was new to the company*: **equipment**, machinery; unit, appliance, fixture, piece of equipment.
4 *a local army installation*: **base**, camp, station, post, depot, centre, facility, establishment, premises; informal outfit, set-up.

instalment noun **1** *they agreed to pay by monthly instalments*: **part payment**, partial payment; instalment plan, instalment-payment plan, deferred payment; Brit. hire purchase, HP; N. Amer. instalment buying; Brit. informal the never-never.
2 *the paper published his letters in weekly instalments*: **part**, portion, section, segment, division, bit; chapter, episode, volume, issue.

instance noun **1** *there was not a single instance of religious persecution*: **example**, occasion, occurrence, case, representative case, typical case, case in point, illustration, specimen, sample, exemplar, exemplification.
2 *criminal investigations are conducted by the police* ***in the first instance***: **place**; stage, step; **initially**, at first, at the start, at the outset, in/at the beginning, to begin with, to start with, originally, in the early stages.
3 formal *proceedings were launched at the instance of the Director of Public Prosecutions*: **instigation**, prompting, suggestion; request, entreaty, solicitation; wish, desire; urging, importuning, pressure; demand, insistence.
▶ verb *as an example of this type of play, I would instance 'Measure for Measure'*: **cite**, quote, refer to, make reference to, mention, allude to, adduce, give, give as an example, point to, point out; specify, name, identify; bring up, invoke, draw attention to, call attention to, put forward, present, offer, advance, propose.

instant adjective **1** *instant access to your money*: **immediate**, instantaneous, on-the-spot, prompt, direct, swift, speedy, rapid, quick, expeditious, express, lightning, sudden, precipitate, abrupt; informal snappy, p.d.q. (pretty damn quick); literary fleet, rathe; rare alacritous.
▷ANTONYMS delayed; long-term.
2 *the additives in instant meals*: **pre-prepared**, ready prepared, ready mixed, pre-cooked, fast, easy/quick to prepare, easy/quick to make, microwaveable, convenience, TV.
▶ noun **1** *there'll never be an instant quite like this again*: **moment**, time, point in time, moment in time, minute, second, hour; stage, phase, juncture, point.
2 *it all happened in an instant*: **short time**, little while, bit, moment, minute, second, split second, trice, twinkling, twinkling of an eye, flash, (less than) no time, no time at all; informal sec, jiffy, jiff, two shakes of a lamb's tail, the blink of an eye; Brit. informal mo, two ticks; N. Amer. informal snap.
▷ANTONYMS eternity.
□ **on the instant** See **instantly**.

instantaneous adjective *it may be difficult for you to make an instantaneous response to what is said*: **immediate**, instant, on-the-spot, prompt, direct, swift, speedy, rapid, quick, expeditious, express, lightning;

sudden, hurried, hasty, precipitate, abrupt; informal snappy, p.d.q. (pretty damn quick); literary fleet, rathe; rare alacritous.
▷ANTONYMS delayed; long-term.

instantly adverb *she fell asleep almost instantly*: **immediately**, at once, straight away, right away, instantaneously, suddenly, abruptly, all of a sudden, on the instant, at a stroke, forthwith, then and there, there and then, here and now, this/that (very) minute, this/that instant; quickly, rapidly, swiftly, speedily, directly, without delay, promptly; in an instant, in a moment, in a (split) second, in a minute, in a trice, in a fraction of a second, in/like a flash, quick as lightning, like a shot, in a wink, in the blink of an eye, in the twinkling of an eye, in two shakes (of a lamb's tail), in (less than) no time, before you know it, on the double, at the speed of light, like an arrow from a bow; French tout de suite; informal in a jiffy, pronto, before you can say Jack Robinson, double quick, in double quick time, p.d.q. (pretty damn quick), like (greased) lightning, toot sweet; Indian informal ekdam; archaic straightway, instanter, forthright.
▷ANTONYMS eventually; slowly.

instead adverb *people should leave their cars at home and travel by train instead*: **as an alternative**, as a substitute, as a replacement, in lieu, alternatively; **rather**, by contrast, for preference, by choice, from choice; on second thoughts; all things being equal, ideally; N. Amer. alternately.
▷ANTONYMS as well.
□ **instead of** *their menus are written in English instead of French*: **as an alternative to**, as a substitute for, as a replacement for, in place of, in lieu of, in preference to; **rather than**, as opposed to, in contrast with, as against, as contrasted with, before.
▷ANTONYMS as well as.

instigate verb **1** *the Commission instigated formal proceedings | he accused union leaders of instigating the disturbances*: **set in motion**, put in motion, get under way, get going, get off the ground, get in operation, start, begin, initiate, launch, institute, lay the foundations of, lay the first stone of, sow the seeds of, set up, inaugurate, found, establish, put in place, organize, get working, get functioning, activate; trigger off, set off, spark off, inspire, foment, kindle, stir up, whip up, actuate, generate, cause, bring about; start/get/set the ball rolling; informal kick off; formal commence.
▷ANTONYMS halt.
2 *the clergy were criticized for instigating men to refuse allegiance*: **incite**, encourage, urge, goad, provoke, spur on, drive on, egg on, entice, stimulate, push, press, prod, prompt, induce, impel, prevail upon, constrain, motivate, make, influence, persuade, sway; arouse, rouse, excite, inflame, stir up, sting, prick; informal put up to; N. Amer. informal root on; Law procure.
▷ANTONYMS dissuade.

instigation noun **1** *the whole team became involved at David's instigation*: **prompting**, suggestion; request, entreaty, solicitation; wish, desire; urging, importuning, pressure, persuasion; demand, insistence; formal instance.
2 *the Interior Ministry spoke of foreign instigation of the disorder*: **initiation**, incitement, provocation, stirring up, whipping up, kindling, fuelling, fomentation, encouragement, inducement; actuation, devising, inception.

instigator noun *Ricardou has been credited as the instigator of this development | the instigators of the revolt*: **initiator**, prime mover, motivator, architect, designer, deviser, planner, shaper, inventor, maker, producer, contriver, mastermind, originator, author, creator, founder, pioneer, father, mother, founding father, agent; inciter, agitator, fomenter, troublemaker, agent provocateur, ringleader, leader; literary begetter.

instil verb **1** *all parents must **instil in** their children the need to be vigilant*: **inculcate**, implant, fix, ingrain, infuse, impress, imprint, introduce; engender, produce, generate, induce, inspire, promote, foster; hammer into, drum into, drive into, drill into, din into.
2 *Boudin instilled Monet with the love of nature*: **imbue**, inspire, infuse, inculcate; brainwash, indoctrinate; teach.
3 *she was told how to instil eye drops*: **administer**, introduce, add gradually, infuse, inject.

instinct noun **1** *Michael showed no instinct to conform | some instinct told me that I must be careful*: **natural tendency**, inborn tendency, inherent tendency, inclination, inner prompting, urge, drive, compulsion, need; **intuition**, natural feeling, sixth sense, second sight, insight, nose.
2 *he already has a good instinct for acting*: **talent**, gift, ability, capacity, facility, faculty, aptitude, skill, flair, feel, genius, knack, bent.

instinctive adjective *an instinctive understanding of machines | his instinctive reaction is to blame someone else*: **intuitive**, natural, innate, inborn, inherent, inbred, instinctual, unconscious, subconscious, subliminal, emotional, intuitional, untaught, unlearned; **automatic**, reflex, knee-jerk, mechanical, spontaneous, involuntary, impulsive, unconditioned, unthinking, unpremeditated; informal gut.
▷ANTONYMS learned; conscious; voluntary.

institute noun *a research institute*: **organization**, establishment, institution, foundation, centre; academy, school, college, university, conservatory, seminary, centre of learning, seat of learning; society, association, federation, group, circle, fellowship, body, league, union, alliance, guild, consortium, concern, corporation.
▶verb **1** *Lowell instituted a search for this unknown planet*: **set in motion**, put in motion, get under way, get going, get off the ground, get in operation, start, begin, initiate, launch, lay the foundations of, lay the first stone of, sow the seeds of, set up, inaugurate, found, establish, put in place, organize, get working, get functioning, activate, actuate, generate, cause, bring about; start/get/set the ball rolling; informal kick off; formal commence.
▷ANTONYMS halt; cancel; end.
2 *he will be instituted as vicar of Saltburn*: **install**, instate, induct, invest, inaugurate, introduce, admit into office, swear in, initiate; ordain, consecrate, anoint; enthrone, crown; appoint, put in, create.
▷ANTONYMS dismiss; defrock.

institution noun **1** *an academic institution | a savings institution*: **organization**, establishment, institute, foundation, centre; academy, school, college, university, conservatory, seminary, centre of learning, seat of learning; society, association, federation, group, circle, fellowship, body, league, union, alliance, guild, consortium, concern, corporation.
2 *young people who have spent most of their lives in institutions*: **home**, residential care organization. See also **home**, **hospital**, **asylum**, **prison**.
3 *the institution of the new rector*: **installation**, instatement, induction, investiture, inauguration, introduction, swearing in, initiation; ordination, consecration, anointing; enthronement, coronation, crowning; appointment, putting in, creation.
▷ANTONYMS dismissal; defrocking.
4 *until 1926 English law did not recognize the institution of adoption*: **practice**, custom, phenomenon, fact, procedure, convention, usage, tradition, rite, ritual, fashion, use, habit, wont; method, system, routine, way, policy, idea, notion, concept; rule, law; Latin modus operandi; formal praxis.
5 *the institution of legal proceedings*: **initiation**, launch, launching, start, starting, beginning, setting in motion, putting in motion, getting under way, getting going, getting off the ground, instigation, setting up, inauguration, founding, foundation, establishment, organization, activation, actuation, generation, origination; formal commencement.
▷ANTONYMS halting; cancellation; ending.

institutional adjective **1** *the new organization would provide an institutional framework for discussions*: **organized**, established, bureaucratic, accepted, orthodox, conventional, procedural, prescribed, set, routine, customary, formal, systematic, systematized, methodical, businesslike, ready, orderly, coherent, structured, regulated; informal establishment.
2 *the school food is OK, if rather institutional*: **unappetizing**, unpalatable, inedible, uneatable, distasteful, unsavoury, insipid, bland, tasteless, flavourless, savourless; unappealing, uninviting, off-putting, unattractive, uninteresting, dull, unpleasant, disagreeable; uniform, unvarying, unvaried, unchanging, monotonous, regimented; informal wishy-washy.
▷ANTONYMS appetizing; attractive.
3 *the house might have remained forever coated in institutional chocolate-coloured paint*: **dreary**, dingy, dismal, gloomy, drab, colourless, grey, grim, cheerless, joyless, sombre, cold, depressing, impersonal, formal, off-putting, unwelcoming, uninviting, forbidding; desolate, austere, severe, stark, spartan, bare, clinical, sterile.
▷ANTONYMS bright; cheerful.

instruct verb **1** *a union may instruct its members to work to rule*: **order**, command, direct, tell, enjoin, give the order to, give orders to, give the command to, require, call on, mandate, charge; dictate; literary bid.
2 *nobody instructed him in how to operate and maintain the baler*: **teach**, school, give lessons to, coach, train, ground, enlighten, illuminate, inform, verse, edify, educate, upskill, tutor, guide, prepare, prime, din something into; drill, discipline, put someone through their paces.
3 *when she reached the age of 16, she exercised her right to instruct solicitors and counsel of her own choice*: **employ**, authorize to act for one, brief, give information to.
4 *I should not have to instruct typists that all my documents are confidential*: **inform**, tell, let someone know, notify, apprise, advise, announce to, impart to, relate to, communicate to; acquaint, familiarize, brief, prime, ground, enlighten, make conversant, make knowledgeable, send word to; informal put in the picture, fill in, clue in/up, put wise.

instruction noun **1** *if a prisoner disobeys an instruction, he will be punished*: **order**, command, directive, direction, decree, edict, injunction, mandate, dictate, commandment, diktat, demand, bidding, requirement, stipulation, charge, ruling, mandate, pronouncement; summons, writ, subpoena, warrant; informal say-so; literary behest; rare rescript.
2 (**instructions**) *read the instructions to find out*: **directions**, key, guide, recipe, specification; handbook, manual, guide, booklet, reference manual, ABC, A to Z, companion; Latin vade mecum; informal bible; rare enchiridion.
3 *an officer in the Royal Engineers provided instruction in demolition work*: **teaching**, tuition, coaching, tutoring, education, schooling, tutelage; lessons, classes, tutorials, lectures; training, drill, drilling, discipline; preparation, grounding, priming; direction, guidance, information, enlightenment, edification.

instructive adjective *a recent study of cooperatives makes instructive reading*: **informative**, instructional, informational, illuminating,

enlightening, revealing, explanatory, telling; educational, educative, edifying, didactic, pedagogic, doctrinal, preceptive, improving, heuristic; moralistic, homiletic; useful, helpful; rare propaedeutic.
▷ANTONYMS unenlightening.

instructor noun *a flying instructor*: **trainer**, teacher, tutor, coach, demonstrator, adviser, counsellor, guide; schoolteacher, schoolmaster, schoolmistress, educator, lecturer, professor; archaic pedagogue, preceptor.
▷ANTONYMS pupil.

instrument noun **1** *the wound appeared to have been made with a sharp instrument*: **implement**, tool, utensil, device, apparatus, contrivance, gadget, contraption, appliance, mechanism; informal gizmo.
2 *when you have climbed to 800 feet you must check all the cockpit instruments again*: **measuring device**, gauge, meter, measure; indicator, dial, display.
3 *drama is both a creative art form and an instrument of learning*: **agent**, agency, catalyst, cause, factor, channel, force, medium, means, mechanism, vehicle, organ.
4 *he was a mere instrument acting under coercion*: **pawn**, puppet, creature, dupe, hostage, counter, cog; tool, cat's paw; informal **stooge**.

instrumental adjective *he was instrumental in developing new diagnostic procedures | the company's record was instrumental in its ultimate failure*: **involved**, active, influential, contributory; helpful, of help/assistance, useful, of use/service; significant, important; (**be instrumental in**) **play a part in**, contribute to, be a factor in, be (partly) responsible for, have a hand in; add to, help, promote, advance, further, forward, oil the wheels of, open the door for, be conducive to, make for; lead to, cause, give rise to; formal conduce to.
▷ANTONYMS uninvolved; obstructive.

i

insubordinate adjective *he soon found a means of dealing with his insubordinate son*: **disobedient**, unruly, wayward, errant, badly behaved, disorderly, undisciplined, delinquent, troublesome, rebellious, defiant, mutinous, recalcitrant, refractory, uncooperative, non-compliant, wilful, unbiddable, intractable, ungovernable, unmanageable, uncontrollable, obstreperous, awkward, difficult, perverse, contrary; naughty, mischievous, impish, roguish, rascally; Brit. informal **bolshie**; archaic or Law contumacious.
▷ANTONYMS obedient.

insubordination noun *a soldier could be shot for insubordination*: **disobedience**, unruliness, waywardness, indiscipline, bad behaviour, misbehaviour, misconduct, delinquency, troublemaking; rebellion, rebelliousness, defiance, mutiny, revolt; recalcitrance, lack of cooperation, non-compliance, wilfulness, intractability, ungovernability, uncontrollability, obstreperousness, awkwardness, perversity, perverseness, contrariness; naughtiness, mischievousness, mischief, impishness, roguery; informal carryings-on, acting-up; archaic or Law contumacy, infraction.
▷ANTONYMS obedience.

insubstantial adjective **1** *these insubstantial structures cannot be converted into satisfactory dwellings*: **flimsy**, slight, light, fragile, breakable, weak, frail, shaky, unstable, wobbly, tottery, rickety, ramshackle, makeshift; **jerry-built**, badly built, thrown together, cheap, shoddy, gimcrack.
▷ANTONYMS sturdy.
2 *insubstantial evidence*: **weak**, flimsy, feeble, poor, inadequate, insufficient, thin, slight, tenuous, insignificant, inconsequential, unsubstantial, unconvincing, implausible, unsatisfactory, paltry, trifling, trivial, shallow.
▷ANTONYMS sound.
3 *she felt worried, in an insubstantial yet unsettling way | the flickering light made her face seem insubstantial*: **intangible**, impalpable, indefinable, indescribable, vague, obscure, unclear, indistinct; untouchable, imperceptible to the touch, unsubstantial, incorporeal; imaginary, imagined, fancied, fanciful, figmental, unreal, non-existent, illusory, illusive, delusive, hallucinatory, phantom, spectral, ghostlike, visionary, chimerical, airy, vaporous; rare immaterial, unbodied, discarnate, phantasmal, phantasmic, inexistent, illusionary.
▷ANTONYMS tangible; real.

insufferable adjective **1** *an insufferable glare of publicity*: **intolerable**, unbearable, unendurable, insupportable, unacceptable, oppressive, overwhelming, overpowering, impossible, not to be borne, past bearing, too much to bear, more than one can stand, more than flesh and blood can stand, enough to try/test/tax the patience of a saint; unspeakable, dreadful, excruciating, grim, outrageous; informal too much.
▷ANTONYMS bearable; congenial.
2 *his triumph had made him insufferable*: **conceited**, arrogant, boastful, cocky, cocksure, full of oneself, above oneself, self-important, immodest, swaggering, strutting; vain, self-satisfied, self-congratulatory, pleased with oneself, self-loving, in love with oneself, self-admiring, self-regarding, smug, complacent; informal swollen-headed, big-headed, too big for one's boots; literary vainglorious; rare peacockish.
▷ANTONYMS modest.

insufficiency noun *there was an insufficiency of evidence*: **lack**, inadequacy, shortage, want, dearth, deficit, shortfall; scarcity, scarceness, scantiness, paucity, absence, undersupply, sparseness, deprivation, meagreness, shortness; rare exiguity, exiguousness.
▷ANTONYMS sufficiency.

insufficient adjective *there was insufficient time available | insufficient resources*: **inadequate**, not enough, too little; too few, too small, deficient, poor, scant, scanty; scarce, sparse, short, in short supply, at a premium; lacking, wanting; paltry, meagre, niggardly; skimpy, sketchy, incomplete, restricted, limited; informal measly, pathetic, piddling; rare exiguous.
▷ANTONYMS sufficient.

insular adjective **1** *a stubbornly insular group of people*: **narrow-minded**, limited, blinkered, restricted, inward-looking, conventional, parochial, provincial, small-town, localist, small-minded, petty-minded, petty, close-minded, short-sighted, myopic, hidebound, dyed-in-the-wool, diehard, set, set in one's ways, inflexible, dogmatic, rigid, entrenched, illiberal, intolerant, prejudiced, bigoted, biased, partisan, sectarian, xenophobic, discriminatory; Brit. parish-pump, blimpish; French borné; N. Amer. informal jerkwater; rare claustral.
▷ANTONYMS broad-minded; tolerant.
2 *an insular community which has few links with the rest of the world*: **isolated**, inaccessible, cut off, closed, separate, segregated, detached, solitary, lonely, insulated, self-contained, self-sufficient.
▷ANTONYMS accessible; cosmopolitan.

insularity noun **1** *he was untrammelled by the insularity which bedevilled the art world*: **narrow-mindedness**, blinkered approach/attitude, parochialism, provincialism, localism, narrowness, small-mindedness, pettiness, short-sightedness, myopia, inflexibility, dogmatism, illiberality, intolerance, prejudice, bigotry, bias, partisanship, sectarianism, xenophobia, discrimination.
▷ANTONYMS broad-mindedness; tolerance.
2 *the valley's insularity has proved a blessing*: **isolation**, inaccessibility, separation, segregation, detachment, solitariness, loneliness, insulation, self-sufficiency.
▷ANTONYMS accessibility.

insulate verb **1** *pipes in the attic must be insulated*: **wrap**, cover, encase, enclose, envelop, swathe, sheathe, bundle up; lag, heatproof, soundproof, muffle, make shockproof, pad, cushion; literary lap.
2 *the Netherlands was largely insulated from the full impact of the Great War*: **protect**, keep safe, keep from harm, save, safeguard, shield, defend, shelter, screen, cushion, cocoon; isolate, segregate, separate, sequester, detach, exclude, cut off, cloister.

insulation noun **1** *his life in Attleborough afforded him insulation from the rigours of inner-city life*: **protection**, defence, shelter, screen, cushion, shield, shielding, safe keeping, safeguarding; isolation, segregation, separation, setting apart, sequestration, closeting, detachment, exclusion, quarantine.
▷ANTONYMS exposure.
2 *lofts should have at least 100mm of insulation*: **lagging**, blanket, jacket, wrap.

insult verb (stress on the second syllable) *you are insulting the woman I love*: **offend**, give/cause offence to, affront, abuse, be rude to, call someone names, slight, disparage, discredit, libel, slander, malign, defame, denigrate, cast aspersions on, impugn, slur, revile, calumniate; hurt, hurt someone's feelings, mortify, humiliate, wound; snub, rebuff, spurn, shun, treat disrespectfully, ignore, cut dead, give someone the cold-shoulder, turn one's back on; informal bad-mouth; Brit. informal **slag off**; N. Amer. informal trash-talk; rare asperse, derogate, miscall.
▷ANTONYMS compliment; flatter.
▸ **noun** (stress on the first syllable) *he hurled insults at us*: **abusive remark**, jibe, affront, slight, snub, barb, slur, backhanded compliment, injury, libel, slander, defamation, abuse, disparagement, depreciation, impugnment, revilement, humiliation, indignity, insolence, rudeness; aspersions; informal dig, put-down, slap in the face, kick in the teeth; archaic contumely.
▷ANTONYMS compliment.

insulting adjective *they directed foul and insulting comments at the referee*: **abusive**, rude, vulgar, offensive, wounding, mortifying, humiliating, disparaging, belittling, derogatory, depreciating, deprecatory, disrespectful, denigratory, uncomplimentary, pejorative, vituperative; disdainful, derisive, scornful, contemptuous; defamatory, slanderous, libellous, scurrilous, blasphemous, discrediting; informal bitchy, catty; archaic contumelious.
▷ANTONYMS complimentary; polite.

Choose the right word **insulting, offensive, derogatory**

See **offensive**.

insuperable adjective *there should be no insuperable obstacle to the purchase*: **insurmountable**, unconquerable, invincible, unassailable; overwhelming, hopeless, impossible.
▷ANTONYMS surmountable.

insupportable adjective **1** *this view appears insupportable*: **unjustifiable**, without justification, indefensible, inexcusable, unforgivable,

unpardonable, unwarrantable, unreasonable; **groundless**, unfounded, without foundation, foundationless, baseless, without basis, unsupported, unsubstantiated, unconfirmed, uncorroborated, invalid, untenable, implausible, weak, shaky, flawed, specious, defective.
▷ANTONYMS justified.
2 *the heat in Cairo was insupportable*: **intolerable**, insufferable, unbearable, unendurable, unacceptable, oppressive, overwhelming, overpowering, impossible, not to be borne, past bearing, too much to bear, more than one can stand, more than flesh and blood can stand; unspeakable, dreadful, excruciating; informal too much.
▷ANTONYMS bearable; congenial.

insurance noun **1** *insurance on his new car was going to cost him £750*: **assurance**, indemnity, indemnification, (financial) protection, security, surety, cover.
2 *the high defence expenditure was considered a reasonable insurance against a third World War*: **protection**, defence, safeguard, safety measure, shelter, security, precaution, provision, preventive measure, immunity; guarantee, warranty; informal backstop.

insure verb *they had failed to insure the building against fire*: **protect**, indemnify, cover, underwrite, assure, guarantee, warrant.

> *Easily confused words* **insure or ensure?**
>
> See **ensure**.

insurgent adjective *insurgent forces have captured the north of the country*: **rebellious**, rebel, revolutionary, mutinous, mutinying; traitorous, renegade, rioting, seditious, subversive; rare insurrectionary, insurrectionist.
▷ANTONYMS loyal; government.
▶ noun *government troops were fighting insurgents*: **rebel**, revolutionary, revolutionist, mutineer, agitator, subversive, guerrilla, anarchist, terrorist, bioterrorist, narcoterrorist, ecoterrorist, cyberterrorist, agroterrorist, rioter; freedom fighter, resistance fighter; traitor, renegade; in Mexico, historical Zapatista; in S. America, historical Montonero; rare insurrectionist, insurrectionary.
▷ANTONYMS loyalist.

insurmountable adjective *there are insurmountable difficulties in ensuring equal opportunities for all pupils*: **insuperable**, unconquerable, invincible, unassailable; overwhelming, hopeless, impossible.
▷ANTONYMS surmountable.

insurrection noun *the leaders of the insurrection surrendered*: **rebellion**, revolt, uprising, mutiny, revolution, insurgence, insurgency, rising, rioting, riot, sedition; civil disobedience, civil disorder, unrest, anarchy, fighting in the streets; coup; French coup d'état, jacquerie; German putsch.

intact adjective *something struck the window but the glass stayed intact | his reputation was intact*: **whole**, entire, complete, unbroken, undamaged, unharmed, uninjured, unimpaired, unflawed, faultless, flawless, unscathed, untouched, unspoilt, unmutilated, unsevered, unblemished, unmarred, unmarked, perfect, pristine, inviolate, unviolated, undefiled, unsullied, in one piece; sound, solid; rare scatheless.
▷ANTONYMS broken; damaged.

intangible adjective **1** *the moonlight made things seem intangible*: **impalpable**, untouchable, imperceptible to the touch, non-physical, bodiless, incorporeal, unembodied, disembodied, abstract, invisible; ethereal, insubstantial, airy, aerial; spiritual, ghostly, spectral, phantom, wraithlike, transcendental, unearthly, supernatural; rare immaterial, unbodied, discarnate, disincarnate, phantasmal, phantasmic.
▷ANTONYMS tangible.
2 *an intangible atmosphere of dread and doom*: **indefinable**, indescribable, inexpressible, nameless; vague, obscure, unclear, hazy, dim, mysterious; indefinite, unanalysable, subtle, elusive, fugitive.
▷ANTONYMS clear.

integral adjective **1** *communicating is an integral part of all human behaviour*: **essential**, fundamental, basic, intrinsic, inherent, constitutive, innate, structural; vital, indispensable, necessary, requisite.
▷ANTONYMS incidental; peripheral.
2 *the travelling hairdryer has integral cord storage*: **built-in**, inbuilt, integrated, incorporated, fitted, component, constituent; rare integrant.
▷ANTONYMS add-on.
3 *an integral approach to users and their needs*: **unified**, integrated, comprehensive, organic, composite, combined, aggregate, undivided, overall, gross, entire, complete, whole, total, full, intact.
▷ANTONYMS fragmented; partial.

integrate verb *he proposes to integrate our reserve forces more closely with the regular forces*: **combine**, amalgamate, merge, unite, join, fuse, blend, mingle, coalesce, consolidate, meld, intermingle, mix, intermix, incorporate, affiliate, unify, assimilate, homogenize, harmonize, mesh, desegregate; literary commingle.
▷ANTONYMS separate.

integrated adjective **1** *an integrated package of support services*: **unified**, united, consolidated, amalgamated, joined, combined, merged, fused, blended, meshed, coherent, homogeneous, homogenized, mutually dependent, assimilated, cohesive, concatenated; federal, federated, confederate, confederated.
▷ANTONYMS unconnected; separate.
2 *an integrated school*: **desegregated**, non-segregated, unsegregated, racially mixed, racially balanced; non-discriminatory.
▷ANTONYMS segregated.

integration noun **1** *the integration of images and text as camera-ready copy*: **combination**, amalgamation, incorporation, unification, consolidation, merger, fusing, blending, meshing, homogenization, homogenizing, coalescing, assimilation, concatenation.
▷ANTONYMS separation.
2 *the report focused attention on the integration of children with special educational needs*: **desegregation**, inclusion.
▷ANTONYMS segregation.

integrity noun **1** *I never doubted his integrity*: **honesty**, uprightness, probity, rectitude, honour, honourableness, upstandingness, good character, principle(s), ethics, morals, righteousness, morality, nobility, high-mindedness, right-mindedness, noble-mindedness, virtue, decency, fairness, scrupulousness, sincerity, truthfulness, trustworthiness.
▷ANTONYMS dishonesty.
2 *internal racial unrest threatened the integrity of the federation*: **unity**, unification, wholeness, coherence, cohesion, undividedness, togetherness, solidarity, coalition.
▷ANTONYMS division.
3 *the structural integrity of the aircraft*: **soundness**, robustness, strength, sturdiness, solidity, solidness, durability, stability, stoutness, toughness.
▷ANTONYMS fragility.

intellect noun **1** *it's a film that appeals more to the intellect than to the gut*: **mind**, brain, brains, head, intelligence, reason, understanding, comprehension, thought, brainpower, sense, judgement, wisdom, wits; informal nous, grey matter, brainbox, brain cells, upper storey; Brit. informal loaf; N. Amer. informal smarts; S. African informal kop.
▷ANTONYMS emotion.
2 *one of the most sophisticated intellects of the century*: **thinker**, intellectual, bluestocking, academic, scholar, sage; mind, brain.

intellectual adjective **1** *he is a man of formidable intellectual capacity*: **mental**, cerebral, cognitive; rational, psychological, abstract, conceptual, theoretical, analytical, logical; academic; rare mindly, phrenic, ratiocinative.
▷ANTONYMS physical.
2 *a remarkably intellectual man*: **intelligent**, clever, academic, well educated, well read, widely read, erudite, cerebral, learned, knowledgeable, literary, bookish, donnish, highbrow, scholarly, studious, cultured, cultivated, civilized, enlightened, sophisticated; informal brainy; archaic lettered, clerkly.
▷ANTONYMS stupid; illiterate.
▶ noun *intellectuals are appalled by the mentality of the popular soap operas*: **intelligent person**, learned person, highbrow, academic, bookworm, bookish person, man of letters, woman of letters, bluestocking, thinker, brain, scholar, sage; **genius**, Einstein, polymath, expert, prodigy, gifted child; mastermind; Hindu pandit; informal egghead, brains, bright spark, whizz, wizard, walking encyclopedia; Brit. informal brainbox, clever clogs, boffin; N. Amer. informal brainiac, rocket scientist, maven, Brahmin, pointy-head; archaic bookman.
▷ANTONYMS dunce.

intelligence noun **1** *a man of great intelligence*: **intellectual/mental capacity**, intellect, mind, brain, brains, brainpower, powers of reasoning, judgement, reason, reasoning, understanding, comprehension, acumen, wit, sense, insight, perceptiveness, perception, perspicaciousness, perspicacity, penetration, discernment, sharpness, quickness of mind, quick-wittedness, smartness, canniness, astuteness, intuition, acuity, alertness, cleverness, brilliance, aptness, ability, giftedness, talent; informal braininess.
▷ANTONYMS stupidity.
2 *the lack of intelligence received from the Eighth Army*: **information**, facts, details, particulars, data, figures, statistics, knowledge, report(s); informal info, gen, dope.
3 *a former agent for British military intelligence*: **information gathering**, surveillance, observation, reconnaissance, spying, espionage, undercover work, infiltration, ELINT, Humint; informal recon.

intelligent adjective **1** *Breuer is an intelligent writer*: **clever**, bright, brilliant, sharp, quick, quick-witted, quick on the uptake, smart, canny, astute, intuitive, thinking, acute, alert, keen, insightful, perceptive, perspicacious, penetrating, discerning; ingenious, inventive; knowledgeable; apt, able, gifted, talented; informal brainy; (**be intelligent**) informal have a good head on one's shoulders, there are no flies on ...; Brit. informal know how many beans make five.
▷ANTONYMS stupid.
2 *an extraterrestrial intelligent being*: **rational**, capable of thought, higher-order.
▷ANTONYMS non-rational.
3 *intelligent machines*: **robotic**, automatic, self-regulating, capable of learning; informal smart.

i

intelligentsia plural noun *there is a distrust of the intelligentsia and of theoretical learning*: **intellectuals**, intelligent people, academics, scholars, learned people, literati, culturati, men and women of letters, cognoscenti, illuminati, highbrows, bluestockings, thinkers, brains; the intelligent; informal eggheads; Brit. informal boffins.
▷ANTONYMS masses.

intelligibility noun *documents of varying degrees of complexity and intelligibility*: **comprehensibility**, ease of understanding, accessibility, digestibility, user-friendliness; lucidity, lucidness, clarity, clearness, coherence, transparency, plainness, simplicity, perspicuity, explicitness, precision, lack of ambiguity, unambiguity.
▷ANTONYMS unintelligibility.

intelligible adjective *statutes were drafted so as to be intelligible only to lawyers*: **comprehensible**, understandable; easy to understand, accessible, digestible, user-friendly; lucid, clear, crystal clear, coherent, transparent, plain, simple, perspicuous, explicit, precise, unambiguous, self-explanatory, penetrable, fathomable, graspable.
▷ANTONYMS unintelligible.

intemperance noun **1** *the friars were frequently criticized for personal intemperance*: **overindulgence**, intemperateness, immoderation, lack of restraint, abandon, lack of self-control; excess, excessiveness, extravagance, prodigality, profligacy, lavishness; self-indulgence, self-gratification; debauchery, decadence, wantonness, dissipation, dissolution, dissoluteness.
▷ANTONYMS moderation.
2 *the Temperance Movement argued that intemperance was a disease*: **drinking**, hard/heavy drinking, alcoholism, alcohol abuse, dipsomania; drunkenness, intoxication, inebriation, insobriety, tipsiness; rare inebriety, sottishness, bibulousness, crapulence.
▷ANTONYMS temperance.

i

intemperate adjective *I drank, I confess, an intemperate amount of beer | his intemperate language*: **immoderate**, excessive, undue, inordinate, unreasonable, unjustified, unwarranted, uncalled for; extreme, unrestrained, unrestricted, uncontrolled, unbridled, uncurbed; self-indulgent, overindulgent, extravagant, lavish, prodigal, profligate, imprudent, reckless, wild, outrageous, egregious; dissolute, debauched, wanton, dissipated, dissipative.
▷ANTONYMS moderate.

intend verb *Charlie intends to buy a bungalow | the goods are intended for export*: **plan**, mean, have the/every intention, have in mind, have in view, have plans, aim, propose, aspire, hope, expect, be looking, be going, be resolved, have resolved, be determined, have set out, purpose, be plotting; desire, want, wish; contemplate, think of, envisage; design, earmark, set apart.

intended adjective *the foul was not intended*: **deliberate**, intentional, calculated, conscious, done on purpose, planned, considered, studied, knowing, wilful, wanton, purposeful, purposive, premeditated, pre-planned, thought out in advance, prearranged, preconceived, predetermined; aforethought; voluntary, volitional; Law, dated prepense.
▷ANTONYMS accidental.
▶noun informal, dated *can you share your inner thoughts with your intended?* **fiancée**, **fiancé**, wife-to-be, husband-to-be, bride-to-be, future wife/husband, prospective wife/husband, prospective spouse; formal betrothed.

intense adjective **1** *the subject of intense interest | intense heat*: **great**, acute, enormous, fierce, severe, extreme, high, exceptional, extraordinary, harsh, strong, powerful, potent, vigorous; major, profound, deep, concentrated, consuming; informal serious.
▷ANTONYMS mild.
2 *a very intense young man*: **passionate**, impassioned, ardent, earnest, fervent, fervid, hot-blooded, zealous, vehement, fiery, heated, feverish, emotional, heartfelt, eager, keen, enthusiastic, excited, animated, spirited, vigorous, strong, energetic, messianic, fanatical, committed; rare perfervid, passional.
▷ANTONYMS apathetic.

intensification noun *the intensification of international competition*: **escalation**, stepping up, boosting, increase, pickup, build-up, sharpening, strengthening, augmentation, concentration, reinforcement; heightening, deepening, broadening, widening, extension, expansion, amplification, magnification, enlargement; aggravation, exacerbation, worsening, deterioration, compounding.
▷ANTONYMS lessening, abatement.

intensify verb *Henry intensified his attack on the church | the violence intensified*: **escalate**, step up, boost, increase, raise, sharpen, strengthen, augment, add to, concentrate, reinforce; gain strength, pick up, build up, heighten, deepen, broaden, widen, extend, expand, amplify, magnify; aggravate, exacerbate, make worse, worsen, inflame, compound.
▷ANTONYMS lessen, abate.

intensity noun **1** *the intensity of the sun*: **strength**, power, powerfulness, potency, vigour, force, forcefulness; severity, ferocity, vehemence, fierceness, violence, harshness; magnitude, greatness, high degree, concentration, extremity, acuteness; seriousness, gravity, graveness, severeness, grievousness.
2 *his eyes seared hers with a glowing intensity*: **passion**, ardour, fervour, fervency, zeal, vehemence, fire, heat, fever, emotion, eagerness, keenness, enthusiasm, excitement, animation, spirit, vigour, earnestness, strength, energy; fanaticism.
▷ANTONYMS apathy; indifference.

intensive adjective *an intensive course in Russian | an intensive search of the area*: **thorough**, in-depth, concentrated, rigorous, exhaustive, all-out, concerted, thoroughgoing; all-embracing, all-encompassing, all-inclusive, comprehensive, complete, full, total, all-absorbing; serious, vigorous, strenuous, detailed, minute, close, meticulous, scrupulous, assiduous, conscientious, painstaking, methodical, careful, sedulous, elaborate, extensive, widespread, sweeping, searching, high-pressure, determined, resolute, persistent, insistent.
▷ANTONYMS superficial; cursory; partial.

intent noun *he tried to divine his father's intent in asking the question*: **aim**, purpose, intention, objective, object, goal, target, end; design, plan, scheme; resolve, resolution, determination; wish, desire, ambition, idea, dream, aspiration, hope.
□ **to all intents and purposes** *to all intents and purposes a newborn human baby is helpless*: **in effect**, effectively, in essence, essentially, virtually, practically, in practical terms, for all practical purposes, in all important respects; more or less, just about, all but, as good as, in all but name, as near as dammit; almost, nearly, verging on, bordering on, well nigh, nigh on; S. African plus-minus; informal pretty much, pretty nearly, pretty well.
▷ANTONYMS fully; by no means.
▶adjective **1** *he was* **intent on** *proving his point*: **bent**, set, determined, insistent, fixed, resolved, hell-bent, keen; firm about, committed to; single-minded about, inflexible about, obsessive about, obsessed with, fanatical about, fixated on; determined to, resolved to, anxious to, impatient to.
▷ANTONYMS half-hearted; reluctant.
2 *she had an intent look on her face*: **attentive**, absorbed, engrossed, fascinated, enthralled, enrapt, rapt, focused, earnest, concentrated, concentrating, intense, studious, fixed, steady, steadfast, occupied, preoccupied, wrapped up, alert, watchful, observant.
▷ANTONYMS vacant.

intention noun **1** *it is his intention to be leader*: **aim**, purpose, intent, objective, object, goal, target, end; design, plan, scheme; resolve, resolution, determination; wish, desire, ambition, idea, dream, aspiration, hope.
2 *Milton manages, with or without intention, to build up a wonderfully vivid and intriguing portrait of Satan*: **deliberateness**, intentionality, intent, design, calculation; premeditation, preconception, forethought, plan, planning, pre-planning, advance planning, prearrangement, malice aforethought.
▷ANTONYMS inadvertency; accident.

intentional adjective *there shall be no intentional physical contact between teams*: **deliberate**, calculated, conscious, done on purpose, intended, planned, meant, considered, studied, knowing, wilful, wanton, purposeful, purposive, purposed, premeditated, pre-planned, thought out in advance, prearranged, preconceived, predetermined; aforethought; voluntary, volitional; Law, dated prepense.
▷ANTONYMS unintentional, accidental.

intentionally adverb *she would never intentionally hurt anyone*: **deliberately**, on purpose, purposely, purposefully, by design, knowingly, wittingly, consciously; premeditatedly, calculatedly, in cold blood, wilfully, wantonly; with malice aforethought.
▷ANTONYMS accidentally.

intently adverb *she listened intently to Harry's story*: **attentively**, closely, keenly, with fascination, raptly, earnestly, concentratedly, hard, studiously, fixedly, steadily, steadfastly, alertly, watchfully, observantly, carefully.
▷ANTONYMS absently; casually.

inter verb *his remains were interred in the new cemetery*: **bury**, lay to rest, consign to the grave, entomb, inurn; earth up; informal put six feet under, plant; N. Amer. informal deep-six; literary sepulchre, ensepulchre, inhume, inearth.
▷ANTONYMS exhume.

intercede verb *several nations offered to intercede on the captives' behalf*: **mediate**, act as an intermediary, intermediate, negotiate, arbitrate, moderate, conciliate, act as honest broker, intervene, interpose, step in, become/get involved, act, take action, take measures, take a hand; plead, petition, entreat, supplicate.

intercept verb *an Italian naval vessel intercepted the gunrunners' boat*: **stop**, head off, cut off; catch, seize, grab, snatch, expropriate, commandeer; obstruct, impede, interrupt, block, check, detain; attack, ambush, take on, challenge, pounce on, swoop down on, waylay, accost, tackle, confront; informal buttonhole.

intercession noun *he made contact with the Austrians through the intercession of the Serbs*: **mediation**, intermediation, negotiation, arbitration, conciliation, intervention, interposition, involvement, action; pleading, petition, entreaty, supplication, good offices, agency, shuttle diplomacy; rare mediatorship.

intercessor noun *they act as priests, intercessors between the people and the gods*: **mediator**, moderator, go-between, negotiator, middleman, intermediary, intervenor, interceder, arbitrator, arbiter; conciliator, reconciler, broker, honest broker, petitioner, supplicant, liaison officer, peacemaker.

interchange verb (stress on the third syllable) **1** *superiors and subordinates freely interchange ideas and information*: **exchange**, trade, swap, change, barter, bandy, reciprocate; archaic truck.
2 *the terms 'tone' and 'colour' are often wrongly interchanged*: **substitute**, transpose, exchange, change, switch, swap (round), reverse, invert, turn about/around, change (round), move (around), rearrange, reorder, replace, supplant.
▶ noun (stress on the first syllable) **1** *the interchange of ideas between the producers and the end users*: **exchange**, trading, trade, swap, swapping, barter, bandying, give and take, traffic, trafficking, reciprocation, reciprocity; archaic truck.
2 *the interchange of the ninth and tenth columns*: **substitution**, transposition, exchange, switch, switching, swap, swapping, reversal, inversion, change, rearrangement, reordering, replacement, replacing; N. Amer. trade.
3 *a motorway interchange*: **junction**, intersection, crossing; turn-off, exit; N. Amer. cloverleaf.

interchangeable adjective **1** *the very latest paint gun has three interchangeable barrels*: **exchangeable**, transposable, replaceable.
▷ANTONYMS incompatible.
2 *you can follow one of two more or less interchangeable roads back into the valley*: **identical**, similar, alike, (exactly) the same, indistinguishable, uniform, twin, undifferentiated, homogeneous, of a piece, cut from the same cloth; corresponding, correspondent, commensurate, equivalent, matching, like, parallel, analogous, comparable, cognate, equal; informal like (two) peas in a pod, much of a muchness, (like) Tweedledum and Tweedledee.
▷ANTONYMS different.

intercourse noun **1** *the market was an important focus of social intercourse*: **dealings**, relations, relationships, association, connections, contact, interchange, communication, intercommunication, communion, correspondence, negotiations, bargaining, transactions, proceedings; **trade**, trading, business, commerce, traffic, trafficking; informal truck, doings.
2 *she did not consent to intercourse with him*: **sexual intercourse**, sex, lovemaking, making love, sex act, act of love, sexual relations, intimate relations, intimacy, coupling, mating, going to bed with someone, sleeping with someone; informal nooky; Brit. informal bonking, rumpy pumpy, a bit of the other, how's your father; S. African informal pata-pata; vulgar slang screwing, fucking; Brit. vulgar slang shagging; formal coitus, coition, copulation; formal fornication; archaic carnal knowledge, (sexual) congress, commerce.

interdict noun *they breached an interdict banning them from organizing mass pickets*: **prohibition**, ban, bar, veto, proscription, interdiction, embargo, moratorium, injunction, restraining order; Brit. exclusion order.
▷ANTONYMS permission.
▶ verb **1** *the Portuguese interdicted all foreign commerce*: **prohibit**, forbid, ban, bar, veto, proscribe, make illegal, place an embargo on, embargo, disallow, debar, outlaw, stop, put a stop to, put an end to, block, suppress; Law enjoin, estop, restrain.
▷ANTONYMS permit.
2 N. Amer. *efforts to interdict the flow of heroin*: **intercept**, stop, head off, cut off; obstruct, impede, interrupt, block, check, detain.

interest noun **1** *the children listened to the story with great interest*: **attentiveness**, undivided attention, absorption, engrossment, heed, regard, notice, scrutiny; curiosity, inquisitiveness; enjoyment, delight.
▷ANTONYMS boredom.
2 *the region has many places of interest to the tourist*: **attraction**, appeal, fascination, charm, beauty, allure, allurement, temptation, tantalization.
3 *this account may only be of interest to those involved*: **concern**, **importance**, import, consequence, moment, momentousness, significance, substance, note, relevance, value, weight, gravity, priority, urgency.
4 *her interests include reading and music*: **hobby**, pastime, leisure activity, leisure pursuit, recreation, entertainment, diversion, amusement, relaxation; passion, enthusiasm; informal thing, bag, scene, cup of tea.
5 *he has a financial interest in the firm*: **stake**, share, portion, claim, investment, stock, equity; involvement, participation, concern.
6 *you must declare your interest in the case*: **involvement**, partiality, partisanship, preference, loyalty; one-sidedness, favouritism, bias, prejudice.
7 *his attorney zealously guarded his interests*: **concern**, business, business matter, matter, care; (**interests**) affairs.
8 *put your cash in a savings account where it will earn interest*: **dividends**, profits, returns; a percentage, a gain.
□ **in someone's interests** *the merger is in the interests of both regiments*: **of benefit to**, to the advantage of, for the sake of, for the benefit of.
▶ verb **1** *write about a topic that interests you*: **be of interest to**, appeal to, attract, be attractive to, intrigue, fascinate; absorb, engross, rivet, grip, hold, captivate; amuse, divert, entertain; arouse one's curiosity, whet one's appetite, hold one's attention, engage one's attention; informal float someone's boat, tickle someone's fancy, light someone's fire.
▷ANTONYMS bore.
2 *can I* **interest** *you* **in** *an aerial photograph of your house?* **arouse someone's interest in**, persuade to buy, sell.

interested adjective **1** *an interested crowd had gathered round the buskers*: **attentive**, intent, absorbed, engrossed, fascinated, riveted, gripped, captivated, rapt, agog, intrigued, enquiring, inquisitive, curious, burning with curiosity; earnest, keen, eager; informal all ears, beady-eyed, nosy, snoopy.
▷ANTONYMS bored, uninterested.
2 *the government must consult with interested bodies before formulating a legislative measure*: **concerned**, involved, implicated, affected, connected, related.
3 *no interested party can judge the contest*: **partisan**, partial, biased, prejudiced, one-sided, preferential, discriminatory.
▷ANTONYMS disinterested.

interesting adjective *it is one of the most interesting novels of its time*: **absorbing**, engrossing, fascinating, riveting, gripping, compelling, compulsive, spellbinding, captivating, engaging, enthralling, entrancing, beguiling; appealing, attractive, amusing, entertaining, stimulating, thought-provoking, diverting, exciting, intriguing, action-packed; informal unputdownable.
▷ANTONYMS boring, uninteresting.

interfere verb **1** *we can't let personal feelings* **interfere with** *our duty*: **impede**, obstruct, get in the way of, stand in the way of, hinder, be a hindrance to, inhibit, restrict, restrain, constrain, hamper, handicap, cramp, check, block, frustrate, thwart, baulk, hold back, hold up; disturb, disrupt, influence, affect, confuse; Brit. informal throw a spanner in the works of; N. Amer. informal throw a monkey wrench in the works of; rare trammel, cumber.
2 *she tried not to* **interfere in** *her children's lives*: **butt into**, barge into, pry into, nose into, be nosy about, intrude into, intervene in, get involved in, intercede in, encroach on, impinge on, impose oneself on; meddle in, tamper with; tread on someone's toes, step on someone's toes; informal poke one's nose into, mess with, horn in on, muscle in on, stick one's oar in, gatecrash; N. Amer. informal kibitz on; archaic entrench on.
3 Brit. euphemistic *he was accused of* **interfering with** *local children*: **sexually abuse**, abuse, sexually assault, indecently assault, assault, molest, grope; harm, damage; informal feel up, touch up, paw, maul.

interference noun **1** *they resent state interference in religious affairs*: **intrusion**, intervention, intercession, involvement, impinging, encroaching, trespass, trespassing, obtrusion; butting in, barging in; meddling, meddlesomeness, tampering, prying, poking around, nosing around; informal horning in, muscling in, gatecrashing.
2 *the cable helps to suppress radio interference*: **disruption**, disturbance, static, fading.

interfering adjective *they wanted to be free from their interfering relatives*: **meddlesome**, meddling, intrusive, intruding, prying, probing, nosy, inquisitive, over-curious, over-interested, busybody; informal nosy-parker, snoopy, snooping; archaic intermeddling; rare obtrusive, busy.

interim noun *in the interim they agreed to carry out further research*: **meantime**, meanwhile, intervening time, interval, interlude; interregnum.
▶ adjective *he appointed an interim advisory committee*: **provisional**, temporary, pro tem, stopgap, short-term, fill-in, caretaker, acting, intervening, transitional, changeover, make-do, makeshift, improvised, impromptu, emergency; Latin pro tempore, ad interim; rare provisory, provisionary.
▷ANTONYMS permanent.

interior adjective **1** *the house has a lovely oak staircase and interior panelling*: **inside**, inner, internal, intramural; on the inside.
▷ANTONYMS exterior.
2 *the interior basin deserts of the western United States*: **inland**, inshore, upcountry, non-coastal, inner, innermost, central; remote, wild.
▷ANTONYMS outer.
3 *he controlled the country's interior affairs*: **internal**, home, domestic, national, state, civil, local.
▷ANTONYMS foreign.
4 *individuals are driven by interior forces*: **inner**, spiritual, mental, psychological, emotional, private, personal, intimate, secret, hidden; instinctive, intuitive, impulsive, involuntary, spontaneous; informal gut.
▶ noun **1** *a hatch led to the interior of the yacht*: **inside**, inner part, inner area, depths, recesses, bowels, belly; centre, middle, nucleus, core, heart; informal innards.
▷ANTONYMS exterior, outside.
2 *he went on treks to the country's interior*: **centre**, heartland, hinterland; wilderness, wilds; in Australia and Africa bush.
▷ANTONYMS borderland.

interject verb **1** *at one point in his story she interjected a comment*: **interpose**, introduce, throw in, insert, interpolate, add.
2 *Christina felt bound to interject before there was open warfare*: **interrupt**, intervene, cut in, break in, butt in, chime in; have one's say, put one's oar in; remark, comment; Brit. informal chip in, put one's pennyworth in; N. Amer. informal put one's two cents in.

interjection noun **1** *there were astonished interjections from the crowd*: **exclamation**, ejaculation, sudden utterance, cry, shout, roar, call; rare vociferation.
2 *the interjection of a question here and there*: **interposition**, interposing, interpolation, interpolating, insertion, inserting, addition, adding, introduction, introducing.

interlock verb *the fixed panel should interlock with the sliding section*: **engage**, interconnect, interlink, mesh, intermesh, fit together, join together, join, unite, connect, yoke, mate, couple.
▷ANTONYMS disengage.

interloper noun *they were a close community and could not abide interlopers*: **intruder**, encroacher, trespasser, invader, infiltrator, unwanted person, unwanted visitor, uninvited guest; outsider, stranger, immigrant, foreigner, alien, newcomer; informal gatecrasher.

interlude noun *a peaceful interlude in her busy day*: **interval**, intermission, break, recess, pause, respite, rest, breathing space, halt, gap, stop, stoppage, hiatus, lull; informal breather, let-up, time out, down time; Austral./NZ informal smoko; archaic surcease.

intermediary noun *they concluded the deal through an intermediary*: **mediator**, go-between, negotiator, intervenor, interceder, intercessor, arbitrator, arbiter, conciliator, peacemaker; middleman, broker, agent, liaison, linkman, linkwoman, linkperson; rare negotiant.

intermediate adjective *an intermediate stage in the cell's development*: **halfway**, in-between, middle, mid, midway, median, intermediary, intervening, interposed, transitional; in the middle, at the halfway point, equidistant between two points/stages; technical medial; rare intermedial.

interment noun *his body was taken for interment*: **burial**, burying, committal, entombment, inhumation; a funeral; funeral rites, obsequies; rare sepulture, exequies.
▷ANTONYMS exhumation.

interminable adjective **1** *Wednesday was a day of interminable meetings*: **seemingly endless**, endless, never-ending, unending, without end, non-stop, everlasting, ceaseless, unceasing, incessant, constant, continual, uninterrupted, unbroken, sustained; monotonous, tedious, wearisome, boring, long-winded, long-drawn-out, overlong, rambling, meandering, laborious, ponderous.
2 *he was back from one of his interminable job interviews*: **countless**, numerous, many, untold, manifold, multitudinous, multifarious, innumerable, numberless, unmeasured, unnumbered, incalculable, indeterminable; literary myriad, legion; rare innumerous, unnumberable.

intermingle verb *the two species of finch rarely intermingle | continue cooking to intermingle the flavours*: **mix**, intermix, mingle, unite, affiliate, associate, fraternize, get together, link up; blend, fuse, merge, combine, amalgamate, compound, marry; rare commingle, commix, admix, interflow.

intermission noun *after the first film there was an intermission | the work goes on without intermission*: **interval**, interlude, entr'acte, break, recess, pause, rest, respite, breathing space, lull, gap, stop, stoppage, halt; cessation, suspension, stopping, pausing, breaking off, discontinuation; informal let-up, breather, time out, down time; Austral./NZ informal smoko; archaic surcease.

intermittent adjective *they heard intermittent bursts of gunfire*: **sporadic**, irregular, fitful, spasmodic, broken, fragmentary, discontinuous, disconnected, isolated, odd, random, patchy, scattered; on again and off again, on and off, in fits and starts; occasional, periodic, cyclic, recurrent, recurring.
▷ANTONYMS continuous, steady.

> *Word toolkit* **intermittent**
>
> See **recurrent**.

intern verb *they have been interned without trial*: **imprison**, incarcerate, impound, jail, put in jail, put behind bars, detain, take into custody, hold in custody, hold captive, hold, lock up, keep under lock and key, confine; Brit. detain at Her Majesty's pleasure; informal put away, put inside, send down; Brit. informal bang up; rare immure.
▷ANTONYMS release.
▶ **noun** N. Amer. *he worked as an intern for a local magazine*: **trainee**, apprentice, probationer, student, novice, learner, beginner; person doing work experience.

internal adjective **1** *the offices faced each other across a large internal courtyard*: **inner**, interior, inside, intramural; central, middle.
▷ANTONYMS external.
2 *she died of internal injuries*: **inside**, inner; within the body, inside the body.
▷ANTONYMS external.
3 *the provinces retain autonomy in their internal affairs*: **domestic**, home, interior, civil, local; national, state; in-house, in-company.
▷ANTONYMS foreign.
4 *she was waging an internal battle with herself*: **mental**, psychological, emotional; personal, private, secret, hidden, intimate.

> *Word links* **internal**
>
> **endo-** related prefix, as in *endoskeleton, endocrine*

international adjective *the international business community | the international flavour of the exhibition*: **global**, worldwide, intercontinental; cosmopolitan, multiracial, multinational, universal, catholic, wide-ranging, far-reaching, all-embracing.
▷ANTONYMS national; local.

internecine adjective *internecine feuds between aspirants to the throne*: **deadly**, bloody, violent, fierce, destructive, ruinous; civil, internal, family.

interplay noun *the interplay between military and civilian populations*: **interaction**, interchange, teamwork, cooperation, reciprocation, reciprocity, give and take, compromises, concessions; flexibility, adaptability.

interpolate verb *the illustrations were interpolated in the text*: **insert**, interpose, introduce, enter, add, incorporate, inset, implant, build, put.

interpose verb **1** *he interposed himself between her and the stairs*: **insinuate**, place, put.
2 *at this point it is necessary to interpose a note of caution*: **introduce**, insert, interject, inject, add, throw in, put in, work in.
3 *the legislature interposed to suppress the custom*: **intervene**, intercede, step in, mediate, involve oneself; interfere, intrude, obtrude, butt in, cut in; informal barge in, horn in, muscle in.

interpret verb **1** *the rabbis interpreted the Jewish laws*: **explain**, elucidate, expound, explicate, clarify, make clear, make plain, illuminate, shed light on, throw light on; gloss, simplify, spell out.
2 *the remark was interpreted as a reference to the government*: **understand**, construe, take to mean, take, read, see, regard, explain.
3 *the symbols are difficult to interpret*: **decipher**, decode, solve, resolve, untangle, unravel, make intelligible; understand, comprehend, make sense of; informal crack.
4 *the book was interpreted for English-speaking readers*: **translate**, transcribe, transliterate, rewrite, convert; paraphrase.
5 *few ballets have so fully interpreted the thoughts of a poet*: **portray**, depict, present, perform, execute, enact, render.

interpretation noun **1** *the interpretation and application of the Bible's teaching*: **explanation**, elucidation, expounding, exposition, explication, exegesis, clarification, definition; simplification.
2 *she did not care what interpretation he put on her haste*: **meaning**, understanding, construal, connotation, reading, explanation, inference, conclusion, supposition.
3 *the interpretation of experimental findings*: **analysis**, reading, evaluation, review, study, examination, diagnosis; decoding, deciphering; rare anatomization.
4 *the interpretation of foreign texts*: **translation**, transcription, transliteration; paraphrasing.
5 *Davis was admirable in his interpretation of the sonata*: **rendition**, rendering, execution, presentation, performance, reading, playing, singing; enactment, portrayal, depiction.

interpreter noun **1** *a fluent Japanese speaker acted as their interpreter*: **translator**, transcriber, transliterator, decipherer; rare dragoman.
2 *she was the most important vocal interpreter of his music*: **performer**, presenter, portrayer, exponent; singer, player.
3 *interpreters of Italian art*: **analyst**, evaluator, reviewer, commentator, annotator; rare exegete, scholiast, glossator.

interrogate verb *the police wished to interrogate her*: **question**, put questions to, cross-question, cross-examine, quiz, probe, catechize, sound out; interview, examine, debrief; informal pump, grill, give someone the third degree, put someone through the third degree, put the screws on, put someone through the wringer, worm something out of someone.

interrogation noun *he was driven to the police station for interrogation*: **questioning**, cross-questioning, cross-examination, quizzing, probing, inquisition, catechism; investigation, interviewing, interview, debriefing; informal pumping, grilling, the third degree; Law examination.

interrogative adjective *he gazed at me with a hard interrogative stare*: **questioning**, enquiring, inquisitive, inquisitorial, probing, searching, quizzing, quizzical, curious, intrigued, investigative; rare catechistic, catechistical.

interrupt verb **1** *she opened her mouth to interrupt | I'm sorry to interrupt your chat*: **cut in (on)**, break in (on), barge in (on), intrude (on), interfere (with), intervene (in); heckle, put one's oar in, have one's say; Brit. put one's pennyworth in; N. Amer. put one's two cents in; informal butt in (on), chime in (on), horn in (on), muscle in (on); Brit. informal chip in (on).

2 *the band had to interrupt their US tour*: **suspend**, adjourn, discontinue, break off, hold up, delay, lay aside, leave off, postpone, put off, put back, defer, shelve; stop, put a stop to, halt, bring to a halt, bring to a standstill, cease, end, bring to an end, bring to a close, cancel, sever, dissolve, terminate; informal take a breather from, put on ice, put on a back burner, put in cold storage.
3 *the coastal plain is interrupted by large lagoons*: **break up**, break, punctuate, intersperse; pepper, strew, dot, scatter.
4 *their view is to be interrupted by a new housing estate*: **obstruct**, impede, block, interfere with, cut off, get in the way of, limit, restrict.

interruption noun **1** *he was not best pleased at her interruption*: **cutting in**, interference, intervention, intrusion, obtrusion, disturbance; informal butting in, barging in, muscling in, horning in, sticking one's oar in.
2 *the system is protected against interruption of the power supply*: **discontinuance**, discontinuation, breaking off, suspension, stopping, halting, ceasing, cessation, termination.
3 *she is returning to education after an interruption in her career*: **interval**, interlude, break, pause, recess, gap, hiatus.

intersect verb **1** *the lines intersect at right angles*: **cross**, criss-cross; converge, meet, connect, join, link up, come together; technical decussate.
2 *the cornfield is intersected by a farm track*: **bisect**, divide, halve, cut in two, cut in half, cut across, cut through; cross, traverse, span.

intersection noun **1** *the intersection of the supply and demand curves*: **crossing**, criss-crossing; convergence, meeting, joining.
2 *the driver stopped at an intersection*: **road junction**, junction, T-junction, interchange, crossroads, crossing; level crossing, railway crossing; Brit. roundabout.

intersperse verb **1** *giant lobelia were interspersed among crags of rock*: **scatter**, distribute, disperse, spread, strew, dot, sprinkle, pepper, litter; literary bestrew.
2 *the beech trees are interspersed with conifers*: **intermix**, mix, mingle; **vary**, diversify, variegate, punctuate.

interstice noun *the interstices between the soil particles*: **space**, gap, interval, aperture, opening, hole, cranny, crevice, chink, slit, slot, crack, breach, vent.

intertwine verb *a wreath of laurel, intertwined with daffodils*: **entwine**, interweave, interlace, interthread, interwind, intertwist, twist, coil, twirl, ravel, lace, braid, plait, knit; rare convolute.

interval noun **1** *I returned to my balcony seat after the interval*: **intermission**, interlude, entr'acte, break, recess, pause, gap; lull, respite; half-time.
2 *polling day was a week away and Baldwin made two speeches in the interval*: **interim**, interlude, intervening time, intervening period, meantime, meanwhile; interregnum.
3 *the rapids have some short intervals of still water*: **stretch**, distance, span, area; space, gap, interspace.

intervene verb **1** *had the war not intervened, they might have married*: **occur**, happen, take place, arise, crop up, materialize, come about; result, ensue, follow, supervene; literary come to pass, befall, betide; archaic hap.
2 *she intervened in the row and drew up new guidelines*: **intercede**, involve oneself, get involved, interpose oneself, insinuate oneself, step in, cut in; mediate, arbitrate, conciliate, negotiate, act as peacemaker, act as an intermediary; interfere, intrude.

intervention noun *they would suffer no state intervention in their private business*: **involvement**, intercession, interceding, interposing, interposition; mediation, mediatorship, arbitration, conciliation, peacemaking; interference, intrusion, meddling; rare arbitrament.

interview noun *all applicants will be called for an interview | the journalists were granted an interview with the bishop*: **meeting**, discussion, conference, question and answer session, examination, evaluation, interrogation; **audience**, talk, dialogue, exchange; talks; informal rap session, confab; formal confabulation, interlocution.
▸ verb *the reporter interviewed him about his book | we interviewed seventy subjects for the survey*: **talk to**, have a discussion with, have a dialogue with, hold a meeting with, confer with; **question**, put questions to, probe, interrogate, cross-examine; poll, canvass, survey, sound out, ascertain the opinions of; informal grill, pump, give the third degree to; Law examine.

interviewer noun *the interviewer had a long list of questions*: **questioner**, interrogator, examiner, evaluator, assessor, appraiser; journalist, reporter, correspondent; rare examinant.

interweave verb **1** *the threads attached to the kite are interwoven*: **intertwine**, entwine, interlace, interthread, splice, braid, plait; twist together, weave together, twine together, wind together; Nautical marry.
2 *their fates were interwoven*: **interlink**, link, connect, associate; intermix, mix, merge, blend, fuse, interlock, knit, bind together.

intestinal adjective *he died from an intestinal complaint*: **enteric**, gastro-enteric, duodenal, coeliac, gastric, ventral, stomach, abdominal, visceral; rare stomachic, stomachical.

intestines plural noun *colic is a sharp pain in a baby's stomach or intestines*: **gut**, guts, entrails, viscera; small intestine, large intestine, bowel, colon; informal insides, innards; Brit. archaic numbles.

> *Word links* **intestines**
>
> **enteric, visceral** relating to the intestines
> **entero-** related prefix
> **enterotomy** incision into the intestine
> **enteritis** inflammation of the intestines

intimacy noun **1** *the sisters instantly re-established their old intimacy*: **closeness**, togetherness, affinity, rapport, attachment, familiarity, confidentiality, close association, close relationship, close attachment, close friendship, friendliness, comradeship, companionship, amity, affection, mutual affection, warmth, warm feelings, understanding, fellow feeling; informal chumminess, palliness; Brit. informal mateyness.
2 *she flushed at the memory of their earlier intimacy*: **sexual relations**, sexual intercourse, sex, intercourse, lovemaking, act of love, carnal knowledge, sexual congress, congress; formal coition, coitus, copulation.

intimate[1] (rhymes with 'ultimate') adjective **1** *an intimate friend of Picasso's*: **close**, bosom, boon, dear, cherished, familiar, confidential, faithful, constant, devoted, fast, firm, favourite, special; informal chummy, pally, as thick as thieves.
▷ANTONYMS distant.
2 *the hotel has an intimate atmosphere*: **friendly**, warm, welcoming, hospitable, harmonious, relaxed, informal, easy; cosy, comfortable, snug; tête-à-tête; informal comfy.
▷ANTONYMS formal; cold.
3 *they divulged their intimate thoughts*: **personal**, private, confidential, secret; innermost, inmost, inner, inward, deep, deepest, darkest, deep-seated; unspoken, undeclared, undisclosed, unvoiced.
4 *he has an intimate knowledge of the coal industry*: **detailed**, thorough, exhaustive, deep, in-depth, profound; experienced, personal, first-hand, direct, immediate.
▷ANTONYMS scant.
5 *he had intimate relations with his friend's wife*: **sexual**, carnal, amorous, amatory, romantic; formal fornicatory.
▸ noun *his background was common knowledge among his intimates*: **close friend**, best friend, bosom friend, constant companion, alter ego, confidant, confidante, close associate; informal chum, pal, buddy, crony, sidekick, cully, spar, main man; Brit. informal mate, mucker, china, oppo, butty; N. English informal marrow, marrer, marra; N. Amer. & S. African informal homeboy, homegirl; S. African informal gabba; Austral./NZ informal offsider; rare fidus Achates.

intimate[2] (rhymes with 'imitate') verb **1** *he intimated to the committee his decision to retire*: **announce**, state, proclaim, set forth, make known, make public, make plain, impart, disclose, reveal, divulge; tell, inform.
2 *Day intimated that the outlook does not look good*: **imply**, suggest, hint at, insinuate, indicate, signal, allude to, refer to, communicate, convey; give someone an inkling of; informal tip someone the wink about, get at, drive at.

intimation noun **1** *the early intimation of training session dates*: **announcement**, statement, communication, notification, notice, report, reporting, publishing, broadcasting, proclamation; disclosure, revelation, divulging; archaic annunciation.
2 *the first* **intimation of** *discord in the family*: **suggestion**, hint, indication, sign, signal, inkling, suspicion, impression; reference to, allusion to, pointer to, clue to, overtone of, undertone of, whisper of.

intimidate verb *he paid them to intimidate his political rivals*: **frighten**, menace, terrify, scare, alarm, terrorize, overawe, awe, cow, subdue, discourage, daunt, unnerve; **threaten**, domineer, browbeat, bully, pressure, pressurize, harass, harry, hound, hector, torment, plague; tyrannize, persecute, oppress; informal push around/about, lean on, bulldoze, steamroller, railroad, twist someone's arm, use strong-arm tactics on; N. Amer. informal bullyrag.

> *Choose the right word* **intimidate, threaten, menace**
>
> See **threaten**.

intimidation noun *there had been blatant intimidation of witnesses*: **frightening**, menacing, terrifying, scaring, alarming, terrorization, terrorizing, cowing, subduing, daunting, unnerving; **threatening**, domineering, browbeating, bullying, pressuring, pressurizing, pressurization, coercion, harassment, harrying, hounding, tormenting, plaguing; tyrannization, persecution, oppression; informal strong-arm tactics, arm-twisting, bulldozing, steamrollering, railroading.

intolerable adjective *the drilling noise had become intolerable*: **unbearable**, insufferable, unsupportable, insupportable, unendurable, beyond endurance, unacceptable, impossible, more than flesh and blood can stand, too much to bear, past bearing, not to be borne, overpowering; informal too much, enough to try the patience of a saint, enough to try the patience of Job.
▷ANTONYMS bearable, tolerable.

intolerance noun **1** *they are protesting at political and religious intolerance*: **bigotry**, narrow-mindedness, small-mindedness, parochialism,

provincialism, insularity, fanaticism, dogmatism, illiberality; prejudice, bias, partiality, partisanship, sectarianism, one-sidedness, inequality, unfairness, injustice, discrimination.
2 *she was tested for lactose intolerance*: **sensitivity**, hypersensitivity, oversensitivity; allergy, allergic reaction.

intolerant adjective **1** *Sophia was intolerant in religious matters*: **bigoted**, narrow-minded, small-minded, parochial, provincial, insular, blinkered, illiberal, inflexible, dogmatic, rigid, uncompromising, unforgiving, unsympathetic; prejudiced, biased, partial, partisan, one-sided, sectarian, discriminatory, unfair, unjust.
2 *limit those foods to which you are intolerant*: **allergic**, sensitive, hypersensitive, oversensitive.

intonation noun **1** *she read the sentence with the wrong intonation | his voice was low with a faint regional intonation*: **inflection**, pitch, tone, timbre, cadence, cadency, lilt, rise and fall, modulation, speech pattern; accentuation, emphasis, stress; accent, brogue.
2 *the intonation of hymns of praise*: **chanting**, incantation, recitation, singing; rare cantillation.

intone verb *grace before the meal was intoned in Gaelic*: **chant**, intonate, sing, recite; rare cantillate.

intoxicate verb **1** *one glass of wine was enough to intoxicate him*: **inebriate**, make drunk, make intoxicated, make inebriated; befuddle, fuddle, stupefy, go to someone's head, make someone's head spin; informal make legless, make woozy.
▷ANTONYMS sober someone up.
2 *he was intoxicated by cinema from the start*: **exhilarate**, thrill, elate, delight, captivate, enthral, entrance, enrapture, invigorate, animate, enliven, excite, stir, rouse, move, inspire, inflame, electrify; fire with enthusiasm, fire someone's imagination; informal give someone a buzz, give someone a kick, bowl over, tickle someone pink; N. Amer. informal give someone a charge.
▷ANTONYMS bore.

intoxicated adjective *he was cautioned for being intoxicated while on duty*: **drunk**, inebriated, inebriate, drunken, tipsy, the worse for drink, under the influence; blind drunk, dead drunk, rolling drunk, roaring drunk, as drunk as a lord, as drunk as a skunk; sottish, gin-soaked; informal tight, merry, the worse for wear, pie-eyed, three sheets to the wind, plastered, smashed, hammered, sloshed, soused, sozzled, well oiled, paralytic, wrecked, wasted, blotto, stewed, pickled, tanked up, soaked, blasted, ratted, off one's face, out of one's head, out of one's skull; Brit. informal legless, bevvied, Brahms and Liszt, half cut, out of it, bladdered, trolleyed, mullered, slaughtered, well away, squiffy, tiddly, out of one's box; Scottish informal fou; N. Amer. informal loaded, trashed, out of one's gourd; Brit. vulgar slang pissed, rat-arsed, arseholed; informal, dated in one's cups, lit up; euphemistic tired and emotional; archaic sotted, foxed, screwed; rare crapulent, crapulous, bibulous, ebriate.
▷ANTONYMS sober.

intoxicating adjective **1** *they abstain from intoxicating drink*: **alcoholic**, containing alcohol; strong, hard, potent, stiff; rare inebriating, intoxicant, spirituous, spiritous, vinous.
▷ANTONYMS non-alcoholic.
2 *an intoxicating sense of freedom prevailed*: **heady**, exhilarating, thrilling, exciting, rousing, stirring, stimulating, invigorating, electrifying, inspiring, galvanizing; strong, powerful, potent; informal mind-blowing.
▷ANTONYMS dull.

intoxication noun *he left the pub in a state of intoxication*: **drunkenness**, inebriation, insobriety, tipsiness, stupefaction; informal tightness; rare inebriety, crapulence.
▷ANTONYMS sobriety.

intractable adjective **1** *their problems have become more acute and intractable*: **unmanageable**, uncontrollable, ungovernable, out of control, out of hand, impossible to cope with; difficult, awkward, complex, troublesome, demanding, burdensome.
▷ANTONYMS manageable.
2 *there was no budging this intractable man*: **stubborn**, obstinate, obdurate, inflexible, unadaptable, unmalleable, unbending, unyielding, uncompromising, unaccommodating, uncooperative, difficult, awkward, perverse, contrary, disobedient, indomitable, refractory, recalcitrant, pig-headed, bull-headed, wilful; N. Amer. rock-ribbed; informal stiff-necked; Brit. informal bloody-minded; N. Amer. informal balky.
▷ANTONYMS compliant; obedient.

intransigent adjective *his intransigent attitude led to the quarrels with his friends*: **uncompromising**, inflexible, unbending, unyielding, unshakeable, unwavering, resolute, unpersuadable, unmalleable, unaccommodating, uncooperative, stubborn, obstinate, obdurate, pig-headed, bull-headed, single-minded, iron-willed, hard-line, hard and fast, diehard, immovable, unrelenting, inexorable, inveterate, rigid, tough, firm, determined, adamant, tenacious; informal stiff-necked; Brit. informal bloody-minded; N. Amer. informal balky; rare indurate.
▷ANTONYMS compliant; flexible.

intrench verb See **entrench**.

intrenched adjective See **entrenched**.

intrepid adjective *the intrepid band braved a precipitous mountain track*: **fearless**, unafraid, undaunted, dauntless, undismayed, unalarmed, unflinching, unshrinking, unblenching, unabashed, bold, daring, audacious, adventurous, dashing, heroic, dynamic, spirited, mettlesome, confident, indomitable; **brave**, courageous, valiant, valorous, stout-hearted, lionhearted, stalwart, plucky; informal gutsy, spunky, game, ballsy, go-ahead, have-a-go; archaic doughty; rare venturous.
▷ANTONYMS fearful; cowardly.

intricate adjective *intricate Arabic patterns | the intricate relationships between plants and animals*: **complex**, complicated, convoluted, tangled, entangled, ravelled, twisted, knotty, maze-like, labyrinthine, winding, serpentine, circuitous, sinuous; elaborate, ornate, detailed; Byzantine, Daedalian, Gordian, involved, mixed up, difficult, hard; informal fiddly; rare involute, involuted.
▷ANTONYMS simple, straightforward.

Word toolkit

intricate	complex	convoluted
design	system	logic
pattern	issue	argument
detail	structure	story
web	interaction	explanation
network	relationship	plot
carving	trait	reasoning
embroidery	mixture	scheme
melody	organism	thinking

intrigue verb (stress on the second syllable) **1** *other people's houses always intrigued her*: **interest**, be of interest to, fascinate, be a source of fascination to, arouse someone's curiosity, engage someone's attention, attract, draw, lure, tempt, tantalize; rivet, absorb, engross, charm, captivate; divert, titillate.
▷ANTONYMS bore.
2 *the ministers were intriguing for their own gains*: **plot**, hatch a plot, conspire, take part in a conspiracy, make secret plans, lay plans, scheme, manoeuvre, connive, collude, work hand in glove; rare complot, cabal, machinate.
▶noun (stress on the first syllable) **1** *the intrigue that accompanied the selection of a new leader | they implicated him in a nasty intrigue*: **plotting**, planning, conspiracy, collusion, conniving, scheming, machination, trickery, sharp practice, double-dealing, unscrupulousness, underhandedness, deviousness, subterfuge; plot, scheme, stratagem, ruse, wile, artifice, manoeuvre; informal dirty tricks; rare complot, cabal, covin.
2 *the king's intrigues with his nobles' wives*: **secret love affair**, affair, affair of the heart, liaison, amour, amorous entanglement, romantic entanglement, fling, flirtation, dalliance; adultery, infidelity, unfaithfulness; informal fooling around, playing around, playing away, hanky-panky; Brit. informal carryings-on, carry-on, bit on the side.

intriguer noun *he was revealed to be a political intriguer*: **conspirator**, co-conspirator, conspirer, plotter, schemer, colluder, collaborator, conniver; manipulator, exploiter; rare machinator, Machiavelli, Machiavellian, cabalist, intrigant(e).

intriguing adjective *a wealth of intriguing stories appear in this book*: **interesting**, fascinating, absorbing, compelling, gripping, riveting, captivating, engaging, enthralling, diverting, titillating, tantalizing; stimulating, thought-provoking.

intrinsic adjective *pride was an intrinsic component of his personal make-up*: **inherent**, innate, inborn, inbred, congenital, natural, native, constitutional, built-in, ingrained, deep-rooted, inseparable, permanent, indelible, ineradicable, ineffaceable; **integral**, basic, fundamental, underlying, constitutive, elemental, essential, vital, necessary; rare connate, connatural.
▷ANTONYMS extrinsic; acquired.

Choose the right word **intrinsic, inherent, essential, innate**

See **inherent**.

introduce verb **1** *he has tried to introduce a new system of joint consultation*: **institute**, initiate, launch, inaugurate, establish, found, instigate, put in place; bring in, bring into being, usher in, set in motion, start, begin, commence, get going, get under way, phase in; organize, develop, originate, pioneer, take the lead in; informal kick off.
▷ANTONYMS abolish.
2 *you can introduce new ideas*: **propose**, put forward, suggest, submit, advance, table, move; raise, broach, bring up, set forth, moot, mention, open, air, ventilate, float.
3 *she* ***introduced*** *Lindsey* ***to*** *the young man*: **present**, present formally, make known; acquaint with, make acquainted with, bring into contact with.
4 *a device used to introduce nitrogen into canned beer*: **insert**, inject, put, place, push, force, drive, shoot, feed.
▷ANTONYMS remove.

5 *she tried to introduce a note of severity into her voice*: **instil**, infuse, inject, add, insert, bring; interpose.
6 *the same presenter introduces the programme each week*: **announce**, present, give an introduction to; preface, precede, lead into, commence, start off, begin, open, launch.

introduction noun **1** *the introduction of democratic reforms*: **institution**, establishment, initiation, launch, inauguration, foundation, instigation; start, commencement, inception; development, origination, pioneering.
▷ANTONYMS abolition.
2 *he wished for an introduction to the king*: **presentation**, formal presentation; meeting, audience, interview, encounter.
3 *he wrote an introduction to the catalogue*: **foreword**, preface, preamble, prologue, prelude, front matter, lead-in; opening, beginning, start, opening statement; informal intro, prelims, curtain-raiser; formal prolegomenon, proem, exordium, prolusion.
▷ANTONYMS afterword, appendix.
4 *the handbook will include an* ***introduction to*** *the history of the period*: **basic explanation of**, brief account of, description of; the basics, the rudiments, the fundamentals, the groundwork.
5 *he had hoped for a gentle introduction to the life of the school*: **initiation**, induction, baptism, inauguration, debut.

introductory adjective **1** *the introductory chapter*: **opening**, initial, starting, commencing, initiatory, first, earliest; prefatory, preliminary, precursory, lead-in; rare prefatorial, precursive, prodromal, prodromic, preambular, preambulatory, preludial, prelusive, prelusory, exordial, proemial, prolegomenal.
▷ANTONYMS final.
2 *a one-day introductory course*: **elementary**, basic, rudimentary, fundamental; initiatory, preparatory, primary; rare rudimental.
▷ANTONYMS advanced.

introspection noun *he wasn't given to introspection*: **brooding**, self-analysis, soul-searching, heart-searching, introversion, self-observation, self-absorption; contemplation, thoughtfulness, pensiveness, thought, thinking, musing, rumination, meditation, pondering, reflection, cogitation; informal navel-gazing.

introspective adjective *a shy and introspective man*: **inward-looking**, self-analysing, self-examining, self-observing, brooding; introverted, introvert, self-contained; contemplative, thoughtful, pensive, musing, ruminative, meditative, reflective; informal navel-gazing; rare indrawn.
▷ANTONYMS outward-looking, extrovert.

introverted adjective *an introverted and thoughtful person*: **shy**, reserved, withdrawn, reticent, diffident, retiring, quiet, timid, timorous, meek, bashful, unsociable; introspective, introvert, inward-looking, self-contained, self-absorbed, self-interested; contemplative, thoughtful, pensive, ruminative, meditative, reflective; rare indrawn.
▷ANTONYMS extroverted.

intrude verb **1** *the press believe they have the right to* ***intrude on*** *people's privacy*: **encroach**, impinge, trespass, infringe, obtrude, thrust oneself in; invade, violate; interfere with, disturb, disrupt; informal horn in, muscle in; archaic entrench.
▷ANTONYMS withdraw.
2 *he intruded his own personality into his work*: **force**, push, introduce, obtrude, impose, thrust.
▷ANTONYMS remove.

intruder noun *the intruder had rifled through drawers*: **trespasser**, interloper, invader, prowler, infiltrator, encroacher, violator; burglar, housebreaker, thief, raider, robber, cat burglar.

intrusion noun *she didn't want his constant* ***intrusion into*** *her life*: **encroachment on**, trespass on, obtrusion into; invasion of, incursion into, violation of, interruption of, intervention in, interference with, disturbance of, disruption of, infringement of, impingement on.
▷ANTONYMS withdrawal.

intrusive adjective **1** *an intrusive journalist*: **intruding**, invasive, obtrusive, interrupting, trespassing, unwanted, unwelcome; meddlesome, meddling, interfering, busybody; inquisitive, prying, curious; informal pushy, nosy.
2 *in those days opinion polls played a much less intrusive role in elections*: **invasive**, impossible to ignore, high-profile, prominent, unavoidable, inescapable, interrupting, disturbing; annoying, irritating, irksome; informal in one's face.
▷ANTONYMS low-key.
3 *some parents reacted badly to the intrusive questions*: **personal**, prying, forward, impudent, impertinent, offensive; informal nosy, nosy-parker, snooping, snoopy.

intuition noun **1** *he works according to intuition*: **instinct**, intuitiveness; sixth sense, divination, clairvoyance, second sight, ESP (extrasensory perception).
▷ANTONYMS intellect.
2 *this confirms an intuition I had*: **hunch**, feeling, feeling in one's bones, gut feeling, funny feeling, inkling, sneaking suspicion, suspicion, impression; premonition, presentiment, foreboding; Buddhism satori; informal feeling in one's water.

intuitive adjective *he had an intuitive grasp of people's moods*: **instinctive**, intuitional, instinctual; innate, inborn, inherent, untaught, unlearned, natural, congenital, inbuilt, built-in, ingrown; automatic, unconscious, subconscious, involuntary, spontaneous, impulsive, unthinking; informal gut.

intumescence noun rare *the intumescence of the abdomen on the right side*. See **swelling**.

inundate verb **1** *many buildings were inundated*: **flood**, deluge, overflow, overrun, swamp, submerge, engulf, drown, immerse, cover; saturate, soak, drench.
2 *we have been inundated by complaints*: **overwhelm**, overpower, overburden, overrun, overload, swamp, bog down, besiege, snow under, bury, bombard, glut.

inundation noun **1** *the annual inundation of the Nile*: **flood**, overflow, deluge, torrent, influx; tidal wave, flash flood, freshet; Brit. spate.
2 *this inundation of classical pedantry soon infected poetry*: **onslaught**, outpouring, flood, deluge, hail, avalanche, flow, barrage, battery, effusion; overabundance, superabundance, plethora, excess, superfluity, surplus, glut; informal tons, heaps.

inure verb *they became inured to poverty*: **harden**, toughen, season, temper, condition; accustom, habituate, familiarize, acclimatize, adjust, adapt, attune; desensitize, dehumanize, brutalize, case-harden; rare indurate.
▷ANTONYMS sensitize.

invade verb **1** *the island was invaded by the Axis powers*: **occupy**, **conquer**, capture, seize, take (over), annex, win, gain, secure; march into, overrun, overwhelm, storm, descend on, swoop on, swarm over, surge over, make inroads on; attack, assail, assault, raid, plunder, maraud.
▷ANTONYMS withdraw from.
2 *I was angry that someone had invaded our privacy*: **intrude on**, violate, encroach on, infringe on, trespass on, obtrude on, burst in on, interrupt, disturb, disrupt; informal horn in on, muscle in on; archaic entrench on.
▷ANTONYMS respect.
3 *the feeling of betrayal that had invaded my being*: **permeate**, pervade, fill, spread through/over, diffuse through, imbue, perfuse, be disseminated through, flow through; assail, attack, take over.

invader noun **1** *the northern frontier was overrun by invaders*: **attacker**, raider, plunderer, pillager, marauder, looter; occupier, conqueror; assailant, assaulter; intruder.
2 *she held herself stiffly, repelling any invader of her personal space*: **intruder**, trespasser, violator, encroacher, infringer.

invalid[1] (stress on the first syllable) adjective See **disabled**.
▶ noun See **disabled**.
▶ verb *an officer invalided by a chest wound*: **disable**, incapacitate, indispose, hospitalize, put out of action, lay up, cripple, paralyse, lame, put on the sick list; injure, wound, hurt, weaken, enfeeble.

invalid[2] (stress on the second syllable) adjective **1** *the by-law was invalid because it infringed rights of common*: **void**, legally void, null, null and void, unenforceable, not binding, inoperative, worthless; illegitimate, incorrect, improper, unacceptable, inapplicable; annulled, nullified, cancelled, revoked, rescinded, abolished, repealed.
▷ANTONYMS valid, binding.
2 *the whole theory is invalid*: **false**, untrue, inaccurate, faulty, fallacious, spurious, inadequate, unconvincing, unsound, weak, wrong, wrongly inferred, wide of the mark, off target; unjustified, unsubstantiated, unwarranted, untenable, baseless, ill-founded, unfounded, groundless; illogical, irrational, unscientific, absurd, preposterous, inconsistent; informal off beam, out, way out, full of holes, bogus.
▷ANTONYMS true, accurate.

invalidate verb **1** *a low turnout invalidated the ballot*: **render invalid**, void, nullify, annul, negate, cancel, quash, veto, overturn, overrule, override, undo, reverse; revoke, rescind, abolish, repeal, repudiate, terminate.
▷ANTONYMS validate.
2 *this case is exceptional, and does not invalidate the general argument*: **disprove**, show/prove to be false, refute, explode, contradict, rebut, negate, gainsay, belie, give the lie to, discredit, expose, debunk, knock the bottom out of, drive a coach and horses through; weaken, undermine, compromise; informal shoot full of holes, shoot down (in flames); formal confute, negative.
▷ANTONYMS validate, support.

invaluable adjective *an invaluable member of the organization*: **indispensable**, crucial, critical, key, vital, irreplaceable, extremely useful, extremely helpful, all-important, vitally important, of the utmost importance.
▷ANTONYMS dispensable, superfluous.

invariable adjective *his routine was invariable*: **unvarying**, unchanging, changeless, unvaried, invariant; constant, stable, set, steady, fast, static, uniform, predictable, regular, consistent, undeviating, unfluctuating, unwavering; unchangeable, unalterable, immutable, fixed.
▷ANTONYMS varied, variable.

invariably adverb *he is invariably described as 'down to earth'*: **always**, every time, each time, on every occasion, at all times, without fail, without exception, whatever happens, universally; everywhere, in all places,

in all cases, in every case, in all instances, in every instance; regularly, consistently, repeatedly, habitually, unfailingly, {day in, day out}, infallibly, inevitably, dependably.
▷ANTONYMS sometimes; never.

invasion noun 1 *the invasion of the islands took place in April*: **occupation**, conquering, capture, seizure, annexation, annexing, takeover, appropriation, expropriation, arrogation; overrunning, overwhelming, storming; attack, incursion, offensive, assailing, assault, onslaught; foray, sortie, raid.
▷ANTONYMS withdrawal.
2 *every year the valley suffers an invasion of cars*: **influx**, inundation, inrush, rush, flood, torrent, deluge, stream, avalanche.
3 *it was a terrible **invasion of** your privacy*: **violation**, infringement, interruption, disturbance, disruption, breach, infraction; intrusion into, encroachment on, trespass on, obtrusion into, interference with.

invective noun *she poured forth a string of invective*: **abuse**, insults, vituperation, expletives, swear words, swearing, curses, bad language, foul language; denunciation, censure, revilement, vilification, castigation, recrimination, reproach, reproval, admonition; informal tongue-lashing; archaic contumely, billingsgate, obloquy.
▷ANTONYMS praise.

inveigh verb *he went on to **inveigh against** pornography and violence in the cinema*: **fulminate**, declaim, protest, rail, rage, remonstrate, storm; denounce, censure, condemn, decry, criticize, complain vehemently about; disparage, denigrate, run down, revile, abuse, vilify, impugn; informal lash, tongue-lash, kick up a fuss about, kick up a stink about, bellyache about, beef about, grouch about, sound off about.
▷ANTONYMS support.

inveigle verb *he was attempting to inveigle them into doing his will*: **cajole**, wheedle, coax, persuade, convince, talk; tempt, lure, allure, entice, ensnare, seduce, flatter, beguile, dupe, fool; informal sweet-talk, soft-soap, butter up, twist someone's arm, con, bamboozle; N. Amer. informal sucker; archaic blandish.

invent verb 1 *Louis Braille invented an alphabet to help blind people*: **originate**, create, innovate, design, devise, contrive, formulate, develop; conceive, think up, come up with, hit on, mastermind, pioneer; discover, find; coin, mint; informal dream up.
2 *he admitted that they invented the story for a laugh*: **make up**, fabricate, concoct, hatch, dream up, trump up, manufacture; informal cook up.

invention noun 1 *the invention of the telescope*: **origination**, creation, innovation, devising, contriving, contrivance, formulation, development, design; conception, masterminding, pioneering, introduction; discovery, finding.
2 *medieval inventions included the spinning wheel*: **innovation**, origination, creation, design, contraption, contrivance, construction, device, gadget, apparatus, machine; discovery; coinage; informal brainchild, gizmo, widget.
3 *his invention was flagging*: **inventiveness**, originality, creativity, creativeness, imagination, imaginativeness, inspiration; ingenuity, ingeniousness, resourcefulness, initiative, enterprise; genius, brilliance, vision.
4 *the movement was never more than a journalistic invention*: **fabrication**, concoction, fiction, piece of fiction, yarn, story, tale, figment of one's imagination; lie, untruth, falsehood, fib, trumped-up story; myth, fantasy; informal tall story, fairy story, fairy tale, cock and bull story, red herring; kidology.

inventive adjective 1 *the most inventive composer of his time*: **creative**, original, innovational, innovative, imaginative, fertile, ingenious, resourceful; artistic, inspired, gifted, talented, virtuoso, accomplished, masterly, skilful, clever.
▷ANTONYMS unimaginative, uninventive.
2 *a fresh, inventive comedy*: **original**, innovative, unusual, fresh, novel, new; experimental, offbeat, quirky, avant garde, forward-looking, groundbreaking; unfamiliar, unorthodox, unconventional, alternative, fringe; N. Amer. left-field.
▷ANTONYMS hackneyed.

inventiveness noun 1 *they valued his vigour and inventiveness*: **creativity**, originality, innovation, invention, imagination, imaginativeness, creative power, creative talent, creative gift, fertility, ingeniousness, resourcefulness, enterprise; artistry, inspiration, giftedness, talent, virtuosity, accomplishment, mastery, skill, cleverness.
▷ANTONYMS unimaginativeness.
2 *the outstanding inventiveness of Irish literature*: **originality**, innovation, unusualness, freshness, novelty, newness, break with tradition; quirkiness, unfamiliarity, unconventionality, unorthodoxy.
▷ANTONYMS unoriginality.

inventor noun *the inventor of the seed drill*: **originator**, creator, innovator; designer, deviser, developer, maker, planner, framer, producer; author, architect; pioneer, mastermind, father, prime mover; scientist, discoverer; informal boffin; literary begetter.

inventory noun *a complete inventory of all their belongings*: **list**, listing, catalogue, directory, record, register, checklist, tally, roster, file, log, account, archive, description, statement.
▶verb *I inventoried his collection of drawings*: **list**, catalogue, record, register, make a list of, file, log, tally.

inverse adjective *inverse snobbery | an inverse correlation between the size and frequency of words*: **reverse**, reversed, inverted, opposite, converse, contrary, counter, antithetical, transposed, retroverted.
▶noun *alkalinity is the inverse of acidity*: **opposite**, converse, obverse, antithesis, other side; informal flip side, other side of the coin.

inversion noun *a hypocrite's inversion of the truth*: **reversal**, transposition, turning about, turning upside down; reverse, contrary, antithesis, converse, transposal; rare contrareity, antipode.

invert verb *the crew inverted the yacht's mast*: **turn upside down**, upturn, upend, turn around, turn about, turn inside out, turn back to front, reverse, flip (over), transpose.

invest verb 1 *he **invested in** a cotton mill*: **put money into**, sink money into, lay out money on, plough money into; provide capital for, spend money on, fund, back, finance, underwrite, subsidize, support, pay for; buy into, buy shares in, buy/take a stake in; informal get a piece of, splash out on.
2 *they invested £18 million to redesign their retail outlets*: **spend**, expend, lay out, put in, plough in, use up, devote; venture, speculate, risk, gamble; contribute, donate, give.
3 *the words were invested with as much sarcasm as she could muster*: **imbue**, infuse, perfuse, charge, steep, saturate, suffuse, pervade, fill, endow.
4 *by virtue of the powers **invested in** me, I grant your request*: **vest in**, endow in, confer on, bestow on, grant to, entrust to, give to, consign to, put in someone's hands.
5 *bishops whom the king had invested*: **admit to office**, instate, install, induct, swear in; ordain, anoint; crown, enthrone.
6 archaic *he proceeded to invest the fort of Arcot*. See **besiege** (sense 1).

investigate verb *police were investigating the death of a woman*: **enquire into**, look into, go into, look over, probe, explore, scrutinize, conduct an investigation into, conduct an enquiry into, make enquiries about, try to get to the bottom of; inspect, analyse, study, examine, consider, research, search/sift the evidence concerning, pore over, delve into; audit, evaluate; follow up; informal check out, suss out, give something the once-over; N. Amer. informal scope out.

investigation noun *this claim requires further investigation | an investigation into the accident*: **examination**, enquiry, study, inspection, exploration, consideration, analysis, appraisal; research, scrutiny, scrutinization, scanning, perusal, sifting, fact-finding; probe, review, survey, search; inquest, hearing, questioning, interrogation, inquisition; audit, evaluation; informal snoop, snooping, post-mortem, recce.

investigator noun *social security fraud investigators*: **inspector**, examiner, enquirer, explorer, analyser; researcher, scrutineer, scrutinizer, factfinder, prober, surveyor, searcher, checker, monitor; detective, questioner, inquisitor.

investiture noun *the investiture of archbishops*: **inauguration**, appointment, installation, instatement, induction, initiation, swearing in; ordination, consecration; crowning, enthroning, enthronement, accession.

investment noun 1 *you can lose money pretty fast by bad investment*: **investing**, speculation; expenditure, outlay, funding, backing, financing, underwriting; buying shares.
2 *I'm satisfied that it's a good investment*: **venture**, speculation, risk, gamble; asset, buy, acquisition, holding, possession; bargain; Brit. informal flutter, punt.
3 *an investment of £305,000*: **stake**, share, portion, interest, money/capital invested; informal ante.
4 *a substantial investment of time and energy*: **sacrifice**, surrender, foregoing, loss, relinquishment, forfeiture.

inveterate adjective 1 *an inveterate gambler*: **confirmed**, hardened, chronic, hard-core, incorrigible; habitual, addicted, compulsive, obsessive, obsessional; informal pathological, hooked.
2 *an inveterate Democrat*: **staunch**, steadfast, committed, devoted, dedicated; deep-dyed, dyed-in-the-wool, thorough, thoroughgoing, out and out, diehard, long-standing.
3 *mankind's inveterate pride and stupidity*: **ingrained**, deep-seated, deep-rooted, deep-set, entrenched, established, long-established, congenital; ineradicable, incurable, irredeemable.

invidious adjective 1 *I didn't want to put her in an invidious position*: **unpleasant**, awkward, difficult; undesirable, unenviable.
▷ANTONYMS pleasant, desirable.
2 *an invidious comparison*: **unfair**, unjust, prejudicial, discriminatory, iniquitous, weighted, one-sided; offensive, objectionable; deleterious, detrimental, unwarranted.
▷ANTONYMS fair.

invigorate verb *we were invigorated by the fresh air*: **revitalize**, energize, refresh, revive, vivify, brace, rejuvenate, enliven, liven up, perk up, wake up, animate, galvanize, electrify, stimulate, motivate, rouse, exhilarate, excite; rally, hearten, uplift, encourage, fortify, strengthen, put new strength/life/heart in; informal buck up, pep up, give a new lease of life to.
▷ANTONYMS tire.

invigorating adjective *we drank in the invigorating cold air*: **revitalizing**, energizing, refreshing, reviving, vivifying, bracing, rejuvenating, enlivening, restorative; galvanizing, electrifying, stimulating, rousing, exhilarating, exciting; rallying, heartening, uplifting, encouraging, fortifying, strengthening, health-giving, healthy, tonic.
▷ANTONYMS tiring.

invincible adjective *an invincible warrior*: **invulnerable**, indestructible, unconquerable, unbeatable, indomitable, unassailable; unyielding, unflinching, unbending, unshakeable, indefatigable, dauntless; impregnable, inviolable, secure, safe.
▷ANTONYMS vulnerable, defenceless.

inviolable adjective *the inviolable right to life*: **inalienable**, absolute, untouchable, unalterable, unchallengeable, unbreakable, impregnable; sacrosanct, sacred, holy, hallowed; rare intemerate.
▷ANTONYMS partial.

inviolate adjective *his home remained inviolate*: **untouched**, undamaged, unhurt, unharmed, unscathed; unmarred, unspoilt, unimpaired, unflawed, unsullied, unstained, undefiled, unpolluted, unprofaned, perfect, pristine, pure, virgin; intact, unbroken, whole, entire, complete, sound, solid; rare scatheless.

invisible adjective *an invisible gas | he lounged in the doorway, invisible in the dark*: **not visible**, unseeable; undetectable, indiscernible, indistinguishable, inconspicuous, unnoticeable, imperceptible; unseen, unnoticed, unobserved, hidden, concealed, obscured, out of sight, secret.
▷ANTONYMS visible.

Word toolkit

invisible	undetectable	veiled
force	levels	threat
man	steroid	reference
barrier	drug	warning
line	changes	criticism
enemy	virus	insult
ink	substances	suggestion
God	concentrations	anger

invitation noun **1** *she'd received an invitation to dinner*: **request**, call, bidding, summons; informal invite.
2 *he left the door open—an invitation to an opportunistic thief*: **encouragement**, provocation, temptation, lure, magnet, bait, enticement, attraction, draw, pull, allure; informal come-on.
▷ANTONYMS discouragement.

invite verb (stress on the second syllable) **1** *they invited us to Sunday brunch*: **ask**, bid, summon; request someone's company at, request someone's presence at, request someone's appearance at, request the pleasure of someone's company, have someone over/round.
2 *applications are invited for the post of director*: **ask for**, request, call for, look for, appeal for, solicit, seek, petition, summon.
▷ANTONYMS refuse.
3 *airing such views in public would invite trouble*: **cause**, induce, provoke, create, generate, engender, foster, encourage, lead to, call forth, make happen; draw, attract, incite, elicit, bring on, bring on oneself, arouse; tempt, court, allure, entice.
▸ **noun** (stress on the first syllable) informal *no one turns down an invite to one of Mickey's parties*. See **invitation** (sense 1).

inviting adjective *an inviting smell of coffee wafted into the room*: **tempting**, enticing, alluring, beguiling, winning; attractive, appealing, pleasant, agreeable, delightful; appetizing, mouth-watering; fascinating, engaging, enchanting, entrancing, bewitching, captivating, intriguing, irresistible, ravishing, seductive, tantalizing.
▷ANTONYMS repellent, offensive.

invocation noun **1** *her invocation of themes favoured by the grass-roots supporters*: **citation**, mention, acknowledgement, calling on; appeal to, reference to, allusion to.
2 *the invocation of rain by tribal people*: **summoning**, bringing, calling, conjuring (up).
3 *an invocation to the Holy Ghost*: **prayer**, request, intercession, supplication, call, entreaty, solicitation, petition, appeal, suit; incantation, chant; archaic orison; rare imploration, adjuration, obsecration, epiclesis.

invoice noun *an invoice for the goods supplied*: **bill**, account, statement, statement of charges, itemization, reckoning, tally; N. Amer. check; informal tab; archaic score.
▸ **verb** *we'll invoice you for the damage*: **bill**, charge, debit, send an invoice/bill to.

invoke verb **1** *he invoked his statutory right to complain to the district auditor*: **cite**, refer to, adduce, instance; resort to, have recourse to, turn to, call into use, use, put into effect/use.
▷ANTONYMS waive.
2 *I closed my eyes and invoked the Madonna*: **pray to**, call on, appeal to, plead with, supplicate, entreat, solicit, beseech, beg, implore, importune, petition; call for, request; rare obtest, obsecrate, impetrate.
3 *she was walking in a circle as though invoking the spirits of the place*: **summon**, call (up), bring, conjure (up).
4 *middle-class moralities invoke peculiar anxieties*: **bring forth**, bring on, elicit, induce, cause, kindle, bring out.

involuntary adjective **1** *she gave an involuntary shudder*: **reflex**, reflexive, automatic, knee-jerk, mechanical, unconditioned; spontaneous, instinctive, instinctual, impulsive, unconscious, unthinking; unintentional, unintended, unplanned, inadvertent, uncontrolled, uncontrollable.
▷ANTONYMS voluntary, deliberate.
2 *a policy of involuntary repatriation*: **compulsory**, obligatory, mandatory, forced, coerced, coercive, compelled, exacted, imposed, demanded, required, constrained, ordained, prescribed; unwilling, unconsenting, against one's will, against one's wishes, reluctant, grudging.
▷ANTONYMS voluntary; optional; willing.

Word toolkit **involuntary**

See **spontaneous**.

involve verb **1** *the research involved the assembly of information on unemployment*: **require**, necessitate, demand, call for; **entail**, mean, imply, presuppose, presume, assume; appertain to, pertain to, relate to, concern.
▷ANTONYMS preclude.
2 *I try to involve everyone in key decisions*: **include**, count in, take in, bring in, draw in, take into account, take account of, take note of, allow for; cover, incorporate, encompass, deal with, touch on; embrace, comprise, contain, comprehend.
▷ANTONYMS exclude.
3 *many drug addicts involve themselves in crime*: **implicate**, incriminate, inculpate; associate, connect, concern; embroil, entangle, enmesh, ensnare; informal mix up.

involved adjective **1** *social workers **involved in** the case*: **associated with**, connected with, concerned with, participating in, taking part in.
▷ANTONYMS unconnected.
2 *he had been involved in burglaries*: **implicated**, incriminated, inculpated, embroiled, entangled, caught up, enmeshed, ensnared; informal mixed up.
3 *a long and involved story*: **complicated**, intricate, complex, elaborate; confused, confusing, bewildering; jumbled, tangled, entangled, convoluted, knotty, mixed up, impenetrable, unfathomable, tortuous, labyrinthine, Byzantine; difficult, hard.
▷ANTONYMS straightforward, simple.
4 *they were both totally **involved in** their work*: **engrossed**, absorbed, immersed, caught up, rapt, interested; preoccupied by, busy with, engaged in/with, riveted by, gripped by, intent on; informal up to one's ears in.
▷ANTONYMS uninterested.

involvement noun **1** *he is in prison for his involvement in a plot to overthrow the government*: **participation**, action, hand; collaboration, collusion, complicity, connivance, implication, incrimination, inculpation; association, connection, attachment, embroilment, entanglement, inclusion.
2 *a nurse has to avoid emotional involvement with the patient*: **attachment**, connection, friendship, intimacy, entanglement; relationship, relations, bond.

invulnerable adjective *no state in the region is invulnerable to attack by another*: **impervious**, insusceptible, immune, insensitive; indestructible, impenetrable, impregnable, unassailable, unattackable, inviolable, invincible, unshakeable, secure, safe, safe and sound, strong; proof against.
▷ANTONYMS vulnerable, defenceless.

inward adjective **1** *a small inward indentation*: **towards the inside**, going in, ingoing; concave.
▷ANTONYMS outward.
2 *he allowed himself an inward smile*: **internal**, inner, interior, inside, innermost; private, personal, hidden, secret, veiled, masked, concealed, unexpressed, unrevealed; intimate, confidential; informal bottled up; archaic privy.
▷ANTONYMS external.
▸ **adverb** *the door opened inward*. See **inwards**.

Word links **inward**

intro- related prefix, as in *introduce, introvert*

inwardly adverb *inwardly, George blamed himself*: **inside**, internally, within, deep down (inside), deep within, at heart, in one's heart (of hearts), in one's mind, to oneself; privately, secretly, confidentially.
▷ANTONYMS outwardly; out loud.

inwards adverb *light spilled inwards from the porch*: **inside**, towards the inside, into the interior, inward, within.

iota noun *nothing she said seemed to make an iota of difference*: **bit**, mite, speck, scrap, shred, ounce, scintilla, atom, jot, tittle, jot or tittle, whit, little bit, tiniest bit, particle, fraction, morsel, grain; French soupçon; informal smidgen, smidge, tad; archaic scruple, scantling.

irascible adjective *an irascible young man*: **irritable**, quick-tempered, short-tempered, bad-tempered, ill-tempered, hot-tempered, thin-skinned, snappy, snappish, tetchy, testy, touchy, edgy, crabby, waspish, dyspeptic; surly, cross, crusty, crabbed, grouchy, crotchety, cantankerous, curmudgeonly, ill-natured, ill-humoured, peevish, querulous, captious, fractious, bilious; informal narky, prickly, ratty, hot under the collar; rare iracund, iracundulous.

irate adjective *an irate customer*: **angry**, very angry, furious, infuriated, incensed, enraged, incandescent, fuming, seething, ireful, cross, mad; raging, ranting, raving, frenzied, in a frenzy, beside oneself, outraged, up in arms; indignant, annoyed, irritated, aggrieved, vexed, exasperated, frustrated, irked, piqued; informal foaming at the mouth, hot under the collar, hacked off; literary wrathful, wroth.
▷ANTONYMS calm, composed.

ire noun literary *the plans provoked the ire of conservationists*: **anger**, rage, fury, wrath, hot temper, outrage, temper, crossness, spleen; annoyance, exasperation, irritation, vexation, displeasure, chagrin, pique; indignation, resentment; literary choler.

Ireland noun Eire, the Republic of Ireland, the Irish Republic, southern Ireland; Northern Ireland; informal the Emerald Isle; Latin Hibernia; literary Erin.

> *Word links* **Ireland**
>
> **Hiberno-** related prefix, as in *Hiberno-English*

i

iridescent adjective *the iridescent films of oil on top of puddles*: **shimmering**, shimmery, glittering, sparkling, dazzling, shining, gleaming, glowing, lustrous, scintillating, dancing, opalescent, opaline; multicoloured, kaleidoscopic, rainbow-like, rainbow-coloured, many-hued, prismatic, colourful, psychedelic; variegated, shot; literary glistering; rare coruscating, coruscant, fulgurating, effulgent, scintillant.

irk verb *her reticence about certain things irked him*: **irritate**, annoy, vex, gall, rattle, pique, rub up the wrong way, exasperate, try someone's patience, put out, displease; anger, infuriate, madden, incense, make someone's blood boil, get on someone's nerves, make angry, make cross; ruffle, ruffle someone's feathers, make someone's hackles rise, raise someone's hackles, discountenance; antagonize, provoke, goad; informal get someone's goat, get/put someone's back up, peeve, miff, rile, aggravate, nettle, needle, get, get to, bug, hack off, get under someone's skin, get up someone's nose, put someone's nose out of joint, give someone the hump, rattle someone's cage, get someone's dander up, drive mad/crazy, drive round the twist, drive up the wall, make someone see red; Brit. informal wind up, brown off, cheese off, nark, get across, get on someone's wick; N. Amer. informal tee off, tick off, burn up, rankle, ride, gravel; vulgar slang piss off; Brit. vulgar slang get on someone's tits; informal, dated give someone the pip.
▷ANTONYMS please.

irksome adjective *an irksome task*: **irritating**, annoying, vexing, vexatious, galling, exasperating, displeasing, grating, disagreeable; tiresome, wearisome, tedious, trying, troublesome, burdensome, bothersome, awkward, inconvenient, difficult, boring, uninteresting; infuriating, maddening; informal pesky, cussed, confounded, infernal, pestiferous, plaguy, pestilent.
▷ANTONYMS pleasant, agreeable.

iron noun **1** *she needed some iron in her soul*: **strength**, toughness, resilience, fortitude, firmness, robustness, hardiness, steel; informal guts, grit, grittiness, spunk.
▷ANTONYMS weakness.
2 *a soldering iron*: **tool**, implement, utensil, device, apparatus, appliance, contrivance, contraption, mechanism.
3 *an iron that is too hot will melt nylon*: **flat iron**, electric iron, steam iron, smoothing iron.
4 (**irons**) *you will be clapped in irons*: **manacles**, shackles, fetters, chains, restraints, handcuffs; informal cuffs, bracelets; rare trammels.
▸ adjective **1** *an iron key*: **made of iron**; ferric, ferrous.
2 *an iron law of politics*: **inflexible**, unbreakable, absolute, unconditional, categorical, unquestionable, incontrovertible, infallible.
▷ANTONYMS flexible.
3 *he ruled over his employees with an iron will*: **uncompromising**, unrelenting, unyielding, unbending, resolute, resolved, determined, firm, rigid, steadfast, unwavering, unvacillating; stern, strict.
▷ANTONYMS weak, flexible.
▸ verb *she even used to iron his shirts*: **press**.
□ **iron something out 1** *John had ironed out all the minor snags*: **resolve**, straighten out, sort out, clear up, settle, put right, set right, set to rights, find a solution to, solve, remedy, heal, cure, rectify; informal patch up, fix, mend, clean up, crack, figure out; archaic compose. **2** *the new directive will iron out differences in national systems*: **eliminate**, eradicate, erase, get rid of, smooth over; harmonize, reconcile.

> *Word links* **iron**
>
> **ferro-** related prefix, as in *ferroconcrete*
> **ferri-** related prefix, as in *ferrimagnetic*
> **sidero-** related prefix, as in *siderophore*

ironic adjective **1** *Edward's tone was ironic*: **sarcastic**, sardonic, dry, caustic, sharp, stinging, scathing, acerbic, acid, bitter, trenchant, mordant, cynical; mocking, satirical, scoffing, ridiculing, derisory, derisive, scornful, sneering; wry, double-edged, backhanded, tongue-in-cheek; Brit. informal sarky.
▷ANTONYMS sincere.
2 *I just wanted to go out and experience life, so it's ironic that I've ended up writing*: **paradoxical**, incongruous, odd, strange, weird, peculiar, unexpected.
▷ANTONYMS logical, to be expected.

> *Choose the right word* **ironic, sarcastic, sardonic, caustic**
>
> See **sarcastic**.

irony noun **1** *that note of irony in her voice*: **sarcasm**, sardonicism, dryness, causticity, sharpness, acerbity, acid, bitterness, trenchancy, mordancy, cynicism; mockery, satire, ridicule, derision, scorn, sneering; wryness, backhandedness; Brit. informal sarkiness.
▷ANTONYMS sincerity.
2 *the irony of the situation hit her*: **paradox**, paradoxical nature, incongruity, incongruousness, peculiarity.
▷ANTONYMS logic.

irradiate verb **1** *the patients were irradiated*: **treat with radiation**, expose to radiation, X-ray.
2 *he was irradiated by a steady glow*: **illuminate**, light up, light, brighten, cast light upon, throw light on, shine on, flood with light; literary illumine.

irrational adjective *she told herself that it was an irrational fear*: **unreasonable**, illogical, groundless, baseless, unfounded, unjustifiable, unsound; absurd, ridiculous, ludicrous, silly, foolish, senseless, nonsensical, laughable, idiotic, stupid, wild; untenable, implausible, unscientific, arbitrary; informal crazy, mad; Brit. informal barmy, daft.
▷ANTONYMS rational, logical.

irreconcilable adjective **1** *the affair revealed irreconcilable views about the duties of government*: **incompatible**, at odds, at variance, incongruous, conflicting, clashing, discordant, antagonistic, mutually exclusive; opposite, contrary, opposing, antithetical, diametrically opposed; different, disparate, variant, dissimilar, poles apart, polar; rare oppugnant.
▷ANTONYMS compatible, similar.
2 *irreconcilable enemies*: **implacable**, unappeasable, uncompromising, inexorable, intransigent, inflexible, remorseless, relentless, unrelenting, hard-line; mortal, bitter, deadly, sworn; informal at each other's throats.

irrecoverable adjective *an irrecoverable bad debt*: **unrecoverable**, unreclaimable, irretrievable, irredeemable, irrevocable, unrestorable, unsalvageable, irremediable, lost, lost and gone, gone for ever, beyond cure, beyond hope, hopeless; written off.
▷ANTONYMS recoverable.

irrefutable adjective *there is irrefutable evidence that there will be a shortfall*: **indisputable**, undeniable, unquestionable, incontrovertible, incontestable, unassailable, impregnable, beyond question, indubitable, beyond doubt, beyond dispute, indisputable; conclusive, definite, definitive, decisive, certain, sure, positive, sound, flawless, watertight, unmistakable, palpable, patent, manifest, obvious, evident, plain, clear, forceful, telling; rare irrefragable, apodictic.
▷ANTONYMS unreliable.

irregular adjective **1** *he had strong, irregular features | an irregular coastline*: **asymmetrical**, non-uniform, uneven, crooked, misshapen, lopsided, contorted, twisted; twisting, serpentine, curving; broken, jagged, ragged, craggy, serrated, sawtooth, saw-edged, notched, nicked, indented.
▷ANTONYMS regular; straight.
2 *use sandpaper to smooth irregular surfaces*: **rough**, bumpy, uneven, coarse; pitted, rutted, rutty, holed, holey; lumpy, knobby, knobbly, gnarled.
▷ANTONYMS regular; smooth.
3 *an irregular heartbeat | an irregular ferry service*: **inconsistent**, unsteady, uneven, shaky, fitful, patchy, variable, varying, changeable, changing, ever-changing, on-and-off, off-and-on, inconstant, erratic, haphazard, unstable, unsettled, spasmodic, sporadic, episodic, intermittent, occasional, unpunctual, wavering, fluctuating, aperiodic, unsystematic, unmethodical, capricious; desultory, casual.
▷ANTONYMS regular; steady.
4 *his appointment was most irregular*: **against the rules**, contrary to the rules, out of order, improper, incorrect, illegitimate, unscrupulous, unethical, unprofessional; unofficial, back-door, grey; not done, unacceptable, wrong, beyond the pale, unorthodox, unconventional, abnormal; informal not on, a bit much, shady; Brit. informal a bit thick, off, not

cricket; Austral./NZ informal over the fence.
▷ANTONYMS above board.
5 *an irregular army*: **guerrilla**, underground; unofficial, paramilitary; resistance, partisan, mercenary.
▷ANTONYMS regular.
▶ **noun** *scruffy, gun-toting irregulars refused to allow traffic through the town*: **guerrilla**, underground fighter; paramilitary; resistance fighter, partisan, mercenary.
▷ANTONYMS regular.

irregularity noun **1** *the irregularity of the coastline*: **asymmetry**, lack of symmetry, non-uniformity, unevenness, crookedness, lopsidedness, contortion, deformity, jaggedness, raggedness, cragginess, indentation.
▷ANTONYMS regularity; straightness.
2 *the irregularity of the road surface*: **roughness**, bumpiness, unevenness, coarseness; lumpiness, knobbliness; rare knobbiness.
▷ANTONYMS regularity; smoothness.
3 *any irregularities in the concrete will be masked by the soft board on top*: **bump**, lump, bulge, hump, knob, knot, projection, prominence, eminence, ridge, protuberance, kink; **hole**, hollow, pit, crater, depression, dip, indentation, trough, dent, dint; gap, space, break, crack, chink, fissure, cranny; informal sticky-out bit; rare concavity.
4 *villagers complained about the irregularity of the bus service*: **inconsistency**, unsteadiness, unevenness, fitfulness, patchiness, haphazardness, inconstancy, instability, variability, changeableness, fluctuation, unpunctuality, unpredictability, unreliability, volatility, fickleness, caprice; casualness, desultoriness; technical aperiodicity; rare erraticism, intermittence, intermittency.
▷ANTONYMS regularity; steadiness.
5 *the monitor showed every little irregularity of her baby's heartbeat*: **fluctuation**, flutter, waver, flicker, falter, quiver, tremor, tremble, hiccup.
6 *there has been irregularity in the conduct of the election | a probe into alleged financial irregularities at the club*: **impropriety**, incorrectness, wrongdoing, misconduct, illegitimacy, dishonesty, corruption, immorality, unscrupulousness, unprofessionalism; inappropriateness, unacceptability, unseemliness, indecorousness, indiscretion, indelicacy; unorthodoxy, unconventionality; informal shadiness, crookedness.
▷ANTONYMS correctness.
7 *staff kept a vigilant watch and noted any irregularity in operation*: **abnormality**, unusualness, uncommonness, strangeness, waywardness, oddness, unexpectedness, singularity, atypicality, anomaly, anomalousness, deviation, divergence, aberrancy, aberration, freakishness, peculiarity, curiousness, eccentricity, idiosyncrasy, quirkiness, unorthodoxy.

irregularly adverb **1** *the first plate is irregularly hexagonal*: **asymmetrically**, unevenly, lopsidedly.
2 *his heart was playing up, beating irregularly*: **erratically**, at irregular intervals, intermittently, in/by fits and starts, on and off, off and on, fitfully, patchily, haphazardly, unsystematically, unmethodically, inconsistently, unsteadily, unevenly, variably, sporadically, spasmodically, episodically, discontinuously, interruptedly, occasionally, piecemeal; rare inconstantly, aperiodically.

irrelevance noun *people are bored at school because of the irrelevance of the curriculum to their own life*: **inapplicability**, unconnectedness, unrelatedness, peripherality, extraneousness; inappropriateness, inappositeness, inaptness; unimportance, inconsequentiality, insignificance; rare impertinence.
▷ANTONYMS relevance.

irrelevant adjective *students must avoid wasting time on irrelevant detail*: **beside the point**, not to the point, immaterial, not pertinent, not germane, off the subject, neither here nor there, unconnected, unrelated, peripheral, tangential, extraneous, inapposite, inapt, inapplicable; unimportant, inconsequential, insignificant, of no matter/moment, of little account, trivial, negligible, minor, trifling, petty, superficial; rare impertinent.
▷ANTONYMS relevant.

irreligious adjective *an irreligious world*: **atheistic**, unbelieving, non-believing, agnostic, sceptical, heretical, faithless, godless, ungodly, unholy, impious, profane, infidel, barbarian, barbarous, heathen, heathenish, idolatrous, pagan; **immoral**, wicked, sinful, morally wrong, evil, bad, iniquitous, corrupt, unrighteous, sacrilegious, blasphemous, irreverent, depraved, degenerate, reprobate, vice-ridden, debauched, dissolute, perverted, dissipated, intemperate, decadent, unprincipled, erring, fallen, impure, sullied, tainted; rare peccable, nullifidian.
▷ANTONYMS pious, religious.

irreparable adjective *if the pump runs dry, irreparable damage can be done*: **irreversible**, irremediable, unrectifiable, irrevocable, irretrievable, irredeemable, unrestorable, irrecoverable, unrecoverable, unrepairable, beyond repair, past mending; hopeless, past hope, beyond hope; written off.
▷ANTONYMS repairable.

irreplaceable adjective *if you make a mistake, you may ruin an irreplaceable recording*: **unique**, unrepeatable, incomparable, unparalleled, priceless, invaluable, beyond price, without price, inestimably precious, of incalculable value/worth, of inestimable value/worth, of immeasurable value/worth, worth its weight in gold; treasured, prized, cherished.
▷ANTONYMS replaceable.

irrepressible adjective **1** *the desire for freedom is irrepressible*: **inextinguishable**, unquenchable, uncontainable, uncontrollable, unstoppable, indestructible, imperishable, undying, unfading, unfailing, enduring, lasting, everlasting, eternal, persistent.
▷ANTONYMS ephemeral; fragile.
2 *his irrepressible personality*: **ebullient**, exuberant, buoyant, sunny, breezy, jaunty, light-hearted, in high spirits, high-spirited, bubbling over, sparkling, effervescent, vivacious, animated, full of life, lively, vigorous, zestful, joyful, cheerful, cheery, merry; informal bubbly, bouncy, peppy, zingy, upbeat, chipper, chirpy, sparky, full of beans; N. Amer. informal peart; dated gay; literary gladsome, blithe, blithesome; archaic as merry as a grig, of good cheer.
▷ANTONYMS gloomy.

irreproachable adjective *he was awarded the medal in recognition of thirty years' irreproachable service*: **impeccable**, exemplary, model, copybook, immaculate, outstanding, exceptional, admirable, meritorious, honourable, consummate, perfect, ideal; above reproach, beyond reproach, blameless, faultless, flawless, guiltless, unimpeachable, unblemished, untarnished, stainless, spotless, pure, sinless, innocent; informal squeaky clean, whiter than white, snow white.
▷ANTONYMS reprehensible.

irresistible adjective **1** *her irresistible smile*: **tempting**, enticing, alluring, inviting, seductive; attractive, desirable, fetching, glamorous, appealing; captivating, ravishing, beguiling, enchanting, fascinating, tantalizing; informal, dated come-hither.
2 *it was an irresistible impulse—I couldn't stop myself*: **uncontrollable**, overwhelming, overpowering, compelling, compulsive, besetting, irrepressible, ungovernable; unavoidable, inescapable, unpreventable, inexorable, driving, forceful, potent, oppressive, imperative, urgent; obsessive.

> *Word toolkit* **irresistible**
>
> See **enchanting**.

irresolute adjective *she stood irresolute outside his door*: **indecisive**, hesitant, tentative, nervous, weak; vacillating, equivocating, dithering, wavering, teetering, fluctuating, faltering, shilly-shallying; ambivalent, divided, in two minds, in a dilemma, in a quandary, torn; doubtful, in doubt, full of doubt, unsure, uncertain; undecided, uncommitted, unresolved, undetermined; informal iffy, blowing hot and cold, sitting on the fence.
▷ANTONYMS decisive.

irresolution noun *'I'll go,' she said after several minutes of irresolution*: **indecisiveness**, indecision, irresoluteness, lack of resolution, hesitancy, hesitation, tentativeness; ambivalence, doubt, doubtfulness, unsureness, uncertainty; vacillation, equivocation, oscillation, wavering, teetering, fluctuation, faltering, second thoughts; delay, hanging back, waiting, shilly-shallying, dithering, stalling, temporizing, temporization; Brit. havering, humming and hawing; Scottish swithering; informal dilly-dallying, blowing hot and cold, sitting on the fence; rare dubiety, incertitude, cunctation.
▷ANTONYMS decisiveness.

irrespective adjective *each member has one vote, **irrespective of** the number of shares held*: **regardless of**, without regard to/for, disregarding, ignoring, notwithstanding, whatever, no matter what, without reference to, without consideration of, setting aside, discounting; informal irregardless of.
▷ANTONYMS according to.

irresponsible adjective **1** *such irresponsible behaviour will not be tolerated*: **reckless**, rash, careless, thoughtless, incautious, unwise, imprudent, ill-advised, ill-considered, injudicious, misguided, heedless, unheeding, inattentive, hasty, overhasty, precipitate, precipitous, wild, foolhardy, impetuous, impulsive, daredevil, devil-may-care, hot-headed, negligent, delinquent, neglectful, remiss, careless of one's duty, lax, slack, uncaring, casual, insouciant; N. Amer. derelict; rare disregardful, inadvertent, oscitant.
▷ANTONYMS responsible; sensible.
2 *if Rose wants to behave like an irresponsible teenager, that's her affair*: **immature**, naive, foolish, hare-brained, feather-brained; carefree, blasé; unreliable, undependable, untrustworthy, flighty, giddy, scatterbrained, erratic; Brit. tearaway; informal harum-scarum, slap-happy.
▷ANTONYMS responsible; serious.

irretrievable adjective *the situation was now irretrievable*: **irreversible**, unrectifiable, irremediable, irrevocable, irredeemable, irrecoverable, unrecoverable, irreparable, unrepairable, beyond repair; irreclaimable, lost, lost and gone, gone forever, hopeless, past hope, beyond hope.
▷ANTONYMS reversible, reparable.

irreverence noun *wacky irreverence is the hallmark of any comedy show worth its salt*: **disrespect**, lack of respect, disdain, scorn, contempt, derision, mockery, ridicule, disparagement; insolence, impudence,

impertinence, cheek, flippancy, insubordination, presumptuousness, presumption, forwardness; rudeness, impoliteness, discourtesy, incivility, abuse; informal lip, nerve.
▷ANTONYMS reverence, respect.

irreverent adjective *an irreverent attitude to tradition*: **disrespectful**, disdainful, scornful, contemptuous, derisive, disparaging; insolent, impudent, impertinent, cheeky, flippant, flip, insubordinate, presumptuous, forward; rude, impolite, discourteous, uncivil, insulting, abusive; informal fresh, lippy.
▷ANTONYMS reverent, respectful.

irreversible adjective *a priority is to stop irreversible damage to the natural environment | an irreversible decision*: **irreparable**, unrepairable, beyond repair, unrectifiable, irremediable, irrevocable; permanent, lasting, enduring, abiding; **unalterable**, unchangeable, invariable, immutable, final, binding, absolute, categorical; Law peremptory, unappealable.
▷ANTONYMS reversible; temporary.

irrevocable adjective *an irrevocable step | an irrevocable commitment*: **irreversible**, unrectifiable, irremediable, irreparable, unrepairable, beyond repair; **unalterable**, unchangeable, immutable, final, binding, absolute, permanent, lasting; Law peremptory, unappealable.
▷ANTONYMS reversible; temporary.

> *Word toolkit* **irrevocable**
>
> See **final**.

i

irrigate verb *the scheme aims to divert water from the river to irrigate agricultural land*: **water**, bring water to; spray, soak, deluge, flood, inundate; make fertile.

irritability noun *apart from occasional irritability, there were no major disagreements among them*: **irascibility**, tetchiness, testiness, touchiness, scratchiness, grumpiness, moodiness, grouchiness, crotchetiness, a (bad) mood, cantankerousness, curmudgeonliness, churlishness, bad temper, ill temper, ill nature, ill humour, peevishness, crossness, pique, impatience, fractiousness, pettishness, crabbiness, waspishness, prickliness, pepperiness, crustiness, spleen, shrewishness, short temper, hot temper, quick temper; informal snappishness, snappiness, chippiness, a short fuse; Brit. informal shirtiness, stroppiness, rattiness; N. Amer. informal crankiness, orneriness, soreheadedness; Austral./NZ informal snakiness; informal, dated miffiness; literary choler.
▷ANTONYMS good humour; placidity.

irritable adjective *being out of work made him irritable*: **bad-tempered**, irascible, tetchy, testy, touchy, scratchy, grumpy, grouchy, moody, crotchety, in a (bad) mood, cantankerous, curmudgeonly, ill-tempered, ill-natured, ill-humoured, peevish, having got out of bed the wrong side, cross, as cross as two sticks, fractious, disagreeable, pettish, crabbed, crabby, waspish, prickly, peppery, crusty, splenetic, shrewish, short-tempered, hot-tempered, quick-tempered, dyspeptic, choleric, bilious, liverish, cross-grained; informal snappish, snappy, chippy, on a short fuse, short-fused; Brit. informal shirty, stroppy, narky, ratty, eggy, like a bear with a sore head; N. Amer. informal cranky, ornery, peckish, soreheaded; Austral./NZ informal snaky; informal, dated waxy, miffy.
▷ANTONYMS good-humoured; easy-going.

irritant noun *in 1966 Vietnam was becoming an irritant to the Labour government*: **annoyance**, irritation, source of irritation, source of vexation, source of annoyance, thorn in someone's side/flesh, pinprick, pest, bother, trial, torment, plague, inconvenience, nuisance, menace; informal aggravation, peeve, pain, pain in the neck, bind, bore, headache, hassle; Scottish informal nyaff, skelf; N. Amer. informal pain in the butt, nudnik, burr in/under someone's saddle; Austral./NZ informal nark; Brit. vulgar slang pain in the arse.
▷ANTONYMS help; pleasure.

irritate verb **1** *if you are feeling slightly down, the smallest things are likely to irritate you*: **annoy**, vex, make angry, make cross, anger, exasperate, bother, irk, gall, pique, put out, displease, get/put someone's back up, antagonize, get on someone's nerves, rub up the wrong way, try someone's patience, ruffle, ruffle someone's feathers, make someone's hackles rise, raise someone's hackles; enrage, infuriate, madden, incense, make someone's blood boil, drive to distraction, goad, provoke; informal aggravate, peeve, hassle, miff, rile, nettle, needle, get, get to, bug, hack off, get under someone's skin, get in someone's hair, get up someone's nose, put someone's nose out of joint, get someone's goat, give someone the hump, rattle someone's cage, get someone's dander up, drive mad/crazy, drive round the bend/twist, drive up the wall, drive bananas, make someone see red; Brit. informal wind up, nark, get across, get on someone's wick; N. Amer. informal tee off, tick off, burn up, rankle, ride, gravel; Brit. informal get on someone's tits; informal, dated give someone the pip; vulgar slang piss off; rare exacerbate, hump, rasp.
▷ANTONYMS pacify.
2 *some sand got into the car and irritated my eyes*: **inflame**, aggravate; hurt, pain; chafe, abrade, fret, gall, rub painfully, rub against, scratch, rasp, scrape, graze, grate; rare excoriate.
▷ANTONYMS soothe.

> *Choose the right word* **irritate, annoy, aggravate, vex, peeve**
>
> See **annoy**.

irritated adjective *she was irritated with herself for having behaved so pettily*: **annoyed**, cross, angry, vexed, exasperated, irked, piqued, displeased, put out, fed up, disgruntled, in a bad mood, in a temper, testy, in high dudgeon, huffy, in a huff, resentful, aggrieved; furious, irate, infuriated, incensed, enraged, wrathful, choleric; informal aggravated, peeved, nettled, miffed, miffy, mad, riled, hacked off, peed off, hot under the collar, foaming at the mouth; Brit. informal browned off, cheesed off, brassed off, narked, ratty, shirty, eggy; N. Amer. informal teed off, ticked off, sore, bent out of shape; Austral./NZ informal snaky, crook; W. Indian informal vex; vulgar slang pissed off; N. Amer. vulgar slang pissed; literary ireful; archaic snuffy, wrath.
▷ANTONYMS contented; good-humoured.

irritating adjective *the railway companies have the irritating habit of addressing passengers as customers*: **annoying**, infuriating, exasperating, maddening, trying, tiresome, vexing, vexatious, irksome, galling, troublesome, bothersome, provoking, displeasing; awkward, difficult, inconvenient; informal aggravating, pesky, cussed, accursed, confounded, infernal, pestiferous, plaguy, pestilent.
▷ANTONYMS helpful; pleasing.

irritation noun **1** *'I found it for myself,' she said, trying not to show her irritation*: **annoyance**, infuriation, exasperation, vexation, indignation, impatience, crossness, displeasure, resentment, gall, chagrin, pique; anger, rage, fury, wrath, outrage, temper; informal aggravation; literary ire.
▷ANTONYMS delight.
2 *I realize my presence here is an irritation for you*: **irritant**, source of irritation, source of vexation, annoyance, source of annoyance, thorn in someone's side/flesh, pinprick, pest, bother, trial, torment, plague, inconvenience, nuisance, bugbear, menace; informal aggravation, peeve, pain, pain in the neck, bind, bore, headache, hassle; Scottish informal nyaff, skelf; N. Amer. informal pain in the butt, nudnik, burr in/under someone's saddle; Austral./NZ informal nark; Brit. vulgar slang pain in the arse.
▷ANTONYMS pleasure.

island noun **isle**, islet; atoll; in the Caribbean key; in Spanish America cay; Brit. ait, holm; Scottish skerry; **(islands)** archipelago, chain, group.
▷ANTONYMS mainland, continent.

> *Word links* **island**
>
> **insular** relating to an island

isolate verb **1** *she tried to isolate herself from her family | the area was evacuated and isolated until the danger had passed*: **separate**, set apart, segregate, detach, cut off, keep apart, cocoon, insulate, quarantine, keep in solitude, sequester, cloister, seclude, divorce, shut away, alienate, distance, exclude, keep out; cordon off, form a ring around, put a cordon sanitaire around, seal off, close off, fence off, rope off, screen off, tape off, curtain off, shut off, partition off.
▷ANTONYMS integrate.
2 *even in a stream of traffic the laser beam can isolate the offending vehicles*: **identify**, single out, pick out, spot, point out, recognize, pinpoint, pin down, put one's finger on, discern, distinguish, discover, find, locate; sort out, filter out, separate out, weed out.
▷ANTONYMS confuse.

isolated adjective **1** *railways are not flexible enough to be able to serve isolated communities*: **remote**, out of the way, outlying, off the beaten track, secluded, in the depths of ..., hard to find, lonely, in the back of beyond, in the hinterlands, off the map, in the middle of nowhere, godforsaken, obscure, inaccessible, cut-off, unreachable; faraway, far-flung; N. Amer. in the backwoods, lonesome; S. African in the backveld, in the platteland; Austral./NZ in the backblocks, in the booay; informal unget-at-able, in the sticks; N. Amer. informal jerkwater, in the tall timbers; Austral./NZ informal Barcoo, beyond the black stump; archaic unapproachable.
▷ANTONYMS accessible.
2 *he lived a very isolated existence and was something of a recluse*: **solitary**, lonely, companionless, unaccompanied, by oneself, on one's own, (all) alone, friendless; secluded, cloistered, sequestered, segregated; protected, cocooned, sheltered, insulated, immune; antisocial, unsociable, withdrawn, reclusive, introverted, hermitic; N. Amer. lonesome.
▷ANTONYMS sociable.
3 *police believe the attack is an isolated incident*: **unique**, single, lone, sole, only, one, solitary, individual; unusual, uncommon, exceptional, anomalous, abnormal, odd, atypical, untypical; random, unrelated, stray, freak; informal one-off.
▷ANTONYMS common; multiple.

isolation noun **1** *there were two single rooms reserved for patients who needed isolation*: **separation**, segregation, setting apart, keeping apart; quarantine; insulation, seclusion, closeting, protection, shielding, partitioning.
2 *the isolation experienced by those bringing up children alone*: **solitariness**,

loneliness, friendlessness, lack of contact, (sense of) exile, aloneness.
▷ANTONYMS contact.
3 *some mental hospitals are considered to be non-viable on the grounds of their isolation*: **remoteness**, seclusion, loneliness, inaccessibility.
▷ANTONYMS accessibility.

issue noun **1** *the committee has yet to meet to discuss the issue*: **matter**, matter in question, affair, business, subject, topic, question, point, point at issue, item, thing, case, concern, theme; proceeding, situation, occasion, circumstance; problem, bone of contention, controversy, argument.
2 *the victory was celebrated with the issue of a special stamp*: **issuing**, issuance, publication, publishing; circulation, distribution, supplying, supply, sending out, delivery; appearance.
3 *the latest issue of our magazine*: **edition**, number, instalment, copy; printing, imprint, impression, version, publication.
4 Law *she died without issue in 1635*: **offspring**, descendants, heirs, successors, children, sons or daughters, progeny, scions, family, youngsters, babies; informal kids; derogatory spawn; archaic seed, fruit, fruit of one's loins.
5 *an issue of blood*: **discharge**, emission, release, outflow, outflowing, outpouring, outrush, rush, flood, deluge, spurt, jet, cascade, stream, torrent, gush; flow, flux, outflux, welling; leakage, escape, drain, drainage; excretion, secretion, ejection, disgorgement, debouchment, emanation, exudation, exuding, venting, effluence, effluent, effusion; technical efflux.
6 dated *his perseverance certainly merited a favourable issue*: **result**, outcome, consequence, end result, net result, upshot, effect, after-effect, aftermath, conclusion, end, denouement; informal pay-off.
□ **at issue** *at issue here is the definition of a work of art*: **in question**, in dispute; being discussed, under discussion, under consideration; on the agenda, for debate, to be discussed, to be decided, unsettled.
□ **take issue** *I take issue with your assertion*: **disagree**, fail to agree, be in dispute, be in contention, be at variance, be at odds, be at loggerheads, not see eye to eye, argue, quarrel; challenge, dispute, question, call into question, oppose, object to, take exception to, protest against, contradict, gainsay, differ from, dissent from, diverge from; archaic disaccord.
▷ANTONYMS agree.
▸ verb **1** *writs were issued against the contractors | the minister issued a statement*: **send out**, put out; release, deliver; publish, announce, proclaim, broadcast, promulgate, communicate, impart, purvey, circulate, distribute, spread, disseminate; literary bruit about/abroad, utter.
▷ANTONYMS withdraw.
2 *the captain* **issued** *the crew* **with** *side arms*: **supply**, provide, furnish, arm, equip, fit out, rig out, kit out, accoutre, outfit, fit up; provision, stock, purvey, accommodate; present, invest, endow, favour; informal fix up.
▷ANTONYMS withdraw.
3 *savoury smells began to issue from the kitchen | soft music issued from overhead speakers*: **emanate**, emerge, proceed, exude, discharge, flow (out/forth), pour (out/forth), gush (out/forth), come (out/forth), seep (out/forth), ooze (out/forth), spread out; be uttered, be emitted, be transmitted.
4 *surprising profits might* **issue from** *the unwinding of a few giant companies*: **result**, follow, ensue, develop, stem, spring, arise, start, derive, evolve, proceed, emerge, emanate, flow; be got, be had, be taken; be caused by, be the result of, be brought on/about by, be produced by, originate in, have its origin in, attend, accompany, be consequent on; Philosophy supervene on.
▷ANTONYMS bring about.

Italy noun

> *Word links* **Italy**
> **Italo-** related prefix
> **Italophobia** hatred or fear of Italian people and things
> **Italophile** lover of Italian people and things

itch noun **1** *scratch my back—I have an itch*: **tingling**, irritation, itchiness, stinging, prickling, tickling; Medicine paraesthesia; rare formication.
2 informal *he had the itch to write fiction*: **longing**, yearning, pining, craving, ache, burning, hunger, thirst, urge, lust, hankering, need, eagerness, zeal, covetousness; wish, fancy, desire; hope, aspiration, dream; informal yen.
▸ verb **1** *the heat made their chilblains itch*: **tingle**, be irritated, be itchy, sting, prickle, tickle.
2 informal *he itched to do something to help | they were* **itching for** *a good game*: **long**, yearn, pine, ache, burn, hanker for/after, hunger, thirst, lust, pant, hope, be eager, be desperate, be consumed with desire, be unable to wait, would give one's eye teeth, wish, have a fancy; crave, need, lust after, dream of, set one's heart on, be bent on, eat one's heart out over, covet; want, desire, fancy, set one's sights on; informal have a yen, be dying, be gagging.

> *Word links* **itch**
> **acarophobia** fear of itching

item noun **1** *an item of farm equipment | earthworms are the main item in a badger's diet*: **thing**, article, object, unit, module, artefact, piece, commodity, product, bit; element, constituent, component, ingredient.
2 *the meeting was ill-prepared to discuss the item*: **issue**, matter, affair, business, subject, topic, question, point, detail, particular, thing, case, concern, consideration, theme, feature; proceeding, situation, occasion, circumstance.
3 *a news item*: **report**, story, account, description, article, piece, write-up, paragraph, column, flash, brief, release, newscast, headline, communication, communiqué, bulletin, feature; message, dispatch, statement; informal scoop.
4 *the exceptional items in the profit and loss account*: **entry**, record, statement, note, listing, thing.

itemize verb **1** *Steinburg itemized thirty-two design faults in the reactor type*: **list**, catalogue, inventory, record, set out, set forth, spell out, document, register, tabulate, detail, particularize, specify, identify, cite, name, mention, give; enumerate, number.
2 *they sent back the bill with a request to itemize it*: **analyse**, break down, split up, dissect, take apart, deconstruct.

iterate verb *the process is iterated until a convincing agreement is reached*: **repeat**, recapitulate, go through again, go over again, run through again, rehearse; say again, restate, reiterate; informal recap; rare reprise, ingeminate.

itinerant adjective *a market for both local and itinerant traders*: **travelling**, peripatetic, wandering, wayfaring, roving, roaming, rambling, touring, nomadic, gypsy, migrant, migratory, ambulatory; vagrant, vagabond, homeless, of no fixed address/abode, displaced; footloose, rootless, drifting, floating, unsettled, restless; globetrotting, jet-setting; archaic errant.
▷ANTONYMS sedentary; settled.
▸ noun *an itinerants' lodging house*: **traveller**, wanderer, wayfarer, roamer, rover, nomad, gypsy, Bedouin; migrant, transient, drifter, vagabond, vagrant, tramp; refugee, displaced person, DP, homeless person; dated bird of passage.

itinerary noun *the ancient university town of Cambridge should be on every visitor's itinerary*: **planned route**, route, journey, way, road, path, course; travel plan, schedule, timetable, programme, travel arrangements, flight plan; tour, circuit, round.

itself pronoun
□ **by itself** See **by oneself** at **by**.

jab verb *he jabbed the Englishman twice in the ribs | he jabbed his forefinger at Melanie*: **poke**, prod, dig, nudge, tap, butt, ram, elbow, shove, punch, jolt; prick; thrust, stab, push, plunge, stick, insert, drive, lunge.
▶ noun *he gave me a jab in my ribs with his rifle butt*: **poke**, prod, dig, nudge, tap, butt, elbow, shove, punch, jolt; prick; thrust, stab, push, plunge, drive, lunge.

jabber verb *they jabbered non-stop to each other over the radio*: **prattle**, babble, chatter, twitter, prate, gabble, go on, run on, rattle on/away, yap, jibber-jabber, patter, blather, maunder, ramble, drivel, blab; talk rapidly, talk incoherently, talk unintelligibly; informal yak, yackety-yak, yabber, yatter, blabber; Brit. informal witter, rabbit, chunter, natter, waffle; Scottish & Irish informal slabber; Austral./NZ informal mag; archaic twaddle, clack, twattle.
▶ noun *stop your jabber and get on with your breakfast*: **prattle**, babble, chatter, chattering, twitter, twittering, prating, gabble, jibber-jabber, patter, blather, rambling, twaddle, drivel; rapid talk, unintelligible talk; informal yak, yackety-yak, yabbering, yatter, blabber; Brit. informal wittering, rabbiting, nattering, waffle, waffling; Austral./NZ informal mag; archaic clack, twattle.

jack verb
□ **jack something in** Brit. informal *I turned professional when I was 17, but I jacked it in*: **give up**, stop, cease, discontinue, desist from, swear off, forbear from, abstain from, cut out, renounce, forswear, forgo, abandon, have done with; resign from, stand down from; informal quit, kick, leave off, knock off, pack in, lay off, chuck, ditch.
▷ANTONYMS take up; continue.
□ **jack something up 1** *thieves jacked up the car and stole the wheels*: **raise**, hoist, lift, lift up, raise aloft, haul up, winch up, lever up, heave up, hike up, hitch up, pull up, take up, upraise, uplift, elevate; rare upheave, uprear, upthrust. **2** informal *he may need to jack up interest rates further*: **increase**, raise, put up, push up, up, mark up, make higher, boost, step up, lift, augment, inflate, escalate; informal hike (up), bump up.
▷ANTONYMS lower.

jacket noun *a jacket for your hot-water tank will save at least £15 a year*: **wrapping**, wrapper, wrap, sleeve, sheath, sheathing, envelope, cover, covering; casing, case, shell, housing, encasement, capsule; technical integument.

jackpot noun *this week's lottery jackpot is over £14 million*: **top prize**, main prize, first prize; kitty, pool, pot, bank, bonanza, windfall.
□ **hit the jackpot** (informal) **win a large prize**, win a lot of money, strike it lucky, make a large profit, make a/one's fortune, make money, be successful, be lucky; informal clean up, strike it rich, rake it in, make a/one's pile, make a killing, make a packet, make a bundle, make a pretty penny, hit the big time; Brit. informal make a bomb; N. Amer. informal make big bucks.

jaded adjective **1** *there are soups exotic enough for the most jaded palate*: **satiated**, sated, surfeited, glutted, cloyed, gorged; **dulled**, blunted, deadened, benumbed.
2 *she has an eye for the detail that a more jaded journalist might overlook*: **tired**, weary, tired out, wearied, worn out, exhausted, fatigued, overtired, sleepy, drowsy, sapped, dog-tired, spent, drained, jet-lagged, debilitated, prostrate, enervated, low; informal all in, done (in/up), dead, dead beat, dead tired, dead on one's feet, asleep on one's feet, ready to drop, played out, fagged out, bushed, pooped, worn to a frazzle, shattered, burnt out; Brit. informal knackered, whacked; N. Amer. informal tuckered out.
▷ANTONYMS fresh.

jag noun *a head of rye, all jags and bristles*: **sharp projection**, point, snag, jagged bit; barb, thorn, tooth, spur; informal sticky-out bit.

jagged adjective *the jagged end of a broken bone*: **spiky**, spiked, barbed, snaggy, nicked, pointed, ragged, craggy, rough, uneven, irregular, broken; serrated, sawtooth, saw-edged, toothed, notched, indented, denticulate.
▷ANTONYMS smooth.

Word toolkit **jagged**

See **spiky**.

jail, gaol noun *he was arrested and thrown into jail*: **prison**, penal institution, place of detention, lock-up, place of confinement, guardhouse, correctional facility, detention centre; young offender institution, youth custody centre; N. Amer. penitentiary, jailhouse, boot camp, stockade, house of correction; informal the clink, the slammer, inside, stir, the jug, the big house, the brig, the glasshouse; Brit. informal the nick; N. Amer. informal the can, the pen, the cooler, the joint, the pokey, the slam, the skookum house, the calaboose, the hoosegow; Brit. informal, dated chokey, bird, quod; historical pound, roundhouse; Brit. historical approved school, borstal, bridewell; Scottish historical tollbooth; French, historical bastille; N. Amer. historical reformatory.
▶ verb *she was jailed for killing her husband*: **imprison**, put in prison, send to prison, incarcerate, lock up, take into custody, put under lock and key, put away, intern, confine, detain, hold prisoner, hold captive, hold, put into detention, constrain, immure, put in chains, put in irons, clap in irons; Brit. detain at Her Majesty's pleasure; informal send down, put behind bars, put inside; Brit. informal bang up.
▷ANTONYMS acquit; release.

jailer, gaoler noun *the jailer had discovered the loss of his prisoners*: **prison officer**, (prison) warder, (prison) wardress, (prison) warden, (prison) guard, keeper, incarcerator, captor, sentry; informal screw; Law detainer; archaic turnkey.

jam[1] verb **1** *he jammed a finger in each ear*: **stuff**, shove, force, ram, thrust, wedge, press, push, stick, squeeze, compress, confine, cram, pack, sandwich, insert.
2 *several hundred friends and celebrities **jammed into** the shop | students soon jammed the streets*: **crowd**, pack, pile, press, squeeze, cram; throng, occupy, fill, overfill, overcrowd; obstruct, block, clog, congest; N. Amer. mob.
3 *the rudder had jammed*: **stick**, become stuck, catch, seize (up), become immobilized, become unable to move, become fixed, become wedged, become lodged, become trapped.
4 *even dust could jam the mechanism*: **immobilize**, paralyse, disable, cripple; deactivate, put out of action, make inoperative; stop, halt, bring to a halt, bring to a standstill.
▷ANTONYMS free.
▶ noun **1** *a traffic jam*: **tailback**, line, stream, hold-up, obstruction, congestion, bottleneck, stoppage; N. Amer. gridlock; informal snarl-up.
2 informal *I'd tell you if we ever got into a real jam*. See **predicament**.

jam[2] noun *raspberry jam*: **preserve**, conserve, jelly, marmalade; N. Amer. dulce; rare confiture, confection.

jamb noun *he leaned against the door jamb*: **post**, doorpost, upright, frame, pillar.

jamboree noun *the world Scout jamboree*: **rally**, gathering, get-together, convention, conference; festival, fête, fiesta, gala, party, carnival, celebration; informal bash, shindig, shindy, jolly, junket.

jammy adjective Brit. informal *that jammy pig's won a million quid!* See **lucky**.

jangle verb **1** *keys jangled at his waist*: **clank**, clink, jingle, tinkle, ding, ping, clang, clash, clatter, rattle, vibrate, ring, chime; rare tintinnabulate.
2 *the sound of merriment jangled her nerves*: **grate on**, jar on, irritate, disturb, assault, fray, rasp, put/set on edge, shred, rub raw, test, rattle, stretch tight, wreak havoc on; informal get on.
▶ noun *the jangle of his chains and bells*: **clank**, clanking, clink, clinking, chink, chinking, jangling, jingle, jingling, clash, clashing, clang, clanging, rattle, rattling, clangour; **cacophony**, din, racket, noise, discord, dissonance, discordance, caterwauling, raucousness, stridency, stridor; rare tintinnabulation.

janitor noun **caretaker**, custodian, porter, concierge, doorkeeper, doorman, steward, warden, watchman; cleaner, maintenance man; N. Amer. superintendent.

jar[1] noun *a jar of honey*: **glass/earthenware container**, pot, crock, urn, pitcher, jug, flask, decanter, carafe, flagon, ewer, drum, canister; vessel, container, receptacle, repository; N. Amer. creamer; historical jorum; archaic reservatory.

jar[2] verb **1** *each step jarred my whole body*: **jolt**, jerk, shake, vibrate; bang.
2 *his daughter's shrill, childish voice **jarred on** him*: **grate on**, set someone's teeth on edge; irritate, annoy, upset, irk, exasperate, nettle, vex, disturb, rattle, discompose; jangle; informal rile, aggravate, get on someone's nerves, get someone's goat.
▷ANTONYMS please.
3 *the play's symbolism **jarred with** the realism of its setting*: **clash**, conflict, be incompatible, be at variance, be at odds, be inconsistent, be incongruous, be in opposition, be in conflict, disagree, contrast, collide; differ from, diverge from; not match, not go, be discordant; informal scream at.
▷ANTONYMS blend; match.

jargon noun *the instructions are written in electrician's jargon*: **specialized language**, technical language, slang, cant, idiom, argot, patter, patois, vernacular; computerese, legalese, bureaucratese, journalese, psychobabble; unintelligible language, obscure language, gobbledegook, gibberish, double Dutch; informal lingo, -speak, -ese, mumbo-jumbo.

jarring adjective *the jarring juxtaposition of opposites*: **clashing**, conflicting, contrasting, incompatible, incongruous; discordant, dissonant, inharmonious; harsh, grating, jangling, strident, shrill, cacophonous; out of place, unsuitable, inappropriate; disagreeable, unpleasant, offensive.
▷ANTONYMS harmonious; pleasing.

jaundiced adjective *a jaundiced view of the world*: **bitter**, resentful, cynical, soured, distorted, disenchanted, disillusioned, disappointed, pessimistic, sceptical, distrustful, suspicious, misanthropic; jealous, envious; narrow-minded, bigoted, prejudiced, intolerant, discriminatory.
▷ANTONYMS optimistic; charitable.

jaunt noun *his wife went off for a jaunt round Oxford*: **trip**, pleasure trip, outing, excursion, expedition, day trip, day out, mini holiday, short break; tour, mystery tour, drive, ride, run, turn, cruise, sally; informal junket, spin, tootle, joyride, tool; Scottish informal hurl.

jaunty adjective *he wore a cap pushed to one side to give him a jaunty air*: **cheerful**, cheery, happy, merry, jolly, joyful, gleeful, glad; **lively**, vivacious, perky, full of life, bright, sunny, buoyant, bubbly, bouncy, breezy, frisky, full of the joys of spring, in good spirits, exuberant, ebullient, effervescent, sparkling, sparkly, sprightly, spry; **carefree**, unworried, untroubled, without a care in the world, blithe, airy, light-hearted, nonchalant, insouciant, happy-go-lucky, free and easy, easy-going, blasé, devil-may-care, casual, relaxed; informal bright-eyed and bushy-tailed, full of beans, sparky, upbeat, go-go, chirpy, chipper, peppy, zippy, zappy, full of vim and vigour; N. Amer. informal peart; dated gay; archaic blithesome, perk, as merry/lively as a grig, wick.
▷ANTONYMS depressed; serious; sedate.

jaw noun **1** *he sustained a broken jaw*: **jawbone**, lower jaw, mandible; maxilla, upper jaw.
2 (**jaws**) *the whale seized a struggling seal pup in its jaws*: **mouth**, maw, muzzle, lips; informal chops.
3 informal *we ought to have a jaw*. See **chat** (noun).
▶ verb informal *Tommaso was the type to jaw about whatever new scheme had taken his fancy*. See **chat** (verb).

> *Word links* **jaw**
>
> **mandibular**, **maxillary** relating to the jaw

jazz verb
□ **jazz something up** informal *why not jazz up your documents with a few unusual typefaces?* **enliven**, liven up, brighten up, make more interesting, make more exciting, put some spirit into, make more attractive, add (some) colour to, wake up, give a lift/boost to, lift, ginger up; improve, enhance, embellish, dress up, beautify, gild, season, leaven, add spice to, spice up, revitalize, vitalize; informal perk up, pep up.

jazzy adjective *their range of ceramic jars uses a jazzy combination of spots and stripes*: **bright**, colourful, brightly coloured, bright-coloured, brilliant, striking, strong, eye-catching, stimulating, exciting, interesting, effective, imaginative, graphic, vivid, lively, vibrant, bold, flamboyant, flashy, glaring, showy, gaudy, lurid, garish; informal (looking) like an explosion in a paint factory.
▷ANTONYMS dull.

jealous adjective **1** *he was jealous of his brother's popularity*: **envious**, covetous, desirous; resentful, grudging, begrudging; jaundiced, bitter, malicious, spiteful; green with envy, green, green-eyed; greedy, selfish, acquisitive; formal emulous.
▷ANTONYMS admiring; proud.
2 *a jealous lover*: **suspicious**, distrustful, mistrustful, doubting, insecure, anxious; apprehensive of rivals, possessive, proprietorial, overprotective, clinging, controlling, dominating.
▷ANTONYMS trusting, understanding.
3 *they are very jealous of their rights*: **protective**, defensive, vigilant, watchful, heedful, mindful, careful, solicitous, attentive.
▷ANTONYMS careless, unconcerned.

> *Word toolkit* **jealous**
>
> See **envious**.

jealousy noun **1** *he was consumed with jealousy at the younger man's superior talents*: **envy**, enviousness, covetousness, desire; resentment, resentfulness, bitterness, discontent, spite, grudge; informal the green-eyed monster.
▷ANTONYMS admiration; pride.
2 *their relationship survived the understandable jealousy of his long-suffering wife*: **suspicion**, suspiciousness, distrust, mistrust, doubt, insecurity, anxiety; apprehension about rivals, possessiveness, overprotectiveness.
▷ANTONYMS trust, understanding.
3 *such hierarchies produce an intense jealousy of status*: **protectiveness**, defensiveness, vigilance, watchfulness, heedfulness, mindfulness, care, solicitousness, attentiveness.
▷ANTONYMS unconcern, carelessness.

> *Word links* **jealousy**
>
> **zelotypophobia** fear of jealousy

jeans plural noun **denims**, blue jeans; cut-offs; trademark Levi's, Wranglers.

jeer verb *the crowd **jeered at** the referee | the demonstrators jeered the police*: **taunt**, mock, scoff at, ridicule, laugh at, sneer at, deride, tease, insult, abuse, jibe (at), scorn, shout disapproval (at); heckle, interrupt, shout at/down, hector, catcall (at), boo (at), hoot at, whistle at, hiss (at), blow raspberries (at); informal knock, give someone a hard time; archaic flout at.
▷ANTONYMS cheer; applaud.
▶ noun *the jeers of the crowd*: **taunt**, sneer, insult, shout, jibe, boo, hiss, catcall; mockery, ridicule, derision, teasing, scoffing, hectoring, shouting, abuse, scorn, disapproval, interruption, heckling, catcalling, booing, hissing; Brit. & Austral./NZ barracking; informal knocking.
▷ANTONYMS cheer; applause; approval.

jejune adjective **1** *their entirely predictable and usually jejune opinions*. See **callow**, **facile** (sense 1).
2 *the following poem now seems to me rather jejune*. See **uninteresting**.

jell verb See **gel**.

jeopardize verb *relocating outside London will jeopardize their competitiveness*: **threaten**, endanger, imperil, menace, risk, put at risk, expose to risk, put in danger, expose to danger, put in jeopardy, put on the line; leave vulnerable, leave unprotected; compromise, prejudice, be prejudicial to; be a danger to, pose a threat to; **damage**, injure, harm, do harm to, be detrimental to; archaic peril.
▷ANTONYMS safeguard.

> *Choose the right word* **jeopardize, endanger, imperil, risk**
>
> See **endanger**.

jeopardy noun *the peace talks are **in jeopardy***: **danger**, peril; at risk; endangerment, imperilment, insecurity; perilousness, riskiness, precariousness, uncertainty, instability, vulnerability, threat, menace.
▷ANTONYMS safety, security.

jerk noun **1** *she gave the reins a jerk*: **yank**, tug, pull, wrench, snatch, heave, drag, tweak, twitch.
2 *he let the clutch in with a jerk*: **jolt**, lurch, bump, start, jar, jog, bang, bounce, shake, shock; rare jounce.
3 informal *I was left behind, feeling a complete jerk*. See **fool**.
▶ verb **1** *she jerked her arm free*: **yank**, tug, pull, wrench, wrest, heave, haul,

j

drag, tweak, twitch, pluck, snatch, seize, rip, tear, whisk; informal whip.
▷ANTONYMS ease.
2 *the car jerked along in the traffic*: **jolt**, lurch, bump, jog, bang, rattle, bounce, shake; rare jounce.
▷ANTONYMS glide.

jerky adjective **1** *the jerky movements of a frightened horse*: **convulsive**, spasmodic, fitful, twitchy, paroxysmal, shaking, shaky, tremulous, uncontrolled, uncontrollable.
▷ANTONYMS fluid, smooth.
2 *the coach drew to a jerky halt*: **jolting**, lurching, bumpy, bouncy, jarring, rough; rare jouncing.
▷ANTONYMS smooth.

jerry-built adjective *they lived in tents and jerry-built shacks*: **shoddy**, badly built, gimcrack, flimsy, insubstantial, rickety, unstable, ramshackle, crude, carelessly built, thrown together, makeshift, defective, faulty, flawed; inferior, poor-quality, second-rate, third-rate, low-grade, cheap, cheapjack; informal tacky, junky; Brit. informal ropy, rubbish, grotty.
▷ANTONYMS well made, sturdy, substantial.

jest noun **1** *the men talk cheerfully and jests are bandied about freely*: **joke**, witticism, funny remark, gag, quip, sally, pun, play on words; French bon mot; informal crack, wisecrack, one-liner, funny, comeback; repartee, banter.
2 *he wished that Lady Lavinia had not practised this jest upon him*: **prank**, joke, practical joke, piece of mischief, hoax, trick, jape; informal leg-pull, put-on, lark; N. Amer. informal dido.
□ **in jest** *he could tell from the others' smirks that it was meant in jest*: **in fun**, as a joke, tongue in cheek, playfully, jokingly, light-heartedly, facetiously, flippantly, frivolously, for a laugh; to tease, teasingly, banteringly, whimsically.
▷ANTONYMS seriously.
▶ verb **1** *'It's good weather when it doesn't snow before half-time,' he jests*: **joke**, crack, quip, gag, sally, pun; tell jokes, crack jokes, banter; informal wisecrack.
2 *she began to fear that they had not been jesting*: **fool**, fool about/around, play a prank, play a practical joke, tease, hoax; informal kid, wind up, have on, pull someone's leg, make a monkey out of; N. Amer. informal pull someone's chain, fun, shuck.

jester noun **1** historical *a court jester*: **fool**, court fool, court jester; clown, harlequin, pantaloon; archaic buffoon, merry andrew, merryman, motley.
2 *teachers don't usually like the class jester*: **joker**, comedian, comic, humorist, wag, wit, funny man/woman, prankster, jokester, clown, buffoon, character; informal card, case, caution, hoot, scream, laugh, kidder, wisecracker, riot, barrel of laughs; Austral./NZ informal hard case.

jet[1] noun **1** *a jet of water went down his neck*: **stream**, spurt, squirt, spray, fountain, spout; gush, outpouring, rush, surge, burst, spill, flow, flood, cascade, torrent, current.
2 *the carburettor jets can get clogged*: **nozzle**, head, spray, rose, atomizer, sprinkler, sprinkler head, spout, nose; technical sparkler, spile.
3 *they found an executive jet to fly me back*: **jet plane**, jetliner; aircraft, plane; Brit. aeroplane.
□ **jet set** *she moves from village life to international jet set*: **the smart set**, the fashionable, the A-list, the wealthy, the beautiful people, the crème de la crème, the beau monde, the haut monde; high society, society, polite society, the elite, the privileged classes; informal the top drawer.
▶ verb **1** *they jetted out of Heathrow last night*: **fly**, travel/go by jet, travel/go by plane, travel/go by air.
2 *little puffs of gas jetted out*: **squirt**, spurt, shoot, spray, fountain, erupt; gush, pour, stream, rush, pump, surge, spew, spill, flow, course, well, spring, burst, issue, emanate; Brit. informal sloosh.

jet[2] adjective *her glossy jet hair*: **black**, jet-black, pitch-black, as black as pitch, pitchy, pitch-dark, inky, ink-black, sloe-black, coal-black, ebony, raven, sable, sooty.

jettison verb **1** *six aircraft jettisoned their loads into the sea*: **dump**, drop, ditch, discharge, eject, throw out, empty out, pour out, tip out, unload, throw overboard, throw over the side.
▷ANTONYMS load.
2 *he sorted out his desk, jettisoning unwanted papers | the scheme was jettisoned*: **discard**, dispose of, throw away, throw out, get rid of, toss out; reject, scrap, dispense with, cast aside/off, abandon, relinquish, drop, have done with, shed, slough off, shrug off, throw on the scrap heap; informal chuck (away/out), fling, dump, ditch, axe, bin, junk, get shut of; Brit. informal get shot of; N. Amer. informal trash.
▷ANTONYMS keep, retain.

jetty noun **pier**, landing stage, landing place, landing, quay, wharf, dock, berth, staithe, stair(s), finger, pontoon, marina, harbour; breakwater, mole, groyne, dyke; N. Amer. dockominium, levee; in Venice traghetto.

Jew noun

> *Word links* **Jew**
>
> **Judaic, Semitic** relating to Jews
> **Judaeo-** related prefix, as in *Judaeo-Christian*

jewel noun **1** *a crown encrusted with priceless jewels*: **gem**, gemstone, precious stone, semi-precious stone, stone, brilliant; baguette, cabochon; informal sparkler, rock; archaic bijou.
2 *the Crown jewels*: **piece of jewellery**, ornament; trinket.
3 *the jewel of his collection | a jewel of a poem*: **finest example/specimen**, choicest example/specimen, best example/specimen, showpiece, pearl, flower, pride, pride and joy, cream, crème de la crème, jewel in the crown, nonpareil, glory, wonder, prize, boast, pick; masterpiece, chef d'oeuvre, pièce de résistance; outstanding example, shining example; Latin ne plus ultra; informal the pick of the bunch.
4 *the girl is a jewel*: **treasure**, saint, angel, paragon, marvel, find, godsend, someone/something worth their weight in gold; darling, dear; informal one in a million, one of a kind, a star, the bee's knees, the tops; archaic nonsuch.

jeweller noun **lapidary**, gemmologist.

jewellery noun **jewels**, gems, gemstones, precious stones, semi-precious stones, bijouterie; treasure, regalia; **ornaments**, trinkets, costume jewellery, diamanté; archaic bijoux.

Jezebel noun **immoral woman**, hussy; seductress, temptress, femme fatale, Delilah; informal **vamp**, **maneater**; N. Amer. informal **roundheel**, **tramp**; informal, derogatory tart; Brit. informal, derogatory **scrubber**, **slapper**, **slag**; dated **scarlet woman**, loose woman, woman of easy virtue, woman of ill repute, fallen woman, wanton, strumpet, trollop; archaic harlot, jade.

jib verb **1** *the horse jibbed at the final fence*: **stop at**, stop short at, baulk at, shy at, retreat from; refuse.
▷ANTONYMS clear.
2 *some struggling farmers jib at paying large veterinary bills*: **baulk at**, fight shy of, shy away from, recoil from, shrink from, draw back from, stop short of; be unwilling to, be reluctant to, demur at, be loath to, not want to; informal boggle at.
▷ANTONYMS be willing to.

jibe noun *the cruel jibes of his former colleagues*: **snide remark**, cutting remark, taunt, sneer, jeer, insult, barb; informal dig, wisecrack, crack, put-down.
▶ verb *'What accomplishments?' Simon jibed in his sarcastic way*: **jeer**, taunt, mock, scoff, sneer.

jiffy noun informal
□ **in a jiffy** *I'll be back in a jiffy*: **very soon**, soon, in a second, in a minute, in a moment, in a trice, in a flash, shortly, directly, any second, any minute, any minute now, in a short time, in an instant, in the twinkling of an eye, in no time, in no time at all, in less than no time, before you know it, before long; N. Amer. momentarily; informal in a sec, in a jif, in two shakes, in two shakes of a lamb's tail, before you can say Jack Robinson, in the blink of an eye, in a blink, in the wink of an eye, in a wink, before you can say knife; Brit. informal in a tick, in two ticks, in a mo; N. Amer. informal in a snap, in jig time; archaic anon.

jig verb *Joan jigged about with excitement*: **bob up and down**, leap up and down, jump up and down, spring up and down, skip, hop; prance, caper, bounce; rare curvet, rollick, capriole, jounce.

jiggle verb **1** *Barrett jiggled his foot, looking anywhere but at Bill*: **shake**, jig, joggle, jog, waggle, wiggle; jerk.
2 *Thomas jiggled excitedly*: **fidget**, wriggle, squirm, move restlessly; informal have ants in one's pants.

jilt verb *the man I thought loved me jilted me and stole my money*: **leave**, walk out on, throw over, finish with, break up with, reject, cast aside; desert, abandon, leave in the lurch, leave high and dry; betray; informal chuck, ditch, dump, drop, run out on, do the dirty on, give someone the push, give someone the old heave-ho, give someone the elbow, give someone the big E; archaic forsake.

jingle noun **1** *the jingle of money in the till*: **clink**, chink, tinkle, jangle, rattle.
2 *the jingle of the bell above the shop door made her jump*: **tinkle**, ring, ding, ping, ting-a-ling, chime; rare tintinnabulation.
3 *advertising jingles*: **slogan**, catchline, catchphrase; **ditty**, song, rhyme, tune, verse; chorus, refrain; limerick, piece of doggerel; N. Amer. tag line.
▶ verb **1** *her bracelets jingled noisily | he jingled the coins in his pocket*: **clink**, chink, tinkle, jangle, rattle, clank.
2 *the bell jingled*: **tinkle**, ring, ding, ping, go ting-a-ling, chime; rare tintinnabulate.

jingoism noun *the jingoism of Hollywood war films*: **extreme patriotism**, blind patriotism, chauvinism, extreme nationalism, flag-waving, excessive loyalty to one's country, xenophobia; isolationism, sectarianism; hawkishness, militarism, warmongering, belligerence, bellicosity.

jinx noun *the jinx struck six days later, when fire gutted the building*: **curse**, spell, hoodoo, malediction, plague, affliction; the evil eye, black magic, voodoo, bad luck, evil fortune; Irish cess; N. Amer. hex; informal the kiss of death; archaic malison.
▶ verb *some people believe the family is jinxed*: **curse**, cast a spell on, put the evil eye on, hoodoo, bewitch; Austral. point the bone at; N. Amer. hex; Austral. informal mozz, put the mozz on; rare accurse.

jitters plural noun informal *a fit of opening-night jitters*. See **nerves** at **nerve** (sense 4 of the noun).

jittery adjective informal See **nervous**.

job noun **1** *my job involves a lot of travelling*: **position of employment**, position, post, situation, place, appointment, posting, placement; **occupation**, profession, trade, career, work, field of work, line of work, line of business, means of livelihood, means of earning a living, walk of life, métier, pursuit, craft; vocation, calling; vacancy, opening; Scottish way; informal berth; Austral. informal grip; archaic employ.
2 *a job that will take him three months to complete*: **task**, piece of work, assignment, project; chore, errand; undertaking, venture, operation, enterprise, activity, business, affair; Military detail.
3 *it's your job to protect her*: **responsibility**, **duty**, charge, concern, task; role, function, contribution, capacity, mission, commission; informal department; Brit. informal pigeon; dated office.
4 informal *it was a job to get here on time*: **difficult task**, problem, trouble, struggle, strain, hard time, trial, bother; informal headache, hassle, performance, pain, hard mountain to climb, hard row to hoe.
5 informal *a series of daring bank jobs*: **crime**, felony; raid, robbery, hold-up, burglary, break-in, theft; informal stick-up, smash-and-grab (raid); N. Amer. informal heist.
□ **just the job** Brit. informal **the very thing**, just the thing, just right, exactly what's needed; informal just what the doctor ordered, just the ticket; Austral. informal just the glassy.

Word links **job**

vocational relating to a job

Choose the right word **job, task, chore, duty**

See **task**.

jobless adjective *sixteen per cent of the town's workforce is jobless*: **unemployed**, out of work, without work, out of a job, without paid employment, unwaged, workless, between jobs, redundant, laid off; N. Amer. on welfare, collecting unemployment; Brit. informal signing on, on the dole, 'resting'; Austral./NZ informal on the wallaby track; N. Amer. informal collecting; rare disemployed.
▷ANTONYMS in work, employed.

jockey noun **rider**, horseman, horsewoman, equestrian; Austral. informal hoop.
▸ verb **1** *I jockeyed the stone into position | he jockeyed himself into a position on the team*: **manoeuvre**, ease, edge, manipulate, work, steer; engineer, inveigle, insinuate, ingratiate, wheedle, coax, cajole; informal finagle.
2 *members of the Cabinet began jockeying for position*: **compete**, contend, vie; **struggle**, fight, tussle, scramble, push, jostle.

jocular adjective *jocular comments | a jocular mood*: **humorous**, funny, witty, comic, comical, amusing, chucklesome, droll, entertaining, diverting, joking, jesting, hilarious, facetious, tongue-in-cheek; playful, light-hearted, jolly, jovial, cheerful, cheery, merry, mirthful, roguish, waggish, whimsical, teasing; informal jokey; dated sportive; rare jocose, ludic.
▷ANTONYMS solemn, serious, earnest.

jocund adjective literary See **cheerful**.

jog verb **1** *he began to jog along the road*: **run slowly**, jogtrot, dogtrot, trot, lope; go jogging.
2 *things seem to be jogging along quite nicely here*: **continue**, proceed, go, go on, carry on.
3 *a hand jogged his elbow*: **nudge**, prod, poke, push, elbow, tap; bump, jar.
4 *I think it was seeing you that jogged her memory*: **stimulate**, prompt, stir, activate, arouse; refresh.
5 *she jogged her foot up and down*: **joggle**, jiggle, bob, bounce, jolt, jerk, shake; rare jounce.
▸ noun *he set off along the bank at a jog*: **run**, jogtrot, dogtrot, trot, lope.

joie de vivre noun French *Mediterranean joie de vivre is not a quality found in the typical Briton*: **gaiety**, cheerfulness, cheeriness, merriment, light-heartedness, happiness, joy, joyfulness, joyousness, delight, pleasure, high spirits, spiritedness, jollity, jolliness, joviality, exuberance, ebullience, liveliness, vivacity, enthusiasm, enjoyment, verve, gusto, relish, animation, effervescence, sparkle, buoyancy, sprightliness, jauntiness, zest, zestfulness; informal pep, zing, get-up-and-go, being full of the joys of spring, perkiness; literary gladsomeness, blitheness, blithesomeness.
▷ANTONYMS depression; sobriety.

join verb **1** *the two parts of the mould are joined with clay*: **connect**, unite, fix, affix, attach, add, annex, fasten, stick, glue, fuse, knit, weld, amalgamate, consolidate, combine, bond, append, link, bridge, secure, lock, make fast, tie, bind, string, lash, couple, marry, pair, yoke, team, chain, merge, dovetail, splice, blend; formal conjoin.
▷ANTONYMS separate.
2 *here the path joins a major road*: **meet**, touch, reach, extend to, abut, adjoin, border (on), converge (with); rejoin.
▷ANTONYMS leave.
3 *I'm off to join the search party*: **become a member of**, help in, participate in, join in, get involved in, contribute to, have a hand in; enlist (in), join up (with), sign up (with), affiliate to, team up (with), join forces (with), play a part (in); band together, get together, ally.
▷ANTONYMS leave.
□ **join up** *he joined up in 1939, becoming an RAF officer*: **enlist**, join; enrol in, sign up for, volunteer for; Brit. archaic take the King's shilling.
▸ noun See **joint**.

joint noun **1** *a leaky joint in the metal guttering*: **join**, junction, juncture, intersection, link, linkage, connection, nexus; weld, knot, seam; coupling, coupler; bracket, brace, hinge; Anatomy commissure, suture.
2 *the hip joint*: technical **articulation**.
3 informal *L'Alouette looked like a pretty classy joint*: **establishment**, restaurant, bar, club, nightclub; informal clip joint, dive; N. Amer. informal honky-tonk; in the US, historical speakeasy.
4 informal *he rolled a joint*: **cannabis cigarette**, marijuana cigarette; informal spliff, reefer, bomb, bomber, stick; S. African zol; black English blunt.
▸ adjective *matters of joint interest | a joint effort*: **common**, shared, communal, collective, corporate; mutual, reciprocal; cooperative, collaborative, concerted, joined, combined, allied, united.
▷ANTONYMS separate, individual.
▸ verb *use a sharp knife to joint the carcass*: **cut up**, chop up, butcher, carve.

Word links **joint**

arthro- related prefix, as in *arthropod, arthroscope*
zygo- related prefix, as in *zygomatic*

jointly adverb *a survey organized jointly by the WWF and the Forestry Commission*: **together**, in partnership, in cooperation, cooperatively, in collaboration, in conjunction, in concert, in combination, as one, mutually; in alliance, in league, in collusion; informal in cahoots.

joke noun **1** *they sat round the table telling jokes*: **funny story**, jest, witticism, quip, pleasantry; pun, play on words; shaggy-dog story, old chestnut, double entendre; in-joke; informal **gag**, wisecrack, crack, funny, one-liner, rib-tickler, killer, knee-slapper, thigh-slapper; N. Amer. informal **boffola**; rare blague.
2 *he was given to playing stupid jokes on people*: **trick**, practical joke, prank, stunt, hoax, jape; informal leg-pull, lark, spoof; Austral. informal goak; N. Amer. informal, dated cutup; archaic quiz; Scottish archaic cantrip.
3 informal *he soon became a joke to most of us because he was so pedantic*: **laughing stock**, figure of fun, source of amusement, object of ridicule; Brit. Aunt Sally.
4 informal *the present system is nothing short of a joke*: **farce**, travesty, waste of time; standing joke; informal laugh; N. Amer. informal shuck.
▸ verb **1** *she laughed and joked with the guests*: **tell jokes**, crack jokes; jest, banter, quip; informal wisecrack, josh.
2 *don't panic—I'm only joking*: **fool**, fool about/around, play a prank, play a trick, play a joke, play a practical joke, tease, hoax, pull someone's leg, mess someone about/around; informal kid, make a monkey out of someone; Brit. informal mess, have someone on, wind someone up; N. Amer. informal fun, shuck someone, pull someone's chain, put someone on.

joker noun *he had a reputation as the family joker*: **humorist**, comedian, comedienne, comic, funny man/woman, wag, wit, jester; prankster, practical joker, hoaxer, trickster, clown; informal card, jokester, wisecracker; archaic quiz, droll, merry andrew; rare quipster, gagster, jokesmith, punster, kidder, farceur.

jolly adjective *a big, jolly woman | he returned home in a jolly mood*: **cheerful**, happy, cheery, good-humoured, jovial, merry, sunny, bright, joyful, light-hearted, in high spirits, in good spirits, sparkling, bubbly, exuberant, effervescent, ebullient, breezy, airy, lively, vivacious, full of life, sprightly, jaunty; glad, cock-a-hoop, gleeful; smiling, grinning, laughing, mirthful, radiant; happy-go-lucky, genial, carefree, unworried, untroubled, without a care in the world, full of the joys of spring, fun-loving, buoyant, optimistic, hopeful, positive; informal chipper, chirpy, perky, smiley, upbeat, peppy, sparky, zippy, zingy, bright-eyed and bushy-tailed, full of beans, full of vim and vigour; N. Amer. informal peart; dated gay; literary gladsome, jocund, joyous, jocose, blithe, blithesome; archaic of good cheer, perk, as merry/lively as a grig; rare Pickwickian.
▷ANTONYMS miserable, gloomy.
▸ verb informal *he tried to jolly her along*: **encourage**, urge, coax, cajole, persuade, wheedle.
▸ adverb Brit. informal *that's a jolly good idea*. See **very**.

jolt verb **1** *the train stopped suddenly, jolting the passengers to one side | he jolted his injured ankle*: **push**, thrust; **jar**, bump, knock, bang, jostle; shake, joggle, jog, nudge.
2 *the car jolted along the rough wet roads*: **bump**, bounce, jerk, rattle, lurch, shudder, vibrate; Brit. judder; rare jounce.
3 *she was jolted out of her reverie | the anger in his tone jolted her*: **startle**, surprise, shock, stun, shake, take aback; astonish, astound, amaze,

stagger, stop someone in their tracks; upset, disturb, perturb, disconcert, discompose, unnerve, throw off balance, set someone back on their heels; galvanize, electrify; informal rock, floor, knock for six, knock sideways.
▶ **noun 1** *a series of sickening jolts that jarred every bone in her body*: **bump**, bounce, shake, jerk, lurch, vibration; impact; Brit. judder; rare jounce.
2 *he woke up with a jolt*: **start**, jerk, jump, abrupt movement, convulsive movement.
3 *the sight of the dagger gave him a jolt*: **fright**, the fright of one's life, shock, scare; informal turn.
4 *it had been an unpleasant jolt, but Susan recovered quickly*: **shock**, surprise, bombshell, bolt from the blue, thunderbolt, rude awakening, eye-opener; blow, upset, setback; informal whammy.

jostle **verb 1** *she stepped aside to avoid being jostled by a crowd of noisy students*: **bump into/against**, knock into/against, bang into, collide with, cannon into, plough into, jolt; **push**, shove, elbow, hustle; mob; N. Amer. informal barrel into.
2 *I jostled my way to the exit*: **push**, thrust, barge, shove, force, squeeze, elbow, shoulder, bulldoze.
3 *people jostled for the best position*: **struggle**, vie, jockey, scramble, crowd one another; informal scrum.

jot **verb** *I've jotted down a few details*: **write down**, note down, make a note of, take down, set down, put down, put on paper, mark down; log, record, list, register, enter; scribble, scrawl.
▶ **noun** *they have not produced a jot of evidence | she didn't care a jot about him*: **iota**, scrap, shred, whit, grain, crumb, ounce, little bit, bit, tiniest bit, jot or tittle, fraction, speck, atom, particle, scintilla, trace, hint, mite; any; rap, hoot, fig; Irish stim; French soupçon; informal smidgen, smidge, tad, damn, tinker's cuss, monkey's; Austral./NZ informal skerrick; archaic scantling, scruple, smitch.

j

journal **noun 1** *a medical journal*: **periodical**, publication, magazine, gazette, digest, professional organ, review, newsletter, news-sheet, bulletin; **newspaper**, paper; daily, weekly, monthly, quarterly.
2 *while abroad, he kept a journal*: **diary**, day-by-day account, daily record, log, logbook, weblog, blog, moblog, yearbook; chronicle, register; notebook, commonplace book; annals, history; N. Amer. daybook.

journalism **noun 1** *a career in journalism*: **the newspaper business**, the newspaper world, the press, the print media, the fourth estate; radio journalism, television journalism; Brit. Fleet Street.
2 *his incisive style of journalism*: **reporting**, writing, reportage, feature writing, news coverage; investigative journalism; articles, reports, features, pieces, stories.

journalist **noun** **reporter**, correspondent, newsman, newswoman, newspaperman, newspaperwoman, columnist, writer, commentator, reviewer, blogger; investigative journalist, photojournalist, war correspondent, lobby correspondent; editor, subeditor, copy editor; paparazzo; Brit. pressman; N. Amer. legman, wireman; Austral. roundsman; informal news hound, hack, hackette, stringer, journo, talking head; N. Amer. informal newsy, thumbsucker; dated publicist; (**journalists**) the commentariat.

journey **noun** *his three-year journey round the world*: **trip**, expedition, period of travelling, tour, trek, voyage, cruise, safari, ride, drive; crossing, passage, flight; travels, wandering, roaming, roving, globetrotting; odyssey, pilgrimage; excursion, outing, jaunt; rare peregrination.
▶ **verb** *they journeyed south*: **travel**, go, voyage, sail, cruise, fly, hike, trek, ride, drive, make one's way, wend one's way; go on a trip, take a trip, go on an expedition, go on an excursion, go on a tour, tour, go on safari; globetrot, backpack; roam, rove, ramble, wander, meander; rare peregrinate.

joust historical **verb** *knights jousted with lances and shields*: **enter the lists**, tourney, tilt, break a lance; fight, spar, contend, clash.
▶ **noun** *a medieval joust*: **tournament**, tourney, tilt, the lists; combat, contest, fight, encounter, duel, passage of arms.

jovial **adjective** *a stout, jovial man | his jovial manner*: **cheerful**, jolly, happy, cheery, good-humoured, convivial, genial, good-natured, friendly, amiable, affable, sociable, outgoing, clubbable; smiling, grinning, laughing, mirthful, merry, sunny, bright, joyful, high-spirited, exuberant, ebullient, lively, vivacious, full of life, sprightly, jaunty, breezy; happy-go-lucky, carefree, unworried, untroubled, without a care in the world, full of the joys of spring, fun-loving, buoyant, optimistic, positive; informal chipper, chirpy, perky, smiley, upbeat, peppy, sparky, bright-eyed and bushy-tailed, full of beans, full of vim and vigour; N. Amer. informal peart; dated gay; literary gladsome, jocund, joyous, jocose, blithe, blithesome; archaic of good cheer, perk, as merry/lively as a grig; rare Pickwickian.
▷**ANTONYMS** miserable, gloomy.

joy **noun 1** *whoops of joy | the look of joy on her face*: **delight**, great pleasure, joyfulness, jubilation, triumph, exultation, rejoicing, happiness, gladness, glee, exhilaration, ebullience, exuberance, elation, euphoria, bliss, ecstasy, transports of delight, rapture, radiance; enjoyment, gratification, felicity; cloud nine, seventh heaven; French joie de vivre; humorous delectation; literary joyousness; rare jouissance, ravishment, jocundity.
▷**ANTONYMS** misery, despair.
2 *it was a joy to be with her*: **pleasure**, source of pleasure, delight, treat, thrill; informal buzz, kick.
▷**ANTONYMS** trial, tribulation.
3 informal *if you still have no joy, you may have to resort to the courts*: **success**, satisfaction, luck, successful result, positive result; accomplishment, achievement.

joyful **adjective 1** *his joyful mood*: **cheerful**, happy, jolly, merry, bright, sunny, joyous, light-hearted, in good spirits, in high spirits, sparkling, bubbly, effervescent, exuberant, ebullient, cock-a-hoop, breezy, airy, cheery, sprightly, jaunty, smiling, grinning, beaming, laughing, mirthful, radiant; jubilant, overjoyed, beside oneself with joy, thrilled, ecstatic, euphoric, blissful, on cloud nine/seven, elated, delighted, glad, gleeful, gratified; jovial, genial, good-humoured, happy-go-lucky, carefree, unworried, untroubled, without a care in the world, full of the joys of spring; buoyant, optimistic, hopeful, full of hope, positive; content, contented; informal upbeat, chipper, chirpy, peppy, smiley, sparky, over the moon, on top of the world; N. Amer. informal peart; dated gay; Austral./NZ informal wrapped; literary jocund, gladsome, blithe, blithesome; archaic of good cheer.
▷**ANTONYMS** sad, miserable.
2 *the joyful news about his forthcoming marriage*: **pleasing**, glad, happy, good, cheering, gladdening, gratifying, welcome, heart-warming, delightful; literary gladsome.
▷**ANTONYMS** distressing.
3 *a joyful occasion*: **happy**, cheerful, merry, jolly, festive, celebratory, joyous; dated gay.
▷**ANTONYMS** sad, depressing.

joyless **adjective 1** *a narrow-minded, joyless man*: **gloomy**, melancholy, morose, lugubrious, glum, sombre, saturnine, sullen, dour, mirthless, humourless; unhappy, sad, miserable, depressed, despondent, sunk in gloom, heavy-hearted, doleful, downcast, dejected, dispirited.
▷**ANTONYMS** cheerful, fun-loving.
2 *a joyless room filled with yellowing oil paintings*: **depressing**, cheerless, gloomy, dreary, bleak, dispiriting, drab, dismal, desolate, wretched, comfortless, austere, stark, sombre, grim; unwelcoming, uninviting, inhospitable; literary drear.
▷**ANTONYMS** pleasant, welcoming.

joyous **adjective** *her joyous expression*. See **joyful**.

jubilant **adjective** *crowds of jubilant fans ran on to the pitch*: **overjoyed**, exultant, triumphant, joyful, jumping for joy, rejoicing, cock-a-hoop, exuberant, elated, thrilled, gleeful, euphoric, ecstatic, beside oneself with happiness, enraptured, in raptures, rhapsodic, transported, walking on air, in seventh heaven, on cloud nine; crowing, gloating, triumphal, triumphalist; informal over the moon, on top of the world, blissed out, on a high, tickled pink; N. Amer. informal wigged out; Austral. informal wrapped.
▷**ANTONYMS** downcast, despondent.

jubilation **noun** *Arlene was unable to conceal her jubilation*: **exultation**, triumph, joy, joyousness, rejoicing, elation, euphoria, ecstasy, rapture, transports of delight, glee, gleefulness, exuberance.
▷**ANTONYMS** despondency.

jubilee **noun** **anniversary**, commemoration; **celebration**, festival, gala, carnival, jamboree, feast day, holiday; festivities, revelry.

Judas **noun** **traitor**, betrayer, back-stabber, double-crosser, false friend; turncoat, quisling, renegade; archaic traditor; rare tergiversator, renegado.

judge **noun 1** *the judge sentenced him to five years*: **justice**, magistrate, His/Her/Your Honour; Law Lord, Lord Justice; (**judges**) the judiciary; in England & Wales **recorder**; in Scotland **sheriff**; in the Isle of Man **deemster**; in the Channel Islands **jurat**; N. Amer. **jurist**, **surrogate**; Spanish **alcalde**; informal **beak**, m'lud; historical **reeve**; Scottish historical **sheriff-depute**, **bailie**.
2 *a distinguished panel of judges will select the winning design*: **adjudicator**, arbiter, assessor, evaluator, appraiser, examiner, moderator; umpire, referee, mediator; expert, connoisseur, authority, specialist, pundit; Latin arbiter elegantiarum.
▶ **verb 1** *I judged that she was simply exhausted | voters were asked what factors they judged to be most important*: **form the opinion**, come to the conclusion, conclude, decide, determine; consider, believe, think, deem, view; deduce, gather, infer, gauge, tell, see, say, estimate, assess, guess, surmise, conjecture; regard as, hold, see as, look on as, take to be, rate as, rank as, class as, count; informal reckon, figure, guesstimate.
2 *other cases were judged by tribunal*: **try**, hear, sit in judgement on; adjudicate, decide, give a ruling/verdict on, pass judgement on.
3 *she was judged innocent of murder*: **adjudge**, pronounce, decree, rule, find.
4 *the competition will be judged by Alan Amey*: **adjudicate**, arbitrate, umpire, referee, mediate, moderate; officiate.
5 *entries will by judged by a panel of experts*: **assess**, appraise, evaluate, weigh up; examine, review, criticize; informal size up.

judgement **noun 1** *the incident showed the extent to which his temper could affect his judgement*: **discernment**, acumen, shrewdness, astuteness, common sense, good sense, sense, perception, perspicacity, percipience, penetration, acuity, discrimination, wisdom, wit, native wit, judiciousness,

prudence, sagacity, understanding, intelligence, awareness, canniness, sharpness, sharp-wittedness, cleverness, powers of reasoning, reason, logic; informal nous, savvy, know-how, horse sense, gumption, grey matter; Brit. informal common; N. Amer. informal smarts; rare sapience, arguteness.
2 *a county-court judgement*: **verdict**, decision, adjudication, ruling, pronouncement, decree, finding, conclusion, determination; sentence.
3 *the critical judgement of work by artists and designers*: **assessment**, evaluation, appraisal; review, analysis, criticism, critique.
4 *the crash had been a judgement on them for their wickedness*: **punishment**, retribution, penalty; just deserts.
□ **against one's better judgement reluctantly**, unwillingly, grudgingly, under protest; despite oneself.
□ **in my judgement** *in my judgement, such things should be forbidden*: **in my opinion**, to my mind, in my view, to my way of thinking, I believe, I think, as I see it, if you ask me, personally, in my book, for my money, in my estimation.

judgemental adjective *I don't like to sound judgemental but it really was a big mistake*: **critical**, fault-finding, censorious, condemnatory, disapproving, disparaging, deprecating, negative, overcritical, hypercritical, scathing.

judicial adjective *a judicial inquiry*: **legal**, judiciary, juridical, judicatory, forensic, jurisdictive; official.

judicious adjective *a judicious course of action*: **wise**, sensible, prudent, politic, shrewd, astute, canny, sagacious, common-sense, commonsensical, sound, well advised, well judged, well thought out, considered, thoughtful, perceptive, discerning, clear-sighted, insightful, far-sighted, percipient, discriminating, informed, intelligent, clever, enlightened, logical, rational; discreet, careful, cautious, circumspect, diplomatic; strategic, expedient, practical, advisable, in one's (best) interests; informal smart, savvy; Scottish & N. English informal pawky; N. Amer. informal heads-up; dated, informal long-headed; rare argute, sapient.
▷ANTONYMS injudicious, foolish, ill-advised.

jug noun **pitcher**, ewer, crock, jar, urn; carafe, flask, flagon, decanter; vessel, receptacle, container; toby jug; N. Amer. creamer; historical amphora, jorum, greybeard.

juggle verb *defence chiefs juggled the figures on bomb tests*: **misrepresent**, tamper with, falsify, misstate, distort, change round, alter, manipulate, rig, massage, fudge; informal fix, doctor, cook the books; Brit. informal fiddle.

juice noun **1** *squeeze the juice from two lemons*: **liquid**, fluid, sap; extract; Winemaking taille.
2 (**juices**) *digestive juices*: **secretions**; serum.
3 (**juices**) *strain the cooking juices into a pan*: **liquid**, liquor.
4 informal *he ran out of juice*. See **petrol**.

juicy adjective **1** *a juicy steak | a juicy peach*: **succulent**, tender, moist; ripe, luscious, lush, sappy; archaic mellow.
▷ANTONYMS dry.
2 informal *juicy gossip*: **very interesting**, fascinating, intriguing, sensational, lurid, thrilling, exciting, colourful, entertaining; **scandalous**, racy, risqué, spicy, piquant, provocative, suggestive; informal hot, shock-horror.
▷ANTONYMS dull.
3 informal *a juicy severance package*: **large**, substantial, sizeable, generous; lucrative, profitable, remunerative; informal fat, tidy, whopping (great), thumping (great); Brit. informal whacking (great).
▷ANTONYMS small.

jumble noun **1** *the books were in a chaotic jumble | a jumble of ideas and impressions*: **untidy heap**, confused heap, clutter, muddle, mess, confusion, welter, disarray, disarrangement, tangle, litter; hodgepodge, hotchpotch, mishmash, miscellany, motley collection, mixture, mixed bag, medley, farrago; informal mash-up; Brit. informal dog's dinner, dog's breakfast; rare gallimaufry, mingle-mangle, congeries, macédoine.
2 Brit. *bags of jumble*: **junk**, bric-a-brac, bits and pieces; Brit. lumber; rare rummage.
▸ verb *the photographs are all jumbled up in an envelope*: **mix up**, muddle up, disarrange, disorganize, disorder, confuse, put in disarray, throw into chaos, make a shambles of; shuffle.

jumbo adjective informal *a jumbo packet of crisps*. See **huge**.

jump verb **1** *the cat jumped off his lap | Flora began to jump about all over the kitchen*: **leap**, spring, bound, hop, bounce; skip, bob, caper, dance, prance, gambol, frolic, frisk, cavort.
2 *the youth jumped the fence and ran across the yard*: **vault (over)**, leap over, clear, sail over, hop over, go over, leapfrog; pole-vault, hurdle.
3 *pre-tax profits jumped from £51,000 to £1.03 million*: **rise**, go up, leap up, shoot up, soar, surge; climb, increase, mount, escalate, spiral; informal skyrocket.
▷ANTONYMS fall, plummet.
4 *an owl hooted nearby, making her jump*: **start**, jerk, jolt, flinch, recoil, twitch, wince; shudder, shake, quiver; informal jump out of one's skin.
5 *Polly **jumped at** the chance to go*: **accept eagerly**, leap at, welcome with open arms, seize on, snap up, grab, snatch, pounce on, go for enthusiastically, show enthusiasm for.
6 informal *he jumped at least seven red lights*: **ignore**, disregard, fail to stop at, drive through, overshoot; informal run.
□ **jump the gun** informal **act prematurely**, act too soon, be overhasty, be precipitate; informal be previous, be ahead of oneself.
□ **jump to it** informal **hurry up**, get a move on, be quick; informal get cracking, get moving, get on with it, shake a leg, look lively, look sharp, get/pull one's finger out, get weaving, rattle one's dags; Brit. informal get one's skates on, stir one's stumps; N. Amer. informal get a wiggle on; Austral./NZ informal get a wriggle on; S. African informal put foot; dated make haste.
▸ noun **1** *in making the short jump across the gully, he lost his balance*: **leap**, spring, vault, bound, hop; bounce, skip.
2 *the horse cleared the last jump with ease*: **obstacle**, barrier; fence, hurdle, rail, hedge, gate.
3 *a fifty-one per cent jump in annual profits*: **rise**, leap, increase, upturn, upsurge, upswing, spiralling, lift, escalation, elevation, boost, advance, augmentation; informal hike.
▷ANTONYMS fall, drop.
4 *I woke up with a jump*: **start**, jerk, sudden movement, involuntary movement, convulsive movement, spasm, twitch, wince; shudder, quiver, shake.

jumpy adjective **1** informal *he was tired and jumpy*: **nervous**, on edge, edgy, tense, anxious, ill at ease, unrelaxed, in a state of nerves, in a state of agitation, fretful, uneasy, restless, fidgety, worked up, keyed up, overwrought, wrought up, strung out, on tenterhooks, on pins and needles, with one's stomach in knots, worried, apprehensive, strained; shaky, shaking, trembling, quivering; Brit. nervy; informal with butterflies in one's stomach, a bundle of nerves, jittery, like a cat on a hot tin roof, twitchy, in a state, in a stew, uptight, wired, het up, all of a dither, all of a doodah, all of a lather, in a tizz/tizzy, stressed out, white-knuckled; Brit. informal strung up, windy, like a cat on hot bricks; N. Amer. informal spooky, squirrelly, antsy; Austral./NZ informal toey; dated overstrung.
▷ANTONYMS calm, relaxed.
2 *jumpy black-and-white footage*: **jerky**, jolting; lurching, bumpy, jarring; fitful, convulsive; rare jouncing.

junction noun **1** *the junction between the roof and the adjoining walls*: **join**, joint, intersection, link, bond, weld, seam, coupling, connection, union, juncture; brace, bracket, hinge; Anatomy commissure, suture, synapse.
2 *the junction of the two rivers*: **confluence**, convergence, meeting, meeting point, conflux, juncture, watersmeet; Indian sangam.
3 *turn right at the next junction*: **crossroads**, crossing, intersection, interchange, T-junction, box junction, gyratory; level crossing; turn, turn-off, exit; Brit. roundabout; N. Amer. turnout, cloverleaf.

juncture noun **1** *at this juncture, I cannot give any further information | a critical juncture in her career*: **point**, point in time, time, moment, moment in time, stage; period, phase.
2 *the juncture of the pipes*. See **junction** (sense 1).
3 *the juncture of the rivers*. See **junction** (sense 2).

jungle noun **1** *the Amazon jungle*: **tropical forest**, (tropical) rainforest; wilderness, wilds, the bush.
2 *the jungle of third world bureaucracy*: **complexity**, confusion, complication, mess, chaos; **labyrinth**, maze, tangle, snarl, web.
□ **the law of the jungle the survival of the fittest**, each/every man for himself, dog-eat-dog.

junior adjective **1** *the junior members of the family*: **younger**, youngest.
▷ANTONYMS senior, older.
2 *a junior minister | part of my function is to supervise those **junior to** me*: **low-ranking**, lower-ranking, subordinate, sub-, lesser, lower, minor, secondary, inferior; beneath, under.
▷ANTONYMS higher-ranking, senior.
3 *John White Junior*: **the Younger**; Brit. minor; N. Amer. II.
▷ANTONYMS Senior.

junk informal noun *an attic full of all kinds of junk*: **useless things, discarded things**, rubbish, clutter, stuff, odds and ends, bits and pieces, bric-a-brac, oddments, flotsam and jetsam, white elephants; garbage, refuse, litter, scrap, waste, debris, detritus, dross; leavings, leftovers, remnants, cast-offs, rejects; Brit. lumber; N. Amer. trash; Austral./NZ mullock; informal dreck; Brit. informal gubbins, odds and sods; vulgar slang crap, shit; archaic rummage.
▸ verb *sort out what can be sold off and junk the rest*: **throw away/out**, discard, get rid of, dispose of, scrap, toss out, jettison, dispense with; informal chuck (away/out), dump, ditch, bin, get shut of; Brit. informal bung away/out, get shot of.

junket noun informal *a media junket organized to stir up interest in the film*. See **party** (sense 1 of the noun), **outing** (sense 1).

junta noun *the military junta took power in a coup last February*: **faction**, group, cabal, clique, party, set, ring, gang, league, confederacy; historical junto; rare camarilla.

jurisdiction noun **1** *an area under French jurisdiction*: **authority**, control, power, dominion, rule, administration, command, sway, leadership, sovereignty, ascendancy, hegemony, mastery; say, influence.
2 *the extradition of criminals from foreign jurisdictions*: **territory**, region,

province, district, area, zone; domain, realm, orbit, sphere; historical soke, leet.

just adjective **1** *a just and democratic society | Max was a just man*: **fair**, fair-minded, equitable, even-handed, impartial, unbiased, objective, neutral, disinterested, unprejudiced, open-minded, non-partisan, non-discriminatory; honourable, upright, upstanding, decent, honest, righteous, ethical, moral, virtuous, principled, full of integrity, good, right-minded, straight, reasonable, scrupulous, trustworthy, incorruptible, truthful, sincere; informal square.
▷ANTONYMS unjust, unfair.
2 *a just reward | his just deserts*: **deserved**, well deserved, well earned, merited, earned; rightful, due, proper, fitting, appropriate, apt, suitable, befitting; formal condign; archaic meet.
▷ANTONYMS undeserved.
3 *just criticism*: **valid**, sound, well founded, well grounded, justified, justifiable, warranted, warrantable, defensible, defendable, legitimate, reasonable, logical; rare vindicable.
▷ANTONYMS unfair, wrongful.
▶ adverb **1** *I just saw him*: **a moment ago**, a second ago, a short time ago, very recently, not long ago, lately, only now.
2 *that's just what I need | she's just right for him*: **exactly**, precisely, absolutely, completely, totally, entirely, perfectly, utterly, wholly, thoroughly, altogether, in every way, in every respect, in all respects, quite; informal down to the ground, to a T, bang on, dead; N. Amer. informal on the money.
3 *we just made it*: **by a narrow margin**, narrowly, only just, by inches, by a hair's breadth, by the narrowest of margins; barely, scarcely, hardly; informal by the skin of one's teeth, by a whisker.
4 *she's just a child | it's just you and me now*: **only**, merely, simply, but, nothing but, no more than; at best, at most; alone, to the exclusion of everyone/everything else, and no one else, and nothing else; N. English nobbut; S. African informal sommer.
5 *the colour's just fantastic*: **really**, absolutely, completely, entirely, totally, altogether, positively, quite, one hundred per cent; indeed, truly.
□ **just about** informal *that's just about all the money I've got left*: **nearly**, almost, practically, all but, virtually, as good as, more or less, close to, nigh on, to all intents and purposes, not far off; not quite; informal pretty much; literary well-nigh.

justice noun **1** *ideas of social justice | I appealed to his sense of justice*: **fairness**, justness, fair play, fair-mindedness, equity, equitableness, even-handedness, egalitarianism, impartiality, impartialness, lack of bias, objectivity, neutrality, disinterestedness, lack of prejudice, open-mindedness, non-partisanship; honour, uprightness, decency, integrity, probity, honesty, righteousness, ethics, morals, morality, virtue, principle, right-mindedness, propriety, scrupulousness, trustworthiness, incorruptibility.
▷ANTONYMS injustice.
2 *the justice of his case*: **validity**, justification, soundness, well-foundedness, legitimacy, legitimateness, reasonableness.
3 *an attempt to pervert the course of justice*: **judicial proceedings**, administration of the law.
4 *an order made by the justices*: **judge**, magistrate, His/Her/Your Honour; Law Lord, Lord Justice; in England & Wales recorder; in Scotland sheriff; in the Isle of Man deemster; in the Channel Islands jurat; N. Amer. jurist, surrogate; Spanish alcalde; informal beak, m'lud; historical reeve; Scottish historical sheriff-depute, bailie.

Word links **justice**

judicial relating to a system of justice
dikephobia fear of justice

justifiable adjective *justifiable criticism*: **valid**, legitimate, warranted, well founded, justified, just, sound, reasonable, sensible; **defensible**, arguable, tenable, able to hold water, defendable, supportable, sustainable, warrantable, vindicable, acceptable, plausible; lawful, legal; explainable, understandable, forgivable, venial.
▷ANTONYMS unjustifiable, indefensible.

justification noun *the justification for government action*: **grounds**, reason, just cause, basis, rationale, premise, rationalization, vindication, warrant, foundation, explanation, excuse; defence, argument, apologia, apology, case.

justify verb **1** *marketing directors were pressed to justify the expenditure*: **give grounds for**, give reasons for, give a justification for, show just cause for, explain, give an explanation for, account for, show/prove to be reasonable, provide a rationale for, rationalize; defend, answer for, vindicate, substantiate, uphold, sustain; establish, legitimize, legitimatize.
2 *the situation was grave enough to justify further investigation*: **warrant**, be good reason for, be a justification for; bear out, confirm, validate.

justly adverb **1** *a man who is justly proud of his achievement*: **justifiably**, with reason, with good reason, legitimately, rightly, rightfully, properly, deservedly, by rights.
▷ANTONYMS unjustifiably.
2 *they deserve to be treated justly*: **fairly**, with fairness, equitably, even-handedly, impartially, without bias, objectively, without prejudice, without fear or favour; by the book, in accordance with the rules; informal fairly and squarely.
▷ANTONYMS unjustly.

jut verb *a rock jutted out from the side of the bank*: **stick out**, project, protrude, poke out, bulge out, overhang, beetle (over), obtrude; extend; rare be imminent, protuberate, impend.

juvenile adjective **1** *juvenile offenders*: **young**, teenage, teenaged, adolescent, junior, under age, pubescent, prepubescent.
▷ANTONYMS adult.
2 *his juvenile behaviour*: **childish**, immature, puerile, infantile, babyish; jejune, inexperienced, callow, green, unsophisticated, naive, foolish, silly, stupid, asinine; N. Amer. sophomoric; informal wet behind the ears.
▷ANTONYMS mature.
▶ noun *cases of assault in which the victims are juveniles*: **young person**, youngster, child, teenager, adolescent, minor, junior; boy, girl, schoolboy, schoolgirl; informal kid.
▷ANTONYMS adult.

Word toolkit **juvenile**

See **youthful**.

juxtapose verb *her work juxtaposes images from serious and popular art*: **place/set side by side**, place/set close to one another, mix; compare, contrast, place/set against one another; Linguistics collocate, colligate.

juxtaposition noun *the juxtaposition of considerable wealth and severe deprivation*: **comparison**, contrast; **proximity**, nearness, closeness; Linguistics collocation, colligation; rare contiguity.

Wordfinder

This section of the ***Oxford Thesaurus of English*** contains word lists that are different to the ordinary thesaurus entries. Instead of giving alternative words that mean the same or a similar thing to the word you have looked up, they are of two further types. Those in section 1, 'Fascinating words', contain words grouped mainly because of their origin or the way they are used, while each list in section 2, 'Thematic lists', gives the names of *types* of a category of things, people, or animals.

Section 1 is essentially for browsing, but affords ample opportunity for enriching your vocabulary. Section 2 is invaluable for solving many word games, and especially crosswords, whether of the 'quick' or cryptic kind. If, for instance, you look up *snake* in the main thesaurus, you will find the synonyms *serpent* and *ophidian*, as well as those which could be used of a person—*traitor*, *cheat*, etc.—but if you look up *snake* in the Wordfinder index, you will be directed to a list of different *types* of snake, including *adder*, *cobra*, *rattlesnake*, *water moccasin*, and many more.

These lists fulfil a function that is not provided by either a dictionary or a conventional thesaurus, whether 'Roget'-style or alphabetical. Because they are grouped thematically—as Animals, Food, Music, etc.—it is easy to find a word if you are not quite sure which category to look under: for example, whether *andante* is under 'Musical forms' or 'Musical directions', it will not take long to find since the two lists are adjacent.

Because the lists will most often be searched for a word of a particular form, each list is arranged alphabetically, as a list of *words* rather than a guide to its subject. This means that alternative names for the same thing are each listed in their own place in alphabetical order; if they were adjacent to each other in order to link them because of their meaning, one or the other would be difficult to find. So although a

Contents

cello and a *violoncello* are the same musical instrument, each name is listed separately in the list of 'Stringed instruments'.

Certain lists, such as those of chemical elements, the Greek alphabet, and suits of cards, are (at least for practical purposes) complete, but most lists are selective, since it would not be possible to include every bird, colour, or weapon, for example. So that they are particularly useful for solving word puzzles, such selective lists do not rigorously list the most common types of their category, but rather include as great a variety of names as possible. Thus, the list of birds, for example, contains many species or families with completely different names, such as *goose*, *plover*, *lyrebird*, and *vulture*, but it omits some which may be just as common but have less distinctive names, such as *grey goose* and *ringed plover*.

Index to thematic lists

1 Fascinating words

Imitative words

Words that imitate a noise (often called 'onomatopoeic') can describe either the noise itself (as with *beep*) or the thing that makes the noise (as with *flip-flop*). These lists group them accordingly and give a sense of the extraordinary variety of words with an imitative origin.

General noises

bang a sudden loud, sharp noise
beep a short, high-pitched sound made by electronic equipment or a vehicle horn
blare a loud, harsh sound
blatter a clatter
bleep a short high-pitched electronic sound
blip a very short high-pitched electronic sound
bloop a short low-pitched electronic sound
boing a clear, reverberating sound, as of a compressed spring being released
bong a low-pitched sound, as of a bell
boom a loud, deep, resonant sound
brattle a sharp rattling sound
burble a continuous murmuring noise
buzz a low, continuous humming or murmuring sound, as of an insect
ching an abrupt high-pitched ringing sound, as of a cash register
chink a light, high-pitched ringing sound, as of glasses or coins striking together
chitter make a twittering or chattering sound
chuff a regular sharp puffing sound, as of a steam engine
chug regular muffled explosive sounds, as of an engine running slowly
clang a loud, resonant metallic sound or series of sounds
clank a loud, sharp sound, as of pieces of metal being struck together
clatter a continuous rattling sound, as of hard objects falling
click a short, sharp sound, as of a switch being operated
clip cut short or trim (hair, vegetation, etc.) with shears or scissors
clip-clop the sound made by a horse's hoofs on a hard surface
clitter make a thin rattling sound
clop the sound made by a horse's hoofs on a hard surface
creak (typically of a wooden object) make a scraping or squeaking sound when moved
crump a sudden, loud, dull sound, as of a bomb
dah a long Morse signal
ding a ringing sound
ding-a-ling a ringing sound
dit a short Morse signal
dong a deep, resonant sound, as of a bell
dump a site for depositing rubbish
fizz the hissing sound of bubbles of gas
fizzle a feeble hissing or spluttering sound
flap (of a bird) move (its wings) up and down
graunch a crunching or grinding noise
gurgle a hollow bubbling sound like that made by water running out of a bottle
gush a rapid and plentiful stream of liquid
hum a low, steady continuous sound like that of a bee
jingle a light ringing sound like metal objects being shaken together
judder a rapid, forceful vibration
ka-ching the sound of a cash register
mewl cry feebly or querulously, as of a baby
parp a honking sound, as of a car horn
peely-wally pale and sickly in appearance (probably from the sound a sickly person might make)
ping an abrupt high-pitched ringing sound
pink (of a vehicle engine) rattle because of over-rapid combustion
pip a short high-pitched sound, especially in a radio time signal
pip pip goodbye (probably imitative of a motor horn)
plash a splashing sound
plink short, sharp, metallic or ringing sound
plock a short, low clicking sound
plop a short sound as of a small, solid object dropping into water without a splash
plump set down heavily or unceremoniously
pop a light explosive sound
popple (of water) flow in a tumbling or rippling way
puff a short burst of breath or wind
purl (of a stream or river) flow with a swirling motion and babbling sound
put-put the sound of a small petrol engine
putter the sound of a small petrol engine
racket a loud unpleasant noise
rattle a rapid succession of short, sharp knocking sounds
ring a clear resonant or vibrating sound
rumble a continuous deep, resonant sound
rustle a soft, muffled crackling sound
scoosh a splash or squirt of liquid
scrunch a loud crunching noise
shatter break suddenly and violently into pieces
shriek a high-pitched piercing sound or shout
sizzle a hissing sound, as of food frying
sloosh a rush of water or an energetic rinsing
smash the violent breaking of something
snap a sharp cracking sound
snip cut (something) with scissors or shears, typically with small quick strokes
splash strike a body of liquid
splatter splash with a liquid, typically a thick or viscous one
splosh a soft splashing sound
splurt a sudden gush of liquid
sputter make a series of soft explosive or spitting sounds
squeak a short, high-pitched sound or cry
squeal a long, high-pitched cry or noise
squelch make a soft sucking sound such as that made by treading heavily through mud
squirt a thin, fast stream or jet of liquid ejected from a small opening
squish a soft squelching sound
swash (of liquid) move with a splashing sound
swish a hissing or rushing sound
swoosh the sound produced by a sudden rush of air or liquid
tac-au-tac a fencing parry combined with a riposte
tang a loud ringing or clanging sound
throb a strong, regular rhythm
thrum a continuous rhythmic humming sound
tick-tock the sound of a large clock ticking
ting a sharp, clear ringing sound
tinkle a light, clear, repeated ringing sound
tinnitus ringing or buzzing in the ears
trickle a small stream of liquid
vroom the roaring sound of a vehicle at high speed
waul a loud plaintive cry like that of a cat
whizz a whistling or buzzing sound caused by moving quickly through the air
whoomph a sudden loud sound, as of a muffled or distant explosion
whoosh the rushing sound of fast movement
whump a dull or muffled thudding sound
wow slow pitch fluctuation in sound reproduction
yawp a harsh or hoarse cry or yelp
yelp a short, sharp cry, especially of pain or alarm
yip a short, sharp cry, especially of excitement or delight
yowl a loud wailing cry, especially of pain or distress
zap destroy or obliterate
zizz a whizzing or buzzing sound
zoom move or travel very quickly

Bodily actions

belch release air from the stomach through the mouth
boohoo cry
burp release air from the stomach through the mouth
chomp munch or chew vigorously
chug consume (a drink) in large gulps without pausing
chumble nibble; chew
clap strike the palms of (one's hands) together
clomp walk with a heavy tread
cough expel air from the lungs with a sudden sharp sound
crunch crush (a hard or brittle foodstuff) with the teeth
flog beat (someone) with a whip or stick
flump fall or sit down heavily
glug pour or drink (liquid) with a hollow gurgling sound
gulp swallow (drink or food) quickly or in large mouthfuls
harrumph clear the throat
hawk clear the throat
hic a hiccup, especially a drunken one
hiccup an involuntary spasm of the diaphragm and respiratory organs
hiss make a sharp sibilant sound as of the letter s
huff blow out air on account of exertion
keck feel as if one is about to vomit; retch
munch eat steadily
pad walk with steady steps making a soft dull sound
piss urinate
pit-a-pat with a sound like quick light steps or taps
poop defecate
pule cry querulously or weakly
quaff drink (something, especially an alcoholic drink) heartily
screech (of a person or animal) give a loud, harsh, piercing cry
screel utter or emit a high-pitched or discordant cry or sound; screech
slobber have saliva dripping copiously from the mouth
slump sit, lean, or fall heavily and limply
smooch kiss and cuddle amorously
sneer a contemptuous or mocking smile, remark, or tone
sniff draw up air through the nose
sniffle sniff slightly or repeatedly
snore a snorting or grunting sound made in one's sleep
snort an explosive sound made by the sudden forcing of breath through the nose
spit eject saliva forcibly from the mouth
splutter make a series of short explosive spitting or choking sounds
suck draw air or liquid into the mouth
tee-hee a giggle or titter
titter a short, half-suppressed laugh
ululate howl or wail as an expression of strong emotion, typically grief
wee urinate
wee-wee urinate
whimper a series of low, feeble sounds expressive of fear, pain, or discontent
whistle a clear, high-pitched sound made by forcing breath between one's lips or teeth
whoop a loud cry of joy or excitement
zizz snooze or doze

Talking or laughter

blah blah boring talk
cachinnate laugh loudly
chunter talk or grumble monotonously
flibbertigibbet a frivolous, flighty, or excessively talkative person
gabble talk rapidly and unintelligibly
gibber talk rapidly and unintelligibly
giggle laugh lightly in a nervous, affected, or silly manner
guffaw laugh loudly and heartily
jabber talk in a rapid, excited, and often incomprehensible way
la-di-da pretentious or snobbish in manner or speech
lisp a speech defect of the sounds s and z
mum silent
mutter say something in a barely audible voice
natter talk casually, especially on unimportant matters
prate talk foolishly or at tedious length
snicker give a smothered or half-suppressed laugh; snigger
squabble a noisy, trivial quarrel
tattle gossip; idle talk
waffle talk or write at length in a vague or trivial manner
whisper talk very softly, using breath instead of one's voice
witter talk at length about trivial matters
yackety-yak a trivial or unduly prolonged conversation
yada yada yada and so on
yak a trivial or unduly prolonged conversation
yatter talk incessantly; chatter
yock a loud hearty laugh

Objects

bleep(er) electronic device that sounds to alert its wearer
bling expensive, ostentatious clothing and jewellery
bomb explosive device
buffer a person or thing that reduces a shock
chincherinchee a white South African lily (from the squeaky sound made by rubbing its stalks together)
choo-choo a child's word for a railway train or locomotive
flip-flop a light sandal with a thong between the big and second toe (from the sound they make when walked in)
frou-frou frills or other ornamentation, particularly of women's clothes (from the sound made by walking in a dress)
hubble-bubble a hookah
ping-pong table tennis
pom-pom a light, quick-firing cannon of the Second World War
slush partially melted snow or ice
tic-tac-toe North American term for noughts and crosses, of which an early version was played with pieces which clicked when placed
zip a fastener for clothes, bags, etc.

Impacts

bam
bash
boff
bonk
bop
bump
clack
clap
clonk
clunk
crash
knap
knock
lash
plonk
plump
pow
prang
rap
rat-tat
skelp
slap
smack
smash
spank
tap
thump
thwack
tonk
whack
wham
whang
whomp
whump
zonk

Music

bada bing an exclamation, imitating a drum roll, to express how easily and predictably something will happen
bebop a type of jazz originating in the 1940s
blare loud, harsh playing by brass instruments
bourdon a low-pitched organ stop
didgeridoo an Australian Aboriginal wind instrument blown to produce a deep, resonant sound
doo-wop a style of pop music using close harmony vocals and nonsense phrases

drum	a percussion instrument consisting of a membrane stretched over an opening
flam	a basic drumming pattern
gong	a circular metal percussion instrument
hurdy-gurdy	a stringed instrument with a droning sound played by turning a handle
kazoo	a small, simple wind instrument with a buzzing sound
mirliton	a musical instrument resembling a kazoo, with a nasal tone
oompah	the rhythmical sound of deep-toned brass instruments in a band
paradiddle	a basic drumming pattern
plink	make short sharp ringing sounds
plunk	play a keyboard or plucked stringed instrument in an inexpressive way
ratamacue	a basic drumming pattern
rataplan	a drumming or beating sound
ruff	a basic drumming pattern
scat	improvised jazz singing in which a voice imitates an instrument
skiffle	a kind of folk music often incorporating improvised instruments such as washboards
skirl	a shrill sound, especially that of bagpipes
strum	play (a guitar or similar instrument) by sweeping the thumb or a plectrum across the strings
tom-tom	a medium-sized cylindrical drum
toot	a short, sharp sound made by a horn, trumpet, or similar instrument
trump	a trumpet or a trumpet blast
twang	a strong ringing sound such as that made by the plucked string of a musical instrument or a released bowstring
wah-wah	device for producing a musical effect on an electric guitar

Animal cries

baa	sheep
bay	dog
bleat	sheep, goat, or calf
caterwaul	cat
champ	horse
chirp	insect
chirr	insect
croak	frog
growl	animal, especially a dog
grunt	animal, especially a pig
hee-haw	donkey or mule
howl	animal such as a dog or wolf
mew	cat
miaow	cat
miaul	cat
moo	cattle
neigh	horse
nicker	horse
oink	pig
peep	young mammal
purr	cat
roar	lion or other large wild animal
snarl	animal such as a dog
whicker	horse
whinny	horse
woof	dog
wuff	dog
yap	dog

Animal names

ai	the three-toed sloth
chickaree	a type of squirrel
cricket	an insect like a grasshopper
dik-dik	a dwarf antelope
gecko	a lizard
gnu	a large antelope
hoolock	a gibbon
quagga	an extinct zebra
tokay	a large gecko
tuco-tuco	a burrowing rodent

Bird calls

cackle	especially hen or goose
caw	rook, crow, etc.
chack	any bird
cheep	young bird
chirp	small bird
cluck	hen
coo	pigeon or dove
croak	crow
crow	cock
gobble	turkeycock
honk	goose
hoot	owl
mew	gull
peep	young bird
quack	duck
squawk	any bird
tu-whit tu-whoo	owl
tweet	small or young bird
twitter	small bird

Bird names

bobolink
bobwhite
bokmakierie
boobook
bulbul
cahow
chachalaca
chat
chickadee
chiffchaff
chook
chough
chuck-will's-widow
crake
cuckoo
curlew
dickcissel
dunkadoo
flicker
garganey
hadada
hoatzin
hoopoe
huia
Jacky Winter
kea
keelie
killdeer
kiskadee
kittiwake
korhaan
mopoke
motmot
owl
peewee
peewit
pewee
phoebe
piapiac
piet-my-vrou
pipit
poor-me-one
poorwill
potoo
quail
quit
rail
rook
shrike
skua
tchagra
tinktinkie
titihoya
toucan
towhee
turtle dove
twite
veery
weka
whaup
whimbrel
whippoorwill
wigeon
willet
yaffle
gaggle

Weird and wonderful words

A selection of colourful, unusual, and obscure words.

aa a kind of volcanic lava that forms jagged masses with a light frothy texture; in an unrelated sense ('a stream') *aa* is the first entry in the *Oxford English Dictionary*

abaya a full-length, sleeveless outer garment worn by Arabs

abomasum the fourth stomach of a ruminant, such as a cow or sheep

absquatulate to leave somewhere abruptly

adscititious additional

afreet a powerful jinn or demon in Arabian and Muslim mythology

Albertopolis a group of museums and other cultural institutions in South Kensington in London, named after Prince Albert

alcazar a Spanish palace or fortress

amphibology a phrase or sentence that is grammatically ambiguous, such as *She sees more of her children than her husband*

amphisbaena a mythical serpent with a head at each end

anfractuous winding or circuitous

anguilliform resembling an eel

apoptosis the death of cells which occurs as a normal part of an organism's growth or development

apple-knocker *US informal* an ignorant or unsophisticated person

argle-bargle copious but meaningless talk or writing

Argus-eyed vigilant, referring to *Argos*, a Greek mythological watchman with a hundred eyes

argute shrewd

ariel a gazelle found in the Middle East and North Africa

aristotle *Austral. rhyming slang* a bottle

aspergillum an implement used for sprinkling holy water in religious ceremonies

astrobleme an eroded remnant of a large, ancient crater made by the impact of a meteorite or comet
Attic salt refined, incisive wit
autotomy the casting off of a limb or other part of the body by an animal under threat, such as a lizard
badmash *Indian* a hooligan
bandoline a sticky preparation used for setting hair
bardolatry *humorous* excessive admiration of Shakespeare ('the Bard of Avon')
Barmecide illusory or imaginary and therefore disappointing
barn burner *N. Amer.* a very exciting or dramatic event, especially a sports contest; first used of an exceptionally good hand at bridge.
bashment *W. Indian* a large party or dance
bawbee *Scottish* a coin of low value
benthos the flora and fauna on the bottom of a sea or lake
bergschrund a type of crevasse
bezoar a small hard, solid mass which may form in the stomachs of animals such as goats or sheep
bibliopole a person who buys and sells books, especially rare ones
bichon frise a breed of toy dog with a fine, curly white coat
bilboes an iron bar with sliding shackles, used to fasten prisoners' ankles
bindlestiff *N. Amer.* a tramp
bingle *Austral. informal* a collision
blatherskite a person who talks at great length without making much sense
bleeding edge the very forefront of technological development
blind pig *N. Amer. informal* a place where alcoholic drinks are sold illegally
bobsy-die a great deal of fuss or trouble
boffola *N. Amer. informal* a joke that gets a loud or hearty laugh
boilover *Austral. informal* a surprise result in a sporting event
borborygmus a rumbling or gurgling noise in the intestines
breatharian a person who believes that it is possible, through meditation, to reach a level of consciousness where one can exist on air alone
Brobdingnagian gigantic, from *Brobdingnag*, a country in Jonathan Swift's *Gulliver's Travels*
bruxism involuntary and habitual grinding of the teeth
bumbo a drink of rum, sugar, water, and nutmeg
burnsides a moustache in combination with whiskers on the cheeks but no beard on the chin
cacoethes an urge to do something inadvisable
callipygian having shapely buttocks
callithumpian like a discordant band or a noisy parade
camisado a military attack carried out at night
canorous melodious or resonant
cantillate to chant or intone a passage of religious text
carphology convulsive or involuntary movements made by delirious patients, such as plucking at the bedclothes
catoptromancy foretelling the future by means of a mirror
cereology the study or investigation of crop circles
cerulean deep sky blue
chad a piece of waste paper produced by punching a hole
chalkdown *S. African informal* a teachers' strike
chanticleer a rooster in a fairy tale
chiliad a thousand things or a thousand years
chump change *N. Amer. informal* a small or insignificant sum of money
claggy *Brit. dialect* sticky or able to form sticky lumps
clepsydra an early clock using the flow of water into or out of a container
colporteur a person who peddles books, newspapers, or other writings, especially bibles and religious tracts
comess *W. Indian* a confused or noisy situation
commensalism an association between two organisms in which one benefits from the relationship and the other derives neither harm nor benefit
comminatory threatening, punitive, or vengeful
concinnity elegance or neatness of literary or artistic style
congius an ancient Roman liquid measure equal in modern terms to about 6 imperial pints
conniption (or **conniption fit**) *N. Amer. informal* a fit of rage or hysterics
constellate to gather together in a cluster or group
coprolalia the involuntary repetitive use of obscene language
coriaceous like leather
couthy *Scottish* (of a person) warm and friendly; (of a place) cosy and comfortable
criticaster a minor or incompetent critic
crore *Indian* ten million
crottle a lichen used in Scotland to make a brownish dye for wool
croze a groove at the end of a cask or barrel in which the head is fixed
cryptozoology the search for and study of animals whose existence is unproven, such as the Loch Ness monster and the yeti
cudbear a purple or violet powder used for dyeing, made from lichen
cupreous of or like copper
cyanic blue; azure
cybersquatting the practice of registering well-known names as Internet domain names, in the hope of reselling them at a profit
dariole a small round metal mould used in French cooking for an individual sweet or savoury dish
deasil clockwise or in the direction of the sun's course
decubitus *Medicine* the posture of someone who is lying down or lying in bed
deedy industrious or effective
defervescence *Medicine* the lessening of a fever
deglutition the action of process of swallowing
degust to taste food or drink carefully, so as to fully appreciate it
deipnosophist a person skilled in the art of dining and dinner-table conversation
deracinate to tear something up by the roots
deterge to cleanse something thoroughly
didi *Indian* an older sister or female cousin
digerati people with expertise or professional involvement in information technology
dight clothed or equipped; also, to make something ready for use
discobolus a discus thrower in ancient Greece
disembogue to emerge or pour out (used of a river or stream)
disenthral to set someone free from enslavement
divagate to stray or digress
divaricate to stretch or spread apart
donkey engine a small auxiliary engine on a ship
donkeyman a man working in a ship's engine room
doryphore a pedantic and annoyingly persistent critic of others
dotish *W. Indian* stupid or silly
douceur a financial inducement or bribe
draff dregs or refuse
dragoman an interpreter or professional guide for travellers, especially one in countries in which Arabic, Turkish, or Persian is spoken
dumbsize to reduce the staff numbers of a company to such low levels that work can no longer be carried out effectively
dwaal *S. African* a dreamy, dazed, or absent-minded state
ecdysiast a striptease performer
edacious having to do with eating or fond of eating
effable able to be described in words. Its opposite, **ineffable**, is more widely used.
emacity fondness for buying things
emmetropia the normal condition of the eye: perfect vision
empasm a perfumed powder sprinkled on the body to prevent sweating or for medicinal purposes
ensorcell to enchant or fascinate someone
entomophagy the eating of insects, especially by people
erf *S. African* a plot of land
ergometer an apparatus which measures energy expended during physical exercise
erubescent reddening or blushing
e-tailer a retailer who sells goods on the Internet
etui a small ornamental case for holding needles, cosmetics, and other articles
eucatastrophe a happy ending to a story
eurhythmic in harmonious proportion
eviternity eternal existence or everlasting duration
exequies funeral rites
exsanguine bloodless or anaemic
extramundane outside or beyond the physical world
eye candy visual images that are superficially attractive and entertaining but intellectually undemanding
eyewater *W. Indian* tears
famulus an assistant or attendant, especially one working for a magician or scholar
fankle *Scottish* to tangle or entangle something
fipple the mouthpiece of a recorder or similar wind instrument
flatline to die
flews the thick pendulous lips of a bloodhound or similar dog
floccinaucinihilipilification the action or habit of estimating something as worthless (a word generally only quoted as a curiosity)
flocculent having or resembling tufts of wool
force-ripe *West Indian* old or mature in certain respects without having developed fully in others
forehanded *chiefly N. Amer.* prudent or thrifty
frondeur a political rebel
fugacious transient or fleeting
funambulist a tightrope walker
furuncle a boil
fuscous dark and sombre in colour
futhark the Scandinavian runic alphabet
futz to waste time or busy oneself aimlessly
gaberlunzie *Scottish archaic* a beggar
gaita a kind of bagpipe played in northern Spain and Portugal
galligaskins a type of loose breeches worn in the 16th and 17th centuries
gallus *Scottish* bold or daring
gasconade extravagant boasting
glabrous (of skin) hairless or (of a leaf) having no down
glaikit *Scottish & N. English* stupid, foolish, or thoughtless
gnathic having to do with the jaws
gobemouche a gullible or credulous listener
goodfella a gangster, especially a member of a Mafia family

guddle *Scottish* to fish with one's hands by groping under the stones or banks of a stream

habile deft or skilful

hallux *Anatomy* the big toe

haruspex a religious official in ancient Rome who inspected the entrails of sacrificial animals in order to foretell the future

higgler *W. Indian* a person who travels from place to place selling small items

hinky *US informal* dishonest, suspect, or unreliable

hoddy-noddy a foolish person

hodiernal of today

hoggin a mixture of sand and gravel, used especially in road-building

hongi a traditional Maori greeting or salutation made by pressing or touching noses

howff *Scottish* a favourite meeting place or haunt, especially a pub

humdudgeon an imaginary illness

hunt-and-peck using only one or two fingers on a computer keyboard

hwyl a stirring feeling of emotional motivation and energy which is associated with the Welsh people

illywhacker *Austral. informal* a small-time confidence trickster

incrassate thickened in form or consistency

incunabula books printed before 1501

ingurgitate to swallow something greedily

inspissate to thicken or congeal

inunct to apply ointment to someone or something

jumbuck *Austral. informal* a sheep

jumentous resembling horse's urine

jungli *Indian* uncultured or wild

karateka a person who performs karate

keek *Scottish* to peep surreptitiously

kenspeckle *Scottish* conspicuous or easily recognizable

kinnikinnick a substance consisting of dried sumac leaves and willow or dogwood bark, smoked by North American Indians

kylie *Austral.* a boomerang

labarum a banner or flag bearing symbolic motifs

lablab a tropical Asian plant of the pea family

lactarium a dairy

liripipe the long dangling tail of a medieval academic hood

loblolly a North American pine tree with very long slender needles

lobola among southern African peoples, the money or cattle given by a bridegroom's family to the bride's family

logomachy an argument about words

lollygag to spend time in an aimless or lazy way

luculent (of speech or writing) clearly expressed

lycanthropy the supernatural transformation of a person into a wolf

macushla *Irish* an affectionate form of address

mallam a learned man or scribe in Nigeria and other parts of Africa

mamaguy *W. Indian* to try to deceive someone by flattering them or telling them lies

martlet *Heraldry* a small, swallow-like bird with tufts of feathers in place of legs and feet

mazel tov a Jewish expression used to congratulate someone or wish them good luck

meacock a coward or effeminate person

merkin an artificial covering of hair for the pubic area

merrythought a bird's wishbone

mim *Scottish* modest or demure in an affected or priggish way

mimsy rather feeble and prim or over-restrained (coined by Lewis Carroll in *Through the Looking Glass*)

minacious menacing or threatening

minibeast *Brit. informal* a small invertebrate animal such as an insect or spider

misogamy the hatred of marriage

mistigris a joker or other extra card played as a wild card in some versions of poker

mixologist *N. Amer. informal* a person who is skilled at mixing cocktails and other drinks

mollitious luxurious or sensuous

momism excessive attachment to or domination by one's mother

monkey's wedding *S. African* simultaneous rain and sunshine

monorchid having only one testicle

moonraker a native of the county of Wiltshire

mouse potato a person who spends large amounts of their leisure or working time on a computer

mudlark a person who scavenges in riverside mud at low tide for anything of value

muktuk the skin and blubber of a whale, eaten by the Inuit people

mumpsimus a traditional custom or notion that is adhered to although it has been shown to be unreasonable

nacarat a bright orange-red colour

nagware computer software which is free for a trial period and thereafter frequently reminds the user to pay for it

nainsook a fine, soft cotton fabric, originally made in the Indian subcontinent

natation swimming

nesh *Brit. dialect* weak, delicate, or feeble

netizen a habitual or keen user of the Internet

noctambulist a sleepwalker

noyade an execution carried out by drowning

nugacity triviality or frivolity

nympholepsy passion or rapture aroused in men by beautiful young girls

obnubilate to darken, dim, or obscure something

ogdoad a group or set of eight

omophagy the eating of raw food, especially meat

omphalos the centre or hub of something

onolatry the worship of donkeys or asses

o-o an endangered Hawaiian bird, a species of honeyeater

operose involving or displaying a lot of effort

opsimath a person who begins to learn or study late in life

orectic having to do with desire or appetite

orrery a clockwork model of the solar system, or the sun, earth, and moon

ortanique a cross between an orange and a tangerine

otalgia earache

oxter *Scottish & N. English* a person's armpit

paludal living or occurring in a marshy habitat

Pantagruelian enormous

panurgic able or ready to do anything

parapente an aerofoil parachute, used for gliding

paraph a flourish after a signature

patulous (of the boughs of a tree, for example) spreading

pavonine to do with or resembling a peacock

pedicular to do with lice

peely-wally *Scottish* looking pale and unwell

peever *Scottish* hopscotch

periapt an item worn as a charm or amulet

petcock a small valve in a steam engine or boiler, used for drainage or for reducing pressure

peterman a person who breaks open and robs safes

pettitoes pig's trotters, especially as food

piacular making or requiring atonement

pilgarlic a bald-headed man, or a person regarded with mild contempt

pinguid resembling fat; oily or greasy

piscatorial connected with fishermen or fishing

pleurodynia severe pain in the muscles between the ribs or in the diaphragm

plew a beaver skin

pneumonoultramicroscopic-silicovolcanoconiosis an invented term said to mean 'a lung disease caused by inhaling very fine ash and sand dust', but rarely used except for its curiosity value

pogey *Canadian informal* unemployment or welfare benefit

pollex *Anatomy* the thumb

pooter a suction bottle for collecting insects and other small invertebrates

portolan a book containing sailing directions with hand-drawn charts and descriptions of harbours and coasts

posology the branch of medicine concerned with the size and frequency of doses of a medicine or a drug

possident a possessor, i.e. a person who owns something

pother a commotion or fuss

pre-loved second-hand

presenteeism the compulsion to spend longer at work than is required or to continue working despite illness

previse to foresee or predict an event

probang a strip of flexible material with a sponge or tuft at the end, used to remove a foreign body from the throat or to apply medication to it

prosopagnosia an inability to recognize the faces of familiar people, typically as a result of brain damage

puddle jumper a small, light aircraft which is fast and highly manoeuvrable and used for short trips

puddysticks *S. African children's word* very easy

pyknic a technical description of a stocky physique with a rounded body and head, thickset trunk, and a tendency to fat

pyroclastic relating to fragments of rock erupted by a volcano

ragtop a convertible car with a soft roof

ratite (of a bird such as the ostrich or emu) unable to fly because of having a flat breastbone, to which no flight muscles are attached

rawky foggy, damp, and cold

razzia a raid carried out by Moors in North Africa

rebirthing a form of therapy involving controlled breathing and intended to simulate the trauma of being born

resurrection man a person who, in past times, illicitly exhumed corpses from burial grounds and sold them to anatomists for dissection

retiform resembling a net

rhinoplasty plastic surgery performed on the nose

rubiginous rust-coloured

rubricate to add elaborate capital letters (typically red ones) or other decorations to a manuscript

rude boy *Jamaican* a lawless or rebellious unemployed urban youth who likes ska or reggae music

rug rat *N. Amer.* a child

rumpot *N. Amer.* a habitual or heavy drinker

sangoma a traditional healer or witch doctor in southern Africa
sarmie *S. African informal* a sandwich
saucier a sauce chef
saudade a feeling of longing or melancholy that is supposedly characteristic of the Portuguese or Brazilian temperament
scofflaw a person who flouts the law
screenager a person in their teens or twenties who has an aptitude for using computers and the Internet
scrippage one's baggage and personal belongings
selkie *Scottish* a mythical sea creature like a seal in water but human on land
serac a pinnacle or ridge of ice on the surface of a glacier
sesquipedalian (of a word) having many syllables or (of a piece of writing) using many long words
shallop a light sailing boat used chiefly for coastal fishing
shamal a hot, dry north-westerly wind that blows across the Persian Gulf in summer and causes sandstorms
shavetail *US military slang* a newly commissioned officer, or any inexperienced person
shippon *Brit. dialect* a cattle shed
shofar a ram's-horn trumpet used in Jewish religious ceremonies and, in ancient times, to sound a battle signal
skanky *N. Amer. informal* revolting
skelf *Scottish* a splinter or sliver of wood
skimmington a kind of procession once undertaken to make an example of a nagging wife or an unfaithful husband
skycap a porter at an airport
snakebitten *N. Amer. informal* unlucky or doomed to misfortune
snollygoster a shrewd or unprincipled person
sockdolager *US informal* a heavy blow
solander a protective box made in the form of a book, for holding items such as botanical specimens, maps, and colour plates
soucouyant a kind of witch, in eastern Caribbean folklore, who is believed to shed her skin by night and suck the blood of her victims
soul case *N. Amer. & W. Indian* the human body
soul catcher a hollowed bone tube used by a North American Indian medicine man to keep a sick person's soul safe while they are sick
spaghettification the process by which (in some theories) an object would be stretched and ripped apart by gravitational forces on falling into a black hole
spitchcock an eel, split and then grilled or fried
splanchnic having to do with the the viscera or internal organs, especially those of the abdomen
spurrier a person who makes spurs
stercoraceous consisting of or resembling dung or faeces
sternutator something that causes sneezing
stiction the frictional force which hinders an object from being moved while in contact with another
strappado a punishment or torture in which the victim was hoisted in the air on a rope and then allowed to fall almost to the ground before being stopped with an abrupt jerk
strigil an instrument with a curved blade used by ancient Greeks and Romans to scrape sweat and dirt from the skin in a hot-air bath or after exercise
struthious having to do with or resembling an ostrich
studmuffin *N. Amer. humorous* a sexually attractive, muscular man
stylite a early Christian ascetic who lived standing on top of a pillar
subfusc the dark formal clothing worn for examinations and ceremonial or formal occasions at some universities.
submontane passing under or through mountains, or situated on the lower slopes of a mountain range
succuss to shake something vigorously, especially a homeopathic remedy
sudd an area of floating vegetation that impedes navigation in a stretch of the White Nile
suedehead a youth like a skinhead but with slightly longer hair and smarter clothes
sun-grazing (of a comet) having an orbit which passes close to the sun
superbious proud and overbearing
superette *N. Amer.* a small supermarket
taniwha a mythical monster which, according to Maori legend, lives in very deep water
tappen the plug by which the rectum of a bear is closed during hibernation
tellurian of or inhabiting the earth, or an inhabitant of the earth
testudo a device used in siege warfare in ancient Rome, consisting of a wheeled screen with an arched roof (literally a 'tortoise')
thalassic relating to the sea
thaumatrope a scientific toy devised in the 19th century. It consisted of a disc with a different picture on each of its two sides: when the disc was rotated rapidly about a diameter, these pictures appeared to combine into one image.
thirstland *S. African* a desert or large arid area
thrutch *N. English* a narrow gorge or ravine
thurifer a person carrying a censer, or **thurible**, of burning incense during religious ceremonies
tiffin *chiefly Indian* a light meal, especially lunch
tigon the hybrid offspring of a male tiger and a lioness (the offspring of a male lion and a tigress being a **liger**)
tokoloshe in African folklore, a mischievous and lascivious hairy water sprite
toplofty *N. Amer. informal* haughty and arrogant
transpicuous transparent
triskaidekaphobia extreme superstition about the number thirteen
triskelion a Celtic symbol consisting of three radiating legs or curved lines, such as the emblem of the Isle of Man
tsantsa a human head shrunk as a war trophy by the Jivaro people of Ecuador
turbary the legal right to cut turf or peat for fuel on common ground or on another person's ground
ulu a short-handled knife with a broad crescent-shaped blade, used by Inuit women.
umbriferous shady
uncinate (of a part of the body) having a hooked shape
uniped a person or animal with only one foot or leg
uroboros a circular symbol depicting a snake (or a dragon) swallowing its tail, intended as an emblem of wholeness or infinity
ustad *Indian* an expert or highly skilled person, especially a musician
vagarious erratic and unpredictable in behaviour or direction
velleity a wish or inclination which is not strong enough to lead one to take action
verjuice a sour juice obtained from crab apples or unripe grapes
vicinal neighbouring or adjacent
vidiot *N. Amer. informal* a habitual, undiscriminating watcher of television or videotapes
vomitous *N. Amer.* nauseating or repulsive
wabbit *Scottish* exhausted or slightly unwell
waitron *N. Amer.* a waiter or waitress
wakeboarding the sport of riding on a short, wide board while being towed behind a motor boat
wayzgoose an annual summer party and outing that used to be held by a printing house for all its employees
winebibber a heavy drinker
wish book *N. Amer. informal* a mail-order catalogue
wittol a man who knows of and tolerates his wife's infidelity
woopie an affluent retired person able to pursue an active lifestyle (from the initials of *well-off older person*)
wowser *chiefly Austral./NZ* a puritanical, prudish person or a killjoy
xenology the scientific study of extraterrestrial phenomena
ylem (in big bang theory) the primordial matter of the universe
zetetic proceeding by inquiry or investigation
zoolatry the worship of animals
zopissa a medicinal preparation made from wax and pitch scraped from the sides of ships
zorro a South American kind of fox
Zyrian a former term for **Komi**, a language spoken in an area of Russia west of the Urals; at present the last entry in the *Oxford English Dictionary*

Wordfinder

British & N. American equivalents

British	North American
aerofoil	airfoil
aeroplane	airplane
agony aunt	advice columnist
anticlockwise	counter-clockwise
articulated lorry	tractor-trailer
asymmetric bars	uneven bars
aubergine	eggplant
black economy	underground economy
blanket bath	sponge bath
bonnet (of car)	hood
boob tube (garment)	tube top
boot (of a car)	trunk
bowls	lawn bowling
brawn (the food)	headcheese
breeze block	cinder block
brent goose	brant goose
bridging loan	bridge loan
bumbag	fanny pack
candy floss	cotton candy
car park	parking lot/garage
central reservation	median strip
chips	French fries
cling film	plastic wrap
common seal	harbor seal
consumer durables	durable goods

British	North American
cornflour	cornstarch
cot	crib
cot death	crib death
cotton bud	cotton swab
cotton wool	absorbent cotton
courgette	zucchini
crash barrier	guardrail
crisps (= potato crisps)	chips *or* potato chips
cross-ply	bias-ply
current account	checking account
cut-throat razor	straight razor
dialling tone	dial tone
double cream	heavy cream
double-declutch	double-clutch
draughts	checkers
drawing pin	thumbtack
drink-driving	drunk driving
driving licence	driver's license
dual carriageway	divided highway
dummy	pacifier
dustbin	trash/garbage can
eat in (of restaurant food)	for here
engaged (of a telephone)	busy
estate agent	realtor (*trademark*) *or* real estate agent
estate car	station wagon
ex-directory	unlisted
eyebath	eyecup
financial year	fiscal year
fire brigade/service	fire company/department
firelighter	fire starter
fringe	bangs
full board	American plan
gear lever	gearshift
gearstick	gearshift
green fingers	green thumb
groundsman	groundskeeper
holidaymaker	vacationer
hundreds and thousands	sprinkles
icing sugar	confectioner's/powdered sugar
indicator (on car)	turn signal
Joe Bloggs	Joe Blow
Joe Public	John Q. Public
jump lead	jumper cable
ladybird	ladybug
level crossing	grade crossing
lift (in building)	elevator
lolly (= lollipop)	Popsicle (*trademark*)
loo	john
maize	corn
mangetout	snow peas
maths	math
monkey tricks	monkeyshines
motorway	expressway/freeway
mum	mom
nappy	diaper
noughts and crosses	tic-tac-toe
number plate	license plate
off-licence	liquor store
opencast	open-pit
paddling pool	wading pool
paracetamol	Tylenol (*trademark*) *or* acetaminophen
pay packet	pay envelope
pedestrian crossing	crosswalk
petrol	gasoline/gas
physiotherapy	physical therapy
plain chocolate	dark chocolate
plain flour	all-purpose flour
plaster *or* sticking plaster	Band-Aid (*trademark*)
post code	zip code
postal vote	absentee ballot
poste restante	general delivery
press-up	pushup
punchbag	punching bag
pushchair	stroller
queue	line
razor shell	razor clam
real tennis	court tennis
recorded delivery	certified mail
registration plate	license plate
reverse the charges	call collect
reversing light	backup light
ringing (of birds)	banding
room only	European plan
roundabout (in road)	traffic circle
rowing boat	rowboat
sailing boat	sailboat
self-raising flour	self-rising flour
Sellotape (*trademark*)	Scotch tape (*trademark*)
shopping trolley	shopping cart
show house/home	model home
skirting board	baseboard
sleeping partner	silent partner
splashback	backsplash
spring onion	green onion
storm in a teacup	tempest in a teapot
surtitle	supertitle
swede	rutabaga
takeaway	takeout *or* carry out *or* to go
terraced house	row house
tick (the symbol)	check *or* check mark
toffee apple	candy apple
trainers	sneakers
tram	streetcar *or* trolley car
transport cafe	truck stop
twelve-bore	twelve-gauge
vest	undershirt
waistcoat	vest
white spirit	mineral spirits
windscreen	windshield
worktop	countertop
zebra crossing	crosswalk
zed	zee

Foreign words and phrases

Over the centuries the English language has assimilated words and phrases from a variety of other languages. In context, those listed here are often printed in italics.

ab initio *Latin* from the beginning

a cappella *Italian* sung without instrumental accompaniment (literally 'in chapel style')

à deux *French* for or involving two people

ad hoc *Latin* made or done for a particular purpose (literally 'to this')

ad infinitum *Latin* endlessly; forever (literally 'to infinity')

ad interim *Latin* for the meantime

ad nauseam *Latin* to a tiresomely excessive degree (literally 'to sickness')

a fortiori *Latin* more conclusively (literally 'from a stronger [argument]')

agent provocateur *French* a person who tempts a suspected criminal to commit a crime so that they can be caught and convicted (literally 'provocative agent')

à huis clos *French* in private (literally 'with closed doors')

al dente *Italian* (of food) cooked so as to be still firm when bitten (literally 'to the tooth')

alfresco *Italian* in the open air (literally 'in the fresh')

amour propre *French* self-respect (literally 'own love')

annus mirabilis *Latin* a remarkable or auspicious year

a posteriori *Latin* based on reasoning from known facts or past events rather than on assumptions or predictions (literally 'from what comes after')

a priori *Latin* based on deduction rather than experience (literally 'from what is before')

au courant *French* well informed; up to date (literally 'in the (regular) course')

au fait *French* having a good or detailed knowledge (literally 'to the point')

au fond *French* basically; in essence (literally 'at the bottom')

au naturel *French* in the most simple or natural way

beau geste *French* a noble and generous act (literally 'fine gesture')

beau idéal *French* the highest standard of excellence (literally 'ideal beauty')

beau monde *French* fashionable society (literally 'fine world')

beaux arts *French* the fine arts

bête noire *French* a person or thing one particularly dislikes (literally 'black beast')

belles-lettres *French* literary works written and read for their elegant style (literally 'fine letters')

billet-doux *French* a love letter (literally 'sweet note')

blitzkrieg *German* an intense, violent military campaign intended to bring about a swift victory (literally 'lightning war')

bona fide *Latin* genuine; real (literally 'with good faith')

bon mot *French* a clever or witty remark (literally 'good word')

bon vivant *French* a person with a sociable and luxurious lifestyle (literally 'person living well')

brasserie *French* an informal or inexpensive restaurant (literally 'brewery')

carpe diem *Latin* make the most of the present time (literally 'seize the day!')

carte blanche *French* complete freedom to act as one wishes (literally 'blank paper')

cause célèbre *French* a controversial issue attracting much public attention (literally 'famous case')

caveat emptor *Latin* the buyer is responsible for checking the quality of goods before purchasing them (literally 'let the buyer beware')

c'est la guerre *French* used as an expression of resigned acceptance (literally 'that's war')

chacun à son goût *French* everyone to their own taste

chef-d'œuvre *French* a masterpiece (literally 'chief work')

cherchez la femme *French* there is certain to be a woman at the bottom of a problem or mystery (literally 'look for the woman')

comme il faut *French* correct in behaviour or etiquette (literally 'as is necessary')

compos mentis *Latin* sane; in full control of one's mind

cognoscenti *Italian* people who are well informed about something (literally 'people who know')

cordon sanitaire *French* a guarded line placed around an area infected by disease to prevent anyone from leaving (literally 'sanitary line')

Cosa Nostra *Italian* a US criminal organization related to the Mafia (literally 'our thing')

coup de foudre *French* love at first sight (literally 'stroke of lightning')

coup de grâce *French* a blow by which a mortally wounded person or thing is mercifully killed (literally 'stroke of grace')

coup de main *French* a sudden surprise attack (literally 'stroke of hand')
coup d'état *French* a sudden violent seizure of power (literally 'blow of state')
cri de cœur *French* a passionate appeal or protest (literally 'cry from the heart')
cui bono? *Latin* who stands to gain? (implying that whoever does may have been responsible for a crime; literally 'to whom (is it) a benefit?')
de facto *Latin* in fact, whether by right or not
Dei gratia *Latin* by the grace of God
déjà vu *French* the sense of having experienced the present situation before (literally 'already seen')
de jure *Latin* rightful; by right (literally 'of law')
de nos jours *French* contemporary (literally 'of our days')
Deo gratias *Latin* thanks be to God
Deo volente *Latin* God willing
de profundis *Latin* expressing one's deepest feelings (literally 'from the depths')
de rigueur *French* obligatory; required by etiquette or current fashion (literally 'of strictness')
dernier cri *French* the very latest fashion (literally 'the last cry')
de trop *French* not wanted; superfluous (literally 'excessive')
deus ex machina *Latin* an unexpected event that saves an apparently hopeless situation (literally 'god from the machinery')
dolce far niente *Italian* pleasant idleness (literally 'sweet doing nothing')
dolce vita *Italian* a life of pleasure and luxury (literally 'sweet life')
doppelgänger *German* an apparition or double of a living person (literally 'double-goer')
double entendre *French* a word or phrase with two possible interpretations (from obsolete French, 'double understanding')
dramatis personae *Latin* the characters in a play (literally 'persons of the drama')
embarras de richesse *French* more options or resources than one knows what to do with (literally 'embarrassment of riches')
éminence grise *French* a person who has power or influence without holding an official position (literally 'grey eminence')
en famille *French* with one's family; in an informal way (literally 'in family')
enfant terrible *French* a person whose behaviour is unconventional or controversial (literally 'terrible child')
en masse *French* all together (literally 'in a mass')
en passant *French* by the way (literally 'in passing')
entente cordiale *French* a friendly understanding between states
entre nous *French* between ourselves
esprit de corps *French* a feeling of pride and loyalty uniting the members of a group (literally 'spirit of body')
ex gratia *Latin* (of payment) given as a favour rather than because of any legal obligation (literally 'from favour')
ex officio *Latin* by virtue of one's position or status (literally 'out of duty')
fait accompli *French* a thing that has been done or decided and cannot now be altered (literally 'accomplished fact')
faute de mieux *French* for want of a better alternative
faux pas *French* an embarrassing blunder or indiscretion (literally 'false step')
femme fatale *French* a seductive woman (literally 'disastrous woman')
fête champêtre *French* an outdoor entertainment; a garden party (literally 'rural festival')
fin de siècle *French* relating to the end of a century
force majeure *French* superior strength
folie de grandeur *French* delusions of grandeur
gîte *French* a small furnished holiday house in France
grande dame *French* a woman who is influential within a particular sphere (literally 'grand lady')
haute couture *French* the designing and making of clothes by leading fashion houses (literally 'high dressmaking')
haute cuisine *French* high-quality cooking (literally 'high cookery')
haut monde *French* fashionable society (literally 'high world')
hors de combat *French* out of action due to injury or damage (literally 'out of the fight')
idée fixe *French* an obsession (literally 'fixed idea')
in absentia *Latin* while not present (literally 'in absence')
in camera *Latin* in private (literally 'in the chamber')
in extremis *Latin* in an extremely difficult situation; at the point of death
in loco parentis *Latin* in the place of a parent
in medias res *Latin* in or into the middle of things
in propria persona *Latin* in his or her own person
in situ *Latin* in the original or appropriate position
inter alia *Latin* among other things
in toto *Latin* as a whole
ipso facto *Latin* by that very fact or act
je ne sais quoi *French* a quality that is hard to describe (literally 'I do not know what')
jeu d'esprit *French* a light-hearted display of wit (literally 'game of the mind')
jeunesse dorée *French* wealthy, fashionable young people (literally 'gilded youth')
joie de vivre *French* exuberant enjoyment of life (literally 'joy of living')
katzenjammer *German* a hangover or a severe headache accompanying a hangover (literally 'cats' wailing')
laissez-faire *French* a non-interventionist policy (literally 'allow to do')
locum tenens *Latin* a temporary deputy or stand-in (literally 'one holding a place')
locus classicus *Latin* the best known or most authoritative passage on a subject (literally 'classical place')
magnum opus *Latin* the most important work of an artist, writer, etc. (literally 'great work')
manqué *French* having failed to become what one might have been (from *manquer* 'to lack')
mea culpa *Latin* an acknowledgement that something is one's fault (literally 'by my fault')
memento mori *Latin* something kept as a reminder that death is inevitable (literally 'remember (that you have) to die')
ménage à trois *French* an arrangement in which a married couple and the lover of one of them live together (literally 'household of three')
modus operandi *Latin* a way of doing something (literally 'way of operating')
modus vivendi *Latin* an arrangement that allows conflicting parties to coexist peacefully (literally 'way of living')
mot juste *French* the most appropriate word or expression
ne plus ultra *Latin* the best example of something (literally 'not further beyond')
nil desperandum *Latin* do not despair
noblesse oblige *French* privilege entails responsibility
nolens volens *Latin* whether one wants or likes something or not (literally 'not willing, willing')
non sequitur *Latin* a conclusion or statement that does not logically follow from the previous statement (literally 'it does not follow')
nouveau riche *French* people who have recently become rich and who display their wealth ostentatiously (literally 'new rich')
objet d'art *French* a small decorative or artistic object
on dit *French* a piece of gossip (literally 'they say')
papabile *Italian* worthy or eligible to be elected pope
par excellence *French* better or more than all others of the same kind (literally 'by excellence')
parti pris *French* a preconceived view; a bias (literally 'side taken')
per annum *Latin* for each year
per capita *Latin* for each person (literally 'by heads')
per se *Latin* by or in itself or themselves
persona non grata *Latin* a person who is not welcome somewhere
pièce de résistance *French* the most important or impressive item (literally 'piece (i.e. means) of resistance')
pied-à-terre *French* a small flat or house kept for occasional use (literally 'foot to earth')
pis aller *French* a last resort (literally 'worse to go')
plat du jour *French* a special dish prepared by a restaurant on a particular day (literally 'dish of the day')
plus ça change *French* used to express resigned acknowledgement of the fact that certain things never change (from *plus ça change, plus c'est la même chose* 'the more it changes, the more it stays the same')
pococurante *Italian* careless or nonchalant (literally 'little caring')
prima facie *Latin* accepted as so until proved otherwise (literally 'at first face')
primus inter pares *Latin* the senior or representative member of a group (literally 'first among equals')
pro rata *Latin* proportional; proportionally (literally 'according to the rate')
proxime accessit *Latin* the person who comes second in an examination or is runner-up for an award (literally 'came very near')
quid pro quo *Latin* a favour or advantage given in return for something (literally 'something for something')
raison d'être *French* the most important reason for someone or something's existence (literally 'reason for being')
reductio ad absurdum *Latin* a method of disproving a premise by showing that its logical conclusion is absurd (literally 'reduction to the absurd')
roman-à-clef *French* a novel in which real people or events appear with invented names (literally 'novel with a key')
sangfroid *French* the ability to stay calm in difficult circumstances (literally 'cold blood')
savoir faire *French* the ability to act appropriately in social situations (literally 'know how to do')
sine die *Latin* (of proceedings) adjourned indefinitely (literally 'without a day')
sine qua non *Latin* a thing that is absolutely essential (literally 'without which not')
soi-disant *French* self-styled; so-called (literally 'self-saying')
sotto voce *Italian* in a quiet voice (literally 'under voice')
sub judice *Latin* being considered by a court of law and therefore not to be publicly discussed elsewhere (literally 'under a judge')
sub rosa *Latin* happening or done in secret (literally 'under the rose')
sui generis *Latin* unique (literally 'of its own kind')
table d'hôte *French* a restaurant meal offered at a fixed price, with few if any choices (literally 'host's table')
tant mieux *French* so much the better
tant pis *French* so much the worse; too bad
terra firma *Latin* dry land; the ground (literally 'firm land')
terra incognita *Latin* unknown territory
tête-à-tête *French* a private conversation (literally 'head-to-head')
tour de force *French* a thing accomplished with great skill (literally 'feat of strength')
tout de suite *French* at once (literally 'quite in sequence')
unheimlich *German* uncanny or weird
verboten *German* forbidden
via media *Latin* a compromise (literally 'middle way')
victor ludorum *Latin* the overall champion in a sports competition (literally 'victor of the games')
vis-à-vis *French* in relation to; as compared with (literally 'face-to-face')
vox populi *Latin* public opinion (literally 'the voice of the people')
zeitgeist *German* the characteristic spirit or mood of a particular historical period (literally 'time spirit')

Archaic words

These words are no longer in everyday use but are sometimes used to impart an old-fashioned flavour to historical novels, for example, or in standard conversation or writing just for a humorous effect. Some, such as *hotchpotch*, reveal the origin of their current meaning, while others reveal the origin of a different modern word, as with *gentle*, the sense of which is preserved in *gentleman*. Some, such as *learn* and *let*, now mean the opposite of their former use.

abroad out of doors
advertisement a notice to readers in a book
ague malaria or a similar illness
aliment food; nourishment
animalcule a microscopic animal
apothecary a person who prepared and sold medicine
asunder apart
audition the power of hearing
aught anything at all
avaunt go away
bane poison
bedlam an asylum
behold see or observe
behoof benefit or advantage
beldam an old woman
betimes in good time; early
bibliopole a dealer in books
billow a large sea wave
blow produce flowers or be in flower
bodkin a dagger
bootless (of a task) ineffectual; useless
breech a person's buttocks
bridewell a prison or reform school for petty offenders
brimstone sulphur
bruit a report or rumour
buck a fashionable and daring young man
bumper a generous glass of an alcoholic drink
burgess a full citizen of a town or borough
buss a kiss
caboose a kitchen on a ship's deck
cadet a younger son or daughter
caducity the infirmity of old age; senility
camelopard a giraffe
carl a man of low birth
ceil line or plaster the roof of (a building)
champaign open level countryside
chapman a pedlar
circumjacent surrounding
cicisbeo a married woman's male companion or lover
cispontine on the north side of the Thames in London
clerk a literate or scholarly person
clew a ball of thread
clout a piece of cloth or clothing
commend entrust someone or something to
commons provisions shared in common; rations
communicant a person who imparts information
compass encircle or surround
con study attentively or learn by heart (a piece of writing)
condition social position
conjure implore (someone) to do something
contemn treat or regard with contempt
contumely insolent or insulting language or treatment
cordwainer a shoemaker (still used in the names of guilds)
corrupt rotten or putrid
cottier a rural labourer living in a cottage
coxcomb a vain and conceited man; a dandy
coz cousin
crinkum-crankum elaborate decoration or detail
crookback a person with a hunchback
crumpet a person's head
cruse an earthenware pot or jar
cully a friendly form of address for a man
cutpurse a pickpocket
dame an elderly or mature woman
damsel a young unmarried woman
dandiprat a young or insignificant person
darbies handcuffs
dark ignorant
degrade reduce to a lower rank, especially as a punishment
degree social or official rank
delate report (an offence)
demoralize corrupt the morals of
dight clothed or equipped
discover divulge (a secret)
dispraise censure or criticize
divers of varying types; several
doit a very small amount of money
dot a dowry from which only the interest or annual income was available to the husband
doxy a lover or mistress
drab a slovenly woman
drought thirst
egad exclamation of surprise, anger, or affirmation
embarrass hamper or impede
embouchure the mouth of a river
ere before (in time)
espousal a marriage or engagement
estate a particular state, period, or condition in life
expectations one's prospects of inheritance
expiry death
fain pleased or willing under the circumstances
fainéant an idle or ineffective person
fair beautiful
fandangle a useless or purely ornamental thing
fare travel
fervent hot or glowing
fie exclamation used to express disgust or outrage
filibeg a kilt
fishwife a woman who sells fish
fizgig a silly or flirtatious young woman
flux diarrhoea or dysentery
forfend avert or prevent (something evil or unpleasant)
forsooth indeed
fourscore eighty
freak a whim
frore frozen or frosty
froward (of a person) difficult to deal with; contrary
fruit offspring
fudge nonsense
furbish polish (a weapon)
gadzooks an expression of surprise or annoyance
gage a valued object deposited as a guarantee
gallant a dashing gentleman
gammer an old woman
garland a literary anthology
garth a yard or garden
gentle noble or courteous
go-cart a baby walker
God's acre a churchyard
goodly attractive, excellent, or virtuous
goody (with a name) an elderly woman of humble position
grateful received with gratitude
grimalkin a cat
gudgeon a credulous person
gyve a fetter or shackle
habiliment clothing
halt lame
handmaid a female servant
hearken listen
hence from here
herbary a herb garden
hereat as a result of this
hereunto to this document
hereupon after or as a result of this
hie go quickly
hight named
hither to or towards this place
horse-coper a person who deals in horses
horseless carriage a car
host an army
hotchpotch a mutton stew with mixed vegetables
howbeit nevertheless
husbandman a farmer
imminent overhanging
indite write; compose
inscribe enter the name of (someone) on a list
intelligence news
intelligencer a person who gathers intelligence
invest surround (a place) in order to besiege or blockade it
iron horse a steam railway locomotive
izzard the letter Z
jade a bad-tempered or disreputable woman
jakes an outdoor toilet
job turn a public office or a position of trust to private advantage

kickshaw a fancy but insubstantial cooked dish
kine cows collectively
king's shilling, take the enlist in the army
knave a dishonest or unscrupulous man
larcener thief
latchet a narrow thong or lace for fastening a shoe or sandal
laud praise
laver a basin or similar container used for washing oneself
learn teach
leech a doctor or healer
leman a lover or sweetheart
let hinder
levant abscond leaving unpaid debts
Levant the eastern part of the Mediterranean
levy a body of enlisted troops
lief as happily; as gladly
lordling a minor lord
love apple a tomato
Lucifer a match
lurdan an idle or incompetent person
lying-in seclusion before and after childbirth
magdalen a reformed prostitute
mage a magician or learned person
maid a girl or young woman
malapert presumptuous and impudent
malison a curse
man-at-arms a soldier
marry an expression of surprise, indignation, or emphatic assertion
mayhap perhaps; possibly
measure a dance
meat food of any kind
mechanical a manual worker
meet suitable or proper
methinks it seems to me
mooncalf a foolish person
morrow, the the following day
mummer an actor in the theatre
natural a person born with impaired intelligence
naught nothing
nay no
neat a bovine animal or animals
nice fastidious
nigh near
nithing a contemptible or despicable person
noise (something) about talk about or make known publicly
nubbing-cheat a gallows

numbles a deer's entrails as food
orison a prayer
orts scraps; remains
otherwhere elsewhere
overleap jump over or across
pale an area within determined bounds or subject to a particular jurisdiction
palfrey a docile riding horse
pate a person's head
peeler a police officer
pelf money, especially when gained dishonestly
peradventure perhaps
perchance by some chance
peregrinate travel or wander from place to place
pest bubonic plague
pestilence a fatal epidemic disease, especially bubonic plague
peterman a thief or safe-breaker
physic medicinal drugs or medical treatment
piepowder a traveller or an itinerant merchant or trader
pismire an ant
pistoleer a soldier armed with a pistol
plight solemnly pledge or promise (faith or loyalty)
pollard an animal that has lost its horns or cast its antlers
poltroon an utter coward
popinjay a parrot
portage the action of carrying or transporting
portion a dowry
portion a person's destiny or lot
posy a short motto or line of verse inscribed inside a ring
pouncet-box a small box with a perforated lid used for holding a substance impregnated with perfume
prithee please
profess teach (a subject) as a professor
progress a state journey or official tour
purfle an ornamental or embroidered edge of a garment
pythoness a woman believed to be possessed by a spirit and to be able to foresee the future
quality high social standing
quean an impudent girl or woman
quick, the the living
quidnunc an inquisitive, gossipy person
quiz look intently at (someone)

quoth said (in *I/he/she quoth*)
rack (of a cloud) be driven by the wind
raiment clothing
rapscallion a mischievous person
rathe-ripe (of fruit) ripening early in the year; (of a person) precocious
receipt a recipe
recipe a medical prescription
recompense punish or reward appropriately
recreant cowardly
rede advice or counsel
reduce besiege and capture (a town or fortress)
relieve make (something) stand out
repair an abode or haunt
repulsive lacking friendliness or sympathy
riband a ribbon
rover a pirate
rude ignorant and uneducated
ruth a feeling of pity, distress, or grief
sacring the consecration of a bishop, a sovereign, or the Eucharistic elements
saddle-bow the pommel of a saddle
salamander a red-hot iron or poker
sanative healing
sanguinary involving or causing much bloodshed
sap make (a building etc.) insecure by removing its foundations
saturnism lead poisoning
scantling a specimen, sample, or small amount
scapegrace a mischievous person; a rascal
scaramouch a boastful but cowardly person
science knowledge
sciolist a person who pretends to be knowledgeable
scold a woman who nags or grumbles constantly
scot a tax-like payment
scurvy worthless or contemptible
sea coal mineral coal
seizing a length of cord or rope on board a ship
sennight a week
shambles a slaughterhouse
shrive (of a priest) absolve (a person making a confession)
silly helpless; defenceless
sippet a small piece of bread or toast for dipping into soup or sauce
skirt an edge, border, or extreme part
slay kill in a violent way
slipshod (of shoes) worn down at the heel

slugabed a lazy person who stays in bed late
small beer weak beer
smite defeat or conquer
soak drink heavily
soft tack bread, especially as rations for sailors or soldiers
soil a stain
sooth truth
sore extremely; severely
speed success; prosperity
spence a larder
statuary a sculptor
steed a horse
stripe a blow with a lash
strumpet a female prostitute or a promiscuous woman
success a good or bad outcome
sugarplum a small round boiled sweet
surety, of/for a for certain
swain a country youth
swash flamboyantly swagger about or wield a sword
sweeting darling
sweetmeat an item of confectionery or sweet food
tantivy a rapid gallop or ride
tapster a person who serves at a bar
tenter a person in charge of something, especially factory machinery
thenceforth from that time, place, or point onward
thereunto to that
therewith with or in the thing mentioned
thither to or towards that place
thrice three times
tilt with engage in a contest with
timbrel a tambourine or similar instrument
'tis it is
tithe a tenth
tocsin an alarm bell or signal
tope drink to excess
top-sawyer a distinguished person
trespass a sin or offence
trig neat and smart
trigon a triangle
troth faith or loyalty when pledged in a solemn undertaking
turnkey a jailer
'tween between
tweeny a maid who assisted both the cook and the housemaid
uncle a pawnbroker
uncommon remarkably
unhand release from one's grasp
up to snuff up to the required standard
usher an assistant teacher

varlet	an unprincipled rogue
venery	hunting
verily	truly; certainly
verse	a line of poetry
very	real; genuine
visionary	existing only in the imagination
wain	a wagon or cart
wait on/upon	pay a respectful visit to
waits	street singers of Christmas carols
wast	second person singular past of *be*
watch	remain awake as religious observance
watchful	wakeful
watchword	a military password
weasand	the oesophagus or gullet
wench	a girl or young woman
whence	from what place or source
whereat	at which
wherefore	for what reason
wherewith	with or by which
whilom	formerly
white goods	domestic linen
whither	to what place or state
wife	a woman, especially an old or uneducated one
wight	a person of a specified kind
wise	manner, way, or extent
withal	in addition
without	outside
wondrous	wonderfully
wont	accustomed
wonted	usual
wool-stapler	a dealer in wool
wright	a maker or builder
yclept	by the name of
ye	you
yea	yes
yoke	the amount of land that one pair of oxen could plough in a day
yonder	over there
zounds	an expression of surprise or indignation

Literary words

These words are used mainly, or with a special meaning, in poetry and other writing in an elevated, 'literary' style.

abode	a home
access	an outburst of an emotion
adieu	goodbye
afar	at a distance
apace	quickly
argosy	a large merchant ship
arrant	utter
asunder	into pieces
atrabilious	melancholy or bad-tempered
aurora	the dawn
bard	a poet
barque	a boat
bedizen	dress gaudily
beget	produce (a child)
behold	see
beseech	ask urgently and fervently
bestrew	scatter
betake oneself	go to
betide	happen
betoken	be a warning of
blade	sword
blithe	happy
bosky	covered by trees or bushes
brand	a sword
brume	mist or fog
celerity	swiftness
circumvallate	surround with a rampart or wall
clarion	loud and clear
cleave to	stick fast to
cockcrow	dawn
coruscate	flash or sparkle
crapulent	relating to the drinking of alcohol
crescent	growing
darkling	relating to growing darkness
deep, the	the sea
dell	a small valley
dingle	a deep wooded valley
divers	of varying types
Dives	a rich man
dolour	great sorrow
dome	a stately building
dulcify	sweeten
effulgent	shining brightly
eld	old age
eminence	a piece of rising ground
empyrean	the sky
ere	before
erne	a sea eagle
espy	catch sight of
ether	the clear sky
evanescent	quickly fading
farewell	goodbye
fervid	hot or glowing
fidus Achates	a faithful friend
finny	relating to fish
firmament	the sky
flaxen	pale yellow
fleer	jeer or laugh disrespectfully
flexuous	full of bends and curves
fulgent	shining brightly
fulguration	a flash like lightning
fuliginous	sooty; dusky
fulminate	explode violently
furbelow	adorn with trimmings
gird	secure with a belt
glaive	a sword
gloaming	dusk
greensward	grassy ground
gyre	whirl or gyrate
hark	listen
horripilation	gooseflesh; hair standing on end
hymeneal	relating to marriage
ichor	blood, or a fluid likened to it
illude	trick someone
imbrue	stain one's hand or sword with blood
impuissant	powerless
incarnadine	colour (something) crimson
ingrate	ungrateful
inhume	bury
inly	inwardly
ire	anger
isle	an island
knell	the sound of a bell
lachrymal	connected with weeping or tears
lacustrine	associated with lakes
lambent	softly glowing or flickering
lave	wash or wash over
lay	a song
lea	an area of grassy land
lenity	kindness or gentleness
lightsome	nimble
limn	represent in painting or words
lucent	shining
madding	acting madly; frenzied
mage	a magician or learned person
main, the	the open ocean
malefic	causing harm
manifold	many and various
marge	a margin
mead	a meadow
mephitic	foul-smelling
mere	a lake or pond
moon	a month
morrow, the	the following day
muliebrity	womanliness
nescient	lacking knowledge; ignorant
nigh	near
niveous	snowy
nocuous	noxious, harmful, or poisonous
noisome	foul-smelling
nymph	a beautiful young woman
orb	an eye
orgulous	proud or haughty
pellucid	translucent
perchance	by some chance
perfervid	intense and impassioned
perfidious	deceitful and untrustworthy
philippic	a bitter verbal attack
plangent	loud and mournful
plash	a splashing sound
plenteous	plentiful
plumbless	extremely deep
poesy	poetry
prothalamium	a song or poem celebrating a wedding
puissant	powerful or influential
pulchritude	beauty
purl	flow with a babbling sound
quidnunc	an inquisitive and gossipy person
realm	a kingdom
refulgent	shining brightly
rend	tear to pieces
repine	be discontented
Rhadamanthine	stern and incorruptible in judgement
roundelay	a short, simple song with a refrain
rubescent	reddening
rutilant	glowing or glittering with red or golden light
sans	without
scribe	write
sea-girt	surrounded by sea
sempiternal	everlasting
serpent	a snake
shade	a ghost
ship of the desert	a camel
shore	country by the sea
slay	kill
slumber	sleep
star-crossed	ill-fated
steed	a horse
stilly	still and quiet
storied	celebrated in stories
strand	a shore
Stygian	very dark
summer	a year of a person's age
supernal	relating to the sky or the heavens
susurration	a whispering or rustling sound
swain	a young lover or suitor

sword, the military power; violence
sylvan wooded
tarry delay leaving
temerarious rash or reckless
tenebrous dark; shadowy
threescore sixty
thrice three times
tidings news; information
toilsome involving hard work
tope drink alcohol to excess
travail painful or laborious effort
troublous full of troubles
tryst a rendezvous between lovers
unman deprive of manly qualities
vestal chaste; pure
vesture clothing
virescent greenish
viridescent greenish or becoming green
visage a person's face
want lack or be short of
wax become larger or stronger
wayfarer a person who travels on foot
wed marry
welkin, the the sky or heaven
whited sepulchre a hypocrite
wind blow (a bugle)
without outside
wondrous inspiring wonder
wont accustomed
wonted usual
wrathful extremely angry
wreathe twist or entwine
yon yonder; that
yore of former ties or long ago
youngling a young person or animal
zephyr a soft, gentle breeze

Useful words for puzzles & games

Abbreviations and proper nouns (the names of individual people, places, or organizations) are not included, since they are not allowed in most word games. A few of the words listed, such as *ad* and *op*, originated as abbreviations but are generally considered to have become words in their own right.

Two-letter words

aa rough cindery lava
ab an abdominal muscle
ad an advertisement
ag *S. African* a general exclamation
ah an exclamation
ai the three-toed sloth
am the present tense of *be*
an a form of the indefinite article
as used to convey relative extent or degree
at expressing location or time
aw an exclamation
ax variant spelling of *axe*
ay variant spelling of *aye*
ba the soul, in Egyptian mythology
be to exist
bi bisexual
bo a kind of fig tree
by beside
da a person's father
do to perform an action
dy a type of sediment
ee dialect form of *oh*
eh an exclamation
El an elevated railway
em a measuring unit in printing
en a measuring unit in printing
er expressing doubt or hesitation
ex a former spouse or partner
fa a musical note
Ga a people in Ghana
gi judo jacket
go to move or travel
ha an exclamation
he a male person or animal
hi a greeting
ho an exclamation
id a part of the mind
if introducing a conditional clause
in within
io a North American moth
is the present tense of *be*
it a thing
ja *S. African* yes
jo *Scottish, archaic* a sweetheart
Ju a kind of Chinese pottery
ka the spirit, in Egyptian mythology
ki a plant of the lily family
la a musical note
li a Chinese unit of distance
lo *archaic* used to draw attention to something
ma a person's mother
me the objective case of the first-person pronoun I
mi a musical note
mo a moment
mu a Greek letter
my belonging to me
né originally called
no not any
nu a Greek letter
ob a type of gene
od a supposed natural force
of belonging to
og *Australian, archaic* a shilling
oh an exclamation
oi used to attract attention
OK used to express assent, agreement, etc.
om a sacred mantra
on supported by or covering
op an operation
or used to link alternatives
os a bone
ou a Hawaiian bird
ow expressing pain
ox a cow or bull
oy = oi
Oz Australia(n)
pa father
pi a Greek letter
po a chamber pot
qi the life force, in Chinese philosophy
ra a moraine, in Norway or Sweden
re a musical note
ri a Japanese unit of length
se a Chinese musical instrument
si = te
so therefore
ta thank you
te a musical note
ti = te
uh expressing hesitation
um expressing hesitation
up towards a higher position
us the objective case of *we*
Wa a people on the borders of China and Burma
we oneself and other people
Wu a dialect of Chinese
xi a Greek letter
xu a Vietnamese unit of money
ye *archaic* the plural form of *thou*
Yi a people in parts of China
yo used as a greeting
yu an ancient Chinese wine container

Three-letter words containing *x* or *z*

axe a chopping tool
biz business
box a container
coz archaic a cousin
cox the person who steers a rowing boat
dux *Scottish* a top pupil at school
dzo a crossbreed of a cow and a yak
fax an electronic copy of a document
fez a type of hat
fix to attach or repair
fox an animal
hex *N. Amer*. to cast a spell on someone
kex cow parsley
lax not strict or careful enough
lox *N. Amer.* smoked salmon
lux a unit of illumination
max maximum
Mex Mexican
mix to blend or combine
nix nothing
pax a call for a truce
pix pictures
pox a disease
pyx a container for Communion bread
Rex the reigning king
sax a saxophone
saz a kind of lute
sex being male or female
six the number
tax money paid to a government
tux a tuxedo
Uzi a type of sub-machine gun
vex to annoy
vox vocals; voice
wax substance used to make candles etc.
wiz = whizz
zag a sharp change of direction
zap to destroy
zed the letter Z
zee *N. Amer.* the letter Z
Zen a type of Buddhism
zig a sharp change of direction
zip a fastener
zit a spot
zol *S. African* a hand-rolled cigarette
zoo a place where wild animals are kept

Words containing *q* not followed by *u*

burqa = burka, a long garment worn by Muslim women
fiqh the theory or philosophy of Islamic law
Iraqi a person from Iraq; relating to Iraq
niqab a Muslim woman's veil
qadi a Muslim judge
qanat an irrigation tunnel
qasida an Arabic or Persian poem
qawwal a qawwali singer
qawwali Muslim devotional music
qi the life force, in Chinese philosophy
qibla the direction towards Mecca
qigong a Chinese system of physical exercises
qin a Chinese musical instrument
qintar an Albanian unit of money
qiviut wool from the musk ox
qwerty the standard layout of a computer keyboard
tariqa the Sufi method of spiritual learning
waqf a Muslim endowment

Words of up to eight letters beginning with *x*

xanthan a polysaccharide
xanthate a chemical compound
xanthene a chemical compound
Xanthian from Xanthus
xanthic yellowish
xanthin a yellow colouring matter
xanthine a biochemical compound
xanthoma a yellow patch on the skin
xebec a sailing ship
xeme a fork-tailed gull
xenia gifts to a guest or guests
xenial relating to hospitality
xenogamy type of flower fertilization
xenolith piece of rock brought in from another area
xenology the study of alien biology
xenon a gaseous chemical element
xenotime a yellowish-brown mineral
xeric very dry
xeroma abnormal dryness of a body part
xerox to photocopy
Xhosa a South African people or their language
xi a Greek letter
Xiang a dialect of Chinese
xiphoid sword-shaped
Xmas Christmas
xoanon a wooden image of a god
xography a photographic process
xu a Vietnamese unit of money
xylan a compound found in wood
xylary of or relating to xylem
xylem plant tissue
xylene a liquid hydrocarbon
xylite a volatile liquid
xylitol a chemical substance
xylol = xylene
xylose: a plant sugar
xyrid a sedge-like herb
xyster a surgical instrument
xyston an ancient Greek spear
xystus an ancient Greek portico

2 Thematic lists

Animals

Amphibians

alpine salamander
amphiuma
bullfrog
caecilian/coecialan
cane toad
cave salamander
clawed frog
crested newt
eft
fire-bellied toad
fire salamander
flying frog
frog
giant salamander
goliath frog
hairy frog
hellbender
horned toad
hyla
leopard frog
lungless salamander
marsh frog
midwife toad
mole salamander
mud puppy
natterjack toad
newt
olm
palmate newt
peeper
platanna
poison-arrow frog
salamander
siren
smooth newt
spadefoot toad
Suriname toad
tiger salamander
toad
toadlet
tree frog
triton
waterdog
Xenopus

Bats

barbastelle
blossom bat
bulldog bat
butterfly bat
Daubenton's bat
disk-wing bat
epauletted fruit bat
false vampire
fisherman bat
flower bat
flying fox
free-tailed bat
fruit bat
funnel-eared bat
ghost bat
golden bat
hairless bat
hammer-headed bat
hog-nosed bat
hollow-faced bat
horseshoe bat
leaf-nosed bat
Leisler's bat
long-eared bat
mastiff bat
mouse-eared bat
mouse-tailed bat
moustached bat
myotis
naked bat
Natterer's bat
noctule
painted bat
particoloured bat
pipistrelle
rousette
sac-winged bat
serotine bat
sheath-tailed bat
short-tailed bat
slit-faced bat
smoky bat
spotted bat
sucker-footed bat
tomb-bat
Trident bat
tube-nosed bat
vampire bat
whiskered bat
white bat

Bears

black bear
brown bear
cinnamon bear
giant panda
grizzly bear
honey bear
Kodiak bear
musquaw
panda
polar bear
red panda
sloth bear
spectacled bear
sun bear

Birds *See also* **Game birds, Breeds of fowl**

adjutant bird
antbird
Arctic tern
auk
avocet
bald eagle
barnacle goose
barn owl
bateleur eagle
Bewick's swan
bird of paradise
bittern
blackbird
blackcap
black swan
bluebird
blue tit
booby
bowerbird
brambling
broadbill
brown owl
budgerigar
bullfinch
bunting
bustard
butcher-bird
buzzard
Canada goose
canary
capercaillie
caracara
cassowary
chaffinch
chicken
chiffchaff
chough
coal tit
cockatiel
cockatoo
condor
coot
cormorant
corncrake
crane
crossbill
crow
cuckoo
curlew
dabchick
darter
dipper
diver
dodo (*extinct*)
dotterel
dove
duck
dunlin
dunnock
eagle
eagle owl
egret
eider duck
emperor penguin
emu
falcon
fantail
fieldfare
finch
flamingo
flycatcher
frigate bird
fulmar
galah
gannet
godwit
goldcrest
golden eagle
goldfinch
goose
goshawk
great auk (*extinct*)
great crested grebe
great tit
grebe
green woodpecker
greenfinch
greenshank
greylag goose
griffon vulture
grouse
guillemot
guineafowl
gull
gyrfalcon
harrier
hawfinch
hawk
hawk owl
hedge sparrow
hen
hen harrier
heron
herring gull
hobby
honeyguide
hooded crow
hoopoe
hornbill
horned owl
house martin
house sparrow
hummingbird
ibis
jackdaw
jay
kestrel
kingfisher
king penguin
kite
kittiwake
kiwi
kookaburra
lammergeier
lanner
lapwing
lark
laughing jackass
linnet
little grebe
little owl
long-tailed tit
lorikeet
lovebird
lyrebird
macaw
magpie
mallard
mandarin duck
marabou stork
marsh harrier
martin
meadowlark
merlin
mistle thrush
moa (*extinct*)
mockingbird
moorhen
mute swan
mynah bird
nighthawk
nightingale
nightjar
noddy
nuthatch
ortolan
osprey
ostrich
ouzel
owl
oystercatcher
parakeet
parrot
partridge
passenger pigeon (*extinct*)
peacock
peafowl
peewit
pelican
penguin
peregrine falcon
petrel
phalarope
pheasant
pigeon
pilot bird
pintail
pipit
plover
ptarmigan
puffin
quail
rail
raven
razorbill
red kite
redpoll
redshank
redstart
redwing
reed bunting
reed warbler
rhea
rhinoceros bird
ringdove
ring ouzel
roadrunner
robin
rook
ruddy duck
ruff
sand martin
sandpiper
scops owl
screech owl
sea eagle
seagull
secretary bird
shag
shearwater
shelduck
shoebill
shoveler
shrike
siskin
skua
skylark
snipe
snow bunting
snow goose
snowy owl
song thrush
sparrow
sparrowhawk
spoonbill
starling
stonechat
stone curlew
stork
storm petrel
sunbird
swallow
swan
swift
tawny owl
teal
tern
thrush
tit
titmouse
toucan
treecreeper
turkey
turkey vulture
turtle dove
vulture
wagtail
wallcreeper
warbler
waxbill
waxwing
weaver bird
wheatear
whinchat
whippoorwill
whitethroat
whooping crane
whydah
wigeon
willow warbler
woodchat
woodcock
woodlark
woodpecker
wood pigeon
wren
wryneck
yellowhammer

Wordfinder

Game birds

black grouse
bobwhite (quail)
capercaillie
duck
francolin
golden pheasant
goose
grouse
guineafowl
hazel grouse
moorfowl
partridge
peafowl
pheasant
ptarmigan
quail
red grouse
ringneck pheasant
ruffed grouse
sage grouse
spurfowl
turkey
waterfowl
willow grouse
woodcock
woodgrouse

Breeds of fowl

Chickens

Ancona
Andalusian
Australorp
Bantam
Booted
Brahmaputra
Bresse
Campine
Cochin
Crèvecour
Croad Langshan
Dorking
Faverolle
Frizzles
Hamburg
Houdan
Indian Game
Ixworth
Jersey Giant
Jubilee Indian Game
La Fleche
Lakenfelder
Leghorn
Malay
Malines
Marans
Marsh Daisy
Minorca
Modern Game
Modern Langshan
Nankin
New Hampshire Red
Norfolk Grey
North Holland Blue
Old English Game
Old English Pheasant Fowl
Orloff
Orpington
Phoenix
Plymouth Rock
Poland
Redcap
Rhode Island Red
Rosecomb
Rumpless
Scots Dumpy
Scots Grey
Sebright
Sicilian Buttercup
Silkie
Spanish
Sultan
Sumatra Game
Sussex
Transylvanian Naked Neck
Welsummer
Wyandotte
Yokohama

Ducks

Aylesbury
Black East Indian
Cayuga
Crested
Indian Runner
Khaki Campbell
Magpie
Muscovy
Orpington
Rouen
Welsh Harlequin
Whalesbury

Geese

Brecon Buff
Chinese
Embden
Pilgrim
Roman
Sebastopol
Toulouse

Guineafowl

Lavender
Pearl Grey
White

Turkeys

Black Norfolk
Bourbon Red
Broad-Breasted Bronze
Broad-Breasted White
Cambridge Bronze
Mammoth Bronze
Narragansett
Nicholas
White Austrian
White Holland

Butterflies

Adonis blue
alpine
angle wings
apollo
arctic
argus
azure
birdwing
blue
brimstone
brown
buckeye
cabbage white
Camberwell beauty
chalkhill blue
checkerspot
cleopatra
clouded yellow
comma
copper
diana
dog face
dryad
Duke of Burgundy
dusky wing
elfin
emperor
festoon
fritillary
gatekeeper
grayling
hairstreak
heath
julia
large blue
map butterfly
marbled white
mazarine blue
meadow brown
metalmark
milkweed
monarch
morpho
mourning cloak
nettle-tree butterfly
nymph
orange tip
owl butterfly
painted lady
peacock butterfly
pearly eye
plain tiger
purple emperor
red admiral
ringlet
satyr
Scotch argus
silver-studded blue
skipper
snout butterfly
speckled wood
sulphur
swallowtail
tortoiseshell
two-tailed pasha
wall brown
white admiral
wood nymph
zebra

Cats

Breeds

Abyssinian
angora
Balinese
Birman
Burmese
Burmilla
chinchilla
colourpoint
Cornish Rex
Devon Rex
ginger cat
Japanese Bobtail
longhair
Maine Coon
Maltese
Manx
marmalade cat
Persian
Ragdoll
Rex
Russian Blue
sealpoint
shorthair
Siamese
smoke Persian
Somali
Sphynx
tabbypoint
Tiffanie
Tonkinese
Turkish Van

Wild cats

bobcat
caracal
catamount
cheetah
clouded leopard
cougar
eyra
fishing cat
Geoffroy's cat
golden cat
jaguar
jaguarundi
jungle cat
leopard
liger
lion
lynx
manul
margay
mountain lion
ocelot
ounce
Pallas's cat
panther
puma
sabre-toothed tiger (*extinct*)
sand cat
serval
snow leopard
Temminck's golden cat
tiger
tigon
wildcat

Cattle

Aberdeen Angus
Afrikander
Andalusian
Ayrshire
Bangus
Barrosã
beefalo
Beef Shorthorn
Belgian Blue
Belted Galloway
Belted Welsh
Blonde d'Aquitaine
Brahmin
British White
Brown Swiss
Charolais
Chianina
Danish Red
Devon
Dexter
Droughtmaster
Durham
Friesian
Galician Blond
Galloway
German Yellow
Guernsey
Hereford
Highland
Holstein
Illawarra shorthorn
Irish Moiled
Jamaica Hope
Jersey
Kerry
Kyloe
Limousin
Lincoln Red
longhorn
Luing
Maine Anjou
Meuse-Rhine-Ijssel
Miranda
Mongolian
Murray Grey
N'Dama
Pinzgauer
Red-and-White Friesian
Red Poll
Romagnola
Sahiwal
Santa Gertrudis
Shetland
shorthorn
Simmental
South Devon
Sussex
Swedish Red-and-White
Texas longhorn
Welsh Black
West Highland
White Galloway
White Park

Wild cattle

anoa
aurochs
banteng
bison
Brahmin
buffalo
dzo/dzho/zho
gaur
gayal
kouprey
musk ox
ox
park cattle
sapi-utan
seladang
takin
tamarau
tsine
water buffalo
wisent
yak
zebu

Crustaceans

acorn barnacle
barnacle
blue crab
Chinese mitten crab
crab
crawdad
crawfish
cray
crayfish
crevette
Cyclops
daphnia
Dungeness crab
edible crab
euphausiid
fairy shrimp
fiddler crab
fish louse
freshwater crayfish
ghost crab
goose barnacle
gribble
hermit crab
horseshoe crab
king crab
king prawn
kreef
krill
land crab
langouste
lobster
mantis shrimp
marron
mitten crab
mudbug
mysid
nipper
Norway lobster
opossum shrimp
pea crab
phyllopod
pill woodlouse
porcelain crab
prawn
robber crab
Sally Lightfoot

sand crab
sandhopper
sea slater
shore crab
shrimp
slater
snow crab
softshell crab
spider crab
spiny lobster
stone crab
swimming crab
tiger prawn
velvet swimming crab
woodlouse
yabby

Deer and antelopes *For goat-antelopes, see* **Goats**

addax
ariel
axis deer
barasingha
beira
beisa
blackbuck
blesbok
bongo
bontebok
brocket
bubal
bushbuck
caribou
chevrotain
Chinese water deer
chinkara
chiru
chital
Clark's gazelle
dama gazelle
dibatag
dik-dik
dorcas gazelle
duiker
eland
elk
fallow deer
gazelle
gemsbok
gerenuk
gnu
goa
grysbok
guemal
hartebeest
hirola
hog deer
impala
klipspringer
kob
kongoni
kudu
lechwe
marsh deer
moose
mouse deer
mule deer
muntjac
musk deer
nilgai
nyala
okapi
oribi
oryx
Père David's deer
pronghorn (antelope)
pudu
puku
red deer
reedbuck
reindeer
rhebok
roan antelope
roe deer
royal antelope
royal stag
rusa
sable (antelope)
saiga
sambar
sasin
scimitar oryx
sika
sitatunga
sorel
springbok
steenbok
steinbock
suni
swamp deer
thamin
Thomson's gazelle
topi
tsessebi
tufted deer
wapiti
waterbuck
water deer
white-tailed deer
wildebeest

Dinosaurs

alamosaurus
albertosaurus
allosaurus
anchiceratops
anchisaurus
ankylosaur
apatosaurus
barosaurus
brachiosaurus
brontosaurus
camarasaurus
camptosaurus
carnosaur
ceratops
ceratosaurus
cetiosaurus
chasmosaurus
coelophysis
coelosaur
compsognathus
conodont
corythosaurus
deinonychus
dilophosaurus
diplodocus
dromaeosaur
dryosaurus
duck-billed dinosaur
edmontosaurus
fabrosaurus
gallimimus
hadrosaur
heterodontosaurus
hypsilophodont
iguanodon
kentrosaurus
leptoceratops
megalosaurus
melanorosaurus
microvenator
monoclonius
ornithischian
ornitholestes
ornithomimus
ornithopod
ostrich dinosaur
oviraptor
pachycephalosaur
parasaurolophus
pentaceratops
plateosaurus
pliosaur
procompsognathus
prosauropod
protoceratops
psittacosaurus
pteranodon
pterodactyl
quetzalcoatlus
raptor
rhamphorhyncoid
riojasaurus
saurischian
saurolophus
sauropod
scelidosaurus
seismosaurus
staurikosaurus
stegoceras
stegosaurus
styracosaurus
syntarsus
tarbosaurus
theropod
thescelosaurus
titanosaurus
torosaurus
triceratops
troodon
tyrannosaurus
ultrasaurus
utahraptor
velociraptor

Dogs

Breeds

Aberdeen terrier
affenpinscher
Afghan hound
Airedale terrier
Akita
Alsatian
Australian terrier
basenji
basset hound
beagle
bearded collie
Bedlington terrier
Belgian sheepdog
Bernese mountain dog
bichon frise
black and tan
Blenheim spaniel
bloodhound
Border collie
Border terrier
borzoi
Boston terrier
bouvier
boxer
Briard
Brussels griffon
bulldog
bull mastiff
bull terrier
cairn terrier
Cape hunting dog
carriage dog
Cavalier King Charles
chihuahua
chow
Clumber spaniel
Clydesdale
coach dog
cocker spaniel
collie
coonhound
corgi
dachshund
Dalmatian
Dandie Dinmont
deerhound
Dobermann pinscher
dray hound
elk hound
English setter
English springer
field spaniel
Finnish spitz
foxhound
fox terrier
French bulldog
German Shepherd
golden retriever
Gordon setter
Great Dane
greyhound
griffon
Groenendael
harrier
husky
Ibizan hound
Irish setter
Irish terrier
Irish wolfhound
Istrian pointer
Ivicene
Jack Russell terrier
keeshond
kelpie
Kerry blue
King Charles spaniel
Komondor
Kuvasz
Labrador retriever
laika
Lakeland terrier
Leonberg
Lhasa apso
malamute/malemute
Maltese dog/terrier
Manchester terrier
mastiff
Mexican hairless
Munsterlander
Newfoundland
Norfolk terrier
Norwich terrier
Old English sheepdog
otter dog/hound
papillon
peke
Pekinese/Pekingese
Pharaoh hound
pit bull terrier
pointer
Pomeranian
poodle
pug dog
puli
Pyrenean mountain dog
Pyrenean sheepdog
Pyrenean wolfhound
Queensland blue heeler
redbone
red setter
retriever
Rhodesian ridgeback
Rottweiler
rough collie
St Bernard dog
saluki
Samoyed
schipperke
schnauzer
Scottie dog
Scottish terrier
Sealyham terrier
setter
Shar Pei
sheepdog
sheltie
Shetland sheepdog
shih-tzu
Skye terrier
sleuth hound
spaniel
Spinone
spitz
springer spaniel
Staffordshire bull terrier
staghound
terrier
Tibetan mastiff
Tibetan spaniel
Tibetan terrier
tosa
vizsla
Weimaraner
Welsh corgi
Welsh hound
Welsh springer
Welsh terrier
West Highland terrier
wheaten terrier
whippet
wolfhound
Yorkshire terrier

Wild dogs

African wild dog
bush dog
Cape hunting dog
coyote
dhole
dingo
dire wolf (*extinct*)
golden jackal
grey wolf
jackal
lobo
maned wolf
raccoon dog
red dog
red wolf
Simien jackal/fox
timber wolf
wolf

Fish *See also* **Sharks**

albacore
alewife
amberjack
anchovy
anemone fish
angelfish
angel shark
anglerfish
archerfish
balloonfish
bandfish
barbel
barracouta
barracuda
barramundi
bass
beluga
bitterling
blackfish
bleak
blenny
blowfish
bluefin
bluefish
boarfish
bonefish
bonito
bowfin
boxfish
bream
brill
brisling
brown trout
bullhead
burbot
butterfly fish
butterfly ray
carp
catfish
charr
chimera
chub
climbing perch
clingfish
clownfish
coalfish
cod
coelacanth
coley
conger eel
cowfish
crappie
dab
dace
damselfish
danio
darter
devil ray
dorado
dory
Dover sole
dragonfish
eagle ray
eel
eelpout
electric eel
electric ray
fighting fish
filefish
flatfish
flathead
flounder
fluke
flying fish
flying gurnard
frogfish
garfish
garpike
glassfish
goatfish

goby
goldfish
goosefish
gourami
grayling
Greenland halibut
grenadier
grey mullet
grouper
grunion
gudgeon
guitarfish
gulper eel
gunnel
guppy
gurnard
haddock
hake
halfbeak
halibut
harlequin fish
herring
hoki
humpback salmon
icefish
John Dory
kingfish
koi carp
labyrinth fish
lamprey
lanternfish
leatherjacket
lemon sole
ling
lionhead
loach
lumpsucker
lungfish
mackerel
manta
marlin
minnow
molly
monkfish
moonfish
moray eel
mudfish
mudminnow
mudskipper
mullet
needlefish
oarfish
orfe
parrotfish
perch
pickerel
pike
pikeperch
pilchard
pilotfish
pipefish
piranha
plaice
pollack
pomfret
porcupine fish
porgy
puffer fish
rabbitfish
rainbow trout
ray
redfish
red mullet
red snapper
remora
ribbonfish
roach
rock bass
rockfish
rockling
roughy
rudd
ruffe
sailfish
salmon
salmon trout
sand eel
sandfish
sardine
sawfish
scad
scorpionfish
sea bass
sea bream
sea horse
sea perch
sea robin
sea trout
shad
shark
shark-sucker
sheepshead
shovelhead
silverside
skate
skipjack tuna
skipper
smelt
snake mackerel
snapper
snipefish
sockeye salmon
sole
sparling
spearfish
sprat
stargazer
stickleback
stingray
stonefish
sturgeon
sucker
sunfish
surgeonfish
swordfish
swordtail
tench
tetra
thornback
threadfin
tilapia
toadfish
triggerfish
trout
tuna
tunny
turbot
walleye
weakfish
weever
whitebait
whitefish
whiting
witch
wolf fish
wrasse
yellowfin
yellowtail
zander

Fossils *See also* Dinosaurs

acanthodian
aepyornis
amber
ammonite
ammonoid
anoplothere
anthracothere
archaeopteryx
archelon
arsinoitherium
arthrodire
baluchitherium
barylambda
belemnite
bioclast
brontops
brontothere
caenolestid
calamite
cave bear
cave lion
cephalaspid
ceratite
chalicothere
condylarth
conodont
coprolite
corallite
creodont
cryptoclidus
cygnognathus
cynodont
deinotherium
diatryma
dicynodont
dimetrodon
dimorphodon
dinocephalian
dinornis
diprotodon
dire wolf
Dryopithecus
elasmosaur
elephant bird
eohippus
eryops
eurypterid
giant elk
glyptodont
gomphotherium
goniatite
graptolite
ground sloth
gryphaea
hesperornis
hyracotherium
ichthyornis
ichthyosaur
ichthyostega
labyrinthodont
lepidodendron
lepidosaur
lepospondyl
litoptern
lycaenops
mammoth
mastodon
megaloceros
megatherium
merychippus
mesohippus
mesosaur
miacid
microfossil
microsaur
moeritherium
morganucodon
moropus
mosasaur
moschops
multituberculate
mylodon
nannofossil
nothosaur
notoungulate
nummulite
Nutcracker man
orthocone
osteostracan
ostracoderm
pantodont
pareiasaur
pelycosaur
phororhacos
phytosaur
placoderm
placodont
plesiadapid
plesiosaur
pliopithecus
pliosaur
propliopithecus
psilophyton
pteranodon
pteridosperm
pterodactyl
pterosaur
quetzalcoatlus
rudist
rugose coral
sabretooth *or* sabre-toothed tiger
seymouria-morph
sivatherium
smilodon
stereospondyl
stigmaria
stone-lily
stromatolite
symmetrodont
synapsid
taeniodont
temnospondyl
thecodont
therapsid
thylacosmilus
tinoceratid
titanothere
toxodont
trilobite
uintatherium
woolly mammoth
woolly rhinoceros
zeuglodont

Foxes

Arctic fox
Azara's fox
bat-eared fox
Blanford's fox
blue fox
Colpeo fox
corsac fox
crab-eating fox
cross fox
fennec
grey fox
hoary fox
kit fox
pale fox
red fox
Samson fox
sand fox
silver fox
swift fox
zorro

Goats

Breeds

Anglo-Nubian
Angora
Apulian
Bagot
Chamois Coloured
Dutch White
French Alpine
Golden Guernsey
Grisons Striped
Kashmiri
Murcian
Nubian
Saanen
Somali
Soviet Mohair
Syrian Mountain
Telemark
Toggenburg
Valais Blackneck

Wild goats

bezoar
ibex
markhor
Spanish ibex
tahr
tur

Goat-antelopes

chamois
goral
mountain goat
musk ox
serow
takin

Horses and ponies

American Saddle Horse
Andalusian
Anglo-Arab
Appaloosa
Arab
Barb
Basuto pony
Breton
brumby
Camargue
Caspian
Cleveland Bay
Clydesdale
Comtois
Conestoga
Connemara pony
criollo
Dales pony
Dartmoor pony
Dutch draught
Dutch warmblood
Exmoor pony
Falabella
Fell pony
Fjord
Friesian
Galiceño
Galloway
Gelderlander
Gotland
Hackney
Haflinger
Hanoverian
Highland pony
Holstein
Huçul
hunter
hyracotherium *or* eohippus (*extinct*)
Iceland pony
Irish draught
Irish hunter
Jutland
Kabardin
Karabakh
Kathiawari
Kazakh
Lipizzaner/ Lippizaner
Lokai
Lundy Island
Mangalarga
Manipur pony
Mérens pony
miniature Shetland
miohippus (*extinct*)
Missouri fox-trotting horse
Morgan
mustang
New Forest pony
Nonius
Noriker
Norwegian racing trotter
Oldenburger
Orlov trotter
Paso Fino
Percheron
Pinto
Pinzgauer
Plateau Persian
pliohippus (*extinct*)
polo pony
pony of the Americas
Przewalski's horse
Quarter Horse
Russ
Russian heavy draught
Russian warmblood
Sable Island
Saddlebred
Salerno
Sandalwood pony
Schleswig
Shetland pony
shire horse
Standardbred
Suffolk Punch
Swedish warmblood
tarpan (*extinct*)
Tartar pony
Tennessee Walking Horse
Tersky
thoroughbred
Timor pony
Trakehner
trotter
Viatka
Waler
warmblood
Welsh cob
Welsh mountain pony
Welsh pony
Welsh pony of cob type
Yorkshire coach horse

Horse family

ass
burro
cuddy
donkey
hinny
horse
hyracotherium
jackass
kiang
kulan
mule
onager
quagga
zebra

Insects *See also* **Butterflies, Moths**

agrion
alderfly
amazon ant
ambrosia beetle
animated stick
anopheles
ant
ant lion
aphid
Argentine ant
army ant
army worm
asparagus beetle
assassin bug
backswimmer
bark beetle
bat fly
bedbug
bee
bee beetle
bee fly
bee louse
beetle
biscuit beetle
biting midge
black ant
black beetle
blackfly
blister beetle
bloodworm
bloody-nosed beetle
blowfly
bluebottle
body louse
boll weevil
bombardier beetle
booklouse
bookworm
borer
botfly
braconid
bristletail
buffalo gnat
bulb fly
bulldog ant
bumblebee
burying beetle
bush cricket
butterfly
cabbage root fly
cabbageworm
caddis fly
cadelle
camel cricket
cankerworm
carabid
cardinal beetle
carpenter ant
carpenter bee
carpet beetle
carrion beetle
carrot fly
chafer
chalcid wasp
cheese fly
chigger
chinch bug
Christmas beetle
churchyard beetle
cicada
cigarette beetle
click beetle
cluster fly
cockchafer
cockroach
Colorado beetle
conehead
corn borer
corn earworm
cotton-leaf worm
cotton stainer
crab louse
crane fly
cricket
cuckoo bee
cuckoo wasp
curculio
cutworm
daddy-long-legs
damsel bug
damselfly
darkling beetle
darner
darter
death-watch beetle
deer fly
demoiselle
devil's coach-horse
digger wasp
diving beetle
dobsonfly
dor beetle
dragonfly
driver ant
drone fly
drosophila
dung beetle
dung fly
earwig
elm bark beetle
emperor dragonfly
fairy fly
field cricket
fig wasp
fire ant
firebrat
firefly
flea
flea beetle
flesh fly
flour beetle
flower beetle
fly
forest fly
frit fly
froghopper
fruit fly
fungus beetle
furniture beetle
gadfly
gall midge
gall wasp
garden chafer
glow-worm
gnat
gold beetle
goliath beetle
grain borer
grain weevil
grasshopper
greenbottle
greenfly
greenhead
ground beetle
groundhopper
harvester ant
hawker
head louse
Hercules beetle
Hessian fly
hide beetle
honey ant
honeybee
honeypot ant
hornet
horntail
hornworm
horsefly
housefly
hoverfly
ichneumon
Japanese beetle
jewel beetle
June bug
katydid
ked
khapra beetle
kissing bug
lace bug
lacewing
lac insect
ladybird
lantern fly
larder beetle
leaf beetle
leafcutter ant
leafcutter bee
leafhopper
leaf insect
leaf miner
leatherjacket
lightning bug
locust
longhorn beetle
louse
louse fly
mantis
Maori bug
mason bee
mason wasp
May bug
mayfly
meal beetle
mealworm
mealy bug
meat ant
midge
mining bee
minotaur beetle
mole cricket
mopane worm
mosquito
moth
mud dauber
museum beetle
musk beetle
nostril fly
oil beetle
onion fly
paper wasp
pharaoh ant
phylloxera
pill beetle
pinhole borer
pismire
plant hopper
plant louse
pond skater
potato beetle
potter wasp
powder-post beetle
praying mantis
rainfly
raspberry beetle
rat-tailed maggot
rhinoceros beetle
robber fly
root fly
rose chafer
rove beetle
St Mark's fly
sandfly
sand wasp
saucer bug
sawfly
sawyer
scale insect
scarab
scorpion fly
screech beetle
screw worm
sexton beetle
shield bug
silverfish
skin beetle
slave-making ant
snake fly
snipe fly
snow flea
soldier beetle
soldier fly
Spanish fly
spider beetle
spider-hunting wasp
spittlebug
springtail
spruce budworm
squash bug
stable fly
stag beetle
stick insect
stilt bug
stink bug
stonefly
stylops
tarantula hawk
tent caterpillar
termite
thrips
thunderbug
thunderfly
tiger beetle
timberman
tobacco beetle
tortoise beetle
treehopper
tsetse fly
tumblebug
turtle bug
vedelia beetle
velvet ant
warble fly
wart-biter
wasp
wasp beetle
water beetle
water boatman
water cricket
water measurer
water scorpion
water strider
weaver ant
web-spinner
webworm
weevil
weta
whirligig
white ant
whitefly
wireworm
witchetty grub
wood ant
woodwasp
woodworm
woolly bear
yellow jacket

Lemurs and other prosimians

angwantibo
aye-aye
bushbaby
colugo
dwarf lemur
flying lemur
galago
indri
lemur
loris
mouse lemur
potto
ring-tailed lemur
ruffed lemur
sifaka
slender loris
slow loris
spectral tarsier
tarsier
tree shrew

Mammals *See also* **Bats, Bears, Cats, Cattle, Deer and antelopes, Dogs, Foxes, Goats, Horses and ponies, Horse family, Lemurs, Marsupials, Monkeys and apes, Pigs, Rabbits and hares, Rodents, Seals, Sheep, Squirrels, Weasels, Whales and dolphins**

aardvark
alpaca
anteater
armadillo
camel
coati
dromedary
duck-billed platypus
dugong
echidna
elephant
giraffe
hippo/hippotamus
hyena
hyrax
kinkajou
laughing hyena
llama
manatee
pangolin
platypus
raccoon
rhinoceros
sea cow
shrew
sloth
spiny anteater
Steller's sea cow
tapir
tenrec
tree shrew

Marsupials

antechinus
bandicoot
bettong
bilby
boodie
brushtail
brush-tailed bettong
brush-tailed possum
cuscus
dasyure
dibbler
dunnart
flying phalanger
glider
honey possum
kangaroo
koala
kowari
kultarr
marsupial cat
marsupial mole
marsupial mouse
marsupial rat
mouse opossum
mulgara
numbat
opossum
pademelon
phalanger
phascogale
planigale
possum
potoroo
pygmy possum
quokka
quoll
rat kangaroo
ringtail
rock wallaby
sminthopsis
Tasmanian devil
thylacine (*or* Tasmanian tiger/wolf)
Virginia opossum
wallaby
wallaroo
wombat
woylie
yapok

Wordfinder

Molluscs

abalone
angel wings
argonaut
ark (shell)
auger (shell)
basket shell
bittersweet shell
bivalve
bubble (shell)
canoe shell
carpet shell
carrier shell
cephalopod
chink shell
chiton
clam
cockle
cone shell
coquina (clam)
cowrie
cuttlefish
date mussel
dog cockle
dog whelk
dove shell
drill
drupe
duck mussel
edible snail
file shell
gaper
gastropod
geoduck
giant clam
hard clam
harp (shell)
helmet (shell)
horn shell
jewel box
jingle (shell)
lamp shell
limpet
lion's paw
mitre (shell)
moon shell
murex
mussel
nautilus
necklace shell
nerite
Noah's ark
nudibranch
octopus
olive (shell)
ormer
otter shell
oyster
pandora
paper nautilus
paua
pearl mussel
pearl oyster
pearly nautilus
pelican's foot shell
pen shell
periwinkle
pheasant shell
piddock
pteropod
quahog
ramshorn snail
razor shell
round clam
scallop
scaphopod
scungille
sea butterfly
sea hare
sea lemon
sea slug
shipworm
slipper limpet
slit limpet
slug
snail
softshell clam
spindle shell
spire shell
squid
sundial (shell)
swan mussel
tellin
teredo
thorny oyster
top shell
tridacna
triton
trough shell
trumpet shell
tulip shell
tun (shell)
turban (shell)
turret (shell)
tusk shell
vase shell
venus
Venus (clam/shell)
wedge shell
wentletrap
whelk
wing oyster
winkle
worm shell
zebra mussel

Monkeys and apes

agile gibbon
baboon
Barbary ape
bonobo
capuchin monkey
chacma baboon
chimpanzee
colobus
Diana monkey
douroucouli
drill
gelada
gibbon
gorilla
green monkey
grivet
guenon
hamadryas
hanuman langur
hoolock
howler monkey
langur
lar gibbon
leaf monkey
macaque
mandrill
mangabey
marmoset
mona monkey
New World monkey
night monkey
Old World monkey
orang-utan
owl-faced monkey
patas monkey
proboscis monkey
rhesus monkey
saki
samango
siamang
spider monkey
squirrel monkey
talapoin
tamarin
titi
uakari
vervet
wanderoo
woolly monkey
woolly spider monkey

Moths

angle shades
atlas moth
bagworm
bogong
brimstone (moth)
brown-tail (moth)
buff-tip
burnet
burnished brass
cabbage moth
cecropia (moth)
cinnabar (moth)
clearwing (moth)
Clifden nonpareil
clothes moth
codling/codlin moth
common heath
corn borer
crescent
dagger
death's head hawkmoth
diamondback moth
drinker (moth)
dun-bar
eggar
emerald (moth)
emperor
ermine (moth)
festoon
flour moth
footman
forester
fox moth
garden carpet
garden tiger
geometer (moth)
geometrid
ghost moth
goat moth
gypsy moth
hawkmoth
heath
hooktip
hornet moth
io moth
Kentish moth
kitten
lackey (moth)
lappet (moth)
leaf miner
leaf roller
leopard moth
lobster moth
luna moth
magpie moth
meal moth
merveille du jour
minor
moon moth
Mother Shipton
noctuid
oak eggar
old lady
owlet
peach blossom
peppered moth
pine beauty
pink bollworm
plume moth
processionary (moth)
prominent (moth)
pug
puss moth
pyralid
rivulet
rustic
sallow
saturniid
shark (moth)
silk moth
silver-line
silver Y
snout (moth)
sphingid
swallow-tailed moth
swift (moth)
tabby
tapestry moth
thorn
tiger moth
tortrix (moth)
triangle
turnip moth
tussock moth
tussore moth
umber
underwing (moth)
vapourer (moth)
wainscot
wax moth
white spot
winter moth
yellow-tail (moth)
yellow underwing
yucca moth

Pigs

Breeds

Berkshire
British Lop
British Saddleback
Chester White
Duroc
Gloucester Old Spot
Hampshire
Landrace
Middle White
Oxford Sandy and Black
Pietrain
Poland China
Saddleback
Tamworth
Vietnamese Pot-Bellied
Welsh

Wild pigs

babirusa
bush pig
hog
peccary
razorback
warthog
wild boar

Rabbits and hares

angora
Arctic hare
Belgian hare
brown hare
chinchilla
cottontail
European rabbit
jackrabbit
mountain hare
pika
snowshoe hare

Reptiles *See also* **Snakes**

agama
alligator
alligator lizard
anole
axolotl
barking gecko
basilisk
bearded dragon
bearded lizard
blindworm
bloodsucker
box turtle
caiman
chameleon
chuckwalla
collared lizard
cooter
crocodile
diamondback terrapin
earless lizard
false gharial
fence lizard
flapshell
flying lizard
freshie
frilled lizard
Galapagos giant tortoise
galliwasp
gecko
gharial
giant tortoise
giant zonure
Gila monster
girdled lizard
glass lizard
goanna
green lizard
green turtle
hawksbill
horned toad
iguana
Jacky lizard
Komodo dragon
land mullet
leatherback
legless lizard
legless skink
leguan
lizard
loggerhead turtle
map turtle
marine iguana
matamata
moloch
monitor lizard
morocoy
mud turtle
mugger
musk turtle
night lizard
Nile crocodile
Nile monitor
padloper
painted turtle
perentie
pond turtle
racerunner
ridley turtle
rock lizard
saltwater lizard
sand lizard
scalyfoot
seps
shingleback
side-necked turtle
skink
slider
slow-worm
snake lizard
snapping turtle
softshell turtle
stinkpot turtle
sungazer
tegu
terrapin
tokay
tortoise
tuatara
turtle
twenty-four hours
viviparous lizard
wall lizard
whiptail
worm lizard
zonure

Rodents *See also* Squirrels

acouchi
agouti
bamboo rat
bandicoot rat
bank vole
beaver
black rat
brown rat
cane rat
capybara
cavy
chinchilla
climbing mouse
common rat
cotton rat
coypu
deer mouse
degu
desert rat
dormouse
field mouse
field vole
gerbil
gopher
grasshopper mouse
guinea pig
gundi
hamster
harvest mouse
hopping mouse
house mouse
hutia
jerboa
jird
jumping mouse
kangaroo mouse
kangaroo rat
lemming
mara
marmot
meadow vole
mole rat
mountain beaver
mouse
muskrat
naked mole rat
Norway rat
paca
pacarana
pine vole
pocket mouse
porcupine
pouched rat
rat
red-backed vole
rice rat
snow vole
spiny mouse
springhaas
springhare
steppe lemming
stick-nest rat
swamp rat
tuco-tuco
vesper rat
viscacha
vole
water rat
water vole
white-footed mouse
white mouse
wood mouse
woodrat

Seals

Baikal seal
bearded seal
common seal
crabeater seal
elephant seal
fur seal
grey seal
harbour seal
harp seal
hooded seal
leopard seal
monk seal
ringed seal
Ross seal
sea elephant
seal
sea lion
walrus
Weddell seal

Sharks

basking shark
blue shark
bonnethead
bramble shark
carpet shark
cat shark
cow shark
dogfish
frilled shark
great white shark
gummy
hammerhead
huss
mako
megamouth
nurse hound
nurse shark
porbeagle
requiem shark
sand shark
sea-angel
selachian
smooth hound
spur-dog
thresher
tiger shark
tope
whaler
whale shark
wobbegong/wobbegon

Sheep

Breeds

Abyssinian
Afrikander
Altai
Askanian
Australian Merino
Awassi
Berber
Bergamo
Beulah Speckled Face
Biella
Blackface
Blackhead Persian
Black Welsh Mountain
Blue-faced Leicester
Border Leicester
Boreray
Bosnian Mountain
Brazilian Woolless
Brecknock Hill Cheviot
British Blue du Maine
British Charollais
British Friesland
British Milksheep
British Oldenburg
British Texel
British Vendéen
Broadtail
Cambridge
Campanian Barbary
Cannock Chase
Castlemilk Moorit
Caucasian
Cheviot
Chios
Clun Forest
Colbred
Columbia
Corriedale
Cotswold
Dalesbred
Dartmoor
Derbyshire Gritstone
Devon Closewool
Devon Longwool
Dorper
Dorset Down
Dorset Horn
Dubrovnik
East Friesland
English Halfbred
English Longwool
Exmoor Horn
Finnish Landrace
French Blackheaded
Galway
Greek Zackel
Hampshire Down
Hebridean
Herdwick
Hexham Leicester
Hill Radnor
Icelandic
Île-de-France
Island Pramenka
Jacob
Karakachan
Karakul
Kent
Kerry Hill
Kivircik
Lacaune
Lacho
Lamon
Leicester
Lincoln Longwool
Llanwenog
Lleyn
Longwool
Lonk
Lourdes
Manech
Manx Loghtan
Masai
Masham
Merino
Mongolian
Mug
Mule
Norfolk Horn
North Country Cheviot
North Ronaldsay
Old Norwegian
Orkney
Oxford Down
Panama
Persian
Poll Dorset
Polwarth
Portland
Précoce
Radnor
Rambouillet
Red Karaman
Rhiw Hill
Romanov
Romeldale
Romney Marsh
Rouge de l'Ouest
Rough Fell
Ryeland
St. Kilda
Sardinian
Scottish Blackface
Scottish Halfbred
Shetland
Shropshire
Sicilian
Soay
South Devon
Southdown
South Wales Mountain
Spanish Merino
Suffolk
Swaledale
Swedish Landrace
Swiss White Alpine
Swiss White Mountain
Talavera
Targhee
Teeswater
Texel
Tibetan
Tsigai
Tyrol Mountain
Welsh Halfbred
Welsh Hill Speckled
Welsh Mountain
Welsh Mountain Badger-faced
Welsh Mule
Wensleydale
Whiteface Dartmoor
Whiteface Woodlands
Wicklow Mountain
Wiltshire Horn

Wild sheep

aoudad
argali
Barbary sheep
bharal
bighorn
blue sheep
Dall/Dall's sheep
mouflon
mountain sheep
urial
white sheep

Shells

abalone
angel wing
ark shell
auger
basket shell
bonnet
bubble shell
canoe shell
carpet shell
carrier shell
cask shell
chambered nautilus
chank
clam
coat-of-mail
cockle
cock's-comb oyster
conch
cone
cowrie
cup-and-saucer
date mussel
dog whelk
dove shell
drill
drupe
ear shell
fighting conch
fig shell
file shell
flamingo tongue
frog shell
furrow shell
gaper
giant clam
hard clam
harp
heart cockle
helmet
hoof shell
horn shell
horse mussel
jewel box
jingle shell
junonia
keyhole limpet
lima
limpet
lion's paw
lucine
marginella
mitre
money cowrie
moon shell
murex
mussel
nautilus
necklace shell
nerite
Noah's ark
nutmeg shell
nut shell
olive
ormer
otter shell
oyster
oyster drill
partridge shell
pearly nautilus
pelican's foot
pen shell
periwinkle
pheasant shell
piddock
puka (shell)
pyramid shell
quahog
queen scallop
razor shell
rock shell
saddle oyster
scallop
sea snail
slipper limpet
slit limpet
slit shell
spider conch
spindle shell
spire shell
staircase shell
sundial
sunset shell
tellin
thorny oyster
tiger cowrie
tooth shell
top shell
tower shell
triton
triton's trumpet
trough shell
trumpet shell
tulip shell
tun
turban
turkey wing
turret shell
tusk shell
umbrella shell
vase shell
venus
Venus shell/clam
violet sea snail
volute
wedge shell
wentletrap
whelk
wing oyster
winkle
worm shell
zebra mussel

Snakes

adder
Aesculapian snake
anaconda
asp
bandy-bandy
black mamba
blind snake
boa
boa constrictor
boomslang
brown snake
bull snake
bushmaster
carpet python
carpet snake
cerastes
coachwhip
cobra
colubrid
constrictor
copperhead
coral snake
corn snake
cottonmouth
death adder
diamondback (rattlesnake)
diamond python
dugite
egg-eating snake
Egyptian cobra
false coral snake
fer de lance
file snake
flowerpot snake
flying snake
Gaboon viper
garter snake
gopher snake
grass snake
green snake
hamadryad
highland moccasin
hognose snake
horned snake
indigo snake
keelback
king cobra
kingsnake
krait
mamba
massasauga
milk snake
night adder
pine snake
pipe snake
pit viper
puff adder
python
racer
rat snake
rattlesnake
reticulated python
rinkhals
rock python
rubber boa
Russell's viper
sea krait
sea snake
shieldtail snake
sidewinder
skaapsteker
smooth snake
spitting cobra
swamp snake
taipan
tiger snake
tree snake
viper
wart snake
water moccasin
water snake
whip snake
wolf snake
woma
worm snake

Spiders and other arachnids

baboon spider
beetle mite
bird-eating spider
black widow
button spider
camel spider
cardinal spider
chigger
cobweb spider
crab spider
diadem spider
false scorpion
funnel-web spider
harvestman
harvest mite
hunting spider
huntsman spider
itch mite
jockey spider
jumping spider
katipo
mite
money spider
mygalomorph
orb weaver
orb-web spider
raft spider
redback
red spider mite
retiary spider
scorpion
scorpion spider
solifuge
spider
spider mite
sun spider
tarantula
tick
trapdoor spider
varroa
violin spider
water scorpion
water spider
whip scorpion
white-tailed spider
wind scorpion
wolf spider
wood tick
zebra spider

Squirrels and related rodents

anomalure
chickaree
chipmunk
flying squirrel
giant squirrel
gopher
grey squirrel
groundhog
ground squirrel
marmot
mountain beaver
palm squirrel
petaurist
pocket gopher
prairie dog
red squirrel
scaly-tailed squirrel
souslik
sun squirrel
tree squirrel
woodchuck

Weasels and similar animals

badger
beech marten
civet
cusimanse
ermine
ferret
ferret-badger
fisher
fossa
genet
glutton
grison
hog badger
honey badger
kolinsky
linsang
marbled polecat
marten
meerkat
mink
mongoose
muishond
otter
palm civet
pine marten
polecat
ratel
sable
sea otter
skunk
stink badger
stoat
suricate
tayra
teledu
toddy cat
weasel
wolverine
zorilla

Whales and dolphins

Amazon dolphin
baleen whale
beaked whale
beluga
blue whale
boto/boutu
bottlenose dolphin
bottlenose whale
bowhead whale
cachalot
dusky dolphin
finback whale
fin whale
grampus
Greenland right whale
grey whale
humpback whale
killer whale
minke whale
narwhal
orca
pilot whale
porpoise
right whale
Risso's dolphin
river dolphin
rorqual
sei whale
sperm whale
spinner dolphin
toothed whale
tucuxi
whalebone whale
white-sided dolphin
white whale

Worms

acanthocephalan
acorn worm
annelid
arrow worm
ascarid
bamboo worm
beard worm
bladder worm
blood fluke
bloodworm
bootlace worm
brandling
bristle worm
catworm
chaetognath
dungworm
earthworm
eelworm
eye worm
fan worm
feather duster (worm)
filaria
fireworm
flatworm
fluke
gapeworm
gordian worm
Guinea worm
hairworm
heartworm
helminth
hookworm
horsehair worm
horseshoe worm
kidney worm
leech
liver fluke
lobworm
lugworm
lungworm
mesozoan
mopane worm
nematode (worm)
nemertean
nereid
oligochaete
paddle worm
palolo worm
parchment worm
peacock worm
peanut worm
phoronid
pinworm
platyhelminth
pognophoran
polychaete
pot worm
proboscis worm
pterobranch
ragworm
rainworm
redworm
rhombozoan
ribbon worm
roundworm
scale worm
sea mouse
serpulid
sipunculid
spiny-headed worm
spoonworm
straw worm
strongyle
tapeworm
thorny-headed worm
threadworm
tongue worm
toxocara
trematode
trichina
tube worm
tubifex
vinegar eel
whipworm
white worm

Male and female animals

Animal	Male	Female
antelope	buck	doe
badger	boar	sow
bear	boar	sow
bobcat	tom	lioness
buffalo	bull	cow
camel	bull	cow
caribou	stag	doe
cat	tom	queen
cattle	bull	cow
chicken	cock	hen
cougar	tom	lioness
coyote	dog	bitch
deer	stag	doe
dog	dog	bitch
donkey	jackass	jenny
duck	drake	duck
elephant	bull	cow
ferret	hob	gill
fish	cock	hen
fox	fox	vixen
giraffe	bull	cow
goat	billygoat	nannygoat
goose	gander	goose
hare	buck	doe
hartebeest	bull	cow
horse	stallion	mare
impala	ram	ewe
jackrabbit	buck	doe
kangaroo	buck	doe
leopard	leopard	leopardess
lion	lion	lioness
lobster	cock	hen

Animal	Male	Female
moose	bull	cow
peafowl	peacock	peahen
pheasant	cock	hen
pig	boar	sow
rhinoceros	bull	cow
seal	bull	cow
sheep	ram	ewe
swan	cob	pen
tiger	tiger	tigress
weasel	boar	cow
whale	bull	cow
wolf	dog	bitch
zebra	stallion	mare

Young animals

Young	Animal
calf	antelope/buffalo/camel/cattle/elephant/elk/giraffe/hartebeest/rhinoceros/seal/whale
chick	chicken/hawk/pheasant
colt	horse
cub	badger/bear/fox/leopard/lion/tiger/walrus/wolf
cygnet	swan
duckling	duck
eaglet	eagle
elver	eel
eyas	hawk
fawn	caribou/deer
filly	horse
foal	horse/zebra
fry	fish
gilt	pig
gosling	goose
joey	kangaroo/wallaby/possum
kid	goat/roedeer
kit	beaver/fox/weasel/ferret/mink
kitten	bobcat/cat/cougar/rabbit/skunk
lamb	sheep
leveret	hare
owlet	owl
parr	salmon
peachick	peafowl
pickerel	pike
piglet	pig
porkling	pig
pup	dog/wolf/seal/rat
puppy	dog/coyote
smolt	salmon
spiderling	spider
squab	pigeon
squeaker	pigeon
tadpole	frog/toad
whelp	dog/wolf

Collective names for animals

shrewdness of **apes**
herd/pace of **asses**
troop of **baboons**
cete of **badgers**
sloth of **bears**
swarm/drift/hive/erst of **bees**
flock/flight/pod of **birds**
herd/gang/obstinacy of **buffalo**
bellowing of **bullfinches**
drove of **bullocks**
army of **caterpillars**
clowder/glaring of **cats**
herd/drove of **cattle**
brood/clutch/peep of **chickens**
chattering of **choughs**
rag/rake of **colts**
covert of **coots**
herd of **cranes**
bask of **crocodiles**
murder of **crows**
litter of **cubs**
herd of **curlew**
herd/mob of **deer**
pack/kennel of **dogs**
school of **dolphins**
trip of **dotterel**
flight/dole/piteousness of **doves**
paddling of **ducks** (on water)
safe of **ducks** (on land)
fling of **dunlins**
herd/parade of **elephants**
herd/gang of **elk**
busyness of **ferrets**
charm of **finches**
shoal/run of **fish**
swarm/cloud of **flies**
skulk of **foxes**
gaggle of **geese** (on land)
skein/team/wedge of **geese** (in flight)
herd of **giraffes**
cloud of **gnats**
flock/herd/trip of **goats**
band of **gorillas**
pack/covey of **grouse**
down/mute/husk of **hares**
cast of **hawks**
siege of **herons**
bloat of **hippopotami**
drove/string/stud/team of **horses**
pack/cry/kennel of **hounds**
flight/swarm of **insects**
fluther/smack of **jellyfish**
mob/troop of **kangaroos**
kindle/litter of **kittens**
desert of **lapwings**
bevy/exaltation of **larks**
leap/lepe of **leopards**
pride/sawt of **lions**
tiding of **magpies**
sord/suit of **mallard**
stud of **mares**
richesse of **martens**
labour of **moles**
troop of **monkeys**
span/barren of **mules**
watch of **nightingales**
parliament/stare of **owls**
yoke of **oxen**
pandemonium of **parrots**
covey of **partridges**
muster of **peacocks**
muster/parcel/rookery of **penguins**
bevy/head of **pheasants**
kit of **pigeons** (in flight)
litter/herd of **pigs**
congregation/stand/wing of **plovers**
rush/flight of **pochards**
pod/school/herd/turmoil of **porpoises**
covey of **ptarmigan**
litter of **pups**
bevy/drift of **quail**
bury of **rabbits**
string of **racehorses**
unkindness of **ravens**
crash of **rhinoceros**
bevy of **roe deer**
parliament/building/rookery of **rooks**
hill of **ruffs**
pod/herd/rookery of **seals**
flock/herd/trip/mob of **sheep**
dopping of **sheldrake**
wisp/walk of **snipe**
host of **sparrows**
murmuration of **starlings**
flight of **swallows**
game/herd of **swans** (on land)
wedge of **swans** (in flight)
drift/herd/sounder of **swine**
spring of **teal**
knot of **toads**
hover of **trout**
rafter of **turkeys**
bale/turn of **turtles**
bunch/knob of **waterfowl**
school/herd/pod/gam of **whales**
company/trip of **wigeon**
sounder of **wild boar**
dout/destruction of **wild cats**
team of **wild ducks** (in flight)
bunch/trip/plump/knob of **wildfowl**
pack/rout of **wolves**
fall of **woodcock**
descent of **woodpeckers**
herd of **wrens**
zeal of **zebras**

Many of these are fanciful or humorous terms which probably never had any real currency but have been popularized in books such as *Sports and Pastimes of England* (1801) by Joseph Strutt.

Animals' homes

Animal	Home
ant	anthill
badger	sett/earth
bear	den
beaver	lodge
bee	beehive/apiary
bird	nest/aviary
cow	byre
dog	kennel
dove	dovecote
eagle	eyrie
fish	aquarium
fox	earth/hole/burrow
hare	form
hen	coop
horse	stable
lion	den
otter	holt
pig	sty
rabbit	burrow/warren
sheep	fold/pen
squirrel	drey
wasp	nest/vespiary

Architecture

Architectural terms *See also the other lists in this group.*

abacus
amphiprostyle
ancon
annulet
architrave
archivolt
astragal
astylar
atlas
baguette
bas-relief
beading
boss
buttress
campanile
capital
capstone
cartouche
caryatid
cavetto
clerestory
colonnade
column
conch
coping
corbel
cornice
cove
coving
cresting
crocket
crow steps
cruck
cupola
cusp
cusping
dado
decastyle
dentil
dipteral
dog-leg stair
dog-tooth
dome
dosseret
double-fronted
dripstone
echinus
egg and dart
embrasure
encrustation
entablature
entablement
entasis
entresol
epistyle
extrados
facade
fascia
fenestration
fillet
finial
flaunching
flute
flying buttress
frieze
frontispiece
gable
gambrel
gargoyle
groin
half-timbered
hammer beam
haunch
hexastyle
hipped roof
hood mould
hypaethral
hypostyle
hypotrachelium
inglenook
intercolumniation
intrados
jerkin head
keystone
king post
lacunar
lancet arch
lantern
linenfold
lintel
loggia
long-and-short work
lunette
machicolation
mansard
manteltree
mezzanine
moulding
mullion
obelisk
octastyle
octofoil
ogee
ogive
onion dome
pediment
pent roof
peripteral
peristyle
perron
pilaster
pillar
plinth
polychromy
porch
portico
prostyle
queen post
quoin
respond
reticulated
rib
rope-moulding
rustication
saddleback
scotia
scroll
scuncheon
sedilia
severy
socle
soffit
spandrel
spandrel wall
springer
squinch
stringboard
string course
stucco
stylobate
talon
tambour
telamon
tetrastyle
tie beam
tracery
transom
trefoil
truss
tympanum
vault
vaulting
vignette
volute
voussoir

Architectural styles

Art Deco
Art Nouveau
baroque
Bauhaus
Beaux Arts
brutalist
Byzantine
Cape Dutch
Carolingian
Churrigueresque
cinquecento
classical
collegiate Gothic
colonial
composite
Corinthian
Decorated
Doric
Early English
Edwardian
Elizabethan
Empire
Federation
flamboyant
functional
Georgian
Gothic
Gothic Revival
Graeco-Roman
Grecian
Greek Revival
international
Ionic
Islamic
Jacobean
mannerist
Manueline
medieval
modernist
Moorish
Moresque
Mozarabic
Mudejar
neoclassical
neo-Gothic
Norman
Palladian
Perpendicular
postmodernist
quattrocento
Queen Anne
rayonnant
Regency
Renaissance
rococo
Roman
Romanesque
Saxon
Spanish-Colonial
Spanish Mission
transitional
Tudor
Tudorbethan
Tuscan
Usonian
vernacular
Victorian Gothic

Homes

adobe
A-frame
apartment
back-to-back
barracks
bastide
bedsit
bedsitter
bed-sitting room
bi-level
black house
blockhouse
bungalow
cabin
caravan
casita
castle
chalet
chateau
condo
condominium
cottage
country house
crannog
dacha
deanery
detached house
donga
duplex
farmhouse
fibro
flat
flatlet
floatel
frame house
gîte
grange
hacienda
hermitage
hogan
homestead
hostel
hotel
house
houseboat
hovel
hut
igloo
jhuggi
lake dwelling
lodge
log cabin
longhouse
maisonette
manoir
manor
manse
mansion
messuage
mobile home
motel
mud hut
palace
park home
parsonage
penthouse
pied-à-terre
pile dwelling
prefab
presbytery
priory
ranch (house)
rancher
rath
rectory
rest home
riad
rondavel
semi
semi-detached house
shack
shanty
side split
single end
skerm
split
stately home
stilted house
studio flat
tenement
tent
tepee
terrace
terraced house
terramare
town house
trailer
tree house
tupik
two-up two-down
vicarage
villa
whare
wigwam
yurt

Rooms

anteroom
assembly room
atrium
attic
ballroom
basement
bathroom
bedchamber
bedroom
bedsit
bed-sitting room
boardroom
boiler room
boudoir
box room
breakfast room
buttery
card room
carrel
casemate
cell
cellar
changing room
chill-out room
classroom
cloakroom
common room
conference room
conservatory
consulting room
cutting room
darkroom
day room
decompression chamber
den
dinette
dining hall
dining room
dormitory
drawing room
dressing room
dungeon
echo chamber
edit suite
engine room
family room
fitting room
Florida room
foyer
front room
gallery
garret
gas chamber
gatehouse
green room
guardroom
guest room
gunroom
hall
kitchen
kitchenette
landing
larder
lavatory
lecture room
library
living room
lobby
locker room
loft
loggia
loo
lounge
lumber room
meeting room
morning room
nursery
office
orderly room
oubliette
pantry
parlour
playroom
presence chamber
pump room
reception room
recreation room
restroom
robing room
rumpus room
sacristy
salon
saloon
sanatorium
schoolroom
scriptorium
scullery
sickbay
sickroom
sitting room
smoking room
snug
solarium
spare room
stateroom
still room
stockroom
storeroom
studio
study

study-bedroom
sun lounge
tack room
tambour
taproom
toilet
torture chamber
utility room
vestiary
vestibule
waiting room
ward
winter garden
withdrawing room
workroom

Windows

arrow slit
bay window
bow window
bullseye
casement
Catherine wheel
clerestory window
compass window
deadlight
dormer window
double-hung window
embrasure
eyelet
fanlight
fenestella
French window
gable window
garret window
grisaille
guichet
Jesse window
lancet window
lattice window
leaded light
lucarne
lunette
mullioned window
oculus
oeil-de-boeuf
opera window
oriel window
oval window
Palladian window
picture window
porthole
quarter-light
roof light
rose window
roundel
sash window
sidelight
skylight
squint
stained-glass window
storm window
top light
transom window
viewport
wheel window

Parts of a theatre

acting area
aisle
apron (stage)
auditorium
backstage
balcony
the boards
box
box office
bridge
catwalk
circle
coulisse
curtain
cut drop
cyclorama
dais
dress circle
dressing room
drop curtain
fire curtain
the flies
floats
fly gallery
fly tower
footlights
forestage
foyer
front of house
gallery
the gods
green room
gridiron
house lights
iron
lighting gallery
loge
mezzanine
orchestra pit
orchestra stalls
parquet
parterre
pass door
picture-frame stage
pit
prompt box
proscenium
proscenium arch
proscenium stage
revolve
revolving stage
safety curtain
scene dock
set
skene
stage
stage door
stalls
tableau curtains
tabs
thrust stage
trap
upper circle
upstage
velarium
vomitorium
vomitory
wings

Parts of a church

aisle
ambo
ambulatory
antechapel
apse
atrium
aumbry
baptistery/baptistry
belfry
buttress
chancel
chantry
chapel
chevet
choir
choir stall
ciborium
clerestory
confessional
crossing
crypt
dome
fenestella
flèche
flying buttress
font
galilee
gallery
Gospel side
high altar
iconostasis
Jesse window
Lady chapel
Lady altar
loft
naos
narthex
nave
organ loft
parclose
parvis/parvise
pew
piscina
predella
presbytery
prothesis
pulpit
retrochoir
rood loft
rood screen
sacrarium
sacristy
sanctuary
sedilia
spire
squint
stall
steeple
tabernacle
tambour
tower
transept
traverse
tribune
triforium
undercroft
vault
vestibule
vestry

Art

Art schools and movements

abstract expressionism
Aesthetic Movement
Art Deco
art nouveau
Arte Povera
Arts and Crafts Movement
Ashcan School
avant-garde
Barbizon School
baroque
Blaue Reiter
Bloomsbury Group
Camden School
chinoiserie
classicism
constructivism
cubism
Dada
Danube School
De Stijl
Euston Road
expressionism
fauvism
Florentine school
futurism
Graecism
Grand Manner
Group of Seven
High Renaissance
Impressionism
International Gothic
intimisme
Jugendstil
magic realism
Mannerism
metaphysical painting
minimalism
modernism
Nabi Group
naive art
naturalism
Nazarenes
neoclassicism
neo-expressionism
neo-Impressionism
neoplasticism
neo-realism
neoromanticism
Neue Sachlichkeit
Norwich School
op art
Orphism
performance art
photorealism
plein-air painting
pop art
post-Impressionism
postmodernism
Precisionism
Pre-Raphaelitism
primitive art
Purism
Rayonism
realism
Renaissance art
rococo
romanticism
seicento
Sezession
Sienese school
socialist realism
social realism
Sturm und Drang
suprematism
surrealism
symbolism
Synchromism
tenebrism
transavant-garde
ukiyo-e
Umbrian school
Venetian school
verism
Vorticism

Art techniques and media

See also **Painting techniques and methods**

airbrushing
aquatint
batik
brass rubbing
calligraphy
cartooning
ceramics
cloisonné
collage
collotype
colour print
Conté
divisionism
drawing
dry-point
enamelling
engineering drawing
engraving
etching
fresco
frottage
grotesque
illumination
intaglio
lino cut
lithography
lost wax
marbling
marquetry
metalwork
mezzotint
montage
mosaic
painting
pastel
photography
photogravure
photomontage
photoprint
screen printing
sculpture
scumbling
sgraffito
silk-screen printing
sketching
soft-ground etching
stained glass
tachism
tapestry
technical drawing
trompe l'œil
wood carving
woodcut
wood engraving
zincography

Painting techniques and methods

acrylic painting
action painting
aquarelle
chiaroscuro
colour-field painting
colour wash
divisionism
encaustic
finger-painting
genre painting
gouache
grisaille
grotesque
impasto
miniature painting
mural painting
oil painting
pointillism
polychromy
sand painting
scumbling
secco
silk painting
spray-can painting
sumi-e
tempera
tenebrism
watercolour
Yamato-e

Types and forms of painting

altarpiece
annunciation
capriccio
cave painting
cityscape
cloudscape
conversation piece
crucifixion
diorama
diptych
Ecce Homo
écorché
fête galante
fresco
half-length
icon
kakemono
landscape
miniature
mural
nativity
nocturne
Noli Me Tangere
nude
old master
panorama
paysage
pietà
polyptych
portrait
predella
retable
riverscape
seascape
skyscape
still life
tondo
townscape
triptych
trompe l'œil
vanitas
wall painting

Body

Bones

astragalus
calcaneum (*or* heel bone)
capitate
carpal
carpus
cervical vertebrae (7)
cheekbone
clavicle (*or* collarbone)
coccygeal vertebrae (4, fused, forming the coccyx)
concha
costa
cranium
cuboid
cuneiform bones
ethmoid
femur (*or* thigh bone)
fibula
floating rib
frontal bone
hamate
humerus
hyoid
ilium
incus (*or* anvil)
innominate bone
ischium
jawbone
lacrimal
lumbar vertebrae (5)
lunate bone
malleus (*or* hammer)
mandible
maxilla
metacarpal
metatarsal
navicular bone
occipital bone
palatine bone
parietal bone
patella (*or* kneecap)
pelvis
phalanx
pisiform bone
pubis
rachis
radius
rib
sacral vertebrae (5, fused)
sacrum
scaphoid
scapula (*or* shoulder blade)
sesamoid bone
skull
sphenoid
spinal column
spine (*or* backbone)
stapes (*or* stirrup)
sternum (*or* breastbone)
talus (*or* ankle bone)
tarsal
tarsus
temporal bone
thoracic vertebrae (12)
tibia (*or* shin bone)
trapezium
trapezoid
triquetral
ulna
vertebra
vertebral column
vomer
zygomatic bone

Parts of the ear

auditory canal
auditory nerve
auricle *or* pinna
basilar membrane
cochlea
eardrum *or* tympanic membrane
endolymph
Eustachian tube
hair cell
incus *or* anvil
inner ear
malleus *or* hammer
middle ear
organ of Corti
outer ear
perilymph
saccule
semicircular canal
stapes *or* stirrup
tectorial membrane
utricle
vestibule

Parts of the eye

aqueous humour
blind spot
central retinal artery
central retinal vein
choroid
ciliary body
cone
conjunctiva
cornea
dilator muscle
extrinsic muscle
eyeball
eyelash
eyelid
fovea
iris
lens
limbus
optic foramen
optic nerve
orbit
pupil
retina
rod
sclera
sinus venosus sclerae
stroma
suspensory ligament
tarsal plate
tear (*or* lacrimal) glands
vitreous humour
zonular ligament

Types of tooth

bicuspid
canine
cuspid
eye tooth
incisor
milk tooth
molar
permanent tooth
premolar
primary tooth
tricuspid
wisdom tooth

Glands

adrenal gland
apocrine gland
Bartholin's gland
Brunner's gland
buccal gland
corpus luteum
Cowper's gland
ductless gland
eccrine gland
endocrine gland
exocrine gland
gastric gland
islets of Langerhans
lacrimal gland
Lieberkühn's gland
liver
mammary gland
meibomian gland
ovary
pancreas
parathyroid gland
parotid gland
pineal gland
pituitary gland
preputial gland
prostate gland
salivary gland
sebaceous gland
sublingual gland
submandibular/submaxillary gland
sweat gland
testis
thyroid gland

Parts of the heart

aortic valve
atrium
epicardium
mitral valve
myocardium
pericardium
pulmonary artery
pulmonary vein
semilunar valve
sino-atrial node
tricuspid valve
upper chamber
vena cava
ventricle
ventricular septum

Muscles

Muscle	Location
biceps	arm
buccinator	cheek
deltoid	shoulder
detrusor	bladder
digastric	jaw
gastrocnemius	leg
gluteus	buttock
gluteus maximus	buttock
gracilis	leg
iliacus	pelvis/groin
intercostal	ribs
latissimus	back
masseter	cheek/jaw
obturator	pelvis
opponent muscle	hand
pectoral	chest
peroneal muscle	leg
psoas	spine/groin
quadriceps	leg
rectus (abdominis)	abdomen
rhomboideus	shoulder
sartorius	leg
scalenus	neck/ribs
soleus	leg
splenius	neck/back
temporalis	jaw
teres	shoulder/arm
trapezius	neck/shoulders
triceps	arm

Veins and arteries

aorta
axillary artery
axillary vein
azygos vein
basilic vein
brachial artery
brachial vein
carotid artery
cephalic artery
cephalic vein
coeliac artery
coronary artery
crural artery
crural vein
cubital vein
digital artery
digital vein
dorsal metatarsal artery
dorsal venous arch
femoral artery
femoral vein
gastric artery
gastroepiploic vein
hepatic artery
hepatic portal vein
iliac artery
iliac vein
inferior vena cava
innominate artery
innominate vein
jugular vein
long thoracic artery
median cubital vein
(inferior/ superior) mesenteric artery
(inferior/ superior) mesenteric vein
ovarian artery
ovarian vein
palmar arch
palmar network
peroneal artery
plantar artery
popliteal artery
popliteal vein
portal vein
pulmonary artery
pulmonary vein
radial artery
renal artery
renal vein
(great/short) saphenous vein
splenic artery
subclavian artery
subclavian vein
superior vena cava
suprarenal vein
testicular artery
testicular vein
tibial artery
ulnar artery
ulnar vein
vena cava
vertebral artery

Early humans

Aegyptopithecus
Australopithecus
Boxgrove man
Cro-Magnon man
Gigantopithecus
Heidelberg man
Homo erectus
Homo habilis
Homo sapiens
Java man
Kabwe man
Lucy
Neanderthal man
Nutcracker man
Paranthropus
Peking man
Pithecanthropus
Proconsul
protohuman
Ramapithecus
Sinanthropus
Zinjanthropus

Clothes

Coats, cloaks, and jackets

achkan
Afghan coat
anorak
baju
balmacaan
Barbour (*trademark*)
bedjacket
biker jacket
blanket coat
blazer
blouson
body warmer
bolero
bomber jacket
British warm
Burberry (*trademark*)
burka
burnous/ burnoose
bush jacket
cagoule/kagoul
cape
capote
Capuchin
car coat
chlamys
coatee
coat of mail
combat jacket
cope
covert coat
cowl
Crombie coat
cutaway
dinner jacket (DJ)
djellaba/jellaba
dolman
domino
donkey jacket
doublet
dreadnought
dress coat
duffel coat
dustcoat
duster (coat)
Eisenhower jacket
Eton jacket
flak jacket
fleece
flying jacket
frock coat
fur coat
gaberdine/ gabardine
gi
gilet
greatcoat
hacking jacket
haik/haick
haori
happi (coat)
Harrington
hoody
hunting jacket
jean jacket
jerkin
jibba/djibba
jumper
kebaya
kirtle
leather jacket
letter jacket
loafer
loden
lumberjacket
mac
macfarlane
mackinaw
mackintosh/ macintosh
mandarin jacket
manteau
mantle
mantlet
Mao jacket
matinee coat
maud
mess jacket
mink
monkey jacket
morning coat
Mother Hubbard
mozzetta
Nehru jacket
Norfolk jacket
nor'wester
oilskin
opera cloak
overcoat
pakamac
pallium
parka
pea jacket
pelerine
pelisse
peplum
pilot jacket
poncho
Puffa (jacket) (*Brit. trademark*)
raglan
raincoat
rainproof
redingote
reefer (jacket)
riding jacket
sack coat
safari jacket
sarape/serape
scapular
shawl
sheepskin
shell jacket
sherwani
shooting coat
shooting jacket
shrug
slicker
smoking jacket
spencer
sportcoat
sports coat/ jacket
suba
surcoat
surtout
swagger coat
swing coat
tabard
tailcoat
tent coat
tippet
topcoat
trench coat
tunic
tux
tuxedo
ulster
undercoat
waistcoat
waterproof
waxed jacket
windbreaker (*US trademark*)
windcheater
workcoat
wrap

Dresses

baby-doll dress
backless dress
ballgown
button-through dress
chemise
cheongsam
coat dress
cocktail dress
dinner gown
dirndl
Empire line dress
evening gown
gymslip
kaftan
kimono
maternity dress
maxidress
minidress
Mother Hubbard
muumuu
overdress
pinafore dress
polonaise
pouf dress
sack dress
sari
sarong
shamma
sheath dress
shift dress
shirt dress
shirtwaister
short waist
skimmer
slip dress
smock
strapless dress
sundress
tea gown
tent dress
tube dress
wedding dress
yukata

Footwear

alpargatas
ankle boots
Arctics
babouches
ballet shoes
balmorals
beetle-crushers
Birkenstocks (*trademark*)
bluchers
boot
bootees
bovver boots
brogans
brogues
brothel creepers
buckskins
buskins
carpet slippers
chappals
Chelsea boots
cleats
clogs
combat boots
court shoes
cowboy boots
crepe-soled shoes
Cuban heels
daps
deck shoes
Derbies
desert boots
Dr Martens (DMs) (*trademark*)
elevator shoes
espadrilles
field boots
flip-flops
galoshes
ghillies
gumboots
half-boots
Hessian boots
high heels
high-lows
high-tops
hobnail boots
huaraches
jackboots
jandals (*NZ trademark*)
jelly shoes
kitten heels
kletterschuhe
lace-ups
loafers
Mary Janes
moccasins
moon boots
mukluks
mules
napoleons
opankas
overboots
overshoes
Oxfords
pattens
peep-toes
penny loafers
platforms
plimsolls
pumps
rubbers
sabots
saddle shoes
sandals
shoe
shoepacks
slingbacks
slip-ons
slippers
sneakers
snow boots
snowshoes
spikes
step-ins
stilettos
stogies
tap shoes
tennis shoe
thigh boots
thongs
top boots
track shoes
trainers
Turkish slippers
waders
walking boots/shoes
wedges
wedgies
wellington boots
winkle-pickers
zoris

Headgear

agal
aigrette
Akubra (*trademark*)
Alice band
amice
babushka
balaclava
balmoral
bandeau
baseball cap
beanie
bearskin
beaver hat
beret
billycock
biretta
boater
bobble hat
bonnet
Borsalino
bowler hat
bucket hat
busby
calash
cap
caubeen
caul
chapeau
chapeau-bras
chaplet
cheese-cutter cap
circlet
cloche
cloth cap
cocked hat
cockscomb
coif
coolie hat
coonskin hat
coronal
coronet
cowl
crash helmet
crown
deerstalker
derby
diadem
doek
Dolly Varden hat
do-rag
dunce's cap
Dutch cap
earmuffs
fedora
fez
fillet
flat cap
forage cap
frontlet
garland
garrison cap
gibus hat
gimme cap
glengarry
hairband
hairnet
hard hat
hat
headband
headscarf
headtie
helmet
high hat
hijab
homburg
hood
jester's cap
jockey cap
Juliet cap
Kangol (*trademark*)
keffiyeh
kepi
kippa
leghorn hat
lum hat
mantilla
mitre
mob cap
mortar board
mutch
nightcap
opera hat
pagri
panama
peaked cap
petasus
Phrygian bonnet
picture hat
pillbox
pixie hat
poke bonnet
pork-pie hat
puggaree
rebozo
sailor hat
shako
shapka
shemagh
shovel hat
skimmer
skullcap
slouch hat
snap-brim hat
snood
sola topi
sombrero
sou'wester
square
Stetson (*US trademark*)
stocking cap
stovepipe hat
sun bonnet
sun hat
sun helmet
taenia
taj
tam
tammy
tam-o'-shanter
tarboosh
ten-gallon hat
terai
tiara
tignon
top hat
topi
topper
toque
tricorne
trilby
triple crown
tuque
turban
veil
velour
watch cap
wideawake
wimple
wreath
yarmulke
zucchetto

Pullovers

cardigan
Cowichan sweater
crew neck
gansey
golfer
guernsey
jersey
jumper
maillot
polo neck
roll-neck
shrug
Siwash sweater
skinny-rib
slipover
sloppy joe
sweater
sweatshirt
turtleneck
V-neck
woolly

Shirts

aloha shirt
blouse
banyan
boiled shirt
button-down
choli
dashiki
dress shirt
evening shirt
grandad shirt
guayabera
hair shirt
kaftan
kurta
long-sleeved shirt
middy blouse
nightshirt
olive-drab shirt
overblouse
overshirt
plastron
polo shirt
sark
short-sleeved shirt
skivvy
smock
sports shirt
sweatshirt
tee
T-shirt

Skirts

A-line skirt
ballet skirt
crinoline
dirndl
divided skirt
filibeg
flared skirt
full skirt
fustanella
gathered skirt
ghaghra
gored skirt
grass skirt
hobble skirt
hoop skirt
hula skirt
kilt
lungi
maxi
midi
mini
miniskirt
overskirt
pencil skirt
piupiu
pleated skirt
puffball skirt
rah-rah skirt
sarong
skort
slit skirt
sports skirt
straight skirt
tennis skirt
tutu
underskirt
wrap-around skirt

Ties

ascot (tie)
bandanna
black tie
bolo tie
bootlace tie
bow tie
cravat
dicky bow
foulard
four-in-hand
kipper tie
neckerchief
old school tie
stock
string tie
white tie
Windsor tie

Trousers

baggies
bags
bell-bottoms
Bermuda shorts
bloomers
board shorts
breeches
breeks
buckskins
capri pants
cargo pants
carpenter trousers
chaparajos/chaps
chinos
churidars
cigarette pants
clamdiggers
combat trousers
cords/corduroys
culottes
cut-offs
cycling shorts
denims
dhoti
drabs
drainpipes
drawstring trousers
ducks

dungarees
flannels
flares
galligaskins
gharara
gym pants
hakama
harem pants
hip-huggers
hipsters
hot pants
jeans
jodhpurs
joggers
jogging pants
khakis
knee breeches
knickerbockers
kuccha
lederhosen
leggings
loons
moleskins
nankeens
overtrousers
Oxford bags
palazzo pants
pantaloons
pedal pushers
pegtops
plus fours
pyjama
riding breeches
salopettes
salwar/shalwar
sharara
shorts
short trousers
ski pants
skort
slacks
slim jims
slops
stirrup pants
sweatpants
toreador pants
Turkish trousers
velveteens
zouaves

Underwear

bikini briefs
bloomers
bodice
body
body stocking
boxer shorts
bra
brassiere
briefs
BVDs (*trademark*)
camiknickers
camisole
chemise
chemisette
choli
chuddies
combination
combs
corselette
corset
crinoline
Directoire drawers
drawers
farthingale
fleshings
foundation garment
French knickers
frillies
girdle
G-string
hold-ups
jockey shorts
jocks
jockstrap
kecks
knickers
liberty bodice
long johns
maillot
Mother Hubbard
nylons
pantalettes
panties
pants
panty girdle
pantyhose
petticoat
posing pouch
roll-on
scanties
semmit
shift
shorts
skivvy
slip
spencer
stays
string vest
suspender belt
suspenders
tanga (briefs)
T-back
teddy
thermals
thong
tights
underpants
undershirt
undershorts
undervest
underwire
union suit
vest
waspie
Y-fronts (*trademark*)

Dance

Dances

allemande
Apache
ballet
ballroom
barn dance
basse danse
beguine
belly dance
black bottom
body popping
bolero
boogaloo
boogie
bop
bossa nova
Boston
bourrée
branle
break-dancing
buck-and-wing
bunny hug
cachucha
cakewalk
cancan
capoeira
carioca
ceroc
cha-cha
cha-cha-cha
chaconne
character dance
charleston
circle dance
clog dance
conga
contradance
contredanse
corroboree
Cossack dance
cotillion
country dance
courante
csardas
cueca
cumbia
Dashing White Sergeant
devil dance
disco
do-si-do
double shuffle
ecossaise
eightsome reel
excuse-me
fan dance
fandango
farandole
farruca
flamenco
fling
folk dance
formation dancing
foxtrot
frug
galliard
gallopade
galop
gavotte
Gay Gordons
gigue
gogo dancing
goombay
gopak
habanera
haka
hay
(Helston) floral dance
(Helston) furry
Highland fling
hoedown
hokey-cokey
hora
hornpipe
hula-hula
hully gully
hustle
Irish jig
Irish reel
jaleo
jazz dance
jig
jitterbug
jive
jota
juba
Kathak
Kathakali
kazachoc
kolo
kwela
lambada
Lambeth Walk
lancers
ländler
lap dancing
limbo
Lindy Hop
lion dance
Macarena
Madison
malagueña
mambo
mashed potato
maxixe
maypole dance
mazurka
merengue
Mexican hat
military two-step
minuet
moonstomp
moonwalk
morris dance
mosh
musette
nautch
old-time
one-step
palais glide
pantsula
pas de deux
pas de quatre
pas de trois
paso doble
passepied
pas seul
pata-pata
Paul Jones
pavane
pole dancing
polka
polonaise
quadrille
quickstep
rain dance
reel
rigadoon
ring-shout
robotic dancing
rock and roll
ronde
round dance
roundelay
rumba
sakkie-sakkie
salsa
saltarello
samba
saraband
seguidilla
sequence dance
shag
shake
Shango
shimmy
shuffle
siciliano/siciliana
Sir Roger de Coverley
skank
slam dance
snake dance
soft-shoe shuffle
square dance
stomp
strathspey
strip the willow
strut
sun dance
sword dance
sytarki
tambourin
tango
tap dance
tarantella
tickey-draai
torch
turkey trot
twist
twosome reel
two-step
veleta
vogueing
volta
waltz
war dance
Watusi
zambra
zapateado

Ballet steps and positions

arabesque
assemblé
attitude
balancé
ballon
balloné
ballotté
battement
battement frappé
battement tendu
batterie
bourrée
brisé
brisé volé
cabriole
chaîné
changement (de pieds)
chassé
dégagé
développé
écarté
échappé
elevation
enchaînement
entrechat
fifth position
first position
fondu
fouetté
fourth position
frappé
glissade
glissé
grand battement
grand batterie
grand jeté
jeté
pas de basque
pas de bourrée
pas de chat
pas de cheval
pas de deux
petit battement
petit batterie
petit jeté
piqué
pirouette
plié
pointe work
port de bras
relevé
retiré
rond de jambe à terre
rond de jambe en l'air
sauté
second position
sissonne
soubresaut
temps
temps levé
third position
tour en l'air

Drinks

Alcoholic drinks *See also* **Beers, Wine and grape varieties, Fortified and dessert wines, Cocktails, Whiskies**

absinthe
advocaat
aguardiente
alcopop
amaretto
anisette
applejack
aquavit
Armagnac
arrack/arak
bourbon
brandy
cachaca
Calvados
cassis
champagne
chartreuse
cherry brandy
cider
cognac
crème de cacao
crème de menthe
curaçao
fine champagne
fraise
framboise
genever
gin
ginger wine
goldwasser
grappa
Hollands
hydromel
kirsch
koumiss
kümmel
kvass
liqueur
makkoli
maraschino
marc
mead
mescal
metheglin
noyau
ouzo
pacharán
palm wine
pastis
perry
pisco
pombe
port
poteen
pulque
raki
ratafia
reposado
rum
sake
sambuca
schnapps
scrumpy
sercial
shochu
slivovitz
sloe gin
tafia
tej
tequila
triple sec
vermouth
vodka
witblits

Beers

ale
barley wine
bitter
bock
brown ale
cask beer
cask-conditioned beer
chicha
craft beer
draught beer
gueuze
heavy
ice beer
India pale ale (IPA)
keg beer
lager
Lambic
light ale
lite
microbrew
mild
milk stout
pale ale
Pils
Pilsner/Pilsener
porter
Rauchbier
real ale
shandy
small beer
spruce beer
stout
top-fermented beer
wheat beer

Wine and grape varieties *See also* **Fortified and dessert wines**

White wines and grapes

Aligoté
Asti
Auslese
Barsac
Beerenauslese
Blanc de blancs
Blanc Fumé
Bourgogne Blanc
Bucelas
Burgundy
Catawba
Cava
Chablis
Champagne
Chardonnay
Chasselas
Chenin Blanc
Clairette
Colombard
Condrieu
Crémant
Eiswein
Entre-Deux-Mers
Frascati
Furmint
Gavi
Gewürztraminer
Graves
Grüner Veltliner
Hárslevelü
Heuriger
Hock
Johannisberg
Jurançon
Kabinett
Kerner
Liebfraumilch
Lutomer Riesling
Mâcon
Mâcon Villages
Malvasia Bianca
Malvoisie
Manseng
Marsanne
Mauzac
Meursault
Minervois
Montrachet
Morio-Muskat
Moselle
Müller-Thurgau *or* Rivaner
Muscadelle
Muscadet
Muscat Blanc
Muscat d'Alexandrie
Muscatel
Niersteiner
Orvieto
Palomino
Pedro Ximenez
Piesporter
Pinot Blanc
Pinot Grigio
Pouilly-Fuissé
Pouilly-Fumé
Retsina
Riesling
Rioja
Roussette
Rueda
sack
Sancerre
Saumur
Sauvignon
Scheurebe
Scuppernong
Sekt
Sémillon
Sercial
Seyval Blanc
Soave
Spätlese
Spumante
Steen
Sylvaner
Symphony
Tocai-Friulano
Tokay
Traminer
Trebbiano
Trockenbeerenauslese
Verdejo
Verdelho
Verdello
Verdicchio
Verduzzo
Vermentino
Vernaccia
Vernaccia di San Gimignano
Villard
Vinho Verde
Viognier
Viura
Vouvray
Welschriesling *or* Olasz Rizling *or* Laski Rizling

Red wines and grapes

Aleatico
Amarone
Aramon
Bandol
Banyuls
Barbaresco
Barbera
Bardolino
Barolo
Beaujolais
Beaune
Blauer Portugieser
Blaufränkisch/Kékfrankos
Bourgogne Rouge
Bourgueil
Brouilly
Brunello de Montalcino
Bull's Blood
Burgundy
Cabernet Franc
Cabernet Sauvignon
Cahors
Carema
Carignan
Chianti
Cinsault
claret
Concord
Corvina
Côtes du Rhône
Crozes-Hermitage
Dão
Dolcetto
Faugères
Fitou
Fleurie
Gaillac
Gamay
Gattinara
Gevrey-Chambertin
Gigondas
Graves
Grenache
Grignolino
Lambrusco
Malbec
Malvasia
Malvoisie Rouge
Mammolo
Mandelaria
Manseng
Margaux
Médoc
Merlot
Meunier
Montepulciano
Mourvèdre
Nebbiolo
Negroamoro
Nuits St George
Pauillac
Pinot Noir
Pinotage
Pomerol
Pommard
Rioja
Rofosco
Saint-émilion
Saint-Estèphe
Sangiovese
Shiraz/Syrah
Tempranillo
Valdepeñas
Valpolicella
Vino Nobile di Montepulciano
Zinfandel
Zweigelt *or* Blauer Zweigelt

Rosé wines

Rosé d'Anjou
Rosé de Syrah
Tavel

Fortified and dessert wines

Bual
canary wine
Grenache
hanepoot
jerepigo
Madeira
malmsey
Marsala
Monbazillac
moscato
muscat
Muscat de Beaumes-de-Venise
muscatel
palomino
Sauternes
Sercial
Tarragona
Verdelho
vin de paille
vin santo

Types of port

crusted
ruby
tawny
vintage

Types of sherry

amontillado
fino
manzanilla
oloroso

Wine bottles

Bottle	Capacity (normal bottles)
magnum	2
jeroboam	4
rehoboam	6
methuselah	8
salmanazar	12
balthazar	16
nebuchadnezzar	20

Cocktails and mixed drinks

Alcoholic

Alaska
Astoria
bee's kiss
Bellini
black velvet
Bloody Friday
Bloody Mary
brandy Alexander
Bronx
Broughton punch
Buck's Fizz
bullshot
caipirinha
Caruso
Castro
champagne cocktail
cobbler
Collins fizz
Collins sour
Copenhagen
cosmopolitan
Cuba libre
Cuban Island
daiquiri
Dom Pedro
egg-flip
egg-nog
El Diablo
Gaelic coffee
Gibson
gimlet
gin and it
gin and tonic (G and T)
gin sling
glögg
gloom raiser
Harvey Wallbanger
highball
horse's neck
Irish coffee
James Bond
John Collins
Kir
Kir royale
Long Island iced tea
mai tai
manhattan
margarita
Martini (*trademark*)
Mary Pickford
Metropolitan
mimosa
mint julep
mojito
monkey gland
moose milk
Moscow mule
negroni
New England iced tea
old-fashioned
orange blossom
pina colada
pink gin
pink lady
planter's punch
Presidente
Prince of Wales
punch
rattlesnake
red-eye
rickey
Rob Roy
rum and black
rusty nail
salty dog
sangria
Sazarac
screwdriver
sea breeze
September morn
Shirley Temple
sidecar
Singapore sling
snakebite
snowball
spritzer
stinger
swizzle
tequila slammer
tequila sunrise
Tom and Jerry
Tom Collins
whisky mac
whisky sour
White Lady
White Russian
yellow bird
yellow fever
zombie

Non-alcoholic

mud
prairie oyster
St Clements
Virgin Mary
zombie

Whiskies

blended whisky
bourbon
corn whisky
grain whisky
Irish whiskey
malt (whisky)
rye (whisky)
Scotch (whisky)
single malt (whisky)
sour mash (whiskey)
vatted malt (whisky)

Non-alcoholic drinks *See also* Cocktails, Teas, Coffee drinks

Water or Water-based

barley water
bitter lemon
carbonated water
cherryade
citron pressé
club soda (*trademark*)
coffee
cola
cordial
cream soda
crush
dandelion and burdock
fruit juice
fruit tea
ginger ale
ginger beer
herbal tea/ infusion
horchata
iced tea
isotonic drink
lemonade
lemon tea
limeade
maté
mineral water
orangeade
orgeat
prairie oyster
pressé
root beer
St Clements
sarsaparilla
seltzer water
sherbet
soda water
sports drink
spring water
squash
tea
tisane
tonic water
Vichy water

Milk or milk-based

buttermilk
cocoa
drinking chocolate
hot chocolate
ice milk
lassi
malted milk
milkshake
smoothie
soya milk

Teas

Assam
black tea
bohea
bush tea
camomile tea
Ceylon
China
congou
Darjeeling
Earl Grey
fruit tea
green tea
gunpowder tea
herbal tea
hyson
iced tea
Indian
jasmine tea
Keemun
Labrador tea
Lapsang Souchong
lemon tea
maté
mint tea
oolong
orange pekoe
pekoe
peppermint tea
post-and-rail tea
pouchong
redbush tea
rooibos tea
rosehip tea
Russian tea
sage tea
souchong
tilleul
tisane
yerba buena
yerba maté

Coffee drinks

café au lait
café noir
caffè latte
caffè macchiato
cappuccino
decaffeinated coffee
drip coffee
espresso
filter coffee
Gaelic coffee
Greek coffee
instant coffee
Irish coffee
latte
latte macchiato
lungo
mocha
mochaccino
percolated (*or* perked) coffee
Turkish coffee

Fashion

Colours

almond
almond green
amaranth
amber
amethyst
anthracite
apple green
apricot
aqua
aquamarine
ash blonde
aubergine
auburn
avocado
azure
baby blue
baby pink
bay
beige
biscuit
bisque
bistre
black
blaze
blonde
blood-red
blue
blush
bottle green
brindle/brindled
bronze
brown
bubblegum pink
buff
burgundy
burnt ochre
burnt sienna
burnt umber
buttermilk
butternut
cadmium yellow
café au lait
Cambridge blue
camel
canary yellow
candy-apple red
caramel
cardinal red
carmine
carnation
carnelian
carrot
celadon
cerise
cerulean
champagne
charcoal
chartreuse
cherry
chestnut
chocolate
cinnabar
cinnamon
citron
clair-de-lune
claret
cobalt blue
cocoa
coffee
Copenhagen blue
copper
coral
cornflower blue
cream
crimson
cyan
cyclamen
daffodil
damask
damson
dove
drab
duck-egg blue
dun
eau de Nil
ebony
ecru
eggshell
electric blue
emerald
fallow
fawn
flame
flesh
fuchsia
gamboge
gentian
ginger
gold
green
greige
grenadine
grey
gunmetal
hazel
heather
heliotrope
henna
honey
ice blue
incarnadine
indigo
iris
iron grey
ivory
jade
jasmine
jet
khaki
kingfisher blue
lapis lazuli
lavender
leaf green
lemon
lilac
lily white
lime green
Lincoln green
liver
lovat green
magenta
magnolia
mahogany
maroon
mauve

mazarine blue
midnight blue
mocha
mouse
mulberry
mushroom
mustard
nankeen
navy blue
Nile blue
Nile green
nut-brown
nutmeg
oatmeal
ochre
off-white
old gold
old rose
olive
opal
orange
oxblood
Oxford blue
oyster pink
oyster white
palomino
pansy
paprika
parchment
peach
peach-bloom
peacock blue
pea green
pearl
periwinkle
perse
petrol blue
pewter
pine green
pink
pistachio
platinum
plum
poppy
powder blue
primrose
puce
purple
putty
raspberry
raven
red
robin's-egg blue
rose
royal blue
royal purple
ruby
russet
rust
sable
saffron
salmon
sand
sanguine
sapphire
saxe blue
scarlet
sea green
seal brown
sepia
shell pink
sienna
silver
sky blue
slate
snow-white
sorrel
spice
steel blue
steel grey
stone
straw
strawberry
strawberry blonde
tan
tangerine
tawny
teak
teal
tea rose
terracotta
Titian
topaz
tortoiseshell
Turkey red
turquoise
Tyrian purple
ultramarine
umber
Venetian red
verditer
vermilion
violet
viridian
walnut
Wedgwood blue
white
wine
yellow

Fabrics and fibres

acetate
Acrilan (*trademark*)
acrylic
Aertex (*trademark*)
aida
alpaca
angora
Antron (*trademark*)
Arnel (*trademark*)
asbestos
astrakhan
bafta
baize
balbriggan
barathea
barège
barkcloth
batiste
beaver (cloth)
Bedford cord
bengaline
blanketing
bobbinet
bobbin lace
bombazine
Botany wool
bouclé
brilliantine
broadcloth
broadtail
brocade
brocatelle
brown holland
buckram
bunting
burlap
butter muslin
byssus
calamanco
calico
Cambrelle (*trademark*)
cambric
camel hair
candlewick
canvas
cashmere
cavalry twill
challis
chambray
Chantilly lace
charmeuse
cheesecloth
chenille
cheviot
chiffon
chinchilla
chino
chintz
ciré
cloqué
coconut matting
coir
CoolMax (*trademark*)
cord
Cordura (*trademark*)
corduroy
cotton
crêpe
crêpe de Chine
crépon
cretonne
crewel
Crimplene (*trademark*)
crinoline
crushed velvet
cupro
Dacron (*trademark*)
damask
denim
devoré
dimity
doeskin
Donegal tweed
drab
Dralon (*trademark*)
drill
drugget
duchesse lace
duchesse satin
duffel
dungaree
dupion
elastane
faille
felt
filoselle
fishnet
flannel
flannelette
flax
fleece
flock
floss silk
foulard
frieze
fustian
gaberdine
gauze
georgette
gimp
gingham
Gore-tex (*trademark*)
gossamer
grasscloth
grenadine
grogram
grosgrain
gros point
guipure
gunny
haircloth
Harris tweed (*trademark*)
hemp
herringbone
hessian
hodden
holland
Honiton lace
hopsack
horsehair
huckaback
ikat
ixtle
jaconet
jacquard
jean
jersey
jute
kalamkari
kapok
karakul
Kasha (*trademark*)
kemp
kenaf
Kendal Green
kente
kersey
kerseymere
khadi
khaki
khanga
kikoi
kincob
kitenge
lace
lambswool
lamé
lampas
lawn
leathercloth
leatherette (*trademark*)
leno
Lincoln green
linen
linsey-woolsey
lint
lisle
loden
Lurex (*trademark*)
lustring
Lycra (*trademark*)
madras
marocain
marquisette
Marseilles
matting
Mechlin
melton
merino
microfibre
micromesh
Milanese silk
modacrylic
mohair
moiré
moleskin
moquette
moreen
mousseline
Moygashel (*trademark*)
mungo
muslin
nainsook
nankeen
Naugahyde (*US trademark*)
needlecord
net
ninon
Nottingham lace
nylon
oakum
oilcloth
oiled silk
oilskin
organdie
organza
organzine
Orlon (*trademark*)
osnaburg
ottoman
Oxford cloth
packthread
paduasoy
paisley
pandanus
panne velvet
paper taffeta
parramatta
pashmina
peau-de-soie
percale
Persian silk
Pertex (*trademark*)
petersham
phulkari
pillow lace
pilot cloth
piqué
plaid
plush
plush velvet
point lace
polycotton
polyester
pongee
poplin
poult
prunella
raffia
ramie
rayon
rep
ripstop
rose-point
sackcloth
sacking
sailcloth
samite
sarsenet
sateen
satin
satinette
saxony
schappe
sea-island cotton
seersucker
sendal
sennit
serge
shahtoosh
shantung
sharkskin
sheer
Shetland wool
shoddy
silk
sisal
slipper satin
slub
Spandex (*trademark*)
spun silk
stammel
stockinet
stroud
suede
sunn
Supplex (*trademark*)
surah
swansdown
tabaret
tabby
taffeta
tailor's twist
tapestry
tarlatan
tarpaulin
tattersall
tatting
Tencel (*trademark*)
terry
Terylene (*Brit. trademark*)
ticking
tiffany
toile
toile de Jouy
toquilla
torchon
towelling
Trevira (*trademark*)
Tricel (*trademark*)
tricot
Tricotine (*US trademark*)
tulle
tussore
tweed
twill
Utrecht velvet
Valenciennes
Velcro (*trademark*)
velour
velvet
velveteen
vicuña
viscose
Viyella (*trademark*)
voile
waxcloth
webbing
whipcord
wild silk
wincey
winceyette
wool
worsted
zari

Sewing techniques and stitches

appliqué
backstitch
bar tack
basting
binding
blackwork
blanket stitch
blind stitch
bullion knot
buttonhole stitch
chain stitch
chikan
couching
crewel work
crocheting
cross stitch
crow's foot
cutwork
darning
dart
drawn work
embroidery
facing
faggoting
feather stitch
fine-drawing
Florentine stitch
French knot
fulling
gathering
gros point
hemstitch
herringbone stitch
ladder stitch
laid work
lazy daisy stitch
lock stitch
loop stitch
mitring
needlepoint
overcasting
overlocking
oversewing
overstitch
patchwork
petit point
pleating
purl
quilting
ruching
ruffling
running stitch
saddle stitch
satin stitch
scalloping
shadow stitch
shirring
slip stitch
smocking
stay stitch
stem stitch
straight stitch
Swiss darning
tacking
tapestry
tent stitch
topstitch
treble
tucking
tufting
whipstitch
whitework
wool work

Knitting stitches

cable stitch
garter stitch
loop stitch
moss stitch
plain stitch
purl stitch
ribbing
shell stitch
slip stitch
stocking stitch
trellis stitch

Hairstyles

Afro
bangs
beehive
big hair
bob
body wave
bouffant
braids
bun
bunches
buzz cut
chignon
combover
cornrows
crew cut
crop
dreadlocks *or* dreads
elf-locks
Eton crop
feathercut
flat-top
French plait
French pleat/roll
French twist
fringe
marcel wave
Mohican/ Mohawk
mullet
number one, two, etc.
pageboy
perm/ permanent
pigtail
plait
pompadour
ponytail
quiff
rat's tails
razor cut
ringlets
shag
shingle
short back and sides
tonsure
topknot
whiffle cut
widow's peak

Jewellery

amulet
anklet
armlet
band
bangle
beads
bijou
bracelet
breastpin
brooch
cameo
chain
charm bracelet
choker
circlet
Claddagh ring
clip
cuff link
diadem
dress watch
ear stud
earring
engagement ring
eternity ring
fibula
friendship bracelet
friendship ring
hair slide
hatpin
hei-tiki
kara
keeper
labret
locket
lunula
manilla
marquise
medallion
mourning ring
necklace
necklet
nose ring
nose stud
pavé
pendant
phalera
pin
posy ring
rakhi
ring
rivière
sautoir
scarf ring
seal ring
signet ring
slave bangle
sleeper
stickpin
strand
stud
tiara
tiepin
toe ring
torc
wedding ring
wristlet

Beans, peas, and lentils

adzuki/aduki bean
asparagus pea
black bean
black-eyed bean
borlotti bean
broad bean
butter bean
cannellini bean
chickpea
cowpea
fava bean
field bean
field pea
flageolet
French bean
garbanzo bean
garden pea
haricot bean
horsebean
jack bean
kidney bean
lentil
lima bean
mangetout
marrowfat pea
masoor
mesquite bean
mung bean
navy bean
partridge pea
pea bean
petit pois
pinto bean
puy lentil
red bean
runner bean
scarlet runner
snap bean
snow pea
soybean
string bean
sugar bean
sugar pea
sugar snap pea
tick bean
waxpod

Biscuits

Bath Oliver (*trademark*)
bourbon
brandy snap
cracknel
cream cracker
crispbread
custard cream
digestive
Florentine
fortune cookie
garibaldi
ginger nut
ginger snap
graham cracker
langue de chat
macaroon
marie biscuit
matzo
Nice biscuit
oatcake
petit beurre
pretzel
ratafia
rusk
saltine
ship's biscuit
shortbread/ shortcake
Shrewsbury biscuit
soda cracker
sweetmeal biscuit
tollhouse cookie
tuile
water biscuit
wholemeal biscuit

Bread and bread rolls

azyme
bagel
baguette
bannock
bap
bara brith
barmbrack
barm cake
barracouta
bialy
billy-bread
bloomer
boxty
bridge roll
brioche
bun
challah
chapatti
ciabatta
cob
cornbread
cottage loaf
crumpet
damper
farl
farmhouse loaf
flatbread
focaccia
French stick
fruit loaf
granary bread (*trademark*)
hoagie
injera
johnnycake
kaiser
kulcha
malt loaf
manchet
matzo
milk loaf
muffin
nan
pan dulce
panettone
panino
pan loaf
paratha
petit pain
pikelet
piki
pitta
platzel
pone
poppadom
potato bread
pumpernickel
puri
quartern loaf
roti
rye bread
soda bread
sourdough
split tin
spoon bread
stollen
stotty
wholemeal

Cakes, puddings, and desserts

almond cake
angel cake
angel food cake
apfelstrudel
apple charlotte
apple pie
baba
baked Alaska
Bakewell tart
baklava
banana split
Banbury cake
banoffi pie
Battenberg
bavarois
beignet
Berliner
black bun
Black Forest gateau
blancmange
bombe
bouchée
brack
brandy snap
bread-and-butter pudding
bread pudding
Brown Betty
brownie
bun
butterfly cake
cabinet pudding
cannoli
cassata
charlotte
charlotte russe
cheesecake
clafoutis
cobbler
college pudding
compote
cream puff
crème brûlée
crème caramel
crêpe
crêpe Suzette
croquembouche
cruller
crumble
crumpet
cupcake
custard pie
Danish pastry
death by chocolate
devil's food cake
Dobos Torte
doughnut/donut
drop scone
dumpling
Dundee cake
Eccles cake
eclair
egg custard
Eskimo pie (*US trademark*)
Eve's pudding
fairy cake
fancy
firni
flapjack
floating island
flummery
fool

frangipane
frozen yogurt
fruit cocktail
fruit salad
frumenty
funnel cake
gateau
gelato
Genoa cake
gingerbread
granita
halwa
hasty pudding
hoecake
hokey-pokey
hot cross bun
ice cream
ice milk
jello
jelly
johnny cake
junket
khir
kissel
Knickerbocker Glory
koeksister
kulfi
lady's finger
lamington
lardy cake
layer cake
macédoine
Madeira cake
madeleine
maid of honour
marble cake
marquise
meringue
milk pudding
millefeuille
mince pie
Mississippi mud pie
moon cake
mousse
mousseline
napoleon
palacsinta
pancake
pandowdy
panettone
panforte
panna cotta
parfait
parkin
pashka
pavlova
peach Melba
petit fours
plum cake
plum duff
plum pudding
popover
pound cake
profiteroles
puftaloon
queen cake
queen of puddings
ras malai
rice pudding
rock cake
roly-poly
Sachertorte
sago pudding
Sally Lunn
sandwich (cake)
savarin
scone
seed cake
semolina
shoo-fly pie
shortcake
simnel cake
singing hinny
snowball
sorbet
soufflé
sponge (cake)
sponge pudding
spotted dick
spumoni
steamed pudding
stollen
streusel
strudel
suet pudding
suji
summer pudding
sundae
Swiss roll
syllabub
tapioca pudding
tart
tarte Tatin
tartlet
tartufo
tipsy cake
tiramisu
torte
treacle tart
trifle
turnover
tutti-frutti
upside-down cake
Victoria sponge
waffle
water ice
whip
yogurt
yule log
zabaglione
zuppa inglese

Cereal crops

barley
blue corn
cockspur grass
corn
durra/dhurra
durum (wheat)
einkorn
emmer
flint corn
mabela
maize
millet
milo
oats
pearl millet
rice
rye
sorghum
spelt
sudan grass
sweet corn
teff
triticale
wheat

Cheeses

Ami du Chambertin
Beaufort
Bel Paese (*trademark*)
blue Brie
blue cheese
blue vinny
Boursin (*trademark*)
Brie
Caerphilly
Cambozola (*trademark*)
Camembert
Cantal
Chaumes
Cheddar
Cheshire
chèvre
Colby
Cotswold
cottage cheese
cream cheese
crowdie *or* crowdy
curd cheese
Danish blue
Derby
Dolcelatte (*trademark*)
Double Gloucester
Dunlop
Edam
Emmental
feta *or* fetta
fontina
fromage blanc
fromage frais
Gervais
Gjetost
Gloucester
Gorgonzola
Gouda
grana
green cheese
Gruyère
halloumi
Ilchester
Jarlsberg (*trademark*)
Lancashire
Leerdammer
Leicester
Liederkranz
Limburger
Liptauer
Livarot
mascarpone
Monterey Jack
mozzarella
Neufchâtel
Oka
paneer *or* panir
Parmesan
Parmigiano Reggiano
pecorino
Pont l'évêque
Port Salut
pot cheese
provolone
quark
reblochon
Red Leicester
ricotta
Romano
Roquefort (*trademark*)
sage Derby
Saint Agur
Sainte Honoré
Saint Nectaire
Samsoe
Stilton
stracchino
taleggio
Tillamook
Tilsit
tomme (de Savoie)
tvorog
Vacherin
vignotte
Wensleydale
Windsor Red

Fruit

ackee
alligator pear
ananas
apple
apricot
Asian pear
avocado
azarole
babaco
bael
bakeapple
banana
beach plum
bilberry
blackberry
blackcurrant
blood orange
blueberry
boysenberry
breadfruit
bullace
cantaloupe
Cape gooseberry
carambola
cashew apple
chayote
checkerberry
cherimoya
cherry
cherry plum
Chinese gooseberry
citron
clementine
cloudberry
coconut
Costard
cowberry
crab apple
cranberry
crowberry
currant
custard apple
damson
date
dewberry
durian
elderberry
feijoa
fig
galia melon
geebung
genip
genipap
gooseberry
gourd
granadilla
grape
grapefruit
greengage
guava
hackberry
honeydew melon
huckleberry
jaboticaba
jackfruit
jamun
jujube
juneberry
kaki
kiwi fruit
kumquat
lemon
lime
lingonberry
loganberry
longan
loquat
lychee
mammee
mandarin
mango
mangosteen
manzanilla
maypop
medlar
melon
minneola
mombin
mulberry
muscat
musk melon
myrobalan
naseberry
nashi
navel orange
nectarine
Ogen melon
olive
orange
ortanique
papaya
partridgeberry
passion fruit
pawpaw
peach
pear
persimmon
physalis
pineapple
pippin
pitahaya
plantain
plum
pomegranate
pomelo
prickly pear
pumpkin
quandong
quince
rambutan
raspberry
redcurrant
roseapple
salmonberry
sapodilla
satsuma
sea grape
serviceberry
sharon fruit
sloe
sorb
soursop
star apple
starfruit
strawberry
sugar apple
sweetsop
tamarillo
tamarind
tangelo
tangerine
tayberry
thimbleberry
tomatillo
tomato
Ugli fruit (*trademark*)
veitchberry
Victoria plum
watermelon
white currant
whortleberry
wineberry
youngberry

Herbs *See also* Spices

angelica
anise
basil
bay leaf
bergamot
borage
camomile
chervil
chicory
chives
cilantro
clary
comfrey
coriander
dandelion greens
dill
dittany
dong quai
fennel
flat-leaf/flat-leaved parsley
hyssop
lavender
lemon balm
lemon grass
lemon mint
lovage
marjoram
mint
oregano
parsley
peppermint
rosemary
rue
saffron
sage
savory
sorrel
spearmint
sweet balm
sweet cicely
tarragon
thyme
vervain
yerba buena

Meals

afternoon tea, banquet, barbecue, barbie, braaivleis, breakfast, brunch, buffet, burgoo, clambake, continental breakfast, cookout, cream tea, cut lunch, dinner, dinner party, elevenses, evening meal, feast, finger buffet, fork supper, harvest supper, high tea, lunch, luncheon, midday meal, packed lunch, picnic, safari supper, smorgasbord, supper, takeaway, tapas, tea, TV dinner, wedding breakfast

Meat cuts and joints

back rib, baron of beef, belly, best end, breast, brisket, chateaubriand, chine, chop, chuck, collar, cutlet, entrecôte, escalope, fillet, flank, fore rib, fricandeau, gigot, hand, hock, hough, knuckle, leg, loin, neck, noisette, porterhouse steak, rack, rib, riblets, round, round steak, rump, saddle, scrag, shank, shin, shoulder, side, silverside, sirloin, skirt, spare rib, T-bone, tenderloin, topside, tournedos, undercut, wing

Meat types and products *See also* Sausages

bacon, beef, beefburger, brains, brawn, bresaola, burger, bushmeat, chicken, chitterlings, corned beef, duck, faggot, fries, game, gammon, goose, grouse, haggis, ham, hamburger, haslet, heart, kidney, lamb, lamb's fry, lights, liver, luncheon meat, mince, mutton, offal, oxtail, tongue, Parma ham, partridge, pâté, pheasant, pig's trotters, pork, poultry, prosciutto, quail, rabbit, rissole, salt pork, sidemeat, spam (*trademark*), steak, sweetbread, tongue, tripe, trotters, turkey, veal, venison

Nuts

acorn, almond, areca nut, beechnut, betel nut, bitternut, Brazil (nut), breadnut, burrawang nut, butternut, candlenut, cashew (nut), chestnut, chincapin, cobnut, coco de mer, coconut, coffee nut, cohune nut, cola nut, conker, coquilla nut, double coconut, dwarf chestnut, earthnut, filbert, groundnut, grugru nut, gum nut, hazelnut, hickory nut, hognut, horse chestnut, ivory nut, lychee nut, macadamia (nut), mockernut, monkey nut, palm nut, peanut, pecan, pine nut, piñon, pistachio (nut), quandong, Queensland nut, sal nut, saouari nut, sweet chestnut, walnut, water chestnut, white walnut

Pasta types

agnolotti, angel hair, annellini, bigoli, bucatini, cannelloni, capelli, capellini, cappelletti, casareccie, conchiglie, cravattine, ditali, ditalini, ditaloni, farfalle, farfalline, fedelini, fettucce, fettuccine, fidelini, fusilli, gramigna, lasagne, linguine, lumache, macaroni, mafalde, manicotti, maruzze, mezzani, mostaccioli, noodles, orecchiette, orzo, paglia e fieno, pappardelle, penne, pipe, radiatori, ravioli, rigatoni, risoni, rotelle, rotini, spaghetti, spaghettini, spaghettone, stelline, tagliatelle, tagliolini, taglioni, tortellini, tortelloni, tortiglioni, trenette, tuffoloni, vermicelli, ziti

Savoury pies

cottage pie, coulibiac, fidget pie, game pie, pirog, pork pie, pot pie, Scotch pie, shepherd's pie, squab pie, stargazy pie, steak and kidney pie, tourtière

Sauces

Alfredo, Amatriciana, aioli, apple sauce, arrabiata, baba ganoush, barbecue sauce, Béarnaise sauce, béchamel sauce, bolognese sauce, bordelaise sauce, bread sauce, brown sauce, carbonara sauce, catsup, chasseur sauce, chaud-froid, chawan mushi, cheese sauce, chilli sauce, cranberry sauce, demi-glace, gravy, harissa, hoisin sauce, hollandaise sauce, horseradish sauce, ketchup, marinara, mayonnaise, milanese sauce, mint sauce, mornay sauce, mousseline sauce, mustard sauce, onion sauce, parsley sauce, pebre, pepper sauce, pesto, pizzaiola sauce, ponzu, puttanesca, ragù, salsa verde, satay sauce, sauce ravigote, sauce remoulade, skordalia, soubise, soy sauce, sweet and sour sauce, Tabasco sauce (*trademark*), tartare sauce, Teriyaki sauce, tomato ketchup, velouté, white sauce, Worcester sauce

Sausages

andouille, baloney/boloney, black pudding, blood pudding, blood sausage, boerewors, bologna, bratwurst, cervelat, chipolata, chorizo, crépinette, Cumberland sausage, frank, frankfurter, kielbasa, knackwurst, merguez, mortadella, pepperoni, salami, saucisson, saveloy, slim jim, summer sausage, weenie, Weisswurst, white pudding, wiener, wurst

Soups

bisque
borscht
bouillabaisse
bouillon
broth
burgoo
callaloo
chowder
cock-a-leekie
congee
consommé
Cullen skink
gazpacho
goulash
gumbo
madrilene
menudo
minestrone
mock turtle soup
mulligatawny
oxtail
petite marmite
pistou
potage
pot-au-feu
rasam
sancoche
Scotch broth
shchi
skilly
stracciatella
vichyssoise

Spices *See also* **Herbs**

ajowan
allspice
black pepper
capers
caraway seeds
cardamom
cassia
cayenne pepper
chilli
cinnamon
cloves
coriander
cumin
curcuma
fennel seeds
fenugreek
five-spice
galangal
garam masala
garlic
ginger
ginseng
grains of Paradise
green pepper
jalapeño (pepper)
juniper berries
mace
mustard
nutmeg
paprika
pepper
pimento
star anise
sumac
turmeric
vanilla
white pepper

Types of sugar

beet sugar
brown sugar
candy (*Brit.*)
cane sugar
caster/castor sugar
crystallized sugar
cube sugar
demerara (sugar)
fruit sugar
golden syrup
granulated sugar
gur
icing sugar
jaggery
lump sugar
maple sugar
molasses
muscovado (sugar)
palm sugar
penuche/panocha
powdered sugar
preserving sugar
refined sugar
syrup
treacle
white sugar

Sweets and confectionery

acid drop
aniseed ball
barley sugar
boiled sweet
brittle
bullseye
burfi
butterscotch
candy cane
candyfloss
caramel
chew
chewing gum
chocolate
chocolate drop
coconut ice
comfit
cracknel
crystallized fruit
dolly mixtures
dragée
Easter egg
fondant
fruit drop
fruit gum
fruit pastille
fudge
gobstopper
gulab jamun
gumball
gumdrop
halva
hazlenut whirl
humbug
jalebi
jelly
jelly baby
jelly bean
jujube
Kendal mint cake
laddu
lemon sherbet
liquorice
liquorice allsort
lollipop
lolly
marshmallow
marzipan
mint
nougat
pastille
patty
pear drop
peppermint
peppermint cream
Pontefract cake
praline
rasgulla
rock
sherbet
sherbet dip
sugared almond
toffee
toffee apple
truffle
Turkish delight
wine gum

Vegetables *See also* **Beans, peas, and lentils**

ackee
acorn squash
adzuki/aduki bean
alfalfa
artichoke
asparagus
aubergine
bamboo shoots
batata
bean
beet
beetroot
black bean
black-eyed bean
borlotti bean
breadfruit
broad bean
broccoli
Brussels sprout
butter bean
buttercup squash
butterhead lettuce
butternut squash
cabbage
cabbage lettuce
calabrese
cannellini bean
capsicum
cardoon
carrot
cassava
cauliflower
cavolo nero
celeriac
celery
chard
chayote
chervil
chickpea
chicory
Chinese artichoke
Chinese cabbage
Chinese leaves
choko
collard
corn on the cob
cos lettuce
courgette
cress
cucumber
curly kale
cush-cush
custard marrow
dishcloth gourd
drumhead
earthnut
eggplant
endive
escarole
fennel
flageolet
French bean
garbanzo
garden pea
garlic
gherkin
globe artichoke
gobo
gourd
green onion
gumbo
haricot bean
iceberg lettuce
Jerusalem artichoke
jicama
kale
kidney bean
kohlrabi
lamb's lettuce
leek
lentil
lettuce
lima bean
lollo rosso
mangetout
manioc
marrow
marrowfat pea
marrow squash
mizuna
mooli
mung bean
mustard
oak leaf (lettuce)
okra
onion
orache
oyster plant
pak choi
parsnip
pattypan (squash)
pea
pea bean
pearl onion
pepper
petits pois
pimiento
pinto bean
plantain
potato
puha
pumpkin
puy lentil
radicchio
radish
red cabbage
romaine
runner bean
rutabaga
salsify
samphire
savoy cabbage
scallion
scorzonera
Scotch kale
sea kale
shallot
snap bean
snow pea
soybean
spinach
spinach beet
spring greens
spring onion
sprue
squash
string bean
succory
sugar bean
sugar snap peas
swede
sweetcorn
sweet pepper
sweet potato
tannia
taro
tiger nut
tomato
turnip
turnip tops/greens
vegetable spaghetti
wasabi
water chestnut
watercress
waxpod
yam
yam bean
zucchini

Vitamins

A	retinol
B1	thiamine
B2	riboflavin
B3	niacin
B6	pyridoxine
B12	cyanocobalamin
B complex	folic acid, pantothenic acid, biotin, inositol, choline, pteroylglutamic acid
C	ascorbic acid
D2	calciferol
D3	cholecalciferol
E	tocopherol
H	biotin
K1	phylloquinone
K2	menaquinone/menadione
M	folic acid
P	citrin, bioflavonoid

Furniture

Furniture types and styles

Bauhaus, Biedermeier, Cape Dutch, Chippendale, Empire, Gothic Revival, Hepplewhite, Jacobean, Louis Quatorze, Louis Quinze, Louis Seize, Louis Treize, Queen Anne, Regency, reproduction, Scandinavian, Shaker, Sheraton

Beds

bassinet, bedstead, berth, bunk bed, camp bed, carrycot, chaise longue, charpoy, cot, couchette, cradle, crib, daybed, divan, feather bed, four-poster, futon, half-tester, hammock, king-size bed, pallet, palliasse, pipe berth/cot, rollaway, shakedown, sleeper, sleigh bed, sofa bed, takht, truckle bed, trundle bed, waterbed, Z-bed

Carpets and rugs

Aubusson, Axminster, broadloom, Brussels, dhurrie, drugget, flokati, hearthrug, ingrain, kaross, Kidderminster, kilim, Kirman, numdah, Persian, prayer mat *or* rug, rag rug, runner, Savonnerie, scatter rug, shagpile, sheepskin, Soumak, tiger-skin, Turkish, Turkoman, twist, vase, velvet, Wilton, Yarkand

Chairs and stools

armchair, BarcaLounger (*US trademark*), barrel chair, bar stool, bath chair, bench, bentwood chair, box seat, bucket seat, buffet, button-back chair, canapé, carver, chaise longue, chesterfield, club chair, comb-back, couch, davenport, deckchair, dining chair, divan, donkey stool, duchesse, easy chair, faldstool, fighting chair, footstool, high chair, ladder-back, lawn chair, Lloyd Loom chair, lounger, love seat, milking stool, Morris chair, music stool, nursing chair, panel-back chair, pew, pouffe, recliner, rocking chair *or* rocker, settee, settle, side chair, slingback chair, sofa, sofa bed, spindle-back chair, stall, stool, studio couch, sugan, swivel chair, tabouret, tailor's chair, throne, tripod, tub chair, tuffet, wheelback chair, wheelchair, Windsor chair, wing chair

Cupboards and chests

almirah, armoire, aumbry, buffet, canterbury, cassone, cellaret/cellarette, chest, chest of drawers, chiffonier, closet, commode, console, credenza, dresser, highboy, hope chest, larder, locker, lowboy, pantry, press, safe, sea chest, sideboard, tabernacle, tallboy, tansu, wardrobe, Welsh dresser, whatnot

Tables and desks

altar, bedside table, billiard table, bonheur du jour, bureau, card table, coffee table, console table, credence table, davenport, dresser, dressing table, drop-leaf table, duchesse, dumb waiter, escritoire, gaming table, gateleg table, kneehole desk, lap desk, lectern, loo table, nightstand, night table, operating table, partners' desk, pedestal table, Pembroke table, piecrust table, pier table, pinball table, prothesis, refectory table, rent table, roll-top desk, secretaire, steam table, tabouret, teapoy, tea table, trestle table, trivet table, vanity table, writing desk

Geography

Map types and projections

atlas, A to Z, azimuthal projection, cadastral map, cartogram, chart, choropleth map, conical/conic projection, contour map, equal-area map, equidistant projection, globe, ichnography, isopleth map, key map, mappemonde, Mercator projection, Mollweide projection, orthomorphic projection, Peters projection, photomap, photomosaic, plane chart, planisphere, plat, relief map, road map, sketch map, street map, topographical map, town plan, weather map/chart, zenithal projection

Geological ages

Archaean/Azoic period
Cambrian period
Carboniferous period
Cenozoic era
Cretaceous period
Devonian period
Eocene epoch
Holocene epoch
Jurassic period
Mesozoic era
Miocene epoch
Oligocene epoch
Ordovician period
Palaeocene epoch
Palaeozoic era
Permian period
Phanerozoic aeon
Pleistocene epoch
Pliocene epoch
Precambrian era
Proterozoic aeon
Quaternary period
Silurian period
Tertiary period
Triassic period

Layers of the Earth's crust

asthenosphere
continental crust
lithosphere
lower mantle
Mohorovičić discontinuity
oceanic crust
sial
transition zone
upper mantle

Layers of the Earth's atmosphere

D-layer
E-layer
exosphere
F-layer
ionosphere
mesosphere
ozone layer
ozonosphere
stratosphere
thermosphere
troposphere

Climatic zones

arid
boreal
continental humid
desert
equatorial rainforest
highland
ice cap
Marine West Coast
Mediterranean
monsoon
polar
semi-arid
steppe
subarctic
subtropical humid
temperate rainy
trade-wind littoral
tropical savannah
tropical wet
tropical wet-dry
tundra

Weather phenomena *See also* **Cloud formations**, **Winds**

anticyclone
blocking high
cold front
cyclone
deep depression
depression
filling depression
frontal system
high pressure
jet stream
low pressure
occlusion
pressure system
ridge
shallow depression
stationary depression
stationary high
temperature inversion
thermal
trough
turbulence
warm front
warm sector

Cloud formations

altocumulus
altostratus
anvil cloud
cirrocumulus
cirrostratus
cirrus
cloud street
cumulonimbus
cumulostratus
cumulus
funnel cloud
lenticular cloud
mackerel sky
mare's tails
nimbostratus
nimbus
noctilucent cloud
rain cloud
storm cloud
stratocirrus
stratocumulus
stratus
thundercloud
thunderhead
wrack

Winds

berg wind
bise
bora
breeze
brickfielder
buran
Cape doctor
chinook
Etesian
föhn/foehn
gale
ghibli
haboob
harmattan
khamsin
levanter
libeccio
maestrale
meltemi
mistral
monsoon
nor'wester
pampero
Perth doctor
shamal
simoom/simoon/samiel
sirocco
solano
southerly buster
storm
trade wind
tramontana
wet chinook
whirlwind
williwaw
willy-willy
zonda

Star types

astrometric binary
binary star
brown dwarf
cepheid
collapsar
dark star
double star
dwarf star
eclipsing binary
flare star
giant
lodestar
magnetar
neutron star
nova
polar
polar star
pulsar
quasar
red dwarf
red giant
supergiant
supernova
variable star
visual binary
white dwarf

Administrative districts

archbishopric
archdeaconry
archdiocese
arrondissement
autonomy
bailiwick
Bantustan
barony
bishopric
borough
canton
century
chapelry
circuit
civil parish
classis
colony
commonwealth
commune
constituency
county
county borough
County Palatine
cure
deme
department
diocese
district
division
dominion
duchy
dukedom
earldom
electorate
emirate
eparchy
exarchate
group area
homeland
hundred
island area
jagir
jurisdiction
krai/kray
Land
manor
marquisate/marquessate
metropolitan county
metropolitan district
minor county
nomarchy
nome
oblast
okrug
palatinate
pargana/pergunnah/pergana
parish
pocket borough
prefecture
presbytery
province
rape
rectory
regality
region
riding
rotten borough
rural district
sanjak
satrapy
seat
see
sheading
shire
shire county
situs
soke
state
stewartry/stewardry
taluk/taluka
tehsil/tahsil
territory
theme
tithing
township
tribe
union
unitary authority
unitary council
urban district
vicus
vilayet
viscounty
wapentake
ward
zamindari/zemindari/zamindary
zilla/zillah

Districts of a city

arrondissement
barrio
block
borough
business park
Cabbagetown
cardboard city
Chinatown
civic centre
clubland
council estate
dockland
downtown
edge city
estate
exurb
exurbia
faubourg
garden suburb
ghetto
group area
hood
housing estate
industrial estate
inner city
jhuggi jhopri
kasbah
liberty
locality
medina
mohalla
nabe
neighbourhood
outskirts
pedestrian precinct
precinct
quarter
quartier
red-light district
rookery
school district
science park
seafront
sector
skid row
slum
smokeless zone
suburb
suburbia
technology park
theatreland
township
trading estate
twilight zone
uptown
village
waterfront

Language and literature

Punctuation marks

accent
 ▸ **Accents**
apostrophe '
asterisk *
asterism ⁂
backslash \
brace { }
bracket [ ] ( )
caret ⁁ ^
colon :
comma ,
dagger †
dash —
diacritical mark
 ▸ **Accents**
double dagger/obelisk/obelus ‡
ellipsis ...
em dash/rule —
en dash/rule –
exclamation mark !
full stop/point .
hyphen -
inverted comma ' " "
obelisk/obelus †
omission mark ...
parenthesis ( )
period .
point .
question mark ?
quotation mark ' " "
semicolon ;
solidus /
square bracket [ ]
stop .
stroke /
swung dash ~
virgule /

Accents

Name	Example in use
acute	é
breve	ŭ
cedilla	ç
circumflex	î
diaeresis/umlaut	ö
grave	è
háček	ř
hook	ę
macron	ā
tilde	ñ

Greek alphabet

Α α alpha
Β β beta
Γ γ gamma
Δ δ delta
Ε ε epsilon
Ζ ζ zeta
Η η eta
Θ θ theta
Ι ι iota
Κ κ kappa
Λ λ lambda
Μ μ mu
Ν ν nu
Ξ ξ xi
Ο ο omicron
Π π pi
Ρ ρ rho
Σ ς, σ sigma
Τ τ tau
Υ υ upsilon
Φ φ phi
Χ χ chi
Ψ ψ psi
Ω ω omega

Hebrew alphabet

א aleph
ב beth
ג gimel
ד daleth
ה he
ו waw
ז zayin
ח heth
ט teth
י yodh
כ kaph
ל lamedh
מ mem
נ nun
ס samekh
ע `ayin
פ pe
צ sadhe
ק qoph
ר resh
שׂ śin
שׁ shin
ת taw

Rhetorical devices and figures of speech

allegory
alliteration
anacoluthon
anadiplosis
anaphora
anastrophe
antiphrasis
antistrophe
antithesis
antonomasia
aporia
apostrophe
assonance
bathos
cacophemism
catachresis
chiasmus
circumlocution
diacope
dysphemism
echoism
ellipsis
enallage
epanalepsis
epanorthosis
epiphora
epistrophe
epizeuxis
euphemism
euphony
euphuism
hendiadys
homeoteleuton
hypallage
hyperbaton
hyperbole
hysteron proteron
innuendo
irony
isocolon
litotes
meiosis
metaphor
metonymy
onomatopoeia
oxymoron
paradox
paralipsis
paronomasia
periphrasis
personification
pleonasm
prolepsis
prosopopoeia
pun
rhetorical question
sarcasm
simile
syllepsis
symploce
synecdoche
tautology
transferred epithet
trope
zeugma

Literary schools, movements, and groups

Acmeism
Aesthetic Movement
Angry Young Men
Augustans
beat generation
Bloomsbury group
Cavalier poets
classicism
Dadaism
existentialism
expressionism
futurism
Georgian poets
Harlem Renaissance
imagism
Kailyard School
Lake poets
Liverpool poets
magic/magical realism
mannerism
medievalism
metaphysical poets
minimalism
modernism
Movement, the
naturalism
neoclassicism
neo-realism
Neue Sachlichkeit
occultism
Parnassians
Pléiade, la

postmodernism
post-structuralism
Pre-Raphaelitism
pre-Romanticism
primitivism
realism
Renaissance humanism
Romanticism
Russian formalism
Scottish Chaucerians
social realism
socialist realism
structuralism
Sturm und Drang
surrealism
symbolism
transcendentalism
verismo
Vorticism

Types of writer

adaptor
agony aunt
amorist
annalist
author
authoress
bard
best-seller
biographer
chronicler
city editor
co-author
columnist
comedist
commentator
continuator
contributor
copywriter
correspondent
crime writer
critic
cub reporter
diarist
draftsman
dramatist
dramaturge
editor
editress
encyclopedist
epilogist
essayist
evangelist
fabulist
farceur
gagster
ghostwriter
glossator
glossographer
hack
hackette
hagiographer
herbalist
humorist
hymnographer
journalist
lexicographer
littérateur
lobby correspondent
lyricist
lyrist
memorialist
Minnesinger
mythographer
necrologist
newsman
newspaperman
novelist
pamphleteer
pastoralist
playwright
poet
poetess
Poet Laureate
pressman
programmer
prosaist
psalmist
publicist
recorder
remembrancer
reporter
reviewer
rhymester
scenarist
screenwriter
scribe
scriptwriter
skald
sob sister
songster
songwriter
sonneteer
speech-writer
story editor
sub
synoptic
synoptist
tragedian
troubadour
trouvère
war correspondent
war poet
wireman
wordsmith
writer-in-residence
Yahwist

Types of poem

aubade
ballad
ballade
bucolic
chanson
clerihew
dirge
dithyramb
dramatic monologue
eclogue
elegy
encomium
epic
epigram
epithalamium
epode
epyllion
georgic
ghazal
haiku
idyll
lay
limerick
lyric
madrigal
monody
nursery rhyme
ode
palinode
pastoral
prothalamium
quatorzain
renga
rondeau
roundel
roundelay
saga
sapphics
satire
sestina
sonnet
tanka
threnody
triolet
vilanelle
virelay

Verse forms

alcaics (*or* alcaic verse)
alexandrine verse
alliterative verse
Anacreontics
ballad
ballade
blank verse
clerihew
dactylics (*or* dactylic verse)
doggerel
dramatic monologue
echo verse
elegy
epic
epigram
epode
epopee
fixed form
free verse
haiku
heroic verse
Horatian ode
iambics (*or* iambic verse)
Leonines
limerick
lyric
macaronics (*or* macaronic verse)
madrigal
monody
ode
ottava rima
pantoum/pantun
Petrarchan sonnet
Pindaric
quatorzain
rhyme royal
ritornello
rondeau
roundel
sapphics
secondary epic
sequidilla
sestina
sonnet
Spenserian stanza
tail rhyme
tanka
terza rima
triolet
triplet
trochaics (*or* trochaic verse)
villanelle
virelay

Verse metres and metrical feet

alexandrine
amphibrach
amphimacer
anapaest/anapest
choree
choriamb/choriambus
cretic
dactyl
decasyllable
dimeter
dipody
distich
disyllable
duple metre
elegiac couplet
elegiac distich
heptameter
heroic couplet
hexameter
iamb/iambus
iambic pentameter
ionic
monometer
octameter
paeon
pentameter
pyrrhic
spondee
tetrameter
tribrach
trimeter
trisyllable
trochee

Types of story and novel

adventure story
Aga saga
allegory
antinovel
autobiography
bedtime story
Bildungsroman
black comedy
blockbuster
bodice-ripper
bonkbuster
cliffhanger
comedy
conte
crime story
detective story/novel
dime novel
epic
epistolary novel
exemplum
fable
fabliau
fairy story
fairy tale
fantasy
folk story
folk tale
ghost story
gothic novel
graphic novel
heartbreaker
historical novel
horror story
just-so story
legend
Märchen
mystery
myth
nancy story
nouveau roman
novelette
novelization
novella
parable
photonovel
picaresque novel
police procedural
policier
roman-à-clef
roman-à-thèse
romance
roman expérimental
roman-fleuve
roman noir
romantic novel
saga
short story
spine-chiller
stream of consciousness
sword and sorcery
tearjerker
techno-thriller
thriller
true story
urban myth
western
whodunnit

Types of play

antimasque
burlesque
closet play
comedy
comedy of manners
commedia dell'arte
docudrama
dumbshow
duologue
fabula
farce
Grand Guignol
Greek drama
harlequinade
improvisation
kabuki
kitchen-sink drama
kyogen
masque
melodrama
mime
miracle play
monodrama
morality play
mummers' play
music drama
mystery play
nativity play
Noh
pantomime
passion play
psychodrama
school drama
sociodrama
teleplay
tragedy
tragicomedy
two-hander
verse drama

Types of newspaper

broadsheet
daily
eveninger
evening paper
extra
final
free sheet
gazette
gutter press
heavy
journal
local paper
national
news-sheet
organ
print
provincial
quality
red top
regional
scandal sheet
special edition
Sunday
tab
tabloid
weekly

Medicine

Branches of medicine

Conventional

allopathy
anaesthesiology
audiology
biosurgery
cardiology
chiropody
community medicine
dermatology
embryology
endocrinology
epidemiology
gastroenterology
geriatrics
gynaecology
haematology
immunology
laryngology
nephrology
neurology
neuropathology
neurosurgery
nuclear medicine
obstetrics
oncology
ophthalmology
orthopaedics
orthotics
paediatrics
parasitology
pathology
pharmacology
physiotherapy
plastic surgery
proctology
prosthetics
psychiatry
psychosurgery
radiology
surgery
therapeutics
trichopathy
urology
venereology
veterinary medicine

Alternative and complementary

acupressure
acupuncture
Alexander technique
aromatherapy
Ayurveda
Bach flower remedies
balneotherapy
Bates method
bioenergetics
bodywork
bush medicine
chiropractic
colour therapy
craniosacral therapy
crystal healing/therapy
electro-acupuncture
eurhythmics
faith healing
Feldenkrais method
Gerson therapy
Hay diet
herbalism
homeopathy
hydropathy
iridology
McTimoney chiropractic
nature cure
naturopathy
neurolinguistic programming
organotherapy
osteopathy
psionic medicine
radionics
rebirthing
reflexology
reiki
Rolfing
shiatsu
thalassotherapy
zone therapy

Physical illnesses and conditions

acne
addiction
ague
Aids (acquired immune deficiency syndrome)
allergy
alopecia
altitude sickness
Alzheimer's disease
anaemia
anaphylaxis
angina
ankylosing spondylitis
ankylosis
anthrax
appendicitis
arc eye
arteriosclerosis
arthritis
asbestosis
asthma
ataxia
atherosclerosis
athlete's foot
avian flu
Bell's palsy
bends
beriberi
bilharzia
bird flu
blackwater fever
blood poisoning
botulism
Bright's disease
Broca's aphasia
bronchitis
brucellosis
bubonic plague
Burkitt's lymphoma
bursitis
cachexia
cancer
cardiomyopathy
carditis
carpal tunnel syndrome (CTS)
cataract
cerebral palsy
chickenpox
chill
cholera
chorea
chronic fatigue syndrome (CFS)
cirrhosis
coeliac disease
cold
colic
colitis
common cold
consumption
coronary heart disease
cough
cowpox
Creutzfeldt-Jakob disease (CJD)
Crohn's disease
croup
cryptosporidiosis
cyanosis
cystic fibrosis (CF)
cystitis
decompression sickness
deep-vein thrombosis (DVT)
deficiency disease
dengue
dermatitis
dermatosis
diabetes
diabetes insipidus
diabetes mellitus
diarrhoea
diphtheria
diverticular disease
double pneumonia
Down's syndrome
Duchenne muscular dystrophy (DMD)
Dupuytren's contracture
dysentery
Ebola
eclampsia
economy-class syndrome
eczema
elephantiasis
emphysema
encephalitis
endocarditis
endometriosis
endometritis
enteritis
epilepsy
ergotism
erysipelas
fetal alcohol syndrome
fever
fibrositis
filariasis
flu
flux
food poisoning
frozen shoulder
full-blown Aids
gangrene
gastric flu
gastritis
gastro-enteritis
German measles
gigantism
gingivitis
glandular fever
glaucoma
glue ear
glycaemia
goitre
gonorrhoea
gout
Gulf War syndrome
Guillain-Barré syndrome
haemophilia
Hansen's disease
hay fever
heat stroke
helminthiasis
hepatitis A/B/C
hepatoma
hernia
herpes
herpes simplex
hives
Hodgkin's disease
hookworm
human variant Creutzfeldt-Jakob disease (hvCJD)
Huntington's disease
hydrocephalus
hydrophobia
hypertension
hypoglycaemia
hypothermia
hypoxia
impetigo
infantile paralysis
influenza
iritis
irritable bowel syndrome (IBS)
ischaemia
jaundice
Kaposi's sarcoma
ketosis
kwashiorkor
laryngitis
Lassa fever
lead poisoning
legionella
legionnaires' disease
leishmaniasis
leprosy
leptospirosis
leukaemia
listeria
listeriosis
lupus
lupus vulgaris
Lyme disease
lymphoma
malaria
mastitis
measles
meningitis
molluscum contagiosum
morning sickness
motor neuron disease
mountain sickness
multiple sclerosis (MS)
mumps
muscular dystrophy
myalgic encephalomyelitis (ME)
myocarditis
nappy rash
narcolepsy
necrotizing fasciitis
nephritis
neuropathy
new variant Creutzfeldt-Jakob disease (nvCJD)
non-Hodgkin's lymphoma
non-specific urethritis
oedema
ophthalmia
orchitis
osteoarthritis
osteomyelitis
osteoporosis
pancreatitis
paratyphoid
Parkinson's disease
parotitis
pellagra
pelvic inflammatory disease
pericarditis
peritonitis
pernicious anaemia
pertussis
phlebitis
pink-eye
plague
pleurisy
pleuropneumonia
pneumoconiosis
pneumocystitis carinii pneumonia (PCP)
pneumonia
poliomyelitis
porphyria
prickly heat
pruritus
psittacosis
psoriasis
puerperal fever
pulmonary emphysema
pyaemia
pyrexia
quinsy
rabies
radiation sickness
rash
repetitive strain injury (RSI)
retinitis
retinopathy
rheumatic fever
rheumatism
rheumatoid arthritis
rhinitis
rickets
ringworm
roseola
rubella
St Vitus's dance
salmonella
sarcoma
scabies
scarlet fever
schizophrenia
sciatica
scleritis
scleroderma
sclerosis
scrofula
scurvy
seasonal affective disorder (SAD)
sepsis
septicaemia
serum hepatitis
severe acute respiratory syndrome (SARS)
sexually transmitted disease (STD)
shingles
sick building syndrome (SBS)
sickle-cell anaemia/disease
silicosis
sinusitis
sleeping sickness
smallpox
Spanish flu
spina bifida
spondylosis
spongiform encephalopathy
strabismus
sudden infant death syndrome
sunburn
sunstroke
swine flu
Sydenham's chorea
synovitis

syphilis
tendinitis
tenosynovitis
tetanus
thrombosis
thrush
tonsillitis
Tourette's syndrome
toxaemia
toxic shock syndrome
toxocariasis
toxoplasmosis
trench foot
trichinosis
trypanosomiasis
tuberculosis (TB)
typhoid
typhus
undulant fever
urethritis
urticaria
vaginismus
variant Creutzfeldt–Jakob disease (vCJD)
venereal disease (VD)
viraemia
virus
vitiligo
Weil's disease
whooping cough
yaws
yellow fever

Viruses

actinophage
adenovirus
alphavirus
arbovirus
arenavirus
bacteriophage
baculovirus
Borna disease virus
coronavirus
Coxsackie virus
cytomegalovirus
Ebola virus
echovirus
enterovirus
Epstein–Barr virus (EBV)
filovirus
hantavirus
herpes simplex virus
herpesvirus
herpes zoster virus
human immuno-deficiency virus (HIV)
human papilloma virus (HPV)
influenza virus
Lassa virus
lentivirus
leukovirus
maedi virus
Marburg virus
mengovirus
morbillivirus
myxovirus
Nipah virus
Norwalk virus
oncornavirus
orbivirus
papillomavirus
papovavirus
parainfluenza virus
paramyxovirus
parvovirus
picornavirus
poliovirus
polyoma virus
poxvirus
reovirus
retrovirus
rhabdovirus
rhinovirus
Ross River virus
rotavirus
Sendai virus
Shope virus
slow virus
tobacco mosaic virus (TMV)
togavirus
tumour virus
ultravirus
varicella virus
West Nile virus

Psychological illnesses and conditions

anorexia nervosa
Asperger's syndrome
attention deficit hyperactivity disorder (ADHD)
autism
bipolar disorder
body dysmorphic disorder
bulimia nervosa
catatonia
combat fatigue
de Clerambault's syndrome
dementia
depression
dysphoria
dysthymia
eating disorder
erotomania
false memory syndrome
gender dysphoria
hebephrenia
hyperactivity
hyperkinesis
hypomania
Korsakoff's syndrome
manic depression
megalomania
multiple-personality disorder
Munchausen's syndrome
Munchausen's syndrome by proxy
obsessive–compulsive disorder
panic disorder
paramnesia
paranoia
paraphilia
pica
post-natal depression
post-traumatic stress disorder (PTSD)
psychosis
schizo-affective disorder
schizophrenia
seasonal affective disorder (SAD)
shell shock

Phobias

Object	Phobia
air travel	aerophobia
American people and things	Americophobia
animals	zoophobia
bacteria	bacteriophobia
beards	pogonophobia
beating	mastigophobia
bed	clinophobia
bees	apiphobia
birds	ornithophobia
blood	haemophobia
blushing	erythrophobia
body odour	bromidrosiphobia
bridges	gephyrophobia
bullets	ballistophobia
burial alive	taphephobia
cancer	carcinophobia
cats	ailurophobia
childbirth	tocophobia
children	paedophobia
Chinese people and things	Sinophobia
church	ecclesiophobia
clouds	nephophobia
coitus	coitophobia
cold	cheimaphobia
colour	chromophobia
comets	cometophobia
computers	cyberphobia
constipation	coprostasophobia
corpses	necrophobia
correspondence	epistolophobia
crowds	demophobia/ochlophobia
dampness	hygrophobia
darkness	scotophobia
dawn	eosophobia
death	thanatophobia
depth	bathophobia
dirt	mysophobia
disease	pathophobia/nosophobia
dogs	cynophobia
dreams	oneirophobia
drink	potophobia
drugs	pharmacophobia
dust	koniophobia
electricity	electrophobia
enclosed places	claustrophobia
English people and things	Anglophobia
everything	panophobia/pantophobia
eyes	ommetaphobia
faeces	coprophobia
failure	kakorrhaphiaphobia
fatigue	kopophobia
fear	phobophobia
feathers	pteronophobia
fever	febriphobia
fire	pyrophobia
fish	ichthyophobia
flesh	selaphobia
floods	antlophobia
flowers	anthophobia
fog	homichlophobia
food	cibophobia/sitophobia
foreigners	xenophobia
freedom	eleutherophobia
French people and things	Francophobia/Gallophobia
fur	doraphobia
German people and things	Germanophobia/Teutophobia
germs	bacteriophobia
ghosts	phasmophobia
glass	nelophobia
God	theophobia
gold	chrysophobia/aurophobia
hair	trichophobia
heart disease	cardiophobia
heat	thermophobia
heaven	uranophobia
hell	hadephobia/stygiophobia
heredity	patroiophobia
high buildings	batophobia
high places	acrophobia/hypsophobia
home	oikophobia
homosexuals	homophobia
horses	hippophobia
ice	cryophobia
ideas	ideophobia
idleness	thassophobia
illness	nosophobia
imperfection	atelophobia
infinity	apeirophobia
injury	traumatophobia
inoculation	trypanophobia/vaccinophobia
insanity	lyssophobia/maniphobia
insects	entomophobia
insect stings	cnidophobia
Italian people and things	Italophobia
itching	acarophobia
jealousy	zelotypophobia
justice	dikephobia
lakes	limnophobia
leprosy	leprophobia
lice	pediculophobia
light	photophobia
lightning	astrapophobia
lists	pinaciphobia/katastichophobia
loneliness	autophobia/ermitophobia
machinery	mechanophobia
magic	rhabdophobia
marriage	gamophobia
men	androphobia
metal	metallophobia
mice	musophobia
microbes	bacillophobia/microbiophobia
mirrors	eisoptrophobia
mites	acarophobia
mobs	ochlophobia
money	chrematophobia
monsters, giving birth to	teratophobia
motion	kinetophobia
music	musicophobia
names	onomatophobia
narrowness	anginophobia
needles	belonephobia
new things	neophobia
night	nyctophobia
nudity	gymnophobia
open places	agoraphobia
pain	algophobia
parasites	parasitophobia
people	anthropophobia
philosophy	philosophobia
pins	enetophobia
places	topophobia
pleasure	hedonophobia
poison	toxiphobia
politics	politicophobia
Pope	papaphobia
poverty	peniaphobia
precipices	cremnophobia
priests	hierophobia
punishment	poinephobia
rabies	hydrophobophobia
rail travel	siderodromophobia
religious works of art	iconophobia
reptiles	batrachophobia

Object	Phobia
responsibility	hypegiaphobia
ridicule	katagelophobia
rivers	potamophobia
robbers	harpaxophobia
ruin	atephobia
Russian people and things	Russophobia
saints	hagiophobia
Satan	Satanophobia
scabies	scabiophobia
Scottish people and things	Scotophobia
sea	thalassophobia
sex	erotophobia
shadows	sciophobia
sharpness	acrophobia
shock	hormephobia
sin	hamartophobia
skin disease	dermatosiophobia/ dermatopathophobia
sleep	hypnophobia
slime	blennophobia
small things	microphobia
smell	olfactophobia/ osmophobia
smothering	pnigerophobia
snakes	ophidiophobia
snow	chionophobia
solitude	eremophobia
sound	acousticophobia
sourness	acerophobia
speech	lalophobia/ laliophobia/ glossophobia/ phonophobia
speed	tachophobia
spiders	arachnophobia
standing	stasophobia
stars	siderophobia
stealing	kleptophobia
string	linonophobia
stuttering	lalophobia/ laliophobia
sun	heliophobia
swallowing	phagophobia
symmetry	symmetrophobia
taste	geumatophobia
technology	technophobia
teeth	odontophobia
telephone	telephonophobia
thinking	phronemophobia
thirteen	triskaidekaphobia
thunder	brontophobia/ tonitrophobia/ keraunophobia
time	chronophobia
touch	haptophobia
travel	hodophobia
tuberculosis	phthisiophobia
tyrants	tyrannophobia
vehicles	ochophobia
venereal disease	syphilophobia
voids	kenophobia
vomiting	emetophobia
water	hydrophobia
waves	cymophobia
weakness	asthenophobia
wind	anemophobia
women	gynophobia
words	logophobia
work	ergophobia
worms	helminthophobia
writing	graphophobia

Operations

Technical name	Procedure
abdominoplasty	removal of excess flesh from abdomen
adenoidectomy	removal of adenoids
angioplasty	repair of blood vessel
appendectomy/ appendicectomy	removal of appendix
arteriotomy	incision of artery
blepharoplasty	repair or reconstruction of eyelid
Caesarean (section)	incision of wall of mother's abdomen to deliver child
cheiloplasty	repair of lips
cholecystectomy	removal of gall bladder
cholecystotomy	incision of gall bladder
colectomy	removal of colon
colostomy	opening of colon
craniotomy	incision of skull
cystectomy	removal of bladder/ removal of cyst
cystoplasty	repair of bladder
cystostomy	opening of bladder
cystotomy	incision of bladder
dermatoplasty	repair of skin
embolectomy	removal of blood clot
enterostomy	opening of small intestine
enterotomy	incision of intestine
episiotomy	incision of vaginal opening
gastrectomy	removal of stomach
gastroplasty	repair of stomach
gastrostomy	opening of stomach
gastrotomy	incision of stomach
glossectomy	removal of tongue
haemorrhoidectomy	removal of haemorrhoids
hepatectomy	removal of liver
hepaticostomy	opening of bile duct
hysterectomy	removal of womb
hysterotomy	incision of womb
keratotomy	incision of cornea
laminectomy	removal of back of vertebra/ vertebrae
laparotomy	incision of abdomen
laryngectomy	removal of larynx
laryngotomy	incision of larynx
lithotomy	removal of kidney stone
lobectomy	removal of lobe of an organ
lobotomy	incision of prefrontal lobe of brain
lumpectomy	removal of breast tumour
mammaplasty	reshaping of breast
mastectomy	removal of breast
myotomy	incision of muscle
nephrectomy	removal of kidney
nephrostomy	opening of kidney
nephrotomy	incision of kidney
neurectomy	removal of nerve
neurotomy	incision of nerve
oesophagectomy	opening of oesophagus
oophorectomy	removal of ovary
orchidectomy	removal of testis
orchidotomy	incision of testis
ostectomy	removal of bone
osteotomy	incision of bone
otoplasty	repair or reshaping of ear
ovariectomy	removal of ovary
ovariotomy	incision of ovary
palatoplasty	repair of cleft palate
pancreatectomy	removal of pancreas
pericardiectomy/ pericardectomy	removal of membrane around heart
pericardiotomy	incision of membrane around heart
perineoplasty	repair of vaginal opening
phalloplasty	repair of penis
pharyngectomy	removal of pharynx
phlebotomy	incision of vein
pleurotomy	incision of pleural membrane
pneumonectomy	removal of lung
polypectomy	removal of polyp
prostatectomy	removal of prostate gland
rhinoplasty	repair of nose
salpingectomy	removal of fallopian tube
salpingostomy	opening of fallopian tube
splenectomy	removal of spleen
tenotomy	incision of tendon
thoracoplasty	repair of thorax
thoracotomy	incision of chest cavity
thrombectomy	removal of blood clot
thymectomy	removal of thymus gland
thyroidectomy	removal of all or part of thyroid gland
tonsillectomy	removal of tonsils
tonsillotomy	incision of tonsil
tracheostomy	opening of windpipe
tracheotomy	incision of windpipe
ureterectomy	removal of ureter
ureterostomy	opening of ureter
ureterotomy	incision of ureter
urethroplasty	repair of urethra
urethrotomy	incision of urethra
vagotomy	incision of vagus nerve
valvotomy	incision of heart valve
varicotomy	removal of varicose vein
vasectomy	removal of vas deferens
vitrectomy	removal of vitreous humour from eyeball

Surgical instruments

bistoury
bougie
burr
cannula
colposcope
curette
depressor
dilator
forceps
gouge
guillotine
haemostat
lancet
laparoscope
osteotome
probe
raspatory
retractor
scalpel
scarificator
scoop
sigmoidoscope
snare
tenaculum
trepan
trephine
trocar

Bone fractures

Colles' fracture, comminuted fracture, compound fracture, greenstick fracture, impacted fracture, march fracture, multiple fracture, open fracture, Pott's fracture, simple fracture, spiral fracture, stress fracture

Medication types

abortifacient, addictive, alpha blocker, anaesthetic, analeptic, analgesic, anaphrodisiac, anodyne, anovulant, antacid, anthelmintic, antibacterial, antibiotic, anticholinergic, anticoagulant, anticonvulsant, antidepressant, antidiarrhoeal, antidote, anti-emetic, anti-epileptic, antifungal, antihistamine, anti-infective, anti-inflammatory, antipruritic, antipsychotic, antipyretic, antiretroviral, antiscorbutic, antiseptic, antispasmodic, antitussive, antiviral, anxiolytic, aperient, aphrodisiac, appetite suppressant, arsenical, beta blocker, booster, bronchodilator, calefacient, calmative, carminative, cathartic, contraceptive, convulsant, counterirritant, curative, cure-all, decongestant, depressant, diaphoretic, digestive, dilator, diuretic, ecbolic, emetic, emollient, euphoriant, evacuant, expectorant, febrifuge, fungicide, germicide, immuno-suppressive, laxative, lenitive, mercurial, muscle relaxant, narcotic, nervine, neuroleptic, nootropic, painkiller, palliative, placebo, preventive, prophylactic, psychotomimetic, psychotropic, relaxant, resolvent, restorative, roborant, sedative, sleeping draught, sleeping pill, soporific, sorbefacient, spasmolytic, steroid, stimulant, stupefacient, sudatory, sudorific, suppressant, sympatholytic, tonic, tranquillizer, vasoconstrictor, vasodilator, vermifuge

Forms of medication

balsam, cachet, caplet, capsule, collyrium, cream, draught, drench, drip, drops, ear drops, enema, eye drops, gargle, hypodermic, inhalant, injectable, linctus, lotion, lozenge, microcapsule, nasal spray, nebulizer, ointment, pastille, pessary, pill, poultice, powder, rub, salve, spray, suppository, syrette, tablet

Narcotic drugs

acid, amphetamine (sulphate), angel dust, basuco, betel, bhang/bang, blow, burley (tobacco), cannabis (resin), cavendish, charas, charlie, chaw, coca, cocaine, crack (cocaine), crystal meth, dagga, designer drug, dope, downer, draw, dynamite, E *or* Es, Ecstasy, eight ball, euphoriant, filler, freebase (cocaine), ganja, gateway drug, gear, GHB, grass, green, H, hashish, hemp, henbane, heroin, hop, horse, ibogaine, junk, kava, khat, kif/kef, kinnikinnick, locoweed, LSD, lysergic acid diethylamide (LSD), marijuana/marihuana, Mary Jane, mescaline/mescalin, meth, meth-amphetamine, methylene dioxymeth-amphetamine (MDMA), muscimol, narceine, nicotine, nose candy, opiate, opium, paan/pan, perique, peyote, peyote buttons, pot, psilocybin, psychedelic drug, rappee, reefer, rock, shag (tobacco), sinsemilla, skag/scag, skunkweed, smack, snow, snuff, speed, speedball, spliff, sugar, tendu leaf, Thai stick, tobacco, toot, upper, wacky baccy, weed, whizz, wild dagga, X, zarda

Contraceptives

barrier method, birth control pill, birth pill, cap, coil, coitus interruptus, combined pill, condom, contraceptive jelly, diaphragm, douche, douche bag, Durex (*trademark*), Dutch cap, female condom, Femidom (*trademark*), French letter, intrauterine device (IUD), johnny, karezza, Lippes loop, mini-pill, morning-after pill, Norplant (*trademark*), oral contraceptive, pessary, the pill, prophylactic, protective, rhythm method, rubber, safe, safety, sheath, spermicidal cream/jelly, spermicide, sponge, sympto-thermal method, withdrawal method

Poisonous substances and gases

aconitine, afterdamp, Agent Orange, aldrin, allyl alcohol, ammonia, antifreeze, arsenic, arsine, atropine, bleach, blister gas, bromine, cacodyl, cacodylic acid, carbon disulphide, carbon monoxide, caustic soda, chlordane, chlorine, coniine, curare, cyanic acid, cyanide, cyanogen, diazomethane, diborane, digitalin, digoxin, dioxane, endrin, ethylene oxide, fluorine, formaldehyde, hydrocyanic acid, hydrogen cyanide, hydrogen sulphide, hyoscyamine, iodine, lewisite, lindane, mercuric chloride, methanol, muscarine, mustard gas, nerve gas, nitric acid, nitrogen dioxide, osmium tetroxide, ouabain, oxalic acid, paraquat, parathion, Paris green, perchloric acid, perchloro-ethylene, phenol, phosgene, quinine, rat poison, ricin, rotenone, santonin, sarin, solanine, strophanthin, strychnine, sulphur dioxide, tartar emetic, tetrodotoxin, turpentine, veratrine, warfarin, white spirit, zinc chromate, Zyklon B

Music

Musical genres *See also* Jazz genres

absolute music
acid house
acid rock
alt.country
ambient
AOR
arioso
bachata
baggy
ballet music
barbershop
baroque
bel canto
benga
bhangra
bluegrass
blues
boogie-woogie
breakbeat
Britpop
calypso
Cantopop
chamber music
chant
choral music
church music
classical music
comic opera
contrapuntal music
country
country and western
country rock
cowpunk
crossover
crunk
cumbia
dance floor
dancehall
death metal
dhrupad
disco
dodecaphonic music
doo-wop
drum and bass
dub
easy listening
electro
emo/emocore
flamenco
folk
funk
funkadelic
fusion
gagaku
galant
gangsta (rap)
garage
glam rock
go-go
gospel
Goth
grand opera
grunge
gumbo
hardcore
heavy metal
highlife
hip hop
house
indie
industrial
jazz
jit
jive
juju
jump blues
jungle
klezmer
Krautrock
kwaito
kwela
light opera
liturgical music
marabi
mariachi
mash
mbaqanga
mento
merengue
minimalism
motet
Motown
multiculti
musique concrète
New Age
New Romantic
new wave
norteño
northern soul
oi
old-time
opera
opera buffa
opera seria
operetta
orbital
orchestral music
Palm Court
parang
pibroch
pogo
pop
popular music
programme music
progressive
psychedelic
psychobilly
punk
qawwali
queercore
ragamuffin/ragga
ragtime
rai
ranchera
rap
rave
reggae
reggaeton
rhythm and blues (R & B)
rock
rockabilly
rock and roll
rocksteady
sacred music
sakkie-sakkie
salsa
serialism
sijo
ska
skiffle
soca
soukous
soul
surf
symphonic music
taarab
talking blues
tasso
techno
technofunk
Tejano
Tex-Mex
thrash (metal)
trance
trip hop
twelve-note/twelve-tone music
vocalese
western swing
world music
zouk
zydeco

Jazz genres

acid jazz
Afro-Cuban
avant-garde
barrelhouse
bebop
bop
cool
Dixieland
free jazz
fusion
Harlem
harmolodics
honky-tonk
hot jazz
jazz funk
mainstream
modern jazz
progressive jazz
razzmatazz
rooty-toot
skiffle
swing
third stream
trad jazz
west coast

Musical forms

air
allemande
anthem
arabesque
aria
arietta
aubade
bagatelle
ballad
ballet
barcarole
berceuse
bourrée
brindisi
cabaletta
calypso
canon
canticle
canzone
canzonetta
capriccio
carol
catch
cavatina
chaconne
chanson
chant
chorale
chorus
concertino
concerto
concerto grosso
coronach
courante
dance
dead march
descant
dirge
ditty
drinking song
duet
dumka
duo
ensemble
entr'acte
entrée
étude
fado
fancy
fanfare
fantasia
fantasy
finale
five-finger exercise
flourish
foxtrot
frottola
fugato
fugue
galop
gavotte
gigue
glee
gradual
hornpipe
humoresque
hymn
impromptu
interlude
intermezzo
introit
jig
jingle
karanga
lament
Lied
lullaby
madrigal
march
mass
medley
minuet
monody
motet
moto perpetuo
movement
musette
musical
nocturne
nonet
octet
opera
operetta
oratorio
overture
partita
part-song
paso doble
passacaglia
passion
pastoral
pavane
pibroch
polka
polonaise
postlude
prelude
psalm
quadrille
quartet
quintet
quodlibet
rag
raga
rap
recitative
reel
refrain
requiem
reverie
rhapsody
ricercar/ricercare
ritornello
romance
rondo
round
roundelay
rumba
samba
sarabande
scena
scherzo
schottische
seguidilla
septet
serenade
serenata
setting
sextet
shanty
shuffle
siciliano/siciliana
signature tune
sinfonia
sinfonia concertante
sinfonietta
Singspiel
solo
sonata
sonatina
song
song cycle
spiritual
stomp
strathspey
study
suite
symphonic poem
symphony
tango
tarantella
terzetto
threnody
thumri
tiento
toccata
tone poem
trio
trio sonata
variation
verset
villanella/villanelle
voluntary
waiata
waltz
zarzuela

Musical directions

Term	Translation
a battuta	return to strict time
a cappella	unaccompanied
accel(erando)	accelerating
adagietto	fairly slowly
adagio	slowly
ad lib(itum)	at will
affettuoso	tenderly

Term	Translation
agitato	agitated
al fine	to the end
allargando	slowing
allegretto	fairly lively
allegro	lively
al segno	as far as the sign
amoroso	tenderly

Term	Translation
andante	moderately slow
andantino	slightly faster than andante
animato	spirited
arco	with the bow
arioso	in a sustained singing style

Term	Translation
assai	very
a tempo	in the original tempo
attacca	continue without a pause
bis	repeat
calando	becoming quieter and slower

Term	Translation
cantabile	in a smooth singing style
capriccioso	freely
coda	final part of a movement
col legno	with the stick of the bow
con amore	tenderly
con brio	with vigour
con fuoco	fiery
con moto	with movement
con sordino	with a mute
cresc(endo)	becoming louder
da capo *or* DC	from the beginning
dal segno *or* DS	from the sign
decresc(endo)	becoming quieter
dim(inuendo)	becoming quieter
dolce	sweetly and softly
dolente	sorrowfully
doppio	double
espressivo	with expression of feeling
fine	end (not at the end of the score)
f(orte)	loudly
forte piano	loudly and then immediately softly
fortissimo *or* ff	very loudly
furioso	furiously and wildly
giocoso	playfully
glissando	sliding
in modo di	in the manner of
larghetto	fairly slowly
largo	very slowly
legato	tied/smoothly
leggiero	lightly
lento	slowly
maestoso	majestically
marcato	accented
marcia	march
meno	less
meno mosso	less quickly
mezza voce	at half vocal strength
mezzo	half
mezzo forte *or* mf	fairly loudly
mezzo piano *or* mp	fairly softly
moderato	at a moderate pace
molto	very
morendo	dying away
mosso	fast and with animation
moto	motion
niente	gradually fading to nothing
nobilmente	nobly
non troppo	not too much
obbligato	not to be omitted
parlando	in the manner of speech
ped.	pedal
pesante	heavily
pianissimo *or* pp	very soft
p(iano)	soft
più	more
pizz(icato)	plucked
poco	a little
portamento	carrying one note into the next
prestissimo	as fast as possible
presto	very fast
rall(entando)	slowing down
ravvivando	quickening
rinforzando *or* rfz	accentuated
rit(ardando)	slowing down
ritenuto	suddenly more slowly
scherzando	playfully
segno	sign
semplice	simply
sempre	always/throughout
senza	without
sf(orzando) *or* sfz	strongly accented
smorzando	dying away
sordino	with a mute
sost(enuto)	sustained
sotto voce	in an undertone
spiccato	bouncing the bow on the strings
stacc(ato)	detached
stretto	in quicker time
stringendo	faster and more intensely
subito	immediately
tacet	voice/instrument remains silent
tanto	too much
tempo	speed/beat
ten(uto)	held
tranquillo	tranquilly
tremolando	trembling
troppo	too much
tutti	all players/singers
una corda	using the soft pedal (on a piano)
vivace	lively
zoppa	syncopated

Stringed instruments

acoustic guitar
aeolian harp
archlute
arpeggione
autoharp
balalaika
bandora/bandura
banjo
banjolele/banjulele
banjolin
baryton
bass guitar
bass lute
bass viol
biwa
bouzouki
cello
Celtic harp
charango
chitarrone
cimbalom
citole
cittern
clarsach
classical guitar
contrabass
cuatro
dobro (*trademark*)
double bass
dulcimer
electric guitar
erhu
fiddle
gamba
gittern
guitar
gusli
harp
Hawaiian guitar
hurdy-gurdy
kanoon
kantele
kithara
kora
koto
lute
lyre
mandola
mandolin
orpharion
oud
pedal steel guitar
pipa
psaltery
rebab
rebec
requinto
samisen
santoor
sarangi
sarod
saz
sitar
steel/steel-string guitar
string bass
tamboura
tamburitza
theorbo
trigon
triple harp
twelve-string guitar
ukulele
veena
vihuela de arco
vihuela de mano
viol
viola
viola bastarda
viola da gamba
viola d'amore
violetta
violin
violoncello
violone
Welsh harp
wind harp
zither

Wind instruments

alpenhorn *or* alphorn
bagpipes
barrel organ
basset horn
bassoon
bombarde
clarinet
contrabassoon
cor anglais
cornetto
didgeridoo
fife
fipple flute
flageolet
flute
harmonica
heckelphone
kazoo
krummhorn
lysarden
melodica
mouth organ
oboe
oboe d'amore
ocarina
piccolo
piffero
pipe
racket
recorder
reed pipe
sarrusophone
saxophone
serpent
shawm
stock-and-horn
tin whistle
whistle

Brass instruments

alto horn
baritone
bombardon
bugle
clarion
cornet
cornopean
euphonium
flugelhorn
French horn
handhorn
helicon
horn
lur
mellophone
ophicleide
post horn
sackbut
sarrusophone
saxhorn
saxotromba
slide trombone
sousaphone
tenor horn
trombone
trumpet
tuba
Wagner tuba
zinke

Percussion instruments

agogo
angel chimes
anvil
balafon
banana drum
barrel drum
bass drum
bells
bhaya
bodhrán
bongos
castanets
celesta
changko
chengcheng
chime bar
Chinese block
clappers
claves
conga drum
cowbell
crotales
cylindrical drums
cymbals
dhol
djembe
drum
dulcimer
frame drum
gamelan
glockenspiel
gong
gong chimes
goombay
handbell
hi-hat (cymbals)
idiophone
Jew's harp
kettledrum
kick drum
lithophone
maracas
mbira
mridangam
piano
rattle
rommelpot
rototom
santoor
saron
scraper
sekere
shaker
side drum
sistrum
sleigh bells
slit drum
snare drum
stamping tube
steel drum
tabla
tabor
taiko
tambour
tambourine
tam-tam
tassa drum
tenor drum
temple block
thumb piano
timbales
timpani
tom-tom
triangle
tubular bells
Turkish crescent
vibraphone
vibraslap
washboard
whip
wobbleboard
wood block
xylophone
xylorimba

Keyboard instruments

accordion
American organ
calliope
carillon
celesta
chamber organ
cinema organ
clavichord
clavicytherium
clavier
computer organ
dulcitone
electric organ
electronic organ
fortepiano
grand piano
Hammond organ (*trademark*)
harmonium
harpsichord
mellotron
melodeon
melodica
Moog synthesizer (*trademark*)
Novachord
ondes martenot
organ
pianino
piano
piano accordion
pianoforte
pianola
pipe organ
player-piano
portative organ
positive organ
reed organ
spinet
stylophone
synthesizer
upright piano
virginals
Wurlitzer (*trademark*)

Organs

American organ
barrel organ
chamber organ
cinema organ
electric organ
electronic organ
Hammond organ (*trademark*)
hand organ
harmonica
harmonium
melodeon
mouth organ
piano organ
pipe organ
portative organ
positive organ
reed organ
steam organ
Wurlitzer (*trademark*)

Orchestral instruments

bass clarinet
bass drum
basset horn
bassoon
bass tuba
celesta
cello
clarinet
contrabassoon
cor anglais
cymbals
double bass
flute
French horn
glockenspiel
harp
kettledrums
oboe
oboe d'amore
piccolo
side drum
snare drum
tam-tam
timpani *or* kettledrums
triangle
trombone
trumpet
tuba
tubular bells
viola
viola d'amore
violin
Wagner tuba

Instrumentalists

Player	Instrument
accordionist	accordion
banjoist	banjo
bassist	bass guitar *or* double bass
bassoonist	bassoon
cellist	cello
clarinettist	clarinet
cornetist	cornet
cymbalist	cymbal
drummer	drum
fiddler	violin
flautist	flute
guitarist	guitar
harper	harp
harpist	harp
harpsichordist	harpsichord
keyboardist	keyboard
lutenist, lutist	lute
lyrist	lyre
mandolinist	mandolin
oboist	oboe
organist	organ
percussionist	percussion
pianist	piano
piper	bagpipes
saxophonist, saxist	saxophone
tambourinist	tambourine
timpanist	timpani
trombonist	trombone
trumpeter	trumpet
vibist, vibraphonist	vibraphone
violinist	violin
violist	viola *or* viol
xylophonist	xylophone

Types of singer

balladeer
choirboy
choirgirl
chorister
chorus boy
chorus girl
coloratura
crooner
diva
folk singer
gleeman
jongleur
Meistersinger
minstrel
opera singer
pop singer
pop star
precentor
prima donna
primo uomo
singer-songwriter
soloist
spinto
troubadour

Types of singing voice

alto
baritone
bass
bass-baritone
basso profundo
boy soprano
castrato
contralto
countertenor
dramatic soprano, tenor, etc.
falsetto
Heldentenor
lyric soprano, tenor, etc.
male soprano
mezzo
mezzo-soprano
soprano
tenor
treble

Mythology

Mythological and fictional creatures *See also* **Nymphs**

Abominable Snowman
amazon
amphisbaena
banshee
basilisk
Bigfoot *or* Sasquatch
bugbear
bunyip
centaur
Cerberus
Charybdis
chimera
cockatrice
dragon
dwarf
dybbuk
elf
Erl King
fairy
firedrake
Frankenstein's monster
the Furies
genie
giant/giantess
gnome
goblin
golem
gorgon
Grendel
griffin
harpy
hippogriff
hobbit
hobgoblin
Hydra
jinn
kelpie
kobold
kraken
kylin
lamia
leprechaun
leviathan
Lilith
Loch Ness monster
lycanthrope
manticore
Medusa
mermaid
merman
Midgard's serpent
Minotaur
naga
ogre/ogress
orc
Pegasus
peri
phoenix
pixie
pooka
roc
Scylla
sea serpent
selkie
simurg
siren
sphinx
taniwha
Tiamat
tokoloshe
troll
unicorn
Valkyrie
vampire
werewolf
windigo
wyvern
yeti
zombie

Nymphs

dryad
hamadryad
naiad
nereid
Oceanid
oread
sprite
sylph
undine

Wordfinder

Plants

Flowering plants and shrubs *See also* Cacti

Aaron's rod
abelia
acacia
acanthus
aconite
African daisy
African violet
agapanthus
agave
agrimony
aloe
alstroemeria
alyssum
amaranth
amaryllis
anemone
angelica
angel's trumpet
aquilegia
arabis
arnica
arrowgrass
arum lily
asphodel
aspidistra
aster
astilbe
astrantia
aubretia
avens
azalea
balsam
baneberry
banksia
barberry
barrenwort
bearberry
bedstraw
begonia
belladonna
bellflower
bergamot
betony
bilberry
bindweed
bird of paradise flower
bird's-foot trefoil
black-eyed Susan
blackthorn
bleeding heart
bluebell
bog asphodel
bog rosemary
boneset
borage
bottlebrush
bougainvillea
bramble
broom
bryony
buckeye
buddleia
bugbane
bugle
bugloss
bulrush
burdock
burnet
busy Lizzie
buttercup
butterfly bush
butterwort
cabbage rose
cactus
calceolaria
calendula
camellia
camomile
campanula
campion
candytuft
canna lily
Canterbury bell
Cape primrose
carnation
catmint
cattleya
ceanothus
celandine
centaury
chaffweed
chervil
chickweed
chicory
chinaberry
Chinese lantern
chives
choisya
chokeberry
Christmas rose
chrysanthemum
cicely
cinchona
cinquefoil
clarkia
clematis
cloudberry
clove pink
clover
cockscomb
coltsfoot
columbine
comfrey
coneflower
convolvulus
coreopsis
cornflower
corydalis
cotoneaster
cottonweed
cow parsley
cowslip
cranesbill
creeping Jenny
crocus
crowfoot
crown imperial
crown of thorns
cuckoo pint
cuckooflower
cyclamen
daffodil
dahlia
daisy
damask rose
dandelion
daphne
deadly nightshade
delphinium
dianthus
dill
dittany
dock
dogbane
dog rose
dog violet
dropwort
duckweed
echinacea
edelweiss
eglantine
elder
evening primrose
eyebright
feverfew
figwort
firethorn
flax
fleabane
forget-me-not
forsythia
foxglove
frangipani
fraxinella
freesia
fritillary
fuchsia
furze
gaillardia
gardenia
gazania
gentian
geranium
gerbera
gillyflower
gladiolus
globeflower
glory-of-the-snow
gloxinia
goat's beard
golden rod
goldilocks
gorse
grape hyacinth
grass of Parnassus
groundsel
guelder rose
gypsophila
harebell
hawkbit
hawksbeard
hawkweed
hawthorn
heartsease
heather
hebe
helianthemum
helianthus
heliotrope
hellebore
helleborine
hemlock
herb Christopher
herb Paris
herb Robert
heuchera
hibiscus
hogweed
holly
hollyhock
honesty
honeysuckle
hop
hosta
hyacinth
hydrangea
ice plant
iris
jacaranda
Jack-by-the-hedge
Jacob's ladder
japonica
jasmine
jonquil
juneberry
kalanchoe
kalmia
kerria
kingcup
knapweed
knotgrass
laburnum
lady's mantle
lady's slipper
lady's smock
lady's tresses
larkspur
lavatera
lavender
lemon balm
leopard lily
lilac
lily
lily of the valley
lobelia
London pride
loosestrife
lords and ladies
lotus
lovage
love-in-a-mist
love-lies-bleeding
lungwort
lupin
madonna lily
magnolia
mahonia
mallow
mandrake
marguerite
marigold
marsh marigold
marshwort
may
mayflower
mayweed
meadow rue
meadow saffron
meadowsweet
Michaelmas daisy
mignonette
milfoil
milkwort
mimosa
mint
mistletoe
mock orange
monkey flower
monkshood
montbretia
moonflower
morning glory
motherwort
musk rose
myrtle
narcissus
nasturtium
nemesia
nettle
nicotiana
nigella
night-scented stock
nightshade
old man's beard
oleander
orchid
ox-eye daisy
oxlip
oyster plant
pansy
Parma violet
parsley
pasque flower
passion flower
pelargonium
pennyroyal
penstemon
peony
peppermint
periwinkle
petunia
pheasant's eye
phlox
pimpernel
pink
pitcher plant
plantain
plumbago
poinsettia
polyanthus
poppy
potentilla
prickly poppy
primrose
primula
privet
pulsatilla
pyracantha
pyrethrum
ragweed
ragwort
rampion
ramsons
rape
red-hot poker
rhododendron
rock rose
rose
rosebay willowherb
rose of Sharon
safflower
St John's wort
salpiglossis
salvia
samphire
sandwort
saxifrage
scabious
scarlet pimpernel
scilla
sedum
shamrock
sheep's-bit
shrimp plant
skimmia
skullcap
snapdragon
snow-in-summer
snowdrop
snowflake
soapwort
Solomon's seal
sorrel
sowthistle
speedwell
spider flower
spider plant
spiderwort
spikenard
spiraea
spurge
spurrey
squill
stargazer lily
star of Bethlehem
starwort
stitchwort
stock
stonecrop
storksbill
strawflower
streptocarpus
sunflower
sweetbriar
sweet cicely
sweet pea
sweet rocket
sweet william
tansy
tea rose
teasel
thistle
thorn apple
thrift
tiger lily
toadflax
tormentil
tradescantia
traveller's joy
trefoil
tuberose
tulip
turnsole
valerian
Venus flytrap
verbena
veronica
vervain
vetch
viburnum
violet
viper's bugloss
wallflower
water lily
water violet
weigela
willowherb
winter jasmine
wintergreen
wintersweet
wisteria/wistaria
witch hazel
wolfsbane
wood anemone
wood avens
woodruff
wood sorrel
woody nightshade
wormwood
yarrow
yerba buena
yucca
zinnia

Trees and shrubs

acacia
acer
ackee
alder
allspice
almond
angelica
anise
annatto
apple
apricot
araucaria
ash
aspen
avocado
azalea
balsa
balsam fir
bamboo
banksia
banyan
baobab
basswood
bay tree
beech
beefwood
bergamot
birch
blackthorn
bluegum
bodh tree
bog oak
bottlebrush
bottle tree
bo tree
box
box elder
breadfruit
bristlecone pine
broom
buckeye
buckthorn
bullace
bur oak
butternut
cacao
calabash
camellia
camphor tree
candelabra tree
candleberry
candlenut
carambola
carob
cashew
cassava
cassia
casuarina
cedar
cherimoya
cherry
cherry laurel
cherry plum
chestnut

chinaberry
cinnamon
citron
clove
coco de mer
coconut palm
coffee
cola
coolibah
copper beech
coral tree
cork oak
coromandel
cottonwood
crab apple
cryptomeria
curry leaf
custard apple
cypress
damson
dawn redwood
dogwood
Douglas fir
dragon tree
ebony
elder
elm
eucalyptus
euonymus
false acacia
fatsia
feijoa
fever tree
ficus
fig
filbert
fir
firethorn
flame tree
frangipani
fuchsia
gean
genipapo
ginkgo
gopherwood
gorse
grapefruit
greengage
guaiacum
guava
gum tree
handkerchief tree
hawthorn
hazel
hemlock fir
hickory
holly
holly oak
holm oak
honey locust
honeysuckle
hornbeam
horse chestnut
hydrangea
ilex
iroko
ironbark
ironwood
jacaranda
jackfruit
jack pine
japonica
jasmine
jojoba
jujube
juniper
kalmia
kapok
kauri (pine)
kermes oak
kola
kumquat
laburnum
lacquer tree
larch
laurel
lemon
Leyland cypress
leylandii
lilac
lime
linden
liquidambar
live oak
locust
lodgepole pine
logwood
Lombardy poplar
London plane
loquat
lychee
macadamia
macrocarpa
madroño
magnolia
mahogany
maidenhair tree
mandarin
mango
mangosteen
mangrove
maple
mastic
maté
may
mimosa
mirabelle
monkey puzzle
mountain ash
mulberry
myrtle
nectarine
Norway spruce
nutmeg
nux vomica
oak
oleaster
olive
osier
pagoda tree
palm
palmyra
papaya
paper mulberry
paperbark
pawpaw
pear
pedunculate oak
persimmon
pine
piñon
pistachio
pitch pine
plane
plum
pomegranate
pomelo
ponderosa (pine)
poplar
privet
pussy willow
quassia
quince
rain tree
rambutan
redbud
red cedar
redwood
rhododendron
robinia
roseapple
rosewood
rowan
royal palm
rubber plant
rubber tree
sallow
sandalwood
sapele
sapodilla
sassafras
satinwood
schefflera
Scots pine
senna
sequoia
service tree
silver birch
Sitka
slippery elm
smoke tree
soapberry
spindle
spruce
star anise
stinkwood
stone pine
storax
sugar maple
sumac
sycamore
tallow tree
tamarind
tamarisk
tangerine
tea
teak
tea tree
thuja
tree of heaven
trembling poplar
tulip tree
tulipwood
umbrella tree
viburnum
walnut
wattle
weeping willow
wellingtonia
whitebeam
willow
witch hazel
wych elm
yew
ylang-ylang

Plant types

algae
angiosperms
bryophytes
clubmosses
conifers
cycads
ferns
fungi
gymnosperms
hornworts
horsetails
lichens
liverworts
mosses
pteridophytes
vascular plants

Plant parts

bark
bract
flower
fruit
guard cell
lateral root
leaf
phloem
root
root cap
root hair
stem
stoma
tap root
vascular bundle
xylem

Flower parts

androecium
anther
calyx
capitulum
carpel
carpophore
catkin
corolla
corymb
cyathium
cyme
dichasium
filament
floret
glume
gynoecium
hypanthium
involucel
involucre
lemma
lip
monochasium
nectary
nucellus
ovary
ovule
palea
panicle
pedicel
peduncle
perianth
petal
pistil
placenta
pollen
pollen grain
pollinium
raceme
rachis
receptacle
sepal
spadix
spathe
spike
spikelet
spur
stamen
stigma
style
tassel
tepal
torus
umbel
whorl

Cacti

cholla
Christmas cactus
epiphyllum
hedgehog cactus
night-blooming cereus
nopal
opuntia
organ pipe cactus
peyote
pitahaya
prickly pear
saguaro
strawberry pear
tuna
Turk's cap

Mushrooms, toadstools, and other fungi

agaric
amethyst deceiver
anise cap
armillaria
artist's fungus
beefsteak fungus
bird's-nest fungus
black bulgar
blewit
blusher
bolete
boletus
bonnet
bootlace fungus
bracket fungus
brain fungus
brown hay cap
brown roll rim
butter cap
button mushroom
Caesar's mushroom
cage fungus
candle snuff fungus
cauliflower fungus
cep
champignon
chanterelle
charcoal burner
chicken of the woods
club foot
coral fungus
coral spot
cramp balls
cup fungus
dead man's fingers
death cap
destroying angel
dryad's saddle
ear pick fungus
earth ball
earth fan
earthstar
elf cup
ergot
fairies' bonnets
fairy ring fungus
false chanterelle
false morel
field mushroom
fly agaric
funnel cap
ghost fungus
giant puffball
grisette
hedgehog fungus
herald of the winter
honey fungus
horn of plenty
horsehair toadstool
horse mushroom
ink cap
jelly babies
jelly fungus
jelly tongue
Jew's ear
King Alfred's cakes
lawyer's wig mushroom
liberty cap
lorchel
meadow mushroom
milk cap
miller
morel
mousseron
old man of the woods
oyster mushroom
panther cap
parasol mushroom
parrot toadstool
penny bun
peppery bolete
plums and custard
poached egg fungus
poison pie
polypore
porcelain fungus
porcini
portobello
prince
puffball
reishi
russet shank
russula
saffron milk cap
St Anthony's fire
St George's mushroom
scarlet elf cup
scarlet hood
shaggy ink cap
shaggy parasol
shiitake
sickener
slimy beech cap
slippery jack
spike cap
stag's-horn fungus
stinkhorn
stinking parasol
straw mushroom
sulphur tuft
tartufo
tawny grisette

tinder fungus
tough shank
truffle
tuckahoe
velvet shank
verdigris agaric
wax cap
weeping widow
white truffle
witches' butter
wood blewit
wood mushroom
wood woolly foot
yellow stainer

Grasses, sedges, and rushes

bamboo
barley
beach grass
beard grass
bent
Bermuda grass
bluegrass
bristle grass
brome
broomcorn
buffalo grass
bulrush
bunch grass
button grass
canary grass
carex
cat's-tail grass
cheat grass
China grass
chufa
clubrush
cocksfoot
cogon
cordgrass
corn
cotton grass
couch grass
crabgrass
cutgrass
cutting grass
danthonia
darnel
deergrass
dogstail
dropseed
durra
elephant grass
esparto
feather grass
fescue
finger grass
fiorin
flowering rush
fog
foxtail
gama grass
hair grass
hare's-tail grass
Indian corn
Job's tears
kangaroo grass
kikuyu grass
lemon grass
lyme grass
maize
marram grass
meadow fescue
meadow grass
melick
millet
milo
moor grass
oat
oat grass
orchard grass
palmarosa
pampas grass
panic grass
papyrus
paspalum
pearl millet
quack grass
quaking grass
quitch grass
razor glass
redtop
reed
reed grass
reed mace
rice
rooigras
rush
rye
ryegrass
sawgrass
sedge
sheep's fescue
small-reed
sorghum
sour grass
spartina
spear grass
spelt
spinifex
squirrel-tail grass
star grass
sugar cane
switchgrass
sword grass
teff
teosinte
timothy grass
tussock grass
twitch grass
umbrella plant
vernal grass
wheat
wild oat
wild rice
wire grass
witch grass
woodrush
Yorkshire fog
zoysia

Religion

Religions and sects

Baha'i

Babism

Buddhism

Falun Gong
Hinayana
Lamaism
Mahayana
Nichiren
Rinzai Zen
Soka Gakkai
Soto Zen
Tantrism
Theravada
Tibetan Buddhism
Zen

Christianity

See also **Christian denominations and movements, Christian religious orders**

Confucianism

neo-Confucianism

Hinduism

Brahmanism
Krishna Consciousness
Saivism
Shaktism/Saktism
Shivaism/Sivaism
Tantrism
Vaishnavism
Vedantism
Vishnuism

Islam

Druzes
Ismailis
Mahdism
Salafi
Senussi
Shia
Sufism
Sunni
Wahhabism

Jainism

Digambara
Svetambara

Judaism

Conservative Judaism
Essenes
Falashas
Hasidism
Kabbalah
Karaism
Messianic Judaism
Orthodox Judaism
Pharisaism
Rabbinism
Reconstructionism
Reform Judaism
Samaritanism
Zionism

Shinto

Sikhism

Taoism

Zoroastrianism

Mazdaism
Parseeism

Other

ancestor worship
animism
candomblé
cargo cult
Druidism
Eleusinian mysteries
Ghost Dance cult
Hau-Hauism
Macumba
Mithraism
Myalism
Neopaganism
Orphism
Paganism
Pocomania
Rastafarianism
Ratana Church
Sabaism
Scientology (*trademark*)
Shamanism
Shango
Spiritualism
Subud
Theosophy
Totemism
Umbanda
Unification Church ('Moonies')
Voodoo
Wicca
Yezidism

Priests, religious officials, and members of religious orders

General

archpriest
cleric
hierarch
hierophant
high priest
preacher
priest
priestess

Ancient Roman

augur
flamen
haruspex
oracle
pontifex
Pythia

Ancient Celtic

Druid
ovate

Buddhist

Dalai Lama
lama
Panchen Lama
pongyi
talapoin

Christian

abbess
abbot
acolyte
almoner
anchoress
anchorite
archbishop
archdeacon
archimandrite
area dean
beadle
bishop
brother
canon
canoness
cantor
cardinal
chaplain
churchwarden
confessor
curate
deacon
deaconess
dean
elder
friar
lay brother
lay sister
mendicant
minister
monk
Monsignor
mother superior
nun
nuncio
padre
patriarch
pope
precentor
prelate
presbyter
primate
prior
prioress
rector
rural dean
sacristan
seminarist/seminarian
sexton
sister
succentor
thurifer
verger
vicar

Hindu

Brahman
guru
mahant
panda
pandit
pujari
rishi

Jewish

cantor
chief rabbi
dayan
hazzan
kohen/cohen
Levite
Maggid
rabbi
rebbe
rebbetzin

Muslim

ayatollah
bilal
caliph
fakir
imam
muezzin
mullah
sheikh

Sikh

guru

Voodoo

houngan
mamaloi
mambo
papaloi

Zoroastrian/Parsee

dastur
magus

Other

santero
witch
witch doctor

Places of worship

abbey
balmyard
baptistery/baptistry
basilica
cathedral
chantry
chapel
chapel of ease
chapel royal
chorten
church
collegiate church
dargah
duomo
fane
feretory
gurdwara
heiau
holy of holies
house of God
joss house
Kingdom Hall
kirk
kiva
mandir
marabout
marae
martyry
masjid
meeting house
minster
Mithraeum
monopteros
mosque
nymphaeum
oracle
oratory
pagoda
pantheon

peculiar
sacrarium
sanctuary
sanctum sanctorum
shrine
shul
stupa
synagogue
tabernacle
temple
teocalli
tirtha/tirth
valhalla
vihara
wat

Prayers

act of contrition
Agnus Dei
Amidah
Ave Maria
benedicite
benediction
Benedictus
bidding prayer
blessing
collect
Confiteor
Creed
decade
doxology
Gloria
grace
Habdalah/ Havdalah
Hail Mary
Kaddish
Kiddush
Kol Nidre
Kyrie (eleison)
Litany
miserere
namaz
Our Father
paternoster
requiescat
rogation
salat
Salve Regina
secret
shahada/ shahadah
suffrages

Christian denominations and movements

Abode of Love
Adventists
African & Afro-Caribbean Churches
African Orthodox Church
Agapemone
Albigenses
Alpha Course
American Baptist Churches
American Orthodox Church
Amish
Amish Mennonites
Anabaptists
Anglican Communion
Anglo-Catholics
Apostolic Brethren
Armenian Church
Assemblies of God
Assumptionists
Assyrian Church
Baptists
Bogomils
Bohemian Brethren
Brethren (Dunkers)
Brethren in Christ
Buchanites
Calvinism
Calvinistic Methodists
Cameronians
Camisards
Catholic Apostolic Church
Catholics
Celtic Church
Chaldaean Christians
Charismatic Movement
Cherubim & Seraphim Churches
Christadelphians
Christian Brethren
Christian Science
Church Army
Churches of Christ
Churches of God
Church in Wales
Church of Christ Scientist
Church of England
Church of Ireland
Church of Jesus Christ of Latter-day Saints
Church of North India
Church of Scotland
Church of South India
Church of the Nazarene
Church of the New Jerusalem
Congregationalists
Conservative Baptists
Coptic Orthodox Church
Countess of Huntingdon's Connexion
Covenanters
Cumberland Presbyterian Church
Disciples of Christ
Doppers
Doukhobors
Dunkers
Dutch Reformed Church
Eastern Orthodox Church
Episcopal Church of Scotland
Episcopal Church of USA
Ethiopian Orthodox Church
Evangelical Churches
Family of Love
Fifth Monarchy Men
Free Church
Free Church of Scotland
Free Presbyterian Church of Scotland
Free Will Baptists
Gideons
Glassites
Gnosticism
Greek Orthodox Church
Huguenots
Hussites
Hutterites
Independent Methodists
Jehovah's Witnesses
Jesus People
Jumpers
Lollards
Lutherans
Malabar Christians
Maronites
Mennonites
Methodists
Millennial Church
Moral Rearmament
Moravian Church
Muggletonians
Nazarenes
Nestorians
New Testament Assembly
Nonconformists
Old Believers
Old Catholics
Opus Dei
Oriental Orthodox Churches
Orthodox Church
Oxford Group
Oxford Movement
Particular Baptists
Paulicians
Pentecostal Churches
Plain People
Plymouth Brethren
Presbyterians
Primitive Methodists
Protestants
Puritans
Quakers
Ranters
Reformed Churches
Religious Society of Friends
River Brethren
Roman Catholics
Rosicrucians
Russian Orthodox Church
Salvation Army
Sandemanians
Seventh-Day Adventists
Shakers
Society of Friends
Southern Baptist Church
Swedenborgians
Syrian Orthodox Church
Tractarians
Trinitarians
Uniates
Unitarians
Unitarian Universalists
Unitas Fratrum
United Church of Christ
United Free Church
United Reformed Church
Waldenses
Wesleyans

Christian religious orders

Antonians
Augustinian Hermits
Austin Friars
Barnabites
Benedictines
Bernardines
Black Friars
Black Monks
Blue Nuns
Bonhommes
Brethren of the Common Life
Brigittines
Brothers Hospitallers
Camaldolites
Canons Regular
Capuchins
Carmelites
Carthusians
Christian Brothers
Cistercians
Cluniacs
Conceptionists
Conventuals
Culdees
Doctrinarians
Dominicans
Franciscans
Friars Minor
Friars Preachers
Gilbertines
Grey Friars
Grey Nuns
Hieronymites
Hospitallers
Ignorantines
Jacobins
Jesuits
Knights Hospitaller
Knights Templar
Little Brothers of Jesus
Marianists
Marists
Minims
Minorites
Norbertines
Oratorians
Passionists
Paulines
Piarists
Poor Clares
Poor Soldiers of the Temple
Premonstratensians
Salesians
Servites
Sisters of Charity
Sisters of the Love of God
Sisters of the Sacred Cross
Somascans
Studites
Sulpicians
Sylvestrines
Templars
Theatines
Trappists
Trinitarians
Ursulines
Visitandines
White Friars

Religious clothing

Christianity

alb
amice
biretta
cassock
chasuble
chimere
clerical collar
cope
cotta
cowl
dalmatic
dog collar
frock
Geneva bands
Geneva gown
habit
hood
infula
maniple
mantle
mitre
mozzetta
pallium
rochet
scapular
shovel hat
skullcap
soutane
stole
superhumeral
surplice
tippet
tunicle
wimple
zucchetto

Islam

burka
chador
hijab
jibba
jilbab
manteau
niqab
turban
yashmak

Judaism

ephod
gaberdine
kippa *or* kipa
pectoral
skullcap
tallith
yarmulke

Sikhism

kangha
kara
kuccha
turban

Science

Branches of science *See also* **Branches of medicine**

acoustics
aerodynamics
agriscience
anatomy
anthropology
astronomy
astrophysics
atomic physics
bacteriology
behavioural science
biochemistry
biology
botany
chemistry
climatology
computer science
conchology
cosmology
cryogenics
crystallography
cybernetics
cytology
dendrology
dynamics
earth science
ecology
economics
electrical engineering
electrodynamics
electronics
engineering
entomology
ethnology
ethology
evolutionary psychology
exobiology
fluid mechanics
forensics
genetic engineering
genetics
geochemistry
geochronology
geography
geology
geomorphology
geophysics
glaciology
herpetology
histology
holography
hydrodynamics
hydrology
hydrostatics
ichthyology
immunology
information technology
limnology
linguistics
marine biology
mathematics
mechanics
medical physics
metallurgy
meteorology
microbiology
mineralogy
molecular biology
mycology
natural history
nephology
neurochemistry
neurology
neuroscience
nuclear chemistry
nuclear physics
oceanography
optics
ornithology
palaeobotany
palaeoclimatology
palaeontology
palynology
particle physics
pedology
petrology
photochemistry
physics
physiography
physiology
phytology
phytopathology
psychology
quantum mechanics
radiochemistry
radiology
robotics
seismology
sociobiology
sociology
soil science
spectroscopy
statistics
stratigraphy
taxonomy
tectonics
thermodynamics
toxicology
virology
volcanology/vulcanology
zoogeography
zoology
zymurgy

Chemical elements and their symbols M = metal R = radioactive

Element	Symbol		
actinium	Ac		R
aluminium	Al	M	
americium	Am	M	R
antimony	Sb	M	
argon	Ar		
arsenic	As		
astatine	At		R
barium	Ba	M	
berkelium	Bk	M	R
beryllium	Be	M	
bismuth	Bi	M	
bohrium	Bh		R
boron	B		
bromine	Br		
cadmium	Cd	M	
caesium	Cs	M	
calcium	Ca	M	
californium	Cf	M	R
carbon	C		
cerium	Ce	M	
chlorine	Cl		
chromium	Cr	M	
cobalt	Co	M	
copper	Cu	M	
curium	Cm	M	R
darmstadtium	Ds		R
dubnium	Db		R
dysprosium	Dy	M	
einsteinium	Es		R
erbium	Er	M	
europium	Eu	M	
fermium	Fm	M	R
fluorine	F		
francium	Fr	M	R
gadolinium	Gd	M	
gallium	Ga	M	
germanium	Ge		
gold	Au	M	
hafnium	Hf	M	
hassium	Hs		R
helium	He		
holmium	Ho	M	
hydrogen	H		
indium	In	M	
iodine	I		
iridium	Ir	M	
iron	Fe	M	
krypton	Kr		
lanthanum	La	M	
lawrencium	Lr	M	R
lead	Pb	M	
lithium	Li	M	
lutetium	Lu		
magnesium	Mg	M	
manganese	Mn	M	
meitnerium	Mt	M	R
mendelevium	Md	M	R
mercury	Hg	M	
molybdenum	Mo	M	
neodymium	Nd	M	
neon	Ne		
neptunium	Np	M	R
nickel	Ni	M	
niobium	Nb	M	
nitrogen	N		
nobelium	No	M	R
osmium	Os	M	
oxygen	O		
palladium	Pd	M	
phosphorus	P		
platinum	Pt	M	
plutonium	Pu		R
polonium	Po	M	R
potassium	K	M	
praseodymium	Pr	M	
promethium	Pm	M	R
protactinium	Pa	M	R
radium	Ra	M	R
radon	Rn		R
rhenium	Re	M	
rhodium	Rh	M	
rubidium	Rb	M	
ruthenium	Ru	M	
rutherfordium	Rf		R
samarium	Sm	M	
scandium	Sc	M	
seaborgium	Sg		R
selenium	Se		
silicon	Si		
silver	Ag	M	
sodium	Na	M	
strontium	Sr	M	
sulphur	S		
tantalum	Ta	M	
technetium	Tc	M	R
tellurium	Te		
terbium	Tb	M	
thallium	Tl	M	
thorium	Th	M	R
thulium	Tm	M	
tin	Sn	M	
titanium	Ti	M	
tungsten	W	M	
uranium	U	M	R
vanadium	V	M	
xenon	Xe		
ytterbium	Yb	M	
yttrium	Y	M	
zinc	Zn	M	
zirconium	Zr	M	

Types of metal *See also* **Alloys**

actinide
alkali metal
alkaline earth (metal)
alloy
amalgam
base metal
heavy metal
lanthanide
noble metal
platinum metal
precious metal
rare earth (metal)
transition metal

Chemicals *See also* **Poisonous substances and gases**

Common name	Chemical name
acetic acid	ethanoic acid
acetone	propanone
acetylene	ethyne
alcohol	ethanol
alum	potash alum
alumina	aluminium oxide
aqua fortis (*archaic*)	nitric acid
baking soda	sodium bicarbonate
baryta	barium hydroxide
bicarbonate of soda	sodium bicarbonate
blue vitriol (*archaic*)	copper sulphate
boracic acid	boric acid
borax	sodium borate
Borazon (*trademark*)	boron nitride
calomel	mercurous chloride
carbolic acid	phenol
carbonic acid gas (*archaic*)	carbon dioxide
carbon tetrachloride	tetrachloromethane
carborundum	silicon carbide
caustic potash	potassium hydroxide
caustic soda	sodium hydroxide
Chile saltpetre	sodium nitrate
chloroform	trichloroethane

Common name	Chemical name
chrome yellow	lead chromate
cinnabar	mercuric sulphide
common salt	sodium chloride
copperas	ferrous sulphate *or* iron(II) sulphate
copper vitriol (*archaic*)	copper sulphate
corrosive sublimate (*dated*)	mercuric chloride
corundum	aluminium oxide
cream of tartar	potassium hydrogen tartrate
cyanide	sodium (*or* potassium) cyanide
dry ice	(solid) carbon dioxide
Epsom salts	magnesium sulphate
ether	diethyl ether
ethyl alcohol	ethanol
firedamp	methane
flowers of zinc	zinc oxide
folic acid	pteroylglutamic acid
formaldehyde	methanal
formic acid	methanoic acid
Glauber's salt	sodium sulphate
glycerine	glycerol
green vitriol (*archaic*)	ferrous sulphate *or* iron(II) sulphate
gypsum	calcium sulphate
jeweller's rouge	ferric oxide
laughing gas	dinitrogen monoxide
litharge	lead monoxide
lithia	lithium oxide
lunar caustic (*archaic*)	silver nitrate
magnesia	magnesium oxide
marsh gas	methane
massicot	lead monoxide
muriatic acid (*archaic*)	hydrochloric acid
nitric oxide	nitrogen monoxide
oil of vitriol (*archaic*)	sulphuric acid
peroxide	hydrogen peroxide
phosphorous acid	phosphoric acid
plaster of Paris	calcium sulphate
potash	potassium carbonate *or* potassium hydroxide
prussic acid (*dated*)	hydrocyanic acid
quicklime	calcium oxide
red lead	lead oxide
sal ammoniac (*dated*)	ammonium chloride
salt	sodium chloride
saltpetre	potassium nitrate
silica	silicon dioxide
slaked lime	calcium hydroxide
soda	sodium carbonate
spirits of salt (*archaic*)	hydrochloric acid *or* hydrogen chloride
strontia	strontium oxide
sugar	sucrose
sugar of lead (*dated*)	lead acetate
sulphuretted hydrogen (*archaic*)	hydrogen sulphide
tartar emetic	potassium antimony tartrate
thoria	thorium dioxide
titanium white	titanium dioxide
verdigris	copper carbonate
vitriol (*archaic*)	sulphuric acid
washing soda	sodium carbonate
white arsenic	arsenic trioxide
white vitriol (*archaic*)	zinc sulphate
xylene	dimethylbenzene
zaffre	cobalt oxide
zirconia	zirconium dioxide

Types of chemical compound

acetate
acid
alcohol
aldehyde
alkaloid
alkane
alkene
alkyne
amine
base
bromide
carbide
carbohydrate
carbonate
chloride
chlorofluorocarbon (CFC)
cyanide
epoxide
ester
fluoride
hydrocarbon
hydroxide
iodide
ketone
nitrate
nitride
nitro compound
oxide
paraffin
phosphate
salt
silicate
silicone
sulphate
sulphide

Types of acid

amino acid
carboxylic acid
dibasic acid
fatty acid
Lewis acid
mineral acid
monobasic acid
nucleic acid
organic acid
tribasic acid

Amino acids

alanine
arginine
asparagine
aspartic acid
cysteine
dopa
gamma-aminobutyric acid
glutamic acid
glutamine
glycine
histidine
homocysteine
isoleucine
leucine
lysine
methionine
ornithine
phenylalanine
proline
sarcosine
serine
taurine
threonine
tryptophan
tyrosine
valine

Gases

acetylene
afterdamp
ammonia
argon
arsine
biogas
blister gas
butadiene
butane
butene
Calor gas (*trademark*)
carbon dioxide
carbon monoxide
chlorine
chlorofluorocarbon (CFC)
coal gas
compressed natural gas (CNG)
CS gas
cyanogen
cyclopropane
diazomethane
diborane
ethane
ethylene
fluorine
formaldehyde
greenhouse gas
halon
helium
hydrogen
isobutane
ketene
krypton
laughing gas
lewisite
liquefied natural gas (LNG)
liquefied petroleum gas (LPG)
marsh gas
methane
mustard gas
natural gas
neon
nerve gas
nitrogen
nitrogen dioxide
nitrous oxide
oil gas
oxygen
ozone
phosgene
phosphine
producer gas
propane
propylene
radon
sarin
silane
soman
steam
sulphur dioxide
tabun
tail gas
tear gas
tetrafluoroethylene
town gas
vinyl chloride
water gas
xenon
Zyklon B

Minerals

actinolite
agate
alabaster
albite
allanite
andalusite
andradite
anhydrite
anorthite
antigorite
apatite
apophylite
aragonite
arsenopyrite
asbestos
augite
autunite
aventurine
azurite
baddeleyite
baryte
bastnaesite
bentonite
beryl
biotite
bloodstone
Blue John
borax
bornite
brucite
bytownite
cairngorm
calcite
carnallite
carnotite
cassiterite
chabazite
chalcedony
chalcopyrite
chiastolite
chlorite
chloritoid
chromite
chrysoberyl
chrysocolla
chrysoprase
chrysotile
cinnabar
clinopyroxene
colemanite
columbite
cordierite
corundum
covellite
crocidolite
crocoite
cryolite
cummingtonite
cuprite
diamond
diopside
dioptase
dolomite
dumortierite
emery
enargite
enstatite
epidote
fayalite
feldspar
ferberite
fluorite
fluorspar
fool's gold
forsterite
gadolinite
galena
garnet
garnierite
geyserite
gibbsite
glauconite
glaucophane
goethite
graphite
greenockite
grossular
gypsum
haematite
halite
hemimorphite
hiddenite
hornblende
hydroxyapatite
hypersthene
iddingsite

idocrase
illite
ilmenite
ilvaite
jacinth
jadeite
jargoon
jasper
kainite
kaolinite
kernite
kieserite
kunzite
kyanite
labradorite
lazurite
lepidocrocite
lepidolite
leucite
limonite
magnesite
magnetite
malachite
manganite
marcasite
mica
microcline
millerite
mimetite
molybdenite
monazite
montmorillonite
muscovite
natron
nepheline
nephrite
oligoclase
olivine
onyx
opal
orpiment
orthoclase
orthopyroxene
pentland
periclase
peridot
perovskite
phlogopite
piemontite
pigeonite
pitchblende
plagioclase
pyrargyrite
pyrites
pyrolusite
pyromorphite
pyroxene
pyrrhotite
quartz
realgar
rhodochrosite
rhodonite
riebeckite
rock salt
rutile
sanidine
sard
scheelite
serpentine
siderite
sillimanite
skutterudite
smaltite
smectite
smithsonite
smoky quartz
sodalite
spectrolite
sphalerite
sphene
spinel
spodumene
staurolite
steatite
stibnite
stishovite
strontianite
sylvite
talc
tantalite
tennantite
tetrahedrite
thenardite
topaz
tourmaline
tremolite
trona
tungstite
tyuyamunite
ulexite
uraninite
vanadinite
verminculite
vesuvianite
vivianite
willemite
witherite
wolframite
wollastonite
wulfenite
wurzite
xenotime
zeolite
zincite
zircon
zoisite

Wordfinder

Rocks

Sedimentary

arenite
argillite
breccia
chalk
chert
claystone
coal
conglomerate
diatomite
dolomite
flint
ironstone
limestone
marl
mudstone
oil shale
oolite
phosphorite
pisolite
radiolarite
rag
rudite
sandstone
shale
siltstone
tillite

Metamorphic

amphibolite
blueschist
eclogite
epidiorite
epidosite
gneiss
granulite
hornfels
lapis lazuli
marble
mica schist
mylonite
phyllite
psammite
pyroxenite
quartzite
schist
serpentinite
slate
verdite

Igneous

andesite
anorthosite
aplite
basalt
breccia
diorite
dolerite
dunite
elvan
felsite
gabbro
granite
greenstone
kimberlite
lamprophyre
lava
monzonite
obsidian
ophiolite
pegmatite
peridotite
phonolite
picrite
porphyry
pumice
rhyolite
syenite
tephrite
tonalite
trachyte
trap
tuff
variolite
vitrophyre

Gems

agate
alexandrite
almandine
amber
amethyst
aquamarine
balas ruby
beryl
bloodstone
cairngorm
carbuncle
carnelian
cat's-eye
chalcedony
chrysolite
chrysoprase
corundum
diamond
emerald
fire opal
garnet
girasol
greenstone
jacinth
jade
jasper
lapis lazuli
marcasite
moonstone
morganite
moss agate
onyx
opal
pyrope
rhodolite
ruby
sapphire
sardonyx
smoky quartz
spessartine
spiderweb
sunstone
tanzanite
topaz
tourmaline
turquoise
uvarovite
zircon

Oils

ajowan
almond oil
arachis oil
attar
baby oil
bergamot oil
brilliantine
cajuput/cajeput
castor oil
chaulmoogra
citronella
coconut oil
cod liver oil
copaiba
corn oil
creosote
croton oil
crude (oil)
Danish oil
diesel oil
drying oil
essential oil
eucalyptus oil
fatty oil
fixed oil
fuel oil
fusel oil
gas oil
geranial
grapeseed oil
grease
heavy oil
jojoba
lavender oil
linseed oil
Macassar
mineral oil
multigrade
naphtha
neat's-foot oil
neroli oil
nut oil
oil of cloves
oil of juniper
oil of turpentine
oil of wintergreen
olive oil
otto
palmarosa oil
palm oil
patchouli
peanut oil
petitgrain
petroleum
rape oil
rapeseed oil
safflower oil
sandalwood oil
sesame oil
shale oil
shea
sperm oil
stand oil
sunflower oil
suntan oil
tanning oil
tar oil
tea oil
train oil
tung oil
turpentine
turps
vanaspati
vegetable oil
vetiver/vetivert
volatile oil
walnut oil
whale oil
white oil
wintergreen
ylang-ylang/ilang-ilang

Types of radiation

alpha radiation
background radiation
backscatter
beta radiation
bremsstrahlung
Cerenkov radiation
coherent radiation
cosmic rays
electromagnetic radiation
gamma radiation
gravitational radiation
Hawking radiation
infrared (IR) radiation
insolation
ionizing radiation
light
microwaves
radar waves
radio waves
submillimetre radiation
synchrotron radiation
ultraviolet (UV) radiation
visible radiation
X-rays

Subatomic particles

antielectron
antineutron
antiparticle
antiproton
antiquark
axion
baryon
boson
electron
fermion
gluon
hadron
Higgs (boson/particle)
hyperon
kaon
lambda particle
lepton
meson
muon
neutrino
neutron
nucleon
photon
pion
positron
proton
psi particle
quark
strange particle
tau particle
WIMP

Flavours and colours of quarks and antiquarks

beauty
blue
bottom
charm
down
green
minus-blue
minus-green
minus-red
red
strangeness
top
truth
up

Society

Political philosophies and systems

absolutism
anarchism
anarcho-syndicalism
authoritarianism
Bolshevism
collectivism
communism
conservatism
democracy
egalitarianism
Eurocommunism
fascism
federalism
imperialism
individualism
laissez-faire
leftism
Leninism
liberalism
libertarianism
Maoism
Marxism
meritocracy
monarchism
nationalism
neo-Marxism
pluralism
plutocracy
populism
republicanism
rightism
situationism
social democracy
socialism
Sovietism
Stalinism
state capitalism
state socialism
statism
syndicalism
technocracy
Thatcherism
theocracy
the third way
timocracy
Titoism
totalitarianism
Trotskyism
utilitarianism
Utopianism

Types and systems of government

autocracy	by an absolute ruler
bureaucracy	by state officials
constitutionalism	according to a constitution
democracy	by elected representatives
despotism	by a despot
diarchy	by two independent authorities
dictatorship	by a dictator
fascism	by a right-wing, nationalistic regime
federalism	according to federal principles
gynarchy	by women
heptarchy	by seven rulers
hierocracy	by priests
imperialism	by an emperor or empire
meritocracy	by people of proven ability
monarchy	by a monarch
monocracy	by one person
ochlocracy	by the populace or mob
octarchy	by eight people
oligarchy	by a small group of people
plutocracy	by the rich
stratocracy	by the army
synarchy	by two or more people or groups
theocracy	by priests representing a deity
timocracy	by property owners
totalitarianism	by an absolute ruler or regime
tyranny	by a tyrant

Rulers' titles

aga
archduke
caesar
caliph
chief
czar
elector
electress
emir
emperor
empress
Führer
grand duke
kaiser
khan
khedive
king
maharaja
mikado
mogul
nawab
negus
nizam
pharaoh
prince
princess
queen
raja
rani
regent
satrap
shah
sheikh
shogun
sultan
tenno
tsar
vicereine
viceroy

Nobles

baron
baroness
baronet
begum
bey
boyar
burgrave
castellan
commander
contessa
count
countess
don
duchess
duke
earl
esquire
grand duke
grandee
hidalgo
Junker
knight
knight commander
life peer
life peeress
maid of honour
marchesa
marchese
marchioness
margrave
margravine
marquesa
marquess
marquis
marquise
Mistress of the Robes
nawab
paladin
palsgrave
prince
rangatira
royal duke
seigneur/seignior
squire
thakur
thane
vicomte
vicomtesse
viscount
viscountess

Police officers and forces

askari
assistant chief constable
bomb squad
Bow Street Runner/Officer
cadet
captain
carabiniere/carabinieri
chief (of police)
chief constable
chief inspector
chief superintendent
CID (Criminal Investigation Department)
commander
commissaire
commissioner
community police officer
constable
constabulary
crime squad
deputy chief constable
desk sergeant
detective chief inspector
detective chief superintendent
detective constable
detective inspector
detective sergeant
detective superintendent
drug/drugs squad
faujdar/faujidar
flying squad
fraud squad
Garda/Gardai
gendarme
gendarmerie
Gestapo
GPU
havildar
Homicide
inspector
investigating officer
Keystone Kops
KGB
LAPD (Los Angeles Police Department)
lieutenant
marshal
master-at-arms
Met
military police (MP)
military policeman/policewoman (MP)
Mountie
murder squad
NKVD
NYPD (New York Police Department)
pointsman
police constable
police department
port police
provost
provost guard
provost marshal
redcap
Royal Canadian Mounted Police
roundsman
Scotland Yard
secret police
Securitate
security police
sepoy
sergeant
snatch squad
SOCO (scene-of-crime officer)
special
special constable
SS
Stasi
station sergeant
strike force
super
superintendent
Sûreté
SWAT team
Sweeney
Texas Ranger
transport police
trooper
vice squad
Vopo
woman police constable

Types of lawyer

advocate
advocate-depute
advocate-general
ambulance-chaser
amicus (curiae)
articled clerk
attorney
Attorney General (AG)
barrister
barrister-at-law
bencher
cadi
canonist
Chief Justice (CJ)
civil lawyer
commissioner for oaths
Common Serjeant
conveyancer
counsel
counselor-at-law
county commissioner
criminal lawyer
Crown prosecutor
custos rotulorum
defence lawyer
defending counsel
Director of Public Prosecutions (DPP)
district attorney (DA)
hakim
high sheriff
judge
judge advocate
Judge Advocate General (JAG)
junior barrister
jurisconsult
jurist
Justice of the Peace (JP)
justiciar
law agent
law lord
Law Officer (of the Crown)

leading counsel
Lord Chancellor
Lord Justice (LJ)
Lord Justice of Appeal
Lord of Session
master
Master of the Rolls (MR)
moulvi
mufti
munsif
notary
notary public (NP)
official (principal)
ordinary
paralegal
proctor
procurator
procurator fiscal
prosecuting counsel
prosecution lawyer
prosecutor
prosecutrix
public defender
public prosecutor
pupil-master
QC
Queen's Counsel
recorder
registrar
resident magistrate (RM)
senator
serjeant-at-law
sheriff
sheriff-depute
silk
solicitor
solicitor General (SG)
Solicitor in the Supreme Court (SSC)
state's attorney
surrogate
trial lawyer
undersheriff
vakil
writer to the Signet

Punishments

attainder
auto-da-fé
banishment
bastinado
belt
birch
blackballing
blacklisting
boxing someone's ears
boycott
branks
cane
capital punishment
confiscation
corporal punishment
Coventry, sending to
crucifixion
cucking stool
damnation
death penalty
debagging
decimation
demotion
detention
ducking
ducking stool
endorsement
excommunication
execution
fatigues
fine
firing squad
flogging
gallows
gating
gauntlet, running the
gibbet
grounding
hanging
hanging, drawing, and quartering
hard labour
hiding
internal exile
jankers
kadaitcha/kurdaitcha
keelhauling
kneecapping
knout
kurbash
lash
lethal injection
life sentence
lines
lynching
mastheading
necktie party
noose
noyade
order mark
ostracism
pack drill
paddle
peine forte et dure
penal servitude
penalty point
penance
perdition
rod
rope
rustication
sanction
scaffold
scourging
self-flagellation
sequestration
six of the best
solitary confinement
spanking
spud-bashing
stocks
strap
strappado
suspended sentence
tarring and feathering
tawse
torture
transportation
wheel
whipping

Taxes

advance corporation tax (ACT)
airport tax
alternative minimum tax (AMT)
capital gains tax (CGT)
capital levy
capital transfer tax (CTT)
capitation
carbon tax
community charge
corporation tax
council tax
countervailing duty
customs (duty)
death duty
estate duty
estate tax
excise
goods and services tax (GST)
groundage
income tax
inheritance tax (IHT)
inland duty
insurance tax
landfill tax
land tax
metage
murage
negative income tax
octroi
pavage
PAYE (pay as you earn)
Peter's pence
poll tax
poor rate
post-war credit
property tax
purchase tax
rates
road tax
sales tax
ship money
stallage
stamp duty
supertax
surtax
taille
tallage
tarrif
tithe
toll
transit duty
uniform business rate (UBR)
VAT (value added tax)
vehicle excise duty (VED)
wealth tax
windfall tax
window tax
withholding tax
zakat

Currency units

afghani
agora
anna
at
avo
baht
baiza
balboa
ban
birr
bolivar
boliviano
butut
cedi
cent
centas
centavo
centesimo
centésimo
centime
centimo
CFA franc
chetrum
colón
cordoba
crore
cruzado
cruzeiro
dalasi
denar
Deutschmark
dinar
diram
DM
D-mark
dobra
dollar
dong
drachma
dram
ecu/ECU
escudo
euro
Eurodollar
European currency unit
eyrir
fen
filler
fils
florin
forint
franc
gopik
gourde
groschen
grosz
guarani
guilder
guinea
gulden
halala
haler
halier
heller
hryvna/hryvnia
inti
jeon
jiao
jun
khoum
kina
kip
kobo
kopek/kopeck/copeck
kopiyka
koruna
krona
krone
kroon
kuna
kurus
kwacha
kwanza
kyat
lari
lat
lek
lempira
leone
lepton
leu
lev/leva
likuta
lilangeni
lipa
lira
litas
loti
luma
lwei
manat
mark
markka
metical
mill
millieme
milreis
mongo
naira
nakfa
ngultrum
ngwee
øre
öre
Ostmark
ouguiya
pa'anga
paisa
para
pataca
pengö
penni
penny
peseta
pesewa
peso
petrodollar
pfennig
piastre
pice
pie
poisha
pound
pul
pula
punt
pya
qintar
quetzal
qursh
rand
rappen
real
Reichsmark
renminbi
rial/riyal
riel
ringgit
rouble
rufiyaa
rupee
rupiah
santim
satang
schilling
sen
sene
seniti
sent
sente
shekel
shilling
simoleon
sol
soldo
som
somoni
sov
stotin
stotinka
sucre
tael
taka
tala
talent
tambala
tein
tenesi
tenge
tetri
thebe
tiyin
toea
tolar
tugrik
vatu
won
xu
yen
yuan
zaire
zloty

Coins *For coins that are also units of currency, such as euro and dinar, see* **Currency units**

angel
as
aureus
bawbee
bezant
chervonets
copper
crown
denarius
denier
dime
double eagle
double napoleon
doubloon
ducat
dupondius
eagle
farthing
florin
follis
groat
groschen
guinea
half-crown
halfpenny
half-sovereign
joey
krugerrand
liard
loonie
louis d'or
maravedi
Maundy money
minim
moidore
napoleon
nickel
noble
obol
picayune

pistole
quarter
scudo
sequin
sestertius
shilling
siliqua
sixpence
soldo
solidus
sou
sovereign
spade guinea
spur royal
stater
stiver
tanner
threepenny bit
tickey

Relatives

aunt
babyfather
babymother
brother
brother-german
brother-in-law
brother uterine
co-parent
cousin
daughter
daughter-in-law
father
father-in-law
first cousin
full brother
full sister
genitor
grandchild
granddaughter
grandfather
grandmother
grandparent
grandson
great-aunt
great-grandchild
great-granddaughter
great-grandfather
great-grandmother
great-grandparent
great-grandson
great-nephew
great-niece
great-uncle
half-brother
half-sister
husband
in-law
mother
mother-in-law
nephew
niece
parallel cousin
parent
sibling
sister
sister-german
sister-in-law
sister uterine
son
son-in-law
spouse
stepbrother
stepchild
stepdaughter
stepfather
stepmother
step-parent
stepsister
stepson
uncle
widow
widower
wife

Restaurants

automat
bistro
brasserie
buffet
cafe
cafe bar
cafeteria
canteen
carry-out
carvery
chophouse
churrascaria
coffee shop
crêperie
cybercafe
diner
drive-in
estaminet
gastropub
grillroom
internet cafe
luncheonette
mess
noodle bar
oyster bar
pizzeria
pull-in
rotisserie
snack bar
steakhouse
supper club
sushi bar
takeaway
tandoori
taqueria
taverna
tea room
tea shop
transport cafe
trattoria
truck stop

Schools

boarding school
board school
charity school
charter school
cheder
choir school
church school
city academy
City Technology College (CTC)
co-educational school
college
community college
comprehensive (school)
conservatory
convent
county school
day school
direct-grant school
elementary school
faith school
farm school
finishing school
first school
free school
grade school
grammar school
grant-maintained school (GM school)
high school
infant school
junior high school
junior school
kindergarten
lower school
madrasa
magnet school
middle school
night school
nursery school
parochial school
preparatory/prep school
pre-school
primary school
private school
public school
residential school
secondary modern (school)
secondary school
seminary
senior high school
separate school
sixth-form centre/college
special school
state school
Talmud Torah
upper school
voluntary school
yeshiva

Sellers of goods

Seller	Goods
apothecary	medicines
baker	bread
bibliopole	books
bowyer	archers' bows
butcher	meat
chandler	candles
cheesemonger	dairy products
chocolatier	chocolate
clothier	clothes
colporteur	books etc.
confectioner	confectionery
cosmetician	cosmetics
costermonger	fruit and vegetables
couturier	clothes
cutler	cutlery
dairyman	dairy products
draper	textile fabrics
druggist	medicinal drugs
fishmonger	fish
fishwife	fish
fletcher	arrows
florist	flowers
flower girl	flowers
fruiterer	fruit
furnisher	furniture
furrier	furs
glazier	glass
greengrocer	fruit and vegetables
grocer	food and small household goods
gunsmith	firearms
haberdasher	sewing items (*Brit.*)
haberdasher	men's clothes (*N. Amer.*)
hatter	hats
herbalist	medicinal herbs
horse-coper	horses
hosier	hosiery
iceman	ice
ironmonger	hardware
jeweller	jewels and jewellery
licensed victualler	alcohol
mercer	fabrics
milkman	milk
milliner	women's hats
newsagent	newspapers
perfumer	perfume
pieman	pies
plumassier	ornamental feathers
poulterer	poultry
salter	salt
seedsman	seeds
ship (*or* ship's) chandler	nautical supplies and equipment
skinner	animal skins
slaver	slaves
stationer	stationery
tobacconist	tobacco
victualler	food
woolman	wool

Specialist shops

Shop	Goods sold
bakery	bread and cakes
bodega	wine and food
boutique	clothes (*Brit.*); specialist goods (*N. Amer.*)
butcher's	meat
cantina	wine
chandlery	candles
charcuterie	cold cooked meats
charity shop	second-hand goods
chemist	medicinal drugs
confectioner's	sweets
convenience store	household goods and groceries
corner shop	household goods and groceries
creamery	dairy products
dairy	dairy products
delicatessen	speciality foods
dime store	cheap merchandise
drugstore	medicinal drugs and toiletries
factory shop/outlet	surplus factory stock
fishmonger	fish
five-and-dime	household goods
florist's	flowers
greengrocer's	fruit and vegetables
grocery	food and household goods
haberdashery	dressmaking and sewing goods (*Brit.*); men's clothing (*N. Amer.*)
heel bar	shoe repairs
ironmonger	tools and household implements
jeweller's	jewels and jewellery
junk shop	second-hand goods
newsagent	newspapers
off-licence	alcoholic drink
parfumerie	perfume
patisserie	pastries and cakes
perfumery	perfume
pharmacy	medicinal drugs

Shop	Goods sold
saddlery	saddles etc.
smoke shop	tobacco and smoking equipment
snackette	snacks and groceries
soda fountain	soft drinks
stationer	stationery
supermarket	food
tabac	tobacco
thrift shop	second-hand goods
tobacconist	tobacco and smoking equipment
tuck shop	sweets

Enthusiasts and collectors

Most enthusiasts and collectors can be described as a ... *fan*, *fanatic*, *lover*, *enthusiast*, *nut*, etc., or a ... *collector*, besides these rarer and informal terms.

Hobby/object of enthusiasm	Enthusiast
amateur radio	ham
arts	culture-vulture
ballet	balletomane
bees	apiarist
birds	birder
boating	boatie
books	bibliophile
cars/motorbikes	petrolhead/motorhead
cats	ailurophile
caves	speleologist
chocolate	chocoholic
climbing buildings	stegophilist
computers	propeller-head/Nethead
crosswords	cruciverbalist
dogs	canophilist
fashion	fashionista
films/cinema	cineaste/cinephile
folk music	folkie
gold	chyrosophilist
good food and drink	epicurean
Greece/Greek culture	philhellene
heavy metal music	headbanger
hi-fi	audiophile
horses	hippophile
horse racing	turfman
jazz	jazzbo
making money	breadhead
malt beer/whisky	malt worm
metal detection	detectorist
mushrooms	mycophile
music	melomane
oysters	ostreophage
parks	parkomane
pigeons	columbarian
photography	shutterbug
railway/trains	gricer
rockets	rocketeer
yachting	yachtie
sport	jock
Star Trek	Trekkie
television	televisionary
trees	dendrophile
tulips	tulipomaniac
wine	oenophile
words	logophile

Thing collected	Collector
antiquarian	antiques
anything	completist
autographs	autographizer
banknotes	notaphilist
beer mats	tegestologist
beetles	coleopterist
birds' eggs	oologist/egger
book plates	ex-librist
butterflies	lepidopterist
cigarette cards/postcards	cartophilist
coins	numismatist
doll's houses	miniaturist
early books	incunabulist
flies	dipterist
gramophone records	discophile
matchboxes or their labels	phillumenist
mineral specimens	rockhound
money boxes	argyrothecologist
old bond and share certificates	scripophilist
postcards	deltiologist
shells	conchologist
sightings of rare birds	twitcher
stamps	philatelist
teddy bears	arctophile

Animals of the Chinese calendar

rat
buffalo
tiger
rabbit/hare
dragon
snake
horse
goat/sheep
monkey
rooster
dog
pig

Sports and games

Sports *See also other lists in this group.*

aerobatics
aerobics
Alpine skiing
angling
aquaplaning
archery
athletics
badminton
ballooning
base-jumping
beagling
BMX
bobsleighing
boxing
bullfighting
bungee jumping
caber tossing
canoe racing
canyoning
caving
clay-pigeon shooting
climbing
coarse fishing
coursing
crossbow archery
cross-country running
curling
cycle racing
cycling
cyclo-cross
darts
dinghy racing
diving
downhill racing
falconry
fencing
figure-skating
fishing
fly-fishing
fowling
freediving
free skating
freestyle skiing
game fishing
gliding
greyhound racing
gymnastics
hang-gliding
hiking
hockey
hydrospeed
ice climbing
ice dancing
ice hockey
ice skating
jet-skiing
kabaddi
kayaking
kiteboarding
kitesurfing
langlauf
luge
match fishing
mountain biking
mountaineering
Nordic skiing
orienteering
parachuting
paragliding
parapente/parapenting
parasailing
parascending
paraskiing
pigeon racing
pistol shooting
potholing
powerboat racing
quoits
rafting
ringette
rock climbing
rollerblading
roller skating
roller skiing
rowing
sailing
sailplaning
scuba-diving
sculling
sea fishing
shinny
shooting
skateboarding
skating
skeet
ski-bob racing
skiing
skijoring
ski jumping
skin diving
skydiving
sky surfing
slalom
sled-dog racing
snorkelling
snowboarding
speed skating
spelunking
sprinting
surfing
swimming
synchronized swimming
tobogganing
trap shooting
wakeboarding
walking
waterskiing
weightlifting
white-water rafting
wildfowling
wild-water racing
windsurfing
wrestling
yacht racing

Athletics events

biathlon
caber, tossing the
cross-country running
decathlon
discus
fell-running
field event
half-marathon
hammer
heptathlon
high jump
hurdles
javelin
long jump
marathon
middle-distance race
pentathlon
pole vault
relay race
shot-put
sprint
steeplechase
tetrathlon
track event
triathlon
triple jump
tug of war
walking

Gymnastics events and disciplines

artistic gymnastics
asymmetric bars
beam
floor exercises
high bar
horse vault
parallel bars
pommel horse
rhythmic gymnastics
rings
side horse vault
sports acrobatics
sports aerobics
trampolining
tumbling

Ball games

American football
Association Football
Australian Rules football
bagatelle
bandy
bar billiards
baseball
basketball
beach volleyball
billiards
bocce
boule/boules
bowling
bowls
broomball
camogie
Canadian football
carom billiards
clock golf
cricket
croquet
crown-green bowls
Eton fives
five-a-side football
fivepin bowling
fives
flat-green bowls
football
French cricket
Gaelic football
goalball
golf
handball
hockey
hurling
jai alai
korfball
lacrosse
lawn tennis
mini rugby
netball
ninepins
paddleball
paddle tennis
pall-mall
pelota
pétanque
polo
pool
rackets
racquetball
real tennis
roller hockey
rounders
Rugby fives
rugby league
rugby union
shinty
short tennis
skittles
snooker
soccer
softball
speedball
squash
stoolball
table tennis
tennis
tenpin bowling
touch football
touch rugby
volleyball
water polo

Equestrian sports

Arab racing
competitive trail riding
cross-country
dressage
endurance riding
eventing
flat racing *or* the flat
gymkhana
harness racing
haute école
horse racing
hunting
marathon driving
one-day eventing
plating
point-to-point
polo
puissance
rodeo
showing
showjumping
skijoring
steeplechasing
three-day eventing
trotting

Martial arts and combat sports

aikido
ba gua
boxing
capoeira
fencing
jousting
judo
ju-jitsu
karate
kendo
kick-boxing
kung fu
pa-kua
Silat
sumo wrestling
tae kwon do
t'ai chi chu'an
tang soo do
Thai boxing
wrestling

Motor sports

autocross
cross-country
demolition derby
dirt-track racing
drag racing
enduro
Formula One (F1)
go-karting
Grand Prix (GP)
hill-climbing
Indy/Indycar
karting
motocross
motorcycle racing
off-roading
rallycross
rallying
scrambling
sidecar racing
speedway
stock-car racing
Tourist Trophy (TT)
trials

Cricket roles and positions

all-rounder
bat
batsman/batswoman
bowler
cover
cover point
deep midwicket
deep square leg
extra cover
fielder
fieldsman
fine leg
gully
keeper
last man
leg-side fielder
leg slip
leg spinner
long field
long leg
long off
long on
longstop
medium pacer
mid-off
mid-on
midwicket
nightwatchman
non-striker
offside fielder
off spinner
opener
opening batsman
pace bowler
paceman
point
runner
seam bowler
seamer
short leg
short midwicket
silly mid-off
silly mid-on
silly point
slip
spin bowler
spinner
square leg
striker
tail-ender
third man
twelfth man
wicketkeeper

Rugby players

attacker
back row
back-row forward
ball carrier
blocker
breakaway
centre
defender
eighthman
five-eighth
flanker
fly half
forward
front row
front-row forward
fullback
halfback
hooker
jumper
left centre three-quarter
left wing three-quarter
lock (forward)
loose forward
loose head (prop)
number eight
prop (forward)
punter
right centre three-quarter
right wing three-quarter
scrum half
second row
second-row forward
stand-off half
three-quarter
tight end
tight head (prop)
winger
wing forward
wing (three-quarter)

Swimming strokes, kicks, and dives

Australian crawl
backcrawl
backstroke
breaststroke
butterfly
crawl
doggy-paddle
dolphin kick
duck-dive
fishtail kick
frog kick
front crawl
jackknife
overarm stroke
recovery stroke
scissors kick
sidestroke
swallow dive
swan dive
trudgen

Tennis strokes

ace
backhand
cross-court
dink
drive
drop shot
forehand
groundstroke
half-volley
lob
overhead
passing shot
serve
slice
smash
stop volley
volley

Golf clubs

brassie, cleek, driver, driving iron, iron, jigger, lofter, mashie, midiron, niblick, putter, sand iron, sand wedge, spoon, wedge, wood

Games

Aunt Sally, bagatelle, bingo, Botticelli, British bulldog, bumble-puppy, charades, chicken, chuck-a-luck, computer game, consequences, crambo, craps, crown and anchor, darts, deck quoits, deck tennis, diabolo, dice, dodgeball, dominoes, dreidel, ducks and drakes, dumb crambo, dungeons and dragons, fan-tan, fantasy football, fivestones, forfeits, frisbee (*trademark*), hazard, housey-housey, jacks, jackstraws, jukskei, kabaddi, keno, liar dice, mah-jong, matador, MUD, mumblety-peg, nim, pachinko, Pac-Man (*trademark*), paintball, panel game, parlour game, pinball, pitch-and-toss, poker dice, pool, quoits, roulette, round game, shove-halfpenny, shovelboard, sic bo, spillikins, spin the bottle, Subbuteo (*trademark*), swy, table football, thimblerig, tiddlywinks, tipcat, trapball, treasure hunt, Trivial Pursuit (*trademark*), tug of war, twenty questions, two-up

Children's games

battleships, blind man's buff, catch, cat's cradle, Chinese whispers, conkers, cops and robbers, follow-my-leader, grandmother's footsteps, hangman, hide-and-seek, hoopla, hopscotch, hunt the slipper, I spy, it, King of the Castle, leapfrog, lotto, marbles, murder in the dark, musical bumps, musical chairs, noughts and crosses, pass the parcel, pat-a-cake, peekaboo, peever, piggy in the middle, Poohsticks, postman's knock, prisoner's base, ring-a-ring o' roses, sardines, Simon Says, statues, tag, taw, tic-tac-toe/tick-tack-toe, tig, tok-tokkie

Board games

backgammon, checkers, chess, Chinese chequers, Chinese chess, Cluedo (*trademark*), draughts, fox and geese, go, halma, kriegspiel, ludo, mah-jong, mancala, Monopoly (*trademark*), nine men's morris, pachisi, peggotty, Pictionary (*trademark*), Risk (*trademark*), Scrabble (*trademark*), shogi, snakes and ladders, solitaire, tric-trac, Trivial Pursuit (*trademark*), wari, wei ch'i

Card games

all fours, auction bridge, baccarat, beggar-my-neighbour, bezique, blackjack, Black Maria, Boston, brag, bridge, canasta, Canfield, cheat, chemin de fer, cooncan, cribbage, donkey, duplicate bridge, écarté, euchre, fan-tan, faro, five hundred, gin rummy, happy families, hearts, high-low, hoy, klobbiyos, Klondike, lansquenet, loo, Michigan, monte, nap, napoleon, Newmarket, old maid, ombre, panguingue, patience, Pedro Sancho, Pelmanism, penny ante, pinochle, piquet, pitch, poker, pontoon, Pope Joan, primero, quinze, racing demon, red dog, rouge et noir, rubber bridge, rummy, Russian Bank, short whist, skat, skin, solitaire, solo whist, strip Jack naked, strip poker, stud poker, thirty-one, three-card monte, trente et quarante, twenty-five, twenty-one, vingt-et-un, whist

Suits of cards

Standard pack	Tarot pack
clubs	cups
diamonds	pentacles/coins/discs
hearts	swords
spades	trumps
	wands/batons

Poker hands

royal flush
straight flush
4 of a kind
full house
flush
straight
3 of a kind
2 pairs
1 pair
high card

Technology

Alloys

aluminium brass
aluminium bronze
babbitt metal
bell metal
bidri
billon
brass
Britannia metal
bronze
constantan
cupro-nickel
Dutch metal
electrum
eureka
German silver
gunmetal
kamacite
magnox
manganese bronze
misch metal
mosaic gold
nickel brass
nitinol
ormolu
permalloy
pewter
phosphor bronze
pinchbeck
platinoid
red gold
shakudo
silver solder
similor
solder
speculum metal
spiegeleisen
stainless steel
steel
terne
tin
tombac
type metal
white gold
white metal
zircaloy

Anchors

bower
Bruce anchor (*trademark*)
Danforth anchor
double-fluked anchor
drag anchor
drift anchor
floating anchor
grapnel
grapple
kedge
killick
mushroom anchor
projectile anchor
sea anchor
sheet anchor
stocked anchor
stockless anchor
stream anchor

Bridges

air bridge
aqueduct
Bailey bridge
bascule bridge
bridge of boats
cantilever bridge
catenary bridge
catwalk
chain bridge
clapper bridge
drawbridge
floating bridge
flyover
footbridge
gangway
girder bridge
humpback bridge
linkspan
overbridge
overpass
pontoon
skew bridge
skyway
suspension bridge
swing bridge
toll bridge
transporter bridge
underbridge
viaduct

Cameras

APS camera
box camera
camcorder
camera phone
cine camera
compact camera
digicam (*trademark*)
digital camera
disc camera
Gatso
instant camera
miniature camera
minicam
movie camera
pinhole camera
Polaroid (*trademark*) camera
reflex camera
rostrum camera
single-lens reflex (SLR)
single-use camera
speed camera
Steadicam (*trademark*)
stereo camera
television camera
twin-lens reflex
video camera
webcam

Clocks and watches

alarm clock
analogue watch/clock
astronomical clock
atomic clock
bracket clock
caesium clock
calendar clock
carriage clock
chronograph
chronometer
clepsydra
clock radio
cuckoo clock
digital watch/clock
egg-timer
fob watch
grandfather clock
grandmother clock
half-hunter watch
hourglass
hunter watch
impulse clock
journeyman clock
lever watch
long-case clock
pendulum clock
pocket watch
quartz-crystal clock
quartz watch/clock
repeater
sandglass
sidereal clock
stem-winder
stopwatch
sundial
tabernacle clock
time clock
travelling clock
turnip
water clock
wristwatch

Computer parts and peripherals

accelerator board/card
acoustic coupler
analogue to digital converter
arithmetic and logic unit (ALU)
bar-code reader
bubblejet printer
bubble memory
buffer
bus
cache memory
card
CD burner
CD-ROM
CD-RW (read-write) disk/drive
CD writer
central processing unit (CPU)
chip
console
control unit
coprocessor
digital to analogue converter
digitizer
DIMM (dual in-line memory module)
disk
disk drive
dongle
drum scanner
DVD burner
DVD (digital videodisc) drive
DVD writer
dynamic memory
dynamic RAM (DRAM)
erasable programmable ROM (EPROM)
expansion card/board
fax modem
firmware
fixed disk
flash drive
flash memory
floating-point unit (FPU)
floppy disk
graphics card
graphics pad
hard disk
hard drive
imagesetter
inkjet printer
input-output device
input-output port
joystick
keyboard
laser printer
LCD (liquid crystal display) screen
light pen
maths coprocessor
memory
Memory Stick (*trademark*)
microprocessor
minidisc
minitower
mobo
modem
monitor
motherboard
mouse
mouse mat
non-volatile memory
optical disk
option card
plotter
port
portable disk drive
printed circuit
printed circuit board (PCB)
printer
processor
random-access memory (RAM)
raster image processor (RIP)
read-only memory (ROM)
register
removable disk
scanner
sequencer
serial port
silicon chip
SIMM (single in-line memory module)
software
solid-state memory
sound card
static RAM (SRAM)
synchronous dynamic RAM (SDRAM)
tape streamer
terminal
TFT (thin film transistor) screen
touch pad
touch screen
trackball
transistor
USB drive
USB port
video card
visual display unit (VDU)
voice synthesizer
wand
Winchester disk
Winchester disk drive
Zip disk (*trademark*)
Zip drive (*trademark*)

Types of computer program

adware
agent
applet
application
application programming interface
assembler
BIOS
bloatware
bot
browser
cancelbot
chatterbot
client
converter
courseware
crawler
cross-assembler
cross-compiler
daemon
database management system
debugger
diagnostic
dialler
disassembler
driver
droid
editor
executable

- expert system
- filter
- firewall
- firmware
- freeware
- garbage collector
- generator
- gopher
- graphic equalizer
- groupware
- hack
- interface
- interpreter
- keylogger
- knowbot
- linker
- loop
- macro
- mailer
- malware
- manager
- microbrowser
- microprogram
- middleware
- nagware
- navigator
- newsreader
- object program
- operating system (OS)
- outliner
- packet sniffer
- parametric equalizer
- parser
- personal information manager
- plug-in
- preprocessor
- rotoscope
- routine
- run-time
- scheduler
- script
- search engine
- servlet
- shareware
- shell program
- shovelware
- simulator
- sniffer
- source program
- spellchecker
- spreadsheet
- spyware
- suite
- telesoftware
- telnet
- text editor
- tool
- translator
- Trojan Horse
- user interface
- utility
- vaccine
- vapourware
- virus
- walk-through
- warez
- word processor
- workalike
- worm

Energy and fuels

- acetylene
- anthracite
- atomic power
- avgas
- benzol
- bio-diesel
- biofuel
- biogas
- biomass energy
- briquette
- butane
- Calor gas (*trademark*)
- chemical energy
- coal
- coal gas
- Coalite (*trademark*)
- coke
- derv
- diesel
- electrical power
- electromagnetic energy
- firewood
- fission energy
- fossil fuel
- four-star petrol
- fuel oil
- fuel rod
- fusion energy
- gas
- gasohol
- gas oil
- gasoline
- geothermal energy
- heat
- hydroelectric power
- hydrogen
- kerosene
- kinetic energy
- leaded petrol
- lead replacement petrol (LRP)
- light
- lignite
- liquefied petroleum gas (LPG)
- methane
- MOX
- natural gas
- nitromethane
- nuclear power
- oil
- Orimulsion (*trademark*)
- paraffin
- peat
- petrol
- petroleum
- photosynthesis
- potential energy
- producer gas
- propane
- renewable energy
- solar energy
- steam power
- Sterno (*US trademark*)
- synfuel
- tidal power
- town gas
- turf
- unleaded petrol
- uranium
- water gas
- water power
- wave power
- whale oil
- wind power

Engines

- aero engine
- auxiliary power unit (APU)
- beam engine
- diesel engine
- donkey engine
- double-acting engine
- dynamo
- electric motor
- external-combustion engine
- flat-four engine
- flathead engine
- four-stroke (engine)
- gas turbine
- generator
- heat engine
- hyperdrive
- inboard
- internal-combustion engine (ICE)
- ion engine
- jato
- jet engine
- linear motor
- magneto
- oil engine
- outboard
- Otto engine
- petrol engine
- piston engine
- prop jet
- pulse jet
- radial engine
- ramjet
- rebore
- reciprocating engine
- rocket engine
- rotary engine
- scramjet
- stationary engine
- steam engine
- steam turbine
- sterndrive
- Stirling engine
- straight-eight
- straight-six
- thruster
- triple expansion engine
- turbine
- turbo diesel
- turbofan
- turbogenerator
- turbojet
- turboprop
- turboshaft
- twin-cam engine
- two-stroke (engine)
- ullage rocket
- V6
- V8
- V12
- Wankel engine

Explosives

- amatol
- blasting gelatin
- cordite
- dynamite
- fuel-air explosive
- gelignite
- guncotton
- gunpowder
- high explosive (HE)
- lyddite
- nitroglycerine
- plastic explosive
- plastique
- RDX
- Semtex
- thermobaric explosive
- trinitrotoluene (TNT)

Farming

Types of farming and cultivation

- agribusiness
- agroforestry
- agro-industry
- animal husbandry
- apiculture
- aquaculture
- arable farming
- arboriculture
- battery farming
- biodynamics
- citriculture
- crofting
- dairy farming
- dairying
- dry-land farming
- extensive farming
- factory farming
- fish farming
- floriculture
- forestry
- horticulture
- hydroponics
- intensive farming
- livestock farming
- mariculture
- market gardening
- monoculture
- orcharding
- organic farming
- pisciculture
- polyculture
- pomiculture
- sericulture
- sharecropping
- share farming
- shifting cultivation/agriculture
- silviculture
- smallholding
- strip cropping
- subsistence farming
- tank-farming
- viniculture
- viticulture

Fireworks

- banger
- Bengal light
- Catherine wheel
- cracker
- firecracker
- fizgig
- fountain
- girandole
- golden rain
- jumping jack
- maroon
- petard
- Pharaoh's serpent
- pinwheel
- rocket
- Roman candle
- skyrocket
- sparkler
- squib
- thunderflash
- torpedo
- volcano
- whizz bang

Glass

Types of Glass

- aventurine
- blown glass
- borosilicate
- bottle glass
- bulletproof glass
- cameo glass
- crown glass
- crystal
- cullet
- cut glass
- favrile glass
- fibreglass
- flint glass
- float glass
- frosted glass
- ground glass
- hobnail
- lace glass
- laminated glass
- latticinio
- lead crystal
- lead glass
- milk glass
- millefiori
- mirror glass
- opal glass
- opaline
- optical glass
- peach-blow
- plate glass
- Pyrex (*trademark*)
- quartz glass
- ruby glass
- safety glass
- sheet glass
- smalt
- stained glass
- toughened glass
- triplex (*trademark*)
- Waterford glass

Parts of a horse's harness or tack

- backband
- bearing rein
- bellyband
- bit
- blinders
- blinkers
- breastband
- breast collar
- breastplate
- breeching
- bridle
- bridoon
- cavesson
- cheekpiece
- cinch
- collar
- crupper
- curb bit
- double bit
- double bridle
- eggbutt snaffle
- frontlet
- girth
- hackamore

halter
hames
head collar
headstall
martingale
noseband
pelham
reins
saddle
saddlepad
snaffle (bit)
surcingle
throatlatch
traces
Weymouth bit

Knots

bend
Blackwall hitch
blood knot
bow
bowknot
bowline
bowline on the bight
carrick bend
cat's paw
clinch knot
clove hitch
diamond knot
Englishman's tie
figure-of-eight knot
fisherman's bend
fisherman's knot
granny knot
half hitch
hangman's knot
harness hitch
hawser bend
Hercules knot
hitch
loop knot
love knot
Matthew Walker
mesh knot
overhand knot
prusik
reef knot
rolling hitch
round turn and two half hitches
running bowline
running knot
sailor's knot
sheepshank
sheet bend
shoulder knot
shroud-knot
slip knot
slippery hitch
square knot
surgeon's knot
swab hitch
thumb knot
timber hitch
true-love knot
Turk's head
wale knot
wall knot
water knot
weaver's knot
Windsor knot

Lamps and lights

Aldis lamp (*trademark*)
anchor light
anglepoise (*trademark*)
arc lamp
Argand lamp
brake light
chandelier
Chinese lantern
Coleman lantern
courtesy light
cross light
crusie/cruisie
Davy lamp
desk lamp
discharge lamp
diya
downlighter
electrolier
fairy lights
fill light
flambeau
flare
flashgun
flash lamp
flashlight
floodlight
floor lamp
fluorescent light
fog lamp/light
follow spot
footlight
gaslight
halogen light
hazard (warning) lights
headlight/headlamp
hurricane lamp
idiot light
indicator
jack light
jack-o'-lantern
klieg
landing lights
lantern
lava lamp
luminaire
mercury vapour lamp
navigation lights
neon light
night light
occulting light
oil lamp
parachute flare
parking light
pendant
penlight
pilot light
pressure lamp
quartz lamp
reversing light
riding light
ring flash
running lights
safelight
safety lamp
sanctuary lamp
searchlight
sidelight
slit lamp
sodium-vapour lamp
spirit lamp
spotlight
standard lamp
stop light/lamp
storm lantern
street light/lamp
strip light
strobe/stroboscope
sunlamp
table lamp
tail light/lamp
tea light
tilley lamp (*trademark*)
torch
track lighting
traffic lights
uplighter
Very light

Locks

barrel lock
Chubb lock (*trademark*)
combination lock
cylinder lock
D-lock
double lock
drawback lock
lever-tumbler lock
mortise lock
night latch
padlock
radial pin-tumbler lock
rim lock
shackle lock
snap-lock
spring lock
stock-lock
time lock
tumbler lock
twist-lock
U-lock
warded lock
Yale lock (*trademark*)

Paints

acrylic
antifouling
cellulose
colour wash
Day-Glo (*trademark*)
distemper
eggshell
emulsion
enamel (paint)
face paint
finger-paint
gloss (paint)
gouache
masonry paint
matt paint
metallic paint
oil paint
poster paint
powder paint
primer
tempera
undercoat
vinyl emulsion
watercolour
whitewash

Types of paper

art paper
blotting paper
bond (paper)
bromide (paper)
brown paper
carbon (paper)
cartridge (paper)
construction paper
crêpe paper
drawing paper
filter paper
flimsy
flypaper
gelatin paper
gift wrap
glassine
glasspaper
graph paper
greaseproof (paper)
India paper
Japanese paper
kitchen paper
kraft (paper)
laid (paper)
lens tissue
litmus paper
Manila (paper)
manuscript paper
mourning paper
notepaper
oaktag
oil paper
onion-skin paper
parchment (paper)
rag paper
ricepaper
sandpaper
satin paper
squared paper
stamp paper
thermal paper
tissue (paper)
toilet paper
tracing paper
transfer paper
vellum
wallpaper
waxed paper
woodchip (paper)
wove (paper)
wrapping paper
writing paper

Patterns

anthemion
argyle
banding
basket weave
bird's-eye
bow tie
chalk-stripe
check
chequers
clock
counterchange
crackle
diaper
dog-tooth
fret
Greek key
herringbone
honeycomb
houndstooth
log cabin
meander
microcheck
millefleurs
mottle
overcheck
paisley
pinstripe
plaid
polka dot
Prince of Wales check
shepherd's plaid
spiral
spreite
starburst
sunburst
swirl
tartan
veining
waffle
woodgrain

Types of pottery and porcelain

Arita
barbotine
basalt
biscuit (ware)
bisque ware
black-figure ware
bone china
Capo di Monte
Castleford ware
celadon
champlevé
Chelsea ware
Chün
cloisonné
Coalport
creamware
Crown Derby
delft
(Royal) Doulton (*trademark*)
Dresden
earthenware
faience
famille jaune/noire/rose/verte
graniteware
greenware
grooved ware
Halaf ware
Imari
ironstone
Iznik ware
jasper/jasperware
Kakiemon ware
Kutani ware
lustreware
maiolica *or* majolica
Martinware
Meissen
Ming
Minton (*trademark*)
Nabeshima ware
Parian ware
pearlware
Peterborough ware
queensware
raku
red-figure ware

Rockingham ware
Samian ware
Satsuma ware
Seto ware
Sèvres
slipware
spatterware
Spode (*trademark*)
Staffordshire ware
stone china
stoneware
terracotta
terra sigillata
Toft ware
transferware
Wedgwood (*trademark*)
willowware
(Royal) Worcester (*trademark*)

Printing processes

autography
autotype
blind stamping/tooling
bubblejet printing
collotype
diazo/diazotype
die-stamping
dry mounting
dyeline
flexography
four-colour process
hot metal
inkjet printing
intaglio
laser printing
letterpress
letterset
linocutting
lithography
nature printing
offset
offset lithography
photogravure
photolithography
photo-offset
planography
process printing
relief printing
rotogravure
screen-printing
serigraphy
sheet printing
silk-screen
thermal printing
thermography
three-colour process
web offset
web printing
xerography
Xerox (*trademark*)
xylography

Ropes

backstay
bobstay
bolt rope
bowline
brace
brail
breeching
buntline
cable
catenary
cord
cordage
downhaul
foot rope
foresheet
forestay
gantline
guest rope
guide rope
guy
halyard
hawser
hobble
inhaul
jackstay
jib sheet
lanyard
lariat
lasso
lazy jack
leg-rope
manrope
marline
noose
outhaul
painter
ratline
rawhide
rode
runner
running rope
seizing
sheet
shroud
slip rope
span
stay
sugan
tack
tackle fall
tether
topping lift
top rope
tow rope
vang
warp

Shapes

Straight-sided shapes

decagon
diamond
dodecagon
hendecagon
heptagon
hexagon
kite
lozenge
nonagon
oblong
octagon
parallelogram
pentagon
pentagram
pentangle
polygon
quadrangle
quadrant
quadrilateral
rectangle
rhomboid
rhombus
square
tetragon
trapezium
trapezoid
triangle
trigon
undecagon

Triangles

acute-angled
circular
congruent triangles
equilateral
isosceles
obtuse-angled
right
right-angled
scalene
similar triangles
spherical

Curves

annulus
arc
Archimedean spiral
bell curve
bow
brachistochrone
cardioid
catenary
characteristic curve
circle
cissoid
conchoid
crescent
Cupid's bow
cycloid
demilune
ellipse
entasis
epicycloid
equiangular spiral
evolute
folium of Descartes
Gaussian curve
half-moon
helix
horseshoe
hyperbola
hypocycloid
involute
lemniscate
logarithmic spiral
logistic curve
normal curve
ogive
oval
ovoid
parabola
polar curve
roulette
roundel
semicircle
sigmoid curve
sine curve/sine wave
sinusoid
solidus
spiral
spline
transition curve
trochoid
whaleback
witch of Agnesi

Telescopes

almucantar
altazimuth telescope
astronomical telescope
Cassegrain telescope
cathetometer
collimator
coudé telescope
Dobsonian telescope
equatorial telescope
finder
Galilean telescope
Gregorian telescope
heliometer
Maksutov telescope
meridian circle
monocular
Newtonian telescope
radio telescope
reflecting telescope
refracting telescope
Schmidt telescope
Schmidt–Cassegrain telescope
space telescope
telescopic sight
terrestrial telescope

Tents

barrel-vaulted tent
bell tent
big top
bivouac
bivvy
box tent
conical tent
dome tent
frame tent
kibitka
lodge
marquee
mat tent
oxygen tent
pandal
pavilion
pup tent
ridge tent
shamiana
tabernacle
tepee/teepee/tipi
touring tent
trailer tent
tunnel tent
tupik
wall tent
wigwam
yurt

Tools See also **Hammers, Saws, Knives**

adze
Allen key (*trademark*)
auger
awl
axe
bastard file
belt sander
bevel (square)
billhook
biscuit jointer
blowlamp
blowtorch
bodkin
borer
brace (and bit)
bradawl
burin
burnisher
burr
capstan lathe
centre bit
centre punch
chisel
chopper
clamp
cleaver
copper bit
cramp
crowbar
croze
cultivator
cutter
dibber
dibble
diestock
dovetailer
drill
drill press
edge tool
edging shears
edging tool
file
flail
float
fly cutter
fork
former
froe
fuller
G-clamp
G-cramp
gimlet
glass cutter
graver
grinder
grouter
grozing iron
hack
hammer
hammer drill
hand-axe
handspike
hatchet
hedge clipper/trimmer
hex key
hob
hoe
(hot-)air gun
jack
jemmy
jointer
knife
lap
lathe
lawnmower
lever
loppers
marlinspike
mattock
mitre
nailer
nail gun
nail punch
needle
nibbler
nippers
paint gun
panga
perforator
pestle
pick
pickaxe
pincers
pitchfork
plane
pliers
pruning hook
punch
rake
ram
rasp
reamer
riddle
riffler
ripper
roller
roulette
router
rule
sander
sandpaper
sash cramp
saw
scarifier
scraper
screwdriver
screw tap
scribe (awl)

scythe
secateurs
shave
shavehook
shears
shovel
sickle
slasher
sley
snarling iron
socket wrench
soldering iron
spade
spanner
spokeshave
square
staple gun
strickle
swage
swingle
tinsnips
torque wrench
trowel
tweezers
vice
wedge
wheel brace
wire cutter
wire stripper
woodcarver
wrecking bar
wrench

Hammers

ball peen/pein (hammer)
beetle
claw hammer
cross peen/pein (hammer)
gavel
jackhammer
Kango (*trademark*)
mallet
plexor
pneumatic hammer
priest
sledge(hammer)
steam hammer
tenderizer
tilt hammer
trip hammer

Saws

bandsaw
bench saw
bowsaw
chainsaw
circular saw
compass saw
coping saw
cross-cut saw
dovetail saw
frame saw
fretsaw
grooving saw
hacksaw
handsaw
hole saw
jigsaw
keyhole saw
padsaw
panel saw
pitsaw
pruning saw
rabbet saw
ripsaw
sawbench
scroll saw
Swede saw
tenon saw
whipsaw

Knives

athame
bayonet
bistoury
bolo
bowie knife
box cutter
bread knife
butter knife
butterfly knife
carver
carving knife
case knife
clasp knife
cleaver
commando knife
craft knife
dagger
dirk
drawknife
fish knife
flensing knife
flesher
flick knife
Frenchman
hunting knife
jackknife
kirpan
kris
kukri
lancet
machete
misericord
panga
paperknife
parang
penknife
pocket knife
poniard
pruning knife
sai
scalpel
scramasax
sheath knife
skean-dhu
Stanley knife (*trademark*)
steak knife
stiletto
Swiss army knife (*trademark*)
switchblade
table knife
tanto
ulu
utility knife
X-acto knife (*trademark*)

Torture instruments

bastinado
boot
branks
cucking-stool
iron maiden
necklace
pilliwinks
rack
scold's bridle
screws
stocks
strappado
thumbscrew
wheel

Toys

action figure
agate
ally
balloon
beanbag
bear
board game
bobskate
box kite
brick
building block
catapult
cuddly toy
diabolo
doll
doll's house
dreidel
Dutch doll
flannelboard
frisbee (*trademark*)
glove puppet
golliwog
hobby horse
hoop
hula hoop
humming top
jack-in-the-box
jigsaw
jumping bean
jumping jack
kaleidoscope
kite
marble
marionette
ocarina
party popper
pea-shooter
pedal car
peery
pegtop
playhouse
Pog
pogo (stick)
popgun
puppet
puzzle
rag doll
rattle
rattlebox
ride-on
rocking horse
Russian doll
scooter
see-saw
skipping rope
slot car
snowstorm
squirt gun
Swanee whistle
tangram
teddy (bear)
teeter-totter
teetotum
thaumatrope
tin soldier
top
train set
tumbler
water gun
water pistol
Wendy house
whipping top
whirligig
windmill
yo-yo
zoetrope

Units of measurement

acre
acre-foot
air mile
ampere
angstrom
are
astronomical unit
atmosphere
atomic mass unit
bale
bar
barleycorn
barn
barrel
bath
baud
becquerel
bel
bigha
bit
board foot
Board of Trade Unit
bovate
brake horsepower
British thermal unit
bushel
butt
byte
cable
calorie
candela
candle
carat
cental
centiare
centigram
centilitre
centimetre
centner
century
chain
cord
coulomb
cran
cubit
cup
cupful
curie
cusec
cycle
dalton
daraf
darcy
day
debye
decade
decalitre
decametre
decibel
decigram
decilitre
decimetre
degree
degree-day
denarius
denier
dessertspoon
dioptre
drachm
dunam
dyne
electronvolt
ell
em
en
ephah
epoch
erg
farad
faraday
fathom
fermi
firkin
fluid drachm
fluid ounce
fluidram
foot
foot-pound
fresnel
furlong
gal
gallon
gamma
gauss
geographical mile
gigabyte
gigaelectronvolt
gigaflop
gigawatt
gilbert
gill
grade
grain
gram
gram-molecular weight
gray
hand
hank
hectare
hectogram
hectolitre
hectometre
henry
hertz
hide
hin
hogshead
Hoppus foot
horsepower
hour
hundredweight
inch
jansky
joule
kelvin
kilderkin
kilo
kilobit
kilobyte
kilocalorie
kilocycle
kilo-electronvolt
kilogram
kilohertz
kilojoule
kilolitre
kilometre
kiloton/kilotonne
kilovolt
kilowatt-hour
kip
knot
lambert
last
lea
league
libra
light year
line
link
litre
lumen
lux
Mach number
magneton
maxwell
megabyte
mega-electronvolt
megaflop
megahertz
megaton
megavolt
megawatt
megohm
metre
metric ton
mho
microfarad
microgram
microlitre
micrometre
micron
microsecond
mil
mile
millennium
milliampere
millibar
milligram
millilitre
millimetre
millimicron
millisecond
millivolt
milliwatt
minim
minute
MIPS
mole

month
morgan
morgen
mutchkin
nail
nanometre
nanosecond
nautical mile
neper
newton
nit
noggin
oersted
ohm
oka/oke
okta
ounce
parsec
pascal
peck
pennyweight
perch
petabyte
phon
phot
pica
pint
pipe
ploughland
point
poise
pole
pound
poundal
probit
puncheon
quantum bit
quart
quarter
quartern
quintal
rad
radian
rem
rod
roentgen
rood
rutherford
sabin
scruple
sea mile
second
section
seer
siemens
sievert
sone
span
spindle
square
stack
stadium
standard
steradian
stere
stilb
stokes
stone
Svedberg
tablespoon
teaspoon
teraflop
terawatt
tesla
therm
tierce
tog
ton
tonne
torr
troy ounce
tsubo
tun
verst
virgate
volt
watt
weber
week
wey
x-unit
yard
year
yoke

Writing Implements

ballpoint
biro
chinagraph pencil
crayon
crow quill
dip pen
felt-tip pen
fibre tip
fountain pen
highlighter
lead pencil
mapping pen
marker (pen)
pen
pencil
propelling pencil
quill
rollerball
slate pencil
stylograph
stylus

Transport

Motor vehicles *See also* Cars, Carriages and carts, Trains and rolling stock

all-terrain vehicle (ATV)
ambulance
armoured car
armoured personnel carrier (APC)
articulated lorry
automobile
autorickshaw
battlebus
beach buggy
Black Maria
bloodmobile
bookmobile
bowser (*trademark*)
bulldozer
bus
cab
camper (van)
car
caravanette
carryall
car transporter
charabanc
coach
combination
crash wagon
delivery truck
digger
dirt bike
dolmus
double-decker bus
DUKW/duck
dumper truck
dump truck
dune buggy
dustcart
earth mover
fire engine
flatbed (truck)
float
forklift truck
four-by-four
four-wheel drive (4WD)
garbage truck
go-kart
golf cart/buggy
gritter
hackney cab
half-track
hearse
heavy goods vehicle (HGV)
horsebox
hot rod
JCB (*trademark*)
Jeep (*trademark*)
juggernaut
kart
large goods vehicle (LGV)
lorry
low-loader
low-rider
lunar roving vehicle (LRV)
milk float
minelayer
moped
motorbike/motorcycle
motor caravan
multi-purpose vehicle (MPV)
off-road vehicle (ORV)
omnibus
pantechnicon
passenger-carrying vehicle (PCV)
people carrier
personnel carrier
pickup (truck)
public service vehicle (PSV)
quad bike
recreational vehicle (RV)
refrigerated van
removal van
roadroller
road train
rover
scooter
scout car
scrambler
semitrailer
shooting brake
skidsteer loader
skimobile
snowcat
snowmobile
snowplough
sport utility vehicle (SUV)
steamroller
streetcar
superbike
tank
tanker
taxi/taxicab
tow truck
tracklayer
tractor
trail bike
trailer
tram
transporter
trolleybus
troop carrier
truck
tuk-tuk
utility
van
wagon/waggon
wrecker

Cars

automatic
bubble car
cabriolet
compact
concept car
convertible
coupé
cruiser
dragster
drophead
estate
fastback
four-wheel drive
GTi
hardtop
hatchback
hot rod
kit car
limousine
low-rider
microcar
minicab
multi-purpose vehicle (MPV)
notchback
off-roader
people carrier
phaeton
racing car
ragtop
rally car
roadster
runabout
saloon
sedan
shooting brake
soft top
sports car
sportster
sport utility vehicle (SUV)
station wagon
stock car
stretch limo
supercar
supermini
targa
taxi
tourer
touring car

Parts of a car

accelerator pedal
air conditioning
alternator
anti-lock braking system (ABS)
anti-roll bar
automatic choke
automatic transmission
axle
battery
bench seat
big end
blinker
bodywork
bonnet
boot
brake
brake disc
brake drum
brake light
brake pad
brake pedal
brake shoe
brush bar
bucket seat
bull bar
bumper
cam belt
camshaft
carburettor
catalytic converter
central locking system
chassis
clutch
clutch pedal
connecting rod
con rod
courtesy light
cowling
crank
crankcase
cruise control
crumple zone
cubbyhole
cylinder
cylinder block
cylinder head
damper
dashboard/dash
differential gear
differential lock
dimmer
dip switch
disc brake
distributor
doorbin
door mirror
drivetrain
driving wheel
drum brake
engine
exhaust pipe
fan
fan belt
fascia
fender
filler cap
final drive
floorpan
flywheel
fog lamp/fog light
footbrake
four-wheel drive
front-wheel drive
fuel gauge
fuel injection pump
fuel tank
gasket
gas tank
gate
gear
gearbox
gear change
gear lever/gearstick
gear shift
generator
glovebox
grille
handbrake
hatch
hazard warning lights
headlight/headlamp
heater
hood
hooter
horn
hubcap
hypoid gear
ignition
ignition key
immobilizer
indicator
injector
instrument panel
kick-down
licence plate
lite
loadspace
manifold
milometer
monocoque
muffler
number plate
odometer
oil gauge
overdrive
overrider
parcel shelf
pedal
petrol tank
piston
pneumatic tyre
points
power brakes
power steering
propshaft/propeller shaft
pushrod

quarter-light
rack-and-pinion
radial tyre
radiator
radiator grille
radius rod
rear-view mirror
rear-wheel drive
reflector
registration plate
rocker
rocker panel
roll bar
roof light
rotor arm
running board
running lights
safety cage
satnav
seat
seat belt
shaft
shift/shifter
shock absorber
sidelight
sidescreen
silencer
sill
solenoid
spare tyre
spare wheel
spark plug
speedometer
spoiler
starter
starter motor
steering column
steering gear
steering rack
steering wheel
stick
stick shift
stop light
subframe
sump
sunroof
suspension
switchgear
tachometer
tag
tailgate
tail light/tail lamp
tailpipe
tappet
thermostat
tie rod
tow bar
track rod
trafficator
transaxle
transmission
trim
trunk
turbocharger
tyre
underframe
valance
valve
vanity mirror
viscous coupling
wheel
wheel nut
windscreen
windscreen washer
windscreen wiper
windshield
windshield washer
windshield wiper
wing
wing mirror
winker
wishbone

Carriages and carts

barouche
brake
breaking cart
britzka
brougham
buckboard
buggy
cab
cabriolet
caleche
caravan
carriole
chaise
chariot
clarence
coach
coach-and-four
Conestoga wagon
coupé
covered wagon
curricle
dog cart
dray
droshky
fiacre
fly
four-in-hand
gharry
gig
hackney
handcart
hansom
haywain
jaunting car
jinker
landau
ox cart
phaeton
post-chaise
prairie schooner
rickshaw
stagecoach
stanhope
sulky
surrey
tarantass
tilbury
trailer
trap
trishaw
tumbril
unicorn
Victoria
vis-à-vis
wagon
wagonette

Parts of a bicycle

bottom bracket
brake
brake block
brake caliper
carrier
cassette
chain
chain gear
chainring
crank
crossbar
derailleur
drop handlebars
dynamo
fork
frame
frameset
freehub
freewheel
gear
gearwheel
groupset
handlebars
headset
hub
hub gear
inner tube
mudguard
pannier
pedal
reflector
saddle
spokes
sprocket
stabilizers
toe clip
twist-grip
tyre
wheel

Roads

A-road
access road
accommodation road
approach road
arterial road/route
artery
Autobahn
autopista
autoroute
autostrada
avenue
B-road
backstreet
beef road
beltway
blind alley
boreen
bottleneck
boulevard
broadway
bypass
byroad
byway
cart track
causeway
clearway
close
concession road
corduroy road
corniche
corso
crescent
cul-de-sac
dead end
divided highway
drag
drive
driveway
drove road
dual carriageway
escape road
expressway
feeder
flyover
freeway
frontage road
hard
haul road
high road
high street
highway
interstate (highway)
lane
loop (road)
main drag
main road
main street
marg
motorway
national road
no through road
off-ramp
one-way street
orbital
overpass
parade
parkway
perimeter road
pike
private road
prospekt
Queen's highway
radial (road)
ramp
rat run
red route
relief road
ridgeway
ring road
Roman road
row
service road
side road
side street
single carriageway
skid road
skyway
slip road
speedway
spur
street
strip
superhighway
terrace
thoroughfare
throughway/thruway
toll road
tollway
trackway
tram road
tramway
trunk road
turnpike (road)
unadopted road
underpass
viaduct
woonerf

Trains and rolling stock

aerotrain
armoured train
baggage car
banker
bi-level carriage
boat train
bogie
boxcar
brake van
buffet car
bullet train
cable car
caboose
car
carriage
chair car
club car
coach
couchette
day coach/car
diesel-electric
diesel-hydraulic
diesel locomotive
diesel multiple unit (DMU)
dining car
double-header
drive-on train
electric train
express
flatcar
freight car
freight train
goods train
goods wagon
guard's van
handcar
high-speed train (HST)
hopper
hospital train
hovertrain
jerkwater train
jigger
light engine
luggage van
maglev
mail coach
mail train
metro
Metroliner
milk train
monorail
Motorail
motor coach
non-smoker
non-stop
observation car
palace car
pannier tank
parlor car
passenger train
Pullman
railbus
railcar
restaurant car
saddle tank
saloon car
shunter
sleeper
sleeping car/carriage
slip carriage
slow train
smoker
steam locomotive
steam train
stopping train
subway train
switcher
tank engine
tender
tilting train
traction unit
the tube
turbotrain
underground train
unit train
wagon-lit

Ships and boats

airboat
aircraft carrier
amphibious assault ship
amphibious landing craft
auxiliary
banker
barge
barque
barquentine
bateau mouche
bathyscaphe
bathysphere
battlecruiser
battleship
bawley
bidarka
bireme
boatel
brig
brigantine
bulk carrier
bumboat
butty
cabin cruiser
cable ship
caique
canal boat
canoe
capital ship
caravel
cargo ship
carrack
catamaran
catboat
chain ferry
chalupa
clipper
coal ship
coaler
coaster
coble
cockboat
cockle
cockleshell
cog
collier
container ship
coracle
corvette
crabber
cruise ship
cruiser
cutter
dahabeeyah
daysailor
destroyer
dhoni
dhow
dinghy
diving bell
dory
double-ender

dragon boat
dreadnought
dredger
drifter
dromond
dugout
DUKW/duck
E-boat
East Indiaman
factory ship
felucca
ferry
flag boat
flagship
flat boat
freighter
frigate
full-rigger
galleon
galley
galliot
gig
gondola
gunboat
helicopter carrier
hermaphrodite brig
hooker
hospital ship
houseboat
hovercraft
hydrofoil
hydroplane
ice-breaker
iceboat
inboard
Indiaman
inflatable dinghy
ironclad
jet ski (*trademark*)
jetboat
jetfoil
johnboat
jolly (boat)
junk
kayak
keelboat
keeler
ketch
laker
landing craft
lapstrake
lateen
launch
liberty boat
life raft
lifeboat
lighter
lightship
liner
longboat
longliner
longship
lugger
mailboat
man-of-war
merchant ship
merchantman
minehunter
minelayer
minesweeper
monitor
monkey-boat
monohull
mosquito boat
motor boat
motor torpedo boat (MTB)
motor yacht
motorsailer
multihull
narrowboat
nuggar
oil tanker
oiler
outboard
outrigger
packet boat
paddle boat
paddle steamer
passenger ship
pedal boat
pedalo
pilot boat
pink
pinnace
pirogue
pitpan
pocket battleship
polacre
pontoon
powerboat
pram
prawner
privateer
proa
PT boat
punt
Q-ship
quinquereme
raft
randan
razee
revenue cutter
RIB
rigger
riverboat
roll-on roll-off
rowing boat
rubber dinghy
sabot
safety boat
sailing boat
sailing ship
sampan
school ship
schooner
scow
scull
sculler
sealer
shallop
sharpie
shell
shikara
ship of the line
ship's boat
showboat
shrimper
side-wheeler
single-hander
ski boat
skiff
skipjack
slaver
sloop of war
sloop
smack
sneakbox
snekkja
speedboat
square-rigger
squirt boat
stake boat
steamboat
steamer
steamship
sternwheeler
submarine
submersible
supertanker
supply ship
surfboat
tall ship
tanker
tartan
tender
three-decker
torpedo boat
trader
traghetto
train ferry
training ship
tramp steamer
trawler
trimaran
trireme
troop carrier
troopship
tub
tug
tugboat
umiak
vaporetto
warship
water bus
water taxi
weekender
whaleboat
whaler
wherry
windjammer
workboat
xebec
yacht
yawl

Parts of a ship *See also* Sails, Rigging

afterdeck
anchor
berth
bilge
bilge keel
bitt
board
boat deck
boiler room
bollard
bow
bridge
brig
bulkhead
bullseye
bulwarks
cabin
caboose
capstan
carline
cathead
cat hole
centreboard
chain locker
chart room
cleat
companion ladder
companionway
counter
crow's nest
daggerboard
davit
dodger
engine room
false keel
figurehead
fin keel
flight deck
forecastle/fo'c'sle
freeboard
funnel
futtock
galley
gangplank
gangway
glory hole
guard rail
gudgeon
gun deck
gunwale/gunnel
half-deck
hatch
hatchway
hawsehole
hawsepipe
hawser
head
hold
keel
keelson
larboard
lazaretto
limber
limber hole
mainmast
maintop
mast
mizzenmast
mizzentop
monkey rail
oar
orlop deck
outboard
outrigger
paddle wheel
painter
pilot house
pintle
planking
Plimsoll line
poop
poop deck
porthole
portside
promenade deck
propeller
propeller shaft
prow
quarter rail
quarters
radio room
rail
riding lamp
rigger
round house
rowlock
rudder
rudderpost
scupper
skeg
spanker
stabilizer
stack
stanchion
starboard
stateroom
stern
sternpost
strake
stretcher
stringer
thole
tiller
transom
trunnion
turtleback
wardroom
washboard
washstrake
waterline
weatherboard
weather deck
wheel
winch
windlass

Sails

course
fore-and-aft sail
fore-course
fore-royal
foresail
forestaysail
fore-topgallant-sail
foretopsail
gaff foresail
gaff topsail
genny
genoa (jib)
gunter
headsail
jib
jigger
kite
lateen sail
lugsail
main course
mainsail
maintopsail
mizzen
moonraker
royal sail
skysail
spanker
spinnaker
spritsail
square sail
staysail
storm sail
studdingsail
topgallant
topsail
trysail

Rigging

backstay
baggywrinkle
bibb
bitt
bobstay
boom
bottlescrew
bowline
brace
brails
bullseye
buntline
burton
chainplate
cheek
claw ring
cleat
cordage
cringle
crossjack
crosstree
crowfoot
deadeye
downhaul
eye
fairlead
foot rope
foresheet
forestay
furling line
gaff
gantline
garland
gasket
gooseneck
halyard
hank
horse
hound
inhaul
jackstay
jibsheet
kicking strap
lanyard
lazy jack
lutchet
mainstay
martingale
mouse
outhaul
parrel
passaree
pendant/pennant
pole
preventer
ratlines
reefing line
reefpoint
sail tie
sheer pole
sheet
shroud
spar
spider
spider hoop
spreader
sprit
stay
step
stirrup
stopper knot
tabernacle
thimble
top
topping lift
track
traveller
trestletree
truck
truss
turnbuckle
uphaul
vangs
wishbone
yard
yardarm
yard sling

Aircraft

aerodyne
aerostat
airliner
airship
amphibian
autogiro
balloon
biplane
blimp
bomber
chopper
convertiplane
delta-wing
dirigible
dive bomber
drone
ekranoplan
fighter
fighter-bomber
floatplane
flying boat
flying wing
freighter
glider
ground-attack aircraft
gunship
gyrocopter
gyroplane
hang-glider
helicopter
hot-air balloon

hydroplane
interceptor
interdictor
jet
jetliner
jet plane
jumbo jet
jump jet
landplane
microlight
minelayer
monocoque
monoplane
multiplane
night fighter
ornithopter
paraglider
paramotor
prop jet
sailplane
seaplane
ski-plane
spaceplane
spotter
spy plane
stealth bomber
stealth fighter
strike fighter
swept-wing
swing-wing
taildragger
tanker
tank killer
taxiplane
towplane
trainer
trijet
triplane
troop carrier
tug
turbofan
turbojet
turboprop
warbird
warplane
water bomber
whirlybird
widebody
Zeppelin

Parts of an aircraft

aerofoil
aileron
air brake
airfoil
airframe
air intake
airscrew
airspeed indicator
altimeter
artificial horizon
astrodome
astrohatch
balance tab
belly
black box
bomb bay
bombsight
bubble canopy
bulkhead
cabin
canard
canopy
cockpit
cockpit voice recorder
collective pitch control
control column
cowl
cowling
cyclic pitch control
delta wing
droop-snoot
drop tank
ejector seat
elevator
elevon
emergency chute
empennage
engine
escape hatch
fairing
fin
firing button
flap
flexwing
flight control
flight deck
flight recorder
float
former
fuel tank
fuselage
glareshield
gondola
hatch
head-up display (HUD)
heat shield
hold
joystick
landing gear
landing lights
leading edge
longeron
mainplane
nacelle
navaid
nose
nose cone
pod
pontoon
porthole
prop
propeller
pylon
radome
rate-of-climb indicator
rib
rotary wing
rotor
rotor blade
rudder
rudder bar
skid
skin
spar
spinner
spoiler
sponson
stabilator
stabilizer
strake
stringer
swept wing
swing-wing
tab
tail
tail boom
tail fin
tailplane
tail rotor
tail skid
throttle
trailing edge
tricycle undercarriage
trim tab
undercarriage
undercart
ventral fin
vertical stabilizer
viewport
wing
winglet
wing tip
yoke

Weapons and armed forces

Types of soldier

archer
artilleryman
banneret
beefeater
blue helmet
bowman
brave
cadet
cannoneer
carabineer
cataphract
cavalier
cavalryman
centurion
chasseur
commando
conscript
cuirassier
doughboy
draftee
dragoon
drum major
enlisted man
ensign
evzone
fencible
foot soldier
freelance
fugleman
fusilier
galloglass
grenadier
guardsman
guerrilla
gunner
halberdier
havildar
hoplite
hussar
infantryman
irregular
janissary
jawan
kern
klepht
knight
lancer
landsknecht
legionary
legionnaire
marine
mercenary
military policeman/policewoman
militiaman
miner
musketeer
non-commissioned officer (NCO)
officer
orderly
other ranks
paratrooper
partisan
pistoleer
point man
ranger
ranker
recruit
redcap
redcoat
regular
reservist
rifleman
sabreur
samurai
sapper
scout
SEAL
sentinel
sentry
sepoy
spahi
spearman
swordsman
Territorial
tirailleur
trooper
uhlan
vedette
yeoman

Military ranks

British Army

Field Marshal
General
Lieutenant General
Major General
Brigadier
Colonel
Lieutenant Colonel
Major
Captain
Lieutenant
Second Lieutenant
Warrant Officer
Staff Sergeant
Sergeant
Corporal/Bombardier
Lance Corporal/Lance Bombardier
Private/Gunner

Royal Navy

Admiral of the Fleet
Admiral
Vice Admiral
Rear Admiral
Commodore
Captain
Commander
Lieutenant Commander
Lieutenant
Sub Lieutenant
Midshipman
Warrant Officer
Chief Petty Officer
Petty Officer
Leading Seaman
Able Seaman
Ordinary Seaman

Royal Air Force

Marshal of the Royal Air Force
Air Chief Marshal
Air Marshal
Air Vice-Marshal
Air Commodore
Group Captain
Wing Commander
Squadron Leader
Flight Lieutenant
Flying Officer
Pilot Officer
Acting Pilot Officer
Warrant Officer
Flight Sergeant
Sergeant
Senior Aircraftman/Aircraftwoman
Leading Aircraftman/Aircraftwoman
Aircraftman/Aircraftwoman

US Army and Air Force

Chief of Staff
General
Lieutenant General
Major General
Brigadier General
Colonel
Lieutenant Colonel
Major
Captain
First Lieutenant
Second Lieutenant
Warrant Officer
Sergeant
Corporal
Private First Class
Private

US Navy

Chief of Naval Operations
Fleet Admiral
Admiral
Vice Admiral
Rear Admiral
Captain
Commander
Lieutenant Commander
Lieutenant
Lieutenant junior grade
Ensign
Warrant Officer
Master Chief Petty Officer
Senior Chief Petty Officer
Petty Officer
Seaman

Guns

ack-ack
air gun/pistol/rifle
AK-47
anti-aircraft gun
anti-tank gun
Armalite (*trademark*)
artillery
assault gun
assault rifle
automatic
bazooka
Big Bertha
blunderbuss
Bofors gun
breech-loader
Bren (gun)
Brown Bess
Browning
burp gun
cannon
carbine
carronade
chain gun
chassepot
Colt (*trademark*)
derringer
double-barrelled gun
duelling pistol
elephant gun
Enfield rifle
express rifle
falconet
field gun
firelock
flintlock
forty-five
fowling piece
fusil
Garand (rifle)
Gatling (gun)
hackbut
handgun
harpoon gun
harquebus/arquebus

Wordfinder

horse pistol
Hotchkiss (gun)
howitzer
Kalashnikov
Lee–Enfield (rifle)
Lewis gun
Luger (*US trademark*)
M-1 (rifle/carbine)
M-16 (rifle)
M-60 (machine gun)
machine gun
magazine rifle
matchlock
Mauser (*trademark*)
Maxim gun
mine-thrower
mortar
musket
muzzle-loader
Oerlikon (*trademark*)
Owen (gun)
Parabellum (*trademark*)
pepperbox
pistol
pistolet
pom-pom
pump-action shotgun
pump gun
rail gun
repeating rifle
revolver
rifle
Saturday night special
sawn-off shotgun
Schmeisser
self-loader
self-loading rifle (SLR)
semi-automatic
shotgun
sidearm
siege gun
six-shooter
small arms
Smith & Wesson (*trademark*)
smooth-bore
Springfield (rifle)
starting pistol
Sten gun
Steyr
sub-machine gun
swivel-gun
thirty-eight
Thompson sub-machine gun
tommy gun
trench mortar
Uzi
Very pistol
Vickers (gun)
Walther
Webley (*trademark*)
Winchester (*trademark*)
zip gun

Bullets and shot

ball
baton round
birdshot
buckshot
canister
cannonball
case-shot
chain shot
dumdum bullet
dust shot
grapeshot
lead shot
pellet
plastic bullet
round-nose
round shot
rubber bullet
shell
slug
soft-nosed bullet
tracer
wadcutter

Projectiles and projectile weapons

Projectiles

arrow
assegai
bolas
bolt
boomerang
brickbat
brinny
bullet
cruise missile
dart
depleted-uranium shell
flare
flechette
flying bomb
gig
Greek fire
guided missile
harpoon
heat-seeking missile
javelin
jerid
kierie
kylie
missile
mortar bomb/shell
pellet
rocket
rocket-propelled grenade (RPG)
shell
shrapnel
shuriken
smoke ball
spear
star shell
torpedo
woomera
whiz-bang

Projectile weapons

See also **Guns**

arbalest
ballista
bazooka
blowpipe
bow
catapult
crossbow
gun
harpoon gun
longbow
mangonel
missile launcher
mortar
rail gun
rocket launcher
rocket-propelled grenade (RPG) launcher
sling
trebuchet

Bombs and mines

A-bomb
acoustic mine
atom/atomic bomb
Bangalore torpedo
blockbuster
booby trap
car bomb
claymore
cluster bomb
CS canister/grenade
daisy-cutter
depth charge
dirty bomb
doodlebug
firebomb
flying bomb
fragmentation bomb/grenade
fuel-air bomb
fusion bomb
gas shell
gelignite
grenade
hand grenade
H-bomb
hydrogen bomb
improvised explosive device (IED)
incendiary bomb
JDAM (joint direct attack munition)
landmine
laser-guided bomb
letter bomb
limpet mine
magnetic mine
mail bomb
Mills bomb
Molotov cocktail
napalm bomb
neutron bomb
nuclear bomb/device
parcel bomb
payload
petard
petrol bomb
pipe bomb
plastic bomb
RPG (rocket-propelled grenade)
satchel charge
shaped charge
smart bomb
smoke bomb
sonic mine
stick grenade
thermobaric bomb
thermonuclear bomb/device
time bomb
vacuum bomb
warhead

Personal weapons *See also* **Guns**, **Knives**

axe
backsword
baseball bat
baton
battleaxe
bayonet
bilbo
bill
blackjack
blade
bludgeon
bowie knife
brass knuckles
broadsword
chopper
claymore
club
commando knife
cosh
cudgel
cutlass
dagger
danda
dirk
épée
falchion
flick knife
foil
gisarme
gun
halberd
harpoon
hatchet
javelin
kierie
kleywang
knife
knobkerrie
knuckleduster
kris
kukri
lance
lathi
life preserver
mace
machete
nulla-nulla
panga
parang
partisan
pike
poleaxe
poniard
quarterstaff
rapier
sabre
scimitar
shillelagh
sjambok
skean
skean-dhu
slung shot
small sword
snickersnee
spear
staff
stave
stick
stiletto
sword
swordstick
tomahawk
truncheon
yataghan

Parts of a suit of armour

basinet
beaver
bracer
brassard
breastplate
brigandine
burgonet
camail
casque
chain mail
chausses
coif
corselet
coutere
cuirass
cuisse
gauntlet
gorget
greave
habergeon
hauberk
helmet
jambeau
lance rest
mail
morion
nasal
neck guard
nosepiece
pectoral
plastron
poleyn
pouldron
rerebrace
sabaton
sallet
solleret
tasses
vambrace
ventail
visor

kaleidoscopic adjective **1** *the branches refracted the light from the street lamps into kaleidoscopic shapes on the pavement*: **multicoloured**, many-coloured, multicolour, many-hued, variegated, particoloured, varicoloured, prismatic, psychedelic, rainbow, rainbow-like, polychromatic, harlequin, motley, many-splendoured; informal (looking) like an explosion in a paint factory.
▷**ANTONYMS** monochrome.
2 *the country's kaleidoscopic political landscape*: **ever-changing**, changeable, shifting, fluid, protean, mutable, variable, varying, inconstant, unstable, fluctuating, mobile, unsteady, unpredictable, ever-moving, chameleon-like, chameleonic, impermanent, indefinite; technical labile; rare changeful.
▷**ANTONYMS** fixed, constant, immutable.
3 *children's questions about the kaleidoscopic world they are living in*: **multifaceted**, many-faceted, varied, manifold, multifarious; **complex**, intricate, complicated, convoluted; confused, chaotic, muddled, disordered, disorganized, disarranged, jumbled, confusing.

kaput informal **adjective** *the TV's kaput*. See **broken** (sense 3).
□ **go kaput** See **break down** (sense 1).

keel verb
□ **keel over 1** *it's going to take more wind to make this boat keel over*: **capsize**, turn turtle, turn upside down, turn topsy-turvy, founder, list, heel over, lean over; overbalance, topple over, overturn, turn over, tip over, fall over. **2** *the slightest activity made him keel over*: **collapse**, faint, fall down in a faint, pass out, black out, lose consciousness; literary swoon.
▸ **noun** *she sat on the upturned keel of the boat*: **base**, bottom, bottom side, underside.

keen[1] adjective **1** *his publishers were* **keen to** *capitalize on his success*: **eager**, anxious, impatient, determined, desirous, longing, wishing, itching, dying, yearning, ambitious, ready; intent on; informal raring.
▷**ANTONYMS** reluctant.
2 *I had been a keen birdwatcher since I was a boy*: **enthusiastic**, avid, eager, ardent, passionate, fervent, fervid, impassioned, wholehearted, zestful, zealous; willing, conscientious, committed, dedicated; diligent, earnest, industrious, assiduous, intent.
▷**ANTONYMS** apathetic, half-hearted.
3 *her sisters are* **keen on** *horses | he had a girl in Kentucky he was* **keen on**: **enthusiastic about**, interested in, passionate about, fascinated by; **attracted to**, fond of, taken with, smitten with, enamoured of, attached to, devoted to, infatuated with; eager for, hungry for; informal struck on, sweet on, gone on, mad about, crazy about, nuts about, into.
▷**ANTONYMS** unenthusiastic, indifferent.
4 *a keen cutting edge*: **sharp**, sharp-edged, sharpened, honed, razor-like, razor-sharp, whetted, fine-edged.
▷**ANTONYMS** blunt.
5 *nimble fingers and keen eyesight are required for the work*: **acute**, sharp, penetrating, discerning, sensitive, perceptive, piercing, clear, observant; powerful.
▷**ANTONYMS** weak, defective.
6 *an able administrator with a keen mind*: **acute**, penetrating, astute, incisive, sharp, perceptive, piercing, rapier-like, razor-like, razor-sharp, perspicacious, shrewd, subtle, finely honed, quick-witted, sharp-witted, discerning, clever, intelligent, brilliant, bright, smart, wise, canny, percipient, insightful, sagacious, sapient; informal brainy.
▷**ANTONYMS** dull, stupid.
7 *the magazines are spoken of with keen derision*: **cutting**, scathing, mordant, caustic, withering, acerbic, stinging, searing, acid, biting, tart, astringent, pointed, trenchant, pungent, incisive, virulent, devastating; sardonic, sarcastic, satirical; rare mordacious.
▷**ANTONYMS** gentle, mild.
8 *a keen wind cut through their coats*: **cold**, icy, freezing, harsh, raw, bitter; penetrating, piercing, biting, sharp, stinging.
9 *there is keen competition for places on these committees | a keen sense of duty*: **intense**, acute, extreme, fierce, violent, passionate, consuming, burning, fervent, fervid, ardent; strong, powerful, profound, deep-seated.

Choose the right word **keen, eager, enthusiastic, avid**

See **eager**.

Choose the right word **keen, acute, penetrating**

Keen is used of sensitive and powerful perception, both physical and mental (*his keen hearing caught the whirring of the tape | he enjoyed exercising his keen intellect in analysing the controversies of the day*); when applied to someone's eyes, it often suggests an appearance of alertness and perceptiveness as well as actual power (*his keen eyes went from Thomas to Ralf*). The impressions or attitudes resulting from *keen* mental perception are intense (*young people show a keen awareness of animal welfare | lawyers with a keen sense of the value of good political connections*).

Someone whose physical or mental perception is **acute** can detect small details that are not readily apparent to others (*young children have a particularly acute sense of smell | Simon's vague manner concealed an agile and acute mind*). An *acute observer* can produce *acute criticism*, identifying central issues and making perceptive points about them. Intense and insistent emotion may be described as *acute* (*acute grief at the loss of her parents*).

Penetrating eyes may or may not have good sight, but they look as though they can see through you (*she was unable to meet his penetrating eyes*). A *penetrating mind* enables one to see deeply into a problem and think up *penetrating questions*, calculated to reveal important truths.

keen[2] verb *the bereaved gathered around the graves to keen*: **lament**, mourn, weep, cry, sob, sorrow, grieve; wail, moan, whine, whimper, groan, howl; Scottish greet; archaic plain; rare ululate.

keenness noun **1** *the company has signalled its keenness to sign a deal*: **eagerness**, willingness, readiness, desire, wish, anxiety, impatience; enthusiasm, fervour, wholeheartedness, zest, zeal, ardour, passion, devotion, avidity; earnestness, diligence, assiduity, conscientiousness, intentness.
▷**ANTONYMS** reluctance.
2 *the keenness of the blade*: **sharpness**, razor-sharpness.
▷**ANTONYMS** bluntness.
3 *keenness of hearing*: **acuteness**, sharpness, sensitivity, perceptiveness, discrimination, clarity.
4 *the keenness of his mind*: **acuity**, sharpness, subtlety, incisiveness, astuteness, perspicacity, perceptiveness, quick-wittedness, sharp-wittedness, shrewdness, penetration, insight, cleverness, discernment, intelligence, brightness, brilliance, canniness, sagacity.

▶ANTONYMS dullness, obtuseness.
5 *the keenness of her wit*: **incisiveness**, causticity, tartness, sharpness, mordancy, acidity, acerbity, trenchancy, pungency, virulence, sarcasm, sardonicism, satire.
▶ANTONYMS gentleness, insipidity.
6 *the keenness of his sense of loss*: **intensity**, acuteness, extremity, strength, power, violence, profundity, depth, ferocity.

keep[1] verb **1** *he kept the ball as a memento of the match | you should keep all the old forms*: **retain**, hold on to, keep for oneself, retain possession of, keep possession of, retain in one's possession, keep hold of, not part with, hold fast to, hold back; **save**, store, store up, save up, hoard, put by, put aside, lay aside, set aside, reserve, keep in reserve, lay down; collect, accumulate, amass, pile up, stockpile, garner; N. Amer. set something by; informal hang on to, stash away.
▶ANTONYMS lose, throw away.
2 *I was trying desperately to keep calm*: **remain**, continue to be, stay, carry on being, go on being, persist in being, not cease to be.
3 *he keeps going on about the murder*: **persist in**, go on, keep on, carry on, continue, do something constantly, do something incessantly, do something continually, not stop doing something, persevere.
▶ANTONYMS give up, stop.
4 *I shan't keep you long*: **detain**, cause to stay, cause to wait, keep waiting, keep back, hold back, restrain; **delay**, hold up, retard, make late, set back, slow down, slow up, hinder, obstruct, check, impede, block, hamper, constrain.
5 *he had to keep his promise | some people kept the rules and some never tried*: **comply with**, obey, respect, observe, conform to, abide by, stick to, act in accordance with, act according to, have regard to, heed, follow, pay attention to, defer to, take notice of; **fulfil**, carry out, act on, make good, be bound by, honour, keep to, redeem, keep faith with, stand by, adhere to; execute, discharge, perform; rare effectuate.
▶ANTONYMS break, disobey.

6 *I like to keep the old traditions*: **preserve**, keep alive, keep going, continue, keep up, carry on, hold on to, perpetuate, maintain, uphold, sustain, conserve, cherish, nurture.
▶ANTONYMS abandon, discard.
7 *the stand where her umbrella was kept*: **store**, house, stow, keep a place for, put away, place, put, deposit, stack, pile.
8 *the shop keeps a good stock of parchment*: **stock**, have in stock, carry, have, have for sale, hold, sell, deal in, trade in, handle, market, supply, provide, offer for sale.
9 *he has to steal to keep his family*: **provide for**, support, provide food for, provide sustenance for, provide board for, feed, keep alive, maintain, sustain, subsidize, finance; take care of, look after, nurture, nourish.
10 *she kept rabbits in the back garden*: **breed**, rear, raise, farm; own, have as a pet, keep as a pet, look after, tend.
11 *his parents kept a shop*: **manage**, run, own, be the proprietor of, be in charge of, administer, organize, direct, keep up, maintain, operate, look after, superintend.
12 *the boy keeps the sheep | 'God keep you,' he muttered*: **tend**, look after, care for, take care of, mind, watch over, have charge of, be responsible for; **protect**, keep safe, keep from harm, preserve, defend, guard, shield, shelter, safeguard, save.
13 *today's consumers do not keep the Sabbath*: **observe**, respect, honour, hold sacred, recognize, acknowledge; celebrate, mark, solemnize, ritualize, ceremonialize, commemorate.
▶ANTONYMS ignore, neglect.

□ **keep at** *start work early and keep at it*: **persevere with**, persist with, be persistent in, keep going with, keep on at, be pertinacious in, show determination in, be resolute in, be steadfast in, not give up, not cease from, not falter in, carry on with, press on with, work away at, continue with, see through, struggle on with; informal stick at, soldier on with, slave away at, peg away at, plug away at, hammer away at, bash on with, plough through.
▶ANTONYMS give up.

□ **keep something back 1** *every week she kept back a portion of the money he gave her*: **reserve**, keep in reserve, put by, save, save up, store up, put aside, lay aside, set aside, hoard, treasure; **retain**, hold back, keep, keep for oneself, hold on to, not part with, keep in one's possession; N. Amer. set by; informal keep for a rainy day, stash away.
2 *she kept back the details from Ann*: **conceal**, keep secret, keep hidden, hide, withhold, suppress, keep quiet about, not tell, not reveal, not divulge, hush up. ▶ANTONYMS disclose, divulge.
3 *she could hardly keep back her tears*: **suppress**, stifle, withhold, choke back, fight back, hold back/in, restrain, repress, check, keep in check, keep under control, contain, curb, smother, swallow, bottle up, bite back.
▶ANTONYMS let out.

□ **keep from** *Dinah bit her lip to keep from screaming*: **refrain from**, stop oneself, restrain oneself from, prevent oneself from, manage not to, forbear from, resist the temptation to, forgo, avoid.

□ **keep someone from something 1** *worry kept her from sleeping | he could hardly keep himself from laughing*: **prevent**, stop, hinder, impede, hamper; **restrain**, check, curb, hold back, halt. ▶ANTONYMS enable, allow.
2 *keep him from harm*: **preserve**, protect, keep safe, afford protection to, guard, shield, shelter, save, safeguard, secure, defend. ▶ANTONYMS endanger.

□ **keep something from someone** *now you know what your mother tried to keep from you*: **keep secret**, keep hidden, hide, conceal, withhold, hush up, not tell, suppress, censor; informal keep dark, not breathe a word of.
▶ANTONYMS tell, divulge.

□ **keep off 1** *he'd tell the boy to keep off private land*: **stay off**, not enter, keep away from, stay away from, not trespass on, remain at a distance from, not go near. ▶ANTONYMS enter.
2 *Maud tried to keep off political subjects*: **avoid**, steer clear of, stay away from, shun, evade, skirt round, sidestep, dodge, pass over, bypass; informal duck. ▶ANTONYMS raise, mention.
3 *the first thing she told me was to keep off alcohol*: **abstain from**, go without, do without, renounce, refrain from, give up, forgo, forswear, resist, turn aside from, swear off, not touch; informal quit. ▶ANTONYMS take up.
4 *it'll be great if the rain keeps off*: **stay away**, hold off, not start, not begin, not come, not happen. ▶ANTONYMS start.

□ **keep on 1** *they preferred to keep on working*: **continue**, go on, carry on, persist in, persevere in, keep going with; soldier on, struggle on, see something through. ▶ANTONYMS stop.
2 *the commander kept on about vigilance*: **talk constantly**, talk endlessly, talk repeatedly, keep talking, go on, go on talking, go on and on, dwell on the subject, refer to repeatedly, repeat oneself, ramble on, rant on; informal harp on, witter on, rabbit on.

□ **keep someone on** *the boss decided to keep the man on*: **continue to employ**, keep employing, carry on employing, retain in one's service, not dismiss, not sack, keep in one's employ, retain the services of.
▶ANTONYMS dismiss.

□ **keep on at** *they kept on at him to hurry up*: **nag**, go on at, keep at, harp on at, badger, chivvy, harass, hound, bully, pester, scold; informal hassle; N. Amer. informal ride.

□ **keep someone/something out** *the doors are closed to keep out any unwelcome visitors*: **exclude**, deny access to, shut out, debar, disbar, bar, ban, prohibit, put an embargo on, embargo; reject, blackball, ostracize, banish; cut out, freeze out; Brit. send to Coventry.
▶ANTONYMS accept, admit.

□ **keep to 1** *I've got to keep to the rules*: **obey**, abide by, observe, follow, comply with, adhere to, act in accordance with, conform to, be governed by, respect, defer to; **honour**, keep, fulfil, act on, stand by, stick to, be bound by, be true to, keep faith with, make good, carry out.
2 *keep to the path by the hedge*: **follow**, follow closely, stick to, stay on.
▶ANTONYMS stray from.
3 *speakers should keep to the point*: **stick to**, restrict oneself to, confine oneself to. ▶ANTONYMS deviate from.

□ **keep someone under** *the local people are kept under by the army*: **keep in subjection**, keep in submission, hold down, keep down, keep under one's thumb, subdue, subject, suppress, repress, oppress, tyrannize over, tyrannize; informal squash, squelch, trample on.

□ **keep up** *he had to run to keep up*: **keep pace**, keep abreast.
▶ANTONYMS lag behind.

□ **keep something up** *keep up the good work | she kept up a continuous conversation*: **continue**, keep on with, continue with, go on with, carry on with, persist with, persevere with; maintain, carry on, keep going, sustain.
▶ANTONYMS cease from.

□ **keep up with 1** *she walked fast to keep up with him*: **keep pace with**, keep abreast of; rival, challenge, compete with, vie with, match, touch, equal. ▶ANTONYMS lag behind.
2 *even while travelling he kept up with events at home*: **keep informed about**, keep up to date with, keep in touch with, not lose track of, keep abreast of, keep an eye on, learn about, retain an interest in; informal keep tabs on, keep a tab on. ▶ANTONYMS lose touch with.
3 *they kept up with him by means of Christmas cards*: **remain in contact with**, stay in touch with, maintain contact with, remain in correspondence with, remain in communication with, keep up one's friendship with, remain acquainted with. ▶ANTONYMS lose touch with.

▶ noun *he had no money to pay for his keep*: **maintenance**, upkeep, support, sustenance, subsistence, board, board and lodging, food, nourishment, nurture; living, livelihood, means.

□ **for keeps** informal *his performance earned him the trophy for keeps*: **forever**, for ever, for all time, for ever and ever, for always, once and for all, for good, for good and all, permanently, in perpetuity; N. Amer. forevermore; informal until kingdom come, until hell freezes over, until doomsday; archaic for aye.
▶ANTONYMS temporarily, for the time being.

keep[2] noun *enemies storming the keep*: **fortress**, fort, stronghold, tower, donjon, castle, citadel, bastion, fortification, fastness; archaic hold, dungeon.

keeper noun **1** *he was made keeper of the archives at court*: **curator**, conservator, custodian, guardian, administrator, overseer; steward,

caretaker, superintendent; governor, warden, attendant.
2 *he was keeper of an inn*: **proprietor**, owner, holder, possessor, master/mistress, landlord/landlady.
3 *she's not a child and you're not her keeper*: **guardian**, protector, defender, guard, bodyguard, escort, minder, attendant, chaperone, carer, nursemaid, nurse.
4 *the prisoners' keepers would sometimes confiscate books*: **jailer**, prison officer, guard, warder, warden, custodian, sentry; informal screw.

keeping noun *the document is in the keeping of the county archivist*: **safe keeping**, care, custody, charge, keep, possession, trust, protection, safeguard; guardianship, trusteeship, tutelage, supervision, protectorship.
□ **in keeping with** *a trend to the left which was in keeping with the political atmosphere of the time*: **consistent with**, in harmony with, in accord with, in accordance with, in agreement with, in line with, in character with, true to, compatible with, congruent with, commensurate with; appropriate to, befitting, as befits, suitable for, suited to.
▷ANTONYMS at odds with.

keepsake noun *she gave him a lock of her hair as a keepsake*: **memento**, token of remembrance, souvenir, reminder, something to remember someone by, remembrance, relic, memorial, token; archaic remembrancer, favour.

keg noun **barrel**, cask, vat, butt, tun, drum, hogshead, firkin, tub, tank, container, vessel.

ken noun *their talk hinted at mysteries beyond my ken*: **knowledge**, awareness, perception, understanding, grasp, comprehension, realization, apprehension, appreciation, consciousness, recognition, notice.

kernel noun **1** *the squirrel cracks the nut's shell and extracts the rich kernel*: **seed**, grain, heart, core, stone; nut; N. Amer. meat.
2 *the foreword contained the kernel of the policy*: **essence**, core, heart, essential part, essentials, quintessence, fundamentals, basics, nub, gist, substance, burden, heart of the matter, marrow, meat, pith, crux; informal nitty-gritty, nuts and bolts, brass tacks.
3 *there may be a kernel of truth in what he says*: **nucleus**, centre, germ, grain, nugget.

key noun **1** *the key to the mystery lay elsewhere* | *customer satisfaction is the key to success*: **answer**, clue, solution, explanation, pointer, cue, lead; **basis of**, foundation for, requisite for; condition, precondition, essential, means, way, route, path, passport, secret, formula; **guide**, gloss, glossary, interpretation, explication, translation, clarification, exposition, annotation, index, legend, code.
2 Music *a song in a minor key*: **tone**, pitch, timbre, tonality, tone colour, modulation.
3 *it was like the sixties all over again, in a more austerely intellectual key*: **style**, character, mood, vein, spirit, feel, feeling, flavour, quality, humour, atmosphere.
▸ adjective *he was a key figure in formulating policy*: **crucial**, central, essential, indispensable, basic, fundamental, pivotal, critical, decisive, dominant, vital, principal, salient, prime, chief, major, leading, main, important, significant.
▷ANTONYMS secondary, peripheral.

keynote noun *the keynote of the paper was 'positive planning'*: **theme**, salient point, point, gist, substance, burden, tenor, heart of the matter, pith, marrow, topic, policy line; essence, heart, core, basis, essential feature/element, defining characteristic, centre, kernel, nucleus.

keystone noun **1** *a carved head formed the keystone of the door*: **cornerstone**, central stone, quoin.
2 *cooperation remains the keystone of the government's security policy*: **foundation**, basis, linchpin, cornerstone, base, principle, guiding principle, core, heart, centre, crux, fundament, mainspring, priority.

kibosh noun informal
□ **put the kibosh on** *his boss put the kibosh on the deal*: **put a stop to**, check, curb, stop, halt, bring to an end, put an end to, nip in the bud, quash, block, cancel, scotch, thwart, frustrate, prevent, quell, suppress; informal squelch, put paid to, scupper, spike, stymie.

kick verb **1** *her attacker punched and kicked her* | *she kicked a box in his direction*: **boot**, punt, strike with the foot; propel, drive, knock, send; Scottish blooter; informal put the boot into.
2 informal *he was struggling to kick his drug habit*: **give up**, break, get out of, abandon, end, escape from; stop, cease, leave off, desist from, renounce, forgo, do without, eschew; informal shake, pack in, lay off, quit.
▷ANTONYMS take up, start.
3 *the gun kicked so hard that he flinched*: **recoil**, spring back, fly back.
□ **kick against** *young people are expected to kick against the establishment*: **resist**, rebel against, oppose, struggle/fight against, refuse to accept; protest against, complain about, rage against, grumble about, object to; defy, disobey, reject, spurn; informal gripe about, grouse about, beef about, bitch about.
▷ANTONYMS accept.
□ **kick someone/something around** informal **1** *we feel we are undervalued and get kicked around*: **abuse**, mistreat, maltreat, treat disrespectfully, treat inconsiderately, push around/about, boss about/around, trample on, take for granted; informal mess about/around, walk all over. **2** *they began to kick around the idea of sending a man into space*: **discuss**, talk over, debate, thrash out, consider, moot, toy with, play with, argue the pros and cons of.
□ **kick back** N. Amer. informal *take a moment to kick back and enjoy an ice cream*: **relax**, unwind, take it easy, rest, take one's ease, slow down, let up, ease up/off, be at leisure, sit back, laze, enjoy oneself; N. Amer. informal chill out, hang loose.
□ **kick off** informal *the festival kicks off on Monday* | *the installation kicks off a three-year project*: **start**, begin, get going, get off the ground, get under way; open, start off, set going, set in motion, launch, put in place, initiate, introduce, inaugurate, usher in, start the ball rolling; informal get the show on the road; formal commence.
□ **kick someone out** informal *he was kicked out of his regiment for insubordination*: **expel**, send away, eject, turn out, throw out, force out, oust, evict, put out, get rid of; dismiss, discharge; informal chuck out, send packing, boot out, show the door to, give someone their marching orders, throw someone out on their ear, sack, fire, give someone the boot, axe; Brit. informal turf out; N. Amer. informal give someone the bum's rush.
▸ noun **1** *he gave the ball a kick*: **boot**, punt.
2 informal *I get a kick out of driving a racing car* | *the murderer was a lunatic who killed for kicks*: **thrill**, excitement, stimulation, tingle; fun, enjoyment, amusement, pleasure, gratification; informal buzz, high; N. Amer. informal charge.
3 informal *caffeine-free cola for those who want the taste without the kick* | *mustard is mixed into the dough to give the roll a delicious kick*: **potency**, stimulant effect, alcoholic effect, strength, power, punch; tang, zest, bite, piquancy, edge, pungency, spice, savour; informal zip, zing, zap, pep, oomph.
4 informal *their parents had gone on a health kick and refused to buy junk food*: **craze**, enthusiasm, obsession, mania, passion, preoccupation, fixation; fashion, vogue, trend; informal fad, jag.

kickback noun **1** *the kickback from the gun punches at your shoulder*: **recoil**, kick, rebound.
2 informal *the businessmen were accused of paying kickbacks to politicians to obtain public contracts*. See **bribe** (noun).

kick-off noun informal *this weekend is the kick-off for Japan's holiday season*: **beginning**, start, outset, opening, starting point, initiation, inception; formal commencement.
▷ANTONYMS end.

kid[1] noun informal *she is married with three kids*: **child**, youngster, little one, young one, baby, toddler, infant, boy/girl, young person, minor, juvenile, adolescent, teenager, youth, stripling; offspring, son/daughter; Scottish bairn, wean; informal kiddie, nipper, tot, tiny, kiddiewink, shaver, young 'un; Brit. informal sprog; N. Amer. informal rug rat; Austral./NZ ankle-biter; derogatory brat, urchin; literary babe.

kid[2] verb informal **1** *the village is called Hell—I'm not kidding*: **joke**, tease, jest, chaff, be facetious; pretend, play, fool about/around; informal pull someone's leg, wind up, have on, rib, josh; N. Amer. informal pull someone's chain, fun, shuck.
2 *why did I kid myself that I'd succeed?* **delude**, deceive, fool, trick, take in, hoodwink, hoax, beguile, dupe, gull, bamboozle; informal con, pull the wool over someone's eyes; literary cozen.

kidnap verb *they attempted to kidnap the president's child*: **abduct**, carry off, capture, seize, snatch, hold to ransom, take as hostage, hijack; run off/away with; informal nobble, shanghai.

kidney noun

> *Word links* **kidney**
>
> **renal, nephritic** relating to kidneys
> **nephro-** related prefix
> **nephrology** branch of medicine concerning the kidneys
> **nephritis** inflammation of the kidneys
> **nephrectomy** removal of kidney
> **lithotomy** removal of kidney stone

kill verb **1** *gangs killed twenty-seven people*: **murder**, cause the death of, take/end the life of, do away with, make away with, assassinate, do to death, eliminate, terminate, dispatch, finish off, put to death, execute; slaughter, butcher, massacre, wipe out, destroy, annihilate, erase, eradicate, exterminate, extirpate, decimate, mow down, shoot down, cut down, cut to pieces; put down, put to sleep; informal bump off, polish off, do in, do for, knock off, top, take out, croak, stiff, blow away, liquidate, dispose of; N. Amer. informal ice, off, rub out, waste, whack, scrag, smoke; literary slay.
2 *media hostility would kill all hopes of progress*: **destroy**, put an end to, bring to an end, be the end of, end, extinguish, dash, quell, quash, ruin, wreck, shatter, smash, crush, scotch; stop, block, frustrate, thwart, put a stop to, prevent, defeat, derail; informal put paid to, do for, put the lid on, put the kibosh on, stymie, queer; Brit. informal scupper, dish.
▷ANTONYMS facilitate.
3 *we had to kill several hours at the airport*: **while away**, use up, fill up, fill in, fill, occupy, beguile, pass, spend, expend; fritter away, waste.

k

4 *you must rest or you'll kill yourself*: **exhaust**, wear out, tire out, overtax, overtire, fatigue, weary, sap, drain, tax, strain, debilitate, enervate, prostrate; informal knock out, fag out, shatter; Brit. informal knacker.
▷ANTONYMS refresh, revitalize.
5 informal *my feet were killing me*: **hurt**, give pain to, cause pain to, cause agony to, pain, torture, torment, cause discomfort to; be agonizing, be excruciating, be painful, be sore, be uncomfortable.
6 informal *the music kills me every time I hear it*: **overwhelm**, take someone's breath away, leave speechless, shake, move, stir, stun, amaze, astonish, stagger, dumbfound; informal bowl over, blow away, knock sideways, blow someone's mind, knock for six, flabbergast.
7 *the captain kept the engines at a low rev to kill the noise*: **muffle**, deaden, stifle, dampen, damp down, smother, reduce, diminish, decrease, suppress, abate, tone down, moderate, silence, mute, still, quieten, soften, quell.
▷ANTONYMS amplify.
8 *she gave me a shot to kill the pain*: **alleviate**, assuage, soothe, allay, take the edge off, mitigate, dull, blunt, mask, deaden, stifle, suppress, subdue, weaken, abate, quell, get rid of, put an end to.
▷ANTONYMS intensify.
9 informal *if a message has been killed, the file contains only the header*: **delete**, wipe out, erase, remove, destroy, rub out, cut out, cut, cancel, get rid of, expunge, obliterate, eliminate; informal zap.
10 informal *Congress killed an anti-tobacco bill*: **veto**, defeat, vote down, rule against, reject, throw out, overrule, stop, block, put a stop to, put an end to, quash, overturn, disallow; informal give the thumbs down to, squash.
▷ANTONYMS pass, accept.
11 informal *Noel parked and killed the engine*: **turn off**, switch off, stop, stop working, shut off, shut down, cut, cut out, deactivate; put out, turn out, extinguish.
▷ANTONYMS start.
▶**noun 1** *the hunter proudly flung down his kill*: **prey**, quarry, victim, bag.
2 *the wolf was moving in for the kill*: **death blow**, killing, act of killing, dispatch; conclusion, ending, finish, end, climax; French coup de grâce.

k

Word links **kill**

-cide person or substance that kills, as in *insecticide*
-cide killing of someone, as in *regicide, suicide*

killer **noun 1** *police are searching for clues to help find the killer*: **murderer**, slaughterer, destroyer, liquidator, exterminator, terminator, executioner; literary slayer; dated homicide.
2 *the major killers are coronary disease, stroke, and cancer*: **cause of death**, fatal/deadly illness, destroyer, threat to life, menace, plague, scourge, peril.

killing **noun** *the community was shocked by the brutal killing*: **murder**, taking of life, assassination, homicide, manslaughter, liquidation, elimination, putting/doing to death, execution, dispatch, martyrdom; **slaughter**, massacre, butchery, carnage, bloodshed, destruction, decimation, extermination, eradication, annihilation, wiping out, extinction; patricide, matricide, parricide, infanticide, filicide; literary slaying.
□ **make a killing** informal *investors are set to make a killing in the sell-off*: **make a large profit**, make a/one's fortune, gain, profit, make money, be successful, be lucky; informal clean up, strike it rich, rake it in, make a/one's pile, make a packet, make a bundle, make a pretty penny; Brit. informal make a bomb; N. Amer. informal make big bucks.
▶**adjective 1** *a killing blow*: **deadly**, lethal, fatal, mortal, death-dealing, causing death, life-threatening, final, destructive, dangerous; murderous, homicidal; literary deathly.
2 informal *the Minister has a killing schedule*: **exhausting**, gruelling, punishing, taxing, draining, wearing, prostrating, sapping, crushing, tiring, fatiguing, debilitating, enervating, arduous, tough, demanding, onerous, strenuous, rigorous, relentless, unsparing, grinding, formidable; informal murderous, back-breaking; Brit. informal knackering.
3 informal *the suspense will be killing*: **unbearable**, intolerable, unendurable, not to be borne, more than one can bear, more than flesh and blood can stand, insupportable, impossible; cruel, heartbreaking, painful, excruciating, agonizing, grievous.
4 informal, dated *'I think he's absolutely killing,' said Muriel*: **hilarious**, hysterically funny, outrageously funny, too funny for words, uproarious, riotous, comic, comical, chucklesome, amusing, laughable, absurd, ludicrous, outrageous; informal priceless, side-splitting, a scream, a hoot, rib-tickling, killingly funny, screamingly funny.

killjoy **noun** *sun worshippers feel the anti-sun lobby are just killjoys*: **spoilsport**, moaner, complainer, mope, prophet of doom, Cassandra, Jeremiah, death's head at a feast; puritan, prig, prude; Austral./NZ wowser; informal wet blanket, party-pooper, misery, dog in the manger.

kilter **noun**
□ **out of kilter** *daylight saving throws everyone's body clock out of kilter*: **awry**, off balance, unbalanced, out of order, not in working order, disordered, confused, disorderly, disorganized, muddled, in poor shape; disharmonious, discordant, out of tune, out of step.

kin **noun** *mothers left their children with grandmothers or other kin*: **relatives**, relations, family, family members, kindred, connections, clan, tribe, kith and kin, one's own flesh and blood, nearest and dearest; kinsfolk, kinsmen/kinswomen; informal folks; dated people.
▶**adjective** *my uncle was kin to the brothers*: **related**, akin, allied, close, connected with, cognate with; rare consanguineous, consanguine.

kind[1] **noun 1** *she brought all kinds of gifts | he named the kinds of bird that could be seen*: **sort**, type, variety, style, form, class, category, genre; genus, species, race, breed, family, strain, order, natural kind; brand, make, model, design, version, line, mark.
2 *the trials were different in kind from any that preceded them | the book was the first of its kind*: **character**, nature, essence, quality, disposition, make-up, calibre; type, style, stamp, manner, description, mould, cast, temperament, ilk, kidney, persuasion; N. Amer. stripe; archaic grain.
□ **kind of** informal *it got kind of cosy*: **rather**, quite, fairly, moderately, somewhat, a little, slightly, a shade; in a way, in a manner of speaking, after a fashion, as one might say; informal sort of, a bit, kinda, pretty, a touch, a thought, a tad, ish.

kind[2] **adjective** *she's a kind girl and often rings me | it was so kind of him to help out*: **kindly**, good-natured, kind-hearted, tender-hearted, warm-hearted, soft-hearted, good-hearted, tender, caring, feeling, affectionate, loving, warm, gentle, mellow, mild; **considerate**, helpful, thoughtful, obliging, unselfish, selfless, altruistic, good, cooperative, accommodating, attentive; compassionate, sympathetic, understanding, big-hearted, benevolent, benign, friendly, neighbourly, courteous, agreeable, pleasant, nice, amiable, hospitable, well meaning, well intentioned, public-spirited, well meant; generous, magnanimous, indulgent, tolerant, charitable, gracious, lenient, humane, merciful, clement, pitying, forbearing, long-suffering, patient; liberal, open-handed, lavish, bountiful, unsparing, unstinting, beneficent, munificent, giving; philanthropic; handsome, princely; Brit. informal decent; literary bounteous; rare benignant.
▷ANTONYMS unkind, inconsiderate, mean, cruel.

kind-hearted **adjective** *she was friendly and kind-hearted*: **kind**, caring, warm-hearted, tender-hearted, soft-hearted, kindly, benevolent, good-natured, good-hearted, mild, tender, warm, feeling, gentle, compassionate, sympathetic, understanding; indulgent, humane, altruistic, patient, tolerant, lenient, merciful, benign, mellow, beneficent, amiable; rare benignant.
▷ANTONYMS hard-hearted.

kindle **verb 1** *he kindled a fire of dry grass*: **light**, **ignite**, set alight, set light to, set on fire, set fire to, put a match to, set burning, get going, start, touch off, spark; informal torch.
▷ANTONYMS douse, extinguish, put out.
2 *it was Elvis who kindled my interest in music*: **rouse**, arouse, wake, waken, awaken, quicken; **stimulate**, inspire, stir up, call forth, call/bring into being, draw forth, bring out, excite, evoke, pique, whet, stir, provoke, spur, fire, inflame, trigger, prompt, induce, encourage, actuate, activate, touch off, spark off, set off, set going, incite, promote, engender, generate; literary enkindle.

kindliness **noun** *she was grateful for his kindliness and care*: **kindness**, benevolence, warmth, benignity, gentleness, mildness, tenderness, care, humanity, humaneness, sensitivity, sympathy, compassion, understanding; generosity, charity, kind-heartedness, warm-heartedness, soft-heartedness, tender-heartedness, thoughtfulness, concern, solicitousness.
▷ANTONYMS unkindness.

kindly **adjective** *the children were adopted by a kindly old lady | he smiled in a kindly manner*: **benevolent**, kind, kind-hearted, warm-hearted, generous, good-natured, humane; **gentle**, warm, mild, compassionate, caring, tender-hearted, soft-hearted, tender, loving, loving and giving, motherly, fatherly, benign, mellow, well meaning, genial; indulgent, understanding, sympathetic, lenient, tolerant, charitable, magnanimous, easy-going, patient; helpful, thoughtful, considerate, good, good-hearted, nice, friendly, neighbourly, pleasant, amiable, agreeable, affable, amicable; Brit. informal decent; rare benignant.
▷ANTONYMS unkind, cruel.
▶**adverb 1** *'Welcome,' she said kindly | someone kindly lent us a car*: **benevolently**, good-naturedly, warmly, affectionately, tenderly, lovingly, compassionately; considerately, thoughtfully, helpfully, obligingly, generously, selflessly, unselfishly, graciously, indulgently, sympathetically, leniently, charitably.
▷ANTONYMS unkindly, harshly.
2 *kindly explain what you mean by that*: **please**, if you please, if you would be so good, if you wouldn't mind, have the goodness to, pray; French s'il vous plaît; archaic prithee.
□ **not take kindly to** *she does not take kindly to criticism*: **resent**, dislike, object to, take umbrage at, take exception to, be offended by, take offence at, be annoyed/irritated by, be displeased by, be affronted by, feel aggrieved about, take something amiss, be upset by, be put out by; informal be miffed at.

kindness **noun 1** *he thanked her for her kindness and support*: **kindliness**, kind-heartedness, warm-heartedness, tender-heartedness, goodwill,

affectionateness, affection, warmth, gentleness, tenderness, concern, care; consideration, considerateness, helpfulness, thoughtfulness, unselfishness, selflessness, altruism, compassion, sympathy, understanding, big-heartedness, benevolence, benignity, friendliness, neighbourliness, hospitality, amiability, courteousness, public-spiritedness; generosity, magnanimity, indulgence, patience, tolerance, charitableness, graciousness, lenience, humaneness, mercifulness; Brit. informal decency; literary bounteousness.
▷ANTONYMS unkindness, meanness.
2 *she has done us many a kindness*: **kind act**, good deed, act of kindness, good turn, favour, act of assistance, service, help, aid.
▷ANTONYMS disservice.

kindred noun **1** *he owed his popularity to his mother's kindred*: **family**, relatives, relations, kin, family members, connections, kith and kin, one's own flesh and blood, clan, tribe, house, lineage; informal folks; dated people; formal kinsfolk, kinsmen/kinswomen.
2 *ties of kindred*: **kinship**, family ties, being related, relationship, relatedness, blood relationship, ties of blood, consanguinity, common ancestry, common lineage.
▶ adjective **1** *the centre collects works on industrial relations and kindred subjects*: **related**, allied, connected, closely connected/related, comparable, similar, like, alike, parallel, associated, corresponding, cognate, analogous, interconnected, affiliated.
▷ANTONYMS unrelated.
2 *she was glad to find a kindred spirit to confide in*: **like-minded**, sympathetic, in sympathy, in harmony, in agreement, in tune, of one mind, akin, similar, like, congenial, compatible, understanding, agreeable; informal on the same wavelength.
▷ANTONYMS uncongenial, unsympathetic, alien.
3 archaic *the tenants were members of an allied and kindred clan*. See **related** (sense 2).

king noun **1** *Edward made a bid to be crowned king of France*: **ruler**, sovereign, monarch, supreme ruler, crowned head, majesty, Crown, head of state, royal personage, emperor, prince, potentate, overlord, liege lord, lord, leader, chief.
2 informal *he has become king of world football*: **star**, leading light, luminary, superstar, mogul, giant, master, kingpin, celebrity, lion; informal supremo, megastar, top dog, VIP, celeb, big name, bigwig, big cheese; N. Amer. informal big wheel.
□ **a king's ransom** *the perfume cost a king's ransom*: **a fortune**, a small fortune, a huge amount, a vast sum, millions, billions; informal a mint, a bundle, a packet, a pretty penny, a tidy sum; Brit. informal a bomb, loadsamoney, shedloads; N. Amer. informal big bucks, big money, gazillions; Austral. informal big bickies.

> *Word links* **king**
>
> **regal** relating to a king

kingdom noun **1** *his kingdom covered many countries*: **realm**, domain, dominion, country, land, nation, state, sovereign state, province, territory; empire, principality, palatinate, duchy.
2 *the third floor was Henry's little kingdom*: **domain**, province, realm, sphere, sphere/field of influence, dominion, area of power, department, territory, field, arena, zone, orbit.
3 *homeopathic remedies are drawn from the plant and mineral kingdoms*: **division**, category, classification, grouping, group; class, family, genus, kind, order, branch.

kingly adjective **1** *kingly power*: **royal**, regal, of a king, monarchical, sovereign, imperial, princely, crowned, supreme, absolute.
2 *kingly robes*: **regal**, **majestic**, stately, august, noble, lordly, proud, dignified, distinguished, courtly; splendid, magnificent, fit for a king, grand, glorious, rich, gorgeous, resplendent, princely, superb, sumptuous, opulent, costly, fine, grandiose, imposing, impressive; informal splendiferous, posh.
3 informal *the kingly sum of 2,500 guineas*. See **handsome** (sense 3).

kink noun **1** *your fishing line should have no kinks or frays*: **curl**, crimp, twist, twirl, ringlet, wave, frizz; knot, tangle, entanglement, coil, loop, crinkle, wrinkle, warp, distortion, irregularity.
2 *go round the kink in the road*: **bend**, corner, angle, dog-leg, crook, twist, turn, curve, loop, zigzag; Brit. hairpin bend.
3 *though the system is making headway, there are still some kinks to iron out*: **flaw**, defect, imperfection, problem, difficulty, complication, hitch, snag, shortcoming, weak point/spot, weakness, catch; informal hiccup, glitch.
4 *I haven't come here to talk about my sartorial kinks*: **peculiarity**, quirk, idiosyncrasy, eccentricity, oddity, foible, whim, whimsy, caprice, vagary, twist, crotchet, mannerism, fad; aberration, irregularity, deviation, perversion, fetish; informal hang-up, thing; rare singularity.

kinky adjective **1** informal *a kinky lover | she was involved in a kinky relationship with a couple of older women*: **abnormal**, unusual, weird, bizarre, peculiar, strange, odd, funny; **perverted**, deviant, unnatural, warped, twisted, depraved, degenerate, perverse, unhealthy, aberrant, sadistic, masochistic, corrupt, immoral; informal sick, pervy, sicko; rare deviative.
2 informal *kinky underwear*: **provocative**, sexy, sexually arousing, sexually exciting, erotic, seductive, suggestive, inviting, tempting, tantalizing, alluring, titillating, indecent, immodest; informal tarty, saucy, naughty.
3 *Catriona's long kinky hair*: **curly**, crimped, curled, curling, frizzy, frizzed, wavy, ringletted, ringletty; twisted, bent, coiled, crinkled.
▷ANTONYMS straight.

kinsfolk noun *his kinsfolk in England*: **relatives**, relations, kin, kindred, family members, family, kith and kin, kinsmen/kinswomen, one's own flesh and blood, blood relatives, connections; informal folks; dated people.

kinship noun **1** *ties of descent and kinship*: **relationship**, relatedness, being related, family ties, family connections, blood relationship, blood ties, common ancestry, common lineage, kindred, connection; formal consanguinity, propinquity.
2 *she could not feel kinship with people who were not decisive*: **affinity**, sympathy, kindred, rapport, harmony, understanding, alliance, association, empathy, closeness, fellow feeling, bond, community, communion, compatibility, link, accord, friendship, togetherness; similarity, likeness, parallel, parallelism, connection, correspondence, concordance, equivalence, agreement, symmetry, analogy, uniformity.

kinsman, kinswoman noun *his namesake and distant kinsman*: **relative**, relation, blood relation/relative, family member, one's own flesh and blood, next of kin; cousin, uncle, nephew, aunt, niece.

kiosk noun *he's buying an ice cream from the kiosk*: **booth**, stand, stall, counter, refreshments kiosk, news-stand, bookstall, telephone kiosk; box, compartment, cubicle, cabin, hut, enclosure.

kismet noun *what chance did I stand against kismet?* **fate**, destiny, fortune, providence, the stars, God's will, what is written in the stars, one's doom, one's portion, one's lot, one's lot in life, karma, predestination, preordination, predetermination, what is to come, the writing on the wall; luck, chance; archaic one's dole; rare predestiny.

kiss verb **1** *he kissed her on the lips | close by a couple were kissing*: **plant a kiss on**, brush one's lips against, blow a kiss to, air-kiss; informal peck, give a peck to, give a smacker to, smooch, canoodle, neck, pet, kiss and cuddle, bill and coo; Brit. informal snog; N. Amer. informal buss; informal, dated spoon; rare osculate.
2 *allow your foot just to kiss the floor*: **brush against**, brush, caress, touch gently, touch lightly, touch, stroke, graze, scrape, shave, skim over, glance off.
▶ noun **1** *she gave him a kiss on the cheek*: air kiss; French kiss, soul kiss; X; informal **peck**, smack, smacker, smackeroo, smooch; Brit. informal snog; N. Amer. informal buss; rare osculation.
2 *the kiss of the flowers against her cheeks*: **gentle touch**, light touch, caress, brush, stroke; **graze**, glance, scrape, shave.

kit noun **1** *his tool kit*: **equipment**, tools, implements, instruments, gadgets, utensils, appliances, tools of the trade, materials, aids, gear, tackle, hardware, paraphernalia, appurtenances; outfit, rig, set of tools, apparatus, set; informal things, stuff, the necessary; Military accoutrements.
2 *boys in football kit*: **clothes**, clothing, rig, outfit, dress, costume, garments, attire, garb; uniform, colours, regimentals, livery, trappings; Brit. strip; informal togs, garms, things, gear, get-up, stuff, duds; Brit. informal rig-out; formal apparel; literary raiment, array, habiliments.
3 *the children were building a model chalet from a kit*: **set of parts**, set of components, set, outfit, DIY kit, do-it-yourself kit, self-assembly set, flat-pack.
4 informal *we packed up all our kit and set off*: **belongings**, luggage, baggage, paraphernalia, effects, supplies, provisions, trappings, appurtenances, impedimenta; informal things, stuff, clobber, gear.
▶ verb
□ **kit someone/something out** *the studio is kitted out with six cameras | we were all kitted out in life jackets*: **equip**, fit, fit out, fit up, fix up, furnish, stock, supply, provide, provision, issue; outfit, get up, rig out, turn out, dress, clothe, array, costume, attire, accoutre, deck out; arm.

kitchen noun *they sat drinking cocoa in the kitchen*: **cooking area**, kitchenette, kitchen-diner, galley, cookhouse, bakehouse, scullery; N. Amer. cookery.

kittenish adjective *girls on radio had to be kittenish and girly*: **playful**, fun-loving, light-hearted, skittish, mischievous, roguish, impish, frisky, lively; coquettish, flirtatious, cute, coy, arch, teasing, cheeky, naughty; frivolous, flippant, superficial, trivial, shallow, giddy, empty-headed, scatterbrained, feather-brained, silly; informal flirty, dizzy; archaic frolicsome, sportive, gamesome, frolic; rare ludic.
▷ANTONYMS serious, solemn, staid.

knack noun **1** *some people have a knack for making money | it takes practice to acquire the knack*: **gift**, talent, flair, genius, instinct, faculty, ability, capability, capacity, aptitude, aptness, bent, forte, facility, dexterity, adroitness, readiness, quickness, ingenuity, proficiency, expertness, competence; **technique**, method, trick, skill, art, secret, approach, way, skilfulness, mastery, expertise, handiness, deftness; informal know-how, the

hang of something.
▷ANTONYMS inability.
2 *he has a knack of getting injured at the wrong time*: **tendency to**, propensity for, habit of, way of, proneness to, aptness to, bent for, liability to, leaning towards, predisposition to, disposition to, inclination to, penchant for, readiness to.

knackered adjective Brit. informal **1** *you look absolutely knackered*. See **exhausted**.
2 *the computer was knackered*. See **broken** (sense 3).

knapsack noun **rucksack**, backpack, haversack, pack, kitbag, duffel bag, satchel, shoulder bag, holdall.

knave noun archaic *don't let yourself by hoodwinked by that knave*. See **villain**.

knavery noun archaic *no system can protect a fool from the knavery of others*. See **villainy**.

knavish adjective archaic *his knavish behaviour*. See **villainous**.

knead verb **1** *turn the dough on to a floured board and knead*: **pummel**, work, pound, squeeze, wring, twist, crush, form, shape, mould, mix, blend; rare malaxate, malax.
2 *she put her hands on his shoulders and kneaded the base of his neck*: **massage**, press, manipulate, palpate, rub, handle, stroke, feel.

kneel verb *they knelt down and prayed*: **fall to one's knees**, get down on one's knees, genuflect, bow, bow down, make obeisance, kowtow, curtsy, show reverence, show deference; crouch, squat, hunch down, hunker down; N. Amer. informal scooch.

knell noun **1** *the knell of the ship's bell*: **toll**, tolling, ringing, chime, clang, dong, peal, stroke, resounding, reverberation, clangour, boom; death knell; archaic knoll, tocsin.
2 *no politician wants to be remembered as the one who sounded the knell for the NHS*: **end**, beginning of the end, presage of the end, death knell; **death sentence**, death warrant; omen, evil omen, ill omen, portent, warning.

knickers plural noun Brit. **underpants**, briefs, bikini briefs, drawers, French knickers, tanga briefs, camiknickers; Brit. **pants**; informal panties, knicks; historical bloomers, Directoire drawers, pantalettes.

knick-knack noun *knick-knacks for the tourist trade*: **ornament**, novelty, gewgaw, piece of bric-a-brac, bibelot, trinket, trifle, bauble, gimcrack, bagatelle, curio, curiosity, plaything, toy; memento, souvenir; N. Amer. kickshaw; French objet, objet d'art; informal oojah, whatnot, thingamajig, thingamabob, dingle-dangle; N. Amer. informal tchotchke, tsatske; Brit. informal doobry, doodah; archaic gaud, folderol, whim-wham, bijou.

knife noun *peel the oranges using a sharp knife*: **cutting tool**, blade, cutter, carver.
▸verb *the victims had been knifed more than seventy times*: **stab**, hack, gash, run through, slash, lacerate, cut, tear, gouge, pierce, spike, impale, transfix, bayonet, spear, skewer, wound.

knight noun *knights in armour*: **chevalier**, cavalier, cavalryman, horseman, equestrian; gallant, champion, paladin, banneret, knight errant; lord, noble, nobleman.
□ **knight in shining armour** *she's still waiting for her knight in shining armour*: **Sir Galahad**, knight on a white charger, protector, rescuer, saviour, preserver, champion, defender, guardian, guardian angel, deliverer, liberator; hero.

knightly adjective **1** *tales of chivalry and knightly deeds*: **gallant**, noble, valiant, heroic, courageous, brave, bold, intrepid, dauntless, fearless, stout-hearted; **chivalrous**, courtly, courteous, gracious, honourable, noble-minded; literary valorous.
▷ANTONYMS ignoble, cowardly, ungallant.
2 *conflict between knightly and non-knightly classes*: **upper-class**, **well born**, high-born, noble, of noble birth, aristocratic, lordly, patrician, blue-blooded, titled; archaic gentle, of gentle birth.
▷ANTONYMS low-born, common.

knit verb **1** *disparate regions had begun to knit together | their experience knitted the men together*: **unite**, become united, unify, become unified, become one, come together, become closer, band together, bond, combine, coalesce, merge, meld, blend, amalgamate, league; bind, weld together, bring together, draw together, ally, link, join, fuse, connect, consolidate.
2 *we expect broken bones to knit*: **heal**, mend, join, fuse, draw together, unite, become whole.
3 *Marcus knitted his brows*: **furrow**, tighten, contract, gather, draw in, wrinkle, pucker, knot, screw up, crease, scrunch up.
▸noun *silky knits in pretty shades*: **knitted garment**, woollen; informal woolly.

knob noun **1** *the drakes have a black bill with a knob at the base*: **lump**, bump, protuberance, projection, protrusion, bulge, swelling, knot, node, nodule, gnarl, growth, outgrowth, excrescence, carbuncle, tumour; boss, stud, ball, knop, nub; technical umbo; rare tumescence.
2 *he fiddled with the knobs on the radio*: **dial**, button, switch, on/off switch, key.
3 *she turned the knob and pushed open the door*: **doorknob**, handle, door handle, grip, pull.
4 *spread a few knobs of butter over the surface*: **nugget**, nub, nubble, lump, pat, cake, ball, cube, chunk, gobbet, dollop, piece, bit, portion, wedge, hunk, bar, slab; Brit. informal wodge, gob.

knock verb **1** *he knocked on the door marked 'Enquiries'*: **bang**, tap, rap, thump, pound, hammer; strike, hit, beat, batter, buffet, pummel.
2 *she knocked her knee painfully on the table*: **bump**, bang, hit, strike, crack; **injure**, hurt, damage, bruise; informal bash, thwack.
3 *he knocked into an elderly man with a walking stick*: **collide with**, bump into, bang into, knock against, hit, strike, be in collision with, run into, crash into, smash into, plough into, slam into, dash against, ram, jolt; N. Amer. impact; informal bash into.
4 informal *I'm not knocking the company—it's first-class*: **criticize**, find fault with, run down, disparage, belittle, depreciate, deprecate, detract from, give a bad press to, cast aspersions on, scoff at, deride, jeer at, carp at, cavil at; lambaste, censure, condemn, denounce, revile, attack; informal slam, pan, bash, pull to pieces, pull apart, pick holes in, maul, savage, flay, throw brickbats at, shoot down, give something a battering, talk something down, have a go at, bad-mouth; Brit. informal slate, rubbish, slag off; N. Amer. informal trash, pummel; Austral./NZ informal bag.
▷ANTONYMS praise.
□ **knock about/around** informal **1** *for a couple of years we knocked around the Mediterranean*: **wander**, roam, rove, range, travel, travel idly, journey, voyage, globetrot, drift, coast, meander, gad about, gallivant, jaunt, take a trip, go on a trip; ramble, stroll, saunter, maunder, amble, traipse, dawdle, potter; traverse, travel round, roam around, range over; rare peregrinate, perambulate, vagabond. **2** *she knocked around with artists*: **associate**, consort, keep company, go around, mix, socialize, have dealings, have to do with, accompany, escort; be friends, be friendly; informal hobnob, hang out, run around, be thick with, chum around, pal around, pal up.
□ **knock someone/something about/around** *her husband was a brute who used to knock her about*: **beat up**, beat, batter, strike, hit, punch, thump, thrash, smack, slap, cuff, buffet, pummel, belabour; **maltreat**, mistreat, abuse, ill-treat, ill-use, treat roughly, assault, attack, maul, manhandle; injure, damage, cause injury to, hurt, harm, wound, bruise; N. Amer. beat up on; informal rough up, do over, lay into, lace into, give someone a hiding, clobber, clout, bash, belt, whack, wallop, sock, plug, deck; archaic smite.
□ **knock something back** informal *she knocked back her gin*: **swallow**, gulp down, drink up, swill down, swill, quaff, guzzle, toss off, consume, finish; informal down, swig; get one's laughing gear round; N. Amer. informal scarf (down/up), snarf (down/up); rare ingurgitate, bib.
□ **knock someone down** *two men knocked him down | their son was knocked down by a car*: **fell**, floor, flatten, bring down, prostrate, topple, knock to the ground, throw to the ground; mug, attack, assault, set upon, beat up; knock over, run over, run down.
□ **knock something down 1** *the shop was closed and knocked down*: **demolish**, pull down, bring down, take down, tear down, destroy; raze, raze to the ground, level, flatten, knock to the ground, topple, fell, bulldoze.
2 informal *the firm has knocked down the prices of its machines*: **reduce**, lower, cut, decrease, bring down, drop, put down, diminish, mark down; informal slash, down.
□ **knock off** Brit. informal *they knock off at 5 o'clock*: **stop work**, finish work, finish working, clock off, close shop, shut down, leave work, finish the working day; take a break, break, break off, rest, pause, stop, halt, finish; informal call it a day, have a breather, take five.
▷ANTONYMS clock on.
□ **knock someone off** informal *the person who slugged me was the one who knocked off Maloney*: **kill**, murder, assassinate, do to death, do away with, make away with, get rid of, dispose of, eliminate, liquidate, terminate, finish off; informal do in, bump off, top, polish off, croak, stiff; N. Amer. informal waste, blow away, ice, off, rub out; literary slay.
□ **knock something off** informal **1** *someone knocked off the video recorder*: **steal**, purloin, take, make off with, abscond with, pilfer, misappropriate; thieve, rob; informal nab, snitch, snaffle, swipe, filch, lift, souvenir; Brit. informal pinch, nick, half-inch, whip, nobble; N. Amer. informal heist, glom; Austral. informal snavel; W. Indian informal tief. **2** *we expect you to knock off three stories a day*: **produce**, make, turn out, create, construct, assemble, fashion, put together, fabricate; complete, finish; mass-produce. **3** *I've always been able to knock off several years from my age*: **deduct**, take off, subtract, take away, dock, debit, remove.
▷ANTONYMS add on.
□ **knock it off!** informal *'Oh, knock it off,' she snapped*: **stop it**; informal cut it out, give it a rest, leave off, pack it in, lay off, quit; Brit. informal give over.
□ **knock someone out 1** *I hit him with the axe and knocked him out*: **stun**, strike unconscious, knock unconscious, render unconscious, knock senseless, stupefy, daze, lay out, floor, prostrate, level; informal KO, kayo, knock cold, put out cold. **2** *England had been knocked out of the World Cup*: **eliminate**; **beat**, defeat, vanquish, overwhelm, overthrow, overcome, get the better of, trounce. **3** informal *walking that far knocked her out*: **exhaust**, wear out, tire out, overtire, overtax, tire, fatigue, weary, enervate, drain, sap, debilitate, enfeeble, prostrate; informal do in, take it out of, fag out, frazzle; Brit. informal knacker; N. Amer. informal poop. **4** informal *the view from my window knocked me out*: **overwhelm**, overpower, stun, stupefy, amaze,

astound, astonish, stagger, take someone's breath away, leave someone open-mouthed, dumbfound, confound, take aback; impress, dazzle, enchant, entrance; informal bowl over, flabbergast, knock sideways, knock for six, hit like a ton of bricks, floor, blow away.
▫ **knock up** *they were knocking up before the tennis match*: **warm up**, practise, have a practice game, hit a ball around.
▫ **knock someone up 1** Brit. informal *we were knocked up at five in the morning*: **wake**, wake up, waken, awaken, call, rouse, arouse, get out of bed, get up; informal give someone a shout. **2** informal *he's going to marry her—he's knocked her up*: **make pregnant**, impregnate, inseminate; informal put in the family way; Brit. informal get in the club; archaic get with child.
▫ **knock something up 1** Brit. informal *I could knock up some frames*: **make quickly**, put together quickly, prepare hastily, build rapidly, whip up, rig up, jerry-build, throw together, cobble together, improvise, devise, contrive; make, prepare, produce, get, get ready, assemble, put together; informal fix, rustle up. **2** informal *Gloucester knocked up their biggest win of the season*: **achieve**, attain, accomplish, gain, win, succeed in making, reach, make, get, obtain; score, chalk up, tally, record; informal clock up, notch up, rack up, bag.
▸ **noun 1** *there was a sharp knock at the door*: **tap**, rap, rat-tat, rat-tat-tat, knocking, bang, banging, beating, pounding, hammering, drumming, thump, thud.
2 *the casing is tough enough to withstand knocks*: **bump**, blow, bang, striking, beating, jolt, jar, jarring, shock; collision, crash, smash, impact.
3 *a knock on the ear*: **blow**, bang, stroke, hit, slap, smack, crack, buffet, punch, cuff, thump, box; informal clip, clout, wallop, thwack, belt, bash.
4 informal *this isn't a knock on Dave, he's the best player we've got*: **criticism**, disparagement, stricture, fault-finding, denigration, censure, reproach, reproval, condemnation, lambasting; informal slamming, panning, slagging off, rubbishing, slating, flak, brickbats.
▷ANTONYMS praise.
5 *life's hard knocks*: **setback**, reversal, reverse of fortune, rebuff, rejection, defeat, failure, difficulty, misfortune, bad luck, stroke of bad luck, mishap, bad experience, blow, body blow, disaster, calamity, disappointment, grief, sorrow, trouble, hardship; informal kick in the teeth, one in the eye, whammy.

knockout noun **1** *forty-three of Rocky's matches were won by a knockout*: **stunning blow**, finishing blow; French coup de grâce; informal KO, kayo.
2 *before the third round knockout punters were growing bored*: **elimination match**, tie, elimination competition.
3 informal *she's nice-looking but not a knockout*: **beauty**, vision, picture, sensation, joy to behold, dream; informal stunner, dish, looker, good-looker, lovely, peach, eyeful, smasher, cracker.
4 informal *the binoculars are a technical knockout*: **masterpiece**, sensation, marvel, wonder, triumph, winner, success, feat, coup, master stroke; smash hit, hit, attraction; French tour de force, coup de maître; informal smasher, cracker.
▷ANTONYMS failure, flop.

knoll noun *she walked up the grassy knoll*: **hillock**, mound, rise, hummock, hill, hump, knob, tor, tump, barrow, outcrop, bank, ridge, dune, elevation, acclivity, eminence; Geology drumlin; Scottish brae; S. African koppie.

knot noun **1** *tie a small knot in the yarn*: **tie**, twist, loop, bow, splice, splicing, join, link, fastening, bond, intertwinement, interlacement, ligature, joint, connection; tangle, entanglement.
2 *a knot in the wood*: **nodule**, gnarl, knurl, node, lump, knob, swelling, growth, gall, protuberance, bump; archaic knar.
3 *there was a knot of people around Catherine*: **cluster**, group, band, huddle, bunch, circle, ring, set, collection; party, gathering, company, crowd, throng, swarm, host, flock, gang, assemblage, mob, pack.
4 *a pretty garden with knots of lavender*: **clump**, tuft, cluster, bunch, tuffet, tussock, bush.
▸ **verb** *their scarves were knotted round their throats*: **tie**, make/tie a knot in, make a bow in, loop, lace; fasten, secure, bind, make fast, tie up, do up, lash, tether.
▷ANTONYMS untie.

knotted adjective *her wild knotted hair*: **tangled**, tangly, knotty, entangled, matted, snarled, ravelled, twisted, entwined, coiled, unkempt, uncombed, tousled; informal mussed up.

knotty adjective **1** *a knotty legal problem*: **complex**, complicated, involved, intricate, convoluted, Byzantine, tangled, tortuous; **difficult**, hard, thorny, taxing, awkward, tricky, problematic, troublesome, perplexing, baffling, mystifying, obscure, unfathomable, unanswerable, insoluble, impenetrable; formal involute, involuted.
▷ANTONYMS straightforward, simple.
2 *knotty roots of gorse bushes*: **gnarled**, knotted, knurled, nodular, knobbly, lumpy, bumpy, rugged, rough, coarse; rare nodulous, nodose.
3 *a knotty piece of thread*: **knotted**, tangled, tangly, twisted, entangled, ravelled, snarled, matted.

know verb **1** *she doesn't know I'm here*: **be aware**, realize, be conscious, have knowledge, be informed, have information; notice, perceive, see, sense, recognize, understand, appreciate; informal savvy, latch on to something.
2 *I would write to him if I knew his address*: **have knowledge of**, be aware of, be cognizant of, be informed of, be apprised of.
3 *he asked whether I knew French | they know the game*: **be familiar with**, be conversant with, be acquainted with, have knowledge of, be versed in, be knowledgeable about, have mastered, have a grasp of, grasp, understand, comprehend, apprehend; have learned, have memorized, have learned by heart; informal be clued up on, have something taped.
4 *I don't know many people here | we know him well*: **be acquainted with**, have met, be familiar with; be friends with, be friendly with, be on good terms with, be close to, be intimate with, socialize with, associate with, have dealings with; understand, have insight into, be in sympathy with, empathize with; Scottish ken; informal be thick with.
5 *a man who had known better times*: **experience**, have experience of, go through, undergo, live through, meet, meet with, encounter, taste.
6 *my brothers don't know a saucepan from a frying pan*: **distinguish**, tell apart, differentiate, tell, tell which is which, discriminate; recognize, pick out, identify, make out, discern, see.

know-all noun informal *you're such a know-all—you tell me!* informal **smart alec**, wise guy, smarty, smarty-pants; Brit. informal clever clogs, clever Dick, smart-arse, smarty-boots; N. Amer. informal know-it-all, smart-ass; archaic wiseacre.

know-how noun informal *know-how in high-tech fields will help build better vehicles*: **knowledge**, expertise, skill, skilfulness, expertness, proficiency, understanding, mastery, art, accomplishment, technique; finesse; ability, capability, competence, capacity, adeptness, dexterity, deftness, aptitude, adroitness, ingenuity, faculty, knack, talent, gift, flair, bent; French savoir faire; N. Amer. informal savvy.
▷ANTONYMS ignorance, incompetence.

knowing adjective **1** *she gave a knowing smile*: **significant**, meaningful, eloquent, expressive, suggestive, speaking; **arch**, sly, cunning, mischievous, impish, teasing, playful; enigmatic.
2 *she's a very knowing child*: **sophisticated**, worldly, worldly-wise, urbane, unprovincial, experienced, seasoned; knowledgeable, well informed, enlightened; shrewd, astute, acute, canny, sharp, wily, aware, perceptive, perspicacious; informal having been around.
▷ANTONYMS ingenuous, innocent.
3 *a knowing infringement of the rules*: **deliberate**, intentional, conscious, intended, calculated, wilful, volitional, purposeful, done on purpose, premeditated, preconceived, pre-planned, planned, aforethought.
▷ANTONYMS accidental.

knowingly adverb *the chairman denied that the company knowingly misled the public*: **deliberately**, intentionally, consciously, wittingly, with full knowledge, in full awareness, with one's eyes open, on purpose, by design, calculatedly, premeditatedly, studiedly, wilfully, purposefully, willingly.
▷ANTONYMS accidentally, unawares.

knowledge noun **1** *his knowledge of history was small | technical knowledge*: **understanding**, comprehension, grasp, grip, command, mastery, apprehension; **expertise**, skill, proficiency, expertness, accomplishment, adeptness, capacity, capability; French savoir faire; informal know-how.
▷ANTONYMS ignorance.
2 *people anxious to display their knowledge*: **learning**, erudition, education, scholarship, letters, schooling, science; wisdom, enlightenment, philosophy.
▷ANTONYMS ignorance, illiteracy.
3 *he slipped away without my knowledge*: **awareness**, consciousness, realization, recognition, cognition, apprehension, perception, appreciation; formal cognizance.
▷ANTONYMS unawareness.
4 *National Trust staff develop an intimate* **knowledge of** *the countryside*: **familiarity with**, acquaintance with, conversance with, intimacy with.
5 *it is your duty to inform the police of your knowledge*: **information**, facts, data, intelligence, news, reports; lore; informal info, gen, low-down.

Word links **knowledge**

gnostic relating to knowledge
epistemology science of knowledge

knowledgeable adjective **1** *a knowledgeable old man*: **well informed**, informed, learned, with great knowledge, well read, well educated, educated, widely read, erudite, scholarly, cultured, cultivated, enlightened, aware.
▷ANTONYMS ignorant.
2 *we need to appoint someone who is* **knowledgeable about** *modern art*: **acquainted with**, familiar with, with a knowledge of, with an understanding of, conversant with, au courant with, au fait with; skilled, expert, competent, proficient; up on, up to date with, abreast of, at home with, no stranger to; experienced in, practised in, well versed in, seasoned; informal clued up about, genned up about, plugged into; Brit. informal switched on to.
▷ANTONYMS ill-informed.

known adjective **1** *a known fact | a known criminal*: **recognized, well known**, widely known, generally known, publicly known, noted, celebrated, notable, notorious; admitted, acknowledged, confessed, self-confessed, avowed, declared, overt, proclaimed, published, revealed, publicized.
▷ANTONYMS secret.
2 *the known world*: **familiar**, known about, well known; studied, investigated.
▷ANTONYMS unknown.
□ **make known** *confidential information should not be made known to a third party*: **disclose**, reveal, divulge, tell, impart, communicate, pass on, vouchsafe, unfold; release, make public, broadcast, publish, report, unveil; leak, betray, let slip, let drop, blurt out, give away; admit, confess; informal let on, blab, spill the beans about, spill, let the cat out of the bag about, blow the lid off, squeal about; Brit. informal blow the gaff; archaic discover, unbosom.

knuckle verb
□ **knuckle under** *bombing does not always make the victims knuckle under*: **surrender**, submit, capitulate, give in, give up, yield, give way, succumb, climb down, back down, quit, admit defeat, lay down one's arms, be defeated, be overcome, acquiesce, accede, accept, defer; informal throw in the towel, raise the white flag, throw in the sponge.
▷ANTONYMS resist.

kowtow verb **1** *they kowtow to her in awe and reverence*: **prostrate oneself**, bow, bow down before, genuflect, do/make obeisance, fall on one's knees before, get down on one's knees before, kneel before; salaam, throw oneself at someone's feet, fall down before someone, curtsy, bow and scrape; pay homage, show reverence, show deference, humble oneself before someone, worship.
2 *she didn't have to* ***kowtow to*** *a boss*: **grovel**, behave obsequiously, be obsequious, be servile, be sycophantic, fawn on, bow and scrape, toady, truckle, abase oneself, humble oneself, prostrate oneself; curry favour with, flatter, court, woo, dance attendance on, make up to, play up to, ingratiate oneself with; informal crawl, creep, suck up to, butter up, be all over, fall all over, lick someone's boots; N. Amer. informal brown-nose; Austral./NZ informal smoodge to; archaic blandish.

kudos noun *much kudos is attached to the position*: **prestige**, cachet, glory, honour, status, standing, distinction, prestigiousness, fame, celebrity, reputation, repute, renown, notability; admiration, respect, esteem, acclaim, acclamation, applause, praise, credit, approbation, tribute.
▷ANTONYMS obscurity, infamy.

label noun **1** *the price is clearly stated on the label*: **tag**, ticket, tab, sticker, marker, docket, chit, chitty, flag, stamp; document, documentation.
2 *they offer both function and fashion under their label*: **brand**, brand name, trade name, trademark, proprietary name, line, make, logo.
3 *I always resented the label of 'shock jock' that the media came up with for me*: **designation**, denomination, description, characterization, identification, tag; name, epithet, nickname, title, sobriquet, pet name, byname; formal appellation, cognomen.
▶ **verb 1** *label each jar with the date*: **tag**, attach labels to, put labels on, tab, ticket, stamp, mark, put stickers on, docket, flag.
2 *tests that will **label** him as an underachiever | he'll always be labelled 'bluesman'*: **categorize**, classify, class, characterize, describe, designate, identify; mark, stamp, pronounce, brand, condemn, pigeonhole, stereotype, typecast, compartmentalize, typify; call, name, term, dub, nickname.

> *Word links* **label**
>
> **phillumenist** matchbox label collector

laborious adjective **1** *tunnelling was a laborious and dangerous job*: **arduous**, hard, heavy, difficult, strenuous, gruelling, murderous, punishing, exacting, tough, formidable, onerous, burdensome, back-breaking, trying, uphill, relentless, stiff, challenging, Herculean; tiring, fatiguing, exhausting, wearying, wearing, taxing, enervating, demanding, wearisome; tedious, boring, irksome; Brit. informal knackering; archaic toilsome; rare exigent.
▷**ANTONYMS** easy, simple.
2 *Doug's slow laborious style*: **laboured**, strained, forced, contrived, affected, studied, stiff, stilted, unnatural, artificial, overdone, overwrought, heavy, ponderous, convoluted, not fluent, elaborate, over-elaborate, intricate, ornate, prolix.
▷**ANTONYMS** effortless, natural.

labour noun **1** *the aristocratic disdain for manual labour*: **work**, toil, employment, exertion, industry, industriousness, toiling, hard work, hard labour, drudgery, effort, the sweat of one's brow, donkey work, menial work; informal slog, grind, sweat, elbow grease; Brit. informal graft; archaic travail, moil.
▷**ANTONYMS** rest, leisure, ease, idleness.
2 *the conflict of interest between capital and labour*: **workers**, employees, workmen, workforce, staff, working people, blue-collar workers, hands, labourers, labour force, hired hands, proletariat, wage-earners, manpower, human resources, personnel; humorous liveware.
▷**ANTONYMS** management.
3 *the labours of Hercules*: **task**, job, chore, undertaking, mission, commission, assignment.
4 *Gina had a long and difficult labour*: **childbirth**, birth, birthing, delivery, nativity; contractions, labour pains, labour pangs, labour throes; technical parturition; archaic confinement, accouchement, lying-in, childbed, travail.
▶ **verb 1** *a project on which he had laboured for many years*: **work (hard)**, toil, slave (away), grub away, plod away, grind away, sweat away, struggle, strive, exert oneself, overwork, work one's fingers to the bone, work like a Trojan/dog/slave, keep one's nose to the grindstone; informal slog away, kill oneself, plug away, put one's back into something, peg away; Brit. informal graft; archaic drudge, travail, moil.
▷**ANTONYMS** rest, relax, laze.
2 *Newcastle laboured to break down the home team's defence*: **strive**, struggle, endeavour, work, try hard, make every effort, do one's best, do one's utmost, do all one can, give (it/something) one's all, go all out, fight, push, be at pains, put oneself out, apply oneself, exert oneself; informal bend/fall/lean over backwards, give it one's best shot, pull out all the stops.
3 *enough has been said, and there is no need to labour the point*: **overemphasize**, belabour, overstress, place/lay too much emphasis on, overdo, strain, over-elaborate, overplay, attach too much importance/weight to, make too much of, exaggerate, dwell on, harp on (about), expound on, expand.
4 *Rex was **labouring under** a misapprehension*: **suffer from**, be a victim of, be burdened by, be overburdened by, be disadvantaged by, be under.

> *Choose the right word* **labour, work, toil**
>
> See **work**.

laboured adjective **1** *his harsh, laboured breathing*: **strained**, difficult, forced, laborious, heavy, awkward.
▷**ANTONYMS** easy.
2 *a rather laboured joke*: **contrived**, stiff, strained, stilted, forced, unnatural, artificial, mannered, studied, affected, overdone, overworked, heavy, ponderous, over-elaborate, over-embellished, long-winded, awkward, clumsy, inelegant, turgid, laborious, overwrought, not spontaneous, unconvincing, convoluted, complex, intricate, ornate, elaborate, prolix.
▷**ANTONYMS** natural.

labourer noun **workman**, worker, working man, hand, manual worker, unskilled worker, blue-collar worker, hired hand, hired man, roustabout, labouring man, drudge, menial; Spanish-American **peon**; Austral./NZ **rouseabout**; Indian **mazdoor**, **khalasi**; dated **navvy**; in Scotland & Ireland, historical **cottar**; in Australia, historical **kanaka**; archaic **mechanic**, **cottier**.

labyrinth noun **1** *a labyrinth of little streets*: **maze**, warren, network, complex, web, coil, entanglement.
2 *the labyrinth of conflicting laws and regulations*: **tangle**, web, morass, jungle, snarl, twist, turn, complexity, confusion, complication, entanglement, convolution, intricacy; jumble, mishmash, hotchpotch, hodgepodge; archaic perplexity.

labyrinthine adjective **1** *the stadium's labyrinthine corridors*: **maze-like**, winding, twisting, serpentine, meandering, wandering, rambling, mazy, sinuous, zigzag.
2 *a labyrinthine criminal justice system*: **complicated**, intricate, complex, involved, tortuous, convoluted, tangled, elaborate, knotty; confusing, puzzling, perplexing, mystifying, bewildering, baffling; inextricable, entangled, impenetrable, thorny, Byzantine, Daedalian, Gordian; rare involute, involuted.
▷**ANTONYMS** straightforward, simple.

lace noun **1** *a dress trimmed with white lace*: **openwork**, lacework, tatting, netting, net, tulle, meshwork, mesh, webbing; Chantilly lace, Brussels lace, fishnet, filigree, passementerie, bobbinet, needlepoint (lace), point lace, filet, bobbin lace, pillow lace, duchesse lace, Honiton lace, Nottingham lace, Shetland lace, guipure, rosaline.
2 *brown shoes with laces*: **shoelace**, bootlace, shoestring, lacing, string, cord, thong, twine, tie; archaic latchet.

▶ **verb 1** *he **laced up** his running shoes*: **fasten**, do up, tie up, secure; bind, knot, truss.
▷ANTONYMS undo.
2 *he laced his fingers into mine*: **entwine**, intertwine, twine, entangle, interweave, interlink, link; criss-cross, braid, plait.
3 *tea laced with rum*: **flavour**, mix (in), blend, fortify, strengthen, stiffen, season, spice (up), imbue, infuse, enrich, enliven, liven up; doctor, adulterate, contaminate, drug; informal spike, boost.
4 *her brown hair was laced with grey*: **streak**, stripe, striate, band, line; mark, smear, daub.
□ **lace into** informal **1** *Danny laced into him and punched him in the stomach*: **set upon**, fall on, attack, assault, assail, beat, thrash, tear into, turn on, set about, lash out at, round on, drub, thump, batter, hammer, pummel, hit out at, strike out at, (let) fly at, weigh into, belabour; informal lay into, light into, sail into, pitch into, paste, let someone have it; Brit. informal have a go at. **2** *the newspaper laced into the prime minister*: **castigate**, censure, condemn, lambaste, criticize, harangue, rant/rave/rail at, attack; scold, berate, upbraid, reprimand, rebuke, chide, reprove, admonish; informal lay into, pitch into; Brit. informal have a go at; N. Amer. informal light into.

lacerate **verb 1** *jagged edges that lacerated their arms*: **cut (open)**, gash, slash, tear, rip, rend, mangle, mutilate, maim, maul, shred, score, scratch, scrape, graze, incise; knife, gouge, split, cleave, hack, stab, tear apart, butcher, savage, wound, injure, hurt, damage.
2 *the author's feelings have been lacerated by criticism*: **hurt**, wound, distress, pain, harrow, torture, torment, crucify, tear to pieces/shreds.

laceration **noun 1** *the laceration of her hand*: **cutting (open)**, gashing, slashing, tearing, ripping, mangling, mutilation, maiming, mauling, scratching, scraping, grazing, incision, splitting, cleaving, hacking, stabbing, tearing apart, butchery, savaging, wounding, injury, damaging.
2 *a bleeding laceration on the animal's back*: **gash**, cut, wound, injury, tear, slash, mutilation, scratch, scrape, abrasion, graze, score, incision, slit, puncture; Medicine lesion, trauma, traumatism.

lachrymose **adjective 1** *she gets quite lachrymose at the mention of his name*: **tearful**, weeping, crying, teary, with tears in one's eyes, close to tears, on the verge of tears, sobbing, snivelling, whimpering; emotional, sad, mournful, woeful, unhappy, depressed, gloomy, melancholy, low-spirited, despondent, downcast, low, glum, morose, sorrowful, joyless, disconsolate, doleful, maudlin, miserable, forlorn, grief-stricken, lugubrious; informal weepy, blubbering, down, down in the mouth, blue; literary dolorous; rare larmoyant.
▷ANTONYMS cheerful, laughing, happy.
2 *a lachrymose novel*: **tragic**, sad, poignant, heart-rending, tear-jerking, moving, melancholy, depressing, plaintive; mawkish, sentimental; Brit. informal soppy.
▷ANTONYMS comic.

lack **noun** *a lack of cash*: **absence**, want, need, deficiency, dearth, insufficiency, shortage, shortfall, scarcity, paucity, unavailability, scarceness, undersupply, deficit, scantiness, sparseness, meagreness, inadequacy, shortness, deprivation, destitution, privation, famine, drought, poverty, non-existence, rareness, infrequency, uncommonness; rare exiguity, exiguousness.
▷ANTONYMS abundance; sufficiency.
▶ **verb** *she's immature and lacks judgement*: **be without**, have need of, be in need of, need, be lacking, require, want, feel the want of, be short of, be deficient in, stand in need of, go without, be bereft of, be deprived of, be low on, be pressed for, not have enough of, be devoid of, have insufficient, cry out for; miss; informal be clean/fresh out of, be strapped for.
▷ANTONYMS have, own, possess, enjoy.

lackadaisical **adjective** *I was lackadaisical about my training*: **careless**, **lazy**, lax, unenthusiastic, half-hearted, uninterested, lukewarm, indifferent, uncaring, unconcerned, casual, offhand, blasé, insouciant, leisurely, relaxed; apathetic, languid, languorous, lethargic, limp, listless, sluggish, enervated, spiritless, aimless, bloodless, torpid, passionless, idle, indolent, shiftless, inert, impassive, feeble; informal laid back, couldn't-care-less, easy going, slap-happy; Brit. vulgar slang half-arsed; rare Laodicean, poco-curante.
▷ANTONYMS enthusiastic, excited.

lackey **noun 1** *lackeys were waiting to help them from their carriage*: **servant**, flunkey, footman, manservant, valet, liveried servant, steward, butler, equerry, retainer, vassal, page, attendant, houseboy, domestic, drudge, factotum; informal skivvy; archaic scullion.
2 *a rich man's lackey*: **toady**, flunkey, sycophant, flatterer, minion, doormat, dogsbody, spaniel, stooge, hanger-on, lickspittle, parasite; tool, puppet, instrument, pawn, subordinate, underling, creature, cat's paw; informal yes-man, bootlicker.

lacking **adjective 1** *proof was lacking*: **absent**, missing, non-existent, not present, unavailable, not to be found.
▷ANTONYMS present, plentiful.
2 *the advocate general found the government lacking on two counts*: **deficient**, defective, inadequate, wanting, limited, flawed, faulty, insufficient, unacceptable, impaired, imperfect, second-rate, restricted, inferior.
▷ANTONYMS perfect.
3 *the game was **lacking in** atmosphere*: **without**, devoid of, bereft of, bankrupt of, destitute of, empty of, deprived of, free from/of; **deficient in**, low on, short on, in need of; informal minus.
▷ANTONYMS full of.

lacklustre **adjective** *a limp and lacklustre speech*: **uninspired**, uninspiring, unimaginative, dull, humdrum, colourless, characterless, bland, insipid, vapid, flat, dry, lifeless, listless, tame, tired, prosaic, mundane, run-of-the-mill, commonplace, spiritless, lustreless, apathetic, torpid, unanimated; uninteresting, boring, monotonous, dreary, tedious, wearisome.
▷ANTONYMS inspired, brilliant.

laconic **adjective 1** *his laconic comment*: **brief**, concise, terse, succinct, short, economical, elliptical, crisp, pithy, to the point, incisive, short and sweet, compendious; abrupt, blunt, curt, clipped, monosyllabic, brusque, pointed, gruff, sharp, tart; epigrammatic, aphoristic, gnomic.
▷ANTONYMS verbose, long-winded.
2 *their laconic press officer*: **taciturn**, of few words, uncommunicative, reticent, quiet, untalkative, reserved, silent, speechless, tight-lipped, unforthcoming, brusque.
▷ANTONYMS loquacious.

lad **noun** informal **1** *a young lad of eight*: **boy**, schoolboy, youth, youngster, juvenile, stripling, young fellow, junior, whippersnapper; informal kid, nipper, shaver; Scottish informal laddie; derogatory brat, urchin.
2 *a hard-working lad trying to make ends meet*: **man**, young man; informal guy, fellow, geezer, customer, gent; Brit. informal chap, bloke; N. Amer. informal dude, hombre; Austral./NZ informal digger; S. African informal oke, ou; Indian informal admi; Brit. informal, dated cove; Scottish archaic carl.

ladder **noun** *I began to edge my way up the academic ladder*: **hierarchy**, scale, set of stages, stratification, pecking order, grading, ranking, spectrum.

laden **adjective** *a tray laden with plates*: **loaded**, burdened, weighed down, overloaded, weighted, piled high, fully charged, encumbered, hampered, oppressed, taxed; full, filled, packed, stuffed, crammed; informal chock-full, chock-a-block.
▷ANTONYMS empty.

la-di-da **adjective** informal *a la-di-da Cambridge graduate*. See **pretentious**, **snobbish**.

ladle **noun** *a soup ladle*: **spoon**, scoop, dipper, bailer.
▶ **verb** *he was **ladling out** the contents of the pot*: **spoon out**, scoop out, dish up/out, serve; bail out.

lady **noun 1** *he gave the ladies presents of flowers from his garden*: **woman**, member of the fair/gentle sex, female; Scottish & N. English lass, lassie; informal biddy, filly; Brit. informal bird, bint; Scottish & N. English informal besom, wifie; N. Amer. informal dame, broad, jane; Austral./NZ informal sheila; archaic maid, damsel; archaic or humorous wench; archaic gentlewoman, petticoat.
2 *lords and ladies and royalty were once entertained at the house*: **noblewoman**, gentlewoman, duchess, countess, peeress, viscountess, baroness, dame, grand dame.

> *Choose the right word* **lady, woman, girl**
>
> See **woman**.

ladylike **adjective** *her antics were considered very undignified by her ladylike peers*: **genteel**, **polite**, refined, well bred, cultivated, polished, decorous, proper, correct, respectable, seemly, well mannered, cultured, sophisticated, courteous, civil, elegant, urbane, civilized, courtly, dignified, gracious; Brit. informal posh.
▷ANTONYMS coarse, unmannerly.

lag **verb** *Elizabeth had not walked over to the villa with the other guests, but lagged behind*: **fall behind**, straggle, fall back, trail (behind), linger, dally, dawdle, hang back, delay, move slowly, loiter, drag one's feet, take one's time, not keep pace, idle, dither, saunter, bring up the rear; informal dilly-dally, shilly-shally; archaic or literary tarry.
▷ANTONYMS lead; keep up; hurry.

laggard **noun** **straggler**, loiterer, lingerer, dawdler, sluggard, snail, delayer, idler, loafer, lounger, shirker, layabout, lagger; informal lazybones, skiver, do-nothing, waster, slacker, slowcoach; N. Amer. informal slowpoke; archaic wastrel; French archaic fainéant.

lagoon **noun** *the yachts on the lagoon*: **inlet**, inland sea, bay, lake, bight, pool, pond, swim; Scottish loch; Anglo-Irish lough; N. Amer. bayou; literary mere.

laid-back **adjective** informal **relaxed**, at ease, easy-going, equable, free and easy, easy, casual, informal, friendly, nonchalant, insouciant, unexcitable, imperturbable, unemotional, unruffled, blasé, blithe, cool, collected, {cool, calm, and collected}, calm, composed, self-possessed, level-headed, self-controlled, unperturbed, unflustered, unworried, unconcerned, placid, peaceful, tranquil, serene, low-key, understated, downbeat; leisurely, unhurried; stoical, phlegmatic, mellow, forbearing, live-and-let-live, tolerant; informal unflappable, together.
▷ANTONYMS tense, edgy, uptight.

laid up adjective *he was laid up for six weeks in the Middlesex Hospital*: **bedridden**, ill in bed, confined to bed, on the sick list, out of action/commission, housebound, immobilized, incapacitated, injured, disabled; ill, sick, unwell, sickly, poorly, infirm, ailing, off colour, afflicted, indisposed.

lair noun **1** *the lair of a large python*: **den**, burrow, hole, lie, covert, tunnel, dugout, hollow, cave, haunt.
2 *the lair of a villain*: **hideaway**, hiding place, hideout, refuge, sanctuary, haven, cache, shelter, retreat; informal hidey-hole.

laissez-faire noun *laissez-faire is an economic system based on individualism and self-interest*: **free enterprise**, private enterprise, free trade, individualism, non-intervention, free-market capitalism, private ownership, market forces, deregulation; non-interference, non-involvement, indifference.
▶ adjective *a belief in laissez-faire economics*: **non-interventionist**, non-interventional, non-interfering, non-restrictive, liberal, libertarian, uninvolved, indifferent, lax, loose, permissive, live-and-let-live; informal hands-off.
▷ANTONYMS interventionist.

lake noun **pond**, pool, tarn, reservoir, lagoon, waterhole, inland sea, swim; Scottish loch, lochan; Anglo-Irish lough; N. Amer. bayou, pothole (lake); NZ moana; Indian sagar; literary mere.

Word links **lake**

lacustrine relating to lakes
limnology study of lakes

lam verb informal *the usher lammed me on the head with his flashlight*. See **hit**.

lambaste verb *the manager fiercely lambasted his team*: **criticize**, castigate, chastise, censure, condemn, take to task, harangue, attack, rail at, rant at, revile, fulminate against, haul/call over the coals; upbraid, scold, reprimand, rebuke, chide, reprove, admonish, berate; informal rap someone's knuckles, slap someone's wrist, lay into, pitch into, tear into, lace into, dress down, give someone a dressing-down, carpet, tell off, bawl out; Brit. informal tick off, have a go at, slag off; N. Amer. informal chew out; rare reprehend, excoriate, objurgate.

lame adjective **1** See **disabled**.
2 *a lame excuse*: **feeble**, weak, thin, flimsy, transparent, poor, puny; **unconvincing**, implausible, unlikely, hollow, hard to believe; informal pathetic, half-baked, hard to swallow.
▷ANTONYMS convincing, persuasive.

lament noun **1** *the widow's laments*: **wail**, wailing, lamentation, moan, moaning, groan, weeping, crying, sob, sobbing, keening, howl, complaint; rare jeremiad, ululation.
2 *he sang a lament for the dead*: **dirge**, requiem, elegy, funeral song/chant, burial hymn, dead march, keen, plaint, knell; Scottish coronach; rare threnody, monody, epicedium.
▶ verb **1** *the mourners lamented a life taken so suddenly*: **mourn**, grieve (for/over), weep for, shed tears for; sorrow, wail, moan, groan, weep, cry, sob, keen, plain, howl, pine for, beat one's breast; rare ululate.
▷ANTONYMS celebrate, rejoice.
2 *he lamented the modernizing of the old buildings*: **bemoan**, bewail, complain about, deplore, regret, rue; protest against, speak out against, object to, oppose, disagree with, fulminate against, inveigh against, rail at, make a fuss about, denounce.

lamentable adjective *a lamentable lack of funds*: **deplorable**, regrettable, tragic, terrible, awful, wretched, woeful, sorrowful, unfortunate, distressing, grievous, dire, disastrous, calamitous, desperate, grave, appalling, dreadful; intolerable, ignominious, pitiful, shameful; rare egregious.

lamentation noun **weeping**, **wailing**, crying, sobbing, moaning, moan, sob, wail, lament, sorrow, complaint, keening, grief, grieving, mourning, howling, howl, plaint; rare ululation.

laminate verb *we will laminate your photos in clear plastic*: **cover**, overlay, coat, surface, face; veneer, glaze.

lampoon verb *he was mercilessly lampooned for his absurd get-ups*: **satirize**, mock, ridicule, make fun of, poke fun at, caricature, burlesque, parody, take off, guy, make a fool of, rag, tease; informal send up; rare pasquinade.
▶ noun *a lampoon of student life in the early twenties*: **satire**, burlesque, parody, skit, caricature, imitation, impersonation, impression, travesty, take-off, mockery, squib; informal send-up, spoof; rare pasquinade.

lance noun *a knight with a lance*: **spear**, pike, javelin, bayonet, shaft; harpoon.
▶ verb *the boil may be lanced to drain the pus*: **cut**, cut open, slit, incise, puncture, prick, nick, notch, pierce, stab, skewer, spike.

land noun **1** *Lyme Park has 1323 acres of land | a campaign to ban fox-hunting on publicly owned land*: **grounds**, ground, fields, open space, open area; property, acres, acreage, estate, estate, lands, realty, real property, real estate, landholding, holding; countryside; unbuilt land, rural area, green area, green belt; archaic demesne.
2 *a small patch of fertile land*: **soil**, earth, loam, sod, dirt, clay, turf, topsoil, humus, marl.
3 (**the land**) *so many people are leaving the land and going to work in the city*: **the countryside**, the country, rural areas, farmland, agricultural land.
4 *Tunisia is a land of variety*: **country**, nation, state, nation state, fatherland, motherland, homeland, realm, kingdom, empire, republic, commonwealth, province, territory, district, region, area, domain.
5 *the lookout sighted land at last*: **terra firma**, dry land, solid ground; coast, coastline, shore.
▷ANTONYMS sea.
▶ verb **1** *Allied troops had landed in France*: **disembark**, reach the shore, go ashore, debark, alight, get off; arrive.
▷ANTONYMS embark.
2 *the ship landed at Le Havre*: **berth**, dock, moor, anchor, drop anchor, tie up, beach, put in, reach the shore, come in to land; arrive.
▷ANTONYMS put to sea, sail, depart.
3 *their plane landed at Chicago airport*: **touch down**, alight, make a landing, come in to land, come down, come to rest, arrive.
▷ANTONYMS take off.
4 *a bird landed on the window sill*: **perch**, settle, come down, come to rest, alight.
▷ANTONYMS fly off.
5 *landing a plane was no problem for me*: **bring down**, make a landing, put down, take down.
6 informal *Nick had landed the job of editor*: **obtain**, get, acquire, procure, secure, be appointed to, gain, net, win, earn, achieve, attain, bag, come by, draw, pick up; carry off, catch, capture, grab, hook; informal get/lay one's hands on, get hold of, get one's mitts on, score, swing, nab, collar, pull down; Brit. informal blag.
7 informal *that habit landed her in juvenile custody*: **bring**, lead, drive, cause to be in, cause to arrive in.
8 informal *she hoped he wouldn't land her with the bill*: **burden**, saddle, encumber, trouble, tax, load; informal dump something on someone; Brit. informal lumber.
9 informal *John tried to land a punch on Brian's chin*: **inflict**, deal, deliver, administer, deposit, dispense, give, catch, mete out; informal fetch.
□ **land up** *many of them land up in prison*: **finish up**, arrive, find oneself, end up, turn up, come, go, appear; informal wind up, fetch up, show up, roll up, blow in.

Word links **land**

terrestrial relating to land

landing noun **1** *during the forced landing the aircraft was substantially damaged | the Apollo 11 moon landing*: **alighting**, arrival, coming in, deplaning; disembarkation, docking; re-entry, touchdown, splashdown; informal greaser.
▷ANTONYMS take-off, departure.
2 *I steered the boat into the south landing*: **harbour**, berth, dock, jetty, landing stage, landing place, pier, quay, wharf, slipway, marina, anchorage, haven, platform.

landlady, landlord noun **1** *the landlord of the pub*: **publican**, licensee, innkeeper, manager, manageress, pub-owner, proprietor; hotel-keeper, hotelier, host, mine host, restaurateur, bar-keeper; barman, barmaid, barperson.
2 *he had just been booted out of his digs because the landlady had objected to the noise*: **property owner**, proprietor, proprietress, lessor, letter, householder, freeholder, landowner, landholder, master, mistress, lady of the house; rare proprietrix.
▷ANTONYMS tenant, lodger.

landmark noun **1** *the spire was once a landmark for ships sailing up the river*: **marker**, mark, indicator, guiding light, leading light, signal, beacon, lodestar, sign.
2 *the Tower of London, one of London's most famous landmarks*: **monument**, distinctive/prominent feature, sight, spectacle.
3 *the landmarks which separated the two states had been removed*: **boundary marker**, demarcator, boundary line, boundary fence, pale, picket; Architecture terminus.
4 *the ruling was hailed as a landmark by human rights activists*: **turning point**, milestone, watershed, critical point, historic event, major achievement; crisis, divide.

landscape noun *the landscape of east Norfolk*: **scenery**, countryside, topography, country, land, terrain, environment; outlook, view, prospect, aspect, vista, panorama, perspective, sweep.

landslide noun **1** *floods and landslides killed several hundred people*: **landslip**, rockfall, mudslide, earthslip, earthfall; avalanche.
2 *the 1906 election produced a Liberal landslide*: **decisive victory**, runaway victory, overwhelming majority, grand slam, triumph, walkover.
▷ANTONYMS narrow victory; hung parliament.

lane noun **1** *she walked along the country lanes*: **byroad**, byway, bridleway, bridle path, path, pathway, footpath, way, towpath, trail, track, road, street, alley, alleyway, roadway, passage, thoroughfare; Scottish vennel; N. English ginnel, snicket, twitten; Scottish & N. English wynd; W. Indian & N. Amer. trace.
2 *cycle lanes | a three-lane highway*: **track**, strip, way, course, channel, road division.

language noun **1** *the grammatical structure of language*: **speech**, **writing**, communication, verbal expression, verbalization, vocalization, conversation, speaking, talking, words, utterance, vocabulary, articulation, enunciation, pronunciation, talk, discourse, interchange, intercourse, interaction; archaic converse.
2 *the English language*: **tongue**, speech, mother tongue, native tongue, dialect, vernacular; Indian bhasha; informal lingo.
3 *the language of tabloid journalism | different varieties of language*: **wording**, diction, phrasing, phraseology, style, vocabulary, terminology, expressions, turns of phrase, parlance, manner of writing/speaking, way of talking, form/mode of expression, usages, locutions, idiolect, choice of words, rhetoric, oratory; speech, dialect, vernacular, regionalisms, provincialisms, localisms, patois, lingua franca, slang, idioms, colloquialisms, jargon, argot, barbarisms, vulgarisms, cant, newspeak; pidgin English, Creole; informal lingo, legalese, journalese, technospeak, gobbledegook.

Word links **language**

-glot related suffix, as in *polyglot*
linguistic relating to language
linguistics scientific study of language

languid adjective **1** *his languid demeanour irritated her | a languid wave of the hand*: **relaxed**, unhurried, languorous, unenergetic, lacking in energy, slow, slow-moving; listless, lethargic, phlegmatic, torpid, sluggish, lazy, idle, slothful, inactive, indolent, lackadaisical, apathetic, indifferent, uninterested, impassive; informal laid back; rare otiose, poco-curante, Laodicean.
▷ANTONYMS energetic, active.
2 *languid days in the Italian sun*: **leisurely**, peaceful, languorous, relaxed, restful, lazy.
▷ANTONYMS energetic, action-packed.
3 *pale, languid individuals*: **sickly**, weak, faint, feeble, frail, delicate, debilitated, flagging, drooping; tired, weary, fatigued, enervated.
▷ANTONYMS energetic, vigorous.

Choose the right word **languid, lethargic, listless**

These words are all used of people who are (or appear to be) lacking in enthusiasm or energy.

Languid is typically used to describe someone other than oneself, or their movements or a part of their body (*the languid and willowy pre-Raphaelite heroine | she lifted a languid hand to push back her flowing hair*). It represents how they appear to an observer rather than how they actually feel. It is typically an attractive quality.

Lethargic is more commonly used to describe a person's own feeling of lacking energy (*he felt lethargic, unable for the moment to move*). It is more common to say that one feels *lethargic* than that one feels *languid* or *listless*, the implication being that *lethargy* tends to be something that one can observe in oneself, while *languor* and *listlessness* are more often observed in others.

A person described as **listless** usually lacks both energy and interest in their surroundings, the suggestion being that their malaise is psychological as well as physical (*a desperate young woman clutching a pale, listless child | she saw youngsters sitting listless and dejected outside their homes*).

languish verb **1** *the plants languished and died*: **weaken**, grow weak, deteriorate, decline, go into a decline; wither, droop, flag, wilt, fade, fail, waste away; informal go downhill.
▷ANTONYMS thrive, flourish.
2 *the general is now languishing in prison*: **waste away**, rot, decay, wither away, moulder, be abandoned, be neglected, be forgotten, suffer; be disregarded, experience hardship.
3 archaic *she still* ***languished after*** *Richard*. See **pine** (sense 2).

languor noun **1** *she clenched her jaw to kill the sultry languor that was stealing over her*: **lassitude**, lethargy, listlessness, tiredness, torpor, fatigue, weariness; laziness, idleness, indolence, inactivity, inertia, sluggishness; sleepiness, drowsiness, somnolence, enervation, lifelessness, apathy.
▷ANTONYMS vigour.
2 *the languor of a hot, breezeless day*: **stillness**, tranquillity, calm, calmness, lull, silence, windlessness, oppressiveness, heaviness.

lank adjective **1** *the man had lank, brown, greasy hair*: **limp**, lifeless, lustreless; straggling, straggly, dull, unkempt, untidy; straight, long; informal ratty.
▷ANTONYMS glossy, lustrous.
2 *his long, lank figure*. See **lanky**.

lanky adjective *a pale-skinned, lanky youth*: **tall**, **thin**, slender, slim, lean, lank, skinny, spindly, spare, gangling, gangly, scrawny, skeletal, scraggy, emaciated, size-zero, bony, gaunt, raw-boned, gawky, rangy, skin-and-bones, angular, pinched, attenuated; informal weedy.
▷ANTONYMS short, fat, stocky.

lap[1] noun *Henry was sitting on his gran's lap*: **knee**, knees, thighs.
□ **in the lap of the gods** *the result is in the lap of the gods now*: **out of one's hands**, beyond one's control, in the hands of fate, open to chance, not one's responsibility.
□ **live in the lap of luxury** *Katie was living in the lap of luxury in Paris*: **lead a very comfortable life**, be very rich, want for nothing, live off the fat of the land; informal live the life of Riley; Irish informal be on the pig's back; N. Amer. informal live high on the hog.

lap[2] noun *Nicky led the race for eight laps*: **circuit**, leg, stretch, tour, circle, revolution, round, part, portion, segment, section, stage, phase, step, loop.
▶verb **1** *she raced around the track, lapping some of the other runners*: **overtake**, overhaul, outstrip, outdistance, leave behind, pass, go past, get/pull ahead of; catch up with.
2 *he was lapped in blankets*: **wrap**, swathe, cover, envelop, enfold, encase, wind, swaddle, twist, surround.

lap[3] verb **1** *the sound of waves lapping against the sea wall*: **splash**, wash, swish, slap, slosh, break, purl; beat, strike, dash, surge, rush, ripple, roll, flow; literary plash.
2 *the dog lapped water out of a puddle*: **drink**, lick up, sip, sup, swallow, slurp, gulp, swill, suck.
□ **lap something up** *he was lapping up the accolades*: **relish**, revel in, savour, delight in, luxuriate in, bask in, wallow in, glory in, enjoy, indulge in.

lapse noun **1** *a momentary lapse of concentration*: **failure**, failing, slip, error, mistake, blunder, fault, omission, oversight, negligence, dereliction; informal slip-up.
2 *his lapse into petty crime*: **decline**, downturn, fall, falling, falling away, slipping, drop, deterioration, worsening, degeneration, dereliction, backsliding, regression, retrogression, decay, descent, sinking, slide, ebb, waning, corruption, debasement, tainting, corrosion, impairment.
3 *after this lapse of time I can look at it more calmly*: **interval**, gap, pause, intermission, interlude, lull, hiatus, break; passage, course, passing, period, term, span, spell.
▶verb **1** *the applicants let the planning permission lapse*: **expire**, become void, become invalid, run out, terminate, become obsolete.
2 *do not let friendships lapse*: **end**, cease, come to an end, stop, terminate, vanish, disappear, pass, fade, fall away, dwindle, wilt, wither, die.
3 *morality has lapsed*: **deteriorate**, decline, fall, fall off, drop, worsen, degenerate, decay, rot, backslide, regress, retrogress, get worse, sink, wane, slump, fail; informal go downhill, go to pot, go to the dogs, go down the toilet, hit the skids.
▷ANTONYMS improve, strengthen.
4 *she lapsed into silence*: **revert**, relapse, fall back; **drift**, slide, slip, sink, subside.

lapsed adjective **1** *a lapsed Catholic*: **non-practising**, lacking faith, backsliding, recidivist, apostate; formal quondam.
▷ANTONYMS practising, devout.
2 *a lapsed season ticket*: **expired**, void, invalid, run out, out of date, terminated, discontinued, unrenewed.
▷ANTONYMS current, valid.

larceny noun **theft**, stealing, robbery, pilfering, thieving, thievery, purloining; burglary, housebreaking, breaking and entering; appropriation, expropriation, misappropriation; informal lifting, filching, swiping; Brit. informal nicking, pinching, half-inching, blagging; rare peculation.

larder noun **pantry**, storage room, storeroom, store, food store, cupboard; cooler, scullery; Brit. buttery, still room, butlery; archaic spence.

large adjective **1** *a large house | large numbers of people*: **big**, great, huge, of considerable size, sizeable, substantial, immense, enormous, colossal, massive, mammoth, vast, goodly, prodigious, tremendous, gigantic, giant, monumental, stupendous, gargantuan, elephantine, titanic, mountainous, monstrous; towering, tall, high, lofty; mighty, epic, inordinate, voluminous, unlimited, king-size, king-sized, giant-size, giant-sized, man-size, man-sized, outsize, oversized, overgrown, considerable, major, Brobdingnagian; cumbersome, unwieldy; informal jumbo, whopping, whopping great, thumping, thumping great, mega, humongous, monster, astronomical, dirty great; Brit. informal whacking, whacking great, ginormous.
▷ANTONYMS small.
2 *a large red-faced man*: **big**, burly, heavy, tall, bulky, thickset, heavyset, chunky, strapping, powerfully built, hefty, muscular, muscle-bound, brawny, muscly, husky, solid, powerful, sturdy, solidly built, broad-shouldered, strong, big and strong, rugged, Herculean; fat, plump, overweight, chubby, stout, weighty, meaty, fleshy, portly, rotund, flabby, well fed, paunchy, Falstaffian, obese, gross, corpulent; buxom; informal hunky, hulking, beefy, roly-poly, tubby, pudgy, porky, well upholstered,

broad in the beam; Brit. informal **podgy**, **fubsy**; N. Amer. informal **zaftig**, **corn-fed**, **lard-assed**.
▷ANTONYMS small; thin.
3 *a large supply of wool*: **abundant**, copious, plentiful, ample, liberal, generous, lavish, profuse, bountiful, bumper, boundless, teeming, overflowing, good, considerable, superabundant, opulent, handsome, galore, sufficient; informal tidy; literary plenteous.
▷ANTONYMS meagre, scanty.
4 *the measure has large economic implications*: **wide-reaching**, far-reaching, wide-ranging, wide, sweeping, large-scale, broad, extensive, comprehensive, exhaustive, wholesale, global.
▷ANTONYMS trivial, petty.
□ **at large 1** *fourteen criminals are still at large*: **at liberty**, free, on the loose, on the run, fugitive; unconfined, unrestrained, roaming, loose, unbound, unrestricted, untied, unchained, unshackled, unfettered, set loose, wild; N. Amer. informal on the lam. ▷ANTONYMS confined, in prison.
2 *society at large*: **as a whole**, as a body, generally, in general, in the main.
▷ANTONYMS in particular, specifically.
3 *he speaks at large of the choroid plexus*: **in detail**, with full details, exhaustively, at length, extensively.
□ **by and large** *the children, by and large, treated him well*: **on the whole**, generally, in general, altogether, all things considered, all in all, taking everything into consideration, for the most part, in the main, as a rule, overall, usually, normally, ordinarily, almost always, customarily, habitually, typically, mainly, mostly, basically, chiefly, predominantly, principally, substantially; on average, in most cases, on balance, to all intents and purposes.

> *Word links* **large**
>
> **macro-** related prefix, as in *macroeconomics, macrocephaly*
> **mega-** related prefix, as in *megalith, megabucks*
> **megalo-** related prefix, as in *megalosaurus, megalomaniac*

largely adverb *the engineer William Jessop was largely responsible for this pioneering work*: **mostly**, mainly, to a large extent, to a great extent, to a great degree, on the whole, chiefly, generally, in general, predominantly, substantially, primarily, overall, for the most part, in the main, principally, in great measure, preponderantly, first and foremost, for all intents and purposes, basically; usually, typically, commonly.

large-scale adjective **1** *a large-scale privatization programme*: **extensive**, wide-reaching, wide-ranging, sweeping, broad, far-reaching, wholesale, comprehensive, exhaustive, expansive, mass, nationwide, global, universal.
▷ANTONYMS small-scale, minor.
2 *a large-scale map*: **enlarged**, blown-up, magnified.

largesse noun **1** *Tupper took advantage of his friend's largesse*: **generosity**, liberality, munificence, bounty, bountifulness, beneficence, benefaction, altruism, charity, philanthropy, magnanimity, benevolence, charitableness, open-handedness, kindness, big-heartedness, great-heartedness, lavishness, free-handedness, unselfishness, selflessness, self-sacrifice, self-denial; historical almsgiving.
▷ANTONYMS meanness, miserliness.
2 *he had distributed largesse to the locals*: **gifts**, presents, donations, handouts, endowments, grants, aid, alms, offerings, favours, contributions; patronage, sponsorship, backing, help.

lark informal noun **1** *I only went along for a lark | we were just having a bit of a lark*: **fun**, amusement, amusing time, laugh, giggle, joke; escapade, prank, trick, game, jape, skylark, practical joke, stunt; informal leg-pull, put-on, gag, crack; (**larks**) **antics**, high jinks, horseplay, fooling about/around, mischief, devilry, roguery, clowning, tomfoolery; informal shenanigans; Brit. informal monkey tricks, monkey business; N. Amer. informal didoes; dated sport.
2 *I've got this snowboarding lark sussed*: **activity**, undertaking, thing to do; hobby, pastime, task; informal business, caper.
▶ verb *he's always joking and larking about*: **fool about/around**, play tricks, indulge in horseplay, make mischief, monkey about/around, footle about/around, clown about/around, have fun, cavort, caper, romp, frolic, skylark; informal mess about/around, play up, act the (giddy) goat; Brit. informal muck about/around, fanny about/around; Brit. vulgar slang bugger about/around, piss about/around, arse about/around; archaic or humorous disport oneself.

larynx noun

> *Word links* **larynx**
>
> **laryngeal** relating to the larynx
> **laryngology** branch of medicine concerning the larynx
> **laryngitis** inflammation of the larynx

lascivious adjective *there was a lascivious glint in his eyes*: **lecherous**, lewd, lustful, licentious, libidinous, goatish, salacious, wanton, lubricious, prurient, dirty, smutty, filthy, naughty, suggestive, indecent, ribald; debauched, depraved, degenerate, dissolute, dissipated, unchaste, loose; informal horny, blue; Brit. informal randy; rare concupiscent, lickerish.
▷ANTONYMS puritanical, ascetic.

lash verb **1** *removing his leather belt, he lashed her repeatedly across buttocks and thighs*: **whip**, flog, beat, thrash, horsewhip, scourge, birch, switch, flay, belt, strap, cane, leather; strike, hit, clout, batter, welt, hammer, pummel, belabour; informal wallop, whack, lam, tan someone's hide, give someone a (good) hiding, larrup; N. Amer. informal whale; archaic smite, stripe, flagellate.
2 *rain lashed the window panes*: **beat against**, dash against, crash against, pound, batter, buffet, smack against, strike, hit, knock.
3 *the tiger began to growl and lash his tail*: **swish**, flick, twitch, switch, whip, wave, wag.
4 *fear lashed them into a frenzy*: **provoke**, incite, arouse, excite, agitate, stir up, whip up, work up, egg on, goad.
5 *two punts were lashed to rings embedded in the stonework*: **fasten**, bind, tie, tie up, tether, hitch, attach, knot, rope, strap, leash, truss, fetter, make fast, secure; chain, pinion, join, connect, couple.
□ **lash out 1** *the president* **lashed out at** *her for publicly opposing his economic policy*: **criticize**, castigate, chastise, censure, attack, condemn, denounce, lambaste, harangue, rant at, rail at, haul over the coals, fulminate against, pillory, let fly; berate, upbraid, scold, rebuke, chide, reprove, reproach, take to task; informal lay into, round on, pitch into, lace into, carpet, bawl out; Brit. informal slate; N. Amer. informal chew out, ream out.
2 *Norman* **lashed out at** *Terry with a chisel*: **hit out**, strike, let fly, take a swing; set upon, set about, turn on, round on, attack, weigh into; informal lay into, tear into, pitch into, lace into, sail into. **3** *he considered lashing out on a taxi*: **spend lavishly**, be extravagant, pay out, spend a lot of money; informal **splash out**, push the boat out, splurge, shell out, squander money, waste money, fritter money away, go on a spending spree, go on a shopping binge.
▶ noun **1** *he brought the lash down upon the prisoner's back*: **whip**, horsewhip, bullwhip, switch, scourge, flagellum, cat-o'-nine-tails, cat, thong, flail, strap, birch, cane; historical knout.
2 *he was sentenced to 50 lashes with a bamboo cane*: **stroke**, blow, hit, strike, welt, bang, thwack, thump; informal swipe, wallop, whack; archaic stripe.

lass noun Scottish & N. English **girl**, young woman, young lady; schoolgirl, miss; Scottish lassie; Irish colleen; informal chick, girlie, filly; Brit. informal bird, bint, popsy; N. Amer. informal dame, babe, doll, gal, broad, patootie, tomato; Austral./NZ informal sheila; derogatory baggage, piece, bit, tart; literary maid, maiden, damsel; archaic or humorous wench.

lassitude noun *prolonged periods of lassitude which she ascribed to the heat*: **lethargy**, listlessness, weariness, languor, sluggishness, enervation, tiredness, exhaustion, fatigue, sleepiness, drowsiness, torpor, torpidity, ennui, lifelessness, sloth, apathy.
▷ANTONYMS vigour, energy.

last[1] adjective **1** *the last woman in the queue*: **rearmost**, rear, hindmost, bringing up the rear, nearest the rear, at the end, furthest back, at the back (of the queue), aftermost, endmost, furthest behind, final, ultimate, most remote, remotest, furthest, utmost, extreme.
▷ANTONYMS first, leading.
2 *Rembrandt spent his last years in Amsterdam*: **closing**, concluding, final, ending, end, finishing, ultimate, terminal, terminating; valedictory; later, latter.
▷ANTONYMS early, initial.
3 *I'd be the last person to say anything against him*: **least likely**, most unlikely, most improbable, most reluctant; least suitable, most unsuitable, most inappropriate, least appropriate, least wanted, least favourite.
▷ANTONYMS first, most likely.
4 *he scored a hat-trick last year*: **previous**, preceding; latest, most recent; prior, former.
▷ANTONYMS next.
5 *this was his last chance to prove it*: **final**, only remaining, only one left.
□ **the last word 1** *you'll marry my daughter over my dead body, and that's my last word*: **final decision**, summation, final statement, definitive statement, conclusive comment; ultimatum. **2** *she turned, determined to leave having had the last word*: **concluding remark**, final remark, final say, closing statement, parting shot, Parthian shot. **3** *the spa is the last word in luxury and efficiency*: **the best**, the peak, the acme, the epitome, the quintessence, the most fashionable, the most up to date, the latest, the newest; the pinnacle, the apex, the apogee, the cream, the ultimate, the height, the zenith, the utmost, the nonpareil, the crème de la crème, the ne plus ultra, the dernier cri, the beau idéal; archaic the nonsuch.
▶ adverb *the candidate coming last is eliminated*: **at the end**, at the rear, in the rear, behind, after.
▶ noun *the most important business was left to the last*: **end**, ending, finish, close, conclusion, completion, finale, termination; bitter end.
▷ANTONYMS beginning, opening.
□ **at last** *at last the storm died away*: **finally**, in the end, eventually, ultimately, at long last, after a long time, after a considerable time, in time, at the end of the day, in the fullness of time; lastly, in conclusion.

last[2] verb **1** *the hearing is expected to last for a number of days*: **continue**, go on, carry on, keep on, keep going, run on, proceed, be prolonged; take; stay, remain, persist, endure.
▷ANTONYMS finish, end, stop.
2 *she managed to* **last out** *until the end of the programme | how long does he reckon he'll last as manager?* **survive**, endure, hold on, hold out, keep going,

persevere, exist; informal stick it out, hang on, stay around, hack it.
3 *the car is built to last*: **endure**, wear well, stand up, keep going, bear up; withstand, resist; informal go the distance.
▷ANTONYMS wear out.

last³ noun *the iron lasts on which he mended our shoes*: **mould**, model, pattern, form, matrix; anvil; N. English hobbing foot/boot.

last-ditch adjective *a last-ditch attempt to save the plan from collapse*: **last-minute**, last-chance, eleventh-hour, last-resort, desperate, frantic, frenzied, wild, struggling, straining, final, extreme, all-out, do-or-die; informal last-gasp.

lasting adjective *a lasting peace*: **enduring**, long-lasting, long-lived, lifelong, abiding, continuing, remaining, long-term, surviving, persisting, permanent, deep-rooted, indelible, ingrained; durable, constant, stable, established, secure, fast, firm, fixed, long-standing; unchanging, never-changing, irreversible, immutable, eternal, undying, everlasting, perennial, perpetual, unending, never-ending, endless, immortal, imperishable, unfading, changeless, indestructible, ceaseless, unceasing, unwavering, unfaltering, non-stop, steady, steadfast, uninterrupted, unbroken, interminable; dependable, reliable; rare sempiternal, perdurable.
▷ANTONYMS short-lived, ephemeral.

lastly adverb *lastly, I would like to thank my parents for making me what I am*: **finally**, in conclusion, to conclude, in closing, to sum up, to end, in drawing things to a close, in winding up, last, ultimately, in fine, last but not least.
▷ANTONYMS firstly.

latch noun *lifting the latch, she pushed the gate open*: **fastening**, catch, fastener; clasp, hasp, hook, bar, bolt, clip; lock, padlock, deadlock; Scottish sneck, snib.
▶ verb *Jess latched the back door*: **fasten**, secure, make fast, bar, bolt; lock, padlock, deadlock; Scottish & Irish sneck, snib.

late adjective **1** *the train was one and a half hours late | he was late for work*: **behind time**, behind schedule, behind, behindhand; not on time, unpunctual, tardy, running late, overdue, belated, delayed; slow, dilatory.
▷ANTONYMS punctual, early, fast.
2 *her late husband*: **dead**, deceased, departed, lamented, passed on/away, lost, expired, gone, extinct, perished.
▷ANTONYMS alive, existing.
3 *he was Minister for Education in the late government*: **previous**, preceding, former, past, prior, earlier, sometime, one-time, ex-, erstwhile, old, defunct, precedent, foregoing, no longer extant; French ci-devant; formal quondam; archaic whilom.
▷ANTONYMS current.
▶ adverb **1** *she had arrived late*: **behind schedule**, behind time, behindhand, unpunctually, belatedly, tardily, at the last minute, at the tail end; dilatorily, slowly, recently.
▷ANTONYMS early, betimes.
2 *I was working late*: **after hours**, after office hours, overtime, past the usual finishing/stopping/closing time.
3 *I won't have you staying out late*: **late at night**, till the early hours of the morning; informal till the wee small hours, till all hours.
□ **of late** *she'd been drinking too much of late*: **recently**, lately, latterly, in the past few days, in the last couple of weeks, in recent times; newly, freshly, not long ago.

lately adverb *divorced people have had a bad press lately*: **recently**, of late, latterly, in the past few days, in the last couple of weeks, in recent times; newly, freshly, not long ago.
▷ANTONYMS long ago.

lateness noun **unpunctuality**, tardiness, belatedness, delay, retardation, dilatoriness.
▷ANTONYMS punctuality, timeliness, earliness.

latent adjective *they have a huge reserve of latent talent*: **dormant**, quiescent, inactive, untapped, unused; **undiscovered**, hidden, unrevealed, unexpressed, concealed, unapparent, indiscernible, imperceptible, invisible, inert, covert, unseen, veiled, masked, lurking, undeveloped, unrealized, unfulfilled, potential, not activated, inoperative, in abeyance, suppressed, repressed; possible, likely, underlying, inherent, innermost, immanent, inchoate, unacknowledged, subconscious, unconscious, sleeping.
▷ANTONYMS manifest, obvious; active.

Word toolkit

latent	potential	dormant
tuberculosis	problems	volcano
infection	benefits	plants
defect	buyers	seeds
factors	investors	account
homosexuality	risk	cells

later adjective *this question will be dealt with in a later chapter*: **subsequent**, following, succeeding, future, upcoming, to come, ensuing, next; archaic after; rare posterior.
▷ANTONYMS earlier, prior.
▶ adverb **1** *later, the film rights were sold*: **subsequently**, eventually, then, next, later on, after this/that, afterwards, following this/that, at a later time, at a later date, at a future time/date, at some point in the future, in the future, in time to come, in due course.
2 *two days later a letter arrived*: **afterwards**, later on, after, after that, subsequently, following; by and by, in a while, in time, after a bit; formal thereafter, thereupon.

lateral adjective **1** *lateral movements*: **sideways**, sidewise, sidelong, sideward, edgewise, edgeways, side, flank, wing, indirect, oblique, slanting.
2 *lateral thinking*: **unorthodox**, inventive, creative, imaginative, original, innovative, ingenious.

latest adjective *the latest fashion*: **most recent**, newest, brand new, just out, just released, fresh, present-day, up to date, up to the minute, state-of-the-art, current, modern, contemporary, modernistic, fashionable, in fashion, in vogue, voguish, bang up to date, in; French à la mode; informal with it, trendy, hip, hot, happening, cool, now.
▷ANTONYMS old, unfashionable.

lather noun **1** *a rich lather of rose-scented suds*: **foam**, froth, suds, soapsuds, bubbles; cream, head; literary spume.
2 *the mare was covered with lather*: **sweat**, perspiration, moisture; technical diaphoresis, hidrosis.
3 informal *Dad was in a right lather*: **panic**, nervous state, state of agitation, state of anxiety, fluster, flutter, fret, fuss, frenzy, fever, pother; informal flap, sweat, tizzy, dither, twitter, state, stew; N. Amer. informal twit.

latitude noun **1** *Toronto shares the same latitude as Nice*: **parallel**, grid line.
▷ANTONYMS longitude, meridian.
2 *he gave them much latitude in day-to-day operations*: **freedom**, **scope**, leeway, elbow room, breathing space, space, room, flexibility, liberty, independence, play, slack, free rein, free play, licence, self-determination, room to manoeuvre, scope for initiative, freedom of action, freedom from restriction, a free hand, margin, leisure, unrestrictedness, indulgence, laxity; French carte blanche.
▷ANTONYMS constraint, restriction.

latter adjective **1** *the latter half of the season*: **later**, hindmost, closing, end, concluding, final.
2 *the latter years of the last century*: **latest**, most recent, modern.
3 *Russia chose the latter option*: **last-mentioned**, second-mentioned, second of the two, second, last, later.
▷ANTONYMS former, prior.

latter-day adjective *a latter-day puritan*: **modern**, present-day, present-time, current, contemporary; French de nos jours.
▷ANTONYMS old-time.

latterly adverb **1** *latterly, she had been in more pain*: **recently**, lately, of late, in the past few days, in the last couple of weeks, in recent times.
▷ANTONYMS formerly.
2 *he worked on the paper for fifty years, latterly as its political editor*: **ultimately**, finally, towards the end, at the end.

lattice noun *honeysuckle was growing up a lattice round the door*: **grid**, latticework, fretwork, open framework, openwork, trellis, trelliswork, network, mesh, web, webbing, netting, net, tracery, interlacing, reticulation, reticulum, grate, grating, grille, grillwork, criss-cross, matrix; espalier, filigree; technical plexus, graticule, reticule, reticle, decussation.

laud verb *the single was lauded by the music press*: **praise**, extol, hail, applaud, acclaim, commend, admire, approve of, make much of, sing the praises of, lionize, speak highly of, pay tribute/homage to, eulogize, sing paeans to; cheer, celebrate, welcome, salute, glorify, exalt, rhapsodize over/about, honour, adore, revere, venerate, idolize; informal put on a pedestal, rave about; black English big someone/something up; dated cry someone/something up; archaic magnify; rare panegyrize.
▷ANTONYMS condemn, criticize.

laudable adjective *a laudable attempt to get more women into Parliament*: **praiseworthy**, commendable, admirable, meritorious, worthy, deserving, creditable, worthy of admiration, estimable, of note, noteworthy, exemplary, reputable, honourable, excellent, sterling; rare applaudable.
▷ANTONYMS blameworthy, shameful.

laudation noun rare *he was singled out for laudation*. See **praise** (sense 1 of the noun).

laudatory adjective *a laudatory front-page endorsement*: **full of praise**, complimentary, congratulatory, praising, extolling, acclamatory, adulatory, commendatory, admiring, approving, approbatory, flattering, celebratory, glorifying, eulogizing, eulogistic, panegyric, panegyrical; fulsome; informal glowing, rave; rare encomiastic, encomiastical.
▷ANTONYMS disparaging, damning.

laugh verb **1** *he started to laugh excitedly*: **chuckle**, chortle, guffaw, giggle, titter, snigger, snicker, cackle, howl, roar, tee-hee, burst out laughing,

roar/hoot with laughter, shake with laughter, be convulsed with laughter, dissolve into laughter, split one's sides, hold one's sides, be doubled up; informal be in stitches, die laughing, be rolling in the aisles, laugh like a drain, bust a gut, break up, be creased up, crease up, fall about, crack up.
▷ANTONYMS cry.
2 *people laughed at Henry and his theories*: **ridicule**, mock, deride, scoff at, jeer at, sneer at, jibe at, make fun of, poke fun at, make jokes about, heap scorn on, scorn, pooh-pooh; lampoon, satirize, caricature, parody; taunt, tease, torment; informal send up, take the mickey out of; Austral./NZ informal poke mullock at; Brit. vulgar slang take the piss out of; dated make sport of.
□ **laugh something off** *she laughed off criticism with good humour*: **dismiss**, make a joke of, make light of, refuse to acknowledge, overlook, turn a blind eye to, discount, ignore, disregard, shrug off, brush aside, scoff at, pooh-pooh, take no notice of, pay no attention to, play down, never mind; informal cock a snook at.
▷ANTONYMS take something to heart.
▶ **noun 1** *he gave a short laugh*: **chuckle**, chortle, guffaw, giggle, titter, ha-ha, tee-hee, snigger, roar of laughter, hoot of laughter, shriek of laughter, peal of laughter, belly laugh.
2 informal *he was a right laugh*: **joker**, comedian, comic, comedienne, humorist, wag, wit, entertainer, clown, funny man, funny woman, jester, prankster, character; informal card, case, caution, hoot, scream, riot, barrel of laughs; Austral./NZ informal hard case.
▷ANTONYMS bore, misery.
3 informal *I entered the contest for a laugh*: **joke**, **prank**, piece of fun, jest, escapade, adventure, caper, romp, practical joke, trick, bit of mischief; shenanigans, horseplay; informal lark, giggle, hoot.

laughable adjective **1** *the idea that nuclear weapons deter anyone is laughable*: **ridiculous**, ludicrous, absurd, risible, preposterous, irrational, worthy of scorn, derisory; foolish, silly, idiotic, daft, stupid, nonsensical, senseless, asinine, fatuous, crazy, insane, hare-brained, scatterbrained, outrageous; informal cock-eyed.
2 *if it wasn't so tragic, it'd be laughable*: **amusing**, funny, humorous, hilarious, uproarious, comical, comic, entertaining, diverting, farcical, droll, side-splitting; informal rib-tickling, jokey, killing, priceless; rare jocose.
▷ANTONYMS serious.

laughing stock noun *they have become the laughing stock of world sport*: **figure of fun**, object of ridicule, dupe, butt, fool, joke, standing joke, everybody's fool, stooge; fair game, everybody's target, victim, Aunt Sally; exhibition, spectacle; informal fall guy; Brit. informal goat.

laughter noun **1** *the sound of conversation and laughter*: **laughing**, chuckling, chortling, guffawing, giggling, tittering, sniggering, howling, convulsions, fits; informal hysterics, hooting; rare cachinnation.
2 *a source of laughter*: **amusement**, entertainment, humour, mirth, merriment, gaiety, hilarity, glee, jollity, jocularity, fun, enjoyment, pleasure, delight, joy, festivity, light-heartedness, blitheness.
▷ANTONYMS despair, gloom, misery.

launch verb **1** *he ordered his crewmen to launch a boat*: **set afloat**, float; put to sea, put into the water, send down the slipway.
2 *they've launched the shuttle*: **send into orbit**, put into orbit; blast off, take off, lift off.
3 *a chair was launched at him*: **throw**, hurl, fling, pitch, lob, toss, cast, let fly, propel, project; fire, shoot; informal chuck, heave, sling.
4 *Amnesty International has launched an emergency appeal*: **set in motion**, get going, get under way, start, begin, embark on, usher in, initiate, put in place, instigate, institute, inaugurate, set up, bring out, organize, introduce, open; establish, found, originate, create, pioneer, lay the foundations of, lay the first stone of, bring into being, activate, mastermind, float, debut, roll out; start the ball rolling; informal kick off; formal commence.
5 *he launched into a tirade against the government*: **start**, burst into, break into, begin, embark on, get going on; formal commence.

launder verb *the used sheets are taken away to be laundered*: **wash**, clean, wash and iron, wash and press, dry-clean.

laundry noun **1** *a big pile of laundry*: **dirty washing**, washing, wash, dirty clothes, clothes to be cleaned; Brit. dated bagwash.
2 *communal accommodation includes a kitchen, a laundry, and two bathrooms*: **washroom**, laundry room, launderette, dry cleaner's, public wash house, Chinese laundry; N. Amer. trademark laundromat.

laurels plural noun *she has rightly won laurels for this perceptive first novel*: **honours**, awards, trophies, prizes, rewards, tributes, praise, plaudits, accolades, decorations, titles; kudos, acclaim, acclamation, commendation, credit, glory, honour, distinction, fame, renown, prestige, recognition; informal brownie points; rare laudation.

lavatory noun **toilet**, WC, water closet, (public) convenience, cloakroom, facilities, powder room, urinal, privy, latrine, outhouse, earth closet, jakes; N. Amer. washroom, bathroom, rest room, men's room, ladies' room, commode, comfort station; French pissoir; Nautical head; informal little girls' room, little boys' room, smallest room; Brit. informal loo, bog, the Ladies, the Gents, khazi, lav, throne, thunderbox; N. English informal netty; N. Amer. informal can, john, honey bucket; Austral./NZ informal dunny, little house; vulgar slang pisser, shithouse, shitter; archaic closet, garderobe.

lavish adjective **1** *he held lavish dinner parties at his home*: **sumptuous**, luxurious, luxuriant, lush, gorgeous, costly, opulent, grand, elaborate, splendid, rich, regal, ornate, expensive; pretentious, showy, fancy; informal posh.
▷ANTONYMS meagre.
2 *he was lavish with his hospitality*: **generous**, liberal, bountiful, open-handed, unstinting, unsparing, ungrudging, free, munificent, handsome; extravagant, prodigal, fulsome; informal over the top.
▷ANTONYMS frugal, mean.
3 *lavish amounts of the best quality olive oil*: **abundant**, copious, ample, superabundant, plentiful, profuse, liberal, prolific, generous; literary plenteous.
▷ANTONYMS scant.
▶ **verb** *she has always lavished money on her children*: **give freely**, spend, expend, heap, shower, pour, deluge, give generously, give unstintingly, bestow freely; informal blow.
▷ANTONYMS economize, begrudge.

law noun **1** *the law of the land*: **rules and regulations**, system of laws, body of laws, constitution, legislation, code, legal code, charter; jurisprudence.
▷ANTONYMS anarchy.
2 *a new law was passed to make divorce easier and simpler*: **regulation**, **statute**, enactment, act, bill, decree, edict, rule, ruling, resolution, promulgation, measure, motion, dictum, command, order, stipulation, commandment, directive, pronouncement, ratification, proclamation, dictate, diktat, fiat, covenant, demand, by-law; N. Amer. ordinance; in Tsarist Russia ukase; in Spain & Spanish-speaking countries pronunciamento.
3 (**the law**) *a career in the law*: **the legal profession**, the bar, barristers and solicitors collectively.
4 *he's got to pay for it, or I'll take him to law*: **litigation**, legal action, legal proceedings, lawsuit, justice.
5 (**the law**) informal *on the run from the law*: **the police**, the officers of the law, the forces of law and order, law-enforcement officers, police officers, policemen, policewomen, the police force, the constabulary; black English derogatory Babylon; informal the cops, the fuzz, the boys in blue, the long arm of the law; Brit. informal the (Old) Bill, the bobbies, the busies, the bizzies, the coppers, the rozzers, the force, plod, PC Plod; N. Amer. informal the heat; informal, derogatory the pigs, the filth.
6 *the laws of the game*: **rule**, regulation, principle, convention, direction, instruction, guideline, practice.
7 *a moral law*: **principle**, rule, precept, directive, direction, injunction, instruction, commandment, prescription, standard, criterion, belief, creed, credo, ethic, maxim, formula, tenet, doctrine, canon; Judaism mitzvah.

Word links **law**
legal, **judicial**, **juridical**, **jural** relating to laws

law-abiding adjective *decent law-abiding citizens*: **well behaved**, lawful, righteous, honest, honourable, correct, upright, upstanding, good, decent, proper, solid, virtuous, moral, ethical; high-minded, right-minded, principled, worthy, orderly, above board, clean-living, peaceable, peaceful, civilized; dutiful, duteous, obedient, compliant, manageable, deferential, respectful, disciplined.
▷ANTONYMS lawless, criminal.

lawbreaker noun **criminal**, felon, wrongdoer, evil-doer, offender, delinquent, malefactor, reprobate, culprit; villain, rogue, ruffian, hoodlum, desperado, outlaw; rascal, transgressor, sinner, trespasser, violator, convict; informal crook, con, jailbird, crim, wrong 'un, baddy; Law malfeasant, infractor; archaic miscreant.

law court noun **court**, court of law, court of justice, tribunal, judicature.

Word links **law court**
judicial, **juridical** relating to law courts

lawful adjective **1** *the jury delivered a verdict of lawful killing*: **legitimate**, legal, licit, just, permissible, permitted, allowable, allowed, rightful, proper, constitutional, legalized, sanctioned, authorized, warranted, justified, justifiable, approved, recognized, admissible, above board, within the law, going by the rules; informal legit, kosher, by the book.
▷ANTONYMS illegal, prohibited.
2 *a lawful political organization*: **law-abiding**, righteous, honourable, good, decent, proper, solid, virtuous, moral, ethical, orderly, well behaved, peacekeeping, peaceful, civilized, dutiful, duteous, obedient, compliant, complying, disciplined.
▷ANTONYMS lawless, criminal.

lawless adjective **1** *an unruly and lawless rabble*: **anarchic**, anarchical, disorderly, ungovernable, unruly, without law and order, disruptive, insurrectionary, insurgent, revolutionary, rebellious, insubordinate, riotous, mutinous, mutinying, seditious, revolting, terrorist.
▷ANTONYMS orderly.

l

2 *any member associated with any subversive or lawless activities shall be expelled*: **illegal**, unlawful, lawbreaking, illicit, illegitimate, criminal, felonious, indictable, delinquent, culpable, villainous, transgressing, violating; informal crooked, shady, bent; archaic miscreant.
▷ANTONYMS law-abiding.

lawlessness noun **anarchy**, disorder, chaos, unruliness, lack of control, lack of restraint, wildness, riot, criminality, crime, rebellion, revolution, mutiny, insurgency, insurrection, misrule.
▷ANTONYMS order.

lawsuit noun **legal action**, suit, suit at law, case, action, cause, legal proceeding, proceedings, judicial proceedings, litigation, trial, legal process, legal dispute, legal contest, bringing to book, bringing of charges, indictment.

lawyer noun **legal practitioner**, attorney, legal officer, legal adviser, legal representative, legal executive, agent, member of the bar; informal brief.

lax adjective *lax discipline in schools*: **slack**, slipshod, negligent, neglectful, remiss, careless, heedless, unmindful, inattentive, slapdash, offhand, casual; easy-going, lenient, permissive, soft, liberal, non-restrictive, indulgent, overindulgent, complaisant, over-tolerant, irresponsible; informal sloppy.
▷ANTONYMS stern, careful.

laxative noun **purgative**, lenitive, aperient, cathartic, evacuant; rare eccoprotic.

lay[1] verb 1 *Curtis laid the empty can on the passenger seat*: **put**, place, set, put down, set down, deposit, rest, situate, sit, settle, stow, balance, station, drop, leave, let fall, throw down, fling down, deploy, locate, position; informal plant, stick, dump, bung, park, plonk, pop, shove.
▷ANTONYMS pick up.
2 *the Act which laid the foundation for the modern education system*: **set in place/position**, put in place/position, set out, position; establish, set up.
3 *I'll **lay money** that Michelle will be there*: **bet**, wager, gamble, stake, hazard, risk, chance, venture; give odds, speculate, game; informal punt, have a flutter.
4 *he had been the first to lay formal charges*: **bring**, bring forward, put forward, submit, advance, present, press, prefer, offer, lodge, register, place, file, table; accuse, charge, indict; N. Amer. impeach.
5 *he **laid the blame for** the crisis firmly at the Prime Minister's door*: **assign**, attribute, ascribe, allocate, allot, impute, attach, impose, fix; hold someone responsible, hold someone accountable, hold someone answerable, condemn, find guilty of, pin the blame on.
▷ANTONYMS exonerate, hold blameless.
6 *we laid plans for the next voyage*: **devise**, arrange, contrive, make, prepare, work out, hatch, concoct, design, plan, scheme, plot, organize, frame, think up, dream up, cook up, brew, conceive, make ready, get ready, put together, draw up, produce, develop, compose, formulate.
7 *the new section laid a responsibility on the court to consider whether financial obligations should be terminated*: **impose**, apply, entrust, vest, place, put; inflict, encumber, saddle, tax, charge, burden.
▷ANTONYMS excuse.
8 *the eagles laid two eggs*: **produce**; technical oviposit.
□ **lay something aside** 1 *payments for farmers who lay aside areas for conservation*: **put aside**, put to one side, keep, save, store, hold in abeyance. 2 *producers must lay aside the conservatism that hindered development in the past*: **abandon**, cast aside, reject, renounce, repudiate, dismiss, disregard, ignore, forget, discard; archaic forsake. ▷ANTONYMS take up.
3 *Protestants opposed it strongly enough to lead the government to lay the idea aside*: **defer**, shelve, hold over, suspend, put on ice, mothball, set aside, put off, put aside, put out of one's mind, wave aside, put back, adjourn; informal put on the back burner, put in cold storage; rare remit.
▷ANTONYMS pursue; promote; progress.
□ **lay something bare** *the secrets of his heart will be laid bare*: **reveal**, disclose, divulge, show, expose, exhibit, bring to light, uncover, unveil, unmask, manifest, express, highlight, pinpoint, put the spotlight on, betray, give away, smoke out, let slip, blurt out, publish, acknowledge, make a clean breast of, make known, make public.
▷ANTONYMS conceal.
□ **lay something down** 1 *he laid down his glass*: **put down**, set down, place down, deposit, drop, station, leave, rest; informal dump, bung down, plonk down. 2 *they were forced to **lay down their weapons***: **relinquish**, surrender, give up, yield, cede, turn over; **disarm**, give in, submit, capitulate, raise/show the white flag, throw in the towel/sponge, demilitarize. 3 *the ground rules laid down by the Civil Aviation Authority*: **formulate**, stipulate, set down, draw up, frame; prescribe, order, command, ordain, dictate, decree, enjoin, assert; pronounce, announce, proclaim, promulgate; enact, pass, direct, decide, determine, impose, establish, institute, specify, fix, codify.
4 *I like to buy young wines and lay them down for a few years*: **store**, put into store, keep for future use, keep, save.
□ **lay down the law** *when his father tried to lay down the law, he rebelled*: **order someone about/around**, tell someone what to do, boss someone about/around, ride roughshod over someone, be dogmatic, be domineering; call the shots, call the tune; informal throw one's weight about/around, push someone about/around.
□ **lay eyes on** informal *I've never laid eyes on him before!* **see**, spot, observe, regard, notice, catch sight of, view, perceive, discern, spy; informal clap/set eyes on, clock; literary behold, espy, descry.
□ **lay hands on** 1 *wait till I lay my hands on you!* **catch**, lay hold of, get one's hands on, get hold of, seize, grab, snatch, clutch, grip, grasp, capture.
▷ANTONYMS let go; leave alone. 2 *it's not easy to lay your hands on decent champagne around here*: **obtain**, acquire, get, come by, find, locate, discover, unearth, uncover, bring to light, run to earth, turn up, pick up, come up with, secure, procure, hit on, ferret out, get one's hands on, encounter, get possession of, buy, purchase; informal get one's mitts on.
3 *the pastor will lay hands on those who come before him*: **bless**, consecrate; confirm; ordain.
□ **lay something in** *Bill proposed that we should lay in a lot of good meat, and keep it for the winter*: **stock up with/on**, stockpile, store (up), amass, heap up, hoard, save, stow, put aside, garner, accumulate, pile up, mass, assemble, stack up, put away, stow away, husband, reserve, preserve, conserve, collect, muster, put by, put by for a rainy day, squirrel away; informal salt away, stash (away).
□ **lay into** informal 1 *a policeman laying into a protestor*: **attack**, assail, hit, strike, let fly at, tear into, lash out at, set about, set upon, fall on, turn on, assault, beat, thrash, pound, pummel, wallop, hammer, pounce on, round on, pelt, drub; informal lace into, sail into, pitch into, let someone have it, get stuck into, paste, do over, knock about/around, rough up; Brit. informal have a go at. ▷ANTONYMS leave in peace.
2 *there was no reason for him to lay into her with a string of insults*: **criticize harshly**, castigate, censure, lambaste, harangue, condemn, pillory, rant at, rave at; berate, upbraid, rebuke, chide, reproach, reprove, scold; informal pitch into, crucify, rubbish, slag off; Brit. informal have a go at; N. Amer. informal light into, bad-mouth, bawl out; rare objurgate.
▷ANTONYMS praise, extol.
□ **lay it on** informal ***lay it on thick** about what you'll do for them*: **exaggerate**, stretch the truth, overdo it, overstate one's case, embellish the truth; flatter, pay extravagant compliments, give fulsome praise, over-praise, soft-soap; informal pile it on, lay it on with a trowel/shovel, ham it up, sweet-talk.
▷ANTONYMS understate.
□ **lay off** informal *you should lay off smoking*: **give up**, stop, refrain from, abstain from, not continue, desist from, leave alone, cut out; N. Amer. quit; informal pack in, leave off, kick, give over, knock off.
▷ANTONYMS start, take up.
□ **lay someone off** *cutbacks forced the museum to lay off 244 employees*: **make redundant**, dismiss, let go, discharge, give notice to, pay off, release; informal sack, give someone the sack, fire, give someone their cards, give someone their marching orders, send packing, give someone the boot, give someone the bullet, give someone the push, give someone the (old) heave-ho, boot out.
▷ANTONYMS take on, hire.
□ **lay something on** *they arrived at the club to find no refreshments laid on*: **provide**, supply, furnish, give, fix up, line up, organize, prepare, produce, come up with, dispense, purvey, bestow, impart, make available; cater.
□ **lay someone out** informal *he belted him, laid him out flat*: **knock out**, knock unconscious, knock down, fell, floor, flatten, prostrate; informal KO, kayo, knock for six.
□ **lay something out** 1 *Robyn laid the plans out on the desk*: **spread out**, set out, arrange, display, exhibit, distribute, line up, order.
▷ANTONYMS fold up, put away. 2 *a pamphlet which tells you how to lay out election leaflets*: **design**, plan, set out, arrange; map out, outline, sketch out, rough out, block out, detail, draw up, formulate, work out, frame, draft, plot out, trace out. 3 informal *he had to lay out $70 on antibiotics*: **spend**, expend, pay, disburse, contribute, part with, invest, put in, devote, use up, donate, give; lavish, squander, waste, dissipate; informal shell out, fork out, dish out, splurge; Brit. informal stump up; N. Amer. informal ante up, pony up.
□ **lay waste** *the army **laid waste to** hundreds of villages*: **devastate**, wipe out, destroy, demolish, annihilate, raze, ruin, leave in ruins, wreck, level, flatten, gut, consume, ravage, pillage, sack, wreak havoc on; literary despoil; rare depredate.

lay[2] adjective 1 *a lay preacher*: **non-clerical**, non-ordained, non-ecclesiastical, secular, temporal; civil, civilian; rare laic, laical.
▷ANTONYMS ordained.
2 *I cannot explain to a lay audience the techniques I used to study these genes*: **non-professional**, amateur, non-specialist, non-technical, untrained, unqualified, inexpert; dilettante.
▷ANTONYMS qualified, professional.

layabout noun **idler**, good-for-nothing, ne'er-do-well, do-nothing, loafer, lounger, shirker, sluggard, laggard, slugabed, malingerer, parasite, leech; informal skiver, waster, slacker, lazybones, lead-swinger, slob, couch potato; Austral./NZ informal **bludger**; Brit. informal, chiefly Military **scrimshanker**; archaic wastrel; French archaic **fainéant**.
▷ANTONYMS workaholic.

layer noun *the walls were topped by a layer of concrete*: **coating**, sheet, coat, surface, film, covering, blanket, skin, veneer, thickness.

layman noun See **layperson**.

lay-off noun *a strike in protest over lay-offs*: **redundancy**, dismissal, discharge; notice; unemployment; informal sacking, firing; marching orders; the sack, the boot, the bullet, the axe, the (old) heave-ho, the elbow, the bounce.
▷ANTONYMS recruitment, hiring.

layout noun **1** *she seems familiar with the layout of the house*: **arrangement**, geography, design, organization, make-up, shape; plan, map.
2 *the magazine's layout and typography give it a stylish look*: **design**, arrangement, presentation, style, format; structure, organization, composition, formation, configuration, set-up; pattern, outline, plan, sketch.

layperson noun **1** *a book for laypeople that explains the church's policies*: **unordained person**, member of the congregation, parishioner; layman, laywoman.
▷ANTONYMS clergyman.
2 *engineering sounds highly specialized to the layperson*: **non-expert**, layman, non-professional, amateur, non-specialist, man in/on the street; dilettante, enthusiast, dabbler.
▷ANTONYMS professional, expert.

laze verb *I was just **lazing around** on beaches*: **relax**, unwind, idle, do nothing, loaf (around/about), lounge (around/about), loll (around/about), lie (around/about), take it easy; waste time, kill time, mark time, while away the hours, fritter away time, twiddle one's thumbs; informal hang around/round, skive, veg (out); Brit. informal hang about; N. Amer. informal bum (around).
▷ANTONYMS work.

laziness noun **idleness**, indolence, slothfulness, sloth, shiftlessness, inactivity, inertia, sluggishness, lethargy, languor, torpidity, slowness, heaviness, dullness; remissness, negligence, slackness, laxity.
▷ANTONYMS industriousness, energy.

lazy adjective **idle**, indolent, slothful, work-shy, shiftless, loafing, inactive, inert, sluggish, lethargic, languorous, listless, torpid, enervated, slow-moving, slow, heavy, dull, plodding; remiss, negligent, slack, lax, lackadaisical, impassive, good-for-nothing, do-nothing; leisurely; informal bone idle; French archaic fainéant; rare otiose.
▷ANTONYMS active, industrious, energetic.

Choose the right word **lazy, idle, indolent**

People described as any of these words are reluctant to expend any energy or go to any trouble over work they have to do.

Lazy is the most general word (*he's too lazy to mow the lawn*). Of the three words, only *lazy* can also be used to describe something done without much effort (*lazy speaking leads to lazy writing*). Uncritically, it can be used of a time when little effort is expended (*what better way to liven up these lazy summer days*) or, figuratively, of inanimate objects (*the Neapolitan Riviera extends in a lazy curve around the coast*).

Idle can be more strongly critical than *lazy* (*you're an idle scrounger*) but is normally used in more formal contexts. Care is sometimes needed to avoid confusion with the sense 'out of work', as in *10.3 per cent of the workforce is now idle*.

Indolent is rarer, and more formal still (*their leaders and functionaries have been indolent, self-serving, or downright corrupt*). It can sometimes indicate slow, even graceful movements (*she moved across the room with an indolent, hip-swaying saunter*).

lazybones noun informal **idler**, loafer, layabout, lounger, good-for-nothing, do-nothing, shirker, sluggard, laggard, slugabed; informal skiver, waster, slacker, slowcoach, slob, couch potato; Austral./NZ informal bludger; archaic wastrel; French archaic fainéant.

leach verb *nitrate is leached from the soil by rainfall*: **drain**, filter, percolate, filtrate, discharge, strain, leak, separate; trickle, dribble, drip, ooze, seep; rare osmose, lixiviate.

lead[1] (rhymes with 'feed') verb **1** *Michelle let them lead her into the porch*: **guide**, conduct, show, show someone the way, lead the way, usher, escort, steer, pilot, marshal, shepherd; accompany, see, take, help, assist.
▷ANTONYMS follow.
2 *we are led to believe that lack of finance is to blame*: **cause**, induce, prompt, move, persuade, sway, influence, prevail on, bring round, make willing, motivate, drive, condition, determine, make, impel, give, force; incline, dispose, predispose, bias.
3 *they feared that the Marshall Plan would **lead to** Germany's industrial revival*: **result in**, cause, bring on, bring about, call forth, give rise to, be the cause of, make happen, create, produce, occasion, effect, engender, generate, contribute to, be conducive to, add to, be instrumental in, have a hand in, have a part in, help, promote, advance; precipitate, hasten, accelerate, quicken, push forward, prompt, expedite, further, speed up; provoke, stir up, spark off, trigger (off), set off, touch off, arouse, rouse, excite, foment, instigate; cost, involve, necessitate, invite, risk, elicit, entail; rare effectuate, conduce to.
4 *he intended to lead a march to the city centre*: **be at the head of**, be at the front of, head, spearhead.
▷ANTONYMS follow.
5 *the Prime Minister led a coalition of republican radicals*: **be the leader of**, be the head of, preside over, hold sway over, head; command, direct, govern, rule, be in charge of, be in command of, be in control of, have control of, have charge of, regulate, supervise, superintend, oversee, chair, run, mastermind, orchestrate, control, conduct, guide, be at the helm of, take the chair of; administer, organize, manage; dominate, master, reign over, domineer, be in power over; informal head up, run the show, call the shots.
▷ANTONYMS serve in.
6 *he fired in breaks of 52 and 65 to lead 8–54*: **be ahead**, be winning, be in front, be out in front, be in the lead, be first, come first.
▷ANTONYMS be losing, lose.
7 *the champion steeplechaser was leading the field as usual*: **be at the front of**, be first in, be ahead of, head; outdistance, outrun, outstrip, outpace, leave behind, get (further) ahead of, draw away from, shake off; outdo, excel, exceed, surpass, outclass, transcend, top, trump, cap, beat, better; widen the gap; informal leave standing, walk away from, run rings around; archaic outrival, outvie.
▷ANTONYMS follow, trail.
8 *right now, all I want is to lead a normal life*: **experience**, have, live, pass, spend, undergo.
9 *a path through the park **leads to** the beach*: **open on to**, give on to, connect with/to, provide a route to, communicate with.
□ **lead something off** *they watched his dramatic announcement lead off the Nine O'Clock News*: **begin**, start, start off, open, get going; informal kick off; formal commence.
▷ANTONYMS end, conclude.
□ **lead someone on** *he knew she was leading him on*: **deceive**, mislead, delude, hoodwink, dupe, trick, take in, fool, pull the wool over someone's eyes, gull; ensnare, entrap, entice, allure, lure, beguile, inveigle, tempt, tantalize, tease, flirt with, seduce; informal **string along**, lead up the garden path, take for a ride, put one over on.
□ **lead the way 1** *he led the way to the kitchen*: **guide**, conduct, show the way. **2** *Britain has often led the way in aerospace technology*: **take the first step**, initiate things, break (new) ground, blaze a trail, lay the foundation, lay the first stone, set in motion, prepare the way, set the ball rolling, take the initiative, make the first move, make a start; develop, introduce, start, begin, launch, instigate, institute, originate.
▷ANTONYMS follow.
□ **lead up to** *she wondered if he was leading up to suggesting that they go together*: **prepare the way for**, pave the way for, open the way for, lay the groundwork for, set the scene for; work round/up to, make overtures about, make advances about, hint at, approach the subject of, introduce the subject of; suggest, hint, imply.
▶ noun **1** *I found myself **in the lead** early in the back straight*: **leading position**, leading place, first place, advance position, van, vanguard; ahead, in front, winning, leading the field, to the fore; informal up front.
▷ANTONYMS last, losing.
2 *they took the lead in the personal computer market*: **first position**, head place, forefront, primacy, dominance, superiority, precedence, ascendancy; pre-eminence, supremacy, advantage, edge, upper hand, whip hand; head start.
▷ANTONYMS last position.
3 *Newcastle built up a 3-0 half-time lead*: **winning margin**, margin, gap, interval.
4 *sixth-formers are supposed to give a lead to younger pupils*: **example**, model, pattern, exemplar, paradigm, standard of excellence; role model.
5 *she is going to be playing the lead in Glen's movie*: **leading role**, star/starring role, star part, title role, principal part; star, principal character, male lead, female lead, leading man, leading lady, hero, heroine, protagonist.
▷ANTONYMS bit part, extra.
6 *a Labrador on a lead*: **leash**, tether, rein, cord, rope, chain, line.
7 *detectives were following up a new lead in their hunt for the killers*: **clue**, pointer, guide, hint, tip, tip-off, suggestion, indication, indicator, sign, signal, intimation, inkling; (**leads**) evidence, information.
▶ adjective *we lost the lead position due to a combination of circumstances*: **leading**, first, top, foremost, front, head; chief, principal, main, most important, premier, paramount, prime, primary.
▷ANTONYMS last.

lead[2] (rhymes with 'bed') noun *he was removing the lead from the man's chest*: **bullet**, pellet, ball, slug; shot, buckshot, ammunition.

Word links **lead**

plumbic, **plumbous** relating to lead
plumb- related prefix, as in *plumbate*

leaden adjective **1** *he levered himself up from the armchair, his eyes leaden with sleep*: **dull**, heavy, weighty; listless, lifeless, inactive, inert.
2 *on leaden feet, he moved back to the staircase*: **sluggish**, heavy, lumbering, plodding, cumbersome, slow, torpid; laboured.
▷ANTONYMS light, springy.
3 *he avoids the leaden prose which so many academics affect*: **boring**, dull, unimaginative, uninspired, uninteresting, tedious, monotonous, insipid, heavy, laboured, stilted, wooden, prosaic, stodgy.
▷ANTONYMS interesting, lively.
4 *a dour and leaden sky*: **grey**, greyish, grey-coloured, black, dark, ashen; **cloudy**, gloomy, overcast, sombre, dim, sunless, starless, louring, oppressive, threatening, dreary, dismal, dingy, bleak, dull, murky, sullen, cheerless, depressing; literary tenebrous; rare Cimmerian, caliginous.
▷ANTONYMS bright, cheerful.

leader noun **1** *the leader of the Democratic Party*: **chief**, head, principal, boss; commander, captain; figurehead, controller, superior, kingpin, headman, mover and shaker; chairman, chairwoman, chairperson, chair, convener, moderator; director, managing director, MD, manager, superintendent, supervisor, overseer, administrator, employer, master, mistress, foreman; president, premier, governor; ruler, monarch, king, queen, sovereign, emperor, tsar, prince, princess, lord, lord and master; elder, patriarch; guru, mentor, authority; informal boss man, skipper, gaffer, guv'nor, top dog, number one, big cheese, big noise, bigwig, big shot; N. Amer. informal honcho, Mister Big, numero uno, sachem, padrone.
▷ANTONYMS follower, supporter.
2 *a world leader in the use of video conferencing*: **pioneer**, front runner, innovator, trailblazer, pathfinder, groundbreaker, trendsetter, leading light, guiding light, torch-bearer, pacemaker, originator, initiator, developer, discoverer, founder, architect.

leadership noun **1** *she won the leadership of the Conservative Party*: **headship**, directorship, direction, governorship, governance, administration, jurisdiction, captaincy, superintendency, control, ascendancy, rule, command, power, mastery, domination, dominion, premiership, sovereignty.
2 *we need firm and committed leadership*: **guidance**, direction, authority, control, management, superintendence, supervision; organization, government, orchestration, initiative, influence.

leading adjective **1** *he played the leading role in his team's narrow victory*: **main**, chief, major, prime, most significant, principal, foremost, key, supreme, paramount, dominant, superior, ruling, directing, guiding, controlling, essential, cardinal, central, focal; momentous, noteworthy, notable; informal number-one.
▷ANTONYMS secondary, subordinate.
2 *the leading industrially developed countries*: **most powerful**, most important, foremost, greatest, chief, outstanding, pre-eminent, richest, principal, dominant, most influential, most illustrious, paramount, top-tier, top-rank, of the first rank, first-rate.
▷ANTONYMS minor, secondary; second-rate.
3 *last season's leading scorer*: **top**, highest, best, first; superlative, unsurpassed, unexcelled, front, in first place, lead, unparalleled, matchless, peerless, incomparable, star, arch-.
▷ANTONYMS last; worst.

leaf noun **1** *sycamore leaves*: **frond**; flag, needle, pad, blade, bract, leaflet; technical cotyledon, foliole.
2 *as he handled the book, a sheaf of loose leaves fell from the back*: **page**, sheet, folio, flyleaf.
□ **turn over a new leaf** *I see fatherhood as a chance to turn over a new leaf*: **reform**, improve, amend; mend one's ways, become a better person, change completely, make a fresh start, change for the better, reconstruct oneself; informal go straight, get back on the straight and narrow.
▷ANTONYMS backslide.
▸ verb **1** *he leafed through a pile of documents*: **flick**, flip, thumb, skim, browse, glance, look, riffle; read, scan, dip into, run one's eye over, have a look at, peruse.
2 *many plants need a period of dormancy before they leaf and flower*: **put out leaves**, bud, burst into leaves; rare foliate.

Word links **leaf**

phyllo- related prefix, as in *phylloxera*
-phyll related suffix, as in *chlorophyll*
foliar relating to leaves
foliaceous resembling leaves
foliate decorated like leaves
folivorous, phyllophagous leaf-eating

leaflet noun **pamphlet**, booklet, brochure, handbill, circular, flyer, handout, advertisement, bulletin, mailshot, bill, notice; N. Amer. folder; informal advert, ad, bumf; N. Amer. & Austral. informal dodger.

league noun **1** *he tried to form a league of chieftains*: **alliance**, confederation, confederacy, federation, union, association, coalition, combine, consortium, affiliation, guild, corporation, conglomerate, cooperative, partnership, fellowship, syndicate, compact, band, group, circle, ring; bloc, faction, axis, congress, entente; brotherhood, society, fraternity, coterie, lodge; rare consociation, sodality.
2 *we won the league last year | the football league*: **championship**, competition, contest; group, band, association.
3 *the store is not in the same league as the major supermarkets*: **class**, group, category, ability group, level of ability, level.
□ **in league with** *they confessed to being in league with foreign powers*: **collaborating with**, cooperating with, in cooperation with, in alliance with, allied with, conspiring with, leagued with, linked with, hand in glove with, in collusion with; informal in cahoots with.
▸ verb *Oscar had **leagued together** with other construction companies*: **ally**, join forces, join together, unite, form an association, band together, affiliate, combine, amalgamate, form a federation, confederate, collaborate, team up, join up.

leak verb **1** *oil leaking from the tanker*: **seep (out)**, escape, ooze (out), exude, discharge, emanate, issue, drip, dribble, drain, bleed; spill, stream, gush (out), spurt, spout, squirt, spew, jet.
2 *ageing underground tanks are leaking gasoline into the area*: **discharge**, exude, emit, eject, release, drip, dribble, pour out, send forth, ooze, excrete, secrete.
3 informal *civil servants who leak information are criticized by politicians for a breach of trust*: **disclose**, divulge, reveal, make known, make public, tell, impart, pass on, relate, communicate, expose, broadcast, publish, release, unveil, give away, betray, admit, confess, let slip, blurt out, bring into the open, bring to light; let on; informal take the lid off, blow wide open, blab, let the cat out of the bag, spill the beans, blow the gaff.
▸ noun **1** *check that there are no leaks in the bag*: **hole**, opening, puncture, perforation, prick, cut, gash, slit, nick, rent, break, rift, crack, crevice, chink, fissure, rupture, aperture.
2 *a gas leak was discovered*: **discharge**, leakage, leaking, oozing, seeping, seepage, drip, percolation; escape, gush, issue, flow, outflow, emanation; technical efflux.
3 informal *a series of leaks to the media*: **disclosure**, revelation, divulgence, uncovering, admission, confession, exposé.

leaky adjective **leaking**, dripping; cracked, split, holed, holey, punctured, perforated; porous, permeable.
▷ANTONYMS watertight.

lean[1] verb **1** *Polly leaned against the door*: **rest**, be propped up, recline, be supported.
2 *a line of palm trees leaning in the wind*: **slant**, incline, bend, tilt, be at an angle, slope, tip, bank, list, heel, careen, cant, bias, veer, sway, angle.
3 *he **leans towards** existentialist philosophy*: **tend**, incline, gravitate, have a tendency; have a propensity for, have a proclivity for, have a preference for, have a penchant for, be partial to, be attracted to, have a liking for, have an affinity with, be prone to.
4 *Jack had always been there, a strong shoulder to **lean on***: **depend**, be dependent, rely, count, bank, pin one's faith; have faith in, trust, have every confidence in, swear by, cling to; not manage without.
5 informal *I got **leaned on** by villains many times*: **intimidate**, coerce, domineer, browbeat, bully, tyrannize, pressurize, threaten, compel, pressure, put pressure on, force, drive, impel, constrain; informal twist someone's arm, put the frighteners on, put the screws on, strong-arm, push around, squeeze, bulldoze.

lean[2] adjective **1** *a tall, lean, aristocratic man*: **slim**, thin, slender, rangy, spare, wiry, slight; lissom, svelte, willowy, sylphlike; skinny, scrawny, scraggy, lanky, lank, bony, gaunt, emaciated, skin and bones, raw-boned, rangy, gangling, spindly, skeletal, size-zero, angular, pinched.
▷ANTONYMS fat.
2 *lean meat*: **non-fatty**, unfatty.
▷ANTONYMS fatty.
3 *a lean harvest*: **meagre**, scanty, sparse, poor, scant, mean, inadequate, insufficient, paltry, limited, restricted, modest, deficient, insubstantial, slight.
▷ANTONYMS abundant, plentiful.
4 *too often in lean times the poorest are asked to make the largest sacrifices*: **unproductive**, unfruitful, unprofitable, unremunerative, arid, barren; hard, bad, difficult, tough, impoverished, poverty-stricken, moneyless.
▷ANTONYMS productive, prosperous.

Word toolkit **lean**

See **thin**.

leaning noun *his early leanings were towards cooking and he went off to become a chef*: **inclination**, tendency, bent, proclivity, propensity, penchant, predisposition, predilection, proneness, partiality, preference, disposition, orientation, bias, attraction, liking, fancy, fondness, taste; weakness, hankering, appetite, thirst.

leap verb **1** *he leapt over the gate*: **jump over**, jump, vault over, vault, spring over, bound over, hurdle, skip (over), cross over, sail over, hop (over),

leapfrog, high jump, clear, negotiate.
2 *Claudia leapt to her feet*: **spring**, jump, jump up, bound, dart; lunge.
3 *we leapt to the rescue*: **rush**, hurry, hasten, hurtle.
4 *she had* **leapt at** *the chance*: **accept eagerly**, grasp, grasp with both hands, grab, take advantage of, seize (on), snatch, jump at, pounce on.
▷**ANTONYMS** reject.
5 *she had* **leapt to** *conclusions which could be hopelessly wide of the mark*: **arrive at hastily**, reach hurriedly, come to overhastily, form hastily, hurry, hasten, jump, rush, reach.
6 *profits leapt by 55%*: **increase rapidly**, soar, rocket, skyrocket, shoot up, escalate, mount, surge, spiral, grow rapidly, rise rapidly.
▷**ANTONYMS** fall, plummet.
▶**noun 1** *he had cleared the brook in an easy leap*: **jump**, vault, spring, bound, hop, skip; Ballet entrechat; rare curvet.
2 *the figures unveiled last week showed a leap of 33%*: **sudden rise**, rapid increase, escalation, soaring, surge, upsurge, upswing, upturn; increment, elevation; revival.
▷**ANTONYMS** drop.
□ **in/by leaps and bounds** *productivity can be improved in leaps and bounds*: **rapidly**, swiftly, quickly, speedily, at an amazing rate, exponentially; informal in no time (at all).
▷**ANTONYMS** slowly.

learn verb **1** *a scheme to encourage people to learn a foreign language*: **acquire a knowledge of**, gain an understanding of, acquire skill in, become competent in, become proficient in, grasp, master, take in, absorb, assimilate, pick up, digest, familiarize oneself with; become expert in, know inside out, know backwards, comprehend; study, read up on, work at, apply oneself to, be taught, have lessons in, pursue; informal get the hang of, get clued up about, get the point of.
2 *if I want to learn a poem I stick it on the fridge*: **memorize**, learn by heart, learn by rote, commit to memory, become word-perfect in, learn word for word, learn parrot-fashion, get off/down pat, have off/down pat, know, retain; informal get off by heart; archaic con.
▷**ANTONYMS** forget.
3 *he learned that the school would shortly be closing*: **discover**, find out, become aware, be made aware, be informed, have it brought to one's attention, hear, be given to understand, get to know, come to know, hear tell; gather, understand, ascertain, establish, realize, determine; informal get wind of the fact, get wise to the fact; Brit. informal suss out; N. Amer. informal dope out.

learned adjective *a learned and formidable intellectual | learned academic books*: **scholarly**, erudite, well educated, knowledgeable, well read, widely read, well versed, well informed, lettered, cultured, cultivated, civilized, intellectual, intelligent, clever, academic, literary, bookish, highbrow, studious, sage, wise, sagacious, discerning, donnish, cerebral, enlightened, illuminated, sophisticated, pedantic; esoteric, obscure, recondite; informal brainy; rare sapient.
▷**ANTONYMS** ignorant, ill-educated.

learner noun **beginner**, trainee, apprentice, pupil, student, mentee, novice, newcomer, starter, probationer, tyro, fledgling, fresher, freshman, freshwoman, neophyte, initiate, new recruit, raw recruit, new boy/girl; N. Amer. tenderfoot, novitiate; informal newbie; N. Amer. informal greenhorn, rookie.
▷**ANTONYMS** veteran, expert.

learning noun **1** *the importance of the library as a centre of learning*: **study**, studying, education, schooling, tuition, teaching, academic work, instruction, training; research, investigation; Brit. informal swotting.
2 *his second book displayed the astonishing range of his learning*: **scholarship**, knowledge, education, erudition, culture, intellect, academic attainment, acquirements, enlightenment, illumination, edification, book learning, insight, information, understanding, sageness, wisdom, sophistication; pedantry; letters.
▷**ANTONYMS** ignorance.

lease noun *they were able to acquire a 15-year lease on a factory*: **leasehold**, rental agreement, hire agreement, charter, contract; **rental**, tenancy, tenure, booking; period of occupancy, period of occupation.
▷**ANTONYMS** freehold.
▶**verb 1** *the film crew leased a large hangar and used it as their headquarters*: **rent**, hire, charter, engage, take, borrow, pay for the use of.
▷**ANTONYMS** buy.
2 *they leased the mill to a reputable family*: **rent out**, rent, let, let out, hire, hire out, sublet, sublease, farm out, charge for the use of.
▷**ANTONYMS** sell.

leash noun **1** *you should always keep your dog on a leash*: **lead**, rein, tether, rope, cord, chain, line, strap; restraint; archaic lyam.
2 *the adolescent Wolfgang found himself off the parental leash*: **control**, restraint, check, curb, rein, hold, discipline.
□ **straining at the leash** *each year some 300 youngsters are straining at the leash to get into professional golf*: **eager**, impatient, anxious, enthusiastic; informal itching, dying, gagging.
▶**verb 1** *she called the dog to heel so that she could leash him*: **put a leash on**, put a lead on, fasten, hitch up, tether, tie up, secure, bind, fetter; confine, restrain.
▷**ANTONYMS** unleash, release.
2 *the ire in her face was barely leashed*: **curb**, control, keep under control, check, restrain, hold back, suppress.
▷**ANTONYMS** unleash, release.

least determiner *I have not the least idea what this phrase could mean*: **slightest**, smallest, minimum, minimal, minutest, tiniest, littlest.
▷**ANTONYMS** greatest, most.
□ **at least** *check in at least one hour before take-off*: **at the minimum**, no less than, not less than; as a conservative estimate, at rock-bottom; more than.

leather noun *his leather jacket | a volume bound in leather*: **skin**, hide.
▶**verb** *he caught me and leathered me black and blue*: **beat**, strap, belt, thrash, flog, whip, lash, scourge, horsewhip, birch, cane, strike, hit, clout, batter, spank; informal wallop, whack, tan someone's hide, give someone a (good) hiding, lather.

leathery adjective **1** *he was about fifty, with soulful eyes and leathery skin*: **rough**, rugged, wrinkled, wrinkly, furrowed, lined, wizened, weather-beaten, callous, hard, hardened, thickened, gnarled, leather-like; technical coriaceous.
2 *leathery sides of beef*: **tough**, hard, hardened, fibrous, gristly, chewy, sinewy, stringy, leather-like; technical coriaceous.

leave[1] verb **1** *I left the hotel*: **depart from**, go away from, go from, withdraw from, retire from, take oneself off from, exit from, take one's leave of, pull out of, quit, be gone from, decamp from, disappear from, abandon, vacate, absent oneself from, evacuate; say one's farewells/goodbyes, make off, clear out, make oneself scarce, check out; abscond from, run away from, flee (from), fly from, bolt from, go AWOL, take French leave, escape (from); informal push off, shove off, cut, cut and run, do a bunk, do a disappearing act, split, vamoose, scoot, clear off, take off, make tracks, up sticks, pack one's bags, flit; Brit. informal sling one's hook.
▷**ANTONYMS** arrive, come, stay.
2 *the next morning we left for Leicester*: **set off**, head, make, begin one's journey, set sail.
3 *he's left his wife*: **abandon**, desert, discard, turn one's back on, cast aside, cast off, jilt, leave in the lurch, leave high and dry, throw over, leave stranded, brush off; informal dump, ditch, chuck, drop, walk out on, run out on, rat on, leave flat; archaic forsake.
▷**ANTONYMS** stay with.
4 *he left his job in November*: **quit**, give up, abandon, move from, resign from, retire from, bow out of, step down from, withdraw from, get out of, pull out of, back out of.
▷**ANTONYMS** stay in.
5 *she left her handbag on a bus*: **leave behind**, omit to take, forget, lose, mislay.
6 *I thought I'd leave it to the experts*: **entrust**, hand over, pass on, refer; delegate; assign, consign, allot, give, commit.
7 *when he died he left her £100,000*: **bequeath**, will, endow, hand down, transfer, convey, make over; Law demise, devise.
8 *the speech left some feelings of disappointment*: **cause**, produce, generate, give rise to, result in.
□ **leave someone in the lurch** *I wouldn't have left the club if it meant leaving them in the lurch*: **leave in trouble**, let down, leave helpless, leave stranded, leave high and dry, abandon, desert, betray; N. Amer. informal bail on; archaic forsake.
▷**ANTONYMS** help, support, come to the aid of.
□ **leave off** informal *I wish he would leave off hanging around with them*: **stop**, cease, finish, desist from, keep from, break off, lay off, give up, discontinue, refrain from, restrain oneself from, hold back from, swear off, resist the temptation to, stop oneself from, withhold from, eschew; conclude, terminate, suspend, bring to an end, renounce, forswear, forbear, relinquish; N. Amer. quit; informal give over, knock off, jack something in.
▷**ANTONYMS** continue, go on.
□ **leave someone/something out 1** *Adam left out the address on the letter*: **miss out**, omit, omit by accident, fail to include, overlook, pass over, neglect to notice, leave unnoticed, forget; skip, miss, jump.
▷**ANTONYMS** include. **2** *he was left out of the England squad*: **exclude**, omit, except, eliminate, drop, count out, disregard, ignore, reject, pass over, neglect, cut out, do away with, bar, debar, keep out.
▷**ANTONYMS** include.

leave[2] noun **1** *the judge granted leave to appeal*: **permission**, consent, authorization, sanction, warrant, dispensation, concession, indulgence, approval, clearance, blessing, agreement, backing, assent, acceptance, confirmation, ratification, mandate, licence, acquiescence, concurrence, liberty, freedom; informal the go-ahead, the green light, the OK, the rubber stamp.
2 *he was on leave from the Royal Engineers*: **holiday**, vacation, break, time off, furlough, sabbatical, leave of absence, a day/week/month off, leisure time, respite, breathing space; half-term, bank holiday, recess; informal hols, vac.

3 *if you will excuse me, I will now take my leave of you*: **departure**, leaving, leave-taking, parting, withdrawal, exit, farewell, goodbye, adieu, valediction.

> *Choose the right word* **leave, permission, consent, authorization**
>
> See **permission**.

> *Choose the right word* **leave, holiday, vacation, break**
>
> See **holiday**.

leaven noun *leaven is added to the dough and the dough is left to rise*: **leavening**, ferment, fermentation agent, raising agent, yeast, barm, baking powder.
▸ verb **1** *the biscuits are light because they use both yeast and baking powder to leaven the flour*: **raise**, make rise, ferment, work, lighten, puff up, expand, swell, inflate.
2 *his humour was sharp, but often leavened with a touch of self-mockery*: **permeate**, infuse, pervade, penetrate, imbue, suffuse, transform, modify; **enliven**, lighten, quicken, inspire, stimulate, liven up, invigorate, vivify, ginger up, energize, electrify, galvanize, perk up, brighten up, cheer up, season, spice; informal buck up, pep up, add zest to, add zing to.

leavings plural noun *the leavings of their hasty meal*: **residue**, remainder, remains, remnants, leftovers, scrapings, scraps, oddments, odds and ends, fragments, cast-offs, excess, surplus, rejects, junk, waste, dregs, refuse, rubbish, litter, debris, sweepings, detritus, lees; rare orts.

lecher noun **lecherous man**, libertine, womanizer, seducer, adulterer, debauchee, rake, roué, profligate, wanton, loose-liver, sensualist, sybarite, voluptuary, Don Juan, Casanova, Lothario, Romeo; pervert; informal lech, dirty old man, DOM, goat, wolf, ladykiller; dated rip; formal fornicator.
▷ANTONYMS puritan.

lecherous adjective *a lecherous old man*: **lustful**, licentious, lascivious, libidinous, prurient, lewd, salacious, lubricious, debauched, dissolute, wanton, loose, fast, impure, unchaste, intemperate, dissipated, degenerate, sinful, depraved, crude, goatish; sensual, libertine, promiscuous, carnal; dirty, filthy, perverted, coarse, corrupt, indecent; informal randy, horny, raunchy, pervy, naughty; rare concupiscent, lickerish.
▷ANTONYMS chaste, pure.

lechery noun **lust**, lustfulness, licentiousness, lasciviousness, lewdness, salaciousness, libertinism, libidinousness, debauchery, dissoluteness, wantonness, intemperance, dissipation, degeneracy, depravity, impurity, unchastity, immorality, looseness, immodesty; promiscuity, carnality, womanizing, rakishness; sensuality, sensualness, sexual desire, desire, sexual appetite, libido; informal randiness, horniness, raunchiness, the hots, leching; rare concupiscence, lubricity, salacity.
▷ANTONYMS chastity.

lecture noun **1** *a lecture on children's literature*: **speech**, talk, address, discourse, disquisition, presentation, oration, lesson, recitation, monologue, sermon, homily.
2 *Dad got a severe lecture for wasting his money*: **scolding**, chiding, reprimand, rebuke, reproof, reproach, remonstration, upbraiding, berating, castigation, tirade, diatribe, harangue, admonition, admonishment, lambasting, obloquy; informal dressing-down, telling-off, talking-to, tongue-lashing; Brit. informal rocket, wigging.
▷ANTONYMS commendation, pat on the back.
▸ verb **1** *he visited schools to lecture on the dangers of drugs*: **give a lecture**, give a talk, talk, give a speech, make a speech, speak, give an address, discourse, expound, hold forth, declaim, expatiate, give a sermon, sermonize, pontificate; informal speechify, preachify, spout, jaw, sound off, spiel, drone on.
2 *she lectures in Communications at Dublin University*: **teach**, tutor in, instruct in, give instruction in, give lessons in.
3 *he was lectured by the headmaster in front of the whole school*: **scold**, chide, reprimand, rebuke, reprove, reproach, remonstrate with, upbraid, berate, castigate, chastise, admonish, lambaste, nag, haul over the coals, take to task, read someone the Riot Act; informal give someone a dressing-down, give someone a talking-to, tell off; Brit. informal tick off, carpet; N. Amer. informal bawl out.

lecturer noun **1** *this year's Reith lecturer is a journalist*: **public speaker**, speaker, speech-maker, orator, declaimer, preacher; rhetorician.
2 *a lecturer in economics*: **university teacher**, college teacher, tutor, reader, instructor, scholar, don, professor, fellow, doctor, researcher; academic, academician, pedagogue, educator, educationalist; informal boffin, egghead; rare preceptor.

ledge noun *she arranged the plants in a row on the ledge* | *a cliff ledge*: **shelf**, sill, mantel, mantelpiece, mantelshelf, shelving; **projection**, protrusion, overhang, extension, ridge, step, prominence, spur, jut, bulge, flange.

ledger noun *a sales ledger*: **book**, account book, record book, register, registry, log; records, archives, books; balance sheet, financial statement.

lee noun *they sat in the lee of the wall*: **shelter**, protection, cover, refuge, safety, security, sanctuary, haven, shield.

leech noun *the smug faces of leeches feeding off the hard-working majority*: **parasite**, clinger, barnacle, bloodsucker, cadger, passenger, layabout; extortioner; sycophant, toady, hanger-on, fawner, yes man; informal **scrounger**, sponger, freeloader, ligger; N. Amer. informal mooch, moocher.

leer verb *Henry* ***leered at*** *her*: **ogle**, look lasciviously, look suggestively, give sly looks to, eye, watch, stare, goggle; informal give someone the glad eye, give someone a/the once-over, lech after/over, drool over, undress someone with one's eyes; Brit. informal gawp, gawk; Austral./NZ informal perv on.
▸ noun *he gave me a sly leer*: **lecherous look**, lascivious look, suggestive look, ogle, sly glance, stare; informal the glad eye, the once-over.

leery adjective informal *he was a bit leery of her from the buffeting she'd given him earlier*. See **wary**.

lees plural noun *the lees in the bottom of the cask*: **sediment**, dregs, deposit, grounds, settlings, residue, remains, accumulation, silt, sludge; technical precipitate, sublimate, residuum; rare draff, grouts.

leeway noun *this has left the police with some leeway to interpret the law for themselves*: **freedom**, **scope**, room to manoeuvre, latitude, elbow room, slack, space, room, liberty, room to spare, room to operate, scope for initiative, freedom of action, freedom from restriction, a free hand, flexibility, independence, licence, self-determination, free rein, free play, unrestrictedness, indulgence, margin, play, give, laxity, leisure; French carte blanche.
▷ANTONYMS constraint, restriction.

left adjective *my left arm*: **left-hand**, sinistral; Nautical port; Nautical, archaic larboard; Heraldry sinister, sinistrous.
▷ANTONYMS right; starboard; dexter.

> *Word links* **left**
>
> **sinistral** relating to the left
> **laevo-**, **sinistro-** related prefixes, as in *laevorotatory*, *sinistrorse*

left-handed adjective **1** *a left-handed golfer*: sinistral; informal southpaw.
▷ANTONYMS right-handed.
2 *a left-handed compliment*: **backhanded**, ambiguous, equivocal, uncertain, double-meaning, double-edged; dubious, indirect, enigmatic, cryptic, paradoxical, ironic, sardonic, insincere, hypocritical.
▷ANTONYMS forthright.

leftover noun **1** *she looks like a leftover from Woodstock in her flowery dress*: **residue**, **survivor**, legacy, vestige, trace.
2 (**leftovers**) *she saves leftovers in a plastic container*: **leavings**, **uneaten food**, remainder, unused supplies, scraps, remnants, remains, scourings, slops, crumbs, dregs; excess, surplus, overage; rejects, offcuts, tail ends, odds and ends, bits and bobs, oddments.
▸ adjective *leftover food*: **remaining**, left; uneaten, unconsumed; excess, surplus, superfluous, extra, additional, unused, unwanted, spare, in reserve, excessive; residual, surviving.

left-wing adjective *a left-wing political group*: **socialist**, **communist**, communistic, Bolshevik, leftist; radical, revolutionary, militant, red; progressive, liberal, reforming, social-democrat, politically correct; Labour, Labourite; Marxist, Leninist, Marxist–Leninist, Trotskyite, Maoist; informal, derogatory Commie, Lefty, pink, bolshie.
▷ANTONYMS right-wing, conservative, reactionary.

leg noun **1** *he broke his leg in a football match*: **lower limb**, shank; limb, member; technical crus; informal stump, peg, pin.
2 *a gilded table leg*: **upright**, support, prop, brace, underpinning, column.
3 *the first leg of a European tour*: **part**, **stage**, portion, segment, section, bit, phase, stretch, lap, step, instalment; passage, subdivision, subsection, juncture.
□ **give someone a leg up** *parents want to give their kids a leg up in the world*: **help/assist someone**, act as someone's support, give someone assistance, lend someone a helping hand, come to someone's aid; give someone a boost, boost, advance, raise, kick-start, give someone a flying start.
□ **on its last legs 1** *your car looked as though it was on its last legs*: **dilapidated**, worn out, rickety, about to break, about to fall apart, about to collapse. ▷ANTONYMS in good condition.
2 *a foundry business that was on its last legs*: **about to fail**, failing, about to go bankrupt, near to ruin, going to the wall; informal **going bust**, going down the toilet. ▷ANTONYMS thriving.
□ **pull someone's leg** *it's all right, Robbie, I was only pulling your leg*: **tease**, rag, make fun of, chaff, trick, joke with, play a joke on, play a trick on, play a practical joke on, taunt, jest; hoax, fool, deceive, misguide, lead on, hoodwink, dupe, beguile, gull; informal kid, have on, rib, wind up, take for a ride, lead up the garden path, take the mickey out of, make a monkey out of; N. Amer. informal put on.
□ **stretch one's legs** *after two days on the bus we were glad of the chance to*

stretch our legs: **go for a walk**, take a walk, go for a stroll, walk, stroll, move about, promenade, get some exercise, get some air, take the air.

▶ verb

□ **leg it** informal **1** *if the dog starts growling, leg it!* **run away**, run, flee, make off, make a break for it, escape, hurry, decamp; informal hightail it, hotfoot it, make a run for it, make tracks, cut and run, skedaddle, vamoose, show a clean pair of heels, split, scoot, scram, hook it; Brit. informal scarper, do a runner, have it away (on one's toes), get cracking, get a move on.
▷ANTONYMS stay. **2** *I am part of a sales team legging it around London*: **walk**, march, tramp, trek, trudge, plod, wander, ramble, go on foot; informal go on Shanks's pony.

Word links **leg**

crural relating to a leg

legacy noun **1** *a legacy from a great aunt had paid for their house*: **bequest**, inheritance, heritage, bequeathal, bestowal, benefaction, endowment, gift, patrimony, heirloom, settlement, birthright, provision; Law devise, hereditament.
2 *the rancorous legacy of the Vietnam war | a legacy of the British Empire*: **consequence**, effect, outcome, upshot, spin-off, repercussion, aftermath, by-product, product, result; residue, fruits.

legal adjective **1** *the Government possessed no legal power to close down this newspaper*: **lawful**, legitimate, licit, within the law, legalized, valid; permissible, permitted, allowable, allowed, above board, admissible, acceptable; authorized, sanctioned, warranted, licensed, official, enforceable, constitutional, statutory, statutable, ex cathedra, binding, bona fide, genuine; right, proper, sound, just, fair, rightful, de jure, honest, upright; informal legit, kosher.
▷ANTONYMS illegal, criminal.
2 *the legal profession*: **judicial**, juridical, jurisdictive, judicatory, forensic.

legality noun *provisions governing the legality of strikes and unions*: **lawfulness**, legitimacy, legitimateness, licitness, validity, rightness, rightfulness, soundness, admissibility, admissibleness, permissibility, constitutionality; justice, fairness, justness, equity, properness.

legalize verb *a campaign to legalize marijuana*: **make legal**, decriminalize, legitimize, legitimatize, legitimate, validate, ratify, permit, allow, admit, accept, authorize, sanction, warrant, license, approve, countenance, pronounce lawful, give the stamp of approval to; regularize, regulate, normalize; informal OK, give the go-ahead to, give the thumbs up to, give the OK to, give the green light to, say the word, give one's blessing to.
▷ANTONYMS prohibit.

legate noun *a papal legate*: **envoy**, emissary, agent, ambassador, representative, nuncio, commissioner, commissary, delegate, proxy, surrogate, deputy, spokesperson, plenipotentiary, messenger; Scottish depute; informal go-between.

legatee noun *his will made her his sole legatee*: **beneficiary**, inheritor, heir, heiress, recipient, receiver, payee, assignee; Law devisee, grantee; Scottish Law heritor.

legation noun **1** *the train carrying the British legation to Istanbul*: **diplomatic mission**, mission, embassy, consulate, ministry, delegation, deputation, representation, contingent, commission; envoys, delegates, deputies, diplomats, aides.
2 *the legations in the capital were besieged*: **embassy**, consulate, diplomatic establishment.

legend noun **1** *the Arthurian legends*: **myth**, saga, epic, folk tale, folk story, traditional story, tale, story, fairy tale, narrative, fable, romance; folklore, lore, mythology, fantasy, oral history, tradition, folk tradition, old wives' tales; technical mythos, mythus; informal yarn.
2 *pop legends like the Beatles*: **celebrity**, star, superstar, icon, famous person, great, genius, phenomenon, luminary, giant, big name; informal celeb, megastar.
3 *'the most distinguished address in Ireland' boasted the legend on the desk notepad*: **caption**, **inscription**, dedication, motto, slogan, device, heading, head, title, wording, subtitle, subheading, rubric, colophon.
4 *the experimental conditions were as described in the legend to Figure 5*: **explanation**, key, code, cipher, table of symbols, guide, glossary.

legendary adjective **1** *the legendary high kings of Ireland*: **fabled**, heroic, ancient, traditional, fairy-tale, storybook, romantic, mythical, mythological.
▷ANTONYMS factual, historical.
2 *a legendary figure in the trade-union movement*: **famous**, **celebrated**, famed, renowned, acclaimed, illustrious, esteemed, honoured, exalted, lauded, lionized, vaunted, venerable, notable, noted, well known, popular, prominent, distinguished, great, eminent, pre-eminent, outstanding, revered, glorious, remembered, immortal, unforgettable.
▷ANTONYMS unknown, obscure, unsung.

legerdemain noun **1** *stage magicians practising legerdemain*: **sleight of hand**, juggling, conjuring, magic, prestidigitation, wizardry, illusion, dexterity; rare thaumaturgy.
2 *a classic piece of management legerdemain*: **trickery**, cunning, artfulness, craftiness, craft, wiles, chicanery, skulduggery, deceit, deception, artifice, cheating, dissimulation, double-dealing, artful argument, specious reasoning, sophistry, humbug, flimflam; Brit. informal jiggery-pokery; archaic stratagem.

legibility noun *type design and layout clearly affect the legibility of the text*: **readability**, clarity, readableness, ease of reading, decipherability, clearness, legibleness, plainness, neatness.

legible adjective *she had large, legible handwriting*: **readable**, easily read, easy to read, decipherable, easily deciphered, clear, distinct, plain, carefully written, neat, sharp, vivid, intelligible, understandable, comprehensible; printed.
▷ANTONYMS illegible.

legion noun **1** *a Roman legion*: **brigade**, regiment, battalion, company, troop, division, squadron, squad, platoon, contingent, unit, force, corps, garrison, section, group, detachment, commando, battery, band, outfit, cohort.
2 *there were legions of photographers and TV cameras*: **horde**, host, throng, multitude, crowd, drove, mass, mob, rabble, gang, swarm, flock, herd, body, pack, score, mountain, army, sea, abundance, profusion.
▶ adjective *her fans, who are legion, will love it*: **numerous**, countless, innumerable, incalculable, immeasurable, untold, endless, limitless, boundless, myriad, many, abundant, plentiful, thick on the ground; informal umpteen.

legislate verb *the parliament will have powers to legislate for Scotland's domestic affairs*: **make laws**, pass laws, enact laws, formulate laws, establish laws, codify laws, ratify laws, constitutionalize, put laws in force; decree, order, ordain, prescribe, authorize, make provision, rule, lay down laws.

legislation noun **1** *it will require legislation to change this situation*: **law-making**, law enactment, law formulation, codification, prescription, ratification.
2 *he demanded the repeal of anti-union legislation*: **law**, body of laws, constitution, rules, rulings, regulations, acts, bills, statutes, enactments, charters, ordinances, measures, canon, code; jurisprudence.

legislative adjective *a legislative assembly*: **law-making**, law-giving, judicial, juridical, jurisdictive, parliamentary, congressional, senatorial, deliberative, governmental, policy-making, administrative; rare legislatorial.

legislator noun **lawmaker**, lawgiver, parliamentarian, politician, representative, minister, statesman, stateswoman; in the UK Member of Parliament, MP; in the US congressman, congresswoman, senator.

legitimate adjective **1** *they have been given permission to run gambling halls, the only legitimate gambling in the area*: **legal**, lawful, licit, legalized, authorized, permitted, permissible, allowable, allowed, admissible, recognized, sanctioned, approved, licensed, statutory, constitutional, within the law, going by the rules, above board, valid, honest, upright; informal legit, by the book.
▷ANTONYMS illegal, illegitimate.
2 *the legitimate heir*: **rightful**, lawful, genuine, authentic, real, true, proper, correct, authorized, sanctioned, warranted, acknowledged, recognized, approved, just; informal legit, kosher, pukka.
▷ANTONYMS false, fraudulent.
3 *these are legitimate grounds for unease*: **valid**, sound, admissible, acceptable, well founded, justifiable, reasonable, sensible, tenable, defensible, supportable, just, warrantable, fair, bona fide, proper, genuine, plausible, credible, believable, reliable, understandable, logical, rational.
▷ANTONYMS invalid, unjustifiable.

legitimize verb *the formal recognition of a union legitimizes workers' resistance to intimidation*: **validate**, legitimate, permit, warrant, authorize, sanction, license, give the stamp of approval to, condone, justify, vindicate, endorse, approve, support, sustain; legalize, pronounce lawful, declare legal, decriminalize, normalize.
▷ANTONYMS outlaw.

leisure noun *whenever Paul had leisure he worked on the manuscript | the trade-off between leisure and work*: **free time**, spare time, spare moments, time to spare, idle hours, time off, freedom, holiday, vacation, breathing space, breathing spell, respite, relief, ease, peace, quiet; **recreation**, relaxation, inactivity, amusement, entertainment, pleasure, diversion, distraction, fun, games, fun and games; informal time to kill, R and R.
▷ANTONYMS work.
□ **at your leisure** *wander at your leisure through the wide selection of shops*: **at your convenience**, when it suits you, in your own (good) time, when you can fit it in, without need for haste, without haste, unhurriedly, without hurry, when you get round to it, when you want to; in due course.

leisurely adjective *the journey was taken at a leisurely pace | a leisurely stroll*: **unhurried**, relaxed, unrushed, easy, easy-going, gentle, sedate, comfortable, restful, effortless, undemanding, slow, lazy, lackadaisical, languid, languorous, lingering; measured, steady; informal laid-back.
▷ANTONYMS brisk, hurried.

lend verb **1** *I'll lend you my towel*: **loan**, give someone the loan of, let someone use, let someone have the use of; **advance**; Brit. informal sub.
▷ANTONYMS borrow; withhold.
2 *these examples lend weight to his assertions*: **add**, impart, give, bestow, confer, provide, grant, supply, furnish, accord, offer, contribute, afford, bring, donate.
▷ANTONYMS detract.
□ **lend an ear listen**, keep one's ears open, prick up one's ears; **pay attention**, take notice, be attentive, attend, concentrate, heed, pay heed, give ear, give one's undivided attention; informal be all ears, pin back one's ears; archaic hearken.
□ **lend a hand** *an agricultural student who had come to lend a hand with the harvest*: **help**, help out, give a helping hand, assist, give assistance, aid, make a contribution, do someone a favour, take part, do one's bit; cooperate; informal pitch in, muck in, get stuck in, get involved.
□ **lend itself to** *the landscape does not lend itself to long-distance walking or riding*: **be suitable for**, be suited to, be appropriate for, be adaptable to, have the right characteristics for, be applicable for, be easily used for, be readily used for, be serviceable for.

length noun **1** *some of these amphibians grew to a length of three or four metres | from the plane she was able to see the whole length of the valley*: **extent**, extent lengthwise, distance, distance lengthwise, linear measure, span, reach; area, expanse, stretch, range, scope.
2 *there has been a tremendous increase in the length of time spent on remand*: **period, duration**, stretch, term, span.
3 *a length of pale blue silk*: **piece**, swatch, portion, section, measure, segment, roll.
4 *MPs criticized the length of the speech*: **protractedness**, lengthiness, extent, extensiveness, elongation; prolixity, prolixness, wordiness, verbosity, verboseness, long-windedness.
▷ANTONYMS conciseness, brevity.
□ **at length 1** *he spoke at length of his suitability for the job*: **for a long time**, for ages, for hours, on and on, interminably, endlessly, incessantly, ceaselessly, constantly, continually, unendingly, eternally, forever.
▷ANTONYMS briefly. **2** *when questioned at length he insisted he had no links with terrorists*: **thoroughly**, fully, in detail, in depth, comprehensively, exhaustively, completely, extensively, to the fullest extent. **3** *his search had led him, at length, to the headquarters in Seattle*: **after a long time**, after a considerable time, eventually, in time, in the long run, in the fullness of time; finally, at last, at long last, lastly, in the end, ultimately, in conclusion. ▷ANTONYMS immediately, straight away.
□ **go to any length(s)** *they'll go to any lengths to obtain money to buy drugs*: **do absolutely anything**, go to any extreme, go to any limits, observe no limits.

lengthen verb **1** *he followed her, lengthening his stride to keep up*: **elongate**, make longer, stretch out, extend; expand, widen, broaden, enlarge.
▷ANTONYMS shorten.
2 *they flower in the spring when the days are lengthening*: **grow longer**, get longer, draw out, stretch.
▷ANTONYMS contract, decrease.
3 *you'll need to lengthen the cooking time*: **prolong**, make longer, increase, extend, expand, protract, stretch out, draw out, drag out, spin out.
▷ANTONYMS curtail, truncate.

lengthy adjective **1** *a lengthy civil war*: **long**, very long, of considerable length, long-lasting, prolonged, extended, extensive.
▷ANTONYMS short.
2 *the board held lengthy discussions on the report*: **protracted**, very long, overlong, long-drawn-out; diffuse, discursive, verbose, wordy, garrulous, prolix, long-winded, ponderous, digressive, rambling, dragged out; **tedious**, boring, interminable, wearisome.
▷ANTONYMS brief, concise.

leniency, lenience noun *the judge rejected pleas for greater leniency*: **mercifulness**, mercy, clemency, lenity, forgiveness; tolerance, forbearance, moderateness, lack of severity, moderation, humanity, charity, indulgence, gentleness, mildness, sufferance, acceptance; pity, sympathy, compassion, understanding, concern, consideration, kindness, kind-heartedness, benevolence; soft-heartedness, permissiveness, liberality, liberalness.
▷ANTONYMS mercilessness, strictness, severity.

lenient adjective *the courts may be more lenient with female offenders*: **merciful**, clement, sparing, forgiving, forbearing, tolerant, moderate, charitable, humane, indulgent, easy-going, magnanimous, sympathetic, compassionate, pitying, kind, kindly, kind-hearted, benevolent, gentle; liberal, permissive, soft, soft-hearted.
▷ANTONYMS merciless, severe, strict.

> *Word toolkit* **lenient**
>
> See **humane**.

leper noun *a social leper*: **outcast**, social outcast, pariah, untouchable, undesirable, exile, reject, non-person, unperson, persona non grata.

leprechaun noun **pixie, goblin**, elf, sprite, fairy, gnome, imp, brownie, puck, devil; (**leprechauns**) the little people.

lesbian noun **homosexual woman**, gay woman; rare tribade, invert; informal les, lesbo, lezzy, butch, femme, dyke, bulldyke; informal, derogatory rug-muncher, carpet-muncher; W. Indian zami.
▷ANTONYMS heterosexual, straight.
▶ **adjective homosexual**, gay, lesbigay, GLBT (gay, lesbian, bisexual, or transgendered); rare tribadic; informal les, lesbo, butch, lezzy, dykey; informal, derogatory queer, bent.
▷ANTONYMS heterosexual, straight.

lesion noun *he lost a lot of weight and the purple-black lesions on his skin began to spread*: **wound**, injury, bruise, abrasion, contusion, scratch, scrape, cut, gash, laceration, tear, puncture; ulcer, ulceration, sore, running sore, abscess, carbuncle, canker; mark; technical trauma.

less pronoun *the fare is* **less than** *£1*: **a smaller amount**; not so much as, not as much as, under, below; informal shy of.
▷ANTONYMS more.
▶ **determiner** *there was less noise now in the town*: **not so much**, not so great, smaller, slighter, shorter, reduced; fewer.
▷ANTONYMS more.
▶ **adverb** *we must consider the alternatives available so we can use the car less*: **to a lesser degree**, to a smaller extent, not so much, not as much; rarely, barely, little, not much.
▷ANTONYMS more.
▶ **preposition** *normally the buyer purchases at list price less 10 per cent*: **minus**, subtracting, excepting, without, lacking.
▷ANTONYMS plus.

> *Easily confused words* **less or fewer?**
>
> In standard English, **less** should be used only with mass nouns, as in *I have less money than I thought*, or with numbers or expressions of time, as in *less than three weeks*. With countable nouns, **fewer** should be used, as in *customers with fewer than five items*.

lessen verb **1** *exercise lessens the risk of coronary heart disease*: **reduce**, **make less**, minimize, make smaller, decrease; allay, assuage, alleviate, attenuate, palliate, ease, dull, deaden, blunt, take the edge off, moderate, mitigate, check, dampen, depress, soften, tone down, dilute, relax, mollify, temper, weaken, tame, erode; narrow, lower, discount; curtail, prune, pare down, truncate; informal slash.
▷ANTONYMS increase, magnify.
2 *the pain in his chest began to lessen*: **grow less**, get less, grow smaller, decrease, diminish, decline, subside, abate, moderate; fade, die down/off, let up, ease off, tail off, drop, drop off/away, fall, dwindle, taper off, peter out, go/come down, shrink, contract; ebb, wane, erode, waste away, flag, attenuate, slacken, lighten, quieten, recede, relent, remit, desist; sink, slump, plummet; informal nosedive.
▷ANTONYMS increase, grow.
3 *his behaviour lessened him in their eyes*: **diminish**, lower, reduce, minimize, degrade, discredit, devalue, belittle, humble.
▷ANTONYMS aggrandize, make more important.

lesser adjective **1** *a lesser offence*: **less important**, minor, secondary, subsidiary, marginal, ancillary, auxiliary, supplementary, supplemental, peripheral; inferior, slighter, insignificant, unimportant, petty; lower, lower-level, lower-grade, second-rate.
▷ANTONYMS greater, primary.
2 *you look down your nose at us lesser mortals*: **subordinate**, minor, inferior, second-class, subservient, lowly, humble, servile, menial, mean; junior.
▷ANTONYMS superior.

lesson noun **1** *a maths lesson*: **class**, session, seminar, tutorial, lecture, period; period of instruction, period of teaching, period of coaching, period of tutoring, period of schooling.
2 *they should be industrious at their lessons*: **exercise**, assignment, school task, drill; (**lessons**) school work, homework.
3 *she would always volunteer to read the lesson in assembly*: **Bible reading**, Bible passage, scripture, text, reading.
4 *Stuart's accident should be a lesson to all parents*: **warning**, deterrent, caution; example, exemplar; message, moral, precept.
5 (**lessons**) *it was a tough time, and it taught her some hard lessons*: **knowledge**, wisdom, enlightenment, experience, truths.

lest conjunction *he cut the remark out of the final programme lest it should offend listeners*: **in case**, just in case, for fear that, in order to avoid, to avoid the risk of.

let verb **1** *let him sleep for now*: **allow**, permit, give permission to, give leave to, authorize, sanction, grant, grant the right to, warrant, license, empower, enable, entitle; assent to, consent to, agree to, acquiesce in, accede to, approve of, tolerate, countenance, suffer, brook, admit of, give one's blessing to, give assent to; cause, make; informal give the green light to, give the go-ahead to, give the thumbs up to, give someone/something the nod, say the magic word, OK.

▷ANTONYMS prevent, prohibit.
2 *Wilcox pushed open the door to let her through*: **allow to go**, permit to pass; make way for.
3 *they hired an agent to let their flat*: **rent out**, let out, rent, lease, hire, hire out, loan, give on loan, sublet, sublease, farm out, contract, charge for the use of.
□ **let someone down** *it's his players who have let the team down*: **fail**, fail to support, fall short of expectation; **disappoint**, disillusion, disenchant; abandon, desert, leave stranded, leave in the lurch, leave high and dry, betray, neglect, jilt; stab in the back; N. Amer. informal bail on; archaic forsake.
▷ANTONYMS support, satisfy; do one's bit.
□ **let something down** *I put on a skirt which Sylvie had let down for me*: **lengthen**, make longer.
▷ANTONYMS take up.
□ **let fly 1** *he let fly with a brick*: **hurl**, fling, throw, propel, pitch, lob, toss, launch, cast, shy, project, catapult, bowl; shoot, fire, blast, discharge; informal chuck, sling, heave. **2** *she* ***let fly at*** *Geoffrey*: **lose one's temper with**, lash out at, scold, criticize, condemn, chastise, chide, rant at, inveigh against, rail against, abuse, revile; explode, burst out, erupt with anger, let someone have it, give free rein to one's emotions, keep nothing back, give vent to one's emotions; informal carpet, give someone a rocket, tear someone off a strip, tear into; rare excoriate.
□ **let go** *apply the brakes before you* ***let go of*** *the pushchair*: **release**, release one's hold on, loose/loosen one's hold on, relinquish, unhand, surrender, give up.
▷ANTONYMS hold tight.
□ **let someone go** *I was upset about letting him go, but he assured me he'd find another job*: **make redundant**, dismiss, discharge, lay off, give notice to, pay off, remove, release; informal sack, give someone the sack, fire, give someone their cards, give someone their marching orders, send packing, give someone the boot, give someone the bullet, give someone the push, give someone the (old) heave-ho, boot out, axe.
▷ANTONYMS retain.
□ **let someone in** *a young lady came to open the gate and let me in*: **allow to enter**, allow in, admit, take in, open the door to, grant entrance to, give access to, allow entry to, permit entry to, give right of entry to; receive, welcome, greet, accept.
▷ANTONYMS refuse admission to.
□ **let someone in on something** *he asked to be let in on the joke*: **include**, count in, admit; **allow to share in**, let participate in, take in, inform about, tell about, bring up to date about.
□ **let something off** *some members of the family let off fireworks in the background*: **detonate**, discharge, explode, set off, fire off.
□ **let someone off 1** *I'll let you off this time, but don't try a trick like that again*: **pardon**, forgive, grant an amnesty to, amnesty; release, discharge; deal leniently with, be lenient on/to, be merciful to, show mercy to, have mercy on; acquit, absolve, exonerate, clear, exculpate, vindicate; let bygones be bygones, bear no malice, harbour no grudge, bury the hatchet; informal let someone off the hook, go easy on. **2** *he let me off work for the day*: **excuse from**, relieve from, exempt from, spare from.
□ **let on** informal **1** *I never let on that Uncle Joe made me feel anxious*: **reveal**, make known, tell, disclose, mention, divulge, let out, let slip, give away, leak, proclaim, blurt out, expose, bring to light, uncover, make public; blab; informal let the cat out of the bag, give the game away, sing, squeal.
▷ANTONYMS conceal, keep quiet about. **2** *they all let on they didn't hear me*: **pretend**, feign, affect, make out, make believe, simulate, fake.
□ **let something out 1** *I let out a cry of triumph*: **utter**, emit, give vent to, produce, give, issue, express, air, voice, verbalize, release, pour out, come out with. ▷ANTONYMS suppress.
2 *she let out that he'd given her a lift home*: **reveal**, make known, tell, disclose, mention, divulge, let slip, give away, let it be known, leak, blurt out, expose, bring to light, uncover, make public, blab. ▷ANTONYMS keep quiet about.
□ **let someone out** *they should never have let Carolyn out of hospital like that*: **release**, liberate, free, set free, let go, discharge; set/turn/let loose, allow to leave, open the door for, grant exit to; uncage, unfetter, unshackle.
▷ANTONYMS imprison.
□ **let up** informal **1** *the rain had let up, so we walked*: **abate**, lessen, decrease, diminish, subside, moderate, decline, relent, slacken, die down/off, ease (off), tail off, taper off, drop off/away, peter out; ebb, wane, dwindle, fade, quieten (down), calm (down), weaken; stop, cease, finish, come to a stop, come to an end, terminate. ▷ANTONYMS continue.
2 *you never let up, do you?* **relax one's efforts**, relax, ease up/off, do less, slow down; **pause**, break (off), take a break, take a breath; adjourn, desist, rest, hold back, stop; informal take a breather.
3 *I promised you I'd* ***let up on*** *him*: **treat less severely**, be more lenient with, be kinder to; informal go easy on. ▷ANTONYMS treat harshly.

let-down noun *it's a big let-down when bonfire parties fizzle out*: **disappointment**, disillusionment, anticlimax, comedown, non-success, non-event, fiasco, setback, frustration, blow; informal washout, damp squib.
▷ANTONYMS triumph, climax.

lethal adjective *a lethal weapon | those pills were lethal*: **fatal**, deadly, mortal, causing death, death-dealing, life-threatening, murderous, homicidal, killing, terminal, final, incurable; poisonous, toxic, virulent, noxious, venomous; dangerous, destructive, harmful, pernicious, malignant, disastrous, calamitous, ruinous; literary deathly, nocuous, mephitic; archaic baneful.
▷ANTONYMS harmless, safe.

lethargic adjective *she became depressed and lethargic*: **sluggish**, inert, inactive, slow, torpid, lifeless, dull; **languid**, listless, lazy, idle, indolent, shiftless, slothful, phlegmatic, apathetic, passive, weary, tired, fatigued, sleepy, drowsy, enervated, somnolent, narcotic.
▷ANTONYMS vigorous, energetic, animated.

> *Choose the right word* **lethargic, languid, listless**
>
> See **languid**.

lethargy noun *with an effort, Miles shook off the lethargy that had been creeping over him since his wife's death*: **sluggishness**, inertia, inactivity, inaction, slowness, torpor, torpidity, lifelessness, dullness, listlessness, languor, languidness, stagnation, laziness, idleness, indolence, shiftlessness, sloth, phlegm, apathy, passivity, ennui, weariness, tiredness, lassitude, fatigue, sleepiness, drowsiness, enervation, somnolence, narcosis; rare hebetude.
▷ANTONYMS vigour, energy, animation.

letter noun **1** *a gold chain which spelled out Zara in half-inch letters*: **alphabetical character**, character, sign, symbol, mark, type, figure, device, rune; technical grapheme.
2 *she received a letter from the king*: **written message**, message, written communication, communication, note, line, missive, epistle, dispatch, report, bulletin; correspondence, news, information, intelligence, word; post, mail.
3 (**letters**) *a man of letters*: **learning**, scholarship, erudition, education, knowledge, book learning, academic training; intellect, intelligence, enlightenment, illumination, wisdom, sagacity, culture, cultivation; literature, books, humanities, belles-lettres.
□ **to the letter** *he followed her instructions to the letter*: **strictly**, precisely, exactly, accurately, closely, faithfully, religiously, punctiliously, literally, with a literal interpretation, with strict attention to detail, word for word, letter for letter, verbatim, in every detail, by the book.
▷ANTONYMS in general terms, approximately.

> *Word links* **letter**
>
> **literal** relating to alphabetical letters
> **epistolary** relating to letters (correspondence)

lettered adjective *my mother was not a lettered woman, but she knew the importance of a good education*: **learned**, erudite, academic, well educated, educated, literate, well read, widely read, knowledgeable, intellectual, schooled, well schooled, enlightened, illuminated, sophisticated, accomplished, versed, cultured, cultivated, civilized, scholarly, scholastic, literary, bookish, highbrow, studious; informal brainy.
▷ANTONYMS ignorant, ill-educated.

let-up noun informal *there can be no let-up in the war against drugs*: **abatement**, lessening, decrease, diminishing, diminution, subsidence, moderation, decline, relenting, remission, slackening, weakening, relaxation, dying down, easing off, tailing off, tapering off, dropping away/off, ebbing, waning, dwindling; respite, break, interval, hiatus, suspension, cessation, stop, pause, breathing space, lull, interlude, intermission.
▷ANTONYMS continuation, escalation.

level adjective **1** *these wallcoverings need to be hung on a smooth and level surface*: **flat**, smooth, even, uniform, plane, flush, plumb, regular, true; (as) flat as a pancake; perfectly horizontal; perfectly vertical.
▷ANTONYMS uneven, bumpy.
2 *he did his best to keep his voice level*: **unchanging**, steady, unvarying, stable, even, uniform, regular, consistent, constant; invariable, unalterable, unaltering, unfluctuating; calm, unemotional, composed, equable, unruffled, serene, tranquil.
▷ANTONYMS unsteady, shaky.
3 *he missed a penalty when the scores were level | just four minutes later Spurs were level*: **equal**, even, drawn, tied, balanced, all square, on a level, in a position of equality; close together, neck and neck, level pegging, nip and tuck, side by side, on a par, evenly matched, with nothing to choose between them; informal even-steven(s).
▷ANTONYMS unequal, uneven.
4 *his eyes were* ***level with*** *hers*: **aligned**, on the same level as, on a level, at the same height as, in line, balanced; abreast, side by side.
▷ANTONYMS above, below, uneven.
▶ noun **1** *the post, which is at research-officer level, will be for two years*: **rank**, standing, status, position; echelon, station, degree, grade, gradation, stage, standard, rung, point, mark, step; class, stratum, group, grouping, set,

classification; level of achievement, degree of competence.
2 *they allowed a high level of employment*: **quantity**, **amount**, extent, measure, degree, volume, size; magnitude, intensity, pitch, strength; proportion.
3 *the lock is being opened so that the level of water is raised allowing a boat to pass through*: **height**, highness, altitude, elevation, distance upward.
4 *the museum tour begins on the sixth level and continues on the floors above*: **floor**, storey, tier, deck.
□ **on the level** informal **genuine**, straight, honest, above board, fair, true, legitimate, sincere, straightforward, proper, honest-to-goodness; informal upfront, kosher; N. Amer. informal on the up and up.
▷ANTONYMS dishonest.
▶ **verb 1** *tilt the tin to level the mixture*: **make level**, level out, level off, make even, even off, even out, make flat, flatten, smooth, smooth out, plane, make uniform, make regular, regularize; polish, face.
2 *they called in air strikes to level the building*: **raze**, raze to the ground, demolish, flatten, gut, topple, lay waste, destroy, wipe out, blow up, blow to bits, bomb; tear down, knock down, pull down, bring down, bulldoze, fell, dismantle, break up, wreck, pulverize, obliterate.
▷ANTONYMS raise, build.
3 *he levelled his opponent with a single blow*: **knock down**, knock to the ground, throw to the ground, lay out, prostrate, flatten, floor, fell, knock out; informal KO, kayo.
4 *Carl levelled the score with an ice-cool goal*: **equalize**, make equal, equal, even, even up, make level.
5 *he levelled his pistol at me*: **aim**, point, direct, train, sight, focus, turn, beam, zero in on, draw a bead on; take aim.
6 *I knew you'd level with me sooner or later*: **be frank**, be open, be honest, be above board, tell the truth, tell all, hide nothing, keep nothing back, be straightforward, put all one's cards on the table; informal be upfront.

Word links **level**

plano- related prefix, as in *planographic*, *planoconcave*

level-headed adjective **sensible**, practical, realistic, prudent, circumspect, pragmatic, wise, reasonable, rational, mature, commonsensical, full of common sense, judicious, sound, sober, businesslike, no-nonsense, sane, composed, calm, cool, collected, {cool, calm, and collected}, serene, relaxed, at ease, confident, well balanced, equable, moderate, unworried, unmoved, unemotional, cool-headed, hard-headed, balanced, self-possessed, unruffled, even-tempered, imperturbable, reliable, dependable, with one's feet on the ground; informal unflappable, together.
▷ANTONYMS excitable.

lever noun **1** *you can insert a lever and prise the rail off*: **crowbar**, bar, handspike, jemmy; crank, arm, shaft, spindle, crankshaft.
2 *he pulled the lever which unlocked the bonnet*: **handle**, grip, pull, switch, joystick, key, knob.
▶ **verb** *he found a crowbar and levered the cottage door open | they levered the inert body up*: **prise**, force, wrench, pull, wrest, twist, rip, strain, tug, jerk, heave, move, shift, dislodge, jemmy; **raise**, lift, hoist, haul; N. Amer. pry, jimmy.

leverage noun **1** *the long handles provide increased leverage*: **grip**, purchase, hold, grasp; contact, attachment, support, anchorage, force, strength; resistance, friction.
2 *the high levels of unionization gave workers significant leverage in workplace negotiations*: **influence**, power, authority, weight, sway, control, say, ascendancy, dominance, advantage, pressure, edge, standing, prestige, rank; informal pull, clout, muscle, teeth, beef.

levitate verb *the casket suddenly levitated a metre above the ground*: **float**, rise into the air, rise, hover, be suspended, glide, waft, drift, hang, defy gravity, fly, soar up.

levity noun **1** *he did much to inject a note of levity into a very hard-working production cycle*: **light-heartedness**, carefreeness, light-mindedness, high spirits, vivacity, liveliness, conviviality, cheerfulness, cheeriness, humour, gaiety, fun, jocularity, hilarity, frivolity, frivolousness, amusement, mirth, laughter, merriment, glee, comedy, funniness, wit, wittiness, jollity, joviality, joking, drollery, good cheer, sportiveness, nonsense, irreverence, facetiousness, flippancy, blitheness, triviality, silliness, foolishness, childishness, giddiness, skittishness.
▷ANTONYMS seriousness, gravity.
2 *he was distressed by the levity of her nature*: **fickleness**, inconstancy, instability, unsteadiness, variability, changeability, unreliability, undependability, inconsistency, flightiness.
▷ANTONYMS constancy.

levy verb **1** *a proposal to levy VAT on fuel*: **impose**, charge, exact, demand, raise, collect, gather; tax; rare mulct.
2 archaic *they levied troops for less grand operations*. See **enlist** (sense 2).
▶ **noun 1** *the troubles had been caused by the levy of taxation for the defence of the realm*: **imposition**, charging, exaction, raising, collection, gathering.
2 *the record industry's call for a levy on blank audio tapes*: **tax**, tariff, toll, excise, duty, fee, imposition, impost, exaction, assessment, tithe, payment; rare mulct; (**levies**) taxation, customs, dues.

lewd adjective **1** *a lewd old man*: **lecherous**, lustful, licentious, lascivious, dirty, prurient, salacious, lubricious, libidinous; immoral, impure, debauched, depraved, degenerate, unchaste, wanton, of easy virtue, decadent, disgusting, dissipated, dissolute, corrupt, perverted, sinful, wicked; bestial, goatish, wolfish; informal horny; Brit. informal **randy**; rare concupiscent, lickerish.
▷ANTONYMS chaste.
2 *a lewd limerick*: **vulgar**, crude, smutty, dirty, filthy, obscene, pornographic, coarse, tasteless, indecorous, indelicate, off colour, unseemly, indecent, salacious, gross, disgusting, sordid, low, foul, vile; rude, racy, risqué, naughty, wicked, arousing, earthy, erotic, sexy, suggestive, titillating, spicy, bawdy, ribald, raw, taboo, explicit, near the bone, near the knuckle; informal blue, raunchy, X-rated, nudge-nudge, porno; euphemistic adult.
▷ANTONYMS decent, clean.

lexicon noun **dictionary**, wordbook, vocabulary list, glossary, word-finder; reference book, phrase book, concordance, thesaurus, encyclopedia.

liability noun **1** *journalists cannot avoid liability for defamation merely by avoiding the naming of names*: **accountability**, **responsibility**, legal responsibility, answerability; incrimination, blame, blameworthiness, culpability, guilt, onus, fault; informal the rap.
▷ANTONYMS immunity.
2 *they have some huge assets and some equally big liabilities*: **financial obligation**, debt, indebtedness, debit; (**liabilities**) **debts**, arrears, dues.
▷ANTONYMS asset.
3 *she had come to be seen as an electoral liability*: **hindrance**, encumbrance, burden, handicap, nuisance, inconvenience; obstacle, impediment, drawback, drag, disadvantage, weakness, shortcoming, problem, weak spot/point; millstone round one's neck, stumbling block, cross to bear, cross, albatross; Achilles heel; informal minus, fly in the ointment; archaic cumber.
▷ANTONYMS asset, advantage.
4 *their liability to the disease*: **susceptibility**, vulnerability, proneness, tendency, predisposition, propensity; risk, chance, likelihood, threat.
▷ANTONYMS immunity.

liable adjective **1** *he held the defendants liable for negligence*: **responsible**, legally responsible, accountable, answerable, chargeable, blameworthy, at fault, culpable, subject, guilty, faulty, censurable.
▷ANTONYMS exempt, unaccountable.
2 *my income is liable to fluctuate wildly*: **likely**, inclined, tending, disposed, apt, predisposed, prone, given; informal on the cards.
▷ANTONYMS unlikely.
3 *you are more* **liable to** *injury when you exercise infrequently*: **exposed**, open, prone, subject, susceptible, vulnerable, in danger of, at risk of, at the mercy of.
▷ANTONYMS immune; above.

liaise verb *social services liaised with the police*: **cooperate**, work together, collaborate; **communicate**, intercommunicate, exchange information, network, interface, link up, hook up.

liaison noun **1** *the Bank of England works in very close liaison with the Treasury*: **cooperation**, contact, association, connection, collaboration; communication, interchange, affiliation, alliance, partnership, link, linkage, tie-up, hook-up.
2 *Dave was my White House liaison and all-round troubleshooter*: **intermediary**, mediator, middleman, contact, contact man/woman/person, link, linkman, linkwoman, linkperson, go-between, representative, agent, interceder, factor.
3 *she abandoned her loyalty to her absent husband in favour of a liaison with William*: **love affair**, affair, relationship, romance, attachment, fling, intrigue, amour, affair of the heart, involvement, amorous entanglement, romantic entanglement, entanglement; flirtation, dalliance; informal hanky-panky; Brit. informal bit on the side, carry-on.

liar noun **deceiver**, fibber, falsifier, teller of lies, teller of untruths, perjurer, false witness, fabricator, equivocator, prevaricator, spinner of yarns; romancer, fabulist; informal storyteller; rare fibster.

Word links **liar**

mythomaniac compulsive liar

libation noun **1** *dressed in their priestly robes, they pour libations into the holy well*: **liquid offering**, offering, tribute, dedication, oblation; sacrifice.
2 humorous *would Madame honour me with her company for a small libation?* **drink**, beverage, alcoholic drink, liquid refreshment, bracer; dram, draught, nip, tot, swallow, sip, gulp; informal swig, tincture, tipple; archaic potation.

libel noun *she sued two national newspapers for libel | a company's reputation could be injured by a libel*: **defamation**, defamation of character, character assassination, calumny, misrepresentation, scandalmongering; aspersions, denigration, vilification, disparagement, derogation, insult, slander, malicious gossip, tittle-tattle, traducement; lie, slur, smear, untruth, false

insinuation, false report, smear campaign, slight, innuendo, rumour; informal mud-slinging; N. Amer. informal bad-mouthing; archaic contumely.
▶ **verb** *she alleged the magazine had libelled her*: **defame**, malign, slander, give someone a bad name, blacken someone's name, sully someone's reputation, speak ill/evil of, write false reports about, traduce, smear, cast aspersions on, fling mud at, drag someone's name through the mud/mire, besmirch, tarnish, taint, do a hatchet job on, tell lies about, spread tales about, spread scandal about, stain, vilify, calumniate, denigrate, disparage, run down, derogate, stigmatize, discredit, slight; N. Amer. slur; rare asperse.

Choose the right word **libel, slander, malign, defame, traduce**

See **malign**.

libellous adjective *we reserve the right to edit correspondence and to remove potentially libellous statements*: **defamatory**, denigratory, vilifying, disparaging, derogatory, aspersive, calumnious, calumniatory, slanderous, false, untrue, misrepresentative, traducing, maligning, insulting, scurrilous, slurring, smearing; informal mud-slinging, muckraking.

liberal adjective **1** *the values of a liberal society*: **tolerant**, unprejudiced, unbigoted, broad-minded, open-minded, enlightened, forbearing; **permissive**, free, free and easy, easy-going, laissez-faire, libertarian, latitudinarian, unbiased, impartial, non-partisan, indulgent, lenient, lax, soft.
▷ANTONYMS narrow-minded, bigoted.
2 *he launched a liberal social agenda*: **progressive**, advanced, modern, forward-looking, forward-thinking, progressivist, go-ahead, enlightened, reformist, radical; left-wing, leftist, freethinking, politically correct, PC; informal right-on.
▷ANTONYMS conservative, reactionary.
3 *the provision of liberal adult education*: **wide-ranging**, broad-based, general, humanistic.
4 *a liberal interpretation of divorce laws*: **flexible**, broad, loose, rough, non-restrictive, free, general, non-literal, non-specific, not literal, not strict, not close; inexact, imprecise, vague, indefinite, ill-defined, unrigorous, unmeticulous.
▷ANTONYMS strict, to the letter.
5 *liberal coatings of paint*: **abundant**, copious, ample, plentiful, generous, lavish, luxuriant, profuse, considerable, prolific, rich; galore; excessive, immoderate, superabundant, overabundant; informal over the top; literary plenteous.
▷ANTONYMS scant.
6 *they had been liberal with their cash*: **generous**, magnanimous, open-handed, unsparing, unstinting, ungrudging, lavish, free, munificent, bountiful, beneficent, benevolent, big-hearted, kind-hearted, kind, philanthropic, charitable, altruistic, unselfish; extravagant, overgenerous, generous to a fault, immoderate, wasteful, overabundant, profligate, prodigal, thriftless, improvident, intemperate, unrestrained, wild; informal over the top; literary bounteous.
▷ANTONYMS miserly, careful.

liberate verb *Lincoln's proclamation liberating the slaves*: **set free**, free, release, let out, let go, discharge, set/let loose, deliver, save, rescue, extricate; unshackle, unfetter, unchain, untie, unmanacle, unbind, unyoke; emancipate, enfranchise, give rights to; ransom; historical manumit; rare disenthral.
▷ANTONYMS confine; enslave, subjugate.

liberation noun **1** *the liberation of prisoners*: **freeing**, release, discharge, deliverance, salvation, rescue, relief, extrication, setting free; loosing, unloosing, unshackling, unfettering, unchaining, untying, unbinding; freedom, liberty; emancipation; ransom; French laissez-aller; historical manumission; rare disenthralment.
▷ANTONYMS confinement; slavery, subjugation.
2 *the battle for women's liberation*: **freedom**, **equality**, equal rights, non-discrimination, emancipation, enfranchisement, independence.
▷ANTONYMS oppression.

liberator noun **rescuer**, saviour, deliverer, freer, emancipator, messiah, champion, knight in shining armour, Good Samaritan; historical manumitter.
▷ANTONYMS enslaver, oppressor.

libertine noun *'Don Giovanni' ends with the unrepentant libertine being dragged down to hell by demons*: **philanderer**, ladies' man, playboy, rake, roué, loose-liver, Don Juan, Lothario, Casanova, Romeo; **lecher**, seducer, womanizer, adulterer, debauchee, sensualist, voluptuary, hedonist; profligate, wanton, reprobate, degenerate; informal stud, skirt-chaser, ladykiller, lech, wolf; dated rip, blood, gay dog; formal fornicator.
▷ANTONYMS puritan.
▶ **adjective** *they were careful to insist that free love was not to be confused with libertine sexual intercourse*: **licentious**, lustful, libidinous, lecherous, lascivious, lubricious, dissolute, dissipated, debauched, immoral, wanton, shameless, degenerate, depraved, debased, profligate, promiscuous, unchaste, lewd, prurient, salacious, indecent, immodest, impure, carnal, intemperate, abandoned, unrestrained, unprincipled, reprobate; rakish, decadent, sensual, voluptuary, hedonistic; informal loose, fast, goatish, randy, horny, raunchy; rare concupiscent, lickerish.
▷ANTONYMS chaste, puritanical.

liberty noun **1** *individuals should enjoy the liberty to pursue their own interests and preferences*: **freedom**, independence, free rein, freeness, licence, self-determination; free will, latitude, option, choice; volition, non-compulsion, non-coercion, non-confinement; leeway, margin, scope, elbow room.
▷ANTONYMS constraint.
2 *parliamentary government is the essence of British liberty*: **independence**, freedom, autonomy, sovereignty, self government, self rule, self determination, home rule; civil liberties, civil rights, human rights; rare autarky.
▷ANTONYMS dependence, subjugation.
3 *no man who was born free would be contented to be penned up and denied the liberty to go where he pleases*: **right**, birthright, opportunity, facility, prerogative, entitlement, privilege, permission, sanction, leave, consent, authorization, authority, licence, clearance, blessing, dispensation, exemption, faculty; French carte blanche.
▷ANTONYMS constraint.
□ **at liberty 1** *he was at liberty for three months before he was recaptured*: **free**, **on the loose**, loose, set loose, at large, unconfined, roaming; unbound, untied, unchained, unshackled, unfettered, unrestrained, unrestricted, wild, untrammelled; escaped, out; informal sprung. ▷ANTONYMS in captivity; imprisoned.
2 *your great aunt was at liberty to divide her estate how she chose*: **free**, **permitted**, allowed, authorized, able, entitled, eligible, fit; unconstrained, unrestricted, unhindered, without constraint. ▷ANTONYMS forbidden.
□ **take liberties** *you've already taken too many liberties with me*: **act with overfamiliarity**, act with familiarity, show disrespect, act with impropriety, act indecorously, be impudent, commit a breach of etiquette, act with boldness, act with impertinence, show insolence, show impudence, show presumptuousness, show presumption, show forwardness, show audacity, be unrestrained; take advantage of, exploit.
▷ANTONYMS be polite; show consideration.

Choose the right word **liberty, freedom, independence**

All these words denote absence of constraint or coercion.

Liberty denotes the desirable state of being free, within society, from oppressive restrictions imposed by authority on one's behaviour or political views (*we believe in civil and religious liberty for everyone*). It may also mean the power or scope to act as one pleases (*individuals should enjoy the liberty to pursue their own preferences*). To be *at liberty* to do something is to be allowed or entitled to do it (*I'm not at liberty to say*).

Freedom is a more general word for the absence of constraint (*decentralization would give local managers more freedom | freedom of expression | freedom to organize their affairs*). *Freedom* can also indicate the absence of a particular evil or constraint (*freedom from fear | freedom from interference*) or the state of being unrestricted in movement (*the shorts have a side split for freedom of movement*). Both *freedom* and *liberty* can also mean the state of not being imprisoned or enslaved (*the teenager committed fifty-six crimes before he lost his freedom | the mayor remained at liberty pending a decision as to his place of confinement*).

The principal meaning of **independence** is the absence of control of a nation or corporate body by an outside power (*recognition of Azerbaijan's independence | the independence of the judiciary*). When used in relation to individuals, *independence* may denote a freedom from commitments (*could she pursue her independence if Chester needed her?*) or the personal quality of not relying on others (*parents should foster their child's independence*).

libidinous adjective *he couldn't come to terms with his own libidinous impulses*: **lustful**, lecherous, lascivious, lewd, carnal; **erotic**, sexual, sensual, venereal, hot, fleshly, voluptuous; salacious, prurient, licentious, libertine, lubricious, dissolute, debauched, depraved, degenerate, decadent, dissipated, wanton, promiscuous, immoral, unchaste, unvirtuous, loose, impure, intemperate, abandoned, incontinent, gross, ruttish, goatish, wolfish; informal horny; Brit. informal randy; rare concupiscent, lickerish.
▷ANTONYMS chaste.

libido noun *in men, heavy drinking can result in loss of libido*: **sex drive**, sexual appetite, sexual passion, sexual urge, sexual longing; sexual desire, desire, passion, sexiness, sensuality, sexuality, lust, lustfulness, carnality, eroticism, ardour; informal horniness, the hots; Brit. informal randiness; rare concupiscence.

licence noun **1** *a driving licence*: **permit**, certificate, document, documentation, authorization, warrant, voucher, diploma, imprimatur; certification, credentials; pass, papers.
2 *I went in dread of the beatings that teachers had licence to administer*: **permission**, authority, discretion, right, a free hand, leave, consent,

authorization, sanction, approval, assent, entitlement, privilege, prerogative, blessing, exemption, mandate; liberty, freedom; power, empowerment, dispensation; French carte blanche; informal a blank cheque; rare warranty.
3 *they manufacture high-fashion footwear under licence*: **franchise**, permission, consent, sanction, warrant, warranty, charter; seal of approval.
4 *the government was criticized for giving the army too much licence*: **freedom**, liberty, free rein, latitude, choice, option, independence, self-determination, scope, impunity, margin, leisure; French carte blanche.
▷ANTONYMS restriction.
5 *he may have used a little poetic licence to embroider a good yarn*: **disregard for the facts**, deviation from the truth, departure from the truth; inventiveness, invention, creativity, imagination, fancy; fancifulness, resourcefulness, ingenuity, inspiration; freedom, looseness.
6 *churchmen and dissenters cooperated against the licence of the age*: **licentiousness**, dissoluteness, dissipation, debauchery, immorality, impropriety, decadence, profligacy, immoderation, intemperateness, indulgence, self-indulgence, excess, excessiveness, lack of restraint, lack of control, irresponsibility, abandon, laxness, laxity, disorder, disorderliness, unruliness, lawlessness, anarchy.
▷ANTONYMS restraint, decorum.

license verb *he was licensed to sell liquor*: **permit**, allow, authorize, grant/give a licence to, grant/give a permit to, grant/give authorization to, grant/give authority to, grant/give the right to, grant/give leave to, grant/give permission to; warrant, certify, accredit, empower, give power to, entitle, enable, validate, charter, franchise, give the stamp of approval to, give approval to, let; recognize, qualify, sanction; informal OK, rubber-stamp.
▷ANTONYMS ban, forbid.

licentious adjective *he was a puritan in a licentious age*: **dissolute**, dissipated, debauched, degenerate, salacious, immoral, wanton, decadent, depraved, profligate, impure, sinful, wicked, corrupt, indecent, libertine; **lustful**, lecherous, lascivious, libidinous, prurient, lubricious, lewd, promiscuous, unchaste, carnal, fleshly, intemperate, abandoned; ribald, risqué, smutty, dirty, filthy, coarse, perverted; informal horny, raunchy, naughty, pervy; Brit. informal randy; rare concupiscent, lickerish.
▷ANTONYMS moral, virtuous.

licit adjective *licit marital sexual intercourse | a warehouse filled with all manner of licit and illicit goods*: **legitimate**, permissible, admissible, allowable, acceptable; **permitted**, valid, allowed, approved, sanctioned, authorized, warranted, recognized, bona fide, genuine, rightful, right, proper, above board, going by the rules; **lawful**, legal, constitutional, statutory, statutable, legalized, within the law, licensed, official; informal legit, kosher, by the book.
▷ANTONYMS illicit, forbidden.

lick verb **1** *the spaniel leapt to lick his face | Pete licked the gravy from his hand*: **tongue**, wet, moisten, wash, clean; taste, lap, slurp.
2 *she sat looking into the flames licking round the coal*: **flicker**, play, flick, flit, dart, ripple, dance.
3 informal *they licked the home side 3-0*. See **defeat** (sense 1 of the verb).
4 informal *the Prime Minister claimed that the government had inflation licked*. See **overcome** (sense 2 of the verb).
▶ noun **1** *the building itself had changed little, apart from a lick of paint here and there*: **dab**, bit, drop, dash, spot, touch, hint, dribble, splash, sprinkle, trickle; little; informal smidgen, tad.
▷ANTONYMS lashings.
2 informal *you came up that last bit at a fair lick*: **speed**, rate, pace, tempo, velocity, momentum; informal clip.

licking noun informal **1** *Arsenal can take a licking as much as any other club*: **defeat**, loss, beating, trouncing, thrashing, drubbing; rout; informal hiding, pasting, caning, hammering, demolition, slaughter, massacre, annihilation; N. Amer. informal shellacking.
▷ANTONYMS victory.
2 *when his father heard what he had done, Ray got the worst licking of his life*: **thrashing**, beating, flogging, whipping, slapping, spanking, thumping; informal walloping, hiding, tanning, pasting, hammering, clobbering, lathering, larruping, working-over; N. Amer. informal whaling.

lid noun *the lid of a saucepan*: **cover**, top, cap, covering; cork, stopper, bung, plug.
□ **put a/the lid on** informal *they're wondering what they've got to do to put a lid on the rumours*: **stop**, control, finish, end, put an end to, be the end of, put a stop to, put paid to, destroy.
□ **lift the lid off/on** informal *lifting the lid on what happened between Jett and Moira all those years ago*: **expose**, reveal, bring to light, make known, make public, bring into the open, leak, disclose, divulge, broadcast, publish, release; informal take the lid off, blow wide open, let the cat out of the bag, spill the beans, blow the gaff, blab.
▷ANTONYMS keep secret.

lie[1] noun *Len's loyalty to his mates had made him tell lies*: **untruth**, falsehood, fib, fabrication, deception, made-up story, trumped-up story, invention, piece of fiction, fiction, falsification, falsity, fairy story/tale, cock and bull story, barefaced lie; (little) white lie, half-truth, exaggeration, prevarication, departure from the truth; yarn, story, red herring, fable, myth, flight of fancy, figment of the imagination; pretence, pretext, sham; (**lies**) misinformation, disinformation, perjury, dissimulation, mendacity, gossip, propaganda; informal tall story, tall tale, whopper; Brit. informal porky, pork pie, porky pie; humorous terminological inexactitude; vulgar slang bullshit; Austral./NZ vulgar slang bulldust.
▷ANTONYMS truth, fact.
□ **give the lie to** *the success of our manufactured exports gives the lie to the Opposition's portrayal of manufacturing*: **disprove**, contradict, negate, deny, refute, rebut, gainsay, belie, invalidate, show/prove to be false, explode, discredit, debunk, quash, knock the bottom out of, drive a coach and horses through; challenge, call into question; informal shoot full of holes, shoot down (in flames); rare controvert, confute, negative.
▷ANTONYMS show to be true, verify, confirm.
▶ verb *he had lied to the police as to his whereabouts*: **say something untrue**, tell an untruth, tell a lie, tell a falsehood, fib, fabricate, invent a story, make up a story, falsify, dissemble, dissimulate, bear false witness; tell a white lie, prevaricate, exaggerate, stretch the truth; perjure oneself, commit perjury, forswear oneself, be forsworn; bluff, pretend, depart from the truth; deceive, delude, mislead, trick, hoodwink, hoax, take in, lead astray, throw off the scent, send on a wild goose chase, put on the wrong track, pull the wool over someone's eyes; informal lie through one's teeth, con; humorous be economical with the truth, tell a terminological inexactitude; vulgar slang bullshit.
▷ANTONYMS tell the truth.

lie[2] verb **1** *he was lying on a bed*: **recline**, lie down, lie back, be recumbent, be prostrate, be supine, be prone, be stretched out, stretch oneself out, lean back, sprawl, rest, repose, relax, lounge, loll, bask.
▷ANTONYMS stand.
2 *her handbag lay on a chair at the other end of the room*: **be placed**, be set, be situated, be positioned, rest, repose, be.
3 *the tiny principality which lies on the border of Switzerland and Austria*: **be situated**, be located, be placed, be positioned, be found, be sited, be established, be.
4 *his body lies in a crypt below our headquarters*: **be buried**, be interred, be laid to rest, rest, be entombed; rare be inhumed, be sepulchred.
5 *the difficulty lies in building real quality into the products*: **consist**, be inherent, inhere, be present, be contained, exist, reside, have its existence/being.
□ **lie heavy on** *it was the loss of human life that lay heavy on him*: **trouble**, worry, bother, torment, oppress, nag, prey on one's mind, plague, niggle at, gnaw at, haunt; be a burden to, burden, press down on, weigh down, be a great weight on, weigh heavily on someone's mind, cause anxiety to; informal bug, aggravate.
□ **lie low** *we'll have to lie low and wait for dark*: **hide**, go into hiding, hide out, find a hiding place, conceal oneself, keep out of sight, keep a low profile, take cover, go to earth, go to ground, go underground, cover one's tracks, lurk, skulk; informal hole up; Brit. informal lie doggo.

liege noun **liege lord**, lord, feudal lord, seigneur, suzerain, overlord, master, chief, chieftain, superior, monarch, sovereign, baron, ruler.

lieutenant noun *he began his criminal career as the lieutenant of a notorious mob boss*: **deputy**, second in command, right-hand man/woman, number two, assistant, aide, henchman, henchwoman, subordinate; informal sidekick.

life noun **1** *only a mother can appreciate the joy of giving life to a child*: **existence**, being, living, animation, aliveness, animateness; entity, sentience, creation, survival, viability; rare esse.
▷ANTONYMS death, non-existence.
2 *armaments that threaten to eliminate life on the planet*: **living things**, living beings, living creatures, the living; human/animal/plant life, fauna, flora, ecosystems, creatures, wildlife; human beings, humanity, humankind, mankind, man, human activity; literary flesh.
3 *inshore fishing isn't an easy life*: **way of life**, way of living, manner of living, lifestyle, situation, position, state, station, condition, set of circumstances, fate, lot; sphere, field, line, career, business.
4 *I hadn't talked to my father for the last nine months of his life*: **lifetime**, life span, days, duration of life, allotted span, course of life, time on earth, existence, one's time, one's career, threescore years and ten, this mortal coil; informal one's born days.
5 *the Parliament Bill introduced a limit of five years for the life of any Parliament*: **duration**, active life, lifetime, existence, functioning period, period of effectiveness, period of usefulness, validity, efficacy.
6 *he is happy and full of life in his new job*: **vivacity**, animation, liveliness, vitality, verve, high spirits, sparkle, exuberance, zest, buoyancy, effervescence, enthusiasm, energy, vigour, dynamism, go, elan, gusto, brio, bounce, spirit, spiritedness, activity, fire, panache, colour, dash, drive, push; business, bustle, hustle and bustle, movement, stir; informal oomph, pizzazz, pep, zing, zip, vim, get-up-and-go.
7 *his mother would be the life of the party*: **moving spirit**, moving force, animating spirit, vital spirit, spirit, vital spark, life force, lifeblood, essence, core, heart, soul, strength, quintessence, substance; French élan vital.
8 *more than 1,500 lives were lost in the accident*: **person**, human being, individual, mortal, soul, creature.

9 *I was reading a life of Chopin*: **biography**, autobiography, life story, life history, memoir, history, profile; diary, journal, confessions; record, chronicle, account, report, portrayal, depiction, portrait; informal biog, bio.
10 *I'll miss you, but there it is, that's life*: **the way of the world**, the world, the way things go, the way of it, the human condition, the times we live in, the usual state of affairs, the school of hard knocks; fate, destiny, providence, kismet, karma, fortune, luck, chance; N. Amer. informal the way the cookie crumbles.
□ **come to life 1** *he could hear the familiar sounds of a barracks coming to life*: **become active**, become lively, come alive, wake up, awaken, waken, show signs of life, arouse, rouse, stir, emerge. ▷ANTONYMS be dormant, be quiescent.
2 *it was as though the carved angel by the lectern had suddenly come to life*: **become animate**, come alive, become a living creature; revive, resurrect.
□ **for dear life** *she was holding on for dear life*: **desperately**, with all one's might, with might and main, urgently, with urgency, vigorously, with as much vigour as possible, for all one is worth, as fast/hard as possible, like the devil.
□ **give one's life 1** *he's devoted to his queen and would give his life for her*: **die**, lay down one's life, sacrifice oneself; die to save, offer one's life, surrender one's life. **2** *he gave his life to the company and could have expected some support from them*: **dedicate oneself**, devote oneself, give oneself, commit oneself, pledge oneself, surrender oneself.

Word links **life**

bio- related prefix, as in *biosphere*
animate having life
vital essential for life

life-and-death adjective *a life-and-death decision*: **vital**, of vital importance, crucial, critical, urgent, pivotal, momentous, of great moment, important, all-important, key, serious, grave, significant, decisive, far-reaching, historic, weighty, consequential, of great consequence, epoch-making, apocalyptic, fateful, portentous; informal earth-shattering, world-shattering, earth-shaking, world-shaking.
▷ANTONYMS trivial, unimportant.

lifeblood noun *fast, accurate information is the lifeblood of the economy*: **life force**, life, essential part/component/constituent, animating spirit, moving force, driving force, dynamic force, vital spark, vital fluid, inspiration, stimulus, centre, animus, essence, crux, heart, soul, core, kernel, marrow, pith; French élan vital; informal guts; Philosophy quiddity.

life-giving adjective *their view of karma as a life-giving force that flows from life to life*: **vitalizing**, animating, vivifying, energizing, invigorating, enlivening, stimulating; life-preserving, life-sustaining.
▷ANTONYMS destructive.

lifeless adjective **1** *they dropped the lifeless body into the shallow grave*: **dead**, deceased, defunct, departed, late, extinct, perished, gone, no more, passed on/away, stiff, cold, (as) dead as a doornail; rare demised, exanimate.
▷ANTONYMS alive.
2 *a lifeless rag doll*: **inanimate**, inorganic, without life, inert, insentient, insensate, wooden, mechanical, abiotic; nerveless.
▷ANTONYMS animate.
3 *a lifeless planet | the lifeless, emotionless city of the future*: **barren**, sterile, bare, desolate, stark, arid, infertile, uncultivated, empty, uninhabited, unoccupied; cold, bleak, joyless, colourless, characterless, soulless.
4 *he spoke in a dull, lifeless voice | a lifeless performance*: **lacklustre**, spiritless, lacking vitality, apathetic, torpid, lethargic; dull, monotonous, boring, tedious, dreary, insipid, unexciting, wearisome, bland, drab, dry, flat, static, stiff, wooden, mechanical, uninspired, inexpressive, expressionless, emotionless, colourless, characterless, two-dimensional, uninspiring.
▷ANTONYMS lively, vibrant.
5 *lifeless hair*: **lank**, lustreless.

lifelike adjective *a lifelike sketch*: **realistic**, true to life, representational, faithful, authentic, exact, precise, detailed, vivid, graphic, natural, naturalistic, convincing, undistorted; photographic, cinematic, filmic; speaking; factual.
▷ANTONYMS unrealistic.

lifelong adjective *a lifelong friendship*: **lasting**, for all one's life, lifetime's, long-lasting, long-standing, long-term, long-running, persisting, prevailing, durable, constant, stable, established, steady, steadfast, secure, fast, firm, fixed, deep-rooted, enduring, continuing, abiding, remaining; permanent, eternal, immutable.
▷ANTONYMS ephemeral, short-lived, temporary.

lifestyle noun *the privileged lifestyle of rich New York youngsters*: **way of life**, way of living, manner of living, life, situation, position, state, station, condition, set of circumstances, fate, lot; conduct, behaviour; customs, habits, ways, mores.

lifetime noun **1** *he made an exceptional contribution to the conservation of nature during his lifetime*: **lifespan**, life, days, duration of life, allotted span, course of life, time on earth, existence, one's time, one's career, one's threescore years and ten, this mortal coil; informal one's born days.
2 *the lifetime of workstations will generally be between three and five years*: **duration**, life, active life, existence, life expectancy, functioning period, period of effectiveness/usefulness/validity/efficacy.
3 *it takes a lifetime to do it properly*: **all one's life**, a very long time, an eternity; hours, days, months, years, aeons, hours/days/months on end; informal ages (and ages), an age.

lift verb **1** *holding the sling in your left hand, lift the pack on to your back*: **raise**, hoist, heave, haul up, uplift, heft, boost, raise up/aloft, upraise, elevate, thrust, hold high, bear aloft; pick up, grab, take up, scoop up, gather up, snatch up; winch up, jack up, lever up; carry, manhandle; informal hump; rare upheave.
▷ANTONYMS drop, put down.
2 *a few cocktails had lifted his flagging spirits*: **boost**, raise, buoy up, elevate, give a lift to, cheer up, perk up, enliven, uplift, brighten up, lighten, ginger up, gladden, encourage, stimulate, arouse, revive, restore; informal buck up, jazz up.
▷ANTONYMS subdue.
3 *they seem able to lift their game for the big occasions*: **improve**, boost, enhance, make better, invigorate, revitalize, upgrade, ameliorate.
▷ANTONYMS worsen, impair.
4 *by now the fog had lifted*: **clear**, rise, disperse, dissipate, disappear, vanish, dissolve, be dispelled, thin out, scatter.
▷ANTONYMS appear.
5 *a draft law lifting the ban on political parties*: **cancel**, raise, remove, withdraw, revoke, rescind, annul, void, discontinue, countermand, relax, end, stop, terminate.
▷ANTONYMS establish, impose.
6 *the end of September is the time to lift and store carrots*: **dig up**, pick, pull up, dig out of the ground, root out, unearth, take up.
▷ANTONYMS plant, sow.
7 *they needed far more supplies than the RAF could lift in the required time scale*: **airlift**, transport by air, transport, move, transfer, fly, convey, shift.
8 *he lifted his voice slightly*: **amplify**, raise, make louder, louden, increase.
▷ANTONYMS soften, quieten.
9 informal *he lifted portions of his book nearly verbatim from a 1986 article*: **plagiarize**, pirate, copy, reproduce, poach, steal, borrow; informal crib, rip off, nick, pinch.
10 informal *he could lift a wallet better than anyone I've ever known*. See **steal** (sense 1 of the verb).
□ **lift off** *the helicopters lifted off at 1030 hours*: **take off**, be launched, blast off, leave the ground, become airborne, take to the air, take wing.
▷ANTONYMS land, touch down.
▶ noun **1** *Alice went up to the second floor in the lift*: **elevator**, hoist; paternoster (lift); dumb waiter.
2 *give me a lift up, Martha*: **push**, hoist, heave, thrust, shove, uplift, a helping hand.
3 *he gave me a lift to the airport*: **car ride**, ride, run, drive, transportation, journey; informal hitch.
4 *he scored an excellent goal, which will give his confidence a real lift*: **boost**, fillip, pick-me-up, stimulus, impetus, encouragement, spur, reassurance, aid, help, push; improvement, enhancement, upgrading, amelioration; informal shot in the arm.
▷ANTONYMS discouragement.

light[1] noun **1** *the houses had only the shadowy light of candles and oil lamps*: **illumination**, brightness, luminescence, luminosity, shining, gleaming, gleam, brilliance, radiance, lustre, glowing, glow, blaze, glare, dazzle; incandescence, phosphorescence; sunlight, moonlight, starlight, lamplight, firelight, electric light, gaslight; ray of light, shaft of light, beam of light; rare effulgence, refulgence, lambency, fulguration.
▷ANTONYMS darkness.
2 *there was a light on in the hall | he shone his light into Oliver's face*: **lamp**, **torch**, flashlight; headlight, headlamp, sidelight; standard lamp, wall light; street light, floodlight; lantern, candle, taper, beacon.
3 *have you got a light?* **match**, **(cigarette) lighter**, flame, spark, source of fire.
4 *don't worry, we'll be driving in the light and we won't have to go fast*: **daylight**, light of day, natural light, sunlight; **daylight hours**, daytime, day, hours of sunlight.
▷ANTONYMS darkness, night-time.
5 *he saw the problem in a different light | the work sheds new light on the early history of the library*: **aspect**, angle, slant, approach, interpretation, viewpoint, standpoint, context, point of view, vantage point; appearance, guise, hue, complexion.
6 *light dawned on Loretta, and she launched herself into her part*: **understanding**, enlightenment, illumination, comprehension, insight, awareness, knowledge, elucidation, explanation, clarification, edification.
▷ANTONYMS ignorance.
7 *an eminent legal light*: **expert**, authority, master, leader, guru; leading light, guiding light, luminary, celebrity, dignitary, public figure, worthy, VIP, big name, star; informal bigwig, big gun, big shot, big noise, celeb.

8 *he served his party loyally according to his lights*: **talent**, skill, ability; intelligence, mental powers, intellect, knowledge, understanding.
□ **bring something to light** *a serious case of corruption within government was first brought to light by an internal audit*: **reveal**, disclose, expose, uncover, show up, lay bare, unveil, manifest, unearth, dig up, dig out, turn up, bring to notice, detect, identify, dredge up, smoke out, root out, ferret out, hunt out, nose out.
▷ANTONYMS hush up, keep secret.
□ **come to light** *the thefts came to light early last year*: **be discovered**, be uncovered, be unearthed, appear, come out, transpire, become known, become apparent, materialize, emerge, crop up, turn up, show up, pop up.
▷ANTONYMS remain secret, remain hidden.
□ **in the light of** *I see no reason, in the light of these reports, to abandon our current policy*: **taking into consideration**, considering, taking into account, bearing in mind, keeping in mind, mindful of, taking note of, in view of.
□ **see the light** *he believed that if he could talk to his opponents, he could make them see the light*: **understand**, realize; informal cotton on, catch on, get the message, get the picture; Brit. informal twig.
□ **throw/cast/shed light on** *no one could shed any light on the mysterious car accident*: **explain**, elucidate, clarify, clear up, offer/give an explanation for/of, make clear, make plain, interpret, comment on.
▸ **verb** *Alan gathered sticks and lit a fire | Rickie lit a cigarette*: **set alight**, set light to, set burning, set on fire, set fire to, put/set a match to, ignite, kindle, burn, spark (off), fire, touch off, start, torch; archaic enkindle.
▷ANTONYMS extinguish, put out.
□ **light up** *the dashboard lit up*: **become bright**, brighten, become brighter, lighten, flash, shine, gleam, flare, blaze, glint, sparkle, flicker, shimmer, glisten, scintillate, glare, beam; rare coruscate, fulgurate.
□ **light something up 1** *a flare lit up the night sky*: **make bright**, brighten, illuminate, make brighter, lighten, throw/cast/shed light on, shine on, irradiate, flood with light, floodlight; literary illumine. **2** *her enthusiasm lit up her face*: **animate**, irradiate, brighten, make cheerful, cheer up, enliven.
▸ **adjective 1** *a cool and light breakfast room adjoins the bar*: **bright**, full of light, well lit, well lighted, well illuminated, sunny, sunshiny, undimmed, brilliant.
▷ANTONYMS dark, gloomy.
2 *a subtle colour scheme of light pastel shades*: **light-coloured**, light-toned, pale, pale-coloured, pastel, pastel-coloured; whitish, faded, faint, weak, bleached.
▷ANTONYMS dark.
3 *a young woman with light hair*: **fair**, light-coloured, blonde, golden, flaxen, yellow.
▷ANTONYMS dark, brunette.

Word links **light**

photo-, lumin-, luc- related prefixes, as in *luminescent, Lucifer*
optics study of behaviour of light
photometry measurement of the intensity of light
photophobia fear of light

light² **adjective 1** *it's light, portable, and you can use it anywhere | you're as light as a feather!* **easy to lift**, not heavy, weighing very little, lightweight; easy to carry, portable, transportable, weightless, insubstantial, airy.
▷ANTONYMS heavy.
2 *a light cotton robe*: **flimsy**, lightweight, insubstantial, thin; delicate, floaty, gauzy, sheer, gossamer, diaphanous, transparent, translucent, see-through.
▷ANTONYMS heavy, thick.
3 *she seemed as light on her feet as a dancer*: **nimble**, deft, agile, lithe, limber, lissom, flexible, supple, adroit, graceful, acrobatic, lively, active, quick, quick-moving, spry, sprightly; light-footed, fleet-footed; informal twinkle-toed, nippy; literary fleet, lightsome.
▷ANTONYMS clumsy.
4 *cotton lavender needs a dry sunny situation in light soil*: **friable**, sandy, easily dug, workable; crumbly, not dense, loose, porous.
▷ANTONYMS dense.
5 *a light dinner*: **small**, modest, scanty, simple, skimpy, frugal, not heavy, not rich, not large; easily digested, digestible.
▷ANTONYMS heavy, rich.
6 *I was put on light duties*: **easy**, simple, undemanding, untaxing, unexacting, not burdensome, moderate, endurable, bearable, tolerable; informal cushy.
▷ANTONYMS hard, burdensome.
7 *his eyes gleamed with light mockery*: **gentle**, mild, moderate, slight; **playful**, light-hearted, easy-going; witty, dry.
▷ANTONYMS serious.
8 *light entertainment | light reading*: **entertaining**, **lightweight**, diverting, recreative, undemanding, easily understood, middle-of-the-road; amusing, humorous, funny, chucklesome, witty, light-hearted; frivolous, unserious, superficial, trivial, trifling.
▷ANTONYMS serious, deep.
9 *I pitched into the chores with a light heart*: **carefree**, light-hearted, cheerful, cheery, happy, merry, jolly, blithe, bright, sunny, untroubled; buoyant, vivacious, bubbly, jaunty, bouncy, breezy, optimistic, positive, upbeat, ebullient, easy-going, free and easy, happy-go-lucky; dated gay.
10 *this is no light matter*: **unimportant**, insignificant, trivial, trifling, petty, worthless, inconsequential, inconsiderable, superficial.
▷ANTONYMS serious, important.
11 *he heard light footsteps | she leaned up and planted a light kiss on Dave's mouth*: **gentle**, **delicate**, soft, dainty, graceful; faint, indistinct.
▷ANTONYMS heavy.
12 *her heart was pounding and her head felt light*: **dizzy**, giddy, light-headed, faint, unsteady; informal woozy, funny; dated queer; rare vertiginous.
□ **make light of something** *I don't want to make light of a serious issue*: **play down**, downplay, understate, underrate, rate too low, not do justice to, do an injustice to, underplay, de-emphasize, underemphasize, trivialize, minimize, diminish, downgrade, reduce, lessen, brush aside, gloss over, shrug off; informal soft-pedal, sell short; rare misprize, minify.

light³ **verb**
□ **light into 1** informal *we started lighting into our attackers*: **assault**, set upon, fall on, attack, assail, turn on, lash out at, round on, strike, beat; thrash, drub, thump, batter, hammer, pummel, hit out at, strike out at, (let) fly at, weigh into, belabour; informal lay into, tear into, sail into, lace into, pitch into, paste, let someone have it; Brit. informal have a go at. **2** *my father really lit into me for being late*: **scold**, berate, upbraid, castigate, censure, condemn, lambaste, criticize, reprimand, rebuke, chide, reprove, admonish, harangue, take to task, lay into, rant at, rave at, rail at, revile, fulminate against, haul/call over the coals; informal pitch into, rap someone's knuckles, slap someone's wrist, dress down, give someone a dressing-down, carpet, tell off, bawl out; Brit. informal tick off, have a go at, slag off; N. Amer. informal chew out; rare reprehend, excoriate, objurgate.
□ **light on/upon** *we will suppose that the author has lighted upon important new material*: **come across**, chance on, hit on, happen on, stumble on/across, blunder on, find, discover, uncover, arrive at, encounter, think of, come up with.

lighten¹ **verb 1** *the sky was beginning to lighten*: **become lighter**, grow brighter, brighten.
▷ANTONYMS darken.
2 *the first touch of dawn lightened the sky*: **make lighter**, make brighter, brighten, light up, illuminate, throw/cast/shed light on, shine on, irradiate, flood with light, floodlight; literary illumine.
▷ANTONYMS darken.
3 *he sometimes used lemon juice to lighten his hair*: **whiten**, make white(r), bleach, peroxide, blanch, make pale(r), remove colour from, fade, wash out, decolour, decolorize.
▷ANTONYMS blacken.
4 rare *it thundered and lightened*: **emit lightning**, flash lightning; rare fulgurate.

lighten² **verb 1** *we intend to lighten the burden of taxation*: **make lighter**, lessen, reduce, decrease, diminish, moderate, soften, ease, temper; alleviate, mitigate, allay, relieve, palliate, assuage, soothe, calm, subdue.
▷ANTONYMS increase, intensify.
2 *an attempt to lighten her spirits*: **cheer (up)**, brighten, gladden, hearten, perk up, lift, ginger up, enliven, boost, buoy (up), elate, inspire, uplift, sweeten, revive, restore, revitalize, stimulate; enhance, improve, leaven; informal jazz up; rare inspirit.
▷ANTONYMS depress.

light-fingered **adjective** *a security system which prevents light-fingered customers from making off with the goods*: **thieving**, thievish, stealing, pilfering, shoplifting, pocket-picking; dishonest; informal crooked, filching, sticky-fingered.
▷ANTONYMS honest.

light-footed **adjective** *these dogs are light-footed and agile*: **nimble**, light on one's feet, agile, deft, graceful, lithe, spry, sprightly, light of foot, limber, lissom, acrobatic; swift, fast, quick, quick-moving; informal twinkle-toed, nippy; literary fleet of foot, fleet-footed.
▷ANTONYMS clumsy, slow.

light-headed **adjective** *the pain had left him feeling light-headed*: **dizzy**, giddy, faint, unsteady, light in the head, weak-headed, muzzy; shaky, reeling, staggering; informal woozy; rare vertiginous.

light-hearted **adjective** *light-hearted banter | a light-hearted comedy*: **carefree**, cheerful, cheery, happy, merry, glad, playful, jolly, jovial, joyful, jocund, gleeful, ebullient, high-spirited, lively, perky, blithe, bright, sunny, buoyant, vivacious, bubbly, effervescent, jaunty, bouncy, breezy; optimistic, positive; easy-going, free and easy, happy-go-lucky, in good spirits, untroubled, genial; entertaining, amusing, funny, comic, humorous, chucklesome, witty, mirthful, diverting; informal chirpy, upbeat; dated gay; archaic frolicsome.
▷ANTONYMS miserable, gloomy, serious, solemn.

lighthouse **noun** **beacon**, pharos, phare, leading light; lightship, floating light, light vessel; light, signal; archaic watchtower, fanal.

lightly adverb **1** *Maisie kissed him lightly on the cheek*: **softly**, gently, faintly, delicately; gingerly, timidly.
▷ANTONYMS hard, heavily.
2 *season very lightly with salt and pepper | lightly cooked salmon*: **sparingly**, slightly, sparsely, moderately, softly, thinly, delicately.
▷ANTONYMS intensely, abundantly.
3 *he has got off lightly*: **without severe punishment**, easily, leniently, mildly.
▷ANTONYMS severely.
4 *her views are not to be dismissed lightly*: **carelessly**, airily, readily, heedlessly, without consideration, uncaringly, indifferently, unthinkingly, thoughtlessly, flippantly, facilely, breezily, frivolously; light-heartedly, gaily, blithely, nonchalantly, cheerfully.
▷ANTONYMS seriously.

lightweight adjective **1** *a comfortable lightweight jacket*: **thin**, light, flimsy, insubstantial; summery; feathery, airy, delicate, fine, floaty, gauzy, sheer, gossamer, diaphanous, transparent, translucent, see-through.
▷ANTONYMS heavy, thick.
2 *snobs will dismiss the show as lightweight, contrived pap*: **trivial**, insubstantial, trifling, frothy, superficial, shallow, unintellectual, undemanding, frivolous, insignificant; of no account, unimportant, of no consequence, inconsequential, minor, paltry, petty, slight, negligible, immaterial, of no merit, of no value, valueless, worthless.
▷ANTONYMS profound, heavyweight.

likable adjective See **likeable**.

like[1] verb **1** *I rather like Colonel Maitland*: **be fond of**, be attached to, have a soft spot for, have a fondness for, have a liking for, have regard for, think well of, look on with favour, hold in esteem, admire, respect, esteem; be attracted to, fancy, find attractive, be keen on, be taken with; informal take a shine to, be into, rate.
▷ANTONYMS dislike, hate.
2 *Maisie likes veal | she likes gardening*: **enjoy**, have a taste for, have a preference for, have a liking for, have a weakness for, be partial to, delight in, find/take pleasure in, be keen on, find agreeable, derive pleasure from, be pleased by, have a penchant for, have a passion for, derive satisfaction from, find enjoyable, take to, appreciate; love, adore, relish, savour, lap up, revel in; informal get a kick from/out of, have a thing about, be into, get off on, go for, be mad about/for, dig, groove on, get a charge from/out of, get a buzz from/out of, get a bang out of, be hooked on, go a bundle on.
▷ANTONYMS dislike, hate.
3 *feel free to say what you like*: **choose**, please, prefer, wish, want, desire, see fit, think fit, care to, fancy, be/feel inclined, will.
▷ANTONYMS reject.
4 *how would she like it if someone did that to her picture?* **feel about**, regard, think about, consider.

like[2] preposition **1** *you're just like a teacher*: **similar to**, the same as, identical to.
▷ANTONYMS unlike.
2 *the figure landed like a cat*: **in the same way as**, in the manner of, in the same manner as, in the same way that, in a similar way to, after the fashion of, along/on the lines of, as, tantamount to.
▷ANTONYMS unlike.
3 *physical decay extends across whole areas of cities like Birmingham, Glasgow, and Leeds*: **such as**, for example, for instance, in particular, as, namely, viz.
▷ANTONYMS except for.
4 *Richard sounded mean and spiteful, which isn't like him*: **characteristic of**, typical of, in character with.
▷ANTONYMS unlike.
▶ noun *well, we shan't see his like again*: **equal**, match, equivalent, counterpart, opposite number, fellow, twin, mate, parallel, peer; rare compeer.
▷ANTONYMS inferior; superior.
▶ adjective *a like situation*: **similar**, much the same, more or less the same, not unlike, comparable, corresponding, correspondent, resembling, alike, approximating, analogous, parallel, equivalent, cognate, related, of a kind, akin, kindred; interchangeable, indistinguishable, identical, same, matching.
▷ANTONYMS different, dissimilar.

> *Word links* **like**
>
> **-esque** related suffix, as in *carnivalesque, Pythonesque*
> **-ish** related suffix, as in *amateurish, girlish*
> **-oid** related suffix, as in *asteroid, rhomboid*

likeable, likable adjective *a lively and very likeable young woman*: **pleasant**, nice, friendly, agreeable, affable, amiable, genial, civil, personable, charming, popular, clubbable, good-natured, engaging, warm, pleasing, appealing, endearing, convivial, congenial, winning, delightful, enchanting, attractive, winsome, fetching, captivating, lovable, adorable, sweet; Scottish couthy; Italian & Spanish simpatico; informal chummy, pally, darling, lovely.
▷ANTONYMS hateful, unpleasant.

likelihood noun *solicitors also fear that the changes could increase the likelihood of a miscarriage of justice*: **probability**, chance, prospect, possibility, likeliness, odds, feasibility, plausibility, conceivability; risk, threat, hazard, danger, fear, peril, liability; hope, opportunity, promise.
▷ANTONYMS unlikeliness.

likely adjective **1** *it seemed likely that a scandal of some sort would eventually break | the likely outcome of the vote*: **probable**, distinctly possible, to be expected, odds-on, on, possible, credible, plausible, believable, within the bounds of possibility, imaginable; expected, anticipated, natural, prospective, predictable, predicted, foreseeable, ten to one, liable; sure, destined, fated; in the wind, in the air; informal on the cards, a pound to a penny.
▷ANTONYMS unlikely, impossible; improbable.
2 *a more likely explanation for the slump can be found in the shaky financial structure of the club*: **plausible**, reasonable, feasible, acceptable, believable, credible, tenable, conceivable.
▷ANTONYMS incredible, unbelievable.
3 ironic *Gone running has he? A likely story!* **unlikely**, implausible, unbelievable, incredible, untenable, unacceptable, inconceivable.
▷ANTONYMS believable.
4 *it was a likely place for a romantic-minded young girl to frequent*: **suitable**, appropriate, apposite, fit, fitting, acceptable, proper, right; reasonable, promising, hopeful.
5 *what would I be needing money for with a likely lad like Tom here to support me?* **likely to succeed**, **promising**, talented, gifted; informal up-and-coming.
▶ adverb *he was most likely dead*: **probably**, in all probability, presumably, no doubt, doubtlessly; informal like enough, (as) like as not.

liken verb *these sculptures have been likened to seashells*: **compare**, equate, show the resemblance/similarity between, analogize, draw an analogy between, make an analogy of/between, draw a parallel between, parallel, correlate, match; link, associate, make connections between, bracket together, think of together, regard as similar, set beside, mention in the same breath; set side by side.
▷ANTONYMS contrast.

likeness noun **1** *her likeness to Anne is quite uncanny*: **resemblance**, similarity, alikeness, sameness, similitude, congruity, affinity, correspondence, analogy, parallelism, agreement, relationship, identity, identicalness, uniformity, conformity, equivalence.
▷ANTONYMS dissimilarity.
2 *the arm of the chair had been carved in the likeness of a naked woman*: **semblance**, guise, appearance, outward form, form, shape, image, aspect, character, mien.
3 *a few coins which bear the likeness of the last president*: **representation**, image, depiction, portrayal, delineation, profile; picture, drawing, sketch, painting, portrait, photograph, study, bust, statue, statuette, sculpture, icon.

likewise adverb **1** *an ambush was out of the question, likewise poison*: **also**, in addition, too, as well, by the same token, to boot; besides, moreover, furthermore, further, into the bargain.
2 *we hope you will continue to support the Society, and encourage your family and friends to do likewise*: **the same**, similarly, correspondingly, in the same way, in like manner, in similar fashion.
▷ANTONYMS the opposite.

liking noun *he had a ruddy complexion due to his liking for port*: **fondness**, love, affection, penchant, attachment; enjoyment, appreciation, taste; preference, partiality, predilection, proclivity, propensity, proneness, predisposition, tendency, bias; desire, fancy, inclination, bent, leaning, hankering, affinity, attraction; passion, longing, urge, itch; informal thing.
▷ANTONYMS dislike, aversion, hatred.

lilt noun *the lilt of his Scottish accent*: **cadence**, rise and fall, inflection, intonation, upswing, emphasis, stress, rhythm, swing, sway, beat, pulse, measure, metre, tempo.

limb noun **1** *he was stretching his sore limbs*: **arm**, **leg**; wing; extremity, appendage, protuberance, projection; archaic member.
2 *the bare limbs of a high tree*: **branch**, bough.
3 *local job centres act as limbs of the Ministry of Employment*: **section**, branch, offshoot, arm, wing, part, subdivision; department, division, office, member.
□ **out on a limb 1** *the portrayal of Scotland as being out on a limb from the rest of Britain*: **isolated**, stranded, segregated, set apart, separate, marooned, cut off; solitary, sequestered, high and dry. ▷ANTONYMS a central part of.
2 *I don't think the government would be prepared to go out on a limb on his behalf*: **in a precarious position**, in a weak position, in a risky situation, vulnerable; informal sticking one's neck out. ▷ANTONYMS in a safe position/situation.

> *Word links* **limb**
>
> **appendicular** relating to a limb

limber adjective *I have to practise to keep myself limber*: **lithe**, **supple**, nimble, lissom, flexible, fit, spry, sprightly, agile, acrobatic, quick-moving, deft, willowy, graceful, loose-jointed, loose-limbed; active, lively, in good condition; informal in good nick.
▷ANTONYMS stiff, unfit.
▶ verb
□ **limber up** *they had been limbering up for their evening's training schedule*: **warm up**, loosen up, get into condition, get into shape, get ready, prepare, practise, train, drill; stretch, exercise, work out.

limbo noun *unbaptized infants are thought to live in limbo*: **oblivion**, void, non-existence, neither heaven nor hell.
□ **in limbo** *the measure has been in limbo since Congress took a 10-day break*: **in abeyance**, unattended to, unfinished, incomplete; suspended, deferred, postponed, put off, pending, in a state of suspension, awaiting action, on ice, in cold storage; unresolved, undetermined, in a state of uncertainty, up in the air, betwixt and between; ongoing, outstanding, hanging fire; abandoned, forgotten, left out, neglected; informal on the back burner, on hold.
▷ANTONYMS in hand, under way, continuing.

limelight noun (**the limelight**) *she couldn't conceal her excitement at being back in the limelight*: **the focus of attention**, public attention, public notice, public interest, the public eye, media attention, media interest; public recognition, publicity, the glare of publicity, prominence, exposure, hype, glare, the spotlight; fame, renown, celebrity, stardom, notability, eminence.
▷ANTONYMS obscurity.

limit noun **1** *a campus outside the city limits*: **boundary**, border, boundary line, bound, bounding line, partition line, frontier, edge, demarcation line, end point, cut-off point, termination; perimeter, outside, outline, confine, periphery, margin, rim, extremity, fringe, threshold, compass.
▷ANTONYMS centre.
2 *for Saturday's match the police have set a limit of 4,500 supporters*: **maximum**, ceiling, limitation, upper limit; restriction, curb, check, control, curtailment, restraint; damper, brake, rein.
▷ANTONYMS minimum.
3 *resources are stretched to the limit*: **utmost**, breaking point, extremity, greatest extent, ultimate, end point, the bitter end.
4 (**the limit**) *that really is the limit!* **the last straw**, the straw that broke the camel's back, enough, more than enough; informal the end, it.
▶ verb *the pressure to limit costs | Congress's power to legislate may be limited by the Constitution*: **restrict**, curb, check, place a limit on, cap, keep within bounds, hold in check, restrain, put a brake on, hold, freeze, peg; regulate, control, govern, delimit, demarcate, circumscribe, ration; arrest, bridle, inhibit, damp (down), fetter, tie down; rare trammel.
▷ANTONYMS increase, allow to grow unchecked.

limitation noun **1** *there have been calls for a limitation on the number of newcomers*: **restriction**, curb, restraint, constraint, control, check, clampdown; hindrance, impediment, obstacle, obstruction, bar, barrier, block, deterrent, inhibition, damper, brake, rein.
▷ANTONYMS extension, increase.
2 *the critic must be aware of his own limitations*: **imperfection**, flaw, defect, failing, shortcoming, weak point, inability, incapability, deficiency, failure, incapacity, frailty, weakness; disability, foible, vice, disadvantage, drawback.
▷ANTONYMS strength, strong point.

limited adjective **1** *the competition for limited resources | space is limited*: **restricted**, **finite**, bounded, little, narrow, tight, lean, slight, slender, in short supply, short; meagre, scanty, sparse, insubstantial, deficient, inadequate, insufficient, paltry, poor, miserly; basic, rudimentary, patchy, sketchy, minimal; cramped, small.
▷ANTONYMS ample, boundless, unlimited.
2 *the limited powers of the council*: **restricted**, curbed, checked, controlled, restrained, constrained, confined; delimited, defined, qualified.
▷ANTONYMS unlimited, absolute.

limitless adjective *he's got limitless ability*: **boundless**, unbounded, unlimited, without limit, illimitable; infinite, endless, never-ending, unending, everlasting, untold, immeasurable, measureless, incalculable, inestimable, bottomless, fathomless; immense, vast, huge, great, extensive; unceasing, unflagging, interminable, without end, inexhaustible, constant, perpetual; literary myriad.
▷ANTONYMS limited, little.

limp[1] verb *she limped out of the house*: **hobble**, walk with a limp, walk with difficulty, walk lamely, walk haltingly, walk unevenly, falter; shuffle, shamble, totter, dodder, stagger, stumble; Scottish hirple.
▶ noun *he walked with a limp*: **lameness**, hobble, uneven gait, shuffle; rare claudication.

limp[2] adjective **1** *a limp handshake | a posy of limp flowers*: **soft**, **flaccid**, loose, slack, lacking firmness, lax, unfirm, pliable, not taut, relaxed; **floppy**, drooping, droopy, sagging, hanging, pendulous.
▷ANTONYMS firm, stiff.
2 *we were all limp with exhaustion*: **tired**, fatigued, weary, exhausted, worn out; lethargic, listless, spiritless, without energy, spent, weak, enervated, flagging.
▷ANTONYMS energetic.
3 *a limp and lacklustre speech*: **uninspired**, uninspiring, insipid, flat, lifeless, vapid, half-hearted.
▷ANTONYMS inspired, stirring.

limpid adjective **1** *a limpid pool | her limpid eyes*: **clear**, transparent, glassy, glass-like, crystal clear, crystalline, see-through, translucent, pellucid, unclouded, uncloudy.
▷ANTONYMS opaque; muddy.
2 *the limpid clarity of his later novels*: **lucid**, clear, plain, understandable, intelligible, comprehensible, perceptible, coherent, explicit, unambiguous, simple, vivid, sharp, direct, clear-cut, crystal clear, luminous, straightforward, distinct, perspicuous; rare luculent.
▷ANTONYMS unintelligible.
3 *it was a limpid, beautiful day*: **calm**, still, serene, tranquil, placid, peaceful, untroubled, fair, fine.
▷ANTONYMS stormy; murky.

line[1] noun **1** *he drew a line through the name | a pattern of wavy lines*: dash, rule, bar, score; underline, underscore, stroke, slash, virgule, solidus; stripe, strip, band, streak, belt, striation; technical stria; Brit. oblique.
2 *there were new lines round her eyes and mouth*: **wrinkle**, furrow, crease, crinkle, crow's foot, groove, corrugation; scar.
3 (usually **lines**) *the classic lines of its exterior*: **contour**, **outline**, configuration, shape, figure, delineation, silhouette, profile, features.
4 *he headed the ball over the line | the county line*: **boundary**, boundary line, limit, border, borderline, bound, bounding line, frontier, partition, demarcation line, dividing line, end point, cut-off point, termination, edge, pale, margin, perimeter, periphery, rim, extremity, fringe, threshold.
5 (usually **lines**) *they were behind enemy lines*: **position**, formation, disposition, front, front line, firing line; trenches.
6 *he put the washing on the line | a fishing line*: **cord**, rope, string, cable, wire, thread, twine, strand, filament, ligature.
7 *a line of soldiers*: **file**, rank, column, string, chain; train, convoy, procession; row, queue; Brit. informal crocodile.
8 *a line of figures*: **column**, row.
9 *it seemed to be the latest in a long line of crass decisions*: **series**, sequence, succession, chain, string, train; progression, course, set, cycle.
10 *it stopped right in the line of flight of some bees*: **course**, route, track, channel, path, way, run; trajectory, bearing, orientation.
11 *they took a very tough line with the industry right from the word go | ministers are obliged to follow the party line*: **course of action**, course, procedure, MO, technique, way, tactic, tack, system, method, process, manner; **policy**, practice, scheme, approach, plan, programme, position, stance, philosophy, argument, avenue; Latin modus operandi.
12 *she had not been listening, but pursuing her own line of thought*: **course**, direction, drift, tack, tendency, trend, bias, tenor.
13 *oh, come on, don't give me that line*: **patter**, story, pitch, piece of fiction, fabrication; informal spiel.
14 (**lines**) *he couldn't seem to remember his lines*: **words**, role, part, script, speech, dialogue.
15 *there are no jobs nowadays in my line*: **line of work**, line of business, business, field, trade, occupation, employment, profession, work, job, calling, vocation, career, pursuit, activity, walk of life; **specialty**, forte, province, department, sphere, area, area of expertise, domain, realm; French métier; informal line of country, game, thing, bag, pigeon, racket.
16 *he's introduced his own line of cologne*: **brand**, kind, sort, type, variety, make, label, trade name, trademark, registered trademark.
17 *a man from a noble line claiming royal descent*: **ancestry**, family, parentage, birth, descent, lineage, extraction, derivation, heritage, genealogy, roots, house, dynasty, origin, background; stock, strain, race, bloodline, blood, breeding, pedigree, succession.
18 *the opening line of Wilfred Owen's 'Anthem for Doomed Youth'*: **sentence**, phrase, group of words, prosodic unit, construction, clause, utterance; passage, extract, quotation, quote, citation, section, piece, part, snippet, sound bite, fragment, portion.
19 *perhaps I should drop Ralph a line*: **note**, letter, card, postcard, message, bulletin, communication, epistle, missive, memorandum, dispatch, report; correspondence, word; informal memo.
□ **draw the line at** *I draw the line at the fish-hook method on humanitarian grounds*: **stop short of**, refuse to accept, draw a line in the sand, baulk at; object to, take issue with, take exception to; informal put one's foot down about.
▷ANTONYMS approve of.
□ **in line 1** *the poor still had to stand in line for food stamps*: **in a queue**, in a row, in a column, in a file. **2** *the adverts are in line with the editorial style of the magazines*: **in agreement**, in accord, in accordance, in harmony, in step, in conformity; in compliance, in obedience. ▷ANTONYMS different, out of step. **3** *hold the front sight directly in line with the bullseye*: **in alignment**, aligned, level, balanced, at the same height, straight; plumb, true; abreast, side by side. **4** *the referee seemed determined to keep him in line*: **under**

control, in order, in check, obedient, conforming with the rules.

□ **in line for** *he was now in line for promotion*: **a candidate for**, in the running for, on the shortlist for, shortlisted for, being considered for, under consideration for, next in succession for, likely to receive, up for, ready for.

□ **lay it on the line** *soon, I'm going to have to lay it on the line, tell them what really has been happening*: **speak frankly**, be direct, speak honestly, pull no punches, be blunt, not mince one's words, call a spade a spade; informal give it to someone straight, tell it like it is.

▷ANTONYMS equivocate, shilly-shally.

□ **on the line** *we should protect police officers whose lives are on the line*: **at risk**, in danger, endangered, imperilled.

□ **toe the line** *sooner or later a boy has to learn to toe the line*: **conform**, obey the rules, comply with the rules, observe the rules, abide by the rules, adhere to the rules, act in accordance with the rules, follow the rules, keep to the rules, stick to the rules; submit, yield; informal play it by the book, play by the rules, keep in step.

▷ANTONYMS misbehave.

▸verb **1** *her face was lined with age*: **furrow**, wrinkle, crease, mark with lines, cover with lines, crinkle, pucker, corrugate.

2 *the driveway was lined by poplars*: **border**, edge, fringe, bound, skirt, hem, rim.

□ **line up** *we entered the building and lined up*: **form a queue**, form a line, form lines, get into rows/columns, file, queue up, group together, fall in, straighten up; Military dress; Brit. informal form a crocodile.

□ **line someone/something up 1** *they lined them up and shot them*: **arrange in a line**, arrange in lines, put in rows, arrange in columns; group, marshal, align, range, straighten up, arrange, array, dispose; Military dress.

2 *we've lined up an all-star cast*: **assemble**, get together, organize, prepare, arrange, lay on; get, obtain, procure, secure, produce, come up with, fix up, prearrange; book, schedule, timetable.

line² verb *a cardboard box lined with a blanket*: **cover**, put a lining in, back, put a backing on, interline, face, panel, inlay, reinforce, encase; paper, decorate; stuff, fill, pack, pad; archaic ceil.

□ **line one's pockets** informal *he had lined his pockets with campaign funds*: **make money**; accept bribes; embezzle money, siphon off money; informal feather one's nest, graft, be on the make, be on the take.

lineage noun *a Dutch nobleman of ancient lineage*: **ancestry**, family, parentage, birth; **descent**, line, extraction, derivation, heritage, genealogy, roots, house, dynasty, origin, background; stock, strain, race, bloodline, blood, breeding, pedigree, succession.

lineaments plural noun *the lineaments of his face*: **distinctive features**, features, distinguishing characteristics, hallmarks, properties, traits; **form**, outline, lines, contours; configuration, physiognomy, profile, face, countenance, visage.

lined¹ adjective **1** *a pad of lined paper*: **ruled**, feint; scored, striped, stripy, banded, streaked, striated.

▷ANTONYMS plain, blank.

2 *his lined, weather-worn face*: **wrinkled**, wrinkly, furrowed, creased, marked with lines, covered with lines, crinkled, wizened, leathery, worn, puckered, grooved, corrugated; scarred.

▷ANTONYMS smooth.

lined² adjective *lined curtains*: **covered**, backed, interlined; faced, panelled, inlaid; reinforced, encased, papered, decorated; stuffed, filled, packed, padded; archaic ceiled.

liner noun **1** *the luxury liner QE II*: **ship**, ocean liner, passenger vessel, boat.

2 *her eyes were ringed with liner*: **eyeliner**, eye pencil, kohl pencil, kohl, eyeshadow, eyebrow pencil, lipliner.

line-up noun **1** *they saw the star-studded line-up as an opportunity to boost viewing figures*: **list of performers**, list, listing, cast, bill, programme.

2 *United's starting line-up*: **list of players**, team, squad, side, selection.

3 *you've got a long line-up of customers at the ticket window*: **queue**, line, row, column; Brit. informal crocodile.

linger verb **1** *the crowd lingered for a long time, until it was almost dark*: **wait around**, stay, remain, stay put, wait; loiter, dawdle, dally, take one's time, lag behind, straggle, dither, potter about/around/round, pause; procrastinate, stall, delay; informal dilly-dally, stick around, hang around/round, hang on, hang back; archaic or literary tarry.

▷ANTONYMS leave.

2 *the infection can linger for many years | ten years later, the memory lingers on*: **persist**, continue, remain, stay; be protracted, endure, carry on, last, keep on/up, hold; survive, abide; informal hang around/round.

▷ANTONYMS vanish, disappear.

> *Choose the right word* **linger, loiter, dawdle**
>
> The idea common to these words is that of prolonging an activity or staying longer than necessary.
>
> A person may **linger** somewhere because they are enjoying being there, not merely because they are wasting time (*just linger over your coffee and liqueurs*). If something such as a person's *fingers, eyes*, or *look* linger, they stay in one place for a long time (*her fingers linger on his | Merrill's gaze lingered on his mouth*). *Linger* is also used of something, typically an abstract noun, that lasts longer than normal or expected (*the memory lingered on*); the adjectival form *lingering* is often used in this sense (*a lingering death*).
>
> **Loiter** is always used in a spatial sense: it is to stay somewhere too long and typically be up to no good (*teenagers loitering in front of a newsagent's, drinking shandy and smoking*).
>
> **Dawdling** is normally used of slow, idle movement (*a handful of people crossed the square, dawdling on their way home*) and often implies that someone is wasting time (*don't dawdle over your breakfast*).

lingerie noun *fine silk lingerie*: **women's underwear**, underclothes, underclothing, undergarments, nightwear, nightclothes; informal undies, frillies, underthings, unmentionables; Brit. informal smalls; rare underlinen.

lingering adjective **1** *there were still some lingering doubts in my mind*: **remaining**, surviving, persisting, abiding, nagging, niggling, gnawing, lasting, residual.

2 *a lingering recession*: **protracted**, persistent, prolonged, long-drawn-out, long-lasting, lasting, dragging, chronic, unabating, long-standing.

▷ANTONYMS short-lived.

lingo informal noun **1** *it doesn't matter if you can't speak the lingo*. See **language** (sense 2).

2 *the hacker lingo makes this magazine indecipherable*. See **language** (sense 3).

linguistic adjective *the meanings of linguistic expressions | a child's linguistic ability*: **language-producing**, semantic, lingual, semasiological; rhetorical, verbal, poetic, expressive.

lining noun *a cape with a fur lining*: **backing**, interlining, facing, inlay, reinforcement, liner; panelling; quilting, cushioning, padding, wadding, stuffing, filling.

link noun **1** *a chain made of steel links*: **loop**, ring, connection, connective, connector, coupling, joint, knot.

2 *the links between transport and the environment*: **connection**, relationship, relatedness, association, linkage, tie-up.

3 *they cultivated their links with the labour movement*: **bond**, tie, attachment, connection, relationship, association, affiliation; mutual interest, liaison; nexus.

4 *one of the links in the organization*: **component**, constituent, element, part, piece, member, division.

▸verb **1** *four boxes were linked together*: **join**, connect, fasten, attach, bind, unite, combine, amalgamate; clamp, secure, fix, affix, tie, stick, hitch, bond, knit, glue, cement, fuse, weld, solder, couple, yoke.

▷ANTONYMS detach, separate.

2 *there wasn't a scrap of evidence linking him with the body*: **associate**, connect, relate, join, bracket, draw a connection between, marry, wed.

lion noun **1** *a lion stands ready to attack*: **big cat**; king of the beasts; lioness.

2 *my lord was a lion amongst men*: **hero**, man of courage, brave man, lionheart, lionhearted man; conqueror, champion, conquering hero, warrior, knight, paladin.

3 *he hobnobbed with all the lions of the symphony hall*: **celebrity**, person of note, dignitary, notable, VIP, personality, public figure, celebutante, pillar of society, luminary; star, superstar, big name, leading light, idol, magnate; informal big shot, bigwig, big noise, big wheel, big cheese, big gun, somebody, celeb, hotshot, megastar.

□ **beard the lion in his den defy danger**, face up to danger, brave danger, confront danger, stand up to danger; court destruction, tempt providence; informal face the music, bell the cat, bite the bullet.

□ **the lion's share** *the lion's share of the profits*: **most**, the majority, the larger part/number, the greater part/number, the best/better part, the main part, more than half, the bulk, the preponderance.

> *Word links* **lion**
>
> **leonine** relating to lions
> **pride, sawt** collective noun
> **den** home

lionhearted adjective *the lionhearted champion of freedom*: **brave**, courageous, valiant, gallant, intrepid, valorous, fearless, bold, daring; stout-hearted, stalwart, staunch, heroic, audacious, resolute, undaunted, dauntless, doughty, plucky, game, mettlesome, assertive; informal gutsy, spunky.

▷ANTONYMS cowardly, timid, mousy.

lionize verb *the band's leader has been lionized by the media*: **celebrate**, fête, glorify, honour, bestow honour on, exalt, acclaim, admire, commend, sing/sound the praises of, praise, extol, applaud, hail, make a fuss of/over, make much of, cry up, venerate, eulogize, sing paeans to, reverence, pay homage to, pay tribute to, put on a pedestal, hero-worship, worship,

idolize, adulate; aggrandize; rare laud, panegyrize.
▷ANTONYMS vilify.

lip noun **1** *the lip of the coffee pot | the lip of the crater*: **edge**, rim, brim, margin, border, verge, brink; boundary, perimeter; mouth.
▷ANTONYMS centre.
2 informal *I'll tan your hide if I have any more of your lip*. See **insolence**.
□ **keep a stiff upper lip keep control of oneself**, not show emotion, appear unaffected, bite one's lip; informal keep one's cool.

Word links **lip**

labial relating to the lips
labio- related prefix, as in *labiodental*

liquefy verb *above a certain temperature it is impossible to liquefy a gas | the wine was warm and the cheese had liquefied*: **make/become liquid**, condense, dissolve, precipitate; liquidize, melt; deliquesce, run.
▷ANTONYMS solidify, coagulate; gasify.

liquid adjective **1** *liquid fuels*: **fluid**, flowing, running; runny, watery, thin, sloppy, aqueous, liquefied; melted, molten, thawed, dissolved, uncongealed; technical hydrous.
▷ANTONYMS solid; gaseous.
2 *her liquid eyes*: **clear**, transparent, limpid, crystal clear, crystalline, see-through; translucent, pellucid, unclouded, uncloudy; bright, shining, brilliant, glowing, gleaming.
▷ANTONYMS cloudy; opaque.
3 *her liquid voice*: **pure**, clear, smooth, fluent, distinct, clarion; **mellifluous**, dulcet, mellow, sweet, sweet-sounding, sweet-toned, soft, melodious, honeyed, soothing, tuneful, musical, lilting, lyrical, harmonious, euphonious; rare mellifluent.
▷ANTONYMS cacophonous, disharmonious.
4 *liquid assets*: **convertible**, negotiable, disposable, usable, realizable, obtainable, spendable.
▷ANTONYMS unavailable, tied up.
▶ noun *a vat of liquid*: **fluid**; moisture, wet, wetness, damp, dampness; liquor; solution; juice, sap, secretion.
▷ANTONYMS solid; gas.

Word links **liquid**

hydraulics science of moving liquids

Choose the right word **liquid, fluid**

Just as these two words are close in their scientific senses, they have similar figurative meanings.

Scientifically, **liquid** is the narrower term, denoting a fluid, such as water or oil, that flows but has constant volume (at constant temperature and pressure). A liquid has no fixed shape and yields easily to external pressure; thus we can talk metaphorically about *liquid assets* (such as shares or commodities) that can easily be converted into cash, while *a liquid market* features much trading and continual price movements. *Liquid* is also used of things that are clear to the eye or ear (*liquid blue eyes | the liquid song of a bird*).

In its scientific sense, **fluid** denotes anything that flows, including gases, which can change shape more dramatically than liquids. In figurative uses, a *fluid situation* is also very volatile, while *fluid pricing*, to which airline flights and package holidays in particular are now subject, means that their prices are varied continually, according to the demand from customers or the cash-flow requirements of the business. *Fluid* is also used to indicate effortless and graceful movement (*in one fluid movement, he picked up the bag and its contents*).

liquidate verb **1** *if the company was liquidated, there would be enough funds released to honour the debts*: **close down**, wind up, put into liquidation, dissolve, break up, disband, terminate.
2 *he would normally have liquidated his share portfolio*: **convert to cash**, convert, cash, cash in, sell off, sell up, realize.
3 *the fund was raided for purposes other than liquidating the public debt*: **pay off**, pay, pay in full, settle, clear, discharge, square, make good, honour, defray, satisfy, account for; remit.
4 informal *nationalist rivals were liquidated in bloody purges*. See **kill**.

liquidize verb *liquidize a large raw carrot to a smooth paste*: **purée**, cream, liquefy, pulp, crush, press; blend, process.
▷ANTONYMS condense.

liquor noun **1** *it is not permitted to sell liquor to a person under 18*: **alcohol**, spirits, alcoholic drink, strong drink, drink, intoxicating liquor, intoxicant; informal booze, hard stuff, shorts, the demon drink, firewater, juice, grog; N. Amer. informal the sauce, hooch.
2 *carefully strain the cooking liquor into the sauce*: **stock**, broth, bouillon, juice, gravy, liquid, infusion, extract, concentrate, decoction.

lissom adjective *she had the lissom body of a dancer*: **supple**, lithe, limber, graceful, elegant, spry, flexible, loose-limbed, agile, nimble, deft, dexterous, fit; **slim**, slender, thin, willowy, sylphlike, sleek, trim.
▷ANTONYMS portly.

list[1] noun *a list of the world's wealthiest people*: **catalogue**, inventory, record, register, roll, file, index, directory, listing, checklist, tally, docket, ticket, enumeration, table, tabulation; series, litany, recital.
▶ verb *the accounts are listed alphabetically*: **record**, register, make a list of, note down, write down, set down, enter; itemize, enumerate, recite, catalogue, file, log, minute, tabulate, categorize, inventory, schedule, chronicle; classify, group, arrange, sort, rank, alphabetize, index.

list[2] verb *the boat listed to one side*: **lean**, lean over, tilt, tip, heel, heel over, careen, cant, pitch, toss, roll, incline, slant, slope, be at an angle, bank, keel over.
▷ANTONYMS be on an even keel.

listen verb **1** *I've just been **listening to** the news*: **hear**, pay attention, be attentive, attend, concentrate on, concentrate on hearing, give ear to, lend an ear to; hang on someone's words; keep one's ears open, prick up one's ears; informal be all ears, pin back one's ears, get a load of, tune in; literary hark, hearken.
2 *policy-makers should **listen to** popular opinion*: **pay attention**, take heed, heed, give heed, take notice, take note, mind, observe, watch, follow, notice, mark, bear in mind, give a thought to, take into consideration, take into account, take to heart, hang on, accept, believe; obey, do as one is told by.
▷ANTONYMS ignore, be deaf to.
□ **listen in** *anyone with the right radio receiver can **listen in on** calls*: **eavesdrop**, spy; overhear, tap, wiretap, bug, monitor; informal snoop.

listless adjective *she was pale and listless | a listless performance*: **lethargic**, enervated, lackadaisical, spiritless, unenergetic, lifeless, vigourless, lacking energy, limp, effete; **languid**, languorous, languishing, inactive, inert, sluggish, torpid, supine, half-hearted, lukewarm, indifferent, uninterested, impassive; indolent, idle, apathetic, shiftless, slothful; passive, dull, heavy.
▷ANTONYMS energetic, lively.

Choose the right word **listless, languid, lethargic**

See **languid**.

litany noun **1** *the lips of others had moved also, repeating the litany*: **prayer**, invocation, petition, supplication, devotion, entreaty; archaic orison.
2 *a litany of complaints*: **recital**, recitation, repetition, enumeration, account, refrain; **list**, listing, catalogue, inventory, roll.

literacy noun *tests of literacy and numeracy*: **ability to read and write**, reading/writing ability, reading/writing proficiency; learning, book learning, education, scholarship, schooling; letters.
▷ANTONYMS illiteracy.

literal adjective **1** *those who believe in the literal truth of the biblical Genesis | it is unique, in the literal sense of that word*: **strict**, **factual**, plain, simple, bare, exact, straightforward, stark; unvarnished, unexaggerated, unembellished, undistorted, unadulterated; objective, narrow, correct, true, truthful, faithful, accurate, genuine, authentic, veritable, veracious, gospel.
▷ANTONYMS metaphorical, figurative; loose, approximate.
2 *a literal translation*: **word-for-word**, verbatim, line-for-line, letter-for-letter; exact, precise, faithful, close, strict, to the letter, undeviating, true, accurate; rare literatim.
▷ANTONYMS loose, liberal, vague.
3 *his literal, unrhetorical manner*: **literal-minded**, down-to-earth, factual, matter-of-fact, no-nonsense, unsentimental, level-headed, hard-headed; prosaic, unimaginative, colourless, pedestrian, tedious, boring, dull, humdrum, uninspired, uninspiring, prosy.
▷ANTONYMS whimsical.
▶ noun *William read through the article, correcting two literals*: **misprint**, error, mistake, slip, slip of the pen, printing/typographical/typesetting/keyboarding/keying/typing error, corrigendum, erratum; informal typo, howler.

literally adverb *their name, translated literally, means 'the river'*: **verbatim**, word for word, line for line, letter for letter, to the letter; exactly, precisely, faithfully, closely, strictly, strictly speaking, accurately, rigorously; rare literatim.
▷ANTONYMS loosely, imprecisely; metaphorically.

literary adjective **1** *an established canon of literary works*: **written**; poetic, artistic, dramatic; published, printed, in print.
2 *her literary friends | a literary magazine*: **scholarly**, learned, intellectual, cultured, erudite, bookish, highbrow, studious, cerebral, lettered, academic, cultivated, civilized; well read, widely read, knowledgeable, educated, well educated; informal brainy.
▷ANTONYMS ill-educated; popular.
3 *literary language*: **formal**, written; **poetic**, dramatic, dignified, solemn;

elaborate, ornate, flowery, purple.
▷ANTONYMS informal, colloquial, vernacular.

literate adjective 1 *their parents were barely literate*: **able to read and write.**
▷ANTONYMS illiterate.
2 *a literate, informed public*: **educated**, well educated, well read, widely read, scholarly, learned, schooled, knowledgeable, intellectual, intelligent, erudite, lettered, cultured, cultivated, sophisticated, well informed.
▷ANTONYMS ignorant.
3 *a literate and readable study*: **well written**, articulate, lucid, eloquent, stylish, polished.
▷ANTONYMS badly written.

literature noun 1 *a lecturer in English literature*: **written works**, writings, (creative) writing, literary texts, compositions, letters, belles-lettres; printed works, published works; humanities, arts, liberal arts.
2 *the literature on prototype theory*: **publications**, published writings, texts, reports, studies, relevant works.
3 *noticeboards have been covered with election literature*: **printed matter**, brochures, leaflets, pamphlets, circulars, flyers, handouts, handbills, mailshots, bulletins, documentation, publicity, blurb, notices, information, data, facts; informal bumf, junk mail.

lithe adjective *his tall lithe figure*: **agile**, graceful, supple, limber, loose-limbed, nimble, deft, spry, flexible, pliant, pliable, lissom, willowy, acrobatic, fit; rare lithesome.
▷ANTONYMS clumsy, stiff.

litigant noun *a litigant in civil proceedings*: **litigator**, opponent in law, opponent, contestant, contender, disputant, plaintiff, claimant, complainant, petitioner, apellant, respondent, party, interest, defendant, accused.

litigation noun *he objected to some passages in the book, but did not resort to litigation*: **legal proceeding(s)**, legal action, lawsuit, legal dispute, legal case, case, legal contest, action, cause, judicial proceeding(s), suit, suit at law, legal process, prosecution, bringing of charges, indictment, trial.

litter noun 1 *always clear up after a picnic and never drop litter*: **rubbish**, refuse, junk, waste, debris, odds and ends, scraps, leavings, fragments, detritus, flotsam, discarded matter, dross, muck; N. Amer. trash, garbage.
2 *she looked at the litter of glasses around her*: **clutter**, jumble, muddle, mess, tangle, heap, disorder, untidiness, confusion, hotchpotch, disarray, disorganization, disarrangement, turmoil; informal shambles; rare olla podrida.
3 *a litter of kittens*: **brood**, family; young, offspring, progeny, issue; rare progeniture.
4 *threshed straw had to be taken from the barns to the horses for use as litter*: **animal bedding**, bedding, straw, floor covering.
5 *he was conveyed the rest of the way in a horse-drawn litter*: **sedan chair**, palanquin; stretcher, portable bed/couch.
▶ verb *clothes and newspapers littered the floor*: **make untidy**, mess up, make a mess of, clutter up, throw into disorder, be strewn about, be scattered about, be jumbled, be disarranged; informal make a shambles of, trash; literary bestrew, besmirch.

little adjective 1 *a little writing desk*: **small**, small-scale, compact; mini, miniature, tiny, minute, minuscule; toy, baby, pocket, undersized, dwarf, midget; bijou, dainty, cute, sweet, dear; Scottish wee; informal teeny, teeny-weeny, teensy, teensy-weensy, itsy-bitsy, tiddly, half-pint, dinky; Brit. informal titchy, ickle; N. Amer. informal little-bitty, vest-pocket.
▷ANTONYMS big, large.
2 *the smile vanished from the little man's face*: **short**, small, slight, thin, petite, diminutive, tiny; squat, stubby; elfin, dwarf, dwarfish, midget, pygmy, bantam, homunculur, Lilliputian; Scottish wee; informal teeny, teeny-weeny, pint-sized, knee high to a grasshopper.
▷ANTONYMS big, large.
3 *my little sister*: **young**, younger, junior, small, baby, infant, minor.
▷ANTONYMS big, old, elder.
4 *I was a bodyguard for a little while*: **brief**, short, short-lived; fleeting, momentary, transitory, transient, ephemeral, evanescent, infinitesimal; fast, quick, hasty, cursory; Scottish wee.
▷ANTONYMS long.
5 *this car does have a few little problems*: **minor**, **unimportant**, insignificant, trivial, trifling, petty, paltry, inconsequential, negligible, inconsiderable, nugatory, of minor importance, of little/no account.
▷ANTONYMS significant, important.
▶ determiner *they have low status and little political influence*: **hardly any**, not much, slight, small, scant, limited, restricted, modest, little or no, minimal, negligible; insufficient, inadequate.
▷ANTONYMS considerable, a great deal of.
□ **a little 1** *if it's too thick, add a little water*: **some**, **a small amount of**, a bit of, a touch of, a soupçon of, a dash of, a taste of, a dab of, a spot of, a modicum of, a morsel of, a fragment of, a snippet of, a tinge of, a particle of, a jot of, a shade of, a suggestion of, a trace of, a hint of, a suspicion of; a dribble of, a splash of, a driblet of; a pinch of, a sprinkling of, a sprinkle of, a grain of, a speck of; informal a smidgen of, a tad of. ▷ANTONYMS a lot of, a great deal of.
2 *after a little, Oliver came in*: **a short time**, a little while, a bit, an interval, a short spell, a short period; a minute, a moment, a second, a split second, an instant, a flash; informal a sec, a mo, a jiffy, a jiff. ▷ANTONYMS a long time.
3 *the whole scene does remind me a little of the Adriatic*: **slightly**, faintly, remotely, vaguely; moderately, somewhat, a little bit, quite, to some degree, fairly; informal sort of, kind of, kinda, ish. ▷ANTONYMS a great deal.
□ **little by little** *little by little, the town was turning into ruins*: **gradually**, slowly, by degrees, by stages, step by step, piecemeal, progressively, bit by bit, inch by inch, inchmeal; subtly, imperceptibly, unnoticeably.
▷ANTONYMS immediately, all at once.
▶ adverb 1 *he is little known as a teacher*: **hardly**, barely, scarcely, not much, only slightly, slightly, only just.
▷ANTONYMS well.
2 *this disease is little seen nowadays*: **rarely**, seldom, infrequently, hardly ever, hardly, scarcely ever, scarcely, not much.
▷ANTONYMS often.

liturgical adjective *liturgical music*: **ceremonial**, ritual, solemn, sacramental, hieratic, church, for use in church.
▷ANTONYMS secular.

liturgy noun *the Anglican liturgy*: **ritual**, worship, service, ceremony, rite, observance, celebration, ordinance, office, sacrament, solemnity, ceremonial; formulation, form, custom, practice, tradition, rubric.

live[1] (rhymes with 'give') verb 1 *he was one of the greatest mathematicians who ever lived*: **exist**, **be alive**, be, have being, have life; breathe, draw breath, walk the earth; be extant; informal be in the land of the living.
▷ANTONYMS die, be dead.
2 *I live in central London | about 38,000 people* ***live in*** *the area*: **reside**, have one's home, have one's residence, be settled; be housed, lodge, board; inhabit, occupy, populate; Scottish stay; informal hang out, hang one's hat, put up; formal dwell, sojourn, be domiciled; archaic bide.
3 *he lived quietly during his remaining years*: **pass one's life**, spend one's life, lead one's life, have a life, have a lifestyle; behave, conduct oneself, comport oneself.
4 *she had lived a difficult life*: **experience**, spend, pass, lead, have, go through, undergo.
5 *old people living on small fixed pensions | Freddy lived by his wits*: **survive**, make a living, earn one's living, eke out a living; subsist, support oneself, sustain oneself; keep alive, stay alive, maintain oneself, make ends meet, keep body and soul together.
6 *couldn't we just forget about work for one afternoon and live a little?* **enjoy oneself**, enjoy life, have fun, be happy, live life to the full; flourish, prosper, thrive, make the most of life.
□ **live it up** informal *those two are living it up in Hawaii*: **live extravagantly**, live in the lap of luxury, live in clover; **carouse**, revel, overindulge, party, enjoy oneself, celebrate, have a good time, roister; informal go on a spree, push the boat out, paint the town red, have a ball, make whoopee, go overboard, make a pig of oneself; N. Amer. informal live high on/off the hog; archaic wassail.
□ **live off/on** *scavenging seabirds live off discarded fish*: **subsist on**, feed on/off, rely for nourishment on, thrive on, depend on; **eat**, consume, use.
□ **live up to** *the drive certainly lived up to my expectations*: **measure up to**, match up to, come up to, reach, satisfy, fulfil, achieve, meet, equal, be equal to, be on a level with, compare with, admit of comparison, bear comparison with; be good enough, fit/fill the bill; informal hold a candle to.
▷ANTONYMS exceed; fall short of.

live[2] (rhymes with 'five') adjective 1 *the use of live bait*: **living**, alive, having life, breathing; animate, organic, biological, sentient; existing, existent, extant; informal in the land of the living, among the living; archaic quick.
▷ANTONYMS dead, inanimate.
2 *this is her first live appearance in Britain | a live radio phone-in*: **in the flesh**, personal, in person, actual; **not pre-recorded**, not recorded, unedited; not delayed, real-time; with an audience.
▷ANTONYMS recorded.
3 *he touched a live rail while working on the track*: **electrified**, charged, powered, connected, active, switched on; informal hot.
▷ANTONYMS inactive.
4 *the fire grate was full of live coals*: **hot**, **glowing**, red hot, aglow, smouldering; burning, alight, flaming, aflame, blazing, fiery, ignited, on fire, afire.
5 *a live grenade*: **unexploded**, explosive, explodable, active; loaded, charged, primed; unstable, volatile.
▷ANTONYMS inactive.
6 *gay rights have become a live issue across America*: **topical**, current, of current interest, contemporary; **burning**, pressing, important, vital; relevant, pertinent; controversial, debatable, unsettled.
□ **live wire** *she's a real live wire*: **energetic person**; informal **ball of fire**, fireball, human dynamo, busy bee, eager beaver, go-getter, whizz-kid, mover and shaker, powerhouse, life and soul of the party, tiger, demon.

livelihood noun *many people in the area relied on the coconut plantations for their livelihood*: **income**, source of income, means of support, means, living, subsistence, keep, maintenance, sustenance, nourishment, daily bread, upkeep; job, work, employment, occupation, trade, profession, career; informal bread and butter.

livelong adjective literary *we decided to hunt and play together the livelong day*: **entire**, whole, total, complete, full, long; unbroken, undivided, continuous.

lively adjective **1** *the bride was an attractive and lively young woman*: **energetic**, active, animated, vigorous, dynamic, full of life, outgoing, spirited, high-spirited, vivacious, enthusiastic, vibrant, buoyant, exuberant, effervescent, cheerful; bouncy, bubbly, perky, sparkling, sprightly, spry, youthful, zesty, zestful, frisky, skittish; fun, fun-loving; informal bright-eyed and bushy-tailed, full of beans, chirpy, go-go, chipper, peppy, zippy, zappy, full of vim and vigour; N. Amer. informal peart.
▷ANTONYMS listless, lifeless, apathetic.
2 *a lively West End bar*: **busy**, crowded, bustling, hectic, swarming, teeming, astir, buzzing, thronging; **vibrant**, boisterous, jolly, festive; informal hopping, jumping, buzzy.
▷ANTONYMS quiet, dead.
3 *a lively debate*: **heated**, vigorous, stimulating, animated, spirited, enthusiastic, forceful; exciting, stirring, interesting, eventful, memorable.
▷ANTONYMS lifeless, dull.
4 *a lively portrait of the local community*: **vivid**, colourful, striking, stirring, graphic, bold, strong, interesting, effective, imaginative.
▷ANTONYMS lifeless, dull.
5 *he bowled at a lively pace*: **brisk**, quick, fast, rapid, swift, speedy, smart, vigorous, fast and furious; informal nippy, snappy.
▷ANTONYMS slow.
6 *the press is making things lively for the Government*: **awkward**, tricky, difficult, challenging; **eventful**, exciting, busy; informal hairy.
▷ANTONYMS easy, peaceful.

> *Word toolkit* **lively**
>
> See **rowdy**.

l

liven verb
□ **liven up** *at this, he seemed to liven up*: **brighten up**, cheer up, perk up, wake up, revive, rally, pick up, become lively, bounce back; informal buck up.
□ **liven someone/something up** *he could do with a drink to liven him up*: **brighten up**, cheer up, enliven, put some life into, animate, put some spark into, raise someone's spirits, perk up, spice up, ginger up, make lively, waken/wake up, hearten, gladden, invigorate, give a boost to, rejuvenate, vitalize, restore, revive, refresh, vivify, put some zest into, galvanize, stimulate, stir up, get going; informal buck up, pep up, jazz up, hot up.
▷ANTONYMS calm someone down.

liver noun

> *Word links* **liver**
>
> **hepatic** relating to the liver
> **hepato-** related prefix, as in *hepatotoxic*
> **hepatitis** inflammation of the liver
> **hepatectomy** removal of the liver

livery noun *pageboys in scarlet and green livery*: **uniform**, regalia, costume, dress, attire, habit, garb, clothes, clothing, outfit, suit, garments, ensemble, robes, finery; informal get-up, gear, togs, clobber, duds, kit; formal apparel; literary raiment, array; archaic vestments.

livid adjective **1** informal *he was livid at finding himself back on the bench*: **furious**, angry, infuriated, irate, fuming, raging, seething, incensed, enraged, angered, beside oneself, wrathful, ireful, maddened, cross, annoyed, irritated, exasperated, indignant; informal mad, boiling, wild, seeing red, hot under the collar, up in arms, foaming at the mouth, on the warpath, steamed up, fit to be tied.
2 *Quinn had a livid bruise on the side of his jaw*: **purplish**, bluish, dark, discoloured, black and blue, purple, greyish-blue; bruised; angry.

living noun **1** *she was cleaning floors for a living*: **livelihood**, income, source of income, means of support, means, subsistence, keep, maintenance, sustenance, nourishment, daily bread, upkeep; job, work, employment, occupation, trade, profession, career; informal bread and butter.
2 *making informed choices about healthy living | urban living*: **way of life**, lifestyle, manner of living, way of living, mode of living, life; conduct, behaviour, activities; customs, habits, ways.
▶adjective **1** *living organisms*: **alive**, live, having life; animate, organic, biological, sentient; breathing, moving; existing, existent; informal in the land of the living, among the living, alive and kicking; archaic quick.
▷ANTONYMS dead, inanimate, extinct.
2 *English, unlike Latin, is a living language*: **current**, contemporary, present; **in use**, operative, active, operating, ongoing, continuing, surviving, extant, persisting, remaining, abiding; existing, existent, in existence.
▷ANTONYMS dead, obsolete, extinct.
3 *he committed to paper a living image of the man*: **exact**, faithful, true to life, speaking, authentic, genuine; close, near, similar, like, alike.
▷ANTONYMS inaccurate.

> *Word toolkit* **living**
>
> See **organic**.

living room noun *the television was on in the living room*: **sitting room**, lounge, parlour, front room, drawing room, morning room, reception room, salon, family room; TV room; common room.

lizard noun

> *Word links* **lizard**
>
> **saurian** relating to lizards

load noun **1** *MacDowell's got a load to deliver | the rear seats can be folded forward to carry larger loads*: **cargo**, freight, freightage, charge, burden; pack, bundle, parcel, bale; consignment, haul, delivery, shipment, batch; goods, merchandise, payload; contents; lorryload, truckload, shipload, boatload, containerload, busload, vanload; archaic lading.
2 informal *I bought **a load of** clothes | a hot dog with **loads of** fried onions*: **a lot**, **a great deal**, a great/large amount, a large quantity, a number, an abundance, a wealth, a profusion, a mountain; many, plenty, reams; ample; informal a heap, a mass, a pile, an ocean, a stack, a ton, lots, heaps, masses, piles, oceans, stacks, tons, oodles, scads; Brit. informal a shedload, lashings; Austral./NZ informal a swag; vulgar slang a shitload.
▷ANTONYMS few.
3 *a heavy teaching load*: **commitment**, responsibility, duty, obligation, onus, charge, weight; burden, encumbrance, cross, millstone, albatross; trouble, worry, strain, pressure.
▶verb **1** *she began to load the washing machine | we quickly loaded the van with our diving gear*: **fill**, fill up, pack, stuff, cram, pile, heap, stack; lade, freight, charge; stock.
▷ANTONYMS unload.
2 *Larry loaded boxes into the jeep*: **pack**, stow, store, stack, bundle, stuff, cram, squeeze, jam, wedge; place, deposit, put away.
▷ANTONYMS unload.
3 *loading the committee with responsibilities means some subjects receive less attention than others*: **burden**, weigh down, weight, saddle, charge; overburden, overwhelm, encumber, hamper, handicap, tax, strain, oppress, trouble, worry; rare trammel.
4 *within a few weeks, Richard was loading Marshal with honours*: **reward**, ply, regale, shower; supply, provide.
5 *he began to load a gun*: **prime**, charge, arm, fill, prepare to fire/use.
▷ANTONYMS unload.
6 *load the cassette into the camcorder*: **insert**, put, place, fit, slide, slot.
▷ANTONYMS remove.
7 *the dice are loaded against him*: **bias**, rig, fix, set up; weight.

loaded adjective **1** *a loaded freight train | a loaded tray*: **full**, filled, laden, packed, burdened, stuffed, crammed, brimming, freighted, stacked; supplied, stocked; informal chock-full, chock-a-block.
▷ANTONYMS empty.
2 *a loaded gun*: **primed**, charged, armed, filled, containing ammunition, ready to fire, ready for use.
▷ANTONYMS unloaded.
3 informal *they could have afforded to buy the stuff—their parents were all loaded*. See **rich** (sense 1).
4 N. Amer. informal *it was an excuse for everyone to get loaded*. See **drunk**.
5 *loaded dice*: **biased**, rigged, fixed; weighted; informal crooked.
▷ANTONYMS honest.
6 *a loaded question | 'green' is a politically loaded word*: **charged**, meaningful, pregnant; tendentious, emotive, sensitive, difficult, delicate.
▷ANTONYMS ingenuous, straightforward.

loaf verb *he was loafing around his father's yards*: **laze**, lounge, loll; do nothing, take things easy, idle, be idle, shirk one's duties; waste time, fritter away time, kill time, while away the time, twiddle one's thumbs, sit on one's hands, dawdle, dally; informal hang around/round, skive; Brit. informal hang about, mooch about/around; N. Amer. informal bum around.
▷ANTONYMS work, toil.

loafer noun **idler**, layabout, good-for-nothing, ne'er-do-well, do-nothing, lounger, shirker, sluggard, laggard, slugabed, malingerer; informal skiver, waster, slacker, cyberslacker, slob, lazybones.

loan noun *a loan to purchase industrial goods*: **credit**, advance; mortgage, overdraft; debenture; **lending**, moneylending, advancing; Brit. informal sub.
▶verb **1** *a friend loaned me £1,500 | works of art will be loaned to the new museum for a period of twenty years*: **lend**, advance, give credit, credit, allow; give on loan, give someone the loan of, let someone have the use of, let out, lease, charter, hire; Brit. informal sub.
▷ANTONYMS borrow.
2 *the majority of exhibits have been loaned from the Kelvingrove Art Gallery*: **borrow**, ask for the loan of, receive/take on loan, use temporarily.

loath adjective *the batsmen were loath to take risks*: **reluctant**, unwilling, disinclined, ill-disposed, not in the mood; hesitant; against, averse, opposed, resistant, hostile, antagonistic; resisting.
▷ANTONYMS willing, eager.

loathe verb *the staff at school loathed him | cats loathe vinegar*: **hate**, detest, abhor, despise, abominate, dislike greatly, execrate; have a strong aversion to, feel repugnance towards, not be able to bear, not be able to stand, shrink from, recoil from, be repelled by, be unable to stomach, find intolerable.
▷ANTONYMS love, like.

loathing noun *his face was filled with loathing for the man in front of him*: **hatred**, hate, detestation, abhorrence, abomination, execration, odium; antipathy, dislike, hostility, animosity, ill will, ill feeling, bad feeling, malice, animus, enmity, aversion; repugnance, disgust, revulsion.
▷ANTONYMS love.

loathsome adjective *a foul and loathsome beast | a loathsome crime against innocent people*: **hateful**, detestable, abhorrent, repulsive, odious, repugnant, repellent, disgusting, revolting, sickening, nauseating, abominable, despicable, contemptible, reprehensible, execrable, damnable; hideous, ghastly, vile, horrible, nasty, frightful, obnoxious, gross, foul, offensive, disagreeable; informal horrid, yucky; literary noisome.
▷ANTONYMS lovable, delightful, pleasant.

lob verb *they lobbed grenades on to the gun platform*: **throw**, toss, fling, pitch, shy, hurl, pelt, sling, loft, cast, let fly with, flip; launch, propel, impel; bowl; informal chuck, bung, heave.

lobby noun **1** *they went into the hotel lobby*: **entrance hall**, hallway, hall, entrance, vestibule, foyer, reception area, outer room, waiting room, anteroom, antechamber, porch; corridor, passage, passageway.
2 *the anti-hunt lobby*: **pressure group**, interest group, interest, movement, campaign, crusade, lobbyists, supporters; faction, camp, bloc, clique; Brit. ginger group.
▶ verb **1** *readers are urged to lobby their MPs on the issue*: **seek to influence**, try to persuade, bring pressure to bear on, importune, persuade, influence, sway; petition, solicit, appeal to, call on, urge, press, pressure, pressurize, push.
2 *a group **lobbying for** better rail services*: **campaign**, crusade, press, push, drum up support, speak, clamour, ask, call, drive; promote, advocate, recommend, speak/plead/argue in favour of, champion, urge, insist on, demand.

local adjective **1** *the local council*: **community**, district, neighbourhood, regional, city, town, municipal, provincial, village, parish, parish-pump, parochial; domestic, internal, home.
▷ANTONYMS national, global.
2 *a local restaurant*: **neighbourhood**, nearby, near, at hand, close by, in the area; accessible, handy, convenient.
3 *a local infection*: **confined**, restricted, contained, limited, localized; circumscribed, delimited, specific, particular.
▷ANTONYMS general.
▶ noun **1** *the police had complaints from the locals*: **local person**, native, inhabitant, resident, parishioner, citizen; humorous denizen, burgher; derogatory, informal local yokel.
▷ANTONYMS outsider.
2 informal *he arranged to meet her at his local*: **pub**, public house, bar, inn, tavern, hostelry, saloon, wine bar; informal boozer, watering hole, drinker.

locale noun *the photography conveys the atmosphere of the locale effectively*: **place**, site, spot, area; position, location, setting, scene, venue, milieu, background, backdrop; neighbourhood, district, region, environs, locality, environment, territory; technical locus.

locality noun **1** *other schools in the locality*: **vicinity**, surrounding area, area, neighbourhood, district, region, environs, zone, locale, territory; community; informal neck of the woods; technical locus.
2 *the locality of the property*: **position**, place, situation, location, spot, point, site, scene, setting; whereabouts, bearings; technical locus.

localize verb *the policy of non-intervention had succeeded in localizing the conflict*: **limit**, restrict, confine, contain, restrain, constrain, circumscribe, concentrate, delimit, delimitate; isolate.
▷ANTONYMS generalize, globalize.

locate verb **1** *he had no difficulty in locating the missing men*: **find**, discover, pinpoint, detect, track down, run to earth, unearth, hit on, come across, reveal, bring to light, sniff out, smoke out, search out, ferret out, turn up, uncover, come up with, lay one's hands on, pin down; light on, stumble across/on, chance on; informal put one's finger on.
2 *a company located near Pittsburgh*: **situate**, site, position, place, base; put, build, establish, found, fix, station, install, lodge, set, settle, seat.

location noun *the property is set in a convenient location*: **position**, **place**, situation, site, locality, locale, spot, whereabouts, point, placement; scene, setting, area, environment; bearings, orientation; venue, address; technical locus.

lock[1] noun *she turned the key in the lock*: **bolt**, catch, fastener, clasp, bar, hasp, latch.
▶ verb **1** *he locked the door behind him*: **bolt**, fasten, bar, secure, make secure, make fast, seal; padlock, latch, chain.
▷ANTONYMS unlock, open.
2 *wedge-shaped pins are driven in to **lock** the parts **together***: **join**, interlock, mesh, engage, link, unite, connect, combine, yoke, mate; couple.
▷ANTONYMS separate, divide.
3 *the wheels locked and the car careered across the road*: **become stuck**, stick, jam, become/make immovable, become/make rigid.
4 *he locked her in an ecstatic embrace*: **clasp**, clench, grasp, embrace, hug, squeeze.
□ **lock horns** *local politicians locked horns with one another*: **quarrel**, disagree, have a dispute, wrangle, bicker, be at odds, be at loggerheads, lock antlers, cross swords; fight, do battle, engage in conflict, contend; challenge; informal have a dust-up, have a scrap, have a barney.
□ **lock something in** *the beach is locked in by headlands at each end*: **enclose**, encircle, surround, encompass, bound, ring, circle, envelop; shut in, hem in, hedge in.
□ **lock someone out** *she was locked out of her office | people locked out of the job market*: **keep out**, shut out, refuse entrance to, deny admittance to; **exclude**, bar, debar, ban, ostracize, banish, exile.
□ **lock someone up** *he was locked up for burglary*: **imprison**, jail, incarcerate, send to prison, put behind bars, put under lock and key, put in chains, put/throw into irons, clap in irons, hold captive; detain, remand, intern, impound, immure, shut up, shut in, confine, cage, pen, coop up, fence in, pen in, wall in, mew (up); informal send down, put away, put inside.

lock[2] noun *a lock of hair*: **tress**, tuft, curl; ringlet, kiss-curl, lovelock, forelock, plait; hank; strand, wisp; snippet.

locker noun *she stowed her shirt in a locker*: **cupboard**, cabinet, chest, safe, box, case, coffer; compartment, storeroom, storage room.

lock-up noun **1** *the old red-brick police station was the site of the village lock-up*: **jail**, prison, cell, police cell, place of detention, place of confinement, detention centre; N. Amer. jailhouse; informal cooler, slammer, jug, can, nick, stir, clink, quod, chokey, pen.
2 *they had some spare space in a lock-up in a basement car park*: **storeroom**, store, warehouse, depository, storage space, garage.

locomotion noun *spider monkeys have prehensile tails used in posture, locomotion, and grasping | steam locomotion*: **movement**, motion, moving, shifting, stirring, action; travel, travelling; mobility, motility; walking, ambulation, perambulation, running; progress, progression, passage, transit, transport, headway.

lodestar noun *she dominated his existence, as chief muse and intellectual lodestar | maximizing profits is management's lodestar*: **guide**, guiding star, guiding light, role model, model, luminary, exemplar, ideal, inspiration; criterion, aim, guiding principle, standard, pattern.

lodge noun **1** *the porter's lodge*: **gatehouse**, cottage, toll house.
2 *a hunting lodge*: **house**, cottage, cabin, chalet; Brit. shooting box.
3 *a beaver's lodge*: **den**, lair, hole, sett; retreat, haunt, shelter.
4 *a Masonic lodge*: **section**, branch, chapter, wing; association, society, group, club, union, guild, fraternity, brotherhood, sorority, alliance, coterie, league; rare sodality.
▶ verb **1** *William lodged at our house*: **reside**, **board**, stay, have lodgings, have rooms, take a room, put up, live, be quartered, stop; occupy; N. Amer. room; informal have digs; formal dwell, be domiciled, sojourn; archaic abide.
2 *Mrs Gould, her maid, and the baby were lodged at an inn in Newcastle*: **accommodate**, provide accommodation for, put up, take in, house, board, billet, quarter, shelter, harbour, provide shelter for; cater for, entertain.
3 *I intend to lodge an official complaint*: **submit**, register, enter, put forward, place, advance, lay, present, press, bring, prefer, tender, proffer, put on record, record, table, file.
4 *the trophy was lodged in the vault of a local bank*: **deposit**, put, bank, entrust, consign; stash, store, stow, put away, lay in, squirrel away; rare reposit.
5 *shrapnel slashed his neck and lodged in his spine*: **become fixed**, embed itself, become embedded, become implanted, get/become stuck, stick, catch, wedge, become caught, become settled, anchor itself, become anchored, come to rest, remain.
6 *the power of the Crown is always lodged in a single person*: **vest**, entrust, place, put, lay, transfer, consign.

lodger noun *she took in a lodger*: **boarder**, paying guest, PG, guest, tenant, resident, inmate; N. Amer. roomer.

lodging noun *she lives in sumptuous lodging in London | he lived alone in a tiny lodging*: **accommodation**, rooms, chambers, living quarters, quarters, apartments; place, place to stay, place of residence, establishment, flat, suite; shelter, board, housing; a roof over one's head; informal digs, pad; formal abode, residence, dwelling, dwelling place, habitation.

lofty adjective **1** *the buildings have lofty towers and spires*: **tall**, high, giant, towering, soaring, sky-high, sky-scraping; imposing, magnificent, majestic.
▷ANTONYMS low, short.
2 *lofty ideals*: **noble**, exalted, high, high-minded, grand, fine, sublime, elevated, worthy.
▷ANTONYMS base, lowly.

3 *he has obtained a lofty position in Hollywood*: **eminent**, prominent, leading, distinguished, illustrious, renowned, celebrated, elevated, esteemed, honoured, respected.
▷ANTONYMS base.
4 *they looked on with lofty disdain*: **haughty**, proud, aloof, arrogant, disdainful, supercilious, condescending, patronizing, scornful, contemptuous, self-important, conceited, snobbish; lordly, grandiose, imperious, pompous, magisterial, overweening, overbearing; informal high and mighty, stuck-up, snooty, snotty, toffee-nosed, uppity, uppish, hoity-toity; literary vainglorious; archaic contumelious.
▷ANTONYMS modest.

log noun **1** *she tripped over a fallen log*: **chunk of wood**, branch, tree trunk, bole, stump; block of wood, billet; timber.
2 *the ship's log | we require a log of calls to be maintained*: **record**, register, logbook, journal, diary, chronicle, daybook, record book, ledger; chart, account, tally; minutes; informal write-up.
▶verb **1** *details of the problem will be logged by the help-desk staff*: **register**, record, make a note of, note down, write down, jot down, book down, set down, put down, put in writing; enter, file, minute, chart, tabulate, catalogue.
2 *the pilot had logged 95 hours*: **attain**, achieve, chalk up, make, do, go, cover.

loggerheads plural noun
□ **at loggerheads** *local councillors have found themselves at loggerheads with the Government*: **in disagreement**, at odds, at variance, in opposition, at cross purposes, out of step, quarrelling, clashing, at outs; in conflict, at war, at daggers drawn, fighting, wrangling, feuding, conflicting, locking horns, estranged; informal at each other's throats, like cat and dog.

logic noun **1** *this case appears to defy all logic | he accepted the logic of the shipowners' argument*: **reason**, judgement, logical thought, rationality, cognition, wisdom, sagacity, sound judgement, sense, good sense, common sense, rationale, sanity; deduction, inference, syllogistic reasoning; coherence, relevance; informal horse sense.
2 *the economic logic of the argument*: **reasoning**, line of reasoning, chain of reasoning, process of reasoning, argument, argumentation.
3 *the study of logic*: **science of reasoning**, science of deduction, science of thought, dialectics, argumentation, ratiocination.

logical adjective **1** *conclusions based on evidence and logical argument | information displayed in a simple and logical fashion*: **reasoned**, well reasoned, rational, sound, cogent, well thought out, valid; lucid, coherent, clear, well organized, systematic, orderly, methodical, articulate, consistent, relevant; syllogistic, deductive, inductive, inferential; informal joined-up.
▷ANTONYMS irrational, illogical.
2 *the move into production seems the logical outcome*: **natural**, unsurprising, only to be expected, understandable, reasonable, sensible; predictable, most likely, likeliest, obvious; right, correct, practical.
▷ANTONYMS unlikely, surprising.
3 *his logical mind*: **reasoning**, thinking, straight-thinking, rational, objective, analytical, cerebral, insightful; intelligent, judicious, wise, sensible, hard-headed.

logistics plural noun *the logistics of deploying forces in foreign territory are daunting*: **organization**, planning, plans, management, arrangement, administration, masterminding, direction, orchestration, regimentation, engineering, coordination, execution, handling, running; strategy, tactics.

logo noun *the company logo*: **emblem**, trademark; device, symbol, design, sign, mark, figure, stamp, monogram; insignia, crest, seal, coat of arms, shield, badge, motif, hallmark, logotype, colophon.

loiter verb **1** *he loitered in the parking lot*: **linger**, potter, wait, skulk; loaf, lounge, idle, laze, waste time, kill time, while away time; informal hang around/round; Brit. informal hang about, mooch about/around; archaic or literary tarry.
2 *the weather had tempted them out to loiter along the river bank*: **dawdle**, dally, stroll, saunter, loll, go slowly, take one's time, go/move at a snail's pace, drag one's feet, delay; informal dilly-dally, mosey; Brit. informal mooch.

> *Choose the right word* **loiter, linger, dawdle**
>
> See **linger**.

loll verb **1** *Louis lolled at ease in one of the deckchairs*: **lounge**, sprawl, drape oneself, stretch oneself, lie, sit, flop; slouch, slump; laze, luxuriate, put one's feet up, lean back, recline, relax, take it easy, repose, rest; loaf, idle, vegetate; informal hang around/round; Brit. informal hang about.
2 *a dog lay down by the side of the building, its tongue* **lolling out** *with thirst*: **hang down**, hang, hang loosely, dangle, droop, sag, flap, flop, drop.

lone adjective **1** *a lone police officer | a lone tree*: **solitary**, single, solo, unaccompanied, unescorted, alone, all alone, by oneself/itself, sole, without companions, companionless; individual, distinct, detached, isolated, unique; lonely.
2 *a lone parent*: **single**, unmarried, unattached, without a partner/husband/wife, partnerless, husbandless, wifeless; separated, divorced, widowed.
3 literary *a cowboy on the lone prairie*. See **deserted** (sense 2).

loneliness noun **1** *he sought refuge in drink because of his loneliness*: **isolation**, friendlessness, lack of friends/companions, forsakenness, abandonment, rejection; unpopularity; sadness, unhappiness, forlornness, despondency; N. Amer. lonesomeness.
2 *the enforced loneliness of a prison cell*: **solitariness**, solitude, lack of company, aloneness, separation.
3 *the loneliness of the village*: **isolation**, remoteness, inaccessibility, seclusion, secludedness; desertedness.

> *Word links* **loneliness**
>
> **autophobia, ermitophobia** fear of loneliness

lonely adjective **1** *a sad and lonely man | I felt very lonely*: **isolated**, alone, all alone, friendless, companionless, without friends/companions, with no one to turn to, outcast, forsaken, abandoned, rejected, unloved, unwanted; unpopular; sad, unhappy, forlorn, despondent; N. Amer. lonesome.
▷ANTONYMS popular.
2 *the lonely life of a writer*: **solitary**, unaccompanied, alone, lone, by oneself/itself, without companions, companionless.
▷ANTONYMS sociable.
3 *a lonely road*: **deserted**, uninhabited, unfrequented, unpopulated, desolate, barren, isolated, remote, out of the way, secluded, sequestered, off the beaten track, in the back of beyond, in the middle of nowhere, godforsaken; literary lone.
▷ANTONYMS populous, crowded.

loner noun *I don't want my child to turn into an antisocial loner*: **recluse**, introvert, lone wolf, hermit, solitary, misanthrope, outsider; maverick, nonconformist, individual; rare eremite, coenobite, anchorite, stylite, solitudinarian.

long[1] adjective **1** *a tall girl with long brown hair | this was followed by a long tense silence*: **lengthy**, of considerable length, extended, prolonged, extensive, stretched out, spread out; long-lasting, lasting.
▷ANTONYMS short.
2 *the white rhinoceros can reach 17 feet long*: **in length**, lengthways, lengthwise.
3 *the couple fought a long battle to get welfare benefits | a long speech*: **prolonged**, protracted, lengthy, overlong, extended, long-drawn-out, drawn-out, spun-out, dragged-out, seemingly endless, lingering, interminable; tedious, boring, wearisome.
▷ANTONYMS short, brief.
▶noun
□ **before long** *before long, others will follow*: **soon**, shortly, presently, in the near future, in a short time, in a little while, in a minute, in a moment; in an instant, in the twinkling of an eye, in (less than) no time, in no time (at all), before you know it, any minute (now); by and by; informal in a jiffy, in two shakes, in two shakes of a lamb's tail, before you can say Jack Robinson; archaic or informal anon; archaic ere long.

long[2] verb *all through the exams I* **longed for** *the holidays | she had longed to be invited to the party*: **yearn**, pine, ache, wish, burn, hanker for/after, hunger, thirst, itch, pant, hope, be eager, be desperate, be consumed with desire, be unable to wait, would give one's eye teeth; crave, need, lust after, dream of, set one's heart on, be bent on, eat one's heart out over, covet; want, desire, set one's sights on; informal have a yen, be dying, yen.

> *Choose the right word* **long, yearn, pine, hanker**
>
> See **yearn**.

long-drawn-out adjective *his trial was a long-drawn-out affair*: **prolonged**, protracted, lengthy, lasting, long-lasting, marathon, overlong, extended, drawn-out, spun-out, dragged-out, dragging, time-consuming, seemingly endless, lingering, interminable; tedious, boring, wearisome.

longing noun *urban dwellers clearly have a longing for the countryside*: **yearning**, pining, craving, ache, burning, hunger, thirst, itch, urge, lust, hankering, need, eagerness, zeal, covetousness; wish, fancy, desire, want; hope, aspiration, dream; informal yen.
▶adjective *a longing look*: **yearning**, desirous, pining, craving, hungry, thirsty, hankering, avid, covetous; wishful, hopeful, wistful.

long-lasting adjective *our long-lasting friendship*: **enduring**, lasting, long-lived, long-running, long-established, long-standing, lifelong; permanent, abiding, surviving, deep-rooted, established; strong, durable, stable, fast, firm, reliable; time-honoured, traditional.
▷ANTONYMS short-lived, ephemeral.

long-lived adjective *the long-lived success of the organization*: **lasting**, enduring, abiding; durable, hardy.
▷ANTONYMS short-lived.

long-standing adjective *a long-standing friendship*: **well established**, long-established, established, fixed; time-honoured, time-hallowed; abiding, enduring, long-lived, surviving, persistent, prevailing, durable,

perennial; firm, constant, deep-rooted, steady, stable, staunch, long-term.
▷ANTONYMS new, recent.

long-suffering adjective *his long-suffering wife*: **patient**, forbearing, tolerant, uncomplaining, with the patience of Job, stoical, resigned; easy-going, indulgent, charitable, accommodating, forgiving; submissive, deferential, acquiescent, meek, docile, compliant, mild.
▷ANTONYMS impatient, complaining.

long-winded adjective *a long-winded speech*: **lengthy**, long, overlong, prolonged, protracted, long-drawn-out, interminable, tedious, wearisome, boring; discursive, diffuse, rambling, meandering, repetitious, tautological, periphrastic, circumlocutory, tortuous, verbose, wordy, prolix; informal windy; rare pleonastic, ambagious, sesquipedalian.
▷ANTONYMS concise, succinct, laconic.

look verb **1** *Mrs. Wright **looked at** him | she looked out of the window*: **glance**, gaze, stare, gape, peer, fix one's gaze, focus; peep, peek, take a look; **watch**, examine, study, inspect, scan, scrutinize, survey, check, contemplate, consider; see, observe, view, regard, pay attention to, take note of, mark; glimpse, spot, spy, lay one's eyes on, catch sight of, eye, take in, ogle; informal take a gander, give someone/something a/the once-over, have a squint, get a load of, rubberneck, recce; Brit. informal take a dekko, take a butcher's, take a shufti, clock, gawp; N. Amer. informal eyeball; archaic behold, espy, descry.
▷ANTONYMS ignore.
2 *a pair of windows looked north over Madison Avenue | the breakfast room looks out on to a small patio*: **command a view**, face, overlook, front.
3 *both visitors looked shocked*: **seem**, seem to be, appear, appear to be, have the appearance/air of being, give the impression of being, give every appearance/indication of being, look to be, present as being, strike someone as being.
□ **look after** *I had to look after my brother after his accident*: **take care of**, care for, attend to, tend, mind, minister to, take charge of, supervise, protect, guard; keep an eye on, keep safe, be responsible for; watch, sit with, nurse, babysit, childmind.
□ **look back on** *I look back on my early teenage years with some amazement*: **reflect on**, think about, remember, recall, bring to mind, muse on, brood on, ponder on, reminisce about, be nostalgic about, hark back to.
□ **look down on** *my mother had social pretensions and looked down on most of our neighbours*: **disdain**, scorn, hold in disdain, regard with contempt, treat with contempt, sneer at, spurn, shun, disparage, pooh-pooh, despise; informal look down one's nose at, turn up one's nose at.
▷ANTONYMS look up to.
□ **look for 1** *she looked for her comb, but couldn't find it | police are looking for two suspects*: **search for**, hunt for, seek, look about/around/round for, cast about/around/round for, try to find, try to track down, forage for, scout out, quest for/after. **2** *Jeremiah and Ezekiel looked for the day when God would forge a new covenant with men*: **anticipate**, expect, await, count on, reckon on, watch for, hope for, look forward to, contemplate, prepare for, envisage.
□ **look forward to** *I was looking forward to seeing Ted*: **await with pleasure**, anticipate, wait for, be unable to wait for, count the days until, long for, hope for; informal lick one's lips over.
▷ANTONYMS dread.
□ **look into** *the authorities promised to look into the complaints*: **investigate**, explore, research, enquire about, make enquiries about, find out about, ask questions about, ask about; probe, search into, go into, delve into, dig into, examine, study, scrutinize, check, analyse, follow up, check up on, pore over, take stock of; vet, audit; N. Amer. check out.
□ **look like** *in his overcoat he looks like an undertaker*: **resemble**, bear a resemblance to, look similar to, have a look of, have the appearance of, remind one of, put one in mind of, make one think of, be the image of, echo, have (all) the hallmarks of, simulate; take after; informal be the spitting image of, be the spit of, be a dead ringer for, favour.
□ **look on/upon** *people he looked on as friends took advantage of him*: **regard**, consider, think of, deem, judge, count, see, view, take, reckon, believe to be.
□ **look out** *you'll be trampled on if you don't look out*: **beware**, watch out, be on (one's) guard, be alert, be wary, be vigilant, be careful, be cautious, pay attention, take heed, heed, keep one's eyes open, keep one's eyes peeled/skinned, keep an eye out, be on the qui vive.
□ **look something over** *he looked over the reports from the engineer*: **inspect**, examine, check, monitor, read through, look through, scan, run through, cast an eye over, leaf through, flick through, flip through, browse, give something/someone a/the once-over, take stock of, view, peruse; informal take a dekko at; N. Amer. check out; N. Amer. informal eyeball.
□ **look right through someone** *the woman, once so friendly, now looked right through her*: **snub**, ignore, slight, spurn, shun, disdain, look past, turn one's back on, give someone the cold shoulder, cold-shoulder, freeze out, steer clear of; Brit. send to Coventry; informal give someone the brush-off, cut, cut dead, knock back, give someone the go-by; Brit. informal blank.
▷ANTONYMS acknowledge.
□ **look through something** *he began to look through the first few pages of the journal*. See **look something over**.
□ **look to 1** *we must look to the future*: **consider**, give thought to, think about, turn one's thoughts to, take heed of, pay attention to, attend to, mind, heed. **2** *they got themselves into trouble and now look to the government for help*: **turn to**, resort to, have recourse to, fall back on, avail oneself of, make use of.
□ **look up** *things are looking up for opera these days*: **improve**, show improvement, get better, pick up, advance, develop, come along/on, progress, make progress, make headway, shape up, perk up, rally, take a turn for the better.
□ **look someone up** informal *Moira said you were going up to Leeds to look up some old friends*: **visit**, pay a visit to, call on, go to see, look in on; N. Amer. visit with, go see; informal drop in on.
□ **look up to** *Jerry looked up to me*: **admire**, have a high opinion of, think highly of, hold in high regard, regard highly, rate highly, respect, hold in esteem, esteem, value; honour, revere, venerate, idolize, worship, hero-worship, adulate, put on a pedestal, lionize.
▷ANTONYMS look down on.
▶noun **1** *have a look at this report*: **glance**, observation, view, examination, study, inspection, scan, survey, sight, peep, peek, glimpse, gaze, stare, gape, ogle; informal eyeful, gander, look-see, once-over, squint, recce; Brit. informal shufti, dekko, butcher's; Austral./NZ informal geek, squiz.
2 *the puzzled look on her face turned to one of irritation*: **expression**, mien.
3 *he had a shifty look about him | the kitchen has that rustic look Mary's so fond of*: **appearance**, air, aspect, bearing, cast, manner, mien, demeanour, features, semblance, guise, facade, impression, effect; atmosphere, mood, quality, ambience, feeling, flavour.
4 *the latest look for this season is lean and elegant*: **fashion**, style, vogue, mode, trend, fad, craze, rage, mania.

> *Word links* **look**
>
> **scopophobia** fear of being looked at

lookalike noun *a Charlie Chaplin lookalike*: **double**, twin, exact likeness, image, living image, mirror image, exact match, replica, clone, imitation, duplicate, copy, facsimile; German Doppelgänger; informal spitting image, spit, spit and image, ringer, dead ringer.

lookout noun **1** *a signal station used as a lookout during the Napoleonic Wars*: **observation post**, lookout point, lookout station, lookout tower, watchtower, tower, post; coastguard station.
2 *the lookout sighted sails on the western horizon*: **watchman**, guard, watch, sentry, sentinel, night watchman, scout, picket; historical vedette.
3 informal *it would be a poor lookout for the men of the fleet if they didn't return to shore before the rain struck*: **outlook**, prospect, view of the future, future; chances, expectations.
4 informal *I doubt if she'll fit in, but that's her own lookout*: **problem**, concern, business, affair, responsibility, worry, difficulty; informal pigeon, funeral, headache.
□ **be on the lookout/keep a lookout** *he kept a sharp lookout for enemy fighters*: **keep watch**, keep/be on one's guard, beware, keep an eye out, keep a vigil, be alert, be observant, be attentive, be on the qui vive; informal keep one's eyes peeled/skinned.

loom verb **1** *ghostly shapes loomed out of the fog*: **emerge**, appear, become visible, come into view, take shape, materialize, reveal itself, appear indistinctly, come to light, take on a threatening shape.
2 *the church **loomed above** him*: **soar**, tower, rise, rise up, mount, rear up; overhang, overshadow, hang over, dominate.
3 *without reforms, disaster looms*: **be imminent**, be on the horizon, impend, be impending, be close, be ominously close, threaten, be threatening, menace, brew, be just around the corner.

loop noun **1** *make a loop in the twine | a loop of rope*: **coil**, hoop, ring, circle, noose, oval, spiral, curl, twirl, whorl, twist, hook, zigzag, helix, convolution, incurvation.
2 *the flex has a loop in it*: **bend**, curve, kink, arc.
▶verb **1** *loop a heavy rope around its hind legs*: **coil**, wind, twist, snake, wreathe, spiral, form a hoop with, form hoops with, make a circle with, make circles with, bend into spirals/whorls.
2 *the driveway looped around the house*: **wind**, curve, bend, twist, turn, snake, meander, coil, spiral, corkscrew; **encircle**, form a ring round, surround, encompass; rare incurvate.
3 *he took two cables and looped them together*: **fasten**, tie, join, connect, knot, bind, secure, tether, lash, leash.

loophole noun **1** *they've taken advantage of a loophole in the regulations*: **means of evasion/avoidance**, means of escape, escape clause, escape route; **ambiguity**, omission, inadequacy, flaw, fault, defect, crack, inconsistency, discrepancy, shortcoming, slip; informal let-out, let-out clause, dodge.
2 historical *loopholes in the walls*: **hole**, gap, opening, aperture, chink, slit, slot.

loose adjective **1** *a loose floorboard*: **not fixed in place**, not secure, insecure, unsecured, unattached; detached, unfastened; wobbly, rickety, unsteady, movable.
▷ANTONYMS secure, tight.

2 *she wore her hair loose*: **untied**, unpinned, unbound, hanging free, down, flowing, floppy.
3 *there's a wolf loose in the woods*: **free**, at large, at liberty, on the loose, escaped; unconfined, untied, unchained, untethered, unsecured, unshackled, unfastened, unrestricted, unbound; freed, let go, liberated, released, set loose.
▷ANTONYMS secure.
4 *the loose interpretation of a particular ruling*: **vague**, indefinite, inexact, imprecise, ill-defined, unrigorous, unmeticulous; broad, general, rough, non-specific, inexplicit; liberal.
▷ANTONYMS literal, narrow.
5 *a loose jacket*: **baggy**, loose-fitting, easy-fitting, generously cut, slack, roomy; oversized, shapeless, bagging, lax, hanging, sagging, sloppy.
▷ANTONYMS tight.
6 dated *a loose woman*. See **promiscuous** (sense 1).
□ **at a loose end** *why don't you stay to eat, if you're at a loose end?* **with nothing to do**, unoccupied, unemployed, at leisure, idle, purposeless, aimless, adrift, with time to kill; bored, twiddling one's thumbs, kicking one's heels.
▷ANTONYMS busy.
□ **break loose** *the tethered horses broke loose*: **escape**, make one's escape, get away, get free, break free, free oneself; run off, run away, make a break for it, make a run for it, bolt, take to one's heels.
□ **let loose 1** *she let the python loose*: **free**, set free, unloose, turn loose, set loose, let go, release, liberate; untie, unchain, unfetter, untether, unfasten, unpen, unleash. **2** *she let loose a graceless snort*: **emit**, give, burst out with, give forth, send forth; shout, yell, bellow.
□ **on the loose** *a serial killer was on the loose*: **free**, at liberty, at large, escaped, set loose, unconfined, unrestrained, roaming, unbound, unrestricted, untied, unchained, unshackled, unfettered; on the run, fugitive; informal on the lam.
▶ **verb 1** *the cattle were loosed on the common*: **free**, set free, unloose, turn loose, set loose, let loose, let go, release, liberate; untie, unchain, unfetter, untether, unfasten, unpen, unleash.
▷ANTONYMS confine.
2 *he loosed the reins a little | the steel fingers loosed their hold*: **relax**, slacken, loosen; weaken, lessen, reduce, diminish, moderate, soften.
▷ANTONYMS tighten.
3 *Brian **loosed off** a shot though the back of the car*: **fire**, discharge, shoot, eject, catapult, let go, let fly with.

loose-limbed adjective *he was loose-limbed and lean*: **supple**, limber, lithe, lissom, willowy, flexible, pliant, pliable, loose-jointed; agile, nimble, deft.

loosen verb **1** *to open it up, you simply loosen two screws*: **make slack**, slacken, slack, unstick; **unfasten**, detach, release, disconnect, undo, unclasp, unlatch, unbolt.
▷ANTONYMS tighten.
2 *her fingers loosened*: **become slack**, slacken, become loose, let go, unbind, ease; work loose, work free.
▷ANTONYMS tighten.
3 *he had loosened his tie and undone his top button*: **unfasten**, undo, release, unhook, slacken, let out.
▷ANTONYMS tighten.
4 *Philip loosened his grip | the extension of the franchise helped loosen the grip of the aristocracy*: **weaken**, relax, slacken, loose, lessen, reduce, moderate, diminish, soften, alleviate, dilute.
▷ANTONYMS tighten.
5 *you need to **loosen up**, get rid of some inhibitions*: **relax**, become relaxed, unwind, ease up/off, become less rigid; informal let up, hang loose, lighten up, go easy.

loot noun *a treasure chest brimming over with loot*: **booty**, spoils, plunder, stolen goods, contraband, pillage; haul, prize; informal swag, the goods, hot goods, ill-gotten gains, boodle.
▶ **verb** *troops rushed in and looted the cathedral*: **plunder**, pillage, ransack, sack, raid, rifle, rob, burgle, steal from; maraud, ravage, devastate, lay waste to, wreak havoc on, vandalize; gut, strip, fleece, clear out; literary despoil; rare depredate, spoliate.

lop verb **1** *workmen have **lopped off** more branches in an effort to save the tree*: **cut**, chop, hack, saw, hew, slice, pare; prune, sever, clip, trim, snip, dock, crop, remove, detach, excise.
2 *it will **lop** an hour **off** journey times to the continent*: **remove**, cut, slash, axe, take, trim, prune, dock, truncate, eliminate.

lope verb *he loped off down the corridor*: **stride**, run, bound; lollop.

lopsided adjective *he gave a rather lopsided grin*: **asymmetrical**, unsymmetrical, uneven, unevenly balanced, unbalanced, off-balance, off-centre, unequal, askew, skew, skewed, squint, tilted, tilting, crooked, sloping, slanted, aslant, one-sided, out of true, out of line, to one side, awry; informal skew-whiff, cock-eyed.
▷ANTONYMS even, level, balanced.

loquacious adjective *he was a loquacious and precocious boy*: **talkative**, garrulous, voluble, over-talkative, long-winded, wordy, verbose, profuse, prolix, effusive, gushing, rambling; communicative; chatty, gossipy, gossiping, chattering, chattery, babbling, blathering, gibbering; informal with the gift of the gab, having kissed the blarney stone, yakking, big-mouthed, gabby, gassy; rare multiloquent, multiloquous.
▷ANTONYMS reticent, taciturn.

loquacity noun *he had a dim recollection of talking with drunken loquacity of his adventures*: **talkativeness**, over-talkativeness, garrulousness, garrulity, volubility, long-windedness, wordiness, prolixity, verbosity, verbiage, effusiveness, profuseness; chattiness, chattering, babble, blathering, gibbering; informal the gift of the gab, yackety-yak, yakking, big mouth, blah-blah, gabbiness, gassiness; rare logorrhoea, multiloquence.
▷ANTONYMS taciturnity, succinctness.

lord noun **1** *lords and ladies were entertained here*: **noble**, nobleman, peer, aristocrat, patrician, grandee; feudal lord, landowner, lord of the manor, seigneur; duke, earl, viscount.
▷ANTONYMS commoner.
2 *leave it to us, my lord | the lord of the manor*: **master**, lord and master, ruler, leader, chief, superior, monarch, sovereign, king, emperor, prince, governor, commander, captain, overlord, suzerain, baron, potentate, liege, liege lord.
▷ANTONYMS servant, inferior.
3 *our Lord's parable of the lost sheep*: **God**, the Father, Jehovah, the Almighty, the Supreme Being, the Deity; **Jesus**, Jesus Christ, Christ, Christ the Lord, the Messiah, the Saviour, the Son of God, the Redeemer, the Lamb of God, the Prince of Peace, the King of Kings.
4 *a press lord*: **magnate**, tycoon, mogul, captain, baron, king, nabob, grandee, mandarin; industrialist, proprietor, entrepreneur, executive, chief, leader; informal big shot, bigwig, honcho; derogatory fat cat; N. Amer. informal big wheel.
▶ **verb**
□ **lord it over someone** *when we were at school, you used to lord it over us*: **order about/around**, boss about/around, give orders to, domineer, dominate, dictate to, pull rank on, tyrannize, bully, browbeat, oppress, repress, ride roughshod over, have under one's thumb; be overbearing, put on airs, swagger; informal throw one's weight about/around, act big.
▷ANTONYMS be submissive.

lordly adjective **1** *the symbols of lordly status | lordly titles*: **noble**, aristocratic, princely, kingly, regal, royal, imperial, courtly, stately; magnificent, majestic, grand, august, lofty, exalted, dignified, imposing, impressive.
▷ANTONYMS lowly.
2 *I called a taxi and in lordly tones asked to be taken to Lansdowne Road*: **imperious**, arrogant, haughty, proud, self-important, swaggering; snobbish, supercilious, disdainful, scornful, contemptuous, condescending, patronizing, cavalier, aloof, superior, high-handed, overbearing, overweening, overconfident, pompous; dictatorial, authoritarian, bossy, peremptory, autocratic, tyrannical; refined; informal high and mighty, stuck-up, snooty, uppity, hoity-toity, toffee-nosed, pushy.
▷ANTONYMS humble.

lore noun **1** *he had a passion for Arthurian legend and lore*: **mythology**, myths, legends, stories, traditions, folklore, culture, beliefs, sayings, superstitions, fantasy, oral tradition; technical mythos, mythus.
2 *cricket lore was passed down from Yorkshire father to son*: **knowledge**, learning, wisdom; informal know-how, how-to.

lorry noun *the lorry was rumbling over Tower Bridge*: **truck**; Brit. juggernaut.

lose verb **1** *I've lost my watch*: **mislay**, misplace, be unable to find; drop, forget, overlook, lose track of, leave (behind), fail to keep/retain, fail to keep sight of.
▷ANTONYMS find.
2 *he's lost a lot of blood but his life is not in danger | she was suffering from flu and had lost her voice*: **be deprived of**, suffer the loss of, no longer have, stop having.
▷ANTONYMS regain.
3 *by this time the fans had managed to lose the police*: **escape from**, evade, elude, dodge, avoid, give someone the slip, shake off, throw off, throw off the scent, duck, get rid of; leave behind, outdistance, outstrip, outrun, outpace, get ahead of; informal ditch; archaic bilk.
4 *she still sometimes **loses her way** in the maze*: **stray from**, wander from, depart from, go astray from, fail to keep to, fail to keep in sight; **get lost**, lose one's bearings.
5 *he never lost an opportunity to poke fun at her*: **neglect**, waste, squander, fail to grasp, fail to take, fail to take advantage of, let pass, miss, forfeit, give up, ignore, disregard; informal pass up, lose out on.
6 *Leeds lost twice to Rangers in the European Cup | he lost the party leadership contest*: **be defeated**, be beaten, suffer defeat, be the loser, be conquered, be vanquished, be trounced, be worsted, be bested by, get/have the worst, come off second-best, lose out, fail, come to grief, meet one's Waterloo; informal come a cropper, go down, take a licking.
□ **lose out** *the town has **lost out on** a major tourist opportunity*: **be unable to take advantage of**, fail to benefit from; be unsuccessful, be defeated, be the loser, be disadvantaged; informal miss out on.
□ **lose out to** *Celtic have lost out to rivals Rangers*: **be defeated by**, be

beaten by, be conquered by, be vanquished by, be trounced by, be worsted by, be bested by, be beaten into second place by.

loser noun **1** *candidates compete against each other, so there are winners and losers*: **defeated person**, also-ran, the defeated, the vanquished; runner-up.
▷ANTONYMS winner.
2 informal *he's a complete loser*: **failure**, nonachiever, underachiever, ne'er-do-well, born loser, dead loss, nonentity, nobody; write-off, has-been; informal flop, dud, non-starter, no-hoper, washout, lemon, two-time loser.
▷ANTONYMS success.

loss noun **1** *the loss of the documents appears to be a serious breach of security*: **mislaying**, misplacement, dropping, forgetting, overlooking.
▷ANTONYMS recovery, finding.
2 *insurance covering loss of earnings | loss of dignity*: **deprivation**, disappearance, losing, privation, forfeiture, waste, squandering, dissipation; **diminution**, erosion, reduction, impoverishment, depletion.
3 *she mourned the loss of her husband*: **death**, **demise**, passing (away/on), decease, end, expiry, expiration; bereavement; rare quietus.
4 (usually **losses**) *they were able to inflict severe losses on enemy troops | British losses in the war were 400,000*: **casualty**, fatality, mortality, victim; dead; missing; **death toll**, number killed/dead/wounded.
5 *the club were facing a loss of £15,000 a year*: **deficit**, debit, debt, indebtedness, lack of profit, deficiency, losing, depletion, minus sum of money; cost, expense, sacrifice.
▷ANTONYMS profit, gain.
□ **at a loss** *I am at a loss to explain this contradiction*: **baffled**, nonplussed, mystified, stumped, stuck, puzzled, perplexed, bewildered, bemused, uncomprehending, (all) at sea, at sixes and sevens, at one's wits' end, without ideas, confused, dumbfounded, blank; informal clueless, flummoxed, bamboozled, discombobulated, fazed, floored, beaten.

lost adjective **1** *they were all searching for her lost keys | a lost cat*: **missing**, strayed, gone missing/astray, mislaid, misplaced, vanished, disappeared, forgotten, nowhere to be found; absent, not present, gone.
2 *his spirit still walks among the hills, searching for lost travellers | I went for a walk in the woods and I got lost*: **stray**, astray, off-course, off-track, off the right track, disorientated, disoriented, having lost one's bearings, adrift, going round in circles, at sea.
3 *a lost opportunity*: **missed**, forfeited, neglected, wasted, squandered, dissipated, gone by the board; informal down the drain.
4 *lost traditional values*: **bygone**, past, former, one-time, previous, old, olden, departed, vanished, forgotten, unremembered, unrecalled, consigned to oblivion, extinct, dead, lost and gone, lost in time; out of date, outmoded; French passé.
5 *a lament over lost species and habitats*: **extinct**, died out, defunct, vanished, gone, perished; **destroyed**, wiped out, ruined, wrecked, crushed, finished, demolished, obliterated, effaced, exterminated, eradicated, annihilated, extirpated.
6 *a lost cause*: **hopeless**, beyond hope, failed, despaired of, beyond remedy, beyond recovery.
7 *lost souls*: **damned**, fallen, cursed, accursed, irredeemable, irreclaimable, irretrievable, past hope, past praying for, condemned, doomed, excommunicated.
8 *he was a person entirely* ***lost to*** *all sense of decency*: **impervious**, immune, closed, unreceptive, unaffected by, unmoved by, untouched by.
9 *Father Reynard was* ***lost in*** *his own thoughts*: **engrossed**, absorbed, rapt, immersed, deep, intent, engaged, wrapped up; preoccupied by, taken up by, spellbound by, distracted by, entranced by, fascinated by, enthralled by, captivated by, riveted by; abstracted, dreamy, distrait, absent-minded, daydreaming, wool-gathering, somewhere else, not there, not with us, in a world of one's own, with one's head in the clouds, in a brown study; informal miles away.
□ **get lost** informal *a woman swore at me and told me to get lost*: **go away**, go, leave, depart, get going, get out, be off with you, shoo; informal scram, be on your way, run along, beat it, skedaddle, split, vamoose, scat, push off, buzz off, shove off, clear off, go (and) jump in the lake; Brit. informal hop it, bog off, naff off, on your bike, get along, sling your hook; N. Amer. informal bug off, light out, haul off, haul ass, take a powder, hit the trail, take a hike; Austral. informal nick off; Austral./NZ informal rack off; S. African informal voetsak, hamba; vulgar slang bugger off, piss off, fuck off; Brit. vulgar slang sod off; literary begone, avaunt.

lot pronoun (**a lot/lots**) *he had obviously spent a lot of money | she had lots of friends*: **a large amount**, a fair amount, a good/great deal, a deal, a great quantity, quantities, an abundance, a wealth, a profusion, plenty, masses; **many**, a great many, a large number, a considerable number, numerous, scores, hundreds, thousands, millions, billions; informal loads, loadsa, heaps, a pile, piles, oodles, stacks, scads, reams, wads, pots, oceans, a mountain, mountains, miles, tons, zillions, gazillions, more ... than one can shake a stick at; Brit. informal a shedload, lashings; N. Amer. informal gobs, a bunch, gazillions, bazillions; Austral./NZ informal a swag; vulgar slang a shitload.
▷ANTONYMS a little, not much; a few, not many.
▶ adverb (**a lot/lots**) *I work in pastels a lot*: **a great deal**, a good deal, to a great extent, much; often, frequently, regularly, many times.
▷ANTONYMS a little, not much.
▶ noun **1** informal *I will not be dictated to by that lot up at the mansion*: **group**, set, crowd, circle, clique, bunch, band, gang, crew, mob, pack, company; Brit. informal shower.
2 *it was auctioned off as a single lot*: **batch**, set, collection, load, group, bundle, bunch, consignment, quantity, assortment, parcel, aggregate.
3 *he was discontented with his lot in life*: **fate**, destiny, fortune, doom; situation, circumstances, state, condition, position, plight, predicament.
4 *they were to have one lot, and one lot only*: **share**, portion, quota, ration, allowance, allocation, percentage, part, piece; informal cut.
5 N. Amer. *some youngsters playing ball in a vacant lot*: **patch of ground**, tract of land, allotment, piece of ground, plot, area, tract, acreage, parcel, building lot; N. Amer. plat.
□ **draw/cast lots** *the players draw lots to decide who goes first*: **decide randomly**, spin/toss a coin, throw dice, draw straws, cut straws, decide on the toss of a coin, decide on the throw of a die, dice, decide on the drawing of straws.
□ **throw in one's lot with** *he threw in his lot with the conspirators*: **join forces with**, join up with, form an alliance with, ally with, align oneself with, link up with, go into league with, combine with, join fortunes with, make common cause with.

lotion noun *she rubbed some lotion into the skin*: **ointment**, cream, salve, balm, rub, emollient, moisturizer, lubricant, unguent, liniment, embrocation, poultice; pomade; hand lotion, body lotion, eye lotion.

lottery noun *Dad had won £7,000 in a lottery*: **raffle**, (prize) draw, sweepstake, sweep, bingo, lotto, tombola, drawing of lots, pools; gamble, speculation, game of chance, competition.

loud adjective **1** *there was loud music in the lounge*: **noisy**, blaring, booming, deafening, roaring, thunderous, thundering, tumultuous, clamorous, blasting, head-splitting, ear-splitting, ear-piercing, piercing; cacophonous, harsh, raucous; strident, resounding, reverberating, reverberant, carrying, clearly audible; sonorous, deep, ringing, lusty, powerful, forceful, stentorian; rowdy; Music forte, fortissimo.
▷ANTONYMS quiet, soft.
2 *the resulting congestion of business led to loud complaints of the law's delays*: **vociferous**, clamorous, insistent, vehement, emphatic, urgent, importunate, demanding.
▷ANTONYMS gentle.
3 *a loud T-shirt*: **garish**, gaudy, flashy, bold, flamboyant, lurid, glaring, showy, ostentatious, obtrusive; vulgar, tasteless; informal flash, naff, kitsch, tacky.
▷ANTONYMS sober, tasteful.

loudly adverb *the audience cheered loudly | music played loudly*: **at the top of one's voice**, **at full volume**, at top volume; **noisily**, blaringly, boomingly, deafeningly, thunderously, thunderingly, tumultuously, clamorously, piercingly; cacophonously, harshly, raucously; stridently, resoundingly; sonorously, deeply, ringingly, lustily, powerfully, forcefully; Music forte, fortissimo; informal as if to wake the dead.
▷ANTONYMS quietly, softly.

loudmouth noun informal **1** *if he wins, the press, who have dismissed him as an untested loudmouth, will have to sit up and take note*: **braggart**, boaster, blusterer, swaggerer; informal windbag, big mouth, blowhard, gasbag, bag of wind, show-off, big-head; N. Amer. informal showboat; vulgar slang bullshitter; literary braggadocio, gasconader.
2 *I approached him in the strictest confidence, but all too quickly I learned that he is just a gin-sodden loudmouth*: **gossip**, gossipmonger, scandalmonger, blabbermouth, blabber, busybody, chatterer, prattler, babbler; N. Amer. blatherskite; informal gasbag.

loudspeaker noun *a muffled announcement was made over the loudspeaker*: **public address system**, PA system, speaker, speaker unit, speaker system, microphone; loud hailer, megaphone; informal mike, mic.

lounge verb *the room was empty except for one man lounging in a comfortable chair | I spent the day lounging around the pool*: **laze**, lie, loll, lie back, lean back, recline, stretch oneself, drape oneself, relax, rest, repose, take it easy, put one's feet up, unwind, luxuriate; sprawl, slump, slouch, flop; loaf, idle, do nothing.
▶ noun **1** *she returned to the lounge to say goodnight*: **living room**, sitting room, parlour, front room, drawing room, morning room, reception room, salon, family room.
2 *the hotel has a lounge, TV room, and cocktail bar*: **public room**, sitting room, common room; cocktail lounge.

lour, lower verb *the lofty statue lours at patients in the infirmary*: **scowl**, frown, look sullen, glower, glare, grimace, give someone black looks, look daggers, look angry; informal give someone dirty looks.
▷ANTONYMS smile.

louring adjective *the louring sky*: **overcast**, dark, leaden, grey, cloudy, clouded, sunless, gloomy, threatening, menacing, promising rain.
▷ANTONYMS sunny, bright.

l

louse noun

> *Word links* **louse**
>
> **pedicular** relating to or infested with lice
> **pediculosis** infestation with lice
> **pediculophobia** fear of lice
> **pediculicide** chemical used to kill lice

lousy adjective **1** informal *he had been a lousy husband*: **awful**, terrible, appalling, abysmal, very bad, atrocious, desperate, unspeakable, frightful, miserable; poor, incompetent, inadequate, unsatisfactory, inferior, not up to scratch, careless, second-rate, shoddy, slovenly; informal rotten, pathetic, useless, hopeless; Brit. informal duff, poxy, rubbish, pants, a load of pants.
▷ANTONYMS good, competent.
2 informal *the lousy, double-crossing snake!* **despicable**, contemptible, dirty, low, mean, base, low-down, hateful, detestable, loathsome, vile, wicked, vicious; informal rotten, no-good.
▷ANTONYMS good, decent.
3 *lousy bedclothes*: **lice-infested**, lice-ridden; rare pedicular, pediculous.
▷ANTONYMS clean, fumigated.
4 informal *Doc Reid dishes me out a few vitamin pills when I'm feeling lousy*: **ill**, unwell, poorly, sick, nauseous, nauseated, queasy, bad; Brit. off, off colour; informal rough, rotten, awful, out of sorts, under the weather; Brit. informal grotty, ropy.
▷ANTONYMS well, healthy.
□ **lousy with** informal *the town is lousy with tourists*: **full of**, crowded with, overrun by, overflowing with, swarming with, teeming with, alive with, crawling with, hopping with, bristling with, thronged with, packed with, rife with, well supplied with, awash with, abounding in, abundant in, knee-deep in, rolling in.
▷ANTONYMS devoid of.

lout noun *a crowd of drunken louts*: **ruffian**, hooligan, thug, boor, oaf, hoodlum, rowdy, bully boy; informal yob, yobbo, tough, roughneck, bruiser, gorilla, yahoo; Brit. informal chav, hoodie; N. Amer. informal lug; Austral. informal ocker; Austral./NZ informal hoon.
▷ANTONYMS smoothie, gentleman.

loutish adjective *a loutish youth | his loutish behaviour*: **uncouth**, rude, impolite, unmannerly, ill-mannered, ill-bred, coarse; **thuggish**, boorish, oafish, rowdy, bullying, uncivilized, wild, rough, vulgar, philistine, common, crass; informal yobbish, slobbish.
▷ANTONYMS polite, well behaved.

lovable adjective *a lovable teddy bear | she was so lovable and funny*: **adorable**, dear, sweet, cute, charming, darling, lovely, likeable, attractive, delightful, captivating, enchanting, engaging, bewitching, pleasing, appealing, winsome, winning, fetching, taking, endearing, cherished; affectionate, warm-hearted, cuddly; Italian & Spanish simpatico; French sympathique; German sympatisch; N. Amer. dated cunning.
▷ANTONYMS hateful, loathsome.

love noun **1** *his friendship with Helen grew into love | she has a great love for her children*: **deep affection**, fondness, tenderness, warmth, intimacy, attachment, endearment; devotion, adoration, doting, idolization, worship; passion, ardour, desire, lust, yearning, infatuation, adulation, besottedness.
▷ANTONYMS hatred.
2 *her love of fashion*: **liking**, weakness, partiality, bent, leaning, proclivity, inclination, disposition; enjoyment, appreciation, soft spot, taste, delight, relish, passion, zeal, appetite, zest, enthusiasm, keenness, predilection, penchant, fondness.
3 *their love for their fellow human beings*: **compassion**, care, caring, regard, solicitude, concern, warmth, friendliness, friendship, kindness, charity, goodwill, sympathy, kindliness, altruism, philanthropy, unselfishness, benevolence, brotherliness, sisterliness, fellow feeling, humanity.
4 *don't fret, my love | he was her one and only true love*: **beloved**, loved one, love of one's life, dear, dearest, dear one, darling, sweetheart, sweet, sweet one, angel, honey; lover, boyfriend, girlfriend, significant other, betrothed, paramour, inamorata, inamorato.
5 *he is confident that their love can survive*: **relationship**, **love affair**, affair, romance, liaison, affair of the heart, intrigue, amour.
6 *my mother sends her love to you*: **best wishes**, regards, good wishes, greetings, kind/kindest regards, felicitations, salutations, compliments, best, respects.
□ **fall in love with** *the moment they met he fell in love with her*: **become infatuated with**, give/lose one's heart to, become smitten with; informal fall for, fall head over heels in love with, be swept off one's feet by, develop a crush on.
□ **in love with** *I'm in love with Gillian*: **besotted with**, infatuated with, enamoured of, smitten with, passionate about, with a passion for, consumed with desire for; captivated by, bewitched by, enthralled by, entranced by; devoted to, doting on; informal mad/crazy/nuts/wild/potty about, bowled over by, carrying a torch for.
▸ **verb 1** *I love you, Rory | she loves her family*: **be in love with**, be infatuated with, be smitten with, be besotted with, be passionate about; **care very much for**, feel deep affection for, hold very dear, adore, think the world of, be devoted to, dote on, cherish, worship, idolize, treasure, prize; informal be mad/crazy/nuts/wild/potty about, have a pash on, carry a torch for.
▷ANTONYMS hate, loathe, detest.
2 *Laura had always loved painting*: **like very much**, delight in, enjoy greatly, have a passion for, take great pleasure in, derive great pleasure from, have a great liking for, be addicted to, relish, savour; have a weakness for, be partial to, have a soft spot for, have a taste for, be taken with, have a predilection for, have a proclivity for, have a penchant for; informal get a kick from/out of, have a thing about/for, be mad for/about, be crazy/nuts/wild/potty about, be hooked on, go a bundle on, get off on, get a buzz from/out of.

> *Word links* **love**
>
> **amatory** relating to love
> **phil(o)-** related prefix, as in *philanthrope, philogynist*
> **-phile** related suffix, as in *bibliophile, Francophile*
> **-philia** related suffix, as in *paedophilia*
> **-phily** related suffix, as in *scripophily*

love affair noun **1** *he had a love affair with a teacher*: **relationship**, affair, romance, liaison, affair of the heart, intrigue, fling, amour, involvement, amorous entanglement, romantic entanglement, entanglement; flirtation, dalliance; French affaire de/du cœur; Brit. informal carry-on.
2 *I have had a love affair with the motor car all of my life*: **enthusiasm**, mania, devotion, passion, liking, appreciation.

loveless adjective *she feels trapped in a loveless marriage*: **passionless**, unloving, unfeeling, heartless, undemonstrative, unresponsive, cold, cold-hearted, icy, frigid.
▷ANTONYMS loving, passionate.

lovelorn adjective *a lovelorn teenager*: **lovesick**, unrequited in love, crossed in love; spurned, jilted, rejected, neglected, forsaken, yearning; pining, moping, languishing, mooning, frustrated, miserable, unhappy.

lovely adjective **1** *a lovely young woman | you look lovely*: **beautiful**, pretty, as pretty as a picture, attractive, good-looking, appealing, handsome, adorable, exquisite, sweet, personable, charming; enchanting, engaging, bewitching, winsome, seductive, gorgeous, alluring, ravishing, glamorous; Scottish & N. English bonny; informal tasty, knockout, stunning, smashing, drop-dead gorgeous; Brit. informal fit; N. Amer. informal cute, foxy; formal beauteous; archaic comely, fair; rare sightly, pulchritudinous.
▷ANTONYMS ugly, hideous.
2 *there's a lovely view across the town*: **scenic**, picturesque, pleasing, easy on the eye; magnificent, stunning, splendid.
3 informal *it was a lovely warm summer's day*: **delightful**, very pleasant, very nice, very agreeable, marvellous, wonderful, sublime, superb, fine, magical, enchanting, captivating; informal terrific, fabulous, fab, heavenly, divine, amazing, glorious.
▷ANTONYMS horrible, disagreeable.

lovemaking noun **sexual intercourse**, sex, intercourse, making love, sexual relations, sex act, act of love, intimate relations, intimacy, sexual union, coupling, sexual congress, congress, mating, going to bed with someone, sleeping with someone; informal it, the other, nooky, rumpy pumpy; Brit. informal bonking, how's your father; vulgar slang fucking, screwing; Brit. vulgar slang shagging; formal coitus, coition, copulation; formal fornication; archaic carnal knowledge.

lover noun **1** *sometimes I think she had a secret lover*: **boyfriend**, **girlfriend**, man friend, woman friend, lady friend, lady-love, beau, loved one, beloved, love, darling, sweetheart; mistress, paramour, other man, other woman; partner, significant other; Italian inamorata, inamorato; informal bit on the side, bit of fluff, toy boy, fancy man, fancy woman, sugar daddy, bird, fella; archaic swain, concubine, doxy, leman, courtesan; rare cicisbeo.
2 *he was a great lover of country sports | a dog lover*: **devotee**, admirer, fan, enthusiast, aficionado, follower, supporter, fanatic, addict, hound; informal buff, freak, nut.

> *Word links* **lover**
>
> **-phile** lover of ..., as in *bibliophile*

lovesick adjective *he was mooning around like a lovesick teenager*: **lovelorn**, pining, languishing, longing, yearning, infatuated; frustrated.

loving adjective **1** *her loving husband*: **affectionate**, fond, devoted, adoring, doting, solicitous, demonstrative; caring, tender, warm, warm-hearted; amorous, ardent, passionate, lustful, amatory.
▷ANTONYMS cold, cold-hearted.
2 *a loving family life*: **caring**, warm, tender, close-knit, close, supportive, nurturing; informal touchy-feely.
▷ANTONYMS cold, cruel.

low[1] adjective **1** *a low fence*: **short**, small, little; squat, stubby, stunted, truncated, dwarfish, knee-high; shallow.
▷ANTONYMS high.

2 *a narrow tract of low land*: **low-lying**, ground-level, sea-level, flat; sunken, depressed, subsided, nether.
▷ANTONYMS high.
3 *the low neckline of her blouse*: **low-cut**, skimpy, revealing; plunging.
4 *grain prices are still low*: **cheap**, inexpensive, low-priced, low-cost, economical, moderate, reasonable, modest, bargain, cut-price, bargain-basement, rock-bottom.
▷ANTONYMS expensive, high.
5 *her money supplies were low*: **scarce**, scanty, scant, skimpy, meagre, sparse, few, little, paltry, measly, trifling; reduced, depleted, diminished; deficient, inadequate, insufficient.
▷ANTONYMS plentiful, abundant.
6 *much of the work was of a very low standard*: **inferior**, substandard, poor, bad, low-grade, low-quality, below par, second-rate, inadequate, unacceptable, unsatisfactory, deficient, defective; wanting, lacking, leaving much to be desired.
▷ANTONYMS superior, high.
7 *a woman of low birth | a man low in the social scale*: **humble**, lowly, low-born, low-bred, low-ranking, plebeian, proletarian, peasant, poor; common, ordinary, simple, plain, unpretentious; inferior, subordinate.
▷ANTONYMS noble, superior.
8 *adults have low expectations of children's ability to explain things*: **unambitious**, unaspiring, modest.
▷ANTONYMS high, ambitious.
9 *most Americans have a low opinion of New York City*: **unfavourable**, poor, bad, adverse, negative, hostile.
▷ANTONYMS good, favourable, high.
10 *she considered it a rather low thing to have done*: **despicable**, contemptible, reprehensible, lamentable, disgusting, shameful, mean, abject, unworthy, shabby, uncharitable, base, dishonourable, unprincipled, ignoble, sordid, wretched; nasty, cruel, foul, bad, wrong, immoral, vile; informal rotten, beastly, low-down; archaic dastardly, scurvy.
▷ANTONYMS admirable, decent.
11 *down-at-heel theatres that put on low comedy*: **crude**, coarse, vulgar, indecent, ribald, smutty, bawdy, suggestive, off colour, rude, rough, unrefined, indelicate, improper; gross, obscene, pornographic, offensive, profane, filthy, dirty; informal blue.
▷ANTONYMS high, exalted.
12 *he was speaking in a low voice*: **quiet**, soft, faint, muted, subdued, muffled, hushed, quietened, whispered, stifled, murmured, gentle, dulcet, indistinct, inaudible.
▷ANTONYMS loud.
13 *going from a low note to a high note without using valves is difficult*: **bass**, low-pitched, deep, deep-toned, low-toned, full-toned, resonant, rich, rumbling, booming, resounding, sonorous.
14 *Fran felt low and unhappy*: **depressed**, dejected, despondent, downhearted, downcast, low-spirited, down, sorrowful, gloomy, glum, unhappy, sad, melancholy, blue, fed up, morose, moody, miserable, dismal, heavy-hearted, mournful, forlorn, woebegone; disheartened, discouraged, crestfallen, dispirited, without energy, enervated, flat, sapped, weary; ill, unwell, poorly, out of sorts; informal down in the mouth, down in the dumps; Brit. informal brassed off, cheesed off.
▷ANTONYMS cheerful.
▶ **noun** *the news caused the dollar to fall to an all-time low*: **nadir**, low point, lowest point, all-time low, lowest level, low-water mark, bottom, rock bottom.
▷ANTONYMS zenith, acme.

low² **verb** *the sound of cattle lowing*: **moo**, bellow.

lowbrow **adjective** *a lowbrow action movie*: **mass-market**, tabloid, pop, popular, intellectually undemanding, lightweight, easy to understand, accessible, unpretentious, simple, simplistic; downmarket, uncultured, unsophisticated, rubbishy, trashy, philistine, plebeian, cheap; informal dumbed-down.
▷ANTONYMS highbrow, intellectual.

low-down informal **adjective** *a dirty low-down trick*: **unfair**, **mean**, despicable, reprehensible, contemptible, lamentable, disgusting, shameful, low, abject, unworthy, shabby, uncharitable, base, dishonourable, unprincipled, ignoble, sordid, wretched, loathsome, odious, treacherous, underhand; nasty, cruel, bad, immoral, wicked, wrong, evil, sinful, vile, foul, vicious, nefarious, heinous; informal rotten, dirty, stinking, beastly; archaic dastardly, scurvy.
▷ANTONYMS kind, altruistic, unselfish.
▶ **noun** (**the low-down**) *he gave us the low-down on his life as Britain's top comedian*: **inside information**, the whole story, the facts; **data**, information, facts and figures, intelligence, the news; **a briefing**, a brief, guidance; informal info, the score, the gen, the latest, the word, the rundown; N. Amer. informal the poop, the dope.

lower¹ (rhymes with 'mower') **adjective 1** *the lower house of the German parliament*: **subordinate**, inferior, lesser, junior, minor, secondary, lower-level, lower-grade, subsidiary, ancillary, second-fiddle, subservient; second-class, second-rate.
▷ANTONYMS upper, senior.
2 *the curtain covers the lower half of the window | Flora stuck out her lower lip*: **bottom**, bottommost, under, underneath, further down, beneath, nether.
▷ANTONYMS top, upper, higher.
3 *you may have to accept a lower price*: **cheaper**, reduced, decreased, lessened, curtailed, pruned, cut, slashed.
▷ANTONYMS higher, increased.

lower² (rhymes with 'mower') **verb 1** *she lowered the mask*: **move down**, let down, take down, haul down, drop, let fall, let sink.
▷ANTONYMS raise, lift up.
2 *the crowd had lowered their voices*: **soften**, modulate, quieten, hush, tone down, muffle, turn down, mute.
▷ANTONYMS raise, intensify.
3 *demand could be stimulated by lowering taxes*: **reduce**, decrease, lessen, bring down, diminish, curtail, prune, pare (down), ease up on, cause to fall, slim down, mark down, cut, slash, axe.
▷ANTONYMS increase.
4 *the water level lowered*: **subside**, fall (off), recede, ebb, wane; abate, die down, let up, moderate, diminish, lessen.
5 *he must really love her to lower himself in this way*: **degrade**, debase, demean, abase, humble, humiliate, downgrade, discredit, shame, dishonour, disgrace; belittle, cheapen, devalue; (**lower oneself**) **condescend**, deign, stoop, sink, descend, vouchsafe.
▷ANTONYMS boost.

lower³ (rhymes with 'power') **verb** See **lour**.

low-grade **adjective** *low-grade coal | low-grade jobs*: **poor-quality**, inferior, substandard, below standard, second-rate; shoddy, cheap, shabby, reject, rubbishy, trashy, junky, bargain-basement, gimcrack; poor, bad, unsatisfactory, not up to par, not up to scratch; mediocre; informal tinpot; Brit. informal duff, ropy, twopenny-halfpenny; N. Amer. informal two-bit, bum, cheapjack, a dime a dozen, low-rent, tinhorn.
▷ANTONYMS top-quality, first-class.

low-key **adjective** *the councils' low-key approach had saved them from widespread media hostility*: **restrained**, modest, understated, muted, subtle, quiet, low-profile, inconspicuous, unostentatious, unobtrusive, discreet, circumspect, played-down, toned-down, self-effacing, relaxed, downbeat, easy-going, modulated, softened; informal laid-back.
▷ANTONYMS ostentatious, showy.

lowly **adjective 1** *it was unheard of for a tradesman of such lowly status to threaten his customers in such a fashion*: **humble**, low, low-born, low-bred, low-ranking, plebeian, proletarian, peasant, poor; common, ordinary, simple, plain; inferior, ignoble, subordinate, obscure.
▷ANTONYMS noble, aristocratic.
2 *I'm just a lowly civil servant*: **average**, modest, simple, plain, ordinary, commonplace, run-of-the-mill; unambitious, unpretentious, unaspiring.

low-spirited **adjective** *she sounded a little low-spirited*: **depressed**, dejected, despondent, downhearted, downcast, low, down, sorrowful, gloomy, glum, unhappy, sad, melancholy, blue, fed up, morose, moody, miserable, dismal, heavy-hearted, mournful, forlorn, woebegone; disheartened, discouraged, crestfallen, dispirited, without energy, enervated, flat; informal down in the mouth, down in the dumps; Brit. informal brassed off, cheesed off.
▷ANTONYMS cheerful.

loyal **adjective** *she was loyal to her country*: **faithful**, true, true-hearted, tried and true, true-blue, devoted; **constant**, steadfast, fast, staunch, dependable, reliable, trusted, trustworthy, trusty, dutiful, unchanging, unwavering, unswerving, dedicated, committed, firm, stable, steady, unfailing; patriotic.
▷ANTONYMS disloyal, treacherous.

> *Choose the right word* **loyal, faithful, constant, true**
>
> See **faithful**.

loyalty **noun** *he owes his primary loyalty to the party*: **allegiance**, faithfulness, fidelity, obedience, fealty, adherence, homage, devotion, bond; trueness, true-heartedness; steadfastness, fastness, staunchness, dependability, reliability, trustiness, trustworthiness, duty, constancy, dedication, commitment; firmness, stability, steadiness; patriotism; archaic troth.
▷ANTONYMS disloyalty, treachery.

lozenge **noun 1** *the patterns comprise mosaics, lozenges, and crosses*: **rhombus**, diamond shape, diamond.
2 *she was always taking throat lozenges and cough mixtures*: **pastille**, tablet, pill, capsule, pilule, drop; **cough sweet**, cough drop, gum, gumdrop, jujube; Medicine troche, bolus; rare trochisk, trochiscus.

lubricant **noun** *the pipe ends had been smeared with lubricant*: **grease**, oil, lubricator, lubrication, emollient, lotion, unguent; lard, fat; moisturizer.

lubricate **verb 1** *lubricate the washer with silicone grease*: **oil**, **grease**, make slippery, make smooth, smear with oil, cover with oil, rub with oil, moisturize, wax, polish.

2 *firms would invite clients in the hope that the goodwill created would lubricate some future deal*: **facilitate**, ease, ready, make smooth, smooth the way for, oil the wheels for, pave the way for.
▷ANTONYMS impede, obstruct.

lucid adjective **1** *a lucid introduction to the philosophy of mind*: **intelligible**, comprehensible, understandable, cogent, coherent, communicative, articulate, eloquent; clear, clear-cut, crystal clear, transparent; plain, simple, direct, vivid, sharp, straightforward, perspicuous, unambiguous, graphic, explicit; informal joined-up.
▷ANTONYMS confusing, unclear, ambiguous.
2 *occasionally she has these lucid moments where she's herself again*: **rational**, sane, in one's right mind, in possession of one's faculties, of sound mind, able to think clearly; normal, balanced, well balanced, sensible, clear-headed, right-minded, sober; Latin compos mentis; informal all there, with all one's marbles.
▷ANTONYMS muddled.
3 literary *the lucid stars*: **bright**, shining, gleaming, luminous, radiant, brilliant, glowing, dazzling, lustrous, luminescent, phosphorescent; literary lucent, lambent; rare effulgent, refulgent.
▷ANTONYMS dark, dull.

luck noun **1** *with luck you'll be in Marseilles tomorrow night | best of luck, John!* **good fortune**, good luck, success, successfulness, prosperity, advantage, advantageousness, felicity; a stroke of luck; informal fluke, a lucky break.
▷ANTONYMS bad luck, misfortune.
2 *she sent up a silent prayer that her luck had changed*: **fortune**, fate, destiny, lot, stars, what is written in the stars, karma, kismet; fortuity, serendipity; chance, accident, a twist of fate, contingency, circumstances; Austral./NZ informal mozzle.
□ **in luck** *I was in luck—the lift was working*: **fortunate**, lucky, blessed, favoured, born under a lucky star; successful, prosperous, happy, opportune, timely, blessed with good luck; Brit. informal jammy.
▷ANTONYMS unlucky, out of luck.
□ **out of luck** *you're out of luck—you've missed the evening edition*: **unfortunate**, unlucky, luckless, hapless, cursed with ill-luck, unsuccessful, disadvantaged, miserable; informal down on one's luck.
▷ANTONYMS lucky, in luck.

luckily adverb *luckily, our ship was not badly damaged*: **fortunately**, happily, providentially, opportunely, by good luck, by good fortune, as luck would have it, propitiously; mercifully, thankfully; thank goodness, thank God, thank heavens, thank the stars.
▷ANTONYMS unfortunately.

luckless adjective *the novel's luckless hero ends tragically without wife, mistress, or home*: **unlucky**, unfortunate, unsuccessful, out of luck, down on one's luck, jinxed, cursed, doomed, hapless, ill-fated, ill-starred, star-crossed; disadvantaged; unhappy, miserable, wretched, forlorn.
▷ANTONYMS lucky, fortunate.

lucky adjective **1** *I'm lucky to have such a caring family | fifty lucky winners have received T-shirts*: **fortunate**, in luck, blessed, blessed with good luck, favoured, born under a lucky star, charmed; successful, prosperous, happy; advantaged, born with a silver spoon in one's mouth; Brit. informal jammy.
▷ANTONYMS unlucky, unfortunate.
2 *I had a lucky escape | it was just a lucky guess*: **providential**, fortunate, advantageous, timely, opportune, serendipitous, expedient, heaven-sent, auspicious, propitious, felicitous, convenient, apt; chance, fortuitous, accidental, unexpected, unanticipated, unforeseen, unlooked-for, coincidental; informal fluky.
▷ANTONYMS unfavourable.

lucrative adjective *a lucrative business*: **profitable**, profit-making, gainful, remunerative, moneymaking, paying, high-income, well paid, high-paying, bankable, cost-effective; productive, fruitful, rewarding, worthwhile, advantageous; thriving, flourishing, successful, booming, going.
▷ANTONYMS unprofitable.

lucre noun *he had seen the inheritance simply as a source of lucre*: **money**, cash, hard cash, ready money, funds, capital, finances, riches, wealth, spoils, ill-gotten gains, Mammon; profit, profits, gain, proceeds, winnings; informal dough, bread, loot, the ready, readies, moolah; Brit. informal dosh, brass, lolly, spondulicks, wonga, ackers; archaic pelf.

ludicrous adjective *a ludicrous idea*: **absurd**, ridiculous, farcical, laughable, risible, preposterous, foolish, idiotic, stupid, inane, silly, asinine, nonsensical; informal crazy, mad, insane; rare derisible.
▷ANTONYMS sensible.

lug verb *they lugged the baskets of laundry upstairs*: **carry**, lift, bear, tote, heave, hoist, shoulder, manhandle; haul, drag, pull, tug, tow, transport, move, take, bring, convey, shift, fetch; informal hump, schlep; Scottish informal humph.

luggage noun *David hauled their luggage off the back seat*: **baggage**, bag and baggage, things, gear, belongings, kit, effects, goods and chattels, impedimenta, paraphernalia, accoutrements, rig, tackle; bags, suitcases, cases, trunks; informal stuff, clobber. See also **bag** (sense 3 of the noun).

lugubrious adjective *his lugubrious expression | a lugubrious hymn*: **mournful**, gloomy, sad, unhappy, doleful, Eeyorish, glum, melancholy, melancholic, woeful, miserable, woebegone, forlorn, despondent, dejected, depressed, long-faced, sombre, solemn, serious, sorrowful, morose, dour, mirthless, cheerless, joyless, wretched, dismal, grim, saturnine, pessimistic; funereal, sepulchral, dirge-like, elegiac; informal down in the mouth, down in the dumps, blue; Brit. informal looking as if one had lost a pound and found a penny; literary dolorous.
▷ANTONYMS cheerful, joyful.

lukewarm adjective **1** *they drank bitter lukewarm coffee*: **tepid**, slightly warm, warmish, blood-hot, blood-warm, at room temperature, at skin temperature; French chambré.
▷ANTONYMS hot; cold.
2 *elsewhere in the country, however, the idea met with a lukewarm response*: **indifferent**, cool, half-hearted, apathetic, unenthusiastic, tepid, uninterested, unconcerned, offhand, lackadaisical, perfunctory, phlegmatic, impassive, dispassionate, emotionless, passionless, limp, non-committal, unresponsive, unmoved; informal laid-back, unenthused, couldn't-care-less; Brit. vulgar slang half-arsed; rare Laodicean.
▷ANTONYMS enthusiastic.

lull verb **1** *the sound of the bells lulled us to sleep*: **soothe**, quiet, hush, lullaby; rock to sleep.
▷ANTONYMS waken, agitate.
2 *he had been unable to lull his wife's anxiety about her fading beauty*: **assuage**, allay, ease, alleviate, pacify, palliate, mitigate, placate, mollify; soothe, quiet, quieten, silence, calm, settle, hush, still, quell, quash, stifle, deaden, repress; temper, reduce, check, diminish.
▷ANTONYMS aggravate.
3 *the noise from the fair had lulled*: **abate**, die down, subside, let up, moderate, slacken, lessen, dwindle, decrease, diminish, ebb, fade away, wane, taper off, lower.
▷ANTONYMS increase.
▶ noun **1** *for two days there had been a lull in the fighting*: **pause**, respite, interval, break, hiatus, suspension, cessation, interlude, intermission, breathing space, moratorium, lacuna; Prosody caesura; informal let-up, breather.
2 *the lull before the storm*: **calm**, calmness, stillness, quiet, quietness, tranquillity, peace, peacefulness, silence, hush.
▷ANTONYMS activity.

lullaby noun *I remembered a lullaby my mother sang to me*: **cradle song**, soothing song, gentle song, quiet song; French berceuse.

lumber[1] verb *she watched him lumber blindly down the steep narrow staircase*: **lurch**, stumble, shamble, shuffle, reel, waddle; **trudge**, clump, stump, plod, tramp, walk heavily/clumsily, stamp, stomp, thump, thud, bang; informal galumph.

lumber[2] noun **1** *a spare room packed with lumber*: **jumble**, clutter, odds and ends, bits and pieces, bits and bobs, rummage, bric-a-brac, oddments, miscellanea, sundries, knick-knacks, flotsam and jetsam, cast-offs, white elephants, stuff, things; rejects, trash, refuse, rubbish, litter; informal junk, odds and sods, gubbins, clobber.
2 *they have diversified into lumber and cattle ranching in the Amazon*: **timber**, wood, planks, planking.
▶ verb Brit. informal *a career would be less easy once she was lumbered with a husband and child*: **burden**, saddle, encumber, hamper, impose on, load, oppress, trouble, tax; informal land, dump something on someone.

lumbering adjective *he was a lumbering bear of a man*: **clumsy**, awkward, heavy-footed, blundering, bumbling, inept, maladroit, uncoordinated, ungainly, oafish, like a bull in a china shop, ungraceful, gauche, lumpish, cumbersome, ponderous, laborious, stolid; informal clodhopping, hulking; archaic lubberly.
▷ANTONYMS nimble, agile.

luminary noun *the luminaries of the art world*: **leading light**, guiding light, inspiration, leader, expert, master, panjandrum, dignitary, VIP; star, superstar, megastar, celebrity, celebutante, big name, household name, somebody, name; notable, public figure, important personage, lion, legend, great, giant; informal bigwig, big shot, big cheese, biggie, celeb.
▷ANTONYMS nobody, pleb.

luminous adjective *a cluster of luminous stars | he checked the luminous dial on his alarm clock*: **shining**, bright, brilliant, radiant, dazzling, glowing, gleaming, scintillating, lustrous, luminescent, phosphorescent, incandescent; vivid, intense, resplendent; lighted, lit, illuminated; literary lambent, lucent; rare coruscating, refulgent, effulgent, candescent, luminiferous.
▷ANTONYMS dark.

lump[1] noun **1** *a lump of coal*: **chunk**, wedge, hunk, piece, mass, block, slab, cake, nugget, ball, brick, cube, dab, pat, knob, clod, gobbet, dollop, wad, clump, cluster, mound, concentration; bit, segment, portion; informal gob, glob.
2 *he had a huge lump on his head*: **swelling**, bump, bulge, protuberance, protrusion, growth, outgrowth, carbuncle, hump, tumour, wen, boil, blister, wart, corn, eruption, node, contusion; rare tumescence.

▸ **verb** *the media tend to* ***lump together*** *women singer-songwriters*: **combine**, put, group, bunch, aggregate, unite, pool, mix, blend, merge, mass, join, fuse, conglomerate, coalesce, consolidate, collect, throw, consider together.

lump[2] informal **verb**
□ **lump it** *we're going to the swimming pool tomorrow, like it or lump it*: **put up with it**, bear it, endure it, take it, tolerate it, suffer it, accept it, make allowances for it, abide it, brook it, weather it, countenance it; Scottish thole it; informal stick it, stomach it, stand it, swallow it, hack it, wear it.

lumpy adjective **1** *a lumpy mattress*: **bumpy**, knobbly, bulging, uneven, covered with lumps, full of lumps.
2 *lumpy custard*: **clotted**, curdled, full of lumps, congealed, coagulated; granular, grainy; rare nodose.

lunacy noun **1** *the survivors descended into despair and lunacy*: **insanity**, madness, mental illness, derangement, dementia, dementedness, insaneness, loss of reason, unsoundness of mind, mental instability, mania, frenzy, psychosis; informal craziness.
▷ANTONYMS sanity.
2 *such an economic policy would be sheer lunacy*: **folly**, foolishness, foolhardiness, stupidity, idiocy, imbecility, irrationality, illogicality, senselessness, nonsense, absurdity, absurdness, madness, insanity; silliness, inanity, ridiculousness, ludicrousness; informal craziness; Brit. informal daftness.
▷ANTONYMS sense, prudence.

lunatic noun **1** *a dangerous lunatic*: **maniac**, madman, madwoman, psychopath, psychotic; informal loony, loon, nut, nutter, nutcase, head case, headbanger, screwball, psycho; Scottish informal radge.
2 *when I'm in a bad mood I drive like a lunatic*: **fool**, idiot, imbecile, moron.
▸ **adjective 1** *a lunatic prisoner*. See **mad**.
2 *a lunatic idea*. See **foolish**.

lung noun

> *Word links* **lung**
>
> **pulmonary** relating to the lungs
> **pneumo-, pneumon-** related prefixes, as in *pneumoconiosis, pneumonitis*
> **pneumonectomy** removal of a lung
> **spirometry** measurement of lung capacity

lunge noun *Harry made a lunge for the dagger*: **thrust**, pounce, dive, jump, spring, leap, rush, sudden movement, grab.
▸ **verb** *McCulloch raised his cudgel and lunged at him*: **thrust**, pounce, dive, launch oneself, jump, spring, leap, rush, charge, move suddenly, make a grab.

lurch verb **1** *he lurched into the kitchen*: **stagger**, stumble, sway, reel, roll, weave, totter, flounder, falter, wobble, slip, move clumsily.
▷ANTONYMS tiptoe.
2 *Scott was hurled across a bulkhead as the ship lurched*: **sway**, reel, list, roll, pitch, toss, keel, veer, labour, flounder, heel, swerve, make heavy weather; Nautical pitchpole.
▸ **noun**
□ **leave someone in the lurch** *up to ninety farmers will be left in the lurch following the decision to stop funding*: **abandon**, desert, leave, leave high and dry, turn one's back on, cast aside, break (up) with; jilt, strand, leave stranded, throw over; informal run/walk out on, dump, ditch; archaic forsake.
▷ANTONYMS stick by.

lure verb *consumers are frequently lured into debt by clever advertising*: **tempt**, entice, attract, induce, coax, persuade, inveigle, allure, seduce, win over, cajole, beguile, bewitch, ensnare, captivate, enrapture; decoy, draw, lead (on); whet someone's appetite.
▷ANTONYMS deter, put off.
▸ **noun** *Les could never resist the lure of the stage*: **temptation**, enticement, attraction, pull, draw, appeal; inducement, allurement, fascination, interest; decoy, incentive, bait, magnet, siren song, drawing card, carrot, snare, trap; informal come-on.

> *Choose the right word* **lure, tempt, entice**
>
> See **tempt**.

lurid adjective **1** *a lurid birthday card*: **brightly coloured**, bright, over-bright, brilliant, glaring, fluorescent, flaming, dazzling, vivid, intense; showy, gaudy, loud.
▷ANTONYMS muted, subtle.
2 *a lurid account of the prostitution trade | lurid details*: **sensational**, sensationalist, melodramatic, exaggerated, overdramatized, extravagant, colourful, trashy, rubbishy, cheap, pulp, tasteless, kitschy; **salacious**, graphic, explicit, unrestrained, prurient, ribald, suggestive, shocking, startling, dirty, filthy; **gruesome**, gory, grisly, macabre, repugnant, revolting, disgusting, ghastly, morbid, unearthly, grotesque, hideous, horrifying, appalling; informal tacky, shock-horror, juicy, full-frontal.
▷ANTONYMS restrained, discreet.

lurk verb *a ruthless killer still lurked in the darkness*: **skulk**, loiter, lie in wait, lie low, hide, conceal oneself, take cover, keep out of sight; sneak, sidle, slink, prowl, steal, move furtively, move with stealth.

luscious adjective **1** *luscious fruits and vegetables*: **delicious**, succulent, lush, juicy, mouth-watering, sweet, tasty, flavourful, flavoursome, appetizing, delectable, palatable, toothsome, choice; informal scrumptious, scrummy, yummy, moreish; N. Amer. informal nummy; literary ambrosial; rare ambrosian, nectareous, nectarean.
▷ANTONYMS unappetizing.
2 *a luscious Swedish beauty*: **sexy**, sexually attractive, nubile, ravishing, gorgeous, desirable, alluring, sultry, sensuous, beautiful, stunning, attractive; voluptuous, curvaceous, shapely, buxom; informal beddable, fanciable, curvy; N. Amer. informal foxy, cute, bootylicious; Austral./NZ informal spunky.
▷ANTONYMS plain; scrawny.

lush adjective **1** *the hills are covered in lush vegetation*: **luxuriant**, rich, abundant, superabundant, profuse, exuberant, riotous, prolific, teeming, flourishing, thriving, vigorous; dense, thick, rank, rampant, overgrown, jungle-like; verdant, green; informal jungly.
▷ANTONYMS barren, meagre.
2 *a lush ripe peach*: **succulent**, luscious, juicy, fleshy, pulpy, soft, tender, ripe, fresh.
▷ANTONYMS shrivelled.
3 *a lush apartment in the best residential section*: **luxurious**, luxury, de luxe, sumptuous, grand, palatial, opulent, lavish, elaborate, extravagant, fancy; informal plush, ritzy, classy, posh, swanky; Brit. informal swish; N. Amer. informal swank.
▷ANTONYMS austere.

lust noun **1** *he was watching her with undisguised lust*: **sexual desire**, sexual appetite, sexual longing, sexual passion, lustfulness, ardour, desire, passion; libido, sex drive, sexuality, biological urge; **lechery**, lecherousness, lasciviousness, lewdness, carnality, licentiousness, salaciousness, prurience; informal horniness, raunchiness, the hots; Brit. informal randiness; rare salacity, concupiscence, nympholepsy.
2 *a lust for power*: **greed**, greediness, desire, craving, covetousness, eagerness, keenness, avidness, avidity, cupidity, longing, yearning, hunger, thirst, appetite, hankering.
▷ANTONYMS aversion.
▸ **verb 1** *he* ***lusted after*** *his employer's wife*: **desire**, be consumed with desire for, find sexually attractive, find sexy, crave, covet, want, wish for, long for, yearn for, hunger for, thirst for, ache for, burn for, pant for; informal have the hots for, lech after/over, fancy, have a thing about/for, drool over, have the horn for.
2 *she* ***lusted after*** *some unbridled adventure*: **crave**, **desire**, be consumed with desire for, covet, have one's heart set on, want, wish for, long for, yearn for, dream of, hanker for, hanker after, hunger for, thirst for, ache for.
▷ANTONYMS be averse to.

lustful adjective *a lustful look*: **lecherous**, lascivious, lewd, libidinous, licentious, lubricious, salacious, goatish; wanton, unchaste, impure, immodest, indecent, dirty, prurient; passionate, ardent, amorous, amatory, hot-blooded, sensual, sexy, erotic; informal horny, randy, raunchy, naughty; rare concupiscent, lickerish.
▷ANTONYMS chaste, pure.

lustily adverb *the crew cheered lustily*: **heartily**, vigorously, loudly, at the top of one's voice, with all one's might, with might and main, powerfully, forcefully, strongly; informal like mad, like crazy.
▷ANTONYMS faintly, quietly.

lustre noun **1** *her hair lost its lustre*: **sheen**, gloss, glossiness, shine, brightness, radiance, burnish, polish, patina, glow, gleam, glimmer, shimmer.
▷ANTONYMS dullness.
2 *the lustre of the Milky Way*: **brilliance**, brightness, sparkle, dazzle, flash, glitter, glint, gleam, radiance, luminousness, luminosity, luminescence, light; rare effulgence, refulgence, lambency, coruscation.
▷ANTONYMS darkness.
3 *the lustre of their achievements*: **honour**, glory, illustriousness, credit, merit, prestige, éclat, distinction, eminence, pre-eminence, notability, consequence, renown, fame.
▷ANTONYMS dishonour.
4 *a ginger jar in pink lustre with embossed flowers*: **glaze**, lacquer, shellac, varnish, enamel, patina, coat, coating, covering, finish.

lustreless adjective *a pallid face and lustreless eyes | lustreless black boots*: **dull**, lacklustre, matt, unburnished, unpolished, tarnished, dingy, dim, dark, drab.
▷ANTONYMS lustrous, bright.

lustrous adjective *lustrous black hair*: **shiny**, shining, satiny, glossy, gleaming, burnished, polished, radiant, bright, brilliant, luminous; dazzling, sparkling, glistening, twinkling, shimmering, scintillating; literary lucent, irradiant; rare effulgent, refulgent.
▷ANTONYMS dull.

> *Word toolkit* **lustrous**
>
> See **glossy**.

lusty adjective **1** *lusty young men*: **healthy**, **strong**, **fit**, vigorous, robust, hale and hearty, hearty, energetic, vital, lively, bursting with good health, blooming, in good condition, in fine fettle; rugged, sturdy, tough, stalwart, brawny, muscular, muscly, strapping, hefty, husky, burly, solidly built, well built, well made, solid, substantial, powerful; virile, red-blooded; informal beefy.
▷ANTONYMS weak.
2 *he sang a few bars in a lusty baritone*: **loud**, vigorous, hearty, strong, powerful, forceful, stentorian; strident.
▷ANTONYMS quiet, weak.

luxuriant adjective *luxuriant green vegetation*: **lush**, rich, abundant, superabundant, profuse, exuberant, prolific, teeming, flourishing, fecund, thriving, vigorous, riotous; dense, thick, rank, rampant, overgrown; verdant, green; informal jungly.
▷ANTONYMS barren, meagre, sparse.

Easily confused words **luxuriant or luxurious?**

See **luxurious**.

luxuriate verb *run a hot bath and **luxuriate in** it*: **revel**, bask, delight, take pleasure, wallow, indulge oneself, enjoy, relish, savour, appreciate, lap up; informal get a kick out of, get a thrill out of, get a charge out of.
▷ANTONYMS dislike, find intolerable.

luxurious adjective **1** *a luxurious New York hotel*: **opulent**, sumptuous, affluent, expensive, rich, costly, de luxe, lush, grand, palatial, splendid, magnificent, lavish, lavishly appointed, well appointed, extravagant, ornate, fancy, stylish, elegant; informal plush, posh, upmarket, classy, ritzy, swanky; Brit. informal swish; N. Amer. informal swank; rare palatian.
▷ANTONYMS poor; austere, spartan.
2 *a luxurious lifestyle*: **self-indulgent**, sensual, pleasure-loving, comfort-seeking, epicurean, hedonistic, sybaritic, lotus-eating, decadent, extravagant, immoderate.
▷ANTONYMS abstemious.

Easily confused words **luxurious or luxuriant?**

You may find *luxuriant foliage* in the conservatory of a *luxurious home*, but the two words have quite different meanings.

Luxurious denotes things that are extremely comfortable, elegant, and pleasurable (usually with a hint that they may be self-indulgent and unnecessarily expensive), as in *the luxurious villas of the rich and famous*.

Luxuriant, on the other hand, is used mainly with reference to the growth of plants (*luxuriant creepers climbed up the wall*), though it may also refer to a person's hair (*she tossed her luxuriant hair back contemptuously*).

luxury noun **1** *we'll live in luxury for the rest of our lives*: **opulence**, luxuriousness, sumptuousness, richness, costliness, grandeur, grandness, splendour, magnificence, lavishness, lap of luxury, bed of roses, milk and honey; comfort, security; affluence, wealth, prosperity, prosperousness, plenty; informal the life of Riley.
▷ANTONYMS austerity; poverty.
2 *the luxury of a long night's rest*: **joy**, delight, bliss, blessing, benefit, advantage, boon; satisfaction, comfort, ease.
3 *a TV is his only luxury*: **indulgence**, extravagance, self-indulgence, treat, extra, non-essential, frill; refinement.
▷ANTONYMS necessity.

lying noun *she was no good at lying*: **untruthfulness**, fabrication, fibbing, perjury, white lies, little white lies; falseness, falsity, dishonesty, mendacity, mendaciousness, perfidy, perfidiousness, lack of veracity, telling stories, invention, misrepresentation, deceit, duplicity, dissimulation, dissembling, pretence, artifice, guile, double-dealing, underhandedness; informal kidology.
▷ANTONYMS telling the truth, honesty.
▸ adjective *he's a lying, cheating snake in the grass*: **untruthful**, false, dishonest, mendacious, perfidious, deceitful, deceiving, deceptive, duplicitous, dissimulating, dissembling, double-dealing, two-faced, guileful, underhand, disingenuous; informal crooked, bent, sneaky, tricky; archaic hollow-hearted.
▷ANTONYMS truthful, honest.

Word links **lying**

mythomania compulsion to lie

lynch verb *six policemen were lynched by angry crowds*: **hang**, hang by the neck; execute, put to death, kill, murder; informal **string up**, do in, bump off, knock off; literary slay; rare gibbet.

lyric adjective **1** *lyric poems of extraordinary beauty*: **melodic**, songlike, musical, melodious, lyrical, rhapsodic, poetic; **expressive**, emotional, deeply felt, personal, subjective, passionate.
2 *lyric voices*: **light**, silvery, clear, lilting, flowing, dulcet, euphonious, sweet, sweet-toned, sweet-sounding, honeyed, mellifluous, mellow, lyrical; rare mellifluent.
▷ANTONYMS harsh, cacophonous.

lyrical adjective **1** *lyrical love poetry*: **songlike**, lyric, melodic, musical, melodious, rhapsodic, poetic; **expressive**, emotional, deeply felt, personal, subjective, passionate.
2 *she was lyrical about her success*: **enthusiastic**, rhapsodic, effusive, rapturous, ecstatic, euphoric, carried away, emotional, passionate, impassioned.
▷ANTONYMS unenthusiastic.

lyrics plural noun *the lyrics of the song*: **words**, libretto, book, text, lines.

macabre adjective **1** *a macabre ritual*: **gruesome**, grisly, grim, gory, morbid, ghastly, unearthly, lurid, grotesque, hideous, horrific, horrible, horrifying, horrid, horrendous, terrifying, frightening, frightful, fearsome, shocking, dreadful, appalling, loathsome, repugnant, repulsive, sickening.
2 *a macabre joke*: **black**, **weird**, unhealthy, sick.

mace noun **staff**, club, cudgel, stick, shillelagh, bludgeon, blackjack, truncheon, cosh, life preserver.

macerate verb *macerate the seeds in a vinegar solution*: **pulp**, mash, squash, soften, liquefy, soak, steep, infuse.

Machiavellian adjective *there were press accusations of Machiavellian deception*: **devious**, cunning, crafty, artful, wily, sly, scheming, designing, conniving, opportunistic, insidious, treacherous, perfidious, two-faced, tricky, double-dealing, unscrupulous, deceitful, dishonest; informal foxy.
▷**ANTONYMS** straightforward, ingenuous.

machinations plural noun *he was cheated by the political machinations of the legislature*: **schemes**, plotting, plots, intrigues, conspiracies, designs, plans, devices, ploys, ruses, tricks, wiles, stratagems, tactics, manoeuvres, manoeuvring, contrivances, expedients; rare complots.

machine noun **1** *a special pincer machine for this work*: **apparatus**, appliance, instrument, tool, utensil, device, unit, contraption, contrivance, gadget, mechanism, engine, motor, lever, pulley; informal gizmo.
2 *a machine can perform these tasks better than a human being*: **robot**, automaton, computer.
3 *an efficient publicity machine*: **organization**, system, structure, arrangement, agency, machinery; informal set-up.

> *Word links* **machine**
>
> **mechanical** relating to machines
> **mechanophobia** fear of machines

machinery noun **1** *a paper mill equipped with modern machinery*: **equipment**, apparatus, hardware, plant, mechanism, gear, tackle, instruments, tools, gadgetry, technology; rare enginery.
2 *the machinery of local government*: **workings**, organization, system, structure, administration, institution, agency, channel, vehicle; informal set-up, nuts and bolts, brass tacks, nitty-gritty.

> *Word links* **machinery**
>
> **mechanophobia** fear of machinery

machinist noun *a machinist in a local paper mill*: **operator**, operative, machine operator, machine-minder, worker.

machismo noun *a woman following her career can challenge a husband's machismo*: **(aggressive) masculinity**, macho, toughness, chauvinism, male chauvinism, sexism, laddishness; virility, manliness.

macho adjective *a macho, non-caring image*: **(aggressively) male**, (unpleasantly) masculine; manly, virile, red-blooded, swashbuckling; informal butch, laddish.
▷**ANTONYMS** wimpish.
▸ **noun 1** *he was a macho at heart*: **red-blooded male**, macho man, muscleman; informal he-man, tough guy, stud; N. Amer. vulgar slang cocksman.
▷**ANTONYMS** wimp, milksop.
2 *macho is out*. See **machismo**.

mackintosh noun **raincoat**, overcoat, gaberdine, trench coat; anorak, cagoule, cape, oilskin, waterproof; Brit. **pakamac**; Brit. informal **mac**; N. Amer. informal **slicker**; trademark **Burberry**, **Drizabone**.

macrocosm noun **1** *the law of the macrocosm*: **universe**, cosmos, world, wide world, globe, creation, solar system, galaxy, outer space.
▷**ANTONYMS** microcosm.
2 *the individual is a microcosm of the social macrocosm*: **system**, structure, totality, entirety, complex.

macula noun **spot**, dot, fleck, mark, speck, speckle, smudge, splash, stain, macule.

mad adjective **1** *he felt he was going mad*: **insane**, mentally ill, certifiable, deranged, demented, of unsound mind, out of one's mind, not in one's right mind, sick in the head, not together, crazy, crazed, lunatic, non compos mentis, unbalanced, unhinged, unstable, disturbed, distracted, stark mad, manic, frenzied, raving, distraught, frantic, hysterical, delirious, psychotic, psychopathic, mad as a hatter, mad as a March hare, away with the fairies, foaming at the mouth; informal mental, off one's head, out of one's head, off one's nut, nuts, nutty, nutty as a fruitcake, off one's rocker, not (quite) right in the head, round the bend, stark staring/raving mad, raving mad, bats, batty, bonkers, dotty, cuckoo, cracked, loopy, loony, bananas, loco, dippy, screwy, schizoid, touched, gaga, up the pole, off the wall, not all there, not right upstairs; Brit. informal barmy, crackers, barking, barking mad, round the twist, off one's trolley, as daft as a brush, not the full shilling; N. Amer. informal buggy, nutsy, nutso; out of one's tree, meshuga, squirrelly, wacko; Canadian & Austral./NZ informal bushed; NZ informal porangi; (**be mad**) informal have a screw loose, have bats in the/one's belfry; Austral. informal have kangaroos in the/one's top paddock.
▷**ANTONYMS** sane.
2 informal *I'm still mad at him for what he did*: **angry**, furious, infuriated, irate, raging, enraged, fuming, blazing, flaming mad, blazing mad, in a towering rage, incensed, wrathful, seeing red, cross, indignant, exasperated, irritated, berserk, out of control, beside oneself; informal livid, spare, wild, aerated; informal, dated waxy, in a wax; N. Amer. informal sore.
▷**ANTONYMS** calm, unruffled.
3 *what sort of mad scheme are you working on?* **foolish**, insane, stupid, lunatic, foolhardy, idiotic, irrational, unreasonable, illogical, zany, senseless, nonsensical, absurd, impractical, silly, inane, asinine, ludicrous, wild, unwise, imprudent, preposterous; informal crazy, daft, crackpot, crackbrained.
▷**ANTONYMS** sensible.
4 informal *he's **mad about** jazz*: **enthusiastic**, passionate, impassioned, keen on; ardent, zealous, fervent, avid, eager, fervid, fanatical, addicted to, devoted to, infatuated with, in love with, hot for; informal crazy, potty, dotty, nuts, wild, hooked on, gone on; N. Amer. informal nutso.
▷**ANTONYMS** indifferent.
5 *we made mad, passionate love*: **unrestrained**, uncontrolled, uninhibited, wild, abandoned, overpowering, overwhelming, excited, frenzied, frantic, frenetic, ebullient, energetic, boisterous.
□ **go mad 1** *he subsequently went mad and threw himself in front of a train*: **become insane**, lose one's reason, lose one's mind, take leave of one's senses, go off one's head, go crazy; informal go doolally (tap), lose one's marbles; Brit. informal go barmy, go off one's trolley, go round the twist, go crackers. **2** informal *when I told her I was going to be an actor, my mother went mad*: **become very angry**, lose one's temper, get in a rage, rant, rant and

rave, fulminate; go crazy; informal explode, burst, go off the deep end, go ape, flip, flip one's lid; Brit. informal do one's nut; N. Amer. informal flip one's wig; vulgar slang go apeshit. **3** *the crowd went mad with excitement*: **become frenzied**, become uncontrollable, lose control, erupt, boil over.
□ **like mad** informal **1** *the two men turned towards me, and I ran like mad*: **fast**, furiously, as fast as possible, as fast as one's legs can carry one, hurriedly, quickly, rapidly, speedily, hastily. **2** *he had to fight like mad to get away*: **energetically**, enthusiastically, madly, with a will, for all one is worth, passionately, intensely, ardently, fervently; informal like crazy, hammer and tongs; Brit. informal, dated like billy-o.

madcap adjective **1** *a madcap scheme*: **reckless**, rash, hot-headed, daredevil, impulsive, wild, daring, adventurous, heedless, thoughtless, incautious, imprudent, indiscreet, ill-advised, hasty, foolhardy, foolish, senseless, impractical, hare-brained; informal crazy, crackpot, crackbrained; Scottish informal radge.
2 *a madcap comedy*: **zany**, eccentric, ridiculous, unconventional, weird.
▸ noun *she was a boisterous madcap*: **eccentric**, crank, madman/madwoman, maniac, lunatic, psychotic; oddity, odd fellow, character, individual; hothead, daredevil; informal crackpot, oddball, weirdo, loony, nut, nutter; N. Amer. informal screwball; Scottish informal radge; Austral./NZ informal dingbat.

madden verb **1** *what maddens people most is his vagueness*: **infuriate**, exasperate, irritate; incense, anger, enrage, send into a rage, inflame, annoy, provoke, upset, agitate, vex, irk, pique, gall, make someone's hackles rise, raise someone's hackles, make someone's blood boil, make someone see red, get someone's back up; informal aggravate, bug, get up someone's nose, make livid; Brit. informal nark.
2 *they were maddened with pain*: **drive mad**, drive insane, derange, unhinge, unbalance; informal drive someone off their head, drive round the bend.

maddening adjective *she put the remaining coins back into her purse with maddening slowness*: **infuriating**, exasperating, irritating, annoying, provoking, upsetting, vexing, irksome, unsettling, disturbing, troublesome, bothersome, vexatious, galling; informal aggravating, pestilential.

made-up adjective **1** *a made-up story*: **invented**, fabricated, trumped-up, concocted, devised, manufactured, fictitious, fictional, false, untrue, unreal, sham, specious, spurious, bogus, apocryphal, imaginary, mythical.
2 *a heavily made-up woman*: **painted**, done up, powdered, rouged.

madhouse noun **1** *his father is shut up in a madhouse*: **mental hospital**, mental institution, psychiatric hospital, asylum; informal nuthouse, funny farm, loony bin; dated lunatic asylum.
2 *the place was a total madhouse*: **bedlam**, mayhem, babel, chaos, pandemonium, uproar, turmoil, wild disarray, scene of confusion, disorder, hurly-burly, tumult, jumble, pell-mell, hullabaloo, hubbub, whirlwind, maelstrom, madness, all hell broken loose; N. Amer. three-ring circus.

m

madly adverb **1** *she was smiling madly*: **insanely**, frantically, hysterically, deliriously, wildly, like a lunatic; informal crazily, barmily.
2 *it was fun, hurtling madly downhill*: **fast**, furiously, hurriedly, quickly, speedily, hastily, energetically; informal like mad, like crazy.
3 informal *Tara is madly in love with you*: **intensely**, fervently, wildly, unrestrainedly, enthusiastically, completely; with all one's heart, to distraction, fantastically.
▹ANTONYMS slightly.
4 informal *his job isn't madly glamorous*: **very**, extremely, exceedingly, excessively, absurdly, ridiculously, fantastically, wildly, outrageously; all that, terribly, terrifically, awfully, tremendously, hugely.

madman, madwoman noun **lunatic**, maniac, psychotic, psychopath, schizophrenic; informal loony, nut, nutter, nutcase, head case, basket case, headbanger, psycho, schizo, crank, crackpot; Scottish informal radge; N. Amer. informal screwball; N. Amer. & Austral./NZ informal dingbat.

madness noun **1** *today madness is called mental illness*: **insanity**, insaneness, dementia, mental illness, derangement, dementedness, instability, unsoundness of mind, lunacy, distraction, depression, mania, hysteria, frenzy, psychosis, psychopathy, schizophrenia, hydrophobia; informal craziness; N. Amer. informal meshugaas; Austral./NZ informal dingbats; rare moon-madness, cynanthropy, deliration, lycanthropy, zoanthropy.
▹ANTONYMS sanity.
2 *it would be madness to do otherwise*: **folly**, foolishness, stupidity, insanity, lunacy, midsummer madness, foolhardiness, idiocy, imprudence, irrationality, unreasonableness, illogicality, senselessness, nonsense, nonsensicalness, absurdness, absurdity, silliness, inanity, ludicrousness, wildness, preposterousness; informal craziness; Brit. informal daftness.
▹ANTONYMS common sense, good sense.
3 *it's absolute madness in here*: **bedlam**, mayhem, chaos, pandemonium, babel, uproar, turmoil, wild disarray, disorder, hurly-burly; scene of confusion, madhouse, tumult, jumble, pell-mell, hullabaloo, hubbub, whirlwind, maelstrom, all hell broken loose; N. Amer. informal three-ring circus.

madrigal noun *a group of five-part madrigals*: **song**, anthem, carol, ballad, canzone, chanson, motet, chant; hymn, psalm.

maelstrom noun **1** *we headed south, with one eye on the maelstrom to starboard*: **whirlpool**, vortex, eddy, swirl; literary Charybdis.
2 *they were caught up in the maelstrom of war*: **turbulence**, tumult, turmoil, uproar, commotion, disorder, jumble, disarray, chaos, confusion, upheaval, seething mass, welter, pandemonium, bedlam, whirlwind, swirl.

maestro noun *the orchestra took to the great maestro | blues maestro Eric Clapton*: **conductor**, director; **virtuoso**, master, expert, genius, wizard, prodigy; informal ace, whizz; Brit. informal dab hand.
▹ANTONYMS tyro, beginner.

magazine noun *she leafed through the magazines*: **journal**, publication, periodical, paper, proceedings; organ, supplement, colour supplement, number, copy, issue, title, weekly, fortnightly, monthly, quarterly, comic; informal glossy, book, rag, mag, 'zine, fanzine; rare magalogue.

magenta adjective **reddish-purple**, purplish-red, crimson, mauvish-crimson, carmine red, fuchsia, fuchsin.

maggot noun **grub**, larva; caterpillar.

magic noun **1** *do you believe in magic?* **sorcery**, witchcraft, wizardry, necromancy, enchantment, spell-working, incantation, the supernatural, occultism, the occult, black magic, the black arts, devilry, divination, malediction, voodoo, hoodoo, sympathetic magic, white magic, witching, witchery; charm, hex, spell, jinx; N. Amer. mojo, orenda; NZ makutu; S. African informal muti; rare sortilege, thaumaturgy, theurgy.
2 *he does magic at children's parties*: **conjuring tricks**, sleight of hand, legerdemain, illusion, prestidigitation, deception, trickery, juggling; informal jiggery-pokery.
3 *the magic of the stage*: **allure**, allurement, attraction, excitement, enchantment, entrancement, fascination, charm, glamour, magnetism, enticement.
▹ANTONYMS dullness.
4 *a taste of soccer magic*: **skill**, skilfulness, brilliance, ability, accomplishment, adeptness, competence, adroitness, deftness, dexterity, aptitude, expertise, expertness, art, finesse, experience, professionalism, talent, cleverness, smartness.
▹ANTONYMS clumsiness, incompetence.
▸ adjective **1** *a magic spell*: **supernatural**, enchanted, occult, Druidical; rare necromantic, thaumaturgic, thaumaturgical, sorcerous.
2 *a magic place*: **fascinating**, captivating, charming, glamorous, magical, enchanting, entrancing, spellbinding, magnetic, irresistible, hypnotic.
3 informal *we had a magic time*. See **marvellous** (sense 2).
□ **magic bullet** informal *there is no magic bullet for successful innovation*: **solution**, answer, resolution, way out; remedy, antidote, cure, nostrum, panacea; informal quick fix.

> *Word links* **magic**
>
> **rhabdophobia** fear of magic

magical adjective **1** *he began uttering magical incantations*: **supernatural**, magic, occult, mystical, mystic, paranormal, preternatural, other-worldly, spectral, ghostly, secret, dark, cryptic, uncanny, cabbalistic, shamanistic; rare necromantic, thaumaturgic, thaumaturgical, sorcerous, extramundane.
2 *the news had an instant and magical effect*: **extraordinary**, remarkable, exceptional, outstanding, incredible, phenomenal, unbelievable, inconceivable, unimaginable, amazing, astonishing, astounding, stunning, staggering, marvellous, magnificent, wonderful, sensational, breathtaking, miraculous, singular, uncommon, unheard of, unique, unparalleled, unprecedented, unusual, unusually good, too good to be true, superlative, prodigious, surpassing, rare; informal fantastic, fabulous, stupendous, out of this world, terrific, tremendous, brilliant, mind-boggling, mind-blowing, awesome, stellar; literary wondrous.
3 *this magical small land in the heart of Europe*: **enchanting**, entrancing, spellbinding, bewitching, beguiling, fascinating, captivating, alluring, enthralling, charming, attractive, appealing, magnetic, irresistible, intriguing, engaging, hypnotic, mesmerizing, mesmeric, intoxicating, heady, seductive, inviting, idyllic, wonderful, magnificent, superb, glorious, sublime, lovely, delightful, beautiful, too good to be true; informal dreamy, heavenly, divine, gorgeous, mind-blowing.
▹ANTONYMS dull, boring.

magician noun **1** *the person the magician wishes to influence*: **sorcerer**, sorceress, witch, wizard, warlock, enchanter, enchantress, necromancer, spell-caster, Druid, shaman, witch doctor, magus, alchemist; in southern Africa sangoma, inyanga; rare thaumaturge, theurgist.
2 *the magician fools his audience with sleight of hand*: **conjuror**, illusionist, juggler, prestidigitator.
3 informal *he is the greatest bowler in modern cricket—a magician*. See **virtuoso** (noun).

magisterial adjective **1** *a magisterial pronouncement*: **authoritative**, masterful, lordly, judgelike.
2 *his magisterial style of questioning*: **domineering**, dictatorial, autocratic, imperious, bossy, overbearing, peremptory, pompous, lofty, overweening, high-handed, arrogant, haughty; confident, self-confident, overconfident, supercilious, patronizing.
▹ANTONYMS hesitant, tentative.

magnanimity noun *Herbert's magnanimity in making do with the smaller bedroom*: **generosity**, charitableness, charity, benevolence, beneficence, open-handedness, big-heartedness, great-heartedness, liberality, humanity, nobility, chivalry, kindness, munificence, bountifulness, bounty, largesse, altruism, philanthropy; **unselfishness**, selflessness, self-sacrifice, self-denial; **clemency**, mercy, leniency, forgiveness, indulgence.
▷ANTONYMS meanness, selfishness.

magnanimous adjective *she was magnanimous in victory*: **generous**, charitable, benevolent, beneficent, open-handed, big-hearted, great-hearted, munificent, bountiful, liberal, handsome, princely, altruistic, kind, kindly, philanthropic, chivalrous, noble; **unselfish**, selfless, self-sacrificing, ungrudging, unstinting; **forgiving**, merciful, lenient, indulgent, clement; literary bounteous.
▷ANTONYMS mean-spirited, selfish.

magnate noun *the real power lay in the hands of a few rich magnates and landowners*: **industrialist**, tycoon, mogul, captain of industry, baron, lord, king, proprietor, entrepreneur, merchant prince, financier, top executive; chief, leader, VIP, notable, magnifico, nabob, grandee, noble, prelate; informal big shot, bigwig, honcho; N. Amer. informal big wheel; derogatory fat cat.
▷ANTONYMS pawn.

magnet noun **1** *the principle of magnets repelling each other*: **lodestone**, magnetite; field magnet, bar magnet, horseshoe magnet, transverse magnet, electromagnet, electret, solenoid, diamagnet, antiferromagnet, magnetoid, wiggler.
2 *the waterfront has become a magnet for tourists*: **attraction**, focus, focal point, enticement, pull, crowd-pleaser, draw, lure, allurement, temptation, invitation, fascination; informal crowd-puller.

magnetic adjective *his magnetic personality*: **alluring**, attractive, fascinating, captivating, enchanting, enthralling, appealing, charming, prepossessing, engaging, entrancing, tempting, tantalizing, seductive, inviting, irresistible, magic, magical, bewitching, charismatic, hypnotic, mesmeric.
▷ANTONYMS repellent.

magnetism noun *the sheer magnetism of his physical presence*: **allure**, attraction, fascination, enchantment, appeal, draw, drawing power, pull, charm, seductiveness, sexual magnetism, animal magnetism, magic, spell, charisma; hypnotism, mesmerism.
▷ANTONYMS repulsion.

Word links **magnetism**

magnetometry measurement of magnetic force

magnification noun **1** *the fine lines were visible only under high magnification*: **enlargement**; increase, augmentation, extension, expansion, amplification, intensification, heightening, deepening, broadening, widening, dilation, boost, enhancement; macrophotography, photomacrography.
▷ANTONYMS reduction.
2 *the magnification of the marginal details in the play*: **exaggeration**, overstatement, amplification, overemphasis, overplaying, dramatization, overdramatization, colouring, embroidery, embellishment, enhancement, extravagance, inflation, hyperbole, aggrandizement; gilding the lily; informal blowing up, blowing up out of all proportion, making a big thing out of something.
▷ANTONYMS understatement.

magnificence noun *the magnificence of eighteenth-century Bath*: **splendour**, resplendence, grandeur, greatness, impressiveness, imposingness, glory, gloriousness, majesty, nobility, pomp, pomp and circumstance, stateliness, sumptuousness, opulence, luxuriousness, luxury, lavishness, richness, brilliance, radiance, dazzle, beauty, elegance, distinction, spectacle, pageantry, splendidness, gorgeousness, éclat, elevation, transcendence, transcendency; informal splendiferousness, ritziness, poshness.
▷ANTONYMS tawdriness, cheapness.

magnificent adjective **1** *a magnificent view of the mountains*: **splendid**, **spectacular**, impressive, striking, glorious, superb, majestic, awesome, awe-inspiring, breathtaking.
▷ANTONYMS uninspiring.
2 *a magnificent apartment overlooking the lake*: **sumptuous**, resplendent, grand, impressive, imposing, monumental, palatial, noble, proud, stately, exalted, royal, regal, kingly, imperial, princely, opulent, fine, luxurious, lavish, rich, brilliant, radiant, dazzling, beautiful, elegant, gorgeous, elevated, transcendent; informal splendiferous, ritzy, posh; rare splendacious, magnolious.
▷ANTONYMS modest, tawdry, cheap.
3 *a magnificent act of heroism*: **admirable**, fine, great, wonderful, notable.
▷ANTONYMS feeble, weak.
4 *a magnificent performance*: **masterly**, skilful, virtuoso, splendid, excellent, impressive, fine, marvellous, wonderful, tremendous; informal terrific, glorious, superb, stellar, brilliant, great, out of this world, (like) a million dollars.
▷ANTONYMS poor, weak.

Easily confused words **magnificent or munificent?**

Magnificent and **munificent** are different in meaning but sometimes confused. *Magnificent* denotes something exceptionally good or beautiful, especially in an impressive or striking style (*a magnificent mansion | a magnificent performance*). *Munificent* means 'extremely generous' (*munificent financial support*). However, there is some overlap between the things to which they apply: a *munificent gift* might well consist of some *magnificent jewellery*.

magnify verb **1** *the image is magnified by an eyepiece*: **enlarge**, boost, enhance, maximize, increase, augment, extend, expand, amplify, intensify, heighten, deepen, broaden, widen, dilate; informal blow up.
▷ANTONYMS reduce.
2 *she tended to magnify the defects of those she disliked*: **exaggerate**, overstate, overemphasize, overplay, dramatize, colour, embroider, embellish, enhance, inflate, amplify, make a mountain out of (a molehill); informal make a big thing out of, blow up, blow up out of all proportion; archaic draw the long bow.
▷ANTONYMS minimize, understate.
3 *my soul doth magnify the lord*: **praise**, bless, worship, venerate, adore, extol.

magniloquence noun **grandiloquence**, loftiness, grandiosity, pompousness, pomposity, pretentiousness, bombast, rhetoric, turgidity, boastfulness, pretension, ornateness; rare orotundity, fustian, braggadocio.

magniloquent adjective *a magniloquent lawyer | his magniloquent phraseology*: **grandiloquent**, high-sounding, high-flown, lofty, heroic, grandiose, ornate, pompous, pretentious, bombastic, overblown, rhetorical, oratorical, orotund, declamatory, sonorous, rotund, stilted, turgid, boastful, bragging, braggart, Falstaffian; informal highfalutin; rare fustian.
▷ANTONYMS terse, crisp.

magnitude noun **1** *they felt daunted by the magnitude of the task*: **immensity**, vastness, hugeness, enormity, enormousness, expanse; size, extent, greatness, largeness, bigness.
▷ANTONYMS smallness.
2 *events of tragic magnitude*: **importance**, import, significance, weight, moment, consequence, mark, notability, note, greatness, distinction, eminence, fame, renown, intensity, power.
▷ANTONYMS triviality.
3 *electorates of less than average magnitude*: **size**, extent, measure, proportions, dimensions, breadth, volume, weight, quantity, mass, bulk; amplitude, capacity, strength, degree, gauge, measurement, extension.
4 *its brightest star is only of magnitude 4.2*: **brightness**, brilliance, radiance, luminosity; absolute magnitude, apparent magnitude.
5 *the magnitude of each economic variable could be determined*: **value**, index, indicator, measure, norm, order, quantity, number, vector, figure.
□ **of the first magnitude of the utmost importance**, of the greatest significance, very important, of importance, of significance, of note, of great moment, of great consequence.

Word links **magnitude**

astrometry measurement of magnitude of stars

maid noun **1** *the maid cleared the table*: **female servant**, maidservant, housemaid, parlourmaid, serving maid, lady's maid, chambermaid, maid-of-all-work, domestic, drudge, menial; help, cleaner, cleaning woman/lady, housekeeper, au pair; Indian amah, bai; Brit. informal daily, skivvy, Mrs Mop; Brit. dated charwoman, charlady, char, cook-general, cook-maid, tweeny; archaic abigail.
2 archaic *a village maid and her swain*. See **girl** (sense 2).
3 archaic *she was no longer a maid*. See **virgin** (noun).

maiden noun archaic See **girl** (sense 2).
▸ adjective **1** *a maiden aunt*: **unmarried**, spinster, unwed, unwedded, single, husbandless, spouseless, celibate.
2 *the maiden voyage of the Titanic*: **first**, initial, inaugural, introductory, initiatory, proving.

maidenhood noun archaic *the loss of her maidenhood*. See **virginity**.

maidenly adjective *her delicate mannerisms and maidenly demeanour*: **virginal**, immaculate, intact, chaste, pure, undefiled, virtuous, unsullied, vestal; **demure**, reserved, retiring, decorous, seemly.
▷ANTONYMS blowsy, tarty.

mail[1] noun *this letter came in the mail*: **post**, letters, packages, parcels, correspondence, communications, airmail; postal system, postal service, post office; registered mail, special delivery, recorded delivery; delivery, collection, mail drop, mailshot, mailing, first class, second class, third class, electronic mail, email, voicemail, Pony Express; informal snail mail; N. Amer. & W. Indian the mails; Indian dak, tappal.
▸ verb *we mailed the six packages*: **send**, post, send by mail/post, dispatch, direct, forward, remit, transmit, email, airmail.

mail² noun historical *warriors in mail shirts*: **armour**, coat of mail, chain mail, chain armour; rare brigandine, hauberk, byrnie, habergeon, camail.

maim verb *they are prepared to kill and maim innocent people in pursuit of their cause*: **injure**, wound, hurt, disable, put out of action, incapacitate, impair, mar, mutilate, lacerate, disfigure, deform, mangle.

main adjective **1** *the main office | the main issue*: **principal**, chief, head, leading, foremost, most important, major, ruling, dominant, central, focal, key, prime, master, premier, primary, first, high, grand, fundamental, supreme, predominant, (most) prominent, pre-eminent, paramount, overriding, cardinal, crucial, vital, critical, capital, pivotal, salient, elemental, essential, staple, intrinsic, urgent.
▷ANTONYMS subsidiary, minor.
2 *they dragged him away by main force*: **sheer**, pure, utter, downright, mere, plain, brute, stark, absolute, out-and-out, direct.
▶ noun literary *the Spanish Main*. See **sea** (sense 1 of the noun).
□ **in the main** See **mainly**.

mainly adverb *the people are mainly visitors*: **mostly**, for the most part, in the main, on the whole, largely, by and large, to a large extent, to a great degree, predominantly, chiefly, principally; generally, usually, typically, commonly, as a rule, on average.

mainspring noun *innovation is the mainspring of the new economy*: **motive**, motivation, impetus, driving force, incentive, impulse, cause, prime mover, reason, origin, fountain, fount, beginning, root, generator, basis.

mainstay noun **1** *agriculture was the mainstay of the economy*: **central component**, centrepiece, prop, linchpin, cornerstone, pillar, bulwark, buttress, chief support, backbone, anchor, foundation, base, bastion.
2 *he is the mainstay of the Arsenal defence*: **tower of strength**, key player, sinew, right-hand man/woman, right arm, Atlas.

mainstream adjective *the author never strays far from mainstream physics*: **normal**, conventional, ordinary, orthodox, conformist, accepted, established, recognized, common, usual, prevailing, popular.

maintain verb **1** *the need to maintain close links between industry and schools*: **continue**, keep, keep going, keep up, keep alive, keep in existence, carry on, preserve, conserve, prolong, perpetuate, sustain, bolster (up), prop up, retain, support, bear.
▷ANTONYMS break off.
2 *the roads are maintained at public expense*: **keep in good condition**, keep in repair, keep up, service, rebuild, conserve, preserve, keep intact, care for, take good care of, look after.
▷ANTONYMS neglect.
3 *the costs of maintaining a family*: **support**, provide for, keep, finance; **nurture**, feed, nourish, sustain.
▷ANTONYMS neglect.
4 *he always maintained his innocence | he maintains that he is innocent*: **insist (on)**, declare, assert, protest, state, aver, say, announce, affirm, avow, profess, claim, allege, contend, argue, swear (to), hold to; rare asseverate.
▷ANTONYMS deny.
5 *the King swears he will maintain the laws of God*: **uphold**, defend, fight for, champion, support, back, advocate.
▷ANTONYMS abandon.

maintenance noun **1** *the maintenance of law and order*: **preservation**, conservation, continuation, continuance, continuity, keeping up, carrying on, prolongation, perpetuation.
▷ANTONYMS breakdown.
2 *a water softener requires regular servicing and maintenance*: **upkeep**, service, servicing, repair(s); improvement, care, aftercare.
▷ANTONYMS neglect.
3 *the maintenance and education of his children*: **nurture**, feeding, life support; **financing**, supporting, support, keeping, upkeep; rare sustentation, alimentation, appanage, corrody.
▷ANTONYMS neglect.
4 *absent fathers are forced to pay maintenance*: **financial support**, child support, alimony, provision, allowance, keep, upkeep, subsistence, living expenses.

majestic adjective *majestic mountain scenery | his father's majestic presence*: **exalted**, august, great, awesome, elevated, sublime, lofty; **stately**, dignified, distinguished, striking, magisterial, solemn, maestoso, magnificent, grand, splendid, resplendent, glorious, sumptuous, impressive, awe-inspiring, monumental, palatial; statuesque, Olympian, imposing, marvellous, sonorous, resounding, heroic, portentous, superb, proud; regal, royal, kingly, queenly, princely, imperial, noble, lordly, sovereign.
▷ANTONYMS pitiful, pathetic.

majesty noun **1** *the majesty of the procession*: **stateliness**, dignity, magnificence, pomp, solemnity, grandeur, grandness, splendour, resplendence, glory, impressiveness, superbness, awesomeness, awe, loftiness, sublimity, regalness, regality, royalty, royalness, kingliness, queenliness, nobility, nobleness, augustness, exaltedness, exaltation, pride.
2 *the majesty invested in the monarch*: **sovereignty**, authority, power, dominion, supremacy.
3 *Your Majesty*: **Royal Highness**, Highness, Serene Highness, Serenity, Magnificence.

major adjective **1** *the major English poets*: **greatest**, **best**, finest, most important, chief, main, prime, principal, capital, cardinal, leading, star, foremost, outstanding, first-rate, top-tier, notable, eminent, pre-eminent, arch-, supreme, uppermost.
▷ANTONYMS minor.
2 *an issue of major importance*: **crucial**, vital, great, considerable, paramount, utmost, prime, extensive.
▷ANTONYMS little; unimportant.
3 *the use of drugs is a major problem*: **important**, big, significant, weighty, crucial, key, sweeping, substantial.
▷ANTONYMS trivial.
4 *major surgery*: **serious**, radical, complicated, difficult.
▷ANTONYMS minor.
□ **major part** See **majority** (sense 1).

majority noun **1** *in the majority of cases*: **larger part/number**, greater part/number, major part, best/better part, main part, most, more than half; bulk, mass, weight, (main) body, preponderance, predominance, generality, lion's share; (**the majority**) (the) people, the masses, the silent majority.
▷ANTONYMS minority.
2 *Labour retained the seat by a large majority*: **(winning) margin**, superiority of numbers/votes; landslide.
3 *a girl who has not yet reached her majority*: **coming of age**, legal age, seniority, adulthood, manhood/womanhood, maturity; age of consent.

make verb **1** *he makes model steam engines*: **construct**, build, assemble, put together, manufacture, produce, fabricate, create, form, fashion, model, mould, shape, forge, bring into existence.
▷ANTONYMS destroy.
2 *she made me drink it*: **force**, compel, coerce, press, drive, pressure, pressurize, oblige, require; have someone do something, prevail on, dragoon, bludgeon, strong-arm, impel, constrain, urge, will, steamroller, browbeat, intimidate, use strong-arm tactics on, bully, hector, blackmail; informal railroad, bulldoze, put the heat on, put the screws on, turn/tighten the screw/screws on.
3 *don't make such a noise*: **cause**, create, give rise to, produce, bring about, generate, engender, occasion, effect, set up, establish, institute, found, develop, originate, frame; literary beget.
4 *she pirouetted and made a little bow*: **perform**, execute, give, do, accomplish, achieve, bring off, carry out, effect, practise, engage in, commit, act, prosecute.
5 *they made him chairman*: **appoint**, designate, name, nominate, select, elect, vote in, install, place, post; induct, institute, invest, ordain, assign, cast as; detail, draft, engage, hire, employ, recruit, retain, enrol, enlist, sign up.
6 *I've made a will and left you everything*: **formulate**, frame, draw up, devise, make out, prepare, compile, compose, put together; draft, write, pen, produce.
7 *I'm sorry, I've* **made a mistake**: **perpetrate**, commit, be responsible for, be guilty of, be to blame for; blunder, err, trip up, put a foot wrong, nod, miscalculate; informal slip up, bloop, make a boo-boo, blow it, foul up, goof (up); Brit. informal boob, drop a clanger; N. Amer. informal screw up, drop the ball.
8 *he had a great talent for making money*: **acquire**, obtain, gain, get, realize, secure, win, earn; gross, fetch, bring in, take (in); take home, pocket, net, clear.
▷ANTONYMS lose.
9 *he made lunch for us all*: **prepare**, get ready, put together, concoct, cook, dish up, throw together, whip up, brew; Brit. informabal mash; N. Amer. informal fix.
10 *parliament makes laws*: **formulate**, draw up, write, frame, draft, form, enact, pass, lay down, establish, institute, found, originate.
▷ANTONYMS repeal.
11 *that makes £100*: **add up to**, amount to, come to, total, count as; Brit. tot up to.
12 *what do you make the total?* **compute**, calculate, work out; estimate, count up, determine, gauge, reckon, put a figure on, give a figure to, forecast, predict.
13 *what do you* **make of** *him?* **think of/about**; appraise, evaluate, assess, size up, adjudge, look on, view, regard, consider, judge, deem; figure (out), value, rate, think, sum up, weigh up.
14 *we've got to make a decision*: **reach**, come to, settle on, determine on, conclude, establish, seal.
15 *I've been asked to make a speech*: **utter**, give, deliver, give voice to, enunciate, recite, pronounce.
16 *he'll make a great leader | the sofa makes a good bed*: **be**, act as, serve as, function as, constitute, perform the function of, do duty for, play the part of, represent, embody, form.
17 *he'll make the first eleven*: **gain a place in**, get into, gain access to, enter; achieve, attain.
18 *he believed he could still make the night train*: **catch**, get, arrive/be in time for, arrive at, reach; get to.
▷ANTONYMS miss.
□ **make as if/though** *he made as if to run away*: **feign**, pretend, give the impression, make a show/pretence of, affect, feint, make out; informal put it on.

m

□ **make away with 1** *he could have made away with her and dumped the body*: **kill**, murder, put to death, slaughter, dispatch, execute, eliminate; informal bump off, do away with, do in, do for, knock off, take out, finish off, top, croak, stiff, liquidate, blow away; N. Amer. informal ice, off, rub out, smoke, waste; literary slay. **2** *they made away with the evidence*: **dispose of**, get rid of, destroy, throw away, jettison, ditch, dump, eliminate; informal do away with.

□ **make believe pretend**, fantasize, indulge in fantasy, daydream, build castles in the air, build castles in Spain, dream, imagine, romance, fancy, play-act, play.

□ **make do 1** *we have very little but we make do*: **scrape by/along**, get by/along, manage, cope, survive, muddle through/along, fare all right, make the best of a bad job, improvise, make ends meet, keep the wolf from the door, keep one's head above water, shift for oneself; informal make out. **2** *you'll have to make do with an old car*: **make the best of**, get by with/on, put to the best use, make the most of.

□ **make for 1** *she made for the door*: **go towards**, head for/towards, aim for, make one's way towards, move towards, direct one's steps towards, steer a course towards, be bound for, set out for, make a beeline for, take to. **2** *constant arguing doesn't make for a happy marriage*: **contribute to**, be conducive to, produce, promote, facilitate, further, advance, forward, foster, favour; formal conduce to.

□ **make fun of** *it is easy to make fun of politicians*: **taunt**, poke fun at, chaff, tease, make jokes about, ridicule, mock, laugh at, guy, mimic, parody, caricature, lampoon, satirize, rag, quiz, be sarcastic about, deride, scoff at, jeer at, jibe at; informal take the mickey out of, send up, rib, josh, wind up, pull someone's leg, make a monkey of; N. Amer. informal goof on, rag on, pull someone's chain, razz; Austral./NZ informal poke mullock at, sling off at; Brit. informal, dated rot, twit; dated make sport of; archaic smoke, rally.

□ **make it 1** *he never really made it as a doctor*: **succeed**, be successful, prosper, distinguish oneself, be a success, get ahead, make good; informal make the grade, arrive, crack it, cut it, find a place in the sun. **2** *she's very ill—is she going to make it?* **survive**, come through, pull through, get better, recover, rally, recuperate.

□ **make love have sex**, have sexual intercourse, go to bed (together), sleep together; Brit. informal bonk, do it, make whoopee, get one's oats; N. Amer. informal get it on; vulgar slang fuck, screw, shag, hump, do the business, have it away/off; Brit. vulgar slang knob, roger; formal copulate, fornicate; dated couple.

□ **make off** *on seeing the police they made off*: **run away/off**, take to one's heels, beat a hasty retreat, flee, make one's getaway, make a quick exit, make a run for it, run for it, take off, take flight, bolt, fly, make oneself scarce, leave, abscond, decamp, do a disappearing act; informal clear off/out, beat it, do a runner, leg it, make tracks, cut and run, skedaddle, vamoose, hightail it, hotfoot it, show a clean pair of heels, fly the coop, split, scoot, scram; Brit. informal scarper, have it away (on one's toes); N. Amer. informal light out, bug out, cut out, peel out, take a powder; Brit. informal, dated hook it.
▷ANTONYMS turn up.

□ **make off with** *burglars made off with all the wedding presents*: **take**, **steal**, purloin, pilfer, abscond with, appropriate, run away/off with, carry off, snatch; kidnap, abduct; informal walk away/off with, swipe, filch, snaffle, nab, lift, 'liberate', 'borrow', snitch; Brit. informal pinch, half-inch, nick, whip, knock off, nobble, bone; N. Amer. informal heist, glom; Austral. informal snavel; W. Indian informal tief; archaic crib, hook.

□ **make out 1** *how did you make out?* **get on**, get along, fare, do, proceed, go, progress, manage, survive, cope, get by. **2** N. Amer. informal *they were making out on the sofa*: **make love**, have sex, have sexual intercourse; kiss and cuddle, caress, French kiss, pet, engage in heavy petting; informal canoodle, neck, smooch; Brit. informal snog, bonk, do it, make whoopee, get one's oats; N. Amer. informal get it on; vulgar slang fuck, screw, hump, do the business, have it away/off; Brit. vulgar slang roger; informal, dated spoon, couple; formal copulate, fornicate.

□ **make something out 1** *I could just make out a figure in the distance*: **see**, discern, distinguish, perceive, pick out, detect, notice, observe, recognize, catch sight of, glimpse, descry; literary descry, espy, behold. **2** *he couldn't make out what she was saying*: **understand**, comprehend, follow, grasp, fathom, work out, figure out, make sense of, interpret, decipher, make head or tail of, get, get the drift of, catch; Brit. informal suss out. **3** *she made out that he was violent*: **allege**, claim, assert, declare, maintain, affirm, aver, suggest, imply, hint, insinuate, indicate, intimate, impute, make as if/though, pretend. **4** *how do you make that out?* **demonstrate**, show to be true, establish, substantiate, prove, verify, validate, authenticate, corroborate. **5** *he made out a receipt for $20*: **write out**, fill out, fill in, complete, draw up, draft, inscribe.

□ **make something over to someone** *he made over the whole property to his son*: **transfer**, sign over, turn over, hand over, hand on, give, hand down, leave, bequeath, bestow, pass on, devolve, transmit, cede, deliver, assign, consign, convey, entrust.

□ **make up** *come now, pet, let's kiss and make up*: **be friends again**, bury the hatchet, declare a truce, make peace, forgive and forget, shake hands, become reconciled, settle one's differences, mend fences, call it quits.
▷ANTONYMS quarrel.

□ **make something up 1** *women make up 56 per cent of the student body*: **comprise**, form, compose, constitute, account for. **2** *he brought another girl with him to make up a foursome*: **complete**, round off, finish. **3** *the pharmacist made up the prescription*: **prepare**, mix, concoct, put together. **4** *I'll have to make up an excuse*: **invent**, fabricate, concoct, dream up, think up, hatch, trump up; devise, manufacture, formulate, frame, construct, coin; informal cook up. **5** *she made up her face carefully*: **apply make-up/cosmetics to**, powder, rouge; (**make oneself up**) informal put on one's face, do one's face, paint one's face, tart oneself up, do oneself up, apply one's warpaint, doll oneself up.

□ **make up for 1** *she tried to make up for what she'd said earlier*: **atone for**, make amends for, compensate for, make recompense for, make reparation for, make redress for, make restitution for, expiate; formal requite. **2** *hard work can more than make up for a lack of intellectual brilliance*: **offset**, counterbalance, counterweigh, counteract, compensate for; balance, neutralize, cancel out, even up, redeem.

□ **make up one's mind** *stop dithering and make up your mind*: **decide**, be decisive, come to a decision, make a decision, reach a decision; determine, resolve, settle on a plan of action, come to a conclusion, reach a conclusion.

□ **make up to** informal *she spent the whole evening making up to Adam*: **flirt with**, chase after, run after, pursue, make romantic advances to, court, woo, vamp; informal chat up, make eyes at, make sheep's eyes at, give the come-on to, come on to, be all over; dated set one's cap at.

□ **make way** *please make way for the king*: **move aside**, clear the way, make a space, make room, stand back; allow to pass, allow through.

▸**noun 1** *a different make of car*: **brand**, marque, model, mark, sort, type, kind, variety, style, label.
2 *a man of a different make from his brother*: **character**, nature, temperament, temper, disposition, cast/turn of mind, humour, make-up, kidney, mould, stamp.

□ **on the make** informal *everyone is on the make, especially the children*: **ambitious**, aspiring, determined, forceful, pushy, enterprising, pioneering, progressive, eager, motivated, enthusiastic, energetic, zealous, committed, go-ahead, go-getting, purposeful, assertive, aggressive, hungry, power-hungry.

> *Word links* **make**
>
> **-facient**, **-faction**, **-fic**, **-genic** suffixes meaning 'making or causing ...', as in *abortifacient, liquefaction, soporific, hallucinogenic*

make-believe noun *if that was make-believe I can't wait to sample the real thing*: **fantasy**, **pretence**, pretending, daydreaming, dreaming, imagination, invention, fancy, dream, unreality, romancing, fabrication, play-acting, charade, masquerade, self-deception, illusion, delusion.
▷ANTONYMS reality.
▸**adjective** *Heather loved reading stories and was always having make-believe adventures*: **imaginary**, imagined, pretended, made-up, fantasy, fantasized, fancied, dream, dreamed-up, unreal, fanciful, fictitious, fictive, mythical, feigned, fake, mock, sham, simulated, pseudo, false, spurious; informal pretend, phoney; S. African play-play.
▷ANTONYMS real, actual.

Maker noun *he had gone to meet his Maker*: **God**, Creator, Prime Mover, master of the universe.

maker noun *the maker's name is stamped on the back*: **creator**, manufacturer, builder, constructor, producer, fabricator, author, architect, designer, framer, originator, inventor, founder, father.

makeshift adjective *a huge makeshift scaffold had been erected in front of the palace*: **temporary**, make-do, provisional, stopgap, standby, rough and ready, substitute, emergency, improvised, ad hoc, impromptu, extemporary, extempore, thrown together, cobbled together; Nautical jury-rigged, jury; informal quick and dirty.
▷ANTONYMS permanent.

make-up noun 1 *she was pale in spite of her excessive make-up*: **cosmetics**, greasepaint; foundation, pancake, panstick, powder, loose powder, pressed powder, blusher, rouge, concealer; mascara, eye make-up, eyeliner, eyeshadow, eyebrow pencil, kohl; lipstick, lip gloss, lip pencil, nail varnish/polish; blackface, whiteface; informal paint, warpaint, face paint, slap; rare maquillage.
2 *the cellular make-up of plants and trees*: **composition**, constitution, configuration, form, arrangement, format, structure, construction, formation, assembly, organization, fabric, framework.
3 *jealousy doesn't seem to be part of his make-up*: **character**, nature, temperament, temper, personality, disposition, constitution, mentality, persona, psyche, psychology, make, stamp, mould, cast/turn of mind; informal kidney, what makes someone tick; archaic humour, grain.

making noun 1 *the making of the cars*: **manufacture**, manufacturing, mass production, building, construction, assembly, production, producing, creation, creating, putting together, modelling, fabrication, invention, forming, formation, moulding, forging, composition.
▷ANTONYMS destruction.
2 (**makings**) *does she have the makings of a champion?* **qualities**, characteristics, ingredients, potential, promise, capacity, capability; **essentials**, essence, beginnings, rudiments, basics, materials, stuff.

□ **in the making** *he was a major heroic actor in the making*: **budding**,

m

burgeoning, coming, emergent, growing, developing, nascent, potential, promising, up and coming, incipient.

maladjusted adjective *a school for maladjusted pupils*: **disturbed**, unstable, ill-adjusted, neurotic, alienated, muddled, confused, unbalanced; informal mixed up, screwed up, untogether, hung up, messed up; vulgar slang fucked up.
▷ANTONYMS well adjusted, together.

maladministration noun *a long battle against maladministration and incompetence*: **mismanagement**, mishandling, misgovernment, misrule, incompetence, inefficiency, bungling, blundering; malpractice, misconduct, corruption, dishonesty; Law malfeasance, misfeasance; rare malversation.
▷ANTONYMS probity, efficiency.

maladroit adjective *both men are unhappy about the maladroit way the matter has been handled*: **bungling**, awkward, inept, clumsy, bumbling, incompetent, unskilful, heavy-handed, ungainly, inelegant, inexpert, graceless, ungraceful, gauche, unhandy, uncoordinated, gawky, cloddish, clodhopping, all fingers and thumbs, flat-footed, lumbering; like a bull in a china shop, tactless, insensitive, thoughtless, inconsiderate, undiplomatic, impolitic, injudicious; informal butterfingered, ham-fisted, ham-handed, cack-handed; archaic lubberly.
▷ANTONYMS adroit, skilful.

malady noun *sea sickness, a malady with no respect for rank or courage*: **illness**, sickness, ailment, disorder, complaint, disease, infection, indisposition, affliction, infirmity; informal lurgy, bug, virus; Austral. informal wog.

malaise noun *a society afflicted by a deep cultural malaise*: **unhappiness**, restlessness, uneasiness, unease, melancholy, depression, despondency, dejection, disquiet, trouble, anxiety, anguish, angst; ailment(s), ills; lassitude, listlessness, languor, weariness, enervation, doldrums; weakness, feebleness, debility, indisposition, infirmity, illness, sickness, disease, discomfort; German Weltschmerz; French ennui.
▷ANTONYMS comfort, well-being.

malapropism noun **wrong word**, **solecism**, error, misuse, misusage, misapplication, infelicity, slip of the tongue.

malapropos adjective **inappropriate**, unsuitable, inapposite, infelicitous, inapt, unseemly, inopportune, ill-timed, untimely, uncalled for, tactless.

malcontent noun *the trouble was caused by a group of malcontents*: **troublemaker**, mischief-maker, agitator, dissentient, dissident, rebel; discontent, complainer, grumbler, moaner, fault-finder, carper; informal stirrer, whinger, grouch, grouser, griper, nit-picker, bellyacher, beefer; N. Amer. informal kvetch.
▶ adjective *a malcontent employee*: **disaffected**, discontented, dissatisfied, disgruntled; **fed up**, restive, unhappy, annoyed, irritated, displeased, vexed, peeved, piqued, put out, malcontented, resentful; rebellious, dissentious, factious, troublemaking, grumbling, complaining, fault-finding, carping; informal nit-picking, bellyaching; Brit. informal browned off, cheesed off, brassed off; N. Amer. informal hacked off, teed off, ticked off; vulgar slang pissed off, peed off.
▷ANTONYMS happy.

m

male adjective *male sexual jealousy*: **masculine**, to do with men, he-; **virile**, manly, macho, red-blooded.
▷ANTONYMS female.
▶ noun See **man**.

Word toolkit

male	manly	mannish
colleague	men	haircut
hybrid	virtues	woman
lion	art	trousers
model	physique	boy

male chauvinist noun **sexist**, chauvinist, anti-feminist, misogynist, woman-hater; informal male chauvinist pig, MCP.

malediction noun *the simple villagers were terrified by his maledictions*: **curse**, oath, imprecation, execration; anathema, voodoo, spell; cursing, damning, damnation; N. Amer. hex; archaic malison.
▷ANTONYMS blessing.

malefactor noun *most malefactors are the victims of their environment*: **criminal**, culprit, wrongdoer, offender, villain, lawbreaker, felon, evil-doer, convict, delinquent, sinner, transgressor, outlaw; scoundrel, wretch, reprobate, rogue, rascal; informal crook, baddy; Austral. informal crim; Law malfeasant, misfeasor; archaic miscreant, trespasser.

malevolence noun *there was a sinister atmosphere, a feeling of oppressive malevolence*: **malice**, **spite**, spitefulness, hostility, hatred, hate, ill will, bitterness, enmity, ill feeling, balefulness, venom, rancour, maliciousness, malignance, malignity, ill nature, vindictiveness, viciousness, revengefulness, vengefulness, cruelty, nastiness, unfriendliness; literary maleficence.
▷ANTONYMS benevolence.

malevolent adjective *she shot a malevolent glare at her companion*: **malicious**, **spiteful**, hostile, evil-minded, baleful, bitter, evil-intentioned, poisonous, venomous, evil, malign, malignant, rancorous, vicious, vindictive, revengeful, vengeful, pernicious; cruel, fierce, nasty, unfriendly, unkind, ill-natured; literary malefic, maleficent.
▷ANTONYMS benevolent.

malformation noun *a congenital malformation of the larynx*: **deformity**, distortion, crookedness, misshapenness, disfigurement, misproportion, abnormality, irregularity, oddity, warp, freak (of nature).

malformed adjective *usually it is the weak, undersized, and malformed beasts that are weeded out*: **deformed**, distorted, crooked, contorted, wry, misshapen, twisted, warped, out of shape, bent, bandy, skewed, asymmetrical, irregular, misproportioned, ill-proportioned, ill-shaped, disfigured, hunchbacked, abnormal, grotesque, monstrous; Scottish thrawn.

malfunction verb *the computer has malfunctioned*: **crash**, develop a fault, go wrong, break down, break, act up, be defective, be faulty, fail, cease to function/work, stop working; informal conk out, go kaput, fall over; Brit. informal play up, pack up.
▶ noun *a major computer malfunction*: **crash**, breakdown, fault, failure, defect, flaw, collapse, impairment; informal glitch.

malice noun *the malice of evil men who hated his good qualities*: **spitefulness**, spite, malevolence, maliciousness, animosity, hostility, ill will, ill feeling, hatred, hate, bitterness, venom, vindictiveness, vengefulness, revenge, malignity, malignance, evil intentions, animus, enmity, devilment, devilry, bad blood, backbiting, gall, rancour, spleen, grudge; informal bitchiness, cattiness; literary maleficence.
▷ANTONYMS benevolence.

malicious adjective *he bore their malicious insults with dignity*: **spiteful**, malevolent, hostile, bitter, venomous, poisonous, evil-intentioned, ill-natured, evil, baleful, vindictive, vengeful, vitriolic, rancorous, malign, malignant, pernicious, mean, nasty, harmful, hurtful, mischievous, destructive, wounding, cruel, unkind, defamatory; informal bitchy, catty; literary malefic, maleficent.
▷ANTONYMS benevolent.

malign verb *he accused them of maligning an innocent man*: **defame**, slander, libel, blacken someone's name/character, smear, run a smear campaign against, vilify, speak ill of, spread lies about, accuse falsely, cast aspersions on, run down, misrepresent, calumniate, traduce, denigrate, disparage, slur, derogate, abuse, revile; informal bad-mouth, knock, drag through the mud/mire, throw/sling/fling mud at, do a hatchet job on; Brit. informal rubbish, slag off; rare asperse, vilipend.
▷ANTONYMS praise.
▶ adjective *a malign influence*: **harmful**, evil, bad, baleful, hostile, inimical, destructive, malevolent, evil-intentioned, malignant, injurious, spiteful, malicious, vicious; literary malefic, maleficent.
▷ANTONYMS beneficial.

Choose the right word **malign, defame, slander, libel, traduce**

All these verbs involve making unfair or damaging critical remarks about someone.

Malign is a non-legal term for making false or unjustifiable criticisms (*teenagers are much maligned, but the support these youngsters gave was tremendous*). One can malign someone unintentionally (*I could be maligning the lad—I haven't seen much of him*).

To **defame** someone is to make an unfair critical or accusatory remark about them which will damage their reputation, even if this is not the intention (*he convinced the jurors that he had been defamed by the article*).

In legal usage, **slander** and **libel** are particular forms of defamation: to *slander* someone is to defame them in speech (*they were accused of insulting and slandering the head of state*), whereas to *libel* someone is to defame them in written form, which is now taken to encompass any 'permanent' form, including broadcasting and the Internet (*Samuelson claims he was libelled in the same article*).

Traduce is a more literary term for the deliberate telling of damaging untruths (*he is traducing his colleagues with his unsubstantiated accusations*).

malignant adjective **1** *a malignant growth in her left kidney*: **cancerous**, non-benign, metastatic.
▷ANTONYMS benign.
2 *a malignant disease*: **virulent**, infectious, invasive, uncontrollable, dangerous, harmful, pernicious; deadly, fatal, life-threatening, lethal, terminal, incurable.
3 *one of the most malignant glares she had ever seen*: **spiteful**, hostile, malevolent, malicious, malign, evil-intentioned, baleful, full of hate, vicious, nasty, poisonous, venomous, acrimonious, rancorous, splenetic, cruel.
▷ANTONYMS benevolent.

malinger verb *the doctor alleged that the plaintiff was malingering*: **pretend to be ill**, feign/fake illness, pretend to be an invalid, sham, shirk, skulk; informal put it on; Brit. informal skive, swing the lead; N. Amer. informal goldbrick.

malingerer noun *patients for whom no specific diagnosis can be made tend to be regarded as malingerers*: **shirker**, slacker, idler, layabout; Brit. informal skiver, lead-swinger; N. Amer. informal gold brick.

mall noun **shopping precinct**, shopping centre, shopping complex, arcade, galleria; N. Amer. plaza, strip mall.

malleable adjective **1** *a malleable substance*: **pliable**, ductile, plastic, pliant, soft, workable, shapable, mouldable, tractile, tensile.
▷ANTONYMS hard.
2 *a malleable young woman*: **easily influenced**, suggestible, susceptible, impressionable, amenable, cooperative, adaptable, compliant, pliable, tractable, accommodating; biddable, docile, obedient, complaisant, manageable, manipulable, persuadable, governable, influenceable, like putty in someone's hands.
▷ANTONYMS intractable.

malnutrition noun *there is a real danger of hunger and even malnutrition*: **undernourishment**, malnourishment, poor diet, inadequate diet, unhealthy diet, lack of food, inanition; starvation, hunger, famine; anorexia.

malodorous adjective *the rubbish was already malodorous despite being in sealed bags*: **foul-smelling**, evil-smelling, fetid, smelly, stinking, stinking to high heaven, reeking, reeky, pungent, acrid, rank, high, putrid, noxious; W. Indian fresh; informal stinky; Brit. informal niffing, niffy, pongy, whiffy, humming; N. Amer. informal funky; literary noisome, mephitic; rare miasmic, miasmal, olid.
▷ANTONYMS fragrant.

malpractice noun *victims of medical malpractice*: **wrongdoing**, dereliction of duty, professional misconduct, breach of ethics, unprofessional behaviour, unprofessionalism, unethical behaviour; negligence, carelessness, incompetence.

maltreat verb *Keith was a bully and occasionally maltreated his wife*: **ill-treat**, mistreat, abuse, ill-use, misuse, treat badly; handle/treat roughly, knock about/around, hit, beat, strike, mishandle, manhandle, maul; bully, torture, injure, harm, hurt, persecute, molest; informal beat up, rough up, do over.

maltreatment noun *the maltreatment and execution of prisoners*: **ill-treatment**, mistreatment, abuse, ill use, ill usage, misuse, bad treatment; rough handling, beating, mishandling, manhandling, mauling; bullying, torture, injury, harm, persecution, molestation.

mammoth adjective *a mammoth task | a crisis of mammoth proportions*: **huge**, enormous, gigantic, giant, colossal, massive, vast, immense, mighty, stupendous, monumental, Herculean, epic, prodigious, mountainous, monstrous, titanic, towering, elephantine, king-sized, king-size, gargantuan, Brobdingnagian; informal mega, monster, whopping great, thumping, thumping great, humongous, jumbo, bumper, astronomical, astronomic; Brit. informal whacking, whacking great, ginormous.
▷ANTONYMS tiny.

man noun **1 male**, adult male, gentleman, youth; informal guy, fellow, geezer, gent, mother's son; Brit. informal bloke, chap, lad; N. Amer. informal dude, bozo, hombre; Austral./NZ informal digger; S. African informal oke, ou, oom; Indian informal admi; Scottish & Irish informal bodach; Brit. informal, dated cove; Scottish archaic carl.
2 *all men are mortal*: **human being**, human, person, mortal, individual, personage, soul.
3 *the evolution of man*: **the human race**, the human species, Homo sapiens, humankind, humanity, human beings, humans, people, mankind.
4 *the men voted to go on strike*: **worker**, workman, labourer, helper, hand, blue-collar worker. See also **staff**.
5 *have you met her new man?* **boyfriend**, partner, husband, spouse, lover, admirer, fiancé, amour, inamorato; common-law husband, escort, live-in lover, significant other, cohabitee; informal fancy man, toy boy, sugar daddy; N. Amer. informal squeeze; S. African informal jong; dated beau, steady, young man; informal, dated intended; archaic leman.
6 *his man brought him a cocktail*: **manservant**, valet, gentleman's gentleman, attendant, retainer; page, footman, flunkey, Jeeves; Military, dated batman; N. Amer. houseman.
□ **man to man frankly**, openly, honestly, directly, candidly, plainly, forthrightly, without beating about the bush; woman to woman.
□ **to a man with no exceptions**, without exception, bar none, one and all, everyone, each and every one, unanimously, as one.
▸ verb **1** *the office is manned from 9 a.m. to 5 p.m.* **staff**, crew, occupy, people.
2 *firemen manned the pumps*: **operate**, work, use, utilize.

> *Word links* **man**
>
> **male**, **masculine**, **virile** relating to men
> **andro-** related prefix
> **androcentric** centred on men
> **androphobia** fear of men
> **misandry** hatred of men
> **androcracy** rule by men

manacle verb *Bosley and Hughes knelt on him and manacled his hands behind his back*: **shackle**, fetter, chain, chain up, put in chains, put/clap in irons, handcuff, restrain; tie, secure; informal cuff.

manacles plural noun *the soldiers were already putting manacles around Rachel's wrists*: **handcuffs**, shackles, chains, irons, fetters, restraints, bonds; informal cuffs, bracelets; archaic darbies, gyves.

manage verb **1** *she manages a staff of 80 people*: **be in charge of**, run, be head of, head, direct, control, preside over, lead, govern, rule, command, superintend, supervise, oversee, administer, organize, conduct, handle, guide, be at the helm of; informal head up.
2 *he's good at managing his money*: **organize**, take care of, administer, regulate, deal with efficiently.
▷ANTONYMS squander.
3 *how much work can you manage this week?* **accomplish**, achieve, do, carry out, perform, undertake, bring about/off, effect, finish, succeed in, contrive, engineer.
4 *will you be able to manage without him?* **cope**, get along/on, make do, be/fare/do all right, carry on, survive, deal with the situation, scrape by/along, muddle through/along, fend for oneself, shift for oneself, make ends meet, weather the storm; informal make out, get by, hack it.
5 *she can't manage that horse*: **control**, handle, master, influence, manipulate; cope with, deal with.

manageable adjective **1** *a manageable amount of work*: **achievable**, **doable**, practicable, possible, feasible, reasonable, attainable, viable.
▷ANTONYMS impracticable, impossible.
2 *a manageable child*: **controllable**, compliant, tractable, pliant, pliable, malleable, biddable, docile, amenable, manipulable, governable, tameable, accommodating, acquiescent, complaisant, yielding, submissive.
▷ANTONYMS unmanageable.
3 *a manageable tool*: **user-friendly**, easy to use, handy; rare wieldy.
▷ANTONYMS unwieldy.

management noun **1** *he's responsible for the management of the firm*: **administration**, running, managing, organization; charge, care, direction, leadership, control, governing, governance, ruling, command, superintendence, supervision, overseeing, conduct, handling, guidance, operation.
2 *the workers are in dispute with the management*: **managers**, employers, directors, board of directors, board, directorate, executives, administrators, administration; owners, proprietors; informal bosses, top brass.
▷ANTONYMS workers.

manager noun **1** *the works manager*: **executive**, head of department, line manager, supervisor, principal, administrator, head, boss, director, managing director, employer, superintendent, foreman, forewoman, overseer; proprietor; informal chief, head honcho, governor; Brit. informal gaffer, guv'nor; N. Amer. informal high muckamuck, straw boss.
2 *the band's manager*: **organizer**, controller, comptroller; impresario.

mandate noun **1** *he called an election to seek a mandate for his policies*: **authority**, approval, acceptance, ratification, endorsement; sanction, authorization.
2 *a mandate from the UN was necessary*: **instruction**, directive, direction, decree, command, order, injunction, edict, charge, commission, bidding, warrant, ruling, ordinance, law, statute, fiat; in Tsarist Russia ukase; in Spanish-speaking countries pronunciamento.

mandatory adjective *the concept of mandatory retirement*: **obligatory**, compulsory, binding, required; inescapable, unavoidable; requisite, necessary, essential, imperative.
▷ANTONYMS optional.

manful adjective *his manful attempt to smile*: **brave**, courageous, bold, plucky, gallant, heroic, intrepid, fearless, valiant, valorous, dauntless, doughty; **resolute**, with gritted teeth, grim, determined, manly, stout, stout-hearted, lionhearted, stalwart; informal gutsy, ballsy, spunky.
▷ANTONYMS cowardly, timorous.

manfully adverb *he began to struggle manfully upwards*: **bravely**, courageously, boldly, gallantly, pluckily, heroically, intrepidly, fearlessly, valiantly, dauntlessly; **resolutely**, determinedly, stoutly, stout-heartedly, stalwartly, hard, strongly, vigorously, with might and main, like a Trojan; with all one's strength, to the best of one's abilities, as best one can, desperately, with desperation, with all the stops out.
▷ANTONYMS timorously.

mange noun **scabies**, scab, itch, rash, eruption, skin infection.

manger noun **trough**, feeding trough, fodder rack, feeder, crib.

mangle verb **1** *the bodies were mangled beyond recognition*: **mutilate**, maim, disfigure, damage, injure, crush, crumple; hack, cut about, lacerate, tear apart, rend, chop (up), butcher, deform, maul, wreck.
2 *he's mangling the English language*: **spoil**, ruin, mar, mutilate, bungle, mess up, make a mess of, wreck; informal murder, make a hash of, muck up, screw up, butcher.

mangy adjective **1** *a mangy cat*: **scabby**, scaly, scabious, diseased.
2 *a mangy old armchair*: **scruffy**, moth-eaten, shabby, worn, unkempt, shoddy, sorry, dirty, squalid, filthy, sleazy, seedy; informal tatty, the worse for wear, scuzzy, grungy, yucky; Brit. informal grotty; N. Amer. informal raggedy.

manhandle verb **1** *he was manhandled by a gang of youths*: **jostle**, shove, hustle, handle roughly, push, pull; **maltreat**, ill-treat, mistreat, abuse, maul, molest, injure, damage, beat, knock about/around, batter; informal paw, beat up, rough up; N. Amer. informal roust.
2 *we manhandled the piano down the stairs*: **heave**, haul, push, shove; pull, tug, drag, move, carry, lift, manoeuvre; informal hump, lug.

manhood noun **1** *the transition from boyhood to manhood*: **maturity**, sexual maturity, adulthood.
2 *an insult to his manhood*: **virility**, manliness, machismo, masculinity, maleness; mettle, spirit, fortitude, resolution, determination, manfulness, bravery, courage, strength, intrepidity, valour, heroism, boldness.

mania noun **1** *she suffered from fits of mania*: **madness**, derangement, dementia, insanity, lunacy, dementedness, psychosis, schizophrenia, mental illness, delirium, frenzy, hysteria, raving, violence, wildness.
2 *he has a mania for gadgets*: **obsession**, compulsion, fixation, fetish, fascination, preoccupation, passion, enthusiasm, desire, urge, craving, craze, fad, rage; informal thing, yen; rare cacoethes.

maniac noun **1** *a homicidal maniac*: **lunatic**, madman, madwoman, mad person, deranged person, psychopath, psychotic; informal loony, fruitcake, nutcase, nut, nutter, psycho, screwball, head case, headbanger, sicko; Scottish informal radge; N. Amer. informal crazy, kook, meshuggener, nutso.
2 informal *a football maniac*: **enthusiast**, fan, addict, devotee, aficionado; informal freak, fiend, nut, buff.

manic adjective **1** *a manic grin*: **mad**, insane, deranged, demented, maniacal, lunatic, crazed, wild, demonic, demoniacal, hysterical, raving, neurotic, unhinged, unbalanced; informal crazy.
▷ANTONYMS sane.
2 *scenes of manic activity*: **frenzied**, feverish, frenetic, hectic, intense; informal hyper, mad.
▷ANTONYMS calm.

manifest verb **1** *she manifested signs of depression*: **display**, **show**, exhibit, demonstrate, betray, present, evince, reveal, indicate, make plain, express, declare.
▷ANTONYMS hide.
2 *disputes and strikes manifest bad industrial relations*: **be evidence of**, be a sign of, indicate, show, attest, reflect, bespeak, prove, establish, evidence, substantiate, corroborate, verify, confirm; literary betoken.
▷ANTONYMS mask; deny.
▶ adjective *his manifest lack of interest in the proceedings*: **obvious**, clear, plain, apparent, evident, patent, palpable, distinct, definite, blatant, overt, glaring, barefaced, explicit, transparent, conspicuous, undisguised, unmistakable, unquestionable, undeniable, noticeable, perceptible, visible, recognizable, observable.
▷ANTONYMS hidden, secret.

manifestation noun **1** *the manifestation of anxiety*: **display**, demonstration, showing, show, exhibition, presentation, indication, illustration, exemplification, exposition, disclosure, declaration, expression, profession.
2 *manifestations of global warming*: **sign**, indication, evidence, proof, token, symptom, testimony, substantiation, mark, symbol, reflection, example, instance.
3 *a supernatural manifestation*: **apparition**, appearance, materialization, visitation.

manifesto noun **policy statement**, platform, programme, declaration, proclamation, pronouncement, announcement, publication, notification; in Spanish-speaking countries pronunciamento.

manifold adjective **many**, numerous, multiple, multifarious, multitudinous, multiplex, legion, diverse, various, several, varied, different, miscellaneous, assorted, sundry, copious, abundant; literary myriad, divers.

> *Word toolkit* **manifold**
>
> See **diverse**.

manipulate verb **1** *the workman manipulated some knobs and levers*: **operate**, handle, work, control, use, employ, utilize.
2 *she used her hands to manipulate the muscles of his back*: **massage**, rub, knead, feel, palpate.
3 *the government tried to manipulate the situation*: **exploit**, **control**, influence, use/turn to one's advantage, manoeuvre, engineer, steer, direct, guide, twist round one's little finger, work, orchestrate, choreograph.
4 *they accused him of manipulating the data*: **falsify**, rig, distort, alter, change, doctor, massage, juggle, tamper with, fiddle with, tinker with, interfere with, misrepresent, fudge, corrupt; informal cook, fiddle.

manipulative adjective **1** *a ruthlessly manipulative woman*: **scheming**, calculating, cunning, crafty, wily, shrewd, devious, designing, conniving, Machiavellian, artful, guileful, slippery, slick, sly, unscrupulous, disingenuous; informal foxy.
▷ANTONYMS ingenuous.
2 *a manipulative skill such as typing*: **manual**, done with one's hands, dexterous.

manipulator noun *a ruthless political manipulator*: **exploiter**, puller of strings, user, manoeuvrer, conniver, intriguer, puppet master, puppeteer, wheeler-dealer; informal operator, thimblerigger.

mankind noun **the human race**, man, humanity, human beings, humans, Homo sapiens, humankind, the human species, people, men and women.

manliness noun **1** *he felt that his manliness was threatened*: **virility**, masculinity, vigour, strength, muscularity, ruggedness, toughness, robustness, powerfulness, brawniness, hardihood; informal hunkiness.
▷ANTONYMS femininity.
2 *they were expected always to exhibit the qualities of 'manliness' and 'pluck'*: **resoluteness**, steadfastness, mettle, spirit, dauntlessness, doughtiness, determination, fortitude, stalwartness; bravery, courage, boldness, valour, fearlessness, pluck, machismo, manhood, manfulness, daring, intrepidity, heroism, gallantry, chivalrousness, stout-heartedness; informal guts, grit, spunk; N. Amer. informal cojones.
▷ANTONYMS cowardice, funk.

manly adjective **1** *his manly physique*: **virile**, masculine, strong, all-male, muscular, muscly, strapping, well built, sturdy, robust, rugged, tough, hardy, powerful, brawny, red-blooded, vigorous; informal hunky.
▷ANTONYMS feminine.
2 *their manly deeds*: **brave**, courageous, bold, valiant, valorous, fearless, plucky, macho, manful, intrepid, daring, lionhearted, heroic, gallant, chivalrous, swashbuckling, adventurous, stout-hearted, stout, dauntless, doughty, mettlesome, resolute, determined, stalwart; informal Ramboesque, gutsy, ballsy, spunky.
▷ANTONYMS effeminate, cowardly, weak.

> *Word toolkit* **manly**
>
> See **male**.

man-made adjective *a blend of 80% wool and 20% man-made fibres*: **artificial**, synthetic, manufactured, fabricated; imitation, ersatz, faux, simulated, mock, fake, plastic.
▷ANTONYMS natural; real.

> *Word toolkit* **man-made**
>
> See **artificial**.

mannequin noun **1** *mannequins in a shop window*: **dummy**, model, figure.
2 *mannequins on the catwalk*: **model**, fashion model, supermodel; informal clothes horse.

manner noun **1** *the matter was dealt with in a very efficient manner*: **way**, fashion, mode, means, method, system, style, approach, technique, procedure, process, methodology, modus operandi, form, routine, practice.
2 *she had a rather unfriendly manner*: **demeanour**, air, aspect, attitude, appearance, look, bearing, cast, deportment, behaviour, conduct; comportment, mien.
3 (**manners**) *the life and manners of Victorian society*: **customs**, habits, ways, practices, conventions, usages.
4 (**manners**) *it's bad manners to stare*: **social behaviour**, behaviour, conduct, way of behaving, form, social habit.
5 (**manners**) *you ought to teach him some manners*: **correct behaviour**, etiquette, social graces, good form, protocol, politeness, decorum, propriety, gentility, civility, formalities, niceties, Ps and Qs, breeding; French politesse; informal the done thing; archaic convenances.
▷ANTONYMS rudeness, bad behaviour.

mannered adjective *Dornford Yates's highly artificial, mannered prose style*: **affected**, pretentious, unnatural, artificial, contrived, stilted, stiff, forced, put-on, insincere, theatrical, elaborate, precious, posed, stagy, camp; informal pseudo.
▷ANTONYMS natural, unpretentious.

mannerism noun *he has the mannerisms of a bishop without actually having become one*: **idiosyncrasy**, quirk, oddity, foible, trait, peculiarity, habit, characteristic, characteristic gesture, trick.

mannerly adjective dated *he woke them up in as mannerly a way as he knew how*. See **polite** (sense 1).

mannish adjective *her gruff, mannish exterior*: **manlike**, masculine, unfeminine, unwomanly, unladylike, Amazonian; informal **butch**, dykey; rare viraginous, viragoish.
▷ANTONYMS feminine, girlish.

> *Word toolkit* **mannish**
>
> See **male**.

manoeuvre verb **1** *I manoeuvred the car into a parking space*: **steer**, guide, drive, negotiate, navigate, pilot, direct, manipulate, move, work, jockey.
2 *he had manoeuvred things to suit himself*: **manipulate**, contrive, manage, engineer, devise, plan, plot, fix, organize, arrange, set up, orchestrate,

choreograph, stage-manage; informal wangle.
3 *he began manoeuvring for the party leadership*: **intrigue**, plot, scheme, plan, lay plans, conspire, pull strings; N. Amer. pull wires; rare machinate.
▶ **noun 1** *a tricky parking manoeuvre*: **operation**, exercise, activity, move, movement, action.
2 *a series of diplomatic manoeuvres*: **stratagem**, **tactic**, gambit, ploy, trick, dodge, ruse, plan, scheme, operation, device, plot, machination, artifice, subterfuge, intrigue, manipulation; French démarche; informal wangle.
3 (**manoeuvres**) *large-scale military manoeuvres*: **training exercises**, exercises, war games, operations.

manse noun Scottish **minister's house**; vicarage, parsonage, rectory, deanery; archaic glebe-house.

manservant noun **valet**, attendant, retainer, equerry, gentleman's gentleman, man, Jeeves; steward, butler, footman, flunkey, page, houseboy, lackey; Military, dated batman; N. Amer. houseman.

mansion noun *a lavish Beverly Hills mansion*: **residence**, hall, abode, stately home, seat, manor, manor house, country house, villa, castle; French château, manoir; Italian palazzo; German schloss; informal palace, pile.
▷ANTONYMS hovel.

manslaughter noun **killing**, murder; literary slaying.

mantle noun **1** *a dark green velvet mantle*: **cloak**, cape, shawl, wrap, stole; rare pelisse, pelerine; S. American poncho, serape; archaic mantlet.
2 *houses covered in a thick mantle of snow*: **covering**, **layer**, blanket, sheet, veil, curtain, canopy, cover, cloak, pall, shroud, screen, mask, cloud, overlay, envelope.
3 *the mantle of leadership*: **role**, burden, onus, duty, responsibility, function, position, capacity, task, job.
▶ **verb** *heavy mists mantled the forest*: **cover**, envelop, veil, cloak, curtain, shroud, swathe, wrap, blanket, screen, cloud, conceal, hide, disguise, mask, obscure, surround, overlay, clothe; literary enshroud.

manual adjective **1** *manual work*: **done with one's hands**, labouring, physical, blue-collar.
2 *a manual typewriter*: **hand-operated**, hand, non-automatic.
▷ANTONYMS automatic, mechanical.
▶ **noun** *a training manual*: **handbook**, set of instructions, instructions, instruction book, guide, companion, reference book, ABC, guidebook; Latin vade mecum; informal bible; rare enchiridion.

manufacture verb **1** *the company manufactures laser printers*: **make**, **produce**, mass produce, build, construct, assemble, put together, create, fabricate, prefabricate, turn out, process, form, fashion, model, mould, shape, forge, engineer.
2 *the story was manufactured by the press*: **make up**, **invent**, fabricate, concoct, hatch, dream up, think up, trump up, devise, formulate, frame, contrive, construct, coin; informal cook up.
▶ **noun** *the manufacture of aircraft engines*: **production**, **making**, manufacturing, mass-production, construction, building, assembly, creation, fabrication, prefabrication, processing, putting together, turning out, engineering, forging.

manufacturer noun **maker**, **producer**, builder, constructor, processor, creator, fabricator; factory owner, industrialist, captain/baron of industry.

manure noun **dung**, muck, droppings, ordure, guano, cowpats; N. Amer. informal cow chips, horse apples; vulgar slang shit, crap.

manuscript noun **document**, text, script, paper, typescript; codex, parchment, palimpsest, vellum, scroll; autograph, holograph.
▷ANTONYMS publication, published work.

> *Word links* **manuscript**
>
> **codicology** study of manuscripts

many determiner & adjective **1** *he has many faults*: **numerous**, a great/good deal of, a lot of, a large/great number of, great quantities of, plenty of, countless, innumerable, scores of, crowds of, droves of, an army of, a horde of, a multitude of, a multiplicity of, multitudinous, numberless, multiple, untold; several, various, sundry, diverse, assorted, multifarious; copious, abundant, profuse, an abundance of, a profusion of; frequent; informal lots of, umpteen, loads of, masses of, stacks of, scads of, heaps of, piles of, bags of, tons of, oodles of, dozens of, hundreds of, thousands of, millions of, billions of, zillions of, more ... than one can shake a stick at; Brit. informal shedload; N. Amer. informal a slew of, gazillions of, bazillions of, gobs of; Austral./NZ informal a swag of; vulgar slang a shitload of; literary myriad, divers.
▷ANTONYMS few.
2 (**the many**) *sacrificing the individual for the sake of the many*: **the people**, the common people, the masses, the multitude, the majority, the populace, the public, the rank and file, the crowd, the commonalty, the commonality; derogatory the hoi polloi, the common herd, the mob, the proletariat, the rabble, the riff-raff, the great unwashed, the canaille, the proles, the plebs.
▷ANTONYMS aristocracy.

> *Word links* **many**
>
> **multi-** related prefix, as in *multicoloured*, *multibuy*
> **poly-** related prefix, as in *polycarbonate*, *polyunsaturated*

map noun **plan**, chart.
▶ **verb** *the region was mapped from the air*: **chart**, plot, delineate, draw, depict, portray, survey.
□ **map something out** *he mapped out a plan of campaign*: **outline**, set out, lay out, sketch out, trace out, rough out, block out, delineate, detail, draw up; formulate, work out, frame, draft, plan, plot out; arrange, design, programme, think out, think through, organize.

> *Word links* **map**
>
> **cartographic** relating to maps
> **cartography** making of maps

mar verb **1** *an ugly scar marred his features*: **spoil**, ruin, impair; **disfigure**, detract from, flaw, blemish, scar, mutilate, deface, deform.
▷ANTONYMS improve, enhance.
2 *the celebrations were marred by violence*: **spoil**, ruin, impair, upset, damage, wreck; **harm**, hurt, blight, taint, tarnish, sully, stain, pollute, vitiate; informal foul up.

maraud verb *bands of robbers crossed the river to maraud*: **plunder**, go looting, go pillaging, foray, raid, ravage, harry, go on forays/raids, freeboot; archaic reave.

marauder noun *they placed chains across the river mouth to keep out marauders*: **raider**, plunderer, pillager, looter, robber, pirate, freebooter, buccaneer, corsair, rover, bandit, brigand, rustler, highwayman, ravager; Scottish historical cateran, mosstrooper; archaic reaver, snaphance.

marauding adjective *reservists are being called up to protect civilians from marauding gunmen*: **predatory**, rapacious, thieving, vulturine, plundering, pillaging, looting, freebooting, piratical; rare plunderous.

marble noun

> *Word links* **marble**
>
> **marmoreal** relating to marble

march verb **1** *a squadron of soldiers marched past*: **stride**, walk, troop, step, pace, tread; footslog, slog, tramp, hike, trudge; parade, file, process, promenade; Brit. informal yomp.
2 *she marched in without even knocking*: **stalk**, strut, stride, flounce, storm, stomp, sweep, swagger.
3 *time marches on*: **move forward**, advance, progress, forge ahead, make headway, go on, continue on, roll on, develop, evolve.
▶ **noun 1** *a 20-mile march across open country*: **hike**, trek, tramp, slog, footslog, walk; route march, forced march; Brit. informal yomp.
2 *a march by veterans and sailors through the centre of the city | a protest march against racism*: **parade**, procession, march past, promenade, cortège; **demonstration**, protest; informal demo; Indian morcha.
3 *the march of technology*: **progress**, advance, progression, passage, continuance, development, evolution, headway.

marches plural noun *the Welsh marches*: **borders**, boundaries, borderlands, frontiers, limits, confines; historical marchlands.

margin noun **1** *the margin of the lake*: **edge**, side, bank, verge, border, perimeter, brink, brim, rim, fringe, boundary, limits, periphery, bound, extremity; literary marge, bourn, skirt.
2 *there was no margin for error*: **leeway**, latitude, scope, room, room for manoeuvre, room to spare, space, allowance, extra, surplus.
3 *they won by a narrow margin*: **gap**, majority, amount, difference, measure/degree of difference.

marginal adjective **1** *the difference is marginal*: **slight**, small, tiny, minute, low, minor, insignificant, minimal, negligible.
▷ANTONYMS vast, gross.
2 *a very marginal case*: **borderline**, disputable, questionable, doubtful.

marijuana noun **cannabis**, hashish, bhang, hemp, kef, kif, charas, ganja, sinsemilla; informal dope, hash, grass, pot, blow, draw, stuff, Mary Jane, tea, the weed, gold, skunkweed, skunk, reefer, rope, smoke, gage, boo, charge, jive, mootah, pod; Brit. informal wacky backy; N. Amer. informal locoweed; S. African dagga, zol; informal, dated green, mezz.

marinate verb *marinate the fruit in the rum for 30 minutes*: **souse**, soak, steep, immerse, marinade.

marine adjective **1** *marine plants*: **saltwater**, seawater, sea, oceanic, aquatic; rare pelagic, thalassic.
▷ANTONYMS freshwater.
2 *a marine insurance company*: **maritime**, nautical, naval, seafaring, seagoing, ocean-going.

mariner noun **sailor**, seaman, seafarer, seafaring man; informal Jack tar, tar, sea dog, salt, bluejacket, matelot, matlow, matlo; N. Amer. informal shellback.

marital adjective *as children leave home marital satisfaction tends to pick up again*: **matrimonial**, married, wedded, conjugal, connubial, nuptial, marriage, wedding; Law spousal; literary hymeneal, epithalamic.

maritime adjective **1** *maritime law*: **naval**, marine, nautical, seafaring, seagoing, sea, ocean-going.
2 *maritime regions*: **coastal**, seaside, littoral.

mark noun **1** *a dirty mark on the tablecloth | a chestnut mare with a white mark on her forehead*: **blemish**, streak, spot, fleck, dot, blot, stain, smear, trace, speck, speckle, blotch, smudge, smut, smirch, fingermark, fingerprint, impression, imprint; bruise, discoloration, scar, pit, pockmark, pock, scratch, dent, chip, notch, nick, line, score, cut, incision, gash; marking, blaze, stripe; birthmark; informal splotch, splodge; technical stigma.
2 *a punctuation mark*: **symbol**, sign, character; exclamation mark, question mark, quotation mark; diacritic, diacritical mark.
3 *he signed his mark in the visitors' book*: **signature**, autograph, cross, X, scribble, squiggle, initials, imprint.
4 *books bearing the mark of a well-known bookseller*: **logo**, seal, stamp, imprint, symbol, emblem, device, insignia, badge, brand, trademark, token, monogram, hallmark, logotype, watermark, label, tag, flag, motto.
5 *unemployment had passed the three million mark*: **point**, level, stage, degree.
6 *the flag was lowered as a mark of respect*: **sign**, token, symbol, indication, badge, emblem, symptom, feature, evidence, proof, clue, hint.
7 *the war left its mark on him*: **impression**, imprint, traces, vestiges, effect, impact, influence.
8 *it is the mark of a civilized society to treat its elderly members well*: **characteristic**, feature, trait, attribute, quality, hallmark, badge, stamp, property, peculiarity, indicator.
9 *he got very good marks for maths and physics*: **grade**, grading, rating, score, percentage; assessment, evaluation.
10 *the bullet missed its mark | his comment hit the mark*: **target**, goal, aim, bullseye, objective, object, end, purpose, intent, intention.
11 *his work hasn't been up to the mark*: **required standard**, standard, norm, par, level, criterion, gauge, yardstick, rule, measure, scale.
□ **make one's mark** *he has made his mark in the financial world*: **be successful, distinguish oneself**, succeed, gain success, be a success, prosper, get ahead, get on, make good, achieve recognition, attain distinction; informal make it, make the grade, find a place in the sun.
□ **quick off the mark alert**, quick, quick-witted, bright, clever, perceptive, sharp, sharp-witted, observant, wide awake; informal on the ball, on one's toes, quick on the uptake.
▷ANTONYMS slow-witted, dozy.
□ **up to the mark** *the team's training is not up to the mark*: **good enough**, up to scratch, up to standard, up to par, satisfactory, acceptable, adequate, passable, sufficient, competent, all right; informal OK, up to snuff.
▷ANTONYMS below standard, unacceptable.
□ **wide of the mark 1** *his answer was wide of the mark*: **inaccurate**, incorrect, wrong, erroneous, inexact, off-target, off-beam, out, fallacious, mistaken, misguided, misinformed; archaic abroad. ▷ANTONYMS spot on.
2 *the observations were wide of the mark*: **irrelevant**, inapplicable, inapposite, inappropriate, inapt, immaterial, not to the point, beside the point, off the subject, extraneous, neither here nor there. ▷ANTONYMS to the point.
▸ verb **1** *be careful not to mark the paintwork*: **discolour**, stain, smear, smudge, streak, blotch, blot, blemish; dirty, smirch, damage, deface, disfigure, pockmark, pit, bruise, scrape, scratch, scar, dent, chip, nick, notch, score, cut, gash; informal splotch, splodge.
2 *all her possessions were clearly marked*: **put one's name on**, name, initial, put one's seal on, label, tag, hallmark, watermark, brand, stamp, earmark.
3 *I've marked the relevant passages | a bronze cross marks the grave*: **indicate**, label, flag, tab, tick, show the position of, show, identify, designate, delineate, denote.
4 *the city held a festival to mark its 200th anniversary*: **celebrate**, observe, recognize, acknowledge, keep, honour, solemnize, pay tribute to, salute, commemorate, remember, memorialize.
5 *two great sea battles marked a new epoch in naval history*: **represent**, signify, be an indication of, be a sign of, indicate, herald.
6 *his style is marked by simplicity and concision*: **characterize**, distinguish, identify, typify, brand, signalize, stamp.
7 *an examiner may have hundreds of papers to mark*: **assess**, evaluate, appraise, correct; N. Amer. grade.
8 *it'll cause trouble, you mark my words!* **take heed of**, pay heed to, heed, listen to, take note/notice of, pay attention to, attend to, note, mind, bear in mind, give (a) thought to, take into consideration, take to heart; archaic regard.
□ **mark something down 1** *prices have been marked down for quick sale*: **reduce**, decrease, lower, cut, put down, take down, discount; informal slash. ▷ANTONYMS increase. **2** *some shops have marked the trainers down*: **lower the price of**, make cheaper, sell at a giveaway price, put in a sale; informal knock down.
▷ANTONYMS mark something up.
□ **mark someone out 1** *his honesty marked him out from the rest of them*: **set apart**, separate, single out, differentiate, distinguish. **2** *she is marked out for fame*: **destine**, ordain, predestine, preordain.
□ **mark something out** *the pitch had already been marked out*: **delineate**, outline, delimit, demarcate, measure out, mark the boundaries/limits of, mark off, define, describe, stake out.
□ **mark something up 1** *they marked up the price by 66 per cent*: **increase**, raise, up, put up, hike (up), escalate; informal jack up. ▷ANTONYMS mark something down. **2** *editors marked up the text in pencil*: **annotate**, correct, label.

marked adjective *a marked deterioration in her health*: **noticeable**, pronounced, decided, distinct, striking, clear, glaring, blatant, unmistakable, obvious, plain, manifest, patent, palpable, considerable, remarkable, prominent, signal, significant, great, substantial, strong, conspicuous, notable, noted, pointed, salient, recognizable, identifiable, distinguishable, discernible, apparent, evident, open, written all over one.
▷ANTONYMS imperceptible, inconspicuous.

markedly adverb *the birth rate declined markedly*: **noticeably**, decidedly, strikingly, distinctly, remarkably, clearly, plainly; blatantly, glaringly, unmistakably, conspicuously, pointedly, obviously, manifestly, patently, palpably, signally, significantly, greatly, considerably, substantially, recognizably, discernibly, notably, apparently, evidently, to a marked extent, to a great extent; informal seriously.
▷ANTONYMS imperceptibly.

market noun **1 shopping centre**, marketplace, mart, retail outlet, flea market, fair, bazaar, piazza, plaza; Arabic souk; historical agora; archaic emporium.
2 *there's no market for such expensive goods*: **demand**, call, want, desire, need, requirement.
3 *the market is sluggish*: **trade**, trading, business, commerce, buying and selling, dealing.
□ **in the market for wishing to buy**, in need of, seeking, wanting, lacking, wishing for, desiring.
□ **on the market on sale**, up for sale, for sale, on offer, purchasable, available, obtainable; N. Amer. on the block.
▸ verb *the product was marketed worldwide*: **sell**, retail, offer for sale, put up for sale, vend, merchandise, trade, peddle, hawk; advertise, promote.

marketable adjective **1** *marketable fruit*: **saleable**, sellable, merchantable; rare vendible.
2 *marketable skills*: **in demand**, sought-after, wanted.

marksman, markswoman noun **sniper**, sharpshooter, good shot; Italian bersagliere; informal crack shot, dead shot; N. Amer. informal deadeye, shootist.

maroon verb *a novel about English schoolboys marooned on a desert island*: **strand**, leave stranded, cast away, cast ashore, abandon, leave behind, leave, leave in the lurch, desert, turn one's back on, leave isolated; informal leave high and dry; archaic forsake.

marriage noun **1** *a proposal of marriage*: **matrimony**, holy matrimony, wedlock, married state, conjugal bond, civil partnership.
2 *the marriage took place at St Margaret's Church*: **wedding**, wedding ceremony, marriage ceremony, nuptials, union; archaic espousal.
▷ANTONYMS divorce, splitting up.
3 *the piece is a marriage of jazz, pop, and gospel*: **union**, alliance, fusion, amalgamation, combination, affiliation, association, connection, coupling, merger, unification; informal hook-up.
▷ANTONYMS sundering, separation.

> *Word links* **marriage**
>
> **marital, matrimonial, nuptial, conjugal, connubial, spousal** relating to marriage
> **gamophobia** fear of marriage
> **gamomania** obsession with marriage

married adjective **1** *a married couple*: **wedded**, wed, joined in marriage, united in wedlock; informal spliced, hitched.
▷ANTONYMS unmarried, single.
2 *married bliss*: **marital**, matrimonial, connubial, conjugal, nuptial, spousal.

marrow noun *the marrow of his statement*: **essence**, core, nucleus, pith, kernel, heart, centre, soul, spirit, quintessence, gist, substance, sum and substance, meat, nub, stuff; informal nitty-gritty, nuts and bolts.

marry verb **1** *the couple married last year*: **get/be married**, wed, be wed, become man and wife, plight/pledge one's troth; informal tie the knot, walk down the aisle, take the plunge, get spliced, get hitched, get yoked, say 'I do'; archaic become espoused.
2 *John wanted to marry her*: **wed**, take to wife/husband, lead to the altar; informal make an honest woman of; archaic espouse, wive.
▷ANTONYMS divorce.
3 *the show marries poetry with art*: **join**, join together, unite, ally, merge, unify, amalgamate, combine, affiliate, associate, link, connect, fuse, weld,

couple, knit, yoke.
▷ANTONYMS split, separate.

marsh noun **swamp**, marshland, bog, peat bog, swampland, morass, mire, quagmire, quag, slough, fen, fenland, wetland, sump; salt marsh, saltings, salina; N. Amer. bayou, pocosin, moor; Scottish & N. English moss; Irish corcass; archaic marish.

> *Word links* **marsh**
>
> **paludal** relating to marshes

marshal verb **1** *the Mercian king marshalled a formidable army*: **gather**, gather together, assemble, collect, muster, mass, amass, call together, draw up, line up, align, array, organize, group, set/put in order, set/put into position, arrange, deploy, position, order; dispose, rank, mobilize, rally, round up; Medicine triage.
▷ANTONYMS disperse, scatter.
2 *guests were marshalled to their seats*: **usher**, guide, escort, conduct, lead, shepherd, steer, take.

marshy adjective **boggy**, swampy, muddy, squelchy, soggy, waterlogged, oozy, squashy, miry, fenny; Scottish & N. English mossy; technical paludal, paludine; rare marish, quaggy, uliginous.
▷ANTONYMS dry; firm.

martial adjective **1** *their martial exploits*: **military**, soldierly, soldier-like, army, naval, fighting, service; courageous, brave, valiant, valorous, heroic.
▷ANTONYMS civil, civilian.
2 *one of the most powerful and martial tribes*: **warlike**, combative, belligerent, bellicose, aggressive, pugnacious, gung-ho, militant, militaristic.
▷ANTONYMS peaceable.

martinet noun **disciplinarian**, slave-driver, stickler for discipline, taskmaster, taskmistress, authoritarian, tyrant; drill sergeant.

martyr verb *she was martyred for her faith*: **put to death**, kill, make a martyr of, martyrize; burn, burn at the stake, stone, immolate, throw to the lions, crucify, put on the rack.
▶ noun
□ **be a martyr to** informal *he's a martyr to migraine*: **suffer from**, be a constant sufferer from, have chronic ...; be seriously affected by, be afflicted with, be troubled by, get.

martyrdom noun **death**, **suffering**, torture, torment, agony, persecution, ordeal, anguish; killing, putting to death, martyrization, sacrifice, crucifixion, immolation, burning, burning at the stake; Portuguese auto-da-fé; archaic passion.
▷ANTONYMS apostasy.

marvel verb *she marvelled at their courage*: **be amazed**, be filled with amazement, be astonished, be surprised, be awed, stand in awe, wonder, be full of wonder, stare, gape, goggle, not believe one's eyes/ears, not know what to say, be dumbfounded; **admire**, applaud, think highly of, respect, venerate, appreciate; informal be flabbergasted.
▷ANTONYMS be indifferent; disregard.
▶ noun *the marvels of technology | I don't know how she did it—she's a marvel*: **wonder**, **miracle**, wonderful thing, amazing thing, sensation, spectacle, phenomenon; genius, miracle worker, prodigy, paragon, virtuoso, wizard; informal something else, something to shout about, something to write home about, eye-opener; whizz, whizz-kid.

marvellous adjective **1** *his solo climb was marvellous*: **amazing**, astounding, astonishing, awesome, breathtaking, sensational, remarkable, spectacular, stupendous, staggering, stunning; phenomenal, prodigious, miraculous, extraordinary, incredible, unbelievable; literary wondrous.
▷ANTONYMS ordinary.
2 *we had marvellous weather*: **excellent**, splendid, wonderful, magnificent, superb, glorious, sublime, lovely, delightful, beautiful, too good to be true; informal super, great, smashing, amazing, fantastic, terrific, tremendous, phenomenal, sensational, heavenly, gorgeous, dreamy, grand, fabulous, fab, fabby, fantabulous, awesome, to die for, magic, ace, cool, mean, bad, wicked, mega, crucial, mind-blowing, far out, A1, sound, out of this world, marvy; black English dope, def, phat; Brit. informal brilliant, brill, bosting; N. Amer. informal neat, badass, bodacious, boss, radical, rad, peachy, boffo, bully, bitching, dandy, jim-dandy; Austral./NZ informal beaut, bonzer; informal, dated groovy, spanking, divine; Brit. informal, dated capital, champion, wizard, corking, ripping, cracking, spiffing, top-hole, topping, beezer; N. Amer. informal, dated swell, keen; S. African informal kif, lank; archaic goodly.
▷ANTONYMS awful.

masculine adjective **1** *a masculine trait*: **male**, manly, manlike, of men, man's, men's, male-oriented.
▷ANTONYMS feminine.
2 *a powerfully masculine man*: **virile**, macho, manly, all-male, muscular, muscly, strong, strapping, well built, rugged, robust, brawny, powerful, red-blooded, vigorous; informal hunky.
▷ANTONYMS weak; timid.
3 *a rather masculine woman*: **mannish**, manlike, unfeminine, unwomanly, unladylike, Amazonian; informal butch, dykey; archaic viraginous, viragoish.
▷ANTONYMS feminine; effeminate.

masculinity noun **virility**, manliness, maleness, vigour, strength, muscularity, ruggedness, toughness, robustness.
▷ANTONYMS femininity.

mash verb *mash the potatoes*: **pulp**, crush, purée, cream, smash, squash, pound, beat, macerate, liquidize, liquefy, whip, grind, mince, soften, mangle, chew.
▶ noun *first pound the garlic to a mash*: **pulp**, purée, mush, paste, pâté, crush, slush, liquid; derogatory pap.

mask noun **1** *she wore a mask to conceal her face*: **disguise**, **veil**, false face, domino, stocking mask, fancy dress; historical visor; archaic vizard.
2 *wear a mask to avoid inhaling dust*: **face mask**, protective mask, gas mask, oxygen mask, fencing mask, iron mask, ski mask, dust mask; safety goggles, welding goggles, welding mask, surgical mask, eye mask, visor.
3 *de Craon had dropped his mask of good humour*: **pretence**, semblance, veil, screen, front, false front, facade, veneer, blind, false colours, disguise, guise, concealment, cover, cover-up, cloak, camouflage.
4 *a mask that blocks out part of the image*: **matte**, photomask, shadow mask, masking, masking tape.
▶ verb *people carried herbs to mask the stench*: **hide**, conceal, disguise, cover up, obscure, screen, cloak, camouflage, veil, mantle, blanket, enshroud.
▷ANTONYMS enhance, reinforce.

masquerade noun **1** *a grand masquerade organized by Lord Tylney at Wanstead House*: **masked ball**, masque, fancy-dress party.
2 *I doubt if he could have kept up the masquerade for much longer*: **pretence**, deception, pose, act, front, facade, disguise, dissimulation, cover-up, bluff, subterfuge, play-acting, make-believe; informal put-on.
▶ verb *a journalist* **masquerading as** *a man in distress*: **pretend to be**, pose as, pass oneself off as, impersonate, disguise oneself as, simulate, profess to be; rare personate.

Mass noun **Eucharist**, Holy Communion, Communion, the Lord's Supper.

mass noun **1** *a thick soggy mass of fallen leaves*: **pile**, heap, stack, clump, cloud, bunch, bundle, lump; concentration, conglomeration, accumulation, aggregation, concretion, accretion, assemblage, collection, stockpile, build-up; rare amassment.
2 *a mass of cyclists*: **large number**, abundance, profusion, multitude, group, crowd, mob, rabble, horde, barrage, throng, huddle, host, troop, army, herd, flock, drove, swarm, pack, press, crush, mountain, flood.
3 *the mass of people voted against*: **majority**, larger part/number, greater part/number, best/better part, major part, most, bulk, main body, preponderance, almost all, lion's share.
4 (**the masses**) **the common people**, the populace, the public, the people, the multitude, the rank and file, the crowd, the commonalty, the commonality, the third estate, the plebeians; derogatory the hoi polloi, the mob, the proletariat, the common herd, the rabble, the riff-raff, the canaille, the great unwashed, the ragtag (and bobtail), the proles, the plebs.
▷ANTONYMS elite, oligarchy.
5 *one tenth of the mass of the star*: **weight**, size, magnitude, bulk, dimensions, capacity, density, extent, scope, greatness, bigness, hugeness, amount, matter.
▶ adjective *mass hysteria*: **wholesale**, universal, widespread, general, large-scale, extensive, pandemic.
▶ verb *both countries began massing troops in the region*: **accumulate**, assemble, amass, collect, gather, gather together, draw together, join together; marshal, muster, round up, mobilize, rally.
▷ANTONYMS disperse, disband.

massacre noun **1** *a cold-blooded massacre of innocent civilians*: **slaughter**, wholesale slaughter, mass slaughter, wholesale killing, indiscriminate killing; murder, murdering, mass murder, mass homicide, execution, mass execution, destruction, mass destruction, annihilation, extermination, liquidation, decimation, carnage, butchery, bloodbath, bloodletting, pogrom, genocide, ethnic cleansing, holocaust, Shoah, night of the long knives; literary slaying; rare battue, hecatomb.
2 informal *the match was an 8–0 massacre*. See **rout** (sense 2 of the verb).
▶ verb **1** *thousands were brutally massacred by the soldiers*: **slaughter**, butcher, murder, kill, annihilate, exterminate, execute, liquidate, eliminate, destroy, decimate, kill off, wipe out, mow down, cut down, cut to pieces, put to the sword, put to death, send to the gas chambers; literary slay.
2 informal *they were absolutely massacred in the final*. See **trounce**.

massage noun **rub-down**, rubbing, rub, kneading, palpation, manipulation, pummelling; technical shiatsu, reflexology, acupressure, hydromassage, Swedish massage, osteopathy, chiropractic treatment, effleurage, tapotement, Rolfing.
▶ verb **1** *he massaged her tired muscles*: **rub**, rub down, knead, palpate, manipulate, pummel, work; rare embrocate.
2 *the statistics have been massaged*: **alter**, tamper with, manipulate, doctor, falsify, juggle, fiddle with, tinker with, distort, change, rig, interfere with, misrepresent; informal fix, cook, fiddle.

massive adjective *these burial chambers were massive structures*: **huge**, enormous, gigantic, very big, very large, great, giant, colossal, mammoth,

vast, immense, tremendous, mighty, stupendous, monumental, epic, prodigious, mountainous, monstrous, titanic, towering, elephantine, king-sized, king-size, gargantuan, Herculean, Brobdingnagian, substantial, extensive, hefty, bulky, weighty, heavy, gross; informal mega, monster, whopping, whopping great, thumping, thumping great, humongous, jumbo, hulking, bumper, astronomical, astronomic; Brit. informal whacking, whacking great, ginormous.
▷ANTONYMS tiny.

mast noun **1** *a ship's mast*: **spar**, boom, yard, gaff, foremast, mainmast, topmast, mizzenmast, mizzen, royal mast; archaic stick.
2 *the mast on top of the building*: **flagpole**, flagstaff, pole, post, rod, support, upright; aerial, transmitter, pylon.

master noun **1** *he acceded to his master's wishes*: **lord**, overlord, lord and master, ruler, sovereign, monarch, liege, liege lord, suzerain; overseer, superintendent, director, manager, controller, leader, governor, commander, padrone, captain, head, headman, boss, principal, employer, foreman; informal chief, top dog, honcho, head honcho, Big Chief, Big Daddy; Brit. informal gaffer, guv'nor; N. Amer. informal kahuna, sachem.
▷ANTONYMS servant; underling.
2 *he's a master of disguise | a chess master*: **expert**, adept, genius, past master, maestro, virtuoso, professional, doyen, authority, pundit, master hand, prodigy, grandmaster, champion, star; informal ace, pro, wizard, whizz, wiz, hotshot; Brit. informal dab hand; N. Amer. informal maven, crackerjack.
▷ANTONYMS amateur, novice.
3 *the dog's pining for his master*: **owner**, keeper.
4 *the master of the ship*: **captain**, skipper, commander.
5 *the geography master*: **teacher**, schoolteacher, schoolmaster, tutor, instructor, pedagogue; rare preceptor.
▷ANTONYMS pupil.
6 *they regarded him as their spiritual master*: **guru**, teacher, spiritual leader, guide, mentor, torch-bearer, swami, Roshi, Maharishi.
▷ANTONYMS acolyte, disciple.
7 *you can make a copy from the master*: **original**, archetype, prototype.
▷ANTONYMS copy.
▸verb **1** *I managed to master my fears*: **overcome**, conquer, beat, quell, quash, suppress, control, repress, restrain, overpower, triumph over, subdue, vanquish, subjugate, prevail over, govern, curb, check, bridle, tame, defeat, get the better of, get a grip on, get over, gain mastery over; informal lick.
▷ANTONYMS give way to.
2 *it took him ages to master the technique*: **learn**, learn thoroughly, become proficient in, know inside out, know backwards, become expert in, acquire, pick up, grasp, understand; informal get the hang of, get clued up about, get off by heart.
▸adjective **1** *a master craftsman*: **expert**, adept, proficient, skilled, skilful, deft, dexterous, adroit, practised, experienced, masterly, accomplished, demon, brilliant; informal crack, ace, mean, wizard; N. Amer. informal crackerjack; vulgar slang shit-hot; archaic or humorous compleat.
2 *the master bedroom*: **principal**, main, chief, leading, prime, predominant, foremost, great, grand, most important, biggest.
3 *his master plan*: **controlling**, ruling, directing, commanding, dominating, overall.

masterful adjective **1** *he looked self-assured and masterful*: **commanding**, powerful, controlling, imposing, magisterial, lordly, authoritative, dominating, domineering, overbearing, overweening, imperious, bossy, peremptory, high-handed, arrogant, autocratic, dictatorial, tyrannical, despotic; informal pushy.
▷ANTONYMS weak, meek, wimpish.
2 *their masterful handling of the situation*: **expert**, adept, clever, masterly; **skilful**, skilled, adroit, proficient, deft, dexterous, accomplished, polished, excellent, superb, superlative, consummate, first-rate, peerless, fine; informal crack, stellar, ace.
▷ANTONYMS incompetent, inept.

> *Easily confused words* **masterful or masterly?**
>
> Some writers use **masterful** only in the sense 'powerful and able to control others' (*a masterful tone of voice*) in order to maintain the distinction from **masterly**. In practice, however, the two words are used almost equally in this sense.

masterly adjective *a masterly analysis of the problem*: **expert**, adept, clever, masterful; **skilful**, deft, adroit, skilled, dexterous, accomplished, polished, excellent, superb, superlative, consummate, first-rate, brilliant, intelligent, fine, talented, gifted; informal crack, stellar, ace.
▷ANTONYMS incompetent, inept.

> *Easily confused words* **masterly or masterful?**
>
> See **masterful**.

mastermind verb *he masterminded the whole campaign*: **control**, **plan**, direct, be in charge of, run, conduct, organize, arrange, administer, regulate, supervise, superintend, preside over, orchestrate, stage-manage, engineer, manage, coordinate, conceive, devise, put together, forge, originate, initiate, think up, create, work out, dream up, frame, hatch, generate, come up with, have the bright idea of; informal be the brains behind.
▸noun *the mastermind behind the project*: **genius**, mind, intellect, author, architect, engineer, director, planner, organizer, deviser, originator, manager, prime mover, initiator, inventor; informal brain, brains, bright spark; Brit. informal brainbox.

masterpiece noun *'La Gioconda' is Leonardo's masterpiece*: **finest work**, best work, masterwork, greatest creation; work of art, object of vertu; Latin magnum opus; French chef-d'œuvre, pièce de résistance, tour de force.
▷ANTONYMS hack work.

master stroke noun **act of genius**, coup, successful manoeuvre, triumph, victory, complete success; French coup de maître.

mastery noun **1** *her mastery of the French language*: **proficiency**, ability, capability; **knowledge**, understanding, comprehension, familiarity, command, grasp, grip.
2 *they played with tactical mastery*: **skill**, skilfulness, expertise, dexterity, finesse, adroitness, virtuosity, prowess, deftness, proficiency; informal know-how.
3 *man's mastery over nature*: **control**, superiority, domination, command, ascendancy, supremacy, pre-eminence, triumph, victory, the upper hand, the whip hand, rule, government, power, sway, authority, jurisdiction, dominion, sovereignty.

masticate verb *this lizard eats a wide variety of plants but does not masticate the food*: **chew**, munch, champ, chomp, crunch, eat; ruminate, chew the cud; technical manducate, triturate; rare chumble.

masturbate verb **practise self-abuse**; informal play with oneself, touch oneself; formal practise onanism; vulgar slang **wank**, jerk off, jack off, toss off, bring oneself off, beat one's/the meat, beat off, frig, whack off.

masturbation noun **auto-eroticism**, self-abuse, self-gratification, self-stimulation; informal playing with oneself; formal **onanism**; vulgar slang **wanking**, wank, handjob, frig, frigging, beating one's/the meat, hand relief.

mat noun **1** *the wooden floor was covered by two mats*: **rug**, runner, carpet, drugget; **doormat**, welcome mat, hearthrug, bath mat, rag rug, scatter rug; bearskin, sheepskin; Indian dhurrie, numdah; Turkish & Persian kilim; Greek flokati; Azerbaijani Soumak; N. Amer. floorcloth; S. African kaross.
2 *he put the casserole on a mat to protect the table*: **table mat**, place mat; **coaster**, beer mat, drip mat, doily.
3 *a thick mat of hair*: **mass**, tangle, knot, mop, thatch, shock, mane, cluster, mesh.
▸verb *his hair was matted with blood*: **tangle**, entangle, knot, ravel, snarl up.

match noun **1** *a football match | a boxing match*: **contest**, **competition**, game, tournament, tie, cup tie, event, fixture, trial, test, test match, meet, bout, fight, duel; quarter-final, semi-final, final, Cup Final; friendly, derby, local derby; play-off, replay, rematch; Canadian & Scottish playdown; N. Amer. split; informal, dated mill; archaic tourney.
2 *he was no match for the champion*: **equal**, rival, equivalent, peer, counterpart; rare compeer.
3 *the vase was an exact match of the one she already owned*: **replica**, copy, lookalike, double, twin, duplicate, equivalent, facsimile, like; mate, fellow, companion, counterpart, pair, complement; informal spitting image, spit and image, spit, dead spit, ringer, dead ringer.
4 *theirs is definitely a love match*: **marriage**, betrothal, relationship, partnership, union, pairing, alliance, compact, contract, affiliation, combination.
5 *he would be a very suitable match for any of their daughters*: **prospective husband/wife**, prospect, candidate; informal catch.
▸verb **1** *the curtains matched the duvet cover*: **go with**, coordinate with, complement, harmonize with, blend with, tone with, team with, be the same as, be similar to, suit.
2 *these socks don't match*: **be a pair**, be a set, be the same, go together.
3 *did their statements match?* **correspond**, be in agreement, tally, agree, match up, coincide, accord, conform, square, harmonize, be consonant, be compatible.
4 *they matched suitable applicants with firms having vacancies*: **combine**, match up, link, bring/put together, unite, marry, pair up, yoke, team, couple, pair, ally; formal conjoin.
5 *no one can match him at chess*: **equal**, be equal to, be the equal of, be a match for, measure up to, compare with, parallel, be in the same league as, be in the same category as, be on a par with, touch, keep pace with, keep up with, emulate, rival, vie with, compete with, contend with; informal hold a candle to.
□ **match against/with** *Spain was matched against France*: **draw against**, set against, pit against, play off against.
□ **match up to** *the film didn't match up to my expectations*: **come up to**, measure up to, meet with, be equal to, be as good as, satisfy, fulfil, answer to.

matching adjective *he picked up a cup and then identified the matching saucer | she was wearing a navy-blue blazer and matching skirt*: **corresponding**, equivalent, parallel, analogous, coordinating,

complementing, complementary, harmonizing, blending, toning, harmonious, the same, paired, twin, coupled, double, duplicate, identical, (all) of a piece, like, like (two) peas in a pod, alike, comparable, similar, correlative, congruent, tallying, agreeing, concordant, consonant.
▷ANTONYMS different, clashing.

matchless adjective *her sister's matchless beauty*: **incomparable**, unrivalled, inimitable, beyond compare, unparalleled, unequalled, without equal, peerless, unmatched, beyond comparison, second to none, unsurpassed, unsurpassable, nonpareil, unique, consummate, perfect, rare, exquisite, transcendent, surpassing, superlative, supreme; rare unexampled.
▷ANTONYMS ordinary, run-of-the-mill.

matchmaker noun **marriage broker**, marriage bureau, dating agency; go-between, pandar, Pandarus; Jewish shadchan.

mate noun **1** Brit. informal *he's gone off to the pub with his mates*: **friend**, companion, boon companion, comrade, intimate, familiar, confidant, alter ego, second self; playmate, classmate, schoolmate, workmate, team-mate, flatmate, room-mate; informal pal, chum, buddy, bosom pal, sidekick, cully, spar, crony, main man; Brit. informal china, mucker, butty, oppo; N. Amer. informal amigo, compadre, paisan, cohort; S. African informal gabba, homeboy; N. English & Scottish informal marrow, marrer; archaic compeer; rare fidus Achates.
2 Brit. informal *see you later, mate*: **man**, my friend; informal pal, chum; Brit. informal cock, squire, matey; Brit. informal, dated old fellow, old bean, old boy, old chap, old fruit; Welsh & Irish informal boyo; N. Amer. informal bud, buster, amigo, Mac, bro, bubba, bo, jack, partner; Austral./NZ informal cobber, digger; Indian informal bhai, yaar; S. African informal jong, okie.
3 *she's finally found her ideal mate*: **partner**, husband, wife, spouse, lover, live-in lover, amour, significant other, inamorato, inamorata, companion, helpmate, helpmeet, consort; informal POSSLQ (person of the opposite sex sharing living quarters), other half, better half, hubby, missus, missis, old man, old lady, old woman; Brit. informal dutch, trouble and strife.
4 *I can't find the mate to this sock*: **match**, fellow, twin, companion, pair, one of a pair, other half, equivalent, counterpart.
5 *a plumber's mate*: **assistant**, helper, apprentice, subordinate; collaborator, accomplice, aider and abetter; informal sidekick.
▸ verb **1** *pandas rarely mate in captivity*: **breed**, couple; formal copulate.
2 *the cow was mated with a Charolais bull*: **couple**, pair, join, bring together.
3 *people tend to* **mate with** *people from their own social class*: **marry**, get married to; wed, pair up, form a relationship; informal shack up.

material noun **1** *the decomposition of organic material*: **matter**, substance, stuff, medium.
2 *the materials for a new building*: **constituent**, raw material, element, component.
3 (**materials**) *cleaning materials*: **things**, items, articles, stuff, necessaries; Brit. informal gubbins.
4 *samples of curtain material*: **fabric**, cloth, stuff, textiles.
5 *she's collecting material for a magazine article*: **information**, data, facts, facts and figures, statistics, evidence, subject matter, ideas, details, particulars; background, notes, documentation, documents, papers; informal info, gen, dope, low-down, dirt.
▸ adjective **1** *the material rather than the spiritual world*: **physical**, corporeal, tangible, non-spiritual, mundane, worldly, earthly, temporal, concrete, real, solid, substantial, secular, lay; rare sublunary.
▷ANTONYMS spiritual, abstract.
2 *she was too fond of material pleasures*: **sensual**, carnal, materialistic, corporal, fleshly, physical, bodily.
▷ANTONYMS aesthetic, intellectual.
3 *the storms caused material damage to the crops*: **significant**, major, important, of consequence, consequential, momentous; weighty, vital, essential, key, meaningful.
▷ANTONYMS unimportant, insignificant, inconsequential.
4 *information that could be material to a murder inquiry*: **relevant**, applicable, pertinent, apposite, germane; apropos, to the point, to the purpose; Latin ad rem; rare appurtenant.
▷ANTONYMS immaterial, irrelevant.

materialistic adjective *a materialistic society that worships consumer goods*: **worldly**, consumerist, money-oriented, money-grubbing; capitalistic, bourgeois; acquisitive, greedy, grasping, avaricious, rapacious; informal, derogatory yuppie.
▷ANTONYMS spiritual, religious, intellectual; aesthetic.

materialize verb **1** *the forecast investment boom did not materialize*: **happen**, occur, come about, take place, come into being, transpire, arise, be realized, take shape; informal come off, shape up; archaic come to pass; rare eventuate.
2 *Harry suddenly materialized at the kitchen door*: **appear**, turn up, arrive, make/put in an appearance, present oneself/itself, come into view/sight, emerge, surface, loom, become visible, show oneself/itself, reveal oneself/itself, show one's face, come to light, pop up; informal show up, fetch up, pitch up, blow in.
▷ANTONYMS disappear.

materially adverb *this will materially affect our plans*: **significantly**, greatly, much, very much, to a great extent, considerably, substantially, a great deal, appreciably, markedly, seriously, gravely, essentially, fundamentally.
▷ANTONYMS negligibly.

maternal adjective **1** *the baby aroused her maternal instincts*: **motherly**, maternalistic; protective, caring, nurturing, loving, devoted, affectionate, fond, warm, tender, gentle, kind, kindly, comforting, compassionate.
2 *his maternal grandparents*: **on one's mother's side**, on the distaff side.
▷ANTONYMS paternal.

maternity noun **motherhood**, parenthood; motherliness.

mathematical adjective **1** **arithmetical**, arithmetic, numerical, statistical, algebraic, geometric, geometrical, trigonometric, trigonometrical, topological.
2 *he arranged everything with mathematical precision*: **rigorous**, meticulous, scrupulous, punctilious, scientific, strict, precise, exact, accurate, pinpoint, correct, careful, unerring.
▷ANTONYMS vague, imprecise.

mating noun *after mating, the female butterfly lays between 50 and 1000 eggs*: **copulation**, copulating, coupling, sexual intercourse, intercourse, sex, procreation; pairing, breeding, union; formal coitus, coition.
▸ adjective *a mating pair of mute swans*: **sexually active**, breeding.

matrimonial adjective *the matrimonial home*: **marital**, conjugal, connubial, married, wedded; shared, jointly owned; Law spousal.

matrimony noun formal *the sacrament of holy matrimony*: **marriage**, wedlock, union; bridal vows, nuptials.
▷ANTONYMS divorce.

matted adjective *his greasy, matted hair*: **tangled**, tangly, entangled, knotted, knotty, tousled, dishevelled, uncombed, unkempt, felted, ratty, greasy, dirty; black English natty.
▷ANTONYMS straight; neat.

matter noun **1** *decaying vegetable matter*: **material**, substance, stuff, medium.
2 *let's get to the heart of the matter*: **affair**, business, proceeding, situation, circumstance, event, happening, occurrence, incident, episode, occasion, experience, thing; **subject**, topic, issue, question, point, point at issue, item, case, concern, theme.
3 *it is of little matter now*: **importance**, consequence, significance, note, import, moment, weight, interest.
4 (**the matter**) *is anything the matter? | what's the matter?* **problem**, trouble, difficulty, upset, distress, worry, bother, complication.
5 *the matter of the sermon*: **content**, subject matter, text, argument, substance, thesis, sense, purport, gist, pith, essentials, burden.
6 *an infected wound full of matter*: **pus**, suppuration, purulence, discharge, secretion; rare sanies.
□ **as a matter of fact actually**, in actual fact, in fact, in point of fact, as it happens, really, believe it or not, in reality, in truth, to tell the truth, truly.
□ **no matter it doesn't matter**, it makes no difference/odds, it's unimportant, never mind, don't apologize, don't worry about it, don't mention it.
▸ verb **1** *it doesn't matter what you wear*: **make any difference**, make a difference, be important, be of importance, be of consequence, signify, be of significance, be relevant, be of account, carry weight, count; informal cut any ice.
2 *she was trying to make an impression on the people who mattered*: **be influential**, have influence, be important.

Word links **matter**
physics science of matter

matter-of-fact adjective **unemotional**, practical, down-to-earth, sensible, realistic, rational, sober, unsentimental, pragmatic, businesslike, commonsensical, level-headed, hard-headed, no-nonsense, factual, literal, straightforward, plain, unembellished, unvarnished, unadorned, prosaic, mundane, unimaginative, uncreative, deadpan, flat, dull, dry, pedestrian, lifeless, humdrum.
▷ANTONYMS airy-fairy.

mature adjective **1** *she is now a mature woman*: **adult**, grown-up, grown, fully grown, full-grown, of age, fully developed, fully fledged, in one's prime, in full bloom, nubile.
▷ANTONYMS immature, growing, adolescent.
2 *he's very mature for his age*: **sensible**, responsible, adult, level-headed, reliable, dependable; discriminating, shrewd, practical, wise, sagacious, experienced, sophisticated.
▷ANTONYMS immature, childish.
3 *mature Cheddar cheese*: **ripe**, ripened, mellow, ready, seasoned, full-flavoured.
▷ANTONYMS fresh, unripe.
4 *on mature reflection, he decided not to go*: **careful**, thorough, deep, considered, methodical.
▷ANTONYMS impulsive, unthinking.
▸ verb **1** *kittens mature when they are about a year old*: **be fully grown**, be

full-grown, be fully developed, develop fully, come of age, become adult, reach adulthood, reach maturity.
2 *he has matured since he left home*: **become more sensible/responsible/adult**, grow up; bloom, blossom.
3 *leave the cheese to mature*: **ripen**, grow ripe, become ripe, mellow, become mellow, age.
4 *their friendship did not have time to mature*: **develop**, grow, evolve, bloom, blossom, flourish, thrive, come to fruition.

maturity noun **1** *her progress from childhood to maturity*: **adulthood**, full growth, majority, coming-of-age, matureness, manhood/womanhood, puberty, pubescence.
▷ANTONYMS childhood, youth.
2 *he displayed a maturity beyond his years*: **sense of responsibility**, sense, level-headedness, responsibleness, matureness, wisdom, adultness; discrimination, shrewdness, practicality, sagacity, sensibleness, sophistication, experience.
▷ANTONYMS childishness.
3 *many fruits change colour when they reach maturity*: **ripeness**, matureness, mellowness.

maudlin adjective **1** *a bout of maudlin self-pity*: **sentimental**, over-sentimental, emotional, overemotional, tearful, lachrymose; informal weepy.
▷ANTONYMS austere, undemonstrative.
2 *a maudlin Irish ballad*: **mawkish**, sentimental, over-sentimental, cloying, sickly, saccharine, sugary, syrupy, sickening, nauseating, banal, trite; Brit. twee; informal mushy, slushy, sloppy, schmaltzy, weepy, cutesy, lovey-dovey, gooey, drippy, sloshy, soupy, treacly, cheesy, corny, icky, sick-making, toe-curling; Brit. informal soppy; N. Amer. informal cornball, sappy, hokey, three-hankie.
▷ANTONYMS understated, dry, prosaic.

maul verb **1** *he had been mauled by a lion*: **savage**, attack, tear to pieces, lacerate, claw, mutilate, mangle, scratch.
2 *she hated being mauled by men*: **molest**, feel, fondle; handle roughly, handle clumsily, manhandle; informal **grope**, paw, touch up, goose.
3 *his book was mauled by the critics*: **criticize**, denigrate, attack, censure, condemn, find fault with, give a bad press to, pillory, lambaste, flay, savage; informal knock, slam, pan, bash, take/pull to pieces, take apart, crucify, hammer, lay into, roast, skewer; Brit. informal slate, rubbish, slag off, monster; N. Amer. informal pummel, cut up; Austral./NZ informal bag; rare excoriate.

m

maunder verb **1** *he maundered on about his problems*: **ramble**, prattle, prate, blather, blether, blither, drivel, rattle, chatter, jabber, gabble, babble; Scottish & Irish slabber; informal gab, yak, yackety-yak, yabber, yatter; Brit. informal rabbit, witter, waffle, natter, chunter; archaic twaddle, clack.
2 *she maundered across the road*: **wander**, drift, meander, amble, dawdle, potter, straggle; Brit. informal mooch.
▷ANTONYMS march.

mausoleum noun **tomb**, sepulchre, crypt, vault, charnel house, burial chamber, catacomb, undercroft.

maverick noun *he was too much of a maverick to fit into any formal organization*: **individualist**, nonconformist, free spirit, unorthodox person, unconventional person, original, trendsetter, bohemian, eccentric, outsider; rebel, dissenter, dissident.
▷ANTONYMS conformist.

maw noun *a gigantic wolfhound with a fearful, gaping maw*: **mouth**, jaws, muzzle, throat, gullet; informal trap, chops, kisser; Brit. informal gob.

mawkish adjective *a long and mawkish poem*: **sentimental**, over-sentimental, overemotional, cloying, sickly, saccharine, sugary, syrupy, sickening, nauseating, maudlin, lachrymose, banal, trite; Brit. twee; informal mushy, slushy, sloppy, schmaltzy, weepy, cutesy, lovey-dovey, gooey, drippy, sloshy, soupy, treacly, cheesy, corny, icky, sick-making, toe-curling; Brit. informal soppy; N. Amer. informal cornball, sappy, hokey, three-hankie.
▷ANTONYMS cool, dry.

maxim noun *'You are what you eat' is a favourite maxim*: **saying**, adage, aphorism, proverb, motto, saw, axiom, dictum, precept, epigram; catchphrase, slogan, byword, watchword; truism, platitude, cliché; French bon mot; rare apophthegm.

maximum adjective *the vehicle's maximum speed*: **greatest**, highest, biggest, largest, top, topmost, most, utmost, supreme, maximal, paramount, extreme.
▷ANTONYMS minimum.
▶ noun *production levels are near their maximum*: **upper limit**, limit, utmost, uttermost, greatest, most, extreme, extremity, peak, height, ceiling, top, summit, pinnacle, crest, apex, vertex, apogee, acme, zenith.

maybe adverb **perhaps**, possibly, conceivably, it could be (that), it is possible (that), for all one knows; N. English happen; literary peradventure, perchance, mayhap, haply; rare percase.

mayhem noun *furious TV bosses watched stunned as the band created mayhem onstage*: **chaos**, disorder, confusion, havoc, bedlam, pandemonium, tumult, uproar, turmoil, madness, madhouse, hullabaloo, all hell broken loose, wild disarray, disorganization, maelstrom, trouble, disturbance, commotion, riot, anarchy, destruction, violence.

maze noun **1** *a maze in the castle grounds*: **labyrinth**, network of paths.
2 *a maze of corridors | a maze of petty regulations*: **complex network**, labyrinth, web, tangle, warren, mesh, jungle, snarl, imbroglio.

meadow noun **field**, pasture, paddock, water meadow, pastureland, grassland; literary lea, mead; Irish & Canadian bawn.

meagre adjective **1** *they were forced to supplement their meagre earnings*: **inadequate**, scanty, scant, paltry, limited, restricted, modest, insufficient, sparse, spare, deficient, negligible, insubstantial, skimpy, short, little, lean, small, slight, slender, poor, miserable, pitiful, puny, miserly, niggardly, beggarly; informal measly, stingy, pathetic, piddling; rare exiguous.
▷ANTONYMS abundant.
2 *a tall, meagre man*: **thin**, thin as a rake, lean, skinny, spare, scrawny, scraggy, gangling, gangly, spindly, stringy, lanky, reedy, bony, raw-boned, gaunt, underweight, emaciated, skeletal, starved, underfed, undernourished, attenuated, wraithlike, cadaverous, wasted, anorexic.
▷ANTONYMS fat.

Choose the right word **meagre, sparse, scanty**

All these words are used when there is less of something than there could or should be.

Meagre is generally used of necessities such as food, money, or something else which is provided or available for people. It suggests that there is not enough (*these men were unable to save out of their meagre earnings*) or that what there is is of poor quality (*prisoners queue for their meagre rations of thin soup*).

Sparse means 'thinly dispersed'—that is, small or few in relation to the area covered or the space to be filled (*a sparse and scattered population*) and therefore, by extension, 'in short supply' (*it was a sparse audience | for the first half of the nineteenth century the evidence is sparse*).

Scanty refers particularly to the smallness of the thing that is inadequate (*there are only scanty remains of any of the great palaces*) and is often used of skimpy or revealing clothing (*the ridiculously scanty nightdress threatened to fall off her shoulders altogether*).

meagreness noun **inadequacy**, scantiness, paucity, paltriness, dearth, limitedness, restrictedness, insufficiency, sparseness, spareness, scarcity, deficiency, slightness, skimpiness, leanness, poorness, poverty, pitifulness, miserliness, puniness, beggarliness; informal measliness, stinginess; rare exiguity.
▷ANTONYMS abundance.

meal noun **repast**, snack; something to eat; informal spread, blowout, bite, bite to eat, nosh, feed; Brit. informal nosh-up, tuck-in; N. Amer. informal **square**; Indian khana; formal collation, refection.

Word links **meal**

prandial relating to meals

mean[1] verb **1** *the flashing lights mean that the road is blocked*: **signify**, convey, denote, designate, indicate, connote, show, express, spell out, stand for, represent, symbolize, imply, purport, suggest, allude to, intimate, hint at, insinuate, drive at, refer to; informal get at; literary betoken.
2 *she didn't mean to break it*: **intend**, aim, plan, design, have in mind, have in view, contemplate, think of, purpose, propose, have plans, set out, aspire, desire, want, wish, expect.
3 *he was hit by a bullet meant for a soldier*: **destine**, predestine, fate, preordain, ordain; intend, design.
4 *the closures will mean a rise in unemployment*: **entail**, involve, necessitate, lead to, result in, give rise to, bring about, cause, engender, produce, effect.
5 *this means a lot to me*: **matter**, have importance, have significance, be important, be significant; have an input on.
6 *a red sky in the morning usually means rain*: **presage**, portend, foretell, augur, promise, foreshadow, herald, signal, bode; rare betoken, foretoken, forebode, adumbrate.

mean[2] adjective **1** *he's too mean to leave a tip*: **miserly**, niggardly, close-fisted, parsimonious, penny-pinching, cheese-paring, ungenerous, penurious, illiberal, close, grasping, greedy, avaricious, acquisitive, Scrooge-like; Austral./NZ & Scottish miserable; informal tight-fisted, stingy, tight, mingy, money-grubbing, skinflinty; N. Amer. informal cheap, grabby; Austral. informal hungry; Brit. vulgar slang tight-arse, tight-arsed, tight as a duck's arse; archaic near, niggard.
▷ANTONYMS generous, extravagant, munificent.
2 *why are you being so mean to me? | that was a mean trick*: **unkind**, **nasty**, spiteful, foul, malicious, malevolent, despicable, contemptible, obnoxious, vile, odious, loathsome, disagreeable, unpleasant, unfriendly, uncharitable, shabby, unfair, callous, cruel, vicious, base, low; informal horrible, horrid, hateful, rotten, low-down; Brit. informal beastly, bitchy, catty; vulgar slang shitty.
▷ANTONYMS kind.
3 *the truth was obvious to even the meanest intelligence*: **inferior**, poor, limited, restricted, meagre.
4 *her flat was mean and cold*: **squalid**, shabby, dilapidated, sordid, seedy,

slummy, sleazy, insalubrious, poor, sorry, wretched, dismal, dingy, miserable, mangy, broken-down, run down, down at heel; informal scruffy, scuzzy, crummy, grungy, ratty, tacky; Brit. informal grotty.
▷ANTONYMS luxurious, palatial.
5 *a man of mean birth*: **lowly**, humble, ordinary, low, low-born, lower-class, modest, common, base, proletarian, plebeian, obscure, undistinguished, ignoble; archaic baseborn.
▷ANTONYMS noble.
6 informal *he's a mean cook*. See **excellent**.

mean[3] **noun** *trying to find a mean between frankness and rudeness*: **middle course**, middle way, mid point, central point, middle, happy medium, golden mean, compromise, balance, median, norm, average.
▶ **adjective** *the mean temperature*: **average**, median, middle, halfway, centre, central, intermediate, medial, medium, normal, standard, middling.

meander **verb 1** *the river meandered gently through the meadow*: **zigzag**, wind, twist, turn, curve, curl, bend, snake.
2 *we meandered along the path*: **stroll**, saunter, amble, wander, roam, ramble, rove, drift, maunder, stray, straggle; Scottish & Irish stravaig; Irish streel; informal mosey, tootle; rare vagabond.
3 *she meandered on about the difficulties*: **ramble**, **prattle**, maunder, prate, blather, blether, blither, drivel, chatter, rattle, drift; Brit. informal witter, waffle, rabbit, natter.
▶ **noun 1** *the river flows in sweeping meanders*: **bend**, loop, curve, twist, turn, turning, coil, zigzag, oxbow, convolution; rare anfractuosity, flexuosity.
2 *a leisurely meander*: **wander**, ramble, stroll, saunter, amble; informal mosey, tootle.

meandering **adjective 1** *a meandering stream*: **winding**, windy, zigzag, zigzagging, twisting, turning, curving, serpentine, sinuous, snaking, snaky, twisty, tortuous; rare anfractuous, flexuous, meandrous.
▷ANTONYMS straight.
2 *meandering reminiscences*: **rambling**, circuitous, roundabout, digressive, discursive, indirect, diffuse, tortuous, convoluted; rare anfractuous.
▷ANTONYMS succinct.

Word toolkit **meandering**

See **serpentine**.

meaning **noun 1** *the poem has a hidden meaning* | *I didn't understand the meaning of his remark*: **significance**, sense, signification, import, thrust, drift, gist, implication, tenor, message, essence, substance, purport, intention.
2 *the word has several different meanings*: **definition**, sense, explanation, denotation, connotation, interpretation, elucidation, explication.
3 *my life has no meaning*: **value**, validity, worth, consequence, account, use, usefulness, significance, point.
4 *his smile was full of meaning*: **expressiveness**, significance, eloquence, implications, intimations, insinuations.
▶ **adjective** *she gave him a meaning look*: **meaningful**, significant, pointed, eloquent, expressive, pregnant, speaking, telltale, revealing, suggestive.
▷ANTONYMS vacant.

Word links **meaning**

semantic relating to meaning
semantics study of meaning

meaningful **adjective 1** *a meaningful remark*: **significant**, relevant, important, consequential, material, telling, pithy, weighty, valid, worthwhile, purposeful.
▷ANTONYMS inconsequential.
2 *a meaningful relationship*: **sincere**, deep, serious, in earnest, significant, important.
3 *a meaningful glance*: **expressive**, eloquent, pointed, significant, meaning; deep, pregnant, speaking, telltale, revealing, suggestive.
▷ANTONYMS meaningless.

meaningless **adjective 1** *a meaningless statement*: **unintelligible**, incomprehensible, incoherent, illogical, senseless, unmeaning, foolish, silly, absurd, fatuous, ridiculous, nonsensical, idle.
▷ANTONYMS meaningful.
2 *she felt her life was meaningless*: **futile**, pointless, aimless, empty, hollow, vain, purposeless, motiveless, valueless, useless, of no use, worthless, trivial, trifling, vacuous, unimportant, insignificant, inconsequential, insubstantial, nugatory, fruitless, profitless, barren, unproductive, unprofitable.
▷ANTONYMS worthwhile.

meanness **noun 1** *his careful attitude towards money bordered on meanness*: **miserliness**, niggardliness, close-fistedness, parsimony, parsimoniousness, penny-pinching, cheese-paring, penury, illiberality, greed, avarice, acquisitiveness; informal stinginess, tight-fistedness, tightness, minginess; N. Amer. cheapness; archaic nearness.
▷ANTONYMS generosity.
2 *the filth and meanness of the place*: **squalor**, squalidness, shabbiness, dilapidation, sordidness, seediness, sleaziness, insalubriousness, wretchedness, dismalness, dinginess, poverty; informal scruffiness, scuzziness, crumminess, grunginess, tackiness; Brit. informal grottiness.
3 *his meanness of temper*: **nastiness**, mean-spiritedness, spitefulness, disagreeableness, unpleasantness, unkindness.

means **plural noun 1** *the drugs were obtained by illegal means* | *modern means of communication such as television*: **method**, way, manner, mode, measure, fashion, process, procedure, technique, expedient, agency, medium, instrument, mechanism, channel, vehicle, avenue, course.
2 *she doesn't have the means to support herself*: **money**, resources, capital, income, finance, funds, cash, the wherewithal, assets; informal dough, bread, dibs, moolah, shekels, gelt, loot, oof, scratch, splosh; Brit. informal dosh, brass, lolly, spondulicks, wonga, ackers; N. Amer. informal dineros, jack, mazuma; Austral./NZ informal Oscar.
3 *a man of means*: **wealth**, riches, affluence, substance, fortune, property, money, capital.
□ **by all means of course**, certainly, definitely, surely, absolutely, naturally, with pleasure, assuredly; N. Amer. informal sure thing.
□ **by means of** *the load was raised by means of a crane*: **using**, utilizing, employing, through, with the help of, with the aid of, as a result of, by dint of, by way of, by virtue of, via.
□ **by no means** *the result is by no means certain*: **not at all**, in no way, not in the least, not in the slightest, not the least bit, not by a long shot, certainly not, absolutely not, definitely not, on no account, under no circumstances; Brit. not by a long chalk; informal no way.

meantime **adverb** See **meanwhile**.

meanwhile **adverb 1** *something will turn up—meanwhile we shall keep an eye on him*: **for now**, for the moment, for the present, for the time being, meantime, in the meantime, in the intervening period, in the interim, in the interval, in the meanwhile, the while, temporarily; Latin pro tem, ad interim; French en attendant.
2 *Moore's old club, meanwhile, are trying to persuade him to rejoin them*: **at the same time**, simultaneously, concurrently, the while.

measurable **adjective 1** *physically measurable aspects of human behaviour*: **quantifiable**, assessable, gaugeable, appraisable, computable, fathomable, resolvable.
2 *a measurable improvement*: **appreciable**, noticeable, significant, visible, tangible, perceptible, obvious, striking, material, moderate, reasonable.
▷ANTONYMS negligible.

m

measure **verb 1** *they measured the length and width of the room*: **take the measurements of**, calculate, compute, estimate, count, meter, quantify, weigh, size, evaluate, rate, assess, appraise, gauge, plumb, measure out, determine, judge, survey.
▷ANTONYMS guess, estimate.
2 *I had better measure my words*: **choose carefully**, select with care, consider, think carefully about, plan, calculate.
3 *she did not need to* ***measure*** *herself* ***against*** *some ideal*: **compare with**, contrast with, put into competition with; pit, set, match, test, judge.
□ **measure something off** *the assistant measured off the required length*: **mark off**, mark the boundaries/limits of, measure out, demarcate, delimit, delineate, outline, describe, define, stake out.
□ **measure something out** *measure out and mix the ingredients*: **pour out**, dole out, deal out; **dispense**, administer, issue.
□ **measure up** *he was sacked because he didn't measure up*: **come up to standard**, achieve the required standard, fulfil expectations, fit/fill the bill, pass muster, do well; be capable, be acceptable, be satisfactory, be adequate, be suitable; informal come up to scratch, make the grade, cut the mustard, be up to snuff.
▷ANTONYMS fall short.
□ **measure something up 1** *I must measure up the windows for some new curtains*: **survey**, quantify, take the measurements of, weigh, appraise, determine; estimate, count, meter. **2** *the two men shook hands and silently measured each other up*: **evaluate**, rate, assess, appraise, judge, adjudge, weigh up, size up, survey.
□ **measure up to** *we didn't measure up to the standards they set*: **achieve**, meet, come up to, equal, be equal to, match, rival, vie with, bear comparison with, be on a level with, serve, satisfy, fulfil, comply with.
▷ANTONYMS fall short of.
▶ **noun 1** *cost-cutting measures*: **action**, act, course, course of action, deed, proceeding, procedure, step, means, expedient; manoeuvre, initiative, programme, operation, control, legal action.
2 *the Senate passed the measure*: **statute**, act, bill, law, legislation.
3 *the original dimensions were in imperial measure, 15 inches on each side*: **system**, **standard**, units, scale.
4 *use a measure to check the size*: **ruler**, **tape measure**, rule, gauge, meter, scale, level, yardstick.
5 *a measure of egg white*: **portion**, **quantity**, amount, quota, ration, allowance, allocation.
6 *the states retain a measure of independence*: **certain amount**, amount, degree, quantity.
7 *sales are the measure of the company's success*: **yardstick**, test, standard,

norm, barometer, touchstone, litmus test, criterion, benchmark.
8 *poetic measure*: **metre**, cadence, rhythm, foot.
9 archaic *now tread we a measure*: **dance**, step, caper, hop.
□ **beyond measure** *it irritates him beyond measure that she is nearly always right*: **immensely**, extremely, vastly, greatly, excessively, immeasurably, incalculably, infinitely, limitlessly, boundlessly, inexhaustibly.
□ **for good measure** *she added a couple of chilli peppers for good measure*: **as a bonus**, as an extra, into the bargain, to boot, in addition, besides, as well.
□ **get/have the measure of** *she wants to get the measure of Kate before they meet at the Olympics*: **evaluate**, assess, gauge, judge, weigh up; understand, fathom, read, be wise to, not be deceived by, see through; informal have someone's number, not fall for, know someone's (little) game.
□ **take measures** *they took measures to improve performance*: **act**, take action, take steps, take measures, take the initiative, move, make a move, react, do something, proceed, go ahead.

measured adjective **1** *the measured tread of the warder in the corridor*: **regular**, steady, even, uniform, rhythmic, rhythmical, unfaltering, constant, sustained, slow, dignified, resolute, stately, sedate, leisurely, unhurried, firm, deliberate, ponderous.
▷ANTONYMS erratic.
2 *he began to speak in carefully measured tones*: **guarded**, studied, thoughtful, careful, carefully chosen, selected with care, well thought out, calculated, planned, considered, judicious, restrained, deliberate, reasoned.
▷ANTONYMS thoughtless, careless.

measureless adjective *Otto turned out to have measureless charm*: **boundless**, limitless, without limit, unlimited, unbounded, untold, immense, vast, great, endless, unending, never-ending, without end, inexhaustible, infinite, interminable, unceasing, everlasting, illimitable, immeasurable, incalculable.
▷ANTONYMS limited, restricted.

measurement noun **1** *measurement of the effect is difficult*: **quantification**, quantifying, computation, calculation, mensuration; estimation, evaluation, assessment, appraisal, gauging; weighing, sizing.
2 *all measurements are given in metric form*: **size**, dimension, proportions, magnitude, amplitude; mass, bulk, volume, capacity, extent, expanse; **value**, amount, quantity, area, length, height, depth, weight, width, range, acreage, footage, mileage, tonnage.

m

> *Word links* **measurement**
>
> **-metry** related suffix, as in *telemetry, calorimetry*
> **-metric** related suffix, as in *volumetric, geometric*
> **metrology** study of measurement

meat noun **1 flesh**, muscle.
2 *meat and drink*: **food**, nourishment, sustenance, provisions, rations, fare, foodstuff(s), nutriment, daily bread, feed; informal grub, eats, chow, nosh, scoff; formal comestibles, provender; archaic victuals, viands, commons; rare aliment.
3 *the meat of the matter*: **substance**, pith, marrow, heart, kernel, core, nucleus, nub; **essence**, essentials, point, gist, fundamentals, basics; informal nitty-gritty, nuts and bolts.

> *Word links* **meat**
>
> **carnivorous** meat-eating

meaty adjective **1** *a tall, meaty young man*: **beefy**, fleshy, brawny, burly, muscular, muscly, powerful, sturdy, rugged, husky, strapping, well built, solidly built, stout, thickset.
▷ANTONYMS weedy, feeble.
2 *the meaty character roles she'd love to play*: **full of interest**, interesting, three-dimensional, stimulating, giving food for thought; **substantial**, pithy, satisfying, meaningful, profound, deep, involved, significant.
▷ANTONYMS insubstantial, one-dimensional.

mechanic noun **technician**, **engineer**, artificer, repairman, serviceman, greaser; informal mech, grease monkey.

mechanical adjective **1** *the invention of the mechanical clock in the fourteenth century*: **mechanized**, machine-driven, automated, automatic, motor-driven, power-driven, self-propelled.
▷ANTONYMS manual.
2 *she stopped the mechanical brushing of her hair*: **automatic**, machine-like, unthinking, unemotional, unconscious, involuntary, instinctive, routine, matter-of-fact, habitual, inattentive; unfeeling, impersonal, inhuman, lifeless, soulless, uninspired, unanimated, casual; perfunctory, cursory, careless, unimaginative, negligent.
▷ANTONYMS conscious, emotional, careful.

mechanism noun **1** *an electrical mechanism for long-distance signalling*: **apparatus**, machine, appliance, tool, device, implement, utensil, instrument, contraption, contrivance, gadget, tackle, structure, system; informal gizmo.
2 *the train's safety mechanism had jammed*: **machinery**, workings, works, movement, motion, action, gear, gears, wheels, components, motor, engine, power source; informal innards, guts.
3 *a formal mechanism for citizens to lodge complaints*: **procedure**, process, system, operation, method, technique, workings, means, medium, agency, channel, channels, vehicle, structure.

mechanize verb *agriculture started to become mechanized*: **automate**, industrialize, motorize, computerize, equip with machines, tool.

medal noun *he won his first gold medal in 1998*: **honour**, **decoration**, ribbon, star, order, badge, pin, laurel, wreath, palm, colours, insignia, plaque, award, trophy; military slang fruit salad; Brit. informal gong.

meddle verb **1** *I don't want him meddling in our affairs*: **interfere**, butt in, intrude, intervene, interlope, pry, poke, nose, busybody, interpose, obtrude, thrust; informal stick one's nose in, horn in, muscle in, snoop, put/stick one's oar in, mess with; N. Amer. informal **kibitz**; archaic intermeddle.
▷ANTONYMS mind one's own business.
2 *you have no right to come in here **meddling with** my things*: **fiddle**, interfere, tamper, tinker, monkey; touch/handle without permission, finger; informal dick around; Brit. informal muck about/around.
▷ANTONYMS leave alone.

meddlesome adjective *a growing demand for more efficient and less meddlesome government*: **interfering**, meddling, intrusive, prying, inquisitive, officious, importunate; informal snooping, nosy; archaic pragmatic, intermeddling; rare obtrusive, busy.

mediate verb **1** *Austria tried to mediate between the belligerents*: **arbitrate**, conciliate, moderate, umpire, referee, act as peacemaker, reconcile differences, restore harmony, make peace, bring to terms, liaise; intervene, step in, intercede, act as an intermediary, interpose; archaic temporize.
2 *a tribunal was set up to mediate disputes*: **resolve**, settle, arbitrate in, umpire, reconcile, mend, clear up, patch up.
3 *he had attempted to mediate a solution to the conflict*: **negotiate**, bring about, effect, make happen; rare effectuate.
4 *the important ministry of mediating the power of the word*: **convey**, transmit, communicate, put across/over, impart, pass on, hand on, relate, reveal.

mediation noun *mediation between victims and offenders*: **conciliation**, arbitration, reconciliation, intervention, intercession, interposition, good offices; negotiation, shuttle diplomacy; archaic temporization.

mediator noun *a mediator in a dispute over teachers' pay*: **arbitrator**, arbiter, negotiator, conciliator, go-between, middleman, intermediary, moderator, intervenor, interceder, intercessor, reconciler, broker, honest broker, liaison officer, peacemaker, umpire, referee, adjudicator, judge.

medicinal adjective *medicinal herbs*: **curative**, healing, curing, remedial, therapeutic, restorative, corrective, health-giving; medical, healthy; rare sanative, analeptic, iatric.

medicine noun **1** *she poured out a dose of medicine for her mother*: **medication**, medicament, remedy, cure, nostrum, patent medicine, quack remedy, panacea, cure-all, placebo, drug, prescription, dose, treatment; archaic physic; rare medicinal.
2 *the remarkable achievements of modern medicine*: **medical science**, practice of medicine, healing, therapeutics, therapy, treatment, healing art.
□ **give someone a dose/taste of their own medicine get even (with)**, get back at, get, let someone see how it feels, have/get/take one's revenge (on), be revenged (on), revenge oneself (on), hit back (at); even the score (with), settle a/the score, settle accounts (with), get one's own back (on), give as good as one gets, play tit for tat (with), pay someone back, repay, reciprocate, retaliate (against), take reprisals (against), exact retribution (on); informal give someone their comeuppance.
□ **take one's medicine accept one's punishment**, take the consequences of one's actions; informal take the rap, take it on the chin.

> *Word links* **medicine**
>
> **pharmaceutical** relating to medicines
> **iatro-** related prefix, as in *iatrogenic, iatrochemistry*
> **pharmacist**, Brit. **chemist**, N. Amer. **druggist** seller of medicines
> **pharmacy**, Brit. **chemist's**, N. Amer. **drugstore** shop selling medicines

medieval adjective **1 of the Middle Ages**, Middle Age, of the Dark Ages, Dark-Age, 11th to 14th century, 6th to 14th century, Gothic, early.
▷ANTONYMS modern.
2 informal *the plumbing's a bit medieval, I'm afraid*. See **crude** (sense 2), **antiquated**.

mediocre adjective *the difference between a world record and a mediocre performance*: **ordinary**, common, commonplace, indifferent, average, middle-of-the-road, middling, medium, moderate, everyday, workaday, tolerable, passable, adequate, fair; **inferior**, second-rate, uninspired, undistinguished, unexceptional, unexciting, unremarkable, run-of-the-mill, not very good, pedestrian, prosaic, lacklustre, forgettable, amateur, amateurish; informal OK, so-so, bog-standard, fair-to-middling, (plain)

vanilla, nothing to write home about, no great shakes, not so hot, not up to much; NZ informal half-pie.
▷ANTONYMS exceptional, excellent.

mediocrity noun 1 *the mediocrity of her work*: **ordinariness**, commonplaceness, lack of inspiration, passableness, adequacy, indifference; **inferiority**, amateurism, amateurishness.
▷ANTONYMS excellence.
2 *a brilliant woman surrounded by mediocrities*: **nonentity**, nobody, nothing, lightweight, cipher, second-rater, amateur; informal no-hoper, non-starter.
▷ANTONYMS star.

meditate verb *he went off to* ***meditate on*** *the idea*: **contemplate**, think about, consider, ponder, cogitate, muse; revolve, weigh up; reflect, deliberate, chew over, ruminate, chew the cud, digest, turn over, pore over, brood, mull over; engage in contemplation, be in a thoughtful state, be in a brown study, be lost in thought, debate with oneself, puzzle, speculate; have in mind, intend, purpose, propose, plan, project, design, devise, scheme, plot; informal put on one's thinking cap; rare cerebrate.

meditation noun *cultivating the presence of God in meditation and prayer*: **contemplation**, thought, thinking, musing, pondering, consideration, reflection, prayer, deliberation, study, rumination, cogitation, brooding, mulling over, reverie, brown study, concentration, speculation; rare cerebration.

meditative adjective *yogic meditative techniques*: **contemplative**, prayerful, reflective, musing, pensive, cogitative, thinking, thoughtful, studious, rapt, introspective, brooding, philosophical, ruminative, deliberative, ruminant, speculative, wistful; rare lucubratory.

medium noun 1 *television is the most powerful medium available*: **means of communication**, means/mode of expression, means, method, way, form, agency, channel, forum; avenue, approach, vehicle; voice, organ, instrument, implement, mechanism, apparatus, instrumentality.
2 *these organisms were growing in their natural medium*: **habitat**, element, environment, surroundings, milieu, setting, conditions, circumstances, ambience, atmosphere.
3 *two mediums told me they could see bags of money over my head*: **spiritualist**, clairvoyant, mind-reader, fortune teller, seer, necromancer; rare spiritist.
4 *a happy medium between what is too easy and what is too difficult*: **middle way**, middle course, middle ground, middle, mean, median, mid point, central point, centre, average, norm, standard; **compromise**, balance, happy medium, golden mean.
▷ANTONYMS extreme.
▸ adjective *he is of medium height*: **average**, middling, medium-sized, middle-sized, moderate, fair, normal, standard, usual.
▷ANTONYMS extreme.

medley noun *a medley of Beatles songs*: **assortment**, miscellany, mixture, melange, blend, variety, mixed bag, mix, diversity, collection, selection, assemblage, combination, motley collection, pot-pourri, conglomeration, jumble, mess, confusion, mishmash, hotchpotch, hodgepodge, ragbag, pastiche, patchwork, farrago, hash; informal scissors-and-paste job, mash-up; rare gallimaufry, omnium gatherum, olio, salmagundi, macédoine.

meek adjective 1 *they used to call her Miss Mouse because she was so meek and mild*: **patient**, long-suffering, forbearing, resigned; **gentle**, quiet, shy, retiring, reverent, peaceful, peaceable, docile, lamblike, mild, demure, modest, humble, lowly, diffident, unassuming, self-effacing, unpretentious, unambitious, unobtrusive.
▷ANTONYMS impatient, assertive.
2 *the meek compliance of our politicians*: **submissive**, yielding, unresisting, obedient, compliant, tame, biddable, tractable, acquiescent, deferential, weak, timid, frightened, spineless, spiritless, unprotesting, like a lamb to the slaughter; informal weak-kneed, wimpish.
▷ANTONYMS assertive, overbearing.

Word toolkit **meek**

See **humble**.

meekness noun *her meekness covers up a precocious intelligence and strength*: **patience**, long-suffering, forbearance, resignation; **gentleness**, mildness, softness, peacefulness, docility, diffidence, modesty, humility, humbleness, unpretentiousness, lowliness; **submissiveness**, submission, self-effacement, self-abasement, lack of resistance, compliance, obedience, acquiescence, tameness, deference; archaic mansuetude.

meet verb 1 *I met an old friend on the train*: **encounter**, meet up with, come face to face with, make contact with, run into/across, come across/upon, chance on, happen on, light on, stumble across/on; informal bump into.
▷ANTONYMS avoid.
2 *she first met Paul at a party*: **get to know**, be introduced to, make the acquaintance of.
3 *the committee will meet on Saturday*: **gather**, assemble, come together, get together, congregate, convene, muster, rally; rare foregather.
▷ANTONYMS disperse.
4 *the curtains don't quite meet*: **come together**, converge, connect, touch, link up, reach, abut, butt, adjoin, join, unite, intersect, cross.
▷ANTONYMS separate.
5 *he met death bravely*: **face**, encounter, undergo, experience, go through, bear, suffer, endure.
6 *the announcement was met with widespread hostility*: **greet**, receive, answer, deal with, handle, treat, face, cope with, approach.
7 *he just does not meet the requirements of the job*: **fulfil**, satisfy, fill, measure up to, match (up to), conform to, come up to, perform, comply with, answer.
8 *shipowners would meet the cost of oil spills*: **pay**, settle, clear, honour, liquidate, satisfy, discharge, pay off, square, account for.
□ **meet someone halfway** See **halfway**.
▸ noun *an international meet in Wales*: **event**, tournament, game, match, contest, competition; bout, fight, encounter, engagement; hunt; gathering, convention, conclave, rally, congress, convocation, muster, quiz.

meeting noun 1 *he stood up to address the meeting*: **gathering**, assembly, conference, congregation, convention, summit, forum, convocation, conclave, council of war; N. Amer. caucus; informal get-together; N. Amer. informal confab.
2 *she demanded a meeting with the housing minister*: **consultation**, audience, interview.
3 *he intrigued her on their first meeting*: **encounter**, contact, introduction, appointment, assignation, rendezvous, tryst.
4 *the meeting of land and sea*: **convergence**, coming together, confluence, conjunction, union, junction, abutment, concourse, intersection, T-junction, crossing.
5 *an athletics meeting*: **event**, meet, rally, competition, match, game, contest.

megalomania noun *demanding changes in the script was an example of the stars' megalomania*: **delusions of grandeur**, obsessionalism, grandiosity, grandioseness; self-importance, egotism, conceit, conceitedness; French folie de grandeur.
▷ANTONYMS modesty, humility.

melancholy adjective *Mozart's exquisitely melancholy clarinet concerto | a tall, bony old man with a long melancholy face*: **sad**, sorrowful, desolate, melancholic, mournful, lugubrious, gloomy, pensive; despondent, dejected, depressed, depressing, down, downhearted, downcast, disconsolate, glum, sunk in gloom, miserable, wretched, dismal, dispirited, discouraged, low, in low spirits, in the doldrums, blue, morose, funereal, woeful, woebegone, doleful, wistful, unhappy, joyless, heavy-hearted, low-spirited, sombre, defeatist, pessimistic; informal down in the dumps, down in the mouth, morbid.
▷ANTONYMS cheerful, happy.
▸ noun *a feeling of melancholy descended on him*: **desolation**, sadness, pensiveness, woe, sorrow, melancholia; unhappiness, dejection, depression, gloom, gloominess, misery, low spirits, moroseness, doldrums, defeatism, pessimism, dejectedness, dispiritedness, despondency; informal the dumps, the blues.
▷ANTONYMS cheerfulness, happiness.

Word toolkit

melancholy	forlorn	miserable
music	hope	life
thoughts	attempt	failure
eyes	cry	existence
lament	lover	experience
tale	victim	conditions

melange noun *the population is a melange of different cultures*: **mixture**, medley, blend, variety, mixed bag, mix, miscellany, diversity, collection, selection, assortment, assemblage, combination, motley collection, pot-pourri, conglomeration, jumble, mess, confusion, mishmash, hotchpotch, hodgepodge, ragbag, pastiche, patchwork, farrago, hash; informal scissors-and-paste job, mash-up; rare gallimaufry, omnium gatherum, olio, salmagundi, macédoine.

melee, mêlée noun *a number of people were trampled to death during the subsequent melee*: **tumult**, disturbance, rumpus, commotion, disorder; **brawl**, fracas, fight, affray, fray, scuffle, breach of the peace, struggle, skirmish, free-for-all, tussle, quarrel; Irish, N. Amer., & Austral. donnybrook; W. Indian bangarang; informal scrap, set-to, ruction, shindy, shindig, punch-up, dust-up; Scottish informal rammy; N. Amer. informal rough house; archaic broil, bagarre.

mellifluous adjective *his low, mellifluous voice was instantly recognizable*: **sweet-sounding**, sweet-toned, dulcet, honeyed, mellow, soft, liquid, soothing, rich, smooth, euphonious, lyric, harmonious, tuneful, musical; rare mellifluent.
▷ANTONYMS cacophonous.

mellow adjective 1 *the splendid mellow brickwork of the Tudor gatehouse*: **seasoned**, conditioned, mature, aged, old; rich in texture, warm.

m

▷ANTONYMS fresh.
2 *the mellow tone of his voice*: **dulcet**, sweet-sounding, tuneful, euphonious, lyric, melodious, mellifluous; fruity, smooth, warm, full, rich, well rounded; rare mellifluent.
▷ANTONYMS harsh.
3 *mellow apples*: **ripe**, mature, soft, lush, juicy, tender, luscious, sweet, full-flavoured, flavoursome.
▷ANTONYMS green, unripe.
4 *I believe you are growing mellow with age*: **easy-going**, tolerant, amicable, amiable, warm-hearted, warm, sympathetic, good-natured, affable, gracious, gentle, pleasant, kindly, kind-hearted.
5 *he was in a mellow mood*: **genial**, jovial, jolly, cheerful, happy, merry.
▷ANTONYMS nasty, irritable.
6 *he was feeling mellow after two glasses of wine*: **tipsy**, slightly drunk, full of well-being; informal happy, merry; Brit. informal tiddly, squiffy.
▶verb 1 *eight years had done nothing to mellow him*: **relax**, calm, settle, mature, improve; soften, sweeten.
2 *age has mellowed the buildings*: **condition**, season, age, improve.

melodious adjective *a quiet melodious voice*: **harmonious**, tuneful, melodic, musical, dulcet, round, sweet-sounding, sweet-toned, silvery, silvery-toned, euphonious, mellifluous, lyrical, soothing; informal easy on the ear; rare mellifluent.
▷ANTONYMS discordant, grating.

melodramatic adjective *he flung the door open with a melodramatic flourish*: **exaggerated**, histrionic, extravagant, overdramatic, overdone, over-sensational, sensationalized, overemotional, sentimental; theatrical, stagy, actressy; informal hammy.
▷ANTONYMS calm, stoical.

melody noun 1 *he's playing the melody from that new film*: **tune**, music, air, strain, theme, subject, line, part, song, refrain, jingle, piece.
2 *his unique gift for melody*: **musicality**, musicalness, melodiousness, tunefulness, lyricism, sweetness, euphony.

melt verb 1 *the snow was beginning to melt | how long does the cheese take to melt?* **liquefy**, thaw, unfreeze, defrost, soften, run, flux, fuse, render, clarify, dissolve, deliquesce.
2 *her charm melted the old lady's heart*: **soften**, touch, disarm, mollify, relax, affect, move.
3 *the crowd melted away | the figure melted into thin air*: **vanish**, vanish into thin air, disappear, fade away; dissipate, disperse, go away, peter out, pass, dissolve, evaporate, evanesce.

m

member noun 1 *a member of the club*: **subscriber**, associate, representative, attender, insider, fellow, comrade, adherent, life member, founder member, card-carrying member; supporter, follower, upholder, advocate, disciple, sectary.
2 *a member of a mathematical set*: **constituent**, element, component, part, portion, piece, unit, factor, feature, attribute.

membership noun 1 *he recently resigned his membership of the Academy*: **belonging**, associateship; community, integration, clanship; shirt, cap, cloth, seat, whip.
2 *less than half the membership bothered to vote*: **members**, subscribers, associates, representatives, attenders, fellows, comrades, followers; fold, congregation, electorate, party, body.

membrane noun **layer**, laminate, sheet, skin, film, veil, diaphragm, partition, drum, tissue, pellicle, integument, overlay, covering, coat; peritoneum, amnion, caul, hymen.

memento noun **souvenir**, keepsake, reminder, remembrance, token, memorial; testimonial, trophy, relic, vestige; archaic memorandum.

memoir noun 1 *her touching memoir of a London childhood in the 1870s*: **account**, historical account, history, record, chronicle, annal(s), commentary, narrative, story, report, portrayal, depiction, sketch, portrait, life, life story, profile, biography.
2 (**memoirs**) *he published his memoirs in 1955*: **autobiography**, life story, life, memories, recollections, personal recollections, reminiscences, experiences, journal, diary, log, weblog, blog, moblog.

memorable adjective **unforgettable**, catchy, haunting, indelible, not/never to be forgotten, signal, special; momentous, significant, historic, notable, noteworthy, important, consequential, remarkable, outstanding, extraordinary, striking, vivid, arresting, impressive, distinctive, distinguished, famous, celebrated, renowned, notorious, illustrious, glorious; immortal, undying, everlasting, eternal, unfading, perpetual, imperishable, timeless; brilliant, supreme, superlative, dazzling, exciting, thrilling, enthralling, wonderful, marvellous; informal out of this world.
▷ANTONYMS forgettable, run-of-the-mill, commonplace.

memorandum noun 1 *the two countries signed a memorandum of understanding*: **record**, minute, note, contract, agreement; aide-memoire, reminder, memory jogger, jotting, chit; N. Amer. informal tickler.
2 *a memorandum from the managing director to all staff*: **message**, communication, note, email, letter, epistle, missive; informal memo.

memorial noun 1 *meet me at the war memorial*: **monument**, shrine, mausoleum, cenotaph; statue, plaque, brass, cairn; tombstone, gravestone, headstone, trophy.
2 *a National Land Fund was established as a memorial to those who lost their lives*: **tribute**, testimonial, remembrance, memento, souvenir.
▶adjective *a memorial service*: **commemorative**, remembrance, celebratory, commemorating, monumental.

memorize verb *Paula listened, memorizing every detail*: **commit to memory**, remember, retain, learn by heart, get by heart, learn off, learn, learn by rote, impress on the memory, study, become word-perfect in, get off pat; archaic con.

memory noun 1 *she is losing her memory*: **ability to remember**, powers of recall, recall, powers of retention, retention, mind.
▷ANTONYMS forgetfulness.
2 *my memory of the events is faint*: **recollection**, remembrance, reminiscence, evocation, reminder, souvenir, echo, impression.
3 *the town built a statue in memory of him*: **commemoration**, remembrance, honour, tribute, recognition, observance, respect.
4 *a computer's memory*: **memory bank**, store, cache, disk, RAM, ROM.

> *Word links* **memory**
>
> **mnemonic** relating to memory

menace noun 1 *an atmosphere full of menace*: **threat**, ominousness, intimidation, warning, ill-omen; rare commination.
2 *it's a menace to British society*: **danger**, peril, risk, hazard, threat; jeopardy, source of apprehension/dread/fright/fear/terror.
3 *the child next door is a menace*: **nuisance**, pest, source of annoyance, annoyance, plague, torment, troublemaker, mischief-maker, a thorn in someone's side/flesh.
▶verb 1 *serious bush fires menaced the suburbs of Sydney*: **threaten**, be a danger to, put at risk, jeopardize, imperil, loom over.
2 *she menaced me with a fire extinguisher*: **bully**, intimidate, issue threats to, threaten, frighten, scare, alarm, terrify; browbeat, cow, terrorize.

> *Choose the right word* **menace, threaten, intimidate**
>
> See **threaten**.

menacing adjective 1 *she shot him a menacing look*: **threatening**, ominous, black, thunderous, glowering, brooding, sinister, intimidating, frightening, terrifying, fearsome, alarming, forbidding, baleful, warning; rare minatory, minacious.
2 *a menacing storm*: **looming**, louring, in the wind, impending, brewing, black, dark, heavy, portentous, ugly, imminent; rare bodeful.
▷ANTONYMS friendly, auspicious.

mend verb 1 *workmen were mending faulty cabling*: **repair**, fix, put back together, piece together, patch up, restore, sew (up), stitch, darn, patch, cobble, botch, vamp (up); rehabilitate, renew, renovate, redevelop, overhaul, recondition, rebuild, refurbish; make whole, make well, cure, heal; N. English **fettle**, **spetch**; Scottish & N. English **ranter**; archaic **clout**, tinker, beet.
▷ANTONYMS break, tear.
2 *'How's Walter?' 'He'll mend.' | foot injuries can take months to mend*: **get better**, get well, recover, be on the road to recovery, pull through, recuperate, convalesce, improve, be well, be cured, be all right, heal, knit, draw together.
▷ANTONYMS worsen.
3 *quarrels could be mended by talking*: **put/set right**, set straight, make up, straighten out, sort out, put in order, rectify, remedy, right, redress, resolve, square, settle, put to rights, correct, amend, emend, retrieve, improve, make better, better, make good, ameliorate, reform.
▷ANTONYMS make worse.
4 *he mended the fire*: **stoke (up)**, make up, charge, fuel.
▶noun
□ **on the mend** *it was tough for a while, but I'm on the mend*: **recovering**, convalescent, on the road to recovery, making progress, progressing, improving.

mendacious adjective *mendacious propaganda*: **lying**, untruthful, dishonest, deceitful, false, dissembling, insincere, disingenuous, hypocritical, fraudulent, double-dealing, two-faced, two-timing, duplicitous, perjured, perfidious; untrue, fictitious, falsified, fabricated, fallacious, invented, made up, hollow; humorous economical with the truth, terminologically inexact; rare unveracious.
▷ANTONYMS truthful.

mendacity noun **lying**, untruthfulness, dishonesty, deceit, deceitfulness, deception, dissembling, insincerity, disingenuousness, hypocrisy, fraud, fraudulence, double-dealing, two-timing, duplicity, perjury, perfidy; untruth, fictitiousness, falsity, falsehood, falseness, fallaciousness, hollowness; informal kidology; Irish informal codology; humorous economy with the truth, terminological inexactitude; rare unveracity.

mendicant noun **beggar**, beggarman, beggarwoman, tramp, vagrant, vagabond, cadger; informal scrounger, sponger; N. Amer. **hobo**; N. Amer. informal

schnorrer, mooch, moocher, bum; rare clochard.
▶ **adjective begging**, cadging; informal scrounging, sponging; N. Amer. informal mooching.

menial adjective *he took a menial job in a factory*: **unskilled**, lowly, humble, low-grade, low-status, routine, humdrum, boring, dull; degrading, mean, inferior, unworthy; N. Amer. blue-collar.
▷ANTONYMS noble, elevated, skilled.
▶ noun *they were treated like menials*: **servant**, domestic servant, domestic, drudge, maid of all work; wage slave, labourer, minion, junior, slave, underling, subordinate, inferior, hireling, vassal, serf, lackey, flunkey, factotum, stooge; hewers of wood and drawers of water; informal dogsbody, skivvy; N. Amer. informal peon, gofer; archaic scullion, servitor.
▷ANTONYMS master.

menstruation noun **period**, menstrual cycle; informal the curse, monthlies, one's/the time of the month, being on the rag; technical **menses**, menarche, show, menorrhoea; archaic time; rare catamenia, flowers.

mensuration noun *for many artisans mensuration was a more necessary skill than writing*: **measurement**, measuring, calculation, computation, estimating, quantification, quantifying, weighing, sizing; evaluation, assessment, appraisal, gauging.

mental adjective **1** *the limits of his mental ability are clear*: **intellectual**, cerebral, brain, rational, psychological, cognitive, abstract, conceptual, theoretical; rare mindly, phrenic.
▷ANTONYMS physical.
2 *mental illness*: **psychiatric**, psychogenic.
3 informal *he's completely mental*. See **mad**.

Word links **mental**

psychometrics measurement of mental capacity

mentality noun **1** *I simply can't understand the mentality of these people*: **way of thinking**, cast of mind, frame of mind, turn of mind, way someone's mind works, mind, mind set, psychology, mental attitude; **outlook**, personality, persona, psyche, disposition, make-up, temperament, temper.
2 *machines can possess mentality*: **intellect**, intellectual capabilities, intelligence, intelligence quotient, IQ, brainpower, brain, brains, mind, comprehension, understanding, wit, wits, reasoning, rationality, powers of reasoning, wisdom, sense, perception, imagination; informal grey matter; Brit. informal loaf; rare ratiocination.

mentally adverb *mentally, I was prepared to deal with the situation*: **in the/one's mind**, in the/one's brain, in the/one's head, inwardly, intellectually, cerebrally, cognitively, psychologically, psychically.
▷ANTONYMS emotionally, spiritually.

mention verb **1** *don't mention the war*: **allude to**, refer to, touch on/upon, speak briefly of, hint at; bring up, raise, broach, introduce, moot.
2 *Nigel mentioned that his father had been a teacher*: **state**, say, let someone/anyone know, declare, disclose, divulge, let out, reveal, intimate, indicate; put forward, advance, present, propound; **tell**, speak about/of, utter, communicate, breathe a word of; informal let on about.
3 *I'll gladly mention your work to my friends*: **recommend**, commend, endorse, advertise, put in a good word for, speak well of; informal puff, hype (up), plug.
□ **don't mention it don't apologize**, it doesn't matter, it makes no difference/odds, it is unimportant, that's all right, never mind, don't worry.
□ **not to mention** *lives may be lost, not to mention the ship*: **in addition to**, as well as; not counting, not including, to say nothing of, aside from, besides.
▶ noun **1** *he made no mention of your request*: **reference to**, allusion to, comment on, remark about; statement, announcement, indication.
2 *a mention in dispatches*: **tribute**, citation, acknowledgement, recognition, honourable mention.
3 *my book got a mention on the show*: **recommendation**, commendation, endorsement, a good word.

mentor noun **1** *one of the prime minister's early political mentors*: **adviser**, guide, confidant, confidante, counsellor, consultant, therapist; master, spiritual leader, rav, rebbe, guru, swami, maharishi, acharya.
2 *regular meetings between mentor and trainee*: **trainer**, teacher, tutor, coach, instructor.

menu noun **bill of fare**, tariff, card; carte du jour, set menu, table d'hôte, specials board; wine list.

mephitic adjective literary *the mephitic, sulphurous stench of the crater*. See **smelly**.

mercantile adjective **1** *the mercantile community of Bordeaux*: **commercial**, trade, trading, business, merchant, sales.
2 *the metaphysical poets expressed discontentment with the mercantile age they lived in*: **profit-oriented**, money-oriented, profit-making, for-profit, mercenary, capitalistic; worldly, greedy, materialistic.
▷ANTONYMS idealistic, unworldly.

mercenary adjective **1** *research suggests that buyers are unashamedly mercenary*: **money-oriented**, grasping, greedy, acquisitive, avaricious, covetous, rapacious, bribable, venal, materialistic; informal money-grubbing.
▷ANTONYMS altruistic, philanthropic.
2 *mercenary soldiers*: **hired**, paid, bought, professional, venal, hireling; historical freelance.
▶ noun *a force of two thousand mercenaries*: **soldier of fortune**, professional soldier, hired soldier, hireling; private army; informal merc, hired gun; historical freelance, condottiere; archaic adventurer, lance-knight.
▷ANTONYMS volunteer; conscript.

merchandise noun *retailers were looking for new merchandise to attract people into their stores*: **goods**, wares, stock, commodities, lines, produce, product; rare vendibles.
▶ verb *such items should be merchandised to form a distinct section of your shop*: **promote**, market, sell, retail, distribute; advertise, publicize, push; informal hype (up), plug, puff, give a puff to.

merchant noun *a wine merchant*: **trader**, dealer, trafficker, wholesaler, broker, agent, seller, buyer, buyer and seller, salesman/saleswoman/salesperson, vendor, retailer, shopkeeper, tradesman, distributor, representative, commercial traveller, marketer, marketeer; magnate, mogul, baron; dated pedlar, hawker.

Word links **merchant**

mercantile, **commercial** relating to merchants

merchantable adjective *the goods must be of merchantable quality*: **saleable**, sellable, marketable, merchandisable; rare vendible.

merciful adjective **1** *she pleads for Titus to be merciful and spare her son*: **forgiving**, compassionate, gracious, lenient, clement, pitying, forbearing, humane, mild, soft-hearted, tender-hearted, kind, kindly, sympathetic; patient, humanitarian, liberal, easy-going, permissive, tolerant, indulgent, generous, magnanimous, beneficent, benign, benignant, benevolent.
▷ANTONYMS merciless, cruel.
2 *her death came as a merciful release*: **welcome**, blessed, acceptable.
□ **be merciful to show mercy to**, have mercy on, have pity on, spare, pardon, forgive, let off, be lenient on/to, deal leniently with; informal go/be easy on.

mercifully adverb *mercifully, the event passed off without incident*: **luckily**, fortunately, happily, thank goodness/God/heavens.

m

merciless adjective *Mithra was merciless to his enemies*: **ruthless**, remorseless, pitiless, unmerciful, unforgiving, uncharitable, unsparing, unpitying, implacable, inexorable, relentless, inflexible, barbarous, inhumane, inhuman, cold-blooded, hard-hearted, stony-hearted, heartless, harsh, callous, cruel, brutal, cut-throat, unsympathetic, unfeeling, illiberal, intolerant, rigid, severe, stern.
▷ANTONYMS merciful, compassionate.

mercurial adjective *a mercurial temperament*: **volatile**, capricious, temperamental, excitable, fickle, changeable, unpredictable, variable, protean, mutable, erratic, quicksilver, inconstant, inconsistent, unstable, unsteady, fluctuating, ever-changing, kaleidoscopic, fluid, wavering, vacillating, moody, flighty, wayward, whimsical, giddy, impulsive; technical labile.
▷ANTONYMS stable, steady, constant.

Word toolkit **mercurial**

See **variable**.

mercy noun **1** *the boy was begging for mercy*: **leniency**, lenience, clemency, compassion, grace, pity, charity, forgiveness, forbearance, quarter, humanity, humaneness, humanitarianism; mildness, soft-heartedness, tender-heartedness, kindness, sympathy, liberality, indulgence, tolerance, generosity, magnanimity, beneficence.
▷ANTONYMS ruthlessness, cruelty, inhumanity.
2 *we must be thankful for small mercies*: **blessing**, godsend, boon, favour, piece/stroke of luck.
□ **at the mercy of 1** *they found themselves at the mercy of the tyrant*: **in the power of**, under/in the control of, in the clutches of, in the palm of someone's hand, under the heel of, subject to. **2** *men who lived and died at the mercy of the violent and unpredictable Australian climate*: **defenceless against**, unprotected against, vulnerable to, threatened by, exposed to, susceptible to, prey to, (wide) open to, an easy target for.

mere adjective **1** *it costs a mere £29.95*: **trifling**, meagre, bare, trivial, paltry, basic, scant, scanty, skimpy, minimal, slender; no more than, just, only.
2 *I was a mere boy at the time*: **no more than**, nothing more than, no better than, no more important than, just, only, merely; unimportant, insignificant, inconsequential.

merely adverb *they were merely exercising their rights*: **only**, purely, solely, simply, entirely, just, but.

meretricious adjective *the meretricious glitter of the whole charade*: **flashy**, pretentious, gaudy, tawdry, trashy, garish, chintzy, Brummagem, loud, tinselly, cheap, tasteless, kitschy; false, artificial, fake, faked, fraudulent, imitation, bogus, spurious, sham, specious, plastic; informal tacky.

> *Easily confused words* **meretricious or meritorious?**
>
> Similar in form, these words are opposite in meaning. **Meretricious** is used of something with a superficial attractiveness that conceals its essential worthlessness (*the artist had been content to churn out meretricious souvenirs for tourists*). **Meritorious**, on the other hand, means 'deserving reward, worthy' (*he received a medal for meritorious conduct*).

merge verb **1** *it needed to merge with another investment bank if it was to survive*: **join (together)**, join forces, amalgamate, consolidate, integrate, unite, unify, combine, incorporate, affiliate, coalesce, meld, agglutinate, team up, link (up), band (together), ally, league, federate.
▷ANTONYMS separate, split.
2 *a decision was taken to merge the two organizations*: **amalgamate**, bring together, join, consolidate, conflate, unite, combine, incorporate, coalesce, meld, pool, link (up), knit, yoke.
3 *the two colours merged*: **mingle**, blend, fuse, run/melt/fade into one another, mix, intermix, intermingle, commingle, converge, integrate, coalesce, compound, homogenize, emulsify, lump (together), mass, conglomerate.

merger noun *a merger between an aerospace company and a car company*: **amalgamation**, combination, merging, union, fusion, coalition, affiliation, coupling, unification, incorporation, coalescence, consolidation, confederation, hook-up, link-up; alliance, association, connection; informal mash-up.
▷ANTONYMS split, break-up.

merit noun **1** *composers of outstanding merit*: **excellence**, goodness, standard, quality, level, grade, high quality, calibre, worth, good, credit, eminence, worthiness, value, virtue, distinction, account, deservingness, meritoriousness.
▷ANTONYMS inferiority.
2 *the merits of the scheme*: **good point**, strong point, advantage, benefit, value, profit, asset, plus, advisability; advantageousness.
▷ANTONYMS fault, disadvantage.
▶ verb *the accusation did not merit a response*: **deserve**, earn, be deserving of, warrant, rate, justify, be worthy of, be worth, be entitled to, have a right to, have a claim to/on, be qualified for.

m

> *Choose the right word* **merit, deserve, earn**
>
> See **earn**.

meritorious adjective *the captain was awarded a medal for meritorious conduct*: **praiseworthy**, laudable, commendable, admirable, estimable, creditable, worthy, worthwhile, deserving, excellent, exemplary, good.
▷ANTONYMS worthless, discreditable.

> *Easily confused words* **meritorious or meretricious?**
>
> See **meretricious**.

merriment noun *her eyes were dancing with merriment*: **high spirits**, high-spiritedness, exuberance; **cheerfulness**, gaiety, fun, effervescence, euphoria, exhilaration, elation, verve, buoyancy, carefreeness, blitheness, levity, zest, sportiveness, liveliness, cheer, joy, joyfulness, joyousness, jolliness, jollity, happiness, gladness, exultation, rejoicing, jocundity, jocularity, conviviality, festivity, merrymaking, revelry, mirth, mirthfulness, glee, gleefulness, laughter, hilarity, light-heartedness, amusement, pleasure; informal larking about.
▷ANTONYMS doom and gloom, misery.

merry adjective **1** *the narrow streets were dense with merry throngs of students*: **cheerful**, cheery, in good spirits, high-spirited, blithe, bright, sunny, light-hearted, buoyant, bubbly, lively, carefree, without a care in the world, joyful, joyous, rejoicing, jolly, jocund, convivial, festive, mirthful, gleeful, happy, glad, laughing; informal chirpy; dated gay; archaic frolicsome, sportive, blithesome.
▷ANTONYMS miserable, sad, gloomy.
2 *after three beers he began to feel quite merry*: **tipsy**, mellow, slightly drunk; Brit. informal tiddly, squiffy.
□ **make merry have fun**, have a good time, enjoy oneself, have a party, party, celebrate, carouse, feast, {eat, drink, and be merry}, revel, roister, rejoice, go on a spree; informal have a ball, make whoopee; dated spree.

merry-go-round noun **carousel**; Brit. roundabout; archaic whirligig.

mesh noun **1** *the wire mesh of a chicken run*: **netting**, net, network, tracery, reticulation; web, webbing, lattice, latticework, lacework, openwork, tatting, filigree, trellis, screen, plexus, tangle, mat.
2 *he was caught in the mesh of political intrigue*: **entanglement**, net, tangle, web, snare, trap.
▶ verb **1** *one gear meshes with the input gear*: **engage**, be engaged, mate, connect, lock, interlock.
2 *I don't want to get meshed in the weeds*: **entangle**, enmesh, ensnare, snare, net, trap, entrap, catch.
3 *our ideas just do not mesh*: **harmonize**, fit together, go together, coordinate, match, be on the same wavelength, dovetail.

mesmerize verb *they were mesmerized by his performance*: **enthral**, spellbind, entrance, hold spellbound, dazzle, bewitch, charm, captivate, enrapture, enchant, fascinate, transfix, transport, grip, magnetize, hypnotize; informal get under someone's skin.

mess noun **1** *please clear up the mess in the kitchen*: **untidiness**, disorder, disarray, clutter, heap, shambles, litter, tangle, jumble, muddle, mishmash, chaos, confusion, disorganization, turmoil; informal muck, fright, sight; Brit. informal dog's dinner/breakfast, tip.
2 *there was cat mess all over the room*: **excrement**, dung, muck, faeces, excreta, dirt.
3 *I've got to get out of this mess*: **plight**, predicament, emergency, tight spot, tight corner, difficulty, straits, trouble, quandary, dilemma, problem, muddle, mix-up, confusion, complication, imbroglio, entanglement, mire; informal jam, fix, pickle, stew, hot water, hole, pretty/fine kettle of fish, scrape.
4 *what a mess he made of the project*: **muddle**, botch, bungle, wreck; informal hash, muck, foul-up, screw-up; Brit. informal cock-up; N. Amer. informal snafu; vulgar slang fuck-up, balls-up.
□ **make a mess of** *she felt she had made a complete mess of her life*: **mismanage**, mishandle, misdirect, misgovern, misconduct, bungle, botch, fluff, fumble, mess up, mar, spoil, ruin, wreck; informal make a hash of, muff, muck up, foul up, screw up, bitch up; Brit. informal make a muck of, make a pig's ear of, make a Horlicks of, cock up; vulgar slang balls up, bugger up, fuck up.
▶ verb
□ **mess about/around potter about**, amuse oneself, pass the time, do nothing very much, fiddle about/around, footle about/around, play about/around, fool about/around; fidget, toy, trifle, tamper, tinker, interfere, meddle, monkey (about/around); informal piddle about/around; Brit. informal muck about/around, lark (about/around), fanny about/around; vulgar slang frig about/around, fuck about/around; Brit. vulgar slang piss about/around, arse about/around, bugger about/around.
□ **mess something up 1** *he had completely messed up my kitchen*: **dirty**, befoul, litter, besmirch, pollute; clutter up, disarrange, jumble, throw into disorder/confusion, muss, dishevel, rumple, tumble. **2** *Eddie has messed things up*: **bungle**, botch, fluff, fumble, make a mess of, mismanage, mishandle, misdirect, misgovern, misconduct, mar, spoil, ruin, mangle, wreck; informal make a hash of, muff, muck up, foul up, screw up, bitch up; Brit. informal make a muck of, make a pig's ear of, make a Horlicks of, cock up; vulgar slang balls up, bugger up, fuck up.

message noun **1** *are there any messages for me?* **communication**, piece of information, news, word, note, memorandum, memo, email, letter, line, missive, report, bulletin, communiqué, dispatch, intelligence, notification, announcement.
2 *a campaign to get the message about home security across*: **meaning**, sense, import, idea; **point**, thrust, gist, essence, spirit, content, subject (matter), substance, implication, tenor, drift, purport, intimation, theme, moral, lesson, precept.
3 Scottish *he would run messages to the pub or the bookie*: **errand**, task, job, commission, chore, mission; shopping.
□ **get the message** *I realized that he'd never get the message—he was too thick*: **understand**, get the point, get the drift, comprehend; take the hint; informal understand what's what, catch on, latch on, get it, get the picture.

messenger noun **message-bearer**, message-carrier, postman, courier, errand boy/girl, runner, dispatch rider, envoy, emissary, agent, go-between, legate, nuncio, herald, harbinger.

Word toolkit

messy	disorderly	chaotic
hair	manner	scene
divorce	fashion	traffic
bedroom	movements	life
handwriting	crowd	event
eater	behaviour	lifestyle
house	conduct	atmosphere

messy adjective **1** *messy oil spills and grease marks* | *messy hair*: **dirty**, filthy, grubby, soiled, grimy, begrimed; mucky, muddy, slimy, sticky, sullied, spotted, stained, smeared, smudged, tarnished; **dishevelled**, blowsy, scruffy, rumpled, matted, unkempt, tousled, bedraggled, tangled, slapdash, slovenly; informal yucky; Brit. informal gungy.
▷ANTONYMS clean.
2 *a messy kitchen*: **disorderly**, disordered, muddled, in a muddle, chaotic, confused, disorganized, in disarray, in turmoil, disarranged; **untidy**, cluttered, littered, in a jumble, jumbled; informal like a bomb's hit it; Brit. informal shambolic.
▷ANTONYMS tidy, orderly.

3 *a messy legal battle*: **chaotic**, convoluted, complex, intricate, tangled, tortuous, confused, confusing, difficult; **unpleasant**, nasty, bitter, acrimonious, spiteful.
▷ANTONYMS straightforward, amicable.

metallic adjective **1** *a metallic sound*: **tinny**, jangling, jangly, jingling, jingly, plinky; grating, harsh, jarring, dissonant, raucous.
2 *metallic paint*: **metallized**, burnished; shiny, gleaming, glossy, lustrous, pearlescent, polished.

metamorphose verb *in the painting Queen Maria Luisa is metamorphosed into a barn owl*: **transform**, change, mutate, transmute, transfigure, convert, alter, vary, modify, remodel, recast, restyle, reconstruct, reorder, reorganize, undergo a sea change, translate; humorous transmogrify; formal transubstantiate.

metamorphosis noun **transformation**, mutation, transmutation, transfiguration, change, alteration, conversion, variation, modification, remodelling, restyling, reconstruction, reordering, reorganization, sea change; humorous transmogrification; formal transubstantiation.

metaphor noun **figure of speech**, figurative expression, image, trope, allegory, parable, analogy, comparison, symbol, emblem, word painting, word picture; literary conceit.

metaphorical adjective *there is no clear line between literal and metaphorical senses*: **figurative**, allegorical, analogous, symbolic, emblematic; imaginative, fanciful, extended; rare parabolic, tropical.
▷ANTONYMS literal.

metaphysical adjective **1** *the metaphysical question of the nature of the mind*: **abstract**, theoretical, conceptual, notional, philosophical, speculative, intellectual, academic; unpractical, abstruse, recondite.
▷ANTONYMS empirical.
2 *Good and Evil are inextricably linked in a metaphysical battle*: **transcendental**, spiritual, supernatural, paranormal; extramundane, unearthly, ethereal, incorporeal.
▷ANTONYMS physical.

mete verb
□ **mete something out** *the judges were unwilling to mete out harsh punishment*: **dispense**, hand out, apportion, distribute, issue, deal out, dole out, measure out, divide out, divide up, parcel out, share out, split up, give out, portion out, dish out, allocate, allot, bestow, assign, administer.

meteor noun **falling star**, shooting star, fireball, meteorite, bolide, meteoroid, comet.

meteoric adjective *her meteoric rise to fame*: **rapid**, lightning, swift, fast, quick, speedy, breakneck, fast-track, accelerated, overnight, instant, whirlwind, mushrooming, sudden, spectacular; momentary, fleeting, transient, ephemeral, evanescent, brief, short-lived.
▷ANTONYMS slow, gradual, long-drawn-out.

meteorologist noun **weather forecaster**, met officer, weatherman, weatherwoman, nowcaster, weather prophet; informal weathergirl, met man.

method noun **1** *they use very old-fashioned methods*: **procedure**, technique, system, practice, routine, modus operandi, method of working, formula, process, means, medium, mechanism; tack, approach, way, line, course of action, route, road; strategy, tactic, plan, recipe, rule.
2 *there's method in his madness*: **order**, orderliness, organization, arrangement, structure, form, system, logic, planning, plan, design, purpose, pattern, routine, discipline.
▷ANTONYMS chaos, disorder.

methodical adjective *a methodical approach to the evaluation of computer systems*: **orderly**, well ordered, well organized, well thought out, planned, well planned, efficient, businesslike, coherent, systematic, scientific, structured, logical, analytic, formal, regular, well regulated, disciplined; meticulous, punctilious, tidy, neat.
▷ANTONYMS disorganized, chaotic, inefficient.

meticulous adjective *meticulous attention to detail*: **careful**, conscientious, diligent, ultra-careful, scrupulous, punctilious, painstaking, demanding, exacting, accurate, correct; **thorough**, studious, rigorous, detailed, perfectionist, fastidious, methodical, particular, strict; pedantic, fussy; archaic nice, laborious.
▷ANTONYMS careless, sloppy, slapdash.

métier noun **1** *he had another métier besides the priesthood*: **occupation**, job, work, profession, specialism, business, employment, employ, career, calling, vocation, mission, trade, craft, walk of life, line (of work), field, province, area; N. Amer. specialty.
2 *television is more my métier*: **forte**, strong point, strength, long suit, strong suit, speciality, talent, skill, gift, bent; informal bag, thing, cup of tea.

metropolis noun **1** *their trip to London gave them nine days in the metropolis*: **capital (city)**, chief town, state/regional/provincial capital, county town, county borough, administrative centre.
2 *compared to Farafra, Bahriyah was a metropolis*: **big city**, conurbation, megalopolis, urban sprawl, concrete jungle; informal big smoke; archaic wen.

mettle noun **1** *Sir Charles, a man of mettle, did not surrender without a struggle*: **spirit**, fortitude, tenacity, strength of character, moral fibre, steel, determination, resolve, resolution, steadfastness, indomitability, backbone, hardihood, pluck, nerve, gameness, courage, courageousness, bravery, gallantry, valour, intrepidity, fearlessness, boldness, daring, audacity; informal guts, grit, spunk; Brit. informal bottle.
2 *Frazer's disciple was of a very different mettle*: **calibre**, character, disposition, nature, temperament, temper, personality, make-up, stamp, kind, sort, variety, mould, kidney, grain.

mettlesome adjective *a rider who likes a mettlesome horse*: **spirited**, game, gritty, intrepid, fearless, courageous, hardy, brave, plucky, gallant, valiant, valorous, bold, daring, audacious, heroic; tenacious, steely, determined, resolved, resolute, steadfast, indomitable.

mew verb **1** *the cat mewed plaintively*: **miaow**, meow, mewl, yowl, cry.
2 *above them, seagulls mewed*: **cry**, screech, squawk.

mewing noun **1** *the mewing of the cat*: **miaowing**, meowing, mewling, yowling; caterwauling, noise.
2 *the mewing of gulls*: **cry**, crying, screech, screeching, squawking.

mewl verb *the baby fretted and mewled*: **whimper**, cry, whine, squall; informal grizzle; literary pule.

miasma noun **stink**, reek, stench, smell, odour, malodour; Brit. informal pong, niff, whiff; Scottish informal guff.

miasmic, miasmal adjective rare *the miasmic smog*. See **smelly**.

microbe noun *microbes which cause dangerous diseases*: **micro-organism**, bacillus, bacterium, virus, germ; informal bug.

> *Word links* **microbe**
> **microphobia**, **bacillophobia** fear of microbes

microscopic adjective *protozoa are microscopic amoeba-like organisms*: **tiny**, very small, minute, infinitesimal, minuscule, nanoscopic, invisible to the naked eye; little, micro, diminutive; Scottish wee; informal teeny, teeny-weeny, teensy, teensy-weensy, weeny, itsy-bitsy, itty-bitty, eensy, eensy-weensy, tiddly, pint-sized, bite-sized, knee-high to a grasshopper; Brit. informal titchy; N. Amer. informal little-bitty.
▷ANTONYMS huge, enormous, gigantic.

midday noun **noon**, twelve noon, twelve midday, twelve o'clock, high noon, noontide, noontime, noonday, twelve hundred, twelve hundred hours, one-two-double-O.
▷ANTONYMS midnight.

> *Word links* **midday**
> **meridional** relating to midday

middle noun **1** *a shallow dish with a spike in the middle*: **centre**, mean, median, mid point, halfway point, dead centre, focal point, focus, hub, nucleus, midst; eye, heart, core, kernel, bosom, interior, depths, thick, bullseye.
▷ANTONYMS outside, circumference.
2 *he had a towel round his middle*: **midriff**, waist, waistline, belly, gut, stomach, paunch, pot belly, beer belly; informal tummy, tum, pot, bread basket.
□ **the middle of nowhere** *it's rural now—out in the middle of nowhere*: **the back of beyond**, the backwoods, the wilds, the hinterland, a backwater; Austral./NZ the back country, the backblocks, the booay; S. African the backveld, the platteland; N. Amer. informal the boondocks, the boonies, the tall timbers; Austral./NZ informal Woop Woop, beyond the black stump.
▶ adjective **1** *the middle point between two extremes*: **central**, mid, mean, medium, medial, median, midway, halfway, equidistant, mesial.
2 *there is a dearth of talent at middle level*: **intermediate**, intermedial, intermediary, inner, inside.

> *Word links* **middle**
> **meso-** related prefix, as in *mesoblast*, *Meso-America*

middleman noun *we give value for money by cutting out the middleman and selling direct*: **intermediary**, go-between; **dealer**, broker, representative, agent, factor, wholesaler, distributor; mediator, liaison officer.

middling adjective *a spa town of the middling kind, neither rich nor poor*: **average**, standard, normal, middle-of-the-road, in-between, medium; moderate, ordinary, common, commonplace, everyday, workaday, tolerable, passable, adequate; run-of-the-mill, fair, indifferent, mediocre, pedestrian, prosaic, uninspired, undistinguished, unexceptional, unexciting, unremarkable, lacklustre, forgettable, inferior, second-rate, amateur, amateurish; informal OK, so-so, bog-standard, fair-to-middling, (plain) vanilla, nothing to write home about, no great shakes, not so hot, not up to much; NZ informal half-pie.

midget noun offensive **small person**, short person, person of restricted growth; offensive dwarf, pygmy; rare homunculus, manikin, Lilliputian.

▶ adjective **1** *a midget lettuce*: **dwarf**, miniature, baby.
2 diminutive, dwarfish, petite, elfin, very small, pocket, toy, pygmy; informal pint-sized, sawn-off.
3 *a midget camera*: **miniature**, pocket.
▷ANTONYMS giant.

Choose the right word **midget**

Although the terms **midget**, **dwarf**, and **pygmy** are usually considered offensive when used to mean 'an unusually small person', there is no term that has been established as an acceptable alternative: **person of restricted growth** has not gained wide currency. The terms **homunculus** or **manikin** are found chiefly in literary or old-fashioned writing.

midnight noun **twelve midnight**, twelve at night, twelve o'clock, dead of night, the middle of the night, zero hours, the witching hour.
▷ANTONYMS midday.

midst noun literary **1** *the anecdote occurs* ***in the midst of*** *a digression*: **middle**, centre, midpoint, halfway point, kernel, nub, focal point; interior, depth(s), thick; **in the course of**, halfway through, at the heart of, at the core of.
2 *a stranger* ***in our midst***: **among us**, between us, amid us, in our group, with us, surrounded by us, in the centre; heart, bosom, core.

midway adverb *he froze in an awkward position midway across the room*: **halfway**, in the middle, at the mid point, in the centre, equidistant; betwixt and between, part-way, at some point.

mien noun *a low-browed, frowning mien*: **appearance**, look, expression, countenance, face, front, aspect, aura, demeanour, comportment, attitude, air, presence, manner, bearing, carriage, deportment, stance.

miffed adjective informal *she was slightly miffed at not being invited*: **annoyed**, displeased, offended, aggrieved, piqued, riled, nettled, vexed, irked, irritated, upset, hurt, pained, put out, in a huff, fed up, chagrined, disgruntled, discontented, resentful; informal peeved, narked, browned off, hacked off; Brit. informal cheesed off; N. Amer. informal sore; vulgar slang pissed off.
▷ANTONYMS pleased.

might noun *she hit him with all her might*: **strength**, force, power; vigour, energy, brawn, sinew, muscularity; stamina, stoutness, mightiness, powerfulness, forcefulness, potency, toughness, robustness, sturdiness.
▷ANTONYMS feebleness.
□ **with might and main with all one's strength**, with everything one has got, to the best of one's ability, as hard as one can, as hard as possible, all out, with maximum force, (with) full force, full blast, with all the stops out, forcefully, powerfully, strongly, vigorously, enthusiastically; informal hammer and tongs, like crazy, like mad.

mightily adverb **1** *he is a mightily impressive election campaigner*: **extremely**, exceedingly, enormously, vastly, immensely, tremendously, hugely, markedly, remarkably, abundantly; awfully, dreadfully; very, very much, most, to a great extent; informal majorly, mega, oh-so; informal, dated devilish; N. Amer. informal mighty, plumb.
2 *Ann and I laboured mightily to no avail*: **strenuously**, energetically, powerfully, heavily, hard, with all one's might, with might and main, all out, heartily, vigorously, with vigour, forcefully, with force, forcibly, with great effort, fiercely, intensely, eagerly, industriously, diligently, assiduously, conscientiously, enthusiastically, sedulously, with application, earnestly, with perseverance, persistently, indefatigably; informal like billy-o, like mad, like crazy.

mighty adjective **1** *a mighty blow to the back of the head*: **powerful**, forceful, violent, ferocious, fierce, brutal, vicious, vigorous, hefty, thunderous, savage, destructive, damaging, painful; lethal, deadly.
▷ANTONYMS feeble.
2 *a mighty warrior*: **fearsome**, ferocious; big, tough, robust, manful, potent, sturdy, muscular, strapping, Herculean; vigorous, energetic, stout.
▷ANTONYMS puny, tiny.
3 *three mighty industrial countries*: **dominant**, influential, strong, powerful, important, leading, authoritative, controlling, predominant, prestigious.
▷ANTONYMS insignificant.
4 *mighty oak trees*: **huge**, enormous, massive, gigantic, big, large, great, giant, colossal, mammoth, vast, immense, tremendous, stupendous, monumental, prodigious, mountainous, monstrous, titanic, towering, elephantine, king-sized, king-size, gargantuan, Brobdingnagian, substantial; informal mega, monster, whopping, whopping great, thumping, thumping great, humongous, jumbo(-sized), hulking, bumper, astronomical, astronomic; Brit. informal whacking, whacking great, ginormous.
▷ANTONYMS tiny.
▶ adverb N. Amer. *I'm mighty pleased to see you*: **extremely**, exceedingly, enormously, vastly, immensely, tremendously, hugely, markedly, remarkably, abundantly, deadly, awfully, dreadfully, mightily, very, very much, most, so, to a great extent; informal majorly, mega, oh-so, way, stinking, bitching; Brit. informal well, jolly; N. Amer. informal plumb; S. African informal lekker; informal, dated frightfully, devilish.

migrant noun *economic migrants*: **immigrant**, **emigrant**, incomer, newcomer, asylum seeker, settler, expatriate, expat, exile; nomad, itinerant, gypsy, traveller, vagrant, transient, rover, wayfarer, wanderer, drifter, displaced person, DP, homeless person.
▶ adjective *the arrival of migrant birds from further south | migrant workers*: **travelling**, wandering, moving, migrating, migratory, expatriate; drifting, nomadic, roving, roaming, itinerant, gypsy, peripatetic, vagrant, transient, floating, unsettled, on the move, displaced, homeless.
▷ANTONYMS indigenous.

migrate verb **1** *rural populations have migrated to urban areas*: **relocate**, resettle, move, move house; emigrate, go abroad, go overseas, be posted, defect, trek; N. Amer. pull up stakes; Brit. informal up sticks, flit; formal remove.
2 *wildebeest migrate around the Serengeti Plains*: **roam**, wander, drift, rove, travel (around), voyage, journey, trek, hike, itinerate, globetrot.

migration noun **1** *new workers were found through migration from the Commonwealth*: **relocation**, resettling, population movement, transhumance, moving, moving abroad, emigration, expatriation, posting, exodus, departure, hegira, defection, trek, diaspora; German Völkerwanderung.
2 *the swallows start flocking before they begin their winter migration*: **departure**, passage; flight, run.

migratory adjective *migratory birds*: **migrant**, migrating, translocating, relocating, moving, travelling.

mild adjective **1** *he continued in the same mild tone of voice*: **gentle**, tender, soft, soft-hearted, tender-hearted, sensitive, sympathetic, warm, warm-hearted, unassuming, conciliatory, placid, meek, modest, docile, calm, tranquil, serene, peaceful, peaceable, pacific, good-natured, amiable, affable, genial, easy, easy-going, mellow.
▷ANTONYMS harsh.
2 *a mild punishment*: **lenient**, clement, light; **compassionate**, pitying, forgiving, merciful, forbearing, humane.
▷ANTONYMS cruel, harsh.
3 *he was eyeing her with mild interest*: **slight**, faint, vague, minimal, half-hearted, paltry, meagre, superficial, nominal, token, feeble, indifferent, imperceptible.
▷ANTONYMS strong.
4 *mild weather*: **warm**, balmy, equable, temperate, gentle, soft, moderate, favourable, clement.
▷ANTONYMS severe, cold.
5 *a mild curry*: **bland**, insipid, flavourless, tasteless, savourless, spiceless; thin, watery, watered down.
▷ANTONYMS spicy.

mildewy adjective *two ounces of mildewy cheese*: **mouldy**, mildewed, blighted, smutty, smutted, musty, fetid, fusty, rotting, rotten, decaying, putrid, putrescent, stale, damp.

mildness noun **1** *there are moments when mildness of manner is not enough*: **gentleness**, tenderness, softness, soft-heartedness, sensitivity, warmth, warmness, compassion, meekness, modesty, docility, calmness, tranquillity, placidity, serenity, peaceableness, amiability, affability, geniality, mellowness.
▷ANTONYMS cruelty, harshness.
2 *the exceptional mildness of the past winter*: **warmth**, balminess, equability, temperateness, gentleness, softness, moderation.
▷ANTONYMS severity.

milieu noun *the social, political, and artistic milieu in Britain*: **environment**, background, backdrop, setting, context, atmosphere, scene; location, locale, conditions, surroundings, habitat, environs; sphere, world, territory, home, domain, preserve, province, circle, element.

militant adjective *the exuberance of his more militant supporters*: **aggressive**, violent, belligerent, bellicose, assertive, pushy, vigorous, forceful, active, ultra-active, fierce, combative, pugnacious; radical, extremist, extreme; enthusiastic, zealous, fanatical.
▷ANTONYMS restrained; apathetic.
▶ noun *the demands of the militants*: **activist**, extremist, radical, enthusiast, supporter, follower, devotee, Young Turk, zealot, fanatic, sectarian, partisan.
▷ANTONYMS centrist, conformist, conservative.

militaristic adjective *the militaristic image of the current leadership*: **warmongering**, war-loving, warlike, martial, hawkish, pugnacious, combative, aggressive, belligerent, bellicose; jingoistic, flag-waving, chauvinistic; informal gung-ho.
▷ANTONYMS peaceable.

military adjective *all forces were put under US military command*: **fighting**, service, army, armed, defence, warrior, soldierly, soldier-like, martial.
▷ANTONYMS civilian.
▶ noun (**the military**) *the zone was set up in 1967 at the insistence of the military*: **armed forces**, army, forces, services, militia, soldiery; navy, air force, marines, special forces.

militate verb *anger may* ***militate against*** *sexual satisfaction*: **tend to prevent**, work against, resist, hinder, discourage, oppose, counter, cancel out, foil, prejudice, operate/work/go/tell against, be detrimental to, be disadvantageous to.
▷ANTONYMS reinforce.

Easily confused words militate or mitigate?

See **mitigate**.

milk noun informal cow juice.
▶ verb **1** *milk a little of the liquid from the cylinder*: **draw off**, siphon, bleed, pump off, tap, drain, extract, withdraw.
2 *phoney psychics can milk their rich clients for years*: **exploit**, take advantage of, cash in on, impose on, bleed, suck dry, fleece, squeeze, wring, blackmail.

Word links milk

dairy, **lactic** relating to milk
lacto- related prefix, as in *lactoprotein, lacto-vegetarian*

milksop noun *would a boy brought up by his mother grow up a milksop?* **namby-pamby**, coward, weakling, Milquetoast; informal drip, mummy's boy, sissy, pansy, jellyfish, wimp, crybaby; Brit. informal **wet**, big girl's blouse, chinless wonder; N. Amer. informal candy-ass, pantywaist, pussy; archaic poltroon.

milky adjective *not a blemish marred her milky skin*: **pale**, white, milk-white, snow-white, whitish, off-white, cream, creamy, chalky, pearly, nacreous, ivory, alabaster, opaque, clouded, cloudy, misty, blanched, bloodless, anaemic, ashen, pallid, drained, pasty, wan, waxen, faded.
▷ANTONYMS swarthy.

mill noun **1** *a paper mill | a steel mill*: **factory**, plant, processing plant, works, workshop, shop, foundry, industrial centre, industrial unit.
2 *a pepper mill*: **grinder**, quern, crusher.
▶ verb *the wheat is milled into flour*: **grind**, pulverize, powder, granulate, kibble; grate, pound, crush, crunch, press; rare comminute, triturate, bray, levigate.
□ **mill around/about** *people were milling about in the streets*: **throng**, swarm, seethe, crowd, stream, surge.

millstone noun *she had become a millstone round his neck*: **burden**, unwanted responsibility, encumbrance, dead weight, load, onus; duty, obligation, liability, trouble, problem, misfortune, affliction; cross to bear, albatross; archaic cumber.

mime noun *he performed a brief mime of someone fencing*: **dumb show**, pantomime, mummery.
▶ verb *she mimed picking up a phone*: **act out**, pantomime, use gestures to indicate, gesture, simulate, represent, indicate by dumb show, indicate by sign language.

Word links mime

Polyhymnia the Muse of mime

mimic verb **1** *she mimicked his broad northern accent*: **imitate**, copy, impersonate, do an impression of, take off, do an impersonation of, do, ape, caricature, mock, make fun of, parody, satirize, lampoon, burlesque, travesty; informal send up, spoof; archaic monkey.
2 *most hoverflies are patterned so as to mimic bees and wasps*: **resemble**, look like, have/take on the appearance of, simulate, mirror, echo; N. Amer. informal make like.
▶ noun *he had a dry wit and was a superb mimic*: **impersonator**, impressionist, imitator, mimicker; parodist, caricaturist, lampooner, lampoonist; copier, copyist; informal copycat; archaic ape, zany; rare epigone.
▶ adjective *they were waging mimic war*: **simulated**, mock, imitation, make-believe, sham, imitative, mimetic; informal pretend, copycat.

mimicry noun *some birds specialize in vocal mimicry*: **imitation**, imitating, impersonation, take-off, impression, copying, aping, caricature, mockery, parody, satire, lampoon, burlesque; informal send-up, spoof; rare apery, pasquinade.

minatory adjective rare *his minatory look*. See **threatening** (sense 1).

mince verb **1** *mince the meat and mix in the remaining ingredients*: **chop up**, cut up, chop/cut into small pieces; **grind**, dice, crumble, cube; N. Amer. hash.
2 *she stood up and minced out of the room*: **walk affectedly**, walk in an affected/dainty way, teeter, waddle, skip; N. Amer. informal sashay.
□ **not mince (one's) words talk straight**, not beat about the bush, call a spade a spade, speak straight from the shoulder, pull no punches, make no bones about something, get to the point; informal tell it like it is; N. Amer. informal talk turkey.

mincing adjective *he had a strange, mincing walk, his hips slightly swaying*: **affected**, fastidious, dainty, effeminate, niminy-piminy, chichi, foppish, dandyish; pretentious, precious; informal camp, sissy, la-di-da, campy, queeny; Brit. informal poncey.

mind noun **1** *my mind was full of dark thoughts | a good teacher must stretch pupils' minds*: **brain**, **intelligence**, intellect, intellectual capabilities, mental capacity, brains, brainpower, wits, wit, powers of reasoning, powers of comprehension, powers of thought, understanding, reasoning, judgement, sense, mentality, perception; head, imagination, subconscious, psyche, ego; informal grey matter, brainbox, brain cells; Brit. informal **loaf**; N. Amer. informal smarts; S. African informal kop; rare ratiocination.
▷ANTONYMS body.
2 *he found it hard to keep his mind on the job*: **attention**, thoughts, concentration, thinking, attentiveness.
3 *the tragedy has affected her mind*: **sanity**, mental balance, mental faculties, senses, wits, reason, reasoning, judgement, rationality; informal marbles.
4 *his words stuck in her mind*: **memory**, recollection, powers of recall.
5 *one of the greatest minds of his time*: **intellect**, thinker, brain, scholar, academic, intellectual, sage.
6 *I've a mind to write in and complain*: **inclination**, desire, wish, urge, notion, fancy, disposition, intention, intent, will, aim, purpose, design.
7 *everyone was of the same mind*: **opinion**, way of thinking, outlook, attitude, view, viewpoint, point of view, belief, judgement, thoughts, feeling, sentiment, persuasion.
□ **be in two minds** *I was in two minds whether to hit him*: **be undecided**, be uncertain, be unsure, be hesitant, be ambivalent, hesitate, waver, vacillate, dither, be on the horns of a dilemma; Brit. haver, hum and haw; Scottish swither; informal dilly-dally, shilly-shally, blow hot and cold.
□ **bear/keep in mind remember**, note, make a mental note of, be mindful of, do not forget, take into account/consideration, consider, take cognizance of, take note of, be cognizant of.
□ **bring/call to mind** *the smell brings to mind past similar experiences | her strong sense of duty called to mind her grandfather*: **remind one of**, cause one to remember, make one think of, cause one to remember, put one in mind of, take one back to, bring/call to mind, awake one's memories of, evoke, call up, conjure up, summon up.
□ **change one's mind** *at the last moment I changed my mind*: think again, think twice, have second thoughts, review one's position, come round, change one's mind; reconsider.
□ **cross one's mind** *it never crossed his mind that this would upset her*: **occur to one**, come to one, come to mind, spring to mind, enter one's mind/head, strike one, hit one, dawn on one, come into one's consciousness, suggest itself.
□ **give someone a piece of one's mind reprimand**, rebuke, scold, reprove, reproach, chastise, castigate, upbraid, berate, read someone the Riot Act, haul over the coals; informal tell off, bawl out, blow up, give someone hell, give someone a talking-to, dress down, give someone a telling-off, give someone a dressing-down, give someone an earful, give someone a roasting, give someone a rocket, give someone a rollicking, give someone a row; Brit. informal tick off, carpet, monster, give someone a mouthful; N. Amer. informal chew out; Brit. vulgar slang bollock; N. Amer. vulgar slang chew someone's ass.
□ **have something in mind** *did you have anything specific in mind?* **think of**, contemplate; intend, aim, plan, design, propose, purpose, aspire, desire, want, wish, set out.
□ **out of one's mind 1** *if you think I'll agree to this you must be out of your mind!* **mad**, insane, deranged, demented, not in one's right mind, non compos mentis, unbalanced, mad as a hatter, mad as a March hare, away with the fairies; informal crazy, mental, off one's head, out of one's head, off one's nut, nuts, nutty, off one's rocker, not (quite) right in the head, round the bend, raving mad, bats, batty, bonkers, cuckoo, loopy, loony, bananas, loco, with a screw loose, touched, gaga, off the wall, not all there, out to lunch, not right upstairs; Brit. informal barmy, crackers, barking, barking mad, round the twist, off one's trolley, not the full shilling; N. Amer. informal buggy, nutsy, nutso, out of one's tree, meshuga, squirrelly, wacko; Canadian & NZ informal bushed; NZ informal porangi. **2** *I've been out of my mind with worry*: **frantic**, beside oneself, berserk, distraught, in a frenzy; informal crazy.
□ **put someone in mind of remind of**, cause to remember, recall, conjure up, suggest, evoke, summon up, call up; **resemble**, look like.
□ **to my mind in my opinion**, in my view, as I see it, (according) to my way of thinking, from my standpoint, personally, in my estimation, in my judgement, in my book, for my money, if you ask me.
▶ verb **1** *do you mind if I smoke? | I don't mind if you're late*: **care**, **object**, be bothered/troubled/annoyed, be upset, be offended, take offence, be affronted, be resentful, disapprove, resent it, dislike it, look askance; informal give/care a damn, give/care a toss, give/care a hoot, give a monkey's, give/care a rap, give a tinker's curse/damn; vulgar slang give a shit.
2 *mind the step!* **be careful of**, **watch out for**, look out for, beware of, take care with, be on one's guard for, be cautious of, be wary of, be watchful of, keep one's eyes open for.
▷ANTONYMS ignore, miss.
3 *mind you wipe your feet before you come in*: **be/make sure (that)**, see (that), take care that; **remember to**, be/make sure to, don't forget to, take care to.
▷ANTONYMS forget.
4 *she left her husband to mind the baby*: **look after**, take care of, keep an eye on, attend to, care for, tend, watch, have/take charge of, guard, protect.
▷ANTONYMS neglect.
5 *mind what your mother says*: **pay attention to**, take heed of, heed, pay heed to, attend to, take note/notice of, be heedful of, note, mark,

concentrate on, listen to, observe, have regard for, respect, be mindful of; obey, follow, comply with, adhere to; archaic regard.
▷ANTONYMS disregard, take no notice of.
□ **mind out** *mind out—there's a car coming*: **take care**, be careful, watch out, look out, beware, be on one's guard, be wary, be watchful, keep one's eyes open, be cautious.
□ **never mind 1** *never mind the cost*: **don't bother about**, pay no attention to, don't worry about, don't concern yourself with, disregard, forget, don't take into consideration, don't give a second thought to, don't think twice about. **2** *never mind, it's all right now*: **don't apologize**, forget it, don't worry about it, it doesn't matter, don't mention it, it's unimportant.

Word links **mind**

mental, cognitive relating to the mind
psychology study of the mind
psychiatry branch of medicine to do with the mind

mindful adjective *he was mindful of the difficulties involved*: **aware of**, conscious of, alive to, sensible of, alert to, awake to, acquainted with, heedful of, watchful of, careful of, wary of, chary of, cognizant of; informal wise to, hip to; rare regardful of, recognizant of.
▷ANTONYMS heedless, oblivious.

mindless adjective **1** *some mindless idiot nearly drove into me*: **stupid**, idiotic, brainless, imbecilic, imbecile, asinine, witless, foolish, empty-headed, vacuous, unintelligent, half-witted, dull, slow-witted, obtuse, weak-minded, feather-brained, doltish, blockish; informal dumb, moronic, pig-ignorant, dead from the neck up, brain-dead, cretinous, thick, thickheaded, birdbrained, pea-brained, pinheaded, dopey, dim, dim-witted, dippy, pie-faced, fat-headed, blockheaded, boneheaded, lamebrained, chuckleheaded, dunderheaded, wooden-headed, damfool, muttonheaded; Brit. informal divvy; Scottish & N. English informal glaikit; N. Amer. informal dumb-ass, chowderheaded; S. African informal dof; W. Indian informal dotish.
▷ANTONYMS intelligent.
2 *mindless acts of vandalism*: **unthinking**, thoughtless, senseless, gratuitous, careless, wanton, indiscriminate, unreasoning, uncalled for, brutish, barbarous, barbaric.
▷ANTONYMS thoughtful, considered, premeditated.
3 *a mindless, repetitive task*: **mechanical**, automatic, routine, robotic; tedious, boring, monotonous, brainless, mind-numbing.
▷ANTONYMS interesting.
□ **mindless of** *she was mindless of the consequences of her actions*: **indifferent to**, heedless of, unaware of, unmindful of, careless of, insensible to, blind to.

m

mine noun **1 pit**, colliery, excavation, quarry, workings, diggings, lode, vein, seam, deposit, shaft, mineshaft; coalfield, goldfield, opencast mine; N. Amer. open-pit mine, strip mine.
2 *the book is a mine of information*: **rich source**, repository, store, storehouse, reservoir, gold mine, mint, treasure house, treasury, reserve, fund, wealth, vein, stock, supply, hoard, accumulation; wellspring.
3 *a mine was built under the fortifications*: **tunnel**; historical sap.
▸ verb **1** *the iron ore was mined from shallow pits*: **quarry**, excavate, dig (up), extract, unearth, remove, draw, scoop out; strip-mine.
2 *medical data was mined for relevant statistics*: **search**, ransack, delve into, rake through, scour, scan, read, look through, survey.
3 *the entrance to the harbour had been mined*: **defend with mines**, protect with mines, lay with mines, sow with mines.

miner noun **pitman**, digger, collier, haulier; faceworker, headsman, surfaceman, topman; tinner; Austral. dry-blower; dated hewer; rare groover.

mingle verb **1** *fact and fiction are skilfully mingled in his novels | the sound of voices mingled with a scraping of chairs*: **mix**, blend, intermingle, commingle, intermix, interweave, interlace, combine, merge, fuse, unite, join, amalgamate, meld, marry, mesh, compound, coalesce, interblend; rare admix, commix, interflow.
▷ANTONYMS separate, be separated.
2 *wedding guests mingled in the marquee*: **socialize**, circulate, fraternize, associate with others, rub shoulders, get together, consort with others; informal hobnob, hang out.
▷ANTONYMS separate, part.

miniature adjective *a miniature railway*: **small-scale**, scaled-down, mini; tiny, little, small, minute, baby, toy, pocket, midget, dwarf, pygmy, minuscule, microscopic, nanoscopic, micro, diminutive, reduced, Lilliputian; Scottish wee; N. Amer. vest-pocket; informal teeny, teeny-weeny, teensy, teensy-weensy, weeny, itsy-bitsy, itty-bitty, eensy, eensy-weensy, tiddly, pint-sized, bite-sized; Brit. informal titchy; N. Amer. informal little-bitty.
▷ANTONYMS giant.

minimal adjective *the committee approved the report with minimal alteration*: **very little**, minimum, the smallest amount of; slightest, least, least possible, minutest, tiniest, littlest; nominal, token, negligible, next to no.
▷ANTONYMS maximal.

minimize verb **1** *the aim is to minimize costs*: **keep down**, keep at/to a minimum, reduce, decrease, cut back on, cut down, lessen, curtail, diminish, prune, pare down, shrink; informal slash.
▷ANTONYMS maximize, increase.
2 *we should not minimize the value of his contribution*: **belittle**, make light of, play down, underestimate, underrate, make little of, downplay, underplay, undervalue, detract from, sell short, de-emphasize, understate, discount, soft-pedal, reduce, lessen, brush aside, gloss over, trivialize, decry, disparage, deprecate, depreciate, denigrate; informal pooh-pooh; archaic hold cheap; rare derogate, misprize, minify.
▷ANTONYMS exaggerate.

minimum noun *operating costs will be kept to the minimum*: **lowest level**, lower limit, bottom level, bottom, base, least, lowest, rock bottom, slightest, depth, nadir.
▷ANTONYMS maximum.
▸ adjective *the minimum amount of effort*: **minimal**, least, smallest, least possible, slightest, lowest, rock-bottom, minutest, littlest.
▷ANTONYMS maximum, most.

minion noun *Inspector Cotton and his minion Sergeant Mack*: **underling**, **henchman**, flunkey, lackey, hanger-on, follower, camp follower, servant, hireling, vassal, stooge, creature, toady, sycophant, flatterer, fawner, lickspittle, myrmidon; informal yes-man, bootlicker; Brit. informal poodle, dogsbody; N. Amer. informal gofer, suck-up, brown-nose; Indian informal chamcha; Brit. vulgar slang arse-licker, bum-sucker; N. Amer. vulgar slang ass-kisser.
▷ANTONYMS peer.

minister noun **1** *a government minister*: **member of the government**, political leader, cabinet minister, secretary of state, secretary, undersecretary, department head, privy counsellor, politician; Indian diwan.
2 *a minister of religion*: **clergyman**, clergywoman, cleric, ecclesiastic, pastor, vicar, rector, priest, parson, father, man/woman of the cloth, man/woman of God, churchman, churchwoman; curate, chaplain, curé, divine, evangelist, preacher; Scottish kirkman; informal reverend, padre, Holy Joe, sky pilot; Austral. informal josser.
3 *the British minister in Egypt*: **ambassador**, chargé d'affaires, plenipotentiary, envoy, emissary, legate, diplomat; consul, delegate, representative, aide, dignitary, official.
▸ verb *doctors were busy* ***ministering to*** *the injured | he selflessly* ***ministered to*** *her needs*: **tend**, care for, take care of, look after, nurse, treat, attend to, see to, administer to, help, assist, succour; cater to, serve, wait on, accommodate, be solicitous of, pander to; informal doctor.

ministrations plural noun *her mother's anxious ministrations*: **attention**, treatment, help, assistance, aid, care, services, succour, relief, support.

ministry noun **1** *the ministry for foreign affairs*: **government department**, department, bureau, agency, office.
2 *he's training for the ministry*: **holy orders**, the priesthood, the cloth, the church.
3 *the life and ministry of Jesus*: **teaching**, preaching, evangelism.
4 *Gladstone's first ministry*: **period of office**, term (of office), administration, incumbency.

minor adjective **1** *minor structural alterations | a relatively minor problem*: **slight**, small; **unimportant**, insignificant, inconsequential, inconsiderable, of little account, peripheral, subsidiary, negligible, trivial, trifling, paltry, petty, footling; N. Amer. nickel-and-dime; informal piffling, piddling.
▷ANTONYMS major.
2 *a minor poet*: **little known**, unknown, lesser; **unimportant**, insignificant, obscure, lightweight, subordinate; N. Amer. minor-league; informal small-time, penny-ante; N. Amer. informal two-bit, picayune, bush-league.
▷ANTONYMS important, considerable.
3 Brit. *Smith minor*: **junior**, younger.
▸ noun *the heir to the throne being a minor, there would have to be a regency*: **child**, infant, youth; adolescent, teenager, boy, girl, lad, lass, schoolboy, schoolgirl; informal kid, kiddie.
▷ANTONYMS adult.

Word toolkit

minor	slight	unimportant
injury	problem	detail
quibble	movement	topic
offence	advantage	information
miracle	exaggeration	stuff
inconvenience	difference	distinction
setback	possibility	paperwork

minstrel noun historical **musician**, **singer**, balladeer; historical bard, troubadour, jongleur; rare joculator.

mint noun **1 coinage factory**, money factory, coining works; rare coinery.
2 (**a mint**) informal *the bank made a mint out of the deal*: **a fortune**, a vast sum of money; millions, billions, a king's ransom; informal a small fortune, pots of money, stacks of money, heaps of money, a tidy sum, a bundle, a wad, a pile; Brit. informal a bomb, a packet, loadsamoney, shedloads; N. Amer. informal big bucks, big money, gazillions; Austral. informal big bickies, motser, motza.

▶ **adjective** *in mint condition*: **brand new**, as new, pristine, perfect, immaculate, unblemished, undamaged, untarnished, unmarked, unmarred, unused, fresh, first-class, excellent; informal spanking.
▶ **verb 1** *the shilling was minted in 1742*: **coin**, stamp, stamp out, strike, cast, punch, die, forge, make, manufacture, produce.
2 *the slogan had been freshly minted for the occasion*: **create**, invent, make up, think up, dream up, hatch, devise, frame, originate, come up with, fabricate, fashion, produce.

minuscule **adjective** *the newsroom was minuscule, not much more than a cubbyhole*: **tiny**, minute, microscopic, nanoscopic, very small, little, micro, diminutive, miniature, baby, toy, midget, dwarf, pygmy, Lilliputian, infinitesimal; Scottish wee; informal teeny, teeny-weeny, teensy, teensy-weensy, weeny, itsy-bitsy, itty-bitty, eensy, eensy-weensy, tiddly; Brit. informal titchy; N. Amer. informal little-bitty.
▷**ANTONYMS** vast, huge.

minute[1] (stress on the first syllable) **noun 1** *it'll only take a minute*: **moment**, short time, little while, second, bit, instant; informal sec, jiffy, jiff; Brit. informal tick, mo, two ticks.
2 *at that minute, Tony walked in*: **point in time**, point, moment, instant, time, juncture, stage.
3 (**minutes**) *their objection was noted in the minutes*: **record(s)**, proceedings, log, notes, transactions, account; transcript, summary, résumé.
□ **at the minute at present**, at the moment, at the present moment/time, now, currently, this minute, presently.
□ **in a minute very soon**, in a moment, in a second, in a trice, in a flash, shortly, any minute, any minute now, in a short time, in an instant, in the twinkling of an eye, in (less than) no time, in no time at all, before you know it, before long; N. Amer. momentarily; informal in a jiffy, in two shakes, in two shakes of a lamb's tail, in the blink of an eye, in a blink, in the wink of an eye, in a wink, before you can say Jack Robinson, before you can say knife; Brit. informal in a tick, in a mo, in two ticks; N. Amer. informal in a snap; archaic or informal anon; archaic ere long.
□ **this minute at once**, immediately, directly, this moment, this second, instantly, straight away, right away, right now, without further/more ado, forthwith; French tout de suite; Latin instanter; informal pronto, straight off, right off, toot sweet; archaic straight.
□ **up to the minute latest**, newest, up to date, modern, fashionable, smart, chic, stylish, all the rage, in vogue, trendsetting, ultra-modern, modish, voguish; French à la mode; informal trendy, with it, in, bang up to date, now, hip.
□ **wait a minute be patient**, wait a moment/second, just a moment/minute/second, hold on; informal **hang on**, hold your horses; Brit. informal hang about.

minute[2] (stress on the second syllable) **adjective 1** *minute particles of gold dust | her handwriting is minute*: **tiny**, minuscule, microscopic, nanoscopic, very small, little, micro, diminutive, miniature, baby, toy, midget, dwarf, pygmy, Lilliputian; Scottish wee; informal teeny, teeny-weeny, teensy, teensy-weensy, weeny, itsy-bitsy, itty-bitty, eensy, eensy-weensy, tiddly, pint-sized, bite-sized, knee-high to a grasshopper; Brit. informal titchy; N. Amer. informal little-bitty.
▷**ANTONYMS** huge.
2 *a minute chance of success*: **negligible**, slight, infinitesimal, minimal, trifling, trivial, paltry, petty, insignificant, inappreciable; informal piffling, piddling; N. Amer. informal picayune.
▷**ANTONYMS** significant.
3 *considering the proposal in minute detail*: **exhaustive**, painstaking, systematic, meticulous, rigorous, scrupulous, punctilious, detailed; close, fine, strict, exact, precise, accurate, critical.
▷**ANTONYMS** superficial, cursory.

> *Word links* **minute**
> **micrometry** measurement of minute objects

minutely **adverb** *every document was examined minutely*: **exhaustively**, painstakingly, systematically, meticulously, rigorously, scrupulously, punctiliously, in detail; closely, finely, precisely, accurately, critically; informal with a fine-tooth comb.

minutiae **plural noun** *the captain cannot be concerned with the minutiae of shipboard life*: **details**, **niceties**, subtleties, finer points, particulars, specifics; trivia, trivialities, trifles, technicalities, non-essentials.

minx **noun tease**, seductress, coquette, trollop, slut, Lolita, loose woman, hussy; informal tramp, floozie, tart, puss; Brit. informal scrubber, madam; N. Amer. informal princess, vamp; vulgar slang cock-teaser, prick-teaser; archaic baggage, hoyden, fizgig, jade, quean, wanton, strumpet.

miracle **noun 1** *his first miracle was to turn water into wine*: **supernatural phenomenon**, mystery, prodigy, sign.
2 *Germany's economic miracle*: **wonder**, marvel, sensation, phenomenon, astonishing feat, amazing achievement.

miraculous **adjective 1** *an attack was repulsed, according to legend, with the miraculous help of St Blaise*: **supernatural**, preternatural, superhuman, inexplicable, unaccountable, fantastic, magical, phenomenal, prodigious; rare thaumaturgic.
2 *it is miraculous that you have finished | a miraculous escape*: **amazing**, astounding, remarkable, extraordinary, incredible, unbelievable, sensational; unparalleled, unprecedented, unheard of, providential, marvellous, wonderful; informal fantastic, fabulous, mind-boggling, mind-blowing.

mirage **noun optical illusion**, hallucination, phantasmagoria, apparition, fantasy, chimera, trick, vision; delusion, figment of the imagination, misconception, pipe dream, day dream; literary phantasm.

mire **noun 1** *when it's wet it's a mire out there*: **swamp**, bog, morass, peat bog, quagmire, quag, slough, sump, quicksand, fen, fenland, swampland, marshland, wetland, salt marsh, saltings, salina; N. Amer. bayou, moor.
2 *her horse was spattered with mire*: **mud**, slime, sludge, dirt, filth, ooze, muck.
3 *they have pulled themselves out of the mire by winning five matches out of six*: **mess**, difficulty, plight, predicament, emergency, tight spot, tight corner, mass of problems, straits, trouble, quandary, dilemma, problem, muddle, mix-up, confusion, complication, imbroglio, entanglement; informal jam, fix, pickle, spot, stew, hot water, hole, pretty/fine kettle of fish, scrape.
▶ **verb 1** *Frank's horse* **got mired** *in a bog hole*: **get bogged down**, sink, sink down, stick in the mud.
2 *the children were mired from playing outside*: **dirty**, soil, muddy, begrime, spatter, smear, make muddy/dirty, cake with dirt/soil.
3 *since his fall from grace he had been mired in lawsuits*: **entangle**, tangle up, embroil, enmesh, catch up, mix up, involve, bog down.

mirror **noun 1** *a quick look in the mirror*: **looking glass**, reflector, reflecting surface; Brit. glass.
2 *he felt that the Frenchman's life was a mirror of his own*: **reflection**, twin, double, exact likeness, image, replica, copy, clone, match, parallel; informal spitting image, spit, dead spit, dead ringer for.
▶ **verb** *pop music mirrored the mood of Britain's desperation | these circumstances are mirrored all over the country*: **reflect**, repeat, match, reproduce, imitate, simulate; reiterate, follow; copy, mimic, echo, parallel, correspond to; impersonate.

> *Word links* **mirror**
> **catoptric, specular** relating to mirrors
> **eisoptrophobia** fear of mirrors

m

mirth **noun** *she giggled, making an effort to control her mirth*: **merriment**, high spirits, mirthfulness, cheerfulness, cheeriness, cheer, hilarity, glee, laughter, jocularity, levity, gaiety, buoyancy, blitheness, euphoria, exhilaration, elation, light-heartedness, joviality, joy, joyfulness, joyousness, fun, enjoyment, amusement, pleasure, merrymaking, jollity, festivity, revelry, frolics, frolicsomeness; dated sport.
▷**ANTONYMS** gloom, misery.

mirthful **adjective merry**, high-spirited, in high spirits, cheerful, cheery, hilarious, gleeful, laughter-filled, jocular, chucklesome, buoyant, carefree, blithe, euphoric, exhilarated, elated, light-hearted, jovial, joyous, fun-filled; enjoyable, amusing, pleasurable, jolly, festive, playful; archaic frolicsome, sportive.
▷**ANTONYMS** miserable, dejected.

mirthless **adjective** *his lips twisted into a mirthless grin*: **humourless**, unamused, grim, glum, moody, sour, surly, dour, sullen, sulky, gloomy, scowling, glowering, sombre, lugubrious, mournful, melancholy, melancholic, doleful, miserable, dismal, grumpy, churlish, grouchy.
▷**ANTONYMS** cheerful, smiling.

miry **adjective** *the roads were miry and troublesome in winter*: **muddy**, oozy, slushy, slimy, swampy, marshy, boggy, fenny, watery, sodden, sopping, saturated, squelchy, waterlogged, soggy, soft, heavy; mucky, dirty, filthy; rare quaggy.

misadventure **noun** *a verdict of death by misadventure | a series of misadventures*: **accident**, **problem**, difficulty, misfortune, mishap, mischance; unfortunate incident, setback, reverse, reverse of fortune, stroke of bad luck, blow; trouble, failure, disaster, tragedy, calamity, woe, trial, tribulation, catastrophe, contretemps, reversal, upset, debacle.
▷**ANTONYMS** piece of good luck.

misanthrope, misanthropist **noun hater of mankind**, cynic, sceptic, churl, grouch, grump, recluse, hermit, anchorite.

misanthropic **adjective** *his misanthropic gloom*: **antisocial**, unsociable, unfriendly, reclusive, uncongenial, unneighbourly, inhospitable, cynical, suspicious, distrustful, sceptical, jaundiced, narrow-minded.
▷**ANTONYMS** sociable.

misanthropy **noun hatred of mankind**, antisocial behaviour, cynicism, scepticism, reclusiveness.

misapply **verb** *the idea of permissiveness has been overstated, exaggerated, or misapplied*: **misuse**, make bad use of, mishandle, misemploy, misappropriate, abuse, exploit, pervert, prostitute; distort, garble, warp, misinterpret, misconstrue, misrepresent; squander, waste, dissipate.

misapprehend verb *I do not think that I misapprehend your meaning*: **misunderstand**, misinterpret, put a wrong interpretation on, misconstrue, misconceive, mistake, misread, miss, confuse, confound, take amiss; miscalculate, err, be mistaken, get the wrong idea, get it/someone wrong, take something the wrong way, receive a false impression, be under a delusion, get (hold of) the wrong end of the stick, be at cross purposes; informal be barking up the wrong tree.

misapprehension noun *you seem to be under the misapprehension that I approve*: **misunderstanding**, mistake, error, misinterpretation, misconstruction, misreading, misjudgement, misconception, misbelief, miscalculation, confusion, mix-up, the wrong idea, false impression, fallacy, illusion, delusion.

misappropriate verb *he confessed to having misappropriated $2.2bn from his clients' portfolios*: **embezzle**, expropriate, steal, thieve, pilfer, swindle, pocket, help oneself to, abscond with, make off with, have one's hand/fingers in the till; informal skim, swipe, lift, filch, rip off, snitch; Brit. informal pinch, half-inch, nick, whip, knock off, bone; rare peculate, defalcate.

misappropriation noun *the alleged misappropriation of funds*: **embezzlement**, expropriation, swindle, stealing, theft, thieving, pilfering, unauthorized removal; rare peculation, defalcation.

misbegotten adjective **1** *it is a disgrace that the hospital is included in this misbegotten scheme*: **ill-conceived**, ill-advised, ill-made, badly planned, badly thought-out, hare-brained, abortive.
2 *you little misbegotten bundle of dog food!* **contemptible**, despicable, wretched, miserable, confounded, blithering, footling, infernal, damned, cursed, accursed, flaming; vulgar slang fucking, frigging, pissing, shitty; N. Amer. vulgar slang chickenshit, pissant.

misbehave verb *the manager appears powerless to prevent his players misbehaving on the field*: **behave badly**, be misbehaved, be bad, be naughty, be disobedient, get up to mischief, get up to no good, misconduct oneself, forget oneself, be guilty of misconduct; be bad-mannered, show bad/poor manners, be rude, fool around; informal carry on, act up.
▷**ANTONYMS** behave oneself.

misbehaviour noun *as soon as the misbehaviour begins, turn away from your child*: **bad behaviour**, misconduct, disorderly conduct, badness, naughtiness, disobedience, mischief, mischievousness, delinquency; misdeed, misdemeanour; bad/poor manners, rudeness, fooling around; informal carryings-on, acting-up, shenanigans.

m

misbelief noun *it is a misbelief that alcohol problems are confined to drinkers*: **false belief**, unorthodoxy, heresy, wrong belief, delusion, illusion, fallacy, error, mistake, misconception, misapprehension.
▷**ANTONYMS** orthodoxy.

miscalculate verb *he had grossly miscalculated the time it would take*: **misjudge**, make a mistake (about), calculate wrongly, estimate wrongly, overestimate, underestimate, overvalue, undervalue; go wrong, err, make an error, blunder, be wide of the mark; informal slip up, make a boo-boo, make a howler; Brit. informal boob.
▷**ANTONYMS** get it right.

miscalculation noun *it is Government miscalculations that are to blame*: **error of judgement**, misjudgement, misreading of the situation, mistake, blunder, faux pas, overestimate, underestimate; informal slip-up, boo-boo; rare misreckoning.

miscarriage noun **1** *she's had a miscarriage*: **spontaneous abortion**, stillbirth.
2 *Gould's impatience stemmed from the miscarriage of a good project | a miscarriage of justice*: **failure**, foundering, ruin, ruination, collapse, breakdown, thwarting, frustration, undoing, reversal, setback, unsuccessfulness, aborting, non-fulfilment, misfiring, mismanagement, perversion.

miscarry verb **1** *the shock caused her to miscarry*: **lose one's baby**, have a miscarriage, abort, have a spontaneous abortion.
2 *our plan miscarried*: **go wrong**, go awry, go amiss, be unsuccessful, fail, misfire, abort, be abortive, founder, come to nothing, come to grief, meet with disaster, fall through, be ruined, fall flat, boomerang, rebound, backfire, recoil; informal flop, bite the dust, go up in smoke, go phut.
▷**ANTONYMS** succeed.

miscellaneous adjective *a variety of miscellaneous tasks*: **various**, varied, different, assorted, mixed, diverse, disparate, sundry, many and different, variegated, diversified, motley, multifarious, jumbled, confused, indiscriminate, heterogeneous; literary divers; rare farraginous.

miscellany noun *a miscellany of poems by several hands*: **assortment**, mixture, melange, blend, variety, mixed bag, mix, medley, diversity, collection, selection, assemblage, combination, motley collection, pot-pourri, conglomeration, jumble, mess, confusion, mishmash, hotchpotch, hodgepodge, ragbag, pastiche, patchwork, farrago, hash; informal scissors-and-paste job; rare gallimaufry, omnium gatherum, olio, salmagundi, macédoine.

mischance noun *we lost it by mischance | a life full of mischances*: **accident**, misfortune, mishap, misadventure, unfortunate incident, setback, failure, disaster, tragedy, calamity, catastrophe, contretemps, reversal, upset, blow, debacle; bad luck, ill fortune.
▷**ANTONYMS** good fortune.

mischief noun **1** *the boys are always getting up to mischief*: **naughtiness**, badness, bad behaviour, misbehaviour, mischievousness, misconduct, misdemeanour, perversity, disobedience, pranks, tricks, larks, capers, nonsense, roguery, devilry, funny business; French diablerie; informal monkey tricks, monkey business, shenanigans, goings-on, hanky-panky; Brit. informal carry-on, carryings-on, jiggery-pokery; archaic deviltry.
▷**ANTONYMS** good behaviour.
2 *he could see mischief in her eyes*: **impishness**, roguishness, devilment; rare rascality.
▷**ANTONYMS** solemnity.
3 informal *be careful, or you'll do yourself **a mischief***: **harm**, hurt, an injury; impairment, damage, detriment, ill, trouble.

mischievous adjective **1** *a mischievous child*: **naughty**, bad, badly behaved, misbehaving, disobedient, troublesome, vexatious, full of mischief; rascally, roguish, prankish, delinquent.
▷**ANTONYMS** well behaved, good.
2 *a mischievous smile*: **playful**, teasing, wicked, impish, puckish, roguish, waggish, arch.
3 *mischievous gossip*: **malicious**, malevolent, hostile, spiteful, bitter, venomous, poisonous, evil-intentioned, ill-natured, evil, baleful, vindictive, vengeful, vitriolic, rancorous, malign, malignant, pernicious, mean, nasty, harmful, hurtful, destructive, wounding, cruel, unkind, defamatory; informal bitchy, catty; literary malefic, maleficent.
▷**ANTONYMS** harmless, well intentioned.

misconceive verb *many lawyers misconceive their own role*: **misunderstand**, misinterpret, put a wrong interpretation on, misconstrue, misapprehend, mistake, misread, miss, confuse, confound, take amiss; miscalculate, err, be mistaken, get the wrong idea, get it/someone wrong, receive a false impression, be under a delusion, be misguided about, get (hold of) the wrong end of the stick, be at cross purposes; informal be barking up the wrong tree.

misconception noun *a popular misconception about science*: **misapprehension**, misunderstanding, mistake, error, mix-up, misinterpretation, misconstruction, misreading, misjudgement, misbelief, miscalculation, false impression, illusion, fallacy, delusion; the wrong idea.

misconduct noun **1** *allegations of misconduct by the security forces*: **wrongdoing**, delinquency, unlawfulness, lawlessness, crime, felony, criminality, sin, sinfulness, evil, evil-doing; unprofessional behaviour, unprofessionalism, unethical behaviour, malpractice, maladministration, dereliction of duty, negligence, breach of ethics, impropriety, immorality, abuse; rare malversation.
2 *misconduct in the classroom was punished by detention*: **misbehaviour**, bad behaviour, misdeeds, misdemeanours, disorderly conduct, badness, mischief, naughtiness, rudeness.

misconstruction noun *his misconstruction of the legislation*: **misunderstanding**, misinterpretation, misapprehension, misconception, misreading, misjudgement, misbelief, miscalculation; mistake, error, mix-up, false impression, illusion, fallacy, delusion; the wrong idea.

misconstrue verb *his indifference can easily be misconstrued as arrogance*: **misunderstand**, misinterpret, put a wrong interpretation on, misconceive, misapprehend, mistake, misread, miss, confuse, confound, take amiss; miscalculate, err, be mistaken, get the wrong idea, get it/someone wrong, receive a false impression, be under a delusion, get (hold of) the wrong end of the stick, be at cross purposes; informal be barking up the wrong tree.

miscreant noun archaic *the village stocks, where miscreants of olden days were pelted with rotten garbage*: **criminal**, culprit, wrongdoer, malefactor, offender, villain, lawbreaker, evil-doer, convict, delinquent, sinner, transgressor, outlaw, trespasser, scoundrel, wretch, reprobate, rogue, rascal; Law malfeasant, misfeasor.

misdeed noun *he repented of his misdeeds and vowed to change his ways*: **wrongdoing**, wrong, evil deed, crime, felony, criminal act, misdemeanour, misconduct, offence, violation, error, peccadillo, transgression, sin; archaic trespass.

misdemeanour noun *he preferred to turn a blind eye to his son's misdemeanours*: **wrongdoing**, evil deed, crime, felony, criminal act; misdeed, misconduct, offence, violation, error, peccadillo, transgression, sin; archaic trespass.

miser noun *a typical miser, he hid his money in the house in various places*: **penny-pincher**, pinchpenny, niggard, cheese-parer, Scrooge; **hoarder**, saver, collector, gatherer, accumulator, magpie, squirrel; ascetic, puritan; informal **skinflint**, meanie, money-grubber, cheapskate; N. Amer. informal tightwad; vulgar slang tight-arse.
▷**ANTONYMS** spendthrift; philanthropist.

miserable adjective **1** *I'm too miserable to eat*: **unhappy**, sad, sorrowful, dejected, depressed, downcast, downhearted, down, despondent, despairing, disconsolate, out of sorts, desolate, bowed down, wretched, glum, gloomy, dismal, blue, melancholy, melancholic, low-spirited, mournful, woeful, woebegone, doleful, forlorn, crestfallen, broken-hearted, heartbroken, inconsolable, luckless, grief-stricken; informal down in

the mouth, down in the dumps.
▷ANTONYMS happy, contented.
2 *their miserable surroundings*: **dreary**, dismal, dark, gloomy, drab, sombre, wretched, depressing, grim, cheerless, godforsaken, bleak, desolate, joyless, uninviting, discouraging, disheartening, unpromising, hopeless, dire, pathetic, tragic, distressing, grievous; mean, poor, shabby, squalid, filthy, foul, sordid, seedy, dilapidated.
▷ANTONYMS luxurious.
3 *those planning day trips face four miserable wet or windy days*: **unpleasant**, disagreeable, displeasing, depressing, uncomfortable; wet, rainy, stormy; informal rotten.
▷ANTONYMS glorious, lovely.
4 *he was a good leader, but a miserable old prune on a bad day*: **grumpy**, sullen, sulky, gloomy, bad-tempered, ill-tempered, in a bad mood, dour, surly, sour, glum, moody, unsmiling, humourless, uncommunicative, taciturn, unresponsive, unsociable, scowling, glowering, ill-humoured, sombre, sober, saturnine, pessimistic, lugubrious, dismal, irritable, churlish, cantankerous, crotchety, cross, crabbed, crabby, grouchy, testy, snappish, peevish, crusty, waspish; N. English informal mardy; informal, dated mumpish.
▷ANTONYMS cheerful, good-natured.
5 *the agricultural working class were forced to work for miserable wages*: **inadequate**, meagre, scanty, scant, paltry, limited, restricted, insufficient, deficient, negligible, insubstantial, skimpy, short, little, lean, small, slight, slender, poor, lamentable, pitiful, puny, niggardly, beggarly; informal measly, stingy, lousy, pathetic, piddling; rare exiguous.
▷ANTONYMS generous, adequate.
6 *all that fuss about a few miserable mushrooms*: **wretched**, **contemptible**, despicable, confounded; informal blithering, flaming, footling, infernal, damned, cursed, accursed.

> *Word toolkit* **miserable**
>
> See **melancholy**.

miserliness noun *miserliness and greed are quickly followed by fear of losing the money*: **avarice**, acquisitiveness, parsimony, parsimoniousness, penny-pinching, cheese-paring, thrift; **meanness**, niggardliness, close-fistedness, closeness, penuriousness, illiberality, greed; asceticism, puritanism, masochism; informal stinginess, minginess, tightness, tight-fistedness; N. Amer. cheapness; archaic nearness.
▷ANTONYMS generosity.

miserly adjective **1** *his miserly great-uncle proved to be worth nearly a million*: **mean**, niggardly, parsimonious, close-fisted; **penny-pinching**, cheese-paring, grasping, greedy, avaricious, Scrooge-like, ungenerous, illiberal, close; ascetic, puritanical, masochistic; informal stingy, mingy, tight, tight-fisted, money-grubbing, money-grabbing; N. Amer. informal cheap; vulgar slang tight-arsed; archaic near.
▷ANTONYMS spendthrift, generous.
2 *the prize for the winner of the women's championship will be a miserly £3,500*: **meagre**, inadequate, paltry, limited, insufficient, deficient, negligible, insubstantial, skimpy, miserable, lamentable, pitiful, puny, niggardly, beggarly; informal measly, stingy, lousy, pathetic, piddling; rare exiguous.
▷ANTONYMS lavish, huge.

misery noun **1** *I went through periods of intense misery*: **unhappiness**, distress, wretchedness, hardship, suffering, affliction, anguish, anxiety, angst, torment, torture, hell, agony, pain, discomfort, deprivation, poverty, grief, heartache, heartbreak, heartbrokenness, despair, despondency, dejection, depression, desolation, gloom, gloominess, low spirits, moroseness, doldrums, melancholy, melancholia, woe, sadness, sorrow; informal the dumps, the blues; literary dolour.
▷ANTONYMS contentment, pleasure.
2 *the miseries of war*: **affliction**, misfortune, difficulty, problem, adversity, ordeal, trouble, hardship, deprivation; pain, sorrow, burden, load, blow, trial, tribulation, woe, torment, catastrophe, calamity, disaster, misadventure, mischance, accident, reverse, reverse of fortune, mishap.
3 Brit. informal *he's a real old misery*: **killjoy**, dog in the manger, damper, dampener, spoilsport, pessimist, prophet of doom, complainer, moaner, mope; informal sourpuss, grouch, grump, wet blanket, party-pooper, doom merchant; rare melancholiac.

misfire verb *his plan had misfired*: **go wrong**, go awry, go amiss, be unsuccessful, fail, abort, be abortive, founder, come to nothing, come to grief, meet with disaster, fall through, be ruined, fall flat; boomerang, rebound, backfire, recoil; informal flop, bite the dust, go up in smoke, go phut.

misfit noun *a refuge for failures, freeloaders, and misfits*: **fish out of water**, square peg in a round hole, round peg in a square hole; **nonconformist**, eccentric, maverick, individualist, deviant, exception, outsider; informal **oddball**, odd fish, weirdo, weirdie, freak; N. Amer. informal screwball, kook.

misfortune noun *they endured many misfortunes*: **problem**, difficulty, trouble, setback, reverse, adversity, reverse of fortune, misadventure, mishap, stroke of bad luck, blow, failure, accident, disaster, tragedy, affliction, sorrow, misery, woe, trial, tribulation, catastrophe, calamity.
▷ANTONYMS piece of luck.

misgiving noun *despite occasional misgivings, he was optimistic*: **qualm**, doubt, reservation, scruple; suspicion, distrust, mistrust, lack of faith, lack of confidence, diffidence, second thoughts; trepidation, scepticism, worry, unease, uneasiness, anxiety, apprehension, uncertainty, niggle, disquiet, disquietude, hesitation, hesitance, hesitancy.
▷ANTONYMS confidence.

misguided adjective **1** *the whole selection policy had been misguided*: **erroneous**, fallacious, unwarranted, unfounded, unsound, misplaced, misconceived, ill-advised, inadvisable, ill-considered, ill-judged, inappropriate, impolitic, unwise, injudicious, imprudent, rash, foolish.
▷ANTONYMS well judged.
2 *the misguided teacher might well believe that self-expression was all that was needed*: **misinformed**, misled, misdirected, labouring under a delusion/misapprehension, wrong, mistaken, deluded, ill-advised, foolish.
▷ANTONYMS well informed.

mishandle verb **1** *he was accused of mishandling the allocation of land for development*: **botch**, bungle, fluff, fumble, make a mess of; **mismanage**, misdirect, misgovern, misconduct, mar, spoil, ruin, mangle, wreck; informal make a hash of, muff, mess up, muck up, foul up, screw up, bitch up; Brit. informal make a muck of, make a pig's ear of, make a Horlicks of, cock up; vulgar slang balls up, fuck up.
2 *he mishandled people and pushed them about*: **bully**, persecute, treat badly, ill-treat, mistreat, maltreat, abuse, ill-use, misuse, knock about/around, hit, beat, strike, manhandle, maul, molest, injure, harm, hurt; informal beat up, rough up, do over.
3 *the equipment could be dangerous if mishandled*: **misuse**, abuse, use inexpertly, misapply, handle/treat roughly.

mishap noun *a fair proportion of major accidents are generated by minor mishaps*: **accident**, trouble, problem, difficulty, setback, reverse, adversity, reverse of fortune, misadventure, misfortune, mischance, stroke of bad luck, blow; failure, disaster, tragedy, affliction, woe, trial, tribulation, catastrophe, contretemps, upset, calamity.

mishmash noun *a bizarre mishmash of colours and patterns*: **jumble**, mess, confusion, hotchpotch, hodgepodge, ragbag, pastiche, patchwork, farrago, hash, assortment, medley, miscellany, mixture, melange, blend, variety, mixed bag, mix, diversity, collection, selection, assemblage, combination, motley collection, pot-pourri, conglomeration; informal scissors-and-paste job, mash-up; rare gallimaufry, omnium gatherum, olio, salmagundi, macédoine.

misinform verb *I'm afraid you have been misinformed*: **mislead**, misguide, misdirect, give wrong information to, delude, take in, deceive, lie to, fool, hoodwink, lead astray, throw off the scent, send on a wild goose chase, put on the wrong track, pull the wool over someone's eyes, pull someone's leg; informal bamboozle, lead up the garden path, take for a ride; N. Amer. informal give someone a bum steer.

misinformation noun *a lot of misinformation was received in Moscow*: **disinformation**, false information, misleading information, deception; lie, fib, false rumour, gossip, red herring, false trail; informal kidology; N. Amer. informal bum steer.

misinterpret verb *he explained that his proposal had been misinterpreted*: **misunderstand**, misconceive, misconstrue, misapprehend, mistake, misread, put a wrong interpretation on; miss, confuse, confound, take amiss; miscalculate, err, be mistaken, get the wrong idea, get it/someone wrong, receive a false impression, be under a delusion, get (hold of) the wrong end of the stick, be at cross purposes; informal be barking up the wrong tree.

misjudge verb *she had misjudged her nearness to the wall and crashed into it*: **get the wrong idea about**, get wrong, get the wrong end of the stick about, judge incorrectly, jump to the wrong conclusion about, estimate wrongly; overestimate, underestimate, overvalue, undervalue, underrate, be wrong about, miscalculate, misconstrue, misread, misapprehend; wrong, do someone an injustice, belittle.

mislay verb *I seem to have mislaid my driving licence*: **lose**, misplace, put in the wrong place, lose track of, miss; drop, forget, be unable to find, be unable to lay one's hands on, forget the whereabouts of, forget where one has put something.
▷ANTONYMS find; keep.

mislead verb *it seemed that Caroline had deliberately misled her*: **deceive**, delude, take in, lie to, fool, hoodwink, lead astray, throw off the scent, send on a wild goose chase, put on the wrong track, pull the wool over someone's eyes, pull someone's leg, misguide, misdirect, misinform, give wrong information to; informal bamboozle, lead up the garden path, take for a ride; N. Amer. informal give someone a bum steer.

misleading adjective *the leaflet was full of misleading statements*: **deceptive**, confusing, deceiving, equivocal, ambiguous, fallacious, specious, spurious, false, mock, pseudo, illusory, delusive, evasive; casuistic, sophistical.

mismanage verb *the campaign had been badly mismanaged*: **botch**, bungle, fluff, fumble, make a mess of, mishandle, misdirect, misgovern, misconduct, mar, spoil, ruin, mangle, wreck; informal **make a hash of**, **muff**, **mess up**, **muck up**, **foul up**, **screw up**, **bitch up**; Brit. informal **make a muck of**, **cock up**, **make a pig's ear of**, **make a Horlicks of**; vulgar slang **fuck up**, **balls up**.

mismatch noun *there is still a mismatch between policy and practice*: **discrepancy**, lack of congruence, inconsistency, contradiction, incongruity, incongruousness, conflict, discord, irreconcilability, misalliance, mismarriage, mésalliance, bad match.

mismatched adjective *mismatched kitchen units*: **ill-assorted**, ill-matched, incongruous, unsuited, incompatible, inharmonious, conflicting, inconsistent, opposed, at odds; out of keeping, clashing, discrepant; uneven, dissimilar, unlike, unalike, different, varying, variant, at variance, disparate, unrelated, divergent, deviating, diverse, various, contrasting, distinct.
▷ANTONYMS matching, compatible.

misogynist noun *a bachelor and renowned misogynist*: **woman-hater**, anti-feminist, male chauvinist, male supremacist, chauvinist, sexist; informal **male chauvinist pig**, **MCP**.

misplace verb *he had misplaced the tickets*: **lose**, mislay, put in the wrong place, lose track of, miss, drop, forget, be unable to find, be unable to lay one's hands on, forget the whereabouts of, forget where one has put something.
▷ANTONYMS find; keep.

misplaced adjective **1** *his comments turned out to be misplaced*: **misguided**, unwise, misconceived, ill-advised, ill-considered, ill-judged; **inappropriate**, unsuitable, untoward, inapt.
2 *her misplaced keys*: **lost**, mislaid, missing, nowhere to be found.

misprint noun *the book is full of misprints*: **mistake**, error, printing mistake/error, typographical mistake/error, typesetting mistake/error, keyboarding mistake/error, keying mistake/error, typing mistake/error, corrigendum, erratum; Brit. **literal**; informal **typo**, **howler**; Brit. informal **boob**.

misquote verb *my original statement has been misquoted*: **misreport**, misrepresent, misstate, quote incorrectly, take/quote out of context, distort, twist, slant, bias, put a spin on, pervert, falsify, garble, muddle, mistranslate; rare misrender.

misrepresent verb *you are misrepresenting the views of the government*: **give a false account of**, give a false idea of, misstate, misreport, misquote, quote/take out of context, garble, misinterpret, put a spin on, falsify, fudge, pervert, belie, distort, warp, strain, colour, manipulate, parody, travesty, conceal, disguise.

misrule noun **1** *the 1484 Act is scathing about the misrule of Edward IV*: **bad government**, misgovernment, mismanagement, misdirection, mishandling, maladministration, negligence, incompetence, malpractice.
2 *the weekly carnival of misrule at contemporary football games*: **lawlessness**, anarchy, disorder, chaos, confusion, mayhem, turmoil, tumult.
▷ANTONYMS order.

miss[1] verb **1** *the shot he fired missed her by inches*: **fail to hit**, be wide of, go wide of, fall short of.
▷ANTONYMS hit.
2 *Mandy missed the catch and flung the ball back rather crossly*: **fail to catch**, drop, fumble, fluff, bungle, mishandle, misfield, mishit.
▷ANTONYMS catch.
3 *I'll miss my bus now*: **be too late for**, fail to catch/get.
▷ANTONYMS catch.
4 *I'm sorry, I missed what you said*: **fail to hear**, fail to take in, mishear, misunderstand.
5 *you can't miss the station because it's so big*: **fail to see/notice**, overlook, pass over, forget.
▷ANTONYMS see, notice.
6 *she never missed a meeting that I remember*: **fail to attend**, be too late for, absent oneself from, be absent from, play truant from, take French leave from, cut, skip, omit; Brit. informal **skive off**.
▷ANTONYMS attend.
7 *don't miss this exciting opportunity!* **fail to take advantage of**, fail to seize/grasp/take, let slip, let go/pass, forfeit, pass up, lose out on, overlook, disregard.
8 *I left my flat early to try to miss the rush-hour traffic*: **avoid**, beat, evade, escape, dodge, sidestep, elude, get round, circumvent, steer clear of, give a wide berth to, find a way round, bypass, skirt, cheat, duck.
▷ANTONYMS get caught up in.
9 *she loved her father and missed him when he was away*: **pine for**, yearn for, ache for, long for, long to see, regret the absence/loss of, feel the loss of, feel nostalgic for, need.
10 *we did not miss the children until darkness fell*: **notice the absence of**, find missing.
□ **miss someone/something out** **leave out**, exclude, fail to include, except, miss, miss off, fail to mention, pass over, skip; Brit. informal **give something a miss**.
▶ noun *one hit and three misses*: **failure**, omission, slip, blunder, error, mistake, fiasco; informal **flop**.
▷ANTONYMS hit.
□ **give something a miss** *if you are not a fan of rock music then I would give it a miss*: **avoid**, keep away from, stay away from, steer clear of, circumvent, give a wide berth to, keep at arm's length, fight shy of.

miss[2] noun *that little miss knows more than she lets on*: **young woman**, young lady, girl, schoolgirl, slip of a girl; girlie, missy, lass, maiden, maid; nymphet, belle, baby doll; Scottish **lassie**; Irish **colleen**; informal **babe**, **chick**, **bit**, **doll**, **teeny-bopper**; Brit. informal **popsy**, **bird**, **bint**, **poppet**; N. Amer. informal **broad**, **dame**, **patootie**; Irish informal **mot**; Austral./NZ informal **sheila**; dated, informal **filly**, **baggage**; N. Amer. dated, informal **bobby-soxer**; literary **damsel**, **nymph**; archaic or humorous **wench**.

misshapen adjective *his bowed legs and misshapen feet*: **deformed**, malformed, distorted, crooked, contorted, wry, twisted, warped, out of shape, bent, bandy, asymmetrical, irregular, misproportioned, ill-proportioned, ill-shaped, disfigured, hunchbacked, abnormal, grotesque, monstrous; Scottish **thrawn**.
▷ANTONYMS well proportioned, well built.

missile noun *a player was hit by a missile thrown by a spectator*: **projectile**; rare trajectile.

missing adjective **1** *his clothes and wallet are also missing*: **lost**, mislaid, misplaced, nowhere to be found, absent, not present, gone, gone astray, unaccounted for.
▷ANTONYMS to hand.
2 *passion was an element that had been* **missing from** *her life for too long*: **absent from**, not present in, not to be found in, lacking in, wanting from; in short supply.
▷ANTONYMS present, plentiful.

mission noun **1** *two Alton drivers are among a team on a mercy mission to Romania*: **assignment**, commission, expedition, journey, trip, errand, undertaking, operation; task, job, labour, work, chore; business, duty, charge, trust; Scottish & Irish **message**.
2 *her mission in life is to heal the sick*: **vocation**, calling, pursuit, goal, aim, quest, undertaking, purpose, function.
3 *a trade mission*: **delegation**, deputation, commission, task force, legation, representation, delegacy.
4 *he returned to southern Africa to work in a mission*: **mission post**, mission station, missionary organization.
5 *a bombing mission*: **sortie**, operation, raid.

missionary noun *he was a missionary in Sierre Leone*: **evangelist**, apostle, proselytizer, preacher, televangelist, minister, priest; **campaigner**, crusader, champion, converter, promoter, advocate, proponent.

missive noun *a missive from the Foreign Office*: **message**, communication, letter, word, note, memorandum, line, report, bulletin, communiqué, dispatch, intelligence, piece of information, news, notification, announcement, greeting, epistle; informal **memo**; literary **tidings**.

misspent adjective *his misspent youth*: **wasted**, dissipated, squandered, thrown away, frittered away, prodigal, misused, misapplied, irregular; idle, profitless, unprofitable.
▷ANTONYMS well regulated, fruitful, profitable.

misstate verb *they were accused of misstating the underlying purpose of the transaction*: **misreport**, misrepresent, take/quote out of context; distort, twist, slant, bias, put a spin on, pervert, falsify; garble, muddle, mistranslate; rare misrender.

mist noun *the mist was clearing and the sun began to peep through*: **haze**, **fog**, smog, murk, cloud, cloudiness, mistiness, Scotch mist, haar, vapour, drizzle, spray; steam, condensation, film; N. English (sea) **fret**; literary **brume**, **fume**.
▶ verb
□ **mist over/up** *her glasses were misting up*: **steam up**, become misty, fog over/up, become covered with condensation, haze over, film over, cloud over, become cloudy, become blurred.

mistake noun **1** *I assumed it had been a mistake on the part of the overworked staff*: **error**, fault, inaccuracy, omission, slip, blunder, miscalculation, misunderstanding, flaw, oversight, misinterpretation, fallacy, gaffe, faux pas, solecism, misapprehension, misconception, misreading; informal **slip-up**, **boo-boo**, **howler**, **boner**; Brit. informal **boob**, **clanger**; N. Amer. informal **goof**; Brit. informal, dated **bloomer**; rare **misreckoning**.
2 *a couple of spelling mistakes*: **misprint**, printing error/mistake, typographical error/mistake, typesetting error/mistake, keyboarding error/mistake, keying error/mistake, typing error/mistake, corrigendum, erratum; Brit. **literal**; informal **typo**.
□ **make a mistake** **go wrong**, err, make an error, blunder, be wide of the mark, go astray, miscalculate; informal **slip up**, **make a boo-boo**, **make a howler**; Brit. informal **boob**.
▶ verb **1** *men were so apt to mistake their own feelings*: **misunderstand**, misinterpret, get wrong, put a wrong interpretation on, misconstrue, misapprehend, misread, miss, take amiss.
2 *children often* **mistake** *vitamin pills* **for** *sweets*: **confuse with**, mix up with, take for, misinterpret as, confound with.
□ **be mistaken** *I'm afraid you are mistaken—I've never been here before*: **be wrong**, be in error, be at fault, be under a misapprehension, be

misinformed, be misguided, be wide of the mark, be barking up the wrong tree, get the wrong end of the stick.
▷ANTONYMS be right.

mistaken adjective *there is a mistaken but widespread belief that manufacturing is still shrinking*: **wrong**, erroneous, inaccurate, incorrect, inexact, off-target, off-beam, out, false, fallacious, unsound, unfounded, misguided, misinformed, wide of the mark.
▷ANTONYMS correct, accurate.

mistakenly adverb **1** *we often mistakenly imagine that when a problem is diagnosed it is solved*: **wrongly**, in error, erroneously, incorrectly, falsely, fallaciously, inaccurately, imprecisely, inappropriately.
▷ANTONYMS correctly, accurately.
2 *Mr Perkins had mistakenly opened a package addressed to the actor*: **by accident**, accidentally, inadvertently, unintentionally, unwittingly, unknowingly, unconsciously, by mistake, by chance, misguidedly.
▷ANTONYMS intentionally.

mistimed adjective *his mistimed floral tribute upset her greatly*: **ill-timed**, badly timed, inopportune, inappropriate, untimely, inconvenient; awkward, unwelcome, unfavourable, unfortunate, inapt; archaic unseasonable.
▷ANTONYMS opportune, timely.

mistreat verb *foreign nationals held hostage in the country had been mistreated*: **ill-treat**, maltreat, abuse, ill-use, misuse, treat badly, handle/treat roughly, knock about/around, hit, beat, strike, mishandle; manhandle, maul, molest, injure, harm, hurt, bully, persecute; informal beat up, rough up, do over.

mistreatment noun *reforms designed to protect detainees from mistreatment or torture*: **ill-treatment**, maltreatment, abuse, ill use, ill usage, beating, rough handling, mishandling, manhandling; molestation, injury, harm, bullying, persecution.

mistress noun *his wife never found out about his mistress*: **lover**, girlfriend, paramour, kept woman, live-in lover; courtesan, concubine, inamorata, hetaera, sultana; informal **fancy woman**, bit on the side, gun moll, (little) bit of fluff; dated lady-love; archaic doxy, leman.

mistrust verb **1** *I mistrust his motives*: **be suspicious of**, be mistrustful of, be distrustful of, be sceptical of, be wary of, be chary of, harbour suspicions about, be uneasy about, distrust, have doubts about, have misgivings about, have reservations about, have qualms about, suspect, wonder about; informal be leery of.
▷ANTONYMS trust.
2 *we are taught to mistrust our impulses*: **question**, challenge, doubt, disbelieve, have no confidence/faith in, query.
▸noun **1** *mistrust of Russia was widespread*: **suspicion**, **distrust**, doubt, misgivings, wariness, circumspection.
▷ANTONYMS trust.
2 *does this reflect* **mistrust of** *David's competence?* **questioning**; lack of confidence/faith in, doubt about, disbelief in.

mistrustful adjective *such youngsters may often be mistrustful of those who try to help them*: **suspicious**, chary, wary, uncertain, unsure, distrustful, untrusting, doubtful, dubious, uneasy, cautious, hesitant, sceptical, unbelieving; informal leery.
▷ANTONYMS trusting.

misty adjective **1** *misty weather*: **hazy**, **foggy**, cloudy, smoggy, steamy, murky, smoky.
▷ANTONYMS clear.
2 *hovering in the darkness was a misty figure*: **blurry**, fuzzy, blurred, dim, indistinct, unclear, vague, obscure, lacking definition, out of focus, nebulous.
▷ANTONYMS sharp.
3 *a few misty memories*: **vague**, unclear, indefinite, obscure, hazy, nebulous; tenuous, slight, rough, approximate, imprecise.
▷ANTONYMS clear.

misunderstand verb *she misunderstood his motives | I must have misunderstood—I thought you were anxious to leave*: **misapprehend**, misinterpret, put a wrong interpretation on, misconstrue, misconceive, mistake, misread, miss, confuse, confound, take amiss; miscalculate, err, be mistaken, get the wrong idea, get it/someone wrong, take something the wrong way, receive a false impression, be under a delusion, get (hold of) the wrong end of the stick, be at cross purposes; informal be barking up the wrong tree.
▷ANTONYMS grasp, understand correctly, get the right idea.

misunderstanding noun **1** *the proposals are based on a fundamental misunderstanding of juvenile crime*: **misinterpretation**, misconstruction, misreading, misapprehension, misconception; mistake, error, misjudgement, misbelief, miscalculation, confusion, mix-up, the wrong idea, false impression, fallacy, illusion, delusion.
2 *there have been misunderstandings but they have been sorted out*: **disagreement**, difference, difference of opinion, variance, clash of views, dispute, disputation, falling-out, quarrel, argument, altercation, squabble, wrangle, row, clash, conflict; informal ruction, spat, scrap, tiff.
▷ANTONYMS harmony.

misuse verb **1** *the mayor was found guilty of misusing public funds*: **put to wrong use**, misapply, misemploy, embezzle, use fraudulently; abuse, exploit, squander, waste, dissipate.
2 *she had been misused by her husband*: **ill-treat**, maltreat, mistreat, abuse, ill-use, treat badly, handle/treat roughly, knock about/around, hit, beat, strike, mishandle, manhandle, maul, molest, injure, harm, hurt, bully, persecute; informal beat up, rough up, do over.
▷ANTONYMS look after, treat well.
▸noun **1** *the misuse of public funds*: **wrong use**, misemployment, embezzlement, fraud; exploitation, squandering, waste, dissipation.
2 *the misuse of drugs*: **illegal use**, wrong use, abuse, misapplication.
3 *only drastic curbs on foreigners would prevent the misuse and injury of the indigenous people*: **ill-treatment**, maltreatment, abuse, ill-use, ill-usage, beating, rough handling, mishandling, manhandling, molestation, injury, harm, bullying, persecution.

mite noun

> *Word links* **mite**
>
> **acarophobia** fear of mites and ticks
> **acarology** study of mites and ticks

mitigate verb *drugs which mitigated the worst symptoms of the disease*: **alleviate**, reduce, diminish, lessen, weaken, lighten, attenuate, take the edge off, allay, ease, assuage, palliate, cushion, damp, deaden, dull, appease, soothe, relieve, help, soften, temper, still, quell, quieten, quiet, tone down, blunt, dilute, moderate, modify, abate, lull, pacify, placate, mollify, sweeten, tranquillize, remit, extenuate, excuse, commute.
▷ANTONYMS aggravate, increase, intensify.

> *Easily confused words* **mitigate or militate?**
>
> **Mitigate** and **militate** are frequently confused on account of their similarity in form, but their meanings are quite different. *Mitigate* means 'make (something bad) less severe', as in *drainage schemes have helped to mitigate this problem*, while *militate* is nearly always used in constructions with *against* to mean 'be a powerful factor in preventing', as in *these disagreements will militate against the two communities coming together*.

mitigating adjective *he would have faced a prison sentence but for mitigating circumstances*: **extenuating**, exonerative, justificatory, justifying, vindicatory, vindicating, exculpatory, palliative, qualifying, moderating, modifying, tempering, lessening.
▷ANTONYMS aggravating.

mitigation noun **1** *the mitigation of the problems of rural unemployment*: **alleviation**, reduction, diminution, lessening, easing, weakening, lightening, assuagement, palliation, cushioning, dulling, deadening; soothing, softening, relief.
▷ANTONYMS intensification.
2 *in mitigation, she said her client had been deeply depressed*: **extenuation**, explanation, excuse; appeasement.

m

mix verb **1** *mix all the ingredients together | oil and water don't mix*: **blend**, mingle, combine, put together, stir, jumble, merge; fuse, unite, unify, join, amalgamate, incorporate, fold in, meld, marry, mesh, compound, alloy, coalesce, homogenize, intermingle, intermix, interweave, interpenetrate, interlace; cross, cross-breed, hybridize, integrate, emulsify, premix; shuffle, shift around; informal blunge; rare admix, commingle, interflow, commix.
▷ANTONYMS separate, divide.
2 *she mixes with all sorts*: **associate**, **socialize**, mingle, meet, get together, have dealings, fraternize, circulate, keep company, rub shoulders, consort, move, go out; N. Amer. rub elbows; informal hang out/around, knock about/around, hobnob; Brit. informal hang about.
▷ANTONYMS keep oneself to oneself.
3 *we're like oil and water—we just don't mix*: **be compatible**, get along/on, go (together), fit together, be in harmony, be like-minded, be of the same mind, be of like mind, see eye to eye, agree; informal hit it off, click, be on the same wavelength.
□ **mix something up 1** *mix up the filler paste with its catalyst*: **blend**, mingle, combine, put together, stir, jumble, merge; fuse, unite, unify, join, amalgamate, incorporate, fold in, meld, marry, mesh, compound, alloy, coalesce, homogenize, intermingle, intermix, interweave, interpenetrate, interlace; cross, cross-breed, hybridize, integrate, emulsify, premix; shuffle, shift around; informal blunge; rare admix, commingle, interflow, commix.
2 *I'm sorry, I mixed up the dates*: **confuse**, get confused, muddle, muddle up, get muddled up, get jumbled up, scramble, mistake.
□ **mixed up in** *I'm sure he was mixed up in this business*: **involved in**, embroiled in, entangled in, drawn into, caught up in, a party to.
▸noun *the decor is a fascinating mix of antique and modern*: **mixture**, blend, mingling, combination, compound, fusion, composition, concoction, brew, alloy, merger, union, amalgamation, amalgam, coalition, cross, hybrid; medley, melange, diversity, collection, selection, assortment, variety, mixed bag, miscellany, assemblage, motley collection, pot-pourri, conglomeration, jumble, mess, confusion, mishmash, hotchpotch,

hodgepodge, ragbag, pastiche, patchwork, farrago, hash; informal scissors-and-paste job, mash-up; rare gallimaufry, omnium gatherum, olio, salmagundi, macédoine.

mixed adjective **1** *a mixed collection of artefacts*: **assorted**, varied, variegated, miscellaneous, different, differing, disparate, diverse, diversified, motley, sundry, jumbled, haphazard, heterogeneous.
▷ANTONYMS homogeneous.
2 *the original chickens were of mixed breed*: **hybrid**, half-caste, half-breed, cross-breed, cross-bred, interbred, mongrel, impure; dated underbred.
▷ANTONYMS pure.
3 *he had mixed reactions*: **ambivalent**, equivocal, unsure, uncertain, doubtful, contradictory, conflicting, confused, muddled.
▷ANTONYMS unequivocal.
□ **mixed bag** *we are given a mixed bag of half-realized ideas*: **assortment**, mixture, variety, array, mix, miscellany, random selection, motley collection, selection, medley, melange, diversity, mishmash, hotchpotch, hodgepodge, ragbag, pot-pourri, jumble, mess, confusion, conglomeration, farrago, patchwork, hash; rare gallimaufry, omnium gatherum, olio, olla podrida, salmagundi, macédoine, motley.

mixed up adjective *she's a crazy mixed-up kid*: **confused**, at sea, befuddled, bemused, bewildered, confounded, muddled, perplexed; maladjusted, ill-adjusted, disturbed, neurotic, unbalanced; informal screwed up, untogether, hung up, messed up; vulgar slang fucked up; archaic mazed. See also **mix**.

mixer noun **1** *a kitchen mixer*: **blender**, food processor, liquidizer, stirrer, beater, churn, whisk.
2 *she was a very private person, never really a mixer*: **sociable person**, socializer, mingler, extrovert, social butterfly, socialite, life and soul of the party.
▷ANTONYMS loner.

mixture noun **1** *every member of the family would stir the pudding mixture*: **blend**, mix, brew, combination, concoction; jumble, fusion, composition, compound, alloy, amalgam.
2 *it's hard to imagine a stranger mixture of people*: **assortment**, miscellany, medley, melange, blend, variety, mixed bag, mix, diversity, collection, selection, assemblage, combination, motley collection, pot-pourri, conglomeration, jumble, mess, confusion, mishmash, hotchpotch, hodgepodge, ragbag, pastiche, patchwork, farrago, hash; informal mash-up; rare gallimaufry, omnium gatherum, olio, salmagundi, macédoine.
3 *other animals were a mixture of genetic strands*: **cross**, cross-breed, mongrel, hybrid, half-breed, half-caste.

mix-up noun *there's been a mix-up over rules governing foreign players*: **confusion**, muddle, misunderstanding, mistake, error, mess, jumble.

moan noun **1** *Katherine's soft moans of pain*: **groan**, wail, whimper, sob, cry, whine, howl, lament, lamentation, keen.
2 *the moan of the wind*: **sough**, sigh, murmur, whisper, groan.
3 *there were moans about the car's feeble ventilation*: **complaint**, complaining, grouse, grousing, moans and groans, grouch, grouching, grumble, grumbling, whine, whining, carping, muttering, murmur, murmuring, whispering; informal gripe, griping, bellyache, bitch, whinge, whingeing, beef, beefing.
▶ verb **1** *the injured man moaned in agony*: **groan**, wail, whimper, sob, cry, whine, howl, keen.
2 *the wind moaned in the trees*: **sough**, sigh, murmur, whisper, groan.
3 *you're always moaning about the weather*: **complain**, grouse, grouch, grumble, whine, carp, mutter, murmur, whisper; informal gripe, bellyache, bitch, beef, whinge; N. English informal mither.

mob noun **1** *troops were called in to disperse the mob*: **crowd**, horde, multitude, rabble, mass, body, throng; group, host, pack, press, crush, jam, gang, gathering, swarm, assemblage; archaic rout.
2 *the mob, the dregs, were to be firmly excluded from political life*: **the common people**, the masses, the populace, the public, the multitude, the rank and file, the commonality, the commonalty, the third estate, the plebeians, the proletariat, the peasantry, the crowd; the hoi polloi, the lower classes, the common herd, the rabble, the riff-raff, the canaille, the great unwashed, the dregs of society, the ragtag (and bobtail), the proles, the plebs.
3 Brit. informal *don't you get any firearms training in your mob?* **group**, set, crowd, lot, circle, coterie, in-crowd, clan, faction, pack, band, ring, fraternity, brotherhood, society, troop, company, team; informal gang, bunch, lads; Brit. informal shower.
▶ verb **1** *he was mobbed by the crowds*: **surround**, swarm around, besiege, jostle; harass, set upon, fall on, worry.
2 *the reporters mobbed the gift shop like a crowd of souvenir-starved tourists*: **crowd (into)**, cram full, fill to overflowing, fill, pack, throng, press into, squeeze into.

> *Word links* **mob**
>
> **demophobia**, **ochlophobia** fear of mobs

mobile adjective **1** *both patients had been mobile up to the day of surgery*: **able to move**, able to move around, moving, walking, ambulant, ambulatory; lively, sprightly, spry, energetic, vigorous; Zoology motile.
▷ANTONYMS immobile, motionless, inert.
2 *her mobile face registered sorrow and concern*: **expressive**, eloquent, suggestive, meaning, speaking, revealing, telltale, animated, changing, ever-changing.
▷ANTONYMS expressionless.
3 *a mobile library*: **travelling**, transportable, transferable, portable, movable, locomotive, manoeuvrable; itinerant, peripatetic, nomadic, peregrine, wandering, roving, rangy; airborne, mechanized, motorized, waterborne, seaborne.
▷ANTONYMS stationary.
4 *these groups consist of highly mobile young people and families*: **adaptable**, flexible, versatile, changing, fluid, moving, on the move, adjustable, transplantable.
▷ANTONYMS static.

mobility noun **1** *elderly people may become socially isolated as a result of restricted mobility*: **ability to move**, movability, moveableness, motility, vigour, strength, potency.
2 *the gleeful mobility of Billy's face*: **expressiveness**, eloquence, animation.
3 *the mobility of the product*: **transportability**, portability, manoeuvrability.
4 *an increasing mobility in the workforce*: **adaptability**, flexibility, versatility, adjustability.

mobilize verb **1** *the government mobilized regular troops and reservists*: **marshal**, deploy, muster, rally, call to arms, call up, summon, assemble, mass, organize, make ready, prepare, ready.
2 *he used the press to mobilize support for his party*: **bring into play**, bring into service, arouse, generate, induce, cause, resort to, awaken, deploy, waken, excite, incite, provoke, foment, prompt, stimulate, stir up, impel, galvanize, urge, encourage, inspire, whip up.

mock verb **1** *the local children taunted and mocked the old people in the home*: **ridicule**, jeer at, sneer at, deride, treat with contempt, treat contemptuously, scorn, make fun of, poke fun at, laugh at, make jokes about, laugh to scorn, scoff at, pillory, be sarcastic about, tease, taunt, make a monkey of, rag, chaff, jibe at; Austral./NZ chiack; informal kid, rib, josh, twit; Brit. informal wind up, take the mickey out of; Brit. vulgar slang take the piss out of; N. Amer. informal goof on, rag on, razz, pull someone's chain; Austral./NZ informal poke mullock at, sling off at; dated make sport of.
2 *they still mock the slow way he speaks*: **parody**, ape, guy, take off, caricature, satirize, lampoon, imitate, mimic; informal send up, spoof.
▶ adjective *a mock leather armchair*: **imitation**, artificial, man-made, manufactured, simulated, synthetic, ersatz, plastic, so-called, fake, false, faux, reproduction, replica, facsimile, dummy, model, toy, make-believe, sham, spurious, bogus, counterfeit, fraudulent, forged, pseudo, pretended; informal pretend, phoney.
▷ANTONYMS genuine.

mockery noun **1** *a note of mockery in his voice*: **ridicule**, derision, jeering, sneering, contempt, scorn, scoffing, joking, teasing, taunting, sarcasm, ragging, chaffing, jibing; Austral./NZ chiacking; informal **kidding**, **kidology**, ribbing, joshing; Brit. informal winding up; taking the mickey; Brit. vulgar slang taking the piss; N. Amer. informal goofing, razzing.
2 *the trial was a mockery*: **travesty**, charade, farce, parody, laughing stock, caricature, lampoon, burlesque, apology, excuse, poor substitute.

> *Choose the right word* **mockery, ridicule, derision**
>
> These three words reflect increasing degrees of scorn.
>
> **Mockery** is the least severe. While it is usually intended to humiliate (*stung by her mockery, Frankie hung his head*), it can also express affectionate amusement (*'Liar,' he said with soft mockery*). It can also mean 'a worthy object of mockery' in the phrase *a mockery of* (*after a mockery of a trial, he was executed*), but the sense is usually considerably weakened, especially (however serious the subject) in the cliché *make a mockery of* (*modern technology has made a mockery of the 1959 Obscene Publications Act*).
>
> **Ridicule** is more intense, the aim being not so much to provoke or tease the victim as to cause others to laugh at them (*Puritans were frequently subjected to ridicule and abuse at the hands of their contemporaries*).
>
> **Derision** is still crueller and more contemptuous (*Eline would forget the hurtful words spoken in derision*). The phrase *of derision* is commonly used to qualify a description of a scornful noise (*the answer was a snort of derision*).

mocking adjective *a mocking smile*: **sneering**, derisive, contemptuous, scornful, sardonic, insulting, satirical, sarcastic, ironic, ironical, quizzical, teasing, taunting.
▷ANTONYMS friendly, open, good-humoured.

mode noun **1** *an extremely informal mode of policing*: **manner**, way, fashion, means, method, system, style, approach, technique, procedure, process, methodology, modus operandi, form, routine, practice.
2 *with the camera in manual mode you can zoom in fast*: **function**, position, operation, role, capacity.
3 *the mode for active wear took hold in the seventies*: **fashion**, **vogue**,

current/latest style, style, look, trend, latest thing, latest taste; craze, rage, fad, general tendency, convention, custom, practice; French dernier cri.

model noun **1** *a working model of a train*: **replica**, copy, representation, mock-up, dummy, imitation, double, duplicate, lookalike, reproduction; **toy**, miniature, facsimile.
2 *the American model of airline deregulation*: **prototype**, stereotype, archetype, type, version, style; mould, template, framework, pattern, design, guide, blueprint, paradigm; sample, example, exemplar.
3 *she was an absolute model as a teacher*: **ideal**, paragon, perfect example, specimen, perfect specimen; personification, embodiment, perfection, acme, the epitome; French beau idéal, nonpareil, crème de la crème; informal pick of the bunch.
4 *she was too small to be a top model*: **fashion model**, supermodel, mannequin; informal clothes horse.
5 *he used his wife as a model for his pictures*: **sitter**, poser, subject, artist's model, photographic model.
6 *he changes his car every year for the latest model*: **version**, type, design, mark, configuration, variety, kind, sort.
7 *this dress is a model, so not for sale, I'm afraid*: **original**, original design, exclusive; informal one-off.
▸ adjective **1** *a competition for model hot-air balloons*: **replica**, **toy**, miniature, mock-up, dummy, imitation, duplicate, lookalike, reproduction, facsimile; artificial, fake, make-believe, sham, false, spurious, bogus, counterfeit; informal pretend, phoney.
2 *ten model farms have been set up as a showcase for alternative production methods*: **prototypical**, prototypal, archetypal, illustrative.
3 *a model teacher*: **ideal**, perfect, exemplary, classic, flawless, faultless, consummate, impeccable.
▷ANTONYMS deficient, imperfect.

moderate adjective **1** *the club enjoyed moderate success*: **average**, modest, medium, middling, ordinary, common, commonplace, everyday, workaday; tolerable, passable, adequate, fair, decent; **mediocre**, indifferent, uninspired, undistinguished, unexceptional, unexciting, unremarkable, run-of-the-mill, lacklustre, forgettable, inferior, second-rate; informal OK, so-so, bog-standard, fair-to-middling, (plain) vanilla, nothing to write home about, no great shakes, not so hot, not up to much; NZ informal half-pie.
▷ANTONYMS great, massive.
2 *moderate demands | moderate prices*: **reasonable**, within reason, acceptable, non-excessive, within due limits; **inexpensive**, low, cheap, bargain-basement, fair, modest; abstemious, temperate, restrained.
▷ANTONYMS outrageous, unreasonable.
3 *a man of moderate views*: **dispassionate**, non-extreme, middle-of-the-road, non-radical, non-reactionary, open to reason, equitable, impartial.
▷ANTONYMS extreme.
4 *moderate behaviour*: **restrained**, controlled, temperate, sober, steady, regular, not given to excesses; easy, even, mild, tolerant, lenient.
▷ANTONYMS unreasonable, immoderate.
▸ verb **1** *the wind has moderated*: **die down**, abate, let up, calm down, lessen, grow less, decrease, diminish, slacken; ebb, recede, dwindle, weaken, subside.
▷ANTONYMS get up, increase.
2 *you can do something to moderate the anger*: **curb**, control, check, keep in check, keep under control, hold in, temper, regulate, restrain, restrict, subdue; still, damp, repress, tame, break, lessen, deaden, decrease, lower, reduce, diminish, remit, mitigate, alleviate, allay, appease, assuage, ease, palliate, soothe, soften, calm, modulate, pacify, mellow, mince, tone down.
▷ANTONYMS exacerbate, aggravate.
3 *the Speaker moderates the assembly*: **chair**, take the chair of, preside over; **arbitrate**, mediate, referee, judge.

moderately adverb *a moderately successful small farmer*: **somewhat**, quite, rather, fairly, reasonably, comparatively, relatively, to a limited extent/degree, to a certain degree, to some extent, within reason, within limits, tolerably, passably, adequately, satisfactorily; informal pretty, kind of, sort of, ish.
▷ANTONYMS massively, hugely.

moderation noun **1** *he was anxious to contrast his moderation with the sabre-rattling of his opponent*: **self-restraint**, restraint, self-control, self-discipline; moderateness, temperateness, temperance, abstemiousness, non-indulgence, leniency, fairness.
▷ANTONYMS extremism.
2 *he called for a moderation of the Government's confrontational style*: **relaxation**, easing (off), reduction, abatement, weakening, slackening, diminution, diminishing, lessening, decrease, lightening, subsidence, contraction; tailing off, waning, decline, modulation, ebb, alleviation, attenuation, modification, mitigation, allaying, appeasement, assuagement, palliation, cushioning, damping, deadening, dulling; soothing, relief, softening, tempering, stilling, quelling, calming, pacification, placation, mollification, remission, extenuation; informal let-up.
▷ANTONYMS stepping up.
□ **in moderation** *wine, if drunk in moderation, can be beneficial to health*: **in moderate quantities**, in moderate amounts, within reasonable limits, within sensible limits, within limits, within bounds, within due limits; moderately, up to a point.

modern adjective **1** *in modern times*: **present-day**, contemporary, present-time, present, current, twenty-first-century, latter-day, recent, latest.
▷ANTONYMS past.
2 *her clothes are very modern*: **fashionable**, in fashion, in, in style, in vogue, up to date, up to the minute, all the rage, trendsetting, stylish, voguish, modish, chic, smart, the latest, new, newest, newfangled, new-fashioned, fresh, modernistic, advanced, progressive, forward-looking; French à la mode; informal trendy, cool, flash, with it, swinging, now, hip, happening, snazzy, natty, nifty, go-ahead; N. Amer. informal tony.
▷ANTONYMS out of date, old-fashioned.

modernity noun **contemporaneity**, contemporaneousness, modernness, modernism, currency, freshness, novelty, fashionableness, vogue; informal trendiness, coolness, snazziness.

modernize verb **1** *the company is investing $9m to modernize its manufacturing facilities*: **update**, bring up to date, bring/drag/lead/march into the twenty-first century, streamline, rationalize, overhaul, develop; **renovate**, rebuild, reindustrialize, remodel, refashion, retouch, remake, redo, refresh, revamp, make over, rejuvenate, redecorate, refurbish; informal do over, tart up.
2 *if we don't modernize, we will lose our competitive edge*: **get up to date**, move with the times, innovate, make changes/alterations; informal get in the swim, drag oneself into the twenty-first century, get on the ball, get with it.

modest adjective **1** *she was always modest about her poetry*: **self-effacing**, self-deprecating, humble, unpretentious, unassuming, unpresuming, unostentatious, low-key, free from vanity, keeping one's light under a bushel; **shy**, bashful, self-conscious, diffident, timid, reserved, retiring, reticent, quiet, coy, embarrassed, shamefaced, blushing, fearful, meek, docile, mild, apologetic; Scottish mim.
▷ANTONYMS boastful, conceited.
2 *a period of modest success*: **moderate**, fair, tolerable, passable, adequate, satisfactory, acceptable, unexceptional, small; light, limited, scanty, skimpy, frugal, meagre, sparse.
▷ANTONYMS great, runaway.
3 *a modest house*: **small**, ordinary, simple, plain, humble, homely; inexpensive, low-cost, cheap, poor; unostentatious, unpretentious, unimposing.
▷ANTONYMS grand, grandiose.
4 *the full-length skirt of her modest navy blue suit*: **decorous**, decent, seemly, demure, sober, severe; coy, proper, discreet, delicate, chaste, virtuous.
▷ANTONYMS immodest, flamboyant.

modesty noun **1** *Hannah's innate modesty cloaks many talents*: **self-effacement**, humility, lack of vanity, lack of pretension, unpretentiousness; **shyness**, bashfulness, self-consciousness, reserve, reticence, timidity, meekness.
▷ANTONYMS boastfulness.
2 *Gandhi's political tactics obscured the modesty of his political aspirations*: **limited scope**, moderation, fairness, acceptability, smallness.
▷ANTONYMS grandeur.
3 *it is appropriate to contrast the modesty of his home with those of more affluent politicians*: **unpretentiousness**, simplicity, plainness, lack of pretension, inexpensiveness, lack of extravagance.
▷ANTONYMS grandeur.
4 *they jeered at her maidenly modesty*: **decorum**, decorousness, decency, seemliness, demureness, sobriety, severity; coyness, propriety, discreetness, delicacy, chasteness, virtue.
▷ANTONYMS immodesty, flamboyance.

modicum noun *people with only a modicum of scientific knowledge*: **little bit**, small amount, particle, degree, speck, fragment, scrap, crumb, grain, morsel, taste, soupçon, shred, mite, dash, drop, pinch, ounce, touch, tinge, dab, jot, iota, whit, tittle, jot or tittle, atom, inch, snippet, sliver, smattering, scintilla, hint, suggestion, whisper, trifle; informal smidgen, smidge, tad; archaic scantling, scruple.

modification noun **1** *the design of the engine is undergoing extensive modification*: **alteration**, adjustment, change, adaptation, improvement, refinement, revision, recasting, reshaping, refashioning, restyling, revamping, reworking, remodelling, remoulding, reconstruction, reorganization; variation, conversion, transformation; tailoring, customization.
2 *the proposal was passed after some minor modifications had been made*: **revision**, refinement, variation, improvement, amendment, adaptation, adjustment, change, alteration.
3 *working class opposition to the tax has led to some modification of this stance*: **softening**, moderation, tempering, qualification, restriction, lessening, reduction, decrease, diminishing, lowering, abatement, mitigation.

modify verb **1** *their economic policy has been substantially modified*: **alter**, make alterations to, change, adjust, make adjustments to, adapt, amend, improve, revise, recast, reform, reshape, refashion, redesign, restyle, revamp, rework, remake, remodel, remould, redo, reconstruct, reorganize,

m

refine, reorient, reorientate, vary, transform, convert; customize, tailor; informal tweak; technical permute; rare permutate.
2 *he was forced to modify his more extreme views*: **moderate**, revise, temper, soften, tone down, blunt, dull, qualify, restrict, limit, lessen, reduce, decrease, diminish, lower, abate, mitigate.

modish adjective **fashionable**, stylish, smart, chic, modern, contemporary, designer, all the rage, in vogue, trendsetting, voguish, up to the minute; French à la mode; informal trendy, cool, with it, in, now, hip, happening, snazzy, natty, nifty; N. Amer. informal kicky, tony; Brit. informal, dated all the go, swagger.

modulate verb **1** *the cells modulate the body's immune response*: **regulate**, adjust, set, attune, balance, harmonize, temper, modify, moderate.
2 *she modulated her voice so as to speak more gently*: **adjust**, change the tone of, vary, inflect.

modus operandi noun Latin **method of working**, method, way, MO, manner, technique, style, procedure, approach, course of action, plan of action, methodology, mode, fashion, process, means, strategy, plan, formula, recipe, practice; rare praxis.

mogul noun *Hollywood movie moguls*: **magnate**, tycoon, VIP, notable, notability, personage, baron, captain, king, lord, grandee, mandarin, nabob; informal bigwig, big shot, big noise, big cheese, big gun, big wheel, big fish, top dog, Big Chief, Big Daddy, biggie, heavy, fat cat; N. Amer. informal kahuna, top banana, big enchilada, macher.

moist adjective **1** *the air was moist and heavy | moist, well-drained soil*: **damp**, dampish, steamy, humid, muggy, clammy, dank, moisture-laden, wet, wettish, rainy, drizzly, drizzling, dewy, dripping, soggy, sweaty, sticky.
▷ANTONYMS dry.
2 *a rich, moist fruit cake*: **succulent**, juicy, soft, spongy.
3 *her dark eyes grew moist*: **tearful**, teary, dewy-eyed, watery, misty.

> *Word toolkit* **moist**
>
> See **ripe**, **wet**.

moisten verb *the compost should be moistened before use*: **dampen**, wet, damp, dew, water, soak, irrigate, humidify; literary bedew; rare sparge, humify, humect, moistify.
▷ANTONYMS dry.

moisture noun *dehumidifiers will remove moisture from the air*: **wetness**, wet, water, liquid, condensation, steam, vapour, dampness, damp, humidity, clamminess, mugginess, dankness, wateriness; rain, dew, drizzle, precipitation, spray; perspiration, sweat.

> *Word links* **moisture**
>
> **hygro-** related prefix
> **hygrometer**, **hygroscope** instrument for measuring moisture in the air

moisturizer noun *a moisturizer which hydrates the skin for up to 12 hours*: **lotion**, cream, balm, emollient, salve, unguent, lubricant; hand lotion, body lotion, baby oil, cold cream, aftershave, aftersun; pomade, pomatum; technical humectant.

mole[1] noun *he had a small mole on his left cheek*: **mark**, freckle, blotch, discoloration, spot, blemish.

mole[2] noun **1** *moles have burrowed under the lawn*: dialect mouldwarp, mouldywarp.
2 *they planted a mole in the other side's operation*: **spy**, agent, secret agent, double agent, undercover agent, operative, plant, infiltrator; N. Amer. informal spook; archaic intelligencer.

> *Word links* **mole**
>
> **labour** collective noun (for the animals)

mole[3] noun *a mole was built to protect the harbour from storms*: **breakwater**, groyne, dyke, pier, jetty, sea wall, embankment, causeway.

molest verb **1** *the crowd were shouting abuse and molesting the police officers*: **harass**, harry, pester, beset, persecute, torment, plague; N. Amer. informal roust.
2 *he was charged with molesting a ten-year-old boy*: **abuse**, sexually abuse, assault, sexually assault, interfere with, rape, violate, attack, hurt, harm, injure; informal maul, grope, paw; dated ravish.

mollify verb **1** *nature reserves were set up to mollify local conservationists*: **appease**, placate, pacify, conciliate, humour, soothe, calm, calm down, still, quieten, propitiate; Austral. square someone off.
▷ANTONYMS enrage.
2 *the government's undertaking mollified the fears of the public*: **allay**, assuage, alleviate, mitigate, ease, lessen, reduce, moderate, lull, temper, tone down, cushion, quell, soften, blunt.
▷ANTONYMS inflame, aggravate.

mollycoddle verb *his parents have mollycoddled him since he was a baby*: **pamper**, cosset, coddle, spoil, indulge, overindulge, pet, baby, wait on hand and foot, wrap in cotton wool, spoon-feed, kill with/by kindness, nanny, nursemaid, feather-bed; archaic cocker.
▶noun *the boy's a mollycoddle!* **milksop**, namby-pamby, crybaby, baby, coward, weakling, Milquetoast; informal sissy, weed, softie, nancy, nancy boy, pansy, ponce; Brit. informal wet, mummy's boy, chinless wonder, jessie; N. Amer. informal pantywaist, cupcake, pussy; Austral./NZ informal sook; S. African informal moffie; archaic poltroon.

molten adjective *a stream of molten metal*: **liquefied**, liquid, fluid, melted, flowing, soft.

> *Word toolkit* **molten**
>
> See **runny**.

moment noun **1** *he thought for a moment before answering*: **little while**, short time, bit, minute, second, instant, split second; informal sec, jiffy, jiff; Brit. informal tick, mo, two ticks.
2 *she would always remember the moment they met*: **point in time**, point, time, hour, juncture, stage.
3 *the issues were of little moment to the voters*: **importance**, import, significance, consequence, substance, note, mark, prominence, value, weight, concern, interest, gravity, seriousness.
□ **at the moment** *I am not very anxious to see you at the moment*: **at present**, just now, right now, at this time, at the present time, currently, presently, at this moment in time.
□ **in a moment very soon**, in a minute, in a second, in a trice, in a flash, shortly, any minute, any minute now, in a short time, in an instant, in the twinkling of an eye, in (less than) no time, in no time at all, before you know it, before long; N. Amer. momentarily; informal in a jiffy, in two shakes, in two shakes of a lamb's tail, before you can say Jack Robinson, in the blink of an eye, in a blink, in the wink of an eye, in a wink, before you can say knife; Brit. informal in a tick, in two ticks, in a mo; N. Amer. informal in a snap; archaic or informal anon; archaic ere long.

momentarily adverb **1** *as he passed her door, he paused momentarily*: **briefly**, temporarily, fleetingly, for a moment, for a second, for an instant, for a minute, for a little while.
2 N. Amer. *my husband will pick me up momentarily*: **(very) soon**, in a minute, in a second, in a trice, in a flash, shortly, any minute, any minute now, in a short time, in an instant, in the twinkling of an eye, in (less than) no time, in no time at all, before you know it, before long; informal in a jiffy, in two shakes, in two shakes of a lamb's tail, before you can say Jack Robinson, in the blink of an eye, in a blink, in the wink of an eye, in a wink, before you can say knife; Brit. informal in a tick, in two ticks, in a mo; N. Amer. informal in a snap; archaic or informal anon; archaic ere long.

momentary adjective *Jamieson didn't see the momentary flash of panic in her eyes*: **brief**, short, short-lived, quick, fleeting, passing, transient, transitory, ephemeral, evanescent, fugitive, temporary, impermanent; rare fugacious.
▷ANTONYMS lengthy, lasting, permanent.

> *Easily confused words* **momentary or momentous?**
>
> **Momentary** and **momentous** are both derived from *moment*, but in different senses. *Momentary* is related to *moment* in the sense 'a very brief time', and means 'lasting only for a very short time' (*after a momentary hesitation she nodded*). *Momentous*, derived from *moment* in the sense of 'importance', means 'of great importance or significance', and applies particularly to events with profound implications for future developments (*a decade of momentous political change*).

momentous adjective *a momentous decision*: **important**, significant, epoch-making, historic, apocalyptic, fateful, portentous, critical, crucial, vital, life-and-death, decisive, pivotal, serious, grave, weighty, consequential, big, great, far-reaching, of importance, of moment, of significance, of consequence; earth-shaking, earth-shattering, world-shaking, world-shattering.
▷ANTONYMS unimportant, trivial, insignificant.

> *Easily confused words* **momentous or momentary?**
>
> See **momentary**.

momentum noun *the vehicle gained momentum as the road dipped*: **impetus**, energy, force, power, strength, drive, thrust, push, driving power, steam, impulse, speed, velocity.

monarch noun **sovereign**, ruler, Crown, crowned head, potentate; king, queen, emperor, empress, prince, princess, tsar.

monarchy noun **1** *the country is a constitutional monarchy*: **kingdom**, sovereign state, principality, empire; realm.
2 *few questioned the moral justification of hereditary monarchy*: **kingship**, sovereignty, autocracy, monocracy, absolutism, absolute power, despotism; royalism, monarchism.

monastery noun **religious house**, religious community; friary, abbey, priory, cloister, convent, nunnery; Buddhism vihara, lamasery; Islam tekke; Indian ashram; historical charterhouse, cell; rare coenobium, coenoby.

monastic adjective **1** *a monastic community*: **cloistered**, conventual, cloistral, claustral, canonical, monastical; rare coenobitic, monachal.
2 *he was a shy man and led a rather monastic existence*: **austere**, ascetic, simple, solitary, monkish, celibate, quiet, cloistered, sequestered, secluded, reclusive, withdrawn, hermit-like, eremitic, anchoritic, hermitic, contemplative, meditative.
▷ANTONYMS sybaritic.

monetary adjective **financial**, fiscal, pecuniary, money, cash, economic, budgetary, capital.

money noun **1** *I haven't got enough money to buy it*: **cash**, hard cash, ready money; **the means**, the wherewithal, funds, capital, finances, (filthy) lucre; banknotes, notes, paper money, coins, change, coin, coinage, silver, copper, currency, legal tender; Brit. sterling; N. Amer. bills; N. Amer. & Austral. roll; informal dough, bread, loot, the ready, readies, shekels, moolah, the necessary, wad, boodle, dibs, gelt, ducats, rhino, gravy, scratch, stuff, oof, folding money; Brit. informal dosh, brass, lolly, spondulicks, wonga, ackers; N. Amer. informal dinero, greenbacks, simoleons, bucks, jack, mazuma; Austral./NZ informal Oscar; informal, dated splosh, green, tin; Brit. dated l.s.d.; N. Amer. informal, dated kale, rocks, shinplasters; formal specie; archaic pelf.
2 *she married him for his money*: **wealth**, riches, fortune, affluence, assets, liquid assets, resources, substance, means, prosperity.
3 *I took the job here because the money was better*: **pay**, salary, wages, remuneration, fee, stipend; rare emolument.
□ **for my money** *for my money, they are the better team*: **in my opinion**, to my mind, in my view, as I see it, (according) to my way of thinking, from my standpoint, personally, in my estimation, in my judgement, in my book, if you ask me.
□ **in the money rich**, wealthy, affluent, well-to-do, well off, prosperous, moneyed, in clover, opulent; informal rolling in it, rolling in money, loaded, stinking rich, well heeled, flush, made of money, in/on easy street; informal, dated oofy; Brit. informal quids in.
□ **money for old rope** informal *I could be one of those TV pundits—money for old rope, if you ask me*: **a cinch**, child's play, a gift, a walkover; informal a doddle, a walk in the park, a piece of cake, a picnic, money for jam, a breeze, kids' stuff, a cushy job/number, a doss, a cakewalk, a pushover; N. Amer. informal duck soup; Austral./NZ informal a bludge; S. African informal a piece of old tackie; dated a snip; Brit. vulgar slang a piece of piss. See also **easy**.

> *Word links* **money**
>
> **pecuniary**, **monetary** relating to money
> **numismatist** collector of notes and coins
> **chrematophobia** fear of money

moneyed adjective *the industrial revolution created a new moneyed class*: **rich**, wealthy, affluent, well-to-do, well off, with deep pockets, prosperous, in clover, opulent, of means, of substance; informal in the money, rolling in it, rolling in money, loaded, stinking/filthy rich, well heeled, flush, made of money, in/on easy street; Brit. informal quids in; informal, dated in the chips, on velvet, oofy.
▷ANTONYMS penniless, poor, impoverished.

money-grubbing adjective informal *his money-grubbing relatives*: **acquisitive**, avaricious, grasping, money-grabbing, greedy, rapacious, mercenary, materialistic; N. Amer. informal grabby; rare quaestuary, Mammonish, Mammonistic.

moneymaking adjective *a moneymaking scheme*: **profitable**, profit-making, remunerative, lucrative, gainful, paying, successful, financially rewarding, productive, thriving, going; commercial, for-profit.
▷ANTONYMS loss-making.

mongrel noun *a rough-haired mongrel with a dash of Airedale*: **cross-breed**, cross, mixed breed, half-breed, hybrid; tyke, cur, mutt; N. Amer. yellow dog; NZ kuri; Asian pye-dog, pariah dog; informal Heinz 57; Austral. informal mong, bitzer; technical bigener.
▶ adjective *a mongrel bitch*: **cross-bred**, of mixed breed, half-breed, hybrid.
▷ANTONYMS pedigree.

monitor noun **1** *a heart monitor | a bank of monitors covered various areas of the building*: **detector**, scanner, recorder; security system, security camera, CCTV.
2 *UN monitors declared that the election had been fair*: **observer**, watchdog, overseer, invigilator, supervisor.
3 *a computer monitor*: **screen**, VDU, visual display unit.
4 Brit. *a school monitor*: **prefect**, praepostor; senior boy, senior girl, senior pupil.
▶ verb *equipment was installed to monitor air quality | his movements were closely monitored*: **observe**, watch, keep an eye on, keep track of, track, keep under observation, keep watch on, keep under surveillance, surveil, check, keep a check on, scan, examine, study, record, note, oversee, supervise, superintend; informal keep tabs on, keep a tab on, keep a beady eye on.

monk noun **brother**, male member of a religious order, religious, contemplative; friar; abbot, prior; novice, oblate, postulant; Benedictine, Black Monk, Cluniac, Carthusian, Cistercian, White Monk, Culdee; Buddhism lama, talapoin; Islam marabout; historical mendicant; rare coenobite, cloisterer, religioner, religieux.

> *Word links* **monk**
>
> **monastic** relating to a monk

monkey noun **1 simian**, primate, ape.
2 *where have you been, you little monkey!* **rascal**, imp, wretch, mischief-maker, devil, rogue; informal scamp, scallywag, horror, tyke, monster; Brit. informal perisher; N. Amer. informal varmint, hellion; informal, dated rip; Brit. informal, dated pickle; archaic scapegrace, rapscallion.
□ **make a monkey (out) of make someone look a fool**, make someone look foolish, make a fool of, make a laughing stock of, ridicule, deride, make fun of, poke fun at; set someone up, play a trick on.
▶ verb informal
□ **monkey about/around** *we were just monkeying around upstairs*: **fool about/around**, play about/around, clown about/around, fiddle-faddle, footle about/around; informal mess about/around, horse about/around, lark (about/around), screw around, puddle about/around; Brit. informal muck about/around, fanny about/around; Brit. vulgar slang piss about/around, arse about/around, bugger about/around.
□ **monkey with** *don't monkey with that lock*: **tamper with**, fiddle with, interfere with, meddle with, tinker with, touch/handle without permission, play with, fool with, trifle with; informal mess with, dick around with; Brit. informal muck about/around with.

> *Word links* **monkey**
>
> **simian** relating to monkeys
> **troop** collective noun

monkey business noun informal *if they try any monkey business with me they'll soon find out who's in charge*: **mischief**, misbehaviour, mischievousness, devilry, devilment, rascality, tomfoolery; dishonesty, trickery, misconduct, misdemeanour, chicanery, skulduggery; informal shenanigans, funny business, hanky-panky, goings-on; Brit. informal monkey tricks, carry-on, carryings-on, jiggery-pokery; N. Amer. informal monkeyshines.

monocle noun **eyeglass**, glass; historical lorgnette, quizzing glass.

monolith noun **standing stone**, menhir, sarsen (stone), megalith.

monolithic adjective **1** *a monolithic building*: **massive**, huge, vast, colossal, gigantic, immense, giant, enormous, mammoth, monumental; **featureless**, characterless, faceless.
2 *he reveals how static and monolithic his thinking really is*: **inflexible**, rigid, unbending, unchanging, intractable, immovable, impenetrable, fossilized, hidebound; undifferentiated, uniform, unitary.

monologue noun *the skilfully varied tone and pace of her 40-minute monologue*: **soliloquy**, speech, address, lecture, oration, sermon, homily; dramatic monologue, interior monologue; informal spiel.

monomania noun *his profound interest in the subject verges on monomania*: **obsession**, fixation, idée fixe, ruling passion, consuming passion, mania, compulsion, fetish, preoccupation, hobby horse; informal bee in one's bonnet, thing.

monopolize verb **1** *the company has monopolized the market*: **corner**, control, take over, gain control/dominance over, have sole/exclusive rights in, exercise a monopoly over; archaic engross.
2 *he has a tendency to monopolize the conversation*: **dominate**, take over, not let anyone else take part in; not let anyone else get a word in edgeways; informal hog.
3 *she monopolized the guest of honour for most of the evening*: **take up all the attention of**, keep to oneself, have all to oneself, not allow to associate with others; informal tie up.
▷ANTONYMS share.

monotonous adjective **1** *a monotonous job*: **tedious**, boring, dull, uninteresting, unexciting, wearisome, tiresome, repetitive, repetitious, unvarying, unchanging, unvaried, lacking variety, without variety, humdrum, ho-hum, routine, mechanical, mind-numbing, soul-destroying, prosaic, run-of-the-mill, uneventful, unrelieved, dreary, plodding, colourless, featureless, dry as dust, uniform, monochrome; informal deadly; Brit. informal samey; N. Amer. informal dullsville.
▷ANTONYMS varied, interesting, exciting.
2 *a monotonous voice*: **toneless**, flat, unvarying, uninflected, droning, soporific.

monotony noun **1** *the monotony of everyday life*: **tedium**, tediousness, lack of variety, dullness, boredom, lack of variation, repetitiveness, repetitiousness, repetition, sameness, unchangingness, uniformity, routine, routineness, wearisomeness, tiresomeness, humdrumness, lack of interest, lack of excitement, prosaicness, uneventfulness, dreariness,

colourlessness, featurelessness; informal deadliness; Brit. informal sameyness.
▷ANTONYMS variety, excitement.
2 *the monotony of her voice*: **tonelessness**, flatness, lack of inflection, drone.

monster noun 1 *legendary sea monsters*: **fabulous creature**, mythical creature.
2 *her husband is an absolute monster*: **brute**, fiend, beast, ogre, devil, demon, barbarian, savage, villain, sadist, animal, bogeyman; informal bastard, swine, pig; Scottish informal radge; vulgar slang shit.
3 *Christian's only a year old, but he's already a little monster*: **rascal**, imp, wretch, mischief-maker, rogue, devil; informal horror, scamp, scallywag, tyke, monkey; archaic rip, scapegrace, rapscallion; Brit. informal perisher; Brit. informal, dated pickle; N. Amer. informal varmint, hellion.
4 *he was huge, a monster of a man*: **giant**, mammoth, colossus, leviathan, behemoth, titan, Brobdingnagian, monstrosity; informal jumbo.
▶adjective *the film is sure to be a monster hit | a monster 16 kg carp*: **huge**, enormous, massive, gigantic, big, large, great, giant, colossal, mammoth, vast, immense, tremendous, mighty, stupendous, monumental, epic, prodigious, mountainous, monstrous, titanic, towering, elephantine, king-sized, king-size, gargantuan, Herculean, Brobdingnagian; informal mega, whopping, whopping great, thumping, thumping great, humongous, jumbo, hulking, bumper, astronomical, astronomic; Brit. informal whacking, whacking great, ginormous.

> *Word links* **monster**
>
> **terato-** related prefix, as in *teratogenic, teratology*

monstrosity noun 1 *the shopping centre was a multi-storey concrete monstrosity*: **eyesore**, horror, blot on the landscape, carbuncle, excrescence.
2 *a biological monstrosity*: **mutant**, mutation, freak, freak of nature, monster, abortion, malformation; Latin lusus naturae; rare abnormity, miscreation.

monstrous adjective 1 *a monstrous creature with great leathery wings and a horny head*: **grotesque**, hideous, ugly, ghastly, gruesome, horrible, horrid, horrific, horrendous, horrifying, grisly, disgusting, repulsive, repellent, revolting, nightmarish, dreadful, frightening, terrifying, fearsome, freakish, malformed, misshapen, unnatural, abnormal, mutant, miscreated; rare teratoid.
▷ANTONYMS lovely, beautiful, normal.
2 *a monstrous tidal wave engulfed the countryside*: **huge**, enormous, massive, great, gigantic, giant, colossal, mammoth, vast, immense, tremendous, mighty, stupendous, monumental, epic, prodigious, mountainous, titanic, towering, elephantine, king-sized, king-size, gargantuan, Herculean, Brobdingnagian, substantial; informal mega, monster, whopping, whopping great, thumping, thumping great, humongous, jumbo, hulking; Brit. informal whacking, whacking great, ginormous.
▷ANTONYMS tiny, minute.
3 *could he be guilty of such monstrous acts?* **appalling**, abhorrent, heinous, evil, wicked, abominable, terrible, horrible, dreadful, hideous, foul, vile; outrageous, shocking, disgraceful, scandalous, atrocious; villainous, nasty, ghastly, odious, loathsome, shameful, infamous, nefarious, iniquitous, unspeakable, intolerable, contemptible, despicable, vicious, cruel, savage, brutish, bestial, barbaric, barbarous, base, inhuman, depraved, fiendish, devilish, diabolical, satanic, ruthless, merciless; Brit. informal beastly; rare egregious, flagitious.
▷ANTONYMS admirable, good, kind.

monument noun 1 *a stone monument was built to mark the site*: **memorial**; statue, pillar, column, obelisk, cross; cairn, dolmen, cromlech, monolith, megalith, henge, stone circle; cenotaph, tomb, mausoleum, shrine, sepulchre, reliquary; Buddhism chorten.
2 *a monument of granite was placed over the grave*: **gravestone**, headstone, tombstone.
3 *the restored airfield is a monument to a past era of aviation | a musical work which is an astonishing monument of skill and industry*: **testament**, record, reminder, remembrance, memorial, commemoration, witness, token; example, exemplar, model, archetype, pattern, nonpareil, paragon.

monumental adjective 1 *a monumental task*: **huge**, great, enormous, gigantic, massive, colossal, mammoth, immense, tremendous, mighty, stupendous, vast, prodigious, Herculean, titanic, gargantuan, staggering, exceptional, extraordinary; Brit. informal ginormous.
2 *a monumental error of judgement*: **terrible**, dreadful, awful, colossal, staggering, huge, enormous; catastrophic, unforgivable, indefensible; informal whopping; rare egregious.
3 *the ballet is one of his most monumental works*: **impressive**, striking, outstanding, remarkable, magnificent, marvellous, majestic, stupendous, prodigious, ambitious, large-scale, grand, awe-inspiring, awesome, important, significant, distinguished, classic, memorable, transcendent, exalted, unforgettable, enduring, lasting, abiding, permanent, immortal, historic, epoch-making.
4 *a monumental inscription*: **commemorative**, memorial, celebratory, commemorating, funerary.

mood noun 1 *she was in a very good mood that morning*: **frame of mind**, state of mind, emotional state, humour, temper; disposition, spirit, tenor, vein.
2 *he's obviously in a mood*: **bad mood**, temper, bad temper, fit of bad/ill temper, sulk, pet, the sulks, fit of pique, low spirits, depression, bout of moping, the doldrums, the blues; informal the dumps, grump; Brit. informal paddy; Brit. informal, dated bate, wax.
3 *the soundtrack captures the mood of the film*: **atmosphere**, feeling, spirit, ambience, aura, character, tenor, flavour, quality, climate, feel, tone, key.
□ **in the mood** *I'm not* ***in the mood for*** *sightseeing | Jane was* ***in the mood*** *to talk*: **in the right frame of mind for/to**, feeling like, ready for/to, wanting to, inclined to, disposed to, minded to, interested in, keen on/to, eager to, enthusiastic about, willing to, game for.

moody adjective *teenagers tend to get a bad name for being moody and irresponsible*: **unpredictable**, temperamental, emotional, volatile, capricious, changeable, mercurial, unstable, fickle, flighty, inconstant, undependable, unsteady, erratic, fitful, impulsive; **sullen**, sulky, morose, gloomy, glum, moping, mopey, mopish, depressed, dejected, despondent, blue, melancholic, doleful, dour, dismal, sour, saturnine, lugubrious, introspective; informal down in the dumps, down in the mouth; N. English informal mardy; informal, dated mumpish; archaic kittle.
▷ANTONYMS cheerful, happy, equable.

moon noun satellite.
▶verb 1 *stop mooning about and get on with some work*: **waste time**, fiddle, loaf, idle, mope, drift, stooge around; Brit. informal mooch; N. Amer. informal lollygag, bat.
2 *he's mooning over her photograph as if he was a schoolboy*: **mope**, pine, languish, brood, daydream, fantasize, be in a reverie, be in a brown study.
□ **many moons ago** informal **a long time ago**, ages ago, years ago; Brit. informal donkey's years ago, yonks ago; S. African before the rinderpest.
□ **once in a blue moon** informal **hardly ever**, almost never, scarcely ever, rarely, very seldom.
□ **over the moon** informal *Eve was over the moon when I broke the news*: **ecstatic**, euphoric, thrilled, overjoyed, elated, delighted, on cloud nine/seven, walking/treading on air, in seventh heaven, jubilant, rapturous, beside oneself with joy, jumping for joy, exultant, transported, delirious, enraptured, blissful, in raptures, as pleased as Punch, cock-a-hoop, as happy as a sandboy, as happy as Larry, like a child with a new toy; informal on top of the world, on a high, tickled pink; N. English informal made up; N. Amer. informal as happy as a clam; Austral. informal wrapped.

> *Word links* **moon**
>
> **lunar** relating to the moon
> **selenology** scientific study of the moon

moonshine noun *David Bates, prosecuting, dismissed the story as moonshine*. See **nonsense** (sense 1).

moor[1] verb *a boat was moored to the end of the dock*: **tie up**, secure, make fast, fix firmly, fasten, anchor, berth, dock; lash, hitch.

moor[2] noun *there was also a good stock of grouse on the moor*: **upland**, moorland, heath, plateau; Brit. fell, wold; grouse moor.

moot adjective *whether the temperature rise is due to the greenhouse effect is a moot point*: **debatable**, open to debate, open to discussion, arguable, questionable, at issue, open to question, open, doubtful, open to doubt, disputable, contestable, controvertible, problematic, problematical, controversial, contentious, vexed, disputed, unresolved, unsettled, up in the air, undecided, yet to be decided, undetermined, unconcluded.
▶verb *the idea was first mooted in the 1930s*: **raise**, bring up, broach, mention, put forward, introduce, advance, present, propose, suggest, submit, propound, air, ventilate.

mop noun 1 *a mop and bucket*: **sponge**, swab, squeegee.
2 *her tousled mop of hair*: **shock**, mane, thatch, tangle, mass, mat.
▶verb *a man was mopping the floor*: **wash**, clean, wipe, swab, sponge, squeegee.
□ **mop something up** 1 *I mopped up the spilt coffee*: **wipe up**, clean up, soak up, absorb, sop up, sponge up. 2 *troops mopped up the last pockets of resistance*: **finish off**, deal with, make an end of, dispose of, account for, take care of, clear up, eliminate, dispatch.

mope verb 1 *it's no use moping—things could be worse*: **brood**, sulk, be miserable, be gloomy, be sad, be despondent, pine, eat one's heart out, fret, grieve, despair; informal be down in the dumps, be down in the mouth; literary repine.
2 *she spends too much time moping about the house*: **languish**, moon, droop, idle, loaf, fiddle, drift, stooge; Brit. informal mooch; N. Amer. informal lollygag, bat.
▶noun *many people regarded her as a mope*: **melancholic**, depressive, pessimist, prophet of doom, killjoy, moaner; informal sourpuss, wet blanket, party-pooper, spoilsport, grouch, grump; Brit. informal misery; rare melancholiac.

moral adjective 1 *moral issues*: **ethical**; social, behavioural; to do with right and wrong.

2 *a very moral man*: **virtuous**, good, righteous, upright, upstanding, high-minded, right-minded, principled, proper, honourable, honest, just, noble, incorruptible, scrupulous, respectable, decent, irreproachable, truthful, law-abiding, clean-living, chaste, pure, blameless, sinless.
▷ANTONYMS immoral, bad, dishonourable.
3 *moral support*: **psychological**, emotional, mental.
▶noun 1 *the moral of the story*: **lesson**, message, meaning, significance, signification, import, point, precept, teaching.
2 (**morals**) *he has no morals and cannot be trusted*: **moral code**, code of ethics, moral standards, moral values, principles, principles of right and wrong, rules of conduct, standards/principles of behaviour, standards, morality, sense of morality, scruples, ideals.

morale noun *morale in the team was higher than it had been for a long time*: **confidence**, self-confidence, self-esteem; spirit, spirits, esprit de corps, team spirit, state of mind; heart, optimism, hope, hopefulness, determination.

moral fibre noun *an ineffectual man with no moral fibre*: **strength of character**, resolution, fortitude, resolve, backbone, spine, mettle, firmness of purpose, toughness of spirit, steel.
▷ANTONYMS weakness, cowardice.

morality noun 1 *the morality of the possession of nuclear weapons*: **ethics**, rights and wrongs, correctness, ethicality.
2 *the past few years have seen a sharp decline in morality*: **virtue**, goodness, good behaviour, righteousness, rectitude, uprightness; morals, principles, honesty, integrity, propriety, honour, justice, fair play, justness, decency, probity, chasteness, chastity, purity, blamelessness.
▷ANTONYMS immorality.
3 *orthodox Christian morality*: **moral standards**, morals, moral code, ethics, principles of right and wrong, rules of conduct, standards/principles of behaviour, ethos, mores, standards, ideals.

moralize verb *doctors should not moralize but simply deal with the patient's medical condition*: **pontificate**, sermonize, philosophize, lecture, preach; informal preachify; rare ethicize.

morass noun 1 *he managed to free himself from the muddy morass*: **quagmire**, swamp, bog, marsh, mire, quag, marshland, peat bog, fen, slough, quicksand; Scottish & N. English moss, carr; Irish corcass; N. Amer. bayou, pocosin, moor; archaic marish.
2 *we were stuck in a morass of procedure and paperwork*: **confusion**, chaos, muddle, tangle, entanglement, imbroglio, mix-up, jumble, clutter; mire, quagmire; W. Indian comess.

moratorium noun *a temporary moratorium on all nuclear testing*: **embargo**, ban, prohibition, suspension, postponement, stay, stoppage, halt, freeze, standstill, respite, hiatus, delay, deferment, deferral, adjournment.

morbid adjective 1 *a morbid fascination with the horrors of contemporary warfare*: **ghoulish**, macabre, unhealthy, gruesome, grisly, grotesque, ghastly, horrible, unwholesome, death-obsessed; informal sick.
▷ANTONYMS wholesome.
2 *during the months leading up to my 40th birthday, I felt decidedly morbid*: **gloomy**, glum, sunk in gloom, melancholy, lugubrious, pessimistic, morose, given to looking on the black side, dismal, funereal, defeatist, sombre, doleful, melancholic, despondent, dejected, sad, blue, depressed, downcast, down, disconsolate, desolate, miserable, unhappy, heavy-hearted, downhearted, dispirited, in low spirits, low-spirited, low, in the doldrums; informal down in the dumps, down in the mouth.
▷ANTONYMS cheerful.
3 *a morbid condition*: **diseased**, pathological.
▷ANTONYMS healthy.

mordant adjective *a mordant sense of humour*: **caustic**, trenchant, biting, cutting, acerbic, sardonic, sarcastic, scathing, acid, sharp, keen, tart, pungent, stinging, astringent, incisive, devastating, piercing, rapier-like, razor-edged; critical, bitter, polemic, virulent, vitriolic, venomous, waspish, corrosive; rare acidulous, mordacious.
▷ANTONYMS vague; uncritical.

more determiner *more water came pouring through the gap | I could do with some more clothes*: **additional**, further, added, extra, increased, fresh, new, other, supplementary, supplemental, spare, alternative.
▷ANTONYMS less, fewer.
▶adverb 1 *he was able to concentrate more on his writing*: **to a greater extent**, further, longer, some more, better.
2 *he was rich, and more, he was handsome*: **moreover**, furthermore, besides, what's more, in addition, also, as well, too, to boot, additionally, on top of that, over and above that, into the bargain; archaic withal, forbye.
▶pronoun *that's not enough—we're going to need more*: **extra**, an additional amount/number, a greater quantity/number; an addition, a supplement, an increase.
▷ANTONYMS less, fewer.
□ **more or less approximately**, roughly, nearly, almost, close to, about, of the order of, in the region of, give or take a few; S. African plus-minus.

moreover adverb **besides**, furthermore, what's more, in addition, also, as well, too, to boot, additionally, on top of that, over and above that, into the bargain, at that, more; archaic withal, forbye.

mores plural noun Latin *factors that shaped the social mores of the community*: **customs**, conventions, ways, way of life, way of doing things, traditions, practices, custom and practice, procedures, habits, usages; formal praxis.

morgue noun *the body, still unidentified, was taken to the morgue*: **mortuary**, funeral parlour, funeral chapel, funeral home; Brit. chapel of rest; archaic charnel house, dead house, lich-house.

moribund adjective 1 *the patient was moribund*: **dying**, expiring, on one's deathbed, near death, near the end, at death's door, breathing one's last, fading/sinking fast, not long for this world, failing rapidly, on one's last legs, in extremis; informal with one foot in the grave.
▷ANTONYMS thriving; recovering.
2 *the country's moribund shipbuilding industry*: **declining**, in decline, on the decline, waning, dying, stagnating, stagnant, decaying, crumbling, atrophying, obsolescent, on its last legs; informal on the way out.
▷ANTONYMS flourishing.

morning noun 1 *I've got a meeting this morning*: **before noon**, before lunch(time), a.m.; literary morn; Nautical & N. Amer. forenoon.
2 *a hint of light showed that morning was on its way*: **dawn**, daybreak, sunrise, break of day, first light; N. Amer. sunup; literary cockcrow, dayspring, dawning, aurora.
□ **morning, noon, and night all the time**, without a break, constantly, continually, always, forever, incessantly, ceaselessly, perpetually, unceasingly; informal 24-7; archaic without surcease.

Word links **morning**

matinal, **matutinal**, **antemeridian** relating to the morning

moron noun informal *why don't you look where you're going, you moron!* See **fool** (sense 1 of the noun).

moronic adjective informal *an endless succession of moronic game shows*. See **stupid** (senses 1 and 2).

morose adjective *Louis sat alone at a table, looking morose*: **sullen**, sulky, gloomy, bad-tempered, ill-tempered, in a bad mood, dour, surly, sour, glum, moody, unsmiling, humourless, uncommunicative, taciturn, unresponsive, unsociable, scowling, glowering, ill-humoured, sombre, sober, saturnine, pessimistic, lugubrious, Eeyorish, mournful, melancholy, melancholic, doleful, miserable, dismal, depressed, dejected, despondent, downcast, unhappy, low-spirited, in low spirits, low, with a long face, blue, down, fed up, grumpy, irritable, churlish, cantankerous, crotchety, cross, crabbed, crabby, grouchy, testy, snappish, peevish, crusty, waspish; informal down in the mouth, down in the dumps; Brit. informal narky; N. English informal mardy; informal, dated mumpish.
▷ANTONYMS cheerful, happy, communicative.

morsel noun **mouthful**, bite, nibble, bit, small piece, soupçon, taste, sample, spoonful, forkful, crumb, grain, particle, fragment, fraction, scrap, sliver, shred, pinch, drop, dollop, whit, atom, granule, segment, spot, modicum, gobbet; titbit, bonne bouche; informal smidgen, smidge; Austral./NZ informal skerrick.

mortal adjective 1 *the coffin held the mortal remains of her uncle | all men are mortal*: **perishable**, physical, bodily, corporeal, fleshly, corporal, earthly; human, earth-born; impermanent, temporal, worldly, transient, ephemeral, passing; rare sublunary.
▷ANTONYMS immortal.
2 *a mortal blow*: **deadly**, fatal, lethal, death-dealing, killing, murderous, destructive, terminal, incurable.
3 *mortal enemies*: **irreconcilable**, deadly, to the death, sworn, bitter, out-and-out, implacable, relentless, unrelenting, unappeasable, remorseless, merciless.
4 *a mortal sin*: **unpardonable**, unforgivable, irremissible.
▷ANTONYMS venial.
5 *parents live in mortal fear of such diseases*: **extreme**, very great, great, enormous, terrible, awful, dreadful, intense, severe, grave, dire, inordinate, unbearable, agonizing.
6 *the punishment is out of all mortal proportion to the offence*: **conceivable**, imaginable, perceivable, possible, earthly.
▶noun *mere mortals*: **human being**, human, person, man/woman, being, creature, individual; earthling; informal, dated body.
▷ANTONYMS immortal, god.

mortality noun 1 *her death filled him with a sense of his own mortality*: **impermanence**, temporality, transience, ephemerality, impermanency, perishability; humanity; corporeality, earthliness; rare corporality.
▷ANTONYMS immortality.
2 *the causes of mortality among infants and young children*: **death**, loss of life, dying.

mortification noun 1 *scarlet with mortification, Leonora looked away*: **embarrassment**, humiliation, chagrin, discomfiture, discomposure, awkwardness, shame, loss of face.
2 *the mortification of the flesh*: **subduing**, suppression, subjugation, control, controlling, restraint; **disciplining**, chastening, punishment, denying.

m

mortify verb **1** *I'd be mortified if my friends found out I was learning ballroom dancing*: **embarrass**, humiliate, chagrin, shame, discomfit, abash, horrify, appal, crush.
▷ANTONYMS be pleased, be proud.
2 *he was mortified at the prospect of being excluded from the meeting*: **hurt**, wound, affront, offend, put out, pique, irk, pain, annoy, displease, vex, gall; informal rile; Brit. informal nark.
▷ANTONYMS gratify.
3 *an ascetic who consistently chooses to mortify the flesh*: **subdue**, suppress, subjugate, control, restrain, get under control; **discipline**, chasten, punish, deny.
▷ANTONYMS indulge.
4 *the cut in his arm had mortified*: **become gangrenous**, fester, putrefy, gangrene, rot, decay, decompose; rare necrose, sphacelate.
▷ANTONYMS heal.

mortuary noun *three of the bodies have been taken to the mortuary*: **morgue**, funeral parlour, funeral chapel, funeral home; Brit. chapel of rest; archaic charnel house, dead house, lich-house.

moss noun

> *Word links* **moss**
>
> **bryology, muscology** study of mosses

most pronoun *she spends most of her time in London | most of the guests brought flowers*: **nearly all**, almost all, the greatest quantity/part/number, the majority, the bulk, the lion's share, the mass, the preponderance.
▷ANTONYMS little, few.
□ **for the most part** *the path for the most part sticks to the coast*: **mostly**, mainly, in the main, on the whole, largely, by and large, to a large extent, to a great degree, predominantly, chiefly, principally, basically, substantially, overall, in general, effectively, to all intents and purposes, especially, primarily, generally, usually, typically, commonly, as a rule, altogether, all in all, on balance, on average.

mostly adverb **1** *the other passengers were mostly businessmen*: **mainly**, for the most part, on the whole, in the main, almost entirely, largely, chiefly, predominantly, principally, primarily, substantially.
2 *I mostly wear jeans and trousers, not skirts*: **usually**, generally, in general, as a general rule, as a rule, ordinarily, normally, commonly, customarily, typically, most of the time, almost always, more often than not, most often.
▷ANTONYMS rarely.

mote noun **speck**, particle, grain, spot, fleck, atom, scintilla, mite.
▷ANTONYMS beam.

moth-eaten adjective *a moth-eaten tweed jacket*: **threadbare**, worn out, well worn, worn, old, shabby, scruffy, decrepit, tattered, ragged, holey, frayed, mangy, unkempt; informal tatty, the worse for wear, ratty, scuzzy, grungy; N. Amer. informal raggedy.

mother noun **1 female parent**, materfamilias, matriarch; biological mother, birth mother, foster mother, adoptive mother, stepmother, surrogate mother; informal ma, mam, mammy, old dear, old lady, old woman; Brit. informal mum, mummy, mumsy; N. Amer. informal **mom**, mommy; Brit. informal, dated mater; dated mama, mamma; Indian Mata; Indian informal amma; rare progenitress, progenitrix.
2 *it was time for the foal to be separated from its mother*: **dam**.
3 *the wish was mother of the deed*: **source**, origin, genesis, fount, fountainhead, inspiration, stimulus; literary wellspring.
▶verb **1** *she mothered her husband, insisting he take cod liver oil*: **look after**, care for, take care of, nurture, nurse, protect, cherish, tend, raise, rear; **pamper**, coddle, cosset, baby, overprotect, fuss over, indulge, spoil.
▷ANTONYMS neglect.
2 *she mothered an illegitimate daughter*: **give birth to**, have, deliver, bear, produce, bring forth; N. Amer. birth; informal drop; archaic be brought to bed of.

> *Word links* **mother**
>
> **maternal** relating to a mother
> **matri-** related prefix, as in *matrilineal*
> **matricide** killing of one's mother

motherly adjective **maternal**, maternalistic, protective, caring, nurturing, loving, devoted, affectionate, fond, warm, tender, gentle, kind, kindly, comforting, understanding, compassionate.

motif noun **1** *a black chenille sweater with a colourful tulip motif*: **design**, pattern, decoration, figure, shape, logo, monogram, device, emblem, ornament.
2 *the room is one of the recurring motifs in Pinter's work*: **theme**, idea, concept, subject, topic, leitmotif, element, motive.

motion noun **1** *the rocking motion of the boat | a planet's motion around the sun*: **movement**, moving, locomotion, rise and fall, shifting, stirring, to and fro, toing and froing, coming and going; **progress**, passage, passing, transit, course, flow, going, travel, travelling; motility, mobility.
2 *she made a little fluttering motion with her hands*: **gesture**, gesticulation, movement, signal, sign, indication; wave, nod; body language, kinesics.
3 *the motion failed to obtain an absolute majority in the Assembly*: **proposal**, proposition, submission, recommendation, suggestion.
□ **go through the motions** *he sounds a bit wooden and like he's going through the motions*: **pretend**, put on an act, put it on, play-act, make believe, fake it.
□ **in motion** *do not distract the driver while the vehicle is in motion*: **moving**, on the move, going, travelling, not at rest, running, functioning, operational; under way.
▷ANTONYMS stationary.
□ **set/put in motion** *the Home Secretary set in motion a review of the law*: **start**, begin, activate, institute, initiate, launch, get under way, get going, get in operation, get working/functioning, get off the ground, start/get/set the ball rolling; trigger off, set off, spark off, generate, cause, bring about; formal commence.
▶verb *he motioned her to sit down*: **gesture**, gesticulate, signal, sign, direct, indicate; wave, beckon, nod.

> *Word links* **motion**
>
> **kinetic** relating to motion
> **kinetophobia** fear of motion

motionless adjective *Rob and Graham remained motionless, not daring to look at each other*: **unmoving**, still, stationary, stock-still, at a standstill, immobile, immovable, static, at rest, halted, stopped, not moving a muscle, rooted to the spot, transfixed, paralysed, frozen, inert, inanimate, quiescent, lifeless.
▷ANTONYMS moving, mobile, active.

> *Word toolkit* **motionless**
>
> See **inert**.

motivate verb **1** *she was primarily motivated by the desire for profit | I asked him what had motivated the theme of his current exhibition*: **prompt**, drive, move, inspire, stimulate, influence, lead, persuade, actuate, activate, impel, push, propel, spur (on); provoke, trigger, cause, bring about, occasion, induce, incite.
2 *it's the teacher's job to motivate the child at school*: **inspire**, stimulate, encourage, spur (on), galvanize, arouse, rouse, excite, stir (up), fire with enthusiasm, fire the imagination of; rare inspirit, incentivize.
▷ANTONYMS demotivate.

motivation noun **1** *the motivation for taking part in the training was often financial*: **motive**, motivating force, incentive, stimulus, stimulation, inspiration, impulse, inducement, incitement, spur, goad, provocation; reason, rationale, ground(s).
2 *keep staff up to date to maintain their interest and motivation*: **enthusiasm**, drive, ambition, initiative, determination, enterprise, sense of purpose; informal get-up-and-go.

motive noun **1** *the motive for the attack is still unknown*: **reason**, motivation, motivating force, rationale, grounds, cause, basis, occasion, thinking, the whys and wherefores, object, purpose, intention, design; incentive, inducement, impulse, incitement, influence, lure, inspiration, stimulus, stimulation, spur, goad, provocation, pressure, persuasion, consideration.
2 *religious motives in art*: **motif**, theme, idea, concept, subject, topic, leitmotif, element.
▶adjective *the machinery supplying the motive power for the hydraulic cranes*: **kinetic**, driving, impelling, propelling, propulsive, operative, moving, motor.

motley adjective **1** *a motley collection of old clothes*: **miscellaneous**, disparate, diverse, assorted, sundry, varied, mixed, diversified, heterogeneous.
▷ANTONYMS homogeneous, uniform.
2 *a motley coat*: **multicoloured**, many-coloured, multicolour, colourful, particoloured, many-hued, variegated, harlequin, kaleidoscopic, rainbow, psychedelic, prismatic, polychromatic; informal (looking) like an explosion in a paint factory.
▷ANTONYMS monochrome.

mottled adjective *her mottled skin | the bird's mottled reddish-brown plumage*: **blotchy**, blotched, spotted, spotty; **speckled**, streaked, streaky, marbled, flecked, freckled, dappled, stippled, piebald, skewbald, pied, brindled, brindle, tabby, marled; patchy, variegated, multicoloured, particoloured; N. Amer. pinto; informal splotchy, splodgy; rare jaspé.

motto noun **1** *he adopted the motto 'work hard and play hard' | their school motto*: **maxim**, saying, proverb, aphorism, adage, saw, axiom, formula, expression, phrase, rule, dictum, precept, epigram, gnome; slogan, catchphrase, watchword, byword, cry, battle cry; truism, cliché, platitude; rare apophthegm.
2 *cracker mottoes*: **joke**, witticism, one-liner.

mould[1] noun **1** *the molten metal is poured into a mould*: **cast**, die, form, matrix, shape, container; **framework**, template, pattern, frame.
2 *an actress in the traditional Hollywood mould*: **pattern**, form, shape, format, structure, configuration, construction, frame, build, model, design, arrangement, organization, formation, figure, cast, kind, brand, make, line, type, cut, style; archetype, paradigm, prototype.
3 *he is a figure of heroic mould*: **character**, nature, temperament, temper, disposition, cast/turn of mind, mettle; calibre, kind, sort, variety, stamp, type, kidney, grain, ilk.
▶ verb **1** *a figure moulded from clay*: **shape**, form, fashion, model, work, construct, frame, make, create, configure, manufacture, design, sculpt, sculpture, throw; forge, cast, stamp, die-cast.
2 *the professionals who were helping to mould US policy*: **determine**, direct, control, guide, lead, influence, shape, form, fashion, affect, make.

mould[2] noun *whitewashed walls stained with mould*: **mildew**, fungus, must, mouldiness, mustiness; blight, smut; dry rot, wet rot.

mould[3] noun *the ground was damp, with old leaves thick in the mould*: **earth**, soil, dirt, loam, humus.

moulder verb *his body still lay mouldering in some forgotten field in France | the buildings had mouldered away*: **decay**, decompose, rot, rot away, go mouldy, perish, go off, go bad, spoil, putrefy; crumble, disintegrate, fall apart, fall to pieces, deteriorate, fall into decay, go to rack and ruin.

mouldy adjective *a lump of mouldy cheese*: **mildewed**, mildewy, musty, mouldering, fusty; blighted, smutty; decaying, decayed, rotting, rotten, bad, spoiled, spoilt, decomposing, decomposed, rancid, rank, putrid, putrescent, putrefying; rare mucid.

mound noun **1** *a mound of leaves and garden rubbish*: **heap**, pile, stack; mass, collection, accumulation, aggregation, assemblage; mountain, pyramid; Scottish, Irish, & N. English rickle; Scottish bing.
2 *he built his castle high on the mound*: **hillock**, hill, knoll, rise, hummock, hump, embankment, bank, ridge, dune, tor, elevation, acclivity; Geology drumlin; Scottish brae; N. Amer. or technical butte; rare tump.
3 *a burial mound | a low mound marks the site of the meeting place*: **barrow**, **tumulus**; motte; Middle East tell; Russian kurgan.
▶ verb *mound up the rice on a serving plate*: **pile**, pile up, heap, heap up.

mount verb **1** *he mounted the stairs*: **go up**, ascend, climb, climb up, scale, clamber up, make one's way up, move up.
▷ANTONYMS descend.
2 *the master of ceremonies mounted the platform*: **climb on to**, jump on to, clamber on to, get on to; board, step aboard.
3 *they mounted their horses and made their way back*: **get astride**, straddle, get on the back of, bestride, get on to, hop on to.
4 *the museum is mounting an exhibition of 16th-century drawings*: **put on display**, display, exhibit, present, put in place, install; organize, put on, stage, prepare.
5 *the company successfully mounted a takeover bid*: **organize**, stage, prepare, arrange, set up, produce, get up; launch, set in motion, put in place, initiate.
6 *their losses mounted rapidly*: **increase**, grow, rise, escalate, soar, spiral, leap up, shoot up, rocket, climb, accumulate, accrue, pile up, build up, multiply, intensify, swell; literary wax.
▷ANTONYMS decrease, diminish.
7 *cameras were mounted above the door*: **install**, place, fix, set, erect, put up, attach, put in position, secure.
▶ noun **1** *he hung on to his mount's bridle*: **horse**; archaic steed.
2 *a decorated photograph mount*: **setting**, backing, support, mounting, fixture, frame, stand, base.

mountain noun **1** **peak**, height, elevation, eminence, prominence, summit, pinnacle, alp, horn; (**mountains**) range, massif, sierra, cordillera, ridge; N. English fell; Scottish ben, Munro; S. African berg; in N. Africa jebel; Geology inselberg; archaic mount.
2 *a mountain of paperwork | mountains of dirty dishes*: **a great deal**, a lot, heap, pile, mound, stack; **profusion**, abundance, quantity; backlog, logjam; informal lots, loads, heaps, piles, tons, masses, oodles, scads; Brit. informal shedload; N. Amer. informal slew, gobs; Austral./NZ informal swag; vulgar slang shitload.
3 *a butter mountain*: **surplus**, surfeit, glut, excess, overabundance, oversupply.
▷ANTONYMS molehill.
□ **make a mountain out of a molehill** informal *she could seldom resist making a mountain out of a molehill*: **exaggerate**, overstate, overemphasize, magnify, amplify, aggrandize, inflate; embellish, embroider, colour, elaborate, over-elaborate, oversell, overdraw, overplay, dramatize; hyperbolize, add colour, stretch the truth; Brit. overpitch; informal pile it on, lay it on thick, lay it on with a trowel/shovel, blow something out of all proportion, make a drama out of a crisis, make a big thing of; Brit. informal shoot a line; archaic draw the longbow.
□ **move mountains 1** *faith can move mountains*: **perform miracles**, work/do wonders, achieve the impossible. **2** *his fans move mountains to catch as many of his performances as possible*: **make every effort**, pull out all the stops, do one's utmost/best; informal bend/lean over backwards.

> *Word links* **mountain**
>
> **oro-** related prefix, as in *orogeny*
> **orographic** relating to mountains

mountainous adjective **1** *a mountainous region | mountainous terrain*: **hilly**, craggy, rocky, alpine, high, steep, precipitous; upland, highland.
▷ANTONYMS flat.
2 *mountainous waves*: **huge**, enormous, gigantic, massive, very big, very large, great, giant, colossal, mammoth, vast, immense, tremendous, mighty, formidable, staggering, monumental, Herculean, epic, prodigious, monstrous, titanic, towering, king-sized, king-size, gargantuan, substantial; informal mega, monster, whopping, whopping great, thumping, thumping great, humongous, jumbo, hulking, astronomical, astronomic; Brit. informal whacking, whacking great, ginormous.
▷ANTONYMS tiny, minute.

mountebank noun **swindler**, charlatan, confidence trickster, confidence man, fraud, fraudster, impostor, trickster, racketeer, hoaxer, sharper, quack, rogue, villain, scoundrel; informal con man, shark, flimflammer, sharp; Brit. informal twister; N. Amer. informal grifter, bunco artist, chiseller; Austral. informal shicer, magsman, illywhacker; rare defalcator.

mourn verb **1** *Isobel mourned her husband*: **grieve for**, sorrow over, lament for, weep for, shed tears for/over, wail/keen over; archaic plain for.
2 *he mourned the loss of the beautiful medieval buildings*: **deplore**, bewail, bemoan, rue, regret, sigh over.
▷ANTONYMS rejoice.

mournful adjective *a mournful expression | mournful music*: **sad**, sorrowful, sorrowing, doleful, melancholy, melancholic, woeful, grief-stricken, miserable, unhappy, heartbroken, broken-hearted, heavy-hearted, gloomy, dismal, tragic, desolate, dejected, despondent, depressed, downcast, disconsolate, woebegone, forlorn, rueful, lugubrious, sombre, joyless, cheerless, mirthless; funereal, elegiac, plaintive, plangent, dirge-like; rare threnodic; literary heartsick, dolorous.
▷ANTONYMS happy, joyful, cheerful.

mourning noun **1** *a period of national mourning*: **grief**, grieving, sorrowing, lamentation, lament, keening, wailing, weeping; sorrow, sadness, misery, melancholy, heartache, anguish, despair, despondency, desolation, woefulness; Judaism shiva; archaic dole.
2 *she was dressed in mourning*: **black clothes**, black; archaic widow's weeds, weeds, sackcloth and ashes, sables.

mouse noun

> *Word links* **mouse**
>
> **murine** relating to mice
> **musophobia** fear of mice

moustache noun informal tash; N. Amer. informal stash; Scottish & N. Amer. mouser.

mousy adjective **1** *mousy hair*: **lightish brown**, brownish, brownish-grey, dun-coloured; colourless, neutral, drab, dull, lacklustre.
2 *he had a small, mousy wife*: **timid**, quiet, meek, fearful, timorous, shy, self-effacing, diffident, ineffectual, unassertive, unconfident, unforthcoming, reticent, shrinking, hesitant, withdrawn, introverted, introvert, unobtrusive.
▷ANTONYMS bold, brazen, ferocious.

mouth noun **1** **lips**, jaws; maw, muzzle; informal trap, chops, kisser, yap; Brit. informal gob, cakehole, mush; N. Amer. informal puss, bazoo.
2 *the mouth of the cave*: **entrance**, opening, entry, way in, entryway, inlet, access, ingress; door, doorway, gateway, gate, portal, aperture, orifice, vent; way out, exit.
3 *the mouth of the bottle*: **opening**, rim, lip.
4 *the mouth of the river*: **outfall**, outlet, debouchment, embouchure, debouchure; **estuary**, firth.
5 *he's not all mouth—he gets results*: **boasting**, bragging, empty talk, idle talk, bombast, fustian; informal hot air, gas; literary braggadocio, rodomontade.
6 *you've got more mouth than any woman I've ever known*: **impudence**, cheek, cheekiness, insolence, impertinence, effrontery, audacity, audaciousness, boldness, presumption, presumptuousness, sauciness, incivility, rudeness, disrespect; informal lip, nerve, neck, brass neck; Brit. informal sauce, backchat; N. Amer. informal sass, sassiness, back talk, smart mouth; archaic malapertness.
□ **down in the mouth** **unhappy**, dejected, sad, miserable, down, downhearted, downcast, depressed, blue, melancholy, gloomy, glum, dispirited, discouraged, disheartened, despondent, disconsolate, with a long face, forlorn, crestfallen, woebegone, subdued, fed up, out of sorts, low, in low spirits, in the doldrums, heavy-hearted; informal down in the dumps; Brit. informal brassed off, cheesed off, browned off, peed off; N. Amer. informal teed off, ticked off; vulgar slang pissed off.
□ **keep one's mouth shut** **say nothing**, keep quiet, not breathe a word, not tell a soul, not give the game away, keep it under one's hat; informal keep mum, play/keep one's cards close to one's chest, not let the cat out of the bag.

m

▸ verb *he mouthed platitudes in soothing tones*: **utter**, speak, say; pronounce, enunciate, articulate, voice, express, vocalize, verbalize; say insincerely, say for form's sake.
□ **mouth off** informal *he was mouthing off about school, teachers, and society in general*: **rant**, spout, declaim, rave, jabber, sound off.

> *Word links* **mouth**
>
> **oral, buccal** relating to the mouth
> **stomatology** scientific study of the mouth

mouthful noun **1** *a mouthful of pizza*: **bite**, nibble, taste, bit, piece; spoonful, forkful, morsel, sample.
2 *a mouthful of beer*: **draught**, sip, swallow, sup, drop, pull, gulp; informal swig, slug, swill.
3 *'sesquipedalian' is a bit of a mouthful*: **tongue-twister**, long word, difficult word.
▷ANTONYMS monosyllable.

mouthpiece noun **1** *the flute's mouthpiece*: **embouchure**.
2 *he's just a mouthpiece for the government*: **spokesperson**, spokesman, spokeswoman, agent, representative, propagandist, organ, voice; negotiator, intermediary, mediator, intermediator.

movable adjective **1** *movable objects*: **portable**, transportable, transferable; mobile; adjustable, flexible, detachable; rare portative.
▷ANTONYMS immovable.
2 *a calendar for all religious feasts, both fixed and movable*: **variable**, changeable, alterable, unfixed, floating.
▷ANTONYMS fixed, immovable.

movables plural noun **possessions**, belongings, effects, property, goods, chattels, things, stuff, paraphernalia, impedimenta; informal gear; rare plenishings.
▷ANTONYMS fixtures, fittings.

move verb **1** *she stood up and moved to the door | stay there—don't move!* **go**, walk, proceed, progress, advance, pass; budge, stir, shift, change position, make a move; rare locomote.
▷ANTONYMS stay put.
2 *he moved the chair closer to the fire*: **carry**, transport, transfer, transpose, shift, switch.
3 *for some people, things were moving too fast*: **progress**, make progress, make headway, advance, develop.
▷ANTONYMS stagnate.
4 *he urged the council to move quickly*: **take action**, act, take steps, make a move, do something, take measures, take the initiative; informal get moving.
▷ANTONYMS do nothing.
5 *she's moved—she lives in Cambridge now*: **relocate**, move house, move away/out, change address/house, leave, go away, decamp; change jobs; migrate, emigrate; Scottish & N. English flit; informal split; Brit. informal up sticks; N. Amer. informal pull up stakes.
6 *I was deeply moved by the story*: **affect**, touch, strike, impress, shake, upset, disturb, hit, disquiet, agitate, stir, make an impression on, have an impact on, tug at someone's heartstrings.
▷ANTONYMS be unaffected (by), be indifferent (to).
7 *she attended a lecture on meditation and was moved to find out more about it*: **inspire**, prompt, stimulate, motivate, provoke, influence, rouse, actuate, incline, persuade, urge, lead, cause, impel, induce, incite, excite.
8 *they are not prepared to move on this issue*: **change**, budge, shift one's ground, change one's tune, sing a different song, change one's mind, change one's opinion, have second thoughts; do a U-turn, do an about-face, reconsider, climb down, back-pedal; Brit. do an about-turn.
9 *she moves in the pop and art worlds*: **circulate**, mix, go round, socialize, fraternize, keep company, associate; informal hang out, hang around; Brit. informal hang about.
10 *I move that we all adjourn to my sitting room*: **propose**, submit, suggest, put forward, advocate, recommend, request, urge.
▸ noun **1** *his eyes followed her every move*: **movement**, motion, action, activity; gesture, gesticulation.
2 *his recent move from Geneva to London*: **relocation**, change of house/address/job, removal, transfer, posting; Scottish & N. English flit, flitting.
3 *the latest move in the war against illegal drugs*: **initiative**, step, action, act, measure, tack, manoeuvre, tactic, stratagem, deed, gambit, ploy, ruse, trick, dodge.
4 *it's your move*: **turn**, go, play; opportunity, chance; informal shot.
□ **get a move on** informal **hurry up**, speed up, move faster; informal get cracking, get moving, make it snappy, step on it, step on the gas, shake a leg, rattle one's dags; Brit. informal get one's skates on, stir one's stumps; N. Amer. informal get a wiggle on; S. African informal put foot; dated make haste.
□ **make a move 1** *each army was waiting for the other side to make a move*: **do something, take action**, act, take measures, take the initiative; informal get moving. **2** *it's getting late—I think I'd better be making a move*: **leave**, take one's leave, take oneself off, be on one's way, get going, depart, be off, set off, take one's farewells; informal push off, skedaddle, scram, shove off, split.
□ **on the move 1** *she's always on the move*: **travelling**, in transit, moving, in motion, journeying, on the road, on the wing; informal on the go.
▷ANTONYMS in one place.
2 *the economy appears to be on the move at last*: **progressing**, making progress, proceeding, advancing, developing, moving/going forward.
▷ANTONYMS stagnating.

movement noun **1** *Rachel made a sudden movement | the scene was almost devoid of movement*: **motion**, move, manoeuvre; gesture, gesticulation, sign, signal; action, activity.
2 *the movement of supplies by foreign military units*: **transportation**, shift, shifting, conveyance, moving, transfer, transferral, relocation, repositioning.
3 *the labour movement*: **political group**, party, faction, organization, grouping, wing, front, lobby, camp; coalition.
4 *a movement to declare war on poverty*: **campaign**, crusade, drive, push.
5 *there have been movements in the financial markets*: **development**, change, fluctuation, rise, fall, variation.
6 *the movement towards greater sexual equality*: **trend**, tendency, drift, swing, current, course.
7 *he believes that some movement in the case will be made by the end of the month*: **progress**, progression, advance, step forward, breakthrough.
8 *a symphony in three movements*: **part**, section, division, passage.
9 *the clock's movement*: **mechanism**, machinery, works, workings, action, wheels, motion; informal innards, guts.

> *Word links* **movement**
>
> **kinetic** relating to movement
> **kinetophobia** fear of movement

movie noun **1** *a horror movie*: **film**, picture, motion picture, feature, feature film; informal flick, talkie; dated moving picture.
2 (**the movies**) *the growth of the movies as mass entertainment*: **the cinema**, the pictures, the silver screen, the big screen; informal the flicks.

moving adjective **1** *the moving parts of the machine | a moving train*: **in motion**, operating, operational, working, going, on the move, active; kinetic; movable, mobile, motile, unfixed.
▷ANTONYMS immobile, fixed, stationary, motionless.
2 *an unforgettable and moving book*: **affecting**, touching, emotive, poignant, heart-warming, heart-rending, emotional, upsetting, disturbing; effective, telling, striking, impressive, inspiring, inspirational, stimulating, arousing, stirring, soul-stirring, exciting, thrilling, dramatic; informal tear-jerking.
▷ANTONYMS unemotional.
3 *he has been the party's moving force since its foundation*: **driving**, motivating, dynamic, impelling, stimulating, inspirational, stimulative.

> *Choose the right word* **moving, touching, affecting**
>
> All three words relate to the arousing of emotions, generally ones in which pleasure and pain are mixed.
>
> The emotions aroused by something **moving** are typically of sadness or sympathy with someone else's suffering (*a moving display of drawings by children in a concentration camp*). They are generally both painful and uplifting (*a moving tribute to the power of the human spirit*), and can be of a religious or artistic nature (*the torchlight procession round the church after Mass was a very moving experience | Philip Bond gives a wonderful and moving portrayal of jaded professor Frank*).
>
> Something **touching** inspires feelings of tenderness, sometimes verging on the sentimental (*there was a touching air of innocence about the boy*). *Touching* is less intense than *moving*. It can also convey gratitude for an unexpected service or tribute (*your concern is most touching*).
>
> **Affecting** is similiar in meaning to *moving* but rarer and more literary (*an infectious and affecting tale of romantic doom*).

mow verb *someone had mown the grass*: **cut**, cut down, scythe, shear, trim; crop, clip.
□ **mow someone/something down** *they were mown down by government troops*: **kill**, gun down, shoot down, cut down, cut to pieces, butcher, slaughter, massacre, decimate, annihilate, exterminate, liquidate, wipe out, destroy; informal blow away; N. Amer. informal smoke; literary slay.

much determiner *did you get much help?* **a lot of**, a great/good deal of, a great/large amount of, plenty of, ample, copious, abundant, plentiful, considerable, substantial; informal lots of, loads of, heaps of, masses of, a pile of, piles of, oodles of, tons of, more ... than one can shake a stick at; Brit. informal lashings of, a shedload of; N. Amer. informal gobs of; vulgar slang a shitload of.
▷ANTONYMS little.
▸ adverb **1** *it didn't hurt much*: **greatly**, to a great extent/degree, a great deal, a lot, exceedingly, considerably, appreciably, decidedly, indeed.
2 *does he come here much?* **often**, frequently, many times, on many/numerous occasions, repeatedly, recurrently, regularly, habitually,

m

customarily, routinely, usually, normally, commonly; for long, for a long time; informal a lot.

▶ **pronoun** *she doesn't eat much | he did so much for our team*: **a lot**, a great/good deal, plenty; informal lots, loads, heaps, masses, oodles, tons.

□ **a bit much** informal *sometimes the pressure can get a bit much*: **unacceptable**, intolerable, insufferable, unsatisfactory, undesirable, unreasonable, objectionable, insupportable; informal not on, a bit much, out of order, out, not quite the done thing, too much; Brit. informal a bit thick, a bit off, off, not cricket.

□ **make much of** *Mr Smith was glad to be made much of*: **flatter**, compliment, praise, commend, admire, express admiration for, pay tribute to, say nice things about; pay court to, pay blandishments to, fawn on, wax lyrical about, make much of; cajole, humour, flannel, blarney; informal sweet-talk, soft-soap, butter up, play up to, suck up to, crawl to, creep to, be all over, fall all over; archaic blandish; rare laud, panegyrize.

□ **much of a muchness very similar**, much the same, more or less the same, very alike, practically identical, practically indistinguishable.

muck noun **1** *I'll just clean the muck off the windscreen*: **dirt**, grime, filth, mud, slime, sludge, scum, mire, mess, rubbish; informal crud, gunk, grunge, gloop, gook, goo, yuck; Brit. informal gunge, grot; N. Amer. informal guck, glop.
2 *the spreading of muck on the fields*: **dung**, manure, ordure, excrement, excreta, droppings, faeces, cowpats, guano, sewage; N. Amer. informal cow chips, horse apples; vulgar slang shit, crap; rare feculence.

▶ **verb**

□ **muck about/around** Brit. informal **1** *he was mucking about with his mates*: **fool about/around**, play about/around, fiddle about/around, amuse oneself, clown about/around, footle about/around; informal mess about/around, horse about/around, lark (about/around), screw around, puddle about/around; Brit. informal fanny about/around; vulgar slang frig about/around, fuck about/around; Brit. vulgar slang piss about/around, arse about/around, bugger about/around. **2** *someone's been mucking about with the video*: **interfere**, fiddle (about/around), play about/around, tamper, meddle, tinker, monkey (about/around); informal mess (about/around), dick around.

□ **muck in** Brit. informal *everyone mucked in and got on with it*: **help out**, help, assist, lend a hand, join in, pitch in, participate, play a part, contribute, do one's bit, chip in, cooperate, collaborate, put one's shoulder to the wheel; Brit. informal get stuck in.

□ **muck something up** informal *I was convinced she would muck the whole thing up*: **make a mess of**, mess up, botch, bungle, spoil, ruin, wreck, mishandle, mismanage; informal make a hash of, muff, fluff, foul up, screw up, louse up, bitch up, blow, foozle; Brit. informal make a muck of, make a pig's ear of, cock up, make a Horlicks of; N. Amer. informal flub, goof up; vulgar slang fuck up, bugger up, balls up.

mucky adjective *a pair of mucky boots*: **dirty**, filthy, grimy, muddy, mud-caked, grubby, messy, soiled, stained, smeared, smeary, scummy, slimy, sticky, sooty, dusty, unclean, foul, begrimed, bespattered, befouled, polluted, squalid, insanitary; informal cruddy, grungy, yucky, icky, gloopy, crummy; Brit. informal manky, gungy, grotty; Austral./NZ informal scungy; literary besmirched; rare feculent.
▷ANTONYMS clean.

mud noun mire, sludge, slush, ooze, silt, clay, gumbo, dirt, soil; Scottish & N. English clart; Irish slob.

muddle verb **1** *the papers seem to have got muddled up*: **confuse**, mix up, jumble, jumble up, disarrange, disorganize, disorder, disturb, throw into disorder, get into a tangle, scramble, mess up.
▷ANTONYMS be in (good) order.
2 *I won't explain—it'll only muddle you*: **bewilder**, confuse, bemuse, perplex, puzzle, baffle, nonplus, mystify, confound, disorientate, disorient, befuddle, daze, addle.
▷ANTONYMS enlighten.

□ **muddle along/through** *we're muddling along as best we can*: **cope**, manage, get by/along, scrape by/along, make do, make the best of a bad job.

▶ **noun 1** *the files are in a bit of a muddle*: **mess**, confusion, jumble, tangle, clutter, hotchpotch, mishmash, mare's nest, chaos, disorder, disarray, welter, disorganization.
2 *a bureaucratic muddle*: **bungle**, mix-up, misunderstanding, mistake; informal hash, foul-up, screw-up; N. Amer. informal snafu; vulgar slang fuck-up; Brit. vulgar slang balls-up.

muddled adjective **1** *a muddled pile of photographs*: **jumbled**, in a jumble, in a muddle, in a mess, chaotic, in disorder, in disarray, topsy-turvy, disorganized, disordered, disorderly, out of place, out of order, mixed up, upside-down, at sixes and sevens, untidy, messy, scrambled, tangled; informal higgledy-piggledy.
▷ANTONYMS orderly.
2 *she felt muddled and couldn't keep track of her thoughts*: **confused**, in a state of confusion, bewildered, bemused, perplexed, disorientated, disoriented, at sea, in a muddle, befuddled, dazed; informal discombobulated; Canadian & Austral./NZ informal bushed.
3 *muddled thinking*: **incoherent**, confused, muddle-headed, woolly, jumbled, disjointed.
▷ANTONYMS clear, lucid.

muddy adjective **1** *we picked our way through the muddy ground*: **waterlogged**, boggy, marshy, swampy, squelchy, squishy, mucky, miry, oozy, slushy, slimy, sodden, spongy, wet, soft, heavy, sloughy; Scottish & N. English mossy, clarty; rare quaggy.
2 *they changed their muddy boots*: **mud-caked**, mud-spattered, muddied, dirty, filthy, mucky, grubby, grimy, soiled, begrimed.
▷ANTONYMS clean.
3 *muddy water*: **murky**, cloudy, muddied, turbid, opaque, impure; N. Amer. riled, roily, roiled.
▷ANTONYMS clear.
4 *the original colours had faded to a muddy pink*: **dingy**, dirty, drab, dull, sludgy, washed out, flat.
5 *some sentences are so muddy that their meaning can only be guessed*: **incoherent**, confused, muddled, jumbled, woolly, vague, fuzzy.

▶ **verb 1** *you can step ashore without muddying your boots*: **make muddy**, cake with mud/dirt, dirty, soil, begrime, grime, mire, spatter, bespatter; literary smirch, besmirch, bemire.
2 *the results muddy rather than clarify the situation*: **make unclear**, **obscure**, confuse, obfuscate, blur, cloud, befog, mix up.
▷ANTONYMS clarify.

muff verb *the administration muffed several of its biggest projects*: **mishandle**, mismanage, mess up, make a mess of, bungle, botch; miss, mishit, fumble; informal make a hash of, fluff, foul up, screw up, louse up, bitch up, blow, foozle; Brit. informal make a muck of, make a pig's ear of, cock up, make a Horlicks of; N. Amer. informal flub, goof up, bobble; vulgar slang fuck up, bugger up, balls up, bollix up.

muffle verb **1** *it was cold and everyone was muffled up in coats and scarves*: **wrap**, wrap up, swathe, swaddle, enfold, envelop, cloak, cover up.
2 *the sound of their footsteps was muffled by the fog | unions fear their voice within the party is being muffled*: **deaden**, dull, dampen, damp down, mute, soften, quieten, hush, silence, still, tone down, mask, stifle, smother, subdue, suppress, gag, muzzle.

muffled adjective *muffled shouts*: **indistinct**, faint, muted, dull, dim, soft, strangled, stifled, smothered, suppressed.
▷ANTONYMS loud, clear.

Word toolkit

muffled	**muted**	**suppressed**
voices	colours	anger
curses	sounds	evidence
footsteps	applause	feelings
thud	television	memories
murmuring	trumpet	desire

mug[1] noun **1** *a china mug*: **beaker**, cup; tankard, glass, stein, flagon, pot, pint pot, toby jug; dated seidel; archaic stoup.
2 informal *I never want to see your ugly mug again*: **face**, features, countenance, physiognomy; informal clock; Brit. informal mush, phiz, phizog, dial; Brit. rhyming slang boat race; Scottish & Irish informal coupon; N. Amer. informal puss, pan; literary visage; archaic front.
3 informal *he's no mug—he's got it all worked out*: **fool**, simpleton, innocent, dupe, gull; informal sucker, soft/easy touch, pushover, chump, noddle, dummy, dope, dimwit, dumbo, nerd, knucklehead, lamebrain, pea-brain, pudding-head, thickhead, wooden-head, pinhead, airhead, birdbrain; Brit. informal muggins, juggins, charlie; N. Amer. informal patsy, sap, schlemiel, pigeon, mark; Austral./NZ informal dill.

▶ **verb** *he was mugged by three youths who stole his bike*: **assault**, attack, set upon, beat up, knock down, rob; informal jump, rough up, lay into, work over, steam; Brit. informal duff up, do over; N. Amer. informal stick up.

mug[2] verb

□ **mug something up** *she's mugging up the Highway Code*: **study**, get up, read up, cram; informal bone up (on); Brit. informal swot; archaic con.

muggy adjective *an unpleasantly muggy evening*: **humid**, close, sultry, sticky, steamy, oppressive, airless, stifling, suffocating, stuffy, clammy, damp, moist, soupy, heavy, fuggy, like a Turkish bath, like a sauna.
▷ANTONYMS fresh, airy.

mulish adjective *George could sometimes be rather mulish*: **obstinate**, stubborn, stubborn as a mule, pig-headed, recalcitrant, refractory, intransigent, intractable, unyielding, inflexible, unbending, bull-headed, stiff-necked, headstrong, difficult, wilful, self-willed, cross-grained; Brit. informal bloody-minded, bolshie; archaic contumacious.
▷ANTONYMS docile, tractable; obliging.

mull verb

□ **mull something over** *Barney sat there for a while, mulling things over*: **ponder**, consider, think over/about, reflect on, contemplate, deliberate, turn over in one's mind, chew over, weigh up, consider the pros and cons of, cogitate on, meditate on, muse on, ruminate over/on, brood on, have one's mind on, give some thought to, evaluate, examine, study, review, revolve; archaic pore on; rare cerebrate.

m

multicoloured adjective **kaleidoscopic**, psychedelic, colourful, multicolour, many-coloured, many-hued, rainbow, jazzy, particoloured, varicoloured, variegated, harlequin, motley, prismatic, polychromatic; pied, piebald, skewbald, dappled, brindled, brindle, tabby; N. Amer. pinto; informal (looking) like an explosion in a paint factory.
▷ANTONYMS monochrome.

multifarious adjective *the multifarious local and ethnic traditions that are found in the USA*: **diverse**, many, numerous, various, varied, diversified, multiple, multitudinous, multiplex, manifold, multifaceted, legion, different, heterogeneous, eclectic, sundry, miscellaneous, assorted, variegated; literary myriad, divers.
▷ANTONYMS homogeneous.

multiple adjective *words with multiple meanings*: **numerous**, many, various, different, diverse, several, sundry, miscellaneous, manifold, multifarious, multitudinous, compound, collective; literary myriad, divers.

Word links **multiple**

multi- related prefix, as in *multidirectional, multibuy*
poly- related prefix, as in *polygon, polyethnic*
-fold related suffix, as in *fourfold*

multiplicity noun *the multiplicity of species found in the rainforests*: **abundance**, scores, mass, host, array, variety, myriad, a lot; range, diverseness, numerousness, heterogeneity, plurality; profusion, quantities; informal lots, loads, stacks, heaps, piles, masses, tons, oodles, hundreds, thousands, millions, billions; Brit. informal shedload; N. Amer. informal slew, gazillions, gobs; Austral./NZ informal swag; vulgar slang shitload.

multiply verb **1** *the difficulties seem to be multiplying by the minute*: **increase**, increase exponentially, grow, become more numerous, accumulate, proliferate, mount up, mushroom, snowball, burgeon, spread, expand; literary wax.
▷ANTONYMS decrease, diminish.
2 *rabbits were introduced here and multiplied*: **breed**, reproduce, procreate, propagate.

multitude noun **1** *a multitude of problems | multitudes of birds*: **a lot**, a great/large number, a great/large quantity, host, horde, mass, mountain, droves, swarm, army, legion, sea, abundance, profusion; scores, quantities; informal lots, loads, masses, stacks, heaps, tons, dozens, hundreds, thousands, millions, billions, zillions; Brit. informal shedload; N. Amer. informal slew, gazillions, bazillions, gobs; Austral./NZ informal swag; vulgar slang shitload.
2 *Father Peter addressed the multitude*: **crowd**, gathering, assembly, group, assemblage, congregation, flock, throng, horde, mob; rare concourse.
3 (**the multitude**) *placing political power in the hands of the multitude*: **the common people**, the populace, the public, the people, the masses, the rank and file, the crowd, the commonality, the commonalty, the third estate, the plebeians; the hoi polloi, the mob, the proletariat, the common herd, the rabble, the riff-raff, the canaille, the great unwashed, the ragtag (and bobtail), proles, plebs.
▷ANTONYMS the elite.

multitudinous adjective *the multitudinous stars*: **numerous**, many, abundant, profuse, prolific, copious, legion, teeming, multifarious, a thousand and one, innumerable, countless, uncounted, infinite, numberless, unnumbered, untold, incalculable; informal umpteen; S. African informal lank; literary divers, myriad; manifold; rare innumerous, unnumberable.

mum[1] noun Brit. informal See **mother**.

mum[2] adjective informal *he was keeping mum about his future plans*: **silent**, quiet, mute, dumb, tight-lipped, close-mouthed, uncommunicative, unforthcoming, reticent, secretive; archaic mumchance.
▶ noun
□ **mum's the word** say nothing, keep quiet, don't breathe a word, don't tell a soul, don't give the game away, keep it secret, keep it to yourself, keep it under your hat, play dumb; Scottish play the daft baddie/lassie; informal don't let on, keep shtum, don't let the cat out of the bag.

mumble verb *the old man shuffled away, mumbling to himself*: **mutter**, murmur, speak indistinctly, talk under one's breath, speak sotto voce, talk to oneself; rare maffle.

mumbo-jumbo noun *the instructions are complete mumbo-jumbo*: **nonsense**, gibberish, claptrap, rubbish, balderdash, blather, blether; rigmarole; **jargon**, unintelligible language, obscure language, hocus-pocus; informal gobbledegook, double Dutch, argle-bargle, bull.

munch verb *he munched his sandwich in a dream*: **chew**, champ, chomp, masticate, crunch, scrunch, eat; rare chumble, manducate, triturate.

mundane adjective **1** *the mundane aspects of daily life*: **humdrum**, dull, boring, tedious, monotonous, tiresome, wearisome, prosaic, unexciting, uninteresting, uneventful, unvarying, unvaried, unremarkable, repetitive, repetitious, routine, ordinary, everyday, day-to-day, quotidian, run-of-the-mill, commonplace, common, workaday, usual, pedestrian, customary, regular, normal; unimaginative, banal, hackneyed, trite, stale, platitudinous; informal typical, vanilla, plain vanilla; rare banausic.
▷ANTONYMS extraordinary, imaginative.
2 *the mundane world*: **earthly**, worldly, terrestrial, material, temporal, secular, non-spiritual, fleshly, carnal, sensual; rare sublunary.
▷ANTONYMS spiritual.

municipal adjective *land use is controlled by the municipal authorities*: **civic**, civil, metropolitan, urban, city, town, borough, community, district, local, council, public; rare oppidan.
▷ANTONYMS rural.

municipality noun *each municipality has its own quota of subsidy*: **borough**, town, city, district, administrative division; N. Amer. precinct, township; Scottish burgh; French arrondissement.

munificence noun *the munificence of our host*: **generosity**, bountifulness, open-handedness, magnanimity, magnanimousness, princeliness, lavishness, free-handedness, liberality, philanthropy, charity, charitableness, largesse, big-heartedness, beneficence, benevolence; literary bounty, bounteousness.
▷ANTONYMS meanness, niggardliness.

munificent adjective *a munificent bequest*: **generous**, bountiful, open-handed, magnanimous, philanthropic, princely, handsome, lavish, unstinting, free-handed, unstinted, liberal, free, charitable, big-hearted, beneficent, ungrudging; literary bounteous.
▷ANTONYMS mean, niggardly, miserly.

Easily confused words **munificent or magnificent?**

See **magnificent**.

murder noun **1** *the brutal murder of a German holidaymaker*: **killing**, homicide, assassination, liquidation, extermination, execution, slaughter, butchery, massacre; manslaughter; patricide, matricide, parricide, fratricide, sororicide, filicide, infanticide, uxoricide, regicide; literary slaying.
2 informal *driving there was murder*: **hell**, hell on earth, a nightmare, an ordeal, a trial, a frustrating/unpleasant/difficult experience, misery, torture, agony.
▶ verb **1** *someone tried to murder him*: **kill**, put/do to death, assassinate, execute, liquidate, eliminate, neutralize, dispatch, butcher, cut to pieces, slaughter, massacre, wipe out, mow down; informal bump off, do in, do away with, do for, knock off, blow away, blow someone's brains out, stiff, take out, top, croak, give someone the works, dispose of, hit, zap; N. Amer. informal ice, rub out, smoke, waste, off, whack, scrag; N. Amer. euphemistic terminate with extreme prejudice; literary slay.
2 informal *Anna was murdering a Mozart sonata*. See **bungle**.
3 informal *he murdered his lacklustre opponent*. See **trounce**.

murderer, murderess noun **killer**, liquidator, terminator, slaughterer; dated homicide; literary slayer.

murderous adjective **1** *a murderous attack*: **homicidal**, brutal, violent, savage, ferocious, fierce, vicious, bloodthirsty, barbarous, barbaric, cruel, inhuman; fatal, lethal, deadly, mortal, killing, death-dealing, bloody; literary fell; archaic sanguinary.
2 informal *the team had a murderous schedule of four games in ten days*: **arduous**, gruelling, strenuous, punishing, hard, onerous, back-breaking, crushing, exhausting, taxing, difficult, hard, laborious, rigorous, stressful, formidable, intolerable, unbearable, harrowing; informal killing, hellish; Brit. informal knackering.
▷ANTONYMS easy, light.

murky adjective **1** *a murky winter afternoon*: **dark**, **gloomy**, grey, leaden, dull, dim, overcast, cloudy, clouded, sunless, foggy, misty, dismal, dreary, bleak, louring, threatening, cheerless, depressing, shadowy, sombre; literary tenebrous, crepuscular; rare caliginous, Cimmerian.
▷ANTONYMS bright, sunny.
2 *murky water*: **dirty**, **muddy**, cloudy, turbid, opaque; N. Amer. riled, roily, roiled.
▷ANTONYMS clear.
3 *a government minister with a murky past*: **questionable**, **suspicious**, suspect, dubious, dark, mysterious, secret; informal shady.
▷ANTONYMS innocent.

murmur noun **1** *his voice was little more than a murmur*: **whisper**, undertone, mutter, mumble.
2 *there were murmurs in Tory ranks*: **complaint**, grumble, moan, grouse; mutter, muttering; informal gripe, beef, bitch.
3 *the murmur of the river*: **burble**, babble, purl, gurgle; literary plash.
4 *the murmur of bees*: **hum**, humming, buzz, buzzing, whirr, thrum, thrumming, drone, sigh; rare susurration, murmuration, susurrus.
▶ verb **1** *he heard them murmuring in the hall*: **mutter**, mumble, whisper, talk under one's breath, speak in an undertone, speak softly, speak sotto voce, speak in hushed tones; breathe, purr.
▷ANTONYMS shout, yell.
2 *no one murmured at the delay*: **complain**, moan, mutter, grumble, grouse, carp, whine, bleat; informal gripe, beef, bitch, whinge; Brit. informal chunter, grizzle; N. English informal mither.
3 *the wind was murmuring through the trees*: **rustle**, whirr, burble, purl, rumble, sigh; literary whisper, breathe.

muscle noun **1** *I've pulled a muscle in my leg*: literary thew.
2 *he had muscle but no brains*: **strength**, power, muscularity, brawn, browniness, burliness, huskiness; informal beef, beefiness; literary thew.
3 *they used financial muscle to secure senior UN posts*: **influence**, power, strength, might, force, forcefulness, weight, potency; informal clout, beef, pull.
▶ verb
▫ **muscle in** *he was determined to* **muscle in** *on the union's affairs*: **interfere with**, force one's way into, elbow one's way in on, butt in on, impose oneself on, encroach on; informal horn in on.

Word links **muscle**

myo- related prefix, as in *myocardial*
orthopaedics branch of medicine to do with muscles
myotomy incision into muscle

muscular adjective **1** *muscular tissue*: **fibrous**, sinewy.
2 *he's tall, blonde, and very muscular*: **strong**, brawny, muscly, sinewy, well built, powerfully built, well muscled, burly, strapping, sturdy, rugged, powerful, broad-shouldered, athletic, well knit, muscle-bound, Herculean, manly; informal hunky, beefy, husky; dated stalwart; literary thewy; Physiology mesomorphic.
3 *a muscular economy*: **vigorous**, robust, strong, powerful, dynamic, potent, energetic, active, aggressive.
▷ANTONYMS weak, puny, feeble.

muse[1] noun *the poet's muse*: **inspiration**, creative influence, stimulus, stimulation; rare afflatus.

muse[2] verb *I* **mused on** *Toby's story as I walked home*: **ponder**, consider, think over/about, mull over, reflect on, contemplate, deliberate, turn over in one's mind, chew over, weigh up, meditate on, ruminate over/on, brood on, give some thought to, cogitate on, evaluate, examine, study, review; think, debate with oneself, be lost in contemplation/thought, be in a brown study, daydream, be in a reverie; archaic pore on; rare cerebrate.

mush noun **1** *she was eating some sort of greyish mush*: **pap**, pulp, slop, paste, purée, slush, swill, mash, pomace; informal gloop, goo, gook; N. Amer. informal glop.
2 *the film's just romantic mush*: **sentimentality**, mawkishness; informal schmaltz, corn, slush, hokum, sob stuff, cheese; N. Amer. informal slop.

mushroom verb *the ecotourism industry mushroomed in the 1980s*: **proliferate**, grow/develop rapidly, burgeon, spread, increase, expand, spring up, shoot up, sprout, burst forth, boom, explode, snowball, rocket, skyrocket; thrive, flourish, prosper.
▷ANTONYMS contract; fail.

mushy adjective **1** *cook until the fruit is mushy*: **soft**, **semi-liquid**, pulpy, pappy, slushy, sloppy, spongy, squashy, squelchy, squishy; informal gooey, gloopy; Brit. informal squidgy; rare pulpous.
▷ANTONYMS hard, firm.
2 *a mushy film*: **sentimental**, mawkish, over-sentimental, emotional, cloying, sickly, saccharine, sugary, syrupy; Brit. twee; informal slushy, sloppy, schmaltzy, weepy, cutesy, lovey-dovey, gooey, drippy, sloshy, soupy, treacly, cheesy, corny, icky, sick-making, toe-curling; Brit. informal soppy; N. Amer. informal cornball, sappy, hokey, three-hankie.
▷ANTONYMS unsentimental, gritty.

music noun

Word links **music**

Euterpe the Muse of flutes
Erato the Muse of hymns
musicophobia fear of music

musical adjective **tuneful**, melodic, melodious, harmonious, sweet-sounding, sweet, mellifluous, dulcet, lyrical, lilting, liquid, euphonious, euphonic; rare mellifluent.
▷ANTONYMS discordant, harsh, grating.
▶ noun **musical comedy**.

musician noun **player**, performer, instrumentalist, accompanist, soloist, virtuoso, maestro, conductor; composer; archaic minstrel.

musing noun **meditation**, thinking, contemplation, deliberation, pondering, reflection, rumination, cogitation, introspection, daydreaming, dreaming, reverie, brown study, abstraction, preoccupation, brooding, wool-gathering; rare cerebration.

muss verb *the wind was* **mussing up** *his hair*: **ruffle**, tousle, dishevel, rumple, mess up, make a mess of, disarrange, make untidy, tumble, put out of place, disorder.
▷ANTONYMS tidy.

must[1] verb *I must go*: **ought to**, should, have to, have got to, need to, be obliged to, be required to, be compelled to, be under an obligation to.
▶ noun informal *this video is* **a must**: **not to be missed**, very good; necessity, essential, necessary thing, sine qua non, requirement, requisite.
▷ANTONYMS option.

must[2] noun *a smell of must*: **mould**, mustiness, mouldiness, mildew, fustiness, decay.

muster verb **1** *they had mustered 50,000 troops*: **assemble**, bring together, call together, marshal, mobilize, rally, round up, raise, summon, gather, gather together, mass, collect, convene, call up, call to arms, recruit, conscript, draft; formal convoke; archaic levy.
▷ANTONYMS disperse.
2 *reporters mustered outside her house*: **congregate**, assemble, gather together, come together, meet, collect together, convene, mass, cluster together, flock together, rally; rare foregather.
3 *mustering her courage, she marched into the office*: **summon up**, summon, screw up, gather together, call up, rally.
▶ noun *the colonel called a muster*: **roll-call**, **assembly**, rally, meeting, round-up, convocation, mobilization, gathering, assemblage, congregation, convention; parade, review.
▫ **pass muster be good enough**, come up to standard, come up to scratch, measure up, be acceptable/adequate, be sufficient, fill/fit the bill, do, qualify; informal make the grade, come/be up to snuff, cut the mustard.

musty adjective **1** *the room smelled musty*: **mouldy**, stale, fusty, damp, dank, mildewed, mildewy, decayed, smelly, stuffy, airless, unventilated; Brit. frowsty; N. Amer. informal funky; rare mucid.
▷ANTONYMS fresh, fragrant.
2 *when I read it again, the play seemed musty*: **unoriginal**, uninspired, unimaginative, hackneyed, derivative, stale, flat, tired, banal, trite, clichéd, dry as dust, old-fashioned, antiquated, antediluvian, out of date, outdated, hoary, moth-eaten, worn out, threadbare, out of fashion, behind the times, obsolete; French passé, vieux jeu; informal old hat.
▷ANTONYMS fresh, modern.

mutable adjective *the mutable nature of fashion*: **changeable**, variable, varying, fluctuating, shifting, inconsistent, unpredictable, inconstant, uncertain, fluid, erratic, irregular, uneven, unsettled, unstable, unsteady, protean, chameleon-like, chameleonic; capricious, fickle, faithless, flighty, unreliable, undependable, mercurial, volatile; technical labile; rare changeful, fluctuant.
▷ANTONYMS constant, invariable.

mutant noun **freak**, freak of nature, deviant, oddity, monstrosity, monster, mutation, variant, variation; Latin lusus naturae; rare miscreation.

mutate verb *rhythm and blues mutated into rock and roll*: **change**, metamorphose, evolve, undergo a sea change; transmute, transform, transfigure, recast, reconstruct, convert; humorous transmogrify.

mutation noun **1** *cells that have undergone mutation*: **alteration**, change, variation, modification, transformation, metamorphosis, transmutation, transfiguration, sea change, evolution; humorous transmogrification.
2 *a genetic mutation*: **mutant**, variant, variation, freak, freak of nature, deviant, monstrosity, monster, deformity; anomaly, departure; Latin lusus naturae; rare miscreation.

mute adjective **1** *although I longed for details, Yasmin remained mute*: **silent**, speechless, dumb, unspeaking, wordless, voiceless, tongue-tied, at a loss for words, tight-lipped, close-mouthed, taciturn, uncommunicative; informal mum; archaic mumchance.
▷ANTONYMS voluble, talkative.
2 *she gazed at him in mute appeal*: **wordless**, silent, dumb, tacit, unspoken, inarticulate, unvoiced, unsaid, unexpressed, unuttered.
▷ANTONYMS spoken.
3 *the church was mute and dark*: **quiet**, silent, noiseless, soundless, hushed.
▷ANTONYMS noisy.
4 *he had been bullied into silence—people wondered if he was actually mute*: **dumb**, unable to speak; technical aphasic, aphonic.
▶ verb **1** *the noise of the traffic was muted by the heavy curtains*: **deaden**, **muffle**, mask, dull, dampen, damp down, soften, quieten, silence; stifle, smother, suppress, lower, reduce, diminish, decrease.
▷ANTONYMS amplify.
2 *Bruce had muted his criticisms*: **restrain**, soften, subdue, tone down, make less intense, moderate, temper, soft-pedal.
▷ANTONYMS intensify.

muted adjective **1** *the muted hum of distant traffic*: **muffled**, faint, indistinct, quiet, soft, softened, low, dull; hushed, whispered, lowered, stifled, suppressed.
▷ANTONYMS amplified.
2 *muted tones of grey and powder blue*: **subdued**, **pastel**, delicate, faded, dusty, subtle, toned down, understated, discreet, unobtrusive, restrained, low-key.
▷ANTONYMS garish.

Word toolkit **muted**

See **muffled**.

mutilate verb **1** *many of the bodies had been mutilated*: **mangle**, maim, disfigure, cut to pieces, cut up, hack up, butcher, dismember, tear limb from limb, tear apart, lacerate.

2 *the 14th-century carved screen had been mutilated*: **vandalize**, damage, deface, spoil, mar, ruin, destroy, wreck, violate, desecrate; N. Amer. informal trash; rare disfeature.

mutilation noun **maiming**, disfigurement, dismembering; damage, vandalization, desecration.

mutinous adjective *mutinous troops seized three military bases*: **rebellious**, insubordinate, subversive, seditious, insurgent, insurrectionary, insurrectionist, rebel, revolutionary; anarchistic, lawless, riotous, rioting, traitorous, factious; disobedient, defiant, wilful, recalcitrant, refractory, restive, disaffected, up in arms, unruly, disorderly, out of control, uncontrollable, ungovernable, unmanageable, unbiddable; Brit. informal bolshie; archaic contumacious.
▷ANTONYMS obedient, compliant.

mutiny noun *the mutiny over pay arrears had spread to the armed forces*: **insurrection, rebellion**, revolt, riot, revolution, uprising, rising, coup, coup d'état, putsch, protest, strike; insurgence, insurgency, subversion, sedition, anarchy, disorder, insubordination, disobedience, resistance, defiance.
▶ verb *thousands of soldiers mutinied*: **rise up, rebel**, revolt, riot, take part in an insurrection/uprising, resist/oppose authority, disobey/defy authority, refuse to obey orders; be insubordinate, protest, strike, go on strike.

mutt noun informal **1** *a long-haired mutt of doubtful pedigree*: **mongrel**, hound, dog, cur, tyke; informal pooch; Austral. informal mong, bitzer.
2 *he pitied the poor mutt who fell for her charms*. See **fool**.

mutter verb **1** *a group of men stood muttering in one corner of the room*: **talk under one's breath**, murmur, mumble, whisper, speak in an undertone, speak sotto voce, speak in hushed tones; talk to oneself.
▷ANTONYMS speak out.
2 *backbenchers muttered about the reshuffle*: **grumble**, moan, complain, grouse, carp, whine, bleat; informal gripe, beef, bitch, whinge, sound off; Brit. informal chunter, grizzle; N. English informal mither; N. Amer. informal kvetch.

mutual adjective *a partnership based on mutual respect and understanding*: **reciprocal**, reciprocated, requited, returned, give-and-take, interchangeable, interactive, complementary, correlative; common, joint, shared.

muzzle noun **1** *she patted the dog's velvety muzzle*: **snout**, nose, mouth, jaws, maw.
2 *the law says that pit bull terriers have to wear a muzzle*: **gag**, restraint.
▶ verb *clumsy attempts to muzzle the media*: **gag**, silence, censor, suppress, stifle, inhibit, restrain, check, curb, fetter.

muzzy adjective **1** *she was shivering and felt muzzy*: **groggy**, light-headed, faint, dizzy, shaky, confused, muddled, fuddled, befuddled, addled, befogged; informal dopey, woozy, not with it.
▷ANTONYMS clear-headed.
2 *a slightly muzzy picture*: **blurred**, blurry, fuzzy, unfocused, unclear, indistinct, ill-defined, woolly, foggy, hazy, faint.
▷ANTONYMS clear.

myopic adjective **1** *thick lenses may restrict a myopic patient's field of view*: **short-sighted**; N. Amer. nearsighted; informal as blind as a bat; archaic purblind.
▷ANTONYMS long-sighted.
2 *the government still has a myopic attitude to public spending*: **unimaginative**, uncreative, unadventurous, narrow-minded, lacking foresight, small-minded, short-term, narrow; insular, parochial, provincial.
▷ANTONYMS far-sighted.

myriad noun *myriads of insects danced around the light*: **multitude**, a large/great number/quantity, a lot, scores, quantities, mass, crowd, throng, host, droves, horde, army, legion, sea, swarm; informal lots, loads, masses, stacks, tons, oodles, hundreds, thousands, millions, billions, zillions, more ... than one can shake a stick at; N. Amer. informal gazillions, bazillions.
▶ adjective *the myriad lights of the city*: **innumerable**, countless, infinite, numberless, unlimited, untold, limitless, unnumbered, immeasurable, multitudinous, numerous, manifold, multiple, legion, several, many, various, sundry, diverse, multifarious; literary divers; rare innumerous, unnumberable.

myself pronoun
□ **by myself** See **by oneself** at **by**.

mysterious adjective **1** *his colleague had vanished in mysterious circumstances*: **puzzling, strange**, peculiar, curious, funny, queer, odd, weird, bizarre, mystifying, inexplicable, baffling, perplexing, bewildering, confusing, uncanny, dark, impenetrable, incomprehensible, unexplainable, unfathomable, Delphic, sibylline, unaccountable, insoluble, obscure; arcane, recondite, secret, esoteric, occult, cryptic, hidden, concealed, supernatural, mystical.
▷ANTONYMS straightforward.
2 *he was being very mysterious about his whereabouts*: **enigmatic**, inscrutable, secretive, sphinx-like, cloak-and-dagger, reticent, non-committal, discreet, evasive, furtive, surreptitious, covert.
▷ANTONYMS open.

> *Word toolkit* **mysterious**
>
> See **secret**.

mystery noun **1** *his death remains a mystery*: **puzzle, enigma**, conundrum, riddle, secret, unsolved problem, problem, question, question mark, closed book; informal poser.
2 *much of her past is shrouded in mystery*: **secrecy**, darkness, obscurity, ambiguity, ambiguousness, uncertainty, impenetrability, vagueness, nebulousness; inscrutability, inscrutableness, unfathomableness, mystique, romance.
3 *a 1920s murder mystery entitled 'The Ghost Train'*: **thriller**, detective story/novel, murder story; informal whodunnit.

mystic, mystical adjective **1** *a mystic experience*: **spiritual**, religious, transcendental, transcendent, paranormal, other-worldly, supernatural, preternatural, non-rational, occult, metaphysical, ineffable.
2 *mystic rites*: **symbolic**, symbolical, allegorical, representational, metaphorical, emblematic, emblematical, non-literal.
3 *a geometric figure of mystical significance*: **cryptic**, concealed, hidden, abstruse, arcane, esoteric, recondite, inscrutable, inexplicable, unfathomable, mysterious, secret, enigmatic, occult, cabbalistic, obscure, unrevealed.

mystify verb *I was completely mystified by his disappearance*: **bewilder**, puzzle, perplex, baffle, confuse, confound, bemuse, obfuscate, nonplus, throw, get; informal flummox, be all Greek to, stump, bamboozle, beat, faze, fox; archaic wilder, gravel, maze.

> *Choose the right word* **mystify, puzzle, perplex, baffle**
>
> See **puzzle**.

mystique noun *a certain mystique still surrounds the family*: **charisma**, glamour, romance, mystery, fascination, magic, spell, charm, appeal, allure, awe.

myth noun **1** *ancient Greek myths*: **folk tale**, story, folk story, legend, tale, fable, saga, allegory, parable, tradition, lore, folklore; technical mythos, mythus.
2 *there are still plenty of myths surrounding pregnancy and childbirth*: **misconception**, fallacy, mistaken belief, false notion, misbelief, old wives' tale, fairy story, fairy tale, fiction, fantasy, delusion, figment of the imagination; invention, fabrication, falsehood, untruth, lie; informal story, tall story, tall tale, fib, cock and bull story, kidology.

> *Word links* **myth**
>
> **mythology** study of myths

mythical adjective **1** *dragons and other mythical beasts*: **legendary**, mythological, fabled, fabulous, folkloric, fairy-tale, storybook, chimerical; fantastical, imaginary, imagined, fictitious; allegorical, symbolic, symbolical, parabolic.
2 *the girl claimed that Tyler was the father of her mythical child*: **imaginary**, fictitious, make-believe, fantasy, fanciful, invented, fabricated, made-up, unreal, untrue, non-existent; informal pretend.
▷ANTONYMS real, actual.

mythological adjective **fabled**, fabulous, folkloric, fairy-tale, legendary, mythical, mythic, heroic, traditional; fictitious, imaginary, imagined; allegorical, symbolic, symbolical, parabolic.

mythology noun **myth(s)**, legend(s), folklore, folk tales, folk stories, lore, tradition, stories, tales; technical mythos.

nab verb informal *police nabbed him when he got back home*. See **catch** (sense 2 of the verb).

nabob noun *a Wall Street nabob*: **very rich person**, tycoon, magnate, millionaire, billionaire, multimillionaire, plutocrat; informal zillionaire, fat cat, moneybags; rare Croesus, Dives.

nadir noun *it was the nadir of his career*: **the lowest point**, the all-time low, the lowest level, low-water mark, the bottom, as low as one can get, rock-bottom, the depths; zero; informal the pits.
▷ANTONYMS zenith, acme, climax.

nag[1] verb **1** *I don't want to nag you but you really should eat something*: **harass**, keep on at, go on at, harp on at, badger, keep after, give someone a hard time, get on someone's back, persecute, chivvy, hound, harry, bully, pick on, criticize, find fault with, keep complaining to, moan (on) at, grumble at, henpeck, carp at, scold, upbraid, berate; informal hassle; N. Amer. informal ride; Austral. informal heavy.
2 *one question has been nagging me for weeks*: **trouble**, worry, bother, plague, torment, niggle, prey on one's mind, gnaw at, hang over, haunt, weigh down, weigh heavily on, lie heavy on, burden, cause anxiety to; annoy, irritate, vex, irk, rankle with; N. English mither; informal bug, aggravate.
▸noun *she's such a nag*: **shrew**, nagger, harpy, termagant, harridan; moaner, complainer, grumbler, fault-finder, carper, caviller; N. Amer. informal kvetch; archaic scold.

nag[2] noun *she can ride any old nag and get the best out of it*: **worn-out horse**, old horse, hack, Rosinante; informal bag of bones; N. Amer. informal plug, crowbait; Austral./NZ informal moke; Brit. informal, dated screw; archaic jade, rip, keffel.

nagging adjective **1** *his nagging wife*: **shrewish**, complaining, grumbling, fault-finding, scolding, carping, cavilling, criticizing.
2 *there was a nagging pain in his chest*: **persistent**, continuous, lingering, niggling, troublesome, unrelenting, unremitting, unabating; aching, painful, distressing, worrying.

nail noun **1 pin**, spike, tack, rivet; hobnail; Brit. panel pin, tin tack; technical brad, sprig, clout nail, sparable.
2 fingernail, thumbnail, toenail; claw, talon, nipper, pincer; technical unguis, chela.
□ **hard as nails callous**, hard-hearted, heartless, with a heart of stone, stony, stony-hearted, unfeeling, unsympathetic, uncaring, insensitive, unsentimental, cold-hearted, cold, hardbitten, tough, unforgiving, lacking compassion, uncharitable, inflexible, unbending, implacable.
□ **on the nail immediately**, at once, without delay, straight away, right away, promptly, on the spot, directly, now, this minute; N. Amer. on the barrelhead.
▸verb **1** *a large blackboard was nailed to the wall*: **fasten**, attach, fix, affix, secure, tack, hammer, pin, post.
2 informal *a device which could help police to nail their suspects*: **catch**, capture, apprehend, arrest, take into custody, seize, take in, bring in; informal collar, nab, pinch, cop, run in, pull in, pick up, bust; Brit. informal nick, nobble.
3 *the paper's exclusive pictures had nailed the lie*: **expose**, reveal, uncover, unmask, bring to light, lay bare, smoke something out, unearth, detect, identify; archaic discover.

Word links **nail**

ungual relating to the nails

naive adjective *I was very naive to begin with, but I learnt fast*: **innocent**, unsophisticated, artless, ingenuous, inexperienced, guileless, unworldly, childlike, trusting, trustful, dewy-eyed, starry-eyed, wide-eyed, fond, simple, natural, unaffected, unpretentious; **gullible**, credulous, easily taken in, easily deceived, unsuspecting, over-trusting, over-trustful, born yesterday, unsuspicious, deceivable, dupable, immature, callow, raw, green, as green as grass, ignorant; informal wet behind the ears.
▷ANTONYMS sophisticated, disingenuous, experienced, worldly.

Choose the right word **naive, artless, ingenuous**

Naive is by far the most common of these adjectives. It is generally used critically or pityingly of people lacking experience, wisdom, or judgement, or of their actions (*the rather naive young man had been totally misled | it may be naive to think that much of the population really believes specific election pledges*). It can, however, also be used more approvingly of a person seen as natural and unaffected (*Andy had a sweet, naive look when he smiled*).

Ingenuous is a more literary term, expressing approval or acceptance of people or actions that are innocent and unsuspecting (*an ingenuous young art student, fresh from college*).

Artless is quite rare and means 'without guile or deception', the opposite of the much more common *artful* (*what she knew of him was picked up from his wife's artless prattle*). Again approvingly, it can mean 'without effort or pretentiousness' (*the children had been directed to give very real, artless performances*). However, an older sense denoting things or actions that are considered to lack aesthetic imagination or practical skill is enjoying a revival (*this awful, artless building*).

naivety noun **innocence**, lack of sophistication, lack of experience, ingenuousness, guilelessness, lack of guile, unworldliness, childlikeness, trustfulness, simplicity, naturalness; **gullibility**, credulousness, credulity, over-trustfulness, lack of suspicion, blind faith, immaturity, callowness, greenness, ignorance.
▷ANTONYMS sophistication.

naked adjective **1** *a naked woman*: **nude**, bare, in the nude, stark naked, with nothing on, stripped, unclothed, undressed, uncovered, in a state of nature, disrobed, unclad, undraped, exposed; French au naturel; informal without a stitch on, in one's birthday suit, in the raw, in the altogether, in the buff, as naked as the day one was born, in the nuddy, mother naked; Brit. informal starkers; Scottish informal in the scud, scuddy; N. Amer. informal bare-assed, buck naked; Austral. informal bollocky; Brit. vulgar slang bollock-naked.
▷ANTONYMS clothed, dressed.
2 *each man was carrying a naked sword | a naked flame*: **unprotected**, uncovered, exposed, open, unguarded; **unsheathed**, drawn.
▷ANTONYMS covered, sheathed.
3 *the naked branches of the trees*: **bare**, barren, stark, denuded, stripped, uncovered; treeless, grassless; rare defoliated.
4 *I felt naked and exposed as I crossed the deserted square*: **vulnerable**, helpless, weak, powerless, defenceless, exposed, unprotected, undefended, open to attack.
5 *the naked truth | naked hostility blazed in his eyes*: **undisguised**, plain, unadorned, unvarnished, unveiled, unqualified, stark, bald, unexaggerated, simple; overt, obvious, open, patent, evident, apparent, manifest, unmistakable, palpable, blatant, glaring, flagrant, barefaced, out-and-out, unmitigated.

Word links **naked**

gymno- related prefix, as in *gymnosophist*
gymnophobia fear of being naked

Choose the right word **naked, nude, bare**

These words are all used to refer to a person's unclothed state.

Naked is the standard word for someone who isn't wearing any clothes. It also has several well-established metaphorical uses, always placed before the noun: *the naked eye* is unaided by a telescope or similar instrument, while a *naked light bulb* is not shielded or dimmed by a shade. *Naked* feelings or behaviour are openly expressed or at least undisguised (*he saw in her eyes naked fear | naked self-interest*).

Nude is slightly more formal or euphemistic than *naked*. It is used especially with reference to paintings and photographs of naked people (*she posed as a nude model in magazines*) or to swimming and sunbathing (*nude bathing is illegal*).

Bare is used typically to refer to just a part of the body (*running about in bare feet*). However, doing something *with your bare hands* implies that you are not using any tools, rather than not wearing gloves. In its metaphorical uses, *bare* suggests the removal of everything that is not absolutely indispensable (*the bare bones of a news story | emissions are kept to a bare minimum*).

nakedness noun **1** *she tried to cover her nakedness*: **nudity**, state of undress, bareness; French déshabillé; informal one's birthday suit.
2 *the nakedness of the landscape*: **bareness**, barrenness, starkness.

namby-pamby adjective *we don't want a club full of namby-pamby bleeding hearts*. See **spineless**.

name noun **1** *her name's Gemma*: **title**, denomination, designation, honorific, tag, epithet, label; Indian naam; informal moniker, handle; formal appellation; rare agnomen, allonym, anonym, appellative.
2 *the top names in the British fashion industry*: **celebrity**, star, superstar, VIP, famous person, important person, leading light, celebutante, big name, luminary, mogul, person of note, dignitary, personage, worthy; expert, authority, lion; informal celeb, somebody, megastar, big noise, big shot, bigwig, big cheese, big gun, big wheel, big fish.
3 *he made his name as one of the greatest steeplechase jockeys of our time | this may damage the good name of the firm*: **reputation**, character, repute, standing, stature, honour, esteem, prestige, cachet, kudos; fame, celebrity, renown, popularity, notability, note, distinction, eminence, prominence; Indian izzat.
□ **give someone/something a bad name** *the gas guzzling machinery that gives the country such a bad name*: **vilify**, disparage, denigrate, defame, cast aspersions on, run down, impugn, revile, belittle, abuse, insult, slight, attack, speak badly of, speak ill of, speak evil of, pour scorn on, criticize, censure, condemn, decry, denounce, pillory; malign, slander, libel, conduct a smear campaign against, spread lies about, blacken the name/reputation of, sully the reputation of, bring into disrepute, discredit, stigmatize, traduce, calumniate, slur; informal bad-mouth, do a hatchet job on, take to pieces, pull apart, throw mud at, drag through the mud, slate, knock, slam, pan, roast, bad-mouth, throw brickbats at; Brit. informal rubbish, slag off, monster; N. Amer. informal pummel, dump on; Austral./NZ informal bag; rare derogate, vituperate, asperse, vilipend.
▸ **verb 1** *they named the child Phoebe*: **call**, give a name to, dub; label, style, term, title, entitle; baptize, christen; archaic clepe; rare denominate.
2 *the driver of the car was later named as Jason Penter*: **identify**, specify, cite, give, mention.
3 *on March 19th, he named his successor*: **choose**, select, pick, decide on, nominate, designate, appoint, delegate, assign.

Word links **name**

nominal, onomastic relating to names
-onym related suffix, as in *pseudonym, synonym*
onomatophobia fear of names

named adjective **1** *a girl named Anne | a condition named 'myasthenic syndrome'*: **called**, by the name of, baptized, christened, known as, under the name of; dubbed, entitled, styled, termed, described as, labelled.
2 *documentary sources able to supply information about named individuals*: **specified**, designated, identified, cited, given, mentioned, selected, nominated, chosen, singled out; rare individuated.

nameless adjective **1** *the pictures were taken by a nameless photographer | a nameless grave*: **unnamed**, unidentified, anonymous, incognito, unspecified, unacknowledged, uncredited; unknown, unheard of, unsung, uncelebrated, inglorious, obscure; untitled, undesignated, unlabelled, untagged; rare innominate.
▷ANTONYMS well known, famous.
2 *he had become a prey to nameless fears*: **unspeakable**, unutterable, inexpressible, unmentionable, indescribable, abominable, horrible, dreadful, appalling, shocking, awful, terrible, frightful; **indefinable**, vague, obscure, unspecified, unspecifiable.
▷ANTONYMS specific.

namely adverb *he has something rare to offer, namely charisma*: **that is**, that is to say, to be specific, specifically, in other words, viz., to wit, sc.; Latin id est, videlicet, scilicet.

nanny noun See **nursemaid**.
▸ **verb** *stop nannying me*. See **mollycoddle** (verb).

nap[1] verb *they arrived to find her napping on the sofa*. See **snooze** (verb).
▸ **noun** *she'd been awake all night and was looking forward to taking a nap*. See **snooze** (noun).
□ **catch someone napping catch off guard**, catch unawares, take by surprise, surprise, catch in an unguarded moment, catch out, find unprepared; informal catch someone with their trousers/pants down; Brit. informal catch on the hop.

nap[2] noun *use a wire brush to raise the nap of the suede*: **pile**, fibres, threads, weave, shag, texture, feel, surface, grain.

nappy noun N. Amer. diaper; Brit. dated napkin.

narcissism noun See **vanity** (sense 1).

narcissistic adjective See **vain** (sense 1).

narcotic noun **soporific drug**, opiate, sleeping pill, soporific; painkiller, pain reliever, analgesic, anodyne, palliative, anaesthetic; tranquillizer, sedative; informal downer; dated sleeping draught; literary nepenthes; rare stupefacient, stupefactive.
▸ **adjective soporific**, sleep-inducing, opiate, hypnotic; painkilling, pain-relieving, analgesic, anodyne, anaesthetic, stupefying, numbing, dulling, tranquillizing, sedative, calming; rare stupefacient, stuporific, stupefactive.

narked adjective Brit. informal *he was just narked that I hadn't told him about it*. See **annoyed**.

narrate verb *the story is narrated by an ageing English butler*: **tell**, relate, recount, give an account of, unfold, set forth/out, describe, detail, sketch out, portray, chronicle, give a report of, report, relay, retail, delineate, rehearse, recite; voice-over.

narration noun **1** *the first chapter is taken up with a narration of past events in his life*: **account**, narrative, story, tale, chronicle, description, portrayal, report, sketch, recital, recitation, rehearsal; telling, relation, story telling, chronicling, detailing; rare recountal.
2 *he introduces the story with a narration that sets the tone for the entire film*: **voice-over**, reading, commentary.

narrative noun *a chronological narrative of Stark's life*: **account**, story, tale, chronicle, history, description, record, portrayal, sketch, portrait, statement, report, rehearsal, recital, rendering.

narrator noun **1** *the narrator of 'the Arabian Nights'*: **storyteller**, teller of tales, recounter, relater, describer, chronicler, romancer, reporter, annalist; raconteur; Austral. informal magsman; rare anecdotist, anecdotalist.
▷ANTONYMS listener, audience.
2 *the film's narrator*: **voice-over**, commentator.

narrow adjective **1** *the path became narrower and more overgrown*: **small**, tapered, tapering, narrowing, narrow-gauged; archaic strait.
▷ANTONYMS wide, broad.
2 *he slid his arm around her narrow waist*: **slender**, slim, lean, slight, spare, attenuated, thin; rare attenuate.
▷ANTONYMS broad.
3 *he eased himself out of the narrow space*: **confined**, cramped, tight, close, restricted, limited, constricted, confining, pinched, squeezed, meagre, scant, scanty, spare; rare incommodious, exiguous, incapacious.
▷ANTONYMS spacious.
4 *a narrow range of products | her experience of life was very narrow*: **limited**, restricted, circumscribed, straitened, small, inadequate, insufficient, deficient, lacking, wanting; select, exclusive.
▷ANTONYMS wide, broad.
5 *a narrow view of the world*. See **narrow-minded**.
6 *this is nationalism in the narrowest sense of the word*: **strict**, literal, exact, precise, close, faithful, true.
7 *a narrow victory | a narrow escape*: **marginal**; lucky.
▸ **verb** *the path narrowed and we had to proceed in single file | it narrowed the gap between rich and poor*: **get/become/make narrower**, get/become/make smaller, taper, diminish, decrease, reduce, contract, shrink, constrict; archaic straiten.

narrowly adverb **1** *one bullet struck the car, narrowly missing him*: **only just**, just, barely, scarcely, hardly, by a hair's breadth, by a very small margin, by the narrowest of margins, by the skin of one's teeth, by a nose; informal by a whisker.
2 *she looked at me narrowly*: **closely**, carefully, searchingly, scrutinizingly, attentively; meticulously, scrupulously, painstakingly.

narrow-minded adjective **intolerant**, illiberal, reactionary, conservative, ultra-conservative, conventional, parochial, provincial, insular, small-town,

localist, small-minded, petty-minded, petty, close-minded, short-sighted, myopic, blinkered, inward-looking, narrow, hidebound, dyed-in-the-wool, diehard, limited, restricted, inflexible, dogmatic, rigid, entrenched, prejudiced, bigoted, biased, partisan, sectarian, discriminatory; prudish, priggish, strait-laced, stuffy, puritanical, moralistic, prim, starchy, prissy, shockable; racist, racialist, chauvinistic, chauvinist, sexist, nationalistic; Brit. parish-pump, blimpish; French borné; N. Amer. informal jerkwater; rare claustral.
▷ANTONYMS broad-minded, tolerant.

narrows plural noun **strait(s)**, sound, neck, channel, waterway, passage, sea passage.

nascent adjective *the nascent economic recovery*. See **emergent**.

nastiness noun **1** *my mother tried to shut herself off from reality and from nastiness*: **unpleasantness**, disagreeableness, offensiveness, vileness, foulness, unsavouriness, ugliness, squalor, filthiness, filth, pollution.
▷ANTONYMS niceness, pleasantness.
2 *he was bewildered by her uncharacteristic nastiness*: **unkindness**, unpleasantness, unfriendliness, disagreeableness, hostility, rudeness, churlishness, spite, spitefulness, malice, maliciousness, meanness, mean-spiritedness, ill temper, ill nature, bad temper, bad-temperedness, viciousness, ill humour, malevolence, venom, venomousness, malignancy, cantankerousness, cruelty, abusiveness; informal bitchiness, cattiness.
▷ANTONYMS niceness, kindness.
3 *for some real nastiness this week, you had to watch 'The Sex Hunters'*: **obscenity**, indecency, offensiveness, impropriety, indelicacy, crudity, vulgarity, grossness, pornography, smuttiness, smut, salaciousness, lewdness, licentiousness.

nasty adjective **1** *there was a nasty smell in the kitchen*: **unpleasant**, disagreeable, disgusting, distasteful, awful, dreadful, horrible, terrible, vile, foul, abominable, frightful, loathsome, revolting, repulsive, odious, sickening, nauseating, nauseous, repellent, repugnant, horrendous, hideous, appalling, atrocious, offensive, objectionable, obnoxious, unpalatable, unsavoury, unappetizing, off-putting, uninviting, dirty, filthy, squalid; noxious, evil-smelling, foul-smelling, smelly, stinking, rank, rancid, fetid, malodorous, acrid; informal ghastly, horrid, gruesome, putrid, diabolical, yucky, sick-making, God-awful, gross, icky, stinky; Brit. informal beastly, grotty, whiffy, pongy, niffy; N. Amer. informal lousy, skanky, funky; Austral. informal on the nose; literary noisome, mephitic; archaic disgustful, loathly; rare miasmal, olid.
▷ANTONYMS nice, delightful, lovely, pleasant.
2 *the weather turned nasty*: **unpleasant**, disagreeable, foul, filthy, inclement; wet, rainy, stormy, cold, foggy, blustery, squally.
▷ANTONYMS fine, sunny.
3 *sometimes, she can be really nasty*: **unkind**, unpleasant, unfriendly, disagreeable, inconsiderate, uncharitable, rude, churlish, spiteful, malicious, mean, mean-spirited, ill-tempered, ill-natured, ill-humoured, bad-tempered, hostile, vicious, malevolent, evil-minded, surly, obnoxious, poisonous, venomous, vindictive, malign, malignant, cantankerous, hateful, hurtful, cruel, wounding, abusive; informal bitchy, catty; vulgar slang shitty.
▷ANTONYMS charming, agreeable, nice, likeable.
4 *her father's had a nasty accident | she's got a nasty cut on her head*: **serious**, dangerous, bad, awful, dreadful, terrible, frightful, critical, severe, grave, alarming, worrying; painful, ugly.
▷ANTONYMS slight, minor.
5 *she had a nasty habit of staring at him*: **annoying**, irritating, infuriating, unwelcome, disagreeable, unpleasant, unfortunate, maddening, exasperating, irksome, vexing, vexatious; informal aggravating, pesky.
6 *they got hold of spray cans and wrote nasty things on the back of the headstones*: **obscene**, indecent, offensive, improper, indelicate, crude, rude, off colour, dirty, filthy, vulgar, foul, vile, gross, disgusting, pornographic, smutty, salacious, risqué, lewd, lascivious, licentious, X-rated; scatological, profane; informal blue, sick.
□ **nasty piece of work** *he was a nasty piece of work and got his just rewards*: **wretch**; informal beast, toad, pig, swine, rat, creep, bastard, louse, snake, skunk, dog, weasel, lowlife, scumbag, heel, stinkpot, stinker, bad lot, no-good, son of a bitch, s.o.b.; Scottish informal scrote; Irish informal spalpeen; N. Amer. informal rat fink, fink, schmuck; Austral. informal dingo; NZ informal kuri; informal, dated rotter, hound, bounder, cad, blighter; black English rass; vulgar slang shit, sod, prick; archaic blackguard, dastard, knave, varlet, whoreson.

nation noun **country**, **state**, land, sovereign state, nation state, kingdom, empire, republic, confederation, federation, commonwealth, power, superpower, polity, domain; fatherland, motherland; people, race, civilization, tribe, society, community, population, body politic, populace, public; Law realm; Latin res publica.

> *Word links* **nation**
>
> **ethnic** relating to a nation or people
> **ethno-** related prefix, as in *ethnocentric, ethnolinguistics*

national adjective **1** *national politics | national and international news*: **state**, public, federal, governmental; civic, civil, domestic, internal, home; popular; ethnic, racial, cultural, tribal, indigenous, native, ethnological.
▷ANTONYMS local; international.
2 *a one-day national strike*: **nationwide**, countrywide, state, coast-to-coast, general, widespread, overall, comprehensive.
▷ANTONYMS local.
▶ noun *a French national*: **citizen**, subject, native, resident, inhabitant; voter.

nationalism noun *the resurgence of nationalism in Europe and in other parts of the world*: **patriotism**, patriotic sentiment, allegiance/loyalty to one's country, loyalism, nationality; **xenophobia**, chauvinism, jingoism, flag-waving, isolationism; ethnocentrism, ethnocentricity.

nationalistic adjective *Russian foreign policy was becoming increasingly nationalistic*: **patriotic**, nationalist, loyal to one's country, pro one's country; **xenophobic**, chauvinistic, jingoistic, flag-waving, isolationist; ethnocentric.

nationality noun **1** *individuals seeking British nationality*: **citizenship**; the right to hold a passport.
2 *all the main nationalities of Ethiopia*: **ethnic group**, ethnic minority, tribe, clan, race, nation; rare ethnos.

nationwide adjective *a nationwide conservation scheme*: **national**, countrywide, state, coast-to-coast, general, widespread, overall, comprehensive, all-embracing, extensive, across the board.

native noun *a native of Sweden | New York in the summer was too hot even for the natives*: **inhabitant**, resident, local; aborigine; **citizen**, national; formal dweller; rare autochthon, indigene.
▷ANTONYMS foreigner, outsider, alien.
▶ adjective **1** *the island's native population*: **indigenous**, aboriginal, original, first, earliest; rare autochthonous, autochthonic.
▷ANTONYMS immigrant.
2 *honey, eggs and other native produce | native plants*: **domestic**, **home-grown**, home-made, home, local; indigenous, endemic.
▷ANTONYMS imported.
3 *his vagueness masked a shrewd native instinct for politics*: **innate**, inherent, inborn, intrinsic, instinctive, instinctual, intuitive, natural, natural-born, deep-seated, deep-rooted; hereditary, inherited, in the blood, in the family, natal, congenital, bred in the bone, inbred, ingrained, built-in; rare connate, connatural.
▷ANTONYMS acquired, learned.
4 *her native tongue*: **mother**, vernacular.

> *Word toolkit* **native**
>
> See **original**.

nativity noun **birth**, childbirth, delivery; technical parturition; rare nascence, nascency.

natter Brit. informal verb & noun See **chat**.

natty adjective *Stephen looked very natty in a lightweight grey suit and shiny black shoes*: **smart**, stylish, fashionable, dapper, debonair, dashing, jaunty, rakish, spruce, well turned out, well dressed, chic, modish, elegant, trim; informal snazzy, trendy, cool, sharp, snappy, with it, nifty, groovy; N. Amer. informal sassy, spiffy, fly, kicky; dated as if one had just stepped out of a bandbox; archaic trig.
▷ANTONYMS scruffy.

natural adjective **1** *a natural occurrence*: **normal**, ordinary, everyday, usual, regular, common, commonplace, typical, routine, standard, established, customary, accustomed, habitual, run-of-the-mill, stock, unexceptional.
▷ANTONYMS abnormal, unnatural, exceptional.
2 *her policy of using fresh, natural produce*: **unprocessed**, organic, pure, wholesome, unrefined, pesticide-free, chemical-free, additive-free, unbleached, unmixed, real, plain, virgin, crude, raw.
▷ANTONYMS artificial, refined.
3 *Alex is a natural leader*: **born**, naturally gifted, untaught.
4 *his natural instincts*: **innate**, inborn, inherent, native, native-born, intrinsic, instinctive, instinctual, intuitive, natural-born, ingrained, built-in; gut; hereditary, inherited, inbred, congenital; rare connate, connatural.
▷ANTONYMS acquired.
5 *she's very natural | the conversation was natural and easy*: **unaffected**, **spontaneous**, uninhibited, straightforward, relaxed, unselfconscious, genuine, open, artless, guileless, ingenuous, unsophisticated, unpretentious, without airs, easy; unstudied, unforced, uncontrived, unmannered, unstilted, unconstrained.
▷ANTONYMS affected, false; stilted, strained; awkward, self-conscious.
6 *it was quite natural for him to think she admired him*: **reasonable**, logical, understandable, unsurprising, expected, (only) to be expected, predictable; inevitable.
▷ANTONYMS unreasonable.
7 *his natural son*: **illegitimate**, born out of wedlock; informal, dated born on the wrong side of the blanket; archaic bastard, misbegotten, baseborn, spurious; rare adulterine.
▷ANTONYMS legitimate.

naturalist noun **natural historian**, **life scientist**, wildlife expert; biologist, botanist, zoologist, ornithologist, entomologist, ecologist, conservationist, environmentalist, preservationist; birdwatcher; N. Amer. birder; informal twitcher.

> *Easily confused words* **naturalist or naturist?**
>
> Unwary **naturalists** might be embarrassed to come across **naturists** when they were looking for specimens. Despite their similar spelling, the two words have quite different meanings: a *naturalist* is someone interested in or knowledgeable about natural history, while *naturist* is a less common term for *nudist*.

naturalistic adjective *naturalistic painting | a naturalistic drama*: **realistic**, real-life, true-to-life, lifelike, vivid, graphic, representational, photographic; factual; French vérité; informal kitchen-sink, warts and all; rare verisimilar, veristic.
▷ANTONYMS abstract.

naturalize verb **1** *he emigrated to London before the Second World War and was naturalized in 1950*: **grant citizenship to**, make a citizen, endow with the rights of citizenship, confer citizenship on, give a passport to, enfranchise; rare endenizen, denizen, citizenize.
2 *coriander has been naturalized in southern Britain*: **establish**, introduce, acclimatize, domesticate; N. Amer. acclimate.
3 *he saw myth as the process by which ideology is naturalized*: **assimilate**, absorb, incorporate, adopt, accept, take in, homogenize; rare acculturate.

naturally adverb **1** *he's naturally shy*: **by nature**, by character, inherently, innately, congenitally, instinctively.
2 *try and act naturally*: **normally**, in a natural manner/way, unaffectedly, spontaneously, genuinely, artlessly, unpretentiously; informal natural.
▷ANTONYMS awkwardly, self-consciously, pretentiously.
3 *naturally, they wanted everything kept quiet*: **of course**, as might be expected, as you/one would expect, needless to say, not unexpectedly, as was anticipated, as a matter of course; obviously, clearly, it goes without saying; informal natch.
▷ANTONYMS surprisingly.

naturalness noun *she was different—she'd lost a certain naturalness*: **unselfconsciousness**, lack of affectation, spontaneity, spontaneousness, lack of inhibition, straightforwardness, genuineness, openness, ingenuousness, simplicity, lack of sophistication, unpretentiousness, lack of pretension.
▷ANTONYMS affectation, awkwardness, self-consciousness, pretentiousness.

n

nature noun **1** *the beauty of nature*: **the natural world**, the living world, Mother Nature, creation, the world, the environment, the earth, Mother Earth, the universe, the cosmos, natural forces; wildlife, flora and fauna, countryside, landscape, scenery.
2 *such crimes are, by their very nature, difficult to hide*: **essence**, inherent/basic/essential characteristics, inherent/basic/essential qualities, inherent/basic/essential attributes, inherent/basic/essential features, sum and substance, character, identity, complexion.
3 *it was not in Daisy's nature to be bitchy*: **character**, personality, disposition, temperament, temper, humour, make-up, cast/turn of mind, persona, psyche, constitution, fibre.
4 *experiments of a similar nature*: **kind**, sort, type, variety, description, category, ilk, class, classification, species, genre, style, cast, order, kidney, mould, stamp, grain; N. Amer. stripe.

naturist noun **nudist**, sun worshipper; informal nudie.
▷ANTONYMS textile.

> *Easily confused words* **naturist or naturalist?**
>
> See **naturalist**.

naught noun archaic *all his efforts will have been for naught*: **nothing**, nothing at all, nought, nil, zero; N. English nowt; informal zilch, sweet Fanny Adams, sweet FA, not a dicky bird, nix; Brit. informal damn all, not a sausage; N. Amer. informal zip, zippo, nada, diddly-squat, a goose egg; Brit. vulgar slang bugger all, fuck all, sod all.
□ **bring to naught** archaic *such recommendations will only bring to naught efforts to increase cooperation*: **ruin**, wreck, destroy, devastate, wreak havoc on, reduce to nothing, blight, smash, shatter, dash, torpedo, scotch, make a mess of, mess up; sabotage, poison; cancel out, neutralize, negate, render ineffective, make of no use or value; informal louse up, screw up, foul up, put the kibosh on, banjax, do for, blow a hole in, nix, queer; Brit. informal scupper, cock up, dish, muller; Austral. informal euchre, cruel; vulgar slang fuck up.
□ **come to naught** *efforts to relocate the event to another seaside resort have so far come to naught*: **fail**, founder, be unsuccessful, not succeed, lack success, fall through, fall flat, break down, abort, miscarry, be defeated, suffer defeat, be in vain, be frustrated, collapse, misfire, backfire, not come up to scratch, meet with disaster, come to grief, come to nothing, miss the mark, run aground, go wrong, go awry, go astray; informal flop, fizzle out, come a cropper, bite the dust, blow up in someone's face, go down like a lead balloon.
▷ANTONYMS succeed.

naughty adjective **1** *a naughty boy*: **badly behaved**, **disobedient**, bad, misbehaved, misbehaving, wayward, defiant, unruly, insubordinate, wilful, self-willed, delinquent, undisciplined, unmanageable, uncontrollable, ungovernable, unbiddable, disorderly, disruptive, mutinous, fractious, refractory, recalcitrant, errant, wild, wicked, obstreperous, difficult, troublesome, awkward, contrary, perverse, exasperating, incorrigible; bad-mannered, rude, impolite; **mischievous**, full of mischief, playful, impish, roguish, puckish, rascally, prankish, tricksy; informal brattish, scampish; Scottish informal gallus; archaic contumacious.
▷ANTONYMS good, well behaved, obedient.
2 *naughty jokes*: **indecent**, **risqué**, rude, racy, ribald, bawdy, broad, spicy, suggestive, titillating, improper, indelicate, indecorous, off colour; vulgar, dirty, filthy, smutty, crude, offensive, salacious, coarse, obscene, lewd, pornographic, X-rated; informal blue, raunchy; Brit. informal fruity, near the knuckle, saucy; N. Amer. informal gamy; euphemistic adult.
▷ANTONYMS decent.

nausea noun **1** *symptoms include a loss of appetite, nausea, and a severe headache*: **sickness**, biliousness, queasiness; vomiting, retching, gagging; travel-sickness, seasickness, carsickness, airsickness, motion sickness, morning sickness, altitude sickness; informal throwing up, puking; rare qualms.
2 *intended to induce a feeling of nostalgia, it only induces in me a feeling of nausea*: **disgust**, revulsion, repugnance, repulsion, distaste, aversion, loathing, abhorrence, detestation, odium; archaic disrelish.

nauseate verb *the smell of the meat nauseated her*. See **sicken** (sense 1).

nauseating adjective *the smell in the compartment was nauseating | his nauseating self-pity*: **sickening**, stomach-turning, stomach-churning, nauseous, emetic, sickly; **disgusting**, revolting, repulsive, repellent, repugnant, offensive, loathsome, abhorrent, odious, obnoxious, nasty, foul, vile, appalling, abominable; N. Amer. vomitous; informal sick-making, ghastly, putrid, horrid, God-awful, gross, gut-churning, yucky; Brit. informal beastly; literary noisome; archaic disgustful, loathly.

nauseous adjective **1** *the thought of food made her feel nauseous*: **sick**, nauseated, queasy, bilious, sick to one's stomach, green, green about/at the gills, ill, unwell, bad; seasick, carsick, airsick, travel-sick; informal about to throw up; N. Amer. informal barfy; rare qualmish.
2 *a nauseous stench | that doesn't mean I have to be involved in this nauseous business*: **sickening**, nauseating, stomach-turning, stomach-churning, emetic, sickly; **disgusting**, revolting, repulsive, repellent, repugnant, offensive, loathsome, abhorrent, odious, obnoxious, nasty, foul, vile, appalling, abominable; N. Amer. vomitous; informal sick-making, ghastly, putrid, horrid, God-awful, gross, gut-churning, yucky; Brit. informal beastly; literary noisome; archaic disgustful, loathly.
▷ANTONYMS charming, pleasing.

nautical adjective **maritime**, marine, naval, seafaring, seagoing, ocean-going; yachting, boating, sailing.

navel noun **1** informal belly button, tummy button; technical umbilicus.
2 *Cyprus was the navel of Byzantine culture*: **centre**, central point, middle, midpoint, hub, nub, focal point, focus, pivot, nucleus, heart, core, eye; rare omphalos.

> *Word links* **navel**
>
> **umbilical** relating to the navel
> **omphalo-** related prefix, as in *omphalocele*

navigable adjective *all of the main tributaries of the Vistula were navigable*: **passable**, negotiable, traversable, able to be sailed/travelled on, crossable; clear, open, free from obstruction, unobstructed, unblocked.

navigate verb **1** *they navigated by the stars*: **steer**; plot a route/course; Nautical helm.
2 *he navigated the yacht across the Atlantic with nothing more than an astrolabe*: **steer**, pilot; guide, manoeuvre, direct, handle, drive; skipper, captain; Nautical con, helm.
3 *the upper reaches of the river are dangerous to navigate*: **sail across/over**, sail, cruise, travel/journey/voyage across/over; cross, traverse, negotiate.
4 *I'll drive—you can navigate*: **map-read**, give directions, plan the route.

navigation noun **1** *the navigation of the ship*: **steering**, piloting, pilotage, sailing, guiding, directing, guidance, manoeuvring.
2 *Cooper learned the skills of navigation*: **helmsmanship**, steersmanship, seamanship, map-reading, chart-reading.

navigator noun **helmsman**, steersman, pilot, guide, seaman, mariner; N. Amer. wheelman.

navvy noun See **labourer**.

navy noun **1** *a 600-ship navy*: **fleet**, flotilla, armada, naval (task) force, squadron.

2 *sober shades of grey, black, and navy*: **navy blue**, dark blue, indigo, midnight blue, ink blue.

nay adverb *it is difficult, nay, impossible, to understand*: **or rather**, and more than that, (and) indeed, and even, in fact, in point of fact, actually, in truth.

near adverb **1** *her children all live near*: **close by**, close, nearby, close/near at hand, not far off/away, in the neighbourhood, in the vicinity, at hand, within reach, within close range, on the doorstep, within earshot, within sight, a stone's throw away, at close quarters, alongside; informal within spitting distance, {a hop, skip, and a jump away}, within sniffing distance; archaic nigh.
▷ANTONYMS far away.
2 *near perfect conditions*: **almost**, just about, nearly, practically, virtually, all but; literary well-nigh.
▶ preposition *a family-run hotel near the seafront*: **close to**, close by, not far (away) from, a short distance from, in the vicinity of, in the neighbourhood of, within reach of, a stone's throw away from, next to, adjacent to, alongside, bordering on, adjoining, abutting, contiguous with; informal within spitting distance of, {a hop, skip, and a jump away from}, within sniffing distance of.
□ **as near as dammit** *that made it as near as dammit a statistical impossibility*: **virtually**, effectively, in effect, all but, more or less, practically, almost, nearly, close to, approaching, not far from, nearing, verging on, bordering on, well nigh, nigh on, just about, as good as, essentially, in essence, in practical terms, for all practical purposes, to all intents and purposes, in all but name; roughly, approximately, not quite; S. African plus-minus; informal pretty much, pretty nearly, pretty well.
□ **near the knuckle** *they were a bit cheeky and quite near the knuckle, but it's all in good fun*: **risqué**, racy, sexy, naughty, spicy, juicy, suggestive, ribald, indelicate, indecorous, indecent, immodest, off colour, dirty, rude, smutty, crude, bawdy, vulgar, salacious, coarse; N. Amer. gamy; informal raunchy, blue, close to the bone, near the bone; Brit. informal fruity, saucy; euphemistic adult.
▶ adjective **1** *they carried her to the nearest house*: **close**, nearby, not far off/away, close/near at hand, at hand, a stone's throw away, within reach, within range, accessible, handy, convenient, local, neighbouring, adjacent, next-door, adjoining, bordering, abutting, contiguous, proximate; informal within spitting distance.
▷ANTONYMS far.
2 *the final judgement is near*: **imminent**, forthcoming, in the offing, close/near at hand, at hand, (just) round the corner, approaching, impending, upcoming, coming, looming.
▷ANTONYMS distant, remote.
3 *a near relation of hers | our nearest and dearest*: **closely related**, close, related, connected.
▷ANTONYMS distant.
4 *apparently it had been a near escape*: **narrow**, close, by a hair's breadth; informal by a whisker.
5 *she's too near to spend that much money*: **mean**, **miserly**, niggardly, close-fisted, penny-pinching, cheese-paring, ungenerous, penurious, illiberal, close, grasping, Scrooge-like, stinting, sparing, frugal; informal tight-fisted, stingy, tight, mingy, money-grubbing, skinflinty; N. Amer. informal cheap; Brit. vulgar slang tight-arsed, tight as a duck's arse.
▶ verb **1** *by dawn the next day we were nearing Moscow*: **approach**, draw near/nearer to, get near/nearer to, get close/closer to, come towards, move towards, advance towards, close in on.
2 *the death toll is nearing 3,000*: **verge on**, border on, approach, get close to, approximate to.

nearby adjective *a boy from one of the nearby villages*: **not far away/off**, close/near at hand, close by, close, near, within reach, at hand, neighbouring, adjacent; accessible, handy, convenient.
▷ANTONYMS faraway.
▶ adverb *her mother lives nearby*: **close by**, not far off/away, close, close/near at hand, near, a short distance away, in the neighbourhood, in the vicinity, at hand, within reach, on the doorstep, (just) round the corner.

Word toolkit

nearby	neighbouring	convenient
hospital	countries	location
park	islands	source
hotel	farms	parking
school	territory	route

nearly adverb *dinner's nearly ready*. See **almost**.

near miss noun *two airliners were involved in a near miss yesterday*: **close thing**, near thing, narrow escape, close call, nasty moment; informal close shave; Brit. informal narrow squeak.

nearness noun **1** *the town's geographical nearness to Rome*: **closeness**, proximity, propinquity, adjacency; accessibility, handiness; rare contiguity, contiguousness, vicinity, vicinage.
2 *the nearness of death focuses the mind*: **imminence**, closeness, immediacy, immediateness.
3 *a marriage is also void on the ground of nearness of relationship*: **consanguinity**, closeness.

nearsighted adjective N. Amer. See **short-sighted** (sense 1).

neat adjective **1** *the bedroom was neat and scrupulously clean*: **tidy**, neat and tidy, as neat as a new pin, orderly, well ordered, in (good) order, well kept, shipshape (and Bristol fashion), in apple-pie order, immaculate, spick and span, uncluttered, straight, trim, spruce; archaic tricksy.
▷ANTONYMS disorderly, untidy.
2 *he's very neat*: **smart**, spruce, dapper, trim, well groomed, well turned out, besuited; organized, well organized, tidy, methodical; fastidious; informal natty; dated as if one had just stepped out of a bandbox; archaic trig.
▷ANTONYMS shabby.
3 *her neat, italic script | the neat white contours of the building*: **well formed**, regular, precise, crisp, clean-cut, elegant, well proportioned, simple, unadorned, unornamented.
4 *this neat little gadget*: **compact**, well designed, well made, handy, easy to use; Brit. informal dinky.
5 *his neat footwork*: **skilful**, deft, dexterous, adroit, adept, expert, practised, accurate, precise, nimble, agile, graceful, stylish; informal nifty.
▷ANTONYMS clumsy.
6 *a neat solution to the problem*: **clever**, ingenious, inventive, resourceful, good, apt, efficient; slick.
7 *a small glass of neat gin*: **undiluted**, straight, unmixed, unadulterated, unblended, pure, uncut; N. Amer. informal straight up.
8 N. Amer. informal *we had a really neat time*. See **wonderful**, **marvellous**.

neaten verb *we neatened ourselves up for dinner*. See **spruce** (verb).

neatly adverb **1** *she was neatly dressed in a tweed suit and a cashmere jersey | neatly arranged papers*: **tidily**, smartly, sprucely; methodically, systematically.
2 *the point was neatly put*: **cleverly**, aptly, nicely, elegantly, well.
3 *a neatly executed back header*: **skilfully**, deftly, adroitly, adeptly, expertly, precisely, nimbly, agilely, gracefully, effortlessly; informal niftily.

neatness noun **1** *I was struck with the neatness of the cottage*: **tidiness**, orderliness, trimness, spruceness, immaculateness, unclutteredness, absence of clutter, straightness.
2 *neatness, grooming, and deportment were important*: **smartness**, spruceness, trimness, tidiness, fastidiousness, simplicity.
3 *the neatness of her movements*: **grace**, gracefulness, nimbleness, precision, deftness, dexterity, adroitness, agility, light-footedness, skill, accuracy, stylishness; literary lightsomeness.

nebulous adjective **1** *the figure was still nebulous—she couldn't quite see it*: **indistinct**, indefinite, unclear, vague, hazy, cloudy, fuzzy, misty, lacking definition, blurred, blurry, out of focus, foggy, faint, shadowy, dim, obscure, shapeless, formless, unformed, amorphous; rare nebulose.
▷ANTONYMS clear.
2 *his nebulous ideas about salvation*: **vague**, ill-defined, unclear, hazy, uncertain, indefinite, indeterminate, imprecise, unformed, muddled, confused, ambiguous, inchoate, opaque, muddy.
▷ANTONYMS well defined.

necessarily adverb **1** *an increase in the money supply will not necessarily have much effect on spending*: **automatically**, as a direct consequence/result, as an automatic consequence/result, as a matter of course, by definition, certainly, surely, definitely, incontrovertibly, undoubtedly, axiomatically.
2 *the timetable may, necessarily, be subject to amendment*: **unavoidably**, of necessity, by force of circumstance, by force majeure, inevitably, inescapably, ineluctably; willy-nilly; Latin nolens volens; informal like it or not; formal perforce.
▷ANTONYMS possibly.

necessary adjective **1** *planning permission is necessary | I don't want to go unless it's absolutely necessary*: **obligatory**, requisite, required, compulsory, mandatory, imperative, demanded, needed, called for, needful; **essential**, indispensable, vital, of the essence, incumbent; French de rigueur.
▷ANTONYMS unnecessary, non-essential, dispensable.
2 *their fate was a necessary consequence of progress*: **inevitable**, unavoidable, certain, sure, inescapable, inexorable, ineluctable, fated, destined, predetermined, predestined, preordained.
▷ANTONYMS possible.
▶ noun (**the necessary**) informal *could you lend me the necessary?* **money**, cash, the wherewithal, funds, finances, capital, means, resources; informal dough, bread, loot, the ready, the readies; Brit. informal dosh. See also **money**.

Choose the right word **necessary, requisite, essential, indispensable**

Something that is **necessary** must be accepted or done, whether we like it or not. The word denotes something without which a condition cannot be fulfilled, often something that is needed for a particular purpose, rather than generally (*carrying out the necessary repairs | a general election was necessary*). *Necessary* is the only one of these words that can be used in the phrase *if necessary* (*do a dummy run if necessary*).

n

Requisite has a very similar meaning to *necessary*, but it is more formal and often refers to something required by regulations rather than an inherent need (*each event must be staffed by the requisite number of officials*). Unlike the other three words here, *requisite* is almost always used before its noun.

Essential is the strongest way to say that something is necessary (*it is essential to keep up-to-date records*). Some uses merge with the older meaning of 'fundamental to the nature of something' (*fibre is an essential ingredient of our diet*): see **inherent.** Of these four words, it is normal to use only *essential* or *necessary* with the anticipatory subject *it* in a construction such as *it is essential to read a daily newspaper*.

Indispensable is typically used of someone or something that is already present, and implies contemplation of having to do without them (*you've been absolutely indispensable to me | electricity is an indispensable source of energy which we take for granted in our everyday lives*).

necessitate verb *such a level of public expenditure would necessitate tax increases*. See **entail**.

necessitous adjective *2.5 tons of dried milk was supplied to necessitous mothers*. See **needy**.

necessity noun **1** *health should not be considered a privilege or even a luxury, but as a necessity and a right*: **essential requirement**, prerequisite, indispensable thing/item, essential, requisite, necessary, fundamental, basic; Latin sine qua non, desideratum.
2 *the necessity of taking expert advice | the necessity for young people to grow up with respect for the law*: **indispensability**, need, needfulness.
3 *political necessity forced him to consider it*: **force/pressure of circumstance**, need, obligation, call, exigency; crisis, emergency, urgency; French force majeure.
4 *the necessity of growing old*: **inevitability**, unavoidability, certainty, inescapability, inexorability, ineluctability.
5 *necessity made them steal*: **poverty**, need, neediness, want, deprivation, privation, penury, destitution, indigence.
□ **of necessity** *such institutional changes will, of necessity, lead to a review of the Arts Council's role*: **necessarily**, inevitably, unavoidably, by force of circumstance, inescapably, ineluctably; by definition, as a matter of course, naturally, automatically, certainly, surely, definitely, incontrovertibly, undoubtedly, axiomatically; willy-nilly; Latin nolens volens; informal like it or not; formal perforce.

neck noun nape, scruff; technical cervix; archaic scrag, halse.
□ **neck and neck** *the six contestants are neck and neck*: **level**, **equal**, tied, nip and tuck, side by side, with nothing to choose between them, close together; Brit. level pegging; informal even-steven(s).
□ **neck of the woods** *this may not reach your neck of the woods until September (if at all)*: **neighbourhood**, district, area, locality, locale, quarter, community, part, region, zone; informal parts; Brit. informal manor; N. Amer. informal hood, nabe.
▶ **verb** informal See **pet**[1] (sense 3 of the verb).

Word links **neck**

cervical, **jugular** relating to the neck

necklace noun **chain**, choker, necklet, beads, pearls, pendant, locket; French rivière, sautoir, lavallière; Maori hei-tiki; historical torc, torque, carcanet, negligée.

necromancer noun See **sorcerer**.

necromancy noun See **sorcery**.

necropolis noun See **cemetery**.

née adjective *Rachel Watts, née Goldstraw*: **born**, formerly, previously; formal heretofore.

need verb **1** *the house still needs a lot of work | do you need money?* **require**, be in need of, stand in need of, have need of, want, be in want of, be crying out for, be desperate for; demand, call for, necessitate, entail, involve; have occasion for/to; lack, be without, be short of, miss.
2 *you needn't come if you don't want to*: **have to**, be under an obligation to, be obliged to, be compelled to, be under a compulsion to; archaic have need to.
3 *she needed him so much that it seemed as if her entire heart and soul were crying out to him*: **yearn for**, pine for, long for, crave for, desire, miss.
▶ **noun 1** *there's no need to apologize | the need to safeguard the environment*: **necessity**, obligation, requirement, call, demand; rare exigency.
2 *the basic human needs of food and shelter*: **requirement**, essential, necessity, want, requisite, prerequisite, wish, demand; Latin desideratum.
3 *a family whose need was particularly pressing*: **neediness**, want, poverty, deprivation, privation, hardship, penury, destitution, indigence, impecuniousness.
4 *please don't abandon me in my hour of need*: **difficulty**, trouble, distress; **crisis**, emergency, urgency, extremity, dire/desperate straits; rare exigency.
□ **in need** *the organization provides food and clothing to people in need*: **needy**, requiring help, deprived, disadvantaged, underprivileged, in want, poor, badly off, unable to make ends meet, in reduced/straitened circumstances, unable to keep the wolf from the door, impoverished, poverty-stricken, destitute, penurious, impecunious, indigent; Brit. on the breadline; rare necessitous.

needed adjective *funds are desperately needed | planning permission is needed*. See **necessary** (sense 1 of the adjective).

needful adjective *I'm willing to do what's needful*. See **necessary** (sense 1 of the adjective).

needle noun **1** *the needle on the meter barely moved*: **indicator**, pointer, marker, arrow, hand.
2 *she lowered the needle on to the record*: **stylus**.
▶ **verb** informal *why had she allowed Leo to needle her into telling him?* **goad**, provoke, bait, taunt, pester, harass, prick, prod, sting; **irritate**, annoy, anger, vex, irk, nettle, pique, exasperate, infuriate, get on someone's nerves, rub up the wrong way, get/put someone's back up, ruffle someone's feathers, try someone's patience; informal aggravate, rile, niggle, get in someone's hair, hassle, get to, bug, miff, peeve, get under someone's skin, get up someone's nose, hack off; Brit. informal wind up, get at, nark, get across; N. Amer. informal ride; vulgar slang piss off; rare exacerbate, hump, rasp.

Word links **needle**

belonephobia fear of needles

needless adjective *there's no point going into needless detail*. See **unnecessary**.
□ **needless to say of course**, as might be expected, as you/one would expect, not unexpectedly, it goes without saying, obviously, naturally, clearly; informal natch.

needlework noun **sewing**, embroidery, needlepoint, needlecraft, tapestry, crocheting, fancy-work, patchwork, wool work, stitching, tatting, crewel work.

needy adjective *the food went to needy families in the area*: **poor**, deprived, disadvantaged, underprivileged, in want, needful, badly off, hard up, in reduced/straitened circumstances, unable to make ends meet, unable to keep the wolf from the door, poverty-stricken, indigent, impoverished, on one's beam-ends, as poor as a church mouse, dirt poor, destitute, penurious, impecunious, penniless, moneyless; Brit. on the breadline, without a penny to one's name; informal on one's uppers, broke, flat broke, strapped for cash, strapped, cleaned out; Brit. informal skint, stony broke, without two pennies/(brass) farthings to rub together, in Queer Street; N. Amer. informal stone broke; rare necessitous, pauperized.
▷**ANTONYMS** wealthy, affluent, rich, well off.

ne'er-do-well noun See **good-for-nothing** (noun).

nefarious adjective *the nefarious activities of the bodysnatchers*. See **villainous**.

negate verb **1** *legislators immediately took steps to negate the effects of the Court's ruling*: **invalidate**, nullify, render null and void, render invalid, make ineffective, neutralize, cancel (out); **undo**, reverse, annul, void, revoke, rescind, abrogate, repeal, retract, countermand, overrule, overturn; Law avoid.
▷**ANTONYMS** confirm, support, validate.
2 *negating the political nature of education*: **deny**, dispute, call into question, contradict, refute, rebut, discredit, disclaim, reject, repudiate; formal gainsay; rare controvert.
▷**ANTONYMS** confirm, ratify.

negation noun **1** *there should be confirmation—or negation—of the findings*: **denial**, contradiction, repudiation, disproving, refutation, refuting, rebuttal, countering, disclaiming; nullification, cancellation, voiding, revocation, rescinding, abrogation, repeal, retraction; Law disaffirmation; rare disproval.
▷**ANTONYMS** confirmation, affirmation, substantiation.
2 *evil is not merely the negation of goodness*: **opposite**, reverse, antithesis, contrary, inverse, converse; absence, lack, want, deficiency.
3 *a life full of negation*: **nothingness**, nothing, nullity, blankness, void, non-existence, vacuity.

negative adjective **1** *the petition produced a negative reply from the Home Office*: **saying 'no'**, in the negative, rejecting, refusing; dissenting, dissentient, contrary, anti-, opposing, opposed; denying; formal gainsaying; rare dissentious.
▷**ANTONYMS** positive, affirmative.
2 *he was criticized for being negative*: **pessimistic**, **defeatist**, gloomy, gloom-ridden, cynical, bleak, fatalistic, dismissive, anti, antipathetic, uncooperative, obstructive; **unenthusiastic**, cool, cold, uninterested, unresponsive, apathetic.
▷**ANTONYMS** positive, optimistic, constructive, enthusiastic.
3 *the crisis had an immediate and negative effect on the economy*: **harmful**, bad, adverse, damaging, detrimental, unfortunate, unfavourable, disadvantageous.
▷**ANTONYMS** favourable, good.

▸ **noun** *he murmured something sufficiently incomprehensible for her to take it as a negative*: '**no**', refusal, rejection, veto; dissension, contradiction; denial.

negativity noun *one person's negativity and intolerance can have a knock-on effect*. See **pessimism**.

neglect verb **1** *she smoked and drank, and neglected the children*: **fail to look after**, fail to care for, fail to provide for, leave alone, abandon; archaic forsake.
▷ANTONYMS cherish, look after, care for.
2 *he's been neglecting his work for the past couple of days*: **pay little/no attention to**, let slide, not attend to, be remiss about, be lax about, leave undone, lose sight of, skimp on, shirk, skip.
▷ANTONYMS concentrate on.
3 *neglect our advice at your peril!* **disregard**, ignore, pay no attention to, take no notice of, pay no heed to, discount, set aside, overlook, turn a deaf ear to, throw to the winds; disdain, pass over, pass by, scorn, slight, spurn, rebuff, turn one's back on.
▷ANTONYMS attend (to), heed.
4 *she's just irritable because I neglected to inform her that you were coming*: **fail**, omit, forget, not remember; archaic pretermit.
▷ANTONYMS remember.
▸ **noun 1** *the whole place had a hopeless air of neglect*: **disrepair**, dilapidation, deterioration, shabbiness, disuse, abandonment; rare desuetude.
2 *her doctor had been guilty of serious neglect*: **negligence**, failure to take proper care, lack of proper care and attention, dereliction of duty, non-performance/non-fulfilment of duty, failure to take proper action, remissness, neglectfulness, carelessness, heedlessness, lack of concern, unconcern, laxity, laxness, slackness, irresponsibility; Scottish Law culpa; formal delinquency.
▷ANTONYMS care.
3 *the relative* **neglect** *of women in studies of redundancy*: **disregard**, ignoring, overlooking, failure to pay attention to, inattention to, indifference to, oversight, heedlessness; disdaining, scorning, slighting, spurning, rebuff.
▷ANTONYMS attention.

neglected adjective **1** *RSPCA officers found more than eighty neglected, underweight, and suffering animals*: **uncared for**, mistreated, abandoned, forsaken.
▷ANTONYMS well cared for.
2 *a neglected 16th-century cottage | the neglected garden behind Merrill's flat*: **run down**, derelict, dilapidated, tumbledown, ramshackle, untended, unmaintained; overgrown, uncultivated, unweeded, wild; rare weedgrown.
▷ANTONYMS neat, well tended.
3 *a neglected masterpiece of seventeenth-century devotional prose*: **disregarded**, **forgotten**, overlooked, ignored, unrecognized, unnoticed, unsung, underestimated, undervalued, unappreciated, passed over, spurned; out in the cold.

neglectful adjective *children whose parents were abusive or neglectful*. See **negligent**.

negligence noun *the company was accused of negligence*: **carelessness**, lack of care, lack of proper care and attention, dereliction of duty, non-performance of duty, non-fulfilment of duty, remissness, neglectfulness, neglect, laxity, laxness, irresponsibility, inattention, inattentiveness, heedlessness, thoughtlessness, unmindfulness, forgetfulness; slackness, sloppiness; Law contributory negligence; Scottish Law culpa; Maritime Law barratry; formal delinquency; rare disregardfulness, inadvertence, inadvertency, oscitation.
▷ANTONYMS conscientiousness, attention to duty.

negligent adjective *she claimed that her solicitor had been negligent*: **careless**, failing to take proper care, remiss, neglectful, lax, irresponsible, inattentive, heedless, thoughtless, unmindful, forgetful; slack, sloppy, slapdash, slipshod; N. Amer. derelict; Maritime Law barratrous; formal delinquent; rare disregardful, inadvertent, oscitant.
▷ANTONYMS careful, attentive, conscientious.

negligible adjective *the damage to the BMW turned out to be negligible*. See **insignificant**.

negotiable adjective **1** *part-time barman required, hours and salary negotiable*: **open to discussion**, subject to discussion, flexible, open to modification, discussable; unsettled, undecided, debatable.
2 *the gulley was negotiable, though it was a tough scramble up the far side*: **passable**, navigable, crossable, traversable; free from obstruction, open, clear, unblocked, unobstructed.
3 *negotiable cheques*: **transferable**, usable as legal tender; valid.

negotiate verb **1** *the government refused to negotiate*: **discuss terms**, hold talks, discuss a settlement, talk, consult together, try to reach a compromise, parley, confer, debate; mediate, intercede, arbitrate, moderate, conciliate, act as honest broker; bargain, haggle, wheel and deal, dicker; informal powwow; formal treat with someone; archaic chaffer, palter.
2 *Peter decided to remain with the company after negotiating a new contract*: **arrange**, **work out**, thrash out, hammer out, reach an agreement on, agree on, come to terms about, reach terms on, broker; settle, clinch, conclude, contract, pull off, bring off, bring about, transact; informal sort out, swing.
3 *he came down, managing with difficulty to negotiate the obstacles on the stairs*: **get round/past/over**, make one's way round/past/over, make it round/past/over, clear, cross, pass over; surmount, overcome, deal with, cope with.

negotiation noun **1** *the negotiations are due to resume in Geneva next week*: **discussion(s)**, talks, consultation(s), parleying, deliberation(s), conference, debate, dialogue; mediation, arbitration, intercession, conciliation; bargaining, haggling, wheeling and dealing, dickering.
2 *the negotiation of the deal*: **working out**, discussing the terms of, arrangement, arranging, thrashing out, hammering out, brokering; settlement, conclusion, completion, clinching, pulling off, bringing off, transaction.

negotiator noun *a team of negotiators from the UN Security Council sought to resolve the situation*: **mediator**, arbitrator, arbiter, moderator, go-between, middleman, intermediary, intercessor, interceder, intervener, conciliator; representative, spokesperson, agent, broker, honest broker, ambassador, diplomat, peacemaker; bargainer, haggler, wheeler-dealer; rare negotiant.

neigh verb **whinny**, bray, nicker, snicker, whicker; Scottish archaic nicher; rare hinny.

neighbourhood noun **1** *a quiet neighbourhood*: **district**, area, locality, locale, quarter, community, part, region, zone; informal neck of the woods, parts; Brit. informal manor; N. Amer. informal hood, nabe.
2 *in the neighbourhood of Canterbury*: **vicinity**, surrounding district/area, environs, purlieus, precincts, proximity; N. Amer. vicinage.
□ **in the neighbourhood of** *the cost was believed to be in the neighbourhood of $4.5m*: **approximately**, about, around, roughly, in the region of, of the order of, not far off, nearly, almost, close to, just about, practically, more or less, or so, there or thereabouts, as near as dammit to; Brit. getting on for; Latin circa; N. Amer. informal in the ballpark of.

neighbouring adjective *the owner of the neighbouring property | neighbouring villages*: **adjacent**, nearest, closest, next-door, next, adjoining, bordering, connecting, abutting, contiguous, proximate; **nearby**, near, very near, close/near at hand, not far away, in the vicinity, in close proximity, surrounding; rare conjoining, approximate, vicinal.
▷ANTONYMS distant, remote, faraway.

> *Word toolkit* **neighbouring**
>
> See **nearby**.

neighbourly adjective **obliging**, helpful, friendly, kind, kindly, amiable, amicable, affable, genial, easy to get on/along with, agreeable, hospitable, sociable, companionable, well disposed, civil, warm, warm-hearted, cordial, convivial, good-natured, nice, pleasant, generous; considerate, thoughtful, accommodating, unselfish, supportive; Brit. informal decent.
▷ANTONYMS unfriendly, unhelpful, curmudgeonly.

neither determiner
□ **neither here nor there** *whether it suits the general public well-being is neither here nor there*: **inconsequential**, insignificant, unimportant, of little/no importance, of little/no consequence, of little/no account, of no moment, incidental, inessential, non-essential, immaterial, irrelevant; negligible, inappreciable, inconsiderable, slight, minor, trivial, trifling, petty, paltry, nugatory, not worth mentioning, not worth bothering about, not worth speaking of, insubstantial, silly, lightweight; informal piddling, fiddling, piffling; N. Amer. informal small-bore, picayune.
▷ANTONYMS significant, important.
□ **neither fish nor fowl** *here's a work that is obscure only because it is neither fish nor fowl*: **ambiguous**, doubtful, unclear, uncertain, indistinct, indefinite, indeterminate, open to question, debatable; mixed, neither one thing nor the other.
□ **neither one thing nor the other** *Sam stands on the cusp, neither one thing nor the other*: **indeterminate**, indefinite, indistinct, insipid, nondescript, neutral, toneless, colourless, dull, drab, washed out; mixed, neither fish nor fowl.

nemesis noun **1** *this could prove to be the bank's nemesis*: **downfall**, undoing, ruin, ruination, destruction, Waterloo.
2 *the nemesis that his crime deserved*: **retribution**, vengeance, retributive justice, punishment, just deserts; fate, destiny.

neologism noun **new word**, new expression, new term, new phrase, coinage, newly coined word, made-up word, invented word, invention, nonce-word; portmanteau word.

neophyte noun **1** *a neophyte of the monastery of St James*: **novice**, novitiate; postulant, proselyte, catechumen.
2 *four-day cooking classes are offered to neophytes and experts alike*: **beginner**, learner, novice, newcomer, new member, new entrant, new recruit, raw recruit, new boy/girl, initiate, tyro, fledgling; trainee, apprentice, probationer; informal rookie, new kid, newbie, newie; N. Amer. informal tenderfoot, greenhorn, punk.

ne plus ultra noun Latin *jeans were the ne plus ultra of the modish and modern*: **the last word**, the ultimate example, the best example, the perfect example, the ultimate, the height, the acme, the zenith, the culmination, the epitome, the quintessence, perfection, the nonsuch; French le dernier cri.

nepotism noun See **favouritism**.

nerd noun informal *it needs care to wear a tie like this without looking like a nerd*: **bore**, dull person; informal dork, dweeb, geek; Brit. informal anorak, spod; N. Amer. informal Poindexter.

nerve noun **1** *the nerves that transmit pain and physical feeling*: **nerve fibre**; technical axon.
2 *the match will be a test of nerve, strength, and skill*: **self-confidence**, confidence, assurance, self-assurance, coolness, cool-headedness, self-possession; courage, bravery, pluck, pluckiness, boldness, courageousness, braveness, intrepidity, intrepidness, fearlessness, valour, daring, dauntlessness, doughtiness, gameness; determination, strength of character, firmness of purpose, will power, spirit, backbone, fortitude, mettle, heart, endurance, tenacity, resolution, resoluteness, stout-heartedness, steadfastness, staunchness, hardihood; informal grit, guts, spunk, gumption, gutsiness; Brit. informal bottle, ballsiness; N. Amer. informal moxie, cojones, sand; vulgar slang balls.
▷ANTONYMS timidity, faint-heartedness.
3 *he had the nerve to try and pick up the casting director at his first audition*: **audacity**, **cheek**, barefaced cheek, effrontery, gall, temerity, presumption, presumptuousness, boldness, brazenness, impudence, impertinence, insolence, pertness, forwardness, front, arrogance, cockiness; informal face, neck, brass neck, brass, sauce; N. Amer. informal chutzpah; informal, dated hide; Brit. informal, dated crust; rare procacity, assumption.
▷ANTONYMS shyness, bashfulness; politeness.
4 (**nerves**) *an attack of pre-wedding nerves*: **anxiety**, **tension**, nervousness, nervous tension, strain, tenseness, stress, worry, cold feet; **apprehensiveness**, apprehension, jumpiness, fright; informal butterflies (in one's stomach), collywobbles, the jitters, the willies, the heebie-jeebies, the shakes, the jumps, jim-jams, the yips; Brit. informal the (screaming) abdabs/habdabs; Austral. rhyming slang Joe Blakes.
▷ANTONYMS calmness, nonchalance.
□ **get on someone's nerves** **irritate**, annoy, irk, anger, bother, vex, provoke, displease, upset, exasperate, infuriate, gall, get/put someone's back up, put out, pique, rankle with, nettle, needle, ruffle someone's feathers, stroke someone's hair the wrong way, make someone's hackles rise, try someone's patience; jar on, grate on; Brit. rub up the wrong way; informal aggravate, get, get to, bug, miff, peeve, rile, get under someone's skin, get in someone's hair, get up someone's nose, hack off, get someone's goat; Brit. informal nark, get on someone's wick, give someone the hump, wind up, get across; N. Amer. informal rankle, ride, gravel; vulgar slang piss off; Brit. vulgar slang get on someone's tits; rare exacerbate, hump, rasp.
▸ verb
□ **nerve oneself** *Morag nerved herself to go on*: **brace oneself**, steel oneself, summon/gather/screw up/muster one's courage, screw one's courage to the sticking place, gear oneself up, prepare oneself, get in the right frame of mind; fortify oneself, bolster oneself; informal psych oneself up; literary gird (up) one's loins.
▷ANTONYMS lose one's nerve.

> *Word links* **nerve**
>
> **neural** relating to nerves in the body
> **neur(o)-** related prefix
> **neuritis** inflammation of a nerve
> **neurology**, **neuropathology**, **neurosurgery** branches of medicine to do with the nerves
> **neurectomy** surgical removal of a nerve
> **neurotomy** surgical cutting of a nerve

nerveless adjective **1** *he took the gun from her suddenly nerveless fingers*: **inert**, lifeless, lacking feeling; weak, powerless, feeble.
2 *a nerveless lack of restraint*: **confident**, self-confident, self-assured, self-possessed, cool, cool-headed, calm, collected, {cool, calm, and collected}, composed, controlled, relaxed.
▷ANTONYMS nervous, worried, anxious.

nerve-racking adjective *meeting him for the first time was nerve-racking to say the least*. See **stressful**.

nervous adjective **1** *a thin, nervous woman who always wore black*: **highly strung**, easily frightened, easily agitated, anxious, edgy, tense, excitable, jumpy, skittish, brittle, neurotic, hysterical; timid, timorous, mousy, shy, fearful, frightened, frightened of one's own shadow, apprehensive, scared; Brit. nervy; informal trepidatious.
▷ANTONYMS calm, relaxed, easy-going.
2 *the day Richard started teaching, he was so nervous he couldn't eat breakfast*: **anxious**, **worried**, **apprehensive**, on edge, edgy, tense, strained, stressed, agitated, in a state of nerves, in a state of agitation, uneasy, restless, worked up, keyed up, overwrought, wrought up, strung out, jumpy, on tenterhooks, with one's stomach in knots, fidgety, fearful, frightened, scared, with one's heart in one's mouth, like a cat on a hot tin roof, quaking, trembling, shaking, shaking in one's shoes, shaky, on pins and needles, in a cold sweat, fevered, febrile; informal with butterflies in one's stomach, jittery, twitchy, in a state, uptight, wired, in a stew, all of a dither, all of a doodah, in a sweat, in a flap, in a tizz/tizzy, all of a lather, het up, in a twitter; Brit. informal strung up, windy, having kittens, like a cat on hot bricks; N. Amer. informal spooky, squirrelly, in a twit; Austral./NZ informal toey; Brit. vulgar slang shitting bricks, bricking oneself; dated overstrung.
▷ANTONYMS cool, calm, relaxed, laid-back.
3 *a nervous disorder*: **neurological**, neural, neuro-.

nervous breakdown noun **mental collapse**, breakdown, collapse, nervous collapse, nervous exhaustion, nervous tension, period of mental illness, crisis, personal crisis, psychological trauma; informal crack-up.

nervousness noun *as he ate, she found herself chattering away to him out of nervousness*. See **anxiety** (sense 1).

nervy adjective Brit. *Harriet isn't the nervy type | when I interviewed Ed, he was very nervy*: **nervous**, **anxious**, **tense**, on edge, edgy, strained, stressed, agitated, apprehensive, in a state of nerves, in a state of agitation, uneasy, restless, worked up, keyed up, overwrought, wrought up, strung out, jumpy, on tenterhooks, with one's stomach in knots, fidgety, fearful, frightened, scared, with one's heart in one's mouth, like a cat on a hot tin roof, quaking, trembling, shaking, shaking in one's shoes, shaky, on pins and needles, in a cold sweat, fevered, febrile; excitable, neurotic, highly strung; informal in a state, uptight, wired, in a stew, all of a dither, in a sweat, in a flap, in a tizz/tizzy, all of a lather, het up, in a twitter; Brit. informal strung up, windy, having kittens, all of a doodah, like a cat on hot bricks; N. Amer. informal spooky, squirrelly, in a twit; Austral./NZ informal toey; Brit. vulgar slang shitting bricks, bricking oneself; dated overstrung.
▷ANTONYMS calm, relaxed, laid-back, easy-going.

nest noun **1** *in May and June, the females build a nest and incubate their eggs*: **roost**, eyrie; nest box, nesting box; N. Amer. bird house.
2 *usually the animals will awake and disperse rapidly from the nest if disturbed*: **lair**, den, drey, lodge, burrow, set, form.
3 *a cosy little love nest*: **hideaway**, hiding place, hideout, retreat, shelter, refuge, snuggery, nook, den, haunt; informal hidey-hole.
4 *the place was a perpetual nest of intrigue*: **hotbed**, den, breeding ground, cradle, seedbed, forcing house.
5 *a nest of tables*: **cluster**, set, group, assemblage.

nest egg noun **savings**, life savings, money put by/saved for a rainy day, cache, funds, reserve.

nestle verb *he nestled up against her*: **snuggle**, cuddle (up), curl up, huddle, nuzzle, settle, lie close, burrow; N. Amer. snug down.

nestling noun **chick**, baby bird, fledgling; Falconry eyas; Scottish archaic gorlin; rare pullus, birdling, broodling.

net[1] noun **1** *a dress of dark green voile and net*: **netting**, meshwork, mesh, webbing, tulle, fishnet, openwork, lace, lacework, latticework, lattice.
2 *one civil servant, at least, managed to escape the net*: **trap**, booby trap, snare; literary toils.
▸ verb *drug busts that netted big criminals both in Panama and America*: **catch**, capture, take captive, trap, entrap, snare, ensnare, bag, hook, land; informal nab, collar.

net[2] adjective **1** *their net earnings*: **after taxes**, **after deductions**, take-home, clear, final; Brit. nett; informal bottom line.
▷ANTONYMS gross.
2 *the net result is difficult to predict*: **final**, end, ultimate, concluding, closing; **overall**, actual, effective.
▸ verb *the once-struggling actress has netted £50,000 from interviews since the news broke*: **earn**, make, get, gain, obtain, acquire, accumulate, take home, bring in, pull in, clear, pocket, realize, make a profit of, be paid; fetch, yield, raise; informal rake in.

nether adjective *the nether reaches of a vast, vaulted interior*: **lower**, low, lower-level, bottom, bottommost, under; underground, basement; technical basal.
▷ANTONYMS upper.

netherworld noun *their souls were forever doomed to wander in the netherworld*: **hell**, the underworld, the infernal regions, the nether regions, the abyss, the land of the dead; the abode of the damned, eternal damnation, perdition; Biblical Gehenna, Tophet, Abaddon; Judaism Sheol; Greek Mythology Hades, Tartarus, Acheron; Brit. the other place; literary the pit; archaic the lower world.
▷ANTONYMS heaven, paradise.

nettle verb **irritate**, annoy, irk, gall, vex, anger, exasperate, infuriate, bother, provoke; **upset**, displease, offend, affront, get/put someone's back up, disgruntle, rankle with, pique, needle, ruffle, get on someone's nerves, try someone's patience, ruffle someone's feathers, make someone's hackles rise, raise someone's hackles, chafe; Brit. rub up the wrong way; N. Amer. rankle, ride, gravel; informal peeve, aggravate, miff, rile, get, get to, bug, get under someone's skin, get in someone's hair, get up someone's nose, hack off, get someone's goat, drive up the wall; Brit. informal nark, get on someone's wick, give someone the hump, wind up, get across someone; N. Amer. informal tick off; vulgar slang piss off; Brit. vulgar slang get on someone's tits; rare exacerbate, hump, rasp.

nettled adjective **irritated**, annoyed, cross, put out, irked, galled, vexed, exasperated, infuriated; **upset**, displeased, offended, affronted, disgruntled, piqued, aggrieved, stung, huffy, in a huff; informal peeved, aggravated, miffed, miffy, riled, hacked off, peed off; Brit. informal cheesed off, browned off, brassed off, narked, eggy; N. Amer. informal teed off, ticked off, sore; W. Indian informal vex; vulgar slang pissed off; archaic snuffy.

network noun **1** *the network of arteries at the base of the brain*: **web**, criss-cross, grid, lattice, net, matrix, mesh, webbing, tracery, trellis; webwork, meshwork, latticework, openwork, filigree, fretwork; French réseau; technical reticulum, plexus, rete, reticulation, reticule, graticule.
2 *a network of narrow, winding lanes*: **maze**, labyrinth, warren, jungle, tangle.
3 *a network of friends and relations*: **system**, complex, interconnected system/structure, complex system/arrangement, nexus, web; neural net; informal grapevine, bush telegraph, old boy network, the old school tie.

neurosis noun *Max was said to be in the grip of some sort of neurosis*: **mental illness**, mental disorder, psychological disorder, mental disturbance, mental derangement, mental instability, psychological maladjustment, psychoneurosis, psychopathy; obsession, phobia, fixation; rare neuroticism.

neurotic adjective **1** *the treatment of anxiety in neurotic patients*: **mentally ill**, mentally disturbed, mentally deranged, unstable, unbalanced, maladjusted, psychoneurotic; psychopathic, phobic.
▷ANTONYMS stable, well balanced.
2 *she seemed a neurotic, self-obsessed woman*: **overanxious**, anxious, nervous, tense, highly strung, jumpy, oversensitive, paranoid; **obsessive**, compulsive, phobic, fixated, hysterical, overwrought, manic, irrational; Brit. nervy; informal twitchy.
▷ANTONYMS calm, laid-back, level-headed.

Word toolkit **neurotic**

See **apprehensive**.

neuter adjective *I did not feel male, but rather, neuter*: **asexual**, sexless, unsexed; **androgynous**; rare androgyne, epicene.
▸ verb *vets encourage owners to have their pets neutered*: **castrate**, geld, cut, emasculate; **spay**, sterilize; fix, desex; N. Amer. & Austral. alter; informal doctor; rare caponize, eunuchize, ovariectomize, oophorectomize.

neutral adjective **1** *Dorothy has no axe to grind. She's completely neutral*: **impartial**, unbiased, unprejudiced, objective, without favouritism, open-minded, non-partisan, non-discriminatory, disinterested, even-handed, equitable, fair, fair-minded, dispassionate, detached, impersonal, unemotional, clinical, indifferent, removed; uninvolved, uncommitted.
▷ANTONYMS biased, partisan.
2 *during the Second World War, Portugal remained neutral*: **unaligned**, non-aligned, unaffiliated, unallied, non-allied, non-participating, uninvolved, non-interventionist; **non-combatant**, non-belligerent, non-combative, non-fighting.
▷ANTONYMS combatant, belligerent.
3 *she racked her brain desperately for a neutral topic of conversation*: **inoffensive**, bland, unobjectionable, unexceptionable, anodyne, unremarkable, ordinary, commonplace, run-of-the-mill, everyday; safe, harmless, innocuous.
▷ANTONYMS provocative, offensive.
4 *a neutral background will make any small splash of colour stand out*: **pale**, pastel, light-toned; beige, cream, taupe, oatmeal, ecru, buff, fawn, grey, greige, sand, stone-coloured, stone, mushroom, putty; colourless, uncoloured, washed out, indefinite, indistinct, indeterminate, neither one thing nor the other, insipid, nondescript, toneless, dull, drab; rare achromatic, achromic.
▷ANTONYMS bright, colourful.

Word toolkit **neutral**

See **equitable**.

neutrality noun **1** *the tradition of civil service neutrality*: **impartiality**, lack of bias, lack of prejudice, objectivity, open-mindedness, disinterestedness, even-handedness, fairness, fair-mindedness, detachment.
▷ANTONYMS partiality, bias.
2 *our long-term interests will be served best by maintaining our neutrality in the war*: **non-alignment**, non-participation, non-involvement, non-intervention, non-interventionism, non-combativeness.
▷ANTONYMS participation, taking sides.

neutralize verb *the strategy of the first half of the campaign was to neutralize the appalling economic news*: **counteract**, offset, counterbalance, balance (out), counterpoise, countervail, compensate for, make up for; **cancel out**, make/render ineffective, nullify, negate, annul, undo, invalidate, be an antidote to, wipe out; equalize, even up, square up; rare negative, counterweigh.

never adverb **1** *his room is never tidy*: **at no time**, not at any time, not ever, not once, on no occasion; literary ne'er.
▷ANTONYMS always, forever.
2 *your mother would never agree to it*: **not at all**, certainly not, not for a moment, not under/in any circumstances, under/in no circumstances, on no account; informal no way, not on your life, not in a million years, not for love or money; Brit. informal not on your nelly.
▷ANTONYMS certainly, definitely.

never-ending adjective **1** *the never-ending noise of the city*: **incessant**, continuous, unceasing, ceaseless, constant, continual, perpetual, unfaltering, permanent, uninterrupted, without interruption, unbroken, steady, unremitting, relentless, persistent, interminable, non-stop, without ceasing, endless, unending, without end, everlasting, eternal.
2 *you need to avoid getting carried away by the never-ending tasks that could fill your day*: **endless**, countless, innumerable, myriad, without number, numberless, infinite, unlimited, untold, limitless, boundless, measureless.

never-never noun
▫ **the never-never** Brit. informal **instalments**, instalment plan/system, instalment-payment plan, credit, finance, deferred payment, easy terms; Brit. hire purchase, HP; N. Amer. instalment buying.

nevertheless adverb *nevertheless, it makes sense to take a few precautions*: **in spite of that/everything**, nonetheless, even so, however, but, still, yet, though, be that as it may, for all that, despite that/everything, after everything, having said that, that said, just the same, all the same, at the same time, in any event, come what may, at any rate, notwithstanding, regardless, anyway, anyhow; informal still and all; archaic howbeit, withal, natheless.

new adjective **1** *Roger used new techniques of measuring and recording growth*: **recently developed**, newly discovered, brand new, up to the minute, up to date, latest, current, state-of-the-art, contemporary, present-day, advanced, recent, modern; newly arrived, newborn.
▷ANTONYMS old, existing.
2 *the committee is generally tolerant of new ideas*: **novel**, fresh, original, unhackneyed, imaginative, creative, experimental, new-fashioned, contemporary, modernist, up to date; newfangled, modish, ultra-modern, avant-garde, futuristic; informal way out, far out.
▷ANTONYMS old-fashioned, stale, hackneyed.
3 *you have to decide whether to buy your boat new or second-hand*: **unused**, brand new, as new, pristine, fresh, mint, in mint condition.
▷ANTONYMS second-hand, used.
4 *new neighbours had recently moved in | she started her new job on Monday*: **different**, another, alternative, changed, unfamiliar, unknown, strange, unaccustomed, untried.
▷ANTONYMS present.
5 *the school has just had a new classroom built*: **additional**, added, extra, increased, more, supplementary, supplemental, further, another, fresh.
▷ANTONYMS existing.
6 *I went into hospital feeling very poorly and came out a new woman*: **reinvigorated**, restored, revived, improved, refreshed, regenerated, reborn, renewed, remodelled.
▫ **breathe new life into** *their visionary clients have successfully breathed new life into old, but steadfast structures | the genre film is injecting new life into the lower end of the market*: **reinvigorate**, revitalize, re-energize, brace, fortify, strengthen, give new strength to, give a boost to, build up, bolster, prop up, help, renew, regenerate, restore, revive, revivify, rejuvenate, reanimate, resuscitate, refresh, reawaken, rekindle, enliven, stimulate, put some spark into, kick-start, uplift; informal give a shot in the arm to, pep up, buck up, get going again.

Word links **new**

neo- related prefix, as in *neonatal, neo-Gothic*
neophobia fear of new things

Word toolkit

new	**recent**	**contemporary**
car	years	art
job	months	music
school	times	society
clothes	studies	issues
friends	research	design
member	events	writer
life	trip	literature
generation	success	architecture

n

newborn adjective *all newborn babies are screened for the condition*: **just born**, newly/recently born.
▸ noun *the bacteria can be fatal to newborns and the elderly*: **newly born child**, new/young/tiny baby, infant, young; technical neonate; literary babe.

newcomer noun **1** *she was a newcomer to the village*: **(new) arrival**, immigrant, settler, stranger, outsider, foreigner, alien, intruder, parvenu, interloper; Brit. incomer; N. English offcomer; informal johnny-come-lately, the new kid on the block; Austral. informal blow-in.
2 *we have some tips for the newcomer to fish photography*: **beginner**, novice, learner, trainee, apprentice, probationer, new recruit, raw recruit, new member, tyro, initiate, neophyte; novitiate, new boy/girl, proselyte; informal rookie, newbie, the new kid on the block, johnny-come-lately; N. Amer. informal tenderfoot, greenhorn.

newfangled adjective *not all hi-fi enthusiasts want newfangled digital technology*: **new**, the latest, modern, novel, the newest, ultra-modern, up to the minute, state-of-the-art, advanced, contemporary, fashionable, new-fashioned, gimmicky; informal trendy, flash, snazzy, nifty.
▹ANTONYMS dated, old-fashioned.

newly adverb *steam and ash began to erupt from a newly formed crater*. See **recently**.

news noun *colleagues were stunned by the news of his death*: **report**, **announcement**, story, account; (news) item, article, news flash, newscast, headlines, press release, communication, communiqué, bulletin; message, dispatch, statement, intelligence; disclosure, revelation, word, talk, notice, intimation, the latest, gossip, tittle-tattle, rumour, scandal, exposé; informal scoop; literary tidings; archaic advices.

newspaper noun **paper**; informal print, rag.

newsworthy adjective *press releases can help to ensure that newsworthy events receive publicity*: **interesting**, topical, notable, noteworthy, important, significant, momentous, historic, remarkable, sensational.
▹ANTONYMS unremarkable.

next adjective **1** *we shall turn to this issue in the next chapter | the first residents move in next week*: **following**, succeeding, to come, upcoming.
▹ANTONYMS previous, preceding.
2 *a brick wall separated the garden of the next house from ours*: **neighbouring**, **adjacent**, adjoining, next-door, bordering, abutting; contiguous, connected, connecting, attached; closest, nearest, proximate.
□ **next of kin** *in the case of childless couples, your next of kin are your parents*: **closest relative**, closest relation, nearest blood relation/relative, closest family member.
□ **the next world/life** *instead of offering salvation in the next world, it offers health and longevity in this one | she passed into the next life a week later*: **the hereafter**, life after death, the afterlife, the life to come, the afterworld, the beyond; immortality, eternity, heaven, paradise.
▸ adverb *people argued about where to go next*: **then**, after this/that, following that/this, after, afterwards, after that time, later, at a later time, subsequently, at a subsequent time; formal thereafter, thereupon.
▹ANTONYMS before.
□ **next to** *she sat down next to a window*: **beside**, next door to, alongside, by/at the side of, abreast of, by, adjacent to, cheek by jowl with, side by side with; close to, near, nearest to, neighbouring, adjoining, abutting; connected to, connecting with, contiguous with, attached to.
▹ANTONYMS away from.
□ **next to nothing** *the market for ponies is poor and they fetch next to nothing | the museum says next to nothing about the region's unique culture and history*: **very small sum**, pittance, trifle, flea-bite, trifling sum, drop in the ocean, insignificant sum, derisory sum, paltry sum; small change, pence; **hardly anything**, very little, the bare minimum; informal peanuts, chicken feed, piddling amount, shoestring; N. Amer. informal chump change; S. African informal tickey.

nibble verb **1** *she sat at her desk, nibbling her sandwich | the monkeys nibbled at mango fruits*: **take small bites (from)**, pick (at), gnaw (at), peck at, pick over, eat listlessly, toy with, eat like a bird; taste, sample; eat between meals, graze (on); informal snack on.
▹ANTONYMS gobble, guzzle.
2 *the bird chirped and nibbled his finger*: **peck**, nip, bite.
▸ noun **1** *the fish enjoyed a nibble on the lettuce*: **bite**, gnaw, peck, taste.
2 *I took a nibble from one of the sandwiches | sherry is perfect with nuts and nibbles*: **morsel**, mouthful, bite, crumb, grain; snack, titbit, a little something, canapé, hors d'oeuvre, bonne bouche; refreshments.

nice adjective **1** *have a nice time | it's a nice part of the country*: **enjoyable**, **pleasant**, pleasurable, agreeable, delightful, satisfying, gratifying, acceptable, to one's liking, entertaining, amusing, diverting, marvellous, good; Scottish bonny, couthy; informal lovely, great; N. Amer. informal neat; S. African informal lekker, mooi; black English, informal irie.
▹ANTONYMS unpleasant.
2 *they were such nice people*: **pleasant**, **likeable**, agreeable, personable, charming, delightful, amiable, affable, friendly, kindly, genial, congenial, good-natured, engaging, gracious, sympathetic, understanding, compassionate, good.
▹ANTONYMS nasty.
3 *he's got very nice manners*: **polite**, courteous, civil, refined, cultivated, polished, genteel, elegant.
▹ANTONYMS unrefined, rough.
4 *that's a rather nice distinction to make*: **subtle**, fine, delicate, minute, precise, exact, accurate, strict, close, careful, meticulous, rigorous, scrupulous, ultra-fine.
▹ANTONYMS rough, approximate.
5 *it's a nice day*: **fine**, dry, sunny, cloudless, warm, mild, pleasant, agreeable.
▹ANTONYMS stormy, nasty, rough.

nicely adverb **1** *the brooch goes nicely with my scarf*: **attractively**, pleasantly, pleasingly, agreeably, delightfully, beautifully, well, enjoyably, amusingly.
▹ANTONYMS badly, so as to clash.
2 *talking to him nicely doesn't work*: **politely**, courteously, civilly.
▹ANTONYMS rudely.
3 *we should manage nicely*: **satisfactorily**, satisfyingly, fittingly, acceptably.

niceness noun **1** *niceness gets you nowhere in the do-or-die modern world*: **pleasantness**, **friendliness**, agreeableness, charm, amiability, affability, kindness, decency, geniality, cordiality, warmth, sympathy, understanding, compassion.
▹ANTONYMS nastiness.
2 *nice chap, right sort of background, but is niceness enough?* **politeness**, courtesy, civility, gentility, refinement, respectability.
▹ANTONYMS rudeness.

nicety noun **1** *legal niceties are wasted on him*: **fine point**, subtlety, nuance, fine distinction, shade, refinement, detail.
2 *great nicety of control was called for*: **precision**, accuracy, exactness, meticulousness, rigour, rigorousness.

niche noun **1** *in a niche in the wall is a statue of St John*: **recess**, alcove, nook, cranny, slot, slit, hollow, bay, cavity, cubbyhole, pigeonhole, opening, aperture; Islam mihrab.
2 *he feels he has found his niche in life*: **ideal position**, calling, vocation, métier, place, function, job, slot, opportunity.

nick noun **1** *there was a slight nick half way up the blade*: **cut**, scratch, abrasion, incision, snick, scrape; notch, chip, score, gouge, gash; dent, indentation; flaw, mark, blemish, defect.
2 Brit. informal *you'll end up in the nick*. See **prison**.
3 Brit. informal *she was down at Lewisham nick, helping police with their enquiries*: **police station**, station; N. Amer. precinct, station house, substation; Indian kotwali, thana; informal cop shop.
4 Brit. informal *the car's in fairly good nick*: **condition**, repair, shape, state, state of health, order, working order, form, fettle, trim.
□ **in the nick of time** *they arrived in the nick of time*: **just in time**, not a moment too soon, almost too late, at the critical moment; N. Amer. informal under the wire; archaic in the Godspeed, in the very nick.
▸ verb **1** *I didn't nick my skin even though I shaved quickly*: **cut**, scratch, abrade, incise, snick, scrape; notch, chip, gouge, gash, score.
2 Brit. informal *he says you nicked his wallet*. See **steal**.
3 Brit. informal *Steve's been nicked*. See **arrest**.

nickname noun **sobriquet**, byname, tag, label, familiar name, epithet; pet name, diminutive, term of endearment, endearment, affectionate name; informal moniker; formal appellation, cognomen; archaic byword, agnomen, eke-name, to-name.

nifty adjective informal **1** *the film has some nifty lenswork*: **skilful**, capable, agile.
▹ANTONYMS clumsy.
2 *the wallpaper trimming wheel is a nifty little gadget*: **useful**, effective, practical.
3 *a nifty Kevlar tracksuit*: **fashionable**, stylish, smart.

niggardliness noun **1** *he condemned the Government's niggardliness about funding*: **meanness**, miserliness, parsimony, parsimoniousness, close-fistedness, penny-pinching, cheese-paring, penury, illiberality; informal stinginess, tight-fistedness, tightness, minginess; N. Amer. cheapness; archaic nearness.
▹ANTONYMS generosity.
2 *he was disappointed at the niggardliness of his reward*: **meagreness**, inadequacy, scantiness, paltriness, limitedness, restrictedness, insufficiency, sparseness, spareness, deficiency, shortness, slightness, skimpiness, leanness, poorness, poverty, pitifulness, puniness, beggarliness; informal measliness; rare exiguity.
▹ANTONYMS lavishness, abundance.

niggardly adjective **1** *the critic must not be niggardly with his advice*: **mean**, miserly, parsimonious, close-fisted, penny-pinching, cheese-paring, penurious, grasping, greedy, avaricious, Scrooge-like, ungenerous, illiberal, close; informal stingy, mingy, tight, tight-fisted, money-grubbing, money-grabbing; N. Amer. informal cheap; vulgar slang tight-arsed; archaic near.
▹ANTONYMS generous.
2 *his men complained of niggardly rations*: **meagre**, inadequate, scanty, scant, paltry, limited, restricted, modest, insufficient, sparse, spare, deficient, negligible, insubstantial, skimpy, short, little, lean, small, slight,

n

slender, poor, miserable, pitiful, puny; informal measly, stingy, pathetic, piddling; rare exiguous.
▷ANTONYMS lavish, abundant.

niggle verb **1** *it does niggle me that we cannot play whenever and wherever we like*: **irritate**, annoy, worry, trouble, bother, provoke, exasperate, upset, gall, irk, rankle with; informal rile, get up someone's nose, hack off, get, get to, bug.
2 *he niggles on about the unemployed*: **complain**, object, moan, fuss, nag, carp, cavil, find fault, grumble, grouse; informal nit-pick.
▸ noun *there were niggles about the lack of trim and equipment on some diesel cars*: **minor criticism**, **quibble**, trivial objection, trivial complaint, adverse comment, moan, grumble, grouse, cavil; informal gripe, beef, grouch, nit-picking; archaic pettifogging.

nigh adverb
□ **nigh on** *highlights are nigh-on impossible to pick out*: **well-nigh**, almost, nearly, just about, more or less, practically, virtually, all but, as good as, next to, close to, near, to all intents and purposes, approaching, bordering on, verging on, nearing, about; roughly, approximately; not quite; informal pretty nearly, pretty much, pretty well.

night noun **darkness**, dark, hours of darkness, night-time, dead of night.
▷ANTONYMS day, light.
□ **night and day** **all the time**, the entire time, around the clock, day and night, {morning, noon, and night}, {day in, day out}, without a break, ceaselessly, endlessly, incessantly, interminably, constantly, unceasingly, perpetually, permanently, continuously, continually, eternally, unremittingly, remorselessly, relentlessly; informal 24-7; archaic without surcease.

Word links **night**
nocturnal relating to night
nyct(o)- related prefix, as in *nyctalopia*
nyctophobia fear of the night

nightclub noun **night spot**, **disco**, discotheque, cabaret, club, supper club, bar; N. Amer. cafe; informal hot spot, niterie.

nightfall noun *we can be back in the city before nightfall*: **dusk**, twilight, sunset, evening, close of day, dark; N. Amer. sundown; literary eventide, gloaming, crepuscule, evenfall.
▷ANTONYMS dawn.

nightly adjective **1** *we were subjected to almost nightly raids*: **every night**, each night, night after night, {night in, night out}.
▷ANTONYMS occasional.
2 *the badgers' nightly wanderings*: **nocturnal**, night-time, at night.
▷ANTONYMS daytime.
▸ adverb *a Tyrolean band plays there nightly*: **every night**, each night, night after night, {night in, night out}.

nightmare noun **1** *she had woken from a nightmare*: **bad dream**, night terrors; archaic incubus; rare ephialtes.
2 *the long journey home was a nightmare | paperwork is most farmers' nightmare*: **ordeal**, horror, torment, trial; burden, curse, bane, bogey, pet hate, dread, phobia; hell, purgatory, misery, agony, torture, murder; French bête noire.

nightmarish adjective *Grant fired at the nightmarish, clawing figure before him*: **unearthly**, monstrous, ghostly, spine-chilling, horrific, macabre, hideous, unspeakable, gruesome, grisly, ghastly, harrowing, hair-raising, disturbing, Kafkaesque; informal scary, creepy; rare phantasmagorical.

nihilism noun **1** *he could not accept Bacon's nihilism, his insistence that man is a futile being*: **negativity**, cynicism, pessimism; rejection, repudiation, renunciation, denial, abnegation; disbelief, non-belief, unbelief, scepticism, lack of conviction, absence of moral values, agnosticism, atheism.
2 *the roots of this decline lay deep in the moral nihilism of the 1960s*: **anarchy**, disorder, chaos, absence of government, lawlessness, mobocracy.

nihilist noun *it is this approach which leads to the denunciation of Derrida as a nihilist*: **disbeliever**, unbeliever, non-believer, sceptic, agnostic, atheist; negativist, cynic, pessimist; anarchist.

nil noun **nothing**, none; **nought**, zero, o; Tennis love; Cricket a duck; N. English nowt; informal zilch, nix, not a dicky bird; Brit. informal damn all, (sweet) Fanny Adams, sweet F.A., not a sausage; N. Amer. informal zip, nada, a goose egg; Brit. vulgar slang bugger all, sod all, fuck all; Computing null character; literary null; dated cipher; archaic naught.

nimble adjective **1** *he was surprisingly nimble on his feet | she tore off the ring with nimble fingers*: **agile**, lithe, sprightly, acrobatic, light-footed, nimble-footed, light, light on one's feet, fleet-footed, spry, lively, active, quick, quick-moving, graceful, supple, limber, lissom, flexible, skilful, deft, dexterous, adroit; informal nippy, zippy, twinkle-toed; literary fleet, lightsome.
▷ANTONYMS stiff, clumsy, lumbering.
2 *the boy had a nimble mind*: **quick-thinking**, quick-witted, quick, nimble-witted; alert, alive, lively, wide awake, ready, quick off the mark, observant, astute, perceptive, perspicacious, penetrating, discerning, shrewd, sharp, sharp-witted; intelligent, bright, clever, gifted, able, brainy, brilliant; informal smart, on the ball, on one's toes, quick on the uptake.
▷ANTONYMS dull.

nimbleness noun *he used his nimbleness to make sure he got on to the sofa first*: **agility**, litheness, sprightliness, light-footedness, nimble-footedness, lightness, spryness, liveliness, activeness, quickness, smartness; grace, gracefulness, suppleness, limberness, lissomness, flexibility, skill, deftness, dexterity, adroitness; informal nippiness, zippiness; literary fleetness, lightsomeness.
▷ANTONYMS clumsiness.

nimbly adverb *she watched him climb nimbly over the wall*: **agilely**, lithely, acrobatically, lightly, easily, spryly, actively, quickly, smartly, briskly; gracefully, supply, lissomly, flexibly, skilfully, deftly, dexterously, adroitly; informal nippily, zippily; literary fleetly, lightsomely.
▷ANTONYMS clumsily.

nincompoop noun *don't be such a nincompoop*. See **fool**, **idiot**.

nine cardinal number **nonet**; rare ennead, ninesome.

Word links **nine**
nona- related prefix, as in *nonagenarian*
nonary relating to nine
nonagon nine-sided figure

nineteen cardinal number
□ **talk nineteen to the dozen** Brit. *the urge to talk incessantly, to jabber nineteen to the dozen*: **prattle**, blather, blether, blither, babble (on), gabble, prate, drivel, rattle on/away, ramble, maunder, go on, run on, talk at length, talk incessantly, talk a lot, chatter, yap; informal jabber, blabber, yatter, jaw, gab, gas, chit-chat, yackety-yak; Brit. informal rabbit, witter, waffle, natter, chunter, talk the hind legs off a donkey; N. Amer. informal run off at the mouth; Austral./NZ informal mag.

nip verb **1** *the dog nipped her ankle*: **bite**, nibble, peck, pinch, tweak, squeeze, grip.
2 Brit. informal *I'll just nip out and see what's going on*: **go**, **rush**, dash, dart, hurry, scurry, scamper; drop by/in/into/round, stop by, visit; informal tootle, pop, whip.
□ **nip something in the bud** *let's nip this unpleasantness in the bud before it goes any further*: **curtail**, cut short, strangle at birth, check, cut off, thwart, beat, frustrate, curb, stop, halt, arrest, stifle, obstruct, impede, block, squash, quash, subdue, quell, crack down on, stamp out; informal squelch, put the kibosh on, clobber.
□ **nip something off** *carefully nip off older flowers on cyclamens and African violets*: **cut off**, snip (off), trim, clip, prune, hack off, chop off, saw off, lop (off), dock, crop, sever, separate, detach, remove, take off.
▸ noun *rockhopper penguins have a strong beak that can deliver a serious nip*: **bite**, nibble, peck, pinch, tweak, squeeze, grip.

nipple noun **teat**, dug; informal tit; technical mamilla; archaic pap, papilla, udder.

Word links **nipple**
mamillary relating to a nipple

nippy adjective informal **1** *so big a man is never going to be exactly nippy*: **agile**, lithe, sprightly, acrobatic, light-footed, nimble-footed, light, light on one's feet, fleet-footed, spry, lively, active, graceful, supple, limber, lissom, flexible, skilful, deft, dexterous, adroit; informal twinkle-toed; literary fleet, lightsome.
▷ANTONYMS lumbering, clumsy.
2 *a nippy three-door hatchback*: **with good acceleration**, **fast**, quick, brisk, lively; informal zippy.
▷ANTONYMS slow.
3 *it's a bit nippy this morning*: **cold**, chilly, icy, bitter, raw.
▷ANTONYMS warm.

nirvana noun *there are no short cuts to nirvana*: **paradise**, heaven, Eden, the promised land; bliss, blessedness, ecstasy, joy, peace, serenity, tranquillity; enlightenment, oblivion.
▷ANTONYMS hell, purgatory.

nit-picking adjective informal *nurses can be driven spare by the nit-picking hierarchies in hospitals*. See **pedantic** (sense 1).

nitty-gritty noun informal *she is no longer involved in the nitty-gritty of running the company*: **basics**, essentials, essence, essential part, main point, fundamental point, fundamentals, substance, heart of the matter, nub, core, heart, centre, quintessence, point, crux, gist, salient point, focal point, nucleus, meat, pith, kernel, marrow, burden; hard work, slog, toil, labour, donkey work, drudgery; informal brass tacks, nuts and bolts.

nitwit noun informal *I want nothing to do with that bunch of nitwits!* See **fool**, **idiot**.

no adverb no indeed, absolutely not, most certainly not, of course not, under no circumstances, by no means, not at all, negative, never, not really, no thanks; Scottish nae; informal nope, nah, not on your life, no way; Brit. informal no fear, not on your nelly; N. Amer. informal no siree; Scottish, N. English, & N. Amer. informal naw; archaic nay.
▷ANTONYMS yes.

nobble verb Brit. informal **1** *he was convicted for nobbling the jury*: **bribe**, corrupt, suborn, buy, buy off, pay off, get at, induce, lure, entice, grease someone's palm, oil someone's palm/hand; **influence**, persuade, win over, secure someone's support, sway, swing, affect, control, manipulate.
2 *a stable lad was persuaded to nobble the horse*: **drug**, dope; tamper with, interfere with, disable, incapacitate, weaken.
3 *what's to stop him nobbling Rose's money?* **steal**, thieve, rob, embezzle.
4 *they would nobble him and throw him on the train*: **abduct**, seize, capture, kidnap, catch, apprehend, arrest, take into custody, take in, bring in; informal **snatch**, nab, nail, pinch, cop, run in, pull in, pick up, collar; Brit. informal nick.

nobility noun **1** *many of the nobility owned property in the area*: **aristocracy**, aristocrats, lords, ladies, peerage, peers, peers of the realm, peeresses, nobles, noblemen, noblewomen, titled men/women/people, members of the aristocracy/nobility/peerage, patricians; informal aristos; Brit. informal nobs.
2 *the nobility of his deed*: **virtue**, goodness, honour, honesty, decency, integrity, magnanimity, generosity, selflessness, bravery.
3 *he lacked any nobility of vision*: **loftiness**, grandness.
4 *this type of trumpet lacks nobility of tone*: **magnificence**, splendour, impressiveness, imposingness, majesty, grandeur, stateliness, dignity, distinction, glory, gloriousness, splendidness.

noble adjective **1** *she came from a noble family*: **aristocratic**, noble-born, of noble birth, titled, patrician, blue-blooded, high-born, well born; archaic gentle, of gentle birth.
▷ANTONYMS humble.
2 *they were fighting for a noble cause*: **righteous**, virtuous, good, honourable, honest, upright, upstanding, decent, worthy, noble-minded, uncorrupted, moral, ethical, reputable, magnanimous, unselfish, generous, self-sacrificing, brave.
▷ANTONYMS dishonourable.
3 *noble thoughts*: **lofty**, exalted, elevated, grand, sublime, imposing.
▷ANTONYMS ignoble, base.
4 *there is nothing more noble than a mature pine forest*: **magnificent**, splendid, grand, stately, imposing, dignified, distinguished, proud, striking, impressive, majestic, glorious, marvellous, awe-inspiring, awesome, monumental, palatial, statuesque, heroic; regal, royal, kingly, queenly, princely, imperial.
▷ANTONYMS unimpressive.
5 *this noble grape variety lends weight and body to the wine*: **excellent**, splendid, marvellous, magnificent, superb, fine, wonderful, exceptional, formidable, sublime, prime, first-class, first-rate, high-grade, grade A, superior, supreme, flawless, choice, select, finest, superlative, model; informal tip-top, A1, top-notch.
▷ANTONYMS poor.
▶noun *seven Scottish nobles were killed in that battle*: **aristocrat**, nobleman, noblewoman, lord, lady, peer, peeress, peer of the realm, patrician, titled man/woman/person; informal aristo; Brit. informal nob.

nod verb **1** *all she could do was nod her head*: **incline**, bob, bow, dip, wag, duck.
2 *he nodded to me to start*: **signal**, gesture, gesticulate, motion, sign, indicate.
3 *even Homer nods*: **make a mistake**, be mistaken, be in error, be wrong, be incorrect, get something wrong, make an error, make a slip, err, trip up, stumble; be careless, be inattentive, be negligent; informal slip up.
□ **nod off** *the audience began to nod off*: **fall asleep**, go to sleep, get to sleep, doze off, drop off; informal go off, drift off, crash out, flake out, go out like a light, conk out; N. Amer. informal sack out, zone out.
▷ANTONYMS stay awake.
▶noun **1** *at a nod from the manager, she dimmed the lights*: **signal**, indication, sign, cue; gesture.
2 *he greeted Ivan with a quick nod of his head*: **inclination**, bob, bow, dip, duck; greeting, acknowledgement.
□ **get the nod** *Clarke got the nod, and really proved himself during the series*: **be selected**, be chosen, be picked, make the grade; Brit. be capped; Austral. informal get a guernsey.
□ **give someone/something the nod 1** *Ronny Johnsen was given the nod in preference to David May*: **select**, choose, pick, go for; Brit. cap.
2 *the chances are that the Lords will give the treaty the nod*: **approve**, agree to, sanction, ratify, endorse, say yes to, give one's approval to, rubber-stamp; informal give something the go-ahead, give something the green light, OK, give something the OK, give something the thumbs up.
▷ANTONYMS reject.

node noun *the intersection of two or more such arteries would become major traffic nodes*: **junction**, fork, branching, intersection, interchange, confluence, convergence, meeting point, crossing, criss-crossing, vertex, apex.

noise noun **sound**, loud sound, din, hubbub, clamour, racket, uproar, tumult, commotion, pandemonium, clangour; crash, clatter, clash, babble, shouting, yelling, babel; W. Indian bangarang; informal **hullabaloo**; Brit. informal row.
▷ANTONYMS silence.
□ **big noise** *her father is a big noise in the army*: **VIP**, important person, notable, notability, personage, dignitary, grandee; celebrity; magnate, mogul; informal somebody, heavyweight, hotshot, big shot, big gun, big cheese, big fish, biggie, big bug, Big Chief, Big Daddy, honcho; Brit. informal brass hat; N. Amer. informal big wheel; Austral./NZ informal joss.
▷ANTONYMS nobody, nonentity.

noisome adjective literary *he had spent six long weeks in this noisome dungeon*. See **offensive** (sense 2 of the adjective).

noisy adjective **1** *cats loathe noisy homes | a noisy crowd*: **rowdy**, rackety, clamorous, boisterous, roisterous, obstreperous, turbulent, brash, clattering, chattering, talkative, vociferous, shouting, screaming, shrieking, bawling.
▷ANTONYMS quiet.
2 *play some sweet music, not noisy pop*: **loud**, fortissimo, blaring, booming, blasting, brassy, deafening, thunderous, tumultuous, clamorous, resounding, reverberating, ear-splitting, piercing, strident, harsh, cacophonous, raucous.
▷ANTONYMS soft.

nomad noun **itinerant**, traveller, migrant, wanderer, wayfarer, roamer, rover, gypsy, Bedouin; transient, drifter, vagabond, vagrant, tramp; refugee, displaced person, DP, homeless person; dated bird of passage.

nominal adjective **1** *the government would be led by a prime minister, along with a president as nominal head of state*: **in name/title only**, titular, formal, official, ceremonial; theoretical, purported, supposed, ostensible; self-styled, so-called, would-be.
▷ANTONYMS real.
2 *agricultural workers have a cottage either free or for a nominal rent*: **token**, symbolic, emblematic, peppercorn; **tiny**, minute, minimal, small, infinitesimal, insignificant, trifling, not worth mentioning, not worth bothering about; informal minuscule, piddling, piffling; N. Amer. informal nickel-and-dime; rare exiguous.
▷ANTONYMS considerable, substantial.

nominate verb **1** *any member of a branch may nominate a candidate*: **propose**, put forward, put up, submit, present, recommend, suggest, name.
2 *he wished to nominate his own assistant*: **appoint**, designate, make, assign, name, dub, delegate, select, choose, decide on, elect, commission, promote.

non-aligned adjective *the non-aligned countries of the Third World*: **neutral**, impartial, non-partisan, uninvolved, unallied, unattached, unaffiliated, uncommitted, floating, independent; informal sitting on the fence.

non-believer noun *I was an absolute non-believer in spiritualism*: **sceptic**, doubter, doubting Thomas, unbeliever, disbeliever, cynic, nihilist; atheist, agnostic, freethinker, libertine; infidel, pagan, heathen; archaic paynim.

nonce noun
□ **for the nonce** *work on the bridge had been suspended for the nonce*: **for the time being**, for the interim, for a while, for now, for the moment, for the present, at present, just now, in the meanwhile, the while, meantime, in the meantime, in the intervening period, provisionally, temporarily, pro tem; Latin ad interim; French en attendant.

nonchalance noun *she shrugged, feigning nonchalance*. See **insouciance**.

nonchalant adjective *he had tried to appear nonchalant about the risks he was taking*. See **insouciant**.

non-combatant adjective *the President sent US armed forces as non-combatant military advisers*: **non-fighting**, non-participating, civilian, non-belligerent, pacifist, neutral, non-aligned.
▷ANTONYMS combatant, fighting.

non-committal adjective *she remained silent, apart from a few non-committal remarks*: **evasive**, equivocal, temporizing, guarded, circumspect, reserved; cautious, wary, careful, prudent; discreet, unrevealing, uncommunicative, politic, tactful, diplomatic, vague; informal cagey.
▷ANTONYMS revealing, careless, indiscreet.
□ **be non-committal** *Alf was non-committal about their chances of success*: **prevaricate**, give nothing away, play one's cards close to one's chest, straddle an issue, dodge the question/issue, sidestep the issue, hedge, fence, pussyfoot, beat about the bush, equivocate, temporize, shilly-shally, vacillate, waver; Brit. hum and haw; informal duck the question, sit on the fence.

non compos mentis adjective Latin *Roger had become non compos mentis through drink and age*. See **mad** (sense 1).

nonconformist noun *if the employees feel industrial action is warranted, they will not tolerate nonconformists*: **dissenter**, dissentient, protester, rebel, renegade, freethinker, apostate, heretic, schismatic, recusant, seceder, individualist, free spirit, maverick, unorthodox person, eccentric,

original, deviant, misfit, hippy, dropout, fish out of water, outsider; informal freak, oddball, odd fish, weirdo, weirdie; N. Amer. informal screwball, kook.
▷ANTONYMS conformist.

nondescript adjective *a little room in a nondescript Victorian terraced house*: **undistinguished**, featureless, characterless, unremarkable, unexceptional, unmemorable, blending into the background; **ordinary**, commonplace, average, mediocre, run-of-the-mill, mundane; uninteresting, boring, uninspiring, dull, colourless, grey, anaemic, insipid, bland; informal bog-standard; Brit. informal common or garden.
▷ANTONYMS distinctive, extraordinary.

none pronoun **1** *none of the fish are unusual*: **not one**, not a one.
▷ANTONYMS all, many, some.
2 *none of this concerns me*: **no part**, not a part, not a bit, not any.
▷ANTONYMS all, some.
3 *none of these five-year-olds could read at that stage | none can know better than you*: **not one**, not a one, never a one, not a soul, not a single person, no one, nobody, no man.
▷ANTONYMS all, many, some.
▶ adverb
□ **none the …** *the family wrote to the Home Secretary for information but were left none the wiser*: **not at all**, not a bit, not the slightest bit, in no way, to no extent, by no means any, not for a moment.
▷ANTONYMS much.

nonentity noun *without bargaining skills, a president will be a nonentity in the White House*: **unimportant person**, person of no importance, person of no account, nobody, cipher, non-person, man of straw, nothing, small fry, lightweight; mediocrity, second-rater; informal no-hoper, non-starter; Brit. informal small beer.
▷ANTONYMS somebody, celebrity, heavyweight.

non-essential adjective *killing seals for non-essential products cannot be justified*: **unnecessary**, inessential, unessential, needless, unneeded, not required, superfluous, uncalled for, redundant, dispensable, expendable, peripheral, unimportant, incidental, optional, extraneous, cosmetic; French de trop; rare supererogatory.
▷ANTONYMS essential, indispensable.

nonetheless adverb *the story behind the rumour is so curious, however, that it is worth telling nonetheless*. See **nevertheless**.

non-existent adjective *she carefully brushed a non-existent piece of lint from her skirt*: **imaginary**, imagined, unreal, fictional, fictitious, made up, invented, hypothetical, suppositional, fancied, fanciful; fantastic, fantasy, mythical, mythological, legendary; illusory, illusive, hallucinatory, chimerical, figmental, notional, shadowy, spectral, ghostly, insubstantial; missing, absent; rare phantasmal, phantasmic; inexistent, illusionary, unsubstantial.
▷ANTONYMS real, actual.

non-intervention noun **laissez-faire**, neutrality, non-alignment, non-participation, non-interference, non-interventionism, non-involvement, a hands-off approach, inaction, passivity; free enterprise, private enterprise, free trade, market forces; live and let live.
▷ANTONYMS interventionism.

non-observance noun *society deems these rules so important as to lay down sanctions for non-observance*. See **violation** (sense 1).

nonpareil adjective *Gould is a nonpareil storyteller*: **incomparable**, matchless, unrivalled, unparalleled, unequalled, without equal, peerless, unmatched, beyond comparison, beyond compare, second to none, unsurpassed, unsurpassable, unbeatable, inimitable; unique, consummate, perfect, rare, exquisite, transcendent, surpassing, superlative, supreme; rare unexampled.
▷ANTONYMS mediocre.
▶ noun *he was a great player, Britain's nonpareil of the 1980s*: **best**, finest, paragon, crème de la crème, peak of perfection, elite, jewel, jewel in the crown, gem; Latin ne plus ultra; informal the best/finest this side of …; archaic nonsuch.
▷ANTONYMS mediocrity.

nonplus verb *young Lewis seemed remarkably nonplussed by the whole affair*: **surprise**, stun, dumbfound, confound, astound, astonish, amaze, take aback, disconcert, stop someone in their tracks, throw, throw/catch off balance; **puzzle**, perplex, baffle, mystify, confuse, bemuse, bewilder; informal faze, flummox, floor, flabbergast, discombobulate, stump, bamboozle, fox.

nonsense noun **1** *don't talk complete nonsense, please!* **rubbish**, balderdash, gibberish, claptrap, blarney, guff, blather, blether; informal hogwash, rot, baloney, tripe, drivel, gobbledegook, bilge, bosh, bull, bunk, hot air, eyewash, piffle, poppycock, phooey, hooey, malarkey, twaddle, dribble; Brit. informal cobblers, codswallop, cock, stuff and nonsense, tosh, double Dutch, flannel, waffle; Scottish & N. English informal havers; N. Amer. informal garbage, flapdoodle, blathers, wack, bushwa, applesauce; informal, dated bunkum, tommyrot, cod, gammon, toffee; vulgar slang shit, bullshit, crap, bollocks, balls; Austral./NZ vulgar slang bulldust.
▷ANTONYMS sense.
2 *modern, mechanized methods would make economic nonsense on a smallholding*: **ridiculousness**, stupidity, absurdity, ludicrousness, inanity, fatuity, pointlessness, foolishness, folly, foolhardiness, silliness, idiocy, senselessness, insanity, madness.
▷ANTONYMS sense, wisdom.
3 *Elaine could not see the villagers putting up with any nonsense from her*: **mischief**, mischievousness, naughtiness, badness; **bad behaviour**, misbehaviour, misconduct, misdemeanour, perversity, pranks, tricks, larks, capers, joking, jesting, clowning, buffoonery, roguery, devilry, funny business; French diablerie; informal tomfoolery, monkey tricks, monkey business, shenanigans, goings-on, hanky-panky; Brit. informal carry-on, carryings-on, jiggery-pokery; archaic deviltry.
□ **no-nonsense** *he pictured his world in a muscular, no-frills, no-nonsense sort of way*: **matter-of-fact**, down-to-earth, practical, sensible, realistic, full of common sense, commonsensical, reasonable, rational, logical, sound, balanced, sober, pragmatic, level-headed, serious-minded, businesslike, hard-headed, responsible, sane, mundane, unromantic, unidealistic.

nonsensical adjective **1** *he would laugh at her soft, nonsensical way of talking*: **meaningless**, senseless, illogical, unmeaning.
▷ANTONYMS logical, rational.
2 *this last comment is really a nonsensical generalization*: **foolish**, insane, stupid, lunatic, idiotic, illogical, irrational, zany, senseless, absurd, silly, inane, asinine, hare-brained, ridiculous, ludicrous, wild, preposterous, fatuous; informal crazy, crackpot, crackbrained, nutty, wacky; Brit. informal daft.
▷ANTONYMS sane, sensible.

non-stop adjective *you can look forward to non-stop fun and entertainment*: **continuous**, incessant, unceasing, ceaseless, constant, continual, perpetual, unfaltering, permanent, uninterrupted, without interruption, round-the-clock, unbroken, steady, unremitting, relentless, persistent.
▷ANTONYMS occasional, intermittent.
▶ adverb *we worked non-stop on the books*: **continuously**, all the time, incessantly, unceasingly, ceaselessly, constantly, continually, perpetually, unfalteringly, permanently, uninterruptedly, without interruption, round the clock, steadily, unremittingly, relentlessly, persistently, without ceasing; informal 24-7.
▷ANTONYMS intermittently.

non-toxic adjective *a non-toxic varnish*: **non-poisonous**, innocuous, harmless, benign, safe, non-irritating, hypoallergenic.
▷ANTONYMS toxic.

> *Word toolkit* **non-toxic**
>
> See **harmless**.

nook noun **1** *he hoped to lose his followers in the bookshop's maze of nooks and crannies*: **recess**, **corner**, alcove, cranny, crevice, niche, hollow, bay, inglenook, cavity, cubbyhole, pigeonhole, opening, gap, aperture.
2 *there are quiet riverside nooks for meditation*: **hideaway**, hiding place, hideout, retreat, refuge, shelter, nest, snuggery, snug, den, haunt; informal hidey-hole.

noon noun *the railway operates between noon and 5 p.m. daily*: **midday**, twelve noon, twelve midday, twelve o'clock, high noon, noontime, noontide, noonday, twelve hundred, twelve hundred hours, one-two-double-O.
▷ANTONYMS midnight.

> *Word links* **noon**
>
> **meridional** relating to noon

no one pronoun *there was no one about*: **nobody**, not a soul, not anyone, not a person, not a single person, never a one, no man, none.
▷ANTONYMS everyone.

norm noun **1** *talks intended to establish norms of diplomatic behaviour*: **convention**, **standard**, criterion, measure, gauge, yardstick, benchmark, point of reference, touchstone, barometer, litmus test, basis, scale, rule, formula, pattern, guide, guideline, model, exemplar, type.
2 (**the norm**) *child protection teams are now the norm in local authorities*: **standard**, **usual**, normal, typical, average, the rule, predictable, unexceptional, par for the course, what one would expect, expected, (only) to be expected.
▷ANTONYMS the exception.

normal adjective **1** *the new library system will issue books in the normal way*: **usual**, standard, typical, stock, common, ordinary, customary, conventional, habitual, accustomed, expected, wonted, everyday, regular, routine, day-to-day, daily, established, settled, set, fixed, traditional, quotidian, prevailing.
▷ANTONYMS unusual.
2 *to anyone looking at them, they must seem like a perfectly normal couple*: **ordinary**, average, run-of-the-mill, standard, typical, middle-of-the-road, common, conventional, mainstream, unremarkable, unexceptional, plain,

n

simple, homely, homespun, workaday; N. Amer. garden-variety; informal bog-standard, vanilla, plain vanilla, a dime a dozen; Brit. informal common or garden; N. Amer. informal ornery.
▷ANTONYMS abnormal.
3 *Mr Lowe was convinced that the man was not normal*: **sane**, in one's right mind, right in the head, of sound mind, in possession of all one's faculties, able to think/reason clearly, lucid, rational, coherent, balanced, well balanced; Latin compos mentis; informal **all there**.
▷ANTONYMS insane, irrational.

normality noun **1** *after yesterday's bomb scare, normality returned to the town centre this morning*: **a normal state of affairs**, business as usual, the daily round, routine, a normal pattern, order, regularity; N. Amer. normalcy.
2 *people begin to wonder about the normality of the sufferer*: **sanity**, soundness of mind, mental health, balance, lucidity, reason, rationality.
▷ANTONYMS insanity.

normally adverb **1** *she wanted to walk normally again*: **as usual**, as normal, ordinarily, naturally, conventionally, regularly.
▷ANTONYMS abnormally.
2 *normally we'd keep quiet about this*: **usually**, ordinarily, commonly, as a rule, as a general rule, generally, in general, in the general run of things, mostly, for the most part, by and large, mainly, most of the time, almost always, more often than not, on the whole; **typically**, habitually, customarily, historically, traditionally, routinely.
▷ANTONYMS exceptionally.

north adjective *the north coast of the island | the north wind*: **northern**, northerly, northwardly, Arctic, polar; technical boreal; literary hyperborean; rare borean, hyperboreal.
▷ANTONYMS south.
▸ adverb *I have to go up north tomorrow*: **to the north**, northward, northwards, northwardly.
▷ANTONYMS south.

nose noun **1** **snout**, muzzle, proboscis, trunk; informal beak, conk, snoot, schnozzle, hooter, sniffer, snitch; Scottish & N. English informal neb; informal, dated bracket; N. Amer. informal, dated bugle.
2 *he has a very good nose*: **sense of smell**, olfactory sense.
3 *he had a nose for scandal*: **instinct**, feeling, gift for discovering/detecting, sixth sense, intuition, insight, perception.
4 *a thin wine with an agreeably fruity nose*: **smell**, bouquet, aroma, fragrance, perfume, scent, odour.
5 *the plane's nose dipped as it started descending*: **tip**, nose cone; bow, prow, front end; Brit. bonnet; N. Amer. hood; informal droop-snoot.
□ **by a nose** *all the appliances tested do the job well, but our best buy wins by a nose*: **just**, only just, barely, narrowly, by a narrow margin, by the narrowest of margins, by a very small margin, by a hair's breadth, by the skin of one's teeth; informal by a whisker.
▷ANTONYMS by miles.
□ **get up someone's nose** informal *it really got up my nose, and it occured to me to wonder why it was so annoying*: **annoy**, aggravate, irritate, exasperate, anger, irk, vex, put out, nettle, provoke, incense, rile, infuriate, antagonize, make someone's blood boil, ruffle someone's feathers, ruffle, try someone's patience, make someone's hackles rise; offend, pique; rankle; informal peeve, needle, make someone see red, get someone's back up, get someone's goat, get under someone's skin, bug, get someone, miff, hack off; Brit. informal wind up, get at, nark, get across, get on someone's wick; N. Amer. informal tick off; vulgar slang piss off.
□ **on the nose** N. Amer. *the van pulled up at ten on the nose*: **exactly**, precisely, sharp, on the dot; **promptly**, prompt, dead (on), on the stroke of ..., on the dot of ...; informal bang (on), spot on ...; N. Amer. informal on the button.
▸ verb **1** *the dog nosed the carcass briefly*: **nuzzle**, nudge, push, prod.
2 *she's always **nosing into** your business*: **pry**, enquire impertinently, be inquisitive, enquire; be curious, poke about/around, mind someone else's business, be a busybody, stick/poke one's nose in; interfere (in), meddle (in), intrude (on); informal be nosy (about), nosy, snoop; Austral./NZ informal stickybeak.
3 *the submarine nosed around the island's waters | he nosed the car out into the traffic*: **move slowly**, ease, inch, edge, move, manoeuvre, steer, slip, squeeze, slide; guide, push, tuck.
□ **nose around/about/round** *the others were no doubt nosing around the wreck*: **investigate**, explore, ferret (about/around) in, rummage in, search, delve into, peer into, prowl around, have a good look at; informal snoop about/around/round.
□ **nose something out** *he has a rare gift of nosing out little-recorded composers*: **detect**, find, search out, discover, disclose, bring to light, track down, dig up, hunt out, ferret out, root out, uncover, unearth, disinter, smell out, sniff out, follow the scent of, scent out, run to earth/ground.

> *Word links* **nose**
>
> **nasal**, **rhinal** relating to the nose
> **naso-**, **rhin(o)-** related prefixes, as in *nasogastric*, *rhinoceros*
> **rhinitis** inflammation in the nose
> **rhinoplasty** surgical repair of the nose
> **otorhinolaryngology** branch of medicine concerning the ears, nose, and throat

nosedive noun **1** *the pilot put the plane into a nosedive and ejected*: **dive**, drop, plunge, descent, plummet.
▷ANTONYMS climb, zoom.
2 informal *sterling took a nosedive*: **sharp fall**, drop, plunge, plummet, tumble, decline, slump; informal crash.
▷ANTONYMS rise.
▸ verb **1** *the engine stopped and the device nosedived to earth*: **dive**, plunge, pitch (down), drop rapidly, swoop, plummet, crash-dive.
▷ANTONYMS soar, climb, zoom.
2 informal *building costs have nosedived*: **fall sharply**, take a nosedive, take a header, drop, sink, plunge, plummet, tumble, slump, go down, decline, subside; informal crash.
▷ANTONYMS rise, soar.

nosegay noun *she carried a nosegay of white roses*. See **posy**.

nosh informal noun **1** *all kinds of lovely nosh*: **food**, sustenance, nourishment, nutriment, fare, daily bread, groceries, rations, iron rations; snacks, titbits, eatables; informal nibbles, eats, grub, bread, chow; Brit. informal scoff; N. Amer. informal chuck; archaic victuals, vittles, meat, viands, commons.
2 *I could have had a nosh in any pub in town*: **meal**, snack; something to eat; informal spread, blowout, bite, bite to eat, nosh-up, feed; Brit. informal, dated tuck-in; N. Amer. informal square.
▸ verb *the privileged can nosh smoked salmon while watching the proceedings*: **eat**, munch (on), ingest, consume, take, partake of, taste, swallow, devour, feast on, gulp (down), gobble (down), wolf (down), scoff (down), tuck in/into, breakfast (on), lunch (on), dine (on); have breakfast, have lunch, have dinner, have tea, have supper; informal get stuck into, get one's laughing gear round; Brit. informal **shift**, gollop, bevvy; N. Amer. informal scarf (down/up), snarf (down/up), inhale; rare ingurgitate, bib.

nostalgia noun *there is a nostalgia for traditional values*: **wistfulness**, longing/yearning/pining for the past, regret, regretfulness, reminiscence, remembrance, recollection, homesickness, sentimentality.

nostalgic adjective *the smell of the sea evoked nostalgic memories of childhood holidays*: **wistful**, evocative, longing/yearning/pining for the past, romantic, sentimental, emotional about the past, regretful, dewy-eyed, maudlin, homesick.

nostrum noun **1** *the pill pedlars will have to show that their nostrums work*: **patent medicine**, quack remedy, potion, elixir, panacea, cure-all, cure for all ills, universal remedy, sovereign remedy, wonder drug, magic bullet; rare catholicon, diacatholicon, panpharmacon.
2 *his successes resulted from such right-wing nostrums as a wage freeze and cutting public spending*: **remedy**, cure, prescription, answer, magic formula, recipe, recipe for success.

nosy adjective *he had to whisper in order to avoid being overheard by their nosy neighbours*: **prying**, inquisitive, curious, busybody, probing, spying, eavesdropping, intrusive; informal snooping, snoopy.

notability noun **1** *the village has always enjoyed a notability out of all relation to its size*: **noteworthiness**, momentousness, memorability, impressiveness, extraordinariness; **prominence**, importance, significance, eminence; **fame**, publicity, renown, notoriety, stature, media attention/interest.
2 *the enterprise enjoyed the patronage of notabilities and aristocrats*: **celebrity**, public figure, important person, VIP, personality, personage, notable, dignitary, leading light, star, superstar, name, big name, famous name, household name; lion, worthy, grandee, luminary, panjandrum; informal celeb, somebody, bigwig, big shot, big noise, big cheese, big gun, big fish, biggie, heavy, megastar; Brit. informal nob; N. Amer. informal kahuna, macher, high muckamuck, high muckety-muck.
▷ANTONYMS nonentity.

notable adjective **1** *there were no notable examples of townships with high unemployment*: **noteworthy**, remarkable, outstanding, important, significant, momentous, memorable, unforgettable, pronounced, marked, striking, glaring, obvious, impressive, uncommon, unusual, particular, special, extraordinary, exceptional, conspicuous, rare, signal.
▷ANTONYMS insignificant, unremarkable.
2 *Dr Butler was a notable headmaster*: **prominent**, important, well known, famous, famed, noted, distinguished, great, eminent, pre-eminent, illustrious, consequential, respected, well thought of, esteemed, honoured, renowned, celebrated, acclaimed, influential, prestigious; in the public eye, of high standing, of distinction, of note, of repute, of mark, of importance, of consequence.
▷ANTONYMS obscure.
▸ noun *the hotel was a favoured haunt for kings, queens, movie stars, authors, and other notables*: **celebrity**, public figure, important person, VIP, personality, personage, notability, dignitary, leading light, star, superstar, name, big name, famous name, household name, lion, worthy, grandee, luminary, panjandrum; informal celeb, somebody, bigwig, big shot, big noise,

n

big cheese, big gun, big fish, biggie, heavy, megastar; Brit. informal nob; N. Amer. informal kahuna, macher, high muckamuck, high muckety-muck.
▷ANTONYMS nonentity.

notably adverb **1** *other industrialized countries, notably the USA, agreed to the measures*: **in particular**, particularly, especially, specially, primarily, principally, above all.
2 *the flightless emu and ostrich are notably short-lived among birds*: **remarkably**, strikingly, impressively, especially, specially, very, extremely, exceptionally, singularly, particularly, peculiarly, distinctly, significantly, unusually, extraordinarily, uncommonly, uniquely, outstandingly, amazingly, incredibly, awfully, terribly, really, markedly, decidedly, surprisingly, conspicuously, spectacularly, signally; informal seriously, majorly, mucho; Brit. informal jolly, dead, well; informal, dated devilish, frightfully.

notation noun **1** *notation is essential for communication*: **system of symbols**, alphabet, syllabary, script; symbols, signs, code, cipher, hieroglyphics.
2 *flicking through, he noticed the notations in the margin*: **annotation**, jotting, inscription, comment, footnote, entry, minute, record, item, memo, gloss, explanation, explication, elucidation; marginalia, exegesis; rare scholium.

notch noun **1** *there was a notch in the end of the arrow for the bowstring*: **nick**, cut, mark, incision, score, scratch, gash, slit, snick, slot, gouge, groove, furrow, cleft, indentation, dent.
2 *her opinion of Nicole dropped a further few notches*: **degree**, step, level, rung, point, mark, measure, grade, gradation, stage.
▸ verb *notch the wood*: **nick**, cut, mark, score, incise, carve, engrave, scratch, gash, slit, slot, snick, gouge, groove, furrow, indent, make an indentation in, dent.
□ **notch something up** *the world champion notched up four wins and five draws*: **score**, achieve, attain, secure, rack up, chalk up, gain, earn, make, register, record.

note noun **1** *she took out her diary and made a note of the time of the meeting*: **record**, account, entry, item, notation, minute, jotting, inscription; memorandum, reminder, aide-memoire; informal memo.
2 (**notes**) *he may be asked to take notes of the meeting*: **minutes**, records, jottings, report, account, commentary, transcript, proceedings, transactions; observations, impressions, details, data; synopsis, precis, summary, sketch, outline.
3 *there were some notes scribbled in the margins*: **annotation**, footnote, commentary, comment, gloss, explanation, explication, exposition, elucidation; marginalia, exegesis; rare scholium.
4 *he dropped me a note the day he left*: **message**, communication, letter, missive, epistle, line; email.
5 Brit. *a £20 note*: **banknote**; N. Amer. bill, greenback; N. Amer. or historical Treasury note; archaic flimsy; (**notes**) paper money.
6 *only two developments are worthy of note*: **attention**, consideration, notice, heed, observation, thought, regard, care, attentiveness, mindfulness.
7 *he was a composer of considerable note*: **distinction**, importance, eminence, pre-eminence, influence, illustriousness, greatness, prestige, fame, acclaim, celebrity, renown, repute, reputation, stature, standing, position, rank, consequence, account.
8 *there was a note of hopelessness in her voice*: **tone**, intonation, inflection, sound, hint, indication, sign, element, streak, strain, vein, suggestion, suspicion.
▸ verb **1** *we shall be delighted to note your suggestion*: **bear in mind**, be mindful of, consider, observe, take into account/consideration, take note of, listen to; heed, take notice of, pay attention to, take in, pay regard to, be guided by.
▷ANTONYMS ignore, disregard.
2 *a final communiqué noted the ministers' concern*: **mention**, make mention of, refer to, allude to, touch on, hint at, indicate, point out, make known, state.
3 *you had better note the date in your diary*: **write down**, put down, jot down, take down, set down, mark down, inscribe, enter, mark, record, register, scribble, scrawl, pencil; put in writing, put down on paper, commit to paper, put in black and white.

notebook noun **notepad**, exercise book, register, logbook, log, diary, daybook, journal, commonplace book, memorandum book, record book, personal organizer; Brit. jotter, pocketbook; N. Amer. scratch pad; French cahier; informal memo pad; trademark Filofax.

noted adjective **1** *a noted French economist*: **eminent**, **famous**, well known, famed, prominent; distinguished, illustrious, great, celebrated, acclaimed, esteemed, august, recognized, pre-eminent, important, of high standing, of distinction, of repute, considerable.
▷ANTONYMS unknown, unheard of, obscure.
2 *the district is noted for its antique shops, boutiques, and restaurants*: **renowned**, **well known**, famous, noteworthy, notable, of note, important, recognized; well thought of, celebrated; notorious.

noteworthy adjective *other noteworthy features include the carved capitals of the chancel arch*: **notable**, worthy of note, interesting, of particular interest, significant, worthy of mention, worth taking a look at, noticeable; **remarkable**, impressive, important, striking, outstanding, memorable, unique, special, prominent, conspicuous; unusual, extraordinary, out of the ordinary, singular, different, rare, uncommon.
▷ANTONYMS unexceptional, boring, insignificant, ordinary.

nothing pronoun **1** *there's nothing I can do about it*: **not a thing**, not a single thing, not anything, nothing at all, nil, zero; N. English nowt; informal zilch, sweet Fanny Adams, sweet FA, nix, not a dicky bird; Brit. informal damn all, not a sausage; N. Amer. informal zip, nada, a goose egg, bupkis; Brit. vulgar slang bugger all, sod all, fuck all; archaic nought, naught.
▷ANTONYMS something.
2 *please forget it, it's nothing*: **a matter of no importance/consequence**, a trifling matter, a trifle, a piece of trivia, a (mere) bagatelle; neither here nor there; informal no big deal.
3 *he seemed to treat her as nothing*: **a person of no importance**, an unimportant person, a person of no account, a nobody, a nonentity, a cipher, a non-person; a lightweight; Brit. small beer.
▷ANTONYMS celebrity.
4 *the value of the shares is unlikely to fall to nothing*: **zero**, nought, o; Tennis love; Cricket a duck.
□ **be/have nothing to do with 1** *it has nothing to do with your enquiries*: **be unconnected with**, be unrelated to; be irrelevant to, be extraneous to, be inapplicable to, be inapposite to, be extrinsic to; rare be malapropos of.
2 *he's a hard, ruthless man and I'll have nothing to do with him*: **avoid**, have no dealings with, have no truck with, avoid dealing with, have no contact with, steer clear of, give a wide berth to.
□ **for nothing 1** *the former TV presenter agreed to host the show for nothing, but then demanded £1,000*: **free**, gratis, without charge, without payment, free of charge, at no cost; informal for free, on the house. **2** *I've taken all this trouble for nothing*: **in vain**, to no avail, to no purpose, with no result, needlessly, pointlessly, futilely; archaic bootlessly.
□ **nothing but** *he was nothing but a nuisance to her*: **merely**, only, just, solely, simply, purely, no more than.

nothingness noun **1** *the total nothingness of death*: **oblivion**, non-existence, non-being, non-life; **nullity**, blankness; void, vacuum; rare nihility.
▷ANTONYMS existence, being.
2 *the nothingness of it all overwhelmed him*: **unimportance**, insignificance, triviality, pointlessness, uselessness, worthlessness, valuelessness.
▷ANTONYMS importance, value, significance.

notice noun **1** *no aspect connected with the running of his companies escaped his notice | two points are worthy of notice*: **attention**, observation, awareness, consciousness, perception, cognizance, heed, note; regard, consideration, scrutiny, interest, thought, mindfulness, watchfulness, vigilance, attentiveness.
2 *a notice was pinned up outside the church*: **information sheet**, bill, handbill, poster, advertisement, announcement, bulletin, broadsheet, circular, flyer, leaflet, pamphlet, sign, placard; card, sticker; handout; French affiche; N. Amer. & Austral. dodger; informal ad; Brit. informal advert.
3 *itineraries are subject to change without notice*: **notification**, (advance) warning, announcement, apprisal, intimation; information, news, communication, intelligence, word.
4 *I handed in my notice yesterday*: **resignation**, letter of resignation.
5 *governors can require the education authority to give notice to a teacher*: **dismissal**, discharge, termination/ending of employment, one's marching orders; informal **the sack**, the boot, the bullet, the axe, the (old) heave-ho, the elbow, the push, the bounce; Brit. informal one's cards, the chop.
6 *the film did not get universally good notices*: **review**, write-up, critique, criticism; French compte rendu; Brit. informal crit.
□ **take no notice (of)** *he took no notice of anything I said*: **pay no attention (to)**, **ignore**, disregard, pay no heed (to), take no account (of), turn a deaf ear (to), brush aside, shrug off, set aside, turn a blind eye (to), shut one's eyes (to), pass over, let pass, let go, overlook, look the other way, pretend not to notice; informal not want to know.
▷ANTONYMS heed, pay attention (to).
▸ verb *I noticed that the front door was open | she slipped back inside, hoping no one would notice her*: **observe**, perceive, note, see, become aware of, discern, detect, spot, distinguish, catch sight of, make out, take notice of, mark, remark; pay attention to, take note of, heed, take heed of, pay heed to; Brit. informal clock; literary behold, descry, espy.
▷ANTONYMS overlook, ignore, disregard.

noticeable adjective *there has been a noticeable shift in public opinion lately*: **perceptible**, discernible, detectable, distinguishable, observable, perceivable, visible, easily seen, appreciable, recognizable, notable, measurable; **distinct**, evident, obvious, apparent, manifest, patent, plain, clear, clear-cut, marked, significant, conspicuous, unmistakable, undeniable, palpable, pronounced, decided, prominent, salient, striking, arresting; archaic sensible.
▷ANTONYMS imperceptible, unobtrusive, inconspicuous.

noticeboard noun **pinboard**, cork board; hoarding, display site, advertisement board; N. Amer. bulletin board.

notification noun **1** *the notification of the victim's next of kin*: **informing**, telling, apprising, apprisal, alerting, warning.
2 *she received notification that her letter had been passed to the chairman of the advisory committee*: **information**, word, notice, advice, news, intelligence; communication, message, report, account, story; literary tidings.
3 *matters relating to the notification of births and deaths*: **announcement**, reporting, declaration, communication, disclosure, divulgence, publication, publishing.

notify verb **1** *we will notify you as soon as possible | parents must be* ***notified of*** *the education authority's decision*: **inform**, tell, advise, apprise, let someone know, put in the picture; alert, warn, caution; acquaint with, send word of.
2 *in the UK, export agreements are meant to be notified to the Office of Fair Trading*: **make known**, report, announce, declare, communicate, give notice of, disclose, reveal, divulge, broadcast, publish.

notion noun **1** *these figures give the lie to the notion that the country is strike-ridden | he had a notion that something very odd was going on*: **idea**, belief, concept, conception, conviction, opinion, view, thought, impression, image, perception, mental picture; assumption, presumption, hypothesis, theory, supposition; feeling, funny feeling, suspicion, sneaking suspicion, hunch.
2 *Claire had no notion of what he meant*: **understanding**, idea, awareness, knowledge, clue, inkling; Brit. informal the foggiest idea.
3 *you can't expect us to fire any of our staff just because you get a notion to come back*: **impulse**, inclination, whim, desire, wish, fancy, caprice, whimsy.

> *Choose the right word* **notion, idea, concept**
>
> See **idea**.

notional adjective *the notional dividing line between the eastern and western zones*. See **theoretical** (sense 2).

notoriety noun *the book earned him undeserved notoriety*: **infamy**, bad reputation/name, disrepute, ill repute, ill fame, dishonour, discredit, obloquy, opprobrium; fame, renown.
▷ANTONYMS anonymity, a low profile.

notorious adjective *the country's most notorious drug trafficker | she was notorious for having lots of love affairs*: **infamous**, of ill repute, with a bad reputation/name, ill-famed, scandalous; **well known**, famous, famed, celebrated, renowned, fabled, legendary, noted, talked about, prominent.
▷ANTONYMS unknown, anonymous, faceless.

n

notwithstanding preposition *notwithstanding his many activities, Alan finds time to be a dedicated husband and father*: **in spite of**, despite, regardless of, for all.
▸ adverb *she tells us she is an intellectual—notwithstanding, she faces the future as unprovided for as a beauty queen*: **nevertheless**, nonetheless, even so, all the same, in spite of this/that, despite this/that, after everything, however, still, yet, be that as it may, having said that, that said, for all that, just the same, anyway, in any event, at any rate, at all events, when all is said and done; archaic withal, howbeit.
▸ conjunction *notwithstanding that Sir Henry had sold much land, his debts were still on the increase*: **although**, in spite of the fact that, despite the fact that, even though, though, for all that.

nought noun **1** *the past forty years have all been for nought*: **nothing**, nothing at all, naught; no point, no purpose, no effect, no end result; N. English nowt; informal zilch, sweet Fanny Adams, sweet FA, not a dicky bird, nix; Brit. informal damn all, not a sausage; N. Amer. informal zip, nada, a goose egg; Brit. vulgar slang bugger all, fuck all, sod all.
2 *Richard Scott went for nought, caught behind by Bishop*: **nil**, zero, o; Tennis love; Cricket a duck; dated cipher.

noun noun

> *Word links* **noun**
>
> **nominal** relating to nouns

nourish verb **1** *it is important that all patients are well nourished prior to surgery*: **feed**, provide for, sustain, maintain; rare nutrify.
▷ANTONYMS starve.
2 *by investing in education we nourish the talents of children*: **promote**, foster, encourage, stimulate, nurture, boost, further, advance, forward, contribute to, be conducive to, assist, help, aid, cultivate, strengthen, enrich.
3 *the hopes Ursula had nourished in his absence had been dashed*: **cherish**, nurture, foster, harbour, nurse, keep in one's mind, entertain, maintain, sustain, hold, have.
▷ANTONYMS repress, discourage.

nourishing adjective *eating regular, nourishing meals is important to keep yourself fit and well*. See **nutritious**.

nourishment noun *she denied wilful neglect by failing to provide the boy with sufficient nourishment*. See **sustenance** (sense 1).

nouveau riche plural noun *the nouveau riche of today buy leather-covered volumes by the metre*: **the new rich**; parvenus, arrivistes, upstarts, social climbers, vulgarians.

novel[1] noun **book**, paperback, hardback; **story**, tale, narrative, romance, work of fiction; best-seller; informal blockbuster; historical yellowback, three-decker.

novel[2] adjective *the practice would not be considered unusual today, but in 1945 it was novel*: **new**, **original**, unusual, unfamiliar, unconventional, unorthodox, different, fresh, imaginative, creative, innovative, innovatory, innovational, inventive, modern, ultra-modern, state-of-the-art, advanced, avant-garde, futuristic, pioneering, groundbreaking, trailblazing, revolutionary; rare, unique, singular, unprecedented, uncommon; experimental, untested, untried, unknown, surprising, strange, exotic, out of the ordinary, newfangled; N. Amer. left-field; rare new-fashioned, neoteric.
▷ANTONYMS old; traditional.

> *Word toolkit* **novel**
>
> See **unfamiliar**.

novelist noun **author**, writer of fiction, creative writer, man/woman of letters; French littérateur; informal penman, scribbler; rare fictionist, fictioneer.

novelty noun **1** *they liked the novelty of our approach*: **originality**, newness, freshness, unconventionality, unfamiliarity, unusualness, difference, imaginativeness, creativity, creativeness, innovativeness, innovation, modernity, modernness, break with tradition.
▷ANTONYMS conservatism.
2 *their products include handmade chocolates, figurines, and seasonal novelties*: **knick-knack**, trinket, bauble, toy, trifle, gewgaw, gimcrack, ornament, curiosity; memento, souvenir; N. Amer. kickshaw; archaic gaud, folderol.

novice noun **1** *a 5-day course during which novices learn enough to skipper a yacht safely*: **beginner**, learner, inexperienced person, neophyte, newcomer, new member, new recruit, raw recruit, new boy/girl, initiate, tyro, fledgling; apprentice, trainee, probationer, student, pupil, mentee; N. Amer. tenderfoot; informal rookie, new kid, newie, newbie; N. Amer. informal greenhorn, punk.
▷ANTONYMS expert, veteran.
2 *a novice who had never achieved ordination*: **novitiate**, postulant, proselyte, catechumen, neophyte.

novitiate noun **1** *in 1868 he began a three-year novitiate*: **probationary period**, probation, trial period, test period, apprenticeship, training period, traineeship, training, initiation.
2 *two young novitiates*: **novice**, neophyte; postulant, proselyte, catechumen.

now adverb **1** *I'm afraid I'm extremely busy now, but I could see you in the morning*: **at the moment**, at present, just now, right now, at the present time, at the present moment, at this time, at this moment in time, currently, here and now; N. Amer. presently; Brit. informal at the minute.
2 *television is now the main source of political information for most people*: **nowadays**, today, these days, in this day and age; in the present climate, things being what they are, in the present circumstances; rare contemporarily.
3 *it would be best if you leave now*: **at once**, straight away, right away, right now, this minute, this instant, immediately, instantly, directly, without further/more ado, promptly, without delay, as soon as possible; French tout de suite; informal pronto, straight off, a.s.a.p., toot sweet; archaic straightway, instanter.
□ **as of now** *as of now, cigarettes are banned in this house*: **from this time on**, from now on/onwards, henceforth, henceforward, from this day forward, in future; formal hereafter.
□ **for now** *that will be all for now, thank you*: **for the time being**, for the moment, for the present, for the meantime, for a little while; archaic for the nonce.
□ **not now** *I promise I will, but not now*: **later**, later on, sometime, one day, some day, one of these days, at some time in the future, at a future time/date, one of these fine days, sooner or later, in due course, by and by, eventually, ultimately.
▷ANTONYMS immediately.
□ **now and again** *I go and stay with my sister now and again*: **occasionally**, now and then, from time to time, sometimes, every so often, (every) now and again, at times, on occasion(s), on the odd occasion, (every) once in a while; at intervals, periodically, on and off; once in a blue moon; archaic ever and anon.

nowadays adverb *nowadays all graduates are computer literate*. See **today** (sense 2 of the adverb).

noxious adjective *the discharge of noxious effluents into streams and rivers | noxious fumes*: **poisonous**, toxic, deadly, virulent; **harmful**, dangerous,

pernicious, damaging, destructive; **very unpleasant**, nasty, disgusting, awful, dreadful, horrible, terrible, vile, revolting, foul, sickening, nauseating, nauseous, appalling, offensive, foul-smelling, evil-smelling, malodorous, fetid, putrid, rancid, unwholesome, unhealthy, insalubrious; informal ghastly, horrid; literary noisome, mephitic; archaic disgustful; rare miasmal, miasmic, nocuous, olid.
▷ANTONYMS innocuous, safe; pleasant.

nuance noun *the expression of subtle nuances of thought*: **fine distinction**, subtle distinction/difference, shade, shading, gradation, variation, modulation, degree; subtlety, nicety, refinement, overtone.

nub noun *the nub of his argument*. See **essence** (sense 1).

nubile adjective *a nubile young girl*: **sexually mature**, marriageable; **sexually attractive**, desirable, sexy, luscious, lush, voluptuous, ripe; informal beddable.

nucleus noun **1** *the nucleus of the international banking world*: **core**, centre, central part, most important part, heart, nub, hub, middle, midpoint, eye, kernel, focus, focal point, pivot, crux; literary navel; rare omphalos.
2 *a nucleus of non-party men were prepared to support him*: **small group**, caucus, cell, coterie, clique, faction, cabal.

nude adjective **naked**, in the nude, stark naked, bare, with nothing on, stripped, unclothed, undressed, uncovered, in a state of nature, disrobed, unclad, undraped, exposed; French au naturel; informal without a stitch on, in one's birthday suit, in the raw, in the altogether, in the buff, as naked as the day one was born, in the nuddy, mother naked; Brit. informal starkers; Scottish informal in the scud, scuddy; N. Amer. informal bare-assed, buck naked; Austral. informal bollocky; Brit. vulgar slang bollock-naked.
▷ANTONYMS dressed, fully clothed.

Word links **nude**

gymnophobia fear of nudity

Choose the right word **nude, naked, bare**

See **naked**.

nudge verb **1** *he nudged Ben in the ribs*: **poke**, elbow, dig, prod, jog, jab, butt.
2 *the canoe nudged a bank of reeds*: **touch**, bump (against), push (against), run into.
3 *enthusiastic reviewers have been known to nudge recalcitrant publishers into action*: **prompt**, encourage, coax, stimulate, prod, jog.
4 *unemployment was nudging 3 million*: **approach**, come/get close to, be verging on, border on, near.
► noun **1** *Maggie gave him a nudge*: **poke**, dig in the ribs, dig, prod, jog, jab, butt, push.
2 *after a little nudge from me, she remembered Lilian*: **reminder**, prompt, prompting, push, prod, encouragement.

nudity noun **nakedness**, bareness, state of undress, undress; French déshabillé; informal one's birthday suit.

nugatory adjective **1** *a nugatory and pointless observation*: **worthless**, of no value, of no importance, unimportant, inconsequential, of no consequence, valueless, trifling, trivial, insignificant, meaningless.
2 *the teacher shortages will render nugatory the hopes of implementing the new curriculum*: **futile**, useless, vain, unavailing, null and void, null, invalid; archaic bootless.

nugget noun *gold nuggets | savoury scones filled with nuggets of potato and cheese*: **lump**, chunk, small piece, hunk, mass, clump, wad, gobbet, globule; Scottish dod; Brit. informal wodge; N. Amer. informal gob; rare nub.

nuisance noun *don't you find these long journeys a nuisance? | I'm terribly sorry to be such a nuisance*: **source of annoyance/irritation**, annoyance, inconvenience, bore, bother, irritant, problem, difficulty, trouble, trial, burden; pest, plague, thorn in one's side/flesh; informal pain, pain in the neck, pain in the backside, headache, hassle, bind, drag, aggravation, menace; Scottish informal nyaff, skelf; N. Amer. informal pain in the butt, nudnik, burr under/in someone's saddle; Austral./NZ informal nark; Brit. vulgar slang pain in the arse; Brit. informal, dated blister; rare infliction.
▷ANTONYMS help, blessing.

null adjective **1** *his previous marriage was declared null*: **invalid**, null and void, void; annulled, nullified, cancelled, abolished, revoked, rescinded, repealed.
▷ANTONYMS valid.
2 *his curiously null life*: **lacking in character**, empty, characterless, blank, colourless, expressionless, vacuous, insipid, vapid, inane.
▷ANTONYMS full, colourful, interesting.

nullify verb **1** *the ANC warned that it would nullify the legislation*: **annul**, declare null and void, render null and void, void, invalidate, render invalid; **repeal**, reverse, rescind, revoke, set aside, cancel, abolish, undo, abrogate; countermand, veto, dissolve, cast aside, do away with, bring to an end, terminate, quash, obliterate; Law vacate; archaic recall; rare disannul.
▷ANTONYMS ratify, validate, confirm.
2 *the costs of preparing the case would more than nullify any tax relief gained*: **cancel out**, neutralize, negate, render ineffective, make of no use or value; rare negative.

nullity noun **1** *nullity of marriage must be carefully distinguished from divorce*: **invalidity**, non-validity; illegality; rare voidness.
▷ANTONYMS validity.
2 *her bright yellow hair contrasted strongly with her pallor and the nullity of her features*: **characterlessness**, emptiness, blankness, expressionlessness, vacuity, insipidity, vapidity, inanity.

numb adjective *his fingers were numb with cold | she felt numb with fear*: **deprived of sensation**, without feeling, numbed, benumbed, dead, deadened, desensitized, insensible, insensate, senseless, unfeeling; anaesthetized, drugged; dazed, stunned, stupefied, in shock, paralysed, petrified, immobilized, frozen, chilled; rare torpefied.
▷ANTONYMS sensitive, responsive.
► verb *the cold had numbed her senses | I sat there, numbed by what had happened*: **deaden**, deprive of sensation, benumb, desensitize, render insensitive, dull; anaesthetize, drug; daze, stun, stupefy, paralyse, petrify, immobilize, freeze, chill; rare torpefy, obtund.
▷ANTONYMS sensitize.

number noun **1** **numeral**, integer, figure, digit; character, symbol; whole number, decimal number, decimal, unit; cardinal number, ordinal number; Roman number, Arabic number; rare cipher.
2 *they received a large number of complaints | the number of accidents involving cyclists has increased*: **amount**, quantity; **total**, sum total, aggregate, tally; quota.
3 *the men were celebrating the wedding of one of their number*: **group**, company, crowd, circle, party, body, band, crew, set; informal gang, tribe.
4 *a copy of the current number of the Society's quarterly magazine*: **edition**, issue, copy; printing, imprint, impression, publication.
5 *in the background she could hear the band performing another number*: **song**, piece of music, musical item, piece, tune, track; turn, item, routine, sketch, dance, act.
□ **a number of** *there are a number of reasons why many crimes are not reported to the police*: **several**, various, quite a few, sundry, diverse; literary divers.
□ **number-one, number one** *heart disease is the number-one cause of death | product knowledge is number one in this business*: **primary**, main, chief, key, prime, central, principal, overriding, **foremost**, first, most important, predominant, paramount, major, ruling, dominant, master, supreme, cardinal, pre-eminent, ultimate; informal top-notch.
▷ANTONYMS secondary, subordinate.
□ **looking after number one** *members are selfish and are looking after number one*: **self-interested**, self-seeking, self-serving, self-regarding, selfish, egocentric, egotistic, egotistical, self-obsessed, self-absorbed, wrapped up in oneself, inward-looking.
► verb **1** *visitors to the cathedral numbered more than 2.25 million last year*: **add up to**, amount to, total, come to.
2 *he numbers the editor of Vogue among his close friends*: **include**, count; reckon, deem, look on.
3 *each paragraph is numbered consecutively*: **assign a number to**, categorize by number, specify by number, mark with a number; itemize, enumerate.
4 *the number of published texts on the subject may be numbered on the fingers of both hands | he numbers the fleet at a thousand*: **count**, add up, total, calculate, compute, enumerate, reckon, tell, tally; assess; Brit. tot up.
5 *his days are numbered*: **limit**, limit in number, restrict, fix.

Word links **number**

numerical relating to numbers

numberless adjective *there are numberless questions to be answered*. See **countless**.

numbing adjective **1** *the menthol in the oil has a slight numbing action on the nerve | a deep, numbing fear*: **deadening**, **desensitizing**, benumbing, anaesthetizing, anaesthetic; paralysing; rare torpefying.
2 *the numbing cold of the bitter wind*: **freezing**, glacial, raw, piercing, cutting, bitter, arctic, polar.
3 *six days of numbing boredom and inactivity*: **stupefying**, mind-numbing, stultifying, paralysing; sleep-inducing, soporific.

numbness noun **lack of sensation**, lack of feeling, deadness, insensibility; paralysis, stupefaction, immobility.
▷ANTONYMS feeling, sensation.

numbskull noun informal *the system seems to be organized and operated exclusively by numbskulls*. See **fool**, **idiot**.

numeral noun **number**, integer, figure, digit; character, symbol, unit; Roman numeral, Arabic numeral; rare cipher.

numerous adjective *numerous studies have been published on the subject*: **many**, a lot of, a great many, very many, countless, scores of, innumerable; several, quite a few, various, diverse; a great number of, a great deal

of, plenty of, copious, a quantity of, quantities of, an abundance of, a profusion of, a multitude of; frequent; informal lots of, umpteen, loads of, masses of, stacks of, heaps of, piles of, bags of, tons of, oodles of, scads of, dozens of, hundreds of, thousands of, millions of, billions of, zillions of, more ... than one can shake a stick at; Brit. informal a shedload of; N. Amer. informal a slew of, a bunch of, gazillions of, bazillions of; Austral./NZ informal a swag of; vulgar slang a shitload of; literary myriad, multitudinous; rare numberless, innumerous.
▷ANTONYMS few, occasional, rare.

nun noun **sister**, novice, abbess, prioress, Mother Superior, Reverend Mother; bride of Christ, religious, conventual, contemplative; Roman Catholic Church canoness; literary vestal; historical anchoress; rare vowess.

nunnery noun See **convent**.

nuptial adjective *the nuptial festivities | moments of nuptial bliss*: **matrimonial**, marital, marriage, wedding, conjugal, connubial, bridal; married, wedded; literary hymeneal, epithalamic; Law spousal.

nuptials plural noun *Queen Sofia arrived in Seville yesterday for her daughter's nuptials*: **wedding**, wedding ceremony, marriage, marriage ceremony, union; archaic espousal, spousals, bridal(s).

nurse noun **1** *a team of skilled doctors and nurses*: **carer**, caregiver, attendant; informal Florence Nightingale, nursey; N. Amer. informal candy-striper.
2 *she had been his nurse when he was a little boy*: **nanny**, childminder, governess, au pair, nursemaid, crèche worker, childcarer, babysitter, nursery nurse; Indian ayah, amah; Jewish metapelot; informal nursey; French, dated bonne.
▸verb **1** *they had nursed smallpox patients*: **care for**, take care of, look after, tend, attend to, minister to.
2 *I nursed my damaged finger*: **treat**, medicate, tend, attend to, cure, heal; dress, bandage, soothe; informal doctor.
3 *Rosa was nursing a baby in her arms*: **breastfeed**, suckle, wet-nurse, feed.
4 *the settlers still nursed old grievances*: **harbour**, foster, entertain, brood over, bear, have, hold (on to), cherish, cling to, maintain, retain.
5 *our political unity needs to be protected and nursed*: **encourage**, nurture, promote, boost, further, advance, contribute to, assist, help, cultivate, stimulate; protect, safeguard, keep alive.
▷ANTONYMS neglect; hinder.

nursemaid noun **nanny**, governess, nursery nurse, nurserymaid, childminder, au pair, childcarer; Indian ayah, amah; Jewish **metapelot**; informal nursey; French, dated **bonne**.

nurture verb **1** *giving birth to children and nurturing them into adulthood*: **bring up**, care for, provide for, take care of, attend to, look after, rear, support, raise, foster, parent, mother, tend; feed, nourish; rare provender.
▷ANTONYMS neglect.
2 *we've nurtured different varieties of plant*: **cultivate**, grow, keep, tend.
3 *my father nurtured my love of art*: **encourage**, promote, stimulate, develop, foster, cultivate, further, advance, boost, forward, contribute to, be conducive to, assist, help, aid, abet, strengthen, advantage, fuel.
▷ANTONYMS hinder.
▸noun **1** *we are all what nature and nurture have made us*: **upbringing**, bringing up, care, fostering, tending, rearing, raising, training, education.
▷ANTONYMS nature, innate disposition, inherited characteristics.
2 *the nurture of ideas*: **encouragement**, promotion, fostering, development, cultivation, boosting, furtherance, advancement.
3 *a good base camp where one may receive nurture and rest*: **food**, nourishment, nutrition, nutriment, diet, sustenance, feeding, subsistence; rare alimentation.

nut noun **1** *nuts in their shells*: **kernel**.
2 informal *he cracked him on the nut with a poker*: **head**, skull, cranium; informal noodle, noddle, nob, noggin, dome; Brit. informal bonce, napper; Scottish & N. English informal **poll**; informal, dated **bean**, **conk**; archaic **pate**, **Costard**, **crumpet**.
3 informal *some nut will pretty soon come up with an appropriate conspiracy theory*: **madman/madwoman**, maniac, lunatic; eccentric; informal loony, nutcase, nutter, fruitcake, head case, basket case, headbanger, schizo, crank, crackpot, oddball, weirdo, weirdie; Brit. informal **odd bod**; Scottish informal radge; N. Amer. informal screwball, crazy, kook, nutso, meshuggener, wacko, wack; N. Amer. & Austral./NZ informal dingbat.
4 informal *he's a movie nut*: **enthusiast**, fan, fanatic, addict, devotee, aficionado; informal freak, fiend, maniac, buff, -head, a great one for; N. Amer. informal geek, jock; S. African informal fundi.

nutriment noun *the egg contains sufficient nutriment for the chick up to the time of hatching*. See **nutrition**.

nutrition noun *the child was not receiving sufficient nutrition*: **nourishment**, nutriment, nutrients, sustenance, food, daily bread; informal grub, chow, nosh; Brit. informal scoff; archaic victuals, vittles, viands; rare aliment.

> *Word links* **nutrition**
>
> **trophic** relating to nutrition

nutritious adjective *porridge is both cheap and nutritious*: **nourishing**, good for one, full of nourishment, full of nutrients, nutritive, wholesome, healthy, health-giving, healthful, beneficial, sustaining, strengthening; rare nutrimental, nutrient, alimentary, alible.
▷ANTONYMS unwholesome.

nuts adjective informal **1** *they must have thought we were nuts*. See **mad** (sense 1), **crazy** (sense 1).
2 *he's still* ***nuts about*** *her*: **very keen on**, devoted to, infatuated with, in love with, smitten with, enamoured of, hot for; enthusiastic, passionate, impassioned, ardent; informal mad, crazy, potty, wild, nutty, hooked on, gone on; Brit. informal dotty, daft; N. Amer. informal nutso.
▷ANTONYMS indifferent.

nuts and bolts plural noun *the nuts and bolts of running an airline*: **practical details**, basic details, fundamentals, basics, practicalities, essentials, mechanics; informal the nitty-gritty, the ins and outs, the brass tacks.

nutshell noun
□ **in a nutshell** *and that, in a nutshell, is the whole movie*: **in short**, briefly, in brief, to put it briefly, to cut a long story short, in a word, to sum up, in sum, to come to the point, in essence, in outline.

nutty adjective informal **1** *they're all as nutty as each other*. See **mad** (sense 1), **crazy** (sense 1).
2 *she confessed that she wasn't as* ***nutty about*** *Elvis as her husband*: **very keen on**, devoted to, infatuated with, in love with, smitten with, enamoured of, hot for; enthusiastic, passionate, impassioned, ardent; informal mad, crazy, potty, nuts, wild, hooked on, gone on; Brit. informal dotty, daft; N. Amer. informal nutso.
▷ANTONYMS indifferent.

nuzzle verb **1** *the horse nuzzled at her coat pocket*: **nudge**, nose, prod, push.
2 *a girl was* ***nuzzling up to*** *her boyfriend*: **snuggle**, cuddle (up), nestle, curl up, settle down, snug down, burrow, embrace, hug, lie close to.

nymph noun **1** *Iris was depicted as a nymph with golden winged sandals*: **sprite**, sylph, wood nymph, water nymph.
2 *a skinny nymph with deep-brown eyes*: **girl**, belle, maiden, maid, nymphet, sylph; young woman, young lady; Scottish & N. English **lass**, **lassie**; Irish **colleen**; Brit. dated **rosebud**; literary **maid**, **maiden**, **damsel**; archaic **demoiselle**.

n

oaf noun *the thoughtless actions of a few loud-mouthed oafs*: **lout**, boor, barbarian, Neanderthal, churl, clown, gawk, hulk, bumpkin, yokel; **fool**, dolt, dullard; Irish bosthoon; informal idiot, imbecile, halfwit, cretin, ass, jackass, goon, jerk, oik, yahoo, ape, gorilla, baboon, bear, lump, clodhopper, clod, blockhead, meathead, bonehead, chucklehead, knucklehead, lamebrain; informal, dated muttonhead, noddy, hobbledehoy; Brit. informal clot, twit, twonk, numpty, muppet, plonker, berk, prat, pillock, wally, git, wazzock, nerk, dork, yob, yobbo, chav; Scottish informal nyaff, sumph, gowk, galoot; Irish informal gobdaw; N. Amer. informal bozo, schmuck, boob, lamer, chowderhead, dumbhead, lummox, klutz, putz, schlemiel, gink, cluck, ding-dong, wiener, weeny, dip, spud, coot, palooka, poop, squarehead, hick, goofus, clunk, dingleberry, turkey, stumblebum; Austral. informal dingbat, alec, galah, nong, bogan, poon, boofhead, drongo, dill; S. African informal skate, mompara; vulgar slang dickhead, fuckwit, fuckhead, shit for brains, dildo; Brit. vulgar slang arsehole, arse, dick, tit, tosser; Irish vulgar slang gobshite; archaic clodpole, lubber.

oafish adjective *her oafish idiot of a son*: **stupid**, foolish, idiotic, cretinous; **ungainly**, loutish, clumsy, awkward, gawkish, lumbering, ape-like, bearish, cloddish, clownish, doltish, Neanderthal, uncouth, uncultured, boorish, lumpen, rough, coarse, crass, brutish, blockish, rough-hewn, ill-mannered, badly behaved, unrefined, unsophisticated; informal clodhopping, blockheaded, moronic, boneheaded, half-witted, dumb, lamebrained, chuckleheaded, thickheaded; Brit. informal yobbish; N. Amer. informal chowderheaded; archaic lubberly.
▷ANTONYMS smart, clever, neat.

oasis noun **1** *the oasis of Bahriyah is over 200 miles from Cairo*: **watering hole**, watering place, water hole, spring; Austral. gnamma, claypan.
2 *a miniature woodland that offers a cool oasis in a hot summer*: **refuge**, haven, safe haven, retreat, sanctuary, sanctum, shelter, resting place, hiding place, harbour, asylum, hideaway, hideout.

oath noun **1** *an oath of allegiance to the king*: **vow**, sworn statement, promise, pledge, avowal, affirmation, attestation, word of honour, word, bond, guarantee, guaranty; archaic troth.
2 *he uttered a stream of unrepeatable oaths*: **swear word**, profanity, expletive, four-letter word, dirty word, obscenity, imprecation, curse, malediction, blasphemy; vulgarism, vulgarity; swearing, bad/foul language, strong language; informal cuss, cuss word.

obdurate adjective *I argued with him but he was obdurate*. See **stubborn** (sense 1).

obedience noun *Louise was so accustomed to obedience that she could not prevent herself from hurrying to carry out his orders*: **compliance**, acquiescence, tractability, tractableness, amenability; **dutifulness**, deference, duty, respect, respectfulness, observance of the law/rules, discipline, biddableness, duteousness; malleability, pliability, conformity, conformance, conformability, submissiveness, submission, docility, tameness, meekness, passivity, passiveness, subservience, obsequiousness, servility.
▷ANTONYMS disobedience, rebellion, recalcitrance.

obedient adjective *Lucinda had always been very obedient*: **compliant**, acquiescent, tractable, amenable; **dutiful**, good, law-abiding, deferential, respectful, duteous, under control, well trained, well disciplined, disciplined, observant, manageable, governable, conformable; **docile**, biddable, submissive, tame, meek, passive, unresisting, malleable, pliable, pliant, yielding, subservient, obsequious, servile.
▷ANTONYMS disobedient, rebellious, unruly.

Choose the right word **obedient, biddable, docile, compliant, dutiful**

Children and animals may be expected to be **obedient**, but nowadays the word is seldom used to describe adults without an implication of subservience (*'I was waiting for you to tell me. The obedient wife,' she said*) except when it is used of obedience to rules, the law, or a faith (*she seeks to be obedient to the Lord*).

The critical note is still stronger in **biddable**: a biddable person (typically a woman or girl) is excessively meek and ready to obey any instruction, without questioning either its wisdom or the authority of the person giving it (*she'd been so meek, so biddable to this man*). It is also used of animals (*the golden retriever is both biddable and intelligent*).

Docile, being used more commonly of animals, has similar implications, but in addition to unquestioning obedience it suggests a general reluctance to complain or rebel, even where such behaviour would be justified (*employers depended on the regime for a cheap and docile workforce*).

Compliant means 'disposed to agree with others or obey rules' and typically has a disparaging tone, criticising the compliant person for not having the willpower to stand up for themselves and show some independence by expressing their own views (*compliant MPs loyally following party policy*).

Even **dutiful**, though applied to a large extent to family members (*daughter, son, wife, parent, mother, father*), may suggest a dull but worthy individual or the perfunctory fulfilment of an obligation (*a dutiful postcard to his mother*).

obeisance noun **1** *they paid obeisance to the Prince | a gesture of obeisance*: **respect**, homage, worship, adoration, reverence, veneration, respectfulness, honour, submission, deference.
2 *she made a deep obeisance*: **bow**, curtsy, bob, genuflection, salaam, salutation; Indian namaskar; Chinese, historical kowtow; archaic reverence.

obelisk noun **column**, pillar, needle, shaft, monolith, monument, memorial.

obese adjective *he ate excessively and became obese*. See **fat** (sense 1 of the adjective).

obesity noun *somehow, his famous charm made one ignore his years and his obesity*. See **fatness**.

obey verb **1** *I was so frightened that I obeyed him without question*: **do what someone says**, take/accept orders from, carry out/follow the orders of, be dutiful to, heed; **submit to**, defer to, be ruled by, bow to, give way/in to, yield to, surrender to, truckle to.
2 *the officer was convicted for refusing to obey an order*: **carry out**, perform, act on, execute, discharge, put into effect, implement, fulfil, meet.
3 *health and safety regulations have to be obeyed*: **comply with**, adhere to, observe, abide by, act in accordance with, conform to, respect, acquiesce in, consent to, agree to, follow, accept, keep to, stick to; play it by the book, toe the line.
▷ANTONYMS disobey, defy, contravene.

obfuscate verb **1** *the debate all too often obfuscates the issue*: **obscure**, confuse, make obscure/unclear, blur, muddle, jumble, complicate, garble, muddy, cloud, befog; muddy the waters.
▷ANTONYMS clarify.
2 *it is more likely to obfuscate people than enlighten them*: **bewilder**, mystify, puzzle, perplex, baffle, confound, bemuse, befuddle, nonplus; informal flummox; archaic wilder, maze, gravel.

obituary noun **death notice**, eulogy; informal obit; rare necrology, necrologue.

object noun (stress on the first syllable) **1** *wooden objects*: **thing**, article, item, piece, device, gadget, entity, body; informal thingamajig, thingamabob, thingummy, whatsit, whatchamacallit, what-d'you-call-it, thingy; Brit. informal doodah, doobry, gubbins; N. Amer. informal doodad, doohickey, doojigger; N. Amer. & S. African informal dingus.
▷ANTONYMS abstract idea, notion.
2 *he became the object of fierce criticism*: **target**, butt, focus, recipient, victim.
3 *the Institute was opened with the object of promoting scientific study*: **purpose**, objective, aim, goal, target, end, end in view, plan, object of the exercise; ambition, design, intent, intention, idea, point.
▸ verb (stress on the second syllable) *some teachers **objected to** the scheme | no reasonable person could have objected*: **protest (against)**, lodge a protest (against), raise/express objections (to), express disapproval (of), express disagreement (with), oppose, be in opposition (to), take exception (to), take issue (with), take a stand against, argue (against), remonstrate (against), make a fuss (about), quarrel with, disapprove (of), condemn, draw the line (at), demur, mind, complain (about), moan (about), grumble (about), grouse (about), cavil (at), quibble (about); beg to differ; informal kick up a fuss/stink (about), beef (about), gripe (about); N. Amer. informal kvetch (about).
▷ANTONYMS approve, accept, acquiesce.

objection noun *the search was carried out regardless of her objections*: **protest**, protestation, demur, demurrer, remonstrance, remonstration, exception, complaint, grievance, moan, grumble, grouse, cavil, quibble, expostulation; **opposition**, argument, counter-argument, demurral, disapproval, dissent, disagreement; informal niggle, gripe, beef, grouch.
▷ANTONYMS approval, acceptance, acquiescence.

objectionable adjective *I thought Randolph was one of the most objectionable people I had ever met*: **offensive**, **unpleasant**, disagreeable, distasteful, displeasing, unacceptable, off-putting, undesirable, obnoxious; **nasty**, disgusting, awful, terrible, dreadful, frightful, repulsive, repellent, repugnant, revolting, abhorrent, loathsome, hateful, detestable, reprehensible, deplorable, appalling, insufferable, intolerable, despicable, contemptible, beyond the pale, odious, vile, obscene, foul, unsavoury, unpalatable, sickening, nauseating, nauseous, noxious; informal ghastly, horrible, horrid, sick-making; Brit. informal beastly; archaic disgustful, loathly; rare exceptionable, rebarbative.
▷ANTONYMS pleasant, agreeable, acceptable.

objective adjective **1** *an interviewer must try to be objective*: **impartial**, unbiased, unprejudiced, non-partisan, disinterested, non-discriminatory, neutral, uninvolved, even-handed, equitable, fair, fair-minded, just, open-minded, dispassionate, detached, impersonal, unemotional, clinical.
▷ANTONYMS biased, partial, prejudiced.
2 *the world of objective knowledge*: **factual**, actual, real, empirical, verifiable, existing, manifest.
▷ANTONYMS subjective.
▸ noun *our objective is to build a profitable business*: **aim**, intention, purpose, target, goal, intent, object, end, end in view, grail, holy grail; idea, design, plan, scheme, ambition, aspiration, desire, hope; the point, the object of the exercise.

objectively adverb *the bank will do all it can to investigate your complaint objectively*: **impartially**, with objectivity, without bias, without prejudice, with impartiality, disinterestedly, even-handedly, with detachment, dispassionately, detachedly, equitably, fairly, justly, open-mindedly, with an open mind, without fear or favour, neutrally.

objectivity noun *the ideals of journalistic accuracy and objectivity*: **impartiality**, absence of bias/prejudice, fairness, fair-mindedness, equitableness, equitability, even-handedness, justness, justice, open-mindedness, disinterest, disinterestedness, detachment, dispassion, dispassionateness, neutrality.
▷ANTONYMS subjectivity, bias, prejudice.

oblation noun *the priest spread his hands over the oblation*. See **offering** (sense 2).

obligate verb *the medical establishment is obligated to take action in the best interests of the public*. See **oblige** (sense 1).

obligation noun **1** *I have an obligation to look after her | he seemed able to fulfil his professional obligations*: **duty**, commitment, responsibility, moral imperative; **function**, task, job, chore, assignment, commission, business, burden, charge, onus, liability, accountability, requirement, debt, engagement; dated office; archaic devoir; literary trust.
2 *she took him in solely out of a sense of obligation*: **duty**, compulsion, indebtedness, duress, necessity, pressure, constraint.
3 *the company's export obligations*: **contract**, agreement, deed, covenant, bond, treaty, deal, pact, compact, understanding, transaction.
□ **under an obligation** *she didn't want to be **under an obligation to** him*: **owing someone a favour**, obliged, beholden, in someone's debt, indebted, obligated, owing someone a debt of gratitude, duty-bound, honour-bound, grateful, owing someone thanks.

obligatory adjective **1** *use of seat belts in cars is now obligatory*: **compulsory**, mandatory, prescribed, required, demanded, statutory, enforced, binding, incumbent; requisite, necessary, imperative, unavoidable, inescapable, essential.
▷ANTONYMS voluntary, optional.
2 *after the obligatory preamble on the weather he got down to business*: **customary**, traditional, usual, accustomed, routine, familiar, regular, habitual; French de rigueur; literary wonted.

oblige verb **1** *courts are obliged to act in accordance with the strict rules of the law | he was obliged to resign*: **require**, compel, bind, make, constrain, obligate, force, put under an obligation, leave someone no option, impel, coerce, pressure, pressurize.
2 *will you **oblige** me **by** filling in this form?* **do someone a favour**, do someone a kindness, do someone a service, accommodate, indulge, gratify, gratify the wishes of, help, assist, serve, humour, meet the wants/needs of, put oneself out for; be kind enough to.

> *Choose the right word* **oblige, compel, force, coerce**
>
> See **compel**.

obliged adjective *if you should hear from her I'd be obliged if you'd let me know*: **thankful**, grateful, appreciative; **beholden**, indebted, in someone's debt, under an obligation, obligated.
□ **much obliged thank you**, thanks, many thanks, thanks a lot, thanks very much, thank you kindly; informal cheers, thanks a million; Brit. informal ta.

obliging adjective *Roger was a cheerful, obliging sort of chap*: **helpful**, eager to help/please, accommodating, willing, cooperative, considerate, complaisant, agreeable, amenable, generous, friendly, kind, neighbourly, hospitable, pleasant, good-natured, amiable, gracious, unselfish, civil, courteous, polite, indulgent, benevolent; Brit. informal decent.
▷ANTONYMS disobliging, obstructive, unhelpful, uncooperative.

oblique adjective **1** *an oblique line*: **slanting**, slanted, sloping, at an angle, angled, diagonal, aslant, slant, slantwise, sloped, inclined, inclining, tilted, tilting, atilt, skew, on the skew, askew; Scottish squint; N. Amer. cater-cornered, catty-cornered, kitty-corner.
▷ANTONYMS straight.
2 *an oblique reference to the president*: **indirect**, inexplicit, roundabout, circuitous, circumlocutory, implicit, implied, elliptical, evasive, backhanded; rare circumlocutionary, ambagious.
▷ANTONYMS direct, explicit.
3 *he cast her an oblique glance*: **sidelong**, sideways, furtive, covert, sly, surreptitious.
▸ noun **slash**, forward slash, solidus, oblique stroke, backslash, diagonal, virgule, slant.

obliquely adverb **1** *the morning sun shone obliquely across the tower*: **diagonally**, at an angle, slantwise, sideways, sidelong, aslant, athwart; literary aslope.
2 *he referred obliquely to the war as 'an unfortunate period'*: **indirectly**, in a roundabout way, circuitously, evasively, not in so many words, not outright.
▷ANTONYMS directly.

obliterate verb **1** *the memory was so painful that he obliterated it from his mind*: **erase**, eradicate, expunge, efface, blot out, rub out, wipe out, remove all traces of, blank out, block out, delete, strike out, cancel, cross out, ink out, score out.
2 *a nuclear explosion that would obliterate a city*: **destroy**, wipe out, annihilate, exterminate, extirpate, demolish, eliminate, eradicate, kill, decimate, liquidate, wipe off the face of the earth, wipe off the map; informal zap.
▷ANTONYMS create, establish.

obliteration noun **1** *the complete and intentional obliteration of a will or any part of it*: **eradication**, erasing, erasure, effacing, rubbing out, blotting out, wiping out, removal, expunging, effacement, blanking out, blocking out, deletion, striking out, cancellation, crossing out, inking out, scoring out; rare expunction, expungement.
2 *pressure from environmentalists has saved one of the country's national parks from obliteration*: **destruction**, wiping out, annihilation, extermination, extirpation, elimination, eradication, killing, decimation, liquidation, demolition; informal zapping.

oblivion noun **1** *he closed his eyes again and sank back into oblivion*: **unconsciousness**, **insensibility**, stupor, stupefaction, senselessness, blankness, darkness; coma, blackout; obliviousness, unawareness, ignorance, amnesia; literary the waters of Lethe.
▷ANTONYMS consciousness, awareness.
2 *their words have been consigned to oblivion | they rescued him from artistic oblivion*: **obscurity**, non-existence, limbo, void, vacuum, nothingness, nihility, nullity, extinction, anonymity, neglect, disregard.
▷ANTONYMS fame.

oblivious adjective *they were clearly oblivious to the danger | she was totally oblivious of her surroundings*: **unaware**, unconscious, heedless, unmindful, insensible, unheeding, ignorant, blind, deaf, unsuspecting, unobservant, disregardful, unconcerned, impervious, unaffected, insensitive,

indifferent, detached, removed; rare incognizant.
▷**ANTONYMS** aware, conscious.

obloquy noun **1** *he endured years of contempt and obloquy*: **vilification**, opprobrium, vituperation, condemnation, castigation, denunciation, abuse, criticism, censure, flak, defamation, denigration, disparagement, derogation, slander, revilement, reviling, calumny, calumniation, execration, excoriation, lambasting, upbraiding, bad press, character assassination, attack, invective, libel, insults, aspersions; informal mud-slinging, bad-mouthing, tongue-lashing; Brit. informal stick, verbal, slagging off; archaic contumely; rare animadversion, objurgation.
▷**ANTONYMS** praise.
2 *conduct to which no moral obloquy could reasonably attach*: **disgrace**, dishonour, shame, discredit, stigma, humiliation, loss of face, ignominy, odium, opprobrium, disfavour, disrepute, ill repute, infamy, notoriety, scandal, stain; rare disesteem.
▷**ANTONYMS** honour.

obnoxious adjective *a thoroughly obnoxious man | the smell was particularly obnoxious*. See **unpleasant**.

obscene adjective **1** *obscene literature | obscene jokes*: **pornographic, indecent**, salacious, smutty, X-rated, lewd, rude, dirty, filthy, vulgar, foul, coarse, crude, gross, vile, nasty, disgusting, offensive, shameless, immoral, improper, immodest, impure, indecorous, indelicate, unwholesome, scabrous, off colour, lubricious, risqué, ribald, bawdy, suggestive, titillating, racy, erotic, carnal, sensual, sexy, lascivious, lecherous, licentious, libidinous, goatish, degenerate, depraved, amoral, debauched, dissolute, prurient; scatological, profane; informal blue, porn, porno, raunchy, sick; Brit. informal near the knuckle, fruity, saucy; euphemistic adult; rare ithyphallic, Fescennine, Cyprian.
▷**ANTONYMS** pure, decent.
2 *it was the most obscene crime he had ever encountered*: **shocking**, scandalous, vile, foul, atrocious, outrageous, heinous, wicked, evil, odious, abhorrent, abominable, disgusting, hideous, repugnant, repulsive, revolting, repellent, obnoxious, offensive, objectionable, loathsome, hateful, nauseating, sickening, awful, dreadful, terrible, frightful, ghastly; archaic disgustful, loathly.

obscenity noun **1** *the book was banned on the grounds of obscenity*: **indecency**, immorality, impropriety, salaciousness, smuttiness, smut, lewdness, rudeness, vulgarity, dirtiness, dirt, filthiness, filth, foulness, coarseness, crudeness, grossness, vileness, nastiness, impurity, immodesty, indelicacy, indecorousness, unwholesomeness, scabrousness, ribaldry, bawdiness, suggestiveness, eroticism, carnality, lasciviousness, lechery, licentiousness, libidinousness, degeneracy, depravity, amorality, debauchery, dissoluteness, prurience; scatology, profanity, profaneness; rare bawdry, salacity, lubricity.
2 *he was an army officer so he knows about the obscenity of war*: **atrocity**, act of brutality, act of savagery, evil, crime, outrage, offence, abomination, enormity.
3 *the men scowled and muttered obscenities*: **curse**, oath, swear word, expletive, profanity, four-letter word, dirty word, blasphemy, imprecation, malediction, vulgarism, vulgarity; swearing, bad/foul language, strong language; informal cuss, cuss word.

obscure adjective **1** *he was born about 1650 though his origins and parentage remain obscure*: **unclear**, uncertain, unknown, in doubt, doubtful, dubious, mysterious, hazy, vague, indeterminate, concealed, hidden.
2 *obscure references to Proust*: **abstruse**, recondite, arcane, esoteric, recherché, occult; enigmatic, mystifying, puzzling, perplexing, baffling, ambiguous, cryptic, equivocal, Delphic, oracular, riddling, oblique, opaque, elliptical, unintelligible, uninterpretable, incomprehensible, impenetrable, unfathomable, inexplicable; unexplained; informal as clear as mud.
▷**ANTONYMS** clear, plain.
3 *an obscure Peruvian painter*: **little known**, unknown, unheard of, undistinguished, insignificant, unimportant, inconsequential, inconspicuous, unnoticed, nameless, anonymous, minor, humble, lowly, unrenowned, unsung, unrecognized, unhonoured, inglorious, forgotten.
▷**ANTONYMS** famous, renowned.
4 *grey and obscure on the horizon rose a low island | the far end of the room was obscure*: **indistinct**, faint, vague, ill-defined, unclear, blurred, blurry, misty, hazy, foggy, veiled, cloudy, clouded, nebulous, fuzzy; dark, dim, unlit, black, murky, sombre, gloomy, shady, shadowy; literary dusky, tenebrous, darkling, crepuscular; rare caliginous, Cimmerian.
▷**ANTONYMS** distinct.
▶verb **1** *grey clouds obscured the sun*: **hide**, conceal, cover, veil, shroud, screen, mask, cloak, cast a shadow over, shadow, envelop, mantle, block, block out, blank out, obliterate, eclipse, overshadow; literary enshroud, bedim, benight; rare obnubilate, adumbrate.
▷**ANTONYMS** reveal.
2 *recent events have obscured rather than illuminated the issue*: **confuse**, complicate, obfuscate, cloud, blur, muddy; muddy the waters; literary becloud, befog.
▷**ANTONYMS** clarify, illuminate.

obscurity noun **1** *he brought the club back to the big time after years of obscurity*: **insignificance**, inconspicuousness, unimportance, anonymity, lack of fame/renown/honour/recognition, non-recognition, ingloriousness, limbo, twilight, oblivion.
▷**ANTONYMS** fame.
2 *poems of impenetrable obscurity*: **incomprehensibility**, impenetrability, unintelligibility, obscureness, complexity, intricacy, opacity, opaqueness, unclearness; abstruseness, reconditeness, arcaneness, deepness, esotericism.
▷**ANTONYMS** clarity.
3 *the obscurities in his poems and plays*: **enigma**, puzzle, mystery, difficulty, problem, complication, intricacy, ambiguity; crux.
4 *the brightness of the light on stage left the recesses of the wings in obscurity*: **darkness**, blackness, dimness, gloom, gloominess, murk, murkiness, shadow, shadowiness; rare tenebrosity.

obsequies plural noun **funeral rites**, funeral service, funeral, burial ceremony/service, burial; interment, entombment, inhumation, last offices; formal exequies; archaic sepulture.

obsequious adjective *an obsequious manservant welcomed them*: **servile**, ingratiating, unctuous, sycophantic, fawning, toadying, oily, oleaginous, greasy, grovelling, cringing, toadyish, sycophantish, subservient, submissive, slavish, abject, Uriah Heepish; informal slimy, bootlicking, smarmy, sucky, soapy; N. Amer. informal brown-nosing; Brit. vulgar slang arse-licking, bum-sucking; N. Amer. vulgar slang kiss-ass, ass-kissing.
▷**ANTONYMS** domineering.

observable adjective *this kind of behaviour is readily observable in all wild and domestic creatures*: **noticeable**, visible, perceptible, perceivable, detectable, discernible, recognizable, obvious, evident, manifest, patent, clear, distinct, plain, overt, conspicuous, palpable, distinguishable, unmistakable, unconcealed, apparent; archaic sensible.
▷**ANTONYMS** hidden.

observance noun **1** *strict **observance of** the rules*: **compliance with**, adherence to, conformity to, obedience to, acquiescence in, accordance with, respect for; keeping, obeying, observation, fulfilment of, following, performance, honouring, heeding; archaic abidance by.
▷**ANTONYMS** disregard.
2 *religious observances*: **rite**, ritual, ceremony, ceremonial, celebration, practice, service, office, festival, tradition, custom, convention, usage, habit, formality, form; formal praxis.
3 *her baby's motionless observance of me*: **scrutiny**, observation, examination, inspection, watching, viewing, eyeing, looking.

observant adjective **1** *lifeguards should be observant and stop risky situations before they start*: **alert**, sharp-eyed, sharp, eagle-eyed, hawk-eyed, with eyes like a hawk, keen-eyed, watchful, on the lookout, on the qui vive, on guard, attentive, vigilant, with one's eyes open/peeled/skinned, awake, heedful, mindful, aware; informal beady-eyed, not missing a trick, on the ball; rare regardful.
▷**ANTONYMS** inattentive, dreamy.
2 *an observant Jew*: **practising**, obedient, dutiful, conformist, conforming; committed, devout, orthodox, law-abiding.

observation noun **1** *she was brought into hospital for observation | detailed observation of the animal's behaviour*: **watching, monitoring**, scrutiny, examination, inspection, scrutinization, viewing, survey, surveillance, surveying, attention, consideration, study, review.
2 *his observations were concise and to the point | record all your observations carefully*: **remark**, comment, statement, utterance, pronouncement, declaration; **opinion**, impression, thought, feeling, reflection; finding, result; note, annotation; Law obiter dictum.
3 *the **observation of** the law*: **observance**, adherence to, compliance with, keeping, conformity to, obeying, heeding, obedience to, fulfilment of, following, honouring, accordance with, respect for, acquiescence in; archaic abidance by.

observe verb **1** *she observed that almost all the chairs were occupied*: **notice**, see, note, perceive, discern, remark, spot, detect, discover, distinguish, make out; literary espy, descry, behold.
▷**ANTONYMS** overlook, fail to see.
2 *Rob stood in the hall, from where he could observe the happenings on the street*: **watch**, see, look at, eye, contemplate, view, survey, regard, witness, keep an eye on, scrutinize, keep under observation, keep watch on, keep under surveillance, monitor, keep under scrutiny, watch like a hawk, keep a weather eye on, spy on, check out, reconnoitre; informal get a load of, keep tabs on, keep a tab on, case, keep a beady eye on; Brit. informal clock, take a dekko/butcher's/gander/shufti at, recce; N. Amer. informal eyeball; archaic twig; rare surveil.
3 *'You look tired,' she observed*: **comment**, remark, say, mention, note, declare, announce, state, utter, pronounce, interpose, interject; formal opine.
4 *the European Council called on the parties involved to observe the ceasefire*: **comply with**, abide by, keep, obey, adhere to, conform to, heed, honour, respect, be heedful of, pay attention to, follow, acquiesce in, consent to, accept, defer to, fulfil, stand by.
▷**ANTONYMS** disregard, ignore, break.
5 *relations gathered to observe the funeral rites*: **participate in**, partake in, be present at, celebrate, keep; commemorate, solemnize, mark, memorialize, remember, recognize.

observer noun **spectator**, onlooker, watcher, looker-on, fly on the wall, viewer, witness, eyewitness, bystander, sightseer; commentator, reporter, blogger, monitor; informal rubberneck; literary beholder.
▷ANTONYMS participant.

obsess verb *thoughts of his own mortality obsessed him*: **preoccupy**, be uppermost in someone's mind, prey on someone's mind, prey on, possess, haunt, consume, plague, torment, hound, bedevil, take control of, take over, become an obsession with, have a hold on, engross, eat up, have a grip on, grip, dominate, rule, control, beset, monopolize.
□ **be obsessed** *she's* ***obsessed with*** *him | he became* ***obsessed by*** *the urge to avenge his friend*: **be fixated**, be preoccupied, be infatuated, be possessed, be haunted, be consumed, be plagued, be tormented, be bedevilled, be eaten up, be gripped, be in the grip of, be dominated, be beset; informal be hung up about/on, have a thing about, have something/someone on the brain, have a bee in one's bonnet; N. Amer. informal be hipped.

obsession noun *the idea grew in his mind until it became an obsession*: **fixation**, ruling/consuming passion, passion, mania, idée fixe, compulsion, preoccupation, enthusiasm, infatuation, addiction, fetish, craze, hobby horse; phobia, complex, neurosis; informal bee in one's bonnet, hang-up, thing, bug.

obsessive adjective *reckless and obsessive love | an obsessive gambler*: **all-consuming**, consuming, compulsive, dominating, controlling, obsessional, addictive, fanatical, fanatic, neurotic, excessive, besetting, gripping, haunting, tormenting, inescapable; informal pathological.

obsolescent adjective *industries regarded by policy makers as obsolescent*: **dying out**, becoming obsolete, going out of use, going out of fashion, on the decline, declining, waning, on the wane, disappearing, past its prime, ageing, moribund, on its last legs, out of date, outdated, old-fashioned, outmoded; informal on the way out, past it.

obsolete adjective *this remarkable aircraft will render all other fighters obsolete*: **out of date**, outdated, outmoded, old-fashioned; **no longer in use**, disused, fallen into disuse, superannuated, outworn, antiquated, antediluvian, anachronistic, discarded, discontinued, old, dated, antique, archaic, ancient, fossilized, extinct, defunct, dead, bygone, out of fashion, out, behind the times; French démodé, passé, vieux jeu; informal old hat, out of the ark, geriatric, prehistoric; Brit. informal past its sell-by date.
▷ANTONYMS contemporary, current, modern, new, up to date.

obstacle noun *lack of childcare provision was cited as a major obstacle for women who wish to participate in training initiatives*: **barrier**, hurdle, stumbling block, bar, block, impediment, hindrance, snag, catch, drawback, hitch, handicap, deterrent, complication, difficulty, problem, disadvantage, baulk, curb, check, stop, interference; obstruction, barricade, blockade; informal fly in the ointment, hiccup, facer; Brit. informal spanner in the works; N. Amer. informal monkey wrench in the works; dated cumber; literary trammel.
▷ANTONYMS advantage, asset, aid.

O

obstinacy noun *Urquhart was irritated by her obstinacy*: **stubbornness**, inflexibility, intransigence, intractability, intractableness, obduracy, mulishness, pig-headedness, bull-headedness, wilfulness, self-will, strong-mindedness, contrariness, perversity, perverseness, uncooperativeness, recalcitrance, refractoriness, unmanageableness, stiffness, rigidity, steeliness, implacability, relentlessness, immovability, persistence, persistency, tenacity, tenaciousness, doggedness, pertinacity, pertinaciousness, single-mindedness, firmness, steadfastness, determination; Brit. informal bloody-mindedness, bolshiness, stroppiness; archaic frowardness, contumaciousness, contumacy; rare induracy.

obstinate adjective *I don't think you'll succeed in changing his mind—he's very obstinate*: **stubborn**, headstrong, wilful, unyielding, inflexible, unbending, intransigent, intractable, obdurate, mulish, stubborn as a mule, pig-headed, bull-headed, self-willed, strong-minded, strong-willed, contrary, perverse, recalcitrant, refractory, uncooperative, unmanageable, cross-grained, stiff-necked, stiff, rigid, steely, iron-willed, uncompromising, implacable, relentless, unrelenting, unpersuadable, immovable, unmalleable, unshakeable, inexorable, with one's toes/feet dug in, persistent, persevering, tenacious, pertinacious, dogged, single-minded, adamant, firm, steadfast, determined; Brit. informal bloody-minded, bolshie, stroppy; N. Amer. informal balky; archaic froward, contumacious; rare contrarious, indurate.
▷ANTONYMS compliant, amenable, tractable.

Choose the right word **obstinate, stubborn, headstrong, wilful**

These words express a more or less exasperated reaction to someone's determination to have their own way in the face of persuasion or pressure to the contrary.

Someone who is **obstinate** resolutely refuses to heed others (*he sensed obstinate refusal rather than a willingness to bargain*) or, occasionally, their own self-interest (*she went to the stake for an obstinate adherence to her views*).

Someone who is **stubborn** is even more obstinate than someone who is *obstinate*. *Stubborn* can imply deliberate or irrational obstructiveness, rather than a mere refusal to comply with persuasion (*you're not in a fit state to drive, but I assumed you'd be stubborn about it*), or it can refer to an obstinacy that has nothing to do with volition (*he tried to make a stubborn mule climb the gangway*). *Stubbornness* can be seen as a good quality, however, or at least as doing no harm to anyone else (*I am quite ill nowadays, but just too stubborn to give up the thrill of the rallies!*).

Whereas *obstinate* and *stubborn* imply refusal to act in accordance with the wishes of others, **headstrong** says little about others but concentrates, sometimes with grudging admiration, on the determination of the person being described, who may not be actually flouting anyone's wishes but is simply ignoring or even completely unaware of them. It is typically used of girls or young women (*how did one stop a person like Harriet, headstrong, independent, beholden to no one?*).

Someone described as **wilful** is being condemned, often as immature, for their determination to do what they want regardless of its effects, especially on others (*she was wilful, determined, exciting, and manipulative*).

obstreperous adjective *obstreperous customers who have had a drop too much to drink*. See **unruly**.

obstruct verb **1** *wheelchairs obstructed the aisles | ensure that air bricks and vents are not obstructed*: **block**, block up, clog, clog up, get/stand in the way of, cut off, shut off, jam, bung up, gum up, choke, barricade, bar, dam up; Brit. informal gunge up; dated cumber; technical occlude, obturate.
▷ANTONYMS clear.
2 *police took him into custody on a charge of obstructing the traffic*: **hold up**, bring to a standstill, stop, halt, block.
3 *environmentalists accused the government of obstructing the passage of the EC pollution laws*: **impede**, hinder, interfere with, hamper, block, interrupt, hold up, hold back, stand in the way of, frustrate, thwart, baulk, inhibit, hamstring, sabotage, encumber, slow, slow down, retard, delay, stonewall, forestall, stall, arrest, check, stop, halt, stay, derail, restrict, limit, curb, put a brake on, bridle, fetter, shackle; informal stymie; N. Amer. informal bork; rare trammel.
▷ANTONYMS facilitate, help, further.

Choose the right word **obstruct, hinder, hamper, impede**

See **hinder**.

obstruction noun *the issue was the major obstruction to progress on the peace process*: **obstacle**, barrier, stumbling block, hurdle, bar, block, impediment, hindrance, snag, difficulty, catch, drawback, hitch, handicap, deterrent, curb, check, stop, baulk, restriction; blockage, stoppage, congestion, bottleneck, hold-up; Medicine occlusion; informal fly in the ointment; Brit. informal spanner in the works; N. Amer. informal monkey wrench in the works; dated cumber.

obstructive adjective *you're being deliberately obstructive!* **making difficulties, unhelpful**, uncooperative, awkward, difficult, unaccommodating, disobliging, unconstructive, perverse, contrary; Scottish thrawn; Brit. informal bloody-minded, bolshie; N. Amer. informal balky; archaic froward, contrarious.
▷ANTONYMS helpful, supportive, cooperative.

obtain verb **1** *the newspaper obtained a copy of the letter*: **get**, acquire, come by, secure, procure, come into possession of, pick up, be given; gain, derive, earn, achieve, attain, win, draw, reap; buy, purchase; informal get/lay hold of, get/lay one's hands on, get one's mitts on, grab, bag, land, net; Brit. informal blag; S. African informal schlenter.
▷ANTONYMS lose, relinquish.
2 *the rules obtaining in other jurisdictions*: **prevail**, be in force, apply, exist, be in use, be established, be customary, be effective, be prevalent, stand, hold, be the case.

obtainable adjective *frozen food is acceptable if fresh vegetables or meat are not obtainable*: **available**, to be had, in circulation, on the market, on offer, in season, at one's disposal, at hand, gettable, procurable, securable, acquirable, realizable, accessible, achievable, attainable, ready; informal up for grabs, on a plate, on tap, get-at-able.

obtrusive adjective *the proposed quarry would be very obtrusive*: **conspicuous**, prominent, noticeable, obvious, pronounced, unmistakable, inescapable; out of place, intrusive; thrusting, protruding, protuberant, sticking out; bold, loud, showy, garish, gaudy, lurid, flashy; informal standing/sticking out a mile, standing/sticking out like a sore thumb.
▷ANTONYMS unobtrusive, inconspicuous.

obtuse adjective *I wondered if he was too obtuse to pick up what I was driving at*. See **stupid** (sense 1).

obviate verb *the settlement obviated the need for the separate cases to be heard in court*: **preclude**, prevent, remove, get rid of, do away with, get round, rule out, eliminate, make unnecessary, take away, foreclose, avoid, avert, counter.

obvious adjective *the reason was blindingly obvious | it's obvious that Bob's keen on her*: **clear**, plain, plain to see, crystal clear, evident, apparent, manifest, patent, conspicuous, pronounced, transparent, clear-cut, palpable, prominent, marked, decided, salient, striking, distinct, bold,

noticeable, perceptible, perceivable, visible, discernible, detectable, observable, tangible, recognizable; unmistakable, indisputable, self-evident, incontrovertible, incontestable, axiomatic, demonstrable, undeniable, as plain as a pikestaff, staring someone in the face, writ large, beyond doubt, beyond question, written all over one, as clear as day, blinding, inescapable; overt, open, undisguised, unconcealed, frank, glaring, blatant, flagrant; informal as plain as the nose on one's face, standing/sticking out like a sore thumb, standing/sticking out a mile, right under one's nose.
▷ANTONYMS imperceptible, inconspicuous, obscure.

obviously adverb *obviously, she didn't want to see you | he was obviously in great pain*: **clearly**, evidently, plainly, patently, visibly, discernibly, manifestly, noticeably; unmistakably, undeniably, indubitably, incontrovertibly, demonstrably, unquestionably, undoubtedly, without doubt; of course, naturally, needless to say, it goes without saying, doubtless.
▷ANTONYMS perhaps.

occasion noun **1** *she consulted him on a number of occasions*: **instance**, time, moment, juncture, point; event, happening, occurrence, affair, incident, episode, experience, situation, case, circumstance.
2 *the perfect venue for a special occasion | family occasions such as weddings*: **social event**, event, affair, function, celebration, party, ceremony, get-together, gathering; informal do, bash; Brit. informal rave-up, thrash, knees-up, jolly, beanfeast, bunfight, beano, lig.
3 *I doubt if the occasion will arise*: **opportunity**, suitable/opportune time, right moment, chance, opening, window.
4 *it's the first time I've had occasion to complain*: **reason**, cause, call, grounds, justification, need, necessity, requirement, excuse, pretext, stimulus, inducement, provocation, motive.
▶ verb *her situation occasioned a good deal of sympathy*: **cause**, give rise to, bring about, result in, lead to, prompt, provoke, evoke, elicit, call forth, produce, create, arouse, make (for), generate, engender, originate, effect, bring on, induce, precipitate, stir up, inspire, spark off, trigger, breed; literary beget; rare effectuate.
□ **on occasion** See **occasionally**.

occasional adjective *there was very little chance of her returning to the village, except for occasional visits*: **infrequent**, intermittent, irregular, periodic, sporadic, odd, random, casual, desultory, incidental, uncommon, episodic, few and far between, fitful, spasmodic, isolated, rare; N. Amer. sometime; dated seldom.
▷ANTONYMS regular, frequent.

occasionally adverb *he's got a flat in London now, though he still comes home occasionally*: **sometimes**, from time to time, (every) now and then, (every) now and again, at times, every so often, (every) once in a while, on occasion, on occasions, on the odd occasion, periodically, at intervals, irregularly, sporadically, spasmodically, infrequently, intermittently, on and off, off and on; archaic ever and anon.
▷ANTONYMS often, frequently.

occlude verb *thick make-up can occlude the pores*. See **block** (sense 1 of the verb).

occlusion noun *the occlusion of a major coronary artery*. See **blockage**.

occult noun **(the occult)** *his sister was a spiritualist with a strong interest in the occult*: **the supernatural**, the paranormal, supernaturalism, magic, black magic, witchcraft, sorcery, necromancy, wizardry, the black arts, Kabbalah, cabbalism, occultism, diabolism, devil worship, devilry, voodoo, hoodoo, white magic, witchery, witching, orenda, mysticism; NZ makutu; rare theurgy.
▶ adjective *occult powers | an occult ceremony*: **supernatural**, magic, magical, mystical, mystic, paranormal, psychic, necromantic, preternatural, transcendental; secret, hidden, dark, concealed, veiled, invisible, obscure, recondite, cryptic, arcane, abstruse, esoteric, cabbalistic; inexplicable, unexplainable, unfathomable, incomprehensible, impenetrable, unrevealed, puzzling, perplexing, mystifying, mysterious, enigmatic, hermetic.

occupancy noun *rents paid by individuals are directly related to their occupancy of council houses*: **occupation**, tenancy, tenure, residence, residency, inhabitation, habitation, lease, possession, holding, owner-occupancy, multi-occupancy, use, term; formal dwelling; rare inhabitancy, habitancy, inhabitance, domiciliation.

occupant noun **resident**, inhabitant, owner, householder, tenant, renter, leaseholder, lessee, lodger, boarder, inmate, user; addressee; incumbent, holder; Brit. occupier, owner-occupier; N. Amer. roomer; formal dweller; humorous denizen; rare indweller.

occupation noun **1** *his father's name and occupation are unknown*: **job**, profession, work, line of work, line of business, trade, employment, position, post, situation, business, career, métier, vocation, calling, craft, skill, field, province, walk of life; Scottish way; informal racket, game; Austral. informal grip; archaic employ.
2 *among her leisure occupations is birdwatching*: **pastime**, activity, leisure activity, hobby, pursuit, interest, entertainment, recreation, diversion, amusement, divertissement; archaic resource.
3 *a property suitable for occupation by older people*: **residence**, residency, habitation, inhabitation, occupancy, tenancy, tenure, lease, living in; possession, use; incumbency, holding; formal dwelling; rare inhabitancy, habitancy, inhabitance, domiciliation.
4 *the Roman occupation of Britain*: **conquest**, capture, invasion, seizure, takeover, annexation, overrunning, subjugation, subjection, appropriation; **colonization**, possession, rule, control, suzerainty.

occupational adjective *the project aims to expand girls' occupational horizons | occupational pensions*: **job-related**, work, professional, vocational, employment, business, career.

occupied adjective **1** *a steady stream of clients kept her occupied until the middle of the afternoon*: **busy**, engaged, working, employed, at work, on the job, hard-pressed, active; absorbed, engrossed, interested, involved, immersed, preoccupied; informal tied up, hard at it, wrapped up, on the go, on the trot; Brit. informal on the hop.
2 *all the tables were occupied*: **in use**, full, engaged, taken, unavailable.
3 *only two of the flats are occupied*: **inhabited**, lived-in, tenanted, settled.
▷ANTONYMS free, idle, vacant, empty.

> *Choose the right word* **occupied, busy, engaged, active**
>
> See **busy**.

occupy verb **1** *Carol occupied the basement flat*: **live in**, inhabit, be the tenant of, tenant, lodge in, be established/ensconced in, establish/ensconce oneself in, take up residence in, make one's home in, settle in, move into; people, populate, settle; Scottish & S. African stay in; formal reside in, dwell in.
2 *two long windows occupied almost the whole of the end wall*: **take up**, fill, fill up, cover, extend over, use up, utilize.
3 *he occupies a senior post at the Treasury*: **hold**, be in, fill, have; informal hold down.
4 *I need something to occupy my mind*: **engage**, busy, employ, distract, absorb, engross, preoccupy, hold, hold the attention of, immerse, interest, involve, entertain, divert, amuse, beguile.
5 *Hamburg was occupied by the French in 1812*: **capture**, seize, take possession of, conquer, invade, overrun, take over, colonize, garrison, annex, dominate, subjugate, hold, commandeer, requisition.
▷ANTONYMS leave, abandon, quit.

occur verb **1** *the accident occurred at about 3.30 p.m.* **happen**, take place, come about, transpire, materialize, chance, arise, crop up, turn out, fall, come, fall out, pass off; N. Amer. informal go down; literary come to pass, befall, betide; archaic hap; rare eventuate.
2 *the disease occurs chiefly in tropical climates*: **be found**, be present, exist, be met with, appear, prevail, present itself, show itself, manifest itself, turn up; formal obtain.
3 *an idea occurred to her | didn't it occur to you that I might have made other arrangements?* **enter one's head/mind**, cross one's mind, come to mind, spring to mind, come to one, strike one, hit one, dawn on one, suggest itself, present itself, come into one's consciousness.

occurrence noun **1** *vandalism used to be a rare occurrence*: **event**, incident, happening, phenomenon, affair, matter, experience, circumstance, development, contingency, eventuality.
2 *the occurrence of cancer increases with age*: **existence**, instance, appearance, manifestation, materialization, development, springing up; frequency, incidence, rate, prevalence; Statistics distribution.

ocean noun **1 (the) sea**; informal the drink; Brit. informal the briny; N. Amer. informal salt chuck; literary the deep, the waves, the main, the foam, the profound; NZ moana.
2 *she had oceans of energy*: **a lot**, a great/large amount, a great/good deal, plenty, quantities, an abundance, a profusion; informal lots, loads, heaps, bags, masses, stacks, oodles, tons, scads; Brit. informal lashings, a shedload; N. Amer. informal gobs; Austral./NZ informal a swag; vulgar slang a shitload.

> *Word links* **ocean**
>
> **oceanic, marine, maritime, pelagic, thalassic** relating to the ocean

odd adjective **1** *the neighbours thought him very odd*: **strange**, peculiar, weird, queer, funny, bizarre, eccentric, unusual, abnormal, idiosyncratic, unconventional, outlandish, offbeat, freakish, quirky, quaint, zany, off-centre; informal wacky, freaky, kooky, screwy, kinky, oddball, cranky; N. Amer. informal off the wall, wacko, bizarro; Austral./NZ informal, dated dilly.
▷ANTONYMS normal, conventional.
2 *quite a few odd things had happened in the last two days*: **strange**, unusual, peculiar, funny, curious, bizarre, weird, uncanny, queer, unexpected, unfamiliar, abnormal, atypical, anomalous, untypical, different, out of the ordinary, out of the way, foreign, exceptional, rare, extraordinary, remarkable, puzzling, mystifying, mysterious, perplexing, baffling, unaccountable, incongruous, uncommon, irregular, singular, deviant, aberrant, freak, freakish; suspicious, dubious, questionable; eerie, unnatural; Scottish unco; French outré; informal fishy, creepy, spooky; Brit. informal rum.
▷ANTONYMS ordinary, usual.

O

3 *odd numbers*: **uneven**, not divisible by two.
4 *we have the odd drink together | he does odd jobs for friends*: **occasional**, casual, irregular, isolated, incidental, random, sporadic, seasonal, periodic, part-time; miscellaneous, various, varied, sundry.
▷ANTONYMS regular.
5 *when you've got an odd five minutes, could I have a word*: **spare**, unoccupied, free, not committed, available; between engagements, between appointments.
6 *he's wearing odd shoes*: **mismatched**, unmatched, unpaired; single, lone, solitary, extra, surplus, leftover, remaining, unused; Scottish orra.
□ **odd man out outsider**, exception, oddity, nonconformist, maverick, individualist, misfit, eccentric, fish out of water, square peg in a round hole, round peg in a square hole; informal freak.

> *Choose the right word* **odd, strange, curious, peculiar**
>
> See **strange**.

oddity noun **1** *she was regarded as a bit of an oddity*: **eccentric**, crank, misfit, fish out of water, square peg in a round hole, round peg in a square hole, maverick, nonconformist, original, rare bird; Latin rara avis; informal character, odd/queer fish, oddball, weirdo, weirdie, crackpot, nut, nutter, freak; Brit. informal odd bod, oner; N. Amer. informal screwball, kook, nutso, wacko, wack; informal, dated case.
▷ANTONYMS conformist.
2 *his most influential work remains an oddity in some respects*: **anomaly**, aberration, curiosity, rarity.
3 *he was struck by the oddity of the collection*: **strangeness**, peculiarity, oddness, curiousness, weirdness, bizarreness, abnormality, unusualness, eccentricity, queerness, freakishness, unnaturalness, incongruity, incongruousness, outlandishness, extraordinariness, unconventionality, singularity, individuality, anomalousness; informal wackiness, kookiness.
4 *the oddities of human nature*: **peculiarity**, idiosyncrasy, eccentricity, quirk, irregularity, twist, kink, crotchet, mannerism.

oddments plural noun **1** *oddments of material*: **scraps**, remnants, odds and ends, bits, pieces, bits and pieces, bits and bobs, leftovers, fragments, snippets, offcuts, ends, shreds, slivers, stubs, tail ends; Brit. informal fag ends.
2 *the cellar was full of oddments he couldn't bring himself to part with*: **odds and ends**, bits and pieces, bits and bobs, stuff, paraphernalia, things, miscellanea, bric-a-brac, sundries, knick-knacks, souvenirs, keepsakes, mementoes, lumber, flotsam and jetsam; informal junk; Brit. informal odds and sods, gubbins, clobber; vulgar slang crap, shit; archaic rummage, truck; rare knick-knackery.

odds plural noun **1** *the odds are that he is no longer alive*: **likelihood**, probability, chances, chance, balance.
2 *the odds are in our favour*: **advantage**, lead, edge, superiority, supremacy, ascendancy.
□ **at odds 1** *he found himself at odds with his colleagues*: **in conflict**, in disagreement, on bad terms, at cross purposes, at loggerheads, quarrelling, arguing, clashing, at daggers drawn, at each other's throats, at outs, estranged; N. Amer. on the outs. **2** *his behaviour is at odds with the interests of the company*: **at variance**, not in keeping, out of keeping, out of line, out of step, in opposition, conflicting, clashing, disagreeing, differing, contrary, incompatible, contradictory, inconsistent, irreconcilable, incongruous, discrepant.
□ **odds and ends bits and pieces**, bits and bobs, bits, pieces, stuff, paraphernalia, things; **sundries**, miscellanea, bric-a-brac, knick-knacks, oddments, fragments, remnants, scraps, offcuts, cuttings, snippets, leftovers, leavings, remains, flotsam and jetsam, debris, detritus, rubbish, litter; informal junk; Brit. informal odds and sods, clobber, gubbins; vulgar slang shit, crap; archaic rummage, truck; rare knick-knackery.

odious adjective *the odious methods they had used to suppress dissent*: **revolting**, repulsive, repellent, repugnant, disgusting, offensive, objectionable, vile, foul, abhorrent, loathsome, nauseating, nauseous, sickening, hateful, detestable, execrable, abominable, monstrous, appalling, reprehensible, deplorable, insufferable, intolerable, unacceptable, despicable, contemptible, beyond the pale, unspeakable, poisonous, noxious, obscene, base, hideous, grisly, gruesome, horrendous, heinous, atrocious, awful, terrible, dreadful, frightful, obnoxious, unsavoury, unpalatable, unpleasant, disagreeable, nasty, distasteful, dislikeable, off-putting, displeasing; informal ghastly, horrible, horrid, gross, putrid, sick-making, yucky, God-awful; Brit. informal beastly; N. Amer. informal skanky; literary noisome; archaic disgustful, scurvy, loathly.
▷ANTONYMS delightful, pleasant, agreeable, charming.

odium noun *his job had made him the target of public hostility and odium*: **disgust**, abhorrence, repugnance, revulsion, repulsion, loathing, detestation, hatred, hate, execration, obloquy, dislike, disapproval, disapprobation, distaste, disfavour, aversion, antipathy, animosity, animus, enmity, hostility, contempt, censure, condemnation; disgrace, shame, opprobrium, discredit, dishonour, disrepute, ill repute, infamy, notoriety, ignominy, stigma, loss of face, humiliation, unpopularity; rare disesteem, reprobation.
▷ANTONYMS approval, delight.

odorous adjective **1** *odorous fumes*: **foul-smelling**, evil-smelling, smelly, stinking, reeking, reeky, malodorous, pungent, acrid, fetid, rank; informal stinky; Brit. informal **pongy**, **whiffy**, **niffy**, **niffing**; N. Amer. informal **funky**; literary noisome, mephitic; rare olid, odoriferous, miasmal, miasmic.
2 *an odorous cloud of damp talcum powder*: **fragrant**, scented, perfumed, aromatic, balmy, tangy, redolent.

odour noun **1** *a delicious odour of coffee | the odour of sweat*: **smell**, scent, aroma, perfume, fragrance, bouquet, savour, nose, tang, essence, redolence; stench, stink, reek, fetor, malodour, miasma; Brit. informal pong, whiff, niff, hum; Scottish informal **guff**; N. Amer. informal **funk**; rare **mephitis**.
2 *an odour of suspicion*: **atmosphere**, air, aura, quality, spirit, flavour, savour, emanation, hint, suggestion, impression, whiff, ambience, tone.

> *Word links* **odour**
>
> **osmic**, **olfactory** relating to odour
> **odorimetry** measurement of intensity of odour

odourless adjective *a clear, odourless gel*: **unscented**, unperfumed, inodorous, deodorized, fragrance-free.

odyssey noun **journey**, voyage, trek, travels, quest, crusade, pilgrimage, wandering, journeying; rare peregrination.

off adverb **1** *the youths scrambled out of the car and ran off*: **away**, to a distance, from here, from there.
2 *David took a day off*: **away**, absent, out, unavailable, not working, not at work, off duty, on holiday, on leave, free, at leisure, idle; N. Amer. on vacation.
▶ adjective **1** *strawberries are off*: **unavailable**, unobtainable, finished, sold out.
▷ANTONYMS available.
2 *due to a waterlogged pitch, the game was called off*: **cancelled**, postponed, called off, abandoned, shelved.
▷ANTONYMS on.
3 *the fish/milk is off*: **rotten**, bad, stale, mouldy, high, sour, rancid, turned, spoiled, putrid, putrescent.
▷ANTONYMS fresh.
4 Brit. *I felt decidedly off*. See **off colour**.
5 informal *his boss deducted the money from his pay, which was a bit off*: **unfair**, unjust, uncalled for, below the belt, unacceptable, unjustified, unjustifiable, unreasonable, unsatisfactory, unwarranted, unnecessary, inequitable; informal a bit much; Brit. informal out of order, a bit thick; Austral./NZ informal over the fence.
▷ANTONYMS fair, reasonable.
6 informal *he was being really off with me*: **unfriendly**, aloof, cool, cold, distant, chilly, frosty, hostile, frigid, unresponsive, unapproachable, uncommunicative; informal stand-offish, offish.
▷ANTONYMS friendly.
□ **off and on** *the book he has been working at, off and on, for over 20 years*: **periodically**, at intervals, on and off, (every) once in a while, every so often, (every) now and then/again, from time to time, occasionally, on occasion, on occasions, on the odd occasion, at times, sometimes, sporadically, spasmodically, erratically, irregularly, intermittently, in/by fits and starts, fitfully, discontinuously, piecemeal; interruptedly.
▷ANTONYMS regularly.

offbeat adjective *the suggestion was a little offbeat but he agreed to put it to his bosses for consideration*: **unconventional**, unorthodox, unusual, eccentric, outré, idiosyncratic, strange, bizarre, weird, peculiar, odd, freakish, outlandish, out of the ordinary, Bohemian, alternative, left-field, hippy, zany, quirky; avant-garde, novel, innovative; informal wacky, freaky, kinky, way-out, far out, kooky, oddball; N. Amer. informal off the wall, bizarro.
▷ANTONYMS ordinary, conventional, run-of-the-mill.

off colour adjective **1** Brit. *I'm feeling a bit off colour*: **unwell**, ill, poorly, bad, out of sorts, indisposed, not oneself, sick, queasy, nauseous, nauseated, peaky, liverish, green about the gills, run down, washed out; Brit. off; informal under the weather, below par, not up to par, funny, peculiar, rough, lousy, rotten, awful, terrible, dreadful, crummy; Brit. informal grotty, ropy; Scottish informal wabbit, peely-wally; Austral./NZ informal crook; dated seedy.
▷ANTONYMS well, fit.
2 *off-colour jokes*: **smutty**, dirty, rude, filthy, crude, suggestive, indecent, indelicate, indecorous, risqué, racy, bawdy, naughty, spicy, blue, vulgar, ribald, broad, salacious, coarse, obscene, pornographic; informal raunchy; Brit. informal fruity, near the knuckle, saucy; euphemistic adult.

offence noun **1** *he denied having committed any offence*: **crime**, illegal/unlawful act, misdemeanour, breach/violation/infraction of the law, felony, wrongdoing, wrong, act of misconduct, misdeed, delinquency, peccadillo, sin, transgression, infringement, act of dereliction, shortcoming, fault, lapse; Law malfeasance; archaic trespass; rare malefaction.
2 *the outcome is an offence to basic justice*: **affront**, slap in the face, insult, outrage, injury, hurt, injustice, indignity, slight, snub.
3 *I do not want to cause offence*: **annoyance**, anger, resentment, indignation, irritation, exasperation, wrath, displeasure, disapproval, dislike, hard/bad/ill feelings, disgruntlement, animosity, pique, vexation,

O

umbrage, antipathy, aversion, opposition, enmity; literary ire.
4 *strategic offence arsenals*: **attack**, offensive, assault, act of aggression, aggression, onslaught, thrust, charge, sortie, sally, invasion, incursion, foray.
□ **take offence** *he went out, making it clear he'd taken offence*: **be/feel offended**, take exception, take something personally, be/feel aggrieved, be/feel affronted, take something amiss, take umbrage, get/be/feel upset, get/be/feel annoyed, get/be/feel angry, be/feel indignant, be/feel put out, be/feel insulted, be/feel hurt, be/feel wounded, feel piqued, be/feel resentful, be/feel disgruntled, get/go into a huff, get huffy; informal be/feel miffed, have one's nose put out of joint, be/feel riled; Brit. informal get the hump.

offend verb **1** *I'm sorry if anything I said offended him*: **hurt someone's feelings**, give offence to, affront, upset, displease, distress, hurt, wound, pain, injure, be an affront to, get/put someone's back up, disgruntle, put out, annoy, anger, exasperate, irritate, vex, pique, gall, irk, provoke, rankle with, nettle, needle, peeve, tread on someone's toes, ruffle, ruffle someone's feathers, rub up the wrong way, make someone's hackles rise, insult, humiliate, embarrass, mortify, scandalize, shock, outrage, spite; informal rile, miff, rattle, aggravate, put someone's nose out of joint, get up someone's nose, get under someone's skin, hack off, get someone's goat, get to, bug; Brit. informal nark, get on someone's wick; N. Amer. informal tick off; vulgar slang piss off.
2 *he didn't smoke and the smell of ash offended him*: **displease**, be displeasing to, be distasteful to, be disagreeable to, be offensive to, cause offence to, upset, put off, disgust, repel, revolt, be repugnant to, repulse, turn someone's stomach, sicken, nauseate, make sick, make someone's gorge rise; informal turn off; N. Amer. informal gross out.
▷ANTONYMS please, delight.
3 *a small hard core of criminals who offend again and again*: **break the law**, commit a crime, do wrong, sin, go astray, fall from grace, err, transgress; archaic trespass.

offended adjective *she was so offended she asked him to leave at once*: **upset**, hurt, wounded, injured, insulted, aggrieved, affronted, pained, displeased, distressed, disgruntled, put out, annoyed, angered, angry, cross, exasperated, indignant, irritated, vexed, piqued, irked, stung, galled, nettled, needled, peeved, ruffled, resentful, in a huff, huffy, in high dudgeon, fed up; W. Indian vex; informal riled, miffed, miffy, rattled, aggravated, peed off, hacked off; Brit. informal narked, eggy, cheesed off, browned off, brassed off; N. Amer. informal sore, teed off, ticked off; vulgar slang pissed off; archaic snuffy.
▷ANTONYMS pleased.

offender noun *one of his main concerns was the problem of persistent offenders*: **wrongdoer**, **criminal**, lawbreaker, malefactor, felon, delinquent, culprit, guilty party, sinner, transgressor, evil-doer, reprobate, outlaw; juvenile delinquent, young offender; informal crook; Austral. informal crim; Law malfeasant, misfeasor; archaic miscreant, trespasser.

offensive adjective **1** *he described the remarks as deeply offensive*: **insulting**, rude, derogatory, disrespectful, hurtful, wounding, abusive, objectionable, displeasing, annoying, exasperating, irritating, vexing, galling, provocative, provoking, humiliating, impertinent, impudent, insolent, personal, discourteous, uncivil, impolite, unmannerly, unacceptable, shocking, scandalous, outrageous; crude, vulgar, coarse, indecent, improper; rare exceptionable.
▷ANTONYMS complimentary, polite.
2 *an offensive smell*: **unpleasant**, disagreeable, nasty, distasteful, displeasing, objectionable, off-putting, uninviting, awful, terrible, dreadful, frightful, obnoxious, abominable, disgusting, repulsive, repellent, repugnant, revolting, abhorrent, loathsome, hateful, detestable, execrable, odious, vile, foul, unsavoury, unpalatable, sickening, nauseating, nauseous, ugly, unsightly; noxious, fetid, rank, rancid, malodorous, mephitic; informal ghastly, horrible, horrid, gross, putrid, sick-making, yucky, God-awful; Brit. informal beastly; Austral. informal on the nose; N. Amer. informal skanky; literary noisome; archaic disgustful, loathly.
▷ANTONYMS pleasant, delightful.
3 *an offensive air action against another country*: **hostile**, **attacking**, aggressive, invading, incursive, combative, threatening, martial, warlike, belligerent, bellicose, antagonistic, on the attack.
▷ANTONYMS defensive.
▸ **noun** *a military offensive against the guerrillas*: **attack**, assault, onslaught, drive, invasion, push, thrust, charge, sortie, sally, foray, raid, offence, act of war, act of aggression, incursion, blitz, campaign.
□ **take the offensive** *security forces took the offensive ten days ago*: **begin to attack**, attack first, be aggressive, strike the first blow, start a war/battle/quarrel; informal be on the warpath.

> *Choose the right word* **offensive, derogatory, insulting**
>
> These words all describe remarks or behaviour that cause offence or distress, unconsciously or intentionally.
>
> **Offensive** remarks or behaviour make someone hurt, upset, or angry, whether or not the speaker realizes or intends this (*the wording was unnecessarily offensive | the work is trite and offensive to women*). An *offensive* term for a person, such as someone of a particular ethnic type, may offend others, not just those of that ethnicity.
>
> A **derogatory** comment is deliberately intended to express a low opinion of someone or something (*derogatory racial remarks | I found myself repelled by the use of derogatory nicknames*).
>
> **Insulting** language or behaviour shows a lack of respect (*the Minister's reply is arrogant and insulting | the cartoon is insulting to men*). It is generally, but not necessarily, intended to upset or annoy.

offer verb **1** *the manager is always at hand to offer advice and information*: **provide**, put forward, give, proffer, present, extend, suggest, recommend, propose, propound, advance, submit, tender, render, come up with.
▷ANTONYMS withdraw, refuse, withhold.
2 *a local man offered to help*: **volunteer**, volunteer one's services, be at someone's disposal, be at someone's service, make oneself available, present oneself, step/come forward, show willing.
3 *the product is offered at a very competitive price*: **put up for sale**, put on the market, sell, market, make available, put under the hammer, ask for bids for; Law vend.
4 *he offered $200*: **bid**, tender, put in a bid of, put in an offer of.
5 *a job offering good career prospects*: **provide**, **afford**, supply, give, furnish, present, give an opportunity for, purvey, make available, hold out.
6 *she offered no resistance when he kissed her firmly on the lips*: **attempt**, try, give, show, express; formal essay.
7 *the birds were occasionally offered to the gods*: **sacrifice**, offer up, immolate, give.
8 *he distinguished himself whenever an occasion offered*: **occur**, present itself, arrive, appear, happen, show itself.
▸ **noun 1** *sympathetic offers of help | a job offer*: **proposal**, proposition, suggestion, submission, approach, overture; literary proffer.
2 *the government rejected the highest offer*: **bid**, tender, bidding price.
□ **on offer** **on sale**, up for sale, on the market, purchasable, available, obtainable, to be had; N. Amer. on the block.

offering noun **1** *you may also place offerings in the charity box*: **contribution**, donation, benefaction, gift, present, handout, widow's mite, subscription; charity; historical alms; rare donative.
2 *during this time, many offerings were made to the goddess of the dead*: **sacrifice**, oblation, burnt offering, peace offering, thank-offering, immolation, libation, first fruits, tribute, dedication; Hinduism prasad, puja; Judaism Omer, sin-offering.

offhand adjective *an offhand comment that she regretted almost immediately*: **indifferent**, **casual**, careless, uninterested, unconcerned, cool, distant, aloof, nonchalant, blasé, insouciant, offhanded, cavalier, glib, perfunctory, cursory, unceremonious, ungracious, curt, abrupt, terse, brusque, dismissive, discourteous, uncivil, impolite, rude; impromptu, off-the-cuff, spontaneous, extempore, unpremeditated, extemporaneous, unthinking, unstudied; informal off, offish, couldn't-care-less, take-it-or-leave-it; rare poco-curante.
▸ **adverb** *I can't think of a better answer offhand*: **without preparation**, on the spur of the moment, without consideration, without checking, extempore, impromptu, ad lib; extemporaneously, without rehearsal, spontaneously; Latin ad libitum; informal off the cuff, off the top of one's head, just like that, at the drop of a hat.

office noun **1** *it was only a few minutes' walk to her office in Aldersgate Street*: **place of business**, place of work, workplace, workroom, studio; headquarters, base, centre.
2 *the Paris office of the New York Herald Tribune*: **branch**, division, section, bureau, department; agency.
3 *he assumed the office of President on May 20*: **post**, position, appointment, job, occupation, role, place, situation, station, function, capacity.
4 *the offices of a nurse*: **chore**, duty, job, task, obligation, assignment, service, responsibility, charge, commission; work, employment.
5 (**offices**) *rescued through the good offices of the Italian Ambassador, he was returned safely to England*: **assistance**, help, aid, services, intervention, intercession, mediation, intermediation, agency, support, backing, patronage, aegis, auspices, advocacy.

officer noun **1** *an officer of the county court*: **representative**, agent, deputy, messenger, envoy.
2 *the officers of the society are under considerable pressure*: **committee member**, **official**, office-holder, office-bearer, board member, public servant, administrator, commissioner, executive, functionary, bureaucrat, dignitary; derogatory apparatchik.
3 *all officers carry warrant cards*: **police officer**, policeman, policewoman, PC, WPC, officer of the law, detective, DC; Brit. constable; N. Amer. roundsman, trooper, peace officer, lawman; French gendarme, flic; informal cop, pig, woodentop; Brit. informal copper, busy, bizzy, plod, rozzer, bobby; N. Amer. informal narc, gumshoe, bear, uniform; Austral./NZ informal demon, walloper, John Hop; informal, dated tec, dick, flatfoot, flattie; archaic peeler, bluebottle, finger, bogey, runner.

official adjective **1** *an official inquiry into the state of the hospital | until probate is granted the will is not official*: **authorized**, accredited, approved, validated, authenticated, authentic, certified, endorsed, documented, sanctioned, licensed, formal, recognized, authoritative, accepted, verified, legitimate, legal, lawful, valid, bona fide, proper, true, ex cathedra, {signed, sealed, and delivered}, signed and sealed; informal kosher.
▷ANTONYMS unofficial, unauthorized.
2 *they were arrayed in all their finery for some official function*: **ceremonial**, formal, solemn, ritualistic, ceremonious; pompous, stiff, bureaucratic, proper; informal stuffed-shirt.
▷ANTONYMS informal.
▸ **noun** *a union official*: **officer**, office-holder, office-bearer, administrator, executive, appointee, functionary; bureaucrat, dignitary, mandarin; representative, agent; derogatory apparatchik; Brit. jack-in-office.

Easily confused words **official or officious?**

See **officious.**

officiate verb **1** *Kathy Dyson* ***officiated at*** *the opening ceremony | he officiated in both World Cups*: **preside (over)**, take charge, be in charge (of), be responsible (for), direct, head (up), manage, oversee, superintend, supervise, conduct, run, lead, chair, take the chair; umpire, referee, judge, adjudicate, moderate, mediate; N. Amer. informal emcee.
2 *the Pope* ***officiated at*** *a public mass on October 11*: **conduct**, perform, celebrate, solemnize, concelebrate.

officious adjective *an officious maître d' told him to wait at the bar*: **self-important**, bumptious, self-assertive, overbearing, overzealous, dictatorial, bossy, domineering, interfering, intrusive, meddlesome, meddling, importunate, forward, opinionated; informal pushy; archaic pragmatic, intermeddling; rare obtrusive, busy.
▷ANTONYMS self-effacing.

Easily confused words **officious or official?**

One may well be unfortunate enough to encounter an **officious** person acting in an **official** capacity; but this is a matter of human nature and does not mean that the words have the same meaning. An *officious* person is excessively fond of asserting his or her authority, especially in relation to trivial matters (*the local bureaucrats are an officious lot*). *Official*, on the other hand, means 'relating to the responsibilities and authority of public office' (*his official duties | the Prime Minister's official engagements*) or 'approved or issued by an authority' (*the official unemployment figures*).

offing noun
□ **in the offing** *important changes were in the offing*: **likely to happen**, on the way, coming soon, coming up, (close) at hand, near, imminent, in prospect, on the horizon, in the wings, just around the corner, in the air, in the wind, brewing, upcoming, forthcoming; informal on the cards.

off-key adjective **1** *a slightly off-key rendition of an old family favourite*: **out of tune**, flat, tuneless, unmusical, unmelodic, discordant, dissonant, unharmonious.
▷ANTONYMS in tune.
2 *some of the cinematic effects are distractingly off-key*: **incongruous**, inappropriate, unsuitable, discordant, out of place, out of keeping, jarring, dissonant, inharmonious.
▷ANTONYMS harmonious.

offload verb **1** *the ship offloaded 500 tonnes of coal ash into the North Sea*: **unload, dump**, jettison, discharge, unship, deposit, empty (out), tip (out), drop, get rid of; archaic unlade; rare disburden.
2 *it's expected that the government will offload most of its BT shares*: **dispose of**, dump, jettison, get rid of, transfer, shift; palm off, foist, fob off.

off-putting adjective *a rather off-putting aroma | while not exactly threatening, her manner was off-putting*: **unpleasant**, unappealing, uninviting, unattractive, disagreeable, offensive, distasteful, unsavoury, unpalatable, unappetizing, objectionable, nasty, disgusting, obnoxious, repellent; **discouraging**, disheartening, demoralizing, dispiriting, daunting, dismaying, forbidding, intimidating, frightening, formidable; informal horrid, horrible; rare rebarbative.

offset verb *profits and losses on each investment tend to offset each other*: **counterbalance**, balance, balance out, cancel, cancel out, even out/up, counteract, counterpoise, countervail, equalize, neutralize, nullify, compensate for, make up for, make good, redeem, indemnify; atone for, redress, make amends for, make restitution for; rare equilibrize.

offshoot noun **1** *the cactus grew some offshoots*: **side shoot**, shoot, sucker, tendril, runner, scion, slip, offset, sprout, sprig, stem, twig, branch, bough, limb, spur; technical stolon.
▷ANTONYMS trunk.
2 *an offshoot of Thomas Cromwell's line*: **descendant**, scion, relation, relative.
3 *offshoots of big firms or finance houses*: **subsidiary**, branch, derivative, adjunct, appendage.
4 *one practical offshoot of the growth of interest in heritage is the growth of tourism*: **outcome**, result, effect, consequence, upshot, product, by-product, spin-off, ramification, development, outgrowth.

offspring noun **1** *anxious parents watching over their offspring*: **children**, sons and daughters, progeny, family, youngsters, babies, brood; descendants, heirs, successors, scions; young, litter, fry; Law issue; informal kids, quiverful; derogatory spawn; archaic seed, fruit, fruit of one's loins.
2 *he obviously had great expectations for his latest offspring*: **child**, baby, infant, son, daughter, youngster, little one, tot, tiny tot; descendant, heir, successor; Scottish & N. English bairn, wean; black English pickney; informal kid, kiddie, kiddiewink, nipper, brat, lad, shaver, munchkin, tiny, chick; Brit. informal sprog; S. African informal outjie, lighty; literary babe.

often adverb *he often asked after you*: **frequently**, many times, many a time, on many/numerous occasions, a lot, in many cases/instances, repeatedly, again and again, time and again, time and time again, time after time, over and over, over and over again, {day in, day out}, {week in, week out}, all the time, regularly, recurrently, continually, usually, habitually, commonly, generally, ordinarily, as often as not; N. Amer. oftentimes; informal lots; literary oft, oft-times.
▷ANTONYMS seldom, rarely, never.

ogle verb *he'd been ogling her ever since she'd entered the room*: **leer at**, stare at, gaze at, eye, make eyes at, make sheep's eyes at; informal eye up, give someone the glad eye, give someone a/the once-over, lech after/over, undress with one's eyes, give someone the come-on; Brit. informal gawp at, gawk at; Austral./NZ informal perv on.

ogre noun **1** *an ogre with two heads*: **monster**, giant, troll, bogeyman, bogey, demon, devil; archaic bugbear.
2 *her friends represented Maclean as an ogre*: **brute, fiend**, monster, beast, devil, demon, barbarian, savage, sadist, animal, tyrant, villain, scoundrel; informal bastard, swine, pig; vulgar slang shit; archaic blackguard.

ogress noun **1 monster**, giantess.
2 *the French teacher was a real ogress*: **harridan**, tartar, termagant, shrew, harpy, gorgon, virago; informal battleaxe.

oil noun *make sure the car has enough oil*: **lubricant**, lubrication, grease; fuel, petroleum; N. Amer. informal black gold; N. Amer. & Austral. informal lube.
▸ **verb** *I'll oil that gate for you tomorrow*: **lubricate**, grease; N. Amer. & Austral. informal lube.

Word links **oil**

oleo- related prefix, as in *oleochemical, oleograph*

oily adjective **1** *his dark oily skin | oily substances*: **greasy**, oleaginous; slippery, slimy; technical sebaceous, pinguid, unctuous.
2 *a plateful of oily moussaka*: **greasy**, fatty, buttery, swimming in oil/fat, oleaginous.
3 *an oily man with plump little hands*: **unctuous**, fawning, ingratiating, smooth, smooth-talking, fulsome, flattering, glib, obsequious, sycophantic, soapy, oleaginous, servile, subservient; informal smarmy, slimy, sucky; rare saponaceous.

ointment noun **lotion**, cream, salve, liniment, embrocation, rub, gel, petroleum jelly, balm, emollient, unguent, balsam; pomade, pomatum; calamine lotion, zinc ointment; Medicine demulcent, humectant; trademark Vaseline, Tiger balm; historical spikenard; archaic unction.

OK, okay informal **exclamation** *OK, I'll go with him*: **all right**, right, right then, right you are, very well, yes, very good, fine, agreed; informal oke, okey-dokey, okey-doke, roger; Brit. informal righto, righty-ho; Indian informal acha.
▸ **adjective 1** *the film was OK | is everything OK?* **satisfactory**, all right, fine, in order, acceptable, up to scratch, up to the mark, up to standard, up to par, competent; adequate, tolerable, passable, reasonable, quite good, fair, decent, not bad, average, middling, moderate, unremarkable, unexceptional; informal hunky-dory, so-so, fair-to-middling, (plain) vanilla; Brit. informal, dated tickety-boo; N. Amer. & Austral./NZ informal jake.
▷ANTONYMS unsatisfactory, unacceptable, inadequate.
2 *Jo's feeling OK now*: **fine**, all right, well, in good shape, in good health, fit, healthy, as fit as a fiddle, as fit as a flea, in fine fettle, up to snuff; informal in the pink; Brit. informal as right as a trivet.
▷ANTONYMS ill, unwell.
3 *is it OK for me to come?* **permissible**, allowable, acceptable, all right, in order, permitted, fine, fitting, suitable, appropriate.
▸ **adverb** *'How's the job going?' 'Okay.'*: **all right**, fine, well, well enough, satisfactorily, passably, tolerably, acceptably.
▸ **noun** *he's just given me* ***the OK***: **authorization**, approval, seal of approval, agreement, consent, assent, permission, endorsement, ratification, sanction, approbation, acquiescence, confirmation, blessing, leave, imprimatur; informal the go-ahead, the green light, the thumbs up, say-so.
▷ANTONYMS refusal, denial.
▸ **verb** *the move must be okayed by the president*: **authorize**, approve, agree to, consent to, sanction, pass, ratify, endorse, allow, give something one's consent, say yes to, accede to, give something one's approval, give something the nod, rubber-stamp; informal give something the go-ahead,

give something the green light, give something the thumbs up, give something one's say-so.
▷ANTONYMS refuse, forbid, veto.

old adjective **1** *old people*: **elderly**, mature, aged, older, senior, advanced in years, up in years, getting on; in one's dotage, long in the tooth, grey, grey-haired, grey-bearded, grizzled, hoary; past one's prime, not as young as one was, ancient, decrepit, doddering, doddery, not long for this world, ripe, senescent, senile, superannuated, venerable, septuagenarian, octogenarian, nonagenarian, centenarian; informal past it, over the hill, no spring chicken; rare longevous.
▷ANTONYMS young.
2 *old farm buildings*: **historic**, antiquated; dilapidated, broken-down, run down, tumbledown, ramshackle, decaying, crumbling, disintegrating.
▷ANTONYMS new, modern.
3 *old clothes*: **worn**, worn out, shabby, threadbare, holey, torn, frayed, patched, tattered, moth-eaten, ragged, yellowed; old-fashioned, out of date, outmoded; cast-off, hand-me-down; French démodé; informal tatty.
▷ANTONYMS new, fashionable.
4 *old cars*: **antique**, veteran, vintage.
▷ANTONYMS new, modern.
5 *she is old for her years | he's an old hand*: **mature**, wise, sensible, experienced, worldly-wise, knowledgeable, well versed, familiar, practised, skilled, skilful, adept, expert, veteran.
▷ANTONYMS young, ingenuous, inexperienced.
6 *in the old days*: **bygone**, past, former, olden, of old, remote, previous, early, earlier, earliest; medieval, ancient, classical, primeval, primordial, prehistoric, antediluvian, forgotten, immemorial.
▷ANTONYMS modern, recent.
7 *political worthies spew out the same old phrases*: **hackneyed**, hack, banal, trite, overused, overworked, cut and dried, tired, worn out, time-worn, stale, stereotyped, clichéd, platitudinous, unoriginal, derivative, unimaginative, commonplace, common, pedestrian, prosaic, run-of-the-mill, stock, conventional; out of date, outdated, old-fashioned, outmoded, archaic, obsolete, defunct, extinct, antiquated, antediluvian, superannuated, hoary; French passé; informal old hat, out of the ark, corny, fuddy-duddy, played out.
▷ANTONYMS fresh, innovative, new.
8 *I love the good old tunes*: **time-honoured**, old-time, long-established, age-old, long-standing, long-lived, enduring, lasting; **familiar**, customary, conventional, established, traditional, ritual, ritualistic, habitual, set, fixed, routine, usual, wonted, historic, folk, old-world, ancestral.
9 *an old girlfriend*: **former**, previous, ex-, one-time, sometime, erstwhile, once, then, lapsed; formal quondam.
▷ANTONYMS new.
□ **old age declining years**, advanced years, elderliness, age, agedness, oldness, winter/autumn of one's life, senescence, senility, dotage.
▷ANTONYMS youth, childhood.
□ **old man 1 senior citizen**, pensioner, OAP, elder, elderly man, grandfather; patriarch; Scottish & Irish bodach; informal greybeard, gaffer, old codger, old boy, old chap, old geezer, old bloke, wrinkly; Brit. informal buffer, josser; N. Amer. informal old coot; archaic grandsire, ancient; literary senex.
▷ANTONYMS youth, boy, young man. **2** informal *her old man was away fighting*: **husband**, man; informal hubby, better half; Brit. informal other half; humorous lord and master; archaic lord. **3** informal *the old man's still on the bridge*: **captain**, **owner**, boss, employer, foreman, manager, overseer, superintendent, director, controller, head, headman, principal; informal head honcho; Brit. informal gaffer, guv'nor; N. Amer. informal sachem.
□ **old person senior citizen**, senior, pensioner, old-age pensioner, OAP, elder, old fogey, dotard, Methuselah; N. Amer. golden ager; informal old stager, old-timer, oldie, wrinkly, crock, crumbly; N. Amer. informal oldster, woopie; offensive geriatric.
▷ANTONYMS youngster.
□ **old woman 1 senior citizen**, pensioner, OAP, elderly woman, crone; Russian babushka; informal old dear; archaic beldam, grandam, gammer, mother.
▷ANTONYMS girl, young woman. **2** informal *his old woman threw him out*: **wife**, spouse, bride; informal old lady, wifey, better half, missus, the little woman; Brit. informal other half, her indoors, (old) dutch, trouble and strife; N. Amer. informal mama, mamma; dated lady, memsahib. **3** informal *my old woman took me to all sorts of doctors when I was a kid*: **mother**; Indian amma; informal mum, mummy, ma, mam, mammy, mumsy, old dear, old lady; N. Amer. informal mom, mommy; dated mama, mamma, mater. **4** *he's such an old woman*: **worrier**, **perfectionist**, stickler, grumbler; informal **fusspot**; N. Amer. informal fussbudget.

Word links **old**

gerontic relating to old age
geriatric relating to old people
geriatrics branch of medicine concerning old people
gerontology study of old age
gerontocracy government by old people
senesce deteriorate with old age
archaeo- related prefix, as in *archaeology, archaeopteryx*
palaeo- related prefix, as in *palaeography, Palaeocene*

old-fashioned adjective *a black-and-white photograph of a woman in old-fashioned clothes*: **out of date**, outdated, dated, out, out of fashion, outmoded, unfashionable, last year's, frumpish, frumpy, out of style, outworn, old, old-time, old-world, behind the times, archaic, obsolescent, obsolete, ancient, antiquated, superannuated, defunct; medieval, prehistoric, antediluvian, old-fogeyish, old-fangled, conservative, backward-looking, quaint, anachronistic, crusted, feudal, fusty, moth-eaten, olde worlde; French passé, démodé, vieux jeu; informal old hat, square, not with it, out of the ark, creaky, mouldy; N. Amer. informal horse-and-buggy, clunky, rinky-dink, mossy; archaic square-toed.
▷ANTONYMS modern, up to date, fashionable.

old-time adjective *old-time dancing*: **old style**, former, past, bygone, historic, heritage, antique, antiquarian, early, classical, traditional, folk, old-world, ancestral, time-honoured, ancient, veteran, vintage, quaint.
▷ANTONYMS modern.

old-world, olde worlde adjective *old-world charm | old-world cottages*: **old-fashioned**, old, archaic, traditional, past, bygone, classical; **picturesque**, quaint.

Olympian adjective *Kerr himself preserved an attitude of Olympian detachment*: **aloof**, distant, remote, stand-offish, unfriendly, unamiable, unaffable, uncongenial, unneighbourly, inhospitable, reclusive, solitary, misanthropic, uncommunicative, unforthcoming, reticent, withdrawn, cold, cool, chilly.
▷ANTONYMS affable, friendly, chummy.

omen noun *the ferocious storm began on our wedding day: perhaps it was an omen of things to come*: **portent**, sign, signal, token, forewarning, warning, foreshadowing, prediction, forecast, prophecy, harbinger, augury; straw in the wind, writing on the wall, indication, hint, auspice, presage, threat, ill omen, menace; literary foretoken.

ominous adjective *ominous black clouds gathered on the horizon*: **threatening**, menacing, baleful, forbidding, sinister, doomy, inauspicious, unpropitious, portentous, unfavourable, dire, unpromising; black, dark, wintry, gloomy, ugly; archaic direful; rare minatory, minacious.
▷ANTONYMS promising, auspicious, propitious.

omission noun **1** *there also appear to be some significant omissions from the Commission's report*: **deletion**, cut, exclusion, gap, blank, lacuna, hiatus; oversight.
▷ANTONYMS addition, inclusion.
2 *the omission of the verb gives the sentence immediacy*: **leaving out**, **exclusion**, exception, non-inclusion, deletion, erasure, cut, excision, elimination, absence; Linguistics aphesis, apheresis, apocope, apostrophe, asyndeton, elision, ellipsis, gapping, haplography, haplology, lipography, syncope; rare expunction.
▷ANTONYMS addition, inclusion.
3 *the damage to the goods was not caused by any act or omission by the carrier*: **negligence**, neglect, neglectfulness, dereliction, forgetfulness, oversight, disregard, non-fulfilment, default, lapse, failure; Law nonjoinder; rare delinquency, misprision.
▷ANTONYMS conscientiousness.

omit verb **1** *they omitted his name from the list*: **leave out**, **exclude**, fail to include, except, shut out, leave off, take out, miss out, miss, fail to mention, pass over, drop, delete, cut, erase, eliminate, elide, expunge, rub out, cross out, strike out, dispense with; informal give something a miss; archaic overleap, pretermit.
▷ANTONYMS add, include.
2 *I am sorry I omitted to mention our guest lecturer*: **forget**, neglect, fail; leave undone, overlook, ignore, skip.
▷ANTONYMS remember.

omnipotence noun *traditional doctrines of divine omnipotence*: **all-powerfulness**, almightiness, supremacy, pre-eminence, supreme power, absolute/unlimited power, undisputed sway, divine right; dictatorship, despotism, totalitarianism, autocracy, autarchy; invincibility.
▷ANTONYMS powerlessness.

omnipotent adjective *an omnipotent deity*: **all-powerful**, almighty, supreme, most high, pre-eminent; dictatorial, despotic, totalitarian, autocratic, autarchic; invincible, unconquerable.

omnipresent adjective *in fairy tales, evil is as omnipresent as virtue*: **present everywhere**, **ubiquitous**, general, universal, worldwide, global, all-pervasive, all-present, infinite, boundless; rife, prevalent, predominant, common, extensive, wide-ranging, far-reaching.

omniscient adjective *the story is told by an omniscient fictional narrator*: **all-knowing**, all-wise, all-seeing.

omnivorous adjective **1** *most duck species are omnivorous*: **eating a mixed/varied diet**, able to eat anything, all-devouring; rare pantophagous, pamphagous, pantophagic, omnivorant.
2 *David was an omnivorous reader*: **undiscriminating**, indiscriminate, unselective, uncritical.

on preposition **1** *there was a book on the table*: **supported by**, resting on, in contact with.
▷ANTONYMS underneath, on the underside of.

2 *she put the book on the table*: **on to**.
▷ANTONYMS off.
▶ adjective *the light was still on*: **functioning**, in operation, working, in use, operating.
▷ANTONYMS off.
▶ adverb *she droned on*: **interminably**, at length, for a long time, continuously, endlessly, ceaselessly, without a pause/break.
□ **on and off** *she had been working on that painting, on and off, for a long time*. See **off and on**.
□ **on and on** *she blabbered on and on*: **for a long time**, for ages, for hours, at (great) length, incessantly, ceaselessly, constantly, continuously, continually, endlessly, unendingly, eternally, forever; **interminably**, unremittingly, relentlessly, indefatigably, without let-up, without a pause/break, without cease.

once adverb 1 *I saw him only once*: **on one occasion**, one time, one single time.
▷ANTONYMS twice, many times.
2 *he did not once help*: **ever**, at any time, on any occasion, at all, under any circumstances, on any account, in a million years.
3 *they were friends once*: **formerly**, previously, in the past, at one time, at one point, once upon a time, on a former occasion, on one occasion, one time, in one case, time was when, in days/times gone by, back in the day, in times past, in the (good) old days, long ago; archaic sometime, erst, erstwhile, whilom; literary in days/times of yore, of yore.
▷ANTONYMS now.
□ **at once 1** *you must leave at once*: **immediately**, right away, right now, this moment/instant/second/minute, now, straight away, instantly, instantaneously, directly, suddenly, abruptly, summarily, forthwith, promptly, without delay/hesitation, without further ado; quickly, as fast as possible, as soon as possible, fast, speedily, with all speed; informal like a shot, in/like a flash, before you can say Jack Robinson, in two shakes (of a lamb's tail). ▷ANTONYMS later, in due course. **2** *all the guests arrived at once*: **at the same time**, at one and the same time, at the same instant/moment, (all) together, simultaneously; as a group, in unison, in concert, in chorus.
▷ANTONYMS singly, in dribs and drabs.
▶ conjunction *he'll be all right once she's gone*: **as soon as**, when, after, immediately after, the instant/moment/second/minute; Brit. informal immediately.
□ **once and for all 1** *you must decide once and for all*: **conclusively**, decisively, finally, positively, absolutely, determinedly, definitely, definitively, irrevocably. **2** *he has gone once and for all*: **for good**, for always, forever, permanently, finally, in perpetuity; informal for keeps.
□ **once in a while** *once in a while a car went past*: **occasionally**, from time to time, (every) now and then/again, every so often, every once in a while, on occasion, on occasions, on the odd occasion, at times, sometimes, off and on, at intervals, periodically, sporadically, spasmodically, erratically, irregularly, intermittently, in/by fits and starts, fitfully, discontinuously, piecemeal; rare interruptedly.

O

oncoming adjective *he lost control on a bend and collided with an oncoming car | the piercing March wind and the oncoming rain*: **approaching**, advancing, coming, nearing, arriving, onrushing; forthcoming, upcoming, on the way, prospective, imminent, impending, looming, gathering, immediate, proximate; close, (close) at hand, about to happen/be, in the offing, in the wind, to come.

one cardinal number **1 unit**, item; technical monad.
2 *only one person came*: **a single**, a solitary, a sole, a lone.
3 *her one concern was her daughter*: **only**, single, solitary, sole.
4 *one day they'll come*: **some**, any, a certain.
5 *they are now one*: **united**, a unit, amalgamated, consolidated, integrated, combined, incorporated, affiliated, allied, federated, linked, joined, unified, in league, in partnership; bound, wedded, married.

Word links **one**

mono- related prefix, as in *monologue, monovalent*
uni- related prefix, as in *unicellular, unicycle*
unitary relating to one
monomania obsession with one thing
sesqui- prefix meaning 'one and a half', as in *sesquicentenary*

onerous adjective *the task proved to be more onerous than she had expected*: **burdensome**, heavy, inconvenient, troublesome, awkward, crushing, back-breaking, oppressive; weighty, arduous, strenuous, uphill, difficult, hard, severe, formidable, laborious, Herculean, exhausting, tiring, taxing, demanding, punishing, gruelling, exacting, wearing, stiff, stressful, wearisome, fatiguing; archaic toilsome; rare exigent.
▷ANTONYMS easy, effortless.

Word toolkit **onerous**

See **arduous**.

oneself pronoun
□ **by oneself** See **by**.

one-sided adjective 1 *foreign publications have been criticized for alleged one-sided reporting*: **biased**, prejudiced, partisan, partial, preferential, discriminatory, coloured, inequitable, unfair, influenced, slanted, unjust, narrow-minded, bigoted.
▷ANTONYMS fair-minded.
2 *a one-sided game*: **unequal**, uneven, unbalanced, lopsided.

one-time adjective *a one-time county cricketer*: **former**, ex-, old, previous, sometime, erstwhile, once, then, lapsed; formal quondam.

ongoing adjective 1 *two laboratories have been refurbished as part of an ongoing programme of modernization*: **in progress**, under way, going on, continuing, happening, occurring, taking place, proceeding, being done, being worked on, being performed, current, extant, existing, existent, progressing, advancing, evolving, growing, developing; pending, outstanding, to be done, unfinished, remaining.
▷ANTONYMS finished, abandoned.
2 *residents face the ongoing problem of shoppers parking outside their homes*: **continuous**, continuing, uninterrupted, unbroken, non-stop, round-the-clock, incessant, unending, constant, ceaseless, unceasing, endless, never-ending, everlasting, eternal, perpetual, unremitting, relentless, unfaltering.
▷ANTONYMS intermittent.

onlooker noun *an onlooker described the scene as one of utter devastation*: **eyewitness**, witness, observer, looker-on, fly on the wall, spectator, watcher, viewer, sightseer, bystander, non-participant; informal rubberneck; literary beholder.
▷ANTONYMS participant.

only adverb 1 *there was only enough for two*: **at most**, at best, (only) just, no/not more than, as little as; no longer ago than, not until; barely, scarcely, hardly, narrowly, by a hair's breadth, by the skin of one's teeth.
2 *he only works on one picture at a time*: **exclusively**, solely, entirely, uniquely, wholly, to the exclusion of everything else.
3 *you're only saying that*: **merely**, simply, just, purely.
▶ adjective *he is their only son*: **sole**, single, one (and only), solitary, lone, unique, only possible, individual, exclusive.

onomatopoeic adjective *'slap' is an onomatopoeic word*: **imitative**, echoic.

onset noun *treatment was administered soon after the onset of symptoms*: **start**, beginning, arrival, (first) appearance, opening, outset, inception; outbreak, dawn, birth, infancy, genesis, creation, day one, emergence, rise; formal commencement.
▷ANTONYMS end, termination.

onslaught noun *the relentless onslaught on the city was taking a heavy toll*: **assault**, attack, offensive, aggression, advance, charge, onrush, rush, storming, sortie, sally, raid, descent, incursion, invasion, foray, push, thrust, drive, blitz, bombardment, barrage, salvo, storm, volley, shower, torrent, broadside; archaic onset.

onus noun *the onus is on the plaintiff to obtain the police report*: **burden**, responsibility, liability, obligation, duty, weight, load, charge, mantle, encumbrance; cross to bear, millstone round one's neck, albatross.

ooze verb 1 *blood oozed from a long scratch on his forehead*: **seep**, discharge, flow, exude, trickle, drip, dribble, issue, filter, percolate, escape, leak, drain, empty, bleed, sweat, well, leach; Medicine extravasate; rare filtrate, transude, exudate.
2 *she was positively oozing charm*: **exude**, **gush**, drip, pour forth, give out, send out, emit, breathe, let loose, display, exhibit, demonstrate, manifest.
▶ noun 1 *the ooze of pus*: **seepage**, seeping, discharge, flow, exudation, trickle, trickling, drip, dribble, filtration, percolation, excretion, escape, leak, leakage, drainage, emptying, bleeding, sweating, welling, leaching, secretion; Medicine extravasation.
2 *the skeletons of zooplankton accumulate in ooze on the ocean floor*: **mud**, slime, alluvium, silt, mire, bog, sludge, slush, muck, dirt, deposit; Scottish & N. English clart; Irish slob.

opacity noun 1 *the opacity of water may arise from a variety of materials in suspension*: **opaqueness**, non-transparency, lack of transparency; cloudiness, filminess, haziness, mistiness, blur, blurredness, dirtiness, dinginess, muddiness, griminess, smeariness.
▷ANTONYMS transparency, translucence, clarity.
2 *the opacity of much philosophical writing*: **lack of clarity**, obscurity, abstruseness, unclearness, density, impenetrability, enigma, unintelligibility, incomprehensibility, reconditeness.
▷ANTONYMS clarity, limpidity.

opalescent adjective *the dress is embroidered with opalescent sequins*: **multicoloured**, many-hued, prismatic, rainbow-like, kaleidoscopic, iridescent, lustrous, shimmering, glittering, sparkling, scintillating, variegated, shot, moiré, opaline, milky, pearly, nacreous, pearlescent.

opaque adjective 1 *the bottle was made of opaque glass so that the contents could not be seen*: **non-transparent**, cloudy, filmy, blurred, smeared, hazy, misty, dirty, dingy, muddy, muddied, grimy, smeary.
▷ANTONYMS transparent, translucent, clear.
2 *federalism renders the decision-making process opaque and bureaucratic*: **obscure**, **unclear**, dense, uncertain, indeterminate, mysterious, puzzling,

perplexing, baffling, mystifying, confusing, enigmatic, inexplicable, unexplained, concealed, hidden, unfathomable, incomprehensible, impenetrable, vague, ambiguous, Delphic, indefinite, indistinct, hazy, foggy, nebulous, equivocal, doubtful, dubious, oblique, elliptical, oracular, cryptic, deep, abstruse, recondite, arcane, esoteric, recherché; informal as clear as mud.
▷ANTONYMS limpid, clear.

open adjective 1 *the door's open*: **not shut**, not closed, unlocked, unbolted, unlatched, off the latch, unfastened, unbarred, unsecured; ajar, wide open, agape, gaping, yawning.
▷ANTONYMS shut, closed.
2 *a blue silk shirt, open at the neck*: **unfastened**, not done up, undone, unbuttoned, unzipped, loose; unbuckled, untied, unlaced.
3 *the council used several tonnes of grit in a bid to keep the main roads open*: **clear**, **passable**, navigable, unblocked, free from obstructions, unobstructed; snow-free, ice-free.
▷ANTONYMS blocked.
4 *an eighteenth-century farmhouse with lovely views over open countryside | her love of open spaces*: **unenclosed**, rolling, sweeping, extensive, wide, wide open, broad, unfenced, exposed, unsheltered; spacious, airy, uncrowded, uncluttered; undeveloped, unbuilt-up.
▷ANTONYMS enclosed, built-up, developed.
5 *a map of the area was open beside him*: **spread out**, unfolded, unfurled, unrolled, straightened out; extended, stretched out.
▷ANTONYMS closed, put away.
6 *the shop is open daily*: **open for business**, open to the public.
▷ANTONYMS shut, closed.
7 *I could keep the position open for a week or two, to give you time to think*: **available**, vacant, free, unfilled, unoccupied; informal on hold, up for grabs.
8 *he criticized the system for being* ***open to*** *abuse*: **at risk of**, vulnerable, subject, susceptible, allowing of, permitting, liable, an easy target for, exposed, at the mercy of.
▷ANTONYMS immune.
9 *she was quite open about her feelings*: **frank**, **candid**, honest, forthright, direct, unreserved, blunt, plain-spoken, outspoken, free-spoken, downright, not afraid to call a spade a spade; straightforward, genuine, natural, ingenuous, innocent, artless, transparent, guileless, simple; communicative, forthcoming, uninhibited; informal upfront; archaic round.
▷ANTONYMS secretive, deep, devious.
10 *they eyed one another with open hostility*: **overt**, obvious, patent, manifest, palpable, conspicuous, plain, undisguised, unconcealed, unhidden, clear, noticeable, visible, apparent, evident; blatant, flagrant, barefaced, brazen.
▷ANTONYMS concealed.
11 *the case is still open*: **unresolved**, not yet settled, yet to be settled, undecided, unsettled, up in the air; open to debate, open for discussion, arguable, debatable, moot.
▷ANTONYMS decided, concluded.
12 *I'm keeping an open mind on the subject*: **impartial**, unbiased, unprejudiced, objective, disinterested, uncommitted, non-partisan, non-discriminatory, neutral, dispassionate, detached.
▷ANTONYMS biased.
13 *I'm always open to suggestions*: **receptive**, amenable, willing/ready/disposed to listen, responsive.
14 *what other options are open to us?* **available**, accessible, on hand, obtainable, on offer.
15 *they are required by law to hold an open meeting*: **public**, general, unrestricted, non-exclusive, accessible to everyone, non-restrictive.
▷ANTONYMS private.
▸verb 1 *she opened the front door*: **unfasten**, unlatch, unlock, unbolt, unbar; throw wide.
▷ANTONYMS close, shut.
2 *when Katherine opened the parcel, she found a copy of 'Daisy Miller'*: **unwrap**, undo, untie, unseal.
3 *shall I open another bottle?* **uncork**, broach, crack (open).
4 *Adam opened the Ordnance Survey map*: **spread out**, unfold, unfurl, unroll, straighten out; extend, stretch out.
▷ANTONYMS close, fold up.
5 *a statement in which he opened his heart as never before*: **reveal**, uncover, expose, lay bare, bare, pour out, exhibit, show, disclose, divulge.
6 *we're hoping to open next month*: **start trading**, open for business, be ready for customers/visitors, admit customers, begin business, set up shop, put up one's plate; N. Amer. informal hang out one's shingle.
7 *Sir Bryan opened the meeting by welcoming the Commissioner | the film opens with a long sex scene*: **begin**, start, initiate, set in motion, launch, get going, get under way, start/get/set the ball rolling, get off the ground; inaugurate; informal kick off, get the show on the road; formal commence.
▷ANTONYMS end, finish.
8 *the lounge* ***opens on to*** *a terrace*: **give access**, give on to, lead, be connected, communicate with; command a view of, face, overlook.

> *Word links* **open**
>
> **agoraphobia** fear of open places

open-air adjective *an open-air swimming pool*: **outdoor**, out-of-doors, outside, alfresco, in the open air; French en plein air; Italian al fresco; rare hypaethral.
▷ANTONYMS inside, indoor.

open-handed adjective *a combination of hard-headed business sense and open-handed philanthropy*: **generous**, magnanimous, charitable, benevolent, beneficent, big-hearted, great-hearted, munificent, bountiful, liberal, handsome, princely; altruistic, kind, kindly, philanthropic, chivalrous, noble, unselfish, selfless, self-sacrificing, generous to a fault, ungrudging, unstinting; literary bounteous.
▷ANTONYMS tight-fisted.

opening noun 1 *the large hall is lit by an opening in the centre of the roof*: **hole**, gap, aperture, space, orifice, vent, slot, window, crack, slit, gash, split, fissure, perforation, cleft, crevice, cut, incision, rent, cavity, cranny, groove, chink, eye, mouth; loophole, spyhole, peephole, judas; interstice; Medicine hiatus, foramen.
2 *she was still heading towards the dark opening in the wall*: **doorway**, gateway, portal, way, entrance, entry, entryway, means of entry, way in, entrée, access, means of access, exit, egress, way out.
3 *United created openings but were unable to score*: **opportunity**, chance, favourable time/occasion/moment, right set of circumstances, moment, occasion, window (of opportunity), possibility, turn, time; informal break, lucky break, shot.
4 *I'm looking for an opening with a stockbroker*: **vacancy**, position, job, opportunity.
5 *the opening of the session had been repeatedly postponed*: **beginning**, start, outset, inception, launch, birth, dawn; introduction, preliminary, preface, prelude, foreword, preamble, prefatory remarks, opening statement, opening remarks, prologue; informal kick-off; formal commencement; rare proem, prolegomenon.
▷ANTONYMS closure, close, end, termination.
6 *he crashes gallery openings for a bite of smoked salmon*: **opening ceremony**, official opening, launch, initiation, inauguration, institution, foundation, establishment, setting up, formation, constitution, opening night, premiere, first night, first showing; private view, vernissage.

openly adverb 1 *dangerous drugs were openly on sale*: **publicly**, in public, in full view of people, for all to see, undisguisedly, blatantly, flagrantly, brazenly, with no attempt at concealment, overtly, boldly, audaciously; unashamedly, shamelessly, unabashedly, wantonly, immodestly.
▷ANTONYMS secretly.
2 *he could no longer speak openly of his problems*: **frankly**, candidly, explicitly, honestly, truly, sincerely, forthrightly, directly, straightforwardly, bluntly, plainly, in plain language, unreservedly, without constraint, truthfully, without dissembling, to someone's face, straight from the shoulder, without beating about the bush, with no holds barred, man to man, woman to woman; informal on the level; Brit. informal straight up.
▷ANTONYMS indirectly, allusively.

open-minded adjective 1 *they have sympathetic, open-minded attitudes to young people*: **unbiased**, unprejudiced, prejudice-free, accepting, non-partisan, neutral, non-aligned, non-judgemental, non-discriminatory, objective, disinterested, dispassionate, detached; **tolerant**, liberal, permissive, broad-minded, undogmatic, unprescriptive.
▷ANTONYMS prejudiced, judgemental.
2 *the musicians have got to be open-minded enough to take some suggestions from the producers*: **receptive**, open, open to suggestions, open to new ideas, amenable, flexible, responsive, willing to change, undogmatic.
▷ANTONYMS narrow-minded, opinionated.

open-mouthed adjective *they stare at us open-mouthed, as if we are completely insane*: **astounded**, amazed, in amazement, surprised, stunned, bowled over, staggered, thunderstruck, aghast, stupefied, dazed, taken aback, shocked, in shock, nonplussed, speechless, dumbfounded, dumbstruck, tongue-tied, at a loss for words, agape, goggle-eyed, wide-eyed, staring; informal flabbergasted; Brit. informal gobsmacked.

operate verb 1 *he can operate the machine*: **work**, make go, run, set off, use, utilize, employ, handle, control, wield, ply, manage, be in charge of; drive, steer, guide, pilot, manipulate, manoeuvre, exercise.
2 *the machine ceased to operate*: **function**, work, go, run, perform, act, be in action, behave, be in working/running order, be operative.
▷ANTONYMS break down, fail.
3 *the research will examine how the law operates in practice*: **take effect**, act, be in effect, be in force, be in operation, stand, apply, be applied, run, be/remain valid, be current, function, be efficacious, hold good, be the case.
4 *Hechstetter continued to operate the mines until about 1634*: **direct**, control, manage, run, conduct, carry on, govern, administer, superintend, head (up), lead, look after, supervise, oversee, preside over, be in control/charge of.
5 *when the results of the X-rays are known, doctors will decide whether to operate on Adis*: **perform surgery**, carry out an operation, intervene; informal put someone under the knife.

operation noun 1 *the slide bars are machined to ensure smooth operation*: **functioning**, working, running, performance, action, behaviour.

O

2 *those responsible for the operation of the factory*: **management**, running, direction, control, governing, administration, supervision.
3 *legislation to curtail the operation of the closed shop*: **effect**, force, potency, power, effectiveness.
4 *a heart bypass operation*: **surgery**, surgical operation, surgical intervention, major surgery, minor surgery.
5 *a carefully planned military operation*: **action**, activity, exercise, affair, business, undertaking, step, enterprise, task, job, process, procedure, manoeuvre, campaign.
6 *the company's South American mining operation*: **business**, enterprise, company, firm, organization, concern; informal outfit, set-up.
□ **in operation** *only the starboard engine was in operation*: **functioning**, working, running, up and running, operative, in use, in action, going; operational, workable, serviceable, functional, usable, in working order/condition, viable; in force, effective, in effect, valid.

operational adjective *the two reactors became operational in 1983*: **up and running**, running, working, functioning, operative, in operation, in use, in action, going; **in working order**, workable, serviceable, functional, usable, viable, ready for action, prepared.
▷ANTONYMS broken, out of order.

operative adjective **1** *although the act has been passed by parliament, it is not operative at the moment*: **in force**, in operation, effective, in effect, valid.
▷ANTONYMS invalid.
2 *the steam railway is still operative*: **functioning**, working, running, up and running, in operation, in use, in action, going; operational, workable, serviceable, functional, usable, in working order/condition, viable.
▷ANTONYMS out of order.
3 *'might' is the operative word*: **key**, significant, relevant, applicable, pertinent, apposite, germane, apropos, crucial, critical, main, chief, major, central, pivotal, fundamental, vital, important, essential.
▷ANTONYMS irrelevant.
▶ **noun 1** *the operatives clean the machines at the end of every shift*: **machinist**, (machine) operator, mechanic, engineer, driver, worker, workman, (factory) hand, artisan, craftsman, craftswoman, blue-collar worker; Brit. machine-minder.
2 N. Amer. *a special operative of the CIA*: **agent**, secret agent, undercover agent, spy, mole, plant, double agent, counterspy; N. Amer. informal spook; archaic intelligencer; archaic, informal beagle.
3 N. Amer. *employ a private operative*: **detective**, private detective, investigator, private investigator, sleuth, shadow; Brit. enquiry agent; informal private eye, tail; N. Amer. informal, dated gumshoe, bogey, dick.

operator noun **1** *a machine operator*: **machinist**, mechanic, operative, engineer, driver, worker; Brit. machine-minder.
2 *a tour operator*: **contractor**, entrepreneur, promoter, impresario, arranger, fixer, trader, dealer, director, manager, partner, businessman, businesswoman, financier, venture capitalist, speculator.
3 *nationalism has always been the ally of the ruthless operator*: **manipulator**, manoeuvrer, mover, worker, string-puller, mover and shaker, wheeler-dealer; N. Amer. wirepuller.

O

opiate noun *six of the patients used an opiate during the radiotherapy*: **drug**, narcotic, mind-altering drug, sedative, tranquillizer, depressant, sleeping pill, soporific, anaesthetic, painkiller, analgesic, anodyne; barbiturate, bromide, morphine, opium, laudanum; Medicine calmative, palliative, stupefacient; informal dope, downer; literary nepenthes; dated sleeping draught.

opine verb *the headmistress opined that the outing would make a nice change*: **suggest**, submit, advance, propose, venture, volunteer, put forward, moot, propound, posit, air, hazard, say, declare, observe, comment, remark; **think**, believe, consider, maintain, imagine, be of the view, be of the opinion, reckon, guess, estimate, conjecture, fancy, suspect, feel, have a/the feeling, assume, presume, take it, suppose, expect, gather; contend, be convinced, be of the conviction, reason, deduce, conclude, theorize, hypothesize, take as a hypothesis; N. Amer. informal allow; archaic ween.

opinion noun *she did not share her husband's opinion*: **belief**, judgement, thought(s), school of thought, thinking, way of thinking, mind, point of view, view, viewpoint, outlook, angle, slant, side, attitude, stance, perspective, position, standpoint; theory, tenet, conclusion, verdict, estimation, thesis, hypothesis, feeling, sentiment, impression, reflections, idea, notion, assumption, speculation, conception, conviction, contention, persuasion, creed, dogma.
□ **a matter of opinion** *whether this is desirable or not is a matter of opinion*: **open to question**, a debatable point, debatable, open to debate, a moot point, open to/for discussion, up to the individual.
□ **be of the opinion** *I'm of the opinion that this is not necessary*: **believe**, think, consider, maintain, imagine, be of the view, reckon, guess, estimate, conjecture, fancy, suspect, feel, have a/the feeling, assume, presume, take it, suppose, expect, gather; contend, put forward, be convinced, be of the conviction, reason, deduce, conclude, theorize, hypothesize, take as a hypothesis; N. Amer. informal allow; formal opine; archaic ween.
□ **in my opinion** *we have very little choice, in my opinion*: **as I see it**, in my view, to my mind, (according) to my way of thinking, from my standpoint, personally, in my estimation, in my judgement, in my book, for my money, if you ask me.

opinionated adjective *the boy was dutiful and punctilious, however opinionated*: **dogmatic**, of fixed views, of preconceived ideas, pontifical, doctrinaire, dictatorial, domineering, assertive, cocksure, pompous, self-important, adamant, arrogant; inflexible, uncompromising, prejudiced, biased, bigoted.
▷ANTONYMS open-minded.

opponent noun **1** *he beat his Republican opponent by a landslide*: **rival**, **adversary**, opposer, the opposition, fellow contestant, (fellow) competitor, other competitor/contestant/player/candidate, enemy, foe, antagonist, combatant, contender, challenger, critic, dissenter, disputant, objector.
▷ANTONYMS ally, partner, colleague.
2 *an opponent of the economic reforms*: **opposer**, objector, dissident, dissenter.
▷ANTONYMS supporter.

opportune adjective *it would seem an opportune moment to impose stricter regulation*: **auspicious**, propitious, favourable, advantageous, heaven-sent, golden, good, right, lucky, happy, fortunate, benign, providential, felicitous; **timely**, well timed, ripe, convenient, expedient, suitable, appropriate, apt, fitting, relevant, applicable, pertinent; archaic seasonable.
▷ANTONYMS disadvantageous, ill-timed.

Choose the right word **opportune, timely, auspicious**

Opportune is used mainly to denote a favourable *time* or *moment* for doing something (*I waited for an opportune moment to discuss the idea*). When applied to actions or events occurring at favourable moments, it can suggest the role of chance in producing a happy outcome (*an opportune visit from the manager allowed him to air his views*).

A **timely** action or event occurs at a moment when it can make the greatest difference to a situation (*the assassins were stopped only by the timely intervention of a patrol*). A *timely reminder* is given when it is much needed, if not overdue.

Auspicious is used where all the circumstances are conducive to the success of a new undertaking, and it is used typically to describe a point in time (*he is waiting for the most auspicious moment to call an election*). It is often used precisely when circumstances are *not* conducive to success, especially when referring to the start of something (*he did not make the most auspicious of starts to the season*).

opportunism noun *many are saying that the early election was prompted by political opportunism*: **expediency**, exploitation, taking advantage, Machiavellianism, manoeuvring, pragmatism, realism, unscrupulousness; striking while the iron is hot, making hay while the sun shines, making the best of a bad job; informal ad-hockery.

opportunity noun *staff will have the opportunity to discuss the matter | it's an opportunity you shouldn't miss*: **chance**, lucky chance, good time, golden opportunity, time, occasion, moment, favourable time/occasion/moment, right set of circumstances, appropriate time/occasion/moment, suitable time/occasion/moment, opportune time/occasion/moment, opening, option, window (of opportunity), slot, turn, go, (clear) run, field day; possibility, scope, freedom, latitude, room to manoeuvre, elbow room; N. Amer. & Austral./NZ show; Canadian a kick at the can/cat; informal shot, break, look-in.

oppose verb *the council received letters of protest from residents who opposed the scheme*: **be against**, object to, be hostile to, be anti, be in opposition to, disagree with, dislike, disapprove of; resist, take a stand against, put up a fight against, stand up to, take on, fight, withstand, defy, set one's face against, stand up and be counted against, go against, counter, cross, confront, challenge, contend with, attack, counterattack, combat, fly in the face of; take issue with, contradict, dispute, rebut, argue with/against, quarrel with; formal gainsay; rare controvert.
▷ANTONYMS support, defend, promote.

opposed adjective **1** *a large proportion of the population is* ***opposed to*** *the construction of nuclear power plants*: **against**, (dead) set against; in opposition, averse, hostile, antagonistic, inimical, antipathetic, unsympathetic, resistant; informal anti.
▷ANTONYMS in favour of, favourably disposed to.
2 *their interests were opposed*: **conflicting**, contrasting, incompatible, irreconcilable, antithetical, contradictory, clashing, contrary, different, differing, at variance, at odds, divergent, dissimilar, disagreeing, opposing, opposite, poles apart, polar; rare oppugnant.
□ **as opposed to** *the concrete as opposed to the abstract*: **in contrast with**, as against, as contrasted with, as an alternative to, rather than, instead of.

opposing adjective **1** *the two opposing points of view*: **conflicting**, contrasting, opposite, incompatible, irreconcilable, contradictory, antithetical, clashing, contrary, different, differing, at variance, at odds, divergent, dissimilar, disagreeing, opposed, poles apart, polar; rare oppugnant.
2 *children whose parents had fought on opposing sides in the war*: **rival**, opposite, combatant, enemy, antagonistic.

▷ANTONYMS allied.
3 *on the opposing page there were two addresses*: **opposite**, facing.

opposite adjective **1** *she and Alice sat opposite each other*: **facing**, face to face with, across from; informal eyeball to eyeball with; archaic fronting.
2 *the drawing on the opposite page*: **facing**, opposing.
3 *other authors have expressed opposite views*: **conflicting**, contrasting, incompatible, irreconcilable, inconsistent, antithetical, converse, contradictory, clashing, contrary, at variance, at odds, different, differing, divergent, dissimilar, unlike, unalike, disagreeing, opposed, opposing, poles apart, polar, obverse; rare oppugnant.
▷ANTONYMS same, identical, like.
4 *opposite sides in a war*: **rival**, opposing, combatant, enemy, antagonistic.
▷ANTONYMS allied.
▶ noun *forecasters expected it to be a year of recovery—in fact the opposite was true | his nature is the opposite of his father's*: **reverse**, converse, antithesis, contrary, inverse, obverse, contradiction; the other extreme, the other side of the coin; Italian per contra; informal flip side; rare antipode, antipodes.

Word links **opposite**

contra- related prefix, as in *contraception, contraflow*
counter- related prefix, as in *counter-attack, counterclockwise*

opposition noun **1** *the proposal met with considerable opposition*: **resistance**, hostility, antagonism, antipathy, enmity, objection, dissent, criticism, defiance, non-compliance, obstruction, obstructiveness, counteraction; dislike, disapproval, demurral.
2 *the home team made short work of the opposition*: **opponents**, opposing side, other side, other team, competition, competitors, opposers, rivals, adversaries, antagonists, enemies; literary foes.
3 *the opposition between the public and the private domains*: **conflict**, clash, difference, contrast, disparity, antithesis, polarity.

oppress verb **1** *the Russians had participated in the dismemberment of Poland and oppressed its people*: **persecute**, abuse, maltreat, ill-treat, treat harshly, be brutal to, be cruel to, tyrannize, crush, repress, suppress, subjugate, subdue, subject, enslave; scourge, exploit, hold down, keep down, grind down, rule with a rod of iron, rule with an iron hand, trample on, trample underfoot, bring someone to their knees, ride roughshod over; informal walk all over.
2 *the gloom in the chapel oppressed her*: **depress**, make gloomy/despondent, weigh down, lie heavy on, weigh heavily on, cast down, dampen someone's spirits, hang over, prey on, burden, crush, dispirit, dishearten, discourage, sadden, make desolate, get down, bring down, trouble, afflict; archaic deject.

oppressed adjective *oppressed racial minorities*: **persecuted**, downtrodden, abused, maltreated, ill-treated, tyrannized, subjugated, repressed, subdued, crushed, enslaved, exploited, victimized, misused; disadvantaged, underprivileged, ground down, browbeaten.

oppression noun *years of violence and oppression*: **persecution**, abuse, maltreatment, ill-treatment, tyranny, despotism, repression, suppression, subjection, subjugation, enslavement, exploitation; cruelty, ruthlessness, harshness, brutality, injustice, hardship, misery, suffering, pain, anguish, wretchedness.
▷ANTONYMS freedom, democracy.

oppressive adjective **1** *an oppressive dictatorship | oppressive laws*: **harsh**, cruel, brutal, repressive, crushing, tyrannical, tyrannous, iron-fisted, domineering, autocratic, dictatorial, despotic, draconian, punitive; ruthless, relentless, merciless, pitiless, severe, inexorable; unjust, unfair, undemocratic.
▷ANTONYMS lenient, humane.
2 *an oppressive sense of despair*: **overwhelming**, overpowering, hard to bear, unbearable, burdensome, unendurable, intolerable, heavy; uncomfortable, grinding.
3 *the day was grey and oppressive*: **muggy**, close, heavy, hot, humid, sticky, steamy, soupy, fuggy, airless, stuffy, stifling, suffocating, sultry, torrid.
▷ANTONYMS fresh, airy.

oppressor noun **persecutor**, tyrant, despot, autocrat, bully, slave-driver, hard taskmaster, iron hand, scourge, dictator, tormentor, torturer, intimidator, subjugator.

opprobrious adjective *a couple of students shouted opprobrious remarks at him*: **abusive**, vituperative, derogatory, disparaging, denigratory, pejorative, deprecatory, insulting, offensive, defamatory, slanderous, libellous, scurrilous, scandalous, vitriolic, venomous; **scornful**, contemptuous, derisive; informal bitchy; archaic contumelious; rare calumnious, calumniatory, aspersive.

opprobrium noun **1** *the government endured months of opprobrium*: **vilification**, abuse, vituperation, condemnation, criticism, censure, castigation, denunciation, defamation, denigration, disparagement, obloquy, derogation, slander, revilement, reviling, calumny, calumniation, execration, excoriation, lambasting, upbraiding, bad press, character assassination, attack, invective, libel, insults, aspersions; informal flak, mud-slinging, bad-mouthing, tongue-lashing; Brit. informal stick, verbal, slagging off; archaic contumely; rare animadversion, objurgation.
▷ANTONYMS praise.
2 *the opprobrium of being associated with gangsters and thugs*: **disgrace**, shame, dishonour, discredit, stigma, humiliation, loss of face, ignominy, odium, obloquy, disfavour, disrepute, ill repute, infamy, notoriety, scandal, stain; rare disesteem.
▷ANTONYMS honour.

opt verb *she **opted for** a cream silk shirt*: **choose**, select, pick, pick out, decide on, go for, settle on, plump for/on, single out, take, fix on; Brit. pitch on.

optimism noun *such statements reflect the growing optimism among members of the profession*: **hopefulness**, hope, confidence, buoyancy, cheer, good cheer, cheerfulness, sanguineness, positiveness, positive attitude.
▷ANTONYMS pessimism.

optimistic adjective **1** *always optimistic, Anne felt sure that she would see him*: **cheerful**, cheery, positive, confident, hopeful, sanguine, bullish, buoyant, bright; disposed to look on the bright side, inclined to look through rose-coloured spectacles, always expecting the best, full of hope, Pollyannaish, Panglossian; informal upbeat; archaic of good cheer.
▷ANTONYMS pessimistic, negative.
2 *the forecast is certainly more optimistic*: **encouraging**, promising, hopeful, bright, rosy, reassuring, favourable, auspicious, propitious.
▷ANTONYMS pessimistic, gloomy, ominous.

Word toolkit **optimistic**

See **confident**.

optimum adjective *the optimum pupil–teacher ratio*: **best**, most favourable, most advantageous, most appropriate, ideal, perfect, prime, optimal, model; finest, superlative, peak, top, supreme, excellent, flawless, first-class; informal tip-top, A1, stellar, top-notch.

option noun *the way I see it, we have two options | she was given the option of resigning or being dismissed*: **choice**, alternative, recourse, possibility, course of action; freedom of choice, power to choose, right to choose; informal bet.

optional adjective *registration was obligatory but voting was optional*: **voluntary**, non-compulsory, at one's discretion, discretionary, not required, up to the individual, elective, non-mandatory, free, open, unforced; Law permissive; rare discretional.
▷ANTONYMS compulsory, obligatory, mandatory, required.

opulence noun **1** *he was taken aback by the sheer opulence of the room*: **luxuriousness**, sumptuousness, lavishness, richness, lushness, luxury, luxuriance, splendour, magnificence, grandeur, splendidness, grandiosity, costliness, fanciness; informal plushness, plushiness, ritziness, swankiness, poshness, classiness.
▷ANTONYMS restraint, simplicity.
2 *a display of opulence*: **wealth**, affluence, wealthiness, richness, riches, prosperity, prosperousness, money, fortune.
▷ANTONYMS poverty.

opulent adjective **1** *his parents' opulent home in Beverly Hills*: **luxurious**, sumptuous, palatial, lavishly appointed, lavish, de luxe, rich, lush, luxuriant, splendid, magnificent, grand, grandiose, costly, expensive, fancy; informal plush, plushy, ritzy, swanky, posh, classy; Brit. informal swish; N. Amer. informal swank.
▷ANTONYMS stark, spartan, restrained, ascetic.
2 *an opulent family*: **wealthy**, rich, affluent, well off, well-to-do, moneyed, with deep pockets, prosperous, of means, of substance; informal well heeled, rolling in it, rolling in money, loaded, in clover, stinking/filthy rich, flush, made of money, in/on easy street; Brit. informal quids in; informal, dated in the chips, oofy, on velvet.
▷ANTONYMS penniless, poor, impoverished, penurious.
3 *he stroked her opulent red hair*: **copious**, abundant, profuse, prolific, plentiful, luxuriant; literary plenteous.
▷ANTONYMS sparse.
4 *the opulent curves of her body*: **voluptuous**, shapely, full, rounded, ample, Rubensesque, lush, luscious, buxom; informal curvaceous, curvy.
▷ANTONYMS thin, emaciated.

opus noun *his acclaimed opus 'In Search of Excellence'*: **composition**, work, work of art, oeuvre, piece, creation, production; rare opuscule.

oracle noun **1** *Hercules consulted the oracle of Apollo*: **prophet**, **prophetess**, sibyl, seer, augur, prognosticator, diviner, soothsayer, wise man, wise woman, sage, fortune teller; rare oracler.
2 *the Colonial Office's oracle on Africa*: **authority**, expert, specialist, pundit, guru, mentor, adviser, mastermind, connoisseur; informal wizard, high priest.

oracular adjective **1** *his every utterance was given oracular significance by his fans*: **prophetic**, prophetical, sibylline, predictive, prescient, prognostic, divinatory, augural; rare vatic, mantic, fatidical, fatidic, haruspical, pythonic.
2 *his hesitation and oracular responses are not good advertisements for privatization*: **enigmatic**, cryptic, abstruse, unclear, obscure, confusing, mystifying, puzzling, perplexing, baffling, mysterious, arcane; ambiguous, equivocal, two-edged, Delphic.

oral adjective *an oral agreement*: **spoken**, verbal, unwritten, by mouth, vocal, viva voce, uttered, said.
▷ANTONYMS written.
▸ noun *a French oral*: **oral examination**; Brit. viva, viva voce.

orate verb *he strode up and down the aisle as he orated*: **declaim**, make a speech, hold forth, speak, discourse, pontificate, preach, sermonize, sound off, spout off; informal spiel, speechify, mouth off; rare perorate.

oration noun *his eloquent funeral oration*: **speech**, address, lecture, talk, homily, sermon, discourse, declamation, recitation, disquisition, peroration, monologue, valedictory, harangue, tirade, diatribe, rant; N. Amer. salutatory; informal spiel; rare allocution, predication.

orator noun *an eloquent and persuasive orator*: **speaker**, public speaker, speech-maker, lecturer, declaimer, rhetorician; informal spieler; historical demagogue, rhetor.

oratorical adjective *he adopted a rather oratorical style*: **rhetorical**, grandiloquent, magniloquent, high-flown, high-sounding, sonorous, lofty, orotund, bombastic, grandiose, pompous, pretentious, overblown, turgid, extravagant, flowery, florid, declamatory, Ciceronian; informal highfalutin; rare epideictic, fustian, euphuistic, aureate, Demosthenic, Demosthenean.
▷ANTONYMS plain-spoken, simple, unadorned.

oratory noun *he whipped the meeting up into a frenzy with his oratory*: **rhetoric**, eloquence, grandiloquence, magniloquence, public speaking, speech-making, declamation, way with words, the gift of the gab, fluency.

orb noun *the red orb of the sun sank beneath the horizon*: **sphere**, globe, ball, circle, ring, spheroid, spherule, round.

orbit noun **1** *the earth's orbit around the sun*: **course**, path, circuit, track, trajectory, rotation, revolution, circle, cycle, round; rare circumgyration.
2 *the problem comes within the Ombudsman's orbit*: **sphere**, sphere of influence, area of activity, range, reach, scope, ambit, compass, sweep, jurisdiction, authority, remit, span of control, domain, realm, province, territory, preserve, department, turf; informal bailiwick.
▸ verb *Mercury orbits the sun*: **revolve round**, circle round, go round, travel round; rare encircle.

orchestra noun **ensemble**; informal band.

orchestrate verb **1** *the piece may have been subsequently orchestrated by Mozart*: **arrange**, adapt, score; rare instrument.
2 *he threatened to orchestrate a campaign of civil disobedience*: **organize**, arrange, put together, plan, set up, bring about, manage, mobilize, mount, stage, stage-manage, mastermind, choreograph, coordinate, direct, engineer; rare concert.

ordain verb **1** *the Church of England voted to ordain women*: **confer holy orders on**, appoint, induct, install, invest, anoint, consecrate; archaic frock.
2 *the path ordained by God*: **predetermine**, predestine, preordain, foreordain, destine, prescribe, fate, will, determine, designate.
3 *it was ordained that anyone hunting in the forest without permission was to pay a fine*: **decree**, rule, order, command, enjoin, lay down, set down, establish, fix, enact, legislate, dictate, prescribe, pronounce.

ordeal noun *both women were understandably shaken by their ordeal*: **painful/unpleasant experience**, trial, tribulation, test, nightmare, trauma, baptism of fire, hell, hell on earth, misery, trouble, difficulty, torture, torment, agony.

order noun **1** *the list is in alphabetical order*: **sequence**, arrangement, organization, disposition, structure, system, series, succession; grouping, classification, categorization, codification, systematization, disposal, form; layout, array, set-up, line-up.
2 *I tried to restore the room to some semblance of order*: **tidiness**, neatness, orderliness, trimness, harmony, apple-pie order.
▷ANTONYMS chaos, disarray, untidiness.
3 *6,000 police were needed to keep order*: **peace**, **control**, lawful behaviour, law and order, law, lawfulness, discipline, calm, quiet, peace and quiet, quietness, peacefulness, peaceableness, tranquillity, serenity.
▷ANTONYMS disorder.
4 *the idea appealed to his sense of order*: **orderliness**, organization, method, system; symmetry, pattern, uniformity, regularity, routine.
5 *all the equipment was in good order*: **condition**, state, repair, shape, situation.
6 *I had no choice but to obey his orders*: **command**, instruction, directive, direction, decree, edict, injunction, mandate, dictate, commandment; law, rule, regulation, ordinance, statute, fiat, diktat; demand, bidding, requirement, stipulation; summons, writ, warrant; in Spanish-speaking countries pronunciamento; in Tsarist Russia ukase; informal say-so; literary behest; rare rescript.
7 *winning the order would mean about £60 million worth of work for the company*: **commission**, purchase order, request, requisition, demand, call; booking, reservation, application.
8 *the upper and lower orders of society*: **class**, level, rank, caste, grade, degree, position, station, category.
9 *the established social order*: **system**, class system, hierarchy, pecking order, grouping, grading, ranking, scale.
10 *the higher orders of insects*: **taxonomic group**, class, subclass, family, species, breed; technical taxon.
11 *the head of a religious order*: **community**, brotherhood, sisterhood.
12 *the Independent Orange Order*: **organization**, association, society, fellowship, body, fraternity, confraternity, sorority, brotherhood, sisterhood, lodge, guild, league, union, club; denomination, sect; rare sodality.
13 *diplomatic skills of a very high order*: **type**, kind, sort, nature, variety, ilk, genre, cast, style, brand, vintage; quality, calibre, standard.
□ **in order 1** *list the points you intend to cover and put them in order*: **in sequence**, in alphabetical order, in numerical order, in order of priority, in order of merit, in order of seniority. **2** *when he switched on the light and went in, he found everything in order*: **tidy**, neat, neat and tidy, orderly, straight, trim, shipshape (and Bristol fashion), in apple-pie order, spick and span; in position, in place. **3** *I think it's in order for me to take the credit, don't you?* **appropriate**, fitting, suitable, right, correct, proper; **acceptable**, all right, permissible, permitted, allowable; French comme il faut; informal okay.
□ **of the order of** *the reduction was of the order of 11 percent*: **roughly**, approximately, about, around, just about, round about, or so, or thereabouts, more or less, in the neighbourhood of, in the region of, in the area of, in the vicinity of, something like, or thereabouts, give or take (a few), in round numbers, rounded up/down; near to, close to, nearly, not far off, almost, approaching; Brit. getting on for; Latin circa; informal pushing, as near as dammit; N. Amer. informal in the ballpark of; archaic nigh.
▷ANTONYMS precisely.
□ **the order of the day** *spectacle is the order of the day for many younger artists*: **predominant**, prevalent, current, customary, established, common, widespread, preponderant, in force, in effect, popular; informal the in thing.
□ **out of order 1** *the lift's out of order*: **not working**, not in working order, not functioning, broken, broken-down, out of service, out of commission, acting up, unserviceable, faulty, defective, non-functional, inoperative, in disrepair; down; informal conked out, bust, (gone) kaput, gone phut, on the blink, gone haywire, shot; Brit. informal knackered, jiggered, wonky; N. Amer. informal on the fritz, out of whack; Brit. vulgar slang buggered. **2** *he wanted to sack her on the spot—that's really out of order*: **unacceptable**, unfair, unjust, unjustified, uncalled for, below the belt, out of turn, not done, unreasonable, unwarranted, unnecessary, wrong, beyond the pale, improper, irregular; informal not on, a bit much; Brit. informal a bit thick, off, not cricket; Austral./NZ informal over the fence.
▸ verb **1** *he ordered me to return at once*: **instruct**, command, direct, enjoin, give the order to, give the command to, tell, require, charge, adjure; literary bid.
2 *Judge Butler ordered that assets worth £23,000 be confiscated under the Drugs Trafficking Act*: **decree**, ordain, rule, legislate, lay down, dictate, prescribe, pronounce, determine; rare enact.
3 *you can order your tickets by phone*: **request**, apply for, send away/off for, write off for, put in an order for, place an order for, requisition; book, reserve; commission, contract for; rare bespeak.
4 *Derek struggled to order his thoughts | the messages are ordered alphabetically*: **organize**, put in order, set in order, arrange, sort out, straighten out, marshal, dispose, lay out, regulate; group, classify, categorize, catalogue, codify, systematize, systemize, tabulate; Medicine triage; rare methodize.
□ **order someone about/around tell someone what to do**, give orders to, boss about/around, bully, lord it over, dictate to, ride roughshod over, dominate, domineer, browbeat; throw one's weight about/around, lay down the law; informal push about/around.

orderly adjective **1** *an orderly room*: **neat**, **tidy**, well ordered, in order, trim, in apple-pie order, as neat as a new pin, spick and span, well kept, straight; Brit. informal, dated shipshape (and Bristol fashion).
▷ANTONYMS disorderly, untidy, chaotic, messy.
2 *Robert had been an orderly man | the orderly presentation of information*: **well organized**, organized, efficient, businesslike, methodical, systematic, careful, meticulous, punctilious; coherent, structured, logical, well planned, well regulated, systematized; French rangé.
▷ANTONYMS disorganized.
3 *the crowd was quiet and orderly*: **well behaved**, law-abiding, disciplined, peaceful, peaceable, non-violent, controlled, restrained, civilized, well mannered, polite, courteous, decorous; archaic ruly.
▷ANTONYMS disorderly, unruly.

ordinance noun **1** *the president issued a series of ordinances in 1944*: **edict**, decree, law, injunction, fiat, command, order, rule, ruling, dictum, dictate, directive, mandate, enactment, statute, act, canon, regulation; in Tsarist Russia ukase; in Spanish-speaking countries pronunciamento.
2 *religious ordinances*: **rite**, ritual, ceremony, sacrament, observance, service, usage, institution, practice.

ordinarily adverb *he ordinarily worked outside Great Britain*: **usually**, normally, as a rule, generally, as a general rule, in general, in the general run of things, for the most part, by and large, mainly, mostly, most of the time, customarily, typically, habitually, commonly, routinely.
▷ANTONYMS exceptionally, unusually.

ordinary adjective **1** *the ordinary course of events*: **usual**, normal, standard, typical, stock, common, customary, habitual, accustomed, expected, wonted, everyday, regular, routine, day-to-day, daily, established, settled, set, fixed, traditional, quotidian, prevailing.
▷ANTONYMS abnormal.

O

2 *he's just an ordinary middle-aged man | my life seemed very ordinary*: **average**, normal, run-of-the-mill, standard, typical, middle-of-the-road, common, conventional, mainstream, unremarkable, unexceptional, unpretentious, modest, plain, simple, homely, homespun, workaday, undistinguished, nondescript, characterless, colourless, commonplace, humdrum, mundane, unmemorable, pedestrian, prosaic, quotidian, uninteresting, uneventful, dull, boring, uninspiring, bland, suburban, hackneyed, stale, mediocre, middling, indifferent; N. Amer. garden-variety; informal OK, so-so, bog-standard, vanilla, plain vanilla, nothing to write home about, a dime a dozen, no great shakes, not up to much; Brit. informal common or garden; N. Amer. informal ornery.
▷ANTONYMS unusual, extraordinary, unique, exceptional.
□ **out of the ordinary** *nothing out of the ordinary happened*: **unusual**, exceptional, remarkable, extraordinary, unexpected, surprising, unaccustomed, uncommon, unfamiliar, abnormal, atypical, unwonted, out of the way, anomalous, different, special, exciting, memorable, striking, noteworthy, unique, singular, unheard of, impressive, outstanding, unconventional, unorthodox, exotic, strange, peculiar, odd, queer, curious, bizarre, offbeat, weird, outlandish.

ordnance noun **guns**, cannon, artillery, weapons, arms, munitions, military supplies, materiel.

ordure noun **excrement**, excreta, dung, manure, muck, droppings, faeces, stools, cowpats, guano, night soil, sewage, dirt, filth, jakes, doings, scat; informal pooh, doo-doo, jobbie; Brit. informal cack, whoopsie, big jobs; N. Amer. informal poop; vulgar slang shit, crap, turds; rare feculence, egesta.

organ noun **1** *the internal organs*: **part of the body**, body part, biological structure.
2 *an article in the official organ of the Salvation Army*: **newspaper**, paper, journal, periodical, magazine, newsletter, gazette, bulletin, publication, means of communication, mouthpiece, voice, forum, vehicle, medium, channel, instrument, agency; informal rag.

organic adjective **1** *organic matter*: **living**, live, animate, biological, natural; technical biotic.
▷ANTONYMS inorganic.
2 *organic vegetables | organic farming*: **pesticide-free**, additive-free, chemical-free, non-chemical, natural.
3 *the love scenes were an organic part of the drama and important in the story telling*: **essential**, fundamental, basic, integral, intrinsic, vital, indispensable, inherent, constitutive, innate, structural.
▷ANTONYMS incidental.
4 *a society is an organic whole*: **structured**, organized, coherent, integrated, coordinated, ordered, systematic, systematized, methodical, orderly, consistent, harmonious, methodized.
▷ANTONYMS disparate.

Word toolkit

organic	biological	living
food	weapons	organisms
vegetables	warfare	creatures
waste	father/mother	cells
fertilizer	diversity	people
chemistry	clock	plants

organism noun **1** *fish and other organisms*: **living thing**, being, creature, animal, plant, structure, life form, entity, body.
2 *parliament is a complex political organism*: **structure**, **system**, organization, entity, whole, set-up.

organization noun **1** *the organization of conferences and seminars*: **planning**, arrangement, coordination, structuring, administration, organizing, running, management, logistics; establishment, formation, development, assembling, assembly, regulation.
2 *the overall organization of the book*: **structure**, arrangement, scheme, plan, pattern, order, form, format, framework, system, composition, constitution, shape, make-up, configuration; systematization, methodization, categorization, classification, codification.
3 *his lack of organization*: **efficiency**, order, orderliness, sense of order, method, system, tidiness, planning.
4 *a large international organization*: **company**, firm, concern, operation, corporation, institution, group, establishment, consortium, conglomerate, combine, syndicate, body, agency, federation, confederation, alliance, coalition, association, movement, society, league, club, network, confederacy; informal outfit, set-up.

organize verb **1** *try to organize your thoughts | our primary objective is to collect, organize, and disseminate information*: **put in order**, order, arrange, sort, sort out, assemble, marshal, put straight, group, dispose, classify, collocate, categorize, catalogue, codify, tabulate, compile, systematize, systemize, regulate, regiment, standardize, structure, shape, mould, lick/knock into shape, pigeonhole; Medicine triage; rare methodize.
▷ANTONYMS jumble, disorganize.
2 *a local man organized a search party | I'll organize the transport*: **make arrangements for**, arrange, coordinate, sort out, put together, fix up, get together, orchestrate, choreograph, be responsible for, be in charge of, take care of, look after, see to, see about, deal with, direct, run, manage, conduct, administrate, set up, mobilize, mastermind, engineer; institute, develop, form, create, establish, found, originate, begin, start; schedule, timetable, programme; rare concert.

organized adjective *a highly organized campaign | she used to be so organized*: **well ordered**, in order, ordered, well run, well regulated, orderly, efficient, neat, tidy, methodical, businesslike, planned, systematic, structured, arranged; informal together.
▷ANTONYMS disorganized, inefficient.

orgiastic adjective *a place remarkable for its wild parties and orgiastic festivals*: **debauched**, wild, riotous, wanton, abandoned, dissolute, depraved, bacchanalian, Bacchic, saturnalian, Dionysiac, Dionysian.
▷ANTONYMS puritanical, ascetic.

orgy noun **1** *a drunken orgy*: **wild party**, debauch, carousal, carouse, revel, revelry, bacchanalia, bacchanal, saturnalia, Dionysiacs; Scottish skite; informal binge, jag, booze-up, bender, spree, drunk, love-in, gang bang; Brit. informal rave-up; N. Amer. informal toot; archaic wassail.
2 *a shopping orgy | an orgy of violence*: **bout**, excess, surfeit, overindulgence; informal spree, splurge, binge.

orient, orientate verb **1** *there were no street names to enable her to orient herself*: **get/find one's bearings**, get the lie of the land, establish one's location, feel one's way.
2 *you will need time to orientate yourself to your new way of life*: **adapt**, adjust, accommodate, familiarize, acclimatize, accustom, attune, habituate, condition, find one's feet; Brit. play oneself in; N. Amer. acclimate.
3 *magazines oriented to the business community*: **aim**, direct, slant, angle, pitch, steer, design, intend.
4 *the fires are oriented in direct line with the midsummer sunset*: **align**, place, position, put, dispose, situate, set.

oriental adjective *his priceless collection of oriental art*: **eastern**, Chinese, Japanese.

Choose the right word **oriental**

The term **oriental** is now regarded as old-fashioned and potentially offensive as a term referring to people from eastern Asia. In US English, **Asian** is the standard accepted term in modern use. In British English, where **Asian** tends to refer to people from the Indian subcontinent, specific terms such as **Chinese** or **Japanese** are preferable, while **South-East Asian** has also emerged as a more general term. The word **Asiatic**, while standard in scientific and technical use, can be offensive when used of individual people and should be avoided in that context.

orientation noun **1** *the orientation of the radar station | a north-easterly orientation*: **positioning**, location, position, situation, lie, bearings, angle, placement, direction, alignment, emplacement, locating, situating.
2 *his orientation to his new way of life*: **adaptation**, adjustment, accommodation, familiarization, acclimatization, settling in.
3 *both studies could be broadly construed as feminist in orientation*: **attitude**, inclination, direction, aim, intention.
4 *only a small fraction of the workforce received any orientation*: **induction**, training, guidance, introduction, initiation, briefing.

orifice noun **opening**, hole, aperture, crack, slot, slit, cleft, cranny, chink, gap, space, vent, breach, break, rent, fissure, mouth, crevice, rift, perforation, pore.

origin noun **1** *the origins of life and the physical universe | social problems that had their origin in the decline in the economy*: **beginning**, start, origination, genesis, birth, dawning, dawn, emergence, inception, launch, creation, birthplace, cradle, early stages, conception, inauguration, foundation, outset; **source**, basis, base, cause, root, roots, spring, mainspring, well head, fountainhead, fountain, fount, head, seat, seed, germ; Latin fons et origo; formal commencement; literary wellspring; rare radix.
▷ANTONYMS end, conclusion, termination.
2 *the Latin origin of the word*: **source**, derivation, root, roots, provenance, etymology; N. Amer. provenience.
3 *his Scottish origins*: **descent**, **ancestry**, parentage, pedigree, lineage, line, line of descent, heritage, birth, extraction, background, family, stock, blood, bloodline, genealogy, beginnings; rare filiation, stirps.

original adjective **1** *the original inhabitants of Canada*: **indigenous**, native, aboriginal; **first**, earliest, early, initial, primary, primordial, primal, primeval, primitive; rare autochthonic, autochthonous.
▷ANTONYMS latest, last.
2 *original Rembrandts*: **authentic**, genuine, actual, real, true, pukka, bona fide, veritable, not copied, archetypal, prototypical, master; informal kosher.
▷ANTONYMS fake.
3 *the film is challenging and highly original*: **innovative**, creative, imaginative, innovatory, innovational, inventive, ingenious; **new**, novel, fresh, refreshing; unusual, unconventional, unorthodox, unfamiliar, unprecedented, groundbreaking, pioneering, avant-garde, seminal, fertile,

O

unique, individual, individualistic, distinctive.
▷ANTONYMS commonplace, conventional, unimaginative.
▶ noun 1 *the portrait may be a copy of the original*: **archetype**, prototype, source, master, paradigm, model, pattern, standard.
2 *he really is an original*: **individualist**, individual, eccentric, nonconformist, free spirit, bohemian, rare bird, maverick, oddity; Latin rara avis; informal character, oddball, odd/queer fish, nut, weirdo, weirdie; Brit. informal one-off, odd bod, oner; N. Amer. informal wacko, wack, screwball, kook; informal, dated card, case.

Word links original

proto-, **ur-** related prefixes, as in *prototype, prototherian, urtext*

Word toolkit

original	native	indigenous
version	language	people
idea	land	culture
design	country	groups
meaning	tongue	species
members	speakers	tribe
owner	habitat	plants
equipment	American	religions

originality noun *the originality of his ideas*: **inventiveness**, ingenuity, creativeness, creativity, innovativeness, innovation, novelty, newness, freshness, imagination, imaginativeness, break with tradition, resourcefulness, cleverness, daring, individuality, unusualness, unconventionality, unprecedentedness, uniqueness, distinctiveness.

originally adverb *the conference was originally scheduled for November*: **at first**, first, in/at the beginning, to begin with, initially, in the first place, at the start, at the outset, in the first instance, from day one; informal from the word go.

originate verb 1 *the disease originates from East Africa*: **arise**, have its origin, derive, begin, start, stem, spring, emerge, develop, grow, rise, flow, emanate, issue.
2 *Bill Levy originated the idea*: **invent**, be the inventor of, create, initiate, devise, think up, dream up, coin, conceive, design, concoct, contrive, formulate, form, evolve, develop, generate, engender, produce, discover, set in motion, set up, put in place, inaugurate, launch, mastermind, pioneer, introduce, establish, institute, bring about, found, give birth to, be the father/mother of; literary beget.
▷ANTONYMS terminate, end.

O

originator noun **inventor**, creator, architect, author, prime mover, father, mother, maker, initiator, innovator, founder, pioneer, mastermind, discoverer, establisher, developer, designer; literary begetter.

ornament noun 1 *small tables covered with ornaments*: **knick-knack**, trinket, bauble, piece of bric-a-brac, bibelot, gewgaw, gimcrack, furbelow, objet, accessory; informal whatnot, dingle-dangle; Brit. informal doobry, doodah; N. Amer. informal tchotchke, tsatske; dated folderol; archaic whim-wham, kickshaw, bijou.
2 *a cream silk dress that had no ornament at all*: **decoration**, adornment, embellishment, ornamentation, trimming, accessories, frills, frippery, finery, enhancement, beautification, garnish, garnishing, garnishment, gingerbread.
▶ verb *the gold ring was exquisitely ornamented with tiny pearls*: **decorate**, adorn, embellish, trim, garnish, bedeck, deck (out), festoon, enhance, beautify, grace, accessorize, dress up; literary bedizen, furbelow.

ornamental adjective *ornamental plasterwork*: **decorative**, fancy, ornate, attractive, pretty, artistic, ornamented, showy, gingerbread, for show, non-functional.

ornamentation noun *she wore simple clothing with no ornamentation*: **decoration**, adornment, embellishment, ornament, finery, frippery, frills, trimmings, accessories, embroidery, garnishing, garnishment, gingerbread; rare fallalery.

ornate adjective 1 *an ornate Venetian gilt mirror*: **elaborate**, decorated, embellished, adorned, ornamented, fancy, over-elaborate, fussy, busy, ostentatious, showy, baroque, rococo, florid, wedding-cake, gingerbread; informal flash, flashy.
2 *ornate, metaphorical language*: **elaborate**, over-elaborate, flowery, florid, flamboyant; **grandiose**, pompous, pretentious, affected, high-flown, high-sounding, orotund, fulsome, magniloquent, grandiloquent, rhetorical, oratorical, bombastic, laboured, strained, overwrought, overblown, overdone, convoluted, stilted, turgid, inflated; informal highfalutin, purple; rare tumid, pleonastic, euphuistic, aureate, Ossianic, fustian, hyperventilated.
▷ANTONYMS plain, austere, simple.

orotund adjective 1 *Halliwell's orotund voice*: **deep**, sonorous, strong, powerful, full, full-toned, rich, fruity, clear, round, resonant, ringing, reverberating, loud, booming, imposing; rare canorous.
2 *the orotund rhetoric of his prose*: **pompous**, pretentious, affected, mannered, fulsome, grandiose, ornate, over-elaborate, overblown, flowery, florid, flamboyant, inflated, high-flown, high-sounding, magniloquent, grandiloquent, declamatory, rhetorical, oratorical, theatrical, rotund, bombastic, overwrought, overdone, convoluted, turgid; informal highfalutin, purple; rare tumid, euphuistic, aureate, Ossianic, fustian, hyperventilated.

orthodox adjective 1 *his views were orthodox in his time*: **conventional**, mainstream, conformist, accepted, approved, received, recognized, correct, proper, established, well established, authorized, authoritative, traditional, traditionalist, prevailing, prevalent, common, popular, customary, usual, normal, regular, standard, canonical, doctrinal, unheretical, conservative, unoriginal, derivative; French bien pensant.
▷ANTONYMS unconventional, unorthodox, nonconformist.
2 *an orthodox Hindu*: **conservative**, traditional, observant, conformist, devout, strict, true, true blue, of the faith, of the true faith.

orthodoxy noun 1 *a pillar of orthodoxy, he challenged the theological liberalism of his time*: **conventionality**, conventionalism, conformism, conservatism, traditionalism, conformity, properness, propriety, correctness, doctrinalism, unoriginality.
2 *the prevailing aesthetic orthodoxies*: **doctrine**, belief, conviction, creed, dogma, credo, theory, view, idea, tenet, teaching, practice, received wisdom, article of faith.

oscillate verb 1 *the pendulum started to oscillate*: **swing**, sway, swing from side to side, swing back and forth, swing backwards and forwards, swing to and fro, vibrate; N. Amer. informal wigwag.
2 *he was oscillating between fear and bravery*: **waver**, swing, fluctuate, alternate, see-saw, veer, yo-yo, sway, go from one extreme to the other, vary, vacillate, teeter, hover; informal wobble, blow hot and cold.

oscillation noun 1 *the oscillation of the pendulum*: **swinging**, swing, swaying, swinging from side to side, swinging backwards and forwards, swinging back and forth, swinging to and fro, vibration.
2 *his oscillation between commerce and art*: **wavering**, fluctuation, see-sawing, vacillation, yo-yoing, variation.

ossify verb 1 *these cartilages may ossify*: **turn into bone**, become bony, harden, solidify, stiffen, rigidify, petrify, fossilize; rare indurate.
2 *past oligarchies have fallen from power because they ossified*: **become inflexible**, become rigid, fossilize, harden, rigidify, stagnate, become unyielding/obdurate, become unprogressive, cease developing.

ostensible adjective *there are of course dangers in taking ostensible motives as real ones*: **apparent**, seeming, outward, surface, superficial, professed, supposed, avowed, presumed, so-called, alleged, declared, claimed, purported, pretended, feigned, specious; rare ostensive.
▷ANTONYMS real, genuine.

ostensibly adverb *it is ostensibly a book about football*: **apparently**, seemingly, on the face of it, to all appearances, on the surface, to all intents and purposes, outwardly, superficially, allegedly, professedly, supposedly, purportedly; rare pretendedly, ostensively.
▷ANTONYMS genuinely, really, truly.

ostentation noun *consumers abandoned the excess and ostentation of the 1980s*: **showiness**, show, showing off, ostentatiousness; **pretentiousness**, pretension, vulgarity, conspicuousness, obtrusiveness, display, flamboyance, gaudiness, garishness, tinsel, brashness, loudness, extravagance, ornateness, theatricality, kitschness, affectation, bad taste, tastelessness, self-advertisement, exhibitionism, flaunting; informal flashiness, flash, flashness, glitz, glitziness, ritziness, swankiness, swank, splashiness.
▷ANTONYMS modesty, unpretentiousness.

ostentatious adjective *an ostentatious display of wealth*: **showy**, **pretentious**, conspicuous, obtrusive, flamboyant, gaudy, garish, tinsel, tinselly, brash, vulgar, loud, extravagant, fancy, ornate, affected, theatrical, overdone, over-elaborate, kitsch, tasteless; informal flash, flashy, fancy-pants, over the top, OTT, glitzy, ritzy, swanky, splashy; N. Amer. informal bling-bling, superfly; US black English dicty.
▷ANTONYMS plain, unobtrusive, restrained, modest.

ostracism noun *the threat of social ostracism*: **exclusion**, rejection, repudiation, shunning, spurning, the cold shoulder, cold-shouldering, boycotting, blackballing, blacklisting, snubbing, avoidance, barring, banishment, exile, expulsion; N. Amer. disfellowship; Christianity excommunication.
▷ANTONYMS acceptance, welcome.

ostracize verb *individuals who took such action risked being ostracized by their fellow workers*: **exclude**, shun, spurn, cold-shoulder, give someone the cold shoulder, reject, repudiate, boycott, blackball, blacklist, cast off, cast out, shut out, avoid, ignore, snub, cut dead, keep at arm's length, leave out in the cold, bar, ban, debar, banish, exile, expel; Brit. send to Coventry; N. Amer. disfellowship; informal freeze out, hand someone the frozen mitt; Brit. informal blank; dated cut; Christianity excommunicate.
▷ANTONYMS welcome, accept, befriend, include.

other adjective 1 *these homes use other fuels only because gas is unavailable*: **alternative**, different, dissimilar, disparate, distinct, separate, contrasting,

unlike, variant.
2 *are there any other questions?* **more**, further, additional, extra, added, supplementary, supplemental.

> *Word links* **other**
>
> **hetero-** related prefix, as in *heterosexual, heteropolar*

otherwise adverb **1** *hurry up, otherwise we'll be late*: **or else**, or, if not.
2 *she's exhausted, but otherwise she's fine*: **in other respects**, in other ways, apart from that.
3 *he could not have acted otherwise*: **differently**, in any other way.

other-worldly adjective *his face was lean with a distant, other-worldly look*: **ethereal**, fey, dreamy, spiritual, mystic, mystical; unearthly, supernatural, preternatural, transcendental; unworldly.

ounce noun *it took every ounce of courage she possessed to board the plane*: **particle**, scrap, bit, speck, iota, whit, jot, trace, atom, shred, crumb, fragment, grain, drop, spot, mite, tittle, jot or tittle, modicum; Irish stim; informal smidgen, smidge, tad; archaic scantling, scruple.

ourselves pronoun
□ **by ourselves** See **by oneself** at **by**.

oust verb *armed forces ousted the new coalition government*: **drive out**, expel, force out, throw out, remove, remove from office/power, eject, get rid of, depose, topple, unseat, overthrow, bring down, overturn, put out, drum out, thrust out, push out, turn out, purge, evict, dispossess, dismiss, dislodge, displace, supplant, disinherit, show someone the door; banish, deport, exile; informal boot out, kick out, give someone the boot; Brit. informal turf out; dated out.

out adjective & adverb **1** *I'm afraid she's out at the moment*: **not here**, not at home, not in, gone away, away, elsewhere, absent, away from one's desk.
▷ANTONYMS in.
2 *the secret was soon out*: **revealed**, in the open, out in the open, common knowledge, public knowledge, known, disclosed, divulged, exposed.
▷ANTONYMS unknown, secret.
3 *the roses are out*: **in flower**, flowering, in bloom, in full bloom, blooming, in blossom, blossoming, open.
▷ANTONYMS in bud.
4 *the book should be out by the end of the month*: **available**, obtainable, in the shops, published, in print, issued.
5 *the fire was nearly out*: **not burning**, extinguished, no longer alight, quenched, doused, dead, defunct.
6 *grunge is out*: **no longer in fashion**, out of fashion, unfashionable, out of style, dated, out of date, outdated, not in, behind the times; French démodé, passé; informal old hat, not with it.
▷ANTONYMS fashionable.
7 *smoking is out and so is too much alcohol*: **forbidden**, not permitted, not allowed, proscribed, taboo, impermissible, unacceptable, not advisable; informal not on.
▷ANTONYMS permitted, ok.
8 *he was slightly out in his calculations*: **mistaken**, inaccurate, incorrect, wide of the mark, wrong, in error, off.
▷ANTONYMS spot on, accurate.
□ **out cold unconscious**, knocked out, out for the count, KO'd, insensible, comatose, senseless; informal kayoed, dead to the world; Brit. informal spark out; rare soporose, soporous.
▶ verb informal *it was not our intention to out him*: **expose**, unmask, uncover.

out-and-out adjective *he really is an out-and-out chauvinist*: **utter**, downright, thoroughgoing, absolute, complete, thorough, through and through, total, unmitigated, outright, real, perfect, consummate, surpassing, sheer, rank, pure, unqualified, inveterate, positive, dyed-in-the-wool, true-blue, undiluted, unalloyed, unadulterated, in every respect, unconditional; blatant, flagrant, overt, naked, barefaced, brazen; N. Amer. full-bore; informal deep-dyed; Brit. informal right; Austral./NZ informal fair; archaic arrant; rare right-down.

outbreak noun **1** *an outbreak of legionnaires' disease | the latest outbreak of hostility*: **eruption**, flare-up, upsurge, outburst, epidemic, breakout, sudden appearance, rash, wave, spate, flood, explosion, burst, blaze, flurry; rare recrudescence, ebullition, boutade.
2 *the outbreak of war*: **start**, beginning, onset, breaking out, opening, outset, day one, inception, dawn, genesis; formal commencement.

outburst noun *outbursts of emotion | a wild outburst of applause*: **eruption**, explosion, burst, outbreak, flare-up, blow-up, blaze, attack, fit, spasm, paroxysm, access, rush, gale, flood, storm, hurricane, torrent, outpouring, surge, upsurge, spurt, effusion, outflow, outflowing, welling up; informal splurt; rare ebullition, boutade.

outcast noun *a social outcast*: **pariah**, persona non grata, reject, leper, untouchable; foundling, waif, stray; exile, refugee, displaced person, DP, evacuee, expatriate, outsider, outlaw, castaway; rare Ishmael.
▷ANTONYMS insider.

outclass verb *he proceeded to win his next nine races, completely outclassing his rivals*: **surpass**, be superior to, be better than, outshine, overshadow, eclipse, outdo, outplay, outmanoeuvre, outdistance, outstrip, outrun, outpace, out-think, get the better of, dwarf, put in the shade, upstage, transcend; top, cap, trump, trounce, beat, defeat, better, put to shame, exceed, leave behind, outrank; informal be a cut above, be head and shoulders above, run rings round, leave standing, walk away from; archaic outrival, outvie.

outcome noun *the future of the industry could hinge on the outcome of next month's election*: **result**, end result, consequence, net result, upshot, effect, after-effect, aftermath, conclusion, sequel, follow-up, issue, product, end product, end, development, offshoot, outgrowth, wake, denouement; Medicine sequelae; informal pay-off; archaic success.

outcry noun **1** *an outcry of spontaneous passion*: **shout**, exclamation, cry, yell, howl, whoop, roar, scream, shriek, screech; informal holler.
2 *the public outcry led to the closure of the bank*: **protest(s)**, protestation(s), complaints, howls of protest, objections, indignation, furore, clamour, clamouring, fuss, commotion, uproar, hue and cry, row, outbursts, tumult, opposition, dissent, vociferation; informal hullabaloo, ballyhoo, ructions, stink.
▷ANTONYMS indifference.

outdated adjective *an outdated rail network*: **old-fashioned**, out of date, outmoded, out of fashion, unfashionable, out of style, dated, out, outworn, old, former, musty, old-time, old-world, behind the times, behindhand, past, bygone, archaic, obsolescent, obsolete, ancient, antiquated, superannuated, defunct, medieval, prehistoric, antediluvian, old-fogeyish, old-fangled, backward-looking, quaint, anachronistic, crusted, feudal, fusty, moth-eaten, olde worlde; French passé, démodé, vieux jeu; informal old hat, square, not with it, out of the ark, creaky, mouldy; N. Amer. informal horse-and-buggy, clunky, rinky-dink, mossy; archaic square-toed.
▷ANTONYMS current, modern, fashionable.

outdistance verb **1** *the colt outdistanced the train at a canter*: **outrun**, outstrip, run faster than, outpace, leave behind, get (further) ahead of, gain on, draw away from, overtake, pass, shake off, throw off, lose, put distance between oneself and someone else, widen the gap between oneself and someone else.
2 *the sugar mill at Torres outdistanced all its rivals in output*: **surpass**, outshine, do better than, outclass, outdo, excel, exceed, transcend, top, cap, trump, beat, better, leave behind, lead; informal leave standing, walk away from; archaic outrival, outvie.

outdo verb *each lady tried to outdo the other in the number of coffee parties given*: **surpass**, outshine, do better than; overshadow, eclipse, outclass, outmanoeuvre, out-think, get the better of, dwarf, put in the shade, upstage, put to shame; **excel**, exceed, transcend, top, cap, trump, beat, better, outdistance, outstrip, outrun, outpace, lead, leave behind, get (further) ahead of, gain on, draw away from, overtake, pass; informal be a cut above, be head and shoulders above, run rings round, leave standing, walk away from; archaic outrival, outvie.

> *Choose the right word* **outdo, excel, surpass**
>
> See **excel**.

outdoor adjective *a popular outdoor activity*: **open air**, out-of-doors, outside, exterior, external; exposed to the elements, not under cover, field; French en plein air, plein-air; Italian al fresco.
▷ANTONYMS indoor, inside.

outer adjective **1** *the outer layer of a vegetable is often the most nutritious*: **outside**, outermost, outward, exterior, external, surface, superficial.
2 *manufacturing industry has moved from inner cities to outer areas*: **outlying**, distant, remote, faraway, furthest, peripheral, fringe, border, marginal, suburban, perimeter.
▷ANTONYMS inner.

outface verb *the Cabinet successfully outfaced the shop stewards' movement*: **stand up to**, face down, cow, overawe, intimidate, browbeat, confront, beard, outstare, stare out/down, defy.

outfit noun **1** *I haven't had a chance to wear this outfit yet*: **costume**, suit, uniform, ensemble, habit, attire, clothes, clothing, dress, garb; regalia, regimentals, rig, livery; accoutrements, trappings, disguise; Brit. kit, strip; informal get-up, gear, togs, garms; Brit. informal rig-out; formal apparel; literary array, raiment.
2 *many photographers require an easy-to-use studio lighting outfit*: **kit**, equipment, tools, utensils, implements, tackle, apparatus, paraphernalia, things, stuff; Military accoutrement; rare turnout.
3 *the company has no intention of setting up a local manufacturing outfit in the UK*: **organization**, set-up, enterprise, company, firm, partnership, house, business, group, band, body, crew, team, coterie, clique; unit, formation, corps, commando, cadre, squad, squadron, patrol, troop, platoon, detachment.
▶ verb *there were enough swords and suits of armour to outfit an army*: **equip**, kit out, fit out/up, rig out, supply, issue, furnish with, provide, provision, stock, arm; dress, attire, clothe, robe, costume, garb, deck out, drape, array, accoutre, get up, turn out, trick out/up; informal doll up; literary bedizen, caparison; archaic apparel, invest, habit, trap out.

outfitter noun **clothier**, **tailor**, **couturier**, couturière, stylist, costumier, dressmaker, garment maker, cutter, seamstress; corsetière, milliner, haberdasher; dated modiste; rare sartor.

outflow noun *the seabed was forced apart by the outflow of lava*: **discharge**, outflowing, outpouring, outrush, rush, flood, deluge, issue, spurt, jet, cascade, stream, torrent, gush, outburst; flow, flux, welling, leakage, escape, drain, drainage, outflux, emanation, effluence, effluent, effusion; technical efflux.

outgoing adjective **1** *children who are outgoing and friendly*: **extrovert**, **uninhibited**, unreserved, demonstrative, affectionate, warm, friendly, genial, cordial, affable, easy-going, easy, hail-fellow-well-met, approachable, sociable, convivial, lively, gregarious; communicative, responsive, open, forthcoming, frank, expansive; talkative, garrulous, loquacious.
▷ANTONYMS reserved, introverted, withdrawn.
2 *the outgoing president*: **departing**, retiring, leaving.
▷ANTONYMS incoming.

outgoings plural noun *monthly outgoings*: **expenses**, expenditure, spending, outlay, money spent, payments, disbursements, costs, overheads.

outgrowth noun **protuberance**, **swelling**, excrescence, growth, knob, lump, bump, bulge, eruption, protrusion, projection, prominence; tumour, cancer, boil, carbuncle, pustule, spot, pimple; technical process; rare tumescence.

outing noun **1** *they would go on family outings to the movies*: **trip**, excursion, jaunt, expedition, pleasure trip, day trip, day out, tour, mystery tour, airing, drive, ride, run, turn, cruise, sally; informal junket, spin, tootle, joyride, tool; Scottish informal hurl.
2 *the outing of public figures by the gay press*: **exposure**, unmasking, uncovering, revelation, exposé.

outlandish adjective *he wears outlandish clothes*: **weird**, queer, offbeat, far out, freakish, grotesque, quirky, zany, eccentric, off-centre, idiosyncratic, unconventional, unorthodox, funny, bizarre, fantastic, unusual, extraordinary, strange, unfamiliar, unknown, unheard of, alien, foreign, peculiar, odd, curious; atypical, irregular, anomalous, deviant, abnormal, quaint, out of the way, ludicrous, preposterous; French outré; informal way-out, wacky, freaky, kooky, screwy, kinky, oddball, cranky; N. Amer. informal off the wall, in left field, bizarro; dated singular.
▷ANTONYMS ordinary, commonplace, conventional.

outlast verb *the buildings outlasted generations of occupants*: **outlive**, survive, live after, remain alive after, live/last longer than, outwear; come through, ride out, weather, withstand, live through.

outlaw noun *bands of outlaws held up trains*: **fugitive**, wanted criminal, outcast, exile, pariah, bandit, desperado, brigand, criminal, robber; informal villain.

O

▶verb **1** *a county council has voted to outlaw fox-hunting on its land*: **ban**, bar, prohibit, forbid, veto, embargo, boycott, make illegal, disallow, proscribe, interdict.
▷ANTONYMS permit, allow.
2 *she kept silent for fear that she would be outlawed*: **banish**, exile, cast out, exclude, expel, shut out; repudiate, condemn, put a price on someone's head.

outlay noun *the project involved comparatively little financial outlay*: **expenditure**, expenses, spending, outgoings, money spent, cost, price, charge, payment, disbursement, investment, injection of capital.

outlet noun **1** *fumes from someone's central-heating outlet*: **vent**, vent hole, way out, exit, egress; **outfall**, opening, channel, trench, culvert, cut, conduit, ditch, mouth, valve, safety valve, blow-off; blowhole; orifice, pore, duct.
2 *ensuring that farmers have an outlet for their crops*: **market**, retail outlet, marketplace, selling place, shop, store.
3 *childless women find an outlet for their mothering instincts through other channels*: **means of expression**, release, means of release, release mechanism, safety valve, vent, avenue, way of harnessing, channel.

outline noun **1** *he could see the rectangular outline of the building*: **silhouette**, **profile**, figure, shape, contour, form, line, lineaments, delineation; configuration, perimeter, circumference, tracing, layout, framework, skeleton, diagram, sketch.
2 *the statement gives an outline of public expenditure for each department*: **rough idea**, thumbnail sketch, (quick) rundown, abbreviated version, summary, synopsis, résumé, precis, abridgement, abstract, reduction, digest; epitome, essence, storyline, storyboard, main points, gist, bones, bare bones, skeleton, draft, plan, sketch, scheme.
▶verb **1** *she could see the budgie outlined against the sky*: **silhouette**, define, demarcate, delimit, mark off; sketch, delineate, trace, pencil.
2 *students can apply some of the techniques outlined in this chapter*: **rough out**, sketch out, block out, indicate, touch on, draft, give a thumbnail sketch of, give a rough idea of, give a quick rundown on, summarize, precis.

outlive verb *she outlived her husband by nearly thirty years*: **live on after**, live longer than, outlast, remain alive after, survive; outwear, come through, ride out, weather, withstand, live through.

outlook noun **1** *the two men were wholly different in character and outlook*: **point of view**, viewpoint, views, slant, angle, interpretation, opinion, thinking, way of thinking, perspective, attitude, standpoint, stance, position, frame of mind.
2 *the house has a lovely open outlook over the golf course*: **view**, vista, prospect, panorama, scene, aspect, exposure, surroundings.
3 *low interest rates had improved the outlook for the economy*: **prospects**, expectations, expectancy, hopes, likely improvement, lookout, future, chances, chances of success.

outlying adjective *customers from outlying areas will be able to contact the main centres by telephone*: **distant**, **remote**, outer, outermost, out of the way, faraway, far-flung, peripheral, provincial, inaccessible, obscure, off the beaten track, unfrequented, backwoods.
▷ANTONYMS central, metropolitan.

outmanoeuvre verb **1** *the English were almost outmanoeuvred by the French army*: **outflank**, circumvent, bypass, shake/throw off, get around.
2 *he hoped to outmanoeuvre his critics*: **outwit**, outsmart, out-think, outplay, be cleverer than, steal a march on, trick, make a fool of, get the better of; informal outfox, pull a fast one on, put one over on, run/make rings round; dated outjockey.

outmoded adjective *an exercise in junking outmoded policies*: **out of date**, **old-fashioned**, outdated, out of fashion, outworn, dated, behind the times, ancient, archaic, antiquated, obsolescent, dead, obsolete, disused, defunct, abandoned, tired, exhausted, stale, hackneyed, superannuated; French passé; informal old hat, out of the ark.
▷ANTONYMS fashionable, modern.

out of date adjective **1** *the precinct is out of date as a modern shopping centre*: **old-fashioned**, outmoded, out of fashion, unfashionable, frumpish, frumpy, out of style, outdated, dated, out, outworn, old, former, musty, old-time, old-world, behind the times, behindhand, past, bygone, archaic, obsolescent, obsolete, ancient, antiquated, superannuated; defunct, medieval, prehistoric, antediluvian, old-fogeyish, old-fangled, backward-looking, quaint, anachronistic, crusted, feudal, fusty, moth-eaten, olde worlde; French démodé, vieux jeu, passé; informal old hat, square, not with it, out of the ark, creaky, mouldy; N. Amer. informal horse-and-buggy, clunky, rinky-dink, mossy; archaic square-toed.
▷ANTONYMS modern, fashionable.
2 *many of the facts in the book are now out of date*: **superseded**, obsolete, no longer current/topical, stale, expired, extinct, lapsed, elapsed, run out, invalid, void, null and void.
▷ANTONYMS current.

out of the way adjective **1** *out-of-the-way places*: **outlying**, outer, outermost; **distant**, remote, faraway, far-flung, peripheral, isolated, sequestered, lonely, godforsaken, secluded, inaccessible, obscure, off the beaten track, unfrequented, backwoods.
▷ANTONYMS accessible, near, handy.
2 *I don't find his methods out of the way*: **strange**, unusual, peculiar, odd, funny, curious, bizarre, weird, uncanny, queer, unexpected, unfamiliar, abnormal; atypical, anomalous, untypical, different, out of the ordinary, foreign, exceptional, rare, extraordinary, remarkable, puzzling, mystifying, mysterious, perplexing, baffling, unaccountable, incongruous, uncommon, irregular, singular, deviant, aberrant, freak, freakish; suspicious, dubious, questionable; eerie, unnatural; Scottish unco; French outré; informal fishy, creepy, spooky; Brit. informal rum; N. Amer. informal bizarro.
▷ANTONYMS run-of-the-mill.

out of work adjective **unemployed**, jobless, out of a job, workless, redundant, laid off, idle, between jobs; Brit. informal on the dole, signing on, 'resting'; Austral. informal on the wallaby track.

outpouring noun *these countries have not significantly curbed the outpouring of sewage*: **outflow**, outflowing, outrush, rush, flood, deluge, discharge, issue, spurt, jet, cascade, stream, torrent, gush, outburst, flow, flux, welling, leakage, escape, drain, drainage, outflux, emanation, effluence, effluent, effusion; technical efflux.

output noun *industrial output fell by 2.8% in the year to November*: **production**, product, amount/quantity produced, yield, harvest, return, volume, gross national product, gross domestic product, out-turn, achievement, accomplishment; works, writings, creation, oeuvre.

outrage noun **1** *there was widespread public outrage at the proposal*: **indignation**, fury, anger, rage, disapproval, wrath, shock, resentment, horror, disgust, amazement.
2 *that young children are starving to death is an outrage*: **affront**, **scandal**, offence, insult, injustice, disgrace, infamy.
3 *no group has yet claimed responsibility for the bomb outrage*: **atrocity**, act of violence/brutality/savagery, evil, abomination, obscenity, act of wickedness, crime, wrong, horror, enormity, violation, brutality, barbarism, barbarity, inhumane act, villainy, disgrace.
▶verb *his remarks outraged his female parishioners*: **enrage**, infuriate, incense, anger, scandalize, offend, give offence to, make indignant, affront, be an affront to, shock, horrify, disgust, revolt, repel, appal, displease.

outrageous adjective **1** *the outrageous burden of taxation*: **shocking**, disgraceful, scandalous, atrocious, appalling, abhorrent, monstrous, heinous; evil, wicked, abominable, terrible, horrible, horrid, horrendous, dreadful, hideous, foul, nauseating, sickening, vile, villainous, nasty,

ghastly, odious, loathsome, shameful, infamous, nefarious, iniquitous, unspeakable, intolerable, insufferable, insupportable, unendurable, unbearable; impossible, exasperating, offensive, maddening, distressing; immoderate, exorbitant, unreasonable; Brit. informal over the top, OTT, steep, beastly.
▷ANTONYMS acceptable, mild, moderate.
2 *we can all sneer at people who are caught out by outrageous offers*: **far-fetched**, unlikely, highly unlikely, doubtful, dubious, questionable, implausible, unconvincing, unbelievable, incredible, ridiculous, preposterous, extravagant, elaborate, high-flown, overdramatic, overdone, sensationalized, excessive, overstated, inflated, highly coloured.
▷ANTONYMS realistic, credible.
3 *pop stars wearing outrageous clothes*: **eye-catching**, startling, striking, flamboyant, showy, flashy, gaudy, ostentatious, dazzling; saucy, shameless, brazen, brash, unspeakable, adventurous, bold, daring, audacious, swashbuckling, defiant, daredevil, shocking.
▷ANTONYMS inconspicuous.

outré adjective *the composer's more outré harmonies*: **weird**, queer, outlandish, offbeat, far out, freakish, grotesque, quirky, zany, eccentric, off-centre, idiosyncratic, unconventional, unorthodox, funny, bizarre, fantastic, unusual, extraordinary, strange, unfamiliar, unknown, unheard of, alien, foreign, peculiar, odd, curious, atypical, irregular, anomalous, deviant, abnormal, quaint, out of the way, ludicrous, preposterous; informal way-out, wacky, freaky, kooky, screwy, kinky, oddball, cranky; N. Amer. informal off the wall, in left field, bizarro; dated singular.
▷ANTONYMS ordinary, normal.

outright adverb 1 *he rejected the proposal outright*: **completely**, entirely, wholly, fully, totally, categorically, absolutely, altogether, utterly, flatly, in every respect, unreservedly, without reservation, without exception, thoroughly, quite.
▷ANTONYMS in part, partially.
2 *I can't bring myself to tell her outright*: **explicitly**, straightforwardly, directly, forthrightly, openly, frankly, candidly, honestly, truly, sincerely, bluntly, plainly, in plain language, unreservedly, without constraint, truthfully, without dissembling, to someone's face, straight from the shoulder, without beating about the bush, with no holds barred, man to man, woman to woman; informal on the level; Brit. informal straight up.
3 *the passengers were killed outright*: **instantly**, instantaneously, immediately, at once, straight away, there and then, then and there, on the spot.
4 *houses could be paid off gradually, but paintings had to be bought outright*: **all at once**, at/in one fell swoop, in one go.
▸ adjective 1 *it was an outright lie*: **out-and-out**, absolute, complete, utter, downright, sheer, stark, thorough, thoroughgoing, categorical, unequivocal, undeniable, unqualified, unmodified, unrestricted, unmitigated, unconditional, positive, simple, wholesale, all-out, rank, consummate, pure; archaic arrant.
2 *the outright winner*: **definite**, unequivocal, clear, unqualified, incontestable, undeniable, unmistakable, categorical, straightforward.

outrun verb *an antelope could easily outrun a lion*: **run faster than**, outstrip, outdistance, outpace, leave behind, get (further) ahead of, gain on, draw away from, overtake, pass, shake off, throw off, lose, put distance between oneself and one's pursuer(s), widen the gap between oneself and one's pursuer(s); informal leave standing, walk away from.

outset noun *it must be stressed at the outset that correct identification is the chief problem*: **start**, starting point, beginning, arrival, (first) appearance, dawn, birth, origin, inception, conception, opening, launch, inauguration, institution, initiation, debut, creation, day one, the first; informal kick-off, the word go; formal commencement.
▷ANTONYMS end, conclusion.

outshine verb *a single large house plant can outshine any number of ornaments*: **surpass**, be superior to, overshadow, eclipse, outclass, dwarf, tower above/over, put in the shade, upstage, put to shame, excel, exceed, transcend, top, cap, trump, beat, better, outstrip, outrun; informal be a cut above, be head and shoulders above, run rings round, leave standing, walk away from; archaic outrival, outvie.

outside noun 1 *the outside of the building is decorated in fine style*: **outer/external surface**, surface, exterior, outer side, case, skin, shell, crust, husk, covering, outer layer, sheath, facade, elevation, front, frontage.
▷ANTONYMS inside.
2 *the outside of the bend*: **outer/longer edge**, edge, the long way round.
▷ANTONYMS inside.
▸ adjective 1 *go and put the outside lights on*: **exterior**, external, outer, outermost, outward, outdoor, out-of-doors.
▷ANTONYMS inside.
2 *this work is to be carried out by outside contractors*: **independent**, consultant, consulting, hired, temporary, freelance, casual, visiting, non-resident, external, extramural, peripatetic; extraneous, extrinsic, outward, alien, foreign.
3 *an outside chance*: **slight**, slender, slim, small, tiny, faint, negligible, marginal, remote, distant, vague, unlikely, improbable; little.
▸ adverb *they went outside | shall we eat outside?* **outdoors**, out of doors, out of the house, on the outside, externally, exteriorly.
▷ANTONYMS inside.

> *Word links* **outside**
>
> **ecto-** related prefix, as in *ectoderm, ectoplasm*
> **exo-** related prefix, as in *exoskeleton, exocrine*
> **extra-** related prefix, as in *extramural, extravehicular*

outsider noun *to an outsider the scene would have appeared normal*: **stranger**, visitor, non-member, odd man out; foreigner, alien, outlander, immigrant, emigrant, émigré; incomer, newcomer, parvenu, arriviste, interloper, intruder, gatecrasher; outcast, misfit, individualist, nonconformist, free spirit, unorthodox person, original, bohemian, eccentric, maverick, rebel, dissenter, dissident.

outsize adjective 1 *she started searching in her outsize handbag*: **huge**, oversized, enormous, gigantic, very big, very large, great, giant, colossal, massive, mammoth, vast, immense, tremendous, monumental, prodigious, mountainous, monstrous, elephantine, king-sized, king-size, gargantuan, Herculean, Brobdingnagian, substantial, extensive, hefty, bulky, weighty, heavy, gross; informal mega, monster, whopping, whopping great, thumping, thumping great, humongous, jumbo, hulking, bumper, astronomical; Brit. informal whacking, whacking great, ginormous.
2 *an outsize and very grand Welsh actor*: **very large**, big, massive, fat, corpulent, gross, obese, overweight, stout, fleshy, heavy, plump, portly, chubby, rotund, podgy, roly-poly, paunchy, pot-bellied, beer-bellied, ample, well upholstered, broad in the beam, bulky, bloated, flabby, Falstaffian; informal porky, pudgy, tubby, blubbery, poddy; Brit. informal fubsy; N. Amer. informal lard-assed; archaic pursy; rare abdominous.

outskirts plural noun *a house on the outskirts of the town*: **outlying districts**, edges, fringes, suburbs, suburbia; purlieus, borders, periphery, margin, boundary; surrounding area/district, environs; French faubourg, banlieue; Spanish barrio.

outsmart verb *buyers and sellers attempt to outsmart each other*: **outwit**, out-think, outmanoeuvre, outplay, be cleverer than, steal a march on, trick, make a fool of, get the better of; informal outfox, pull a fast one on, put one over on, run/make rings round; dated outjockey.

outspoken adjective *an outspoken critic of the government*: **forthright**, direct, candid, frank, straightforward, honest, open, straight, straight from the shoulder, plain, plain-spoken, vociferous, vocal; explicit, point-blank, round, blunt, abrupt, bluff, brusque, unequivocal, free, unreserved, uninhibited, unceremonious; archaic free-spoken.
▷ANTONYMS diplomatic, reticent, evasive.

> *Choose the right word* **outspoken, candid, frank, forthright, blunt**
>
> See **candid**.

O

outspread adjective *the kestrels were soaring with outspread wings*: **fully extended**, outstretched, stretched out, spread out, fanned out, splayed out, expanded, unfolded, unfurled, open, open wide, wide open, opened out.

outstanding adjective 1 *an outstanding painter*: **excellent**, marvellous, magnificent, superb, fine, wonderful, superlative, exceptional, formidable, first-class, first-rate, virtuoso, skilful, masterful, masterly; informal great, terrific, tremendous, super, smashing, amazing, fantastic, sensational, stellar, fabulous, fab, ace, crack, A1, mean, awesome, magic, bad, wicked, out of this world; Brit. informal brilliant, brill, bosting; N. Amer. informal neat, badass, boss; Austral. informal bonzer; Brit. informal, dated wizard, spiffing, ripping, topping, champion, capital, top-hole; N. Amer. informal, dated swell, keen; vulgar slang shit-hot.
▷ANTONYMS mediocre.
2 *the site has outstanding views*: **remarkable**, extraordinary, exceptional, striking, eye-catching, vivid, arresting, impressive, distinctive, unforgettable, catchy, haunting, indelible, not/never to be forgotten, memorable, signal, special, momentous, monumental, significant, historic, notable, noteworthy, important, consequential, distinguished, pre-eminent, eminent, well known, famous, famed, celebrated, renowned, notorious, illustrious; informal out of this world.
▷ANTONYMS unexceptional.
3 *how much work is still outstanding?* **to be done**, undone, not done, neglected, omitted, unattended to, unfinished, incomplete, left, remaining, pending, ongoing.
▷ANTONYMS complete, finished.
4 *outstanding debts*: **unpaid**, unsettled, owing, owed, to be paid, payable, receivable, due, overdue, undischarged, in arrears, in the red; N. Amer. delinquent, past due.
▷ANTONYMS paid, settled.

outstrip verb 1 *speeding at 90 mph, he outstripped police cars for an hour*: **go faster than**, outrun, outdistance, outpace, leave behind, get (further) ahead of, gain on, draw away from, overtake, pass, shake off, throw off, lose, put distance between oneself and someone else, widen the gap between oneself and someone else; informal leave standing, walk away from. **2** *demand far outstrips supply*: **surpass**, exceed, be more than, go beyond, better, beat, top, overshadow, eclipse, put to shame.

outward adjective *she put on an outward appearance of sadness*: **external**, outer, outside, outermost, exterior; extrinsic, surface, superficial, visible, observable, noticeable, perceptible, discernible, seeming, apparent, ostensible, evident, obvious.
▷ANTONYMS inward, inner, internal.

outwardly adverb *the house is outwardly no different from any of the others*: **externally**, on the outside, on the surface, superficially, on the face of it, at first sight/glance, to/from all appearances, to the casual eye/observer, as far as one can see/tell/judge, to all intents and purposes, apparently, ostensibly, seemingly, evidently.
▷ANTONYMS inwardly.

outweigh verb **1** *Dixon was outweighed by nearly two stone and was knocked down twice in the second round*: **be heavier than**.
2 *the costs outweigh the benefits*: **be greater than**, exceed, be superior to, take precedence/priority over, prevail over, have the edge on/over, preponderate over, override, tip/turn the scales/balance against, supersede, offset, cancel out, (more than) make up for, outbalance, overbalance, compensate for, redress.

outwit verb *constant vigilance is needed to outwit enemy infiltrators*: **outsmart**, out-think, outmanoeuvre, outplay, be cleverer than, steal a march on, trick, gull, make a fool of, get the better of; informal outfox, pull a fast one on, put one over on, run/make rings round; dated outjockey.

outworn adjective *many of his doctrines are outworn today*: **out of date**, outdated, old-fashioned, out of fashion, outmoded, dated, behind the times, ancient, archaic, antiquated, obsolescent, dead, obsolete, disused, defunct, tired, exhausted, stale, hackneyed, superannuated; French passé; informal old hat, out of the ark.
▷ANTONYMS up to date, fresh, original.

oval adjective **egg-shaped**, ovoid, ovate, oviform, elliptical, ellipsoidal; technical obovate.

ovation noun *the show ended with an ovation from the audience*: **round of applause**, applause, handclapping, clapping, cheering, cheers, bravos, acclaim, standing ovation, acclamation, praise, plaudits, laurels, tribute, accolade, bouquets; informal (big) hand; rare laudation, extolment.

oven noun **stove**, kitchen stove, microwave (oven), (kitchen) range; roaster, kiln; Indian tandoor; NZ hangi; archaic caboose.

over preposition **1** *there will be cloud over most of the country*: **above**, on top of, higher than, higher up than, atop.
▷ANTONYMS under, below.
2 *a view over the lake | he walked over the grass*: **across**, on to, around, throughout, all through, throughout the extent of, everywhere in, in all parts of.
3 *he has three people over him at work*: **superior to**, above, higher up than, more powerful than, in charge of, responsible for, commanding.
4 *over 200,000 people now live in the area*: **more than**, above, in excess of, exceeding, upwards of, beyond, greater than.
5 *this led to further discussion over what constitutes success*: **on the subject of**, about, concerning, apropos of, with reference to, speaking of, with regard/respect to, regarding, as regards, relating to, respecting, in connection with, as for, re; Latin in re.
□ **over and above** *she had an allowance from her father over and above her paltry salary*: **in addition to**, on top of, over and beyond, plus, as well as, besides, not to mention, along with, let alone.
▶ adverb **1** *a flock of geese flew over*: **overhead**, above, on high, aloft, past, by.
2 *the relationship is over*: **at an end**, finished, concluded, terminated, no more, ended, extinct, gone, dead, a thing of the past, ancient history.
3 *he paid all his bills and still had some money over*: **left over**, left, remaining, unused, surplus, superfluous, in excess, extra, in addition.
□ **over and over** *he is a crashing bore who tells the same old jokes over and over*: **repeatedly**, again and again, over and over again, time and again, time and time again, many times over, on many/several occasions, often, frequently, recurrently, constantly, continually, persistently, regularly, habitually, ad nauseam.

> *Word links* **over**
>
> related prefixes: **super-**, as in *superstructure, superlunary*; **sur-**, as in *surtitle, surtax*; **supra-**, as in *suprarenal, supranational*; **hyper-**, as in *hypersonic, hyperlink*

overact verb *she's a weepy actress with a strong tendency to overact*: **exaggerate**, overdo it, overplay it; informal **ham it up**, camp it up, pile it on, lay it on thick, lay it on with a trowel.

overall adjective *the overall cost of a project*: **all-inclusive**, general, comprehensive, universal, all-embracing, gross, net, final, inclusive; master, ruling, sweeping, wholesale, complete, blanket, across the board, umbrella, global, worldwide, international, pandemic, nationwide, countrywide, coast-to-coast, company-wide.
▶ adverb *overall, things have improved*: **generally**, in general, generally speaking, altogether, all in all, on balance, on average, for the most part, mostly, in the main, on the whole, largely, by and large, to a large extent, to a great degree; predominantly, mainly, chiefly, as a rule, principally, basically, substantially.

overawe verb *Jane was often overawed by her landlady*: **intimidate**, daunt, cow, take someone's breath away, awe, disconcert, blind someone with something, unnerve, discourage, subdue, abash, dismay, frighten, alarm, scare, deter, terrify, terrorize, browbeat, bully; informal psych out; N. Amer. informal buffalo.

overbalance verb *she turned round so fast that she almost overbalanced*: **fall over**, topple over, lose one's balance, lose one's footing, tip over, keel over, capsize, overturn, turn turtle; **push over**, upend, upset.

overbearing adjective *he was at the mercy of his overbearing wife*: **domineering**, dominating, autocratic, tyrannical, despotic, heavy-handed, oppressive, high-handed, bullying, high and mighty, lordly, lording it, officious, masterful, dictatorial, bossy, imperious, pontifical, pompous, peremptory, arrogant, cocksure, proud, over-proud, overweening, presumptuous, opinionated, dogmatic; informal pushy, throwing one's weight about, cocky.

overblown adjective *an overblown piece of writing*: **overwritten**, extravagant, florid, grandiose, pompous, over-elaborate, flowery, overwrought, pretentious, high-flown, turgid, bombastic, oratorical, grandiloquent, magniloquent, orotund; informal highfalutin, over the top, OTT; rare euphuistic, fustian, aureate, hyperventilated.
▷ANTONYMS simple, plain.

overcast adjective *the sky was murky and overcast*: **cloudy**, clouded, clouded over, overclouded, sunless, darkened, dark, grey, black, leaden, heavy, dull, murky, dirty, misty, hazy, foggy, louring, threatening, menacing, promising rain, dismal, dreary, cheerless, sombre.
▷ANTONYMS bright, clear.

overcharge verb **1** *clients feel that they are being overcharged for an inadequate service*: **swindle**, charge too much, cheat, defraud, gazump, fleece, short-change, surcharge; informal rip off, sting, screw, soak, rob, diddle, do, rook, clip; N. Amer. informal gouge; Brit. informal, dated rush.
▷ANTONYMS undercharge.
2 *the decoration is overcharged with statues and other accessories*: **overstate**, overdo, exaggerate, over-colour, over-embroider, over-embellish, embroider, embellish; overwrite, overdraw; informal pile it on, lay it on thick, lay it on with a trowel.

overcome verb **1** *neither team was strong enough to overcome the other*: **defeat**, beat, best, conquer, trounce, thrash, rout, vanquish, overwhelm, overpower, destroy, drub, get the better of, triumph over, prevail over, gain a victory over, win over/against, outdo, outclass, outstrip, surpass, excel, worst, subdue, quash, crush; informal slaughter, murder, kill, clobber, hammer, whip, lick, paste, crucify, demolish, tank, wipe the floor with, make mincemeat of, blow out of the water, take to the cleaners, walk (all) over, run rings around; Brit. informal stuff; N. Amer. informal shellac, skunk.
2 *a one-day course which helps people overcome their fear of flying*: **get the better of**, prevail over, control, get control of, get/bring under control, bridle, tame, master, gain mastery over, deal with, conquer, defeat, vanquish, beat, solve, triumph over, best, worst, overpower, overwhelm; get over, get a grip on, curb, subdue, subjugate, repress, quell, quash; informal lick.
▶ adjective *I was overcome, half-suffocated by the sadness*: **overwhelmed**, emotional, moved, affected, struck, choky, speechless, at a loss for words, shaken, disturbed; informal bowled over.

overconfident adjective *her downfall came through being overconfident*: **cocksure**, smug, conceited, self-assured, self-assertive, unabashed, brash, swaggering, blustering, overbearing, overweening, presuming, presumptuous, riding/heading for a fall, foolhardy; informal cocky, too big for one's boots; rare hubristic.
▷ANTONYMS diffident, shy, unsure of oneself.

overcritical adjective *overcritical parents*: **fault-finding**, hypercritical, captious, carping, cavilling, quibbling, hair-splitting, hard to please, over-censorious, over-particular; fussy, finicky, fastidious, meticulous, pedantic, over-exacting, overscrupulous, punctilious, perfectionist; informal nit-picking, pernickety; archaic overnice.
▷ANTONYMS uncritical.

overcrowded adjective *pupils are forced to share textbooks in overcrowded classrooms*: **overfull**, overflowing, full to overflowing/bursting, crammed full, cram-full, jammed, packed like sardines, congested, choked, overloaded, overpopulated, overpeopled, overrun, crowded, thronged, swarming, teeming; informal bursting/bulging at the seams, full to the gunwales, jam-packed, like the Black Hole of Calcutta.
▷ANTONYMS deserted, empty, vacant.

overdo verb **1** *if you overdo the atmosphere, the effect is likely to be comic*: **exaggerate**, overstate, do to death, overemphasize, overplay, go overboard with, dramatize, overdramatize; colour, embroider, embellish, inflate, amplify, magnify, make a mountain out of a molehill, blow up, blow up out of all proportion; informal ham up, camp up, make a (big) thing of/about, pile on, lay it on thick, lay it on with a trowel, make a production of, make a big

deal out of; archaic pull the longbow.
▶ANTONYMS understate, play down.
2 *don't overdo the drink*: **have/do/use/drink too much** ..., overindulge in, have/use/do/eat/drink to excess, carry too far, carry to extremes, not know when to stop, be intemperate.
3 *they always overdid beef*: **overcook**, overbake, burn, burn to a cinder/crisp; informal burn to a frazzle.
□ **overdo it work too hard**, overwork, do too much, work like a Trojan/horse/slave, work day and night, burn the midnight oil, burn the candle at both ends, strain oneself, sweat, sweat blood, overtax oneself, overtax one's strength, overburden oneself, overload oneself, drive/push oneself too hard, work/run oneself into the ground, wear oneself to a shadow, work one's fingers to the bone, wear oneself out, have too many irons in the fire, have too many balls in the air, burn oneself out, bite off more than one can chew; informal kill oneself, knock oneself out; vulgar slang work/sweat one's balls off.

overdone adjective **1** *the flattery was overdone*: **excessive**, too much, undue, immoderate, inordinate, disproportionate, inflated, beyond the pale, overstated, overworked, laboured, exaggerated, over-elaborate, overemphasized, extravagant, over-enthusiastic, effusive, over-effusive, gushing, fulsome, highly coloured, sensationalistic, forced, affected; theatrical, melodramatic, stagy; informal a bit much, over the top, OTT, hyped up, laid on with a trowel, camp.
▶ANTONYMS understated.
2 *overdone food*: **overcooked**, overbaked, dried out, burnt, burnt to a cinder/crisp; informal burnt to a frazzle.
▶ANTONYMS underdone.

overdue adjective **1** *the ship is overdue*: **late**, not on time, behind schedule, behindhand, behind time, delayed, belated, tardy, unpunctual.
▶ANTONYMS early, punctual, on time.
2 *an automatic right to claim interest on overdue payments*: **unpaid**, unsettled, owing, owed, to be paid, payable, receivable, due, outstanding, undischarged, in arrears, in the red; N. Amer. delinquent, past due.

overeat verb *most of us are inclined to overeat occasionally*: **eat too much**, be greedy, eat like a horse, gorge (oneself), overindulge, overindulge oneself, surfeit, guzzle, feast; informal binge, stuff one's face, stuff oneself, pack it away, put it away, make a pig of oneself, pig oneself, pig out; N. Amer. informal scarf out; rare gourmandize, gluttonize.
▶ANTONYMS fast, diet.

overemphasize verb *the importance of appropriate design methods cannot be overemphasized*: **overstress**, exaggerate, attach too much importance/weight to, make too much of, overplay, overdo, overdramatize, belabour, labour, dwell on, harp on, make something out of nothing, make a mountain out of a molehill; informal make a big thing about/of, blow up out of all proportion.
▶ANTONYMS understate, play down.

overflow verb *cream overflowed the edges of the shallow dish*: **spill over**, flow over, run over, brim over, well over, slop over, slosh over, pour forth, stream forth, flood, discharge, surge, debouch.
▶ noun **1** *a ball valve failure would lead to tank overflow in the loft*: **overspill**, spill, spillage, flood, flooding, inundation, excess water.
2 *to accommodate the overflow, five more offices have been built*: **surplus**, excess, additional people/things, extra people/things, remainder, overabundance, overspill.

overflowing adjective *the floods were caused by overflowing rivers*: **overfull**, full to overflowing/bursting, spilling over, running over, crammed full, cram-full, jammed, overcrowded, packed like sardines, congested, choked, overloaded, overpopulated, overpeopled, overrun, crowded, thronged, swarming, teeming; informal bursting/bulging at the seams, full to the gunwales, jam-packed, like the Black Hole of Calcutta.

overhang verb *the shrubs overhang the lawn | the crag below us overhung*: **stick out (over)**, stand out (over), extend (over), project (over), protrude (over), jut (over), jut out (over), poke out (over), beetle (over), bulge out (over), loom (over), hang over, cantilever out (over); archaic be imminent; rare impend, protuberate.

overhaul verb **1** *I've been overhauling the gearbox*: **service**, maintain, repair, mend, fix up, patch up, rebuild, renovate, revamp, recondition, remodel, refit, refurbish, modernize; regulate, adjust; check, check out, check over, check up on, give something a check-up, investigate, inspect, examine, survey; revise, update, reconsider, rework, restructure, realign, shake up; N. English fettle; informal do up.
2 *Kenyon was the only man who could have overhauled him in the world title race*: **overtake**, pass, get past, go past, go by, go faster than, get/pull ahead of, outdistance, outstrip; gain on, catch up with, draw level with.

overhead adverb *another burst of thunder erupted overhead*: **above**, up above, high up, (up) in the sky, on high, above/over one's head, in flight, aloft.
▶ adjective *the proposed 400,000-volt overhead line and its pylons*: **aerial**, elevated, raised, suspended, projecting, overhanging.
▶ANTONYMS underground.

overheads plural noun **running costs**, operating costs, fixed costs, budget items, costs, expenses; Brit. oncosts.
▶ANTONYMS variable costs, cost of sales.

overindulge verb **1** *it's all too easy to overindulge at Christmas*: **drink/eat too much**, overeat, drink like a fish, overdrink, be greedy, be immoderate, be intemperate, overindulge oneself, overdo it, not know when to stop, drink/eat/go to excess, gorge (oneself), surfeit, guzzle, feast; informal binge, go on a binge, stuff one's face, stuff oneself, pack it away, put it away, paint the town red, push the boat out, go overboard, live it up, make a pig of oneself, pig oneself; N. Amer. informal scarf out; archaic tope; rare gourmandize, gluttonize.
2 *his mother had overindulged him*: **spoil**, give in to, indulge, humour, pander to, cosset, pamper, mollycoddle, baby, spoon-feed, feather-bed; informal spoil rotten.

overindulgence noun *overindulgence in food and drink*: **intemperance**, immoderation, excess, overeating, overdrinking, prodigality, lack of restraint, gorging, surfeit, debauch, debauchery, dissipation, dissoluteness, greed, gluttony, orgy; informal binge.
▶ANTONYMS temperance.

overjoyed adjective *Ms Bailey was overjoyed at the birth of her daughter*: **ecstatic**, euphoric, thrilled, elated, delighted, on cloud nine/seven, walking/treading on air, in seventh heaven, jubilant, rapturous, beside oneself with joy, jumping for joy, exultant, transported, delirious, enraptured, blissful, in raptures, as pleased as Punch, cock-a-hoop, as happy as a sandboy, as happy as Larry, like a child with a new toy; informal over the moon, on top of the world, on a high, tickled pink; N. English informal made up; N. Amer. informal as happy as a clam; Austral. informal wrapped.
▶ANTONYMS dejected, depressed; impassive, unmoved.

overlay verb *the area was concreted and overlaid with green, red, and white mosaic marble*: **cover**, face, surface, veneer, inlay, laminate; carpet, blanket, swathe, cloak, veil, shroud; overspread, encrust, smear, daub, bedaub, coat, plaster, plate, varnish, glaze, wash, suffuse.
▶ noun *the joists must be protected with an overlay of glass-fibre insulation*: **covering**, layer, face, surface, veneer, lamination, encrustation, carpet, blanket, sheet, curtain, canopy, cover, cloak, veil, pall, shroud, screen, mask, cloud, envelope; coat, smear, daub, plating, varnish, glaze, wash.
▶ANTONYMS underlay, base.

overload verb **1** *iron has to be carried in alternate holds to avoid overloading the ship*: **overburden**, put too much in, overcharge, encumber, burden, weigh down; rare surcharge.
2 *you should take care not to overload the electrical wiring*: **strain**, impose excessive strain on, overtax, stretch, overwork, overuse; deluge, swamp, oversupply, overwhelm, clog, snow under, beset.
▶ noun *there was an overload of demands on government*: **excess**, overabundance, superabundance, profusion, glut, surfeit, surplus, superfluity, more than enough, too many, too much; avalanche, deluge, flood, abundance, plethora, overkill, backlog.

overlook verb **1** *he overlooked a mistake on the first page*: **miss**, fail to notice, fail to observe, fail to spot, fail to see, leave, leave unnoticed; informal slip up on.
▶ANTONYMS spot, notice.
2 *his work has been overlooked by modern authors*: **disregard**, neglect, ignore, pay no attention/heed to, turn a blind eye, turn a deaf ear to, pass over, omit, skip (over), gloss over, leave out, leave undone, forget.
3 *it is a shortcoming that many are willing to overlook*: **deliberately ignore**, not take into consideration, disregard, take no notice of, take no account of, make allowances for, let pass, turn a blind eye to, wink at, blink at, connive at, excuse, pardon, forgive, condone, let someone off with, let go, sink, bury, let bygones be bygones; informal let something ride.
▶ANTONYMS punish.
4 *the breakfast room overlooks a peaceful garden*: **have a view of**, afford a view of, look over/across, look on to, look out on/over, face, front on to, give on to, give over, open out over, command a view of, command, dominate.

overly adverb *these guitars aren't cheap, but they're not overly expensive either*: **unduly**, excessively, inordinately, too, to too great an extent/degree, immoderately, exceedingly; wildly, absurdly, ridiculously, outrageously, unreasonably, exorbitantly, impossibly.

overpower verb **1** *the prisoners might rebel and overpower the crew*: **gain control over**, overwhelm, prevail over, get the better of, get the upper hand over, gain mastery over, master, control, overthrow, overturn, upset, subdue, suppress, subjugate, repress, quell, quash, crush, finish, bring someone to their knees, break, conquer, defeat, vanquish, beat, be victorious over, gain a victory over, triumph over, best, worst, trounce, rout; informal thrash, lick, clobber, whip, wipe the floor with, drub, tank, blow out of the water.
2 *he was overpowered by grief*: **overcome**, overwhelm, sweep over, move, stir, affect, touch, impress, sweep someone off their feet, strike, stun, shake, disturb, devastate, take aback, daze, leave speechless, spellbind, dazzle, floor; informal bowl over, blow away, knock/hit for six, knock sideways, get to.

overpowering adjective **1** *overpowering grief*: **overwhelming**, burdensome, oppressive, weighty, unbearable, unendurable, intolerable,

O

shattering, intimidating, overbearing, dominating; informal mind-blowing.
2 *an overpowering smell*: **stifling**, suffocating, pervasive, penetrating, strong, pungent, powerful; nauseating, nauseous, sickly, offensive, acrid, astringent, sharp, bitter, fetid, cloying, mephitic; heady, aromatic.
3 *overpowering evidence*: **irrefutable**, undeniable, unquestionable, indisputable, incontestable, incontrovertible, compelling, conclusive, forceful, telling.
▷ANTONYMS mild, slight.

overrate verb *it is easy to overrate what Frederick achieved*: **assess too highly**, overestimate, overvalue, rate/prize too highly, think too much of, exaggerate the worth of, attach too much importance to; praise too highly, exaggerate the merits of, over-praise, oversell, glorify, magnify; informal blow up; rare over-prize.
▷ANTONYMS underrate, underestimate.

overreach verb
□ **overreach oneself** *he waited for his opponents to overreach themselves*: **try to do too much**, overestimate one's ability, overdo it, overstretch oneself, strain oneself, wear/burn oneself out, go too far, try to be too clever/smart, bite off more than one can chew, be too clever by half, have too many irons in the fire, have too many balls in the air, defeat one's own ends, have one's scheme backfire on one, have one's scheme boomerang on one, be hoist with one's own petard.

overreact verb *parents should set children a good example rather than overreact*: **get upset over nothing**, react disproportionately, get overexcited, go too far, act irrationally, lose one's sense of proportion, exaggerate, make something out of nothing, make a mountain out of a molehill, blow something up out of all proportion; informal press/push/hit the panic button; Brit. informal go over the top.
▷ANTONYMS be impassive, be cool.

override verb **1** *the court could not override her decision*: **disallow**, overrule, countermand, veto, set aside, quash, overturn, overthrow; cancel, reverse, rescind, rule against, revoke, withdraw, retract, take back, repeal, repudiate, recant, annul, nullify, declare null and void, invalidate, negate, void, abrogate; Law vacate; archaic recall.
▷ANTONYMS allow, accept.
2 *the government can override all opposition*: **disregard**, pay no heed to, take no account of, close one's mind to, turn a deaf ear to, discount, ignore, ride roughshod over, trample on.
▷ANTONYMS listen to, take notice of.
3 *such a positive attitude will override any negative thoughts*: **outweigh**, supersede, take precedence over, take priority over, be more important than, tip/turn the scales/balance against, offset, cancel out, (more than) make up for, outbalance, overbalance, compensate for, redress.

overriding adjective *safety was the overriding consideration*: **most important**, of greatest importance, of prime importance, of supreme importance, of greatest significance, uppermost, top, supreme, first, first and foremost, highest, pre-eminent, outstanding, predominant, dominant, prevailing, preponderant, principal, leading, primary, paramount, chief, main, major, most prominent, cardinal, foremost, central, key, focal, pivotal, essential; informal number-one.
▷ANTONYMS insignificant, irrelevant.

O

overrule verb *this ban was overruled by a federal court*: **countermand**, cancel, reverse, rescind, repeal, revoke, retract, withdraw, take back, rule against, disallow, override, veto, set aside, quash, overturn, overthrow, repudiate, recant, annul, nullify, declare null and void, invalidate, negate, void, abrogate; Law vacate; archaic recall.
▷ANTONYMS allow, accept.

overrun verb **1** *guerrillas overran the principal military barracks*: **invade**, storm, march into, occupy, infest, swarm over, surge over, flow over, inundate, swamp, overwhelm, permeate, penetrate, spread over, spread like wildfire over, run riot over, overgrow, grow over.
2 *the talks overran the deadline for an agreement*: **exceed**, go beyond, go over, last longer than, overshoot, run over.

oversee verb *it was decided to appoint a project manager to oversee the building work*: **supervise**, superintend, be in charge of, be responsible for, run, look after, keep an eye on, inspect, administer, organize, manage, direct, guide, control, be in control of, preside over, head (up), lead, chair, umpire, referee, judge, adjudicate, moderate, govern, rule, command.

overseer noun **supervisor**, foreman, forewoman, chargehand, team leader, controller, manager, manageress, line manager; boss, head, head of department, superintendent, captain; Scottish grieve; informal chief, head honcho, governor, super; Brit. informal gaffer, guv'nor; N. Amer. informal straw boss; Austral. informal pannikin boss; Mining overman.

overshadow verb **1** *a massive hill overshadows the town*: **shade**, darken, conceal, obscure, block out, obliterate, eclipse, screen, shroud, veil, mantle, cloak, mask; dominate, command, overlook.
2 *it is easy to let this feeling of tragedy overshadow his story*: **cast gloom over**, blight, take the pleasure out of, bring a note of sadness to, take the edge off, mar, spoil, ruin.
3 *he was always overshadowed by his brilliant elder brother*: **outshine**, eclipse, put in the shade, surpass, exceed, excel, be superior to, outclass, outstrip, outdo, top, cap, trump, transcend, tower above/over, dwarf, upstage, shame, put to shame, outdistance, lead; informal be head and shoulders above, be a cut above; archaic extinguish.

oversight noun **1** *I must apologize for this stupid oversight*: **mistake**, error, fault, failure, omission, lapse, inaccuracy, slip, blunder, faux pas, miscalculation; informal slip-up, boo-boo; Brit. informal boob; N. Amer. informal goof.
2 *the omission was not due to oversight or ignorance*: **carelessness**, inattention, neglect, negligence, forgetfulness, inadvertence, laxity, dereliction, neglectfulness.
3 *school governors have oversight of the curriculum*: **supervision**, surveillance, superintendence, inspection, charge, care, administration, management, government, direction, control, command, handling, custody.

overstate verb *he admitted that he had perhaps overstated his case*: **exaggerate**, overdo, overemphasize, overplay, dramatize, colour, embroider, embellish, enhance, magnify, inflate, amplify, make a mountain out of a molehill; informal make a big thing out of, blow up, blow up out of all proportion; archaic draw the long bow.
▷ANTONYMS understate.

overstatement noun *it is not an overstatement to say that a crisis is imminent*: **exaggeration**, overemphasis, magnification, amplification, overplaying, dramatization, colouring, embroidery, embellishment, enhancement, inflation, extravagance, hyperbole, excessiveness, overestimation, overvaluation, aggrandizement.
▷ANTONYMS restraint.

overt adjective *there was little overt opposition to parliamentary government*: **undisguised**, unconcealed, plain to see, plainly seen, plain, clear, apparent, conspicuous, unmistakable, obvious, noticeable, observable, visible, manifest, patent, open, public, above board; blatant, glaring, shameless, brazen.
▷ANTONYMS covert, hidden.

overtake verb **1** *a green car overtook the taxi*: **pass**, get past, go past, go by, overhaul, get/pull ahead of, leave behind, outdistance, outstrip; gain on, catch up with, draw level with, go faster than.
2 *tourism overtook coffee as the main earner of foreign currency*: **outstrip**, surpass, overshadow, eclipse, outshine, outclass; dwarf, put in the shade, put to shame, excel, exceed, transcend, top, cap, trump, beat, better; informal leave standing, walk away from; archaic outrival, outvie.
3 *the calamity which overtook us*: **befall**, happen to, come upon, hit, strike, fall on, overwhelm, overpower, overcome, be visited on, engulf, sweep over, take by surprise, surprise, catch unawares, catch unprepared, catch off guard; literary betide, whelm.

overthrow verb **1** *the President was overthrown in a bloodless coup*: **remove (from office/power)**, bring down, bring about the downfall of, topple, bring low, undo, depose, oust, displace, supplant, unseat, subvert, dethrone, disestablish, dissolve.
2 *a deliberate attempt to overthrow the established order*: **put an end to**, defeat, conquer, displace, break up, subvert, annihilate, dissolve.
▶ noun **1** *the overthrow of King Richard*: **removal (from office/power)**, downfall, fall, collapse, toppling, undoing, deposition, ousting, displacement, supplanting, unseating, subversion, dethronement, disestablishment, dissolution.
2 *their aim was the overthrow of capitalism*: **ending**, defeat, displacement, fall, rout, collapse, downfall, demise, break-up, subversion, annihilation, dissolution.

overtone noun **connotation**, hidden meaning, secondary meaning, implication, association, undercurrent, undertone, echo, vibrations, hint, suggestion, insinuation, intimation, flavour, colouring, smack, suspicion, feeling, aura, atmosphere, nuance, trace, murmur, touch, vein; rare subcurrent.

overture noun **1** *the overture to Don Giovanni*: **prelude**, introduction, opening, introductory movement, voluntary; rare verset.
2 *the talks were no more than the overture to a long debate*: **preliminary**, prelude, curtain-raiser, introduction, lead-in, precursor, forerunner, harbinger, herald, start, beginning; informal opener.
3 *the enemy were making peace overtures*: **opening move**, conciliatory move, move, approach, advances, feeler, signal, proposal, proposition, pass, offer, tender, suggestion.

overturn verb **1** *the boat overturned*: **capsize**, turn turtle, keel over, tip over, topple over, turn over, overbalance, turn topsy-turvy; Nautical pitchpole.
2 *I overturned a full supermarket trolley on to my leg*: **upset**, tip over, topple over, turn over, throw over, overthrow, knock over, upend, invert, turn topsy-turvy; informal roll; archaic overset.
3 *the Senate may yet overturn this ruling*: **cancel**, reverse, rescind, repeal, revoke, retract, countermand, withdraw, take back, rule against, disallow, override, overrule, veto, set aside, quash, overthrow, repudiate, recant, annul, nullify, declare null and void, invalidate, negate, void, abrogate; Law vacate; archaic recall.
▷ANTONYMS allow, accept.

overused adjective **hackneyed**, overworked, worn out, time-worn, worn, tired, played out, stereotyped, clichéd, threadbare, stale, trite, banal, stock,

hack, unoriginal, derivative, platitudinous.
▷ANTONYMS fresh, original.

overweening adjective **overconfident**, conceited, cocksure, cocky, smug, haughty, supercilious, disdainful, lofty, patronizing, arrogant, proud, vain, vainglorious, self-important, egotistical, high-handed, magisterial, cavalier, imperious, domineering, dictatorial, overbearing, presumptuous, lordly, peremptory, pompous, officious, blustering, boastful, self-assertive, opinionated, bold, forward, insolent; informal high and mighty, throwing one's weight about/around, uppish; rare hubristic.
▷ANTONYMS modest, diffident, unassuming.

overweight adjective *Allen was in his early fifties and somewhat overweight*: **fat**, obese, stout, corpulent, gross, fleshy, plump, portly, chubby, rotund, podgy, roly-poly, paunchy, pot-bellied, beer-bellied, bloated, flabby, Falstaffian, big, large, ample, well fed, well upholstered, well padded, broad in the beam, bulky, outsize, massive, heavy; informal porky, pudgy, tubby, blubbery, poddy; Brit. informal fubsy; N. Amer. informal lard-assed; archaic pursy; rare abdominous.
▷ANTONYMS skinny, scrawny, thin, undernourished.

overwhelm verb **1** *advancing sand dunes could overwhelm built-up areas | they were overwhelmed with work*: **swamp**, submerge, engulf, bury, deluge, flood, inundate; clog, saturate, glut, overload, beset, overburden, snow under.
2 *Spain overwhelmed Russia in the hockey*: **defeat (utterly/heavily/easily)**, trounce, rout, beat, beat hollow, conquer, vanquish, be victorious over, gain a victory over, prevail over, get the better of, triumph over; best, worst, gain mastery over, master, overpower, overcome, overthrow, subdue, suppress, subjugate, repress, quell, quash, crush, finish, bring someone to their knees, break; informal thrash, lick, clobber, whip, wipe the floor with, drub, tank, blow out of the water.
3 *she was overwhelmed by a sense of tragedy*: **overcome**, move, stir, affect, touch, impress, sweep someone off their feet, strike, stun, make emotional, dumbfound, shake, disturb, devastate, take aback, daze, spellbind, dazzle, floor, leave speechless, take someone's breath away, stagger; informal bowl over, blow away, knock/hit for six, knock sideways, blow someone's mind, get to.

overwhelming adjective **1** *an overwhelming number of players declared themselves unavailable for the competition*: **very large**, profuse, enormous, immense, inordinate, massive, huge, formidable, stupendous, prodigious, fantastic, staggering, shattering, devastating, sweeping; informal mind-boggling, mind-blowing.
▷ANTONYMS small.
2 *we have overwhelming public support*: **very strong**, forceful, profound, uncontrollable, irrepressible, irresistible, unbearable, overpowering, oppressive, unutterable, compelling, irrefutable.

overwork verb **1** *the school doctor says that we should work hard, but not overwork*: **work too hard**, work like a Trojan/horse/slave, work/run oneself into the ground, wear oneself to a shadow, work one's fingers to the bone, drive oneself into the ground, sweat, sweat blood, work day and night, burn the candle at both ends, burn the midnight oil, overtax oneself, overtax one's strength, kill oneself, burn oneself out, do too much, overdo it, strain oneself, overburden oneself, overload oneself, drive/push oneself too hard; informal knock oneself out, work one's tail off; vulgar slang work/sweat one's balls off.
▷ANTONYMS be idle.
2 *my colleagues did not want to overwork me*: **exploit**, drive (too hard), drive into the ground, tax, overtax, sweat, overburden, put upon, impose on, oppress; be a slave driver, be a hard taskmaster.

overworked adjective **1** *a mistake on the part of overworked staff*: **stressed**, under stress, stressed out, stress-ridden, strained, overtaxed, overburdened, overloaded, exhausted, fatigued, worn out.
2 *'new' must be one of the most overworked words in an advertising agency*: **hackneyed**, overused, worn out, worn, tired, played out, stereotyped, clichéd, threadbare, stale, trite, banal, platitudinous, stock, hack, unoriginal, derivative.

overwrought adjective **1** *this must have been a shock, and you're overwrought*: **tense**, agitated, nervous, on edge, edgy, keyed up, worked up, highly strung, neurotic, overexcited, beside oneself, distracted, distraught, under a strain, frantic, frenzied, hysterical, panicky, restless, jittery, fidgety, jumpy; Brit. nervy; informal in a state, in a tizzy, uptight, twitchy, wound up, wired, het up; Brit. informal throwing a wobbly, strung up.
▷ANTONYMS calm, cool, laid-back.
2 *the painting is technically brilliant but overwrought*: **excessively ornate**, over-ornate, over-elaborate, over-embellished, overblown, exaggerated, overdone, florid, busy, fussy, contrived, overworked, strained, laboured, baroque, rococo.
▷ANTONYMS plain, understated.

owe verb *I still owe him £200*: **be in debt (to)**, be indebted (to), be in arrears (to), be under an obligation (to), be obligated (to), be beholden to; be in debit, be overdrawn (by), be in the red; informal be in debt to the tune of.
▷ANTONYMS settle up.

owing adjective *no rent was owing*: **unpaid**, unsettled, to be paid, payable, receivable, due, overdue, undischarged, owed, outstanding, in arrears, in the red; N. Amer. delinquent, past due.
▷ANTONYMS paid, settled.
□ **owing to** *our train was halted owing to an air raid in the region*: **because of**, as a result of, on account of, on grounds of, due to, as a consequence of, thanks to, through, by reason of, by/in virtue of, for the sake of, in view of, after, following, in the wake of.

own adjective *he has his own reasons*: **personal**, individual, particular, private, personalized, idiosyncratic, characteristic, unique; rare especial.
▷ANTONYMS shared, common.
▶ pronoun
□ **get one's own back** *we'll* ***get our own back on*** *them for the way they have treated us*: **have/get/take one's revenge (on)**, be revenged (on), revenge oneself (on), hit back, get back at, get, get even (with), even the score (with), settle a/the score, settle accounts (with), give as good as one gets, play tit for tat, repay, pay someone back, give someone their just deserts, reciprocate, retaliate (against/on), take reprisals (against), exact retribution (on), let someone see how it feels, give someone a taste of their own medicine.
□ **hold one's own** *Britain has begun to hold its own in world markets*: **stand firm**, stand one's ground, maintain/keep one's position, keep one's end up, keep one's head above water, compete, survive, manage, cope, get through, get on, get along, get by.
▷ANTONYMS go under.
□ **on one's own 1** *she's not here now and I am all on my own*: **alone**, all alone, (all) by oneself, in a solitary state, single, solitary, unaccompanied, companionless, partnerless, unattended, unescorted, unchaperoned, solo; informal by one's lonesome; Brit. informal on one's tod, on one's lonesome, on one's jack, on one's Jack Jones. ▷ANTONYMS in company.
2 *she works well with tasks she has to achieve on her own*: **unaided**, unassisted, without help, without assistance, (all) by oneself, (all) alone, by one's own efforts, under one's own steam, independently, single-handed(ly), standing on one's own two feet, off one's own bat, on one's own initiative. ▷ANTONYMS jointly, with help.
▶ verb **1** *I own this house*: **be the owner of**, possess, be the (proud) possessor of, have in one's possession, have to one's name, count among one's possessions, have, keep, retain, maintain, hold, be blessed with, enjoy, boast.
2 *she had to own that she felt a little that way herself*: **admit**, allow, concede, grant, accept, accede, acknowledge, recognize, agree, confess.
□ **own up** *we so often feel guilty and are afraid to own up | he still couldn't own up to the lie*: **confess (to)**, admit to, admit guilt, plead guilty, accept blame/responsibility, acknowledge (that), tell the truth (about), make a clean breast of it, tell all; informal come clean (about), spill the beans, get something off one's chest.
▷ANTONYMS hush up, conceal.

> *Word links* **own**
>
> **idio-** related prefix, as in *idiolect, idiotype*

owner noun **possessor**, holder, proprietor/proprietress, homeowner, freeholder, landlord, landlady, master/mistress, keeper; rare proprietrix.

> *Word links* **owner**
>
> **proprietary** relating to an owner

ownership noun **possession**, right of possession, holding, freehold, proprietorship, proprietary rights, title.

ox noun **bull**, bullock, steer, beef; beast of burden, draught animal.

pace noun **1** *he stepped back a pace*: **step**, stride, footstep.
2 *they continued their steady slow pace*: **gait**, stride, walk, tread, march; rhythm.
3 *he had driven home at a furious pace*: **speed**, rate, swiftness, quickness, rapidity, velocity, tempo, momentum; informal clip, lick.
▶ verb *she paced up and down | the chauffeur paced the forecourt anxiously*: **walk**, stride, tread, march, pound, patrol, walk up and down, walk back and forth, cross, traverse.

pacific adjective **1** *there were demonstrations in the normally pacific community*: **peace-loving**, peaceable, pacifist, non-violent, non-aggressive, non-belligerent, non-combative, mild, gentle, equable, dovelike, dovish; rare pacifistic.
▷ANTONYMS hostile, aggressive, belligerent.
2 *he raised his right hand, palm forward, as a sign of his pacific intentions*: **conciliatory**, peacemaking, placatory, placating, propitiatory, appeasing, mollifying, calming, mediatory, mediating, diplomatic; rare irenic.
▷ANTONYMS warmongering.
3 *pacific waters*: **calm**, still, motionless, smooth, tranquil, placid, waveless, unruffled, undisturbed, like a millpond; quiet, peaceful, at peace.
▷ANTONYMS stormy.

pacifism noun **peacemaking**, conscientious objection(s), passive resistance, love of peace, peace-mongering; dovishness, non-violence; rare satyagraha.

pacifist noun **peace-lover**, conscientious objector, passive resister, peacemaker, peace-monger, appeaser, pacifier; informal dove, peacenik; Brit. informal conchie; rare satyagrahi.
▷ANTONYMS warmonger.

pacify verb *Gregory tried to think of a way of pacifying his wife*: **placate**, appease, calm, calm down, conciliate, propitiate, assuage, mollify, soothe, tranquillize, content, still, quieten, silence, relax, compose.
▷ANTONYMS provoke, enrage, inflame.

pack noun **1** *a pack of cigarettes*: **packet**, container, package, box, crate, carton, parcel.
2 *he could climb two or three peaks a day carrying a 50-pound pack*: **backpack**, rucksack, knapsack, kitbag, duffel bag, bag, satchel, load, luggage.
3 *a pack of wolves*: **group**, herd, troop.
4 *a pack of youngsters who spent all their time together*: **crowd**, mob, group, band, troupe, party, set, club, clique, coterie, gang, rabble, horde, throng, huddle, multitude, mass, assembly, gathering, collection, host, contingent; informal crew, bunch.
▶ verb **1** *she helped pack the hamper*: **fill**, fill up, put things in, load, stuff, cram.
2 *it took only a few minutes to pack their belongings*: **stow**, put away, store, box up, crate; put in a case/trunk.
3 *the glasses were packed tightly in straw*: **wrap (up)**, package, parcel, tie (up), swathe, swaddle, encase, enfold, envelop, cloak, bale, bundle, cover (up), protect.
4 *Christmas shoppers packed the store*: **throng**, crowd (into), fill (to overflowing), cram full, mob, cram, jam, press into, squash into, squeeze into.
5 *wet the cloth and pack it against the wall*: **compress**, **press**, squash, squeeze, jam, tamp, ram, thrust, force, wedge, crush, flatten.
□ **pack something in** informal **1** *one of the models has packed in her day job*: **resign from**, **leave**, give up, drop, abandon, renounce, relinquish; informal quit, chuck, jack in. **2** *he might have to pack in smoking*: **give up**, abstain from, drop, desist from, refrain from, steer clear of, give a wide berth to, reject, eschew, forswear, avoid, discontinue; informal quit, leave off, kick; archaic forsake.
□ **pack someone off** informal *the best thing is to pack the kiddies off to Grandma*: **send off**, **dispatch**, dismiss, bundle off; informal send packing.
□ **pack up** informal **1** *something electrical is bound to pack up over Christmas*: **break down**, **stop working**, cease to work/function, fail, give out, stall, come to a halt, develop a fault, malfunction, go wrong, break, act up, be defective/faulty, crash; informal conk out, go kaput, go phut; Brit. informal play up. **2** *there's no point worrying—if you do, it's time to pack up*: **stop**, call it a day, break off, quit, desist, not continue, halt, finish, cease; informal leave off, knock off, pack/jack it in.
□ **pack something up** *in the morning, she packed up her belongings*: **put away**, tidy up/away, clear up/away, store, stow.

package noun **1** *69,000 packages of asparagus*: **parcel**, **packet**, container, box, carton.
2 *an annual subscription charge for a complete package of services*: **collection**, bundle, lot; combination, conglomeration, raft, package deal.
▶ verb *goods packaged in recyclable materials*: **wrap**, wrap up, gift-wrap; pack, pack up, parcel, parcel up, box, case, encase, bundle, bundle up.

packaging noun *avoid products with excessive packaging*: **wrapping**, wrappers, packing, cover, covering.

packed adjective *an audience of 500 in the packed conference hall*.
See **crowded**.

packet noun **1** *a packet of cigarettes*: **pack**, **carton**, box, cardboard box, container, case, package, parcel, padded bag; trademark Jiffy bag.
2 (**a packet**) informal *that must have cost a packet*: **a fortune**, a considerable/vast/large sum of money, a king's ransom; informal a small fortune, millions, billions, lots/pots/heaps of money, a mint, a bundle, a wad, a pile, a stack, a heap, a tidy sum, a killing, a pretty penny, telephone numbers; Brit. informal a bomb, loadsamoney, a shedload, shedloads; N. Amer. informal big bucks, big money, gazillions; Austral. informal big bickies, motser, motza.

pact noun *the guerrilla group made a peace pact with the government*: **agreement**, **treaty**, entente, protocol, deal, contract, settlement, arrangement, bargain, compact, obligation, understanding, covenant, bond, concord, concordat, convention; armistice, truce; alliance, league.

pad[1] noun **1** *Sister will put a pad over your eye for the time being*: **dressing**, compress, pack, padding, wadding, wad, stuffing.
2 *the chair comes with a loose seat pad*: **cushion**, squab, pillow, bolster; filling, stuffing, upholstery.
3 *he was making notes on a pad*: **notebook**, notepad, writing pad, memo pad, jotter, tablet, block, sketch pad, sketchbook; N. Amer. scratch pad.
▶ verb *a quilted jacket padded with duck feathers for extra warmth*: **stuff**, fill, pack, line, wad, upholster, cushion.
□ **pad something out** *don't pad out your answer to make it seem impressive*: **spin out**, fill out, augment, amplify, increase, add to, stretch out, eke out, flesh out, lengthen, overdo, protract, elaborate.
▷ANTONYMS tighten up; condense.

pad[2] verb *I make no noise as I pad along towards the bedroom*: **walk quietly**, tread softly, walk barefoot, walk in stockinged feet, walk in slippers, shuffle, soft-shoe.

padding noun **1** *the boots have padding around the ankle*: **wadding**, cushioning, stuffing, packing, upholstery, filling, filler, lining.
2 *write in a concise manner with no padding*: **verbiage**, verbosity, verboseness, wordiness, prolixity, prolixness; Brit. informal waffle, wittering, flannel; rare logorrhoea.

paddle[1] noun *use the paddles to row ashore*: **oar**, scull, sweep, blade, spoon, spade.
▸ verb *we paddled out another hundred yards*: **row gently**, pull, scull.

paddle[2] verb *a few children were paddling in the shallow water*: **splash about**, wade; dabble, slop, squelch.

paddock noun **field**, meadow, pasture; enclosure for horses, yard, pen, pound, stockade; N. English park; Scottish parrock; N. Amer. corral; French parc fermé; S. African kraal; in S. America potrero.

paddy noun Brit. informal *you know what Bert's like when he's in a paddy*. See **temper** (sense 1 of the noun).

padlock verb *you should padlock ladders to something secure*: **lock**, lock up, fasten, chain, bolt; secure.

padre noun **priest**, chaplain, minister (of religion), pastor, father, parson, clergyman, cleric, ecclesiastic, man of God, man of the cloth, churchman, vicar, rector, curate, curé, divine, evangelist, preacher; Scottish kirkman; informal reverend, Holy Joe, sky pilot; Austral. informal josser.

paean noun *Moses leads the people in a great paean of triumph | paeans of praise for everybody's wisdom*: **song of praise**, hymn, psalm, anthem, shout of praise, alleluia; praise, plaudit, exaltation, glorification, eulogy, tribute, testimonial, extolment, encomium, panegyric, accolade, acclamation, commendation, compliment, bouquet.

pagan noun *in prehistoric times, pagans used to worship the sun gods*: **heathen**, infidel, idolater/idolatress, atheist, irreligious person, agnostic, sceptic, heretic, apostate; archaic paynim.
▹ANTONYMS believer.
▸ adjective *the great pagan festival of the solar solstice*: **heathen**; ungodly, irreligious, infidel, idolatrous, atheistic, agnostic, sceptical, faithless, impious; rare paganistic, paganish, apostatical, nullifidian, heathenish, heathenistic.

page[1] noun **1** *a book of 672 pages*: **folio**, sheet, side, leaf; recto, verso.
2 *a glorious page in this distinguished writer's life*: **period**, time, episode, stage, phase, epoch, era, chapter; event, incident, point.

page[2] noun **1** *a page in a hotel*: **errand boy**, pageboy, messenger boy; N. Amer. bellboy, bellhop; Brit. informal, dated Buttons.
2 *a page at a wedding*: **attendant**, pageboy, train-bearer.
▸ verb *could you please page Mr Johnson in the dining room?* **call (for)**, ask for, broadcast for, summon, send for.

pageant noun *the Queen attended a 1000-horse pageant and re-creation of the coronation parade*: **parade**, procession, cavalcade, scene, play, representation, tableau, tableau vivant; display, spectacle, extravaganza, show.

pageantry noun *the trooping of the colour brings Londoners out for a historic day of military pageantry*: **spectacle**, display, ceremony, ceremoniousness, magnificence, pomp, glory, splendour, grandeur, glamour, flourish, glitter, theatricality, drama, show, showiness; informal pizzazz, razzle-dazzle, razzmatazz; rare grandezza.

pain noun **1** *it seemed impossible that anyone could endure such pain for so long*: **suffering**, agony, affliction, torture, torment, discomfort, soreness.
2 *she had a dull pain in her stomach*: **ache**, aching, soreness, hurt, throb, throbbing, smarting, pricking, sting, stinging, twinge, shooting pain, stab, pang, spasm; stitch, cramp; discomfort, irritation, stiffness, tenderness.
3 *the pain of losing a loved one*: **sorrow**, grief, heartache, heartbreak, sadness, unhappiness, distress, desolation, misery, wretchedness, despair, desperation, mental suffering, emotional suffering, trauma; bitterness, anguish, affliction, tribulation, vexation, woe, agony, torment, torture.
4 *that child is a pain*: **nuisance**, pest, bother, vexation, irritant, source of irritation/annoyance, worry, problem, inconvenience, trial, tribulation, plague, source of aggravation, bore, thorn in the flesh, the bane of one's life; informal pain in the neck, drag; vulgar slang pain in the arse.
5 (**pains**) *he took great pains to hide his feelings*: **care**, effort, bother, trouble, labour, exertion, strain, struggle.
□ **be at pains** *they were at pains to put him at ease*: **try hard**, make a great effort, make an effort, make every effort, spare no effort, take (great) pains, take care, put oneself out, apply oneself, exert oneself; strive, endeavour, try, struggle, battle, labour, toil, strain, work, aim; do one's best, do all one can, do one's utmost, give (it) one's all, go all out; informal bend/fall/lean over backwards, give it one's best shot.
▸ verb **1** *her foot is still paining her*: **hurt**, cause pain, be painful, be sore, ache, throb, smart, burn, prickle, sting, pinch, twinge, cause discomfort, be tender; informal kill; Brit. informal play up.
2 *the memory of the event still pains her*: **sadden**, grieve, distress, make miserable/wretched, trouble, worry, bother, perturb, disturb, oppress, harrow, cause anguish to, afflict; cut to the quick, mortify, torment, torture, wound, sting, gnaw at.

> *Word links* **pain**
>
> **-algia** pain in a part of the body, as in *neuralgia*
> **analgesic** medicine for reducing pain
> **anaesthetic** drug making one unable to feel pain
> **anaesthesiology** branch of medicine concerning insensitivity to pain

pained adjective *she stared at Hebden with a pained expression on her face*. See **hurt** (sense 2 of the adjective).

painful adjective **1** *a painful arm*: **sore**, hurting, hurt, tender, aching, throbbing, smarting, burning, irritating, agonizing, excruciating; informal gut-wrenching.
2 *a painful experience*: **distressing**, unpleasant, nasty, bitter, awful, disquieting, disturbing, upsetting, traumatic, miserable, wretched, sad, heartbreaking, heart-rending, agonizing, harrowing, mortifying; unendurable, unbearable, torturous, cruel, uncomfortable, disagreeable; rare distressful.
▹ANTONYMS pleasant, agreeable.

painfully adverb *the whole affair had been painfully embarrassing*: **distressingly**, worryingly, upsettingly, disturbingly, sadly, pitifully, unfortunately, agonizingly, harrowingly, excruciatingly, chillingly, alarmingly, insufferably, unendurably, unbearably, torturously, cruelly, uncomfortably, embarrassingly, disconcertingly, unenviably, unpleasantly; woefully, dreadfully, terribly, awfully, horribly; dated frightfully.

painkiller noun **analgesic**, pain reliever, anodyne, anaesthetic, narcotic, embrocation, liniment; rare palliative, demulcent.

painless adjective **1** *any killing of animals should be painless*: **pain-free**, under anaesthetic.
▹ANTONYMS painful.
2 *getting rid of him proved painless*: **easy**, trouble-free, effortless, undemanding, unexacting, simple, uncomplicated, smooth, plain sailing; informal as easy as pie, as easy as falling off a log, as easy as ABC, a piece of cake, child's play, a cinch; dated a snip.
▹ANTONYMS difficult, demanding.

painstaking adjective **careful**, meticulous, thorough, assiduous, sedulous, attentive, diligent, industrious, laborious, hard-working, conscientious, ultra-careful, punctilious, scrupulous, demanding, exacting, searching, close, elaborate, minute, accurate, correct, studious, rigorous, particular; religious, strict; pedantic, fussy.
▹ANTONYMS careless, negligent, slapdash.

paint noun **colouring**, colourant, tint, dye, stain, pigment, wash, colour; varnish.
▸ verb **1** *simply paint the ceiling*: **colour**, apply paint to, decorate, tint, dye, stain, distemper, whitewash, emulsion, gloss, spray, spray-paint, airbrush, roller, coat, cover.
2 *soldiers arrested three men who had been painting slogans on a wall*: **daub**, smear, plaster, spray, spray-paint, airbrush.
3 *he was twelve when Modigliani painted him*: **portray**, picture, paint a picture of, depict, delineate, draw, sketch, represent, catch (a likeness of); reproduce, illustrate, render.
4 *you paint a very stark picture of the suffering*: **tell**, recount, narrate, set forth/out, outline, sketch, detail, unfold, describe, depict, characterize, evoke, conjure up.
□ **paint the town red** **celebrate**, carouse, enjoy oneself, make merry, have a good/wild time, party, have a party; N. Amer. step out; informal go out on the town, whoop it up, make whoopee, have a night on the tiles, live it up, have a ball, push the boat out; dated go on a spree.

painting noun **picture**, illustration, portrayal, depiction, delineation, representation, likeness, image, sketch, cartoon, artwork; oil painting, oil, watercolour, canvas.

pair noun **1** *a pair of gloves*: **set of two**, set, matching set, matched set, two of a kind.
2 *the pair were arrested on Saturday | a pair of pheasants*: **two**, couple, duo, brace, twosome; twins; archaic twain; rare duplet, dyad, duad, doubleton.
3 *a pair of lines in Chaucer's first fabliau*: **couplet**, distich.
4 *a coach and pair*: **two horses**, team, yoke, span.
5 *they drank a toast of long life and many babies to the happy pair*: **couple**, man and wife, husband and wife, partners, lovers.
▸ verb *a cardigan paired with a matching skirt*: **match**, put together, couple, twin, partner, marry up.
□ **pair off/up** *Rachel paired up with Tommy*: **get together**, join up, link up, team up, unite, form a partnership, form a couple, make a twosome.

pal informal noun **friend**, companion, comrade, intimate, familiar, confidant, alter ego, second self; playmate, classmate, schoolmate, workmate; informal chum, buddy, bosom pal, sidekick, cully, spar, crony, mucker, butty, main man; Brit. informal mate, oppo, china; N. English informal marrow, marrer, marra; N. Amer. informal amigo, compadre, paisan; N. Amer. & S. African informal homeboy, homegirl; S. African informal gabba; archaic compeer; rare fidus Achates.
▸ verb
□ **pal up** *I palled up with Alan*: **become friendly**, make friends, become

friends, form a friendship; informal get in; N. Amer. informal buddy up; informal, dated chum up.

palace noun **royal/official residence**, castle, mansion, stately home; in France château; in Italy palazzo; in German-speaking countries schloss; in Spain alcazar; in Turkey, historical seraglio.

> *Word links* **palace**
>
> **palatial** like a palace

palatable adjective **1** *a very palatable local red wine | palatable meals*: **tasty**, appetizing, pleasant-tasting; eatable, edible, drinkable, flavourful, flavoursome, savoury, delicious, delectable, enjoyable, mouth-watering, luscious, toothsome, succulent, dainty; informal scrumptious, finger-licking, yummy, scrummy, nummy, moreish, delish, yum-yum; literary ambrosial; rare comestible, flavorous, ambrosian, sapid, nectarean, nectareous.
▷ANTONYMS tasteless, insipid, unpalatable.
2 *he gives us the truth—not all of it is palatable*: **pleasant**, acceptable, satisfactory, pleasing, agreeable, easy to take, to one's liking, pleasurable, nice; rare sapid.
▷ANTONYMS disagreeable, unpalatable, unpleasant.

palate noun **1** *the tea was so hot it burned her palate*: **roof of the mouth**; hard palate, soft palate.
2 *the spicy menus have been toned down to suit the tourist palate*: **sense of taste**, taste, taste buds; appetite, stomach.
3 *a wine with a zingy, peachy palate*: **flavour**, taste, savour; rare goût.

> *Word links* **palate**
>
> **palatoplasty** repair of cleft palate

> *Easily confused words* **palate, palette, or pallet?**
>
> These unrelated words may be confused because of their similar pronunciation. A person's **palate** is their sense of taste and discrimination (*this dish may be too exotic for the British palate*). Literally, the word denotes the roof of the mouth. **Palette**, on the other hand, literally denotes an artist's board for mixing colours, but is also used to refer to the range of colours used (*gold, burnt orange, stone, and mink are used to create a warm palette*). **Pallet** has no common figurative uses, and means either a crude bed, a platform on which goods are stacked for transport, or a vertical strip on a heraldic shield.

palatial adjective *a palatial five-star hotel*. See **luxurious** (sense 1).

palaver noun *what was all that palaver about?* **fuss**, fuss and bother, bother, commotion, trouble, rigmarole, folderol, ado; informal song and dance, performance, to-do, carry-on, carrying-on, kerfuffle, hoo-ha, hullabaloo, ballyhoo, business, pantomime, hoopla; NZ informal bobsy-die.
▸ verb *don't stand there palavering all day*: **chatter**, gossip, prattle, prate, babble, blather, blether, blither, maunder, gabble, jabber, tittle-tattle; Scottish & Irish slabber; informal chit-chat, jaw, gas, gab, yak, yackety-yak, yabber, yatter; Brit. informal natter, rabbit, witter, chunter, waffle, chinwag; archaic twaddle, clack.

pale[1] noun **1** *the pales of a fence*: **stake**, post, pole, paling, picket, upright; palisade.
2 *a woman who stands outside the pale of family and community life*: **boundary**, confines, bounds, limits.
□ **beyond the pale** *his behaviour was beyond the pale*: **unacceptable**, unseemly, improper, indiscreet, unsuitable, irregular, unreasonable, intolerable, disgraceful, deplorable, outrageous, scandalous, shocking, insupportable, objectionable, offensive, distasteful; informal not on, not the done thing, out of order, out of line; dated not quite the thing; Austral./NZ informal over the fence; rare exceptionable.

pale[2] adjective **1** *his pale skin | she looked pale and drawn*: **white**, pallid, pasty, pasty-faced, wan, colourless, anaemic, bloodless, washed out, peaky, peakish, ashen, ashen-faced, ashy, chalky, chalk-white, grey, whitish, white-faced, whey-faced, waxen, waxy, blanched, drained, pinched, green, ghastly, sickly, sallow, as white as a sheet, as white as a ghost, deathly pale, cadaverous, corpse-like, looking as if one had seen a ghost; milky, creamy, cream, ivory, milk-white, alabaster; informal like death warmed up; Scottish informal peely-wally; rare etiolated, lymphatic.
▷ANTONYMS flushed, rosy.
2 *pale colours*: **light**, light-coloured, pastel, neutral, light-toned, muted, subtle, soft, low-key, restrained; faded, bleached, dusty, whitish, washed out, insipid.
3 *the pale light of morning*: **dim**, faint, weak, feeble, thin, watery, wan.
▷ANTONYMS dark; bright.
4 *a pale imitation of the real thing*: **inferior**, poor, feeble, weak, insipid, wishy-washy, vapid, bland, puny, flat, inadequate, ineffectual, ineffective, half-hearted; lame, tame, uninspired, unimaginative, lacklustre, spiritless, lifeless, anaemic, bloodless; informal pathetic; rare etiolated.
▸ verb **1** *his face paled*: **go/turn white**, grow/turn/become pale, blanch, blench, lose colour; whiten, lighten.
2 *everything else pales by comparison*: **decrease in importance**, lose significance, pale into insignificance; fade, dwindle, diminish, lessen, dim, lose lustre.

palisade noun **fence**, paling, enclosure, defence, barricade, stockade, fortification, bulwark.

pall[1] noun **1** *the coffin lay under a rich velvet pall*: **funeral cloth**, coffin covering.
2 *a pall of black smoke hung over the quarry*: **cloud**, covering, cloak, mantle, veil, shroud, layer, blanket, sheet, curtain, canopy.
□ **cast a pall over** *the news cast a pall over the occasion*: **spoil**, take the fun/enjoyment/pleasure out of, cast a shadow over, overshadow, envelop in gloom, darken, cloud, put a damper on, mar, blight.

pall[2] verb *two years of pandering to bloated businessmen began to pall*: **become/grow tedious**, become/grow boring, become/grow tiresome, lose its/their interest, lose attraction, wear off, cloy; bore, tire, fatigue, weary, sicken, nauseate; irritate, irk.

palliate verb **1** *the treatment works by palliating symptoms*: **alleviate**, ease, relieve, soothe, take the edge off, assuage, allay, dull, soften, lessen, moderate, temper, mitigate, diminish, decrease, blunt, deaden, abate; rare lenify.
2 *if only there were some way to palliate his dirty deed*: **disguise**, hide, gloss over, conceal, whitewash, cover, cover up, camouflage, cloak, mask, paper over, varnish over; excuse, justify, extenuate, minimize, mitigate, make light of, tone down, play down, downplay.

palliative adjective *the role of these drugs is essentially palliative*: **soothing**, alleviating, sedative, calmative, calming; rare alleviative, alleviatory, lenitive, demulcent, assuasive, mitigatory, mitigative, paregoric.
▸ noun *antibiotics and palliatives*: **painkiller**, analgesic, pain reliever, sedative, tranquillizer, anodyne, calmative, opiate, bromide; rare lenitive, demulcent, mitigative, paregoric.

pallid adjective **1** *his skin was damp and pallid | a pallid child*: **pale**, white, pasty, pasty-faced, wan, colourless, anaemic, bloodless, washed out, peaky, peakish, peaked, whey-faced, ashen, ashen-faced, ashy, chalky, chalk-white, grey, whitish, white-faced, waxen, waxy, blanched, drained, pinched; green; ghastly, sickly, sallow, deathly pale, cadaverous, corpse-like; informal like death warmed up; Scottish informal peely-wally; rare etiolated, lymphatic.
▷ANTONYMS flushed, rosy.
2 *pallid watercolours of the better-known beauty spots of Norfolk*: **insipid**, uninspired, colourless, uninteresting, feeble, dull, boring, tedious, tired, unexciting, unimaginative, lifeless, spiritless, sterile, anaemic, bloodless, bland, vapid, wishy-washy.
▷ANTONYMS vivid, lively.

pallor noun *her dark hair accentuated her pallor*: **paleness**, pallidness, lack of colour, whiteness, colourlessness, wanness, ashen hue, pastiness, peakiness, greyness, sickliness, sallowness; rare etiolation.

pally adjective **friendly**, on good terms, close, familiar, affectionate, intimate; informal as thick as thieves, thick, matey, buddy-buddy, palsy-walsy, chummy.

palm[1] verb
□ **palm something off** *they palmed off their shoddiest products on the tourists*: **foist**, fob off, offload, get rid of, dispose of; informal unload.
▸ noun
□ **grease someone's palm bribe**, buy off, buy, corrupt, suborn, give an inducement to; informal give a backhander to, give a sweetener to, square.
□ **have someone in the palm of one's hand have control over**, have power over, have influence over, have someone at one's mercy, have someone in one's clutches, have someone eating out of one's hand, have someone on a string; N. Amer. have someone in one's hip pocket.

> *Word links* **palm**
>
> **volar** relating to the palm of the hand

palm[2] noun *she holds the palm for absent-mindedness*: **prize**, trophy, award, crown, wreath, laurel wreath, laurels, bays; honour, glory, fame, victory, triumph, success, accolade.

palmist noun *she was told by a palmist that she would die in her thirties*: **fortune teller**, palm-reader, clairvoyant, chiromancer; rare chirosophist, palmister.

palmistry noun **fortune telling**, palm-reading, clairvoyancy, chiromancy; rare chirosophy, chirognomy.

palmy adjective *the palmy days of the 1960s*: **happy**, fortunate, glorious, prosperous, halcyon, golden, flourishing, successful, thriving, rosy, roaring, booming, triumphant.

palpable adjective **1** *a palpable bump at the bridge of the nose*: **tangible**, touchable, noticeable, detectable, solid, concrete, material, substantial, real.
2 *his reluctance was palpable*: **perceptible**, perceivable, visible, noticeable, appreciable, discernible, detectable, observable, tangible, recognizable, notable, unmistakable, transparent, indisputable, self-evident,

incontrovertible, incontestable, undeniable; **obvious**, clear, plain, plain to see, evident, apparent, manifest, patent, marked, conspicuous, pronounced, striking, distinct; as plain as a pikestaff, as plain as the nose on one's face, standing/sticking out like a sore thumb, standing/sticking out a mile, right under one's nose, staring one in the face, writ large, beyond doubt, beyond question, written all over someone, as clear as day, blinding, inescapable, overt, open, undisguised, unconcealed, glaring, blatant, flagrant, barefaced, gross, stark.
▷ANTONYMS intangible, imperceptible.

Word toolkit **palpable**
See **perceptible**.

palpitate verb **1** *her heart began to palpitate*: **beat rapidly**, pound, throb, pulsate, pulse, thud, thump, hammer, flutter, pitter-patter, go pit-a-pat, quiver, pump, race, pant, thrill; rare quop.
2 *she was palpitating with terror*: **tremble**, quiver, quake, shake, shake like a leaf, shiver, shudder; rare quave.

paltry adjective **1** *a paltry sum of money | a paltry 41p*: **small**, meagre, trifling, insignificant, negligible, inadequate, insufficient, scant, scanty, derisory, pitiful, pitiable, pathetic, miserable, sorry, wretched, puny, trivial, niggardly, beggarly, mean, ungenerous, inappreciable, mere; informal measly, piddling, piffling, mingy, poxy, dinky; rare exiguous.
▷ANTONYMS considerable, substantial.
2 *naval glory struck him as paltry*: **worthless**, petty, trivial, unimportant, insignificant, inconsequential, of little account/consequence, meaningless, negligible, nugatory, minor, footling, contemptible; informal penny-ante; Brit. informal twopenny, twopenny-halfpenny; N. Amer. informal nickel-and-dime, picayune.
▷ANTONYMS important, significant, valuable.

Word toolkit **paltry**
See **inconsequential**.

pamper verb *Trevor's big sister pampered him*: **spoil**, **indulge**, overindulge, cosset, mollycoddle, coddle, baby, pet, wait on someone hand and foot, cater to someone's every whim, feather-bed, wrap in cotton wool; humour, pander to; archaic cocker.

pamphlet noun **brochure**, leaflet, booklet, circular, flyer, handbill, handout, bill, notice, tract; N. Amer. mailer, folder; N. Amer. & Austral. dodger.

pan¹ noun **1** *heat the olive oil in a heavy pan*: **saucepan**, frying pan, pot, casserole, wok, skillet, bain-marie, fish kettle, pressure cooker, poacher, chafing dish; container, cooking utensil; Indian karahi.
2 *the evaporation of sea water in salt pans*: **hollow**, pit, basin, depression, dip, indentation, crater, cavity, concavity.
▸ verb **1** informal *the movie was panned by the critics*: **criticize**, censure, attack, lambaste, condemn, find fault with, give a bad press to, flay, savage, shoot down, bring under fire; informal knock, take to pieces, take/pull apart, crucify, hammer, slam, bash, give something a battering; roast, skewer, maul, throw brickbats at; Brit. informal slate, rubbish, slag off, monster; N. Amer. informal trash, pummel; Austral./NZ informal bag.
▷ANTONYMS praise, commend, applaud.
2 *prospectors panned for gold*: **sift for**, search for, look for.
□ **pan out 1** *Harold's idea had been a good one even if it hadn't panned out*: **succeed**, be successful, work, turn out well, work out; informal do the trick.
2 *the deal panned out badly*: **turn out**, work out, conclude, end (up), result, come out, fall out, develop, evolve; rare eventuate.

pan² verb *the camera panned to the building*: **swing (round)**, sweep, track, move, turn, circle.

panacea noun *a panacea for the country's economic problems*: **universal cure**, cure-all, cure for all ills, universal remedy, sovereign remedy, heal-all, nostrum, elixir, wonder drug, perfect solution, magic formula, magic bullet; rare catholicon, diacatholicon, panpharmacon.

panache noun *they played with panache and authority*: **flamboyant confidence**, flamboyance, confidence, self-assurance, style, stylishness, flair, elan, dash, flourish, verve, zest, spirit, brio, éclat, vivacity, vigour, gusto, animation, liveliness, vitality, enthusiasm, energy; informal pizzazz, oomph, zip, zing.

pancake noun **crêpe**, drop scone, galette, waffle, griddle cake, batter cake, flannel cake; N. Amer. flapjack, slapjack; Russian blini; Mexican tortilla, tostada; Indian chapatti, dosa; Jewish latke, blintze.

pandemic adjective *the disease is pandemic in Africa*: **widespread**, prevalent, pervasive, rife, rampant, epidemic; universal, global.

pandemonium noun *we heard a massive bang and then there was complete pandemonium*. See **uproar** (sense 1).

pander verb
□ **pander to** *David was always there to pander to her every whim*: **indulge**, gratify, satisfy, cater to, give in to, fulfil, yield to, bow to, humour, please, accommodate, comply with, go along with.

pane noun **sheet of glass**, panel, windowpane.

panegyric noun *he finished up with a panegyric on the Vice-Chancellor*: **eulogy**, **speech of praise**, paean, accolade, tribute, testimonial; commendation, acclamation.

panel noun **1** *a control panel*: **console**, instrument panel, fascia, board, dashboard; instruments, controls, dials.
2 *a panel of judges*: **group**, advisory group, team, body, committee, jury, council, board, commission.

pang noun **1** *hunger pangs*: **pain**, sharp pain, shooting pain, twinge, stab, spasm, ache, cramp.
2 *Melissa felt a pang of remorse*: **qualm**, misgiving, scruple, twinge, prick, dart, twitch, gnawing.

panic noun *she felt a wave of panic | he ran outside in a panic*: **alarm**, anxiety, nervousness, fear, fright, trepidation, dread, terror, horror, agitation, hysteria, consternation, perturbation, dismay, disquiet, apprehension, apprehensiveness; informal flap, fluster, state, cold sweat, funk, tizzy, tizz; N. Amer. informal swivet.
▷ANTONYMS calm, calmness.
▸ verb **1** *there's no need to panic*: **be alarmed**, be scared, be nervous, be afraid, overreact, become panic-stricken, take fright, be filled with fear, be terrified, be agitated, be hysterical, lose one's nerve, be perturbed, get overwrought, get worked up, go/fall to pieces, lose control, fall apart; informal flap, get in a flap, lose one's cool, get the jitters, get into a tizzy/tizz, run around like a headless chicken, freak, freak out, get in a stew, get the willies, get the (screaming) heebie-jeebies; Brit. informal get the wind up, go into a (flat) spin, have kittens, lose one's bottle, throw a wobbly, have an attack of the wobblies.
2 *talk of love panicked her*: **frighten**, alarm, scare, unnerve, fill with panic, agitate, horrify, terrify; informal throw into a tizzy/tizz, freak, freak out, spook; Brit. informal put the wind up.
▷ANTONYMS relax.

panic-stricken adjective See **scared**.

panoply noun **1** *the full panoply of America's military might*: **array**, range, collection.
2 *all the panoply of Western religious liturgy*: **trappings**, regalia, apparatus; splendour, spectacle, show, display; ceremony, ritual.

panorama noun **1** *stopping the car, he surveyed the panorama*: **view**, vista, wide view, aerial view, bird's-eye view, scenic view, prospect, perspective, outlook, aspect, scene, scenery, landscape, seascape.
2 *a panorama of the contemporary art scene*: **overview**, overall picture, survey, review, perspective, presentation, appraisal.

panoramic adjective **1** *a panoramic view of Manhattan*: **sweeping**, wide, extensive, bird's-eye, scenic, commanding.
2 *a panoramic look at 20th century German art*: **wide-ranging**, extensive, broad, far-reaching, overall, comprehensive, sweeping, all-encompassing, all-embracing, inclusive, general.
▷ANTONYMS restricted, narrow, limited.

pant verb **1** *the Brigadier was panting a little as they reached the top of the slope*: **breathe heavily**, breathe hard, breathe quickly, puff, huff and puff, puff and blow, gasp, wheeze, heave, blow.
2 *the track has the sort of subtle start that makes you pant for more*: **yearn for**, long for, crave, hanker after/for, pine for, ache for, hunger for, thirst for, be hungry for, be greedy for, be thirsty for, itch for, sigh for, be dying for, cry out for, wish for, desire, be consumed with desire for, want, covet; informal have a yen for; archaic be athirst for, suspire for.
▸ noun *Robyn was breathing in shallow pants*: **gasp**, puff, wheeze, breath.

panting adjective **out of breath**, breathless, short of breath, puffed out, puffing, huffing and puffing, puffing and blowing, gasping, gasping for breath, wheezing, wheezy, winded, short-winded; informal out of puff.

pantry noun **larder**, storage room, store, storeroom; Brit. buttery, butlery, still room; archaic spence.

pants plural noun **1** Brit. **underpants**, briefs, Y-fronts, boxer shorts, boxers, long johns, knickers, French knickers, bikini briefs; G-string, thong; Brit. tanga briefs, camiknickers; N. Amer. shorts, undershorts; informal panties, undies, frillies; Brit. informal kecks, smalls; dated drawers, bloomers; N. Amer. dated step-ins; historical pantalettes, Directoire drawers.
2 N. Amer. **trousers**.

pap noun **1** *a plateful of tasteless pap*: **soft food**, mush, semi-liquid food, baby food, slop, slush, swill, pulp, purée, mash, paste; informal goo, gloop, gook; N. Amer. informal glop.
2 *an aspiring writer sees his profound drama turned into commercial pap by Hollywood*: **trivia**, pulp, pulp fiction, rubbish, trash, nonsense, froth; Brit. candyfloss; informal dreck, drivel, twaddle, rot; rare pabulum, pablum.

paper noun **1** *a sheet of paper*: **writing paper**, notepaper.
2 *the story made the front page of the local paper*: **newspaper**; informal print, rag.
3 *the paper was peeling off the walls*: **wallpaper**, wallcovering; Brit. woodchip; trademark Anaglypta, Lincrusta.
4 *toffee papers*: **wrapper**, wrapping.

P

5 *we had to sit a three-hour paper*: **exam**, examination, test.
6 *he published a paper which proved to be a landmark in the evolution of macroeconomic ideas*: **essay**, article, composition, monograph, thesis, work, dissertation, treatise, study, report, analysis, tract, critique, exegesis, review, disquisition, discourse, piece of writing; N. Amer. theme.
7 (**papers**) *the personal papers of major political figures*: **documents**, certificates, forms, letters, files, deeds, records, dossiers, diaries, archives, legal papers, paperwork, documentation; informal treeware; rare muniments, instruments, assignments.
8 (**papers**) *two men stopped us and asked us for our papers*: **identification papers**, identification documents, identity card, ID, credentials, bona fides.
□ **on paper 1** *he's putting a few thoughts down on paper*: **in writing**, written down, in black and white, in print, on record; recorded, documented, printed. **2** *the combatants were, on paper at least, evenly matched*: **in theory**, theoretically, hypothetically, in the abstract, supposedly.
▸ **verb** *we papered the walls and put up curtains to match*: **wallpaper**, hang wallpaper on, line; decorate.
□ **paper over something** *the unions tried to paper over their differences*: **cover up**, hide, conceal, disguise, camouflage, gloss over, whitewash, varnish over, draw a veil over.

papery adjective *papery leaves | dry, papery skin*: **thin**, paper-thin, gossamer-thin, ultra-thin, flimsy, delicate, insubstantial, fragile, frail, light, lightweight; rare papyraceous, chartaceous.

par noun
□ **below par 1** *the team's performances have been consistently below par*: **substandard**, inferior, not up to standard, not up to scratch, under par, below average, lacking, wanting, second-rate, mediocre, middling, poor, bad, inadequate, unsatisfactory, uninspired, undistinguished; informal not up to snuff; N. Amer. informal bush-league. **2** *I'm feeling a bit below par this evening*: **slightly unwell**, not (very) well, not oneself, not in good shape, out of sorts; ill, ailing, unwell, poorly, indisposed; unhealthy, unfit, washed out, run down, tired, fatigued, peaky, liverish; sick, queasy, nauseous; Brit. off, off colour; informal under the weather, not up to snuff, funny, peculiar, crummy, lousy, rough; Brit. informal ropy, grotty; Scottish informal wabbit; Austral./NZ informal crook; dated seedy, queer.
□ **on a par with** *a degree of training on a par with the best cathedral choirs England has to offer*: **as good as**, comparable with, in the same class/league as, equivalent to, much the same as, equal to, a match for, on a level with, on an equal footing with, of the same standard as.
□ **par for the course** *long hours are par for the course in catering*: **normal**, typical, standard, usual, predictable, what one would expect, only to be expected.
□ **up to par** *those students whose grades are up to par*: **good enough**, up to the mark, satisfactory, acceptable, adequate, passable, up to scratch, all right; informal OK, up to snuff.

parable noun *the parable of the prodigal son*: **allegory**, moral story, moral tale, fable, lesson, exemplum; Judaism Haggadah; rare apologue.

parade noun **1** *a St George's Day parade | a military parade*: **procession**, march, cavalcade, motorcade, cortège, ceremony, spectacle, display, pageant, concours, file, train, column; array, review, muster, dress parade, tattoo; Brit. march past; Indian jatha, yatra, rath yatra; W. Indian mas.
2 *his daughter made a great parade of doing the housework*: **exhibition**, show, display, performance, production, spectacle, demonstration; fuss, bother, to-do, commotion, ado; informal hoo-ha.
3 *she walked along the parade as far as the pier*: **promenade**, walk, walkway, esplanade, mall; N. Amer. boardwalk; Brit. informal prom; Spanish alameda.
▸ **verb 1** *the teams will parade through the city with a police escort*: **march**, process, file, troop, go in columns, pass in formation, promenade.
2 *she paraded up and down her office*: **strut**, swagger, swank, stride, stalk, prance; N. Amer. informal sashay.
3 *he was keen to parade his knowledge*: **display**, exhibit, make a show of, flaunt, show, show off, demonstrate, draw attention to, air.

> *Choose the right word* **parade, strut, swagger**
>
> See **strut**.

paradigm noun *the institutional arrangements of a particular society cannot serve as a paradigm for all others*. See **example** (sense 2).

paradisal adjective **heavenly**, idyllic, blissful, divine, sublime, Elysian, perfect; literary Arcadian; rare paradisiacal, paradisical.

paradise noun **1** *the pagan belief that the soul of a murdered person never entered paradise*: **heaven**, the kingdom of heaven, the promised land, the heavenly kingdom, the City of God, the celestial city, the abode of God, the abode of the saints, Zion, Abraham's bosom; Christianity the New Jerusalem; Classical Mythology Elysium, the Elysian Fields, the Islands of the Blessed; Scandinavian Mythology Valhalla; Arthurian Legend Avalon.
2 *Adam and Eve's expulsion from Paradise*: **the Garden of Eden**, Eden.
3 *Bali is a lush tropical paradise*: **Utopia**, fairyland, Shangri-La, heaven, idyll, nirvana; literary Arcadia.
4 *the sun rising slowly above the mountains—sheer paradise!* **bliss**, heaven, ecstasy, rapture, delight, joy, happiness, nirvana, seventh heaven, heaven on earth.
▷ANTONYMS hell.

paradox noun *the apparent paradox of simultaneous unemployment and skilled-labour shortages*: **contradiction**, contradiction in terms, self-contradiction, inconsistency, incongruity, anomaly, conflict; absurdity, oddity, enigma, puzzle, mystery, conundrum; rare oxymoron, antinomy.

paradoxical adjective *it was paradoxical that a government dedicated to privatization should produce a bill to nationalize the legal profession*: **contradictory**, self-contradictory, inconsistent, incongruous, anomalous, conflicting; improbable, impossible, odd, illogical, confusing, absurd, puzzling, baffling, bewildering, incomprehensible, inexplicable; rare oxymoronic.

paragon noun *a paragon of fortitude and cheerfulness | your cook is a paragon*: **perfect example**, shining example, good example, model, epitome, archetype, ideal, exemplar, nonpareil, paradigm, embodiment, personification, quintessence, standard, prototype, apotheosis, the crème de la crème, the beau idéal, acme; jewel, gem, flower, angel, treasure; a perfect example of its kind; informal one in a million, the bee's knees, something else, the tops; archaic a nonsuch.

paragraph noun **1** *the letter's concluding paragraph*: **section**, subdivision, part, subsection, division, portion, segment, bit, passage, clause.
2 *appointments which rate a paragraph in the more serious newspapers*: **report**, article, item, piece, notice, write-up, note, mention.

parallel adjective **1** *parallel lines*: **side by side**, aligned, collateral, equidistant.
2 *problems parallel to those we discussed earlier*: **similar**, analogous, comparable, corresponding, like, resembling, much the same, of a kind, akin, related, kindred, equivalent, correspondent, homologous, analogical, cognate, coequal, matching, duplicate.
3 *a parallel universe*: **coexisting**, coexistent, concurrent; contemporaneous, simultaneous, synchronous.
▷ANTONYMS different, dissimilar, divergent.
▸ **noun 1** *it is difficult to find an exact parallel*: **counterpart**, analogue, equivalent, likeness, correspondent, match, twin, duplicate, equal, coequal, mirror; rare homologue.
2 *there is an interesting parallel between these figures and those of 1994*: **similarity**, likeness, resemblance, analogy, correspondence, equivalence, correlation; comparison, relation, symmetry, parity, parallelism, similitude, coequality.
▸ **verb 1** *his experiences parallel mine in many ways*: **resemble**, be similar to, be like, bear a resemblance to; correspond to, be analogous to, be comparable/equivalent to, compare with, equate with/to, correlate with, imitate, echo, remind one of, duplicate, mirror, repeat, recreate, follow, match, be in harmony with, chime (in) with; coincide with, keep pace with.
2 *her performance has never been paralleled*: **equal**, match, rival, emulate, touch.

paralyse verb **1** *both of his legs were temporarily paralysed*: **disable**, immobilize, render/make powerless, incapacitate, debilitate, numb, deaden, benumb, dull; rare obtund, torpefy.
2 *Maisie seemed to have been paralysed by the sight of him*: **immobilize**, transfix, become rooted to the spot, freeze, stun, render motionless, become horror-struck/horror-stricken, petrify; rare gorgonize.
3 *the regional capital was paralysed by a general strike*: **bring to a standstill**, immobilize, bring to a (grinding) halt, halt, stop, freeze, cripple, disable, put out of action/commission, render inoperative, deactivate; rare disenable.

paralysed adjective immobilized, incapacitated, powerless; Medicine paraplegic, quadriplegic, tetraplegic, monoplegic, hemiplegic, paretic, paraparetic; dated palsied.

paralysis noun **1** *the disease can cause paralysis*: **immobility**, powerlessness, lack of sensation, numbness, deadness, incapacity, debilitation; Medicine paraplegia, quadriplegia, tetraplegia, monoplegia, hemiplegia, diplegia, paresis, paraparesis; dated palsy.
2 *strike leaders claimed an almost complete paralysis of the ports*: **shutdown**, immobilization, stoppage, halt, standstill, stopping.

paralytic adjective **1** *her hands became paralytic*. See **paralysed**.
2 Brit. informal *a leaving party which left everyone paralytic*. See **drunk**.
▷ANTONYMS sober.

parameter noun *they set the parameters of the debate*: **framework**, variable, limit, boundary, limiting factor, limitation, restriction, specification, criterion, guideline; technical constant.

paramount adjective *the safety of the staff is paramount | children's needs should be of paramount importance*: **most important**, of greatest importance, of prime importance, of supreme importance; uppermost, supreme, chief, overriding, predominant, cardinal, foremost, first and foremost, prime, primary, principal, pre-eminent, highest, utmost, main, key, central, leading, major, top, topmost, dominant; informal number-one.

paramour noun *his stepfather's paramour*. See **lover** (sense 1).

paranoia noun **persecution complex**, delusions, obsession, megalomania, monomania; psychosis.

paranoid adjective *they probably don't mean me at all—I'm probably just being paranoid*: **irrationally anxious**, over-suspicious, paranoiac, suspicious, mistrustful, distrustful, fearful, insecure; Brit. informal para.

parapet noun **1** *Marian leaned over the parapet of the bridge*: **balustrade**, barrier, wall, railing, fence.
2 *the sandbags that made up the parapet had been blown away*: **barricade**, rampart, bulwark, bank, embankment, fortification, defence, breastwork, earthwork, bastion; battlement, castellation; rare bartizan.

paraphernalia plural noun *the paraphernalia necessary for home improvements*: **equipment**, stuff, things, apparatus, tackle, kit, implements, tools, utensils, material(s), appliances, rig, outfit, accoutrements, appurtenances, impedimenta, miscellaneous articles, odds and ends, bits and pieces, bits and bobs, trappings, accessories; informal gear, junk, rubbish, the necessary, dunnage, traps; Brit. informal clobber, gubbins, odds and sods; archaic equipage.

paraphrase verb *you can either quote or paraphrase literary texts*: **reword**, rephrase, put/express in other words, put/express in one's own words, express differently, rewrite, restate, rehash, interpret, gloss.
▸ noun *this paraphrase of St Paul's words*: **rewording**, rephrasing, rewriting, rewrite, restatement, restating, rehash, rendition, rendering, version, interpretation, gloss; rare paraphrasis.

parasite noun *Sam was a parasite with no interest in anything but drink and gambling*: **hanger-on**, cadger, leech, passenger, drone; informal bloodsucker, sponger, sponge, scrounger, freeloader; Brit. informal ligger; N. Amer. informal moocher, mooch; Austral./NZ informal bludger.

Word links **parasite**

parasitophobia fear of parasites
parasitology branch of medicine concerning parasitic organisms

parasitic adjective *the parasitic behaviour of some bureaucrats*: **exploitative**, parasitical; informal bloodsucking, sponging, freeloading.

parcel noun **1** *a parcel of food and clothes*: **package**, packet; pack, carton, bundle, box, case, bale; archaic fardel.
2 *a 21-acre parcel of land*: **plot**, piece, patch, tract, area, section, allotment; N. Amer. lot, plat.
3 *a parcel of rogues*: **group**, band, pack, gang, crowd, mob, company, collection, horde, party, troop; informal crew, bunch.
▸ verb **1** *she parcelled up the papers*: **pack**, pack up, package, wrap, wrap up, gift-wrap, tie up, do up, box, box up, bundle up, fasten together.
2 *parcelling out commercial farmland in small plots will reduce productivity*: **divide up**, portion out, distribute, share out, allocate, allot, apportion, hand out, give out, deal out, dole out, mete out, dispense, split up, carve up; informal divvy up, dish out.

parched adjective **1** *the parched earth*: **dry**, as dry as a bone, bone dry, dried up, dried out, arid, waterless, desiccated, dehydrated, sun-baked, baked, burned, scorched, seared, withered, shrivelled; literary sear, adust; rare exsiccated.
▷ANTONYMS wet, soaking.
2 *Can I have a drink, please? I'm parched*: **thirsty**, dehydrated, dry; informal gasping; Austral./NZ informal spitting chips; archaic athirst; rare thirstful, droughty, sitient.

parching adjective *the parching southern sun*: **searing**, scorching, blistering, flaming, blazing (hot), baking (hot), burning, fiery, torrid, withering; informal boiling, boiling hot, sizzling, roasting, sweltering.

pardon noun **1** *he obtained pardon for his sins*: **forgiveness**, absolution, remission, clemency, mercy, lenience, leniency, condonation; historical indulgence.
2 *he offered a full pardon to the five convicted men*: **reprieve**, free pardon, general pardon, amnesty, exoneration, exculpation, release, acquittal, discharge; rare oblivion.
▸ verb **1** *I know she will pardon me*: **forgive**, absolve, have mercy on, be merciful to, deal leniently with; **excuse**, condone, overlook; rare remit.
▷ANTONYMS blame.
2 *the convicted men were subsequently pardoned*: **exonerate**, acquit, amnesty, exculpate; **let off**, grant a pardon to, reprieve, release, free, spare.
▷ANTONYMS punish.
▸ exclamation *'Pardon?' I said, cupping a hand to my ear*: **what did you say**, what, eh, I beg your pardon, beg pardon, sorry, excuse me, say again; N. Amer. pardon me; informal come again.

Choose the right word **pardon, forgive, excuse, condone**

See **forgive**.

pardonable adjective *a pardonable error*: **excusable**, forgivable, allowable, condonable, understandable, minor, slight, venial, not serious, permissible.
▷ANTONYMS inexcusable.

pare verb **1** *pare 4 strips of zest from the lemon | pare the mangoes*: **cut (off)**, trim (off), peel (off), shave (off), strip (off), clip (off), skin; technical decorticate, excoriate.
2 *the company's domestic operations have been pared down*: **reduce**, diminish, decrease, cut, cut back/down, make cutbacks in, whittle away/down, trim, slim down, prune, lower, lessen, retrench, curtail.

parent noun **1** *her parents divorced when she was seven*: **mother**, **father**; birth/biological parent, adoptive mother/father, surrogate mother, foster-parent, foster-mother, foster-father, step-parent, stepmother, stepfather, guardian; single parent, lone parent, co-parent; informal one's old man, one's old woman, one's old lady; rare begetter, procreator, progenitor, progenitress, progenitrix, genitor, pater.
2 *rhythm and blues, the parent of rock and roll*: **source**, origin, genesis, originator, root, fountain, cause, author, architect; **precursor**, forerunner, predecessor, antecedent, forebear, ancestor; literary wellspring; rare radix.
▸ verb *all children are special to those who parent them*: **bring up**, be the parent of, look after, take care of, rear, raise, nurture.

Word links **parent**

parricide killing of one's parent

parentage noun *a young woman of African parentage*: **origins**, extraction, birth, family, ancestry, lineage, heritage, pedigree, descent, line of descent, line, blood, bloodline, stock, paternity, roots, derivation; rare filiation, stirps.

parenthetical adjective *parenthetical remarks*: **incidental**, supplementary, by-the-way, by-the-by, in parentheses, parenthetic, in brackets; explanatory, qualifying, inserted, interposed, extraneous.

parenthetically adverb **incidentally**, **by the way**, by the by(e), in passing, en passant, by way of explanation, in parenthesis; informal BTW.

parenthood noun **childcare**, child-rearing, motherhood, fatherhood, parenting, mothering, fathering.

pariah noun *they were treated as social pariahs*: **outcast**, persona non grata, leper, reject, untouchable, undesirable; rare unperson.

parings plural noun **peelings**, clippings, peel, rind, cuttings, trimmings, shavings, strips, pieces, slivers, fragments, shreds.

parish noun **1** *the parish of Poplar in East London*: **district**, community.
2 *a vicar must do nothing that would scandalize the parish*: **parishioners**, churchgoers, church, congregation, flock, fold, community.

Word links **parish**

parochial relating to a parish

parish-pump adjective *a major league performer showing the parish-pump locals how to run their affairs*: **provincial**, unsophisticated, small-town, parochial, parish-pump, insular, inward-looking, limited, blinkered, bourgeois, middle-class, conservative, petty, close-minded, myopic, introverted, illiberal, hidebound, intolerant.
▷ANTONYMS cosmopolitan, broad-minded, liberal.

parity noun *parity of incomes between rural workers and those in industrial occupations*: **equality**, equivalence, uniformity, sameness, consistency, correspondence, congruity, congruence, levelness, unity, coequality, parallelism, evenness.

park noun **1** *Yvonne and her friends were playing in the park*: **public garden**, recreation ground, playground, play area, public/municipal park.
2 *a property set in fifty acres of park*: **parkland**, grassland, woodland, garden(s), lawns, grounds, estate; literary greensward.
3 *he was the liveliest player on the park*: **playing field**, football field, field, pitch.
▸ verb **1** *he parked his car outside Emma's house*: **leave**, station, position; stop, pull up.
2 *park your bag by the door*: **put**, put down, place, deposit, set, set down, leave, stick, shove, dump, plump; informal plonk, plunk; Brit. informal bung.
□ **park oneself** *he parked himself in the seat opposite*: **sit down**, seat oneself, settle (oneself), install oneself, plant oneself, ensconce oneself, plump oneself, plop oneself, flump, perch; informal plonk oneself.

parlance noun *a Munro, in climbing parlance, is a Scottish mountain exceeding 3000 feet in height*. See **idiom** (sense 2).

parley noun *a peace parley*: **negotiation**, talk(s), meeting, conference, summit, discussion, dialogue, conclave, consultation, deliberation, colloquy; informal confab, powwow; formal confabulation; dated palaver.
▸ verb *the two parties were willing to parley*: **discuss terms**, talk, hold talks, speak to each other, confer, consult with each other, negotiate, deliberate; informal powwow.

parliament noun **1** *the Queen's speech to Parliament*: **the Houses of Parliament**, Westminster, the House of Commons, the House of Lords, the Commons, the Lords, the House, the Lower House, the Upper House, the Mother of Parliaments.
2 *the Russian parliament*: **legislature**, legislative assembly, congress, senate, chamber, house, upper house, lower house, upper chamber, lower

chamber, second chamber, convocation, diet, council, assembly, Chamber of Deputies.

parliamentary adjective *parliamentary assemblies*: **legislative**, law-making, lawgiving, deliberative, governmental, congressional, senatorial, democratic, elected, representative; rare legislatorial.

parlour noun **1** *they had tea in the parlour*: **sitting room**, living room, lounge, front room, best room, drawing room, morning room, salon; Brit. reception room.
2 *a beauty parlour*: **salon**, shop, establishment, store.

parlous adjective archaic or humorous *the parlous state of the industry*: **bad**, dire, dreadful, awful, terrible, appalling, frightful, grave, serious, desperate, precarious, uncertain, touch-and-go, difficult, unsafe, perilous, dangerous, risky; pitiful, wretched, sorry, poor, lamentable, woeful, hopeless; informal dicey, hairy, lousy; Brit. informal dodgy, chronic.

parochial adjective *parochial attitudes*: **narrow-minded**, small-minded, provincial, insular, narrow, small-town, inward-looking, limited, restricted, localist, conservative, conventional, short-sighted, petty, close-minded, blinkered, myopic, introverted, illiberal, hidebound, intolerant; Brit. parish-pump; N. Amer. informal jerkwater, hick.
▷**ANTONYMS** cosmopolitan, broad-minded, liberal.

parochialism noun **narrow-mindedness**, **localism**, provincialism, insularity, narrowness, small-mindedness.

parody noun **1** *a parody of the gothic novel*: **satire**, burlesque, lampoon, pastiche, caricature, take-off, skit, imitation, mockery; informal spoof, send-up; W. Indian informal pappyshow; Brit. vulgar slang piss-take; rare pasquinade, pasticcio.
2 *an appalling* ***parody of*** *the truth*: **distortion**, travesty, poor imitation, caricature, mockery, misrepresentation, perversion, corruption, debasement; apology for.
▶ verb *his speciality was parodying schoolgirl fiction*: **satirize**, burlesque, lampoon, caricature, mimic, imitate, ape, copy, do, do an impression of, make fun of, travesty, take off; informal send up; Brit. vulgar slang take the piss out of.

paroxysm noun *violent paroxysms of coughing | a paroxysm of rage*: **spasm**, attack, fit, burst, bout, convulsion, seizure, outburst, outbreak, eruption, explosion, flare-up, access; throes; rare ebullition, boutade.

parrot verb *they parroted slogans without appreciating their significance*: **repeat mindlessly**, repeat, repeat mechanically, echo, say again.

Word links **parrot**
psittacine relating to parrots

parrot-fashion adverb *his wife had just repeated the phrase parrot-fashion*: **mechanically**, by rote, mindlessly, without thinking, unthinkingly, automatically.

parry verb **1** *Sharpe parried the blow*: **ward off**, fend off, stave off, turn aside; **deflect**, hold off, block, avert, counter, rebuff, repel, repulse, hold/keep at bay.
2 *I parried her constant questions about my job-hunting activities*: **evade**, sidestep, avoid, dodge, answer evasively, field, fend off, deflect, circumvent, steer clear of, fight shy of; informal duck.

parsimonious adjective **mean**, miserly, niggardly, close-fisted, penny-pinching, cheese-paring, ungenerous, penurious, illiberal, close, grasping, Scrooge-like, stinting, sparing, frugal; informal tight-fisted, stingy, tight, mingy, money-grubbing, skinflinty; N. Amer. informal cheap; Brit. vulgar slang tight-arsed, tight as a duck's arse; archaic near.
▷**ANTONYMS** generous, extravagant, lavish.

parsimony noun **meanness**, miserliness, parsimoniousness, niggardliness, close-fistedness, closeness, penuriousness, penny-pinching, cheese-paring, illiberality, frugality; informal stinginess, minginess, tightness, tight-fistedness; N. Amer. cheapness; archaic nearness.
▷**ANTONYMS** generosity.

parson noun **vicar**, rector, clergyman, member of the clergy, cleric, chaplain, pastor, curate, churchman, man of the cloth, man of God, ecclesiastic, minister, priest, preacher, divine; French curé; informal reverend, padre, Holy Joe, sky pilot; Austral. informal josser.

part noun **1** *the last part of the cake | a large part of life is spent at the workplace*: **bit**, slice, chunk, lump, hunk, wedge, fragment, scrap, segment, piece; portion, share, proportion, percentage, fraction, division, section.
▷**ANTONYMS** whole, entirety.
2 *some car parts are now assembled by people working at home*: **component**, bit, constituent, element, unit, module, ingredient.
3 *some of pigs' body parts are very much like ours*: **organ**, limb, member, biological structure.
4 *this chapter links the second and third parts of the book*: **section**, division, component, volume, chapter, passage, act, scene, episode, instalment.
5 *her parents lived in another part of the country*: **district**, neighbourhood, quarter, section, area, region, sector, zone, belt, territory, locality; informal neck of the woods.
6 *one of the boy actors played the part of Juliet*: **role**, theatrical role, character, persona, representation, portrayal, depiction.
7 *I don't care how long he's had to learn the part*: **lines**, words, script, dialogue, speech, libretto, book, lyrics, score.
8 *he was jailed for his part in the affair*: **involvement**, role, function, hand, job, task, work, responsibility, capacity, post, position, office, participation, bit, contribution, concern, province.
□ **for the most part** See **most**.
□ **in part** *inflation is caused in part by indirect tax increases*: **to a certain extent/degree**, to a limited extent/degree, to some extent/degree, partly, partially, half, in some measure, relatively, comparatively, moderately, (up) to a point, a little, somewhat; not totally, not wholly, not entirely, not fully, incompletely; slightly, fractionally; informal ish.
▷**ANTONYMS** completely.
□ **on the part of** *there is increased interest in these coins on the part of collectors*: **by**, made by, done by, carried out by, caused by, from, in, of; for which someone is responsible.
□ **in good part** See **good**.
□ **take part** *anyone interested is welcome to take part*: **participate**, join in, get involved, enter, go in for something, throw oneself into something, share in something, play a part, play a role, be a participant, partake, contribute, be associated, associate oneself, have a hand, have something to do with something, be (a) party to something, cooperate, help, assist, lend a hand; informal get in on the act, pitch in.
□ **take part in** *the cadets are obliged to take part in adventurous training*: **participate in**, engage in, enter into, join in, get involved in, go in for, throw oneself into, share in, play a part in, play a role in, be a participant in, partake in, contribute to, be associated with, associate oneself with, have a hand in, have something to do with, be (a) party to.
□ **take someone's part** *an attack would drive Count William to take his son's part*: **support**, give one's support to, take the side of, side with, be on the side of, stand by, stand up for, stick up for, be supportive of, encourage, back, back up, give one's backing to, uphold, be loyal to, defend, come to the defence of, champion, ally (oneself) with, associate oneself with, favour, abet, aid and abet.
▷**ANTONYMS** turn against.
▶ verb **1** *the curtains parted and the show began | he knelt down and parted the heather with his hands*: **separate**, **divide**, divide in two, split, split in two, break up; move apart; rare disjoin.
▷**ANTONYMS** join.
2 *if we part like this I may never see him again*: **leave**, take one's leave, say goodbye/farewell/adieu, say one's goodbyes, say/make one's farewells, separate, break up, go one's (separate) ways, take oneself off, set off, be on one's way, go, go away, get going, depart, be off; informal split, push off, hit the road, skedaddle, scram, shove off.
▷**ANTONYMS** arrive; meet.
□ **part company with** *here we will again part company with the consensus*: **disagree with**, fail to agree with, express disagreement with, be at variance/odds with, argue with, take issue with; decline/refuse to support, not ratify, protest against, object to, dispute, challenge, quibble over.
□ **part with** *she had no wish to part with any of her land*: **give up**, relinquish, forgo, surrender, hand over, deliver up, let go of, renounce, give away, dispose of, discard, abandon, sacrifice, yield, cede.
▷**ANTONYMS** acquire.
▶ adjective *a part payment is refundable*: **incomplete**, partial, half, semi-, demi-, near, moderate, limited, slight, inadequate, insufficient, unfinished.
▷**ANTONYMS** complete.
▶ adverb *the engine components can be supplied part finished*: **to a certain extent/degree**, to a limited extent/degree, to some extent/degree, partly, partially, in part, half, in some measure, relatively, comparatively, moderately, (up) to a point, a little, somewhat; not totally, not wholly, not entirely, not fully, incompletely, nearly, very nearly, almost, just about, all but; slightly, barely, scarcely, fractionally, inadequately, insufficiently, not nearly.
▷**ANTONYMS** completely.

partake verb **1** *video conferencing allows executives to* ***partake in*** *negotiations abroad*: **participate in**, take part in, engage in, enter into, join in, get involved in, share in, play a part in, contribute to, have a hand in, have something to do with.
2 *she had* ***partaken of*** *a cheese sandwich and a cup of coffee*: **consume**, have, eat, drink, take, devour, polish off, ingest; informal tuck into, wolf down, dispose of, get outside of, get one's laughing gear round.
3 *Bohemia is where eastern and western Europe meet,* ***partaking of*** *both, part of neither*: **have the qualities/attributes of**, suggest, evoke, be characterized by, hint at, evince, manifest.

partial adjective **1** *the partial recovery of the economy*: **incomplete**, limited, qualified, restricted, imperfect, fragmentary, unfinished.
▷**ANTONYMS** complete, total, whole.
2 *the paper gave a distorted and very partial view of the situation*: **biased**, prejudiced, partisan, one-sided, slanted, skewed, coloured, interested, parti pris, discriminatory, preferential, jaundiced; unjust, unfair, inequitable, unbalanced.

P

▷ANTONYMS unbiased, impartial, disinterested.
□ **be partial to** *Celeste was partial to bacon sandwiches*: **like**, love, enjoy, have a liking for, be fond of, be keen on, have a fondness for, have a weakness for, have a soft spot for, have a taste for, be taken with, care for, have a predilection/proclivity/penchant for, be enamoured of; informal adore, be mad about/on, have a thing about, be crazy about, be potty about, be nutty about; N. Amer. informal cotton to, be nutso over/about; Austral./NZ informal be shook on.

Choose the right word **partial, biased, prejudiced**

See **biased**.

partiality noun **1** *the president had shown partiality towards the group's cause*: **bias**, prejudice, favouritism, favour, partisanship, unfair preference, discrimination, unjustness, unfairness, inequity.
2 *his partiality for brandy and soda was notorious*: **liking**, love, fondness, taste, weakness, soft spot, keenness, inclination, predilection, predisposition, proclivity, penchant, fancy, relish, passion.

partially adverb *the plan was only partially successful*: **to a limited extent/degree**, partly, to a certain extent/degree, to some extent/degree, in part, not totally, not wholly, not entirely, not fully, relatively, moderately, (up) to a point, half, somewhat, in some measure, comparatively, fractionally, slightly, incompletely; informal ish.

participant noun **participator**, contributor, sharer, party, member, partaker; entrant, competitor, player, contestant, contender, candidate.

participate verb *400,000 people* ***participated in*** *the peaceful demonstration*: **take part**, engage, join, get involved, share, play a part, play a role, be a participant, partake; cooperate, help, assist, lend a hand; go in for, contribute to, be associated with, associate oneself with, have a hand in, have something to do with, be (a) party to; informal get in on the act, pitch in.

participation noun *the government's participation in the peace talks*: **involvement**, taking part, part, engagement, contribution; sharing, association, partaking, joining in.

particle noun **1** *minute particles of rock*: **bit**, tiny bit, piece, tiny piece, speck, spot, fleck, dot, atom, molecule; mote, fragment, sliver, splinter.
2 *he never showed a particle of sympathy for her*: **iota**, jot, whit, bit, scrap, shred, crumb, morsel, mite, atom, drop, hint, touch, trace, suggestion, whisper, suspicion, scintilla, grain, tittle, jot or tittle; any; Irish stim; informal smidgen, smidge, tad; archaic scantling, scruple.

particular adjective **1** *the action seems to discriminate against a particular group of companies*: **specific**, certain, distinct, separate, isolated; single, individual, peculiar, discrete, definite, express, precise.
▷ANTONYMS general.
2 *an issue of particular importance*: **special**, extra special, especial, exceptional, unusual, marked, singular, uncommon, notable, noteworthy, remarkable, outstanding, unique; formal peculiar.
▷ANTONYMS ordinary.
3 *he was particular about what he ate*: **fussy**, fastidious, meticulous, punctilious, discriminating, selective, painstaking, exacting, demanding, critical, over-particular, over-fastidious, finicky, faddish, finical, dainty; informal pernickety, choosy, picky; Brit. informal faddy; archaic nice.
▷ANTONYMS careless, easy-going, laid-back.
4 *he gave a long and particular account of his journey*: **detailed**, blow-by-blow, itemized, item-by-item, thorough, minute, exact, explicit, precise, faithful, close, circumstantial, painstaking, meticulous, punctilious, particularized.
▶ **noun** *the two contracts will be the same in every particular*: **detail**, item, point, fine point, specific, specification, element, aspect, respect, regard, particularity, fact, feature, circumstance, thing.
□ **in particular 1** *she wasn't talking about anyone in particular*: **specific**, special. **2** *beer drinkers in particular were hit by prices rising faster than inflation*: **particularly**, specifically, to be specific, especially, specially.

particularity noun **1** *the particularity of each human being*: **individuality**, distinctiveness, uniqueness, singularity, originality, peculiarity.
2 *parties must present their case with some degree of particularity*: **detail**, precision, exactness, accuracy, thoroughness, scrupulousness, meticulousness.
3 *local and personal particularities*: **feature**, trait, characteristic, idiosyncrasy, peculiarity, quirk, detail, item, circumstance, point, property.

particularize verb *the indictment particularized several incidents*: **specify**, detail, itemize, list, enumerate, spell out, be specific about, cite, stipulate, instance, distinguish; rare individuate.

particularly adverb **1** *the acoustics in the church are particularly good*: **especially**, specially, very, extremely, exceptionally, singularly, peculiarly, distinctly, unusually, extraordinarily, extra, uncommonly, uniquely, remarkably, strikingly, outstandingly, amazingly, incredibly, awfully, terribly, really, notably, markedly, decidedly, surprisingly, conspicuously; N. English powerful, right; informal seriously, majorly, mucho; Brit. informal jolly, dead, well; informal, dated devilish, frightfully.
2 *he particularly asked that I should help you*: **specifically**, explicitly, expressly, in particular, especially, specially.

parting noun **1** *it was an emotional parting*: **farewell**, leave-taking, goodbye, adieu, departure, leaving, going (away); valediction.
2 *he and his wife kept their parting quiet from the press*: **separation**, **break-up**, splitting up, split, split-up, breaking up, divorce, rift, breach, parting of the ways, estrangement, rupture; Brit. informal bust-up.
3 *the parting of the Red Sea*: **division**, dividing, separation, separating, splitting, breaking up/apart, severance, disjoining, detachment, partition, partitioning.
▶ **adjective** *a parting kiss*: **farewell**, goodbye, departing, leaving, last, final, closing, concluding, valedictory; deathbed, dying.

partisan noun **1** *Conservative partisans claimed that television news was biased against their party*: **supporter**, follower, adherent, devotee, champion, backer, upholder, promoter, fanatic, fan, enthusiast, stalwart, zealot, disciple, votary; N. Amer. booster, cohort; N. Amer. informal rooter; rare janissary, sectary.
2 *the partisans opened fire from the woods*: **guerrilla**, freedom fighter, resistance fighter, member of the resistance, underground fighter, irregular soldier, irregular; terrorist.
▶ **adjective** *the government had adopted a blatantly partisan attitude*: **biased**, prejudiced, one-sided, coloured, discriminatory, preferential, partial, interested, parti pris, bigoted, sectarian, factional, unjust, unfair, inequitable, unbalanced.
▷ANTONYMS impartial, unbiased.

partisanship noun **bias**, prejudice, one-sidedness, discrimination, favouritism, favour, unfair preference, partiality, sectarianism, factionalism; injustice, unfairness, inequity.

partition noun **1** *the partition of Palestine in 1947*: **dividing up**, partitioning, separation, division, dividing, subdivision, splitting, splitting up, split-up, breaking up, break-up, parting, segregation, severance; rare partitionment.
2 *the room was divided by partitions*: **screen**, **divider**, room divider, dividing wall, barrier, wall, fence, panel, separator.
▶ **verb 1** *the resolution partitioned Palestine into two states*: **divide**, divide up, subdivide, separate, split, split up, cut up, carve up, break up, sever, segregate; share, share out, parcel out, portion, portion out.
2 *the huge halls and corridors have been partitioned*: **subdivide**, **separate**, divide, divide up; separate off, section, section off, screen off, wall off, fence off.

partly adverb *the book is partly autobiographical*: **to a certain extent/degree**, to some extent/degree, to a limited extent/degree, in part, partially, a little, somewhat, not totally, not wholly, not entirely, not fully, relatively, moderately, (up) to a point, half, in some measure, comparatively, slightly; informal ish.
▷ANTONYMS completely, wholly.

partner noun **1** *two former business partners*: **colleague**, associate, co-worker, fellow worker, co-partner, collaborator, ally, comrade, companion, teammate; French confrère; Brit. informal oppo; Austral./NZ informal offsider; archaic compeer; rare consociate.
2 *his partner in crime*: **accomplice**, confederate, accessory, collaborator, fellow conspirator, right hand, right-hand man/woman, helper, abetter; N. Amer. cohort; informal sidekick.
3 *are you worried about your relationship with your partner?* **spouse**, husband, wife, consort, helpmate, helpmeet; **lover**, girlfriend, boyfriend, fiancé, fiancée, significant other, live-in lover, cohabitee, common-law husband/wife, man, woman, mate; Italian inamorato, inamorata; informal hubby, old man, old lady, old woman, missus, missis, better half, other half, WAGs (wives and girlfriends), POSSLQ (person of the opposite sex sharing living quarters); Brit. informal dutch, her indoors; Brit. rhyming slang trouble and strife; dated beau, young man, lady; informal, dated intended.

partnership noun **1** *the close partnership between Britain and the US*: **cooperation**, association, collaboration, coalition, alliance, union, compact, league, confederation, co-partnership, affiliation, relationship, fellowship, connection; rare consociation.
2 *the partnership now owns twenty-two department stores*: **company**, firm, business, corporation, organization, association, consortium, establishment, house, cooperative, concern, operation, undertaking, conglomerate, combine, syndicate; informal outfit, set-up.

parturition noun **childbirth**, giving birth, birth, birthing, delivery, labour; archaic confinement, childbed, accouchement, travail.

party noun **1** *150 people attended the party*: **social gathering**, gathering, social occasion, social event, social function, function, get-together, celebration, reunion, festivity, jamboree, reception, at-home, soirée, social; dance, ball, ceilidh, frolic, carousal, carouse; N. Amer. fête, hoedown, shower, bake, cookout, levee; Austral./NZ corroboree; W. Indian bashment; Hawaiian luau; Spanish tertulia; Jewish simcha; informal bash, shindig, shindy, rave, blowout, beer-up, disco, do, shebang, bop, hop, whoopee, after-party; Brit. informal rave-up, thrash, knees-up, beanfeast, beano, bunfight, jolly, lig; Irish informal hooley, crack; N. Amer. informal blast, wingding, kegger; Austral./NZ informal shivoo, rage, ding, jollo, rort; S. African informal jol; dated squash, squeeze, ding-dong.

2 *a party of British tourists arrived*: **group**, company, body, gang, band, crowd, pack, contingent; informal bunch, crew, gaggle, posse, load.
3 *left-wing parties were highly critical of the proposals*: **faction**, political party, group, grouping, side, alliance, affiliation, association, coalition, movement, cabal, junta, bloc, camp, set, caucus, sect.
4 *a certain party's name is not to be mentioned*: **person**, individual, human being, somebody, someone; informal character.
5 *the trial judge must apportion blame between the parties*: **litigant**, plaintiff, defendant; participant.
□ **be a party to** *I am not going to be a party to their plan for nabbing you*: **get involved in/with**, be associated with, concern/involve oneself in, be a participant in, touch, handle.
▶ **verb** *let's party!* **celebrate**, have fun, enjoy oneself, have a party, have a good/wild time, rave it up, carouse, make merry; informal go out on the town, paint the town red, whoop it up, let one's hair down, make whoopee, have a night on the tiles, live it up, have a ball, go on a bender, push the boat out, go on a spree; S. African informal jol.

parvenu **noun** **upstart**, social climber, arriviste, vulgarian; the nouveau riche, the new rich.

pass[1] **verb** **1** *the traffic passing through the village*: **go**, **proceed**, move, progress, make one's way, travel, drive, fly; run, flow, course, stream, roll, drift, sweep.
▷**ANTONYMS** halt, stop.
2 *every time a car passed him, he worried it might be the police*: **overtake**, go past, move past, go by, get ahead of, pull ahead of, go ahead of; outstrip, outdistance, lap, leave behind; Brit. overhaul.
3 *as time passed, my feelings towards him slowly changed*: **elapse**, go by, go past, proceed, progress, advance, wear on, slip by, slip away, roll by, glide by, tick by.
4 *he passed the time writing letters*: **occupy**, spend, fill, use (up), employ, devote, take up, while away, beguile; kill, waste, fritter, dissipate.
5 *pass me the salt, please*: **hand**, let someone have, give, hand over, hand round, reach; transfer, convey, deliver; throw, toss; informal chuck, bung.
6 *he passed the ball back to the goalkeeper*: **kick**, hit, throw, head, lob, loft.
7 *on her death in 1865, the estate passed to her grandson*: **be transferred**, be made over, be turned over, be signed over, go, devolve, be left, be bequeathed, be handed down/on, be given, be consigned, be passed on.
8 *his death passed almost unnoticed*: **happen**, occur, take place, come about, transpire; literary befall; rare eventuate.
9 *the storm passed as quickly as it had begun*: **come to an end**, cease to exist, fade, fade away, melt away, blow over, run its course, ebb, die out, evaporate, vanish, peter out, draw to a close, disappear, finish, end, cease, terminate; rare evanish.
10 *God's peace passes all human understanding*: **surpass**, exceed, go beyond, transcend, outdo, surmount, outstrip.
11 *he passed the entrance exam*: **be successful in**, succeed in, gain a pass in, get through, come through, meet the requirements of, pass muster in; qualify, graduate; informal come up to scratch in, come up to snuff in, sail through, scrape through.
▷**ANTONYMS** fail.
12 *the Senate passed the defence bill by seventy votes to sixteen*: **approve**, vote for, accept, ratify, adopt, carry, agree to, authorize, sanction, endorse, validate, legalize, put into effect, enact; informal OK.
▷**ANTONYMS** reject.
13 *there was no way she could let that comment pass*: **go unnoticed**, go unheeded, stand, go, be accepted, go unremarked, go undisputed, go uncensored.
14 *I'm hardly in a position to pass judgement on her*: **declare**, pronounce, utter, express, deliver, issue, set forth.
15 *he felt a stinging sensation every time he passed urine*: **discharge**, excrete, eliminate, evacuate, expel, emit, void, release, let out.
□ **come to pass** *such a moment came to pass one fateful Saturday back in 1985*: **happen**, come about, occur, transpire, arise; literary befall.
□ **pass away/on** *she passed away peacefully in her sleep*. See **die**.
□ **pass as/for** *she could easily pass for someone half her age*: **be mistaken for**, be taken for, be regarded as, be accepted as.
□ **pass off 1** *the rally passed off peacefully*: **take place**, go off, happen, occur, be carried though, be completed, be brought to a conclusion, be accomplished; turn out, fall out, pan out; N. Amer. go down. **2** *when the dizziness passed off he sat up and looked at his watch*: **wear off**, come to an end, fade, fade away, pass, disappear, vanish, die down, ebb.
□ **pass someone off** *he added Natasha's name to his passport, passing her off as his daughter*: **misrepresent**, falsely represent, give a false identity to; disguise, dress up.
□ **pass out** *she probably banged her head when she passed out*: **faint**, collapse, lose consciousness, black out, keel over; informal flake out, conk out; literary swoon.
□ **pass something over** *the court cannot possibly pass over these offences*: **disregard**, overlook, ignore, avoid considering, not take into consideration, forget, pay no attention to, let pass, let go, gloss over, take no notice of, pay no heed to, take no account of, close one's eyes to, turn a deaf ear to, turn a blind eye to, omit, skip; archaic overleap.
□ **pass something up** *I can't pass up a bargain like this, can I?* **fail to take advantage of**, turn down, reject, refuse, decline, deny oneself, give up, forgo, let go by, let pass, miss, miss out on, ignore, brush aside, dismiss, waive, spurn, neglect, abandon; informal give something a miss.
▶ **noun 1** *you can only get in if you have a pass*: **permit**, warrant, authorization, licence; passport, visa, safe conduct, exeat; free ticket, free admission, complimentary ticket; rare laissez-passer.
2 *a cross-field pass*: **kick**, hit, throw, shot, header.
□ **come to a pretty pass** *things have come to a pretty pass if the tabloids are influencing England's selection policy*: **reach a regrettable/bad state (of affairs)**, be in a worrying state, be in a sad plight, be in troubled circumstances, be in dire straits; informal be in a pickle/hole.
□ **make a pass at** *I bet he made a pass at Elizabeth*: **make sexual advances to**, make advances to, make sexual overtures to, proposition, make a sexual approach to; informal come on to, make a play for; N. Amer. informal hit on, make time with, put the make on; dated make love to.

pass[2] **noun** *a pass through the mountains*: **route**, way, road, narrow road, passage, cut, gap, gorge, canyon, ravine, gully, defile, col, couloir; Scottish bealach; N. Amer. notch.

passable **adjective 1** *the beer was passable*: **adequate**, all right, fairly good, acceptable, sufficiently good, sufficient, satisfactory, moderately good, not (too) bad, average, tolerable, fair, decent, respectable, presentable, admissible, allowable; mediocre, middling, ordinary, run-of-the-mill, workaday, indifferent, unremarkable, undistinguished, unexceptional; informal OK, so-so, fair-to-middling, nothing to write home about, no great shakes, not up to much, not much cop, bog-standard, vanilla, plain vanilla; NZ informal half-pie.
▷**ANTONYMS** unacceptable; excellent.
2 *the road is still passable*: **navigable**, traversable, negotiable, crossable, able to be travelled on/along, unblocked, unobstructed, open, clear, usable.
▷**ANTONYMS** impassable.

passably **adverb** *a passably good dinner*: **quite**, rather, somewhat, fairly, reasonably, moderately, comparatively, relatively, after a fashion, to a limited extent/degree, to a certain degree, to some extent, tolerably; adequately, satisfactorily; informal pretty, ish.

passage **noun 1** *only one incident marred their passage through the country | the passage of sound through water*: **transit**, progress, passing, movement, moving, motion, going, crossing, travelling, traversal, traverse.
2 *the passage of time*: **passing**, advance, course, march, moving on, flow.
3 *they obtained a passage to Ajaccio from the French Minister of Culture*: **safe conduct**, entry, admission, access; permission/authorization to travel through, leave to travel in; warrant, visa.
4 *the overnight passage to Aberdeen was wild and stormy*: **voyage**, crossing, trip, cruise, sail; journey, tour, trek.
5 *police officers cleared a passage to the front door*: **way**, way through, route, path, course.
6 *a small passage led to the kitchen*: **corridor**, passageway, hall, hallway, entrance hall, entrance, walkway, aisle, gangway.
7 *a passage between the buildings*: **alley**, alleyway, lane, path, pathway, way, footpath, track, trackway, road, thoroughfare; Scottish & N. English ginnel, snicket, vennel, wynd, twitten; N. Amer. areaway; W. Indian & US trace; Indian gully.
8 *food and air passages | the nasal passages*: **duct**; orifice, opening, aperture, hole, channel; inlet, outlet.
9 *an abrupt passage from the darkness of the Middle Ages to the light of the Renaissance*: **transition**, development, progress, progression, move, change, shift, conversion, metamorphosis.
10 *the passage of a Private Member's Bill*: **enactment**, passing, ratification, acceptance, approval, adoption, authorization, sanction, validation, legalization, endorsement.
11 *a passage from 'Macbeth'*: **extract**, excerpt, quotation, quote, citation, cite, reading, section, piece, selection, part, snippet, fragment, portion; text, paragraph, verse, stanza, canto, line, sentence, phrase.

passageway **noun 1** *the house was full of secret passageways*: **corridor**, hall, passage, hallway, walkway, gangway, aisle.
2 *her hotel was at the end of a narrow passageway off the main street*: **alley**, alleyway, lane, path, pathway, way, footpath, track, trackway, road, thoroughfare; Scottish & N. English ginnel, snicket, vennel, wynd, twitten; N. Amer. areaway; W. Indian & US trace; Indian gully.

passé **adjective** French *this type of film has long been denounced as passé*: **out of date**, outdated, out, dated, unfashionable, out of fashion, old-fashioned, outmoded, out of style, behind the times, outworn, archaic, obsolescent, obsolete, ancient, antiquated, superannuated, defunct, dead, old-fogeyish, old-fangled, quaint, anachronistic, olde worlde, medieval; French démodé; N. Amer. horse-and-buggy; informal old hat, square, not with it, out of the ark, creaky, mouldy, square-toed; N. Amer. informal clunky, rinky-dink, mossy.
▷**ANTONYMS** fashionable.

passenger **noun 1** *more than fifty passengers escaped injury when the train was derailed*: **traveller**, commuter, voyager, rider, fare payer, fare; deck passenger, foot passenger.
2 *all departments have their share of passengers*: **hanger-on**, drone, idler, parasite; informal freeloader.

passing adjective **1** *his death was of only passing interest*: **fleeting**, transient, transitory, ephemeral, evanescent, brief, short-lived, short, temporary, momentary, fading, impermanent; rare fugacious.
▷ANTONYMS permanent, lasting.
2 *the sculpture is worth more than a passing glance*: **hasty**, rapid, hurried, brief, quick; **cursory**, superficial, casual, perfunctory, desultory, incidental, summary, glancing.
▷ANTONYMS careful.
▶noun **1** *the passing of time has done little to improve the situation*: **passage**, course, progress, advance, process, flow.
2 *it was with much regret that I learned of Jack's passing | the passing of 'traditional' art*: **death**, **demise**, passing away, passing on, end, expiry, loss, expiration, decease; disappearance, vanishing, dying out; rare quietus.
3 *the passing of the government's new Heritage Bill*: **enactment**, passage, ratification, acceptance, approval, adoption, authorization, sanction, validation, legalization, endorsement.
□ **in passing** *he mentioned in passing that you had a lot of female visitors*: **incidentally**, by the by, by the way, as it happens, in the course of conversation, en passant, parenthetically.

passion noun **1** *the passion with which voters attach themselves to a particular political party*: **fervour**, ardour, intensity, enthusiasm, eagerness, zeal, zealousness, vehemence, vigour, avidity, avidness, feeling, emotion, fire, heat, fieriness, fierceness, excitement, energy, animation, gusto, zest, zestfulness, spirit, spiritedness, commitment, fanaticism, violence; rare fervency, ardency, passionateness.
▷ANTONYMS indifference, apathy.
2 *he gradually worked himself up into a passion*: **rage**, blind rage, fit of rage/anger/temper, temper, towering rage, outburst of anger, tantrum, fury, frenzy, paroxysm, fever; Brit. informal paddy; Brit. informal, dated wax, bate, paddywhack.
3 *Roman's deep voice was husky with passion*: **love**, desire, sexual love, sexual desire, lust, ardour, hunger, yearning, longing, craving, adoration, infatuation, lasciviousness, lustfulness; French amour fou; rare concupiscence, nympholepsy.
4 *his passion for football*: **enthusiasm**, love, mania, keen interest, fascination, obsession, fanaticism, fixation, predilection, compulsion, appetite, relish, partiality, liking, interest, weakness, penchant, addiction, fondness; informal thing, yen; rare appetency.
5 *English literature is something of a passion with me*: **obsession**, preoccupation, craze, mania, rage, hobby horse.
6 *the Passion of Christ*: **crucifixion**, pain, suffering, agony, martyrdom; rare martyrization.

passionate adjective **1** *a passionate entreaty | passionate hatred*: **intense**, impassioned, ardent, fervent, zealous, vehement, fiery, heated, feverish, emotional, heartfelt, eager, excited, animated, spirited, vigorous, strong, energetic, messianic, fanatical, frenzied, wild, fierce, consuming, violent, tumultuous, flaming, raging, burning, uncontrollable, ungovernable; rare perfervid, fervid, passional.
▷ANTONYMS apathetic, half-hearted.
2 *McGregor is **passionate about** sport*: **very keen on**, very enthusiastic about, addicted to, devoted to, infatuated with; informal mad about, crazy about, hooked on, nuts about, nutty about, gone on; N. Amer. informal nutso over; Austral./NZ informal shook on.
3 *a passionate lover | a passionate kiss*: **amorous**, ardent, hot-blooded, red-blooded, warm-blooded, aroused, loving, on fire, sexy, sensual, erotic, lustful, sultry, torrid; informal steamy, sizzling, hot, red-hot, turned on.
▷ANTONYMS cold, passionless.
4 *Christina was passionate and given to terrible tantrums*: **excitable**, emotional, intense, fiery, volatile, mercurial, quick-tempered, hot-headed, highly strung, hot-blooded, impulsive, temperamental, tempestuous, dramatic, melodramatic.
▷ANTONYMS phlegmatic, placid.

passionless adjective **1** *he was not as passionless as they made out*: **unemotional**, cold, cold-blooded, emotionless, frigid, cool, unfeeling, unloving, unresponsive, undemonstrative, impassive, withdrawn, unapproachable, aloof, detached, distant, dispassionate, remote.
▷ANTONYMS passionate.
2 *the whole movie seems oddly passionless*: **dull**, boring, lacking in vitality, spiritless, lifeless, soulless, wooden, dry, desiccated, flat, uninspired, unimpassioned, insipid, lacklustre, colourless, anaemic, bloodless, vapid.
▷ANTONYMS exciting.

passive adjective **1** *he played only a passive role in the proceedings*: **inactive**, non-active, non-participative, non-participating, uninvolved, dormant, quiescent, inert.
2 *the women were portrayed as passive victims*: **submissive**, acquiescent, unresisting, yielding, unassertive, non-resistant, compliant, complaisant, pliant, resigned, obedient, docile, tractable, malleable, pliable, meek, subdued, deferential, forbearing, long-suffering, patient, lamblike, non-violent, supine; non-aggressive; archaic resistless.
▷ANTONYMS active, assertive.
3 *the woman's face was passive*: **emotionless**, impassive, indifferent, unemotional, unmoved, unconcerned, dispassionate, passionless, detached, unresponsive, undemonstrative, remote, aloof, calm, apathetic, phlegmatic, lifeless.

passport noun **1** **travel document**, travel papers, papers, travel permit, visa, identity card, ID, laissez-passer.
2 *good qualifications are the passport to success*: **key**, path, way, route, avenue, means of access, door, doorway, entry, entrée, admission, admittance, open sesame.

password noun **word of identification**, sign, signal, word; open sesame; Military, archaic watchword, countersign, parole.

past adjective **1** *memories of times past | writers from past centuries*: **gone by**, over, over and done with, no more, gone, done, dead and buried, finished, ended, forgotten, bygone, former, old, of old, earlier, long-ago, ancient, defunct, extinct; literary of yore, olden, foregone.
2 *the past few months*: **last**, recent, preceding, latter.
3 *a past chairman of the society*: **previous**, former, prior, foregoing, late, erstwhile, one-time, sometime, ex-; formal quondam; archaic whilom.
▷ANTONYMS present; future.
▶noun *she gave little away about her past*: **history**, background, life story, life, experience, career to date, biography.
□ **in the past** *some of the shelters may have been habitation sites in the past*: **formerly**, previously, in days/years/times gone by, in bygone days, back in the day, in former times, in the (good) old days, at one time, in days of old, in the olden days, in olden times; before, hitherto, once, once upon a time, time was when, in auld lang syne, long ago, in antiquity; literary in days of yore, of yore, in yesteryear.
▶preposition **1** *she walked past the cafe*: **in front of**, by, beyond.
2 *he's well past retirement age*: **beyond**, beyond the limits of, in excess of.
□ **past it** informal *I was told I was past it when I was 28*: **past one's prime**, not as young as one was, not as young as one used to be; in one's dotage, long in the tooth, as old as the hills; elderly, old, aged, senior, ancient, venerable; decrepit, doddering, doddery, not long for this world; informal over the hill, no spring chicken; formal senescent.
▶adverb *they averted their eyes and hurried past*: **along**, by, on.

paste noun **1** *blend the ingredients to a paste*: **purée**, mixture, pulp, mush, pap, blend; informal goo.
2 *wallpaper paste*: **adhesive**, glue, gum, fixative; N. Amer. mucilage.
3 *fish paste*: **spread**, pâté.
▶verb *a notice was pasted on the door*: **glue**, stick, fasten, gum, fix, affix.

pastel adjective *pastel colours*: **pale**, soft, delicate, light, light-coloured, light-toned, muted, subtle, subdued, faint, soft-hued, low-key, understated.
▷ANTONYMS dark; bright, vivid.

pastiche noun **1** *a pastiche of literary models and sources*: **mixture**, blend, medley, melange, miscellany, mixed bag, pot-pourri, mosaic, patchwork, mix, compound, composite, collection, motley collection, assortment, conglomeration, hotchpotch, hodgepodge, jumble, ragbag, mishmash, farrago, hash; informal mash-up; rare gallimaufry, olio, olla podrida, salmagundi, omnium gatherum, macédoine, motley.
2 *the operetta is a pastiche of 18th century style*: **imitation**, parody, take-off; rare pasticcio.

pastille noun **lozenge**, sweet, gumdrop, drop, gum; tablet, pill; rare dragée, jujube, troche.

pastime noun **hobby**, leisure activity/pursuit, sport, game, recreation, amusement, avocation, diversion, divertissement, distraction, relaxation, pleasure, entertainment, fun, interest, sideline, enthusiasm, passion, fad, craze, mania, obsession; informal bug, thing.

past master noun *the manager was a past master at recharging faltering spirits*: **expert**, virtuoso, master, wizard, genius, artist, old hand, adept, professional, doyen, veteran, maestro, connoisseur, authority, grandmaster, master hand, skilled person; informal ace, buff, pro, star, whizz, hotshot; Brit. informal dab hand; N. Amer. informal maven, crackerjack.

pastor noun **priest**, minister (of religion), parson, clergyman, cleric, chaplain, padre, father, ecclesiastic, man of God, man of the cloth, churchman, preacher; Scottish kirkman; N. Amer. dominie; informal reverend, Holy Joe, sky pilot; Austral. informal josser.

pastoral adjective **1** *a pastoral scene*: **rural**, country, countryside, countrified, outdoor, rustic, agricultural, agrarian, provincial, grassy, green, verdant; simple, innocent, idyllic, unspoilt; literary bucolic, sylvan, Arcadian; rare exurban, georgic.
▷ANTONYMS urban.
2 *his pastoral duties*: **priestly**, clerical, ecclesiastical, ministerial; rare hieratic, sacerdotal, vicarial, parsonical, rectorial, churchly, prelatic, apostolic.

pastry noun *I've come to get some pastries for tea*: **tart**, tartlet, pie, pasty, patty, turnover, slice.

pasture noun **grazing land**, grazing, grassland, grass, pastureland, pasturage, range, ley, paddock, croft; meadow, field, water meadow, sheepwalk; Scottish & N. English shieling, bent; literary lea, mead, greensward, sward; Irish & Canadian bawn; Austral./NZ run; S. African veld; in Switzerland alp; in France bocage; in S. America potrero.

Word links pasture

pastoral relating to pasture

pasty adjective *people with pasty faces*. See **wan** (sense 1).

pat¹ verb *Brian patted her absent-mindedly on the shoulder*: **tap**, slap lightly, clap, dab; touch, stroke, pet, caress, fondle, rub.
□ **pat someone on the back congratulate**, praise, sing the praises of, express approval of, take one's hat off to; **commend**, compliment, applaud, acclaim, give someone a pat on the back, throw bouquets at.
□ **pat oneself on the back boast**, brag, crow, swagger, swank, blow one's own trumpet, congratulate oneself; preen oneself, pride oneself; informal talk big.
▸ **noun 1** *a pat on the cheek*: **tap**, light blow, clap, dab; caress, stroke, fondle, touch.
2 *a pat of butter*: **piece**, dab, lump, portion, knob, mass, cake, chunk, wedge, hunk, gobbet, ball, curl; rare clod, gob.
□ **a pat on the back** *you owe me a pat on the back for a job well done*: **praise, congratulations**, commendation, applause, salutes, honour, acclaim, acclamation, tribute, cheers, ovation, accolade, plaudits, felicitations; approval, admiration, approbation, compliments, kudos, adulation, homage; eulogy, encomium, panegyric, bouquets, laurels, testimonial; rare extolment, laudation, eulogium.

pat² adjective *up to now, he has given pat, perfunctory answers*: **glib**, simple, simplistic, facile, slick, smooth, unconvincing, perfunctory.
▸ **adverb** *his reply came rather pat*: **opportunely**, conveniently, advantageously, at just/exactly the right moment, expediently; usefully, beneficially, favourably, profitably, appropriately, fittingly, suitably, aptly, timely, auspiciously, luckily, happily, providentially, felicitously, seasonably, propitiously.
□ **off pat** *in time he'll have the jargon off pat*: **word-perfect**, by heart, by rote, word for word, parrot-fashion, verbatim, by memory, memorized.
□ **get something off pat memorize**, commit to memory, remember, retain, learn by heart, learn, learn by rote, impress on the memory, become word-perfect in; archaic con.

patch noun **1** *an old jacket with patches on the elbows*: **piece of cloth/material/fabric/leather**, reinforcement; piece sewn on.
2 *he had a patch over one eye*: **cover**, eyepatch, covering, pad, shield.
3 *a small reddish patch on her wrist*: **blotch**, mark, spot, smudge, dot, speck, speckle, smear, stain, streak, stripe, blemish; birthmark, port wine stain, strawberry mark; informal splodge, splotch; technical naevus.
4 *a patch of ground*: **plot**, area, piece, strip, row, lot, tract, parcel; bed, border, allotment.
5 *Adam and his wife are going through a difficult patch*: **period**, time, spell, phase, stretch, interval; stint, run, term, span, extent; Brit. informal spot.
▸ **verb** *her jeans were neatly patched*: **mend**, repair, put a patch on, cover, sew, sew up, stitch, stitch up.
□ **patch something up 1** *the remaining houses were either being patched up or demolished*: **repair**, mend, fix hastily, do a makeshift repair on, repair/fix temporarily; cobble, botch; Nautical jury-rig. **2** *he's trying to patch things up with his wife*: **reconcile**, make up, settle, conciliate; **remedy**, put to rights, rectify, clear up, set right, heal, mend, cure, make good, resolve, square, harmonize.

patchwork noun *work that was a patchwork of different styles*: **assortment**, miscellany, mixture, melange, medley, blend, variety, mixed bag, mix, diversity, collection, selection, assemblage, combination, motley collection, pot-pourri, conglomeration, jumble, mess, confusion, mishmash, hotchpotch, hodgepodge, ragbag, pastiche, farrago, hash; informal scissors-and-paste job; rare gallimaufry, omnium gatherum, olio, salmagundi, macédoine.

patchy adjective **1** *a stretch of patchy grass | their first aid teaching has been patchy*: **uneven**, bitty, varying, variable, variegated, dappled, mottled, speckled, multicoloured; intermittent, fitful, occasional, fluctuating, sporadic, erratic, irregular, random.
▷ANTONYMS uniform, constant.
2 *we have only patchy evidence*: **fragmentary**, deficient, inadequate, insufficient, lacking, rudimentary, limited, sketchy.
▷ANTONYMS complete, comprehensive.

Word toolkit patchy

See **blotchy**.

patent noun *a company has since taken out a patent on the chemical*: **copyright**, licence, legal protection, right, performing right, permit, privilege, charter, franchise, registered trademark.
▸ **adjective 1** *the idea is patent nonsense*: **obvious**, clear, plain, evident, apparent, manifest, self-evident; distinct, definite, transparent, overt, discernible, visible, conspicuous, blatant, downright, barefaced, flagrant, palpable, glaring, glaringly obvious, undisguised, unconcealed, unmistakable, unequivocal, unquestionable, undeniable.
▷ANTONYMS unobtrusive, inconspicuous.
2 *patent medicines*: **proprietary**, patented, licensed, protected, branded, brand-name, own-brand, own-label, designer-label.

paternal adjective **1** *some employers felt paternal concern for their workers*: **fatherly**, fatherlike, patriarchal; protective, vigilant, concerned, solicitous, kindly, warm, friendly, benevolent, compassionate, sympathetic.
2 *his paternal grandfather*: **on one's father's side**, patrilineal, patrimonial.
▷ANTONYMS maternal.

paternity noun *he refused to admit paternity of the child*: **fatherhood**; rare fathership.

path noun **1** *a much-trodden path led down to the beach*: **footpath**, pathway, footway, pavement, track, jogging track, trail, trackway, bridleway, bridle path, ride, riding, towpath, walk, walkway, promenade, esplanade, avenue, lane, alley, alleyway, passage, passageway, byway, sidetrack, berm, causeway, right of way; cycle path, cycle track, cycleway; N. Amer. sidewalk, bikeway; W. Indian & US trace; French pavé.
2 *dozens of journalists blocked his path*: **route**, way, course, approach, road; direction, bearing, line, track, beat, round, run; orbit, trajectory.
3 *good quality consultation may be one path to consider*: **course of action**, route, road, avenue, procedure, direction, line, approach, tack, method, system, scheme, strategy, tactic, plan, formula.

pathetic adjective **1** *he made a small, pathetic groan*: **pitiful**, pitiable, piteous, to be pitied, moving, touching, poignant, plaintive, stirring; affecting, distressing, disquieting, disturbing, upsetting, miserable, heartbreaking, heart-rending, agonizing, harrowing, mortifying, sad, wretched, poor, forlorn, tragic, doleful, mournful, woeful; rare distressful.
▷ANTONYMS comical; cheerful.
2 informal *he made some pathetic excuse about the train being delayed*: **feeble**, woeful, sorry, poor, pitiful, lamentable, deplorable, miserable, wretched, contemptible, despicable, inadequate, meagre, paltry, insufficient, negligible, insubstantial, unsatisfactory, worthless.
▷ANTONYMS admirable, excellent.

pathfinder noun *she sees herself as a pathfinder for her daughter's generation*: **pioneer**, trailblazer, groundbreaker, experimenter, trendsetter, front runner, leader, leading light, guiding light, torch-bearer, pacemaker, originator, instigator, initiator, innovator, avant-gardist, developer, creator, discoverer, founder, founding father, architect.

pathological adjective **1** *a pathological condition*: **morbid**, diseased.
2 informal *a pathological liar*: **compulsive**, obsessive, inveterate, habitual, persistent, chronic, clinical, hardened, confirmed, unreasonable, irrational, illogical.

pathos noun *the pathos of Antoine's predicament*: **poignancy**, tragedy, sadness, pitifulness, piteousness, pitiableness, plaintiveness, sorrowfulness.

patience noun **1** *she tried everyone's patience to the limit*: **forbearance**, tolerance, restraint, self-restraint, resignation, stoicism, fortitude, sufferance, endurance; calmness, composure, even temper, even-temperedness, equanimity, equilibrium, serenity, tranquillity, imperturbability, unexcitability, understanding, indulgence, lenience, kindness, consideration; rare longanimity, inexcitability.
2 *a task requiring patience*: **perseverance**, persistence, endurance, tenacity, diligence, assiduity, application, staying power, indefatigability, doggedness, determination, resolve, resolution, resoluteness, obstinacy, insistence, singleness of purpose, purposefulness, pertinacity.
▷ANTONYMS impatience.

patient adjective **1** *I must ask you to be patient with my navigation*: **forbearing**, uncomplaining, tolerant, long-suffering, resigned, stoical; calm, composed, serene, even-tempered, tranquil, imperturbable, unexcitable, accommodating, understanding, indulgent, kind, considerate; informal unflappable, cool; rare longanimous, equanimous, inexcitable.
2 *a good deal of dogged, patient work*: **persevering**, persistent, tenacious, diligent, assiduous, indefatigable, dogged, determined, resolved, resolute, obstinate, insistent, single-minded, purposeful, pertinacious.
▸ **noun** *the trust between doctor and patient*: **sick person**, case, sufferer, victim; **invalid**, convalescent, outpatient, day patient, inpatient, hospital patient; the sick, the infirm; rare valetudinarian.

patio noun **terrace**, courtyard, veranda, loggia, court, plaza, quadrangle, quad, cloister; N. Amer. sun deck, deck, porch; Austral./NZ sleepout; S. African stoep; Hawaiian lanai; technical peristyle.

patois noun **vernacular**, dialect, local parlance, local speech/talk/usage/idiom/slang/tongue, local variety, regional language, non-standard language/variety, jargon, argot, patter, cant, -speak; informal (local) lingo.

patriarch noun *the respected patriarch of the household*: **senior figure**, father, paterfamilias, leader, elder, grandfather; guiding light, guru.

patrician noun *the great patricians of the Empire*: **aristocrat**, grandee, noble, nobleman, noblewoman, lord, lady, peer, peeress, peer of the realm, titled man/woman/person, landowner; landowning class, landed gentry/aristocracy; informal top person; Brit. informal nob, chinless wonder.
▸ **adjective** *the patrician families of Bordeaux*: **aristocratic**, noble, noble-born, of noble birth, titled, blue-blooded, high-born, well born, upper-class, elite,

landowning, landed, born with a silver spoon in one's mouth; Brit. county, upmarket; informal upper-crust, top-drawer, {huntin', shootin', and fishin'}; archaic gentle, of gentle birth.

patrimony noun *constant wars and invasions have destroyed the country's cultural patrimony*: **heritage**, inheritance, birthright; property, riches, wealth, possessions; legacy, bequest, endowment, estate, bequeathal; Law devise, hereditament.

patriot noun *a great patriot who had died for his country*: **nationalist**, loyalist; chauvinist, jingoist, jingo, flag-waver, isolationist, xenophobe.
▷ANTONYMS traitor.

patriotic adjective **nationalist**, nationalistic, loyalist, loyal; chauvinistic, jingoistic, jingo, flag-waving, isolationist, xenophobic; N. Amer. dated spreadeagle.
▷ANTONYMS traitorous.

patriotism noun *a national flag or anthem has the power to instil patriotism*: **nationalism**, patriotic sentiment, allegiance/loyalty to one's country, loyalism; chauvinism, jingoism, flag-waving, isolationism, xenophobia.
▷ANTONYMS treachery.

patrol noun **1** *anti-poaching patrols have ceased*: **vigil**, guard, watch, monitoring, policing, beat, beat-pounding, patrolling, round, sentry duty; reconnoitre, surveillance, survey, examination; informal recce.
2 *at 2.20 the patrol reached the jeeps*: **patrolman/patrolwoman**, sentinel, sentry, garrison, defender; detail, scout, scouting party, task force, escort, convoy.
▸ verb *a security guard was attacked patrolling a housing estate | they patrolled behind enemy lines*: **keep guard (on)**, guard, keep watch (on); police, walk the beat (of), pound the beat (of), make the rounds (of), walk along/round, range (over), perform sentry duty (on); picket, stand guard (over), keep a vigil (on), keep a lookout (over), cover, monitor, defend, safeguard; cruise, pound, prowl, rove, roam.

patron noun **1** *a patron of the arts*: **sponsor**, backer, financier, subsidizer, underwriter, guarantor, benefactor/benefactress, contributor, subscriber, donor; philanthropist, promoter, friend, helper, supporter, upholder, advocate, champion, protector; informal angel; rare Maecenas.
2 *patrons of shops, restaurants, and clubs*: **customer**, client, frequenter; shopper, buyer, purchaser, consumer, diner, user, visitor, guest, member of the audience/crowd; (**patrons**) clientele; informal regular.

patronage noun **1** *art patronage does not come cheap*: **sponsorship**, backing, funding, financing, philanthropy, promotion, furtherance, help, aid, assistance, support, guaranty, encouragement, championship, advocacy, defence, protection, guardianship, aegis, auspices.
2 *the abuse of political patronage*: **power of appointment**, right of appointment, favouritism, nepotism, partisanship, partiality, preferential treatment; the old boy network.
3 *that form of address implies slight patronage*: **condescension**, patronizing, deigning, stooping, disdain, disrespect, scorn, contempt, mockery; snobbery, snobbishness; rare patronization.
4 *bus patronage was declining*: **custom**, trade, business, commerce, trafficking; shopping, buying, purchasing.

patronize verb **1** *don't patronize me!* **treat condescendingly**, treat with condescension, condescend to, look down on, talk down to, put down, humiliate, treat like a child, treat as inferior, treat with disdain, treat scornfully/contemptuously, be snobbish to, look down one's nose at.
2 *they patronized the local tradesmen*: **do business with**, buy from, shop at, be a customer of, be a client of, bring trade/custom to, deal with, trade with; frequent, haunt, attend, visit; subscribe to, join, become a member of, support; informal hang out at.
3 *Joseph Bonaparte patronized a national museum of painting*: **sponsor**, back, fund, finance, be a patron of, promote, further, foster, help, aid, assist, support, encourage, champion, protect.

patronizing adjective **condescending**, supercilious, superior, imperious, haughty, lofty, lordly, magisterial, disdainful, scornful, contemptuous, cavalier, snobbish, pompous; informal uppity, high and mighty, snooty, stuck-up, fancy-pants; Brit. informal toffee-nosed.
▷ANTONYMS friendly; humble.

patter[1] verb **1** *raindrops pattered against the wooden shutters*: **pitter-patter**, tap, drum, clatter, beat, pound, rattle, throb, pulsate, rat-a-tat, go pit-a-pat, pit-a-pat, clack, click-clack, thrum; archaic bicker, clacket.
2 *she pattered across the floor*: **scurry**, scuttle, skip, trip, tiptoe, walk lightly, walk on tiptoe.
▸ noun *the rain had stopped its vibrating patter above him*: **pitter-patter**, tapping, pattering, drumming, drumbeat, clatter, beat, beating, tattoo, pounding, throb, pulsation, rat-a-tat, pit-a-pat, clack, click-clack, clacketing, thrum, thrumming.

patter[2] noun **1** *this witty gentleman's patter is now issued on a cassette*: **rambling(s)**, **prattle**, prating, blather, blither, drivel, chatter, jabber, gabble, babble, glib talk, monologue; Scottish blether; informal gab, yak, yackety-yak, yabbering, yatter; Brit. informal rabbiting, wittering, waffle, chuntering; archaic twaddle, clack.
2 *the salesmen's patter was good*: **(sales) pitch**, sales talk, line, spiel.
3 *the patter of the local peasantry*: **way/manner of speaking**, speech, language, idiom, vocabulary, jargon, parlance, argot, patois, cant, -speak, dialect, vernacular, idiolect, phraseology, terminology; French façon de parler; informal lingo.
▸ verb *she pattered on incessantly*: **prattle**, ramble, prate, blather, blether, blither, drivel, rattle, chatter, jabber, gabble, babble; informal gab, yak, yackety-yak, yabber, yatter; Brit. informal rabbit, witter, waffle, natter, chunter; Austral. informal mag; archaic twaddle, clack.

pattern noun **1** *the pattern on the wallpaper*: **design**, decoration, motif, marking, ornament, ornamentation, device, figure.
2 *the ants' behaviour pattern*: **system**, order, arrangement, method, sequence, structure, scheme, plan, form, format, framework, composition, constitution, shape, make-up, configuration.
3 *such a step would set the pattern for at least a generation*: **model**, example, criterion, standard, basis, point of reference, gauge, norm, formula, guide, scale, guideline, yardstick, touchstone, benchmark, ideal, exemplar, paradigm, canon; blueprint, archetype, prototype, original, design; template, mould, cast, matrix, last, layout, outline, sketch, draft, stencil, sample, specimen, specification, shape, plan, style, source, type.
4 *a book of textile patterns*: **sample**, specimen, swatch.
▸ verb *there is a dread that someone else is patterning your life*: **shape**, influence, form, model, fashion, mould, style; affect, determine, direct, control, guide, lead.

patterned adjective **decorated**, ornamented, figured, tessellated, mosaic; goffered, crimped, watered, moiré, fancy, adorned, embellished, intricate.
▷ANTONYMS plain.

paucity noun *a paucity of evidence*. See **inadequacy** (sense 1).

paunch noun **pot belly**, fat/protruding stomach/belly/abdomen, beer belly, stomach, belly, middle, midriff, waist, waistline; informal beer gut, gut, tummy, tum, pot, breadbasket; dated, humorous corporation.

pauper noun **poor person**, indigent, bankrupt, insolvent; beggar, mendicant, down-and-out; informal have-not. See also **poor**.

pause noun *there was a pause in the conversation*: **stop**, **cessation**, break, halt, stoppage, standstill, interruption, check, lull, respite, stay, breathing space, discontinuation, discontinuance, hiatus, gap, lapse (of time), interlude, intermission, interval, entr'acte; adjournment, suspension, moratorium, interregnum; rest, time out, stopover, delay, hold-up, wait; hesitation, beat, caesura; informal let-up, breather.
▸ verb *Hannah paused for a moment before answering*: **stop**, cease, halt, discontinue, break off, take a break, take a breath; adjourn, desist, rest, hold back, wait, delay, hesitate, hang back, pull up, mark time, falter, waver; informal let up, take a breather.
▷ANTONYMS continue, proceed.

pave verb *the centre of the garden was to be paved*: **cover**, surface, floor, top, finish, concrete (over), asphalt, flag, tile, tar, tarmac, metal.
□ **pave the way for** *a consultative document that could pave the way for legislation*: **prepare for**, prepare the way for, clear the way for, open the way for, make preparations for, make provision for, get ready for, lay the foundations for, do the groundwork for, work round/up to, approach/introduce the subject of, put things in order for, set the scene for, smooth the path of, usher in, herald, show in, harbinger, precede, be the forerunner/precursor of.

pavement noun *I had parked blocking the pavement*: **footpath**, paved path, pedestrian way, walkway, footway; N. Amer. sidewalk.

paw noun **foot**, pad; forepaw, hind paw.
▸ verb **1** *their offspring were yammering and pawing each other*: **poke**, handle roughly/carelessly/clumsily, finger, thumb, pull, grab, maul, manhandle, mangle, mess up.
2 *some Casanova had tried to paw her*: **fondle**, feel, maul, molest; informal grope, feel up, touch up, goose.

pawn[1] verb *he pawned his watch to buy some clothes*: **pledge**, deposit with a pawnbroker, put in pawn, give as security, put up as security/collateral, use as collateral, mortgage; informal hock, put in hock; Brit. informal pop.

pawn[2] noun *she was a pawn in the battle for the throne*: **puppet**, dupe, hostage, counter, cog; tool, cat's paw, instrument; informal stooge.

pay verb **1** *I must pay him for his work*: **reward**, reimburse, recompense, give payment to, settle up with, remunerate, tip, indemnify.
2 *the public would prefer to pay a few pounds more council tax*: **spend**, expend, pay out, lay out, part with, disburse, hand over, remit, render; informal dish out, shell out, fork out, cough up; N. Amer. informal ante up, pony up.
3 *the company was unable to pay its debts*: **discharge**, settle, pay off, pay in full, meet, clear, square, defray, honour, satisfy, make good, liquidate.
4 *our reputation for quality and service will pay dividends*: **yield**, pay out, return, produce, bring in; informal rake in.
5 *he has made the buses pay*: **be profitable**, make money, make a profit, be remunerative, make a return, provide a living.
6 *it may pay you to drop all your sails while you anchor*: **be advantageous to**, **benefit**, be of advantage to, be of benefit to, be beneficial to, be profitable

P

to, be worthwhile to, repay, serve.
7 *he had always found it difficult to pay Martha compliments*: **bestow**, present, grant, give, hand out, extend, offer, proffer, render, afford.
8 *I'll make him pay for his mistakes*: **suffer**, suffer the consequences, be punished, pay a penalty, atone, make atonement, pay the price, get one's deserts, take one's medicine; informal get one's comeuppance.
□ **pay someone back** *I'll pay you back for what you've done!* **get one's revenge on**, be revenged on, revenge oneself on, give someone their just deserts, reciprocate, punish, avenge oneself on, hit back at, get back at, get, get even with, settle a/the score with, settle accounts with, pay someone out, retaliate against, take reprisals against, exact retribution on; let someone see how it feels, give someone a taste of their own medicine.
□ **pay something back** *they did eventually pay me back the money*: **repay**, pay off, give back, return, remunerate, compensate, make restitution/amends to, reimburse, recoup, refund, restore, make good, indemnify, requite.
□ **pay for** *he had just enough money to pay for the meal*: **defray the cost of**, settle up for; **finance**, endow, donate/leave money for; support, back, stake, fund, capitalize, provide finance/capital for, furnish credit for, subsidize, sponsor; treat someone to; informal foot the bill for, shell out for, fork out for, cough up for; N. Amer. informal ante up for, pony up for.
□ **pay someone off 1** *the taxi had gone before Tunney could pay off the driver*: **pay what one owes**; dismiss, discharge. **2** *arrangements were made to pay off the police and hush it all up*: **bribe**, suborn, buy, buy off, get at, induce, lure, entice, grease someone's palm, oil someone's palm/hand.
□ **pay something off** *you use the proceeds to pay off your loan*: **pay in full**, pay, settle, discharge, meet, clear, square, honour, satisfy, make good, liquidate.
□ **pay off** *his hard work paid off*: **meet with success**, be successful, succeed, be effective, work, get results, be profitable.
□ **pay someone out** *this was to pay Emma out, to make her feel guilty*: **get one's revenge on**, be revenged on, revenge oneself on, repay, give someone their just deserts, reciprocate, punish, avenge oneself on, hit back at, get back at, get, get even with, settle a/the score with, settle accounts with, pay someone back, retaliate on/against, take reprisals against, exact retribution on; let someone see how it feels, give someone a taste of their own medicine.
□ **pay something out** *she had to pay out £300 for treatment*: **spend**, expend, pay, lay out, put up, part with, hand over, remit, furnish, supply, disburse, contribute, give, donate, invest, advance, pledge; informal dish out, shell out, fork out/up, cough up.
□ **pay up** *he has been allowed a week to pay up*: **make payment**, pay, settle up, pay in full, meet one's obligations, come up with the money; informal fork out/up, come across, cough up; Brit. informal stump up.
▷ANTONYMS withhold.
▶ **noun** *equal pay for women*: **salary**, **wages**, wage, take-home pay, gross/net pay, payment; earnings, fee(s), remuneration, stipend, emolument(s), honorarium, allowance, handout(s), recompense, compensation, reimbursement, reward, income, revenue, profit(s), proceeds, takings, gain, lucre.

P

payable adjective *capital gains tax is payable if the shares are sold*: **due**, to be paid, owed, owing; outstanding, unpaid, unsettled, receivable, overdue, undischarged, in arrears, in the red; N. Amer. delinquent, past due.

payment noun **1** *a seller may offer discounts for early payment*: **remittance**, remission, settlement, discharge, clearance, liquidation, reckoning.
2 *twelve monthly payments*: **instalment**, premium, amount, remittance; deposit, retainer, subscription.
3 *they offer extra payment for good performance*: **salary**, **wages**, wage, pay, earnings, fee(s), remuneration, take-home pay, gross/net pay; rate, price, hire, stipend, emolument(s), honorarium, allowance, handout, recompense, compensation, reimbursement, reward, income, revenue, profit(s), proceeds, takings, gain, lucre.

pay-off noun informal **1** *the lure of enormous pay-offs in hard currency could prove irresistible*: **payment**, payout, reward, recompense, consideration; **bribe**, inducement, 'incentive', enticement; N. Amer. payola; informal kickback, sweetener, carrot, backhander, hush money, slush fund, cut, graft; Brit. informal **bung**, **dropsy**; N. Amer. informal **plugola**, **schmear**; Austral. informal **sling**; rare douceur, drop.
2 *sales are forecast to produce a pay-off of £160,000*: **return**, return on investment, yield, payback, reward, profit, gain, income, revenue, interest, dividend, percentage.
3 *the murderer is finally unmasked in a dramatic pay-off*: **outcome**, **denouement**, culmination, conclusion, development, result, consequence, out-turn, end result, upshot, aftermath; archaic success.

peace noun **1** *can't a man get any peace around here?* **tranquillity**, **calm**, calmness, restfulness, peace and quiet, peacefulness, quiet, quietness, quietude, silence, soundlessness, hush, noiselessness, stillness, still; privacy, privateness, seclusion, solitude, isolation, retirement, lack of disturbance/interruption, freedom from interference.
▷ANTONYMS noise; irritation.
2 *those who have guilty secrets rarely enjoy true peace of mind*: **serenity**, peacefulness, tranquillity, equanimity, calm, calmness, composure, placidity, placidness, rest, repose, ease, comfort, contentment, content, contentedness, security; bliss, joy, nirvana.
▷ANTONYMS agitation, distress.
3 *we pray for peace in the province*: **law and order**, lawfulness, order, peacefulness, peaceableness, harmony, harmoniousness, accord, concord, amity, amicableness, goodwill, friendship, cordiality, non-aggression, non-violence; ceasefire, respite, lull.
▷ANTONYMS conflict.
4 *the envoy hopes to set the seal on a lasting peace today*: **treaty**, **truce**, ceasefire, armistice, end/cessation/suspension of hostilities, moratorium, agreement, alliance, concord, appeasement, reconciliation.
▷ANTONYMS war.

> *Word links* **peace**
>
> **irenic** intended to bring about peace

peaceable adjective **1** *a calm, quiet, and peaceable man*: **peace-loving**, unwarlike, non-belligerent, non-violent, non-combative, non-aggressive, easy, easy-going, placid, gentle, meek, mild, inoffensive, good-natured, even-tempered, amiable, amicable, friendly, affable, genial, civil, cooperative, conciliatory, pacific, pacifist, dovelike, dovish; rare irenic, pacifistic.
▷ANTONYMS aggressive, belligerent.
2 *a peaceable society*: **peaceful**, **strife-free**, harmonious, amicable, amiable, friendly, cordial; well behaved, law-abiding, disciplined, orderly, civilized; archaic ruly.
▷ANTONYMS unruly, warring.

peaceful adjective **1** *the cottage is in a peaceful setting*: **tranquil**, **calm**, restful, pleasant, quiet, still, relaxing, soothing, sleepy, silent, soundless, hushed, noiseless, undisturbed, untroubled, private, secluded, solitary, isolated, free from disturbance/interruption/interference.
▷ANTONYMS bustling, noisy.
2 *his peaceful, contemplative mood vanished*: **serene**, calm, tranquil, composed, placid, at peace, at rest, at ease, in repose, reposeful, undisturbed, untroubled, unworried, unruffled, anxiety-free, content, blissful, secure.
▷ANTONYMS agitated.
3 *peaceful conditions between the two countries*: **harmonious**, at peace, strife-free, peaceable, on good terms, amicable, friendly, cordial, non-violent, unwarlike; orderly, disciplined.
▷ANTONYMS hostile, warring.

> *Choose the right word* **peaceful, calm, serene, tranquil, placid**
>
> See **calm**.

peacemaker noun **arbitrator**, arbiter, mediator, negotiator, conciliator, go-between, middleman, intermediary, moderator, intervenor, interceder, intercessor, reconciler, broker, honest broker, liaison officer, pacifier, appeaser; umpire, referee, adjudicator, judge; peace-monger, pacifist, conscientious objector, passive resister, peace-lover, dove; informal peacenik; rare satyagrahi.

peak noun **1** *there was snow on the very peaks of the mountains*: **summit**, top, crest, pinnacle, spire, heights, brow, apex, crown, tip, cap, vertex, acme, zenith, apogee.
2 *the highest unclimbed peak in the Karakoram*: **mountain**, hill, height, alp, aiguille, serac, puy, crag, tor, inselberg; bluff, scarp, escarpment, eminence, prominence, elevation; ridge, range, massif, sierra, cordillera; Scottish ben, Munro; S. African berg; Arabic **jebel**; archaic mount.
3 *the peak of a cap*: **brim**, visor.
4 *he is at the peak of his career as a singer*: **height**, high point/spot, pinnacle, summit, top, highlight, climax, culmination, consummation, epitome, apex, zenith, ascendancy, crowning point, peak of perfection; acme, meridian, apogee, prime, heyday, ne plus ultra, nonpareil, best part, perfection, top form, highest level.
▷ANTONYMS bottom, nadir, trough.
▶ **verb** *Labour support may have peaked last week*: **reach its highest point**, reach the high point; **climax**, reach a climax, come to a climax, culminate, reach the zenith, come to a head.
▶ **adjective** *storage capacity has to be adequate to meet peak loads*: **maximum**, maximal, top, greatest, highest, utmost, uttermost, extreme; ultimate, best, optimum.
▷ANTONYMS minimum.

peaky adjective *you're looking a bit peaky*. See **pale²** (sense 1 of the adjective).

peal noun **1** *just then, a peal of bells rings out*: **chime**, carillon, ring, ringing, knell, toll, tolling, sound, sounding, death knell, clang, boom, resounding, reverberation, change, touch; archaic tocsin; rare tintinnabulation.
2 *Ross burst into peals of laughter*: **shriek**, shout, scream, howl, gale, fit, eruption, ripple, roar, hoot.
3 *a peal of thunder crashed directly overhead*: **rumble**, roar, boom,

rumbling, crash, clap, crack, resounding, reverberation.
▶ **verb 1** *the bell pealed again*: **ring**, ring out, chime, chime out, clang, toll; sound, clash, bong, clink, ding, jingle; boom, resound, reverberate.
2 *the lightning flashed and the thunder pealed*: **rumble**, roar, boom, crash, resound, reverberate.

peasant **noun 1** *the peasants were driving their cows to market*: **agricultural worker, small farmer**, rustic, son of the soil, countryman, countrywoman, farmhand, swain, villein, serf; French paysan; Russian muzhik, kulak; Spanish campesino, paisano; Italian contadino; Egyptian fellah; Indian ryot; archaic carl, cottier, kern, hind.
2 *he refused to sit with people he called peasants*: **lout**, boor, oaf, clown, churl, yokel, bumpkin, country bumpkin, village idiot, provincial, barbarian; Irish culchie, bosthoon, bogman; informal clod, clodhopper, yahoo; N. Amer. informal hayseed, hick, rube, hillbilly; Austral. informal ocker; Austral./NZ informal hoon; rare bucolic.

peccadillo **noun misdemeanour**, minor offence, petty offence, delinquency; indiscretion, lapse, misdeed, infraction, error, slip; informal slip-up.

peck **verb 1** *the cockerel tried to peck my heel*: **bite**, nip, strike, hit, tap, rap, jab, poke, prick.
2 *he pecked her on the cheek*: **kiss**, plant a kiss, give someone a peck; informal give someone a smacker.
3 informal *the old lady* **pecked at** *her food*: **nibble**, pick at, pick over, take very small bites from, eat listlessly, toy with, play with, eat like a bird, show no appetite for, eat sparingly of.

peculiar **adjective 1** *something even more peculiar began to happen*: **strange**, unusual, odd, funny, curious, bizarre, weird, uncanny, queer, unexpected, unfamiliar, abnormal, atypical, anomalous, untypical, different, out of the ordinary, out of the way; exceptional, rare, extraordinary, remarkable; puzzling, mystifying, mysterious, perplexing, baffling, unaccountable, incongruous, uncommon, irregular, singular, deviant, aberrant, freak, freakish; suspicious, dubious, questionable; eerie, unnatural; Scottish unco; French outré; informal fishy, creepy, spooky; Brit. informal rum; N. Amer. informal bizarro.
▷**ANTONYMS** normal, ordinary.
2 *his peculiar behaviour at the airport*: **bizarre**, eccentric, strange, odd, weird, queer, funny, unusual, abnormal, idiosyncratic, unconventional, outlandish, offbeat, freakish, quirky, quaint, droll, zany, off-centre; informal wacky, freaky, kooky, screwy, kinky, oddball, cranky; N. Amer. informal off the wall, wacko; Austral./NZ informal, dated dilly.
3 informal *I still feel a bit peculiar*: **unwell**, ill, poorly, bad, out of sorts, indisposed, not oneself, sick, queasy, nauseous, nauseated, peaky, liverish, green about the gills, run down, washed out; Brit. off, off colour; informal under the weather, below par, not up to par, funny, rough, lousy, rotten, awful, terrible, dreadful, crummy, seedy; Brit. informal grotty, ropy; Scottish informal wabbit, peely-wally; Austral./NZ informal crook; rare peaked, peakish.
4 *attitudes and mannerisms* **peculiar to** *the islanders*: **characteristic of**, typical of, representative of, belonging to, indicative of, symptomatic of, suggestive of, exclusive to, like, in character with.
5 *Elena added her own peculiar contribution*: **distinctive**, characteristic, distinct, different, individual, individualistic, distinguishing, typical, special, specific, representative, unique, idiosyncratic, personal, private, essential, natural; identifiable, unmistakable, conspicuous, notable, remarkable; rare singular.

> *Choose the right word* **peculiar, strange, odd, curious**
>
> See **strange**.

peculiarity **noun 1** *the problems arise from a legal peculiarity*: **oddity**, anomaly, abnormality, twist, quirk, eccentricity, trick.
2 *it was a strange physical peculiarity of his*: **idiosyncrasy**, mannerism, quirk, foible, caprice, whimsy; rare singularity.
3 *a peculiarity of Phaistos is its two sets of royal apartments*: **characteristic**, feature, (essential) quality, nature, property, trait, particularity, aspect, attribute, mark, badge, stamp, hallmark, trademark, distinction, point.
4 *he points out the peculiarity of this notion*: **strangeness**, peculiarness, oddness, bizarreness, weirdness, queerness, abnormality, unexpectedness, unfamiliarity, atypicality, anomalousness, curiosity, mystery, incongruity, uncommonness, irregularity, deviancy, aberrance, aberrancy, freakishness, suspiciousness, dubiousness, questionableness; eeriness, unnaturalness; informal fishiness, creepiness, spookiness; rare dubiety, singularity.
5 *I see you have noticed a certain peculiarity about my appearance*: **outlandishness, bizarreness**, unconventionality, idiosyncrasy, weirdness, oddness, eccentricity, unusualness, abnormality, queerness, peculiarness, strangeness; grotesqueness, freakishness, quirkiness, quaintness, drollness, zaniness; informal wackiness, freakiness, kookiness, kinkiness, crankiness; N. Amer. informal screwiness.

pecuniary **adjective** *he was free from all pecuniary anxieties*: **financial**, monetary, money, fiscal, economic, capital, commercial, budgetary.

pedagogic **adjective** See **educative**.

pedagogue archaic or humorous **noun** See **teacher**.

pedant **noun** *pedants insist that the 21st century starts with 2001*: **dogmatist**, purist, literalist, formalist, doctrinaire; precisionist, perfectionist; quibbler, hair-splitter, casuist, sophist, fault-finder, caviller, carper; informal nit-picker; archaic pettifogger; rare precisian, Dryasdust.

pedantic **adjective 1** *a pedantic interpretation of the rules*: **overscrupulous**, scrupulous, precise, exact, over-exacting, perfectionist, precisionist, punctilious, meticulous, fussy, fastidious, finical, finicky; dogmatic, purist, literalist, literalistic, formalist, scholastic; casuistic, casuistical, sophistic, sophistical; captious, hair-splitting, quibbling, pettifogging, fault-finding, hypercritical, cavilling, carping; informal nit-picking, pernickety; archaic overnice.
2 *pedantic words like 'irriguous'*: **learned**, cerebral, didactic, bookish, pedagogic, donnish, highbrow, ivory-tower, pretentious, pompous; intellectual, academic, scholastic, scholarly, literary; informal egghead.

pedantry **noun 1** *keeping the two distinct is more than mere pedantry*: **dogmatism**, purism, literalism, formalism; overscrupulousness, scrupulousness, precision, exactness, perfectionism, fastidiousness, punctiliousness, meticulousness, finickiness, finicality; captiousness, quibbling, hair-splitting, fault-finding, cavilling, carping, casuistry, sophistry; informal nit-picking; archaic pettifogging, pettifoggery.
2 *the book lacks the creaking pedantry of many such works*: **pretentiousness**, pomposity, pompousness, dullness, tedium; intellectualism, academicism, scholasticism, scholarliness, erudition, studiousness, didacticism, bookishness, pedagogism, donnishness.

peddle **verb 1** *they are peddling water filters*: **sell**, sell from door to door, hawk, tout, vend, offer for sale; carry, stock, offer, market, merchandise, trade, trade in, deal in, traffic in; informal push; Brit. informal flog.
2 *the unorthodox views peddled by independent research institutes*: **advocate**, suggest, urge, recommend, champion; preach, present, put forward, advance, offer, introduce, spread, proclaim, propound, promote.

pedestal **noun** *a bust of Shakespeare on a pedestal*: **plinth**, base, support, bottom, bed, foot, substructure, mounting, platform, stand, foundation, pillar, column, pier; Architecture podium, socle.
□ **put someone on a pedestal** *at an early age one puts one's father on a pedestal*: **idealize**, exalt, lionize, heroize, aggrandize; look up to, respect, hold in high regard, think highly of, have a high opinion of, hold in admiration, admire; esteem, revere, glorify, adulate, worship, hero-worship, adore, reverence, venerate, deify.

pedestrian **noun** *a collision between a pedestrian and a car*: **walker**, person on foot, hiker, rambler, stroller, wayfarer, footslogger; rare foot traveller.
▷**ANTONYMS** driver.
▶ **adjective** *the cup final was a pedestrian affair*: **dull**, plodding, boring, tedious, monotonous, uneventful, unremarkable, tiresome, wearisome, uninspired, uncreative, unimaginative, unexciting, uninteresting, lifeless, dry; unvarying, unvaried, repetitive, repetitious, routine, commonplace, average, workaday; ordinary, everyday, unoriginal, derivative, mediocre, run-of-the-mill, flat, prosaic, matter-of-fact, turgid, stodgy, mundane, humdrum; informal OK, so-so, bog-standard, vanilla, plain vanilla, nothing to write home about, not so hot, not up to much; Brit. informal common or garden; NZ informal half-pie.
▷**ANTONYMS** inspired, exciting.

pedigree **noun** *Hereford cattle have a long pedigree*: **ancestry**, descent, lineage, line, line of descent, genealogy, family tree, extraction, derivation, origin, heritage, parentage, paternity, birth, family, dynasty, house, race, strain, stock, breed, blood, bloodline, history, background, roots; rare stirps, filiation, stemma.
▶ **adjective** *a pedigree cat*: **pure-bred**, thoroughbred, pure, pure-blooded, full-blooded.

pedlar, peddler **noun 1** *we saw pedlars of watches and compact discs*: **travelling salesman**, door-to-door salesman; street trader; Brit. barrow boy; W. Indian higgler; Brit. informal fly-pitcher; dated hawker; archaic chapman, packman; rare huckster, crier, colporteur.
2 *a drug pedlar*: **trafficker**, dealer; informal pusher.

peek **verb 1** *one of the models had peeked at the audience from behind the curtains*: **peep**, have a peep, have a peek, take a secret look, spy, take a sly/stealthy look, sneak a look, glance, cast a brief look, look hurriedly, look, peer; Scottish keek; informal take a gander, have a look-see, give someone/something a/the once-over, have a squint; Brit. informal have a dekko, have/take a butcher's, take a shufti.
2 *the deer's antlers* **peeked out** *from a clump of aspen trees*: **appear (slowly/partly)**, show, come into view/sight, make an appearance, put in an appearance, present oneself/itself, become visible, emerge, issue, peep, peer out, surface, loom, show one's/its face, come to light, spring up, pop up.
▶ **noun** *she sneaked a peek at the map*: **secret look**, sly look, stealthy look, sneaky look, peep, glance, glimpse, brief/hurried/quick look, look, peer; Scottish keek; informal gander, look-see, squint, eyeful; Brit. informal dekko; butcher's, shufti.

peel **verb 1** *peel and core the fruit*: **pare**, skin, take the skin/rind off, strip, shave, trim, flay; hull, shell, husk, shuck; technical decorticate.

P

2 *a long knife peels the veneer from a round log*: **trim (off)**, peel off, pare, strip (off), shave (off), remove, take off, flay; technical excoriate.
3 *the paper on the ceiling had started to peel*: **flake (off)**, peel off, come off in layers/strips; blister; technical exfoliate, desquamate.
□ **keep one's eyes peeled** *keep your eyes peeled for bandits*: **keep a (sharp) lookout**, be on the lookout, look out, keep one's eyes open, keep an eye out/open, observe, watch (closely), keep watch, be watchful, be on the watch, be alert, be on the alert, be on the qui vive, be on guard; beware, mind out, be vigilant, be wary, be careful, pay attention, take heed; Brit. keep one's eyes skinned; informal keep one's peepers peeled.
□ **peel something off** *he peeled off his wet clothes*: **take off**, strip off, cast off, remove, discard, throw off; dated doff, divest oneself of.
▸ **noun** *orange peel*: **rind**, **skin**, covering, zest; hull, pod, crust, shuck, capsule, outer layer; technical epicarp, pericarp, exocarp; rare integument.

peep[1] **verb 1** *I peeped through the keyhole*: **look quickly**, cast a brief look, take a secret look, spy, take a sly/stealthy look, sneak a look, peek, have a peek, glance, peer; Scottish keek; informal take a gander, have a look-see, give someone/something a/the once-over, have a squint; Brit. informal have a dekko, have/take a butcher's, take a shufti.
2 *the moon peeped through a chink in the clouds*: **appear (slowly/partly)**, show, come into view/sight, make an appearance, put in an appearance, present oneself/itself, become visible, emerge, issue, peek, peer out, surface, loom, show one's/its face, come to light, spring up, pop up.
▸ **noun** *I'll just take a peep at it*: **quick look**, brief look, sly look, stealthy look, sneaky look, peek, glance, glimpse, look, peer; Scottish keek; informal gander, look-see, squint, eyeful; Brit. informal dekko, butcher's, shufti.

peep[2] **noun 1** *one morning I heard a telltale peep*: **cheep**, chirp, chirrup, tweet, twitter, chirr, pipe, piping, warble, squeak, chatter.
2 *there's been not a peep out of the children*: **sound**, noise, cry, utterance, word; informal cheep.
3 *a looted painting was sold without a peep*: **complaint**, grumble, moan, mutter, murmur, grouse, objection, protest, protestation, outcry, demur, argument, remonstrance, remonstration, exception, grievance, cavil, quibble, word, sound; informal niggle, gripe, grouch, beef.
▸ **verb** *the fax peeped and began to flutter out the papers*: **cheep**, chirp, chirrup, tweet, twitter, chirr, squeak.

peephole noun opening, gap, cleft, spyhole, slit, crack, chink, keyhole, aperture, orifice, crevice, cranny, fissure; Architecture arrow slit, embrasure, squint; rare judas (hole).

peer[1] **verb** *he swivelled his head to peer in our direction*: **squint**, look closely/earnestly, try to see, look through narrowed eyes, narrow one's eyes, screw up one's eyes; peep, peek, pry, spy, look, gawp, gaze, stare, gape; scrutinize, survey, examine, view, eye, scan, observe, study, regard, contemplate; informal snoop; rare squinny.

peer[2] **noun 1** *hereditary and life peers*: **aristocrat**, lord, lady, peer of the realm, peeress, noble, nobleman, noblewoman, titled man/woman/person, patrician, member of the aristocracy/nobility/peerage.
2 *the quality of medical work can only be reviewed by a doctor's peers*: **equal**, fellow, co-worker, match, like, rival; French confrère; rare compeer, co-equal.
3 *he looks older than his peers*: **contemporary**, person of the same age; rare coeval.

peerage noun aristocracy, nobility, peers and peeresses, lords and ladies, the House of Lords, the Lords, titled nobility/class, titled men/women/people, landed gentry; rare patriciate.

peerless adjective *a peerless performance*: **incomparable**, matchless, unrivalled, inimitable, beyond compare, unparalleled, unequalled, without equal, unmatched, beyond comparison, second to none, unsurpassed, unsurpassable, nonpareil; unique, consummate, perfect, rare, exquisite, transcendent, surpassing, superlative, supreme; rare unexampled.

peeve verb informal *the surprise early closing of the bar peeved more than one punter*. See **irritate** (sense 1).

> *Choose the right word* **peeve, annoy, irritate, aggravate, vex**
>
> See **annoy**.

peeved adjective informal *she was peeved that he had succeeded*. See **irritated**.

peevish adjective *the remark came out sounding peevish and sensitive*. See **irritable**.

peg noun spike, pin, nail, dowel, skewer, rivet, brad, screw, bolt, hook, stick, nog, spigot; Nautical fid; Curling hack; Quoits hob; Mountaineering piton; Golf tee; Rowing thole (pin); rare knag, spile.
□ **take someone down a peg or two humble**, humiliate, mortify, bring/take down, bring low, demean, show up, shame, put to shame, make ashamed, discomfit, disgrace, discredit, downgrade, debase, degrade, devalue, dishonour, embarrass, put someone in their place, make a fool of, chasten, subdue, get the better of, have the last laugh on, abash, abase, crush, squash, quash, deflate, flatten, make someone eat humble pie; informal put down, settle someone's hash, cut down to size; N. Amer. informal make someone eat crow.
▸ **verb 1** *the flysheet is draped over and pegged to the ground*: **fix**, pin, attach, fasten, secure, make fast.
2 *we decided to peg our prices*: **hold down**, keep down, fix, set, hold, control, freeze, limit.
□ **peg away** informal *I am going to peg away with this novel*: **work hard**, work away, hammer away, grind away; persevere, persist, exert oneself, apply oneself, keep at it, plod, soldier on; informal slog, beaver (away), plug (away), stick at, stick with it; Brit. informal graft, get one's head down.

pejorative adjective disparaging, derogatory, denigratory, deprecatory, defamatory, slanderous, libellous, abusive, insulting, slighting, vituperative, disapproving, contemptuous; informal bitchy; rare invective, contumelious.
▷**ANTONYMS** complimentary, approbatory.

> *Word toolkit* **pejorative**
>
> See **abusive**.

pellet noun 1 *millions of blind worker ants each carry a tiny pellet of mud*: **little ball**, little piece; technical prill.
2 *pellet wounds inflicted by shotguns*: **bullet**, shot, lead shot, buckshot.
3 (usually **pellets**) *rabbit pellets*: **excrement**, excreta, dropping, faeces, dung, stool, dirt, mess, motion.

pell-mell adverb 1 *the sparrows fly pell-mell up the hedgerow*: **helter-skelter**, headlong, (at) full tilt, hotfoot, post-haste, hurriedly, hastily; wildly, impetuously, recklessly, rashly, precipitately, impulsively; informal slap bang; archaic hurry-scurry.
2 *the words slipped pell-mell into one another*: **in disorder**, in confusion, in a muddle/jumble, in disarray, in a disorganized manner, untidily, in a mess, in a heap, anyhow; informal all over the place, every which way; Brit. informal all over the shop, shambolically; N. Amer. informal all over the map, all over the lot.

pellucid adjective 1 *the pellucid Caribbean waters | a pellucid singing tone*: **translucent**, transparent, clear, crystal clear, crystalline, bright, glassy, limpid, unclouded.
2 *pellucid prose*: **easily understood**, easily grasped, comprehensible, understandable, intelligible, articulate, coherent, lucid, clear, crystal clear, crystalline; graspable, fathomable, digestible, straightforward, direct, simple, plain, well constructed, graphic, explicit, unambiguous, user-friendly.

pelt[1] **verb 1** *they **pelted** him **with** snowballs*: **bombard**, shower, attack, assail, batter, pepper, strafe, rake, sweep, enfilade, blitz; throw at, rain something down on, fire a broadside at; archaic cannonade, fusillade.
2 *the rain was now **pelting down***: **pour**, teem, stream; rain cats and dogs, rain hard; Brit. informal bucket down, come down in stair rods, rain stair rods.
3 informal *they pelted into the factory*: **run**, race, leap, sprint, dash, rush, speed, streak, shoot, whizz, whoosh, buzz, zoom, flash, blast, charge, stampede, chase, career, bustle, hare, fly, wing, kite, skite, dive, jump, skip, scurry, scud, scutter, scramble, hurry, hasten; informal belt, scoot, scorch, tear, zap, zip, whip; Brit. informal bomb, bucket, shift; N. Amer. informal boogie, hightail, clip; N. Amer. vulgar slang drag/tear/haul ass; informal, dated cut along.

pelt[2] **noun** *a man who used to hunt otters for their pelts*: **skin**, hide, fleece, coat, fur, fell.

pen[1] **verb** *he penned a great number of articles*: **write**, write down, jot down, note, set down, take down, inscribe, scribble, scrawl, pencil, compose, draft, formulate, draw up, dash off, put in writing, put down on paper, commit to paper, put in black and white.

pen[2] **noun** *the sheep in the pen behind the barn*: **enclosure**, fold, sheepfold, pound, compound, paddock, stockade, sty, coop, cage, stall, lock-up; N. Amer. corral; Scottish parrock; S. African kraal; in S. America potrero.
▸ **verb** *you should ask the owners to **pen up** their dogs | the use of interlocking metal barricades to **pen** protesters **in***: **confine**, enclose, impound, shut in, fence in; hurdle, rail in, coop (up), immure, mew up, box up/in, lock up/in, cage, imprison, intern, hold captive, incarcerate; encircle, surround, ring, encompass, hem in, close in, hedge in, trap; N. Amer. corral.

penal adjective 1 *a penal institution*: **disciplinary**, punitive, corrective, correctional, retributive.
2 *he avoided borrowing at penal rates of interest*: **exorbitant**, extortionate, excessive, outrageous, preposterous, immoderate, unreasonable, inordinate, iniquitous, inflated, sky-high, expensive, gross.

penalize verb 1 *he promised to penalize parents whose children missed school*: **punish**, discipline, inflict a penalty on, exact a penalty from, deal with, mete out punishment to, sentence, impose a sentence on, chastise, castigate, correct, chasten.
▷**ANTONYMS** reward.
2 *an enterprise culture penalizes those at the bottom of the income pile*: **handicap**, inflict a handicap on, unfairly disadvantage, put at an unfair disadvantage, put in an unfavourable position, cause to suffer, put a stumbling block in the way of, put a hindrance/impediment in the way of.
▷**ANTONYMS** favour, help.
3 *Section 18 penalizes the possession of a firearm with intent to commit a crime*: **prohibit**, forbid, ban, outlaw, bar, veto, embargo, declare something

a punishable offence, make something punishable, make illegal, disallow, proscribe, interdict.
▷ANTONYMS legalize.

penalty noun **1** *increased penalties for dumping oil at sea*: **punishment**, sanction, punitive action, retribution, penance; **fine**, forfeit, sentence; rare mulct.
▷ANTONYMS reward.
2 *for some, the economic penalties of motherhood outweigh its attractions*: **disadvantage**, difficulty, drawback, handicap, snag, downside, minus, detriment, unpleasant aspect; trial, torment, bane, tribulation, affliction, suffering, burden, trouble, worry; deprivation, cost, undesirable consequence.
▷ANTONYMS advantage.

penance noun *self-awareness is the necessary ingredient for penance | penances for a variety of sins*: **atonement**, expiation, self-punishment, self-mortification, self-abasement, reparation, amends, penalty, punishment.
□ **do penance** *you must do penance for the crimes in your life*: **atone**, make amends/reparation/recompense/restitution, make up, redeem oneself, pay the penalty, pay, recompense, pay the price, expiate, redress, compensate.

penchant noun *he has a penchant for champagne*. See **taste** (sense 4 of the noun).

pencil noun *a pencil of light*: **beam**, ray, shaft, finger, gleam.
▶ verb **1** *she pencilled slogans on an envelope*: **write**, write down, jot down, note, set down, take down, inscribe; **scribble**, rough out, write roughly, scrawl, pen, compose, draft; formulate, draw up, dash off, put in writing, put down on paper, commit to paper, put in black and white.
2 *pencil a line along the top of the moulding*: **draw**, trace, plot, chart, sketch, outline.
□ **pencil something in** *they have pencilled in 1 May for a family day out*: **arrange provisionally**, make as a provisional arrangement, arrange subject to confirmation, forecast tentatively.

pendant noun *he slipped the pendant over his neck*: locket, medallion, drop, stone; necklace, chain.

pendent adjective *pendent catkins*: **hanging**, suspended, supported from above, dangling, pendulous, drooping, droopy, flaccid, swinging, swaying, trailing, flowing, falling, tumbling; rare pendant, pensile.

pending adjective **1** *dismissal of all other litigation pending between them*: **unresolved**, undecided, unsettled, unconcluded, uncertain, awaiting decision, awaiting action, undetermined, (still) open, hanging fire, (up) in the air, in limbo, in the balance, on ice, in reserve, in abeyance, ongoing, awaiting attention, outstanding, to be done, undone, not done, unattended to, unfinished, incomplete, left, remaining; informal on the back burner.
2 *her rumoured pending marriage*: **imminent**, impending, about to happen/be, forthcoming, upcoming, on the way, coming, approaching, looming, gathering, prospective, near, nearing, close, close at hand, in the offing, in the wind, to come, -to-be, anticipated, expected.
▶ preposition *the two boys were released on bail pending another hearing next week*: **awaiting**, waiting for, until, till, before, until there is/are.

pendulous adjective *this magnolia produces large, white, pendulous flowers*: **drooping**, dangling, droopy, sagging, saggy, floppy; hanging, suspended, supported from above, pendent; swinging, swaying, falling, tumbling, trailing, flowing, loose, relaxed; rare pensile.

penetrable adjective **1** *vines grow best in a penetrable subsoil*: **permeable**, pervious, porous, open; honeycombed, cellular, holey; sieve-like, leaky; pierceable; accessible.
▷ANTONYMS impervious; impenetrable.
2 *the translation makes the original text penetrable*: **understandable**, fathomable, graspable, approachable; easy to understand; comprehensible, intelligible, accessible.
▷ANTONYMS incomprehensible.

penetrate verb **1** *the sharp point of the spear did not penetrate his throat*: **pierce**, puncture, make a hole in, perforate, stab, prick, probe, gore, spike, stick, impale, transfix, bore (through), drill (through), lance.
2 *the oil has penetrated into the stones*: **seep**, soak, percolate, filter, infiltrate, spread, diffuse; enter, make one's way into/through, pass/move/flow into, get into.
3 *they penetrated the enemy territory via a gap cut in the fence*: **infiltrate**, slip into, sneak into, creep into, insinuate oneself into, worm one's way into, make inroads into, invade, intrude on, overrun.
4 *I am allowing the healing energy to penetrate my digestive organs*: **permeate**, pervade, fill, spread throughout, imbue, suffuse, diffuse through, seep through, steep, impregnate, inform, infuse, saturate, charge, drench, inundate; influence, infect, excite, stimulate, inspire.
5 *humans' efforts to penetrate the enigma of their beginnings*: **understand**, comprehend, apprehend, fathom, grasp, perceive, discern, get to the bottom of, solve, resolve, make out, make sense of, interpret, puzzle out, work out, figure out, unravel, decipher, make head or tail of; informal crack, get, tumble to, latch on to, cotton on to; Brit. informal suss out, twig.
6 *Douglas was at the door before Jamieson's words penetrated*: **be understood**, be comprehended, be taken in, be grasped, become clear; **register**, make an impression, get through, sink in, fall into place, dawn, come home; informal click.
7 *I don't think the implication penetrated my mind all that quickly*: **get through to**, be understood/comprehended by, register on, make an impression on, have an impact on.

penetrating adjective **1** *a penetrating wind*: **piercing**, cutting, stinging, biting; **keen**, sharp, acute, numbing, harsh, fierce, raw; frosty, freezing, frigid, chill, chilling, glacial, arctic, wintry, cold, bitterly/intensely cold, nippy; Brit. informal parky; rare nipping.
▷ANTONYMS gentle, mild.
2 *a penetrating voice*: **shrill**, strident, piercing, carrying, clearly audible, loud, strong, high, high-pitched, piping, ear-piercing, ear-splitting, screechy, intrusive.
▷ANTONYMS mellow, soft.
3 *a penetrating smell*: **pungent**, pervasive, strong, powerful, suffocating, stifling; sharp, acrid, acid, sour, biting, stinging, burning, smarting, irritating, nauseating, nauseous, sickly, offensive, astringent, bitter, fetid, cloying; heady, aromatic, flowery, fragrant; literary mephitic.
▷ANTONYMS mild.
4 *penetrating eyes*: **observant**, searching, intent, alert, shrewd, perceptive, probing, piercing, sharp, keen.
5 *a penetrating analysis*: **perceptive**, insightful, keen, sharp, sharp-witted, quick-witted, intelligent, clever, smart, incisive, piercing, knife-like, razor-edged, trenchant, astute, shrewd, subtle, quick, ready, clear, acute, discriminating, percipient, perspicacious, discerning, sensitive, thoughtful, penetrative, deep, profound.
▷ANTONYMS dull.
6 *penetrating questions*: **enquiring**, searching, sharp, incisive, probing, deep, inquisitive, analytic, in-depth.

Choose the right word **penetrating, keen, acute**

See **keen**[1].

penetration noun **1** *skin penetration by infective larvae*: **perforation**, piercing, puncturing, puncture, riddling, stabbing, prick, pricking, probing, goring, spiking, sticking, impaling, impalement, transfixing, transfixion, boring, drilling, lancing, tapping.
2 *rot that is attributable to rain penetration*: **infiltration**, entry, inflow, spread, spreading, diffusion, percolation, filtering, seepage, soaking, soakage.
3 *remarks of great penetration*: **insight**, **discernment**, perception, perceptiveness, intelligence, sharp-wittedness, quick-wittedness, cleverness, smartness, incisiveness, keenness, sharpness, trenchancy, astuteness, shrewdness, acuteness, subtlety, clarity, acuity, discrimination, sensitivity, thoughtfulness, profundity, percipience, perspicacity, perspicuity, sagacity.
▷ANTONYMS dullness.

peninsula noun **cape**, promontory, point, head, headland, foreland, ness, horn, bill, bluff, limb; Scottish mull; archaic half-island, half-isle, demi-island.

penis noun **phallus**, (male) member, (male) organ, sex, erection; N. Amer. informal pee-pee; Irish informal mickey; humorous lunch box; vulgar slang cock, dick, prick, knob, chopper, tool, equipment, dipstick, ding-a-ling, dong, (one-eyed) trouser snake, shaft, ramrod, root, boner, length, meat, pudding, pego, John Thomas, Johnson, machine, manhood, thing, winkle, middle leg, third leg, old man, joystick, pencil, pisser, prong, putz, rig, rod, Roger, stalk, stiffy, tonk, tube, weapon, yard; Brit. vulgar slang willy, horn, how's your father, peter, plonker, todger; Irish vulgar slang langer; N. Amer. vulgar slang dork, pecker, weenie, wiener, schlong, whang, whanger; technical intromittent organ; archaic membrum virile, virile member, nerve, person, propagator, tarse, verge, pizzle; archaic, vulgar slang loom, needle, pillicock, pintle, runnion.

penitence noun *the writer prays to God in penitence*: **repentance**, contrition, compunction, regret, remorse, remorsefulness, ruefulness, pangs of conscience, self-reproach, contriteness, self-accusation, shame, sorrow, guilt.

penitent adjective *she stood with her hands joined below her waist like a penitent child*: **repentant**, contrite, regretful, remorseful, sorry, apologetic, conscience-stricken, rueful, ashamed, shamefaced, abject.
▷ANTONYMS impenitent, unrepentant.

Word toolkit **penitent**

See **apologetic**.

pen-name noun **pseudonym**, assumed name, incognito, alias, stage name, professional name, false name, sobriquet, nickname; French nom de plume, nom de guerre; rare allonym, anonym.

pennant noun *pennants fly from the towers*: **banner**, banderole, streamer, flag, standard, ensign, jack, pennon, colour(s); Brit. pendant; Nautical burgee; rare gonfalon, guidon, labarum.

penniless adjective *Van Gogh died penniless*: **poor**, indigent, impoverished, penurious, impecunious, in penury, moneyless, without a sou, as poor as a church mouse, poverty-stricken, destitute, necessitous; bankrupt, bust,

P

insolvent; needy, in need/want, badly off, in reduced circumstances, in straitened circumstances, hard up, on one's beam-ends, unable to make ends meet, underprivileged; Brit. on the breadline, without a penny (to one's name); informal broke, flat broke, cleaned out, strapped for cash, strapped, on one's uppers, without two pennies/(brass) farthings to rub together; Brit. informal stony broke, skint, in Queer Street; N. Amer. informal stone broke; rare pauperized, beggared.
▷ANTONYMS wealthy, affluent.

penny noun
□ **a pretty penny** informal *I bet this costs a pretty penny*: **a lot of money**, a fortune, a considerable/vast sum of money, millions, billions, a king's ransom, a killing, a windfall, a bonanza; informal a small fortune, lots/pots/heaps of money, a mint, a bundle, a packet, a wad, a pile, a stack, a heap, a tidy sum; telephone numbers; Brit. informal a bomb, shedloads, a shedload; N. Amer. big bucks, big money, gazillions; Austral. informal big bickies, motser, motza.
□ **two/ten a penny** *nursing homes are two a penny in Devon*: **numerous**, abundant, thick on the ground, profuse, plentiful, prolific, copious, legion, innumerable, countless, infinite, numberless; in large numbers, by the gross, in strength, by the yard; very common, widespread, popular, universal, ubiquitous; literary myriad, innumerous, manifold.

penny-pincher noun **skinflint**, miser, Scrooge, niggard, cheese-parer; informal meanie, money-grubber, cheapskate; N. Amer. informal tightwad; vulgar slang tight-arse.
▷ANTONYMS spendthrift; philanthropist.

penny-pinching adjective **mean**, miserly, niggardly, parsimonious, close-fisted, cheese-paring, penurious, scrimping, grasping, greedy, avaricious, Scrooge-like, ungenerous, illiberal, close; informal stingy, mingy, tight, tight-fisted, money-grubbing, money-grabbing; vulgar slang tight-arsed; archaic near.
▷ANTONYMS generous, liberal, munificent.

pension noun **1** *they will get a pension when they retire*: **annuity**, superannuation; retirement pension, old-age pension, state pension, company pension, occupational pension, employer's pension, contributory pension, non-contributory pension, supplementary pension, graduated pension, earnings-related pension, index-linked pension, personal pension, private pension, portable pension.
2 *a disability pension*: **welfare payment**, allowance, benefit, support, welfare, assistance; widow's pension, war pension, disablement/disability pension, invalidity pension.

pensioner noun **retired person**, old-age pensioner, OAP, senior citizen; N. Amer. senior, retiree; rare retirer, pensionary.

pensive adjective **thoughtful**, thinking, reflective, contemplative, musing, meditative, introspective, prayerful, philosophical, cogitative, ruminative, absorbed, engrossed, rapt, preoccupied, deep/immersed/lost in thought, in a brown study, broody, serious, studious, solemn, dreamy, dreaming; wistful, brooding, melancholy, sad; rare ruminant.

> *Word toolkit* **pensive**
>
> See **wistful**.

P

pent-up adjective *a release of pent-up emotion*: **repressed**, suppressed, stifled, smothered, restrained, constrained, confined, bottled up, held in/back, kept in check, curbed, bridled.

penurious adjective **1** *a penurious student*: **poor**, as poor as a church mouse, poverty-stricken, destitute, necessitous, in penury, impecunious, impoverished, indigent, needy, in need/want, badly off, in reduced circumstances, in straitened circumstances, hard up, on one's beam-ends, unable to make ends meet, underprivileged, penniless, without a sou, moneyless, bankrupt, bust, insolvent; Brit. on the breadline, without a penny (to one's name); informal broke, flat broke, cleaned out, strapped for cash, strapped, on one's uppers; Brit. informal stony broke, skint, without two pennies/(brass) farthings to rub together, in Queer Street; N. Amer. informal stone broke; rare pauperized, beggared.
▷ANTONYMS wealthy.
2 *a penurious old skinflint*: **mean**, miserly, niggardly, parsimonious, penny-pinching, close-fisted, cheese-paring, scrimping, grasping, greedy, avaricious, Scrooge-like, ungenerous, illiberal, close; informal stingy, mingy, tight, tight-fisted, money-grubbing, money-grabbing; vulgar slang tight-arsed; archaic near.
▷ANTONYMS generous.

penury noun **extreme/dire poverty**, pennilessness, impecuniousness, impoverishment, indigence, need, neediness, want, destitution, privation, deprivation, hardship, beggary, bankruptcy, insolvency, ruin, reduced circumstances, straitened circumstances; rare pauperism, pauperdom, mendicity.
▷ANTONYMS wealth, affluence.

people plural noun **1** *crowds of people*: **human beings**, persons, individuals, humans, mankind, humankind, the human race, Homo sapiens, humanity, the human species, mortals, (living) souls, personages, {men, women, and children}; informal folk, peeps.
2 *the British people have not been told the truth*: **citizens**, subjects, electors, voters, taxpayers, residents, inhabitants, (general) public, citizenry, nation, population, populace, community, society.
3 *a man of the people*: **the proletariat**, the common people, the masses, the populace, the multitude, the rank and file, the commonality, the commonalty, the third estate, the plebeians, the crowd; derogatory the hoi polloi, the common herd, the rabble, the mob, the riff-raff, the canaille, the great unwashed, the ragtag (and bobtail), the proles, the plebs.
4 *her people don't live far away*: **family**, parents, relatives, relations, folk, kinsmen, kin, kith and kin, next of kin, one's (own) flesh and blood, blood relatives/relations, nearest and dearest; informal folks; formal kinsfolk, kinfolk.
5 singular *the peoples of Africa*: **race**, tribe, clan, (ethnic) group, strain, stock, caste, nation, country, population, populace; archaic breed, folk, seed.
▸ verb *the Indians who once peopled Newfoundland*: **populate**, settle (in), colonize, establish oneself in, inhabit, live in, occupy; formal be, reside in, domiciled in, dwell in.

> *Word links* **people**
>
> **demotic**, **plebeian** relating to (ordinary) people
> **demo-** related prefix, as in *democratic, demography*
> **ethnic** relating to a people
> **anthropology** study of people
> **ethnology** study of different peoples
> **anthropophobia** fear of people
> **ethnocide** killing of a people

pep informal noun *full of pep after the holidays*: **dynamism**, life, go, energy, spirit, liveliness, animation, bounce, sparkle, effervescence, fizz, verve, spiritedness, ebullience, high spirits, enthusiasm, initiative, vitality, vivacity, fire, dash, panache, elan, snap, zest, zeal, exuberance, vigour, gusto, drive, push, brio; informal feistiness, get-up-and-go, gumption, oomph, pizzazz, vim, zing, zip.
▸ verb
□ **pep something up** *the turbocharger is designed to pep up performance*: **improve**, **enliven**, animate, liven up, put some/new life into, invigorate, vitalize, revitalize, vivify, ginger up, energize, electrify, galvanize, put some spark into, stimulate, get something going, add zest to, perk up, brighten up, cheer up; season, spice, add spice to, pepper, leaven, flavour, add flavouring to; informal buck up.
▷ANTONYMS subdue.

pepper verb **1** *salt and pepper the potatoes*: season, flavour, spice, spice up.
2 *a sprinkle of stars peppered the desert skies*: **sprinkle**, fleck, intersperse, dot, spot, bespatter, dab, bestud, stipple, pock, freckle, scatter; literary befleck, bestrew.
3 *another burst of enemy bullets peppered the tank*: **bombard**, pelt, shower, rain down on, attack, assail, batter, fire a broadside at, strafe, rake, sweep, enfilade, blitz, hit; archaic cannonade, fusillade.

peppery adjective **1** *this salami is very peppery*: **spicy**, spiced, peppered, hot, highly seasoned, pungent, fiery, gingery, piquant, sharp.
▷ANTONYMS mild, bland.
2 *retired generals are expected to be peppery*: **irritable**, peevish, cross, crabbed, crabby, crotchety, cantankerous, hot-tempered, irascible, fiery, quick-tempered, impatient, complaining, querulous, curmudgeonly, bitter, acerbic, sour, caustic, moody, grumpy, huffy, brusque, surly, curt, gruff, scratchy, ill-tempered, bad-tempered, short-tempered, ill-natured, ill-humoured, touchy, sharp-tongued, testy, tetchy, snappish, snarling, waspish, prickly, crusty, bilious, liverish, dyspeptic, splenetic, choleric; informal snappy, chippy, grouchy, cranky; Brit. informal narky, ratty, eggy, like a bear with a sore head; N. Amer. informal peckish, sorehead, soreheaded; Austral./NZ informal snaky; informal, dated miffy.
▷ANTONYMS easy-going.

perceive verb **1** *Belinda immediately perceived the flaws in her story*: **discern**, recognize, become cognizant of, become aware of, become conscious of, get/come to know, tell, distinguish, grasp, understand, take in, make out, find, identify, hit on, comprehend, apprehend, figure out, deduce, conclude, see, discover, learn, appreciate, realize, ascertain, sense, divine, intuit; informal catch on to; Brit. informal twig; rare cognize.
2 *sharks and rays cannot perceive colour*: **see**, make out, pick out, discern, detect, catch sight of, spot, observe, glimpse, notice, recognize, identify; hear, smell, sniff (out), scent, nose out, feel, taste, sense.
3 *he was perceived as too negative*: **look on**, view, regard, consider, think of, judge, deem, appraise, assess, adjudge, figure (out), size up, value, rate, suppose, think, sum up, weigh up.

perceptible adjective **noticeable**, perceivable, detectable, discernible; appreciable, visible, observable, recognizable; obvious, evident, manifest, patent, clear, distinct, plain, overt, conspicuous, distinguishable, unmistakable, unconcealed, transparent, apparent; significant, measurable, tangible, palpable.
▷ANTONYMS imperceptible, inconspicuous.

Word toolkit

perceptible	palpable	appreciable
shift	tension	difference
nod	fear	effect
form	presence	increase
risk	relief	number
bias	excitement	extent
rise	desire	degree
noise	anger	benefit
movement	sensation	quantity

perception noun **1** *our perception of our own limitations | his perception of the world*: **discernment**, appreciation, recognition, realization, cognizance; **awareness**, consciousness, knowledge, acknowledgement, grasp, understanding, comprehension, interpretation, apprehension; impression, sense, sensation, feeling, observation, picture, notion, thought, belief, conception, idea, judgement, estimation.
2 *he talks with great perception on all matters theatrical*: **insight**, perceptiveness, percipience, perspicacity, perspicuity, understanding, keenness, sharpness, sharp-wittedness, quick-wittedness, intelligence, intuition, cleverness, incisiveness, trenchancy, wit, astuteness, shrewdness, acuteness, acuity, subtlety, clarity, discrimination, discernment, sensitivity, penetration, thoughtfulness, profundity.

perceptive adjective **insightful**, discerning, responsive, sensitive, observant; piercing, penetrating, percipient, perspicacious, penetrative, intelligent, clever, canny, keen, sharp, sharp-witted, quick-witted, astute, shrewd, subtle, quick, ready, clear, acute, discriminating; intuitive, thoughtful, deep, profound.
▷ANTONYMS obtuse, unobservant, dull.

perch noun *the budgerigar shuffled along its perch*: **pole**, rod, branch, roost, rest, resting place.
▸ verb **1** *three swallows perched on the telegraph wire*: **roost**, sit, rest; **alight**, settle, land, come to rest.
2 *she perched a pair of pince-nez on her nose*: **put**, place, set, rest, balance.
□ **be perched** *the church is perched on a hill above Florence*: **be located**, be situated, be positioned, be sited, stand.

perchance adverb literary **1** *if perchance he arrives on time*: **by chance**, by any chance, by some chance, as it may be, as it may happen, as things may turn out.
2 *perchance the outlook is not as bleak as she imagines*: **maybe**, perhaps, possibly, for all one knows, it could be (that), it is possible (that), conceivably; N. English happen; literary peradventure, mayhap, haply; rare percase.

percipience noun **perceptiveness**, perception, discernment, astuteness, shrewdness, insight, penetration, perspicacity, perspicaciousness, sharpness, sharp-wittedness, quick-wittedness, keen-wittedness, acuteness, acuity, discrimination, clear-sightedness, far-sightedness, intelligence, cleverness, canniness, wit, intuition, intuitiveness, alertness, judiciousness, judgement, wisdom, sagacity, sageness, understanding, sensitivity; N. Amer. informal savvy; rare sapience, arguteness.

percipient adjective *a percipient political commentator*: **astute**, perceptive, shrewd, discerning, perspicacious, sharp, sharp-witted, acute, penetrating, discriminating, clear-sighted, clear-eyed, far-sighted, intelligent, clever, canny, intuitive, quick, alert, sensible, judicious, wise, sagacious, sage, incisive, sharp-sighted, far-seeing, open-eyed, understanding, responsive, sensitive; informal on the ball, smart, downy; Brit. informal suss; Scottish & N. English informal pawky; N. Amer. informal heads-up; dated long-headed; rare argute.
▷ANTONYMS obtuse, stupid.

percolate verb **1** *water that has percolated through the soil*: **filter**, drain, drip, ooze, seep, trickle, dribble, strain, leak, leach; rare filtrate, transude.
2 *a few of these technological marvels began to slowly percolate into the countryside*: **spread**, be disseminated, filter, pass, go; penetrate, permeate, pervade, infiltrate.
3 *he put some coffee on to percolate*: **brew**; informal perk.

percussion noun *the clattering percussion of objects striking the walls and the shutters*: **crash**, bang, smash, clash, bump, thump, thwack, whack; impact, collision, striking, beating, shock, knock.

perdition noun **damnation**, eternal punishment; **hell**, hellfire, spiritual destruction, doom, ruin, ruination, condemnation, destruction, downfall.

peregrinations plural noun *his European peregrinations*: **travels**, wanderings, journeys, voyages, expeditions, explorations, perambulations, odysseys, trips, treks, excursions; globetrotting, travelling, wandering, journeying, roving, roaming, wayfaring, trekking.

peremptory adjective **1** *'Just do it!' came the peremptory reply*: **brusque**, imperious, high-handed, brisk, abrupt, summary, commanding, authoritative, overbearing, dogmatic, autocratic, dictatorial, bossy, domineering, arbitrary, arrogant, overweening, lordly, tyrannical, despotic, imperial, magisterial, authoritarian; emphatic, firm, insistent, imperative, positive.
2 *a peremptory order of the court*: **incontrovertible**, irreversible, binding, absolute, final, conclusive, decisive, definitive, categorical, irrefutable, unconditional, unchallengeable; Law unappealable.

perennial adjective *the perennial fascination with crime*: **everlasting**, perpetual, eternal, continuing, unending, never-ending, endless, undying, ceaseless, abiding, enduring, lasting, persisting, permanent, constant, continual, unfailing, unchanging, never-changing.

perfect adjective (stress on the first syllable) **1** *she strove to be the perfect wife*: **ideal**, model, without fault, faultless, flawless, consummate, quintessential, exemplary, best, best-example, ultimate, copybook.
2 *it was a perfect holiday*: **superb**, exquisite, superlative, excellent, wonderful, marvellous, beautiful, sublime, magnificent, idyllic, blissful, Utopian; unrivalled, unequalled, matchless, unparalleled, beyond compare, without equal, second to none, too good to be true, unmatched, incomparable, nonpareil, peerless, inimitable, unexcelled, unsurpassed, unsurpassable; informal out of this world, terrific, fantastic, fabulous, great, super, heavenly, glorious, gorgeous, stellar, divine, phenomenal, sensational, dreamy, fab, fabby, fantabulous, awesome, to die for, magic, ace; Brit. informal brilliant, brill, bosting; rare unexampled, indefectible.
3 *an E-type Jaguar in perfect condition*: **flawless**, mint, as good as new, pristine, impeccable, immaculate, superb, superlative, optimum, prime, optimal, peak, excellent, faultless, as sound as a bell, unspoilt, unblemished, undamaged, spotless, unmarred, unimpaired; informal tip-top, A1.
4 *a perfect copy*: **exact**, precise, accurate, faithful, correct, unerring, right, close, true, strict; Brit. informal spot on; N. Amer. informal on the money.
▷ANTONYMS imperfect, faulty, defective.
5 *the perfect Christmas present for golfers everywhere*: **ideal**, just right, right, appropriate, fitting, fit, suitable, apt, made to order, tailor-made; very; Brit. informal spot on, just the job.
6 *she felt a perfect idiot*: **absolute**, complete, total, real, out-and-out, thorough, thoroughgoing, downright, utter, sheer, consummate, unmitigated, unqualified, veritable, in every respect, unalloyed; Brit. informal right; Austral./NZ informal fair; archaic arrant.
▸ verb (stress on the second syllable) *he's busy perfecting his bowling technique*: **improve**, make perfect, bring to perfection, better, polish (up), burnish, hone, refine, consummate, put the finishing/final touches to, ameliorate, brush up, fine-tune; rare meliorate.

perfection noun **1** *the satiny perfection of her skin*: **flawlessness**, **excellence**, superbness, sublimity, exquisiteness, magnificence, perfectness, faultlessness, impeccability, immaculateness, exemplariness.
2 *for her, he was still perfection*: **the ideal**, a paragon, the ne plus ultra, the beau idéal, a nonpareil, the crème de la crème, the last word, the ultimate, a dream; informal one in a million, the tops, the best/greatest thing since sliced bread, the bee's knees; archaic a nonsuch.
3 *the perfection of new mechanisms of economic management*: **improvement**, betterment, refinement, refining, perfecting, polishing, amelioration; rare melioration.

perfectionist noun **purist**, stickler for perfection, idealist, pedant, precisionist, formalist; archaic precisian.

perfectly adverb **1** *a perfectly cooked meal | things have worked out perfectly*: **superbly**, superlatively, excellently, flawlessly, faultlessly, to perfection, without fault, ideally, wonderfully, marvellously, magnificently, sublimely, admirably, inimitably, incomparably, impeccably, immaculately, exquisitely, consummately; N. Amer. to a fare-thee-well; informal like a dream, to a T, terrifically, fantastically.
▷ANTONYMS badly.
2 *I think we understand each other perfectly*: **absolutely**, utterly, completely, altogether, entirely, wholly, totally, thoroughly, fully, quite, in every respect.
3 *you know perfectly well that is not what I meant*: **very**, quite, full; informal damn, damned; Brit. informal jolly, bloody; N. Amer. informal darned; archaic or N. English right.

perfidious adjective *a perfidious lover*: **treacherous**, duplicitous, deceitful, disloyal, faithless, unfaithful, traitorous, treasonous, false, untrue, double-dealing, dishonest, two-faced, untrustworthy; rare false-hearted, double-faced, truthless, Punic.
▷ANTONYMS faithful, loyal.

perfidy noun *the perfidy of her lover*: **treachery**, duplicity, deceit, perfidiousness, deceitfulness, disloyalty, infidelity, faithlessness, unfaithfulness, betrayal, treason, falseness, falsity, double-dealing, dishonesty, two-facedness, untrustworthiness, breach of trust; rare false-heartedness, Punic faith.
▷ANTONYMS faithfulness, loyalty.

perforate verb *fragments of an explosive bullet perforated his intestines*: **pierce**, penetrate, enter, puncture, prick, bore through, riddle, hole, make/punch/put holes in.

perforce adverb formal *amateurs, perforce, have to settle for less expensive solutions*: **necessarily**, of necessity, inevitably, unavoidably, by force of circumstances, needs must; Latin nolens volens; informal like it or not.

perform verb **1** *I have my duties to perform | your agent cannot perform miracles for you*: **carry out**, do, execute, discharge, bring about, bring

P

off, accomplish, achieve, fulfil, complete, conduct, effect, dispatch, work, implement; informal pull off; archaic acquit oneself of; rare effectuate.
▷ANTONYMS neglect, omit.
2 *the car performs well at low speeds*: **function**, work, operate, run, go, respond, behave, act, acquit oneself/itself.
3 *the play has already been performed in Britain*: **stage**, put on, present, mount, enact, act, represent, do, produce.
4 *the band will be performing live in Hyde Park*: **appear**, play, be on stage.

performance noun **1** *there are two evening performances*: **show**, production, showing, presentation, entertainment, staging, act; concert, recital; Brit. house; informal gig.
2 *their performance of Mozart's concerto in E flat was beautifully judged*: **rendition**, rendering, interpretation, account, playing, acting, representation, staging.
3 *the continual performance of a single task reduces a man to the level of a machine*: **carrying out**, execution, discharge, conducting, conduct, effecting, accomplishment, achievement, completion, fulfilment, dispatch, implementation; rare effectuation.
4 *the tests assess the performance of the processor*: **functioning**, working, operation, running, behaviour, capabilities, capability, capacity, power, potential.
5 *he made a great performance of telling her about it*: **fuss**, fuss and bother, production, palaver, parade, scene, display, exhibition; informal song and dance, to-do, hoo-ha, ballyhoo, business, pantomime, hoopla; Brit. informal carry-on; NZ informal bobsy-die.

performer noun **actor**, **actress**, thespian, artiste, artist, entertainer, trouper; star, superstar; rare executant; (**performers**) troupe, company, cast.

perfume noun **1** *a bottle of perfume*: **scent**, fragrance, eau de toilette, toilet water, eau de cologne, cologne, spray, aftershave.
2 *the heady perfume of lilacs*: **smell**, odour, aroma, scent, fragrance, bouquet, redolence.

perfumed adjective *perfumed soap*: **sweet-smelling**, sweet-scented, scented, fragrant, aromatic, sweet; rare fragranced, aromatized, perfumy.

perfunctory adjective *the guards gave a perfunctory look up and down the carriage*: **cursory**, desultory; **quick**, brief, hasty, hurried, rapid, passing, fleeting, summary; token, casual, superficial, uninterested, careless, half-hearted, unthinking, sketchy, mechanical, automatic, routine, offhand, indifferent, inattentive; dismissive.
▷ANTONYMS careful, thorough.

perhaps adverb *perhaps he'll come tomorrow*: **maybe**, for all I know, for all you know, it could be (that), it may be (that), it is possible (that), possibly, conceivably, feasibly; N. English happen; literary peradventure, perchance, mayhap, haply; rare percase.

peril noun *a situation fraught with peril | the perils of alcohol abuse*: **danger**, jeopardy, risk, riskiness, hazard, insecurity, uncertainty, menace, threat, perilousness; pitfall, problem.
▷ANTONYMS safety, security.

p

> *Choose the right word* **peril, danger, hazard, risk**
>
> See **danger**.

perilous adjective *a perilous journey through the mountains | the economy remained in a perilous state*: **dangerous**, fraught with danger, hazardous, risky, unsafe, treacherous; precarious, vulnerable, uncertain, insecure, critical, desperate, exposed, at risk, in jeopardy, in danger, touch-and-go; problematic, difficult; informal hairy, dicey; N. Amer. informal gnarly; archaic or humorous parlous.
▷ANTONYMS safe, secure.

perimeter noun **1** *the perimeter of a circle*: **circumference**, outside, outer edge.
2 *the perimeter of the vast estate*: **boundary**, border, frontier, limits, outer limits, bounds, confines, edge, margin, fringe(s), periphery, borderline, verge; literary bourn, marge, skirt; rare ambit.
▷ANTONYMS centre, middle, heart.

period noun **1** *he had long periods of depression | a six-week period*: **time**, spell, interval, stretch, term, span, phase, session, bout, run, space, duration, chapter, stage; while; Brit. informal patch.
2 *the post-war period | the period of the French Revolution*: **era**, age, epoch, time, days, years, aeon; generation, date.
3 *a double maths period*: **lesson**, class, session.
4 *women who suffer from painful periods*: **menstruation**, menstrual flow; informal the curse, monthlies, time of the month; technical menses; archaic time; rare flowers.
5 N. Amer. *a comma instead of a period*: **full stop**, full point, point, stop.
6 *it's a hard job, period*: **and that's that**, and that is the end of the matter, full stop, finis.

periodic adjective *Michael had to make periodic visits to the hospital*: **regular**, periodical, at fixed intervals, recurrent, recurring, repeated, cyclical, cyclic, seasonal; occasional, infrequent, intermittent, sporadic, spasmodic, odd.

periodical noun *articles in specialist periodicals*: **journal**, publication, magazine, newspaper, paper, review, digest, gazette, newsletter, organ, serial, annual, quarterly, monthly, bimonthly, fortnightly, weekly, biweekly; informal mag, book, glossy.
▸ adjective See **periodic**.

peripatetic adjective *his peripatetic way of life*: **nomadic**, itinerant, travelling, wandering, roving, roaming, migrant, migratory, ambulatory, unsettled, vagabond, vagrant.

peripheral adjective **1** *some of the city's peripheral housing estates*: **outlying**, outer, on the edge/outskirts, outermost, fringe, border, surrounding; rare circumferential, perimetric.
2 *fund raising by the school is peripheral to the main business of teaching | peripheral issues*: **secondary**, **subsidiary**, incidental, tangential, marginal, minor, unimportant, lesser, inessential, non-essential, immaterial, superficial, ancillary, borderline; irrelevant, beside the point, of little account, extraneous.
▷ANTONYMS central, vital.

periphery noun *rambling estates on the periphery of the city*: **edge**, outer edge, margin, fringe, boundary, border, perimeter, circumference, rim, verge, borderline; outskirts, outer limits/regions/reaches, bounds; literary bourn, marge, skirt; rare ambit.
▷ANTONYMS centre, middle, heart.

periphrastic adjective *the periphrastic nature of legal syntax*: **circumlocutory**, circuitous, roundabout, indirect, tautological, prolix, verbose, wordy, long-winded, rambling, wandering, tortuous, diffuse, discursive; rare pleonastic, circumlocutionary, ambagious.

perish verb **1** *millions of young British soldiers perished*: **die**, lose one's life, be killed, fall, expire, meet one's death, be lost, lay down one's life, breathe one's last, draw one's last breath, pass away, go the way of all flesh, give up the ghost, go to glory, meet one's maker, go to one's last resting place, cross the great divide; informal bite the dust, kick the bucket, cash in one's chips, croak, turn up one's toes, shuffle off this mortal coil, go the way of the dinosaurs, conk out, buy it; Brit. informal snuff it, peg out, pop one's clogs, hop the twig/stick; N. Amer. informal bite the big one, buy the farm, check out, hand in one's dinner pail; Austral./NZ informal go bung; literary exit; archaic decease, depart this life.
2 *must these hopes perish so soon?* **come to an end**, die (away), be destroyed, cease to exist, disappear, vanish, fade, dissolve, evaporate, melt away, pass into oblivion, wither.
▷ANTONYMS live, survive.
3 *the potatoes had all perished | an abandoned tyre whose rubber had perished*: **go bad**, go off, spoil, rot, go mouldy, moulder, putrefy, decay, decompose; deteriorate, disintegrate, fall apart, crumble.

perishable adjective **liable to rot**, easily spoilt, decomposable, biodegradable; rare putrescible, decayable, putrefiable.

perjure verb
▫ **perjure oneself** *Colum had tried to make her perjure herself to give him an alibi*: **lie under oath**, lie, commit perjury, give false evidence/testimony, forswear oneself, be forsworn, bear false witness/testimony, swear falsely.

perjury noun *the jury found him guilty of theft, perjury, and fraudulent trading*: **lying under oath**, violation of an oath, giving false evidence/testimony, bearing false witness/testimony, forswearing oneself, making false statements, wilful falsehood; mendacity, mendaciousness.

perk[1] verb
▫ **perk up** *as he thought about the evening ahead he perked up slightly | the economy has been slow to perk up*: **cheer up**, brighten (up), become more cheerful, become livelier, feel happier, take heart, be heartened, liven up, revive; improve, get better, recover, rally, take a turn for the better, look up, pick up, bounce back, be on the mend; informal buck up.
▫ **perk someone/something up** *you look as though you could do with something to perk you up*: **cheer up**, liven up, brighten up, make more cheerful/lively, make happier, raise someone's spirits, give someone heart, give someone a boost/lift, revitalize, invigorate, energize, enliven, ginger up, put new life/heart into, add some zest to, put some spark into, rejuvenate, refresh, vitalize, vivify, wake up; informal buck up, pep up; rare inspirit.

perk[2] noun *your contract may offer a variety of perks, such as private health care*: **fringe benefit**, additional benefit, benefit, advantage, bonus, dividend, extra, plus, premium, consideration, reward; N. Amer. lagniappe; informal freebie; Brit. informal golden hello; formal perquisite; rare appanage.

perky adjective *I felt much more perky after I put the phone down*.
See **bouncy** (sense 3).

permanence noun *our craving for some sense of permanence in a rapidly changing world*: **stability**, durability, persistence, permanency, fixity, fixedness, changelessness, immutability, endurance, dependability, constancy, continuance, continuity, immortality, indestructibility, perpetuity, endlessness; rare lastingness, everlastingness, eternalness, eternality, perdurability, perenniality, imperishability, inalterability, unchangeableness, unchangeability.

permanent adjective **1** *a permanent ban on the dumping of nuclear waste at sea | permanent brain damage*: **lasting**, enduring, indefinite, continuing,

perpetual, everlasting, eternal, abiding, constant, persistent, irreparable, irreversible, lifelong, indissoluble, indelible, standing, perennial, unending, endless, never-ending, immutable, unchangeable, unalterable, invariable, unchanging, changeless, undying, imperishable, indestructible, ineradicable; rare perdurable.
2 *a permanent job*: **long-term**, long-lasting, lasting, stable, fixed, established, sound, secure, solid, firm, continuing, durable.
▷ANTONYMS temporary, fleeting, ephemeral.

permanently adverb **1** *the container is then permanently sealed*: **for all time**, forever, for good, for always, for good and all, for ever and ever, (for) evermore, in perpetuity, lastingly, indelibly, immutably, inalterably, invariably, until the end of time, everlastingly, enduringly, abidingly; N. Amer. forevermore; informal for keeps, until the cows come home, until hell freezes over, until doomsday, until kingdom come; archaic for aye.
▷ANTONYMS temporarily.
2 *I was permanently hungry*: **continually**, constantly, perpetually, perennially, always, forever, ever, invariably, eternally, persistently.

permeable adjective **porous**, pervious, penetrable, spongy, absorbent, absorptive.
▷ANTONYMS impermeable, watertight.

permeate verb **1** *the delicious smell emanating from the kitchen permeated the entire flat*: **pervade**, spread through, fill, filter through, diffuse through, imbue, penetrate, pass through, percolate through, perfuse, extend throughout, be disseminated through, flow through, charge, suffuse, run through, steep, impregnate, inform, infiltrate.
2 *these resins are able to permeate partly decayed timber*: **soak through**, **penetrate**, seep through, saturate, percolate through, leach through, pass through, spread through.

permissible adjective *permissible levels of atmospheric pollution*: **permitted**, allowable, allowed, acceptable, legal, lawful, legitimate, admissible, licit, authorized, sanctioned, within accepted bounds, tolerated, tolerable, proper, all right, in order; excusable, pardonable, venial; informal legit, OK.
▷ANTONYMS forbidden, unacceptable.

permission noun *you must get permission from your manager for all absences*: **authorization**, consent, leave, authority, sanction, licence, dispensation, assent, acquiescence, agreement, approval, seal of approval, approbation, endorsement, blessing, imprimatur, clearance, acceptance, allowance, tolerance, sufferance, empowerment, freedom, liberty; informal the go-ahead, the thumbs up, the OK, the green light, say-so; rare permit.

Choose the right word **permission, authorization, consent, leave**

Permission is generally given by someone wielding power by reason of position, authority, or ownership, who does not usually intend to participate in the activity for which it is sought (*they are seeking planning permission for a supermarket on the site | he has permission to leave school early*).

Superiors within some institution or system give **authorization**, which often involves an actual delegation of authority (*authorization of credit card transactions in the UK typically takes about 3 to 5 seconds | authorization to attend courses must be obtained from the education chairman*).

Consent is typically used when what is at issue is not a difference in power, but whether someone is able or allowed to make a free choice that is informed by at least some knowledge of possible alternatives and consequences (*in English law, a woman may not be given in marriage without her consent*). *Consent*, constituting agreement, has acquired two special uses in relation to the law regarding sexual intercourse and medical procedures (*the raising or lowering of the age of consent | you should not be tested without your consent, except in cases of extreme medical emergency*). *Consent* can also be used for official permission (*the absence of planning consent*).

In legal or parliamentary contexts, **leave** denotes permission to inaugurate an official procedure (*an application for leave to appeal*). Elliptically, it is used for permission to be absent from military duty (*shore leave*) or from any job (*25 days' annual leave*).

permissive adjective *the permissive society of the 1960s*: **liberal**, broad-minded, open-minded, non-restrictive, free, free and easy, easy-going, live-and-let-live, latitudinarian, laissez-faire, libertarian, unprescriptive, unrestricted, tolerant, forbearing, indulgent, lenient; overindulgent, lax, soft.
▷ANTONYMS intolerant, strict.

permit verb (stress on the second syllable) *no company would permit an unqualified accountant to audit its books*: **allow**, let, authorize, give someone permission/authorization/leave, sanction, grant, grant someone the right, license, empower, enable, entitle, qualify; **consent to**, assent to, give one's consent/assent to, give one's blessing to, give someone/something the nod, acquiesce in, agree to, accede to, approve of, tolerate, countenance, suffer, brook, admit of; legalize, legitimatize, legitimate; informal give the go-ahead to, give the thumbs up to, OK, give the OK to, give the green light to, say the word.
▷ANTONYMS ban, forbid, prohibit.
▶ noun (stress on the first syllable) *I need to see your permit*: **authorization**, licence, pass, voucher, ticket, warrant, document, certification; passport, visa; rare triptyque, carnet, laissez-passer, firman.

permutation noun *all the possible permutations were explored*.
See **disposition** (sense 3).

pernicious adjective *a pernicious influence on society*: **harmful**, damaging, destructive, injurious, hurtful, detrimental, deleterious, dangerous, adverse, inimical, unhealthy, unfavourable, bad, evil, baleful, wicked, malign, malevolent, malignant, noxious, poisonous, cancerous, corrupting, ruinous, deadly, lethal, fatal; literary malefic, maleficent; archaic pestilent, pestilential, baneful, pestiferous.
▷ANTONYMS beneficial, benign, favourable.

pernickety adjective informal **fussy**, difficult to please, difficult, finicky, over-fastidious, fastidious, over-particular, particular, faddish, finical, dainty, punctilious, hair-splitting, exacting, demanding, critical, overcritical; informal nit-picking, choosy, picky; Brit. informal faddy; N. Amer. informal persnickety; archaic nice, overnice.
▷ANTONYMS easy-going, laid-back.

peroration noun **1** *the blazing peroration with which the speech ended*: **closing remarks**, conclusion, ending, close, final section, summation, summing-up, recapitulation, reiteration; informal recap, recapping.
2 *a perfectly dreadful hour-long peroration*: **speech**, lecture, talk, address, oration, sermon, disquisition, discourse, declamation, harangue, diatribe; informal spiel.

perpendicular adjective **1** *the shadows of the perpendicular stones lay parallel to one another*: **upright**, vertical, erect, plumb, straight (up and down), on end, standing, upended.
▷ANTONYMS horizontal.
2 *lines perpendicular to each other*: **at right angles**, at 90 degrees, square.
3 *the perpendicular hillside*: **steep**, sheer, precipitous, abrupt, bluff, vertiginous; rare scarped, acclivitous, declivitous.

perpetrate verb *right-wing elements perpetrated a series of attacks and assaults*: **commit**, carry out, perform, execute, do, effect, bring about, be guilty of, be to blame for, be responsible for, accomplish, inflict, wreak; informal pull off, pull; rare effectuate.

perpetual adjective **1** *deep caves in perpetual darkness*: **everlasting**, never-ending, eternal, permanent, unending, endless, without end, lasting, long-lasting, constant, abiding, enduring, perennial, timeless, ageless, deathless, undying, immortal; unfailing, unchanging, never-changing, changeless, unvarying, unfading, invariable, immutable, indissoluble, indestructible, imperishable; rare sempiternal, perdurable.
▷ANTONYMS transitory, temporary.
2 *the population lived in a perpetual state of fear*: **constant**, permanent, uninterrupted, continuous, unremitting, unending, unceasing, persistent, unbroken.
▷ANTONYMS intermittent.
3 *Clara could recall her mother's perpetual nagging at her father*: **interminable**, incessant, ceaseless, endless, without respite, relentless, unrelenting, persistent, frequent, continual, continuous, non-stop, never-ending, recurrent, repeated, unremitting, sustained, round-the-clock, habitual, chronic, unabating; informal eternal.

perpetuate verb *a monument to perpetuate the memory of those killed in the war*: **keep alive**, keep going, keep in existence, preserve, conserve, sustain, maintain, continue, extend, carry on, keep up, cause to continue, prolong; immortalize, commemorate, memorialize, eternalize; literary eternize.

perpetuity noun
□ **in perpetuity** *the complete archive will be preserved in perpetuity as a unified collection*: **forever**, permanently, for always, for good, for good and all, perpetually, (for) evermore, for ever and ever, for all (future) time, until the end of time, eternally, for eternity, everlastingly; N. Amer. forevermore; informal for keeps, until hell freezes over, until doomsday; archaic for aye.

perplex verb *she was perplexed by her husband's moodiness*: **puzzle**, baffle, mystify, bemuse, bewilder, confound, confuse, nonplus, disconcert, dumbfound, throw, throw/catch someone off balance, get, exercise, worry, befuddle, fuddle, addle, fog; informal flummox, be all Greek to, discombobulate, stump, bamboozle, floor, beat, faze, make someone scratch their head, fox; archaic wilder, distract, gravel, maze, pose, cause to be at a stand.

Choose the right word **perplex, puzzle, mystify, baffle**

See **puzzle**.

perplexed adjective *her perplexed expression*: **puzzled**, baffled, mystified, bemused, bewildered, confused, nonplussed, disconcerted, dumbfounded, worried, at a loss, at sea, befuddled, fuddled, addled; informal **flummoxed**, bamboozled, discombobulated, stumped, fazed, beaten; Canadian & Austral./NZ informal bushed; archaic wildered, distracted, mazed.

P

perplexing adjective **puzzling**, baffling, mystifying, mysterious, bewildering, confusing, disconcerting, worrying, unaccountable, difficult to understand, inexplicable, impenetrable, unfathomable, paradoxical, peculiar, funny, strange, weird, odd, beyond one; complex, complicated, difficult, hard, taxing, knotty, thorny, ticklish, involved, intricate, convoluted, labyrinthine, Byzantine; informal spiny, mind-bending; archaic wildering.

perplexity noun **1** *he scratched his head in perplexity*: **confusion**, bewilderment, puzzlement, bafflement, incomprehension, lack of comprehension, mystification, bemusement, befuddlement; quandary, nonplus; informal bamboozlement, discombobulation; rare disconcertion, disconcertment.
2 *the perplexities of international relations*: **complexity**, complication, intricacy, problem, difficulty, dilemma, mystery, puzzle, enigma, paradox, obscurity; obfuscation.

perquisite noun formal See **perk**[2].

per se adverb *possessing a knife was not per se an unlawful act*: **in itself**, of itself, by itself, as such, intrinsically; by its very nature, in essence, by definition, essentially.

persecute verb **1** *no one should be persecuted for their religious beliefs*: **oppress**, abuse, victimize, ill-treat, mistreat, maltreat, discriminate against, punish, inflict pain/suffering on, tyrannize, afflict, torment, torture, martyr.
2 *she complained of being persecuted by the press*: **harass**, hound, plague, badger, harry, bait, intimidate, pick on, trouble, molest, tease, pester, bother, worry, annoy, bedevil, bully, victimize, terrorize; N. Amer. devil; informal hassle, give someone a hard time, get on someone's back, make it/things hot for someone, get/stick the knife into; Austral. informal heavy; US black slang vamp on.

persecution noun **1** *victims of religious persecution*: **oppression**, victimization, maltreatment, ill-treatment, mistreatment, abuse, ill-usage, discrimination, tyranny, tyrannization, punishment, torment, torture, pogrom; informal witch hunt; N. Amer. informal red-baiting.
2 *the persecution I endured at school got worse as I got older*: **harassment**, hounding, harrying, badgering, teasing, bullying, molestation.

perseverance noun *medicine is a field which requires dedication and perseverance*: **persistence**, tenacity, determination, resolve, resolution, resoluteness, staying power, purposefulness, firmness of purpose; patience, endurance, application, diligence, sedulousness, dedication, commitment, doggedness, pertinacity, assiduity, assiduousness, steadfastness, tirelessness, indefatigability, stamina; intransigence, obstinacy; German Sitzfleisch; informal stickability; N. Amer. informal stick-to-it-iveness; archaic continuance; rare perseveration.

persevere verb *she always perseveres in spite of discouraging setbacks*: **persist**, continue, carry on, go on, keep on, keep going, not give up, struggle on, hammer away, be persistent, be determined, see/follow something through, keep at it, show determination, press on/ahead, stay with something, not take no for an answer, be tenacious, be pertinacious, be patient, stand one's ground, stand fast/firm, hold on, hold out, go the distance, stay the course, plod on, plough on, grind away, stop at nothing, leave no stone unturned; informal soldier on, hang on, plug away, peg away, stick to one's guns, stick at it, stick it out, hang in there, bash on.
▷ANTONYMS give up, stop, quit.

persist verb **1** *Corbett persisted with his questioning*: **persevere**, continue, carry on, go on, keep at it, keep on, keep going, keep it up, not give up, be persistent, be determined, see/follow something through, show determination, press on/ahead, plod on, plough on, stay with something, not take no for an answer; be tenacious, be pertinacious, insist, be patient, be diligent, stand one's ground, stand fast/firm, hold on, hold out, go the distance, stay the course, grind away, struggle on, hammer away, stop at nothing, leave no stone unturned; informal plug away, peg away, stick at it, soldier on, hang on, stick to one's guns, stick it out, hang in there, bash on.
▷ANTONYMS abandon, stop.
2 *if dry weather persists, water the lawn thoroughly*: **continue**, hold, carry on, last, keep on, keep up, remain, linger, stay, endure, survive.

persistence noun *he had risen to his present position by dint of hard work and sheer persistence*: **perseverance**, tenacity, determination, resolve, resolution, resoluteness, staying power, purposefulness, firmness of purpose, patience, endurance, application, diligence, sedulousness, dedication, commitment, doggedness, persistency, pertinacity, assiduity, assiduousness, steadfastness, tirelessness, indefatigability, stamina; intransigence, obstinacy; German Sitzfleisch; informal stickability; N. Amer. informal stick-to-it-iveness; archaic continuance; rare perseveration.

persistent adjective **1** *he's a very persistent man*: **tenacious**, persevering, determined, resolute, purposeful, dogged, single-minded, tireless, indefatigable, pertinacious, patient, diligent, assiduous, sedulous, unflagging, untiring, unwavering, insistent, importunate, relentless, unrelenting; stubborn, intransigent, obstinate, obdurate.
▷ANTONYMS irresolute.
2 *persistent rain will affect many areas*: **continuing**, constant, continual, continuous, non-stop, lasting, never-ending, steady, uninterrupted, unbroken, interminable, incessant, unceasing, endless, unending, perpetual, unremitting, unrelenting, relentless, unrelieved, sustained.
▷ANTONYMS intermittent, occasional.
3 *a persistent cough*: **chronic**, permanent, lingering, nagging, frequent, repeated, habitual.

person noun *you were probably the last person to see Glynn alive | he's an aggressive person*: **human being**, individual, man/woman, human, being, living soul, soul, mortal, creature, fellow; figure, personage; informal character, type, sort, beggar, cookie, customer, critter, bunny, fella; Brit. informal bloke, chap, bod, geezer, gent; N. Amer. informal guy, gal, dame, dude, hombre; Austral. informal bastard; informal, dated body, dog; Brit. informal, dated cove; Brit. vulgar slang sod, bugger; archaic wight.
□ **in person** *the Queen was unable to be there in person*: **physically**, in the flesh, personally, bodily, actually; oneself; Latin in propria persona; informal as large as life; archaic in one's own person.

> *Word links* **person**
>
> **homicide** killing of a person

persona noun *his brash public persona is a facade for a very vulnerable man*: **image**, face, public face, character, personality, identity, self, front, facade, mask, guise, exterior, role, part.

personable adjective *a personable young man*. See **likeable**.

personage noun *a succession of Hollywood personages*: **important person**, VIP, luminary, celebrity, celebutante, personality, name, famous name, household name, public figure, star, mogul, leading light, dignitary, notable, notability, person of note, worthy, panjandrum; person; informal celeb, somebody, big shot, big noise, big gun, hotshot, big cheese, bigwig, big fish; Brit. informal nob; N. Amer. informal big wheel, kahuna, macher, high muckamuck, high muckety-muck.

personal adjective **1** *a highly personal style*: **distinctive**, characteristic, unique, individual, one's own, particular, private, peculiar, exclusive, idiosyncratic, individualized, personalized; rare especial.
▷ANTONYMS public, general.
2 *the President made personal campaign appearances*: **in person**, in the flesh, actual, live, physical.
3 *our manager will give personal attention to your enquiry*: **individual**, particular, special, in person.
4 *I'm sick of you prying into my personal life!* **private**, confidential, one's own business, intimate, secret.
5 *I count him as a personal friend*: **intimate**, close, dear, great, bosom.
6 *they have personal knowledge of the situation*: **direct**, empirical, first-hand, immediate, experiential.
7 *how dare you make personal remarks!* **derogatory**, disparaging, belittling, insulting, critical, rude, slighting, disrespectful, offensive, pejorative.

> *Easily confused words* **personal or personnel?**
>
> Despite their similar spelling, these words are quite different in meaning. The adjective **personal** denotes things relating or belonging to an individual (*personal belongings should be clearly marked*). One's *personal life* is private; the expression generally denotes a person's emotions and relationships as distinct from their career. **Personnel**, on the other hand, is a noun denoting the staff employed by an organization (*no major salary increases for personnel are likely*).

personality noun **1** *her cheerful and vibrant personality*: **character**, nature, disposition, temperament, make-up, persona, psyche, identity.
2 *she's always had loads of personality*: **charisma**, magnetism, strength of personality, force of personality, character, powers of attraction, charm, presence, individuality, attractiveness.
3 *an official opening by a famous personality*: **celebrity**, VIP, star, superstar, celebutante, name, famous name, household name, big name, somebody, leading light, notable, personage, luminary, notability, worthy; informal celeb, televisionary.

personalize verb **1** *all these products can be personalized to the client's exact requirements*: **customize**, individualize, give a personal touch to, make distinctive, make to order.
2 *attempts to personalize God*: **personify**, humanize, anthropomorphize.

personally adverb **1** *I will deal personally with any queries*: **in person**, oneself.
2 *personally, I think he made a very sensible move*: **for my (own) part**, for myself, according to my way of thinking, to my mind, in my estimation, as far as I am concerned, in my (own) view/opinion, from my own point of view, from where I stand, from my standpoint, as I see it, if you ask me, for my money, in my book; privately.
□ **take something personally** *don't take it personally if they turn you down*: **take something as an insult**, regard something as a slight, take something amiss, take offence at, be offended by; **be upset**, be aggrieved, be affronted, take umbrage, take exception, be indignant, feel insulted, feel hurt.

personification noun *he was the very personification of British pluck and diplomacy*: **embodiment**, incarnation, epitome, quintessence, essence, type, symbol, soul, picture, model, symbolization, exemplification, exemplar, image, representation, likeness, manifestation; rare avatar.

personify verb **1** *in the poem, the oak trees are personified*: **humanize**, anthropomorphize, personalize.
2 *you personify every foreigner's image of the perfect English gentleman*: **epitomize**, embody, be the embodiment/incarnation of, typify, exemplify, represent, symbolize, stand for, give human form/shape to, body forth, incarnate, be representative of, encapsulate, manifest; rare image.

personnel noun *sales personnel*: **staff**, employees, workforce, workers, labour force, manpower, human resources, people, men and women; crew, team, force, organization; informal liveware.

> *Easily confused words* **personnel or personal?**
>
> See **personal**.

perspective noun **1** *her perspective on everything had been changing*: **outlook**, view, viewpoint, point of view, standpoint, position, stand, stance, angle, slant, attitude, frame of mind, frame of reference, approach, way of looking/thinking, vantage point, interpretation.
2 *a perspective of the whole valley*: **view**, vista, panorama, prospect, bird's-eye view, sweep, outlook, aspect; archaic lookout.

perspicacious adjective *his more perspicacious advisers recommended caution*. See **shrewd**.

perspicacity noun *Adam was surprised at the perspicacity of Mary's comments*. See **shrewdness**.

perspicuous adjective *a detailed and perspicuous explanation*. See **limpid** (sense 2).

perspiration noun **sweat**, moisture, dampness, wetness; a lather; sweating; informal a muck sweat; technical diaphoresis, hidrosis.

perspire verb **sweat**, be dripping/pouring with sweat, glow, be damp, be wet, break out in a sweat; informal be in a muck sweat; rare sudate.

persuadable adjective **easily persuaded**, amenable, adaptable, accommodating, cooperative, malleable, pliable, compliant, flexible, acquiescent, tractable, pliant, yielding, biddable, complaisant, like putty in one's hands, impressionable, manageable, manipulable, influenceable, suggestible, susceptible; rare persuasible, suasible, convincible, susceptive.

persuade verb **1** *he tried to persuade her to come with him*: **prevail on**, talk someone into, coax, convince, make, get, press someone into, induce, win someone over, bring someone round, argue someone into, pressure someone into, pressurize someone into, coerce, influence, sway, prompt, inveigle, entice, tempt, lure, cajole, wheedle someone into, get round, blarney, prod someone into, reason someone into; Law procure; informal sweet-talk, smooth-talk, soft-soap, twist someone's arm.
▷ANTONYMS dissuade, discourage, deter.
2 *shortage of money persuaded them to abandon the scheme*: **cause**, lead, move, dispose, incline, motivate, induce.

> *Choose the right word* **persuade, convince, induce**
>
> See **convince**.

persuasion noun **1** *Monica needed plenty of persuasion before she actually left*: **coaxing**, persuading, coercion, inducement, convincing, blandishment, encouragement, urging, prompting, inveiglement, temptation, cajolery, enticement, wheedling, pressure, moral pressure; informal sweet-talking, smooth-talking, soft-soaping, arm-twisting; rare suasion.
2 *varying political and religious persuasions*: **group**, grouping, sect, denomination, party, camp, side, faction, religion, cult, affiliation, school of thought, belief, creed, credo, faith, philosophy.
3 *she entertained a strong persuasion that her brother would one day return*: **belief**, opinion, conviction, faith, certainty, certitude, view.

persuasive adjective *a persuasive argument | he was so persuasive*: **convincing**, effective, cogent, compelling, potent, forceful, eloquent, impressive, weighty, influential, sound, valid, powerful, strong, effectual, efficacious, winning, telling, plausible, credible; silky, smooth-tongued, silver-tongued, slick, glib, not taking no for an answer; informal smooth-talking; rare suasive, assuasive, suasory.
▷ANTONYMS unconvincing, weak.

pert adjective **1** *a pert little hat with a feather*: **jaunty**, neat, trim, stylish, smart, spruce, perky, rakish; informal natty; N. Amer. saucy.
2 *a young girl with dark hair and a pert manner*: **impudent**, impertinent, cheeky, irreverent, forward, insolent, disrespectful, flippant, familiar, presumptuous, audacious, bold, bold as brass, brazen, cocky, out of line, shameless; informal fresh, flip, lippy, mouthy, smart-arsed; Brit. informal saucy; N. Amer. informal sassy, nervy, smart-assed; archaic malapert; rare tossy.

pertain verb **1** *developments pertaining to the economy*: **concern**, relate to, be related to, be connected with, be relevant to, have relevance to, apply to, be pertinent to, have reference to, refer to, have a bearing on, appertain to, bear on, affect, involve, cover, touch; archaic regard.
2 *the shop premises and stock and all assets pertaining to the business*: **belong to**, be a part of, be an adjunct of, go along with, be included in.
3 *salaries which are much lower than those that pertain in Western Europe*: **exist**, be the order of the day, obtain, be in effect, be the case, be prevalent, prevail, be current, be established.

pertinacious adjective *she was very pertinacious in her questions*: **determined**, tenacious, persistent, persevering, assiduous, purposeful, resolute, dogged, indefatigable, insistent, single-minded, unrelenting, relentless, implacable, uncompromising, unyielding, tireless, unshakeable, importunate, stubborn, stubborn as a mule, mulish, obstinate, obdurate, strong-willed, headstrong, inflexible, unbending, intransigent, intractable, pig-headed, bull-headed, stiff-necked, with one's toes/feet dug in, wilful, refractory, contrary, perverse; Brit. informal bloody-minded; rare indurate.
▷ANTONYMS irresolute, tentative.

pertinent adjective *she asked me a lot of very pertinent questions*: **relevant**, to the point, apposite, appropriate, suitable, fitting, fit, apt, applicable, material, germane, to the purpose, apropos; Latin ad rem; rare appurtenant.
▷ANTONYMS irrelevant, inappropriate.

pertness noun *a Liverpool-born lass renowned for pertness*: **impudence**, impertinence, cheek, cheekiness, sauciness, effrontery, irreverence, insolence, disrespect, disrespectfulness, flippancy, presumption, presumptuousness, audacity, audaciousness, boldness, brazenness, forwardness, cockiness, shamelessness; informal mouth, neck, brass neck, nerve; Brit. informal sauce; Scottish informal snash; N. Amer. informal sassiness, sass, chutzpah, a smart mouth; archaic malapertness; rare procacity.

perturb verb *David's appearance perturbed his parents*: **worry**, upset, unsettle, disturb, concern, trouble, make anxious, make uneasy, make fretful, disquiet; discompose, disconcert, discomfit, unnerve, alarm, bother, distress, dismay, gnaw at, agitate, fluster, ruffle, discountenance, exercise; informal rattle, faze; archaic pother.
▷ANTONYMS reassure.

perturbed adjective *she didn't seem perturbed at the noises around her*: **upset**, worried, unsettled, disturbed, concerned, troubled, anxious, ill at ease, uneasy, fretful, disquieted; disconcerted, discomposed, unnerved, alarmed, bothered, distressed, dismayed, apprehensive, nervous, restless, agitated, flustered, ruffled, shaken, flurried, discountenanced, uncomfortable; informal twitchy, rattled, fazed, discombobulated; N. Amer. informal antsy; rare unquiet.
▷ANTONYMS unperturbed, calm, composed.

perusal noun *I continued my perusal of the instructions*. See **reading** (sense 1).

peruse verb *as he sipped his coffee, he perused the newspaper*. See **read** (sense 1 of the verb).

pervade verb *a strong smell of floor polish pervaded the house | her whole being seemed pervaded by a dreamy languor*: **spread through**, permeate, fill, suffuse, be diffused through, diffuse through, imbue, penetrate, pass through, filter through, percolate through, infuse, perfuse, extend throughout, be disseminated through, flow through, run through; charge, steep, saturate, impregnate, inform, infiltrate, invade, affect.

pervasive adjective *a pervasive smell of staleness | ageism is pervasive in our society*: **prevalent**, penetrating, pervading, permeating, extensive, ubiquitous, omnipresent, present everywhere, rife, widespread, general, common, universal, pandemic, epidemic, endemic, inescapable, insidious; immanent; rare permeative, suffusive, permeant.

perverse adjective **1** *he is being deliberately perverse*: **awkward**, contrary, difficult, unreasonable, uncooperative, unhelpful, obstructive, disobliging, unaccommodating, troublesome, tiresome, annoying, vexatious, obstreperous, disobedient, unmanageable, uncontrollable, recalcitrant, refractory, rebellious; wilful, headstrong, self-willed, capricious, wayward, cross-grained, stubborn, obstinate, obdurate, pertinacious, mulish, pig-headed, bull-headed, intractable, intransigent, inflexible; Scottish thrawn; informal cussed; Brit. informal **bloody-minded**, bolshie, stroppy; N. Amer. informal balky; archaic froward, contumacious; rare contrarious.
▷ANTONYMS accommodating, cooperative.
2 *juries often come up with a verdict that is manifestly perverse*: **illogical**, irrational, unreasonable, contradictory, wrong, wrong-headed, incorrect, irregular, inappropriate, unorthodox.
▷ANTONYMS reasonable.
3 *an evil life dedicated to perverse pleasure*: **perverted**, depraved, unnatural, abnormal, deviant, degenerate, immoral, warped, twisted, corrupt; wicked, base, evil; informal kinky, sick, pervy, sicko.

perversion noun **1** *a twisted perversion of the truth*: **distortion**, misrepresentation, falsification, travesty, misinterpretation, misconstruction, twisting, corruption, subversion, misuse, misapplication, debasement.
2 *his book revolutionized ideas about sexual perversion*: **deviance**, deviancy, deviation; unnaturalness, corruption, depravity, degeneracy, debauchery, vice, wickedness, immorality, aberration, abnormality, perversity, irregularity; informal kinkiness.

perversity noun **1** *some streak of perversity made her refuse his offer*: **contrariness**, perverseness, awkwardness, unreasonableness, difficultness, waywardness, capriciousness, wilfulness, refractoriness, stubbornness, obstinacy, obduracy, mulishness, pig-headedness; informal cussedness;

Brit. informal **bloody-mindedness**; archaic frowardness.
2 *the perversity of the decision*: **unreasonableness**, irrationality, illogicality, wrong-headedness, irregularity, inappropriateness.

pervert verb (stress on the second syllable) **1** *people who attempt to pervert the rules for their own gain*: **distort**, warp, corrupt, subvert, twist, bend, abuse, divert, deflect, misapply, misuse, misrepresent, misinterpret, misconstrue, falsify, garble.
2 *potentially great men can be perverted and destroyed by power*: **corrupt**, lead astray, deprave, make degenerate, debauch, debase, warp, vitiate, pollute, poison, contaminate; archaic demoralize.
▸ noun (stress on the first syllable) *a sexual pervert*: **deviant**, degenerate, debauchee, perverted person, depraved person; informal perv, perve, dirty old man, sicko, weirdo.

perverted adjective *it's impossible to understand the perverted mentality of someone who could do such a thing*: **unnatural**, **deviant**, warped, corrupt, twisted, abnormal, unhealthy, depraved, perverse, aberrant, distorted, immoral, corrupted, debauched, debased, degenerate, sadistic, evil, wicked, vile, amoral, rotten, wrong, bad; informal sick, kinky, pervy, sicko.

pessimism noun *formerly he had been prone to pessimism, full of gloomy predictions about the future*: **defeatism**, negative thinking, negativity, expecting the worst, doom and gloom, gloom, gloominess; **hopelessness**, lack of hope, cynicism, fatalism, depression, despair, melancholy, despondency, dejection, angst, distrust, doubt; German Weltschmerz; informal looking on the black side.

pessimist noun *pessimists attempted to paint a picture of a nation in decline*: **defeatist**, fatalist, alarmist, prophet of doom, cynic, doomsayer, doomster, gloom-monger, doom-monger, doomwatcher, Cassandra; sceptic, doubter, doubting Thomas; misery, killjoy, worrier, Job's comforter; informal doom and gloom merchant, wet blanket; N. Amer. informal gloomy Gus.
▷ANTONYMS optimist.

pessimistic adjective *a pessimistic outlook on life*: **gloomy**, negative, defeatist, downbeat, gloom-ridden, cynical, bleak, fatalistic, dark, black, despairing, despondent, depressed, dejected, demoralized, hopeless, melancholy, glum, lugubrious, suspicious, distrustful, doubting, alarmist; informal given to looking on the black side.
▷ANTONYMS optimistic, hopeful, cheerful.

pest noun *that child is a real pest*. See **nuisance**.

pester verb *I've been pestered by reporters for days*: **badger**, hound, annoy, bother, harass, trouble, plague, irritate, irk, chivvy, keep after; persecute, torment, molest, bedevil, besiege, harry, worry, beleaguer, nag, dun, importune; informal hassle, bug, aggravate, give someone a hard time, get on someone's nerves, drive round the bend, drive up the wall, get in someone's hair, get up someone's nose, get at, get on someone's back; N. English mither; N. Amer. informal ride, devil.

pestilence noun *Londoners fled in time of pestilence*: **plague**, bubonic plague, the Black Death; disease, contagious disease, contagion, infection, sickness, epidemic, pandemic; archaic the pest, lues.

pestilential adjective **1** *pestilential fever*: **plague-like**, contagious, communicable, epidemic, pestilent, dangerous, injurious, harmful, destructive, virulent, pernicious; toxic, venomous; malign, fatal, deadly; informal catching; literary pestiferous.
2 *what a pestilential man!* **annoying**, irritating, infuriating, exasperating, maddening, troublesome, bothersome, tiresome, irksome, vexing, vexatious; informal aggravating, pesky, infernal, pestiferous, plaguy, pestilent.

pet[1] noun *the others teased him and called him teacher's pet*: **favourite**, darling, the apple of one's eye, idol; Brit. informal blue-eyed boy/girl; N. Amer. informal fair-haired boy/girl.
▸ adjective **1** *a pet lamb*: **tame**, domesticated, domestic, tamed; Brit. house-trained; N. Amer. housebroken.
2 *his pet theory*: **favourite**, favoured, cherished, prized, dear to one's heart, preferred, particular, special, chosen, personal, treasured, precious.
□ **pet name affectionate name**, term of endearment, endearment, nickname, diminutive; rare hypocorism, hypocoristic.
▸ verb **1** *the cats came to be petted*: **stroke**, caress, fondle, pat.
2 *an only child, she had always been petted by her parents*: **pamper**, spoil, mollycoddle, coddle, cosset, baby, indulge, overindulge, dote on, wrap in cotton wool; archaic cocker.
3 *she watched the couples petting in their cars*: **kiss and cuddle**, kiss, cuddle, embrace, caress; informal canoodle, neck, smooch, bill and coo; Brit. informal snog; N. Amer. informal make out, get it on, play kissy-face; informal, dated spoon.

pet[2] noun *Mum's in a pet*: **bad mood**, mood, bad temper, temper, sulk, fit of the sulks, ill temper, ill humour, fit of pique, huff, tantrum; informal grump; Brit. informal paddy, strop; N. Amer. informal blowout, hissy fit; Brit. informal, dated bate, wax; archaic paddywhack, miff, the pouts.

peter verb
□ **peter out** *the economic recovery is in danger of petering out*. See **vanish** (sense 2).

petite adjective *she was dark, petite, and sophisticated*: **small**, dainty, diminutive, slight, little, tiny, elfin, delicate, small-boned; Scottish wee; informal pint-sized; Brit. informal dinky.

petition noun **1** *about 7,000 people signed a petition objecting to the scheme*: **appeal**, round robin, list of signatures/protesters.
2 *a steady stream of petitions to Allah were audible*: **entreaty**, supplication, plea, prayer, appeal, request, application, invocation, suit; archaic orison; rare imploration.
▸ verb *human rights activists petitioned the king to release the hunger strikers*: **appeal to**, request, ask, call on, entreat, beg, implore, beseech, plead with, make a plea to, pray, apply to, solicit, press, urge, adjure, present one's suit to, importune; rare obsecrate.

petrified adjective **1** *she looked absolutely petrified*: **terrified**, terror-stricken, terror-struck, horrified, horror-stricken, horror-struck, scared/frightened out of one's wits, scared witless, scared/frightened to death, aghast, appalled; paralysed, stunned, stupefied, transfixed, benumbed, frozen.
2 *the petrified remains of prehistoric animals*: ossified, fossilized; rare lapidified.

petrify verb *the thought of speaking in public petrified her*: **terrify**, horrify, frighten, scare, scare to death, scare someone out of their wits, scare witless, scare the living daylights out of, frighten the life out of, strike terror into, fill with fear, put the fear of God into, make someone's blood run cold, chill someone's blood, panic, throw into a panic, alarm, appal; paralyse, stun, stupefy, transfix; informal scare the pants off; Brit. informal throw into a blue funk, put the wind up; Irish informal scare the bejesus out of; archaic affright.

petrol noun **fuel**; unleaded, superunleaded, diesel; N. Amer. gasoline, gas; informal juice.

petticoat noun **slip**, underskirt, half-slip, underslip, undergarment; historical crinoline, farthing, hoop petticoat; archaic kirtle.

petty adjective **1** *a maze of petty regulations*: **trivial**, trifling, minor, small, slight, unimportant, insignificant, inessential, inconsequential, inconsiderable, negligible, paltry, footling, fiddling, niggling, pettifogging, nugatory, of little account; informal piffling, piddling, penny-ante; Brit. informal twopenny-halfpenny; N. Amer. informal nickel-and-dime, picayune; N. Amer. vulgar slang chickenshit.
▷ANTONYMS important, serious, major.
2 *they took other forms of revenge which were no less petty*: **small-minded**, narrow-minded, mean, ungenerous, grudging, shabby, spiteful.
▷ANTONYMS magnanimous, generous.

> *Word toolkit* **petty**
>
> See **inconsequential**.

petulance noun **peevishness**, bad temper, ill temper, pettishness, pique, impatience, irritability, moodiness, sulkiness, snappishness, touchiness, waspishness, irascibility, tetchiness, testiness, querulousness, fractiousness, cantankerousness, grumpiness, grouchiness, crabbiness, ill humour, spleen; sullenness, surliness, sourness, churlishness, ungraciousness; N. English mardiness; informal whinginess; N. Amer. informal crankiness, a sore head.

petulant adjective *he sounded as petulant as a spoiled child*. See **querulous**.

phantasmagorical adjective *phantasmagorical figures and landscapes*. See **dreamlike**.

phantom noun **1** *a phantom who haunts lonely roads*: **ghost**, apparition, spirit, spectre, wraith, shadow; Scottish & Irish bodach; W. Indian duppy; informal spook; literary phantasm, shade, revenant, wight; rare eidolon, manes.
2 *he tried to clear the phantoms from his head and grasp reality*: **figment of the imagination**, delusion, hallucination, illusion, chimera, vision, fantasy, mirage; rare phantasm.

Pharisaic adjective *a mean-spirited, Pharisaic bunch of suburbanites*: **self-righteous**, sanctimonious, Pharisaical, holier-than-thou, pietistic, moralizing, priggish, self-satisfied, smug, hypocritical, insincere, Pecksniffian, canting; Scottish unco guid; informal preachy, goody-goody.

phase noun **1** *the final phase of the election campaign*: **stage**, period, chapter, episode, part, step, point, time, juncture.
2 *he's going through a difficult phase*: **period**, stage, time, spell; Brit. informal patch.
3 *the phases of the moon*: **aspect**, shape, form, appearance, state, condition.
▸ verb
□ **phase something in introduce gradually**, incorporate by stages, begin using, ease in, start using.
□ **phase something out eliminate gradually**, withdraw/remove/replace gradually, discontinue, get rid of by stages, stop using, ease off, run down, wind down, wind up, deactivate, finish, end.

phenomenal adjective *sales growth has been nothing short of phenomenal*: **exceptional**, extraordinary, remarkable, outstanding, amazing, astonishing, astounding, stunning, staggering, marvellous, magnificent, wonderful, sensational, breathtaking, miraculous, singular; incredible, unbelievable, inconceivable, unimaginable, uncommon, unheard of; unique, unparalleled, unprecedented, unusual, unusually good, too good

to be true, superlative, prodigious, surpassing, rare; informal fantastic, fabulous, stupendous, out of this world, terrific, tremendous, brilliant, mind-boggling, mind-blowing, awesome, stellar; literary wondrous.
▷ANTONYMS ordinary, usual, run-of-the-mill.

phenomenon noun **1** *war was not a rare phenomenon in the 18th century*: **occurrence**, event, happening, fact, situation, circumstance, experience, case, incident, episode, sight, appearance, thing.
2 *the band was a pop phenomenon*: **marvel**, sensation, wonder, prodigy, miracle, rarity, nonpareil, curiosity, spectacle; informal something else, something to write home about, something to shout about; N. Amer. informal standout; rare oner.

philander verb *he had no time or inclination to philander*: **womanize**, have affairs/an affair, flirt, trifle/toy/dally with someone's affections; informal play around, carry on, play the field, sleep around; N. Amer. informal fool around; vulgar slang screw around; rare be a carpet knight, coquet.

philanderer noun *everyone warned me he was a philanderer*: **womanizer**, Casanova, Don Juan, Lothario, flirt, ladies' man, playboy, Romeo, seducer, rake, roué, libertine, debauchee; informal stud, skirt-chaser, ladykiller, wolf; informal, dated gay dog.

philanthropic adjective *a philanthropic desire to improve the lot of other people | a philanthropic millionaire*: **charitable**, generous, benevolent, humanitarian, public-spirited, altruistic, socially concerned, magnanimous, munificent, open-handed, bountiful, liberal, ungrudging, unstinting, generous to a fault, beneficent, benignant, caring, compassionate, solicitous, unselfish, selfless, humane, kind, kind-hearted, big-hearted; literary bounteous; rare eleemosynary.
▷ANTONYMS selfish, mean, miserly.

philanthropist noun *the trust was founded by an American philanthropist*: **benefactor**, benefactress, humanitarian, patron, patroness, donor, contributor, giver, sponsor, backer, helper, altruist, good Samaritan; do-gooder, Lady Bountiful; archaic almsgiver; rare philanthrope, Maecenas.

philanthropy noun *he acquired a considerable fortune and was noted for his philanthropy*: **benevolence**, generosity, humanitarianism, public-spiritedness, altruism, social conscience, social concern, charity, charitableness, brotherly love, fellow feeling, magnanimity, munificence, liberality, largesse, open-handedness, bountifulness, beneficence, benignity, unselfishness, selflessness, humanity, kindness, kind-heartedness, big-heartedness, compassion, humaneness; patronage, sponsorship, backing, help; historical almsgiving; literary bounty, bounteousness.

philippic noun *Viscount Castlereagh was the butt of Shelley's philippic*. See **tirade**.

philistine noun *she was no philistine, but an artist herself*: **lowbrow**, anti-intellectual, materialist, bourgeois; **boor**, ignoramus, lout, oaf, barbarian, primitive, savage, brute, yahoo, vulgarian.
▶ adjective *a philistine effort to destroy culture*: **crass**, **tasteless**, uncultured, uncultivated, uneducated, untutored, unenlightened, unread, commercial, materialist, bourgeois, unsophisticated, unrefined; boorish, barbarian, barbarous, barbaric, primitive, savage, brutish, loutish, oafish, uncivilized, uncouth, vulgar, coarse, rough.

philosopher noun **thinker**, theorist, theorizer, theoretician, philosophizer, metaphysicist, metaphysician, epistemologist, dialectician, logician; speculator, hypothesizer, seeker after truth, dreamer; scholar, intellect, intellectual, learned person, sage, wise man, Solomon, guru, pundit.

philosophical adjective **1** *a philosophical question*: **theoretical**, **analytical**, rational, metaphysical, logical, reasoned, esoteric, scholarly, erudite.
2 *in a philosophical mood*: **thoughtful**, thinking, reflective, pensive, meditative, musing, contemplative, introspective, prayerful, cogitative, ruminative, brooding, broody, serious, studious, solemn, dreamy, dreaming; rare ruminant.
▷ANTONYMS active, practical.
3 *training officers have learnt to be philosophical about such mishaps*: **calm**, composed, cool, collected, {cool, calm, and collected}, self-possessed, serene, tranquil, placid, stoical, impassive, sober, dispassionate, detached, unemotional, phlegmatic, unperturbed, imperturbable, equable, unruffled, patient, forbearing, long-suffering, tolerant, accommodating, indulgent, easy-going, even-tempered, restrained, fatalistic, unexcitable, resigned, rational, logical, realistic, practical; informal unflappable.
▷ANTONYMS emotional, upset.

philosophize verb *he paused for a while to philosophize on racial equality*: **theorize**, moralize, sermonize, pontificate, preach.

philosophy noun **1** *a lecturer in philosophy*: **thinking**, **reasoning**, thought, wisdom, knowledge.
2 *I'd like to see your philosophy in action*: **beliefs**, credo, faith, convictions, ideology, ideas, thinking, notions, theories, doctrine, tenets, values, principles, ethics, attitude, line, view, viewpoint, outlook, world view, school of thought; German Weltanschauung.

phlegm noun **1 mucus**, catarrh, mucous secretion.
2 *British phlegm and perseverance carried them through many difficult situations*: **self-control**, calmness, calm, coolness, composure, sangfroid, level-headedness; **equanimity**, serenity, tranquillity, placidity, placidness, impassivity, self-possession, self-confidence, self-assurance, stolidity, stolidness, imperturbability, impassiveness, dispassionateness; informal cool, unflappability.

phlegmatic adjective *a phlegmatic attitude to every crisis*. See **imperturbable**.

phobia noun **abnormal fear**, irrational fear, obsessive fear, fear, dread, horror, terror, dislike, hatred, loathing, detestation, distaste, aversion, antipathy, revulsion, repulsion; spectre, bugbear, bogey, nightmare, bête noire; complex, fixation, preoccupation, idée fixe, mania, neurosis, anxiety, obsession; informal thing, hang-up.

phone noun **1** *she spent hours on the phone*: **telephone**, mobile phone, mobile, cellphone, car phone, radio-telephone, cordless phone, videophone, extension; N. Amer. speakerphone; Brit. informal blower; Brit. rhyming slang dog and bone.
2 *pick up the phone and dial 999*: **handset**, earpiece, receiver.
3 *give me a phone sometime*: **phone call**, telephone call, call, ring; informal buzz; Brit. informal tinkle, bell.
▶ verb *maybe I should phone the police*: **telephone**, call, call up, give someone a call/ring, ring, ring up, get someone on the phone, get on the phone to, get, reach, dial, make/place a call (to); informal buzz, give someone a buzz; Brit. informal bell, give someone a bell/tinkle, get on the blower to; N. Amer. informal get someone on the horn.

phoney adjective *he gave a phoney address*: **bogus**, not genuine, sham, false, fake, fraudulent, forged, feigned, counterfeit, so-called, spurious, pseudo; imitation, man-made, mock, ersatz, artificial, synthetic, manufactured, simulated, reproduction, replica, facsimile, dummy, model, toy; make-believe, pretended, contrived, affected, insincere; informal pretend, put-on; Brit. informal, dated cod.
▷ANTONYMS authentic, genuine.
▶ noun **1** *the doctor's a phoney*: **impostor**, sham, fake, fraud, mountebank, quack, cheat, swindler, fraudster, confidence trickster, defrauder, hoaxer, bluffer, pretender, masquerader, charlatan, rogue, scoundrel; informal con man, con artist; dated confidence man.
2 *the diamond's a phoney*: **counterfeit**, fake, forgery, sham, hoax, imitation, copy, reproduction, replica, facsimile, dummy, model, toy.

photocopy noun *he sent me a photocopy of the article*: **reproduction**, copy, mimeograph, mimeo, facsimile, fax, duplicate; trademark Xerox, photostat.
▶ verb *you can photocopy the entry form*: **copy**, mimeograph, mimeo, xerox, photostat, fax, duplicate, reproduce, make a Xerox of.

photograph noun *a photograph of her father*: **picture**, photo, shot, snap, snapshot, likeness, image, portrait, study, print, slide, transparency, negative, positive, plate, film, bromide, frame, exposure, still, proof, enlargement; Brit. enprint.
▶ verb *the Princess was photographed leaving the castle*: **take someone's picture/photo**, take/get a picture of, take/get a snapshot/snap of, take, snap, shoot, take/get a shot of, take a likeness of, record, film, capture/record on film/celluloid.

photographer noun lensman, paparazzo, documentarian; cameraman; informal snapper; N. Amer. informal shutterbug; rare photographist.

photographic adjective **1** *a photographic display*: **in photographs**, pictorial, graphic; cinematic, filmic.
2 *a photographic memory*: **detailed**, graphic, exact, precise, accurate, minute, faithful, lifelike, vivid, realistic, naturalistic, cinematic, filmic.

phrase noun *the man who coined the phrase 'desktop publishing'*: **expression**, group of words, word group, construction, clause, locution, wording, term, turn of phrase, idiom, idiomatic expression, set phrase, phrasal idiom, phrasal verb; remark, comment, saying, utterance, witticism, tag; quotation, quote, citation; line, sentence.
▶ verb *how could I phrase the question?* **express**, put into words, put, word, style, formulate, couch, frame, set forth, utter, say, tell, articulate, verbalize, communicate, convey, get/put across.

phraseology noun **wording**, choice of words, phrasing, usage, idiom, diction, parlance, words, language, vocabulary, terminology; jargon, patter, cant, -speak, dialect, vernacular, argot, patois, style, way of speaking/writing, manner of speaking/writing, style of speech/writing, mode of speech/writing; French façon de parler; informal lingo; rare idiolect.

physical adjective **1** *mental and physical well-being*: **bodily**, corporeal, corporal, fleshly, in the flesh; rare somatic.
▷ANTONYMS mental.
2 *hard physical work*: **manual**, labouring, blue-collar.
▷ANTONYMS clerical; intellectual.
3 *our spiritual relationship affects our physical relationship*: **earthly**, worldly, terrestrial, earthbound, non-spiritual, unspiritual, material; carnal, fleshly, sensual; mortal, human, temporal; brutish, bestial, animal, base, sordid; secular, lay, mundane.
▷ANTONYMS spiritual.
4 *everything physical in the universe*: **material**, substantial, solid, concrete, tangible, palpable, visible, real, actual.
▷ANTONYMS abstract, intangible.

physician noun **doctor**, doctor of medicine, MD, medical practitioner, medical man/woman/person; Navy surgeon; informal doc, medic, medico, quack; archaic leech, sawbones.

physiognomy noun *his physiognomy was European*. See **countenance** (sense 1 of the noun).

physique noun **body**, build, figure, frame, anatomy, constitution, shape, form, proportions, (physical) make-up, physical/body structure, physical development, muscles, musculature, skeleton, flesh; informal vital statistics, bod, carcass, chassis; rare soma.

pick verb **1** *he lives on a fruit farm and helps to pick apples*: **harvest**, gather (in), collect, take in, pluck, pull, dig, crop, reap, bring home; literary glean, garner, cull.
2 *pick the time that suits you best*: **choose**, select, pick out, single out, include, hand-pick, decide on, settle on, fix on; sift out, sort out, take, prefer, favour, opt for, plump for, vote for, elect, name, nominate, adopt, designate, assign, appoint, allot, identify, specify, mention, cite.
▷ANTONYMS reject, discard.
3 *Beth only **picked at** her food*: **nibble**, peck, eat listlessly, toy with, play with, take very small bites from, push one's food around (on) one's plate, eat like a bird, show no appetite for, eat sparingly of.
4 *people were singing and picking guitars*: **strum**, twang, thrum, pluck, finger.
5 *he had taught them how to pick a lock*: **force open**, break open, prise open, open without a key, break into; informal jemmy, crack.
6 *she was trying to pick a fight with him*: **provoke**, start, cause, incite, invite, foment, stir up, whip up, encourage, kindle, instigate, excite, prompt, bring about.
□ **pick holes in** *the judge picked holes in the prosecution's case*: **find fault with**, quarrel with, fault, criticize, argue with/against, take exception to, attack, take issue with, find lacking, impugn, contradict, dispute, rebut, complain about, cavil at, carp at, object to, be hostile to; informal knock; formal gainsay; rare controvert.
□ **pick someone/something off** *the soldiers were picked off by a sniper*: **shoot (down)**, gun down, fire at, hit, put a bullet in; fell, bring down, take out, kill, bag, wound, injure; informal pot, zap, plug; literary slay.
□ **pick on** *why don't you pick on somebody else?* **bully**, victimize, tyrannize, torment, persecute; criticize, grumble at, discriminate against; badger, bait, goad, tease; informal get at, have it in for, have a down on, be down on, needle.
□ **pick something out 1** *it's impossible to pick out any single painting for praise*: **choose**, select, pick, single out, hand-pick, decide on, settle on, fix on; sift out, sort out, take, prefer, favour, opt for, plump for, vote for, elect, name, nominate, adopt, designate, assign, appoint, allot, identify, specify, mention, cite. **2** *it was difficult to pick out anything in the torrential rain*: **see**, discern, spot, distinguish, perceive, make out, detect, notice, observe, recognize, identify, catch sight of, glimpse, discover; literary espy, behold, descry.
□ **pick up 1** *the Japanese economy will soon pick up again*: **improve**, get better, recover, mend, be on the road to recovery, rally, make a comeback, bounce back, perk up, look up, take a turn for the better, turn the/a corner, be given/take on a new lease of life, be on the mend, develop, make headway, progress, make progress, advance. **2** *the wind began to pick up*: **get stronger**, strengthen, become more powerful, blow up.
□ **pick someone/something up** *bend at the knees to pick up a bulky object*: **lift**, take up, raise, hoist, scoop up, gather up, seize, snatch up, grab.
□ **pick someone up 1** *be sure to pick up Kirsty from school*: **fetch**, **collect**, go to get, go/come and get, call for, go/come for; give someone a lift, give someone a ride. **2** informal *he was picked up by the police for questioning*: **arrest**, apprehend, detain, take into custody, take prisoner, seize, capture, catch, take in; informal collar, nab, run/pull in, nick, pinch, bust, nail, do, feel someone's collar. **3** informal *he thought of going to a nightclub and picking up a girl*: strike up a casual acquaintance/relationship with, take up with; make advances to; informal get off with, pull, cop off with.
□ **pick something up 1** *not the most obvious place to pick up a bargain*: **find**, discover, locate, come across, stumble across, happen on, chance on, unearth, obtain, come by, come to have, get, receive, procure; secure, take/get possession of, acquire; purchase, buy; informal get hold of, get/lay one's hands on, get one's mitts on, bag, land, net. **2** *he picked up the story in the 1950s*: **begin again**, begin, take up, start again, start, resume, recommence, carry on, go on, continue. **3** *Georgiana began picking up Spanish*: **learn**, get to know, acquire (a knowledge of), acquire skill in, become competent/proficient in, master; digest, imbibe, assimilate, absorb, take in; informal get the hang of. **4** *she has picked up a virus*: **catch**, contract, get, become infected with, become ill with, go/come down with. **5** *he was full of gossip picked up from the ships he visited*: **hear**, hear tell, find out, get to know, get wind of, be informed of, be told, learn, be made aware of, be given to understand; glean, discern, become conscious/aware of, observe, notice, perceive. **6** *we've picked up a distress signal*: **receive**, detect, get, hear.
□ **pick up the tab** informal *the company picked up the tab for the meal | we are picking up the tab for their externalities in the form of disease*: **pay**, pay up, pay out, pay the bill, settle up; bail someone out; informal foot the bill, cough up, fork out, shell out, come across, chip in; Brit. informal stump up; N. Amer. informal ante up, pony up, pick up the check.
▸ noun **1** *please take your pick*: **choice**, selection, option, decision; preference, favourite.
2 *the pick of the crop*: **best**, finest, top, choice, choicest, prime, cream, flower, prize, treasure, pearl, gem, jewel, the jewel in the crown, the crème de la crème, elite, elect; informal the tops.

picket noun **1** *forty pickets were arrested*: **striker**, **demonstrator**, protester, objector, picketer; strike picket, flying picket.
2 *they decided to organize a picket*: **demonstration**, picket line, blockade, boycott; picketing, secondary picketing.
3 *a glider can be secured by tying it down with pickets*: **stake**, **peg**, post, paling; upright, stanchion, pier, piling, palisade.
▸ verb *over 200 people picketed the factory*: **demonstrate at**, form a picket at, man the picket line at, launch a demonstration at, protest at, form a protest group at; blockade, isolate, surround, cordon off.

pickle noun **1** *cheese and pickle sandwiches*: **relish**, chutney, chow chow, piccalilli, sauerkraut; Indian achar; Japanese tsukemono.
2 *steep the vegetables in pickle*: **marinade**, brine, vinegar.
3 informal *they got into an awful pickle*: **plight**, predicament, mess, difficulty, trouble, crisis, dire/desperate straits, ticklish/tricky situation, problem, quandary, dilemma; informal tight corner, tight spot, jam, fix, stew, scrape, bind, hole, hot water, pretty/fine kettle of fish; Brit. informal spot of bother.
▸ verb *the olives are ready for pickling*: **preserve**, souse, marinate, conserve; bottle, tin, can, pot.

pick-me-up noun **1** *we have grown accustomed to using tea or coffee as a pick-me-up*: **tonic**, restorative, energizer, stimulant, antidepressant, refresher; informal pep pill, upper, reviver, bracer; Medicine analeptic, roborant.
2 *his winning goal was a perfect pick-me-up*: **boost**, boost to the spirits, fillip, uplift, reviver, stimulant, stimulus, invigoration; informal shot in the arm.

pickpocket noun **thief**, petty thief, sneak thief; bag-snatcher, purse-snatcher; archaic cutpurse, pickpurse, pocket-picker, purse-picker, finger, dipper, reefer.

pickup noun **1** *David brought the wardrobe home in his pickup*: pickup truck, utility vehicle/truck; monster truck; S. African bakkie; Austral./NZ informal ute.
2 *a pickup in the housing market*: **improvement**, recovery, revival, upturn, upswing, rally, comeback, resurgence, renewal, reinvigoration, advancement, betterment; a turn for the better.
▷ANTONYMS slump, downturn.

picnic noun **1** *a picnic on the beach*: **outdoor meal**, alfresco meal, barbecue; garden party; informal barbie; French fête champêtre, déjeuner sur l'herbe; N. Amer. clambake, cookout, burgoo; NZ hangi; S. African braaivleis.
2 informal *diving in the North Sea has never been a picnic*: **easy task**, easy job, child's play, five-finger exercise, gift, walkover, nothing, sinecure, gravy train; informal doddle, walk in the park, piece of cake, money for old rope, money for jam, cinch, breeze, sitter, kids' stuff, cushy job/number, doss, cakewalk, pushover; N. Amer. informal duck soup, snap; Austral./NZ informal bludge, snack; S. African informal a piece of old tackie; Brit. vulgar slang a piece of piss; dated snip.

pictorial adjective *a pictorial history of Gateshead*: **illustrated**, with illustrations, with pictures, with drawings, with sketches; in pictures, in picture form, in photographs, photographic, graphic; representational, depictive, illustrative, drawn.

picture noun **1** *one of his pictures stood on an easel in the centre of the room*: **painting**, **drawing**, sketch, print, canvas, delineation, cartoon, portrait, portrayal, illustration, artwork, depiction, likeness, representation, image, icon.
2 *I would not let the photographer take the picture*: **photograph**, photo, shot, snap, snapshot, image, portrait, study; print, slide, transparency, negative, positive, plate, film, bromide, frame, exposure, still, proof, enlargement; Brit. enprint.
3 *they have a picture of the sort of person the child should be*: **concept**, idea, impression, mental picture, view, (mental) image, vision, visualization, notion, theory, abstraction.
4 *the picture of health*: **personification**, embodiment, epitome, essence, perfect example, soul, model; rare exemplar, archetype, quintessence.
5 *a picture starring Robert De Niro*: **film**, movie, feature film; Brit. cinema film; N. Amer. motion picture; informal flick; dated moving picture.
6 (**the pictures**) *Julie took me to the pictures on Saturday*: **the cinema**, the movies, the silver screen, the big screen; N. Amer. a motion picture house; informal the flicks.
□ **get the picture** *she got the picture and rubbed her hands in anticipation*: **understand the situation**, work out what's going on, see the light, see daylight, get the point; fathom, grasp, understand, follow, see, take in, realize, perceive, apprehend; informal understand/see what's what, catch on, latch on, get the drift, get the message, get it.
□ **put someone in the picture** *the museums all help to put the visitor in the picture* **inform**, fill in, give details to, explain the situation to, give information to, explain the circumstances to, describe the state of affairs to, bring up to date, update, brief, keep posted; informal clue in, bring up to speed.

▸ verb 1 *this child was pictured at a feeding centre*: **photograph**, take/get a photograph/photo of, take someone's picture/photo, take/get a picture of, take/get a snapshot/snap of, take, snap, shoot, take/get a shot of; record, film, capture/record on film/celluloid.
2 *in the drawing they were pictured against a snowy background*: **paint**, **draw**, paint a picture of, sketch, depict, delineate, portray, catch (a likeness of), show, illustrate, reproduce, render, represent.
3 *Anne still pictured Richard as he had been*: **visualize**, see in one's mind, see in one's mind's eye, conjure up a picture of, conjure up an image of, imagine, conceive, call to mind, image, see, evoke; fantasize about, dream about; rare envision.

picturesque adjective 1 *a picturesque maze of narrow streets*: **attractive**, **pretty**, beautiful, lovely, scenic, charming, quaint, pleasing, delightful, romantic.
▷ANTONYMS ugly, drab.
2 *a picturesque description*: **vivid**, graphic, colourful, impressive, striking.
▷ANTONYMS dull.

Word toolkit **picturesque**

See **graphic**.

piddling adjective informal *a piddling little incident | they were bought for piddling sums*. See **trivial** (sense 1).

pie noun **pastry**, tart, tartlet, quiche, pasty, patty, turnover.
□ **pie in the sky** informal *their dreams of travel are pie in the sky*: **false hope**, illusion, delusion, unrealizable dream, fantasy, pipe dream, daydream, reverie, mirage, castle in the air, castle in Spain.

piebald adjective **black and white**, brown and white, pied, skewbald; dappled, brindled, brindle, spotted, marked, mottled, speckled, flecked, patchy, blotchy, blotched, variegated, multicoloured, multicolour, particoloured, tabby; N. Amer. pinto; rare marled, jaspé.

piece noun 1 *a piece of cheese | a piece of wood*: **bit**, section, slice, chunk, segment, lump, hunk; wedge, slab, knob, block, cake, bar, tablet, brick, cube, stick, length; offcut, sample, particle, fragment, flake, sliver, splinter, wafer, chip, crumb, grain, speck, scrap, remnant, shred, shard, snippet, mite; mouthful, morsel; Brit. informal wodge.
2 *his ability to take a clock to pieces*: **component**, part, bit, section, segment, constituent, element; unit, module.
3 *a piece of furniture | a vital piece of evidence*: **example**, specimen, sample, instance, illustration, occurrence, case.
4 *he gets $16 million plus a piece of the profit*: **share**, slice, portion, quota, part, bit, percentage, amount, quantity, ration, fraction, division, subdivision; allocation, allotment, measure, apportionment; informal cut, whack, rake-off; rare quantum, moiety.
5 *one of the finest pieces is a Tuscan vase | a piece of music*: **work of art**, work; musical work, composition, creation, production, opus.
6 *the reporter who wrote the piece*: **article**, item, story, report, essay, study, review, composition, paper, column.
7 *the pieces on a chess board*: **token**, counter, man, disc, chip, marker.
□ **come/fall to pieces** *one large transport came to pieces in space | it splintered loudly and fell to pieces under his weight*: **break up**, break, break open/apart, shatter, splinter, fracture, burst apart, explode, blow apart, implode; disintegrate, fall apart, collapse, break down, tumble down; smash, smash to smithereens; informal bust; technical spall; rare shiver.
□ **give a piece of one's mind to** *I'm going to confront my brother and give him a piece of my mind*: **reprimand**, rebuke, scold, admonish, reprove, upbraid, chastise, chide, censure, castigate, lambaste, berate, lecture, criticize, take to task, read the Riot Act to, haul over the coals; informal tell off, give someone a telling-off, dress down, give someone a dressing-down, bawl out, pitch into, lay into, lace into, blow up at, give someone an earful, give someone a roasting, give someone a rocket, give someone a rollicking; Brit. informal have a go at, carpet, tear someone off a strip, give someone what for, let someone have it; N. Amer. informal chew out, ream out; Brit. vulgar slang bollock, give someone a bollocking.
□ **go/fall to pieces** *he went to pieces when his wife died*: **have a (mental/nervous) breakdown**, break down, go out of one's mind, crack, snap, lose control, lose one's head, fall apart; informal crack up, come/fall apart at the seams, disintegrate, freak, freak out, get in a stew; Brit. informal go into a (flat) spin.
□ **in one piece** 1 *I checked my camera to see if it was still in one piece*: **unbroken**, entire, whole, intact, undamaged, unharmed, unmarked, untouched, unspoilt. 2 *I'll bring her back in one piece*: **unhurt**, uninjured, unscathed, safe, safe and sound.
□ **in pieces** 1 *the dish lay in pieces on the floor*: **broken**, in bits, shattered, smashed, in smithereens; informal bust. 2 *this man's only ambition appeared to be to cut him in pieces*: **apart**, up, to pieces; literary asunder.
□ **(all) of a piece** *the rounded-off curves of the figure's body make her seem of a piece with the curlicued chair | the first three objections are all of a piece*: **similar**, alike, (exactly) the same, indistinguishable, undistinguishable, identical, uniform, of the same kind, twin, interchangeable, undifferentiated, homogeneous, cut from the same cloth, consistent, unvarying; corresponding, correspondent, commensurate, equivalent, matching, like, parallel, analogous, comparable, cognate, equal; informal like (two) peas in a pod, much of a muchness, (like) Tweedledum and Tweedledee.
▷ANTONYMS different, unlike.
□ **piece of the action** *when great new technologies come along, everybody wants a piece of the action*: **share**, portion, bit, cut, quota, percentage; commission, dividend; informal whack, slice of the cake, rake-off.
□ **piece of cake** informal *a career is a piece of cake compared to this | being a single mother isn't the piece of cake she thought it would be*: **easy task**, easy job, child's play, nothing, five-finger exercise, gift, walkover, sinecure; informal breeze, doddle, walk in the park, picnic, money for old rope, money for jam, cinch, sitter, kids' stuff, cushy job/number, doss, cakewalk, pushover; N. Amer. informal **duck soup**, snap; Austral./NZ informal bludge, snack; S. African informal a piece of old tackie; Brit. vulgar slang a piece of piss; dated snip.
□ **tear/pull someone/something to pieces** *theatre critics would tear the production to pieces*: **criticize**, attack, censure, condemn, denigrate, find fault with, give a bad press to, pillory, maul, lambaste, flay, savage; informal knock, slam, pan, bash, take apart, crucify, hammer, lay into, roast, skewer; Brit. informal slate, rubbish, slag off, monster; N. Amer. informal pummel, cut up; Austral./NZ informal bag; rare excoriate.
▸ verb
□ **piece something together** *it might be possible to piece the photographs together | investigators are now trying to piece together what happened*: **put together**, assemble, compose, construct, join up, fit together, join, unite, reassemble, reconstruct, put back together, mend, repair, patch up, sew (up); build up a picture/impression of.

pièce de résistance noun French **masterpiece**, magnum opus, masterwork, tour de force, showpiece, prize, gem, jewel, jewel in the crown, speciality, special, claim to fame, forte; French chef-d'œuvre.

piecemeal adverb *the reforms were implemented piecemeal*: **a little at a time**, piece by piece, bit by bit, gradually, slowly, in stages, in steps, step by step, little by little, by degrees, in/by fits and starts, in bits; bittily, irregularly, erratically, unevenly, discontinuously, disjointedly, unsystematically; rare inchmeal.

pied adjective *pied horses*. See **piebald**.

pier noun 1 *I left my boat tied up to the pier*: **jetty**, quay, wharf, dock, landing, landing stage, landing place, slipway, marina, waterfront, breakwater, mole, groyne, dyke, sea wall, embankment.
2 *the piers of the bridge*: **support**, cutwater, pile, piling, plinth, pedestal, foot, footing, abutment, buttress, stanchion, prop, stay, upright, pillar, post, column.

pierce verb 1 *be careful not to pierce the skin | pierce a hole with a skewer*: **make a hole in**, penetrate, puncture, punch, perforate, riddle, stab, prick, probe, gore, spike, stick, impale, transfix, bore (through), drill (through), lance, tap.
2 *her father's anguish had pierced her to the quick*: **hurt**, wound, pain, grieve, sadden, distress, make miserable/wretched, upset, trouble, harrow, cause anguish to, afflict, perturb, disturb; cut to the quick; affect, move, sting, mortify, sear, torment, torture, gnaw at, vex, gall.
3 *shafts of bright sunlight pierced the smoke*: **penetrate**, pass through, burst through, percolate, pervade, permeate, filter through, light up.

piercing adjective 1 *a piercing shriek*: **shrill**, ear-piercing, ear-splitting, high-pitched, air-rending, penetrating, shattering, strident, loud, strong; sharp, intrusive, screechy, squawky.
2 *the piercing cold*: **freezing**, frosty, frigid, chill, chilling, glacial, arctic, wintry, sharp, keen, biting, stinging, cutting, penetrating, numbing, harsh, fierce, raw, bitter; Brit. informal parky; rare nipping.
3 *a piercing pain*: **intense**, excruciating, agonizing, sharp, stabbing, shooting, stinging, severe, extreme, fierce, harrowing, searing, penetrating, racking, insufferable, unbearable, unendurable, torturous; rare exquisite.
4 *a piercing glance*: **shrewd**, discerning, perceptive, probing, searching, observant, penetrating, penetrative, sharp, keen, alert, intent, inquisitive.
5 *a piercing intelligence*: **perceptive**, percipient, perspicacious, penetrating, discerning, discriminating, intelligent, quick-witted, sharp, sharp-witted, shrewd, insightful, keen, acute, astute, clever, smart, incisive, knife-like, razor-edged, trenchant, subtle, quick, ready, clear, sensitive, thoughtful, deep, profound.

piety noun 1 *the piety of a saint*: **devoutness**, devotion, piousness, religiousness, religion, holiness, godliness, sanctity, sanctitude, saintliness, devotion to God, veneration, reverence, faith, religious duty, spirituality, sacredness, religious zeal, fervour, pietism, religiosity.
2 *the strict code of filial piety*: **dutifulness**, obedience, deference, duty, respect, respectfulness, compliance, acquiescence, tractability, tractableness; submissiveness, submission, subservience.
▷ANTONYMS impiety.

piffle noun informal *you don't actually believe this piffle, do you?* **nonsense**, rubbish, garbage, claptrap, balderdash, blather, blether, moonshine; foolishness, silliness; informal rot, tripe, hogwash, baloney, drivel, bilge, bosh, bull, bunk, guff, eyewash, poppycock, phooey, hooey, malarkey, twaddle, dribble; Brit. informal cobblers, codswallop, stuff and nonsense, tosh, cack; Scottish & N. English informal havers; Irish informal codology; N. Amer. informal flapdoodle, blathers, applesauce, wack, bushwa; informal, dated bunkum, tommyrot, cod, gammon, toffee; vulgar slang bullshit, crap, balls; Brit. vulgar slang bollocks; Austral./NZ vulgar slang bulldust.

piffling adjective *Mummy gives me such a piffling allowance*: **inadequate**, insufficient, tiny, small, minimal, trifling, paltry, pitiful; miserly, miserable; negligible, token, nominal; insulting, derisory, contemptible, outrageous; ridiculous, laughable, ludicrous, risible, preposterous, absurd; informal measly, stingy, lousy, pathetic, piddling, mingy, poxy; N. Amer. informal nickel-and-dime.

pig noun **1** *she decided to keep pigs*: **hog**, boar, sow, porker, swine, piglet; children's word piggy; rare baconer, cutter, grunter.
2 informal *he's eaten the lot, the pig*: **glutton**, guzzler, gobbler, gorger, gourmand, gourmandizer; informal greedy pig, hog, greedy guts, guts; Brit. informal gannet.
3 informal *what an absolute pig he was this evening*: **brute**, monster, devil; scoundrel, rogue, wretch; informal **bastard**, beast, louse, swine, rat, son of a bitch, s.o.b., low life; Brit. informal toerag, scrote; informal, dated bounder, rotter, heel, stinker, blighter; dated cad; vulgar slang shit, sod, bugger.
□ **make a pig's ear of** Brit. informal *engineers seem to have made a pig's ear of the design*: **bungle**, mess up, make a mess of, botch, spoil, mar, ruin, mishandle, mismanage; informal make a hash of, muff, fluff, foul up, screw up, louse up, bitch up, blow, foozle; Brit. informal make a muck of, cock up, make a Horlicks of; N. Amer. informal flub, goof up, bobble; vulgar slang fuck up, bugger up, balls up, bollix up.
▸ verb *I was **pigging myself** on lamb on the spit and other Greek food | I could **pig out** at a buffet for hours*: **overeat**, eat too much, be greedy, eat like a horse, gorge (oneself), overindulge, overindulge oneself, surfeit, guzzle, feast; informal binge, stuff one's face, stuff oneself, pack it away, put it away, make a pig of oneself, pig out; N. Amer. informal scarf out; rare gourmandize, gluttonize.

Word links **pig**

boar male
sow female
piglet young
porcine relating to pigs
sty home

pigeon noun

Word links **pigeon**

squab young

pigeonhole noun **1** *there was a note in my pigeonhole*: **cubbyhole**, compartment, slot, locker, niche.
2 *he had to supply information about his identity so he could be put in the right bureaucratic pigeonhole*: **category**, categorization, compartment, class, classification, group, grouping, grade, grading, designation, set, section, division.
▸ verb **1** *people everywhere wish to pigeonhole you*: **categorize**, compartmentalize, classify, characterize, label, brand, tag, designate, grade, codify, sort, rank, rate.
2 *a plan for new intercity trains was pigeonholed last year*: **postpone**, put off, put back, defer, shelve, delay, hold over, put on one side, lay aside, adjourn, suspend, put on ice, mothball, put in cold storage; N. Amer. table; informal put on the back burner.

pig-headed adjective **obstinate**, stubborn, stubborn as a mule, mulish, bull-headed, obdurate, headstrong, self-willed, wilful, perverse, contrary, recalcitrant, refractory, stiff-necked; tenacious, dogged, single-minded, inflexible, uncompromising, adamant, intractable, intransigent, unyielding, unmalleable, unpersuadable.

pigment noun **colouring matter**, colouring agent, colouring, colourant, colour, tint, dye, dyestuff, stain.

pile[1] noun **1** *a pile of stones*: **heap**, stack, mound, pyramid, mass, quantity, bundle, clump, bunch, jumble; collection, accumulation; assemblage, store, stockpile, aggregation; hoard, load, tower, rick; N. Amer. cold deck; Scottish, Irish, & N. English rickle; Scottish bing.
2 *I've a pile of work to do*: **great deal**, lot, great/large amount, large quantity, abundance, superabundance, cornucopia, plethora, wealth, profusion, mountain; quantities, reams, plenty; informal load, heap, mass, ocean, stack, ton; Brit. informal shedload; N. Amer. informal slew; Austral./NZ informal swag; vulgar slang shitload.
3 informal *he wants to make his pile as quickly as possible*: **fortune**, considerable/vast/large sum of money, millions, billions; informal small fortune, mint, lots/pots/heaps/stacks of money, bomb, packet, killing, bundle, wad, tidy sum, pretty penny, telephone numbers; Brit. informal shedloads, loadsamoney; N. Amer. informal big bucks, big money, gazillions; Austral. informal big bickies, motser, motza.
4 *his recently inherited stately pile*: **mansion**, stately home, hall, manor, big house, manor house, country house, castle, palace; edifice, impressive building/structure, residence, abode, seat; French château, manoir; Italian palazzo.
▸ verb **1** *he piled up brushwood*: **heap (up)**, stack (up), make a heap/pile/stack of; accumulate, assemble, put together.
2 *he piled his plate with the fried eggs*: **load**, heap, fill (up), lade, pack, stack, charge, stuff, cram; smother, stock.
3 *news was meanwhile piling up*: **increase**, grow, rise, mount, escalate, soar, spiral, leap up, shoot up, rocket, climb, accumulate, accrue, build up, multiply, intensify, swell; literary wax.
4 *they piled up the points*: **amass**, accumulate, collect, gather (in), pull in, assemble, stockpile, heap up, store up, garner, lay by/in, put by; bank, deposit, husband, save (up), squirrel away, salt away; informal stash away.
5 *half a dozen of us piled into an old station wagon*: **crowd**, climb, charge, tumble, stream, flock, flood, pack, squeeze, push, shove, jostle, elbow, crush, jam.
□ **pile it on** informal *it was a sad case but he really piled it on*: **exaggerate**, overstate the case, make a mountain out of a molehill, overdo, overplay, dramatize, overdramatize; informal lay it on thick, lay it on with a trowel, ham it up, blow up out of all proportion, give someone a sob story.

pile[2] noun *a wall supported by timber piles*: **post**, rod, pillar, column, support, foundation, piling; plinth, pedestal, foot, footing, base, substructure, underpinning, bed, subfloor, abutment, pier, cutwater, buttress, stanchion, prop, stay, upright; rare underprop.

pile[3] noun *a carpet with a short pile*: **fibres**, threads, loops; nap, velvet, shag, plush; fur, hair; soft surface, surface.

pile-up noun *a pile-up on the motorway*: **crash**, multiple crash, car crash, collision, multiple collision, smash, car smash, accident, car accident, road accident, traffic accident; bump; Brit. RTA (road traffic accident); N. Amer. wreck; informal smash-up; Brit. informal shunt, prang.

pilfer verb *the gun was part of a cache pilfered from the air force three years ago*. See **thieve**.

pilgrim noun **visitor to a shrine**, worshipper, devotee, believer, traveller, wayfarer, crusader; Islam haji, alhaji; historical palmer.

pilgrimage noun **religious journey**, holy expedition, crusade, mission, trip, journey, excursion; Indian yatra; Islam hajj.

pill noun *a sleeping pill*: **tablet**, capsule, caplet, pellet, lozenge, pastille; rare jujube, bolus, troche, pilule.

pillage verb **1** *the abbey was pillaged*: **ransack**, steal from, plunder, rob, raid, loot, rifle, sack; dispossess, strip, deprive, denude, devastate, lay waste, ravage, harry, maraud; literary despoil; archaic spoil, reave, rape; rare depredate, spoliate, forage.
2 *windows and columns pillaged from a more ancient town*: **steal**, pilfer, thieve, rob, take, snatch, purloin, loot, rifle, abscond with, carry off; informal walk off/away with, run away/off with, swipe, nab, rip off, lift, 'liberate', 'borrow', filch, snaffle, snitch; Brit. informal pinch, half-inch, nick, whip, knock off, nobble, bone; N. Amer. informal heist, glom; Austral. informal snavel; W. Indian informal tief; archaic crib, hook, reave.
▸ noun *they believed the rebellious peasants to be intent on pillage*: **robbery**, robbing, raiding, pillaging, plunder, plundering, looting, sacking, sack, ransacking, ravaging, laying waste, devastation, depredation, rape, harrying, marauding; literary despoiling, rapine; archaic spoliation, reaving.

pillar noun **1** *eight stone pillars supported a dome*: **column**, post, pole, support, upright, vertical, baluster, pier, pile, piling, pilaster, stanchion, standard, prop, buttress; rod, shaft, leg, mast, tower, pylon; obelisk, monolith; technical newel, caryatid, telamon, herm.
2 *he was a pillar of his local community*: **stalwart**, mainstay, strength, tower of strength, bastion, rock; leading light, worthy, backbone, support, upholder, champion, torch-bearer.

pillory noun *offenders were punished by being put in the pillory*: **stocks**.
▸ verb **1** *he was savagely pilloried by the press*: **attack**, criticize, censure, condemn, denigrate, find fault with, give a bad press to, lambaste, flay, savage, brand, stigmatize, cast a slur on, denounce; informal knock, slam, pan, bash, take to pieces, take apart, crucify, monster, hammer, lay into, slate, rubbish, slag off, roast, skewer; N. Amer. informal pummel; Austral./NZ informal bag; archaic slash; rare excoriate.
2 *his children were pilloried at school and his wife humiliated*: **ridicule**, jeer at, sneer at, deride, show up, hold up to shame, mock, hold up to ridicule, heap scorn on, treat with contempt, scorn, make fun of, poke fun at, laugh at, make jokes about, scoff at, be sarcastic about, tease, taunt, rag, chaff, jibe at, twit; informal kid, rib, josh, wind up, take the mickey out of, make a monkey of; N. Amer. informal goof on, rag on, razz, pull someone's chain; Austral./NZ informal chiack, poke mullock at, sling off at; Brit. vulgar slang take the piss (out of); archaic quiz, flout (at).

pillow noun *his head rested on the pillow*: **cushion**, **bolster**, headrest, pad, support, rest.
▸ verb *she pillowed her head on folded arms*: **lay**, cushion, cradle, rest, support, prop (up).

pilot noun **1** *a fighter pilot*: **airman/airwoman**, flyer, aeronaut; captain, commander, co-pilot, first/second officer, wingman; aircrew; informal skipper;

dated aviator, aviatrix; N. Amer. informal jock, fly boy.
2 *a harbour pilot*: **navigator**, helmsman, guide, steersman, coxswain; leader, director, usher, escort, attendant.
3 *a pilot for a possible TV series*: **trial episode**, pilot episode, pilot programme; sample, experiment.
▸ **adjective** *the scheme will begin with a pilot project*: **experimental**, exploratory, trial, test, sample, model, tentative, speculative, preliminary.
▸ **verb 1** *he piloted the jet*: **fly**, be at the controls of, control, handle, manoeuvre, drive, operate, steer, regulate, monitor, direct, captain; informal skipper; rare aviate.
2 *he had piloted the ship through the night*: **navigate**, guide, steer, direct, sail, usher, shepherd, show the way to, lead, conduct, escort, convoy.
3 *the enclosed questionnaire has been piloted in a number of institutions*: **test**, trial, put to the test, try out, carry out trials on, experiment with, assess, investigate, examine, appraise, evaluate, check out.

pimp noun *the pimp forced the girl back on to the streets*: **procurer**, procuress; go-between; brothel-keeper, madam; French souteneur; Brit. informal ponce; Austral. informal hoon; rare pander, panderess, mack, bawd, fancy man.

pimple noun **spot**, pustule, blackhead, boil, swelling, eruption, carbuncle, wen, cyst, abscess, **blister**; acne; informal whitehead, zit; Scottish informal plook; technical comedo; rare papule, bleb, blain, whelk.

pin noun **1** *fasten the hem with a pin*: **tack**, safety pin, nail, staple, skewer, spike, brad, fastener.
2 *a broken pin in the machine*: **peg**, **bolt**, rivet, dowel, screw, set screw; rare thole.
3 *they wore pins that read 'Kindness to all animals'*: **badge**, brooch, sticker.
□ **on pins and needles** *I'll be on pins and needles till they get here*: **in suspense**, waiting with bated breath; **anxious**, nervous, apprehensive, worried, worried sick, on edge, edgy, tense, strained, stressed, agitated, in a state of nerves, in a state of agitation, fretful, restless, worked up, keyed up, overwrought, wrought up, strung out, jumpy, with one's stomach in knots, with one's heart in one's mouth, like a cat on a hot tin roof, fidgety; Brit. nervy; informal with butterflies in one's stomach, jittery, twitchy, in a state, uptight, wired, in a stew, in a dither, all of a dither, in a sweat, in a flap, in a tizz/tizzy, all of a lather, het up, in a twitter, waiting for the axe to fall; Brit. informal strung up, windy, having kittens, all of a doodah; N. Amer. informal spooky, squirrelly, in a twit; Austral./NZ informal toey; Brit. vulgar slang shitting bricks, bricking oneself; dated overstrung.
▸ **verb 1** *she pinned the brooch to her dress*: **attach**, fasten, affix, fix, stick, tack, nail, staple, clip, join, link, secure.
2 *they had to pin me to the ground*: **hold**, restrain, press, pinion, constrain, hold fast, hold down, immobilize.
□ **pin someone/something down 1** *your supporting troops can just as easily pin down the enemy from a distance*: **confine**, **trap**, hem in, corner, close in, shut in, hedge in, pen in, restrain, entangle, enmesh, immobilize.
2 *she tried to pin him down to something definite*: **make someone commit themselves**, constrain, force, compel, pressure, put pressure on, pressurize, tie down, nail down. **3** *it evoked some distant memory but he couldn't quite pin it down*: **define**, put one's finger on, put into words, put words to, express in words, express, designate, name, specify, identify, pinpoint, place, home in on.
□ **pin something on** *he was scared they'd pin the crime on him*: **blame something on**, lay the blame for something on, attribute something to, impute something to, ascribe something to; blame someone for something, hold someone responsible for something, lay something at someone's door; informal stick something on.
□ **pin one's hopes/faith on** *I didn't pin my hopes on anything as I know what men can be like*: **rely on**, count on, depend on, place reliance on, lean on, bank on, trust, be sure of, trust in, place one's trust in, have (every) confidence in, believe in, put one's faith in, swear by, take for granted, take on trust, take as read.

pinch verb **1** *he pinched my arm harder*: **nip**, **tweak**, squeeze, compress, grasp.
2 *my new shoes pinch my big toe*: **hurt**, cause pain to, pain; **squeeze**, crush, cramp, chafe, confine; be uncomfortable, cause discomfort, be painful.
3 *if I scraped and pinched a bit, I might manage*: **economize**, be economical, scrimp, scrimp and save, cut corners, reduce wastage, skimp, stint, be sparing, be frugal, cut back, tighten one's belt, draw in one's horns, retrench, cut expenditure, cut one's coat according to one's cloth; be niggardly, be tight-fisted, be close; informal be stingy, be tight, be mingy.
4 informal *he was pinched for drink-driving*: **arrest**, take into custody, apprehend, take prisoner, detain, seize, capture, catch, lay hold of, take in, haul in; informal collar, nab, pick up, run/pull in, nick, bust, nail, do, feel someone's collar.
5 Brit. informal *you shouldn't have pinched his biscuits*: **steal**, thieve, rob, take, snatch, pilfer, purloin, loot, rifle, abscond with, carry off; embezzle, misappropriate; informal walk off/away with, run away/off with, swipe, nab, rip off, lift, 'liberate', 'borrow', filch; Brit. informal nick, half-inch, whip, knock off, nobble, bone; N. Amer. informal heist, glom; Austral. informal snavel; W. Indian informal tief; archaic crib, hook.
▸ **noun 1** *he gave her arm a pinch*: **nip**, **tweak**, squeeze.
2 *dissolve the yeast in the water with a pinch of sugar*: **small quantity**, bit, touch, dash, spot, trace, soupçon, speck, taste; informal smidgen, smidge, tad.
□ **at a pinch** *there's room for four adults, five at a pinch*: **if necessary, with difficulty**, in case of necessity, if need be, in an emergency, just possibly; N. Amer. in a pinch; Brit. informal at a push.
□ **feel the pinch** *the recession hit us hard and many of our customers have been feeling the pinch*: **suffer hardship**, have less money, be short of money, be poor, be impoverished, suffer poverty, suffer adversity.
□ **if it comes to the pinch if things get bad**, if it comes to the push, in an emergency, in a crisis, in times of hardship, if one is in difficulty, in time of need, in case of necessity, if necessary.
□ **take something with a pinch of salt** informal *take these figures with a pinch of salt in an election year*: **disbelieve**, not believe, not credit, give no credence to, discredit, discount, doubt, distrust, mistrust, be suspicious of, have no confidence/faith in, be incredulous of, be unconvinced about; not accept, reject, repudiate, question, challenge, contradict.
▷**ANTONYMS** believe.

pinched adjective *their pale, pinched faces, dulled with years of lost endeavour*: **strained**, stressed, fraught, tense, taut, tired, worn, drained, sapped; wan, peaky, pale, pallid, pasty, pasty-faced, colourless, anaemic, washed out, ashen, ashen-faced, grey, blanched; thin, drawn, haggard, gaunt, wizened, cadaverous, hollow-cheeked, hollow-eyed, emaciated.
▷**ANTONYMS** healthy, glowing, chubby.

pine verb **1** *she thinks I am pining away from love*: **languish**, decline, go into a decline, lose strength, weaken, waste away, dwindle, wilt, wither, fade, flag, sicken, droop, brood, mope, moon; archaic peak.
2 *Leopold was clearly **pining for** his son*: **yearn**, long, ache, sigh, hunger, thirst, itch, languish, carry a torch; miss, mourn, lament, grieve over, cry/weep over, fret about, shed tears for, bemoan, rue, regret the loss/absence of, hanker for/after, eat one's heart out over, cry out for.

> *Choose the right word* **pine, yearn, long, hanker**
>
> See **yearn**.

pinion verb *he was pinioned to the ground*: **hold down**, pin down, press down, restrain, constrain, hold fast, immobilize; **tie**, bind, rope, fasten, secure, shackle, fetter, tether, lash, truss (up), chain (up), hobble, manacle, handcuff; informal **cuff**.

pink adjective **rosy**, rose, rose-coloured, rosé, pale red, salmon, salmon-pink, shell-pink; flesh-coloured, flushed, blushing.
▸ **noun** *those who are in the pink of condition*: **prime**, perfection, best, finest, top form, height, highest level, upper limit, limit; utmost, peak of perfection, uttermost, greatest, extreme, extremity, ceiling; epitome, apex, zenith, acme, bloom, blossoming, flowering, full flowering; Latin ne plus ultra.
□ **in the pink in good health**, in perfect health, very healthy, very well, hale and hearty, bursting with health, in rude health; blooming, flourishing, thriving, vigorous, strong, lusty, robust, bounding, in fine fettle, fit, (as) fit as a flea, (as) fit as a fiddle, in tip-top condition, in excellent shape.

pinnacle noun **1** *soaring pinnacles of rock*: **peak**, needle, crag, tor, summit, top, crest, apex, tip, vertex; French aiguille, serac, puy; N. Amer. hoodoo; technical inselberg.
2 *the intricate pinnacles of the clock tower*: **turret**, minaret, spire, belfry, obelisk, needle, pyramid, cone, finial, shikara, mirador; rare bartizan.
3 *the brothers have reached the pinnacle of the sport*: **highest level**, peak, height, high point/spot, summit, top, climax, crowning point, peak of perfection, apex, vertex, zenith, apogee, ascendancy, upper limit, acme, meridian.
▷**ANTONYMS** nadir, trough.

pinpoint noun *a pinpoint of light from a torch*: **point**, spot, speck, dot, fleck; dapple, speckle; source.
▸ **adjective** *pinpoint accuracy was necessary*: **precise**, strict, rigorous, meticulous, scrupulous, punctilious; scientific, mathematical, exact, accurate, correct, careful, unerring.
▸ **verb** *pinpoint the cause of the trouble*: **identify**, discover, determine, distinguish, find, locate, detect, track down, run to earth, spot, diagnose, recognize, name, single out, pick out, pin down, home in on, zero in on, nail down, put one's finger on.

pint-sized adjective informal *he is constantly being upstaged by his pint-sized co-star*. See **small** (sense 2).

pioneer noun **1** *the pioneers of the Wild West*: **settler**, colonist, colonizer, frontiersman/frontierswoman, explorer, trailblazer, discoverer.
2 *a pioneer of motoring*: **developer**, innovator, groundbreaker, trailblazer, pathfinder, front runner, founder, founding father, architect, experimenter, instigator, avant-gardist, creator; avant-garde, spearhead.
▸ **verb** *he pioneered the sale of motor insurance through high-street shops*: **develop**, **introduce**, evolve, start, begin, launch, instigate, initiate, put in place, take the initiative in, take the lead in, spearhead, institute, establish, found, give birth to, be the father/mother of, originate, set in motion, create, open up, lay the groundwork for, lead the way for, prepare the way

P

for, lay the foundations of; blaze a trail, set the ball rolling, break new ground, make the first move.

pious adjective **1** *a pious family*: **religious**, devout, devoted, dedicated, reverent, God-fearing, churchgoing, spiritual, prayerful, holy, godly, saintly, faithful, dutiful, righteous.
▷ANTONYMS impious, irreligious.
2 *a pious platitude*: **sanctimonious**, hypocritical, insincere, self-righteous, holier-than-thou, pietistic, churchy; for form's sake, to keep up appearances; informal goody-goody, pi; rare religiose, Pharisaic, Pharisaical.
▷ANTONYMS sincere.
3 *a pious hope*: **sincere**, **forlorn**, vain, desperate, despairing, doomed, hopeless, lost; unlikely, unduly optimistic, unrealistic.

Choose the right word **pious, religious, devout**

See **religious**.

pip noun *grapes with the pips removed*: **seed**, stone, pit.

pipe noun **1** *a central-heating pipe*: **tube**, conduit, hose, main, duct, line, channel, canal, conveyor, pipeline, drain, tubing, piping, siphon, cylinder; Medicine fistula.
2 *he smokes a pipe*: **tobacco pipe**, briar (pipe), meerschaum, clay pipe; Brit. churchwarden; Scottish & N. English cutty; Anglo-Irish dudeen; rare calabash, calumet, chibouk, hookah, narghile, calean, hubble-bubble, bong, chillum.
3 *someone was playing a pipe*: **whistle**, penny whistle, flute, recorder, fife; chanter, drone; wind instrument.
4 (**pipes**) *Scottish regimental pipes and drums*: **bagpipes**; pan pipes; Irish uillean pipes.
▸verb **1** *the beer is piped into barrels*: **convey**, channel, siphon, run, feed, lead, bring.
2 *the programmes will be piped in from London*: **transmit**, feed, lead, patch.
3 *he heard a tune being piped*: **play on a pipe**; play the pipes, tootle, whistle; literary flute.
4 *outside a curlew piped | a voice piping away in French*: **chirp**, cheep, chirrup, twitter, chatter, warble, trill, peep, sing, shrill, squeal, squeak.
□ **pipe down** informal **be quiet**, quieten down, be silent, fall silent, hush, stop talking, hold one's tongue; informal shut up, shut one's face/mouth/trap/gob, button up, button it/one's lip, belt up, wrap up, wrap it up, put a sock in it.

pipe dream noun **fantasy**, false hope, illusion, delusion, daydream, unrealizable dream, reverie, mirage, castle in the air, castle in Spain, chimera; informal pie in the sky.

pipeline noun *a gas pipeline*: **pipe**, conduit, main, line, duct, channel, tube, conveyor.
□ **in the pipeline** *there are more changes in the pipeline*: **on the way**, in preparation, being prepared, in production, under way, coming, forthcoming, upcoming, imminent, about to happen, near, close, brewing, in the offing, in the wind, anticipated, expected.

pipsqueak noun informal *I won't have some nineteen-year-old pipsqueak telling me what to do*: **insignificant person**, nobody, nonentity, non-person, gnat, insect, cipher, pygmy; upstart; informal squirt, stripling; Brit. informal nerk, johnny, squit, whippersnapper; Scottish informal nyaff; N. Amer. informal bozo, picayune, pisher, snip; dated puppy, pup; archaic, informal dandiprat.
▷ANTONYMS somebody.

piquancy noun **1** *when added to certain dishes, the herb gives a tantalizing piquancy*: **spiciness**, tang, spice, tastiness, savouriness, pungency, edge, sharpness, tartness, pepperiness, saltiness, bite, zest; informal zing, kick, punch; archaic relish.
2 *the play retains much of its original piquancy*: **interest**, fascination, excitement, vigour, vitality, liveliness, spirit, colour, sparkle, zest, spice, spiciness, sharpness, raciness, saltiness, provocativeness, bite, edge; informal zing, pizzazz.

piquant adjective **1** *a piquant sauce of tamarind, chillis, and garlic*: **spicy**, tangy, spiced, peppery, hot; tasty, flavoursome, flavourful, appetizing, highly seasoned, savoury, pungent, sharp, tart, zesty, strong, salty; rare sapid, flavorous.
2 *a particularly piquant story*: **intriguing**, stimulating, interesting, fascinating, colourful, exciting, arresting, lively, sparkling, spirited, witty, spicy, provocative, racy, salty; informal juicy.
▷ANTONYMS bland, insipid, dull.

pique noun *he left in a fit of pique*: **irritation**, annoyance, resentment, anger, displeasure, indignation, temper, bad temper, wounded/hurt pride, wounded/hurt feelings, petulance, ill humour, peevishness, offence, umbrage, vexation, exasperation, disgruntlement, discontent, discontentment.
▸verb **1** *his scientific curiosity was piqued*: **stimulate**, arouse, rouse, provoke, whet, awaken, excite, kindle, stir, spur, intrigue, galvanize.
2 *she was piqued by Stephen's neglect of her*: **irritate**, annoy, bother, vex, provoke, displease, upset, offend, affront, anger, exasperate, infuriate, gall, irk, get someone's back up, disgruntle, nettle, needle, ruffle, get on someone's nerves, ruffle someone's feathers, make someone's hackles rise, rub up the wrong way; informal peeve, aggravate, miff, rile, get, get to, bug, get under someone's skin, get in someone's hair, get up someone's nose, hack off, get someone's goat, wind up; Brit. informal nark, get on someone's wick, give someone the hump, get across; N. Amer. informal tick off, rankle, ride, gravel; vulgar slang piss off; rare exacerbate, hump, rasp.

piracy noun **1** *piracy on the high seas*: **robbery at sea**, freebooting; historical buccaneering.
2 *software companies are reluctant to say how much piracy costs them*: **illegal reproduction**, plagiarism, illegal copying, copyright infringement, bootlegging, stealing, theft.

pirate noun **1** *pirates boarded the ship*: **freebooter**; marauder, raider; historical buccaneer, privateer; archaic corsair, rover, sea rover; rare picaroon, filibuster, sea thief, sea robber, water thief, sea wolf, sea rat, water rat, marooner.
2 *software pirates*: **copyright infringer**, plagiarist, plagiarizer.
▸verb *designers may pirate good ideas*: **reproduce illegally**, infringe the copyright of, copy illegally, plagiarize, poach, steal, appropriate, bootleg; informal crib, lift, rip off; Brit. informal nick, pinch.

pirouette noun *Sandra performed a little pirouette*: **spin**, twirl, whirl, turn, gyration, revolution.
▸verb *she pirouetted before the wardrobe mirror*: **spin round**, twirl, whirl, turn round, gyrate, revolve, pivot.

piss Brit. vulgar slang **noun pee**, wee, piddle, widdle; Brit. informal wee-wee, Jimmy (Riddle), slash, wazz.
□ **piss-take** *it is a hilarious piss-take of social stereotypes*: **take-off**, **satire**, send-up, burlesque, lampoon, pastiche, caricature, skit, squib, imitation, impression, impersonation, mockery, mimicry, travesty; informal spoof, mickey-take; W. Indian informal pappyshow; rare pasquinade, pasticcio.
▸**verb pass water**, go to the loo, go to the toilet, go to the lavatory, relieve oneself; wet one's bed/pants, wet oneself; cock/lift its leg; informal go, do it, spend a penny, have/take a leak, shake hands with an old friend, answer the call of nature, pee, pee oneself, pee one's pants, piddle, have a piddle, widdle, have a widdle, tinkle, have a tinkle; Brit. informal wee, have a wee, wee-wee, have a Jimmy (Riddle), have a slash, have a wazz; N. Amer. informal whizz, take a whizz; vulgar slang have a piss; technical micturate.
□ **piss off 1** *his girlfriend seems to be with him just to piss off her parents*: **annoy**, aggravate, irritate, exasperate, anger, irk, vex, put out, nettle, provoke, incense, rile, infuriate, antagonize, get on someone's nerves, rub up the wrong way, make someone's blood boil, ruffle someone's feathers, ruffle, try someone's patience, make someone's hackles rise; offend, pique; informal peeve, needle, make someone see red, get someone's back up, get someone's goat, get under someone's skin, get up someone's nose, bug, get someone, miff, hack off; Brit. informal wind up, get at, nark, get across, get on someone's wick; N. Amer. informal tick off. **2 verb** *why don't we all piss off overseas | now piss off—I 'm tired*: **go away**, depart, leave, take yourself off, take off, get out, get out of my sight; go, go your way, get going, get moving, move off, be off, set off, set out, start out, make a start, take your leave, decamp, duck out, take wing, walk out, walk off, absent yourself; be off with you!, shoo!; informal hit the road, fly, skedaddle, split, vamoose, scat, make yourself scarce, be on one's way, run along, beat it, get, get lost, push off, shove off, buzz off, clear off, skip off, pop off, go (and) jump in the lake; on your bike!, go and chase yourself!; Brit. informal get along, push along, get stuffed, sling your hook, hop it, hop the twig/stick, bog off, naff off; N. Amer. informal bug off, light out, haul off, haul ass, take a powder, hit the trail, take a hike; Austral. informal nick off; Austral./NZ informal rack off; vulgar slang bugger off, fuck off; Brit. vulgar slang sod off; literary begone, avaunt.
□ **pissed off** *we've all got pissed off at someone at least once in our lifetime*: **dissatisfied**, discontented, aggrieved, resentful, fed up, displeased, disgruntled, unhappy, disappointed, disaffected, malcontent; angry, irate, annoyed, cross, exasperated, indignant, vexed, irritated, piqued, irked, put out, out of temper; sulky, sullen, petulant, peevish, grumpy, churlish, testy; informal peeved, miffed, aggravated, hacked off, riled, peed off, hot under the collar, in a huff; Brit. informal cheesed off, browned off, narked, eggy; N. Amer. informal sore, teed off, ticked off; W. Indian informal vex; N. Amer. vulgar slang pissed; archaic snuffy.

pistol noun **revolver**, gun, handgun, side arm; automatic pistol, six-shooter, thirty-eight, derringer, Browning automatic; informal gat; N. Amer. informal piece, shooting iron, Saturday night special, rod, roscoe; trademark Colt, Webley, Luger.

pit[1] noun **1** *a rectangular pit dug in the ground*: **hole**, ditch, trench, trough, hollow, shaft, mineshaft, excavation, cavity, pothole, rut; abyss, chasm, gulf, crater.
2 *controversy over plans for pit closures*: **coal mine**, colliery, quarry, workings, diggings.
3 *the ugly pits stood out on her skin*: **pockmark**, pock, mark, hollow, indentation, depression, dent, dint, concavity, dimple.
□ **the pits** informal *this place really is the pits*: **the worst**, the lowest of the low; rock-bottom, extremely bad, awful, terrible, dreadful, wretched, unspeakable, deplorable; informal appalling, lousy, abysmal, dire; Brit. informal chronic, grotty, pants, a load of pants.
▸verb **1** *his skin had been pitted by acne*: **mark**, pockmark, scar, blemish, disfigure.

P

2 *rain poured down, pitting the bare earth*: **make holes in**, make hollows in, hole, dent, indent, depress, dint, pothole.

□ **pit someone/something against** *a chance to pit your wits against the world champions*: **set against**, match against, put in opposition to, put in competition with, measure against; compete with/against, contend with, vie with, grapple with, wrestle with; informal pitch against.

pit² noun *cherry pits*: **stone**, pip, seed.

pit-a-pat adverb

□ **go pit-a-pat** *my heart was going pit-a-pat all the time*: **beat rapidly**, palpitate, pound, throb, pulsate, pulse, thud, thump, hammer, flutter, pitter-patter, quiver, pump, race, pant, thrill; rare quop.

pitch¹ noun **1** *the umpires declared the pitch unfit for first-class cricket*: **playing field**, field, ground, sports field; stadium, arena; Brit. close, park.
2 *her voice rose in pitch*: **tone**, timbre, sound, key, tonality, modulation, frequency.
3 *the pitch of the roof*: **steepness**, angle, gradient, slope, slant, tilt, incline, cant, rake, dip, inclination.
4 *her frustration reached such a pitch that she screamed*: **level**, intensity, point, degree, height, extent.
5 *a pitch of the ball*: **throw**, cast, fling, hurl, toss, delivery, lob; informal chuck, heave.
6 *his sales pitch*: **patter**, talk; informal spiel, line.
7 *the street traders had already reserved their pitches*: **site**, place, spot, station; Scottish stance; Brit. informal patch.
8 *the pitch of the ship*: **lurch**, pitching, lurching, roll, rolling, plunging, reeling, swaying, rocking, list, wallowing, labouring; rare keeling.
□ **make a pitch for** *he made a clear pitch for the support of the left of the party*: **try to obtain**, try to acquire, try to get, bid for, make a bid for.
▸ verb **1** *he crumpled the page up and pitched it into the fireplace*: **throw**, toss, fling, hurl, cast, lob, launch, flip, shy, dash, aim, direct, propel, bowl; informal chuck, sling, heave, buzz, whang, bung; N. Amer. informal peg; Austral. informal hoy; NZ informal bish.
2 *he pitched overboard*: **fall**, fall headlong, tumble, topple, plunge, plummet, dive, take a nosedive, nosedive.
3 *they pitched their tents for the night*: **put up**, set up, erect, raise, position, fix in position, place, locate; set up camp.
4 *the boat pitched sharply*: **lurch**, toss (about), plunge, roll, reel, sway, rock, flounder, keel, list, wallow, labour; Nautical pitchpole.
□ **pitch in** *everyone pitched in to complete the task*: **help out**, help, assist, lend a hand, join in, participate, play a part, contribute, do one's bit, chip in, cooperate, collaborate, put one's shoulder to the wheel; Brit. informal muck in, get stuck in.
□ **pitch into** *he pitched into the youths with such fury that they ran off*: **attack**, turn on, lash out at, set upon, assault, fly at, lunge at, let fly at, tear into, weigh into, belabour; informal lay into, sail into, lace into, let someone have it, take a pop at; N. Amer. informal light into.

pitch² noun *the cement is coated with pitch*: **bitumen**, asphalt, tar.

> *Word links* **pitch**
>
> **piceous** relating to pitch

pitch-black adjective *the sky was pitch-black | her pitch-black hair*: **black**, dark, pitch-dark, black as pitch; inky, pitchy, starless, moonless, unilluminated, unlighted; jet-black, coal-black, jet, ebony, raven, sooty; literary sable, Stygian; rare Cimmerian.

pitcher noun *a pitcher of iced water*: **jug**, ewer, jar, crock; N. Amer. creamer; historical jorum.

piteous adjective *a piteous cry/sight*. See **pitiful** (sense 1).

pitfall noun *the pitfalls of setting up an office at home*: **hazard**, danger, risk, peril, difficulty, catch, snag, stumbling block, drawback; informal banana skin.

pith noun **1** *the pith of the argument*: **essence**, essential part, main point, fundamental point, heart, substance, heart of the matter, nub, core, quintessence, point, crux, gist, salient point, focal point, nucleus, meat, kernel, marrow, burden; informal nitty-gritty.
2 *he writes with a combination of pith and exactitude*: **succinctness**, conciseness, concision, pithiness, economy of language, brevity; vigour, cogency, weight, depth, force, forcefulness, power, strength.

pithy adjective *pithy comments*. See **succinct**.

pitiful adjective **1** *two children in a very pitiful state*: **distressing**, sad, piteous, to be pitied, pitiable, pathetic, disturbing, heart-rending, heartbreaking, saddening, moving, affecting, touching, tear-jerking, plaintive, poignant, forlorn, poor, sorry, wretched, abject, miserable, tragic, woeful, lamentable, grievous; rare distressful.
2 *they earn a pitiful $50 a month*: **paltry**, miserable, meagre, beggarly, insufficient, insignificant, trifling, negligible, pitiable, derisory; informal pathetic, measly, piddling, piffling, mingy; Brit. informal poxy; N. Amer. informal dinky.
3 *his performance was pitiful*: **dreadful**, awful, terrible, lamentable, hopeless, wretched, sorry, poor, bad, feeble, well below par, pitiable, woeful, inadequate, contemptible, deplorable, despicable, laughable, worthless; informal pathetic, useless, rotten, appalling, lousy, abysmal, dire, the pits; Brit. informal chronic, pants, a load of pants.

pitiless adjective *a pitiless executioner*. See **callous**.

> *Choose the right word* **pitiless, relentless, remorseless, ruthless**
>
> See **relentless**.

pittance noun *the musicians were paid a pittance*: **a very small amount**, a tiny amount, an insufficient amount, next to nothing, very little; informal peanuts, chicken feed, slave wages, a shoestring; N. Amer. informal chump change.

pitted adjective **1** *his skin was sallow and pitted*: **pockmarked**, pocked, scarred, blemished, marked; archaic pocky.
▹ANTONYMS smooth.
2 *the pitted lane*: **potholed**, rutted, rutty, holey, bumpy, rough, uneven, eaten away; dented, indented.

pitter-patter noun *the pitter-patter of brushed drums*: **patter**, tapping, pattering, drumming, drumbeat, clatter, beat, beating, tattoo, pounding, throb, pulsation, rat-a-tat, pit-a-pat, clack, click-clack, clacketing, thrum, thrumming.
▸ verb *their little feet pitter-pattered across the house*: **patter**, tap, drum, clatter, beat, pound, rattle, throb, pulsate, rat-a-tat, go pit-a-pat, pit-a-pat, clack, click-clack, thrum; archaic bicker, clacket.

pity noun **1** *her voice was full of pity*: **compassion**, commiseration, condolence, sorrow, regret, sadness, distress, sympathy, fellow feeling, understanding, feeling, emotion; archaic ruth, rue.
▹ANTONYMS indifference, cruelty.
2 *it's a pity he never had any children of his own*: **shame**, crying shame, cause for regret/disappointment, source of regret, sad thing, unfortunate thing, bad luck, misfortune; informal crime, bummer, sin.
□ **take pity on** *Amanda looked so upset that Jean took pity on her*: **feel sorry for**, relent, show sympathy for, show compassion towards, be compassionate towards, be sympathetic/charitable towards, have mercy on, show mercy to, help, help out, put someone out of their misery.
▸ verb *I could see from their faces that they pitied me*: **feel sorry for**, feel pity for, feel for, feel sympathy for, sympathize with, be sympathetic towards, empathize with, commiserate with, have compassion for, be compassionate towards, take pity on, be moved by, bleed for, have one's heart go out to, condole with, weep for, grieve for.

pivot noun **1** *the machine turns on a pivot*: **central shaft**, fulcrum, axis, axle, swivel, pin, hub, spindle, hinge, pintle, kingpin, gudgeon, trunnion.
2 *his financial methods became the pivot of government policy*: **centre**, focal point, focus, central point, hub, heart, nucleus, raison d'être, crux, keystone, cornerstone, linchpin, kingpin.
▸ verb **1** *a large panel in the side pivots inwards*: **rotate**, turn, revolve, spin, swivel, twirl, whirl, wheel, oscillate.
2 *the government's reaction* **pivoted on** *the response of the prime minister*: **depend**, hinge, turn, centre, hang, rely, rest, be contingent; revolve around.

pivotal adjective *Japan's pivotal role in the world economy*: **central**, crucial, vital, critical, focal, essential, key, significant, important, determining, decisive, deciding.

pixie noun **elf**, fairy, sprite, imp, brownie, puck, leprechaun, hobgoblin, peri; literary faerie, fay; rare nix, nixie, elfin, hob.

placard noun *placards with slogans that read 'Stop the War'*: **notice**, poster, public notice, sign, bill, sticker, advertisement; banner; French affiche; informal ad; Brit. informal advert.

placate verb *John did his best to placate her*. See **conciliate** (sense 1).

placatory adjective *a placatory gesture*. See **conciliatory**.

place noun **1** *the hotel is an ideal place to have pre-dinner cocktails*: **location**, site, spot, scene, setting, position, point, situation, area, region, whereabouts, locale; venue; technical locus.
2 *she gets to visit millions of foreign places every year*: **town**, **city**, village, hamlet; country, state, area, region; **locality**, district, neighbourhood, quarter, section; literary clime.
3 *at last she had a place of her own*: **home**, house, flat, apartment, a roof over one's head; accommodation, establishment, property; rooms, quarters, lodgings; French pied-à-terre; informal pad, digs; Brit. informal gaff; formal residence, abode, dwelling, dwelling place, domicile, habitation.
4 *I think if I were in your place, I'd agree*: **situation**, position, circumstances, condition; informal shoes.
5 *a place was reserved for her in the front row*: **seat**, chair, position, space.
6 *I offered him a place in the company*: **job**, position, post, appointment, situation, office; employment; informal berth; archaic employ.
7 *I know my place*: **status**, position, station, standing, grade, rank, footing, niche; dated estate.
8 *she decided it was not her place to make such suggestions*: **responsibility**, duty, job, task, role, function, part, concern, affair, mission, charge; right,

privilege, prerogative.
□ **in place 1** *the full length veil was held in place by a band of pearls*: **in position**, in situ. **2** *contingency plans should be in place*: **ready**, set up, established, arranged, in order, all set.
□ **in place of** *use lemon juice in place of salt | maybe Newman can go in my place*: **instead of**, as an alternative for, rather than, as a substitute for, as a replacement for, in exchange for, in lieu of; in someone's stead.
□ **out of place 1** *I never saw her with a hair out of place*: **out of position**, out of order, in disorder, disarranged, in disarray, disorganized, in a mess, messy, topsy-turvy, muddled. **2** *he has never said anything to me that was out of place*: **inappropriate**, unsuitable, unseemly, improper, untoward, inapposite, out of keeping, unbecoming, unfit, misplaced, wrong. **3** *such a glamorous woman seemed out of place in a launderette*: **incongruous**, out of one's element, like a fish out of water, uncomfortable, ill at ease, uneasy.
□ **put someone in his/her place humiliate**, take down a peg or two, deflate, crush, squelch, squash, humble, mortify, make someone eat humble pie, take the wind out of someone's sails; informal cut down to size, settle someone's hash; N. Amer. informal make someone eat crow.
□ **put something in place** *the rules which we shall put in place in the months ahead meet these criteria*: **establish**, set up, start, begin, get going, initiate, institute, form, found, create, bring into being, inaugurate, organize, lay the foundations of, build, construct, install, plant.
□ **take place** *people laid flowers at the spot where the crash took place*: **happen**, occur, come about, transpire, crop up, materialize, arise, chance, fall out; N. Amer. informal go down; literary come to pass, befall, betide.
□ **take the place of** *Lucy stepped in at very short notice to take Joan's place*: **replace**, stand in for, be a substitute for, substitute for, act for, fill in for, cover for; take over from, relieve.
▸ **verb 1** *newspapers and magazines were placed on the table*: **put down**, **put**, set, set down, lay down, deposit, position, plant, rest, stand, sit, settle, station, situate, leave, stow, prop, lean; arrange, set out, array; informal stick, dump, bung, park, plonk, pop; N. Amer. informal plunk.
2 *I would never betray the trust you placed in me*: **put**, lay, set, pin, invest.
3 *a survey placed the company 13th for achievement*: **rank**, order, put in order, grade, group, arrange, sort, class, classify, categorize; put, set, assign.
4 *she seemed familiar, but Joe couldn't quite place her*: **identify**, recognize, remember, put one's finger on, put a name to, pin down, locate, pinpoint.
5 *the agency had placed 3,000 people in work | the children were placed with foster-parents*: **find employment for**, find a job for; **find a home for**, accommodate, find accommodation for; allocate, assign, appoint.

placement noun **1** *the placement of the chairs around the fire*: **positioning**, placing, putting in place, arrangement, position, arranging, deployment, location, disposition, disposal, emplacement, installation, install, stationing.
2 *teaching practice placements*: **job**, assignment, posting, position, appointment, engagement.

placid adjective **1** *she's normally very placid*: **even-tempered**, **calm**, equable, tranquil, imperturbable, unexcitable, peaceable, peaceful, serene, mild, gentle, quiet, cool, cool-headed, collected, {cool, calm, and collected}, composed, self-possessed, poised, easy-going, temperate, level-headed, steady, unruffled, unmoved, undisturbed, unperturbed, unemotional, phlegmatic, stolid, bovine; informal unflappable; rare equanimous.
▷ANTONYMS excitable, temperamental.
2 *the placid waters of a small lake | a placid village*: **quiet**, calm, tranquil, still, peaceful, motionless, smooth, waveless, pacific, unruffled, undisturbed, like a millpond; restful, sleepy.
▷ANTONYMS stormy, rough.

Choose the right word **placid, peaceful, calm, serene, tranquil**

See **calm**.

plagiarism noun *there were accusations of plagiarism*: **copying**, infringement of copyright, piracy, theft, stealing, poaching, appropriation; informal cribbing.

plagiarize verb *he was fined for plagiarizing a song*: **copy**, **pass off as one's own**, infringe the copyright of, pirate, steal, poach, borrow, appropriate; informal rip off, lift, crib; Brit. informal pinch, nick.

plague noun **1** *an outbreak of plague | they died of the plague*: **disease**, sickness; bubonic plague, pneumonic plague, the Black Death; contagious disease, contagion, epidemic, pandemic; archaic pestilence, the pest, murrain.
2 *another hot summer has produced a plague of cat fleas*: **huge number**, infestation, epidemic, invasion, influx, swarm, multitude, host.
3 *staff theft is usually the plague of restaurants*: **bane**, curse, scourge, affliction, blight, cancer, canker.
▸ **verb 1** *he has been plagued by poor health*: **afflict**, bedevil, cause suffering to, torture, torment, trouble, beset, dog, curse, rack.
2 *he was plaguing her with questions*: **pester**, harass, badger, bother, torment, persecute, bedevil, harry, hound, disturb, trouble, be a nuisance to, keep after, irritate, worry, nag, annoy, vex, molest; N. English mither; informal hassle, bug, aggravate, give someone a hard time, drive up the wall, drive round the bend; N. Amer. informal devil, ride.

plain adjective **1** *it was plain that something was very wrong*: **obvious**, clear, crystal clear, as clear as crystal, evident, apparent, manifest, patent, visible, discernible, perceptible, perceivable, noticeable, detectable, recognizable, observable, unmistakable, transparent, palpable, distinct, pronounced, marked, striking, conspicuous, overt, self-evident, indisputable; as plain as a pikestaff, staring someone in the face, writ large, written all over someone, as plain as day, plain to see, beyond (a) doubt, beyond question; informal as plain as the nose on one's face, standing/sticking out like a sore thumb, standing/sticking out a mile.
2 *put it in plain English*: **intelligible**, comprehensible, understandable, coherent, accessible, uncomplicated, lucid, perspicuous, unambiguous, clear, simple, straightforward, clearly expressed, clear-cut, direct, digestible, user-friendly.
▷ANTONYMS unclear, obscure.
3 *there were indrawn breaths at such plain speaking*: **candid**, frank, outspoken, forthright, plain-spoken, direct, honest, truthful, blunt, downright, unvarnished, bald, straight from the shoulder, explicit, unequivocal; informal upfront; archaic round, free-spoken.
4 *her plain black dress*: **simple**, ordinary, unadorned, undecorated, unembellished, unornamented, unpretentious, unostentatious, unfussy, homely, homespun, basic, modest, unsophisticated, penny plain, without frills; stark, severe, spartan, austere, chaste, bare, uncluttered, restrained, muted, unpatterned, patternless, everyday, workaday.
▷ANTONYMS fancy, elaborate.
5 *a rather plain girl*: **unattractive**, unprepossessing, as plain as a pikestaff, ugly, ill-favoured, unlovely, ordinary-looking; N. Amer. homely; informal not much to look at; Brit. informal no oil painting.
▷ANTONYMS attractive, beautiful, good-looking.
6 *a plain, honest man with no nonsense about him*: **straightforward**, unpretentious, simple, ordinary, average, unassuming, unaffected, honest-to-goodness, ingenuous, artless, guileless, sincere; N. Amer. cracker-barrel.
▷ANTONYMS pretentious, affected.
7 *it was plain bad luck*: **sheer**, pure, downright, out-and-out, unmitigated, rank, nothing other than.
□ **plain sailing** *getting their products onto the market has not been plain sailing*: **uncomplicated**, straightforward, simple, easy, effortless, painless, undemanding, unexacting; elementary, a five-finger exercise, child's play; routine; informal as easy as falling off a log, as easy as pie, as easy as ABC, a piece of cake, a cinch, a snip, easy-peasy, no sweat, a doddle, money for old rope, money for jam, kids' stuff, a breeze, a doss, a cakewalk; N. Amer. informal duck soup, a snap; Austral./NZ informal a bludge, a snack; S. African informal a piece of old tackle.
▸ **adverb** *this is just plain stupid*: **downright**, utterly, absolutely, completely, totally, really, thoroughly, positively, profoundly, categorically, simply, incontrovertibly, unquestionably, undeniably; informal plumb.
▸ **noun** *the vast treeless plains of North America*: **grassland**, **flatland**, lowland, pasture, meadowland, open country, prairie, savannah, steppe; in S. America tableland, tundra, pampas, campo, llano, vega; in southern Africa veld; Geology pediplain; literary champaign.

plain-spoken adjective *he was well known for being plain-spoken*. See **frank**[1] (sense 1).

plaintive adjective *a plaintive cry*: **mournful**, sad, wistful, doleful, pathetic, pitiful, piteous, melancholy, melancholic, sorrowful, unhappy, wretched, woeful, grief-stricken, broken-hearted, heartbroken, desolate, heart-rending, forlorn, woebegone, disconsolate; literary plangent, heartsick, dolorous.

Word toolkit **plaintive**

See **wistful**.

plan noun **1** *he had a new plan for raising money*: **scheme**, plan of action, idea, master plan, game plan, proposal, proposition, ploy, suggestion, project, programme, system, method, procedure, strategy, stratagem, formula, recipe, scenario, arrangement, schedule, agenda; way, means, measure, tactic, tack, plot, device, manoeuvre, ruse; archaic shift.
2 *her plan was really just to find the hotel*: **intention**, aim, idea, intent, objective, object, goal, target, hope, aspiration, ambition.
3 *plans for the clubhouse have been drawn up by a local architect*: **blueprint**, drawing, scale drawing, diagram, sketch, chart, map, layout; illustration, representation, delineation; N. Amer. plat.
▸ **verb 1** *plan your route in advance | oil workers were planning strike action*: **organize**, arrange, work out, think out, design, line up, outline, sketch out, map out, chalk out, draft, prepare, schedule, programme, formulate, frame, project, develop, set up, fix up, shape, build, devise, concoct, contrive; plot, scheme, cook up, hatch, brew, mastermind, orchestrate, choreograph; N. Amer. slate; rare excogitate.
2 *he plans to buy an apartment in the city*: **intend**, make plans, aim, propose, mean, be resolved, have in mind, hope, want, wish, desire, contemplate, envisage, foresee, envision, expect; formal purpose.
3 *there are many things to bear in mind when planning a new garden*: **design**,

p

draw up a plan of, make a drawing of, draw up a layout of, sketch out, make a map of, map out, make a representation of; N. Amer. plat.

plane[1] noun **1** *a horizontal plane*: **flat surface**, level surface; the flat, horizontal.
2 *trying to reach a higher plane of achievement*: **level**, stage, degree, standard, stratum; position, rung, echelon, footing.
▶ **adjective** *a plane surface*: **flat**, level, horizontal, even, flush, levelled, true; smooth, regular, uniform; technical planar; rare homaloidal.
▶ **verb 1** *seagulls swooped and planed overhead*: **soar**, glide, float, drift, wheel.
2 *boats planing across the water*: **skim**, glide.

plane[2] noun *the plane crashed close to the airport*: **aircraft**, craft, flying machine; Brit. aeroplane; N. Amer. airplane, ship; informal bird; Brit. informal, dated kite.

> *Word links* **plane**
>
> **aeronautics** science of flight

plangent adjective literary *from somewhere outside came a plangent keening*: **melancholy**, mournful, plaintive; sonorous, reverberant, reverberating, resonant, loud.

plank noun *rough wooden planks*: **board**, floorboard, beam, timber, stave, deal.

planning noun *the planning should be every bit as enjoyable as the event itself*: **preparation(s)**, organization, arrangement, forethought, design, designing, drafting, working out, setting up, groundwork.

plant[1] noun **1** *a pot plant | garden plants*: **herb**, flower, vegetable, shrub, weed; (**plants**) greenery, flora, vegetation, undergrowth; rare herbage, verdure.
2 *we thought he was a CIA plant spreading disinformation*: **spy**, informant, informer, undercover agent, secret agent, agent, mole, infiltrator, operative; N. Amer. informal spook.
▶ **verb 1** *plant the seeds this autumn and they will flower next summer*: **sow**, scatter, seed, put in the ground; bed out, set out, transplant.
2 *he planted his feet more firmly on the ground*: **put**, **place**, set, position, station, situate, settle, stick, fix; informal plonk.
3 *someone had planted the idea in Alexander's mind*: **insert**, impress, imprint, instil, put, place; implant, introduce, sow the seeds of, fix, establish, embed, root, lodge.
4 *the letters might have been planted there to embarrass the government*: **hide**, place secretly, conceal, secrete.

> *Word links* **plant**
>
> **phyto-** related prefix, as in *phytoplankton*
> **-phyte** related suffix, as in *epiphyte*
> **botany** study of plants
> **herbivorous** plant-eating
> **herbicide** substance used to kill plants

plant[2] noun **1** *the plant commenced production in June*: **factory**, works, foundry, mill, workshop, shop, yard, industrial unit.
2 *there has been inadequate investment in new plant*: **machinery**, machines, equipment, apparatus, appliances, gear.

plaque noun *a commemorative plaque*: **memorial tablet**, plate, stone plate, metal plate, tablet, panel, sign, brass, medallion, plaquette, cartouche.

plaster noun **1** *he stripped away the plaster to expose the bare brick*: **plasterwork**, stucco; trademark Artex; rare pargeting, parging.
2 *a statuette made of plaster*: **plaster of Paris**, gypsum.
3 *waterproof plasters*: **sticking plaster**, adhesive dressing, dressing, bandage; trademark Elastoplast, Band-Aid.
▶ **verb 1** *home-made bread plastered with butter*: **cover thickly**, smother, spread, smear, cake, coat, daub, bedaub, overlay; literary besmear.
2 *he arrived late, his hair **plastered down** with sweat*: **flatten (down)**, smooth down, slick down, sleek down.

plastic adjective **1** *at very high temperatures, rocks may become plastic*: **malleable**, mouldable, shapable, pliable, pliant, ductile, flexible, soft, workable, supple, bendable; informal bendy; rare fictile.
▷ANTONYMS rigid.
2 *the plastic minds of young children*: **impressionable**, malleable, easily influenced, responsive, receptive, mouldable, pliable, pliant, flexible, compliant, tractable, manageable, controllable, docile, biddable, persuadable, susceptible, manipulable, influenceable; unformed, inexperienced; rare ductile, persuasible, suasible.
▷ANTONYMS intractable.
3 *she smiled a little plastic smile*: **artificial**, false, synthetic, fake, superficial, pseudo, sham, bogus, ersatz, assumed, spurious, specious, unnatural, insincere; informal phoney, pretend.
▷ANTONYMS genuine.

plasticity noun *the plasticity of the clay*: **malleability**, softness, pliancy, pliability, flexibility, suppleness, ductility.

plate noun **1** *he pushed his empty plate to one side*: **dish**, platter, bowl, salver; dinner plate, side plate, soup plate; Scottish & N. English **ashet**; archaic trencher, charger; rare paten.
2 *a plate of spaghetti*: **plateful**, helping, portion, serving, platter.
3 *the ship's hull was made of overlapping steel plates*: **panel**, sheet, layer, lamina, leaf, pane, slab.
4 *a brass plate on the door*: **plaque**, nameplate, door plate, tablet, sign, brass, medallion, plaquette, cartouche.
5 *the book contains sixty colour plates*: **picture**, print, illustration, photograph, photo, engraving, lithograph; rare vignette.
▶ **verb** *the roof was plated with steel*: **cover**, coat, overlay, laminate, veneer; electroplate, anodize, galvanize, gild, platinize, silver, tin, nickel.

plateau noun **1** *a windswept plateau*: **upland**, tableland, elevated plain, mesa, highland, table.
2 *house prices have reached a plateau*: **level**, stage; period of little change, quiescent period, levelling-off period; let-up, break, respite, lull.

platform noun **1** *another official climbed on the platform and spoke to the crowd*: **stage**, **dais**, stand, rostrum, podium, soapbox; Indian mandapam.
2 *the Democratic Party's platform*: **policy**, **programme**, party line, manifesto, plan, plan of action, principles, tenets, objectives, aims.

platitude noun *a string of empty platitudes*: **cliché**, truism, commonplace, hackneyed/trite/banal/overworked saying, banality, old chestnut; bromide, inanity, tag.

platitudinous adjective *politicians delivering platitudinous sound bites*: **hackneyed**, overworked, overused, clichéd, banal, trite, commonplace, stock, stereotyped, stereotypical, set, well worn, stale, tired, vapid, inane, unimaginative, unoriginal, derivative, vieux jeu, dull, flat, conventional; informal corny, old hat; rare truistic, bromidic.
▷ANTONYMS original, fresh.

platonic adjective *our relationship is purely platonic*: **non-sexual**, non-physical, chaste; spiritual, intellectual, friendly.
▷ANTONYMS physical, sexual.

platoon noun *a platoon of British Royal Marines*: **unit**, patrol, troop, squad, team, squadron, company, group, corps, division, outfit, detachment, contingent.

platter noun *the meat was arranged on silver platters*: **plate**, dish, serving plate, serving dish, salver, tray; Scottish & N. English **ashet**; archaic charger, trencher; rare paten.

plaudits plural noun *the president will win plaudits from most economists if he carries through his plans*: **praise**, acclaim, acclamation, commendation, congratulations, encomiums, approval, approbation, accolades, compliments, cheers, tributes, salutes, bouquets; a pat on the back, kudos, good press; applause, a round of applause, a standing ovation; informal a (big) hand; rare laudation.
▷ANTONYMS condemnation, criticism.

plausible adjective *a plausible explanation*: **credible**, reasonable, believable, likely, feasible, probable, tenable, possible, conceivable, imaginable, within the bounds of possibility, convincing, persuasive, cogent, sound, rational, logical, acceptable, thinkable; smooth-talking, smooth-tongued, smooth, glib, specious; rare verisimilar, colourable.
▷ANTONYMS unlikely, improbable.

play verb **1** *the children were playing with toys on the floor*: **amuse oneself**, entertain oneself, enjoy oneself, have fun, have a good time, relax, rest, be at leisure, occupy oneself, divert oneself, play games, frolic, frisk, gambol, romp, cavort, caper; informal mess about/around, lark (about/around); dated sport; archaic or humorous disport oneself.
2 *I used to play football*: **take part in**, participate in, engage in, be involved in, join in, compete in, do.
3 *Liverpool play Sheffield United on Wednesday*: **compete against**, contend against, oppose, take on, challenge, vie with, rival.
4 *he was about to play Macbeth*: **act the part of**, play the part of, act, take the role of, enact, represent, perform, appear as, portray, depict, impersonate, pretend to be, execute, render, interpret; rare personate.
5 *he never learned to play a musical instrument*: **perform on**, make music on; blow, sound, strum.
6 *his hair gleamed as the sunlight played on it*: **move lightly**, dance, flit, dart, ripple, lick, touch.
□ **play around** informal *I played around a bit but now I've settled down*: **womanize**, philander, have affairs/an affair, flirt, dally, trifle/toy with someone's affections; informal carry on, mess about/around, play the field, play away, sleep around, swing, be a maneater; N. Amer. informal fool around; vulgar slang screw around; rare coquet.
□ **play at** *like a dictator he will play at being kind and good*: **pretend to be**, give the appearance of, assume/affect the role of, pass oneself off as, masquerade as, profess to be, pose as, impersonate, make out, fake, feign, simulate, affect, go through the motions of; N. Amer. informal make like.
□ **play ball** informal *if you play ball, I can help you*: **cooperate**, collaborate, play along, play the game, go along with the plan, show willing, be willing, help, lend a hand, assist, be of assistance, contribute, reciprocate, respond; informal pitch in.

P

□ **play something down** *ministers sought to play down the extent of the damage*: **make light of**, make little/nothing of, set little/no store by, gloss over, de-emphasize, underemphasize, downplay, understate, underplay, minimize, shrug off; soft-pedal, tone down, diminish, downgrade, trivialize, detract from, underrate, underestimate, undervalue, think little of, disparage, decry, deprecate, talk down, belittle, slight, scoff at, sneer at; informal pooh-pooh; rare derogate.
▷ANTONYMS exaggerate.
□ **play for time use delaying tactics**, stall, temporize, gain time, hang back, hang fire, hold back, procrastinate, beat about the bush, drag one's feet, delay, filibuster, stonewall.
□ **play havoc with** *dust will play havoc with electrical systems*: **disturb**, disrupt, disorder, disorganize, disarrange, interfere with, upset, unsettle, convulse; obstruct, impede, hamper; hold up, delay, retard, slow (down); throw into confusion, throw into disorder, throw into disarray, cause confusion/turmoil in, derange, turn upside-down, make a mess of; **ruin**, wreck, spoil, undo, mar, frustrate, blight, crush, quell, quash, dash, scotch, shatter, devastate, demolish, sabotage; informal mess up, screw up, louse up, foul up, make a hash of, do in, put paid to, put the lid on, put the kibosh on, stymie, queer, nix, banjax, blow a hole in; Brit. informal scupper, dish, throw a spanner in the works of; N. Amer. informal throw a monkey wrench in the works of; Austral. informal euchre, cruel.
□ **play it by ear improvise**, extemporize, rise to the occasion, ad lib; take it as it comes; Latin ad libitum; informal busk it, wing it.
□ **play on** *it is despicable to play on the fears of ordinary people*: **exploit**, take advantage of, use, make use of, turn to (one's) account, profit by, capitalize on, impose on, trade on, milk, abuse, misuse; informal walk all over.
□ **play out 1** *the position of the sub-tropical jet stream across North America will determine how winter plays out*: **turn out**, work out, conclude, end (up), result, come out, fall out, develop, evolve. **2** *this scenario plays out all across the country*: **happen**, occur, take place, come about, come to pass, crop up, turn up, arise, chance, ensue, befall, be realized, take shape, transpire; rare eventuate.
□ **play something out** *the simmering tension between them is played out against the sweep of world events*: **portray**, represent, depict, characterize, describe, present; enact, perform, render, act, stage; express, give expression to, communicate, set forth, articulate.
□ **played out** informal *the melodrama is a little played out to be entirely satisfying*: **stale**, hackneyed, well-worn, clichéd, stock, trite, banal, worn out, time-worn, threadbare, hoary, tired, overused, obsolete, antiquated, finished, old; informal clapped out, old hat.
□ **play a part in** *historical events have also played a part in directing these efforts*: **contribute to**, be instrumental in, be a factor in, be partly responsible for, have a hand in, be conducive to, make for, lead to, cause, give rise to; help, promote, advance, further, forward, oil the wheels of, open the door for, add to; formal conduce to.
▷ANTONYMS stand in the way of.
□ **play the fool clown about/around**, act the clown, act the fool, fool about/around, mess about/around, monkey about/around, footle about/around, joke, play pranks, indulge in horseplay; informal horse about/around, screw around, puddle about/around, act the goat, lark about/around; Brit. informal muck about/around, fanny about/around; Brit. vulgar slang piss about/around, arse about/around; dated play the giddy goat.
□ **play the game** *I don't trust them—they don't always play the game*: **play fair**, be fair, play by the rules, abide by the rules, follow the rules, conform, be a good sport, toe the line, keep in step.
□ **play up 1** *there were some boys that really did play up*: **misbehave**, be misbehaved, behave badly, be bad, be naughty, be mischievous, get up to mischief, be disobedient, be awkward, give/cause/make trouble; Brit. informal be stroppy, be bolshie. **2** Brit. informal *the boiler's playing up again*: **not work properly**, be defective, be faulty, malfunction, act up, give trouble; informal be/go on the blink. **3** Brit. informal *his injured leg was playing up*: **be painful**, hurt, ache, be sore, cause pain, cause discomfort, cause trouble, annoy; informal kill someone, give someone gyp.
□ **play something up** *the press has played up the problems*: **emphasize**, put/lay emphasis on, accentuate, bring/draw/call attention to, focus attention on, point up, underline, underscore, highlight, spotlight, foreground, feature, give prominence to, bring to the fore, heighten, stress, accent.
□ **play up to** *he's been playing up to her the whole time*: **ingratiate oneself with**, seek the favour of, try to get on the good side of, curry favour with, court, fawn on/over, make up to, keep someone sweet, toady to, crawl to, grovel to, pander to, be obsequious towards, truckle to, flatter; informal soft-soap, suck up to, butter up, be all over, lick someone's boots; N. Amer. informal brown-nose; vulgar slang lick/kiss someone's arse.

▶ **noun 1** *one must strike a balance between work and play*: **amusement**, entertainment, relaxation, recreation, enjoyment, pleasure, diversion, distraction, leisure, fun, games, fun and games; playfulness, horseplay, skylarking, larks, a good time, jollification, junketing, merrymaking, revelry; informal living it up; dated sport.
▷ANTONYMS work.
2 *a play by Shakespeare*: **drama**, stage play, stage show, theatrical work, theatrical piece, radio play, television play, teleplay, screenplay, comedy, tragedy, farce, sketch; production, performance, spectacle, show.
3 *they have understood the play of the real world*: **action**, activity, operation, movement, motion, agency, employment, working, function, functioning, exercise, interaction, interplay.
4 *the steering rack was loose, and there was a little play*: **movement**, freedom of movement, free motion, slack, give; room to manoeuvre, room to operate, scope, latitude, elbow room, space, margin.
5 *we enable people to give full play to their energy and abilities*: **scope**, range, latitude, liberty, licence, freedom, indulgence, free rein, release.
□ **bring into play** *all of these factors are brought into play in the strategic planning process*: **use**, employ, exercise, make use of, utilize, avail oneself of, put to use; **practise**, apply, bring to bear, implement, exert, wield.
□ **play on words** *its very title turns out to be a play on words*: **pun**, wordplay, double entendre, double meaning, innuendo, witticism, quip, quibble; rare paronomasia, equivoque, amphibology, pivot, calembour, carriwitchet, clench, clinch, conundrum, nick, pundigrion, whim.

playboy noun *Nigel isn't the marrying type—he's just a playboy*: **socialite**, pleasure seeker, sybarite; ladies' man, womanizer, philanderer, rake, roué; rich man about town; informal ladykiller, gay dog; W. Indian informal saga boy.

player noun **1** *a tournament enjoyed by both players and spectators*: **participant**, **contestant**, competitor, contender, team member; sportsman, sportswoman, sportsperson, athlete.
2 *the younger players in the orchestra*: **musician**, performer, instrumentalist, soloist, virtuoso, artist, artiste.
3 *the players of the Royal Shakespeare Company*: **actor**, **actress**, performer, thespian, entertainer, artist, artiste, trouper.

playful adjective **1** *she was in a playful mood*: **frisky**, jolly, fun-loving, lively, full of fun, high-spirited, spirited, in high spirits, exuberant, perky, skittish, coltish, kittenish; mischievous, impish, devilish, puckish, roguish, rascally, tricksy, prankish; informal full of beans, frolicky; dated gay; archaic frolicsome, gamesome, sportive; rare ludic.
▷ANTONYMS solemn.
2 *a playful remark*: **light-hearted**, in fun, in jest, joking, jokey, teasing, humorous, jocular, jesting, good-natured, tongue-in-cheek, facetious, frivolous, flippant, arch, waggish, flirtatious, whimsical; rare jocose.
▷ANTONYMS serious.

playground noun **play area**, park, playing field, recreation ground, amusement park; Brit. adventure playground.

playmate noun **friend**, playfellow, companion; informal chum, pal, buddy; Brit. informal mate.

plaything noun *a child's plaything*: **toy**, game, amusement.

playwright noun **dramatist**, writer, tragedian; scriptwriter, screenwriter, scenarist; rare dramaturge, dramaturgist, comedist.

plea noun **1** *a desperate plea for aid*: **appeal**, entreaty, supplication, petition, prayer; request, call, solicitation, invocation, suit; rare imploration, adjuration.
2 *her plea of a headache was not entirely false*: **claim**, explanation, defence, justification, vindication; excuse, pretext.

plead verb **1** *he had pleaded with her to stay*: **beg**, entreat, beseech, implore, appeal to, petition, supplicate, importune, pray to, request, ask earnestly, call on, adjure; apply to, solicit; rare obsecrate.
2 *his accomplice pleaded ignorance | she pleaded her case to no avail*: **claim**, use as an excuse, assert, allege; **argue**, state, present, put forward.

pleasant adjective **1** *a very pleasant evening*: **enjoyable**, pleasing, pleasurable, nice, agreeable, satisfying, gratifying, welcome, good, acceptable, to one's liking; entertaining, amusing, diverting; delightful, charming, inviting, attractive, beautiful; fine, balmy, salubrious; Scottish bonny, couthy; informal lovely, great; N. Amer. informal neat; S. African informal lekker, mooi.
2 *the staff are always pleasant*: **friendly**, agreeable, amiable, affable, nice, genial, likeable, amicable, lovely, good-humoured, personable, congenial, hospitable, approachable, good-natured, companionable; gracious, courteous, polite, cordial, obliging, helpful, considerate; cheerful, warm, charming, engaging, winning, delightful, sweet, as nice as pie, sympathetic; German gemütlich; N. English & Scottish canny; Scottish couthy; archaic fair-spoken.
▷ANTONYMS unpleasant, disagreeable, nasty.

pleasantry noun **1** (usually **pleasantries**) *we exchanged the usual pleasantries*: **banter**, badinage; inconsequential remark, friendly/good-natured remark, polite remark, casual remark; N. Amer. informal josh.
2 *he laughed at his own pleasantry*: **joke**, **witticism**, quip, jest, gag, witty remark, sally; French bon mot; informal wisecrack, crack.

please verb **1** *he'd do anything to please her*: **make happy**, give pleasure to, make someone pleased/glad/content, make someone feel good, delight, charm, amuse, divert, entertain, be agreeable to, gladden, cheer up; satisfy, gratify, humour, oblige, content, suit; informal tickle pink.
▷ANTONYMS displease, annoy.
2 *guests are urged to do as they please*: **like**, want, wish, desire, see/think fit, choose, be inclined, will, prefer, opt.
▶ **adverb** *let me know as soon as possible, please | please sit down*: **if you please**, if you wouldn't mind, if you would be so good; kindly, have the goodness to, pray; archaic prithee.

pleased adjective *Edward seemed really pleased to see me*: **happy**, glad, delighted, gratified, grateful, thankful, content, contented, satisfied, well pleased, thrilled, elated, as pleased as Punch, overjoyed, cock-a-hoop, like a dog with two tails, like a child with a new toy; informal over the moon, tickled pink, on cloud nine/seven; Brit. informal chuffed; N. English informal made up; Austral. informal wrapped; derogatory complacent, smug; humorous gruntled.
▷ANTONYMS unhappy, dissatisfied.
□ **pleased with oneself** *I was rather pleased with myself, and was really trying to keep that smug look off my face*: **self-satisfied**, smug, complacent, self-congratulatory, superior, puffed up, self-approving, well pleased, proud of oneself; informal goody-goody; Brit. informal like the cat that's got the cream, I'm-all-right-Jack; N. Amer. informal wisenheimer; N. Amer. vulgar slang shit-eating.

pleasing adjective **1** *a very pleasing day*: **nice**, **agreeable**, pleasant, pleasurable, satisfying, gratifying, welcome, good, acceptable, to one's liking, enjoyable, entertaining, amusing, delightful, fine; informal lovely. See also **pleasant** (sense 1).
2 *her pleasing manner*: **friendly**, **amiable**, pleasant, agreeable, affable, nice, genial, likeable, good-humoured, charming, engaging, winning, delightful; informal lovely. See also **pleasant** (sense 2).

pleasurable adjective *a pleasurable experience*. See **agreeable** (sense 1).

pleasure noun **1** *she smiled with pleasure*: **happiness**, delight, joy, gladness, rapture, glee, satisfaction, gratification, fulfilment, contentment, contentedness, enjoyment, amusement; humorous delectation.
2 *watercolour painting is one of his greatest pleasures*: **joy**, delight, source of pleasure, enjoyment, amusement, diversion, recreation, pastime, divertissement; treat, thrill.
3 *he doesn't believe in mixing business and pleasure*: **enjoyment**, fun, entertainment, amusement, diversion, recreation, leisure, relaxation; informal jollies; Brit. informal beer and skittles.
4 *they were indolent and addicted to a life of pleasure*: **sensual gratification**, **hedonism**, indulgence, self-indulgence, self-gratification, lack of self-restraint, lotus-eating; rare sybaritism.
5 *what's your pleasure?* **wish**, **desire**, preference, will, inclination, choice, option.
□ **take pleasure in** *even the youngest children take pleasure in music*: **enjoy**, delight in, love, like, adore, be entertained by, be amused by, be pleased by, appreciate, relish, savour, revel in, glory in; informal get a kick out of, get a thrill out of.
□ **with pleasure** *'Would you mind telling me the way to the station?' 'With pleasure.'*: **gladly**, willingly, happily, readily, cheerfully, by all means, of course; archaic fain.
▷ANTONYMS displeasure, sorrow, pain.

Word links **pleasure**

hedonism pursuit of pleasure

pleat noun *a pleat at the edge of the curtain*: **fold**, tuck, crease, gather, pucker, crimp; rare plication.
▶ verb *the garment is softly pleated at the front*: **fold**, tuck, crease, gather, pucker, crimp; rare plicate.

plebeian noun *the hostility towards him was shared by plebeians and gentry alike*: **proletarian**, **commoner**, common person, man/woman/person in the street, working-class person, worker, working person; peasant; informal, derogatory pleb, prole.
▷ANTONYMS aristocrat, noble, patrician.
▶ adjective **1** *people of plebeian descent*: **lower-class**, low-class, working-class, proletarian, common, peasant, mean, humble, lowly, low, of low birth, low-born, low-ranking, ignoble, undistinguished; archaic baseborn.
▷ANTONYMS aristocratic, noble, patrician.
2 *a man of plebeian tastes*: **uncultured**, uncultivated, unrefined, lowbrow, philistine, uneducated, unpolished, provincial, rustic; coarse, uncouth, crass, common, vulgar, base, boorish, gross; informal plebby; Brit. informal non-U; rare illiberal.
▷ANTONYMS refined, cultivated, sophisticated.

plebiscite noun *a plebiscite for the approval of constitutional reforms*: **vote**, referendum, ballot, poll.

pledge noun **1** *he fulfilled his election pledge to end the war*: **promise**, undertaking, vow, word, word of honour, commitment, assurance, oath, covenant, bond, agreement, guarantee, warrant.
2 *he had given the object as a pledge to a creditor*: **surety**, **bond**, security, collateral, guarantee, deposit, pawn; archaic gage, earnest.
3 *take this as a pledge of my sincerity*: **token**, **symbol**, sign, mark, testimony, proof, evidence, badge.
▶ verb **1** *the president had publicly pledged that he would root out corruption*: **promise**, give one's word, vow, swear, give an assurance, give an undertaking, undertake, take an oath, swear an oath, engage, contract, commit oneself, bind oneself, declare, affirm, avow, state; rare asseverate.
2 *Japan pledged $100 million in aid*: **undertake to give**, promise (to give), donate, contribute, give, make a gift of, put oneself down for, put up; Brit. covenant.
3 *even his home is pledged as security against the loans*: **mortgage**, put up as collateral, guarantee, pawn; archaic gage, plight.

plenary adjective **1** *the council has plenary powers to administer the agreement*: **unconditional**, unlimited, unrestricted, unqualified, absolute, complete, sweeping, comprehensive; plenipotentiary.
2 *a plenary session of the European Parliament*: **full**, fully constituted, general, complete, entire, open.

plenipotentiary noun *his last posting was as plenipotentiary in Paris*: **diplomat**, representative; ambassador, minister, emissary, chargé d'affaires, chargé, envoy, legation; archaic legate.

plenitude noun *Croft Farm boasts a plenitude of animals and birds*. See **profusion**.

plenteous adjective literary See **plentiful**.

plentiful adjective *a plentiful supply of food*: **abundant**, copious, ample, profuse, rich, lavish, liberal, generous, bountiful, large, huge, great, bumper, flush, overflowing, superabundant, infinite, inexhaustible, opulent, prolific, teeming; informal a gogo, galore; S. African informal lank; literary bounteous, plenteous.
▷ANTONYMS scarce, meagre.
□ **be plentiful be abundant**, abound, be numerous, exist in abundance, proliferate, be thick on the ground; informal grow on trees; Brit. informal be two/ten a penny.

plenty noun *we live in times of plenty*: **prosperity**, affluence, wealth, opulence, comfort, well-being, luxury; plentifulness, abundance, fruitfulness, profusion; literary plenteousness.
▶ pronoun *there are **plenty of** books available on the subject*: **a lot of**, many, a great deal of, a good deal of, a large number/amount of, a plethora of, quantities of, enough, more than enough, enough and to spare, no lack of, sufficient, a wealth of, a feast of, a cornucopia of; informal loads of, lots of, heaps of, bags of, stacks of, piles of, masses of, tons of, oodles of, oceans of, a raft of, a hatful of, more ... than one can shake a stick at; Brit. informal lashings of; N. Amer. informal scads of, a slew of, gobs of, gazillions of; Austral./NZ informal a swag of; vulgar slang a shitload of, shitloads of; archaic a deal of, a mickle of, a peck of.

plethora noun *a plethora of newspaper opinion polls*. See **profusion**.

pliability noun *the pliability of leather*: **flexibility**, pliancy, elasticity, whippiness, suppleness, malleability, plasticity, springiness, ductility, bendability.

pliable adjective **1** *quality leather is pliable*: **flexible**, easily bent, bendable, pliant, elastic, supple, stretchable, malleable, workable, plastic, whippy, springy, limber, ductile, tensile; informal bendy; archaic flexile.
▷ANTONYMS rigid.
2 *pliable teenage minds*: **malleable**, easily influenced, impressionable, flexible, adaptable, pliant, compliant, docile, biddable, tractable, like putty in one's hands, yielding, manageable, governable, controllable, amenable, accommodating, susceptible, suggestible, influenceable, persuadable, manipulable, responsive, receptive; rare persuasible, suasible, susceptive.
▷ANTONYMS intractable, obdurate.

pliant adjective **1** *the tsar had replaced him with a more pliant successor*: **compliant**, biddable, docile, tractable, yielding, malleable, manageable, governable, controllable, amenable, accommodating, susceptible, suggestible, easily influenced, influenceable, persuadable, manipulable, like putty in one's hands, responsive, receptive; rare persuasible, suasible, susceptive.
2 *memories of Isabelle lying pliant in his arms*: **supple**, soft, loose-limbed, willowy, lissom, lithe, limber.

plight noun *an attempt to highlight the plight of the homeless*. See **predicament**.

plod verb **1** *Melissa plodded wearily up the stairs*: **trudge**, walk heavily, clump, stomp, stump, tramp, drag oneself, lumber, slog; Brit. informal trog.
2 *I suppose I'll just have to plod through the whole book*: **work one's way**, wade, plough, toil, trawl, soldier (on), proceed laboriously, labour; informal slog.

plot noun **1** *a plot to overthrow the government*: **conspiracy**, intrigue, secret plan/scheme, stratagem; machinations; rare cabal, complot, covin.
2 *the plot of her next novel*: **storyline**, story, chain of events, scenario, action, thread; rare diegesis, mythos.
3 *a three-acre plot*: **piece of ground**, patch, area, location, parcel, tract, allotment, acreage; N. Amer. lot, plat; N. Amer. & Austral./NZ homesite; S. African stand, yard, erf.
▶ verb **1** *he was found guilty of plotting the downfall of the government*: **plan**, scheme, arrange, organize, lay, hatch, concoct, devise, frame, think up, dream up, cook up, brew, conceive.
2 *the president's brother was accused of plotting against him*: **conspire**, scheme, participate in a conspiracy, intrigue, collude, connive, manoeuvre; rare machinate, cabal, complot.
3 *the position of the fifty-three sites was plotted*: **mark**, chart, map, indicate, represent, graph.

P

plotter noun *the plotters had intended to assassinate the president*: **conspirator**, co-conspirator, schemer, intriguer; planner; rare machinator, conspirer, Machiavellian, cabalist.

plough verb **1** *the fields had been ploughed*: **cultivate**, till, work, furrow, harrow, ridge, break up, turn up.
2 *the car overturned and ploughed into a lamp post*: **career**, plunge, crash, smash, bulldoze, hurtle, cannon, lurch, drive, run, careen; N. Amer. informal barrel.
3 *they ploughed their way through deep snow*: **trudge**, plod, toil, clump, push one's way, wade, flounder, press, move laboriously; informal slog; Brit. informal trog.
□ **plough into** *it begins to look as though the plane will plough into the water*: **crash into**, smash into, collide with, be in collision with, hit, strike, ram, smack into, slam into, bang into, meet head-on, run into, drive into, bump into, crack into/against; dash against; N. Amer. impact.
□ **plough something into** *profits from sales of the work are ploughed into further commissions*: **invest in**, put money into, sink money into, lay out money on; provide capital for, spend money on, fund, back, finance, underwrite, subsidize, support, pay for; buy into, buy shares in, buy/take a stake in; informal get a piece of, splash out on.
□ **plough on** *she ploughed on nonetheless and cleared her plate*: **persevere**, persist, continue, carry on, go on, keep at it, keep on, keep going, keep it up, not give up, be persistent, be determined, see/follow something through, show determination, press on/ahead, plod on, stay with something, not take no for an answer; be tenacious, be pertinacious, insist, be patient, be diligent, stand one's ground, stand fast/firm, hold on, hold out, go the distance, stay the course, grind away, struggle on, hammer away, stop at nothing, leave no stone unturned; informal plug away, peg away, stick at it, soldier on, hang on, stick to one's guns, stick it out, hang in there, bash on.

ploy noun *perhaps this had been a ploy to revive her husband's fading interest*. See **stratagem**.

pluck verb **1** *Jane plucked a thread from the lapel of his coat*: **remove**, **pick off**, pick, pull, pull off/out, extract, take, take off.
2 *she plucked at his T-shirt*: **pull (at)**, tug (at), clutch (at), snatch (at), take hold of, grab, seize, catch (at), tweak, twitch, jerk; informal yank.
3 *the turkeys are plucked and cleaned*: **remove the feathers from**, strip of feathers; rare deplume, displume.
4 *he picked up the guitar and began to pluck the strings*: **strum**, pick, thrum, twang, plunk, finger; play pizzicato.
▸ noun *it must have taken a lot of pluck to go there alone*: **courage**, bravery, nerve, pluckiness, boldness, courageousness, braveness, backbone, spine, daring, spirit, intrepidness, intrepidity, fearlessness, mettle, determination, fortitude, resolve, resolution, stout-heartedness, hardihood, dauntlessness, valour, doughtiness, heroism, audacity; informal grit, guts, spunk, gutsiness, gumption; Brit. informal bottle, ballsiness; N. Amer. informal moxie, cojones, sand; vulgar slang balls.

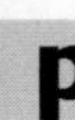

plucky adjective *plucky staff defeat armed raiders*: **brave**, courageous, bold, daring, fearless, intrepid, spirited, game, valiant, valorous, lionhearted, heroic, gallant, stout-hearted, stout, dauntless, resolute, determined, gritty, stalwart, undaunted, indomitable, unflinching, audacious, unafraid, doughty, mettlesome; informal gutsy, ballsy, spunky, have-a-go, feisty.
▷ANTONYMS cowardly, timid, timorous.

plug noun **1** *she pulled out the plug and the liquid drained away*: **stopper**, bung, cork, seal, spigot, spile; N. Amer. stopple.
2 *a plug of tobacco*: **wad**, quid, twist, chew; N. Amer. informal chaw; rare pigtail, cud, cake.
3 informal *he put in a plug for his new book*: **piece of publicity**, favourable mention, advertisement, promotion, recommendation, mention, good word, commercial; informal hype, push, puff, ad, boost, ballyhoo; Brit. informal advert.
□ **pull the plug on** informal *we pulled the plug on the new product line and laid off about 90 employees*: **discontinue**, wind up, stop, end, terminate, abort, bring to an end, put an end to, put a stop to, finish, bring to a halt, call a halt to, cancel, drop, dispense with, do away with, get rid of, abolish; suspend, interrupt, break off, phase out, withdraw; abandon, give up, cease, refrain from; informal cut, axe, scrap, give something the chop, knock something on the head, leave off, pack in; N. Amer. informal quit; rare intermit.
▸ verb **1** *plug the holes with dowels*: **stop (up)**, seal (up/off), close (up/off), cork, stopper, bung, block (up/off), dam (up), fill (up), pack, stuff; N. Amer. stopple.
2 informal *he plugged his new film*: **publicize**, promote, give publicity to, advertise, mention, give a mention to, write up, build up, beat/bang the drum for, commend, draw attention to; informal hype, hype up, push, puff, boost.
3 informal *don't say a word or I'll plug you*: **shoot**, hit, shoot down, gun down, pick off; informal blast, pump full of lead.
□ **plug away** informal *he plugged away at his writing*: **toil**, labour, toil away, plod away, work away, slave away, soldier on with, persevere with, persist with, keep on with, plough on with, hammer away, grind away; informal slog away, beaver away, peg away; archaic drudge away.

plum adjective *a plum job*: **excellent**, very good, wonderful, marvellous, choice, best, prize, first-class; informal great, terrific, cushy; Brit. informal plummy.

plumb[1] verb *the actor's attempt to plumb the twisted psyche of Richard III*: **explore**, probe, delve into, search, examine, investigate, scrutinize, inspect, sound out, go into, understand, fathom, get to the bottom of, penetrate, unravel.
□ **plumb the depths** *she had* ***plumbed the depths of*** *depravity*: **find**, reach the lowest possible level, reach the lowest point, get down to the bottom, reach the nadir, experience the worst extremes, reach rock bottom.
▸ adverb **1** *the bullets went plumb through the middle of the screen*: **right**, exactly, precisely, directly, dead, straight, without interruption; informal bang, slap, slap bang, smack.
2 *they must both be plumb crazy*: **utterly**, absolutely, completely, downright, totally, entirely, wholly, quite, altogether, thoroughly, stark.
3 *the bell hangs plumb within the tower of the church*: **vertically**, perpendicularly, straight up, straight up and down.
▸ adjective *the bird's flight ends with a plumb drop*: **vertical**, perpendicular, straight.

plumb[2] verb *he had* ***plumbed in*** *a washing machine*: **install**, put in, fit, put/set in place.

plume noun *black ostrich plumes*: **feather**, crest, quill; technical plumule; literary pinion.
▸ verb
□ **plume oneself** *he plumed himself on his latest innovation*: **congratulate oneself**, pat oneself on the back, pride oneself, preen oneself, feel proud about, feel self-satisfied about, boast about; archaic pique oneself.

plummet verb **1** *the plane plummeted to the ground*: **plunge**, fall headlong, hurtle, nosedive, dive, drop, crash, descend rapidly.
2 *share prices plummeted*: **fall steeply/sharply**, plunge, tumble, drop/decrease rapidly, go down, sink, slump; informal crash, nosedive, take a nosedive.

plummy adjective Brit. informal *a plummy voice*: **upper-class**, refined, aristocratic, affected, Home Counties, fruity, grand; Scottish Kelvinside, Morningside; Brit. informal posh, Sloaney; S. African informal larney.

plump[1] verb **1** *exhausted, Jack plumped down on to a chair*: **flop**, **collapse**, sink, fall, drop, slump, plop oneself; informal plonk oneself; N. Amer. informal plank oneself.
2 *she plumped her bag on the table*: **put**, put down, set, set down, deposit, dump, stick, place; informal plonk; Brit. informal bung; N. Amer. informal plunk.
3 *I* ***plumped for*** *a fixed-rate mortgage*: **choose**, decide on, go for, opt for, pick, pick out, settle on, select, take, elect, fix on, come down in favour of, vote for, single out, prefer; Brit. pitch on.

plump[2] adjective *a plump, rosy-faced girl*: **chubby**, **fat**, stout, rotund, buxom, well upholstered, well covered, well padded, of ample proportions, ample, roly-poly, round, rounded, well rounded, full, fattish, dumpy, chunky, broad in the beam, portly, overweight, fleshy, paunchy, bulky, corpulent; informal tubby, pudgy, beefy, porky, blubbery, poddy; Brit. informal podgy, fubsy; N. Amer. informal zaftig, corn-fed, lard-assed; archaic pursy; rare abdominous.
▷ANTONYMS thin, slender, skinny.

plumpness noun *his wife was inclined to plumpness*: **fat**, fatness, chubbiness, stoutness, dumpiness, portliness, fleshiness, corpulence; informal tubbiness, pudginess, porkiness; Brit. informal podginess; rare embonpoint.

plunder verb **1** *the invaders plundered the countryside*: **pillage**, loot, rob, raid, ransack, strip, fleece, ravage, lay waste, devastate, maraud, sack, rape; literary despoil; archaic spoil, pirate, reave; rare depredate, spoliate, forage.
2 *millions of pounds plundered from pension funds*: **steal**, take illegally, purloin, seize, thieve, rob, pillage, carry off; make off with, misappropriate, embezzle.
▸ noun **1** *the plunder of the villages*: **looting**, pillaging, plundering, robbery, robbing, raiding, ransacking, devastation, depredation, laying waste, sacking, marauding; literary despoiling, rapine, ravin; rare spoliation.
2 *the army sacked the city and carried off huge quantities of plunder*: **booty**, **loot**, stolen goods, spoils, prizes, ill-gotten gains, haul, takings, pickings; informal, dated swag, boodle.

plunge verb **1** *Joy stripped her clothes off and plunged into the sea*: **jump**, **dive**, hurl oneself, throw oneself, fling oneself, launch oneself, catapult oneself, cast oneself, pitch oneself.
2 *the aircraft plunged to the ground*: **crash**, **plummet**, pitch, drop, fall, fall headlong, tumble, nosedive, take a nosedive, crash-dive, descend.
3 *the car turned, plunging down a bumpy alley*: **charge**, **hurtle**, career, plough, cannon, lurch, careen, rush, dash, tear; N. Amer. informal barrel.
4 *world oil prices plunged in the 1980s*: **fall steeply/sharply**, plummet, drop rapidly, go down, tumble, sink, slump; informal crash, nosedive, take a nosedive.
5 *he plunged the dagger into the man's back*: **thrust**, stick, ram, drive, jab, stab, push, shove, force, sink.
6 *plunge the pears into a bowl of cold water*: **immerse**, submerge, sink, dip, dunk, douse, duck.

7 *the room was plunged into darkness*: **throw**, cast, pitch.
8 *the boat plunged*: **lurch**, pitch, roll, reel, toss about, keel, list, wallow, labour, flounder, make heavy weather; Nautical pitchpole.
▶ noun 1 *a plunge into the deep end of the pool*: **jump**, **dive**; nosedive, fall, pitch, drop, plummet, descent, tumble; archaic plump.
2 *the bank declared a 76% plunge in its profits*: **fall**, **drop**, tumble, slump; informal nosedive, crash.
□ **take the plunge** *he decided to take the plunge and become a full-time professional musician*: **commit oneself**, go for it, throw caution to the wind(s), give it one's all, give it all one has, go all out; informal jump in at the deep end, go for broke.

plurality noun *a plurality of religious traditions*: **wide variety**, large number, lot, diversity, range; multitude, multiplicity, galaxy, wealth, profusion, abundance, quantity, quantities, score, plethora, host; informal load, stack, heap, pile, mass, ton; Brit. informal shedload; N. Amer. informal slew; Austral./NZ informal swag.

plus preposition 1 *three plus three makes six*: **and**, **added to**, increased by, with the addition of.
2 *he wrote forty-seven novels plus various other books*: **as well as**, together with, along with, in addition to, added to, and, not to mention, besides, coupled with, with.
▷ANTONYMS minus.
▶ noun *one of the pluses of the job is having really supportive colleagues*: **advantage**, good point, plus point, asset, pro, benefit, added advantage, additional benefit, fringe benefit, bonus, extra, added extra, perk, dividend, attraction, attractive feature, beauty; formal perquisite.
▷ANTONYMS disadvantage, drawback, minus.

plush adjective *a plush hotel in the south of France*. See **sumptuous**.

plutocrat noun *champagne-swilling plutocrats*: **rich person**, capitalist, tycoon, magnate, nabob, millionaire, billionaire, multimillionaire, nouveau riche, person of means; informal fat cat, moneybags, zillionaire; rare Midas, Croesus, Dives.

ply[1] verb 1 *the gondolier plied his single oar*: **use**, wield, work, work with, employ, operate, utilize, manipulate, handle.
2 *for three years he plied a profitable export trade*: **engage in**, carry on, be engaged in, pursue, conduct, follow, practise, work at, occupy oneself with, busy oneself with; archaic prosecute.
3 *ferry boats ply between all the resorts on the lake*: **go regularly**, travel regularly, make regular journeys, travel, go back and forth, shuttle, commute.
4 *she plied me with tea and scones*: **provide**, supply, keep supplying, lavish, shower, regale, load, heap.
5 *he plied her with questions about her visit*: **bombard**, assail, besiege, beset, pester, plague, harass, importune; informal hassle.

ply[2] noun *tiles that have a black PVC ply in the lamination*: **layer**, thickness, strand, sheet, leaf, fold, insertion.

poach verb 1 *old Hector's been poaching salmon again*: **hunt illegally**, catch/trap/kill illegally, plunder.
2 *employers risk having their newly trained workers poached by other firms*: **steal**, appropriate, purloin, misappropriate, take; informal nab, swipe; Brit. informal nick, pinch.
3 *they resented foreign film-makers trying to poach on their territory*: **encroach on**, trespass on, invade, infringe on, intrude on.

pocket noun 1 *a roomy, padded bag with pockets on either side*: **compartment**, pouch, receptacle, sack, cavity.
2 *all the jewellery was far beyond her pocket*: **means**, budget, resources, financial resources, finances, funds, money, capital, assets, wherewithal; N. Amer. pocketbook.
3 *there were pockets of disaffection in parts of the country*: **area**, **patch**, small area, isolated area, district, region, island, cluster, centre.
▶ adjective *a pocket dictionary*: **small**, little, miniature, mini, compact, concise, abridged, potted, portable; N. Amer. vest-pocket; informal pint-sized.
▶ verb *he was arrested and charged with pocketing $900,000 of his followers' money*: **steal**, take for oneself, help oneself to, appropriate, misappropriate, thieve, purloin, embezzle, expropriate; informal filch, swipe, snaffle, lift, rip off, skim; Brit. informal pinch, nick, half-inch, whip, nobble; rare peculate, defalcate.

pockmark noun *his face was covered with pockmarks*: **scar**, **pit**, pock, pitted scar, mark, blemish.

pod noun *pea pods*: **shell**, husk, hull, case, seed vessel; N. Amer. shuck; technical pericarp, capsule, legume.

podgy adjective *she's a bit podgy*: **chubby**, plump, fat, fattish, stout, rotund, buxom, well upholstered, well covered, well padded, of ample proportions, ample, roly-poly, round, rounded, well rounded, full, chunky, broad in the beam, dumpy, portly, overweight, fleshy, paunchy, bulky; informal tubby, pudgy, porky, blubbery, poddy; Brit. informal fubsy; N. Amer. informal zaftig, corn-fed, lard-assed; archaic pursy, abdominous.
▷ANTONYMS thin, skinny, slender.

podium noun **platform**, stage, dais, rostrum, stand, soapbox; Indian mandapam.

poem noun **verse**, song, rhyme, piece of poetry, verse composition, metrical composition; rare verselet.

poet noun **verse writer**, versifier, verse-maker, rhymester, rhymer, sonneteer, lyricist, lyrist, elegist; laureate; literary **bard**, **swan**; derogatory poetaster; historical troubadour, balladeer; archaic **rhymist**; rare **metricist**, ballad-monger, idyllist, Parnassian, poeticule.

poetic adjective 1 *poetic compositions*: **in verse**, verse, metrical, rhythmical; poetical, lyrical, lyric, elegiac, rhapsodic; rare Parnassian.
2 *his rather poetic language*: **expressive**, figurative, symbolic, flowery, moving, aesthetic, artistic, tasteful, graceful, elegant, elevated, fine, beautiful; sensitive, imaginative, creative.

poetry noun **poems**, **verse**, verses, versification, metrical composition, rhythmical composition, rhymes, rhyming, balladry; Welsh **penillion**; literary poesy, Parnassus.

> *Word links* **poetry**
>
> **Calliope**, **Erato**, **Terpsichore** Muses of poetry

pogrom noun **massacre**, slaughter, wholesale slaughter, mass slaughter, mass killing, mass murder, mass homicide, mass execution, night of the long knives, annihilation, extermination, decimation, carnage, bloodbath, bloodletting, butchery, genocide, holocaust, Shoah, ethnic cleansing, megadeath; persecution, witch-hunt, destruction, victimization.

poignancy noun *the fact that he was soon to die gave his words a special poignancy*: **pathos**, **sadness**, pitifulness, piteousness, sorrow, mournfulness, wretchedness, misery, bitterness, pain, painfulness, distress, tragedy.

poignant adjective *the father of the murder victim bade a poignant farewell to his son*: **touching**, moving, sad, saddening, affecting, pitiful, piteous, pitiable, pathetic, sorrowful, mournful, tearful, wretched, miserable, bitter, painful, distressing, disturbing, heart-rending, heartbreaking, tear-jerking, plaintive, upsetting, tragic.

point[1] noun 1 *the point of a knitting needle*: **tip**, sharp end, tapered end, end, extremity; prong, spike, tine, nib, barb.
2 *the dark surface of the ocean was studded with points of light*: **pinpoint**, dot, spot, speck, fleck, mark.
3 *a prearranged meeting point*: **place**, position, location, site, spot, area, locality, locale; technical locus.
4 *at this point in her life, what she needs is a bit of romance*: **time**, stage, juncture, period, phase; moment in time, moment, instant.
5 *when it came to the point he would probably do what was expected of him*: **decisive moment**, critical moment, moment of truth, point of no return, crunch, crux, zero hour.
6 *tension between them had reached such a point that they barely spoke*: **level**, degree, stage, pitch, extent, height.
7 *you have ignored a number of important points*: **detail**, item, particular, fact, thing, piece of information, idea, argument, consideration, factor, element, aspect, regard, respect; subject, issue, topic, question, matter.
8 *it took her a long time to get to the point*: **most important fact**, main point, central point, essential point, essence, nub, focal point, salient point, heart of the matter, keynote, core, pith, marrow, meat, crux; meaning, significance, signification, import, gist, substance, drift, thrust, burden, theme, sense, moral, relevance, tenor; informal brass tacks, nitty-gritty.
9 *what's the point of telling me this?* **purpose**, aim, object, objective, goal, intention, end, design, reason, use, utility, sense, motive, value, advantage.
10 *she had to admit he had his good points*: **attribute**, characteristic, feature, trait, quality, property, aspect, facet, side; streak, peculiarity, idiosyncrasy.
□ **beside the point** *his comments seem to me to be beside the point*: **irrelevant**, immaterial, unimportant, not to the point, neither here nor there, nothing to do with it, not pertinent, not germane, off the subject, inapposite, inconsequential, incidental, pointless, out of place, wide of the mark, unconnected, peripheral, tangential, extraneous, extrinsic.
□ **case in point** *a good case in point is distance learning*: **example**, instance, case, representative case, typical case, illustration, specimen, sample, exemplar, exemplification, occasion, occurrence.
□ **in point of fact** *in point of fact nothing at all has been laid on*: **in fact**, as a matter of fact, actually, in actual fact, really, in reality, as it happens, in truth, to tell the truth, truly.
□ **make a point of** *he made a point of reading all the reviews*: **make an effort to**, go out of one's way to, put/place emphasis on.
□ **on the point of** *she was on the point of saying something, but changed her mind*: **just about to**, **on the verge of**, about to, going to, on the brink of, ready to, all set to.
□ **point of view** 1 *they expressed different points of view*: **opinion**, view, belief, attitude, feeling, sentiment, way of thinking, way of looking at it, thoughts, ideas. 2 *try and see things from his point of view*: **position**, perspective, viewpoint, standpoint, angle, slant, outlook, stand, stance, vantage point, side, frame of reference.
□ **to the point** *his observations were concise and to the point*: **relevant**, pertinent, apposite, germane, applicable, apropos, appropriate, apt, fitting, suitable, material, connected, related, linked; Latin ad rem; rare appurtenant.

P

▫ **up to a point** *this is true, but only up to a point*: **partly, to some extent**, to a certain extent, to some degree, to a certain degree, in part, somewhat, partially, not totally, not entirely, not wholly; informal ish.

▸ **verb 1** *she drew a revolver and pointed it at him*: **aim**, direct, level, train; N. Amer. draw/get a bead on.

2 *all the evidence **pointed to** his guilt*: **indicate**, suggest, be evidence of, evidence, signal, signify, denote, be symptomatic of, be a sign/symptom of, reveal, manifest; literary bespeak, betoken.

▫ **point the finger at** informal *this is not to point the finger at any one political leader*: blame, accuse, denounce, inform against, blacken the name of; incriminate, implicate, involve; entrap; informal frame, set up, stick/pin the blame on, grass on, rat on; Brit. informal fit up; archaic inculpate.

▫ **point something out** *the flaws in the plan have already been pointed out*: **identify**, show, designate, draw/call attention to, direct attention to, indicate, specify, detail, mention, refer to, allude to, touch on.

▫ **point something up** *studies are pointing up the value of specific vitamins*: **emphasize**, **highlight**, draw attention to, accentuate, underline, underscore, turn the spotlight on, spotlight, foreground, put/lay emphasis on, stress, give prominence to, play up, focus attention on, accent, bring to the fore.

point² **noun** *the ship rounded the point*: **promontory**, headland, head, foreland, cape, peninsula, bluff, ness, horn, bill.

point-blank **adverb 1** *Waxman fired the pistol point-blank at Clyde*: **at very close range**, at point-blank range, close up, close to.

2 *she couldn't say so point-blank to Alison*: **bluntly**, **directly**, straight, straightforwardly, frankly, candidly, forthrightly, openly, explicitly, unequivocally, unambiguously, unmistakably, plainly, clearly, flatly, positively, certainly, decisively, categorically, outright.

▸ **adjective** *a point-blank refusal*: **blunt**, **direct**, straight, straightforward, straight from the shoulder, frank, candid, forthright, open, explicit, unequivocal, unambiguous, unmistakable, plain, clear, clear-cut, crystal clear, well defined, flat, positive, certain, decisive, unqualified, categorical, outright, downright.

pointed **adjective 1** *the pointed end of the stick*: **sharp**, spear-like, needle-like, spear-shaped, V-shaped, tapering, tapered, cone-shaped, conic, conical, acute, sharp-cornered, wedge-shaped, sharp-edged, edged, jagged, spiky, spiked, barbed; informal pointy; technical acicular, lanceolate, acuminate, subulate, mucronate, aculeate; rare cuspidate, cusped, conoid.

2 *a pointed remark*: **cutting**, trenchant, biting, incisive, acid, acerbic, tart, caustic, scathing, mordant, razor-edged, venomed, venomous, piercing, penetrating; N. Amer. informal snarky; rare acidulous, mordacious.

pointer **noun 1** *the pointer moved to 'start engines'*: **indicator**, needle, arrow, hand.

2 *the met officer used a pointer on the chart*: **stick**, rod, cane, pole, laser pointer, cursor.

3 *the politicians' mood is a pointer to the outcome of the election*: **indication**, indicator, clue, hint, lead, sign, signal, evidence, symptom, implication, intimation, inkling, suggestion.

4 *perhaps I can give a few pointers to anyone just starting up*: **tip**, hint, piece of advice, suggestion, guideline, recommendation, warning.

pointless **adjective** **senseless**, **futile**, hopeless, fruitless, useless, needless, wasted, in vain, unavailing, aimless, idle, to no purpose, purposeless, worthless, valueless, unproductive, unprofitable; absurd, insane, nonsensical, stupid, silly, irrelevant, footling, fatuous, foolish, hollow, inane, ridiculous.

▷ANTONYMS useful, valuable.

> *Choose the right word* **pointless, futile, fruitless, vain**
>
> See **futile**.

poise **noun 1** *poise and good deportment can be cultivated*: **balance**, equilibrium, control, grace, gracefulness, presence.

2 *in spite of this setback she retained her poise*: **composure**, equanimity, self-possession, aplomb, presence of mind, assurance, self-assurance, self-control, nerve, calmness, coolness, sangfroid, countenance, collectedness, serenity, dignity, imperturbability, suaveness, urbanity, elegance; informal cool, unflappability.

▸ **verb 1** *the dancer was poised on one foot* | *a world poised between peace and war*: **balance**, hold (oneself) steady, steady oneself, be suspended, hang suspended, remain motionless, hang in mid-air, hang, hover.

2 *the president was poised for decisive action*: **position oneself**, ready oneself, prepare oneself, brace oneself, get into position, gear oneself up, stand by; balance, steady.

poised **adjective** *a very poised young woman*: **self-possessed**, self-assured, composed, assured, self-controlled, cool-headed, calm, cool, {cool, calm, and collected}, at ease, tranquil, serene, unperturbed, unruffled, impassive, nonchalant, confident, self-confident, dignified, equable, imperturbable, suave, urbane, elegant; informal together, unfazed, unflappable; rare equanimous.

▷ANTONYMS excited, flustered; inelegant.

poison **noun 1** **toxin**, venom; archaic bane; rare toxicant.

2 *Marianne would waste no time in spreading her poison*: **malice**, maliciousness, ill will, hate, malevolence, malignity, malignancy, balefulness, embitterment, embitteredness, spite, spitefulness, venom, acrimony, acrimoniousness, rancour; bad influence, blight, bane, contagion, cancer, canker, corruption, pollution.

▸ **verb 1** *her stepmother poisoned her*: **administer poison to**, give poison to; murder.

2 *a blackmailer had been poisoning baby foods*: **contaminate**, put poison in, adulterate, tamper with, spike, lace, doctor.

3 *the Amazon basin is being poisoned by mercury*: **pollute**, contaminate, taint, foul, befoul, dirty, blight, spoil.

4 *his mind was poisoned against her*: **prejudice**, bias, jaundice, colour, embitter, sour, envenom, warp, corrupt, subvert.

> *Word links* **poison**
>
> **toxi-**, **toxico-**, **toxo-** related prefixes, as in *toxigenic, toxicodendron, toxocariasis*
> **toxicology** study of poisons

poisonous **adjective 1** *a poisonous snake*: **venomous**, deadly.

▷ANTONYMS harmless.

2 *a poisonous chemical*: **toxic**, deadly, fatal, lethal, mortal, death-dealing, virulent, noxious.

▷ANTONYMS harmless, non-toxic.

3 *he shot a poisonous glance towards Rickie*: **malicious**, malevolent, hostile, vicious, spiteful, bitter, venomous, evil-intentioned, ill-natured, vindictive, vengeful, vitriolic, rancorous, malign, malignant, pernicious, mean, nasty, harmful, hurtful, wounding; slanderous, libellous, defamatory; informal bitchy, catty; literary malefic, maleficent.

▷ANTONYMS benevolent.

poke **verb 1** *they poked him in the ribs* | *he poked the baton hard into the man's stomach*: **prod**, jab, dig, nudge, tap, butt, ram, shove, punch, prick, jolt; thrust, stab, push, plunge, stick, insert, drive, lunge.

2 *leave the cable **poking out** of the wall*: **stick out**, jut out, stand out, protrude, project, extend, loom; rare protuberate.

▫ **poke about/around** *you've no right to go poking around in that cupboard*: **search**, hunt, rummage (around), forage, scrabble, grub, root about/around, scavenge, fish about/around, rake around, feel around, grope around, nose around, ferret (about/around); pry into, ransack, rake through, sift through, go through, shuffle through, rifle through, scour, comb, explore, probe; Brit. informal rootle (around).

▫ **poke fun at** *they giggled and poked fun at Eleanor*: **mock**, make fun of, laugh at, make jokes about, ridicule, jeer at, sneer at, deride, treat with contempt, treat contemptuously, scorn, laugh to scorn, scoff at, pillory, be sarcastic about, satirize, lampoon, burlesque, parody, tease, taunt, rag, make a monkey of, chaff, jibe at; informal send up, kid, rib, josh; Brit. informal wind up, take the mickey out of; N. Amer. informal goof on, rag on, razz, pull someone's chain; Austral./NZ informal poke mullock at, sling off at, chiack; Brit. informal, dated twit, rot; Brit. vulgar slang take the piss (out of); dated make sport of; archaic joke, quiz, flout.

▫ **poke one's nose into** *she was poking her nose into something that did not concern her*: **pry into**, **interfere in**, nose around in, intrude on, butt into, meddle with, tamper with; informal snoop into.

▸ **noun 1** *Carrie gave him a poke*: **prod**, jab, dig, elbow, nudge, tap, butt.

2 *a poke in the eye with a stick*: **thrust**, push, jab, shove, plunge, insertion.

poker-faced **adjective** *the poker-faced Gilels betrays hardly a trace of emotion throughout the performance* | *the book presents the script, together with a poker-faced foreword*: **expressionless**, inscrutable, unexpressive, inexpressive, impassive, dispassionate, blank, unresponsive, stony, wooden, empty, vacant, glazed, fixed, lifeless; **deadpan**, straight-faced.

poky **adjective** *a poky room*: **small**, little, tiny; **cramped**, confined, restricted, narrow, tight, uncomfortable, cell-like, boxy; informal with no room to swing a cat; euphemistic 'compact', 'bijou', 'easy to maintain/clean', 'well planned'; archaic strait; rare incommodious.

▷ANTONYMS spacious, roomy, palatial.

polar **adjective 1** *polar weather conditions*: **Arctic**, **Antarctic**; **cold**, frozen, freezing, frigid, chill, chilling, icy, icy-cold, glacial, gelid, Siberian; rare boreal, hyperborean, circumpolar, brumal, borean, hyperboreal.

2 *the two polar types of interview*: **opposite**, opposed, opposing, oppositional, diametrically opposed, extreme, contrary, contradictory, antithetical, antagonistic, conflicting, counterbalancing; rare antitypical, antonymous, antipodal, contrarious, dichotomous, oppositive.

polarity **noun** *the polarity between social and biological explanations*: **difference**, separation, opposition, contradiction, contradictoriness, antithesis, duality, antagonism, conflict, dichotomy; rare contrariety, antonymy.

pole¹ **noun** *the notice was pinned on a wooden pole*: **post**, pillar, stanchion, standard, paling, pale, stake, stick, picket, palisade, support, prop, batten, mast, bar, shaft, rail, rod, beam, spar, crosspiece, upright, vertical; staff, stave, cane, spike, baton, truncheon.

□ **up the pole** informal *a disgusted England fan went up the pole when Portugal beat them*: **mad**, crazy, insane, out of one's mind, deranged, demented, distracted; informal mental, off one's head, out of one's head, off one's nut, nutty, off one's rocker, round the bend, raving mad, stark staring/raving mad, bats, batty, bonkers, bananas, loco; Brit. informal barmy, crackers, round the twist; N. Amer. informal buggy, nutsy, nutso.

pole[2] noun *our points of view are at opposite poles*: **extremity**, extreme, limit; rare antipode.

□ **poles apart** *our views are poles apart*: **completely different**, as different as they could be, widely separated, directly opposed, antithetical, incompatible, irreconcilable, miles/worlds apart, at opposite extremes/poles, like night and day; Brit. like chalk and cheese; rare antipodal.

Word links **pole**

bipolar relating to both the North and South Poles

polemic noun **1** *this is not just a polemic against injustice*: **diatribe**, invective, denunciation, denouncement, rant, tirade, broadside, attack, harangue, verbal onslaught; condemnation, brickbats, criticism, admonishment, admonition, abuse, stream of abuse, stricture, tongue-lashing, castigation, reprimand, rebuke, reproof, reproval, upbraiding; informal knocking, blast; Brit. informal slating; rare philippic.

2 (**polemics**) *skilled in polemics*: **argumentation**, argument, debate, contention, dispute, disputation, discussion, controversy, altercation, faction, wrangling; formal contestation.

▸ adjective See **polemical**.

polemical adjective *Brunner published a polemical tract against Barth*: **critical**, hostile, bitter, polemic, virulent, vitriolic, venomous, waspish, corrosive, biting, caustic, trenchant, cutting, acerbic, sardonic, sarcastic, scathing, acid, sharp, keen, tart, pungent, stinging, astringent, incisive, devastating, piercing; rare acidulous, mordacious.

police noun **police force**, police officers, policemen, policewomen, officers of the law, the forces of law and order, law-enforcement officers, law-enforcement agency; Brit. **constabulary**; Scottish & Irish **polis**; French **gendarmerie**; German **Polizei**; Italian **carabinieri**; historical **watch**; informal the cops, the fuzz, the law, the Man, the boys in blue, the long arm of the law; Brit. informal the (Old) Bill; coppers, rozzers, bobbies, busies, bizzies, the force, plod, PC Plod; N. Amer. informal the heat, ...'s finest; informal, derogatory pigs, the filth; black English, derogatory Babylon.

▸ verb **1** *it would not be possible to police the area effectively*: **maintain law and order in**, keep the peace in, keep guard over, keep watch on, watch over, guard, protect, defend, patrol, make the rounds of.

2 *the cost of policing the demonstration*: **control**, keep in order, keep under control, regulate.

3 *the regulations will be policed by Environmental Health officers*: **enforce**, regulate, implement, oversee, check (up on), supervise, monitor, observe, watch.

police officer noun **policeman**, **policewoman**, officer of the law, law-enforcement officer/agent, officer; Brit. constable; N. Amer. patrolman, trooper, roundsman, peace officer; Indian kotwal, jawan; French gendarme; informal cop, jack, uniform; Brit. informal copper, bobby, rozzer, busy, bizzy, plod, PC Plod; N. Amer. informal bear; Austral./NZ informal walloper, demon; French informal flic; informal, derogatory pig; informal, dated flatfoot, bogey, flattie, woodentop; archaic peeler, runner, bluebottle, finger.

policy noun **1** *government policy on international trade*: **plans**, **strategy**, proposed action, blueprint, approach, scheme, stratagem, programme, schedule, code, system, guidelines, intentions, notions, theory, line, position, stance, attitude.

2 *it was good policy to listen politely*: **practice**, custom, procedure, wont, way, tack, routine, matter of course, style, pattern, convention, mode, rule.

polish verb **1** *I polished his shoes*: **shine**, wax, buff, rub up, rub down; gloss, burnish, brighten, smooth; varnish, oil, glaze, lacquer, enamel, japan, shellac; archaic furbish.

2 *it's time to **polish up** your essay*: **perfect**, refine, improve, hone, embellish, enhance, put the finishing/final touches to; brush up, revise, copy-edit, correct, emend, rewrite, rephrase, go over, touch up, finish off; informal clean up.

□ **polish something off 1** *he had polished off an apple pie and a strawberry milkshake*: **eat up**, **finish**, consume, devour, eat greedily, guzzle, feast on, wolf down, down, bolt; drink up, empty, drain, quaff, gulp (down); informal binge on, stuff one's face with, stuff oneself with, get outside of, murder, pack away, put away, scoff (down), shovel down, pig oneself on, pig out on, sink, swill, knock back, get one's laughing gear round; Brit. informal shift, gollop, bevvy; N. Amer. informal scarf (down/up), snarf (down/up), inhale; rare ingurgitate, bib. **2** *a third enemy plane tried to polish him off*: **destroy**, put an end to, finish off, dispatch, dispose of, do away with, eliminate, kill, liquidate; informal bump off, knock off, do in, blow away, take out; N. Amer. informal rub out. **3** *I'll polish off the last few pages*: **complete**, finish, deal with, wrap up, accomplish, execute, discharge, do, get done, fulfil, achieve, attain, end, conclude, close, bring to a conclusion/end/close, finalize, stop, cease, terminate, round off, wind up; informal sew up, have something sewn up.

▸ noun **1** *shoe polish | nail polish*: **wax**, **varnish**, glaze, lacquer, enamel, japan, shellac.

2 *this process achieves a good surface polish*: **shine**, gloss, lustre, sheen, sparkle, patina, finish, smoothness.

3 *he had changed, with all his polish and scholarship*: **sophistication**, refinement, urbanity, suavity, suaveness, elegance, style, grace, finish, accomplishment, finesse, subtlety, distinction, taste, cultivation, culture, politeness, civility, gentility, breeding, courtesy, courteousness, (good) manners; informal class.

polished adjective **1** *a polished table*: **shiny**, shining, bright, glossy, gleaming, lustrous; smooth, level, glassy, slippery; waxed, buffed, burnished, sanded, ground, varnished, glazed, lacquered, enamelled, japanned, shellacked; archaic furbished.

▸ANTONYMS dull, tarnished; rough.

2 *a polished performance of Mozart's Divertimento in D*: **expert**, accomplished, masterly, masterful, skilful, skilled, clever, proficient, adept, deft, adroit, dexterous, impeccable, flawless, faultless, perfect, consummate, exquisite, outstanding, excellent, superb, superlative, remarkable, first-rate, fine, talented, gifted; informal ace, stellar, class.

▸ANTONYMS inexpert.

3 *polished manners*: **refined**, cultivated, civilized, civil, well bred, polite, courteous, well mannered, genteel, decorous, proper, respectable, courtly, urbane, suave, sophisticated, seemly.

▸ANTONYMS gauche, ill-bred.

polite adjective **1** *we were too polite to comment*: **well mannered**, civil, courteous, respectful, deferential, well behaved, well bred, gentlemanly, ladylike, chivalrous, gallant, genteel, cultivated, gracious, urbane, well brought up; tactful, considerate, thoughtful, discreet, diplomatic; dated mannerly.

▸ANTONYMS rude, impolite.

2 *the picture outraged polite society*: **civilized**, refined, cultured, sophisticated, genteel, well bred, urbane, elegant, courtly.

▸ANTONYMS savage, uncivilized.

Choose the right word **polite, civil, courteous**

These three adjectives all describe people or actions that are considerate and exhibit good manners.

Polite is the most common word and is used in general social rather than commercial settings (*he was always polite on the phone | I only asked a polite question*); compare *courteous* below. Sometimes *polite* actions are just the minimum required or done purely for the sake of good manners (*I tried to make polite conversation*). It can also mean 'civilized and cultured' since politeness can involve glossing over subjects that are socially unacceptable because they are coarse or embarrassing (*this is not what passes for humour in polite society*).

Civil behaviour is formal and rather reserved and may be only the absolute minimum required to avoid actually being rude (*his replies were civil, but scarcely welcoming*).

Courteous either suggests a particularly graceful and charming politeness (*a courteous regard for the lady's feelings*) or is used in commercial contexts (*friendly and courteous staff*).

politeness noun *I have been treated with great politeness*: **courtesy**, civility, respect, deference, good breeding, manners, good manners, chivalry, gallantry, gentility, cultivation, grace, urbanity; tact, tactfulness, consideration, considerateness, thoughtfulness, discretion, diplomacy; dated mannerliness.

▸ANTONYMS rudeness.

politic adjective *I did not think it politic to express my reservations*: **wise**, prudent, sensible, judicious, canny, well judged, sagacious, expedient, shrewd, astute, discreet, tactful, diplomatic; recommended, advantageous, beneficial, profitable, gainful, desirable, advisable; appropriate, suitable, fitting, apt, timely, opportune, propitious, provident.

▸ANTONYMS inadvisable, injudicious, unwise.

political adjective **1** *the political affairs of the nation*: **governmental**, government, local government, ministerial, parliamentary, party political, diplomatic, legislative, policy-making, constitutional, public, civic, state, administrative, bureaucratic.

2 *he certainly wasn't a political animal*: **activist**, active, militant, factional, partisan, party, party political.

politician noun **legislator**, Member of Parliament, MP, representative, minister, statesman, stateswoman, political leader, lawmaker, public servant, elected official, office-bearer; in the US senator, congressman, congresswoman; informal politico; N. Amer. informal pol.

politics noun **1** *a career in politics*: **government**, local government, affairs of state, public affairs, diplomacy, party politics.

2 *he studies politics*: **political science**, civics, statecraft, statesmanship; rare polity.

3 *what are his politics?* **political views/beliefs/leanings/sympathies**, party politics, political alliance.

4 *office politics*: **power struggle**, manipulation, machination(s), manoeuvring, jockeying for position, wheeler-dealing, machiavellianism, opportunism, realpolitik.

poll noun **1** *the electoral rules provided for a second-round poll*: **vote**, **ballot**, show of hands, straw vote/poll, referendum, plebiscite, election.
2 *apathy might cause the poll to be unduly low*: **voting figures**, vote, returns, count, tally.
3 *they may conduct a poll to investigate whether people enjoyed their holidays*: **survey**, opinion poll, canvass, market research, sampling, census.
▶ **verb 1** *57% of the people polled supported his action*: **canvass**, **survey**, ask, question, interview, ballot, sample.
2 *she polled 119 votes*: **get**, gain, register, record, return.

pollute verb **1** *fish farms will pollute the lake*: **contaminate**, adulterate, taint, poison, befoul, foul, dirty, soil, blight, make filthy, infect.
▷ANTONYMS clean, purify.
2 *the propaganda that polluted this nation*: **corrupt**, poison, warp, pervert, deprave, defile, blight, debauch, sully, besmirch, desecrate, violate.
▷ANTONYMS purify.

pollution noun **1** *pollution caused by vehicle emissions*: **contamination**, contaminating, adulteration, adulterating, tainting, impurity, fouling, befouling, foulness, dirtiness, dirtying, soiling, filthiness, infection, infecting.
▷ANTONYMS purity.
2 *research into the pollution of young minds*: **defilement**, **corruption**, corrupting, poison, poisoning, blight, warping, depravation, depravity, sullying, besmirching, desecration, violation.

pomp noun *the pomp and popular jubilation accompanying his arrival*: **ceremony**, ceremoniousness, ceremonial, solemnity, ritual, display, spectacle, pageantry, pageant; show, showiness, ostentation, splendour, grandeur, grandness, magnificence, majesty, stateliness, glory, gloriousness, sumptuousness, opulence, lavishness, richness, brilliance, radiance, dazzle, theatricality, drama, flourish, glitter, style, éclat, resplendence, splendidness; informal pizzazz, razzle-dazzle, razzmatazz.
▷ANTONYMS simplicity.

pomposity noun **1** *Musgrave was inclined to pomposity*: **self-importance**, imperiousness, pompousness, sententiousness, grandiosity, affectation, stiffness, airs, pretentiousness, pretension, arrogance, vanity, haughtiness, pride, conceit, egotism, superciliousness, condescension, affectedness; informal snootiness, uppishness, uppitiness.
▷ANTONYMS modesty, humility.
2 *he seems to equate pomposity with profundity*: **bombast**, loftiness, pompousness, turgidity, grandiloquence, magniloquence, ornateness, portentousness, pedantry, boastfulness, boasting, bragging, sonorousness, windiness; rare fustian, euphuism, orotundity.

pompous adjective **1** *a pompous official who kept quoting the rules*: **self-important**, imperious, overbearing, domineering, magisterial, pontifical, sententious, grandiose, affected, stiff, pretentious, puffed up, arrogant, vain, haughty, proud, conceited, egotistic, supercilious, condescending, patronizing; informal snooty, uppity, uppish.
▷ANTONYMS modest, humble, self-effacing.
2 *pompous language*: **bombastic**, high-sounding, high-flown, lofty, turgid, grandiloquent, magniloquent, ornate, overblown, inflated, rhetorical, oratorical, declamatory, sonorous, portentous, pedantic, boastful, boasting, bragging, braggart, Falstaffian; informal highfalutin, windy; rare fustian, euphuistic, orotund.

pond noun **pool**, puddle, lake, tarn, reservoir, waterhole, lagoon, inland sea, swim; Brit. stew; Scottish loch, lochan; Anglo-Irish lough; N. Amer. pothole, bayou, tank; NZ moana; literary mere, plash.

ponder verb *she had plenty of time to* ***ponder over*** *the incident*: **think about**, give thought to, consider, review, reflect on, mull over, contemplate, study, meditate on, muse on, deliberate about, cogitate on, dwell on, brood on/over, ruminate about/on, chew over, puzzle over, speculate about, weigh up, turn over in one's mind; be in a brown study; informal put on one's thinking cap about; archaic pore on; rare cerebrate.

ponderous adjective **1** *a mechanical doll performed a ponderous dance*: **clumsy**, **slow**, heavy, awkward, lumbering, slow-moving, cumbersome, heavy-footed, ungainly, graceless, maladroit, uncoordinated, blundering, like a bull in a china shop; informal clodhopping, clunky; archaic lubberly; rare cumbrous.
▷ANTONYMS light, graceful, elegant.
2 *his ponderous sentences*: **laboured**, laborious, dull, awkward, clumsy, forced, stilted, unnatural, artificial, turgid, stodgy, stolid, lifeless, plodding, pedestrian, boring, uninteresting, solemn, serious, tedious, monotonous, dry, dreary, pedantic; ornate, elaborate, over-elaborate, intricate, convoluted, verbose, long-winded, windy, prolix.
▷ANTONYMS lively.

pontifical adjective *such explanations were greeted with pontifical disdain*: **pompous**, cocksure, self-important, arrogant, superior; **opinionated**, dogmatic, doctrinaire, dictatorial, authoritarian, domineering; intolerant, prejudiced, biased, bigoted; adamant, obstinate, stubborn, pig-headed, bull-headed, obdurate, of fixed views, headstrong, wilful, single-minded, rigid, inflexible, uncompromising, unyielding.
▷ANTONYMS open-minded; humble.

pontificate verb *he began to pontificate about life and art*: **hold forth**, expound, declaim, preach, lay down the law, express one's opinion (pompously), sound off, spout (off), dogmatize, sermonize, moralize, pronounce, lecture, expatiate; informal preachify, mouth off, spiel; rare perorate.

pooh-pooh verb informal *this idea was pooh-poohed by the scientific community*: **dismiss**, reject, brush aside, play down, spurn, rebuff, repudiate, disregard, discount, wave aside, make light of, make little of, belittle, treat with contempt, ridicule, deride, mock, hold up to scorn, scoff at, sneer at; N. Amer. informal slam-dunk; Austral./NZ informal wipe.

pool[1] noun **1** *pools of water in the fields after the rain*: **puddle**, pond.
2 *the hotel has its own pool*: **swimming pool**, baths, lido, piscina, plunge pool; Brit. swimming bath(s); N. Amer. rare natatorium.

pool[2] noun **1** *a car pool | a pool of skilled labour*: **supply**, common supply, reserve(s), store, reservoir, stock, stockpile, accumulation, storehouse, hoard, cache, fund, backlog.
2 *the cash would come from the pool of money set aside for such incidents*: **fund**, reserve, kitty, pot, bank, purse; jackpot, ante, stakes.
▶ **verb** *the members pool their skills and their grants*: **combine**, put together, amalgamate, group, join, unite, lump together, merge; fuse, conglomerate, agglomerate, coalesce, integrate; share.

poor adjective **1** *a poor family*: **poverty-stricken**, impoverished, necessitous, beggarly, in penury, penurious, impecunious, indigent, needy, needful, in need/want, badly off, in reduced circumstances, in straitened circumstances, destitute, hard up, short of money, on one's beam-ends, unable to make ends meet, underprivileged, deprived, penniless, without a sou, as poor as a church mouse, moneyless; bankrupt, bust, insolvent, in debt, in the red; Brit. on the breadline, without a penny (to one's name); informal broke, flat broke, cleaned out, strapped for cash, strapped, on one's uppers, without two pennies/(brass) farthings to rub together; Brit. informal stony broke, skint, in Queer Street; N. Amer. informal stone broke; rare pauperized, beggared.
▷ANTONYMS rich, wealthy.
2 *poor workmanship*: **substandard**, below standard, below par, bad, deficient, defective, faulty, imperfect, inferior, mediocre; abject, appalling, abysmal, atrocious, awful, terrible, dismal, dreadful, unsatisfactory, low-grade, second-rate, third-rate, jerry-built, shoddy, crude, tinny, trashy, rubbishy, miserable, wretched, lamentable, deplorable, pitiful, inadequate, insufficient, unacceptable, execrable, frightful; informal crummy, dire, bum, diabolical, rotten, sad, tatty, tenth-rate; Brit. informal ropy, duff, rubbish, pants, a load of pants, grotty; vulgar slang crap, crappy; archaic direful; rare egregious.
▷ANTONYMS superior.
3 *a poor crop of apples*: **meagre**, scanty, scant, paltry, limited, disappointing, restricted, reduced, modest, insufficient, inadequate, sparse, spare, deficient, negligible, insubstantial, skimpy, short, little, lean, small, slight, slender; miserable, lamentable, pitiful, puny, niggardly, beggarly; informal measly, stingy, pathetic, piddling; rare exiguous.
▷ANTONYMS satisfactory, good.
4 *poor soil*: **unproductive**, barren, unyielding, unfruitful, uncultivatable; depleted, exhausted, bare, arid, sterile; rare infecund; N. Amer. rare hardscrabble.
▷ANTONYMS fertile, productive.
5 *tropical oceanic waters are generally* ***poor in*** *nutrients*: **deficient in**, lacking (in), wanting (in), short of/on, low on, missing, with an insufficiency of, with too few/little ....
▷ANTONYMS rich in.
6 *you poor thing*: **unfortunate**, unlucky, luckless, unhappy, hapless, ill-fated, ill-starred, pitiable, pitiful, wretched.
▷ANTONYMS lucky.

poorly adverb *the text is poorly written*: **badly**, deficiently, defectively, faultily, imperfectly, unsuccessfully, incompetently, inexpertly, abjectly, appallingly, abysmally, atrociously, awfully, terribly, dismally, dreadfully; crudely, shoddily, inadequately, unsatisfactorily, unacceptably, execrably, frightfully; informal crummily, diabolically.
▶ **adjective** Brit. *she felt poorly yesterday*: **ill**, unwell, indisposed, ailing, not (very) well, not oneself, not in good shape, out of sorts, not up to par, under/below par, peaky, liverish; sick, queasy, nauseous; Brit. off, off colour; informal under the weather, not up to snuff, funny, peculiar, crummy, lousy, rough; Brit. informal ropy, grotty; Scottish informal wabbit; Austral./NZ informal crook; dated queer, seedy.

pop verb **1** *champagne corks were popping*: **go bang**, go off with a bang, go off, crack, snap, burst, explode.
2 *I'm just popping upstairs*: **go**, drop by/in/into/round, stop by, visit; informal tootle, whip; Brit. informal nip.
3 *pop a clear polythene bag over the pot*: **put**, place, slip, slide, push, stick, rest, deposit, set, lay, settle, locate, install, drop, shove, hang, position, arrange.
□ **pop one's clogs** Brit. informal *he died of a heart attack, and was overweight when he popped his clogs*. See **die** (sense 1).

▫ **pop up** *many familiar faces pop up during the twenty-six episodes*: **appear**, appear suddenly/unexpectedly/abruptly, occur suddenly/abruptly, come into view/sight, materialize, arrive, make/put in an appearance; come along, happen, emerge, arise, crop up, turn up, present itself, come on the scene, come to light, manifest itself; informal show up.

▸ **noun 1** *the balloons burst with a pop*: **bang**, crack, snap, boom, explosion, report.
2 informal *a bottle of pop*: **fizzy drink**, soft drink, carbonated drink; N. Amer. soda; Scottish informal scoosh.

pope noun **pontiff**, sovereign/supreme pontiff, Bishop of Rome, Holy Father, Vicar of Christ, His Holiness.

> *Word links* **pope**
>
> **papal, pontifical** relating to a pope
> **papacy** position of pope

pop music noun **pop**, popular music, chart music.

poppycock noun informal *Tory MPs dismissed Labour's claims as poppycock*: **nonsense**, rubbish, garbage, claptrap, balderdash, blather, blether, moonshine; foolishness, silliness; informal rot, tripe, hogwash, baloney, drivel, bilge, bosh, bull, bunk, guff, eyewash, piffle, phooey, hooey, malarkey, twaddle, dribble; Brit. informal cobblers, codswallop, stuff and nonsense, tosh, cack; Scottish & N. English informal havers; N. Amer. informal flapdoodle, blathers, applesauce, wack, bushwa; informal, dated bunkum, tommyrot, cod, gammon, toffee.

populace noun **population**, inhabitants, residents, natives, occupants, occupiers; community, country, public, people, nation; common people, general public, man/woman in the street, masses, multitude, rank and file, commonality, commonalty, third estate, plebeians, proletariat, crowd; N. Amer. man/woman on the street; informal folk, common folk; Brit. informal Joe Public, Joe Bloggs; N. Amer. informal John Doe; humorous denizens; derogatory the hoi polloi, common herd, rabble, mob, riff-raff, the canaille, the great unwashed, ragtag (and bobtail), proles, plebs; rare indigenes.

popular adjective **1** *the most popular boy around | the restaurant is very popular*: **well liked**, liked, favoured, in favour, well received, approved, admired, accepted, welcome, sought-after, in demand, desired, wanted; commercial, marketable, saleable, fashionable, in fashion, in vogue, voguish, all the rage, hot; informal in, cool, big; Brit. informal, dated all the go.
▷ANTONYMS unpopular.
2 *popular science | the popular press*: **non-specialist**, non-technical, non-professional, amateur, lay, lay person's, general, middle-of-the-road; accessible, approachable, simplified, plain, simple, easy, straightforward, understandable, readily understood, easy to understand, intelligible; mass-market, middlebrow, lowbrow, pop, bland, cheap.
▷ANTONYMS highbrow.
3 *policy-makers should listen to popular opinion*: **widespread**, general, common, current, prevalent, prevailing, customary, universal, standard, stock, shared, in circulation, rife; **ordinary**, usual, accepted, established, acknowledged, recognized, conventional, orthodox, conformist.
4 *a popular movement for independence*: **mass**, general, communal, collective, social, societal, collaborative, group, civil, public, civic; democratic, representative.

popularity noun **1** *the growing popularity of the city as a holiday destination*: **fashionableness**, vogue, stylishness; approval, favour, admiration, regard, acceptance, acclaim, welcome, demand; commerciality, marketability, saleability; adoration, adulation, idolization, lionization; informal coolness, trendiness.
2 *the new popularity of collectivist ideas*: **currency**, prevalence, commonness, universality, recognition.

popularize verb **1** *tobacco-smoking was popularized by Sir Walter Raleigh*: **make popular/fashionable**, bring into vogue, create a fashion for; market, publicize, hype.
2 *he popularized the subject, writing fourteen books for the layman*: **simplify**, make accessible, give mass-market appeal to, familiarize; vulgarize.
3 *the report popularized the notion that the world was running out of oil*: **give currency to**, spread, propagate, give credence to, universalize, generalize.

popularly adverb **1** *it was popularly believed that every strange old woman was a witch*: **widely**, generally, universally, commonly, by many/most/all, usually, regularly, customarily, habitually, conventionally, ordinarily, traditionally, as a rule.
2 *the Carboniferous is popularly known as the 'Age of Amphibians'*: **informally**, unofficially, simply, non-technically; by lay people, by non-specialists.
3 *the President is popularly elected for a five-year term*: **democratically**, by the people, universally, by universal suffrage.

populate verb **1** *the island is populated by some 40,000 people*: **inhabit**, live/reside in, occupy, people; formal dwell in.
2 *we are trying to populate a land which has been derelict*: **settle (in)**, colonize, people, move into, occupy, take up residence in, make one's home in, open up, pioneer, overrun.

population noun **inhabitants**, residents, people, citizens, citizenry, public, community, populace, society, natives, occupants, occupiers; informal folk, common folk; humorous denizens.

> *Word links* **population**
>
> **demo-** related prefix, as in *demography, democracy*

populous adjective *the country's second most populous city*: **densely populated**, heavily populated, thickly populated, heavily settled, crowded, congested, packed, jammed, crammed, teeming, swarming, seething, crawling, full; informal jam-packed.
▷ANTONYMS uninhabited, deserted.

porch noun **vestibule**, foyer, entrance, entrance hall, entry, portal, portico, lobby, anteroom; N. Amer. ramada, stoop; Austral./NZ sleepout; Indian mandapam; Architecture lanai, narthex, galilee, peristyle, stoa, colonnade, porte cochère, tambour.

pore[1] noun *sweat poured from every pore in his body*: **opening**, orifice, aperture, hole, outlet, inlet, vent; technical stoma, hydathode, ostiole, ostium, foramen.

pore[2] verb *they* **pored over** *a map of Eastern Europe*: **study**, read intently, peruse, be absorbed in, scrutinize, scan, examine, go over/through.

pornographic adjective **obscene**, indecent, improper, indelicate, crude, lewd; **erotic**, titillating, arousing, suggestive, sexy, risqué; coarse, vulgar, gross, dirty, ribald, smutty, filthy, bawdy, earthy, corrupting, exploitative, prurient, salacious, immoral; off-colour, adult, X-rated, hard-core, soft-core; informal porn, porno, blue, skin; rare rank.
▷ANTONYMS decent, pure, wholesome.

pornography noun **erotica**, pornographic material, pornographic literature/films/videos, hard-core pornography, soft-core pornography, dirty books; smut, filth, vice; informal porn, hard porn, soft porn, porno, skin/girlie magazines, cheesecake, pornies; dated, rare facetiae; curiosa.

porous adjective **permeable**, penetrable, pervious; absorbent, sponge-like, spongy, sieve-like, leaky, honeycombed, cellular, open, holey; technical absorptive; rare percolative, cavernulous, leachy, porose, poriferous, spongiose, foraminous, pory.
▷ANTONYMS impermeable.

port[1] noun **1** *the German port of Kiel*: **seaport**, port city/town; French entrepôt.
2 *shells exploded down by the port*: **harbour**, dock, docks, haven, mooring, jetty, pier, marina; anchorage, roads; archaic hithe; rare moorage, harbourage, roadstead.

port[2] noun *push the water supply pipes into the correct ports in the shower*: **aperture**, **opening**, outlet, inlet, socket, vent, passage, porthole, trap, embrasure, door, gate.

portable adjective **transportable**, movable, mobile, transferable, easily carried, easy to carry, conveyable, travelling, travel; lightweight, compact, handy, convenient, manageable; rare portative.

portal noun *he walked up to the portal of the palazzo*: **doorway**, gateway, entrance, way in, way out, exit, egress, opening; door, gate, threshold; N. Amer. entryway.

portend verb *the sound of the death-watch beetle was thought to portend the death of someone in the house*: **presage**, augur, foreshadow, foretell, prophesy; **be a sign of**, be a warning of, warn of, be an omen of, be an indication of, be a harbinger of; indicate, herald, signal, bode, announce, promise, threaten, point to, mean, signify, spell, denote; literary betoken, foretoken, forebode, harbinger.

portent noun **1** *here was a striking portent of things to come*: **omen**, sign, indication, presage, warning, forewarning, harbinger, augury, signal, promise, threat, menace, ill omen, forecast, prediction, prognostication, prophecy, straw in the wind, writing on the wall, hint, auspice; premonition, presentiment, feeling, vague feeling, funny feeling, feeling in one's bones, foreboding, misgiving; literary foretoken.
2 *the word 'plague' carries terrifying portent*: **significance**, importance, import, consequence, meaning, meaningfulness, moment, momentousness, weight, weightiness, cruciality.

portentous adjective **1** *portentous signs had been seen*: **ominous**, warning, foreshadowing, predictive, premonitory, prognosticatory, momentous, fateful; threatening, menacing, foreboding, sinister, ill-omened, inauspicious, unpropitious, unpromising, gloomy, unfavourable.
2 *Dr Chen muttered some portentous dialogue*: **pompous**, bombastic, self-important, pontifical, ponderous, solemn, sonorous, grandiloquent, declamatory, overblown, inflated, rhetorical, oratorical.

porter[1] noun *she asked a porter to help with their bags*: **carrier**, bearer, baggage carrier, baggage bearer; Sherpa; stretcher bearer; N. Amer. redcap, skycap; Indian khalasi; Spanish cargador.

porter[2] noun Brit. *some elegant blocks of flats have a full-time porter on the front door*: **doorman**, doorkeeper, door attendant, commissionaire, gatekeeper; caretaker, janitor, concierge.

P

portion noun **1** *the upper portion of the chimney | he could repeat large portions of Shakespeare*: **part**, piece, bit, section, chunk, segment, slice, fragment; wedge, lump, slab, hunk, parcel, tranche; Brit. informal wodge.
2 *she wanted the right to decide how her portion of the allowance should be spent*: **share**, slice, quota, part, bit, percentage, amount, quantity, ration, piece, fraction, division, subdivision, allocation, allotment, measure, apportionment; informal cut, whack, rake-off; rare quantum, moiety.
3 *a generous portion of chips*: **helping**, serving, amount, quantity, piece; plateful, bowlful.
4 *disease and hopeless poverty were certain to be his portion*: **destiny**, lot, fate, fortune, luck, kismet; what is written in the stars; archaic dole, cup, heritage.
▸ verb *her mother **portioned out** the food*: **share out**, allocate, apportion, distribute, hand out, deal out, dole out, give out, dish out, parcel out, divide out, allot, dispense, measure out, mete out; informal divvy up.

portly adjective *a portly, florid-faced man*: **stout**, plump, fat, overweight, heavy, corpulent, fleshy, paunchy, pot-bellied, beer-bellied, of ample build, ample, well upholstered, well padded, broad in the beam, rotund, roly-poly, round, rounded, stocky, bulky, Falstaffian; informal tubby, beefy, porky, pudgy, blubbery, poddy; Brit. informal podgy, fubsy; N. Amer. informal lard-assed, corn-fed; archaic pursy; rare abdominous.
▹ANTONYMS slim, thin.

portrait noun **1** *a portrait of King George III*: **painting**, picture, drawing, sketch, likeness, image, study, representation, portrayal, depiction, canvas; miniature, self-portrait, kit-cat portrait; informal oil; formal portraiture.
2 *she turned to photography, taking portraits for the Sunday Times*: **photograph**, photo, studio portrait, picture, shot, study, still, snap, snapshot, vignette; historical daguerreotype, carte de visite.
3 *the book paints a vivid portrait of contemporary Italy*: **description**, portrayal, representation, depiction, impression, account, story, chronicle; thumbnail sketch, vignette, profile, characterization.

portray verb **1** *many artists choose to portray Windermere in sunny weather*: **paint**, draw, paint/draw a picture of, picture, sketch, depict, represent, illustrate, present, show, render; literary limn.
2 *the ineffectual Oxbridge dons portrayed by Evelyn Waugh*: **describe**, depict, characterize, represent, delineate, present, show, paint in words, evoke.
3 *an article which portrays her as the victim of a loveless marriage*: **represent**, depict, characterize, describe, present.
4 *the actor portrays a spy*: **play the part of**, play, act the part of, take the role of, act, represent, appear as; rare personate.

portrayal noun **1** *a portrayal of an Imperial Amazon parrot*: **painting**, picture, drawing, portrait, sketch, representation, depiction, study, rendering.
2 *her acute and witty portrayal of adolescence*: **representation**, characterization, depiction, description, delineation, presentation, study, evocation.
3 *Brando's famous* **portrayal of** *Vito Corleone in 'The Godfather'*: **performance as**, acting, playing, enacting, representation, interpretation; rare personation.

pose verb **1** *pollution levels pose a threat to people's health*: **constitute**, present, create, cause, produce, give rise to, lead to, result in.
2 *the question posed in Chapter 1 remains unanswered*: **put forward**, raise, ask, put, set, submit, advance, propose, propound, posit, broach, suggest, postulate, moot.
3 *he asked her to come to his studio and pose for him*: **be a model**, model, sit, take up a position, assume an attitude, strike a pose.
4 *he posed her on the sofa*: **position**, place, put, arrange, lay out, set out, dispose, locate, situate; archaic posture.
5 *a bunch of fashion victims stood posing at the bar*: **behave affectedly**, strike an attitude, strike a pose, posture, attitudinize, put on airs, put on an act; informal show off; N. Amer. informal cop an attitude.
□ **pose as** *a gang posing as police officers hijacked the lorry*: **pretend to be**, impersonate, pass oneself off as, be disguised as, masquerade as, profess to be, purport to be, set oneself up as, assume/feign the identity of, pass for, represent oneself as; rare personate.
▸ noun **1** *a photograph of a glamorous brunette in a sexy pose*: **posture**, position, stance, attitude, bearing.
2 *she found her pose of aggrieved innocence hard to keep up*: **pretence**, act, affectation, facade, show, front, display, masquerade, posture; play-acting, attitudinizing, dissimulation.

poser[1] noun *'How are we going to get there?' This was a bit of a poser*: **difficult question**, awkward problem, knotty problem, vexed question, tough one, puzzle, mystery, conundrum, puzzler, enigma, riddle; informal dilemma, facer, toughie, tough/hard nut to crack, brain-teaser, stumper, cruncher.

poser[2] noun *he's such a poser*: **exhibitionist**, poseur, poseuse, self-publicist; informal show-off, pseud; rare attitudinizer, posturer.

poseur noun See **poser**[2].

posh adjective **1** informal *a posh Beverly Hills hotel*: **smart**, stylish, upmarket, fancy, high-class, fashionable, chic, luxurious, luxury, de luxe, exclusive, select, sumptuous, opulent, lavish, grand, rich, elegant, ornate, ostentatious, showy; N. Amer. high-toned; informal classy, swanky, snazzy, plush, plushy, ritzy, flash, la-di-da, fancy-pants; Brit. informal swish; N. Amer. informal swank, tony; S. African informal larney; US black English dicty; Brit. informal, dated swagger; derogatory chichi; archaic swell; rare sprauncy.
2 Brit. informal *her posh accent*: **upper-class**, aristocratic, upmarket, Home Counties; informal upper-crust, top-drawer; Brit. informal plummy, Sloaney, U.

posit verb *there are those who posit a purely biological basis for this phenomenon*: **postulate**, put forward, advance, propound, submit, predicate, hypothesize, take as a hypothesis, set forth, propose, pose, assert; presuppose, assume, presume.

position noun **1** *radars determine the aircraft's position*: **location**, place, situation, spot, site, locality, locale, scene, setting, area, point; whereabouts, bearings, orientation; Austral./NZ slang possy; technical locus.
2 *she levered herself into a standing position*: **posture**, stance, attitude, pose; set, arrangement, disposition, placement.
3 *the company's financial position is dire*: **situation**, state, condition, circumstances, set of circumstances, state of affairs, case; predicament, plight, pass, strait(s).
4 *all the political parties were jockeying for position*: **advantage**, pole position, advantageous position, favourable position, the upper hand, the edge, the whip hand, primacy; N. Amer. informal the catbird seat; Austral./NZ informal the box seat.
5 *people's awareness of their position in society*: **status**, place, level, rank, grade, grading, rating, standing, station, footing; stature, prestige, influence, reputation, repute, importance, consequence, class.
6 *I'm looking for a secretarial position*: **job**, post, situation, appointment, role, occupation, employment; office, capacity, duty, function; opening, vacancy, niche, opportunity, placement; informal berth; Austral. informal grip; archaic employ.
7 *the chancellor was asked to clarify the government's position on the matter*: **point of view**, viewpoint, opinion, way of thinking, outlook, attitude, stand, standpoint, stance, posture, angle, perspective, approach, slant, thinking, policy, thoughts, ideas, sentiments, feelings.
▸ verb *he pulled out a chair and positioned it between them*: **put**, place, locate, situate, set, site, stand, station; lay, lie, rest, prop, plant, stick, install, settle; arrange, dispose, array, range, lay out, deploy; orient, orientate; informal plonk, park; rare posit.

positive adjective **1** *I am confident of getting a positive response from the commission*: **affirmative**, favourable, approving, in the affirmative, good, constructive, enthusiastic, supportive, reassuring, encouraging, corroborative.
▹ANTONYMS negative.
2 *the results of the blood test were positive*: **showing a reaction**, affirmative.
▹ANTONYMS negative.
3 *do something positive about your problems*: **constructive**, practical, useful, pragmatic, productive, helpful, worthwhile, beneficial, effective, efficacious.
4 *she seems a lot more positive these days*: **optimistic**, hopeful, confident, forward-looking, cheerful, sanguine, buoyant, assured; informal upbeat.
▹ANTONYMS pessimistic.
5 *in spite of these positive signs, economists are not predicting a recovery*: **favourable**, good, pleasing, welcome, promising, encouraging, heartening, propitious, auspicious.
▹ANTONYMS negative.
6 *positive proof of identification must be produced*: **definite**, conclusive, certain, categorical, unequivocal, incontrovertible, indisputable, undeniable, incontestable, unmistakable, unambiguous, indubitable, unquestionable, irrefutable, beyond question, beyond a doubt, absolute, reliable, persuasive, convincing, concrete, tangible, clear, clear-cut, precise, direct, explicit, express, firm, decisive, real, actual; informal as sure as eggs is eggs.
▹ANTONYMS doubtful, disputable.
7 *I am positive that he's not coming back*: **certain**, sure, convinced, confident, satisfied, free from doubt, assured, persuaded.
▹ANTONYMS uncertain, unsure.
8 *the journey was a positive nightmare*: **utter**, complete, sheer, absolute, real, total, perfect, out-and-out, pure, outright, thoroughgoing, thorough, downright, unmitigated, unqualified, consummate, veritable, rank, unalloyed; Brit. informal right, bloody; Austral./NZ informal fair.

> *Choose the right word* **positive, sure, certain, convinced, definite**
>
> See **sure**.

positively adverb **1** *this is positively my last word on the matter*: **emphatically**, confidently, firmly, categorically, definitely, with certainty, conclusively, without qualification, certainly, beyond question, unquestionably, undoubtedly, indisputably, unmistakably, indubitably, assuredly.
2 *he looked positively livid*: **absolutely**, really, downright, simply, thoroughly, completely, utterly, totally, perfectly, extremely, to a marked degree, decidedly, fairly; informal plain, plumb.

possess verb **1** *the hat was the only one she possessed*: **own**, have, be the owner of, have in one's possession, be in possession of, be the possessor of, have to one's name, hold.
2 *he did not possess a sense of humour*: **have**, be blessed with, be endowed with, be gifted with, be possessed of, be born with; enjoy, boast, benefit from; archaic participate of.
3 *it was almost as though some supernatural force had possessed him*: **take control of**, have power over, take over, have mastery over, cast a spell over, bewitch, enchant, enthral, control, dominate, influence; madden, drive mad; rare bedevil.
4 *she was possessed by a burning need to talk to him*: **obsess**, dominate, haunt, preoccupy, consume; eat someone up, prey on someone's mind, become an obsession with, be uppermost in someone's mind, take control of.
□ **possess oneself of** *he possessed himself of a loaded shotgun*: **acquire**, obtain, get, get hold of, procure, secure, take, seize, take/gain possession of, get one's hands on; informal get one's mitts on.

possessed adjective *he ran towards the door like a man possessed*: **mad**, demented, insane, crazed, maddened, berserk, out of one's mind; bewitched, enchanted, under a spell, obsessed, haunted; rare bedevilled.

possession noun **1** *the estate came into the possession of the Heslerton family*: **ownership**, proprietorship, control, hands, keeping, care, custody, charge, hold, title, guardianship.
2 *an attempt to drive the tenant out of her possession of the premises*: **occupancy**, tenure, occupation, holding, tenancy.
3 *that photograph was Bert's most precious possession*: **asset**, thing, article, item owned, chattel.
4 (**possessions**) *he loaded Francesca and all her possessions into his car*: **belongings**, things, property, worldly goods, goods, personal effects, effects, stuff, assets, accoutrements, paraphernalia, impedimenta, bits and pieces, luggage, baggage, bags and baggage, chattels, movables, valuables; Law goods and chattels; informal gear, junk, dunnage, traps; Brit. informal clobber; S. African informal trek; vulgar slang shit, crap.
5 *France's former colonial possessions*: **colony**, dependency, territory, holding, dominion, protectorate.
□ **take possession of** seize, appropriate, impound, expropriate, sequestrate, sequester, confiscate; take, get, acquire, obtain, secure, procure, possess oneself of, get hold of, get one's hands on, help oneself to; occupy, conquer, capture, commandeer, requisition; Law distrain, attach, disseize; Scottish Law poind; informal get one's mitts on.

possessive adjective **1** *he was very possessive—he wanted me to spend every minute with him*: **proprietorial**, overprotective, clinging, controlling, dominating, jealous.
2 *one of those possessive women who wants to grab everything within reach*: **grasping**, greedy, acquisitive, covetous, selfish; N. Amer. informal grabby.

possibility noun **1** *there was still a possibility that he might be found alive*: **chance**, likelihood, probability, prospect, hope; risk, hazard, danger, fear.
2 *they discussed the possibility of launching a major research project on the theme*: **feasibility**, practicability, chances, odds, attainability, achievability, potentiality, conceivability, probability; opportunity, scope; rare workableness.
3 *buying a smaller house is one possibility*: **option**, alternative, choice, course of action, solution, recourse; informal bet.
4 (**possibilities**) *he had distinct possibilities as a player*: **potential**, potentiality, promise, prospects; capability, ability, aptitude, capacity; informal what it takes.

possible adjective **1** *it's not possible to check the accuracy of the figures*: **feasible**, able to be done, practicable, viable, within the bounds/realms of possibility, attainable, achievable, realizable, within reach, workable, manageable; informal on, doable.
▷ANTONYMS impossible.
2 *there was another possible reason for his disappearance*: **conceivable**, plausible, imaginable, thinkable, believable, likely, potential, probable, credible, tenable, odds-on; informal on the cards.
▷ANTONYMS unlikely.
3 *he was a possible future leader of the party*: **potential**, prospective, likely, probable, could-be, would-be, aspiring.

possibly adverb **1** *possibly he took the boy with him*: **perhaps**, maybe, it may/could be, it is possible, it is conceivable, for all one knows, feasibly, very likely; hopefully, God willing; N. English happen; literary peradventure, perchance, mayhap, haply; rare percase.
2 *you can't possibly refuse*: **conceivably**, under any circumstances, by any means, at all, in any way.
3 *could you possibly spare me a few moments?* **please**, kindly, be so good as to; by any chance, if possible.

post[1] noun *a high roof supported by wooden posts*: **pole**, stake, upright, shaft, prop, support, picket, strut, pillar, pale, paling, column, piling, standard, stanchion, pylon, stave, rod, newel, baluster, jamb, bollard, mast; fence post, gatepost, finger post, king post; N. Amer. & Austral. milepost; historical palisade; technical puncheon, shore.
▶ verb **1** *he studied the notice posted on the wall*: **affix**, attach, fasten, hang, display, pin (up), put up, stick (up), tack (up), nail (up).
2 *the group posted a net profit of $1.1 million*: **announce**, report, make known, advertise, publish, publicize, circulate, broadcast.

post[2] noun Brit. **1** *the winners will be notified by post*: **mail**, the postal service/system; airmail, surface mail, registered mail, special delivery; informal snail mail; N. Amer. & W. Indian the mails; Indian dak, tappal.
2 *did we get any post?* **letters**, cards, correspondence; parcels, packages, packets; mail, junk mail, direct mail.
3 *what time is the last post?* **postal delivery/collection**, mail delivery/collection.
▶ verb **1** Brit. *post the order form today*: **send**, send off, mail, put in the post/mail, get off, send/dispatch by post, transmit, remit, convey, consign, forward, redirect; airmail.
2 *post the transaction in the second column*: **record**, **write in**, enter, fill in, register, note, list.
□ **keep someone posted** *I'll keep you posted about his progress*: **keep informed**, inform, keep up to date, keep in the picture, keep briefed, brief, give someone the latest information, update, fill in, let someone know, advise, notify, apprise, report to; informal clue in, keep up to speed.

post[3] noun **1** *there were seventy candidates for the post*: **job**, position, appointment, situation, place, office, assignment, employment, placing; vacancy, opening; informal berth; Austral. informal grip; archaic employ.
2 *'Back to your posts!' he commanded*: **assigned position**, area of duty; position, place, location, station, observation post, base, beat.
▶ verb **1** *he'd been posted to Berlin*: **send**, send to take up an appointment, assign to a post, dispatch.
2 *armed guards were posted beside the exit door*: **put on duty**, station, position, put, situate, set, locate, install, establish, base, garrison.

poster noun *a poster advertising his latest film*: **notice**, placard, public notice, bill, sign, advertisement, announcement, affiche, playbill, sticker; Brit. fly-poster; China dazibao; informal ad; Brit. informal advert.

posterior adjective **1** *the posterior part of the skull*: **rear**, hind, back, hinder, rearward; technical dorsal, caudal, posticous.
▷ANTONYMS anterior, front.
2 formal *a date posterior to the first Reform Bill*: **later than**, subsequent to, following, succeeding, after.
▷ANTONYMS previous.
▶ noun humorous *her plump posterior*: **buttocks**, **behind**, backside, rear, rear end, rump, seat, haunches, hindquarters, cheeks; Brit. bottom; French derrière; German Sitzfleisch; informal sit-upon, stern, BTM, tochus; Brit. informal bum, botty, prat, jacksie; Scottish informal bahookie; N. Amer. informal butt, fanny, tush, tushie, tail, duff, buns, booty, caboose, heinie, patootie, keister, tuchis, bazoo, bippy; W. Indian informal batty; black English rass, rusty dusty; Brit. vulgar slang arse; N. Amer. vulgar slang ass; technical nates; humorous fundament; archaic breech.

posterity noun **1** *the names of those who died are recorded for posterity on a framed scroll*: **future generations**, succeeding generations, those who come after us; the future.
2 archaic *God appeared to Abraham with a promise that his posterity should inhabit the land*: **descendants**, heirs, successors, offspring, children, family, progeny, scions; Law issue; archaic seed.

post-haste adverb *he departed post-haste for Venice*: **as quickly as possible**, without delay, (very) quickly, speedily, swiftly, without further/more ado, with all speed, promptly, immediately, at once, straight away, right away, directly, forthwith; informal double quick, p.d.q. (pretty damn quick), pronto, before you can say Jack Robinson, straight off; archaic straight, instanter.

postman, postwoman noun **postal worker**; N. Amer. mailman, letter carrier, mail carrier; Brit. informal postie.

post-mortem noun **1** *the hospital will want to carry out a post-mortem*: **autopsy**, post-mortem examination, PM, dissection, necropsy.
2 *the very last thing she needed was a post-mortem of her failed relationship*: **analysis**, evaluation, assessment, appraisal, examination, review, investigation, breakdown, critique, study; rare anatomization.

postpone verb *he had to postpone his scheduled trip to South Africa*: **put off**, delay, defer, put back, hold over/off, carry over, reschedule, adjourn, stay, shelve, stand over, pigeonhole, keep in abeyance, suspend, mothball; N. Amer. put over, table, take a rain check on; N. Amer. Law continue; informal put on ice, put on the back burner, put in cold storage; rare remit, respite.
▷ANTONYMS advance, bring forward.

postponement noun *a further postponement of the trial*: **deferral**, deferment, delay, putting off/back, rescheduling, adjournment, shelving, suspension; stay, respite; Law moratorium; N. Amer. Law continuance; rare put-off.

postscript noun **1** *handwritten at the bottom of the letter was a postscript*: **afterthought**, PS, additional remark; rare subscript.
2 *he translated, reprinted, or edited works, adding postscripts of his own*: **addendum**, supplement, appendix, codicil, afterword, addition, adjunct; rare postlude, subscript.

postulate verb *such hypotheses have been postulated by highly reputable geologists*: **put forward**, **suggest**, advance, posit, hypothesize, take as a hypothesis, propose, assume, presuppose, suppose, presume, predicate, take for granted, theorize.

p

posture noun **1** *the priest quietly resumed his kneeling posture*: **position**, pose, attitude, stance.
2 *she took ballet lessons to improve her posture*: **bearing**, carriage, comportment, way of standing/sitting, stance; Brit. deportment.
3 *trade unions adopted a more militant posture in wage negotiations*: **attitude**, stance, stand, standpoint, view, point of view, viewpoint, opinion, position, way of thinking, frame of mind, outlook, angle, slant, perspective.
▶ verb *Keith postured, flexing his biceps for Douglas to see*: **pose**, strike an attitude, put on airs, attitudinize, behave affectedly, strut; informal show off; N. Amer. informal cop an attitude, hot-dog.

posy noun *a posy of snowdrops and violets*: **bouquet**, bunch, bunch of flowers, spray, nosegay, corsage; buttonhole, boutonnière; rare tussie-mussie.

pot noun **1** *from below came the rattling of pots in the kitchen*: **cooking utensil**, container, receptacle, vessel; pan, saucepan, casserole, stewpot, stockpot, skillet, dixie, chafing dish, cauldron, crucible, crock, basin, bowl; S. African potjie; Indian lota, surahi; archaic pipkin, cruse, pottle, Dutch oven, gallipot.
2 *glazed earthenware pots filled with geraniums and petunias*: **flowerpot**, planter, jardinière.
3 *Jim raked in half the pot*: **bank**, kitty, pool, purse, stakes, ante, jackpot.
4 informal *a man with a florid face and a big pot*. See **pot belly**.
□ **go to pot** *the foundry was allowed to go to pot in the seventies*: **deteriorate**, decline, degenerate, go to (rack and) ruin, go downhill, go to seed, decay, fall into disrepair, become dilapidated, run down, rot, slide; informal go to the dogs, go down the tubes, hit the skids; Austral./NZ informal go to the pack.

pot-bellied adjective **paunchy**, beer-bellied, portly, rotund, roly-poly, stout, overweight, corpulent, Falstaffian; informal porky, tubby.

pot belly noun **paunch**, belly, beer belly, gut, fat/protruding stomach; informal beer gut, pot, tummy, spare tyre, middle-aged spread; N. Amer. informal bay window; informal, dated corporation.

potency noun **1** *the sheer potency of poetry*: **power**, powerfulness, vigour, strength, might, mightiness, force, forcefulness; influence, dominance, energy, potential; literary puissance.
2 *the potency of his words*: **forcefulness**, force, effectiveness; **persuasiveness**, cogency, impressiveness, strength, authoritativeness, authority; power, powerfulness.
3 *the potency of the drugs*: **strength**, powerfulness, power; headiness; **efficacy**, effectiveness, efficaciousness; informal kick.

potent adjective **1** *the party could be a potent political force in the future*: **powerful**, strong, vigorous, mighty, formidable, influential, commanding, dominant, forceful, dynamic, redoubtable, overpowering, overwhelming; literary puissant.
▷**ANTONYMS** weak, impotent.
2 *one of the most potent arguments was marshalled by defence contractors*: **forceful**, **convincing**, cogent, compelling, persuasive, powerful, strong, effective, effectual, eloquent, impressive, telling, sound, well founded, valid, weighty, authoritative, irresistible.
3 *two doses of a very potent drug | a potent alcoholic brew*: **strong**, powerful, effective, efficacious; **intoxicating**, heady, hard, stiff, spiritous.
▷**ANTONYMS** weak.

potentate noun *diplomatic missions to foreign potentates*: **ruler**, head of state, monarch, sovereign, king, queen, emperor, empress, prince, tsar, crowned head, mogul, dynast, overlord, leader.

potential adjective *a potential source of conflict*: **possible**, likely, prospective, future, probable, budding, in the making; latent, embryonic, developing, dormant, inherent, unrealized, undeveloped.
▶ noun *the economic potential of the area | he obviously has great potential*: **possibilities**, potentiality, prospects; promise, capability, capacity, ability, power; aptitude, talent, flair; informal what it takes.

> *Word links* **potential**
>
> **potentiometry** measurement of electrical potential

> *Word toolkit* **potential**
>
> See **latent**.

potion noun *Dotty concocted strange potions from the herbs in her tiny garden*: **concoction**, mixture, brew, elixir, philtre, drink, decoction; medicine, tincture, tonic; archaic potation; literary draught.

pot-pourri noun *this book is a pot-pourri of curious animal stories*: **mixture**, assortment, collection, selection, assemblage, medley, miscellany, melange, mix, variety, motley collection, mixed bag, patchwork, pastiche, blend; smorgasbord, ragbag, hotchpotch, hodgepodge, mishmash, jumble, farrago; rare gallimaufry, omnium gatherum, olio, olla podrida, salmagundi, pasticcio, macédoine, motley.

potter verb *we pottered down to the library*: **amble**, wander, meander, stroll, saunter, maunder; informal mosey, tootle, toddle; Brit. informal **mooch**; N. Amer. informal putter.
□ **potter about/around** *I spent Monday at home, just pottering about*: **do nothing much**, amuse oneself, tinker about/around, fiddle about/around, footle about/around, do odd jobs; informal mess about/around, piddle about/around, puddle about/around; Brit. informal muck about/around, fanny about/around; N. Amer. informal putter about/around, lollygag.

pottery noun **china**, crockery, ceramics, ware.

> *Word links* **pottery**
>
> **ceramic**, **fictile** relating to pottery

potty adjective **1** *I must be going potty*: **mad**, insane, out of one's mind, deranged, demented, not in one's right mind; informal crazy, mental, off one's head, nuts, off one's rocker, round the bend, bats, bonkers; Brit. informal barmy, crackers.
▷**ANTONYMS** sane.
2 *she's **potty about** you*: **infatuated with**, very keen on, devoted to, in love with, smitten with, enamoured of, addicted to; enthusiastic about, passionate about; informal mad about, crazy about, nuts about.
▷**ANTONYMS** indifferent.

pouch noun **1** *he took a small leather pouch from his pocket*: **bag**, purse, wallet, sack, sac, pocket, container, receptacle; Scottish poke, sporran; historical reticule.
2 *a kangaroo's pouch*: technical **marsupium**.

pounce verb *two men pounced on him, demanding cash*: **jump on**, spring on, leap on, swoop (down) on, dive at, drop down on, lunge at, bound at, fall on, set on, make a grab for, take by surprise, take unawares, catch off-guard, attack suddenly; ambush, mug; informal jump.
▶ noun *with a sudden pounce, the cheetah's jaws fastened on the gazelle's throat*: **leap**, spring, jump, swoop, dive, lunge, bound.

pound[1] verb **1** *the two bigger men pounded him with their fists*: **beat**, strike, hit, batter, thump, pummel, punch, rain blows on, belabour, hammer, thrash, set on, tear into, weigh into, bang, crack, drub, welt, thwack; informal bash, clobber, wallop, beat the living daylights out of, give someone a (good) hiding, whack, biff, bop, lay into, pitch into, lace into, let someone have it, knock into the middle of next week, sock, lam, whomp; Brit. informal stick one on, slosh; N. Amer. informal boff, bust, slug, light into, whale; Austral./NZ informal dong, quilt; literary smite, swinge.
2 *40ft waves pounded the seafront*: **beat against**, crash against, batter, dash against, crack into/against, lash, strike, hit, buffet.
3 *US gunships pounded the capital*: **bombard**, bomb, shell, blitz, strafe, torpedo, pepper, fire on, attack; archaic cannonade.
4 *pound the cloves with salt and pepper until smooth*: **crush**, grind, pulverize, beat, mill, pestle, mash, pulp, bruise, powder, granulate; technical triturate, comminute; archaic bray, levigate; rare kibble.
5 *I heard him pounding along the gangway*: **walk/run heavily**, stomp, lumber, clomp, clump, tramp, trudge; thunder; N. Amer. tromp.
6 *she leaned weakly against the door, her heart pounding*: **throb**, thump, thud, hammer, pulsate, pulse, pump, palpitate, race, beat heavily, go pit-a-pat, pitter-patter, vibrate, drum; literary pant, thrill; rare quop.

pound[2] noun *every Christmas she sent the girls ten pounds each*: **pound sterling**, £; Brit. informal **quid**, smacker, smackeroo, nicker, oner, oncer; Brit. historical sovereign.

pound[3] noun *the dog ended up in the local pound*: **enclosure**, compound, pen, yard; Brit. greenyard; historical pinfold.

pour verb **1** *blood was pouring from his nose*: **stream**, flow, run, gush, cascade, course, spout, jet, spurt, flood, surge, spill, rush, well, spew, discharge; Brit. informal sloosh; rare disembogue.
2 *Amy poured more wine into his glass*: **tip**, let flow, dribble, drizzle, splash, spill, decant, discharge; informal slosh, glug, slop; archaic circumfuse.
3 *the sky was black and it was pouring with rain*: **rain heavily/hard**, teem down, pelt down, tip down, beat down, lash down, sheet down, come down in torrents/sheets, rain cats and dogs; informal be chucking it down; Brit. informal bucket down, come down in buckets/bucketloads, come down by the bucketful, come down in stair rods, tipple down; N. Amer. informal rain pitchforks; Brit. vulgar slang piss down.
4 *people poured off the train*: **throng**, crowd, swarm, stream, flood, gush, teem.
□ **pour out** *the words were just pouring out and I didn't know how to control them*: **gush out**, spew out, spurt out, spout out; erupt; **flow**, issue, emerge, come out, come forth, come.
□ **pour something out 1** *the remaining liquid is poured out*: **drain**, decant, pour off, draw off, siphon off, tap, tip, discharge, transfer; disgorge, discharge, eject, emit, expel, evacuate, empty, spit out, spew out, belch forth, spout; vomit, regurgitate, throw up; archaic regorge. **2** *Tchaikovsky poured out his innermost feelings in hundreds of letters*: **express**, voice, vent, give vent to, give expression to, vocalize, give voice to, put in words, give utterance to, communicate, declare, state, set forth, bring into the open,

make public, assert, divulge, reveal, proclaim, announce, raise, table, air, ventilate, mention, talk of, point out, go into; utter, say, speak, articulate, enunciate, pronounce, mouth; informal come out with.

pout verb *'But everyone else is going,' said Crystal, pouting*: **look petulant**, pull a face, look sulky, purse one's lips, make a moue, turn the corners of one's mouth down; scowl, glower, sulk; rare mop and mow.
▸ noun *a childish pout*: **petulant expression**, sulky expression, moue, face, scowl, glower.

poverty noun **1** *they experienced years of relentless poverty*: **penury**, destitution, indigence, pennilessness, privation, deprivation, impoverishment, neediness, need, want, hardship, impecuniousness, impecuniosity, hand-to-mouth existence, beggary, pauperism, straitened circumstances, bankruptcy, insolvency; Economics primary poverty; rare pauperdom.
▷ANTONYMS wealth.
2 *the poverty of choice meant that many left-wing voters read right-wing papers*: **scarcity**, deficiency, dearth, shortage, paucity, insufficiency, inadequacy, absence, lack, want, deficit, meagreness, limitedness, restrictedness, sparseness, sparsity; rare exiguity.
▷ANTONYMS abundance.
3 *the poverty of her imagination*: **inferiority**, mediocrity, poorness, barrenness, aridity, sterility.

> *Word links* **poverty**
>
> **peniaphobia** fear of poverty

poverty-stricken adjective *his family was poverty-stricken and starving*: **extremely poor**, impoverished, destitute, penniless, on one's beam-ends, as poor as a church mouse, without a sou, dirt poor, in penury, penurious, impecunious, indigent, needy, needful, in need/want, unable to make ends meet, down and out, necessitous, beggarly, moneyless, bankrupt, in straitened circumstances; Brit. on the breadline, without a penny (to one's name); informal broke, flat broke, cleaned out, strapped for cash, strapped, on one's uppers; Brit. informal stony broke, skint, without two pennies/farthings to rub together, in Queer Street; N. Amer. informal stone broke; rare pauperized, beggared.

powder noun **dust**, fine particles, fine grains; talcum powder, talc; archaic pulvil, pulvilio; rare pounce.
▸ verb **1** *give lipstick staying power by lightly powdering your lips first*: **dust**, sprinkle/dredge/cover with powder, talc.
2 *the rose petals are dried and powdered*: **crush**, grind, pulverize, pound, mill, granulate; technical comminute, triturate; archaic bray, levigate.

powdered adjective *powdered milk*: **dried**, freeze-dried, dehydrated; technical lyophilized.

powder room noun **lavatory**, toilet; Brit. the Ladies, cloakroom, (public) convenience; N. Amer. ladies' room, restroom, bathroom, washroom, comfort station; Brit. informal loo.

powdery adjective **1** *a powdery residue*: **fine**, dry, fine-grained, powder-like, dusty, chalky, floury, mealy, sandy, crumbly, friable, granulated, granular; ground, crushed, pulverized; rare pulverulent, levigated.
2 *her pale powdery cheeks*: **powder-covered**, powdered.

power noun **1** *my mother suffered a stroke and lost the power of speech | I'll do everything within my power to help*: **ability**, capacity, capability, potential, potentiality, faculty, property, competence, competency.
▷ANTONYMS inability, incapacity.
2 *the unions wield enormous power in party affairs*: **control**, authority, influence, dominance, mastery, domination, rule, command, ascendancy, supremacy, dominion, sovereignty, jurisdiction, sway, weight, leverage, hold, grasp, say; informal clout, pull, beef, teeth; N. Amer. informal drag; literary puissance.
3 *police do not have the power to stop and search*: **authority**, right, authorization, warrant, licence, prerogative, faculty; informal say-so.
4 *in the eighteenth century Russia became a major European power*: **state**, country, nation, world power, superpower.
5 *he hit the ball with as much power as he could | the sheer physical power of the man*: **strength**, powerfulness, might, force, forcefulness, mightiness, weight, vigour, energy, intensity, potency; brawn, browniness, muscle; informal punch; Brit. informal welly; literary thew.
6 *the power of his arguments*: **forcefulness**, powerfulness, potency, strength, force, eloquence, effectiveness, cogency, persuasiveness, impressiveness, authoritativeness; informal punch.
▷ANTONYMS weakness, impotence.
7 *the new engine has more power*: **driving force**, horsepower, hp, acceleration; informal poke, oomph; N. Amer. informal grunt.
8 *generating power from waste*: **energy**, electrical power, nuclear power, solar power, steam power, water power; informal juice.
9 informal *the holiday in Tenerife did him **a power of** good*: **a great deal of**, a lot of, much; informal lots of, loads of, heaps of, masses of, tons of; dated a deal of.
□ **have someone in/under one's power** have control over, have influence over, have under one's thumb, have at one's mercy, have in one's clutches, have in the palm of one's hand, have eating out of one's hand, have on a string, have one's claws into; N. Amer. have in one's hip pocket; informal have over a barrel.
□ **the powers that be** *the powers that be did nothing to diffuse the situation*: **the authorities**, the people in charge, the establishment, the government, the administration, the men in (grey) suits.

> *Word links* **power**
>
> **megalomania** obsession with power

powerful adjective **1** *his powerful shoulders bulged under his suit*: **strong**, muscular, muscly, sturdy, strapping, robust, mighty, hefty, brawny, burly, husky, athletic, manly, well built, Herculean, tough, solid, substantial, lusty; informal beefy, hunky; dated stalwart; literary stark, thewy.
▷ANTONYMS weak.
2 *a powerful local aperitif*: **intoxicating**, heady, hard, strong, stiff; rare spirituous, intoxicant.
3 *a powerful blow across the face*: **violent**, forceful, heavy, hard, mighty, vigorous, hefty, thunderous.
▷ANTONYMS gentle.
4 *he felt a powerful desire to kiss her*: **intense**, keen, acute, fierce, violent, passionate, ardent, burning, consuming, strong, irresistible, overpowering, overwhelming, fervent, fervid.
5 *a powerful nation*: **influential**, strong, high-powered, important, controlling, dominant, commanding, potent, forceful, vigorous, dynamic, formidable, redoubtable; informal big, high-octane; literary puissant.
▷ANTONYMS weak, powerless.
6 *a powerful and detailed critique of current thinking in social research*: **cogent**, compelling, convincing, persuasive, eloquent, impressive, striking, telling, influential; forceful, strong, effective; dramatic, passionate, graphic, vivid, moving, potent, authoritative, great, weighty, vigorous, forcible, irresistible, substantial.
▷ANTONYMS ineffective.

> *Choose the right word* **powerful, strong**
>
> On the face of it, these two words are very similar in meaning: a *powerful argument* is much the same as a *strong argument*. However, *powerful* is rarely used of drink, for example, or *strong* of an engine: one talks of *strong drink* and *powerful engines*, because *powerful* tends to imply dynamic force—an ability to exert it while performing actions—while *strong* tends to imply static force, or an ability to resist it. So, with many nouns that can be described as either *powerful* or *strong*, the two words mean different things: a *powerful nation* is one that has influence abroad, while a *strong nation* has a sense of nationhood that can resist outside pressure. A *powerful tool* can perform a lot of useful work (*the steam hammer is an extremely powerful tool for working iron*), while a *strong tool* will stand heavy use or pressure without breaking (*the resulting forged tool is far stronger than a cheap two-part construction*).

powerless adjective *we felt intimidated and powerless | police are powerless to prosecute the offenders*: **impotent**, helpless, without power, ineffectual, inadequate, ineffective, with no say, useless, defenceless, vulnerable, weak, feeble, paralysed; unable, not able, incapable; literary impuissant; archaic resistless.
▷ANTONYMS powerful, strong.

practicability noun *we expressed doubts about the practicability of the scheme*. See **feasibility**.

practicable adjective *it is important that all practicable steps be taken to prevent violence breaking out*. See **feasible**.

practical adjective **1** *they have practical experience of language-teaching methods*: **empirical**, hands-on, pragmatic, real, actual, active, applied, experiential, experimental, non-theoretical, in the field; informal how-to; technical heuristic; rare empiric.
▷ANTONYMS theoretical.
2 *the opposition have failed to put forward any practical alternatives*: **feasible**, practicable, realistic, viable, workable, possible, within the bounds/realms of possibility, reasonable, sensible, useful, helpful, constructive; informal doable; rare accomplishable.
3 *do you want your clothes to be practical or frivolous?* **functional**, serviceable, sensible, useful, utilitarian, utility, everyday, workaday, ordinary; suitable, appropriate.
4 *I'm just being practical—we must find a ground-floor flat*: **realistic**, sensible, down-to-earth, pragmatic, businesslike, matter-of-fact, reasonable, rational, commonsensical, hard-headed, no-nonsense, with one's/both feet on the ground; informal hard-nosed.
▷ANTONYMS impractical.
5 *it was a practical certainty that he would try to raise more money*: **virtual**, effective, in effect.

practicality noun **1** *we asked an architect to consider the practicality of cleaning the stonework*: **feasibility**, possibility, practicability, viability, workability; utility, usefulness, use, value.

2 *the table is a masterpiece of elegance and practicality*: **functionalism**, functionality, serviceability; usefulness, utility.
3 *he spoke with calm practicality*: **common sense**, sense, realism, pragmatism, matter-of-factness.
4 *the practicalities of army life*: **practical details**, mechanics; informal nitty gritty, nuts and bolts.

practical joke noun **trick**, joke, prank, jape, hoax; informal leg-pull; N. Amer. informal dido; Austral. informal goak; dated cutup, rag; archaic quiz.

practically adverb **1** *the cinema was practically empty*: **almost**, nearly, very nearly, virtually, just about, all but, more or less, not far from, close to, in effect, as good as, to all intents and purposes, approaching, verging on, bordering on, next to, essentially, basically; informal pretty much, pretty nearly, pretty well; literary well-nigh.
2 *'You can't afford it,' he pointed out practically*: **realistically**, sensibly, reasonably, pragmatically, matter-of-factly, rationally, with common sense.

practice noun **1** *the principles and practice of radiotherapy*: **application**, exercise, use, operation, implementation, execution, enactment, action, doing.
2 *it has become common practice to employ women lawyers for the defence in rape trials*: **custom**, procedure, policy, convention, tradition, fashion, habit, wont, method, system, routine, institution, way, rule; Latin modus operandi; formal praxis.
3 *it takes lots of practice to get this technique right | the team's final practice on Friday evening*: **training**, rehearsal, repetition, preparation, exercise, drill, study; practice session, dummy run, run-through, try-out, warm-up; informal dry run.
4 *such was his disillusionment that he gave up the practice of medicine*: **profession**, career, business, work, pursuit, occupation, following.
5 *small legal practice seeks reliable receptionist/secretary*: **business**, firm, office; partnership; company, enterprise; informal outfit.
□ **in practice** *your proposal is all very well in theory, but in practice it will not work*: **in reality**, actually, in real life, realistically, practically, effectively.
□ **out of practice** **rusty**, unpractised.
□ **put something into practice** *I wondered if I would ever be able to put my professional training into practice*: **use**, make use of, put to use, utilize, apply, employ, exercise, put into effect/operation, draw on, bring into play.

practise verb **1** *once they'd selected the songs he practised them every day*: **rehearse**, run through, go through, go over, work on, work at, repeat; polish, refine, perfect.
2 *performers were practising for the air show*: **train**, rehearse, prepare, exercise, drill, work out, warm up, go through one's paces, keep one's hand in, get into shape, do exercises, study; Brit. informal knock up.
3 *we still practise some of these rituals today*: **carry out**, perform, do, observe, put into practice, execute, follow, exercise.
4 *she practised medicine for three years*: **work at**, pursue a career in, have a career in, go in for, engage in, specialize in, ply, follow; N. Amer. hang out one's shingle; archaic prosecute.

P

practised adjective *Sam was a practised judge of character*: **expert**, **experienced**, seasoned, skilled, skilful, accomplished, proficient, talented, able, capable, adept, adroit, consummate, master, masterly, veteran; trained, qualified, well trained, well versed; informal crack, ace, mean, demon, wizard; N. Amer. informal crackerjack; archaic or humorous compleat.

pragmatic adjective *my father was entirely pragmatic in his response to difficult situations*. See **practical** (sense 4).

praise verb **1** *the police praised Parveen for her courage*: **commend**, express approval of, express admiration for, applaud, pay tribute to, speak highly of, eulogize, compliment, congratulate, celebrate, sing the praises of, praise to the skies, rave about, go into raptures about, heap praise on, wax lyrical about, say nice things about, make much of, pat on the back, take one's hat off to, throw bouquets at, lionize, admire, hail, cheer, flatter; N. Amer. informal ballyhoo; black English big someone/something up; dated cry someone/something up; rare laud, panegyrize.
▷ANTONYMS criticize, condemn.
2 *we praise God for past blessings*: **worship**, glorify, honour, exalt, adore, pay tribute to, pay homage to, give thanks to, venerate, reverence, hallow, bless; archaic magnify; rare laud.
▸ noun **1** *James was full of praise for the medical teams | he left Washington with the President's praises ringing in his ears*: **approval**, acclaim, admiration, approbation, acclamation, plaudits, congratulations, commendation, applause, flattery, adulation; tribute, accolade, cheer, compliment, a pat on the back, eulogy, encomium, panegyric, ovation, bouquet, laurels; N. Amer. puffery; rare laudation, eulogium.
2 *give praise to God*: **honour**, **thanks**, glory, glorification, worship, devotion, exaltation, adoration, veneration, reverence, tribute.

> *Word links* **praise**
>
> **laudatory** expressing praise

praiseworthy adjective *the government's praiseworthy efforts to improve efficiency in health and education*: **commendable**, **laudable**, admirable, creditable, worthy, worthy of admiration, meritorious, deserving, honourable, estimable, exemplary, excellent, sterling, fine; rare applaudable.
▷ANTONYMS blameworthy, disgraceful.

pram noun Brit. pushchair; N. Amer. baby carriage, stroller, pushcart; Brit. trademark baby buggy; formal perambulator.

prance verb *he was prancing around in his underpants*: **cavort**, dance, jig, trip, caper, jump, leap, spring, bound, skip, hop; parade, strut, swagger, swank; frisk, gambol, romp, frolic, curvet; N. Amer. informal sashay, cut a/the rug; rare peacock, rollick, capriole.

prank noun *a silly student prank*: **practical joke**, trick, mischievous act, piece of mischief, joke, escapade, stunt, caper, jape, game, hoax, antic; informal lark, leg-pull; N. Amer. informal dido; Austral. informal goak; informal, dated rag, cutup; archaic quiz; rare frolic, freak, gambado, gambade, rig, prat.

prattle verb *he loved to prattle on about his friends' affairs*: **chatter**, babble, prate, blather, blether, ramble, gabble, jabber, twitter, go on, run on, rattle on/away, blither, maunder, drivel, patter, gossip, tittle-tattle, tattle, yap, jibber-jabber, cackle; Scottish & Irish slabber; informal chit-chat, jaw, gas, gab, blabber, yak, yackety-yak, yabber, yatter, shoot one's mouth off; Brit. informal witter, rabbit, chunter, natter, waffle; N. Amer. informal run off at the mouth; Austral./NZ informal mag; archaic twaddle, clack, twattle.
▸ noun *do you intend to keep up this childish prattle?* **chatter**, babble, talk, prating, blather, blether, rambling, gabble, jabber, drivel, palaver, tattle; informal gab, yak, yackety-yak, yabbering, yatter, twaddle; Brit. informal wittering, waffle, waffling, natter, chuntering; archaic clack, twattle.

pray verb **1** *let us pray | he prayed to God*: **say one's prayers**, be at prayer, make one's devotions; offer a prayer/prayers, commune with.
2 *she prayed God to give her enlightenment | I prayed for forgiveness*: **invoke**, call on, implore, appeal to, entreat, beseech, beg, ask/request earnestly, plead, crave, petition, solicit, supplicate, importune; rare obsecrate.

prayer noun **1** *she stood in the chapel listening to the priest's murmured prayers*: **invocation**, intercession, devotion; archaic orison.
2 *Shannon sent up a quick prayer that she wouldn't bump into him en route*: **appeal**, plea, entreaty, petition, solicitation, supplication, request, suit, invocation; rare obsecration, imploration, adjuration.
□ **not have a prayer** informal **have no hope**, **not have/stand a chance**, have/stand no chance, not have/stand the ghost of a chance; informal not have a hope in hell, not have a cat in hell's chance, not have a dog's chance, not have/stand an earthly, not have a snowball's chance (in hell); Austral./NZ informal not have Buckley's (chance).

prayer book noun **service book**; Church of England Book of Common Prayer; Roman Catholic Church **missal**, breviary; Judaism **Machzor**, **Siddur**; historical **ordinal**, primer; rare formulary, euchologion, euchology.

preach verb **1** *he preached to a large congregation*: **give a sermon**, deliver a sermon, sermonize, spread the gospel, evangelize, address, speak; rare gospelize.
2 *a church that preaches the good news*: **proclaim**, teach, spread, propagate, expound, explain, make known.
3 *my parents have always preached toleration*: **advocate**, recommend, advise, urge, exhort, teach, counsel, champion, inculcate, instil.
4 *who are you to preach at me?* **moralize**, be moralistic, sermonize, pontificate, lecture, harangue; informal preachify; rare ethicize.

> *Word links* **preach**
>
> **homiletic** relating to preaching
> **homiletics** art of preaching

preacher noun **minister (of religion)**, parson, clergyman, clergywoman, member of the clergy, priest, man/woman of the cloth, man/woman of God, cleric, churchman, churchwoman, evangelist, apostle, missionary, revivalist, evangelical, gospeller, sermonizer, spreader of the faith, crusader, proselytizer, moralizer; Scottish kirkman; N. Amer. televangelist, dominie; informal reverend, padre, Holy Joe, sky pilot, hot gospeller; N. Amer. informal preacher man, preach; Austral. informal josser; rare predicant, pulpiteer, homilist.

preaching noun *large crowds came to hear his preaching*: **religious teaching**, instruction, message; sermons, sermonizing, homilies, evangelism, homiletics; rare pulpitry, kerygma.

preachy adjective informal *her speeches can sometimes sound preachy*: **moralistic**, moralizing, sanctimonious, self-righteous, holier-than-thou, priggish, sententious, pietistic, didactic, dogmatic; Scottish unco guid; rare Pharisaic, Pharisaical.

preamble noun *Lord Denning's preamble to the report*: **introduction**, preliminary/preparatory/opening remarks, preliminary/preparatory/opening statement, preliminaries, preface, lead-in, overture, prologue; foreword, prelude, front matter, forward matter; informal intro, prelims; rare proem, prolegomenon, exordium, prolusion, prodrome.

prearranged adjective *they met at prearranged meeting points in the city*: **arranged beforehand/in advance**, arranged, agreed, predetermined, pre-established, pre-planned, set, fixed.

precarious adjective *the club's precarious financial position*: **uncertain**, insecure, unreliable, unsure, unpredictable, undependable, risky, hazardous, dangerous, unsafe, hanging by a thread, hanging in the balance, perilous, treacherous, on a slippery slope, on thin ice, touch-and-go, built on sand, doubtful, dubious, delicate, tricky, problematic; unsettled, unstable, unsteady, shaky, rocky, wobbly; informal dicey, chancy, hairy, iffy; Brit. informal dodgy; archaic or humorous parlous.
▷ANTONYMS safe, secure.

precaution noun *have your car regularly serviced as a precaution against mechanical breakdowns*: **safeguard**, preventative/preventive measure, safety measure, insurance, defence, provision; informal backstop.

precautionary adjective *keeping him in overnight was just a precautionary measure*: **preventative**, preventive, safety, protective; rare precautional.

precede verb **1** *a clever advertising campaign preceded the film*: **go/come before**, go in advance of, lead up to, lead to, pave the way for, prepare the way for, set the scene for, herald, introduce, usher in, antecede, predate, antedate; archaic forego, prevene.
▷ANTONYMS follow, succeed.
2 *he opened the door and allowed Catherine to precede him into the studio*: **go ahead of**, go in front of, go before; go first, lead the way.
3 *he preceded the book with a collection of poems*: **preface**, prefix, introduce, begin, open, launch.

precedence noun *quarrels over precedence among the Bonaparte family*: **priority**, pre-eminence, rank, seniority, superiority, primacy, first place, pride of place, eminence, supremacy, ascendancy, preference.
□ **take precedence over** *artistic integrity should take precedence over economic considerations*: **take priority over**, be considered more important/urgent than, outweigh, supersede, prevail over, come before.

precedent noun *there are few precedents for this sort of legislation | we hope to set a legal precedent*: **model**, exemplar, example, pattern, previous case, prior case, previous instance/example, prior instance/example; paradigm, criterion, yardstick, standard, lead, guide.

preceding adjective *this discussion amplifies many of the issues raised in the preceding chapters*: **foregoing**, previous, prior, former, precursory, earlier, above, above-mentioned, aforementioned, above-stated, above-named, antecedent; rare anterior, prevenient, precedent, precursive, supra.

precept noun **1** *the precepts of Orthodox Judaism*: **principle**, rule, tenet, canon, code, doctrine, guideline, working principle, law, ordinance, statute, command, order, decree, mandate, dictate, dictum, directive, direction, instruction, injunction, prescription, commandment; Judaism mitzvah; rare prescript.
2 *precepts that her grandmother used to quote*: **maxim**, saying, adage, axiom, aphorism, saw, proverb, motto; rare apophthegm.

precinct noun **1** *the main pedestrian precinct*: **area**, zone, sector, district, section, quarter, region.
2 (**precincts**) *within the hallowed precincts of the City of London*: **bounds**, boundaries, limits, confines; surrounding area, environs, surroundings, purlieus, surrounds, neighbourhood, vicinity, locality.
3 *they entered the cathedral precinct*: **enclosure**, close, quadrangle, court, courtyard; informal quad.

precious adjective **1** *precious works of art*: **valuable**, costly, expensive, high-priced, dear; invaluable, priceless, beyond price, of incalculable value/worth; rare, choice, fine, exquisite, irreplaceable, inestimable.
2 *the photograph album was her most precious possession*: **valued**, cherished, treasured, prized, favourite, dear, dearest, beloved, darling, adored, loved, special, esteemed, worth its weight in gold, revered, venerated, hallowed.
▷ANTONYMS worthless, cheap.
3 *his exaggerated, precious manners*: **affected**, over-refined, artificial, studied, pretentious, chichi, flowery, mannered, contrived, effete; informal twee, la-di-da, fancy-pants; Brit. informal poncey; rare alembicated.

precipice noun **cliff face**, steep cliff, rock face, sheer drop, cliff, crag, bluff, height, escarpment, scarp, escarp, scar; Scottish linn; S. African krantz; literary steep.

precipitate verb **1** *the incident precipitated a political crisis*: **bring about**, bring on, cause, lead to, occasion, give rise to, trigger, spark, touch off, provoke, hasten, accelerate, expedite, speed up, advance, quicken, push forward, further, instigate, induce.
2 *the crampon failed, precipitating them both down the mountain*: **hurl**, catapult, throw, plunge, launch, project, fling, cast, heave, propel.
▸ adjective **1** *we should not make precipitate cuts to our conventional forces*: **hasty**, overhasty, rash, hurried, rushed; **impetuous**, impulsive, spur-of-the-moment, precipitous, incautious, imprudent, injudicious, ill-advised, heedless, reckless, hare-brained, foolhardy; informal harum-scarum, previous; rare temerarious.
2 *a precipitate decline in the party's fortunes*. See **precipitous** (sense 2).

Choose the right word **precipitate, headlong, impetuous, impulsive**
See **impetuous**.

precipitous adjective **1** *the road became narrower, the drop on each side more precipitous*: **steep**, sheer, high, perpendicular, abrupt, sharp, dizzy, vertiginous, vertical, bluff; rare acclivitous, declivitous.
2 *his fall from power was precipitous*: **sudden**, **rapid**, swift, abrupt, meteoric, headlong, speedy, quick, fast, hurried, breakneck, violent, precipitate, unexpected, without warning, unanticipated, unforeseen; rare precipitant.
3 *he was arguably too precipitous*. See **precipitate** (sense 1 of the adjective).

precis noun *a precis of the report*: **summary**, synopsis, résumé, abstract, outline, summarization, summation; **abridgement**, digest, condensation, abbreviation, survey, overview, rundown, run-through, sketch; French tour d'horizon; N. Amer. wrap-up; Law headnote, brief; rare conspectus, summa, epitome, compendium.
▸ verb *another strategy for improving your writing skills is to precis a passage*: **summarize**, sum up, give a summary/synopsis/precis of, give the main points of; **abridge**, condense, shorten, synopsize, abstract, outline, compress, abbreviate; rare epitomize.

precise adjective **1** *precise measurements*: **exact**, **accurate**, correct, error-free, pinpoint, specific, detailed, explicit, clear-cut, unambiguous, meticulous, close, strict, definite, particular, express; minute, faithful.
▷ANTONYMS imprecise, inaccurate.
2 *at that precise moment the car stopped*: **exact**, **particular**, very, specific, actual, distinct.
3 *the attention to detail is very precise*: **meticulous**, careful, exact, scrupulous, punctilious, conscientious, particular, exacting, methodical, strict, rigorous; mathematical, scientific.
▷ANTONYMS loose, careless.

Choose the right word **precise, accurate, exact**
See **accurate**.

precisely adverb **1** *at 2 o'clock precisely, the phone rang | she lives precisely in the centre of Canada*: **exactly**, sharp, on the dot; **promptly**, prompt, dead (on), on the stroke of ..., on the dot of ...; right, directly, squarely; informal bang (on), spot on, smack, slap, slap bang, plumb; N. Amer. on the button, on the nose, smack dab.
2 *Toby is precisely the kind of man I have been looking for*: **exactly**, absolutely, just, in all respects, in every way, entirely, altogether; informal to a T.
3 *fertilization can be timed precisely*: **accurately**, exactly, carefully, to a nicety; clearly, distinctly, strictly.
4 *'You mean it was a conspiracy?' 'Precisely'*: **yes**, exactly, quite, absolutely, right, that's right, just so, quite so, indubitably, without a doubt, definitely; informal you bet, I'll say.

precision noun *the deal was planned and executed with military precision*: **exactness**, exactitude, accuracy, accurateness, correctness, preciseness, clarity, clearness, distinctness; faithfulness, fidelity; care, carefulness, meticulousness, scrupulousness, punctiliousness, particularity, methodicalness, perfection, rigour, rigorousness, nicety.

preclude verb *his difficulties preclude him from leading a normal life*: **prevent**, make it impossible for, make it impracticable for, rule out, put a stop to, stop, prohibit, debar, interdict, block, bar, hinder, impede, inhibit, exclude, disqualify, forbid; Law estop.

precocious adjective *some of the boys were extremely precocious*: **advanced**, old beyond one's years, forward, ahead of one's peers, mature, prematurely developed, ahead, gifted, talented, clever, intelligent, quick; informal smart; rare rathe-ripe.
▷ANTONYMS backward, slow.

preconceived adjective *some people tend to have preconceived ideas about us*: **predetermined**, prejudged; prejudiced, biased.

preconception noun *they had no preconceptions about his personality or his politics*: **preconceived idea/notion**, presupposition, assumption, presumption, prejudgement, expectation, prepossession; prejudice, bias; French parti pris.

precondition noun *political stability is a precondition for economic revival*: **prerequisite**, necessary condition, obligatory condition, essential condition, condition, requirement, necessity, essential, necessary thing, imperative, stipulation, proviso; Latin sine qua non; informal must.

precursor noun **1** *the precursors of the Expressionist movement | a three-stringed precursor of the guitar*: **forerunner**, predecessor, forefather, father, parent, antecedent, ancestor, forebear, progenitor; pioneer, trailblazer.
2 *lapses in form are often a precursor of disasters to come*: **harbinger**, herald, prelude, sign, signal, indication, portent, omen.

precursory adjective *a precursory version of 'Lolita' | precursory seismic activity*: **preliminary**, prior, previous, antecedent, preceding, introductory, preparatory, prefatory; warning, premonitory; rare anterior, precursive, preludial, prelusive, prevenient.

predatory adjective **1** *predatory birds*: **predacious**, carnivorous, hunting, raptorial, ravening; of prey; rare raptatorial.
2 *I could see a predatory gleam in his eyes*: **exploitative**, wolfish, rapacious,

greedy, acquisitive, avaricious, vulturine; rare vulturous.
3 *a warlike and predatory clan*: **marauding**, plundering, pillaging, ravaging, looting, robbing, thieving, rapacious; rare plunderous.

predecessor noun **1** *the Prime Minister learned from his predecessor's mistakes*: **former/previous holder of the post**, forerunner, precursor, antecedent.
▷ANTONYMS successor.
2 *our Victorian predecessors*: **ancestor**, forefather, forebear, progenitor, antecedent.
▷ANTONYMS descendant.

predestined adjective *some people claim that everything is predestined*: **preordained**, ordained, foreordained, destined, predetermined, fated; rare predestinated.

predetermined adjective **1** *they are expected to manage their departments with a predetermined budget*: **prearranged**, arranged/established in advance, set, fixed, preset, pre-agreed, pre-established, pre-planned, pre-decided, agreed, settled.
2 *our predetermined fate*: **predestined**, preordained, foreordained, fated.

predicament noun *I really cannot understand how you could have allowed yourself to get into such a predicament*: **difficult situation**, **awkward situation**, mess, difficulty, problematic situation, plight, quandary, trouble, muddle, mare's nest, crisis; informal hole, fix, jam, sticky situation, pickle, scrape, bind, tight spot/corner, spot, corner, dilemma, hot/deep water, kettle of fish, how-do-you-do.

predicate verb *all the social sciences are predicated on the notion that individuals are not isolated*: **base**, **be dependent**, found, establish, rest, build, ground, premise.

predict verb *it is difficult to predict what the outcome will be*: **forecast**, foretell, foresee, prophesy, divine, prognosticate, anticipate, see, say, tell in advance, project, speculate, envision, envisage, imagine, picture, estimate, conjecture, guess, hazard a guess; archaic augur, previse, presage, foreshow; Scottish archaic spae; rare vaticinate, auspicate.

predictable adjective *Guido's reaction was predictable | a novel described as 'drearily predictable'*: **foreseeable**, (only) to be expected, expected, par for the course; **unsurprising**, anticipated, probable, likely, foreseen; formulaic, formularized, obvious; informal inevitable, on the cards.

prediction noun *seven months later, his prediction came true*: **forecast**, prophecy, divination, prognosis, prognostication, augury; bet, projection, conjecture, guess; rare vaticination, prognostic, auspication.

predilection noun *her predilection for married men*: **liking**, fondness, preference, partiality, taste, penchant, weakness, soft spot, fancy, inclination, leaning, bias, propensity, bent, proclivity, proneness, predisposition, tendency, affinity, appetite, love; archaic gusto.
▷ANTONYMS dislike, disinclination.

predispose verb **1** *lack of exercise may predispose an individual to high blood pressure*: **make susceptible**, make liable, make prone, lay open, make vulnerable, put at risk of, leave open, make subject.
2 *attitudes and opinions predispose people to behave in a certain way*: **lead**, incline, move, persuade, influence, sway, induce, prompt, dispose, make, make of a mind to; bias, prejudice.

predisposed adjective **1** *the audience were young and predisposed to like the film*: **inclined**, prepared, ready, of a mind, disposed, minded, willing, not unwilling, in the mood, liable, susceptible; biased, prejudiced.
2 *some of us are* ***predisposed to*** *cardiovascular disease*: **susceptible**, vulnerable, liable, inclined, prone, given, subject, disposed, open; likely to have/get, apt to get, with a tendency to get, at risk of, in danger of getting.

predisposition noun **1** *those who have a hereditary predisposition to heart disease*: **susceptibility**, proneness, tendency, liability, inclination, disposition, vulnerability, weakness; Homeopathy miasm.
2 *differences in public perceptions of the news were associated with people's political predispositions*: **preference**, predilection, inclination, leaning, propensity, bent, proclivity, penchant, liking; bias, prejudice; rare velleity.

predominance noun **1** *there are other reasons for the predominance of women carers*: **prevalence**, dominance, greater number/amount, preponderance, majority, bulk; rare predomination.
2 *defence planners naturally consider military predominance to be a major strength*: **supremacy**, mastery, control, power, ascendancy, dominance, sway, pre-eminence, superiority, leadership, hegemony, sovereignty; upper hand, edge; rare predomination, paramountcy, prepotence, prepotency, prepollency.

predominant adjective **1** *the predominant objectives of the organization*: **main**, chief, principal, most important, of greatest importance, primary, prime, overriding, uppermost, central, cardinal, leading, top-tier, foremost, key, paramount, preponderant, prevailing; most obvious, most noticeable, most prominent; informal number-one, top-priority.
▷ANTONYMS subsidiary, minor.
2 *the predominant political forces*: **controlling**, in control, dominant, predominating, more/most powerful, more/most important, pre-eminent, ascendant, superior, in the ascendancy, ruling, leading, principal, chief, main, supreme, prevalent; rare prepotent, prepollent.

predominantly adverb *although predominantly a disease of older men, it is not unknown in people of his age*: **mainly**, mostly, for the most part, chiefly, principally, primarily, predominately, preponderantly, in the main, on the whole, largely, by and large, to a large extent, to a great degree, typically, in general, generally, usually, commonly, as a rule.

predominate verb **1** *small-scale producers predominate in the south*: **be in the majority**, preponderate, be predominant, be greater/greatest in amount/number, be prevalent, prevail, dominate, reign, be the order of the day; be most prominent, be most noticeable, stand out, stick out.
2 *private interest was not allowed to* ***predominate over*** *the public good*: **prevail**, dominate, be dominant, hold sway, have/get the upper hand, carry most weight, be in control, rule; override, overshadow, outweigh.

pre-eminence noun *his pre-eminence as a historian*: **superiority**, supremacy, greatness, excellence, distinction, prominence, predominance, eminence, peerlessness, transcendence, importance, prestige, stature, fame, renown, celebrity; rare supereminence.

pre-eminent adjective *the country's pre-eminent environmentalist*: **greatest**, leading, foremost, best, finest, chief, outstanding, excellent, distinguished, prominent, eminent, important, major, star, top, top-tier, topmost, famous, renowned, celebrated, illustrious, towering, supreme, superior, exceptional, unrivalled, unsurpassed, unequalled, inimitable, incomparable, matchless, peerless, unmatched, arch-, transcendent; N. Amer. marquee; rare supereminent.
▷ANTONYMS unknown, undistinguished; inferior.

pre-eminently adverb *the novel is pre-eminently a realistic genre | he was pre-eminently qualified to act as peace broker*: **primarily**, principally, above all, chiefly, mostly, mainly, in particular; particularly, par excellence, especially, manifestly, eminently, supremely, conspicuously, notably, signally, singularly, emphatically, uniquely, outstandingly, incomparably, inimitably.

pre-empt verb **1** *he seized on the claims, determined to preempt any political criticism of his government*: **forestall**, prevent; steal a march on, anticipate, get in before; informal get one's retaliation in first.
2 *many tables were already pre-empted by family parties*: **commandeer**, take possession of, occupy, seize, arrogate, appropriate, take over, take, acquire, secure, reserve.

preen verb **1** *a robin sat on a low branch, preening its feathers*: **clean**, **tidy**, groom, smooth, arrange; archaic plume, prink.
2 *his wife preened before the mirror*: **admire oneself**, primp oneself, primp, prink oneself; pretty oneself, prettify oneself, smarten oneself, beautify oneself, make oneself pretty/smart/beautiful, groom oneself, tidy oneself, spruce oneself up; informal titivate oneself, doll oneself up; Brit. informal tart oneself up; N. Amer. informal gussy oneself up; archaic plume oneself, trig oneself.
□ **preen oneself** *he's busy preening himself on acquiring such a pretty girlfriend*: **congratulate oneself**, be pleased with oneself, pride oneself, be proud of oneself, pat oneself on the back, give oneself a pat on the back, feel self-satisfied; archaic pique oneself.

preface noun *Sartre's famous preface to de Beauvoir's first novel*: **introduction**, foreword, preamble, prologue, prelude, preliminary/prefatory/opening remarks; front matter, forward matter; informal prelims, intro; rare proem, exordium, prolegomenon, prolusion, prodrome.
▸ verb *the catalogue is prefaced by a memoir of the artist*: **precede**, introduce, prefix, begin, open, start, launch, lead up to, lead into; rare prologue, premise.

prefatory adjective *three further prefatory remarks are necessary*: **introductory**, preliminary, opening, initial, preparatory, explanatory, lead-in, initiatory, precursory, prior, antecedent; rare prefatorial, precursive, prodromal, prodromic, preambular, preambulatory, preludial, prelusive, prelusory, exordial, proemial, prolegomenal.
▷ANTONYMS final, closing.

prefect noun Brit. *a school prefect*: **monitor**; Brit. praepostor, prepostor.

prefer verb **1** *I prefer white wine to red | those who prefer to travel by rail*: **like better**, would rather (have), would sooner (have), favour, be more partial to, lean/incline towards, think preferable; choose, select, pick, opt for, go for, vote for, plump for, single out, elect, wish, desire, want; informal fancy.
2 formal *do you want to prefer charges?* **bring**, press, file, lodge, tender, present, place, lay, submit, put forward, proffer, offer, propose.
3 archaic *he was preferred to the post in 1589*: **promote**, upgrade, advance, raise, move up, elevate, aggrandize.

preferable adjective *personal pension plans may be preferable if you change jobs frequently*: **better**, best, more desirable, more suitable, more advisable, advantageous, superior, preferred, recommended, favoured, nicer, more expedient; rare predilect.
▷ANTONYMS undesirable.

preferably adverb *applicants should be graduates, preferably with some relevant experience*: **ideally**, if possible, for preference, by preference, from choice, by choice, as a matter of choice, much rather, rather; much sooner, sooner.

preference noun **1** *my mother was a little put out by my preference for boys' games*: **liking**, partiality, predilection, proclivity, fondness, taste, inclination, leaning, bias, bent, penchant, predisposition, desire, wish.
2 *I like most types of music, but my preference is rock*: **favourite**, first choice, top of the list, choice, selection, pick; informal cup of tea, bag, thing; N. Amer. informal druthers.
3 *preference will be given to applicants with some proficiency in Japanese*: **priority**, favour, precedence, advantage, preferential treatment, favoured treatment, favouritism.
□ **in preference to** *the thief chose their home in preference to others*: **rather than**, instead of, in place of, sooner than, above, before, over.

preferential adjective *regular blood donors do not receive preferential treatment when they themselves need a transfusion*: **special**, **better**, privileged, superior, favoured, advantageous, favourable; partial, discriminatory, partisan, biased.

preferment noun *superior qualifications were by no means a guarantee of preferment*. See **advancement** (sense 2).

prefigure verb *his work prefigures that of the magic realists*: **foreshadow**, be an early indication of, presage, be a presage of, be a harbinger of, herald, suggest, indicate, point to; literary foretoken.

pregnancy noun gestation; rare gravidity, parturiency.

> *Word links* **pregnancy**
>
> **antenatal**, **prenatal**, **gestational**, **gestatory** relating to pregnancy

pregnant adjective **1** *when I told Chris I was pregnant, I expected him to panic*: **expecting a baby**, having a baby, with a baby on the way, having a child, expectant, carrying a child; French enceinte; informal expecting, in the family way, expecting a happy event, preggers, preggy, with a bun in the oven, with one in the oven, up the pole; Brit. informal in the club, up the duff, in the pudding club, up the spout, up the stick; N. Amer. informal knocked up, having swallowed a watermelon seed; Austral. informal preggo, clucky, with a joey in the pouch; informal, dated in trouble, in pod; archaic with child, heavy/big with child, in a delicate condition, in an interesting condition, childing, on the way; technical gravid, parturient; rare impregnate; N. Amer. rare infanticipating, storked; (**be pregnant with**) expect, carry, bear.
2 *a sacred rite, **pregnant with** religious significance*: **filled**, charged, heavy, fraught, replete, teeming; full of, abounding in, rich in.
3 *there was a pregnant pause*: **meaningful**, significant, eloquent; **suggestive**, expressive, loaded, meaning, charged, pointed, telling, revealing, weighty.

prehistoric adjective **1** *prehistoric times*: **primitive**, primeval, primordial, primal, earliest, ancient, early, antediluvian; rare pristine, primigenial.
2 *the special effects in the film now look prehistoric*: **out of date**, outdated, outmoded, old-fashioned, passé, ancient, antiquated, archaic, antique, superannuated, anachronistic, outworn, behind the times, primitive, medieval, quaint, old-fangled, obsolescent, obsolete, antediluvian, fossilized; informal out of the ark, old hat, creaky, mouldy; N. Amer. informal horse-and-buggy, mossy, clunky.
▷ANTONYMS modern.

> *Word links* **prehistoric**
>
> **archaeo-** related prefix, as in *archaeology, archaeopteryx*
> **palaeo-** related prefix, as in *Palaeolithic, palaeography*

Word toolkit

prehistoric	ancient	primordial
man	Greece	slime
creatures	city	ooze
cave paintings	history	sea
fish	Egyptians	swamp
ancestors	cultures	jungle
monster	civilization	germ cells

prejudge verb *it is wrong to prejudge an issue on the basis of speculation*: **judge prematurely**, anticipate; jump to conclusions about; rare forejudge, prejudicate.

prejudice noun **1** *male prejudices about women*: **preconceived idea**, preconception, preconceived notion; prejudgement.
2 *he claimed that his opponents were motivated by prejudice*: **bigotry**, **bias**, partisanship, partiality, intolerance, discrimination, a jaundiced eye, preference, one-sidedness, unfairness, inequality, inequity; racism, racialism, anti-Semitism, chauvinism, sexism, ageism, heterosexism, classism, fattism; US Jim Crowism.
3 *without prejudice to the interests of other countries*: **detriment**, harm, disadvantage, damage, injury, hurt, impairment, loss.
▸ verb **1** *it was felt that the article would prejudice the jury*: **bias**, influence, sway, predispose, make biased, make partial, make partisan, colour, poison, jaundice, warp, twist, slant, distort; rare prepossess.
2 *this could prejudice his chances of victory in the November election*: **damage**, be detrimental to, be prejudicial to, be disadvantageous to, injure, harm, hurt, mar, spoil, impair, undermine, be deleterious to, hinder, compromise.

prejudiced adjective *his prejudiced views*: **biased**, bigoted, discriminatory, partisan, partial, one-sided, jaundiced, intolerant, narrow-minded, unfair, unjust, inequitable, non-objective, unobjective, blinkered, parti pris, coloured, distorted, warped, loaded, weighted; racist, racialist, anti-Semitic, chauvinistic, chauvinist, sexist, heterosexist, ageist, disablist, classist, fattist.
▷ANTONYMS unbiased, impartial, fair.

> *Choose the right word* **prejudiced, biased, partial**
>
> See **biased**.

prejudicial adjective *disclosure of the information would be prejudicial to the interests of the company*: **detrimental**, damaging, injurious, harmful, disadvantageous, unfavourable, hurtful, inimical, deleterious, counterproductive; rare prejudicious.
▷ANTONYMS beneficial, advantageous.

preliminary adjective **1** *the discussions are still at a preliminary stage*: **preparatory**, introductory, initial, opening, prefatory, prior, preceding, lead-in, initiatory, precursory; early, advance, exploratory, pilot, test, trial, experimental, explorative; rare precursive, prodromal, prodromic, preludial, prelusive, prelusory.
▷ANTONYMS concluding.
2 *the preliminary rounds of the European Cup*: **qualifying**, eliminating.
▷ANTONYMS closing, final.
□ **preliminary to** *the geese gather in the estuaries, preliminary to their flight southwards*: **in preparation for**, before, in advance of, prior to, ahead of, preparatory to.
▸ noun **1** *without any preliminaries, he began interrogating me*: **introduction**, preamble, opening, opening/prefatory remarks, formalities.
2 *political activity was seen as a necessary preliminary to the resumption of the military campaign*: **prelude**, preparation, preliminary/preparatory measure, preliminary action, overture, groundwork, first round.

prelims plural noun informal *the publisher usually provides the prelims and the jacket copy*: **front matter**, introductory material, preliminary material, prefatory material, forward matter, introduction, foreword, preface, preamble; informal intro; rare proem, prolegomenon, exordium.

prelude noun **1** *a ceasefire was agreed as a prelude to full peace negotiations*: **preliminary**, overture, opening, preparation, introduction, start, beginning, curtain-raiser, lead-in, precursor, forerunner, harbinger, herald; informal opener; formal commencement; rare prolusion.
2 *the piece begins with an orchestral prelude*: **overture**, introductory movement, introduction, opening, voluntary; rare verset.
3 *the whole passage forms a prelude to Part III*: **introduction**, preface, prologue, foreword, preamble; informal intro; rare proem, exordium, prolegomenon, prodrome.
▷ANTONYMS conclusion, postscript.

P

premature adjective **1** *Jenks' term of office was cut short by his premature death*: **untimely**, early, too soon, too early, before time; archaic unseasonable.
▷ANTONYMS overdue.
2 *a premature baby*: **preterm**; informal prem; N. Amer. informal preemie.
▷ANTONYMS overdue, late.
3 *she felt that such a step would be premature*: **rash**, overhasty, hasty, too soon, precipitate, precipitous, impulsive, impetuous, ill-timed, ill-considered; informal jumping the gun, previous.

prematurely adverb **1** *Sam was born three months prematurely*: **too soon**, too early, before the usual time, ahead of time, before one's time; preterm.
2 *his main concern was not to act prematurely*: **rashly**, overhastily, hastily, too soon, too early, precipitately, precipitously; informal at half-cock, half-cocked; archaic untimely.

premeditated adjective *premeditated murder*: **planned**, intentional, intended, deliberate, pre-planned, calculated, cold-blooded, conscious, done on purpose, wilful, prearranged, preconceived, considered, studied, purposive; Law, dated prepense.
▷ANTONYMS accidental, unintentional; spontaneous.

premeditation noun *it looks as if he wore gloves and that would point to premeditation*: **planning**, intent, forethought, pre-planning, advance planning, prearrangement, deliberation; criminal intent, malice aforethought, scheming, plotting; Law mens rea.

premier adjective *one of Britain's premier chefs*: **leading**, foremost, chief, principal, head, top-ranking, top, top-tier, prime, primary, first, highest, second to none, pre-eminent, main, senior, outstanding, master; N. Amer. ranking; informal top-notch, crack.
▸ noun *the Italian premier*: **head of government**, prime minister, PM, president, chief minister, chancellor.

premiere noun *the new musical is having its world premiere at the Haymarket Theatre tonight*: **first performance**, first showing, first night, opening, opening night, debut, launch.

premise noun *a philosophy based on the premise that human life consists of a series of choices*: **proposition**, assumption, hypothesis, thesis, presupposition, postulation, postulate, supposition, presumption, surmise, conjecture, speculation, datum, argument, assertion, belief, thought; Brit. premiss.
▸ verb *one school of thought premised that the cosmos is indestructible*: **postulate**, hypothesize, conjecture, posit, theorize, suppose, presuppose, surmise, assume, predicate, argue, state, assert; rare hypothecate.

premises plural noun *the company has moved to new premises in Gloucester*: **building(s)**, property, site, establishment, office, place.

premiss noun Brit. See **premise**.

premium noun **1** *a 25-year policy with monthly premiums of £30*: **insurance charge**, insurance payment, regular payment, instalment.
2 *customers are reluctant to pay a premium for organic fruit*: **surcharge**, additional payment, extra amount/charge, additional fee.
3 *you may receive a foreign service premium and a cost of living allowance*: **bonus**, extra, percentage, perk, recompense, remuneration, prize, reward; incentive, inducement; formal perquisite; historical bounty.
□ **at a premium** *parking space is at a premium in Japanese cities*: **scarce, in great demand**, like gold dust, hard to come by, in short supply, thin on the ground, few and far between, not to be had, rare, rare/scarce as hen's teeth; informal not to be had for love or money.
□ **put/place a premium on 1** *I place a high premium on the historic relationship between the United States and Britain*: **value greatly**, attach great/special importance to, set great store by, regard as particularly valuable/important, put a high value on, hold in high regard, appreciate greatly. **2** *the huge increase in the price of oil put a premium on the coal industry*: **make valuable**, make invaluable, put a high value on, make essential, make important.
▸ adjective *the quality of premium American table wines improves every year*: **superior**, premier, high-end, top-end, exclusive, elite, top, select, choice, de luxe, luxurious, classy, prime, first-rate, high-quality, top-quality, high-grade, five-star, fine, finest; Brit. upmarket.
▷ANTONYMS inferior.

premonition noun See **foreboding** (sense 2).

preoccupation noun **1** *in spite of my preoccupation I enjoyed the journey*: **pensiveness**, concentration, engrossment, absorption, self-absorption, musing, thinking, thinking of other things, deep thought, brown study, brooding; abstraction, absent-mindedness, absence of mind, distraction, forgetfulness, inattentiveness, wool-gathering, inadvertence, heedlessness, dream, reverie, daydreaming, oblivion, obliviousness.
2 *their main preoccupation is providing winter feed for their cattle*: **obsession**, concern, fixation; fascination, passion, enthusiasm, hobby horse, pet subject, compulsion, fetish, complex, neurosis, mania; French idée fixe; informal bee in one's bonnet, hang-up, thing, bug.

P

preoccupied adjective **1** *officials **preoccupied with** their careers*: **obsessed**, concerned; passionate about, absorbed in, engrossed in, interested in, intent on, involved in, wrapped up in, sunk in, immersed in, taken up.
2 *she looked worried and preoccupied*: **lost in thought**, deep in thought, immersed in thought, in a brown study, pensive, brooding, absent-minded, distracted, abstracted, distrait, heedless, far away, oblivious.

preoccupy verb *the issues which currently preoccupy environmentalists*: **engross**, concern, absorb, dominate, take up someone's whole attention, take up all of someone's time, distract, obsess, occupy, grip, enthral, consume, haunt, prey on someone's mind, become an obsession with, be uppermost in someone's mind, take control of.

preordain verb *he believes that everything we do is preordained*: **predestine**, destine, foreordain, ordain, fate, doom, foredoom, predetermine, determine, mark out, prescribe.

preparation noun **1** *the preparation of contingency plans*: **devising**, putting together, thinking up, drawing up, construction, composing, composition, editing, fashioning, concocting, production, getting ready, making ready, arrangement, development, assembling, assembly.
2 (**preparations**) *preparations for the conference will begin almost immediately*: **arrangements**, planning, plans, provision, preparatory measures, preliminaries, necessary steps, groundwork, spadework, foundation, gearing up.
3 *too much of the curriculum was taken up with preparation for exams*: **instruction**, teaching, education, coaching, training, tutoring, inculcation, grooming, disciplining, drilling, priming, briefing, guiding, direction.
4 *a preparation such as benzyl benzoate is needed to kill off the mites*: **mixture**, compound, concoction, composition, blend, amalgam, solution, suspension, emulsion, tincture, medicine, potion, cream, ointment, lotion.

preparatory adjective *there is much preparatory work to be done*: **preliminary**, initial, prior, introductory, prefatory, opening, basic, elementary, fundamental, rudimentary, preparative, precursory, initiatory.
□ **preparatory to** *she touched up her make-up preparatory to leaving*: **in preparation for**, in advance of, before, prior to, previous to, in anticipation of, in expectation of, leading up to.

prepare verb **1** *I want you to prepare a plan of action for me*: **make ready**, get ready, put together, draw up, produce, arrange, develop, assemble, construct, compose, edit, devise, work out, think up, conceive, formulate, concoct, fashion, work up, lay.
2 *the meal was easy to prepare*: **cook**, make, get, put together, assemble, muster, dish up, concoct, blend, infuse, brew; informal fix, rustle up; Brit. informal knock up.
3 *if you want peace, prepare for war*: **get ready**, make preparations, arrange things, make provision, get everything set, take the necessary steps, do the necessary, lay the groundwork, do the spadework, gear oneself up, gird up one's loins, fit oneself out, kit oneself out, rig oneself out, provide, arm oneself; face up to; informal psych oneself up.
4 *the top teams prepare for such an event all year*: **train**, get into shape, practise, exercise, warm up; get ready, get set.
5 *we enable employees to prepare for exams*: **study**, work, do preparation, revise, do homework; Brit. informal swot.
6 *this course is written specifically to prepare students for these exams*: **instruct**, teach, educate, coach, train, tutor, inculcate, groom, discipline, drill, prime, brief, guide, direct, put in the picture.
7 *you must prepare yourself for a shock*: **brace**, make ready, tense, steel, steady, buttress, strengthen, fortify; literary gird.

prepared adjective **1** *he will need to be well prepared for the task*: **ready**, set, all set, equipped, primed, in a fit state; waiting, available, on hand, fixed, poised, in position.
2 *you've got to be prepared to cut your price*: **willing**, ready, disposed, predisposed, inclined, favourably inclined, of a mind, minded, in the mood, agreeable.

preponderance noun **1** *the preponderance of women among older people*: **prevalence**, predominance, dominance.
2 *the preponderance of evidence indicates that such is likely to be the case*: **bulk**, **majority**, greater quantity, larger part, best/better part, main part, most, almost all, more than half, mass, weight, (main) body, lion's share, predominance, generality.
3 *many members were dissatisfied with the preponderance of the trade unions*: **predominance**, dominance, ascendancy, leadership, mastery, supremacy, control, sway, power; advantage, upper hand, edge; rare paramountcy.

preponderant adjective *the Western states remained militarily preponderant in the region*: **dominant**, predominant, prevalent, in control, more/most powerful, superior, supreme, ascendant, in the ascendancy; controlling, more/most important, pre-eminent, predominating, ruling, leading, principal, chief, main; rare prepotent, prepollent.

prepossessing adjective **attractive**, beautiful, pretty, handsome, good-looking, fetching, striking, pleasing, pleasant, agreeable, appealing, likeable, lovable, amiable, charming, delightful, engaging, inviting, alluring, magnetic, winning, enchanting, captivating, bewitching, fascinating; dated taking; archaic fair.
▷ANTONYMS ugly, unprepossessing.

preposterous adjective **absurd**, ridiculous, foolish, stupid, ludicrous, farcical, laughable, comical, risible, hare-brained, asinine, inane, nonsensical, pointless, senseless, insane, unreasonable, irrational, illogical; outrageous, shocking, astonishing, monstrous, unbelievable, incredible, unthinkable; informal crazy.
▷ANTONYMS reasonable, sensible.

prerequisite noun *training is a prerequisite for competence*: **necessary condition**, precondition, condition, essential, requirement, requisite, necessity, proviso, qualification, imperative, basic, rudiment, obligation, duty; Latin sine qua non; informal must.
▷ANTONYMS non-essential.
▸ adjective *the student must have the prerequisite knowledge*: **necessary**, needed, required, called for, essential, requisite, vital, basic, of the essence, indispensable, imperative, obligatory, mandatory, compulsory; French de rigueur; rare needful.
▷ANTONYMS unnecessary, non-essential.

prerogative noun **entitlement**, right, privilege, advantage, due, birthright; liberty, authority, authorization, power, licence, permission, dispensation, leave, consent, warrant, charter, franchise, sanction; exemption, immunity, indemnity; French carte blanche; Law, historical droit.

presage verb *the owl's hooting was thought to presage death*: **portend**, augur, foreshadow, foretell, prophesy, be an omen of, herald, be a sign of, be the harbinger of, be a warning of, give a warning of, warn of, be an indication of, indicate, be a presage of, signal, bode, announce, promise, threaten; point to, mean, signify, spell, denote, add up to, amount to; literary betoken, foretoken, forebode, harbinger.
▸ noun *these symptoms were a sombre presage of his final illness*: **omen**, sign, indication, portent, warning, forewarning, harbinger, foreshadowing, augury, signal, promise, threat, ill omen, forecast, prediction, prognostication, prophecy, straw in the wind, writing on the wall, hint; literary foretoken; archaic auspice.

prescience noun *with the uncanny prescience of children, they had divined that he was a fake*: **far-sightedness**, foresight, foreknowledge; psychic powers, clairvoyance; prediction, prognostication, divination, prophesy, augury; insight, vision, intuition, perception, percipience; Hinduism & Buddhism third eye; rare vaticination, haruspication, pythonism, prevision, psychism, adumbration.

prescient adjective *much of what happened was predicted in Leonard's prescient article*: **prophetic**, predictive, visionary; psychic, clairvoyant; far-seeing, far-sighted, with foresight, prognostic, divinatory, oracular, sibylline, apocalyptic, fateful, revelatory; insightful, intuitive, perceptive, percipient; rare foreknowing, previsional, vatic, mantic, vaticinal, vaticinatory, prognosticative, augural, adumbrative, fatidic, fatidical, haruspical, pythonic.

prescribe verb **1** *your doctor may prescribe an antibiotic*: **order**, advise, authorize, direct.
2 *traditional values prescribe a life of domesticity*: **advise**, recommend, advocate, commend, urge, suggest, subscribe to, endorse, support, back, champion, argue for, promote.
3 *two rules prescribe the nature of that duty*: **stipulate**, lay down, dictate, specify, impose, set down, determine, establish, fix, formulate, appoint, decree, order, command, pronounce, ordain, require, direct, enjoin, make provision for, promulgate.

Easily confused words **prescribe or proscribe?**

Prescribe is sometimes confused with **proscribe**, but their meanings are totally different. *Prescribe* is a much commoner word and means either 'issue a medical prescription' or 'recommend with authority', as in *the doctor prescribed antibiotics*. *Proscribe*, on the other hand, is a formal word meaning 'condemn or forbid', as in *gambling was strictly proscribed by the authorities*.

prescription noun **1** *the doctor wrote her a prescription for more sedatives*: **instruction**, order, direction, authorization; informal script; archaic recipe.
2 *he was asked to fetch a prescription from the chemist*: **medicine**, drug, medication, remedy, cure, dose, treatment, preparation, mixture; archaic physic; rare medicament, medicinal, nostrum.
3 *a painless prescription for improvement*: **method**, measure; **recommendation**, suggestion, advice, recipe, formula, direction.

prescriptive adjective *guidelines must avoid being too prescriptive*: **dictatorial**, authoritarian, tyrannical, despotic; arbitrary, oppressive, repressive, coercive; insistent, dogmatic, pontifical; binding, enforceable; limiting, narrow, rigid; informal bossy.
▷**ANTONYMS** free and easy; optional.

presence noun **1** *presence of a train on a section of track was indicated electrically*: **existence**, being there.
▷**ANTONYMS** absence.
2 *I would like to request the presence of an adjudicator*: **attendance**, attending, appearance, residence, occupancy; company, companionship; informal turning up, showing, showing up.
▷**ANTONYMS** absence.
3 *he was impressed by her presence*: **bearing**, carriage, stance, deportment, comportment, attitude, posture, manner, air, guise; **demeanour**, mien, behaviour, conduct, dignified air/demeanour, dignified bearing, dignity.
4 *a woman of presence*: **aura**, charisma, personality, strength/force of personality, individuality, magnetism, attraction; poise, self-assurance, self-possession, self-confidence.
5 *she felt a presence in the castle*: **ghost**, spirit, spectre, phantom, vision, wraith, shadow, poltergeist, manifestation, apparition, supernatural being; Scottish & Irish bodach; W. Indian duppy; informal spook; literary shade, visitant, revenant; archaic eidolon.
□ **presence of mind composure**, equanimity, self-possession, level-headedness, aplomb, poise, assurance, self-assurance, self-control, nerve, calmness, sangfroid, countenance, collectedness, imperturbability; alertness, quickness, quick-wittedness; informal cool, unflappability.

present[1] (stress on the first syllable) adjective **1** *a doctor must be present at the ringside*: **in attendance**, attending, here, there, near, nearby, at hand, close/near at hand, adjacent, available, ready; accounted for.
▷**ANTONYMS** absent.
2 *organic compounds are present in the waste*: **in existence**, existing, existent, extant.
▷**ANTONYMS** absent.
3 *in the present climate jobs are hard to come by*: **current**, present-day, existing, contemporary, immediate; archaic instant.
▷**ANTONYMS** past; future.
▶ noun (**the present**) *forget the past and think about the present*: **now**, today, the present time, the here and now, this day and age, the present moment, the time being.
▷**ANTONYMS** past; future.
□ **at present** *at present he is very angry*: **at the moment**, just now, right now, at this time, at the present time, currently, presently, at this moment in time; in this day and age, nowadays.
□ **for the present** *for the present she stayed where she was*: **for the time being**, for now, for the moment, for a while, in the meanwhile, in the meantime, provisionally, temporarily, pro tem; rare for the nonce.
□ **the present day modern times**, the present age/time, nowadays, now.

present[2] (stress on the second syllable) verb **1** *Eddy will present the cheque to the winner*: **hand over**, give, give out, dispense, hand out, confer, bestow, award, grant, donate, gift, accord, extend, entrust, furnish.
2 *the committee finally presented its report*: **submit**, set forth, put forward, put up, proffer, offer, show, tender, advance, propose, propound, suggest, venture, bring up, broach, moot, air, ventilate, table, register, lay, lodge, introduce, move, volunteer.
3 *may I present my wife?* **introduce**, make known, acquaint someone with, make acquainted with.
4 *I called to present my warmest compliments*: **offer**, give, express, extend.
5 *they presented their new product at an exhibition last month*: **demonstrate**, show, put on show/display/view, exhibit, display, introduce, launch, unveil; parade, flaunt.
6 *they have a reputation for presenting good quality opera*: **stage**, put on, put before the public, produce, mount, organize; perform, render, act.
7 *she is to present a breakfast TV show*: **host**, introduce, announce, compère, anchor, be the presenter of; N. Amer. informal emcee.
8 *the authorities sought to present him as a common criminal*: **represent**, describe, portray, depict, characterize.
□ **present itself** *make the most of opportunity when it presents itself*: **occur**, arise, happen, transpire, emerge, come about, appear, materialize, come up, crop up, pop up, turn up.
□ **present oneself** *he was ordered to present himself at the office at ten*: **be present**, make an appearance, appear, attend, turn up, arrive.

present[3] (stress on the first syllable) noun *I got him this tie as a birthday present*: **gift**, donation, offering, contribution, handout, presentation, bestowal; largesse, alms, charity, bonus, award, premium, bounty, boon, favour; bequest, legacy, settlement; subsidy, grant, endowment, benefaction; tip, gratuity; in the Middle and Far East baksheesh; French pourboire; informal prezzie, freebie, perk, sweetener; formal perquisite; archaic conferment.

presentable adjective **1** *I'm trying to make the place look presentable*: **tidy**, **neat**, fit to be seen, orderly, straight, clean, spick and span, in good order, shipshape (and Bristol fashion), in apple-pie order.
2 *you'd better make yourself presentable*: **smartly dressed**, tidily dressed, smart, tidy, of smart appearance, well groomed, dapper, elegant, trim, spruce; informal natty.
3 *they have produced one or two quite presentable videos*: **fairly good**, passable, decent, respectable, adequate, all right, satisfactory, moderately good, not (too) bad, average, tolerable, fair; informal OK.

presentation noun **1** *the presentation of his certificate took place at the conference*: **awarding**, presenting, giving, handing over, dispensing, handing out, conferral, bestowal, granting, donation, award, according, extending, entrusting, furnishing.
2 *the presentation of foods in the supermarket*: **appearance**, arrangement, organization, packaging, exposition, disposition, display, layout.
3 *let's decide what you're going to wear for your presentation to the Queen*: **introduction**, making known, acquainting; dated debut, coming out.
4 *the presentation of drastic proposals for economic reform*: **submission**, proffering, offering, tender, tendering, advancing, proposal, propounding, suggestion, venturing, broaching, mooting, airing, ventilating, tabling, registering, introduction, moving, volunteering.
5 *a sales presentation*: **demonstration**, talk, lecture, address, speech, show, exhibition, display, introduction, launch, launching, unveiling, parading.
6 *a Radio 4 presentation of his latest play*: **staging**, production, performance, mounting, organizing, showing, show, representation, rendition.

present-day adjective **current**, present, contemporary, latter, latter-day, present-time, twenty-first-century, modern, latest, existing, extant, recent; up to date, up to the minute, fashionable, trendsetting, voguish, modish, the latest, new, newest, newfangled, new-fashioned; informal mod, trendy, cool, now.
▷**ANTONYMS** past; future.

presentiment noun *I understood that you had some sort of presentiment of disaster*: **premonition**, foreboding, intuition, feeling, hunch, suspicion, sneaking suspicion, feeling in one's bones, funny feeling, vague feeling, inkling, idea, sixth sense; misgiving, worry, anxiety, apprehension, apprehensiveness, fear, dread; archaic presage.

presently adverb **1** *I shall see you presently*: **soon**, shortly, directly, quite soon, in a short time, in a short/little while, at any moment/minute/second, in a moment/minute/second, in less than no time (at all), in next to no time, before long, by and by; N. Amer. momentarily; S. African just now; informal pretty soon, any moment now, before you know it, before you can say Jack Robinson, in a jiffy, in two shakes of a lamb's tail; Brit. informal in a mo; archaic or informal anon; literary ere long.
2 *he is presently abroad*: **at present**, currently, at the/this moment, at the present moment/time, now, nowadays, these days, today, in this day and age; Brit. informal at the minute.

P

preservation noun **1** *waste tar was used in wood preservation*: **conservation**, protection, maintenance, care, safeguarding, keeping.
2 *the ruling classes were bent on preservation of the status quo*: **continuation**, conservation, keeping up, keeping alive, keeping going, maintenance, upholding, sustaining, prolongation, perpetuation.
3 *the preservation of food | the preservation of dead bodies*: **conserving**, bottling, tinning, canning, potting, chilling, freezing, freeze-drying, quick-freezing, drying, desiccation, dehydration; curing, smoking, kippering, salting, pickling, marinating, sousing, corning, jellying, candying; embalming, mummification.

preserve verb **1** *the oil helps to preserve the wood*: **conserve**, protect, maintain, care for, take care of, look after, save, safeguard, keep.
▷ANTONYMS damage; neglect.
2 *the employers wished to preserve the status quo*: **continue**, conserve, keep up, keep alive, keep going, maintain, continue with, uphold, sustain, prolong, perpetuate.
▷ANTONYMS discontinue, abandon.
3 *she wanted to preserve him from harassment*: **guard**, protect, keep, defend, safeguard, secure, shelter, shield, screen, watch over.
4 *spices enabled us to preserve food | I preserved the worm in alcohol*: **conserve**, bottle, tin, can, pot, chill, freeze, freeze-dry, quick-freeze, dry, desiccate, dehydrate; cure, smoke, kipper, salt, pickle, marinate, souse, corn, jelly, candy; embalm, mummify.
▷ANTONYMS consume, use.
▶ noun **1** *strawberry preserve*: **jam**, jelly, marmalade, conserve, confection; N. Amer. dulce; French confiture.
2 *high culture remains the preserve of an educated middle-class minority*: **domain**, area, field, sphere, orbit, arena, realm, province, speciality, specialism, territory, department; informal thing, turf, bailiwick.
3 *an animal preserve*: **sanctuary**, reserve, reservation, game reserve.

preside verb *a chairman has to be elected to* ***preside at*** *the meeting*: **chair**, take the chair, be chairman/chairwoman/chairperson, officiate (at); conduct, run, lead, guide, moderate.
□ **preside over be in charge of**, be responsible for, be accountable for, be at the head/helm of, head, be head of, manage, administer, organize, be in control of, control, direct, lead, run, govern, rule, be boss of, head up, conduct, command, supervise, superintend, oversee, handle; informal be in the driving/driver's seat, be in the saddle, pull the strings, call the shots/tune.

president noun **1** *the president of the United States*: **head of state**, chief of state, elected head of a country.
2 *the president of the society*: **head**, chief, director, leader, governor, principal, master, chancellor, vice-chancellor, dean, rector, warden, provost, captain, figurehead; N. Amer. informal prexy, prex.
3 *the president of the company*: **chairman**, chairwoman; managing director, MD, chief executive (officer), CEO, director.

press verb **1** *press the paper firmly on to the type*: **push (down)**, press down, thumb, depress, bear down on, lean on, lower, pin, pinion, hold down, force, ram, thrust, cram, squeeze, compress, wedge.
2 *the brown suit had been brushed and pressed*: **smooth**, iron, smooth out, remove creases from, put creases in; steam, calender.
3 *tips on how to press flowers*: **flatten**, make flat, smooth out.
4 *friends come in to help us gather and press the grapes*: **crush**, squeeze, squash, compress, mash, pulp, reduce, clamp, pack down, tamp, condense, compact, trample, stamp, tread, grind, mill, pound, pulverize, macerate.
5 *she pressed the child to her bosom*: **clasp**, hold close, hug, cuddle, squeeze, crush, enfold, clutch, grasp, embrace.
6 *Winnie pressed his hand*: **squeeze**, give something a squeeze, grip, clutch, pinch.
7 *the crowd* ***pressed round*** *for a better view*: **cluster**, gather; converge, congregate, flock, push forward, swarm, throng, crowd, seethe, surge, rush.
8 *the government was able to press its claim for recognition*: **plead**, urge, advance insistently, file, prefer, lodge, tender, present, place, lay, submit, put forward.
9 *you should* ***press*** *him* ***to*** *undertake the most careful inquiry*: **urge**, pressure, put pressure on, pressurize, force, drive, impel, push, coerce, nag; lean on, prevail on; dragoon into, steamroller into, browbeat into, use strong-arm tactics on, have someone do something; informal put the heat on, put the screws on, twist someone's arm, railroad into, bulldoze into.
10 *workers were pressed into accepting new contracts*: **pressurize**, pressure, push, goad, dragoon, steamroller, browbeat, importune, wheedle, cajole, sway, argue, talk; informal railroad, bulldoze.
11 *our campaigns include* ***pressing for*** *a ban on the ivory trade*: **call**, ask, clamour, push, make a claim, campaign; insist on, demand.
□ **be pressed for** *you should never need to arrange interviews when you are pressed for time*: **have too little**, be short of, have barely enough, have an insufficiency of, have insufficient, lack, be lacking (in), be wanting, be deficient in, be deprived of, be low on, need, be/stand in need of; informal be strapped for.
□ **press on** *the team regrouped and pressed on*: **proceed, keep going**, continue, carry on, move forward, move along, advance, make progress, make headway, press ahead, forge on/ahead, push on, go on, keep on, not give up, struggle on, hammer away, be persistent, be pertinacious, persevere, persist, keep at it, be determined, show determination, stay with it, be tenacious, go the distance, stay the course, plod on, plough on, grind away, see/follow something through; informal soldier on, hang on, plug away, peg away, stick at it, stick it out, hang in there.
▶ noun **1** *he printed his poems on his own press*: **printing press**, printing machine.
2 *a private press prints solely what it chooses to print*: **publishing house**, publishing company, printing establishment/firm/business/house.
3 (**the press**) *rumours began to appear in the press | the freedom of the press*: **the media**, **the newspapers**, the papers, the news media, journalism, the newspaper world, the newspaper business, the print media, the fourth estate; journalists, newspapermen, newsmen, newspaper women, reporters, columnists, commentariat, pressmen, presswomen; informal journos, hacks, hackettes, news hounds; N. Amer. informal newsies; dated publicists; Brit. dated Fleet Street.
4 *the company has had its share of bad press*: **reports**, press treatment, press coverage, press reporting, press articles, press reviews, press write-ups.

pressing adjective **1** *a pressing problem*: **urgent**, critical, crucial, acute, desperate, serious, grave, dire, drastic, burning, extreme, life-and-death.
▷ANTONYMS non-urgent.
2 *I have a pressing engagement*: **important**, of the utmost importance, high-priority, pivotal, critical, crucial, compelling, demanding, necessary, key, vital; imperative, essential, of the essence; inescapable.
▷ANTONYMS unimportant.
3 *a pressing invitation to dinner*: **insistent**, persistent, determined, resolute, tenacious, obstinate, dogged, unrelenting, importunate; repeated, unremitting, continuous, incessant, demanding, entreating, clamorous; rare exigent.

pressure noun **1** *a confined gas exerts a constant pressure on the wall of its container*: **(physical) force**, load, stress, thrust; compression, compressing, squeezing, crushing, weight, heaviness.
2 *we shall not put pressure on you to borrow money*: **coercion**, force, compulsion, constraint, duress, oppression, enforcement, insistence, demand, entreaty, goading, pestering, provocation, harassment, nagging, harrying, badgering, intimidation, arm-twisting, pressurization, persuasion, influence.
3 *she had a lot of pressure from work*: **strain**, stress, tension, heat, burden, load, weight, drain, trouble, care, adversity, difficulty; informal hassle.
▶ verb *it might be possible to* ***pressure*** *him* ***into*** *resigning*: **coerce**, pressurize, press, push, persuade, influence, force, squeeze, bulldoze, hound, harass, nag, harry, badger, goad, prod, pester, browbeat, brainwash, bully, bludgeon, intimidate, dragoon, twist someone's arm, strong-arm; bring pressure to bear on, use pressure on, put pressure on, lean on; N. Amer. blackjack; informal railroad, put the screws/squeeze on; N. Amer. informal hustle, fast-talk.

> *Word links* **pressure**
>
> **baro-** related prefix, as in *barotrauma*
> **barometer**, **barograph** device for measuring atmospheric pressure
> **sphygmomanometer** instrument for measuring blood pressure

pressurize verb *he never tried to* ***pressurize*** *Buffy* ***into*** *buying the apple*: **coerce**, pressure, press, push, persuade, influence, force, squeeze, bulldoze, hound, harass, nag, harry, badger, goad, prod, pester, browbeat, brainwash, bully, bludgeon, intimidate, dragoon, twist someone's arm, strong-arm; use pressure on, put pressure on, lean on, prevail on; N. Amer. blackjack; informal railroad, put the screws/squeeze on; N. Amer. informal hustle, fast-talk.

prestige noun *he experienced a tremendous increase in prestige following his victory*: **status**, standing, stature, prestigiousness, reputation, repute, regard, fame, note, renown, honour, esteem, estimation, image, account, rank, celebrity, importance, prominence, consequence, class, distinction, influence, weight, authority, supremacy, eminence, superiority; laurels, kudos, cachet; NZ mana; Indian izzat; informal clout, brownie points.

prestigious adjective **1** *his work appeared in prestigious journals of physics*: **reputable**, distinguished, respected, esteemed, estimable, eminent, august, honoured, of high standing, of note, highly regarded, well thought of, acclaimed, authoritative, well known, in the public eye, celebrated, illustrious, leading, renowned, famed, famous.
▷ANTONYMS disreputable; obscure.
2 *a prestigious job*: **impressive**, conferring prestige, important, prominent, exalted, high-ranking, influential, imposing, powerful, glamorous; well paid, high-end, expensive; Brit. upmarket.
▷ANTONYMS minor, humble, lowly.

presumably adverb *presumably he'll get the job*: **I assume**, I expect, I believe, I presume, I take it, I suppose, I imagine, I dare say, I would have thought, it is to be presumed, I guess, in all probability, probably, in all likelihood, all things being equal, all things considered, as likely/like as not, doubtless, undoubtedly, no doubt, without doubt; on the face of it, apparently, seemingly.

presume verb **1** *I presume that it had once been an attic*: **assume**, suppose, dare say, imagine, take it, expect, believe, think, surmise, guess, judge,

trust, conjecture, speculate, postulate, posit, hypothesize, deduce, divine, infer, conclude, presuppose, take for granted, take as read.
2 *let me* ***presume*** *to give you a word of advice*: **venture**, dare, have the temerity, have the audacity, have the effrontery, be so bold as, make so bold as, go so far as; take the liberty of.
□ **presume on** *he was wary of presuming on their friendship*: **take advantage of**, take unfair advantage of, exploit, take liberties with; rely on, depend on, count on, bank on, reckon on, place reliance on, trust.

presumption noun **1** *this presumption may be easily rebutted*: **assumption**, supposition, presupposition, belief, thought, guess, expectation, judgement, surmise, conjecture, speculation, hypothesis, postulation, premise, generalization, inference, deduction, conclusion.
2 *he apologized for his presumption in arriving without warning*: **brazenness**, audacity, boldness, audaciousness, temerity, arrogance, egotism, front, presumptuousness, pertness, forwardness; cockiness, shamelessness, insolence, impudence, bumptiousness, impertinence, effrontery, face, cheek, cheekiness, gall; rudeness, incivility, impoliteness, disrespect, disrespectfulness, familiarity, freshness; informal nerve, neck, brass neck, chutzpah; N. Amer. informal sass, sassiness; archaic assumption.

presumptive adjective **1** *dating of these structures can only be presumptive*: **conjectural**, speculative, tentative, suppositional, notional, hypothetical; theoretical, academic, unproven, unconfirmed.
▷**ANTONYMS** definitive.
2 *the heir presumptive*: **probable**, likely, prospective, assumed, supposed, expected, predictable, awaited, anticipated; odds-on, plausible, foreseeable.

presumptuous adjective *it's rather presumptuous to judge my character on such short acquaintance*: **brazen**, **overconfident**, arrogant, egotistical, overbold, bold, audacious, pert, forward, familiar, impertinent, fresh, free, insolent, impudent, cocksure; cheeky, rude, impolite, uncivil, bumptious; **overhasty**, hasty, premature, previous, precipitate, impetuous; informal cocky; N. Amer. informal sassy; archaic presumptive, assumptive.
▷**ANTONYMS** timid, unassuming.

presuppose verb **1** *the following course of action presupposes the existence of a policy-making group*: **require**, necessitate, imply, entail, mean, involve, assume, suppose, have as a necessary condition, have as a precondition.
2 *I had presupposed that theme parks make people happy*: **presume**, assume, take it for granted, take it, take it as read/given, suppose, surmise, think, accept, consider, postulate, posit.

presupposition noun *he challenged the presupposition that all enzymes are proteins*: **presumption**, assumption, preconception, preconceived idea/notion, supposition, hypothesis, surmise, speculation, guess, prediction, thesis, theory, premise, belief, suspicion, thought, argument, postulation, prejudgement.

pretence noun **1** *cease this pretence and be true to yourself*: **make-believe**, act, putting on an act, acting, dissembling, shamming, sham, faking, feigning, simulation, falsification, dissimulation, invention, imagination, self-deception, play-acting, posturing, posture, posing, pose, cant, attitudinizing; deception, deceit, deceitfulness, fraud, hoax, fraudulence, fabrication, duplicity, artifice, subterfuge, treachery, trickery, dishonesty, hypocrisy, falsity, lying, mendacity, lack of veracity; Brit. false colours; informal kidology; rare simulacrum.
▷**ANTONYMS** reality; honesty.
2 *he made a pretence of being unconcerned*: **false show**, show, semblance, affectation, false appearance, appearance, outward appearance, impression, image, front, false front, guise, colour, facade, display, posture, pose, masquerade, mask, cloak, veil, veneer, smokescreen, camouflage, cover, travesty, parody, charade; archaic snivel.
3 *she herself had long since dropped any pretence to faith*: **claim**, aspiration, purporting, profession.
4 *he was absolutely without pretence*: **pretentiousness**, display, ostentation, affectation, showiness, flaunting, posturing, posing, humbug.
5 *he abducted the queen on the pretence of seeking to protect her*: **pretext**, false excuse, guise, sham, ruse, wile, trickery; lie, falsehood.

pretend verb **1** *they just* ***pretend to*** *listen*: **make as if**, profess, affect; dissimulate, dissemble, pose, posture, put it on, put on a false front, go through the motions, sham, fake it; informal kid.
2 *if you like, I'll pretend to be the dragon*: **put on an act**, make believe, play at, act, play-act, pass oneself off as, bluff, impersonate.
3 *it was useless to pretend innocence*: **feign**, sham, fake, simulate, put on, counterfeit, affect.
4 *he did not even* ***pretend to*** *a crushing burden of work*: **claim**, lay claim to, make a claim to, purport to have, profess to have, go through the motions of having.
▸ **adjective** informal *she picked up the phone and had a pretend conversation*: **imaginary**, imagined, pretended, make-believe, made-up, fantasy, fantasized, fancied, dream, dreamed-up, unreal, fanciful, invented, fictitious, fictive, mythical, feigned, fake, mock, imitative, sham, simulated, artificial, ersatz, dummy, false, faux, spurious, bogus, counterfeit, fraudulent, forged, pseudo; informal phoney; S. African informal play-play.

pretended adjective *her eyes widened in pretended astonishment*: **fake**, faked, affected, assumed, professed, purported, spurious, ostensible, quasi-, contrived, in name only; insincere, hypocritical, mock, imitation, simulated, so-called, make-believe, pseudo, sham, false, bogus; counterfeit, fraudulent, forged; informal pretend, phoney.

pretender noun *a pretender to the throne*: **claimant**, aspirant, claimer.

pretension noun **1** *the author firmly denies any pretension to exhaustive coverage | literary pretensions*: **aspiration**, claim, assertion, pretence, profession, purporting.
2 *I dislike the pretension of her style*: **pretentiousness**, affectation, affectedness, ostentation, ostentatiousness, artificiality, attitudinizing, airs, posing, posturing, showing off, hypocrisy, snobbery, show, flashiness; pomposity, pompousness, floweriness, grandiosity, grandness, grandiloquence, magniloquence, elaborateness, extravagance, heroics, flamboyance, ornateness, bombast, turgidity, rhetoric, pedantry; informal la-di-da; Brit. informal **side**; Austral./NZ informal **guyver**; rare fustian, flatulence.

pretentious adjective *Clytemnestra is a pretentious name for a dog*: **affected**, ostentatious, chichi, showy, flashy, tinselly, conspicuous, flaunty, tasteless, kitschy; overambitious, pompous, artificial, flatulent, inflated, overblown, fustian, hyperventilated, mannered, high-flown, high-sounding, flowery, grandiose, big, grand, elaborate, extravagant, heroic, flamboyant, ornate, grandiloquent, magniloquent, bombastic, turgid, orotund, rhetorical, oratorical; N. Amer. sophomoric; informal highfalutin, la-di-da, fancy-pants, posey, pseud, pseudo; Brit. informal poncey, toffee-nosed; US black English dicty.
▷**ANTONYMS** natural, unaffected.

preternatural adjective *autumn had arrived with preternatural speed*: **extraordinary**, out of the ordinary, exceptional, unusual, uncommon, rare, singular, signal, peculiar, unprecedented, outstanding, remarkable, phenomenal, abnormal, anomalous, inexplicable, unaccountable; supernatural, paranormal, mystical, unearthly, unworldly, other-worldly, fantastic, magical, prodigious, wonderful, wondrous, miraculous; strange, mysterious, odd, weird.

pretext noun *he called at her house on the pretext of enquiring after Mr Bradshaw*: **excuse**, false excuse, ostensible reason, alleged reason, plea, supposed grounds; guise, ploy, pretence, ruse, semblance, show, blind, pose, masquerade, mask, cloak, veil, veneer, smokescreen, camouflage, cover, travesty, parody, charade.

prettify verb *the landscape had been tamed and weakened by man's attempts to prettify nature*: **beautify**, make attractive, make pretty, pretty up, titivate, dress up, adorn, ornament, embellish, trick out, decorate, smarten (up), glamorize, prink, preen, primp; informal doll up, do up, give something a facelift; Brit. informal tart up.
▷**ANTONYMS** uglify.

pretty adjective *a pretty child*: **attractive**, lovely, good-looking, nice-looking, fetching, prepossessing, appealing, charming, delightful, nice, engaging, pleasing; darling, sweet, dear, adorable, lovable; winning, winsome, cute, as pretty as a picture, dainty, graceful; handsome, well favoured, personable, beautiful, glamorous, gorgeous, ravishing, stunning, bewitching, alluring; chocolate-box; Scottish & N. English bonny; informal easy on the eye; literary beauteous; archaic fair, comely.
▷**ANTONYMS** plain; ugly.
□ **pretty penny** informal *it must have cost a pretty penny to lure this talented actor back*: **a huge amount**, a small fortune, a king's ransom, a vast sum, a large sum of money, a lot, a fortune, millions, billions; informal a packet, a mint, a bundle, a pile, a wad, an arm and a leg, a tidy sum, a killing; Brit. informal a bomb, loadsamoney, shedloads; N. Amer. informal big bucks, big money, gazillions; Austral. informal big bickies.
▸ **adverb** *a pretty large sum of money*: **quite**, rather, somewhat, fairly, reasonably, moderately, comparatively, relatively, tolerably, passably, adequately, satisfactorily, decently, respectably; informal kind of, sort of.
□ **pretty much/well** informal *by mid-October the growing season is pretty much complete | his old cloth cap was pretty well worn out*: **nearly**, almost, just about, about, more or less, practically, virtually, all but, as good as, next to, close to, near, nigh on, not far from, not far off, to all intents and purposes, approaching, bordering on, verging on, nearing; roughly, approximately; not quite; informal pretty nearly; literary well-nigh.
▸ **verb** *she's prettying herself*: **beautify**, make attractive, make pretty, prettify, pretty up, adorn, ornament, embellish, smarten, glamorize, prink, preen, primp; put make-up on; informal do oneself up; Brit. informal tart oneself up.

prevail verb **1** *we can only hope that common sense will prevail*: **win**, win out, win through, triumph, be victorious, be the victor, gain the victory, carry the day, carry all before one, finish first, come out ahead, come out on top, succeed, prove superior, conquer, overcome, gain/achieve mastery, gain ascendancy; take the crown, gain the palm, rule, reign.
2 *the excellent conditions that prevailed in the 1950s*: **exist**, be in existence, be present, be the case, hold, obtain, occur, be prevalent, be current, be rife, be rampant, be the order of the day, be customary, be established, be common, be widespread, be in force, be in effect; abound, hold sway, predominate, preponderate; endure, survive, persist.
□ **prevail on/upon** *Jane had prevailed on Dorothy to come*: **persuade**, induce, talk someone into, coax, convince, make, get, press someone into, win someone over, sway, bring someone round, argue someone into, urge,

P

pressure someone into, pressurize someone into, bring pressure to bear on, coerce, influence, prompt; inveigle, entice, tempt, lure; cajole, wheedle someone into, get round, prod someone into, reason someone into; Law procure; informal sweet-talk, soft-soap, twist someone's arm, smooth-talk.

prevailing adjective *a research project examined prevailing attitudes in the classroom*: **current**, existing, prevalent, usual, common, most usual, commonest, most frequent, general, mainstream; widespread, rife, in circulation; set, recognized, established, customary, acknowledged, accepted, ordinary; popular, fashionable, in fashion, in style, in vogue.

prevalence noun *the prevalence of smoking among teenagers*: **commonness**, currency, widespread presence, generality, pervasiveness, universality, extensiveness, ubiquity, ubiquitousness; rampancy, rifeness; frequency, regularity; familiarity, acceptance; popularity, fashionableness.

prevalent adjective *the work attitudes still prevalent in the UK*: **widespread**, prevailing, frequent, usual, common, general, universal, pervasive, extensive, ubiquitous, ordinary; endemic, rampant, rife; recognized, established, accepted; current, popular, fashionable, in fashion, in style, in vogue.
▷ANTONYMS uncommon, rare.

prevaricate verb *he seemed to prevaricate when journalists asked pointed questions about his involvement*. See **equivocate**.

prevent verb **stop**, put a stop to, avert, nip in the bud, fend off, turn aside, stave off, ward off, head off, shut out, block, intercept, halt, arrest, check, stay; hinder, impede, hamper, obstruct, baulk, foil, thwart, obviate, cheat, frustrate, forestall, counteract, inhibit, hold back, curb, restrain, preclude, pre-empt, save, help, suppress; disallow, prohibit, forbid, proscribe, exclude, debar, bar, deter; archaic let.
▷ANTONYMS allow; cause; encourage.

preventive, preventative adjective **1** *preventive maintenance is the key to dependability*: **inhibitory**, deterrent, pre-emptive, obstructive; **precautionary**, protective.
2 *preventive medicine*: **prophylactic**, disease-preventing, precautionary, protective.
▶ noun **1** *a preventive against crime*: **precautionary measure**, deterrent, preventive/protective measure, safeguard, security, protection, defence, hindrance, block, check, impediment, curb, restraint, obstruction.
2 *substances that have value as disease preventives*: **prophylactic**, prophylactic device, prophylactic medicine, preventive drug.

previous adjective **1** *the previous five years | her previous boyfriend*: **foregoing**, preceding, precursory, antecedent, above; old, earlier, prior, former, ex-, past, last, sometime, one-time, erstwhile; formal quondam; archaic whilom; rare anterior.
▷ANTONYMS following, next.
2 informal *I admit I may have been previous*: **overhasty**, hasty, premature, precipitate, impetuous, too early, too soon, untimely, presumptuous; informal ahead of oneself.
□ **previous to** *previous to this everything was fine*: **before**, prior to, until, till, up to, earlier than, preceding, leading up to, in advance of, ahead of, ante-, pre-; rare anterior to.
▷ANTONYMS after, as a result of.

previously adverb **formerly**, earlier, earlier on, before, until now/then, hitherto, once, at one time, in the past, in days gone by, in years gone by, in times gone by, in bygone days, in times past, in former times, time was when; in advance, in readiness, ahead of time, sooner, already, beforehand; formal heretofore.

prey noun **1** *lions tend to kill prey their own size*: **quarry**, game, kill.
▷ANTONYMS predator, hunter.
2 *an opposing Counsel will find you easy prey in his cross-examination*: **victim**, target, dupe, fool, innocent, gull; informal sucker, soft/easy touch, pushover, chump; Brit. informal muggins, charlie; N. Amer. informal patsy, sap, schlemiel, pigeon, mark; Austral./NZ informal dill; Brit. informal, dated juggins.
□ **be prey to** *Paris was prey to yet another cholera epidemic*: **succumb to**, be overcome by, be overwhelmed by; be stricken with, fall victim to, fall ill with, become infected with, catch, develop, contract, pick up; informal come/go down with.
▶ verb
□ **prey on 1** *most hoverfly larvae prey on aphids*: **hunt**, catch, seize; eat, devour, feed on, live on, live off. **2** *it is a callous thing to do, to prey on a vulnerable elderly woman*: **exploit**, victimize, molest, pick on, intimidate, harass, hound, take advantage of; trick, swindle, cheat, hoodwink, fleece; attack, terrorize; blackmail, bleed; informal con. **3** *the unfinished Requiem had begun to* ***prey on*** *his mind*: **oppress**, weigh on, weigh heavily on, lie heavy on, burden, be a burden on/to, hang over, gnaw at; **trouble**, worry, beset, disturb, depress, distress, haunt, nag, torment, plague, obsess, take over, take control of.

price noun **1** *the purchase price of a car*: **cost**, asking price, selling price, charge, fee, terms, payment, rate, fare, levy, toll, amount, sum, total, figure; worth, (monetary) value; outlay, expense, expenses, expenditure, bill; valuation, quotation, estimate; informal damage.
2 *she accepted spinsterhood as the price of her career*: **consequence**, result, cost, toll, penalty, sacrifice, forfeit, forfeiture; downside, snag, drawback, disadvantage, minus; trial, torment, bane, tribulation, affliction, suffering, burden, trouble, worry, deprivation, undesirable consequence.
▷ANTONYMS reward; advantage.
3 *he had a price on his head*: **reward**, bounty, premium; recompense, compensation.
□ **at a price** *the software is available, but at a price*: **at a high price/cost**, at considerable cost, for a great deal of money.
□ **at any price** *it's not for sale at any price | my father was a gentle person, wanting peace at any price*: **whatever the price**, whatever the cost, at whatever cost, no matter (what) the cost, cost what it may, regardless.
□ **beyond price** *the Crown Jewels are of course beyond price*: **of incalculable value/worth**, of inestimable value/worth, of immeasurable value/worth, invaluable, priceless, without price, worth its weight in gold, worth a king's ransom; irreplaceable, incomparable, unparalleled, expensive, costly, high-priced, at a premium, rich, dear, rare, choice, fine, exquisite, precious, treasured, prized, cherished.
▶ verb *a family day ticket is priced at £5.00*: **fix/set the price of**, put a price on, cost, value, rate, evaluate, assess, estimate, appraise, assay.

priceless adjective **1** *a fabulous house full of priceless works of art*: **of incalculable value/worth**, of inestimable value/worth, of immeasurable value/worth, invaluable, beyond price, without price, worth its weight in gold, worth a king's ransom; rare, irreplaceable, incomparable, unparalleled, expensive, costly, high-priced, at a premium, rich, dear, choice, fine, exquisite, treasured, prized, precious, cherished.
▷ANTONYMS worthless, cheap.
2 informal *Jim thought this was priceless and laughed loudly*: **hilarious**, extremely amusing, very funny, comic, comical, riotous, uproarious, screamingly/hysterically funny, too funny for words, side-splitting, rib-tickling, absurd, ridiculous; informal a scream, a hoot; dated killing, killingly funny.

pricey adjective informal **expensive**, dear, costly, high-priced, high-cost, high-end; overpriced, exorbitant, excessive, extortionate, outrageous, inflated; lavish, extravagant; Brit. upmarket, over the odds; informal steep.
▷ANTONYMS cheap.

prick verb **1** *prick the potatoes all over with a fork*: **pierce**, puncture, make/put a hole in, stab, perforate, rupture, riddle, penetrate, nick, spear, slit, incise, knife, bore, spike, skewer, spit, stick, punch, pin, needle, jag, jab; rare pink, transpierce.
2 *his eyes began to prick in the smoke*: **sting**, smart, burn, tingle, prickle, itch; hurt, be sore, be irritated.
3 *his conscience began to prick him*: **trouble**, worry, distress, cause someone distress, perturb, disturb, oppress, harrow, harass, cause someone anguish, afflict, torment, plague, prey on, gnaw at, cut, touch, stab, pain, cause someone pain.
4 *ambition pricked him on to greater effort*: **goad**, prod, incite, provoke, urge, spur, sting, whip, prompt, stimulate, encourage, inspire, motivate, push, propel, impel.
5 *the horse* ***pricked up*** *its ears*: **raise**, erect, point.
□ **prick up one's ears listen carefully**, pay attention, become attentive, begin to take notice, attend, concentrate on hearing, lend an ear, pin one's ears back; informal be all ears; literary hark.
▶ noun **1** *the patient will feel a prick in the back*: **jab**, sting, pinprick, stab, nick, jag.
2 *he could still see the prick of that vanished drawing pin in the plaster*: **hole**, puncture, perforation, pinhole; nick, wound, cut, gash.
3 *Juliet felt the prick of tears behind her eyelids*: **sting**, stinging, smart, smarting, burning, tingle, tingling, itch, itching, soreness, irritation.
4 *the prick of conscience*: **pang**, pricking, twinge, stab, gnawing.

prickle noun **1** *the cactus is covered with prickles*: **thorn**, needle, barb, spike, point, spine, quill, spur, bristle, prong, tine; technical spicule.
2 *Willie felt a cold prickle crawl up his back*: **tingle**, tingling sensation, tingling, prickling sensation, chill, thrill, itching, creeping sensation, gooseflesh, goose pimples, pins and needles; Medicine paraesthesia; rare formication.
▶ verb **1** *the thought made her prickle with excitement*: **tingle**, itch, have a creeping sensation, have goose pimples, have gooseflesh, have goosebumps, have pins and needles.
2 *its tiny spikes prickled his skin*: **make something tingle**, make something smart, make something itch; sting, prick.

prickly adjective **1** *the hedgehog curled up into a prickly ball*: **spiky**, spiked, thorny, barbed, spiny, pronged, bristled, bristly; briary, brambly, burry, rough, scratchy, sharp; technical spiculate, spicular, aculeate, barbellate, spinose, spinous, muricate, setaceous.
2 *my skin feels all prickly*: **tingly**, tingling, prickling, stinging, smarting, itching, itchy, creeping, crawling.
3 *Mr Griffith was a prickly character*: **irritable**, irascible, peevish, fractious, fretful, cross, crabbed, crabby, crotchety, cantankerous, curmudgeonly, disagreeable, miserable, morose, petulant, pettish, peppery, on edge, edgy, impatient, complaining, querulous, bitter, moody, huffy, grumpy, scratchy, ill-tempered, bad-tempered, ill-natured, ill-humoured, sullen, surly, sulky, sour, churlish, touchy, testy, tetchy, grouchy, snappish, waspish, crusty, bilious, liverish, dyspeptic, splenetic, choleric; informal snappy, chippy,

cranky, whingeing, whingy; Brit. informal narky, ratty, eggy, stroppy, shirty; N. Amer. informal peckish, soreheaded; Austral./NZ informal snaky; informal, dated miffy, waxy.
▷ANTONYMS affable, easy-going.
4 *the prickly question of compensation*: **problematic**, awkward, ticklish, tricky, delicate, sensitive, difficult, hard, baffling, perplexing, knotty, thorny, tough, troublesome, bothersome, trying, taxing, irksome, vexatious, worrying; complicated, complex, intricate, convoluted, involved; informal sticky; Brit. informal dodgy.

pride noun 1 *the triumphs of war were a source of pride to them*: **self-esteem**, dignity, honour, self-respect, ego, self-worth, self-image, self-identity, self-regard, pride in oneself, pride in one's abilities, belief in one's worth, faith in oneself; French amour propre.
▷ANTONYMS shame.
2 *many craftsmen take pride in a good job well done*: **pleasure**, joy, delight, gratification, fulfilment, satisfaction, sense of achievement; comfort, content, contentment.
3 *he refused her offer out of sheer pride*: **arrogance**, vanity, self-importance, hubris, self-conceit, conceit, conceitedness, self-love, self-glorification, self-adulation, self-admiration, narcissism, egotism, presumption, superciliousness, haughtiness, snobbery, snobbishness; disdain, disdainfulness, condescension, pretentiousness; French hauteur; informal big-headedness, swollen-headedness; literary vainglory.
▷ANTONYMS modesty, humility.
4 *the six-year-old bull is the pride of the herd*: **best**, finest, top, cream, pick, choice, choicest, most select, elite, prize, jewel, the jewel in the crown, flower, gem, pearl, treasure, paragon, leading light, glory; French crème de la crème.
▷ANTONYMS dregs.
5 *the large vegetable garden was the pride of the hospital gardener*: **source of satisfaction**, pride and joy, darling, apple of someone's eye, treasured possession, admiration, object of admiration, joy, delight, marvel.
▸ verb
□ **pride oneself on** *she prided herself on her sincerity*: **be proud of**, be proud of oneself for, take pride in, take satisfaction in, congratulate oneself on, flatter oneself on, preen oneself on, pat oneself on the back for, revel in, glory in, delight in, exult in, rejoice in, triumph over; feel self-satisfied about, vaunt, boast about, brag about, crow about, gloat over; archaic pique oneself on/in.

priest noun **clergyman**, **clergywoman**, minister (of religion), cleric, ecclesiastic, pastor, parson, churchman, churchwoman, man/woman of the cloth, man/woman of God, father; Scottish kirkman; N. Amer. dominie; informal reverend, padre, Holy Joe, sky pilot; Austral. informal josser.

> *Word links* **priest**
>
> **clerical**, **hieratic**, **sacerdotal** relating to priests
> **hierophobia** fear of priests

priestly adjective **clerical**, pastoral, priestlike, canonical, ecclesiastical; archaic vicarial; rare sacerdotal, hieratic, Aaronic, rectorial, presbyteral.

prig noun **prude**, puritan, killjoy, Mrs Grundy, Grundy, pedant, old maid, schoolmarm, Pharisee, hypocrite, pietist, priggish person; N. Amer. bluenose; informal goody-goody, Goody Two-Shoes, holy Joe, holy Willie, Miss Prim, stuffed shirt; literary Tartuffe; archaic precisian.

priggish adjective **self-righteous**, holier-than-thou, smug, sanctimonious, moralistic, sententious, prudish, puritanical, prim, strait-laced, tight-laced, stuffy, starchy, prissy, Victorian, schoolmarmish, schoolmistressy, old-maidish, narrow, narrow-minded, censorious, Pecksniffian, Pharisaic, hypocritical; informal goody-goody; rare Grundyish.
▷ANTONYMS broad-minded, permissive.

prim adjective *a prim, fastidious woman*: **demure**, proper, prim and proper, formal, stuffy, strait-laced, prudish; prissy, mimsy, priggish, puritanical, niminy-piminy, Victorian, old-maid, old-maidish, schoolmistressy, schoolmarmish, governessy; Brit. po-faced; informal starchy; archaic square-toed; rare Grundyish.
▷ANTONYMS uninhibited; informal.

primacy noun *the primacy of industry over agriculture*: **greater importance**, priority, precedence, pre-eminence, preference, superiority, first place, pride of place, weighting, supremacy, ascendancy, sovereignty, dominance, dominion, leadership; rare paramountcy.

prima donna noun 1 *this solo was added to give the prima donna another aria*: **leading soprano**, leading lady, diva, (opera) star, protagonist, heroine, principal singer, female lead.
2 *the sport's overpaid prima donnas would throw tantrums on court*: **temperamental person**, unpredictable person, self-important person.

primal adjective 1 *they ignore their primal masculine instincts*: **basic**, fundamental, essential, elemental, primary, vital, central, intrinsic, indispensable, inherent, cardinal; characteristic.
▷ANTONYMS peripheral.
2 *the sea is the primal source of all living things on earth*: **original**, initial, early, earliest, first, primitive, primeval, primary.
▷ANTONYMS subsequent; derivative.

primarily adverb 1 *the bishop was primarily a leader of the local community*: **first and foremost**, first, firstly, essentially, in essence, fundamentally, in the first place, most importantly, principally, predominantly, predominately, basically, elementally, above all, especially, particularly.
2 *such work is undertaken primarily for large institutional clients*: **mostly**, for the most part, chiefly, mainly, in the main, on the whole, largely, by and large, to a large extent, to a great degree, substantially, overall, in general, effectively, especially, generally, usually, typically, commonly, as a rule.

primary adjective 1 *the police believe that crime detection is their primary role*: **main**, chief, key, prime, central, principal, foremost, first, most important, predominant, paramount, overriding, major, ruling, dominant, master, supreme, cardinal, pre-eminent, ultimate; informal number-one.
▷ANTONYMS secondary, subordinate.
2 *you must start by removing the primary cause of the trouble*: **original**, earliest, initial, beginning, first; **essential**, fundamental, basic.
▷ANTONYMS secondary.

prime[1] adjective 1 *his prime reason for going to America*: **main**, chief, key, primary, central, principal, foremost, first, most important, paramount, major, dominant, supreme, overriding, cardinal, pre-eminent, ultimate; informal number-one.
▷ANTONYMS secondary, subordinate.
2 *deforestation is the prime cause of flooding*: **fundamental**, basic, essential, elemental, primary, vital, central.
▷ANTONYMS secondary.
3 *extensive areas of prime agricultural land*: **top-quality**, highest quality, top, top-tier, best, first-class, first-rate, high-grade, grade A, superior, supreme, flawless, choice, select, finest, superlative, peak, optimal, model; excellent, marvellous, magnificent, superb, fine, wonderful, exceptional, formidable; informal tip-top, A1, stellar, top-notch.
▷ANTONYMS inferior.
4 *the NHS remains the prime example of a public health service*: **archetypal**, prototypical, typical, classic, ideal, excellent, standard, stock, conventional, characteristic, quintessential.
▸ noun *he was, in his prime, the most famous man in the world*: **heyday**, best days/years, day, time, prime of one's life, maturity; youth, springtime, salad days, bloom, flowering, full flowering, perfection; peak, pinnacle, height, high point/spot, zenith, ascendancy.

prime[2] verb 1 *he grabbed a gun from a nearby rack and primed it*: **prepare**, load, set up, ready, make ready, get ready, equip, gear up.
2 *Mischa knew what to say, as Lucy had primed him carefully*: **brief**, give information to, fill in, prepare, supply with facts, put in the picture, inform, advise, notify, tell, instruct, coach, drill; informal clue in, give someone the low-down; Brit. informal gen up.

prime minister noun **premier**, first minister, head of the government; Brit. First Lord of the Treasury.

primeval adjective 1 *one of Europe's last areas of primeval forest*: **ancient**, earliest, first, prehistoric, antediluvian, antique, primordial, primitive, primal; pristine, original, untouched by humans; aboriginal, indigenous; rare autochthonous, autochthonic, primigenial.
▷ANTONYMS modern.
2 *all sorts of primeval fears*: **instinctive**, primitive, basic, primal, primordial, intuitive, intuitional, involuntary, inborn, innate, inherent, inbred, natural, congenital, hereditary, inherited, in the blood, ingrained.

primitive adjective 1 *primitive times | some of these primitive insects learned to fly*: **ancient**, earliest, first, prehistoric, antediluvian, antique, primordial, primeval, primal, primary, lower, original, proto-, ur-; aboriginal, indigenous; rare autochthonous, autochthonic, primigenial.
▷ANTONYMS modern, recent; developed.
2 *idealization of the way of life of primitive peoples must be avoided*: **preliterate**, non-industrial; simple, unsophisticated.
▷ANTONYMS advanced, literate, industrial.
3 *the quarrier worked with primitive tools*: **crude**, simple, rough, basic, elementary, rough-hewn, rudimentary, undeveloped, unrefined, unsophisticated, rude, rough and ready, makeshift; old-fashioned, obsolete, archaic.
▷ANTONYMS sophisticated, advanced.
4 *primitive art*: **simple**, natural, unsophisticated, naive, unaffected, undeveloped, childlike, innocent, artless, unpretentious; untaught, untrained, untutored.
▷ANTONYMS sophisticated, refined.

primordial adjective 1 *these primordial chunks of dust and ice lie in the very fringes of the solar system*: **ancient**, earliest, first, prehistoric, antediluvian, antique, primeval, primitive, primal; rare autochthonous, autochthonic, primigenial.
▷ANTONYMS modern.
2 *the primordial desire for earthly happiness*: **instinctive**, primitive, basic, primal, primeval, intuitive, intuitional, involuntary, inborn, innate, inherent, inbred, natural, congenital, hereditary, inherited, in the blood, ingrained.

Word toolkit **primordial**

See **prehistoric**.

primp verb *Fran primped her hair | they passed a few women primping at the mirrors.* See **preen** (sense 2).

prince noun *the prince of a neighbouring state*: **ruler**, **sovereign**, lord, overlord, dynast, leader, monarch, crowned head; royal duke, king, emperor, tsar, grand duke, elector, potentate, suzerain, crown prince, princeling, prince regent, mogul, baron, liege (lord); emir, sheikh, sultan, maharaja, raja; historical atheling.

princely adjective **1** *the Cathedral is flanked by princely buildings*: **magnificent**, grand, impressive, imposing, splendid, superb, majestic, glorious, striking, spectacular, awe-inspiring, breathtaking; sumptuous, opulent, fine, luxurious, de luxe, lavish, resplendent; monumental, palatial, august, distinguished, noble, proud, stately, dignified, exalted, great, royal, regal, kingly, imperial; rich, brilliant, beautiful, elegant, gorgeous; informal splendiferous, ritzy, posh; rare splendacious, magnolious.
2 *this will cost the Treasury the princely sum of £11m*: **huge**, enormous, generous, handsome, massive, gigantic, very big, very large, great, giant, colossal, mammoth, vast, immense, tremendous, mighty, stupendous, monumental, prodigious, mountainous, monstrous, substantial; informal mega, monster, whopping, whopping great, thumping, thumping great, humongous, jumbo, hulking, bumper, astronomical; Brit. informal whacking, whacking great, ginormous.

principal adjective *vehicle emissions are the principal cause of bad air*: **main**, chief, primary, leading, foremost, first, most important, predominant, dominant, (most) prominent; key, crucial, vital, essential, basic, staple, critical, pivotal, salient, prime, central, focal; premier, paramount, major, ruling, master, supreme, overriding, cardinal, capital, pre-eminent, ultimate, uppermost, highest, utmost, top, topmost, arch-; informal number-one.
▷ANTONYMS minor, subordinate, subsidiary.
▶ noun **1** *the principal of the firm of contractors*: **boss**, chief, chief executive (officer), CEO, chairman, chairwoman, managing director, MD, president, director, manager, employer, head, leader, ruler, controller; informal head honcho; Brit. informal gaffer, governor, guv'nor.
2 *the school's principal*: **head teacher**, head, headmaster, headmistress, director; dean, rector, warden, chancellor, vice-chancellor, president, provost, governor; N. Amer. informal prexy, prex.
3 *she is currently a principal in a soap opera*: **leading actor/actress**, leading player/performer, leading man/lady, lead, star; protagonist, hero, heroine, leading role, title role; prima donna, diva, prima ballerina.
4 *no repayment of the loan's principal is required for the first few years*: **capital sum**, capital, capital funds, working capital, financial resources; money, debt, loan.

Easily confused words **principal or principle?**

See **principle**.

principally adverb *the decline is principally due to overfishing*: **mainly**, mostly, chiefly, for the most part, in the main, on the whole, largely, by and large, to a large extent, to a great degree, predominantly, predominately, above all, first and foremost, basically, substantially, overall, in general, effectively, especially, particularly, primarily, generally, usually, typically, commonly, as a rule.

principle noun **1** *the most elementary principles of physics*: **truth**, proposition, concept, idea, theory, postulate; assumption, basis, fundamental, essence, essential; philosophy.
2 *they stuck to the principle of laissez-faire*: **doctrine**, belief, creed, credo, attitude, rule, golden rule, guideline, formula, standard, criterion, tenet, truism, code, ethic, maxim, motto, axiom, aphorism, notion, dictum, dogma, canon, law.
3 *a woman of principle | he was applauded for sticking to his principles*: **morals**, morality, moral standards, moral values, ethics, code of ethics, beliefs, credo, ideals, standards, integrity, uprightness, high-mindedness, righteousness, virtue, probity, rectitude, sense of honour, honour, decency, conscience, sense of duty, scruples.
□ **in principle 1** *there is no reason, in principle, why we couldn't work together*: **in theory**, theoretically, on paper, in an ideal world; French en principe. **2** *he has accepted the idea in principle*: **in general**, **on balance**, generally, in essence, by and large, on the whole, all in all, in the main, all things considered, taking everything into consideration.

Easily confused words **principle or principal?**

Although the words **principle** and **principal** are pronounced in the same way, they do not have the same meaning. *Principle* is a noun meaning 'a fundamental basis of a system of thought or belief', as in *this is one of the basic principles of democracy*. *Principal*, on the other hand, is normally an adjective meaning 'main or most important', as in *one of the country's principal cities*.
Principal can also be a noun, where it is used to refer to the most senior or most important person in an organization or other group (*the deputy principal*).

principled adjective *she took a principled feminist stance*: **moral**, ethical, good, virtuous, righteous, upright, upstanding, high-minded, right-minded, proper, correct, honourable, honest, just, noble, incorruptible, scrupulous, conscientious, respectable, decent.
▷ANTONYMS unprincipled.

prink verb *he prinked himself in front of the mirror*: **groom**, tidy, arrange, brush, comb, smooth, smarten (up), spruce up, freshen (up), beautify, pretty, preen, primp; informal titivate, doll up; Brit. informal tart up; N. Amer. informal gussy up; archaic plume, trig (up).

print verb **1** *four newspapers are printed in the town*: **set in print**, send to press, run off, preprint, reprint, pull, proof, copy, reproduce; Computing list, dump; informal put to bed, litho.
2 *patterns of birds, flowers, and trees were printed on the cloth*: **imprint**, impress, stamp, mark.
3 *they printed 30,000 copies of the offending magazine*: **publish**, issue, release, disseminate, circulate, propagate, purvey.
4 *one particular incident is indelibly printed on her memory*: **register**, record, note, impress, imprint, engrave, etch, stamp, mark, brand, set, ingrain.
▶ noun **1** *the print was very small*: **type**, printing, letters, lettering, characters, type size, typeface, face, font; Brit. fount.
2 *there were fresh prints of the deceased's left hand on the bottle*: **impression**, fingerprint, mark; footprint.
3 *the picture was supposed to be a print of the Coventry tapestry*: **reproduction**, copy, replica, imitation, facsimile, duplicate.
4 *there was a print of a hunting scene on one wall*: **picture**, design, engraving, etching, lithograph, silk screen, linocut, monoprint, plate, cut, woodcut, vignette.
5 *the processor sends you the prints and negatives*: **photograph**, photo, snap, snapshot, shot, picture; positive, still, proof, enlargement; Brit. enprint.
6 *our room was luxuriously furnished with soft floral prints*: **printed material/cloth/fabric**, patterned material/cloth/fabric, chintz.
□ **in print 1** *he looks forward to seeing his work in print*: **printed**, in black and white, on paper; published, out, on the streets. **2** *they continued to keep the book in print and supply it*: **published**, printed, available in bookshops, obtainable in the shops, in circulation, on the market, on the shelves.
□ **out of print** *this volume is now out of print*: **no longer available**, unavailable, unobtainable, o.p., no longer published/printed, not on the market.

prior adjective *visitors can tour the mill by prior arrangement*: **earlier**, previous, preceding, foregoing, antecedent, advance, preparatory, preliminary, initial; rare anterior, precedent.
▷ANTONYMS later, subsequent.
□ **prior to** *prior to the seventeenth century clocks were made by blacksmiths*: **before**, until, till, up to, previous to, earlier than, preceding, leading up to, in advance of, ahead of, ante-, pre-; rare anterior to.
▷ANTONYMS after, following.

priority noun **1** *pioneering new forms of surgery should be a priority for the National Health Service*: **prime concern**, first concern, most important consideration, most pressing matter, matter of greatest importance, primary issue.
2 *the government's commitment to give priority to primary education*: **precedence**, greater importance, preference, precedency, pre-eminence, first/highest place, predominance, primacy, the lead, weighting, weight.
3 *traffic already on the roundabout has priority*: **right of way**.

priory noun **religious house**, religious community, abbey, cloister; monastery, friary; convent, nunnery; rare coenobium, coenoby, beguinage.

prise verb **1** *Joe was trying to prise the cap off a bottle of painkillers*: **lever**, **force**, wrench, pull, wrest, twist; jemmy; N. Amer. pry, jimmy.
2 *it shouldn't have been necessary to prise information from them*: **extract/obtain with difficulty**, worm out; Brit. winkle out.

prison noun **jail**, penal institution, place of detention, lock-up, place of confinement, guardhouse, detention centre; Brit. young offender institution; N. Amer. penitentiary, correctional facility, jailhouse, boot camp, stockade, house of correction; informal the clink, the slammer, inside, stir, the jug, the big house, the brig, the glasshouse; Brit. informal the nick; N. Amer. informal the can, the pen, the cooler, the joint, the pokey, the slam, the skookum house, the calaboose, the hoosegow; Brit. informal, dated the chokey, bird, quod; historical pound, roundhouse; Brit. historical youth custody centre, approved school, borstal, bridewell; Scottish historical tollbooth; French, historical bastille; N. Amer. historical reformatory.

Word links **prison**

carceral, **custodial** relating to prison

prisoner noun **1** *a prisoner serving a life sentence*: **convict**, inmate; trusty; informal jailbird, con, lifer; Brit. informal (old) lag; N. Amer. informal **yardbird**; archaic transport.

2 *the army took several hundred prisoners*: **prisoner of war**, POW; hostage, captive, detainee, internee.

prissy adjective *he hated it when she swore, but he didn't like to sound prissy*: **prudish**, priggish, prim, prim and proper, niminy-piminy, strait-laced; formal, proper, stuffy, mimsy, namby-pamby, Victorian, old-maidish, schoolmistressy, schoolmarmish, governessy; Brit. po-faced; informal goody-goody, starchy; rare square-toed, Grundyish.
▷ANTONYMS broad-minded.

pristine adjective *a pristine white handkerchief*: **immaculate**, in perfect condition, perfect, in mint condition, as new, unspoilt, spotless, flawless, clean, fresh, new, virgin, pure, unused; unmarked, unblemished, untarnished, untouched, unsullied, undefiled.
▷ANTONYMS dirty, sullied.

Word toolkit **pristine**

See **impeccable**.

privacy noun *a walled garden ensures complete privacy*: **seclusion**, privateness, solitude, isolation, retirement, peace, peace and quiet, peacefulness, quietness, lack of disturbance, lack of interruption, freedom from interference; rare sequestration, reclusion.

private adjective 1 *his private plane*: **personal**, **one's own**, individual, particular, special, exclusive, privately owned.
▷ANTONYMS public.
2 *his private talks with the UK prime minister*: **confidential**, strictly confidential, secret, top secret, classified, unofficial, off the record, not for publication, not to be made public, not to be disclosed, closet; backstage, offstage, privileged, one-on-one, tête-à-tête; covert, clandestine, surreptitious; Latin in camera; informal hush-hush.
▷ANTONYMS open, public.
3 *their private thoughts on the subject*: **intimate**, personal, secret; innermost, inward, unspoken, undeclared, undisclosed, unvoiced, sneaking, hidden.
4 *he was a very private man*: **reserved**, introvert, introverted, self-contained, reticent, discreet, uncommunicative, non-communicative, unforthcoming, secretive, retiring, ungregarious, unsocial, unsociable, withdrawn, solitary, insular, reclusive, hermit-like, hermitic.
▷ANTONYMS extrovert.
5 *he hustled her away, searching for some private spot*: **secluded**, secret, quiet, undisturbed, concealed, hidden, remote, isolated, out of the way, sequestered.
▷ANTONYMS busy, crowded.
6 *we can phone from the library—we'll be private in there*: **undisturbed**, uninterrupted, without disturbance, without interruption; alone, by ourselves.
7 *he would continue to represent her in a private capacity as advisor and confidant*: **unofficial**, **personal**, non-official, non-public.
▷ANTONYMS official.
8 *80 per cent of the funding came from private industry*: **independent**, non-state-controlled, non-state-run, privatized, denationalized, non-public, commercial, private-enterprise.
▷ANTONYMS public, nationalized, state-controlled.
▶ noun *a private in the army*: **private soldier**, common soldier; infantryman, foot soldier, trooper; Brit. sapper, ranker; in the US GI, enlisted man; French poilu; Indian jawan; Brit. informal Tommy, squaddie, Tommy Atkins; N. Amer. informal grunt, buck private; Austral./NZ informal digger; S. African informal troopie; archaic swad, swaddy.
□ **in private** *the inquiry will be held in private*: **in secret**, secretly, in secrecy, privately, behind closed doors, in camera, with no one else present; in confidence, confidentially, between ourselves, off the record; Latin sub rosa; French entre nous, à huis clos.
▷ANTONYMS in public.

private detective noun **private investigator**, detective, operative; Brit. enquiry agent; informal private eye, PI, sleuth, snoop; N. Amer. informal private dick, peeper, shamus, gumshoe; informal, dated hawkshaw, sherlock; N. Amer. dated Pinkerton.

privately adverb 1 *I wanted the opportunity to talk to you privately*: **in private**, with no one else present, behind closed doors, between ourselves, confidentially, in confidence, discreetly, in secret, secretly; French entre nous; Latin in camera.
▷ANTONYMS publicly.
2 *privately, MPs were disturbed by the news*: **secretly**, inwardly, deep down, personally, unofficially.
3 *they lived their lives very privately*: **out of the public eye**, out of public view, in seclusion, in solitude, alone, without being disturbed, without being interrupted.

private parts plural noun **genitals**, genitalia, sexual organs, reproductive organs, pudenda, nether regions, crotch groin; informal privates, bits, naughty bits, dangly bits.

privation noun *years of rationing and privation*: **deprivation**, hardship, poverty, penury, indigence, destitution, impoverishment, want, need, neediness; disadvantage, austerity; suffering, affliction, distress, misery; rare impecuniousness, impecuniosity.
▷ANTONYMS plenty; luxury.

privilege noun 1 *he sought to reduce the legal privileges of the unions*: **advantage**, right, benefit, prerogative, entitlement, birthright, due; concession, freedom, liberty.
2 *it was a privilege to meet her*: **honour**, pleasure, source of pleasure/pride/satisfaction.
3 *a breach of parliamentary privilege*: **immunity**, exemption, dispensation.

privileged adjective 1 *she comes from a privileged background*: **wealthy**, rich, affluent, prosperous; **lucky**, fortunate, special, elite, favoured, select; advantaged, socially advantaged.
▷ANTONYMS underprivileged, disadvantaged.
2 *he accused me of giving away privileged information*: **confidential**, private, secret, top secret, restricted, classified, not for publication, off the record, inside; informal hush-hush; archaic privy.
3 *the MP is privileged but the reporter and the publisher could face civil action*: **immune (from prosecution)**, protected, exempt, excepted.

privy adjective *she was not* ***privy to*** *any information contained in those letters*: **aware of**, acquainted with, in on, informed of, advised of, apprised of, in the know about, cognizant of; informal genned up on, clued in on, clued up on, wise to, hip to.

prize noun 1 *Britain's most prestigious prize for contemporary art | a £2,500 cash prize*: **award**, reward, premium; trophy, cup, medal, plate, shield; honour, accolade, crown, laurels, bays, palm; jackpot, bonanza, purse, winnings, sweepstake; informal pot; dated garland; archaic guerdon; Biblical prey.
2 *the prizes of war*: **spoils**, booty, plunder, loot, pickings, profits, takings.
▶ adjective 1 *a prize bull can father thousands of cows*: **champion**, award-winning, prize-winning, winning, top, top-class, top-tier, first-class, first-rate, choice, quality, select, best.
▷ANTONYMS second-rate.
2 *a prize example of how well organic farming can function*: **outstanding**, excellent, superlative, superb, supreme, very good, prime, fine, magnificent, marvellous, wonderful; informal great, terrific, tremendous, fantastic, top-notch, A1.
3 *you must think I'm a prize idiot*: **utter**, complete, total, absolute, real, perfect, positive, veritable; Brit. informal right, bloody; Austral./NZ informal fair; archaic arrant.
▶ verb *this was the era when honesty was prized above all other virtues*: **value**, set/place a high value on, set great store by, rate highly, attach great importance to, esteem, hold in high regard, think highly of, treasure, cherish, hold dear, appreciate greatly.

prized adjective *his prized collection of soccer memorabilia*: **treasured**, precious, valued, cherished, much loved, beloved.

prizewinner noun **champion**, winner, medallist, cup winner, prizeman, victor; Brit. victor ludorum; informal champ.

pro preposition Latin
□ **pro bono (publico)** *architects and engineers were all working pro bono for the nonprofit museum | he will act as pro bono advisor to the company*: **free**, gratis, unpaid, unrewarded, unsalaried, free of charge, without charge, for nothing, at no cost, without payment, for the common good; gratuitous, complimentary, voluntary, volunteer; informal for free, on the house; Brit. informal buckshee.
□ **pro tem** *he allows his son to move back home, pro tem, after his house is destroyed in a fire*: **temporarily**, for the time being, for the moment, for now, for the present, in the interim, for the nonce, in/for the meantime, in the meanwhile; for a short time, for a short/little while, briefly, momentarily, fleetingly; provisionally; Latin pro tempore, ad interim; French en attendant.
▷ANTONYMS permanently.

probability noun 1 *the probability of higher mortgage rates*: **likelihood**, likeliness, prospect, expectation, chance, chances, odds, possibility.
2 *relegation back to the Second Division looks like a distinct probability*: **probable event**, prospect, possibility, good/fair/reasonable bet.

probable adjective *it is probable that the economic situation will deteriorate further*: **likely**, most likely, odds-on, expected, to be expected, anticipated, predictable, foreseeable, ten to one, presumed, potential, credible, quite possible, possible, feasible; informal on the cards, a good/fair/reasonable bet.
▷ANTONYMS improbable, unlikely.

probably adverb *I knew I would probably never see her again*: **in all likelihood**, **in all probability**, as likely as not, very likely, most likely, likely, as like as not, ten to one, the chances are, doubtless, no doubt, all things considered, taking all things into consideration, all things being equal, possibly, perhaps, maybe, it may be, presumably, on the face of it, apparently; archaic like enough, belike.

probation noun *clerks were only paid a proper salary after the first three years of probation*: **trial period**, test period, experimental period, trial; apprenticeship, traineeship, training, novitiate.

probationer noun **trainee**, novice, apprentice, inexperienced worker, new recruit, learner, beginner, tyro, neophyte; informal rookie, greenhorn; N. Amer. informal probie.

probe noun *a probe into alleged financial irregularities at the club*: **investigation**, enquiry, enquiry, examination, scrutiny, inquest, exploration, study, research, analysis, scrutinization.
▸ verb 1 *hands probed his body from top to bottom*: **examine**, feel, feel around, explore, prod, poke, check.
2 *a lengthy public enquiry probed the cause of the disaster*: **investigate**, conduct an investigation into, enquire/enquire into, look into, study, conduct an enquiry/enquiry into, examine, scrutinize, go into, carry out an inquest into, research, analyse, dissect, search into, delve into, dig into; sound, plumb.

probity noun *the chancellor exuded competence and fiscal probity*: **integrity**, honesty, uprightness, decency, morality, rectitude, goodness, virtue, right-mindedness, trustworthiness, truthfulness, honour, honourableness, justice, fairness, equity; principles, ethics.
▷ANTONYMS untrustworthiness.

problem noun 1 *he's been under increasing stress due to business and personal problems | they ran into a problem*: **difficulty**, trouble, worry, complication, difficult situation, mess, muddle, mix-up; snag, hitch, drawback, stumbling block, obstacle, hurdle, hiccup, setback, catch; catch-22, vexed question, quandary, the rub; predicament, plight, can of worms, hornets' nest, Gordian knot; misfortune, mishap, misadventure; informal dilemma, headache, prob, hassle, pickle, fix, tight spot, fly in the ointment, how-do-you-do, job, gremlin, facer; N. Amer. informal katzenjammer; rare nodus.
2 *'I don't want to be a problem,' Lucy said*: **nuisance**, source of difficulty, bother, pest, source of trouble, irritant, thorn in one's side/flesh, vexation; informal drag, pain, pain in the neck; vulgar slang pain in the arse.
3 *arithmetical problems*: **puzzle**, question, poser, enigma, riddle, conundrum; informal teaser, brain-teaser.
▸ adjective *a problem child*: **troublesome**, difficult, unmanageable, unruly, disobedient, uncontrollable, ungovernable, intractable, recalcitrant, intransigent, refractory; delinquent, maladjusted, disturbed.
▷ANTONYMS well behaved, manageable.

problematic adjective *the piece is among the most problematic of all his major works*: **difficult**, hard, problematical, taxing, troublesome, tricky, awkward, controversial, ticklish, complicated, complex, knotty, thorny, prickly, involved, intricate, vexed; paradoxical, puzzling, baffling, perplexing; informal sticky; Brit. informal dodgy.
▷ANTONYMS easy, simple, straightforward.

procedure noun *the council agreed a procedure for dealing with future breaches of the law*: **course of action**, line of action, plan of action, policy, series of steps, plan, method, system, strategy, stratagem, way, approach, formula, mechanism, methodology, MO (modus operandi), SOP (standard operating procedure), technique, means, measure, process, proceeding, operation, agenda; routine, drill, practice.

proceed verb 1 *after almost six weeks, she was still uncertain how to proceed*: **begin**, make a start, get going, move, set something in motion; **take action**, act, go on, take steps, take measures, go ahead, make progress, make headway.
2 *he turned off the road and proceeded down the long drive*: **go**, **make one's way**, advance, move, move forward, move along, progress, carry on, press on, push on.
▷ANTONYMS stop.
3 *the government confirmed its decision to* **proceed with** *the investigations*: **go ahead**, carry on, go on, continue, keep on, get on, get ahead; pursue, prosecute.
4 *there is not enough evidence to* **proceed against** *him*: **take to court**, start proceedings against, take proceedings against, begin an action against, start an action against, sue.
5 *his claim that all power proceeded from God*: **originate**, have its origin, spring, stem, come, derive, arise, issue, flow, emanate, descend, result, follow, ensue, begin, emerge, start.

proceeding noun 1 *have they any idea of the danger of such a proceeding?* **course of action**, action, step, measure, move, operation, manoeuvre, procedure, process, act, deed, undertaking, initiative, venture, transaction.
2 (**proceedings**) *she began to enjoy the evening's proceedings*: **events**, activities, business, affairs, happenings, goings-on, doings.
3 (**proceedings**) *the proceedings of the meeting are to be published later*: **report(s)**, transactions, minutes, account(s), record(s), business; annals, archives; French procès-verbal.
4 (**proceedings**) *in 1989 he began libel proceedings against the paper*: **legal action**, legal proceedings, judicial proceedings, lawsuit, suit, case, action, litigation.

proceeds plural noun *the event starts at 1pm and all proceeds will go to Animal Welfare*: **profits**, takings, earnings, receipts, returns, income, revenue, gain, yield; Sport gate, gate money, gate receipts; N. Amer. take.

process (stress on the first syllable) noun 1 *faxing a seventy page document is an expensive process*: **procedure**, operation, action, activity, exercise, affair, business, job, task, undertaking, proceeding.
2 *the development of a new canning process*: **method**, procedure, system, technique, means, practice, way, approach.
3 *they may find themselves, in the process of time, caring for their elderly parents*: **course**, advance, progress, progression, unfolding, evolution.
4 Law *the person on whom the process is to be served*: **summons**, writ, subpoena; N. Amer. citation.
□ **in the process of** *the company is in the process of moving into new premises in Palo Alto*: **in the course of**, in the middle of, in the midst of.
▸ verb *I'll make sure that your application is processed quickly*: **deal with**, attend to, see to, sort out, handle, take care of, action, organize, manage.

procession noun 1 *a ceremonial procession through the town*: **parade**, march, cavalcade, motorcade, cortège; column, file, train; march past; Indian jatha, yatra; W. Indian mas.
2 *he employed a procession of nubile young secretaries*: **series**, succession, stream, steady stream, string, sequence, chain, run.

proclaim verb 1 *four of the five men arrested proclaimed their innocence*: **declare**, announce, pronounce, state, make known, give out, advertise, publish, broadcast, promulgate, trumpet, blazon, blaze, shout something from the rooftops; profess, assert, maintain, protest.
2 *he proclaimed himself president*: **declare**, pronounce, announce.
3 *the very shape and design of the new schools proclaimed acceptance of a new way of thinking*: **demonstrate**, indicate, show, signify, reveal, testify to, manifest, betray.

proclamation noun 1 *the rector issued a proclamation forbidding such practices*: **decree**, order, edict, command, rule, ruling, announcement, declaration, pronouncement, statement; in Spanish-speaking countries pronunciamento.
2 *the shooting resulted in the proclamation of a state of emergency*: **announcement**, declaration, pronouncement, notification, advertisement, publishing, broadcasting, promulgation; literary blazoning.

proclivity noun *his sexual proclivities are none of your business*: **liking**, inclination, tendency, leaning, disposition, propensity, bent, bias, penchant, predisposition, predilection, partiality, preference, taste, fondness, weakness, proneness; rare velleity.

procrastinate verb *fear of failure is often the reason why people procrastinate*: **delay**, put off doing something, postpone action, defer action, be dilatory, use delaying tactics, stall, temporize, play for time, play a waiting game, dally, drag one's feet/heels, take one's time; hesitate, vacillate, dither, be indecisive, be undecided, waver; Brit. haver, hum and haw; Scottish swither; informal dilly-dally, shilly-shally.

procrastination noun **dithering**, delaying tactics, dilatoriness, stalling, temporizing, hesitation, vacillation; Brit. humming and hawing; informal dilly-dallying, shilly-shallying.

procreate verb *the biological imperative to procreate*: **produce offspring**, reproduce, multiply, propagate, breed; bring young into the world, father offspring, sire offspring; literary beget offspring.

procure verb 1 *vegetables and fruit were not easy to procure*: **obtain**, acquire, get, find, come by, secure, pick up, get possession of; buy, purchase; informal get hold of, get one's hands on, get one's mitts on.
2 archaic or Law *his uncle procured his death by means of a poisoned drink*: **bring about**, cause, contrive, effect.
3 *the police found that he was procuring*: **be a pimp**, be pimping; Brit. informal ponce; N. Amer. informal hustle.

prod verb 1 *Cassie prodded him in the chest*: **poke**, jab, dig, nudge, elbow, butt, push, stab.
2 *the campaign was intended to prod the government into action*: **spur**, stimulate, stir, rouse, prompt, drive, push, galvanize, move, motivate, encourage, persuade, urge, chivvy, impel, actuate; incite, goad, egg on, provoke.
▸ noun 1 *a sharp prod in the ribs*: **poke**, jab, dig, nudge, butt, push, shove, thrust.
2 *you need a gentle prod to remind you that life is only what you make it*: **stimulus**, push, prompt, reminder, prompting, spur, motivation; incitement, goad.
3 *an electric cattle prod*: **goad**, stick, spike.

prodigal adjective 1 *prodigal habits die hard*: **wasteful**, extravagant, spendthrift, improvident, imprudent, immoderate, profligate, thriftless, excessive, intemperate, irresponsible, self-indulgent, reckless, wanton.
▷ANTONYMS thrifty, economical; parsimonious.
2 *a composer who is prodigal with his talents*: **generous**, **lavish**, liberal, unstinting, unsparing, bountiful; copious, profuse; abundant in, abounding in, rich; literary bounteous.
▷ANTONYMS mean.

prodigious adjective 1 *prodigious quantities of food | his prodigious talent*: **enormous**, huge, colossal, immense, vast, great, massive, gigantic, mammoth, tremendous, considerable, substantial, large, sizeable, inordinate, monumental, mighty, gargantuan; amazing, astonishing, astounding, staggering, stunning, marvellous, remarkable, wonderful, phenomenal, terrific, miraculous, impressive, striking, startling, sensational, spectacular, extraordinary, exceptional, breathtaking, incredible, unbelievable, unusual; informal humongous, stupendous,

fantastic, fabulous, fantabulous, mind-boggling, mind-blowing, flabbergasting, mega, awesome; Brit. informal ginormous; literary wondrous.
▷ANTONYMS small; unexceptional.
2 *prodigious apparitions were seen*: **unnatural**, monstrous, grotesque, abnormal.

prodigy noun **1** *he was a child prodigy, giving his first concert at the age of nine*: **child genius**, genius, wonder child, mastermind, virtuoso; German wunderkind; informal whizz-kid, whizz, wizard, Einstein.
2 *Germany seemed a prodigy of industrial discipline*: **model**, classic example, paragon, paradigm, epitome, exemplar, ideal, prototype, archetype, type.

produce verb (stress on the second syllable) **1** *the plant is currently scheduled to produce 1,100 cars a day*: **manufacture**, make, construct, build, fabricate, put together, assemble, turn out, bring out, process, create; mass-produce; informal churn out.
2 *the vineyards in the Val d'Or produce excellent wines*: **yield**, grow, give, supply, provide, furnish, bear, bring forth.
3 *she produced a litter of ten puppies*: **give birth to**, bear, breed, bring into the world, give life to, spawn.
4 *the garden where the artist produced many of his flower paintings*: **create**, compose, originate, develop, fashion, turn out.
5 *she dug into her bag and produced her card | no evidence was produced to support the allegation*: **present**, offer, proffer, show, display, exhibit; pull out, bring out, draw out, fish out, extract; provide, furnish, advance, put forward, bring forward, come up with, set forth, bring to light.
6 *direct communication between the two countries will produce greater understanding*: **give rise to**, bring about, cause, occasion, generate, engender, lead to, result in, effect, induce, initiate, start, set off; contribute to, make for, be conducive to, foster, promote; provoke, precipitate, breed, spark off, trigger; literary beget.
7 *a group of young women committed to producing quality drama*: **stage**, put on, mount, present, put before the public, show, perform.
▸ noun (stress on the first syllable) *organically grown produce*: **food**, foodstuff(s); crops, fruit, vegetables, greens; goods, products, commodities, staples, wares; Brit. greengrocery; N. Amer. rare truck.

Word links **produce**

-facient, **-fic**, **-genic** suffixes meaning '-producing', as in *abortifacient, soporific, hallucinogenic*

producer noun **1** *the company is the largest European car producer*: **manufacturer**, maker, builder, fabricator, creator.
2 *Tanzanian coffee producers*: **grower**, farmer.
3 *a producer and director of musical films*: **impresario**, manager, administrator, promoter, regisseur.

product noun **1** *new electronic products | household products*: **artefact**, commodity, manufactured item/article/thing; creation, invention; goods, wares, merchandise, produce.
2 *her fear was a product of her emotional insecurity*: **result**, consequence, outcome, effect, upshot, fruit, by-product, spin-off, legacy, issue.

production noun **1** *the production of nuclear weapons*: **manufacture**, manufacturing, making, producing, construction, building, fabrication, assembly, creation; mass production.
2 *the production of literary works*: **creation**, composition, origination, development, fashioning.
3 *literary productions of the 1980s*: **work**, publication, book, novel, composition, piece, creation, opus; work of art, painting, picture.
4 *areas affected by acid rain had seen a fall in agricultural production*: **output**, yield, fruits; productivity.
5 *ticket concessions are available to students on production of suitable identification*: **presentation**, offering, proffering, showing, display, exhibition.
6 *a new production of 'The Merchant of Venice'*: **performance**, staging, mounting.
7 *she took a starring role in a recent production by the St Albans Theatrical Society*: **play**, drama, film, concert, musical; show, performance, presentation, piece.

productive adjective **1** *few small towns can have had so productive a group of artists*: **prolific**, inventive, creative; dynamic, energetic, vigorous, effective.
▷ANTONYMS unproductive.
2 *the talks were said to have been long and productive*: **useful**, constructive, profitable, fruitful, gainful, valuable, effective, worthwhile, beneficial, helpful, rewarding, gratifying.
▷ANTONYMS unproductive.
3 *productive agricultural land*: **fertile**, fruitful, rich, fecund, high-yielding.
▷ANTONYMS sterile, barren.

productivity noun **1** *workers have boosted productivity by 30 per cent*: **efficiency**, production, productiveness, work rate, output, yield, capacity, productive capacity.
2 *the productivity of the soil*: **fruitfulness**, fertility, productiveness, fecundity, richness.

profane adjective **1** *a talk that tackled subjects both sacred and profane*: **secular**, lay, non-religious, non-church, temporal, worldly, earthly; unsanctified, unconsecrated, unhallowed; rare laic.
▷ANTONYMS religious, sacred.
2 *a profane, unprincipled man*: **irreverent**, ungodly, godless, impious, disrespectful, irreligious, unbelieving, disbelieving, sacrilegious, idolatrous.
3 *he was famous for his wildly profane language*: **obscene**, **blasphemous**, foul, vulgar, crude, filthy, dirty, smutty, coarse, rude, offensive, scurrilous, off colour, indecent, indecorous; rare Fescennine, Cyprian.
▷ANTONYMS decorous.
▸ verb *it was a serious matter to profane a tomb*: **desecrate**, violate, defile, treat with disrespect, debase, degrade, contaminate, pollute, taint.

profanity noun **1** *he led her away, hissing profanities in her ear | an outburst of profanity*: **oath**, swear word, expletive, curse, obscenity, four-letter word, dirty word, execration, imprecation; blasphemy, swearing, foul language, bad language, cursing; informal cuss, cuss word.
2 *some traditional festivals were irremediably tainted with profanity*: **idolatry**, sacrilege, irreligiousness, ungodliness, impiety, unholiness, profaneness, blasphemy, irreverence, disrespectfulness, disrespect.

profess verb **1** *he professed his undying love for her*: **declare**, announce, proclaim, assert, state, affirm, avow, maintain, protest, aver, vow; rare asseverate.
2 *she thrived on the publicity she professed to loathe*: **claim**, pretend, purport, allege, make a pretence of, lay claim, make out that; informal let on that.
3 *in 325 the Emperor himself professed Christianity*: **state/affirm one's faith in**, affirm one's allegiance to, make a public declaration of, declare publicly, avow, confess, acknowledge publicly.

professed adjective **1** *their professed commitment to human rights*: **supposed**, ostensible, alleged, claimed, so-called, soi-disant, self-styled, apparent, pretended, purported, would-be.
2 *a professed and active Christian*: **declared**, self-acknowledged, self-confessed, confessed, sworn, avowed, confirmed, certified.

professedly adverb *the government is threatening to break one of its professedly sacred principles*: **supposedly**, ostensibly, allegedly, apparently, avowedly, purportedly, by one's own account.

profession noun **1** *his chosen profession of teaching | the legal profession*: **career**, occupation, calling, vocation, line of work, line of employment, line, métier; business, trade, craft, walk of life, sphere; job, position; Scottish way; informal racket; archaic employ.
2 *a profession of allegiance*: **declaration**, affirmation, statement, announcement, proclamation, assertion, avowal, vow, claim, allegation, protestation; acknowledgement, admission, confession; rare asseveration, averment.

professional adjective **1** *people in professional occupations*: **white-collar**, executive, non-manual.
▷ANTONYMS manual.
2 *a professional tennis player*: **paid**, salaried, non-amateur, full-time.
▷ANTONYMS amateur.
3 *I think we gave a thoroughly professional performance*: **expert**, accomplished, skilful, adept, masterly, masterful, excellent, fine, polished, finished, skilled, proficient, competent, capable, able, efficient, experienced, practised, trained, seasoned, slick, businesslike, deft, dexterous; informal ace, crack, stellar, top-notch.
▷ANTONYMS amateurish, incompetent, inept.
4 *it's really not professional of me to comment on these things*: **appropriate**, ethical, fitting, in order, correct; French comme il faut.
▸ noun **1** *affluent young professionals*: **white-collar worker**, professional worker, office worker.
2 *it's his first season as a professional*: **professional player**, non-amateur, paid player; informal pro.
3 *she was a real professional on stage*: **expert**, master, maestro, past master, trooper, adept, virtuoso, old hand, skilled person, authority; informal pro, ace, whizz, hotshot; Brit. informal dab hand, wizard; N. Amer. informal maven, crackerjack; rare proficient.
▷ANTONYMS amateur.

professor noun *a former professor of French at Oxford University*: **holder of a chair**, chair, head of faculty, head of department; Regius professor, emeritus professor; don, academic; N. Amer. full professor, academician; informal prof.

proffer verb *Coleman proffered his resignation*: **offer**, tender, present, extend, give, submit, volunteer, suggest, propose, put forward; hold out.
▷ANTONYMS refuse, withdraw.

proficiency noun *her proficiency was obvious to everyone who sailed with her*: **skill**, skilfulness, expertise, experience, ability, capability, capacity, competence, competency, adeptness, adroitness, excellence, mastery, prowess, professionalism, aptitude, deftness, dexterity, finesse, facility, effectiveness, accomplishment, aptness, expertness, talent; informal know-how.
▷ANTONYMS incompetence.

proficient adjective *a proficient horsewoman*: **skilled**, skilful, expert, accomplished, experienced, practised, trained, seasoned, well versed, adept, adroit, deft, dexterous, able, capable, competent, professional, effective, apt, handy, talented, gifted, masterly, consummate, master; good, great, excellent, brilliant; informal crack, ace, mean, wicked; Brit. informal wizard; N. Amer. informal crackerjack; vulgar slang shit-hot; archaic or humorous compleat.
▷ANTONYMS inept, inexpert, incompetent.

profile noun **1** *she looked up at his handsome profile silhouetted against the dark sky*: **side view**, outline, silhouette, contour, shape, form, figure, lines.
2 *she wrote a profile of Martin Luther King*: **description**, account, study, portrait, portrayal, depiction, rundown, sketch, outline.
□ **keep a low profile lie low**, keep quiet, keep out of the public eye, avoid publicity, keep oneself to oneself, keep out of sight.
▸ verb *he was profiled in the Irish Times*: **describe**, write about, write an article about, give an account of, characterize, portray, depict, outline, sketch.

profit noun **1** *no one can guarantee a profit on stocks and shares*: **financial gain**, gain, return(s), payback, dividend, interest, yield, surplus, excess; gross profit, net profit, operating profit; N. Amer. take; informal killing, pay dirt, bottom line; Brit. informal bunce.
▷ANTONYMS loss.
2 *Stevenson decided that there was little profit in going on*: **advantage**, benefit, value, use, gain, good, avail, worth, usefulness; informal mileage, percentage; archaic behoof.
▷ANTONYMS disadvantage.
▸ verb **1** *many local people believe that the development will profit them*: **benefit**, be beneficial to, be of benefit to, be advantageous to, be of advantage to, be of use to, be of value to, do someone good, help, be helpful to, be of service to, serve, assist, aid, stand someone in good stead, further the interests of, advance, promote.
2 *certain sectors of society had visibly profited*: **make money**, make a killing, make a profit; informal rake it in, clean up, make a packet, make a bundle, line one's pockets; N. Amer. informal make big bucks, make a fast/quick buck.
□ **profit from** *loopholes in the law allowed landlords to profit from the situation*: **benefit from, take advantage of**, obtain an advantage from, derive benefit from, reap the benefit of, capitalize on, make the most of, turn to one's advantage, put to good use, do well out of, utilize, exploit, make capital out of, maximize, gain from; informal cash in on, milk.

profitable adjective **1** *a profitable venture*: **moneymaking**, profit-making, commercial, successful, commercially successful, money-spinning, sound, solvent, in the black, cost-effective, fruitful, gainful, remunerative, financially rewarding, paying, lucrative, bankable.
▷ANTONYMS unprofitable, loss-making.
2 *working with Kelly had been a profitable experience for him*: **beneficial**, useful, advantageous, helpful, of use, of service, valuable, productive, worthwhile; rewarding, fruitful, enriching, illuminating, informative, well spent, salutary.
▷ANTONYMS fruitless, useless.

P

profiteer verb *the companies are thus removed from the common temptation to profiteer*: **overcharge**, racketeer, make an excessive/illegal profit; informal make a fast/quick buck, make a quick killing.
▸ noun *letters in the paper denounced capitalist profiteers*: **extortionist**, extortioner, racketeer, exploiter, black marketeer; in Japan yakuza; informal bloodsucker; Austral. informal urger.

profiteering noun **extortion**, racketeering, exploitation; Brit. Rachmanism.

profitless adjective *further argument would be profitless*: **pointless**, useless, to no purpose, (of) no use, unprofitable, futile, vain, in vain, to no avail, to no effect, fruitless, senseless, unproductive, purposeless, idle, worthless, valueless, ineffective, unavailing, unrewarding, thankless; archaic bootless.

profligate adjective **1** *profligate local authorities*: **wasteful**, extravagant, spendthrift, improvident, prodigal, immoderate, excessive, thriftless, imprudent, reckless, irresponsible.
▷ANTONYMS thrifty, frugal.
2 *he succumbed to drink and a profligate lifestyle*: **dissolute**, degenerate, dissipated, debauched, corrupt, depraved, reprobate, unprincipled, immoral; promiscuous, loose, wanton, licentious, lascivious, lecherous, libertine, lewd, decadent, rakish, shameless, abandoned, unrestrained, fast; sybaritic, voluptuary.
▷ANTONYMS moral, upright.
▸ noun **1** *an out-and-out profligate, darting from one partner to the next*: **libertine**, debauchee, degenerate, reprobate, roué, lecher, rake, loose-liver, dissolute person; sybarite, voluptuary, sensualist; informal lech; dated rip.
2 *he's a gambler and a drunkard—a profligate in every way*: **spendthrift**, prodigal, squanderer; informal waster; archaic wastrel.

profound adjective **1** *a sigh of profound relief*: **heartfelt**, intense, keen, great, very great, extreme, sincere, earnest, deep, deepest, deeply felt, wholehearted, acute, overpowering, overwhelming, deep-seated, deep-rooted, fervent, ardent.
▷ANTONYMS superficial; mild.
2 *the silence was so profound that I could hear my heart beating*: **complete**, utter, total, absolute, extreme, pronounced.
3 *the implications of this discovery are profound*: **far-reaching**, radical, extensive, exhaustive, thoroughgoing, sweeping.
4 *a profound analysis of the problems*: **wise**, learned, clever, intelligent, with/showing great knowledge, knowledgeable, intellectual, scholarly, sage, sagacious, erudite, discerning, penetrating, perceptive, astute, thoughtful, full of insight, insightful, percipient, perspicacious, philosophical, deep; rare sapient.
▷ANTONYMS superficial, stupid.
5 *expressing profound truths in simple language*: **complex**, abstract, deep, weighty, serious, difficult; **abstruse**, recondite, esoteric, metaphysical, impenetrable, unfathomable, mysterious, obscure, dark.

profoundly adverb **1** *she was profoundly grateful that none of her colleagues could see her*: **extremely**, very, deeply, exceedingly, greatly, immensely, enormously, terribly, tremendously, awfully, intensely, heartily, keenly, acutely, from the bottom of one's heart, painfully, thoroughly, sincerely, so; informal well, jolly, seriously, majorly, oh-so; informal, dated devilish; N. Amer. informal mighty, plumb; S. African informal lekker; literary sore, thrice.
2 *he spoke profoundly on the subject*: **discerningly**, penetratingly, wisely, sagaciously, thoughtfully, philosophically, weightily, seriously, learnedly, eruditely.

profundity noun **1** *the simplicity and profundity of the message*: **wisdom, (deep) insight**, intelligence, sagacity, acuity, depth, profoundness, perceptiveness, penetration, perception, percipience, perspicuity, discernment, thoughtfulness; rare sapience.
2 *the profundity of her misery*: **intensity**, depth, extremity, severity, keenness, profoundness, strength.

profuse adjective **1** *she telephoned me with profuse apologies for the misunderstanding*: **copious**, prolific, abundant, ample, extravagant, lavish, liberal, unstinting, fulsome, effusive, gushing, immoderate, unrestrained, excessive, inordinate; informal over the top, gushy.
2 *so profuse are the flowers that you could imagine you were in a tropical garden*: **luxuriant**, plentiful, copious, abundant, lush, rich, exuberant, riotous, teeming, overabundant, superabundant, rank, rampant; informal jungly.
▷ANTONYMS meagre, sparse.

profusion noun *a profusion of shrubs and flowers*: **abundance**, lot, mass, host, plenitude, cornucopia, riot; plethora, superfluity, superabundance, glut, surplus, surfeit; quantities, scores, millions, multitude; informal sea, wealth; lots, heaps, masses, stacks, piles, loads, bags, mountains, tons, oodles; Brit. informal shedload; Austral./NZ informal swag; rare nimiety.

progenitor noun **1** *he was the progenitor of an illustrious family*: **ancestor**, forefather, forebear, parent; archaic begetter; rare primogenitor, procreator, stirps.
2 *the progenitor of modern jazz*: **originator**, founder, instigator, source; forerunner, predecessor, precursor, antecedent.

progeny noun **1** *physical characteristics are passed on from parents to their progeny by genes*: **offspring**, children, young, family, brood; Law issue; derogatory spawn; rare progeniture, quiverful.
2 *the progeny of the Scottish settlers who settled there in the mid-1800s*: **descendants**, successors, heirs, stock, scions, lineage; archaic seed, posterity.

prognosis noun *it is very difficult to make an accurate prognosis*: **forecast**, prediction, projection, prognostication, prophecy; rare prognostic.

prognosticate verb *the economists were prognosticating financial Armageddon*: **forecast**, predict, prophesy, foretell, divine; archaic presage, augur, previse; Scottish archaic spae; rare vaticinate, auspicate.

prognostication noun *their prognostications had proved remarkably accurate*: **prediction**, forecast, prophecy, divination, prognosis, projection; rare vaticination, auspication, prognostic.

programme noun **1** *an action-packed programme of events*: **schedule, agenda**, calendar, timetable; order of events, list of events, order of the day, line-up, list, listing; bill, menu, bill of fare.
2 *a government programme to rescue the ailing economy*: **scheme**, plan, plan of action, series of measures, project, strategy.
3 *the programme attracted an audience of almost twenty million*: **broadcast**, production, show, presentation, transmission, performance, telecast, simulcast; documentary, play, comedy, film, docudrama, newscast, chat show, magazine (programme), phone-in; episode, instalment; informal prog.
4 *a programme of study*: **course**, syllabus, curriculum.
5 *shall I buy a programme?* **guide**, list of performers/players/artistes; N. Amer. playbill.
▸ verb **1** *she tried to programme her day into housework and study*: **arrange, organize**, schedule, plan, map out, lay out, timetable, line up, prearrange; N. Amer. slate.
2 *some hotels programme their canned music in 24-hour cycles*: **set**, fix, arrange.

progress noun (stress on the first syllable) **1** *ceaseless rain made further progress impossible*: **forward movement**, onward movement, progression, advance, advancement, headway, passage; going.
2 *the progress of medical science | little progress was reported during the*

peace talks: **development**, advance, advancement, headway, step(s) forward, progression, improvement, betterment, growth; breakthrough.
□ **in progress** *a game of cricket was in progress*: **under way, going on**, ongoing, happening, occurring, taking place, proceeding, being done, being performed, continuing, in operation; awaiting completion, not finished, not completed, on the stocks; N. Amer. in the works.
▸ **verb** (stress on the second syllable) **1** *they progressed slowly back along the grass*: **go**, make one's way, move, move forward, go forward, proceed, continue, advance, go on, make progress, make headway, press on, gain ground, push forward, go/forge ahead, work one's way.
▷**ANTONYMS** return.
2 *the practice has a strong commercial base and has progressed steadily*: **develop**, make progress, advance, make headway, take steps forward, make strides, get better, come on, come along, move on, get on, gain ground, shape up, improve, thrive, prosper, blossom, flourish; grow, expand, increase, mature, evolve; informal be getting there.
▷**ANTONYMS** regress, deteriorate.

progression noun **1** *a progression of calm, still days and nights*: **succession**, series, sequence, string, stream, parade, chain, concatenation, train, row, order, course, flow, cycle.
2 *antiviral drugs appear to halt progression of the disease*: **development**, progress, process, continuation, continuance, advance, advancement, movement, forward movement, onward movement, passage, career, march; evolution, growth, evolvement.

progressive adjective **1** *the progressive deterioration of the social conditions of farm labourers*: **continuing**, continuous, increasing, growing, developing, ongoing, intensifying, accelerating, escalating; gradual, step by step, cumulative.
2 *a teacher with progressive views on primary education*: **modern**, liberal, advanced, forward-looking, forward-thinking, go-ahead, enlightened, enterprising, innovative, up-and-coming, new, dynamic, avant-garde, modernistic; radical, left-wing, reforming, reformist, revolutionary, revisionist, progressivist.
▷**ANTONYMS** conservative, reactionary.
▸ **noun** *people present themselves as progressives or traditionalists*: **innovator**, reformer, reformist, liberal, libertarian, progressivist, progressionist, leftist, left-winger.

prohibit verb **1** *a law to prohibit the dumping of nuclear waste at sea*: **forbid**, ban, bar, interdict, veto, proscribe, make illegal, place an embargo on, embargo, disallow, outlaw; taboo; Law enjoin, restrain.
▷**ANTONYMS** permit, authorize.
2 *his old age and illness prohibited him from attending*: **prevent**, stop, rule out, preclude, make impossible, hinder, impede, hamper, obstruct, restrict, constrain.
▷**ANTONYMS** allow, facilitate.

> *Choose the right word* **prohibit, forbid, ban**
>
> See **forbid**.

prohibited adjective *smoking is prohibited in many public places in Britain*: **forbidden**, banned, not allowed, not permitted, illegal, illicit, against the law, barred, vetoed, proscribed, embargoed, disallowed, outlawed, contraband; taboo; Latin non licet; German verboten; Islam haram; NZ tapu; informal no go.

prohibition noun **1** *the prohibition of cannabis*: **banning**, forbidding, prohibiting, barring, debarment, vetoing, proscription, disallowing, disallowance, interdiction, outlawing, making illegal.
2 *a prohibition on the sale of food containing pesticide residues*: **ban**, bar, interdict, veto, embargo, injunction, proscription, boycott, moratorium.

prohibitive adjective **1** *production costs have been prohibitive*: **excessively high**, extortionate, excessive, exorbitant, sky-high, preposterous, outrageous, scandalous, out of the question, beyond one's means, more than one can afford, unreasonable, impossible, overinflated; informal steep, criminal.
2 *prohibitive regulations*: **proscriptive**, prohibitory, restrictive, suppressive, repressive, restraining, inhibitory.

project noun (stress on the first syllable) **1** *a project to reforest the country's coastal areas*: **scheme**, plan, plan of action, programme, enterprise, undertaking, venture, activity, operation, campaign; proposal, proposition, idea, conception.
2 *he's doing some sort of history project*: **assignment**, piece of work, homework, piece of research, task.
▸ **verb** (stress on the second syllable) **1** *substantial growth of over six per cent is projected for 1993 and 1994*: **forecast**, predict, estimate, calculate, gauge, reckon, expect, extrapolate.
2 *his projected book on Greenland was never completed*: **intend**, plan, propose, map out, devise, design, outline.
3 *balconies projected over the lake*: **stick out**, jut out, jut, protrude, extend, stand out, hang over, overhang, bulge out, poke out, lap over, ride over, thrust out, obtrude, cantilever; archaic be imminent, protuberate.
4 *they projected missiles at each other from behind their barricades*: **throw**, cast, fling, hurl, toss, lob, launch, discharge, propel, shoot; informal chuck, sling, bung, heave.
5 *the one light projected azure shadows on the wall*: **cast**, throw, send, shed, let fall, reflect, shine.
6 *he projected an unassuming and non-threatening image*: **convey**, put across, put over, communicate, present, promote; present oneself as.
7 *it's not me who's unhappy—she's projecting her own problems on to me!* **attribute**, ascribe, impute, assign; externalize.

projectile noun **missile**; rare trajectile.

projecting adjective *she had projecting teeth | a projecting bay window*: **sticking out**, protuberant, protruding, prominent, jutting, jutting out, overhanging, standing out, proud, bulging, bulbous; technical obtrusive, extrusive; rare protrusive, protrudent, excrescent, exsertile.

projection noun **1** *the company claims it has exceeded its initial sales projection*: **estimate**, forecast, prediction, calculation, prognosis, prognostication, reckoning, expectation; forecasting, estimation, computation; extrapolation.
2 *tiny projections on the chalk face of the cliffs*: **protuberance**, protrusion, sticking-out bit, overhang, ledge, shelf, ridge, prominence, spur, outcrop, outgrowth, jut, bulge, jag, snag; flange, eminence.

proletarian adjective *those from less privileged, proletarian backgrounds*: **working-class**, plebeian, cloth-cap, common, ordinary.
▸ **noun** *a growing mass of disaffected proletarians*: **working-class person**, worker, working person, plebeian, commoner, ordinary person, man/woman/person in the street; informal Joe Bloggs; derogatory prole.

proletariat noun **the workers**, working-class people, wage-earners, the labouring classes, the common people, the ordinary people, the lower classes, the masses, the commonalty, the rank and file, the third estate, the plebeians; derogatory the hoi polloi, the plebs, the proles, the great unwashed, the mob, the rabble, the canaille.
▷**ANTONYMS** aristocracy, nobility.

proliferate verb *the debate continued and articles in the media proliferated*: **increase rapidly**, grow rapidly, multiply, become more numerous, mushroom, snowball, burgeon, escalate, rocket, run riot.
▷**ANTONYMS** decrease, dwindle.

proliferation noun *the proliferation of missiles and missile technology*: **rapid increase**, growth, multiplication, spread, escalation, expansion, build-up, buildout, burgeoning, snowballing, mushrooming.
▷**ANTONYMS** decrease.

prolific adjective **1** *the plant bears a prolific crop of large, firm tomatoes*: **plentiful**, abundant, bountiful, profuse, copious, luxuriant, rich, lush, proliferative; fertile, fruitful, fecund; rife, rank; literary plenteous, bounteous; rare proliferous.
2 *he was enormously prolific, writing 263 solo cantatas and arias*: **productive**, creative, inventive, fertile.

prolix adjective *his prolix speeches could often be tiresome*: **lengthy**, long-winded, long-drawn-out, overlong, prolonged, protracted, interminable, laborious, ponderous, endless, unending, verbose, wordy, full of verbiage, verbal, diffuse, discursive, digressive, rambling, wandering, circuitous, meandering, maundering, periphrastic, circumlocutory; informal windy; rare ambagious, pleonastic, circumlocutionary, logorrhoeic.

prologue noun *the prologue to his book on the harrowing contemporary history of Cambodia*: **introduction**, foreword, preface, preamble, prelude, preliminary; informal intro; rare exordium, proem, prolegomenon, prooemium, prooemion.
▷**ANTONYMS** epilogue.

prolong verb *unwilling to prolong the conversation, Kate said her goodbyes*: **lengthen**, make longer, extend, extend the duration of, draw out, drag out, protract, spin out, stretch out, string out, elongate; carry on, continue, keep up, keep something going, go on with, perpetuate, sustain; archaic wire-draw.
▷**ANTONYMS** shorten.

promenade noun **1** *they strolled along the tree-lined promenade*: **esplanade**, front, seafront, parade, walk, boulevard, avenue, walkway, mall; N. Amer. boardwalk; in Spanish-speaking countries alameda; Brit. informal prom.
2 *our nightly promenade up and down the road*: **walk**, stroll, saunter, turn, wander, amble, breather, airing; N. Amer. paseo; Italian passegiata; informal mosey; dated constitutional; rare perambulation.
▸ **verb** *people were promenading along the pavements and down the pier*: **walk**, stroll, saunter, wander, amble, stretch one's legs, take a walk/stroll, go for a walk/stroll, take the air; informal mosey; rare perambulate.

prominence noun **1** *his rise to prominence was meteoric*: **fame**, celebrity, eminence, pre-eminence, importance, distinction, greatness, note, notability, prestige, stature, standing, position, rank, renown, repute, illustriousness, acclaim, influence, account, consequence, visibility.
2 *the US and UK press gave prominence to the reports*: **good coverage**, close attention, importance, precedence, weight, a high profile, top billing, noticeability.
3 *the steep rocky prominence resembled a snow-capped mountain*: **hillock**, hill, hummock, mound, outcrop, spur, rise, tor, ridge, peak, pinnacle,

elevation; promontory, cliff, crag, headland, height; French arête.
4 *bony prominences in the arm and leg*: **protuberance**, projection, swelling, bump, bulge, lump; technical process, bulla.

prominent adjective **1** *a prominent member of the Royal College of Surgeons*: **important, well known**, leading, eminent, pre-eminent, distinguished, notable, noteworthy, noted, public, outstanding, foremost, of mark, illustrious, celebrated, famous, renowned, acclaimed, famed, honoured, esteemed, respected, well thought of, influential, prestigious, big, top, great, chief, main; N. Amer. major-league.
▷ANTONYMS unimportant, obscure, unknown.
2 *his cheekbones were high and prominent*: **protuberant**, protruding, projecting, jutting, jutting out, standing out, sticking out, proud, bulging, bulbous; raised, elevated; rare protrusive, protrudent, excrescent.
3 *the rectangular fields and straight lanes that are now such a prominent feature of the landscape*: **conspicuous**, noticeable, easily seen, obvious, evident, discernible, recognizable, distinguishable, unmistakable, eye-catching, pronounced, salient, striking, outstanding, dominant, predominant; obtrusive.
▷ANTONYMS inconspicuous.

promiscuity noun *allegations of alcoholism and sexual promiscuity*: **licentiousness**, lack of sexual discrimination, promiscuousness, immorality, wantonness, debauchery, dissoluteness, dissipation, libertinism, profligacy, incontinence; informal sleeping around; dated looseness.
▷ANTONYMS chastity, celibacy.

promiscuous adjective **1** *despite what you seem to think, I have never been promiscuous*: **licentious**, sexually indiscriminate, immoral, unchaste, debauched, dissolute, dissipated, profligate, of easy virtue, fast; libertine, wanton, abandoned, unrestrained, uncontrolled, incontinent; informal easy, swinging; N. Amer. informal roundheeled; W. Indian informal slack; informal, derogatory sluttish, whorish, tarty, slaggy; dated loose, fallen; archaic light; rare riggish.
▷ANTONYMS chaste; moral, pure.
2 *the promiscuous popping of antibiotics hasn't helped his T-cell count*: **indiscriminate**, undiscriminating, unselective, random, irresponsible, haphazard, thoughtless, unthinking, unconsidered, casual, careless.
▷ANTONYMS careful, selective.

promise noun **1** *if I don't go I'll be breaking my promise*: **word of honour**, word, assurance, pledge, vow, guarantee, oath, bond, undertaking, agreement, commitment, contract, covenant, compact.
2 *Derek showed considerable promise in a number of sports*: **potential**, ability, aptitude, capability, capacity, potentiality; talent, flair.
3 *dawn came with a promise of fine weather*: **indication**, hint, suggestion, sign.
▸**verb 1** *she promised to keep it a secret*: **give one's word**, swear, pledge, vow, undertake, guarantee, assure, contract, engage, give an undertaking, give an assurance, commit oneself, bind oneself, cross one's heart (and hope to die), swear/take an oath, covenant; archaic plight.
2 *the skies promised a blissful day of warm summer sunshine*: **indicate**, give an/every indication of, lead one to expect, give good grounds for expecting, point to, denote, signify, be a sign of, be evidence of, show signs of, hint at, suggest, give hope of, hold out hopes of, bespeak, presage, be a presage of, augur, herald, bode, foreshadow, portend; literary betoken, foretoken, forebode; rare harbinger.

P

promising adjective **1** *he made a promising start to his cricketing career*: **good**, encouraging, favourable, hopeful, full of promise, auspicious, propitious, optimistic, positive, bright, rosy, likely-looking, heartening, reassuring.
▷ANTONYMS unfavourable, inauspicious, ominous.
2 *a promising young actor*: **with potential**, budding, up-and-coming, rising, coming, in the making; talented, gifted, able, apt.

promontory noun **headland**, point, cape, head, foreland, horn, spit, hook, bill, ness, naze, peninsula; bluff, cliff, precipice, prominence, projection, overhang, height, ridge, spur; Scottish mull.

promote verb **1** *she's been promoted—she's head of her department now*: **advance**, upgrade, give promotion to, give a higher position to, elevate, move up, raise, improve the position/status of, aggrandize; informal kick upstairs; archaic prefer.
▷ANTONYMS demote.
2 *an organization promoting racial equality*: **encourage**, further, advance, assist, aid, help, contribute to, foster, nurture, develop, boost, stimulate, forward; advocate, recommend, urge, support, back, endorse, champion, speak for, proselytize, sponsor, espouse, push for, work for.
▷ANTONYMS obstruct, impede.
3 *she went over to America to promote her new book*: **advertise**, publicize, give publicity to, beat/bang the drum for, popularize, sell, market, merchandise; informal push, plug, give a plug to, hype, hype up, give a puff to, puff, puff up, boost, flog; N. Amer. informal ballyhoo, flack, huckster.

promoter noun *promoters of alternative tourism point to its contribution to economic growth*: **advocate**, champion, supporter, backer, upholder, proponent, exponent, protagonist, campaigner; N. Amer. booster.

promotion noun **1** *his promotion to the rank of Brigadier*: **preferment**, upgrading, move up, elevation, advancement, advance, step up, step up the ladder, aggrandizement; informal kick upstairs.
2 *the promotion of competition in our domestic economy*: **encouragement**, furtherance, furthering, advancement, assistance, aid, help, contribution to, fostering, boosting, stimulation, development; advocacy, recommendation, urging, support, backing, endorsement, championship, sponsoring, espousal; N. Amer. informal boosterism.
3 *two tiring weeks of promotion for his first English-language movie*: **advertising**, publicity, marketing, selling, advertising/publicity campaign, propaganda, publicization; informal hard sell, hype, plugging, puff, puffery; N. Amer. informal ballyhoo.

prompt verb **1** *a sense of alarm prompted her to knock again*: **induce**, make, move, cause, motivate, lead, dispose, persuade, incline, encourage, stimulate, prod, impel, spur on, urge, inspire; provoke, incite.
▷ANTONYMS discourage.
2 *the move could prompt a rise in UK base lending rates*: **give rise to**, bring about, cause, occasion, result in, lead to, elicit, produce, bring on, engender, induce, call forth, evoke, precipitate, trigger, spark off, provoke, instigate.
▷ANTONYMS deter, restrain.
3 *the bridegroom could not follow the marriage service and had to be prompted by the impatient clergyman*: **remind**, cue, give someone a cue, help out, coach, feed; jog someone's memory, refresh someone's memory.
▸**adjective** *I should be grateful for a prompt reply*: **quick**, swift, rapid, speedy, fast, direct, immediate, instant, instantaneous, expeditious, early, punctual, in good time, on time, timely; ready, willing, eager, unhesitating; archaic rathe.
▷ANTONYMS slow, late; unwilling.
▸**adverb** *he set off at 3.30 prompt*: **exactly**, precisely, sharp, on the dot, dead, dead on, promptly, punctually, on the nail; informal bang on, spot on; N. Amer. informal on the button, on the nose; Austral./NZ informal on the knocker.
▸**noun** *he stopped, and Julia supplied a prompt*: **reminder**, cue, feed.

prompting noun *Gilbert needed no prompting and moved quickly towards her*: **encouragement**, reminder(s), reminding, cue(s), prodding, pushing, persuasion, hint(s), advice, suggestion(s), assistance, inducement.

promptly adverb **1** *William arrived promptly at 7.30*: **punctually**, on time, on the dot, on the nail; informal bang on, spot on; N. Amer. informal on the button; Austral./NZ informal on the knocker.
2 *I expect the matter to be dealt with promptly*: **quickly**, swiftly, rapidly, speedily, fast, as soon as possible, expeditiously; at once, immediately, straight away, right away, now, without delay, without hesitation, forthwith, directly, instantly, instantaneously, by return, unhesitatingly; N. Amer. momentarily; informal pronto, a.s.a.p., p.d.q. (pretty damn quick), in double quick time.

promptness noun *he acted with commendable promptness*: **speed**, swiftness, speediness, rapidity, promptitude, alacrity, dispatch, quickness, expeditiousness, expedition, immediacy, instantaneousness, readiness, willingness, eagerness; punctuality.

promulgate verb **1** *ideas which Ruskin had been the first to promulgate*: **make known**, make public, publicize, spread, communicate, propagate, disseminate, circulate, broadcast, promote, announce, proclaim; literary bruit about.
2 *the new law was promulgated on December 19*: **put into effect**, enact, implement, enforce, pass.

prone adjective **1** *tired, malnourished people are* **prone to** *infection*: **susceptible**, vulnerable, liable, inclined, given, subject, disposed, predisposed, open; likely to have/get, apt to get, with a tendency to get, at risk of, in danger of getting.
▷ANTONYMS resistant, immune.
2 *he was stretched prone on the ground*: **(lying) face down**, face downwards, on one's stomach, on one's front; **lying flat**, lying down, flat, horizontal, prostrate; rare procumbent.
▷ANTONYMS upright; supine.

proneness noun *her proneness to anxiety*: **susceptibility**, liability, tendency, inclination, disposition, predisposition, vulnerability, openness, propensity, proclivity; Homeopathy miasm.

prong noun **tine**, point, tip, spike, projection.

pronounce verb **1** *his name is difficult to pronounce*: **say**, enunciate, articulate, utter, express, voice, vocalize, get one's tongue round, sound; rare enounce.
2 *the judge pronounced that he would be sentenced to sixteen years' imprisonment*: **announce**, proclaim, declare, rule, decree, ordain, adjudicate, lay down, affirm, assert, state, judge; rare asseverate.

pronounced adjective *a strong voice with a pronounced German accent*: **noticeable**, marked, strong, conspicuous, striking, distinct, decided, definite, prominent, notable, unmistakable, inescapable, obvious, evident, plain, clear, recognizable, identifiable; broad, thick.
▷ANTONYMS faint, inconspicuous, indefinite.

pronouncement noun *his public pronouncements were brilliantly timed and phrased*: **announcement**, proclamation, declaration, formal statement, assertion, judgement, ruling, adjudication, decree, edict, ordinance, dictum, promulgation, deliverance; in Tsarist Russia ukase; in Spain & Spanish-speaking countries pronunciamento; Latin ipse dixit; rare asseveration.

pronunciation noun *her Merseyside pronunciation | the dictionary includes a guide to the pronunciation of difficult and foreign words*: **accent**, manner of speaking, speech pattern, speech, diction, delivery, elocution, intonation, modulation; articulation, enunciation, saying, uttering, utterance, sounding, voicing, vocalization; rare orthoepy.

Word links **pronunciation**

orthoepy study of correct pronunciation

proof noun **1** *the last thing she wanted was proof of Luke's betrayal*: **evidence**, verification, corroboration, authentication, confirmation, certification, validation, attestation, demonstration, substantiation, witness, testament; documentation, facts, data, testimony; ammunition.
2 *a desk strewn with the proofs of a book he was correcting*: **page proof**, galley proof, galley, pull, slip, trial print; revise.
▸ adjective *their battle armour is proof against most weapons*: **resistant**, impenetrable, impervious, repellent; proofed, treated; waterproof, windproof, rainproof, leakproof, damp-proof, weatherproof, bulletproof, bombproof, fireproof, soundproof, childproof, tamper-proof; rare imperviable.

prop noun **1** *steel props support the 1.5 km long underpass construction*: **pole**, post, beam, support, upright, brace, buttress, stay, shaft, strut, stanchion, shore, pier, vertical, pillar, pile, piling, bolster, truss, column, rod, stick; French point d'appui; Mining sprag.
2 *he found himself becoming the emotional prop of the marriage*: **mainstay**, pillar, anchor, rock, backbone, support, cornerstone; supporter, upholder, sustainer.
▸ verb **1** *he propped his bike against the garage wall*: **lean**, rest, set, stand, position, place, lay, balance, steady.
2 *the longest branches were initially* **propped up** *with planks*: **hold up**, shore up, bolster up, buttress, support, brace, underpin, reinforce, strengthen; archaic underprop.
3 *the government's attempt to* **prop up** *their loss-making state airline*: **subsidize**, underwrite, fund, finance, maintain; **support**, give support to, bolster (up), shore up, buttress; help, aid, assist, revitalize.

propaganda noun *regulations restricting political propaganda were relaxed*: **information**, promotion, advertising, advertisement, publicity, advocacy; spin, newspeak, agitprop, disinformation, counter-information, brainwashing, indoctrination, the big lie; informal info, hype, plugging.

propagandist noun *an enthusiastic propagandist for the government's reforms*: **advocate**, champion, supporter, promoter, proponent, exponent, campaigner, crusader, publicist, evangelist, apostle, proselytizer, indoctrinator; informal plugger, spin doctor.

propagandize verb **1** *political concepts propagandized by the West*: **advocate**, champion, support, promote, publicize, propagate, promulgate, campaign for, proclaim, preach.
2 *they should not be propagandized into spending beyond their means*: **persuade**, convince, brainwash, indoctrinate, proselytize.

propagate verb **1** *the plant can be easily propagated by taking leaf cuttings*: **breed**, grow, cultivate, generate; technical layer, pipe.
2 *the wild flowers and herbs get cut before they have a chance to flower and propagate*: **reproduce**, multiply, proliferate, breed, procreate, increase, spawn; self-seed, self-sow.
3 *the advanced ideas drawn from the West or propagated by other leading democrats*: **spread**, disseminate, communicate, pass on, put about, make known, promulgate, circulate, transmit, distribute, broadcast, publish, publicize, proclaim, preach, promote; propagandize.

propel verb **1** *a long fishing boat propelled by six oars*: **push/move forwards**, move, set in motion, get moving, drive.
2 *he propelled the ball vertically into the air*: **throw**, thrust, toss, fling, hurl, lob, let fly, launch, pitch, project, send, shoot; informal chuck, sling, bung.
3 *confusion propelled her into action*: **spur**, drive, prompt, precipitate, catapult, motivate, force, impel.

propeller noun **screw**, airscrew, rotor, vane, propulsor; informal prop.

propensity noun *her propensity to jump to conclusions | his propensity for accidents*: **tendency**, inclination, predisposition, proneness, proclivity, readiness, susceptibility, liability, disposition; aptness, penchant, leaning, predilection, bent, habit, weakness.

proper adjective **1** *Dan hadn't had a proper job for over ten years*: **real**, genuine, actual, true, bona fide; informal kosher.
2 *they didn't apply through the proper channels*: **right**, correct, accepted, orthodox, conventional, established, official, formal, regular, acceptable; appropriate, suitable, fitting, apt, due; French de règle; archaic meet.
▷ANTONYMS inappropriate, wrong.
3 *her parents' view of what was proper for a well-bred girl | Sally-Anne was very prim and proper*: **respectable**, decorous, seemly, decent, refined, ladylike, gentlemanly, genteel; formal, conventional, correct, orthodox, polite, punctilious, sedate, modest, demure, virtuous; becoming, befitting, fit, done; French comme il faut.
▷ANTONYMS improper, unconventional.
4 Brit. informal *you've made a proper fool of yourself*: **complete**, absolute, real, perfect, total, thorough, thoroughgoing, utter, out-and-out, positive, unmitigated, consummate; Brit. informal right; Austral./NZ informal fair; archaic arrant.
5 *the formalities* **proper to** *her age and position*: **belonging**, relating, pertaining, related, relevant, unique, peculiar; associated with.

Choose the right word **proper, fitting, suitable, appropriate**

See **appropriate**.

property noun **1** *a widower who left all his property to his housekeeper*: **possessions**, belongings, things, goods, worldly goods, effects, personal effects, stuff, chattels, movables; resources, assets, valuables, fortune, capital, riches, wealth, holdings, securities, patrimony; Law personalty, goods and chattels; informal gear; S. African informal trek.
2 *a growing number of Germans are buying property in Denmark | empty council properties*: **building(s)**, premises, house(s), land, estates, acres, acreage; freehold, leasehold; Law real property, realty; N. Amer. real estate.
3 *garlic has been known for its healing properties for more than 5,000 years*: **quality**, attribute, characteristic, feature, power, trait, mark, hallmark.

prophecy noun **1** *her prophecy is coming true*: **prediction**, forecast, prognostication, prognosis, divination, augury; rare prognostic.
2 *the gift of prophecy*: **foretelling the future**, forecasting the future, fortune telling, crystal-gazing, prediction, second sight, clairvoyance, prognostication, divination, soothsaying; rare vaticination, augury, sortilege, auspication.

prophesy verb *many commentators prophesied disaster*: **predict**, foretell, forecast, foresee, forewarn of, prognosticate, divine; archaic augur, presage, previse, foreshow, croak; Scottish archaic spae; rare vaticinate, auspicate.

prophet, prophetess noun **seer**, soothsayer, forecaster of the future, fortune teller, clairvoyant, prognosticator, prophesier, diviner; oracle, augur, sibyl; Scottish spaewife, spaeman; rare haruspex, vaticinator, oracler.
□ **prophet of doom pessimist**, doom-monger, doom merchant, Cassandra, Jeremiah, doomster, doomsayer; informal doom and gloom merchant.

prophetic adjective *his words proved prophetic—in less than a week he was dead*: **prescient**, predictive, prophetical, far-seeing, prognostic, divinatory, oracular, sibylline, apocalyptic, fateful, revelatory, inspired; rare vatic, mantic, vaticinal, vaticinatory, prognosticative, augural, adumbrative, fatidic, fatidical.

prophylactic adjective *prophylactic measures should be taken*: **preventive**, preventative, precautionary, protective, disease-preventing, pre-emptive, counteractive, preclusive, anticipatory, inhibitory, deterrent.
▸ noun **1** *vaccination remains one of the greatest prophylactics the world has ever known*: **preventive measure**, precaution, safeguard, safety measure; preventive medicine.
2 N. Amer. *a packet of prophylactics*: **condom**, sheath; female condom; Brit. trademark Durex, Femidom; informal Frenchy; Brit. informal johnny, something for the weekend; N. Amer. informal rubber, safe, safety, skin; Brit. informal, dated French letter; dated protective.

prophylaxis noun *the use of HRT as a prophylaxis against osteoporosis*: **preventive treatment**, prevention, protection.

propinquity noun **1** *discussion of family support often seems to assume geographical propinquity*: **proximity**, closeness, nearness, adjacency; rare contiguity, contiguousness, vicinity, vicinage.
2 *propinquity of descent*: **close kinship**, close relationship, family connection, blood ties, consanguinity.

propitiate verb *George's attempt to propitiate his father did not succeed*: **appease**, placate, mollify, pacify, make peace with, conciliate, make amends to, soothe, calm, humour, win over, satisfy; pour oil on troubled waters; Austral. square someone off.

propitious adjective *the timing for such a meeting seemed propitious*: **favourable**, auspicious, promising, providential, advantageous, fortunate, lucky, optimistic, bright, happy, rosy, full of promise, heaven-sent, hopeful, beneficial; opportune, suitable, apt, fitting, timely, well timed.
▷ANTONYMS inauspicious, unfortunate.

proponent noun *a radical Roman Catholic priest and outspoken proponent of liberation theology*: **advocate**, supporter, upholder, exponent, promoter, adherent, endorser, champion, defender, backer, subscriber, patron, espouser, friend, apostle, apologist, pleader, proposer, propounder, spokesperson, spokesman, spokeswoman; enthusiast, propagandist.

proportion noun **1** *only a small proportion of the land can be farmed*: **part**, portion, amount, quantity, bit, piece, percentage, section, segment, share, quota, division, fraction, measure.
2 *the proportion of water to alcohol*: **ratio**, distribution, relative amount/number; relationship.
3 *serious photographers interested in line and proportion should find the exhibition instructive*: **balance**, symmetry, harmony, correspondence, correlation, congruity, agreement, concord.

P

4 (**proportions**) *men of huge proportions | an achievement of quite extraordinary proportions*: **size**, **dimensions**, magnitude, measurements; mass, volume, bulk; expanse, extent, width, breadth, scale, scope, range.
□ **in proportion to** *the amount of land in proportion to our needs is still large*: **relative to**, proportionate to, proportional to, commensurate with, corresponding to.
□ **out of (all) proportion** *they had an impact out of all proportion to their size*: **incommensurate with**, disproportionate to, relatively too large/small for, not appropriate for; out of keeping with, at odds with; insufficient, inadequate; excessive, inordinate, unreasonable.

proportional adjective *an increase in working hours unaccompanied by a proportional increase in wages*: **corresponding**, proportionate, comparable, in proportion, pro rata, commensurate, equivalent, consistent, relative, correlated, correlative, analogous, analogical; rare commensurable.
▷ANTONYMS disproportionate.

proposal noun 1 *the Select Committee gave the proposal a very mixed reception*: **scheme**, plan, project, programme, manifesto, motion, bid, proposition, presentation, submission, approach, suggestion, overture, draft, recommendation, tender, terms; rare proffer.
2 *the proposal of a flexible school leaving age*: **putting forward**, **suggesting**, proposing, advancing, offering, presentation, submitting, submission, preferring, filing, lodging, tabling, introduction, initiation, tendering, bidding, projecting, recommendation, advocacy, propounding, proffering, positing.
▷ANTONYMS withdrawal.

propose verb 1 *we could propose a simpler system*: **put forward**, **suggest**, advance, offer, present, move, submit, prefer, file, lodge, table, initiate, bring, bring forward, come up with, tender, bid, project, recommend, advocate, propound, proffer, posit.
▷ANTONYMS withdraw.
2 *how do you propose to raise the money?* **intend**, have the intention, mean, plan, have plans, set out, have in mind/view, resolve, be resolved, aim, purpose, contemplate, think of, aspire, desire, want, wish, expect.
3 *it is premature to propose Mr Lang for canonization*: **nominate**, put forward, put up, name, suggest, submit, present, recommend.
▷ANTONYMS withdraw.
4 *first he must propose to Emily*: **ask someone to marry you**, make an offer of marriage, offer marriage, ask for someone's hand in marriage; informal pop the question.

proposition noun 1 *they advanced the proposition that investors prefer high earnings growth*: **theory**, **hypothesis**, thesis, argument, premise, postulation, theorem, concept, idea, statement.
2 *I have a business proposition to put to you*: **proposal**, **scheme**, plan, project, programme, manifesto, motion, bid, presentation, submission, suggestion, recommendation, approach.
3 *I'm not in the market for your sort of proposition*: **sexual advance**, sexual overture, indecent proposal, improper suggestion, soliciting; informal pass, come-on.
4 *getting cold water into the attic is no problem, but hot water is a different proposition*: **task**, job, undertaking, venture, activity, problem, affair.
▸ verb *he never dared proposition her*: **propose sex with**, make sexual advances to, make sexual overtures to, make an indecent proposal to, make an improper suggestion to; informal give someone the come-on.

propound verb *the theory of relativity was first propounded by Albert Einstein in 1905*: **put forward**, advance, offer, present, set forth, submit, tender, suggest, come up with, broach, moot, bring up, mention, introduce, postulate, propose, pose, discuss, hypothesize, peddle, spread, promote, advocate, proffer, posit.

proprietor, proprietress noun **owner**, possessor, holder, keeper, freeholder, landowner, squire, landlord/landlady, master/mistress; innkeeper, hotel-keeper, hotelier, licensee, patron, shopkeeper; title-holder, deed-holder; rare proprietrix.

propriety noun 1 *he always behaves towards me with the utmost propriety*: **decorum**, respectability, decency, correctness, appropriateness, good manners, courtesy, politeness, rectitude, civility, modesty, demureness; sobriety, refinement, decorousness, seemliness, becomingness, discretion, gentility, etiquette, breeding, conventionality, orthodoxy, formality, protocol; formal probity; archaic tenue.
▷ANTONYMS impropriety, indecorum.
2 (**proprieties**) *he was careful to preserve the proprieties in public*: **etiquette**, social conventions, social grace(s), social niceties, one's Ps and Qs, protocol, decorum, standards, civilities, ceremony, formalities, rules of conduct, accepted behaviour, conventionalities, good manners, good form, the done thing, the thing to do, punctilio, attention to detail; archaic convenance(s).
3 *they question the propriety of certain investments made by the council*: **correctness**, rightness, fitness, suitability, suitableness, appropriateness, aptness, morality, ethicality.
▷ANTONYMS impropriety.

propulsion noun *these seabirds use their wings for propulsion under water*: **thrust**, **motive force**, propelling force, impelling force, impetus, impulse, drive, driving force, actuation, push, surge, pressure, momentum, power.

prosaic adjective 1 *flowers are given variously poetic or prosaic names*: **unimaginative**, uninspired, matter-of-fact, dull, dry, humdrum, mundane, pedestrian, heavy, plodding, lifeless, dead, spiritless, lacklustre, undistinguished, stale, jejune, bland, insipid, vapid, vacuous, banal, hackneyed, trite, literal, factual, unpoetic, unemotional, unsentimental, clear, plain, unadorned, unembellished, unvarnished, monotonous, deadpan, flat.
▷ANTONYMS imaginative, inspired.
2 *Bloomwater's present owner was a more prosaic figure*: **ordinary**, everyday, usual, common, conventional, straightforward, routine, humdrum, commonplace, run-of-the-mill, workaday, businesslike, pedestrian, tame, mundane, dull, dreary, tedious, boring, ho-hum, uninspiring, monotonous.
▷ANTONYMS interesting.

proscribe verb 1 *gambling was proscribed*: **forbid**, prohibit, ban, bar, disallow, rule out, embargo, veto, make illegal, interdict, outlaw, taboo.
▷ANTONYMS allow, permit.
2 *a case was made for precisely the sort of intervention which the Report proscribed*: **condemn**, denounce, attack, criticize, censure, denigrate, damn, reject.
▷ANTONYMS authorize, accept.
3 historical *the pedlar appeals to the local authorities who proscribe Buckley as a highwayman*: **outlaw**, boycott, black, blackball, exclude, ostracize; exile, expel, expatriate, evict, deport; Christianity excommunicate.

> *Easily confused words* **proscribe or prescribe?**
>
> See **prescribe**.

proscription noun 1 *the proscription of the sale of alcohol on Sundays*: **prohibition**, prohibiting, forbidding, banning, ban, barring, bar, disallowing, ruling out, embargo, embargoing, vetoing, veto, making illegal, interdicting, interdict, outlawing, tabooing.
▷ANTONYMS allowing.
2 *composers began to find ways of circumventing the proscription on opera*: **condemnation**, denunciation, attack, criticism, censure, denigration, damning, rejection.

prosecute verb 1 *they were going to prosecute the offender*: **take to court**, bring/institute legal proceedings against, bring an action against, take legal action against, accuse, cite, summons, sue, try, bring to trial, put on trial, put in the dock, bring a charge against, bring a criminal charge against, charge, prefer charges against, bring a suit against, indict, arraign; N. Amer. impeach; informal have the law on, do; N. Amer. informal jug; rare implead.
▷ANTONYMS defend; let off, pardon.
2 *we have to prosecute this war to a successful conclusion*: **pursue**, carry on, conduct, direct, engage in, work at, proceed with, continue, continue with, keep on with, go ahead with; fight, wage.
▷ANTONYMS give up.

proselyte noun **convert**, new believer, catechumen, recruit, neophyte, newcomer, initiate, tyro, novice.

proselytize verb 1 *I'm not here to proselytize*: **evangelize**, convert, seek/make converts, bring to God/Christ, bring into the fold, spread the gospel/word (to), propagandize, preach (to), win over, recruit; brainwash.
2 *they are preoccupied with proselytizing a liberal view*: **promote**, present, spread, proclaim, peddle, propound, preach, back, urge, suggest, support, advocate, endorse, champion, sponsor, espouse, advance, further, assist, aid, help, contribute to, foster, boost.

prospect noun (stress on the first syllable) 1 *there is little prospect of success*: **likelihood**, hope, expectation, anticipation, (good/poor) chance, chances, odds, probability, possibility, likeliness, promise, lookout; dream; fear, danger, hazard.
2 (**prospects**) *she would have better job prospects with a postgraduate qualification*: **possibilities**, potential, promise, expectations, outlook, future, scope.
3 *finding schools abroad may be a daunting prospect for employees*: **vision**, **thought**, idea, contemplation; task, undertaking.
4 *Jimmy, who plays in midfield, is an exciting prospect*: **candidate**, possibility; informal catch.
5 *guests are greeted with a pleasant prospect from the ground-floor lounge*: **view**, vista, outlook, perspective, panorama, aspect, scene; scenery, sweep, landscape, seascape, townscape, cityscape, surroundings; picture, spectacle, sight; archaic lookout.
□ **in prospect** *further job losses are in prospect*: **coming soon**, on the way, in the pipeline, likely to happen, to come, coming up, at hand, close/near at hand, near, imminent, in the offing, in view, in store, on the horizon, in the wings, just around the corner, in the air, in the wind, brewing, upcoming, forthcoming, impending, approaching; informal on the cards.
▸ verb (stress on the second syllable) 1 *the mining companies never got to prospect the area*: **inspect**, survey, make a survey of, explore, search, scout, reconnoitre, examine, check out.
2 *he obtained rights to* ***prospect for*** *minerals*: **search**, look, seek, hunt, go after, dowse.

P

prospective adjective *the prospective buyer should always endeavour to negotiate*: **potential**, possible, probable, likely, future, eventual, -to-be, soon-to-be, in the making, destined, intended; **intending**, aspiring, would-be; forthcoming, approaching, coming, imminent; presumptive, designate.

prospectus noun *a school or company prospectus*: **brochure**, description, announcement, advertisement; syllabus, curriculum, catalogue, programme, list, scheme, particulars, schedule, outline, synopsis; pamphlet, literature.

prosper verb *the European personal computer market continued to prosper*: **do well**, get on well, go well, fare well; **thrive**, flourish, flower, bloom, blossom, burgeon, grow vigorously, shoot up; boom, expand, spread, pick up, improve, come on; succeed, be successful, make it, do all right for oneself, get ahead, progress, make progress, make headway, advance, get on in the world, go up in the world, arrive, fly high, make one's mark, make good, become rich, strike gold/oil, be in clover; informal go places, go great guns, make the big time, be in the pink, be fine and dandy, be on easy street, live the life of Riley; archaic make good speed.
▷ANTONYMS fail, collapse, crash.

> *Choose the right word* **prosper, flourish, thrive**
>
> See **flourish**.

prosperity noun *Britain's prosperity depends on its exports*: **wealth**, **success**, profitability, affluence, riches, opulence, the good life, (good) fortune, ease, plenty, welfare, comfort, security, well-being; luxury, life of luxury, milk and honey, a bed of roses; prosperousness, successfulness; archaic speed, Godspeed.
▷ANTONYMS hardship; failure.

prosperous adjective *a prosperous family shipping firm*: **thriving**, doing well, prospering, buoyant, expanding, flourishing, successful, strong, vigorous, productive, profitable, booming, burgeoning, fruitful, roaring, golden, palmy; **affluent**, wealthy, rich, moneyed, with deep pockets, well off, well-to-do, opulent, substantial, fortunate, lucky, in clover; informal on a roll, on the up and up, rolling in it, rolling in money, in the money, loaded, stinking rich, well heeled, flush, made of money, on easy street; Brit. informal quids in; informal, dated oofy.
▷ANTONYMS depressed; poor.

prostitute noun **whore**, sex worker, call girl, white slave; male prostitute, rent boy, call boy, gigolo; euphemistic model, escort, masseuse; Brit. tom; French fille de joie; Spanish puta; N. Amer. sporting girl/woman/lady, chippy; informal tart, pro, moll, tail, brass nail, grande horizontale, woman on the game, working girl, member of the oldest profession, renter, toy boy; N. Amer. informal hooker, hustler; black English ho; vulgar slang bumboy; dated streetwalker, woman of the streets, lady/woman of the night, scarlet woman, cocotte; archaic courtesan, strumpet, harlot, trollop, woman of ill repute, lady of pleasure, Cyprian, doxy, drab, quean, trull, wench; rare sing-song girl, succubus.
▶verb *they couldn't bring themselves to prostitute their art by copying others*: **betray**, sacrifice, profane, sell, sell out, debase, degrade, demean, devalue, cheapen, lower, misapply, misemploy, misuse, pervert, squander, waste; abandon one's principles, be untrue to oneself.

prostitution noun **whoring**, the sex industry, streetwalking, Mrs Warren's profession, white slavery, sex tourism; informal the oldest profession, the game, the trade; rough trade; N. Amer. informal hooking, hustling, the life; dated whoredom; archaic courtesanship, harlotry, Magdalenism, the social evil.

prostrate adjective (stress on the first syllable) **1** *they surged forward around the prostrate figure on the ground*: **prone**, **lying flat**, lying down, flat, stretched out, spreadeagled, sprawling, horizontal, recumbent, on one's front; rare procumbent.
▷ANTONYMS upright.
2 *his wife was prostrate with shock*: **overwhelmed**, overcome, overpowered, brought to one's knees, crushed, stunned, dazed; speechless, helpless, paralysed, laid low, impotent; informal knocked/hit for six.
3 *the fever which had just left me prostrate*: **worn out**, exhausted, fatigued, tired out, overtired, weary, sapped, dog-tired, spent, drained, played out, debilitated, enervated, low; informal all in, done (in/up), dead, dead beat, dead tired, dead on one's feet, ready to drop, fagged out, bushed, whacked, worn to a frazzle, burnt-out; Brit. informal knackered; N. Amer. informal pooped.
▷ANTONYMS fresh.
▶verb (stress on the second syllable) *she expected to find Kathleen prostrated by the tragedy in her family*: **overwhelm**, overcome, overpower, bring someone to their knees, crush, devastate, make helpless, paralyse, lay low, make powerless, debilitate, incapacitate, weaken, enfeeble, devitalize, enervate, handicap, immobilize, hamstring, make impotent, wear out, exhaust, tire out, fatigue, weary, make weary, drain, sap, wash out, take it out of, tax, overtax, undermine; informal knacker, whack, frazzle, do in, knock out, fag out; N. Amer. informal poop.
□ **prostrate oneself** *he prostrated himself on the altar mat*: **throw oneself flat**, throw oneself down, lie down, stretch oneself out, bow low, throw oneself at someone's feet; dated measure one's length.

prostration noun *he was left exhausted, sometimes near to prostration*: **collapse**, weakness, debility, lassitude, exhaustion, fatigue, tiredness, enervation, emotional exhaustion; paralysis; desolation, despair, despondency, dejection, depression, helplessness.

protagonist noun **1** *the very first line of the play is spoken by the protagonist*: **chief character**, central/principal/main/leading character, chief/central/principal/main/leading participant, principal, hero/heroine, leading man/lady, title role, lead, star, (leading/key) player, (leading) figure, leading light.
▷ANTONYMS minor character.
2 *the EC is a great protagonist of deregulation*: **supporter**, upholder, adherent, backer, proponent, advocate, promoter, champion, exponent, standard-bearer, torch-bearer, prime mover, moving spirit, mainstay, spokesman/spokeswoman/spokesperson.
▷ANTONYMS opponent.

protean adjective **1** *the diverse and protean nature of mental disorders*: **ever-changing**, **variable**, changeable, mutable, kaleidoscopic, erratic, quicksilver, inconstant, inconsistent, unstable, unsteady, shifting, uneven, unsettled, fluctuating, chameleon-like, chameleonic; fluid, wavering, vacillating, mercurial, volatile, unpredictable, wayward, unreliable, undependable; technical labile; rare stayless, changeful.
▷ANTONYMS constant, consistent.
2 *Shostakovich was a remarkably protean composer*: **versatile**, adaptable, flexible, all-round, multifaceted, multitalented, many-sided, resourceful, malleable.
▷ANTONYMS limited.

protect verb *the men fought hand-to-hand to protect their women and children*: **keep safe**, keep from harm, save, safeguard, shield, preserve, defend, cushion, shelter, screen, secure, fortify, guard, mount/stand guard on; watch over, look after, take care of, care for, tend, keep, mind, afford protection to, harbour, house, hedge, inoculate, insulate.
▷ANTONYMS expose, neglect; attack, harm.

protected adjective *the nation's largest protected wetland*: **secured**, sheltered, in safe hands, safe, guarded, out of danger, safeguarded, preserved.

Word toolkit

protected	guarded	secure
area	gates	access
species	compound	employment
rights	border	parking
speech	entrance	website
wildlife	house	transaction

protection noun **1** *physical fitness provides considerable protection against stress*: **defence**, shielding, shelter, preservation, conservation, safe keeping, safeguarding, safety, security, sanctuary, refuge, lee, immunity, insurance, indemnity.
2 *he remains in hiding under the protection of the United States*: **safe keeping**, care, charge, keeping, protectorship, guidance, aegis, auspices, umbrella, guardianship, support, patronage, championship, providence.
3 *a good education is not a protection against the hazards of life*: **barrier**, buffer, shield, screen, hedge, cushion, preventive, preventative, armour, safeguard; refuge, bulwark, bastion, wall.

protective adjective **1** *firefighters wear special protective clothing*: **preservative**, protecting, safeguarding, shielding, defensive, safety, precautionary, preventive, preventative, covering; waterproof, fireproof, heatproof, insulating; shatterproof, toughened, armoured.
2 *he felt protective towards the girl*: **solicitous**, **caring**, mindful, careful, wary, watchful, vigilant, warm, paternal/maternal, fatherly/motherly, gallant, chivalrous; overprotective, possessive, jealous, clinging.

protector noun **1** *his wife was always his chief protector*: **defender**, preserver, bodyguard, minder, guardian, guard, champion, watchdog, ombudsman, knight in shining armour, guardian angel, patron, chaperone, escort, keeper, custodian; informal hired gun.
2 *I encounter men drilling the roads without wearing ear protectors*: **guard**, shield, pad, buffer, cushion, screen; protection.

protégé, protégée noun **pupil**, student, trainee, apprentice; **disciple**, follower, discovery, ward, dependant, charge, mentee; archaic fosterling.

protest noun (stress on the first syllable) **1** *voters humiliated the government as a protest against high public spending*: **objection**, exception, complaint, disapproval, disagreement, opposition, challenge, dissent, demurral, remonstration, expostulation, fuss, outcry; railing, inveighing, fulmination, protestation.
▷ANTONYMS support, approval.
2 *women staged a protest outside the gates*: **demonstration**, march, protest march, peace camp, rally, sit-in, human chain, occupation, sleep-in, dirty protest, write-in, non-cooperation; work-to-rule, industrial action, stoppage, strike, walkout, mutiny, picket, boycott; Indian morcha, gherao, hartal; informal demo.

P

▸ **verb** (stress on the second syllable) **1** *people began to protest at the development of nuclear power*: **express opposition**, raise objections, object, make a protest, dissent, take issue, make/take a stand, put up a fight, kick, take exception, complain, express disapproval, disagree, express disagreement, demur, remonstrate, expostulate, make a fuss; cry out, speak out, rail, inveigh, fulminate; oppose, challenge, denounce; informal kick up a fuss/stink.
▹**ANTONYMS** acquiesce.
2 *two dozen people protested outside the cathedral*: **demonstrate**, march, hold a rally, sit in, form a human chain, occupy somewhere, sleep in, stage a dirty protest, refuse to cooperate; work to rule, take industrial action, stop work, down tools, strike, go on strike, walk out, mutiny, picket somewhere; boycott something.
3 *Richardson has always protested his innocence*: **insist on**, claim, maintain, declare, announce, profess, proclaim, assert, affirm, argue, vow, avow, aver, pledge, swear, swear to, testify to; rare asseverate.

protestation noun **1** *police poured scorn on the bombers' protestations of regret*: **declaration**, announcement, statement, profession, assertion, insistence, claim, affirmation, assurance, attestation, oath, vow, pledge, avowal; rare maintenance, asseveration.
2 *no amount of protestations will make you change your mind*: **objection**, protest, statement of opposition, exception, complaint, disapproval, opposition, challenge, dissent, demurral, remonstration, fuss, outcry; railing, inveighing, fulmination; informal stink.

protester noun **1** *a spokesman for the council admitted losing protesters' letters*: **objector**, opposer, opponent, complainer, dissenter, dissident, nonconformist; rare dissentient.
2 *sixty protesters were arrested for wire-cutting*: **demonstrator**, protest marcher, human chain; striker, mutineer, picket.

protocol noun **1** *he was always a stickler for protocol*: **etiquette**, conventions, formalities, customs, rules of conduct, procedure, ritual, code of behaviour, accepted behaviour, conventionalities, propriety, proprieties, one's Ps and Qs, decorum, manners, courtesies, civilities, good form, the done thing, the thing to do, punctilio; French politesse.
2 *the two countries signed a protocol on defence and security*: **agreement**, treaty, entente, concord, concordat, convention, deal, pact, contract, compact, settlement, arrangement; armistice, truce; rare engagement.

prototype noun *he was working on the prototype of an inexpensive but effective ventilator*: **original**, first example, first model, master, mould, template, framework, mock-up, pattern, type; **design**, guide, blueprint; sample, example, paradigm, archetype, exemplar.

protract verb *the Opposition will try to protract the discussion*. See **prolong**.

protracted adjective *his appointment followed weeks of protracted negotiations*. See **lengthy** (sense 2).

protrude verb *a handle protrudes from the motor housing*: **stick out**, jut, jut out, poke out, project, stand out, come through, peek, poke, stick up, hang out, loom (out), extend, obtrude; balloon, bulge (out), swell (out), pouch (out); N. Amer. informal pooch (out); rare protuberate.

P

protruding adjective *he had protruding teeth*: **sticking out**, jutting, jutting out, standing out, prominent, protuberant, proud, obtrusive; overhanging, projecting; bulging, bulbous, swollen, distended; informal goofy; rare protrusive, outjutting, excrescent, gibbous.
▹**ANTONYMS** sunken; inconspicuous.

protrusion noun **1** *the neck vertebrae have short vertical protrusions*: **bump**, lump, knob, hump, jut, projection, prominence, protuberance, overhang, eminence, ledge, shelf, ridge; swelling, bulge, excrescence, outgrowth, growth, carbuncle; technical process; rare tumescence, intumescence, tumefaction.
2 *a phonetician would comment on protrusion of the lips*: **sticking out**, jutting, projection, projecting, obtrusion, obtruding, prominence, protuberance; swelling, bulging; rare tumescence, tumefaction.

protuberance noun **1** *some of the duck-billed dinosaurs evolved protuberances on top of their heads*: **bump**, lump, knob, hump, jut, projection, prominence, protrusion, overhang, eminence, ledge, shelf, ridge, swelling, bulge, excrescence, outgrowth, growth, carbuncle; rare tumescence, intumescence, tumefaction.
2 *the protuberance of the incisors in the species suggests that they were extremely important*: **sticking out**, jutting, projection, projecting, obtrusion, obtruding, prominence, protrusion; swelling, bulging; rare tumescence, tumefaction.

protuberant adjective *his eyes are a little protuberant*: **bulging**, bulbous, popping, swelling, swollen, distended, sticking out, jutting, jutting out, protruding; projecting, prominent, proud, humped, obtrusive; informal goggle; rare protrusive, outjutting, excrescent, gibbous.
▹**ANTONYMS** sunken.

proud adjective **1** *Moira was a delight to her proud parents | we are very proud of our herb garden*: **pleased (with)**, glad (about/at), happy (about/at/with), delighted (about/at/with), joyful (at), overjoyed (at/over), thrilled (at/about/by/with), well pleased (with), satisfied (with), gratified (at), content (at), appreciative (of).
▹**ANTONYMS** ashamed.
2 *it's a proud day for all of our workers*: **pleasing**, gratifying, satisfying, fulfilling, rewarding, cheering, heart-warming; happy, good, memorable, notable, red-letter, glorious, splendid, wonderful, marvellous.
▹**ANTONYMS** shameful.
3 *they were poor but proud*: **self-respecting**, dignified, noble, worthy; independent.
▹**ANTONYMS** humble.
4 *he is too proud to admit to being in the wrong*: **arrogant**, conceited, vain, self-important, full of oneself, narcissistic, egotistical, puffed up, jumped-up, boastful, smug, complacent, disdainful, condescending, pretentious, scornful, supercilious, snobbish, imperious, pompous, overbearing, bumptious, lordly, presumptuous, overweening, haughty, high and mighty, high-handed; informal cocky, big-headed, swollen-headed, too big for one's boots, stuck-up, uppity, snooty, toffee-nosed, highfalutin; informal, dated too big for one's breeches; literary vainglorious; rare hubristic.
▹**ANTONYMS** modest, humble.
5 *she took a final look down the proud granite staircase*: **magnificent**, splendid, resplendent, grand, noble, stately, imposing, dignified, distinguished, august, illustrious, striking, impressive, majestic, glorious, sumptuous, marvellous, awe-inspiring, awesome, monumental, palatial, statuesque, heroic; superb, regal, royal, kingly, queenly, princely, imperial.
▹**ANTONYMS** unimpressive.
6 *fill the holes slightly proud to allow for sanding smooth*: **projecting**, sticking out/up, jutting, jutting out, protruding, prominent, raised, convex, elevated.
▹**ANTONYMS** concave; flush.

prove verb **1** *even this argument would not prove that everyone benefits from the reform*: **demonstrate**, show, show beyond doubt, show to be true, manifest, produce/submit proof, produce/submit evidence, establish evidence, evince; witness to, give substance to, determine, demonstrate the truth of, substantiate, corroborate, verify, ratify, validate, authenticate, attest, certify, document, bear out, confirm.
▹**ANTONYMS** disprove.
2 *the rumour proved to be correct*: **turn out**, be found, happen.
□ **prove oneself demonstrate one's abilities/qualities/courage**, show one's (true) mettle, show what one is made of.
□ **prove someone wrong** *if you can prove me wrong let me know and I'll update the review*: **refute**, show to be wrong, rebut, confute, give the lie to, demolish, discredit; informal shoot full of holes, shoot down (in flames), blow sky-high; rare controvert, negative.

provenance noun *the police were suspicious about the provenance of the paintings*: **origin**, source, place of origin; birthplace, spring, wellspring, fount, roots, history, pedigree, derivation, root, etymology; N. Amer. provenience; rare radix.

proverb noun **saying**, adage, saw, maxim, axiom, motto, aphorism, epigram, gnome, dictum, precept; words of wisdom; catchphrase, slogan, byword, watchword; truism, platitude, cliché; French bon mot; rare apophthegm.

proverbial adjective *the pirate's greed was as proverbial as his cowardice*: **well known**, famous, famed, renowned, traditional, time-honoured, legendary; notorious, infamous.

provide verb **1** *the government refused to provide money for the project*: **supply**, give, issue, furnish, lay out, come up with, dispense, bestow, impart, produce, yield, bring forth, bear, deliver, donate, contribute, pledge, advance, spare, part with, allocate, distribute, allot, assign, put forward, put up, proffer, present, extend, render; informal fork out; N. Amer. informal ante up, pony up.
▹**ANTONYMS** refuse; withhold.
2 *please provide her with the necessary documents*: **equip**, furnish, issue, supply, outfit; fit out, rig out, kit out, arm, array, attire, accoutre, provision, stock, purvey, accommodate, bestow, favour, endow, present; informal fix up.
▹**ANTONYMS** deprive.
3 *the work at least enabled him to **provide for** his family*: **feed**, nurture, nourish, give food to, provide board for; **support**, maintain, keep, sustain, provide sustenance for, fend for, finance, endow; take care of, care for, look after.
▹**ANTONYMS** neglect.
4 *this procedure can provide an opportunity for testing opinion*: **make available**, present, offer, afford, accord, give, add, bring, yield, impart, bestow, confer, lend.
5 *we have **provided for** further restructuring*: **prepare**, allow, make provision, make preparations, be prepared, anticipate, arrange, make arrangements, get ready, plan, make plans, cater.
6 *the forces of nature which no human foresight can **provide against***: **take precautions**, take steps/measures, guard, forearm oneself; make provision for.
7 *the contract provides that the tenants are responsible for house repairs*: **stipulate**, lay down, have as a condition, make it a condition, require, order, ordain, demand, prescribe, state, set out, specify.

provided conjunction *the clove-pink needs no special cultivation, provided it has well-drained soil*: **if, on condition that**, providing (that), provided that, presuming (that), assuming (that), on the assumption that, as long as, given (that), with the provision/proviso that, with/on the understanding that, if and only if, contingent on, in the event that, allowing that.

providence noun **1** *her life was mapped out for her by providence*: **fate**, destiny, nemesis, kismet, God's will, divine intervention, predestination, predetermination; astral influence, the stars; fortune, fortuity, serendipity, chance, luck, accident, circumstances, coincidence; one's lot (in life); archaic one's portion.
2 *it was considered a duty to encourage providence*: **prudence**, **foresight**, forethought, far-sightedness, judgement, judiciousness, shrewdness, circumspection, wisdom, sagacity, common sense, precaution, caution, care, carefulness; good management, careful budgeting, thrift, thriftiness, economy; N. Amer. forehandedness.

provident adjective **prudent**, far-sighted, judicious, shrewd, circumspect, forearmed, wise, sagacious, sensible, commonsensical, politic, cautious, careful, thrifty; N. Amer. forehanded; rare forethoughtful.
▷ANTONYMS improvident.

providential adjective **1** *the battle was won with the aid of a providential wind*: **opportune**, advantageous, favourable, auspicious, propitious, heaven-sent, welcome, golden, good, right, lucky, happy, fortunate, benign, felicitous, timely, well timed, ripe, convenient, expedient; archaic seasonable.
▷ANTONYMS inopportune.
2 *shooting stars are not providential signs*: **divine**, heaven-sent, miraculous.

provider noun *the state is still the main provider of welfare*: **supplier**, donor, giver, contributor, source, mainstay.

providing conjunction *the public are admitted to the galleries, providing they make a small donation*: **if**, **on condition that**, provided (that), providing that, presuming (that), assuming (that), on the assumption that, as long as, given (that), with the provision/proviso that, with/on the understanding that, if and only if, contingent on, in the event that, allowing that.

province noun **1** *Egypt was still a province of the Ottoman Empire*: **territory**, region, state, department, canton, area, district, sector, zone, division, administrative district/division/unit/area; colony, settlement, dominion, fief, protectorate, mandate, dependency, possession, holding, satellite state.
2 (**the provinces**) *wages were higher in London than in the provinces*: **non-metropolitan areas/counties**, the rest of the country, middle England/America, rural areas/districts, the countryside, the backwoods, the wilds, the wilderness, the back of beyond; informal the sticks, the middle of nowhere; N. Amer. informal the boondocks.
3 *that's outside my province, I'm afraid*: **area of responsibility**, area of activity, area of interest, area of knowledge, area, department, responsibility, sphere, world, realm, field, discipline, domain, territory, orbit, preserve, business, affair, line of business, line, speciality, forte, line of country, charge, concern, worry, duty, jurisdiction, authority; informal pigeon, bailiwick, turf.

provincial adjective **1** *the provincial government*: **regional**, state, territorial, district, local; sectoral, zonal, cantonal, county, parochial; colonial.
▷ANTONYMS national.
2 *both the London and provincial press*: **non-metropolitan**, small-town, non-city, non-urban, outlying, rural, country, rustic, backwoods, backwater; informal one-horse; N. Amer. informal hick, freshwater.
▷ANTONYMS national; metropolitan; cosmopolitan.
3 *pompous bankers and their dull, provincial wives*: **unsophisticated**, **narrow-minded**, parochial, small-town, suburban, insular, parish-pump, inward-looking, limited, restricted, localist, conservative, narrow; small-minded, petty, blinkered, illiberal, inflexible, bigoted, prejudiced, intolerant; N. Amer. informal jerkwater, corn-fed.
▷ANTONYMS sophisticated; broad-minded.
▶ **noun** *those who did not know what it took were dismissed as provincials*: **(country) bumpkin**, country cousin, rustic, yokel, village idiot, peasant, churl, lout, boor, oaf, clown, barbarian, yahoo; Irish, derogatory culchie, bogman; informal clod, clodhopper; Brit. informal yob, yobbo, plonker; N. Amer. informal schlub, hayseed, hick, rube, hillbilly; Austral. informal ocker; rare bucolic.

provision noun **1** *the President condemned the provision of weapons to guerrillas*: **supplying**, supply, providing, purveying, delivery, furnishing, equipping, giving, donation, allocation, distribution, presentation.
2 *there has been limited provision for gifted children in the past*: **facilities**, services, amenities, resource(s), equipment, arrangements; means, offering, funds, benefits, assistance, allowance(s), concession(s), opportunities.
3 (**provisions**) *the English troops were tired and running out of provisions*: **supplies**, food and drink, food, stores, stocks, groceries, foodstuff(s), rations, iron rations, eatables, edibles, fare, daily bread, staples; Scottish vivers; informal grub, bread, eats, chow, nosh, scoff; N. Amer. informal chuck; archaic victuals, vittles, viands, commons, meat; rare sustenance, provender, comestibles, aliment, viaticum, commissariat.
4 *he never made any sort of provision for the future*: **preparations**, plans, planning, prearrangement, arrangements, precautions, precautionary steps/measures, contingency.
5 *nearly everyone will be covered by the provisions of the Act*: **term**, clause, requirement, specification, stipulation; proviso, condition, rider, qualification, restriction, reservation, caveat, limitation.

provisional adjective *a provisional government | provisional results from the election*. See **interim** (adjective).

provisionally adverb *he was appointed provisionally for one year*. See **temporarily**.

proviso noun *he let his house out for the year, with the proviso that his own staff should remain to run it*: **condition**, stipulation, provision, clause, rider, qualification, restriction, reservation, caveat, limitation; strings.

provocation noun **1** *he remained calm despite severe provocation*: **goading**, prodding, egging on, incitement, rousing, stirring, stimulation, prompting, inducement, encouragement, urging, inspiration, stimulus, pressure; **annoyance**, irritation, nettling, agitation, vexation, being rubbed up the wrong way; harassment, plaguing, molestation; teasing, taunting, torment; affront, insults; informal hassle, aggravation.
2 *without provocation, Jones punched Mr Cartwright*: **justification**, excuse, pretext, occasion, call, motivation, motive, cause, grounds, reason, purpose, need.

provocative adjective **1** *he was making provocative remarks guaranteed to drive her into a fury*: **annoying**, irritating, exasperating, infuriating, provoking, maddening, goading, vexing, galling; affronting, insulting, offensive, inflaming, rousing, arousing, inflammatory, incendiary, controversial; informal aggravating, in-your-face; rare instigative, agitative.
▷ANTONYMS soothing, calming.
2 *provocative dress does not constitute an invitation to sexual assault*: **sexy**, sexually arousing, sexually exciting, alluring, seductive, tempting, suggestive, inviting, tantalizing, titillating; indecent, pornographic, indelicate, immodest, shameless; erotic, sensuous, slinky, passionate, sexual, piquant, racy, juicy, risqué, raunchy, steamy, coquettish, amorous, flirtatious, come-hither; informal kinky, tarty; vulgar slang fuck-me.
▷ANTONYMS modest, decorous.

provoke verb **1** *a planned golf course has provoked anger among locals*: **arouse**, produce, evoke, cause, give rise to, occasion, call forth, draw forth, elicit, induce, inspire, excite, spark off, touch off, kindle, generate, engender, instigate, result in, lead to, bring on, contribute to, make for, foster, promote, breed, precipitate, prompt, trigger; literary beget, enkindle.
▷ANTONYMS allay.
2 *he might be provoked into making remarks he'd regret*: **goad**, spur, prick, sting, prod, egg on, hound, badger, incite, rouse, stir, move, stimulate, motivate, excite, inflame, work/fire up, impel, pressure, pressurize, prompt, induce, encourage, urge, inspire.
▷ANTONYMS deter.
3 *he thought that I was trying to provoke him*: **annoy**, make angry, anger, incense, enrage, send into a rage, irritate, infuriate, exasperate, exacerbate, madden, pique, nettle, get/take a rise out of, bother, upset, agitate, vex, irk, gall, get/put someone's back up, get on someone's nerves, ruffle, ruffle someone's feathers, make someone's hackles rise, raise someone's hackles, make someone's blood boil, rub up the wrong way, put someone out; harass, harry, plague, molest; tease, taunt, torment; affront, insult, offend; informal peeve, aggravate, hassle, miff, rile, needle, get, get to, bug, hack off, get under someone's skin, get in someone's hair, get up someone's nose, get someone's goat, get across someone; Brit. informal get on someone's wick, give someone the hump, wind up, nark; N. Amer. informal rankle, ride, gravel; vulgar slang piss off; Brit. vulgar slang get on someone's tits.
▷ANTONYMS pacify, appease.

provoking adjective *really, you can be most provoking*: **annoying**, irritating, exasperating, infuriating, provocative, maddening, goading, vexing, galling, affronting, insulting, offensive; inflaming, inflammatory, incendiary, controversial; informal aggravating, in-your-face; rare instigative, agitative.

prow noun *the prow of a ship*: **bow**, bows, stem, fore, forepart, front, head, nose, cutwater; informal sharp end; rare fore-end, stem-post, beak, beak-head.

prowess noun **1** *his prowess as a winemaker*: **skill**, skilfulness, expertise, effectiveness, mastery, facility, ability, capability, capacity, talent, genius, adroitness, adeptness, aptitude, dexterity, deftness, competence, competency, professionalism, excellence, accomplishment, experience, proficiency, expertness, finesse, know-how; French savoir faire.
▷ANTONYMS inability, ineptitude.
2 *the knights were famed for their prowess in battle*: **courage**, bravery, gallantry, valour, heroism, intrepidness, intrepidity, nerve, pluck, pluckiness, doughtiness, hardihood, braveness, courageousness, dauntlessness, gameness, manfulness, boldness, daring, audacity, spirit, fearlessness; mettle, determination, fortitude, steadfastness, stoutness, resolve, resolution, backbone, spine, stout-heartedness; informal bottle, grit, guts, spunk, gutsiness, gumption, ballsiness; N. Amer. informal moxie, cojones, sand; vulgar slang balls; archaic valiance.
▷ANTONYMS cowardice.

prowl verb *youths have been prowling around the back of the flats*: **move stealthily**, slink, skulk, steal, nose, pussyfoot, sneak, sidle, stalk, creep; roam, range, rove, cruise, hunt, scavenge; informal snoop.

proximity noun *their minds were concentrated by the proximity of the enemy*: **closeness**, nearness, presence, juxtaposition, propinquity, adjacency; accessibility; rare contiguity, vicinity, vicinage.

proxy noun *any member is entitled to appoint another person as his proxy to attend and vote instead of him*: **deputy**, representative, substitute, delegate, agent, surrogate, stand-in, attorney, ambassador, emissary, go-between, envoy; rare factor, procurator.

prude noun **puritan**, prig, killjoy, moral zealot/fanatic, moralist, Mrs Grundy, Grundy, old maid, schoolmarm, pietist, Victorian, priggish person; N. Amer. bluenose; informal goody-goody, Goody Two-Shoes, holy Joe, holy Willie, Miss Prim.

prudence noun **1** *foresters argue about the prudence of drastic thinning*: **wisdom**, judgement, good judgement, judiciousness, sagacity, shrewdness, advisability, common sense, sense.
▷ANTONYMS folly.
2 *an elder counselled prudence*: **caution**, cautiousness, care, carefulness, canniness, chariness, wariness, circumspection; far-sightedness, foresight, forethought; discretion.
▷ANTONYMS recklessness.
3 *thanks to his father's prudence, a fortune was made*: **thrift**, thriftiness, providence, good management, careful budgeting, economy, canniness, frugality, abstemiousness; N. Amer. forehandedness; rare sparingness.

prudent adjective **1** *it is not always prudent to approach strangers found in desolate spots*: **wise**, well judged, judicious, sagacious, sage, shrewd, advisable, well advised, politic, sensible, commonsensical.
▷ANTONYMS unwise, imprudent.
2 *a prudent approach to borrowing*: **cautious**, careful, canny, chary, wary, circumspect, far-sighted, forearmed; N. Amer. forehanded; rare forethoughtful.
▷ANTONYMS incautious, imprudent.
3 *Phyllis was a prudent shopper*: **thrifty**, provident, economical, canny, sparing, frugal, abstemious, scrimping.
▷ANTONYMS extravagant, imprudent.

prudish adjective *his grandmother was a rather prudish woman*: **puritanical**, puritan, priggish, prim, prim and proper, formal, moralistic, strait-laced, prissy, mimsy, stuffy, niminy-piminy, Victorian, old-maid, old-maidish, schoolmistressy, schoolmarmish, governessy; informal goody-goody, starchy; rare Grundyish.
▷ANTONYMS permissive, liberal, broad-minded.

prune verb **1** *it will soon be time to prune the apple trees*: **cut back**, trim, thin, thin out, pinch back, crop, clip, shear, pollard, top, dock; shape, even up, neaten, tidy (up).
2 *prune lateral shoots of wisteria*: **cut off**, lop (off), chop off, hack off, clip, snip (off), nip off, dock, sever, detach, remove.
3 *companies are pruning their headquarters teams in an attempt to save money*: **reduce**, cut, cut back, cut down, cut back on, pare, pare down, slim down, make reductions in, make cutbacks in, trim, whittle away/down, decrease, diminish, axe, shrink, minimize; eliminate, get rid of, do away with; informal slash.

prurient adjective *obscene material deals with sex in a manner appealing to prurient interest*: **salacious**, licentious, voyeuristic, lascivious, lecherous, lustful, lewd, libidinous, lubricious; depraved, debauched, degenerate, dissolute, dissipated; rare concupiscent.

pry verb *she might start **prying into** his private affairs | I don't mean to pry*: **enquire impertinently into**, investigate impertinently, be inquisitive about, be curious about, poke about/around in, ferret (about/around) in, delve into, eavesdrop on, listen in on; mind someone else's business, be a busybody, tap someone's phone; spy on, interfere in, meddle in, intrude on; scrutinize, probe; informal stick/poke one's nose in/into, be nosy (about), nose into, snoop about/around/round in; Austral./NZ informal stickybeak.
▷ANTONYMS mind one's own business.

prying adjective *their prying neighbours*: **inquisitive**, curious, busybody, probing, spying, eavesdropping, impertinent, interfering, meddling, meddlesome, intrusive; informal **nosy**, snooping, snoopy; rare busy.

psalm noun **sacred song**, hymn, song of praise, religious song, anthem, carol, chant, plainsong, canticle, antiphon, introit, prayer; psalmody, psalter; rare paean, lay, miserere.

pseud noun *what a pseud to tell her she had a Pre-Raphaelite face!* **pretentious person**, poser, poseur, show-off, sham, fraud; informal phoney.

pseudo adjective *there is something pseudo about him | a pseudo science*: **bogus**, sham, phoney, imitation, artificial, mock, ersatz, quasi-, fake, feigned, pretended, false, faux, spurious, counterfeit, fraudulent, deceptive, misleading, assumed, contrived, affected, insincere; informal pretend, put-on; Brit. informal cod.
▷ANTONYMS genuine.

pseudonym noun *Hanbury wrote a novel under the pseudonym of James Aston*: **pen-name**, assumed name, incognito, alias, false name, professional name, sobriquet, stage name, nickname; French nom de plume, nom de guerre; rare allonym, anonym.

psych verb informal
□ **psych someone out unsettle**, upset, agitate, disturb, make nervous, put off, put off balance, put someone off their stroke, intimidate; outstare, stare down, outface, stand up to, daunt, cow, deter, awe, disconcert, unnerve, discourage, subdue, abash, dismay; frighten, alarm, scare, terrify, terrorize, browbeat, pressure, pressurize; N. Amer. informal buffalo.
□ **psych oneself up** *we had to psych ourselves up for the race*: **nerve oneself**, steel oneself, summon/gather/screw up one's courage, prepare, prepare oneself, gear oneself up, arm oneself, brace oneself, get ready, urge oneself on, gird (up) one's loins, get in the mood, get in the right frame of mind.

psyche noun *Laura saw clearly the effect of beautiful surroundings on the psyche*: **soul**, spirit, (inner) self, innermost self, (inner) ego, true being, essential nature, life force, vital force, inner man/woman, persona, identity, personality, individuality, make-up, subconscious, mind, intellect; technical anima, pneuma; Ancient Egypt ka; Hinduism atman.
▷ANTONYMS body.

psychiatrist noun **psychoanalyst**, **psychologist**, psychopathologist, psychotherapist, therapist, counsellor; mind doctor, head doctor; N. Amer. alienist; informal **shrink**, headshrinker, trick cyclist; men in white coats.

psychic adjective **1** *there may be psychic effects, such as poltergeist activity*: **supernatural**, paranormal, other-worldly, supernormal, preternatural, metaphysical, extrasensory, transcendental, magic, magical, mystical, mystic, occult; rare necromantic.
2 *you have to tell me—I'm not psychic*: **clairvoyant**, telepathic, telekinetic, spiritualistic, with second sight, with a sixth sense.
3 *psychoanalysts argue that motherhood is important for psychic development*: **emotional**, spiritual, inner; cognitive, psychological, intellectual, mental, psychiatric, psychogenic; rare psychical, mindly, phrenic.
▶noun *the planchette is used by psychics and mediums*: **clairvoyant**, fortune teller, prophet, seer, soothsayer, forecaster of the future, crystal-gazer, astrologer, prognosticator, prophesier, oracle, augur, sibyl, Cassandra, mind-reader, palmist, palm-reader, chiromancer, medium, telepathist, spiritualist, spiritist; rare necromancer, chirosophist, palmister.

psychological adjective **1** *other drugs can do much more psychological damage*: **mental**, emotional, intellectual, inner, non-physical, cerebral, brain, rational, cognitive, abstract, conceptual, theoretical; rare psychical, mindly, phrenic.
2 *it was concluded that her pain was psychological*: **(all) in the mind**, psychosomatic, emotional, irrational, subjective, subconscious, subliminal, unconscious; imaginary, unreal.
▷ANTONYMS physical.

psychology noun **1** *she has a degree in psychology*: **study of the mind**, science of the mind, science of the personality, study of the mental processes.
2 *research on the psychology of the road user*: **mindset**, mind, mental processes, thought processes, way of thinking, cast of mind, frame of mind, turn of mind, mentality, persona, psyche, (mental) attitude(s), make-up, character, disposition, temperament, temper, behaviour; informal what makes someone tick.

psychopath noun *Rick was a dangerous psychopath who might kill again*: **madman/madwoman**, mad person, deranged person, maniac, lunatic, psychotic, sociopath; informal loony, fruitcake, nutcase, nut, nutter, psycho, schizo, head case, headbanger, sicko, crank, crackpot; Scottish informal radge; N. Amer. informal screwball, crazy, kook, meshuggener, nutso.

psychopathic adjective *could she have been attacked by some psychopathic killer?* **severely mentally ill**, mentally ill, insane, mad, certifiable, deranged, demented, of unsound mind, out of one's mind, not in one's right mind, not together, crazed, maniac, maniacal, lunatic, unbalanced, unhinged, unstable, disturbed, distracted, stark mad, manic, frenzied, raving, distraught, frantic, hysterical, delirious, mad as a hatter, mad as a March hare; Latin non compos mentis; informal crazy, mental, off one's head, out of one's head, off one's nut, nuts, nutty, nutty as a fruitcake, off one's rocker, not (quite) right in the head, round the bend, stark staring/raving mad, raving mad, bats, batty, bonkers, cuckoo, loopy, loony, bananas, loco, dippy, screwy, with a screw loose, schizoid, touched, gaga, up the pole, not all there, not right upstairs, away with the fairies, foaming at the mouth; Brit. informal barmy, crackers, barking, barking mad, round the twist, off one's trolley, daft, as daft as a brush, not the full shilling; N. Amer. informal buggy, off the wall, nutsy, nutso, out of one's tree, meshuga, squirrelly, wacko; Canadian & Austral./NZ informal bushed; NZ informal porangi; technical psychotic, sociopathic, psychopathological.

psychosomatic adjective *a diagnosis of psychosomatic illness should not be made lightly*: **(all) in the mind**, psychological, irrational, stress-related, stress-induced, subjective, subconscious, unconscious.

psychotic adjective *he was attacked by his psychotic cell mate*: **severely mentally ill**, insane, mad, certifiable, deranged, demented, of unsound mind, out of one's mind, not in one's right mind, not together, crazed, lunatic, unbalanced, unhinged, unstable, disturbed, distracted, stark mad, maniac, maniacal, manic, frenzied, raving, distraught, frantic, hysterical, delirious, mad as a hatter, mad as a March hare; Latin non compos mentis;

informal crazy, mental, off one's head, out of one's head, off one's nut, nuts, nutty, nutty as a fruitcake, off one's rocker, not (quite) right in the head, round the bend, raving mad, bats, batty, bonkers, cuckoo, loopy, loony, bananas, loco, screwy, with a screw loose, touched, gaga, up the pole, not all there, not right upstairs, away with the fairies, foaming at the mouth; Brit. informal barmy, crackers, barking, barking mad, round the twist, off one's trolley, daft, as daft as a brush, not the full shilling; N. Amer. informal buggy, off the wall, nutsy, nutso, out of one's tree, meshuga, squirrelly, wacko; Canadian & Austral./NZ informal bushed; NZ informal porangi; technical psychopathic, psychopathological, sociopathic.

Word toolkit

psychotic	**demented**	**crazed**
disorder	old man	fan
episode	soul	gunman
killer	minds	animal
rage	comedy	genius

pub noun Brit. See **inn**.

puberty noun *the onset of puberty may occur as early as eleven or twelve*: **adolescence**, pubescence, sexual maturity, growing up; youth, young adulthood, teenage years, teens, the awkward age; rare juvenescence.

public adjective **1** *the public sector of the economy*: **state**, national, federal, government; constitutional, democratic, civic, civil, official, social, municipal, community, local; communal, nationalized; urban, metropolitan.
▷ANTONYMS private.
2 *there is a great public demand for information on food*: **popular**, general, common, communal, collective, shared, joint, universal, widespread.
3 *Stukeley was already a well-known physician and public figure*: **prominent**, well known, in the public eye, leading, important, eminent, pre-eminent, recognized, distinguished, notable, noteworthy, noted, outstanding, foremost, of mark; illustrious, celebrated, famous, renowned, acclaimed, famed, honoured, esteemed, respected, well thought of, influential, prestigious.
▷ANTONYMS obscure, unknown.
4 *plans are afoot to ban smoking in public places*: **open (to the public)**, **communal**, not private, not exclusive, accessible to all, available, free, unrestricted, community.
▷ANTONYMS private, restricted.
5 *he never made his views public*: **known**, widely known, overt, plain, obvious, in circulation, published, publicized, exposed.
▷ANTONYMS secret.
□ **the public eye** *an individual may be momentarily in the public eye, but such notoriety rarely lasts*: **the spotlight**, the limelight, the glare of publicity, prominence; the focus of interest, the focus of attention.
▸ noun **1** *the opinion polls do not reflect the true opinions of the British public*: **people**, citizens, subjects, general public, electors, electorate, voters, taxpayers, ratepayers, residents, inhabitants, citizenry, population, populace, community, society, country, nation, world; everyone.
2 *he was adored by his public and his pupils*: **audience**, spectators, followers, following, fans, devotees, aficionados, admirers; patrons, clientele, market, consumers, buyers, customers, readers; informal buffs, freaks.
□ **in public publicly**, in full view of people/the public, openly, in the open, for all to see, undisguisedly, blatantly, flagrantly, brazenly, with no attempt at concealment, overtly, boldly, audaciously, unashamedly, shamelessly, unabashed, wantonly, immodestly; Latin coram populo.
▷ANTONYMS secretly.

Word links **public**

agoraphobia fear of public places

publication noun **1** *he is the author of numerous publications*: **book**, volume, hardback, paperback, title, work, tome, opus, treatise, manual, register, almanac, yearbook, compendium; newspaper, paper, magazine, periodical, part-work, newsletter, gazette, bulletin, journal, report, daily, weekly, fortnightly, monthly, quarterly, annual, comic, organ, booklet, brochure, catalogue, magalogue; informal glossy, rag, mag, 'zine, fanzine.
2 *she was in England for the publication of her new book*: **issuing**, announcement, publishing, printing, notification, reporting, declaration, communication, proclamation, broadcasting, publicizing, advertising, distribution, spreading, dissemination, promulgation, issuance, appearance, emergence.

publicity noun **1** *the blaze of publicity surrounding him vanished overnight*: **public attention**, public interest, public notice, media attention/interest, exposure, glare, limelight, fuss, commotion; fame, renown, celebrity, stardom, notability, notoriety; informal to-do.
2 *clever publicity has created a wave of enthusiasm*: **promotion**, advertising, propaganda; boost, push, fanfare; informal hype, ballyhoo, puff, puffery, build-up, razzmatazz; plug.

publicize verb **1** *the king's itinerary was normally publicized in advance*: **make known**, make public, bring to public notice/attention, announce, report, communicate, impart, disclose, reveal, divulge, leak, publish, broadcast, transmit, issue, put out, distribute, spread, unfold, disseminate, circulate, air, blazon, herald, proclaim, promulgate.
▷ANTONYMS conceal, suppress.
2 *he hit the talk show circuit to publicize his new diet book*: **advertise**, promote, build up, talk up, push, beat the drum for, boost, merchandise; informal hype, plug, puff (up).

public-spirited adjective *the debris was left for public-spirited citizens to remove*: **community-minded**, socially concerned, philanthropic, charitable, helpful to others; **altruistic**, humanitarian, generous, unselfish, selfless.

publish verb **1** *we want to publish good-quality literary works*: **issue**, bring out, produce, print.
2 *it would be useful to publish his comments*: **make known**, make public, publicize, bring to public notice/attention, announce, report, declare, post, communicate, impart, broadcast, transmit, issue, put out, distribute, spread, promulgate, propagandize, disseminate, circulate, air, blazon, herald, proclaim; disclose, reveal, divulge, leak.

pucker verb *I find a zigzag stitch tends to pucker the fabric*: **wrinkle**, crinkle, cockle, crumple, rumple, ruck up, scrunch up, corrugate, ruffle, screw up, crease, shrivel, furrow, crimp, gather, draw, tuck, pleat; Brit. rare ruckle.
▸ noun *cotton thread can produce a pucker in the sewing with shrinkage*: **wrinkle**, fold, crinkle, crumple, corrugation, furrow, line, gather, tuck, pleat.

puckish adjective *he had very a puckish sense of humour*. See **impish**.

pudding noun *Pete had given up on the stew and was eating the pudding*: **dessert**, sweet, sweet course/dish, second course, last course; Brit. informal afters, pud.

puddle noun *puddles of water*: **pool**, spill, splash; literary plash.

puerile adjective *it was the cause of many a puerile pub argument*. See **childish** (sense 1).

puff noun **1** *a puff of wind*: **gust**, blast, rush, squall, gale, whiff, breath, flurry, draught, waft, breeze, blow; literary zephyr.
2 *he took a puff at his cigar*: **pull**; informal drag.
3 informal *the publishers expected a puff in our literary column*: **favourable mention**, piece of publicity, favourable review, advertisement, promotion, recommendation, commendation, mention, good word, commercial; informal push, ad, boost; Brit. informal advert.
4 informal *extravagant statements are accepted as part of a salesman's puff*: **publicity**, advertising, promotion, marketing, propaganda, push, puffery, build-up, boosting; patter, line, pitch, sales talk, presentation; informal **spiel**, hype, ballyhoo.
▸ verb **1** *he reached the top of the stairs, puffing a little*: **breathe heavily**, breathe loudly/rapidly/quickly, pant, puff and pant, puff and blow, blow; **gasp**, fight for breath, catch one's breath.
2 *Hauser **puffed at** his cigarette*: **smoke**, draw on, pull on, drag on, suck at/on.
3 informal *the royal family may not be used to puff commercial products*: **advertise**, promote, give publicity to, publicize, push, recommend, commend, endorse, put in a good word for, beat the drum for; informal give a puff to, hype (up), plug; rare merchandise.
□ **puff out/up** *if she went for a walk her ankles puffed up*: **bulge**, swell (out), stick out, distend, belly (out), balloon (up/out), expand, inflate, enlarge; rare tumefy, intumesce.
□ **puff something out/up** *he puffed out his cheeks*: **distend**, stick out, cause to swell, cause to bulge, belly (out), balloon (up/out), expand, dilate, inflate, blow up, pump up, enlarge, bloat.

puffed adjective **1** *I'll be too puffed to dance properly*: **out of breath**, breathless, short of breath, puffed out, panting, puffing, huffing and puffing, puffing and blowing, gasping, gasping for breath, wheezing, wheezy, winded, short-winded; informal out of puff.
2 *he was just another **puffed-up** tinpot dictator*: **self-important**, conceited, arrogant, bumptious, self-assertive, full of oneself, pompous, overbearing, (self-)opinionated, cocky, presumptuous, forward, imperious, domineering, magisterial, pontifical, sententious, grandiose, affected, stiff, vain, haughty, proud, egotistic; supercilious, condescending, patronizing; informal snooty, uppity, uppish.

puffy adjective *her eyes were puffy from crying*: **swollen**, puffed up, distended, enlarged, full, inflated, dilated, bloated, engorged, bulging, baggy; rare tumid, turgescent, tumescent, tumefied, oedematous, ventricose.

Word toolkit

puffy	**swollen**	**bloated**
eyes	glands	bureaucracy
clouds	lips	corpse
face	ankles	ego
sleeves	feet	belly
cotton ball	river	budget

P

pugilism noun **boxing**, prizefighting, bare-knuckle boxing/fighting, fisticuffs, sparring; the ring; archaic the noble art/science (of self-defence).

pugilist noun **boxer**, fighter, prizefighter, sparring partner; informal bruiser, pug; rare ringster.

pugnacious adjective *the bouncer that night was a pugnacious 42-year-old from East London*: **combative**, **aggressive**, antagonistic, belligerent, bellicose, warlike, quarrelsome, argumentative, contentious, disputatious, defiant, hostile, threatening, truculent; irascible, fiery, hot-tempered, ill-tempered, bad-tempered, rough.
▷**ANTONYMS** peaceable; friendly.

puke verb *he sank to his knees and puked again*. See **vomit** (sense 1 of the verb).

pukka adjective **1** *it wouldn't be considered the pukka thing to do*: **respectable**, decorous, proper, genteel, formal, polite, conventional, right, correct, accepted, presentable, decent, smart; French comme il faut; Brit. informal posh, top-notch, tip-top.
▷**ANTONYMS** improper.
2 *their old van was up against pukka racing cars*: **genuine**, authentic, proper, actual, real, true, bona fide, veritable, original, not copied, legitimate; informal kosher, the real McCoy.
▷**ANTONYMS** imitation.

pull verb **1** *he pulled a small plastic box towards him*: **tug**, haul, drag, draw, trail, tow, heave, lug, strain at, jerk, lever, prise, wrench, wrest, twist; N. Amer. pry; informal yank.
▷**ANTONYMS** push.
2 *I'll let you pull the next bad tooth*: **pull out**, draw out, take out, extract, remove, root out.
3 *he still feels pain in his back where he has pulled a muscle*: **strain**, sprain, turn, wrench, rick, stretch, tear; dislocate, put out of joint, damage.
4 *before World War II, race days here pulled big crowds*: **attract**, draw, pull in, bring in, lure, charm, engage, enchant, captivate, bewitch, seduce, catch the eye of, entice, tempt, beckon, interest, fascinate.
▷**ANTONYMS** repel.
□ **pull something apart** *it is wise to pull the gearbox apart only when absolutely necessary*: **dismantle**, disassemble, take/pull to pieces, take/pull to bits, take apart, strip down; demolish, destroy, break up.
▷**ANTONYMS** build, assemble.
□ **pull back** *the army was forced to pull back behind the canal*: **withdraw**, retreat, draw back, fall back, retire, disengage, pull out, back off, give way/ground; flee, take flight, turn tail, beat a (hasty) retreat.
▷**ANTONYMS** advance.
□ **pull something down** *several old buildings were pulled down*: **demolish**, knock down, take down, tear down, dismantle, raze, raze to the ground, level, flatten, bulldoze, destroy, lay waste.
▷**ANTONYMS** build, erect.
□ **pull a fast one on** informal *he is a car salesman who will try to pull a fast one on his co-conspirators*: **outsmart**, outwit, out-think, outmanoeuvre, outplay, be cleverer than, steal a march on, trick, gull, make a fool of, get the better of; informal outfox, put one over on, run/make rings round; dated outjockey.

□ **pull in** *a police car pulled in behind*: **stop**, halt, come to a stop/halt, park, arrive, pull over, draw in, draw up.
□ **pull someone/something in 1** *comedies continued to pull in the biggest audiences*: **attract**, draw, pull, bring in, lure, charm, engage, enchant, captivate, bewitch, seduce, catch the eye of, entice, tempt, beckon, interest, fascinate.
2 informal *the police pulled him in for questioning*: **arrest**, apprehend, detain, take into custody, take prisoner, seize, capture, catch, take in; informal collar, nab, nick, pinch, pick up, run in, bust, nail, do, feel someone's collar.
▷**ANTONYMS** release.
3 informal *the company has pulled in £70m from disposals*: **earn**, be paid, make, get, bring in, rake in, clear, collect, net, gross, pocket, take home.
□ **pull someone's leg** **tease**, fool, play a trick on, make fun of, joke with, rag, chaff, twit, pull the wool over someone's eyes; informal kid, bamboozle, lead up the garden path, take for a ride, rib, take the mickey out of, get/take a rise out of; Brit. informal wind up, have on.
□ **pull something off** *they pulled off a daring crime*: **achieve**, fulfil, succeed in, accomplish, bring off, bring about, carry out, carry off, execute, perform, perpetrate, discharge, complete, conduct, negotiate, clinch, work out, fix, effect, establish, engineer.
□ **pull out 1** *one of their star players has pulled out with stomach trouble*: **withdraw**, resign, leave, retire, step down, get out, quit, back out, bow out.
2 *the French* ***pulled out of*** *the agreement*: **retreat from**, leave, quit, abandon, give up, stop participating in, get out of, back out of, bow out of, renege on. ▷**ANTONYMS** join, engage in.
□ **pull something out** *Goetz pulled out a gun and fired*: **take out**, draw, pull, draw out, bring out, get out, withdraw, fish out, produce.
□ **pull out all the stops** informal *the disc's producers have pulled out all the stops for this tiny cult classic*: **make an effort**, exert oneself, try hard, strive, endeavour, apply oneself, do one's best, do all one can, do one's utmost, give one's all, make every effort, spare no effort, be at pains, put oneself out; struggle, labour, toil, strain, push oneself, drive oneself, work hard, work like a Trojan; rack/cudgel one's brains; informal give it one's best shot, go all out, bend/lean over backwards, put one's back into it, knock oneself out, do one's damnedest, move heaven and earth, beaver away, slog away, keep one's nose to the grindstone, work one's socks off, break sweat; N. Amer. informal do one's darnedest/durnedest, bust one's chops; Austral. informal go for the doctor.
□ **pull over** *I decided to pull over on to the hard shoulder*: **stop**, halt, come to a stop/halt, pull in, pull off the road, draw in, park, arrive, draw up.
□ **pull the strings** informal *these are the people that pull the strings behind the scenes*: **manage**, direct, control, operate, regulate, conduct, handle, run, orchestrate, organize, supervise, superintend, oversee, preside over, boss, be the boss of, govern, rule, administer, lead, head, guide, steer, pilot; exercise control over, be in control of, be in charge of, be in command of, take care of, look after, be responsible for, be at the helm of, hold sway over; informal head up, call the shots, call the tune, run the show, be in the driving seat, be in the saddle.
□ **pull through** *she has serious injuries, but we are all praying for her to pull through*: **get better**, get well again, improve, recover, rally, survive, come through, recuperate; get over something; be all right.
□ **pull together** *in tough times we must pull together*: **collaborate**, cooperate, work together, work side by side, act together, act jointly, band together, come together, get together, join forces, team up, unite, combine, merge, amalgamate, pool resources, club together, make common cause, form an alliance; coordinate with each other, liaise with each other; conspire, connive, collude, be in collusion, work hand in glove; informal gang up; rare coact.
□ **pull something to pieces 1** *can I trust you not to pull my radio to pieces?* **dismantle**, disassemble, take to pieces, take/pull to bits, take/pull apart, strip down, demolish, destroy, break up. **2** *we should look at those draft guidelines and be prepared to pull them to pieces*: **criticize**, attack, censure, condemn, denigrate, find fault with, pillory, maul, lambaste, flay, savage; informal knock, slam, pan, bash, take apart, crucify, hammer, lay into, roast, skewer; Brit. informal slate, rubbish, monster, slag off; N. Amer. informal pummel, cut something up; Austral./NZ informal bag; archaic slash; rare excoriate.
□ **pull oneself together** **regain one's composure**, regain one's self-control, regain control of one's emotions, recover, get a grip/hold on oneself, get over it, become one's old self; informal snap out of it, get one's act together, buck up.
□ **pull up** *a van pulled up with six men inside*: **stop**, draw up, come to a stop/halt, halt, come to a standstill, brake, park; arrive.
□ **pull someone up** *he grinned unabashedly when his mother pulled me up*: **reprimand**, rebuke, scold, chide, chastise, upbraid, berate, castigate, reprove, reproach, censure, take to task, tear into, admonish, lecture, lambaste, read someone the Riot Act, haul over the coals; informal tell off, give someone a telling-off, bawl out, dress down, give someone hell, give someone a talking-to, give someone a dressing-down, give someone an earful, give someone a piece of one's mind, blow up, give someone a roasting, give someone a rocket, give someone a rollicking, give someone a row; Brit. informal tick off, carpet, give someone a mouthful; N. Amer. informal chew out; Austral. informal monster; rare reprehend, excoriate.
▸ noun **1** *give the chain one sharp downward pull*: **tug**, haul, jerk, heave; informal yank.
2 *she took a huge pull on her beer*: **gulp**, draught, drink, swallow, mouthful, sip, sup; informal swill, swig, slug.
3 *he took a long pull on the cigarette*: **puff**; informal drag.
4 *she felt the pull of the tranquillity of the place*: **attraction**, lure, allurement, enticement, drawing power, draw, magnetism, influence, enchantment, magnet, temptation, invitation, fascination, appeal.
5 *he could get you a job—he has a lot of pull*: **influence**, sway, strength, power, authority, say, prestige, standing, weight, leverage, muscle, teeth; informal clout, beef.

pulp noun **1** *he kneaded the fungus into a pulp*: **mash**, mush, purée, cream, pressé, pap, slop, paste, slush, mulch, swill, slurry, semi-liquid, semi-fluid, mess; baby food; informal gloop, goo, gook; N. Amer. informal glop; technical triturate; rare pomace.
2 *monkeys suck the sweet pulp off cocoa seeds*: **flesh**, soft part, fleshy part, marrow, meat.
▸ verb *then pulp the gooseberries through a sieve*: **mash**, purée, cream, crush, press, smash, liquidize, liquefy, sieve, shred, squash, pound, beat, macerate, mill, grind, mince, soften, mangle; technical comminute, triturate; archaic levigate, bray, powderize.
▸ adjective *perhaps pulp fiction is your métier rather than poetry?* **trashy**, rubbishy, cheap, sensational, lurid, tasteless, kitschy; informal tacky.

pulpit noun **stand**, lectern, platform, podium, stage, staging, dais, rostrum; soapbox, stump; box, dock; Islam minbar; rare ambo, tribune.

pulpy adjective *cook the rhubarb slowly until it is soft and pulpy*: **mushy**, soft, semi-liquid, pappy, slushy, sloppy, spongy, squashy, squelchy, squishy, succulent, juicy; informal gooey, gloopy; Brit. informal squidgy; rare pulpous.

pulsate verb *the flesh of the clam pulsates gently as water is pumped through it*: **palpitate**, pulse, throb, vibrate, pump, undulate, surge, heave, rise and fall, ebb and flow; beat, pound, thud, thump, hammer, drum, thrum, oscillate, reverberate; tick, flutter, pitter-patter, go pit-a-pat, quiver; rare quop.

pulse noun **1** *she could feel the pulse at the base of her neck*: **heartbeat**, pulsation, pulsing, throb, throbbing, vibration, pounding, thudding, thud, thumping, thump, drumming.
2 *the pulse of the train wheels*: **rhythm**, beat, rhythmical flow/pattern, measure, metre, tempo, cadence.
3 *a dolphin emits short pulses of ultrasound*: **burst**, blast, spurt, eruption, impulse, surge; informal splurt.
▸ verb *loud music pulsing throughout the building*: **throb**, pulsate, vibrate, palpitate, beat, pound, thud, thump, hammer, drum, thrum, oscillate, reverberate; pitter-patter, go pit-a-pat, quiver; rare quop.

Word links **pulse**
sphygmo- related prefix
sphygmology study of the pulse
sphygmograph instrument for recording the pulse

pulverize verb **1** *mustard seeds may be pulverized into flour*: **grind**, crush, pound, crumble, powder, turn to dust; mill, crunch, squash, press, pulp, mash, sieve, mince, mangle, chew, shred, macerate; technical comminute, triturate; archaic levigate, bray, powderize.
2 informal *he could have pulverized the opposition*: **defeat utterly**, annihilate, beat hollow, trounce, rout, crush, smash, break, overwhelm, vanquish; informal hammer, clobber, thrash, whip, lick, paste, pound, crucify, demolish, destroy, drub, tank, take to the cleaners, wipe the floor with, make mincemeat of, blow out of the water, murder, slaughter, massacre, flatten, turn inside out; Brit. informal stuff, marmalize; N. Amer. informal blow out, cream, skunk.

pummel verb *he felt like a boxer who had been pummelled mercilessly*.
See **batter** (sense 1).

pump verb **1** *an engine pumped air out of the tube*: **force**, drive, push, send, transport, raise, inject; suck, draw, tap, milk, siphon, withdraw, expel, extract, bleed, drain.
2 *I fetched the bike and* ***pumped up*** *the back tyre*: **inflate**, blow up; swell, aerate, fill up, enlarge, distend, expand, dilate, bloat, puff up; rare tumefy.
▷ANTONYMS deflate.
3 *one man was still alive, with blood pumping from his leg*: **spurt**, spout, squirt, jet, surge, spew, gush, stream, flow, flood, pour, spill, rush, well, cascade, run, course, discharge; Brit. informal sloosh; rare disembogue.
4 informal *I started pumping them for information*: **ask**, question (persistently/intensely), quiz, interrogate, probe, put questions to, sound out, cross-examine, catechize; informal grill, put the screws on, give someone the third degree, put someone through the third degree, put someone through the wringer/mangle, worm something out of someone.

pun noun **play on words**, wordplay, double entendre, double meaning, innuendo, witticism, quip; French bon mot, jeu de mots; rare paronomasia, equivoque, amphibology, pivot, calembour, carriwitchet, clench, clinch, conundrum, nick, pundigrion, whim, quibble.

punch[1] verb *Jimmy punched him in the face*: **hit**, strike, knock, thump, thwack, jab, cuff, clip, smash, slam, welt; batter, buffet, thrash, pound, pummel, rain blows on, drub, box someone's ears; informal sock, slug, biff, bop, wallop, clobber, bash, whack, clout, crown, poke, lick, let someone have it, knock into the middle of next week, lam, whomp, deck, floor; Brit. informal stick one on, dot, slosh; N. Amer. informal boff, bust, whale; Austral./NZ informal dong, quilt, king-hit; literary smite, swinge.
▸ noun **1** *he landed a punch on Lorrimer's nose*: **blow**, hit, knock, thump, thwack, box, jab, fist, cuff, clip, smash, slam, welt, straight, uppercut, hook, body blow; informal sock, slug, biff, bop, wallop, bash, whack, clout, poke, lick, belt; N. Amer. informal boff, bust, whale; Austral./NZ informal dong, king-hit, stoush; dated buffet; archaic plug.
2 *strong and full of punch, this album is one of their best*: **vigour**, vigorousness, liveliness, vivacity, vitality, force, forcefulness, drive, strength, zest, animation, verve, panache, enthusiasm, impact, bite, kick, effectiveness, influence; informal oomph, pizzazz, zing, zip.

punch[2] verb *Flora handed him her ticket, which he punched*: **make a hole in**, put/punch holes in, perforate, puncture, pierce, prick, hole, riddle, spike, skewer, spit, stick, pin, needle; rare pink, transpierce.

punch-up noun *Mark quit the band after a punch-up at a Beverly Hills party*.
See **brawl** (noun).

punchy adjective *passionate, punchy acting*: **forceful**, incisive, strong, powerful, vigorous, vivacious, zestful, animated, dynamic, enthusiastic, effective, impressive, striking, telling, influential, cogent, compelling, convincing, persuasive, eloquent, dramatic, passionate, graphic, vivid, moving, potent, authoritative, great, forcible, aggressive, irresistible, effectual; informal zappy, in-your-face.
▷ANTONYMS feeble, ineffectual.

punctilio noun **1** *a relaxation of the extreme punctilio of earlier generations was now to be seen*: **conformity**, scrupulousness, meticulousness, conscientiousness, punctiliousness, exactitude, precision, strictness, nicety; **etiquette**, protocol, ceremony, conventions, formalities, customs, rules of conduct, procedure, ritual, code of behaviour, accepted behaviour, propriety, proprieties, one's Ps and Qs, decorum, manners, courtesies, civilities, conventionalities, good form, the done thing, the thing to do; French politesse.
▷ANTONYMS informality.
2 *both counsel and judges follow the punctilios of court procedure*: **detail**, finer point, nicety, particular, subtlety, nuance, refinement, distinction.

punctilious adjective *his punctilious implementation of orders impressed the King*: **meticulous**, conscientious, careful, diligent, attentive, ultra-careful, scrupulous, painstaking, exact, precise, accurate, correct, thorough, studious, rigorous, mathematical, detailed, perfectionist, methodical, particular, religious, strict; **fussy**, fastidious, hair-splitting, finicky, finical, demanding, exacting, pedantic; informal nit-picking, pernickety; N. Amer. informal persnickety; archaic nice, overnice, laborious.
▷ANTONYMS careless, easy-going, slapdash.

punctual adjective *Mrs Marsh liked her guests to be punctual*: **on time**, prompt, to/on schedule, in good time, in time, when expected, timely, well timed; informal on the dot; Brit. informal bang/spot on time.
▷ANTONYMS late, early.

punctually adverb *please arrive punctually | Edward arrived there punctually at nine*: **promptly**, **on time**, at the proper time, at the right time, dead on time; prompt, sharp, exactly, precisely, to the minute, to the second, dead; Brit. informal bang on time, spot on time, bang on, spot on.

punctuate verb **1** *pupils should be shown how to set out and punctuate direct speech*: **add punctuation to**, put punctuation marks in, dot; archaic point, apostrophize, accentuate.
2 *slides were used to punctuate the talk*: **break up**, interrupt, intersperse, pepper, sprinkle, scatter, strew, dot.

punctuation noun **punctuation marks**, points.

puncture noun **1** *the back offside tyre developed a puncture*: **hole**, perforation, prick, rupture, cut, nick, slit, leak.
2 *my bike has got a puncture*: **flat tyre**; informal flat.
▸ verb **1** *he deliberately punctured another child's bicycle tyre*: **make a hole in**, pierce, penetrate, rupture, perforate, riddle, stab, cut, nick, slit, prick, spike, stick, impale, transfix, bore (through), drill (through), lance, tap; decompress, depressurize, deflate.
2 *she knows how to puncture the wordiness of his speeches*: **put an end to**, cut short, reverse, prick, deflate, flatten, reduce.

pundit noun *a leading pundit predicts a further interest-rate cut this year*: **expert**, authority, adviser, member of a think tank, member of a policy unit, specialist, consultant, doyen, master, mentor, guru, sage, savant; informal buff, whizz, boffin.

pungent adjective **1** *the pungent smell of the horses*: **strong**, powerful, pervasive, penetrating, suffocating, stifling; **sharp**, acrid, acid, sour, biting, stinging, burning, smarting, irritating; nauseating, nauseous, sickly, offensive, astringent, bitter, fetid, cloying; literary mephitic.
▷ANTONYMS bland, mild.
2 *the marinade is more pungent than soy sauce*: **sour**, acid, biting, bitter, tart, vinegary, tangy; highly flavoured, aromatic, spicy, spiced, piquant, peppery, hot, fiery.
▷ANTONYMS bland, mild.
3 *pungent remarks*: **caustic**, biting, trenchant, cutting, acerbic, sardonic, sarcastic, scathing, acrimonious, pointed, barbed, acid, sharp, keen, tart, stinging, astringent, incisive, devastating, piercing, penetrating, rapier-like, razor-edged, critical, bitter, polemic, virulent, vitriolic, venomous, waspish, corrosive, mordant, stringent; rare acidulous, mordacious.
▷ANTONYMS bland, mild.

Word toolkit

pungent	**aromatic**	**spicy**
smell	herbs	Thai food
odour	oil	sauce
aroma	wine	burrito
smoke	candle	sausage
cheeses	rice	soup

punish verb **1** *some parents punish their children harder than they should*: **penalize**, **discipline**, mete out punishment to, bring someone to book, teach someone a lesson, make an example of; tan/whip someone's hide; informal get, scalp, murder, wallop, thump, give it to someone, throw the book at, come down on (like a ton of bricks), have someone's guts for garters, skin alive; Brit. informal drop on, give someone what for; N. Amer. informal tear down; dated chastise; archaic chasten, recompense, visit.
▷ANTONYMS pardon, exonerate.
2 *Boro's in-form strikers will be quick to punish any mistakes by United's defence*: **exploit**, take advantage of, put to advantage, use, make use of, turn to (one's) account, profit by/from, capitalize on, cash in on, trade on; informal walk all over.
3 *a new rise in prescription charges would punish the poor*: **treat harshly/unfairly**, be unfair to, unfairly disadvantage, put at an unfair disadvantage, put in an unfavourable position, handicap, do a disservice to, make someone suffer, hurt, wrong, ill-use, maltreat.

P

punishable adjective *money-laundering is a punishable offence*: **illegal**, unlawful, illegitimate, criminal, felonious, actionable, prosecutable, indictable, penal, blameworthy, dishonest, fraudulent, unauthorized, unsanctioned, outlawed, banned, forbidden, barred, prohibited, interdicted, proscribed.

punishing adjective *she went on a punishing schedule of visits to the US*. See **arduous**.

punishment noun **1** *judicial ideology stresses the punishment of the guilty*: **penalizing**, punishing, disciplining; retribution, damnation; dated chastising, chastisement.
2 *the teacher may impose reasonable punishments*: **penalty**, discipline, correction, retribution, penance, sentence, reward, one's just deserts, medicine, the price, the rap, requital, vengeance, justice, judgement, sanction; informal comeuppance; Brit., Military jankers; dated chastisement.
3 *both boxers gave and took punishment*: **battering**, thrashing, beating, thumping, pounding, pummelling, hammering, buffeting, drubbing; informal walloping, bashing, roughing up, hiding, belting.
4 *domestic ovens are not constructed to take continual punishment*: **maltreatment**, mistreatment, ill-treatment, abuse, ill-use, rough handling, mishandling, manhandling; injury, damage, harm.

Word links **punishment**

punitive, **penal** relating to punishment
penology study of punishment
poinephobia fear of punishment

punitive adjective **1** *truancy rates would decline if tougher punitive measures against parents were taken*: **penal**, disciplinary, corrective, correctional, retributive; in retaliation, in reprisal; rare penitentiary, punitory, castigatory.
2 *the government plans to announce punitive taxes on imports*: **harsh**, severe, stiff, austere, cruel, savage, stringent, burdensome, demanding, draconian, drastic, swingeing, crushing, crippling; high, sky-high, inflated, exorbitant, extortionate, excessive, outrageous, inordinate, iniquitous, immoderate, unreasonable.

punter noun Brit. informal **1** *each punter has a 1:39 chance of a win*: **gambler**, backer, staker, speculator; N. Amer. bettor; informal plunger; N. Amer. informal high roller; Austral./NZ informal spieler.
2 *you have to get the punters to pack in*: **customer**, client, patron; buyer, purchaser, shopper, consumer, user, visitor, guest; member of the audience/crowd; (**punters**) clientele, patronage, audience, following, trade, business, market; Brit. informal bums on seats.
3 *imagine her pimp sending her a punter at this time of day*: **customer**, client, kerb-crawler; informal john, trick, score.

puny adjective **1** *we grew up puny, with bad chests*: **undersized**, underdeveloped, undernourished, underfed, stunted, slight, small, little, diminutive, dwarfish, pygmy; **weak**, feeble, weakly, sickly, delicate, frail, fragile; informal weedy, pint-sized.
▷ANTONYMS strong, sturdy.
2 *the men were jeering at the villagers' puny efforts to save their homes*: **pitiful**, pitiable, inadequate, negligible, insufficient, scant, scanty, derisory, miserable, sorry, wretched, meagre, paltry, trifling, trivial, insignificant, inconsequential, petty; informal pathetic, measly, piddling, piffling, mingy, poxy, dinky; rare exiguous.
▷ANTONYMS significant, sizeable, substantial.

pupil noun **1** *they are former pupils of the school*: **student**, schoolchild, schoolboy, schoolgirl, scholar.
2 *will you take me on as your pupil?* **disciple**, follower, learner, student, protégé, apprentice, trainee, mentee, probationer, novice, recruit, beginner, tyro, neophyte.

puppet noun **1** *a puppet show*: **marionette**, glove puppet, hand puppet, finger puppet, rod puppet, shadow puppet.
2 *he was little more than a puppet of his aides*: **pawn**, tool, instrument, cat's paw, poodle, creature, hostage, counter, cog, dupe; mouthpiece, minion, figurehead; informal flunkey, lackey, stooge.

purchase verb *the school decided to purchase the software*: **buy**, acquire, obtain, pick up, snap up, take, secure, procure, come by, pay for, shop for, invest in, put money into; informal get hold of, get one's hands on, get one's mitts on, score.
▷ANTONYMS sell, market.
▶noun **1** *if you are not delighted with your purchase, we will give you a full refund*: **acquisition**, investment, buy, order, deal, bargain, property, asset, possession, holding; shopping, goods.
▷ANTONYMS sale.
2 *his hand fought for purchase on the smooth wall*: **grip**, firm contact, attachment, hold, foothold, footing, toehold, fingerhold, anchorage, support, grasp; resistance, friction, leverage, advantage.

purchaser noun **buyer**, shopper, customer, consumer, client, patron, investor, user; clientele, patronage, public, trade, market; Law vendee; rare emptor.

pure adjective **1** *every coin was of pure gold*: **unmixed**, unalloyed, unadulterated, unblended, uncontaminated, sterling, solid, refined, one hundred per cent, 100%; clarified, clear, filtered, distilled, processed, neat, straight, undiluted; flawless, perfect, genuine, authentic, real, actual, bona fide, veritable, pukka, true.
▷ANTONYMS impure, adulterated.
2 *they have their health because the air is so pure*: **clean**, clear, fresh, crisp, refreshing, sparkling, unpolluted, untainted, unadulterated, uncontaminated; wholesome, natural, healthy, health-giving, healthful, good for you; salubrious, sanitary, uninfected, disinfected, germ-free, sterile, sterilized, pasteurized, aseptic.
▷ANTONYMS impure, dirty, polluted.
3 *she did so want to be pure in body and mind*: **virtuous**, moral, ethical, good, righteous, angelic, saintly, pious, honourable, reputable, wholesome, clean, honest, upright, upstanding, exemplary, above reproach, irreproachable, innocent; chaste, pure as the driven snow, virginal, maidenly; decent, worthy, noble, blameless, guiltless, sinless, stainless, spotless, unsullied, unblemished, unspoilt, unaffected, uncorrupted, undefiled; informal squeaky clean; Christianity immaculate, impeccable.
▷ANTONYMS immoral.
4 *a system that emphasized practical rather than pure research*: **theoretical**, abstract, conceptual, academic, hypothetical, philosophical, speculative, conjectural, non-practical, non-technical; informal blue-sky.
▷ANTONYMS applied, practical.
5 *three hours of pure magic—a show not to be missed*: **sheer**, utter, simple, absolute, downright, out-and-out, rank, complete, thorough, total, perfect, consummate, unmitigated, unqualified, palpable, patent; archaic arrant.

pure-bred adjective *only pure-bred dogs can take part in shows*: **pedigree**, thoroughbred, full, full-bred, pure-blooded, blooded, pedigreed, pure, genuine.
▷ANTONYMS hybrid, mixed, mongrel.

purely adverb *he seemed to regard the exchange purely as a joke*: **entirely**, completely, absolutely, totally, wholly, exclusively, uniquely, solely, only, simply, just, merely; no more than.

purgative adjective *I took some purgative medicine*: **laxative**, aperient, lenitive, cathartic, evacuant, purging; archaic eccoprotic.
▶noun *orris root was once used medicinally as a purgative*: **laxative**, enema, aperient, lenitive, cathartic, evacuant; dated purge; archaic eccoprotic.

purgatory noun *the pre-med year was a necessary term of purgatory*: **torment**, torture, misery, suffering, affliction, anguish, agony, wretchedness, woe, tribulation, hell, hell on earth; an ordeal, a nightmare, a hellhole, an abyss; trials and tribulations.
▷ANTONYMS paradise, bliss.

purge verb **1** *the experience has purged them of the desire to doubt*: **cleanse**, clear, purify, wash, shrive, absolve, free someone from; make someone pure; rare lustrate.
2 *the party was purged of the so-called 'capitalist roaders'*: **rid**, clear, cleanse, empty, strip, scour, void; rare depurate.
3 *human rights violators would be purged from the army*: **remove**, get rid of, clear out, sweep out, expel, eject, exclude, evict, dismiss, sack, oust, axe, depose, eradicate, root out, weed out, scour.
▶noun *the purge of the dissidents from the party*: **removal**, expulsion, ejection, exclusion, eviction, clearance, clear-out, discharge, dismissal, sacking, ousting, deposition, eradication, rooting out, weeding out; rare deposal.

purify verb **1** *trees help purify the air*: **clean**, make pure, refine, cleanse, decontaminate; filter, sieve, strain, sift, clarify, clear, freshen, deodorize; boil, distil, sanitize, disinfect, sterilize, pasteurize, fumigate; technical autoclave, liquate, rectify; rare depollute, filtrate.
▷ANTONYMS pollute, contaminate.
2 *for months he lived there purifying himself*: **purge**, cleanse, clear, free, unburden, deliver, relieve; redeem, shrive, exorcize, sanctify; rare lustrate.
▷ANTONYMS corrupt, defile.

Word links **purify**

lustral relating to ceremonial purification

purist noun *the purist will point out that every aircraft accident results from human error of some kind*: **pedant**, precisionist, perfectionist, formalist, literalist, stickler, traditionalist, doctrinaire, quibbler, hair-splitter, dogmatist, casuist, sophist, fault-finder, caviller, carper, pettifogger; informal nit-picker; rare precisian, Dryasdust.

puritan noun *today's puritans impede frank talk about sexuality*: **moralist**, pietist, prude, prig, moral zealot/fanatic, killjoy, Mrs Grundy, Grundy, old maid, schoolmarm, Victorian, priggish person, ascetic; informal goody-goody, Goody Two-Shoes, holy Joe, holy Willie, Miss Prim; N. Amer. informal bluenose.

puritanical adjective *the region's farmers are insular and puritanical*: **moralistic**, pietistic, strait-laced, tight-laced, stuffy, starchy, prissy, prudish, puritan, prim, priggish, Victorian, schoolmarmish, schoolmistressy, old-maidish, narrow-minded, censorious, sententious; austere, severe, spartan, ascetic, hair-shirt, abstemious; informal goody-goody; rare Grundyish.
▷ANTONYMS permissive, broad-minded.

purity noun **1** *the purity of our tap water*: **cleanness**, clearness, clarity, freshness, freedom from adulteration/contamination, lack of pollution, untaintedness; wholesomeness, naturalness, healthiness, healthfulness, salubrity; sterility, salubriousness.
▷ANTONYMS impurity, pollution.
2 *perhaps in a foul world these men were seeking purity*: **virtue**, virtuousness, lack of corruption, morality, goodness, righteousness, rectitude, saintliness, piety, honour, honesty, integrity, uprightness, decency, worthiness, nobility of soul/spirit, ethicality; blamelessness, guiltlessness, innocence, chastity, sinlessness, stainlessness, spotlessness, irreproachableness, immaculateness, impeccability.
▷ANTONYMS immorality.

purloin verb *they crash cars through storefronts to purloin merchandise*. See **thieve**.

purport verb (stress on the second syllable) *this work purports to be authoritative*: **claim**, lay claim, profess, pretend; set oneself up (as), appear, seem; allege/maintain/assert/proclaim/imply that one is, be apparently, be ostensibly, pose as, impersonate, pass oneself off as, be disguised as, masquerade as, feign the identity of, pass for, represent oneself as; rare personate.
▸ noun (stress on the first syllable) **1** *the purport of his remarks is already familiar*: **gist**, substance, drift, implication, intention, meaning, significance, signification, sense, essence, import, tenor, thrust, message, spirit.
2 *the purport of the attack was to prove him wrong*: **intention**, purpose, intent, object, objective, aim, goal, target, end, plan, scheme, design, idea, ambition, desire, wish, hope.

purpose noun **1** *the main purpose of his visit*: **motive**, motivation, grounds, cause, impetus, occasion, reason, point, basis, justification.
2 *the trade unions insisted that their purpose was not to subvert the market economy*: **intention**, aim, object, objective, goal, end, plan, scheme, target; ambition, aspiration, desire, wish, hope.
3 *I cannot see any purpose in just saying no*: **advantage**, benefit, good, use, usefulness, value, merit, worth, gain, profit, avail, result, outcome, effect; informal mileage, percentage; archaic behoof, boot.
4 *the original purpose of this large porch was to shelter pilgrims*: **function**, role; French raison d'être.
5 *Middlesbrough had started the game with more purpose and menace*: **determination**, resoluteness, resolution, resolve, firmness (of purpose), steadfastness, backbone, drive, push, thrust, enthusiasm, ambition, initiative, enterprise, motivation, single-mindedness, commitment, conviction, dedication; informal get-up-and-go.
□ **on purpose** *her mother made a terrible clatter with the plates on purpose*: **deliberately**, intentionally, purposely, by design, wilfully, calculatedly, premeditatedly, wittingly, knowingly, consciously; in cold blood, of one's own volition; **expressly**, explicitly, specifically, especially, specially.
□ **to the purpose** *it would not be to the purpose to take this figure as the standard*: **pertinent**, applicable, apposite, material, apropos, to the point, germane, admissible, relevant; appropriate, apt, fitting, suitable, proper; connected, related, linked; Latin ad rem; rare appurtenant.
▷ANTONYMS irrelevant.
▸ verb formal *they purposed to reach the summit that night*: **intend**, mean, aim, plan, design, have the intention, have in mind, have a mind; **decide**, resolve, determine, propose, have plans, set out, aspire, desire, want, wish, expect, hope; set one's sights on, have in view, contemplate, think of.

purposeful adjective *I sense a more purposeful attitude towards clients*: **determined**, resolute, resolved, firm, steadfast, single-minded; enthusiastic, ambitious, enterprising, motivated, committed, dedicated, persistent, persevering, tenacious, dogged, unfaltering, unwavering, unshakeable.
▷ANTONYMS aimless, irresolute.

purposely adverb *Whitlock purposely fired wide | had Amanda done that purposely to horrify them?* **deliberately**, intentionally, on purpose, by design, wilfully, calculatedly, premeditatedly, wittingly, knowingly, consciously, in cold blood, of one's own volition; **expressly**, explicitly, specifically, especially, specially, just; Law with malice aforethought; rare purposefully.
▷ANTONYMS accidentally.

purse noun **1** *Mother opened her handbag and fished for her purse*: **wallet**, pouch, money bag; N. Amer. change purse, pocketbook.
2 N. Amer. *the many things that go into a woman's purse*: **handbag**, bag, clutch bag, shoulder bag, evening bag, pochette; N. Amer. pocketbook; historical reticule, scrip.
3 *the cost of running the schools is borne by the public purse*: **fund**, funds, resources, money, kitty, pool, coffers, bank, treasury, exchequer, finances, wealth, reserves, cash, capital, assets; N. Amer. fisc.
4 *the fight in Berlin will net him a $75,000 purse*: **prize**, award, reward; prize money, winnings, stake(s).
▸ verb *the doctor pursed his lips in thought*: **press together**, compress, contract, tighten, pucker, screw up, wrinkle, pout.

pursuance noun **1** *he has been arrested in pursuance of section 7 of this Act*: **execution**, discharge, implementation, performance, carrying out, conducting, conduct, effecting, doing, accomplishment, achievement, completion, fulfilment, dispatch, pursuing, prosecution, enforcement, following.
2 *their **pursuance of** militant expansion*: **seeking of**, search for, pursuit of; quest for, hunt for, mission to acquire.

pursue verb **1** *I pursued him down the garden*: **go after**, run after, follow, chase, give chase to; hunt, stalk, track, trail, trace, shadow, dog, hound, course; informal tail.
▷ANTONYMS avoid, flee.
2 *it would be unprofitable to pursue the goal of political union*: **strive for**, push towards, work towards, try for, seek, search for, quest (after), be intent on, aim at/for, have as a goal, have as an objective, aspire to.
▷ANTONYMS eschew.
3 *he was desperate to impress a woman he had been pursuing for weeks*: **woo**, court, pay court to, pay suit to, chase after, chase, run after; informal make up to; dated make love to, romance, set one's cap at, seek the hand of, pay addresses to.
4 *she also pursued a political career*: **engage in**, be engaged in, be occupied in, participate in, take part in, work at, practise, follow, prosecute, conduct, ply, apply oneself to, go in for, take up.
▷ANTONYMS shun.
5 *the appointee will be encouraged to pursue his or her own research*: **conduct**, undertake, follow, carry on, devote oneself to, go on with, proceed with, go ahead with, keep/carry on with, continue with, continue, take further, prosecute, persist in, stick with/at.
6 *he decided not to pursue the matter*: **investigate**, research, enquire into, look into, examine, study, review, check, scrutinize, analyse, delve into, dig into, probe.
▷ANTONYMS give up.

pursuit noun **1** *within France the gendarmerie remains responsible for law enforcement and the **pursuit of** criminals*: **chasing**, pursuing, stalking, tracking, trailing, shadowing, dogging, hounding; chase after, hunt for; informal tailing.
2 *the organization is devoted to the **pursuit of** profit*: **striving towards**, push towards, aspiration for, quest after/for, search for; aim of, goal of, objective of, dream of.
3 *redirect your energies to a worthwhile pursuit*: **activity**, leisure activity, leisure pursuit, leisure interest, hobby, pastime, diversion, avocation, recreation, relaxation, divertissement, sideline, entertainment, amusement, sport, game; **occupation**, trade, calling, vocation, craft, business, line, work, job, employment.

purvey verb **1** *he had acquired a massive fortune purveying a health drink*: **sell**, supply, provide, furnish, cater, retail, deal in, trade, carry, handle, stock, offer, auction, have for sale, put on the market, peddle, hawk, tout, traffic in; informal flog.
2 *the majority of newspapers purvey typically right-wing attitudes*: **pass on**, transmit, broadcast, disseminate, spread, put round, put about, circulate, communicate, make known, publicize, publish; provide, supply, furnish, make available, peddle.

purveyor noun *a local purveyor of gourmet sandwiches*: **seller**, vendor, trader, retailer, supplier, provider, stockist, tout, trafficker; dated pedlar, hawker.

pus noun *the boil may be lanced to drain the pus*: **matter**, suppuration, discharge, secretion; rare sanies.

Word links **pus**

purulent relating to pus
pyo- related prefix, as in *pyogenic*

push verb **1** *she tried to push him away*: **shove**, thrust, propel, impel; send, press, drive, plunge, stick, force, shoot, ram, bump, knock, strike, hit, jolt, butt, prod, poke, nudge, elbow, shoulder; bulldoze, sweep, jostle, bundle, hustle, hurry, rush, manhandle.
▷ANTONYMS pull.
2 *he tried to push his way into the flat*: **force (one's way)**, shove, thrust, squeeze, jostle, elbow, shoulder; thread, wind, work, inch.
3 *he managed to push a silent panic button*: **press (down)**, push down, depress, exert pressure on, bear down on, hold down, squeeze; **operate**, activate, actuate.
4 *don't **push** her **to** join in if she doesn't want to*: **urge**, press, pressure, put pressure on, pressurize, force, drive, impel, coerce, nag; lean on, prevail on; dragoon into, steamroller into, browbeat into, use strong-arm tactics on; informal put the heat on, put the screws on, twist someone's arm, railroad into, bulldoze into.
5 *the manufacturers of each fuel push their own products*: **advertise**, publicize, promote, give publicity to, beat/bang the drum for, popularize; sell, market, merchandise; informal plug, give a plug to, hype, hype up, give a puff to, puff, puff up, boost, flog; N. Amer. informal ballyhoo, flack, huckster.

□ **push someone around bully**, domineer, boss about/around, ride roughshod over, trample on, tread on, bulldoze, abuse, mistreat, maltreat, kick around/about, browbeat, lean on, tyrannize, intimidate, threaten, torment, terrorize, victimize, pick on.
□ **push for** *the trade unions will be likely to push for wage increases*: **demand**, insist on, clamour for, ask/call for, request, press for, campaign for, work for, lobby for, speak for, drum up support for, sponsor, urge, promote, advocate, recommend, champion, espouse.
□ **push off** informal *push off, will you—I'm busy*: **go away**, depart, leave, take oneself off, take off, get out, get out of my sight; go, go your way, get going, get moving, be off, take your leave, decamp, absent yourself; be off with you, shoo; informal hit the road, fly, skedaddle, split, vamoose, scat, scram, make yourself scarce, be on your way, run along, beat it, get, get lost, shove off, buzz off, clear off, skip off, pop off, go (and) jump in the lake; on your bike, go and chase yourself; Brit. informal get stuffed, sling your hook, hop it, bog off, naff off; N. Amer. informal bug off, light out, haul off, haul ass, take a powder, hit the trail, take a hike; Austral./NZ informal rack off, nick off; S. African informal voetsak, hamba; vulgar slang bugger off, piss off, fuck off; Brit. vulgar slang sod off; literary begone, avaunt.
▷ANTONYMS stay, remain.
□ **push on** *I decided to push on towards the coast*: **continue one's journey**, continue on one's way, carry on, advance, press on, progress, make progress, proceed, go on, make headway, gain ground, push forward, go/forge ahead; resume one's journey, start off again.
□ **push the boat out** informal *you could push the boat out and go for the top of the range*: **be extravagant**, go on a spending spree, splash out, splurge, spare no expense, spend lavishly, spend a lot of money; informal lash out, go mad, go on a shopping binge, indulge in some retail therapy.
▶ **noun 1** *I felt a push in the back*: **shove**, thrust, ram, bump, knock, hit, jolt, butt, prod, poke, elbow, nudge, shoulder, jostle.
2 *the enemy's eastward push had overrun Dutch positions*: **advance**, drive, thrust, charge, attack, assault, onslaught, onrush, offensive, sortie, foray, raid, sally, invasion, incursion, blitz, campaign; archaic onset.
□ **at a push** Brit. informal *at a push, you could use a disk editor to recover files*: **if necessary**, in case of necessity, if need be, if needs must, if forced, if all else fails, in an emergency.
□ **give someone the push** informal *council chiefs gave him the push for looking too old*: **throw out**, remove, eject, expel, turn out, turf out, fling out, force out, drive out, evict, dislodge, oust; dismiss, discharge; informal chuck out, kick out, send packing, boot out, give someone the boot, give someone their marching orders, throw someone out on their ear, show someone the door, sack, fire, give someone the (old) heave-ho; N. Amer. informal give someone the bum's rush.

pushing adjective *I don't want to seem pushing or jealous*. See **pushy**.

pushover noun **1** *if the panel withdrew its report, word would soon get about that it was a pushover*: **weakling**, not a force to be reckoned with, feeble opponent, unworthy opponent, man of straw; easy meat, easy game; informal soft/easy touch, easy mark.
2 *this course is no pushover, even for experts*: **easy task**, easy job, five-finger exercise, gift, walkover, sinecure, gravy train; child's play, nothing; informal doddle, walk in the park, piece of cake, picnic, money for old rope, money for jam, cinch, breeze, sitter, kids' stuff, cushy job/number, doss, cakewalk; N. Amer. informal duck soup, snap; Austral./NZ informal bludge, snack; S. African informal a piece of old tackie; Brit. vulgar slang a piece of piss; dated snip.

pushy adjective *behind every successful child there is a pushy parent*: **assertive**, thrusting, pushing, ambitious, aggressive, forceful, forward, obtrusive, bold, brash, bumptious, arrogant, officious, bossy, presumptuous, full of oneself, self-assertive, overbearing, domineering, confident, overconfident, cocksure; loud, obnoxious, offensive; informal cocky; rare pushful.
▷ANTONYMS retiring.

pusillanimous adjective *the President's increasingly pusillanimous stance on social issues*. See **cowardly**.

pussyfoot verb **1** *you can't pussyfoot around with children's welfare*: **equivocate**, be evasive, be non-committal, evade/dodge/sidestep/fudge the issue, prevaricate, quibble, parry questions, hedge, fence, vacillate, shuffle about, beat about the bush; Brit. hum and haw; informal duck the question, sit on the fence, shilly-shally, blow hot and cold; rare tergiversate.
2 *I had to pussyfoot over the crunchy gravel*: **creep**, move stealthily, tiptoe, pad, soft-shoe, steal, sneak, nose, sidle, stalk, prowl, slink, skulk, tread warily.

pustule noun **pimple**, spot, blackhead, boil, swelling, eruption, carbuncle, wen, cyst, abscess, blister; informal whitehead, zit; Scottish informal plook; technical comedo; rare papule, bleb, blain, whelk.

put verb **1** *she put the parcel on a chest in the hall*: **place**, set, put down, set down, lay, lay down, deposit, situate, position, settle; leave, stow, prop, lean, plant, pose; informal stick, dump, bung, park, plonk, pop; N. Amer. informal plunk; rare posit.
2 *Preston didn't see that he could be* **put in** *either category*: **assign to**, consign to, allocate to, place in; classify with, categorize with, bracket with.
3 *don't try and* **put** *the blame* **on** *me*: **lay**, pin, place, impose, fix; attribute to, impute to, attach to, assign to, allocate to, ascribe to.
4 *the proposals* **put to** *the Finance Committee on 9 December*: **submit**, present, tender, offer, proffer, advance, suggest, propose; set before, lay before.
5 *to put it bluntly, he gets on my nerves*: **express**, word, phrase, frame, formulate, render, convey, couch; state, say, utter, voice, speak, articulate, pronounce.
6 *legal experts put the cost of bringing the case to court at more than £8,000*: **estimate**, calculate, reckon, gauge, assess, evaluate, value, judge, measure, compute, establish, fix, set, guess; informal guesstimate.
□ **put something about** *the rumour had been deliberately put about by the authorities*: **spread (about/around)**, circulate, make public, make known, disseminate, broadcast, publicize, pass on, propagate, announce, give out, bandy about; literary bruit abroad.
□ **put about** *the ship put about*: **turn round**, change direction, come/go about, change course, alter course.
□ **put something across/over** *the party needs to put across its message more efficiently and effectively*: **communicate**, get across/over, convey, explain, make clear, make understood, express, spell out, clarify; bring something home to someone, get through to someone.
□ **put something aside 1** *we've got a little bit put aside in the bank*: **save**, put/lay by, put away, set/lay aside, put to one side, deposit, reserve, keep in reserve, keep, store, stockpile, hoard, stow away, cache; informal salt away, squirrel away, stash away. **2** *politicians put aside their differences in pursuit of a peaceful political solution*: **disregard**, set aside, ignore, pay no heed to, forget, discount, shrug off, bury, consign to oblivion.
□ **put someone away** informal **1** *they've got enough on him to put him away for life*: **put in prison**, put behind bars, imprison, jail, lock up/away, shut up/away, incarcerate, confine; informal cage; Brit. informal bang up, send down; N. Amer. informal send up, jug. **2** *you're trying to convince me I'm senile—you want me put away!* **commit**, certify, section, hospitalize, institutionalize.
□ **put something away 1** *I put away some money every week*: **save**, put aside, put/lay by, set/lay aside, put to one side, reserve, keep in reserve, deposit, keep, store, stockpile, hoard, stow away, cache; informal salt away, squirrel away, stash away. **2** *she doesn't seem to put anything away—there are clothes everywhere*: **replace**, put back, return to its place, tidy away, tidy up, clear away. **3** informal *did you see how much food she put away?* **eat**, consume, devour, down, gobble up, bolt, wolf down, guzzle; **drink**, gulp down; informal polish off, tuck away, demolish, get outside of, pack away, scoff (down), shovel down, pig out on, sink, knock back, get one's laughing gear round; Brit. informal **shift**, gollop, bevvy; N. Amer. informal scarf (down/up), snarf (down/up), inhale; rare ingurgitate, bib.
□ **put something back 1** *he put the books back carefully*: **replace**, return to its place, restore, put away, tidy away. **2** *they have put back the film's release date to September*: **postpone**, defer, delay, put off, adjourn, hold over, reschedule, table; N. Amer. put over, lay something on the table.
□ **put someone down 1** informal *he put me down in front of my own staff*: **criticize**, belittle, disparage, deprecate, denigrate, take down a peg or two, slight, humiliate, show up, mortify, shame, crush, squash, deflate; informal have a go at, cut down to size, settle someone's hash; N. Amer. informal make someone eat crow. **2** *I put him down as shy*: **consider to be**, judge to be, reckon to be, take to be; regard, categorize, mark down, have down, take for.
□ **put something down 1** *he put his ideas down on paper*: **write down**, put in writing, note down, make a note of, jot down, take down, set down, put in black and white, list, record, register, log, enter. **2** *security forces put down the rebellion*: **suppress**, put an end to, crush, quash, quell, overthrow, stamp out, squash, repress, check, subdue. **3** *the horse's condition deteriorated and he had to be put down*: **destroy**, put to sleep, put out of its misery, put to death, kill; N. Amer. euthanize. **4** *I can't imagine what came over me—put it down to the heat*: **attribute**, ascribe, set down, chalk up, impute, assign; blame on.
□ **put something forward** *recently, another explanation has been put forward* | *he put himself forward for the post*: **propose**, offer, advance, submit, present, tender, move, introduce, proffer, set forth, table; suggest, nominate, put up, name, recommend.
□ **put something in** *Dr Kailey put in a claim for compensation*: **submit**, present, make, file, enter, lodge.
□ **put in for** *some people put in for voluntary redundancy*: **apply for**, put in an application for, request, seek, ask for, try for.
□ **put someone off 1** *the smell put Lisa off*: **deter**, discourage, dishearten, demoralize, dissuade, daunt, unnerve, intimidate, scare off; offend, repel, disgust, revolt, repulse, sicken, nauseate; informal turn off. **2** *the players weren't put off by the disturbance*: **distract**, put someone off their stroke, disturb someone's concentration, cause someone to lose their concentration, divert someone's attention, sidetrack.
□ **put something off** *it's very easy to put off difficult decisions*: **postpone**, defer, delay, put back, adjourn, hold over, reschedule, shelve, table; N. Amer. put over, lay on the table, take a rain check on; informal put on ice, put on the back burner.
□ **put it on** *he laughed but Olivia thought he was putting it on*: **pretend**, put on an act, play-act, make believe, fake it, go through the motions.
□ **put something on 1** *she put on jeans and a black T-shirt*: **get dressed in**, dress in, don, clothe oneself in, pull on, climb into, fling on, throw on, pour

oneself into, slip into, change into, rig oneself out in; informal tog oneself up/out in, doll oneself up in. **2** *I put the landing light on*: **switch on**, turn on, flick on, power up; activate. **3** *the obvious solution was for the company to put on an additional train*: **provide**, lay on, supply, furnish, make available, run; informal sort out, fix up. **4** *the museum is putting on an exhibition of Monet's paintings*: **organize**, stage, mount, present, produce; perform. **5** *Adam put on an American accent*: **feign**, fake, sham, simulate, affect, assume. **6** *he put a fiver on Thetford Queen and it won*: **bet**, gamble, stake, wager, place, lay, risk, chance, hazard.

□ **put one over on** informal *they've been trying to put one over on us and they won't get away with it*: **deceive**, trick, hoodwink, mislead, lead astray, delude, fool, take in, dupe, outwit, steal a march on, throw off the scent, put on the wrong track; informal pull a fast one on, pull the wool over someone's eyes, take for a ride, con, bamboozle, lead up the garden path, slip something over on, sell a pup to; N. Amer. informal give someone a bum steer; Austral. informal pull a swifty on.

□ **put someone out 1** *Maria was put out by the slur on her character*: **annoy**, anger, irritate, offend, affront, displease, exasperate, infuriate, provoke, irk, vex, pique, nettle, gall, upset; informal rile, miff, peeve, aggravate, hack off; Brit. informal nark; vulgar slang piss off. **2** *I'm sure she wouldn't want to put you out, especially when you're feeling unwell*: **inconvenience**, trouble, bother, impose on, cause inconvenience to, create difficulties for, put someone to any trouble, disoblige; informal put someone on the spot; rare discommode, incommode.

□ **put something out 1** *firemen put out the blaze*: **extinguish**, quench, douse, stamp out, smother, beat out; blow out, snuff out; Scottish dout. **2** *he put out a press release explaining his decision*: **issue**, publish, release, bring out, broadcast, circulate, make known, make public, publicize, post.

□ **put paid to** *a disastrous fire put paid to their pioneering exploits*: **forestall**, thwart, frustrate, baulk, stand in the way of; scotch, derail, foil, smash, dash; stop, check, block, prevent, defeat, impede, obstruct, snooker, oppose, hinder, hamper; informal put the stopper on, put the kibosh on, do for, stymie; Brit. informal scupper, put the mockers on, nobble.

□ **put together** *the company has put together a bankruptcy plan*: **assemble**, compile, make up, collate, compose, marshal, organize, arrange, sort out, systematize, systemize, anthologize; gather, collect, accumulate, amass.

□ **put someone up 1** *we're going to put him up for a few days*: **give accommodation to**, provide with accommodation, accommodate, house, take in, give a roof to, give a bed to, lodge, quarter, billet. **2** *the SDLP are expected to put up a candidate*: **nominate**, propose, put forward, recommend.

□ **put something up 1** *the building was put up about 100 years ago*: **build**, construct, erect, raise, set up. **2** *she put up a poster advertising the concert*: **display**, pin up, stick up, hang up, nail up, post. **3** *they asked local architects to put up alternative schemes*: **propose**, put forward, present, submit, recommend, suggest, tender. **4** *unless the economy recovers, they will be forced to put up taxes*: **increase**, raise, lift; informal jack up, hike, bump up. **5** *union leaders put up 90% of the funding*: **provide**, supply, furnish, give, come up with, contribute, donate, pledge, pay, advance; informal fork out, cough up, shell out, dish out; N. Amer. informal ante up, pony up.

□ **put upon** informal *his eagerness to please ensured that he was put upon*: **take advantage of**, impose on, take for granted, exploit, use, misuse; informal walk all over.

□ **put someone up to** informal *Is this some kind of seduction scene? Did Shirley put you up to it?* **persuade to**, encourage to, urge to, spur on to, egg on to, incite to, goad to.

□ **put up with** *Harriet told him she was not prepared to put up with such behaviour*: **tolerate**, take, stand (for), accept, stomach, swallow, endure, bear, brook, support, submit to, take something lying down; informal stick, abide, lump it; Brit. informal wear, be doing with; archaic suffer.

putative adjective *the putative father of her child*. See **supposed** (sense 1).

put-down noun *he was still smarting from the put-down*: **snub**, **disparaging remark**, insult, slight, affront, rebuff, sneer, disparagement, humiliation, slap in the face, barb, jibe, criticism; informal dig, brush-off.

putrefy verb **decay**, rot, decompose, go bad, go off, perish, spoil, deteriorate, fester, moulder; gangrene, mortify; rare necrose, sphacelate.

putrescent adjective **decaying**, rotting, putrefying, decomposing, festering, going bad, going off; rare putrefactive, putrefacient.

putrid adjective *putrid meat | a putrid smell*: **decomposing**, decomposed, decaying, decayed, rotting, rotten, bad, off, putrefied, putrescent, rancid, mouldy, spoilt; foul, fetid, stinking, rank; rare putrefacient, putrefactive, olid.

puzzle verb **1** *Isabelle's apparent change of heart puzzled me*: **perplex**, **confuse**, bewilder, bemuse, baffle, mystify, confound, nonplus, throw, set someone thinking; informal flummox, discombobulate, faze, stump, beat, make someone scratch their head, fog; archaic wilder, gravel, maze, pose; rare obfuscate.
2 *she lay awake for some time, **puzzling over** the problem*: **think hard about**, give much thought to, rack one's brains about, mull over, muse over, ponder, brood about, contemplate, meditate on, consider, reflect on, deliberate on, chew over, turn over in one's mind, cogitate on, wonder about, ask oneself about; archaic pore on.
3 *Amanda was trying to **puzzle out** what her father had meant*: **work out**, understand, comprehend, think out, think through, sort out, reason out, solve, make sense of, get to the bottom of, make head or tail of, unravel, untangle, decipher, decode, find the key to, piece together; informal figure out, suss out, crack.

▸ **noun** *the meaning of the poem has always been a puzzle*: **enigma**, mystery, paradox, conundrum, poser, riddle, question, question mark, problem; informal stumper.

> *Choose the right word* **puzzle, perplex, mystify, baffle**
>
> These four verbs describe different degrees of puzzlement. All are commonly used as participial adjectives (*puzzling, puzzled*, etc.).
>
> **Puzzle** is used of relatively mild problems that typically do not cause serious worries or are likely to be resolved. It is a fairly neutral word (*one remark he made puzzled me | that was the most puzzling aspect of the whole affair*).
>
> **Perplex** is a more literary word than *puzzle* and can be used of more difficult or intractable problems (*Ruth was perplexed by her husband's moodiness | he was in a very perplexing situation*).
>
> **Mystify** describes even greater puzzlement, with the suggestion that the cause is likely to remain a mystery (*the disease that is mystifying doctors and spreading rapidly | the figure melted into thin air, leaving the foreman completely mystified*).
>
> **Baffle** is the most emphatic word, suggesting extreme puzzlement (*skincare products bearing baffling scientific claims*). It is also beloved of journalists (*police are baffled after a gang stole 150 T-shirts*).

puzzled adjective *Fiona looked puzzled*: **perplexed**, **confused**, bewildered, bemused, baffled, mystified, confounded, nonplussed, at a loss, at sea; informal flummoxed, discombobulated, stumped, fazed, clueless, without a clue; Canadian & Austral./NZ informal bushed; archaic wildered, gravelled, mazed.

puzzling adjective *his explanation was rather puzzling*. See **baffling**.

pygmy noun **1** offensive **very small person**, person of restricted growth; informal shrimp, pint-sized person; offensive midget, dwarf, runt; rare homunculus, manikin, Lilliputian, fingerling, thumbling.
2 *he saw his brother as a poetic giant among literary pygmies*: **insignificant person**, lightweight, mediocrity, nobody, gnat, insect, cipher; (**pygmies**) small fry; informal pipsqueak, squirt; Brit. informal nerk, johnny, squit, whippersnapper; Scottish informal nyaff; N. Amer. informal bozo, picayune, pisher, snip; archaic, informal dandiprat; N. Amer. vulgar slang pissant.
▹ANTONYMS giant.

pyromaniac noun **arsonist**, incendiary, firebomber; Brit. fire-raiser; informal firebug, pyro; N. Amer. informal torch.

P

quack noun **1** *the man is a quack selling fake medicines*: **swindler**, charlatan, mountebank, confidence trickster, fraud, fraudster, impostor, trickster, racketeer, hoaxer, sharper, rogue, villain, scoundrel; informal con man, shark, flimflammer, sharp; Brit. informal twister; N. Amer. informal grifter, bunco artist, chiseller; Austral. informal shicer, magsman, illywhacker; dated confidence man; rare defalcator.
2 *get the quack to examine you*: **doctor**, physician, medical practitioner, medical man/woman/person; Navy surgeon; informal doc, medic, medico; archaic leech, sawbones.
▶ adjective *a quack doctor | a quack cancer therapy*: **bogus**, false, fraudulent, unqualified, not genuine; spurious, sham, imitation, mock, fake, feigned, simulated, dummy, make-believe, so-called, forged, counterfeit, pseudo, pretended; informal phoney, pretend; Brit. informal cod.

quadrangle noun **courtyard**, quad, court, cloister, precinct, square, plaza, piazza, enclosure, close.

quaff verb *Suzy quaffed glass after glass of white wine | miners quaffed from decorated pottery beakers*: **drink**, swallow, gulp (down), guzzle, slurp, attack, down, drink up/down, force down, get down, finish off, polish off, drain, empty, imbibe, have, take, partake of, ingest, consume, sup, sip, lap; take alcohol, indulge, tipple, carouse, overdrink, overindulge, tope; informal booze, sink, kill, glug, swig, swill, slug, hit, knock back, dispose of, toss off, get one's laughing gear round; take a drop, wet one's whistle, hit the bottle, take to the bottle, crack a bottle, drink like a fish, get tanked up; Brit. informal get outside (of), shift, murder, neck, bevvy; N. Amer. informal bend one's elbow, chug, snarf (down), scarf (down); archaic bib, sot.

quagmire noun **1** *the rains arrived and the area was transformed into a red quagmire*: **swamp**, morass, bog, peat bog, marsh, mire, quag, marshland, fen, slough, quicksand; Scottish & N. English moss; Irish corcass; N. Amer. bayou, pocosin, moor; archaic marish, carr.
2 *the case has become a judicial quagmire*: **muddle**, mix-up, mess, predicament, unfortunate/difficult/awkward situation, mare's nest, quandary, entanglement, tangle, jumble, imbroglio; trouble, confusion, difficulty; corner, tight corner/spot; informal sticky situation, pickle, hole, stew, dilemma, fix, bind, jam, scrape, kettle of fish, how-do-you-do, hot/deep water; W. Indian comess.

quail verb *his supporters quailed at the size of the army ranged against them*: **cower**, cringe, waver, falter, get cold feet; flinch, shrink, recoil, start, shy (away), pull back, back away, draw back; shudder, shiver, tremble, shake, quake, blench, blanch.

quaint adjective **1** *narrow streets lead to a quaint bridge over the river*: **picturesque**, charming, sweet, attractive, pleasantly old-fashioned, old-fashioned, old-world, toytown; N. Amer. cunning; Brit. informal twee, arty-crafty; pseudo-archaic olde, olde worlde.
▷ANTONYMS modern; ugly.
2 *Polybius comments on the quaint customs of the Romans*: **unusual**, different, out of the ordinary, out of the way, unfamiliar, curious, eccentric, quirky, bizarre, zany, whimsical, fanciful, idiosyncratic, unconventional, outlandish, offbeat, off-centre; French outré.
▷ANTONYMS normal, ordinary.

quake verb **1** *the ground quaked as they walked on it*: **shake**, tremble, quiver, shiver, shudder, sway, rock, wobble, move, heave, convulse.
2 *we quaked every time we saw police or soldiers*: **tremble**, shake, shake with fear, shake like a leaf, shudder, shiver; blench, blanch, flinch, shrink, recoil, start, shy (away), pull back, back away, draw back, cower, cringe, waver, falter, get cold feet.

> *Choose the right word* **quake, shake, tremble, shiver, quiver**
>
> See **shake**.

qualification noun **1** *a professional teaching qualification | qualification for the pension was to be determined by a committee*: **certificate**, diploma, degree, licence, document, warrant; **eligibility**, acceptability, adequacy, suitableness, suitability, preparedness, fitness; proficiency, skill, ability, quality, skilfulness, adeptness, capability, capacity, aptitude.
2 *I have difficulty in accepting that submission without some qualification*: **modification**, limitation, restriction, reservation, stipulation, allowance, adaptation, alteration, adjustment, amendment, revision, refinement, moderation, tempering, softening, lessening, reduction, mitigation; condition, proviso, provision, caveat, rider.

qualified adjective **1** *he was a fully qualified engineer*: **certified**, certificated, chartered, licensed, professional; **trained**, fit, equipped, prepared, competent, knowledgeable, accomplished, proficient, skilled, skilful, adept, practised, experienced, expert, seasoned, capable, able.
2 *the report received qualified approval from the colleges*: **limited**, conditional, restricted, bounded, contingent, circumscribed, reserved, guarded, cautious, hesitant, tentative, equivocal; modified, adapted, amended, adjusted, moderated, refined, tempered, lessened, reduced.

qualify verb **1** *you may qualify for free prescriptions*: **be eligible**, meet the requirements; be entitled to, be allowed, be permitted.
2 *to qualify as tourists they are required to carry at least the equivalent of $1500 in spending money*: **count**, be counted, be considered, be designated, be characterizable, be eligible; meet the requirements of.
3 *she qualified as a doctor*: **gain qualifications**, gain certification, be certified, be licensed, be authorized; pass, graduate, make the grade, succeed, get through, come through with flying colours, pass muster.
4 *the students had taken a course which qualified them to teach children*: **authorize**, allow, permit, license, empower, fit, equip, prepare, arm, make ready, train, upskill, educate, coach, teach.
▷ANTONYMS disqualify.
5 *the authors later qualified their findings*: **modify**, limit, make conditional, restrict, add reservations to, add to, make additions to, add a rider to; moderate, temper, soften, tone down, modulate, mitigate, reduce, lessen, decrease, diminish, lower, abate.

quality noun **1** *the system will compress digital TV signals while retaining most of the original quality | a poor quality of life*: **standard**, grade, class, classification, calibre, status, condition, character, nature, constitution, make-up, form, rank, worth, value, level; sort, type, kind, variety.
2 *work of such quality remains a rarity*: **excellence**, superiority, merit, worth, value, virtue, calibre, eminence, pre-eminence, supremacy, transcendence, distinction, refinement, incomparability, account; talent, skill, skilfulness, virtuosity, expertise, brilliance, craftsmanship, flair, finish, mastery.
3 *they have many good qualities*: **feature**, trait, attribute, characteristic, point, aspect, facet, side, streak, property, peculiarity, idiosyncrasy, quirk; mark, badge, stamp, hallmark, trademark.

qualm noun **1** *I have no qualms about going to Japan*: **misgiving**, doubt, reservation, second thought, worry, concern, anxiety; (**qualms**) hesitation, hesitance, hesitancy, demur, reluctance, disinclination, apprehension, trepidation, disquiet, disquietude, unease, uneasiness.
▷ANTONYMS confidence.
2 *shameless politicians have no qualms about their misdeeds*: **scruple**, pang of conscience, twinge of conscience/remorse; (**qualms**) compunction, remorse.

quandary noun *George was in a quandary*: **dilemma**, plight, predicament, state of uncertainty, state of perplexity, unfortunate situation, difficult situation, awkward situation; trouble, muddle, mix-up, mare's nest, mess, confusion, difficulty, impasse, stalemate; Brit. cleft stick; informal sticky situation, pickle, hole, stew, fix, bind, jam.

quantity noun **1** *the quantity of food collected | the quantity of animals killed was quite dramatic*: **amount**, **number**, total, aggregate, sum, quota, group, size, mass, weight, volume, bulk, load, consignment, expanse, extent, length, area; quantum, proportion, portion, part; dose, dosage.
2 *police divers recovered a quantity of ammunition | quantities of empty drinks cans have been found in the building*: **an amount**, **a number**, a good number/few, a lot, a large amount, (a) good/great deal; quite a number, scores, many, considerable amounts, plenty; several, numerous, countless, innumerable, ample, copious, abundant, plentiful, considerable, substantial; informal a pile, piles, oodles, tons, lots, loads, heaps, masses, stacks, scads, bags, more ... than one can shake a stick at; Brit. informal lashings, a shedload, shedloads; N. Amer. informal gobs; vulgar slang a shitload.

quarrel noun *there was a quarrel about how much my father was paid*: **argument**, row, fight, disagreement, difference of opinion, dissension, falling-out; **dispute**, disputation, contention, squabble, contretemps, clash, altercation, exchange, brawl, tussle, disturbance, conflict, affray, brouhaha, commotion, uproar, tumult, war of words, shouting match, fracas, feud; wrangle, tangle, misunderstanding; Irish, N. Amer., & Austral. donnybrook; informal tiff, set-to, shindig, shindy, stand-up, run-in, spat, scrap, dust-up, ruction; Brit. informal barney, bunfight, ding-dong, bust-up, ruck, slanging match; Scottish informal rammy; N. Amer. informal hassle; archaic broil, miff; French archaic tracasserie(s).
▷ANTONYMS reconciliation, agreement.
▶verb *I should be sorry to quarrel over it*: **argue**, have a row/fight, row, fight, disagree, fail to agree, differ, be at odds, have a misunderstanding, be at variance, fall out; dispute, bicker, squabble, brawl, chop logic; wrangle, spar, bandy words, cross swords, lock horns, be at each other's throats, be at loggerheads; informal scrap, argufy, spat; archaic altercate.
□ **quarrel with** *it is difficult to quarrel with the verdict*: **find fault with**, fault, criticize, argue with/against, object to, be hostile to, censure, condemn, be against, be anti, oppose, be in opposition to, take exception to, attack, take issue with, find lacking, pick holes in, impugn, contradict, dispute, rebut, complain about, cavil at, carp at; informal knock; formal gainsay; rare controvert.
▷ANTONYMS agree with.

Choose the right word **quarrel, argue, wrangle, dispute, bicker**

Quarrel is used of people having an angry argument (*he married her for her money, so now they're always quarrelling*). One may also dispassionately *quarrel with* something in the sense of disagreeing with or objecting to it (*there was nothing in this document with which he could quarrel*).

Arguing involves two people staunchly, possibly also acrimoniously, defending two different and incompatible points of view (*he and Martin used to argue for hours about the paranormal*).

Wrangle suggests a long, complex, and sometimes intense debate or argument, often a legal or political one (*the party is facing internal wrangling and a cash crisis | after considerable wrangling a compromise was reached*).

People who **dispute** are expected to show more reasoned argument than if they are merely quarrelling. *Dispute* is mainly used of denying or arguing against a specified view, and the matter of contention is typically a direct object (*people who dispute the official interpretation of their rights*).

Bicker represents an argument as childish, on account of either the logic employed or the triviality of the issue disputed (*those who had fought together for the overthrow of Charles I now bickered amongst themselves | there was no point in bickering over trifles*).

quarrelsome adjective *he was pleased to be leaving his quarrelsome neighbours behind*: **argumentative**, disputatious, disputative, contentious, confrontational, captious, factious, cavilling, pugnacious, combative, ready for a fight, defiant, hostile, antagonistic, bellicose, belligerent, militant, warring, fighting, battling; threatening, litigious; irascible, cantankerous, irritable, petulant, truculent, fiery, quick-tempered, hot-tempered, ill-tempered, bad-tempered, choleric; bickering, wrangling; Brit. informal stroppy; N. Amer. informal scrappy.
▷ANTONYMS peaceable.

quarry noun *he had no intention of allowing his quarry to elude him*: **prey**, victim; the hunted; prize, object, goal, target, kill; wild fowl, game, big game.

quarter noun **1** *the Latin quarter of Paris*: **district**, area, region, part, side, neighbourhood, precinct, locality, sector, section, zone, tract, belt; ghetto, community, colony; pocket, enclave, territory, province, parish, ward.
2 *help came from an unexpected quarter*: **source**, direction, place, point, spot, location; person.
3 (**quarters**) *rooms that had once been servants' quarters*: **accommodation**, lodgings, rooms, chambers, place of residence, home, shelter; French pied-à-terre; Brit. informal digs; informal, dated pad, billet; formal abode, dwelling, dwelling place, residence, domicile, habitation.
4 *the riot squads gave no quarter, using their batons liberally*: **mercy**, leniency, clemency, lenity, compassion, pity, charity, forbearance, indulgence, kindness, sympathy, tolerance.
▶verb **1** *they were quartered in a sumptuous villa*: **accommodate**, house, board, lodge, give accommodation to, provide with accommodation, put up, take in, give a bed to, install, give a roof to, put a roof over someone's head, shelter; informal, dated billet.
2 *I started to quarter the streets, eyes peeled for the car*: **patrol**, range over, tour, reconnoitre, traverse, survey, inspect, spy out, scout; Brit. informal recce.

quash verb **1** *the Court of Appeal may quash the sentence*: **cancel**, reverse, rescind, repeal, revoke, retract, countermand, withdraw, take back, rule against, disallow, overturn, override, overrule, veto, set aside, overthrow, repudiate, annul, nullify, declare null and void, invalidate, render invalid, negate, void, abrogate; Law vacate; archaic recall.
▷ANTONYMS validate.
2 *we want to quash these horrible suggestions*: **put an end to**, stamp out, put a stop to, end, finish, get rid of, crush, put down, check, crack down on, curb, nip in the bud, thwart, frustrate, squash, quell, subdue, suppress, repress, quench, extinguish, stifle, abolish, terminate; beat, overcome, defeat, rout, destroy, demolish, annihilate, wipe out; informal squelch, put the kibosh on, clobber; rare extirpate.
▷ANTONYMS bring about, prompt.

quasi- combining form **1** *she had problems with drugs, alcohol, and a quasi-religious cult*: **supposedly**, seemingly, apparently, allegedly, reportedly, professedly, ostensibly, on the face of it, to all appearances, on the surface, to all intents and purposes, outwardly, superficially, purportedly, nominally, by one's/its own account, on paper; pseudo-; rare pretendedly, ostensively.
2 *diplomacy was then a quasi-profession, in which family connections counted for much*: **supposed**, seeming, apparent, alleged, reported, ostensible, purported, nominal, so-called, would-be, pseudo-; bogus, sham, phoney, imitation, artificial, mock, ersatz, fake, forged, feigned, pretended, simulated, false, spurious, counterfeit, fraudulent, deceptive; informal pretend, put-on; Brit. informal cod; rare ostensive.
3 *a quasi-autonomous non-governmental organization*: **partly**, partially, in part, part, to a certain extent/degree, to a limited extent/degree, to some extent/degree, half, in some measure, relatively, comparatively, moderately, (up) to a point, a little, somewhat; **almost**, nearly, very nearly, just about, all but, not totally, not wholly, not entirely, not fully, incompletely.

quaver verb *his voice quavered with emotion*: **tremble**, quiver, shake, flutter, vibrate, pulsate, oscillate, fluctuate, waver, ripple, falter, trill, twitter, warble.

quay noun **dock**, wharf, pier, harbour, berth, jetty, landing, landing stage, landing place, slipway, marina, waterfront, sea wall, embankment.

queasy adjective *he still felt queasy and he was grateful for the fresh air*: **nauseous**, nauseated, bilious, sick; seasick, carsick, trainsick, airsick, travel-sick, suffering from motion sickness, suffering from altitude sickness; ill, unwell, poorly, bad, out of sorts, dizzy, peaky, liverish, green about the gills; Brit. off, off colour; N. Amer. sick to one's stomach; informal funny, peculiar, rough, lousy, rotten, awful, terrible, dreadful, crummy; Austral./NZ informal crook; rare peakish.

queen noun **1** *the Queen waved and smiled*: **monarch**, sovereign, head of state, ruler, Crown, Her Majesty; king's consort, queen consort, queen mother.
2 informal *the queen of soul music*: **doyenne**, star, leading light, celebrity, big name, superstar, top dog, queen bee, mistress, prima donna, idol, heroine, favourite, darling; goddess, belle, pin-up.
3 See **homosexual**.

queer adjective **1** *it seemed queer to see the windows all dark*: **odd**, strange, unusual, funny, peculiar, curious, bizarre, weird, outlandish, eccentric, unconventional, unorthodox, uncanny, unexpected, unfamiliar, abnormal, anomalous, atypical, untypical, different, out of the ordinary, out of the way, extraordinary, remarkable, puzzling, mystifying, mysterious, perplexing, baffling, unaccountable, incongruous, uncommon, irregular, outré, offbeat, singular, deviant, aberrant, freak, freakish; suspicious, dubious, questionable; eerie, unnatural; Scottish unco; informal fishy, creepy, spooky, freaky; Brit. informal rum; N. Amer. informal off the wall; bizarro.
▷ANTONYMS ordinary, conventional, normal.

q

2 *there's something queer going on up there*: **suspicious**, suspect, irregular, questionable, dubious, doubtful, funny, mysterious, murky, dark, criminal, dishonest, corrupt, nefarious, crafty, deceitful, shifty, underhand, dishonourable, unscrupulous, unprincipled, fraudulent, illegal, unlawful; informal fishy, shady, bent.
3 Brit. informal, dated *you just feel queer because you're packed full of drugs*: **ill**, unwell, poorly, bad, out of sorts, indisposed, not oneself, sick, queasy, nauseous, nauseated, peaky, liverish, green about the gills, run down, washed out, faint, dizzy, giddy; Brit. off, off colour; informal under the weather, below par, not up to par, funny, peculiar, rough, lousy, rotten, awful, terrible, dreadful; Brit. informal grotty, ropy; Scottish informal wabbit, peely-wally; Austral./NZ informal crook; dated seedy; rare peaked, peakish.
▷ANTONYMS well.
4 See **homosexual**.
□ **queer fish** informal *they have invariably chosen the queer fish in preference to the more or less recognisable member of the human race*: **eccentric**, oddity, odd fellow, unorthodox person, character, individualist, individual, free spirit, misfit; informal oddball, weirdo, weirdie, freak, nut, nutter, nutcase, case, head case, crank, crackpot, loony, loon; Brit. informal one-off, odd bod; N. Amer. informal wacko, wack, screwball, kook; Austral./NZ informal dingbat.
□ **in queer street** Brit. informal *if it wasn't for my pension I'd be in queer street*: **impoverished**, poor, penniless, penurious, in penury, indigent, insolvent, impecunious, moneyless, hard up, poverty-stricken, needy, in need, in want, destitute; poor as a church mouse, without a sou, in straitened circumstances, on one's beam ends, unable to make ends meet; Brit. on the breadline, without a penny (to one's name); informal broke, flat broke, strapped for cash, cleaned out, strapped, on one's uppers, without two pennies/brass farthings to rub together; Brit. informal skint, boracic, stony broke; N. Amer. informal stone broke; rare pauperized, beggared.
▶ **noun** See **homosexual**.
▶ **verb** *trying to crash the party would probably queer the whole deal*: **spoil**, damage, impair, harm, be detrimental to, mar, wreck, destroy, devastate, smash, shatter, scupper, scotch, disrupt, undo, thwart, hinder, foil, ruin, blight, injure, cripple, hurt, jeopardize, endanger, imperil, threaten, put at risk, undermine, prejudice, be prejudicial to, be disadvantageous to, play havoc with, be deleterious to, compromise; informal botch, blow, put the kibosh on.

quell **verb 1** *troops were called in to quell the unrest*: **put an end to**, stamp out, put a stop to, end, finish, get rid of, crush, put down, check, crack down on, curb, nip in the bud, thwart, frustrate, squash, quash, subdue, suppress, repress, quench, extinguish, stifle, abolish, terminate, beat, overcome, defeat, rout, destroy, demolish, annihilate, wipe out, extirpate; informal squelch, put the kibosh on, clobber.
▷ANTONYMS bring about, prompt.
2 *he managed to quell his initial misgivings*: **calm**, soothe, pacify, settle, quieten, quiet, put at rest, lull, silence, put behind one, rise above, allay, appease, stay, assuage, abate, deaden, dull, tranquillize, mitigate, moderate, palliate.
▷ANTONYMS succumb to.

quench **verb 1** *they quenched their thirst with local wine and spring water | his answer had not quenched my curiosity at all*: **satisfy**, slake, sate, satiate, gratify, relieve, assuage, take the edge off, appease, meet, fulfil, indulge; **lessen**, deaden, decrease, lower, reduce, diminish, curb, check, still, damp; **suppress**, extinguish, smother, stifle, overcome.
2 *the flames were quickly quenched with buckets of water*: **extinguish**, put out, snuff out, smother, douse, dampen down.

q

querulous **adjective** *there'll be no rest for me with a querulous adolescent*: **petulant**, complaining, pettish, touchy, testy, tetchy, waspish, prickly, crusty, peppery, fractious, fretful, irritable, cross, crabbed, crabby, crotchety, cantankerous, curmudgeonly, disagreeable, miserable, morose, on edge, edgy, impatient, bitter, moody, in a bad mood, grumpy, huffy, scratchy, out of sorts, out of temper, ill-tempered, bad-tempered, ill-natured, ill-humoured, sullen, surly, sulky, sour, churlish, bilious, liverish, dyspeptic, splenetic, choleric; informal snappish, snappy, chippy, grouchy, cranky, whingeing, whingy; Brit. informal narky, ratty, eggy, like a bear with a sore head; N. Amer. informal sorehead, soreheaded, peckish; Austral./NZ informal snaky; informal, dated miffy.

query **noun 1** *we are happy to answer any queries about our products*: **question**, enquiry; interrogation, examination; Brit. informal quiz, quizzing.
2 *there was a query as to who actually owned the hotel*: **doubt**, uncertainty, question, question mark, reservation, suspicion; scepticism.
▶ **verb 1** *'Why do they all wear yellow?' queried Isabel*: **ask**, enquire, question; Brit. informal quiz.
2 *folk may query the authenticity of this*: **question**, call in/into question, doubt, raise/entertain doubts about, throw doubt on, have/harbour/express suspicions about, suspect, feel uneasy about, have/harbour/express reservations about, challenge, dispute, cast aspersions on, object to, raise objections to.

quest **noun 1** *nothing will stop their quest for her killer*: **search**, hunt, pursuit; pursuance of, investigation into.
2 *Sir Galahad was nearing the end of his quest*: **expedition**, adventure, journey, voyage, trek, travels, odyssey, wandering, journeying, exploration, venture, search, undertaking; crusade, mission, pilgrimage, errand; rare peregrination.
□ **in quest of** *I telephoned Downing Street in quest of the Prime Minister*: **searching for**, after, seeking, looking for, on the lookout for, in search of, in pursuit of, chasing after.
▶ **verb** literary *his eyes quested to left and right*: **search**, seek, look, hunt, pursue, investigate, explore, probe, inspect.

question **noun 1** *you didn't answer my question*: **enquiry**, query; interrogation, examination; Brit. informal quiz, quizzing.
▷ANTONYMS answer, response.
2 *there is no question that he is ill*: **doubt**, dispute, argument, debate, uncertainty, dubiousness, controversy, reservation; rare dubiety.
▷ANTONYMS certainty.
3 *it is a question of trust | he wrote essays on the principal political questions of the day*: **issue**, matter, business, problem, point at issue, point, concern, subject, topic, theme, item, case, proposal, proposition, debate, argument, dispute, bone of contention, controversy.
□ **beyond question 1** *her loyalty is really beyond question*: **undoubted**, beyond doubt, without doubt, certain, indubitable, indisputable, irrefutable, incontestable, incontrovertible, unquestionable, undeniable, unmistakable, clear, patent, manifest, obvious, palpable.
▷ANTONYMS in doubt. **2** *the results demonstrated beyond question that gas accumulated in some quantity*: **indisputably**, irrefutably, incontestably, incontrovertibly, unquestionably, undeniably, undoubtedly, beyond doubt, without doubt, certainly, indubitably, unmistakably, clearly, patently, manifestly, obviously, palpably.
□ **in question** *the matter in question*: **at issue**, being discussed, under discussion, under consideration, on the agenda, for debate, to be discussed, to be decided.
□ **out of the question** *going back to the railway station was out of the question*: **impossible**, beyond the bounds of possibility, impracticable, unattainable, unachievable, not feasible, not worth considering, unworkable, unobtainable, inconceivable, unthinkable, unimaginable, unrealizable, unsuitable; beyond one, hopeless, absurd, ridiculous, preposterous, outrageous, ludicrous, beyond the realm of reason; informal not on.
▶ **verb 1** *the magistrate may question the suspect and other witnesses*: **interrogate**, ask questions of, put questions to, cross-examine, cross-question, quiz, probe, canvass, catechize, interview, debrief, sound out, examine, give the third degree to; informal grill, pump.
2 *she should question his motives*: **query**, call in/into question, doubt, raise/entertain doubts about, throw doubt on, have/harbour/express suspicions about, suspect, feel uneasy about, have/harbour/express reservations about, challenge, dispute, cast aspersions on, object to, raise objections to.

> *Word links* **question**
>
> **interrogative** relating to questions

questionable **adjective 1** *it is questionable whether such an attack could be effective | he indulges in jokes of questionable taste*: **controversial**, contentious, open to question, open to doubt, in doubt, doubtful, dubious, uncertain, unsure, debatable, in dispute, in question, arguable, problematic, problematical; unverified, unprovable, unresolved, unsettled, undecided, equivocal, unconvincing, implausible, improbable, not definite, unclear, not obvious, apocryphal, spurious, borderline, marginal, moot; informal iffy; Brit. informal dodgy.
▷ANTONYMS certain, indisputable.
2 *some of his questionable financial dealings have been investigated*: **suspicious**, suspect, under suspicion, irregular, dubious, doubtful, odd, queer, strange, not quite right, mysterious, murky, dark, shifty, unsavoury, disreputable, potentially dishonest, potentially illegal; informal funny, fishy, shady, iffy; Brit. informal dodgy.

questionnaire **noun question sheet**, set of questions, survey form, form, test, exam, examination, quiz, opinion poll; technical questionary, personality inventory.

queue **noun 1** *there was a queue of people waiting for the bus*: **line**, row, column, file, chain, string, stream; procession, train, succession, progression, cavalcade, sequence, series; waiting list, reserve list; N. Amer. breadline, wait list, backup, waiting line; Brit. informal crocodile.
2 *he was sitting in a taxi, stuck in a queue along Knightsbridge*: **traffic jam**, jam, tailback, line, stream, gridlock; informal snarl-up, traffic snarl.
▶ **verb** *we queued for ice creams*: **line up**, stand in a queue, form a queue, queue up, wait in line, form a line, form lines, get into rows/columns, fall in, file, walk/move in line; Brit. informal form a crocodile.

quibble **noun 1** *apart from that quibble, it was fine*: **minor criticism**, trivial objection, trivial complaint, adverse comment, protest, query, argument, exception, moan, grumble, grouse, cavil; informal niggle, gripe, beef, grouch, nit-picking; archaic pettifogging.
2 *I ignored his ridiculous quibbles about interest rates*: **evasion**, dodge; (**quibbles**) avoidance, equivocation, prevarication, hedging, fudging.
▶ **verb 1** *no one would* **quibble with** *the subtitle*: **find fault with**, raise trivial

objections to, complain about, object to, cavil at, carp about; split hairs, chop logic; criticize, query, fault, pick, holes in; informal nit-pick; archaic pettifog.
2 *he's always quibbling, so it is difficult to get a straight answer out of him*: **be evasive**, equivocate, avoid the issue, prevaricate, hedge, fudge, be ambiguous; informal beat about the bush.

quick adjective **1** *John was generally a quick worker*: **fast**, swift, rapid, speedy, high-speed, expeditious; brisk, lively, sprightly, nimble, prompt; lightning, meteoric, overnight, whirlwind, fast-track, whistle-stop, breakneck, smart; informal nippy, zippy; Brit. informal cracking; literary fleet; rare tantivy, alacritous, volant.
▷ANTONYMS slow.
2 *she took a quick look behind her*: **hasty**, hurried, cursory, perfunctory, superficial, desultory, incidental, summary, glancing; **brief**, short, fleeting, passing, transient, transitory, short-lived, flying, lightning, momentary, temporary.
▷ANTONYMS long, careful.
3 *there was no quick end to the recession*: **sudden**, instantaneous, immediate, instant, abrupt, sharp, precipitate, breakneck, headlong.
4 *she isn't as quick as the others, but she works hard*: **intelligent**, bright, clever, gifted, able, brilliant, astute, quick-witted, sharp-witted, ready, quick off the mark; observant, alert, sharp, wide awake, receptive, perceptive; informal brainy, smart, on the ball, on one's toes, quick on the uptake.
▷ANTONYMS stupid.

quicken verb **1** *his pulse quickened | she unconsciously quickened her pace*: **speed up**, accelerate, step up, hasten, hurry, hurry up; informal gee up.
▷ANTONYMS slow.
2 *the film quickened his interest in wild life*: **stimulate**, excite, stir up, arouse, rouse, waken, animate, activate, incite, galvanize, instigate, whet, inspire, kindle, fan, refresh, strengthen, invigorate, reanimate, reactivate, revive, revitalize, resuscitate, revivify; titillate, tempt.
▷ANTONYMS dull.

quickly adverb **1** *he began to walk quickly*: **fast**, swiftly, rapidly, speedily, at high speed, with all speed, at (full) speed, at the speed of light, at full tilt, as fast as one's legs can carry one, at a gallop, briskly, at the double, post-haste, with all possible haste, like a whirlwind, like an arrow from a bow, at breakneck speed, expeditiously, madly, hotfoot, with dispatch; informal double quick, in double quick time, p.d.q. (pretty damn quick), nippily, like (greased) lightning, hell for leather, at warp speed, like mad, like crazy, like blazes, like the wind, like a bomb, like nobody's business, like a scalded cat, like the deuce, a mile a minute, like a bat out of hell, like a bullet out of a gun; Brit. informal like the clappers, at a rate of knots, like billy-o; N. Amer. informal lickety-split; literary apace.
▷ANTONYMS slowly.
2 *sensing her discomfort, he quickly went on | the apartments were sold quite quickly*: **immediately**, directly, at once, now, straight away, right away, instantly, forthwith, as soon as possible, shortly, without delay, without further/more ado, instantaneously, expeditiously, suddenly, abruptly; soon, soon after, promptly, early; N. Amer. momentarily; informal like a shot, a.s.a.p. (as soon as possible), pronto, before you can say Jack Robinson, before the ink is dry on the page, before you can say knife, straight off; archaic straight, instanter.
3 *he calmed the animal and quickly inspected it*: **briefly**, fleetingly, briskly; **hastily**, in haste, precipitately, hurriedly, in a hurry, cursorily, perfunctorily, superficially, desultorily.

quick-tempered adjective *they tend to be impulsive and quick-tempered*: **irritable**, irascible, hot-tempered, short-tempered, fiery, touchy, volatile; peevish, cross, crabbed, crabby, crotchety, cantankerous, impatient, grumpy, huffy, brusque, ill-tempered, bad-tempered, ill-natured, ill-humoured, testy, tetchy, snarling, waspish, prickly, crusty, peppery, bilious, liverish, dyspeptic, splenetic, choleric; informal snappish, snappy, chippy, cranky, grouchy, on a short fuse; Brit. informal narky, ratty, eggy, like a bear with a sore head; N. Amer. informal peckish, soreheaded; Austral./NZ informal snaky; informal, dated miffy.
▷ANTONYMS placid, calm.

quick-witted adjective **alert**, astute, perceptive, quick, quick-thinking, sharp-witted, sharp, shrewd, penetrating, discerning, perspicacious; wide awake, ready, quick off the mark, observant; intelligent, bright, clever, gifted, able, brainy, brilliant; informal smart, on the ball, on one's toes, quick on the uptake.
▷ANTONYMS stupid, slow.

quid pro quo noun *a congressman's support for the president on a particular issue may not represent a straightforward quid pro quo*: **exchange**, trade, trade-off, swap, switch, barter, substitute, substitution, reciprocity, reciprocation, return, payment, remuneration, amends, compensation, indemnity, recompense, restitution, reparation, satisfaction; rare requital.

quiescent adjective *the volcano is in a quiescent state*: **inactive**, inert, latent, fallow, passive, idle, at rest, inoperative, deactivated, in abeyance, quiet; still, motionless, immobile, stagnant, dormant, asleep, slumbering, sluggish, lethargic, torpid.
▷ANTONYMS active.

quiet adjective **1** *the whole pub went quiet*: **silent**, still, hushed, noiseless, soundless; mute, dumb, speechless, voiceless, unspeaking.
2 *she spoke in a quiet voice*: **soft**, low, lowered, muted, muffled, faint, indistinct, inaudible, dull; hushed, whispered, stifled, suppressed.
▷ANTONYMS loud.
3 *a quiet village | he liked the quiet life*: **peaceful**, sleepy, tranquil, calm, still, relaxing, soothing, pleasant, restful, undisturbed, free from disturbance, free from interruption, free from interference, untroubled; unfrequented, private, secluded, sequestered, retired, isolated, out of the way, off the beaten track, solitary.
▷ANTONYMS busy.
4 *I thought we'd better have a quiet word together before the kids come*: **private**, confidential, secret, discreet, unofficial, off the record, between ourselves, between you and me (and the bedpost/gatepost/doorpost/wall).
▷ANTONYMS public.
5 *he's a very quiet, private person*: **calm**, equable, serene, composed, {cool, calm, and collected}, placid, untroubled, peaceful, peaceable, tranquil, gentle, mild, phlegmatic, imperturbable, unexcitable; moderate, reserved, uncommunicative, unresponsive, taciturn, secretive, withdrawn, silent; meek, mousy, retiring, reticent, unforthcoming, shy, self-effacing, diffident, modest, temperate, restrained, unassuming, unassertive, unemotional; informal unflappable; rare equanimous.
6 *I've always preferred quiet colours*: **unobtrusive**, unostentatious, unpretentious, restrained, reserved; soft, pale, pastel, muted, understated, subdued, subtle, low-key, conservative, sober, plain, ordinary.
▷ANTONYMS loud.
7 *you can't keep a mass murder quiet for long*: **secret**, top secret, confidential, strictly confidential, classified, unrevealed, undisclosed, unpublished, untold, unknown, uncommunicated, under wraps, unofficial, off the record, not for publication/circulation, not to be made public, not to be disclosed, clandestine, surreptitious; Latin sub rosa; informal hush-hush, mum.
▷ANTONYMS public.
8 *business is quiet today*: **slow**, slow-moving, stagnant, slack, sluggish, inactive, not busy, idle.
▶ **noun** *after London, the quiet of the country was almost tangible*: **peacefulness**, peace and quiet, peace, restfulness, calm, calmness, tranquillity, serenity; silence, quietness, stillness, still, quietude, hush, noiselessness, soundlessness; privacy, privateness, seclusion, solitude, isolation, retirement, lack of disturbance/interruption, freedom from interference.
□ **on the quiet** *doing good works on the quiet for impoverished congregations*: **in secret**, secretly, furtively, stealthily, sneakily, slyly, surreptitiously, covertly, clandestinely, on the sly, on the side, behind someone's back, under cover; under the counter; informal on the q.t..
▷ANTONYMS openly.

quieten verb **1** *the teacher had to stop to quieten the children down*: **silence**, make quieter, hush, shush, quiet, still; informal shut up.
2 *her travelling companions had quietened*: **fall silent**, stop talking, break off, become quiet, quieten down, grow silent, shush, hold one's tongue; informal shut up, clam up, shut it, pipe down, shut one's mouth/face/trap, put a sock in it, button one's lip, button it, cut the cackle; Brit. informal wrap up; N. Amer. informal save it.
3 *he tried using lithium salts to quieten manic patients*: **calm**, calm down, pacify, soothe, subdue, tranquillize, cool, content, silence, relax, comfort, compose.
4 *Dexter yearned for a cigarette and could not quieten the urge*: **allay**, appease, assuage, mollify, palliate, ease, lessen, reduce, abate, mitigate, moderate, stifle, dull, deaden, lull, temper, subjugate, repress, quell, quash, overcome, rise above.

quietly adverb **1** *she quietly absorbed the lovely surroundings*: **silently**, in silence, noiselessly, soundlessly, inaudibly; mutely, dumbly, tacitly; literary stilly.
2 *he spoke quietly so as not to disturb anyone*: **softly**, making little noise, in a low voice, in low/hushed/muted/subdued tones, in a whisper/murmur/mumble, murmuringly, under one's breath, in an undertone, sotto voce, gently, faintly, weakly, feebly.
▷ANTONYMS loudly, audibly.
3 *some bonds were sold quietly to Club members*: **discreetly**, privately, confidentially, secretly, unofficially, off the record, between ourselves, between you and me (and the bedpost/gatepost/doorpost/wall).
▷ANTONYMS publicly.
4 *Mrs Wilson dressed quietly in grey or black*: **unobtrusively**, unostentatiously, unpretentiously, with restraint, with reserve, conservatively, soberly, modestly, demurely, plainly.
▷ANTONYMS loudly.
5 *she is quietly confident*: **calmly**, patiently, placidly, serenely, undemonstratively, unemotionally, unassumingly.

quietness noun *she was glad of the quietness of her surroundings*: **peacefulness**, peace and quiet, peace, restfulness, calm, calmness, tranquillity, serenity; silence, stillness, still, quiet, quietude, hush, noiselessness, soundlessness.

quilt noun **duvet**, continental quilt, counterpane, bedspread, cover, coverlet, Durham quilt; Brit. eiderdown; Scottish, trademark downie; French plumeau; N. Amer. comforter, puff; Austral./NZ trademark Doona; Indian rezai; Turkish yorgan; archaic pourpoint.

quintessence noun **1** *Wemmick's cottage is the quintessence of the Victorian home*: **perfect example**, exemplar, prototype, stereotype, picture, epitome, embodiment, personification, paragon, ideal; best, cream, elite, flower, jewel, gem, pick, prime, last word, acme of perfection; French crème de la crème, beau idéal.
2 *they wanted to know how our brains function and thereby discover the quintessence of intelligence*: **essence**, soul, spirit, ethos, nature, core, heart, centre, crux, nub, nucleus, kernel, marrow, pith, substance, sum and substance; informal nitty-gritty; Philosophy quiddity, esse.

quintessential adjective *skiing was the quintessential 1980s yuppie holiday*: **typical**, prototypical, stereotypical, archetypal, classic, model, essential, standard, stock, representative, true to type, conventional; ideal, consummate, exemplary, best, ultimate, supreme, absolute.

quip noun *the quip failed to provoke a smile*: **joke**, witty remark, witticism, jest, pun, sally, pleasantry, epigram, aphorism; (**quips**) repartee, banter; French bon mot; informal one-liner, gag, crack, wisecrack, funny.
▸ verb *'There's no accounting for taste,' I quipped*: **joke**, jest, pun, sally, banter; informal gag, wisecrack.

quirk noun **1** *he likes working with people he knows because they know his quirks*: **idiosyncrasy**, peculiarity, oddity, eccentricity, foible, whim, whimsy, notion, conceit, vagary, caprice, fancy, kink, crotchet, mannerism, habit, characteristic, trait, feature, obsession, fad; French idée fixe; informal hang-up, thing; rare singularity.
2 *by a quirk of history they were related to seven American presidents*: **chance**, **fluke**, freak, anomaly, unusual occurrence, turn, peculiar turn of events, twist, twist of fate.

quirky adjective *he had this quirky sense of humour*: **eccentric**, **idiosyncratic**, unconventional, unorthodox, unusual, strange, bizarre, weird, peculiar, odd, freakish, outlandish, offbeat, out of the ordinary, Bohemian, alternative, zany; French outré; informal wacky, freaky, kinky, way-out, far out, kooky, oddball, off the wall; N. Amer. informal in left field; bizarro.
▷ANTONYMS conventional.

> *Word toolkit* **quirky**
>
> See **eccentric**.

quisling noun **collaborator**, fraternizer, colluder, sympathizer; **traitor**, turncoat, betrayer, informer, back-stabber, double-crosser, double-dealer, renegade, defector, deserter, apostate, Judas, snake in the grass, fifth columnist; informal two-timer; Austral. informal dog.

quit verb **1** *let us assume he quit the lay-by at about 12.30*: **leave**, go away from, depart from, vacate, evacuate, move out of, exit from, withdraw from, abandon, desert.
▷ANTONYMS arrive at; occupy.
2 informal *he's decided to quit his job | this defeat will increase the calls for the manager to quit*: **resign (from)**, leave, hand in one's notice, give notice, stand down (from), give up, bow out, relinquish, depart from, vacate, walk out (on), retire (from), abdicate; informal chuck, pack in.
▷ANTONYMS take up.
3 informal *she has to quit living in the past | the best advice to smokers is to quit*: **give up**, stop, finish, cease, discontinue, not continue, drop, leave off, break off, abandon, abstain from, renounce, desist (from), refrain (from), eschew, forbear from, avoid, forgo, do without; call it a day; informal pack (it) in.
▷ANTONYMS start; continue.

quite adverb **1** *there are in fact two quite different types*: **completely**, fully, entirely, totally, wholly, absolutely, utterly, outright, thoroughly, altogether, in every respect, in all respects, without reservation, without exception.
2 *it was quite common in the last century*: **fairly**, rather, somewhat, a bit, a little, slightly, relatively, comparatively, moderately, after a fashion, reasonably, to some extent/degree, to a certain extent; informal pretty, kind of, sort of, ish.

quiver verb **1** *I sat quivering with terror until dawn*: **tremble**, shake, shiver, quaver, quake, shudder, convulse.
2 *the bird runs along, quivering its wings*: **flutter**, agitate, vibrate, flap, beat.
▸ noun *Mr Beckenham could hear a quiver in her voice*: **tremor**, tremble, shake, shaking, shakiness, shiver, frisson, chill, vibration, quaver, quake, shudder, flutter, oscillation, fluctuation, waver, ripple, falter.

> *Choose the right word* **quiver, shake, quake, tremble, shiver**
>
> See **shake**.

quixotic adjective *the 1000-storey building is a vast, exciting and perhaps quixotic project*: **idealistic**, unbusinesslike, romantic, extravagant, starry-eyed, visionary, Utopian, perfectionist, unrealistic, unworldly; **impracticable**, unworkable, impossible, non-viable, inoperable, unserviceable; useless, ineffective, ineffectual, inefficacious.

Word toolkit

quixotic	idealistic	visionary
attempt	youth	leadership
quest	dream	leader
campaign	rhetoric	work
gesture	student	artist
venture	belief	thinker
pursuit	philosophy	poet
mission	generation	architect

quiz noun **1** *the talk was followed by a gardening quiz*: **test of knowledge**, competition, panel game, quiz game, quiz show.
2 *jockey faces new quiz over pub killings*: **interrogation**, questioning, cross-examination, cross-questioning, interview, catechism, examination; informal grilling, pumping, the third degree.
▸ verb *a man was being quizzed by police last night*: **question**, interrogate, put questions to, probe, sound out, interview, examine, cross-examine, catechize; informal grill, put the screws on, pump, give someone the third degree, put someone through the third degree, put someone through the wringer/mangle, worm something out of someone.

quizzical adjective *'To do what?' he asked with a cool, quizzical look*: **puzzled**, perplexed, baffled, questioning, enquiring, mystified, curious, sceptical; **amused**, sardonic, supercilious, mocking, teasing.

quota noun *he rarely took his full quota of holiday*: **allocation**, share, allowance, limit, ration, portion, apportionment, assignment, dispensation, slice, slice of the cake; percentage, commission, measure, proportion, part, piece, fraction, division, subdivision, bit, amount, number, range, quantity; informal cut, whack, rake-off.

quotation noun **1** *a quotation from Dryden*: **citation**, quote, reference, mention, allusion, excerpt, extract, selection, passage, line, cutting, clip, clipping, snippet, reading, section, piece, part, fragment, portion, paragraph, verse, stanza, canto, sentence, phrase; N. Amer. cite; informal, dated gobbet.
2 *the company will then give you a quotation for the work*: **estimate**, estimated price, price, quote, tender, bid, cost, charge, rate, figure.

quote verb **1** *he quoted a sentence from a speech by Lord Denning*: **recite**, repeat, say again, reproduce, restate, retell, echo, iterate, parrot; take, extract, excerpt, derive; misquote; archaic ingeminate.
2 *Russell quoted one case in which a person had died in a fire*: **cite**, mention, refer to, make reference to, give, name, instance, specify, identify; relate, recount, enumerate, list, itemize, spell out, allude to, adduce, exemplify, put forward, point out, call attention to, present, offer, advance, propose.
3 *he quoted £900 for building a staircase*: **estimate**, state, set, tender, bid, offer; price something at.

quotidian adjective **1** *the car sped off through the quotidian traffic*: **daily**, everyday, occurring each/every day, day-to-day; rare diurnal, circadian.
2 *they took me home in Gillian's dreadfully quotidian motor car*: **ordinary**, average, normal, run-of-the-mill, everyday, standard, typical, middle-of-the-road, common, conventional, mainstream, unremarkable, unexceptional, unpretentious, modest, plain, simple, workaday, undistinguished, nondescript, characterless, colourless, commonplace, humdrum, mundane, unmemorable; pedestrian, prosaic, uninteresting, uneventful, dull, boring, uninspiring, homely, homespun; Brit. common or garden; N. Amer. garden-variety; informal OK, so-so, bog-standard, nothing to write home about, a dime a dozen, no great shakes, not up to much; N. Amer. informal ornery.
▷ANTONYMS unusual, exciting.

rabbit noun Brit. coney; children's word bunny (rabbit).

Word links **rabbit**

buck male
doe female
warren, burrow, hutch home

rabble noun **1** *a rabble of noisy, angry youths*: **mob**, (disorderly) crowd, throng, gang, swarm, host, horde, pack, press, crush, jam, gathering, assemblage, multitude, mass, body, group; archaic rout.
2 *democracy was often taken to mean rule by the rabble*: **the common people**, the masses, the populace, the public, the multitude, the rank and file, the commonality, the commonalty, the third estate, the plebeians, the proletariat, the peasantry, the crowd, the hoi polloi, the lower classes, the common herd, the riff-raff, the canaille, the great unwashed, the dregs of society, the ragtag (and bobtail), the proles, the plebs.
▷**ANTONYMS** aristocracy, nobility.

rabble-rouser noun *a group of rabble-rousers conducted a public protest*. See **demagogue**.

Rabelaisian adjective *a Rabelaisian novel*: **ribald**, racy, bawdy, vulgar, coarse, earthy, risqué, lewd, blue, spicy; **exuberant**, uninhibited, vigorous, lively; satirical, parodic, irreverent, disrespectful; informal raunchy.
▷**ANTONYMS** boring, tame, strait-laced.

rabid adjective **1** *a rabid anti-royalist*: **extreme**, fanatical, overzealous, over-enthusiastic, extremist, violent, maniacal, wild, passionate, fervent, diehard, uncompromising; intolerant, unreasonable, illiberal, bigoted, prejudiced, biased, partisan, one-sided; informal raving, gung-ho; literary perfervid.
▷**ANTONYMS** moderate, liberal, half-hearted.
2 *she was bitten by a rabid dog*: **rabies-infected**, mad, foaming at the mouth, hydrophobic.

race[1] noun **1** *Dave won the race and Andy came second*: **contest**, competition; relay, event, fixture, heat, rally, trial, time trial, head-to-head.
2 *the race for naval domination accelerated*: **competition**, contest, rivalry, contention, quest.
3 *the brook was diverted into the mill race*: **channel**, waterway, watercourse, conduit, sluice, spillway, aqueduct.
▶ **verb 1** *Jimmy will race in the semi-finals*: **compete**, take part in a race, run, contend.
2 *dogs would race the train furiously*: **compete against**, have a race with, run against, be pitted against, try to beat.
3 *Cally raced after him*: **hurry**, dash, run, rush, sprint, bolt, dart, gallop, career, charge, shoot, hurtle, hare, bound, fly, speed, zoom, go hell for leather, pound, streak, scurry, scuttle, scamper, scramble, make haste, hasten, lose no time, spank along, really move; informal tear, belt, pelt, scoot, zap, zip, whip, step on it, get a move on, hotfoot it, leg it, steam, put on some speed, go like a bat out of hell, burn rubber; Brit. informal bomb, bucket, put one's foot down; Scottish informal wheech; N. Amer. informal boogie, hightail it, clip, barrel, get the lead out; informal, dated cut along; N. Amer. vulgar slang drag/tear/haul ass; literary fleet; archaic post, hie, haste.
4 *she tried to calm herself, but her heart was racing*: **beat rapidly**, pound, throb, pulsate, pulse, thud, thump, hammer, palpitate, flutter, pitter-patter, go pit-a-pat, quiver, vibrate, pump, pant, thrill; rare quop.

race[2] noun **1** *the school has pupils of many different races*: **ethnic group**, racial type, (ethnic) origin.
2 *we Scots were a bloodthirsty race then*: **people**, nation.
3 *a new race of novelists had appeared*: **group**, type, sort, class, kind, variety, ilk, genre, cast, style, brand, vintage, order, breed, species, generation.
4 literary *a prince of the race of Solomon*: **family**, line, lineage, house, dynasty, stock, blood, folk, clan, tribe; ancestry, descent, bloodline; progeny, offspring, issue.

Word links **race**

ethnocide, genocide killing of a race

racial adjective *he suggests that modern racial differences have a long evolutionary history*: **ethnic**, race-related, ethnological; cultural, national, tribal, folk.

racism noun **racial discrimination**, racialism, racial prejudice/bigotry, xenophobia, chauvinism, bigotry, bias, intolerance; anti-Semitism; in S. Africa, historical apartheid.

racist noun *the party organizer was exposed as a racist*: **racial bigot**, racialist, xenophobe, chauvinist; anti-Semite.
▶ **adjective** *a racist society*: **(racially) discriminatory**, racialist, prejudiced, bigoted, biased, intolerant, illiberal; anti-Semitic.
▷**ANTONYMS** multicultural, tolerant.

rack noun *turn the cake out on to a wire rack to cool*: **framework**, frame, stand, holder, shelf, form, trestle, support, bin, box, bunker, container, structure.
□ **on the rack under pressure**, under stress, under a strain, in distress; suffering, going through torture, in agony, in pain, racked with pain; in trouble, in difficulties, having problems.
▶ **verb** *she was racked with guilt* | *the pain racked his whole body*: **torment**, afflict, torture, pain, agonize, cause agony/suffering/pain to, harrow, pierce, stab, wound, crucify; plague, bedevil, persecute, harass, distress, trouble, worry; convulse; literary rend.
□ **rack one's brains** *she racked her brains, but there was nothing she could tell him*: **think hard**, put one's mind to something, give much thought to something, concentrate, try to remember, puzzle over something, cudgel one's brains, furrow one's brow; informal scratch one's head.
□ **rack up** informal *the privately-held chain racks up sales of $3.3 million*: **achieve**, attain, accomplish, gain, earn, win, succeed in making, reach, make, get, obtain; accumulate, amass; score, tally, record, register, log; informal chalk up, clock up, knock up, notch up, turn in, bag.

racket noun **1** *the engine makes the most incredible racket*: **noise**, din, hubbub, clamour, row, uproar, hullabaloo, tumult, commotion, rumpus, fracas, pandemonium, clangour, brouhaha, disturbance; crash, clatter, clash, babble, shouting, yelling, babel; W. Indian bangarang.
2 informal *he was accused of masterminding a gold-smuggling racket*: **criminal activity**, illegal scheme/enterprise, fraud, fraudulent scheme, swindle, bit of sharp practice; informal game, scam, rip-off; Brit. informal ramp; N. Amer. informal shakedown.

raconteur noun **storyteller**, teller of tales, spinner of yarns, narrator, relater, recounter; Austral. informal magsman; rare anecdotist, anecdotalist.

racy adjective *the show included a rather racy striptease revue*. See **ribald**.

raddled adjective *he had begun to look quite raddled*: **haggard**, gaunt, hollow-eyed, drawn, with sunken cheeks, pinched, tired, fatigued, drained, exhausted, worn out, washed out; unwell, unhealthy, below/under par, on

one's last legs; informal the worse for wear.
▷ANTONYMS healthy.

radiance noun **1** *the radiance of the sun*: **light**, shining, brightness, brilliance, luminosity, radiation, beams, rays, illumination, blaze, glow, luminousness, gleam, lustre, glitter, sparkle, flash, dazzle, shimmer, glare; luminescence, incandescence, fluorescence, phosphorescence; rare irradiance, lucency, lambency, effulgence, refulgence, coruscation.
▷ANTONYMS darkness.
2 *her face flooded with radiance as she saw him*: **joy**, joyfulness, elation, jubilance, ecstasy, rapture, euphoria, delirium, happiness, delight, pleasure.
▷ANTONYMS gloom, misery.
3 *her skin had the unmistakable radiance of youth*: **splendour**, resplendence, magnificence, brilliance, dazzle, beauty, vividness, glory, gloriousness.

radiant adjective **1** *the radiant moon*: **shining**, bright, illuminated, lit, lighted, brilliant, gleaming, glowing, ablaze, luminous, luminescent, lustrous, incandescent, glittering, sparkling, dazzling, flashing, shimmering; literary irradiant, lucent, lambent, splendent; rare effulgent, refulgent, coruscating.
▷ANTONYMS dark, dull.
2 *flushed and radiant, she smiled up at him*: **joyful**, elated, thrilled, overjoyed, jubilant, in raptures, enraptured, rapturous, ecstatic, beside oneself with joy, euphoric, deliriously happy, blissfully happy, in seventh heaven, on cloud nine/seven, delighted, joyous, pleased, happy, beaming, glowing, transported, in transports of joy/pleasure/delight; informal on top of the world, over the moon, blissed out; Austral. informal wrapped.
▷ANTONYMS gloomy.
3 *the opening chorus is another radiant piece*: **splendid**, magnificent, brilliant, dazzling, scintillating, vivid, intense, beautiful, gorgeous, transcendent, resplendent, impressive, spectacular, striking, stunning, glorious, superb, majestic, great, breathtaking, ravishing, sumptuous, fine; informal splendiferous; rare splendacious, magnolious.

radiate verb **1** *the hot stars radiate energy*: **emit**, give off/out, send out/forth, discharge, scatter, diffuse; shed, cast, beam out.
2 *a faint light radiated from the cage*: **shine**, be diffused, beam, emanate.
3 *their faces radiate interest and hope*: **display**, show, exhibit, demonstrate; transmit, emanate, breathe, be a/the picture of.
4 *four spokes radiate from the hub*: **spread out**, fan (out), ray (out), branch (out/off), diverge, extend, separate, split off, issue; technical divaricate, ramify.

radical adjective **1** *radical reform is long overdue*: **thoroughgoing**, thorough, complete, total, entire, absolute, utter, comprehensive, exhaustive, root-and-branch, sweeping, far-reaching, wide-ranging, extensive, profound, drastic, severe, serious, major, desperate, stringent, violent, forceful, rigorous, draconian.
▷ANTONYMS superficial.
2 *the apparently radical differences between logic and natural language*: **fundamental**, basic, essential, quintessential; inherent, innate, structural, deep-seated, intrinsic, organic, constitutive, root.
▷ANTONYMS minor.
3 *a radical political movement*: **revolutionary**, progressive, reforming, reformist, revisionist, progressivist; leftist, left-wing, socialist; extreme, extremist, fanatical, militant, diehard; informal red; derogatory Bolshevik.
▷ANTONYMS conservative, reactionary; moderate.
▶noun *he was by no means a radical*: **revolutionary**, progressive, reformer, revisionist; leftist, left-winger, socialist; militant, zealot, extremist, fanatic, diehard; informal ultra, red; derogatory Bolshevik, Bolshevist.
▷ANTONYMS conservative, reactionary; moderate.

raffish adjective *his cosmopolitan, raffish air*: **rakish**, jaunty, dapper, dashing, sporty, flashy; unconventional, bohemian; devil-may-care, casual, careless; louche, disreputable, dissolute, dissipated, debauched, decadent; informal flash.

raffle noun *she won the car in a raffle*: **lottery**, (prize) draw, sweepstake, sweep, tombola, ballot; Brit. trademark Instants; N. Amer. lotto, numbers game/pool/racket; Austral./NZ tote, pakapoo.

rag[1] noun **1** *he wiped his hands on an oily rag*: **piece of cloth**, bit/scrap/fragment of cloth, cloth; N. Amer. informal schmatte; archaic clout.
2 (**rags**) *a man dressed in rags*: **tattered clothes**, torn clothing, tatters, old clothes, cast-offs, hand-me-downs.

rag[2] noun Brit. *students caused a ninety-minute traffic jam during their rag week*: **fund-raising event**, charity event, charitable event, collection.
▶verb informal *the President is now ragged mercilessly on national television*. See **tease**.

ragamuffin noun **urchin**, guttersnipe, waif; informal scarecrow; dated gamin, gamine; historical mudlark; archaic street Arab, wastrel, tatterdemalion.

ragbag noun *a ragbag of products of all shapes and sizes*: **jumble**, hotchpotch, hodgepodge, mishmash, mess, confusion, hash, pastiche, farrago; **assortment**, mixture, miscellany, medley, motley, motley collection, mixed bag, melange, mix, blend, variety, diversity, collection, selection, assemblage, combination, conglomeration, pot-pourri; rare mingle-mangle, gallimaufry, omnium gatherum, olio, salmagundi, macédoine.

rage noun **1** *Keith's rage is caused by frustration*: **fury**, anger, wrath, outrage, indignation, passion, hot temper, spleen, resentment, pique, annoyance, vexation, exasperation, displeasure, bitterness, rancour, antagonism, hostility; literary ire, choler.
▷ANTONYMS calmness.
2 *Toby flew into a rage at this remark*: **temper**, fit of rage/fury/anger/temper, fit of bad/ill temper, towering rage, bad temper, pet, fit of pique, tantrum, fury, frenzy of rage/anger, rampage, paroxysm of rage/anger, passion, bad mood, mood; informal grump, strop, state; N. Amer. informal blowout, hissy fit; Brit. informal, dated bate, wax, skid; archaic paddywhack.
3 *the current rage for portable computing*: **craze**, passion, fashion, taste, desire, craving, appetite, trend, vogue, fad, enthusiasm, love, obsession, compulsion, weakness, fondness, fixation, fetish, mania, fascination, preoccupation; informal thing, yen; rare cacoethes.
□ **(all) the rage** *for today's children, video and computer games are all the rage*: **very popular**, in fashion, in style, in vogue, (all) the fashion, the (latest) craze, the (latest) thing, (all) the vogue, in (great) demand, much sought-after, ultra-fashionable; French le dernier cri; informal in, the in thing, cool, big, trendy, hot, hip; Brit. informal, dated all the go.
▶verb **1** *she raged silently all the way back to the cottage*: **be angry**, be furious, be enraged, be incensed, be infuriated, seethe, be beside oneself, have a fit, boil, be boiling over, rant, rave, rant and rave, storm, fume, spit, breathe fire, burn; informal be livid, be wild, jump up and down, froth/foam at the mouth, be steamed up, have steam coming out of one's ears; Brit. informal do one's head/nut in, spit feathers.
2 *he* ***raged against*** *the carving-up of the land*: **protest strongly at**, complain vociferously about, disagree violently with, oppose strongly, denounce; **fulminate**, storm, inveigh, rail, kick, expostulate, make a fuss about; informal kick up a fuss/stink about.
3 *a tropical storm was raging*: **be violent**, be at its height, be turbulent, be tempestuous, be uncontrollable, thunder, rampage.

ragged adjective **1** *a pair of ragged jeans*: **tattered**, in tatters, torn, ripped, split, in holes, holey, moth-eaten, frayed, worn, worn out, well worn, worn to shreds, falling to pieces, threadbare, the worse for wear, patched, scruffy, shabby, decrepit, old; informal tatty; literary rent.
2 *a ragged child*: **dressed in rags**, shabby, unkempt; Brit. down at heel.
▷ANTONYMS smart.
3 *a ragged coastline*: **jagged**, craggy, rugged, uneven, rough, irregular, broken; serrated, sawtooth, saw-edged, notched, nicked, indented; technical crenulate, crenulated, denticulate, denticulated, dentate, crenate, crenated, serrate, serrulate.
4 *the ragged remnants of an expedition sought refuge in the village*: **disorganized**, **in disarray**, confused, in confusion, disordered, disorderly; muddled, jumbled, in a muddle/jumble, straggling, straggly, fragmented.

raging adjective **1** *a raging mob*: **angry**, furious, enraged, incensed, infuriated, irate, wrathful, seething, fuming, blazing, flaming mad, blazing mad, mad, ranting, raving, beside oneself; informal livid, wild; Brit. informal, dated waxy.
▷ANTONYMS calm, placid.
2 *raging seas | a raging storm*: **stormy**, violent, strong, wild, turbulent, tempestuous, blustery.
▷ANTONYMS calm.
3 *a raging headache*: **excruciating**, agonizing, very painful, searing, harrowing, throbbing, acute, very bad, sharp.
4 *her raging thirst*: **severe**, extreme, huge, excessive, very great, inordinate.

raid noun **1** *the raid on Dieppe*: **surprise attack**, hit-and-run raid, tip-and-run raid, assault, descent, blitz, incursion, foray, sortie; sally, inroad, onslaught, onrush, storming, charge, thrust, offensive, invasion; German blitzkrieg; Italian razzia.
2 *clothing worth £40,000 has been stolen in a raid on a shop in Bond Street*: **robbery**, burglary, hold-up, break-in; mugging, robbing, pillaging, looting, plunder, plundering, ransacking, sack, sacking, marauding; informal snatch, smash-and-grab; Brit. informal blag; N. Amer. informal heist, stick-up.
3 *police discovered stolen ammunition during a raid on the flat*: **swoop**, surprise search; N. Amer. informal bust, takedown.
▶verb **1** *the aim was to raid shipping in Benghazi harbour*: **attack**, make a raid on, assault, set upon, descend on, swoop on, harass, harry, blitz, make inroads on, assail, storm, rush, charge.
2 *they live as outlaws, raiding villages and towns for food and clothing*: **plunder**, steal from, pillage, loot, rifle, maraud, strip, ransack, sack; literary despoil; archaic reave, spoil; rare depredate, spoliate, forage.
3 *they had raided the electrical store next door*: **rob**, steal from, hold up, break into, make a raid on; N. Amer. informal stick up.
4 *homes and offices in Merseyside were raided by police*: **search**, make a search of, swoop on, make a raid on; N. Amer. informal bust.

raider noun *armed raiders escaped with several thousand pounds of jewellery*: **attacker**, assailant; **robber**, burglar, thief, housebreaker; plunderer, pillager, looter, marauder, ransacker, sacker, invader; archaic reaver.

rail verb *Johnson* ***rails against*** *injustice and oppression*: **protest strongly at**, make a protest against, fulminate against, inveigh against, rage against, thunder against, declaim against, remonstrate about, expostulate about, make a fuss about, speak out against, express disapproval of, criticize severely, denounce, censure, condemn; **object to**, raise objections to, take issue with, oppose strongly, complain vociferously/bitterly about, disagree violently with, kick against, take great exception to, make/take a stand against, put up a fight against, challenge; informal kick up a fuss/stink about.

railing noun **fence**, fencing, rail(s), paling, palisade, balustrade, banister, hurdle, barrier, parapet.

raillery noun *the affectionate raillery from her fellow workers*: **teasing**, good-humoured mockery, chaff, banter, ragging, badinage, japing; informal leg-pulling, ribbing, joshing, kidding, kidology; N. Amer. informal josh; rare persiflage.

railroad verb
□ **railroad someone into** informal *they were being railroaded into accepting an unfavourable agreement*: **coerce**, force, compel, pressure, pressurize, badger, hustle, pester, hound, harass, nag, harry, urge, goad, prod, spur; browbeat, bludgeon, bulldoze, steamroller, dragoon, prevail on, strong-arm; Brit. informal bounce; N. Amer. informal fast-talk.

rain noun **1** *the rain had almost stopped*: **rainfall**, precipitation, raindrops, rainwater, wet weather; the wet, a fall of rain; sprinkle, drizzle, mizzle, Scotch mist, shower, rainstorm, cloudburst, torrent, downpour, deluge, squall, thunderstorm.
2 *a rain of hot ash | a rain of blows*: **shower**, deluge, flood, torrent, spate, avalanche, outpouring, rush, flurry; volley, storm, hail, barrage, broadside, salvo.
▸ verb **1** *it was raining heavily*: **pour (down)**, pelt down, tip down, teem down, beat down, lash down, sheet down, come down, come down in torrents/sheets, rain cats and dogs; fall, shower, drizzle, spit; informal be chucking it down; Brit. informal bucket down, come down in buckets/bucketloads, come down in stair rods, tipple down; Brit. vulgar slang piss down.
2 *bombs rained on the city's crowded streets*: **fall**, pour/rain down, drop, shower.
3 *guerrillas rained mortar bombs on the capital*: **shower**, pour, drop; bombard someone with, pepper someone with, pelt someone with.

Word links **rain**
pluvial, pluvious, hyetal relating to rain

rainy adjective *rainy weather*: **wet**, showery, drizzly, damp, inclement.
▷ANTONYMS dry.

raise verb **1** *Arthur raised a hand in greeting | the remains of the ship were eventually raised*: **lift**, lift up, raise aloft, elevate; uplift, upraise, hoist, haul up, heave up, lever up, hitch up, take up; Brit. informal hoick up; rare upheave, uprear, upthrust.
2 *he raised the child to a sitting position*: **set upright**, place vertical, set up, put up, stand (up), upend, stand on end; pitch.
▷ANTONYMS knock over, lay down.
3 *there was no alternative but to raise prices*: **increase**, put up, push up, up, mark up, step up, lift, augment, escalate, inflate, swell, add to; informal hike (up), jack up, bump up.
▷ANTONYMS lower, reduce.
4 *I really hope they can raise their game*: **improve**, boost, lift, enhance, make better, ameliorate, upgrade.
5 *he raised the volume of his voice slightly | they were able to raise public awareness of the issues involved*: **increase**, heighten, make higher, lift, augment, amplify, magnify, intensify, boost, step up, turn up, add to; make louder, louden.
▷ANTONYMS lower.
6 *the temple was raised in about 900 BC*: **build**, construct, erect, assemble, put up.
▷ANTONYMS demolish, raze.
7 *the yeast created enough gas to raise the thick bread dough*: **cause to rise**, make rise, leaven, ferment; puff up, dilate, inflate.
8 *how do you propose to raise the money?* **get**, obtain, acquire; accumulate, amass, scrape together, collect; fetch, realize, yield, net, make.
▷ANTONYMS distribute, spend.
9 *the city had raised troops to fight for the Government*: **recruit**, enlist, sign up, conscript, call to arms, call up, muster, mobilize, levy, rally, press, get/gather together, collect, assemble, call together; N. Amer. draft.
▷ANTONYMS stand down, demobilize.
10 *stamp duty is a tax raised on transfers of ownership*: **levy**, impose, exact, demand, charge.
11 *he raised one objection after another*: **bring up**, introduce, advance, broach, mention, allude to, touch on, suggest, moot, put forward, bring forward, pose, present, table, propose, submit; air, ventilate.
▷ANTONYMS withdraw, keep quiet about.
12 *the disaster raised doubts about the safety of nuclear power*: **give rise to**, occasion, cause, bring into being, bring about, produce, engender, draw forth, elicit, create, set going, set afoot, result in, lead to, prompt, awaken, arouse, excite, summon up, activate, evoke, induce, kindle, incite, stir up, trigger, spark off, provoke, instigate, foment, whip up; literary beget, enkindle.
▷ANTONYMS allay, end.
13 N. Amer. *most parents manage to raise their children successfully*: **bring up**, rear, nurture, look after, care for, take care of, provide for, mother, parent, tend, protect, cherish; educate, train, foster.
14 *he raised cattle in Nebraska*: **breed**, rear, nurture, keep, tend.
15 *wheat is also raised in considerable quantity*: **grow**, farm, cultivate, produce, propagate, bring on; plant.
16 *he was raised to the peerage*: **promote**, advance, upgrade, elevate, prefer, ennoble, aggrandize, exalt, give a higher rank to, give advancement to; informal kick upstairs.
▷ANTONYMS demote.
17 *raids across the border raised the spectre of civil war*: **cause to appear**, call up, call forth, invoke, summon (up), conjure up.
▷ANTONYMS lay.
18 *Alfonso at once raised the siege of Saragossa*: **end**, stop, bring to an end, put an end to, terminate, abandon, lift.
▷ANTONYMS start, impose.
19 Brit. informal *see if you can raise them on the radio*: **contact**, get in touch with, get hold of, reach, communicate with; phone, radio, call; Brit. get on to.
□ **raise hell** informal See **hell**.
▸ noun N. Amer. *he wanted a raise and some extra holiday*: **rise**, pay/wage/salary increase, increment.

raised adjective *the plate bears an inscription in raised letters*: **embossed**, relief, relievo, cameo, die-stamped, thermographed, ribbed.
▷ANTONYMS engraved.

rake[1] verb **1** *another man was raking the clippings into a sack*: **scrape up/together**, collect, gather.
2 *she raked the gravel meticulously*: **smooth**, smooth out, level, even out, flatten, comb.
3 *the cat raked his face with its claws*: **scratch**, lacerate, scrape, rasp, graze, abrade, grate, bark; technical excoriate.
4 *she raked a hand through her hair*: **drag**, pull, scrape, draw, tug.
5 *Dempster raked through his pockets*: **rummage**, search, hunt, sift, rifle; ransack, comb, turn upside down, scour, go through with a fine-tooth comb.
6 *machine-gun fire raked the streets*: **sweep**, enfilade, pepper, strafe; archaic cannonade, fusillade.
7 *her eyes raked the room*: **search**, scan, look around/round/over, survey, study, inspect, scour, scrutinize, examine, explore; N. Amer. informal scope.
□ **rake something in** informal *the movie raked in over $300 million*: **earn**, make, get, gain, get paid, obtain, acquire, accumulate, bring in, gather in, pull in, haul in, pocket, realize, make a profit of, fetch, return, yield, raise, clear, net, gross.
□ **rake something up** *I was afraid that someone had raked up the past*: **remind people of**, revive the memory of, recollect, remember, call to mind; drag up, dredge up, speak out about.

rake[2] noun *the third earl had the reputation of being something of a rake*: **playboy**, libertine, profligate; degenerate, roué, debauchee, dissolute man, loose-liver; lecher, seducer, ladies' man, womanizer, philanderer, adulterer, Don Juan, Lothario, Casanova; informal ladykiller, lech; dated gay dog, rip, blood; archaic rakehell; rare dissolute.

rake-off noun informal *he demanded a 10 per cent rake-off*. See **whack** (sense 2 of the noun).

rakish adjective *his moustache gave him a slightly rakish look*: **dashing**, debonair, sporty, jaunty, devil-may-care, breezy; stylish, fashionable, dapper, spruce; raffish, disreputable, louche; informal sharp.

rally verb **1** *the hard-pressed French troops rallied and held their position*: **reassemble**, regroup, re-form, reunite, gather together again, get together again; round up.
▷ANTONYMS disperse.
2 *the exiled monarch rallied an Irish Catholic army*: **muster**, marshal, mobilize, raise, call up, call to arms, recruit, enlist, conscript, draft; assemble, bring together, call together, summon, gather, gather together, round up, mass, collect; formal convoke; archaic levy.
▷ANTONYMS demobilize, disband.
3 *ministers rallied in a concerted effort to denounce rumours of the rift*: **come/get together**, band together, assemble, group, join, join together, join forces, link (up), combine, unite, ally, collaborate, cooperate, work together, act together, pull together.
▷ANTONYMS separate, split up.
4 *he tried to rally support for more radical policies*: **gather**, accumulate, collect, assemble, amass, muster, marshal, organize, round up, garner, harvest; get up, raise, mobilize, whip up.
5 *the shock grew less and her spirits rallied | share prices have rallied*: **recover**, improve, get better, pick up, revive, come back, make a comeback, rebound, bounce back, perk up, look up, take a turn for the better, turn the/a corner, be given a new lease of life, take on a new lease of life; emerge from something, get over something, shake something off; informal come up smiling.
▷ANTONYMS deteriorate.
▸ noun **1** *there was a rally in support of the strike*: **meeting**, mass meeting, gathering, assembly; **demonstration**, march, protest march, parade; informal get-together, demo.

2 *blizzards caused a short-lived rally in oil prices*: **recovery**, upturn, improvement, revival, comeback, rebound, resurgence, renewal, a turn for the better, reaction; technical dead cat bounce.
▷ANTONYMS slump.

ram verb **1** *he rammed his sword back into its sheath*: **force**, thrust, plunge, stab, push, sink, dig, stick, cram, jam, stuff, pack, compress, squeeze, wedge, press, tamp, pound, drive, hammer, bang.
2 *a stolen van was used to ram the police car*: **hit**, strike, crash into, collide with, be in collision with, meet head-on, run into, slam (into), smash into, dash against, crack into/against, bump (into), bang (into), knock into, butt; N. Amer. impact.

ramble verb **1** *we rambled around the Cornwall countryside*: **walk**, take a walk, go for a walk, hike, tramp, backpack, trek; wander, stroll, saunter, amble, drift, roam, range, rove, traipse, jaunt; Scottish & Irish stravaig; informal mosey, tootle; Brit. informal pootle; rare vagabond, perambulate, peregrinate.
2 *I'm not going to ramble on about environmental issues*: **chatter**, babble, prattle, prate, blather, blether, gabble, jabber, twitter, go on, run on, rattle on/away, blither, maunder, drivel; informal jaw, gas, gab, yak, yackety-yak, yabber, yatter, shoot one's mouth off; Brit. informal witter, rabbit, chunter, natter, waffle; N. Amer. informal run off at the mouth; Austral./NZ informal mag; archaic twaddle, clack, twattle.
▶ noun *I had looked forward to a leisurely ramble amongst the hills*: **walk**, hike, trek; wander, stroll, saunter, amble, roam, traipse, jaunt, promenade, trip, excursion, tour; informal mosey, tootle; Brit. informal pootle; rare perambulation, peregrination.

rambler noun **walker**, hiker, stroller, saunterer, wanderer, roamer, rover, drifter, traveller, wayfarer.

rambling adjective **1** *a long, rambling speech*: **long-winded**, garrulous, verbose, wordy, prolix; digressive, wandering, maundering; roundabout, circuitous, diffuse, discursive, circumlocutory, oblique, periphrastic; disconnected, disjointed, ill-thought-out, incoherent, illogical.
▷ANTONYMS concise, pithy.
2 *a maze of narrow, rambling streets*: **winding**, twisting, twisty, labyrinthine; **sprawling**, spreading, straggling.
3 *a rambling rose*: **trailing**, creeping, straggling, vining, prostrate.

ramification noun *the political ramifications of shutting the factory would be immense*: **consequence**, result, aftermath, outcome, effect, upshot, issue, sequel; complication, development, implication; product, by-product, outgrowth, spin-off.

ramp noun *there was a ramp down to a double garage on basement level*. See **incline** (noun).

rampage verb *stone-throwing mobs rampaged through the streets*: **rush wildly/madly**, riot, run riot, go on the rampage, run amok, go berserk, storm, charge, tear; rave; informal steam.
▶ noun
□ **on the rampage** *a sacked chef went on the rampage in his kitchen*: **berserk**, out of control, wild, violent, frenzied, running amok, rioting, riotous, destructive, rampaging; N. Amer. informal postal.

rampant adjective **1** *the rampant inflation of the mid-1970s*: **uncontrolled**, unrestrained, unchecked, unbridled, widespread, pandemic, epidemic, pervasive; out of control, out of hand, rife, spreading like wildfire.
▷ANTONYMS controlled, under control.
2 *that first interested glance had been replaced by one of rampant dislike*: **vehement**, strong, violent, forceful, raging, wild, intense, fanatical, passionate.
▷ANTONYMS mild.
3 *rampant vegetation*: **luxuriant**, exuberant, lush, rank, rich, riotous, profuse, lavish, vigorous, productive; informal jungly.
4 Heraldry *two large stone pillars surmounted by rampant lions*: **upright**, standing (up), erect, rearing, vertical, perpendicular, upended, on end.

rampart noun **defensive wall**, embankment, earthwork, parapet, breastwork, battlement, stockade, palisade, bulwark, bastion, barbican, outwork, fortification; Latin vallum; rare bartizan, circumvallation.

ramshackle adjective *a ramshackle cottage*: **tumbledown**, dilapidated, derelict, ruinous, falling to pieces, decrepit, neglected, gone to rack and ruin, run down, crumbling, decaying, disintegrating, rickety, shaky, unsteady, broken down, unsound, unsafe; informal shambly, geriatric; N. Amer. informal shacky.
▷ANTONYMS well maintained, sturdy.

rancid adjective *the smell of rancid butter*: **sour**, stale, turned, rank, putrid, foul, rotten, bad, off, old, tainted; gamy, high, fetid, stinking, malodorous, foul-smelling, evil-smelling; unpleasant, noxious, revolting, nasty, sickening, offensive; literary noisome, mephitic; rare miasmic, miasmal, olid.
▷ANTONYMS fresh.

rancorous adjective *the campaign became increasingly rancorous as it progressed*: **bitter**, spiteful, hateful, resentful, acrimonious, malicious, malevolent, malign, malignant, hostile, antipathetic, venomous, poisonous, vindictive, evil-intentioned, ill-natured, baleful, vengeful, vitriolic, virulent, pernicious, mean, nasty; informal bitchy, catty; literary malefic, maleficent.
▷ANTONYMS amicable.

rancour noun *an atmosphere of festering rancour and distrust*: **bitterness**, spite, hate, hatred, resentment, malice, ill will, malevolence, malignancy, animosity, antipathy, enmity, hostility, acrimony, venom, poison, vindictiveness, balefulness, vengefulness, vitriol, virulence, perniciousness, meanness, nastiness; informal bitchiness, cattiness; literary maleficence.
▷ANTONYMS amicability.

random adjective *random spot checks | a random sample of eighty-six people*: **unsystematic**, arbitrary, unmethodical, haphazard, unarranged, unplanned, undirected, casual, indiscriminate, non-specific, stray, erratic; chance, accidental, hit-and-miss; serendipitous, fortuitous, contingent, adventitious; non-linear, entropic, fractal; rare aleatory, stochastic.
▷ANTONYMS systematic, planned.
□ **at random** *five schools were chosen at random*: **unsystematically**, arbitrarily, randomly, without prearrangement, without method, unmethodically, haphazardly, without conscious choice, leaving things to chance; out of a hat, by lot.
▷ANTONYMS systematically.

range noun **1** *it was beyond his range of vision | the age range of all patients was 39–97*: **span**, scope, compass, radius, scale, gamut, reach, sweep, extent, area, field, orbit, ambit, province, realm, domain, horizon, latitude; limits, bounds, confines, parameters.
2 *a range of mountains*: **row**, chain; **sierra**, cordillera, ridge, massif; line, file, rank, string, series.
3 *the toucan eats a very wide range of fruits | a new range of quality foods*: **assortment**, variety, diversity, mixture, collection, array, set, selection, choice, pick; kind, sort, type, class, rank, order, genus, species.
4 *Bertha put the dish into the range to cook*: **stove**, cooking stove, kitchen stove; trademark Aga.
5 *cows grazed on open range*: **pasture**, pasturage, pastureland, grass, grassland, grazing land, ley, paddock, croft; literary lea, mead, greensward, sward; Scottish & N. English **shieling**, **bent**; Irish & Canadian **bawn**; Austral./NZ **run**; S. African **veld**; in Switzerland **alp**; in France **bocage**; in S. America **potrero**.
▶ verb **1** *annual charges range from 0.5% to 1%*: **vary**, fluctuate, differ; extend, stretch, reach, cover, go, run, pass.
2 *on the long stalls are ranged all sorts of fresh farm products*: **line up**, align, draw up, put/set in order, order, place, position, arrange, dispose, set out, array, rank.
3 *herdsmen ranged over the steppes*: **roam**, rove, traverse, travel, journey, wander, stray, drift, ramble, meander, amble, stroll, traipse, walk, hike, trek, backpack; rare peregrinate.
4 *the pupils were ranged according to ability*: **classify**, class, categorize, type, rank, order, sort, bracket, group, rate, grade, size, graduate, pigeonhole, designate; break down, codify, catalogue, file, list, label, tabulate, index.

> *Choose the right word* **range, wander, roam, rove, stray**
>
> See **wander**.

rangy adjective *his rangy figure*: **long-legged**, long-limbed, leggy, tall, slender, slim, lean; thin, gangling, gangly, lanky, spindly, skinny, size-zero, spare, scrawny, bony, gaunt.
▷ANTONYMS stocky.

rank[1] noun **1** *a former civil servant elevated to ministerial rank*: **position**, **grade**, level, echelon, gradation, point on the scale, rung on the ladder; class, stratum, status, station, standing.
2 *the girl must come from a family of rank*: **high standing**, nobility, aristocracy, blue blood, high birth, eminence, distinction, prestige; prominence, influence, importance, consequence, power.
3 *the first rank of riflemen was instructed to lie down*: **row**, line, file, column, series, succession, string, train, procession; queue.
□ **the rank and file 1** *both the officers and the rank and file*: **other ranks**, soldiers and NCOs, lower ranks; common/ordinary/private soldiers, soldiers, men, troops. **2** *the rank and file of the organization*: **ordinary members**; grass roots. **3** *a speech redolent with phrases designed to warm the hearts of the rank and file*: **the people**, the proletariat, the common people, the masses, the populace, the multitude, the commonality, the commonalty, the third estate, the plebeians, the crowd; derogatory the hoi polloi, the common herd, the rabble, the mob, the riff-raff, the canaille, the great unwashed, the ragtag (and bobtail), the proles, the plebs.
▶ verb **1** *the plant is ranked as endangered*: **classify**, class, categorize, rate, grade, type, order, sort, bracket, group, pigeonhole, designate; codify, catalogue, file, list, tabulate; Medicine triage.
2 *Swainson felt that an illustrator ranked below a real man of science*: **have a rank**, **be graded**, be placed, be positioned, have a status, be classed, be classified, be categorized; belong.
3 *rows of tulips were ranked like guardsmen*: **line up**, align, draw up, put/set in order, order, place, position, arrange, dispose, set out, array, range.

rank[2] adjective **1** *rank vegetation*: **abundant**, lush, luxuriant, dense, profuse, flourishing, exuberant, vigorous, productive, spreading, overgrown; informal jungly.
▷ANTONYMS sparse.

r

2 *a rank smell*: **offensive**, unpleasant, nasty, disagreeable, revolting, sickening, obnoxious, noxious; foul-smelling, evil-smelling, fetid, smelly, stinking, reeking, reeky, high, off, rancid, putrid, malodorous, ill-smelling, fusty, musty, stale; Brit. informal niffy, pongy, whiffy, humming; literary noisome, mephitic; rare miasmic, miasmal, olid.
▷ANTONYMS pleasant.
3 *rank stupidity*: **downright**, utter, outright, out-and-out, absolute, complete, sheer, stark, thorough, thoroughgoing, categorical, unequivocal, undeniable, unqualified, unmodified, unrestricted, unmitigated, unconditional, positive, simple, wholesale, all-out, perfect, consummate, patent, pure, total, entire, flat, direct, dead, final, conclusive; archaic arrant; rare right-down.

rankle verb *their insults still rankle with Martin*: **cause resentment to**, cause annoyance to, annoy, upset, anger, irritate, offend, affront, displease, exasperate, infuriate, provoke, irk, vex, pique, nettle, gall, gnaw at, eat away at, grate on; fester; informal rile, miff, peeve, aggravate, hack off; Brit. informal nark; N. Amer. informal tick off; vulgar slang piss off.

ransack verb **1** *burglars had ransacked the place*: **plunder**, pillage, steal from, raid, rob, loot, rifle, sack, strip, denude; ravage, maraud, lay waste, devastate; literary despoil; archaic reave; rare depredate, spoliate.
2 *she ransacked the wardrobe for something to wear*: **rummage through**, hunt through, search (through), rake through, scour, rifle, look all round, go through, comb, scrabble around in, poke around in, rummage around in, hunt around in, explore, turn inside out, turn over.

ransom noun **1** *the kidnappers demanded a huge ransom*: **pay-off**, payment, price.
2 *the ransom of the prisoners*: **release**, freedom, setting free, deliverance, liberation, rescue, redemption, restoration.
▸verb *the girl was subsequently ransomed for £4 million*: **obtain the release of**, exchange for a ransom, buy the freedom of, release, free, deliver, liberate, rescue, redeem, restore to freedom.

rant verb *she was still ranting on about the unfairness of it all*: **hold forth**, go on and on, deliver a tirade, rant and rave, fulminate, sound off, spout, pontificate, trumpet, bluster, declaim; shout, yell, roar, bellow; informal mouth off; rare vociferate.
▸noun *he went into a rant about the people who were annoying him*: **tirade**, harangue, diatribe, broadside, verbal onslaught; rare philippic.

rap[1] verb **1** *he stood up and rapped the table | she rapped his fingers with a ruler*: **hit**, strike, bang, thump, knock; informal whack, thwack, bash, wallop; literary smite.
2 *I rapped on the open door of his office*: **knock**, tap; bang, hammer, batter, pound.
3 informal *banks are to be rapped for delaying interest rate cuts*. See **rebuke**.
▸noun **1** *she gave her son a rap on the shoulder*: **blow**, hit, knock, bang, crack, thump; informal whack, thwack, bash, wallop.
2 *there was a rap at the door*: **knock**, knocking, tap, bang, banging, hammering, battering, pounding, rat-tat.
□ **rap over the knuckles** informal *she will get a rap over the knuckles and be fined*: **rebuke**, reprimand, reproach, reproof, admonishment, admonition, reproval, remonstration, lecture, upbraiding, castigation, lambasting, criticism, censure; informal telling-off, scolding, dressing-down, earful, roasting, bawling-out, caning, blast, row; Brit. informal ticking-off, carpeting, rollicking, wigging; Brit. vulgar slang bollocking; dated rating.
□ **take the rap** informal *I don't want him to take the rap for something he didn't do*: **be punished**, **be blamed**, take the blame, pay, suffer, suffer the consequences, pay the price; answer for something; informal be for it; Brit. informal carry the can.
▷ANTONYMS get off scot-free.

rap[2] noun *they didn't care a rap about me*: **whit**, iota, jot, hoot, scrap, bit, fig; one bit, even a little bit, two hoots, the smallest amount, the tiniest bit; informal damn, tinker's cuss/curse, brass farthing, monkey's.

rapacious adjective *rapacious landlords*: **grasping**, **greedy**, avaricious, acquisitive, covetous, mercenary, materialistic, insatiable, predatory, voracious, usurious, extortionate; informal money-grubbing; N. Amer. informal grabby.
▷ANTONYMS generous.

rapacity noun **greed**, avarice, rapaciousness, acquisitiveness, covetousness, materialism, predatoriness, voracity, voraciousness, graspingness, mercenariness, usury, extortion.
▷ANTONYMS unselfishness.

rape noun **1** *the man was charged with rape*: **sexual assault**, sexual abuse; date rape, gang rape; N. Amer. acquaintance rape; informal gang bang; archaic or humorous a fate worse than death; archaic ravishment, defilement.
2 *people everywhere decry the rape of rainforest*: **destruction**, violation, vandalizing, ravaging, pillaging; **plundering**, raiding, desecration, defilement; marauding, ransacking, sacking, sack; literary despoilment, rapine; rare despoliation, spoliation.
3 archaic *the rape of the Sabine women*: **abduction**, carrying off, kidnapping, seizure, capture.
▸verb **1** *he raped her at knifepoint*: **sexually assault**, violate, force oneself on, abuse sexually; date-rape, gang-rape; informal gang-bang; euphemistic have one's (evil) way with; archaic ravish, defile, dishonour.
2 *they raped our country*: **ravage**, plunder, pillage, violate, desecrate, defile; lay waste, ransack, sack; maraud over, raid; literary despoil; archaic spoil, reave; rare depredate, spoliate.
3 archaic *the Romans raped the Sabine women*: **abduct**, carry off, kidnap, seize, capture, make off with.

rapid adjective *his rapid rise to stardom | they made a rapid exit*: **quick**, fast, swift, speedy, high-speed, expeditious, express, brisk, lively, prompt, flying, fleeting, lightning, meteoric, overnight, whirlwind, fast-track, whistle-stop; sudden, instantaneous, immediate, instant, hurried, hasty, abrupt, sharp, precipitate, breakneck, headlong; informal p.d.q. (pretty damn quick); literary fleet; rare alacritous, volant.
▷ANTONYMS slow, leisurely.

rapidity noun **quickness**, swiftness, speed, speediness, briskness, expeditiousness, alacrity, dispatch, velocity, promptness, promptitude; suddenness, immediacy, instantaneousness, hurriedness, haste, hastiness, abruptness, precipitateness; literary fleetness, celerity.

rapidly adverb *he drove rapidly to the scene of the accident*: **quickly**, fast, swiftly, speedily, at (full) speed, at the speed of light, post-haste, hotfoot, at full tilt, as fast as one's legs can carry one, at a gallop, expeditiously, briskly, promptly; hurriedly, in a hurry, fast and furious, hastily, in haste, in a rush, precipitately, abruptly; informal like a shot, double quick, p.d.q. (pretty damn quick), before one can say Jack Robinson, in a flash, hell for leather, at warp speed, pronto, at the double, like a bat out of hell, like (greased) lightning, like a madman/madwoman, like mad, like crazy, like blazes, like a streak, like the wind, like a bomb, like nobody's business, like a scalded cat, like the deuce, a mile a minute, before the ink is dry on the page, before one can say knife; Brit. informal like the clappers, at a rate of knots, like billy-o; N. Amer. informal lickety-split; literary apace.
▷ANTONYMS slowly.

rapport noun *the gift of quiet spiritual rapport with an audience*: **affinity**, close/special relationship, (mutual) understanding, bond, empathy, harmony, sympathy, link, accord.
□ **have a rapport with** *she had an instant rapport with animals*: **relate to**, get on (well) with, respond to, sympathize with, feel sympathy with, feel for, identify with, empathize with, connect with, understand, speak the same language as, be in tune with, be on the same wavelength as; informal hit it off with.

rapprochement noun *growing political and diplomatic rapprochement between the two countries*. See **reconciliation** (sense 3).

rapt adjective **1** *the rapt teenage audience*: **fascinated**, enthralled, spellbound, captivated, riveted, gripped, mesmerized, enchanted, entranced, charmed, bewitched, transported, enraptured; thrilled, ecstatic, rapturous; informal blissed out.
▷ANTONYMS uninterested, inattentive.
2 *she stood motionless for a second, as if rapt in thought*: **engrossed**, absorbed, lost, preoccupied, in a brown study, intent.

rapture noun *she gazed up at him in rapture*: **ecstasy**, bliss, euphoria, elation, exaltation, joy, joyfulness, joyousness, cloud nine, seventh heaven, transport, rhapsody, enchantment, delight, exhilaration, happiness, pleasure, ravishment; informal the top of the world; humorous delectation.
▷ANTONYMS boredom, indifference.
□ **go into raptures** *the critics went into raptures about her performance*: **enthuse**, rhapsodize, rave, gush, wax lyrical, express intense pleasure/enthusiasm; heap praise on, praise to the skies, make much of; informal go wild/mad/crazy.

rapturous adjective *he was given a rapturous reception by a flag-waving crowd*: **ecstatic**, joyful, joyous, elated, euphoric, enraptured, on cloud nine, in seventh heaven, transported, in transports, in raptures, beside oneself with joy/happiness, rhapsodic, ravished, enchanted, enthusiastic, delighted, thrilled, overjoyed, blissful, happy; informal over the moon, on top of the world, blissed out; Austral. informal wrapped.
▷ANTONYMS bored, indifferent.

rara avis noun Latin *a man of integrity in high office is something of a rara avis*: **rarity**, rare person/thing, rare bird, wonder, marvel, nonpareil, nonsuch, one of a kind, find; anomaly, curiosity, oddity, aberration, freak; Brit. informal one-off, oner.

rare adjective **1** *their rare moments of privacy*: **infrequent**, few and far between, scarce, sparse, scattered, thin on the ground, golden, like gold dust, as scarce as hen's teeth; occasional, limited, odd, isolated, sporadic, intermittent, unaccustomed, unwonted; Brit. out of the common.
▷ANTONYMS common, frequent.
2 *a collector of rare stamps and coins | one of Britain's rarest birds*: **unusual**, uncommon, unfamiliar, out of the ordinary, atypical, singular, remarkable, recherché, special, precious.
▷ANTONYMS ordinary, commonplace.
3 *he's a man of rare talent*: **exceptional**, outstanding, unparalleled, peerless, matchless, unique, unequalled, incomparable, unrivalled, inimitable, beyond compare, beyond comparison, without equal, second to none, unsurpassed, surpassing, exquisite, superb, consummate, superior, superlative, first-class, first-rate, special, choice, excellent, very fine; informal

A1, stellar, top-notch; rare unexampled.
▷ANTONYMS common, everyday.

rarefied adjective *the academic or rarefied nature of much of their work*: **esoteric**, exclusive, select, private, cliquish; elevated, exalted, lofty.
▷ANTONYMS commonplace.

rarely adverb *she rarely mentions her late husband*: **seldom**, infrequently, on rare occasions, hardly ever, scarcely ever, hardly, scarcely, almost never, once in a while, only now and then, not often, only occasionally, sporadically; informal once in a blue moon.
▷ANTONYMS often, frequently.

raring adjective *he was raring to get back in the ring*: **eager**, keen, enthusiastic, full of enthusiasm, impatient, longing, champing/chafing at the bit, desperate; ready, willing; informal dying, itching, gagging.

rarity noun **1** *the rarity of earthquakes there has lulled people into a false sense of security*: **infrequency**, rareness, unusualness, uncommonness, singularity, uniqueness; scarcity, scarceness, sparseness.
2 *steam locomotives are now becoming something of a rarity*: **collector's item**, rare person/thing, rare bird, marvel, wonder, nonpareil, one of a kind, find, conversation piece; curiosity, oddity, anomaly, freak; Latin rara avis; Brit. informal one-off, oner.

rascal noun **1** *what's the little rascal been up to now?* **scallywag**, scamp, devil, imp, monkey, mischievous person, mischief-maker, wretch; informal horror, monster; Brit. informal perisher; Irish informal spalpeen; N. English informal tyke, scally; N. Amer. informal varmint, hellion; dated rip; archaic rapscallion, scapegrace.
2 *a double-dealing rascal*: **scoundrel**, rogue, ne'er-do-well, good-for-nothing, reprobate; informal villain, rat; Brit. informal scrote; informal, dated rotter, bounder; dated cad; archaic miscreant, blackguard, knave, vagabond, varlet, wastrel.

rash[1] noun **1** *next day, he broke out in a rash*: **spots**, skin eruption, breakout; hives, heat rash, nettle rash, nappy rash; technical erythema, exanthema, urticaria, papules, roseola, purpura, pompholyx; rare efflorescence.
2 *the incident provoked a rash of articles in the press*: **series**, succession; **spate**, wave, flood, deluge, torrent; outbreak, plague, epidemic, explosion, run, flurry; rare boutade.

rash[2] adjective *he cursed himself for being so rash | a rash decision*: **reckless**, impetuous, impulsive, hasty, overhasty, foolhardy, incautious, precipitate, precipitous, premature, careless, heedless, thoughtless, imprudent, foolish, headstrong, adventurous, over-adventurous, hot-headed, daredevil, devil-may-care, overbold, audacious, indiscreet; ill-considered, unconsidered, unthinking, ill-advised, injudicious, ill-judged, misguided, spur-of-the-moment, unthought-out, hare-brained, unwary, unguarded, wild, madcap; informal harum-scarum; rare temerarious.
▷ANTONYMS careful, cautious, prudent.

> *Choose the right word* **rash, reckless, foolhardy**
>
> All these adjectives are used to criticize actions or people for a lack of proper caution.
>
> **Rash** suggests an overhasty judgement that one might regret (*now isn't the time for us to make rash statements | he would be rash to expect everyone to obey him all the time*).
>
> **Reckless** typically describes something more serious: a *reckless* act is that of a person who simply does not care what damage they cause to themselves or others (*reckless consumption of the earth's resources | he could be convicted of causing death by reckless driving*).
>
> **Foolhardy**, as the word suggests, refers to foolish daring, and a *foolhardy* act is most likely to harm the *foolhardy* person themselves (*old mines were not to be left open as an invitation to any foolhardy visitor*).

rasp verb **1** *enamel is rasped off the edges of the horse's teeth*: **scrape**, file, rub, abrade, grate, sand, sandpaper, scratch, scour; technical excoriate.
2 *'What's going on?' he rasped*: **croak**, say/utter hoarsely, squawk, shrill, caw.
3 *her hard, metallic voice rasped his nerves*: **grate on**, jar on, irritate, irk; get on someone's nerves, set someone's teeth on edge; Brit. informal rub up the wrong way.
▸ noun *the rasp of the engine*: **grinding**, grating, scraping, scrape, scratching, scratch.

rasping adjective *a dry, rasping sound | his father's rasping voice*: **harsh**, grating, jarring, raspy, discordant, dissonant, scratchy, creaky; hoarse, rough, gravelly, croaky, croaking, gruff, husky, throaty, guttural; rare stridulant.

rat noun **1** *her rat of a husband cheated her*: **scoundrel**, wretch, rogue; informal beast, pig, swine, bastard, creep, louse, snake, snake in the grass, bum, lowlife, scumbag, heel, skunk, dog, weasel; Brit. informal scrote; N. Amer. informal rat fink; Irish informal sleeveen; Austral. informal dingo; dated rotter, cad, bounder; vulgar slang shit.
2 *the most famous rat in mob history*: **informer**, betrayer, stool pigeon; informal snitch, finger, squealer, nose; Brit. informal grass, supergrass, nark, snout; Scottish & N. Irish informal tout; N. Amer. informal fink, stoolie; Austral. informal fizgig, pimp, shelf; archaic intelligencer, beagle.
▸ exclamation *Rats! I've lost my ticket!* **damn**, damnation, blast, hell, heck, Gordon Bennett; Brit. bother; informal drat, sugar, botheration, flip, flipping heck/hell; Brit. informal dash, blooming heck/hell, blinking heck/hell; N. Amer. informal doggone it, shucks, shoot, tarnation; Indian informal arré; dated confound it, pish.
▸ verb informal
□ **rat on 1** *we may have been poor but ratting on our friends was something we didn't do*: **inform on/against**, betray, be disloyal to, be unfaithful to, break one's promise to, break faith with, sell out, stab someone in the back; informal tell on, sell down the river, blow the whistle on, squeal on, stitch up, peach on, do the dirty on; Brit. informal grass on, shop; N. Amer. informal rat out, finger, drop a/the dime on; Austral. informal pimp on, pool, put someone's pot on. **2** *he accused the government of ratting on an earlier pledge*: **break**, renege on, go back on, back out of, default on, welsh on; break one's word.

rate noun **1** *a fixed rate of interest | the maximum rate of taxation*: **percentage**, ratio, proportion, scale, standard.
2 *boats can be hired for a reasonable daily rate | an hourly rate of $30*: **charge**, price, cost, tariff, hire, fare, figure, amount, outlay; tax, duty, levy, toll; fee, remuneration, pay, payment, wage, allowance; informal damage.
3 *the rate of change was very fast*: **speed**, pace, tempo, velocity, momentum; gait; informal clip, lick.
□ **at a rate of knots** informal *it is obviously improving at a rate of knots*: **rapidly**, speedily, swiftly, quickly, fast, post-haste, at (full) speed, at the speed of light, at full tilt, as fast as one's legs can carry one, at a gallop; promptly, immediately, briskly; hastily, hurriedly, precipitately; informal p.d.q. (pretty damn quick), double quick, at a lick, hell for leather, pronto, at the double, at wasp speed, a mile a minute, like the wind, like a bomb, like a bat out of hell, like a scalded cat, like the deuce, like nobody's business, like (greased) lightning, like a madman/madwoman; Brit. informal like the clappers, like billy-o; N. Amer. informal lickety-split; literary apace.
▷ANTONYMS slowly.
□ **at any rate** *at any rate, I think I'm in with a chance*: **in any case**, anyhow, anyway, at all events, in any event, nevertheless; whatever happens, no matter what happens, come what may, regardless, notwithstanding.
▸ verb **1** *they were asked to rate their ability at different driving manoeuvres*: **assess**, evaluate, appraise, weigh up, judge, estimate, calculate, compute, gauge, measure, adjudge, value, put a value on; grade, rank, classify, class, categorize, position, place.
2 *the scheme was rated as no more than moderately effective*: **consider to be**, judge to be, reckon to be, think to be, hold to be, deem to be, find to be; regard, account, esteem, mark down as, look on, count.
3 *his statement rated only a brief mention near the end of the report*: **merit**, deserve, warrant, be worthy of, be worth, be entitled to, be deserving of, have a claim to, have a right to.
4 informal *I think he's okay, but Benny doesn't rate him*: **think highly of**, have a high opinion of, admire, think much of, set much store by, hold in esteem, esteem, value, hold in high regard.

rather adverb **1** *I'd rather you went*: **by preference**, sooner, preferably, from/by choice, more willingly, more readily; N. Amer. if I had my druthers.
2 *it all sounds rather complicated*: **quite**, a bit, a little, fairly, slightly, somewhat, relatively, to some degree/extent, comparatively, moderately; informal pretty, sort of, kind of, kinda, ish.
3 *she was finally forced to confront her true feelings for him—or rather, her lack of feelings*: **more precisely**, to be precise, to be exact, strictly speaking, correctly speaking.
4 *she seemed indifferent **rather than** angry*: **more**, more truly; as opposed to, instead of.
5 *the judgement was not impulsive, but rather a carefully thought-out decision*: **on the contrary**, quite the opposite, instead.

ratify verb *both countries were due to ratify the treaty by the end of the year*. See **confirm** (sense 3).

rating noun *the hotel's four-star rating*: **grade**, classification, class, grading, ranking, rank, category, categorization, designation, position, standing, status, placing; assessment, evaluation, appraisal; mark, score.

ratio noun **proportion**, comparative number/extent, quantitative relation, correlation, relationship, correspondence, balance; percentage, fraction, quotient.

ration noun **1** *she allowed herself a daily ration of chocolate*: **allowance**, allocation, quota, fixed amount, amount, quantity, share, portion, helping, allotment, measure, part, lot, proportion, percentage; rare apportionment, quantum, moiety.
2 (**rations**) *the garrison had run out of rations*: **supplies**, provisions, food, food and drink, foodstuffs, eatables, edibles; necessaries, necessities, stores; Scottish vivers; informal grub, eats; N. Amer. informal chuck; archaic victuals, vittles, viands, meat, commons; rare comestibles, provender, aliment, viaticum.
▸ verb **1** *coal and petrol were also rationed*: **control**, limit (to a fixed amount), restrict (the consumption of), conserve, budget.
2 *they **rationed out** the water*: **distribute**, share out, measure out, divide

out/up, apportion, give out, deal out, issue, allocate, allot, dispense, hand out, pass out, dole out, parcel out; rare admeasure.

rational adjective **1** *a rational approach to the problem*: **logical**, reasoned, well reasoned, sensible, reasonable, cogent, coherent, intelligent, wise, judicious, sagacious, astute, shrewd, perceptive, enlightened, clear-eyed, clear-sighted, commonsensical, common-sense, well advised, well grounded, sound, sober, prudent, circumspect, politic; down-to-earth, practical, pragmatic, matter-of-fact, hard-headed, with both one's feet on the ground, unidealistic; informal joined-up.
▷ANTONYMS irrational, illogical.
2 *she was not fully rational at the time of signing the agreement*: **lucid**, coherent, sane, in one's right mind, able to think/reason clearly, of sound mind, in possession of all one's faculties; normal, balanced, well balanced, clear-headed; Latin compos mentis; informal all there.
▷ANTONYMS insane.
3 *man is a self-conscious, rational being*: **intelligent**, thinking, discriminating, reasoning; cognitive, mental, cerebral, logical, analytical, conceptual; rare ratiocinative.

rationale noun *the government's rationale for introducing such radical legislation*: **reason(s)**, reasoning, thinking, (logical) basis, logic, grounds, sense; principle, theory, philosophy, hypothesis, thesis, argument, case; motive, motivation, the whys and wherefores, explanation, justification, excuse, vindication; French raison d'être.

rationalize verb **1** *as soon as Mary had gone he began to rationalize his behaviour*: **justify**, explain (away), account for, defend, vindicate, excuse, make excuses for, make allowances for, give an explanation for, provide a rationale for, make acceptable; rare extenuate.
2 *they embarked on a series of attempts to rationalize the industry*: **streamline**, make more efficient, improve the running of, trim, slim down, hone, make economies in, reduce wastage in, simplify; make cutbacks in, cut back on, prune, retrench on; reorganize, modernize, update.
3 *Parliament should seek to rationalize the country's court structure*: **reorganize**; clarify, make consistent, apply logic/reasoning to; rare pragmatize.

rattle verb **1** *we were awakened by the sound of stones rattling against the window*: **clatter**, bang, clang, clank, clink, clunk.
2 *he put his hand in his pocket and rattled his small change*: **jingle**, jangle, clink, tinkle.
3 *the bus rattled along the bumpy streets*: **jolt**, bump, bounce, shake, vibrate, jar; Brit. judder; rare jounce.
4 *the government were clearly rattled by the campaign*: **unnerve**, disconcert, disturb, fluster, shake, perturb, discompose, discomfit, discountenance, make nervous, put off, throw off balance, ruffle, agitate, put off one's stroke, upset, frighten, scare; informal faze, throw, get to.
□ **rattle someone's cage** informal *if that corporate caveat really rattled your cage, there's more bad news*: **anger**, annoy, antagonize, provoke, vex, irritate, offend; informal aggravate, rile, needle, get someone's back up, make someone's hackles rise, rub up the wrong way, ruffle someone's feathers, get up someone's nose, get in someone's hair, get someone's dander up, get under someone's skin; Brit. informal nark, get on someone's wick.
▷ANTONYMS pacify, placate.
□ **rattle something off** *she rattled off the names of films he had directed*: **reel off**, **recite**, list rapidly, fire off, run through, enumerate; informal spiel off.
□ **rattle on/away** *she found herself rattling on about the meaning of life*: **prattle**, babble, chatter, gabble, prate, go on, run on, jabber, jibber-jabber, gibber, blether, blather, blither, ramble, maunder, drivel, twitter; informal gab, yak, yackety-yak, yap, yabber, yatter; Brit. informal witter, rabbit, chunter, waffle; Scottish & Irish informal slabber; N. Amer. informal run off at the mouth; archaic twaddle, clack, twattle.
▶ noun **1** *the rattle of bottles as he stacked the crates*: **clatter**, clattering, clank, clanking, clink, clinking, clanging; jingle, jingling, jangle, jangling.
2 *there was a choking rattle in his throat*: **death rattle**; technical rale.

ratty adjective Brit. informal *'don't bother!' he repeated, sounding ratty*. See **irritated**.

raucous adjective **1** *outbursts of raucous laughter*: **harsh**, strident, screeching, squawky, squawking, sharp, grating, discordant, dissonant, inharmonious, unmelodious, jarring, brassy; rough, rasping, husky, hoarse, scratchy; noisy, loud, piercing, shrill, ear-splitting, penetrating, clamorous, cacophonous.
▷ANTONYMS soft, dulcet.
2 *a hilariously raucous hen night*: **rowdy**, noisy, boisterous, roisterous, unruly, disorderly, wild.
▷ANTONYMS peaceful, quiet, restrained.

raunchy adjective informal *the show went on for a long time and it was fairly raunchy*. See **sexy** (sense 2).

ravage verb *the inhabitants of the country had been decimated, their land ravaged*: **lay waste**, **devastate**, ruin, leave in ruins, destroy, wreak havoc on, leave desolate, level, raze, demolish, wipe out, wreck, damage; pillage, plunder, harry, maraud, ransack, sack, loot; literary despoil, rape; archaic spoil, havoc; rare depredate, spoliate.

ravaged adjective *a ravaged landscape*: **devastated**, ruined, wrecked, desolate; war-torn, battle-scarred.

ravages plural noun **1** *skin that showed the ravages of time*: **damaging effects**, ill effects, scars.
2 *few places these days are untouched by the ravages of man*: **acts of destruction**, destruction, damage, devastation, ruin, havoc, depredation(s), wreckage; literary rape.

rave verb **1** *the old man was raving about Armageddon and the fires of hell*: **talk wildly**, babble, jabber, ramble, maunder; talk incoherently, be delirious.
2 *I was angry as hell—I raved and swore at them*: **rant**, rant and rave, rage, explode in anger, lose one's temper, be beside oneself, storm, fulminate, deliver a tirade/harangue, go into a frenzy, lose control; shout, roar, thunder, bellow; be very angry, be furious, be enraged, be incensed, fume; informal fly off the handle, flip one's lid, blow one's top, go up the wall, blow a fuse, go off the deep end, hit the roof, go through the roof, be livid, have a fit, lose one's cool, go mad, go bananas, go wild, freak out, have steam coming out of one's ears, foam/froth at the mouth, go ape, be fit to be tied; Brit. informal go spare, go crackers; N. Amer. informal flip one's wig; vulgar slang go apeshit.
3 *he **raved about** her talent and predicted she'd win all the Oscars*: **praise enthusiastically**, go into raptures about/over, wax lyrical about, sing the praises of, praise to the skies, heap praise on, rhapsodize over, enthuse about/over, gush about/over, throw bouquets at, express delight over, acclaim, eulogize, extol; informal go wild about, be mad about, go on about; N. Amer. informal ballyhoo; black English big someone/something up; dated cry someone/something up; rare laud, panegyrize.
▷ANTONYMS criticize, condemn.
▶ noun informal **1** *the imaginative menu won raves from the local food critics*: **enthusiastic/lavish praise**, a rapturous reception, tribute, plaudits, encomiums, bouquets; acclaim, applause.
▷ANTONYMS criticism, condemnation.
2 *their annual fancy-dress rave*. See **party**.
3 *TV news reports have depicted raves as all-night drug parties*: **warehouse party**, acid house party; informal all-nighter.
▶ adjective informal *his big break came when a critic gave him a rave review*: **very enthusiastic**, rapturous, glowing, ecstatic, full of praise, rhapsodic, laudatory, eulogistic, panegyrical, excellent, highly favourable.

raven adjective *her thick raven hair*: **black**, glossy black, jet-black, coal-black, ebony, inky, sooty; literary sable.

Word links **raven**

corvine relating to ravens
unkindness collective noun

ravenous adjective **1** *I'm absolutely ravenous—I missed lunch*: **very hungry**, starving, starved, famished; informal with one's stomach cleaving to one's backbone; rare sharp-set, esurient.
▷ANTONYMS full.
2 *her ravenous appetite*: **voracious**, insatiable, ravening, wolfish; greedy, gluttonous, gannet-like; literary insatiate; rare edacious.

rave-up noun Brit. informal *festive rave-ups*. See **party**.

ravine noun See **gorge** (noun).

raving adjective **1** *she's raving mad*. See **mad**.
2 *she'd never been a raving beauty*: **very great**, considerable, remarkable, extraordinary, singular, striking, outstanding, stunning.

ravings plural noun *he dismissed her words as the ravings of a hysterical woman*: **gibberish**, rambling, babbling, wild talk, incoherent talk.

ravish verb **1** *I'm sorry I kissed you, but I swear I've no intention of ravishing you*: **rape**, sexually assault/abuse, violate, force oneself on, molest; seduce; euphemistic take advantage of, have one's (wicked) way with; archaic dishonour, defile.
2 *those who adore the steely, mineral style of Chablis will be ravished by this wine*: **enrapture**, send into raptures, enchant, fill with delight, delight, charm, entrance, enthral, captivate, bewitch, spellbind, fascinate, transport, overjoy; informal blow away; rare rapture.

ravishing adjective *you look utterly ravishing*: **very beautiful**, gorgeous, stunning, wonderful, exquisite, lovely, striking, magnificent, dazzling, radiant, delightful, charming, enchanting, entrancing, captivating, bewitching; informal incredible, amazing, sensational, fantastic, fabulous, terrific, smashing, heavenly, divine, out of this world, fab, drop-dead gorgeous, knockout, delectable, scrumptious; N. Amer. informal babelicious, bodacious.
▷ANTONYMS hideous.

raw adjective **1** *a piece of raw carrot | raw fish*: **uncooked**, fresh; underdone.
▷ANTONYMS cooked.
2 *the cost of raw materials is likely to rise | raw silk*: **unprocessed**, untreated, unrefined, crude, natural, unmilled, unprepared, unfinished; green.
▷ANTONYMS refined, processed.
3 *a group of raw recruits*: **inexperienced**, new, lacking experience,

untrained, unskilled, unpractised, untried, untested, unseasoned, untutored, unschooled; callow, immature, green, ignorant, naive, unsophisticated; informal wet behind the ears.
▷ANTONYMS experienced, skilled.
4 *his skin was raw in places*: **sore**, red, inflamed, painful, sensitive, tender; abraded, chafed, skinned, open, exposed, unhealed, bloody; technical excoriated.
5 *it was a raw morning with a bitter east wind*: **bleak**, cold, chilly, chilling, chill, freezing, icy, icy-cold, wintry, bitter, biting, piercing, penetrating, sharp, keen, damp, wet; informal nippy; Brit. informal parky.
▷ANTONYMS warm, balmy.
6 *the raw emotions depicted in such stories*: **strong**, intense, passionate, fervent, vehement, powerful, violent, acute; **undisguised**, unconcealed, unrestrained, uninhibited.
7 *raw, contemporary images of Latin America*: **realistic**, true to life, unembellished, unvarnished, gritty, naked, bare, brutal, harsh; **frank**, candid, honest, forthright, straightforward, direct, blunt, outspoken; informal warts and all.
▷ANTONYMS unrealistic, idealized.
8 *raw but authentic artistic power*: **unsophisticated**, crude, rough, unpolished, unrefined, undeveloped.
□ **in the raw** informal *I slept in the raw*. See **naked**.

raw-boned adjective **thin**, as thin as a rake, lean, gaunt, bony, angular, skinny, size-zero, spare, lanky, scrawny, scraggy, hollow-cheeked; underfed, underweight, emaciated, skeletal, half-starved; dated spindle-shanked.
▷ANTONYMS plump, well padded.

ray noun **1** *misty rays of light shone through the trees*: **beam**, shaft, streak, bar, pencil, finger, stream, gleam, flash, glint, glimmer, flicker, twinkle, shimmer.
2 *there was just one small ray of hope*: **glimmer**, flicker, spark, glint, trace, hint, indication, suggestion, sign, scintilla, whisper.
▸ verb *Fran leaned forward, her fair hair raying out in the water*: **spread out**, fan out, radiate out.

raze verb *during the campaign, 80,000 people were killed and 440 villages razed*: **destroy**, demolish, raze to the ground, tear down, pull down, knock down, knock to pieces, level, flatten, bulldoze, fell, wipe out, lay waste, ruin, wreck.

re preposition *correspondence re the formation of neighbourhood watch schemes*: **about**, concerning, regarding, with regard to, relating to, apropos (of), on the subject of, respecting, in respect of, with respect to, with reference to, as regards, in the matter of, in connection with, referring to, touching on; Scottish anent.

reach verb **1** *Travis reached out a hand and pulled her towards him*: **stretch out**, hold out, extend, outstretch, thrust out, stick out; literary outreach.
2 informal *reach me that book*: **pass**, hand, give, let someone have.
3 *by the time she reached Helen's house she was exhausted*: **arrive at**, get to, get as far as, come to, make it to, gain; end up at, land up at, set foot on; informal make, hit.
4 *the temperature reached 94°F | his political popularity had reached a new low*: **attain**, get to, amount to; **rise to**, climb to; **fall to**, sink to, drop to; run to; informal hit.
5 *the two governments failed to reach an agreement*: **achieve**, attain, gain, accomplish; work out, draw up, put together, strike, negotiate, thrash out, hammer out.
6 *one of their solicitors has been trying to reach you all day*: **get in touch with**, contact, get through to, get, communicate with, make contact with; speak to, talk to; informal get hold of; Brit. informal raise.
7 *their central concern is to reach more people at all levels of society*: **influence**, sway, carry weight with, get through to, get to, make an impression on, have an effect on, have an impact on, register with.
▸ noun **1** *Bobby moved out of his reach*: **grasp**, range.
2 *set yourself small goals which are within your reach*: **capabilities**, capacity.
3 *they may be beyond the reach of the law*: **jurisdiction**, authority, sway, control, command, influence; **scope**, range, compass, ambit, orbit, latitude; sphere, area, field, territory.

react verb **1** *Ginny wondered how he would react if she told him the truth*: **behave**, act, take it, conduct oneself, proceed; **respond**, reply, answer; retaliate; rare comport oneself.
2 *it was perhaps no wonder that he* **reacted against** *this spartan, puritanical environment*: **rebel against**, oppose, revolt against, rise up against.

reaction noun **1** *his reaction had bewildered her | the reaction from listeners was encouraging*: **response**; answer, reply, rejoinder, retort, riposte; feedback; informal comeback.
2 *during the 1960s there was a reaction against this kind of sociology*: **backlash**, counteraction, recoil.
3 *the forces of reaction which spring up in the face of change*: **conservatism**, ultra-conservatism, the right, the right wing, the extreme right; counter-revolution, revanchism.

reactionary adjective *government policy became increasingly reactionary*: **right-wing**, conservative, rightist, ultra-conservative; blimpish, diehard; traditionalist, conventional, traditional, old-fashioned, unprogressive; N. Amer. Birchite.
▷ANTONYMS radical, progressive.
▸ noun *he was later to become an extreme reactionary*: **right-winger**, conservative, rightist, diehard, Colonel Blimp; traditionalist, conventionalist; N. Amer. Birchite; informal stick-in-the-mud.
▷ANTONYMS radical.

Word toolkit

reactionary	traditionalist	conventional
forces	Catholic	weapons
elements	Muslim	methods
policies	Anglican	medicine
politics	priest	warfare
agenda	doctrine	thinking
regime	Conservative	techniques
ideology	supporters	morality
nationalism	parish	standards

read verb **1** *he sat reading the evening newspaper*: **peruse**, study, scrutinize, look through; pore over, devour, be absorbed in, bury oneself in; wade through, plough through; run one's eye over, cast an eye over, leaf through, scan, glance through, flick through, skim through, thumb through, flip through, browse through, dip into; archaic con.
2 *'Listen to this,' he said and read a passage of the letter*: **read out**, read aloud, say aloud, recite, declaim.
3 *I can't read my own writing*: **decipher**, make out, make sense of, interpret, understand, comprehend.
4 *his remark could be read as a dig at Forsyth*: **interpret**, take, take to mean, construe, see, explain, understand.
5 *the thermometer read 0°C*: **indicate**, register, record, display, show, have as a reading, measure.
6 *I can't read your future, you know*: **foresee**, predict, forecast, foretell, prophesy, divine, prognosticate; archaic augur, presage.
7 *he went on to read modern history at Oxford*: **study**, do, take; N. Amer. & Austral./NZ major in.
□ **read something into something** *officials cautioned against reading too much into the statistics*: **infer from**, interpolate from, assume from, attribute to; read between the lines, get hold of the wrong end of the stick.
□ **read someone the riot act** *they read me the riot act on fighting and grounded me*: **reprimand**, rebuke, scold, admonish, reprove, upbraid, chastise, chide, censure, castigate, lambaste, berate, lecture, criticize, take to task, give a piece of one's mind to, haul over the coals; informal tell off, give someone a telling-off, dress down, give someone a dressing-down, bawl out, pitch into, lay into, lace into, blow up at, give someone an earful, give someone a roasting, give someone a rocket, give someone a rollicking; Brit. informal have a go at, carpet, tear someone off a strip, give someone what for, let someone have it; N. Amer. informal chew out, ream out; Brit. vulgar slang bollock, give someone a bollocking.
□ **read up on** *Chris had read up on this particular method of teaching children to write*: **study**, get up; informal bone up on; Brit. informal mug up on, swot; archaic con.
□ **take as read** *it is taken as read that our products must be good*: **presuppose**, take for granted, presume, assume, take it, suppose, surmise, think, accept, consider, postulate, posit.
▸ noun *I settled down for a read of 'The Irish Press'*: **perusal**, study, scan, scrutiny; look (at), browse (through), glance (through), leaf (through), flick (through), skim (through).

Word links **read**

legible readable
illegible unreadable
literacy ability to read
illiteracy inability to read

readable adjective **1** *the inscription is still perfectly readable*: **legible**, easy to read, decipherable, easily deciphered, clear, intelligible, understandable, comprehensible, easy to understand.
▷ANTONYMS illegible, indecipherable.
2 *her novels are immensely readable*: **enjoyable**, entertaining, interesting, absorbing, engaging, gripping, enthralling, engrossing, compulsive, stimulating; worth reading, well written; informal unputdownable.
▷ANTONYMS boring, unreadable.

readily adverb **1** *Durkin readily offered to drive him*: **willingly**, without hesitation, unhesitatingly, gladly, happily, cheerfully, with pleasure, with good grace, without reluctance, ungrudgingly, voluntarily; eagerly, promptly, quickly; freely.
▷ANTONYMS reluctantly.
2 *the island is readily accessible from the mainland*: **easily**, with ease, without difficulty, effortlessly.
▷ANTONYMS with difficulty.

r

readiness noun **1** *their readiness to accept new technology*: **willingness**, inclination, enthusiasm, eagerness, keenness, gameness; promptness, quickness, alacrity; ease, facility; dated address.
2 *we need to maintain our forces in a state of readiness*: **preparedness**, preparation, fitness.
3 *I was surprised at the readiness of his reply*: **promptness**, quickness, rapidity, swiftness, speed, speediness, punctuality, timeliness; **cleverness**, sharpness, astuteness, shrewdness, keenness, discernment, aptness, adroitness, deftness, skill, skilfulness.
□ **in readiness** *there were candles in readiness, and Anne quickly lit them* | *the troops were in readiness for a possible battle*: **ready**, at the ready, available, on hand, accessible, handy, at one's fingertips; **prepared**, primed, on standby, standing by, on stand-to, on call, on full alert; informal on tap.

reading noun **1** *a cursory reading of the financial pages*: **perusal**, study, scan, scanning, scrutiny; browse (through), look (through), glance (through), leaf (through), flick (through), skim (through).
2 *a man of wide reading*: **learning**, book learning, scholarship, education, erudition, knowledge (of literature).
3 *readings from the Bible*: **passage**, lesson; section, piece, selection; recital, recitation.
4 *a one-sided reading of the situation*: **interpretation**, construal, understanding, account, explanation, analysis, construction; version; informal take.
5 *the reading on the gas meter*: **record**, figure, indication, read-out, display, measurement.

ready adjective **1** *are you ready to go now?* | *she'd gone too far—he wasn't ready for this*: **prepared**, all set, set, organized, in a fit state, equipped, primed; informal fit, psyched up, geared up, up for it, hot to trot.
▶ANTONYMS unprepared, taken by surprise.
2 *supper's ready* | *at last everything was ready*: **completed**, finished, prepared, organized, done, arranged, fixed, in readiness; ripe; informal done and dusted.
▶ANTONYMS incomplete, in preparation.
3 *he's always ready to help*: **willing**, prepared, pleased, inclined, agreeable, disposed, predisposed, minded, of a mind, in the mood, apt, prone, given, likely; **eager**, keen, happy, glad; informal game.
▶ANTONYMS reluctant, unwilling.
4 *she looked* **ready to** *collapse*: **about to**, on the point of, on the verge of, on the brink of, close to, as if one is going to, in danger of, liable to, likely to.
5 *the early settlers found a ready supply of flints in the chalk cliffs*: **easily available**, available, accessible; **handy**, close at hand, at hand, to hand, on hand, near at hand, convenient, within reach, at the ready, near, at one's fingertips, at one's disposal; on call; informal on tap.
6 *she had a ready answer to this challenge* | *Sir Vivien is blessed with great charm and a ready wit*: **prompt**, quick, rapid, swift, speedy, fast, immediate, unhesitating; timely; **clever**, sharp, astute, shrewd, keen, acute, perceptive, discerning, resourceful, smart, bright, alert, apt, adroit, deft, agile, skilful; archaic rathe.
□ **at the ready** *a group of parents stood on the sidelines, camcorders at the ready*: **in position**, poised, ready for use, ready for action, waiting; all systems go; N. Amer. on deck.
□ **make ready** *the crew were busily making ready for the departure*: **prepare**, make preparations, make provisions, get everything ready, take the necessary steps, do the necessary, gear up for; gear oneself up.
▶ **verb** *seven other vessels were readied and armed* | *he wanted time to ready himself*: **prepare**, get ready, make ready, organize, equip, put together, fix; prime, set; gear oneself up, arm oneself; informal psych oneself up; literary gird oneself, gird up one's loins.

ready-made adjective **1** *ready-made clothing*: **ready to wear**, off the shelf; Brit. off the peg; N. Amer. off the rack.
▶ANTONYMS bespoke, tailor-made.
2 *ready-made meals*: **pre-cooked**, oven-ready, TV, frozen, convenience.

real adjective **1** *she treats fictional characters as if they were real people*: **actual**, existent, non-fictional, non-fictitious, factual; historical; material, physical, tangible, concrete, palpable, corporeal, substantial; rare unimaginary, veridical.
▶ANTONYMS unreal, imaginary.
2 *do you think it could be real gold?* **genuine**, authentic, bona fide, pukka; informal honest-to-goodness, your actual, kosher.
▶ANTONYMS imitation, fake.
3 *it's not my real name*: **true**, actual.
4 *there were tears of real grief in his eyes*: **sincere**, genuine, true, unfeigned, unpretended, heartfelt, from the heart, unaffected, earnest, wholehearted, fervent, honest, truthful.
▶ANTONYMS false.
5 *he was a real man with manly pursuits*: **proper**, true, rightly so called; informal regular; archaic very.
6 *you made me look a real idiot*: **complete**, utter, thorough, absolute, total, prize, perfect, veritable; Brit. informal right, proper; Austral./NZ informal fair; archaic arrant.
▶ **adverb** N. Amer. informal *that was real good of you*. See **very**.

realism noun **1** *his optimism was tinged with realism*: **pragmatism**, practicality, matter-of-factness, common sense, level-headedness, clear-sightedness.
2 *both stories show life in a mining town with some degree of realism*: **authenticity**, fidelity, verisimilitude, truthfulness, faithfulness, naturalism; informal telling it like it is.

realistic adjective **1** *you've got to be realistic and accept what has happened*: **practical**, pragmatic, matter-of-fact, down-to-earth, sensible, commonsensical; rational, logical, reasonable, level-headed, clear-sighted, hard-headed, businesslike, sober, unromantic, unsentimental, unidealistic, tough-minded, robust, hard-boiled, unemotional; informal with both/one's feet on the ground, hard-nosed, no-nonsense.
▶ANTONYMS unrealistic, idealistic.
2 *a regional settlement remains an important and realistic aim*: **achievable**, attainable, feasible, practicable, within the bounds of possibility, viable, reasonable, sensible, logical, workable; informal doable.
▶ANTONYMS impracticable.
3 *the film was not intended to be a realistic portrayal of the war*: **true to life**, lifelike, true, truthful, faithful, real-life, close, naturalistic, authentic, genuine, representational, graphic, convincing; French vérité; informal kitchen-sink, warts and all; rare verisimilar, veristic, speaking.
▶ANTONYMS imaginative, fictional.

reality noun **1** *he is unable to distinguish between fantasy and reality*: **the real world**, real life, actuality; truth; physical existence, corporeality, substantiality, materiality.
▶ANTONYMS fantasy.
2 *the harsh realities of life*: **fact**, actuality, truth, verity.
3 *the reality of Marryat's detail*: **verisimilitude**, authenticity, realism, fidelity, faithfulness.
▶ANTONYMS idealism.
□ **in reality** *she sounded sympathetic but in reality she was furious*: **in fact**, in actual fact, in point of fact, as a matter of fact, actually, really, in truth, if truth be told; in practice; archaic in sooth.

realization noun **1** *the growing realization that many of these diseases were intimately related to people's lifestyles*: **awareness**, understanding, comprehension, consciousness, apprehension, cognizance, appreciation, recognition, perception, discernment.
2 *the realization of our dreams surpassed our wildest expectations*: **actualization**, **fulfilment**, achievement, accomplishment, attainment, bringing to fruition, bringing into being, consummation, effecting; rare effectuation, reification.

realize verb **1** *it took him a moment to realize what she meant* | *I realized someone was watching me*: **register**, perceive, discern, be/become aware of (the fact that), be/become conscious of (the fact that), notice; understand, grasp, take in, comprehend, see, recognize, work out, fathom (out), appreciate, ascertain, apprehend, be/become cognizant of, know, conceive; discover, find; see the light; informal latch on to, cotton on to, catch on to, tumble to, get, figure out, get a fix on, wrap one's mind around, get the message, get the picture; Brit. informal twig, suss; N. Amer. informal savvy; rare cognize.
2 *he realized a 15-year dream by restoring the castle to its original glory*: **fulfil**, achieve, accomplish, make real, make a reality, make happen, make concrete, bring to fruition, bring about, bring off, consummate, perform, carry out, carry through, execute, actualize, effect; rare effectuate, reify.
3 *he had been able to realize significant trading profits for his companies*: **make**, obtain, clear, acquire, gain, bring in, reap; earn, return, produce.
4 *when the goods were put up for sale by auction, they realized £3000*: **be sold for**, sell for, fetch, go for, get, make, net.
5 *he realized other assets and used the money to subsidize the business*: **cash in**, convert into cash; liquidate, capitalize.

really adverb **1** *although he lived in a derelict house, he was really very wealthy*: **in fact**, in actual fact, actually, in reality, in point of fact, as a matter of fact, in truth, if truth be told, to tell the truth, in actuality; archaic in sooth.
2 *he really likes her* | *I really appreciate what you've done*: **genuinely**, truly, honestly; undoubtedly, without a doubt, indubitably, certainly, surely, assuredly, unquestionably, undeniably; indeed; archaic verily.
3 *I bet this place is really spooky late at night* | *they were really kind to me*: **very**, extremely, thoroughly, decidedly, awfully, terribly, frightfully, dreadfully, fearfully, exceptionally, exceedingly, immensely, uncommonly, remarkably, eminently, extraordinarily, most, positively, downright; heartily; Scottish unco; N. Amer. quite; French très; informal terrifically, tremendously, right, devilishly, ultra, too ... for words, mucho, mega, seriously, majorly, oh-so, stinking; Brit. informal jolly, ever so, dead, well, fair; N. Amer. informal real, mighty, awful, plumb, powerful, way, bitching; S. African informal lekker; informal, dated devilish; archaic exceeding, sore.
4 *his career is really over*: **for all practical purposes**, to all intents and purposes, virtually, just about, almost.
▶ **exclamation** *'Apparently they've split up.' 'Really?'*: **is that so**, is that a fact, well I never, well I never did; go on, you don't say; informal well knock/blow me down with a feather; Brit. informal well I'll be blowed; N. Amer. informal well what do you know about that; archaic go to.

realm noun **1** *his prime concern was to promote peace in the realm*: **kingdom**, sovereign state, monarchy; empire, principality, palatinate, duchy; country,

land, domain, dominion, nation, province.
2 *the realm of academic research*: **domain**, sphere, area, field, department, arena; world, region, province, territory, zone, orbit.

reap verb **1** *the corn was reaped in two stages*: **harvest**, garner, gather in, bring in, take in; cut, crop.
2 *it may be some time before the company reaps the benefits of its current investments*: **receive**, obtain, get, acquire, secure, bring in, realize, derive, procure.

rear[1] verb **1** *I was born and reared in Newcastle*: **bring up**, care for, look after, nurture, parent; educate, train, instruct; N. Amer. raise.
2 *he reared cattle and sheep*: **breed**, raise, keep, tend.
3 *laboratory-reared plantlets*: **grow**, cultivate.
4 *Harry stiffened and reared his head*: **raise**, lift (up), hold up, uplift, upraise.
5 *Creagan Hill reared up before them*: **rise**, rise up, tower, soar, loom.

rear[2] noun **1** *a door at the rear of the building*: **back**, back part, hind part, back end, other end; Anatomy occiput; Nautical stern.
▷ANTONYMS front.
2 *Sophie and I brought up the rear of the queue*: **end**, tail end, rear end, back end, tail; N. Amer. tag end; Nautical aft, after.
▷ANTONYMS front, vanguard; bow.
3 *he slapped her on the rear*: **buttocks**, backside, behind, rear end, rump, seat, haunches, hindquarters, cheeks; Brit. bottom; French derrière; German Sitzfleisch; informal sit-upon, stern, BTM, tochus; Brit. informal bum, botty, prat, jacksie; Scottish informal bahookie; N. Amer. informal butt, fanny, tush, tushie, tail, duff, buns, booty, caboose, heinie, patootie, keister, tuchis, bazoo, bippy; W. Indian informal batty; humorous posterior, fundament; black English rass, rusty dusty; Brit. vulgar slang arse; N. Amer. vulgar slang ass; technical nates.
▶ adjective *the car's rear bumper*: **back**, end, rearmost, endmost; hind, hinder, hindmost; technical posterior, caudal.
▷ANTONYMS front, foremost.

rearrange verb **1** *the curtains had been drawn, the furniture rearranged*: **reposition**, move round, change round, arrange differently, regroup, switch round, swap round.
2 *Tony had rearranged his work schedule*: **reorganize**, alter, adjust, change (round), reorder, reschedule, rejig, reshuffle; informal jigger.

reason noun **1** *he cited a lack of funds as the main reason for his decision*: **cause**, grounds, ground, basis, rationale; **motive**, motivation, purpose, point, aim, intention, objective, goal, occasion, impetus, inducement, incentive; **explanation**, justification, case, argument, defence, apology, vindication, excuse, pretext, rationalization; warrant; the whys and wherefores; Latin apologia.
2 *a rising crescendo of postmodern voices today rail against reason and science*: **rationality**, logic, logical thought, scientific thinking, reasoning, thought, cognition; the mind, intellect, intelligence, intellectuality; Philosophy nous; rare ratiocination.
▷ANTONYMS emotion, feeling.
3 *he was afraid of losing his reason*: **sanity**, mind, mental faculties, mental health, soundness of mind; senses, wits; informal marbles.
4 *he continues, against reason, to love the woman passionately*: **good sense**, good judgement, common sense, sense, judgement, understanding, wisdom, sagacity; reasonableness, moderation, propriety; practicality, practicability, advisability.
□ **by reason of** *those incapable of supporting themselves by reason of age, infirmity, or disease*: **because of**, on account of, as a result of, as a consequence of, owing to, due to, by virtue of, thanks to, through.
□ **with reason** *he was anxious, with reason, about his own political survival*: **justifiably**, justly, legitimately, rightly, properly, reasonably.
▶ verb **1** *such a child, left to himself, grows up unable to express himself and unable to reason*: **think rationally**, think logically, think straight, use one's mind, use one's common sense, use one's head, use one's brain, think things through, cogitate; intellectualize; informal put on one's thinking cap; rare cerebrate, ratiocinate, logicize.
2 *Scott reasoned that if Annabel were having a heart attack, she wouldn't be able to talk on the telephone*: **calculate**, come to the conclusion, conclude, reckon, think, consider, be of the opinion, be of the view, judge, deduce, infer, surmise; N. Amer. informal figure.
3 *she was growing too tired to **reason it out***: **work out**, find an answer/solution to, think through, come to a conclusion about, sort out, make sense of, get to the bottom of, puzzle out, solve; informal figure out.
4 *her husband tried to **reason with** her, but she refused to listen*: **talk round**, bring round, win round, persuade, coax, prevail on, convince; show someone the error of their ways, make someone see the light.

Word links **reason**
rational relating to reason

reasonable adjective **1** *a reasonable man | it seemed a reasonable explanation*: **sensible**, rational, open to reason, full of common sense, logical, fair, fair-minded, just, equitable, decent; intelligent, wise, level-headed, practical, realistic; based on good sense, sound, judicious, well thought out, well grounded, reasoned, well reasoned, valid, commonsensical, advisable, well advised; tenable, plausible, feasible, credible, acceptable, admissible, believable, viable.
▷ANTONYMS unreasonable, illogical.
2 *you must take all reasonable precautions to ensure the safety of your property*: **within reason**, practicable, sensible; appropriate, suitable, fitting, proper.
▷ANTONYMS excessive, obsessional.
3 *most hire cars are in reasonable condition*: **fairly good**, acceptable, satisfactory, average, adequate, respectable, fair, decent, all right, not bad, tolerable, passable; informal OK, fair-to-middling.
▷ANTONYMS bad, poor.
4 *good hot food at reasonable prices*: **inexpensive**, moderate, low, low-cost, low-priced, modest, within one's means, economical, cheap, budget, bargain; competitive.
▷ANTONYMS expensive, inflated.

reasoned adjective *reasoned argument*: **logical**, rational, well thought out, clear, lucid, coherent, cogent, systematic, methodical, organized, well organized, well expressed, well presented, considered, sensible, intelligent.
▷ANTONYMS illogical, unsystematic.

reasoning noun *I can't quite follow your reasoning | the reasoning behind their decisions*: **thinking**, line of thought, train of thought, thought, thought process, logic, reason, rationality, analysis, interpretation, explanation, deduction, rationalization, argumentation; reasons, rationale, arguments, premises, case; supposition, hypothesis, thesis; Philosophy dialectics; rare cerebration, ratiocination, mentation.

reassure verb *Daniel patted his wife's arm and tried to reassure her*: **put/set someone's mind at rest**, dispel someone's fears, restore/bolster someone's confidence, raise someone's spirits, put someone at ease, encourage, hearten, buoy up, cheer up; comfort, soothe; rare inspirit.
▷ANTONYMS alarm, unnerve.

rebate noun *you will be entitled to a 20 per cent rebate*: **refund**, partial refund, repayment; discount, deduction, reduction, decrease; allowance, concession.

rebel noun (stress on the first syllable) **1** *the rebels took control of the capital*: **revolutionary**, insurgent, revolutionist, mutineer, agitator, subversive, guerrilla, anarchist, terrorist; freedom fighter, resistance fighter; traitor, renegade; in Mexico, historical Zapatista; in S. America, historical Montonero; rare insurrectionist, insurrectionary.
2 *the modernist concept of the artist as a rebel, challenging society's norms*: **nonconformist**, dissenter, dissident, iconoclast, maverick; heretic, recusant, apostate, schismatic.
▶ verb (stress on the second syllable) **1** *the citizens of the town rebelled*: **revolt**, mutiny, riot, rise up, rise up in arms, take up arms, stage/mount a rebellion, take to the streets, defy the authorities, refuse to obey orders, be insubordinate.
2 *his stomach rebelled at the mere thought of food*: **recoil**, show/feel repugnance; shrink (from), flinch (from), shy away (from), pull back (from).
3 *most teenagers go through a stage of **rebelling against** their parents*: **defy**, disobey, refuse to obey, flout, kick against, challenge, oppose, resist, be at odds with, refuse to accept the authority of, repudiate; dissent; fly in the face of, kick over the traces.
▷ANTONYMS obey, conform.
▶ adjective (stress on the first syllable) **1** *the rebel officers who led the abortive coup*: **insurgent**, revolutionary, mutinous, rebellious, mutinying; traitorous, renegade; rare insurrectionary, insurrectionist.
2 *rebel MPs | rebel clergymen*: **rebellious**, defiant, disobedient, insubordinate, subversive, disaffected, malcontent, resistant, dissentient, recalcitrant, unmanageable, ungovernable; nonconformist, maverick, iconoclastic; heretical, recusant, apostate, schismatic; archaic contumacious.
▷ANTONYMS obedient, compliant.

rebellion noun **1** *troops were sent into the area to suppress the rebellion*: **uprising**, revolt, insurrection, mutiny, revolution, insurgence, insurgency, rising, rioting, riot; civil disobedience, civil disorder, unrest, anarchy, fighting in the streets; coup, regime change; French coup d'état, jacquerie; German putsch.
2 *in the 1950s and 60s listening to rock'n'roll was an act of rebellion*: **defiance**, disobedience, rebelliousness, insubordination, mutinousness, subversion, subversiveness, resistance, dissent, nonconformity; heresy, apostasy, schism, recusancy; archaic contumacy.
▷ANTONYMS obedience.

rebellious adjective **1** *rebellious troops*: **rebel**, insurgent, mutinous, disorderly, lawless, out of control, mutinying, rebelling, rioting, riotous, revolutionary, seditious, subversive; breakaway, traitorous, renegade; rare insurrectionary, insurrectionist.
▷ANTONYMS obedient, law-abiding.
2 *a rebellious adolescent*: **defiant, disobedient**, insubordinate, unruly, ungovernable, unmanageable, uncontrollable, turbulent, mutinous, wayward, obstreperous, recalcitrant, refractory, intractable, resistant, dissentient, disaffected, malcontent; nonconformist; Brit. informal bolshie; archaic contumacious.
▷ANTONYMS conformist, compliant.

r

Word toolkit **rebellious**

See **unruly**.

rebirth noun *the rebirth of black nationalism | his spiritual rebirth*: **revival**, renaissance, renascence, resurrection, reawakening, renewal, resurgence, regeneration, restoration, new beginning; revitalization, rejuvenation, revivification; reincarnation.

rebound verb **1** *the ball rebounded off the wall*: **bounce**, bounce back, spring back, ricochet, boomerang, glance, recoil; N. Amer. carom; rare resile.
2 *sterling rebounded and closed half a pfennig higher*: **recover**, rally, bounce back, pick up, make a recovery, make a comeback.
3 *Thomas's tactics **rebounded on him***: **backfire on**, misfire on, boomerang on, have an adverse effect on, have unwelcome repercussions for, come back on, be self-defeating for, cause one to be hoist with one's own petard; informal score an own goal; archaic redound on.

rebuff verb *his offer was immediately rebuffed | she rebuffed the prince on several occasions*: **reject**, turn down, spurn, refuse, decline, repudiate, disdain; snub, slight, repulse, repel, dismiss, brush off, turn one's back on; give someone the cold shoulder, cold-shoulder, ignore, cut (dead), look right through; informal give someone the brush-off, tell someone where to get off, put down, freeze out, stiff-arm; Brit. informal knock back; N. Amer. informal give someone the bum's rush, give someone the brush; Austral. informal snout; informal, dated give someone the go-by.
▷**ANTONYMS** accept, welcome.
▶ noun *the rebuff did little to dampen his ardour*: **rejection**, snub, slight, repulse, cut; refusal, spurning, repudiation, repulsion, cold-shouldering, discouragement; informal brush-off, knock-back, put-down, kick in the teeth, slap in the face, smack in the face, smack in the eye.

rebuild verb *they must have spent a colossal amount rebuilding the stadium*: **reconstruct**, renovate, restore, refashion, remodel, revamp, remake, reassemble; recondition; N. Amer. informal rehab.
▷**ANTONYMS** demolish.

rebuke verb *however much she hated seeing him drink, she never rebuked him in front of others*: **reprimand**, reproach, scold, admonish, reprove, remonstrate with, chastise, chide, upbraid, berate, take to task, pull up, castigate, lambaste, read someone the Riot Act, give someone a piece of one's mind, haul over the coals, criticize, censure; informal tell off, give someone a talking-to, give someone a telling-off, dress down, give someone a dressing-down, give someone an earful, give someone a roasting, give someone a rocket, rap, rap over the knuckles, slap someone's wrist, let someone have it, bawl out, give someone hell, come down on, blow up, pitch into, lay into, lace into, give someone a caning, slap down, blast, rag, keelhaul; Brit. informal tick off, have a go at, carpet, monster, give someone a mouthful, tear someone off a strip, give someone what for, give someone a rollicking, wig, give someone a wigging, give someone a row, row; N. Amer. informal chew out, ream out; Brit. vulgar slang bollock, give someone a bollocking; N. Amer. vulgar slang chew someone's ass, ream someone's ass; dated call down, rate, give someone a rating, trim; rare reprehend, objurgate.
▷**ANTONYMS** praise, compliment, commend.
▶ noun *Damian sat down, completely silenced by the rebuke*: **reprimand**, reproach, reproof, scolding, admonishment, admonition, reproval, remonstration, lecture, upbraiding, castigation, lambasting, criticism, censure; informal telling-off, rap, rap over the knuckles, dressing-down, earful, roasting, bawling-out, caning, blast, row; Brit. informal ticking-off, carpeting, rollicking, wigging; Brit. vulgar slang bollocking; dated rating.
▷**ANTONYMS** praise, compliment, commendation.

rebut verb *the shadow chancellor rebutted the prime minister's allegations*: **refute**, deny, disprove, prove wrong, prove false; invalidate, negate, contradict, counter, discredit, give the lie to, drive a coach and horses through, quash, explode, shoot down, destroy; informal shoot full of holes, blow sky-high; rare controvert, confute, negative.
▷**ANTONYMS** confirm.

rebuttal noun *a point-by-point rebuttal of the accusations*: **refutation**, denial, disproving, counter-argument, countering, invalidation, negation, contradiction; Law counterstatement, surrejoinder, rebutter, surrebutter, replication; rare confutation, disproval.
▷**ANTONYMS** confirmation.

recalcitrant adjective *a class of recalcitrant fifteen-year-olds*. See **defiant**.

recall verb **1** *he recalled his student days at Harvard*: **remember**, recollect, call to mind, think of; think back on/to, look back on, cast one's mind back to, reminisce about, hark back to; Scottish mind.
▷**ANTONYMS** forget.
2 *their daring exploits and the nobility of their spirit recall the legendary days of chivalry*: **bring to mind**, call to mind, put one in mind of, call up, summon up, conjure up, evoke, echo, allude to.
3 *the Panamanian ambassador was recalled from Peru*: **summon back**, order back, call back, bring back.
▷**ANTONYMS** dissolve, prorogue.
4 formal *he sent another note to Lord Grey, recalling his earlier communication*: **revoke**, rescind, cancel, retract, countermand, take back, withdraw, repeal, veto, overrule, override, abrogate; annul, invalidate, nullify, declare null and void, void; rare disannul, negate.
▷**ANTONYMS** ratify, confirm.
▶ noun **1** *the recall of the ambassador*: **summoning back**, ordering back, calling back; summons.
2 *most people find they can improve their recall of dreams with practice*: **recollection**, memory, remembrance; technical anamnesis.
3 formal *the Chancery Division may possess power to order the recall of probate*: **revocation**, rescinding, cancellation, cancelling, retraction, retracting, countermanding, withdrawal, abrogation, repeal, vetoing, veto; annulment, invalidation, nullification; rare rescission.

recant verb **1** *he was forced to recant his position, and was subjected to imprisonment*: **renounce**, forswear, disavow, deny, repudiate, renege on, abjure, relinquish, abandon; archaic forsake.
▷**ANTONYMS** reaffirm.
2 *he was charged with heresy, refused to recant, and was put to death*: **change one's mind**, be apostate, defect, renege; rare apostatize, tergiversate.
3 *he recanted his testimony*: **retract**, take back, withdraw, disclaim, disown, recall, unsay.

recantation noun **renunciation**, renouncement, disavowal, denial, repudiation, retraction, withdrawal; apostasy; rare abjuration, retractation.

recapitulate verb *I will recapitulate some of the main points of the argument*: **summarize**, sum up; **restate**, state again, repeat, reiterate, go over, run over, run through, review; enumerate, recount, list; informal recap; rare epitomize.

recede verb **1** *the flood waters receded | her footsteps receded down the stairs*: **retreat**, go back, move back, move further off, move away, withdraw; ebb, subside, go down, abate, fall back, sink; rare retrocede.
▷**ANTONYMS** advance, approach.
2 *I stood on the deck watching the harbour lights recede into the distance*: **disappear from view**, gradually disappear, fade into the distance, be lost to view, pass from sight, grow less visible.
3 *by May 23, fears of widespread violence had receded*: **diminish**, lessen, grow less, decrease, dwindle, fade, abate, subside, ebb, wane, fall off, taper off, peter out, shrink; rare de-escalate.
▷**ANTONYMS** grow, intensify.

receipt noun **1** *the receipt of his letter threw Clara into ecstasy*: **receiving**, reception, getting, obtaining, gaining; acceptance; arrival, delivery; rare recipience.
2 *always make sure you get a receipt*: **proof of purchase**, sales slip, sales ticket, till receipt; stub, counterfoil, voucher, slip, docket; Law, dated acquittance.
3 (**receipts**) *receipts from council house sales*: **proceeds**, takings, money/payment received, income, revenue, earnings, turnover; gate; profits, gains, financial return(s), return(s); N. Amer. take.

receive verb **1** *Tony received his award at a gala lunch in London | they received £650 in damages*: **be given**, be presented with, be awarded, collect, accept, have conferred on one; get, obtain, gain, acquire, secure, come by, pick up, be provided with, take; derive; win, be paid, earn, gross, net, accrue; inherit, come into; informal cop.
▷**ANTONYMS** give, present.
2 *she received a letter from the council threatening court action*: **be sent**, be in receipt of; accept delivery of, accept, take into one's possession.
▷**ANTONYMS** send.
3 *Alec received the news on Monday afternoon*: **be told**, be informed of, be notified of, be made aware of, hear, discover, find out (about), learn, gather, get wind of.
4 *he received her suggestion with a complete lack of interest*: **hear**, listen to; respond to, react to, take; meet, greet.
5 *she received a serious head injury*: **experience**, sustain, undergo, meet with, encounter, go through, be subjected to, come in for; **suffer**, bear, endure.
6 *the young couple looked radiant as they received their guests*: **greet**, welcome, say hello to, show in, usher in, admit, let in.
7 *she's not receiving visitors*: **entertain**, be at home to.

receiver noun **1** *the receiver of a gift*: **recipient**, beneficiary, donee; legatee; Law grantee, devisee.
▷**ANTONYMS** donor.
2 *a telephone receiver*: **handset**, apparatus; headset, earpiece.

recent adjective **1** *recent research*: **new**, the latest, late, current, fresh, modern, contemporary, present-day, up to date, up to the minute, latter-day, latter; rare neoteric.
▷**ANTONYMS** old.
2 *his recent visit*: **not long past**, occurring/appearing recently; immediate, just gone.
▷**ANTONYMS** former.

Word toolkit **recent**

See **new**.

recently adverb *Kate recently published her first novel*: **not long ago**, a short time ago, in the last few days/weeks/months, in the past few days/weeks/months, a little while back; lately, of late, latterly; just now; newly, freshly.

receptacle noun **container**, holder, vessel, repository; box, tin, bin, can, canister, drum, case, chest, casket, crate, tank; basin, pan, pot, dish, bowl; bag, pouch, purse, basket; archaic reservatory.

reception noun **1** *the reception of the goods*: **receipt**, receiving, getting, acceptance; rare recipience.
2 *the reception of foreign diplomatic representatives*: **greeting**, welcome, welcoming, entertaining.
3 *they met with a chilly reception from my mother*: **response**, reaction, treatment; acknowledgement, recognition.
4 *there was a small reception after the preview*: **(formal) party**, function, social occasion, social event, entertainment, soirée, gathering, get-together, celebration; N. Amer. levee; informal do, bash; Brit. informal rave-up, thrash, knees-up, jolly, beanfeast, bunfight, beano.

receptive adjective *a receptive audience*: **open-minded**, ready/willing to consider new ideas, open to new ideas, open to suggestions, open, responsive, amenable, sympathetic, well disposed, interested, attuned, flexible, willing, favourable, approachable, accessible, friendly, welcoming; susceptible, impressionable, suggestible, pliable, pliant; rare susceptive, acceptive, acceptant.
▷ANTONYMS resistant, unresponsive.

recess noun **1** *two recesses fitted with floor-to-ceiling bookshelves*: **alcove**, bay, niche, nook, corner, inglenook; hollow, cavity; apse; Japanese tokonoma; technical oriel, aumbry, exedra; archaic tabernacle.
2 (**recesses**) *the deepest recesses of Broadcasting House*: **innermost parts/reaches**, remote/secret places, dark corners, heart, inner sanctum, interior; depths, bowels; informal innards; rare penetralia.
3 *the Commons rises for the Christmas recess on Thursday*: **adjournment**, break, interlude, interval, rest, intermission, respite, temporary closure, temporary cessation of business; holiday, vacation, time off; informal breather, time out.
▶ verb *we'll recess for lunch and reconvene at 2 pm*: **adjourn**, suspend proceedings, take a recess, break, stop, take a break; informal knock off, take five, take time out.

recession noun *the country is in the depths of a recession*: **economic decline**, downturn, depression, slump, slowdown, trough, credit crunch, credit squeeze; stagnation, stagflation; hard times; informal bust.
▷ANTONYMS boom, upturn.

recherché adjective *most of the titles are recherché and long out of stock*: **obscure**, **rare**, esoteric, abstruse, arcane, recondite, little known; exotic, strange, unusual, unfamiliar, out of the ordinary.
▷ANTONYMS commonplace.

recipe noun **1** *try our quick and tasty recipe for beef goulash*: **cooking directions**; archaic receipt.
2 *low local taxes are not always a* **recipe for** *electoral success*: **means/way of achieving**, means/way of ensuring; **prescription**, formula, method, technique, system, procedure, plan; likely cause of, source of; MO, process, means, way; blueprint; Latin modus operandi.

recipient noun *the recipient of the prize*: **beneficiary**, receiver, donee, legatee; Law grantee, devisee.
▷ANTONYMS donor.

reciprocal adjective **1** *reciprocal, passionate love*: **given/felt in return**, corresponding; **requited**, returned, reciprocated.
2 *reciprocal obligations and duties*: **mutual**, common, shared, joint, corresponding, correlative, give-and-take, exchanged, complementary; rare reciprocatory, reciprocative, commutual.

reciprocate verb **1** *Karen had done her bit for me, and I was more than happy to reciprocate*: **do the same (in return)**, respond in kind, return the favour; give as good as one gets, give tit for tat.
2 *a hopeless love that could not possibly be reciprocated*: **requite**, return, feel/give in return, repay, give back; match, equal.

recital noun **1** *he gave his first recital at the age of 16*: **concert**, performance, musical performance, public performance, solo performance, solo, show; informal gig.
2 *her recital of Adam's failures and shortcomings | his recital of the events of the night*: **enumeration**, list, litany, catalogue, listing, detailing, itemizing, specification; **account**, report, description, narrative, narration, record, story, tale, chronicle, history; recapitulation, rehearsal, run through; recounting, telling, relation; rare recountal.
3 *a recital of the Lord's Prayer in French*: **recitation**, saying aloud, reading aloud, repetition, declaiming, declamation, rendition, rendering.

recitation noun **1** *the recitation of his poem*: **recital**, saying aloud, reading aloud, declaiming, declamation, rendering, rendition, delivery, performance.
2 *do not respond to the question with a recitation of your life story*: **account**, description, narration, narrative, story, tale, history; recapitulation, rehearsal, run through; rare recountal.
3 *those who could do so entertained the others with songs and recitations*: **reading**, passage, piece, something known off by heart; poem, verse, monologue; informal one's party piece.

recite verb **1** *we used to have great fun reciting poetry to each other*: **repeat from memory**, say aloud, read aloud, declaim, quote, speak, deliver, render; intone, chant; spout, parrot, say parrot-fashion; Judaism daven; rare cantillate, intonate, bespout.
2 *sometimes, if he got bored, he would just stand up and start reciting*: **give a recitation**, say a poem, perform; informal do one's party piece.
3 *once again, Sir John recited the facts they knew*: **enumerate**, list, detail, itemize, reel off, rattle off; **recount**, relate, describe, narrate, give an account of, run through, recapitulate, repeat, rehearse, specify, particularize, spell out.

reckless adjective *he was angry with himself and that made him reckless*: **rash**, careless, thoughtless, incautious, heedless, unheeding, inattentive, hasty, overhasty, precipitate, precipitous, impetuous, impulsive, daredevil, devil-may-care, hot-headed; **irresponsible**, wild, foolhardy, headlong, over-adventurous, over-venturesome, audacious, death-or-glory; ill-advised, injudicious, misguided, hare-brained, madcap, imprudent, unwise, ill-considered, unconsidered, ill-conceived, unthinking, indiscreet, mindless, negligent; Brit. tearaway; informal harum-scarum, bull-in-a-china-shop; rare temerarious.
▷ANTONYMS careful, cautious, prudent.

> *Choose the right word* **reckless, rash, foolhardy**
>
> See **rash²**.

reckon verb **1** *the cost to the company was reckoned at £6,000 | Pat reckoned up the cost*: **calculate**, compute, work out, put a figure on, figure, number, quantify; **count (up)**, add up, total, tally; Brit. tot up.
2 *Anselm reckoned Hugh among his friends*: **include**, count, number; consider to be, deem to be, regard as, look on as, take to be.
3 informal *I reckon she had her eye on him from the start*: **believe**, think, be of the opinion, be of the view, be convinced, suspect, dare say, have an idea, have a feeling, imagine, fancy, guess, suppose, assume, surmise, conjecture, consider; N. Amer. informal figure; archaic ween.
4 *category A prisoners are reckoned the most dangerous*: **regard as**, consider, judge, hold to be, view, think of as, look on as; deem, rate, evaluate, gauge, count, estimate; repute.
5 *when I spend that much I* **reckon to** *get good value for money*: **expect**, anticipate, hope to, be looking to; **count on**, rely on, depend on, bank on, calculate on, be sure of, trust in, take for granted, take as read; N. Amer. informal figure on.
□ **to be reckoned with** *Michael Ryan was still a force to be reckoned with*: **important**, of considerable importance, not to be ignored, significant, considerable; influential, powerful, strong, potent, formidable, redoubtable, dominant, commanding; informal a hard nut to crack.
□ **reckon with 1** *it's her mother you'll have to reckon with*: **deal with**, cope with, contend with, handle, face, face up to. **2** *they hadn't reckoned with her burning ambition to win*: **take into account**, take into consideration, bargain for, bargain on, allow for, anticipate, foresee, be prepared for, plan for; bear in mind, consider, take cognizance of, take note of.
□ **reckon without** *unfortunately he had reckoned without sniffer dogs*: **overlook**, ignore, fail to take account of, fail to anticipate, disregard, lose sight of, fail to notice.
▷ANTONYMS take into account.

reckoning noun **1** *by the judge's reckoning, this comes to close on $2 million*: **calculation**, estimation, computation, working out, summation, counting; addition, total, tally, score.
2 *by her reckoning, it was high time her luck changed*: **opinion**, view, judgement, evaluation, way of thinking, estimate, estimation, appraisal, consideration.
3 *the terrible reckoning that he deserved*: **retribution**, fate, doom, nemesis, judgement, punishment, what is coming to someone.
□ **day of reckoning judgement day**, day of judgement, day of retribution, final accounting, final settlement; Christianity doomsday.

reclaim verb **1** *travelling expenses can be reclaimed*: **get back**, claim back, have returned, recover, take back, regain, retrieve, recoup; rare recuperate.
▷ANTONYMS forfeit.
2 *Henrietta had reclaimed him from a life of vice*: **save**, rescue, redeem, win back; reform.
▷ANTONYMS abandon.

recline verb *his mother was reclining on the sofa*: **lie**, lie down, lie back, lean back; be recumbent, be prone; **rest**, relax, repose; **loll**, lounge, sprawl, stretch out, drape oneself over; literary couch.
▷ANTONYMS stand; sit up.

recluse noun **1** *a religious recluse*: **hermit**, ascetic; monk, nun; Islam marabout, santon; rare eremite, anchorite, anchoress, stylite, coenobite.
2 *a natural recluse who found all human relationships difficult*: **loner**, solitary, lone wolf; introvert, misanthrope; rare solitudinarian, solitaire, solitarian, isolate.

r

reclusive adjective *she lived a reclusive life and was hardly ever seen*: **solitary**, secluded, isolated, hermit-like, cloistered, sequestered, withdrawn, retiring, shut away; introverted, unsociable, antisocial, misanthropic; rare seclusive, eremitic, eremitical, hermitic, anchoritic.
▷ANTONYMS gregarious, sociable.

recognition noun **1** *he stared at her, but there was no sign of recognition on his face*: **identification**, recollection, recall, remembrance.
2 *his recognition of his lack of political experience*: **acknowledgement**, acceptance, admission, conceding, concession, granting; realization, awareness, consciousness, knowledge, perception, appreciation, understanding, apprehension, cognizance.
3 *the organization will seek recognition by the International Rugby Board*: **official approval**, certification, accreditation, endorsement, sanctioning, validation, ratification.
4 *the team deserve recognition for the tremendous job they are doing*: **appreciation**, gratitude, thanks, congratulations, a pat on the back, credit, commendation, acclaim, acclamation; tributes, acknowledgement, reward, honour, homage, applause, a round of applause, accolades; a mention; informal bouquets, brownie points.

recognizable adjective *he spoke with a faint but recognizable Irish lilt*: **identifiable**, noticeable, perceptible, discernible, appreciable, detectable, distinguishable, observable, perceivable; visible, notable, measurable; **distinct**, marked, conspicuous, unmistakable, clear, apparent, evident; archaic sensible.
▷ANTONYMS imperceptible.

recognize verb **1** *Hannah recognized him at once*: **identify**, place, know, know again, pick out, put a name to; **remember**, recall, recollect, call to mind; know by sight; Scottish & N. English ken; rare agnize.
▷ANTONYMS forget.
2 *he had never liked Marler, though he recognized his ability*: **acknowledge**, **accept**, admit, concede, allow, grant, confess, own; **realize**, be aware of, be conscious of, perceive, discern, appreciate, understand, apprehend, see, be cognizant of; informal take on board; rare cognize.
▷ANTONYMS overlook.
3 *psychotherapists recognized by the British Psychological Society*: **officially approve**, certify, accredit, endorse, sanction, put the seal of approval on; **acknowledge**, validate, accept as valid, ratify, uphold, support.
4 *the Trust recognized the hard work of those involved in the project*: **pay tribute to**, show appreciation of, appreciate, give recognition to, show gratitude to, be grateful for, acclaim, commend, salute, applaud, take one's hat off to, reward, honour, pay homage to.

recoil verb (stress on the second syllable) **1** *as he leaned towards her, she instinctively recoiled*: **draw back**, jump back, spring back, jerk back, pull back; **flinch**, shy away, shrink (back), blench, start, wince, cower, quail.
2 *he pictured them in his mind and **recoiled from** the thought*: **feel revulsion at**, feel disgust at, feel abhorrence at, be unable to bear, be unable to stomach, shrink from, shy away from, baulk at, hesitate at.
3 *his rifle recoiled*: **kick (back)**, jerk back, spring back, fly back, jump back.
4 *his attempts to discredit them will eventually **recoil on** him*: **rebound on**, come back on, affect badly; misfire, backfire, boomerang, go wrong, fail to work out, be unsuccessful, go amiss, come to grief, meet with disaster; archaic redound on.
▶ noun (stress on the first syllable) *the recoil of the gun*: **kickback**, kick.

recollect verb *he grimaced as he recollected the incident*: **remember**, recall, call to mind, think of; think back to, cast one's mind back to, look back on; reminisce about, hark back to, summon up, revive the memory of; Scottish mind; archaic bethink oneself of.
▷ANTONYMS forget.

recollection noun *Leonard's recollections of his early childhood are vague*: **memory**, remembrance, mental image, impression, reminiscence; technical anamnesis.

recommend verb **1** *his former employer recommended him for the post*: **advocate**, endorse, commend, approve, suggest, put forward, propose, advance, nominate, put up, mention; speak favourably of, speak well of, put in a good word for, beat the drum for, vouch for, look with favour on; informal push, plug; black English big something up.
▷ANTONYMS reject, veto.
2 *the committee recommended a cautious approach*: **advise**, counsel, urge, exhort, enjoin, prescribe, speak in favour of, speak for, argue for, back, support, offer as one's opinion; suggest, advocate, propose.
▷ANTONYMS argue against.
3 *however little else there was to recommend her, she could at least cook*: **have in one's favour**, render appealing/attractive/desirable, endow with appeal/attraction, give an advantage to; informal have going for one.

recommendation noun **1** *the government accepted the advisory group's recommendations*: **advice**, counsel, guidance, direction, exhortation, enjoinder, advocacy; suggestion, proposal, submission; Law, Brit. rider.
2 *a personal recommendation is best when you are looking for an agent*: **commendation**, endorsement, good word, favourable mention, special mention, testimonial; suggestion, tip; praise, words of approval/approbation; informal plug.
3 *some forsaken place whose only recommendation is that it has lots of men and very few women*: **advantage**, good point/feature, thing in one's/its favour, appealing/favourable aspect, benefit, blessing, asset, boon, attraction, appeal, selling point.

recompense verb **1** *the Home Secretary contended that offenders should recompense their victims*: **compensate**, indemnify, repay, reimburse, pay money to, make reparation to, make restitution to, make amends to.
2 *she wanted to recompense him in some way*: **reward**, pay, pay back; archaic guerdon.
3 *she still hadn't received much to recompense her loss*: **make up for**, compensate for, make amends for, make restitution for, make reparation for, redress, make good, satisfy.
▶ noun *substantial damages were paid in recompense*: **compensation**, reparation, restitution, indemnification, indemnity; reimbursement, repayment, reward, redress, satisfaction; Latin quid pro quo; archaic guerdon, meed; rare solatium.

reconcilable adjective *I believe the two sets of findings are reconcilable*: **compatible**, consistent, congruous, congruent, consonant.

reconcile verb **1** *the news reconciled us*: **reunite**, bring (back) together (again), restore friendly relations between, restore harmony between, make peace between, resolve differences between, bring to terms; pacify, appease, placate, propitiate, mollify; rare conciliate.
▷ANTONYMS estrange, alienate.
2 *it wasn't easy trying to reconcile his religious beliefs with his career*: **make compatible**, harmonize, square, make harmonious, synthesize, make congruent, cause to be in agreement, cause to sit happily/easily with; adjust, balance, attune; rare syncretize.
3 *the quarrel was reconciled*: **settle**, resolve, patch up, sort out, smooth over, iron out, put to rights, mend, remedy, heal, cure, rectify.
4 *the creditors had to **reconcile themselves to** drastic losses of income and capital*: **accept**, come to accept, resign oneself to, come to terms with, learn to live with, get used to, make the best of, submit to, accommodate oneself to, adjust oneself to, become accustomed to, acclimatize oneself to; grin and bear it; informal like it or lump it.

reconciliation noun **1** *the reconciliation of the disputants*: **reuniting**, reunion, bringing (back) together (again), conciliation, reconcilement; pacification, appeasement, placating, propitiation, mollification.
▷ANTONYMS estrangement, alienation.
2 *a reconciliation of their differences*: **resolution**, settlement, rectification; settling, resolving, mending, remedying.
3 *there was little hope of reconciliation between the two groups*: **restoration of friendly relations**, restoration of harmony, agreement, compromise, understanding, peace, an end to hostilities, amity, concord; French rapprochement, détente; informal fence-mending.
▷ANTONYMS feud.
4 *the reconciliation of scientific philosophy with clinical practice*: **harmonizing**, harmonization, synthesis, squaring, adjustment, balancing; rare syncretization.
▷ANTONYMS incompatibility.

recondite adjective *the recondite realms of Semitic philology*: **obscure**, abstruse, arcane, esoteric, little known, recherché, abstract, deep, profound, cryptic, difficult, complex, complicated, involved; over/above one's head, incomprehensible, unfathomable, impenetrable, opaque, dark, mysterious, occult, cabbalistic, secret, hidden; rare Alexandrian.
▷ANTONYMS straightforward, simple, familiar.

recondition verb *the engine had been completely reconditioned*: **overhaul**, rebuild, renovate, restore, repair, fix up, reconstruct, remodel, renew, refit, refurbish, make over; informal do up, revamp, vamp up.

reconnaissance noun *he took some marines to make a reconnaissance of the island*: **preliminary survey**, survey, exploration, observation, investigation, examination, inspection, probe, scrutiny, scan; patrol, search, expedition; reconnoitring, scouting (out), spying out; informal recce; Brit. informal shufti; N. Amer. informal recon.

reconnoitre verb *a survey plane was dispatched to reconnoitre the area*: **survey**, make a reconnaissance of, explore, scout (out), make a survey of, make an observation of; find out the lie of the land, see how the land lies; investigate, examine, spy out, scrutinize, scan, inspect, observe, take a look at, take stock of; patrol; informal recce, make a recce of, case, case the joint, check out; Brit. informal take a shufti round, suss out; N. Amer. informal recon.

reconsider verb *the government might be forced to reconsider its decision*: **rethink**, review, revise, re-examine, re-evaluate, reassess, reappraise, think better of, think over, take another look at, look at in a different light, have another think about; change, alter, modify; think again, think twice, have second thoughts, review one's position, come round, change one's mind.

reconsideration noun *a reconsideration of the case*: **review**, re-examination, reassessment, re-evaluation, reappraisal, rethink, another look, a fresh look.

reconstruct verb **1** *the building had to be substantially reconstructed | a pressing need to reconstruct the war-damaged economy*: **rebuild**, restore, renovate, recreate, remake, reassemble, remodel, refashion, revamp, recondition, refurbish; regenerate, breathe new life into, reform, make

over, overhaul, re-establish, reorganize; N. Amer. informal rehab.
2 *an effort to reconstruct the events of that day*: **recreate**, build up a picture/impression of, form a picture/impression of, piece together, re-enact, build up; see in one's mind's eye.

record noun (stress on the first syllable) **1** *written records of the past | fraud squad officers want to examine his bank records*: **account(s)**, document(s), documentation, data, file(s), dossier(s), information, evidence, report(s); annal(s), archive(s), chronicle(s); note(s), minutes, transactions, proceedings, transcript(s); certificate(s), deed(s), instrument(s); diary, journal, memoir; register, log, logbook; yearbook, almanac; inventory, list, catalogue; case history, case study, casebook; French procès-verbal; dated act(s); rare muniment(s).
2 *I spent a lot of time listening to records*: **album**; vinyl; tape, cassette, disc, compact disc, CD; recording, release; dated gramophone record, LP, long-player, single, forty-five, twelve-inch (single), EP (extended-play); seventy-eight, 78; Brit. dated black disc; N. Amer. dated phonograph record.
3 *Cameron would have faced a High Court sentence had it not been for his good record*: **previous conduct/performance**, track record, previous achievements/accomplishments, career to date, history, past, life history, background; reputation; Latin curriculum vitae.
4 *he's got a record as long as my arm*: **criminal record**, police record, list of offences, list of previous convictions; previous; history of crime; Military crime sheet; Brit. informal form; N. Amer. informal rap sheet.
5 *it was my greatest race and a British record*: **best performance**, highest achievement, star performance; best time, fastest time, furthest distance; personal best; world record.
6 *a personal and lasting record of what they have achieved*: **reminder**, memorial, souvenir, memento, token, token of remembrance, remembrance, keepsake, testimony, testament, testimonial, witness, monument.
□ **off the record 1** *he was at pains to emphasize that his comments were off the record*: **unofficial**, **confidential**, in (strict) confidence, not for publication, not for public consumption, not to be made public, not for circulation, not to be disclosed, not to be mentioned, private, secret, classified, (to be kept) under wraps. ▷ANTONYMS official.
2 *senior opposition figures are beginning to admit, off the record, that they made a mistake*: **unofficially**, **privately**, in (strict) confidence, confidentially, between ourselves; Latin sub rosa; Italian in petto; French entre nous; informal between you, me, and the bedpost/gatepost; archaic under the rose. ▷ANTONYMS officially, publicly.
▶ **adjective** (stress on the first syllable) *the company announced record pre-tax profits*: **record-breaking**, best ever, its/one's best, optimum, unbeaten, unsurpassed, unparalleled, unequalled, superlative, second to none, never previously achieved.
▷ANTONYMS worst.
▶ **verb** (stress on the second syllable) **1** *the doctor recorded her blood pressure on a chart*: **write down**, set down, put in writing, put down, take down, note, make a note of, jot down, put down on paper, commit to paper; **document**, put on record, post; enter, minute, register, chronicle, file, put on file, chart, docket, log; inscribe, transcribe; list, catalogue, make an inventory of; rare diarize.
2 *the thermometer recorded a temperature of 99°F*: **indicate**, register, read, show, display.
3 *the team recorded their fourth away win of the season*: **achieve**, accomplish, gain, earn, chalk up, notch up, turn in; informal clock up.
4 *the recital was recorded live at the Schleswig-Holstein Music Festival*: **make a record/recording of**, tape, tape-record; video-record, videotape, video, audiotape; telerecord.
5 *he took time out from working with the band to record a new solo album*: **make**, produce, cut, put on disc/tape; informal lay down, put on wax.

recorder noun **1 tape recorder**, cassette recorder; video cassette recorder, VCR, video recorder, videotape recorder, video.
2 record keeper; registrar, archivist, annalist, diarist, chronicler, historian; scribe, clerk; rare chronologer, chronologist, chronographer.

recount verb *she listened incredulously to the chain of events recounted by her sister*: **tell**, relate, narrate, give an account of, describe, portray, depict, paint, unfold, set forth, present, report, outline, delineate, retail, recite, repeat, rehearse, relay, convey, communicate, impart; detail, enumerate, list, specify, itemize, cite, particularize, catalogue.

recoup verb *the club managed to recoup £300*: **get back**, regain, recover, win back, retrieve, repossess, redeem, make good; rare recuperate.

recourse noun *surgery may be the only recourse*: **option**, possibility, alternative, possible course of action, resort, way out, place/person to turn to, source of assistance, available resource, hope, remedy, choice, expedient; refuge.
□ **have recourse to** *all three countries had recourse to the IMF for standby loans*: **resort to**, make use of, use, avail oneself of, utilize, employ, turn to, call on, draw on, bring into play, bring into service, look to, appeal to; fall back on, run to.

recover verb **1** *he's still recovering from a heart attack*: **recuperate**, get better, get well, convalesce, regain one's strength, regain one's health, get stronger, get back on one's feet, feel oneself again, get back to normal, return to health; be on the mend, be on the road to recovery, pick up, rally, respond to treatment, make progress, improve, heal, take a turn for the better, turn the corner, get out of the woods, get over something, shake something off, pull through, bounce back, revive; Brit. pull round; informal perk up.
▷ANTONYMS deteriorate, worsen, go downhill.
2 *the FTSE 100 share index recovered to end the day down 30.5 points*: **rally**, improve, pick up, make a recovery, rebound, bounce back, come back, make a comeback.
3 *around £385,000-worth of the stolen material had now been recovered*: **retrieve**, regain (possession of), get back, win back, take back, recoup, reclaim, repossess, recapture, retake, redeem; find (again), track down, trace; claw back; Law replevin, replevy; rare recuperate.
▷ANTONYMS lose.
4 *gold coins and bars recovered from the wreck of a seventeenth-century galleon*: **salvage**, save, rescue, retrieve, reclaim, redeem.
□ **recover oneself** *she recovered herself, grateful that he had not noticed how nervous she had been*: **pull oneself together**, regain one's composure/self-control, regain control of oneself, take a hold of oneself, steady oneself; informal get a grip (on oneself), get one's act together, snap out of it.

recovery noun **1** *she could face lengthy physiotherapy and her recovery may be slow*: **recuperation**, convalescence, return to health, process of getting better, rehabilitation, healing, rallying.
▷ANTONYMS relapse.
2 *the Polish economy was beginning to show signs of recovery*: **improvement**, rallying, picking up, betterment, amelioration; rally, upturn, upswing, comeback, revival, renewal, a turn for the better.
▷ANTONYMS deterioration.
3 *the recovery of the stolen works of art*: **retrieval**, regaining, repossession, getting back, recapture, reclamation, recouping, retaking, redemption; Law replevin; rare recoupment, recuperation.
▷ANTONYMS loss.

recreation noun **1** *cycling is becoming more popular, both for recreation and for travel to work*: **pleasure**, leisure, relaxation, fun, enjoyment, entertainment, amusement, refreshment, restoration, distraction, diversion; play, sport; informal R and R, jollies; Brit. informal beer and skittles; N. Amer. informal rec; archaic disport.
▷ANTONYMS work.
2 *his favourite recreations were skating and fishing*: **pastime**, hobby, leisure activity, leisure pursuit, leisure interest, entertainment, diversion, divertissement, distraction, avocation.

recrimination noun *tears and bitter recriminations followed | she told herself that nothing was to be gained by recrimination*: **accusation(s)**, mutual accusation(s), counter-accusation(s), countercharge(s), counterattack(s), retaliation(s); quarrelling, squabbling, bickering; Brit. informal rowing.

recruit verb **1** *a special unit of Portuguese-speaking soldiers was recruited*: **enlist**, sign up, enrol, engage, take on, round up; call up, conscript; N. Amer. draft, muster in, induct; historical press, press-gang, shanghai; archaic levy, impress, list, conscribe, crimp, attest.
2 *a king's power depended on his capacity to recruit armies and to lead them*: **muster**, form, raise, gather/bring together, assemble, mobilize, marshal, round up, call to arms.
▷ANTONYMS demobilize, disband.
3 *the company is planning to recruit a thousand new staff*: **hire**, employ, take on, take into one's employ; **enrol**, sign up, get, obtain, acquire.
▷ANTONYMS dismiss, lay off.
▶ **noun 1** *thousands of recruits had been enlisted*: **conscript**, new soldier; N. Amer. draftee, inductee; Brit. informal sprog; N. Amer. informal plebe, buck private, yardbird.
▷ANTONYMS veteran.
2 *the profession continues to attract a flow of top-quality recruits*: **new member**, new entrant, newcomer, new boy/girl, initiate; **trainee**, apprentice; beginner, novice, learner, tyro, neophyte, proselyte; N. Amer. tenderfoot, hire; informal rookie, new kid, newbie, cub; N. Amer. informal greenhorn.

rectify verb *mistakes made now cannot be rectified later*: **correct**, put/set/make right, right, put to rights, sort out, deal with, amend, revise, remedy, repair, fix, cure, heal, make good, reform, harmonize, retrieve, improve, better, ameliorate, adjust, resolve, settle, redress, square; informal patch up.

rectitude noun *local worthies rarely challenged the rectitude of the chief constable*: **righteousness**, goodness, virtue, moral virtue, morality, honour, honourableness, integrity, principle, probity, honesty, right-mindedness, trustworthiness, truthfulness, uprightness, upstandingness, good character, scrupulousness, decency, fairness, equity, justice; principles, ethics.
▷ANTONYMS infamy, dishonesty.

rectum noun

Word links **rectum**

procto- related prefix, as in *proctology*

r

recumbent adjective *he stepped over the recumbent body*: **lying**, flat, horizontal, stretched out, sprawled, spreadeagled, reclining, resting, lounging, prone, prostrate, supine; lying down, lying flat, (flat) on one's back, on one's stomach/front, (flat) on one's face; rare procumbent.
▷ANTONYMS erect, standing, upright.

recuperate verb **1** *he fell ill that summer and travelled to the south of France to recuperate*: **get better**, recover, convalesce, get back to normal, get well, regain one's strength/health, get back on one's feet, get over something; be on the road to recovery, be on the mend, improve, mend, pick up, rally, revive, perk up, pull through, bounce back.
2 *he won an appeal and recuperated the money*: **get back**, regain, recover, win back, recoup, retrieve, reclaim, repossess, have something returned, be reunited with, find, redeem, rescue.

recur verb *they cannot guarantee that the problem will not recur*: **happen again**, reoccur, occur again, be repeated, repeat (itself); happen repeatedly, come and go; come back (again), return, come round (again); reappear, appear again, flare up; rare recrudesce.

recurrent adjective *virtue is a recurrent theme in court poetry*: **repeated**, recurring, repetitive, reiterative, periodic, happening at intervals, cyclical, cyclic, seasonal, perennial, regular, habitual, chronic, continual, frequent; intermittent, sporadic, spasmodic, odd.
▷ANTONYMS isolated, single, unique.

Word toolkit

recurrent	repeated	intermittent
theme	attempts	rain
dream	calls	treatment
nightmare	use	periods
role	warnings	fever
motif	exposure	symptoms
images	appeals	electricity
injury	assurances	flashes

recycle verb *all our stores now collect and recycle cardboard boxes*: **reuse**, reprocess, convert into something, reclaim, recover; salvage, save.

red adjective **1** *a red dress*: scarlet, vermilion, ruby, ruby-red, ruby-coloured, cherry, cherry-red, cerise, cardinal, carmine, wine, wine-red, wine-coloured, claret, claret-red, claret-coloured, blood-red; flame, flaming, coral, cochineal, rose, rosy; brick-red, maroon, rusty, foxy, rufous; reddish; literary damask, vermeil; Heraldry sanguine, gules; rare rufescent.
2 *he was somewhat red in the face from his exertions*: **flushed**, reddish, pink, pinkish, florid, high-coloured, rubicund, roseate; ruddy, healthy-looking, rosy, glowing; burning, flaming, feverish; embarrassed, shamefaced; archaic sanguine; rare erubescent, rubescent.
3 *the chlorine in the water made his eyes red*: **bloodshot**, red-rimmed, inflamed; swollen, sore.
4 *the lady with the red hair*: reddish, flaming red, flame-coloured, auburn, Titian, chestnut, carroty, ginger, sandy, foxy.
▶noun informal, derogatory *in this film the war is against drug barons rather than Reds*: **Communist**, Marxist, socialist, left-winger, leftist, Bolshevik, revolutionary; informal Commie, lefty.
□ **in the red** *his account is still in the red*: **overdrawn**, in debt, in debit, in deficit, owing money, in arrears, showing a loss.
▷ANTONYMS in the black.
□ **see red** informal *she saw red and hit him with the hammer*: **become very angry**, become enraged, go into a rage, lose one's temper; informal go/get mad, go crazy, go wild, go bananas, hit the roof, go through the roof, go up the wall, go off the deep end, fly off the handle, blow one's top, blow a fuse/gasket, lose one's rag, go ape, flip, flip one's lid, go non-linear, go ballistic, go psycho; Brit. informal go spare, go crackers, do one's nut; N. Amer. informal flip one's wig, blow one's lid/stack; vulgar slang go apeshit.
□ **red herring** *it's more of a red herring than a legitimate plot element*: **bluff**, blind, ruse, feint, deception, subterfuge, hoax, trick, ploy, device, wile, sham, pretence, artifice, cover, smokescreen, distraction, expedient, contrivance, machination; informal dodge, put-on, put-up job.

Word links **red**

rhodo- related prefix, as in *rhodonite*
erythro- related prefix, as in *erythrocyte*

red-blooded adjective *like any attractive red-blooded man he's had his share of romances*: **manly**, masculine, all-male, virile, macho; strong, strapping, rugged, robust, powerful, vigorous; informal hunky.

redden verb **1** *the rain reddened our faces*: **make/colour red**; rare mantle.
2 *Sean felt his cheeks redden*: **go/turn red**, go/turn pink/crimson/scarlet, blush, flush, colour, colour up, crimson, burn; rare mantle.

redeem verb **1** *one feature alone redeems the book*: **save**, compensate for the defects of, rescue, justify, vindicate.
2 *he fell in that race but fully redeemed himself next time out*: **vindicate**, save/free from blame, absolve, remove guilt from.
3 *he had decided to stop trying to redeem the sins of America*: **atone for**, make amends for, make restitution for.
4 *she committed herself to redeeming sinners*: **save**, free/save/deliver from sin, turn from sin, convert, purge/absolve of sin.
5 *Billy has to redeem his drums from the pawnbrokers*: **retrieve**, regain, recover, get back, reclaim, repossess, have something returned, rescue; buy back, repurchase.
6 *this voucher can be redeemed at any branch of the shop*: **exchange**, give in exchange, swap, barter, cash in, convert, turn in, return, trade in.
7 *Parliament absolved the King from all obligation to redeem this debt*: **pay off**, pay back, clear, discharge, square, honour, make good.
8 *the government made no effort to redeem this promise*: **fulfil**, carry out, discharge, make good, execute; keep, keep to, stick to, hold to, adhere to, abide by, heed, obey, be faithful to, honour, meet, satisfy.

redeeming adjective *his work is not without redeeming features*: **compensating**, compensatory, extenuating, offsetting, qualifying, redemptive; rare extenuatory.

redemption noun **1** *God's redemption of his people*: **saving**, saving/freeing from sin, vindication, absolution.
2 *cash must be available for the redemption of possessions*: **retrieval**, recovery, reclamation, repossession, recoupment, return, rescue; repurchase.
3 *the redemption of credit vouchers*: **exchange**, swapping, bartering, cashing in, conversion, return, trade-in.
4 *the redemption of the mortgage*: **paying off**, paying back, discharge, clearing, squaring, honouring; archaic quittance.
5 *the redemption of his obligations*: **fulfilment**, carrying out, discharge, making good, execution, performing, accomplishment, achievement, observance, honouring, meeting, satisfying, adherence to.

red-handed adjective *the thief was caught red-handed*: **in the act**, with one's fingers/hand in the till; Latin in flagrante delicto; informal dead to rights; Brit. informal bang to rights; with one's trousers down; N. Amer. informal with one's pants down.

redolent adjective **1** *an old village church is redolent of everything that is England*: **evocative**, suggestive, reminiscent, remindful.
2 *the air was redolent of patchouli*: **smelling of**, reeking of; scented with, fragrant with, perfumed with.

redoubtable adjective *he had already proved himself a redoubtable commander of troops*: **formidable**, awe-inspiring, fearsome, daunting, alarming; impressive, commanding, tremendous, indomitable, invincible, resolute, doughty, mighty, strong, powerful.

redound verb **1** formal *he must hope that his diplomatic effort will still* ***redound to his credit***: **contribute to**, be conducive to, result in, lead to, effect; have an effect on, affect; formal conduce to.
2 archaic *the unimagined consequences of the detonation* ***redounded upon*** *them*: **rebound on**, have an adverse effect on, come back on, recoil on; misfire, backfire.

redress verb **1** *people no longer take to the barricades to redress wrongs*: **rectify**, correct, put/set/make right, right, put to rights, compensate for, sort out, deal with, amend, remedy, repair, fix, cure, heal, make good, reform, harmonize, retrieve, improve, better, ameliorate, adjust, resolve, settle, square; informal patch up.
2 *bad news is drowning out the good news, but we aim to redress the balance*: **even up**, regulate, adjust, equalize, make level, regularize, correct.
▶noun *their best hope of redress lay in court action*: **compensation**, reparation, restitution, recompense, repayment, damages, indemnity, indemnification; requital, retribution, satisfaction, remedy, comeback; justice, atonement, amends.

reduce verb **1** *the aim is to reduce pollution*: **lessen**, make less, make smaller, lower, bring down, decrease, turn down, diminish, take the edge off, minimize; shrink, narrow, contract, shorten, foreshorten, truncate, taper, close, abbreviate, condense, concentrate, abridge; deplete, axe, cut, cut back/down, make cutbacks in, scale down, trim, slim (down), prune, chop, curtail, limit; moderate, lighten, ease, dilute, mitigate, commute, qualify, alleviate, relax, abate; Finance amortize.
▷ANTONYMS increase, enlarge.
2 *he succeeded in reducing her to tears*: **bring to**, bring to the point of, force into, drive into.
3 *he was jailed for five years and reduced to the ranks*: **demote**, downgrade, lower, lower in rank/status; abase, humble, demean, belittle, humiliate, bring low; N. Amer. informal bust.
▷ANTONYMS promote.
4 *ribs of beef have been reduced to £1.88 a pound*: **make cheaper**, lower the price of, lower/cut in price, cheapen, cut, mark down, discount, put on sale, offer at a giveaway price; informal slash, knock down.
▷ANTONYMS put up.
□ **in reduced circumstances** **impoverished**, in straitened circumstances, ruined, bankrupt, bankrupted, bust, insolvent; **poor**, indigent, penurious, impecunious, in penury, moneyless, without a sou, as poor as a church mouse, poverty-stricken, destitute, necessitous; needy, in need/want,

badly off, hard up, on one's beam-ends, unable to make ends meet, underprivileged; Brit. on the breadline, without a penny (to one's name); informal broke, flat broke, cleaned out, strapped for cash, strapped, on one's uppers; Brit. informal stony broke, skint, without two pennies/(brass) farthings to rub together, in Queer Street; N. Amer. informal stone broke; rare pauperized, beggared.

reduction noun **1** *a reduction in pollution*: **lessening**, lowering, decrease, diminution, minimizing.
▷ANTONYMS increase, enlargement.
2 *the closure of those offices led to a reduction in staff*: **depletion**, cut, cutting, cutback, scaling down, trimming, slimming (down), pruning, axing, chopping, curtailment, limiting.
3 *there will be some reduction in the pressure to keep costs down*: **easing**, lightening, moderation, dilution, mitigation, commuting, qualification, alleviation, relaxation, abatement.
4 *a reduction in status*: **demotion**, downgrading, lowering; abasement, humbling, demeaning, belittling, humiliation, bringing low.
▷ANTONYMS promotion.
5 *substantial reductions on children's clothes*: **discount**, markdown, deduction, (price) cut, pullback, concession, allowance; informal slash.
▷ANTONYMS increase.

redundancy noun **1** *there is a great deal of redundancy in language*: **superfluity**, unnecessariness, expendability, uselessness, excess.
2 *they know redundancy is in the offing | a hospital has announced 300 redundancies*: **sacking**, dismissal, lay-off, discharge, notice; unemployment; Brit. one's cards; informal marching orders.

redundant adjective **1** *many churches have become redundant over the last twenty years*: **unnecessary**, not required, inessential, unessential, needless, unneeded, uncalled for, dispensable, disposable, expendable, unwanted, useless; **surplus**, surplus to requirements, superfluous, too much/many, supernumerary, excessive, in excess, extra, additional, spare; French de trop; informal needed like a hole in the head.
▷ANTONYMS essential, necessary.
2 *2,000 workers were **made redundant***: **sacked**, dismissed, laid off, discharged; **unemployed**, idle, jobless, out of work, out of a job; rare disemployed.
▷ANTONYMS in work, employed.

reef noun *waves crashed over the reef*: **shoal**, bar, sandbar, sandbank, spit; ridge, ledge, shelf, atoll, key; barrier reef, fringing reef; Scottish skerry; in Spanish America cay.

reek verb *the whole place reeked of cheap perfume*: **stink**, smell, smell bad/disgusting, give off a bad smell, stink/smell to high heaven.
▶ **noun** *the reek of cattle dung*: **stink**, bad smell, foul smell, stench, taint, effluvium; Brit. informal niff, pong, whiff, hum; Scottish informal **guff**; N. Amer. informal, dated funk; rare miasma, mephitis, malodour, fetor.

reel verb **1** *Cormack reeled as the ship began to roll*: **stagger**, lurch, sway, rock, stumble, totter, wobble, falter, waver, swerve, pitch, roll.
2 *the Government was still **reeling from** the currency crisis*: **be shaken by**, be stunned by, be in shock after, be shocked by, be numb from, be dazed by, be taken aback by, be staggered by, be aghast at, be dumbfounded at, be dumbstruck at, be upset by, be bowled over by, feel giddy/dizzy from, feel confused by.
3 *she closed her eyes and the room reeled*: **go round**, go round and round, whirl, spin, revolve, gyrate, swirl, twirl, turn, wheel, swim.
□ **reel something off** *he reeled off a choice string of unpleasant epithets*: **recite**, rattle off, loose off, fire off, list rapidly, run through, enumerate, detail, itemize; informal spiel off.

r

refer verb **1** *he **referred to** errors in the article*: **mention**, make mention of, make reference to, allude to, touch on, speak of/about, talk of/about, write about, cite, name, comment on, deal with, go into, treat (of), note, point out, call attention to, bring up, raise, broach, introduce; rare advert to, moot.
2 *the matter has been referred to my insurers*: **pass**, hand on, send on, transfer, remit, direct, leave, commit, entrust, assign, hand over.
3 *these figures **refer** only to 2001*: **apply to**, **be relevant to**, have relevance to, concern, relate to, belong to, be about, have to do with, be connected with, have reference to, pertain to, appertain to, be pertinent to, have a bearing on, bear on, affect, involve, cover, touch, touch on; archaic regard.
4 *the name is an ancient word **referring to** a Saxon village*: **denote**, describe, indicate, mean, depict, symbolize, signify, designate, stand for, represent.
5 *the constable **referred to** his notes | please **refer to** your manager for the correct password*: **consult**, turn to, look at, look up (in), seek information from, search in, have recourse to, call on; seek advice from, call in, take counsel from, ask.

referee noun **1** *the referee blew his whistle for a penalty*: **umpire**, judge, adjudicator, arbitrator, arbiter, mediator; informal ref.
2 *applications should include a curriculum vitae and the names of two referees*: **supporter**, character witness, backer, advocate.
▶ **verb 1** *he refereed the Scotland v Spain game*: **umpire**, judge, adjudicate, run, be in control of.
2 *they asked him to referee in the dispute*: **arbitrate**, mediate, act as arbitrator/arbiter/mediator/negotiator.

reference noun **1** *his journal contains many **references to** railways*: **mention of**, allusion to, comment on, remark about; citation of, instance of.
2 *some references are given in the bibliography to this chapter*: **source**, information source, citation, authority, credit; note, footnote; bibliographical data, bibliography.
3 *this was an appropriate case for a reference to the European Court of Justice*: **referral**, transfer, passing on, handover, direction, remission.
4 *his employer gave him a glowing reference*: **testimonial**, character reference, recommendation, good word, backing; credentials; dated character.
□ **with reference to apropos**, with regard to, regarding, as regards, with respect to, on the subject of, in the matter of, re; in relation to, relating to, in connection with.

referendum noun *he called for a referendum on the death penalty*: **public vote**, **plebiscite**, popular vote, ballot, poll.

refine verb **1** *we were losing this valuable fibre by refining our cereal foods and sugar*: **purify**, clarify, clear, cleanse, strain, sift, filter, rarefy, distil, concentrate, process, treat; technical rectify.
▷ANTONYMS adulterate.
2 *the supporting documents help students to refine their English language skills*: **improve**, perfect, polish (up), hone, temper, fine-tune, elaborate, touch up, revise, edit, copy-edit; complete, finish, finish off, put the final/finishing touches to, crown, consummate; informal tweek.
▷ANTONYMS lose.

refined adjective **1** *refined sugar*: **purified**, pure, clarified, clear, strained, sifted, filtered, rarefied, distilled, concentrated, processed, treated, polished; technical rectified.
▷ANTONYMS crude, raw.
2 *a refined lady*: **cultivated**, cultured, polished, civilized, stylish, elegant, sophisticated, urbane; civil, polite, gracious, courtly, well mannered, well bred, gentlemanly, ladylike, genteel; informal couth.
▷ANTONYMS boorish, coarse.
3 *she is a woman of refined taste*: **discriminating**, discerning, selective, fastidious, sensitive, perceptive; sophisticated, cultured, educated, enlightened; exquisite, impeccable, delicate, fine.

refinement noun **1** *the refinement of sugar*: **purification**, refining, clarifying, clarification, cleansing, straining, sifting, filtering, filtration, rarefaction, distillation, concentration, processing, treatment, treating; technical rectification.
▷ANTONYMS adulteration.
2 *all programs have bugs and need endless refinement*: **improvement**, perfection, polishing, honing, fine-tuning, touching up, revision, editing, copy-editing; completion, finishing, finishing off, the final/finishing touches, crowning, consummation; informal tweeking.
3 *a woman who spoke with self-conscious refinement*: **style**, elegance, finesse, polish, finish, sophistication, urbanity; civility, politeness, grace, graciousness, courtliness, good manners, good breeding, gentility; cultivation, culture, taste, discrimination; French politesse.

reflect verb **1** *the snow reflects a great deal of light*: **send back**, throw back, cast back, give back, bounce back, shine back, return, mirror.
▷ANTONYMS absorb.
2 *their facial expressions reflected their feelings*: **indicate**, show, display, demonstrate, be evidence of, register, reveal, betray, evince, disclose, exhibit, manifest; express, bespeak, communicate, bear out, attest, prove, evidence; result from.
3 *he **reflected on** his responsibilities as a teacher*: **think about**, give thought to, consider, give consideration to, review, mull over, contemplate, study, cogitate about/on, meditate on, muse on, deliberate about/on, ruminate about/on/over, dwell on, brood on/over, agonize over, worry about, chew over, puzzle over, speculate about, weigh up, revolve, turn over in one's mind, be in a brown study; informal put on one's thinking cap; archaic pore on; rare cerebrate.
□ **reflect badly on** *the incident reflected badly on the government*: **discredit**, do discredit to, be a discredit to, disgrace, shame, put in a bad light, damage, damage/tarnish/blemish the reputation of, give a bad name to, bring into disrepute, become a stain/blot of the escutcheon of, detract from.

reflection noun **1** *the colours seen in soap bubbles are caused by reflection of light*: **sending back**, throwing back, casting back, mirroring, backscattering.
▷ANTONYMS absorption.
2 *she glanced at her own reflection in the mirror*: **image**, mirror image, likeness; echo.
3 *your hands and nails are a reflection of your well-being*: **indication**, display, demonstration, manifestation; expression, attestation, proof, evidence.
4 *the sale is not any reflection on the business*: **slur**, aspersion, imputation, censure, reproach, shame, criticism, source of discredit, derogation.
5 *after some reflection, he turned the offer down*: **thought**, thinking, consideration, contemplation, study, deliberation, pondering, meditation, musing, rumination, cogitation, brooding, agonizing; rare cerebration.

6 *write down your reflections on the subject*: **opinion**, thought, view, viewpoint, belief, feeling, idea, impression, conclusion, judgement, assessment, estimation; **comment**, observation, remark, statement, utterance, pronouncement, declaration.

reflex adjective *sneezing is a reflex action*: **instinctive**, automatic, mechanical, involuntary, knee-jerk, reflexive, impulsive, intuitive, spontaneous, unconscious, subliminal, unthinking, unpremeditated, unconditioned, untaught, unlearned, unintentional, unwitting, inadvertent, accidental.
▷ANTONYMS conscious, voluntary, learned.

reform verb **1** *a comprehensive plan to reform the health-care system*: **improve**, make better, better, ameliorate, refine, mend, rectify, correct, rehabilitate; **alter**, make alterations to, change, adjust, make adjustments to, adapt, amend, revise, recast, reshape, refashion, redesign, restyle, revamp, renovate, rework, redo, remake, rebuild, reconstruct, remodel, make over, remould, reorganize, revolutionize, reorient, reorientate, vary, transform, convert; customize, tailor; technical permute; rare permutate.
▷ANTONYMS preserve, maintain.
2 *after his marriage he reformed*: **mend one's ways**, change for the better, change completely, make a fresh start, turn over a new leaf, become a new person, reconstruct oneself, improve, go straight, get back on the straight and narrow.
▷ANTONYMS worsen.
▶ noun *the reform of the prison system*: **improvement**, betterment, amelioration, refinement, rectification, correction, rehabilitation; **alteration**, change, adjustment, adaptation, amendment, revision, recasting, reshaping, refashioning, redesigning, restyling, revamp, revamping, renovation, reworking, redoing, remake, rebuilding, reconstruction, remodelling, makeover, remoulding, reorganizing, reorganization, reorienting, reorientation, transformation, conversion; customizing, tailoring.

refractory adjective *a refractory child*: **obstinate**, stubborn, stubborn as a mule, mulish, bull-headed, pig-headed, obdurate, headstrong, self-willed, wayward, wilful, perverse, contrary, recalcitrant, obstreperous, disobedient, insubordinate, rebellious, mutinous, defiant, stiff-necked, intractable, intransigent, unyielding, unmalleable, unmanageable, ungovernable, unpersuadable; Scottish thrawn; informal cussed; Brit. informal **bloody-minded**, bolshie, stroppy; N. Amer. informal balky; archaic contumacious, froward; rare contrarious.
▷ANTONYMS obedient, manageable.

refrain verb *he appealed to the protestors to **refrain from** violence*: **abstain**, desist, hold back, stop oneself, withhold; forbear, forgo, do without, dispense with, resist the temptation to, avoid, steer clear of, give a wide berth to, have nothing to do with, fight shy of, eschew, shun, renounce, forswear, abjure, leave alone, not touch, reject; stop, cease, finish, discontinue, give up, break off, drop; informal quit, leave off, kick, swear off; Brit. informal jack in; archaic forsake.

refresh verb **1** *the cool air will refresh me*: **reinvigorate**, revitalize, revive, restore, brace, fortify, strengthen, give new strength to, enliven, perk up, stimulate, freshen, energize, exhilarate, reanimate, wake up, resuscitate, revivify, rejuvenate, regenerate, renew, breathe new life into; blow away the cobwebs; informal buck up, pep up; rare inspirit.
▷ANTONYMS weary.
2 *let me refresh your memory*: **jog**, stimulate, prompt, prod, activate, rouse, arouse; cue, help out, give someone a cue.
3 N. Amer. *I refreshed his glass*: **refill**, top up, replenish, recharge.

refreshing adjective **1** *a refreshing drink | a refreshing breeze*: **invigorating**, revitalizing, reviving, restoring, bracing, fortifying, enlivening, stimulating, freshening, energizing, exhilarating, reanimating, revivifying, rejuvenating; thirst-quenching; rare inspiriting.
2 *these latest proposals are a refreshing change of direction*: **welcome**, **stimulating**, new, novel, creative, fresh, imaginative, original, different, innovative, innovatory, innovational, inventive, ingenious, inspired, resourceful, unusual, unconventional, unorthodox, unfamiliar, unprecedented, groundbreaking, pioneering, avant-garde, unique, individual, individualistic, distinctive; not just another.

refreshment noun **1** *the hotel provided refreshment at reasonable prices | refreshments will be available in the interval*: **food and drink**, sustenance, fare, liquid refreshment; snacks, titbits, eatables, a bite, drinks; informal nibbles, eats, grub, bread, nosh, chow, booze; Brit. informal scoff; N. Amer. informal chuck; formal comestibles, provender; archaic victuals, vittles, viands, meat, commons; rare aliment, pabulum.
2 *spiritual refreshment*: **invigoration**, revitalizing, revival, restoring, strengthening, enlivening, perking up, stimulation, freshening, energizing, reanimation, resuscitation, revivification, rejuvenation, regeneration, renewal.

refrigerate verb *refrigerate the dough for an hour*: **keep cold**, cool, cool down, chill; freeze, deep-freeze, ice.
▷ANTONYMS heat; defrost.

refuge noun **1** *many homeless people were seeking refuge in subway stations*: **shelter**, protection, safety, security, asylum, sanctuary; preservation, safe keeping.
2 *the park serves as a refuge for mountain gorillas*: **sanctuary**, place of shelter, shelter, place of safety, haven, safe haven, sanctum, safe house, harbour, port in a storm, ark; retreat, bolt-hole, foxhole, hiding place, hideaway, hideout, fastness; Spanish querencia.

refugee noun *she had fled to England as a refugee*: **displaced person**, DP, escapee, fugitive, asylum seeker, runaway, exile, émigré, stateless person, outcast, returnee; Austral. informal reffo.

refund verb (stress on the second syllable) **1** *we guarantee to refund your money if you're not entirely satisfied with your order*: **repay**, **give back**, return, pay back, restore; replace, make good.
2 *there was no alternative but to refund the subscribers*: **reimburse**, compensate, recompense, square accounts with, settle up with, make restitution/amends to, recoup, remunerate, indemnify.
▶ noun (stress on the first syllable) *if you are not entirely satisfied, return the goods within 14 days for a full refund*: **repayment**, reimbursement, restitution, reparation; rebate, indemnity, indemnification.

refurbish verb *millions of pounds are needed to refurbish the conference and exhibition halls*: **renovate**, recondition, rehabilitate, revamp, make over, overhaul, restore, renew, develop, redevelop, rebuild, reconstruct, remodel; redecorate, brighten up, freshen up, spruce up; improve, upgrade, refit, fix up, re-equip; modernize, update, bring up to date, bring into the twenty-first century; N. Amer. bring up to code; informal do up; N. Amer. informal rehab.

refusal noun **1** *we have had only one refusal to our invitation*: **non-acceptance**, no, dissent, demurral, negation, rebuff, turndown; regrets; informal knock-back, brush-off; rare declinature.
▷ANTONYMS acceptance.
2 *you can have first refusal*: **option**, choice, consideration, opportunity to purchase.
3 *the Council's refusal of planning permission*: **withholding**, failure to grant, denial, veto, turndown; informal the thumbs down.
▷ANTONYMS granting.

refuse[1] (stress on the second syllable) verb **1** *he refused their invitation to lunch*: **decline**, **turn down**, say no to; reject, spurn, scorn, rebuff, disdain, repudiate, dismiss, repulse; shake one's head, send one's regrets; baulk at, demur at, protest at, jib at, draw the line at; informal pass up; Brit. informal knock back.
▷ANTONYMS accept.
2 *the Council refused planning permission*: **withhold**, not grant, disapprove, deny, discountenance; informal give the thumbs down to.
▷ANTONYMS grant.

> *Choose the right word* **refuse, decline, reject, spurn**
>
> These words all share the basic meaning of saying 'no' to something, but they can also convey how or why it was said.
>
> **Refuse** is the most neutral word for simply saying 'no' to a request, suggestion, or offer (*I refused to answer their questions | he must refuse any food offered him*). *Refuse* is the only one of these words that can have two objects (*the USA had refused him an entry visa*).
>
> To **decline** something is to refuse it politely and rather formally (*I am sorry to have to decline your offer*). *Decline* and *refuse* are the only two of these words that can followed by an infinitive (*he declined to speculate about a cancer cure*).
>
> **Reject** suggests that what is on offer is felt to be not good enough (*an article which her editor had rejected*). It is also used, especially in official contexts, when a request is not granted (*the coroner rejected a request to submit a technical report*). *Reject* is also used of the body's immune system response to a transplanted organ.
>
> **Spurn** suggests disdain or contempt (*the opposition spurned an invitation to participate in a coalition government | she cut herself off from us and spurned our forgiveness*), although nowadays journalists often use it in a weaker sense (*pensions managers may spurn equities*). Both *spurn* and *reject* are also used of refusing affection to someone who used to be or might be expected to be the object of it (*a spurned lover | he was reared on the bottle, having been completely rejected by his mother*).

refuse[2] (stress on the first syllable) noun *dogs nosed around in piles of refuse*: **rubbish**, waste, debris, litter, garbage, discarded matter, detritus, dross, landfill, scrap, rubble, slag, spoilage, sullage, sewage, slop; dregs, lees, leavings, leftovers, sweepings; N. Amer. trash; Austral./NZ **mullock**; informal dreck, junk; Brit. informal gash; Archaeology debitage; rare draff, raffle, raff.

refute verb **1** *attempts to refute Einstein's theory of relativity*: **disprove**, prove wrong/false, show/prove to be wrong/false, rebut, confute, give the lie to, demolish, explode, debunk, drive a coach and horses through, discredit, invalidate; informal shoot full of holes, shoot down (in flames), blow sky-high; rare controvert, negative.
▷ANTONYMS confirm.
2 *a spokesman totally refuted the allegation of bias*: **deny**, reject, repudiate, rebut, declare to be untrue; contradict; formal gainsay.
▷ANTONYMS accept.

r

Easily confused words **refute or deny?**

The core meaning of **refute** is 'prove (a statement or theory) to be wrong', as in *attempts to refute Einstein's theory*. In the second half of the 20th century, a sense developed in which *refute* is treated as synonymous with **deny**, as in *I absolutely refute the charges made against me*, where no evidence or argument to show that the charges are untrue is given. Traditionalists object to the second use, but it is now widely accepted in standard English.

regain verb **1** *government troops regained control of the area | he did not regain consciousness*: **recover**, get back, win back, recoup, retrieve, reclaim, repossess, have something returned, be reunited with, rescue, salvage; take back, retake, recapture, reconquer.
2 *it would be easier to regain the glacier by traversing the mountain*: **return to**, get back to, find one's way back to, reach again, reattain, rejoin.

regal adjective **1** *a regal feast was laid before him*: **majestic**, fit for a king/queen/prince/princess, grand, impressive, imposing, splendid, superb, magnificent, noble, proud, stately, dignified, exalted, glorious, striking, spectacular, awe-inspiring, breathtaking, sumptuous, opulent, fine, luxurious, de luxe, lavish, resplendent, monumental, palatial, august, distinguished, great; informal splendiferous, ritzy, posh; rare splendacious, magnolious.
2 *his regal forebears*: **royal**, kingly, queenly, princely, sovereign, crowned.
▷**ANTONYMS** plebeian.

regale verb **1** *the carol-singers were regaled with refreshment at most houses*: **supply lavishly**, entertain lavishly/sumptuously, ply, wine and dine, fête, feast, cater for, serve, feed.
2 *he regaled her with a colourful account of that afternoon's meeting*: **entertain**, amuse, divert, delight, fascinate, captivate, beguile; treat to.

regard verb **1** *we regard these results as encouraging*: **consider**, look on, view, see, hold, think, think of, contemplate, count, judge, deem, estimate, evaluate, interpret, appraise, assess, make of, find, put down as, take for, account, reckon, treat, adjudge, size up, value, rate, gauge, sum up, weigh up.
2 *he regarded her with a cold stare*: **look at**, contemplate, eye, gaze at, stare at; watch, observe, view, survey, scan; examine, inspect, study, scrutinize; literary behold.
3 archaic *he seldom regards her advice*: **heed**, pay heed to, pay attention to, attend to, listen to, mind, take notice of, take into consideration, take into account.
▸ **noun 1** *he has no regard for human life*: **consideration**, care, concern, sympathy, thought, mind, notice, heed, attention, interest.
2 *doctors are held in high regard by society*: **esteem**, respect, high opinion, acclaim, admiration, approval, approbation, popularity, appreciation, estimation, favour, deference, reverence, veneration, liking, affection, love.
3 (**regards**) *Jamie sends his regards*: **best wishes**, good wishes, greetings, kind/kindest regards, felicitations, salutations, respects, compliments, best, love; archaic remembrances, devoirs.
4 *she was aware of his steady regard*: **look**, gaze, stare, fixed look, intent look; observation, contemplation, examination, inspection, study, scrutiny.
5 *in this regard I disagree with you*: **respect**, aspect, facet, consideration, point, item, characteristic, particular, detail, specific, particularity, fact; matter, issue, topic, question, circumstance.
□ **with regard to** *I am writing with regard to an article in your November edition*. See **regarding**.

r

regarding preposition *further details regarding this scheme are available from the Council*: **concerning**, as regards, with regard to, in regard to, with respect to, in respect of, with reference to, relating to, respecting, as for, as to, re, about, apropos, on the subject of, in connection with; French vis-à-vis; Latin in re.

regardless adverb *he decided to go, regardless*: **anyway**, anyhow, in any case, nevertheless, nonetheless, notwithstanding, despite everything, in spite of everything, for all that, after everything, no matter what, even so, just the same, all the same, be that as it may, in any event, come what may, (come) rain or shine, whatever the cost; informal still and all, irregardless.
□ **regardless of** *the Commission should promote equal opportunities for people regardless of age*: **irrespective of**, without regard to, without reference to, disregarding, unmindful of, heedless of, careless of/about, indifferent to, unconcerned about, without consideration of, negligent of, setting aside, discounting, ignoring, notwithstanding, no matter, despite, in spite of, for all; informal irregardless of.
▷**ANTONYMS** mindful of, heedful of.

regenerate verb *government grants have helped to regenerate many of our inner-city areas*: **revive**, **revitalize**, renew, restore, breathe new life into, revivify, rejuvenate, reanimate, resuscitate, reawaken, rekindle, kick-start, uplift, change radically, improve, amend; reorganize, reconstruct, renovate, overhaul; informal give a shot in the arm to.

regime noun **1** *the military regime controls very carefully what is written*: **government**, authorities, system of government, rule, reign, dominion, sovereignty, jurisdiction, authority, control, command, administration, establishment, direction, management, leadership.
2 *a favourable tax regime | many people who start a health regime stop it too early*: **system**, arrangement, scheme, code; apparatus, mechanism; order, pattern, method, procedure, routine, policy, practice, course, plan, programme; diet, regimen.

regiment noun *the regiment was fighting somewhere in France*: **unit**, outfit, force; army, group, corps, division, brigade, battalion, squadron, company, commando, battery, platoon, section, crew, detachment, contingent, band, legion, cohort.
▸ **verb** *every aspect of their life is strictly regimented*: **organize**, order, systematize, control, manipulate, regulate, manage, discipline, keep a tight rein on, bring into line, rule with a rod of iron; rare methodize.

regimented adjective *the regimented environment of the ward*: **strict**, strictly regulated, organized, disciplined, controlled, ordered, systematic, neat, tidy, orderly; uniform, unvarying, unvaried, unchanging, even, unbroken, monotonous, dull.
▷**ANTONYMS** free, varied.

region noun *the western region of the country*: **district**, province, territory, division, area, section, sector, zone, belt, tract, stretch, expanse, terrain, part, quarter, locality, locale; informal parts; Brit. informal patch.
□ **in the region of** *a population in the region of 1,400*: **approximately**, about, around, roughly, in the neighbourhood of, in the area of, of the order of, something like, some, round about, close to, near to, just about, practically, more or less; or so, or thereabouts, there or thereabouts, give or take a few, plus or minus a few, give or take a bit, in round numbers; not far off, nearly, almost, approaching; Brit. getting on for; Latin circa; informal as near as dammit to; N. Amer. informal in the ballpark of.

regional adjective **1** *there was considerable regional variation*: **geographical**, topographical, zonal, territorial, topical; by region, from one region to another.
2 *a regional parliament*: **local**, localized, devolved; state, territorial, provincial, sectoral, zonal, cantonal, county, district, parochial; native, vernacular.
▷**ANTONYMS** national.

register noun **1** *the register of electors*: **official list**, listing, roll, roster, index, directory, catalogue, schedule, inventory, tally, calendar.
2 *her death was recorded in the parish register*: **record**, chronicle, diary, journal, log, logbook, ledger, archive; annals, files.
3 *the lower register of the piano*: **range**, area, region, reaches, sweep; voice, notes, octaves.
▸ **verb 1** *the car is registered in his name | I wish to register a complaint*: **record**, put on record, enter, file, lodge, post, set down, inscribe, write down, put in writing, submit, report, take down, note, minute, list, log, catalogue.
2 *it is not too late to **register for** the conference*: **enrol**, put one's name down, enlist, enter, sign on, sign up, apply; go in for; check in.
3 *the dial registered much more than half an ounce*: **indicate**, read, record, show, display.
4 *her face registered gathering anger*: **display**, show, express, exhibit, evince, betray, disclose, evidence, reveal, manifest, demonstrate, reflect, bespeak, testify to; literary betoken.
5 *the content of her statement did not register*: **make an impression**, get through, sink in, fall into place, penetrate, have an effect, dawn, strike home, be understood; strike someone.

regress verb *he regressed to his former state of madness*: **revert**, retrogress, relapse, lapse, backslide, go backwards, slip back, drift back, subside, sink back; **deteriorate**, decline, worsen, degenerate, get worse, fall, fall off, fall away, drop, ebb, wane, slump; informal go downhill, go to pot, go to the dogs; rare recidivate, retrograde.
▷**ANTONYMS** progress, improve.

regret verb **1** *they may come to regret their decision*: **be sorry about**, feel contrite about, feel apologetic about, feel remorse about/for, be remorseful about, rue, repent (of), feel repentant about, be regretful at/about, have a conscience about, blame oneself for.
▷**ANTONYMS** applaud, welcome.
2 *it made him regret the passing of his youth*: **mourn**, grieve for/over, feel grief at, weep over, sigh over, fret about, pine over; feel sad about, be regretful at/about, lament, feel sorrow at, sorrow for, be upset/disappointed about, deplore.
▸ **noun 1** *it was an injudicious action, and both players later expressed regret*: **remorse**, sorrow, contrition, contriteness, repentance, penitence, pangs of conscience, guilt, compunction, remorsefulness, ruefulness, shame, self-reproach, self-accusation, self-condemnation; rare sorriness.
▷**ANTONYMS** satisfaction.
2 (**regrets**) *please give your grandmother my regrets as I have to leave*: **apology**, apologies, expression of regret; refusal, non-acceptance.
3 *the family left London with genuine regret*: **sadness**, sorrow, disappointment, dismay, unhappiness, dejection, lamentation, grief, mourning, mournfulness.
▷**ANTONYMS** happiness, gladness.

regretful adjective **1** *she sounded genuinely regretful*: **sorry**, remorseful, contrite, repentant, rueful, penitent, conscience-stricken, apologetic, abject, guilty, guilt-ridden, ashamed, shamefaced, sheepish, in sackcloth

and ashes, afraid; rare compunctious.
▷ANTONYMS unrepentant.
2 *there was no time to feel regretful when Greg and his family left*: **sad**, unhappy, sorrowful, dejected, depressed, downcast, miserable, downhearted, down, despondent, despairing, disconsolate, out of sorts, desolate, wretched, glum, gloomy, dismal, blue, melancholy, melancholic, low-spirited, mournful, woeful, woebegone, doleful, forlorn, crestfallen; informal down in the mouth, down in the dumps.
▷ANTONYMS glad.

regrettable adjective *a regrettable lack of foresight was at the root of it*: **undesirable**, unfortunate, unwelcome, sad, sorry, woeful, disappointing, distressing, too bad; deplorable, lamentable, reprehensible, shameful, disgraceful, blameworthy, ill-advised, dreadful, terrible, awful; rare egregious.
▷ANTONYMS desirable, welcome.

regular adjective 1 *he had to plant the flags at regular intervals*: **uniform**, even, consistent, constant, unchanging, unvarying, orderly, systematic, fixed; symmetrical.
▷ANTONYMS irregular, erratic.
2 *a poem with a very regular beat*: **rhythmic**, steady, even, uniform, constant, unchanging, unvarying; smooth.
▷ANTONYMS irregular, unsteady.
3 *the reprocessing plant has been the subject of regular protests*: **frequent**, repeated, continual, recurrent, periodic, habitual, constant, perpetual, oft repeated, repetitive, numerous.
▷ANTONYMS occasional.
4 *in their haste to be rich they deviated from safe and regular methods of business*: **established**, conventional, orthodox, proper, formal, official, fixed, stated, approved, sanctioned, bona fide, standard, usual, traditional, classic, time-honoured, tried and tested, tried and trusted.
▷ANTONYMS irregular, experimental.
5 *you should have a regular procedure for taking and recording attendance*: **methodical**, systematic, structured, well ordered, well organized, orderly, efficient, smooth-running, streamlined, well regulated, disciplined, planned, well planned, businesslike, meticulous, punctilious.
▷ANTONYMS haphazard.
6 *his regular route to work*: **usual**, normal, customary, habitual, routine, typical, everyday, accustomed, established, expected, wonted, ordinary, daily, common.
▷ANTONYMS unusual.
7 informal, dated *he's a regular charmer*: **utter**, real, absolute, complete, thorough, thoroughgoing, total, unmitigated, outright, out-and-out, perfect, consummate, surpassing, sheer, rank, pure, unqualified, inveterate, positive, dyed-in-the-wool, true-blue, undiluted, unalloyed, unadulterated, in every respect; N. Amer. full-bore; informal deep-dyed; Brit. informal right, proper; Austral./NZ informal fair; archaic arrant; rare right-down.

regulate verb 1 *the flow of the river has been regulated with sluices*: **control**, adjust, manage, balance, set, synchronize, modulate, tune.
2 *businesses that are regulated under the Financial Services Act*: **supervise**, oversee, police, superintend, monitor, check (up on), keep an eye on, inspect, administer, be responsible for; **control**, manage, direct, guide, govern, rule, order; informal keep tabs on, keep a tab on, keep a beady eye on.

regulation noun 1 *EC regulations regarding health and safety in the workplace*: **rule**, ruling, order, directive, act, law, by-law, statute, edict, canon, ordinance, pronouncement, mandate, dictate, dictum, decree, fiat, proclamation, command, injunction, procedure, requirement, prescription, precept, guideline; in Tsarist Russia ukase; in Spanish-speaking countries pronunciamento.
2 *chromium is thought to play a very important part in the regulation of blood sugar*: **adjustment**, control, management, balancing, setting, synchronization, modulation, tuning.
3 *the regulation of financial services*: **supervision**, **policing**, overseeing, superintendence, monitoring, inspection, administration; **control**, management, responsibility for, direction, guidance, government, rule, ordering.
▶ adjective *regulation dress went by the board in such extreme conditions*: **official**, prescribed, set, fixed, required, mandatory, compulsory, obligatory; correct, acceptable, appropriate, proper, fitting, standard, normal, usual, customary.
▷ANTONYMS non-standard, unofficial, informal.

regurgitate verb 1 *a ruminant continually regurgitates food from its stomach*: **vomit**, bring up, disgorge; archaic regorge.
2 *I knew how to regurgitate facts for examinations*: **repeat**, say again, restate, recapitulate, iterate, reiterate, recite, rehearse, parrot; informal trot out.

rehabilitate verb 1 *efforts are made to rehabilitate patients after treatment*: **restore to health/normality**, reintegrate, readapt, retrain; N. Amer. informal rehab.
2 *with the fall of the government, many former dissidents were rehabilitated*: **reinstate**, reinstall, restore, bring back, re-establish; **pardon**, absolve, exonerate, exculpate, forgive.
3 *the authority has an excellent reputation for rehabilitating vacant housing*: **recondition**, restore, renew, renovate, refurbish, revamp, make over, make fit for habitation/use, overhaul, develop, redevelop, convert, rebuild, reconstruct, remodel; redecorate, brighten up, freshen up, spruce up; improve, upgrade, refit, fix up, re-equip; modernize, update, bring up to date, bring into the twenty-first century; N. Amer. bring something up to code, rehab; informal do up.

rehearsal noun 1 *we've got a rehearsal for the school concert*: **practice**, practice session, try-out, trial performance, read-through, sing-through, walk-through, run-through, going-over, drill; informal dry run.
2 *they would interrupt speakers with lengthy rehearsals of facts and figures*: **enumeration**, listing, itemization, detailing, spelling out, setting out, specification, naming, cataloguing, recitation, rattling off, presentation; list, catalogue.

rehearse verb 1 *I had rehearsed this role for years*: **prepare**, practise, try out, read through, sing through, walk through, run through/over, go over; N. Amer. informal run down.
2 *he was rehearsing with the rest of the band*: **practise**, have a practice session, prepare, have a trial performance, go through one's paces.
3 *I recall him rehearsing the Vienna Philharmonic in two works by Tchaikovsky*: **train**, drill, prepare, coach, tutor, groom, put someone through their paces, teach, instruct, school, direct, guide, inculcate.
4 *this carefully worded document rehearsed the arguments for making the joint award*: **enumerate**, list, itemize, detail, spell out, set out, present, specify, name, give, describe, delineate, catalogue, recite, rattle off; **restate**, repeat, reiterate, recapitulate, recount, go over, run through, review; informal recap.

reign verb 1 *Robert II reigned for nineteen years*: **be king/queen**, be monarch, be sovereign, sit on the throne, occupy the throne, wear the crown, wield the sceptre, hold sway, rule, govern, be in power.
2 *chaos reigned for a few moments*: **prevail**, exist, be in existence, be present, be the case, hold, obtain, occur, be prevalent, be current, be rife, be rampant, be the order of the day, be customary, be established, be common, be widespread, be in force, be in effect; abound, predominate, preponderate, be supreme, hold sway; endure, survive, persist.
▶ noun 1 *the later years of Henry's reign*: **rule**, sovereignty, monarchy.
2 *during his reign as manager*: **period in office**, incumbency, tenancy, managership, leadership; period as champion.

> *Word links* **reign**
>
> **regnal** relating to a reign

reigning adjective 1 *the reigning monarch*: **ruling**, regnant; on the throne.
2 *the reigning world champion*: **incumbent**, current, in office, presiding, in power.
3 *the reigning legal conventions*: **prevailing**, existing, extant, contemporary, present, current, modern, latest; usual, common, set, recognized, established, accepted, ordinary, popular, fashionable; general, pervasive, ubiquitous, widespread, rampant, universal; in force, in fashion, in style, in vogue.

reimburse verb 1 *it is usual for companies to reimburse travel costs*: **repay**, refund, return, pay back, give back, restore, replace, make good.
2 *we'll reimburse you out of petty cash*: **compensate**, recompense, refund, repay, square accounts with, settle up with.

rein noun *he has no rein on his own behaviour*: **restraint**, check, curb, constraint, restriction, limitation, control, bridle, brake.
▶ verb *he* ***reined in*** *his horse | he made no attempt to* ***rein back*** *costs*: **restrain**, check, curb, constrain, hold back, keep in check, keep under control, hold in, regulate, restrict, control, bridle, put the brakes on, slow down, curtail, limit, stop, arrest.
□ **free rein** *you'd be given free rein to run the show how you wanted it*: **freedom**, scope, a free hand, leeway, latitude, elbow room, space, room, flexibility, liberty, independence, play, slack, free play, leisure, licence, room to manoeuvre, scope for initiative, freedom of action, freedom from restriction, indulgence, laxity, margin; French carte blanche.
□ **keep a tight rein on** **exercise strict control over**, keep on a tight rein, allow little freedom to, regulate, manage, discipline, regiment, keep in line, rule with a rod of iron.

reincarnation noun **rebirth**, transmigration of the soul, metempsychosis; Hinduism & Buddhism **samsara**; rare **transanimation**.

reinforce verb 1 *experts constructed a new stone wall to reinforce the dam*: **strengthen**, fortify, bolster up, shore up, buttress, prop up, underpin, brace, stiffen, toughen, support, hold up; archaic underprop.
2 *the scheme reinforces the links between colleges and companies*: **strengthen**, fortify, bolster up, shore up, buttress, prop up, underpin, support; cement, uphold, defend, maintain, back (up), buoy up; boost, give a boost to, aid, assist, help, promote, encourage, deepen, broaden, enrich, enhance, intensify, improve; underline, heighten, emphasize, stress.
3 *the USA would have as little as two weeks to reinforce NATO troops*: **augment**, increase, add to, supplement, boost, swell, build up, top up.

reinforcement noun 1 *the proposed directive would require reinforcement of the landing gear*: **strengthening**, fortification, bolstering, shoring up,

r

propping up, buttressing, underpinning, bracing, stiffening, supporting, holding up.
2 *reinforcement of the heavy bomber force was continuing*: **augmentation**, increase, supplementing, boosting, swelling, building up, build-up, topping up.
3 (**reinforcements**) *they were forced into a temporary retreat but returned later with reinforcements*: **additional troops**, fresh troops, additional police, supplementaries, auxiliaries, reserves; support, backup, help; archaic succours.

reinstate verb *he was reinstated as President on 21 August*: **restore**, return to a former position, return to power, put back, replace, bring back, reinstitute, reinstall, rehabilitate, re-establish.

reinstatement noun *the reinstatement of the legitimate government*: **restoration**, return to a former position, return to power, bringing back, reinstitution, reinstallation, rehabilitation, re-establishment.

reiterate verb *he reiterated his opposition to abortion*: **repeat**, say again, restate, retell, recapitulate, go over (and over), iterate, rehearse, belabour, dwell on, harp on, hammer away at; N. Amer. informal do over; archaic ingeminate.

reject verb (stress on the second syllable) **1** *the miners rejected the government's offer to negotiate their demands*: **turn down**, refuse, decline, say no to; dismiss, spurn; informal give the thumbs down to, give the red light to, give something a miss; Brit. informal knock back; rare negative.
▷ANTONYMS accept.
2 *she had been deeply in love with Jamie, but he rejected her*: **rebuff**, spurn, repudiate, cut off, cast off, cast aside, discard, jettison, abandon, desert, turn one's back on, have nothing (more) to do with, wash one's hands of, cast out, shut out, exclude, shun, cold-shoulder, give someone the cold shoulder; ostracize, blackball, blacklist, avoid, give a wide berth to, ignore, snub, cut dead, keep at arm's length, leave out in the cold; Brit. send to Coventry; N. Amer. disfellowship; informal give someone the brush-off, kick someone in the teeth, freeze out, hand someone the frozen mitt; informal, dated give someone the go-by; Brit. informal blank; dated cut; Christianity excommunicate; archaic forsake.
▷ANTONYMS welcome.
▶ noun (stress on the first syllable) **1** *I got it cheap—it is only a reject*: **substandard article**, discard, second; (**rejects**) substandard goods.
2 *even a reject like him could be of use in such a godforsaken spot*: **failure**, loser, incompetent; (**rejects**) flotsam.

Choose the right word **reject, refuse, decline, spurn**

See **refuse**[1].

rejection noun **1** *the chairman is expected to issue a rejection of the offer*: **refusal**, non-acceptance, declining, turning down, no, dismissal, spurning, rebuff; informal knock-back.
▷ANTONYMS acceptance.
2 *it took a long while before he got over Madeleine's rejection of him*: **repudiation**, rebuff, spurning, abandonment, forsaking, desertion, shutting out, exclusion, shunning, cold-shouldering, ostracizing, ostracism, blackballing, blacklisting, avoidance, ignoring, snubbing, snub, cutting dead; Brit. sending to Coventry; informal brush-off, a kick in the teeth; Christianity excommunication.
▷ANTONYMS welcome.

rejoice verb **1** *palaeontologists rejoiced when they discovered a complete dinosaur skeleton*: **be joyful**, be happy, be pleased, be glad, be delighted, be elated, be ecstatic, be euphoric, be overjoyed, be as pleased as Punch, be cock-a-hoop, be jubilant, be rapturous, be in raptures, be transported, be beside oneself with joy, be delirious, be thrilled, jump for joy, be on cloud nine, be walking/treading on air, be in seventh heaven, exult, glory, triumph; celebrate, cheer, revel, make merry; informal be over the moon, be on top of the world, be blissed out, whoop it up; Austral. informal be wrapped; archaic joy, jubilate.
▷ANTONYMS mourn, lament.
2 *he **rejoiced in** his success*: **take delight in**, find/take pleasure in, find/take satisfaction in, feel satisfaction at, find joy in, enjoy, appreciate, revel in, glory in, bask in, delight in, exult in, triumph over, relish, savour, luxuriate in, wallow in; **be/feel proud of**, feel proud about, be proud of oneself for, congratulate oneself on, flatter oneself on, preen oneself on, pat oneself on the back for, give oneself a pat on the back for; **crow about**, feel self-satisfied about, vaunt, boast about, brag about, gloat over; archaic pique oneself on/in.

rejoicing noun *this should be an occasion for rejoicing*: **happiness**, pleasure, joy, gladness, delight, elation, cheer, jubilation, euphoria, delirium, ecstasy, rapture, transports of delight, exuberance, exultation, glory, triumph, celebration, revelry, merrymaking, festivity, feasting.
▷ANTONYMS mourning.

rejoin[1] verb *the side road rejoins the main road further on*: **return to**, be reunited with, come/get/go back to, join again, find one's way back to, reach again, regain, reattain.

rejoin[2] verb *Eugene rejoined that you couldn't expect to see him in the dark*: **answer**, reply, respond, return, retort, riposte, come back, counter.

rejoinder noun *the smart rejoinder to a put-down usually occurs to me on the bus on the way home*: **answer**, reply, response, retort, riposte, counter, sally; informal comeback.

rejuvenate verb *the leadership change was seen as an attempt to rejuvenate the party*: **revive**, revitalize, renew, regenerate, restore, breathe new life into, make someone feel young again, revivify, reanimate, resuscitate, refresh, reawaken, rekindle, put new life into, put new heart into, add some zest to, put some spark into, kick-start, uplift; reorganize, reconstruct, renovate, overhaul, revamp, modernize; informal give a shot in the arm to, pep up, buck up.

relapse verb **1** *although most children remain well after this procedure, a few relapse*: **get ill/worse again**, have/suffer a relapse, worsen, deteriorate, degenerate, take a turn for the worse, sicken, weaken, fail, sink.
▷ANTONYMS recover, improve.
2 *the old woman relapsed into silence*: **revert**, lapse; regress, retrogress, backslide, fall back, go backwards, slip back, slide back, drift back, degenerate; rare recidivate, retrograde.
▶ noun **1** *one of the patients later suffered a relapse*: **deterioration**, worsening of someone's condition, turn for the worse, setback, weakening; **recurrence**, repetition.
▷ANTONYMS recovery, improvement.
2 *he foresaw a relapse into an excessively objective kind of theology*: **decline**, lapse, deterioration, worsening, degeneration, backsliding, recidivism, reversion, regression, retrogression, downturn, fall, falling, falling away, slipping, drop, descent, sinking, slide.

relate verb **1** *he goes on to relate many other such stories*: **tell**, recount, narrate, give an account of, describe; portray, depict, paint, unfold, set forth, present, report, chronicle, outline, delineate, retail, recite, repeat, rehearse, relay, convey, communicate, impart, spin; detail, enumerate, list, specify, itemize, cite, particularize, catalogue.
2 *they found that mortality is **related to** unemployment levels | the infant cannot yet relate cause and effect*: **connect (with)**, associate (with), link (with), correlate (with), ally (with), couple (with), bracket (with); bring together, find/establish a connection between, find/establish a relationship between, find/establish a link between, find/establish an association between, find/establish a correspondence between.
3 *the charges **relate to** offences allegedly committed on 4 August*: **apply to**, be relevant to, have relevance to, concern, refer to, have reference to, belong to, pertain to, be pertinent to, have to do with, bear on, have a bearing on, appertain to, affect, involve, cover, touch; archaic regard.
4 *many adolescents find it hard to **relate to** a stepfather*: **have a rapport with**, get on (well) with, respond to, sympathize with, feel sympathy with, feel for, identify with, empathize with, connect with, understand, speak the same language as, be in tune with, be on the same wavelength as; informal hit it off with.

related adjective **1** *an amalgam of several related ideas*: **connected**, interconnected, associated, linked, coupled, correlated, allied, affiliated, accompanying, concomitant, corresponding, analogous, kindred, parallel, comparable, equivalent, homologous, incidental.
▷ANTONYMS unconnected, separate.
2 *are you two related?* **of the same family**, kin, akin, kindred, of the same blood, with a common ancestor/forebear, connected; rare agnate, consanguineous, cognate.
▷ANTONYMS unrelated.

relation noun **1** *he understood the **relation between** religion and life*: **connection**, relationship, association, link, correlation, correspondence, parallel, tie-in, tie-up, alliance, bond, interrelation, interconnection; interdependence of.
2 *such information had no **relation to** national security*: **relevance**, applicability, application, reference, pertinence, bearing on, regard.
3 *are you a relation of his?* **relative**, member of someone's/the family, one's (own) flesh and blood, next of kin; (**relations**) family, kin, kith and kin, kindred; formal kinsman, kinswoman.
4 (**relations**) *he sought to improve relations with India*: **dealings**, associations, communication, relationship, connections, contact, interaction, intercourse.
5 (**relations**) formal *all thought of **sexual relations** was abhorrent to her*. See **sex**.

relationship noun **1** *the relationship between diet and diabetes*: **connection**, relation, association, link, correlation, correspondence, parallel, tie-in, tie-up, alliance, bond, interrelation, interconnection; interdependence of.
2 *we have evidence here of some direct relationship with the Marquesses of Bath*: **family ties**, family connections, blood relationship, blood ties, kinship, affinity, consanguinity, common ancestry, common lineage, connection; technical propinquity.
3 *he reacted badly to the end of his relationship with his girlfriend*: **romance**, love affair, affair, affair of the heart, love, amorous entanglement, flirtation, liaison; French affaire de/du cœur, amour.

relative adjective **1** *the relative importance of each factor*: **comparative**, respective, comparable, correlative, parallel, corresponding, reciprocal.
▷ANTONYMS absolute.

2 *a kitten requires three times more nourishment,* ***relative to*** *body weight, than a fully grown cat*: **proportionate**, proportional, in proportion, commensurate, corresponding, dependent on, based on.
▷ANTONYMS disproportionate.
3 *Semtex was able to be smuggled with relative ease*: **moderate**, reasonable, a fair degree of, considerable, some; comparative, qualified, modified; in/by comparison.
▷ANTONYMS great, complete.
▶ **noun** *he's a relative of mine*: **relation**, member of someone's/the family, one's (own) flesh and blood, next of kin; formal kinsman, kinswoman; (**relatives**) **family**, kin, kith and kin, kindred; informal folks; formal kinsfolk; dated people.

Word links **relative**

parricide killing of a near relative

relatively adverb *the roads were still relatively clear*: **comparatively**, in comparison, by comparison, proportionately; **quite**, fairly, reasonably, rather, somewhat, to a limited extent/degree, to a certain extent/degree, to some extent/degree, to an extent, to a degree, within reason, within limits, tolerably, passably, adequately, satisfactorily; informal pretty, kind of, sort of, ish.

relax verb 1 *yoga or meditation may be helpful in learning to relax*: **unwind**, loosen up, ease up/off, let up, slow down, de-stress, unbend, rest, repose, put one's feet up, take it easy, take time off, take time out, slack off, be at leisure, take one's leisure, take one's ease, laze, luxuriate, do nothing, sit back, lounge, loll, slump, flop, idle, loaf, enjoy oneself, amuse oneself, play, entertain oneself; informal let it all hang out, let one's hair down, unbutton, veg out; N. Amer. informal hang loose, stay loose, chill out, kick back.
▷ANTONYMS be tense, psych oneself up.
2 *a walk will relax you*: **calm**, calm down, unwind, loosen up, make less tense/uptight, quieten, tranquillize, soothe, pacify, compose.
▷ANTONYMS psych someone up.
3 *he relaxed his grip on the mug*: **loosen**, loose, slacken, unclench, weaken, lessen, let up, reduce, diminish.
▷ANTONYMS tighten.
4 *she felt her tense muscles relax*: **become less tense**, become less stiff/rigid, loosen, slacken, ease, unknot.
▷ANTONYMS tighten, contract.
5 *the ministry relaxed some of the restrictions*: **moderate**, modify, temper, make less strict/formal, ease, ease up on, loosen, lessen, lighten, slacken; alleviate, mitigate, qualify, dilute, weaken, reduce, diminish, decrease; informal let up on.
▷ANTONYMS tighten up.

relaxation noun 1 *a state of relaxation*: **mental repose**, composure; calm, tranquillity, peacefulness, calming oneself, loosening up, unwinding, winding down.
▷ANTONYMS anxiety.
2 *I just play for relaxation nowadays*: **recreation**, enjoyment, amusement, entertainment, diversion, distraction, fun, pleasure, rest, refreshment, relief, respite, leisure, leisure activity/pursuit; informal R and R.
3 *skills for coping with anxiety include muscle relaxation*: **loosening**, slackening, loosing, easing.
▷ANTONYMS tightening, contraction.
4 *relaxation of censorship rules*: **moderation**, modification, easing, loosening, lessening, lightening, slackening; alleviation, mitigation, qualification, dilution, weakening, diminution, reduction; informal letting up.
▷ANTONYMS tightening up.

relay noun *an uninterrupted relay of the performance*: **broadcast**, transmission, programme, communication, telecast, show, feed.
▶ **verb** *it is better for individuals to talk directly to each other rather than relay messages through a third party*: **pass on**, hand on, transfer, repeat, retail, impart, communicate, send, transmit, broadcast, feed, disseminate, make known, publish, spread, circulate.

release verb 1 *the government released some 150 prisoners*: **free**, set free, let go, allow to leave, set/let/turn loose, let out, liberate, set at liberty, deliver, rescue, ransom, emancipate; historical manumit.
▷ANTONYMS imprison.
2 *Burke released the animal*: **untie**, undo, loose, let go, unhand, unloose, unbind, unchain, unleash, unfetter, unclasp, unshackle, unmanacle, extricate, unhitch, unbridle, detach, disentangle.
▷ANTONYMS tie up.
3 *this enabled vast numbers of troops to be released for the other front*: **make available**, free, free up; contribute, put at someone's disposal, supply, furnish, provide; deploy.
▷ANTONYMS detain.
4 *Stephen was released from his promise*: **let off**, excuse, exempt, discharge, deliver; clear, exculpate, absolve, acquit, exonerate.
▷ANTONYMS hold someone to.
5 *police released news of his arrest yesterday*: **make public**, make known, bring to public notice/attention, issue, break, announce, declare, report, post, reveal, divulge, disclose, publish, publicize, print, broadcast, air, transmit, put out, circulate, communicate, impart, disseminate, distribute, spread, propagate, purvey.
▷ANTONYMS suppress, withhold.
6 *another series has just been released on video cassette*: **launch**, put on the market, market, put on sale, offer for sale, bring out, unveil, present, make available, distribute.
▶ **noun** 1 *the government ordered the release of 106 political prisoners*: **freeing**, liberation, deliverance, ransom, emancipation; freedom, liberty; historical manumission.
2 *continuous consultation took place regarding the release of the news*: **issuing**, breaking, announcement, declaration, reporting, posting, revealing, divulging, disclosure, publishing, publication, printing, broadcasting, airing, transmission, putting out, circulation, communication, imparting, dissemination, distribution, spreading, propagation, purveying.
3 *a press release*: **announcement**, bulletin, newsflash, briefing, dispatch, publication, proclamation.
4 *the group's last release was a big seller*: **CD**, disc, record, single, album; video, film; book.
5 *the next release of the network operating system*: **version**, edition, issue, model, mark, draft, form, impression, publication.

relegate verb *she was relegated to the status of mere spokesperson*: **downgrade**, lower, lower in rank/status, put down, move down; consign, banish, exile; demote, degrade, declass, strip someone of their rank, reduce to the ranks, disrate, drum out; N. Amer. bust.
▷ANTONYMS upgrade, promote.

relent verb 1 *the Government considered making everybody pay the tax but relented*: **change one's mind**, do a U-turn, back-pedal, back down, give way, give in, capitulate, yield, accede, come round, acquiesce; soften, melt, weaken, unbend, become merciful, become lenient, have/show pity, have/show mercy, give quarter; agree to something, allow something, concede something, admit something; Brit. do an about-turn.
▷ANTONYMS harden.
2 *by early evening the rain relented*: **ease off**, slacken, let up, ease, ease up, relax, abate, drop, fall off, die down, lessen, decrease, diminish, moderate, subside, weaken, tail off.
▷ANTONYMS strengthen, worsen.

relentless adjective 1 *their relentless pursuit of quality*: **persistent**, continuing, constant, continual, continuous, non-stop, lasting, never-ending, steady, uninterrupted, unabated, unabating, unbroken, interminable, incessant, unstoppable, unceasing, endless, unending, perpetual, unremitting, unrelenting, unrelieved, sustained; **unfaltering**, unflagging, untiring, unwavering, unswerving, undeviating, persevering, determined, resolute, purposeful, dogged, single-minded, tireless, indefatigable, patient, diligent, assiduous, sedulous, tenacious, pertinacious, insistent, importunate; stubborn, intransigent, obstinate, obdurate.
▷ANTONYMS short-lived, irresolute, intermittent.
2 *a relentless taskmaster*: **harsh**, grim, fierce, cruel, severe, strict, punishing, remorseless, merciless, pitiless, ruthless, unmerciful, unsparing, heartless, hard-hearted, hard, stony-hearted, stony, with a heart of stone, cold-blooded, cold-hearted, unforgiving, unfeeling, uncaring, unsympathetic, uncharitable, lacking compassion, unpitying; **inflexible**, unbending, uncompromising, obdurate, unyielding, unmoved, inexorable, implacable.
▷ANTONYMS lenient, merciful.

Choose the right word **relentless, remorseless, ruthless, pitiless**

These words all apply to people or processes that are not affected by anyone's wishes or entreaties. They differ chiefly in the extent to which they emphasize continuing activity or the attitude with which it is carried out.

A **relentless** action or process cannot be stopped (*the relentless march of rainforest destruction*) and is unvaryingly intense or severe (*the ships were subjected to relentless air attack*). When applied to a person, it means 'inflexible or uncompromising' but does not necessarily imply a lack of pity or humanity (*a patient but relentless taskmaster*).

Remorseless is used of a process that will not be stopped or deflected however great the suffering or distress it causes (*the company continued the remorseless cost-cutting drive*). When used of a person, the word marks them out as having no regret or guilt about the distress they have caused (*a remorseless killer*).

A **ruthless** person has no pity or compassion for others (*ruthless killers had set the building alight*) and is usually determined to continue regardless (*a ruthless operator whose sole ambition is to have a place in political history*).

Whereas a *ruthless* person is generally ruthless in pursuit of some goal, the emphasis of **pitiless**, a rarer word, is on a more intrinsic absence of pity itself (*his cold pitiless voice*).

relevant adjective *make a note of the relevant page numbers*: **pertinent**, applicable, apposite, material, apropos, to the point, to the purpose, germane, admissible; appropriate, apt, fitting, suitable, proper; connected, related, linked; Latin ad rem; rare appurtenant.
▷ANTONYMS irrelevant.

reliable adjective **1** *reliable evidence*: **dependable**, good, well founded, well grounded, authentic, definitive, attested, valid, genuine, from the horse's mouth, sound, true; Brit. copper-bottomed.
▷ANTONYMS unreliable.
2 *a reliable friend*: **trustworthy**, dependable, good, true, faithful, devoted, steady, steadfast, staunch, unswerving, unwavering, constant, loyal, trusty, dedicated, committed, unfailing, infallible, certain, sure; truthful, honest.
▷ANTONYMS unreliable, untrustworthy.
3 *the new bikes have reliable V-brakes*: **dependable**, **safe**, fail-safe, tried and tested, well built, well engineered, good.
▷ANTONYMS unreliable.
4 *a reliable firm*: **reputable**, dependable, trustworthy, honest, responsible, established, proven, stable, sound, solid, secure, safe, safe as houses.
▷ANTONYMS unreliable, dodgy.

reliance noun **1** *saving for a pension reduces* ***reliance on*** *the state*: **dependence**, dependency; seeking support from, leaning on.
2 *he displayed a lack of* ***reliance on*** *his own judgement*: **trust in**, confidence in, faith in, credence in, belief in, conviction in; credit.

relic noun **1** *a Viking relic which was more than a thousand years old*: **artefact**, historical object, ancient object, antiquity, antique, heirloom, object of virtu, curio; fossil.
2 (**relics**) *a shrine containing the saint's relics*: **remains**, body parts, bones; corpse, dead body, cadaver; holy/sacred objects; Latin reliquiae.

relief noun **1** *it was such a relief to share my secret worries with her | I found relief in desperately scribbling poetry*: **reassurance**, **consolation**, comfort, solace, calmness, relaxation, repose, ease.
2 *the relief of pain*: **alleviation**, alleviating, relieving, mitigation, mitigating, assuagement, assuaging, palliation, allaying, appeasement, soothing, easing, dulling, lessening, reduction, abatement.
▷ANTONYMS intensification.
3 *she just needed relief from her burden of bags*: **freedom**, release, liberation, deliverance, exemption, discharge.
4 *how she needed a little light relief!* **respite**, remission, lightening, brightening; amusement, diversion, entertainment, jollity, jollification, recreation; interruption, break; informal let-up.
▷ANTONYMS seriousness, solemnity.
5 *the coming of the rains brought no physical relief to the besieged*: **help**, aid, assistance, succour, care, sustenance; subsidy, benefit, charity, gifts, donations, financial assistance, debt remission; a helping hand, a leg up.
6 *his relief arrived to take over*: **replacement**, substitute, deputy, reserve, standby, stopgap, cover, stand-in, supply, fill-in, locum, locum tenens, understudy, proxy, surrogate.
□ **throw something into relief** *this brief account throws into sharp relief the differences between the rival theories*: **highlight**, spotlight, give prominence to, foreground; set off, point up, throw up, show up; emphasize, bring out, stress, accent, underline, underscore, accentuate; heighten, intensify, increase, enhance.
▷ANTONYMS mask, play down.

r

relieve verb **1** *a battery-powered device which helps relieve pain*: **alleviate**, mitigate, assuage, allay, soothe, soften, palliate, appease, ease, dull, reduce, lessen, diminish.
▷ANTONYMS aggravate.
2 *his studies helped to relieve the boredom*: **counteract**, reduce, alleviate, mitigate, brighten, lighten, sweeten, bring respite to, make something bearable; interrupt, punctuate, vary, break up, stop, bring an end to, cure, dispel; prevent.
▷ANTONYMS exacerbate, emphasize.
3 *there was no shortage of helpers to relieve us for breaks*: **replace**, take over from, take the place of, stand in for, act as stand-in for, fill in for, substitute for, act as a substitute for, deputize for, be a proxy for, cover for, provide cover for, act as locum for, hold the fort for, do something in someone's place/stead.
4 *this* ***relieves*** *the teacher* ***of*** *a heavy load of formal teaching*: **free of/from**, set free from, release from, liberate from, exempt from, excuse from, absolve from, let off, extricate from, discharge from, unburden of, disburden of, disencumber of; deliver from, rescue from, save from; rare disembarrass of.
▷ANTONYMS put an extra burden on.
□ **relieve oneself** See **urinate**, **defecate**.

relieved adjective *I'll be relieved when it's all over*: **glad**, thankful, grateful, pleased, happy; put at one's ease, easy/easier in one's mind, comforted, cheered, reassured.
▷ANTONYMS worried, anxious.

religion noun *the right to freedom of religion | what religion are you?* **faith**, belief, divinity, worship, creed, teaching, doctrine, theology; **sect**, cult, religious group, faith community, church, denomination, body, following, persuasion, affiliation.

religious adjective **1** *he was a very religious person*: **devout**, pious, reverent, believing, godly, God-fearing, dutiful, saintly, holy, prayerful, churchgoing, practising, faithful, devoted, committed.
▷ANTONYMS atheistic, irreverent.
2 *it was against her religious beliefs | religious music*: **spiritual**, theological, scriptural, doctrinal, church, churchly, ecclesiastical, holy, divine, celestial, heavenly, sacred, devotional, sanctified, consecrated, dedicated, hallowed; schismatic, sectarian.
▷ANTONYMS secular, civil.
3 *pay religious attention to detail*: **scrupulous**, conscientious, meticulous, sedulous, punctilious, zealous, strict, rigid, rigorous, exact, close, unfailing, unswerving, undeviating; **fussy**, pedantic, fastidious, nit-picking, finicky, finical.
▷ANTONYMS slapdash.

Word links **religious**

divinity, **theology** study of religion

Choose the right word **religious, devout, pious**

Religious basically means 'relating to a religion' (*the patriotic and religious duty of any Jew*) or 'believing in a religion' (*the word is regarded by many religious people with considerable disapproval*), and both senses are neither critical nor approving. Only in the second sense can *religious* be used after the verb *to be*, or be qualified by an adverb, to express the degree of someone's commitment (*he wasn't a churchgoer, but very religious*). Sometimes it is used in an extended sense to suggest that someone attaches particular importance to a secular object or pursuit; there may be a critical suggestion that such devotion is misplaced (*he always had a religious obsession with fame*).

Devout is used to indicate a deep and genuine religious commitment (*he was a devout Quaker and would not allow a pub in the village*), and is an approving word. It is also used to convey total or uncritical enthusiasm for or commitment to a secular object (*a devout soccer fan*).

Pious, too, can convey religious commitment (*donations to the Church from pious laymen*) but is now mainly used pejoratively to denote hypocritical religiosity (*I know what's under that pious face of yours*).

relinquish verb **1** *he relinquished control of the company to his sons*: **renounce**, give up, part with, give away; **hand over**, turn over, lay down, let go of, waive, resign, abdicate, yield, cede, surrender, sign away.
▷ANTONYMS keep, retain.
2 *he offered to relinquish his post as acting President*: **leave**, resign from, stand down from, bow out of, walk out of, retire from, give up, depart from, vacate, pull out of, abandon, abdicate; informal **quit**, chuck, jack in; archaic forsake.
3 *he relinquished his pipe-smoking*: **discontinue**, stop, cease, give up, drop, desist from; avoid, steer clear of, give a wide berth to; reject, eschew, forswear, refrain from, abstain from, forbear from, forgo; informal **quit**, leave off, kick; archaic forsake.
▷ANTONYMS continue.
4 *she relinquished her grip on the door*: **let go**, release, loose, unloose, loosen, relax.

relish noun **1** *he dug into his plate of food with relish*: **enjoyment**, gusto, delight, pleasure, glee, rapture, satisfaction, contentment, contentedness, gratification, happiness, exhilaration, excitement, titillation, appreciation, liking, fondness, enthusiasm, appetite, zest; humorous delectation.
▷ANTONYMS dislike.
2 *the sauce is ideal served as hot relish with beefburgers*: **condiment**, accompaniment, sauce, dressing, flavouring, seasoning, dip.
▶ verb **1** *he was relishing his moment of glory*: **enjoy**, delight in, love, like, adore, be pleased by, take pleasure in, rejoice in, appreciate, savour, revel in, luxuriate in, glory in; **gloat over**, feel self-satisfied about, crow about; informal get a kick out of, get a thrill out of.
▷ANTONYMS dislike.
2 *I don't relish the drive, but we could go by train*: **look forward to**, fancy, anticipate with pleasure, await with pleasure, lick one's lips over, be unable to wait for, count the days until, long for, hope for.
▷ANTONYMS dread.

reluctance noun *she sensed his reluctance to continue*: **unwillingness**, disinclination, lack of enthusiasm; hesitation, hesitance, hesitancy, diffidence, timidity, timorousness, trepidation, backwardness (in coming forward); demurral, wavering, vacillation, foot-dragging, resistance; doubts, second thoughts, scruples, qualms, pangs of conscience, misgivings; archaic disrelish.
▷ANTONYMS willingness, eagerness.

reluctant adjective **1** *she persuaded her reluctant parents to buy her a cat*: **unwilling**, disinclined, unenthusiastic, grudging, resistant, resisting, opposed, antipathetic; hesitant.
▷ANTONYMS willing, eager.
2 *Hilary gave a reluctant smile*: **shy**, bashful, coy, retiring, diffident,

reserved, restrained, withdrawn, shrinking, timid, timorous, sheepish, unconfident, insecure, unsure, suspicious, unassertive; apprehensive, fearful; rare costive.
▷ANTONYMS eager, ready.
3 *the man was* ***reluctant to*** *leave*: **loath**, unwilling, disinclined, not in the mood, indisposed, sorry, averse, slow; chary of, not in favour of, against, opposed to; hesitant about, diffident about, bashful about, shy about, coy about; ashamed to, afraid to.
▷ANTONYMS willing, eager, ready.

rely verb **1** *I think we can* ***rely on*** *his discretion*: **depend**, count, bank, place reliance, bargain, plan, reckon; anticipate, expect, pin one's hopes on, hope for, take for granted, take on trust, trust; be confident of, have (every) confidence in, be sure of, believe in, have faith in, pin one's faith on, trust in, cling to, swear by; N. Amer. informal figure on.
▷ANTONYMS distrust.
2 *law centres have had to* ***rely on*** *government funding to keep going*: **be dependent**, depend, lean, hinge, turn, hang, rest, pivot, be contingent; be unable to manage without, have recourse to, resort to, fall back on.

remain verb **1** *unless that is sorted out, the problem will remain*: **continue to exist**, endure, last, abide, go on, carry on, persist, hang in the air, stay around/round, stand, be extant, hold out, prevail, survive, live on.
▷ANTONYMS cease to exist.
2 *he would have to remain in hospital for around a month*: **stay**, stay behind, stay put, wait, wait around, linger, be left, hold on, hang on, rest, stop; informal hang around/round; Brit. informal hang about; formal sojourn; archaic bide, tarry.
▷ANTONYMS go, depart, leave.
3 *union leaders remain sceptical*: **continue to be**, stay, keep, persist in being, carry on being, go on being.
4 *I think we should leave them alone for the few minutes that remain*: **be left**, be left over, be still available, be unused; have not yet passed, have not yet expired.

remainder noun *eighty-seven members are elected directly, and the remainder by proportional representation*: **residue**, **balance**, remaining part/number/quantity, part/number/quantity (that is) left over, rest, others, those left, remnant, remnants, rump, surplus, difference, extra, excess, superfluity, overflow, overspill, additional people/material/things, extra people/material/things; technical residuum.

remaining adjective **1** *the cutbacks will help protect the jobs of the remaining 160 workers | he still had 4,300 pounds of fuel remaining*: **residual**, surviving, left, left over, unused; extra, surplus, spare, superfluous, excess, in excess, in addition.
2 *he settled his remaining debts*: **unsettled**, outstanding, unresolved, unfinished, incomplete, to be done, undone, not done, unattended to; unpaid.
3 *those are my only remaining memories of my first five years*: **surviving**, **lasting**, enduring, continuing, persisting, lingering, abiding, long-lived, (still) existing, extant, in existence, living, lifelong, long-term, perennial.
▷ANTONYMS short-lived.

remains plural noun **1** *she downed the remains of her drink in one go*: **remainder**, residue, remaining part/number/quantity, part/number/quantity (that is) left over, rest, remnant, remnants; leftovers, leavings, scraps, debris, detritus; technical residuum.
2 *Pula's Roman remains include the public baths and a triumphal arch*: **antiquities**, relics; inheritance, heritage; Latin reliquiae.
3 *Saint Ubaldo's remains are housed in the basilica*: **corpse**, dead body, body, cadaver, carcass; body parts, bones, skeleton.

remark verb **1** *'You're very quiet,' he remarked, breaking into her thoughts*: **comment**, say, observe, mention, reflect, state, declare, announce, pronounce, assert; interpose, interject; come out with; formal opine.
2 *many critics remarked on the rapport between the two stars*: **comment on**, mention, refer to, speak of, pass comment on, say something about, touch on.
3 *he remarked the absence of policemen*: **note**, notice, observe, take note of, mark, perceive, discern.
▶ noun **1** *Soanes claimed that his remarks had been misinterpreted*: **comment**, statement, utterance, observation, declaration, pronouncement; reflection, thought, opinion; (**remarks**) words.
2 *these discrepancies were thought worthy of remark*: **attention**, notice, comment, mention, observation, consideration, heed, acknowledgement, recognition.

remarkable adjective *a remarkable coincidence | the remarkable achievements of modern medicine*: **extraordinary**, exceptional, amazing, astonishing, astounding, marvellous, wonderful, sensational, stunning, incredible, unbelievable, miraculous, phenomenal, prodigious; **striking**, outstanding, momentous, impressive, singular, signal, pre-eminent, memorable, unforgettable, never to be forgotten, unique, arresting, eye-catching, conspicuous, noteworthy, notable, great, considerable, distinctive, important, distinguished, prominent; out of the ordinary, unusual, uncommon, rare, surprising, curious, strange, odd, peculiar, uncanny; Scottish unco; informal fantastic, terrific, tremendous, stupendous, awesome, out of this world, unreal; literary wondrous.
▷ANTONYMS ordinary, commonplace, run-of-the-mill.

> *Word toolkit* **remarkable**
>
> See **exceptional**.

remediable adjective *surgically remediable diseases*: **curable**, treatable, medicable, operable; able to be put right, capable of solution, solvable, soluble, reparable, repairable, rectifiable, resolvable, retrievable; rare corrigible.
▷ANTONYMS irremediable, incurable.

remedy noun **1** *traditional herbal remedies*: **treatment**, cure, medicine, medication, medicament, drug, restorative; antidote, prophylactic; nostrum, panacea, cure-all; therapy; archaic physic, specific.
2 *marriage is sometimes prescribed as a remedy for all kinds of life problems*: **solution**, answer, cure, antidote, corrective, curative, nostrum, panacea, cure-all, heal-all, palliative, balm, magic formula; countermeasure; informal magic bullet.
3 *the company is not liable and he has no effective remedy against them*: **(means of) redress**, (means of) reparation, comeback.
▶ verb **1** *little has been done to remedy the situation*: **put right**, set right, set to rights, put to rights, right, rectify, retrieve, solve, fix, sort out, put in order, straighten out, resolve, deal with, correct, repair, mend, redress, make good; improve, amend, ameliorate, make better, better.
2 *anaemia can be remedied by iron tablets*: **cure**, treat, heal, make better, counteract, control; relieve, ease, alleviate, soothe, palliate.

remember verb **1** *she smiled wistfully, remembering happy times*: **recall**, call to mind, recollect, think of; put a name to, place; reminisce about, think back to, look back on, hark back to, cast one's mind back to, summon up, muse on; take a trip down memory lane; Scottish mind; archaic bethink oneself of.
▷ANTONYMS forget.
2 *do you think you can remember all that or shall I write it down?* **memorize**, commit to memory, retain; learn off by heart, get off pat.
▷ANTONYMS forget.
3 *you must remember that she's still only five years old*: **bear in mind**, keep in mind, not lose sight of the fact, not forget, be mindful of the fact; take into account, take into consideration.
▷ANTONYMS overlook.
4 ***remember to*** *feed the cat*: **don't forget**, be sure, be certain; mind that you, make sure that you.
▷ANTONYMS neglect.
5 *please* ***remember me to*** *Alice*: **send one's best wishes to**, send one's regards to, give one's love to, send greetings from, send one's compliments to, say hello to; archaic commend oneself to.
6 *yesterday the nation remembered those who gave their lives in times of conflict*: **commemorate**, pay tribute to, honour, salute, celebrate, pay homage to, pay one's respects to, memorialize, keep alive the memory of; spare a thought for.
7 *she had remembered them in her will*: **bequeath something to**, leave something to, make someone a gift, give something to, bestow something on.

remembrance noun **1** *his face took on a faint expression of remembrance*: **recollection**, reminiscence, nostalgia; remembering, recalling, recollecting, reminiscing; technical anamnesis.
2 *she smiled at the remembrance*: **memory**, recollection, reminiscence, echo from the past, mental image, thought.
3 *we sold poppies in remembrance of all those who died*: **commemoration**, memory, recognition.
4 *take this ring as a remembrance of my father*: **memento**, reminder, keepsake, souvenir, token, commemoration, memorial, relic, something to remember someone by; archaic remembrancer.

remind verb **1** *I left a note on the cooker to remind him*: **jog someone's memory**, refresh someone's memory, help someone remember, cause someone to remember; prompt, nudge, give someone a cue.
2 *the song* ***reminded*** *me* ***of*** *my ex-wife*: **make one think of**, cause one to remember, put one in mind of, take one back to, bring/call to mind, awake one's memories of, evoke, call up, conjure up, summon up.

reminder noun *Granny sometimes needed the odd reminder*: **prompt**, prompting, cue, nudge; aide-memoire, mnemonic.

reminisce verb *Duncan and I reminisced about the last time we'd worked together*: **remember (with pleasure)**, cast one's mind back to, think back to, look back on, be nostalgic about, hark back to, recall, recollect, reflect on, call to mind, review; exchange memories, take a trip down memory lane, indulge in reminiscence, dwell on the past.

reminiscences plural noun *her reminiscences of a wartime childhood*: **memories**, recollections, reflections, remembrances, anecdotes; memoirs.

reminiscent adjective *a highly sophisticated style* ***reminiscent of*** *Italian art of the same period*: **similar to**, comparable with, inviting/bearing comparison with, tending to make one think of; **evocative of**, suggestive of, redolent of; rare remindful of.

remiss adjective *I can see that I have been very remiss*: **negligent**, neglectful, irresponsible, careless, thoughtless, heedless, unthinking, unmindful, lax, slack, slipshod, lackadaisical, forgetful, inattentive, unheeding; lazy,

dilatory, indolent; N. Amer. derelict; informal sloppy; formal delinquent; Maritime Law barratrous; archaic disregardful, oscitant.
▷ANTONYMS careful, diligent, painstaking.

remission noun **1** *the remission of all taxation on export sales for ten years*: **cancellation**, setting aside, suspension, revocation, repeal, rescinding, abrogation.
2 Brit. *he was released within three years after remission for good behaviour*: **reduction in sentence**, reduced sentence; allowance, deduction.
3 *spontaneous remission of acute leukaemia is unusual*: **respite**, abeyance; **diminution of intensity**, diminution of severity, period of temporary recovery.
4 *the wind howled that night without remission*: **respite**, lessening, abatement, easing, moderation, decrease, reduction; diminution, slackening, dying down, dwindling, lull, ebbing, waning; informal let-up.
5 *the remission of sins*: **forgiveness**, pardoning, absolution, exoneration, exculpation; historical indulgence.
6 *the remission of the matter to a subcommittee*: **referral**, passing on, transfer, redirection.

remit verb (stress on the second syllable) **1** *the fines imposed on the Earl of Lancaster were remitted*: **cancel**, set aside, revoke, repeal, rescind, abrogate, suspend.
2 *they refused to remit customs duties to the federal authorities*: **send**, dispatch, forward, transmit, convey; **pay**, hand over, make payment of.
3 *the case was remitted to the Court of Appeal*: **pass (on)**, refer, send on, transfer, hand on, direct, assign, commit, entrust.
4 *we remitted all further discussion until he sent me a copy of his letter*: **postpone**, defer, put off, put back, shelve, delay, hold over/off, stand over, suspend, prorogue, reschedule, keep in abeyance; N. Amer. put over, lay on the table, table; N. Amer. Law continue; informal put on the back burner, put on ice, put in cold storage; rare respite.
5 *remitting their sins*: **pardon**, forgive; excuse, overlook, pass over.
6 *the fever remitted*: **diminish**, lessen, decrease, ease (up), abate, moderate, dwindle, wane, ebb, subside.
7 *she remitted her efforts*: **slacken**, relax, reduce, decrease, diminish, lessen; cease, stop, halt, desist from.
▶ **noun** (stress on the first syllable) *his remit includes administering the consumer credit licensing system*: **area of responsibility**, area of activity, sphere, orbit, scope, ambit, province, territory, realm, department, turf; brief, instructions, orders; informal bailiwick.

remittance noun **1** *complete the booking form and send it together with your remittance*: **payment**, settlement, money, fee; cheque, money order, transfer of funds; technical negotiable instrument; formal monies.
2 *he gets a remittance once every three months*: **allowance**, sum of money, consideration.

remnant noun **1** *they cleared up the remnants of the picnic*: **remains**, remainder, leftovers, leavings, residue, rest; stub, butt, end, tail end; dregs, lees; technical residuum.
2 *remnants of cloth*: **scrap**, piece, bit, fragment, shred, offcut, oddment.

remonstrate verb **1** *'I'm not a child!' he remonstrated* | *I* ***remonstrated with*** *him but he just laughed in my face*: **protest**, complain, expostulate; argue with, take issue with, take to task, make a protest to; reprimand, reproach, reprove, upbraid, berate, scold; rare reprehend, objurgate.
2 *pro-reform deputies* ***remonstrated against*** *this proposal*: **object strongly to**, complain vociferously about, protest against, lodge a protest against, argue against, take a stand against, oppose strongly, take exception to, take issue with, make a fuss about, challenge, raise objections to, express disapproval of, express disagreement with, speak out against; deplore, condemn, denounce, criticize; informal kick up a fuss/stink about.
▷ANTONYMS accept.

remorse noun *he was filled with remorse*: **contrition**, deep regret, repentance, penitence, guilt, feelings of guilt, bad/guilty conscience, compunction, remorsefulness, ruefulness, contriteness, sorrow, shame, self-reproach, self-accusation, self-condemnation; pangs of conscience.
▷ANTONYMS indifference.

remorseful adjective *many parents feel very remorseful after punishing their children*: **sorry**, full of regret, regretful, sad, contrite, repentant, penitent, guilt-ridden, conscience-stricken, guilty, ashamed, chastened, shamefaced, self-reproachful, rueful, apologetic; rare compunctious.
▷ANTONYMS unrepentant.

remorseless adjective **1** *a remorseless killer*: **heartless**, pitiless, merciless, ruthless, callous, cruel, hard-hearted, stony-hearted, with a heart of stone, cold-hearted, harsh, inhumane, unmerciful, unforgiving, unfeeling, unpitying, uncompromising, unkind; rare marble-hearted.
▷ANTONYMS merciful, compassionate.
2 *the company continued its remorseless cost-cutting drive*: **relentless**, unrelenting, unremitting, unabating, inexorable, implacable, unstoppable.

Choose the right word **remorseless, relentless, ruthless, pitiless**

See **relentless**.

remote adjective **1** *doctors who practise in areas remote from hospitals* | *the remote past*: **faraway**, **distant**, far, far off, far removed; dim and distant.
▷ANTONYMS close, near.
2 *a remote mountain village*: **isolated**, out of the way, outlying, off the beaten track, secluded, in the depths of ..., hard to find, lonely, in the back of beyond, in the hinterlands, off the map, in the middle of nowhere, godforsaken, obscure, inaccessible, cut-off, unreachable; faraway, far-flung; N. Amer. in the backwoods, lonesome; S. African in the backveld, in the platteland; Austral./NZ in the backblocks, in the booay; informal unget-at-able, in the sticks; N. Amer. informal jerkwater, in the tall timbers; Austral./NZ informal Barcoo, beyond the black stump; literary lone; archaic unapproachable.
▷ANTONYMS central.
3 *the parables may seem somewhat* ***remote from*** *modern times*: **irrelevant to**, unrelated to, unconnected to, unconcerned with, not pertinent to, inapposite to, immaterial to, unassociated with, inappropriate to; foreign to, alien to; rare extrinsic to.
▷ANTONYMS relevant.
4 *up to now, the possibility had seemed so remote as not to need consideration*: **unlikely**, improbable, implausible, doubtful, dubious, far-fetched; faint, slight, slim, small, slender, minimal, marginal, negligible, insignificant, inconsiderable.
▷ANTONYMS likely, strong.
5 *when I was a child, she wasn't so remote*: **aloof**, distant, detached, impersonal, withdrawn, reserved, uncommunicative, unforthcoming, unapproachable, unresponsive, indifferent, unconcerned, preoccupied, abstracted; unfriendly, unsociable, stand-offish, cool, chilly, cold, haughty; introspective, introvert, introverted.
▷ANTONYMS friendly, approachable.

Choose the right word **remote, distant, faraway, far off**

See **distant**.

removal noun **1** *the removal of heavy artillery from towns and villages*: **taking away**, moving, carrying away, shifting, transfer, transporting; confiscation.
▷ANTONYMS installation.
2 *opposition parties demanded his immediate removal from office*: **dismissal**, eviction, ejection, expulsion, throwing out, ousting, dislodgement, displacement, purging, unseating, deposition; dethronement, dethroning; N. Amer. ouster; informal sacking, firing.
▷ANTONYMS appointment.
3 *the removal of customs barriers within the EC*: **withdrawal**, **abolition**, elimination, doing away with, taking away.
▷ANTONYMS introduction, bringing in.
4 *the removal of errors*: **deletion**, elimination, erasing, rubbing out, erasure, effacing, obliteration.
5 *removal of weeds is important*: **uprooting**, eradication, destruction.
6 *regular removal of old branches from the base will encourage newer growth*: **cutting off**, chopping off, hacking off, amputation, excision.
7 *her removal to France*: **move**, transfer, relocation; Scottish & N. English flit, flitting.
8 *the removal of a gang member by a rival*: **killing**, murder, disposal, elimination, termination, assassination; informal liquidation.

remove verb **1** *switch off the power and remove the plug*: **detach**, unfasten, separate; **pull out**, take out, disconnect.
▷ANTONYMS attach.
2 *he took the box and removed the lid*: **take off**, undo, unfasten.
▷ANTONYMS put on.
3 *he pulled out his wallet and removed a twenty dollar bill*: **take out**, **produce**, bring out, get out, draw out, withdraw, extract, pull out, fish out.
▷ANTONYMS insert.
4 *police searched his flat, removing fifteen bags of clothing*: **take away**, carry away, move, shift, convey, transport; confiscate, take possession of; informal cart off.
▷ANTONYMS replace, put back.
5 *in the bathroom, Sheila soon removed the mud*: **clean off**, wash off, wipe off, rinse off, scrub off, sponge out.
6 *Henry removed his coat*: **take off**, pull off, peel off, shrug off, discard, divest oneself of, shed, fling off, fling aside, climb out of, slip out of; undo, unfasten, unbutton, unzip; dated doff.
▷ANTONYMS don, put on.
7 *he was removed from his post as head of the security department*: **dismiss**, discharge, get rid of, dislodge, displace, throw out, evict, eject, expel, oust, purge, unseat, depose, topple, supplant; dethrone; informal sack, fire, kick out, boot out, give someone the boot, give someone their marching orders, show someone the door; Brit. informal turf out; dated out.
▷ANTONYMS install, appoint.
8 *tax relief on life assurance premiums was removed*: **withdraw**, **abolish**, eliminate, get rid of, do away with, take away, stop, put an end to, cut; informal axe.
▷ANTONYMS introduce, bring in.
9 *Gabriel carefully removed the last two words*: **delete**, erase, rub out, cross

out, strike out, ink out, score out, block out, blue-pencil, cut out, eliminate, efface, obliterate.
▷ANTONYMS add.
10 *weeds have to be removed and a good general weedkiller applied*: **uproot**, take out, pull out, eradicate, destroy.
11 *sometimes it may be necessary to remove branches of the tree*: **cut off**, chop off, lop off, hack off, amputate, excise.
12 dated *in 1800 he removed to Edinburgh*. See **move** (sense 5 of the verb).
13 *mobsters like that could simply have you removed if they didn't like you*: **kill**, murder, put to death, get rid of, dispose of, assassinate, eliminate, execute, wipe out; informal bump off, do away with, do in, do for, knock off, take out, top, stiff, croak, liquidate, blow away, give someone the works, wipe off the face of the earth; N. Amer. informal rub out, waste, smoke, ice, off; N. Amer. euphemistic terminate with extreme prejudice.
▸ **noun** *it is almost impossible, at this remove, to reconstruct the impact of the incident*: **distance**, space of time, interval.

removed adjective *the programme was described as a fairy story completely* ***removed from*** *reality*: **distant**, remote, disconnected, different; unrelated to, unconnected to, foreign to, alien to.

remunerate verb *lawyers should be fairly remunerated for work done*: **pay**, reward, reimburse, recompense, give payment to; rare fee.

remuneration noun *it's a demanding job which deserves adequate remuneration*: **payment**, pay, salary, wages; earnings, fee(s), stipend, emolument(s), honorarium, remittance, consideration, reward, recompense, reimbursement, repayment.

remunerative adjective *he left to take up a more remunerative post elsewhere*: **lucrative**, **well paid**, financially rewarding, financially worthwhile, moneymaking, paying, gainful; profitable.

renaissance noun *the renaissance of Byzantine art and scholarship*. See **rebirth**.

rend verb *a crisis which threatened to rend the Atlantic alliance apart*: **tear/rip apart**, tear/rip in two, tear/rip to pieces, split, rupture, sever, separate; literary cleave, tear/rip asunder, sunder, rive; rare dissever.

render verb **1** *her fury rendered her temporarily speechless*: **make**, cause to be/become, leave.
2 *Burcham was quickly surrounded by people anxious to render assistance*: **give**, provide, supply, furnish, make available, contribute; **offer**, extend, proffer.
3 *the invoices rendered by the accountants amounted to £11,690*: **send in**, present, tender, submit.
4 *it was about an hour before the jury rendered their verdict*: **deliver**, return, hand down, bring in, give, announce, pronounce, proclaim.
5 *a sailor was bound to render instant obedience to a midshipman*: **show**, display, exhibit, evince, manifest.
6 *her paintings are rendered in wonderfully vivid colours*: **paint**, draw, depict, portray, represent, reproduce, execute; literary limn.
7 *the French songstress had just rendered all three verses of the Marseillaise*: **perform**, play, sing, execute, interpret.
8 *the characters are vividly rendered*: **act**, perform, play, depict; interpret.
9 *the phrase is almost impossible to render into English*: **translate**, put, express, transcribe, convert; rephrase, reword; transliterate; dated construe.
10 *he was called upon to* ***render up*** *the stolen money*: **give back**, return, restore, pay back, repay, hand over, give up, surrender, relinquish, deliver, turn over, yield, cede.
11 *the fat can be rendered and used for cooking*: **melt down**, clarify, purify.

rendezvous noun **1** *Edward turned up late for their rendezvous*: **meeting**, appointment, engagement, assignation; informal date; literary tryst.
2 *you'd be welcome to use my place as a rendezvous*: **meeting place**, venue, place of assignation; literary trysting place.
▸ **verb** *at seven o'clock she reached the wine bar where they had agreed to rendezvous*: **meet**, come together, get together, gather, assemble.

rendition noun **1** *a muted rendition of Beethoven's Fifth*: **performance**, rendering, interpretation, presentation, execution, delivery; playing, singing, reading, recitation, recital.
2 *the artist's rendition of Adam and Eve mourning the dead Abel*: **depiction**, portrayal, representation, delineation.
3 *the flatbread is my rendition of the classic Italian focaccia*: **version**, variation, take on.
4 *an interpreter's rendition of a message*: **translation**, transliteration, transcription; interpretation, version, reading, construction.

renegade noun *he was denounced as a renegade*: **traitor**, defector, deserter, turncoat, betrayer; rebel, mutineer; quisling, fifth columnist; rare renegado, tergiversator.
▷ANTONYMS follower.
▸ **adjective** *350 army mutineers led by a renegade colonel*: **treacherous**, traitorous, disloyal, perfidious, treasonous, rebel, mutinous, rebellious.
▷ANTONYMS loyal, faithful.

renege verb *he* ***reneged on*** *a campaign promise to keep taxes down*: **default on**, fail to honour, go back on, break, back out of, pull out of, withdraw from, retreat from, welsh on, backtrack on; repudiate, retract; go back on one's word, break one's word, break one's promise, do an about-face; informal cop out of, rat on.
▷ANTONYMS keep, honour.

renew verb **1** *I renewed my search for Frankie*: **resume**, return to, pick up again, take up again, come back to, reopen, begin again, start again, restart, recommence; continue (with), carry on (with), proceed with; re-establish.
2 *they renewed their vows at a cathedral service in Chicago*: **reaffirm**, reassert, confirm; repeat, reiterate, restate, say again, iterate; rare ingeminate.
3 *she needed something to renew her interest in life*: **revive**, regenerate, revitalize, reinvigorate, restore, breathe new life into, resurrect, resuscitate, awaken, wake up, rejuvenate, stimulate; archaic renovate.
4 *the hotel was completely renewed in 1990*: **renovate**, restore, modernize, redecorate, refurbish, revamp, make over, improve, recondition, rehabilitate, overhaul, redevelop, rebuild, reconstruct, remodel; update, bring up to date; refit, re-equip, refurnish; N. Amer. bring something up to code; informal do up, fix up, give something a facelift, vamp up; Brit. informal tart up; N. Amer. informal rehab.
5 *the station renewed Jackie's contract after three months*: **extend**, prolong.
6 *I had to run to the store to renew my supply of toilet paper*: **replenish**, stock up, restock, resupply, refill, top up; replace.

renewal noun **1** *the renewal of our friendship*: **resumption**, recommencement; continuation; re-establishment.
2 *the landscapes of the Lake District were a lifelong source of spiritual renewal*: **regeneration**, restoration, revival, reinvigoration, revitalization, rejuvenation; archaic renovation.
3 *the comprehensive renewal of older urban areas*: **renovation**, restoration, modernization, improvement, reconditioning, rehabilitation, regeneration, overhauling, redevelopment, rebuilding, reconstruction; gentrification; repair, mending.

renounce verb **1** *Edward renounced his claim to the French throne*: **give up**, relinquish, abandon, resign, abdicate, surrender, sign away, waive, forgo; Law disclaim; rare abnegate, demit.
▷ANTONYMS assert, reassert.
2 *Hungary renounced the 1977 agreement on environmental grounds*: **reject**, refuse to abide by, refuse to recognize, repudiate.
▷ANTONYMS accept, abide by.
3 *she had renounced her family*: **repudiate**, deny, discard, reject, give up, forswear, abandon, wash one's hands of, turn one's back on, have nothing more to do with, have done with; disown, cast off, cast aside, disinherit, cut off, throw off, spurn, shun; archaic forsake.
▷ANTONYMS embrace.
4 *by renouncing champagne, Eliot felt that he was exercising a measure of self-denial*: **abstain from**, give up, go without, do without, desist from, refrain from, swear off, keep off, eschew, reject, cease to indulge in; informal quit, leave off, pack in, kick, lay off.
▷ANTONYMS turn to.
□ **renounce the world become a recluse**, become a hermit, turn one's back on society, retreat, withdraw, cloister oneself, hide oneself away, shut oneself off/away, cut oneself off.

renovate verb *the hotel has been completely renovated*: **modernize**, restore, redecorate, refurbish, revamp, make over, recondition, rehabilitate, overhaul, repair, redevelop, rebuild, reconstruct, remodel; update, bring up to date, improve; upgrade, gentrify; refit, re-equip, refurnish; N. Amer. bring something up to code; informal do up, fix up, give something a facelift, vamp up; Brit. informal **tart up**; N. Amer. informal **rehab**.

renovation noun *the renovation of council properties*: **modernization**, restoration, redecoration, refurbishment, revamping, makeover, reconditioning, rehabilitation, overhauling, repair, redevelopment, rebuilding, reconstruction, remodelling, updating, improvement; gentrification, upgrading; refitting; informal facelift.

renown noun *a number of them achieved political renown*: **fame**, distinction, eminence, pre-eminence, prominence, repute, reputation, prestige, acclaim, celebrity, note, notability, mark, consequence, standing, stature, account; glory, illustriousness.
▷ANTONYMS obscurity, anonymity.

renowned adjective *Satyajit Ray, the renowned Indian film maker*: **famous**, celebrated, famed, eminent, distinguished, acclaimed, illustrious, pre-eminent, prominent, great, esteemed, well thought of, of note, of consequence, of repute, of high standing; well known, much publicized, noted, notable, prestigious; fabled, legendary, proverbial; informal on the map.
▷ANTONYMS unknown, obscure, unsung.

> *Choose the right word* **renowned, famous, celebrated, well known**
>
> See **famous**.

rent[1] noun *I can't afford to pay the rent*: **hire charge**, rental; fee, cost, price, rate, tariff.
▸ **verb 1** *she rented a car at the airport*: **hire**, lease, charter.

r

2 *I'm hoping to rent a house in Hampstead for a few weeks*: **occupy temporarily**, live in temporarily; take.
3 *if you don't want to sell it, why don't you* **rent** *it* **out***?* **let (out)**, lease (out), hire (out); sublet, sublease.

rent² noun **1** *his knee poked through the rent in his trousers*: **rip**, tear, split, hole, gash, slash, slit, opening, perforation.
2 *a vast rent in the Andes, about 2000 feet deep*: **gorge**, chasm, fault, rift, fissure, crevasse; cleft, crack, breach; break, fracture, rupture.

renunciation noun **1** *Henry III's renunciation of his rights to Normandy*: **relinquishment**, giving up, abandonment, resignation, abdication, surrender, signing away, waiving, forgoing; Law disclaimer; rare abnegation, demission.
▷ANTONYMS assertion, reassertion.
2 *his* **renunciation of** *luxury*: **abstention from**, refraining from, going without, doing without, giving up of, eschewal of, rejection of.
3 *an unconditional renunciation of war*: **repudiation**, rejection, abandonment, forsaking, forswearing, disavowal, denial; rare abjuration.

reorganize verb *the company reorganized its manufacturing and distribution operations*: **restructure**, change, make alterations to, make adjustments to, alter, adjust, transform, shake up, rationalize, reshuffle, redeploy, rearrange, reshape, refashion, recast, overhaul, rebuild, reconstruct; reschedule, rejig, reorder.

repair¹ verb **1** *the car was taken to a garage to be repaired*: **mend**, fix (up), put right, set right, restore, restore to working order, make as good as new, patch up, put back together, overhaul, service, renovate, recondition, rehabilitate, rebuild, reconstruct, refit, adjust, regulate; N. English fettle; informal see to.
2 *an army of seamstresses repaired costumes and cut new ones*: **mend**, darn, sew up, stitch up, patch up; archaic clout.
3 *the government repaired relations with several other countries*: **put/set right**, put to rights, patch up, mend, fix, sort out, straighten out, make better, improve, right, heal, cure, remedy, retrieve.
▷ANTONYMS wreck, worsen, destroy.
4 *she sought to repair the wrong she had done*: **rectify**, make good, put right, correct, right, redress, make up for, make amends for, make reparation for, compensate for.
▷ANTONYMS compound.
▶ noun **1** *the building is in urgent need of repair*: **restoration**, fixing (up), renovation, rebuilding, reconstruction; mending, servicing; improvement, adjustment; archaic reparation.
2 *a virtually invisible repair*: **mend**; darn, patch.
3 *are the tools in good repair?* **condition**, working order, state, shape, form, fettle; Brit. informal nick.
□ **beyond repair** *their relationship may well be beyond repair*: **irreparable**, irreversible, past mending, irretrievable, hopeless, past hope, beyond hope, irremediable, irrecoverable, incurable, beyond cure; written off.
▷ANTONYMS reparable, rectifiable.

repair² verb formal *relax in the stylish bar before* **repairing to** *the dining room*: **go to**, adjourn to, head for, wend one's way to; retire to, withdraw to, retreat to; set off for, take off for, leave for, depart for; formal remove to; literary betake oneself to.

reparable adjective *I think the situation is still reparable*: **rectifiable**, remediable, able to be put/set right, curable, restorable, recoverable, retrievable, salvageable; rare corrigible.
▷ANTONYMS beyond repair.

reparation noun *there is a range of ways in which offenders may make reparation to their victims*: **amends**, restitution, redress, compensation, recompense, repayment, atonement; indemnification, indemnity, damages; rare solatium.

repartee noun *an evening of wit and repartee*: **banter**, badinage, witty conversation, bantering, raillery, witticism, crosstalk, wordplay, patter; witty remarks, witticisms, ripostes, sallies, quips; joking, jesting, teasing, chaff, chaffing, drollery; French bons mots; rare persiflage.

repast noun formal *they sat down to a sumptuous repast*: **meal**, feast, banquet; snack; informal spread, feed, bite, bite to eat; Brit. informal nosh, nosh-up; formal collation, refection.

repay verb **1** *I'm making an effort to repay customers who have been cheated*: **reimburse**, refund, pay back, recompense, compensate, remunerate, square accounts with, settle up with, indemnify, pay off; rare recoup.
2 *community care grants do not have to be repaid*: **pay back**, return, refund, reimburse, give back.
3 *I'd like to be able to repay her generosity*: **reciprocate**, return, requite, recompense, reward; return the favour, return the compliment; archaic guerdon.
4 *there are a number of interesting books on this subject that would repay further study*: **be well worth**; be worth one's while, be worthwhile, be useful, be advantageous.

repayment noun **1** *without that certificate, the charity cannot obtain the repayment of the basic rate tax*: **refund**, reimbursement, paying back.
2 *I would prefer them to keep this as some repayment for all they have done*: **recompense**, reward, compensation, reparation, restitution.

repeal verb *the Act was repealed in 1990*: **revoke**, rescind, cancel, reverse, abrogate, annul, nullify, declare null and void, make void, void, invalidate, render invalid, quash, abolish, set aside, countermand, retract, withdraw, overrule, override; Law vacate, avoid; archaic recall; rare disannul.
▷ANTONYMS introduce, enact, ratify.
▶ noun *the repeal of Protective Custody Law*: **revocation**, rescinding, cancellation, reversal, annulment, nullification, voiding, invalidation, quashing, abolition, abrogation, setting aside, countermanding, retraction, withdrawal, rescindment, overruling, overriding; archaic recall; rare rescission, disannulment.
▷ANTONYMS introduction, enactment, ratification.

repeat verb **1** *she repeated her story in a flat monotone*: **say again**, restate, reiterate, go through again, go over again, run through again, iterate, rehearse, recapitulate; informal recap; rare reprise, ingeminate.
2 *children can remember and repeat large chunks of text*: **recite**, quote, reproduce; **echo**, parrot, regurgitate; say again, restate; informal trot out.
3 *Steele had been invited to repeat his work in a scientific environment*: **do again**, redo, replicate, duplicate, perform again.
4 *the episodes from the first two series were constantly repeated*: **rebroadcast**, rerun, reshow, replay.
□ **repeat itself** *now history has repeated itself*: **reoccur**, occur again, happen again, recur, reappear.
▶ noun **1** *the ladies' final was a repeat of the previous year's fixture*: **repetition**, duplication, replication, rerun; duplicate, replica, copy; echo; rare ditto.
2 *he's the highest-paid US showbiz star, thanks to repeats of his TV show*: **rerun**, replay, rebroadcast, reshowing.

repeated adjective *he made repeated complaints about the noise*: **recurrent**, frequent, persistent, unremitting, sustained, continual, incessant, constant, ceaseless; regular, periodic, many, numerous, a great many, very many, countless; informal more ... than one can shake a stick at.
▷ANTONYMS occasional, sporadic.

> *Word toolkit* **repeated**
>
> See **recurrent**.

repeatedly adverb *she tried repeatedly to bring up the subject of money*: **frequently**, often, again and again, over and over (again), time and (time) again, time after time, many times, on many occasions, many a time, many times over; {day in, day out}, day after day, {week in, week out}, night and day, all the time; persistently, recurrently, constantly, continually, regularly; N. Amer. oftentimes; Latin ad nauseam; informal 24-7; literary many a time and oft, oft, oft-times.
▷ANTONYMS never, seldom.

repel verb **1** *the rebels were repelled by army units*: **fight off**, repulse, drive back/away, put to flight, force back, beat back, push back, thrust back, hold off, ward off, fend off, stand off, stave off, parry, keep at bay, keep at arm's length; foil, check, frustrate; Brit. see off; informal send packing; archaic rebut.
2 *the polypropylene cover will repel water*: **be impervious to**, be impermeable to, keep out, be resistant to, resist.
▷ANTONYMS attract; absorb; let through.
3 *the thought of kissing him repelled me*: **revolt**, disgust, repulse, sicken, nauseate, make someone feel sick, turn someone's stomach, be repulsive to, be extremely distasteful to, be repugnant to, make shudder, make someone's flesh creep, make someone's skin crawl, make someone's gorge rise, put off, offend, horrify; informal turn off, give someone the creeps, give someone the heebie-jeebies, make someone want to throw up; N. Amer. informal gross out.
▷ANTONYMS delight.

repellent adjective **1** *a repellent stench | critics found the film pretentious and repellent*: **revolting**, repulsive, disgusting, repugnant, sickening, nauseating, stomach-turning, stomach-churning, nauseous, emetic, vile, nasty, foul, appalling, abominable, hideous, horrible, awful, dreadful, terrible, obnoxious, loathsome, offensive, objectionable, off-putting, distasteful, disagreeable, uninviting; abhorrent, despicable, reprehensible, contemptible, odious, heinous, obscene, hateful, execrable; gruesome, grisly; N. Amer. vomitous; informal sick-making, ghastly, putrid, horrid, God-awful, gross, gut-churning, yucky, icky, cringe-making; Brit. informal beastly; literary noisome; archaic disgustful, loathly; rare rebarbative.
▷ANTONYMS delightful, lovely.
2 *the detergent forms a repellent coating | water-repellent leather*: **impermeable**, impervious, resistant; -proof; rare imperviable.

repent verb *he later* **repented of** *what he had done | her stubbornness and pride would not allow her to repent*: **feel remorse for**, regret, be sorry for, rue, reproach oneself for, be ashamed of, feel contrite about, wish that one had not done something; be penitent, see the error of one's ways, be regretful, be remorseful, be repentant, be conscience-stricken, be guilt-ridden, wear sackcloth and ashes.

repentance noun *her apparent lack of repentance made me even angrier*: **remorse**, contrition, contriteness, penitence, sorrow, sorrowfulness, regret, ruefulness, remorsefulness, pangs of conscience, prickings of conscience, shame, guilt, self-reproach, self-condemnation, compunction;

Christianity conversion; archaic rue; rare sorriness.

repentant adjective *Nancy looked suitably repentant and said she was sorry*: **penitent**, contrite, regretful, full of regret, sorrowful, rueful, remorseful, apologetic, conscience-stricken, ashamed, guilt-ridden, chastened, self-reproachful, shamefaced, guilty; rare compunctious.
▷ANTONYMS unrepentant, impenitent.

repercussion noun *the political repercussions of the scandal were devastating*: **consequence**, result, effect, outcome, by-product; reverberation, backlash, ripple, shock wave; aftermath, fallout.

repertoire noun *his repertoire of quotes and quips*: **collection**, stock, range, repertory; reserve, store, repository, supply, stockpile.

repetition noun **1** *statistics have already been quoted and they bear repetition*: **reiteration**, repeating, restatement, retelling, iteration, recapitulation; recital, rehearsal; informal recap; rare reprise, iterance.
2 *the repetition of words just heard*: **repeating**, echoing, parroting, quoting, copying; Psychiatry echolalia.
3 *she drew back, fearful of a repetition of the scene in the kitchen*: **recurrence**, reoccurrence, repeat, rerun, replication, duplication; echo.
4 *there is some repetition, but not enough to detract from the valuable information the book contains*: **repetitiousness**, repetitiveness, redundancy, superfluity, tautology.

repetitious adjective *boring, repetitious work*. See **repetitive**.

repetitive adjective *he spent day after day doing the same repetitive tasks*: **monotonous**, tedious, boring, uninteresting, humdrum, mundane, tiresome, wearisome, dreary, soul-destroying, mind-numbing; **unvaried**, unchanging, unvarying, undiversified, lacking variety, recurrent, recurring, repeated, repetitious, routine, mechanical, automatic, clockwork; Brit. informal samey.
▷ANTONYMS varied, interesting.

rephrase verb *perhaps I should rephrase the question*: **reword**, put differently, put another way, put in other words, express differently, recast; paraphrase.

repine verb literary *even if I die, I doubt that he'll repine*: **fret**, be/feel unhappy, mope, languish, eat one's heart out, be/feel miserable, be/feel upset, be/feel despondent, brood; lament, grieve, mourn, sorrow, pine, agonize.

replace verb **1** *Adam replaced the receiver thoughtfully*: **put back**, return, return to its place, restore.
▷ANTONYMS remove.
2 *a new chairman was brought in to replace him*: **take the place of**, succeed, be a replacement for, take over from, supersede, follow after, come after; supplant, oust; stand in for, substitute for, act as stand-in for, deputize for, act for, stand in lieu of, fill in for, cover for, relieve, act as locum for, understudy; step into the breach, hold the fort; informal fill someone's shoes/boots, step into someone's shoes/boots, sub for.
3 *she took away his empty cereal bowl and* **replaced** *it* **with** *a plate piled high with toast*: **substitute**, **exchange**, change; give in place of, give as a replacement for, give in return/exchange for, swap for.

> *Choose the right word* **replace, supersede, supplant**
>
> All three words are used when one person or thing takes the place of another, but each has different connotations.
>
> **Replace** is the most neutral term. One person or thing may replace another as part of a normal process (*the interim government was replaced by an elected one*) or in an emergency (*Heslop replaces Underwood, who has a broken jaw*).
>
> Something that has been **superseded** has had its place taken by something more up to date or otherwise preferable (*the older mainframes are being superseded by more powerful, more compact systems*); the emphasis is on the fact of being replaced rather than on the new person or thing, since the word is typically used in the passive, and it is common not to mention the replacement (*current models may be superseded in due course*).
>
> There is emphasis on the person or thing that **supplants** another, as they are mentioned more often than with *supersede* or *replace*, and *supplant* is normally used in the active (*another invention or discovery could supplant the original finding*). There may be a sense of injustice if the new person or thing is seen as a poor substitute (*vast, impersonal motorways supplanted the agreeably irregular network of real roads*).

replacement noun **1** *the nanny was taken ill and we had barely a week to find a replacement*: **successor**, someone else; **substitute**, stand-in, fill-in, locum, understudy, proxy, surrogate; relief, cover, stopgap; Latin locum tenens.
▷ANTONYMS predecessor.
2 *the wiring was in urgent need of replacement*: **renewal**, replacing; substitution.

replenish verb **1** *she went to the drinks cabinet to replenish their glasses*: **refill**, top up, fill up, recharge, reload; N. Amer. freshen; Scottish plenish.
▷ANTONYMS empty.
2 *the organization's supplies were replenished by a new airlift of weaponry*: **stock up**, restock, restore, fill up, make up; replace, renew.
▷ANTONYMS exhaust, use up.

replete adjective **1** *the guests, replete with roast lamb and chocolate mousse, lingered over coffee*: **well fed**, **sated**, satiated, full, full up, full to bursting, satisfied; glutted, gorged; informal stuffed; archaic satiate, surfeited.
2 *a sumptuous environment replete with European antiques*: **filled**, full, well stocked, well supplied, well provided, crammed, crowded, packed, jammed, stuffed, teeming, overflowing, bursting, brimful, brimming, loaded, overloaded, thick, solid, charged, abounding; informal jam-packed, chock-a-block, chock-full, chocker.

replica noun **1** *I cannot confirm whether it is a replica or a real firearm at this stage*: **copy**, **model**, duplicate, reproduction, replication; **dummy**, imitation; carbon copy, facsimile; informal knock-off, dupe.
▷ANTONYMS original, genuine article.
2 *Amelie was physically a replica of her mother*: **perfect likeness**, exact likeness, double, lookalike, living image, mirror image, image, picture, twin, clone; German Doppelgänger; informal spitting image, dead ringer, ringer, dead spit, spit and image.

replicate verb *the technology would be very hard to replicate*: **copy**, reproduce, duplicate, make a copy of, make a replica of; recreate, repeat, perform again; clone.

reply verb **1** *Rachel didn't bother to reply*: **answer**, respond; acknowledge, write back; take the bait, rise to the bait, come back.
2 *'No, I didn't,' he replied, defensively*: **respond**, answer, say in response, rejoin, return; retort, counter, fling back, hurl back, retaliate, come back; rare riposte.
▸ noun *he did not wait for a reply*: **answer**, response, acknowledgement, rejoinder, return, reaction; retort, riposte; informal comeback.

report verb **1** *the government reported the biggest fall in manufacturing output since 1981*: **announce**, describe, give an account of, tell of, detail, delineate, outline; communicate, pass on, relay; divulge, disclose, reveal; make public, publish, circulate, set out, set forth, put out, post, broadcast; blazon, herald, proclaim, declare, publicize, promulgate; document, record, chronicle; formal adumbrate.
2 *many magazines happily* **report on** *the titillating activities of the stars*: **investigate**, look into, enquire into, survey, research, study; **write about**, write an account of, broadcast details of, cover, describe, give details of, write up; commentate on.
3 *I reported him to the police*: **make a complaint against**, make a charge against, inform on, tattle on, accuse; informal blow the whistle on, grass on, shop, tell on, squeal on, rat on, split on, peach on; rare delate on.
4 *Juliet reported for duty at 8.30*: **present oneself**, arrive, appear, turn up, clock in, sign in; make oneself known, announce oneself, come, be present; Brit. clock on; N. Amer. punch in, punch the (time) clock; informal show up.
▸ noun **1** *I've asked James for a full report of the meeting*: **account**, review, record, description, exposition, statement, delineation; transactions, proceedings, transcripts, minutes; French compte rendu, procès-verbal; Military, informal sitrep.
2 *police received reports of drug dealing in the area*: **news**, **information**, word, intelligence, intimation; literary tidings; archaic advices.
3 *I followed his progress through television and newspaper reports*: **story**, account, description; **article**, piece, item, column, feature, write-up, exposé; **bulletin**, communiqué, dispatch, communication.
4 Brit. *his last school report had been good*: **assessment**, evaluation, appraisal; marks; N. Amer. report card, grades.
5 *reports of his imminent resignation circulated*: **rumour**, whisper, piece of gossip, piece of hearsay; French on dit; informal buzz; rare bruit.
6 archaic *those who are true, and honest, and of good report*: **reputation**, repute, regard, character, name, standing, stature.
7 *they heard the report of a gun*: **bang**, blast, crack, pop, shot, gunshot; explosion, detonation, boom; crash, noise, sound, echo, reverberation.

reporter noun **journalist**, correspondent, newspaperman, newspaperwoman, newsman, newswoman, columnist, writer, blogger; broadcaster, newscaster, news commentator, announcer, presenter; investigative journalist, photojournalist, war correspondent, lobby correspondent; Brit. pressman; N. Amer. legman, wireman; Austral. roundsman; informal news hound, hack, hackette, stringer, journo, talking head; N. Amer. informal newsy, thumbsucker.

repose noun **1** *in repose, her face still showed signs of the strain she had been under*: **rest**, **relaxation**, inactivity, restfulness, stillness, idleness; sleep, slumber.
▷ANTONYMS work, activity.
2 *true repose can never be found in that house*: **peace**, peace and quiet, peacefulness, quiet, quietness, quietude, calm, calmness, tranquillity, stillness; leisure, ease, respite, time off, breathing space.
▷ANTONYMS stress, strain.
3 *such a depth of repose in so young a man*: **composure**, calmness, serenity, tranquillity, equanimity, peace of mind; poise, self-possession, aplomb, self-assurance, dignity.
▷ANTONYMS agitation.
▸ verb **1** *the diamond reposed on a bed of plum velvet*: **lie**, be placed, be set, be situated, be positioned, be supported, rest.

2 literary *perhaps Jessica had not realized how much trust he had reposed in her*: **put**, place, lay, lodge, set, consign, invest, entrust.
3 *the beds on which we were to repose*: **lie**, lie down, recline, stretch out; **rest**, relax, sleep, slumber, take one's ease; literary couch.

repository noun *a permanent repository for spent nuclear fuel | he's a veritable repository of musical knowledge*: **store**, storing place, storehouse, depository; reservoir, bank, cache, treasury, treasure house, treasure trove, fund, mine, archive, repertory; warehouse, depot, storeroom, safe; container, receptacle.

reprehensible adjective *his conduct was morally reprehensible*: **deplorable**, disgraceful, discreditable, disreputable, despicable, blameworthy, culpable, wrong, bad, shameful, dishonourable, ignoble, erring, errant, objectionable, odious, opprobrious, repugnant, inexcusable, unpardonable, unforgivable, insufferable, indefensible, unjustifiable, regrettable, unacceptable, unworthy, remiss; criminal, sinful, scandalous, iniquitous; condemnable, reprovable, blameable, reproachable, censurable; rare exceptionable.
▷ANTONYMS creditable, praiseworthy, good.

represent verb **1** *many of Dickens' characters represent a single idea or quality*: **symbolize**, **stand for**, personify, epitomize, typify, be symbolic of; embody, be the embodiment/incarnation of, give human form/shape to, body forth, illustrate, incorporate, reflect; rare incarnate, image.
2 *the initials which represent her myriad qualifications*: **stand for**, correspond to; designate, denote, mean; literary betoken.
3 *Hathor, the Egyptian sky goddess, is represented as a woman with cow's horns*: **depict**, portray, render, picture, delineate, show, illustrate, characterize, paint, draw, sketch; exhibit, display; literary limn.
4 *she sacked him for* ***representing*** *himself* ***as*** *the owner of the factory*: **describe as**, present as, profess to be, purport to be, claim to be, set oneself up as, pass oneself off as, pose as, pretend to be, masquerade as.
5 *for many people, ageing represents a threat to their independence*: **constitute**, be, amount to, mean, be regarded as.
6 *a fifteen-member panel was chosen to represent a cross section of the public*: **be a typical sample of**, be representative of, typify, stand for.
7 *Rachel will represent Hampshire at Havant this Saturday*: **play for**, appear for; be a member of the team.
8 *MPs representing Scottish constituencies*: **be elected by**, be the councillor/MP for, have the vote of.
9 *his solicitor represented him in court*: **appear for**, act for, speak for, act/speak on behalf of, be spokesperson for, be the representative of.
10 *the Queen was represented by Lord Lewin*: **deputize for**, act as a substitute for, substitute for, stand in for, take the place of, replace.
11 *I represented the case to him as I saw it*: **point out**, state, indicate, present, set forth, put forward.
12 *the vendors have represented that such information is accurate*: **claim**, maintain, state, say, affirm, allege, contend; rare asseverate.

representation noun **1** *Rossetti's representation of women*: **portrayal**, **depiction**, delineation, presentation, rendition, rendering, characterization, description.
2 *the earliest representations of the human form*: **likeness**, **painting**, **drawing**, picture, portrait, illustration, sketch, diagram; image, model, figure, figurine, statue, statuette, bust, head, effigy, icon; simulacrum, reproduction.
3 *anyone who wishes to make representations to the council should make them in writing*: **statement**, deposition, allegation, claim; declaration, account, exposition, report, argument; protestation, remonstrance, expostulation.

representative adjective **1** *a representative sample of British society*: **typical**, prototypical, characteristic, illustrative, indicative; archetypal, paradigmatic, exemplary.
▷ANTONYMS atypical, unrepresentative.
2 *Britannia, a female figure allegorically representative of Britain*: **symbolic**, emblematic, evocative.
3 *a system of representative government*: **elected**, elective, chosen, democratic, popular, nominated, appointed, commissioned; delegated, authorized, accredited, official.
▷ANTONYMS totalitarian.
▸ noun **1** *a representative of the Royal Pharmaceutical Society*: **spokesperson**, spokesman, spokeswoman, agent; officer, official; mouthpiece.
2 *a sales representative*: **commercial traveller**, travelling salesman, salesman, saleswoman, agent, traveller; informal rep, knight of the road; N. Amer. informal drummer; Brit. archaic commercial.
3 *the Cambodian representative at the UN*: **delegate**, commissioner, ambassador, attaché, envoy, emissary, chargé, chargé d'affaires, commissary, deputy, aide; Scottish depute; Canadian & Austral. agent general; Roman Catholic Church nuncio; archaic legate, factor.
4 *our representatives in parliament*: **Member of Parliament**, MP, Member; councillor; N. Amer. Member of Congress, congressman, congresswoman, senator.
5 *he acted as his father's representative*: **deputy**, substitute, stand-in, proxy, surrogate.
6 *fossil representatives of lampreys and hagfishes*: **example**, **specimen**; exemplar, exemplification, type, archetype, illustration.

repress verb **1** *the rebellion was successfully repressed*: **suppress**, quell, quash, subdue, put down, put an end to, crush, squash, extinguish, stamp out, put a stop to, stop, end, nip in the bud; defeat, conquer, rout, overpower, overwhelm, triumph over, trounce, vanquish, get the better of; contain, gain control over, gain mastery over; informal squelch.
2 *a ruling class which repressed and exploited workers and peasants*: **oppress**, subjugate, hold down, keep down, rule with a rod of iron, rule with an iron hand, dominate, intimidate, master, domineer over, tyrannize, subject, crush, overpower, overcome.
3 *in later childhood these emotions may well be repressed*: **restrain**, hold back, keep back, hold in, bite back, suppress, fight back, keep in check, check, control, keep under control, curb, rein in, contain, silence, muffle, stifle, smother, swallow, choke back, strangle, gag; conceal, hide, bottle up, inhibit, frustrate; informal button up, keep the lid on, cork up.
▷ANTONYMS release, express.

repressed adjective **1** *a repressed country*: **oppressed**, subjugated, subdued, tyrannized, ground down, downtrodden.
▷ANTONYMS free, democratic.
2 *repressed feelings of hostility*: **restrained**, suppressed, held back, held in, kept in check, muffled, stifled, smothered, pent up, bottled up; concealed, hidden, subconscious, unconscious; unfulfilled, latent.
▷ANTONYMS overt, expressed.
3 *a reclusive, emotionally repressed man*: **inhibited**, frustrated, restrained, self-restrained, withdrawn, introverted; informal uptight, hung up.
▷ANTONYMS uninhibited, relaxed.

repression noun **1** *the brutal repression of the peaceful protests*: **suppression**, quelling, quashing, subduing, crushing, squashing, stamping out; informal squelching.
2 *20 years of militarism and political repression*: **oppression**, subjugation, suppression, domination, tyranny, subjection, despotism, dictatorship, authoritarianism; censorship.
▷ANTONYMS freedom, liberty.
3 *the repression of sexual urges*: **restraint**, restraining, holding back, keeping back, biting back, suppression, keeping in check, control, keeping under control, stifling, smothering, bottling up; inhibition, frustration.
▷ANTONYMS expression.

repressive adjective *a repressive military regime*: **oppressive**, authoritarian, despotic, tyrannical, tyrannous, dictatorial, fascist, autocratic, totalitarian, dominating, coercive, draconian, iron-fisted, harsh, severe, strict, tough, cruel, brutal; undemocratic, illiberal; rare suppressive.
▷ANTONYMS democratic, liberal.

reprieve verb **1** *she was sentenced to death, but was reprieved*: **grant a stay of execution to**, cancel/postpone/commute/remit someone's punishment; pardon, spare, acquit, grant an amnesty to, amnesty; informal let off, let off the hook; archaic respite.
▷ANTONYMS charge, punish.
2 *the accident and emergency unit has also been reprieved*: **save**, rescue, grant a stay of execution to, give a respite to; informal take off the hit list.
▸ noun *he was saved by a last-minute reprieve*: **stay of execution**, cancellation of punishment, postponement of punishment, remission, suspension of punishment, respite; pardon, amnesty, acquittal; N. Amer. Law continuance; informal let-off.

reprimand verb *he was publicly reprimanded for his behaviour*: **rebuke**, admonish, chastise, chide, upbraid, reprove, reproach, scold, remonstrate with, berate, take to task, pull up, castigate, lambaste, read someone the Riot Act, give someone a piece of one's mind, haul over the coals, lecture, criticize, censure; informal tell off, give someone a talking-to, give someone a telling-off, dress down, give someone a dressing-down, give someone an earful, give someone a roasting, give someone a rocket, give someone a rollicking, rap, rap over the knuckles, slap someone's wrist, send someone away with a flea in their ear, let someone have it, bawl out, give someone hell, come down on, blow up, pitch into, lay into, lace into, give someone a caning, put on the mat, slap down, blast, rag, keelhaul; Brit. informal tick off, have a go at, carpet, give someone a mouthful, tear someone off a strip, give someone what for, give someone some stick, wig, give someone a wigging, give someone a row, row; N. Amer. informal chew out, ream out; Austral. informal monster; Brit. vulgar slang bollock, give someone a bollocking; N. Amer. vulgar slang chew someone's ass, ream someone's ass; dated call down, rate, give someone a rating, trim; rare reprehend, objurgate.
▷ANTONYMS praise, commend, compliment.
▸ noun *they received a severe reprimand from the Office of Fair Trading*: **rebuke**, reproof, admonishment, admonition, reproach, reproval, scolding, remonstration, upbraiding, castigation, lambasting, lecture, criticism, censure; informal telling-off, rap, rap over the knuckles, slap on the wrist, flea in one's ear, dressing-down, earful, roasting, tongue-lashing, bawling-out, caning, blast; Brit. informal ticking-off, carpeting, wigging, rollicking, rocket, row; Austral./NZ informal serve; Brit. vulgar slang bollocking; dated rating.
▷ANTONYMS praise, commendation.

reprisal noun *he declined to be named for fear of reprisal*: **retaliation**, counterattack, counterstroke, comeback; revenge, vengeance, retribution, requital, recrimination, an eye for an eye, a tooth for a tooth, tit for tat, getting even, redress, repayment, payback; Latin lex talionis; informal a taste of one's own medicine; rare ultion, a Roland for an Oliver.

reproach verb *Albert reproached him for being late*: **rebuke**, reprove, scold, chide, reprimand, admonish, chastise, upbraid, remonstrate with, berate, take to task, pull up, castigate, lambaste, read someone the Riot Act, give someone a piece of one's mind, haul over the coals, lecture, criticize, find fault with, censure, express disapproval of; informal tell off, give someone a talking-to, give someone a telling-off, dress down, give someone a dressing-down, give someone an earful, give someone a roasting, give someone a rocket, give someone a rollicking, rap, rap someone over the knuckles, slap someone's wrist; Brit. informal tick off, have a go at, carpet, give someone a mouthful, tear someone off a strip, give someone what for, give someone some stick, wig, give someone a wigging, give someone a row, row; dated call down, rate, give someone a rating, trim; rare reprehend, objurgate, reprobate.
▷ANTONYMS praise, commend.
▸ noun 1 *he reddened in acknowledgement of her reproach*: **rebuke**, reproof, reproval, admonishment, admonition, scolding, reprimand, remonstration, lecture, upbraiding, castigation, lambasting, criticism, censure, disapproval, disapprobation; informal telling-off, rap, rap over the knuckles, slap on the wrist, dressing-down, earful, roasting, rollicking; Brit. informal ticking-off, carpeting, wigging; Austral./NZ informal serve; dated rating.
▷ANTONYMS praise, commendation.
2 *this party is **a reproach to** the British political system*: **disgrace**, discredit, source of shame, outrage; blemish on, stain on, blot on, blot on the escutcheon of, slur on; scandal, stigma; literary smirch.
▷ANTONYMS credit.
□ **beyond/above reproach** *her public image had to be beyond reproach*: **perfect**, beyond criticism, blameless, above suspicion, without fault, faultless, flawless, irreproachable, exemplary, unimpeachable, impeccable, immaculate, unblemished, spotless, untarnished, stainless, unstained, pure, as pure as the driven snow, whiter than white, sinless, guiltless, unsullied; informal squeaky clean.
▷ANTONYMS blameworthy.

reproachful adjective *Angela gave him a reproachful look but he persisted*: **disapproving**, reproving, full of reproof, critical, censorious, disparaging, disappointed, withering, accusatory, admonitory, condemnatory, castigatory, fault-finding.
▷ANTONYMS approving.

reprobate noun *even a hardened reprobate like myself has some standards to adhere to*: **rogue**, rascal, scoundrel, good-for-nothing, villain, wretch, unprincipled person, rake, profligate, degenerate, debauchee, libertine; troublemaker, mischief-maker, wrongdoer, evil-doer, transgressor, sinner; French roué, vaurien; informal scallywag, bad egg; N. Amer. informal scofflaw, hellion; informal, dated rotter, bounder; dated cad, ne'er-do-well; archaic miscreant, blackguard, knave, rapscallion, varlet, wastrel, rakehell, scapegrace.
▸ adjective *reprobate behaviour*: **unprincipled**, roguish, bad, wicked, rakish, shameless, immoral, profligate, degenerate, dissipated, debauched, depraved, corrupt; incorrigible, hardened, unregenerate; informal scoundrelly, rascally; archaic knavish.
▷ANTONYMS upright, virtuous, principled.
▸ verb archaic *they reprobated his conduct*: **criticize**, condemn, censure, denounce, express strong disapproval of; rare reprehend.
▷ANTONYMS praise, commend.

reproduce verb 1 *each artwork is reproduced in full colour on a single page*: **copy**, produce a copy of, make a facsimile of, duplicate, replicate; photocopy, xerox, photostat, mimeograph, mimeo, print; transcribe; clone; forge, counterfeit; trademark make a Xerox of.
2 *this work has not been reproduced in other laboratories*: **repeat**, replicate, recreate, redo, perform again, reconstruct, remake; simulate, imitate, emulate, mirror, parallel, match, echo, mimic, ape, follow.
3 *some forms of animals and plants reproduce prolifically*: **breed**, produce offspring, bear young, procreate, propagate, multiply, proliferate, give birth, spawn, increase.

reproduction noun 1 *the reproduction of copyrighted material*: **copying**, duplication, duplicating, replication, replicating; photocopying, xeroxing, photostatting, printing; transcription, cloning, forging, counterfeiting.
2 *a photostatic reproduction of the original*: **print**, **copy**, reprint, duplicate, replica, facsimile, carbon copy; photocopy, mimeograph, mimeo; imitation, fake, forgery, counterfeit; informal dupe; trademark Xerox, photostat; rare ectype.
▷ANTONYMS original.
3 *marine invertebrates are not always restricted to one method of reproduction*: **breeding**, producing young, procreation, multiplying, propagation, proliferation, spawning.

reproductive adjective *reproductive organs | reproductive ability*: **generative**, procreative, propagative; **sexual**, genital, sex; rare progenitive, procreant, conceptive.

reproof noun *he muttered a reproof | he clicked his tongue at her in mock reproof*: **rebuke**, reprimand, reproach, admonishment, admonition, reproval, remonstration; **disapproval**, disapprobation, criticism, censure, blame, condemnation, fault-finding; informal telling-off, rap over the knuckles, slap on the wrist, dressing down, blast; Brit. informal ticking-off, wigging; Austral./NZ informal serve; Brit. vulgar slang bollocking; dated rating; rare reprehension.
▷ANTONYMS approval, praise.

reprove verb *he annoyed the new chauffeur by reproving him for grinding the gears*: **reprimand**, rebuke, reproach, scold, admonish, remonstrate with, chastise, chide, upbraid, berate, take to task, pull up, castigate, lambaste, read someone the Riot Act, give someone a piece of one's mind, haul over the coals, criticize, censure; informal tell off, give someone a talking-to, give someone a telling-off, dress down, give someone a dressing-down, give someone an earful, give someone a roasting, give someone a rocket, give someone a rollicking, rap, rap over the knuckles, slap someone's wrist, let someone have it, send someone away with a flea in their ear, bawl out, give someone hell, come down on, pitch into, lay into, lace into, give someone a caning, put on the mat, slap down, blast, rag, keelhaul; Brit. informal tick off, have a go at, carpet, give someone a mouthful, tear someone off a strip, give someone what for, give someone some stick, wig, give someone a wigging, give someone a row, row; dated call down, rate, give someone a rating, trim; rare reprehend, objurgate.
▷ANTONYMS praise, compliment.

reptile noun

> *Word links* **reptile**
>
> **-saur**, **-saurus** related suffixes, as in *ichthyosaur*, *stegosaurus*
> **herpetology** study of reptiles and amphibians

reptilian adjective 1 *reptilian species*: **reptile**; cold-blooded; saurian, ophidian, crocodilian; technical poikilothermic; rare reptiloid, reptiliform, reptant, repent.
2 *a reptilian smirk twisted his features | the reptilian young reception clerk*: **unpleasant**, distasteful, nasty, disagreeable, unappealing, unattractive, off-putting, horrible, horrid; unctuous, ingratiating, fulsome, oily, oleaginous; untrustworthy, devious, sly, underhand, crafty; informal smarmy, slimy, creepy, sneaky.
▷ANTONYMS nice, pleasant, attractive.

repudiate verb 1 *a world that repudiated aggression and violence as a way of resolving disputes | they have repudiated the founder of the party*: **reject**, renounce, abandon, forswear, give up, turn one's back on, have nothing more to do with, wash one's hands of, have no more truck with, abjure, disavow, recant, desert, discard, disown, cast off, lay aside, cut off, rebuff; archaic forsake; rare disprofess.
▷ANTONYMS embrace.
2 *Cranham repudiated the allegations*: **deny**, refute, contradict, rebut, dispute, disclaim, disavow; dismiss, brush aside; formal gainsay; rare controvert, negate.
▷ANTONYMS confirm, acknowledge.
3 *Egypt repudiated the treaty*: **cancel**, set aside, revoke, rescind, reverse, retract, overrule, override, overturn, invalidate, nullify, declare null and void, abrogate; refuse to fulfil, disregard, ignore, disobey, dishonour, renege on, go back on, backtrack on; Law disaffirm, avoid, vacate.
▷ANTONYMS ratify, accept, abide by.
4 *he repudiated his first wife*: **divorce**, end one's marriage to.
▷ANTONYMS marry.

repudiation noun 1 *the repudiation of one's religious heritage*: **rejection**, renunciation, renouncement, abandonment, forsaking, forswearing, giving up, disavowal, recantation, desertion, discarding, disowning, casting aside; rare abjuration.
2 *his repudiation of the allegations*: **denial**, refutation, contradiction, rebuttal, rejection, disclaimer, disavowal; dismissal; rare negation.
▷ANTONYMS confirmation, acknowledgement.
3 *a repudiation of the contract*: **cancellation**, revocation, rescindment, reversal, abrogation, retraction, invalidation, nullification; Law disaffirmation, disaffirmance, defeasance, avoidance; rare rescission.
▷ANTONYMS ratification, acceptance.

repugnance noun *a look of repugnance crossed Michael's features*: **revulsion**, **disgust**, abhorrence, repulsion, nausea, loathing, horror, hatred, detestation, aversion, abomination, distaste, antipathy, dislike, contempt, odium; archaic disrelish; rare repellency, repellence.
▷ANTONYMS delight, liking.

repugnant adjective 1 *the idea of cannibalism may seem repugnant to us*: **abhorrent**, revolting, repulsive, repellent, disgusting, offensive, objectionable, vile, foul, nasty, loathsome, sickening, nauseating, nauseous, hateful, detestable, execrable, abominable, monstrous, appalling, reprehensible, deplorable, insufferable, intolerable, unacceptable, despicable, contemptible, beyond the pale, unspeakable, noxious, obscene, base, hideous, grisly, gruesome, horrendous, heinous, atrocious, awful, terrible, dreadful, frightful, obnoxious, unsavoury, unpalatable, unpleasant, disagreeable, distasteful, dislikeable, off-putting, displeasing; informal ghastly, horrible, horrid, gross, putrid, sick-making, yucky, God-awful; Brit. informal beastly; N. Amer. informal skanky; literary noisome; archaic disgustful, scurvy, loathly; rare rebarbative.

r

▷**ANTONYMS** attractive, agreeable, pleasant.
2 formal *the restriction is* ***repugnant to*** *the nature of the tenancy*: **incompatible with**, in conflict with, contrary to, at variance with, contradictory to, inconsistent with, alien to, opposed to; rare oppugnant to.

repulse verb **1** *the rebels made another assault on the Secretariat and were again repulsed*: **repel**, **drive back**, drive away, fight back, fight off, put to flight, force back, beat off, beat back, push back, thrust back; ward off, hold off, stave off, fend off; foil, check, frustrate; Brit. see off; informal send packing; archaic rebut.
2 *she tried to show him affection, but was repulsed*: **rebuff**, reject, spurn, snub, disdain, give someone the cold shoulder, cold-shoulder; informal give someone the brush-off, freeze out, stiff-arm; Brit. informal knock back; N. Amer. informal give someone the bum's rush, give someone the brush; Austral. informal snout; informal, dated give someone the go-by.
▷**ANTONYMS** welcome.
3 *his bid for the company was repulsed*: **reject**, turn down, refuse, decline, say no to; informal give the thumbs down to.
▷**ANTONYMS** accept.
4 *the concept of being with a man repulsed her*: **revolt**, disgust, repel, sicken, nauseate, make someone feel sick, turn someone's stomach, be repulsive to, be extremely distasteful to, make shudder, be repugnant to, make someone's flesh creep, make someone's skin crawl, make someone's gorge rise, offend, horrify; informal turn off, give someone the creeps, make someone want to throw up; N. Amer. informal gross out.
▷**ANTONYMS** delight.
▶ noun **1** *the repulse of the Austrian attack*: **repelling**, driving back, putting to flight; warding off, holding off; **defeat**, check, foiling, frustration; rare repulsion.
2 *he was, no doubt, mortified by this repulse*: **rebuff**, rejection, snub, slight, repudiation, spurning, cold-shouldering, discouragement; informal brush-off, knock-back, kick in the teeth, slap/smack in the face, smack in the eye.

repulsion noun *she shuddered with repulsion*: **disgust**, revulsion, abhorrence, repugnance, nausea, loathing, horror, hatred, detestation, aversion, abomination, distaste, antipathy, dislike, contempt, odium; archaic disrelish; rare repellency, repellence.
▷**ANTONYMS** delight, liking.

repulsive adjective *Gleeson was so repulsive that surely no one would be interested in him*: **revolting**, disgusting, abhorrent, repellent, repugnant, offensive, objectionable, vile, foul, nasty, loathsome, sickening, nauseating, stomach-churning, stomach-turning, hateful, detestable, execrable, abominable, monstrous, appalling, reprehensible, deplorable, insufferable, intolerable, despicable, contemptible, beyond the pale, unspeakable, noxious, horrendous, heinous, atrocious, awful, terrible, dreadful, frightful, obnoxious, unsavoury, unpleasant, disagreeable, distasteful, dislikeable, off-putting, uninviting, displeasing; ugly, as ugly as sin, hideous, grotesque, gruesome, unsightly, reptilian; N. Amer. vomitous; informal ghastly, horrible, horrid, God-awful, gross, putrid, sick-making, sick, yucky, icky; Brit. informal beastly; N. Amer. informal skanky; literary noisome; archaic disgustful, scurvy, loathly; rare rebarbative.
▷**ANTONYMS** delightful, pleasant, attractive.

reputable adjective *if you decide to have an alarm fitted, make sure it is done by a reputable company*: **well thought of**, highly regarded, well respected, respected, respectable, with a good reputation, of repute, of good repute, creditable, esteemed, prestigious, estimable; established, well known; reliable, dependable, trusted, trustworthy, tried and trusted, honest, honourable, principled, above board, legitimate, upright, virtuous, irreproachable, worthy, good, excellent, conscientious; informal legit; Brit. informal copper-bottomed; archaic of good report.
▷**ANTONYMS** disreputable, untrustworthy.

reputation noun *her reputation has been seriously damaged by the scandal*: **name**, **good name**, character, repute, standing, stature, status, position, rank, station; fame, celebrity, renown, esteem, eminence, prestige; image, stock, credit; Indian izzat; N. Amer. informal rep, rap; archaic honour, report; rare reputability.

repute noun **1** *a woman of ill repute | Ramsay knew her only by repute*: **reputation**, name, character; archaic report.
2 *a firm of international repute*: **fame**, renown, celebrity, distinction, high standing, stature, eminence, prominence, note, prestige, account; good reputation, good name.
▷**ANTONYMS** obscurity, infamy.

reputed adjective **1** *they are reputed to be amongst the richest men in France*: **thought**, said, reported, rumoured, believed, held, considered, regarded, deemed, judged, estimated; alleged, purported.
▷**ANTONYMS** known.
2 *his reputed father | the reputed flatness of the Middle West*: **supposed**, putative; apparent, ostensible; rare suppositious; rare reputative.
▷**ANTONYMS** actual.
3 *he had been elevated from obscurity to the status of reputed naturalist*: **well thought of**, well respected, respected, highly regarded, with a good reputation, of good repute; well known, widely known.
▷**ANTONYMS** unknown, obscure.

reputedly adverb *the yew trees are reputedly the oldest in Europe*: **supposedly**, by all accounts, according to popular belief, so the story goes, so I'm told, so people say, by repute, allegedly, putatively, apparently, seemingly, ostensibly; rare reputatively, putatitiously.

request noun **1** *we received several urgent requests for assistance*: **appeal**, entreaty, plea, petition, solicitation, supplication, prayer, invocation; application; demand, call, summons, requisition; literary behest; rare imploration, adjuration, obtestation, impetration, obsecration.
2 *Charlotte insisted, at Ursula's request, on driving him to the station*: **bidding**, asking, entreaty, pleading, solicitation, petitioning, supplication, begging; demand, instance.
3 *please indicate your requests on the booking form*: **requirement**, wish, want, desire; choice; Latin desideratum.
▶ verb *the government requested foreign military aid | I requested him to inform Charles immediately*: **ask for**, appeal for, call for, seek, solicit, plead for, put in a plea for, pray for, petition, sue for, supplicate for; apply for, put in an application for, put in for, place an order for, put in an order for, order; demand, require, requisition; **call on**, beg, beseech, entreat, implore, importune, adjure; invite, bid; rare obtest, impetrate, obsecrate.

require verb **1** *the youngest child required further hospital treatment*: **need**, be in need of, stand in need of, have need of; be crying out for.
2 *it was a situation that required patience*: **necessitate**, demand, call for, involve, entail, take.
3 *unquestioning faith and obedience is required*: **demand**, insist on, call for, ask for, request, order, command, decree; exact; expect, look for.
4 *she was required to pay over £10,000 in costs*: **order**, instruct, command, enjoin, oblige, bid, compel, constrain, charge, make, force.
5 *do you require anything else, sir?* **want**, wish, wish to have, desire; lack, be short of, be without, find oneself in need of.

required adjective **1** *the book is required reading for everyone interested in philosophical thought*: **essential**, vital, indispensable, necessary, needed, called for, requisite, prerequisite; compulsory, obligatory, mandatory, prescribed, statutory; recommended, set; French de rigueur.
▷**ANTONYMS** optional, inessential.
2 *cut the cable to the required length*: **desired**, preferred, chosen, selected; **correct**, proper, right.

requirement noun *it's essential to assess your requirements carefully before you buy*: **need**, wish, demand, want, necessity, essential, necessary/essential item; prerequisite, requisite, precondition, condition, stipulation, specification; Latin desideratum, sine qua non; informal must.

requisite adjective *he lacks the requisite communication skills*: **necessary**, **required**, prerequisite, essential, indispensable, vital, needed, needful; compulsory, obligatory, mandatory, stipulated, demanded, called-for, imperative; French de rigueur.
▷**ANTONYMS** optional, unnecessary, non-essential.
▶ noun **1** *she sold all sorts of goods, from vegetables to toilet requisites*: **requirement**, need, necessity, essential, want, necessary/essential item.
2 *a university degree has become a requisite for any successful career in this field*: **necessity**, essential requirement, prerequisite, essential, precondition, specification, stipulation; qualification; Latin desideratum, sine qua non; informal must.
▷**ANTONYMS** non-essential.

> *Choose the right word* **requisite, necessary, essential, indispensable**
>
> See **necessary**.

requisition noun **1** *in mid-1946, the Air Ministry placed its first requisition for an atomic bomb*: **order**, purchase order, request, call, application; claim, demand, summons; Brit. indent.
2 *the illegal requisition of cultural treasures*: **appropriation**, commandeering, possession, takeover, taking over, occupation; seizure, confiscation, expropriation, sequestration.
▶ verb **1** *the house was requisitioned by the army*: **commandeer**, appropriate, take, take over, take possession of, occupy; seize, confiscate, expropriate, sequestrate, sequester.
2 *she requisitioned statements and demanded the material that was missing*: **request**, order, call for, apply for, put in a claim for, put in for; demand.

requital noun **1** *take this from me in requital of your kindness*: **repayment** reward, return, payment, recompense, reparation.
2 *punishment ought not to be inflicted by the victim as a means of personal requital*: **revenge**, vengeance, retribution, retaliation, redress, satisfaction; Latin quid pro quo.

requite verb **1** *the king promised to requite his hospitality*: **return**, reciprocate, match; reward, repay, recompense; archaic guerdon.
2 *Drake had requited the wrongs inflicted on them*: **avenge**, exact revenge for, revenge, retaliate for, pay someone back for; get/have/take one's revenge, take reprisals, settle old scores, settle the score with someone, take an eye for an eye (and a tooth for a tooth), give tit for tat, get even, give someone their just deserts, give someone a dose/taste of their own medicine, give as good as one gets, give like for like.

3 *she did not requite his love*: **reciprocate**, return, feel/give in return.

rescind verb *the court has the power to rescind a bankruptcy order*: **revoke**, repeal, cancel, reverse, abrogate, overturn, overrule, override, annul, nullify, declare null and void, make void, void, invalidate, render invalid, quash, abolish, set aside, countermand, retract, withdraw; Law vacate, avoid; archaic recall; rare disannul.
▷ANTONYMS enforce, enact.

rescission noun *the rescission of the contract*: **revocation**, repeal, cancellation, rescindment, reversal, abrogation, annulment, nullification, invalidation, voiding, setting aside, retraction; archaic recall; rare disannulment.
▷ANTONYMS enforcement.

rescue verb **1** *an attempt was made to rescue the hostages*: **save**, save from danger, save the life of, come to the aid of; **set free**, free, release, liberate, extricate, get someone out; deliver, redeem, ransom, emancipate, relieve; bail someone out; Nautical bring someone off; informal save someone's bacon, save someone's neck, save someone's skin.
▷ANTONYMS endanger, jeopardize; imprison; abandon.
2 *Boyd bent hastily to rescue his papers*: **retrieve**, recover, salvage, get back; pick up, gather up, scoop up.
▶ noun *the rescue of 10 crewmen from a ship which had run aground on the Shetland Isles*: **saving**, rescuing; release, freeing, liberation, extrication; deliverance, delivery, redemption, ransom, emancipation, relief.
□ **come to someone's rescue help**, assist, aid, lend a helping hand to, lend a hand to, bail out; be someone's knight in shining armour; informal save someone's bacon, save someone's neck, save someone's skin, get someone out of a tight spot.

research noun **1** *a group set up to oppose the use of animals in medical research*: **investigation**, experimentation, testing, exploration, analysis, fact-finding, examination, scrutiny, scrutinization, probing; groundwork; rare indagation.
2 (**researches**) *he could no longer afford to continue his researches*: **experiments**, experimentation, tests, enquiries, studies, analyses, work.
▶ verb **1** *the phenomenon has been widely researched*: **investigate**, conduct investigations into, study, enquire into, make enquiries into, look into, probe, explore, analyse, examine, scrutinize, inspect, review, assess.
2 *I researched all the available material on the subject*: **study**, read, read up on, pore over, delve into, dig into, sift through; informal check out.

resemblance noun *any resemblance between their reports is purely coincidental*: **similarity**, likeness, alikeness, similitude; correspondence, congruity, congruence, coincidence, concurrence, conformity, agreement, equivalence; comparability, comparableness, comparison, parallelism, parity, analogy, affinity, closeness, nearness; sameness, identicalness, uniformity; archaic semblance.
▷ANTONYMS dissimilarity.

resemble verb *the woman resembled Jackie Kennedy | her views resemble those of the right-wing tabloid press*: **look like**, be similar to, be like, bear a resemblance to, remind one of, put one in mind of, take after, favour, have a look of, make one think of; approximate to, smack of, have (all) the hallmarks of, correspond to, be not dissimilar to, be not unlike; echo, mirror, duplicate, parallel; Zoology & Botany mimic; archaic bear semblance to.
▷ANTONYMS differ from.

resent verb *the girls resented the fact that Peter got so much attention*: **begrudge**, feel aggrieved at/about, feel bitter about, grudge, be annoyed at/about, be angry at/about, be resentful of, dislike, be displeased at/about, take exception to, object to, be offended by, take amiss, take offence at, take umbrage at; envy, feel envious of, feel jealous of; bear/harbour a grudge about; archaic take something ill.
▷ANTONYMS like, welcome, be pleased by.

resentful adjective *constant criticism will make your partner feel resentful*: **aggrieved**, indignant, irritated, exasperated, piqued, put out, in high dudgeon, displeased, dissatisfied, disgruntled, discontented, malcontent, offended, bitter, hostile, acrimonious, rancorous, spiteful, jaundiced; envious, jealous, grudging, begrudging; sullen, sulky, sour, fed up, huffy, in a huff, irked; informal miffed, miffy, peeved, mad, aggravated; Brit. informal narked; N. Amer. informal sore; W. Indian informal vex; vulgar slang pissed off; archaic snuffy, wroth.
▷ANTONYMS satisfied, contented.

resentment noun *the proposal aroused deep resentment among many party members*: **bitterness**, **indignation**, irritation, pique, displeasure, dissatisfaction, disgruntlement, discontentment, discontent, resentfulness, bad feelings, hard feelings, ill feelings, acrimony, rancour, animosity, hostility, jaundice, antipathy, antagonism, enmity, hatred, hate; envy, jealousy, malice, ill will; grudge, grievance, a chip on one's shoulder; literary ire.
▷ANTONYMS contentment, happiness.

reservation noun **1** *the British government expressed grave reservations about the proposals*: **doubt**, qualm, scruple; **misgivings**, scepticism, unease, hesitation, hesitancy, demur, reluctance; objection; Law demurrer.
▷ANTONYMS confidence.
2 *groups of ten or more should make reservations*: **advance booking**, booking, prior arrangement; charter/hire arrangements; dated engagement.
3 *Ms Jones wrote, confirming the reservation of the room*: **booking**, ordering, arrangement, prearrangement, securing; charter, hire; dated engagement, engaging.
4 *the Yanomami Indian reservation*: **reserve**, preserve, enclave, sanctuary, area, territory; homeland.
□ **without reservation** *Mr McNeill apologized without reservation*: **wholeheartedly**, **unreservedly**, without qualification, without reserve, without demur, fully, completely, categorically, totally, entirely, wholly, in every respect; implicitly, unconditionally; informal all the way; N. Amer. informal flat out.

reserve verb **1** *ask your newsagent to reserve you a copy*: **put to one side**, put aside, set aside, lay aside, keep back; **keep**, save, hold, keep in reserve, hold back, retain, conserve, preserve, put away, withhold, earmark; informal hang on to.
▷ANTONYMS use up.
2 *that evening, he reserved a table at Chez Jacques*: **book**, make a reservation for, order, arrange in advance, arrange for, prearrange for, secure; charter, hire; informal bag; dated engage; rare bespeak.
3 *the management reserves the right to alter the advertised programme if necessary*: **retain**, keep, hold, secure.
4 *I'd advise you to reserve your judgement on him until you get to know him a little better*: **defer**, postpone, put off, delay, withhold; N. Amer. take something under advisement.
▶ noun **1** *Harriet had used up some of her precious reserves of petrol for this journey*: **stock**, store, supply, stockpile, reservoir, pool, fund, bank, accumulation; hoard, cache.
2 *the men were stationed as a central reserve ready to be transported wherever necessary*: **backup**; (**reserves**) **reinforcements**, extras, auxiliaries.
3 *a 2,500 acre nature reserve*: **national park**, **animal sanctuary**, preserve, reservation, conservation area; safari park.
4 *Carrie found it very difficult to penetrate his reserve*: **reticence**, self-restraint, restraint, self-containment; uncommunicativeness, unwillingness to open up, unapproachability, detachment, distance, remoteness, coolness, lack of warmth, aloofness, stand-offishness, constraint, formality, guardedness, unresponsiveness, secretiveness, taciturnity, silence; shyness, diffidence, timidity, self-effacement, inhibitedness, inhibition; coldness, frigidity; French froideur.
▷ANTONYMS friendliness, openness, approachability.
5 *she trusted him without reserve*: **reservation**, qualification, condition, limitation, proviso; hesitation, doubt, qualm, scruple.
□ **in reserve** *the army had only one fresh regiment in reserve*: **available**, at hand, to hand, on hand, on call, ready, in readiness, for use when needed, set aside; obtainable, accessible, at one's disposal, on tap; spare.
▶ adjective *United's reserve goalkeeper*: **substitute**, stand-in, second-string, relief, replacement, fallback, emergency; in reserve, spare, extra, auxiliary, secondary.

reserved adjective **1** *as a young man, Sewell was rather reserved*: **reticent**, self-restrained, restrained, quiet, private, self-contained; uncommunicative, unforthcoming, undemonstrative, unsociable, formal, constrained, cool, aloof, stand-offish, detached, distant, remote, unapproachable, unfriendly, withdrawn, guarded, secretive, close, silent, taciturn, close-mouthed; shy, retiring, diffident, timid, demure, self-effacing, shrinking, inhibited, introverted; unemotional, cold, chilly, frigid; archaic retired; rare Olympian.
▷ANTONYMS outgoing, open.
2 *the corner table is reserved, I'm afraid*: **booked**, taken, spoken for, prearranged; chartered, hired; dated engaged; rare bespoken.
▷ANTONYMS free.

reservoir noun **1** *large numbers of birds frequent the reservoir*: **pool**, lake, pond; water supply; technical waterbody; Scottish loch; Indian & Austral./NZ tank; Mexican Spanish cenote.
2 *the toner reservoir is housed within a single-piece cartridge*: **receptacle**, container, holder, repository, tank; sump.
3 *companies that fail to promote women are cutting their reservoir of managerial talent by half*: **stock**, store, stockpile, reserve(s), supply, accumulation, bank, pool, fund; cache, hoard.

reshuffle verb (stress on the second syllable) *the prime minister reshuffled his cabinet*: **reorganize**, restructure, change, change around, change the line-up of, shake up, rearrange, interchange, shuffle, regroup, rejig, redistribute, realign; informal jigger.
▶ noun (stress on the first syllable) *the company announced a management reshuffle*: **reorganization**, restructuring, upheaval, change, rearrangement, regrouping, redistribution; informal shake-up.

reside verb **1** *a number of students* ***reside in*** *flats and other lodgings in Coleraine*: **live in**, occupy, inhabit, have one's home in, be settled in, have taken up residence in, have established oneself in; stay in, lodge in; informal hang out in; N. Amer. informal hang one's hat in; formal dwell in, be domiciled in, sojourn in; archaic bide in.
▷ANTONYMS visit.
2 *the Lewis Papers now reside in an air-conditioned vault in the suburbs of*

r

Chicago: **be situated**, be placed, be found, be located, lie, repose.
3 *a unitary state in which executive power* ***resides in*** *the president*: **belong to**, be vested in, be bestowed on, be conferred on, be entrusted to, be in the hands of.
4 *the distinctive qualities that* ***reside within*** *each individual*: **be inherent in**, be intrinsic to, be present in, inhere in; **exist in**, rest in, lie in, dwell in, abide in; consist in, subsist in; rare indwell.

residence noun **1** formal *his private residence*: **home**, house, flat, apartment, place of residence, address, accommodation, place; quarters, lodgings; seat; French pied à terre; informal pad, digs; formal dwelling, dwelling place, domicile, abode, habitation.
2 *his last known place of residence*: **occupancy**, habitation, residency, inhabitation, tenancy, stay; formal abode, sojourn; rare inhabitancy, inhabitance, domiciliation, habitancy.

resident noun **1** *the residents of New York City*: **inhabitant**, local; householder, homeowner, houseowner; citizen, native, townsman, townswoman, taxpayer; occupant, occupier, tenant; humorous denizen, burgher; formal dweller; rare residentiary, indweller.
2 Brit. *at present, the hotel bar is open to residents only*: **guest**, person staying, boarder, lodger, client.
▷ANTONYMS non-resident.
3 *residents at a nursing home near Middleton St George*: **patient**, inmate.
▶ adjective **1** *trustees resident in the UK*: **living**, residing, in residence, staying, remaining; formal dwelling; archaic biding; rare residentiary.
2 *a resident nanny*: **live-in**, living in.
3 *the resident registrar in obstetrics and gynaecology*: **permanent**, incumbent; French en poste.
▷ANTONYMS visiting.
4 *the health-care needs of the resident population*: **local**, neighbourhood.

residential adjective *a residential area*: **suburban**; commuter, dormitory; rare exurban.

residual adjective **1** *this machine has five programmes, and uses the residual heat to dry the dishes*: **remaining**, leftover, unused, unconsumed; surplus, extra, excess, superfluous; technical residuary, remanent.
2 *she still seemed to feel some residual affection for her errant husband*: **lingering**, lasting, enduring, abiding, persisting, surviving, vestigial.

residue noun *the residue of his estate was divided equally among them*: **remainder**, remaining part, part leftover, rest, remnant, remnants; surplus, extra, excess, balance; remains, leftovers, leavings, dregs, lees, sediment, grounds, settlings; technical residuum, precipitate, sublimate; Commerce overage.

resign verb **1** *the senior management resigned after the losses were announced*: **leave**, go, hand in one's notice, give in one's notice, give notice, stand down, step down, bow out, walk out; informal **quit**, call it a day.
2 *19 MPs resigned their parliamentary seats*: **give up**, leave, vacate, stand down from, retire from; informal quit, pack in, jack in; archaic demit.
▷ANTONYMS take up.
3 *he had resigned his right to the title*: **renounce**, relinquish, give up, abandon, surrender, forgo, cede, abdicate, sign away; Law disclaim; archaic forsake.
▷ANTONYMS claim, assert, keep.
4 *we* ***resigned ourselves to*** *a long wait*: **reconcile oneself to**, become resigned to, become reconciled to, have no choice but to accept, come to terms with, learn to live with, get used to the idea of; give in to the inevitable, grin and bear it.
▷ANTONYMS refuse to accept.

resignation noun **1** *his resignation from his government post | the resignation of his ministerial portfolio*: **departure**, leaving, standing down, stepping down, retirement; giving up, vacating, relinquishment, renunciation, surrender, abdication; informal quitting; archaic demission.
2 *she toyed with the idea of handing in her resignation*: **notice**, notice to quit, letter of resignation.
3 *he confronted the indignities of old age with his usual resignation*: **patience**, forbearance, tolerance, stoicism, endurance, fortitude, sufferance, lack of protest, lack of complaint, acceptance of the inevitable, fatalism, acceptance, acquiescence, compliance, passivity, passiveness, non-resistance, submission, docility, phlegm; rare longanimity.
▷ANTONYMS resistance.

resigned adjective *'What time?' he asked, with a resigned sigh*: **patient**, long-suffering, uncomplaining, forbearing, tolerant, stoical, philosophical, unprotesting, reconciled, fatalistic; **acquiescent**, compliant, unresisting, non-resistant, passive, submissive, subdued, docile, phlegmatic; rare longanimous.
▷ANTONYMS resistant.

resilience noun **1** *he uses different types of vertical and cross strings in his rackets for added resilience*: **flexibility**, pliability, suppleness, plasticity, elasticity, springiness, spring, give; **durability**, ability to last, strength, sturdiness, toughness.
▷ANTONYMS rigidity; fragility.
2 *she displayed an indomitable resilience in the face of misfortune*: **strength of character**, strength, toughness, hardiness; **adaptability**, buoyancy, flexibility, ability to bounce back; informal bouncebackability.
▷ANTONYMS vulnerability, weakness.

resilient adjective **1** *remember that the more resilient the underlay, the more it will prolong the life of your carpet*: **flexible**, pliable, pliant, supple, plastic, elastic, springy, rubbery; **durable**, hard-wearing, stout, strong, sturdy, tough.
▷ANTONYMS inflexible, rigid; fragile.
2 *he was still young and resilient*: **strong**, tough, hardy; **quick to recover**, quick to bounce back, buoyant, difficult to keep down, irrepressible; **adaptable**, flexible.
▷ANTONYMS vulnerable, sensitive.

resist verb **1** *the vine's hard wood helps it resist cold winters*: **withstand**, be proof against, hold out against, combat, counter; weather, endure, outlast; repel, be resistant to, be impervious to, be impermeable to, keep out.
▷ANTONYMS be harmed by, be susceptible to.
2 *those resisting attempts to upgrade the building may be evicted*: **oppose**, fight against, refuse to accept, be hostile to, object to, be anti, take a stand against, defy, go against, set one's face against, kick against, baulk at; **obstruct**, impede, hinder, block, thwart, frustrate, inhibit, restrain; stop, halt, prevent, check, stem, curb; dig in one's heels; archaic reluct.
▷ANTONYMS accept, welcome.
3 *I resisted the urge to retort*: **refrain from**, abstain from, keep from, forbear from, desist from, forgo, avoid; not give in to, restrain oneself from, prevent oneself from, stop oneself from, check oneself.
▷ANTONYMS succumb to, give in to.
4 *she tried to resist him, but she hadn't the strength*: **struggle with/against**, fight (against), put up a fight against, battle against, stand up to, withstand, stand one's ground against, hold one's ground against, hold off, hold out against, contend with, confront, face up to; fend off, keep at bay, ward off, keep at arm's length.
▷ANTONYMS submit, yield.
□ **cannot resist** *he is a man who cannot resist a challenge*: **love**, adore, relish, be addicted to, have a weakness for, be very partial to, be very keen on, be very fond of, like; delight in, enjoy, take great pleasure in; informal have a thing about, be mad about, be hooked on, get a kick out of, get a thrill out of.
▷ANTONYMS hate.

resistance noun **1** *they displayed a narrow-minded* ***resistance to*** *change*: **opposition to**, hostility to, aversion to, refusal to accept, unwillingness to accept, disinclination to accept, reluctance to accept, lack of enthusiasm for.
▷ANTONYMS acceptance, receptivity.
2 *James put up a spirited resistance*: **opposition**, fight, battle, stand, struggle, confrontation, defiance.
▷ANTONYMS submission, surrender.
3 *tobacco lowers the body's* ***resistance to*** *disease*: **ability to fight off**, ability to counteract, ability to withstand, immunity from, defences against; resilience.
4 *he joined the resistance*: **underground**, freedom fighters, partisans, guerrillas; in France, historical Maquis.

resistant adjective **1** *a reinforced PVC membrane which is* ***resistant to*** *water | people are more* ***resistant to*** *infection if they have an adequate diet*: **impervious to**, proof against, unaffected by, repellent of; unsusceptible to, immune to, invulnerable to; water-resistant, waterproof, impenetrable; rare imperviable to.
▷ANTONYMS susceptible to.
2 *she is very* ***resistant to*** *change*: **opposed to**, averse to, hostile to, inimical to, against, anti, unwilling to accept, disinclined to accept, reluctant to accept, unenthusiastic about.
▷ANTONYMS receptive to.

resolute adjective *France's resolute defence of Verdun*: **determined**, purposeful, purposive, resolved, decided, adamant, single-minded, firm, unswerving, unwavering, undaunted, fixed, set, intent, insistent; steadfast, staunch, stalwart, earnest, manful, deliberate, unfaltering, unhesitating, unflinching, persevering, persistent, pertinacious, indefatigable, tenacious, bulldog, strong-minded, strong-willed, unshakeable, unshaken, steely, four-square, dedicated, committed, constant; stubborn, dogged, obstinate, obdurate, inflexible, relentless, intransigent, implacable, unyielding, unbending, immovable, unrelenting; spirited, brave, bold, courageous, plucky, stout, stout-hearted, mettlesome, indomitable, strenuous, vigorous, gritty, stiff; N. Amer. rock-ribbed; informal gutsy, spunky; rare perseverant, indurate.
▷ANTONYMS irresolute, half-hearted.

> *Word toolkit* **resolute**
>
> See **staunch**[1].

resolution noun **1** *despite her resolution to remain calm, Shannon could feel her temper rising*: **intention**, resolve, decision, intent, aim, aspiration, design, purpose, object, plan; commitment, pledge, promise, undertaking.
2 *the committee passed the resolution by 26 votes to 12*: **motion**, proposal,

r

proposition, plan; ruling, verdict, judgement, finding, adjudication, decision, declaration, decree; N. Amer. resolve; Law determination.
3 *she handled the work with resolution*: **determination**, purpose, purposefulness, resolve, resoluteness, single-mindedness, strength of will, strength of character, will power, firmness, firmness of purpose, fixity of purpose, intentness, decision, decidedness; steadfastness, staunchness, manfulness, perseverance, persistence, indefatigability, tenacity, tenaciousness, staying power, strong-mindedness, backbone, dedication, commitment, constancy, the bulldog spirit, pertinacity, pertinaciousness; stubbornness, doggedness, obstinacy, obdurateness, obduracy, inflexibility; spiritedness, braveness, bravery, boldness, courage, pluck, courageousness, pluckiness, stout-heartedness; German Sitzfleisch; informal guts, spunk, grit, stickability; N. Amer. informal stick-to-it-iveness; archaic intension; rare perseveration.
▷ANTONYMS irresolution, half-heartedness.
4 *it is hoped that the proposals will pave the way for a satisfactory* ***resolution of*** *the problem*: **solution to**, answer to, end to, explanation to; resolving, settlement, settling, solving, sorting out, working out, rectification, unravelling, disentanglement, clarification, conclusion, ending; informal cracking.
▷ANTONYMS continuation, prolonging.

resolve verb **1** *the government seems to think that the matter can be resolved overnight*: **settle**, sort out, solve, find a solution to, find an answer to, fix, work out, straighten out, deal with, put right, set right, put to rights, rectify, iron out, reconcile; answer, explain, fathom, unravel, disentangle, clarify, clear up, throw light on; informal sew up, hammer out, thrash out, patch up, crack, figure out.
2 *Charity resolved not to think about him any longer*: **determine**, decide, make up one's mind, take a decision, reach a decision, conclude, come to the conclusion; settle on a plan of action.
3 *the committee resolved that the council should proceed*: **vote**, pass a resolution, rule, move, decide formally, agree, undertake.
4 *these compounds can be resolved into their active constituents by various methods*: **break down**, break up, separate, reduce, decompose, divide; disintegrate, dissolve.
▷ANTONYMS combine.
5 *one of the most important of a lawyer's accomplishments is the ability to resolve facts into their legal categories*: **analyse**, dissect, break down, anatomize.
6 *the shore came closer, the grey smudge* ***resolving into*** *green fields and a sandy beach*: **turn into**, **be transformed into**, become clearly visible as, change into, metamorphose into, be transmuted into.
7 *all my doubts were resolved*: **dispel**, remove, allay, dissipate, clear up, banish, put an end to.
▷ANTONYMS reinforce.
▶ noun **1** *attempts to intimidate him merely strengthened his resolve*: **determination**, resolution, firmness of purpose, fixity of purpose, purpose, purposefulness, resoluteness, single-mindedness, strength of will, strength of character, will power, firmness, intentness, decision, decidedness; steadfastness, staunchness, manfulness, perseverance, persistence, indefatigability, tenacity, tenaciousness, staying power, strong-mindedness, backbone, dedication, commitment, constancy, the bulldog spirit, pertinacity, pertinaciousness; stubbornness, doggedness, obstinacy, obdurateness, obduracy, inflexibility; spiritedness, braveness, bravery, boldness, courage, courageousness, pluck, pluckiness, stout-heartedness; German Sitzfleisch; informal guts, spunk, grit, stickability; N. Amer. informal stick-to-it-iveness; archaic intension; rare perseveration.
▷ANTONYMS indecision.
2 *he made a resolve not to go there alone next time*: **decision**, resolution, commitment, intention; conclusion.

> *Choose the right word* **resolve, decide, determine**
>
> See **decide**.

resolved adjective *he was* ***resolved to*** *marry her*: **determined to**, bent on, hell bent on, set on, intent on, insistent on, committed to the idea of.

resonant adjective **1** *a resonant voice with an attractive Welsh lilt*: **deep**, low, sonorous, full, full-bodied, vibrant, rich, clear, ringing, orotund; bass, baritone, basso; loud, carrying, booming, thunderous, thundering; plangent; rare pear-shaped, canorous.
▷ANTONYMS faint, thin, weak.
2 *alpine valleys resonant with the sound of church bells*: **reverberating**, ringing, resounding, echoing, filled; vibrating, pulsating.
3 *that most resonant of all English four-letter words—home*: **evocative**, suggestive, expressive, redolent, moving, poignant, haunting.

resort noun **1** *a English seaside resort*: **holiday destination**, holiday centre, tourist centre, centre, spot, retreat, haunt; spa, watering place; informal tourist trap, honeypot.
2 *it is desirable that the matter be settled without* ***resort to*** *legal proceedings*: **recourse to**, turning to, the use of, utilizing; application to, appealing to, looking to.
3 *strike action should only be used as a last resort*: **expedient**, measure, possible course of action, step, recourse, alternative, option, choice, source of help, source of assistance, someone/something to turn to, possibility, hope, remedy.
□ **in the last resort ultimately**, in the end, at the end of the day, finally, in the long run, eventually; when all is said and done; informal when push comes to shove.
▶ verb
□ **resort to** *I don't have to resort to such underhand tricks*: **have recourse to**, fall back on, turn to, look to, make use of, use, utilize, avail oneself of, employ, bring into play/service, press into service, call on; adopt, exercise; stoop to, descend to, sink to.

resound verb **1** *an explosion of thunder resounded round the silent street*: **echo**, re-echo, reverberate, ring out, fill the air, boom, peal, thunder, rumble.
2 *a large building resounding with the clang of hammers*: **reverberate**, echo, re-echo, resonate, ring; vibrate, pulsate.
3 *whatever they do next will not resound in the way their earlier achievements did*: **be acclaimed**, be celebrated, be renowned, be famed, be noted, be glorified, be proclaimed, be trumpeted, be talked about, be on everyone's lips.
▷ANTONYMS sink into obscurity.

resounding adjective **1** *a resounding bass voice*: **reverberant**, reverberating, resonant, resonating, echoing, vibrant, ringing, sonorous, deep, rich, clear; loud, booming, thunderous, deafening.
▷ANTONYMS faint.
2 *the show was a resounding success*: **enormous**, huge, massive, very great, tremendous, terrific, colossal; **emphatic**, decisive, conclusive, striking, impressive, outstanding, unmistakable, notable, noteworthy, memorable, remarkable, phenomenal, monumental; informal whopping, thumping, fantastic; Brit. informal ginormous.

resource noun **1** (usually **resources**) *is the company using its resources efficiently?* **assets**, funds, wealth, money, riches, capital; staff, people; supplies, materials, store(s), stock(s), reserve(s), holding(s); supply, reservoir, pool, fund, stockpile, accumulation, hoard.
2 *your tutor is there as a resource*: **facility**, amenity, aid, help, service, support; convenience, advantage, benefit.
3 *so often her only resource is tears*: **expedient**, resort, means, measure, method, course, way, scheme, plan, plot, stratagem, manoeuvre, machination, agency, trick, ruse, artifice, device, tool.
4 *a person of resource*: **initiative**, resourcefulness, enterprise, imagination, imaginativeness, ingenuity, inventiveness; quick-wittedness, cleverness, native wit, talent, ability, capability; spirit, spiritedness, enthusiasm, drive, zest, dash, ambition, energy, vigour, vitality; informal gumption, get-up-and-go, go, push, oomph, pizzazz, pep, zip, vim.

resourceful adjective *somebody proved how resourceful they were by organizing the help of three local firemen*: **ingenious**, imaginative, inventive, creative; quick-witted, clever, bright, sharp, talented, gifted, able, capable; spirited, enthusiastic, ambitious, energetic, vigorous.
▷ANTONYMS unimaginative.

respect noun **1** *the respect due to a great artist*: **esteem**, regard, high regard, high opinion, acclaim, admiration, approbation, approval, appreciation, estimation, favour, popularity, recognition, veneration, awe, reverence, deference, honour, praise, homage.
▷ANTONYMS contempt.
2 *he speaks to the old lady with respect*: **due regard**, consideration, thoughtfulness, attentiveness, politeness, courtesy, civility, deference.
▷ANTONYMS disrespect.
3 (**respects**) *it was normal to pay one's respects to the local military commander on arriving*: **regards**, kind/kindest regards, compliments, greetings, best wishes, good wishes, felicitations, salutations; archaic remembrances; French, archaic devoirs.
4 *the report turned out to be accurate in every respect*: **aspect**, regard, facet, feature, way, sense, characteristic, particular, point, detail, question, matter, connection.
□ **with respect to/in respect of concerning**, regarding, as regards, in/with regard to, with reference to, relating to, respecting, as for, as to, re, about, apropos, on the subject of, in the matter of, in connection with; French vis-à-vis; Latin in re.
▶ verb **1** *as a teacher he was highly respected for his industry and patience*: **esteem**, admire, think highly of, have a high opinion of, hold in high regard, hold in (high) esteem, think much of, approve of, appreciate, cherish, value, set (great) store by, prize, treasure, look up to, pay homage to, venerate, revere, reverence, adulate, worship, idolize, put on a pedestal, lionize, hero-worship, honour, applaud, praise, favour.
▷ANTONYMS despise.
2 *at least they respect your privacy*: **show consideration for**, show regard for, take into consideration, take into account, make allowances for, take cognizance of, observe, pay heed/attention to, bear in mind, be mindful of, be heedful of, remember; archaic regard.
▷ANTONYMS scorn.
3 *her father respected her wishes | democrats must respect the law*: **abide by**, comply with, follow, adhere to, conform to, act in accordance with,

acquiesce to, assent to, consent to, accord to, yield to, submit to, defer to, bow to, obey, observe, hold to, keep (to), stick to, stand by, heed.
▷ANTONYMS ignore, disobey.

respectable adjective **1** *she came from a highly respectable middle-class background*: **reputable**, of good repute, upright, honest, honourable, trustworthy, above board, worthy, decent, good, virtuous, admirable, well bred, clean-living, proper, decorous; genteel, accepted, presentable; French comme il faut.
▷ANTONYMS disreputable, unworthy.
2 *he earns a respectable salary*: **fairly good**, passable, decent, fair, reasonable, presentable, moderately good, not bad; **substantial**, considerable, ample, sizeable; informal not to be sneezed at, OK.
▷ANTONYMS paltry, small.

respectful adjective *a uniformed attendant gave them a respectful salute*: **deferential**, reverent, admiring, humble, reverential, dutiful, subservient; **polite**, well mannered, civil, courteous, chivalrous, gallant, gracious, considerate, obliging, solicitous, thoughtful, attentive; dated mannerly; rare regardful.
▷ANTONYMS disrespectful, rude.

respective adjective *the girls had gone back to their respective boarding schools*: **separate**, personal, own, particular, individual, specific, special, corresponding, relevant, appropriate, different, various, several.

respite noun **1** *the thought of a brief respite was tempting*: **rest**, break, breathing space, interval, intermission, interlude, recess, lull, pause, time out, hiatus, halt, stop, stoppage, cessation, discontinuation, standstill; relief, relaxation, repose; informal breather, let-up.
2 *granting respite from debts was a means of encouraging men to serve in the army*: **postponement**, deferment, delay, stay, stay of execution, reprieve, remission, suspension, adjournment, moratorium; N. Amer. Law continuance.

resplendent adjective *the General was resplendent in his uniform and military ribbons*: **splendid**, magnificent, brilliant, dazzling, glittering, glowing, radiant, gorgeous, transcendent, impressive, imposing, spectacular, striking, stunning, glorious, superb, majestic, great, awe-inspiring, breathtaking, fine; informal splendiferous; rare splendacious, magnolious.

respond verb **1** *they do not* ***respond to*** *questions*: **answer**, reply to, say something in response to; acknowledge, greet, counter; make a response, make a rejoinder, make a riposte, make reply, come back.
▷ANTONYMS ask; ignore.
2 *'No,' she responded*: **say in response**, answer, reply, rejoin, retort, return, riposte, counter, fling back, hurl back, retaliate, come back.
3 *Western countries have been slow to* ***respond to*** *appeals*: **react to**, act in response to, make a response; hit back at, take the bait, rise to the bait, reciprocate, return the favour, retaliate, give as good as one gets, give tit for tat.
▷ANTONYMS make, ignore.

response noun **1** *there was laughter at his response to the question*: **answer**, reply, acknowledgement, rejoinder, retort, return, riposte, sally, counter; informal comeback.
▷ANTONYMS question.
2 *the Chancellor's move drew an angry response from opposition MPs*: **reaction**, reply, reciprocation, retaliation; feedback; informal comeback.

responsibility noun **1** *it was his responsibility to find witnesses*: **duty**, task, function, job, role, place, charge, business, onus, burden, liability, accountability, answerability, province; Brit. informal pigeon.
2 *the organization denied responsibility for the bomb attack at the airport*: **blame**, fault, guilt, culpability, blameworthiness, liability.
3 *teenagers may not be showing enough sense of responsibility to be safely granted privileges*: **trustworthiness**, level-headedness, rationality, sanity, reason, reasonableness, sense, common sense, stability, maturity, adultness, reliability, dependability, competence.
4 *we train those staff who show an aptitude for managerial responsibility*: **authority**, control, power, leadership, management, influence; duty.

responsible adjective **1** *the Home Office is* ***responsible for*** *prisons*: **in charge of**, in control of, at the helm of, accountable for, liable for, charged with; (**be responsible for**) **manage**, oversee, superintend, supervise, conduct, run, look after, organize, produce, see to.
2 *those* ***responsible for*** *the mistake have been dealt with*: **accountable**, answerable, to blame; behind, at the bottom of, guilty of, culpable of; blameworthy, at fault, in the wrong.
▷ANTONYMS guiltless.
3 *Margaret holds a responsible position in marketing*: **important**, powerful, authoritative, executive, decision-making, high.
▷ANTONYMS lowly.
4 *he is* ***responsible to*** *the president*: **answerable**, accountable; supervised by, managed by.
5 *Mr Smith is likely to prove a respectable and responsible tenant*: **trustworthy**, capable of being trusted, trusty, level-headed, rational, sane, reasonable, sensible, sound, stable, mature, adult; reliable, dependable, conscientious.
▷ANTONYMS irresponsible, untrustworthy.

responsive adjective *the industry must become more responsive to consumer needs*: **quick to react**, reactive, receptive, open to suggestions, amenable, flexible, accessible, approachable, forthcoming, sensitive, perceptive, sympathetic, well disposed, susceptible, impressionable, open, alive, awake, aware.
▷ANTONYMS apathetic, insensitive.

rest[1] verb **1** *he needed to rest and think*: **relax**, take a rest, ease up/off, let up, slow down, pause, have/take a break, unbend, repose, laze, idle, loaf, do nothing, take time off, slack off, unwind, recharge one's batteries, be at leisure, take it easy, sit back, sit down, stand down, lounge, luxuriate, loll, slump, flop, put one's feet up, lie down, go to bed, have/take a nap, nap, catnap, doze, have/take a siesta, drowse, sleep; informal de-stress, take five, have/take a breather, veg out, snooze, snatch forty winks, get some shut-eye; Brit. informal kip, have a kip, get some kip; N. Amer. informal chill out, kick back, catch some Zs; literary slumber.
2 *his hands rested on the small rucksack he carried*: **lie**, be laid, recline, repose, be, be placed, be positioned; be supported by, be propped up by.
3 *she rested her basket on the ground*: **support**, prop (up), steady, balance, lean, lay, set, sit, stand, position, place, put.
4 *the film script* ***rests on*** *an improbable premise*: **be based on**, be grounded in, be founded on, depend on, be dependent on, rely on, hinge on, turn on, hang on, pivot on, be contingent on, revolve around, centre on.
▶ noun **1** *get some rest, or you won't be fit for tomorrow | Robbie was ready for a rest and some food*: **repose**, relaxation, leisure, ease, inactivity, respite, time off, time out, breathing space; **sleep**; **period of relaxation**, period of repose, nap, doze, siesta; informal shut-eye, snooze, lie-down, forty winks; Brit. informal kip; literary slumber.
2 *I was in need of a short rest from work*: **holiday**, vacation, recess; break, breathing space, pause, interval, interlude, intermission; time off, time out; informal breather.
3 *she took the poker from its rest*: **stand**, base, holder, support, stay, prop, brace, rack, hook, frame, shelf, bracket, trestle, tripod, plinth, pedestal, foundation, bed, foot, substructure.
4 *our landing was cushioned by the snow, and we came to rest 100 metres lower*: **a standstill**, a halt, a stop; stationary.

rest[2] noun *only the chairman has been elected—the rest are appointees*: **remainder**, residue, balance, remaining part/number/quantity, part/number/quantity (that is) left over, others, those left, remains, remnant, remnants, rump, surplus, difference, extra, excess, superfluity, overflow, overspill, additional people/material/things, extra people/material/things; technical residuum.
▶ verb *you may rest assured that he is there*: **remain**, continue to be, stay, keep, persist in being, carry on being, go on being.

restaurant noun **eating place**, eating house; informal eatery.

restful adjective *I hope you have had a restful weekend*: **relaxed**, relaxing, quiet, calm, calming, tranquil, soothing, peaceful, placid, reposeful, comfortable, leisurely, easy-going, undisturbed, free from disturbance/interruption/interference, untroubled, unhurried.
▷ANTONYMS exciting, noisy.

> *Word toolkit* **restful**
>
> See **sleepy**.

restitution noun **1** *the claims were for restitution of land allegedly seized by the occupying power*: **return**, restoration, handing back, replacement, surrender, yielding, recovery.
▷ANTONYMS seizure, occupation.
2 *he was ordered to pay $50,000 in restitution for the damage caused*: **compensation**, recompense, reparation, damages, indemnification, indemnity, reimbursement, repayment, remuneration, reward, redress, satisfaction; quid pro quo; archaic guerdon, meed; rare solatium.

restive adjective **1** *I haven't done anything about supper—Edward will be getting restive*: **restless**, fidgety, edgy, on edge, tense, uneasy, ill at ease, worked up, nervous, agitated, anxious, on tenterhooks, keyed up, apprehensive, unquiet, impatient; Brit. nervy; informal jumpy, jittery, twitchy, uptight, wired, like a cat on a hot tin roof; Brit. informal like a cat on hot bricks.
▷ANTONYMS calm.
2 *the militants are increasingly restive*: **unruly**, disorderly, out of control, uncontrollable, unmanageable, ungovernable, unbiddable, disobedient, defiant, up in arms, wilful, recalcitrant, refractory, insubordinate, disaffected, dissentious, riotous; **rebellious**, mutinous, seditious, insurgent, insurrectionary, insurrectionist, revolutionary; Brit. informal bolshie; archaic contumacious.
▷ANTONYMS biddable, peaceable.

restless adjective **1** *she was restless, moving uneasily about the hut*: **uneasy**, ill at ease, restive, fidgety, edgy, on edge, tense, worked up, nervous, agitated, anxious, on tenterhooks, keyed up, apprehensive, unquiet, impatient; Brit. nervy; informal jumpy, jittery, twitchy, uptight, wired, like a cat on a hot tin roof; Brit. informal like a cat on hot bricks.
▷ANTONYMS calm.
2 *he had spent a restless night*: **sleepless**, wakeful, insomniac; fitful, broken,

r

disturbed, troubled, unsettled, uncomfortable; tossing and turning; archaic watchful; rare insomnolent.
▷ANTONYMS peaceful.

restlessness noun 1 *at lunch there was an odd restlessness among his pupils*: **unease**, restiveness, fidgetiness, edginess, tenseness, nervousness, agitation, anxiety, fretfulness, discomposure, jitteriness, apprehension, unquietness, disquiet, disquietude, impatience.
▷ANTONYMS calm.
2 *a walk outside might help night restlessness*: **sleeplessness**, insomnia, wakefulness; archaic watchfulness.
▷ANTONYMS repose, sleep.

restoration noun 1 *an opposition rally demanded the restoration of democracy*: **reinstatement**, reinstitution, re-establishment, reimposition, reinstallation, rehabilitation, return, putting back, replacing.
▷ANTONYMS abolition.
2 *the restoration of derelict housing*: **repair**, repairing, fixing, mending, refurbishment, reconditioning, rehabilitation, rebuilding, reconstruction, remodelling, redecoration, revamping, revamp, makeover, overhaul; redevelopment, renovation, modernization, updating, bringing up to date; upgrading, gentrification; informal facelift; N. Amer. informal rehab.
▷ANTONYMS neglect.

restore verb 1 *his aim was to restore democracy in the country*: **reinstate**, put back, replace, bring back, reinstitute, reimpose, reinstall, rehabilitate, re-establish, return to a former position/state.
▷ANTONYMS abolish.
2 *we'll try to restore it to its rightful owner*: **return**, give back, hand back, take back, remit.
▷ANTONYMS keep.
3 *the building has been carefully restored*: **repair**, fix, mend, refurbish, recondition, rehabilitate, rebuild, reconstruct, remodel, redecorate, revamp, make over, overhaul; put back into its original condition; redevelop, renovate, modernize, update, bring up to date; upgrade, gentrify; refit, re-equip, refurnish; N. Amer. bring up to code; informal do up, fix up, give a facelift to; N. Amer. informal rehab.
▷ANTONYMS neglect.
4 *sleep can be just as effective in restoring us physically*: **reinvigorate**, revitalize, revive, refresh, energize, reanimate, resuscitate, brace, fortify, strengthen, give new strength to, build up, revivify, rejuvenate, regenerate, renew, breathe new life into, enliven, stimulate, freshen.

restrain verb 1 *Charles restrained his anger*: **control**, keep under control, check, hold/keep in check, curb, suppress, repress, contain, keep within bounds, limit, regulate, restrict, moderate, dampen, put a brake on, subdue, smother, choke back, stifle, bridle, leash, bit, muzzle, bottle up, cork, rein back, rein in, keep in; informal keep the lid on.
▷ANTONYMS provoke, encourage.
2 *she had to* ***restrain*** *herself* ***from*** *slamming the receiver down*: **prevent**, stop, keep, hold back; hinder, impede, hamper, restrict, constrain, obstruct; archaic hold.
▷ANTONYMS force.
3 Law *a court could* ***restrain*** *a doctor* ***from*** *continuing treatment*: **prohibit**, ban, bar, disallow, interdict; forbid, veto, proscribe; Law enjoin.
▷ANTONYMS compel, encourage.
4 *the insane used to be restrained with straitjackets*: **tie up**, bind, strap, truss, pinion, lash, tether, chain (up), fetter, shackle, manacle, put in irons, handcuff.

restrained adjective 1 *compared with her exuberant father, Julie was quite restrained*: **self-controlled**, controlled, self-restrained, moderate, not given to excesses, sober, steady, phlegmatic, unemotional, inhibited, undemonstrative, unassuming, quiet, calm, thoughtful, reticent, discreet, guarded.
▷ANTONYMS immoderate, emotional.
2 *the restrained elegance of their new floral wallpapers*: **muted**, soft, pale, subdued, discreet, subtle, quiet, unobtrusive, unostentatious, understated, artistic, tasteful, graceful.
▷ANTONYMS garish, loud, extravagant.

restraint noun 1 *he acts as a restraint on their impulsiveness*: **constraint**, check, control, restriction, limitation, curtailment; rein, bridle, brake, damper, deterrent, hindrance, impediment, obstacle, retardant, inhibition; informal clampdown, wet blanket.
▷ANTONYMS incitement.
2 *the customary restraint of the British police*: **self-control**, self-restraint, self-discipline, control, moderation, temperateness, abstemiousness, non-indulgence, prudence, judiciousness.
▷ANTONYMS abandon.
3 *the dining room has been decorated with commendable restraint*: **subtlety**, mutedness, understatedness, taste, tastefulness, delicacy, delicateness, discretion, discrimination.
▷ANTONYMS excess, indulgence.
4 *her restraint puts people off*: **reserve**, self-restraint, self-control, self-possession, lack of emotion, sobriety, coldness, formality, aloofness, detachment, reticence, uncommunicativeness.
▷ANTONYMS forwardness, outspokenness.
5 *a warrant for the release of the person under restraint*: **confinement**, captivity, custody, detention, imprisonment, internment, incarceration, constraint, committal, quarantine, arrest; archaic duress; rare detainment.
6 *children must wear an approved child restraint*: **belt**, harness, strap.

restrict verb 1 *a busy working life restricted his leisure activities*: **limit**, set/impose limits on, keep within bounds, keep under control, regulate, control, moderate, cut down on.
2 *the cuff supports the ankle without restricting movement*: **hinder**, interfere with, impede, hamper, obstruct, block, slow, check, curb, retard, handicap, straitjacket, tie, cramp.
3 *he managed to* ***restrict himself to*** *a 15-minute speech*: **confine**, limit; make do with only, be happy with.

restricted adjective 1 *this may be the result of cramming so much into a restricted space*: **cramped**, confined, constricted, small, narrow, compact, tight, poky, minimal, sparse, inadequate; archaic strait; rare incommodious.
▷ANTONYMS roomy.
2 *people on a restricted calorie intake*: **limited**, controlled, regulated; reduced, curbed; moderate, modest; deficient.
▷ANTONYMS unlimited, unrestricted.
3 *she parked in a restricted zone*: **out of bounds**, off limits; private, closed off, regulated; secret, top secret, privy, classified; exclusive, reserved, privileged; informal hush-hush.
▷ANTONYMS unrestricted, public.

restriction noun 1 *there will be no restriction on the number of places available*: **limitation**, limit, constraint, control, check, curb; regulation, condition, provision, proviso, stipulation, requirement, qualification, demarcation, rider, strings.
2 *the restriction of personal freedom*: **reduction**, limitation, diminution, curtailment, cutback, cut, scaling down.
3 *the infection led to restriction of eye movement*: **hindrance**, impediment, hampering, blocking, slowing, handicapping, straitjacket, reduction, limitation; interference with.

result noun 1 *stress is often the result of overwork*: **consequence**, outcome, upshot, out-turn, sequel, effect, reaction, repercussion, reverberation, ramification, end, conclusion, termination, culmination, corollary, concomitant, aftermath, fruit(s), product, produce, by-product; Medicine sequelae; informal pay-off; dated issue; archaic success.
▷ANTONYMS cause.
2 *the result of this addition*: **answer**, solution, calculation; sum, total, aggregate, product, quotient.
3 *his exam results*: **mark**, score, percentage, grade, grading, rating, place, placing, position, rank, ranking; assessment, appraisal, evaluation.
4 *he was dissatisfied with the result of the recent trial*: **verdict**, decision, outcome, conclusion, opinion, determination, judgement, adjudication, arbitration, findings, ruling, pronouncement, decree, settlement, order.
▶ verb 1 *differences between species could result from differences in their habitat*: **follow**, ensue, develop, stem, spring, arise, derive, evolve, proceed, emerge, emanate, issue, flow; occur, happen, take place, come about, supervene; be caused by, be brought about by, be produced by, originate in, attend, accompany, be consequent on; Philosophy supervene on.
▷ANTONYMS cause.
2 *the shooting* ***resulted in*** *the deaths of five people*: **end in**, culminate in, finish in, terminate in, involve, lead to, prompt, elicit, precipitate, trigger, spark off, provoke; **cause**, bring about, occasion, effect, bring to pass, create, give rise to, produce, engender, generate, induce; formal redound to; literary beget.

resume verb 1 *the government agreed to resume negotiations*: **restart**, recommence, begin again, start again, reopen; take up again, renew, reinstitute, return to, continue with, carry on with; proceed with, go on with, push on with, pick up where one left off.
▷ANTONYMS suspend, abandon.
2 *the priest quietly resumed his kneeling posture*: **return to**, come back to, take up again, reoccupy, occupy again.
▷ANTONYMS leave.
3 *the seller can resume possession of the goods*: **take back**, recover, take up again, assume again, re-establish.
▷ANTONYMS renounce.

résumé noun 1 *this is a brief résumé of the problems*: **summary**, precis, synopsis, abstract, outline, summarization, summation; abridgement, digest, condensation, abbreviation, survey, overview, rundown, run-through, review, sketch; French tour d'horizon; N. Amer. wrap-up; Law headnote, brief; rare conspectus, summa, epitome, compendium.
2 N. Amer. *a few Saturdays in a veterinary hospital might look great on her résumé*: **CV**, life history, biography, details; Latin **curriculum vitae**; N. Amer. vita, bio.

resumption noun *the minister called for a resumption of negotiations*: **restart**, restarting, recommencement, reopening, reinstitution; continuation, carrying on, taking up again, renewal, return to.
▷ANTONYMS suspension, abandonment.

resurgence noun *there has been a resurgence of interest in jazz*: **renewal**, revival, recovery, rally, upturn, comeback, reinvigoration, reawakening,

r

resurrection, reappearance, re-emergence, rejuvenation, regeneration, new birth, rebirth, renaissance, new dawn, new beginning; **resumption**, recommencement, continuation, re-establishment; Italian risorgimento; rare renascence, recrudescence, rejuvenescence.

resurrect verb **1** *on the third day Jesus was resurrected*: **raise from the dead**, restore to life, bring back to life, revive.
2 *it gives him a chance to resurrect his career*: **revive**, restore, regenerate, revitalize, breathe new life into, give the kiss of life to, give a new lease of life to, reinvigorate, renew, resuscitate, awaken, wake up, rejuvenate, stimulate, re-establish, relaunch; archaic renovate.

resurrection noun **1** *the resurrection of Jesus*: **raising from the dead**, restoration to life; rising from the dead, return from the dead.
2 *the promised resurrection of the cottage hospital*: **revival**, restoration, regeneration, revitalization, reinvigoration, renewal, resuscitation, awakening, rejuvenation, stimulation, re-establishment, relaunch, reintroduction, reinstallation, reappearance, rebirth, renaissance, renascence, comeback.

resuscitate verb **1** *medics tried to resuscitate him*: **bring round**, revive, bring back, bring (back) to life, bring someone (back) to their senses, bring back to consciousness, rescue, save, bring back from the edge of death; give artificial respiration to, give the kiss of life to, give cardiac massage to, defibrillate.
2 *measures to resuscitate the economy*: **revive**, resurrect, restore, regenerate, revitalize, breathe new life into, give the kiss of life to, give a new lease of life to, reinvigorate, renew, awaken, wake up, rejuvenate, stimulate, re-establish, relaunch; archaic renovate.

retain verb **1** *the government retained a minority share in the privatized industries*: **keep**, keep possession of, keep hold of, hold on to, hold fast to, keep back, hang on to, cling to; literary cleave to.
▷ANTONYMS give up, lose.
2 *existing footpaths are to be retained*: **maintain**, keep, continue, preserve, reserve, conserve, perpetuate, cherish.
▷ANTONYMS abolish, discontinue, alter.
3 *some students retain facts easily*: **remember**, memorize, keep in one's mind, keep in one's memory; **learn**, learn by heart, get by heart, commit to memory, get off pat, learn by rote, impress on the memory, become word-perfect in; **recall**, call to mind, recollect, think of, succeed in remembering; archaic con.
▷ANTONYMS forget.
4 *the solicitor will retain a barrister when necessary*: **employ**, commission, contract, pay, keep on the payroll, have in employment; **hire**, engage, appoint, recruit, put on the payroll, secure the services of, sign on, sign up, take on, take into one's employ.
▷ANTONYMS dismiss.

retainer noun **1** *you're paid a retainer every month to keep me informed*: **retaining fee**, fee, periodic payment, partial payment, deposit, advance, subscription, standing charge.
2 *a faithful family retainer*: **attendant**, follower, servant, hireling, hanger-on, escort, minion, lackey, flunkey, vassal, dependant, domestic, valet, footman.

retaliate verb *they could torment him without his being able to retaliate*: **fight back**, strike back, hit back, respond, react, reply, reciprocate, counterattack, return fire, return the compliment, put up a fight, take the bait, rise to the bait, return like for like, get back at someone, get, give tit for tat, give as good as one gets, let someone see how it feels, give someone a dose/taste of their own medicine; **have/get/take one's revenge**, take/exact/wreak revenge, be revenged, revenge oneself, avenge oneself, take reprisals, get even, even the score, settle a/the score, settle accounts, pay someone back (in their own coin), pay someone out, repay someone, exact retribution, take an eye for an eye (and a tooth for a tooth); informal give someone their comeuppance; Brit. informal get one's own back; rare give someone a Roland for an Oliver.
▷ANTONYMS turn the other cheek.

retaliation noun *the bombing was in retaliation for a rebel raid on two border villages*: **revenge**, vengeance, reprisal, retribution, requital, recrimination, an eye for an eye (and a tooth for a tooth), getting even, redress, repayment, payback; **response**, reaction, reply, reciprocation, counterattack, counterstroke, comeback, tit for tat, measure for measure, blow for blow; Latin lex talionis; rare ultion, a Roland for an Oliver.

retard verb *the worst thing that governments can do is to retard this admittedly painful process*: **delay**, **slow down**, slow up, hold back, set back, keep back, hold up, postpone, put back, detain, decelerate, put a brake on; **hinder**, hamper, obstruct, inhibit, impede, handicap, hamstring, curb, check, restrain, restrict, arrest, interfere with, interrupt, encumber, clog; Brit. informal throw a spanner in the works of; N. Amer. informal throw a monkey wrench in the works of; literary stay, trammel, cumber.
▷ANTONYMS accelerate, expedite.

retch verb **1** *he was sick in the road and stayed there for several minutes, retching*: **gag**, heave, dry-heave, reach, convulse, almost vomit, have nausea, feel nauseous; informal keck.
2 *he retched all over the table*: **vomit**, cough up, bring something up, regurgitate; Brit. be sick; N. Amer. get sick; informal puke (something up), chunder, chuck up, hurl, spew, do the technicolor yawn; Brit. informal honk, sick something up; Scottish informal boke; N. Amer. informal spit up, barf, upchuck, toss one's cookies.

reticence noun *she overcame her usual reticence and talked about their married life*: **reserve**, introversion, restraint, inhibition, diffidence, shyness, modesty, distance, undemonstrativeness; **uncommunicativeness**, unresponsiveness, quietness, taciturnity, silence, secretiveness, secrecy.
▷ANTONYMS expansiveness.

reticent adjective *Smith was extremely reticent about his personal affairs*: **reserved**, withdrawn, introverted, restrained, inhibited, diffident, shy, modest, unassuming, shrinking, distant, undemonstrative, wouldn't say boo to a goose; **uncommunicative**, unforthcoming, unresponsive, tight-lipped, close-mouthed, close-lipped, quiet, taciturn, silent, guarded, secretive, private, playing one's cards close to one's chest; informal mum.
▷ANTONYMS expansive, garrulous.

retinue noun *Sir James ordered one of his retinue to stable the horses*: **entourage**, escort, company, court, attendant company, staff, personnel, household, cortège, train, suite, following, bodyguard; aides, associates, members of court, companions, attendants, servants, retainers, followers, camp followers, hangers-on; informal groupies; archaic rout.

retire verb **1** *he retired two years ago*: **give up work**, stop working, stop work; reach retirement age.
2 *we've retired him on full pension*: **pension off**, force to retire, force to give up work; informal put out to grass.
3 *Gillian retired to her own office*: **go off**, **withdraw**, go away, go out, exit, make an exit, take oneself off, depart, decamp, adjourn, leave for; shut oneself away in, absent oneself; literary betake oneself; formal repair.
4 *every diplomatic effort was made to get him and his army to retire*: **retreat**, withdraw, pull back, fall back, pull out, disengage, back off, give way, give ground, flee, take flight, turn tail, beat a (hasty) retreat.
▷ANTONYMS advance.
5 *everyone retired early that night*: **go to bed**, go to one's room, call it a day, go to sleep; informal turn in, hit the hay, hit the sack.

retired adjective *Thomas is a retired schoolteacher*: **former**, ex-, emeritus, past, in retirement, pensioned, pensioned off; superannuated, elderly.
▸ noun (**the retired**) *a development of apartments for the retired*: **retired people**, pensioners, old-age pensioners, OAPs, senior citizens, old people, the elderly; N. Amer. seniors, retirees; rare retirers, pensionaries.

retirement noun **1** *they are just coming up to retirement*: **giving up work**, stopping working, stopping work; Scottish retiral.
2 *he spent nearly the whole of his retirement there*: **life after one retires**, retired years, post-work years.
3 *life in retirement in an English village*: **seclusion**, retreat, solitude, loneliness, isolation, privacy, obscurity.

retiring adjective **1** *a cut-glass bowl was presented to the retiring president*: **departing**, outgoing.
▷ANTONYMS incoming.
2 *he was such a quiet, retiring man*: **shy**, diffident, bashful, self-effacing, shrinking, unassuming, unassertive, reserved, reticent, quiet, timid, timorous, nervous, modest, demure, coy, meek, humble; private, secret, secretive, withdrawn, reclusive, unsociable; rare seclusive, eremitic, eremitical, hermitic, anchoritic.
▷ANTONYMS bold, outgoing.

retort verb *'Oh, sure,' she retorted*: **answer**, reply, respond, say in response, acknowledge, return, counter, rejoin, riposte, retaliate, hurl back, fling back, snap back; round on someone, come back.
▸ noun *he wanted to make some sarcastic retort about her being bossy*: **answer**, reply, response, acknowledgement, return, counter, rejoinder, riposte, sally, retaliation; informal comeback.

retract verb **1** *the sea otter can retract the claws on its front feet*: **pull in**, draw in, pull back, sheathe, put away.
▷ANTONYMS extend.
2 *he apologized and retracted his allegation*: **take back**, withdraw, unsay, recant, disown, disavow, disclaim, abjure, repudiate, renounce, reverse, revoke, rescind, annul, cancel, go back on, backtrack on, do a U-turn on; eat one's words; Brit. do an about-turn on.
▷ANTONYMS assert, confirm.

retreat verb **1** *the army retreated*: **withdraw**, retire, draw back, pull back, pull out, fall back, give way, give ground, recoil, flee, take flight, beat a retreat, beat a hasty retreat, run away, run off, make a run for it, run for it, make off, take off, take to one's heels, make a break for it, bolt, make a quick exit, clear out, make one's getaway, escape, head for the hills; informal beat it, vamoose, skedaddle, split, cut and run, leg it, show a clean pair of heels, turn tail, scram, hook it, fly the coop, skip off, do a fade; Brit. informal do a runner, scarper, do a bunk; N. Amer. informal light out, bug out, cut out, peel out, take a powder, skidoo; Austral. informal go through, shoot through; archaic fly, levant.
▷ANTONYMS advance; dig in.
2 *the tide was retreating*: **go out**, ebb, recede, flow out, fall, go down.
▷ANTONYMS come in.
3 *the government had to retreat over the plan*: **change one's decision**,

r

change one's mind, change one's attitude, change one's plans; **back down**, climb down, do a U-turn, backtrack, back-pedal, retract, reconsider, eat one's words, eat humble pie, give in, concede defeat, shift one's ground; Brit. do an about-turn.
▶ noun **1** *a counteroffensive caused the retreat of the imperial army*: **withdrawal**, pulling back, flight; rare katabasis.
▷ANTONYMS advance.
2 *Democrats welcomed the President's retreat on the tax issue*: **climbdown**, backdown, retraction, concession, about-face, U-turn; Brit. about-turn.
3 *she invited us to her retreat in rural Sweden*: **refuge**, haven, resort, asylum, sanctuary, sanctum sanctorum; hideaway, hideout, hiding place; cottage, dacha, shelter, cabin, den, lair, nest; informal hidey-hole.
4 *a period of retreat from the world for spiritual regeneration*: **seclusion**, withdrawal, retirement, solitude, isolation, hiding, privacy, sanctuary; rare sequestration, reclusion.

retrench verb **1** *not all the directors wanted to retrench*: **economize**, cut back, make cutbacks, make savings, make economies, reduce expenditure, be economical, be sparing, be frugal, budget, tighten one's belt, husband one's resources, draw in one's horns, save, scrimp and save, cut corners.
2 *welfare services will have to be retrenched*: **reduce**, cut, cut back, cut down, cut back on, pare, pare down, slim down, bring down, make reductions in, make cutbacks in, trim, prune, whittle away/down, take off, decrease, lower, lessen, shorten, curtail, truncate, shrink, diminish, minimize; informal slash, axe.

retribution noun *the assassins were cornered, awaiting inevitable retribution*: **punishment**, penalty, nemesis, fate, doom, one's just deserts, due reward, just reward, wages; **justice**, retributive justice, poetic justice, judgement, reckoning; **revenge**, reprisal, requital, retaliation, payback, vengeance, an eye for an eye (and a tooth for a tooth), tit for tat, measure for measure; **redress**, reparation, restitution, recompense, repayment, damages, satisfaction, remedy, comeback, atonement, amends; informal one's comeuppance; archaic measure.

retrieve verb **1** *we made a laborious descent to retrieve our skis*: **get back**, recover, regain (possession of), win back, recoup, reclaim, repossess, redeem, have returned; salvage, rescue, fetch, bring back; Law replevy; rare recuperate.
2 *they were working hard to retrieve the situation*: **put right**, set right, set to rights, put to rights, rectify, remedy, restore, solve, sort out, straighten out, resolve, deal with, correct, repair, mend, fix, redress, make good; improve, amend, ameliorate, make better, better.

retro adjective *a retro restaurant with a Fifties-style lunch counter*: **in period style**, period, nostalgic, evocative, of yesteryear, olde worlde; dated, old-fashioned, backward-looking, retrogressive, out of date, passé.

retrograde adjective **1** *the closure of the factory is a retrograde step*: **for the worse**, regressive, negative, downhill, unwelcome, unprogressive; worsening, deteriorating, degenerate, declining.
▷ANTONYMS positive, forward-looking.
2 *the retrograde motion of the planets*: **backward**, backwards, reverse, rearward, directed backwards, retreating, retrogressive.
▷ANTONYMS forward.

retrospect noun
□ **in retrospect** looking back, thinking back, on reflection, on re-examination, in/with hindsight.

retrospective adjective *the Government introduced retrospective legislation to change the rules*: **backdated**, retroactive, ex post facto, backward-looking.

return verb **1** *he returned to London*: **go back**, **come back**, get back, arrive back, arrive home, come home, come again.
▷ANTONYMS depart, set out.
2 *the symptoms returned after a few days*: **happen again**, recur, reoccur, occur again, be repeated, repeat (itself), come round (again); **reappear**, appear again, flare up; rare recrudesce.
▷ANTONYMS disappear.
3 *he would have to return the money he had been given*: **give back**, send back, hand back, take back, carry back; pay back, repay, remit.
▷ANTONYMS keep; throw away.
4 *Peter returned the book to its place on the shelf*: **restore**, put back, replace, reinstate, reinstall.
5 *he just managed to return the volley*: **hit back**, send back; throw back.
▷ANTONYMS miss.
6 *the party faithful welcomed her, and she returned the compliment*: **reciprocate**, requite, feel/give in return, repay, send/give in response, give back; match, equal; wish someone the same.
▷ANTONYMS ignore.
7 *'Later,' returned Isabel coldly*: **answer**, reply, respond, say in response; acknowledge, counter, rejoin, riposte, retort, retaliate, hurl back, fling back, snap back; round on someone; N. Amer. come back.
8 *the jury returned a unanimous verdict*: **deliver**, bring in, hand down, render, submit, announce, pronounce, proclaim.
9 *the club returned a small profit*: **yield**, bring in, earn, make, realize, secure, net, gross, clear, pay out, fetch, pocket.
10 *the official Labour candidate was returned with 53% of the vote*: **elect**, vote in, put in power, choose, opt for, select, pick, adopt.
▶ noun **1** *failing health forced his return to Paris*: **homecoming**, travel back.
▷ANTONYMS departure.
2 *a buffer against the return of hard times*: **recurrence**, reoccurrence, repeat, rerun, repetition; reappearance, flare-up; revival, rebirth, renaissance, resurrection, reawakening, re-emergence, resurgence; rare recrudescence, renascence.
▷ANTONYMS disappearance.
3 *I displayed notices requesting the return of books*: **giving back**, handing back, replacement, restoration, reinstatement, reinstallation, restitution; rare reinstalment.
4 *it might be worth checking with the box office for returns*: **returned item**, unsold item, unwanted item/ticket, reject, exchange.
5 *two returns to London, please*: **return ticket/fare**; N. Amer. round trip ticket/fare.
▷ANTONYMS single.
6 *the company hoped for a quick return on its investment*: **yield**, profit, returns, gain, income, revenue, interest, dividend, percentage; Brit. informal bunce.
7 *a census return*: **statement**, report, submission, account, paper, record, file, dossier, write-up, data, information, log, journal, diary, register, summary; document, form.
□ **in return for** *they were offered a reduction of their prison sentences in return for confessions to crimes*: **in exchange for**, in consideration of; in response to, as a reward for, against, as a compensation for.

revamp verb *they plan to revamp the kitchen*: **renovate**, redecorate, refurbish, recondition, rehabilitate, rebuild, reconstruct, overhaul, make over; **modernize**, update, bring up to date, renew; improve, upgrade; refit, re-equip, refurnish; brighten up, freshen up, spruce up; remodel, refashion, redesign, restyle, rejig, rework, redo, remould, reorganize; N. Amer. bring up to code; informal do up, fix up, give something a facelift, vamp up; Brit. informal tart up; N. Amer. informal rehab.

reveal verb **1** *for operational reasons the police can't reveal his whereabouts*: **divulge**, disclose, tell, let out, let slip, let drop, let fall, give away, give the game/show away, blurt (out), babble, give out, release, leak, betray, open up, unveil, bring out into the open; go public on/with, make known, make public, bring to public notice/attention, broadcast, air, publicize, publish, circulate, disseminate, pass on, report, declare, post, communicate, impart, unfold, vouchsafe; **confess**, admit, lay bare; informal let on, spill, blab, let the cat out of the bag, dish the dirt, take/blow the lid off, blow wide open, come clean about; Brit. informal cough, blow the gaff; archaic discover.
▷ANTONYMS hide, conceal.
2 *he let the garage door slide up to reveal a new car*: **show**, display, exhibit, disclose, uncover, expose to view, allow to be seen, put on display, put on show, put on view, bare; literary uncloak, unclothe; rare unclose.
▷ANTONYMS hide.
3 *the data can be used to reveal a good deal about the composition of Anglo-Norman households*: **bring to light**, uncover, turn up, expose to view, lay bare, unearth, dig up, excavate, unveil, unmask, detect, betray, be evidence of, indicate, demonstrate, manifest, evince, make clear, make plain; literary uncloak.

revel verb **1** *with their exams out of the way they revelled all night*: **celebrate**, make merry, have a party, party, feast, {eat, drink, and be merry}, carouse, roister, have fun, have a good time, enjoy oneself, go on a spree; informal live it up, whoop it up, have a fling, have a ball, make whoopee, rave, paint the town red; Brit. informal push the boat out; dated spree.
▷ANTONYMS mourn.
2 *he* **revelled in** *the applause which greeted him*: **enjoy**, delight in, love, like, adore, be entertained by, be amused by, be pleased by, take pleasure in, appreciate, relish, lap up, savour, luxuriate in, bask in, wallow in, glory in; **gloat over**, feel self-satisfied about, crow about; informal get a kick out of, get a thrill out of.
▷ANTONYMS hate.
▶ noun *there are a few spots in town for night revels*: **celebration**, festivity, jollification, merrymaking, carousal, carouse, spree, debauch, bacchanal; **party**, jamboree; informal rave, shindig, bash, jag; Brit. informal do, rave-up, knees-up, jolly, thrash, beano, beanfeast; Irish informal hooley, crack; N. Amer. informal wingding, blast; Austral. informal shivoo, rage, ding, jollo.

revelation noun **1** *Washington has been rocked by the further revelation that the alleged killer is a respected economist*: **disclosure**, surprising fact, divulgence, declaration, utterance, announcement, report, news, leak, avowal; acknowledgement, admission, confession.
2 *the plot hinges on the revelation of a secret*: **divulging**, divulgence, telling, disclosure, disclosing, letting slip, letting out, letting drop, giving away, giving out, leaking, leak, betrayal, unveiling, making known, making public, bringing to public notice/attention, broadcasting, airing, publicizing, publication, publishing, circulation, dissemination, passing on, proclamation, announcing, announcement, reporting, report, declaring, declaration, posting, communication, imparting, unfolding, vouchsafing; admission, confession; rare divulgation.
▷ANTONYMS keeping.

3 *new revelations of government corruption*: **uncovering**, turning up, exposure, exposing, bringing to light, unearthing, digging up, unveiling, unmasking, smoking out, detecting, detection.
▷ANTONYMS covering up.

reveller noun *residents feared disturbances from late-night revellers*: **merrymaker**, partygoer, carouser, roisterer, good-time boy/girl, pleasure seeker; archaic wassailer; rare celebrator, bacchanal, bacchant.

revelry noun *a night of beer-swilling revelry*: **celebration(s)**, partying, parties, revels, festivity/festivities, jollification, merrymaking, carousing, carousal, roistering, debauchery, frolics; informal junketing.

revenge noun **1** *she is seeking revenge for the murder of her husband*: **vengeance**, retribution, retaliation, reprisal, requital, recrimination, an eye for an eye (and a tooth for a tooth), tit for tat, measure for measure, getting even, redress, satisfaction, repayment, payback; Latin lex talionis; rare ultion.
2 *they were so filled with revenge that they shot his father*: **vengefulness**, vindictiveness, vitriol, virulence, spite, spitefulness, malice, maliciousness, malevolence, malignancy, ill will, animosity, antipathy, enmity, hostility, acrimony, venom, poison, hate, hatred, rancour, bitterness; literary revengefulness, maleficence.
▶ verb **1** *he was determined to revenge his brother's murder*: **avenge**, take/exact revenge for, make retaliation for, retaliate for, exact retribution for, take reprisals for, get redress for, get satisfaction for; requite.
2 ***I'll be revenged on*** *the whole pack of you*: **take revenge on**, exact/wreak revenge on, get one's revenge on, avenge oneself on, take vengeance on, get even with, settle a/the score with, get, pay back, pay out, retaliate on/against, take reprisals against, exact retribution on, let someone see how it feels, give someone their just deserts, give someone a dose/taste of their own medicine, give as good as one gets; give/return like for like, give tit for tat, take an eye for an eye (and a tooth for a tooth); informal give someone their comeuppance; Brit. informal get one's own back on; archaic recriminate; rare give someone a Roland for an Oliver.

revenue noun *15% of all revenue is generated by a single product*: **income**, takings, receipts, proceeds, earnings; **profit**, profits, returns, return, rewards, yield, interest, gain; Brit. informal bunce.
▷ANTONYMS outgoings, expenditure.

reverberate verb *her voice reverberated around the classroom*: **resound**, echo, re-echo, repeat, resonate, pulsate, vibrate, ring, peal, boom, rumble, roll, pound, thump, drum, thrum.

reverberation noun **1** *electronic musical instruments are totally free from any natural reverberation*: **resonance**, echo, echoing, re-echoing, resounding, pulsation, vibration, ringing, peal, boom, booming, rumble, rumbling, roll, pound, pounding, thump, thumping, drumming, thrumming.
2 (usually **reverberations**) *the scandal's political reverberations*: **repercussions**, ramifications; **consequence**, result, effect, upshot, outcome, out-turn, by-product; aftermath, fallout, backlash, ripple, shock wave.

revere verb *the president is revered as a national hero*: **respect**, **admire**, think highly of, have a high opinion of, hold in high regard, esteem, hold in (high) esteem, think much of, approve of, appreciate, cherish, value, set (great) store by, prize, treasure, look up to; **worship**, pay homage to, venerate, reverence, adulate, hold in awe, idolize, put on a pedestal, lionize, hero-worship, honour, love.
▷ANTONYMS despise.

r

reverence noun *reverence for the countryside runs deep in this intensely respectful country*: **high esteem**, high regard, great respect, acclaim, admiration, approbation, approval, appreciation, estimation, favour, recognition; **worship**, veneration, awe, homage, adoration, deference, honour, praise; liking, affection, love; Roman Catholic Church dulia.
▷ANTONYMS scorn.
▶ verb *they reverence modern jazz*: **revere**, respect, admire, think highly of, have a high opinion of, hold in high regard, esteem, hold in (high) esteem, think much of, approve of, appreciate, cherish, value, set (great) store by, prize, treasure, look up to; **worship**, pay homage to, venerate, adulate, hold in awe, idolize, put on a pedestal, lionize, hero-worship, honour, love.
▷ANTONYMS despise.

reverent adjective *there was a reverent silence*: **respectful**, reverential, worshipping, worshipful, adoring, loving, admiring, devoted, devout, dutiful, awed; deferential, submissive, humble, meek.
▷ANTONYMS irreverent, cheeky.

reverie noun *she was startled out of her reverie by a loud crash*: **daydream**, daydreaming, trance, fantasy, vision, fancy, hallucination, musing; inattention, inattentiveness, wool-gathering, preoccupation, obliviousness, engrossment, absorption, self-absorption, absent-mindedness, abstraction, lack of concentration, lack of application; Scottish dwam.

reversal noun **1** *there was to be no reversal of the British attitude*: **turnaround**, turnround, turnabout, about-face, volte-face, change of heart, U-turn, sea change, swing, shift, swerve, backtracking; Brit. about-turn; rare tergiversation.
2 *there will have to be a reversal of roles*: **swap**, **exchange**, change, swapping, trade, trading, interchange, transposition, inversion.
3 *the reversal of the decision followed intense public criticism*: **alteration**, changing; **countermanding**, undoing, setting aside, upsetting, overturning, overthrow, disallowing, overriding, overruling, veto, vetoing, repudiation, revocation, repeal, abrogation, cancellation, rescinding, rescindment, annulment, nullification, voiding, invalidation, negation, quashing; withdrawal, recanting, retraction; archaic recall; rare rescission, disannulment.
4 *a late penalty was the only reversal suffered by the New Zealanders*: **setback**, reverse, upset, check, non-success, failure, misfortune, mishap, misadventure, accident, disaster, tragedy, catastrophe, blow, disappointment, adversity, hardship, affliction, vicissitude, defeat, rout; ill luck, bad luck, distress, tribulation, woe, hard times.

reverse verb **1** *the car reversed into a lamp post*: **back**, go back/backwards, drive back/backwards, move back/backwards, send back/backwards; back-pedal.
▷ANTONYMS go forwards.
2 *you can reverse the bottle in the ice bucket to cool the wine in the neck first*: **turn upside down**, turn over, upend, upturn, put bottom up, flip over, turn topsy-turvy, invert, capsize; archaic overset.
3 *when climbing on rough rock I reverse the jacket to protect the outer layer*: **turn inside out**; technical evert, introvert, evaginate, invaginate.
4 *it may be a good idea to reverse the roles*: **swap**, swap round, change, change round, exchange, interchange, switch, switch round, trade, transpose, invert, turn about/around.
▷ANTONYMS keep to.
5 *the crowd were clamouring for the umpire to reverse the decision*: **alter**, change; **countermand**, undo, set aside, upset, overturn, overthrow, rule against, disallow, override, overrule, veto, repudiate, revoke, repeal, cancel, rescind, annul, nullify, declare null and void, void, invalidate, negate, abrogate, quash; withdraw, take back, recant, retract, back-pedal on, backtrack on, do a U-turn on; eat one's words; Brit. do an about-turn on; Law vacate; archaic recall.
▷ANTONYMS uphold, stick to.
▶ adjective **1** *I would probably have a completely reverse opinion*: **opposite**, contrary, converse, counter, inverse, obverse, opposing, contrasting, antithetical.
▷ANTONYMS same.
2 *here are the results in reverse order*: **backward**, backwards, reversed, inverted, transposed, from bottom to top.
▷ANTONYMS forwards.
▶ noun **1** *the reverse is the case*: **opposite**, contrary, converse, inverse, obverse, antithesis, opposite/other extreme.
2 *a varied picture of successes and reverses*: **setback**, reversal, upset, check, non-success, failure, misfortune, mishap, misadventure, accident, disaster, tragedy, catastrophe, blow, disappointment, adversity, hardship, affliction, vicissitude, defeat, rout; ill luck, bad luck, distress, tribulation, woe, hard times.
▷ANTONYMS success.
3 *the deadlines are listed on the reverse of this page*: **other side**, reverse side, back, rear, underside, wrong side, flip side, B-side, verso.
▷ANTONYMS front, recto.

revert verb **1** *life will soon* ***revert to*** *normal*: **return**, go back, come back, change back, retrogress, regress, default; fall back into, relapse into, lapse into, drift back into; archaic retrograde.
2 *at the end of the lease the property reverts to the landlord*: **be returned**; Law fall, escheat.

review noun **1** *the Council is to undertake a review of its property portfolio*: **analysis**, evaluation, assessment, appraisal, examination, investigation, scrutiny, enquiry, exploration, probe, inspection, study, audit; rare anatomization.
2 *the rent is due for review*: **reconsideration**, re-examination, reassessment, re-evaluation, reappraisal, moderation, rethink, another look, a fresh look; **change**, alteration, modification, revision.
3 *he began to write reviews of local stage plays*: **criticism**, critique, write-up, notice, assessment, evaluation, judgement, rating, commentary; piece, article, column; Brit. informal crit.
4 *a recent scientific review contained the following article*: **journal**, periodical, magazine, organ, publication, proceedings, annual, quarterly, monthly.
5 *the authority's latest annual review of the local economy*: **survey**, report, study, account, record, description, exposition, statement, delineation, overview, rundown, breakdown, overall picture; French compte rendu, procès-verbal; Law summing-up; Military, informal sitrep.
6 *in a traditional military review, the visiting leader inspects the soldiers up close*: **inspection**, parade, display, demonstration, field day, tattoo, array, muster, procession; Brit. march past.
▶ verb **1** *I shall first review the empirical evidence*: **survey**, study, research, consider, take stock of, analyse, audit, examine, scrutinize, enquire into, make enquiries into, explore, look into, probe, investigate, conduct investigations into, inspect, assess, appraise, size up; Law sum up; rare anatomize.
2 *the referee reviewed the decision he'd made*: **reconsider**, re-examine, reassess, re-evaluate, reappraise, moderate, rethink, think over, take

another look at, take a fresh look at, look at in a different light, have another think about; **change**, alter, modify, revise.
▷ANTONYMS stick by.
3 *once in bed, he reviewed the day*: **remember**, recall, recollect, reflect on, think through, go over in one's mind, cast one's mind back to, think back on, look back on; hark back to, call to mind, summon up, evoke.
4 *the Commander-in-Chief reviewed his troops*: **inspect**, view, scrutinize; parade, muster, march past.
5 *John Daly reviewed the novel for the Times*: **comment on**, discuss, evaluate, assess, appraise, judge, weigh up, rate, write up, critique, criticize.

reviewer noun *one reviewer remarked on the production's 'refreshing spontaneity'*: **critic**, **commentator**, connoisseur, judge, observer, pundit, analyst, arbiter.

revile verb *he was arrested and reviled as a traitor*: **criticize**, censure, condemn, attack, inveigh against, rail against, lambaste, flay, savage, brand, stigmatize, denounce; blacken someone's reputation, defame, smear, slander, libel, traduce, cast aspersions on, cast a slur on, malign, vilify, calumniate, besmirch, run down, abuse; informal knock, slam, pan, bash, take to pieces, take apart, crucify, hammer, lay into, slate, roast, skewer, bad-mouth; Brit. informal slate, rubbish, slag off, monster; N. Amer. informal pummel; Austral./NZ informal bag; rare vituperate against, excoriate.
▷ANTONYMS praise, extol.

revise verb **1** *she wasn't about to revise her opinion*: **reconsider**, review, re-examine, reassess, re-evaluate, reappraise, rethink, think over, take another look at, take a fresh look at, look at in a different light, have another think about; **change**, alter, modify, disconfirm.
▷ANTONYMS retain, confirm.
2 *the editor has completely revised the text*: **amend**, emend, correct, alter, change, adapt, edit, copy-edit, rewrite, redraft, recast, rephrase, rework, update, revamp.
▷ANTONYMS preserve.
3 Brit. *revise your lecture notes | he's revising for his exams*: **go over**, reread, run through, study, memorize; cram; informal bone up on; Brit. informal swot up (on), mug up (on), swot.

revision noun **1** *the conference called for revision of the Prayer Book*: **emendation**, correction, alteration, changing, adaptation, editing, copy-editing, rewriting, redrafting, recasting, rephrasing, reworking, updating, revamping.
2 *this revision is much more readable*: **version**, corrected version, edition, rewrite, reworking; variant, form, update, reading, rendition, adaptation.
▷ANTONYMS first edition, first draft.
3 *a major revision of the system*: **reconsideration**, review, re-examination, reassessment, re-evaluation, reappraisal, rethinking, rethink, thinking over; **change**, alteration, modification.
4 *he was doing some revision for his exam*: **rereading**, studying, memorizing, cramming; Brit. informal swotting.

revitalize verb *the plan would reduce inflation and revitalize the economy*: **reinvigorate**, re-energize, brace, fortify, strengthen, give new strength to, give a boost to, build up, bolster, prop up, help, renew, regenerate, restore, revive, revivify, rejuvenate, reanimate, resuscitate, refresh, reawaken, rekindle, put new life into, breathe new life into, enliven, stimulate, put some spark into, kick-start, uplift; informal give a shot in the arm to, pep up, buck up, get going again.
▷ANTONYMS depress.

revival noun **1** *a revival in the economy*: **improvement**, rallying, picking up, betterment, amelioration, turn for the better; advance, rally, upturn, upswing, comeback, resurgence, renewal.
▷ANTONYMS downturn.
2 *new interest has resulted in the revival of old traditional crafts*: **comeback**, bringing back, re-establishment, reintroduction, restoration, reappearance, resurrection, resuscitation, relaunch, reinstallation, regeneration, revitalization, reinvigoration, awakening, rejuvenation, stimulation, rebirth, renaissance, renascence.
▷ANTONYMS disappearance.

revive verb **1** *attempts to revive the woman failed*: **resuscitate**, bring round, bring to life, bring back, bring someone (back) to their senses, bring back to consciousness, bring back from the edge of death; rescue, save; give artificial respiration to, give the kiss of life to, give cardiac massage to, defibrillate.
2 *the man soon revived*: **regain consciousness**, recover consciousness, come round, come to life, come to one's senses, recover, awake, wake up.
3 *a cup of tea revived her*: **reinvigorate**, revitalize, refresh, energize, reanimate, resuscitate, brace, fortify, strengthen, revivify, rejuvenate, regenerate, renew, breathe new life into, enliven, stimulate, freshen.
▷ANTONYMS torpefy.
4 *the man who revived the Orient Express*: **reintroduce**, re-establish, restore, resurrect, relaunch, bring back, reinstall, regenerate, revitalize, resuscitate, breathe new life into, give a new lease of life to; reinvigorate, renew, awaken, wake up, rejuvenate, stimulate; archaic renovate.
▷ANTONYMS abolish.

revoke verb *the Board has the power to revoke the licence of a bank*: **cancel**, repeal, rescind, reverse, abrogate, annul, nullify, declare null and void, make void, void, invalidate, render invalid, quash, abolish, set aside, countermand, retract, withdraw, overrule, override; Law vacate, avoid; archaic recall; rare disannul.
▷ANTONYMS introduce, enact; ratify.

revolt verb **1** *the people revolted against colonial rule*: **rebel**, rise up, rise, take to the streets, take up arms, riot, mutiny, take part in an uprising, show resistance; resist/oppose authority, disobey/defy authority, refuse to obey orders, be insubordinate.
2 *the sight and smell revolted him*: **disgust**, sicken, nauseate, make someone sick, make someone feel sick, make someone's gorge rise, turn someone's stomach, upset, be repugnant to, repel, repulse, be repulsive to, make someone's flesh crawl, make someone shudder, put off, offend, be offensive to, cause offence to, shock, horrify; informal turn off; N. Amer. informal gross out.
▶ noun *there was an armed revolt in progress*: **rebellion**, revolution, insurrection, mutiny, uprising, riot, rioting, rising, insurgence, insurgency, coup, overthrow, seizure of power, regime change, subversion, sedition, anarchy, disorder, protest, strike, act of resistance, act of defiance; French coup d'état, jacquerie; German putsch.

revolting adjective *the sink was covered in a revolting green scum*. See **repulsive**.

revolution noun **1** *the French Revolution*: **rebellion**, revolt, insurrection, mutiny, uprising, riot, rioting, rising, insurgence, insurgency, coup, overthrow, seizure of power, regime change; subversion, sedition, anarchy, disorder, protest, strike, act of resistance, act of defiance; French coup d'état; German putsch; rare jacquerie.
2 *there has been a revolution in printing techniques*: **dramatic change**, radical change, drastic/radical alteration, complete shift, sea change, metamorphosis, transformation, conversion, innovation, breakaway; reorganization, restructuring, reformation, remodelling, rearrangement, reorientation, regrouping, redistribution; upheaval, upset, disruption, convulsions, cataclysm; informal shake-up; N. Amer. informal **shakedown**; humorous transmogrification.
3 *the prop shaft turns 4.7 times for one revolution of a road wheel*: **single turn**, turn, rotation, circle, whirl, twirl, spin, wheel, roll, round, cycle, circuit, lap.
4 *the rate of revolution of the earth*: **turning**, gyration, rotation, circumrotation, wheeling, turning around, circling, whirling, twirling, spinning, swivelling, rolling, orbital motion, orbiting, orbit; rare circumgyration.

revolutionary adjective **1** *revolutionary troops*: **rebellious**, rebel, insurgent, rioting, mutinous, mutinying, renegade, insurrectionary, seditious, factious, insubordinate, subversive; rabble-rousing, inflammatory, extremist, anarchic; rare revolting, insurrectionist.
▷ANTONYMS moderate, law-abiding.
2 *a society undergoing revolutionary change*: **thoroughgoing**, thorough, complete, total, entire, absolute, utter, comprehensive, exhaustive, sweeping, far-reaching, wide-ranging, extensive, profound; drastic, severe, serious, major, desperate, stringent, violent, forceful, rigorous, draconian.
3 *a revolutionary kind of wheelchair*: **new**, novel, original, unusual, unfamiliar, unconventional, unorthodox, different, fresh, imaginative, creative, innovative, innovatory, innovational, inventive, ingenious, modern, ultra-modern, state-of-the-art, advanced, avant-garde, futuristic, pioneering, groundbreaking, trailblazing; rare, unique, singular, unprecedented, uncommon; experimental, untested, untried, unknown, surprising, strange, exotic, out of the ordinary, newfangled; N. Amer. left-field; rare unhackneyed, new-fashioned, neoteric.
▷ANTONYMS conventional, orthodox.
▶ noun *his actions were not those of a revolutionary*: **rebel**, insurgent, revolutionist, Bolshevik, mutineer, insurrectionary, agitator, subversive, guerrilla, anarchist; freedom fighter, resistance fighter; rare insurrectionist; French, rare frondeur.

revolutionize verb *aerial photography revolutionized archaeology*: **transform**, alter dramatically, transfigure, make far-reaching changes in, shake up, stir up, turn upside down, restructure, reorganize, rejig, reform, recast, reshape, remould, transmute, metamorphose; humorous transmogrify.

revolve verb **1** *overhead, the fan revolved slowly*: **go round**, turn round, rotate, spin, whirl, pirouette, wheel.
2 *the moon revolves around the earth*: **circle**, go, travel, orbit, gyrate, circulate, loop, wheel; rare encircle.
3 *a man whose life* ***revolves around*** *cars*: **be concerned with**, be preoccupied with, be absorbed in, focus on, concentrate on, centre around, hang on, rely on, rest on, pivot on.
4 *they were revolving various thoughts in their minds*: **think about**, give thought to, consider, reflect on, mull over, contemplate, study, meditate on, muse on, think over, think on, deliberate about/on, cogitate about/on, dwell on, brood on/over, agonize over, worry about, ruminate about/on/over, chew over, puzzle over, speculate about, weigh up, review, turn over; archaic pore on.

revulsion noun *he spoke of the country's revulsion at the bombing*: **disgust**, repulsion, abhorrence, repugnance, nausea, loathing, horror, hatred, detestation, aversion, abomination, distaste, antipathy, dislike, contempt, odium; archaic disrelish; rare repellency, repellence.
▷ANTONYMS delight, liking.

reward noun **1** *the dog's owners have offered a reward for its safe return*: **recompense**, prize, prize money, winnings, purse, award, honour, decoration, profit, advantage, benefit, bonus, plus, premium; **bounty**, price; present, gift, tip, gratuity, inducement, carrot, payment, consideration, return, requital; informal pay-off, cut, perk; formal perquisite; archaic guerdon, meed.
2 *he thought his reward cruel after such loyal service*: **treatment**, handling, service, reception.
▸ verb *they were to be well rewarded for their work*: **recompense**, pay, remunerate, give a bounty to, give a present to, make something worth someone's while, tip, honour, decorate, give an award to, recognize, requite; archaic guerdon.
▷ANTONYMS punish.

rewarding adjective *pilgrims found their journey a highly rewarding experience*: **satisfying**, gratifying, pleasing, fulfilling, enriching, edifying, beneficial, illuminating, informative, worthwhile, advantageous, productive, fruitful, valuable.
▷ANTONYMS unrewarding.

reword verb *the rules were reworded in 1986*: **rewrite**, rephrase, recast, put differently, put another way, put in other words, express differently, redraft, rework, revise, edit; paraphrase.

rewrite verb *pupils are asked to rewrite a document from an opposite point of view*: **revise**, recast, rework, reword, rephrase, redraft.

rhetoric noun **1** *he was considered to excel in this form of rhetoric*: **oratory**, eloquence, power of speech, command of language, expression, way with words, delivery, diction.
2 *there is a good deal of rhetoric in this field*: **bombast**, loftiness, turgidity, grandiloquence, magniloquence, ornateness, portentousness, pomposity, boastfulness, boasting, bragging, heroics, hyperbole, extravagant language, purple prose, pompousness, sonorousness; windiness, wordiness, verbosity, prolixity; informal hot air; rare tumidity, fustian, euphuism, orotundity.

rhetorical adjective **1** *the skilful use of such rhetorical devices like metaphor*: **stylistic**, oratorical, linguistic, verbal.
2 *he had a tendency to engage in rhetorical hyperbole*: **extravagant**, grandiloquent, magniloquent, high-flown, high-sounding, sonorous, lofty, orotund, bombastic, grandiose, pompous, pretentious, overblown, oratorical, turgid, flowery, florid, declamatory, Ciceronian; informal highfalutin; rare tumid, epideictic, fustian, euphuistic, aureate, Demosthenic, Demosthenean.

rhyme noun *the words of a famous rhyme were going through her head*: **poem**, piece of poetry, verse, ditty, ode, limerick, song, jingle, verse composition, metrical composition; (**rhymes**) poetry, versification, rhyming, doggerel; rare verselet.

rhythm noun **1** *the rhythm of the rock music thumped relentlessly*: **beat**, cadence, tempo, time, pace, pulse, throb, lilt, swing; technical periodicity.
2 *poetic features such as rhythm, rhyme, and alliteration*: **metre**, measure, pattern, stress, accent, pulse, time, flow, cadence.
3 *part of the normal rhythm of daily life*: **pattern**, flow, tempo, regular features, recurrent nature.

r

rhythmic adjective *a rhythmic orchestral accompaniment*: **pulsing**, with a steady pulse, rhythmical, metrical, measured, throbbing, beating, pulsating, cadenced, lilting, repeated, periodic, regular, steady, even, paced.
▷ANTONYMS smooth, irregular.

rib noun

> *Word links* **rib**
>
> **costal** relating to ribs
> **intercostal** between ribs

ribald adjective *the more ribald the men's remarks, the faster she walked*: **bawdy**, indecent, risqué, rude, racy, broad, earthy, Rabelaisian, spicy, suggestive, titillating, improper, naughty, indelicate, indecorous, off colour, locker-room; vulgar, dirty, filthy, smutty, crude, offensive, salacious, coarse, obscene, lewd, pornographic, X-rated; informal blue, raunchy; Brit. informal fruity, near the knuckle, saucy; N. Amer. informal gamy; euphemistic adult.

ribaldry noun *not for him the slightly raucous ribaldry with which most of the chaps used to greet us*: **bawdy remarks/jokes/songs, bawdiness**, indecency, rudeness, raciness, broadness, earthiness, spiciness, suggestiveness, titillation, impropriety, naughtiness, indelicacy, indecorousness; **obscenity**, vulgarity, dirt, filth, filthiness, smut, smuttiness, crudeness, salaciousness, coarseness, lewdness, pornography; informal blueness, raunchiness; Brit. informal fruitiness, sauciness; rare bawdry, salacity.

rich adjective **1** *rich people pay higher rates of tax*: **wealthy**, affluent, moneyed, well off, well-to-do, with deep pockets, prosperous, opulent, substantial, propertied; N. Amer. silk-stocking; informal rolling in money, rolling in it, in the money, loaded, stinking rich, filthy rich, well heeled, flush, made of money, quids in, worth a packet, worth a bundle, on easy street; informal, dated oofy.
▷ANTONYMS poor.
2 *the castle houses rich furnishings and tapestries*: **sumptuous**, opulent, luxurious, luxury, de luxe, palatial, lavish, lavishly appointed, gorgeous, splendid, magnificent, resplendent, lush, plush, costly, expensive, upmarket, fancy, stylish, elegant, exquisite, grandiose; informal posh, ritzy, swanky, plushy, classy, glitzy; Brit. informal swish; N. Amer. informal swank; rare palatian, Lucullan.
▷ANTONYMS plain, austere, cheap.
3 *the walled garden was already **rich in** spring flowers*: **abounding in**, well provided with, well supplied with, well stocked with, replete with, abundant in, rife with, crammed with, crowded with, packed with, jammed with, stuffed with, teeming with, swarming with, overflowing with, bursting with, brimful with, brimming with, loaded with, overloaded with, thick with, solid with; informal jam-packed with, chock-a-block with, chock-full of; Austral./NZ informal chocker with.
4 *the town offers a rich supply of coffee shops and restaurants*: **plentiful**, abundant, copious, ample, profuse, lavish, liberal, generous, bountiful, large, huge, great, bumper, overflowing, superabundant, infinite, inexhaustible, prolific; S. African informal lank; literary bounteous, plenteous.
▷ANTONYMS meagre, poor.
5 *blackcurrant bushes require fairly rich soil*: **fertile**, productive, fecund, fruitful, lush, arable.
▷ANTONYMS barren.
6 *mussels should not be bathed in a rich sauce*: **creamy**, fatty, buttery, heavy, full-flavoured.
▷ANTONYMS light, delicate.
7 *a lovely, rich, oaky wine*: **full-bodied**, heavy, luscious, robust, opulent, big, fruity, fat.
▷ANTONYMS light.
8 *the rich colours of autumn*: **strong**, deep, full, intense, vivid, brilliant, warm, vibrant, graphic.
▷ANTONYMS delicate, pastel.
9 *her rich contralto voice*: **sonorous**, full, resonant, ringing, vibrant, deep, clear, mellow, mellifluous, melodious, full-bodied, strong, booming, fruity; rare mellifluent.
▷ANTONYMS thin, reedy.
10 informal *that's rich, coming from you*: **preposterous**, outrageous, unreasonable, absurd, ironic, ridiculous, ludicrous, laughable, risible; informal a bit much, a joke, a laugh, priceless; Brit. informal over the top, OTT, a bit thick.

riches plural noun **1** *he may decide to invest some of his new-found riches here*: **money**, wealth, finance(s), funds, cash, hard cash, (filthy) lucre, wherewithal, means, assets, liquid assets, capital, resources, reserves; opulence, gold, property, treasure, affluence, substance, prosperity; informal dough, bread, loot, the ready, readies, shekels, moolah, the necessary, boodle, dibs, gelt, ducats, rhino, gravy, scratch, stuff, oof; Brit. informal dosh, brass, lolly, spondulicks, wonga, ackers; N. Amer. informal greenbacks, simoleons, bucks, jack, mazuma, dinero; Austral./NZ informal Oscar; informal, dated splosh, green, tin; Brit. dated l.s.d.; N. Amer. informal, dated kale, rocks, shinplasters; archaic pelf.
2 *we were able to see many of the underwater riches of the island*: **resources**, treasure(s), bounty, jewels, gems, valuables, masterpieces, pride, cornucopia.

richly adverb **1** *he gazed round the richly furnished audience chamber*: **sumptuously**, opulently, luxuriously, palatially, lavishly, gorgeously, splendidly, magnificently, resplendently, plushly, expensively, fancily, stylishly, elegantly, exquisitely, grandiosely; informal poshly, ritzily, swankily, classily, glitzily; Brit. informal swishly.
▷ANTONYMS meanly, shabbily.
2 *Anne is finding the joy that she richly deserves*: **fully**, thoroughly, in full measure, well, completely, wholly, totally, entirely, absolutely, altogether, amply, utterly, perfectly, quite, in every respect, in all respects.

rickety adjective *we went carefully up the rickety stairs*: **shaky**, unsteady, unsound, unsafe, tottering, crumbling, decaying, disintegrating, tumbledown, broken-down, dilapidated, ramshackle, derelict, ruinous, falling to pieces, decrepit; informal shambly, geriatric; N. Amer. informal shacky.

rid verb *they had rid the building of all asbestos*: **clear**, free, make free, cleanse, purge, purify, empty, strip, scour, void, relieve, deliver.
□ **get rid of 1** *we'll have to get rid of some of our stuff*: **dispose of**, do away with, throw away, throw out, toss out, clear out, discard, scrap, remove, dispense with, lose, dump, bin, unload, jettison, dismiss, expel, eject, weed out, root out; informal chuck (away), ditch, junk, get shut of; Brit. informal get shot of, see the back of; N. Amer. informal shuck off. **2** *hawks were introduced to get rid of the rats*: **destroy**, abolish, eliminate, banish, annihilate, obliterate, wipe out, kill; N. Amer. informal nuke.

riddle[1] noun *they hope for an answer to the riddle of why he was killed*: **puzzle**, conundrum, brain-teaser, Chinese puzzle, problem, unsolved problem, question, poser, enigma, mystery, quandary, paradox; Zen Buddhism koan; informal stumper.

riddle² verb **1** *his car was riddled by sniper fire*: **perforate**, hole, make/put/ punch holes in, pierce, penetrate, puncture, honeycomb, pepper; prick, gore, bore through, transfix.
2 *he died eight months later, riddled with cancer*: **permeate**, **suffuse**, fill, pervade, spread through, imbue, inform, charge, saturate, overrun, take over, overspread, infiltrate, run through, filter through, be diffused through, invade, beset, pester, plague.
3 *when sowing small seeds, the soil must be riddled*: **sieve**, sift, strain, screen, filter, purify, refine, winnow; archaic bolt, griddle.

ride verb **1** *she can ride a horse*: **sit on**, mount, be mounted on, bestride; **manage**, handle, control, steer.
2 *two men were riding round the town on stolen motor bikes*: **travel**, go, move, progress, proceed, make one's way; drive, cycle; trot, canter, gallop.
□ **ride roughshod over** *they rode roughshod over normal disciplinary procedures*: **treat with contempt**, disregard, set at naught, trample over, show no consideration for, treat inconsiderately, treat disrespectfully, ignore, discount, encroach on, infringe, abuse, do violence to.
▶ noun *he took us for a ride in his car*: **trip**, journey, drive, run, expedition, excursion, outing, jaunt, tour, airing, turn, sally; lift; informal junket, spin, tootle, joyride, tool; Scottish informal hurl.

ridicule noun *he was subjected to ridicule by his colleagues*: **mockery**, derision, laughter, scorn, scoffing, contempt, jeering, sneering, sneers, jibes, jibing, joking, teasing, taunts, taunting, ragging, chaffing, twitting, raillery, sarcasm, satire, lampoon, burlesque, caricature, parody; informal kidding, kidology, ribbing, joshing; Brit. informal winding up, taking the mickey; N. Amer. informal goofing, razzing, pulling someone's chain; Austral./NZ informal chiacking; archaic sport; Brit. vulgar slang taking the piss.
▷ANTONYMS praise, respect.
▶ verb *it was easy to ridicule him in his battered old hat*: **deride**, mock, laugh at, heap scorn on, hold up to shame, hold up to ridicule, expose to ridicule, jeer at, jibe at, sneer at, show up, treat with contempt, scorn, make fun of, poke fun at, make jokes about, laugh to scorn, scoff at, pillory, be sarcastic about, satirize, lampoon, burlesque, caricature, parody, tease, taunt, rag, chaff, twit; informal kid, rib, josh, wind up, take the mickey out of; N. Amer. informal goof on, rag on, razz, pull someone's chain; Austral./NZ informal chiack, poke mullock at, sling off at; Brit. vulgar slang take the piss (out of); dated make sport of; archaic quiz, flout (at).
▷ANTONYMS praise.

Choose the right word **ridicule, mockery, derision**

See **mockery**.

ridiculous adjective **1** *the car looked ridiculous with a yellow child's cot strapped to the roof*: **laughable**, absurd, comical, funny, hilarious, humorous, risible, derisory, droll, amusing, entertaining, diverting, chucklesome, farcical, slapstick, silly, facetious, ludicrous, hysterical, riotous, side-splitting; informal crazy, priceless; dated killing; rare derisible.
▷ANTONYMS serious.
2 *it was a ridiculous suggestion*: **pointless**, senseless, silly, foolish, foolhardy, stupid, inane, nonsensical, fatuous, childish, puerile, half-baked, hare-brained, scatterbrained, feather-brained, ill-thought-out, ill-conceived, crackpot, idiotic, brainless, mindless, witless, vacuous, asinine, moronic; informal half-witted.
▷ANTONYMS sensible.
3 *this is a ridiculous exaggeration*: **absurd**, preposterous, stupid, ludicrous, farcical, laughable, comical, risible, nonsensical, pointless, senseless, insane, unreasonable, irrational, illogical, outrageous, shocking, astonishing, monstrous, unbelievable, incredible, unthinkable; informal crazy.
▷ANTONYMS reasonable.

rife adjective **1** *violence is rife in our cities*: **widespread**, general, common, universal, extensive, ubiquitous, global, omnipresent, everywhere, present everywhere, pandemic, epidemic, endemic, inescapable, insidious, prevalent, penetrating, pervading, pervasive, permeating, immanent; rare permeative, suffusive, permeant.
▷ANTONYMS scarce, unknown.
2 *the village was* ***rife with*** *gossip*: **overflowing**, bursting, alive, swarming, teeming, seething, lousy; **abounding in**, abundant in, overrun by, full of.
▷ANTONYMS devoid of.

riff-raff noun informal *she said that she thought my friends were riff-raff*: **rabble**, scum, refuse, garbage, rubbish, trash, vermin, the lowest of the low, in the underclass, the dregs of society, good-for-nothings, undesirables; informal peasants; Brit. informal as common as muck.
▷ANTONYMS elite, high-class.

rifle verb **1** *she* ***rifled through*** *the contents of her wardrobe*: **rummage**, search, hunt, forage, sift, rake; ransack, comb, turn upside down, scour.
2 *the man kept her talking while an accomplice rifled her home*: **burgle**, rob, steal from, loot, raid, plunder, sack, ransack, pillage.

rift noun **1** *a deep rift in the Antarctic ice*: **crack**, fault, flaw, split, break, breach, fissure, fracture, cleft, crevice, gap, cranny, slit, chink, interstice, cavity, opening, space, hole, aperture.
2 *a rift between the government and the presidency*: **breach**, division, split; quarrel, squabble, disagreement, difference of opinion, falling-out, fight, row, altercation, argument, war of words, dispute, conflict, contretemps, clash, wrangle, tussle, feud, battle royal; estrangement, alienation, schism; informal run-in, spat, scrap; Brit. informal ding-dong, bust-up.

rig¹ verb **1** *these vessels were rigged with a single square sail*: **equip**, kit out, fit out/up, supply, outfit, furnish, accoutre, array, provide, provision, stock, arm.
2 *I* ***rigged*** *myself* ***out*** *in all-American gear*: **dress**, attire, clothe, robe, garb, array, deck out, drape, accoutre, outfit, costume, get up, turn out, trick out/up; informal doll up; literary bedizen, caparison; archaic apparel, invest, habit, trap out.
3 *Alfred will rig up a bit of shelter*: **set up hastily**, erect hastily, assemble hastily, throw together, cobble together, put together, whip up, improvise, devise, contrive, jury-rig; Brit. informal knock up.
▶ noun **1** *he had left his CB radio rig switched on*: **apparatus**, appliance, piece of equipment, tool, machine, device, tackle, gear, mechanism, outfit, plant, kit, implement, utensil, instrument, contraption, contrivance, gadget, structure, system; informal gizmo.
2 *an officer in the rig of the American Army Air Corps*: **uniform**, costume, ensemble, outfit, suit, livery, attire, clothes, clothing, garments, dress, garb, regimentals, accoutrements, regalia, finery, trappings, disguise; Brit. kit, strip; informal get-up, gear, togs; Brit. informal rig-out; formal apparel; archaic array, raiment, habit, habiliments, vestments.

rig² verb *he will not need to rig the election or buy voters*: **manipulate**, arrange fraudulently, interfere with, influence, gerrymander, juggle, massage, distort, misrepresent, pervert, manoeuvre, tamper with, tinker with, doctor; **falsify**, forge, fake, engineer, trump up; informal fix, cook; Brit. informal fiddle.

right adjective **1** *I do not believe that it would be right to reverse this decision*: **just**, fair, equitable, good, upright, righteous, virtuous, proper, moral, morally justified, ethical, honourable, honest, principled; lawful, legal.
▷ANTONYMS wrong, unjust.
2 *he was first to give the right answer | you haven't gone about it the right way*: **correct**, accurate, without error, unerring, exact, precise; accepted, proper, valid, orthodox, conventional, established, official, formal, regular; informal on the mark; Brit. informal spot on; French de règle; archaic meet.
▷ANTONYMS wrong, inaccurate.
3 *the right person for the job*: **suitable**, appropriate, acceptable, fitting, fit, correct, proper, desirable, preferable, ideal; well suited, well qualified.
▷ANTONYMS wrong, unsuitable.
4 *you've come at just the right moment*: **opportune**, advantageous, favourable, auspicious, propitious, promising, heaven-sent, golden, good, lucky, happy, fortunate, benign, providential, felicitous, timely, well timed, ripe, convenient, expedient, suitable, appropriate, apt, fitting; archaic seasonable.
▷ANTONYMS wrong, inopportune.
5 *unfortunately he is not quite right in the head*: **sane**, in one's right mind, of sound mind, in possession of all one's faculties, able to think/reason clearly, lucid, rational, coherent, balanced, well balanced; Latin compos mentis; informal all there.
▷ANTONYMS insane, of unsound mind.
6 *John's face does not look right*: **healthy**, in good health, fine, hale, in good shape, in trim, in good trim, well, fit, fighting fit, normal, sound, up to par; informal up to scratch, in the pink.
▷ANTONYMS wrong, unhealthy.
7 *my right hand*: **right-hand**; Nautical starboard; Heraldry dexter.
▷ANTONYMS left; port; sinister.
8 informal *the library is a right mess*: **absolute**, complete, total, real, out-and-out, thorough, thoroughgoing, downright, perfect, utter, sheer, consummate, unmitigated, unqualified, veritable, in every respect, unalloyed; Austral./NZ informal fair; archaic arrant.
▶ adverb **1** *she was right at the limit of her patience*: **completely**, fully, entirely, totally, wholly, absolutely, altogether, utterly, thoroughly, quite; all the way, to the maximum extent, to the hilt, in all respects, in every respect.
2 *the hotel is right in the middle of the village*: **exactly**, precisely, directly, immediately, just, squarely, square, dead; informal bang, slap bang, smack, slap, plumb; N. Amer. informal smack dab.
3 *keep going* ***right on*** *till you come to a blue house*: **straight**, directly, in a straight line, as the crow flies.
▷ANTONYMS indirectly.
4 informal *he'll be right down*: **straight**, **immediately**, instantly, at once, straight away, right away, now, right now, this/that (very) minute, this/that instant, in/like a flash, directly, on the spot, forthwith, without further/more ado, promptly, quickly, without delay, then and there, there and then, here and now, a.s.a.p., as soon as possible, as quickly as possible, with all speed; N. Amer. in short order; French tout de suite; informal straight off, toot sweet, double quick, in double quick time, p.d.q. (pretty damn quick), pronto, before you can say Jack Robinson; N. Amer. informal lickety-split; Indian informal ekdam; archaic straightway, instanter, forthright.

▷ANTONYMS sometime, later, not now.
5 *I think I heard right*: **correctly**, accurately, properly, exactly, precisely, aright, rightly, perfectly, unerringly, faultlessly, truly.
▷ANTONYMS wrong, imperfectly.
6 *you get treated right there*: **justly**, fairly, equitably, impartially, well, properly, morally, ethically, honourably, honestly, lawfully, legally.
▷ANTONYMS unjustly.
7 *things usually turn out right in the end*: **well**, for the better, for the best, favourably, happily, advantageously, to one's advantage, beneficially, profitably, providentially, luckily, opportunely, conveniently, to one's satisfaction.
▷ANTONYMS badly, for the worse.
□ **right away** *I'll go and find them right away*: **at once**, straight away, now, right now, this/that (very) minute, this/that instant, immediately, instantly, in/like a flash, directly, on the spot, forthwith, without further/more ado, promptly, quickly, without delay, then and there, there and then, here and now, a.s.a.p., as soon as possible, as quickly as possible, with all speed; N. Amer. in short order; French tout de suite; informal straight off, toot sweet, double quick, in double quick time, p.d.q. (pretty damn quick), pronto, before you can say Jack Robinson, from the word go; N. Amer. informal lickety-split; Indian informal ekdam; archaic straight, straightway, instanter, forthright.
▷ANTONYMS sometime, later, not now, in due course.
▶**noun 1** *the difference between right and wrong*: **goodness**, rightness, righteousness, virtue, virtuousness, integrity, rectitude, uprightness, principle, propriety, morality, truth, truthfulness, honesty, honour, honourableness, justice, justness, fairness, equity, equitableness, impartiality; lawfulness, legality.
▷ANTONYMS wrong.
2 *everyone has the right to say no*: **entitlement**, prerogative, privilege, advantage, due, birthright, liberty, authority, authorization, power, licence, permission, dispensation, leave, consent, warrant, charter, franchise, sanction, exemption, immunity, indemnity; French carte blanche; Law, historical droit.
□ **by rights** *by rights, these young people should have been destined for college or university*: **properly**, in fairness, correctly, legally, technically, in (all) conscience; Law de jure.
▷ANTONYMS unfairly.
□ **in the right** *technically he is in the right*: **justified**, vindicated, borne out, with right on one's side, with the law on one's side, right.
▷ANTONYMS in the wrong.
□ **put something to rights remedy**, put right, set right, set to rights, rectify, retrieve, solve, fix, resolve, sort out, put in order; **straighten out**, deal with, correct, repair, mend, redress, make good; **improve**, amend, ameliorate, make better, better.
□ **within one's rights** *she was within her rights to do this*: **entitled**, permitted, allowed, at liberty, empowered, authorized, qualified, licensed, justified.
▶**verb 1** *you must be able to right a capsized dinghy*: **turn the right way up again**, turn back over, set upright again, stand upright again.
▷ANTONYMS invert, capsize.
2 *he would do what was necessary to right the situation*: **remedy**, put right, set right, put to rights, set to rights, rectify, retrieve, solve, fix, resolve, sort out, put in order; **straighten out**, deal with, correct, repair, mend, redress, make good; **improve**, amend, ameliorate, make better, better.
▷ANTONYMS worsen.
3 *my bill seeks to right this serious wrong*: **rectify**, correct, put right, set right, make right, sort out, deal with, remedy, repair, fix, cure, resolve, settle, square, make amends for; avenge, vindicate.

Word links **right**

dextral relating to the right-hand side
dextro- related prefix, as in *dextrorotatory*

righteous adjective **1** *the scriptures contain rules for righteous living*: **good**, virtuous, upright, upstanding, decent, worthy; **ethical**, **principled**, moral, high-minded, law-abiding, just, honest, innocent, faultless, honourable, blameless, guiltless, irreproachable, sinless, uncorrupted, saintly, angelic, pure, noble, noble-minded, pious, God-fearing.
▷ANTONYMS wicked, sinful.
2 *a look of righteous anger came over his face*: **justifiable**, justified, legitimate, defensible, supportable, just, rightful; well founded, sound, valid, admissible, allowable, understandable, excusable, acceptable, reasonable, sensible.
▷ANTONYMS unjustifiable.

righteousness noun *the successful are always tempted to regard their success as a reward for righteousness*: **goodness**, virtue, virtuousness, uprightness, decency, integrity, worthiness, rectitude, probity, morality, ethicalness, high-mindedness, justice, honesty, honour, honourableness, innocence, blamelessness, guiltlessness, irreproachability, sinlessness, saintliness, purity, nobility, noble-mindedness, piety, piousness.
▷ANTONYMS wickedness, sinfulness.

rightful adjective **1** *I intend to return it to its rightful owner*: **legal**, lawful, licit, sanctioned; **real**, true, proper, correct, recognized, genuine, warranted, authentic, acknowledged, approved, licensed, statutory, constitutional, valid; Latin bona fide; Law de jure; informal legit, kosher.
▷ANTONYMS wrongful.
2 *women have long been denied their rightful place in society*: **deserved**, well deserved, merited, earned, well earned; **due**, just, right, fair, proper, fitting, appropriate, apt, suitable, reasonable.
▷ANTONYMS undeserved.

right-wing adjective *the right-wing opposition party*: **conservative**, rightist, ultra-conservative; blimpish, diehard; reactionary, traditionalist, conventional, traditional, old-fashioned, unprogressive; N. Amer. Birchite.
▷ANTONYMS left-wing, radical.

rigid adjective **1** *sandwiches are best packed in a rigid container*: **stiff**, hard, firm, inflexible, non-flexible, unbending, unyielding, inelastic; taut, tight; rare impliable, unmalleable.
▷ANTONYMS flexible, plastic.
2 *many dog owners establish a rigid routine for feeding*: **fixed**, set, firm, inflexible, unalterable, unchangeable, immutable, unvarying, invariable, hard and fast, cast-iron.
▷ANTONYMS flexible.
3 *poorer nations warned against a rigid approach to IMF funding*: **strict**, severe, stern, stringent, rigorous, inflexible, uncompromising, resolute, determined, immovable, unshakeable; unrelenting, intransigent, unyielding, unwavering, unswerving, obdurate, unadaptable, adamant.
▷ANTONYMS flexible, lenient.

rigmarole noun **1** *she went through all the rigmarole of dressing and making up*: **lengthy process**, **fuss**, fuss and bother, bother, commotion, trouble, folderol, ado, pother; informal palaver, song and dance, performance, to-do, carry-on, carrying-on, kerfuffle, hoo-ha, hullabaloo, ballyhoo, business, pantomime, hassle, hoopla; NZ informal bobsy-die.
2 *that rigmarole about the house being haunted was just to keep people away*: **lengthy story/explanation**, saga, yarn, recitation, burble, burbling, maundering, shaggy-dog story; informal spiel, banging on, palaver.

rigorous adjective **1** *their rigorous attention to detail paid off*: **meticulous**, punctilious, conscientious, careful, diligent, attentive, ultra-careful, scrupulous, painstaking, exact, precise, accurate, correct, thorough, studious, exhaustive, mathematical, detailed, perfectionist, methodical, particular, religious, strict; **fussy**, fastidious, hair-splitting, finicky, finical, demanding, exacting, pedantic; informal nit-picking, pernickety; N. Amer. informal persnickety; archaic nice, overnice, laborious.
▷ANTONYMS slapdash.
2 *the rigorous enforcement of minor school rules*: **strict**, severe, stern, stringent, austere, spartan, tough, hard, harsh, rigid, cruel, savage, relentless, unsparing, inflexible, authoritarian, despotic, draconian, intransigent, uncompromising, demanding, exacting.
▷ANTONYMS lax.
3 *rigorous yachting conditions*: **harsh**, severe, bad, bleak, extreme, inclement; unpleasant, disagreeable, foul, nasty, filthy; stormy, blustery, squally, wild, tempestuous, storm-tossed, violent, heavy, heaving, raging, choppy, agitated.
▷ANTONYMS gentle, mild.

rigour noun **1** *the mines were operated under conditions of some rigour*: **strictness**, severity, sternness, stringency, austerity, toughness, hardness, harshness, rigidity, inflexibility; cruelty, savagery, relentlessness, unsparingness, authoritarianism, despotism, intransigence.
▷ANTONYMS laxness.
2 *a speech noted for its intellectual rigour*: **meticulousness**, thoroughness, carefulness, attention to detail, diligence, scrupulousness, exactness, exactitude, precision, accuracy, correctness, strictness, punctiliousness, conscientiousness; archaic nicety.
▷ANTONYMS carelessness.
3 (**rigours**) *she could not face the rigours of the journey*: **hardship**, harshness, severity, adversity, suffering, privation, ordeal, misery, distress, trial; discomfort, inconvenience.
▷ANTONYMS pleasures.

rig-out noun Brit. informal *some of her rig-outs are gorgeous*. See **outfit** (sense 1 of the noun).

rile verb informal *he had a sceptical air guaranteed to rile Ursula*: **irritate**, annoy, bother, vex, provoke, displease, upset, offend, affront, anger, exasperate, infuriate, gall, irk, get/put someone's back up, disgruntle, pique, rankle with, nettle, needle, ruffle, get on someone's nerves, ruffle someone's feathers, make someone's hackles rise, raise someone's hackles, rub up the wrong way; informal peeve, aggravate, miff, get, get to, bug, get under someone's skin, get in someone's hair, get up someone's nose, hack off, get someone's goat; Brit. informal nark, get on someone's wick, give someone the hump, wind up, get across; N. Amer. informal tick off, rankle, ride, gravel; vulgar slang piss off; Brit. vulgar slang get on someone's tits; rare exacerbate, hump, rasp.
▷ANTONYMS conciliate, soothe.

rim noun **1** *she stared at him over the rim of her cup*: **brim**, edge, lip.
2 *the limestone formed a jagged rim along the lake*: **edge**, **border**, side,

r

verge, margin, brink, fringe, boundary, perimeter, circumference, limits, periphery, bound, extremity; literary marge, bourn, skirt.

rind noun *add the grated rind of one lemon*: **skin**, peel, covering, zest; hull, pod, shell, husk, crust, shuck, capsule, outer layer, bark; hide; technical epicarp, pericarp, exocarp; rare integument.

ring[1] noun **1** *a ring round the moon means rain*: **circle**, circlet, band, round, loop, hoop, circuit, halo, disc.
2 *she wasn't wearing a ring*: **wedding ring**, band of gold, marriage token.
3 *a circus ring | a boxing ring*: **arena**, enclosure, area, field, ground, platform; amphitheatre, colosseum, stadium.
4 *a ring of onlookers forms around them*: **circle**, group, knot, cluster, bunch, band, gathering, throng, crowd, flock, assemblage, mob, pack.
5 *a large spy ring existed right under their noses*: **gang**, syndicate, cartel, mob, band, organization, confederation, confederacy, federation, union, association, circle, society, combine, consortium, alliance, league, cabal, cell, coterie, crew, junta.
▸ verb *riot police ringed the building*: **circle**, encircle, circumscribe, encompass, loop, gird, girdle, enclose, surround, embrace, form a ring round, go around, hem in, fence in, confine, seal off.

Word links **ring**

annular ring-shaped

ring[2] verb **1** *the vicar arranged to ring the church bells | she rang the doorbell*: **toll**, sound, strike, peal; press, set off; rare tintinnabulate.
2 *church bells rang all day*: **chime**, ring out, chime out, toll, peal, knell; sound, clang, bong, clink, ding, jingle, tinkle.
3 *the whole cellar rang with laughter*: **resound**, reverberate, resonate, echo, re-echo; vibrate, pulsate.
4 *I'll ring you tomorrow*: **telephone**, phone, call, call up, ring up, give someone a ring, give someone a call, get someone on the phone, get on the phone to, get, reach, dial, make/place a call (to); informal buzz, give someone a buzz; Brit. informal bell, give someone a bell, give someone a tinkle, get on the blower to; N. Amer. informal get someone on the horn.
□ **ring something in** *the bells were beginning to ring in the new year*: **herald**, signal, announce, proclaim, usher in, introduce, launch, celebrate, mark, signify, indicate, give notice of; literary betoken, harbinger, knell.
▸ noun **1** *there was the sharp ring of a bell from the gate*: **ringing**, chime, carillon, toll, tolling, peal, knell; sound, sounding, clang, clanging, clink, clinking, ding, dinging, jingle, jingling, tinkle, tinkling; archaic tocsin; rare tintinnabulation.
2 *I'll give Chris a ring*: **call**, telephone call, phone call; informal buzz; Brit. informal bell, tinkle.

rinse verb *he rinsed out a couple of mugs | Jean rinsed the crumbs off the plates*: **wash**, wash out, wash lightly, clean, cleanse, bathe, dip, drench, splash, hose down, swill, sluice; flush out/away, wash off.

riot noun **1** *there was a riot when he was arrested*: **uproar**, rampage, furore, tumult, commotion, upheaval, disturbance, street fight, melee, row, scuffle, fracas, fray, affray, brawl, free-for-all; violent disorder, violence, mob violence, street fighting, vandalism, frenzy, mayhem, turmoil, lawlessness, anarchy; N. Amer. informal wilding.
2 *the garden was a riot of colour*: **mass**, sea, lavish display, splash, extravagance, extravaganza, flourish, show, exhibition.
□ **run riot 1** *family rooms are useful for letting noisier children run riot*: **go on the rampage**, rampage, riot, run amok, go berserk, get out of control, run free, go undisciplined; informal raise hell. **2** *in rainforest, the daily downpours let vegetation run riot*: **grow profusely**, spread uncontrolled, increase rapidly, grow rapidly, luxuriate, spread like wildfire, burgeon, prosper; multiply, mushroom, snowball, escalate, rocket.
▸ verb *the miners rioted and attacked the local Party HQ*: **rampage**, go on the rampage, run riot, take to the streets, fight in the streets, start a fight, raise an uproar, cause an affray, run/go wild, run amok, go berserk, fight, brawl, scuffle; informal raise hell.

riotous adjective **1** *the match was abandoned after a demonstration in the National Stadium turned riotous*: **unruly**, rowdy, disorderly, disruptive, out of control, rioting, uncontrollable, ungovernable, unmanageable, unbiddable, insubordinate, undisciplined, turbulent, uproarious, tumultuous; violent, wild, ugly, brawling, lawless, anarchic.
▷ANTONYMS law-abiding, peaceable, calm.
2 *a riotous party*: **boisterous**, lively, loud, noisy, rip-roaring, unrestrained, uninhibited, roisterous, uproarious, unruly, rollicking; abandoned, orgiastic, debauched, depraved; Brit. informal rumbustious; N. Amer. informal rambunctious; archaic robustious.
▷ANTONYMS restrained, quiet.

rip verb **1** *the man threatened to rip the posters down*: **tear**, snatch, jerk, tug, wrench, wrest, prise, force, heave, haul, drag, pull, twist, peel, pluck, grab, seize; informal yank.
2 *she ripped Leo's note into tiny pieces*: **tear**, slit, cut, gash, cleave, slash, claw, savage, mangle, mutilate, hack; literary rend.
□ **rip off** informal *if our guests felt they'd been ripped off, we'd hear about it*: **swindle**, fleece, cheat, defraud, deceive, trick, dupe, hoodwink, double-cross, gull; short-change; exploit, take advantage of, victimize; informal do, diddle, con, bamboozle, rob, shaft, sting, have, bilk, rook, gyp, finagle, flimflam, put one over on, pull a fast one on, take for a ride, lead up the garden path, sell down the river, pull the wool over someone's eyes; N. Amer. informal sucker, snooker, goldbrick, gouge, stiff, give someone a bum steer; Austral. informal pull a swifty on; archaic cozen, chicane, sell.
▸ noun *a green corduroy jacket with a rip in the sleeve*: **tear**, slit, split, rent, laceration, cut, gash, slash.

ripe adjective **1** *a ripe tomato*: **mature**, ripened, fully developed, full grown, ready to eat, soft, lush, juicy, tender; luscious, sweet, full-flavoured, mellow.
▷ANTONYMS unripe, green.
2 *the former dock is ripe for development*: **ready**, fit, suitable, right.
▷ANTONYMS unready, unsuitable.
3 *he lived to the ripe old age of ninety*: **advanced**, hoary, venerable, old.
▷ANTONYMS young, early.
4 *the time is ripe for his return*: **opportune**, advantageous, favourable, auspicious, propitious, promising, heaven-sent, good, right, fortunate, benign, providential, felicitous, well timed, convenient, expedient, suitable, appropriate, apt, fitting; archaic seasonable.
▷ANTONYMS unsuitable.

Word toolkit

ripe	succulent	moist
tomatoes	leaves	cake
berries	flavour	chicken
peaches	morsels	salmon
cheese	roast	bread

ripen verb **1** *tomatoes ripen faster when placed on a window ledge*: **become ripe**, mature, come to maturity, mellow; become tender.
2 *to ripen melons, keep them at room temperature for a few days*: **make ripe**, mature, bring to maturity, mellow.

rip-off noun informal *another victim of the pension rip-off*: **fraud**, swindle, fraudulent scheme, confidence trick, mare's nest; overcharging; informal con, con trick, scam, flimflam, gyp, kite; Brit. informal ramp, twist, swizz, daylight robbery; N. Amer. informal rip, shakedown, hustle, grift, bunco, boondoggle; Austral. informal rort; Brit. archaic, informal do, flanker, have.

riposte noun *his mother forestalled his indignant riposte by replacing the receiver*: **retort**, counter, rejoinder, sally, return, retaliation, answer, reply, response; informal comeback.
▸ verb *'And heaven help you,' riposted Sally*: **retort**, counter, rejoin, return, retaliate, hurl back, fling back, snap back, answer, reply, respond, say in response; round on someone, come back.

ripple noun *he blew ripples in the surface of his coffee*: **wavelet**, wave, undulation, ripplet, ridge, crease, wrinkle, ruffle, pucker.
▸ verb *before her the sea rippled placidly | a breeze rippled the surface of the lake*: **form ripples (on)**, flow in wavelets, undulate, popple, lap, purl, babble; form something into ridges, crease, wrinkle, ruffle, pucker.

rise verb **1** *the sun rose across the bay*: **move up/upwards**, come/go up, make one's/its way up, arise, ascend, climb, climb up, mount, soar.
▷ANTONYMS fall, descend, set.
2 *the mountains rising above us*: **loom**, tower, soar, rise up, rear (up), stand high, reach high.
3 *prices rose by over 3%*: **go up**, get higher, increase, grow, advance, soar, shoot up, surge (up), leap, jump, rocket, escalate, spiral.
▷ANTONYMS drop.
4 *living standards have risen substantially*: **improve**, get better, advance, go up, get higher, soar, shoot up.
▷ANTONYMS worsen.
5 *his voice rose in anger*: **get higher**, grow, increase, become louder, swell, intensify.
▷ANTONYMS drop.
6 *he rose from his chair*: **stand up**, get/rise to one's feet, get up, jump up, leap up, spring up; become erect, straighten up; literary arise.
▷ANTONYMS sit.
7 *he rises every day at dawn*: **get up**, get out of bed, rouse oneself, stir, bestir oneself, be up and about; informal rise and shine, shake a leg, surface; literary arise.
▷ANTONYMS go to bed, retire.
8 *the court rose at midday*: **adjourn**, recess, be suspended, suspend proceedings, pause, break off, take a break; informal knock off, take five.
▷ANTONYMS continue, resume.
9 *he rose through the ranks to become managing director*: **make progress**, make headway, make strides, forge ahead, come on, climb, advance, get on, make/work one's way, be promoted.
10 *he refused to rise to the bait*: **react to**, respond to, take.
11 *I have seen the dead rise, lepers healed, water flow like wine*: **come back to life**, be raised from the dead, come back from the dead, be resurrected, be restored to life, revive, be revived.
▷ANTONYMS die.

12 *the dough was starting to rise*: **swell**, expand, enlarge, puff up; ferment.
13 *the nation would eventually rise against its oppressors*: **rebel**, revolt, mutiny, riot, rise up (in arms), take up arms, stage/mount a rebellion, take to the streets.
▷ANTONYMS kowtow.
14 *the River Rhine rises in the Swiss Alps*: **originate**, begin, start, emerge, appear; issue from, spring from, flow from, emanate from; formal commence.
▷ANTONYMS disgorge.
15 *the sickness lightened a little and her spirits rose*: **lift**, improve, cheer up, grow buoyant, become optimistic/hopeful, brighten, take a turn for the better; informal buck up.
16 *the ground rose gently away from the river*: **slope upwards**, slant upwards, go uphill, incline, climb, get higher.
▷ANTONYMS shelve, drop away.
▸ **noun 1** *a price rise*: **increase**, hike, advance, growth, leap, upsurge, upswing, ascent, climb, jump, escalation, spiralling.
2 *the managing director got a rise of 11.3%*: **pay increase**, salary/wage increase, hike, increment; N. Amer. raise.
3 *a rise in standards*: **improvement**, amelioration, advance, upturn, leap, jump.
4 *her rise to power*: **progress**, climb, progression, advancement, promotion, elevation, aggrandizement.
5 *we began to walk up the rise*: **(upward) slope**, incline, elevation, acclivity, rising ground, eminence, hillock, hill.

risible adjective *their irresponsibility would be risible were it not so dangerous*: **laughable**, **ridiculous**, absurd, comical, comic, amusing, funny, chucklesome, hilarious, humorous, droll, entertaining, diverting, farcical, slapstick, silly, facetious, ludicrous, hysterical, uproarious, riotous, side-splitting, zany, grotesque; informal rib-tickling, crazy, priceless; dated killing; rare derisible.
▷ANTONYMS serious.

risk noun **1** *to publish the story was indeed a risk | there is a certain amount of risk involved*: **chance**, **uncertainty**, unpredictability, precariousness, instability, insecurity, perilousness, riskiness, gamble, venture.
▷ANTONYMS safety.
2 *do not use the stove inside a tent because of the risk of fire*: **possibility**, chance, probability, likelihood, danger, peril, threat, menace, fear, prospect.
▷ANTONYMS impossibility.
3 *they're putting their own lives at risk*: **danger**, peril, jeopardy, hazard, threat, menace.
▸ **verb 1** *a father risked his life to save his twin babies from a fire*: **endanger**, put at risk, put in danger, expose to danger, put on the line, take a chance with, imperil, jeopardize, put in jeopardy, hazard, gamble (with), bet, wager, chance, venture.
2 *in a tweed coat you risk getting cold and wet*: **chance**, venture, take the risk of, stand a chance of.

> *Choose the right word* **risk, danger, peril, hazard**
>
> See **danger**.

> *Choose the right word* **risk, endanger, imperil, jeopardize**
>
> See **endanger**.

r

risky adjective *risky sports like skindiving and hang-gliding are not covered*: **dangerous**, fraught with danger, high-risk, hazardous, perilous, unsafe, insecure, exposed, defenceless, precarious, touch-and-go, tricky, treacherous; uncertain, unpredictable, speculative; informal chancy, dicey, sticky, hairy; Brit. informal dodgy; N. Amer. informal gnarly; archaic or humorous parlous.
▷ANTONYMS safe.

risqué adjective *the girls would giggle and tell risqué stories*: **bawdy**, indecent, ribald, rude, racy, broad, earthy, Rabelaisian, spicy, suggestive, titillating, improper, naughty, indelicate, indecorous, off colour, locker-room; vulgar, dirty, filthy, smutty, crude, offensive, salacious, coarse, obscene, lewd, pornographic, X-rated; informal blue, raunchy; Brit. informal fruity, near the knuckle, saucy; N. Amer. informal gamy; euphemistic adult.

rite noun *coronation has long been a religious rite*: **ceremony**, ritual, ceremonial, observance, service, sacrament, liturgy, worship, office, celebration; performance, act, practice, order, custom, tradition, convention, institution, procedure.

ritual noun *the official thanksgiving was an elaborate civic ritual*: **ceremony**, rite, ceremonial, observance; service, sacrament, liturgy, worship; office, celebration, performance, act, practice, order, custom, tradition, convention, institution, formality, procedure, protocol.
▸ **adjective** *the ritual burial was to ward off evil spirits*: **ceremonial**, ritualistic, prescribed, set, formal, stately, solemn, dignified, celebratory, sacramental, liturgical; customary, traditional, conventional, routine, usual, habitual.

ritzy adjective informal *his ritzy $4 million oceanside mansion*: **luxurious**, luxury, de luxe, plush, sumptuous, palatial, lavish, lavishly appointed, gorgeous, opulent, splendid, magnificent, lush, glamorous, glittering, rich, costly, expensive, upmarket, fancy, stylish, grandiose; informal posh, swanky, plushy, classy, glitzy, fancy-pants; Brit. informal swish; N. Amer. informal swank; rare palatian, Lucullan.
▷ANTONYMS plain, austere.

rival noun **1** *his chief rival for the nomination*: **competitor**, **opponent**, contestant, contender, challenger; adversary, antagonist, enemy, foe; rare corrival, vier.
▷ANTONYMS partner, ally.
2 *in terms of versatility the tool has no rival*: **equal**, match, peer, equivalent, fellow, counterpart, like; rare compeer.
▸ **verb** *few countries can rival Slovakia for mountain scenery*: **compete with**, vie with, match, be a match for, equal, emulate, measure up to, come up to, compare with, bear comparison with, be comparable to/with, parallel, be in the same league as, be in the same category as, be on a par with, be on a level with, touch, keep pace with, keep up with; challenge; informal hold a candle to.
▸ **adjective** *the rival candidates*: **competing**, in competition, opposing, opposed, in opposition, contending, conflicting, in conflict; rare corrival.

rivalry noun *the growing rivalry between the two groups*: **competitiveness**, competition, contention, vying; opposition, conflict, struggle, strife, feuding, dissension, discord, antagonism, friction, enmity; informal keeping up with the Joneses.

riven adjective *the country was riven by civil war*: **torn apart**, split, rent, ripped apart, ruptured, severed; literary cleft, torn asunder, ripped asunder; rare dissevered.

river noun **1** **watercourse**, waterway, stream, tributary, brook, inlet, rivulet, rill, runnel, streamlet, freshet; canal, channel; Scottish & N. English burn; N. English beck; S. English bourn; N. Amer. & Austral./NZ creek; Austral. billabong; rare rillet.
2 *a river of molten lava*: **stream**, torrent, flood, deluge, cascade; spate, wave.
□ **sell someone down the river** informal **cheat**, trick, swindle, defraud, dupe, hoodwink; double-cross, betray, deceive, sell out, stab in the back; exploit, take advantage of; informal do, con, take for a ride, sell, diddle, bamboozle, finagle, bilk, rip off, fleece.

> *Word links* **river**
>
> **fluvial**, **potamic**, **riparian**, **riverine** relating to rivers
> **fluvio-** related prefix, as in *fluviometer, fluvioglacial*
> **potamo-** related prefix, as in *potamoplankton*
> **potamology** study of rivers
> **potamophobia** fear of rivers

riveted adjective **1** *he walked away, leaving her riveted to the spot*: **fixed**, rooted, frozen; unable to move, motionless, unmoving, immobile, stock-still, as still as a statue, as if turned to stone.
2 *he was riveted by the newsreels*: **fascinated**, engrossed, gripped, captivated, enthralled, intrigued, spellbound, rapt, mesmerized, transfixed.
▷ANTONYMS bored, uninterested.
3 *the children's eyes were* **riveted on** *the headmistress*: **fixed on**, fastened on, focused on, concentrated on, pinned on, locked on, directed at.

riveting adjective *a riveting book*: **fascinating**, gripping, engrossing, very interesting, very exciting, thrilling, absorbing, captivating, enthralling, intriguing, compelling, compulsive, spellbinding, mesmerizing, hypnotic, transfixing; informal unputdownable.
▷ANTONYMS boring, dull.

road noun **1** *the roads were crowded with holiday traffic*: **highway**, thoroughfare, roadway; road surface; N. Amer. pavement.
2 *the road to economic recovery*: **way**, path, route, direction, course.
3 *there seemed an almost endless queue of freighters and tankers waiting in the roads*: **anchorage**, channel, haven; rare roadstead.
□ **on the road** *the band have been on the road all year*: **on tour**, touring, travelling, doing the rounds, on the circuit.

roam verb *a tramp who had roamed the country for nine years*: **wander**, rove, ramble, meander, drift, maunder; walk, traipse; prowl; range, travel, tramp, traverse, trek through; Scottish & Irish stravaig; Irish streel; informal knock about/around, cruise, mosey, tootle; Brit. informal pootle, swan; rare perambulate, peregrinate, circumambulate, vagabond.

> *Choose the right word* **roam, wander, rove, range, stray**
>
> See **wander**.

roar noun **1** *the roars of the crowd increased in intensity*: **shout**, bellow, yell, cry, howl, shriek, scream, screech; clamour, clamouring; N. Amer. informal holler; rare vociferation, ululation.
▷ANTONYMS whisper.
2 *the deafening roar of the wind and the sea*: **loud noise**, boom, booming, crash, crashing, rumble, rumbling, roll, thundering, peal, crack, clap, thunderclap.
3 *his claims were greeted with roars of laughter*: **guffaw**, howl, hoot, shriek; gale, peal.

▶ **verb 1** *'Get out!' roared Angus*: **bellow**, yell, shout, bawl, howl, cry, shriek, scream, screech; N. Amer. informal holler; rare vociferate, ululate.
▷ANTONYMS whisper.
2 *thunder roared and lightning flashed*: **boom**, rumble, crash, roll, thunder, peal.
3 *the movie has left preview audiences roaring*: **guffaw**, laugh heartily, roar/howl/shriek with laughter, laugh hysterically, laugh uproariously, be convulsed with laughter, burst out laughing, hoot; informal split one's sides, be rolling in the aisles, be doubled up, crack up, laugh like a drain, be in stitches, die laughing; Brit. informal crease up, fall about.
▷ANTONYMS weep.
4 *a motorbike roared past*: **speed**, zoom, whizz, flash; informal belt, tear, vroom, scorch, zap, zip, burn rubber; Brit. informal bomb.

roaring adjective **1** *a roaring fire*: **blazing**, burning, red-hot.
2 informal *last week's 70s night was a roaring success*: **enormous**, huge, massive, (very) great, tremendous, terrific; complete, unqualified, out-and-out, thorough, unmitigated; informal rip-roaring, whopping, thumping, fantastic.

roast verb **1** *potatoes roasted in olive oil*: **cook**, bake, grill; spit-roast, pot-roast; N. Amer. broil.
2 informal *they roasted Lavelle for eating at exclusive restaurants at the company's expense*. See **criticize**.

roasting informal **adjective** *a roasting day in London*: **extremely hot**, baking (hot), blazing (hot), sweltering, scorching, blistering, searing, torrid; informal sizzling, boiling (hot).
▶ **noun** *the manager hauled him in and gave him a roasting*. See **lecture** (sense 2 of the noun).

rob verb **1** *the gang were convicted of robbing Barclays Bank in Kelvedon*: **burgle**, steal from, hold up, break into; raid, loot, ransack, plunder, pillage, sack; N. Amer. burglarize; informal do, turn over, steam, knock off, stick up; archaic spoil, reave.
2 *police are hunting a man who robbed an old woman at gunpoint last night*: **steal from**; informal **mug**, jump, roll; N. Amer. informal clip.
3 *he was robbed of his savings*: **cheat**, swindle, defraud, fleece, dispossess; informal bilk, do out of, con out of, rook out of, skin, steal someone blind; N. Amer. informal **stiff**; rare mulct.
4 informal *my suit cost £70, and he thinks I was robbed*: **overcharge**, charge too much; informal rip off, screw, sting, do, diddle; N. Amer. informal gouge; Brit. informal, dated rush.
5 *defeat robbed him of his chance of regaining the world No 1 ranking*: **deprive**, strip, divest; deny.
6 informal *I didn't buy it—I robbed it*. See **steal**.

robber noun **burglar**, thief, housebreaker, cat burglar, sneak thief, mugger, shoplifter, stealer, pilferer; raider, looter, plunderer, pillager, marauder; bandit, brigand, pirate, highwayman; Indian dacoit; informal crook, cracksman, steamer; Brit. informal, dated **drummer**; N. Amer. informal yegg, second-story man/worker; W. Indian informal tief; Brit. rhyming slang tea leaf.

robbery noun **1** *they were arrested for robbery | a spate of robberies*: **burglary**, theft, thievery, stealing, breaking and entering, housebreaking, larceny, shoplifting, pilfering, filching, embezzlement, misappropriation, swindling, fraud; hold-up, break-in, raid; looting, pillage, plunder; informal mugging, smash-and-grab, steaming, snatch; Brit. informal blag; N. Amer. informal heist, stick-up.
2 *Six quid? That's robbery*: **extortion**, exorbitant, expensive; informal a rip-off, steep; Brit. informal daylight robbery.

robe noun **1** *the women were draped from head to toe in heavy black robes*: **cloak**, wrap, mantle, cape, kaftan; N. Amer. wrapper; Arabic **dishdasha**, **djellaba**; Turkish **dolman**; African **kanzu**; Hawaiian **muumuu**.
2 (**robes**) *coronation robes*: **garb**, regalia, costume, livery, finery, trappings; garments, clothes; formal apparel; archaic raiment, habiliments, vestments, vesture, habit.
3 *his priestly robes*: **vestment**, surplice, cassock, rochet, alb, dalmatic, chasuble; canonicals, pontificals.
4 *a short towelling robe*: **dressing gown**, bathrobe, housecoat, negligee, kimono; French **peignoir**, robe de chambre; N. Amer. wrapper.
▶ **verb** *I went into the vestry and robed for the Mass*: **dress oneself**, dress, get dressed, attire oneself, enrobe; archaic apparel oneself.

robot noun **automaton**, android, machine, golem; informal bot, droid.

robust adjective **1** *a large and robust man*: **strong**, vigorous, sturdy, tough, powerful, powerfully built, solidly built, as strong as a horse/ox, muscular, sinewy, rugged, hardy, strapping, brawny, burly, husky; **healthy**, fit, fighting fit, as fit as a fiddle/flea, bursting with health, hale and hearty, hale, hearty, lusty, in fine fettle, in good health, in good shape, in trim, in good trim, aerobicized, able-bodied; Brit. in rude health; informal beefy, hunky; dated stalwart; literary thewy, stark.
▷ANTONYMS weak, frail.
2 *these knives are more robust and better at cutting*: **durable**, resilient, tough, hard-wearing, long-lasting, well made; **sturdy**, strong, strongly made.
▷ANTONYMS fragile.
3 *Libby took her usual robust view of the matter*: **down-to-earth**, hard-headed, sensible, practical, realistic, pragmatic, common-sense, commonsensical, matter-of-fact, businesslike, level-headed, unromantic, unsentimental, unidealistic; tough-minded, forceful, vigorous; informal no-nonsense, hard-nosed.
▷ANTONYMS impractical, romantic.
4 *a robust red wine*: **strong**, full-bodied, flavourful, full-flavoured, flavoursome, full of flavour, rich; rare sapid.
▷ANTONYMS insipid, tasteless.

rock[1] verb **1** *the ship rocked on the water*: **move to and fro**, move backwards and forwards, move back and forth, sway, swing, see-saw; roll, pitch, plunge, toss, lurch, reel, list; wobble, undulate, oscillate; Nautical pitchpole.
2 *the building began to rock on its foundations*: **shake**, vibrate, quake, tremble.
3 *Wall Street was rocked by the news and shares fell 4.3 per cent*: **stun**, shock, stagger, astound, astonish, amaze, startle, surprise, dumbfound, daze, shake, shake up, set someone back on their heels, take aback, throw, unnerve, disconcert.

rock[2] noun **1** *a narrow gully strewn with rocks*: **boulder**, stone; Austral. informal goolie.
2 *a castle built on a rock*: **crag**, cliff, tor, outcrop, outcropping.
3 *he was the rock on which his whole family relied*: **foundation**, cornerstone, support, prop, mainstay, backbone; tower of strength, pillar of strength, bulwark, anchor, source of protection, source of security.
4 informal *she was wearing a massive rock on her fourth finger*: **diamond**, precious stone, jewel.
□ **on the rocks** informal **1** *Sue's marriage was on the rocks*: **in difficulty**, in trouble, breaking down, practically over, heading for divorce, heading for the divorce courts; in tatters, in pieces, destroyed, shattered, ruined, beyond repair; informal kaput, done for, toast. **2** *he ordered a Scotch on the rocks*: **with ice**, on ice.

> *Word links* **rock**
>
> **litho-** related prefix, as in *lithography*
> **petro-** related prefix, as in *petroleum*
> **-lite** related suffix, as in *hyalite*
> **lithology**, **petrology**, **petrography** study of rocks

rocket noun **1** *guerrillas fired five rockets at the capital yesterday*: **missile**, projectile; rare trajectile.
2 Brit. informal *he got a rocket from the director*. See **lecture** (sense 2 of the noun).
▶ **verb 1** *prices have rocketed during the last ten years*: **shoot up**, soar, increase rapidly, rise rapidly, escalate, spiral upwards; informal go through the ceiling, go through the roof, skyrocket.
▷ANTONYMS fall, plummet.
2 *they rocketed into the alley ahead of the police car*: **speed**, zoom, shoot, roar, whizz, career, go hell for leather; informal scorch, tear, go like a bat out of hell; Brit. informal **bomb**; N. Amer. informal **barrel**, hightail it.

rocky[1] adjective *damp leaves covered the rocky path | Malta is naturally rocky and treeless*: **stony**, rock-strewn, pebbly, shingly, rough, bumpy, rugged, hard; craggy, mountainous.
▷ANTONYMS smooth, flat.

rocky[2] adjective **1** *that table's a bit rocky*: **unsteady**, shaky, unstable, wobbly, tottery, rickety, flimsy; Irish bockety.
▷ANTONYMS steady.
2 *the couple had a rocky marriage*: **difficult**, up and down, problematic, precarious, unsteady, unstable, uncertain, unsure, unreliable, undependable, built on sand; informal iffy.
▷ANTONYMS solid, stable.

rococo adjective *rococo Victorian wrought ironwork*: **ornate**, fancy, very elaborate, curlicued, over-elaborate, extravagant, baroque, fussy, busy, ostentatious, showy, wedding-cake, gingerbread; flowery, florid, flamboyant, high-flown, high-sounding, magniloquent, grandiloquent, orotund, rhetorical, oratorical, bombastic, overwrought, overblown, overdone, convoluted, turgid, inflated; informal highfalutin, purple; rare tumid, pleonastic, euphuistic, aureate, Ossianic, fustian, hyperventilated.
▷ANTONYMS plain, simple.

rod noun **1** *an iron rod*: **bar**, stick, pole, baton, staff; shaft, strut, rail, spoke; cane, birch, switch; historical knout.
2 *the ceremonial rod of the House of Commons*: **staff**, wand, mace, sceptre; Greek Mythology caduceus.
3 (**the rod**) *instruction in these subjects was brisk and accompanied by the rod*: **corporal punishment**, the cane, the lash, the birch, the belt, the strap; beating, flogging, caning, birching.

> *Word links* **rod**
>
> **rhabdoid** rod-shaped

rodent noun

> *Word links* **rodent**
>
> **rodenticide** substance used to kill rodents

r

rogue noun **1** *you are a rogue, Colin, without ethics or scruples*: **scoundrel**, villain, reprobate, rascal, good-for-nothing, wretch; Spanish picaro; informal rat, bastard, son of a bitch, s.o.b., nasty piece of work, dog, cur, louse, crook; Brit. informal scrote; Irish informal spalpeen; N. Amer. informal slicker; W. Indian informal scamp; informal, dated rotter, bounder, hound, blighter, vagabond; dated cad, ne'er-do-well; archaic miscreant, blackguard, dastard, knave, varlet, wastrel, mountebank, picaroon.
2 *we were at school together—he was a right little rogue*: **scamp**, rascal, imp, devil, monkey, mischief-maker; informal scallywag, monster, horror, terror, holy terror; Brit. informal perisher; N. English informal tyke, scally; N. Amer. informal hellion, varmint; archaic scapegrace, rapscallion.

roguish adjective **1** *a roguish and untrustworthy character*: **unprincipled**, dishonest, deceitful, unscrupulous, untrustworthy, reprobate, shameless, wicked, villainous; incorrigible, unregenerate; informal shady, scoundrelly, rascally; archaic knavish.
▷ANTONYMS honest, honourable.
2 *a roguish grin*: **mischievous**, playful, teasing, cheeky, naughty, wicked, impish, puckish, devilish, arch, waggish, rakish, raffish; rare ludic.
▷ANTONYMS serious.

roister verb *the mansions in which the nobility of the city had once roistered*: **enjoy oneself**, celebrate, revel, carouse, frolic, romp, have fun, have a good time, make merry, have a party, party, {eat, drink, and be merry}, go on a spree; informal live it up, whoop it up, have a fling, have a ball, make whoopee, paint the town red; dated spree; rare rollick.

role noun **1** *he had a small role in Coppola's 'Dracula'*: **part**, character; title role; bit part, walk-on part, non-speaking part.
2 *his success in his role as President of the European Community*: **capacity**, position, job, post, office, task, duty, responsibility, mantle, place, situation; **function**, part, contribution, hand.

roll verb **1** *the empty bottle rolled down the pavement*: **turn round and round**, go round and round, turn over and over, spin, rotate; bowl.
2 *waiters rolled in trolleys laden with food*: **wheel**, push, trundle.
3 *we rolled past endless rows of shacks*: **travel**, go, move, pass, cruise, be carried, be conveyed, sweep.
4 *the months rolled by*: **pass**, go by/past, slip by/past, slide by/past, sail by/past, glide by/past, fly by/past, elapse, wear on, steal by/past, march on.
5 *tears were rolling down her cheeks*: **flow**, run, course, stream, pour, spill, trickle.
6 *mist rolled here and there in thick white clouds*: **billow**, undulate, rise and fall, toss, tumble; literary welter.
7 *he rolled his handkerchief into a ball*: **wind**, coil, furl, fold, curl; twist.
8 *roll out the pastry on a floured surface*: **flatten**, level, smooth; even out.
9 *they were rolling about with laughter*: **stagger**, lurch, reel, sway, pitch, totter, teeter, wobble.
10 *the ship began to roll*: **lurch**, toss, rock, pitch, plunge, sway, reel, list, keel, wallow, labour, make heavy weather.
11 *the sky had darkened and thunder rolled in the west*: **rumble**, reverberate, echo, re-echo, resound, boom, peal, roar, grumble.
□ **roll in** informal **1** *since the appeal, money has been rolling in*: **pour in**, flood in, flow in, stream in; informal arrive by the truckload. **2** *he rolled in about 9.00*: **arrive**, turn up, appear, walk in, make/put in an appearance, show one's face; informal show up, pitch up, fetch up, roll up, blow in.
▷ANTONYMS leave.
□ **rolling in it** informal **rich**, wealthy, affluent, moneyed, well off, well-to-do, prosperous, substantial, propertied; informal in the money, loaded, stinking rich, filthy rich, well heeled, flush, made of money, quids in, worth a packet, worth a bundle, on easy street; informal, dated oofy.
▷ANTONYMS penniless.
□ **roll something out 1** *she rolled out her towel*: **unroll**, spread out, unfurl, unfold, open (out), unwind, uncoil, lay out. ▷ANTONYMS roll up.
2 *the Union is to roll out a series of courses for mid-career journalists*: **launch**, introduce, organize, start, begin, embark on, usher in, initiate, put in place, instigate, institute, inaugurate, set up, bring out, open, get under way, set in motion, get going; establish, found, originate, create, pioneer, lay the foundations of, lay the first stone of, bring into being, activate, mastermind, float, debut; start the ball rolling; informal kick off; formal commence.
□ **roll something up** *she rolled up her pyjamas*: **fold (up)**, furl, wind up, coil (up), bundle up.
▷ANTONYMS unroll, roll out.
□ **roll up** informal *at that moment, the police rolled up*: **arrive**, come, turn up, appear, make/put in an appearance, show one's face; informal show up, pitch up, fetch up, roll in, blow in.
▷ANTONYMS leave.
▶ noun **1** *a roll of wrapping paper*: **cylinder**, tube, scroll; bolt.
2 *a roll of film*: **reel**, spool.
3 *a thick roll of notes*: **wad**, bundle.
4 *a roll of the dice*: **throw**, toss; turn, rotation, revolution, spin.
5 *the roll of the ship*: **rocking**, tossing, lurching, pitching, plunging, swaying.
6 *the parish has just 100 people on its electoral roll*: **list**, register, listing, directory, record, file, index, catalogue, inventory; census.
7 *a roll of thunder* | *a roll of drums*: **rumble**, reverberation, echo, boom, thunder, thunderclap, clap, crack, roar, grumble; tattoo, rataplan.

rollicking[1] noun Brit. informal *I got a rollicking for turning up late*. See **lecture** (sense 2 of the noun).

rollicking[2] adjective *a rollicking party*: **lively**, boisterous, exuberant, frisky, spirited; riotous, noisy, rip-roaring, wild, unrestrained, uninhibited, rowdy, roisterous, unruly; Brit. informal rumbustious; N. Amer. informal rambunctious; archaic frolicsome, robustious.
▷ANTONYMS restrained, quiet.

rolling adjective *the rolling waves*: **undulating**, surging, heaving, tossing, rippling, rising and falling, swelling; billowing, billowy; rare undulant.
▷ANTONYMS flat.

roly-poly adjective *a roly-poly man with a walrus moustache*: **chubby**, plump, fat, stout, rotund, buxom, well upholstered, well covered, well padded, of ample proportions, ample, round, rounded, well rounded, full, fattish, dumpy, chunky, broad in the beam, portly, overweight, fleshy, paunchy, bulky, corpulent; informal tubby, pudgy, beefy, porky, blubbery, poddy; Brit. informal podgy, fubsy; N. Amer. informal zaftig, corn-fed, lard-assed; archaic pursy; rare abdominous.
▷ANTONYMS thin, slender, skinny.

romance noun **1** *despite the age gap, romance blossomed*: **love**, passion, ardour, adoration, devotion; affection, fondness, intimacy, attachment.
2 *he's had his share of romances*: **love affair**, affair, affair of the heart, relationship, liaison, courtship, amorous/romantic entanglement, intrigue, attachment; flirtation, dalliance; French amour, affaire, affaire de/du cœur.
3 *a best-selling author of historical romances*: **love story**; novel; romantic fiction, light fiction, sentimental fiction; informal tear jerker.
4 *the romance of Paris in the 1930s*: **mystery**, **glamour**, excitement, colourfulness, colour, exoticism, mystique; appeal, allure, fascination, charm.

romantic adjective **1** *he's very handsome, and so romantic*: **loving**, amorous, passionate, tender, tender-hearted, fond, affectionate; informal lovey-dovey.
2 *the disc jockey kept the romantic records for the end of the night*: **sentimental**, hearts-and-flowers; mawkish, over-sentimental, cloying, sickly, saccharine, sugary, syrupy; informal slushy, mushy, sloppy, schmaltzy, weepy, cutesy, gooey, drippy, sloshy, soupy, treacly, cheesy, corny, icky, sick-making, toe-curling; Brit. informal soppy; N. Amer. informal cornball, sappy, hokey, three-hankie; trademark Mills and Boon.
▷ANTONYMS unsentimental, gritty.
3 *a beautiful cottage in a romantic setting*: **idyllic**, picturesque, fairy-tale; beautiful, lovely, charming, delightful, pretty.
4 *romantic notions of rural communities*: **idealistic**, idealized, unrealistic, head-in-the-clouds, out of touch with reality; starry-eyed, optimistic, hopeful, visionary, utopian, fairy-tale, fanciful, dreamy, ivory-towered; impractical, unpractical, unworkable, improbable, unlikely; rare Micawberish, Panglossian.
▷ANTONYMS realistic, practical, down-to-earth.
5 *she found him an intensely romantic figure*: **fascinating**, **glamorous**, attractive, interesting, mysterious, exotic, exciting, quixotic.
▶ noun *the guy is an incurable romantic*: **idealist**, sentimentalist, romanticist; dreamer, visionary, utopian, Don Quixote, fantasist, fantasizer; archaic fantast.
▷ANTONYMS realist.

Romeo noun *no Italian Romeo with an over-active libido was going to catch her*: **ladies' man**, Don Juan, Casanova, Lothario, womanizer, playboy, lover, seducer, philanderer, flirt; gigolo; informal wolf, ladykiller, stud, skirt-chaser; informal, dated gay dog; archaic gallant.

romp verb **1** *two fox cubs romped playfully on the bank*: **play**, frolic, frisk, gambol, jump about/around, spring about/around, bound about/around, skip, prance, caper, sport, cavort; rare rollick, curvet.
2 *South Africa romped to a six-wicket win over India*: **sweep**, sail, coast; win easily, win hands down, run away with it; informal win by a mile, walk it.

roof noun
□ **hit the roof** informal *Ron will hit the roof when he sees this*: **be very angry**, be furious, lose one's temper, go into a rage, breathe fire; informal go mad, go crazy, be hopping mad, be livid, go wild, go bananas, have a fit, blow one's top, blow a fuse, blow a gasket, do one's nut, go through the roof, go up the wall, go off the deep end, go ape, flip, flip one's lid, lose one's rag, be fit to be tied, go non-linear; Brit. informal go spare, go crackers, get one's knickers in a twist; N. Amer. informal flip one's wig.

Word links **roof**

tectiform roof-shaped

rook verb informal *police files are overflowing with complaints from people who've been rooked*. See **swindle**.

room noun **1** *there isn't much room*: **space**, free space; headroom, legroom; area, territory, expanse, extent, volume; informal elbow room.
2 *there's always room for improvement*: **scope**, capacity, margin, leeway,

r

latitude, freedom; occasion, opportunity, chance.
3 *he wandered around the room*: archaic **chamber**.
4 (**rooms**) *he had rooms in the Pepys building, overlooking the River Cam*: **lodgings**, quarters; accommodation, a place, a place to stay, a billet; suite, apartments; Brit. informal digs; formal abode.
▸ verb *he had roomed there since September*: **lodge**, board, have rooms; live, stay; be quartered, be housed, be billeted; formal dwell, reside, be domiciled, sojourn.

roomy adjective *the accommodation was roomy and warm | a roomy coat*: **spacious**, commodious, capacious, sizeable, generous, big, large, broad, wide, extensive; voluminous, ample, loose-fitting; rare spacey.
▷ANTONYMS cramped, tiny, poky; tight-fitting.

root noun **1** *the fungus attacks a plant's roots*: **radicle**, rhizome, rootstock, tuber, tap root, rootlet; rare radicel.
2 *the root of the problem*: **source**, origin, starting point, seed, germ, beginnings, genesis; **cause**, reason; base, basis, foundation, bottom, seat, fundamental; core, nucleus, heart, kernel, nub, essence; Latin fons et origo; literary fountainhead, wellspring, fount; rare radix.
3 (**roots**) *he has rejected his roots*: **origins**, beginnings, family, ancestors, predecessors; heritage; birthplace, native land, motherland, fatherland, homeland, native country, native soil.
□ **put down roots** *they married and put down roots in Britain*: **settle**, become established, establish oneself, make one's home, set up home.
□ **root and branch 1** *the whole ghastly superstructure should be brought down and got rid of, root and branch*: **completely**, entirely, wholly, totally, utterly, thoroughly; radically. **2** *the party wanted a root-and-branch reform of the electoral system*: **complete**, total, entire, utter, thorough; radical.
□ **take root 1** *leave the plants to take root over the next couple of weeks*: **begin to germinate**, begin to sprout, establish, strike, take.
2 *environmentalism had taken root as a political movement in Europe*: **become established**, establish itself, become fixed, take hold; develop, thrive, flourish.
▸ verb **1** *give the shoot a gentle tug to see if it has rooted*: **take root**, grow roots, become established, establish, strike, take.
2 *June is a good month to begin rooting cuttings*: **plant**, bed out, sow.
3 *he rooted around in the cupboard and brought out a packet of biscuits*: **rummage**, hunt, search, rifle, delve, forage, dig, nose, poke; Brit. informal rootle.
□ **root for** informal *the clamour of baseball fans rooting for their team*: **cheer**, applaud, cheer on, support, encourage, urge on, shout for.
□ **root something out 1** *the hedge was rooted out*: **uproot**, tear something up by the roots, pull something up, grub something out; rare deracinate.
▷ANTONYMS plant. **2** *his main purpose was to root out corruption in the judiciary*: **eradicate**, get rid of, eliminate, weed out, remove, destroy, put an end to, do away with, wipe out, stamp out, extirpate, abolish, extinguish.
▷ANTONYMS establish. **3** *are you hoping to root out some dark secret from Joseph's past?* **unearth**, dig up, dig out, turn up, bring to light, uncover, discover, dredge up, ferret out, hunt out, nose out, expose.

> *Word links* **root**
> **radical** relating to roots
> **rhizo-** related prefix, as in *rhizomorph*

rooted adjective **1** *such views are rooted in Indian culture*: **embedded**, fixed, firmly established, implanted; deep-rooted, entrenched, ingrained, ineradicable.
2 *Nell was* **rooted to the spot**: **unable to move from**, frozen to, riveted to, paralysed to, glued to, fixed to; stock-still, as still as a statue, as if turned to stone, motionless, unmoving.

rootless adjective *once she had been proud of being rootless*: **itinerant**, unsettled, drifting, roving, footloose; **homeless**, without family ties, of no fixed abode, without a settled home, vagabond.

rope noun **cord**, cable, line, strand, hawser; string.
□ **know the ropes** informal **know what to do**, know the procedure, know the routine, know one's way around, know one's stuff, know what's what, understand the set-up, be experienced, be an old hand, know all the ins and outs; informal know the drill, know the score.
▷ANTONYMS be a beginner.
▸ verb *his feet were roped together*: **tie**, bind, lash, truss, pinion; secure, moor, fasten, make fast, attach; hitch, tether, lasso.
□ **rope someone in/into** *they tried to rope me into helping out*: **persuade to/into**, talk into, inveigle into; enlist, engage; informal drag in/into.

> *Word links* **rope**
> **funicular** relating to ropes

ropy adjective **1** Brit. informal *I feel a bit ropy, actually*. See **ill**.
2 Brit. informal *the Italians were helped by some ropy defending from the home team*. See **substandard**.
3 *ropy strands of sticky lava*: **viscous**, gelatinous, viscid, sticky, glutinous, mucilaginous, thick; **stringy**, thready, fibrous, filamentous.

roster noun *according to the roster, he was due to work today*: **list**, listing, register, schedule, agenda, calendar, roll, directory, table; Brit. **rota**.

rostrum noun **dais**, platform, podium, stage; soapbox; Indian mandapam; rare tribune.

rosy adjective **1** *her rosy cheeks | a rosy complexion*: **pink**, pinkish, rose-pink, rose-coloured, roseate, red, reddish, rose-red; glowing, healthy-looking, fresh, radiant, blooming; blushing, flushed; ruddy, high-coloured, rubicund, florid; rare erubescent, rubescent.
▷ANTONYMS pale, pallid, sallow.
2 *Ian's future looks rosy*: **promising**, full of promise, optimistic, auspicious, hopeful, full of hope, encouraging, favourable, bright, sunny, golden, cheerful, happy; informal upbeat.
▷ANTONYMS bleak, dismal, depressing.

rot verb **1** *the floorboards in the centre of the room had rotted*: **decay**, decompose, disintegrate, crumble, become rotten; corrode, perish.
2 *the meat was beginning to rot*: **go bad**, go off, spoil; go sour, moulder, go mouldy, taint; putrefy, fester, become gangrenous, mortify; rare necrose, sphacelate.
3 *poor city neighbourhoods have been left to rot for years*: **deteriorate**, degenerate, decline, decay, fall into decay, go to rack and ruin, become dilapidated, go to seed, go downhill, languish, moulder; informal go to pot, go to the dogs, go down the toilet.
▷ANTONYMS recover, improve.
▸ noun **1** *the leaves were turning black with rot*: **decay**, decomposition; corrosion; mould, mouldiness, mildew, blight, canker; putrefaction, putrescence; wet rot, dry rot.
2 *staunch defenders of traditionalism argued that the rot set in with Van Gogh and Gauguin*: **deterioration**, decline; corruption, canker, cancer.
3 informal *stop talking rot*: **nonsense**, rubbish, balderdash, gibberish, claptrap, blarney, blather, blether; informal hogwash, baloney, tripe, drivel, bilge, bosh, bull, bunk, hot air, eyewash, piffle, poppycock, phooey, hooey, malarkey, twaddle, guff, dribble; Brit. informal cobblers, codswallop, cock, stuff and nonsense, tosh; Scottish & N. English informal havers; N. Amer. informal garbage, flapdoodle, blathers, wack, bushwa, applesauce; informal, dated bunkum, tommyrot, cod, gammon.
▷ANTONYMS sense.

> *Word links* **rot**
> **sapro-** related prefix, as in *saprogenic*

rota noun Brit. **roster**, list, schedule, register, timetable, calendar.

rotary adjective *rotary motion*: **rotating**, rotatory, rotational, revolving, turning, spinning, gyrating, gyratory, whirling.

rotate verb **1** *the wheels had to rotate continually to provide power*: **revolve**, go round, turn, turn round, move round, spin, gyrate, wheel, whirl, twirl, swivel, circle, pirouette, pivot, reel.
2 *many nurses rotate between high risk and low risk areas during the course of their work*: **alternate**, take turns, take it in turns, work/act in sequence, trade places, change, switch, interchange, exchange, swap; pass from one to another in rotation, move around.

rotation noun **1** *the rotation of the wheels*: **revolving**, turning, spinning, gyration, wheeling, whirling, twirling, swivelling, circling.
2 *one rotation of the Earth*: **turn**, revolution, spin, whirl, orbit.
3 *each member state acts as president of the council for six months in rotation*: **sequence**, succession; alternation, cycle.

> *Word links* **rotation**
> **gyro-** related prefix, as in *gyroscope, gyrocompass*

rote noun
□ **by rote** *they were able to recite Newton's laws by rote*: **mechanically**, automatically, without thinking, unthinkingly, parrot-fashion, mindlessly; **from memory**, by heart.

rotten adjective **1** *the smell of rotten meat*: **decaying**, decayed, rotting, bad, off, decomposed, decomposing, putrid, putrescent, spoiled, spoilt, tainted, perished, mouldy, mouldering, mildewy, sour, rancid, rank, festering, fetid, stinking, smelly, unfit for human consumption; addled; maggoty, worm-eaten, wormy, flyblown.
▷ANTONYMS fresh.
2 *the wooden floor was rotten in places*: **disintegrating**, crumbling, falling to pieces, decomposing, decaying; corroding.
▷ANTONYMS sound.
3 *he had the most disgusting rotten teeth*: **decaying**, decayed, crumbling, carious, black; rare caried.
4 *a New York detective who's rotten to the core*: **corrupt**, unprincipled, dishonest, dishonourable, unscrupulous, untrustworthy, immoral, villainous, bad, wicked, evil, sinful, iniquitous, vicious, base, amoral, debauched, degenerate, dissolute, dissipated, depraved, perverted, wanton;

r

venal; informal crooked, warped; Brit. informal bent.
▷ANTONYMS honourable, decent, incorruptible.
5 informal *it was a rotten thing to do*: **nasty**, unkind, unpleasant, foul, bad, obnoxious, vile, contemptible, despicable, wretched, shabby; spiteful, mean, malicious, poisonous, mean-spirited, cruel, hateful, hurtful; unfair, uncharitable, uncalled for, below the belt, unacceptable, unwarranted; informal dirty, filthy, dirty rotten, low-down, off; Brit. informal beastly, out of order; vulgar slang shitty.
▷ANTONYMS nice, pleasant, kind.
6 informal *he was a rotten journalist*: **bad**, poor, dreadful, awful, terrible, frightful, atrocious, hopeless, inadequate, inferior, unsatisfactory, laughable, substandard; informal crummy, pathetic, useless, lousy, appalling, abysmal, dire; Brit. informal duff, chronic, poxy, rubbish, pants, a load of pants; N. Amer. vulgar slang chickenshit.
▷ANTONYMS good, accomplished.
7 informal *you can keep your rotten job for all I care!* **wretched**, horrible, unspeakable; informal damn, damned, blasted, blessed, flaming, precious, confounded; Brit. informal flipping, blinking, blooming, bloody, bleeding, effing, chuffing; N. Amer. informal goddam; Austral./NZ informal plurry; Brit. informal, dated bally, ruddy, deuced; vulgar slang fucking, frigging; Brit. vulgar slang sodding; Irish vulgar slang fecking.
8 informal *she's had a pretty rotten time*: **unpleasant**, disagreeable, miserable, awful, dreadful, terrible, frightful, bad, vile, grim, horrid, horrible, ghastly; disappointing, regrettable, unfortunate, unlucky; informal lousy, beastly, diabolical; Brit. informal shocking.
▷ANTONYMS delightful, good, nice.
9 informal *I feel rotten about it—I've ruined his life*: **guilty**, conscience-stricken, remorseful, guilt-ridden, ashamed, chastened, contrite, sorry, full of regret, regretful, repentant, penitent, shamefaced, self-reproachful, apologetic.
10 Brit. informal *I felt rotten and couldn't eat for two days*: **ill**, unwell, poorly, bad, out of sorts, indisposed, not oneself, sick, queasy, nauseous, nauseated, peaky, liverish, green about the gills, run down, washed out, faint, dizzy, giddy, light-headed; Brit. off, off colour; informal under the weather, below par, not up to par, funny, peculiar, rough, lousy, awful, terrible, dreadful, crummy; Brit. informal grotty, ropy; Scottish informal wabbit, peely-wally; Austral./NZ informal crook; dated queer, seedy; rare peaked, peakish.
▷ANTONYMS well, okay.
▶ **adverb** informal *he fancies you* ***something rotten***: **very much**, **a lot**, a great deal; really.

rotter **noun** informal *we had decided that all men were rotters*: **scoundrel**, rogue, villain, wretch, reprobate; informal beast, pig, swine, rat, creep, bastard, louse, snake, snake in the grass, skunk, dog, weasel, scumbag, heel, stinker, stinkpot, bad lot, nasty piece of work; Brit. informal scrote; Irish informal spalpeen; N. Amer. informal rat fink, fink; Austral. informal dingo; informal, dated hound, bounder, blighter; vulgar slang son of a bitch, s.o.b., shit; dated cad; archaic blackguard, dastard, vagabond, knave, varlet.

rotund **adjective 1** *a small, rotund man in his late thirties*: **plump**, chubby, fat, stout, roly-poly, fattish, portly, dumpy, chunky, broad in the beam, overweight, heavy, pot-bellied, beer-bellied, paunchy, Falstaffian; buxom, well upholstered, well covered, well padded, of ample proportions, ample, round, rounded, well rounded, full; flabby, fleshy, bulky, corpulent, obese; informal tubby, pudgy, beefy, porky, blubbery, poddy; Brit. informal podgy, fubsy; N. Amer. informal zaftig, corn-fed, lard-assed; archaic pursy; rare abdominous.
▷ANTONYMS thin, slender, skinny.
2 *huge stoves bearing rotund cauldrons*: **round**, bulbous, spherical; rare rotundate, spheral, spheric, spherular, orbicular.
3 *his splendidly rotund tone*: **sonorous**, full-toned, full-bodied, round, rich, deep, mellow, resonant, reverberant; magniloquent, grandiloquent, orotund; rare pear-shaped, canorous.
▷ANTONYMS thin, reedy.

roué **noun** *he had lived the life of a roué in the fleshpots of London and Paris*: **libertine**, rake, debauchee, dissolute man, loose-liver, degenerate, profligate; lecher, seducer, ladies' man, womanizer, philanderer, adulterer, Don Juan, Lothario, Casanova, playboy; sensualist, sybarite, voluptuary; informal ladykiller, lech, dirty old man, goat, wolf, skirt-chaser; dated gay dog, rip, blood; archaic rakehell; rare dissolute.

rough **adjective 1** *she stumbled on the rough ground*: **uneven**, irregular, bumpy, stony, rocky, broken, rugged, jaggy, craggy; rutted, pitted, rutty.
▷ANTONYMS flat, smooth.
2 *the terrier's coat is rough and thick*: **coarse**, bristly, scratchy, prickly; **shaggy**, hairy, hirsute, bushy, fuzzy.
▷ANTONYMS smooth, sleek.
3 *the tree has a rough, purplish-brown bark*: **gnarled**, knotty, lumpy, knobbly, nodular; rare nodulous, nodose.
4 *the cream brings immediate relief to rough skin*: **dry**, leathery, weather-beaten; **chapped**, chafed, calloused, scaly, scabrous; technical furfuraceous.
▷ANTONYMS smooth.
5 *his voice was rough with barely controlled anger*: **gruff**, hoarse, harsh, rasping, raspy, husky, throaty, gravelly, guttural.
▷ANTONYMS soft.
6 *down the hall, a noise of rough laughter and shouting could be heard*: **raucous**, discordant, cacophonous, grating, jarring, strident, harsh, dissonant, unmusical, inharmonious, unmelodious.
▷ANTONYMS dulcet.
7 *a bottle of rough red wine*: **sharp-tasting**, sharp, sour, acidic, acid, vinegary; rare acidulous.
▷ANTONYMS sweet, mellow.
8 *he tends to get rough when he's drunk*: **violent**, brutal, vicious; **aggressive**, belligerent, pugnacious, thuggish; **boisterous**, rowdy, disorderly, unruly, unrestrained, wild, riotous, undisciplined, unmanageable; informal ugly; Scottish informal radge.
▷ANTONYMS gentle, passive.
9 *a robust machine, able to withstand rough handling*: **careless**, clumsy, inept, unskilful.
▷ANTONYMS careful.
10 *Sophie disliked his rough manners*: **boorish**, loutish, oafish, brutish, coarse, crude, uncouth, rough-hewn, roughcast, vulgar, unrefined, unladylike, ungentlemanly, uncultured, ill-bred, ill-mannered, unmannerly, impolite, churlish, discourteous, uncivil, ungracious, rude, brusque, blunt, curt.
▷ANTONYMS cultured, civilized, refined.
11 *rough seas*: **turbulent**, stormy, storm-tossed, tempestuous, violent, heavy, heaving, raging, choppy, agitated.
▷ANTONYMS calm.
12 *the weather was really rough*: **stormy**, wild, tempestuous, squally, wet, rainy, windy, blustery; foul, filthy, nasty, inclement, unpleasant, disagreeable.
▷ANTONYMS fine.
13 informal *they gave him a very rough time*: **difficult**, hard, tough, bad, unpleasant, demanding, arduous.
▷ANTONYMS easy, pleasant.
14 Brit. informal *you were a bit rough on her*: **harsh**, hard, tough, stern, sharp, abrasive, severe, unfair, unjust, unrelenting, unfeeling, insensitive, nasty, cruel; **unkind**, unsympathetic, inconsiderate, brutal, heartless, savage, merciless, extreme.
▷ANTONYMS kind, gentle.
15 informal *'How are you feeling?' 'Pretty rough'*: **ill**, unwell, poorly, bad, out of sorts, indisposed, not oneself, sick, queasy, nauseous, nauseated, peaky, liverish, green about the gills, run down, washed out, faint, dizzy, giddy, light-headed; Brit. off, off colour; informal under the weather, below par, not up to par, funny, peculiar, lousy, rotten, awful, terrible, dreadful, crummy; Brit. informal grotty, ropy; Scottish informal wabbit, peely-wally; Austral./NZ informal crook; dated seedy; rare peaked, peakish.
▷ANTONYMS well, okay.
16 *she cobbled together a rough draft and then rewrote it*: **preliminary**, hasty, quick, sketchy, cursory, basic, crude, rudimentary, rough and ready, raw, unpolished, unrefined; incomplete, unfinished, uncompleted.
▷ANTONYMS finished, perfected.
17 *this is only a rough estimate*: **approximate**, inexact, estimated, imprecise, vague, general, hazy; N. Amer. informal ballpark.
▷ANTONYMS exact, accurate, precise.
18 *I'm afraid the accommodation is rather rough*: **plain**, **basic**, simple, rough and ready, rustic, rude, crude, primitive, spartan, uncomfortable.
▷ANTONYMS luxurious.
▶ **noun 1** *the artist's initial roughs are very important*: **preliminary sketch**, draft, outline, mock-up, model.
2 Brit. *a bunch of roughs attacked him*: **ruffian**, thug, lout, hooligan, hoodlum, rowdy, bully boy, brawler; Austral. larrikin; informal tough, roughneck, bruiser, gorilla, yahoo; Brit. informal yob, yobbo, bovver boy, lager lout, chav; Scottish informal radge; Scottish & N. English informal keelie, ned; Austral./NZ informal roughie, lout.
▶ **verb** *rough the surface with sandpaper*: **roughen**, make rough.
□ **rough something out** **draft**, sketch out, outline, block out, mock up; suggest, delineate, give a brief idea of; formal adumbrate.
□ **rough someone up** informal **beat up**, beat, attack, assault, knock about/around, maltreat, mistreat, abuse, batter, manhandle; informal do over, bash up, work over, beat the living daylights out of; Brit. informal **duff up**; N. Amer. informal beat up on.

rough and ready **adjective** *a somewhat rough and ready solution to the problem*: **basic**, simple, crude, unrefined, unpolished, unsophisticated; makeshift, make-do, thrown together, cobbled together, provisional, stopgap, improvised, extemporary; hurried, sketchy; Latin ad hoc.
▷ANTONYMS sophisticated.

rough and tumble **noun 1** *the row started a real rough and tumble*: **scuffle**, struggle, fight, brawl, fracas, rumpus, melee, free-for-all, scrimmage; Irish, N. Amer., & Austral. donnybrook; Law, dated affray; informal scrap, dust-up, punch-up, shindy; N. Amer. informal rough house.
2 *the boisterous rough and tumble of four three-year-olds*: **fun and games**, horseplay, play, high jinks, romping.

roughly **adverb 1** *he shoved her roughly away from him*: **violently**, forcefully, forcibly, abruptly, unceremoniously.
▷ANTONYMS gently.

r

2 *they treated him roughly*: **harshly**, unkindly, severely, unsympathetically; brutally, violently, savagely, inhumanly, mercilessly, cruelly, heartlessly.
▷ANTONYMS kindly, gently.
3 *a deal worth roughly £2.4 million*: **approximately**, about, around, round about, in the region of, something like, in the area of, in the neighbourhood of, of the order of, or so, or thereabouts, there or thereabouts, more or less, give or take a few, plus or minus a few; nearly, close to, as near as dammit, not far off, approaching; Brit. getting on for; S. African plus-minus; Latin circa; N. Amer. informal in the ballpark of.
▷ANTONYMS exactly, precisely.

roughneck noun informal See **ruffian**.

round adjective **1** *a small round window | a round glass ball*: **circular**, disc-shaped, disk-like; ring-shaped, hoop-shaped, hoop-like, annular; **spherical**, globular, ball-shaped, globe-shaped, orb-shaped, orb-like, cylindrical, bulbous, bulb-shaped, balloon-like; convex, curved, curvilinear, rounded, rotund; technical cycloidal, discoid, discoidal, spheroid, spheroidal; rare globate, globose, orbicular, orbiculate.
2 *a short round man with a loud voice*: **plump**, chubby, fat, stout, rotund, roly-poly, fattish, portly, dumpy, chunky, broad in the beam, overweight, heavy, pot-bellied, beer-bellied, paunchy, Falstaffian; buxom, well upholstered, well covered, well padded, of ample proportions, ample, rounded, well rounded, full; flabby, fleshy, bulky, corpulent, obese; informal tubby, pudgy, beefy, porky, blubbery, poddy; Brit. informal podgy, fubsy; N. Amer. informal zaftig, corn-fed, lard-assed; archaic pursy; rare abdominous.
▷ANTONYMS thin, slender, skinny.
3 *his deep, round voice went down well with the listeners*: **sonorous**, resonant, rich, full, full-toned, full-bodied, mellow, mellifluous, rounded, reverberant, orotund; rare pear-shaped, canorous.
▷ANTONYMS harsh, thin, reedy.
4 *a round dozen*: **complete**, entire, whole, full, undivided, unbroken.
5 archaic *she berated him in round terms*: **candid**, frank, direct, honest, truthful, straightforward, plain, plain-spoken, blunt, outspoken, forthright, downright, unvarnished, bald, straight from the shoulder, explicit, unequivocal; informal upfront, not pulling any punches, not beating about the bush; archaic free-spoken.
▷ANTONYMS evasive.
▶noun **1** *divide the dough into 2 oz pieces and mould into rounds*: **circle**, disc, circlet; **ring**, hoop, band; **ball**, sphere, globe, orb, bead; technical annulus.
2 *the local policeman was on his rounds*: **circuit**, beat, course, route; tour, turn.
3 *the first round of the World 500cc championship*: **stage**, level; **heat**, game, lap, bout, contest.
4 *an endless round of late-night parties*: **succession**, sequence, series, cycle.
5 *the gun can fire 30 rounds a second*: **bullet**, cartridge, shell, shot.
▶preposition & adverb **1** *there's a maze of alleys round the station*: **around**, about, encircling, enclosing; near, in the neighbourhood of, in the vicinity of, in the area of; orbiting.
2 *casinos dotted round the south of France*: **throughout**, all over, here and there in, everywhere in.
□ **round about** *he earns round about £40,000 a year*: **approximately**, about, around, roughly, in the neighbourhood of, in the area of, of the order of, just about, something like, more or less, as near as dammit to, close to, near to, practically; or so, or thereabouts, there or thereabouts, give or take a few, plus or minus a few, give or take a bit, in round numbers; not far off, nearly, almost, approaching; Brit. getting on for; S. African plus-minus; Latin circa; N. Amer. informal in the ballpark of.
▷ANTONYMS precisely, exactly.
□ **round the bend** informal **mad**, insane, out of one's mind, deranged, demented, not in one's right mind, certifiable, of unsound mind, crazed, lunatic, unbalanced, unhinged, unstable, disturbed, frenzied, raving, distraught, mad as a hatter, mad as a March hare; Latin non compos mentis; informal crazy, mental, off one's head, out of one's head, off one's nut, nuts, nutty, nutty as a fruitcake, off one's rocker, not (quite) right in the head, raving mad, bats, batty, bonkers, cuckoo, loopy, loony, bananas, loco, dippy, screwy, touched, gaga, doolally, up the pole, not all there, out to lunch, not right upstairs, away with the fairies; Brit. informal barmy, crackers, barking, barking mad, round the twist, off one's trolley, as daft as a brush, not the full shilling, two sandwiches short of a picnic; N. Amer. informal buggy, off the wall, nutsy, nutso, out of one's tree, meshuga, squirrelly, wacko, gonzo; Canadian & Austral./NZ informal bushed; NZ informal porangi.
▷ANTONYMS sane.
□ **round the clock 1** *I've got a team working round the clock*: **day and night**, night and day, all the time, {morning, noon, and night}, the entire time, continuously, non-stop, uninterruptedly, without interruption, without a break, steadily, unremittingly; informal all the hours God sends, 24-7.
▷ANTONYMS intermittently.
2 *she needs round-the-clock supervision*: **continuous**, constant, non-stop, continual, uninterrupted, without interruption, unbroken, steady.
▷ANTONYMS intermittent.
▶verb *the ship rounded the point*: **go round**, move round, travel round, sail round, circumnavigate; orbit; skirt.
□ **round something off 1** *the square edges were rounded off*: **smooth off**, plane off, sand off, level off. **2** *the annual Christmas party rounded off a hugely successful year for the company*: **complete**, finish off, crown, cap, top off, conclude, close, bring to a close/end, end. ▷ANTONYMS begin.
□ **round on** *Guido rounded on Rosie, as though she were to blame*: **snap at**, attack, turn on, set upon, weigh into, fly at, let fly at, lash out at, hit out at, lambaste; informal bite someone's head off, jump down someone's throat, lay into, wade into, lace into, pitch into, tear into; Brit. informal have a go at; N. Amer. informal light into.
□ **round someone/something up gather together**, herd together, drive together, bring together, muster, marshal, rally, assemble, collect, group; N. Amer. corral, wrangle.
▷ANTONYMS disperse, scatter.

> *Word toolkit* **round**
>
> See **circular**.

roundabout adjective **1** *the bus took a very long and roundabout route to Linby*: **circuitous**, indirect, meandering, winding, serpentine, tortuous; rare anfractuous.
▷ANTONYMS straight.
2 *I did ask him, in a roundabout sort of way*: **indirect**, oblique, circuitous, circumlocutory, periphrastic; meandering, discursive, digressive, long-winded; evasive; rare circumlocutionary, ambagious.
▷ANTONYMS direct.
▶noun Brit. **1** *go straight on at the roundabout*: N. Amer. rotary, traffic circle.
2 *an old-fashioned roundabout with painted wooden horses*: **merry-go-round**, carousel; archaic whirligig.

roundly adverb **1** *the 13 per cent pay increase was roundly condemned*: **vehemently**, emphatically, fiercely, forcefully, sharply, bitterly, severely; **bluntly**, outspokenly, forthrightly, baldly, plainly, frankly, candidly.
▷ANTONYMS mildly, gently.
2 *she was roundly defeated by a ratio of two votes to one*: **utterly**, completely, totally, thoroughly, decisively, conclusively, heavily, soundly.
▷ANTONYMS narrowly.

round-up noun **1** *a cattle round-up*: **gathering together**, collecting up, collection, assembly, assembling, rally, rallying, muster, mustering, marshalling; herding together; N. Amer. rodeo, corralling, wrangling.
▷ANTONYMS dispersal.
2 *the Monday sports round-up*: **summary**, synopsis, overview, review, survey, outline, summarization, digest, recapitulation; French precis, tour d'horizon; N. Amer. wrap-up; informal recap.

rouse verb **1** *he roused Ralph at dawn*: **wake**, wake up, awaken, waken, arouse; call, get up; informal give someone a shout, knock up.
2 *she roused and looked around*: **wake up**, wake, awaken, come to, get up, get out of bed, rise, bestir oneself; formal arise.
▷ANTONYMS go to sleep.
3 *he roused the crowd with a speech*: **stir up**, excite, galvanize, electrify, stimulate, inspire, move, fire up, fire the enthusiasm of, fire the imagination of, get going, whip up, inflame, agitate, goad, provoke; incite, egg on, spur on; N. Amer. light a fire under; rare inspirit.
▷ANTONYMS calm.
4 *he's got quite a nasty temper when he's roused*: **provoke**, **annoy**, anger, make angry, infuriate, send into a rage, madden, incense, vex, irk, work up, exasperate; informal aggravate.
▷ANTONYMS pacify, appease.
5 *the letter's disappearance roused my suspicions*: **arouse**, awaken, give rise to, prompt, provoke, stimulate, pique, stir up, trigger, spark off, touch off, kindle, elicit; literary beget, enkindle.
▷ANTONYMS allay.

rousing adjective *Mr Edmonds made a rousing speech*: **stirring**, inspiring, exciting, stimulating, moving, electrifying, invigorating, enlivening, animating, energizing, exhilarating; **enthusiastic**, vigorous, hearty, energetic, lively, spirited, animated; inflammatory; N. Amer. informal stem-winding; rare anthemic, inspiriting.
▷ANTONYMS dull; half-hearted.

rout noun **1** *the army's offensive turned into an ignominious rout*: **disorderly retreat**, retreat, flight, headlong flight.
2 *Newcastle scored 13 tries in the 76–4 rout*: **crushing defeat**, overwhelming defeat, defeat, trouncing, annihilation; debacle, fiasco; informal licking, hammering, clobbering, thrashing, pasting, drubbing, hiding, caning, demolition, going-over, pounding, massacre; N. Amer. informal shellacking.
▷ANTONYMS victory.
▶verb **1** *his army was routed at the Battle of Milvian Bridge*: **put to flight**, put to rout, drive off, dispel, scatter; defeat, beat, conquer, vanquish, crush, overpower, overwhelm, overthrow, subjugate.
2 *the German star routed the defending champion*: **beat hollow**, trounce, defeat utterly, annihilate, triumph over, win a resounding victory over, be victorious over, best, get the better of, worst, bring someone to their knees; informal lick, hammer, clobber, thrash, paste, pound, pulverize, crucify, demolish, destroy, drub, give someone a drubbing, cane, wipe the floor

with, walk all over, give someone a hiding, take to the cleaners, blow out of the water, make mincemeat of, murder, massacre, slaughter, flatten, turn inside out, tank; Brit. informal **stuff, marmalize**; N. Amer. informal **blow out, cream, shellac, skunk, slam.**
▷ANTONYMS lose.

route noun *he walked back by a different route*: **way, course**, road, path, avenue, direction; circuit, round, beat; passage, journey, flight path.
▸ verb *the system will ensure that specialist enquiries are routed to the most appropriate staff*: **direct**, send, convey, dispatch, forward.

routine noun **1** *his early morning routine never varied*: **procedure**, practice, pattern, drill, regime, regimen, groove; programme, schedule, plan; formula, method, system, order; ways, customs, habits, usages; wont; Latin modus operandi; formal praxis.
2 *his stand-up routine depends heavily on improvisation*: **act**, performance, number, turn, piece, line; informal shtick, spiel, patter.
▸ adjective **1** *a routine health check*: **standard**, regular, customary, accustomed, normal, usual, ordinary, established, natural, unexceptional, typical; everyday, common, commonplace, conventional, day-to-day, habitual, wonted, familiar.
▷ANTONYMS unusual.
2 *a routine urban-action movie*: **boring**, tedious, tiresome, wearisome, monotonous, humdrum, run-of-the-mill, prosaic, dreary, pedestrian, menial; unvarying, unchanging; predictable, workaday, hackneyed, stock, unexciting, uninteresting, uninspiring, unimaginative, unoriginal, derivative, banal, trite; uneventful.
▷ANTONYMS exciting.

rove verb *for ten years I roved about*: **wander**, roam, ramble, drift, meander, go hither and thither, maunder; range, travel about; gallivant; Scottish stravaig; Irish streel; rare vagabond, circumambulate, peregrinate.

> *Choose the right word* **rove, wander, roam, range, stray**
>
> See **wander**.

rover noun **wanderer**, traveller, globetrotter, drifter, bird of passage, roamer, itinerant, transient; nomad, gypsy, Romany; tramp, vagrant, vagabond; N. Amer. hobo; informal gadabout; Scottish archaic landloper.

row[1] (rhymes with 'go') noun **1** *rows of small children*: **line, column**, file, cordon; queue; procession, chain, string, series, succession; informal crocodile.
2 *the middle row of seats*: **tier**, line, rank, bank.
□ **in a row** *three days in a row*: **consecutively**, one after the other, in succession; running, straight; informal on the trot.

row[2] (rhymes with 'cow') Brit. informal noun **1** *have you and Peter had a row?* **argument**, quarrel, squabble, fight, contretemps, disagreement, difference of opinion, dissension, falling-out, dispute, disputation, contention, clash, altercation, shouting match, exchange, war of words; informal tiff, set-to, run-in, spat; Brit. informal barney, slanging match, bunfight, ding-dong, bust-up; N. Amer. informal rhubarb; archaic broil, miff; Scottish archaic threap, collieshangie; French, archaic tracasserie(s).
▷ANTONYMS reconciliation, agreement.
2 *Zach could hardly hear because of the row the crowd was making*: **din**, noise, racket, clamour, uproar, tumult, hubbub, commotion, disturbance, brouhaha, ruckus, rumpus, pandemonium, babel; informal ruction, hullabaloo; N. Amer. informal foofaraw.
3 *if Ted spotted you at it, he'd give you a row*: **reprimand**, rebuke, reproof, admonition, reproach, reproval, scolding, remonstration, upbraiding, castigation, lambasting, lecture, criticism, censure; informal rap, rap over the knuckles, telling-off, slap on the wrist, flea in one's ear, dressing-down, roasting, tongue-lashing, bawling-out, caning, blast; Brit. informal ticking-off, carpeting, wigging, rollicking, rocket; Austral./NZ informal serve; Brit. vulgar slang bollocking; dated rating.
▸ verb *lots of couples row about money*: **argue**, quarrel, squabble, bicker, have a row/fight, fight, fall out, disagree, fail to agree, differ, be at odds, have a misunderstanding, be at variance, have words, dispute, spar, wrangle, bandy words, cross swords, lock horns, be at each other's throats, be at loggerheads; informal scrap, go at it hammer and tongs, argufy; archaic altercate, chop logic; Scottish archaic fratch.

rowdy adjective *gangs of rowdy youths*: **unruly**, disorderly, badly behaved, obstreperous, riotous, unrestrained, undisciplined, ill-disciplined, unmanageable, uncontrollable, ungovernable, uncontrolled, disruptive, out of hand, out of control, rough, wild, turbulent, lawless; boisterous, irrepressible, uproarious, rollicking, roisterous, rackety, noisy, loud, clamorous; Brit. informal rumbustious; N. Amer. informal rambunctious; archaic rampageous.
▷ANTONYMS peaceful, quiet, restrained.
▸ noun *the pub was filling up with rowdies*: **ruffian**, troublemaker, lout, thug, hooligan, bully boy, hoodlum, brawler; Brit. tearaway; Scottish & N. English keelie, ned; Austral. larrikin; informal tough, bruiser, yahoo; Brit. informal rough, yob, yobbo, bovver boy, lager lout, chav, hoodie; Austral./NZ informal roughie, lout.

> *Word toolkit*

rowdy	boisterous	lively
behaviour	laughter	debate
crowd	applause	discussion
bunch	children	music
bar	celebration	atmosphere
drunks	comedy	dance
sailors	cheers	game

royal adjective **1** *a royal wave | the royal prerogative*: **regal**, kingly, queenly, kinglike, queenlike, princely; sovereign, monarchical.
2 *tourists can expect a royal welcome*: **excellent**, fine, marvellous, magnificent, splendid, superb, wonderful, first-rate, first-class; informal fantastic, terrific, great, tremendous, grand.
3 informal *she's a royal pain in the neck*: **complete**, utter, total, real, absolute, thorough, veritable; informal flaming, damn, damned, blasted, blessed, confounded; Brit. informal proper, right, flipping, blinking, blooming, bloody, bleeding, effing, chuffing; Austral./NZ informal plurry; Brit. informal, dated bally, ruddy; vulgar slang fucking, frigging.

rub verb **1** *Polly rubbed the back of her neck*: **massage**, knead; stroke, pat.
2 *Rodney was rubbing suntan lotion on Sophie's back*: **apply**, put on, smear, smooth, spread, work in, cream in.
3 *badly fitting shoes can rub painfully*: **chafe**, pinch, scrape, abrade; hurt, be sore, be painful.
□ **rub along** Brit. informal *we rubbed along as best as we could*: **manage**, cope, get along/on, make do, be/fare/do all right, muddle along/through, shift; informal make out, get by.
□ **rub something down** *the horses were unsaddled and rubbed down*: **clean**, sponge, wash; dry; groom; smooth.
□ **rub it in** informal **emphasize**, stress, underline, highlight; **keep going on about**, harp on, dwell on, make an issue of; informal rub someone's nose in it.
□ **rub off on** *my father had a strong contempt for science which rubbed off on me*: **be transferred to**, be passed on to, be transmitted to, be communicated to; affect, influence, have an effect on.
▷ANTONYMS have no effect on; be water off a duck's back to.
□ **rub someone out** N. Amer. informal See **kill**.
□ **rub something out erase**, delete, scrub out, wipe off, remove, efface, obliterate, expunge.
▷ANTONYMS add, leave.
□ **rub shoulders with associate with**, mingle with, fraternize with, socialize with, mix with, keep company with, consort with; N. Amer. rub elbows with; informal hang around/out with, hobnob with, run around with, knock about/around with, pal around with, chum around with; Brit. informal hang about.
□ **rub something up** *the top of the stove was rubbed up every day*: **polish**, buff up, burnish, shine, wax; clean, wipe, scrub, scour.
□ **rub someone up the wrong way** informal **irritate**, annoy, irk, vex, provoke, displease, exasperate, infuriate, get on someone's nerves, get/put someone's back up, put out, pique, upset, nettle, needle, ruffle someone's feathers, make someone's hackles rise, try someone's patience; jar on, grate on; informal aggravate, get, get to, bug, miff, peeve, rile, get under someone's skin, get in someone's hair, get up someone's nose, hack off, get someone's goat; Brit. informal nark, get on someone's wick, give someone the hump, wind up, get across; N. Amer. informal rankle, ride, gravel; vulgar slang piss off; Brit. vulgar slang get on someone's tits; rare exacerbate, hump, rasp.
▷ANTONYMS charm.
▸ noun **1** *she gave my back a rub*: **massage**, rub-down.
2 *I gave my shoes a final rub*: **polish**, buffing; wipe, clean.
3 *that's the rub—will busy managers contemplate reading such a large amount of material?* **problem, difficulty**, trouble, drawback, hindrance, obstacle, obstruction, impediment; snag, hitch, catch.

> *Word links* **rub**
>
> **tribo-** related prefix, as in *triboelectricity*
> **tribology** study of friction

rubber stamp noun *few believe it is anything more than a place where legislation gets a rubber stamp*: **authorization**, permission, approval, assent, consent, sanction; leave, clearance, warranty, agreement, imprimatur, one's blessing, green light, the seal/stamp of approval; authority, licence, dispensation, empowerment, freedom, liberty; informal the OK, the go-ahead, the thumbs up, the say-so, the nod; rare permit, nihil obstat.
▷ANTONYMS the red light; refusal.
▸ verb *officers have been making the decisions, with the councillors just rubber-stamping them*: **approve**, give one's seal/stamp of approval to, agree to, consent to, assent to, acquiesce in, concur in, accede to, give one's blessing to, bless, say yes to, accept; ratify, sanction, endorse, authorize, mandate, license, warrant, validate, pass; confirm, support, back; give one's permission/leave; informal give the go-ahead to, give the green light to, give the OK to, OK, give the thumbs up to, give the nod,

say the word, buy.
▷**ANTONYMS** refuse.

rubbish noun **1** *a more environmentally friendly way of disposing of rubbish*: **refuse**, waste, garbage, litter, discarded matter, debris, detritus, scrap, dross; flotsam and jetsam, lumber; sweepings, leavings, leftovers, scraps, dregs, offscourings, odds and ends; muck; N. Amer. trash; Austral./NZ mullock; informal dreck, junk; Brit. informal grot, gash; Archaeology debitage; rare draff, raffle, raff, cultch, orts.
2 *she's talking a load of rubbish*: **nonsense**, balderdash, gibberish, claptrap, blarney, blather, blether, moonshine; informal hogwash, baloney, tripe, drivel, bilge, bosh, bull, bunk, rot, hot air, eyewash, piffle, poppycock, phooey, hooey, malarkey, twaddle, guff, dribble; gobbledegook; Brit. informal codswallop, cock, cobblers, stuff and nonsense, tosh, taradiddle, cack; Scottish & N. English informal havers; Irish informal codology; N. Amer. informal garbage, flapdoodle, blathers, wack, bushwa, applesauce; informal, dated bunkum, tommyrot, cod, gammon, toffee; vulgar slang shit, crap, bullshit, balls; Austral./NZ vulgar slang bulldust.
▷**ANTONYMS** sense.
▸ **verb** Brit. informal *he seems to spend a lot of his time rubbishing trade unions*. See **criticize**.
▸ **adjective** Brit. informal *they're a rubbish team*. See **hopeless** (sense 4).

rubbishy adjective informal *a crop of delightfully named but rubbishy books*: **worthless**, valueless, trashy, inferior, unsatisfactory, substandard, second-rate, third-rate, poor-quality, low-quality, low-grade, cheap, shoddy, tawdry, gimcrack, twopenny-halfpenny; **bad**, poor, dreadful, awful, terrible, frightful, atrocious; informal crummy, appalling, abysmal, lousy, dire, tacky; Brit. informal duff, chronic, rubbish, poxy, pants, a load of pants; vulgar slang crap, crappy, chickenshit.
▷**ANTONYMS** high-quality.

rubble noun *at the moment we are still trying to dig people out of the rubble*: **debris**, remains, ruins, wreckage; broken bricks.

ruck verb
□ **ruck up** *he pushed back his chair so that it rucked up the carpet*: **scrunch up**, wrinkle, crinkle, cockle, crumple, rumple, pucker, corrugate, ruffle, screw up, crease, shrivel, furrow, crimp, gather, draw, tuck, pleat; Brit. rare ruckle.

ruction noun informal *what's that ruction going on outside?* | *the painting caused ructions at the National Gallery*: **disturbance**, noise, racket, din, commotion, fuss, pother, uproar, furore, hue and cry, rumpus, ruckus, fracas; altercation, quarrel; (**ructions**) an outcry, trouble, the devil to pay, hell to pay; informal to-do, carry-on, hullabaloo, hoo-ha, ballyhoo, stink; Brit. informal row, kerfuffle; N. Amer. informal foofaraw.

ruddy adjective **1** *he was tall and fair with a ruddy complexion*: **reddish**, red, rosy, rosy-cheeked, pink, pinkish, roseate, rubicund; healthy-looking, glowing, fresh; flushed, blushing; florid, high-coloured; archaic sanguine; rare erubescent, rubescent.
▷**ANTONYMS** pale, unhealthy.
2 *the ruddy glow of the low sun*: **red**, reddish, scarlet, vermilion, crimson, blood-red, rose-red, pink, roseate.
3 Brit. informal *you ruddy idiot!* **complete**, total, utter; informal damn, damned, blasted, blessed, flaming, confounded, blithering; Brit. informal flipping, blinking, blooming, bloody, bleeding, effing, chuffing; N. Amer. informal goddam, doggone; Austral./NZ informal plurry; Brit. informal, dated bally; vulgar slang fucking, frigging; Irish vulgar slang fecking.

rude adjective **1** *a rude, arrogant young man*: **ill-mannered**, bad-mannered, impolite, discourteous, impertinent, insolent, impudent, cheeky, audacious, presumptuous, uncivil, disrespectful, unmannerly, ill-bred, churlish, crass, curt, brusque, blunt, ungracious, graceless, brash, unpleasant, disagreeable, offhand, short, sharp; **offensive**, insulting, derogatory, disparaging, abusive; tactless, undiplomatic, uncomplimentary, uncharitable, unchivalrous, ungallant, ungentlemanly, unladylike; archaic malapert, contumelious; rare underbred, mannerless.
▷**ANTONYMS** polite, civil, chivalrous.
2 *some of the boys made rude jokes about her shapely figure*: **vulgar**, coarse, smutty, dirty, filthy, crude, lewd, obscene, offensive, indelicate, improper, indecorous, salacious, off colour, tasteless, in bad taste; risqué, naughty, ribald, bawdy, racy, broad, spicy, colourful, suggestive; informal blue, raunchy, nudge-nudge; Brit. informal fruity, near the knuckle, saucy; N. Amer. informal gamy; euphemistic adult.
▷**ANTONYMS** clean.
3 *if they expected a friendly atmosphere, they were in for a rude awakening*: **abrupt**, sudden, sharp, startling; **unpleasant**, disagreeable, nasty, harsh.
4 *everything in the rude cabin was filthy*: **primitive**, crude, rudimentary, rough, rough-hewn, rough and ready, simple, basic, makeshift.
▷**ANTONYMS** sophisticated, classy.

rudeness noun *I wanted to apologize for my rudeness the other day*: **discourteousness**, discourtesy, lack of manners, bad manners, impoliteness, impertinence, impudence, insolence, effrontery, audacity, presumptuousness, cheek, cheekiness, incivility, disrespect, disrespectfulness, churlishness, crassness, curtness, brusqueness, bluntness, ungraciousness, brashness, sharpness, abusiveness; tactlessness, lack of tact, lack of diplomacy, ungentlemanly behaviour, unladylike behaviour, boorishness, uncouthness; informal lip; Brit. informal sauce, backchat; N. Amer. informal back talk, smart mouth, sass; archaic malapertness, contumely.
▷**ANTONYMS** politeness, good manners.

rudimentary adjective **1** *a simple device which can be constructed by anyone with rudimentary carpentry skills*: **basic**, elementary, introductory, early, primary, initial, first; fundamental, essential; rare rudimental.
▷**ANTONYMS** advanced.
2 *the equipment in all the workshops was rudimentary*: **primitive**, **crude**, simple, unsophisticated, rough, rough and ready, makeshift, rude.
▷**ANTONYMS** sophisticated.
3 *spider monkeys have four long fingers, but only a rudimentary thumb*: **vestigial**, undeveloped, incomplete, embryonic, immature; non-functional; technical abortive, primitive, obsolete.
▷**ANTONYMS** developed.

rudiments plural noun *the rudiments of statistics and probability theory*: **basic principles**, basics, fundamentals, elements, essentials, first principles; beginnings, foundation; informal nuts and bolts, ABC.

rue verb *she might live to rue this impetuous decision*: **regret**, be sorry about, feel apologetic/remorseful about, feel remorse for, repent of; reproach oneself for, kick oneself for; deplore, lament, bemoan, bewail.

rueful adjective *'I've been pretty stupid, haven't I?' Harry said, with a rueful smile*: **sorrowful**, regretful, apologetic, sorry, remorseful, shamefaced, sheepish, hangdog, contrite, repentant, penitent, conscience-stricken, self-reproachful; woebegone, woeful, sad, melancholy, mournful; rare compunctious.
▷**ANTONYMS** happy; unrepentant.

ruffian noun *she was set upon by a gang of young ruffians*: **thug**, scoundrel, villain, rogue, rascal, lout, hooligan, hoodlum, vandal, delinquent, rowdy, bully boy, bully, brute; Austral. larrikin; informal tough, bruiser, heavy, gorilla, yahoo; Brit. informal rough, yob, yobbo, bovver boy, lager lout, chav, hoodie; Scottish & N. English informal keelie, ned; N. Amer. informal hood, goon; Austral./NZ informal roughie, hoon; archaic miscreant; rare myrmidon.

ruffle verb **1** *Patrick kissed her on the cheek and ruffled her hair*: **disarrange**, tousle, dishevel, rumple, run one's fingers through, make untidy, tumble, riffle, disorder; mess up, make a mess of, tangle; N. Amer. informal muss, muss up.
▷**ANTONYMS** smooth.
2 *a light wind ruffled the water*: **make ripples in**, ripple, riffle, roughen.
▷**ANTONYMS** smooth.
3 *'Keep calm,' she told herself, 'don't let him ruffle you'*: **annoy**, irritate, irk, vex, nettle, needle, anger, exasperate; **disconcert**, unnerve, fluster, flurry, agitate, harass, upset, disturb, discomfit, put off, put someone off their stroke, throw off balance, make nervous, discompose, discountenance, cause someone to lose their composure, perturb, unsettle, bother, affect, ruffle someone's feathers, worry, disquiet, trouble, confuse; informal rattle, faze, throw, get to, put into a flap, throw into a tizz, rile, niggle, aggravate, bug, miff, peeve, discombobulate, shake up; Brit. informal wind up, nark, get across.
▷**ANTONYMS** soothe, calm.
▸ **noun** *a very full shirt with ruffles down the front*: **frill**, flounce, ruff, ruche, jabot, furbelow.

rug noun **1** *Charles and Elaine were sitting on the rug in front of the fire*: **mat**, carpet; N. Amer. floorcloth.
2 *his legs were wrapped in a tartan rug*: **blanket**, coverlet, throw, wrap; travelling rug; N. Amer. lap robe, steamer rug.
3 informal *he's still wearing that ridiculous rug*: **toupee**, wig, hairpiece; rare merkin.

rugged adjective **1** *the rugged coast path meanders among tall cliffs*: **rough**, uneven, bumpy, rocky, stony, irregular, pitted, broken up, jagged, craggy, precipitous.
▷**ANTONYMS** smooth.
2 *the sort of conditions which could tear a wheel off a less rugged vehicle*: **durable**, robust, sturdy, strong, strongly made, hard-wearing, built to last, tough, resilient.
▷**ANTONYMS** flimsy, fragile.
3 *up on the scaffolding, two rugged manly types whistled at her*: **well built**, burly, strong, big and strong, muscular, muscly, brawny, strapping, chunky, husky, broad-shouldered, powerfully built, muscle-bound; tough, hardy, robust, sturdy, vigorous, hale and hearty, lusty, solid, mighty; informal hunky, beefy, hulking; dated stalwart; literary thewy, stark.
▷**ANTONYMS** frail, weedy, skinny.
4 *Drew's rugged features*: **strong**, craggy, rough-hewn, rough-textured, manly, masculine; irregular; weather-beaten, weathered.
▷**ANTONYMS** delicate, pretty.
5 *a rugged outdoor life*: **austere**, tough, harsh, spartan, exacting, taxing, demanding, difficult, hard, arduous, rigorous, strenuous, onerous.
▷**ANTONYMS** easy.
6 *the region is a bastion of rugged individualism*: **uncompromising**, unwavering, unflinching, firm, tenacious, determined, resolute.
▷**ANTONYMS** ineffectual, feeble.

ruin noun **1** *these handsome red-brick buildings may now be saved from ruin*: **disintegration**, decay, disrepair, dilapidation, falling to pieces,

r

decrepitude, ruination; **destruction**, devastation, damage, demolition, wreckage.
▷ANTONYMS reconstruction, preservation.
2 (**ruins**) *the ruins of an ancient church*: **remains**, remnants, fragments, relics, remainder, rubble, debris, detritus, wreckage; wreck.
3 *the situation was thought to spell electoral ruin for Labour*: **downfall**, collapse, defeat, overthrow, undoing, fall, failure, breakdown, break-up, disintegration, devastation, ruination; Waterloo; rare labefaction.
▷ANTONYMS triumph, success.
4 *despite extra sales, many shopkeepers are facing ruin*: **bankruptcy**, insolvency, penury, poverty, destitution, impoverishment, indigence, beggary, financial failure; disaster, catastrophe, calamity; rare pauperism, pauperdom, mendicity.
▷ANTONYMS wealth, success.
□ **in ruins 1** *today, the abbey is in ruins*: **derelict**, ruined, gone to rack and ruin, in disrepair, falling to pieces, falling apart, dilapidated, tumbledown, ramshackle, broken-down, decrepit, decaying, ruinous; neglected, uncared-for. ▷ANTONYMS intact.
2 *he was a bitter man, his career in ruins*: **destroyed**, ruined, in pieces, in ashes, falling down about one's ears; over, finished, at an end; informal in tatters, in shreds, on the rocks, done for, toast.
▷ANTONYMS flourishing.
▸ verb **1** *a confrontation now would ruin all my plans*: **wreck**, destroy, devastate, wreak havoc on, reduce to nothing, damage, spoil, mar, injure, blast, blight, smash, shatter, dash, torpedo, scotch, make a mess of, mess up; sabotage, poison; informal louse up, screw up, foul up, put the kibosh on, banjax, do for, blow a hole in, nix, queer; Brit. informal scupper, cock up, dish, muller; Austral. informal euchre, cruel; vulgar slang fuck up; archaic bring to naught.
▷ANTONYMS restore, save.
2 *the bank's collapse was believed to have ruined nearly 2,000,000 people*: **bankrupt**, make bankrupt, cause to go bankrupt, make insolvent, impoverish, reduce to penury/destitution, bring to ruin, bring someone to their knees, wipe out, break, cripple; rare pauperize, beggar.
3 *a country that was ruined by decades of civil war*: **destroy**, devastate, lay waste, leave in ruins, wreak havoc on, ravage, leave desolate; raze, demolish, blast, wreck, wipe out, flatten, level, crush; archaic waste.
▷ANTONYMS rebuild, repair.

ruined adjective **1** *a fascinating medieval town with a ruined castle*: **derelict**, in ruins, gone to rack and ruin, dilapidated, ruinous, tumbledown, ramshackle, broken-down, decrepit, in disrepair, falling to pieces, falling apart, crumbling, decaying, disintegrating; neglected, uncared-for; informal shambly; N. Amer. informal **shacky**; literary blasted.
▷ANTONYMS intact, well maintained.
2 *he finds his reputation as an art dealer ruined*: **destroyed**, in ruins, in pieces, in ashes, falling down about one's ears; over, finished, at an end; informal in tatters, in shreds, on the rocks, done for, toast.
▷ANTONYMS flourishing.

ruinous adjective **1** *the spectre of a ruinous trade war loomed*: **disastrous**, devastating, catastrophic, calamitous, cataclysmic, crippling, crushing, dire, injurious, damaging, destructive, harmful; costly.
▷ANTONYMS beneficial.
2 *lending money at ruinous interest rates*: **extortionate**, exorbitant, excessively high, sky-high, outrageous, inflated, more than can be afforded; Brit. over the odds; informal criminal, steep.
3 *a little to the west of the house is an old, ruinous chapel*: **derelict**, in ruins, ruined, gone to rack and ruin, dilapidated, tumbledown, ramshackle, broken-down, decrepit, in disrepair, falling to pieces, falling apart, crumbling, decaying, disintegrating; neglected, uncared-for; informal shambly; N. Amer. informal shacky.
▷ANTONYMS intact, well maintained.

rule noun **1** *you should follow any health and safety rules which apply to your workplace*: **regulation**, ruling, directive, order, court order, act, law, by-law, statute, edict, canon, ordinance, pronouncement, mandate, command, dictate, dictum, decree, fiat, proclamation, injunction, commandment, prescription, stipulation, requirement, precept, guideline, direction; in Tsarist Russia ukase; in Spain & Spanish-speaking countries pronunciamento.
2 *the general rule is that problems are referred upwards through the organization*: **procedure**, practice, protocol, convention, standard, norm, form, routine, custom, habit, wont; formal praxis.
3 *moderation in all things—that's the golden rule*: **precept**, principle, standard, axiom, truth, truism, maxim, aphorism.
4 *Punjab came under British rule in 1849*: **control**, jurisdiction, command, power, sway, dominion, government, administration, sovereignty, leadership, ascendancy, supremacy, authority, direction, mastery, hegemony, regime, influence; Indian raj; archaic regiment.
□ **as a rule usually**, generally, in general, normally, ordinarily, customarily, almost always, for the most part, on the whole, by and large, in the main, mainly, mostly, more often than not, commonly, typically, on average, in most cases.
▸ verb **1** *El Salvador was ruled by Spain until 1821*: **govern**, preside over, control, have control of, be in control of, lead, be the leader of, dominate, run, head, direct, administer, manage, regulate; literary sway.
2 *Mary ruled for only six years*: **be in power**, be in control, hold sway, be in authority, be in command, be in charge, govern, be at the helm; **reign**, sit on the throne, wear the crown, wield the sceptre, be monarch, be sovereign.
3 *a High Court judge ruled that the children should be sent back to their father*: **decree**, order, direct, pronounce, make a judgement, judge, adjudge, adjudicate, lay down, ordain; decide, find, determine, resolve, settle, establish, hold; rare asseverate.
4 *up in the shanty towns, subversion ruled*: **prevail**, obtain, be the order of the day, predominate, hold sway, be supreme.
□ **rule something out exclude**, eliminate, reject, dismiss, disregard; preclude, prohibit, prevent, obviate, disallow.

Word links **rule**

-cracy related suffix, as in *democracy*
-archy related suffix, as in *oligarchy*

ruler noun **leader**, **sovereign**, monarch, potentate, crowned head, head of state; overlord, chief, chieftain, lord; dynast; despot, dictator, tyrant, autocrat; rare tetrarch, ethnarch, autarch.
▷ANTONYMS subject.

ruling noun *the judge's ruling was slammed by medical experts and union leaders*: **decision**, pronouncement, resolution, decree, determination, injunction; **judgement**, adjudication, finding, verdict; sentence.
▸ adjective **1** *the ruling monarch*: **reigning**, sovereign, on the throne; rare regnant.
2 *the secretary general of Japan's ruling party*: **governing**, in charge, leading, dominant, controlling, commanding, supreme, most powerful, ascendant, in the ascendancy; rare prepotent, prepollent.
3 *in the early 1950s football remained the ruling passion of working men*: **main**, chief, principal, major, prime, most important, dominating, foremost; prevalent, predominant, widespread, general, popular; central, focal; informal number-one; rare regnant.
▷ANTONYMS subsidiary, minor.

rum adjective Brit. informal *she's a rum one, and no mistake*: **odd**, strange, peculiar, unusual, funny, bizarre, queer, weird, curious, abnormal, singular; suspicious, suspect, dubious, questionable; Scottish unco; informal funny peculiar.
▷ANTONYMS ordinary, normal.

rumble verb *thunder rumbled high above us*: **boom**, thunder, roll, roar, resound, reverberate, echo, grumble, growl.

rumbustious adjective Brit. informal *rumbustious football fans*: **boisterous**, unrestrained, irrepressible, exuberant, uproarious, rollicking, roisterous, rackety, noisy, loud, clamorous; **unruly**, disorderly, rowdy, badly behaved, riotous, undisciplined, ill-disciplined, unmanageable, uncontrollable, ungovernable, uncontrolled, obstreperous, disruptive, wild, rough; N. Amer. informal rambunctious; archaic rampageous; rare robustious.
▷ANTONYMS restrained, quiet.

ruminate verb **1** *we sat ruminating on the nature of existence*: **think about**, contemplate, consider, give thought to, give consideration to, mull over, meditate on, muse on, ponder on/over, deliberate about/on, cogitate about/on, dwell on, brood on/over, agonize over, worry about, chew over, puzzle over; turn over in one's mind; archaic pore on.
2 *cows emit more methane when they are ruminating*: **chew the cud**.

rummage verb *Nancy* ***rummaged in*** *her bag for her cigarettes*: **search (through)**, hunt through, scrabble about/around in, root about/around in, ferret (about/around) in, fish about/around in, poke around in, dig in, grub about in, delve in, go through, explore, sift through, rifle through, scour, ransack, turn over; Brit. informal rootle around in; Austral./NZ informal fossick through; rare roust around in.

rumour noun **1** *rumour has it that they have been dabbling in the black arts*: **gossip**, hearsay, talk, tittle-tattle; informal the grapevine, the word on the street; Brit. informal goss; N. Amer. informal **scuttlebutt**, **poop**; Austral./NZ informal furphy; archaic fame.
2 *she had already heard rumours about the couple's problems*: **piece of gossip**, report, story, whisper, canard; speculation; information, word, news; French on dit; informal buzz; rare bruit.
▷ANTONYMS hard facts.

rumoured adjective *a prominent politician is* ***rumoured to be*** *among the customers*: **said to be**, reported to be; reportedly, reputedly, allegedly, apparently, by all accounts, so the story goes.

rump noun **1** *he removed his hand from Shirley's rump*: **buttocks**, behind, backside, rear, rear end, seat, haunches, cheeks; hindquarters, croup; Brit. bottom; French derrière; German Sitzfleisch; informal sit-upon, stern, BTM, tochus; Brit. informal **bum**, **botty**, **prat**, **jacksie**; N. Amer. informal **butt**, **fanny**, **tush**, tushie, tail, duff, buns, booty, caboose, heinie, patootie, keister, tuchis, bazoo, bippy; W. Indian informal batty; humorous fundament, posterior; black English rass, rusty dusty; Brit. vulgar slang arse; N. Amer. vulgar slang ass; technical **nates**; archaic breech.
2 *the rump of the army*: **remainder**, remaining part/number, rest, remnant, remnants, remains; those left.

rumple verb **1** *one bed was empty, the sheet rumpled*: **crumple**, crease, wrinkle, tumble, crush, crinkle, ruck, ruck up, scrunch up, disorder; Brit. rare ruckle.
▷ANTONYMS smooth (out).
2 *Ian rumpled her hair*: **ruffle**, disarrange, tousle, dishevel, run one's fingers through, riffle; make untidy, mess up, make a mess of; N. Amer. informal muss, muss up.
▷ANTONYMS smooth.

rumpus noun informal *there's a terrible rumpus going on outside*: **disturbance**, commotion, uproar, confusion, furore, brouhaha, hue and cry, ruckus, fuss, fracas, melee, tumult, riot, brawl, free-for-all, scuffle, struggle, altercation, quarrel; noise, racket, din, outcry; Irish, N. Amer., & Austral. donnybrook; informal to-do, carry-on, ruction, shindig, shindy, hullabaloo, hoo-ha, ballyhoo, dust-up, scrap, stink; Brit. informal row, kerfuffle; Scottish informal stooshie; N. Amer. informal foofaraw, rough house; Law, dated affray; archaic broil; rare bagarre.

run verb **1** *she jumped out of her car and ran across the road*: **sprint**, race, dart, rush, dash, hasten, hurry, scurry, scuttle, scamper, hare, bolt, bound, fly, gallop, career, charge, pound, shoot, hurtle, speed, streak, whizz, zoom, sweep, go like lightning, go hell for leather, go like the wind, flash, double; jog, lope, trot, jogtrot, dogtrot; informal tear, pelt, scoot, hotfoot it, leg it, belt, zip, whip, go like a bat out of hell, step on it, get a move on, get cracking, put on some speed, stir one's stumps; Brit. informal hop it, bomb; N. Amer. informal boogie, hightail it, barrel, get the lead out; informal, dated cut along; archaic post, hie.
▷ANTONYMS dawdle.
2 *the other three men turned and ran*: **flee**, run away, run off, make a run for it, run for it, take flight, make off, take off, take to one's heels, make a break for it, bolt, beat a (hasty) retreat, make a quick exit, make one's getaway, escape, head for the hills, do a disappearing act; informal beat it, clear off, clear out, vamoose, skedaddle, split, cut and run, leg it, show a clean pair of heels, turn tail, scram; Brit. informal do a runner, scarper, do a bunk; N. Amer. informal light out, bug out, cut out, peel out, take a powder, skidoo; Austral. informal go through, shoot through; vulgar slang bugger off; archaic fly.
▷ANTONYMS stay.
3 *he decided to run in the marathon*: **compete**, take part, participate; enter, be in.
4 *my horse ran second to Suave Dancer in this race last year*: **finish**, come in, come.
5 *a shiver ran down my spine | the ball ran towards the green*: **go**, pass, move, travel; roll, coast.
6 *Grant ran his eye down the column of figures*: **cast**, pass, skim, flick, slide.
7 *a narrow, twisting road which runs the length of the Duddon valley*: **extend**, stretch, reach, range, continue, go.
8 *rainwater ran from the eaves*: **flow**, pour, stream, gush, flood, glide, cascade, spurt, jet, issue; roll, course, slide, spill, trickle, seep, drip, dribble, leak; Brit. informal sloosh.
9 *the walls were **running with** condensation*: **stream with**, drip with, be covered with, be wet with; be flooded by.
10 *my nose was running*: **stream**, drip, exude/secrete/ooze liquid.
11 *a courtesy bus runs to Sorrento three times a day*: **travel**, **ply**, shuttle, go, make a regular journey.
12 *I'll run you back to your hotel*: **drive**, give someone a lift, take, bring, ferry, chauffeur; transport, convey.
13 *he runs a transport company*: **be in charge of**, manage, administer, direct, control, be in control of, be the boss of, boss, head, lead, govern, supervise, superintend, oversee, look after, organize, coordinate, regulate; operate, conduct, carry on, own; preside over, officiate at.
14 *he could no longer afford to run a car*: **maintain**, keep, own, possess, have, drive.
15 *they ran a series of tests*: **carry out**, do, perform, fulfil, execute.
16 *he left the engine running | her car runs well*: **operate**, function, work, go, be in operation; tick over, idle; perform, behave.
17 *the lease runs for twenty years*: **be valid**, last, be in effect, operate, be in operation, be operative, be current, continue, be effective, have force, have effect.
18 *the show ran in the West End for two years*: **be staged**, be presented, be performed, be on, be put on, be produced; be mounted; be screened; last.
19 *he first **ran for** president in 1984*: **stand for**, stand for election as, stand as a candidate for, be a contender for, put oneself forward for, put oneself up for.
20 *the Guardian ran the story on Friday*: **publish**, print, feature, carry, put out, release, issue.
21 *they run drugs for the cocaine cartels*: **smuggle**, traffic in, deal in.
22 *they were run out of town*: **chase**, drive, hunt, hound, put to flight.
□ **run across** *we ran across David when we were playing in LA*: **meet (by chance)**, come across, run into, chance on, stumble on/across, happen on; informal bump into; archaic run against.
□ **run after** informal *ever since his school days, girls have been running after him*: **pursue**, chase, make romantic advances to, flirt with; informal make up to, make eyes at, give the come-on to, come on to, be all over; N. Amer. informal vamp; dated set one's cap at.
□ **run along** informal *run along now, can't you see I'm busy?* **go away**, be off with you, shoo, on your way, make yourself scarce; informal scram, buzz off, skedaddle, scat, beat it, get lost, shove off, clear off; Brit. informal hop it; S. African informal hamba, voetsak; literary begone, avaunt.
□ **run away 1** *she screamed and the men ran away*: **flee**, run off, make a run for it, run for it, take flight, make off, take off, take to one's heels, make a break for it, bolt, beat a (hasty) retreat, make a quick exit, make one's getaway, escape, head for the hills; informal beat it, clear off, clear out, vamoose, skedaddle, split, cut and run, leg it, show a clean pair of heels, turn tail, scram, hook it, fly the coop, skip off, do a fade; Brit. informal do a runner, scarper, do a bunk; N. Amer. informal light out, bug out, cut out, peel out, take a powder, skidoo; Austral. informal go through, shoot through; archaic fly, levant.
▷ANTONYMS stay. **2** *the administration has tried to **run away from** its responsibilities*: **evade**, dodge, get out of, shirk; avoid, disregard, ignore, take no notice of, pay no attention to, turn one's back on; informal shut one's eyes to, duck, cop out of.
▷ANTONYMS face up to, deal with. **3** *Doyle **ran away with** another man's wife*: **run off with**, elope with. **4** *Mario Andretti ran away with the championship*: **win easily**, win hands down; informal win by a mile, walk it, romp home.
□ **run down** *he was dismayed to discover how much the farm had run down*: **decline**, degenerate, go downhill, become dilapidated, go to seed, fall into decay, decay, go to rack and ruin; informal go to pot, go to the dogs.
▷ANTONYMS recover, improve.
□ **run someone/something down 1** *the boy was run down by joyriders*: **run over**, knock down, knock over, knock to the ground; hit, strike. **2** *she began to run him down in front of other people*: **criticize**, denigrate, belittle, disparage, deprecate, speak badly off, speak ill of, find fault with; revile, vilify; informal put down, knock, bad-mouth, have a go at; Brit. informal rubbish, slag off; rare derogate, asperse.
▷ANTONYMS praise.
□ **run something down 1** *she finally ran a copy of the book down in Covent Garden*: **find**, discover, locate, track down, trace, run to earth, unearth, hunt out, ferret out. **2** *employers should run down their labour forces gradually*: **reduce**, cut back on, cut, downsize, decrease, pare down, trim; phase out, wind down, wind up.
▷ANTONYMS increase.
□ **run for it** **flee**, make a run for it, run away, run off, take flight, make off, take off, take to one's heels, make a break for it, bolt, beat a (hasty) retreat, make a quick exit, make one's getaway, escape, head for the hills, take oneself off, decamp, abscond, do a disappearing act; informal beat it, clear off, clear out, vamoose, skedaddle, split, cut and run, leg it, show a clean pair of heels, scram, hook it, fly the coop, do a fade; Brit. informal do a runner, scarper, do a bunk; N. Amer. informal light out, bug out, cut out, peel out, take a powder, skidoo.
□ **run high** *patriotic fervour was running high*: **be strong**, be vehement, be fervent, be passionate, be intense.
□ **run in** *he has a history of heart disease, which runs in the family*: **be common in**, be frequently found in, be inherent in.
□ **run someone in** informal **arrest**, take into custody, apprehend, detain, take in, take prisoner, put in jail, throw in jail; informal pick up, pull in, haul in, pinch, bust, nab, nail, do, collar, feel someone's collar; Brit. informal nick.
□ **run into 1** *the plane was badly damaged when it ran into a parked aircraft*: **collide with**, be in collision with, hit, strike, crash into, smash into, knock into, plough into, barge into, meet head-on, ram; N. Amer. impact.
▷ANTONYMS miss. **2** *I ran into Hugo the other day*: **meet (by chance)**, run across, chance on, stumble on/across, happen on; informal bump into; archaic run against. **3** *the negotiators immediately ran into a problem*: **experience**, encounter, meet with, be faced with, run up against, be confronted with, come face to face with. **4** *Peter had been left with debts running into six figures*: **reach**, extend to, be as high/much as.
□ **run low** *food supplies were running low*: **dwindle**, diminish, become depleted, get less, be used up, become exhausted, be short, be in short supply, be tight.
▷ANTONYMS be plentiful.
□ **run off 1** *three youths scrambled out of the car and ran off*: **flee**, run away, make a run for it, run for it, take flight, make off, take off, take to one's heels, make a break for it, bolt, beat a (hasty) retreat, make a quick exit, make one's getaway, escape, head for the hills, make oneself scarce, decamp, abscond, do a disappearing act; informal beat it, clear off, clear out, vamoose, skedaddle, split, cut and run, leg it, show a clean pair of heels, scram, hook it, skip off; Brit. informal do a runner, scarper, do a bunk, have it away (on one's toes); N. Amer. informal light out, bug out, cut out, peel out, take a powder, skidoo; Austral. informal go through, shoot through; vulgar slang bugger off; archaic fly, levant. ▷ANTONYMS stay.
2 informal *his wife **ran off with** one of the doctors*: **run away with**, elope with, go off with.
3 informal *he **ran off with** the £1000 in the appeal fund*: **steal**, take, snatch, purloin, abscond with, help oneself to; **pilfer**, embezzle, misappropriate; informal walk off/away with, swipe, nab, rip off, lift, 'liberate', 'borrow', filch, snaffle, snitch; Brit. informal pinch, half-inch, whip, knock off, nobble; N. Amer. informal heist, glom; Austral. informal snavel; W. Indian informal tief.
□ **run something off 1** *Sophie, would you just run off a list of all the*

outstanding accounts, please? **copy**, photocopy, xerox, duplicate, print, photostat, mimeograph; make, produce, do. **2** *run off some of the water that has been standing in the pipes*: **drain**, drain off, bleed off, draw off, pump out.
□ **run on 1** *the call ran on for two and a quarter hours*: **continue**, go on, carry on, last, keep going, extend, stretch. **2** *your mother does run on, doesn't she?* **talk incessantly**, talk a lot, rattle on, go on, chatter on, gabble on, ramble on; informal yak, gab, yackety-yak, yap, yabber, yatter; Brit. informal rabbit on, witter on, natter on, chunter on, talk the hind leg off a donkey; Scottish & Irish slabber on; N. Amer. informal run off at the mouth; Austral./NZ informal mag; archaic twaddle, twattle, clack. **3** *my thoughts ran too much on death*: **be preoccupied with**, be concerned with, dwell on, focus on, be focused on, revolve around, centre around, be dominated by, be fixated with.
□ **run out 1** *food supplies were running out*: **be used up**, dry up, be exhausted, be finished, give out, peter out, fail; exhaust.
▷ANTONYMS be plentiful. **2** *they've run out of cash*: **have none left**, have no more of, be out of; use up, exhaust one's supply of, consume, eat up; sell out of; informal be fresh out of, be cleaned out of. **3** *her contract was due to run out*: **expire**, come to an end, end, terminate, finish; lapse, be no longer valid.
□ **run out on someone** informal **desert**, abandon, leave in the lurch, jilt, leave high and dry, discard, cast aside, throw over, turn one's back on; informal walk out on, dump, ditch, leave someone holding the baby, leave flat; archaic forsake.
□ **run over 1** *the bathwater's running over*: **overflow**, spill over, spill, brim over; rare overbrim. **2** *the project ran wildly over budget*: **exceed**, go over, go beyond, overshoot, overreach.
□ **run someone/something over run down**, knock down, knock over, knock to the ground, hit, strike.
□ **run something over** *he quickly ran over the story*: **recapitulate**, repeat, run through, go over, go through, reiterate, review; **look through**, look over, read through; informal recap.
□ **run rings around someone** informal *in a demonstration of classy centre-forward play he ran rings round the opposition*: **surpass**, outshine, outclass, overshadow, eclipse, exceed, excel, transcend, cap, top, outstrip, outdo, put to shame, make look pale by comparison, put in the shade, be better than, beat, outplay, outperform, upstage, dwarf; informal be head and shoulders above, be a cut above, leave standing; archaic outrival, outvie.
□ **run the show** informal **be in charge**, be in control, be the boss, be at the helm, be in the driving seat, be in the driver's seat, be at the wheel, be in the saddle, pull the strings, be responsible; informal call the shots.
□ **run through 1** *her husband had long ago run through their money*: **squander**, fritter away, spend, spend like water, throw away, dissipate, waste, go through, consume, use up; informal blow. **2** *the markedly sceptical attitude that runs through his writings*: **pervade**, permeate, suffuse, imbue, inform, go through. **3** *he ran through his notes again*: **go over**, go through, look over, look through, cast one's eye over, take a look at, run over; read, study, scan, peruse, review, examine, inspect; informal give something a/the once-over. **4** *okay, let's run through scene three again*: **rehearse**, practise, go through, go over, repeat, do again; recapitulate; N. Amer. run down; informal recap.
□ **run someone through** *Campbell threatened to run him through with his sword*: **stab**, pierce, transfix, impale.
□ **run to 1** *the original bill ran to £22,000*: **reach**, extend to, be as high as, be as much as; **amount to**, add up to, total, come to, equal. **2** *sorry, we can't run to champagne*: **afford**, stretch to, manage, have money for. **3** *he was running to fat*: **tend to**, show a tendency to; become, get, grow.
□ **run up** *his loose way of living ran up such big debts that he had to get out of town*: **accumulate**, accrue, amass, collect, gather, stockpile, heap up, rack up, build up, scrape together, hoard, lay in/up, garner; Brit. tot up.
▶ **noun 1** *his early morning run along the Embankment*: **sprint**, race, dash, gallop, rush, spurt; **jog**, trot.
2 *she volunteered to do the school run*: **route**, way, course, journey; circuit, round, beat.
3 *we went out for a run in the car*: **drive**, ride, turn; **trip**, excursion, outing, jaunt, short journey, airing; informal spin, joyride, tootle; Scottish informal hurl.
4 *the current run of unseasonably hot weather | an unbeaten run of eleven home victories*: **period**, spell, stretch, spate, bout; patch, interval, time; **series**, succession, sequence, string, chain, streak.
5 *the budget accelerated a **run on** sterling*: **demand for**, rush for, sudden request for, clamour for.
6 *Margaret gave them **the run of** her home*: **unrestricted/free use of**, unrestricted access to; a free hand in, a free rein in.
7 *it's certainly different from the usual run of East European cafes*: **type**, kind, sort, variety, class, category, order.
8 *against the run of play, Mytchett scored a second goal*: **trend**, tendency, course, direction, movement, drift, tide, current; tenor.
9 *the wire mesh of a chicken run*: **enclosure**, pen, coop, compound.
10 *a steep run with 10 cm of fresh snow*: **slope**, piste, track; bump run; N. Amer. trail.
11 *she had a run in her nylons*: **ladder**, rip, tear, snag, hole.
□ **in the long run eventually**, in the end, ultimately, when all is said and done, in the final analysis, in the fullness of time; Brit. informal at the end of the day.
□ **on the run 1** *a con man on the run*: **on the loose**, at large, loose; **running away**, fleeing, in flight, fugitive; informal AWOL; N. Amer. informal on the lam.
2 *I've been on the run all day*: **busy**, rushing about, rushed off one's feet, dashing about, hurrying about, in a rush, in a hurry, on the move, active; informal on the go.
□ **the runs** informal See **diarrhoea**.

> *Word links* **run**
>
> **-drome** place for running or racing

runaway noun *a 16-year-old runaway*: **fugitive**, escaper, escapee; refugee; truant; absconder, deserter; archaic runagate.
▶ **adjective 1** *a runaway horse*: **out of control**, escaped, loose, on the loose; riderless.
2 *a runaway 6–3 victory*: **easy**, effortless; informal as easy as pie.
3 *prices were heavily increased by runaway inflation*: **rampant**, out of control, uncontrolled, unchecked, unbridled, unsuppressed.
▷ANTONYMS controlled.

rundown noun **1** *let me give you a brief rundown of the situation*: **analysis**, review, overview, briefing, brief, sketch, thumbnail sketch, outline, rough idea; **summary**, résumé, synopsis, precis, recapitulation, run-through, summarization, summation; French tour d'horizon; informal low-down, recap; rare conspectus, summa.
2 *the rundown of NATO forces in the area*: **reduction**, cut, cutback, decrease, curtailment, drop, decline, diminution.

run down adjective **1** *a run-down area of East London*: **dilapidated**, tumbledown, ramshackle, derelict, ruinous, falling to pieces, decrepit, gone to rack and ruin, in ruins, broken-down, crumbling, decaying, disintegrating; **neglected**, uncared-for, unmaintained, depressed, down at heel, seedy, shabby, dingy, slummy, insalubrious, squalid; informal shambly, crummy; Brit. informal grotty; N. Amer. informal shacky.
▷ANTONYMS smart.
2 *by eating more leafy green vegetables you can avoid feeling run down and tense*: **unwell**, ill, poorly, out of sorts, unhealthy, peaky, not oneself, below par, in bad shape; **tired**, debilitated, drained, exhausted, fatigued, enervated, weak, worn out, washed out; Brit. off, off colour; informal under the weather, crummy; Brit. informal not (feeling) up to snuff, ropy, knackered; Scottish informal wabbit; Austral./NZ informal crook; dated seedy, queer; rare peaked, peakish.
▷ANTONYMS healthy, well.

run-in noun informal *his latest run-in with the authorities*: **disagreement**, argument, dispute, difference of opinion, altercation, confrontation, contretemps, quarrel; brush, encounter, tangle; fight, clash, skirmish, tussle; informal set-to, dust-up, shindig, shindy, spat, scrap; Brit. informal row; Scottish informal rammy.

runner noun **1** *seven runners were limbering up*: **athlete**; sprinter, hurdler, racer, long-distance runner, cross-country runner; jogger; competitor, contender, participant, entrant; informal miler.
2 *a strawberry runner*: **shoot**, offshoot, sprout, tendril, sprig, sucker; technical stolon, flagellum.
3 *bookmakers employed runners who ran round picking up bets*: **messenger**, courier, errand boy, messenger boy; scout; agent, collector; N. Amer. informal gofer.
□ **do a runner** Brit. informal See **run away**.

running noun **1** *it was his running between the wickets that really caught the eye*: **sprinting**, sprint, racing; jogging, jog.
2 *the day-to-day running of the school*: **administration**, management, managing, organization, coordination, orchestration, handling, direction, conduct, overseeing, controlling, control, regulation, supervision, charge.
3 *the smooth running of her department*: **operation**, working, functioning, performance.
□ **in the running** *he's in the running for a Nobel Prize*: **likely to win/get/receive**, in contention for, a candidate for, in line for, on the shortlist for, being considered for, up for.
□ **out of the running** *Downpatrick are out of the running for championship honours this season*: **out of contention**, out of the competition, out of the contest, no longer a candidate for.
▶ **adjective 1** *the sound of running water*: **flowing**, streaming, gushing, rushing, moving.
2 *a running argument*: **continuous**, ongoing, sustained, unceasing, incessant, ceaseless, uninterrupted, constant, perpetual, unbroken; **recurrent**, recurring, perennial.
3 *I'm not going to wear the same thing two days running*: **in succession**, in a row, in sequence, one after the other, consecutively; straight, together; informal on the trot.

runny adjective *runny egg yolk*: **liquefied**, liquid, fluid, melted, molten, flowing; thin, watery, diluted; S. African slap.
▷ANTONYMS solid, viscous.

r

Word toolkit

runny	molten	watery
nose	metal	soup
eyes	rock	beer
cheese	lava	coffee
eggs	lead	oatmeal
mascara	glass	mustard
paste	globule	discharge

run-of-the-mill adjective *the match was a pretty run-of-the-mill affair*: **ordinary**, average, standard, middle-of-the-road, unremarkable, unexceptional, undistinguished, unmemorable, forgettable, commonplace, humdrum, mundane, nondescript, characterless, colourless, conventional, normal, pedestrian, prosaic, uninspired, uninspiring, quotidian, uninteresting, uneventful, dull, boring, routine, bland, lacklustre, tame, mediocre, middling, indifferent, unimpressive; N. Amer. garden-variety; informal OK, so-so, bog-standard, vanilla, plain vanilla, nothing to write home about, nothing to get excited about, nothing special, a dime a dozen, no great shakes, not up to much; Brit. informal common or garden; N. Amer. informal ornery; NZ informal half-pie.
▷ANTONYMS remarkable, extraordinary, exceptional.

rupture noun **1** *a recent series of pipeline ruptures*: **break**, fracture, crack; **burst**, split, fissure, blowout.
2 *the rupture was due more to personal than to intellectual differences*: **rift**, estrangement, break-up, breach, split, severance, separation, parting, division, alienation; disagreement, quarrel, feud; schism; informal falling-out, bust-up; Brit. informal row.
3 *ruptures are most common in the very young or very old*: **hernia**.
▶ verb **1** *the steel drum enclosing the reactor core might rupture*: **break**, fracture, crack, breach; **burst**, split, tear, puncture; informal bust.
2 *the situation threatened to rupture their relationships*: **sever**, break, cut off, break off, breach, disrupt; separate, divide; literary tear asunder, cleave, rend, sunder, rive; rare dissever.

rural adjective *an idealized view of rural life | rural areas of Britain*: **country**, countryside, pastoral, rustic, bucolic; agricultural, farming, agrarian; literary Arcadian, sylvan; rare georgic, agrestic, exurban.
▷ANTONYMS urban, city, town.

ruse noun *a ruse to throw would-be pursuers off the scent*: **ploy**, stratagem, tactic, move, device, scheme, trick, gambit, cunning plan, manoeuvre, contrivance, expedient, dodge, subterfuge, machination, game, wile, smokescreen, red herring, blind; the oldest trick in the book; Brit. informal wheeze; archaic shift.

rush verb **1** *Simone rushed back into the house*: **hurry**, dash, run, race, sprint, bolt, dart, gallop, career, charge, shoot, hurtle, hare, bound, fly, speed, zoom, go hell for leather, pound, plunge, dive, whisk, streak, scurry, scuttle, scamper, scramble, make haste, hasten, bustle, bundle; stampede; informal tear, belt, pelt, scoot, zap, zip, whip, step on it, get a move on, hotfoot it, leg it, steam, put on some speed, go like a bat out of hell; Brit. informal bomb, bucket; Scottish informal wheech; N. Amer. informal boogie, hightail it, clip, barrel, get the lead out; informal, dated cut along; N. Amer. vulgar slang drag/tear/haul ass; literary fleet; archaic post, hie, haste.
▷ANTONYMS dawdle.
2 *the noise of water rushing along gutters*: **flow**, pour, gush, surge, stream, cascade, shoot, swirl, run, course; spout, spurt, pump, jet; Brit. informal sloosh.
3 *the tax was rushed through parliament*: **send rapidly**, pass rapidly, hurry, push, hasten, speed, hustle, press, steamroller, force; informal railroad.
4 *some demonstrators rushed the cordon of tanks and troops*: **attack**, charge, run at, fly at, assail; storm, attempt to capture.
▶ noun **1** *the men made a rush for the exit*: **dash**, run, sprint, dart, bolt, charge, scramble, bound, break; stampede.
2 *the lunchtime rush gathered pace*: **hustle and bustle**, commotion, bustle, hubbub, hurly-burly, flurry of activity, stir; archaic hurry scurry.
3 *travel agents say there's been a last minute rush for holidays abroad*: **demand**, clamour, call, request, run (on).
4 *Peacock was in no rush to leave Tyneside*: **hurry**, haste, dispatch; urgency.
5 *a rush of adrenalin | he felt a rush of excitement*: **surge**, flow, gush, stream, flood, spurt; dart, thrill, flash, flush, blaze, stab.
6 *a rush of cold night air*: **gust**, draught, flurry.
7 *I made a sudden rush at him*: **charge**, onslaught, attack, sortie, sally, assault, onrush.
▶ adjective *a rush job*: **urgent**, high-priority, top-priority, emergency; hurried, hasty, fast, quick, rapid, swift; N. Amer. informal hurry-up.

rushed adjective **1** *a rushed divorce from his wife was arranged*: **hasty**, fast, speedy, quick, swift, rapid, hurried, brisk, expeditious; precipitate.
2 *he had been too rushed in Rome to enjoy his stay*: **in a hurry**, running about, run off one's feet, rushing about, dashing about, pushed for time, pressed for time; **busy**, hectic, frantic.

rust verb *the pipe is wrapped with special tape to prevent it from rusting*: **corrode**, oxidize, become rusty, tarnish; crumble away, decay, rot.

Word links rust

ferruginous containing rust

rust-coloured adjective *his rust-coloured hair and beard*: **reddish-brown**, tawny, chestnut, russet, coppery, copper, auburn, Titian, reddish, ginger, gingery, rusty, rufous; brick-red, brick; rare rufescent.

rustic adjective **1** *a rustic setting*: **rural**, country, countryside; countrified; pastoral, bucolic; agricultural, agrarian; literary Arcadian, sylvan; rare georgic, agrestic, exurban.
▷ANTONYMS urban, city, town.
2 *rustic wooden tables*: **plain**, simple, homely, unsophisticated, homespun; peasant; rough and ready, rough, rude, crude.
▷ANTONYMS fancy, elaborate.
3 *rustic peasants*: **unsophisticated**, uncultured, unrefined, uncultivated, simple, plain, homely, artless, unassuming, guileless, naive, ingenuous; coarse, rough, uncouth, graceless, awkward, cloddish, boorish, lumpen; N. Amer. backwoods, hillbilly, hick; archaic clownish.
▷ANTONYMS sophisticated, cultured, urbane.
▶ noun *they paused to watch the rustics dancing and carousing*: **countryman**, **countrywoman**, peasant, son/daughter of the soil, country bumpkin, bumpkin, yokel, country cousin; French paysan; Spanish campesino; Italian contadino, paisano; Russian muzhik, kulak; Egyptian fellah; Indian ryot; Irish informal culchie, bogman; N. Amer. informal hillbilly, hayseed, hick, rube; Austral./NZ informal bushy; archaic clown, villein, swain, hind, carl, cottier; rare bucolic.

rustle verb **1** *the wind rustled lightly through the cottonwoods | her dress of white satin rustled as she walked*: **swish**, whisper, sigh, whoosh; rare susurrate.
2 *he was making a lucrative living rustling cattle*: **steal**, thieve, take, abduct, kidnap.
□ **rustle something up** informal **prepare hastily**, produce, make, put together; informal fix; Brit. informal knock up.
▶ noun *he could hear the soft rustle of her skirt*: **swish**, swishing, whisper, whispering, rustling; rare susurration, susurrus.

rusty adjective **1** *rusty barbed wire*: **rusted**, rust-covered, corroded, oxidized; tarnished, discoloured; rare aeruginous.
2 *his hair was a vibrant rusty colour*: **reddish-brown**, chestnut, auburn, tawny, russet, coppery, copper, Titian, rust-coloured, reddish, rufous; brick-red, brick; rare rufescent.
3 *my French is a little rusty*: **out of practice**, not as good as it used to be, below par; unpractised, not what it was, neglected, deficient, impaired, weak.

rut noun **1** *the Land Rover bumped across the ruts*: **wheel track**, furrow, groove, track, trough, ditch, trench, gutter, gouge, crack, hollow, hole, pothole, cavity, crater.
2 *Julian felt he was stuck in a rut*: **boring routine**, humdrum existence, routine job, same old round, groove, grind, daily grind, treadmill, dead end, assembly line.

ruthless adjective *a ruthless killer | his ruthless determination*: **merciless**, pitiless, cruel, heartless, hard-hearted, hard, stony-hearted, stony, with a heart of stone, cold-blooded, cold-hearted, harsh, callous, severe, unmerciful, unrelenting, unsparing, unforgiving, unfeeling, uncaring, unsympathetic, uncharitable, lacking compassion; **relentless**, remorseless, unbending, inflexible, inexorable, implacable, unpitying, unremitting, steely; brutal, inhuman, inhumane, barbarous, barbaric, savage, bloodthirsty, sadistic, vicious, fierce, ferocious, cut-throat, dog-eat-dog; archaic inclement, fell; rare marble-hearted.
▷ANTONYMS merciful, compassionate, gentle.

Choose the right word ruthless, remorseless, pitiless, relentless

See **relentless**.

Ss

sable adjective *a sable curtain starred with gold*: **black**, jet-black, jet, pitch-black, pitch-dark, pitch, black as pitch, pitchy, ebony, raven, sooty, dusky, ink-black, inky, black as ink, coal-black, black as coal, black as night; literary ebon.

sabotage noun **1** *the fire may have been an act of sabotage*: **wrecking**, deliberate damage, vandalism, destruction, obstruction, disruption, crippling, impairment, incapacitation; rare ecotage.
2 *this procedure is open to sabotage by an awkward participant*: **disruption**, spoiling, ruining, wrecking, undermining, filibustering, impairment, damage, subversion; Brit. informal a spanner in the works; N. Amer. informal a monkey wrench in the works.
▸ **verb 1** *a guerrilla group sabotaged the national electricity grid*: **wreck**, deliberately damage, vandalize, destroy, obstruct, disrupt, cripple, impair, incapacitate.
2 *it would be very easy for me to sabotage your plans*: **disrupt**, spoil, ruin, wreck, undermine, filibuster, impair, damage, threaten, subvert; Brit. informal throw a spanner in the works of, muller; N. Amer. informal throw a monkey wrench in the works of.

sac noun *cephalopods have an ink sac*: **bag**, pouch, bladder, blister; technical bursa, acinus, follicle, cyst, saccule, utricle, vesicle, vesica, vesicula, theca, liposome.

saccharine adjective *some saccharine love songs*: **sentimental**, over-sentimental, over-emotional, mawkish, cloying, sickly, sugary, syrupy, sickening, nauseating, maudlin, lachrymose, banal, trite; informal mushy, slushy, sloppy, schmaltzy, weepy, cutesy, lovey-dovey, gooey, drippy, sloshy, soupy, treacly, cheesy, corny, icky, sick-making, toe-curling; Brit. informal soppy, twee; N. Amer. informal cornball, sappy, hokey, three-hankie.

sack[1] noun **1** *a sack full of flour*: **bag**, pack, pouch, pocket; N. Amer. & Indian gunny; Scottish poke.
2 (**the sack**) informal *I'd better get on with my work now or I'll get the sack*: **dismissal**, discharge, redundancy, termination of employment, one's marching orders; informal the boot, the bullet, the axe, the (old) heave-ho, the elbow, the push, the bounce; Brit. informal one's cards, the chop.
3 (**the sack**) informal *you don't stay long in the sack*: **bed**; Scottish kip; Brit. informal pit.
□ **hit the sack** informal **go to bed**, retire, go to one's room, call it a day, go to sleep; informal turn in, hit the hay.
▷ANTONYMS get up.
▸ **verb** informal *she was sacked for refusing to work on Sundays*: **dismiss**, give someone their notice, throw out, get rid of, lay off, make redundant, let go, discharge, cashier; informal fire, kick out, boot out, give someone the sack, give someone the boot, give someone the bullet, give someone the (old) heave-ho, give someone the elbow, give someone the push, give someone their marching orders, show someone the door, send packing; Brit. informal give someone their cards, turf out; dated out.
▷ANTONYMS hire, take on.

sack[2] verb *Edward I sacked the town in 1296*: **ravage**, lay waste, devastate, ransack, strip, fleece, plunder, pillage, loot, rob, raid; literary despoil; archaic spoil, reave; rare depredate, spoliate, forage.
▸ **noun** *after the sack of the city the cathedral fell into decay*: **laying waste**, ransacking, plunder, plundering, sacking, looting, ravaging, pillage, pillaging, devastation, depredation, stripping, robbery, robbing, raiding; literary despoiling, rape, rapine, ravin; rare spoliation.

sackcloth noun **1** *both clergy and laity wore an extremely uncomfortable black sackcloth*: **hessian**, sacking, hopsack, hopsacking, burlap; N. Amer. & Indian gunny; East Indies tāt; historical poldavy, stramin, sugarsack.
2 *she walked through the town barefoot in the frost, clad in sackcloth*: **penitential garb**, hair shirt; **mourning clothes**, mourning, funeral clothes.
□ **in/wearing sackcloth and ashes penitent**, contrite, regretful, full of regret, sorrowful, rueful, remorseful, apologetic, conscience-stricken, ashamed, guilt-ridden, chastened, shamefaced, self-reproachful, guilty; rare compunctious.
▷ANTONYMS unrepentant.

sacred adjective **1** *only the priest was allowed to approach this most sacred place*: **holy**, hallowed, blessed, blest, consecrated, sanctified, dedicated, venerated, revered.
▷ANTONYMS unconsecrated, cursed.
2 *sacred music*: **religious**, spiritual, devotional, church, churchly, ecclesiastical.
▷ANTONYMS secular, profane.
3 *Coronation Hill was sacred to an Aboriginal group*: **sacrosanct**, inviolable, inviolate, unimpeachable, invulnerable, untouchable, inalienable, protected, defended, secure, safe, unthreatened.

Word links **sacred**

hiero- related prefix, as in *hierogram, hierocracy*

Word toolkit **sacred**

See **holy**.

sacrifice noun **1** *initiation ceremonies include the sacrifice of animals*: **ritual slaughter**, hecatomb, immolation, offering, oblation; self-sacrifice, self-immolation.
2 *Abraham set out to offer Isaac as a sacrifice*: **(votive) offering**, gift, oblation, victim, burnt offering.
3 *the agreement has been achieved without any sacrifice of sovereignty*: **giving up**, abandonment, surrender, foregoing, renouncing, renunciation, renouncement, forfeiture, loss, relinquishment, resignation, abdication, signing away, yielding, ceding, waiving.
4 *many parents **make sacrifices** to send their children to independent schools*: **renunciation**, relinquishment, loss, self-sacrifice; sacrifice something, give up things.
▸ **verb 1** *an ox and two goats were sacrificed*: **offer up**, immolate, slaughter.
2 *he hadn't sacrificed his humanitarian principles*: **give up**, abandon, surrender, forgo, renounce, forfeit, relinquish, resign, abdicate, sign away, yield, cede, waive; prostitute, betray.

sacrificial adjective *the altar may have been used for sacrificial offerings*: **votive**, atoning, expiatory, oblatory, oblational, propitiatory.

sacrilege noun *the sacrilege of committing a murder on holy ground*: **desecration**, profanity, profaneness, profanation, blasphemy, impiety, impiousness, sin, irreverence, irreligion, irreligiousness, godlessness, unholiness, disrespect.
▷ANTONYMS piety, respectfulness.

sacrilegious adjective *he condemned the book as a vicious, sacrilegious attack on their faith*: **profane**, blasphemous, impious, sinful, irreverent, irreligious, godless, ungodly, unholy, disrespectful.
▷ANTONYMS pious, respectful.

sacrosanct adjective *the rights of parents are sacrosanct for this government*: **sacred**, hallowed, respected, inviolable, inviolate, unimpeachable, unchallengeable, invulnerable, untouchable, inalienable, set apart, protected, defended, secure, safe, unthreatened.

sad adjective **1** *every one of us felt sad at having to part company*: **unhappy**, sorrowful, dejected, regretful, depressed, downcast, miserable, downhearted, down, despondent, despairing, disconsolate, out of sorts, desolate, bowed down, wretched, glum, gloomy, doleful, dismal, blue, melancholy, melancholic, low-spirited, mournful, woeful, woebegone, forlorn, crestfallen, broken-hearted, heartbroken, inconsolable, grief-stricken; informal down in the mouth, down in the dumps.
▷ANTONYMS happy, cheerful.
2 *people who knew her sad story have helped her*: **tragic**, unhappy, unfortunate, awful, sorrowful, miserable, cheerless, wretched, sorry, pitiful, pitiable, grievous, traumatic, upsetting, depressing, distressing, dispiriting, heartbreaking, heart-rending, agonizing, harrowing; rare distressful.
▷ANTONYMS cheerful, amusing, comic.
3 *this is a sad state of affairs*: **unfortunate**, regrettable, sorry, wretched, deplorable, lamentable, pitiful, pitiable, pathetic, shameful, disgraceful.
▷ANTONYMS fortunate.

sadden verb *I was saddened by the number of casualties*: **depress**, dispirit, dishearten, grieve, desolate, discourage, upset, get down, bring down, cast down, dash, dampen someone's spirits, cast a gloom on, bring tears to someone's eyes, break someone's heart, make someone's heart bleed; archaic deject.
▷ANTONYMS cheer up.

saddle verb *they were unwilling to be saddled with children*: **burden**, encumber, lumber, hamper, weigh down, land, charge; inflict something on, impose something on, thrust something on, unload something on, fob something off on to.
▶ **noun**
□ **in the saddle** *the president is firmly in the saddle*: **in charge**, in command, in control, responsible, at the top, in authority, in the seat of authority, at the wheel, in the driving seat, at the helm; **managing**, running, administering, directing, supervising, overseeing, controlling, commanding, leading, heading up; informal holding the reins, running the show, pulling the strings, calling the shots.

sadism noun *these incidents displayed a streak of sadism*: **schadenfreude**; **callousness**, barbarity, bestiality, perversion, viciousness, brutality, cruelty, savagery, fiendishness, cold-bloodedness, inhumanity, ruthlessness, heartlessness, mercilessness, pitilessness.

sadistic adjective *we learned that a sadistic killer was on the loose in the area*: **callous**, barbarous, bestial, perverted, vicious, brutal, cruel, savage, fiendish, cold-blooded, inhuman, ruthless, heartless, merciless, pitiless.

sadness noun *there will be great sadness at this news*: **unhappiness**, sorrow, dejection, regret, depression, misery, cheerlessness, downheartedness, despondency, despair, desolation, wretchedness, glumness, gloom, gloominess, dolefulness, melancholy, low spirits, mournfulness, woe, broken-heartedness, heartache, grief; informal down; rare disconsolateness, disconsolation, dismalness.
▷ANTONYMS happiness.

safe adjective **1** *the children are safe in bed | the jewels are safe in the bank*: **protected from harm/danger**, shielded, sheltered, guarded, defended, secure, safe and sound, out of harm's way, all right.
▷ANTONYMS unsafe, insecure, at risk.
2 *the missing children are all safe*: **unharmed**, all right, alive and well, well, unhurt, uninjured, unscathed, in one piece, undamaged, out of danger, out of the wood(s); informal OK.
▷ANTONYMS in danger.
3 *the building is quite safe | it was a safe place to hide*: **secure**, sound, risk-free, riskless, impregnable, unassailable, invulnerable.
▷ANTONYMS dangerous.
4 *he's a safe person to be with*: **trustworthy**, capable of being trusted, trusty, faithful, reliable, dependable, responsible; level-headed, rational, sane, reasonable, sensible, sound, stable, mature, discreet, adult; capable, competent, conscientious; reputable, upright, honest, honourable.
▷ANTONYMS unreliable.
5 *he's a safe driver | on the safe side*: **cautious**, circumspect, prudent, chary, attentive; **timid**, unadventurous, conservative, unenterprising; informal leery.
▷ANTONYMS reckless.
6 *the makers of the drug say it is safe for most people*: **harmless**, innocuous, non-toxic, non-poisonous, non-irritant, benign, wholesome, mild.
▷ANTONYMS harmful.
▶ **noun** *I'm proud of my medal and keep it in a safe*: **strongbox**, safety-deposit box, safe-deposit box, coffer, casket, money chest, cash box, repository, depository, locker; strongroom, vault.

safe conduct noun **1** *UN inspectors had been guaranteed safe conduct*: **freedom of movement**, freedom to travel, free access; immunity.
2 *the Scottish envoys had safe conducts to travel to Nottingham*: **(travel) permit**, pass, passport, transit visa, authority, authorization, credentials; French laissez-passer.

safeguard noun *early warning provides a safeguard against operational crises*: **protection**, defence, guard, shelter, screen, buffer, preventive, precaution, prophylactic, provision, security, safety measure, surety, cover, insurance, indemnity.
▶ **verb** *the contract will safeguard about 1000 jobs*: **protect**, afford protection to, shield, screen, defend, guard, keep safe, shelter; **preserve**, conserve, look after, save, secure.
▷ANTONYMS jeopardize.

safe keeping noun *the document was deposited in the bank vaults for safe keeping | the cash is placed in the safe keeping of the head teacher*: **protection**, **preservation**, safety; custody, care, charge, keeping, surveillance, supervision, guardianship, trusteeship, tutelage, wardship.

safety noun **1** *she is still driving too fast for the safety of local residents*: **welfare**, well-being, protection, security.
▷ANTONYMS danger.
2 *research into the safety of roll-on roll-off ferries*: **security**, soundness, secureness, dependability, reliability, impregnability.
3 *they had to reach the safety of open water*: **shelter**, sanctuary, refuge.
4 *the safety of medicines*: **harmlessness**, lack of side effects.

sag verb **1** *he sagged back in his chair*: **sink**, **subside**, slump, crumple, loll, flop.
2 *the house is very old and the floors all sag*: **curve down**, hang down, dip, droop, swag, bulge, bag.
3 *his spirits sagged as the team suffered yet another defeat*: **falter**, weaken, languish, flag, fade, wilt, shrivel, wither, fail, fall.
4 *industrial production has sagged*: **decline**, fall, go down, drop, drop/fall off, turn down, decrease, diminish, reduce, sink; slump, plummet, tumble; informal crash, take a nosedive, nosedive.

saga noun **1** *the Celts' tribal sagas abound with mythical figures*: **epic**, chronicle, legend, folk tale, romance, traditional story, history, narrative, adventure, fairy story, myth; French roman-fleuve.
2 *the embarrassed staff related the sorry saga of how the seats had been removed*: **rigmarole**, **story**, lengthy story/statement/explanation; chain of events, catalogue of disasters; informal spiel, palaver.

sagacious adjective *the President sent his most sagacious aide to help Republican candidates*: **wise**, clever, intelligent, with/showing great knowledge, knowledgeable, sensible, sage; discerning, judicious, canny, penetrating, perceptive, acute, astute, shrewd, prudent, politic, thoughtful, full of insight, insightful, percipient, perspicacious, philosophical, profound, deep; informal streetwise; rare sapient.
▷ANTONYMS stupid, foolish.

sagacity noun *a man of great sagacity*: **wisdom**, **(deep) insight**, intelligence, understanding, judgement, acuity, astuteness, insight, sense, canniness, sharpness, depth, profundity, profoundness, perceptiveness, penetration, perception, percipience, perspicuity, discernment, erudition, learning, knowledgeability, thoughtfulness; rare sapience.
▷ANTONYMS stupidity.

sage noun *the Chinese sage Confucius*: **wise man/woman**, learned man/woman, man/woman of letters, philosopher, scholar, thinker, savant, Solomon, Nestor, Solon; pandit, authority, expert, guru, maharishi, mahatma, elder, teacher, guiding light, mentor.
▷ANTONYMS fool.
▶ **adjective** *he makes some very sage comments in his book*: **wise**, learned, clever, intelligent, with/showing great knowledge, knowledgeable, sensible, intellectual, scholarly, sagacious, erudite; discerning, judicious, canny, penetrating, perceptive, acute, astute, shrewd, prudent, politic, thoughtful, full of insight, insightful, percipient, perspicacious, philosophical, profound, deep; rare sapient.
▷ANTONYMS foolish.

sagging adjective *we slept on sagging cots*: **drooping**, saggy, bowed, bowing; hanging limply, dangling; droopy, wilting.

Word toolkit

sagging	**droopy**	**dangling**
breasts	eyes	feet
bed	head	chain
roof	eyelids	thread
belly	shoulders	cigarette
flesh	branches	earrings

sail noun *the upright rig means more sail is presented to the wind*: **canvas**.
▶ **verb 1** *we sailed across the Atlantic*: **go by water**, go by sea, go on a sea voyage, voyage, steam, navigate, cruise, ride the waves.
2 *you can learn to sail here*: **yacht**, boat, go sailing; crew, helm, skipper a boat.
3 *we sail tonight*: **set sail**, **put to sea**, put out (to sea), leave port, leave dock, leave harbour, hoist sail, raise sail, weigh anchor, put off, shove off.
4 *he is sailing the ship*: **steer**, captain, pilot, skipper, navigate, con, helm.
5 *untidy grey clouds were sailing past a pale moon*: **glide**, drift, float, flow, slide, slip, sweep, skim, coast, skate, breeze, flit.

S

6 *a pencil sailed past his ear*: **whizz**, speed, streak, shoot, whip, whoosh, buzz, zoom, flash, blast, career, fly, wing, kite, skite, scud; informal scorch, tear, zap, zip.
7 *the ball sailed high into the air*: **soar**, wing, wing its way, take to the air, fly, ascend, mount, climb, arc, curve.
□ **sail into** *he really sailed into the driver of the other car*: **attack**, set upon, set about, fall on, assault, assail, tear into, weigh into, lay into, light into, pitch into, turn on, lash out at, hit out at, strike out at, (let) fly at, lash, round on, drub, thump, batter, hammer, pummel, beat, paste, thrash, belabour, lambaste, berate, abuse; informal let someone have it; Brit. informal have a go at.
□ **sail through** *she sailed through GCSE | he sailed through the Royal Grammar School*: **succeed easily at**, gain success in easily, pass easily, romp through, walk through.
▷ANTONYMS fail, scrape through.

sailor noun *I want to be a sailor and go to sea*: **seaman**, seafarer, seafaring man, mariner; boatman, yachtsman, yachtswoman; hand, crew member; informal (old) salt, sea dog, bluejacket; Brit. informal matelot, matlow, matlo; informal, dated tar, Jack Tar, hearty; **(sailors) crew**, complement.

saint noun

> *Word links* **saint**
>
> **hagio-** related prefix, as in *hagiography*
> **hagiophobia** fear of saints

saintliness noun *one could only admire the bishop's courage and saintliness*: **holiness**, godliness, piety, devoutness, spirituality, blessedness; **virtue**, righteousness, purity, goodness, morality, sanctity, unworldliness, innocence, lack of corruption, ethicality, blamelessness, stainlessness, spotlessness, irreproachableness, guiltlessness, sinlessness.
▷ANTONYMS ungodliness, sinfulness.

saintly adjective *he was a saintly but somewhat ineffective archbishop*: **holy**, godly, pious, God-fearing, religious, devout, spiritual, prayerful, blessed; **virtuous**, righteous, good, moral, ethical, unworldly, innocent, sinless, blameless, guiltless, irreproachable, stainless, spotless, uncorrupted, pure, sainted, saintlike, angelic.
▷ANTONYMS unholy, sinful.

sake noun **1** *some parts of the mechanism are omitted from the diagram* ***for the sake of*** *clarity*: **cause**, purpose, reason, aim, end, objective, object, goal, motive; **for purposes of**, for, in the interests of, in the cause of, in the furtherance of, in order to achieve, with something in mind.
2 *she knew she had to be brave* ***for the sake of*** *her daughter*: **benefit**, advantage, good, well-being, welfare, interest, gain, profit; in someone's interests, to someone's advantage.

salacious adjective **1** *a piece of salacious writing*: **pornographic**, obscene, indecent, improper, indelicate, crude, lewd, erotic, titillating, arousing, suggestive, sexy, risqué, coarse, vulgar, gross, dirty, ribald, smutty, filthy, bawdy, earthy; corrupting, exploitative, prurient, immoral; off colour, nasty, adult, X-rated, low, hard-core, soft-core; informal porn, porno, blue, skin; rare rank.
2 *our father told us to stay away from salacious women*: **lustful**, lecherous, licentious, lascivious, libidinous, prurient, lewd; lubricious, debauched, dissolute, wanton, loose, fast, impure, unchaste, intemperate, dissipated, degenerate, sinful, depraved, crude, goatish; sensual, libertine, promiscuous, carnal; informal randy, horny, raunchy, pervy, naughty; rare concupiscent, lickerish.

S

salary noun *his annual salary was £35,000*: **pay**, earnings, remuneration, fee(s), emolument(s), stipend, honorarium, hire, wages, wage, gross pay, payment, earned income; take-home pay, net pay.

sale noun **1** *a law to curb the sale of firearms*: **selling**, vending, disposal; dealing, trading, bargaining.
▷ANTONYMS purchase.
2 *they chalk up a sale every two seconds*: **deal**, **transaction**, bargain, disposal.
▷ANTONYMS purchase.
□ **for sale** *is that picture for sale?* **on the market**, on sale, on offer, available for purchase, able to be bought/purchased, purchasable, obtainable, in the shops.

salesperson noun *she worked as a salesperson for a time*: **salesman**, **saleswoman**, sales assistant, assistant, shop assistant, saleslady, salesgirl, seller, negotiator, representative, sales representative, agent; reseller, auctioneer, travelling salesperson/salesman/saleswoman, shopkeeper, trader, merchant, dealer; N. Amer. sales clerk; informal counter-jumper, rep, knight of the road; dated shop boy, shop girl, shopman, traveller, commercial traveller, pedlar, hawker.

salient adjective *the salient points stuck out clearly in her mind*: **important**, main, principal, major, chief, primary, notable, noteworthy, outstanding, arresting, conspicuous, striking, noticeable, obvious, remarkable, signal, prominent, pronounced, predominant, dominant, key, crucial, vital, essential, basic, staple, critical, pivotal, prime, central, focal, paramount.
▷ANTONYMS unimportant, inconspicuous.

saliva noun *saliva ran down his chin*: **spit**, spittle, dribble, drool, slaver, slobber, sputum.

sallow adjective *his lips were blue with the cold and his cheeks sunken and sallow*: **yellowish**, jaundiced, pallid, wan, pale, waxen, anaemic, bloodless, colourless, pasty, pasty-faced; unhealthy-looking, sickly, sickly-looking, washed out, peaky, peakish, peaked; informal like death warmed up; Scottish informal wabbit, peely-wally; rare etiolated, lymphatic.
▷ANTONYMS rosy, glowing.

sally noun **1** *a week later the garrison made a sally against us*: **charge**, sortie, foray, thrust, drive, offensive, attack, raid, assault, descent, blitz, incursion, invasion, onset, inroad, onslaught, rush, onrush; German blitzkrieg; Italian razzia.
2 *he sent a dutiful report on his fruitless sally into North Wales*: **expedition**, excursion, trip, outing, jaunt, run, visit, tour, escapade, airing.
3 *he looked round, delighted with his sally*: **witticism**, witty remark, smart remark, quip, barb, pleasantry, epigram, aphorism; joke, pun, jest; **retort**, riposte, counter, rejoinder, return, retaliation; French bon mot; informal one-liner, gag, wisecrack, crack, funny, comeback.

salon noun **1** *a hairdressing salon*: **shop**, parlour, establishment, place, premises, building, place of business, boutique, store.
2 *the famous mirrored salon in the Chateau de Chavigny*: **reception room**, drawing room, morning room, sitting room, living room, lounge, front room, best room, parlour.

salt noun **1** *the temptation to add more salt to food should be resisted*: **sodium chloride**; table salt, sea salt, marine salt, rock salt.
2 literary *he described danger as the salt of pleasure*: **zest**, spice, spiciness, sharpness, raciness, saltiness; flavour, piquancy, pungency, tang, bite, edge; liveliness, vigour, vitality, spirit, colour, sparkle; informal zing, zip, punch, pizzazz.
3 informal *the bay was angry, as old salts would say*. See **seaman**.
□ **with a pinch of salt** *you have to take what she says with a pinch of salt*: **with reservations**, with misgivings, with a grain of salt, sceptically, cynically, mistrustfully, doubtfully, doubtingly, suspiciously, disbelievingly, questioningly, quizzically, incredulously.
▷ANTONYMS credulously, as gospel.
▶ adjective *salt water*: **salty**, salted, saline, briny, brackish.
▷ANTONYMS fresh.
▶ verb
□ **salt something away** informal *she had salted money away in Brazil*: **save**, **put aside**, put away, put by, lay by, set aside, lay aside, put to one side, reserve, keep in reserve, deposit, keep, store, stockpile, hoard, stow away, cache; informal squirrel away, stash away.

salty adjective **1** *salty water | the bacon was quite salty*: **salt**, salted, saline, briny, brackish; piquant, tangy; over-salted.
▷ANTONYMS fresh, bland.
2 *the Princess has a salty sense of humour*: **lively**, vigorous, spirited, colourful, sparkling; zesty, zestful, spicy, sharp; **racy**, piquant, pungent, tangy, biting; informal punchy.

salubrious adjective **1** *I anticipate that I shall find the climate eminently salubrious*: **healthy**, health-giving, healthful, beneficial, good for one's health, wholesome, salutary.
▷ANTONYMS unhealthy.
2 *we managed to move to a more salubrious area of London*: **pleasant**, agreeable, nice, select, upmarket, high-class, leafy, fashionable, expensive, luxurious, grand, fancy; informal posh, swanky, plushy, classy, glitzy; Brit. informal swish; N. Amer. informal swank.
▷ANTONYMS unpleasant, downmarket.

salutary adjective **1** *those incidents are a salutary reminder of the dedication of police officers*: **beneficial**, good, good for one, advantageous, profitable, productive, helpful, useful, of use, of service, valuable, worthwhile, practical; relevant, timely.
▷ANTONYMS unwelcome; irrelevant.
2 *the salutary Atlantic air*: **healthy**, health-giving, healthful, salubrious, beneficial, good for one's health, wholesome.
▷ANTONYMS unhealthy, unwholesome.

salutation noun *her early morning salutation was delivered with chilly sangfroid*: **greeting**, salute, address, hail, welcome, toast, tribute, homage, obeisance.

salute noun **1** *he gave the Brigadier a smart salute*: **gesture of respect**, greeting, salutation, address, hail, welcome, tribute, wave; homage, obeisance, acknowledgement.
2 *the awards were described as an American* ***salute to*** *British courage*: **tribute**, testimonial, honour, homage, toast, compliment, bouquet, eulogy; recognition of, celebration of, acknowledgement of.
▶ verb **1** *the Emperor saluted the assembled ambassadors*: **greet**, address, hail, welcome, acknowledge, pay one's respects to, toast, make obeisance to, wave to, accost.
2 *we salute a truly great photographer*: **pay tribute to**, pay homage to, honour, recognize, celebrate, acknowledge, take one's hat off to.

salvage verb **1** *all attempts to salvage the Danish cargo vessel have been called off*: **rescue**, save, recover, retrieve, raise, reclaim, get back, restore, reinstate.

2 *his first goal salvaged a precious point for his club*: **retain**, preserve, conserve; **regain**, win back, recoup, recapture, redeem, snatch.
▸ noun 1 *the salvage operation is taking place 400 miles off the coast of Newfoundland*: **rescue**, saving, recovery, raising, reclamation, restoration, salvation.
2 *I bought an old car from a salvage dealer*: **scrap**, waste, waste material, waste paper, remains.

salvation noun 1 *we are here to bring you to salvation by way of repentance*: **redemption**, deliverance, saving, help, reclamation.
▷ANTONYMS damnation, downfall, destruction.
2 *she clung to that conviction, knowing it was her salvation*: **lifeline**, preservation, conservation, means of escape.

salve noun *lip salve*: **ointment**, cream, balm, unction, unguent, balsam, pomade, rub, embrocation, emollient, liniment.
▸ verb *she promised him lunch to salve her conscience*: **soothe**, lighten, alleviate, assuage, comfort, ease, allay, dull, mollify, mitigate, palliate.

salver noun *he offered her caviar from a silver salver*: **platter**, plate, dish, tray; Scottish & N. English ashet; archaic trencher, charger; rare paten.

same adjective 1 *it turned out that we were staying at **the same** hotel*: **the identical**, the very same, selfsame, one and the same, the very.
▷ANTONYMS another, different.
2 *all three patients had **the same** symptoms*: **matching**, identical, alike, duplicate, carbon-copy, twin, paired, coupled, double, indistinguishable, interchangeable, corresponding, equivalent, parallel, (all) of a piece, like, like (two) peas in a pod, comparable, similar, correlative, congruent, tallying, agreeing, concordant, consonant.
▷ANTONYMS different, dissimilar.
3 *the Allied landings took place that same month*: **selfsame**, aforesaid, aforementioned.
▷ANTONYMS another.
4 *international hotels tend to provide **the same** menu worldwide*: **unchanging**, unchanged, changeless, unvarying, unvaried, invariable, constant, consistent, uniform, regular.
▷ANTONYMS different, varying.
▸ noun *Louise would have said **the same***: **the same thing**, the aforementioned, the aforesaid, the above-mentioned.
□ **all the same** 1 *I was frightened all the same*: **in spite of that/everything**, nevertheless, nonetheless, even so, however, but, still, yet, though, be that as it may, for all that, despite that/everything, after everything, having said that, just the same, at the same time, in any event, come what may, at any rate, notwithstanding, regardless, anyway, anyhow; informal still and all; archaic howbeit, withal, natheless. 2 *it's all the same to me—see if I care*: **immaterial**, of no importance, of no consequence, inconsequential, unimportant, of no matter/moment, of little account, irrelevant, insignificant, trivial, petty, slight, inappreciable.
▷ANTONYMS of great importance.

Word links **same**

hom(e)o- related prefix, as in *homosexual, homeopathy*

Word toolkit **same**

See **identical**.

sameness noun 1 *a tyranny of sameness is sweeping the earth*: **similarity**, **uniformity**, resemblance, likeness, alikeness, similitude, closeness, comparability, correspondence, indistinguishability, consistency, equality, equalness, parity, equivalence, interchangeability, parallelism; **monotony**, changelessness, invariability, standardization, lack of variety, tedium, tediousness, routine, routineness, humdrum, predictability, repetition, duplication; archaic semblance.
▷ANTONYMS variety, difference, contrast.
2 *the sameness of the force on two electrons explains why they accelerate at the same rate*: **identity**, identicalness, oneness, selfsameness, congruity, congruence.
▷ANTONYMS difference.

sample noun 1 *they each sent a sample of the soil from their district*: **specimen**, example, bit, snippet, illustration, demonstration, exemplification, instance, selection, representative piece; model, prototype, pattern, dummy, swatch, test piece, pilot, trailer, trial, indication, foretaste, taste, taster, tester, smear; archaic scantling.
2 *the survey was carried out on a sample of 10,000 people nationwide*: **cross section**, variety, sampling, test.
▸ verb *plenty of people turned up to sample the culinary offerings*: **try out**, try, taste, sip, nibble, test, put to the test, dip into, experiment with, experience, inspect, examine, check out, appraise, evaluate.
▸ adjective 1 *the sample group is very small*: **representative**, illustrative, selected, specimen, test, trial, typifying, typical.
2 *a sample copy can be obtained at a special price of £2.50*: **specimen**, test, trial, pilot, dummy.

sanatorium noun *he spent long periods in the sanatorium undergoing treatment*: **infirmary**, clinic, sickbay, sickroom, medical centre, hospital, hospice, nursing home, convalescent home, rest home; N. Amer. sanitarium; informal san.

sanctify verb 1 *a small shrine was built to sanctify the site*: **consecrate**, make holy, make sacred, bless, hallow, set apart, dedicate to God, anoint, ordain, canonize, beatify.
2 *they sanctified themselves*: **purify**, cleanse, free from sin, absolve, unburden, redeem, exculpate, wash someone's sins away; rare lustrate.
3 *we must not sanctify this outrageous state of affairs*: **approve**, sanction, give the stamp of approval to, underwrite, condone, justify, vindicate, endorse, support, back, ratify, confirm, warrant, permit, allow, accredit, authorize, legitimize, legitimatize.

sanctimonious adjective *one tries to set a bit of an example, if that's not too sanctimonious*: **self-righteous**, holier-than-thou, churchy, pious, pietistic, moralizing, unctuous, smug, superior, priggish, mealy-mouthed, hypocritical, insincere, for form's sake, to keep up appearances; informal goody-goody, pi; rare religiose, Pharisaic, Pharisaical, Tartuffian.

sanction noun 1 (usually **sanctions**) *codes of practice should be accompanied by sanctions for offenders | trade sanctions*: **penalty**, punishment, deterrent; punitive action, discipline, penalization, correction, retribution; **embargo**, ban, prohibition, boycott, barrier, restriction, tariff.
▷ANTONYMS reward.
2 *the scheme is to receive the sanction of the court*: **authorization**, consent, leave, permission, authority, warrant, licence, dispensation, assent, acquiescence, agreement, approval, seal/stamp of approval, approbation, recognition, endorsement, accreditation, confirmation, ratification, validation, blessing, imprimatur, clearance, acceptance, allowance; informal the go-ahead, the thumbs up, the OK, the green light, say-so; rare permit.
▷ANTONYMS prohibition, ban.
▸ verb 1 *the rally was sanctioned by the government*: **authorize**, consent to, permit, allow, give leave for, give permission for, warrant, accredit, license, give assent to, endorse, agree to, approve, accept, give one's blessing to, back, support; informal give the thumbs up to, give the green light to, OK; N. Amer. rare approbate.
▷ANTONYMS prohibit, ban.
2 *the penalties for water pollution are frail in comparison with those available to sanction traditional crime*: **punish**, discipline someone for.

sanctity noun 1 *few could attain the sanctity of St Francis*: **holiness**, godliness, sacredness, blessedness, saintliness, sanctitude, spirituality, piety, piousness, devoutness, devotion, righteousness, goodness, virtue, virtuousness, purity.
▷ANTONYMS wickedness.
2 *gone is the sanctity of the family meal*: **sacrosanctity**, ultimate importance, inviolability; rare paramountcy.

sanctuary noun 1 *the sanctuary at Delphi was dedicated to Apollo*: **holy place**, temple, shrine, tabernacle, altar, sanctum, inner sanctum, holy of holies, sacrarium, bema, naos, adytum; Latin sanctum sanctorum; Architecture presbytery.
2 *the island was a sanctuary, untouched by the mad modern world*: **refuge**, haven, harbour, port in a storm, oasis, shelter, retreat, bolt-hole, foxhole, hideout, hiding place, hideaway, den, asylum, safe house, fastness; Spanish querencia.
3 *around a thousand abused women and children were given sanctuary*: **safety**, safe keeping, protection, shelter, security, immunity, asylum.
4 *a bird sanctuary*: **reserve**, park, wildlife reserve, nature reserve, reservation, preserve, home, shelter.

sanctum noun 1 *the carving is done in that portion of the temple designed to be the sanctum*: **holy place**, shrine, sanctuary, altar, inner sanctum, holy of holies; Latin sanctum sanctorum.
2 *the inner bar remained a private sanctum for the regulars*: **refuge**, retreat, bolt-hole, foxhole, hideout, hiding place, hideaway, study, den; Spanish querencia.

sand noun *she came bounding across the sand*: **beach**, sands, shore, seaside, seashore, foreshore, (sand) dunes, sandhills, desert; literary strand.

sane adjective 1 *an accused person is presumed to be sane until they can prove the contrary*: **of sound mind**, right in the head, in one's right mind, in possession of all one's faculties, able to think/reason clearly, lucid, clear-headed, rational, coherent, balanced, well balanced, stable, normal; Latin compos mentis; informal all there.
▷ANTONYMS insane, mad.
2 *who would think it sane to use nuclear weapons?* **sensible**, practical, advisable, responsible, realistic, full of common sense, prudent, circumspect, pragmatic, wise, reasonable, rational, mature, level-headed, commonsensical, judicious, politic, sound, balanced, sober.
▷ANTONYMS foolish.

sangfroid noun *he recovered his usual sangfroid*: **composure**, equanimity, self-possession, level-headedness, equilibrium, aplomb, poise, assurance, self-assurance, self-control, nerve, calmness, coolness, countenance, collectedness, imperturbability, presence of mind; informal cool, unflappability.

S

sanguine adjective **1** *he is sanguine about the remorseless advance of information technology*: **optimistic**, bullish, hopeful, buoyant, positive, disposed to look on the bright side, confident, cheerful, cheery, bright, assured; informal upbeat; archaic of good cheer.
▷ANTONYMS pessimistic, gloomy.
2 archaic *a sanguine complexion*. See **florid**.

> *Word toolkit* **sanguine**
>
> See **confident**.

sanitary adjective *improvements in health are also the result of more sanitary conditions*: **hygienic**, clean, germ-free, antiseptic, aseptic, sterile, sterilized, uninfected, disinfected, unpolluted, uncontaminated, salubrious, healthy, pure, wholesome.
▷ANTONYMS insanitary.

sanitize verb **1** *the best way to sanitize a chiller is to let boiling water flow through it*: **sterilize**, disinfect, clean, cleanse, cauterize, purify, fumigate, pasteurize, decontaminate; technical autoclave; rare depollute.
2 *sometimes she would depart from her official schedule and visit some village that had not been sanitized in advance*: **make presentable**, make acceptable, make palatable, clean up; **purge**, expurgate, bowdlerize, censor, emasculate, blue-pencil, water down.

sanity noun **1** *she wondered if she was losing her sanity*: **soundness of mind**, mental health, mental faculties, balance, balance of mind, stability, reason, rationality, saneness, lucidity, lucidness, sense, senses, wits, normality, right-mindedness.
▷ANTONYMS insanity.
2 *we are delighted that sanity has prevailed*: **sense**, common sense, good sense, wisdom, prudence, judiciousness, practicality, reasonableness, rationality, soundness, sensibleness.
▷ANTONYMS insanity.

sap[1] noun **1** *these insects suck the sap from the roots of trees*: **plant fluid**, vital fluid, life fluid, juice, secretion, liquor, liquid.
2 *people full of sap and ready to go*: **vigour**, energy, gusto, drive, push, brio, dynamism, life, go, spirit, liveliness, animation, bounce, sparkle, effervescence, fizz, verve, spiritedness, ebullience, high spirits, enthusiasm, initiative, vitality, vivacity, fire, dash, panache, elan, snap, zest, zeal, exuberance; informal feistiness, get-up-and-go, gumption, oomph, pizzazz, vim, zing, zip.
▶ verb **1** *the great loss of life had sapped the will of the troops to attack*: **erode**, wear away, wear down, deplete, reduce, lessen, lower, attenuate, undermine, exhaust, impair, drain, bleed, consume.
2 *the confirmation of his friend's guilt sapped him of all energy*: **drain**, empty, exhaust, deprive, milk.

sap[2] noun informal *he realized that he'd just made a sap of himself*. See **idiot**.

sarcasm noun *his voice was heavy with sarcasm*: **derision**, mockery, ridicule, satire, irony, scorn, sneering, scoffing, gibing, taunting; trenchancy, mordancy, acerbity; rare causticity, mordacity.

sarcastic adjective *I've had enough of your sarcastic comments*: **sardonic**, ironic, ironical, satirical; derisive, scornful, contemptuous, mocking, ridiculing, sneering, jeering, scoffing, taunting, snide; caustic, scathing, trenchant, mordant, cutting, sharp, stinging, acerbic, tart, acid; Brit. informal sarky; rare mordacious, acidulous.

> *Choose the right word* **sarcastic, sardonic, ironic, caustic**
>
> A **sarcastic** comment expresses the opposite of what it literally means, thus mocking the person on the receiving end, while possibly entertaining others (*'That's nice,' Broomhead said in his most sarcastic manner | the youngsters gave a sarcastic cheer*).
>
> **Sardonic** suggests a grimmer, more cynical amusement. It is used of actual utterances less frequently than the other three words, so people typically give a *sardonic smile* or *grin*, display *sardonic amusement*, or *raise a sardonic eyebrow*.
>
> As with *sarcasm*, **ironic** remarks convey the opposite of their literal meaning, but more subtly and with an effect of wry amusement rather than blatant mockery (*Annie Lennox's first solo LP 'Diva', which she claims is an ironic title*).
>
> A **caustic** remark is cruellest of all; it is straightforward, but scathing or bitter (*she longed to hurl some caustic retort at him*).

sardonic adjective *his sardonic wit*: **mocking**, satirical; **sarcastic**, ironical, ironic, cynical, scornful, contemptuous, derisive, derisory, sneering, jeering, scoffing, taunting; scathing, caustic, trenchant, mordant, cutting, sharp, stinging, acerbic, tart, acid; wry, dry; Brit. informal sarky; rare mordacious, acidulous.

> *Choose the right word* **sardonic, sarcastic, ironic, caustic**
>
> See **sarcastic**.

sash noun **belt**, cummerbund, waistband, girdle; Japanese obi; archaic cincture, zone.

satanic adjective *how could ordinary people have committed such satanic atrocities?* **diabolical**, fiendish, devilish, demonic, demoniac, demoniacal, Mephistophelian; hellish, infernal, accursed, wicked, evil, sinful, iniquitous, nefarious, vile, foul, abominable, unspeakable, loathsome, monstrous, atrocious, heinous, hideous, odious, horrible, horrifying, shocking, appalling, dreadful, awful, terrible, ghastly, abhorrent, despicable, damnable, villainous, depraved, perverted, ungodly, dark, black, black-hearted, immoral, amoral; vicious, cruel, savage, brutish, bestial, barbaric, barbarous; rare cacodemonic, egregious, flagitious, facinorous.

sate verb **1** *he rested, his passion temporarily sated*: **satiate**, fully satisfy; slake, quench, take the edge off.
▷ANTONYMS starve, deprive, dissatisfy.
2 *the children were sated with blackberries*: **gorge**, stuff, fill, overfill, overfeed, surfeit, glut, cloy.

satellite noun **1** *the European Space Agency's ERS-1 satellite*: **space station**, space capsule, spacecraft; artificial satellite, communications satellite, weather satellite, television satellite; sputnik, COBE, IRAS; informal Comsat.
2 *the two small satellites of Mars*: **moon**, secondary planet.
3 *Bulgaria was then a Russian satellite*: **dependency**, colony, protectorate, dominion, possession, holding; historical fief, tributary.
4 *many were Hollywood people, writers and actors and their satellites*: **acolyte**, follower, camp follower, disciple, hanger-on, shadow; henchman, sidekick, lackey, flunkey, minion, underling, hireling, vassal; puppet, stooge, creature; toady, sycophant, parasite; dependent, dependant; Brit. poodle; N. Amer. **cohort**; informal **yes-man**, **bootlicker**; N. Amer. informal **gofer**, suck-up, brown-nose; Indian informal **chamcha**; Brit. vulgar slang **arse-licker**, bum-sucker; N. Amer. vulgar slang **ass-kisser**; archaic retainer, client.
▶ adjective *a satellite state*: **dependent**, subordinate, subsidiary, ancillary; puppet, vassal; historical tributary.

satiate verb *he leaned back against the cushions, satiated by the Christmas fare*: **fill**, fully satisfy, sate; slake, quench; gorge, stuff, overfill, overfeed, surfeit, glut, cloy; sicken, nauseate.
▷ANTONYMS starve, deprive, dissatisfy.

satiety noun *a commercial culture that exhorted one to consume to the point of satiety and well beyond*: **satiation**, satisfaction, sufficiency, repleteness, repletion, fullness; over-fullness, surfeit.
▷ANTONYMS hunger.

satiny adjective *the satiny, honey-coloured wood*: **smooth**, shiny, glossy, shining, gleaming, lustrous, sleek, silky, sheeny; polished, patinated; slippery, glassy; rare nitid.

> *Word toolkit* **satiny**
>
> See **glossy**.

satire noun **1** *a stinging satire on American politics*: **parody**, burlesque, caricature, lampoon, skit, take-off, squib, travesty; informal spoof, send-up; Brit. vulgar slang piss-take; rare pasquinade, pasticcio.
2 *in recent years, the phenomenon has become the subject of satire*: **mockery**, ridicule, derision, scorn, caricature; irony, sarcasm.

satirical adjective *a collection of satirical essays on English social life*: **mocking**, ironic, ironical, satiric, sarcastic, sardonic, scornful, derisive, ridiculing, taunting; caustic, trenchant, mordant, biting, cutting, sharp, pointed, keen, stinging, acerbic, pungent, cynical; critical, irreverent, disparaging, disrespectful, Rabelaisian; rare Hudibrastic, mordacious.

satirize verb *a strip cartoon satirizing middle-aged, middle-class liberals*: **mock**, ridicule, hold up to ridicule, deride, make fun of, poke fun at, parody, lampoon, burlesque, caricature, take off, travesty; criticize, censure, pillory; informal send up; Brit. informal take the mickey out of; Brit. vulgar slang take the piss out of; archaic squib; rare pasquinade.

satisfaction noun **1** *he smiled with satisfaction*: **contentment**, contentedness, content, pleasure, gratification, fulfilment, happiness, sense of well-being, pride, sense of achievement, delight, joy, enjoyment, relish, triumph; self-satisfaction, smugness, complacency; archaic self-content.
▷ANTONYMS dissatisfaction, displeasure, discontent.
2 *the satisfaction of consumer needs and wants*: **fulfilment**, gratification; appeasement, assuagement.
3 *investors may have to turn to the courts for satisfaction*: **compensation**, recompense, reparation, restitution, repayment, payment, settlement, reimbursement, indemnification, indemnity, damages; redress, amends, atonement; justice; requital, retribution; Latin quid pro quo.
▷ANTONYMS loss.

satisfactory adjective *David Kerslake made a satisfactory debut for Leeds*: **adequate**, all right, acceptable, good enough, sufficient, sufficiently good, fine, in order, up to scratch, up to the mark, up to standard, up to par, competent, reasonable, quite good, fair, decent, not bad, average, tolerable, passable, middling, moderate; presentable; suitable, convenient; informal OK, so-so, fair-to-middling; N. Amer. & Austral./NZ informal jake.
▷ANTONYMS unsatisfactory, inadequate, unacceptable, poor.

satisfied adjective **1** *Henry felt satisfied with the day's work | there was a satisfied smile on her face*: **pleased**, well pleased, happy, content, contented;

proud, triumphant; smug, self-satisfied, pleased with oneself, complacent; Brit. informal like the cat that's got the cream; N. Amer. vulgar slang shit-eating; humorous gruntled.
▷ANTONYMS dissatisfied, unhappy.
2 *the pleasure of satisfied desire*: **fulfilled**, gratified, appeased, assuaged; archaic satiate.
▷ANTONYMS unfulfilled.
3 *I am quite satisfied that most of my staff are happy with their conditions of employment*: **convinced**, certain, sure, positive, free from doubt, persuaded, easy in one's mind.
▷ANTONYMS uncertain, unconvinced.

satisfy verb **1** *he wanted one last chance to satisfy his hunger for romance*: **fulfil**, gratify, meet, fill, serve, provide for, supply; indulge, cater to, pander to; appease, assuage; quench, slake, satiate, sate, take the edge off; rare satisfice.
▷ANTONYMS frustrate.
2 *his role was a creative one, and it satisfied him up to a point*: **please**, content, make happy.
▷ANTONYMS dissatisfy, frustrate.
3 *she satisfied herself that it had been an accident*: **convince**, persuade, assure, make certain; reassure, put someone's mind at rest, dispel someone's doubts.
4 *products which satisfy the EC's criteria will be awarded a special eco label*: **comply with**, meet, fulfil, answer, conform to; match up to, measure up to, come up to; suffice, be good enough, fit/fill the bill; Law perfect; informal make the grade, cut the mustard.
5 *there was insufficient collateral to satisfy the loan*: **repay**, pay, pay off, pay in full, settle, make good, discharge, square, liquidate, clear.

satisfying adjective **1** *it's hard work, but very satisfying*: **fulfilling**, rewarding, gratifying, pleasing, enjoyable, pleasurable, to one's liking; worthwhile, constructive, productive, valuable, beneficial.
▷ANTONYMS dissatisfying, frustrating, pointless.
2 *potatoes are satisfying and provide good value for money*: **filling**.
3 *a satisfying explanation*: **satisfactory**, reasonable, acceptable; convincing, persuasive; reassuring.
▷ANTONYMS unsatisfactory.

saturate verb **1** *heavy autumn rain saturated the ground*: **soak**, drench, waterlog, wet through, wet; souse, steep, douse, impregnate; technical ret; Scottish & N. English drouk; archaic sop.
▷ANTONYMS dry out.
2 *the air was saturated with the stench of joss sticks*: **permeate**, impregnate, suffuse, imbue, pervade, steep, charge, infuse, inform, fill, spread throughout.
3 *Japan's electronics industry began to saturate the world markets*: **flood**, glut, swamp, oversupply, overfill, overload.
▷ANTONYMS starve.

saturated adjective **1** *his trousers were saturated*: **soaked**, soaking, soaking wet, wet through, sopping, sopping wet, sodden, dripping, dripping wet, wringing wet, drenched, streaming wet; soaked to the skin, like a drowned rat.
▷ANTONYMS bone dry.
2 *the saturated ground*: **waterlogged**, soggy, squelchy, heavy, muddy, swampy, boggy.

saturnine adjective **1** *he was a rather saturnine individual who never spoke an unnecessary word*: **gloomy**, sombre, melancholy, melancholic, moody, miserable, lugubrious, dour, glum, unsmiling, humourless, grumpy, bad-tempered; taciturn, uncommunicative, unresponsive.
▷ANTONYMS cheerful, jovial.
2 *his saturnine good looks*: **swarthy**, dark, dark-skinned, dark-complexioned; mysterious, mercurial, moody.

sauce noun **1** *serve with a piquant sauce and redcurrant jelly*: **relish**, dressing, condiment, ketchup, flavouring; dip; French jus, coulis.
2 Brit. informal *'I'll have less of your sauce,' said Aunt Edie*: **impudence**, impertinence, cheek, cheekiness, effrontery, irreverence, sauciness, pertness, freshness, flippancy, insolence, rudeness, disrespect, disrespectfulness, familiarity, presumption, presumptuousness, audacity, audaciousness, boldness, brazenness, forwardness, cockiness, shamelessness; informal mouth, lip, neck, brass neck, nerve, face; Brit. informal backchat; Scottish informal snash; N. Amer. informal sassiness, sass, chutzpah, smart mouth, back talk; archaic malapertness, contumely; rare procacity.
▷ANTONYMS politeness, respectfulness.
3 N. Amer. informal *she's been on the sauce for years*: **alcohol**, liquor, alcoholic drink, strong drink, intoxicating drink, spirits; informal booze, the bottle, the hard stuff, mother's milk, hooch; Brit. informal wallop; N. English & Irish informal sup; N. Amer. informal juice; Austral./NZ informal grog.

saucepan noun **cooking utensil**, pan, pot, casserole, skillet, stockpot, stewpot; steamer, double boiler; billy, billycan, dixie; N. Amer. trademark Crockpot; Provençal tian; S. African potjie.

saucy adjective informal **1** *saucy seaside postcards*: **suggestive**, titillating, risqué, rude, bawdy, racy, ribald, spicy; informal raunchy, smutty; Brit. informal fruity; N. Amer. informal gamy.
▷ANTONYMS demure, prim.
2 *you saucy little minx!* **cheeky**, impudent, impertinent, irreverent, forward, insolent, disrespectful, flippant, familiar, presumptuous, audacious, bold, bold as brass, brazen, cocky, out of line, shameless; informal fresh, flip, lippy, mouthy, smart-arsed; N. Amer. informal sassy, nervy, smart-assed; archaic malapert; rare tossy.
▷ANTONYMS polite, respectful.
3 *her cap sat at a saucy angle on her black hair*: **jaunty**, rakish, sporty, raffish; pert, perky, stylish, dashing, dapper; informal natty, snazzy, snappy; N. Amer. informal spiffy, sassy; dated gay.

saunter verb *they sauntered back to the car*: **stroll**, amble, wander, meander, drift, maunder, potter, walk, promenade, ramble; go for a walk, go for a stroll, take a walk, stretch one's legs, take the air; Scottish & Irish stravaig; Irish streel; informal mosey, tootle; Brit. informal pootle; rare perambulate.
▸ noun *a quiet saunter down the road*: **stroll**, amble, wander, meander, walk, turn, constitutional, ramble, airing, promenade, breather; N. Amer. paseo; Italian passegiata; informal mosey, tootle; Brit. informal pootle.

> *Choose the right word* **saunter, stroll, amble**
>
> See **stroll**.

sausage noun Brit. informal banger; Austral. informal snag.
□ **not a sausage** Brit. informal *there's not a sausage I can do about it*: **nothing**, not a thing, not a single thing, not anything, nothing at all, nil, zero; N. English nowt; informal zilch, sweet Fanny Adams, sweet FA, nix, not a dicky bird; Brit. informal damn all; N. Amer. informal zip, nada, a goose egg, bupkis; Brit. vulgar slang bugger all, sod all, fuck all; archaic nought, naught.

savage adjective **1** *packs of savage dogs roamed the streets*: **ferocious**, fierce; **wild**, untamed, undomesticated, feral; predatory, ravening.
▷ANTONYMS tame.
2 *James died after a savage assault at his home near Blackpool*: **vicious**, brutal, cruel, sadistic, ferocious, fierce, violent, bloody, murderous, homicidal, bloodthirsty, bestial, brutish, barbaric, barbarous, merciless, ruthless, pitiless, heartless, inhuman, harsh, callous, cold-blooded; archaic fell, sanguinary.
3 *Calvert launched a savage attack on European free-trade policy*: **fierce**, blistering, scathing, searing, stinging, devastating, mordant, trenchant, caustic, cutting, biting, withering, virulent, vitriolic.
▷ANTONYMS mild, gentle.
4 *a savage race*: **primitive**, uncivilized, unenlightened, non-literate, in a state of nature, heathen; wild, barbarian, barbarous, barbaric; archaic rude.
▷ANTONYMS civilized.
5 *the most savage landscape you are likely to see in the Pyrenees*: **rugged**, rough, wild, inhospitable, uninhabitable.
6 *the decision was a savage blow for the town*: **severe**, crushing, devastating, crippling, terrible, awful, dreadful, dire, catastrophic, calamitous, ruinous; mortal, lethal, fatal.
▸ noun **1** *Sheila had expected mud huts and savages*: **barbarian**, wild man, wild woman, primitive, heathen; cannibal; Caliban.
2 *the mother of one of the victims has described his assailants as savages*: **brute**, beast, monster, barbarian, ogre, demon, sadist, animal.
▸ verb **1** *11-year-old Kelly was savaged by two Rottweilers*: **maul**, attack, tear to pieces, lacerate, claw, bite, mutilate, mangle; worry.
2 *British critics savaged the film*: **criticize severely**, attack, lambaste, condemn, flay, shoot down, pillory, revile; informal jump on, tear to pieces, take to pieces, take/pull apart, lay into, pitch into, hammer, slam, bash, do a hatchet job on, crucify, give something a battering, roast, skewer, throw brickbats at, knock; Brit. informal slate, rubbish, slag off, monster; N. Amer. informal bad-mouth, pummel; Austral./NZ informal trash, bag, give someone bondi; archaic excoriate, slash.
▷ANTONYMS praise, commend, applaud.

savagery noun *the appalling savagery of the attack*: **brutality**, ferocity, fierceness, violence, viciousness, cruelty, sadism, barbarity, barbarousness, murderousness, bloodthirstiness, brutishness, mercilessness, ruthlessness, pitilessness, inhumanity, heartlessness; rare ferity.
▷ANTONYMS mildness, gentleness.

savant noun *Sir Isaiah Berlin, the Oxford savant*: **intellectual**, scholar, sage, philosopher, thinker, learned person, wise person, Solomon; guru, master, authority; Indian mahatma, maharishi, pandit.
▷ANTONYMS ignoramus, fool.

save verb **1** *the captain was saved by his crew when a windscreen blew out during the flight*: **rescue**, come to someone's rescue, save someone's life, come to someone's aid; set free, free, liberate, deliver, extricate, snatch; bail out; Nautical bring off; informal save someone's bacon, save someone's neck, save someone's skin.
▷ANTONYMS endanger.
2 *the fifteenth century farmhouse has been saved from demolition*: **preserve**, keep safe, keep, protect, safeguard, guard, conserve; salvage, retrieve, reclaim, rescue.
3 *we've saved enough for a deposit on a house | start saving newspapers to use for wrapping china*: **put aside**, set aside, lay aside, put by, put to one side, lay by, keep, retain, reserve, keep in reserve, conserve, stockpile, store,

S

hoard, save for a rainy day, keep for future use, put in a safe place; collect, amass; N. Amer. set by; informal salt away, squirrel away, stash away, hang on to.
▷ANTONYMS waste, fritter away, use up.
4 *I suppose I'll have to start saving*: **economize**, be (more) economical, make economies, scrimp, scrimp and scrape; be thrifty, be frugal, tighten one's belt, cut back, make cutbacks, budget, retrench, husband one's resources, cut costs, cut expenditure, draw in one's horns, watch one's pennies; N. Amer. pinch the pennies; black English rake and scrape.
▷ANTONYMS spend, be extravagant.
5 *if I'd known this a few days ago, it would have saved a lot of trouble*: **prevent**, obviate, forestall, spare; stop; avoid, avert; make unnecessary, rule out.
▷ANTONYMS cause.
▸ **preposition & conjunction** *no one needed to know save herself | the kitchen was empty save for Boris*: **except (for)**, apart from, but (for), other than, besides, aside from, with the exception of, bar, barring, excluding, omitting, leaving out, saving; informal outside of.

saving noun 1 *this resulted in a considerable saving in development costs*: **reduction**, cut, decrease, economy.
2 *after five years of scrimping and saving we bought a modest house*: **economizing**, economy, frugality, thrift, thriftiness, retrenchment, cutting back, belt-tightening, penny-pinching; carefulness, prudence.
3 (**savings**) *he wanted to know how to invest his savings*: **nest egg**, money put by for a rainy day, life savings; capital, assets, funds, resources, reserves.

saving grace noun *the bungalow's only saving grace was a room with spectacular views of the sea*: **redeeming feature**, compensating feature, good point, thing in its/one's favour, appealing/attractive aspect, advantage, asset, selling point; mitigating/extenuating feature.

Saviour noun *in the centre of the mosaic, the Saviour is depicted, attended by two archangels*: **Christ**, Jesus, Jesus Christ, the Redeemer, the Messiah, Our Lord, the Lamb of God, the Son of God, the Son of Man, the Prince of Peace, the King of Kings, Emmanuel.

saviour noun *to many Frenchmen, de Gaulle appeared to be the saviour of France | luckily my saviour, Larry, was on hand to help me*: **rescuer**, liberator, deliverer, emancipator; champion, knight in shining armour, friend in need, Good Samaritan; salvation.

savoir faire noun French *he had been faced with a situation that even his charm and savoir faire were unable to resolve*: **social skill**, social grace(s), urbanity, urbaneness, suaveness, suavity, finesse, sophistication, poise, aplomb, grace, adroitness, accomplishment, polish, style, smoothness, tact, tactfulness, diplomacy, discretion, delicacy, sensitivity; assurance, confidence, knowledge, know-how; French savoir vivre; informal savvy.
▷ANTONYMS awkwardness, gaucheness.

savour verb 1 *I savoured each delicious mouthful | she wanted to savour every moment of the evening*: **relish**, enjoy, enjoy to the full, taste to the full, appreciate, delight in, take pleasure in, revel in, smack one's lips over, luxuriate in, bask in, drool over; informal smack one's chops over.
2 *such a declaration would **savour of** immodesty*: **suggest**, smack of, have the hallmarks of, have all the signs of, give the impression of, seem like, have the air of, have a suggestion of, be indicative of, hint at, have overtones of.
▸ **noun 1** *the subtle savour of wood smoke*: **taste**, flavour, tang, smack; **smell**, aroma, fragrance, scent, perfume, bouquet, odour, whiff; archaic relish; rare sapidity.
2 *a savour of bitterness seasoned my feelings towards him*: **trace**, hint, suggestion, touch, smack.
3 *her usual diversions had lost their savour*: **piquancy**, interest, attraction, fascination, flavour, spice, zest, excitement, enjoyment, joy; informal zing.

savoury adjective 1 *cloves can be used to flavour both sweet and savoury dishes*: **salty**, **spicy**, piquant, tangy.
▷ANTONYMS sweet.
2 *a rich, savoury aroma was wafting from the kitchen*: **appetizing**, mouth-watering, delicious, delectable, aromatic, luscious; tasty, flavoursome, flavourful, palatable, toothsome; informal scrumptious, finger-licking, yummy, scrummy, nummy, moreish, delish, yum-yum; literary ambrosial; rare flavorous, ambrosian, sapid, nectarean, nectareous.
▷ANTONYMS unappetizing, unpalatable.
3 *everyone knew it was a front for less savoury operations*: **acceptable**, pleasant, palatable, wholesome, respectable, honourable, proper, seemly, creditable.
▷ANTONYMS unpleasant, unacceptable, dishonourable.
▸ **noun** *a tray of cocktail savouries*: **canapé**, hors d'oeuvre, appetizer, titbit; French amuse-gueule.

savvy informal noun *much will depend on his political savvy*: **shrewdness**, astuteness, sharp-wittedness, sharpness, acuteness, acumen, acuity, intelligence, wit, canniness, common sense, discernment, insight, understanding, penetration, perception, perceptiveness, perspicacity, perspicaciousness, knowledge, sagacity, sageness; informal nous, horse sense; rare sapience, arguteness.
▷ANTONYMS inexperience, ignorance.
▸ **verb** *he knew she had been making a fool of him, but he didn't quite savvy how*: **realize**, understand, comprehend, grasp, see, know, apprehend; informal get, get a fix on, catch on, latch on, cotton on; Brit. informal twig, suss.
▸ **adjective** *Bob is a savvy veteran who knows all the tricks*: **shrewd**, astute, sharp-witted, sharp, acute, intelligent, clever, canny, perceptive, perspicacious, sagacious, sage; informal on the ball, smart, streetwise; Scottish & N. English informal **pawky**; N. Amer. informal **heads-up**; rare long-headed, sapient, argute.
▷ANTONYMS stupid, gullible.

saw noun *spare me the old saw about eggs and omelettes*: **saying**, maxim, proverb, aphorism, axiom, adage, motto, epigram, dictum, gnome; expression, phrase; platitude, cliché, truism; rare apophthegm.

say verb 1 *she felt her stomach flutter as he said her name*: **speak**, utter, voice, pronounce, give utterance to, give voice to, vocalize.
2 *'I must go,' she said*: **declare**, state, announce; **remark**, observe, mention, comment, note, add; reply, respond, answer, rejoin; whisper, mutter, mumble, mouth; informal come out with.
3 *Newall says he's innocent*: **claim**, maintain, assert, hold, insist, contend, aver, affirm, avow; allege, profess; formal opine; rare asseverate.
4 *I can't conjure up the words to say how I feel | what are you trying to say, Inspector?* **express**, put into words, phrase, articulate, communicate, make known, get across, put across, convey, verbalize, render, tell; reveal, divulge, impart, disclose; imply, suggest, signify, denote, mean.
5 *they sang hymns and said a prayer*: **recite**, repeat, utter, deliver, perform, declaim, orate.
6 *the lighted dial of her watch said one twenty*: **indicate**, show, read.
7 *I'd say about 90 per cent of my stories are off the top of my head*: **estimate**, judge, guess, hazard a guess, dare say, predict, speculate, surmise, conjecture, venture; imagine, think, believe; informal reckon.
8 *let's say you'd just won a million pounds*: **suppose**, assume, imagine, presume, take as a hypothesis, hypothesize, postulate, posit.
9 *she determined to find something to say in his favour*: **adduce**, propose, advance, bring forward, offer, plead.
□ **be said** *it **is said** that she lived to be over a hundred | his widow was said to be inconsolable*: **be reported**, be thought, be believed, be alleged, be rumoured, be reputed, be put about; be described, be asserted; apparently, seemingly, it seems that, it appears that, (so) they say, (so) the story goes, by all accounts, rumour has it, the rumour is.
□ **that is to say** *people emigrated for economic reasons—that is to say, because they were poor*: **in other words**, to put it another way, to rephrase it; i.e., that is, to wit, viz., namely, sc.; Latin id est, scilicet, videlicet.
□ **to say the least** *his performance was disappointing to say the least*: **to put it mildly**, putting it mildly, without any exaggeration, at the very least, as an understatement.
▸ **noun 1** *Miss Honey was determined to have her say*: **right/chance/turn to speak**, right/chance/turn to express one's opinion, vote, opinion, view, voice; informal one's twopence worth, one's twopenn'orth.
2 *don't I have any say in the matter?* **influence**, sway, weight, authority, voice, input, share, part; informal clout.

saying noun *you know the old saying about all work and no play?* **proverb**, maxim, aphorism, axiom, adage, saw, tag, motto, precept, epigram, epigraph, dictum, gnome, pearl of wisdom; expression, phrase, formula; slogan, catchphrase; platitude, cliché, commonplace, truism; rare apophthegm.
□ **it goes without saying** **of course**, naturally, needless to say, it is taken for granted, it is understood/assumed, it is taken as read, it is accepted, it is unquestionable, it is an accepted fact; obviously, self-evidently, manifestly; informal natch.

say-so noun *Kathleen ran things around here and nothing could be done without her say-so*: **authorization**, approval, seal of approval, agreement, consent, assent, permission, endorsement, sanction, ratification, approbation, acquiescence, confirmation, blessing, leave; informal OK, the go-ahead, the green light, the thumbs up.
▷ANTONYMS refusal, denial.

scald verb *the boiling water scalded his skin*: **burn**, scorch, sear; technical cauterize.

scalding adjective *a jet of scalding water*: **extremely hot**, burning, blistering, searing, red-hot; piping hot; informal **boiling (hot)**, sizzling.

scale[1] noun 1 *all reptiles have scales covering the skin*: **plate**; technical lamella, lamina, squama, scute, scutum.
2 *the disease causes scales on the skin*: **flake**; (**scales**) scurf, dandruff; technical furfur.
3 *scale is bad enough in kettles, but can have a disastrous effect on the insides of boilers*: **limescale**; deposit, encrustation, coating; Brit. fur.

scale[2] noun 1 *the Celsius scale of temperature*: **calibrated system**, calibration, graduated system, system of measurement, measuring system, register.
2 *two men at opposite ends of the social scale*: **hierarchy**, ladder, ranking, pecking order, order, spectrum, progression, succession, sequence, series.
3 *the number of points needed to represent the line will depend on the scale of the map*: **ratio**, proportion, relative size.

4 *no one foresaw the scale of the disaster*: **extent**, **size**, scope, magnitude, dimensions, range, breadth, compass, degree, reach, spread, sweep.
▸ verb *thieves scaled an 8ft high fence*: **climb**, ascend, go up, go over, clamber up, shin (up), scramble up, mount; N. Amer. shinny (up); rare escalade.
□ **scale something down** *manufacturing capacity has been scaled down*: **reduce**, cut down, cut back, cut, make cutbacks in, decrease, lessen, lower, trim, slim down, prune, curtail.
□ **scale something up** *the departments intend to scale up their activities*: **increase**, expand, augment, build up, add to; step up, boost, escalate.

scales plural noun **weighing machine**, balance, pair of scales; steelyard.

scaly adjective 1 *the dragon's scaly hide*: technical squamate, squamose, squamous, lamellate, lamellar, lamelliform, lamellose; rare squamulose.
2 *scaly patches of dead skin*: **dry**, **flaky**, flaking, peeling, scurfy, rough, scabrous, mangy, scabious; technical furfuraceous, lepidote.

scam noun informal *the scam involved a series of bogus reinsurance deals*: **fraud**, swindle, fraudulent scheme, racket, trick, diddle; informal con, con trick, flimflam, gyp, kite; Brit. informal ramp, twist; N. Amer. informal hustle, grift, shakedown, bunco, boondoggle; Austral. informal rort.

scamp noun *he was a little scamp in those days*: **rascal**, monkey, devil, imp, rogue, wretch, mischief-maker, troublemaker, prankster; informal scallywag, horror, monster, terror, holy terror; Brit. informal perisher, pickle; Irish informal spalpeen; N. English informal tyke, scally; N. Amer. informal varmint, hellion; dated rip; archaic rapscallion, scapegrace.

scamper verb *the boy scampered off | his dogs scampered around the yard*: **scurry**, scuttle, dart, run, rush, dash, race, sprint, hurry, hasten, make haste; romp, frolic, gambol; Brit. scutter; informal scoot, beetle.

scan verb 1 *Adam scanned the horizon | his eyes were scanning her face*: **study**, **examine**, scrutinize, inspect, survey, search, scour, sweep, rake; look at, look someone/something up and down, stare at, gaze at, eye, watch, contemplate, regard; take stock of; Hunting glass; informal check out, recce; N. Amer. informal scope; archaic con.
2 *he pulled out a leather-bound diary and scanned the pages*: **glance through/over**, look through/over, have a look at, run/pass/cast one's eye over, skim, flick through, flip through, riffle through, leaf through, thumb through, read quickly, browse through; peruse.
▹ANTONYMS pore over.
▸ noun 1 *a careful scan of the terrain*: **inspection**, scrutiny, examination, survey, search.
2 *a quick scan through the 'For Sale' pages*: **glance**, look, flick, browse, skim.
3 *a brain scan*: **examination**, screening; ultrasound (scan).

scandal noun 1 *he was forced out of office because of a sex scandal*: **outrageous wrongdoing**, outrageous behaviour, immoral behaviour, unethical behaviour, discreditable behaviour, shocking incident/series of events, impropriety, misconduct, wrongdoing; offence, transgression, crime, sin; skeleton in the closet; informal business, affair, -gate.
2 *unmarried motherhood at that time was fraught with scandal*: **shame**, dishonour, disgrace, disrepute, discredit, infamy, ignominy, embarrassment; odium, opprobrium, censure, obloquy; stigma.
3 *it's a scandal that the disease is not yet being adequately treated*: **disgrace**, outrage, injustice; shame, pity, crying shame; affront, insult, reproach.
4 *you know what scandals were spread about me*: **malicious gossip**, malicious rumour(s), slander, libel, scandalmongering, calumny, defamation, aspersions, muckraking, smear campaign; informal dirt.

scandalize verb *Henry is said to have been scandalized by William's conduct*: **shock**, appal, outrage, horrify, disgust, revolt, repel, sicken, nauseate; offend, give offence to, affront, insult, cause raised eyebrows.
▹ANTONYMS impress.

scandalmonger noun **gossip**, muckraker, tattler; rare quidnunc, calumniator.

scandalous adjective 1 *it is scandalous that elderly patients should be treated in that way*: **disgraceful**, shocking, outrageous, monstrous, criminal, wicked, sinful, shameful, atrocious, appalling, terrible, dreadful, disgusting, abhorrent, despicable, deplorable, reprehensible, obscene, iniquitous, inexcusable, intolerable, insupportable, unforgivable, unpardonable; rare egregious.
▹ANTONYMS acceptable, praiseworthy.
2 *a series of scandalous liaisons*: **discreditable**, disreputable, dishonourable, improper, unseemly, sordid.
▹ANTONYMS seemly, proper.
3 *she loved to spread scandalous rumours*: **scurrilous**, malicious, slanderous, libellous, defamatory; rare calumnious, calumniatory, aspersive.

scant adjective *he paid scant attention to these wider issues | there is only scant evidence to support this hypothesis*: **little**, little or no, minimal, hardly any, limited, negligible, barely sufficient, meagre; insufficient, too little, not enough, inadequate, deficient; rare exiguous.
▹ANTONYMS abundant, ample, sufficient.

scanty adjective 1 *they paid whatever they could out of their scanty wages to their families | details of his life are scanty*: **meagre**, scant, minimal, limited, modest, restricted, sparse; tiny, small, paltry, negligible, insufficient, inadequate, deficient, sketchy, too small/little/few, not enough, poor; thin, thinning; scarce, in short supply, thin on the ground, few and far between; informal measly, piddling, mingy, pathetic; rare exiguous.
▹ANTONYMS abundant, ample, plentiful.
2 *her ridiculously scanty nightdress threatened to fall off altogether*: **skimpy**, revealing, short, brief; low, low-cut; indecent.
▹ANTONYMS modest.

> *Choose the right word* **scanty, sparse, meagre**
>
> See **meagre**.

scapegoat noun **whipping boy**, victim, Aunt Sally; N. Amer. goat; informal fall guy; N. Amer. informal patsy.

scar noun 1 *a tall dark man with a scar on his left cheek*: **cicatrix**; **mark**, blemish, disfigurement, discoloration, defacement; pockmark, pock, pit; wound, lesion, burn; birthmark, naevus; (**scars**) Christianity stigmata.
2 *behind the smile there were deep psychological scars*: **trauma**, damage, shock, injury, suffering, upset.
▸ verb 1 *Antony lost a lot of blood and is likely to be scarred for life*: **disfigure**, mark, blemish, blotch, discolour; pockmark, pit; Christianity stigmatize.
2 *the scenic red-rock vistas have been scarred by strip mining*: **damage**, spoil, mar, deface, injure; rare disfeature.
3 *he remained deeply scarred by his wartime experiences*: **traumatize**, damage, injure, wound; distress, disturb, upset.

scarce adjective 1 *the drought means that the crops have failed and food is scarce | scarce financial resources*: **in short supply**, short, scant, scanty, meagre, sparse, hard to find, hard to come by, not enough, too little, insufficient, deficient, inadequate, lacking, wanting; at a premium, like gold dust, not to be had, scarcer than hen's teeth; paltry, negligible, thin; informal not to be had for love nor money; rare exiguous.
▹ANTONYMS plentiful, abundant.
2 *birds that prefer dense forest interiors are becoming scarcer*: **rare**, few and far between, thin on the ground, seldom seen/found; uncommon, unusual, infrequent; Brit. out of the common.
▹ANTONYMS common.

scarcely adverb 1 *she could scarcely hear what he was saying*: **hardly**, barely, only just; almost not.
2 *I **scarcely ever** see him*: **rarely**, seldom, infrequently, not often, hardly ever, almost never, on rare occasions, every once in a while; informal once in a blue moon.
▹ANTONYMS often.
3 *this could scarcely be accidental*: **surely not**, not, hardly, certainly not, definitely not, not at all, on no account, under no circumstances, by no means; N. Amer. noway.

scarcity noun 1 *the scarcity of affordable housing*: **shortage**, dearth, lack, want, undersupply, insufficiency, paucity, scarceness, scantness, meagreness, sparseness, scantiness, poverty; deficiency, inadequacy, limitedness; unavailability, absence; rare exiguity, exiguousness.
▹ANTONYMS abundance, excess, surplus.
2 *the bird's current scarcity is the result of a lack of appropriate food*: **rarity**, rareness, infrequency, sparseness, uncommonness, unusualness.
▹ANTONYMS commonness.

scare verb *the thought of what might happen scared her*: **frighten**, make afraid, make fearful, make nervous, panic, throw into a panic; terrify, petrify, scare/frighten to death, scare/frighten someone out of their wits, scare stiff, scare witless, scare/frighten the living daylights out of, scare/frighten the life out of, scare the hell out of, strike terror into, fill with fear, put the fear of God into, make someone jump (out of their skin), make someone's hair stand on end, give someone goose pimples, make someone's blood run cold, chill someone's blood, send into a cold sweat, make someone shake in their shoes; **startle**, alarm, give someone a fright, give someone a turn; shock, appal, horrify; intimidate, daunt, unnerve; informal give someone the heebie-jeebies, scare the pants off, scarify, make someone's hair curl; Brit. informal throw into a blue funk, put the wind up; Irish informal scare the bejesus out of; N. Amer. informal spook; vulgar slang scare shitless, scare the shit out of; archaic fright, affright.
▹ANTONYMS reassure.
▸ noun *you gave me a scare—how did you get here?* **fright**, shock, start, turn, jump; informal the heebie-jeebies.

> *Choose the right word* **scare, frighten, startle**
>
> See **frighten**.

scared adjective *it was growing dark and she began to feel scared*: **frightened**, afraid, fearful, nervous, panicky, agitated, alarmed, worried, intimidated; terrified, petrified, horrified, panic-stricken, scared stiff, frightened/scared out of one's wits, scared witless, frightened/scared to death, terror-stricken, terror-struck, horror-stricken, horror-struck, frantic, hysterical, beside oneself; with one's heart in one's mouth, shaking in one's shoes, shaking like a leaf, shaky; Scottish feart; informal in a cold sweat, in a (blue) funk, jumpy, jittery; Brit. informal funky, windy; N. Amer. informal spooked; vulgar slang scared shitless, shit scared, shitting bricks, bricking oneself; dialect frit; archaic afeared, affrighted.
▹ANTONYMS confident, laid-back, calm.

scaremonger noun **alarmist**, prophet of doom, Cassandra, voice of doom, doom-monger; pessimist; informal doom and gloom merchant.

S

scarf noun **muffler**; headscarf, headsquare, square; stole, tippet; neckerchief, kerchief, cravat, bandanna; N. Amer. babushka; dated comforter; in Spanish-speaking countries mantilla, rebozo.

scarper verb Brit. informal *they left the stuff where it was and scarpered.* See **run away**.

scary adjective informal *we set off for the graveyard—it was really scary*: **frightening**, scaring, hair-raising, terrifying, petrifying, spine-chilling, blood-curdling, chilling, horrifying, alarming, appalling, daunting, formidable, fearsome, nerve-racking, unnerving; eerie, sinister; informal creepy, spine-tingling, spooky, hairy.

scathing adjective *the shadow trade and industry spokesman launched a scathing attack on the government*: **devastating**, withering, blistering, extremely critical, searing, scorching, fierce, ferocious, savage, severe, stinging, biting, cutting, mordant, trenchant, virulent, caustic, vitriolic, scornful, sharp, bitter, acid, harsh, unsparing; rare mordacious.
▷ANTONYMS mild, gentle; complimentary.

scatter verb **1** *he broke the slices of bread into pieces and scattered them over the lake | scatter the seeds as evenly as possible*: **throw**, strew, toss, fling; **sprinkle**, spread, distribute, sow, broadcast, intersperse, disseminate; shower, spatter, spray; literary bestrew.
▷ANTONYMS collect, gather.
2 *the police fired over their heads and the crowd scattered | he spurred his horse forward, scattering onlookers in all directions*: **disperse**, break up, disband, separate, move/go in different directions, go separate ways; dissipate, disintegrate, dissolve; drive, send, put to flight, chase.
▷ANTONYMS assemble, converge, congregate.
3 *the sky above them was scattered with stars*: **fleck**, stud, dot, cover, sprinkle, stipple, spot, pepper; litter; literary bestud.

> *Choose the right word* **scatter, disperse, dissipate**
>
> These words all describe the spreading out or elimination of something or a group of things that originally formed a concentrated or closely knit whole.
>
> **Scatter** emphasizes the random distribution of something over a wide area (*the occupants had scattered far and wide | sow thinly in rows, rather than scattering the seeds randomly*).
>
> With **disperse**, the emphasis is primarily on the parting and spreading out of people or things rather than on where they all go (*troops were deployed to disperse the protesters*), but the result will probably be more even or organized than with *scatter*. Unlike *scatter*, *disperse* can refer to the thinning of mist, cloud, and similar concentrations of small particles (*the blanket of fog above their heads began to disperse*).
>
> With **dissipate**, the emphasis is more on the actual loss of a commodity, substance, or form of energy than on the manner of its going: something that is *dissipated* is spread out so thinly that it is no longer detectable or usable (*the semiconductor has low power requirements, thereby dissipating little heat*). *Dissipate* can also describe the thinning of mist or cloud; unlike *disperse*, it is extended to the fading away of emotions, especially unpleasant ones (*she waited a moment for her exasperation to dissipate*). If money or resources are *dissipated*, they are squandered on something or other (*he turned out to be a waster and dissipated his fortune*).

scatterbrained adjective *a scatterbrained young woman*: **absent-minded**, forgetful, with a mind like a sieve, disorganized, unsystematic; dreamy, wool-gathering, with one's head in the clouds, feather-brained, feather-headed, birdbrained, empty-headed, erratic, giddy; informal scatty, dizzy, dippy, not with it.
▷ANTONYMS organized, together.

S

scattering noun *a scattering of freckles across the bridge of her nose*: **handful**, few, one or two, not many, a small number; **sprinkling**, dusting, smattering, smatter.

scavenge verb *pigs and poultry scavenged for food around the farm*: **rummage**, search, hunt, look, forage, root about/around, scratch about/around, grub about/around; rare mudlark.

scenario noun **1** *Walt wrote scenarios for a major Hollywood studio*: **plot**, outline, storyline, framework, structure, scheme, plan, layout; screenplay, script; synopsis, summary, precis; technical schema; rare diegesis.
2 *every possible scenario must be explored*: **sequence of events**, course of events, chain of events, series of developments, situation.
3 *this film has a more contemporary scenario*: **setting**, background, context, scene, milieu.

scene noun **1** *others were treated at the scene of the accident for cuts and bruises*: **location**, site, place, position, point, spot; locale, whereabouts; arena, stage, set; technical locus.
2 *tapestries and shields adorned the wall, setting the scene for the conference | the scene is London, in the late 1890s*: **background**, setting, context, milieu, backdrop; French mise en scène.
3 *there had been terrible scenes of violence in Europe*: **incident**, event, episode, happening, moment.
4 *an impressive mountain scene*: **view**, vista, outlook, panorama, prospect, sight; landscape, scenery; picture, tableau, spectacle.
5 *she made an embarrassing scene outside the bank*: **fuss**, exhibition of oneself, performance, tantrum, outburst, commotion, disturbance, row, upset, contretemps, furore, brouhaha; informal song and dance, to-do; Brit. informal carry-on.
6 *Michael never joined in—I don't think it was his scene | the Irish music scene*: **area of interest**, field of interest, field, interest, speciality, territory, province, preserve; sphere, world, milieu, realm, domain; informal thing.
7 *the last scene of the play*: **subdivision**, division, section, segment.
8 *a scene from a Laurel and Hardy film*: **section**, segment, part, clip, sequence.
□ **behind the scenes 1** *informal discussions continued behind the scenes*: **secretly**, in secret, privately, in private, behind closed doors, clandestinely, surreptitiously; confidentially, off the record; informal on the quiet, on the q.t..
▷ANTONYMS publicly. **2** *behind-the-scenes diplomatic activity*: **secret**, private, clandestine, surreptitious; confidential.
▷ANTONYMS public.

scenery noun **1** *the beautiful scenery of central and west Wales*: **landscape**, countryside, country, terrain, topography, setting, surroundings, environment; view, vista, panorama, prospect, outlook; cityscape, townscape, roofscape, riverscape, seascape, waterscape, snowscape.
2 *we had all helped with the scenery and costumes*: **stage set**, set, flats, backdrop, drop curtain; setting, background, decor; Brit. backcloth; French coulisse, mise en scène.

scenic adjective *the most scenic route from Florence to Siena*: **picturesque**, pretty, pleasing, attractive, lovely, beautiful, charming, pretty as a picture, easy on the eye; impressive, striking, spectacular, breathtaking; panoramic.
▷ANTONYMS dreary, unattractive.

scent noun **1** *the scent of freshly cut hay*: **smell**, fragrance, aroma, perfume, redolence, savour, odour, whiff; bouquet, nose.
▷ANTONYMS stink, stench.
2 *she brushed her hair and sprayed scent over her body*: **perfume**, fragrance, toilet water, lavender water, cologne; French parfum, eau de toilette, eau de cologne; informal scoosh.
3 *the hounds picked up the scent of a hare*: **spoor**, trail, track; Hunting foil, wind.
4 *the day was gloomy and cold with a scent of rain on the air*: **hint**, suggestion, trace, whiff.
▶verb **1** *a shark can scent blood from well over half a kilometre away*: **smell**, detect the smell of, pick up the smell of, get a whiff of.
2 *Rose looked at him, scenting a threat*: **sense**, become aware of, become conscious of, detect, discern, perceive, recognize, get wind of, sniff out, nose out.

scented adjective *scented soap | scented pine woods*: **perfumed**, fragranced, perfumy; **sweet-smelling**, fragrant, aromatic; rare aromatized.
▷ANTONYMS smelly, malodorous.

sceptic noun **1** *sceptics said the marriage wouldn't last*: **cynic**, doubter, questioner, scoffer; pessimist, prophet of doom; rare Pyrrhonist, minimifidian.
2 *empowered by that Spirit, sceptics have found faith*: **agnostic**; atheist, unbeliever, non-believer, disbeliever, doubting Thomas; rationalist; rare nullifidian.
▷ANTONYMS believer.

sceptical adjective *they were sceptical about the Treasury's forecast of inflation dropping to 3 per cent*: **dubious**, doubtful, having reservations, taking something with a pinch of salt, doubting, questioning; cynical, distrustful, mistrustful, suspicious, disbelieving, misbelieving, unconvinced, incredulous, hesitant, scoffing; pessimistic, defeatist; informal iffy; rare Pyrrhonist, minimifidian.
▷ANTONYMS certain, convinced; optimistic.

scepticism noun **1** *members of the organization greeted his ideas with scepticism*: **doubt**, doubtfulness, dubiousness, a pinch of salt, lack of conviction; **disbelief**, cynicism, distrust, mistrust, suspicion, misbelief, incredulity; pessimism, defeatism; rare dubiety, Pyrrhonism, scepsis, minimifidianism.
▷ANTONYMS conviction.
2 *a vague kind of scepticism is one of the commonest spiritual diseases in this generation*: **agnosticism**, doubt; atheism, unbelief, non-belief; rationalism.
▷ANTONYMS belief, faith.

schedule noun **1** *until that decision is made we cannot begin to draw up an engineering schedule*: **plan**, programme, timetable, scheme.
2 *I have a very busy schedule for the next few days*: **timetable**, agenda, diary, calendar, appointment book, list of appointments, social calendar; itinerary.
3 *ring us for a schedule of all our courses*: **list**, catalogue, inventory; syllabus.
□ **behind schedule** *the project is three months behind schedule*: **late**, running late, overdue, behind time, not on time, behind, behindhand, behind target.
▶verb *another meeting was scheduled for April 20*: **arrange**, organize, plan, programme, timetable, fix a time for, make arrangements for, book, set up, line up, slot in, time; N. Amer. slate.

schematic adjective **1** *this concept is shown in schematic form in Figure 1*: **simplified**; **diagrammatic**, representational, illustrative, graphic, delineative; symbolic.
2 *his rather schematic notions of what marriage can be*: **simplistic**, oversimplified, oversimple, formulaic, formularized, unimaginative; facile, shallow.

scheme noun **1** *adventurous fund-raising schemes*: **plan**, project, plan of action, programme, strategy, stratagem, game plan; enterprise, venture, measure, move, course of action, line of action; system, procedure, design, formula, recipe; device, tactic, contrivance; proposal, proposition, suggestion, idea, blueprint; Brit. informal wheeze; Austral. informal lurk; archaic shift.
2 *police uncovered a scheme to steal paintings worth more than $250,000*: **plot**, intrigue, conspiracy, secret plan; ruse, ploy, stratagem, manoeuvre, subterfuge; machinations; informal game, racket, scam, dodge; S. African informal schlenter.
3 *the sonnet's rhyme scheme*: **arrangement**, system, organization, configuration, pattern, format, layout, disposition; technical schema.
▸ verb *he schemed to bring about the collapse of the government*: **plot**, hatch a plot, conspire, take part in a conspiracy, intrigue, connive, manoeuvre, plan, lay plans; rare machinate, cabal, complot.

schemer noun **plotter**, conspirator, intriguer, intrigant, intrigante, conniver; tactician, strategist, planner; rare machinator, conspirer, Machiavellian, cabalist.

scheming adjective *at long last he had seen his scheming wife for what she really was*: **cunning**, crafty, calculating, devious, designing, conniving, wily, sly, tricky, artful, guileful, slippery, slick; **manipulative**, Machiavellian, unscrupulous, disingenuous; duplicitous, deceitful, underhand, treacherous; informal foxy; S. African informal slim; archaic subtle.
▹ANTONYMS ingenuous, honest, artless.

schism noun *the widening schism between church leaders and politicians*: **division**, **split**, rift, breach, rupture, break, separation, severance, estrangement, alienation, detachment; chasm, gulf; discord, disagreement, dissension, disunion; rare scission.

schismatic adjective *the proliferation of schismatic religious movements over the previous few years*: **separatist**, heterodox, dissident, dissentient, dissenting, heretical; **breakaway**, splinter.
▹ANTONYMS mainstream, orthodox.

schmaltzy adjective informal *the record's schmaltzy love songs*: **sentimental**, over-sentimental, mawkish, cloying, sickly, saccharine, sugary, syrupy; Brit. twee; informal **slushy**, sloppy, mushy, weepy, cutesy, lovey-dovey, gooey, drippy, sloshy, soupy, treacly, cheesy, corny, icky, sick-making, toe-curling; Brit. informal soppy; N. Amer. informal cornball, sappy, hokey, three-hankie.

scholar noun **1** *a leading French biblical scholar*: **academic**, intellectual, learned person, professor, man of letters, woman of letters, mind, intellect, savant, polymath, highbrow, bluestocking; authority, expert, pundit, mastermind; Hindu pandit; Jewish rabbi; informal egghead; N. Amer. informal pointy-head; archaic bookman.
2 archaic *after two or three months there were 28 scholars*: **pupil**, student, schoolchild, schoolboy, schoolgirl, learner.

scholarly adjective **1** *an earnest, scholarly man*: **learned**, erudite, academic, well read, widely read, intellectual, literary, lettered, well educated, knowledgeable, cultured, cultivated, highbrow; studious, bookish, donnish, bluestocking, cerebral; informal egghead; N. Amer. informal pointy-headed; archaic clerkly.
▹ANTONYMS uneducated, illiterate, ignorant.
2 *a young woman aspiring to a scholarly career*: **academic**, educational, scholastic, professorial, pedagogic, pedagogical.
3 *a scholarly account of the period*: **well researched**, painstaking, studious, thorough, detailed, thoroughgoing, comprehensive, exhaustive; well argued, well informed, well reasoned, authoritative.

scholarship noun **1** *Prague became one of the centres of medieval scholarship | a woman of great scholarship*: **learning**, book learning, knowledge, erudition, education, letters, culture, academic study, academic achievement, intellectual attainment; wisdom, lore.
2 *a scholarship of £200 per term*: **grant**, award, endowment, payment; fellowship; Brit. bursary, bursarship, exhibition.

scholastic adjective **1** *Walter's scholastic achievements*: **academic**, educational, school, scholarly.
2 *scholastic attempts to distinguish between the various religious denominations*: **scholarly**, learned, academic, erudite, donnish; pedantic, over-subtle, over-precise, hair-splitting, precisionist; informal nit-picking; archaic overnice.

school noun **1** *the school caters for children with learning difficulties*: **educational institution**, centre of learning; academy, college; Latin alma mater; rare phrontistery.
2 *the University's School of English*: **department**, faculty, division.
3 *he painted in oils, in a manner strongly reminiscent of the Barbizon School*: **group**, set, circle, clique, faction, sect; followers, following, disciples, apostles, pupils, students, admirers, devotees, votaries; proponents, adherents, imitators, copiers, emulators; rare epigones.
4 *the school of linguistics associated with his ideas*: **way of thinking**, school of thought, persuasion, creed, credo, doctrine, belief, faith, outlook, opinion, point of view; denomination; **approach**, method, style; informal ism.
▸ verb **1** *he was born in Paris and schooled in Lyon*: **educate**, teach, instruct.
2 *he schooled her in horsemanship | she had schooled herself to be patient*: **train**, teach, tutor, coach, instruct, upskill, drill, discipline, direct, guide, prepare, groom, mould, shape, form; prime, verse; indoctrinate, inculcate.

> *Word links* **school**
>
> **scholastic** relating to schools

schooling noun **1** *his parents paid for his schooling*: **education**, teaching, tuition, instruction, tutoring, tutelage; lessons; learning, book learning.
2 *the schooling of horses*: **training**, coaching, instruction, drill, drilling, discipline, disciplining; preparation, guidance.

schoolteacher noun **teacher**, schoolmaster, schoolmistress, instructor, tutor, educationist; Brit. master, mistress; Scottish informal dominie; N. Amer. informal schoolmarm; Austral./NZ informal chalkie, schoolie; rare preceptor, pedagogue.

science noun *the science of criminology*: **branch of knowledge**, body of knowledge/information/facts, area of study, discipline, field.

scientific adjective **1** *scientific research | the scientific establishment in Britain*: **technological**, technical; research-based, factual, knowledge-based, empirical; chemical, biological, medical.
2 *you need to approach it in a more scientific way*: **systematic**, **methodical**, organized, well organized, ordered, orderly, meticulous, rigorous, exact, precise, accurate, mathematical, regulated, controlled; analytical, rational.
▹ANTONYMS unsystematic, random.

scientist noun **researcher**, technologist; Brit. informal boffin.

scintilla noun *there is not the faintest scintilla of truth in it*: **particle**, iota, jot, whit, atom, speck, bit, trace, ounce, shred, crumb, morsel, fragment, grain, drop, spot, mite, tittle, jot or tittle, modicum, hint, touch, suggestion, whisper, suspicion; informal smidgen, smidge, tad; Irish informal stim; archaic scantling, scruple.

scintillate verb *the brilliant stones scintillated in the sunlight*: **sparkle**, shine, gleam, glitter, flash, shimmer, twinkle, glint, glisten, wink, blink; literary glister; rare coruscate, fulgurate, effulge, luminesce, phosphoresce, incandesce.

scintillating adjective **1** *a scintillating diamond necklace*: **sparkling**, shining, bright, brilliant, gleaming, glittering, twinkling, flashing, shimmering, shimmery; rare scintillant.
▹ANTONYMS dull, matte.
2 *his scintillating closing speech | the team produced a scintillating second-half performance*: **brilliant**, dazzling, exciting, exhilarating, stimulating, invigorating; vivacious, sparkling, effervescent, lively, vibrant, animated, ebullient, bright; witty, clever; rare coruscating.
▹ANTONYMS boring, dull, pedestrian.

scion noun **1** *the process involves grafting a scion of the chosen tree on to rootstock of the same species*: **cutting**, graft, slip; shoot, offshoot, twig.
2 *the scion of an aristocratic Massachusetts family*: **descendant**, offshoot; heir, successor; child, issue, offspring.
▹ANTONYMS ancestor, predecessor.

scoff[1] verb *she told Jack it was a bad omen, but he* **scoffed at** *her superstitions*: **mock**, deride, ridicule, sneer at, be scornful about, treat contemptuously, jeer at, jibe at, make fun of, poke fun at, laugh at, scorn, laugh to scorn, dismiss, pooh-pooh, make light of, belittle; taunt, tease, make a fool of, rag; informal thumb one's nose at, take the mickey out of; Austral./NZ informal poke mullock at; Brit. vulgar slang take the piss out of; dated make sport of; rare fleer at, bite one's thumb at, scout at.

scoff[2] Brit. informal verb *I bet he's scoffed all the chips*: **eat**, devour, consume, guzzle, gobble, wolf down, polish off, finish off, gulp down, bolt; informal put away, nosh, get outside of, pack away, demolish, shovel down, stuff (down), stuff one's face with, stuff oneself with, pig oneself on, pig out on, sink, get one's laughing gear round; Brit. informal gollop, shift; N. Amer. informal scarf (down/up), snarf (down/up), inhale; rare ingurgitate.
▸ noun *ice cream was seen as suitable scoff to keep the under-tens quiet*: **food**, fare, eatables, refreshments; informal grub, nosh, chow, eats, feed; Brit. informal tuck; N. Amer. informal chuck; archaic victuals, vittles, meat.

scold verb *Mum took Anna away, scolding her for her bad behaviour*: **rebuke**, reprimand, reproach, reprove, admonish, remonstrate with, chastise, chide, upbraid, berate, take to task, pull up, castigate, lambaste, read someone the Riot Act, give someone a piece of one's mind, go on at, haul over the coals, criticize, censure; informal tell off, give someone a talking-to, give someone a telling-off, dress down, give someone a dressing-down, give someone an earful, give someone a roasting, give someone a rocket, give someone a rollicking, rap, rap over the knuckles, slap someone's wrist, let someone have it, send someone away with a flea in their ear, bawl out, give someone hell, come down on, blow up, pitch into, lay into, lace into, give someone a caning, put on the mat, slap down, blast, rag, keelhaul; Brit. informal tick off, have a go at, carpet, monster, give someone a mouthful, tear someone off a

strip, give someone what for, give someone some stick, wig, give someone a wigging, give someone a row, row; N. Amer. informal **chew out**, **ream out**, **take to the woodshed**; Brit. vulgar slang **bollock**, **give someone a bollocking**; N. Amer. vulgar slang **chew someone's ass**, **ream someone's ass**; dated **call down**, **rate**, **give someone a rating**, **trim**; rare **reprehend**, **objurgate**.
▷**ANTONYMS** praise, compliment.
▸ **noun** archaic *she is turning into a scold*: **nag**, nagger, shrew, fishwife, harpy, termagant, harridan; complainer, moaner, grumbler, fault-finder, carper; N. Amer. informal **kvetch**; rare **Xanthippe**.

scolding noun *Joe meekly accepted her scolding*: **rebuke**, reprimand, reproach, reproof, admonishment, admonition, reproval, remonstration, lecture, upbraiding, castigation, lambasting, criticism, censure; informal **telling-off**, **rap**, **rap over the knuckles**, **dressing-down**, **earful**, **roasting**, **bawling-out**, **caning**, **blast**, **row**; Brit. informal **ticking-off**, **carpeting**, **rollicking**, **wigging**; Brit. vulgar slang **bollocking**; dated **rating**.
▷**ANTONYMS** praise, compliment, commendation.

scoop noun **1** *a measuring scoop is provided*: **spoon**, ladle, dipper; bailer.
2 *add a scoop of vanilla ice cream*: **spoonful**, ladleful, portion, lump, ball; informal **dollop**.
3 informal *reporters at the three tabloid papers competed for scoops*: **exclusive (story)**, inside story, exposé, revelation; coup; the latest.
▸ **verb 1** *a hole was **scooped out** in the floor*: **hollow out**, gouge out, dig, excavate, cut out.
2 *halve the potatoes, **scoop out** the flesh and mash it with the yogurt mixture*: **remove**, take out, spoon out, scrape out, ladle out; bail out.
3 *she **scooped up** armfuls of clothes and dumped them on the bed*: **pick up**, gather up, lift, sweep up, catch up, take up; snatch up, grab; remove, clear away.
▷**ANTONYMS** drop.

scoot verb informal *Hilary panicked and scooted down the corridor*: **dash**, dart, run, sprint, race, rush, hurry, hasten, hare, hurtle, bolt, shoot, charge, career, speed, fly, whizz, zoom; scuttle, scurry, scamper, skip, skitter, trot; Brit. **scutter**; informal **tear**, **pelt**, **zip**, **belt**, **beetle**; archaic **post**, **hie**; rare **skirr**.
▷**ANTONYMS** amble, stroll.

scope noun **1** *we widened the scope of our investigation | a study of the subject is beyond the scope of this book*: **extent**, range, breadth, width, reach, sweep, purview, span, stretch, spread, horizon; area, sphere, field, realm, compass, orbit, ambit, terms of reference, field of reference, jurisdiction, remit; confine, limit; gamut, competence.
2 *the scope for major change is always limited by political realities*: **opportunity**, freedom, latitude, leeway, capacity, liberty, room, room to manoeuvre, elbow room, play; possibility, chance.

scorch verb **1** *the buildings around us were scorched by the fire*: **burn**, sear, singe, char, blacken, discolour; rare **torrefy**.
2 *grass scorched by the sun*: **dry up**, desiccate, parch, wither, shrivel; burn, bake, roast.
3 informal *to get to New York you have to scorch along sixteen-lane highways*: **speed**, zoom, whizz, blast; informal **zap**, **zip**, **burn**, **burn rubber**, **belt**, **vroom**; Brit. informal **bomb**, **bucket**, **put one's foot down**, **blind**; N. Amer. informal **barrel**, **lay rubber**.

scorching adjective **1** *the scorching July sun*: **extremely hot**, red-hot, unbearably hot, baking (hot), blazing, flaming, fiery, burning, blistering, searing, sweltering, torrid, tropical, like an oven, like a furnace, like a blowtorch; parching, withering; N. Amer. **broiling**; informal **boiling (hot)**, **sizzling**.
▷**ANTONYMS** freezing.
2 *he faced scorching criticism*: **fierce**, savage, scathing, withering, blistering, searing, devastating, stringent, severe, harsh, stinging, biting, mordant, trenchant, caustic, virulent, vitriolic.
▷**ANTONYMS** mild.

score noun **1** *the final score was 4–3*: **result**, outcome; **number of goals/runs/points**, total, sum total, tally, count.
2 *an IQ score of 161*: **rating**, grade, mark, percentage.
3 *check the shaft for rust, scores, and any other types of damage*: **scratch**, nick, notch, snick, scrape, groove, chip, cut, gouge, incision, slit, gash; mark; archaic **scotch**.
4 *I've got a score to settle with you*: **grievance**, bone to pick, axe to grind, grudge, complaint; dispute, bone of contention; rare **crow to pluck**.
5 (**the score**) informal *he knew the score before he got here*: **the situation**, the position, the facts, the truth of the matter, the (true) state of affairs, the picture, the story, how things stand, the lie of the land; Brit. **the state of play**; N. Amer. **the lay of the land**; informal **the set-up**, **what's what**.
6 *he had resigned on the score of ill health*: **grounds**, reason, basis, count; cause, motive, rationale.
7 (**scores**) *police have received scores of complaints | scores of people attended his funeral*: **a great many**, a lot, a great/good deal, a large/great number/amount, great quantities, plenty, a host, hosts, a crowd, crowds, droves, a bevy, bevies, an army, armies, a horde, hordes, a flock, flocks, herds, a throng, throngs, legions, a multitude, multitudes, a swarm, swarms; copious, abundant, profuse, an abundance, a profusion; informal **lots**, **umpteen**, **loads**, **masses**, **stacks**, **scads**, **heaps**, **piles**, **bags**, **tons**, **oodles**, **dozens**, **hundreds**, **thousands**, **millions**, **billions**, **zillions**, **more ... than one can shake a stick at**; Brit. informal **shedloads**, **a shedload**; N. Amer. informal **a slew**, **a bunch**, **gazillions**, **gobs**, **bazillions**; Austral./NZ informal **a swag**; vulgar slang **a shitload**; literary **myriad**, **divers**.
▷**ANTONYMS** few.
□ **on this/that score** *there were no complaints on that score*: **on this/that subject**, as/so far as this/that is/was concerned, in this/that respect, about this/that, on this/that matter, as regards this/that.
□ **pay off/settle old scores** *he can't resist settling old scores—the book is full of retaliatory digs and sneers*: **take (one's) revenge**, hit back at someone, get back at someone, retaliate, get even, get one's own back, pay someone back, give someone a dose/taste of their own medicine, pay someone back in their own coin.
▸ **verb 1** *he has already scored 13 goals for Aston Villa this season*: **get**, gain, chalk up, win, achieve, attain, make; record; informal **notch up**, **bag**, **knock up**, **rack up**.
2 *when I was your age I spent every summer weekend scoring for my father's village cricket team*: **keep (the) score**, keep count, keep a record, keep a tally.
3 informal *his new movie really scored*: **be successful**, be a success, achieve success, win, triumph, make an impression, have an impact, go down well, get an enthusiastic reception; informal **be a hit**, **be a winner**, **be a sell-out**, **go down a storm**.
4 *the Quartet Suite was scored for flute, violin, viola da gamba, and continuo*: **orchestrate**, arrange, set, adapt; write, compose; rare **instrument**.
5 *score the wood in criss-cross patterns*: **scratch**, cut, make a notch/notches in, make a groove/grooves in, notch, incise, scrape, nick, snick, chip, gouge, slit, gash; mark; cross-hatch; carve, engrave; archaic **scotch**.
□ **score points off** *Harry was continually seeking ways to score points off Sam*: **get the better of**, gain an advantage over, outdo, best, worst, have the edge over; have the last laugh on, make a fool of, humiliate; informal **get/be one up on**, **get one over on**.
□ **score something out/through** *she scored out the last word*: **cross out**, strike out, put a line through, ink out, blue-pencil, scratch out; **delete**, obliterate, expunge.

scorn noun *he was unable to hide the scorn in his voice*: **contempt**, derision, contemptuousness, disdain, derisiveness, scornfulness, mockery, sneering, scoffing; archaic **contumely**, **despite**.
▷**ANTONYMS** admiration, respect.
□ **pour scorn on** *he pours scorn on the idea that any such thing could really exist*: **disparage**, denigrate, run down, deprecate, depreciate, downgrade, play down, belittle, trivialize, minimize, make light of, treat lightly, undervalue, underrate, underestimate; scoff at, sneer at, laugh at, laugh off, mock, ridicule, deride, dismiss, scorn, cast aspersions on, discredit; N. Amer. **slur**; informal **do down**, **do a hatchet job on**, **take to pieces**, **pull apart**, **pick holes in**, **drag through the mud**, **have a go at**, **hit out at**, **knock**, **slam**, **pan**, **bash**, **bad-mouth**, **pooh-pooh**, **look down one's nose at**; Brit. informal **rubbish**, **slate**, **slag off**; archaic **hold cheap**; rare **asperse**, **derogate**, **misprize**, **minify**.
▸ **verb 1** *critics scorned the painting, but it was very popular with those who attended the exhibition | his father was a man who scorned tradition*: **deride**, be contemptuous about, hold in contempt, treat with contempt, pour/heap scorn on, be scornful about, look down on, look down one's nose at, disdain, curl one's lip at, mock, scoff at, sneer at, sniff at, jeer at, laugh at, laugh out of court; disparage, slight; dismiss, cock a snook at, spit in the eye/face of, spit on, thumb one's nose at; informal **turn one's nose up at**, **blow raspberries at**; N. Amer. informal **give the Bronx cheer to**; Brit. vulgar slang **piss on/over**; archaic **contemn**; rare **misprize**, **scout**.
▷**ANTONYMS** admire, respect.
2 *'I am a woman scorned,' she thought*: **spurn**, rebuff, reject, ignore, shun, snub.
3 *even at her lowest ebb, she would have **scorned to** stoop to such tactics*: **refuse to**, refrain from, not lower oneself to; be above, consider it beneath one.

scornful adjective *Isabel ignored his scornful remarks*: **contemptuous**, full of contempt, derisive, derisory, withering, mocking, scoffing, sneering, jeering, scathing, snide, disparaging, slighting, supercilious, disdainful, superior, dismissive; informal **sniffy**, **snotty**; archaic **contumelious**.
▷**ANTONYMS** admiring, respectful.

scornfully adverb *'How would she know?' said Anne scornfully*: **contemptuously**, with contempt, derisively, witheringly, mockingly, with a sneer, scathingly, snidely, disparagingly, superciliously, disdainfully, dismissively; informal **sniffily**, **snottily**.
▷**ANTONYMS** admiringly, respectfully.

scotch verb *their plans were scotched by the Pentagon*: **put an end to**, put a stop to, bring to an end, nip in the bud, put the lid on; ruin, wreck, scupper, destroy, devastate, smash, shatter, demolish, queer; frustrate, thwart; informal **put paid to**, **blow**, **put the kibosh on**, **clobber**; Brit. informal **dish**.

scot-free adverb *the real criminals behind the racket are getting away scot-free*: **unpunished**, without punishment, unreprimanded; unscathed, unhurt, unharmed, without a scratch, uninjured, undamaged, safe; rare **scatheless**.

S

Scotland noun Brit. north of the border; Scottish the land o' the leal; Latin Caledonia; informal the land of cakes.

scoundrel noun *the lying scoundrel admitted that he was married to another woman*: **rogue**, rascal, good-for-nothing, reprobate, unprincipled person; cheat, swindler, fraudster, trickster, charlatan; informal villain, bastard, beast, son of a bitch, s.o.b., rat, louse, swine, dog, hound, skunk, heel, snake, snake in the grass, wretch, scumbag, bad egg, stinker; Brit. informal scrote; Irish informal sleeveen, spalpeen; N. Amer. informal rat fink; informal, dated rotter, bounder, blighter; vulgar slang shit, bugger; N. Amer. vulgar slang motherfucker, mother, mofo; dated cad, ne'er-do-well; archaic blackguard, miscreant, knave, dastard, vagabond, varlet, wastrel, rapscallion, whoreson.

scour[1] verb *she scoured the cooker and cleaned out the kitchen cupboards*: **scrub**, rub, clean, wash, cleanse, wipe; polish, buff (up), shine, burnish; abrade; Scottish & N. English dight; archaic furbish.

scour[2] verb *Christina scoured the antique shops until she found the perfect piece*: **search**, comb, hunt through, rummage through, sift through, go through with a fine-tooth comb, root through, rake through, leave no stone unturned, mine, look all over, look high and low in; ransack, turn upside-down, turn over; drag; Austral./NZ informal fossick through.

scourge noun **1** historical *he was beaten with a scourge*: **whip**, horsewhip, lash, strap, birch, switch, flail; N. Amer. bullwhip, rawhide; historical cat-o'-nine-tails, knout; rare flagellum, quirt, blacksnake.
2 *inflation was the scourge of the mid-1970s | the scourge of war*: **affliction**, bane, curse, plague, menace, evil, misfortune, burden, cross to bear, thorn in one's flesh/side, bitter pill, trial, nuisance, pest; torment, torture, misery, suffering; blight, cancer, canker; punishment, penalty, visitation.
▷**ANTONYMS** blessing, godsend.
▶ **verb 1** historical *he was publicly scourged*: **flog**, whip, beat, horsewhip, lash, flagellate, flail, strap, birch, cane, thrash, belt, leather; N. Amer. bullwhip; informal give someone a hiding, tan someone's hide, lather, take a strap to, beat the living daylights out of; N. Amer. informal whale; archaic switch, stripe, thong; rare quirt.
2 *scurvy was a disease which scourged the English for centuries*: **afflict**, plague, torment, torture, curse, cause suffering to, oppress, burden, bedevil, beset; devastate; punish.

scout noun **1** *scouts reported that the enemy were massing at two points ahead*: **lookout**, lookout man/woman, outrider, advance guard, vanguard, spy; French avant-courier.
2 *I returned from a lengthy scout round the area*: **reconnaissance**, reconnoitre; exploration, search, expedition; informal recce; Brit. informal shufti; N. Amer. informal recon.
3 *Brock slid the ball in from 14 yards, impressing watching scouts*: **talent spotter**, talent scout, recruiter; N. Amer. informal bird dog.
▶ **verb 1** *I scouted around for some logs*: **search**, look, hunt, cast about/around/round, ferret (about/around), root about/around.
2 *a night patrol was sent to **scout out** the area*: **reconnoitre**, explore, take a look at, make a reconnaissance of, inspect, investigate, spy out, survey, make a survey of; examine, scan, study, observe; see how the land lies, find out the lie of the land; informal recce, make a recce of, check out, case, case the joint; Brit. informal take a shufti round, suss out; N. Amer. informal recon.

scowl noun *she stamped into the room with a scowl on her face*: **frown**, glower, glare, grimace, black look; informal dirty look; Scottish archaic glunch.
▷**ANTONYMS** smile, grin.
▶ **verb** *she **scowled at him** defiantly*: **glower**, frown, glare, lour, look daggers at, look angrily at, give someone a black look; make a face, pull a face, turn the corners of one's mouth down, pout; informal give someone a dirty look; archaic mop and mow, glout; Scottish archaic glunch.
▷**ANTONYMS** smile, grin, beam.

scrabble verb *she scrabbled around in the sandy earth*: **scratch**, grope, rummage, root, pole, grub, scavenge, fumble, feel, clamber, scramble; archaic grabble.

scraggy adjective *a scraggy mongrel*: **scrawny**, thin, thin as a rake, skinny, skin-and-bones, size-zero, gaunt, bony, angular, gawky, rangy, raw-boned, skeletal, emaciated, pinched; lean, slim, slender, lanky, spindly, gangly, gangling; dated spindle-shanked.
▷**ANTONYMS** fat, plump.

scram verb informal *scram or I'll call the police*: **go away**, depart, leave, take yourself off, take off, get out, get out of my sight; go, go your way, get going, get moving, move off, be off, set off, set out, start out, make a start, take your leave, decamp, duck out, take wing, walk out, walk off, absent yourself; be off with you!, shoo!; informal hit the road, fly, skedaddle, split, vamoose, scat, make yourself scarce, be on one's way, run along, beat it, get, get lost, push off, shove off, buzz off, clear off, skip off, pop off, go (and) jump in the lake; on your bike!, go and chase yourself!; Brit. informal get along, push along, get stuffed, sling your hook, hop it, hop the twig/stick, bog off, naff off; N. Amer. informal bug off, light out, haul off, haul ass, take a powder, hit the trail, take a hike; Austral. informal nick off; Austral./NZ informal rack off; S. African informal voetsak, hamba; vulgar slang bugger off, piss off, fuck off; Brit. vulgar slang sod off; literary begone, avaunt.

scramble verb **1** *we scrambled over the boulders to inspect the rapids below*: **clamber**, climb, crawl, claw one's way, scrabble, grope one's way; N. Amer. shinny.
2 *he scrambled for shelter behind a heap of rubble*: **struggle**, **hurry**, scurry, scud, scutter, hasten, rush, race, run.
3 *the children scrambled for new pennies thrown down from the tower*: **jostle**, scuffle, scrimmage, tussle, battle, struggle, strive, compete, contend, vie, jockey.
4 *his stage fright scrambled the lines in his head*: **muddle**, confuse, mix up, jumble (up), disarrange, disorganize, disorder, disturb, throw into disorder, throw into confusion, get into a tangle, mess up.
▶ **noun 1** *a short scramble over the rocks takes you to our secret spot*: **clamber**, climb, ascent, trek.
2 *it was a scramble to get there on time*: **struggle**, **hurry**, rush, race, scurry.
3 *I lost Tommy in the scramble for a seat*: **tussle**, jostle, scrimmage, scuffle, battle, struggle, free-for-all, competition, contention, vying, jockeying; **muddle**, confusion, melee.

scrap[1] noun **1** *he scribbled Pamela's address on a scrap of paper*: **fragment**, piece, bit, offcut, oddment, snippet, snip, tatter, wisp, shred, remnant.
2 *there wasn't a scrap of evidence to link him with the body*: **bit**, speck, iota, particle, ounce, whit, jot, atom, shred, crumb, morsel, fragment, grain, drop, hint, touch, trace, suggestion, whisper, suspicion, scintilla, spot, mite, tittle, jot or tittle, modicum; Irish stim; informal smidgen, smidge, tad; archaic scantling, scruple.
3 (**scraps**) *between jobs he slept rough and lived on scraps*: **leftovers**, uneaten food, leavings, crumbs, scrapings, slops, dregs, scourings, offscourings, remains, remnants, residue, odds and ends, bits and pieces, bits and bobs; pieces, bits.
4 *the whole thing was made from bits of scrap*: **waste**, refuse, garbage, rubbish, litter, discarded matter, debris, detritus, dross; flotsam and jetsam, lumber; N. Amer. trash; Austral./NZ mullock; informal dreck, junk; Brit. informal grot, gash; rare draff, raffle, raff, cultch, orts.
▶ **verb 1** *the government intended to scrap sixty-two naval ships*: **throw away**, throw out, dispose of, get rid of, do away with, toss out, throw on the scrap heap, clear out, discard, remove, dispense with, lose, eliminate, dump, bin, jettison, shed, dismiss, expel, eject, weed out, root out; decommission, recycle, break up, demolish, write off; **destroy**, annihilate, obliterate; informal chuck (away/out), ditch, junk, get shut of; Brit. informal get shot of, see the back of; N. Amer. informal trash, shuck off, wreck.
▷**ANTONYMS** keep, preserve.
2 *campaigners are calling for the plans to be scrapped*: **abandon**, drop, abolish, withdraw, throw out, do away with, give up, stop, put an end to, cancel, eliminate, cut, jettison; informal axe, ditch, dump, junk, chuck in.
▷**ANTONYMS** keep, restore.

scrap[2] informal **noun** *he would always win a scrap with Stephen*: **quarrel**, argument, row, fight, disagreement, difference of opinion, dissension, falling-out, dispute, disputation, contention, squabble, contretemps, clash, altercation, exchange, brawl, tussle, conflict, affray, war of words, shouting match, fracas, wrangle, tangle, misunderstanding, passage of/at arms, battle royal; Irish, N. Amer., & Austral. donnybrook; informal tiff, set-to, run-in, shindig, shindy, stand-up, spat, dust-up, ruction; Brit. informal barney, bunfight, ding-dong, bust-up, ruck, slanging match; Scottish informal rammy; N. Amer. informal hassle; archaic broil, miff; Scottish archaic threap, collieshangie; French archaic tracasserie(s).
▶ **verb** *the older boys started scrapping with me*: **quarrel**, argue, have a row/fight, row, fight, disagree, fail to agree, differ, be at odds, have a misunderstanding, be at variance, fall out, dispute, squabble, brawl, bicker, chop logic, spar, wrangle, bandy words, cross swords, lock horns, be at each other's throats, be at loggerheads; informal argufy; archaic altercate.

scrape verb **1** *the men only had to scrape the ship and overhaul her rigging*: **abrade**, grate, sand, sandpaper, scour, scratch, rub, file, rasp.
2 *she scraped the earth back and saw something blue buried there*: **rake**, drag, push, brush, sweep.
3 *their boots scraped along the floor*: **grate**, creak, grind, jar, rasp, scratch, drag, rub, squeak, screech, grit, set someone's teeth on edge.
4 *the stag first scrapes a hole in the ground*: **scoop out**, hollow out, dig out, dig, excavate, gouge out, quarry, make.
5 *Ellen had scraped her shins on the wall*: **graze**, scratch, abrade, scuff, rasp, skin, rub raw, cut, lacerate, bark, chafe, strip, flay, wound; technical excoriate.
□ **scrape by** *students have to scrape by on an inadequate grant*: **manage**, cope, survive, muddle through/along, scrape along, make ends meet, get by/along, make do, manage to live with difficulty, barely/scarcely manage to live, barely/scarcely have enough to live on, keep the wolf from the door, keep one's head above water, scrimp, scrape a living; informal make out.
□ **scrape through** *he managed to scrape through the exam*: **just pass**, pass and no more, pass by a narrow margin, just succeed in, narrowly achieve.
□ **scrape something together** *we scraped together enough coins to buy some tea*: **collect**, amass, gather, rake together, rake up, dredge up, get hold of, raise, muster, accumulate, build up.
▶ **noun 1** *he heard the scrape of a stool being dragged across the floor*: **grate**, grating, creak, creaking, grind, grinding, jar, jarring, rasp, rasping, scratch, scratching, rub, rubbing, squeak, squeaking, screech, screeching.
2 *the shopkeeper sustained scrapes to his knee and hand in the struggle*: **graze**, scratch, abrasion, cut, laceration, wound.
3 informal *he's always getting into scrapes because he trusts the wrong people*:

predicament, plight, tight corner, tight spot, ticklish/tricky situation, problem, quandary, dilemma, crisis, mess, muddle; informal jam, fix, stew, bind, hole, hot water, a pretty/fine kettle of fish; Brit. informal spot of bother; (**scrapes**) trouble, difficulty, straits, dire/desperate straits, distress.

scrappy adjective *the match was a scrappy affair*: **disorganized**, untidy, disjointed, unsystematic, thrown together, uneven, bitty, sketchy, superficial, perfunctory, slipshod, inadequate, imperfect, incoherent, piecemeal; fragmentary, incomplete, unfinished, unpolished, deficient, defective.

scratch verb **1** *take care not to scratch the surface on plastic baths*: **score**, abrade, scrape, roughen, scuff (up), lacerate, groove, gash, engrave, incise, gouge.
2 *thorns scratched her tender skin*: **graze**, scrape, abrade, rasp, skin, rub raw, cut, lacerate, bark, chafe, strip, flay, wound; technical excoriate.
3 *he scratched the back of his neck*: **rub**, claw (at), scrape, tear at.
4 *many names had been* ***scratched out*** *or overwritten*: **cross out**, strike out, score out, delete, erase, remove, strike off, eliminate, cancel, expunge, obliterate.
5 *due to a knee injury she was forced to* ***scratch from*** *the race*: **withdraw**, pull out (of), back out (of), bow out (of), stand down, give up, leave, quit.
□ **scratch about/around** *the authority had scratched around for every spare penny over the years*: **search**, hunt (around), cast about/around/round, rummage (around), forage (about), poke around/about, scrabble, grub about/around, root (around), scavenge, fish about/around, rake around, feel around, grope (around), nose around/about/round, ferret (about/around).
▸ noun **1** *he had two scratches on his cheek*: **graze**, scrape, abrasion, cut, laceration, wound.
2 *there was a large dent in the panel and a scratch in the paint*: **score**, mark, line, abrasion, scrape, scuff, laceration, groove, gash, gouge.
□ **up to scratch** *the workmanship once again is up to scratch*: **good enough**, up to the mark, up to standard, up to par, satisfactory, acceptable, adequate, passable, sufficient, competent, all right; informal OK, up to snuff.
▷ANTONYMS below standard, unacceptable.

scrawl verb *he scanned the page, then scrawled his name at the bottom*: **scribble**, write hurriedly, write untidily, write illegibly, scratch, doodle, dash off, jot (down).
▸ noun *you might wonder how pharmacists decipher a doctor's scrawl*: **scribble**, hurried handwriting, untidy handwriting, illegible handwriting, squiggle(s); archaic cacography.

scrawny adjective *he was small, scrawny, and hairless*: **skinny**, thin, thin as a rake, skin-and-bones, gaunt, bony, size-zero, angular, gawky, scraggy, rangy, raw-boned, skeletal, emaciated, pinched; lean, slim, slender, lanky, spindly, gangly, gangling; dated spindle-shanked.
▷ANTONYMS plump, fat.

scream verb *he screamed in pain*: **shriek**, screech, yell, howl, shout, bellow, bawl, cry out, call out, yawp, yelp, squeal, wail, squawk, squall, caterwaul, whoop; N. Amer. informal holler.
▷ANTONYMS whisper.
▸ noun **1** *a scream of pain*: **shriek**, screech, yell, howl, shout, bellow, bawl, cry, yawp, yelp, squeal, wail, squawk, squall, caterwaul, whoop; N. Amer. informal holler.
▷ANTONYMS whisper.
2 informal *the whole thing's a scream*: **laugh**; hoot, comedy; informal gas, giggle, lark, riot, bundle of fun, bundle of laughs; informal, dated yell. See also **funny**.
3 informal *he's an absolute scream*: **wit**, hoot, comedian, comic, entertainer, joker, clown, buffoon; informal character, gas, giggle, riot; Austral./NZ informal hard case; informal, dated caution, case, card, yell.
▷ANTONYMS bore.

screech verb *'Look what you've made me do!' she screeched | the car screeched to a halt*: **shriek**, squeal, squawk, howl, shout, yell, bellow, bawl, cry out, call out, yawp, yelp, wail, squall, caterwaul, whoop; N. Amer. informal holler.
▷ANTONYMS whisper.
▸ noun *the wailing rose in pitch to an awful screech*: **shriek**, squeal, squawk, howl, shout, yell, bellow, bawl, cry, yawp, yelp, wail, squall, caterwaul, whoop; N. Amer. informal holler.
▷ANTONYMS whisper.

screen noun **1** *he dressed hurriedly behind the screen*: **partition**, (room) divider, dividing wall, separator, curtain, arras, blind, awning, shade, shutter, canopy, windbreak.
2 *the computer comes with a 15-inch screen*: **display**, monitor, visual display unit, VDU, cathode-ray tube, CRT.
3 *every window has a screen here because of the mosquitoes*: **mesh**, net, netting.
4 *the hedge acts as a screen against the wind*: **buffer**, protection, shield, shelter, guard, safeguard.
5 *the earth must be put through a screen*: **sieve**, riddle, sifter, strainer, colander, filter, winnow; archaic griddle.
▸ verb **1** *the far end of the hall had been* ***screened off*** *as a waiting room*: **partition off**, divide off, separate off, curtain off.
2 *during the experiment the speaker was screened from the children's view*: **conceal**, hide, mask, shield, shelter, shade, protect, guard, safeguard, veil, cloak, camouflage, disguise.
3 *the security is excellent and the staff are very tightly screened*: **vet**, check, check up on, check out, evaluate, assess, scrutinize, test.
4 *health-care workers who had had contact with the patient were screened for diphtheria*: **check**, test, examine, investigate, scan.
5 *coal used to be screened by hand*: **sieve**, riddle, sift, strain, filter, sort, winnow; archaic bolt, griddle.
6 informal *the programme is screened on Thursday evenings at 7.30*: **show**, present, air, broadcast, transmit, televise, put out, put on the air, telecast, relay.

screw noun **1** *fit the shelf to its supports with the screws provided*: **bolt**, fastener; nail, pin, tack, spike, rivet, brad.
2 *the handle needs a couple of screws to tighten it*: **turn**, twist, wrench, lever, heave.
3 *the ship's twin screws*: **propeller**, rotor.
□ **put the screws on** informal **pressurize**, put pressure on, use pressure on, pressure, press, bring force to bear on, force, drive, impel, coerce, urge, push, nag; lean on, prevail on; dragoon, steamroller, browbeat, use strong-arm tactics on, have someone do something; hold/put a gun/pistol to someone's head; informal put the heat on, put the squeeze on, twist someone's arm, railroad, bulldoze.
□ **with a screw loose** *it really needs to be a person with a screw loose to commit violence*: **unstable**, unbalanced, of unsound mind, mentally ill, deranged, demented, crazed, troubled, disturbed, unhinged, insane, mad, mad as a hatter, mad as a March hare, raving mad, out of one's mind, not in one's right mind, neurotic, psychotic; Latin non compos mentis; informal crazy, loopy, loony, mixed up, nuts, nutty, nutty as a fruitcake, bananas, cracked, crackpot, daft, dippy, screwy, batty, dotty, cuckoo, bonkers, potty, mental, screwed up, not all there, off one's head, out of one's head, out to lunch, a bit lacking, round the bend, round the twist, away with the fairies; Brit. informal barmy, crackers, barking, barking mad, off one's trolley, off one's rocker, daft as a brush, not the full shilling; N. Amer. informal nutsy, nutso, squirrelly, wacko, buggy; dated touched.
▸ verb **1** *he screwed the lid back on the jar*: **tighten**, turn, twist, wind, work.
2 *I screwed the boards down tightly*: **fasten**, secure, fix, attach, clamp, bolt, rivet, batten.
3 *she intended to* ***screw*** *money* ***out of*** *them*: **extort**, force, extract, wrest, wring, squeeze; informal bleed someone of something.
4 informal *they screwed him at least once, so now he doesn't trust them at all*: **cheat**, swindle, defraud, gazump, fleece; overcharge, short-change; informal rip off, bilk, diddle, do, sting, soak, rob, clip, gyp, skin; N. Amer. informal stiff, gouge; Brit. informal, dated rush; archaic cozen; rare mulct.
□ **screw something up 1** *Christina screwed up her face in disgust*: **wrinkle (up)**, pucker, crumple, crease, furrow, contort, distort, twist, purse.
2 informal *they'll screw up the whole economy*: **wreck**, ruin, destroy, devastate, wreak havoc on, reduce to nothing, damage, spoil, mar, injure, blast, blight, smash, shatter, dash, torpedo, scotch, make a mess of, mess up; informal louse up, foul up, put the kibosh on, banjax, do for, blow a hole in, nix, queer; Brit. informal scupper, cock up, dish; Austral. informal euchre, cruel; vulgar slang fuck up; archaic bring to naught.
▷ANTONYMS sort out.

screwy adjective informal *are the cases you work on always this screwy?* See **strange**, **crazy**.

scribble verb *he scribbled a few lines on a scrap sheet*: **write hurriedly**, write untidily, write illegibly, scratch, scrawl, doodle, dash off, jot (down).
▸ noun *the postman would never have been able to decipher your scribble*: **illegible handwriting**, hurried handwriting, untidy handwriting, squiggle(s), jottings; rare cacography.

scribe noun **1** historical *if he wished to send a letter he would have to get a scribe to write it for him*: **clerk**, secretary, copyist, transcriber, amanuensis, recorder, record keeper; in Africa mallam; informal pen-pusher; N. Amer. informal pencil-pusher; archaic penman, scrivener, writer.
2 informal *he'd been corresponding with a local cricket scribe before the trip*: **writer**, author, penman, journalist, reporter; informal hack.

scrimmage noun *seventeen hecklers were thrown out after terrific scrimmages in the audience*: **fight**, battle, struggle, tussle, brawl, fracas, rumpus, melee, free-for-all, rough and tumble; Irish, N. Amer., & Austral. donnybrook; Law, dated affray; informal scrap, dust-up, punch-up, set-to, shindy; Brit. informal scrum; N. Amer. informal rough house.

scrimp verb *she scrimped for six months to buy a pair of evening gloves*: **economize**, skimp, be (more) economical, make economies, scrimp and scrape, save; be thrifty, be frugal, tighten one's belt, cut back, make cutbacks, budget, retrench, husband one's resources, cut costs, cut expenditure, draw in one's horns, watch one's pennies, look after the pence; N. Amer. pinch the pennies; black English rake and scrape.
▷ANTONYMS spend.

script noun **1** *it was written in a careful script*: **handwriting**, writing, hand, autograph, pen, letters, longhand, penmanship, calligraphy, chirography; scribble, scrawl; informal fist.
2 *the script of the play*: **text**, book, screenplay, libretto, lyrics, score, lines, parts, dialogue, words, manuscript.

S

scripture noun *he appeals solely to scripture for his authority*: **sacred text**, Holy Writ, the Bible, the Holy Bible, the Gospel, the Good Book, the Word of God, the Book of Books.

Scrooge noun *he is depicted as a Scrooge keeping tight hold of the purse strings*: **miser**, penny-pincher, pinchpenny, niggard, cheese-parer, hoarder, saver; informal skinflint, meanie, money-grubber, cheapskate; N. Amer. informal tightwad; vulgar slang tight-arse.
▷ANTONYMS spendthrift; philanthropist.

scrounge verb *they were always scrounging food from the tourists*: **beg**, borrow; informal cadge, sponge, bum, touch someone for; Brit. informal scab; Scottish informal sorn on someone for; N. Amer. informal mooch; Austral./NZ informal bludge.

scrounger noun *the unemployed are often depicted as scroungers*: **beggar**, borrower, parasite, scrounge, cadger; informal sponger, freeloader; Scottish informal sorner; N. Amer. informal mooch, moocher, schnorrer; Austral./NZ informal bludger.

scrub[1] verb **1** *he scrubbed the kitchen floor*: **scour**, rub, brush, sponge, swab, clean, cleanse, wash, wipe.
2 informal *you could only save that much by scrubbing the Navy*: **abolish**, scrap, throw out, abandon, drop, do away with, give up, discontinue, take away, stop, put an end to, cancel, call off, eliminate, cut, jettison, discard, forget (about), abort; informal axe, ditch, dump, junk.
▷ANTONYMS keep, restore.

scrub[2] noun *there the buildings ended and the scrub began*: **brush**, brushwood, scrubland, undergrowth, coppice, copse, thicket.

scruffy adjective *he wore scruffy jeans*: **shabby**, worn, down at heel, shoddy, ragged, tattered, mangy, sorry, run down, disreputable; **untidy**, unkempt, bedraggled, messy, dishevelled, ungroomed, ill-groomed, sleazy, seedy, slatternly, slovenly; **dirty**, squalid, filthy; informal tatty, the worse for wear, scuzzy, grungy, yucky; Brit. informal grotty; N. Amer. informal raggedy.
▷ANTONYMS smart, tidy, clean.

scrumptious adjective informal *a piece of scrumptious gateau*: **delicious**, gorgeous, tasty, good, mouth-watering, appetizing, inviting, palatable, delectable, delightful, succulent, rich, sweet, choice, dainty, savoury, flavoursome, flavourful, piquant, luscious, toothsome; informal delish, scrummy, yummy, yum-yum; Brit. informal moreish; N. Amer. informal finger-licking, nummy; literary ambrosial; rare ambrosian, nectareous, nectarean.
▷ANTONYMS inedible, unpalatable.

scrunch verb *I had **scrunched up** the pages and stuffed them into the gaps*: **crumple (up)**, crunch (up), crush, rumple, screw up, squash (up), twist (up), mash (up), squeeze, compress, chew (up); informal squidge.

scruple verb *they would not **scruple to** cut his throat*: **hesitate**, be reluctant, be loath, have qualms about, have scruples about, have misgivings about, have reservations about, stick at, think twice about, baulk at, demur about/from, mind doing something; recoil from, shrink from, hang back from, shy away from, flinch from, drag one's feet/heels over, waver about, vacillate about; informal boggle at; archaic disrelish something.
▷ANTONYMS jump at the chance.

scruples plural noun **1** *he had no scruples about eavesdropping*: **qualms**, twinge of conscience, compunction, hesitation, reservations, second thoughts, doubt(s), misgivings, pangs of conscience, uneasiness, reluctance.
2 *I respect your scruples*: **principles**, standards, values, morals, morality, moral concern, ethics, conscience, creed, beliefs.

scrupulous adjective **1** *the research has been carried out with scrupulous attention to detail*: **careful**, meticulous, painstaking, thorough, assiduous, sedulous, attentive, diligent, conscientious, ultra-careful, punctilious, searching, close, elaborate, minute, studious, rigorous, particular; religious, strict; pedantic, fussy.
▷ANTONYMS careless, slapdash.
2 *the finances were in the hands of one of our most scrupulous colleagues*: **honest**, honourable, upright, upstanding, high-minded, righteous, right-minded, moral, ethical, good, virtuous, principled, proper, correct, just, noble, incorruptible, conscientious, respectable, decent.
▷ANTONYMS dishonest, unscrupulous.

scrutinize verb *Basil scrutinized the painting*: **examine carefully**, **inspect**, survey, scan, study, look over, peruse; search, investigate, explore, probe, research, enquire into, go over, go over with a fine-tooth comb, check, audit, review, sift, analyse, dissect.
▷ANTONYMS glance at.

scrutiny noun *Frick continued his scrutiny of the room*: **careful examination**, **inspection**, survey, scan, study, perusal; search, investigation, exploration, research, probe, enquiry, check, audit, review, analysis, dissection; informal going-over, look-see, once-over.
▷ANTONYMS glance, cursory look.

scud verb *a few dark clouds scudded across the sky*: **speed**, race, sail, streak, shoot, sweep, skim, whip, whizz, whoosh, buzz, zoom, flash, blast, career; hare, fly, wing, kite, skite, scurry, flit, scutter, hurry, hasten, rush; informal belt, scoot, scorch, tear, zap, zip; Brit. informal bomb, bucket, shift; N. Amer. informal boogie, hightail, clip; N. Amer. vulgar slang drag/tear/haul ass; informal, dated cut along.

scuff verb *the girl scuffed the toe of her shoe in the gravel*: **scrape**, rub, drag, brush, scratch, graze, abrade, rasp, lacerate, chafe, roughen.

scuffle noun *there was a scuffle outside the pub*: **fight**, struggle, tussle, brawl, fracas, rumpus, melee, free-for-all, rough and tumble, scrimmage, disturbance, brouhaha, commotion; Irish, N. Amer., & Austral. donnybrook; Law, dated affray; informal scrap, dust-up, punch-up, set-to, shindy; N. Amer. informal rough house.
▶ verb *tempers flared as the supporters scuffled with other passengers*: **fight**, struggle, tussle, exchange blows, come to blows, brawl, grapple, clash, scrimmage; informal scrap, have a dust-up, have a punch-up, have a set-to; N. Amer. informal rough-house.

sculpt verb *the Minoans were adept at sculpting human figures from ivory*: **carve**, **model**, chisel, sculpture, fashion, form, shape, cast, cut, hew; rare sculp.

sculptor noun *a bronze statue by the fifth-century sculptor Polyclitus*: **carver**, modeller.

sculpture noun *a Michelangelo sculpture of the Madonna*: **carving**, **model**, statue, statuette, figure, figurine, effigy, bust, head, image, likeness.
▶ verb *the west doorway is richly decorated with sculptured figures*: **sculpt**, carve, chisel, model, fashion, form, shape, cast, cut, hew; rare sculp.

scum noun **1** *it is important that the scum on the surface is not disturbed*: **film**, layer, covering, froth, foam, suds, dross, dirt.
2 informal *the glorious traditions of the Service meant nothing to scum like that*: **despicable person/people**, rabble, riff-raff, refuse, garbage, trash, vermin, good-for-nothing(s), undesirable(s), the lowest of the low, the dregs of society; Brit. trog(s); informal dirt, dirty dog(s), rat(s), louse(s), toad(s), worm(s), scumbag(s), crud(s), cur(s), no-good(s); N. Amer. informal pond scum, scuzzball(s), sleazeball(s); archaic dastard(s).

scupper verb **1** *the captain decided to scupper the ship*: **sink**, scuttle, submerge, send to the bottom, open the seacocks in.
▷ANTONYMS float, raise.
2 informal *he denied trying to scupper the agreement*: **ruin**, wreck, destroy, devastate, wreak havoc on, damage, spoil, mar, injure, blast, blight, smash, shatter, dash, torpedo, scotch, mess up; sabotage, poison; informal louse up, screw up, foul up, put the kibosh on, banjax, do for, blow a hole in, nix, queer; Brit. informal cock up, dish; Austral. informal euchre, cruel; vulgar slang fuck up; archaic bring to naught.
▷ANTONYMS further, promote.

scurrility noun *this scurrility is aimed at provoking controversy*: **abuse**, scurrilousness, disparagement, denigration, deprecation, insult, defamation, slander, libel, scandal, calumny, aspersions, invective, opprobrium, vituperation, vitriol, venom; informal bitchiness; archaic contumely; dated billingsgate.

scurrilous adjective *a scurrilous attack on her character*: **abusive**, vituperative, derogatory, disparaging, denigratory, pejorative, deprecatory, insulting, offensive, defamatory, slanderous, libellous, scandalous, opprobrious, vitriolic, venomous; **unfounded**, ill-founded, groundless, baseless, unsubstantiated, unwarranted, unsupported, insupportable, uncorroborated, unjustified, unjustifiable; informal bitchy; rare contumelious, calumnious, calumniatory, aspersive, invective.

scurry verb *waiters scurry to and from their cafes*: **scamper**, scuttle, bustle, skip, trot, hurry, hasten, make haste, rush, race, dash, run, sprint; Brit. scutter; informal scoot, beetle.
▷ANTONYMS amble, stroll.
▶ noun **1** *there was a scurry to get out*: **rush**, race, dash, run, sprint; scamper, scampering, scuttle, scuttling, scramble, scrambling, bustle, bustling, trot, hurry; Brit. scutter, scuttering.
▷ANTONYMS stroll.
2 *none of these people speak a word of English, hence the scurry of interpreters*: **swarm**, cloud, flock, horde, throng, bustle, maelstrom, turmoil, flurry, whirl, flood.

scurvy noun

> *Word links* **scurvy**
>
> **antiscorbutic** preventing scurvy

scuttle verb *there were men scuttling across the upper deck*: **scamper**, scurry, scramble, bustle, skip, trot, hurry, hasten, make haste, rush, race, dash, run, sprint; Brit. scutter; informal scoot, beetle.
▶ noun *there was the soft scuttle of rats*: **scamper**, scampering noise, scurry, scurrying; bustle, bustling, trot, hurry, haste, rush, race, dash, run, sprint; rustle, rasp, scratching noise; Brit. scutter, scuttering.

sea noun **1** *the sea sparkled in the sun*: **(the) ocean**, the waves; informal the drink; Brit. informal the briny; N. Amer. informal salt chuck; literary the deep, the main, the foam; NZ rare moana.
▷ANTONYMS land, dry land; fresh water.
2 *there were very heavy seas and the boat overturned*: **wave**, breaker, roller, comber, billow; Austral. bombora; informal boomer; N. Amer. informal kahuna; **(seas) swell**, white horses, white caps.

3 *the ground was now a sea of glutinous mud | I saw a sea of roofs and turrets*: **expanse**, stretch, span, area, tract, sweep, blanket, sheet, carpet, mass; multitude, host, profusion, abundance, plethora.
□ **at sea** *as teachers we may leave our students completely at sea*: **confused**, perplexed, puzzled, baffled, mystified, bemused, bewildered, nonplussed, disconcerted, disoriented, dumbfounded, at a loss, at sixes and sevens, adrift; informal flummoxed, bamboozled, discombobulated, stumped, fazed, beaten; Canadian & Austral./NZ informal bushed; archaic wildered, distracted, mazed.
▷ANTONYMS clear, enlightened.
▸ adjective *outstanding apartments with magnificent sea views | microscopic sea creatures*: **marine**, ocean, oceanic; salt, saltwater, seawater, watery, pelagic; ocean-going, seagoing, seafaring, afloat; maritime, naval, nautical; rare thalassic, pelagian.
▷ANTONYMS land, shore; freshwater.
□ **sea change** *it indicated a sea change in American attitudes*: **transformation**, change, alteration, modification, variation, conversion, revision, amendment, metamorphosis, transfiguration, evolution, mutation; remodelling, reshaping, remoulding, redoing, reconstruction, rebuilding, recasting, reorganization, rearrangement, reordering, reshuffling, restyling, rejigging, reworking, renewal, renewing, revamping, renovation, overhaul, remaking; revolutionizing, revolution, transmutation; humorous transmogrification.

Word links **sea**

marine, **maritime**, **nautical** relating to the sea
submarine under the sea
hydrography surveying of the sea
thalassophobia fear of the sea

seafaring adjective *an ancient seafaring people*: **maritime**, nautical, naval, seagoing, pelagic, sea; rare pelagian.

seal[1] noun **1** *the seal round the bath has come unstuck*: **sealant**, sealer, adhesive.
2 *the king put his seal on the letter*: **emblem**, symbol, insignia, device, badge, crest, coat of arms, token, mark, monogram, stamp.
3 *the Energy Minister gave his* ***seal of approval*** *to the project*: **ratification**, assurance, attestation, confirmation, guarantee, authentication, warrant, warranty; charter, licence, imprimatur, validation; **blessing**, stamp of approval, approval, consent, agreement, permission, sanction, authority, endorsement, clearance, approbation.
□ **set the seal on** *parliament assembled at York to set the seal on the royalist victory*: **endorse**, confirm, guarantee, ratify, validate; **authorize**, certify, warrant, authenticate, seal, put the seal on, cap, clinch, wind up, close; informal sew up.
▸ verb **1** *he read the letter and sealed the envelope | she quietly sealed the door behind her*: **fasten**, secure, shut, close up, lock, bolt, board up.
2 *seal each bottle while it is hot*: **stop up**, seal up, make airtight, make watertight, close, shut, cork, stopper, stop, plug, block, block up, bung up, clog, clog up, choke, occlude, fill.
3 *police* ***sealed off*** *the High Street*: **close off**, shut off, cordon off, fence off, form a ring around, put a cordon sanitaire round, isolate, quarantine, segregate.
4 *he held out his hand to seal the bargain*: **clinch**, secure, settle, conclude, complete, establish; set the seal on, cap, wind up, close; informal sew up.

seal[2] noun

Word links **seal**

bull male
cow female
pup, **calf** young
rookery collective noun
phocine relating to seals

seam noun **1** *I use small stitches so that the seam is not obvious*: **join**, stitching, joint, junction, closure, line; Surgery suture.
2 *a seam of coal*: **layer**, stratum, vein, lode, deposit.
3 *the seams of his face*: **furrow**, crease, corrugation, fold, groove, crinkle, pucker, line, ridge, wrinkle, crow's foot, scar.

seaman noun *Captain Bligh was a superb seaman | he joined a cargo ship as a mere seaman*: **sailor**, seafarer, seafaring man, mariner, boatman, hand, crew member, rating; informal (old) salt, sea dog, bluejacket; Brit. informal matelot, matlow, matlo; informal, dated tar, Jack Tar, hearty; (**seamen**) **crew**, complement.
▷ANTONYMS landlubber.

seamy adjective *he seemed very knowledgeable about the seamy side of life*: **sordid**, disreputable, seedy, sleazy, corrupt, shameful, low, dark, squalid, unwholesome, unsavoury, rough, mean, nasty, unpleasant.
▷ANTONYMS salubrious.

sear verb **1** *the heat of the muzzle blast seared his face*: **scorch**, burn, singe, scald, char; **dry up**/**out**, parch, desiccate, dehydrate, wither, shrivel; discolour, brown, blacken, carbonize; Medicine cauterize; rare exsiccate.
2 *sear the meat before adding the rest of the ingredients*: **flash-fry**, seal, brown, fry/grill quickly, toast.
3 *his betrayal had seared her terribly*: **distress**, grieve, sadden, make miserable/wretched, upset, trouble, harrow, cause anguish to, afflict, perturb, disturb; hurt, wound, pain, cut to the quick; affect, move, sting, mortify, torment, torture, gnaw at, vex, gall.

search verb **1** *we* ***searched for*** *clues*: **hunt**, look, explore, forage, fish about/around, look high and low, cast about/around/round, ferret (about/around), root about/around, rummage about/around; seek, scout out, pursue.
2 *he searched the house thoroughly*: **look around**/**round**, explore, probe, hunt through, look through, scrabble about/around in, root about/around in, ferret (about/around) in, rummage about/around in, rummage in/through, forage through, fish about/around in, poke around in, dig in, grub about/around in, delve in, go through, sift through, rifle through, scour, comb, ransack, turn over, go through with a fine-tooth comb; turn upside down, turn inside out, leave no stone unturned in; Brit. informal rootle around in; Austral./NZ informal fossick through; rare roust around in.
3 *these statutes enable the police to stop and search suspects*: **examine**, inspect, check, frisk; informal give someone a/the once-over.
□ **search me!** informal **I don't know**, how should I know?, why ask me?, it's a mystery, I haven't an inkling/clue, I haven't the least idea, I've no idea; informal dunno, don't ask me, I haven't the faintest/first/foggiest (idea/notion), it beats me, ask me another.
▸ noun *we continued our* ***search for*** *a hotel*: **hunt**, look, exploration, scout, probe, dig, digging, forage, foraging, scavenge, scavenging, ferreting (about/around), rummage, rummaging about/around, rooting about/around, rifling, scouring, quest, pursuit of, seeking after.
□ **in search of** *they are forced to travel in search of food*: **searching for**, hunting for, after, seeking, looking for, on the lookout for, in quest of, in pursuit of, on the track of, questing after, chasing after.

searching adjective **1** *a searching look*: **observant**, penetrating, piercing, probing, curious, discerning, incisive, keen, alert, perceptive, shrewd, sharp, intent, minute, thorough.
▷ANTONYMS casual.
2 *searching questions*: **penetrating**, probing, incisive, inquisitive, analytic, deep, in-depth, enquiring.
▷ANTONYMS cursory, vague.

searing adjective **1** *the searing heat of the flames*: **scorching**, blistering, flaming, blazing (hot), baking (hot), burning, fiery, torrid, parching, withering; informal boiling, boiling hot, sizzling, roasting, sweltering.
2 *she winced with the searing pain*: **intense**, excruciating, agonizing, sharp, stabbing, shooting, stinging, severe, extreme, fierce, harrowing, piercing, penetrating, racking, insufferable, unbearable, unendurable, torturous; rare exquisite.
3 *she made national headlines with her searing attack on the President*: **fierce**, savage, blistering, scathing, stinging, devastating, mordant, trenchant, caustic, cutting, biting, withering, virulent, vitriolic.

seaside noun *a day out at the seaside*: **coast**, shore, coastal region, seashore, seaboard, sea coast, waterside; beach resort, beach, sand, sands, foreshore; technical littoral; literary strand.

season noun *the rainy season | the opera season*: **period**, active period, time, time of year, spell, term, phase, stage.
□ **in season** *strawberries are in season*: **available**, obtainable, readily available/obtainable, to be had, on offer, on the market, growing, common, plentiful, abundant.
▷ANTONYMS out of season.
▸ verb **1** *remove the bay leaves and season the casserole to taste*: **flavour**, add flavouring to, add salt/pepper to, spice, add spices/herbs to; informal pep up, add zing to.
2 *his albums include standard numbers seasoned with a few of his own tunes*: **enliven**, leaven, add spice to, enrich, liven up, animate, augment; informal pep up, add zest/zing to.
3 *oak should be well seasoned*: **mature**, age, mellow, condition, acclimatize, temper, prepare, prime, ripen.

seasonable adjective *seasonable weather*: **usual**, expected, predictable, normal for the time of year, appropriate to the time of year.
▷ANTONYMS unseasonable.

Easily confused words **seasonable or seasonal?**

Something **seasonable** is appropriate to a particular occasion or time of year (*surprise your Christmas guests with variations on seasonable recipes*). **Seasonal** is a more common word, and means 'varying with or determined by the time of year' (*a seasonal climate | seasonal employment*). A *seasonal crop*, ripening at a particular time of year, might also be seen as *seasonable* in the sense of being characteristic of that time; and from this connection, together with the similarity between the words, a use of *seasonal* in the sense 'appropriate to the time of year' has developed (*there's not much seasonal goodwill in evidence*).

seasoned adjective *seasoned travellers*: **experienced**, practised, well versed, expert, knowledgeable, sophisticated, established, habituated, long-serving, time-served, veteran, hardened, battle-scarred, consummate, well trained.
▷ANTONYMS inexperienced, callow, green.

seasoning noun *stir in the bean sprouts, garlic, soy sauce, and seasoning*: **flavouring**, salt and pepper, herbs, spices, condiments, dressing, relish.

seat noun **1** *enough seats for the audience/spectators*: **chair**, place, space; (**seats**) seating, seating accommodation, room.
2 *the patient can then move his seat or legs*: **buttocks**, behind, backside, rear, rear end, rump, haunches, hindquarters, cheeks; Brit. bottom; French derrière; German Sitzfleisch; informal sit-upon, stern, BTM, tochus; Brit. informal bum, botty, prat, jacksie; Scottish informal bahookie; N. Amer. informal butt, fanny, tush, tushie, tail, duff, buns, booty, caboose, heinie, patootie, keister, tuchis, bazoo, bippy; W. Indian informal batty; humorous fundament, posterior; black English rass, rusty dusty; Brit. vulgar slang arse; N. Amer. vulgar slang ass; technical nates; archaic breech.
3 *the seat of government*: **headquarters**, location, site, whereabouts, place, base, centre, nerve centre, nucleus, centre of operations/activity, hub, focus, focal point, heart.
4 *the family had a country seat in Surrey*: **residence**, ancestral home, mansion, stately home, abode.
▸ verb **1** *they seated themselves round the table | he was seated next to Margaret*: **position**, put, place, stand, station; install, settle, arrange, dispose, array, range, deploy; informal plonk, park; rare posit.
2 *the hall seats 500*: **have room for**, contain, take, sit, hold, accommodate.

seating noun *the theatre has seating for 600*: **seats**, room, places, chairs, seating accommodation, accommodation.

seaweed noun

> *Word links* **seaweed**
>
> **phyco-** related prefix, as in *phycocyanin*
> **phycology** study of seaweed

secede verb *the Southern states **seceded from** the Federal Union*: **withdraw from**, break away from, break with, separate (oneself) from, sever relations with, leave, quit, split with, split off from, disaffiliate from, defect from, resign from, pull out of, drop out of, have nothing more to do with, turn one's back on, repudiate, reject, renounce, desert; form a splinter group.
▷ANTONYMS join.

secession noun *the republic's secession from the Soviet Union*: **withdrawal**, break, breakaway, separation, severance, schism, apostasy, leaving, quitting, split, splitting, disaffiliation, resignation, pulling out, dropping out, desertion, defection.
▷ANTONYMS joining; unification.

secluded adjective *the house overlooks a quiet, secluded garden*: **sheltered**, **private**, concealed, hidden, undisturbed, unfrequented, sequestered, tucked away.
▷ANTONYMS public, busy, accessible.

seclusion noun *he spends much of his time in seclusion at his mountain cottage*: **isolation**, solitude, retreat, privacy, privateness, retirement, withdrawal, purdah, an ivory tower, concealment, hiding, secrecy, peace, peace and quiet, peacefulness, quietness, lack of disturbance, lack of interruption, freedom from interference; rare sequestration, reclusion.

second[1] (stress on the first syllable) adjective **1** *the second day of the trial*: **next**, following, after the first, subsequent, ensuing, succeeding, coming.
▷ANTONYMS first, preceding.
2 *would you like a second helping?* **additional**, extra, fresh, another, further, repeat, supplementary, supplemental.
▷ANTONYMS first.
3 *he keeps a second pair of glasses in his office*: **spare**, extra, additional, alternative, another, backup, relief, fallback, substitute, auxiliary, ancillary; redundant, surplus, superfluous; N. Amer. alternate.
▷ANTONYMS primary, principal.
4 *Malcolm is dropping down to captain the second team*: **secondary**, lower, subordinate, subsidiary, lesser, minor, subservient, supporting, lower-grade, inferior.
▷ANTONYMS first, top.
5 *there was a fear that the conflict would turn into a second Vietnam*: **another**, duplicate, reproduction, twin, double, new, replicate, matching; repeat of, copy of, carbon copy of.
▷ANTONYMS original.
□ **have second thoughts** *I had second thoughts about the original review myself*: **rethink**, reconsider, review, revise, re-examine, re-evaluate, reassess, reappraise, think better of, think over, take another look at, look at in a different light, have another think about; change, alter, modify; think again, think twice, review one's position, come round, change one's mind.
□ **second thoughts** *not all of them come to the decision easily, and their nervousness and second thoughts are a natural result*: **qualm**, misgivings, doubt, reservation, scruple; suspicion, distrust, mistrust, lack of faith, lack of confidence, diffidence; trepidation, scepticism, worry, unease, uneasiness, anxiety, apprehension, uncertainty, niggle, disquiet, disquietude, hesitation, hesitance, hesitancy.
□ **second to none** *the hotel offers a level of service that is second to none*: **incomparable**, matchless, unrivalled, inimitable, beyond compare, unparalleled, without parallel, unequalled, without equal, unmatched, in a class of its own, beyond comparison, peerless, unsurpassed, unsurpassable, nonpareil, unique; **perfect**, consummate, rare, exquisite, transcendent, surpassing, superlative, supreme; rare unexampled.
▸ noun **1** *Eva had been working as his second*: **assistant**, attendant, helper, aide, supporter, backer, auxiliary, right-hand man/woman, girl/man Friday, second in command, number two, deputy, vice-, understudy, subordinate, adjutant, subaltern, henchman; informal sidekick.
2 (**seconds**) informal *he enjoyed the pie so much he asked for seconds*: **a second helping**, a further helping, more.
3 (**seconds**) *sometimes factory shops sell seconds*: **imperfect goods**, faulty goods, defective goods, flawed goods, inferior goods, rejects, export rejects, discards.
▸ verb *George Beale seconded the motion*: **formally support**, give one's support to, announce one's support for, vote for, back, back up, approve, give one's approval to, endorse, promote, commend.

> *Word links* **second**
>
> **deuter(o)-** related prefix, as in *deuterium, Deuteronomy*

second[2] (stress on the first syllable) noun *I'll only be gone for a second*: **moment**, bit, little while, short time, instant, split second; informal sec, jiffy, jiff; Brit. informal mo, tick, two ticks.
□ **in a second** *you'll see in a second*: **(very) soon**, in a minute, in a moment, in a trice, in a flash, shortly, any minute, any minute now, in a short time, in an instant, in the twinkling of an eye, in (less than) no time, in no time at all, before you know it, before long; N. Amer. momentarily; informal in a jiffy, in two shakes, in two shakes of a lamb's tail, before you can say Jack Robinson, in the blink of an eye, in a blink, in the wink of an eye, in a wink, before you can say knife; Brit. informal in a tick, in two ticks, in a mo; N. Amer. informal in a snap.

second[3] (stress on the second syllable) verb *personnel are sometimes seconded to charities*: **assign temporarily**, lend; transfer, move, shift, relocate, assign, reassign, send, attach, allocate, detail, appoint.

secondary adjective **1** *'women's issues' have often been seen as secondary*: **subordinate**, lesser, lower, lower-level, minor, peripheral, incidental, tangential, marginal, ancillary, subsidiary, subservient, non-essential, inessential, of little account, unimportant, less important.
▷ANTONYMS primary, central.
2 *primary sources are not necessarily more accurate than secondary sources*: **indirect**, non-primary, derived, derivative, resulting, resultant, concomitant, accompanying, consequential, contingent, second-hand.
▷ANTONYMS primary, direct.
3 *they bombed their secondary target instead*: **alternative**, spare, extra, additional, another, backup, supporting, relief, fallback, substitute, auxiliary; N. Amer. alternate.
▷ANTONYMS primary, main.

second-class adjective *we were treated like second-class citizens*: **second-rate**, second-best, low-class, inferior, lesser, unimportant.

second-hand adjective **1** *a second-hand car*: **used**, old, nearly new, worn, pre-owned, handed-down, cast-off; informal hand-me-down, reach-me-down.
▷ANTONYMS new.
2 *they shouldn't have to rely on second-hand information*: **indirect**, secondary, derivative, derived, vicarious.
▷ANTONYMS first-hand.
▸ adverb *the information was invariably gathered second-hand*: **indirectly**, at second hand, on the bush/jungle telegraph; informal on the grapevine.
▷ANTONYMS directly.

second in command noun *he left it to his second in command to sort out the details*: **deputy**, number two, subordinate, assistant, right-hand man/woman, vice-, understudy, lieutenant, adjutant, subaltern; informal sidekick.

secondly adverb *firstly it is wrong and secondly it is difficult to implement*: **furthermore**, also, moreover; second, in the second place, next; secondarily.

second-rate adjective *he replied tetchily that he never made second-rate films*: **substandard**, below standard, below par, bad, deficient, defective, faulty, imperfect, inferior, mediocre; abject, poor, appalling, abysmal, atrocious, awful, terrible, dismal, dreadful, unsatisfactory, low-grade, third-rate, jerry-built, shoddy, crude, tinny, trashy, rubbishy, miserable, wretched, lamentable, deplorable, pitiful, inadequate, insufficient, unacceptable, execrable, frightful; informal crummy, dire, bum, diabolical, rotten, sad, tatty, tacky, tenth-rate; Brit. informal ropy, duff, rubbish, pants, a load of pants, grotty; vulgar slang crap, crappy; archaic direful; rare egregious.
▷ANTONYMS first-rate, excellent.

secrecy noun **1** *there is no guarantee that the secrecy of the material will be maintained*: **confidentiality**, classified nature, privateness.
2 *you must make him understand the need for secrecy*: **clandestineness**, furtiveness, surreptitiousness, secretiveness, stealth, stealthiness, covertness, cloak and dagger, mystery.
3 *in the secrecy of that room, her eyes now betrayed all*: **seclusion**, privacy, concealment, shelter, solitariness, loneliness, retirement, isolation, remoteness, privateness; rare sequestration.

secret adjective **1** *they have a secret plan*: **confidential**, strictly confidential, top secret, classified, restricted, unrevealed, undisclosed, unpublished, untold, unknown, uncommunicated, behind someone's back, under wraps, unofficial, off the record, not for publication/circulation, not to be made public, not to be disclosed; Latin sub rosa; informal hush-hush, mum.
▷ANTONYMS known, public.
2 *there is a secret drawer in the table*: **hidden**, concealed; camouflaged, disguised; unnoticeable, invisible, inconspicuous.
▷ANTONYMS visible.
3 *a secret operation to infiltrate terrorist groups*: **clandestine**, covert, undercover, underground, hidden, shrouded, conspiratorial, surreptitious, stealthy, cloak-and-dagger, hole-and-corner, closet; sneaky, sly, underhand, shifty, furtive; informal hush-hush.
▷ANTONYMS overt.
4 *a secret message | a secret code*: **cryptic**, encoded, coded, enciphered, hidden, mysterious, abstruse, recondite, arcane, esoteric, cabbalistic.
▷ANTONYMS open.
5 *a secret place*: **secluded**, **private**, concealed, hidden, sheltered, undisturbed, unfrequented, solitary, lonely, sequestered, out of the way, remote, isolated, off the beaten track, tucked away, cut-off.
▷ANTONYMS known about, public.
6 *he's a very secret person*: **uncommunicative**, secretive, unforthcoming, reticent, taciturn, silent, non-communicative, quiet, tight-lipped, close-mouthed, close, playing one's cards close to one's chest, clamlike, reserved, introvert, introverted, self-contained, discreet.
▷ANTONYMS open, communicative, chatty.
▶noun **1** *he just can't keep a secret*: **confidential matter**, confidence, private affair, skeleton in the cupboard.
▷ANTONYMS public knowledge.
2 *the secrets of the universe*: **mystery**, enigma, problem, paradox, puzzle, conundrum, poser, riddle, question, question mark.
▷ANTONYMS known fact.
3 *the secret of their success*: **recipe**, formula, blueprint, magic formula, key, answer, solution.
□ **in secret** *groups of MPs met in secret over the summer*: **secretly**, without anyone knowing, in private, privately, in confidence, confidentially, behind closed doors, behind the scenes, behind someone's back, under cover, under the counter, discreetly, unobserved, quietly, furtively, stealthily, on the sly, on the quiet, privily, conspiratorially, covertly, clandestinely, on the side; Latin sub rosa, in camera; informal on the q.t..
▷ANTONYMS openly.

Word links **secret**

crypto- prefix denoting something secret, as in *cryptogram*

Word toolkit

secret	**arcane**	**mysterious**
agent	knowledge	man/woman
ballot	language	circumstances
society	rules	death
location	art	disappearance
life	ritual	illness
meeting	symbols	power
information	matters	forces
admirer	science	figure

S

secret agent noun *his tutor might have been a British secret agent*: **spy**, agent, double agent, counterspy, field agent, undercover agent, operative, plant, infiltrator, mole; N. Amer. informal spook; archaic intelligencer.

secretary noun *he asked his secretary to place a call through to England*: **assistant**, personal assistant, PA, administrator, clerk, clerical assistant, amanuensis, girl/man Friday; typist, shorthand typist, copyist, keyboarder, stenographer.

secrete[1] verb *the gland can become enlarged and secrete excess levels of the hormone*: **produce**, **discharge**, emit, excrete, exude, ooze, leak, leach, emanate, give off, release, send out; Medicine extravasate.
▷ANTONYMS absorb.

secrete[2] verb *Bert and I were to secrete ourselves behind the curtains*: **conceal**, hide, cover up, veil, shroud, disguise, screen, bury, stow away, sequester, cache; informal stash away.
▷ANTONYMS reveal, show.

secretion noun *histamine promotes the secretion of gastric acid | a secretion produced by the thoracic gland*: **production**, **discharge**, emission, excretion, exudation, ooze, oozing, leakage, leaching, emanation, giving off, release, sending out; Medicine extravasation.

secretive adjective *a secretive person*: **uncommunicative**, secret, unforthcoming, reticent, taciturn, silent, non-communicative, quiet, tight-lipped, close-mouthed, close, playing one's cards close to one's chest, clamlike, reserved, introvert, introverted, self-contained, discreet.
▷ANTONYMS open, communicative, chatty.

secretly adverb **1** *the microphones had been used for secretly recording conversations*: **covertly**, without anyone knowing, in secret, in private, privately, in confidence, confidentially, behind closed doors, behind the scenes, behind someone's back, under cover, under the counter, discreetly, unobserved, quietly, furtively, stealthily, on the sly, on the quiet, privily, conspiratorially, clandestinely, on the side; Latin sub rosa, in camera; informal on the q.t..
▷ANTONYMS publicly.
2 *I think he was secretly jealous of Bartholomew*: **privately**, in one's heart, in one's heart of hearts, in one's innermost thoughts.
▷ANTONYMS openly.

sect noun *he joined a rather weird religious sect*: **(religious) cult**, religious group, faith community, denomination, persuasion, religious order; splinter group, faction, schism, schismatic group/religion/church, heretical movement.

sectarian adjective *years of sectarian violence*: **factional**, schismatic, cliquish, clannish, partisan, parti pris; denominational; **doctrinaire**, dogmatic, extreme, fanatical, rigid, inflexible, bigoted, hidebound, narrow-minded.
▷ANTONYMS tolerant, liberal, broad-minded.
▶noun *he was attacked by sectarians within the world of modern art*: **separatist**, dissenter, dissident, nonconformist, free thinker, renegade, recusant, schismatic, revisionist; unbeliever, sceptic, agnostic, atheist; zealot, Young Turk, extremist, radical, activist, militant; bigot, dogmatist, partisan, devotee.

section noun **1** *I unscrewed every section of the copper pipe*: **segment**, part, component, division, piece, portion, length, element, module, unit, constituent, bit, slice, fraction, fragment.
2 *this last section of the questionnaire relates solely to training*: **subdivision**, part, chapter, subsection, division, portion, component, bit, passage, clause, act, scene, episode, instalment.
3 *the reference section of your local library*: **department**, part, division, branch, sector, wing, compartment.
4 *a residential section of the capital*. See **sector** (sense 2).

sectional adjective *there are universal principles that transcend sectional interests*: **individual**, **group**, separate, divided, special, personal, private, exclusive, local, provincial, regional, national, sectarian, factional, party, party political, class, racial, partisan, partial, selfish.
▷ANTONYMS collective, universal.

sector noun **1** *every sector of the industry is affected*: **part**, branch, arm, division, subdivision, area, department, category, field, sphere, layer, stratum, corner.
2 *the north-eastern sector of the town*: **district**, quarter, part, section, zone, precinct, borough, locality, neighbourhood, side; province, territory, division, region, area, belt, tract, locale; N. Amer. informal hood.

secular adjective *secular music | a secular building*: **non-religious**, lay, non-church, temporal, worldly, earthly, profane; unsanctified, unconsecrated, unhallowed; rare laic.
▷ANTONYMS holy, religious, sacred.

secure adjective **1** *check to ensure that all nuts and bolts are secure*: **tight**, firm, taut, fixed, secured, done up; closed, shut, locked, sealed.
▷ANTONYMS loose, unlocked.
2 *make sure that the ladder you are working on is secure*: **stable**, fixed, secured, fast, safe, steady, immovable, unshakeable, dependable; anchored, moored, jammed, rooted, braced, cemented, riveted, nailed, tied; strong, sturdy, solid, sound.
▷ANTONYMS precarious, rocky.
3 *jars kept secure in a pantry may survive for several generations | children need an environment in which they can feel secure*: **protected from harm/danger**, free from danger, sheltered, shielded, guarded, unharmed, undamaged, safe and sound, safe, out of harm's way, in a safe place, in safe hands, invulnerable, immune, impregnable, unassailable; **at ease**, unworried, reassured, relaxed, happy, comfortable, confident.
▷ANTONYMS vulnerable, threatened, unsettled.
4 *few young people face a secure future*: **certain**, assured, reliable, dependable, settled, fixed, established, solid, sound.
▷ANTONYMS uncertain, insecure.
▶verb **1** *pins secure the handle to the main body*: **fix**, attach, fasten, affix, link, hitch, join, connect, couple, bond, append, annex, stick, pin, tack, nail, staple, clip.
2 *the doors had not been properly secured*: **fasten**, **close**, shut, lock, bolt, chain, seal, board up.

3 *Athens was seeking to secure herself from a lightning invasion from the west*: **protect**, make safe, make sound, make invulnerable, make immune, make impregnable, fortify, strengthen, shelter, shield, guard.
4 *he killed the engine, then leapt out to secure the boat*: **tie up**, moor, make fast, lash, hitch, berth; anchor.
5 *a written constitution would secure the rights of the individual*: **assure**, ensure, insure, guarantee, warrant, protect, indemnify, confirm, establish.
6 *the company has already secured two million pounds' worth of business*: **obtain**, acquire, gain, get, find, come by, pick up, procure, get possession of; buy, purchase; informal get hold of, land, get one's hands on, lay one's hands on, get one's mitts on.
▷ANTONYMS lose, let slip.

Word toolkit **secure**

See **protected**.

security noun **1** *the security of the nation's citizens is our highest responsibility*: **safety**, freedom from danger; protection, safe keeping, shielding, guarding, care; invulnerability, impregnability, unassailability.
▷ANTONYMS vulnerability, danger.
2 *he could give her the security she needed*: **feeling of safety**, feeling of ease, absence of worry/anxiety, peace of mind, freedom from doubt, certainty, happiness, comfort, confidence.
▷ANTONYMS disquiet.
3 *employees have an interest in the security of their jobs*: **certainty**, safe future, assured future, safety, reliability, dependability, solidness, soundness.
4 *the two accused men appeared in court amid tight security*: **safety measures**, safeguards; guards, surveillance, defence, protection.
5 *additional security for your loan may be required*: **guarantee**, collateral, surety, pledge, bond; hostage, pawn, backing, bail; archaic gage, earnest.

sedate[1] verb *the patient had to be sedated heavily*: **tranquillize**, give a sedative to, put under sedation, calm down, quieten, pacify, soothe, relax, dope, drug, administer drugs/narcotics/opiates to, knock out, anaesthetize; stupefy.
▷ANTONYMS invigorate, energize.

sedate[2] adjective **1** *sedate suburban domesticity*: **calm**, tranquil, placid, composed, serene, steady, unruffled, imperturbable, unflappable; **dignified**, serious, serious-minded, formal, decorous, proper, prim, demure, sober, earnest, staid, stiff, stuffy, boring; informal starchy, stick-in-the-mud.
▷ANTONYMS exciting, wild.
2 *they continued at a more sedate pace*: **slow**, unhurried, relaxed, leisurely, unrushed, slow-moving, slow-going, slow and steady, easy, easy-going, gentle, comfortable, restful, undemanding, lazy, languid, languorous, plodding, dawdling, leisured, measured, steady; informal laid-back.
▷ANTONYMS fast.

sedative adjective *he took a combination of sedative drugs*: **tranquillizing**, calming, depressant, soothing, calmative, relaxing, soporific; Medicine neuroleptic.
▶ noun *the doctor gave him a sedative*: **tranquillizer**, calmative, depressant, sleeping pill, soporific, narcotic, opiate; Medicine neuroleptic; informal trank, sleeper, downer.

sedentary adjective *a sedentary job*: **sitting**, seated, desk-bound, desk, inactive, still, stationary.
▷ANTONYMS active, mobile.

sediment noun *there is a thick layer of sediment on the bottom*: **dregs**, lees, deposit, grounds, settlings, residue, remains, accumulation, silt, sludge, alluvium; technical precipitate, sublimate, residuum; rare draff, grouts.

sedition noun *advocating multiparty democracy is considered sedition*: **incitement (to riot/rebellion)**, agitation, rabble-rousing, fomentation (of discontent), troublemaking, provocation, inflaming; **rebellion**, revolt, insurrection, rioting, mutiny, insurgence, insurgency, subversion, civil disorder, insubordination, disobedience, resistance, defiance.

seditious adjective **1** *a seditious speech*: **rabble-rousing**, inciting, agitating, fomenting, troublemaking, provocative, inflammatory.
2 *the interior minister issued a decree outlawing seditious groups*: **revolutionary**, rebellious, insurrectionist, mutinous, insurgent, subversive, insubordinate, civil disobedience, dissident, defiant, disloyal, treasonous.

Word toolkit **seditious**

See **unfaithful**.

seduce verb **1** *he took her to his tent where he seduced her*: **persuade someone to have sexual intercourse**, take away someone's innocence; rape, violate, debauch; lead astray, corrupt, deprave; informal bed, pop someone's cherry, tumble; euphemistic have one's (wicked) way with, take advantage of; literary ravish, deflower; archaic dishonour, ruin.
2 *people are seduced by the packaging of inferior products*: **attract**, allure, lure, tempt, entice, beguile, cajole, wheedle, ensnare, charm, captivate, enchant, hypnotize, mesmerize, tantalize, titillate, bewitch, ravish, inveigle, lead astray, trap; manoeuvre, deceive, dupe.

seducer noun *the man was an accomplished seducer*: **womanizer**, philanderer, deceiver, adulterer, Romeo, Don Juan, Lothario, Casanova, playboy, lecher, ladies' man; informal ladykiller, lech, dirty old man, goat, wolf, skirt-chaser.

seduction noun **1** *he had engaged in gambling, drinking, and the seduction of women*: **persuading someone to have sexual intercourse**, taking away someone's innocence; rape, violation, debauching, corruption; informal bedding, tumbling; archaic dishonouring, ruin; dated ravishment, defloration.
2 *the seduction of ambition | the more cerebral seductions of art and literature*: **temptation**, **attraction**, lure, allure, call, pull, draw, charm, bait, decoy, magnet; **(seductions) appeal**, attractiveness, fascination, interest, glamour, drawing power, magnetism, enchantment, enticement; informal come-on.

seductive adjective **1** *she appears in the guise of a seductive temptress*: **sexy**, sexually arousing, sexually exciting, alluring, tempting, suggestive, tantalizing, fascinating, ravishing, captivating, bewitching, immodest, shameless, erotic, sensuous, sultry, slinky, passionate, raunchy, steamy, coquettish, amorous, flirtatious, provocative, come-hither; informal come-to-bed, tarty; vulgar slang fuck-me.
▷ANTONYMS repulsive.
2 *she crept towards the seductive warmth of the stove*: **attractive**, appealing, inviting, alluring, tempting, enticing, beguiling, engaging, winning, irresistible.
▷ANTONYMS repellent, off-putting.

seductress noun *the story of an innocent art student who becomes a wanton seductress*: **temptress**, siren, femme fatale, enchantress, sorceress, Delilah, Circe, Lorelei, Mata Hari; **flirt**, coquette, Lolita, loose woman; informal tart; N. Amer. informal vamp; archaic fizgig, wanton, strumpet.

sedulous adjective *he picked a spine from his leg with sedulous care*: **diligent**, careful, meticulous, thorough, assiduous, attentive, industrious, laborious, hard-working, conscientious, ultra-careful, punctilious, scrupulous, painstaking, searching, close, elaborate, minute, studious, rigorous, particular; religious, strict; pedantic, fussy.
▷ANTONYMS nonchalant.

see[1] verb **1** *I can see the house*: **discern**, perceive, glimpse, catch/get a glimpse of, spot, notice, catch sight of, sight; **make out**, pick out, spy, distinguish, identify, recognize, detect, note, mark; informal clap/lay/set eyes on, clock; literary behold, descry, espy.
2 *they saw a television programme on Hong Kong*: **watch**, look at, view, observe, catch.
3 *would you like to* **see over** *the house?* **inspect**, view, see round, look around/round, look through, have a look around/round, have a tour of, go on a tour of, tour, survey, scrutinize; informal give something a/the once-over.
4 *I can't see how this helps us*: **understand**, grasp, comprehend, follow, take in, realize, appreciate, recognize, work out, get the drift of, make out, conceive, perceive, fathom (out), become cognizant of; informal get, latch on to, cotton on to, catch on to, tumble to, figure out, get the hang of, get a fix on, get one's head round/around, get the message, get the picture; Brit. informal twig, suss; N. Amer. informal savvy; rare cognize.
5 *I must go and see what Victor is up to*: **find out**, discover, learn, ascertain, get to know, determine, establish; ask, enquire, make enquiries as to, investigate; Brit. informal suss out.
6 *let me see*: **think**, consider, contemplate, reflect, deliberate, have a think, meditate, muse, ponder, cogitate, brood, agonize; give it some thought, mull it over, chew it over, puzzle over it, turn it over in one's mind, revolve it in one's mind; rare cerebrate.
7 *he checked to see that all of his desk drawers were locked | see that you do it now*: **make sure**, make certain, see to it, check, verify, take care, mind, satisfy oneself, ensure; remember to, be/make sure to, not forget to.
8 *I see trouble ahead*: **foresee**, predict, forecast, prophesy, prognosticate, anticipate, envisage, envision, picture, visualize; archaic augur, previse, presage, foreshow.
9 *about a year later, I saw a friend in town*: **meet (by chance)**, encounter, run into, run across, stumble on/across, happen on, chance on, come across; informal bump into; archaic run against.
10 *they see each other from time to time*: **meet (by arrangement)**, meet up with, get together with, have a meeting, have meetings, meet socially, make a date with.
11 *I'd better see a doctor about it*: **consult**, confer with, talk to, speak to, seek advice/information from, take counsel from, have recourse to, call on, call in, turn to, ask.
12 *the doctor will see you now*: **interview**, give an interview to, give a consultation to, give an audience to, give a hearing to, receive, talk to; examine, treat.
13 *he's seeing someone else now*: **go out with**, **be dating**, take out, be someone's boyfriend/girlfriend, keep company with, go with, be with, court, have a fling with, have an affair with, dally with; informal go steady with; Brit. informal, dated walk out with; N. Amer. informal, dated step out with.
14 *he saw her to her car*: **escort**, accompany, show, walk, conduct, lead, take, usher, guide, shepherd, attend.

◻ **see about** *I'll go and see about fixing a meal*: **arrange**, make arrangements for, see to, deal with, take care of, look after, attend to, sort out; organize, be responsible for, take responsibility for, be in charge of, direct.
◻ **see the light** *even the Vatican has seen the light and is using the technology to manage its library*: **understand**, comprehend, realize, find out, see daylight, work out what's going on, get the point; informal cotton on, catch on, tumble, latch on, get the picture, get the message, get the drift, get it, get wise, see what's what, savvy; Brit. informal twig.
◻ **see through** *I can see right through your little plot | I saw through you from the start*: **not be deceived by**, not be taken in by, be wise to, get/have the measure of, read like a book, fathom, penetrate, realize, understand; informal not fall for, have someone's number, know someone's (little) game.
▶ANTONYMS be hoodwinked by.
◻ **see someone through** *it was Francine's devotion which saw him through*: **sustain**, encourage, buoy up, cheer along, keep going, keep someone's head above water, tide over; **support**, give strength to, be a source of strength to, be a tower of strength to, comfort, help (out), assist.
▶ANTONYMS let someone down.
◻ **see something through** *I want to see the job through*: **bring to completion**, continue to the end, bring to a finish; **persevere with**, persist with, continue (with), carry on with, go on with, keep at, keep on with, keep going with, keep up, not give up with, follow through, press on/ahead with, plod on through, plough on through, stay with; not take no for an answer; informal plug away at, peg away at, stick at, soldier on with, stick something out, stick to one's guns, hang in there.
▶ANTONYMS give up (on).
◻ **see to** *I'll go and see to the sitting-room fire*: **attend to**, deal with, see about, take care of, look after, sort out, fix up, get together, organize, arrange, be responsible for, be in charge of, direct, run, manage, conduct, administer, administrate.

Word links **see**
scopophobia fear of being seen

see² noun *a bishop's see*: **diocese**, bishopric.

seed noun **1** *a liqueur made from grape seeds and skins*: **pip**, stone, pit, nut, kernel, germ; technical ovule.
2 *the male of the species supplies the seed for reproduction*: **semen**, sperm, spermatic fluid, seminal fluid, milt, ejaculate, emission; Biology spermatozoa; vulgar slang come, cum, jism, jissom, jizz; Brit. vulgar slang spunk.
3 *each war contains within it the seeds of a fresh war*: **genesis**, source, origin, root, starting point, germ, beginnings, potential (for); **cause**, reason, motivation, motive; base, basis, foundation, bottom, seat, fundamental; core, nucleus, heart, kernel, nub, essence; Latin fons et origo; literary fountainhead, wellspring, fount.
4 archaic *Abraham and his seed*: **descendants**, heirs, successors, scions; **offspring**, children, sons and daughters, progeny, family, youngsters, babies, brood; Law issue; informal kids, quiverful; derogatory spawn; archaic fruit, fruit of someone's loins.
◻ **go to seed** *with the ferry gone and the road traffic diverted the place has gone to seed*: **deteriorate**, degenerate, decline, decay, fall into decay, run to seed, go to rack and ruin, become dilapidated, go downhill, break down, waste away, wither away, languish, moulder, rot; informal go to pot, go to the dogs, go down the toilet.

Word links **seed**
seminal relating to seeds

S

seedy adjective **1** *he began hanging out at a seedy bar*: **sordid**, disreputable, seamy, sleazy, corrupt, shameful, low, dark, squalid, unwholesome, unsavoury, rough, mean, nasty, unpleasant.
▶ANTONYMS classy.
2 *the live-in caretaker of a seedy block of flats*: **dilapidated**, tumbledown, ramshackle, derelict, ruinous, falling to pieces, decrepit, gone to rack and ruin, in ruins, broken-down, crumbling, decaying, disintegrating; **neglected**, uncared-for, unmaintained, depressed, run down, down at heel, shabby, dingy, slummy, insalubrious, squalid; informal shambly, crummy; Brit. informal grotty; N. Amer. informal shacky.
▶ANTONYMS high-class, fashionable.
3 dated *feeling rather seedy*. See **ill** (sense 1 of the adjective).

seek verb **1** *six bombers took off and flew southwards to seek the enemy*: **search for**, try to find, look for, look about/around/round for, cast about/around/round for, be on the lookout for, be after, hunt for, be in quest of, quest (after), be in pursuit of.
2 *the new regime sought his extradition*: **try to obtain**, pursue, go after, strive for, go for, push towards, work towards, be intent on, aim at/for, have as a goal, have as an objective.
3 *you may need to seek the advice of a specialist*: **ask for**, request, solicit, call on, invite, entreat, beg for, petition for, appeal for, apply for, put in for.
4 *we constantly seek to improve the service*: **try**, attempt, endeavour, strive, work, aim, aspire, do one's best, set out; formal essay.

seem verb *she seemed annoyed at this*: **appear**, appear to be, have the appearance/air of being, give the impression of being, look, look like, look as though one is, look to be, have the look of, show signs of; come across as, strike someone as, give someone the feeling that one is, sound.

seeming adjective **1** *there is a seeming contradiction here*: **apparent**, outward, surface.
▶ANTONYMS actual, real.
2 *you can't simply kill him, even with a seeming accident*: **pretended**, feigned, specious, professed, supposed, presumed, avowed, so-called, alleged, declared, claimed, purported, ostensible; rare ostensive.
▶ANTONYMS genuine.

seemingly adverb *he stared down the seemingly endless corridor*: **apparently**, on the face of it, to all appearances, as far as one can see/tell, on the surface, to all intents and purposes, outwardly, evidently, superficially, supposedly, avowedly, allegedly, professedly, purportedly; rare pretendedly, ostensively.
▶ANTONYMS genuinely.

seemly adjective *it was not thought seemly to look in a mirror in those days*: **decorous**, proper, decent, becoming, fitting, suitable, appropriate, apt, apposite, meet, in good taste, genteel, polite, conventional, the done thing, right, correct, acceptable; French comme il faut.
▶ANTONYMS unseemly, unbecoming, unsuitable.

seep verb *oil continued to seep out of the sunken vessel*: **ooze**, trickle, exude, drip, dribble, flow, issue, discharge, excrete, escape, leak, drain, bleed, sweat, well, leach, filter, percolate, permeate, soak; Medicine extravasate; rare filtrate, transude, exudate.

seepage noun *the clay soil has slowed down the seepage of radioactive material into the groundwater*: **oozing**, seeping, trickle, trickling, drip, dribble, flow, issuance, discharge, excretion, escape, leak, leakage, drainage, bleeding, sweating, welling, leaching, filtration, percolation, secretion; Medicine extravasation; archaic transudation, exudation.

seer noun *a seer had foretold that the earl would assume the throne*: **prophet**, **prophetess**, sibyl, augur, soothsayer, wise man, wise woman, sage, oracle, prognosticator, prophesier, forecaster of the future, diviner, fortune teller, crystal-gazer, clairvoyant, psychic, spiritualist, medium; Scottish spaeman, spaewife; rare haruspex, vaticinator, oracler.

see-saw verb *the market see-sawed as rumours spread*: **fluctuate**, swing, go from one extreme to the other, go up and down, rise and fall, oscillate, alternate, yo-yo, teeter, be unstable, be unsteady, vary, shift, sway, ebb and flow.

seethe verb **1** *the brew foamed and seethed*: **boil**, bubble, simmer, foam, froth, rise, ferment, fizz, effervesce.
2 *the shallow water seethed with creatures*: **teem**, swarm, boil, bubble, foam, ferment, swirl, convulse, churn, whirl, surge.
3 *I was still seething at the injustice of it*: **be angry**, be furious, be enraged, be incensed, be infuriated, be beside oneself, have lost one's temper, have/throw a fit, boil, simmer, be boiling over, chafe, rage, be in a rage, rant, rave, rant and rave, storm, fume, smoulder, spit, breathe fire, burn; informal be livid, be wild, jump up and down, froth/foam at the mouth, be steamed up, be hot under the collar, have steam coming out of one's ears; Brit. informal do one's head/nut in, throw a wobbly, spit feathers.

see-through adjective *a see-through plastic map pouch | a dress with see-through sleeves*: **transparent**, translucent, clear, limpid, crystal clear, crystalline, pellucid, glassy; thin, light, lightweight, flimsy, sheer, diaphanous, filmy, gossamer, gossamer-like, gossamer-thin, chiffony, cobwebby, gauzy, gauze-like, ultra-fine.
▶ANTONYMS opaque, substantial.

segment noun (stress on the first syllable) **1** *arrange the orange segments on top of the filling*: **piece**, part, bit, section, chunk, division, portion, slice, fragment, component, wedge, lump, slab, hunk, parcel, tranche; Brit. informal wodge.
▶ANTONYMS whole.
2 *economic growth would bring benefits to all segments of society*: **subdivision**, division, fraction, part, portion, section, constituent, element, unit, module, ingredient, slice, department, compartment, sector; branch, wing.
▶ANTONYMS whole.
▶ verb (stress on the second syllable) *they plan to segment the company's 22% market share into four sections*: **divide**, divide up, subdivide, separate, split, split up, cut up, carve up, slice up, break up, dismember; sever, segregate, divorce, partition, section, compartment; **share out**, portion out, distribute.
▶ANTONYMS amalgamate.

segregate verb *he campaigns for routes which segregate cycles from motor vehicles*: **separate**, set apart, keep apart, sort out; isolate, quarantine, insulate, exclude, closet, protect, shield, partition; **divide**, detach, disconnect, sever, divorce, dissociate, cut off; sequester.
▶ANTONYMS amalgamate.

segregation noun *they recommend the full segregation of vehicles and pedestrians in the town centre*: **separation**, setting apart, keeping apart, sorting out; isolation, quarantine, insulation, exclusion, closeting,

protection, shielding, partitioning; **division**, detachment, disconnection, dissociation; sequestration, partition; in S. Africa, historical **apartheid**.
▷ANTONYMS integration.

seize verb **1** *a protester seized the microphone*: **grab**, grasp, snatch, seize hold of, grab hold of, take hold of, lay hold of, lay (one's) hands on, get one's hands on, take a grip of, grip, clutch, take, pluck.
▷ANTONYMS let go of.
2 *army rebels seized an air force base*: **capture**, take, overrun, annex, occupy, take possession of, conquer, take over, subjugate, subject, colonize.
▷ANTONYMS relinquish, retreat from; liberate.
3 *the drugs were seized by customs officers at Kennedy Airport*: **confiscate**, impound, commandeer, requisition, appropriate, expropriate, take possession of, sequester, sequestrate, take away, take over, take; Law distrain, attach, disseize; Scottish Law **poind**.
▷ANTONYMS release.
4 *kidnappers seized his wife*: **kidnap**, abduct, take captive, take prisoner, take hostage, hold to ransom; hijack; informal snatch; Brit. informal **nobble**, **nab**.
▷ANTONYMS release, ransom.
□ **seize on** *governments have seized on recycling as the best way to reduce rubbish*: **grasp**, grasp with both hands, grab (at), leap at, snatch, jump at, pounce on, exploit.
▷ANTONYMS overlook, fail to take advantage of.

seizure noun **1** *Napoleon's seizure of Spain*: **capture**, occupation, takeover, overrunning, annexation, annexing, invasion, conquering, subjugation, subjection, colonization.
▷ANTONYMS restitution; liberation.
2 *the authorities resorted to the seizure of defaulters' property*: **confiscation**, impounding, commandeering, requisitioning, appropriation, expropriation, sequestration; Law distraint, distrainment, attachment, disseizin; Scottish Law **poind**.
▷ANTONYMS restitution.
3 *the rumoured seizure of UN observers by guerrillas*: **kidnapping**, kidnap, abduction, hostage-taking; hijacking; informal snatching; Brit. informal **nobbling**.
▷ANTONYMS release, ransoming.
4 *the baby suffered a seizure on the plane*: **convulsion**, spasm, paroxysm, collapse, sudden illness, attack, fit, bout; stroke, apoplexy; Medicine **ictus**.

Word links **seizure**

ictal (Medicine) relating to a seizure

seldom adverb *he was seldom absent*: **rarely**, infrequently, on rare occasions, hardly ever, scarcely ever, hardly, scarcely, almost never, (every) once in a while, only now and then, not often, only occasionally, sporadically; informal once in a blue moon.
▷ANTONYMS often, frequently.

select verb *the important thing is to select the correct tool for the job*: **choose**, pick, hand-pick, single out, pick out, sort out, take, opt for, decide on, settle on, set, fix, fix on, adopt, determine, designate, name, nominate, appoint, elect, specify, stipulate, prefer, favour.
▶ adjective **1** *a small and select group of SAS members*: **choice**, hand-picked, carefully chosen, prime, first-rate, first-class, high-grade, grade A, superior, finest, best, high-quality, top-quality, top-class, supreme, superb, excellent, rare, prize, prize-winning, award-winning; informal tip-top, A1, stellar, top-notch.
▷ANTONYMS inferior, mediocre.
2 *the concert was a very fashionable occasion with a select audience*: **exclusive**, elite, favoured, limited, rarefied, privileged, cliquish, private; informal **posh**.
▷ANTONYMS common.

selection noun **1** *Jed had made his selection of toys*: **choice**, pick, option, preference, election.
2 *we offer a wide selection of dishes*: **range**, array, diversity, display, variety, assortment, mixture, line-up, set, repertoire.
3 *the publication of a selection of his poems*: **anthology**, assortment, choice, miscellany, medley, pot-pourri, collection, assemblage.

selective adjective *he is very selective in his reading*: **discriminating**, discriminatory, discerning, critical, exacting, demanding, particular, hard to please; fussy, fastidious, faddish, careful, cautious; informal **choosy**, pernickety, picky; Brit. informal **faddy**; archaic **nice**.
▷ANTONYMS indiscriminate.

self noun *these whispers come from our inner self*: **ego**, I, oneself, persona, person, identity, character, personality, psyche, soul, spirit, mind, intellect, inner man/woman/person, inner self, one's innermost feelings, one's heart of hearts.
▷ANTONYMS other.

Word links **self**

auto- related prefix, as in *autobiography, automobile*
ego- related prefix, as in *egosurfing*
egomania, **egotism**, **egocentrism** obsession with oneself
suicide killing oneself

self-assembly noun *the artist can buy easel kits for self-assembly*: **do-it-yourself**, DIY, self-build.
▶ adjective *self-assembly furniture*: **flat-pack**, in kit form, kit, do-it-yourself, DIY, self-build.

self-assurance noun *such courses provide them with the training and self-assurance they need*: **self-confidence**, confidence, belief in oneself, positiveness, assertiveness, assurance, self-reliance, self-possession, composure, nerve, poise, presence, aplomb.
▷ANTONYMS diffidence, unsureness.

self-assured adjective *a stubborn and self-assured lady*: **self-confident**, confident, believing in oneself, positive, assertive, assured, authoritative, commanding, self-reliant, self-possessed, composed, poised.
▷ANTONYMS diffident, unsure.

self-centred adjective *your father's too self-centred to care what you do*: **egocentric**, egotistic, egotistical, egomaniacal, self-regarding, self-absorbed, self-obsessed, self-seeking, self-interested, self-serving, wrapped up in oneself, inward-looking, introverted, selfish, self-loving, narcissistic, vain; **inconsiderate**, thoughtless, unthinking, uncaring, uncharitable, unkind; informal looking after number one.
▷ANTONYMS considerate.

self-confidence noun *she took care to build up his self-confidence by involving him in the planning*: **morale**, confidence, self-assurance, belief in oneself, positiveness, assertiveness, assurance, self-reliance, self-possession, composure, nerve, poise, presence, aplomb.
▷ANTONYMS diffidence, unsureness.

self-confident adjective *they were now the self-confident, responsible young ladies they had been trained to be*: **self-assured**, confident, believing in oneself, positive, assertive, assured, authoritative, commanding, self-reliant, self-possessed, composed, poised.
▷ANTONYMS diffident, unsure.

self-conscious adjective *he gave me a self-conscious grin*: **embarrassed**, uncomfortable, ill at ease, uneasy, nervous, tense, edgy; unnatural, inhibited, gauche, awkward, strained; modest, shy, diffident, bashful, blushing, timorous, timid, retiring, shrinking.
▷ANTONYMS confident, natural.

self-contained adjective **1** *each train was a self-contained unit*: **complete**, independent, separate, free-standing, enclosed.
▷ANTONYMS linked.
2 *a very self-contained child*: **independent**, standing on one's own two feet, self-sufficient, self-reliant, introverted, undemonstrative, quiet, private, aloof, insular, reserved, unemotional, uncommunicative, reticent, secretive.
▷ANTONYMS dependent; forthcoming, outgoing.

self-control noun *he had recovered his self-control*: **self-discipline**, self-restraint, restraint, control, self-mastery, self-possession, will power, strength of will, composure, coolness; moderation, temperateness, temperance, abstemiousness, abstention, non-indulgence; informal cool; rare countenance.
▷ANTONYMS loss of control, indiscipline.

self-denial noun *a farm built up over the years by hard work and self-denial*: **self-sacrifice**, selflessness, unselfishness, altruism, self-discipline, asceticism, abnegation, self-abnegation, self-deprivation, abstemiousness, abstinence; moderation, austerity, temperance, abstention, renunciation; celibacy, chastity; teetotalism; rare continence.
▷ANTONYMS self-indulgence.

self-discipline noun *his observance of his diet was a show of tremendous self-discipline*: **self-control**, self-mastery, control; restraint, self-restraint; will power, strength of will, firmness, firmness of purpose, purposefulness, strong-mindedness, resolution, resolve, moral fibre; doggedness, persistence, determination, tenacity; informal grit.

self-employed adjective *a self-employed painter and decorator*: **freelance**, independent, one's own boss, working for oneself, casual; consultant, consulting; temporary, part-time, jobbing, visiting, non-resident, outside, external, extramural, peripatetic.
▷ANTONYMS staff, in-house, employed.

self-esteem noun *assertiveness training for those with low self-esteem*: **self-respect**, self-regard, pride in oneself/one's abilities, faith in oneself, pride, dignity, morale, self-confidence, confidence, self-assurance, assurance; French amour propre.
▷ANTONYMS lack of self-confidence, self-deprecation.

self-evident adjective *the reason for this is self-evident*: **obvious**, clear, plain, evident, apparent, manifest, patent; distinct, definite, transparent, overt, discernible, visible, conspicuous, palpable, glaringly obvious, undisguised, unconcealed, unmistakable, unequivocal, unquestionable, undeniable.
▷ANTONYMS unclear.

self-explanatory adjective *this paragraph is largely self-explanatory*: **easily understood**, readily comprehensible, intelligible, straightforward, unambiguous, unproblematic, accessible, clearly expressed, user-friendly, simple, self-evident, obvious, clear, crystal clear.
▷ANTONYMS impenetrable.

S

self-governing adjective *Singapore became a self-governing state in 1959*: **independent**, sovereign, autonomous, non-aligned, free; self-legislating, self-determining.
▷ANTONYMS dependent, subservient.

self-government noun *Senegal achieved self-government in 1958*: **independence**, self-rule, home rule, self-legislation, self-determination, sovereignty, autonomy, non-alignment, freedom.
▷ANTONYMS hegemony, colonialism.

self-important adjective *he was given the nickname Colonel because he was so self-important*: **conceited**, arrogant, bumptious, self-assertive, full of oneself, puffed up, swollen-headed, pompous, overbearing, (self-)opinionated, cocky, swaggering, strutting, presumptuous, forward, imperious, domineering, magisterial, pontifical, sententious, grandiose, vain, haughty, overweening, proud, egotistic, egotistical; supercilious, condescending, patronizing; informal snooty, uppity, uppish.
▷ANTONYMS humble.

self-indulgence noun *there is also the chance for some self-indulgence, such as taking breakfast in bed*: **hedonism**, indulgence, pursuit of pleasure, pleasure-seeking, luxury, lotus-eating, epicureanism, self-gratification; lack of self-restraint, intemperance, intemperateness, immoderation, overindulgence, excess, extravagance, the high life, high living, licence, licentiousness, sensualism, voluptuousness, dissipation, dissoluteness, decadence; rare sybaritism.
▷ANTONYMS abstemiousness, restraint.

self-indulgent adjective *it was regarded as an ailment contracted by women who led an idle, self-indulgent life*: **pleasure-seeking**, **hedonistic**, sybaritic, indulgent, luxurious, lotus-eating, epicurean; unrestrained, intemperate, immoderate, overindulgent, excessive, extravagant, licentious, sensual, voluptuous, dissipated, dissolute, decadent.
▷ANTONYMS abstemious, restrained.

self-interest noun *laissez-faire is an economic system based on individualism and self-interest*: **self-seeking**, self-serving, self-obsession, self-absorption, self-regard, egocentrism, egotism, egomania, introversion, selfishness; **lack of consideration**, inconsiderateness, thoughtlessness, unthinkingness; informal looking after number one.
▷ANTONYMS altruism; generosity.

self-interested adjective *it is necessary for people to think and act not simply as self-interested individuals*: **self-seeking**, self-serving, self-obsessed, self-absorbed, self-regarding, wrapped up in oneself, egocentric, egotistic, egotistical, egomaniacal, inward-looking, introverted, selfish; **inconsiderate**, thoughtless, unthinking, uncaring; informal looking after number one.
▷ANTONYMS altruistic, considerate; generous.

selfish adjective *he is just selfish by nature*: **egocentric**, egotistic, egotistical, egomaniacal, self-centred, self-regarding, self-absorbed, self-obsessed, self-seeking, self-serving, wrapped up in oneself, inward-looking, introverted, self-loving; **inconsiderate**, thoughtless, unthinking, uncaring, heedless, unmindful, regardless, insensitive, tactless, uncharitable, unkind; mean, miserly, grasping, greedy, mercenary, money-grubbing, acquisitive, opportunistic, out for what one can get; informal looking after number one, on the make.
▷ANTONYMS unselfish, selfless, altruistic, considerate, generous.

selfishness noun *selfishness is one of the biggest problems in marriages*: **egocentrism**, egotism, egomania, introversion, self-seeking, self-serving, self-obsession, self-absorption, self-regard, self-interest, self-love; **lack of consideration**, inconsiderateness, thoughtlessness, unthinkingness, heedlessness, regardlessness, insensitivity, insensitiveness, tactlessness, uncharitableness, unkindness; **meanness**, miserliness, greed, acquisitiveness, opportunism; informal looking after number one.
▷ANTONYMS unselfishness, altruism; generosity.

S

selfless adjective *an act of selfless devotion*: **unselfish**, altruistic, self-sacrificing, self-denying; **considerate**, compassionate, kind, decent, noble, public-spirited; **generous**, magnanimous, ungrudging, unstinting, charitable, benevolent, liberal, open-handed, philanthropic.
▷ANTONYMS selfish, egoistic, inconsiderate, mean.

self-possessed adjective *a girl who has been shy or awkward can become quite self-possessed as she cares for her new baby*: **assured**, self-assured, calm, cool, {cool, calm, and collected}, composed, at ease, tranquil, serene, unperturbed, unruffled, impassive, nonchalant, confident, self-confident, sure of oneself, poised, dignified, equable, imperturbable, suave, urbane, elegant; informal together, unfazed, unflappable; rare equanimous.
▷ANTONYMS unsure, nervous.

self-possession noun *she had recovered her usual self-possession*: **composure**, assurance, self-assurance, self-control, calmness, coolness, cool head; ease, tranquillity, serenity, imperturbability, impassivity, equanimity, nonchalance, confidence, self-confidence, sureness, poise, dignity, aplomb, presence of mind, nerve, sangfroid, countenance, collectedness, suaveness, urbanity, elegance; informal cool, unflappability.
▷ANTONYMS nervousness.

self-reliance noun *a commitment to greater European self-reliance in defence matters*: **self-sufficiency**, self-support, self-sustenance, self-standing, independence; rare autarky.
▷ANTONYMS dependence.

self-reliant adjective *ineligible for social security, they have to be entirely self-reliant*: **self-sufficient**, self-supporting, self-sustaining, self-standing, able to stand on one's own two feet, living on one's hump; self-contained, independent, self-made; rare autarkic, autarkical.
▷ANTONYMS dependent.

self-respect noun *she lost her self-respect when her husband was attracted to her colleague*: **self-esteem**, self-regard, pride in oneself/one's abilities, faith in oneself, pride, dignity, morale, self-confidence, confidence, self-assurance, assurance; French amour propre.
▷ANTONYMS self-deprecation.

self-restraint noun *with great self-restraint, he did not grab the rod from his friend's hand*: **self-control**, restraint, control, self-discipline, self-mastery, self-possession, will power, strength of will, moderation, temperateness, temperance, abstemiousness, abstention, non-indulgence; informal cool; rare countenance.
▷ANTONYMS self-indulgence.

self-righteous adjective *you're too self-righteous to see your own frailties*: **sanctimonious**, holier-than-thou, self-satisfied, smug, priggish, complacent, too good to be true, pious, pietistic, moralizing, unctuous, superior, mealy-mouthed, hypocritical; informal goody-goody; rare Pharisaic, Pharisaical, Tartuffian.
▷ANTONYMS humble.

self-righteousness noun *his diary records the incident in a tone of self-righteousness*: **sanctimoniousness**, sanctimony, self-satisfaction, smugness, superiority, priggishness, complacency, piety, unctuousness, hypocrisy; rare pietism, Pharisaism, Tartufferie.
▷ANTONYMS humility.

self-sacrifice noun *self-sacrifice involved giving up her fine mansion and living in cheap lodgings*: **self-denial**, selflessness, unselfishness, altruism, self-discipline, asceticism, abnegation, self-abnegation, self-deprivation, abstemiousness, abstinence, moderation, austerity, temperance, abstention, renunciation; celibacy, chastity; teetotalism; rare continence.

self-satisfaction noun *the cosy self-satisfaction of the educated classes*: **complacency**, self-congratulation, smugness, superiority, self-approval, self-approbation.
▷ANTONYMS humility.

self-satisfied adjective *Janice climbed into the Mercedes and looked around her with a self-satisfied smile*: **complacent**, self-congratulatory, smug, superior, puffed up, pleased with oneself, self-approving, well pleased, proud of oneself; informal goody-goody, I'm-all-right-Jack; Brit. informal like the cat that's got the cream; N. Amer. informal wisenheimer; N. Amer. vulgar slang shit-eating.
▷ANTONYMS humble.

self-seeking adjective *Duncan was far from being a self-seeking assassin*: **self-interested**, self-serving, self-obsessed, self-absorbed, self-regarding, wrapped up in oneself, egocentric, egotistic, egotistical, egomaniacal, inward-looking, introverted, selfish; **inconsiderate**, thoughtless, unthinking, uncaring; informal looking after number one.
▷ANTONYMS altruistic.

self-styled adjective *the self-styled 'General' is in fact the biggest obstacle to peace in the region*: **would-be**, **self-appointed**, so-called, self-titled, professed, self-confessed, confessed, sworn, avowed; French soi-disant; rare self-named.

self-sufficiency noun *the drought undermined the country's self-sufficiency in rice*: **independence**, self-reliance, self-support, self-sustenance, self-standing; rare autarky.
▷ANTONYMS dependence.

self-sufficient adjective *the economy became nearly self-sufficient in many foodstuffs*: **independent**, self-supporting, self-sustaining, self-reliant, self-standing, able to stand on one's own two feet, living on one's hump; self-contained, self-made; rare autarkic, autarkical.
▷ANTONYMS dependent.

self-supporting adjective *the remaining one third of Pomeranian farmers had rather larger, self-supporting farms*: **self-sufficient**, self-sustaining, self-reliant, self-standing, able to stand on one's own two feet, living on one's hump; self-contained, independent, self-made, autarkic, autarkical.
▷ANTONYMS dependent.

self-willed adjective *she was a bossy, self-willed creature*: **wilful**, contrary, perverse, uncooperative, wayward, headstrong, stubborn, stubborn as a mule, obstinate, obdurate, pig-headed, mulish, intransigent, recalcitrant, refractory, stiff-necked, intractable, unpersuadable, ungovernable, difficult, disobedient, insubordinate, naughty; informal cussed; Brit. informal bloody-minded; archaic contumacious.
▷ANTONYMS obedient, easily led.

sell verb **1** *they are trying to sell their house*: **dispose of**, get rid of, vend, auction (off); put up for sale, offer for sale, put on sale; trade, barter, exchange, part-exchange, give in part-exchange.
▷ANTONYMS buy.

2 *he sells fruit and vegetables*: **trade in**, deal in, be in the business of, traffic in, stock, carry, offer for sale, handle, peddle, hawk, retail, market, advertise, promote.
3 *the book should sell well*: **be bought**, be purchased, go; sell like hot cakes, move, be in demand.
4 *the kit **sells for** £79.95*: **be priced at**, sell at, retail at, go for, be, be found for, be trading at, cost.
5 *the President still has to sell the deal to Congress*: **persuade someone to accept**, convince someone of the merits of, talk someone into, bring someone round to, win someone over to, get acceptance for, win approval for, get support for, get across, promote.
□ **sell someone down the river** informal See **river**.
□ **sell out 1** *the garage **had sold out of** petrol*: **have none left**, be out of stock of, have run out of, have sold all one's ...; informal be fresh out of, be cleaned out of. ▷ANTONYMS have plenty of.
2 *the English edition sold out very quickly*: **be bought up**, be depleted, be exhausted. ▷ANTONYMS flop.
3 *he does not see himself as having sold out*: **abandon one's principles**, prostitute oneself, sell one's soul, betray one's cause/ideals, be untrue to oneself, go over to the other side, play false, sacrifice oneself, debase oneself, degrade oneself, demean oneself.
□ **sell someone out** *you sold me out to the cops, didn't you?* **betray**, inform on/against; be disloyal to, be unfaithful to, desert, break one's promise to, double-cross, break faith with, stab in the back; informal tell on, sell down the river, blow the whistle on, squeal on, stitch up, peach on, do the dirty on; Brit. informal grass on, shop; N. Amer. informal rat out, finger, drop a/the dime on; Austral. informal pimp on, pool, put someone's pot on.
□ **sell someone short 1** *she is always selling herself short*: **undervalue**, underrate, underestimate, disparage, deprecate, belittle; rare derogate.
2 *shopkeepers were selling people short*: **swindle**, cheat, give short measure to, defraud, fleece; short-change, overcharge.

seller noun *sellers of fruit and vegetables*: **vendor**, **retailer**, purveyor, shopkeeper, supplier, stockist, trader, merchant, dealer; salesperson, salesman, saleswoman, sales assistant, assistant, shop assistant, travelling salesperson/salesman/saleswoman, representative, sales representative, agent, negotiator, reseller, auctioneer; N. Amer. sales clerk; informal counter-jumper, rep, knight of the road; dated saleslady, salesgirl, shop boy, shop girl, shopman, pedlar, hawker, traveller, commercial traveller; archaic chapman.
▷ANTONYMS buyer.

selling noun **1** *the selling of property*: **vending**, selling off, auctioning, trading, trade (in); traffic, trafficking, barter, bartering, exchange, exchanging, part-exchange, part-exchanging.
2 *a career in selling*: **salesmanship**, sales, marketing, merchandising, promotion, advertising.

semblance noun *there remained at least a semblance of discipline*: **appearance**, outward appearance, approximation, show, air, guise, pretence, facade, front, veneer.

semen noun *the rapist was identified by a semen sample*: **sperm**, spermatic fluid, seminal fluid, seed, milt, ejaculate, emission; technical spermatozoa; vulgar slang come, cum, jism, jissom, jizz; Brit. vulgar slang spunk.

> *Word links* **semen**
>
> **seminal** relating to semen

seminal adjective **1** *her paper is still considered a seminal work on the subject*: **influential**, formative, groundbreaking, pioneering, original, creative, innovative; imaginative, productive, major, important.
▷ANTONYMS irrelevant, unimportant.
2 *seminal fluid*: **spermatic**, sperm, seed; technical spermatozoal, spermatozoan.

seminar noun **1** *these suggestions were discussed at a seminar attended by education authority officials*: **discussion**, symposium, meeting, conference, congress, convention, forum, awayday, convocation, colloquy, summit, synod, conclave, consultation.
2 *teaching is usually in the form of seminars*: **study group**, workshop, tutorial, lecture, session, class, lesson, period.

seminary noun *he went to a seminary to study for the priesthood*: **theological college**, rabbinical college, Talmudical college, academy, training college, training institute, school, high school, conservatory.

send verb **1** *she said she'd send me a letter*: **dispatch**, post, mail, put in the post/mail, address, get off, convey, consign, direct, forward, redirect, send on, remit, airmail.
▷ANTONYMS receive.
2 *they sent a message to headquarters*: **transmit**, convey, communicate; telephone, phone, broadcast, televise, telecast, radio, fax, email, upload, ISDN, FTP; dated telegraph, wire, cable.
▷ANTONYMS receive.
3 *we have **sent for** a doctor*: **call**, call for, call in, summon, ask to come, request, request the presence/attendance of, order, contact, fetch.
4 *I squeezed the plastic bottle and sent a jet of petrol out of it*: **propel**, project, send forth, eject, deliver, discharge, spout, fire, shoot, blast, catapult, launch, release, force, push, impel, ram; throw, fling, toss, lob, hurl, shy, cast, let fly; informal chuck, sling, bung.
5 *the empty barrels **send off** evil-smelling fumes*: **emit**, give off, discharge, exude, send out, send forth, eject, release, leak.
6 *it's enough to send one mad*: **make**, drive, cause to be/become.
7 informal *it's the spectacle and music that send us, not the words*: **excite**, stimulate, move, rouse, stir, thrill, electrify, intoxicate, enrapture, enthral, grip, ravish, charm, delight, give pleasure to, titillate; informal turn on, blow away, give someone a buzz/kick, stoke.
□ **send someone down 1** Brit. *she was sent down from Cambridge*: **expel**, exclude; Brit. rusticate. ▷ANTONYMS admit; readmit.
2 *he pleaded guilty and was sent down for life*: **send to prison**, sentence to imprisonment, imprison, jail, incarcerate, lock up, confine, detain, intern, immure; informal put away; Brit. informal bang up.
▷ANTONYMS release; let off.
□ **send someone off** Sport *Miller was sent off for a second bookable offence*: **order off**, tell to leave the field, dismiss; show someone the red card; informal red-card, send for an early bath, give someone their marching orders, sin-bin.
□ **send someone packing** informal *they decided they'd had enough of him, and sent him packing*: **expel**, send away, eject, turn out, throw out, force out, oust, evict, put out, get rid of; dismiss, discharge; informal chuck out, kick out, boot out, show the door to, give someone their marching orders, throw someone out on their ear, sack, fire, give someone the boot, axe; Brit. informal turf out; N. Amer. informal give someone the bum's rush.
□ **send someone to Coventry** Brit. *all three have been sent to Coventry for not treading the party line*: **ostracize**, exclude, shun, spurn, cold-shoulder, give someone the cold shoulder, reject, repudiate, boycott, blackball, blacklist, cast off, cast out, shut out, avoid, ignore, snub, cut dead, keep at arm's length, leave out in the cold, bar, ban, debar, banish, exile, expel; N. Amer. disfellowship; informal freeze out, hand someone the frozen mitt; Brit. informal blank; dated cut.
□ **send someone/something up** informal *we used to send him up something rotten*: **satirize**, **ridicule**, make fun of, parody, lampoon, mock, caricature, imitate, ape; informal take off, spoof, take the mickey out of; archaic monkey; Brit. vulgar slang take the piss out of.

send-off noun *she was given a rousing send-off at her retirement party*: **farewell**, goodbye, adieu, leave-taking, valediction, going-away party; funeral; Latin vale.
▷ANTONYMS welcome.

send-up noun *a good-natured French send-up of the Hollywood private-eye film*: **satire**, burlesque, lampoon, pastiche, caricature, take-off, skit, squib, imitation, impression, impersonation, mockery, mimicry, travesty; informal spoof, mickey-take; W. Indian informal pappyshow; Brit. vulgar slang piss-take; rare pasquinade, pasticcio.

senile adjective *she couldn't cope with her senile husband*: **doddering**, doddery, decrepit, aged, long in the tooth, senescent, failing, declining, infirm, feeble, unsteady, in one's dotage, losing one's faculties, in one's second childhood, mentally confused, suffering from Alzheimer's (disease), suffering from senile dementia; informal past it, gaga, soft in the head; rare anile.
▷ANTONYMS in the prime of life.

senility noun *he was declared unfit for office on grounds of senility*: **decrepitude**, infirmity, feebleness, unsteadiness, senescence, decline, old age, dotage, second childhood, confusion, Alzheimer's (disease), senile dementia; informal softening of the brain; rare caducity, anility.
▷ANTONYMS the prime of life.

senior adjective **1** *senior school pupils*: **older**, elder; more grown up.
▷ANTONYMS junior, younger.
2 *you mustn't say that to a senior officer*: **higher-ranking**, highest-ranking, high-ranking, superior, top, chief, more/most important; N. Amer. ranking.
▷ANTONYMS junior, subordinate.
3 *Albert Saul Senior*: **the Elder**; Brit. major; N. Amer. I, (the First).

senior citizen noun *a Christmas treat for the senior citizens of the village*: **retired person**, (old-age) pensioner, OAP; old person, elderly person, elder, old fogey, dotard, Methuselah, patriarch; N. Amer. senior, retiree, golden ager; informal old stager, old-timer, oldie, ancient, wrinkly, crock, crumbly; Brit. informal buffer, josser; N. Amer. informal oldster, woopie; offensive geriatric; literary senex; rare retirer, pensionary.

seniority noun *the Chief Clerk was next in seniority*: **rank**, standing, primacy, superiority, precedence, priority, longer service, age; greater age, higher rank.

sensation noun **1** *excessive pressure on the eyeball causes a sensation of light*: **feeling**, sense, awareness, consciousness, perception, impression, tickle, tingle, prickle.
2 *I caused something of a sensation by announcing that this boat would cost £1m*: **commotion**, stir, uproar, furore, outrage, scandal, impact; interest, excitement, agitation; informal splash, to-do, hullabaloo.
3 *the new cars were a sensation when they first appeared*: **great success**, sell-out, triumph, star attraction, talking point; informal smash, smash hit, hit, box-office hit, show-stopper, winner, crowd-puller, wow, knockout, biggie.

sensational adjective **1** *a sensational murder trial*: **amazing**, startling, astonishing, staggering, shocking, appalling, horrifying, scandalous; stirring, exciting, thrilling, electrifying; fascinating, interesting, notable, noteworthy, important, significant, remarkable, momentous, historic, newsworthy.
▷ANTONYMS run-of-the-mill.
2 *the newspapers ran sensational stories about kids indulging in drugs*: **overdramatized**, dramatic, melodramatic, exaggerated, sensationalist, sensationalistic, graphic, explicit, unrestrained, lurid; rubbishy, trashy, cheap, tasteless, kitschy, yellow, pulp, garish, full-frontal; informal shock-horror, tacky, juicy; N. Amer. informal whiz-bang.
▷ANTONYMS dull, understated.
3 informal *she looked sensational in her new evening dress*: **gorgeous**, stunning, wonderful, exquisite, lovely, magnificent, dazzling, radiant, delightful, charming, enchanting, entrancing, captivating, bewitching; **striking**, spectacular, remarkable, outstanding, impressive, memorable, unforgettable, unique, arresting, eye-catching; marvellous, superb, excellent, exceptional, fine, superlative, formidable, first-class, first-rate, virtuoso, skilful, masterful, masterly; informal great, terrific, tremendous, super, smashing, fantastic, stupendous, stellar, fabulous, fab, heavenly, divine, drop-dead gorgeous, knockout, delectable, scrumptious, ace, A1, mean, awesome, magic, bad, wicked, out of this world, unreal; Brit. informal brilliant, brill; N. Amer. informal neat, babelicious, bodacious; Austral. informal bonzer; Brit. informal, dated wizard, spiffing, ripping, topping, champion, capital, top-hole; N. Amer. informal, dated swell, keen; vulgar slang shit-hot.
▷ANTONYMS ordinary, unremarkable.

sense noun **1** *the sense of touch*: **sensory faculty**, feeling, sensation, perception; sight, hearing, touch, taste, smell, sixth sense; Zoology, dated sensibility.
2 *she felt a sense of guilt*: **awareness**, **feeling**, sensation, consciousness, perception, recognition.
3 *a sense of humour*: **appreciation**, awareness, understanding, comprehension, discernment, acknowledgement.
4 *the driver had the sense to press the panic button*: **wisdom**, **common sense**, good sense, practicality, sagacity, sharpness, discernment, perception; native wit, mother wit, wit, level-headedness, intelligence, cleverness, astuteness, shrewdness, judgement, soundness of judgement, understanding, reason, logic, brain, brains; informal gumption, nous, horse sense, savvy; Brit. informal loaf, common; N. Amer. informal smarts.
▷ANTONYMS stupidity, mindlessness.
5 *I can't see the sense in leaving all the work to you*: **purpose**, point, reason, aim, object, motive, use, utility, value, advantage, benefit.
6 *here there are two different senses of 'exist'*: **meaning**, definition, import, denotation, signification, significance, purport, implication, intention, nuance, drift, gist, thrust, tenor, burden, theme, message, essence, spirit, substance.
▶ verb *she could sense their hostility to her | he sensed that disaster was imminent*: **discern**, feel, observe, notice, get the impression of, recognize, pick up, be/become cognizant of, be/become aware of, be/become conscious of, get/come to know, tell, distinguish, make out, find, identify, comprehend, apprehend, see, discover, learn, appreciate, realize, suspect, have a funny feeling, have a hunch, just know, divine, intuit, conceive; informal catch on to; Brit. informal twig; rare cognize.

senseless adjective **1** *he was punched and kicked senseless by a gang of thugs*: **unconscious**, out cold, out, cold, stunned, numb, numbed, insensible, insensate, comatose, knocked out, out for the count; informal KO'd, kayoed, laid out, dead to the world, out like a light; Brit. informal spark out; rare soporose, soporous.
▷ANTONYMS conscious, aware.
2 *a senseless waste of life*: **pointless**, **futile**, hopeless, fruitless, useless, needless, wasted, in vain, unavailing, aimless, idle, to no purpose, purposeless, worthless, meaningless, valueless, unproductive, unprofitable; **absurd**, foolish, mad, insane, asinine, moronic, imbecilic, nonsensical, stupid, idiotic, silly, irrelevant, footling, fatuous, hollow, inane, ridiculous, ludicrous, mindless, unintelligent, unwise, irrational, illogical; informal daft.
▷ANTONYMS sensible, wise.

sensibility noun **1** *the study of literature leads to a growth of intelligence and sensibility*: **sensitivity**, sensitiveness, finer feelings, delicacy, subtlety, taste, discrimination, discernment; understanding, insight, empathy, appreciation, awareness of the feelings of others; feeling, intuition, intuitiveness, responsiveness, receptivity, receptiveness, perceptiveness, awareness.
2 (**sensibilities**) *the wording was changed because it might offend people's sensibilities*: **feelings**, emotions, finer feelings, delicate sensitivity, sensitivities, susceptibilities, moral sense, sense of outrage.

sensible adjective *isn't this the sensible thing to do? | she's a very sensible person*: **practical**, realistic, responsible, full of common sense, reasonable, rational, logical, sound, circumspect, balanced, sober, no-nonsense, pragmatic, level-headed, serious-minded, thoughtful, commonsensical, down-to-earth, wise, prudent, mature; judicious, sagacious, sharp, shrewd, far-sighted, intelligent, clever.
▷ANTONYMS foolish.

sensitive adjective **1** *as people get older, their bodies often grow less sensitive to changes in external temperature*: **responsive to**, quick to respond to, sensitized to, reactive to, sentient of; aware of, conscious of, alive to; susceptible to, easily affected by, vulnerable to; attuned to, tuned in to; rare susceptive of.
▷ANTONYMS unresponsive, impervious, insensitive.
2 *don't use facial scrubs if your skin is sensitive | his innocent words touched sensitive spots within her own heart*: **delicate**, easily damaged, fragile; tender, sore, painful, raw.
▷ANTONYMS resilient, tough.
3 *these matters will need sensitive handling by the social services | a poignant, sensitive movie*: **tactful**, careful, thoughtful, diplomatic, delicate, subtle, finely tuned, kid-glove; **sympathetic**, compassionate, understanding, empathetic, intuitive, feeling, responsive, receptive; perceptive, discerning, acute, insightful.
▷ANTONYMS insensitive, clumsy, like bull in a china shop.
4 *I didn't realize he was so sensitive | her father was sensitive about his bald patch*: **easily offended**, easily upset, easily hurt, thin-skinned, touchy, oversensitive, hypersensitive, defensive; emotional, volatile, temperamental; paranoid, neurotic; informal twitchy, uptight; rare umbrageous.
▷ANTONYMS thick-skinned.
5 *a politically sensitive issue*: **difficult**, delicate, tricky, awkward, problematic, ticklish, precarious; controversial, emotive; informal sticky.
▷ANTONYMS uncontroversial.

sensitivity noun **1** *many commonly prescribed drugs increase the sensitivity of the skin to ultraviolet light*: **responsiveness**, sensitiveness, reactivity; susceptibility, vulnerability; rare reactiveness, susceptivity, susceptibleness.
▷ANTONYMS imperviousness.
2 *introducing change calls for patience and sensitivity*: **consideration**, care, thoughtfulness, tact, diplomacy, delicacy, subtlety, finesse, finer feelings; understanding, empathy, awareness of the feelings of others, sensibility, feeling, intuition, intuitiveness, responsiveness, receptivity, receptiveness; perceptiveness, perception, discernment, insight; French savoir faire.
▷ANTONYMS insensitivity.
3 *Shiona's sensitivity on the subject of boyfriends*: **touchiness**, oversensitivity, hypersensitivity, thin skin, defensiveness; informal twitchiness.
4 *the sensitivity of the issue*: **delicacy**, trickiness, awkwardness, difficulty, ticklishness.

sensual adjective **1** *sensual pleasure*: **physical**, physically gratifying, carnal, bodily, fleshly, animal; hedonistic, epicurean, sybaritic, voluptuary, Dionysiac; rare appetitive.
▷ANTONYMS spiritual, mental.
2 *a beautiful, sensual woman | his touch was warm and sensual*: **sexually attractive**, sexy, voluptuous, sultry, seductive, passionate; sexually exciting/arousing, erotic, sexual.
▷ANTONYMS ascetic, frigid, passionless.

> *Easily confused words* **sensual or sensuous?**
>
> The words **sensual** and **sensuous** are frequently used interchangeably to mean 'gratifying the senses', especially in a sexual sense. Some people maintain a distinction, according to which *sensuous* is a more neutral term, meaning 'relating to the senses rather than the intellect', as in *swimming is a beautiful, sensuous experience*, while *sensual* relates to gratification of the senses, especially sexually, as in *a sensual massage*. In practice, however, the connotations are such that it is difficult to distinguish the words in this way.

sensualist noun **hedonist**, pleasure lover, pleasure seeker, sybarite, voluptuary; epicure, epicurean, gastronome, gastronomist; French bon vivant, bon viveur.
▷ANTONYMS puritan.

sensuality noun *her heavy eyelids gave her face an air of sleepy sensuality*: **sexiness**, sexual attractiveness, voluptuousness, sultriness, seductiveness, passion; sexuality, eroticism; physicality, carnality.
▷ANTONYMS asceticism.

sensuous adjective **1** *big, richly coloured, sensuous canvases | his sensuous love of music*: **aesthetically pleasing**, aesthetic, pleasurable, gratifying, rich, sumptuous, luxurious; affective; sensory, sensorial.
2 *her full, sensuous lips*: **sexually attractive**, sexy, seductive, voluptuous, luscious, lush.

> *Easily confused words* **sensuous or sensual?**
>
> See **sensual**.

sentence noun **1** *Jones showed no emotion as the judge passed sentence*: **judgement**, ruling, pronouncement, decision, determination, decree; verdict; punishment.
2 *her husband is serving a three-year sentence for fraud*: **prison term**, prison sentence, jail sentence, penal sentence; life sentence, suspended sentence;

S

informal time, stretch, stint; Brit. informal porridge; N. Amer. informal rap; rhyming slang bird.
▶ verb *the men will be sentenced at a later date | two of the accused were sentenced to death*: **pass judgement on**, impose a sentence on, pronounce sentence on, mete out punishment to, punish, convict; condemn, doom.

sententious adjective *his sententious remarks were unbearable*: **moralistic**, moralizing, sanctimonious, self-righteous, pietistic, pious, priggish, Pecksniffian, judgemental, canting; pompous, pontifical, self-important; Scottish unco guid; informal preachy, preachifying; Brit. informal pi.

sentient adjective *I fail to see any sound moral justification for treating sentient creatures as mere commodities*: **feeling**, capable of feeling, living, live; conscious, aware, responsive, reactive.
▷ANTONYMS insentient.

sentiment noun **1** *the comments in today's Daily Telegraph echo my own sentiments*: **view**, point of view, way of thinking, feeling, attitude, thought, opinion, belief, idea.
2 *overpowered by an intense sentiment of horror, I leapt up*: **feeling**, emotion.
3 *many of the appeals rely on treacly sentiment | there's no room for sentiment at the hard edge of professional sport*: **sentimentality**, mawkishness, over-sentimentality, emotionalism, overemotionalism, sentimentalism; **emotion**, sensibility, finer feelings, tender feelings, tenderness, softness, soft-heartedness, tender-heartedness; Brit. tweeness; informal schmaltz, mush, slush, sob stuff, slushiness, sloppiness, slop, goo, corn, corniness, hokum, cheese; Brit. informal soppiness; N. Amer. informal sappiness, hokeyness.

sentimental adjective **1** *she felt a sentimental attachment to the place creep over her | I wanted to hold on to one of the vases for sentimental reasons*: **nostalgic**, tender, emotional, dewy-eyed, misty-eyed, affectionate, loving.
▷ANTONYMS dispassionate, practical.
2 *the film is unfocused and sentimental*: **mawkish**, over-sentimental, overemotional, cloying, sickly, saccharine, sugary, sugar-coated, syrupy; romantic, hearts-and-flowers, touching, pathetic; Brit. twee; informal slushy, sloppy, mushy, weepy, tear-jerking, schmaltzy, cutesy, lovey-dovey, gooey, drippy, sloshy, soupy, treacly, cheesy, corny, icky, sick-making, toe-curling; Brit. informal soppy; N. Amer. informal cornball, sappy, hokey, three-hankie; trademark Mills-and-Boon.
▷ANTONYMS gritty, unsentimental, realistic, hard-headed.
3 *Hannah had always been sentimental about animals*: **soft-hearted**, tender-hearted, soft, soft-centred; informal soppy.

sentimentality noun *a romantic fiction of unashamed sentimentality*: **mawkishness**, over-sentimentality, sentimentalism, emotionalism, overemotionalism; nostalgia, pathos; romanticism; kitsch; Brit. tweeness; informal schmaltz, mush, slush, sob stuff, slushiness, sloppiness, slop, corn, corniness, hokum, cheese; Brit. informal soppiness; N. Amer. informal sappiness, hokeyness.

sentry noun **guard**, sentinel, lookout, watch, watchman, patrol, picket; historical vedette.

separable adjective *body and soul are not separable*: **divisible**, distinguishable, distinct, independent; detachable, removable, severable; technical scissile.

separate adjective **1** *he had kept his personal life quite separate from his job | they went their separate ways*: **unconnected**, unrelated, different, discrete, distinct, disparate; detached, divorced, disconnected, independent, autonomous; respective, individual, particular, several.
▷ANTONYMS interdependent, connected; same.
2 *the infirmary was* **separate from** *the main building*: **set apart from**, unattached to, not attached to, not joined to, disjoined from; fenced off from, cut off from, segregated from, isolated from, shut off from; free-standing, by itself, alone; self-contained, detached.
▷ANTONYMS attached, joined.
▶ verb **1** *police were trying to separate two rioting mobs | the twins were separated at birth*: **part**, split (up), break up, move apart, divide; archaic sunder.
▷ANTONYMS unite, bring together.
2 *the connectors come in two parts, which can be easily separated*: **disconnect**, pull apart, break apart, detach, disengage, uncouple, unyoke, disarticulate, disassemble, disunite, disjoin, disaffiliate; split in two, divide in two, sever; disentangle, unravel.
▷ANTONYMS join, connect, combine.
3 *the second stage of the rocket failed to separate*: **become detached**, become disconnected, come apart, come away, uncouple, break off.
▷ANTONYMS link up with.
4 *he led Cleo through the kitchen gardens to the wall that separated the two estates*: **divide**, partition, lie between, come between, stand between, keep apart; bisect, intersect.
▷ANTONYMS link, bridge.
5 *the west end of the south aisle was* **separated off**: **isolate**, partition off, divide off, section off; close off, shut off, cordon off, fence off, curtain off, screen off.
6 *they separated at the airport*: **part company**, part, go their separate ways, go different ways, split, split up, say goodbye/farewell/adieu, say one's goodbyes; disperse, disband, scatter.
▷ANTONYMS meet.
7 *the road separated and ran around both sides of the immense lawn*: **fork**, divide, branch, bifurcate, diverge, go in different directions; rare divaricate.
▷ANTONYMS converge, merge.
8 *after her parents separated, she was brought up by her mother*: **split up**, break up, part, stop living together, part company, reach a parting of the ways, become estranged; divorce, get divorced, get a divorce.
▷ANTONYMS get together; marry.
9 *the skins are separated from the juice before fermentation | we need to separate fact from fiction*: **isolate**, set apart, put to one side, segregate; sort out, sift out, winnow out, filter out, remove, weed out; distinguish, differentiate, dissociate.
▷ANTONYMS mix.
10 *individuals who* **separate themselves from** *a society of which they have formerly been members*: **break away from**, break with, secede from, sever relations with, withdraw from, delink from, leave, quit, split with, dissociate oneself from, disaffiliate oneself from, resign from, pull out of, drop out of, have nothing more to do with, repudiate, reject, desert.
▷ANTONYMS join.

separated adjective *his parents are separated*: **living separately**, no longer together, apart, living apart, parted; estranged.
▷ANTONYMS together.

separately adverb *I'll have to interview you all separately | the passengers will be returning separately*: **individually**, one by one, one at a time, singly; **apart**, not together, independently, alone, by oneself, on one's own, personally; formal severally.

separation noun **1** *according to tradition, death represents the separation of the soul from the body | the separation of BT from the Post Office in 1981*: **disconnection**, detachment, severance, uncoupling, dissociation, disassociation, disjunction, disunion, disaffiliation, segregation; partition; literary sundering; rare disseverment.
▷ANTONYMS unification.
2 *presumably you were the cause of Rachel and Florian's separation*: **break-up**, split, split-up, parting, estrangement, parting of the ways, rift, rupture, breach; divorce, legal separation, judicial separation; Brit. informal bust-up.
▷ANTONYMS marriage.
3 *the separation between art and life*: **distinction**, difference, differentiation, division, dividing line; polarity; gulf, gap, chasm.
▷ANTONYMS connection.

septic adjective *a septic finger | his leg went septic*: **infected**, festering, suppurating, pus-filled, putrid, putrefying, putrefactive, purulent, poisoned, diseased; inflamed, angry, red, hot, swollen; rare pussy.

sepulchral adjective *'There's been an accident,' he said in sepulchral tones*: **gloomy**, lugubrious, sombre, melancholy, melancholic, sad, sorrowful, mournful, doleful, mirthless, cheerless, joyless, funereal, dismal; literary dolorous.
▷ANTONYMS cheerful, happy.

sepulchre noun **tomb**, vault, burial place, burial chamber, crypt, catacomb, mausoleum, sarcophagus, pyramid; grave; Archaeology mastaba; rare undercroft.

sequel noun **1** *the film was successful enough to inspire a sequel*: **follow-up**, continuation.
2 *the immediate sequel was an armed uprising in several cities*: **consequence**, result, upshot, outcome, development, issue, end, conclusion, postscript; effect, after-effect, aftermath; Medicine sequelae; informal pay-off; archaic success; rare sequent.

sequence noun **1** *the sequence of events became clear*: **succession**, order, course, series, chain, concatenation, train, string, cycle, progression; arrangement, pattern; chronology; flow.
2 *a sequence from his new film*: **excerpt**, clip, scene, extract, episode, section, segment.

sequester verb **1** *he* **sequestered himself** *from the world*: **isolate oneself**, hide oneself away, shut oneself away, seclude oneself, cut/shut oneself off, set oneself apart, segregate oneself; closet oneself, withdraw oneself, remove oneself, retire.
2 *the government sequestered all his property*: **confiscate**, seize, sequestrate, take possession of, take, appropriate, expropriate, impound, commandeer, arrogate; Law distrain, attach, disseize; Scottish Law poind.

sequestered adjective *she wondered if she had been unwise to shut herself away in this sequestered spot*: **secluded**, cloistered, hidden away, concealed, tucked away, hard to find; **isolated**, out of the way, off the beaten track, remote, cut off; unfrequented, lonely; quiet, private, secret; archaic retired.
▷ANTONYMS busy; central, public.

sequestrate verb *in November 1956 the property was sequestrated by the Egyptian authorities*: **confiscate**, seize, take possession of, take, sequester, appropriate, expropriate, impound, commandeer, arrogate; Law distrain, attach, disseize; Scottish Law poind.

seraphic adjective *he listened with an expression of seraphic contentment on his face*: **blissful**, beatific, sublime, rapturous, ecstatic, joyful, rapt; **serene**, ethereal; pure, innocent, cherubic, saintly, angelic; celestial, heavenly, holy, divine.
▷ANTONYMS demonic.

serendipitous adjective *their diligent efforts were coupled with the joys of serendipitous discovery*: **chance**, accidental; **lucky**, fortuitous; unexpected, unanticipated, unforeseen, unlooked-for; coincidental; informal fluky.

serendipity noun *technical innovation may be the result of pure serendipity*: **chance**, happy chance, accident, happy accident, fluke; **luck**, good luck, good fortune, fortuity, fortuitousness, providence; coincidence, happy coincidence.

serene adjective **1** *on the surface I might have seemed serene, but underneath I was panicking*: **calm**, composed, collected, {cool, calm, and collected}, as cool as a cucumber, tranquil, peaceful, at peace, pacific, untroubled, relaxed, at ease, poised, self-possessed, unperturbed, imperturbable, undisturbed, unruffled, unworried, unexcitable, placid, equable, even-tempered; N. Amer. centered; informal together, unflappable.
▷ANTONYMS anxious, nervous, agitated.
2 *Trentino is a labyrinth of deep valleys and serene lakes*: **peaceful**, tranquil, quiet, still, restful, relaxing, soothing, undisturbed, untroubled.
▷ANTONYMS turbulent, noisy.
3 *the serene western sky*: **cloudless**, unclouded, clear, bright, sunny.
▷ANTONYMS cloudy, stormy.

> *Choose the right word* **serene, calm, tranquil, placid, peaceful**
>
> See **calm**.

serenity noun **1** *she radiated an air of serenity*: **calmness**, calm, composure, tranquillity, peacefulness, peace of mind, peace, peaceableness, collectedness, poise, aplomb, self-possession, sangfroid, imperturbability, equanimity, equableness, ease, placidity, placidness; informal togetherness, unflappability; rare ataraxy, ataraxia.
▷ANTONYMS anxiety, agitation.
2 *the garden is an oasis of serenity amidst the bustling city*: **peace**, peace and quiet, peacefulness, tranquillity, calm, quiet, quietness, quietude, stillness, restfulness, repose.
▷ANTONYMS disruption.
3 *the serenity of the sky*: **cloudlessness**, clearness, brightness, sunniness.
▷ANTONYMS cloudiness, storminess.

serf noun historical **bondsman**, slave, servant, menial, villein, thrall, helot, ceorl; vassal, liegeman.
▷ANTONYMS freeman, master.

series noun **1** *detectives are investigating a series of burglaries in the area | a series of lectures on modern art*: **sequence**, succession, string, chain, concatenation, train, run, chapter, round, progression, procession; **spate**, wave, stream, rash, outbreak; set, course, cycle; row, line, bank, battery, arrangement, order.
2 *a new drama series*: **set of programmes**, programme, production, serial; situation comedy, soap opera; informal sitcom, soap.

serious adjective **1** *he had a serious expression on his face | Prudence was a thin, pale, serious young woman*: **solemn**, earnest, grave, sober, sombre, unsmiling, poker-faced, stern, grim, dour, humourless, stony-faced; **thoughtful**, preoccupied, deep in thought, pensive, meditative, ruminative, contemplative, introspective; staid, sedate, studious, bookish.
▷ANTONYMS light-hearted, cheerful, jovial.
2 *we have some serious decisions to make*: **important**, significant, consequential, of consequence, momentous, of moment, key, grave, weighty, far-reaching, major; urgent, pressing, crucial, critical, vital, life-and-death, high-priority; no joke, no laughing matter.
▷ANTONYMS trivial, unimportant.
3 *the president should give serious consideration to this advice*: **careful**, detailed, in-depth, deep, profound, meaningful.
▷ANTONYMS superficial.
4 *a serious play about Art and Life*: **intellectual**, **highbrow**, heavyweight, deep, profound, literary, learned, scholarly, cultured; classical; informal heavy.
▷ANTONYMS light, lowbrow, populist.
5 *four of the victims received serious injuries | he appealed for emergency foreign aid to combat the serious shortages of foodstuff and medicines*: **severe**, grave, bad, critical, acute, alarming, worrying, grievous, dreadful, terrible, dire, extreme, dangerous, perilous, precarious; archaic or humorous parlous.
▷ANTONYMS minor, negligible.
6 *is the government serious about developing decent employment opportunities for women?* **in earnest**, earnest, sincere, wholehearted, genuine, meaning what one says; committed, firm, resolute, resolved, determined.
▷ANTONYMS uncommitted, half-hearted, flippant.
7 informal *she spends serious sums of money*. See **considerable**.

seriously adverb **1** *Faye nodded seriously, biting her lower lip*: **solemnly**, earnestly, gravely, soberly, sombrely, without smiling, with a poker face, sternly, grimly, dourly, humourlessly; thoughtfully, pensively, meditatively, ruminatively, contemplatively.
▷ANTONYMS cheerfully, jovially.
2 *one woman died and another was seriously injured*: **severely**, gravely, badly, critically, acutely, sorely, grievously, desperately, alarmingly, dangerously, perilously.
▷ANTONYMS slightly.
3 *do you seriously expect me to believe that?* **really**, actually, honestly.
4 *seriously, I'm very pleased that you're staying*: **joking aside/apart**, to be serious, honestly, without joking, no joking, truthfully, truly, I mean it; informal Scout's honour; Brit. informal straight up; dated honest Injun.
5 informal *'I've handed in my notice.' 'Seriously?'*: **really?**, is that so? is that a fact? you're joking! well I never, well I never did, go on, you don't say; informal you're kidding! well knock/blow me down with a feather; Brit. informal well I'll be blowed; N. Amer. informal well what do you know about that?; archaic go to.
6 informal *he was seriously rich*: **extremely**, very, really, dreadfully, terribly, awfully, fearfully, incredibly, amazingly, exceptionally, exceedingly, immensely, uncommonly, remarkably, extraordinarily; Scottish unco; French très; informal terrifically, tremendously, right, ultra, mega, mucho, stinking, majorly, oh-so, madly; Brit. informal jolly, ever so, dead, well; N. Amer. informal real, mighty, awful, powerful, way, bitching; S. African informal lekker; informal, dated devilish, frightfully; archaic exceeding.

seriousness noun **1** *in spite of the seriousness of his expression, Rostov was amused*: **solemnity**, solemnness, earnestness, graveness, gravity, gravitas, soberness, sobriety, sombreness, sternness, grimness, dourness, humourlessness; **thoughtfulness**, preoccupation, pensiveness.
▷ANTONYMS cheerfulness, joviality.
2 *I stressed the seriousness of the matter*: **importance**, significance, consequence, momentousness, moment, weightiness, weight; urgency, crucialness, vitalness.
▷ANTONYMS triviality, unimportance.
3 *he tried to play down the seriousness of his injuries*: **severity**, severeness, gravity, graveness, acuteness, grievousness, extremity, danger, dangerousness, perilousness.
4 *I doubt his seriousness*: **earnestness**, sincerity, wholeheartedness, genuineness; commitment, firmness, resolution, resolve, determination.

sermon noun **1** *he preached a sermon based on a text from the Book of Wisdom*: **homily**, address, speech, talk, discourse, oration; lesson; preaching, teaching; rare peroration.
2 *he realized that if he said any more he would have to listen to another lengthy sermon*: **lecture**, tirade, harangue, diatribe; speech, disquisition, monologue, declamation, exhortation; reprimand, reproach, reproof, scolding, admonishment, admonition, reproval, remonstration, upbraiding, castigation, lambasting, criticism, censure; informal spiel, telling-off, talking-to, rap over the knuckles, dressing-down, earful, roasting, bawling-out, blast, row; Brit. informal ticking-off, carpeting, rollicking, wigging; Brit. vulgar slang bollocking; dated rating.
▷ANTONYMS commendation, pat on the back.

> *Word links* **sermon**
>
> **homiletic** relating to sermons
> **homiletics** art of preaching sermons

serpentine adjective **1** *a narrow, serpentine path wound down through woods of cedar and pine*: **winding**, windy, zigzag, zigzagging, twisting, twisty, turning, meandering, curving, sinuous, snaking, snaky, tortuous; rare anfractuous, flexuous, meandrous, serpentiform.
▷ANTONYMS straight.
2 *Labour's serpentine leadership election rules*: **complicated**, intricate, complex, involved, tortuous, convoluted, tangled, elaborate, knotty, confusing, bewildering, baffling; inextricable, entangled, impenetrable, Byzantine, Daedalian, Gordian; rare involute, involuted.
▷ANTONYMS straightforward, simple.

Word toolkit

serpentine	meandering	winding
lines	river	road
tail	path	staircase
canyon	thoughts	driveway
curves	narrative	corridor

serrated adjective *a ten-inch hunting knife with a serrated blade*: **jagged**, sawtoothed, sawtooth, saw-edged, zigzag, notched, indented, toothed; technical serrate, serrulate, serrulated, serriform, serratiform, crenulated, crenate, denticulate, denticulated.
▷ANTONYMS smooth, straight.

serried adjective *the serried mass of dark conifers | serried ranks of soldiers*: **close together**, packed together, close-set, dense, tight, compact; massed,

assembled, tiered.
▷ANTONYMS scattered.

servant noun **1** *an army of servants were cleaning the hall after the previous night's banquet*: **attendant**, retainer; domestic help, domestic worker, domestic, help, cleaner, cleaning woman/lady, helper; lackey, flunkey, minion; maid, housemaid, maidservant, lady's maid, handmaid, parlour maid, scullery maid, serving maid, girl, maid-of-all-work; footman, page, page boy, valet, butler, man, gentleman's gentleman, batman, manservant, houseman, houseboy, boy; housekeeper, steward, major domo; coachman, postilion, equerry; menial, drudge, hireling, slave; N. Amer. hired help; in Spanish-speaking countries mozo; Indian bearer, chokra, amah, bai; Brit. dated charwoman, charlady, char, boots; S. African, chiefly historical jong; Brit. informal Mrs Mop, daily woman, daily, skivvy; Brit. university slang scout, bedder, gyp; archaic seneschal, abigail, servitor, scullion, tweeny, servingman, servingwoman, serving wench, turnspit, varlet, vassal, serf; rare famulus.
▷ANTONYMS master, mistress.
2 *he was a great servant of the Labour Party*: **helper**, supporter, follower.

serve verb **1** *they have served their political masters faithfully for the past 40 years*: **work for**, be in the service of, perform duties for, be employed by, have a job with; obey, be obedient to, carry out the wishes of.
2 *I decided that I wanted to work somewhere where I could serve the community*: **be of service to**, be of use to, help, give help to, assist, give assistance to, aid, lend a hand to, give a helping hand to, do a good turn to, make a contribution to, do one's bit for, do something for, benefit; minister to, succour.
3 *altogether she had* ***served on*** *the committee for 11 years*: **be a member of**, work on, be on, sit on, have/hold a place on, perform duties on, carry out duties on.
4 *California is limiting the number of terms a politician can serve in office | Lewis served his apprenticeship in Scotland*: **carry out**, perform, do, fulfil, complete, discharge; spend, go through.
5 *serve the soup hot with lots of crusty bread | dinner is served at candlelit tables*: **dish up/out**, give out, distribute, set out, plate up, spoon out, ladle out; present, provide, supply, make available.
6 *Elizabeth walked off to serve another customer*: **attend to**, give one's attention to, attend to the requirements of, deal with, see to; **assist**, help, look after, take care of.
7 *the landlord's daughter served at table*: **act as waiter/waitress**, wait, distribute food/refreshments; N. Amer. informal sling hash, sling plates.
8 *they were just about to* ***serve*** *him* ***with*** *a writ*: **deliver to**, present with, give to, hand over to, cause to accept.
9 *she stabbed the cigarette out in a saucer* ***serving as*** *an ashtray*: **act as**, function as, fulfil the function of, do duty as, do the work of, act as a substitute for.
10 *official forms are obtainable that, with minor adaptation, will serve in all but a few cases*: **suffice**, be adequate, be good enough, be all right, fit/fill the bill, do, answer; be useful, serve a purpose, meet requirements, suit.
11 *Cornish householders wonder if they are being fairly served*: **treat**, deal with, act towards, behave towards, conduct oneself towards, handle.

service noun **1** *there has been an improvement in pay and conditions of service*: **work**, employment, employ, labour, performance of one's duties.
2 *he has done us a great service | Josie offered her services as a babysitter*: **act of assistance**, good turn, favour, kindness, helping hand; **(services) assistance**, help, aid, offices, ministrations.
3 *both the food and the service were excellent*: **waiting**, waitressing, waiting at table, serving of food and drink, attendance, serving.
4 *high quality products which will give many years of reliable service*: **use**, usage.
5 *he took his car in for a service*: **overhaul**, servicing, maintenance check, routine check, check.
6 *he will be cremated tomorrow after a private funeral service | the first words of the marriage service*: **ceremony**, ritual, rite, observance, ordinance; liturgy, sacrament, office.
7 *the provision of a wide range of local services | the national telephone service*: **amenity**, facility, resource, utility; system.
8 **(the services)** *if you're about to leave the services, the prospect of Civvy Street can be daunting*: **armed forces**, armed services, forces, military; army, navy, air force, marines.
□ **be of service** *a close liaison between mathematics and computer science can* ***be of service to*** *an archaeologist*: **help**, assist, benefit, be helpful, be of assistance, be beneficial, be advantageous, be of benefit, serve, advantage, be useful, be of use, be profitable, profit, be valuable, be of worth, do someone a good turn.
□ **out of service** *one of the elevators is out of service*: **out of order**, not working, not in working order, not functioning, broken, broken-down, out of commission, acting up, unserviceable, faulty, defective, non-functional, inoperative, in disrepair; down; informal conked out, bust, (gone) kaput, gone phut, on the blink, gone haywire, shot; Brit. informal knackered, jiggered, wonky; N. Amer. informal on the fritz, out of whack; Brit. vulgar slang buggered.
▶**verb** *ensure that gas appliances are serviced regularly*: **overhaul**, check, check over, go over, give a maintenance check to, maintain, keep in good condition; repair, mend, recondition.

serviceable adjective **1** *an ageing but still serviceable water supply system*: **in working order**, working, functioning, functional, operational, operative; usable, workable, viable, useful, of use.
▷ANTONYMS outworn, non-functioning, unusable.
2 *sturdy, serviceable lace-up shoes*: **functional**, utilitarian, sensible, practical, non-decorative, plain, unadorned; **hard-wearing**, durable, lasting, long-lasting, tough, strong, robust, wear-resistant.
▷ANTONYMS decorative, impractical.

servile adjective *his attitude towards Mandeville can only be described as servile*: **obsequious**, sycophantic, excessively deferential, subservient, fawning, toadying, ingratiating, unctuous, oily, oleaginous, greasy, grovelling, cringing, toadyish, slavish, abject, craven, humble, Uriah Heepish, self-abasing; informal slimy, bootlicking, smarmy, sucky, soapy, forelock-tugging; N. Amer. informal brown-nosing, apple-polishing; Brit. vulgar slang arse-licking, bum-sucking; N. Amer. vulgar slang kiss-ass, ass-kissing.
▷ANTONYMS bossy, assertive.

servility noun *Lovat was used to servility—he couldn't remember when anyone had last disagreed with him*: **obsequiousness**, sycophancy, excessive deference, subservience, submissiveness, fawning, toadyism, toadying, grovelling, cringing, unctuousness, oiliness, abjectness, abjection, cravenness, slavishness, humility, self-abasement; informal smarminess, sliminess, bootlicking; N. Amer. informal apple-polishing; Brit. vulgar slang arse-licking, bum-sucking; N. Amer. vulgar slang ass-kissing.
▷ANTONYMS bossiness, assertiveness.

serving noun *a large serving of spaghetti*: **portion**, helping, plateful, platter, plate, bowlful; amount, quantity, ration.

servitude noun *Indian slaves were bought and sold and kept in servitude*: **slavery**, enslavement, bondage, subjugation, subjection, domination; literary thraldom; historical serfdom, vassalage.
▷ANTONYMS freedom, liberty.

session noun **1** *a special session of the OECD Environment Committee*: **meeting**, sitting, assembly, conclave, plenary; hearing; conference, discussion, forum, symposium; Scottish sederunt, diet; N. Amer. & NZ caucus.
2 *I'll arrange some training sessions*: **period**, time, spell, stretch, bout.
3 informal *we had a bit of a session last night*: **drinking bout**, binge; informal sesh, booze-up, beer-up, liquid lunch, drunk, blind, souse; Scottish informal skite; N. Amer. informal jag; Brit. vulgar slang piss-up; archaic fuddle, potation.
4 *the college is recognized by the Government and the next session begins on 1st August*: **academic year**, school year; **term**, school term; N. Amer. semester, trimester.

set[1] verb **1** *Beth set the two bags on the kitchen table*: **put**, place, put down, lay, lay down, deposit, position, settle, station; leave, stow, prop, lean, stand, plant, pose, dispose; informal stick, dump, bung, park, plonk, plump, pop; N. Amer. informal plunk; rare posit.
2 **(be set)** *the cottage was set on a hill at the back of the village*: **be situated**, be located, lie, stand, be sited, be perched; be found.
3 *the bright red benches were attached to the ground by bolts set in concrete | a huge square cut emerald set in platinum*: **fix**, embed, insert; mount.
4 *an enamelled gold figurine set with precious stones*: **adorn**, ornament, decorate, embellish, deck, bedeck; literary bejewel.
5 *I'll go and set the table*: **lay**, prepare, arrange, make ready.
6 *to find out if attitudes really have changed, we set three couples five everyday tasks*: **assign**, allocate, give, allot, deal, prescribe.
7 *anyone can lose weight if they set their mind to it*: **apply**, address, direct, aim, turn, focus, concentrate.
8 *the government had still not set a date for the election*: **decide on**, select, choose, arrange, schedule; fix, fix on, determine, designate, name, appoint, specify, stipulate; settle, resolve on, agree on, confirm.
9 *he spun round in surprise and then he set his horse towards her*: **direct**, steer, orientate, point, aim, train.
10 *his time in the 25m freestyle set a national record*: **establish**, set up, create, provide, institute.
11 *Mr Crump set his watch by the clock in the hall*: **adjust**, regulate, synchronize, coordinate, harmonize; calibrate; put right, correct; technical collimate.
12 *have you set the alarm?* **programme**, activate; switch on, turn on.
13 *the adhesive will set hard in about an hour | pour the mixture on top of the jelly and leave it to set*: **solidify**, harden, become solid, become hard, stiffen, thicken, gel; cake, congeal, coagulate, clot; freeze, crystallize; rare gelatinize.
▷ANTONYMS melt.
14 *the sun was setting and a warm, red glow filled the sky*: **go down**, sink, dip below the horizon; vanish, disappear, subside, decline.
▷ANTONYMS rise.
□ **set about 1** *Mike set about raising £5000 to pay for the boy's medical treatment | she set about her task with vigour*: **begin**, start, make a start on, go about, set to, get to work on, get down to, get going on, embark on, tackle, attack, address oneself to, buckle down to, undertake; put/set the wheels in motion, get down to business, get/set the ball rolling, put one's shoulder to the wheel, put one's hand to the plough, roll up one's sleeves, get things moving; informal get cracking, get one's finger out, get weaving; formal commence. **2** *he was pushed up against the wall as the youths set about him*: **attack**, assail, assault, hit, strike, beat, give someone a beating, thrash,

S

pound, pummel, wallop, hammer, tear into, set upon, fall on, turn on, let fly at; informal lay into, lace into, beat the living daylights out of, sail into, pitch into, let someone have it, get stuck into, paste, do over, work over, rough up, knock about/around; Brit. informal duff up, have a go at; N. Amer. informal beat up on, light into.

□ **set something against something else** *these figures need to be set against the incomes of the other social groups*: **compare**, juxtapose, place side by side with; **offset**, set off against; contrast.

▷ANTONYMS take in isolation.

□ **set someone against someone else** *he wants to set you against me*: **alienate from**, estrange from, cause to dislike; drive a wedge between, cause hostility between, sow dissension, set at odds.

▷ANTONYMS reconcile.

□ **set someone apart distinguish**, differentiate, mark off, mark out, single out, make different, separate, demarcate.

□ **set something apart** *one pew was set apart from the rest*: **isolate**, separate, segregate, put to one side.

□ **set something aside 1** *set aside some money each month for emergencies*: **save**, put by, put aside, put away, lay aside, lay by, put to one side, keep, reserve, keep in reserve; store, stockpile, hoard, stow away, cache, put in a safe place, put down; earmark, withhold, keep for oneself; N. Amer. set by; informal salt away, squirrel away, stash away, hang on to. ▷ANTONYMS use, use up, spend.

2 *he set aside his half-empty cup and strode towards the door*: **put down**, put to one side, discard, abandon, dispense with, cast aside, drop.

▷ANTONYMS pick up.

3 *can't you set aside your differences for now?* **disregard**, put aside, put to one side, ignore, forget, discount, shrug off, bury, consign to oblivion.

4 *the Court of Appeal set aside the High Court decision*: **overrule**, overturn, reverse, revoke, countermand, rule against, nullify, render null and void, annul, cancel, quash, dismiss, reject, repudiate, abrogate, remit; Law vacate, disaffirm; archaic recall. ▷ANTONYMS uphold, confirm.

□ **set someone back** informal *that must have set you back a bit!* **cost**; Brit. informal knock back.

□ **set someone/something back** *we'll have to re-advertise the position, which will set us back another six months | the growth of American trade unionism was set back by the economic depression*: **delay**, hold up, hold back, slow down, slow up, retard, put a brake on, check, decelerate; **hinder**, impede, obstruct, hamper, inhibit, interfere with, frustrate, thwart; Brit. informal throw a spanner in the works of; N. Amer. informal throw a monkey wrench in the works of; archaic stay.

▷ANTONYMS speed up, expedite.

□ **set something down 1** *that evening, he set down his thoughts*: **write down**, put in writing, put down, put down on paper, put in black and white, jot down, note down, make a note of; record, register, log, catalogue, tabulate. **2** *the Association set down a code of practice for all members to comply with*: **formulate**, draw up, establish, frame; **lay down**, determine, fix, stipulate, specify, codify, prescribe, impose, ordain. **3** *I set it down to the fact that he'd had no experience with girls*: **attribute**, put down, ascribe, assign, chalk up; blame on, impute, lay at the door of.

□ **set forth** *accompanied by a large entourage, she set forth for Framlingham*: **set out**, set off, start out, sally forth, begin one's journey, leave, depart, set sail; archaic set forward.

▷ANTONYMS arrive.

□ **set something forth** *the policy paper of March 2 sets forth the core of Labour's programme*: **present**, describe, set out, detail, delineate, explain, expound, give an account of, rehearse, catalogue, particularize; state, declare, announce; submit, offer, put forward, advance, propose, propound.

□ **set free** *there wasn't enough evidence to hold the suspects and they were set free*: **release**, free, let go, allow to leave, set/let/turn loose, let out, liberate, set at liberty, deliver, emancipate; literary disenthral; historical manumit.

▷ANTONYMS imprison.

□ **set in** *the pilot was winched to safety before bad weather set in*: **begin**, start, arrive, come, develop, become established, get under way, settle in; formal commence.

□ **set something in motion** See **motion**.

□ **set off** *on the appointed day, we set off for Heathrow*: **set out**, start out, set forth, sally forth, begin one's journey, leave, depart, embark, set sail; informal hit the road; archaic set forward.

▷ANTONYMS arrive.

□ **set something off 1** *police don't know how the bomb was set off*: **detonate**, explode, blow up, touch off, trigger; ignite, light.

▷ANTONYMS defuse.

2 *the announcement set off a wave of protest*: **give rise to**, cause, lead to, set in motion, occasion, bring about, bring on, begin, start, initiate, precipitate, prompt, trigger (off), spark (off), touch off, provoke, incite, stimulate; formal commence. ▷ANTONYMS bring to an end.

3 *a velvet dress in a deep royal blue which set off her auburn hair*: **enhance**, bring out, emphasize, show off, throw into relief, point up; complement; heighten, intensify, increase. ▷ANTONYMS clash with.

□ **set on** *he and his friends were set on by a gang*: **attack**, assail, assault, hit, strike, beat, give someone a beating, thrash, pound, pummel, wallop, hammer, tear into, set about, set upon, fall on, turn on, let fly at; informal lay into, lace into, beat the living daylights out of, sail into, pitch into, let someone have it, get stuck into, paste, do over, work over, rough up, knock about/around; Brit. informal duff up, have a go at; N. Amer. informal beat up on, light into.

□ **set one's heart on** *Marilyn had set her heart on white satin and four bridesmaids*: **want desperately**, wish for, desire, long for, yearn for, be consumed with desire for, hanker after/for, ache for, hunger for, thirst for, lust after/for, sigh for, burn for, itch for, be dying for, die for.

□ **set out 1** *he set out early next morning*: **start**, make a start, start out, set off, set forth, begin one's journey; depart, leave, get under way, sally forth, embark, set sail; informal hit the road; archaic set forward. ▷ANTONYMS arrive.

2 *well, you've achieved what you set out to achieve*: **aim**, intend, mean, seek, have in mind; hope, aspire, want; set one's sights on.

□ **set something out 1** *the gifts were set out on trestle tables*: **arrange**, lay out, spread out, array, dispose, present, put out; display, exhibit. **2** *they set out a series of guidelines*: **present**, describe, set forth, detail; **explain**, expound, delineate; state, declare, announce; submit, offer, put forward, advance, propose, propound.

□ **set someone up 1** *his father set him up in business*: **establish**; finance, fund, back, subsidize. **2** *after my operation the doctor recommended a cruise to set me up again*: **restore to health**, make better, make stronger, strengthen, build up, invigorate, energize, fortify; rehabilitate. **3** informal *suppose Lorton had set him up for Newley's murder?* **falsely incriminate**, frame, fabricate evidence against, trap, entrap; Brit. informal fit up.

□ **set something up 1** *a monument to her memory was set up in Gloucester Cathedral*: **erect**, put up, construct, build, raise, elevate; **place**, put (in position). **2** *she set up the business with a £4,000 bank loan*: **establish**, start, begin, get going, initiate, institute, found, create, bring into being, inaugurate, lay the foundations of. **3** *I'll ask my secretary to set up a meeting with him*: **arrange**, organize, fix, fix up, fix a time for, schedule, timetable, sort out, line up.

set[2] **noun 1** *an envelope containing a set of colour postcards*: **group**, **collection**, series, complete series; assortment, selection, compendium, batch, number, combination, grouping, assemblage; arrangement, array.

2 *it was a fashionable haunt of the literary set*: **clique**, coterie, circle, crowd, group, lot, crew, band, company, pack, ring, camp, fraternity, school, clan, faction, party, sect, league, cabal; informal gang, bunch.

3 *a chemistry set*: **kit**, **apparatus**, equipment, rig, outfit.

4 *a set of cutlery*: **canteen**; box, case.

5 *a set of Coalport china*: **service**.

6 *although he's in the bottom set, he's doing quite well*: **class**, form, study group; **stream**, band.

7 *something in the set of his shoulders suggested that he was uneasy*: **posture**, position, cast, attitude; bearing, carriage.

8 *her husband's brow furrowed as he noted the set of her face*: **expression**, look; determined expression, fixed look.

9 *sponsorship was necessary to defray the costs of building and painting the set*: **stage furniture**, stage set, stage setting, setting, scenery, backdrop, wings, flats; French mise en scène.

set[3] **adjective 1** *we have set procedures for dealing with such matters | a staid man with a set routine*: **fixed**, established, hard and fast, determined, predetermined, arranged, prearranged, prescribed, scheduled, specified, defined, appointed, decided, agreed; unvarying, unchanging, invariable, unvaried, unchanged, rigid, inflexible, cast-iron, strict, settled, predictable; routine, standard, customary, regular, normal, usual, habitual, accustomed, wonted, conventional.

▷ANTONYMS changing, variable, unpredictable.

2 *she had set ideas about bringing up children*: **inflexible**, rigid, fixed, firm, deep-rooted, deep-seated, ingrained, entrenched, unchangeable.

▷ANTONYMS flexible.

3 *he had a number of set speeches for such occasions*: **stock**, standard, routine, rehearsed, well worn, formulaic, unspontaneous, unoriginal, derivative, conventional, stale, hackneyed, stereotyped, overused.

▷ANTONYMS fresh, original.

4 *I was all set for the evening | get set for a long, cold winter*: **ready**, prepared, organized, equipped, primed; informal fit, geared up, psyched up, up for it.

▷ANTONYMS unprepared.

5 *he's set on marrying that girl*: **determined to**, intent on, bent on, hell bent on, committed to the idea of, resolved to, resolute about, insistent about/on.

▷ANTONYMS uncertain.

6 *last night you were dead* ***set against*** *the idea*: **opposed to**, averse to, hostile to, in opposition to, resistant to, antipathetic to, unsympathetic to; informal anti.

setback noun *Alexander was faced with one setback after another and most people would have given up*: **problem**, difficulty, hitch, complication, upset, disappointment, misfortune, mishap, piece of bad luck, unfortunate development, reversal, reverse, reverse of fortune; blow, body blow, knock; stumbling block, hindrance, impediment, obstruction; delay, hold-up, check; informal glitch, hiccup, (double) whammy, kick in the teeth, knock-back, one in the eye; archaic foil.

▷ANTONYMS breakthrough, step forward.

S

settee noun **sofa**, couch, divan, chaise longue, love seat, chesterfield; sofa bed; Brit. put-you-up; French canapé, tête-à-tête; N. Amer. davenport, day bed, studio couch, sectional; rare squab.

setting noun **1** *a converted barn in a beautiful rural setting | it was an unlikely setting for a marriage proposal*: **surroundings**, position, situation, environment, background, backdrop, milieu, environs; habitat; spot, place, location, locale, site, scene; context, frame; area, neighbourhood, region, district; French mise en scène; technical locus.
2 *a garnet in a heavy gold setting*: **mounting**, mount, fixture, surround.

setting up noun *the setting up of a national information centre*: **establishment**, establishing, organization, institution, creation, formation, foundation, founding, initiation, inauguration, inception, origination, constitution.
▷ANTONYMS abolition.

settle verb **1** *every effort was made to settle the dispute*: **resolve**, sort out, reach an agreement about, find a solution to, find an answer to, solve, clear up, bring to an end, fix, work out, iron out, smooth over, straighten out, deal with, put right, set right, put to rights, rectify, remedy, reconcile; informal patch up; archaic compose.
▷ANTONYMS prolong.
2 *Joyce settled their affairs in London*: **put in order**, sort out, straighten out, tidy up, order, arrange, organize, adjust, clear up, set to rights, regulate, systematize.
3 *they had not yet* **settled on** *a date for the wedding*: **decide on**, set, fix, come to a decision about, agree on, name, determine, establish, arrange, arrive at, appoint, designate, assign; confirm; choose, select, pick.
4 *she went down to the lobby to settle her bill*: **pay**, pay in full, settle up, discharge, square, clear, defray, liquidate, satisfy.
5 *the union* **settled for** *a 4.2% pay increase this autumn*: **accept**, agree to, accede to, acquiesce in, assent to; compromise on.
6 *in 1863, the family* **settled in** *London*: **make one's home**, set up home, take up residence, put down roots, establish oneself; go to live, move to, emigrate to; N. Amer. set up housekeeping in; formal become domiciled in.
▷ANTONYMS move away from.
7 *European immigrants settled much of Australia*: **colonize**, establish a colony in, occupy; people, inhabit, populate.
8 *Catherine* **settled down to** *her work*: **apply oneself to**, turn one's attention to, address oneself to, get down to, set about, set to work on, begin to tackle, attack; concentrate on, focus on, devote oneself to.
9 ***settle down****, all of you!* **calm down**, quieten down, be quiet, be still, relax.
10 *a small brandy had helped to settle her nerves*: **calm**, calm down, quieten, quiet, soothe, compose, pacify, lull, subdue, quell; sedate, tranquillize.
▷ANTONYMS agitate, disturb.
11 *he settled into an armchair*: **sit down**, seat oneself, install oneself, plant oneself, ensconce oneself, plump oneself, flump; informal park oneself, plonk oneself.
▷ANTONYMS stand up.
12 *come and read to Tom while I settle him*: **make comfortable**, tuck in, bed down.
13 *a butterfly settled on the flower*: **land**, come to rest, come down, alight, light, descend, perch.
▷ANTONYMS take off.
14 *sediment settles near the bottom of the tank*: **sink**, subside, fall, gravitate; precipitate out.
▷ANTONYMS rise.

settlement noun **1** *unions succeeded in reaching a pay settlement*: **agreement**, deal, arrangement, resolution, accommodation, bargain, understanding, pact; compromise; decision, conclusion, determination.
2 *the settlement of the dispute*: **resolution**, sorting out, settling, solution, solving, bringing to an end, working out, smoothing over, reconciliation; successful arbitration/mediation/brokering; informal patching up; archaic composition.
3 *a remote frontier settlement*: **community**, colony, outpost, encampment; trading post, post; village, hamlet; kibbutz, commune; American Indian pueblo, rancheria; S. African werf; NZ kainga; Archaeology terramare; historical plantation.
4 *the settlement of the area*: **colonization**, settling, populating, peopling; historical plantation.
5 *the settlement of his debt*: **payment**, discharge, defrayal, liquidation, settling, settling up, clearance, clearing, satisfaction; archaic reckoning.

settler noun **colonist**, colonizer, frontiersman, frontierswoman, pioneer; immigrant, newcomer; Brit. incomer; N. Amer. historical homesteader, habitant, redemptioner, squatter.

set-to noun informal *when he came on the scene, there was a right old set-to*. See **argument** (sense 1).

set-up noun **1** *their current telecommunications set-up*: **system**, structure, organization, arrangement, framework, format, layout, configuration, composition; situation, conditions, circumstances.
2 *a set-up called Film International*: **organization**, group, body, concern, agency, association, syndicate, operation, movement; company, firm; society, league, club; informal outfit.
3 informal *the whole thing was a set-up*: **trick**, trap; conspiracy; informal put-up job, frame-up, frame.

seven cardinal number **septet**, septuplets; Poetry heptameter, septenarius; technical heptad; rare sevensome, septenary.

> *Word links* **seven**
>
> **hept(a)-** related prefix, as in *heptathlon*
> **sept(i)-** related prefix, as in *septivalent*
> **septenary** relating to seven
> **heptagon** seven-sided figure
> **septennial** relating to seven years

sever verb **1** *the head had been completely severed from the body*: **cut off**, chop off, lop off, hack off, cleave, hew off, shear off, slice off, split; break off, tear off; divide, separate, part, detach, disconnect; amputate, dock; literary rend; archaic sunder; rare dissever.
▷ANTONYMS join, attach.
2 *she had died from a single knife wound which had severed the artery*: **cut**, cut through, rupture, split, pierce, rip, tear.
3 *neither country has expressly severed diplomatic ties*: **break off**, discontinue, suspend; bring to an end, end, put an end to, terminate, stop, cease, conclude, dissolve.
▷ANTONYMS maintain, establish, initiate.

several adjective **1** *several people arrived early*: **some**, a number of, a few, not very many, a handful of, a small group of, various, a variety of, assorted, sundry, diverse; literary divers.
▷ANTONYMS a lot, many.
2 *the two levels of government must sort out their several responsibilities*: **respective**, individual, own, particular, specific; **separate**, different, diverse, disparate, divergent, distinct, discrete; various, sundry.
▷ANTONYMS joint.

severally adverb formal *a three-person board, the members of which would be severally nominated by the company*: **separately**, individually, singly, discretely; respectively.
▷ANTONYMS jointly.

severe adjective **1** *severe shortages of basic foodstuffs | the victim sustained severe head injuries*: **acute**, very bad, serious, grave, critical, dire, drastic, grievous, extreme, dreadful, terrible, awful, frightful, appalling, sore; alarming, worrying, distressing, dangerous, perilous, life-threatening; Medicine peracute, profound; archaic or humorous parlous.
▷ANTONYMS minor, negligible.
2 *the severe storms which battered Orkney this year*: **fierce**, violent, strong, wild, powerful, forceful, intense; tempestuous, turbulent, tumultuous.
▷ANTONYMS gentle.
3 *it was an exceptionally severe winter*: **harsh**, hard, bitter, bitterly cold, cold, bleak, freezing, icy, arctic, polar, Siberian, extreme, nasty.
▷ANTONYMS mild.
4 *Maria complained of a severe headache*: **excruciating**, agonizing, violent, intense, dreadful, awful, terrible, frightful, unbearable, intolerable, unendurable; stabbing, shooting; informal splitting, thumping, pounding.
▷ANTONYMS slight.
5 *their traumatic experiences meant that the further five-mile walk would be a severe test of their remaining stamina*: **very difficult**, demanding, hard, tough, arduous, formidable, taxing, exacting, rigorous, punishing, onerous, gruelling, burdensome, heavy; back-breaking, uphill, stiff.
▷ANTONYMS easy, simple.
6 *the government's economic policies came in for severe criticism*: **harsh**, scathing, sharp, strong, fierce, ferocious, stringent, savage, blistering, searing, stinging, scorching, devastating, mordant, trenchant, caustic, biting, cutting, withering, rigorous, unsparing; smart, sound.
▷ANTONYMS mild.
7 *a campaign against severe tax penalties*: **extortionate**, excessive, unreasonable, inordinate, outrageous, sky-high, harsh, stiff; **punitive**, punishing, penal; Brit. swingeing.
8 *army service offered poor living conditions, low pay, and severe discipline | Ceauşescu singled out this minority for especially severe treatment*: **strict**, stern, rigorous, harsh, hard, inflexible, uncompromising, inexorable, implacable, rigid, unbending, relentless, unrelenting, unyielding, merciless, pitiless, ruthless, draconian, oppressive, repressive, punitive, rough, nasty; tyrannical, iron-fisted, iron-handed, brutal, inhuman, cruel, savage; Austral./NZ informal solid.
▷ANTONYMS lenient, lax.
9 *his severe expression softened*: **stern**, dour, grim, grim-faced, forbidding, disapproving, tight-lipped, unsmiling, unfriendly, sombre, grave, sober, serious, austere, stiff, flinty, stony, steely, glowering, frowning; cold, aloof, frosty, icy, frigid.
▷ANTONYMS genial, friendly.
10 *the severe style of early Classical Greek architecture*: **plain**, simple, restrained, unadorned, undecorated, unembellished, unornamented, austere, chaste, spare, stark, ultra-plain, unfussy, without frills, spartan, ascetic, monastic, puritanical; functional, clinical, uncluttered; classic.
▷ANTONYMS ornate, fancy.

severely adverb **1** *Picher was severely injured*: **very badly**, extremely badly, seriously, gravely, critically, grievously, acutely, sorely; dangerously; fatally.
▷ANTONYMS slightly.
2 *he was severely criticized by the chairman*: **sharply**, roundly, soundly, fiercely, scathingly, savagely; informal like a ton of bricks.
▷ANTONYMS mildly.
3 *the view that rapists should be treated more severely was repeated in the editorial*: **harshly**, strictly, sternly, rigorously, relentlessly, mercilessly, pitilessly, oppressively, repressively, roughly, sharply, with an iron hand, with a rod of iron; **brutally**, cruelly, savagely.
▷ANTONYMS leniently.
4 *she looked severely at Harriet*: **sternly**, grimly, dourly, disapprovingly, sombrely, gravely, seriously, stiffly; coolly, coldly, frostily, icily.
▷ANTONYMS genially.
5 *a stout woman dressed severely in black*: **plainly**, simply, austerely, without adornment, without frills, starkly, spartanly, monastically; classically.

severity noun **1** *the severity of the disease*: **acuteness**, seriousness, gravity, graveness, severeness, grievousness, extremity; danger, dangerousness.
2 *global warming was blamed for an increase in the severity of storms | the pain increased in severity*: **strength**, **intensity**, ferocity, fierceness, violence, power, powerfulness, force, forcefulness.
3 *the severity of the winter may have killed the grass*: **harshness**, severeness, cold, coldness, bleakness, extremity.
▷ANTONYMS mildness.
4 *the Emperor was often on bad terms with his younger brothers, whom he treated with great severity | the severity of the sentence caused surprise*: **harshness**, strictness, hardness, sternness, toughness, rigorousness, rigour, stringency, inflexibility, relentlessness, pitilessness, ruthlessness; **brutality**, inhumanity, cruelty, savagery.
▷ANTONYMS leniency.
5 *Robyn flinched at the severity of his expression*: **sternness**, dourness, grimness, sombreness, unfriendliness, graveness, gravity, soberness, seriousness, austereness, austerity, stiffness, flintiness, stoniness, steeliness; coldness, frostiness, iciness, frigidity.
▷ANTONYMS geniality.
6 *a white, filmy gown that contrasted with the black severity of her own attire*: **plainness**, simplicity, restraint, lack of adornment, lack of decoration, lack of ornament, lack of embellishment, austerity, spareness, starkness; functionalism.
▷ANTONYMS elaboration.

sew verb *her aunt sewed the last seams of the tunic | I sewed black armbands to their coats*: **stitch**, machine stitch; embroider; seam, hem, tack, baste; attach, fasten.
▷ANTONYMS unpick, remove.
□ **sew something up 1** *no sooner was one tear sewn up than another appeared*: **darn**, mend, repair, patch; archaic clout.
▷ANTONYMS rip, tear.
2 informal *last week, the company sewed up a deal with IBM*: **secure**, clinch, pull off, bring off, settle, conclude, bring to a successful conclusion, complete, finalize, tie up, seal, set the seal on; informal swing.
▷ANTONYMS lose.

sewing noun **needlework**, needlecraft, fancy-work, stitching.

> *Word links* **sewing**
>
> **sutorial**, **sutorian** relating to sewing

S

sex noun **1** *a group of teenage boys sat around the table talking about sex*: **sexual intercourse**, intercourse, lovemaking, making love, sex act, sexual relations, sexual/vaginal/anal penetration; mating; informal nooky; Brit. informal bonking, rumpy pumpy, a bit of the other, how's your father; S. African informal pata-pata; vulgar slang screwing, fucking; Brit. vulgar slang shagging; formal coitus, coition, copulation; archaic fornication, carnal knowledge, congress, commerce.
2 *you can learn how to teach your children about sex*: **the facts of life**, sexual reproduction, reproduction; informal the birds and the bees.
3 *adults of both sexes*: **gender**.
□ **have sex (with) have sexual intercourse (with)**, **make love (to)**, sleep with/together, go to bed with/together; mate (with); seduce, rape, ravish; informal do it, do the business, go all the way, make whoopee, have one's way with, bed, know in the biblical sense, tumble; Brit. informal bonk, get one's oats; N. Amer. informal boff, get it on (with); euphemistic be intimate (with); vulgar slang fuck, screw, bang, lay, get one's leg over, shaft, dick, frig, do, have, hump, poke, shtup, dip one's wick, ride, service, tup; Brit. vulgar slang have it away (with), have it off (with), shag, knob, get one's end away, knock someone off, give someone one, roger, grind, stuff; Scottish vulgar slang podger; N. Amer. vulgar slang ball, jump, jump someone's bones, bone, pork, diddle, nail; Austral./NZ vulgar slang root; formal copulate (with); archaic fornicate (with), possess, lie with/together, couple (with), swive, know.

> *Word links* **sex**
>
> **carnal** relating to sex
> **erotomania**, **nymphomania** obsession with sex
> **erotophobia** fear of sex

sex appeal noun *she just oozes sex appeal*: **sexiness**, seductiveness, sexual attractiveness, desirability, sensuality, sexuality; magnetism, charisma; informal it, oomph, SA.

sexism noun *he admitted that the company had been accused of sexism*: **chauvinism**, **discrimination**, prejudice, bias; machismo, laddishness.

sexless adjective *she's very thin, so thin that she looks almost sexless*: **asexual**, non-sexual, neuter; **androgynous**, epicene; technical parthenogenetic.

sexual adjective **1** *the sexual organs*: **reproductive**, genital, sex, procreative.
2 *sexual pleasure | sexual activity*: **carnal**, erotic, coital, venereal; sensual.
3 *she's so sexual, don't you think?* **sexy**, sexually attractive, seductive, desirable, alluring, inviting, sensual, sultry, slinky, provocative, tempting, tantalizing; nubile, voluptuous, shapely, luscious, lush; feline; informal fanciable, beddable, come-hither, come-to-bed; Brit. informal **fit**; N. Amer. informal foxy, cute; Austral. informal spunky.

sexual intercourse noun See **sex**.

sexuality noun **1** *there was no doubting the fact that this woman had a powerful sexuality*: **sensuality**, sexiness, seductiveness, desirability; **sexual appetite**, sexual instincts, sexual urges, passion, desire, lust; eroticism, physicality.
2 *I've always been pretty open about my sexuality*: **sexual orientation**, orientation, sexual preference, leaning, persuasion; heterosexuality, homosexuality, lesbianism, bisexuality; transsexuality, omnisexuality, pansexuality.
3 *sexuality within holy matrimony was only justified as a necessary part of reproduction*: **sexual activity**, reproductive activity, procreation, sexual intercourse, sex, intercourse, sexual relations.

sexy adjective **1** *she's so sexy | her dark, sexy eyes*: **sexually attractive**, seductive, desirable, alluring, inviting, sensual, sultry, slinky, provocative, tempting, tantalizing; nubile, voluptuous, shapely, luscious, lush; feline; bedroom; flirtatious, coquettish; informal fanciable, beddable, come-hither, come-to-bed; Brit. informal fit; N. Amer. informal foxy, cute, bootylicious; Austral. informal spunky; vulgar slang fuck-me.
▷ANTONYMS undesirable.
2 *a TV show featuring sexy home videos*: **erotic**, arousing, exciting, stimulating, hot; **sexually explicit**, titillating, suggestive, racy, risqué, provocative, spicy, juicy, adult, X-rated; rude, coarse, smutty, pornographic, vulgar, crude, lewd, lubricious; informal raunchy, steamy, naughty, horny, porno, blue, skin; Brit. informal saucy, fruity; N. Amer. informal gamy.
▷ANTONYMS family.
3 *neither of them was feeling sexy*: **aroused**, sexually excited, amorous, lustful, passionate; informal horny, hot, turned on, sexed up; Brit. informal randy; N. Amer. informal squirrelly; rare concupiscent.
4 *sales promotion is fast becoming an area that product managers see as sexy*: **exciting**, stimulating, interesting, appealing, intriguing; fashionable; informal trendy.
▷ANTONYMS dull, boring.

shabby adjective **1** *a shabby little bar in Paddington*: **run down**, down at heel, scruffy, uncared-for, neglected, dilapidated, in disrepair, ramshackle, tumbledown; **dingy**, seedy, slummy, insalubrious, squalid, sordid, mean, wretched, miserable; informal crummy, scuzzy, tacky, grungy, shambly, beat-up; Brit. informal grotty; N. Amer. informal shacky.
▷ANTONYMS smart, upmarket.
2 *an old lady in a shabby grey coat*: **scruffy**, well worn, worn, old, worn out, threadbare, moth-eaten, mangy, ragged, frayed, tattered, battered, decrepit, having seen better days, falling apart at the seams; faded, dowdy; dirty, grubby; informal tatty, ratty, the worse for wear; N. Amer. informal raggedy, raggedy-ass; Austral. informal warby; rare out at elbows.
▷ANTONYMS new, in good condition.
3 *it's pretty hard to come to terms with Angela's shabby treatment of Rick*: **contemptible**, despicable, dishonourable, disreputable, discreditable, mean, mean-spirited, base, low, dirty, shameful, sorry, ignoble, unfair, unworthy, ungenerous, unkind, ungentlemanly, cheap, shoddy, unpleasant, nasty; informal rotten, low-down, hateful; Brit. informal beastly; vulgar slang shitty; archaic scurvy.
▷ANTONYMS decent, honourable.

shack noun **hut**, shanty, cabin, log cabin, lean-to, shed; hovel; Scottish bothy, shieling, shiel; Canadian tilt; S. African hok; Austral. gunyah, mia-mia, humpy; NZ whare; American Indian hogan, wickiup; in Brazil favela; N. Amer. archaic shebang.
▶ **verb**
□ **shack up with** informal *he's been shacking up with a girl for months*: **cohabit**, live with, live together, share a house; informal, dated live in sin, live over the brush.

shackle verb **1** *the prisoner was shackled to the heavy steel chair in the centre of the room*: **chain**, fetter, manacle; secure, tie (up), bind, tether, hobble;

put in chains, put/clap in irons, handcuff; archaic gyve.
▷ANTONYMS free.
2 *investigative journalists could soon be shackled by a new European directive on data protection*: **restrain**, restrict, limit, constrain; hamper, hinder, impede, obstruct, handicap, hamstring, encumber, inhibit, check, curb, tie down; tie someone's hands, cramp someone's style; rare trammel.
▷ANTONYMS give someone free rein.

shackles plural noun 1 *the men filed through their shackles and made a desperate bid for freedom*: **chains**, fetters, irons, leg irons, manacles, handcuffs; bonds, tethers, ropes, restraints; informal cuffs, bracelets; archaic darbies, gyves, bilboes.
2 *the shackles of bureaucracy*: **restrictions**, trammels, restraints, constraints, straitjacket; impediments, hindrances, obstacles, barriers, encumbrances, obstructions, checks, curbs; ball and chain.

shade noun 1 *they sat in the shade of a large oak tree*: **shadow**, shadiness, shadows; coolness, cool; shelter, cover.
▷ANTONYMS light, glare.
2 *light rain began falling and* ***the shades of evening*** *drew on*: **darkness**, gathering darkness, dimness, dusk, semi-darkness, twilight; gloom, gloominess, murkiness, murk; literary gloaming.
▷ANTONYMS sunlight, daylight.
3 *fabrics in autumnal shades | various shades of blue*: **colour**, hue; **tone**, tint, tinge; intensity.
4 *a word with many shades of meaning*: **nuance**, gradation, modulation, shading, degree, difference, variation, variety; nicety, subtlety; undertone, overtone.
5 *there was* ***a shade*** *of wistfulness in his tone | her skirt was* ***a shade*** *too short*: **a little**, a bit, a trace, a touch, a dash, a modicum, a soupçon, a suspicion, a hint, a suggestion, a tinge, a smack; slightly, rather, somewhat; informal a tad, a smidgen.
6 (**shades**) *the film is about a celebrity being stalked by an obsessed man—shades of 'The Bodyguard'*: **echoes**, a reminder, memories, intimations, suggestions, hints.
7 *she saw a crouching figure silhouetted against the window shade*: **blind**, curtain, venetian blind; **screen**, shield, cover, covering, protection; awning, canopy.
8 informal *he was wearing shades and a string vest*: **sunglasses**, dark glasses; Austral. informal sunnies; trademark Polaroids, Raybans.
9 literary *he confronted the shade of his lost love*: **ghost**, spectre, phantom, apparition, spirit, wraith, phantasm, shadow; Scottish & Irish bodach; informal spook; literary revenant, wight; rare manes, eidolon.
□ **put someone/something in the shade** *stunts that put his previous daredevilry in the shade*: **surpass**, outshine, outclass, overshadow, eclipse, exceed, excel, transcend, cap, top, outstrip, outdo, put to shame, make look pale by comparison, be better than, beat, outplay, outperform, upstage, dwarf; informal run rings around, be head and shoulders above, be a cut above, leave standing; archaic outrival, outvie.
▸ verb 1 *vines shaded a garden filled with fountains and citrus trees*: **cast a shadow over**, shadow, shut out the light from, block off the light to; darken, dim; shelter, cover, screen.
2 *the shaded area of the diagram | she* ***shaded in*** *the outline of a chimney*: **darken**, colour in, pencil in, block in, fill in; cross-hatch.
3 *the sky shaded from turquoise to night blue | at times, self-consciousness can shade into actual fear*: **change gradually**, transmute, turn, go, become; **merge**, blend.

shadow noun 1 *a dim night light cast her shadow against the closed double doors*: **silhouette**, outline, shape, contour, profile; penumbra, umbra.
2 *the north side of the cathedral was deep in shadow | a stranger slowly approached from the shadows*: **shade**, shadowiness, darkness, gathering darkness, dimness, semi-darkness, twilight; gloom, gloominess, murkiness, murk, obscurity; literary gloaming; rare tenebrosity, umbrage.
3 *for years, unemployment has cast a dark shadow over the area | the shadow of war fell across Europe*: **cloud**, black cloud, pall; gloom, gloominess, blight; threat.
4 *she knew without any shadow of doubt that he was lying*: **slightest bit**, trace, scrap, shred, crumb, particle, ounce, atom, iota, scintilla, jot, whit, grain, tittle, jot or tittle; Irish stim; informal smidgen, smidge, tad; archaic scantling, scruple.
5 *a shadow of a smile creased her mouth*: **trace**, hint, suggestion, suspicion, ghost, glimmer, flicker.
6 *he's a shadow of his former self | the band were a pale shadow of the Beatles*: **inferior version**, poor imitation, apology, travesty; ghost, spectre, phantom; remnant.
7 *he had become her shadow, staying constantly by her side*: **constant companion**, inseparable companion, alter ego, second self, Siamese twin; close friend, bosom friend, intimate; informal bosom pal; rare fidus Achates.
8 *no matter where Johnson went, his shadow stayed with him*: **follower**; informal **tail**.
▸ verb 1 *the market is shadowed by St Margaret's church*: **overshadow**, cast a shadow over, envelop in shadow, shade, block off the light to; darken, dim.
2 *he had been up all night shadowing a team of poachers*: **follow**, trail, track, dog someone's footsteps, keep watch on; stalk, pursue, hunt; informal tail, keep tabs on, keep a tab on.

Word links **shadow**

sciophobia fear of shadows

shadowy adjective 1 *a long shadowy corridor | the shadowy garden*: **dark**, dim, gloomy, murky; shady, shaded, sunless; literary tenebrous, crepuscular; rare tenebrious, umbrageous, umbrose, umbriferous, umbrous, caliginous, Cimmerian.
▷ANTONYMS bright, sunny.
2 *a shadowy figure appeared through the mist*: **indistinct**, hazy, indefinite, lacking definition, out of focus, vague, nebulous, ill-defined, faint, blurred, blurry, unclear, indistinguishable, unrecognizable, indeterminate, unsubstantial; ghostly, phantom, spectral, wraithlike; rare nebulose.
▷ANTONYMS distinct, clear.

shady adjective 1 *a shady corner of the garden*: **shaded**, shadowy, dark, dim, sunless; sheltered, screened, covered, protected, shrouded; leafy, arboured; cool; literary bosky, bowery, tenebrous; rare umbrageous, umbriferous, Cimmerian.
▷ANTONYMS bright, sunny.
2 *shady deals*: **suspicious**, suspect, questionable, dubious, doubtful, of dubious character, disreputable, untrustworthy, dishonest, dishonourable, devious, slippery, tricky, underhand, unscrupulous, irregular, potentially illegal, unethical; N. Amer. snide; informal shifty, fishy, murky; Brit. informal dodgy; Austral./NZ informal shonky.
▷ANTONYMS reputable, honest.

shaft noun 1 *a wooden shaft about a yard long | the shaft of a golf club*: **pole**, stick, rod, staff, shank, upright; **handle**, hilt, butt, stock, stem; historical pikestaff, thill; rare helve.
2 *the shaft of a feather*: **quill**; technical rachis.
3 *shafts of early sunlight*: **ray**, beam, gleam, streak, pencil, finger, bar; literary lance.
4 *shafts of criticism*: **cutting remark**, barb, gibe, taunt, sting; informal dig.
5 *the main shaft was impassable | a ventilation shaft*: **mineshaft**, tunnel, passage, pit, adit, downcast, upcast; **borehole**, bore; duct, air shaft, well, light well, flue, vent; rare winze.

shaggy adjective *his shaggy beard | a shaggy wolfhound lay in front of the fire*: **hairy**, hirsute, bushy, thick, woolly, fleecy, long-haired, unshorn, uncut, shock-headed; tangled, tousled, unkempt, dishevelled, untidy, matted; rare crinose, hispid.
▷ANTONYMS sleek; close-cropped.

shake verb 1 *the whole building seemed to shake*: **vibrate**, tremble, quiver, quake, shiver, shudder, judder, jiggle, wobble, rock, sway, swing, roll, oscillate; convulse.
2 *I was shaking with fear*: **tremble**, quiver, quake, shiver, shudder, shake like a leaf; rare quave.
3 *she stood in the hall and shook her umbrella | I shook the sauce bottle*: **jiggle**, joggle, wave from side to side; agitate; informal waggle.
4 *he shook his stick at the old man*: **brandish**, wave, flourish, swing, wield; raise.
5 *it was the crazed look in his eyes that really shook her*: **upset**, distress, disturb, unsettle, perturb, disconcert, discompose, disquiet, unnerve, trouble, take aback, throw off balance, agitate, fluster; shock, alarm, frighten, scare, worry, dismay; informal rattle, get to, do someone's head in; N. Amer. informal mess with someone's head.
▷ANTONYMS soothe, reassure.
6 *the escalation in costs is certain to shake the confidence of private investors*: **weaken**, undermine, damage, impair, harm, hurt, injure, have a bad effect on; reduce, diminish, decrease, lessen.
▷ANTONYMS strengthen.
□ **shake a leg** informal **hurry up**, get a move on, be quick, speed up; informal get cracking, get moving, make it snappy, step on it, step on the gas, rattle one's dags; Brit. informal get one's skates on, stir one's stumps; N. Amer. informal get a wiggle on; S. African informal put foot; dated make haste.
□ **shake someone off** *Manville thought he had shaken off his pursuer*: **get away from**, escape, elude, give someone the slip, leave behind, throw off, throw off the scent, dodge, lose, get rid of, rid oneself of; outdistance, outstrip; Brit. informal get shot of.
□ **shake something off** *he has shaken off his back trouble | Simon has finally shaken off her pernicious influence*: **recover from**, get over, get better after; get rid of, free oneself from, lose; Brit. informal get shot of, see the back of; N. Amer. informal shuck off.
□ **shake someone/something up 1** *the accident really shook him up.* See **shake** (sense 5 of the verb). **2** *he presented plans to shake up the legal profession*: **reorganize**, restructure, revolutionize, alter dramatically, make far-reaching changes in, transform, reform, overhaul, update; reshuffle.
3 *I hired you because I thought you might shake the place up a bit*: **put some life into**, enliven, put some spark into, liven up, stir up, rouse, get going.
▸ noun 1 *she removed his wet coat and gave it a shake*: **jiggle**, joggle, jerk; informal waggle.
2 *a shake of his thick forefinger*: **flourish**, brandish, wave.
3 (**the shakes**) *I had a bad case of the shakes | I wouldn't go in there, it gives me the shakes*: **a fit of trembling**, delirium tremens, tremors; the horrors;

informal the DTs, the jitters, the willies, the heebie-jeebies, the jim-jams, the jumps, the yips; Austral. rhyming slang Joe Blakes.
4 informal *police switchboards were flooded with requests for information on the shake*: **earthquake**, earth tremor, aftershock, convulsion; informal quake; N. Amer. informal tremblor.
□ **in two shakes (of a lamb's tail)** informal *I'll be back in two shakes*: **in a moment**, in a second, in a flash, in a minute, shortly, any minute, any minute now, in a short time, (very) soon, in an instant, in the twinkling of an eye, in (less than) no time, in no time at all, before you know it, before long; N. Amer. momentarily; informal in a jiffy, before you can say Jack Robinson, in the blink of an eye, in a blink, in the wink of an eye, in a wink, before you can say knife; Brit. informal in a tick, in two ticks, in a mo; N. Amer. informal in a snap.
□ **no great shakes** informal *it's no great shakes as a piece of cinema*: **not very good**, undistinguished, unmemorable, forgettable, unexceptional, uninspired, uninspiring, uninteresting, indifferent, unimpressive, lacklustre; informal nothing to write home about, nothing to get excited about, nothing special, not up to much; NZ informal half-pie.
▷ANTONYMS exceptional.

> *Choose the right word* **shake, tremble, shiver, quiver, quake**
>
> **Shake** is the most general term (*buildings shook in Sacramento*): the others denote shaking of various degrees of intensity, and when used of a person, indicate more often than *shake* that it results from weakness or emotion. *Shake* and *quiver* are the only ones that can be used transitively (*a severe earthquake shook the area*).
>
> To **tremble** is to shake uncontrollably with slight, rapidly repeated movements. Trembling is especially associated with fear or weakness (*the boy spoke cockily, but his voice trembled | she held the letter with trembling hands*).
>
> **Shiver** denotes a similar slight and uncontrollable shaking, but, unlike *tremble*, it can be used only of bodies and other physical objects, not, for example, of voices (*the spectators shivered and drew their coats firmly about them*). Shivering is most commonly caused by cold or horror (*Katherine shivered and drew her coat more tightly round her | she shivered at the threat in his quiet voice*).
>
> To **quiver** is to move lightly and rapidly and often results from strong emotion (*Anthea's eyelids quivered | 'Don't you love me any more?' I asked, quivering my bottom lip*).
>
> To **quake** is to shake violently (*the rumbling vibrations set the whole valley quaking*). Applied to people, *quake* indicates extreme fear and is typically used figuratively (*those words should have them quaking in their boots*).

shake-up noun *the company's boardroom shake-up followed a £365m pre-tax loss*: **reorganization**, restructuring, rearrangement, change, reshuffle, regrouping, redistribution, overhaul, revamp, makeover; upheaval; N. Amer. informal shakedown.

shaky adjective **1** *she walked over to him on shaky legs*: **trembling**, shaking, tremulous, quivering, quivery, unsteady, wobbly, weak; quavery; informal trembly.
▷ANTONYMS steady.
2 *he levered himself to his feet and took a few shaky steps*: **faltering**, unsteady, uncertain, tentative, wobbly, wobbling, tottering, tottery, teetering, doddering, doddery, shaking, staggering.
3 *I still feel a bit shaky*: **faint**, dizzy, light-headed, giddy; weak, weak-kneed, weak at the knees, wobbly, quivery, unsteady, groggy, muzzy; informal trembly, all of a tremble, all of a quiver, with rubbery legs, woozy; rare vertiginous.
4 *a room furnished with two iron beds and a shaky table*: **unsteady**, unstable, wobbly, precarious, rocky, rickety, flimsy, frail; decrepit, ramshackle, dilapidated, on its last legs; informal teetery; Brit. informal wonky, dicky.
▷ANTONYMS stable.
5 *the evidence against him is distinctly shaky*: **unreliable**, untrustworthy, questionable, dubious, doubtful, tenuous, suspect, unsubstantial, flimsy, weak, nebulous, unsound, undependable, unsupported, unsubstantiated, ungrounded, unfounded; informal iffy; Brit. informal dodgy.
▷ANTONYMS sound, strong.

shallow adjective *a shallow analysis of contemporary society*: **superficial**, facile, glib, simplistic, oversimplified, schematic, slight, flimsy, insubstantial, lightweight, empty, trivial, trifling; surface, skin-deep; frivolous, foolish, silly, unintelligent, unthinking, unscholarly, ignorant.
▷ANTONYMS profound, serious; in-depth.

sham noun **1** *all the tenderness he had shown her had been nothing more than a sham*: **pretence**, fake, act, fiction, simulation, imposture, fraud, feint, lie, counterfeit; putting on an act, faking, feigning, play-acting, dissembling; humbug; informal a put-up job.
▷ANTONYMS the real McCoy, the genuine article.
2 *he was a sham, totally unqualified for his job as a senior doctor*: **charlatan**, fake, fraud, impostor, pretender, masquerader, dissembler, wolf in sheep's clothing; quack, mountebank; informal phoney.
▶ **adjective** *she didn't want any more pretend closeness, any more sham togetherness*: **fake**, pretended, feigned, simulated, false, artificial, bogus, synthetic, spurious, ersatz, insincere, not genuine, manufactured, contrived, affected, plastic, make-believe, fictitious; imitation, mock, counterfeit, fraudulent; informal pretend, put-on, phoney, pseudo; Brit. informal, dated cod.
▷ANTONYMS real, genuine.
▶ **verb 1** *she shams indifference*: **feign**, fake, pretend, put on, make a pretence of, simulate, counterfeit, affect, imitate.
2 *was he ill or was he shamming?* **pretend**, fake, dissemble; malinger; informal put it on; Brit. informal swing the lead.

shaman noun **medicine man**, medicine woman, healer; witch doctor; North American Indian **powwow, pawaw**; South American Indian **peai, peaiman**; in Hawaii **kahuna**; in Greenland **angekok**; in Malaysia & Indonesia **pawang**; in SE Asia **dukun**.

shamble verb *he shambled off down the corridor*: **shuffle**, lumber, totter, dodder, stumble; scuff/drag one's feet; hobble, limp.
▷ANTONYMS run, sprint, bound.

shambles noun **1** *he called an emergency summit of ED leaders to sort out the shambles*: **chaos**, mess, muddle, confusion, disorder, disarray, disorganization, havoc, mare's nest; Brit. informal dog's dinner, dog's breakfast.
2 *the room was a shambles*: **complete mess**, pigsty; N. Amer. **pigpen**; informal disaster area; Brit. informal tip.

shambling adjective *a big, shambling bear of a man*: **ungainly**, lumbering, shuffling, awkward, clumsy, uncoordinated, heavy-footed.
▷ANTONYMS dapper, neat, trim, petite.

shambolic adjective Brit. informal *he accused the party headquarters of running a shambolic campaign*: **chaotic**, disorganized, muddled, confused, in (total) disarray, at sixes and sevens, unsystematic, haphazard, hit-or-miss, scrappy, fragmented, inefficient; informal all over the place; Brit. informal all over the shop; N. Amer. informal all over the map, all over the lot.
▷ANTONYMS efficient, organized.

shame noun **1** *Lily walked in front of him, her face scarlet with shame*: **humiliation**, mortification, chagrin, ignominy, loss of face, shamefacedness, embarrassment, indignity, abashment, discomfort, discomfiture, discomposure.
▷ANTONYMS pride.
2 *I felt a pang of shame at telling Alice a lie*: **guilt**, remorse, contrition, compunction.
▷ANTONYMS indifference.
3 *the incident had brought shame on the family*: **disgrace**, dishonour, discredit, degradation, ignominy, disrepute, ill-repute, infamy, scandal, odium, opprobrium, obloquy, condemnation, contempt; rare disesteem, reprobation, derogation.
▷ANTONYMS honour, glory.
4 *it's a shame she never married*: **pity**, misfortune, crying shame, cause for regret, source of regret, sad thing, unfortunate thing; bad luck, ill luck; informal bummer, crime, sin.
5 *this situation is a* **shame to** *our country*: **discredit to**, disgrace to, stain on, blemish on, blot on, blot on the escutcheon of, slur on, reproach to, bad reflection on; stigma, scandal, outrage; literary smirch on.
▷ANTONYMS credit.
□ **put someone/something to shame outshine**, outclass, overshadow, eclipse, surpass, excel, be superior to, outstrip, outdo, put in the shade, upstage, leave behind; show up, humble; informal run rings around, be head and shoulders above, leave standing, knock into a cocked hat; Brit. informal knock spots off; archaic outrival, outvie; rare put to the blush.
▷ANTONYMS not be a patch on.
▶ **verb 1** *you have shamed your family's name*: **disgrace**, dishonour, discredit, bring into disrepute, degrade, debase, defame, stigmatize, taint, sully, tarnish, besmirch, stain, blacken, drag through the mud/mire, give a bad name to, put in a bad light.
▷ANTONYMS honour, do credit to, enhance the reputation of.
2 *he had been shamed in public*: **humiliate**, mortify, make someone feel ashamed, chagrin, embarrass, abash, chasten, humble, put someone in their place, take down a peg or two, cut down to size, show up; N. Amer. informal make someone eat crow.

> *Choose the right word* **shame, ignominy, disgrace, dishonour**
>
> See **disgrace**.

shamefaced adjective *Giles looked shamefaced*: **ashamed**, abashed, sheepish, guilty, conscience-stricken, guilt-ridden, contrite, sorry, remorseful, repentant, penitent, hangdog, regretful, rueful, apologetic; **embarrassed**, mortified, red-faced, chagrined, humiliated, uncomfortable, discomfited; in sackcloth and ashes; informal with one's tail between one's legs; rare compunctious.
▷ANTONYMS proud, unrepentant.

shameful adjective **1** *no one can justify such shameful behaviour*: **disgraceful**, deplorable, despicable, contemptible, dishonourable, discreditable, reprehensible, base, mean, low, blameworthy, unworthy,

ignoble, shabby, inglorious, infamous, unprincipled, shocking, scandalous, outrageous, abominable, atrocious, appalling, disgusting, vile, odious, monstrous, heinous, unspeakable, loathsome, sordid, bad, wicked, immoral, nefarious, indefensible, inexcusable, unforgivable; informal low-down, hateful; archaic knavish, dastardly, scurvy; rare egregious, flagitious.
▷ANTONYMS admirable, honourable, laudable.
2 *are you saying that my father had a shameful secret of some sort?*: **embarrassing**, mortifying, shaming, humiliating, degrading, ignominious; informal blush-making.
▷ANTONYMS praiseworthy.

shameless adjective **1** *O'Brien marvelled at his shameless self-promotion*: **flagrant**, blatant, barefaced, overt, brazen, brash, audacious, outrageous, undisguised, unconcealed, transparent; unabashed, unashamed, without shame, unembarrassed, unblushing, unrepentant; archaic arrant.
▷ANTONYMS reticent, diffident.
2 *I suppose you think me shameless for telling you I want you so much*: **brazen**, bold, forward, immodest, indecorous, wanton, abandoned.
▷ANTONYMS demure, modest.

shanty noun **shack**, hut, cabin, lean-to, shed; hovel; Scottish **bothy**, **shieling**, **shiel**; Canadian **tilt**; S. African **hok**; in Brazil **favela**; N. Amer. dated **shebang**.

shape noun **1** *the sweater was too big for her but did not disguise the shape of her body | the rectangular shape of the dining table*: **form**, appearance, configuration, formation, structure; figure, build, physique, body; contours, lines, outline, silhouette, profile; design, format; cut, pattern, mould.
2 *a woman was drowned in the lough and now haunts the area in the shape of a fox*: **guise**, likeness, semblance, form, appearance, image, aspect.
3 *you're in pretty good shape, Donald*: **condition**, state, health, state of health, trim, fettle, order, repair; Brit. informal **nick**.
4 *dressmaking shapes*: **pattern**, model.
□ **take shape** *a glorious idea began to take shape in her brain*: **become clear**, become definite, become tangible, crystallize, gel, come together, fall into place.
▸ verb **1** *an alloy of two metals that could be shaped into knives and tools*: **form**, fashion, make, create, mould, model, cast, frame, sculpt, sculpture, block; carve, cut, hew, whittle.
2 *current attitudes were shaped by Bowlby's influential report to the World Health Organization*: **determine**, create, produce, form, fashion, mould, define, develop, build, construct; influence, affect.
□ **shape up 1** *the 20-year-old is shaping up nicely*: **improve**, show improvement, get better, make headway, make progress, progress, show promise; develop, take shape, come on, come along, turn out, go. **2** *simple ideas to help you shape up while you're getting a tan*: **get fit**, get into shape, tone up; slim, lose weight, get thinner.

> *Word links* **shape**
>
> **morpho-** related prefix, as in *morphometry*
> **-morph** related suffix, as in *polymorph, ectomorph*
> **morphology** study of the shapes of things

shapeless adjective **1** *these shapeless lumps are called sea squirts*: **formless**, amorphous, unformed, indefinite, nebulous; misshapen.
2 *Alison was wearing a shapeless grey woollen dress*: **baggy**, badly cut, sack-like, tent-like, oversized, sagging, saggy, ill-fitting, ill-proportioned, inelegant, unshapely, formless.
▷ANTONYMS tailored.

shapely adjective *Katherine's shapely figure was swathed in blue silk*: **well proportioned**, well formed, well shaped, attractive, clean-limbed; **curvaceous**, voluptuous, sexy, opulent, full-figured, Junoesque, rounded, buxom, full-bosomed; informal **curvy**; archaic **comely**; rare **sightly**, **well turned**, **gainly**.
▷ANTONYMS misshapen.

shard noun *shards of glass flew in all directions*: **piece**, fragment, bit, sliver, splinter, shiver, chip, particle, scrap; paring, shaving.

share noun *her share of the profits from the original television show*: **portion**, part, division, bit, quota, allowance, ration, allocation, allotment, lot, measure, due; percentage, commission; dividend; stake, interest, equity; helping, serving; informal **cut**, **whack**, **slice**, **piece/slice of the cake**, **piece of the action**, **rake-off**; Brit. informal **divvy**; rare **apportionment**, **quantum**, **moiety**.
▸ verb **1** *we were a real eighties couple—we shared the bills and the shopping*: **split**, divide, go halves in/with; informal **go fifty-fifty in**, **go Dutch**.
2 *they* ***shared out*** *the peanuts*: **apportion**, portion out, divide up, allocate, ration out, give out, distribute, dispense, hand out, dish out, deal out, dole out, parcel out, measure out; carve up; informal **divvy up**.
3 *a tutorial is an opportunity for a student to* ***share in*** *the learning process*: **participate in**, take part in, play a part in, have a role in, be involved in, contribute to, have a hand in, have something to do with, partake in; have a share in, have a percentage of, have a stake in.
▷ANTONYMS be excluded from.

shark noun

> *Word links* **shark**
>
> **squaloid** relating to sharks

sharp adjective **1** *you will need a very sharp knife*: **keen**, sharp-edged, razor-sharp, razor-edged; sharpened, honed, whetted; serrated, knife-like, cutting, edged; rare **acute**.
▷ANTONYMS blunt.
2 *he winced as a sharp pain shot through his left leg*: **excruciating**, agonizing, intense, violent, piercing, stabbing, shooting, stinging, severe, acute, keen, fierce, searing; exquisite.
3 *Danish Blue has a distinctively sharp taste*: **tangy**, piquant, strong; **acidic**, acid, acidy, sour, tart, vinegary, pungent, bitter; N. Amer. **acerb**; rare **acidulous**, **acetic**, **acetous**.
▷ANTONYMS mild, mellow, bland.
4 *the air still had a sharp sooty smell*: **acrid**, burning, pungent.
▷ANTONYMS sweet.
5 *Isabel couldn't repress a sharp cry of pain | a sharp crack of thunder*: **loud**, **piercing**, shrill, high-pitched, high, penetrating, harsh, strident; ear-splitting, deafening, thunderous, booming, head-splitting.
▷ANTONYMS quiet, soft.
6 *it was growing dark and a sharp wind was blowing off the sea*: **cold**, chilly, chill, brisk, keen, piercing, penetrating, biting, cutting, icy, bitter, freezing, glacial, raw, harsh; informal **nippy**; Brit. informal **parky**.
▷ANTONYMS warm, balmy.
7 *some sharp words were exchanged*: **harsh**, bitter, hard, cutting, scathing, caustic, biting, barbed, trenchant, mordant, acrimonious, acerbic, tart, acid, sarcastic, sardonic, ill-tempered, spiteful, venomous, malicious, vitriolic, vicious, hurtful, nasty, unkind, severe, cruel, wounding, abusive; curt, brusque, abrasive; N. Amer. **acerb**; informal **bitchy**, **catty**; rare **mordacious**, **acidulous**.
▷ANTONYMS kind, amicable.
8 *she was achingly aware of a sharp sense of loss*: **intense**, acute, keen, strong, bitter, fierce, searing, piercing, heartfelt, very great, overpowering.
9 *her face was thin and her nose sharp | each leaf ends in a sharp point*: **pointed**, tapering, tapered, needle-like, spiky; informal **pointy**; technical **acicular**, **lanceolate**, **acuminate**, **subulate**, **mucronate**, **aculeate**; rare **cuspidate**, **cusped**, **conoid**.
▷ANTONYMS rounded.
10 *the lens brings the rays of all the different colours into sharp focus | there was a sharp difference of opinion between them*: **distinct**, clear-cut, clear, well defined, well focused, crisp; stark; obvious, marked, definite, pronounced, evident, manifest.
▷ANTONYMS blurred, indistinct.
11 *a sharp increase in interest rates*: **sudden**, abrupt, rapid; steep, precipitous, precipitate.
▷ANTONYMS gradual.
12 *a large articulated lorry was turning the sharp corner*: **hairpin**, tight, angular.
13 *Moore set off at a sharp pace*: **brisk**, rapid, quick, fast, smart, swift, speedy, vigorous, spirited, lively; informal **snappy**.
▷ANTONYMS slow.
14 *the edge of the gully had a very sharp drop*: **steep**, sheer, abrupt, precipitous, vertical, vertiginous; rare **acclivitous**, **declivitous**.
▷ANTONYMS gentle, gradual.
15 *his sharp eyes had seen a figure moving in the darkness*: **keen**, perceptive, observant, acute, sharp-sighted, beady, hawklike.
▷ANTONYMS weak.
16 *his mind was as sharp as it had ever been | she was sharp and witty*: **perceptive**, discerning, percipient, perspicacious, penetrative, piercing, penetrating, discriminating, sensitive, incisive, keen, keen-witted, acute, sharp-witted, quick, quick-witted, clever, shrewd, astute, intelligent, intuitive, bright, agile, nimble, nimble-witted, alert, quick off the mark, ready, apt, fine, finely honed, rapier-like, probing, searching, insightful, knowing; informal **smart**, **on the ball**, **quick on the uptake**, **not missing a trick**, **savvy**, **with all one's wits about one**, **downy**; Brit. informal **suss**, **knowing how many beans make five**; Scottish & N. English informal **pawky**; N. Amer. informal **cute**, **heads-up**; rare **long-headed**, **argute**.
▷ANTONYMS slow, dull, stupid.
17 *it sounds as if he's a sharp operator*: **clever**, shrewd, canny, smart; **cunning**, wily, crafty, artful, guileful, unscrupulous, dishonest; informal **slick**; Brit. informal **fly**.
▷ANTONYMS naive, ingenuous.
18 *they were greeted by a young man in a sharp suit*: **smart**, stylish, fashionable, chic, modish, elegant, spruce; informal **trendy**, **cool**, **snazzy**, **classy**, **flash**, **snappy**, **natty**, **nifty**, **dressy**; N. Amer. informal **fly**, **spiffy**, **sassy**, **kicky**; archaic **trig**.
▷ANTONYMS shabby, scruffy.
□ **sharp practice** *spin has become associated with sharp practice and associated in the public mind with sleaze*: **trickery**, chicanery, deception, deceit, deceitfulness, duplicity, dishonesty, unscrupulousness, underhandedness, subterfuge, fraud, fraudulence, legerdemain, sophistry,

S

skulduggery, swindling, cheating, duping, hoodwinking; deviousness, guile, intrigue, craft, craftiness, artfulness, slyness, wiles; misleading talk; informal crookedness, monkey business, funny business, hanky-panky, shenanigans, flimflam; Brit. informal jiggery-pokery; N. Amer. informal monkeyshines; Irish informal codology; archaic management, knavery.
▸ **adverb 1** *I'll pick you up at nine o'clock sharp*: **precisely**, exactly, on the dot; **promptly**, prompt, punctually, dead on, on the stroke of ...; N. Amer. informal on the button, on the nose; Austral./NZ informal on the knocker.
▷ANTONYMS approximately, roughly.
2 *the world stock market hiccup of October 1987 pulled people up sharp*: **abruptly**, suddenly, sharply, all of a sudden, unexpectedly, without warning.

sharpen verb **1** *first sharpen the carving knife*: **make sharp/sharper**, hone, whet, strop, grind, file; rare edge, acuminate.
▷ANTONYMS blunt.
2 *the world's top players are* ***sharpening up*** *their grass court skills before Wimbledon*: **improve**, brush up, polish up, better, enhance; hone, refine, fine-tune, perfect.

sharp-eyed adjective *a sharp-eyed witness contacted the police with details of a car spotted nearby*: **observant**, perceptive, sharp-sighted, eagle-eyed, with eyes like a hawk, hawk-eyed, keen-eyed, lynx-eyed, gimlet-eyed; watchful, vigilant, alert, on the alert, on the lookout, on the qui vive, with one's eyes/open/peeled/skinned; informal beady-eyed; rare Argus-eyed.
▷ANTONYMS unobservant.

sharpness noun **1** *the pain came again, with a sharpness that made her cry out*: **intensity**, severity, acuteness, keenness, violence, fierceness, ferocity.
2 *she felt thankful for her jacket's protection against the sharpness of the wind*: **chilliness**, chill, briskness, coldness, keenness, iciness, bitterness, harshness.
▷ANTONYMS warmth, balminess.
3 *he winced slightly at the sharpness in her voice*: **harshness**, asperity, bitterness, acerbity, acidity, tartness, edge.
▷ANTONYMS kindness, friendliness.
4 *focusing needs to be done carefully to obtain maximum sharpness*: **clarity**, definition, precision, crispness.
▷ANTONYMS blurriness.
5 *the sharpness of his mind*: **acuity**, acuteness, keenness, sharp-wittedness, quick-wittedness, perceptiveness, discernment, percipience, penetration, discrimination, cleverness, shrewdness, astuteness, intelligence, intuitiveness, agility, nimbleness; informal savvy.
▷ANTONYMS dullness.

shatter verb **1** *one of the shots had shattered his windscreen | the wine spilt and the glasses shattered*: **smash**, smash to smithereens, break, break into pieces, burst, blow out; explode, implode; splinter, crack, fracture, fragment, disintegrate; informal bust; rare shiver.
2 *the announcement shattered hopes of an early release for the foreign hostages*: **destroy**, wreck, ruin, dash, crush, devastate, demolish, wreak havoc with, blast, blight, wipe out, overturn, torpedo, scotch; burst someone's bubble; informal put the kibosh on, banjax, do for, blow a hole in, nix, put paid to, queer; Brit. informal scupper, dish; archaic bring to naught.
3 *everyone was shattered by the news*: **devastate**, shock, stun, daze, dumbfound, traumatize, crush, overwhelm, greatly upset, distress; informal knock for six, knock sideways, knock the stuffing out of.
▷ANTONYMS please, excite.

shattered adjective **1** *we couldn't believe how bad the reviews were—Michael was absolutely shattered*: **devastated**, shocked, stunned, dazed, staggered, dumbfounded, traumatized, crushed, overwhelmed; heartbroken, broken-hearted; informal knocked/hit for six, knocked sideways.
▷ANTONYMS pleased, thrilled.
2 informal *I feel too shattered to do more than crawl into bed*. See **exhausted**.

S

> *Word toolkit* **shattered**
>
> See **cracked**.

shattering adjective *the death of her elder son from tuberculosis was a shattering blow*: **devastating**, crushing, staggering, severe, savage, overwhelming, traumatic, very great, dreadful, terrible, awful.

shave verb **1** *he had* ***shaved off*** *his beard | his hair was closely shaved at the sides*: **cut off**, snip off; crop, trim, barber, tonsure.
2 *the electric version can* ***shave off*** *excess wood quickly and easily*: **plane off**, pare off, shear off, whittle off, scrape off.
3 *shave Parmesan over the top*: **grate**, shred.
4 *he fought the seat at the last two elections, shaving the majority to 2,000 in 1992*: **reduce**, cut, bring down, lessen, decrease, make smaller, prune, pare down, shrink, slim down, whittle down.
5 *Dad said the shortcut would* ***shave*** *at least 20 miles* ***off*** *the trip*: **take off**, remove from, lop off, cut off.
6 *his shot shaved the post*: **touch lightly**, brush, brush against, graze, glance off, kiss.

sheaf noun *he sat down at the table with a sheaf of papers*: **bundle**, bunch, stack, pile, heap, mass, armful, collection; informal load, wodge.

sheath noun **1** *he slid the gleaming sword out of its sheath*: **scabbard**, case.
2 *an optical fibre has a core and a cladding encased in a tough protective plastic sheath*: **covering**, cover, case, casing, envelope, sleeve, wrapper; technical tunica, capsule, fascia, neurilemma, epimysium, perimysium, perineurium, sarcolemma; coleoptile, coleorhiza, ochrea.
3 *a barrier method of contraception such as a sheath*: **condom**; contraceptive; N. Amer. prophylactic; Brit. trademark Durex; Brit. informal johnny, something for the weekend; N. Amer. informal rubber, safe, safety, skin; Brit. informal, dated French letter, Frenchy; dated protective.

shed[1] noun *guinea pigs and rabbits should be kept in sheds or garages*: **hut**, lean-to, outhouse, outbuilding, shack; potting shed, woodshed; cattle shed, cow-house; Brit. lock-up; N. Amer. barn, smokehouse; Austral./NZ woolshed; N. English shippon; S. English linhay; archaic hovel.

shed[2] verb **1** *tall beech trees shed their leaves over a disused tennis court*: **let fall**, let drop, drop; scatter, spill, shower.
2 *the caterpillar has to shed its skin four or five times to allow it to grow*: **slough off**, cast, cast off, moult; technical exuviate.
▷ANTONYMS grow.
3 *we shed our jackets*: **take off**, remove, pull off, peel off, shrug off, discard, divest oneself of, doff, fling off, fling aside, climb out of, slip out of; undo, unfasten, unbutton, unzip.
▷ANTONYMS don, put on.
4 *too much blood has been shed*: **spill**, pour forth, let flow, discharge.
5 *the two firms are each to shed ten workers*: **make redundant**, dismiss, let go, discharge, give someone their notice, get rid of, discard; informal sack, give someone the sack, fire, give someone their cards, give someone their marching orders, send packing, give someone the boot, give someone the bullet, give someone the push, give someone the (old) heave-ho, boot out.
▷ANTONYMS hire, take on.
6 *the revolutionaries must shed their populist illusions*: **discard**, get rid of, dispose of, do away with, drop, abandon, throw out, jettison, lose, scrap, cast aside/off, dump, have done with, reject, repudiate; informal ditch, junk, get shut of; Brit. informal get shot of, see the back of; N. Amer. shuck off.
▷ANTONYMS adopt, keep.
7 *the moon shed a watery light on the scene*: **cast**, send forth, send out, radiate, give out, diffuse, disperse, scatter.
□ **shed tears** *a number of the pupils shed tears as they read the many messages of sympathy*: **weep**, cry, sob, blubber; lament, grieve, mourn, bewail, wail; Scottish greet; informal blub, boohoo; literary pule.

sheen noun *her hair, once so dark and lustrous, had lost its sheen*: **shine**, lustre, gleam, patina, gloss, shininess, burnish, polish, shimmer, glimmer, sparkle, brightness, brilliance, radiance.
▷ANTONYMS dullness.

sheep noun ram, ewe, lamb, wether, bellwether; Brit. tup; Austral. informal jumbuck, woolly.

> *Word links* **sheep**
>
> **ram** male
> **ewe** female
> **lamb** young
> **ovine** relating to sheep
> **flock, herd** collective noun

sheepish adjective *Sam looked sheepish and apologetic*: **embarrassed**, uncomfortable, hangdog, self-conscious; shamefaced, ashamed, abashed, mortified, chastened, chagrined; remorseful, contrite, rueful, regretful, penitent, repentant; shy, bashful, diffident.
▷ANTONYMS unabashed.

sheer[1] adjective **1** *he whistled at the sheer audacity of the plan*: **utter**, complete, absolute, total, pure, perfect, downright, out-and-out, thorough, thoroughgoing, through and through, consummate, patent, surpassing, veritable, unqualified, unmitigated, unalloyed, unadulterated, unmixed; stark, rank; plain, simple, mere; Brit. informal proper; Austral./NZ informal fair; archaic arrant; rare right-down.
2 *there was a terrifying sheer drop to the sea*: **precipitous**, very steep, perpendicular, vertical, abrupt, bluff, sharp, vertiginous; rare acclivitous, declivitous, scarped.
▷ANTONYMS gradual.
3 *a dress of sheer white silk chiffon*: **diaphanous**, gauzy, filmy, floaty, very thin, translucent, transparent, see-through, gossamer, gossamer-like, chiffony, insubstantial, ultra-fine, fine.
▷ANTONYMS thick, heavy.

sheer[2] verb **1** *the boat* ***sheered off*** *to beach further along the coast*: **swerve**, swing, veer, slew, skew, change course, drift, yaw.
▷ANTONYMS stay on course.
2 *her mind* ***sheered away from*** *images she didn't want to dwell on*: **turn away**, flinch, recoil, shy away; refuse to contemplate, avoid, evade.
▷ANTONYMS face up to.

sheet noun **1** *she changed the sheets and tidied the room*: **(sheets) bed linen**, linen, bedclothes.
2 *the lake was covered with a sheet of ice*: **layer**, stratum; covering, blanket, coating, coat, overlay, lamina, lamination, veneer, film, skin, membrane.
3 *a sheet of glass*: **pane**, panel, piece, plate; slab.
4 *she ripped out the paper and put in a fresh sheet*: **piece of paper**, leaf, page, folio.
5 *the glistening sheet of water*: **expanse**, area, stretch, sweep.

shelf noun **1** *she put Frank's card on the shelf*: **ledge**, bracket, sill, rack; bookshelf, mantelshelf, mantelpiece; shelving; in a church or monastery predella, retable.
2 *the waters above the shelf*: **sandbank**, sandbar, bank, bar, reef, shoal.
□ **on the shelf** *the tangled love life of a 30-year old woman who fears she will be left on the shelf*: **unmarried**, single, without a partner/spouse, without a husband/wife, unattached, on one's own; lonely, unloved, neglected; archaic sole.
▷ANTONYMS married.

shell noun **1** *the shell of a crab*: **carapace**, outside, exterior; armour.
2 *peanuts roasted in their shells*: **pod**, casing, case, husk, hull; integument, cover, covering; N. Amer. shuck.
3 *the sound of shells passing overhead*: **projectile**, bomb; grenade; bullet, cartridge, shot; rare trajectile.
4 *the metal shell of the car*: **framework**, frame, chassis, skeleton, basic structure; hull, exterior.
▸ verb **1** *they were shelling peas*: **extract**; husk, hull, pod; N. Amer. shuck.
2 *rebel artillery began to shell the city*: **bombard**, fire on, open fire on, shoot at, attack, pound, bomb, blitz, strafe; archaic cannonade.
□ **shell something out** informal *they shelled out £3.3 million for the England striker*. See **pay**.

> *Word links* **shell**
>
> **conch(o)-** related prefix, as in *conchometer*
> **conchology** study or collection of shells

shellfish noun **crustacean**, bivalve, mollusc.

shelter noun **1** *the plants provide shelter for animals*: **protection**, shield, cover, a roof, screen, shade; safety, security, defence, refuge, sanctuary, asylum, safe keeping, safeguarding.
▷ANTONYMS danger, exposure.
2 *she runs a shelter for battered cats*: **sanctuary**, place of shelter, refuge, accommodation, housing, home, place of safety, haven, safe haven, sanctum, safe house; harbour, port in a storm, ark; retreat, bolt-hole, foxhole, hiding place, hideaway, hideout, fastness; Spanish querencia.
▸ verb **1** *the hut sheltered him from the cold wind*: **protect**, keep safe, shield, cover, screen, shade, keep from harm, afford protection to, provide protection for, save, safeguard, wrap, cover for, preserve, conserve, defend, cushion, secure, guard, hedge; inoculate, insulate.
▷ANTONYMS endanger, expose.
2 *the anchorage where convoys sheltered in bad weather*: **take shelter**, take refuge, seek protection, seek refuge, seek sanctuary, take cover; informal hole up.

sheltered adjective **1** *a sheltered stretch of water lying between the coast and the peninsula*: **protected**, screened, shielded, covered, calm; shady, shaded, cool; cosy, snug, warm.
▷ANTONYMS exposed.
2 *their daughter had led a sheltered life*: **secluded**, withdrawn, isolated, protected, immune, cloistered, unworldly, sequestered, retired, reclusive; privileged, secure, safe, quiet, cosy, comfortable.

shelve verb *plans to reopen the school have been shelved*: **put to one side**, lay aside, pigeonhole, stay, stand over, keep in abeyance, suspend, mothball; **postpone**, put off, delay, defer, put back, hold over/off, carry over, reschedule, do later, adjourn; put off the evil day/hour; **abandon**, drop, abolish, withdraw, throw out, do away with, give up, take away, stop, put an end to, cancel, eliminate, cut, jettison; N. Amer. put over, table, lay on the table, take a rain check on; N. Amer. Law continue; informal put on ice, put on the back burner, put in cold storage, axe, ditch, dump, junk, chuck in; rare remit, respite.
▷ANTONYMS carry out, execute, implement; revive.

shepherd noun *he worked as a shepherd*: **herdsman**, herdswoman, shepherd boy, shepherdess; N. Amer. sheepman.
▸ verb *police shepherded thousands of workers away from the area*: **guide**, conduct, usher, convoy, marshal, steer, herd, lead, take, escort, accompany, walk; show, see, attend, chaperone.

shield noun **1** *using his shield to fend off blows*: **buckler**, target; in Australia hielaman; Heraldry escutcheon; Mythology aegis; archaic targe.
2 *a protective coating of grease provides a shield against abrasive dirt*: **protection**, guard, defence, cover, screen, shade, safety, security, shelter, safeguard, support, bulwark, protector.
▸ verb *he pulled his cap lower to shield his eyes from the glare* | *these people have been completely shielded from economic forces*: **protect**, keep safe, cover, screen, shade, keep from harm, afford protection to, provide protection for, save, safeguard, wrap, preserve, conserve, defend, cushion, secure, guard, inoculate, insulate.
▷ANTONYMS expose, endanger.

shift verb **1** *Lawton had already shifted some chairs to form a barricade*: **move**, carry, transfer, transport, convey, take, bring, bear, lug, cart, haul, fetch, switch, move around, transpose, relocate, reposition, rearrange, displace.
2 *her foot began to tingle and she shifted her position* | *they cannot be trusted; they shift their position from day to day*: **change**, alter, adjust, make adjustments to, adapt, amend, recast, vary, modify, revise, reverse, retract, do a U-turn on; eat one's words; Brit. do an about-turn on.
▷ANTONYMS keep, stick to.
3 *the cargo has shifted*: **move**, slide, slip, move around, be displaced.
4 *the wind has shifted*: **veer**, alter, change, back, vary, fluctuate, turn, swing, change direction.
5 Brit. *a small rubber brush with large prongs really shifts the dirt*: **get rid of**, take out, get off, remove, budge, lift, expunge.
□ **shift for oneself** *the least and the most able being left to shift for themselves*: **cope (on one's own)**, manage (by oneself), survive, manage without help/assistance, make it on one's own, fend for oneself, take care of oneself, make do, get by/along, scrape by/along, muddle through/along; make ends meet, keep the wolf from the door, stand on one's own two feet, keep one's head above water; informal paddle one's own canoe, make out.
▸ noun **1** *the shift of people into south of the country has slowed substantially*: **movement**, move, shifting, transference, transport, conveyance, switch, transposition; **relocation**, repositioning, rearrangement.
2 *a shift in public opinion*: **change**, alteration, adjustment, adaptation, amendment, recasting, variation, modification, revision, reversal, retraction, sea change, U-turn; Brit. about-turn.
3 *they worked three shifts—morning, afternoon, and evening*: **work period**, stint, spell of work, stretch.
4 *the night shift goes home at 8 a.m.* **group**, crew, gang, team, squad, patrol.
5 *he had to resort to dubious shifts to make enough money to live on*: **stratagem**, scheme, subterfuge, expedient, dodge, trick, ruse, wile, artifice, deception, strategy, device, plan.

shiftless adjective *he thought the whole family shiftless and dishonest*: **lazy**, idle, indolent, slothful, lethargic, lackadaisical; spiritless, apathetic, improvident, aimless, worthless, feckless, good-for-nothing, ne'er-do-well; inefficient, incompetent, inept, unambitious, unenterprising.
▷ANTONYMS enthusiastic, enterprising.

shifty adjective informal *he had a shifty look about him*: **devious**, evasive, slippery, duplicitous, false, deceitful, underhand, untrustworthy, double-dealing, two-faced, dishonest, shady, wily, crafty, cunning, tricky, sneaky, furtive, treacherous, artful, sly, scheming, contriving; N. Amer. snide, snidey; informal foxy, iffy; Austral./NZ informal shonky.
▷ANTONYMS honest, open, trustworthy.

shilly-shally verb *the government shilly-shallied about the matter*: **dither**, be indecisive/irresolute, be undecided, be uncertain, be unsure, be doubtful, vacillate, waver, teeter, hesitate, oscillate, fluctuate, falter, drag one's feet; Brit. haver, hum and haw; Scottish swither; informal dilly-dally, blow hot and cold, sit on the fence.

shimmer verb *the glow of the lanterns shimmered on the water*: **glint**, glisten, flicker, twinkle, sparkle, flash, scintillate, flare, glare, gleam, glow, glimmer, glitter, dance, blink, wink; rare coruscate, fulgurate.
▸ noun *the wet streets reflected the shimmer of lights from never-ending traffic*: **glint**, glistening, flicker, twinkle, sparkle, flash, scintillation, flare, glare, gleam, glow, glimmer, lustre, glitter, dancing, blinking, winking; rare coruscation, fulguration.

shin verb *he* **shinned up** *a tree* | *she* **shinned down** *the rope*: **climb (up/down)**, clamber up/down, scramble up/down, scrabble up/down, swarm up/down, shoot up/down, go up/down; mount, ascend, scale, claw one's way up; descend, slide down, drop down; N. Amer. shinny.

shine verb **1** *the sun shone through the window*: **emit light**, give off light, beam, radiate, gleam, glow, glint, glimmer, sparkle, twinkle, flicker, glitter, glisten, shimmer, flash, dazzle, flare, glare, fluoresce; literary glister; rare coruscate, fulgurate, effulge, luminesce, incandesce, phosphoresce.
2 *she would even shine his shoes for him*: **polish**, burnish, buff, wax, gloss, brighten, brush, smooth, rub up.
3 *they shone at university*: **excel**, be outstanding, be brilliant, be excellent, be very good, be successful, be expert, stand out, be pre-eminent.
▸ noun **1** *he flinched at the sight of the ravaged face now caught in the shine of the moon*: **light**, brightness, gleam, glow, glint, glimmer, sparkle, twinkle, flicker, glitter, glisten, shimmer, flash, dazzle, beam, flare, glare, radiance, illumination, luminescence, luminosity, incandescence, phosphorescence, fluorescence; rare refulgence, lambency, effulgence, fulguration.
2 *linseed oil helps restore the shine to a dull surface*: **polish**, burnish, gleam, gloss, lustre, sheen, patina.

shining adjective **1** *a shining expanse of water*: **gleaming**, bright, illuminated, lit, lighted, ablaze, brilliant, lustrous, glowing, glinting, sparkling, twinkling, flickering, glittering, glistening, shimmering,

flashing, dazzling, glaring, luminous, luminescent, incandescent, phosphorescent, fluorescent; literary glistering, irradiant, lucent, lucid, lambent; rare effulgent, refulgent, coruscating, fulgurating.
▷ANTONYMS dark.
2 *she had an eager, shining face*: **glowing**, beaming, radiant, blooming, healthy, happy.
▷ANTONYMS gloomy.
3 *a new folding chair made of shining chromium tubes*: **shiny**, bright, polished, burnished, gleaming, glossy, glassy, satiny, sheeny, lustrous, smooth; rare nitid.
▷ANTONYMS matt.
□ **a shining example** *a shining example of British enterprise*: **paragon**, model, epitome, archetype, ideal, exemplar, nonpareil, paradigm, embodiment, personification, quintessence, standard, prototype, apotheosis, the crème de la crème, the beau idéal, acme, jewel, gem, flower, angel, treasure, an outstanding example, a perfect example of its kind; informal one in a million, the bee's knees, something else, the tops; archaic a nonsuch.
▷ANTONYMS poor example.

shiny adjective *a shiny red mackintosh*: **glossy**, glassy, bright, polished, burnished, gleaming, satiny, sheeny, lustrous, smooth; rare nitid.
▷ANTONYMS matt.

ship noun *a ship's hull*: **vessel**, craft, boat.

> *Word links* **ship**
>
> **marine**, **maritime**, **nautical**, **naval** relating to ships

shipshape adjective *volunteers will shovel out dirt, grass, and weeds to get the village looking shipshape for summer*: **neat and tidy**, orderly, well ordered, in (good) order, well kept, spick and span, in apple-pie order, as neat as a new pin, immaculate, uncluttered, straight, trim, spruce; spotless, as fresh as paint; Brit. dated informal shipshape and Bristol fashion; archaic tricksy.
▷ANTONYMS disorderly, untidy.

shirk verb **1** *she was brave and would not shirk any task*: **evade**, dodge, avoid, get out of, sidestep, shuffle off, run away from, shrink from, shun, slide out of, play truant from, skip, miss, not attend; **neglect**, let slide, not attend to, pay little/no attention to, be remiss about, be lax about, leave undone, lose sight of, skimp on; informal duck, duck out of, cop out of; Brit. informal skive off, funk; N. Amer. informal cut; Austral./NZ informal duck-shove.
2 *discipline was strict and no one shirked*: **evade one's duty**, be remiss, be negligent, skulk, play truant, malinger; Brit. informal skive (off), wag, dodge the column, swing the lead, scrimshank, slack; N. Amer. informal goof off, goldbrick, play hookey; Austral./NZ informal bludge, play the wag.

shirker noun **dodger**, truant, (habitual) absentee, malingerer, layabout, loafer, idler; informal slacker, cyberslacker; Brit. informal skiver, wag, scrimshanker; Austral./NZ informal duck-shover; archaic shirk.

shiver[1] verb *she was shivering with fear*: **tremble**, quiver, shake, shudder, quaver, quake, vibrate, palpitate, flutter, convulse.
▸ noun *she gave a shiver as the door opened*: **tremble**, trembling, quiver, quivering, shake, start, shudder, shuddering, quaver, quake, vibration, tremor, palpitation, flutter, convulsion, twitch, jerk.

> *Choose the right word* **shiver, shake, tremble, quiver, quake**
>
> See **shake**.

S

shiver[2] noun *a shiver of glass*: **splinter**, sliver, fragment, chip, shard, paring, shaving, shred, smithereen, particle, bit, piece.

shivery adjective *she felt sick and shivery*: **trembling**, trembly, quivering, quivery, shaking, shaky, shuddering, shuddery, quavering, quavery, quaking; **cold**, chilly, chilled.

shoal noun *three ships ran aground on the shoal*: **sandbank**, bank, mudbank, bar, sandbar, tombolo, shallow, shelf, sands; in Latin America cay.

shock[1] noun **1** *the news of the murder came as a shock*: **blow**, upset, disturbance, source of distress, source of amazement/consternation; **surprise**, revelation, a bolt from the blue, a bolt out of the blue, thunderbolt, bombshell, rude awakening, eye-opener; informal whammy.
2 *you really gave me a shock then*: **fright**, scare, jolt, start, state of agitation/perturbation, distress, consternation, panic; informal turn.
3 *she was taken to hospital suffering from shock after the accident*: **trauma**, a state of shock, traumatism, prostration, stupor, stupefaction, collapse, breakdown.
4 *the first shock of a great earthquake*: **vibration**, shaking movement, reverberation, shake, jolt, jar, jarring, jerk; bump, impact, blow, collision, crash, clash.
▸ verb *her savage murder shocked the nation*: **appal**, horrify, scandalize, outrage, repel, revolt, disgust, nauseate, sicken, offend, give offence to, traumatize, make someone's blood run cold, distress, upset, perturb, disturb, disquiet, unsettle, discompose, agitate; stun, rock, stagger, astound, astonish, amaze, startle, surprise, dumbfound, daze, shake, shake up, jolt, set someone back on their heels, take aback, throw, unnerve, disconcert, bewilder.

shock[2] noun *a shock of red hair*: **mass**, mane, mop, thatch, head, crop, bush, cloud, frizz, fuzz, foam, curls, tangle, chaos, cascade, quiff, halo.

shocking adjective *it was the next day before they heard the shocking news*: **appalling**, horrifying, horrific, dreadful, awful, frightful, terrible, horrible, scandalous, outrageous, disgraceful, vile, abominable, ghastly, foul, monstrous, unspeakable, abhorrent, hideous, atrocious, repellent, revolting, odious, repulsive, repugnant, disgusting, nauseating, sickening, grisly, loathsome, offensive, distressing, upsetting, perturbing, disturbing, disquieting, unsettling, agitating; stunning, staggering, amazing, astonishing, startling, stupefying, overwhelming, bewildering, unnerving, surprising.
▷ANTONYMS admirable, wonderful, delightful.

shoddy adjective **1** *we're not paying good money for shoddy goods*: **poor-quality**, inferior, second-rate, third-rate, low-grade, cheap, cheapjack, tawdry, rubbishy, trashy, gimcrack, jerry-built, crude, tinny; informal tacky, tatty, junky; Brit. informal ropy, duff, rubbish, grotty.
▷ANTONYMS well made.
2 *shoddy workmanship*: **careless**, slapdash, sloppy, slipshod, scrappy, untidy, messy, hasty, hurried, negligent, cursory.
▷ANTONYMS careful.

shoemaker noun **cobbler**, bootmaker; Scottish & N. English souter; archaic cordwainer, snob, snab; rare broguer, clogger.

shoot verb **1** *he went out to shoot rabbits*: **gun down**, shoot down, mow down, hit, wound, injure, cut down, bring down; put a bullet in, pick off, bag, fell, kill; execute, put before a firing squad; informal pot, blast, pump full of lead, plug, zap; literary slay.
2 *the men began to **shoot at** the enemy*: **fire (at/on)**, open fire (at/on), aim at, snipe at, let fly (at), blaze away; bombard, shell.
3 *faster than a machine gun can shoot bullets*: **discharge**, fire, launch, let off, loose off, let fly, send forth, emit.
4 *a police car shot past*: **race**, hurry, hasten, flash, dash, dart, rush, speed, hurtle, streak, really move, spank along, whirl, whizz, go like lightning, go hell for leather, whoosh, buzz, zoom, swoop, blast, charge; stampede, gallop, chase, career, bustle, sweep, hare, fly, wing, scurry, scud, scutter; informal belt, scoot, scorch, tear, zap, zip, whip (along), get cracking, get a move on, step on it, burn rubber, go like a bat out of hell; Brit. informal bomb, bucket, shift, put one's foot down; N. Amer. informal clip, boogie, hightail, barrel, lay rubber; literary fleet; N. Amer. vulgar slang drag/tear/haul ass; archaic post, hie.
5 *some years one or other plant fails to shoot*: **sprout**, put forth shoots, put forth buds, bud, burgeon, germinate; technical pullulate.
6 *the film was shot on location in Tunisia*: **film**, photograph, take/get a photograph/photo of, take/get photographs of, take/get a picture of, take/get pictures of, take someone's picture/photo, take/get a snapshot/snap of, take, snap, capture/record on film/celluloid; make a film of, televise, video.
▸ noun *I nip off the new shoots to make the plant bush out*: **sprout**, offshoot, scion, sucker, bud, spear, runner, tendril, sprig, cutting; technical stolon, flagellum, bine, ratoon.

shop noun **1** *a shop selling all sorts of goods*: **store**, retail store, outlet, retail outlet, reseller, cash and carry; boutique, salon, parlour; establishment, emporium, department store, supermarket, hypermarket, superstore, warehouse club, warehouse, factory outlet, chain store, mall, shopping mall, shopping centre, retail centre, megastore, bargain basement, concession, market, mart, stall, stand, booth, counter, trading post; Brit. multiple (shop/store), lock-up; N. Amer. minimart, convenience store, mini-mall; informal shed; N. Amer. informal big box.
2 *he works in the machine shop*: **workshop**, workroom, plant, factory, works, manufacturing complex, industrial unit, mill, foundry, yard, garage, atelier, studio; Brit. shop floor; archaic manufactory.
▸ verb **1** *we shop twice a week | he was going to **shop for** spices in the market*: **go shopping**, do the shopping, buy what one needs/wants, buy things, go to the shops; buy, purchase, get, acquire, obtain, pick up, snap up, procure, stock up on, get in supplies of, look to buy, be in the market for.
2 Brit. informal *the police got him to shop his fellow bank raiders*: **inform on/against**, betray, sell out, tell tales on, be disloyal to, be unfaithful to, break one's promise to, break faith with, stab in the back; informal tell on, rat on, put the finger on, squeal on, stitch up, snitch on, peach on, sing about, sell down the river, blow the whistle on, do the dirty on; Brit. informal grass on, split on; N. Amer. informal rat out, finger, fink on, drop a/the dime on; Austral./NZ informal pimp on, pool, put someone's pot on.

shopkeeper noun *the shopkeeper was counting some change out on the counter*: **shop-owner**, **shop manager**, shop proprietor, retailer, dealer, seller, trader, trafficker, wholesaler, broker, salesman, saleswoman, salesperson, tradesman, distributor, agent, vendor; N. Amer. storekeeper; Brit. dated shopman.

shopper noun *supermarkets helping the shopper to make more informed choices*: **buyer**, purchaser, customer, consumer, client, patron; (**shoppers**) **clientele**, patronage, public, trade, market; Law vendee; rare emptor.

shopping centre noun *Florida's largest shopping centre has over 200 shops*: **shopping precinct**, shopping complex, (shopping) mall, (shopping) arcade, galleria, (shopping) parade; marketplace, mart, flea market, fair, bazaar, piazza; N. Amer. plaza, strip mall; Arabic souk; historical agora; archaic emporium.

shore[1] noun *his friends swam out from the shore*: **seashore**, seaside, beach, coast, coastal region, seaboard, sea coast, bank, lakeside, verge, edge, shoreline, waterside, front, shoreside, foreshore, sand, sands; technical littoral; literary strand.

> *Word links* **shore**
>
> **littoral** relating to a shore

shore[2] verb *rescue workers had to* ***shore up*** *the building*: **prop up**, hold up, bolster up, support, brace, buttress, strengthen, fortify, reinforce, underpin, truss, stay; archaic underprop.

short adjective **1** *a short piece of string*: **small**, little, tiny, minuscule; informal teeny, teeny-weeny.
▷ANTONYMS long.
2 *the problem for short people was to see over the crowd*: **small**, little, petite, tiny, squat, stocky, dumpy, stubby, elfin, dwarfish, diminutive, Lilliputian; Scottish wee; informal pint-sized, teeny, teeny-weeny, pocket-sized, knee-high to a grasshopper; Brit. informal fubsy.
▷ANTONYMS tall.
3 *there is a female redwing in the short scrubby bushes*: **low**, squat, stubby, miniature, dwarf; Scottish wee.
▷ANTONYMS tall.
4 *the 'Times' published a short report of the affair*: **concise**, brief, succinct, to the point, compact, terse, curt, summary, economical, crisp, short and sweet, pithy, epigrammatic, laconic, pointed, thumbnail, abridged, abbreviated, condensed, synoptic, compendious, summarized, contracted, curtailed, truncated.
▷ANTONYMS long, overlong, verbose.
5 *for a short time | a short look at the instruments*: **brief**, momentary, temporary, short-lived, impermanent, short-term, cursory, fleeting, passing, fugitive, flying, lightning, transitory, transient, ephemeral, evanescent, fading, quick, meteoric; rare fugacious.
6 *let's take the short route*: **direct**, straight.
▷ANTONYMS roundabout.
7 *money is a bit short at the moment | there is only a short supply of food*: **scarce**, in short supply, scant, scanty, meagre, sparse, hard to find, hard to come by, not enough, too little, insufficient, deficient, inadequate, lacking, wanting; at a premium, like gold dust, not to be had, scarcer than hen's teeth; paltry, negligible, thin; informal not to be had for love nor money; rare exiguous.
▷ANTONYMS plentiful.
8 *he was rather short with her*: **curt**, sharp, abrupt, blunt, brusque, terse, offhand, gruff, ungracious, graceless, surly, snappy, testy, tart, rude, discourteous, uncivil, impolite, ill-mannered, bad-mannered.
▷ANTONYMS patient, courteous.
9 *short pastry*: **crumbly**, crispy, crisp, brittle, friable; shortcrust; fatty.
□ **in short** *in short, then, the government is being called to account for the economic disaster*: **briefly**, to put it briefly/succinctly/concisely, in a word, in a nutshell, in a few words, in precis, in essence, to cut a long story short, to come to the point; in conclusion, summarizing, in summary, to sum up, in sum.
▷ANTONYMS in full.
□ **short of 1** *holidays or sickness may leave a ward short of nurses*: **deficient in**, lacking (in), wanting (in), in need of, low on, short on, missing, with an insufficiency of, with too few/little ...; informal strapped for, pushed for, minus. **2** *short of interning suspects without trial, there is little the security forces can do*: **apart from**, other than, in any other way than, aside from, besides, except (for), excepting, without, without going so far as, excluding, leaving out, not counting, disregarding, save (for).
▶ adverb *Iris headed for the kitchen, then stopped short*: **abruptly**, suddenly, sharply, all of a sudden, all at once, unexpectedly, without warning, out of the blue.

shortage noun *the shortage of people with adequate training*: **scarcity**, sparseness, sparsity, dearth, paucity, poverty, insufficiency, deficiency, inadequacy, famine, lack, want, meagreness, scantiness, limitedness, restrictedness, deficit, shortfall, rarity, rareness; rare exiguity.
▷ANTONYMS abundance.

shortcoming noun *he was fully aware of his own shortcomings*: **defect**, fault, flaw, imperfection, deficiency, limitation, blemish, failing, drawback, weakness, weak point, foible, fallibility, frailty, vice, infirmity.
▷ANTONYMS strength.

shorten verb **1** *you can shorten your essay without losing its balance | an invention that helped shorten the war*: **make shorter**, abbreviate, abridge, condense, precis, synopsize, contract, compress, reduce, lessen, shrink, decrease, diminish, cut, cut down, cut short, dock, trim, clip, crop, pare down, prune; **curtail**, truncate; turn up, take up.
▷ANTONYMS lengthen, extend, elongate.
2 *the days are shortening*: **get shorter**, grow shorter, grow less, contract, compress, shrink.
▷ANTONYMS lengthen.

> *Choose the right word* **shorten, abbreviate, abridge, truncate, curtail**
>
> **Shorten** is the most general term for reducing the length of duration of something (*the reforms had made progress in shortening hospital waiting lists | we are not allowed to give drugs to shorten life*).
>
> The most common thing to be **abbreviated** is a word or phrase (*Hybrid Perpetual, abbreviated to H.P.*). Something that does not last as long as was planned may be described as *abbreviated*, especially if the shortening is forced by circumstances and is seen as excessive or undesirable (*his abbreviated stay in Princeton*), and the word can also be used of clothes created shorter than usual (*tight or abbreviated shorts are unacceptable*).
>
> A text or other work that has been **abridged** has been made shorter by cutting out details while preserving the proportions or basic character of the original (*the editor reserves the right to abridge letters*).
>
> To **truncate** something is to cut off one end (*a truncated pyramid*). There is usually a sense that the item is mutilated as a result (*Tolkien found that the Old English being dished up was in a grossly truncated form*), or that something has been brought to an end too soon (*further discussion was truncated by the arrival of tea*).
>
> Something that is **curtailed** is typically restricted in scope, especially in freedom of action (*ill health probably curtailed his activities | contemporaries sought to curtail the influence of the Court*), but the word is also used for an unplanned shortening in time (*rain forced us to curtail our visit*).

short-lived adjective *this was a short-lived setback*: **brief**, short, momentary, temporary, impermanent, short-term, cursory, fleeting, passing, fugitive, flying, lightning, transitory, transient, ephemeral, evanescent, fading, quick, meteoric; rare fugacious.
▷ANTONYMS long-lived.

shortly adverb **1** *she will be with you shortly*: **soon**, directly, presently, quite soon, in a short time, in a short/little while, at any moment/minute/second, in a moment/minute/second, in less than no time (at all), in next to no time, before long, by and by; N. Amer. momentarily; S. African just now; informal pretty soon, any time/day/minute/second/moment now, before one knows it, before one can say Jack Robinson, in a jiffy, in two shakes of a lamb's tail; Brit. informal in a mo, sharpish; archaic or informal anon; literary ere long.
2 *'I know that,' he replied shortly*: **curtly**, sharply, abruptly, bluntly, brusquely, tersely, in an offhand manner, gruffly, ungraciously, gracelessly, surlily, snappily, testily, tartly, rudely, discourteously, uncivilly, impolitely.
▷ANTONYMS patiently, courteously.

short-sighted adjective **1** *a short-sighted neighbour asked me what the flowers were*: **myopic**; N. Amer. nearsighted; informal as blind as a bat; archaic purblind.
▷ANTONYMS long-sighted; normal-sighted.
2 *short-sighted critics will no doubt dismiss this film as trash*: **narrow-minded**, narrow, unimaginative, lacking foresight, improvident, unadventurous, small-minded, short-term, insular, parochial, provincial.
▷ANTONYMS far-sighted, imaginative.

short-staffed adjective *we're rather short-staffed what with Christmas and everything*: **understaffed**, short-handed, undermanned, below strength.
▷ANTONYMS overstaffed.

short-tempered adjective *she found she was short-tempered with shop assistants*: **irritable**, irascible, hot-tempered, quick-tempered, fiery, peevish, cross, crabbed, crabby, crotchety, cantankerous, impatient, grumpy, huffy, brusque, ill-tempered, bad-tempered, ill-natured, ill-humoured, touchy, volatile, testy, tetchy, snarling, waspish, prickly, crusty, peppery, bilious, liverish, dyspeptic, splenetic, choleric; informal snappish, snappy, chippy, grouchy, cranky, on a short fuse; Brit. informal narky, ratty, eggy, like a bear with a sore head; N. Amer. informal peckish, soreheaded; Austral./NZ informal snaky; informal, dated miffy.
▷ANTONYMS placid, calm, easy-going, phlegmatic.

shot[1] noun **1** *a shot rang out*: **report**, crack, bang, blast, explosion, discharge; (**shots**) gunfire.
2 *the cannon have run out of shot*: **ball**, bullet, cannonball, slug, projectile; pellets, ammunition.
3 *his partner pulled off a winning backhand shot*: **stroke**, hit, strike; kick, throw, pitch, roll, bowl, lob, fling, hurl, shot-put.
4 *Mike was an excellent shot*: **marksman**, markswoman, shooter, rifleman; rare shootist.
5 *here's a shot of us on holiday*: **photograph**, photo, snap, snapshot, picture, likeness, image, portrait, study, print, slide, transparency, negative, positive, plate, film, bromide, frame, exposure, still, proof, enprint, enlargement.
6 informal *it's nice to get a shot at steering*: **attempt**, try, effort, endeavour;

S

turn, chance, opportunity; guess; informal go, stab, crack, bash, whack; formal essay.
7 *you need typhoid and cholera shots*: **injection**, inoculation, immunization, vaccination, revaccination, booster; Medicine venepuncture; informal jab, fix, hype.
□ **a shot in the arm** informal *the improvements will provide a shot in the arm for thousands of small businesses*: **boost**, fillip, pick-me-up, tonic, stimulus, spur, push, impetus, encouragement.
▷ANTONYMS blow.
□ **a shot in the dark** *Cunliffe admitted that his figure was little more than a shot in the dark*: **guess**, random guess, wild guess, surmise, supposition, conjecture, speculation, theorizing.
□ **like a shot** informal *he would take the job like a shot*: **without hesitation**, unhesitatingly, very willingly, eagerly, enthusiastically, gladly; **immediately**, at once, right away, right now, quickly, straight away, instantly, instantaneously, directly, forthwith, promptly, without delay; informal in/like a flash, before one can say Jack Robinson, before one can say knife.
□ **not by a long shot** *he is not yet out of the woods, not by a long shot*: **by no means**, by no manner of means, not at all, in no way, not in the least, not in the slightest, not the least bit, certainly not, absolutely not, definitely not, on no account, under no circumstances; Brit. not by a long chalk; informal no way.

shot[2] adjective
□ **get shot of** Brit. informal *the group also got shot of its brewing interests*: **dispose of**, do away with, throw away, throw out, toss out, clear out, discard, scrap, remove, dispense with, lose, dump, bin, unload, jettison, dismiss, expel, eject, weed out, root out; informal get rid of, chuck (away), ditch, junk, get shut of; Brit. informal see the back of; N. Amer. informal shuck off. *shot silk*: **variegated**, mottled, watered, moiré; multicoloured, many-coloured, varicoloured; iridescent, opalescent, lustrous, shimmering.

shoulder noun
□ **give someone the cold shoulder** snub, shun, cold-shoulder, ignore, turn one's back on, cut, cut dead, look right through, rebuff, dismiss, reject, brush off, turn down, spurn, disdain, refuse, decline, repudiate, ostracize; informal give someone the brush-off, tell someone where to get off, put down, freeze out, stiff-arm; Brit. informal knock back, send to Coventry; N. Amer. informal give someone the bum's rush, give someone the brush; Austral. informal snout; informal, dated give someone the go-by.
□ **put one's shoulder to the wheel get (down) to work**, apply oneself, set to work, fall to, buckle down, get down to business, put one's hand to the plough, roll up one's sleeves, get things moving, start the ball rolling; work hard, make an effort, strive, be industrious/diligent/assiduous, exert oneself; informal give it one's best shot, get cracking, get one's finger out, get weaving, get the show on the road, get off one's backside; Brit. informal get stuck in; dated buckle to.
□ **shoulder to shoulder 1** *the regiment lined up shoulder to shoulder in three columns*: **side by side**, abreast, alongside (each other), level, beside each other, cheek by jowl. **2** *he fought off the attack on economic internationalism, shoulder to shoulder with City bankers*: **united**, together, jointly, working together, in partnership, in collaboration, in cooperation, cooperatively, side by side, arm in arm, hand in hand, in unity, in unison, in alliance, in league, in concert, concertedly, conjointly, as one.
▸ verb **1** *Britain shouldered the primary responsibility for the stability of the area*: **take on**, take on oneself, undertake, accept, assume; bear, carry, support, sustain, be responsible for.
2 *another lad shouldered him aside | he shouldered his way through the crowd*: **push**, shove, thrust, propel, jostle, elbow, force, crowd, prod, poke, nudge, knock, ram, bulldoze, sweep, bundle, hustle, hurry, rush, manhandle.

shout verb *'Help,' he shouted*: **yell**, cry, cry out, call, call out, roar, howl, bellow, bawl, call at the top of one's voice, clamour, bay, cheer, yawp, yelp, wail, squawk, shriek, scream, screech, squeal, squall, caterwaul, whoop; raise one's voice; N. Amer. informal holler; rare vociferate.
▷ANTONYMS whisper.
▸ noun *a shout of pain*: **yell**, cry, call, roar, howl, bellow, bawl, clamour, bay, cheer, yawp, yelp, wail, squawk, shriek, scream, screech, squeal, squall, caterwaul, whoop; N. Amer. informal holler; rare vociferation.
▷ANTONYMS whisper.

shove verb **1** *she shoved him back into the chair*: **push**, thrust, propel, impel; send, press, drive, plunge, stick, force, shoot, ram, barge, bump, knock, strike, hit, jolt, butt, prod, poke, nudge, elbow, shoulder; bulldoze, sweep, jostle, bundle, hustle, hurry, rush, manhandle.
2 *she shoved past him and ran off*: **push (one's way)**, force one's way, barge (one's way), elbow (one's way), shoulder one's way, muscle, bludgeon one's way, plunge, crash, bulldoze, sweep, bundle, hustle, hurry, rush.
□ **shove off** informal *shove off—I don't want you here*: **go away**, depart, leave, take off, get out, get out of my sight; go, go your way, get going, take oneself off, get moving, move off, be off, set off, set out, start out, make a start, take one's leave, decamp, duck out, take wing, walk out, walk off; be off with you!, shoo!; informal hit the road, fly, skedaddle, split, vamoose, scat, scram, make oneself scarce, be on one's way, run along, beat it, get, get lost, push off, buzz off, clear off, skip off, pop off, go (and) jump in the lake; on your bike!, go and chase yourself!; Brit. informal get along, push along, get stuffed, sling your hook, hop it, hop the twig/stick, bog off, naff off; N. Amer. informal bug off, light out, haul off, haul ass, take a powder, hit the trail, take a hike; Austral. informal nick off; Austral./NZ informal rack off; S. African informal voetsak, hamba; vulgar slang bugger off, piss off, fuck off; Brit. vulgar slang sod off; literary begone, avaunt.
▸ noun *she gave him a hefty shove*: **push**, thrust, barge, ram, bump, bang, jolt, butt, knock, prod, poke, nudge, elbow, shoulder, jostle.

shovel noun *the turf had been dug up by vandals using a pick and shovel*: **spade**, scoop; Austral./NZ banjo; archaic peel.
▸ verb *supporters tried to shovel snow off the pitch*: **scoop (up)**, spade, dig, excavate, move, shift, heap, spoon, ladle, toss.

show verb **1** *the dropped stitches can be left if they do not show*: **be visible**, be seen, be in view, manifest; appear, be revealed, be obvious.
▷ANTONYMS be invisible.
2 *the first-floor gallery shows pictures of Gandhiji in London*: **display**, **exhibit**, put on show, put on display, put on view, expose to view, unveil, present; launch, introduce, air, demonstrate, set out, set forth, arrange, array, flaunt, parade, uncover, reveal.
▷ANTONYMS conceal.
3 *it was Frank's turn to show his frustration*: **manifest**, make manifest, exhibit, reveal, convey, communicate, make known; indicate, express, proclaim, intimate, make plain, make obvious, signify, evince, evidence, disclose, betray, divulge, give away.
▷ANTONYMS suppress.
4 *I'll show you how to make a daisy chain*: **demonstrate to**, point out to, explain to, describe to, expound to; clarify, make clear, illustrate, explicate, expound, elucidate; teach, instruct someone in, give instructions in, give an idea of, tutor someone in, indoctrinate someone in.
5 *recent events show this to be true*: **prove**, demonstrate, confirm, show beyond doubt, manifest, produce/submit proof, produce/submit evidence, establish evidence, evince; witness to, give substance to, determine, demonstrate the truth of, convince someone, substantiate, corroborate, verify, establish, ratify, validate, authenticate, attest, certify, testify, document, bear out.
6 *a young woman showed them to their seats*: **escort**, accompany, take, walk, conduct, lead, usher, bow, guide, direct, steer, shepherd, attend, chaperone.
7 informal *we were waiting for them, but they never showed*: **appear**, arrive, come, get here, get there, be present, put in an appearance, make an appearance, materialize, turn up, present oneself, report, clock in, sign in; Brit. clock on; N. Amer. punch in, punch the (time) clock; informal show up.
□ **show off** informal *he was showing off, trying to make a really big impression*: **behave affectedly**, put on airs, put on an act, give oneself airs, boast, brag, crow, trumpet, gloat, glory, swagger around, swank, bluster, strut, strike an attitude, strike a pose, posture, attitudinize; draw attention to oneself, blow one's own trumpet; N. Amer. informal cop an attitude; Austral./NZ informal skite, big-note oneself.
□ **show something off** *the easel was commonly used to show off a painting*: **display**, show to advantage, exhibit, demonstrate; parade, make a show of, draw attention to, flaunt, wave, dangle, brandish, vaunt.
□ **show up 1** *modern-day swabs do show up on X-rays*: **be visible**, be obvious, be seen, be revealed, be conspicuous, stand out, catch the eye.
▷ANTONYMS be invisible. **2** informal *only two waitresses showed up for work*. See **show** (sense 7 of the verb).
□ **show someone/something up 1** *the sun showed up the faded shabbiness of the room*: **expose**, reveal, bring to light, lay bare, make visible, make obvious, manifest, highlight, pinpoint, put the spotlight on.
▷ANTONYMS conceal. **2** *they showed him up in front of his friends*: **humiliate**, humble, mortify, bring/take down, bring low, demean, expose, show in a bad light, shame, put to shame, discomfit, disgrace, discredit, downgrade, debase, degrade, devalue, dishonour, embarrass; put someone in their place, make a fool of, chasten, subdue, get the better of, have the last laugh on; abash, abase, crush, squash, quash, deflate, flatten, make someone eat humble pie; informal put down, settle someone's hash, cut down to size; N. Amer. informal make someone eat crow. ▷ANTONYMS put someone in a good light.
▸ noun **1** *a spectacular show of bluebells*: **display**, array, arrangement, exhibition, presentation, exposition, spectacle.
2 *the Paris motor show*: **exhibition**, demonstration, display, exposition, fair, presentation, extravaganza, spectacle, pageant; N. Amer. exhibit.
3 *they decided to take in a show while they were up in London*: **performance**, public performance, theatrical performance, production, staging; play, drama, film, concert, musical, piece; informal gig.
4 *she's only doing it for show*: **appearance**, display, impression, ostentation, affectation, image, window dressing.
5 *Drew made a show of looking around for firewood*: **pretence**, outward appearance, false appearance, front, false front, air, guise, semblance, false show, illusion, pose, affectation, profession, parade.
6 informal *I don't run the show*: **undertaking**, affair, operation, proceedings, enterprise, business, venture, organization, establishment.

S

showdown noun *the government was contemplating a future showdown with the miners*: **confrontation**, deciding event, clash, face-off, moment of truth, crisis.

shower noun **1** *a shower of rain*: **fall**, light fall, drizzle, flurry, sprinkling, mizzle; downpour, deluge.
2 *a shower of arrows*: **volley**, cascade, hail, rain, storm, salvo, bombardment, barrage, fusillade, broadside, cannonade.
3 *he was pleased by the shower of awards*: **avalanche**, **deluge**, rush, flood, spate, torrent, cluster, flurry, wave, outbreak, outpouring; **profusion**, abundance, plethora, superabundance, glut; large number, large quantity, mass.
▷**ANTONYMS** trickle; dearth.
▶ **verb 1** *confetti showered down on us*: **rain**, fall, drizzle, spray, mizzle, hail.
2 *she showered them with gifts*: **deluge**, flood, inundate, swamp, submerge, engulf, bury; overwhelm, saturate, glut, overload, beset, overburden, snow under.
3 *Macmillan showered political honours on his backbenchers*: **lavish**, pour, load, heap, bestow freely; give freely, give generously; waste, squander; informal blow.

showing noun **1** *another showing of the three-part series*: **presentation**, appearance, broadcast, airing, televising, staging, playing, production, demonstration, performance.
2 *on its present showing in the polls the party doesn't stand a chance*: **performance**, track record, record, results, success, achievement, conduct, reputation.

showman noun **1** *a travelling showman at a fair*: **impresario**, stage manager, publicist; ringmaster, host, compère, master of ceremonies, MC; presenter, anchorman, anchorwoman, anchorperson; N. Amer. informal emcee.
2 *he is a great talker and showman*: **entertainer**, performer, player, artist, artiste, trouper, star, virtuoso, extrovert, self-publicist, show-off.

show-off noun *he was a show-off, with a big flashy car*: **exhibitionist**, extrovert, poser, poseur, poseuse, peacock, swaggerer, egotist, bragger, braggart, boaster, self-publicist; informal pseud, trendy, swanker; N. Amer. informal blowhard; rare attitudinizer, posturer.

showy adjective *showy costume jewellery*: **ostentatious**, **conspicuous**, pretentious, obtrusive, flamboyant, gaudy, garish, brash, vulgar, loud, extravagant, fancy, ornate, affected, theatrical, overdone, over-elaborate, kitsch, tasteless; informal flash, flashy, over the top, OTT, glitzy, fancy-pants, ritzy, swanky, splashy; N. Amer. informal superfly, bling-bling; US black English dicty.
▷**ANTONYMS** discreet, restrained, plain.

shred noun **1** *her beautiful dress was torn to shreds*: **tatter**, scrap, strip, ribbon, rag, snippet, snip, remnant, fragment, sliver, splinter, chip, bit, tiny bit, piece, tiny piece, wisp.
2 *we have not a shred of evidence to go on*: **scrap**, bit, tiny amount, speck, iota, particle, ounce, whit, jot, atom, molecule, crumb, morsel, fragment, grain, drop, hint, touch, trace, suggestion, whisper, suspicion, scintilla, spot, mite, tittle, jot or tittle, modicum; Irish stim; informal smidgen, smidge.
▶ **verb** *you can use the grating blade of a food processor to shred the vegetables*: **chop finely**, cut up, tear up, rip up, grate, rub into pieces, mince, mangle, chew, macerate, grind, granulate, pulverize.

shrew noun *Matilda has the reputation of being a shrew*: **virago**, dragon, termagant, vixen, cat, fishwife, witch, hellcat, she-devil, tartar, spitfire, hag, gorgon, harridan, fury, ogress, harpy; informal battleaxe, old bag, old bat, bitch; archaic scold; rare Xanthippe.

shrewd adjective *a shrewd businessman | a shrewd career move*: **astute**, sharp-witted, sharp, acute, intelligent, clever, alert, canny, perceptive, perspicacious, observant, discriminating, sagacious, sage, wise, far-seeing, far-sighted; cunning, artful, crafty, wily, calculating, disingenuous; informal on the ball, smart, savvy; Brit. informal suss; Scottish & N. English informal pawky; N. Amer. informal heads-up; rare long-headed, sapient, argute; (**be shrewd**) have all one's wits about one.
▷**ANTONYMS** stupid, unwise; ingenuous.

shrewdly adverb *she had invested the money shrewdly*: **astutely**, acutely, intelligently, cleverly, smartly, alertly, with all one's wits about one, cannily, perceptively, perspicaciously, observantly, discriminatingly, sagaciously, sagely, wisely, far-sightedly; cunningly, artfully, craftily, wilily, calculatingly, disingenuously.
▷**ANTONYMS** unwisely.

shrewdness noun *his bombast concealed considerable political shrewdness*: **astuteness**, sharp-wittedness, sharpness, acuteness, acumen, acuity, intelligence, cleverness, smartness, alertness, wit, canniness, common sense, discernment, insight, understanding, penetration, perception, perceptiveness, perspicacity, perspicaciousness, discrimination, knowledge, sagacity, sageness; cunning, artfulness, craftiness, wiliness, calculation, calculatedness; informal nous, horse sense, savvy; rare sapience, arguteness.
▷**ANTONYMS** stupidity.

shrewish adjective *orphaned at birth, he was brought up by his shrewish sister*: **bad-tempered**, quarrelsome, nasty, mean, spiteful, sharp-tongued, scolding, nagging, peevish, catty, snappy, vindictive, aggressive; venomous, rancorous, bitchy, snide, backbiting, petulant, vixenish, cattish; complaining, grumbling, fault-finding, carping, cavilling, criticizing, captious.

shriek verb *she shrieked with laughter*: **scream**, **screech**, squeal, squawk, roar, howl, bellow, bawl, shout, yell, cry, cry out, call, call out, call at the top of one's voice, clamour, bay, cheer, yawp, yelp, squall, caterwaul, whoop, wail; raise one's voice; N. Amer. informal holler.
▷**ANTONYMS** sigh, whisper.
▶ **noun** *a shriek of laughter*: **scream**, **screech**, squeal, squawk, roar, howl, bellow, bawl, shout, yell, cry, call, clamour, bay, cheer, yawp, yelp, squall, caterwaul, whoop, wail; N. Amer. informal holler.

shrill adjective *a shrill scream rent the air*: **high-pitched**, **piercing**, high, sharp, ear-piercing, ear-splitting, air-rending, penetrating, shattering, strident, loud, strong, intrusive, screeching, shrieking, screechy, squawky.
▷**ANTONYMS** low, soft, dulcet.

shrine noun **1** *the shrine of St James*: **holy place**, temple, church, chapel, tabernacle, altar, sanctuary, sanctum; Buddhism stupa, tope; Islam dargah, marabout; Hinduism tirtha; in Tibet chorten; in ancient Rome sacrarium, nymphaeum; archaic fane; rare martyry, ciborium, feretory.
2 *Davis has turned his home into a shrine to the jockey*: **memorial**, monument, cenotaph, cairn, place dedicated to ....
3 *the abbey was built around the shrine of Saint Alban*: **tomb**, burial chamber, sepulchre, mausoleum, crypt, vault, catacomb, reliquary, charnel house; rare feretory.

shrink verb **1** *a sweater that shrank in the wash | the workforce has shrunk to less than a thousand*: **get smaller**, become/grow smaller, contract, diminish, lessen, reduce, decrease, dwindle, narrow, shorten, slim, decline, fall off, drop off, condense, deflate, shrivel, wither.
▷**ANTONYMS** expand, increase.
2 *the summer sun had shrunk and dried the wood*: **make smaller**, contract, lessen, reduce, decrease, narrow, shorten, truncate, abbreviate, condense, slim down, pare down, concentrate, abridge, compress, squeeze, deflate, shrivel, wither.
▷**ANTONYMS** expand, increase.
3 *he shrank back against the wall*: **draw back**, recoil, jump back, spring back, jerk back, pull back, start back, back away, retreat, withdraw; **flinch**, shy away, blench, start, wince, cringe, cower, quail.
4 *he doesn't **shrink from** naming names*: **recoil**, shy away, hang back, demur, flinch; **have scruples about**, scruple about, have misgivings about, have qualms about, be loath to, be reluctant to, be unwilling to, be disinclined to, be indisposed to, be sorry to, be averse to, be slow to; be chary of, fight shy of, not be in favour of, be against, be opposed to, be hesitant to, be diffident about, be bashful about, be shy about, be coy about, be ashamed to, be afraid to, hesitate to, hate to, not like to, not have the heart to, drag one's feet/heels over, waver about, vacillate about, think twice about, baulk at, quail at, mind doing something; informal boggle at; archaic disrelish something.
▷**ANTONYMS** confront, be eager to.

shrivel verb *full sun is likely to shrivel the leaves | the bark of affected trees turns black and shrivels*: **wither**, wrinkle, pucker up, shrink; wilt; **dry up**, desiccate, dehydrate, parch, frazzle, scorch, sear, burn; literary blast; rare exsiccate.
▷**ANTONYMS** plump up.

shrivelled adjective *she was clutching the remnants of the shrivelled flowers*: **withered**, dry, dried up, desiccated, dehydrated, wrinkled, puckered, wizened, faded; **parched**, frazzled, scorched, seared, burnt; literary blasted, sear; rare exsiccated.
▷**ANTONYMS** fresh, plump, juicy.

shroud noun **1** *the Turin Shroud*: **winding sheet**, grave clothes, burial clothes, cerements, chrisom.
2 *a shroud of mist | governments are cloaking the operation in a shroud of secrecy*: **covering**, cover, pall, cloak, mask, mantle, blanket, sheet, layer, overlay, envelope, cloud, veil, screen, curtain, canopy.
▶ **verb** *a sea mist shrouded the jetties*: **cover**, envelop, veil, cloak, curtain, swathe, wrap, blanket, screen, cloud, mantle, conceal, hide, disguise, mask, obscure, surround, overlay, clothe; literary enshroud.

shrub noun *this eucalyptus can be encouraged to grow as a shrub*: **bush**, woody plant; (**shrubs**) undergrowth, shrubbery.

shrug verb
□ **shrug something off** *he shrugged off suggestions that he was keen to quit politics*: **disregard**, dismiss, take no notice of, ignore, set aside, pay no heed to, forget, not trouble about, gloss over, play down, talk down, make light of, make little/nothing of, minimize, discount, diminish, downgrade, trivialize.

shudder verb *she still shuddered at the thought of him*: **shake**, shiver, tremble, quiver, quaver, vibrate, palpitate, flutter, quake, heave, convulse.
▶ **noun** *another great shudder racked his body*: **shake**, shiver, tremor, tremble, trembling, quiver, quivering, quaver, start, vibration, palpitation, flutter, convulsion, spasm, twitch, jerk.

shuffle verb **1** *they shuffled along the passage towards the headmaster's study*: **shamble**, drag one's feet, stumble, lumber; stagger, teeter, totter, dodder, reel, lurch; hobble, limp.
2 *she looked down and shuffled her feet inanely*: **scrape**, drag, scratch, grind, scuffle, scuff.
3 *he shuffled the cards and began to deal*: **mix**, mix up, mingle, intermix; shift about, rearrange, reorganize, jumble.

shun verb *he shunned publicity | everyone seemed to shun her*: **avoid**, evade, eschew, steer clear of, shy away from, fight shy of, recoil from, keep away from, keep one's distance from, give a wide berth to, have nothing to do with, leave alone, not touch; **snub**, give someone the cold shoulder, cold-shoulder, ignore, turn one's back on, cut, cut dead, look right through; **reject**, rebuff, dismiss, brush off, turn down, spurn, disdain, refuse, decline, repudiate, ostracize; informal give someone the brush-off, tell someone where to get off, put down, freeze out, stiff-arm; Brit. informal knock back, send to Coventry; N. Amer. informal give someone the bum's rush, give someone the brush; Austral. informal snout; informal, dated give someone the go-by.
▷ANTONYMS accept; seek; welcome.

shut verb *please shut the door*: **close**, draw/pull/push to, slam, fasten; put the lid on, bar, lock, latch, padlock, secure, seal; put up the shutters.
▷ANTONYMS open, unlock.
□ **shut someone/something away** *she supposes that Mrs. Tilney was shut away in her bedroom chamber*: **confine**, isolate, cloister, sequester, seclude, closet, immure.
□ **shut down** *the factory has shut down*: **cease activity**, close, close down, cease production, cease operating, come to a halt, go on strike, cease trading, collapse, fail, crash, go under, go to the wall, go bankrupt, become insolvent, go into receivership, go into liquidation, be liquidated, be wound up, be closed (down), be shut (down); informal go bust, go bump, fold, flop, go broke, go belly up.
□ **shut something down 1** *they have shut down the factory*: **close**, close down, discontinue, put into receivership, liquidate, put into liquidation.
▷ANTONYMS open, open up. **2** *the correct way to shut the machine down is to type 'exit'*: **switch off**, power down, stop, halt.
▷ANTONYMS switch on, start.
□ **shut someone/something in** *she pushed the dogs into the breakfast room and shut them in*: **confine**, enclose, impound, shut up, pen (in/up), fence in, hedge in; hurdle, rail in, coop (up), mew up, immure, box up/in, wall in/up, lock up/in, cage, imprison, intern, hold captive, incarcerate, encircle, surround, ring, encompass, hem in, close in, trap; N. Amer. corral; rare gird, compass.
□ **shut something off** *a door pivots to shut off the gallery*: **close off**, seal off, tape off, fence off, rope off, screen off, curtain off, cordon off, partition off, separate off, isolate, segregate, blockade, quarantine; seal, close, turn off, cut, stop, halt; enclose, encircle, surround.
□ **shut someone/something out 1** *he had accidentally shut me out of the house*: **lock out**, keep out, exclude, leave out, refuse entrance to, deny admittance to. ▷ANTONYMS let in.
2 *she tried to shut out those memories*: **block**, suppress, halt, stop, forget.
▷ANTONYMS call up, recall.
3 *the bamboo shut out the light as effectively as the forest canopy*: **keep out**, block out, screen, cover up, hide, conceal, veil. ▷ANTONYMS let in.
□ **shut up** informal *just shut up and listen*: **be quiet**, keep/stay quiet, be/keep/stay silent, hold one's tongue, keep one's lips sealed; **stop talking**, say no more, quieten (down), fall silent, dry up; informal keep mum, button one's lip, button it, cut the cackle, pipe down, clam up, shut it, shut your face/mouth/trap, keep your face/mouth/trap shut, belt up, put a sock in it, give it a rest; Brit. informal wrap up, wrap it up, shut your gob; N. Amer. informal save it.
▷ANTONYMS speak up.
□ **shut someone/something up 1** *I haven't shut the hens up yet*: **confine**, enclose, impound, pen (in/up), fence in, hedge in; hurdle, rail in, coop (up), mew up, box up/in, wall in/up, immure, lock up/in, cage, imprison, intern, hold captive, incarcerate, encircle, surround, ring, encompass, hem in, close in, shut in, trap; N. Amer. corral; rare gird, compass. **2** informal *that should shut them up*: **quieten (down)**, silence, hush, shush, quiet, still, gag, muzzle.

S

shutter noun *Ianthe went over to the window and flung open the shutters*: **screen**, louvre, blind, roller blind, venetian blind, curtain, shade, awning, canopy; French jalousie, persiennes.

shuttle verb **1** *minibuses shuttle between the centre and the car park*: **ply**, run, commute, alternate, come and go, go/travel back and forth, go/travel to and fro.
2 *he works as a pilot shuttling planes between a Greek island and the mainland*: **ferry**, take/run back and forth, chauffeur.

shy¹ adjective *as a teenager I was painfully shy*: **bashful**, **diffident**, timid, sheepish, reserved, reticent, introverted, retiring, self-effacing, shrinking, withdrawn, timorous, mousy, fearful, apprehensive, nervous, hesitant, reluctant, doubting, insecure, wary, suspicious, chary, unconfident, inhibited, constrained, repressed, self-conscious, embarrassed, coy, demure, abashed, modest, humble, meek.
▷ANTONYMS bold, brash, confident.
▶verb
□ **shy away from** *don't shy away from saying what you think*: **flinch**, demur, recoil, hang back; have scruples about, scruple about, have misgivings about, have qualms about, be averse to, be chary of, not be in favour of, be against, be opposed to, be diffident about, be bashful about, be shy about, fight shy of, be coy about; be loath to, scruple to, be reluctant to, be unwilling to, be disinclined to, not be in the mood to, be indisposed to, be sorry to, be slow to, be hesitant to, be ashamed to, be afraid to, hesitate to, hate to, not like to, not have the heart to, drag one's feet/heels over, waver about, vacillate about, think twice about, baulk at, quail at, mind doing something; informal be cagey about, boggle at; archaic disrelish.

> *Choose the right word* **shy, bashful, diffident, timid**
>
> A **shy** person lacks confidence and is uncertain how to behave or what to say in the presence of other people (*the British are supposed to be a staid, shy, retiring lot | I was inordinately shy of girls*). *Shy* is also used of people who try to avoid someone or something about which they feel uneasy (*people can be very shy about giving compliments | small investors remained shy of the stock market*).
>
> **Bashful** denotes a nervous reluctance to draw attention to oneself (*many men are bashful about discussing their feelings out in the open*). The word can have a faintly old-fashioned or humorous tinge to it.
>
> **Diffident** describes someone who is so modest or hesitant that they have difficulty in putting themselves forward (*'Aren't you Sergei Rozanov?' she enquired in a soft, diffident voice | he was very diffident about working with classical actors*).
>
> **Timid** means 'lacking normal confidence or courage'. It stems from fear, resulting in excessive nervousness in the presence of others (*I was too timid to ask for what I wanted | she gave him a timid smile*). It can also imply an unwillingness to take risks; thus a *timid* action is often inadequate, half-hearted, or piecemeal (*the history of the UN's peacekeeping operations shows what can go wrong when timid measures are tried*).

shy² verb *they began shying stones at him*: **throw**, toss, fling, hurl, cast, lob, launch, flip, pitch, dash, aim, direct, propel, bowl; informal chuck, heave, sling, buzz, whang, bung; N. Amer. informal peg; Austral. informal hoy; NZ informal bish.

shyness noun *overcome with shyness, she looked down at her feet*: **bashfulness**, **diffidence**, sheepishness, reserve, reservedness, introversion, reticence, timidity, timidness, timorousness, fearfulness, nervousness, mousiness, apprehension, hesitancy, hesitation, reluctance, doubt, insecurity, wariness, suspicion, chariness, lack of confidence, inhibitedness, constraint, repression, self-effacement, self-consciousness, embarrassment, coyness, demureness, modesty, humility, meekness.

sibling noun *the birth of a sibling is a stressful event in the life of a child*: **brother or sister**; (**siblings**) brothers and/or sisters.

> *Word links* **sibling**
>
> **siblicide** killing of a sibling, by an animal

sick adjective **1** *half of children in the class are sick*: **ill**, unwell, poorly, ailing, indisposed, laid up, bad, out of sorts, not oneself; Brit. off, off colour; informal under the weather, on the sick list; Austral./NZ informal crook.
▷ANTONYMS well, healthy.
2 *he was starting to feel sick*: **nauseous**, nauseated, queasy, bilious, sick to one's stomach, green, green about the gills; seasick, carsick, airsick, travel-sick, suffering from motion sickness, suffering from altitude sickness, suffering from radiation sickness; informal about to throw up; N. Amer. informal barfy; rare qualmish.
3 informal *we're sick about the closure plans*: **disappointed**, miserable, depressed, dejected, despondent, downcast, disconsolate, unhappy, low-spirited, distressed; **angry**, cross, enraged, annoyed, disgusted, displeased, disgruntled, fed up, grumpy; Brit. informal cheesed off.
▷ANTONYMS glad.
4 *I'm thoroughly sick of this music*: **fed up with**, bored with/by, tired of, weary of, jaded with/by, surfeited with/by, satiated with, glutted with/by; (**be sick of**) have had enough of; informal have had a basinful of, have had it up to here with; have had something up to here.
▷ANTONYMS fond.
5 *a sick joke*: **macabre**, black, ghoulish, morbid, perverted, gruesome, sadistic, cruel, offensive.
▷ANTONYMS in good taste.
□ **be sick** Brit. *he was sick in a bucket*: **vomit**, **throw up**, retch; cough up, bring up, regurgitate; heave, gag; N. Amer. get sick; informal chunder, chuck up, hurl, spew, do the technicolor yawn, keck, ralph; Brit. informal honk, sick up; Scottish informal boke; N. Amer. informal spit up, barf, upchuck, toss one's cookies.

sicken verb **1** *the stench of blood sickened him*: **nauseate**, make someone feel nauseous, make someone sick, turn someone's stomach, make someone's gorge rise, make someone's stomach rise, revolt, disgust, appal, repel, repulse, be repugnant to, offend; informal make someone want to throw up; N. Amer. informal gross out.

2 *his little sister had sickened and died*: **become ill**, fall ill, be taken ill, be taken sick, catch something; **relapse**, have/suffer a relapse, worsen, deteriorate, weaken, fail, sink.
▷ANTONYMS recover.
3 *I think I'm* ***sickening for*** *something*: **become ill with**, fall ill with, be taken ill with, show symptoms of, become infected with, get, catch, develop, pick up, contract, come down with, be struck down with, be stricken with; Brit. go down with; informal take ill with; N. Amer. informal take sick with.
▷ANTONYMS recover from, get over.
4 *they are afraid they will* ***sicken of*** *each other*: **tire**, weary, become/get tired of, become/get fed up with, become/get bored with/by, become/get satiated with, feel jaded with, have had a surfeit of, have had a glut of; informal become/get bored of, have had something up to here.

sickening adjective *there were some sickening photographs of the dead boys*: **nauseating**, stomach-turning, stomach-churning, repulsive, revolting, disgusting, repellent, repugnant, appalling, abominable, hideous, horrible, awful, dreadful, terrible, obnoxious, nauseous, vile, nasty, foul, loathsome, offensive, objectionable, off-putting, distasteful, disagreeable, uninviting; abhorrent, despicable, reprehensible, contemptible, odious, heinous, obscene, hateful, execrable; gruesome, grisly; N. Amer. vomitous; informal sick-making, ghastly, putrid, horrid, God-awful, gross, gut-churning, yucky, icky, cringe-making; Brit. informal beastly; N. Amer. informal skanky; literary noisome; archaic disgustful, loathly; rare rebarbative.
▷ANTONYMS wholesome, delightful.

sickle noun

> *Word links* **sickle**
>
> **falcate** sickle-shaped

sickly adjective **1** *a sickly child*: **unhealthy**, in poor health, chronically ill, often ill, always ill; **delicate**, frail, weak, feeble, puny.
▷ANTONYMS healthy, robust.
2 *the foul streets and the sickly faces he encountered*: **pale**, wan, pasty, colourless, sallow, pallid, white, waxen, ashen; ashen-faced, anaemic, bloodless, peaky, peakish, languid, listless, washed out; informal like death warmed up; Scottish informal peely-wally; rare etiolated, lymphatic.
▷ANTONYMS healthy-looking.
3 *his hotel room had been repainted a sickly green*: **bilious**, nauseating, distasteful, unattractive; lurid, garish, loud, violent.
▷ANTONYMS muted, subtle.
4 *sickly love songs*: **sentimental**, over-sentimental, overemotional, mawkish, cloying, sugary, syrupy, saccharine, sickening, nauseating, maudlin, lachrymose, banal, trite; Brit. twee; informal mushy, slushy, sloppy, schmaltzy, weepy, cutesy, lovey-dovey, gooey, drippy, sloshy, soupy, treacly, cheesy, corny, icky, sick-making, toe-curling; Brit. informal soppy; N. Amer. informal cornball, sappy, hokey, three-hankie.

sickness noun **1** *she was absent through sickness | an incurable sickness*: **illness**, disease, disorder, ailment, complaint, affliction, infection, malady, infirmity, indisposition; informal lurgy, bug, virus; Austral. informal wog.
2 *a wave of sickness swept over her*: **nausea**, biliousness, queasiness.
3 *he suffered sickness and diarrhoea for five days*: **vomiting**, retching, gagging, upset stomach, stomach upset; travel-sickness, seasickness, carsickness, airsickness, motion sickness, morning sickness, altitude sickness; informal throwing up, puking; rare qualms.

side noun **1** *at the side of the road | the eastern side of the lake*: **edge**, border, verge, boundary, margin, fringe, fringes, flank, brink, bank, brim, rim, lip, perimeter, circumference, extremity, periphery, limit, outer limit, limits, bound, bounds; hand; literary marge, bourn, skirt.
▷ANTONYMS centre, heart; end.
2 *he was driving on the wrong side of the road | the left side of the brain*: **half**, part; carriageway, lane; hemisphere.
3 *on the east side of the city*: **district**, quarter, area, region, part, neighbourhood, precinct, locality, sector, section, zone, tract, belt, ghetto, community, colony, pocket, enclave, territory, province, parish, ward.
4 *manuscripts should be typed, on one side of the paper only*: **surface**, face, plane, part, facet, aspect, facade.
5 *he felt he should put his side of the argument*: **point of view**, viewpoint, view, perspective, opinion, way of thinking, mind, standpoint, stance, stand, position, attitude, posture, outlook, frame of reference, slant, aspect, angle, facet.
6 *his family was ruined by backing the losing side in the civil war*: **faction**, camp, bloc, clique, caucus, entente, axis, ring, party, wing, splinter group, sect, clan, set.
7 *there was a mixture of old and young players in their side*: **team**, squad, line-up, crew.
8 Brit. informal *she has all the money in the world, but there's absolutely no side about her*: **pretension**, pretentiousness, affectation, affectedness, ostentation, ostentatiousness, artificiality, attitudinizing, airs, airs and graces, superciliousness, posing, posturing, showing off, boasting, boastfulness, hypocrisy, snobbery, show, flashiness; pomposity, pompousness, flatulence, grandiosity, grandness; informal snootiness; Austral./NZ informal guyver; rare fustian.
□ **side by side 1** *they cycled along side by side*: **alongside (each other)**, beside each other, abreast, level, shoulder to shoulder, cheek by jowl, together, close together. **2** *most transactions proceed side by side*: **at the same time**, at one and the same time, at the same instant/moment, simultaneously, contemporaneously; (all) together, as a group.
▷ANTONYMS in line.
□ **take the side of** *any who took the side of the enemy would be treated as enemies themselves*: **support**, give one's support to, take the part of, side with, be on the side of, stand by, stand up for, stick up for, be supportive of, encourage, back, back up, give one's backing to, uphold, take to one's heart, be loyal to, defend, come to the defence of, champion, ally (oneself) with, associate oneself with, sympathize with, favour, prefer, abet, aid and abet.
▷ANTONYMS oppose.
▸ adjective **1** *the frame had elaborately carved side pieces*: **lateral**, wing, flank, flanking.
▷ANTONYMS front.
2 *this is just a side issue*: **subordinate**, lesser, lower, lower-level, secondary, minor, peripheral, incidental, tangential, marginal, ancillary, subsidiary, subservient, non-essential, inessential, immaterial, borderline, irrelevant, beside the point, of little account, extraneous, unimportant, less important.
▷ANTONYMS central, primary.
3 *a side look*: **sidelong**, sideways, sideward, oblique, indirect.
▷ANTONYMS straight.
▸ verb *the British tend to* ***side with*** *the underdog*. See **take the side of**.

> *Word links* **side**
>
> **lateral** relating to the side of something
> **-gon** figure with a given number of sides, as in *pentagon*

sideline noun *he founded the fast-food company as a sideline to his petrol station*: **secondary occupation**, second job, subsidiary; **hobby**, leisure activity/pursuit, recreation, diversion, distraction.
□ **on the sidelines** *he is biding his time on the sidelines, ready to step in*: **without taking part**, without getting involved.

sidelong adjective *he gave her a sidelong glance*: **indirect**, oblique, sideways, sideward, side; **surreptitious**, furtive, covert, sly.
▷ANTONYMS straight, overt.
▸ adverb *he looked sidelong at her*: **indirectly**, obliquely, sideways, out of the corner of one's eye; **surreptitiously**, furtively, covertly, slyly; archaic askance.

side-splitting adjective informal *side-splitting anecdotes*: **hilarious**, extremely amusing, very funny, very humorous, comic, riotous, uproarious, screamingly/hysterically funny, too funny for words, rib-tickling, comical, absurd, ridiculous; informal a scream, a hoot, priceless; dated killing, killingly funny.

sidestep verb *he neatly sidestepped the questions about crime*: **avoid**, evade, dodge, escape, elude, circumvent, skirt round, give a wide berth to, find a way round, bypass, steer clear of, get out of, shirk; informal duck.
▷ANTONYMS tackle, meet something head on.

sidetrack verb *he allows himself to be constantly sidetracked by minor problems*: **distract**, divert, deflect, draw away, lead away, turn aside, head off.

sideways adverb **1** *I slid off the horse sideways*: **to the side**, laterally, crabwise; athwart.
2 *the expansion slots are mounted sideways*: **edgewise**, sidewards, side first, edgeways, end on.
3 *he looked sideways at her*: **obliquely**, indirectly, sidelong; covertly, furtively, surreptitiously, slyly; archaic askance.
▸ adjective **1** *there is little sideways force on the mast*: **lateral**, sideward, on the side, side to side.
2 *a sideways look*: **oblique**, indirect, sidelong, side; covert, furtive, surreptitious, sly.

sidle verb *she sidled into the room apologetically*: **creep**, sneak, slink, slip, slide, skulk, prowl, steal, edge, inch, ease, worm, nose, move furtively, move with stealth, tread warily.
▷ANTONYMS march, stride.

siege noun **blockade**, beleaguerment, encirclement; archaic investment; rare besiegement.
▷ANTONYMS relief, raising.

siesta noun *after lunch they would take a siesta*: **afternoon sleep**, nap, catnap, doze, drowse, rest; informal snooze, lie-down, forty winks, a bit of shut-eye; Brit. informal kip, zizz; literary slumber.

sieve noun *use a sieve to strain the mixture*: **strainer**, sifter, filter, colander, riddle, screen, muslin cloth; archaic griddle.
▸ verb **1** *sieve the mixture into a bowl*: **strain**, sift, screen, filter, riddle; archaic bolt, griddle.
2 *a hoard of coins was carefully sieved from the ash*: **separate out**, filter out, sift, sort out, isolate, divide, part, segregate, put to one side, weed out, remove, extract.

sift verb **1** *sift the flour into a large bowl*: **sieve**, strain, screen, filter, riddle, purify, refine, winnow; archaic bolt, griddle.
2 *we first sift out those applications which are unlikely to succeed*: **separate out**, filter out, sort out, isolate, divide, part, segregate, put to one side, weed out, get rid of, remove.
3 *crash investigators have been **sifting through** the wreckage | until we sift the evidence ourselves, we can't comment objectively*: **search through**, look through, rummage through, root about/around in, ferret (about/around) in, poke around in, go through, turn over, explore, examine, inspect, scrutinize, pore over, investigate, conduct investigations into, enquire into, conduct an enquiry into, delve into, go into, analyse, screen, sieve, probe, dissect, review, assess; Brit. informal rootle around in; Austral./NZ informal fossick through; rare roust around in.

sigh verb **1** *she sighed with relief*: **breathe out**, exhale; groan, moan; rare suspire.
2 *the wind sighed in the trees*: **rustle**, whisper, murmur, sough.
3 *he **sighed for** days gone by*: **yearn**, long, pine, ache, languish, carry a torch; **grieve over**, cry/weep for/over, fret about, shed tears for; bemoan, rue, miss, mourn, lament, regret the loss/absence of, hanker for/after, eat one's heart out over, hunger/thirst for; cry out for, pant for, crave, have a yen for, dream of.

sight noun **1** *she has excellent sight*: **eyesight**, vision, eyes, faculty of sight, power of sight, ability to see, visual perception, observation.
2 *her first sight of it gave her a severe shock*: **view**, glimpse, seeing, glance at, look at.
3 *he was almost within sight of the enemy*: **range of vision**, field of vision, view.
4 *we are all equal in the sight of God*: **perception**, judgement, belief, opinion, point of view, view, viewpoint, outlook, observation; thought(s), thinking, way of thinking, mind, perspective, standpoint; verdict, estimation, feeling, sentiment, impression, idea, notion.
5 *the town's historic sights*: **landmark**, place of interest, thing worth seeing, (distinctive/prominent) feature, monument, spectacle, scene, view, area, landscape, display, show, exhibition, curiosity, rarity, beauty, marvel, wonder, splendour; informal something to write home about.
6 informal *I changed so quickly into these clothes I must be a sight*: **eyesore**, spectacle, monstrosity, horror, mess; informal fright, blot on the landscape.
□ **catch sight of** *they turned off the main road and caught sight of the cottage*: **glimpse**, catch/get a glimpse of, see, spot, spy, notice, observe, make out, discern, pick out, sight, detect, have sight of; informal clap/lay/set eyes on; literary espy, behold, descry.
□ **out of sight** *a camera should be kept out of sight as it is seen as a tool of espionage*: **hidden**, concealed, not visible, unseen, invisible, screened, covered, disguised, camouflaged, obscured, secret; inconspicuous, unnoticeable; private, privy; secreted, tucked away.
□ **set one's sights on** *she set her sights on a teaching career*: **aspire to**, aim at/for, try for, strive for/towards, work towards, be after, want, seek, have in view, think of, hope for.
▸ verb *one of the helicopters has sighted wreckage in the area*: **glimpse**, catch/get a glimpse of, catch sight of, see, spot, spy, notice, observe, make out, pick out, detect, have sight of; informal clap/lay/set eyes on; literary espy, behold, descry.

Word links **sight**

optical, **visual** relating to sight

sightseer noun **1** *a car park for sightseers to the estate*: **tourist**, visitor, tripper, holidaymaker, traveller, globetrotter; Brit. informal emmet, grockle; rare excursionist.
2 *get those gawping sightseers off the bridge*: **busybody**, gawker, ghoul; informal rubberneck; Brit. informal gawper.

sign noun **1** *flowers are often given as a sign of affection*: **indication**, signal, symptom, hint, pointer, suggestion, intimation, mark, manifestation, demonstration; **token**, testimony, evidence, attestation, proof; rare sigil.
2 *it may have been a sign of things to come*: **portent**, omen, warning, forewarning, augury, presage; promise, threat, hint.
3 *Sir Edmund made a sign, and the soldiers followed him*: **gesture**, signal, wave, gesticulation, cue, nod; action, movement, motion; body language, kinesics.
4 *there were signs saying 'keep out'*: **notice**, signpost, signboard, warning sign, road sign, traffic sign; placard, board, plate, pointer, arrow, marker, waymark, indicator; poster, bill, sticker, advertisement; informal ad; Brit. informal advert.
5 *the dancers were daubed with signs which I assumed were messages to their gods*: **symbol**, mark, cipher, letter, character, numeral, figure, type, code, hieroglyph; signifier, ideogram, logogram, graph; rune, diacritic, representation, emblem, device, badge, insignia, arms, coat of arms, crest, logo; (**signs**) writing, hieroglyphics.
▸ verb **1** *he signed the letter and put it in the envelope*: **autograph**, endorse, witness, initial, put one's mark on, countersign, re-sign; Law set one's hand to, subscribe; archaic underwrite, style; rare chirographate.
2 *the government was unwilling to sign the agreement*: **endorse**, **validate**, certify, authenticate, authorize, sanction, legalize, put into effect, enact; **agree to**, approve, ratify, adopt, say yes to, give one's approval to, rubber-stamp; informal give something the go-ahead, give something the green light, OK, give something the OK, give something the thumbs up.
▹ANTONYMS repudiate.
3 *he merely signed his name at the bottom*: **write**, inscribe, pen, pencil, scribble, scrawl, dash off, put, add; archaic underwrite.
4 *we have signed a very talented player*: **recruit**, hire, engage, employ, take on, appoint, take into one's employ, take into employment, contract, put on the payroll, sign on/up, enrol, enlist; dated take into service.
▹ANTONYMS dismiss.
5 *she then signed to Susan to leave*: **gesture**, signal, give a sign to, indicate, direct, motion, gesticulate; wave, beckon, nod.
□ **sign away** *he had signed away the rights to his music for next to nothing*: **relinquish**, renounce, waive, give up, abandon, reject, surrender, yield, cede, hand over, turn over, do without, dispense with, set/put aside, abdicate, abjure, sacrifice, refuse, turn down, spurn.
□ **sign on/up** *he signed on for a permanent career in the Air Force*: **enlist**, take a job, sign, join (up), join the forces/services, enrol, register, volunteer, put one's name down, become a member; dated take service, go into service; archaic take the King's/Queen's shilling.
▹ANTONYMS resign.
□ **sign someone on/up** *Chapman had signed on new players in July*: **recruit**, hire, engage, employ, take on, appoint, take into one's employ, take into employment, contract, put on the payroll, sign, enrol, enlist; dated take into (one's) service.
▹ANTONYMS dismiss.
□ **sign something over** *they have signed over ownership of the animals to the RSPCA*: **transfer**, turn over, make over, hand over, hand on, give, hand down, leave, bequeath, bestow, pass on, devolve, transmit, cede, deliver, assign, consign, convey, entrust.
▹ANTONYMS keep; accept.

signal[1] noun **1** *the policeman raised his hand as a signal to stop*: **gesture**, sign, wave, gesticulation, cue, prompt, indicator, indication, communication, message; alert, warning, tip-off; action, movement, motion; body language, kinesics.
2 *the move by their rival was a clear signal that the company was in trouble*: **indication**, sign, symptom, hint, pointer, suggestion, intimation, clue, manifestation, demonstration; token, testimony, evidence, attestation, proof.
3 *the encroaching dark is a signal for people to emerge to dump their trash*: **cue**, prompt, occasion, green light, incentive, impetus, impulse, stimulus; informal go-ahead.
▸ verb **1** *a lorry driver signalled to her to cross the road*: **gesture**, sign, give a sign to, indicate, direct, motion, gesticulate; wave, beckon, nod.
2 *the Community could signal displeasure by refusing to cooperate*: **indicate**, show, express, communicate; announce, proclaim, declare, pronounce.
3 *his death signals the end of an era*: **mark**, signify, mean, be a sign of, spell, add up to, amount to, be evidence of, denote, imply, be symptomatic of, be a symptom of, reveal, manifest, designate; **foretell**, herald, bode, announce, be an indication of, indicate, point to, warn of, be a warning of, give a warning of, be an omen of, promise, threaten, presage, augur, portend, foreshadow, prophesy; literary betoken, foretoken, forebode, harbinger.

signal[2] adjective *although a signal failure, the campaign produced one benefit for the Allies*: **notable**, noteworthy, remarkable, striking, glaring, outstanding, significant, momentous, memorable, unforgettable, pronounced, marked, obvious; impressive, distinguished, uncommon, unusual, particular, special, extraordinary, exceptional, conspicuous, rare.

significance noun **1** *tourism is of considerable significance in this area*: **importance**, import, noteworthiness, consequence, substance, seriousness, gravity, weight, weightiness, magnitude, moment, momentousness; memorableness, unforgettableness, pronounced nature, remarkableness, outstanding nature, markedness, obviousness, conspicuousness, strikingness, distinction, impressiveness, uncommonness, unusualness, rarity, extraordinariness, exceptionalness, specialness; rare cruciality.
▹ANTONYMS insignificance.
2 *the significance of his remarks was not lost on Scott*: **meaning**, sense, signification, import, thrust, drift, gist, burden, theme, implication, tenor, message, essence, substance, relevance, purport, intention, spirit, point.

significant adjective **1** *a significant increase in sales*: **notable**, noteworthy, worthy of attention, remarkable, outstanding, important, of importance, of consequence, consequential; serious, crucial, weighty, material, appreciable, momentous, of moment, memorable, unforgettable, pronounced, marked, considerable, obvious, conspicuous, striking, glaring, signal, impressive, uncommon, unusual, rare, extraordinary, exceptional, particular, special.
▹ANTONYMS insignificant, minor.
2 *he gave her a significant look*: **meaningful**, expressive, eloquent, informative, revealing, indicative, suggestive, symbolic, relevant, pregnant, knowing, telling, pithy, valid, purposeful.
▹ANTONYMS meaningless.

S

significantly adverb **1** *this is a significantly better car than the old model*: **notably**, remarkably, outstandingly, importantly, seriously, crucially, materially, appreciably; memorably, unforgettably, pronouncedly, markedly, considerably, obviously, conspicuously, strikingly, glaringly, signally, impressively, unusually, extraordinarily, exceptionally, particularly, specially.
▷ANTONYMS slightly.
2 *he paused significantly*: **meaningfully**, expressively, eloquently, informatively, revealingly, indicatively, suggestively; relevantly, knowingly, tellingly, purposefully; pregnantly.
▷ANTONYMS meaninglessly.

signify verb **1** *this decision signified a fundamental change in their priorities*: **be evidence of**, be a sign of, mark, signal, mean, spell, add up to, amount to, denote, be symptomatic of, be a symptom of, reveal, manifest, designate; announce, herald, be an indication of, indicate, point to; literary betoken.
2 *the symbol of an egg signifies life*: **mean**, denote, designate, represent, symbolize, stand for, correspond to, be equivalent to, imply; literary betoken.
3 *signify your agreement by signing the letter below*: **express**, indicate, show, communicate, intimate; announce, proclaim, declare, pronounce.
▷ANTONYMS withhold; keep secret.
4 *the locked door doesn't necessarily signify*: **mean anything/something**, be of importance, be of consequence, be important, be significant, be of significance, carry weight, be of account, count, matter, be relevant; informal cut any ice.

silence noun **1** *the sound of falling stones broke the silence of the night*: **quietness**, quiet, quietude, still, stillness, hush, tranquillity, noiselessness, soundlessness, peace, peacefulness, peace and quiet.
▷ANTONYMS sound, noise.
2 *she was reduced to silence*: **speechlessness**, wordlessness, voicelessness, dumbness, muteness; taciturnity, reticence, uncommunicativeness, unresponsiveness.
▷ANTONYMS speech; loquacity.
3 *politicians keep their silence on the big issues*: **secretiveness**, secrecy, reticence, taciturnity, uncommunicativeness, concealment.
▷ANTONYMS communication, communicativeness.
▶ verb **1** *he silenced her with a kiss | Barnes has failed to silence his critics*: **quieten**, quiet, hush, shush, still; **gag**, muzzle, censor, stifle.
2 *the ventilator also silences outside noises*: **muffle**, deaden, soften, mute, smother, dampen, damp down, tone down, mask, suppress, reduce, abate; extinguish, kill.
▷ANTONYMS amplify.
3 *cheap nuclear power would silence complaints from industry*: **stop**, put an end to, put a stop to, cut short, suppress.
▷ANTONYMS occasion, encourage.

silent adjective **1** *the night was silent*: **completely quiet**, still, hushed, inaudible, noiseless, soundless, peaceful, tranquil, so quiet you could hear a pin drop.
▷ANTONYMS audible, noisy.
2 *you have the right to remain silent*: **speechless**, quiet, unspeaking, wordless, voiceless, dumb, mute, taciturn, reticent, uncommunicative, unforthcoming, tight-lipped, close-mouthed, untalkative, tongue-tied, saying nothing, at a loss for words, struck dumb; informal mum.
▷ANTONYMS loquacious.
3 *we gave silent thanks that no one else had the right money for the jukebox*: **unspoken**, wordless, unsaid, unstated, undeclared, unexpressed, unmentioned, unpronounced, unvoiced, tacit, implicit, understood, implied, taken for granted.
▷ANTONYMS spoken.

silently adverb **1** *Nancy took off her shoes and crept silently up the stairs*: **quietly**, inaudibly, noiselessly, soundlessly, in silence.
▷ANTONYMS audibly, noisily.
2 *they drove on silently for a few minutes*: **without a word**, saying nothing, speechlessly, quietly, in silence, unspeakingly, wordlessly, voicelessly, dumbly, mutely, taciturnly, reticently, uncommunicatively.
▷ANTONYMS while talking, in conversation.
3 *I silently said goodbye*: **without words**, wordlessly, in one's head, tacitly, implicitly; rare subvocally, unspokenly.
▷ANTONYMS aloud.

silhouette noun *the silhouette of St Peter's is dominated by Michelangelo's dome*: **outline**, contour(s), profile, delineation, form, shape, figure, shadow, features, lines, curves, configuration.
▶ verb *the castle was silhouetted against the sky*: **outline**, etch, delineate, define, demarcate, delimit, mark off, trace; (**be silhouetted**) stand out.

silky adjective *she had long, silky hair*: **smooth**, soft, sleek, lustrous, fine, glossy, satiny, silken, velvety.

silly adjective **1** *don't be so silly*: **foolish**, **stupid**, unintelligent, idiotic, brainless, mindless, witless, imbecilic, imbecile, doltish; imprudent, thoughtless, rash, reckless, foolhardy, irresponsible; mad, erratic, unstable, scatterbrained, feather-brained; flighty, frivolous, giddy, fatuous, inane, immature, childish, puerile, half-baked, empty-headed, half-witted, slow-witted, weak-minded; informal daft, crazy, dotty, scatty, loopy, screwy, soft, brain-dead, cretinous, thick, thickheaded, birdbrained, pea-brained, pinheaded, dopey, dim, dim-witted, dippy, pie-faced, fat-headed, blockheaded, boneheaded, lamebrained, chuckleheaded, dunderheaded, wooden-headed, muttonheaded, damfool; Brit. informal divvy; Scottish & N. English informal glaikit; N. Amer. informal dumb-ass, chowderheaded; S. African informal dof; W. Indian informal dotish; dated tomfool.
▷ANTONYMS sensible, rational.
2 *that was a silly thing to do*: **unwise**, imprudent, thoughtless, foolish, stupid, idiotic, senseless, mindless, fatuous; rash, reckless, foolhardy, irresponsible, inadvisable, injudicious, ill-considered, misguided, inappropriate, illogical, irrational, unreasonable; hare-brained, absurd, ridiculous, ludicrous, laughable, risible, farcical, preposterous, asinine; informal daft, crazy.
▷ANTONYMS sensible, rational.
3 *he would brood about silly things*: **trivial**, trifling, frivolous, footling, petty, niggling, small, slight, minor, insignificant, unimportant, inconsequential, of little account; informal piffling, piddling; N. Amer. informal small-bore.
▷ANTONYMS important.
4 *he often drank himself silly*: **senseless**, insensible, unconscious, stupid, dopey, into a stupor, into oblivion, into senselessness, into a daze; numb, dazed, stunned, stupefied, groggy, muzzy.
▶ noun informal *come on, silly*: **nincompoop**, dunce, simpleton; informal nitwit, ninny, dimwit, dope, dumbo, dummy, chump, goon, jackass, fathead, bonehead, chucklehead, knucklehead, lamebrain, clod, pea-brain, pudding-head, thickhead, wooden-head, pinhead, airhead, birdbrain, scatterbrain, noodle, donkey; Brit. informal silly billy, stupe, nit, clot, twit, berk, twerp; Scottish informal nyaff, sumph, gowk, balloon; N. Amer. informal bozo, boob, schlepper, goofball, goof, goofus, galoot, lummox, dip, simp, spud, coot, palooka, poop, yo-yo, dingleberry; Austral./NZ informal drongo, dill, alec, galah, nong, bogan, poon, boofhead; S. African informal mompara; informal, dated muttonhead, noddy; archaic clodpole, spoony, mooncalf.

Word toolkit **silly**

See **foolish**.

silt noun *the annual flooding brought more silt*: **sediment**, deposit, alluvium, mud, slime, ooze, sludge; sand, clay.
▶ verb *the old harbour had silted up*: **become blocked**, become choked, become clogged, fill up (with silt), become filled, become dammed.

silver noun **1** *the table was laden with freshly polished silver*: **silverware**, (silver) plate; dishes, plates, flatware; cutlery, {knives, forks, and spoons}.
2 *Fred reached into his pocket and took out a handful of silver*: **coins**, coinage, specie; change, small change, loose change; informal shrapnel.
▷ANTONYMS notes.
3 *she won three silvers*: **silver medal**, second prize.
▶ adjective **1** *a man with silver hair*: **grey**, greyish, white, greyish-white, whitish-grey, light.
2 *the silver water*: **silvery**, shining, lustrous, bright, gleaming; literary argent.
▶ verb *a silvered bracelet*: **plate with silver**, coat with silver, overlay with silver, laminate with silver, back with silver; plate, electroplate.

similar adjective **1** *the two of you are very similar*: **alike**, (much) the same, indistinguishable, close, near, almost identical, homogeneous, interchangeable; kindred, akin, related; informal much of a muchness.
▷ANTONYMS dissimilar, different.
2 *northern India and similar areas*: **comparable**, like, corresponding, homogeneous, parallel, equivalent, analogous, matching.
3 *other parts of the region were* ***similar to*** *Wales*: **like**, much the same as, comparable to, close to, near (to), in the nature of.
▷ANTONYMS dissimilar to, unlike.
□ **be similar to resemble**, look like, have the appearance of, correspond to, simulate, mimic.
▷ANTONYMS differ from.

similarity noun *the similarity between him and his daughter was startling*: **resemblance**, likeness, sameness, similar nature, similitude, comparability, correspondence, comparison, analogy, parallel, parallelism, equivalence; interchangeability, closeness, nearness, affinity, homogeneity, agreement, indistinguishability, uniformity; community, kinship, relatedness; archaic semblance.
▷ANTONYMS dissimilarity, difference.

similarly adverb **likewise**, in similar fashion, in like manner, comparably, correspondingly, uniformly, indistinguishably, closely, analogously, homogeneously, in parallel, equivalently, in the same way, the same, identically, by the same token.
▷ANTONYMS differently, the opposite way.

similitude noun *Conrad uses a range of constructions which express or imply similitude*: **resemblance**, similarity, likeness, sameness, similar nature, comparability, correspondence, comparison, analogy, parallel, parallelism, equivalence; interchangeability, closeness, nearness, affinity, homogeneity, agreement, indistinguishability, uniformity; community, kinship, relatedness; archaic semblance.
▷ANTONYMS dissimilarity, difference.

S

simmer verb **1** *a pan of vegetable soup was simmering on the stove | simmer the apple until it is tender*: **boil gently**, not quite boil, cook gently, stew, poach; bubble; rare seethe.
2 *she was simmering with resentment*: **be furious**, be enraged, be angry, be incensed, be infuriated, be beside oneself, have lost one's temper, have a fit, boil, seethe, be boiling over, chafe, rage, be in a rage, rant, rave, rant and rave, storm, fume, smoulder, spit, breathe fire, burn; informal be livid, be wild, jump up and down, froth/foam at the mouth, be steamed up, be hot under the collar, have steam coming out of one's ears; Brit. informal do one's head/nut in.
□ **simmer down** *he stormed out of the theatre in a rage but soon simmered down*: **become less angry**, cool off, cool down, be placated, let someone smooth one's ruffled feathers, contain oneself, control oneself, become calmer, calm down, become quieter, quieten down, loosen up, settle (down).
▷**ANTONYMS** get steamed up.

simper verb *she simpered, looking pleased with herself*: **smile affectedly**, smile coquettishly, giggle, titter, smirk, look coy.

simple adjective **1** *it sounds difficult I know, but it's really pretty simple*: **straightforward**, **easy**, uncomplicated, uninvolved, effortless, painless, manageable, undemanding, unexacting, elementary, child's play, plain sailing, a five-finger exercise, nothing; informal as easy as falling off a log, as easy as pie, as easy as ABC, a piece of cake, a cinch, a snip, easy-peasy, no sweat, a doddle, a pushover, money for old rope, money for jam, kids' stuff, a breeze, a doss, a cakewalk; N. Amer. informal duck soup, a snap; Austral./NZ informal a bludge, a snack; S. African informal a piece of old tackle; Brit. vulgar slang a piece of piss.
▷**ANTONYMS** difficult, hard, demanding, complicated.
2 *the chapter on finance explains in simple language how a profit and loss account is compiled*: **clear**, plain, straightforward, clearly expressed, intelligible, comprehensible, uncomplicated, understandable, (words) of one syllable, lucid, coherent, unambiguous, direct, accessible, uninvolved; informal user-friendly.
▷**ANTONYMS** complex.
3 *a simple white blouse | a simple, square house in Bath stone*: **plain**, unadorned, undecorated, unembellished, unornamented, without ornament/ornamentation, unelaborate, unpretentious, unostentatious, unfussy, no-nonsense, basic, modest, unsophisticated, penny plain, without frills, honest, homely, homespun, everyday, workaday; stark, severe, spartan, austere, chaste, spare, bare; muted, unpatterned, patternless; classic, understated, uncluttered, clean, restrained; N. Amer. homestyle; informal no-frills.
▷**ANTONYMS** fancy, elaborate.
4 *the simple fact is that stray dogs are a menace | she was overcome at last by simple exhaustion*: **basic**, fundamental; **mere**, sheer, pure, pure and simple.
5 *she wondered how he would react if she told him the simple truth*: **candid**, frank, honest, direct, sincere, plain, absolute, unqualified, bald, stark, naked, blunt, unadorned, unvarnished, unembellished.
6 *simple country people*: **unpretentious**, unsophisticated, ordinary, unaffected, unassuming, natural, honest-to-goodness, modest, homely, wholesome, humble, quiet, lowly, rustic; innocent, artless, guileless, childlike, naive, ingenuous, gullible, inexperienced; N. Amer. cracker-barrel; informal green.
▷**ANTONYMS** pretentious, affected.
7 *simple chemical substances*: **non-compound**, non-complex, uncompounded, uncombined, unmixed, unblended, unalloyed, pure, basic, single, elementary, fundamental.
▷**ANTONYMS** compound.

simpleton noun *there will always be those in business who persist in treating their customers like simpletons*: **fool**, nincompoop, dunce, dullard, ignoramus; informal idiot, imbecile, moron, cretin, halfwit, thicko, thickhead, nitwit, dope, dimwit, dumbo, dummy, donkey, stupid, stupe; Brit. informal twit, nit, numpty, twerp, clot, muggins, juggins, silly billy; Scottish informal nyaff, sumph, gowk; Irish informal gobdaw; N. Amer. informal sap, schmuck, lamer. See also **fool**.

simplicity noun **1** *recipes will be judged on taste, appearance, simplicity, and appeal*: **straightforwardness**, ease, easiness, simpleness, lack/absence of complication, effortlessness, manageability.
▷**ANTONYMS** difficulty.
2 *the simplicity of the everyday language*: **clarity**, clearness, plainness, simpleness, intelligibility, comprehensibility, understandability, lucidity, lucidness, coherence, directness, straightforwardness, accessibility; informal user-friendliness.
▷**ANTONYMS** complexity, intricacy.
3 *the charm of the building lies in its simplicity*: **plainness**, lack/absence of adornment, lack/absence of decoration, lack/absence of ornament/ornamentation, lack/absence of embellishment, unpretentiousness; starkness, austereness, austerity, spareness, severity; classic lines, clean lines, lack/absence of clutter, restraint, purity.
▷**ANTONYMS** ornateness, fanciness.
4 *the simplicity of their lifestyle*: **unpretentiousness**, ordinariness, lack of sophistication, lack of affectation, naturalness, modesty, homeliness, wholesomeness, quietness; innocence, guilelessness, naivety, ingenuousness.
▷**ANTONYMS** pretentiousness, affectation.

simplify verb *the government intends to simplify existing environmental legislation | this information is simplified in Figure 4.1*: **make simple/simpler**, make easy/easier to understand/do, make plainer, clarify, make more comprehensible, make more intelligible, remove the complexities from, disentangle, untangle, unravel; paraphrase, put in words of one syllable, make more accessible, popularize; streamline, reduce to essentials, rationalize; N. Amer. informal dumb down.
▷**ANTONYMS** complicate.

simplistic adjective *the proposed solutions are far too simplistic | an irritatingly simplistic film*: **facile**, superficial, oversimple, oversimplified, schematic, black and white; shallow, pat, glib, jejune, naive; N. Amer. informal dime-store, bubblegum.

simply adverb **1** *he spoke simply and forcefully*: **straightforwardly**, directly; **clearly**, plainly, intelligibly, lucidly, unambiguously.
2 *she was dressed simply in a white blouse and dark skirt*: **plainly**, without adornment, without decoration, without ornament/ornamentation, without embellishment, soberly, unfussily, unelaborately, unostentatiously, without frills; severely, austerely, starkly, with restraint, monastically; classically, without clutter.
3 *they lived simply*: **unpretentiously**, modestly, naturally, quietly.
4 *people like her are accepted in society simply because they have enormous sums of money*: **merely**, just, purely, solely, only, for no other reason.
5 *Mrs Marks was simply livid*: **utterly**, absolutely, completely, positively, really, totally; informal plain, plumb.
6 *it's simply the best thing ever written on the subject*: **without doubt**, unquestionably, undeniably, incontrovertibly, altogether, unreservedly, certainly, unconditionally, categorically, entirely, wholly; easily.

simulate verb **1** *it was impossible to force a smile, to simulate pleasure*: **feign**, pretend, fake, sham, affect, put on, counterfeit, go through the motions of, give the appearance of.
2 *this stage aims to simulate the actual conditions on the production line*: **imitate**, reproduce, replicate, duplicate, mimic, parallel, be a mock-up of.

simulated adjective **1** *she howled in simulated anguish*: **feigned**, fake, mock, pretended, affected, assumed, counterfeit, sham, insincere, not genuine, false, bogus, spurious; informal pretend, put-on, phoney; Brit. informal, dated cod.
▷**ANTONYMS** genuine, real.
2 *a simulated leather handbag*: **artificial**, imitation, fake, false, faux, mock, synthetic, man-made, manufactured, ersatz, plastic.
▷**ANTONYMS** real.

simultaneous adjective *officers carried out simultaneous raids on homes across the city*: **concurrent**, happening at the same time, done at the same time, contemporaneous, concomitant, coinciding, coincident, synchronous, synchronized, synchronic; coexistent, parallel, side by side.
▷**ANTONYMS** asynchronous.

simultaneously adverb *Alison and Frank spoke simultaneously*: **at the same time**, at one and the same time, at the same instant/moment, at once, concurrently, concomitantly; together, all together, in unison, in concert, in chorus, as a group; rare synchronously.
▷**ANTONYMS** singly.

sin noun **1** *a sin in the eyes of God*: **immoral act**, wrong, wrongdoing, act of evil/wickedness, transgression, crime, offence, misdeed, misdemeanour, error, lapse, fall from grace; archaic trespass.
2 *the human capacity for sin*: **wickedness**, wrongdoing, wrong, evil, evil-doing, sinfulness, ungodliness, unrighteousness, immorality, vice, transgression, crime, error, iniquity, irreligiousness, irreverence, profanity, blasphemy, impiety, impiousness, sacrilege, profanation, desecration.
▷**ANTONYMS** virtue, good.
3 informal *the way they spend money—it's a sin*: **scandal**, crime, disgrace, outrage.
▶ verb *I sinned and brought down shame on us*: **commit a sin**, offend against God, commit an offence, transgress, do wrong, commit a crime, break the law, misbehave, go astray, stray from the straight and narrow, go wrong, fall from grace; archaic trespass.

sincere adjective **1** *my wife and I would like to express our sincere gratitude for what you did*: **heartfelt**, wholehearted, profound, deep, from the heart; **genuine**, real, unfeigned, unaffected, true, honest, bona fide, earnest, cordial, fervent, ardent, devout; rare full-hearted.
▷**ANTONYMS** perfunctory, token.
2 *Jean is such a sincere person*: **honest**, genuine, truthful, unhypocritical, meaning what one says, straightforward, direct, frank, candid; artless, guileless, ingenuous; informal straight, upfront, on the level; N. Amer. informal on the up and up; Austral./NZ informal **dinkum**.
▷**ANTONYMS** insincere, hypocritical, disingenuous, two-faced.

S

Choose the right word **sincere, genuine, unfeigned, unaffected**

These words are all used to indicate that someone or something can be trusted to be what they appear to be.

Sincere is used of emotions that are free from pretence or deceit (*a sincere concern for the future of Britain*), and can also be used of a person (*a sincere and generous man*). It can also apply to the results of such genuine feelings (*very bad but sincere poems | please accept my sincere condolences*).

A feeling described as **genuine** is truly that feeling and not a hypocritical imitation of it (*a man with a genuine love of his country*). When used of a person, *genuine* can have two quite different senses, depending on the noun and the context: 'truly what they are said or appear to be' (*no genuine police officers will demand cash on the spot for speeding offences*) or 'having emotions that are what they appear to be' (*most of the people in the regiment were hard-working, genuine people*).

Unfeigned is a rarer, more literary word, used only for emotions, not people (*a broad smile of unfeigned delight*).

Unaffected is used either of a person who behaves naturally and simply, without trying to impress with artificiality or insincerity (*what a pretty, unaffected girl she was, full of life and fun*) or of their emotions (*taking unaffected pleasure in his friend's good fortune*).

sincerely adverb *I sincerely hope that this scheme will succeed*: **genuinely**, honestly, really, with all sincerity, truly, truthfully, wholeheartedly, with all one's heart, from the bottom of one's heart, earnestly, fervently, seriously; without pretence, without feigning, in good faith.
▷ANTONYMS insincerely.

sincerity noun *there seems no reason to doubt the sincerity of her apology*: **honesty**, **genuineness**, truthfulness, good faith, lack of deceit, integrity, probity, trustworthiness; wholeheartedness, seriousness, earnestness; straightforwardness, openness, candour, candidness, guilelessness, ingenuousness; Latin bona fides.
▷ANTONYMS insincerity.

sinecure noun *Connie's job was a sinecure that could be done by anyone*: **easy job**, soft option; informal cushy number, money for old rope, money for jam, picnic, doddle, walk in the park, cinch, gravy train; Austral. informal bludge.

sinewy adjective *he was tall, blonde, and sinewy*: **muscular**, well muscled, muscly, brawny, well built, powerfully built, burly, strapping, sturdy, rugged, strong, powerful, broad-shouldered, athletic, well knit, muscle-bound, Herculean, manly; informal hunky, beefy, husky; dated stalwart; literary thewy; Physiology mesomorphic.
▷ANTONYMS puny, weedy.

sinful adjective **1** *he warned her that such talk was sinful | sinful men*: **immoral**, **wicked**, wrong, morally wrong, wrongful, evil, bad, iniquitous, corrupt, ungodly, godless, unholy, irreligious, unrighteous, sacrilegious, profane, blasphemous, impious, irreverent, criminal, nefarious, depraved, degenerate, perverted, erring, fallen, impure, sullied, tainted; rare peccable.
▷ANTONYMS sinless, virtuous, godly, innocent.
2 *a sinful waste of money*: **reprehensible**, scandalous, disgraceful, deplorable, shameful, criminal, iniquitous.
▷ANTONYMS admirable.

sinfulness noun **immorality**, **wickedness**, sin, wrongdoing, evil, evilness, evil-doing, iniquitousness, corruption, turpitude, ungodliness, godlessness, unholiness, irreligiousness, sacrilegiousness, profanity, blasphemy, impiety, impiousness, irreverence, impurity, depravity, degeneracy, vice, perversion, pervertedness; rare peccability, peccancy.
▷ANTONYMS virtue.

sing verb **1** *Miguelito began to sing a traditional Spanish folk song*: **chant**, intone, croon, carol, chorus, warble, trill, pipe, quaver; yodel; render, perform; informal belt out; rare troll.
2 *the birds were singing in the chestnut trees*: **warble**, trill, twitter, chirp, chirrup, cheep, peep.
3 *he sang out a greeting*: **call out**, call, cry, cry out, shout, yell, trumpet, bellow, roar; informal holler, cooee.
4 informal *maybe he's going to sing to the police*: **inform (on someone)**, tell tales (on someone); informal squeal, rat on someone, blow the whistle on someone, peach (on someone), snitch (on someone), put the finger on someone, sell someone down the river; Brit. informal grass (on someone), shop someone; N. Amer. informal rat someone out, finger someone, fink on someone, drop a/the dime on someone; Austral. informal pimp on someone.

singe verb *sparks burnt holes in my shirt and the fire singed my sleeve*: **scorch**, burn, sear, char, blacken.

singer noun **vocalist**, soloist, songster, songstress; French chanteuse.

single adjective **1** *a single red rose | the lobby was empty except for a single security guard*: **one**, one only, sole, lone, solitary, isolated, by itself; unique, exclusive; unaccompanied, by oneself, alone, solo; odd.
▷ANTONYMS double, multiple.
2 *she wrote down every single word | alcohol is the single most important cause of violence*: **individual**, separate, distinct, particular.
3 *is she single?* **unmarried**, unwed, unwedded, unattached, free, without a partner/husband/wife, wifeless, husbandless, spouseless, partnerless, a bachelor, a spinster; on the shelf; archaic sole.
▷ANTONYMS married.
▶ verb
□ **single someone/something out** *the prime minister singled him out for promotion when he was a junior whip*: **select**, pick out, fix on, choose, decide on; target, earmark; mark out, distinguish, differentiate, separate out, set apart/aside, put aside; cull.

Word links **single**

mono- related prefix, as in *monochrome, monophagous*
uni- related prefix, as in *unicycle, unicuspid*
haplo- related prefix, as in *haplology, haplotype*
monomania obsession with a single thing

single-handed adverb *he's been running the place single-handed*: **by oneself**, alone, on one's own, solo, unaided, unassisted, without help, by one's own efforts, independently; under one's own steam.
▷ANTONYMS jointly, with help.

single-minded adjective *I've never met anyone so ambitious and single-minded*: **determined**, full of determination, hell-bent, committed, unswerving, unwavering, undeviating, resolute, purposeful, set, fixed, devoted, dedicated, uncompromising, persevering, tireless, tenacious, persistent, pertinacious, indefatigable; obsessive, fanatical, dogged, monomaniacal; obstinate, stubborn, unyielding, intransigent, pig-headed, inflexible, obdurate.
▷ANTONYMS half-hearted, lackadaisical.

singly adverb *we should interview people singly and discreetly*: **one by one**, one at a time, one after the other, individually, separately, by oneself, on one's own; apart; independently; Latin seriatim; formal severally.
▷ANTONYMS together, simultaneously.

sing-song adjective *he began to recite in a sing-song voice*: **chanting**, chant-like; **monotonous**, monotone, droning, toneless.

singular adjective **1** *the success of the appeal demonstrates the gallery's singular capacity to attract sponsors*: **remarkable**, extraordinary, exceptional, outstanding, striking, signal, eminent, especial, particular, notable, noteworthy, conspicuous, distinctive, impressive; rare, unique, unparalleled, unprecedented, superior, superlative, amazing, astonishing, phenomenal, astounding, sensational, spectacular; informal tremendous, awesome, fantastic, fabulous, terrific, stupendous, unreal.
▷ANTONYMS ordinary, run-of-the-mill.
2 *Lydia wondered why Betty was behaving in so singular a fashion*: **strange**, unusual, odd, peculiar, funny, curious, extraordinary, bizarre, eccentric, weird, queer, outlandish, offbeat, unexpected, unfamiliar, abnormal, aberrant, atypical, unconventional, out of the ordinary, incongruous, unnatural, anomalous, untypical, puzzling, mystifying, mysterious, perplexing, baffling, unaccountable; French outré; N. Amer. informal off the wall.
▷ANTONYMS normal, unsurprising.

singularity noun **1** *the anthology communicates both the singularity and the universality of women's deepest concerns*: **uniqueness**, distinctiveness, difference, individuality, particularity.
2 *his psychological singularities*: **idiosyncrasy**, quirk, trait, foible, peculiarity, oddity, eccentricity, abnormality.

singularly adverb *I have to admit it was a singularly foolish thing to do*: **remarkably**, extraordinarily, exceptionally, very, extremely, really, outstandingly, strikingly, signally, eminently, especially, particularly, incredibly, awfully, terribly, decidedly, supremely, peculiarly, distinctly, conspicuously; amazingly, astonishingly, phenomenally, astoundingly, spectacularly, prodigiously, unusually, uncommonly, extra; N. English right; informal tremendously, seriously, majorly, fantastically, terrifically, stupendously; Brit. informal jolly, dead, well; N. Amer. informal powerful.

sinister adjective **1** *there was a sinister undertone in his words*: **menacing**, threatening, ominous, forbidding, baleful, frightening, eerie, alarming, disturbing, disquieting, dark, black, suggestive of evil, evil-looking; ill-omened, inauspicious, unpropitious, portentous; Scottish eldritch; informal spooky, scary, creepy; rare minatory, minacious, minatorial, bodeful, direful.
2 *we need not assume a sinister motive for these meetings*: **evil**, wicked, bad, criminal, corrupt, nefarious, villainous, base, vile, malevolent, malicious, malign; underhand; informal shady.
▷ANTONYMS innocent, good.

sink verb **1** *he saw the coffin sink below the surface of the waves*: **become submerged**, be engulfed, go down, drop, fall, descend; disappear, vanish.
▷ANTONYMS rise, float.
2 *500 passengers and crew were saved after the luxury cruise liner sank yesterday*: **founder**, go under, submerge, capsize.
3 *they sank their ships, rather than let them fall into enemy hands*: **scupper**, scuttle, send to the bottom, open the seacocks in.
4 *the Bank of England sank lingering hopes of an imminent recovery*: **destroy**, ruin, wreck, put an end to, be the ruin/ruination of, wreak havoc

S

on, demolish, devastate, blast, blight, smash, shatter, dash, torpedo, scotch, sabotage; informal put the kibosh on, put the skids under, put paid to, banjax, do for, blow a hole in, nix; Brit. informal scupper, dish, throw a spanner in the works of; N. Amer. informal throw a monkey wrench in the works of; Austral. informal euchre, cruel; archaic bring to naught.
5 *they agreed to sink their differences*: **ignore**, overlook, disregard, forget, put aside, set aside, put to one side, bury, consign to oblivion.
6 *I sank myself in the communal life of the place*: **immerse oneself in**, plunge oneself into, lose oneself in, bury oneself in, absorb oneself, occupy oneself with.
7 *the plane sank towards the small airstrip*: **descend**, drop, go down/downwards, come down/downwards, go lower; fall, plunge, plummet, pitch, fall headlong, nosedive.
▷ANTONYMS ascend.
8 *the sun was sinking in a red glow*: **set**, go down/downwards, dip beneath the horizon, descend.
▷ANTONYMS rise.
9 *Loretta sank into an armchair*: **lower oneself**, flop, collapse, drop down, slump, plump oneself; informal plonk oneself, plop oneself; N. Amer. informal plank oneself.
▷ANTONYMS stand up.
10 *her voice sank to a confidential whisper*: **fall**, drop, become/get lower, become/get quieter, become/get softer.
▷ANTONYMS rise.
11 *whatever she is guilty of, she would never sink to your level*: **stoop**, lower oneself, descend, be reduced; demean oneself, debase oneself.
12 *his breathing was laboured—he was clearly sinking fast*: **deteriorate**, decline, fade, fail, weaken, grow weak, flag, languish, degenerate, decay, waste away; be at death's door, be on one's deathbed, be breathing one's last, be about to die, be approaching death, be slipping away, have one foot in the grave, be in extremis, become moribund; informal go downhill, be on one's last legs, be giving up the ghost.
▷ANTONYMS recover, improve.
13 *sink 3-inch pots of good soil into the ground | screws sunk beneath the surface of the wood*: **embed**, insert; **drive**, place, put down, plant, position.
14 *they planned to sink a gold mine in Oklahoma*: **dig**, excavate, bore, drill.
15 informal *after sinking five pints of lager, he decided it was time to leave*: **drink**, quaff, gulp down; informal down, swill, knock back, polish off, dispose of, shift; Brit. informal get outside of, neck, bevvy; N. Amer. informal chug, scarf down.
16 *many investors sank their life savings into the company*: **invest**, put, venture, risk, plough.
□ **sink in** *Peter read the letter twice before its meaning sank in*: **register**, penetrate, be understood, be comprehended, be realized, be taken in, be grasped, become clear, get through.
▸ **noun** *he washed himself as best he could at the sink in the bathroom*: **basin**, washbasin, handbasin, wash-hand basin; dated lavabo.

sinless adjective *she was asleep, looking as careless and sinless as a child*: **innocent**, pure, virtuous, faultless, unsullied, undefiled, as pure as the driven snow, whiter than white, uncorrupted, unblemished, untainted, untarnished; irreproachable, blameless, guiltless; informal squeaky clean; Theology immaculate, impeccable.
▷ANTONYMS sinful, wicked.

sinner noun **wrongdoer**, evil-doer, transgressor, offender, criminal; archaic miscreant, trespasser, reprobate.

sinuous adjective **1** *a small town with a slow-moving, sinuous river*: **winding**, windy, serpentine, curving, twisting, meandering, snaking, snaky, zigzag, zigzagging, turning, bending, curling, coiling, undulating; tortuous; technical sinuate, ogee; rare anfractuous, flexuous, meandrous, serpentiform.
▷ANTONYMS straight.
2 *she got to her feet in one sinuous movement*: **lithe**, supple, agile, graceful, loose-limbed, limber, lissom, willowy; informal slinky; literary lithesome.
▷ANTONYMS clumsy.

sip verb *Amanda sipped her coffee*: **drink slowly**, drink, taste, sample; dated sup.
▸ **noun** *he took another sip of whisky*: **mouthful**, swallow, drink, drop, dram, nip; taste; informal slurp, swig; dated sup.

siren noun **1** *the wail of an air-raid siren*: **alarm**, alarm bell, warning bell, danger signal; whistle, horn; Brit. hooter; archaic tocsin.
2 *seamed stockings are the trademark of a true siren*: **seductress**, temptress, femme fatale, Mata Hari, enchantress, Circe, Lorelei, Delilah; **flirt**, coquette, Lolita; informal mantrap; N. Amer. informal vamp.

sissy informal **noun** *I'd hate the other boys to think he was a sissy*: **coward**, weakling, milksop, Milquetoast, namby-pamby, crybaby, baby; informal weed, softie, nancy, nancy boy, pansy, ponce, mollycoddle, chicken; Brit. informal wet, mummy's boy, big girl's blouse, jessie, yellow-belly, funk; N. Amer. informal pantywaist, cupcake, pussy; Austral./NZ informal sook; S. African informal moffie; archaic poltroon.
▸ **adjective** *he felt sure his father would think the whole idea was sissy*: **cowardly**, weak, feeble, spineless, effeminate, effete, limp-wristed, womanish, unmanly, soft; informal wet, weedy, wimpish, wimpy, sissyish, queeny, sissified, swishy, yellow, yellow-bellied; N. Amer. informal candy-assed.

sister noun **1** *I had nine brothers and sisters*: **female sibling**; informal sis; Brit. rhyming slang skin and blister.
2 *working together with our European brothers and sisters in the struggle against fascism*: **comrade**, friend, partner, associate, colleague.
3 *Mother Mary Bernadette is one of nine sisters in the convent*: **nun**, novice, abbess, prioress, Mother Superior, Reverend Mother; bride of Christ, religious, conventual, contemplative; Roman Catholic Church canoness; literary vestal; historical anchoress, ancress; rare vowess.

> *Word links* **sister**
>
> **sororal** relating to a sister
> **sorori-** related prefix, as in *sorority*
> **sororicide**, Law **fratricide** killing of one's sister

sit verb **1** *you'd better* **sit down** *| Lily sat on the window seat to read the letters*: **take a seat**, seat oneself, settle down, be seated, take a chair; perch, install oneself, ensconce oneself, plant oneself, plump oneself, flop, collapse, sink down, flump; informal take the load/weight off one's feet, park oneself, plonk oneself; Brit. informal take a pew.
▷ANTONYMS stand, rise.
2 *she sat the package on the table*: **put**, place, set, put down, set down, lay, deposit, rest, leave, stand; informal stick, bung, dump, park, plonk, pop, plant.
▷ANTONYMS lift.
3 *the chapel sat about 3,000 people*: **hold**, seat, have seats for, have space for, have room for, accommodate, take.
4 *Walter Deverell asked her to sit for him*: **pose**, model.
5 *an attractive hotel sitting on the west bank of the River Dee*: **be situated**, be located, be positioned, be sited, be placed, perch, rest, stand.
6 *normally, the Appeals Committee sits on Saturday*: **meet**, assemble, convene, be in session.
7 *they were determined that women jurists should* **sit on** *the tribunal*: **serve on**, have a seat on, hold a seat on, be a member of, carry out duties on, work on.
8 *his shyness doesn't sit easily with Hollywood tradition*: **be harmonious**, go, fit in, harmonize, mesh.
9 *I wonder if she'll be able to get Mrs Hillman to sit*: **babysit**, babymind, childmind.
□ **sit back** *sit back and enjoy the music*: **relax**, unwind, lie back, loosen up; informal let it all hang out, lighten up, veg out; N. Amer. informal hang loose, stay loose, chill out, kick back.
□ **sit in for** *he's sitting in for the regular disc jockey*: **stand in for**, fill in for, take the place of, cover for, substitute for, be a substitute for, act as stand-in for, deputize for; hold the fort; informal sub for; N. Amer. informal pinch-hit for.
□ **sit in on** *I sat in on a training session for therapists*: **attend**, be present at, be an observer at, observe, watch; N. Amer. audit.
□ **sit tight** informal **1** *this shouldn't take long—just sit tight*: **stay put**, stay there, wait there, remain in one's place. **2** *we're advising our clients to sit tight and neither buy nor sell*: **take no action**, wait, hold back, hang back, be patient, bide one's time, play a waiting game; informal hold one's horses.

site noun **1** *the site of the Battle of Flodden*: **location**, place, position, situation, locality, whereabouts, locale, spot, scene, setting; technical locus.
2 *a building site*: **plot**, lot, area; N. Amer. plat.
▸ **verb** *175 weapons have been dumped in bins sited at police stations*: **place**, put, position, situate, locate, set, install.

sitting noun *all-night sittings of Parliament*: **session**, meeting, assembly, plenary; hearing; consultation; Scottish sederunt, diet; N. Amer. & NZ caucus.
▸ **adjective** *a sitting position*: **sedentary**, seated.
▷ANTONYMS standing.

sitting room noun **living room**, lounge, front room, drawing room, morning room, reception room, salon, family room; S. African sitkamer; dated parlour, withdrawing room.

situate verb *hypermarkets are usually situated on the outskirts of towns*: **locate**, site, set, position, place, base; build, establish; install; station, post.

situation noun **1** *the club's financial situation had deteriorated*: **circumstances**, set of circumstances, state of affairs, affairs, state, condition, case; predicament, plight; informal kettle of fish, ball game.
2 *have a drink—it'll give me a chance to fill you in on* **the situation**: **the facts**, the picture, how things stand, the lie of the land, what's going on; Brit. the state of play; N. Amer. the lay of the land; informal what's what, the score, the set-up.
3 *the hotel enjoys a pleasant situation on the south bank of the River Swale*: **location**, place, position, spot, site, locality, locale; setting, environment; Austral./NZ informal possy; technical locus.
4 *he had recently been offered a situation in America*: **job**, post, position, place, appointment; employment; informal berth; Austral. informal grip; archaic employ.
5 archaic *he was much above my sister's situation in life*: **status**, station, position, standing, footing, rank, degree.

six cardinal number **sextet**, sextuplets; Poetry sestet, sestina, senarius, sixain; technical hexad; rare sixsome.

□ **at sixes and sevens** *he was at sixes and sevens about how to describe what was going on in education*: **chaotic**, disorganized, disordered, disorderly, untidy, messy, jumbled, muddled, confused, unsystematic, irregular, cluttered, littered; out of order, out of place, in disarray, in a mess, in a jumble, in a muddle, upside-down, higgledy-piggledy, haywire, haphazard; informal all over the place, like a bomb's hit it; Brit. informal shambolic, all over the shop; N. Amer. informal all over the map, all over the lot; rare orderless.

Word links **six**

hexa-: *hexameter*, **sex(i)-:** *sexivalent* related prefixes
senary relating to six
hexagon six-sided figure
sexennial relating to six years

sixth adjective
□ **sixth sense** *none of us were born with that sixth sense for handling audiences*: **instinct**, intuition, intuitiveness; clairvoyance, second sight, divination, ESP (extrasensory perception).

size noun *the room was of medium size | she seemed slightly awed by the size of the building*: **dimensions**, measurements, proportions, magnitude, largeness, bigness, bulk, area, expanse, square footage, footage, acreage; breadth, width, length, height, depth; extent, scope, range, scale; volume, capacity, mass, weight, avoirdupois; immensity, amplitude, hugeness, vastness.
▶ verb *the drills are sized in millimetres*: **sort**, categorize, classify.
□ **size someone/something up** *having sized up the competition, I was confident that I had nothing to fear*: **assess**, appraise, form an estimate of, measure up, take the measure of, weigh up, estimate, judge, take stock of, evaluate, gauge, rate; Brit. informal suss out.

sizeable adjective *sizeable sums of money*: **fairly large**, substantial, considerable, respectable, significant, largish, biggish, decent, decent-sized, generous, handsome; Scottish & N. English bonny; informal tidy, not to be sneezed at, serious; archaic goodly.
▷ANTONYMS small, tiny.

sizzle verb *thick slabs of bacon sizzled in the pan*: **crackle**, frizzle, sputter, hiss, spit, fry.

sizzling adjective informal **1** *the sizzling summer temperatures*: **extremely hot**, red-hot, unbearably hot, baking (hot), blazing, flaming, fiery, burning, scorching, blistering, searing, sweltering, torrid, tropical, like an oven, like a furnace, like a blowtorch; parching, withering; N. Amer. broiling; informal boiling (hot).
▷ANTONYMS freezing.
2 *that was the start of a sizzling affair*: **passionate**, torrid, amorous, ardent, sexy, lustful, erotic; informal steamy, hot, red-hot.

skedaddle verb informal *when he saw us, he skedaddled*. See **run away**.

skeletal adjective **1** *a tall, skeletal man*: **emaciated**, very thin, as thin as a rake, cadaverous, skin-and-bones, hollow-cheeked, scrawny, scraggy, skinny, size-zero, bony, angular, stick-like, raw-boned, lantern-jawed, gaunt, haggard, wasted; starved, half-starved, undernourished, underfed; shrunken, wizened, fleshless; informal looking like a bag of bones, anorexic, anorectic; dated spindle-shanked; archaic starveling.
▷ANTONYMS fat, obese.
2 *a rather skeletal account of the phenomenon*: **lacking in detail**, incomplete, outline, inadequate, insufficient, fragmentary, sketchy, patchy, bitty, scrappy, broad-brush, superficial, perfunctory; thumbnail.
▷ANTONYMS detailed, full, thorough.

skeleton noun **1** *she was no more than a skeleton at the end*: **skin and bone**, stick, scrag; informal bag of bones; Scottish informal skinnymalinks; archaic starveling.
2 *the concrete skeleton of an unfinished building*: **framework**, basic structure, frame, shell; chassis.
3 *the skeleton of a report*: **outline**, draft, abstract, plan, blueprint; main points, bones, bare bones; sketch, rough draft.
▶ adjective *there was only a skeleton staff on duty*: **minimum**, minimal, smallest possible, basic, reduced; essential.

Word links **skeleton**

osteology study of the skeleton

sketch noun **1** *a quick sketch of the proposed design*: **drawing**, preliminary drawing, outline; diagram, representation, delineation, design, plan; tracing; informal rough; technical underdrawing, cartoon, maquette, ébauche, esquisse, croquis.
2 *she slipped next door and gave May a rough sketch of what had happened*: **outline**, brief idea, rundown, run-through, main points, thumbnail sketch, bones, bare bones, skeleton; **summary**, synopsis, brief description, recapitulation, summarization, abstract, precis, résumé; French tour d'horizon; N. Amer. wrap-up; informal recap.
3 *a biographical sketch*: **description**, portrait, vignette, cameo, profile, portrayal, depiction; potted biography.
4 *a hilarious sketch from their latest BBC series*: **skit**, scene, piece, performance, act, item, turn, routine, number; playlet.
▶ verb **1** *as they talked, he began to sketch the garden*: **draw**, make a drawing of, draw a picture of, depict, portray, represent, delineate, pencil; rough out, outline.
2 *the company **sketched out** its plans for tackling the problem*: **describe**, outline, give a brief idea of, give a rundown of, give a thumbnail sketch of, rough out, block out, trace out, chalk out, map out, delineate, indicate; **summarize**, give a summary of, give an abstract/precis/résumé of, precis, recapitulate.

sketchily adverb *this idea is only sketchily outlined in the prologue*: **perfunctorily**, cursorily, superficially, scantily, skimpily; incompletely, imperfectly, patchily, scrappily; vaguely, imprecisely, roughly, crudely; hastily, hurriedly, in a hurry.
▷ANTONYMS thoroughly, exhaustively, fully.

sketchy adjective *he has only been able to provide the police with sketchy details of the youths*: **incomplete**, inadequate, limited, patchy, scrappy, bitty, fragmentary, rudimentary; **superficial**, cursory, perfunctory, slight, scanty, skimpy, meagre, insufficient; **vague**, imprecise, fuzzy; hurried, hasty, provisional; informal on the back of an envelope.
▷ANTONYMS detailed, exhaustive, full.

skew-whiff adjective & adverb Brit. informal *his tie was skew-whiff*. See **crooked** (sense 4).

skilful adjective *he was also a skilful diplomat*: **expert**, accomplished, skilled, masterly, virtuoso, master, consummate, proficient, talented, gifted, adept, adroit, deft, dexterous, able, good, competent, capable, efficient, experienced, trained, practised, professional, polished, well versed, versed, smart, clever, ingenious, brilliant, ready, apt, handy, artful; informal great, mean, wicked, nifty, crack, ace, wizard; Brit. informal a dab hand at; N. Amer. informal crackerjack; vulgar slang shit-hot; archaic or humorous compleat; rare habile.
▷ANTONYMS incompetent, inept, amateurish.

skill noun **1** *once again, he demonstrated his skill as a politician*: **expertise**, skilfulness, expertness, adeptness, adroitness, deftness, dexterity, ability, prowess, mastery, competence, competency, capability, efficiency, aptitude, artistry, art, finesse, flair, virtuosity, experience, professionalism, talent, cleverness, smartness, ingenuity, versatility, knack, readiness, handiness; informal know-how.
▷ANTONYMS incompetence.
2 *bringing up a family gives you many skills*: **accomplishment**, strength, gift, forte.

skilled adjective *more than 170 skilled engineers are employed on the project*: **experienced**, trained, qualified, professional, proficient, practised, seasoned, accomplished, expert, skilful, master, talented, gifted, adept, adroit, deft, dexterous, able, good, competent, capable, efficient, well versed, versed, smart, clever; informal crack; N. Amer. informal crackerjack.
▷ANTONYMS unskilled, inexperienced.

skim verb **1** *as the scum rises, skim it off*: **remove**, take off, scoop off, spoon off, ladle off; cream.
2 *the boat skimmed over the waters of the loch*: **glide**, move lightly, slide, sail, plane, scud, skate, float, coast; aquaplane, skid.
3 *he bent to pick up a small pebble, skimming it across the water*: **throw**, toss, fling, cast, pitch; bounce, skip.
4 *she **skimmed through** the newspaper*: **glance through**, flick through, flip through, leaf through, thumb through, read quickly, scan, look through, have a quick look at, run one's eye over, dip into, browse through.
▷ANTONYMS pore over.
5 *Hannah had **skimmed over** this part of the story as she told it to the policeman*: **mention briefly**, make only brief mention of, pass over quickly, skate over, gloss over; skip.
▷ANTONYMS elaborate on.

skimp verb **1** *whatever fabric you buy, don't **skimp on** the amount*: **stint on**, scrimp on, be sparing with, be economical with, economize on, be frugal with, cut back on; **be mean with**, be parsimonious with, be niggardly with; cut corners, pinch pennies; informal be stingy with, be mingy with, be tight with.
▷ANTONYMS squander, lavish.
2 *the process cannot be skimped*: **do hastily**, do carelessly, dash off, cut corners with; rare scamp.

skimpy adjective **1** *Judy wriggled into a skimpy black dress*: **revealing**, short, brief, scanty, insubstantial; low, low-cut; flimsy, thin, see-through, indecent.
▷ANTONYMS modest.
2 *the information on second-home ownership is rather skimpy*: **meagre**, scanty, scant, sketchy, limited, restricted, inadequate, insufficient, paltry, deficient, negligible, insubstantial, small, sparse; rare exiguous.
▷ANTONYMS comprehensive, exhaustive.

skin noun **1** *these chemicals could damage the skin*: **epidermis**, dermis; technical cuticle, cutis, corium, derma, derm, integument, tegument.
2 *Mary's fair skin*: **complexion**, colouring, skin colour, skin tone, pigmentation.

3 *until recent years, leopard skins fetched high prices*: **hide**, pelt, fleece; Austral. greenhide; technical crop, kip; archaic fell.
4 *a banana skin*: **peel**, rind, outside; technical integument.
5 *the coffee was cold, with a skin on it | the water was covered by a thin skin of ice*: **film**, coating, coat, layer, overlay; sheet; membrane; technical pellicle.
6 *the plane's skin was ripped apart by the force of the explosion*: **casing**, cover, covering, exterior, pod.
□ **by the skin of one's teeth** *he won, but only by the skin of his teeth*: **only just**, just, narrowly, by a hair's breadth, by a very small margin, by the narrowest of margins, barely, by a nose; informal by a whisker.
□ **get under someone's skin 1** *it was the sheer effrontery of them which got under my skin*: **irritate**, annoy, gall, irk, get/put someone's back up, pique, rankle with, nettle, needle, bother, vex, provoke, displease, upset, offend, affront, anger, exasperate, disgruntle, ruffle, get on someone's nerves, ruffle someone's feathers, make someone's hackles rise, raise someone's hackles, rub up the wrong way; informal peeve, aggravate, miff, get, get in someone's hair, get up someone's nose, hack off, get someone's goat; Brit. informal nark, get on someone's wick, give someone the hump, wind up, get across; N. Amer. informal tick off, rankle, ride, gravel; vulgar slang piss off; Brit. vulgar slang get on someone's tits; rare exacerbate, hump, rasp. **2** *she's got under my skin—I can't stop thinking about her*: **obsess**, intrigue, captivate, interest greatly, charm; enthral, enchant, fill someone's mind, mesmerize, hypnotize, entrance.
□ **it's no skin off my nose** informal *it's no skin off my nose—I never wanted to go to Germany in the first place*: **I don't care**, I don't mind, I'm not bothered, it doesn't bother me, it doesn't matter to me, it's of no concern to me, it's of no importance to me; informal I don't give/care a damn/hoot/toss/rap, I don't give a monkey's; vulgar slang I don't give a shit.
▶ **verb 1** *scald and skin the tomatoes*: **peel**, pare, hull; technical decorticate.
2 *he slipped and skinned his knee*: **graze**, scrape, abrade, bark, cut, rub something raw, chafe; technical excoriate.
3 informal *Dad would* ***skin me alive*** *if I forgot it*: **punish severely**, tan/whip someone's hide; informal murder, scalp, thump, give it to someone, come down on someone (like a ton of bricks), have someone's guts for garters; Brit. informal give someone what for.

> *Word links* **skin**
>
> **cutaneous** relating to the skin
> **dermato-** related prefix
> **subcutaneous** under the skin
> **dermatology** branch of medicine concerning the skin
> **dermatoglyphics** study of skin markings
> **dermatoplasty** surgical repair of skin

skin-deep adjective *their left-wing attitudes were only skin-deep*: **superficial**, on the surface, surface, external, outward; shallow, empty, artificial, meaningless.
▷**ANTONYMS** deep, heartfelt.

skinflint noun informal *don't be such a skinflint—you earn more than she does*: **miser**, penny-pincher, Scrooge, pinchpenny, niggard, cheese-parer; informal meanie, money-grubber, cheapskate; N. Amer. informal tightwad; vulgar slang tight-arse.
▷**ANTONYMS** spendthrift.

skinny adjective *a tall, skinny man*: **thin**, scrawny, scraggy, bony, angular, raw-boned, hollow-cheeked, gaunt, as thin as a rake, skin-and-bones, stick-like, size-zero, emaciated, skeletal, pinched, undernourished, underfed; **slim**, lean, slender, rangy; lanky, spindly, gangly, gangling, gawky; informal looking like a bag of bones, anorexic, anorectic; dated spindle-shanked; rare starveling, macilent.
▷**ANTONYMS** fat, plump, obese.

skip verb **1** *she began to skip down the path*: **caper**, prance, trip, dance, bound, jump, leap, spring, hop, bounce, gambol, frisk, romp, cavort, bob; rare curvet.
▷**ANTONYMS** trudge.
2 *if you don't mind, I'd rather we skipped the biographical stuff*: **omit**, leave out, miss out, dispense with, do without, pass over, bypass, skim over, steer clear of, disregard, ignore; informal give something a miss.
▷**ANTONYMS** include.
3 *I skipped school to visit my mother*: **fail to attend**, play truant from, miss, absent oneself from, take French leave from; N. Amer. cut; Brit. informal skive off, wag; N. Amer. informal play hookey from, goof off; Austral./NZ informal play the wag from.
▷**ANTONYMS** attend.
4 *I'll* ***skip through*** *the magazine first*: **glance at**, have a quick look at, flick through, flip through, leaf through, scan, run one's eye over.
▷**ANTONYMS** pore over.
5 informal *I'm not giving them a chance to* ***skip off*** *again*: **run off**, run away, do a disappearing act, make off, take off; informal beat it, clear off, vamoose, skedaddle, split, cut and run, fly the coop, do a fade; Brit. informal do a runner, do a bunk, scarper; N. Amer. informal light out, cut out, take a powder; Austral. informal go through, shoot through; vulgar slang bugger off.
▷**ANTONYMS** stay, stay put.

skirmish noun **1** *the unit was caught up in several skirmishes*: **fight**, battle, clash, conflict, encounter, confrontation, engagement, fray, contest, combat, tussle, scrimmage, fracas, affray, melee; archaic rencounter.
2 *there was a skirmish over the budget*: **argument**, quarrel, squabble, contretemps, disagreement, difference of opinion, dissension, falling-out, dispute, disputation, contention, clash, altercation, exchange, war of words; Irish, N. Amer., & Austral. donnybrook; informal tiff, set-to, run-in, spat, dust-up; Brit. informal row, barney, ding-dong, bust-up, bit of argy-bargy, ruck; Scottish informal rammy; archaic broil, miff; Scottish archaic threap, collieshangie.
▶ **verb** *they* ***skirmished*** *briefly* ***with*** *soldiers from Fort Benton*: **fight**, do battle with, battle with, engage with, close with, combat, clash with, come to blows with, exchange blows with, struggle with, tussle with; informal scrap with.

skirt ▶ **verb 1** *he did not go through the city but skirted it*: **go round**, move round, walk round, circle, circumnavigate.
2 *the fields that skirted the highway were full of cattle*: **border**, edge, flank, fringe, line, lie alongside.
3 *he had carefully* ***skirted round*** *the subject of Elise*: **avoid**, evade, steer clear of, sidestep, dodge, circumvent, bypass, pass over, fight shy of; ignore, overlook, gloss over, fail to mention; informal duck; Austral./NZ informal duck-shove.

skit noun *an old vaudeville skit | a skit on daytime magazine programmes*: **comedy sketch**, act, piece, turn, item, routine, number; **parody**, take-off, pastiche, burlesque, satire, travesty, squib; informal spoof, send-up; Brit. vulgar slang piss-take; rare pasquinade.

skittish adjective **1** *she joined in the drinking and afterwards grew skittish*: **playful**, lively, high-spirited, frisky, coltish; flirtatious, kittenish, coquettish; informal flirty; archaic frolicsome, sportive, gamesome, frolic, wanton.
▷**ANTONYMS** solemn, staid.
2 *Cranston's mount was skittish*: **restive**, excitable, nervous, easily frightened; skittery, jumpy, fidgety, highly strung.
▷**ANTONYMS** calm.

skive verb Brit. informal *they'll think I'm skiving | I skived off school*: **malinger**, pretend to be ill, feign/fake illness; play truant, truant; **avoid work**, evade one's duty, shirk, skulk, idle; N. Amer. cut; Brit. informal bunk off, swing the lead, wag, scrimshank, dodge the column; Irish informal mitch off; N. Amer. informal goldbrick, play hookey, goof off; Austral./NZ informal play the wag.

skiver noun Brit. informal **malingerer**, shirker, work-dodger, idler, layabout; informal do-nothing, slacker, cyberslacker, passenger; Brit. informal lead-swinger, scrimshanker; N. Amer. informal gold brick, goof-off; Austral./NZ informal bludger; French archaic fainéant.

skulduggery noun *there is no evidence to support any allegations of skulduggery*: **trickery**, swindling, fraudulence, double-dealing, sharp practice, unscrupulousness, underhandedness, chicanery, machinations; informal shenanigans, funny business, hanky-panky, monkey business; Brit. informal monkey tricks, jiggery-pokery; N. Amer. informal monkeyshines.

skulk verb *he spent most of his time skulking about the corridors*: **lurk**, loiter, hide, conceal oneself, lie in wait, keep out of sight; **creep**, sneak, slink, move furtively, sidle, slope, pad, prowl, tiptoe, pussyfoot.

skull noun

> *Word links* **skull**
>
> **cranial** relating to the skull
> **cranio-** related prefix, as in *craniotomy*
> **phrenology** study of skull shape as supposed indicator of character
> **craniology** study of the skull
> **craniometry** measurement of the skull
> **craniotomy** incision into skull

sky noun *they lay on the grass, gazing up at* ***the sky***: **the atmosphere**, the stratosphere, the skies, airspace; literary **the heavens**, the firmament, the vault of heaven, the blue, the (wide) blue yonder, the welkin, the ether, the empyrean, the azure, the upper regions, the sphere.
□ **to the skies** *he wrote to his sister praising Lizzie to the skies*: **effusively**, profusely, very highly, very enthusiastically, unreservedly, without reserve, ardently, fervently; fulsomely, extravagantly, inordinately, excessively, immoderately.

> *Word links* **sky**
>
> **celestial**, **supernal**, **empyrean** relating to the sky

slab noun *slabs of concrete | a chipped saucer containing a slab of soap*: **piece**, block, hunk, chunk, lump; portion; cake, tablet, brick, wodge.

slack adjective **1** *she heard a splash and the rope went slack*: **loose**, limp, not taut, not tight, hanging, flapping; relaxed, flexible, pliant.
▷**ANTONYMS** tight, taut, stretched.
2 *try these tips to tone and tighten slack, unattractive skin*: **flaccid**, flabby, loose, sagging, saggy, drooping, droopy, soft.

S

▷ANTONYMS taut, toned, firm.
3 *she was wearing a slack blue dress*: **baggy**, loose-fitting, loose, not tight, generously cut, roomy; shapeless, sack-like, oversized, ill-fitting, bagging, hanging, flapping, saggy.
▷ANTONYMS tight, tailored.
4 *business had never been so slack*: **sluggish**, slow, quiet, slow-moving, not busy, inactive, flat, depressed, stagnant.
▷ANTONYMS busy, thriving.
5 *some slack defensive play by Villa*: **lax**, negligent, neglectful, remiss, careless, slapdash, slipshod, lackadaisical, lazy, inefficient, incompetent, inattentive, offhand, casual, disorderly, disorganized; N. Amer. derelict; informal sloppy, slap-happy, do-nothing, asleep at the wheel; Brit. vulgar slang half-arsed; formal delinquent; rare otiose, poco-curante.
▷ANTONYMS meticulous, diligent.
▶ **noun 1** *the rope had just enough slack in it to allow her to reach him*: **looseness**, play, give.
2 *as domestic demand starts to flag, foreign demand will help pick up the slack*: **surplus**, excess, residue, spare capacity.
3 *he slept deeply, refreshed by a little slack in the daily routine*: **lull**, pause, respite, spell of inactivity, interval, break, hiatus, breathing space; informal let-up, breather.
▶ **verb 1** *the horse slacked his pace*: **reduce**, lessen, slacken, slow, ease up/off.
▷ANTONYMS increase.
2 Brit. informal *okay, carry on with this painting and no slacking*: **idle**, shirk, be inactive, be lazy, be indolent, sit back and do nothing, waste time, lounge about; Brit. informal skive, bunk off; N. Amer. informal goof off.
▷ANTONYMS work hard.
□ **slack off 1** *the rain had slacked off to a soft drizzle*: **decrease**, lessen, subside, get less, let up, ease off, abate, moderate, diminish, dwindle, die down, fall off, drop off, taper off, ebb, recede, wane. ▷ANTONYMS intensify.
2 *I told him to slack off a bit*: **relax**, take things easy, let up, ease up/off, do less, loosen up, slow down, be less active; N. Amer. informal hang loose, stay loose, chill out. ▷ANTONYMS work harder.
□ **slack up** *the horse didn't slack up until he reached the trees*: **slow down**, slow, decelerate, reduce speed, drop speed, put the brakes on.
▷ANTONYMS speed up, accelerate.

slacken **verb 1** *he slackened his grip | the straps can be slackened to allow greater freedom of movement*: **loosen**, make looser, release, relax, loose; lessen, reduce, weaken; Nautical, dated veer.
▷ANTONYMS tighten.
2 *her footsteps slackened | he slackened his pace a little*: **become/get/make slower**, slow down, slow, decelerate, reduce in speed, slack.
▷ANTONYMS speed up, quicken.
3 *I think the rain might just be slackening*: **decrease**, lessen, subside, ease up/off, get less, let up, abate, moderate, become less intense, slack off, diminish, dwindle, die down, fall off, drop off, taper off, ebb, recede, wane.

slacker **noun** informal **layabout**, idler, shirker, loafer, malingerer, work-dodger, clock-watcher, good-for-nothing, sluggard, laggard; informal passenger, lazybones, slugabed, couch potato, cyberslacker; Brit. informal skiver, lead-swinger, scrimshanker; N. Amer. informal gold brick, goof-off; Austral./NZ informal bludger; French, archaic fainéant.
▷ANTONYMS workaholic.

slag **verb** Brit. informal
□ **slag someone/something off** See **criticize**.

slake **verb** *slake your thirst with a citron pressé*: **quench**, satisfy, take the edge off, sate, satiate, relieve, assuage, gratify.

slam **verb 1** *he left the room, slamming the door behind him*: **bang**, shut/close with a bang, shut/close noisily, shut/close with a crash, shut/close with force, fling shut.
▷ANTONYMS pull something to, close gently.
2 *the car mounted the pavement, **slamming into** a lamp post*: **crash into**, smash into, smack into, collide with, be in collision with, hit, strike, ram, plough into, meet head-on, run into, bump into, crack into/against; N. Amer. impact.
▷ANTONYMS miss.
3 informal *he was slammed by the critics for his first-half performance*. See **criticize**.

slander **noun** *he'd sue me for slander if I made the accusation publicly*: **defamation**, defamation of character, character assassination, misrepresentation of character, calumny, libel; scandalmongering, malicious gossip, muckraking, smear campaigning, disparagement, denigration, derogation, aspersions, vilification, traducement, obloquy, backbiting, scurrility; lie, slur, smear, untruth, false accusation, false report, insult, slight; informal mud-slinging; N. Amer. informal bad-mouthing; archaic contumely.
▷ANTONYMS acclamation, praise.
▶ **verb** *they were accused of slandering the head of state*: **defame**, defame someone's character, blacken someone's name, give someone a bad name, tell lies about, speak ill/evil of, drag through the mud/mire, throw/sling/fling mud at, sully someone's reputation, libel, smear, run a smear campaign against, cast aspersions on, spread scandal about, besmirch, tarnish, taint, misrepresent; **malign**, traduce, vilify, calumniate, disparage, denigrate, decry, run down; N. Amer. slur; Brit. informal do a hatchet job on; rare derogate, asperse, vilipend.
▷ANTONYMS acclaim, praise.

> *Choose the right word* **slander, malign, libel, defame, traduce**
>
> See **malign**.

slanderous **adjective** *you have no right to make such slanderous accusations*: **defamatory**, denigratory, disparaging, derogatory, libellous, pejorative, false, untrue, lying, misrepresentative, damaging, injurious, scurrilous, scandalous, poisonous, vicious, opprobrious, malicious, abusive, insulting; informal dirty, mud-slinging; rare calumnious, calumniatory, aspersive, aspersory.

> *Word toolkit* **slanderous**
>
> See **abusive**.

slang **noun** **informal language**, colloquialisms, idioms, patois, argot, cant, dialect; jargon, terminology; rhyming slang, back slang; informal lingo.

slanging match **noun** Brit. informal *the decision provoked a slanging match between all three major parties*. See **quarrel**.

slant **verb 1** *he felt as though the floor was beginning to slant*: **slope**, tilt, incline, be at an angle, angle, tip, cant, be askew, skew, lean, dip, pitch, shelve, list, bank, heel.
2 *it doesn't automatically follow that their findings will be slanted in favour of their own beliefs*: **bias**, distort, twist, skew, colour, weight, spin, angle, orient, give a slant to, give a bias to.
▶ **noun 1** *the slant of the roof*: **slope**, incline, tilt, ramp, gradient, pitch, angle, rake, cant, camber, skew, leaning, inclination, shelving, listing.
2 *some of the essays have a feminist slant*: **point of view**, viewpoint, standpoint, stance, angle, perspective, approach, view, opinion, attitude, position, frame of reference; bias, leaning, partiality, prejudice, twist, bent; spin.

slanting **adjective** *the slanting angle of the deck*: **oblique**, sloping, at an angle, angled, not straight, on an incline, inclined, tilting, tilted, atilt, slanted, aslant, slantwise, diagonal, canted, cambered, leaning, dipping, shelving, listing; crooked, askew, skew; Scottish squint; N. Amer. cater-cornered, catty-cornered, kitty-corner.
▷ANTONYMS straight.

slap **verb 1** *he slapped her hard across the face*: **hit**, strike, smack, crack, clout, cuff, thump, punch, thwack, spank, rap, beat; informal whack, wallop, biff, swipe, clip, bop, belt, bash, sock; Brit. informal slosh; N. Amer. informal boff, slug, bust; Austral./NZ informal dong, quilt; archaic smite.
2 *he slapped a £10 note down on the table*: **fling**, throw, toss, sling, slam, bang; informal bung, plonk.
3 *all you need to do is slap on a coat of paint*: **daub**, plaster, spread; apply.
4 informal *the United States slapped a huge tax on European wine imports*: **impose**, levy, put on, add.
□ **slap someone down** informal *Uncle Max was always slapping me down for being big-headed*: **reprimand**, rebuke, reproach, scold, admonish, take to task; squash, squelch, put down, put someone in their place, take down a peg or two, deflate; informal tell off; Brit. informal tick off, have a go at.
▶ **noun** *he gave her a slap across the cheek*: **smack**, blow, thump, cuff, clout, punch, crack, thwack; spank, rap, bang; informal whack, wallop, clip, biff, swipe, bop, belt, bash, sock.
□ **a slap in the face** *his remarks were a slap in the face for the local community*: **rebuff**, rejection, snub, insult, affront, put-down, humiliation, a blow to one's pride.
▷ANTONYMS praise.
□ **a slap on the back** *they deserve a hearty slap on the back for their efforts*: **congratulations**, commendation, approbation, approval, accolades, encomiums, compliments, tributes, a pat on the back, praise, acclaim, acclamation, a round of applause; informal a (big) hand; rare laudation.
▷ANTONYMS condemnation, criticism.
□ **a slap on the wrist** *this was not a question, but a slap on the wrist*: **reprimand**, rebuke, reproof, scolding, admonition, admonishment, reproval; informal telling-off, rap over the knuckles, dressing-down; Brit. informal ticking-off, wigging; Austral./NZ informal serve; Brit. vulgar slang **bollocking**.
▶ **adverb** informal *the bypass goes slap through Oxford's green belt*: **straight**, right, directly, squarely, dead, plumb, point-blank; **exactly**, precisely; informal smack, bang, slap bang; N. Amer. informal spang, smack dab.

slapdash **adjective** *this can lead to slapdash, irresponsible journalism*: **careless**, slipshod, lackadaisical, hasty, hurried, disorganized, haphazard, unsystematic, untidy, messy, thrown together, last-minute, hit-or-miss, offhand, thoughtless, heedless, negligent, neglectful, remiss, cursory, perfunctory, lax, slack; informal sloppy, shambolic, all over the place, slap-happy; Brit. informal all over the shop.
▷ANTONYMS careful, meticulous, painstaking.

slap-happy adverb informal **1** *Drysdale's slap-happy friend*: **happy-go-lucky**, devil-may-care, carefree, cheerful, breezy, easy-going, nonchalant, insouciant, blithe, airy, casual, irresponsible.
▷ANTONYMS serious, solemn.
2 *the slap-happy way the tests were carried out*. See **slapdash**.
3 *she's a bit slap-happy after such a narrow escape*: **dazed**, stupefied, punch-drunk, unsteady, wobbly.

slap-up adjective Brit. informal *a slap-up dinner*: **lavish**, sumptuous, elaborate, expensive, no-expense-spared, fit for a king, princely; excellent, splendid, magnificent, marvellous, superb, first-class.
▷ANTONYMS meagre.

slash verb **1** *her car had been scratched and the tyres slashed | she threatened to slash her wrists*: **cut (open)**, gash, slit, split open, lacerate, knife, hack, make an incision in, score; rip, tear; literary rend.
2 informal *the company was forced to slash prices*: **reduce**, cut, drop, bring down, mark down, lower, put down.
▷ANTONYMS raise, put up.
3 informal *they have threatened to slash 10,000 jobs worldwide*: **get rid of**, axe, cut, shed, lose.
▷ANTONYMS create.
▶noun **1** *he staggered over with a crimson slash across his temple*: **cut**, gash, laceration, slit, hack, score, incision; wound, injury; rip, tear, rent.
2 *sentence breaks are indicated by slashes*: **solidus**, **oblique**, backslash, diagonal, virgule, slant.

slashing adjective informal *a slashing attack by the newspapers*: **devastating**, withering, blistering, extremely critical, searing, scorching, fierce, ferocious, savage, severe, stinging, biting, cutting, incisive, mordant, trenchant, virulent, caustic, vitriolic, scornful, sharp, bitter, acid, harsh, unsparing; rare mordacious.
▷ANTONYMS mild, gentle; complimentary.

slate verb Brit. informal *his work was slated by the critics*: **criticize harshly**, attack, pillory, lambaste, condemn, flay, savage, shoot down, revile, vilify; informal pan, knock, tear/pull/take to pieces, take/pull apart, crucify, hammer, slam, do a hatchet job on, bash, give something a battering, roast, skewer, maul, throw brickbats at; Brit. informal rubbish, slag off, monster; N. Amer. informal trash, pummel; Austral./NZ informal bag; archaic slash; rare excoriate.
▷ANTONYMS praise, commend, applaud.

slatternly adjective *a slatternly girl wearing cardigans and a thick scarf*: **slovenly**, untidy, messy, scruffy, unkempt, ill-groomed, dishevelled, frowzy, blowsy; dirty, grubby; sluttish; N. Amer. informal raggedy; archaic draggle-tailed.

slaughter verb **1** *more than 150 bison were slaughtered to provide meat*: **kill**, butcher.
2 *innocent civilians are being slaughtered*: **massacre**, murder, butcher, kill, kill off, annihilate, exterminate, execute, liquidate, eliminate, destroy, decimate, wipe out, mow down, cut down, cut to pieces, put to the sword, put to death, send to the gas chambers; literary slay.
3 informal *the first team were slaughtered*: **defeat utterly**, **trounce**, annihilate, beat hollow, drub, give a drubbing to, crush, rout; informal hammer, clobber, thrash, paste, pound, pulverize, massacre, crucify, demolish, destroy, wipe the floor with, take to the cleaners, make mincemeat of, murder, flatten, turn inside out; Brit. informal stuff, marmalize; N. Amer. informal shellac, blow out, cream, skunk.
▶noun **1** *the slaughter of 20 peaceful demonstrators*: **massacre**, **murder**, murdering; mass murder, mass killing, wholesale killing, indiscriminate killing, mass homicide, execution, mass execution, destruction, mass destruction, annihilation, extermination, liquidation, decimation, carnage, butchery; pogrom, genocide, ethnic cleansing, holocaust, Shoah, night of the long knives; literary slaying; rare battue, hecatomb.
2 *a scene of slaughter*: **carnage**, bloodshed, indiscriminate bloodshed, bloodletting; bloodbath.
3 informal *a desperate attempt to avoid their imminent electoral slaughter*: **crushing defeat**, annihilation, drubbing, trouncing, rout; informal massacre, hammering, thrashing, caning, demolition, going-over, licking, pasting, pounding; N. Amer. informal shellacking.

slaughterhouse noun **abattoir**; Brit. butchery, knacker's yard; archaic shambles, butcher-row.

slave noun **1** historical *most of the work on the land was done by slaves*: **bondsman**, bondswoman, bondservant, bondslave, serf, vassal, thrall; historical helot, odalisque, blackbird, hierodule.
▷ANTONYMS freeman, master.
2 *Anna was attracted to him and within 24 hours was his willing slave*: **drudge**, servant, general factotum, man/maid of all work, lackey, minion; Brit. informal skivvy, dogsbody, slavey, poodle, fag; N. Amer. gofer; rare slaveling.
▶verb *I'm sick of slaving away for a pittance*: **toil**, labour, grind, sweat, work one's fingers to the bone, work day and night, work like a Trojan/dog, keep one's nose to the grindstone, exert oneself, grub, plod, plough; informal work one's guts out, work one's socks off, kill oneself, sweat blood, knock oneself out, plug away, slog away; Brit. informal graft, fag; Austral./NZ informal bullock; Brit. vulgar slang work one's balls/arse/nuts off; N. Amer. vulgar slang work one's ass/butt off; archaic drudge, travail, moil.
▷ANTONYMS relax; skive.

Word links **slave**

servile like a slave

slave-driver noun **(hard) taskmaster**, (hard) taskmistress, tyrant.

slaver verb *the Labrador was slavering at the mouth*: **drool**, slobber, dribble, salivate; Scottish & Irish slabber; archaic drivel.

slavery noun **1** historical *thousands had been sold into slavery*: **bondage**, enslavement, servitude, subjugation, thraldom, thrall, serfdom, vassalage, enthralment, yoke; captivity, bonds, chains, fetters, shackles; US History peculiar institution.
▷ANTONYMS freedom, liberty, emancipation.
2 *working here is sheer slavery*: **drudgery**, toil, (hard) slog, hard labour, grind, sweated labour; Austral./NZ informal (hard) yakka; archaic travail, moil.
▷ANTONYMS sinecure, soft option, money for old rope.

slavish adjective **1** *they were reviled as slavish lackeys of the government*: **servile**, subservient, fawning, obsequious, sycophantic, excessively deferential, toadying, ingratiating, unctuous, grovelling, cringing, toadyish, sycophantish, abject, craven, humble, Uriah Heepish, self-abasing; informal slimy, bootlicking, sucky, soapy, forelock-tugging; N. Amer. informal brown-nosing, apple-polishing; Brit. vulgar slang arse-licking, bum-sucking; N. Amer. vulgar slang kiss-ass, ass-kissing, suckholing.
▷ANTONYMS independent, assertive.
2 *a slavish copying of medieval motifs*: **unoriginal**, uninspired, unimaginative, uninventive, non-innovative, imitative, derivative.
▷ANTONYMS original, imaginative.

slay verb **1** *8,000 men from the regiment were slain*: **kill**, murder, put to death, do to death, put to the sword, butcher, cut down, cut to pieces, slaughter, massacre, shoot down, gun down, mow down, assassinate, execute, dispatch, destroy, eliminate, annihilate, exterminate, dispose of; informal wipe out, take out, bump off, do in, do for, rub out, top, wipe off the face of the earth, blow away, liquidate, stiff; N. Amer. informal waste, smoke, ice, off.
2 informal *you slay me, you really do*: **amuse greatly**, convulse with mirth/laughter, entertain greatly, make someone laugh; informal have people rolling in the aisles, make someone crack up, kill, knock dead, be the death of, wow, be a hit with; Brit. informal crease up.

slaying noun *the gruesome slaying of eleven youngsters*: **murder**, killing, homicide, putting to death, execution, butchery, slaughter, massacre, assassination, dispatch, destruction, extermination; informal liquidation; rare mactation.

sleazy adjective **1** *a series of deals involving sleazy arms dealers and middlemen*: **corrupt**, immoral, sordid, unsavoury, unpleasant, disreputable; informal shady, sleazoid, sleazo.
▷ANTONYMS reputable, principled.
2 *a sleazy tenpin bowling alley*: **squalid**, seedy, seamy, sordid, slummy, insalubrious, unpleasant, unprepossessing, mean, cheap, low-class, run down, down at heel; informal scruffy, scuzzy, tacky, crummy, grungy, ratty; Brit. informal grotty; N. Amer. informal skanky.
▷ANTONYMS upmarket, smart.

sledge noun **toboggan**, bobsleigh, sleigh; N. Amer. sled; in Canada carriole; in Russia kibitka; in Labrador komatik; historical travois.

sleek adjective **1** *his sleek dark hair*: **smooth**, **glossy**, shiny, shining, gleaming, lustrous, silken, silky, satiny, velvety, sheeny; well brushed, polished, burnished.
▷ANTONYMS dull, rough.
2 *he ran his hand lingeringly over the car's sleek lines*: **streamlined**, trim, aerodynamic; elegant, graceful, flowing, smooth.
3 *a group of sleek young men in city suits*: **well groomed**, stylish, wealthy-looking, prosperous-looking.
▷ANTONYMS unkempt, slovenly.

sleep noun *why don't you go and lie down and have a sleep?* **nap**, doze, rest, siesta, drowse, catnap; beauty sleep; informal snooze, forty winks, a bit of shut-eye, power nap; Brit. informal kip, zizz; children's language bye-byes; literary slumber.
□ **go to sleep** *I went to sleep almost as soon as my head hit the pillow*: **fall asleep**, get to sleep; informal drop off, nod off, go off, drift off, crash out, go out like a light, flake out, conk out; N. Amer. informal sack out, zone out.
□ **put something to sleep** *the horse's condition deteriorated and he was put to sleep*: **put down**, destroy, put out of its misery.
▶verb *she slept for about an hour*: **be asleep**, doze, rest, take a siesta, nap, take a nap, catnap, drowse; sleep like a log/top; informal snooze, snatch forty winks, get some shut-eye, be in the land of Nod; Brit. informal kip, have a kip, get one's head down, zizz, get some zizz, doss (down); N. Amer. informal catch some Zs; literary slumber, be in the arms of Morpheus.
▷ANTONYMS wake up.

S

Word links **sleep**

hypno- related prefix, as in *hypnotherapy*
narco- related prefix, as in *narcolepsy*
somn- related prefix, as in *somnambulism*
sedative, **hypnotic**, **soporific** causing sleep
hypnophobia fear of sleep

sleepiness noun **drowsiness**, tiredness, somnolence, languor, languidness, doziness; lethargy, sluggishness, inactivity, heaviness, lassitude, enervation, torpor, torpidity; Medicine narcosis, narcolepsy; rare somnolency, comatoseness, oscitancy, oscitation.

sleepless adjective *she spent a sleepless night agonizing over what had happened | he lay sleepless until dawn*: **wakeful**, restless, disturbed, without sleep; **awake**, wide awake, unsleeping, tossing and turning; insomniac; archaic watchful; rare insomnolent.

sleeplessness noun *sleeplessness can lead to irritability and aggression*: **insomnia**, wakefulness.

sleepwalker noun **somnambulist**, noctambulist; rare night-walker.

sleepwalking noun **somnambulism**, noctambulism; rare somnambulation, noctambulation, night-walking.

sleepy adjective **1** *it was a hot day and she felt very sleepy*: **drowsy**, tired, somnolent, languid, languorous, heavy-eyed, dozy, nodding, asleep on one's feet, yawning; lethargic, sluggish, inactive, enervated, torpid, comatose; informal snoozy, dopey, yawny; literary slumberous; rare oscitant, slumbersome.
▷ANTONYMS awake, alert.
2 *the sleepy heat of the afternoon*: **soporific**, sleep-inducing, somnolent, hypnotic.
▷ANTONYMS energizing, invigorating.
3 *a sleepy little fishing village*: **quiet**, peaceful, tranquil, placid, slow-moving, inactive; dull, boring, backwater, backwoods; informal one-horse.
▷ANTONYMS busy.

Word toolkit

sleepy	**tranquil**	**restful**
town	setting	sleep
backwater	atmosphere	night
seaside	beauty	slumber
hamlet	oasis	holiday
suburb	existence	break
morning	lake	weekend
summer	garden	activities

sleight of hand noun **1** *she rolled a cigarette with impressive sleight of hand*: **dexterity**, adroitness, deftness, nimbleness of fingers, skill.
2 *this is financial sleight of hand of the worst sort*: **deception**, deceit, dissimulation, double-dealing, chicanery, trickery, sharp practice, legerdemain.

slender adjective **1** *her tall slender figure*: **slim**, lean, willowy, sylphlike, svelte, lissom, graceful, snake-hipped, rangy; slight, slightly built, delicate; thin, skinny, size-zero, spare, attenuated, lanky, spindly; rare gracile, attenuate.
▷ANTONYMS fat, plump.
2 *a notion based on slender evidence*: **meagre**, limited, slight, modest, scanty, scant, sparse, small, little, paltry, inconsiderable, insubstantial, inadequate, insufficient, deficient, negligible, trifling; rare exiguous.
▷ANTONYMS considerable, substantial, abundant.
3 *the chances of recruiting enough people seemed slender*: **faint**, remote, feeble, flimsy, tenuous, fragile, slim; outside, distant, unlikely, improbable.
▷ANTONYMS good, strong.

sleuth noun informal **private detective**, detective, private investigator, investigator; Brit. enquiry agent; informal private eye, PI, snoop, sleuth-hound; N. Amer. informal private dick, dick, peeper, shamus, gumshoe; informal, dated hawkshaw, sherlock; N. Amer. dated Pinkerton.

slice noun **1** *a slice of fruit cake | thick slices of chicken*: **piece**, portion, wedge, chunk, hunk, lump, slab, segment; rasher, collop; sliver, wafer, shaving; helping; Brit. round; Cookery escalope, scallop, scaloppina, fricandeau; Brit. informal wodge; rare hunch.
2 *local authorities control a huge slice of public spending*: **share**, part, portion, tranche, piece, bit, parcel, proportion, allotment, allocation, percentage; ration, quota; informal cut, whack, rake-off.
▶ verb **1** *slice the cheese as thinly as possible*: **cut**, cut up, carve, divide, segment, section.
2 *one man had his ear **sliced off** in the fight*: **cut off**, sever, chop off, hack off, shear off; separate; rare dissever.

slick adjective **1** *a slick advertising campaign*: **efficient**, **smooth**, smooth-running, polished, well organized, well run, streamlined; skilful, deft, adroit, dexterous, masterly, professional, clever, smart, sharp, shrewd.
▷ANTONYMS amateurish, clumsy, inexpert.
2 *his slick use of the written word*: **glib**, smooth, fluent, plausible, neat, pat, superficial; disingenuous, insincere, specious, meretricious, shallow.
▷ANTONYMS profound, thoughtful.
3 *the slick manager of the Berkeley Chase Hotel*: **suave**, urbane, sophisticated, polished, assured, self-assured, smooth-talking, smooth-spoken, smooth-tongued, silver-tongued, glib; unctuous, oily, ingratiating; informal smarmy.
▷ANTONYMS unsophisticated, gauche.
4 *her slick brown hair*: **shiny**, glossy, shining, sleek, smooth, silky, silken; oiled, plastered down, Brylcreemed.
5 *the pavements were slick with rain*: **slippery**, slithery, wet, greasy, oily, icy, glassy, smooth; informal slippy, skiddy; rare lubricious.
▷ANTONYMS dry, rough.
▶ verb *his black hair was slicked down*: **smooth**, sleek, flatten; plaster, grease, oil, gel; informal smarm.

Choose the right word **slick, glib, smooth, urbane**

See **glib**.

slide verb **1** *the glass slid across the table | the car slid across the road*: **glide**, move smoothly, slip, slither, skim, skate, glissade, coast, plane; **skid**, slew, aquaplane.
2 *tears slid down her cheeks*: **trickle**, run, flow, pour, stream, course, spill.
3 *four men slid out of the shadows*: **creep**, steal, slink, slip, glide, tiptoe, sidle, ease, edge.
4 *the country is sliding into recession*: **sink**, fall, drop, descend; decline, degenerate, deteriorate.
□ **let something slide** **neglect**, pay little/no attention to, not attend to, be remiss about, be lax about, shirk, skimp on, let something go downhill, let something go to seed.
▶ noun **1** *the current slide in house prices*: **fall**, decline, drop, slump, tumble, downturn, downswing; informal nosedive.
▷ANTONYMS rise.
2 *David placed the slide back in its case*: **transparency**, diapositive, mount.

slight adjective **1** *the chance of success is slight*: **small**, modest, little, tiny, minute, inappreciable, imperceptible, infinitesimal, hardly worth mentioning, negligible, inconsiderable, insignificant, minimal, marginal; remote, scant, slim, outside; faint, vague, subtle, gentle; informal minuscule; rare exiguous.
▷ANTONYMS big, considerable.
2 *the book is a slight work by his usual standards*: **minor**, inconsequential, trivial, trifling, unimportant, lightweight, superficial, shallow, of little account, petty, paltry; informal penny-ante; Brit. informal twopenny-halfpenny; N. Amer. informal nickel-and-dime.
▷ANTONYMS major, substantial.
3 *Elizabeth's slight figure*: **slim**, slender, slightly built, petite, diminutive, small, delicate, dainty, small-boned, elfin; thin, skinny, size-zero, spare, puny, undersized, frail, weak; Scottish wee; informal pint-sized, pocket-size; rare gracile, attenuate.
▷ANTONYMS sturdy, burly, muscular.
4 *slight, flat-bottomed boats made only of timber*: **flimsy**, insubstantial, fragile, frail, rickety, jerry-built.
▷ANTONYMS strong, robust.
▶ verb *he was convinced that he had been socially slighted*: **insult**, **snub**, rebuff, repulse, spurn, treat disrespectfully, give someone the cold shoulder, cold-shoulder, brush off, turn one's back on, keep at arm's length, disregard, ignore, cut (dead), neglect, take no notice of, disdain, scorn; informal give someone the brush-off, freeze out, stiff-arm, knock back; informal, dated give someone the go-by; rare misprize, scout.
▷ANTONYMS respect, welcome.
▶ noun *she often started rows in response to what she saw as slights on Nicky's part*: **insult**, affront, slur, disparaging remark; **snub**, rebuff, rejection; spurning, cold-shouldering, disregard, rudeness, disrespect, disdain, scorn; informal put-down, dig, brush-off, kick in the teeth, slap in the face.
▷ANTONYMS compliment.

Word toolkit **slight**

See **minor**.

slighting adjective *slighting references to foreigners*: **insulting**, disparaging, belittling, derogatory, disrespectful, denigratory, uncomplimentary, pejorative, abusive, offensive, defamatory, slanderous, libellous, scurrilous; disdainful, scornful, contemptuous; informal bitchy; archaic contumelious.
▷ANTONYMS complimentary.

slightly adverb *she felt slightly ill at ease*: **a little**, a bit, somewhat, rather, moderately, to some degree, to a certain extent, to a slight extent, faintly, vaguely, obscurely; marginally, a shade; informal sort of, kind of, kinda, ish.
▷ANTONYMS very.

slim adjective **1** *she was tall and slim with long blonde hair*: **slender**, lean, willowy, sylphlike, svelte, lissom, graceful, snake-hipped, rangy,

S

clean-limbed, trim, slight, slightly built; thin, as thin as a reed, skinny, size-zero, spare, attenuated, lanky, spindly; rare gracile, attenuate.
▷ANTONYMS fat, plump.
2 *a slim silver bracelet*: **narrow**, slender, slimline.
▷ANTONYMS broad.
3 *there was only a slim chance of escape*: **slight**, small, slender, faint, feeble, poor, flimsy, tenuous, fragile, negligible, marginal, minimal; outside, remote, distant, unlikely, improbable.
▷ANTONYMS good, strong.
▸verb 1 *if you eat only wholefoods, it should be easy to slim*: **lose weight**, get thinner, lose/shed some pounds, lose some inches, get into shape, shape up, reduce, diet, go on a diet; N. Amer. slenderize.
▷ANTONYMS put on weight.
2 *the number of staff had been* ***slimmed down*** *from 32 to 24*: **reduce**, cut, cut down/back, make cutbacks in, scale down, trim, decrease, diminish, pare down, whittle away, prune; rationalize, downsize.
▷ANTONYMS increase.

slime noun *the steps were covered in green and black slime*: **ooze**, sludge, muck, mud, mire; mucus; informal goo, gunk, yuck, gook, gloop; Brit. informal gunge, grot; N. Amer. informal guck, glop.

slimy adjective 1 *the floor was cold and slimy*: **slippery**, slithery, greasy, oozy, muddy, mucky, sludgy, miry; clammy, wet; sticky, viscous, viscid, mucilaginous, glutinous, mucous, mucoid; informal slippy, gunky, gooey, gloopy, gummy.
2 *her slimy press agent*: **obsequious**, sycophantic, excessively deferential, subservient, fawning, toadying, ingratiating, unctuous, oily, oleaginous, greasy, reptilian, grovelling, cringing, toadyish, sycophantish, slavish, abject, craven, humble, Uriah Heepish, self-abasing; informal bootlicking, smarmy, sucky, soapy, forelock-tugging; N. Amer. informal brown-nosing, apple-polishing; Brit. vulgar slang arse-licking, bum-sucking; N. Amer. vulgar slang kiss-ass, ass-kissing, suckholing.

sling noun 1 *she had her arm in a sling*: **support bandage**, support, bandage, strap.
2 *700 men armed only with slings*: **catapult**, slingshot; Austral./NZ shanghai.
▸verb 1 *a hammock was slung between two trees | she noticed the binoculars slung round his neck*: **hang**, suspend, string, dangle, swing, drape.
2 informal *she took off her jacket and slung it on the sofa*: **throw**, toss, fling, hurl, cast, pitch, lob, launch, flip, shy, catapult, send flying, let fly with; informal chuck, bung, heave, buzz, whang; N. Amer. informal peg; Austral. informal hoy; NZ informal bish.

slink verb *she slunk past the open door of the living room*: **creep**, sneak, steal, slip, slide, sidle, edge, move furtively, tiptoe, pussyfoot, pad; skulk, lurk; prowl.

slinky adjective informal 1 *a slinky black evening dress*: **tight**, clinging, tight-fitting, close-fitting, figure-hugging, skintight, sheath-like; sexy; informal sprayed on.
▷ANTONYMS baggy.
2 *the outfit gave her a slinky, model-like elegance*: **sinuous**, feline, willowy, graceful, sleek.

slip[1] verb 1 *she slipped on the ice*: **slide**, skid, slither, glide; **fall over**, fall, lose one's balance, lose/miss one's footing, stumble, tumble, trip.
2 *the envelope slipped through Luke's fingers*: **fall**, drop, slide.
3 *we slipped out by a back door*: **creep**, steal, sneak, slide, sidle, slope, slink, pad, tiptoe, pussyfoot, edge, move stealthily/quietly, insinuate oneself.
4 *many people feel standards have slipped*: **decline**, deteriorate, degenerate, worsen, get worse, fall, fall off, drop, decay, backslide, regress; informal go downhill, go to the dogs, go to pot, go down the tube/tubes, go down the toilet, hit the skids.
▷ANTONYMS improve.
5 *the bank's shares slipped 1.5p to 227p*: **drop**, go down, sink, slump, tumble, plunge, plummet, decrease, depreciate; informal crash, nosedive.
▷ANTONYMS rise.
6 *the hours* ***slipped by*** *so quickly that she had no time to brood*: **pass**, elapse, go by/past, roll by/past, glide by/past, slide by/past, fly by/past, steal by/past, tick by/past, wear on.
7 *she slipped the map into her pocket*: **put**, tuck, stow, insert; informal pop, stick, shove, stuff.
▷ANTONYMS remove.
8 *Sarah* ***slipped into*** *a black velvet skirt*: **put on**, pull on, don, dress/clothe oneself in, get into, climb into, fling on, throw on; pour oneself into; change into; informal tog oneself up/out in, doll oneself up in.
▷ANTONYMS take off.
9 *in the bathroom she quickly* ***slipped out of*** *her clothes*: **take off**, remove, pull off, peel off, shrug off, discard, shed, divest oneself of, doff, fling off, fling aside, climb out of; undo, unfasten, unbutton, unzip.
▷ANTONYMS put on.
10 *he was already slipping the knot of his tie*: **untie**, unfasten, undo, loosen, disentangle, untangle, unsnarl.
▷ANTONYMS tie, do up.
□ **let something slip reveal**, disclose, divulge, let out, give away, come out with, blurt out, leak; give the game away; informal let on, blab, let the cat out of the bag, spill the beans; Brit. informal blow the gaff; archaic discover.
▷ANTONYMS keep something secret.
□ **slip away 1** *how did they manage to slip away?* **escape**, make one's escape, get away, break free, make one's getaway, abscond, decamp; disappear, vanish; informal fly the coop; Brit. informal do a bunk, do a runner; N. Amer. informal take a powder. **2** *she slipped away in her sleep at two o'clock in the morning*: **die**, pass away, pass on, expire, breathe one's last, go, go to meet one's maker, shuffle off this mortal coil, go to one's last resting place, go the way of all flesh, cross the Styx; informal pop off, snuff it, croak, kick the bucket, give up the ghost, turn up one's toes, cash in one's chips, conk out, flatline; Brit. informal pop one's clogs, peg out, hop the twig/stick; N. Amer. informal check out, hand in one's dinner pail; Austral./NZ informal go bung; archaic decease, depart this life, exit.
□ **slip up** informal *we can't afford to slip up like that again*: **make a mistake**, blunder, make a blunder, get something wrong, miscalculate, make an error, trip up, err, go wrong; informal make a bloomer, make a boo-boo, screw up, make a howler, muff something up; Brit. informal boob, cock something up, drop a clanger; N. Amer. informal goof up.
▸noun 1 *a single slip could send them plummeting down the mountainside*: **false step**, misstep, slide, skid, fall, trip, tumble.
2 *I may have made a slip I can never forgive myself for*: **mistake**, error, blunder, miscalculation, gaffe, faux pas, slip of the tongue/pen; oversight, omission; indiscretion, impropriety, lapse; inaccuracy, fault, defect; informal slip-up, boo-boo, boner, howler; Brit. informal boob, clanger, bloomer; N. Amer. informal goof, blooper, bloop; Latin lapsus linguae, lapsus calami.
3 *a silk slip*: **underskirt**, petticoat, underslip, half-slip.
□ **give someone the slip** informal *we gave them the slip at the station*: **escape from**, get away from, evade, dodge, elude, lose, shake off, throw off, throw off the scent, get clear of, get rid of, get free from, break away from, leave behind; informal ditch; Brit. informal get shot of; archaic bilk.

slip[2] noun 1 *she wrote the number down on a slip of paper*: **piece of paper**, scrap of paper, paper, sheet, note; chit, coupon, voucher; informal stickie; trademark Post-it (note).
2 *they took seeds or slips from rare and threatened plants*: **cutting**, graft; scion, shoot, offshoot, sprout, sprig, runner.
□ **a slip of a ...** *it amazed him that such a slip of a girl could be so strong*: **small**, slender, slim, slight, slightly built, petite, little, tiny, diminutive, elfin, dainty, delicate, frail; Scottish wee; informal pint-sized.

slipper noun 1 *he slid out of bed and pulled on his slippers*: **mule**, moccasin, house shoe; N. Amer. slipperette; rare pantofle, pantable, panton.
2 *she wore a white organdie dress and high-heeled satin slippers*: pump, mule.

slipperiness noun 1 *the slipperiness of the path*: **smoothness**, slickness, greasiness, oiliness, iciness, glassiness; sliminess, wetness; informal slippiness.
2 *his campaign has been hurt not so much by scandal, but by his slipperiness*: **evasiveness**, unreliability, unpredictability; deviousness, craftiness, cunning, wiliness, trickiness, artfulness, guilefulness, slickness, untrustworthiness, duplicitousness, dishonesty, treachery, two-facedness; informal shadiness, shiftiness; rare tergiversation.

slippery adjective 1 *heavy rain had made the roads slippery*: **slithery**, greasy, oily, icy, glassy, smooth, slick; slimy, wet; informal slippy, skiddy; rare lubricious.
▷ANTONYMS dry, rough.
2 *Martin's a slippery customer*: **evasive**, unreliable, unpredictable, hard to pin down; **devious**, crafty, cunning, wily, tricky, artful, guileful, slick, sly, sneaky, scheming, contriving, untrustworthy, deceitful, deceptive, duplicitous, dishonest, treacherous, false, two-faced; N. Amer. snide; informal shady, shifty, foxy, iffy; Brit. informal dodgy; Austral./NZ informal shonky.
▷ANTONYMS open, reliable, trustworthy.

slipshod adjective *he blamed unprofessionalism and a slipshod approach for the club's performance*: **careless**, lackadaisical, slapdash, disorganized, unorganized, haphazard, hit-or-miss, last-minute, untidy, messy, unsystematic, unmethodical, casual, offhand, thoughtless, heedless, negligent, neglectful, remiss, lax, slack, slovenly; informal sloppy, all over the place, slap-happy; Brit. informal all over the shop.
▷ANTONYMS careful, meticulous, painstaking.

slip-up noun informal *it was all down to a simple clerical slip-up*: **mistake**, slip, error, blunder, miscalculation, oversight, omission, gaffe, faux pas, slip of the tongue/pen, lapse; inaccuracy, fault, defect; informal boo-boo, boner, howler; Brit. informal boob, clanger, bloomer, cock-up; N. Amer. informal goof, blooper, bloop; Latin lapsus linguae, lapsus calami.

slit noun 1 *make three diagonal slits in each side of the trout and season generously*: **cut**, incision, split, slash, gash, laceration; rip, tear, rent; vent, placket.
2 *Henry saw a face peeping through a slit in the curtains*: **opening**, gap, chink, space, crack, cranny, aperture, slot; peephole.
▸verb *he threatened to slit her throat*: **cut**, slash, split open, slice open, gash, lacerate, make an incision in; tear, rip; pierce, knife, lance; literary rend.

slither verb *Ben and I slithered down the bank | a green snake slithered silently across the grass*: **slide**, slip, glide, glissade; squirm, wriggle, snake, worm, slink, creep, crawl; skid.

S

sliver noun *slivers of glass | a sliver of cheese*: **splinter**, shard, shiver, chip, flake, shred, scrap, slither, shaving, paring; slice, wafer; piece, fragment, bit; Scottish skelf; technical rove.

slob noun informal *her no-good slob of a husband*: **layabout**, good-for-nothing, sluggard, laggard; lout, oaf; informal slacker, couch potato, pig; Brit. informal slummock, yob, chav; N. Amer. informal schlump, bum, lardass; archaic sloven, lurdan.

slobber verb **drool**, slaver, dribble, salivate, water at the mouth; Scottish & Irish slabber; archaic drivel.

slog verb **1** *they were slogging away to meet a deadline*: **work hard**, toil, labour, work one's fingers to the bone, work like a Trojan/dog, work day and night, exert oneself, keep at it, keep one's nose to the grindstone, grind, slave, grub, plough, plod, peg; informal beaver, plug, put one's back into something, work one's guts out, work one's socks off, knock oneself out, sweat blood, kill oneself; Brit. informal graft, fag; Austral./NZ informal bullock; Brit. vulgar slang work one's balls/arse/nuts off; N. Amer. vulgar slang work one's ass/butt off; archaic drudge, travail, moil.
▷ANTONYMS skive, take it easy.
2 *the three of them slogged around the streets of the capital in the July heat*: **trudge**, tramp, traipse, toil, plod, trek, footslog, drag oneself; Brit. informal trog, yomp; N. Amer. informal schlep.
▸ noun **1** *writing the book took 10 months' hard slog*: **hard work**, toil, toiling, labour, struggle, effort, exertion, grind, {blood, sweat, and tears}, drudgery; Herculean task; informal sweat, elbow grease; Brit. informal graft; Austral./NZ informal (hard) yakka; archaic travail, moil.
▷ANTONYMS leisure, relaxation.
2 *a steady uphill slog*: **trudge**, tramp, traipse, plod, trek, footslog; Brit. informal trog, yomp; N. Amer. informal schlep.

slogan noun *well-known advertising slogans*: **catchphrase**, catchline, catchword, jingle, saying, formula, legend; watchword, motto, mantra, rallying cry; shibboleth; N. Amer. informal tag line.

slop verb *water slopped over the edge of the sink*: **spill**, flow, overflow, run, slosh, splash, splatter, spatter.
□ **slop around/about** Brit. informal *at weekends he would slop about in his oldest clothes*: **laze (around/about)**, lounge (around/about), do nothing, loll (around/about), loaf (around/about), slouch (about/around), vegetate; informal hang around, veg out; Brit. informal hang about, mooch about/around, slummock around; N. Amer. informal bum around, bat around/about, lollygag.

slope noun **1** *the roof should have a slope sufficient for proper drainage*: **gradient**, incline, angle, slant, inclination, pitch, decline, ascent, declivity, acclivity, rise, fall, downward, upward, downslope, upslope, ramp, rake, tilt, tip, dip, camber, cant, bevel; N. Amer. grade, downgrade, upgrade.
2 *a steep, grassy slope*: **hill**, hillside, hillock, bank, rise, escarpment, scarp; Scottish brae; technical glacis, versant, adret, ubac, bajada, piedmont; literary steep.
3 *a ten-minute cable-car ride delivers you to the slopes*: **piste**, run, track; nursery slope, dry slope, dry-ski slope; N. Amer. trail.
▸ verb *the garden sloped down to a stream*: **slant**, incline, tilt; drop away, fall away, decline, descend, sink, shelve, lean, dip; rise, ascend, climb.
□ **slope off** informal *they gathered up their belongings and sloped off*: **leave**, go away, go, slip away, take oneself off, make oneself scarce, take one's leave, make off, steal away, slink off, creep off, sneak off; informal push off, clear off.
▷ANTONYMS arrive.

sloping adjective *a sloping floor*: **at a slant**, on the slant, at an angle, not straight, slanting, slanted, slantwise, slant, oblique, leaning, inclining, inclined, angled, cambered, canted; askew, skew, lopsided, crooked, tilting, tilted, atilt, dipping, out of true, out of line; Scottish squint; rare declivitous, declivous, acclivitous, acclivous.
▷ANTONYMS level, straight.

sloppy adjective **1** *they sat round the table eating a sloppy chicken curry*: **runny**, watery, thin, liquid, semi-liquid, mushy, soupy; wet, soggy, slushy, sludgy; S. African slap; informal gloopy.
▷ANTONYMS dry, solid.
2 *we gave away a goal through sloppy defending*: **careless**, slapdash, slipshod, lackadaisical, disorganized, haphazard, unmethodical, unsystematic, hit-or-miss, untidy, messy, thoughtless, inattentive, heedless, hasty, hurried; thrown together, last-minute, cursory, perfunctory, negligent, neglectful, remiss, lax, slack, slovenly; amateurish, unprofessional; informal shambolic, all over the place, slap-happy; Brit. informal all over the shop.
▷ANTONYMS careful, meticulous.
3 *sloppy T-shirts*: **baggy**, loose-fitting, loose, generously cut, not tight, roomy; shapeless, sack-like, slack, oversized, ill-fitting, bagging.
▷ANTONYMS tight, tailored.
4 *sloppy letters from a boy she had met on holiday*: **sentimental**, mawkish, over-sentimental, overemotional, cloying, sickly, saccharine, sugary, sugar-coated, syrupy; romantic, hearts-and-flowers; Brit. twee; informal slushy, mushy, weepy, tear-jerking, schmaltzy, cutesy, lovey-dovey, gooey, drippy, sloshy, soupy, treacly, cheesy, corny, icky, sick-making, toe-curling; Brit. informal soppy; N. Amer. informal cornball, sappy, hokey, three-hankie; trademark Mills-and-Boon.
▷ANTONYMS unemotional, gritty.

slosh verb **1** *he slammed the glass on the table and beer sloshed over the side*: **spill**, slop, splash, flow, overflow, splatter, spatter.
2 *workers sloshed round in rubber boots*: **splash**, swash, squelch, wade; informal splosh.
3 *she sloshed more wine into her glass*: **pour**, slop, splash; informal glug.
4 Brit. informal *Gary sloshed him*: **hit**, strike, thump, slog, punch, cuff, smack, thwack, box someone's ears; informal whack, belt, bash, biff, bop, clout, wallop, swipe, sock, lam, crown, whomp, deck, floor; Brit. informal stick one on, dot; N. Amer. informal boff, bust, slug, whale; Austral./NZ informal dong, quilt; literary smite, swinge.

slot noun **1** *he slid a coin into the slot of the jukebox*: **aperture**, slit, crack, hole, opening, groove, notch.
2 *the programme's mid-morning slot*: **spot**, time, period; place, position, niche, space; informal window.
▸ verb *he slotted a cassette into the tape machine*: **insert**, put, place, fit, slide, slip.

sloth noun *sloth and bad organization seem to be to blame*: **laziness**, idleness, indolence, slothfulness, inactivity, inertia, sluggishness, apathy, accidie, listlessness, lassitude, passivity, lethargy, languor, torpidity, slowness, heaviness, dullness, shiftlessness; French, archaic fainéance; rare hebetude.
▷ANTONYMS industriousness, energy.

slothful adjective *fatigue made him slothful*: **lazy**, idle, indolent, work-shy, inactive, inert, sluggish, apathetic, lethargic, listless, languid, torpid, slow-moving, slow, heavy, dull, enervated, shiftless, lackadaisical; informal bone idle, do-nothing; French, archaic fainéant; rare otiose.
▷ANTONYMS active, industrious, energetic.

slouch verb *Nicky slouched back in his chair*: **slump**, hunch; loll, droop, sag, stoop.

slough verb *the nudibranch sloughed its armour and acquired a new set of biological and chemical defences | in a matter of seconds, he **sloughs off** the image of a carefree billionaire*: **dispose of**, discard, throw away, throw out, get rid of, toss out; shed, jettison, scrap, cast aside/off, repudiate, abandon, relinquish, drop, dispense with, have done with, reject, shrug off, throw on the scrap heap; informal chuck (away/out), fling away, dump, ditch, axe, bin, junk, get shut of; Brit. informal get shot of; N. Amer. informal trash; archaic forsake.
▷ANTONYMS keep; acquire.

slovenly adjective **1** *he was upbraided for his slovenly appearance*: **scruffy**, untidy, messy, unkempt, ill-groomed, slatternly, dishevelled, bedraggled, tousled, rumpled, frowzy, blowsy, down at heel; dirty, grubby; sluttish; informal slobbish, slobby; N. Amer. informal raggedy, schlumpy, raunchy; archaic draggle-tailed.
▷ANTONYMS tidy, neat.
2 *his work is slovenly and his manners are unsatisfactory*: **careless**, slapdash, slipshod, disorganized, unorganized, unsystematic, unmethodical, haphazard, hit-or-miss, untidy, messy, thoughtless, negligent, neglectful, lax, lackadaisical, slack; informal sloppy, slap-happy, couldn't-care-less.
▷ANTONYMS careful, meticulous, painstaking.

slow adjective **1** *a slow pace | their slow walk back to the village*: **unhurried**, leisurely, measured, moderate, deliberate, steady, sedate, slow-moving, slow-going, easy, relaxed, unrushed, gentle, undemanding, comfortable; ponderous, plodding, laboured, dawdling, loitering, lagging, laggard, sluggish, sluggardly, snail-like, tortoise-like, leaden-footed, leaden, creeping; N. Amer. informal lollygagging.
▷ANTONYMS fast, rapid, brisk.
2 *a slow process*: **long-drawn-out**, time-consuming, lengthy, long-lasting, protracted, prolonged, interminable; gradual, progressive.
▷ANTONYMS brief, short.
3 *he didn't guess—he can be so slow*: **obtuse**, stupid, unperceptive, imperceptive, blind, uncomprehending, unimaginative, insensitive, bovine, stolid, slow-witted, dull-witted, unintelligent, doltish, witless, blockish; informal dense, dim, dim-witted, thick, slow on the uptake, dumb, dopey, not with it, boneheaded, blockheaded, lamebrained, wooden-headed, muttonheaded; Brit. informal dozy; Scottish & N. English informal glaikit; N. Amer. informal dumb-ass, chowderheaded; S. African informal dof.
▷ANTONYMS astute, bright, perceptive.
4 *the objectors were not **slow to** voice their opinions*: **reluctant**, unwilling, disinclined, loath, averse, indisposed; hesitant about, afraid of, chary of, shy of.
5 *an attempt by the industry to boost sales in a slow season*: **sluggish**, slack, quiet, slow-moving, not busy, inactive, flat, depressed, stagnant, dead; unproductive.
▷ANTONYMS busy, hectic.
6 *a slow and mostly aimless narrative*: **dull**, boring, uninteresting, unexciting, uneventful, tedious, tiresome, wearisome, dry, as dry as dust, monotonous, plodding, tame, dreary, lacklustre; informal ho-hum.
▷ANTONYMS gripping, exciting, action-packed.
7 *Stratford's too small, too slow—I've got to get away*: **quiet**, sleepy, unprogressive, behind the times, backward, backwoods, backwater; informal dead, one-horse, dead-and-alive; N. Amer. informal dullsville.

S

▶ **verb 1** *the traffic forced him to* ***slow down****:* **reduce speed**, go slower, decelerate, lessen one's speed, brake, put the brakes on, slack off.
▷ANTONYMS accelerate, speed up.
2 *Paula, you really need to* ***slow down****:* **take it easy**, relax, ease up/off, take a break, take some time off, slack off; informal let up; N. Amer. informal chill out, hang loose, kick back.
▷ANTONYMS work harder.
3 *he'll only* ***slow us up*** *| such a development would* ***slow down*** *economic growth in Europe:* **hold back**, hold up, keep back, delay, detain, retard, set back; restrict, restrain, limit, put the brakes on, check, curb, rein in, interfere with, inhibit, impede, obstruct, hinder, hamper, get in the way of, handicap; archaic stay.
▷ANTONYMS speed up.

Word links **slow**

bradycardia abnormally slow heart action

slowly adverb **1** *Rose walked off slowly:* **unhurriedly**, without hurrying, at a leisurely pace, at a slow pace, leisurely, steadily, taking one's time, in one's own good time; at a snail's pace, ploddingly, with heavy steps, with leaden steps, heavily; Music adagio, lento, largo, larghetto, adagietto.
▷ANTONYMS fast, quickly, rapidly.
2 *her health is improving slowly:* **gradually**, bit by bit, by degrees, little by little, slowly but surely, step by step, inchmeal.
▷ANTONYMS by leaps and bounds.

sludge noun *the channel had become silted up with layer upon layer of sludge:* **mud**, muck, mire, ooze, silt, alluvium, dirt, slime, slush, slurry; sediment, lees, dregs, deposit, grounds, settlings, precipitate, residue; Scottish & N. English clart; Irish slob; informal gunk, crud, gloop, grunge, gook, goo; Brit. informal gunge, grot; N. Amer. informal guck, glop; rare grouts.

sluggish adjective **1** *Alex woke late, feeling tired and sluggish:* **lethargic**, listless, lacking in energy, unenergetic, lifeless, inert, inactive, slow, torpid, dull, languid, apathetic, passive, unresponsive, weary, tired, fatigued, sleepy, half asleep, drowsy, heavy-eyed, enervated, somnolent; lazy, idle, indolent, slothful, sluggardly; phlegmatic, bovine; Medicine asthenic, neurasthenic; informal dozy, dopey, yawny; N. Amer. informal logy; archaic lymphatic.
▷ANTONYMS vigorous, energetic, active.
2 *the sluggish global economy:* **inactive**, quiet, slow, slow-moving, slack, flat, depressed, stagnant, static.
▷ANTONYMS busy, brisk.

sluggishness noun **1** *Rob put down his sluggishness to over-exuberant birthday celebrations:* **lethargy**, inertia, listlessness, lack of energy, lifelessness, inactivity, inaction, slowness, languor, languidness, torpor, torpidity, dullness, heaviness, apathy, passivity, weariness, tiredness, lassitude, fatigue, sleepiness, drowsiness, enervation, somnolence, laziness, idleness, indolence, sloth, slothfulness; phlegm; Medicine asthenia, neurasthenia, anergia; informal doziness, dopeyness; rare hebetude.
▷ANTONYMS vigour, energy, animation.
2 *they are having difficulties exporting because of the sluggishness of other economies:* **lack of activity**, quietness, slowness, slackness, flatness, stagnation.
▷ANTONYMS briskness.

sluice verb **1** *crews sluiced down the decks of their ship:* **wash**, wash down, rinse, swill down, clean, cleanse, flush.
2 *the water sluiced out through the open door:* **pour**, flow, run, gush, cascade, stream, course, spout, jet, spurt, flood, surge, spill, rush, well, spew, discharge; Brit. informal sloosh; rare disembogue.

S

slum noun hovel; (**slums**) ghetto, shanty town; in Brazil favela; Indian jhuggi, jhuggi jhopri, bustee; Canadian informal Cabbagetown; rare rookery.

slumber literary verb *the child slumbered fitfully against his chest:* **sleep**, be asleep, doze, rest, take a siesta, nap, take a nap, catnap, drowse; sleep like a log/top; informal snooze, snatch forty winks, get some shut-eye, be in the land of Nod; Brit. informal kip, have a kip, get one's head down, zizz, get some zizz, doss (down); N. Amer. informal catch some Zs; literary be in the arms of Morpheus.
▷ANTONYMS wake up.
▶ **noun** *he drifted off into an uneasy slumber:* **sleep**, nap, doze, rest, siesta, drowse, catnap; beauty sleep; informal snooze, forty winks, a bit of shut-eye; Brit. informal kip, zizz.

slummy adjective *a slummy area of town:* **seedy**, insalubrious, squalid, sleazy, seamy, sordid, dingy, mean, wretched; **run down**, down at heel, shabby, dilapidated, in disrepair, neglected, uncared-for, unmaintained, depressed; informal crummy, scruffy, scuzzy, grungy; Brit. informal grotty; N. Amer. informal shacky, skanky.
▷ANTONYMS smart, upmarket.

slump verb **1** *he slumped into a chair:* **sit heavily**, flop, flump, collapse, sink, fall, subside; sag, slouch; informal plonk oneself, plop oneself.
▷ANTONYMS stand up, sit up.
2 *houses prices slumped:* **fall steeply**, plummet, plunge, tumble, drop, go down, slide, decline, decrease; reach a new low; informal crash, nosedive, take a nosedive, go into a tailspin.
▷ANTONYMS rise, soar.
3 *the reading standards of 7-year-olds have slumped:* **decline**, deteriorate, degenerate, worsen, get worse, slip, lapse; informal go downhill, go to pot, go to the dogs, nosedive, take a nosedive.
▷ANTONYMS improve.
▶ **noun 1** *a slump in annual profits:* **steep fall**, plunge, drop, collapse, tumble, plummet, downturn, downswing, slide, decline, falling off, decrease, lowering, devaluation, depreciation; meltdown; informal nosedive.
▷ANTONYMS rise.
2 *higher interest rates would drive the country into a slump:* **recession**, economic decline, depression, slowdown, trough, credit crunch; stagnation, stagflation; hard times; informal bust.
▷ANTONYMS boom, upturn.

slur verb *she was slurring her words:* **mumble**, speak unclearly, garble, stumble over, stammer; rare misarticulate.
▷ANTONYMS enunciate.
▶ **noun** *it is a gross slur on a highly respected and honest man:* **insult**, slight, slander, slanderous statement, libel, libellous statement, misrepresentation, defamation, aspersion, calumny, smear; allegation, imputation, insinuation, innuendo.

slush noun **1** *he wiped the slush off his shoes:* **melting snow**, wet snow; muck, mush, mud, sludge.
2 informal *the slush of Hollywood's romantic fifties films:* **sentimentality**, mawkishness, over-sentimentality, emotionalism, overemotionalism, sentimentalism, banality, triteness; Brit. tweeness; informal schmaltz, mush, sob stuff, slushiness, sloppiness, slop, goo, corn, corniness, hokum, cheese; Brit. informal soppiness; N. Amer. informal sappiness, hokeyness.

slut noun **promiscuous woman**; prostitute, whore; slattern; euphemistic model, escort, masseuse; French poule; informal **tart**, floozie, bike, pro; Brit. informal scrubber, slag, slapper; N. Amer. informal tramp, hooker, hustler, roundheel, chippy, skank, puta; black English ho; dated scarlet woman, loose woman, hussy, woman of ill repute, streetwalker, trollop; archaic harlot, strumpet, wanton, drab, doxy, trull, sloven.

sly adjective **1** *she's getting sly in her old age:* **cunning**, crafty, clever, wily, artful, guileful, tricky, conniving, scheming, devious, designing, deceitful, duplicitous, dishonest, disingenuous, underhand, sneaky, untrustworthy; manipulative, calculating, Machiavellian; informal foxy, shifty; Brit. informal fly; Austral./NZ informal shonky; S. African informal slim; archaic subtle; rare carny.
▷ANTONYMS honest, artless.
2 *he gave her a sly grin:* **roguish**, mischievous, impish, puckish, playful, teasing, naughty, wicked, waggish; arch, knowing; Scottish & N. English informal pawky.
3 *she took a sly sip of water:* **surreptitious**, furtive, stealthy, covert, secret.
▶ **noun**
□ **on the sly** *is she meeting some other guy on the sly?* **in secret**, secretly, furtively, stealthily, sneakily, slyly, surreptitiously, covertly, clandestinely, on the quiet, on the side, behind someone's back, under cover; under the counter; informal on the q.t..
▷ANTONYMS openly.

smack[1] noun **1** *she gave Mark a smack across the face:* **slap**, blow, spank, cuff, clout, thump, punch, rap, swat, thwack, crack; informal whack, clip, biff, wallop, swipe, bop, belt, bash, sock.
2 *the parcel landed with a solid smack on the terrace below:* **bang**, crash, thud, thump, wham.
3 informal *she gave him a quick smack on the cheek:* **kiss**, peck; informal smacker.
□ **a smack in the face/eye** *this could only be seen as a smack in the face for the government:* **rebuff**, rejection, repulse, snub, insult, affront, put-down, humiliation, blow to one's pride, slap in the face; informal brush-off.
▶ **verb 1** *he lost his temper and smacked her:* **slap**, hit, strike, spank, cuff, clout, thump, punch, rap, swat, thwack, crack; put someone over one's knee, make someone feel the back of one's hand, box someone's ears; informal whack, clip, wallop, biff, swipe, bop, belt, bash, sock, give someone a hiding, warm someone's bottom, give someone a hot bottom; Brit. informal slosh; Scottish & N. English informal skelp, scud; N. Amer. informal boff, slug, bust; Austral./NZ informal dong, quilt; archaic smite.
2 *the waiter smacked a plate on the table:* **bang**, slam, crash, thump, sling, fling; informal bung, plonk; N. Amer. informal plunk.
▶ **adverb** informal *I ran smack into the back of a parked truck | our mother's house was smack in the middle of the city:* **straight**, right, directly, squarely, headlong, dead, plumb, point-blank; **exactly**, precisely; informal slap, bang, slap bang, smack bang; N. Amer. informal spang, smack dab.

smack[2] verb
□ **smack of 1** *the tea smacked strongly of tannin:* **taste of**, have the flavour of, have the savour of. **2** *I didn't want to engage in anything that smacked of self-promotion:* **suggest**, hint at, have overtones of, have a suggestion of, have the air of, give the impression of, have the hallmark of, have the stamp of, resemble, seem like; smell of, reek of.
▶ **noun 1** *anything with even a modest smack of hops dries the palate:* **taste**, flavour, savour; archaic relish.
2 *there was more than a smack of bitterness in his words:* **trace**, tinge,

touch, suggestion, hint, scintilla, impression, overtone, air, suspicion, whisper, whiff.

small adjective **1** *a small flat in Fulham | he put his hand in his jacket and pulled out a small package*: **little**, small-scale, compact, bijou; portable; tiny, miniature, mini, minute, microscopic, nanoscopic, minuscule; toy, baby; poky, cramped, boxy; Scottish wee; informal tiddly, teeny, weeny, teeny-weeny, teensy, teensy-weensy, itsy-bitsy, itty-bitty, eensy, eensy-weensy, pocket-sized, half-pint, dinky, ickle, with no room to swing a cat; Brit. informal titchy; N. Amer. informal little-bitty, vest-pocket.
▷ANTONYMS big, large.
2 *he was a very small man*: **short**, little, slight, slightly built, small-boned, petite, diminutive, elfin, tiny; puny, undersized, stunted; squat, stubby; dwarf, bantam; a slip of a ...; Scottish wee; informal teeny, teeny-weeny, pint-sized; rare homuncular, Lilliputian.
▷ANTONYMS heavily built, tall, large.
3 *we may have to make a few small changes*: **slight**, minor, unimportant, trifling, trivial, insignificant, inconsequential, inappreciable, inconsiderable, negligible, nugatory, paltry, infinitesimal; informal minuscule, piffling, piddling.
▷ANTONYMS major, substantial.
4 *small helpings of vegetables*: **inadequate**, meagre, insufficient, ungenerous, not enough; informal measly, stingy, mingy, pathetic.
▷ANTONYMS generous, ample.
5 *they had succeeded in making him feel small*: **foolish**, stupid, insignificant, unimportant; embarrassed, humiliated, uncomfortable, mortified, chagrined, ashamed; deflated, crushed.
▷ANTONYMS proud.
6 *the captain had been paying small attention*: **hardly any**, not much, scant, little or no, little, minimal.
7 *a small farmer*: **small-scale**, small-time; modest, unpretentious, humble, lowly, simple.
▷ANTONYMS large-scale, substantial.

Word links **small**

micro- related prefix, as in *microscope, microbrewery*
mini- related prefix, as in *minidisc, minibeast*
nano- related prefix, as in *nanotechnology, nanosecond*

small change noun **coins**, change, coppers, silver, cash; formal specie.

small-minded adjective *a bunch of small-minded bigots*: **narrow-minded**, petty-minded, petty, mean, mean-spirited, mean-minded, uncharitable, ungenerous, grudging, close-minded, short-sighted, myopic, blinkered, inward-looking, narrow, conventional, unimaginative, parochial, provincial, insular, small-town, localist; intolerant, illiberal, reactionary, conservative, hidebound, dyed-in-the-wool, diehard, limited, restricted, set in one's ways, inflexible, dogmatic, rigid, entrenched, prejudiced, bigoted, biased, partisan; Brit. parish-pump, blimpish; French borné; N. Amer. informal jerkwater; rare claustral.
▷ANTONYMS broad-minded, tolerant, open-minded.

small-time adjective *small-time crooks | a small-time printer*: **minor**, small-scale, small; petty, unimportant, insignificant, of no account, of no consequence, inconsequential; N. Amer. minor-league; informal penny-ante, piddling; N. Amer. informal two-bit, no-account, bush-league, picayune.
▷ANTONYMS major, important, big-time.

smarminess noun informal *I just can't bear his smarminess*: **unctuousness**, smoothness, slickness, oiliness, greasiness, fulsomeness, obsequiousness; informal sliminess; rare unctuosity.

smarmy adjective informal *he's too smarmy*: **unctuous**, ingratiating, smooth, slick, oily, greasy, fulsome, flattering, obsequious, sycophantic, fawning; informal slimy, sucky, soapy.

smart adjective **1** *you look very smart | a pair of smart black shoes*: **well dressed**, well turned out, fashionably dressed, fashionable, stylish, chic, modish, elegant, neat, besuited, spruce, trim, dapper, debonair; shiny, gleaming, bright, spotless, clean, spick and span; French soigné; informal snazzy, natty, snappy, sharp, nifty, cool, with it; N. Amer. informal sassy, spiffy, fly, kicky; dated as if one had just stepped out of a bandbox; Brit. informal, dated swagger; archaic trig.
▷ANTONYMS scruffy.
2 *a smart restaurant*: **fashionable**, stylish, high-class, exclusive, chic, fancy; Brit. upmarket; N. Amer. high-toned; informal trendy, posh, ritzy, plush, plushy, classy, swanky, glitzy, fancy-pants; Brit. informal swish; N. Amer. informal swank, tony; S. African informal larney; US black English dicty; derogatory chichi.
▷ANTONYMS unfashionable, downmarket.
3 informal *Joey will know what to do—he's the smart one*: **clever**, bright, intelligent, sharp, sharp-witted, quick-witted, nimble-witted, shrewd, astute, acute, apt, able; well educated, well read; perceptive, percipient, discerning; informal brainy, savvy, streetwise, on the ball, quick on the uptake.
▷ANTONYMS stupid.
4 *he set off at a smart pace*: **brisk**, quick, fast, rapid, swift, lively, spanking, energetic, spirited, vigorous, jaunty; informal snappy, cracking, rattling.
▷ANTONYMS slow.
5 *he gave the animal a smart blow on the snout*: **sharp**, severe, forceful, violent; painful.
▷ANTONYMS gentle.
□ **look smart** Brit. *come up here and look smart about it!* **be quick**, hurry up, speed up; informal make it snappy, get cracking, get moving, step on it, step on the gas, rattle one's dags; Brit. informal get one's skates on, stir one's stumps; N. Amer. informal get a wiggle on; S. African informal put foot.
▸ **verb 1** *her eyes were smarting from the smoke*: **sting**, burn, tingle, prickle; hurt, ache.
2 *she had smarted at Jenny's accusations*: **feel annoyed**, feel upset, feel offended, take offence, feel aggrieved, feel indignant, feel put out, feel hurt, feel wounded, feel resentful.

smart alec noun informal **wise guy**, smarty-pants, smarty; Brit. informal **know-all**, clever clogs, clever Dick, smart-arse, smarty-boots; N. Amer. informal know-it-all, smart-ass; archaic wiseacre.

smarten verb **1** *the cottages had been* ***smartened up***: **spruce up**, make smarter, clean up, tidy up, make neater, make tidy, put in order; redecorate, refurbish, brighten up, modernize; informal do up; Brit. informal tart up, posh up; N. Amer. informal gussy up.
2 *Ellie* ***smartened herself up***: **groom oneself**, spruce oneself up, freshen oneself up, preen oneself, primp oneself, prink oneself, pretty oneself, beautify oneself; informal titivate oneself, doll oneself up; Brit. informal tart oneself up; archaic plume oneself, trig oneself.

smash verb **1** *one of the men smashed a window | drinks fell and glasses smashed*: **break**, break to pieces, smash to smithereens, shatter; splinter, crack, disintegrate; informal bust; rare shiver.
2 *she's smashed the car*: **crash**, wreck; Brit. write off; Brit. informal prang; N. Amer. informal total.
3 *the car* ***smashed into*** *a brick wall*: **crash into**, collide with, be in collision with, hit, strike, ram, smack into, slam into, bang into, plough into, meet head-on, run into, drive into, bump into, crack into/against; dash against; N. Amer. impact.
4 *Donald smashed him over the head*: **hit**, strike, thump, punch, cuff, smack, thwack; informal whack, belt, bash, biff, bop, clout, wallop, swipe, sock, lam, crown, whomp, deck, floor; Brit. informal stick one on, slosh, dot; N. Amer. informal boff, bust, slug, whale; Austral./NZ informal dong, quilt; literary smite, swinge.
5 *he smashed the club's hopes of FA Cup glory*: **destroy**, wreck, ruin, shatter, dash, crush, devastate, demolish, blast, blight, wipe out, overturn, torpedo, scotch; burst someone's bubble; informal put the kibosh on, banjax, do for, blow a hole in, nix, put paid to, queer; Brit. informal scupper, dish; archaic bring to naught.
▸ **noun 1** *he heard the smash of glass*: **breaking**, shattering, crashing, crash.
2 *a motorway smash*: **crash**, multiple crash, car crash, collision, multiple collision, accident, car accident, road accident, traffic accident, road traffic accident, bump; Brit. RTA; N. Amer. wreck; informal pile-up, smash-up; Brit. informal prang, shunt.
3 informal *a box-office smash*: **great success**, sensation, sell-out, triumph; French succès fou; informal hit, smash hit, winner, crowd-puller, knockout, wow, biggie.

smashing adjective *tell Anna we had an absolutely smashing day*: **wonderful**, **marvellous**, excellent, splendid, magnificent, superb, glorious, sublime, lovely, delightful; informal super, great, amazing, fantastic, terrific, tremendous, phenomenal, sensational, heavenly, stellar, gorgeous, dreamy, grand, fabulous, fab, fabby, fantabulous, awesome, magic, ace, cool, mean, bad, wicked, mega, crucial, mind-blowing, far out, A1, sound, out of this world, marvy, spanking; Brit. informal brilliant, brill, bosting; N. Amer. informal peachy, dandy, jim-dandy, neat, badass, boss, radical, rad, boffo, bully, bitching; Austral./NZ informal beaut, bonzer; S. African informal kif, lank; black English dope, def, phat; informal, dated groovy, divine; Brit. informal, dated capital, champion, wizard, corking, cracking, ripping, spiffing, top-hole, topping, beezer; N. Amer. informal, dated swell, keen; archaic goodly.

smattering noun *an audience with a smattering of classical education*: **bit**, small amount, little, modicum, touch, soupçon; superficial knowledge, nodding acquaintance, passing acquaintance, rudiments, elements, basics; informal smidgen, smidge, tad.

smear verb **1** *the table was smeared with grease*: **streak**, smudge, stain, mark, soil, dirty; blur; informal splotch, splodge; literary besmirch.
2 *smear the meat with olive oil*: **cover**, coat, grease, lard; anoint; literary bedaub.
3 *she smeared sunblock on her skin*: **spread**, rub, daub, slap, slather, smother, plaster, cream, slick; apply, put on, dab; literary besmear.
4 *it's a campaign by people who are trying to smear our reputation*: **sully**, tarnish, besmirch, blacken, drag through the mud/mire, stain, taint, damage, defame, discredit, defile, vilify, malign, slander, libel, stigmatize, calumniate; N. Amer. slur; informal do a hatchet job on; literary smirch; rare asperse, vilipend.
▸ **noun 1** *a smear of yellow paint | smears of blood*: **streak**, smudge, daub, dab, spot, patch, blotch, blob; stain, mark; informal splotch, splodge.
2 *there were a number of press smears about some of his closest aides*: **false accusation**, false report, false imputation, slander, libel, lie, untruth, slur, defamation, calumny, vilification; stain, taint.

smell noun **1** *there was a smell of burning in the air*: **odour**, whiff.
2 *the smell of new-mown grass*: **aroma**, fragrance, scent, perfume, redolence, tang, savour; bouquet, nose.
3 *27 cats lived there—you can imagine the smell*: **stench**, stink, reek, fetidness, effluvium, miasma; Brit. informal pong, niff, whiff, hum; Scottish informal guff; N. Amer. informal funk; rare fetor, malodour, mephitis.
▶ verb **1** *Peter smelled her perfume*: **get a whiff of**, scent, get a sniff of, detect the smell of.
2 *the dogs smelled each other*: **sniff**, nose.
3 *the room was dirty and it smelled*: **stink**, stink to high heaven, reek, have a bad smell, be stinking, be malodorous; Brit. informal pong, hum.
4 *it smells like a hoax to me*: **give the impression of**, smack of, savour of, have the hallmarks of, have all the signs of, seem/appear like, have the air of, suggest.

> *Word links* **smell**
>
> **osmic** relating to smell
> **odorimetry** measurement of intensity of a smell
> **olfactory** relating to the sense of smell

smelly adjective *the tunnel was damp and smelly* | *smelly fish*: **foul-smelling**, evil-smelling, stinking, stinking to high heaven, reeking, fetid, malodorous, pungent, acrid, rank, putrid, noxious; off, gamy, high; musty, fusty; Brit. frowsty; W. Indian fresh; informal stinky, reeky; Brit. informal niffing, niffy, pongy, whiffy, humming; N. Amer. informal funky; literary noisome, mephitic; rare olid, miasmic, miasmal.

smile verb *Joseph looked up at her and smiled*: **grin**, beam, grin like a Cheshire cat, grin from ear to ear, twinkle; informal be all smiles.
▶ noun *she gave him a warm smile*: **grin**, beam; smirk, simper; leer.
▷ANTONYMS frown, scowl.

smirk verb *she turned and smirked at Edward*: **smile smugly**, simper, snigger; leer; Scottish archaic smicker, smirtle.

smitten adjective **1** *he was smitten with cholera*: **struck down with**, laid low with, prostrated with, suffering from, affected by, afflicted by, plagued with; archaic stricken with.
2 *you know Jane's* ***smitten with you?*** **infatuated with**, besotted with, in love with, head over heels in love with, hopelessly in love with, obsessed with, enamoured of, very attracted to, very taken with, devoted to, charmed by, captivated by, enchanted by, enthralled by, bewitched by, beguiled by, under someone's spell; informal bowled over by, swept off one's feet by, struck on, crazy about, mad about, wild about, potty about, very keen on, gone on, sweet on, into; literary ensorcelled by.
▷ANTONYMS indifferent.

smog noun **exhaust fumes**, fumes, smoke, pollution, gas; fog, haze, vapour; Brit. informal pea-souper.

smoke verb **1** *the peat fire was smoking*: **smoulder**, emit smoke, emit fumes; archaic reek.
2 *Henry lay back in the chair and smoked his cigarette*: **puff on**, draw on, pull on; inhale; light up; informal take a drag of, drag on.
3 *they smoke their own salmon*: **cure**, preserve, dry.
▶ noun *the smoke from the bonfire*: **fumes**, exhaust, gas, vapour; smog.

smoky adjective **1** *the smoky atmosphere*: **smoke-filled**, smoggy, hazy, foggy, murky, thick; smelly; informal reeky; Brit. informal fuggy.
▷ANTONYMS fresh, airy.
2 *the walls were smoky*: **smoke-stained**, sooty, discoloured, grimy, dirty, begrimed.
▷ANTONYMS clean.
3 *her wide smoky eyes*: **grey**, dark grey, slate grey, sooty, black, dark.

S

smooth adjective **1** *they lay down to sunbathe on the smooth flat rocks*: **even**, level, flat, as flat as a pancake, plane, flush, unwrinkled, featureless; polished, burnished, glossy, shiny, glassy, sheeny, lustrous, sleek, silky, satiny; rare unrough.
▷ANTONYMS uneven, rough, dull.
2 *his face was smooth and youthful*: **clean-shaven**, smooth-shaven, hairless.
▷ANTONYMS rough, hirsute.
3 *a lovely smooth sauce*: **creamy**, whipped, velvety, of an even consistency.
▷ANTONYMS lumpy.
4 *a smooth sea*: **calm**, still, tranquil, placid, serene, undisturbed, unruffled, even, flat, glassy, mirror-like, waveless, dead calm, like a millpond.
▷ANTONYMS rough, choppy.
5 *electronic and other high-tech components ensure the smooth running of the equipment*: **steady**, regular, rhythmic, uninterrupted, unbroken, flowing, frictionless, fluid, fluent.
▷ANTONYMS irregular, jerky.
6 *the smooth working of the world economy*: **straightforward**, easy, effortless, trouble-free, untroubled, well ordered, simple; plain sailing.
▷ANTONYMS fraught.
7 *a smooth wine*: **mellow**, mild, agreeable, pleasant, bland, soft, soothing.
▷ANTONYMS harsh, bitter.
8 *Mozart loved the smooth, resonant tone of the clarinet*: **dulcet**, soft, soothing, mellow, sweet, sweet-sounding, sweet-toned, pretty, silvery, honeyed, mellifluous, melodious, musical, lilting, lyrical, harmonious, euphonious; rare mellifluent.
▷ANTONYMS raucous.
9 *Hogan was a smooth, confident Foreign Office man*: **suave**, urbane, sophisticated, polished, debonair, courteous, gracious, smooth-tongued, glib, persuasive, slick, oily, ingratiating, unctuous; informal smarmy.
▷ANTONYMS gauche.
▶ verb **1** *pour the mixture into the lined tin and smooth the surface* | *she stood up and* ***smoothed out*** *her dress*: **flatten**, make flat, level, make level, level out, level off, make even, even off, even out, press (down), roll, steamroll, iron, plane, make uniform, make regular, regularize.
2 *the diplomats have apologized and made every effort to* ***smooth over*** *the situation*: **settle**, resolve, patch up, sort out, iron out, put to rights, mend, remedy, heal, cure, rectify.
3 *a plan for smoothing the conversion of the power stations from coal to gas*: **ease**, make easy, make easier, facilitate, clear the way for, pave the way for, smooth the way for, open the door for, expedite, assist, aid, help, help along, oil, oil the wheels of, lubricate.

> *Choose the right word* **smooth, urbane, slick, glib**
>
> See **glib**.

smoothly adverb **1** *her hair was combed smoothly back from her forehead*: **evenly**, level, flat, flush, as flat as a pancake, horizontally.
▷ANTONYMS roughly.
2 *the door closed smoothly behind them*: **steadily**, frictionlessly, fluidly, fluently, without bumping, without jerking; quietly; regularly, rhythmically.
▷ANTONYMS jerkily.
3 *he was happy that the day had gone smoothly*: **without a hitch**, like clockwork, with no trouble, without difficulty, easily, effortlessly, as planned, (according) to plan, swimmingly, satisfactorily, very well; informal like a dream, like magic.
▷ANTONYMS disastrously.
4 *'All taken care of,' he said smoothly*: **suavely**, urbanely, calmly, evenly, placidly; glibly, persuasively, slickly, ingratiatingly, unctuously; informal smarmily; rare oilily.
▷ANTONYMS abrasively.

smoothness noun **1** *the smoothness of the road surfaces*: **evenness**, levelness, flatness, plainness.
▷ANTONYMS unevenness, roughness.
2 *his dress shirt gleamed white against the tanned smoothness of his freshly shaved skin*: **clean-shavenness**, smooth-shavenness, hairlessness.
▷ANTONYMS roughness, hirsuteness.
3 *the strength of glass is usually down to its surface smoothness*: **glossiness**, gloss, shine, shininess, gleam, glassiness, sheen, lustre, brightness, sleekness, silkiness, polish, burnish.
▷ANTONYMS dullness.
4 *this fat substitute has the smoothness associated with fat*: **creaminess**, even consistency.
▷ANTONYMS lumpiness.
5 *the smoothness of the sea*: **calmness**, stillness, tranquillity, placidness, serenity, evenness, flatness, glassiness.
▷ANTONYMS roughness, choppiness.
6 *the engine has a V12-style smoothness*: **steadiness**, smooth running, regularity, rhythm, rhythmicity, freedom from interruption, flow, frictionlessness, fluidity, fluency.
▷ANTONYMS irregularity, jerkiness.
7 *this system was cumbersome but worked with reasonable smoothness*: **straightforwardness**, ease, easiness, effortlessness, simplicity.
▷ANTONYMS trouble.
8 *the strength of champagne is belied by its smoothness of flavour*: **mellowness**, mildness, pleasantness, blandness, softness.
9 *the smoothness of the sounds*: **softness**, mellowness, sweetness, sweet sound, sweet tone, prettiness, silveriness, mellifluousness, melodiousness, musicality, lilt, lyricism, harmony, euphony.
▷ANTONYMS raucousness.
10 *she was irritated by his smoothness*: **suaveness**, urbaneness, urbanity, sophistication, polish, finish, courteousness, grace, smooth talking, glibness, persuasiveness, slickness, oiliness, ingratiation, unctuousness; informal smarminess.
▷ANTONYMS gaucheness.

smooth-talking adjective *a smooth-talking gang conned an elderly woman into giving her bank cash card away*: **persuasive**, plausible, credible, silver-tongued, smooth-tongued, smooth-spoken, slick, glib, eloquent, fast-talking, suave, ingratiating, silky, unctuous, obsequious, fawning, sycophantic, flattering; informal smarmy.
▷ANTONYMS no-nonsense, blunt.

smother verb **1** *a teenage mum tried to smother her baby in hospital*: **suffocate**, stifle, asphyxiate, choke, throttle, strangle, strangulate.

2 *police officers tried to smother the flames with their jackets*: **extinguish**, put out, snuff out, dampen, damp down, stamp out, douse, choke.
3 *we smothered the children with suncream*: **smear**, daub, bedaub, spread, cover; literary besmear.
4 *it's time for you to leave the house—she'll smother you if you remain*: **overwhelm**, inundate, envelop, trap, surround, cocoon.
5 *she smothered a sigh*: **stifle**, muffle, strangle, gag, restrain, repress, suppress, hold back, keep back, fight back, choke back, bite back, swallow, contain, bottle up, conceal, hide; bite one's lip; informal button up, keep the lid on, cork up.

smoulder verb **1** *the bonfire still smouldered*: **burn slowly**, smoke, glow; archaic reek.
2 *she was smouldering with resentment*: **seethe**, boil, fume, burn, simmer, be boiling over, be beside oneself; informal be livid, be wild, jump up and down, froth/foam at the mouth.
3 *discontent had been smouldering for years*: **exist unseen**, burn, seethe, simmer, fester, lie dormant.

smudge noun *there was a thick smudge of blood on his car*: **streak**, smear, mark, dirty mark, spot, fleck, speck, stain, blotch, stripe, dot, blot, blob, dab, blur, smut, fingermark; informal splotch, splodge; literary smirch.
▸ verb **1** *her face and arms were smudged with dust*: **streak**, mark, dirty, spot, soil, muddy, fleck, speck, blotch, blacken, smear, stripe, dot, blot, blob, daub, bedaub, stain; informal splotch, splodge; literary besmirch.
2 *she dabbed her eyes, careful not to smudge her make-up*: **smear**, streak, blur, mess up.

smug adjective *he was feeling smug after his win*: **self-satisfied**, complacent, self-congratulatory, superior, puffed up, pleased with oneself, self-approving, well pleased, proud of oneself; informal goody-goody; Brit. informal like the cat that's got the cream, I'm-all-right-Jack; N. Amer. informal wisenheimer; N. Amer. vulgar slang shit-eating.

> *Word toolkit* **smug**
>
> See **conceited**.

smuggle verb *they smuggled drugs into Britain*: **bring/take illegally**, run, sneak.

smuggler noun *a convicted cocaine smuggler*: **contrabandist**, runner, courier, bootlegger; informal mule; N. Amer. informal moonshiner.

smutty adjective *his humour is of the smutty adolescent variety*: **vulgar**, dirty, rude, filthy, crude, offensive, salacious, coarse, obscene, indecent, lewd, pornographic, X-rated, risqué, racy, broad, earthy, bawdy, Rabelaisian, spicy, suggestive, titillating, improper, naughty, indelicate, indecorous, ribald, off colour, locker-room; informal blue, raunchy; Brit. informal fruity, near the knuckle, saucy; N. Amer. informal gamy; euphemistic **adult**.
▹ANTONYMS pure.

snack noun *this makes a snack for two or a substantial meal for one*: **light meal**, something to eat, sandwich, supper, treat, refreshments, nibbles, canapés, titbit(s); informal bite, bite to eat, a little something; Brit. informal elevenses.
▸ verb *don't* **snack on** *sugary foods and drinks during the day*: **eat between meals**, nibble, munch; informal graze.

snaffle verb informal *Ginny took a fancy to my gardening shorts and snaffled them*: **steal**, thieve, rob, take, purloin, help oneself to, abscond with, run off with, carry off; pilfer, embezzle, misappropriate; informal walk off/away with, run away/off with, swipe, nab, rip off, lift, 'liberate', 'borrow', filch, snitch; Brit. informal nick, pinch, half-inch, whip, knock off, nobble, bone, scrump, blag; N. Amer. informal heist, glom; Austral. informal snavel; W. Indian informal tief; archaic crib, hook.

snag noun **1** *the snag is that a stronger economy might mean higher inflation*: **obstacle**, difficulty, complication, catch, hitch, stumbling block, pitfall, unseen problem, problem, barrier, impediment, hindrance, inconvenience, setback, hurdle, disadvantage, downside, drawback, minus; informal hiccup.
2 *the wooden rails become smooth over time, with no snags or rough corners*: **sharp projection**, jag, jagged bit; thorn, spur; informal sticky-out bit.
3 *she got a snag in her tights*: **tear**, rip, rent, ladder, run, hole, gash, slash, slit.
▸ verb **1** *she wouldn't want cats' claws snagging her tights*: **tear**, rip, ladder, gash.
2 *the zip runs freely and doesn't* **snag on** *the fabric*: **catch (in)**, hook, jag; get caught in/on.

snake noun **1** literary serpent; Zoology **ophidian**; Austral. rhyming slang Joe Blake.
2 *that man is a cold-blooded snake*: **traitor**, turncoat, betrayer, informer, back-stabber, double-crosser, double-dealer, quisling, Judas; **cheat**, swindler, fraudster, trickster, charlatan, viper, serpent, snake in the grass; informal two-timer, creep, rat, beast, pig, swine, skunk, dog, weasel, bastard; Brit. informal twister, scrote; Brit. informal, dated bounder, rotter; N. Amer. informal rat fink; Irish informal sleeveen; Austral. informal dingo; vulgar slang shit; dated heel, cad, blackguard.
▸ verb *the road snakes inland*: **twist**, wind, twist and turn, meander, zigzag; curl, coil, wreathe, spiral, twine, loop, curve, corkscrew.

> *Word links* **snake**
>
> **colubrine**, **ophidian**, **serpentine**, **anguine** relating to snakes
> **ophiology** study of snakes
> **ophidiophobia** fear of snakes

snap verb **1** *the safety rope snapped and Davis was sucked under the water*: **break**, break in/into two, fracture, splinter, separate, come apart, part, split, crack; informal bust.
▹ANTONYMS hold.
2 *she claims she snapped after years of violence*: **lose one's self-control**, crack, freak, freak out, get overwrought, go to pieces, get hysterical, get worked up, flare up; informal crack up, lose one's cool, blow one's top, fly off the handle; Brit. informal throw a wobbly.
3 *a white Range Rover passed, the Union flag snapping from a small mast on the bonnet*: **crack**, flick, click, crackle; **flutter**, wave, flap, quiver, vibrate.
4 *a dog was* **snapping at** *his heels*: **bite**, gnash its teeth; try to bite, try to nip.
5 *'I'm not that old!' Anna snapped | there's no need to* **snap at** *me—I'm only trying to help*: **say/speak roughly**, say/speak brusquely, say/speak nastily, say/speak abruptly, say/speak angrily, bark, snarl, growl, fling, hurl; lash out at; retort, rejoin, riposte, retaliate, snap back; round on someone; informal jump down someone's throat, fly off the handle at.
6 *they could see photographers snapping the royal shooting party*: **photograph**, take/get a photograph/photo of, take someone's picture/photo, take/get a picture of, picture, take/get a snapshot/snap of, take, shoot, take/get a shot of, take a likeness of, record, film, capture/record on film/celluloid.
□ **snap out of it** informal *you've had a bad time, and now you're snapping out of it*: **recover**, recover/regain control of oneself, recover/regain control of one's emotions, recover/regain one's composure, recover/regain one's calm, recover/regain one's self-control, get/take a grip/hold on oneself, pull oneself together, get over it, become one's old self, get better, cheer up, become cheerful, perk up; informal get one's act together, buck up.
▹ANTONYMS mope.
□ **snap something up** *people are snapping up bargains all over the place*: **buy eagerly/quickly**, jump at, accept eagerly, snatch at, take advantage of, grab (at), snatch, seize (on), grasp, grasp with both hands, pounce on, swoop down on.
▹ANTONYMS pass up.
▸ noun **1** *she closed her purse with a snap*: **click**, crack, pop, clink, tick, report, smack, whack, crackle.
2 *there was a sudden cold snap immediately after Christmas*: **period**, spell, time, interval, season, stretch, run; Brit. informal patch, spot.
3 *the snap of the dialogue*: **dynamism**, life, go, energy, spirit, vigour, vigorousness, liveliness, sparkle, vivacity, vitality, sprightliness, force, forcefulness, drive, strength, animation, verve, panache, elan, enthusiasm, exuberance, gusto, brio, zest, bite; informal oomph, pizzazz, zing, zip, feistiness.
▹ANTONYMS inertia, lethargy.
4 *Mark showed me his holiday snaps of Barbados*: **photograph**, picture, photo, shot, snapshot, likeness, image, portrait, study, print, slide, transparency, negative, positive, plate, film, bromide, frame, exposure, still, proof, enprint, enlargement.

snappy adjective informal **1** *he's in a snappy mood*: **irritable**, irascible, short-tempered, hot-tempered, quick-tempered, fiery, peevish, cross, crabbed, crabby, crotchety, cantankerous, impatient, grumpy, huffy, brusque, ill-tempered, bad-tempered, ill-natured, ill-humoured, touchy, volatile, testy, tetchy, snarling, waspish, prickly, crusty, peppery, bilious, liverish, dyspeptic, splenetic, choleric; informal snappish, chippy, grouchy, cranky, on a short fuse; Brit. informal narky, ratty, eggy, like a bear with a sore head; N. Amer. informal peckish, soreheaded; Austral./NZ informal snaky; informal, dated miffy.
▹ANTONYMS good-natured, peaceable.
2 *a snappy catchphrase*: **concise**, succinct, memorable, catchy, neat, clever, crisp, pithy, witty, incisive, brief, short, short and sweet, sharp, terse, curt, laconic, aphoristic, epigrammatic.
▹ANTONYMS long-winded.
3 *a snappy dresser*: **smart**, well dressed, well turned out, besuited, fashionably dressed, fashionable, stylish, chic, modish, elegant, neat, spruce, trim, dapper, debonair; French soigné; informal snazzy, natty, sharp, nifty, cool, with it; N. Amer. informal sassy, spiffy, fly, kicky; dated as if one had just stepped out of a bandbox; Brit. informal, dated swagger; archaic trig.
▹ANTONYMS slovenly.
□ **make it snappy** *into bed with you, and make it snappy!* **hurry**, hurry (it) up, be quick (about it), get a move on, come along, look lively, speed up, move faster; informal get moving, get cracking, step on it, step on the gas, move it, buck up, shake a leg; Brit. informal get one's skates on; Brit. informal, dated stir one's stumps; N. Amer. informal get a wiggle on; Austral./NZ informal rattle your dags; S. African informal put foot; dated make haste.
▹ANTONYMS dilly-dally.

snare noun **1** *he came upon a hare struggling in an illegal snare*: **trap**, gin, net, noose; rare springe.
2 *prudent people can avoid the snares of the Football Act by not walking on*

S

the pitch: **pitfall**, trick, trap, tangle, web, mesh, catch, danger, hazard, peril; literary toils.
▸**verb 1** *cats were snared by people who look after game birds*: **trap**, catch, net, bag, ensnare, entrap; rare springe.
2 *Havvie had already managed to snare one Yankee heiress*: **entrap**, ensnare, trap, catch, get hold of, seize, capture, bag, hook, land.

snarl[1] **verb 1** *a pack of snarling wolves*: **growl**, show its teeth.
2 *'Shut your mouth!' he snarled | I used to* ***snarl at*** *anyone I disliked*: **say/speak roughly**, say/speak brusquely, say/speak nastily, say/speak angrily, bark, snap, growl, fling, hurl; lash out at; round on someone; informal jump down someone's throat, fly off the handle at.

snarl[2] **verb**
□ **snarl something up 1** *the trailing lead got snarled up in a bramble bush*: **tangle**, entangle, entwine, enmesh, ravel, knot, twist, intertwine, jumble, muddle, foul. ▷ANTONYMS untangle.
2 *a heavy backlog of cases has snarled up the court process*: **complicate**, confuse, muddle, jumble, throw into disorder, embroil, make difficult; informal mess up. ▷ANTONYMS sort out, facilitate.

snarl-up **noun** informal **1** *Edinburgh's daily traffic snarl-ups*: **traffic jam**, jam, tailback, line, stream, gridlock.
2 *the main cause of the brouhaha is a snarl-up in terminology*: **muddle**, mess, tangle, jumble, entanglement, imbroglio; misunderstanding, misinterpretation, misconstruction, misapprehension, misconception, the wrong idea, false impression, confusion; mistake, error, mix-up, bungle; W. Indian comess; informal hash, mess-up, foul-up, screw-up; N. Amer. informal snafu; vulgar slang fuck-up; Brit. vulgar slang balls-up.

snatch **verb 1** *she snatched the last sandwich from the plate*: **grab**, seize, seize hold of, grab hold of, take hold of, lay hold of, lay (one's) hands on, get one's hands on, take, pluck; take a grip of, grip, grasp, clutch.
2 informal *someone snatched my handbag on a bus*: **steal**, thieve, rob, take, pilfer, purloin, loot, rifle, abscond with, carry off; embezzle, misappropriate; informal walk off/away with, run away/off with, swipe, nab, rip off, lift, 'liberate', 'borrow', filch, snaffle, snitch; Brit. informal pinch, half-inch, nick, whip, knock off, nobble, bone; N. Amer. informal heist, glom; Austral. informal snavel; W. Indian informal tief; archaic crib, hook.
3 informal *she posed as a childminder and snatched Julie from her home*. See **abduct**.
4 *Fogdoe skied a brilliant second run to snatch victory in the men's slalom*: **achieve**, secure, obtain, seize, pluck, wrest, scrape.
5 *I* ***snatched at*** *the chance*: **accept eagerly**, jump at, take advantage of, grab (at), snap up, seize (on), grasp, grasp with both hands, pounce on, swoop down on; buy eagerly/quickly.
▸**noun 1** *brief snatches of sleep*: **period**, spell, time, fit, bout, interval, duration, season, term, stretch, span, phase, run; Brit. informal patch, spot.
2 *he heard a snatch of their conversation*: **fragment**, snippet, smattering, bit, scrap, piece, part, extract, excerpt, portion, section, selection.
3 informal *her snatch of £3 million in used notes has been described as 'the perfect crime'*. See **theft**.

snazzy **adjective** *they look good in those snazzy little silk dresses*: **stylish**, smart, attractive, lovely, glamorous, gorgeous, stunning; fashionable, dapper, debonair, dashing, jaunty, rakish, spruce; chic, modish, elegant, trim; informal trendy, cool, sharp, snappy, with it, swinging, nifty, natty, groovy; N. Amer. informal sassy, spiffy, fly, kicky; dated as if one had just stepped out of a bandbox, gay; Brit. informal, dated swagger; archaic trig.
▷ANTONYMS dowdy.

S

sneak **verb 1** *I sneaked out by the back exit*: **creep**, slink, steal, slip, slide, sidle, edge, move furtively, tiptoe, pussyfoot, pad, prowl.
2 *someone sneaked a camera inside*: **bring/take surreptitiously**, bring/take secretly, bring/take illicitly, smuggle, spirit, slip.
3 *she sneaked a glance at her watch | he sneaked a doughnut while no one was looking*: **snatch**, take a furtive/stealthy/surreptitious ..., get furtively/stealthily/surreptitiously, steal.
4 Brit. informal *it felt wrong, like sneaking to an adult | a little squirt called Ollie Bogwhistle* ***sneaked on*** *me*: **inform (on/against)**, act as an informer, tell tales (on), report, give someone away, be disloyal (to), sell someone out, stab someone in the back; informal squeal (on), rat (on), blow the whistle (on), peach (on), snitch (on), put the finger on, sell someone down the river, stitch someone up; Brit. informal grass (on), split (on), shop; Scottish informal clype (on); N. Amer. informal rat someone out, finger, fink on, drop a/the dime on; Austral. informal pimp on, pool, put someone's pot on.
▸**noun** Brit. informal *Ethel was the form sneak and goody-goody*: **informer**, betrayer, stool pigeon; informal snitch, finger, squealer, rat, whistle-blower, nose; Brit. informal grass, supergrass, nark, snout; Scottish informal clype; Scottish & N. Irish informal tout; N. Amer. informal fink, stoolie; Austral. informal fizgig, pimp, shelf; archaic intelligencer, beagle.
▸**adjective** *a sneak thief | a sneak preview*: **furtive**, secret, stealthy, sly, surreptitious, clandestine, covert; private, quick, surprise.

sneaking **adjective 1** *she had a sneaking admiration for him*: **secret**, private, hidden, concealed, innermost, inward, unexpressed, unvoiced, undisclosed, undeclared, undivulged, unconfessed, unavowed.
2 *I have a sneaking feeling I may have broken a bone in my right hand*: **niggling**, nagging, lurking, insidious, lingering, gnawing, unrelenting, slight but persistent, worrying.

sneaky **adjective** *it was a sneaky trick and I fell for it*: **sly**, crafty, cunning, wily, clever, artful, scheming, devious, guileful, tricky, conniving, designing, deceitful, duplicitous, dishonest, disingenuous, underhand, untrustworthy, unscrupulous, double-dealing; **furtive**, secretive, secret, stealthy, surreptitious, sneaking, skulking, slinking, clandestine, hidden, covert, cloaked, conspiratorial, under the table; informal dirty, foxy, shifty; Brit. informal fly; Austral./NZ informal shonky; S. African informal slim; archaic subtle; rare carny.
▷ANTONYMS honest, open.

sneer **noun 1** *I spent a lot of time watching daytime television with a sneer on my face*: **curl of the/one's lip**, disparaging smile, contemptuous smile, smug smile, conceited smile, cruel smile, mirthless smile, smirk, snicker, snigger.
2 *I was oblivious to the sneers of others*: **jibe**, barb, jeer, taunt, insult, cutting remark, slight, affront, slur, insinuation; **(sneers) scorn**, scoffing, contempt, disdain, mockery, ridicule, derision; informal dig.
▸**verb 1** *he looked me right in the face and sneered*: **curl one's lip**, smile disparagingly, smile contemptuously, smile smugly, smile conceitedly, smile cruelly, smile mirthlessly, smirk, snicker, snigger.
2 *it is easy to* ***sneer at*** *the credulous pilgrims*: **scoff at**, scorn, be contemptuous of, treat with contempt, hold in contempt, disdain, mock, jeer at, gibe at, ridicule, deride, taunt, insult, make cutting remarks about, slight, affront; N. Amer. slur; N. Amer. informal jive.

sneeze **verb**
□ **not to be sneezed at** informal *the average saving of £550 was not be sneezed at*: **worth having**, considerable, substantial, sizeable, fairly large, largish, biggish, significant; fairly good, passable, reasonable, moderately good, not bad, worth taking into account; informal OK.

snicker **verb** *she is a woman they all love to snicker at*: **snigger**, sneer, smirk, simper; titter, giggle, chortle.
▸**noun** *he could not evoke a snicker with his jokes*: **snigger**, sneer, smirk, simper; titter, giggle, chortle.

snide **adjective** *I'm fed up with your snide remarks*: **disparaging**, derogatory, deprecating, deprecatory, denigratory, insulting, vituperative, disapproving, contemptuous; mocking, taunting, ridiculing, sneering, jeering, scoffing; scornful, derisive, sarcastic, caustic, biting, bitchy, shrewish, spiteful, hurtful, nasty, mean; Brit. informal sarky; rare mordacious.
▷ANTONYMS complimentary, sympathetic.

> *Word toolkit* **snide**
>
> See **dismissive**.

sniff **verb 1** *Maria sniffed and wiped her nose | he sniffed the morning air*: **inhale**, snuffle, breathe in, snuff (up).
2 *carefully she sniffed the fruit*: **smell**, test the smell of, nose at; detect the smell of, pick up the smell of, catch the scent of, scent, get a whiff of.
□ **sniff at** *the working mothers were all sniffed at by the uniformed nannies*: **scorn**, disdain, hold in disdain, show contempt for, be contemptuous of, treat/regard with contempt, hold in contempt, treat as inferior, be snobbish to, despise, look down on, pour/heap scorn on, sneer at, scoff at; informal turn one's nose up at, look down one's nose at.
□ **sniff something out** informal *journalists who sniff out sensation or scandal*: **detect**, find, search out, discover, disclose, bring to light, track down, dig up, hunt out, ferret out, root out, uncover, unearth, disinter, smell out, nose out, follow the scent of, scent out, run to earth/ground.
▸**noun 1** *she gave a loud sniff*: **snuffle**.
2 *the sniff of lunch was everywhere | I haven't had a sniff of fresh air*: **smell**, scent, whiff; lungful.
3 informal *they're off at the first sniff of trouble*: **indication**, hint, intimation, whiff, inkling, suggestion, suspicion, whisper, trace, signal, sign, clue, gleam, wind.

sniffy **adjective** informal *some people are sniffy about tea bags*: **contemptuous**, scornful, full of contempt, derisive, derisory, withering, mocking, scoffing, sneering, jeering, scathing, snide, disparaging, slighting, supercilious, disdainful, superior, dismissive; informal snotty, fancy-pants; archaic contumelious.
▷ANTONYMS friendly, complimentary.

snigger **verb** *the boys at school were sure to snigger at him behind his back*: **give a suppressed laugh**, snicker, sneer, smirk, simper; titter, giggle, chortle.
▸**noun** *it was a good joke, but it got hardly a snigger*: **suppressed laugh**, snicker, sneer, smirk, simper; titter, giggle, chortle.

snip **verb 1** *an usher neatly snips your ticket in two*: **cut**, clip, cut into, slit, nick, gash, notch, incise, snick.
2 *always have your secateurs in hand to snip faded flowers*: **cut off**, snip off, trim (off), clip, prune, hack off, chop off, saw off, lop (off), dock, crop, sever, separate, detach, remove, take off.

▶ **noun 1** *make snips along the length up to this line*: **cut**, clip, trim; slit, nick, gash, notch, incision, snick.
2 *the collage consists of snips of wallpaper*: **scrap**, cutting, shred, strip, ribbon, rag, snippet, remnant, fragment, sliver, splinter, chip, bit, tiny bit, piece, tiny piece, speck, crumb, spot, fleck, wisp.
3 Brit. informal *at £1 million, the goalkeeper has turned out to be* ***a snip***: **bargain**, good buy, cheap buy; (good) value for money, surprisingly cheap; informal giveaway, steal.
▷**ANTONYMS** rip-off.
4 informal *the job was* ***a snip***: **easy task**, **easy job**, child's play, five-finger exercise, gift, walkover, nothing, sinecure, gravy train; informal doddle, walk in the park, piece of cake, picnic, money for old rope, money for jam, cinch, breeze, sitter, kids' stuff, cushy job/number, doss, cakewalk, pushover; N. Amer. informal duck soup, snap; Austral./NZ informal bludge, snack; S. African informal a piece of old tackie; Brit. vulgar slang a piece of piss.

snippet **noun** *snippets of information*: **piece**, bit, scrap, fragment, morsel, particle, shred, snatch, excerpt, extract.

snivel **verb 1** *they found him slumped in a chair, snivelling*: **sniffle**, snuffle, run at the nose, have a runny/running nose; **whimper**, whine, weep, cry, shed tears, sob, howl, mewl, bawl; Scottish greet; informal blub, blubber, boohoo; Brit. informal grizzle.
2 *if you get caught, you shouldn't snivel about what you get*: **complain**, moan, mutter, grumble, grouse, groan, grouch, growl, carp, bleat, whine, object, make a fuss; Scottish & Irish gurn; informal gripe, beef, bellyache, bitch, whinge, sound off, go on; Brit. informal chunter, create, be on at someone; N. English informal mither; N. Amer. informal kvetch; S. African informal chirp; Brit. dated crib, natter.

snobbery **noun** *there was a complete lack of snobbery about staff mingling with guests*: **affectation**, **pretentiousness**, condescension, affectedness, pretension, elitism, snobbishness, arrogance, pride, haughtiness, airs, airs and graces, disdain, disdainfulness, superciliousness, exclusiveness; informal snootiness, uppitiness; Brit. informal side.

snobbish **adjective** *the snobbish distinction between art and craft*: **elitist**, snobby, superior, supercilious, exclusive; arrogant, proud, haughty, disdainful; patronizing, condescending; pretentious, affected; informal snooty, uppity, high and mighty, la-di-da, fancy-pants, stuck-up, hoity-toity, snotty; Brit. informal toffee-nosed; N. Amer. informal high-hat, toplofty.

snoop informal **verb 1** *you shouldn't* ***snoop into*** *our affairs*: **pry**, enquire impertinently, be inquisitive (about), enquire, do some detective work; be curious, poke about/around, mind someone else's business, be a busybody, nose into, stick/poke one's nose in/into; interfere (in/with), meddle (in/with), intrude (on); informal be nosy (about), nosy; Austral./NZ informal stickybeak.
2 *they decided to* ***snoop around*** *the building*: **investigate**, explore, ferret (about/around) in, rummage in, search, delve into, peer into, prowl around, nose around/about/round, have a good look at.
▶ **noun 1** *White went off for a snoop around, as policemen do*: **search**, nose, look, prowl, ferret, poke, exploration, investigation.
2 *the broadcast was intercepted by radio snoops*. See **snooper**.

snooper **noun** *a snooper employed by her ex-husband's lawyer*: **eavesdropper**, pryer, interferer, meddler, busybody; investigative journalist; **investigator**, detective, private detective, private investigator, operative; Brit. enquiry agent; informal snoop, nosy parker, Paul Pry, private eye, PI, sleuth; N. Amer. informal private dick, peeper, shamus, gumshoe; Austral./NZ informal stickybeak; informal, dated hawkshaw, sherlock; N. Amer. dated Pinkerton.

snooty **adjective** *they thought that I was too snooty to be friends with them*: **arrogant**, proud, haughty, conceited, lofty, aloof, disdainful, superior, self-important, supercilious, exclusive; **snobbish**, patronizing, condescending, affected, pretentious, elitist, snobby; informal uppity, high and mighty, la-di-da, fancy-pants, stuck-up, hoity-toity, snotty; Brit. informal toffee-nosed; N. Amer. informal high-hat, toplofty.
▷**ANTONYMS** friendly, modest.

snooze informal **noun** *a sandy bank looked a good place for a snooze*: **sleep**, nap, doze, rest, siesta, drowse, catnap; beauty sleep; informal forty winks, a bit of shut-eye; Brit. informal kip, zizz; literary slumber.
▶ **verb** *her eyes finally stayed closed as she gently snoozed*: **sleep**, be asleep, doze, rest, take a siesta, nap, take a nap, catnap, drowse; sleep like a log/top; informal snatch forty winks, get some shut-eye, be in the land of Nod; Brit. informal kip, have a kip, get one's head down, zizz, get some zizz, doss (down); N. Amer. informal catch some Zs; literary be in the arms of Morpheus, slumber.
▷**ANTONYMS** be awake.

snout **noun** *the spiny anteater has a long pointed snout*: **muzzle**, face; nose, proboscis, trunk; mouth, jaws, maw; beak; Scottish & N. English neb.

snow **noun** **snowflakes**, flakes, snowdrift, snowfield, snowpack; snowfall, snowstorm, blizzard; sleet, hail, soft hail; avalanche; N. Amer. snowslide.
▶ **verb** *I am not in a position to bind myself in any way, as we are rather* ***snowed under*** *with commitments*: **inundate**, overwhelm, overload, overrun, flood, swamp, deluge, engulf; shower, bombard.

> *Word links* **snow**
>
> **niveous, nival** relating to snow
> **chionophobia** fear of snow

snub **verb** *they were accused of snubbing their hosts by missing two official functions*: **insult**, slight, affront, humiliate, treat disrespectfully; rebuff, spurn, repulse, cold-shoulder, brush off, disdain, scorn, give someone a slap in the face, give someone the cold shoulder, turn one's back on, keep someone at arm's length; cut (dead), ignore, take no notice of; N. Amer. stiff; informal give someone the brush-off, freeze out, stiff-arm, knock back, put down; informal, dated give someone the go-by; rare misprize, scout.
▶ **noun** *she was angry and humiliated at her very public snub*: **rebuff**, **insult**, repulse, slight, affront, slap in the face, humiliation; informal brush-off, put-down.

snuff **verb** *a breeze* ***snuffed out*** *the candle*: **extinguish**, put out, douse, smother, choke, stamp out, blow out, quench, stub out, turn out, dampen, damp down.
▷**ANTONYMS** light, ignite. **noun**
□ **up to snuff** informal *while the animation is up to snuff, the storyline is thin*: **adequate**, competent, acceptable, satisfactory, reasonable, fair, decent, good enough, sufficiently good, not bad, all right, average, tolerable, passable, moderate, middling; up to scratch, up to the mark, up to par; informal OK, okay, so-so, fair-to-middling.
▷**ANTONYMS** inadequate.

snug **adjective 1** *our tents were snug and dry*: **cosy**, comfortable, warm, homely, cheerful, welcoming, friendly, congenial, hospitable, relaxed, restful, reassuring, intimate, sheltered, secure; informal comfy.
▷**ANTONYMS** bleak, unwelcoming.
2 *a snug black minidress*: **tight**, close-fitting, figure-hugging, skintight, slinky, close, sheath; informal sprayed on.
▷**ANTONYMS** loose.

snuggle **verb** *I* ***snuggled down*** *in my sleeping bag | Tess* ***snuggled up*** *to him*: **nestle**, curl up, huddle (up), cuddle up (to), nuzzle (up to), settle, ensconce oneself, lie close to; embrace, hug; N. Amer. snug down.

soak **verb 1** *soak the beans overnight in water*: **immerse**, steep, submerge, submerse, dip, sink, dunk, bathe, wet, rinse, douse, marinate, souse, pickle, ret.
2 *we got soaked by the rain*: **drench**, wet through, saturate, waterlog, deluge, inundate, submerge, drown, swamp; archaic sop.
3 *the sweat* ***soaked through*** *his clothes*: **permeate**, penetrate, percolate, soak into, seep into/through, spread through, infuse, impregnate, imbue, pervade.
4 *use clean tissues to* ***soak up*** *any droplets of water*: **absorb**, suck up, draw up/in, blot (up), mop (up), sponge up, sop up, take in/up.

soaking **adjective** *get your jacket off, it's soaking*: **drenched**, soaked, soaked to the skin, like a drowned rat, wet through, soaked through, sodden, soggy, waterlogged, saturated, sopping (wet), dripping (wet), wringing (wet), streaming.
▷**ANTONYMS** parched, bone dry.

soap **noun**

> *Word links* **soap**
>
> **saponaceous** relating to soap

soar **verb 1** *the bird spread its wings and soared into the air*: **fly up**, wing, wing its way; take off, take flight, take to the air; ascend, climb, rise, mount.
▷**ANTONYMS** plummet.
2 *the gulls soared on the summery winds*: **glide**, plane, float, drift, wheel, hang, hover.
3 *the cost of living continued to soar*: **increase rapidly**, shoot up, rise rapidly, escalate, spiral upwards; informal go through the ceiling, go through the roof, skyrocket.

sob **verb** *he broke down and sobbed like a child*: **weep**, cry, shed tears, snivel, whimper, whine, howl, mewl, bawl; Scottish greet; informal blub, blubber, boohoo; Brit. informal grizzle.

sober **adjective 1** *they were drunk more often than sober*: **not drunk**, not intoxicated, clear-headed, as sober as a judge; **teetotal**, abstinent, non-drinking; abstemious, temperate, moderate; informal on the wagon, dry.
▷**ANTONYMS** drunk.
2 *a sober view of life*: **serious**, sensible, solemn, thoughtful, grave, sombre, severe, earnest, sedate, staid, dignified, steady, level-headed, serious-minded, businesslike, down-to-earth, commonsensical, pragmatic, self-controlled, restrained, conservative; strict, puritanical; Scottish douce.
▷**ANTONYMS** light-hearted, frivolous.
3 *a sober account of the trial*: **unemotional**, dispassionate; factual, realistic, objective; low-key, matter-of-fact, prosaic, no-nonsense, rational, logical, straightforward, well considered, plain.
▷**ANTONYMS** sensational, emotional.
4 *a sober grey suit*: **sombre**, **restrained**, subdued, severe, austere;

conventional, traditional, staid, unadventurous; dark, dark-coloured, quiet, drab, plain.
▷ANTONYMS flamboyant.
▶ verb 1 *I ought to* ***sober up*** *a bit*: **become sober**, become clear-headed; informal dry out.
2 *that coffee* ***sobered him up***: **make sober**, clear someone's head; informal dry out.
3 *he smiled at her, but then his expression sobered*: **become (more) serious**, settle (down), relax, soften, steady, cool.
4 *his expression sobered her*: **make (more) serious**; subdue, calm down, quieten, steady; bring to, bring down to earth, make reflective/pensive, make someone stop and think, give someone pause for thought.

sobriety noun 1 *he hated her more in his sobriety than when he was drunk*: **soberness**, clear-headedness; **abstinence**, teetotalism, non-indulgence, non-drinking; abstemiousness, temperance, moderation, moderateness.
2 *his daughter had always been a model of sobriety*: **seriousness**, solemnness, solemnity, thoughtfulness, gravity, graveness, sombreness, severity, earnestness, sedateness, staidness, dignity, dignified demeanour, steadiness, level-headedness, serious-mindedness, common sense, pragmatism, practicality, practicalness, self-control, self-restraint, conservatism, strictness, puritanism.

so-called adjective *many so-called critics are in fact told what to write*: **inappropriately named**; supposed, alleged, presumed, ostensible, reputed, pretended, feigned, artificial, synthetic, counterfeit; nominal, in title/name only, titular; self-styled, self-titled, professed, would-be, self-appointed; French soi-disant; rare self-named.

soccer noun **Association Football**; Brit. football, the beautiful game.

sociability noun **friendliness**, affability, amiability, amicability, cordiality, neighbourliness, companionability, gregariousness, conviviality, clubbability; warmness, warmth, warm-heartedness, good nature, niceness, pleasantness, geniality, civility, liveliness; communicativeness, responsiveness, forthcomingness, openness, extroversion, approachability, accessibility; informal chumminess, clubbiness; archaic hospitableness, good-naturedness.
▷ANTONYMS unsociability, unfriendliness, uncommunicativeness, solitariness.

sociable adjective *being a sociable person, Eva loved entertaining*: **friendly**, affable, amicable, cordial, neighbourly, hospitable, companionable, gregarious, convivial, clubbable; warm, warm-hearted, good-natured, genial, easy to get on/along with, lively; communicative, responsive, forthcoming, open, outgoing, extrovert, easy-going, easy, hail-fellow-well-met, approachable, accessible; informal chummy, clubby; Brit. informal matey; N. Amer. informal regular; rare conversable.
▷ANTONYMS unsociable, unfriendly; solitary.

social adjective 1 *alcoholism is a major social problem*: **communal**, community, community-based, collective, group, general, popular, civil, civic, public, societal; endemic, pandemic.
▷ANTONYMS individual.
2 *a social club*: **recreational**, entertainment, amusement, leisure.
3 *the mountain gorilla is a uniquely social animal | many venomous animals live in social groups*: **gregarious**, organized, civilized, interactional.
▶ noun *the club has a social once a month*: **party**, gathering, social gathering, social occasion, social event, social function, function, get-together, celebration, reunion, festivity, jamboree, reception, at-home, soirée; informal bash, shindig, shindy, do; Brit. informal rave-up, knees-up, beanfeast, beano, bunfight, jolly, thrash.

socialism noun **leftism**, Fabianism, syndicalism, consumer socialism, utopian socialism, welfarism; communism, Bolshevism; radicalism, militancy; progressivism, social democracy; labourism; Marxism, Leninism, Marxism–Leninism, neo-Marxism, Trotskyism, Maoism.
▷ANTONYMS conservatism.

S

socialist adjective *the socialist movement*: **left-wing**, Fabian, syndicalist, utopian socialist; communist, communistic, Bolshevik, leftist; radical, revolutionary, militant, red; progressive, progressivist, reforming, social-democrat; Labour, Labourite, labourist; Marxist, Leninist, Marxist–Leninist, Trotskyite, Maoist; informal, derogatory lefty, pink, pinko, Bolshie, Commie.
▷ANTONYMS conservative.
▶ noun *she was a socialist*: **left-winger**, Fabian, syndicalist, utopian socialist; communist, Bolshevik, leftist; radical, revolutionary, militant, red; progressive, progressivist, reformer, social democrat; Labourite, labourist; Marxist, Leninist, Marxist–Leninist, Trotskyite, Maoist; informal, derogatory lefty, pink, pinko, Bolshie, Commie.
▷ANTONYMS conservative.

socialize verb *guests can socialize in a real holiday atmosphere*: **interact**, converse, be sociable, mix, mingle, get together, meet, keep company, fraternize, consort; entertain, have people round; get out (and about), go out, meet people; informal hobnob.
▷ANTONYMS keep oneself to oneself.

society noun 1 *drugs, crime, and other dangers to society*: **the community**, the public, the general public, the people, the population; civilization, the world at large, humankind, mankind, humanity.
2 *a modern industrial society*: **culture**, group, community, civilization, nation, population.
3 *Lady Angela will teach you all you need to know to enter society*: **polite society**, high society, the aristocracy, the gentry, the nobility, the upper classes, the elite, the privileged classes, the county set; the smart set, the fashionable, the A-list, the wealthy, the beautiful people, the crème de la crème, the beau monde, the haut monde; informal the upper crust, the top drawer, the jet set; Brit. informal nobs, toffs; informal, dated swells.
4 *a local history society*: **association**, club, group, band, circle, fellowship, body, guild, college, lodge, order, fraternity, confraternity, brotherhood, sisterhood, sorority, league, federation, union, alliance, affiliation, institution, coterie; rare sodality.
5 *she shunned the society of others*: **company**, companionship, fellowship, friendship, comradeship, camaraderie, social intercourse.

> *Word links* **society**
>
> **socio-** related prefix, as in *socio-economic, sociopath*
> **sociology** study of society

sodden adjective 1 *his clothes were sodden*: **soaking**, soaking wet, soaked, soaked through, wet through, saturated, drenched, sopping (wet), dripping (wet), wringing (wet), streaming.
2 *the sodden ground*: **waterlogged**, soggy, saturated, sopping (wet); boggy, swampy, miry, fenny, oozy, marshy; heavy, squelchy, soft; rare quaggy.
▷ANTONYMS dry, arid.

sodomy noun **anal intercourse**, anal sex, buggery, pedication; formal intercourse per anum; N. Amer. vulgar slang reaming; gay slang a bit of ring.

sofa noun **settee**, couch, divan, chaise longue, love seat, chesterfield, Knole sofa; sofa bed; Brit. put-you-up; French canapé, tête-à-tête; N. Amer. davenport, day bed, studio couch, sectional; rare squab.

soft adjective 1 *soft margarine*: **mushy**, squashy, pulpy, pappy, slushy, sloppy, squelchy, squishy, oozy, doughy, semi-liquid; informal gooey, gloopy; Brit. informal squidgy; rare pulpous.
▷ANTONYMS hard.
2 *soft ground*: **swampy**, marshy, boggy, miry, fenny, oozy; heavy, squelchy; rare quaggy.
▷ANTONYMS firm.
3 *a soft cushion*: **supple**, elastic, springy, pliable, pliant, squashy, resilient, cushiony, spongy, compressible, flexible, ductile, malleable, tensile, plastic.
▷ANTONYMS hard.
4 *soft fabric*: **velvety**, smooth, cushiony, fleecy, downy, leathery, furry, silky, silken, satiny, suede-effect; informal like a baby's bottom.
▷ANTONYMS harsh, rough.
5 *a soft wind*: **gentle**, light, mild, moderate, calm, balmy, delicate, zephyr-like.
▷ANTONYMS strong.
6 *soft light*: **dim**, low, faint, shaded, subdued, muted, mellow.
▷ANTONYMS harsh.
7 *soft colours*: **pale**, pastel, muted, washed out, understated, restrained, subdued, subtle.
▷ANTONYMS lurid.
8 *he spoke in soft tones*: **quiet**, low, faint, muted, subdued, muffled, hushed, quietened, whispered, stifled, murmured, gentle, dulcet, indistinct, inaudible.
▷ANTONYMS strident, clear.
9 *the soft outlines of the trees*: **blurred**, vague, hazy, misty, foggy, veiled, cloudy, clouded, nebulous, fuzzy, blurry, ill-defined, indistinct, unclear, flowing, fluid.
▷ANTONYMS sharp.
10 *he seduced her with soft words*: **kind**, gentle, mild, sympathetic, soothing, tender, sensitive, affectionate, loving, warm, warm-hearted, sweet, sentimental, mushy, romantic; informal slushy, schmaltzy.
▷ANTONYMS harsh.
11 *many teachers are too soft with their pupils*: **lenient**, easy-going, tolerant, forgiving, forbearing, indulgent, generous, clement, permissive, liberal, lax; **tender-hearted**, soft-hearted.
▷ANTONYMS strict.
12 informal *he must be going soft in the head*. See **stupid** (sense 1).

soften verb 1 *he could reduce interest rates to soften the blow of tax increases*: **alleviate**, ease, relieve, soothe, take the edge off, assuage, allay, dull, cushion, lessen, moderate, temper, mitigate, palliate, diminish, decrease, blunt, deaden, abate, tone down; rare lenify.
2 *the winds softened*: **die down**, abate, subside, moderate, let up, calm down, lessen, grow less, decrease, diminish, slacken, dwindle, weaken.
□ **soften someone up** 1 *they used long-range shelling to soften up defensive positions*: **weaken**, undermine someone's resistance, reduce someone's defensive capability. 2 *he would soften up potential buyers in the pub before a sale*: **charm**, win over, persuade, influence, undermine someone's resistance, disarm, work on, sweeten, butter up, soft-soap; Brit. informal nobble.

soft-hearted adjective *you ought to have turned her away but you were always soft-hearted*: **kind**, tender-hearted, kind-hearted, mild, tender, kindly, gentle, sympathetic, affectionate, generous, charitable, compassionate, indulgent, humane, lenient, merciful, beneficent, benign, benignant, benevolent.
▷ANTONYMS hard-hearted.

softly-softly adjective informal *we tried a softly-softly approach originally because we didn't want to push them too hard*: **cautious**, circumspect, discreet, gentle, gradual, calm, restrained, patient, tactful, diplomatic.
▷ANTONYMS clumsy.

soft-pedal verb *they soft-pedal the news because they worry she'll take it personally*: **play down**, make light of, make little/nothing of, set little/no store by, gloss over, de-emphasize, underemphasize, downplay, understate, underplay, minimize, shrug off.
▷ANTONYMS emphasize; exaggerate.

soft spot noun *Fabia had a **soft spot for** dogs*: **liking**, love of, fondness, taste, weakness, keenness on, inclination, partiality, predilection, predisposition for/towards, proclivity for/towards, penchant, bias towards, fancy.
▷ANTONYMS dislike, aversion.

soggy adjective *the thick, soggy mass of fallen leaves*: **soft and wet**, mushy, squashy, pulpy, pappy, slushy, sloppy, squelchy, squishy, oozy, doughy, semi-liquid, over-moist; swampy, marshy, boggy, miry, fenny; soaking, soaked, soaked through, wet through, saturated, drenched, sopping (wet), dripping (wet), wringing (wet); informal gooey, gloopy; Brit. informal squidgy; rare quaggy, pulpous.

soil[1] noun **1** *blueberries need very acid soil*: **earth**, loam, sod, ground, dirt, clay, turf, topsoil, mould, humus, marl, dust.
2 *the existence of American bases on British soil*: **territory**, land, space, terra firma; domain, dominion, orbit, jurisdiction, region, country.

soil[2] verb **1** *he might soil his expensive suit*: **dirty**, get/make dirty, get/make filthy, blacken, grime, begrime, stain, muddy, splash, spot, spatter, splatter, smear, smudge, sully, spoil, defile, pollute, contaminate, foul, befoul; informal make mucky, muck up.
▷ANTONYMS keep clean; clean.
2 *the reputation of the company is being soiled by sinister elements*: **damage**, **sully**, injure, stain, blacken, tarnish, taint, besmirch, blemish, defile, blot, smear, bring discredit to, dishonour, drag through the mud.

sojourn formal **noun** *his sojourn in France*: **stay**, visit, stop, stopover, residence; holiday; N. Amer. vacation.
▶ **verb** *I sojourned in California before settling in the Midwest*: **stay**, live; put up, stop, stop over, break one's journey, lodge, room, board, have rooms, be quartered, be housed, be billeted; holiday; N. Amer. vacation; archaic bide, abide, tarry.

solace noun *they tried to find solace in pictures of their little girl as they wanted to remember her*: **comfort**, consolation, cheer, support, relief.
▶ **verb** *Miss Wharton was driven home to be solaced with tea and sympathy*: **comfort**, give solace to, console, cheer, support, relieve, soothe, calm.

soldier noun *thirty soldiers died during the operation*: **fighter**, serviceman, servicewoman, fighting man, fighting woman, comrade-in-arms, warrior, trooper; (**soldiers**) cannon fodder; in the US GI, enlisted man; Brit. informal squaddie; Brit. military slang pongo; archaic man-at-arms.
▶ **verb**
□ **soldier on** informal *Graham wasn't enjoying this, but he soldiered on*: **persevere**, persist, carry on doggedly, keep on, keep going, not give up, struggle on, hammer away, be persistent, be determined, see/follow something through, keep at it, show determination, press on/ahead, stay with something, not take no for an answer, be tenacious, be pertinacious, stand one's ground, stand fast/firm, hold on, hold out, go the distance, stay the course, plod on, plough on, grind away; informal hang on, plug away, peg away, stick to one's guns, stick at it, stick it out, hang in there, bash on.

> *Word links* **soldier**
>
> **military** relating to soldiers

sole[1] noun

> *Word links* **sole**
>
> **plantar**, **volar** relating to the sole of the foot

sole[2] adjective *my sole aim was to contribute to the national team*: **only**, one (and only), single, solitary, lone, unique, only possible, individual, exclusive, singular.

solecism noun **1** *the poems are marred by solecisms*: **(grammatical) mistake**, error, blunder; informal howler, boob; Latin lapsus linguae, lapsus calami; archaic cacology.
2 *it would have been a solecism to answer the question*: **faux pas**, gaffe, breach of etiquette, impropriety, piece of indecorum, social indiscretion, inappropriate behaviour, infelicity, slip, error, blunder, miscalculation, lapse; French gaucherie; informal slip-up, boo-boo; Brit. informal boob, clanger, bloomer; Brit. informal, dated floater; N. Amer. informal goof, blooper, bloop.

solely adverb *people are appointed solely on the basis of merit*: **only**, simply, just, merely, uniquely, exclusively, entirely, completely, absolutely, totally, wholly, alone, no more than, to the exclusion of everything/everyone else.

solemn adjective **1** *a solemn occasion*: **dignified**, ceremonious, ceremonial, stately, courtly, majestic, imposing, impressive, awe-inspiring, portentous, splendid, magnificent, grand, important, august, formal.
▷ANTONYMS frivolous.
2 *Tim looked very solemn*: **serious**, earnest, grave, sober, sombre, unsmiling, poker-faced, stern, grim, dour, humourless, glum, gloomy, moody, stony-faced; **thoughtful**, preoccupied, deep in thought, pensive, meditative, ruminative, contemplative, introspective; staid, sedate, studious, bookish, owlish.
▷ANTONYMS light-hearted.
3 *a solemn promise*: **sincere**, earnest, honest, genuine, firm, committed, unconditional, heartfelt, wholehearted, sworn, formal.
▷ANTONYMS insincere.

solemnity noun **1** *the solemnity of the occasion*: **dignity**, ceremony, stateliness, courtliness, majesty, impressiveness, portentousness, splendour, magnificence, grandeur, importance, augustness, formality; solemnness.
2 *he paused and looked at Mike with great solemnity*: **seriousness**, earnestness, gravity, sobriety, sombreness, sternness, grimness, dourness, humourlessness, glumness, gloominess, moodiness; **thoughtfulness**, preoccupation, pensiveness, meditativeness; staidness, sedateness, studiousness, bookishness, owlishness; solemnness.
3 (usually **solemnities**) *the law requires certain solemnities to make a contract binding*: **formalities**, proceedings, business, rigmarole, ado, ceremony, rite, ritual, celebration, festivity; informal palaver, performance.

solemnize verb *their weddings were solemnized in the Dutch Reformed Church*: **perform**, **celebrate**, ceremonialize; **formalize**, officiate at.

solicit verb **1** *Phil had been trying to solicit his help all morning*: **ask for**, request, apply for, put in for, seek, beg, plead for, sue for, crave, canvass, call for, drum up, press for; rare impetrate.
2 *they are endlessly solicited for their opinions*: **ask**, beg, beseech, implore, plead with, entreat, appeal to, apply to, lobby, petition, importune, canvass, supplicate, call on, press, pressure; rare obsecrate.
3 *prostitutes gather in the centre of the city to solicit*: **work as a prostitute**, engage in prostitution, accost people, make sexual advances, tout (for business); N. Amer. informal hustle.

solicitor noun Brit. *they sued the company through their solicitor*: **lawyer**, legal representative, legal practitioner, legal executive, notary (public), advocate, attorney; Brit. commissioner for oaths, articled clerk, Solicitor General, Attorney General, Official Solicitor; in England & Wales Recorder; in Scotland law agent; in Scotland, historical writer to the Signet; informal brief.

solicitous adjective *she was always solicitous about the welfare of her students*: **concerned**, caring, attentive, mindful, interested, considerate, thoughtful; anxious, worried; archaic tender.

> *Word toolkit* **solicitous**
>
> See **humane**.

solicitude noun *it may be that their solicitude for the boy was slightly harmful*: **concern**, care, attentiveness, mindfulness, consideration, considerateness, thoughtfulness, solicitousness, carefulness; **anxiety**, worry; archaic concernment.

solid adjective **1** *the stream was frozen solid*: **hard**, rock-hard, rigid, firm, solidified, set, frozen, jellied, congealed, concrete.
▷ANTONYMS liquid, gaseous.
2 *a pendant made of solid gold*: **pure**, 24-carat, unalloyed, unmixed, unadulterated, genuine, complete.
▷ANTONYMS alloyed; plated; hollow.
3 *a solid line of people | for a solid hour*: **continuous**, uninterrupted, unbroken, non-stop, unremitting, incessant, constant, consecutive, undivided.
▷ANTONYMS broken.
4 *good solid houses*: **well built**, well constructed, sound, substantial, strong, sturdy, stout, durable, stable.
▷ANTONYMS flimsy.
5 *a solid argument*: **well founded**, well grounded, valid, sound, reasonable, logical, weighty, authoritative, convincing, cogent, plausible, credible, reliable.
▷ANTONYMS untenable, incoherent.
6 *a solid friendship*: **dependable**, reliable, firm, unshakeable, trustworthy, stable, steadfast, unfailing, staunch, constant, unwavering.
▷ANTONYMS unreliable.
7 *the family have established themselves in this country as solid citizens*: **sensible**, level-headed, dependable, trustworthy, down-to-earth, decent, law-abiding, upright, upstanding, worthy.

8 *the company is very solid and will come through the current recession*: **financially sound**, secure, creditworthy, of good financial standing, in funds, profit-making, able to pay its debts, debt-free, solvent, in credit, not in debt, out of debt, in the black; Finance ungeared, unlevered; rare unindebted.
9 *they received solid support from their colleagues*: **unanimous**, united, uniform, consistent, undivided; of one mind, of the same mind, in unison; rare consentient.
▷ANTONYMS divided.

solidarity noun *there was a great feeling of solidarity between us all*: **unanimity**, unity, like-mindedness, agreement, accord, harmony, consensus, concord, concurrence, singleness of purpose, community of interest, mutual support, cooperation, cohesion, team spirit, camaraderie, esprit de corps.

solidify verb *these droplets of liquefied rock solidify rapidly*: **harden**, go hard, set, freeze, ice over/up, gel, thicken, stiffen, congeal, clot, coagulate, curdle, cake, dry, bake, consolidate, ossify, fossilize, petrify; rare gelatinize.
▷ANTONYMS liquefy, melt, thaw, gasify.

soliloquy noun *Viola ends the scene with a soliloquy*: **monologue**, speech, address, lecture, oration, sermon, homily, stand-up, aside; dramatic monologue, interior monologue; informal spiel.
▷ANTONYMS dialogue.

solitary adjective **1** *I live a pretty solitary life*: **lonely**, companionless, unaccompanied, by oneself/itself, on one's/its own, (all) alone, friendless; **antisocial**, unsociable, withdrawn, reclusive, cloistered, introverted, hermitic; N. Amer. lonesome.
▷ANTONYMS sociable.
2 *solitary farmsteads were sparingly dotted about*: **isolated**, remote, out of the way, outlying, off the beaten track, in the depths of ..., hard to find, lonely, in the back of beyond, in the hinterlands, off the map, in the middle of nowhere, godforsaken, obscure, inaccessible, cut-off, tucked away, unreachable; faraway, far-flung; secluded, hidden, concealed, private, unfrequented, unvisited, undisturbed, sequestered, desolate; N. Amer. in the backwoods, lonesome; S. African in the backveld, in the platteland; Austral./NZ in the backblocks, in the booay; informal unget-at-able, in the sticks; N. Amer. informal jerkwater, in the tall timbers, in the boondocks; Austral./NZ informal Barcoo, beyond the black stump; literary lone; archaic unapproachable.
▷ANTONYMS accessible, busy.
3 *we have not a solitary shred of evidence to go on*: **single**, lone, sole, unique, only, one, individual; odd.
▶ noun *at school he remained a solitary*: **loner**, lone wolf, introvert, recluse, hermit; rare eremite, anchorite, anchoress, stylite, coenobite.

solitude noun **1** *she savoured her few hours of freedom and solitude*: **loneliness**, solitariness, remoteness, isolation, seclusion, retirement, withdrawal, purdah, privacy, privateness, peace, peace and quiet, desolation; N. Amer. lonesomeness; rare sequestration, reclusion.
▷ANTONYMS company.
2 *solitudes like the area around the loch are becoming more and more precious*: **wilderness**, undisturbed area, unspoilt area, rural area, wilds, backwoods, the back of beyond; desert, emptiness, wasteland, no-man's-land; in Australia the bush, the outback; N. Amer. & Austral./NZ backcountry; S. African the backveld; informal the sticks, the middle of nowhere; N. Amer. informal the boondocks; archaic retirement.

> *Word links* **solitude**
>
> **eremophobia** fear of solitude

S

solo adjective *a solo flight*: **unaccompanied**, single-handed, companionless, unescorted, unattended, unchaperoned, independent, lonely, solitary; alone, all alone, on one's own, by oneself/itself, without companions, in a solitary state; archaic single, sole.
▷ANTONYMS accompanied.
▶ adverb *she'd spent most of her life flying solo*: **unaccompanied**, alone, all alone, on one's own, single-handed, single-handedly, by oneself/itself, without companions, companionless, unescorted, unattended, unchaperoned, unaided, by one's own efforts, independently, under one's own steam, in a solitary state.
▷ANTONYMS accompanied, in company, with help.

solution noun **1** *there is no easy solution to this problem*: **answer**, result, resolution, way out, panacea; key, formula, guide, clue, pointer, gloss; explanation, explication, clarification, interpretation, elucidation, exposition.
2 *a solution of ammonia in water*: **mixture**, mix, blend, compound, suspension, tincture, infusion, emulsion, colloid, gel, fluid; Chemistry aerosol.

solve verb *that doesn't solve our immediate problem*: **find an/the answer to**, find a/the solution to, answer, resolve, work out, puzzle out, fathom, find the key to, decipher, decode, break, clear up, interpret, translate, straighten out, get to the bottom of, make head or tail of, unravel, disentangle, untangle, unfold, piece together, explain, expound, elucidate; informal figure out, suss out, crack.
▷ANTONYMS encode, complicate, obfuscate.

solvent adjective *although the business was solvent, Chambers asked his bank for an overdraft facility*: **financially sound**, able to pay one's debts, debt-free, not in debt, out of debt, in the black, in funds, in credit, creditworthy, of good financial standing, solid, secure, profit-making; Finance ungeared, unlevered; rare unindebted.
▷ANTONYMS in debt.

sombre adjective **1** *it was the custom to wear very sombre clothes to a funeral*: **dark**, dark-coloured, dull, dull-coloured, drab, dingy, shady; restrained, subdued, sober, funereal, severe, austere.
▷ANTONYMS bright.
2 *he looked at her with a sombre expression*: **solemn**, earnest, serious, grave, sober, unsmiling, poker-faced, stern, grim, dour, humourless, stony-faced; **gloomy**, depressed, sad, melancholy, dismal, doleful, mournful, joyless, cheerless, lugubrious, funereal, sepulchral.
▷ANTONYMS cheerful.

somebody noun *nobody was going to stop her becoming a somebody*: **important person**, VIP, personage, public figure, notable, notability, dignitary, pillar of society, pillar of the community, worthy; someone, name, big name, famous name, household name, personality, celebrity, celebutante, leading light, star, superstar; lion, heavyweight, grandee, luminary, panjandrum; magnate, mogul; informal celeb, bigwig, big shot, big noise, big cheese, big gun, big fish, biggie, heavy, hotshot, megastar.
▷ANTONYMS nonentity.

some day adverb *some day I'll live in the countryside*. See **sometime** (sense 1 of the adverb).

somehow adverb *I knew that I had to be involved somehow*: **by some means**, by any means (whatsoever), in some way, (in) one way or another, no matter how, somehow or other, by fair means or foul, by hook or by crook, come what may, come hell or high water.

sometime adverb **1** *we must visit her sometime*: **some day**, one day, one of these days, at some time/point in the future, at a future time/date, one of these fine days, sooner or later, by and by, in due course, in the fullness of time, in the long run.
▷ANTONYMS immediately; never.
2 *the break-in happened **sometime on** Sunday afternoon*: **at some time**, at some point; during, in the course of.
▶ adjective *the sometime editor of the paper*: **former**, past, previous, prior, foregoing, late, erstwhile, one-time, ex-; formal quondam; archaic whilom.

sometimes adverb *he sometimes talks nonsense*: **occasionally**, from time to time, (every) now and then/again, every so often, (every) once in a while, on occasion, on occasions, on the odd occasion, at times, off and on, at intervals, periodically, sporadically, spasmodically, erratically, irregularly, intermittently, in/by fits and starts, fitfully, discontinuously, piecemeal; rare interruptedly.

somewhat adverb **1** *matters have improved somewhat since then*: **a little**, a bit, a little bit, to a limited extent/degree, to a certain degree, to some extent, to some degree, (up) to a point, in some measure, rather, quite, within limits; N. Amer. informal some; informal kind of, sort of, ish.
▷ANTONYMS massively, hugely.
2 *a somewhat thicker book*: **slightly**, relatively, comparatively, moderately, fairly, marginally, a shade, rather, quite, within limits.

somnolent adjective **1** *he was feeling decidedly somnolent after his lunch*: **sleepy**, drowsy, tired, languid, languorous, heavy-eyed, dozy, nodding, groggy, half asleep, asleep on one's feet, yawning; lethargic, sluggish, inactive, enervated, torpid, comatose; informal snoozy, dopey, yawny; literary slumberous; rare oscitant, slumbersome.
2 *the film's action took place in a somnolent northern village*: **quiet**, restful, tranquil, calm, peaceful, pleasant, relaxing, soothing, undisturbed, untroubled, isolated.

> *Easily confused words* **somnolent or soporific?**
>
> See **soporific**.

son noun **male child**, boy, son and heir; descendant, offspring; informal lad.

> *Word links* **son**
>
> **filial** relating to a son
> **filicide** killing of one's son or daughter

song noun **1** *a beautiful song*: **air**, strain, ditty, melody, tune, popular song, pop song, number, track; literary lay.
2 *all sounds were muffled except the song of the birds*: **call(s)**, calling, chirp(s), chirping, cheep(s), cheeping, peep(s), peeping, chirrup(s), chirruping, warble(s), warbling, trill(s), trilling, twitter, twittering, whistling, piping, birdsong.
□ **song and dance** informal *she would be sure to make a song and dance about her aching feet*: **fuss**, fuss and bother, bother, commotion, trouble, rigmarole, folderol, ado, pother; informal palaver, performance, to-do, carry-on, carrying-on, kerfuffle, hoo-ha, hullabaloo, ballyhoo, business, pantomime, hoopla; Indian tamasha; NZ informal bobsy-die.

songster noun *talented songsters from all over Merseyside took pubs by storm*: **singer**, vocalist, soloist, songstress, crooner, warbler, melodist, artiste; French chanteuse; informal popster, soulster, folkie.

sonorous adjective **1** *he read aloud with a sonorous and musical voice*: **resonant**, rich, full, round, ringing, booming, vibrant, deep, clear, mellow, mellifluous, melodious, full-toned, orotund, full-bodied, fruity, strong, resounding, reverberating, reverberant, vibrating, pulsating; rare canorous.
2 *he relished the sonorous words of condemnation*: **impressive**, imposing, majestic, extravagant, grandiloquent, magniloquent, high-flown, high-sounding, lofty, rotund, orotund, bombastic, grandiose, pompous, pretentious, overblown, oratorical, rhetorical, turgid, flowery, florid, declamatory, Ciceronian; informal highfalutin; rare tumid, epideictic, fustian, euphuistic, aureate, Demosthenic, Demosthenean.

soon adverb **1** *she'll be there soon*: **in a short time**, shortly, presently, in the near future, before long, in a little while, in a minute, in a moment, in an instant, in a twinkling, in the twinkling of an eye, before you know it, any minute (now), any day (now), any time (now), by and by; informal pronto, in (less than) no time, in no time (at all), in a jiffy, in two shakes, in two shakes of a lamb's tail, before you can say Jack Robinson; Brit. informal sharpish, in a tick, in two ticks; dated directly; archaic or informal anon; literary ere long.
2 *how soon can you get here?* **early**, quickly, promptly, speedily, punctually; by when.

sooner adverb **1** *he should have done it sooner*: **earlier**, before, beforehand, in advance, in readiness, ahead of time, already.
2 *I would sooner stay*: **rather**, by preference, preferably, from/by choice, more willingly, more readily; N. Amer. if I had my druthers.

soot noun

> *Word links* **soot**
>
> **fuliginous** relating to soot

soothe verb **1** *Rachel patted his hand to soothe him*: **calm**, calm down, quiet, pacify, subdue, settle, settle down, comfort, hush, lull, tranquillize, appease, win over, conciliate, make peace with, mollify, propitiate; Brit. quieten (down).
▷ANTONYMS agitate, disturb.
2 *it contains a mild local anaesthetic to soothe the pain*: **alleviate**, ease, relieve, take the edge off, assuage, allay, dull, soften, lessen, moderate, temper, palliate, mitigate, diminish, decrease, blunt, deaden, abate; rare lenify.
▷ANTONYMS aggravate.

soothing adjective **1** *soothing music*: **relaxing**, restful, quiet, calm, calming, reassuring, tranquil, peaceful, placid, reposeful, tranquillizing, soporific.
2 *a soothing ointment*: **palliative**, mild, calmative, alleviating; rare alleviative, alleviatory, lenitive, demulcent, assuasive, mitigatory, mitigative, paregoric.

soothsayer noun *a soothsayer had promised him he should die there*. See **prophet**.

sophisticated adjective **1** *sophisticated production techniques*: **advanced**, highly developed, innovatory, trailblazing, revolutionary; modern, ultra-modern, futuristic, avant-garde, state of the art, the latest, new, the newest, up to the minute; complex, complicated, elaborate, intricate, subtle, delicate; gimmicky.
▷ANTONYMS crude, backward.
2 *a chic, sophisticated woman*: **worldly**, worldly-wise, experienced, enlightened, cosmopolitan, knowledgeable; suave, urbane, cultured, cultivated, civilized, polished, smooth, refined, elegant, stylish; informal cool.
▷ANTONYMS naive, unsophisticated.

sophistication noun *despite his jeans, there was still an air of sophistication about him*: **worldliness**, experience; suaveness, urbanity, urbaneness, culture, civilization, polish, smoothness, refinement, elegance, style, poise, finesse; French savoir faire; informal cool.
▷ANTONYMS naivety, uncouthness.

sophistry noun **1** *to claim that patients differ in any more fundamental way is pure sophistry*: **specious reasoning**, the use of fallacious arguments, sophism, casuistry, quibbling, equivocation, fallaciousness.
2 *he went along with this sophistry, but his heart clearly wasn't in it*: **fallacious argument**, sophism, fallacy, quibble; Logic paralogism.

soporific adjective *soporific drugs | soporific music*: **sleep-inducing**, somnolent, sedative, calmative, tranquillizing, narcotic, opiate, drowsy, sleepy, somniferous; boring, dull, deadly dull, monotonous; Medicine hypnotic; rare somnific.
▷ANTONYMS invigorating.
▶noun *she was given a soporific*: **sleeping pill**, sleeping potion, sedative, calmative, tranquillizer, narcotic, opiate; Medicine hypnotic.
▷ANTONYMS stimulant.

> *Easily confused words* **soporific or somnolent?**
>
> Strictly speaking, these words apply to cause and effect. **Soporific** means 'causing sleepiness' (*the motion of the train had a soporific effect on Mr. Wishart*), while **somnolent** means 'inclined to sleep' (*the lunch had rendered some of the elders somnolent*).

soppy adjective Brit. informal **1** *I find love songs really soppy*: **sentimental**, over-sentimental, overemotional, mawkish, cloying, sickly, saccharine, sugary, sugar-coated, syrupy; romantic, hearts-and-flowers; Brit. twee; informal slushy, sloppy, mushy, weepy, tear-jerking, schmaltzy, cutesy, lovey-dovey, gooey, drippy, sloshy, soupy, treacly, cheesy, corny, icky, sick-making, toe-curling; N. Amer. informal cornball, sappy, hokey, three-hankie; trademark Mills-and-Boon.
2 *my little sisters were too soppy for our adventurous games*: **silly**, foolish, soft, feeble, namby-pamby, cowardly, spineless; informal sissy, sissified, drippy, wimpish, wimpy, weedy, daft; Brit. informal wet.

sorcerer, sorceress noun **wizard**, **witch**, (black) magician, warlock, diviner, occultist, voodooist, enchanter, enchantress, necromancer, magus, medicine man, medicine woman, shaman, witch doctor; in southern Africa sangoma; Irish pishogue; N. Amer. & W. Indian conjure woman; rare thaumaturge, thaumaturgist, theurgist, spell-caster, mage, magian.

sorcery noun **(black) magic**, the black arts, witchcraft, wizardry, the occult, occultism, enchantment, spell, incantation, necromancy, divination, voodooism, voodoo, hoodoo, witching, medicine, shamanism; rare thaumaturgy, theurgy, witchery, demonry.

sordid adjective **1** *I'm not interested in your sordid little affairs*: **sleazy**, seedy, seamy, unsavoury, shoddy, vile, foul, tawdry, louche, cheap, base, low, low-minded, debased, degenerate, corrupt, dishonest, dishonourable, disreputable, despicable, discreditable, contemptible, ignominious, ignoble, shameful, wretched, abhorrent, abominable, disgusting; informal sleazoid.
▷ANTONYMS high-minded, respectable.
2 *the lane was a narrow, sordid little gully, chock-full of rubbish*: **dirty**, filthy, mucky, grimy, muddy, grubby, shabby, messy, soiled, stained, smeared, smeary, scummy, slimy, sticky, sooty, dusty, unclean, foul, squalid, flea-bitten, slummy; informal cruddy, grungy, yucky, icky, crummy, scuzzy; Brit. informal manky, gungy, grotty; Austral./NZ informal scungy; literary besmirched.
▷ANTONYMS immaculate.

> *Word toolkit* **sordid**
>
> See **dirty**.

sore adjective **1** *a sore leg*: **painful**, in pain, hurting, hurt, aching, throbbing, smarting, stinging, burning, irritating, irritated, agonizing, excruciating; inflamed, angry, red, reddened, sensitive, tender, delicate, chafed, raw, bruised, wounded, injured.
▷ANTONYMS healthy.
2 N. Amer. informal *I didn't even know they were sore at us*: **upset**, **angry**, annoyed, cross, angered, furious, enraged, in a temper, bothered, vexed, displeased, disgruntled, dissatisfied, indignant, exasperated, irritated, galled, irked, put out, aggrieved, offended, affronted, resentful, piqued, nettled, ruffled, in high dudgeon; informal aggravated, miffed, peeved, riled, hacked off, peed off; Brit. informal narked, eggy, cheesed off, browned off, brassed off; N. Amer. informal teed off, ticked off, steamed; vulgar slang pissed off.
▷ANTONYMS happy.
3 *we are in sore need of you*: **dire**, urgent, pressing, desperate, critical, crucial, acute, grave, serious, intense, crying, burning, compelling, drastic, extreme, life-and-death, great, very great, terrible; archaic or humorous parlous; rare exigent.
▷ANTONYMS some, slight.
▶noun *a sore on his leg*: **inflammation**, swelling, lesion; wound, scrape, abrasion, chafe, cut, laceration, graze, contusion, bruise; running sore, ulcer, ulceration, boil, abscess, carbuncle, canker.

sorrow noun **1** *he felt genuine sorrow at what had happened*: **sadness**, unhappiness, dejection, regret, depression, misery, cheerlessness, downheartedness, despondency, despair, desolation, wretchedness, glumness, gloom, gloominess, heaviness of heart, dolefulness, melancholy, low spirits, mournfulness, woe, broken-heartedness, heartache, grief; informal down; literary dolorous; rare disconsolateness, disconsolation, dismalness.
▷ANTONYMS joy.
2 *the joys and sorrows of life*: **trouble**, difficulty, problem, adversity, misery, woe, affliction, trial, tribulation, misfortune, reverse of fortune, misadventure, mishap, stroke of bad luck, setback, reverse, blow, failure, accident, disaster, tragedy, catastrophe, calamity.
▶verb *they stood sorrowing over the grave of their niece*: **be sad**, feel sad, be miserable, be despondent, despair, suffer, ache, agonize, anguish, be wretched, be dejected, be heavy of heart, pine, weep, shed tears, grieve, mourn, lament, wail.
▷ANTONYMS rejoice.

sorrowful adjective **1** *she looked at him with sorrowful eyes*: **sad**, unhappy, dejected, regretful, depressed, downcast, miserable, downhearted, down, despondent, despairing, disconsolate, desolate, bowed down, wretched, glum, gloomy, doleful, dismal, blue, melancholy, melancholic, low-spirited, mournful, woeful, woebegone, forlorn, crestfallen, broken-hearted, heartbroken, inconsolable, grief-stricken; informal down in the mouth, down in the dumps.
▷ANTONYMS happy, cheerful.
2 *the sorrowful news of his father's death*: **tragic**, sad, unhappy, awful, miserable, wretched, sorry, pitiful, pitiable, grievous, traumatic, upsetting, depressing, distressing, disturbing, disquieting, dispiriting, heartbreaking, heart-rending, agonizing, harrowing; rare distressful.
▷ANTONYMS cheerful, comic.

sorry adjective **1** *I was sorry to hear about his accident*: **sad**, unhappy, sorrowful, distressed, upset, depressed, downcast, miserable, downhearted, disheartened, dejected, down, despondent, despairing, disconsolate, broken-hearted, heartbroken, inconsolable, grief-stricken.
▷ANTONYMS glad.
2 *he couldn't help feeling sorry for her*: **full of pity**, sympathetic, pitying, compassionate, moved, commiserative, consoling, empathetic, caring, concerned, understanding.
▷ANTONYMS unsympathetic.
3 *I'm sorry if I was a bit brusque*: **regretful**, remorseful, contrite, repentant, rueful, penitent, conscience-stricken, apologetic, abject, guilty, guilt-ridden, self-reproachful, bad, ashamed, shamefaced, sheepish, in sackcloth and ashes, afraid; rare compunctious.
▷ANTONYMS unrepentant.
4 *he looks a sorry sight | we keep quiet about the whole sorry business*: **pitiful**, pitiable, heart-rending, distressing; **unfortunate**, wretched, unhappy, unlucky, disastrous, calamitous, regrettable, mortifying, shameful, awful; rare distressful.

sort noun **1** *what sort of book do you like reading?* **type**, kind, variety, class, category, classification, style; description, condition, calibre, quality, nature, manner, design, shape, form, pattern, group, set, bracket, genre, species, rank, genus, family, order, breed, race, strain, generation, vintage, make, model, brand, stamp, ilk, kidney, cast, grain, mould; N. Amer. informal stripe.
2 informal *he was a good sort*: **person**, individual, soul, creature, human being; man, woman, boy, girl; informal fellow, chap, bloke, lad, guy, geezer, gent, kid, brat, character, type, beggar, cookie, customer; Brit. informal bod; N. Amer. informal dude, hombre; Austral. informal bastard; informal, dated body, dog; Brit. informal, dated cove; Brit. vulgar slang sod, bugger; archaic wight.
□ **out of sorts 1** *she is feeling a bit out of sorts*: **unwell**, ill, poorly, bad, indisposed, not oneself, sick, queasy, nauseous, nauseated, peaky, liverish, green about the gills, run down, washed out; Brit. off, off colour; informal under the weather, below par, not up to par, not up to the mark, funny, peculiar, rough, lousy, rotten, awful, terrible, dreadful, crummy; Brit. informal grotty, ropy; Scottish informal wabbit, peely-wally; Austral./NZ informal crook; dated seedy. **2** *she may have been out of sorts but she meant every word*: **irritable**, irascible, peevish, fractious, fretful, cross, crabbed, crabby, crotchety, cantankerous, curmudgeonly, disagreeable, petulant, pettish; on edge, edgy, impatient, complaining, querulous, peppery, bitter, moody, grumpy, huffy, scratchy, ill-tempered, bad-tempered, ill-natured, ill-humoured, sullen, surly, sulky, sour, churlish, touchy, testy, tetchy, snappish, waspish, crusty, bilious, liverish, dyspeptic, splenetic, choleric; informal snappy, chippy, grouchy, cranky, whingeing, whingy; Brit. informal narky, ratty, eggy, stroppy, shirty; N. Amer. informal peckish, sorehead, soreheaded; Austral./NZ informal snaky; informal, dated miffy. **3** *Tim says you've been out of sorts and would like to have a chat*: **unhappy**, dejected, sad, miserable, down, downhearted, downcast, depressed, blue, melancholy, morose, gloomy, glum, dispirited, discouraged, disheartened, despondent, disconsolate, with a long face, forlorn, crestfallen, woebegone, subdued, fed up, low, in low spirits, in the doldrums, heavy-hearted; informal down in the dumps, down in the mouth; Brit. informal brassed off, cheesed off, browned off, peed off; N. Amer. informal teed off, ticked off; vulgar slang pissed off.
□ **sort of** informal **1** *those people look sort of familiar*: **slightly**, faintly, remotely, vaguely; **somewhat**, moderately, quite, rather, fairly, reasonably, comparatively, relatively, to a limited extent/degree, to a certain degree, to some extent; informal pretty, kind of, kinda, ish. ▷ANTONYMS very.
2 *then he sort of pirouetted and fell over*: **as it were**, in a (strange) kind of way, somehow.
▶ verb **1** *the children soon got the idea and sorted things of similar size and shape*: **classify**, class, categorize, catalogue, grade, rank, group, divide, sort out; **organize**, arrange, order, put in order, marshal, assemble, collocate, codify, tabulate, systematize, systemize, structure, pigeonhole; Medicine triage; rare methodize.
2 *the problem with the port engine was soon sorted*: **resolve**, settle, sort out, solve, find a solution to, find an answer to, fix, work out, straighten out, deal with, put right, set right, put to rights, rectify, iron out; answer, explain, fathom, unravel, disentangle, clarify, clear up, throw light on; informal sew up, hammer out, thrash out, patch up, crack, figure out.
□ **sort something out 1** *she sorted out the clothes, some to be kept, some to be thrown away*: **organize**, arrange, sort, put in order, set in order, straighten out, marshal, dispose, lay out, regulate; group, classify, categorize, catalogue, codify, systematize, systemize, tabulate; rare methodize. **2** *she started sorting out the lettuce from the spinach*: **separate (out)**, pick out, divide, isolate, remove, segregate, sift, sieve, weed out, winnow; keep apart; put to one side. **3** *the teacher helps the children to sort out their problems*. See **sort** (sense 2 of the verb).

sortie noun **1** *the inhabitants made several sorties against their besiegers*: **foray**, sally, charge, offensive, attack; raid, thrust, drive, assault, onset, inroad, onslaught, rush, onrush; German blitzkrieg; Italian razzia.
2 *he was already a veteran of twelve bomber sorties*: **raid**, flight, operational flight, mission, operation.

so-so adjective *he's only a so-so golfer*: **mediocre**, indifferent, average, middle-of-the-road, middling, medium, moderate, everyday, workaday, ordinary, tolerable, passable, adequate, fair; **inferior**, second-rate, uninspired, undistinguished, unexceptional, unexciting, unremarkable, run-of-the-mill, not very good, pedestrian, prosaic, lacklustre, forgettable, amateur, amateurish; informal bog-standard, fair-to-middling, (plain) vanilla, nothing to write home about, no great shakes, not so hot, not up to much; NZ informal half-pie.
▷ANTONYMS outstanding.

soul noun **1** *painting is the art of reaching the soul through the eyes*: **spirit**, psyche, (inner) self, innermost self, (inner) ego, inner being, true being, essential nature, animating principle, life force, vital force, inner man/woman; persona, identity, personality, individuality, make-up, subconscious; technical anima, pneuma; in ancient Egypt ka; Hinduism atman.
2 *he is the very soul of discretion*: **embodiment**, personification, incarnation, epitome, quintessence, essence; type, symbol, picture, model, symbolization, exemplification, exemplar, image, representation, likeness, manifestation; rare avatar.
3 *there was not a soul in sight*: **person**, human being, individual, man, woman, {man, woman, or child}, human, being, living soul, mortal, creature, body.
4 *their interpretation lacked soul*: **inspiration**, feeling, emotion, passion, animation, intensity, fervour, ardour, enthusiasm, eagerness, warmth, energy, vitality, vivacity, spirit, spiritedness, commitment; rare fervency, ardency, passionateness.

soulful adjective *she gave him a soulful glance*: **emotional**, deep, deeply felt, profound, fervent, heartfelt, sincere, passionate; meaningful, significant, eloquent, expressive; moving, inspiring, stirring, uplifting; sad, mournful, doleful.
▷ANTONYMS matter-of-fact.

soulless adjective **1** *the team quickly attempted to stamp its personality on the soulless office space*: **characterless**, featureless, bland, dull, colourless, dreary, drab, uninspiring, unremarkable, unexceptional, undistinguished, unmemorable, grey, anaemic, insipid; ordinary, mundane, commonplace, average, mediocre, run-of-the-mill.
2 *it was soulless, non-productive work*: **boring**, dull, deadly dull, tedious, dreary, routine, humdrum, ho-hum, tiresome, wearisome, uninteresting, uninspiring, unexciting, soul-destroying, mind-numbing, lifeless, dry; monotonous, unvarying, repetitive, repetitious, mechanical.
▷ANTONYMS exciting.

sound[1] noun **1** *she heard the sound of the car driving away*: **noise**, note, din, racket, row, bang, report, hubbub, resonance, reverberation.
▷ANTONYMS silence.
2 *she did not make a sound*: **utterance**, cry, word, noise, peep; informal cheep.
3 *the sound of the flute*: **music**, tones, note, chord.
4 *they do not like the sound of her plans*: **idea**, thought, concept, impression, prospect, description.
5 *the cemetery nestled beneath the cliffs, within sound of the sea*: **hearing distance**, hearing, distance, earshot, range.
▶ verb **1** *the buzzer sounded*: **go (off)**, **resonate**, resound, reverberate, blow, blare; ring, chime, peal, toll, ding, clang.
2 *engine drivers must sound their whistle*: **operate**, set off; play, blow, blast, toot, blare; ring, chime, peal, toll, ding, clang; literary wind.
3 *do you sound the 'h' in 'Doha'?* **pronounce**, verbalize, voice, enunciate, articulate, vocalize, say; rare enounce.
4 *a Labour backbencher sounded a warning*: **utter**, express, voice, speak, pronounce, declare, announce, deliver, put into words, intone.
5 *it sounds a crazy idea*: **appear to be**, appear, look, look to be, look like, seem, seem to be, have the appearance/air of being, give/create the impression of being, strike someone as being, give every indication of being.
6 *you sound as though you really believe that*: **appear**, look, seem; give/create the impression that, strike someone that, give every indication that; informal look like.
□ **sound off** *he sounds off on the human costs of offshoring*: **speak at length**, talk at length, speak, talk, go on, hold forth; **declaim**, discourse, spout, expatiate, pontificate, orate, preach, sermonize; lecture, harangue, fulminate, rant; informal spiel, speechify, preachify, drone on; rare perorate.

Word links **sound**

acoustic, sonic, aural, audio relating to sound
audio- related prefix, as in *audio-visual*
sono- related prefix, as in *sonogram*
acoustiphobia fear of sound

sound[2] adjective **1** *your heart is as sound as a young man's | he was not of sound mind*: **healthy**, in good condition, toned, fit, physically fit, hale and hearty, in good shape, in fine fettle, in trim, disease-free, undamaged, uninjured, unimpaired.
▷ANTONYMS unhealthy.
2 *it is a very sound building*: **well built**, solid, well constructed, substantial, strong, sturdy, stout, durable, stable, intact, whole, undamaged, unimpaired.
▷ANTONYMS unsafe, flimsy.
3 *that is very sound advice*: **well founded**, well grounded, valid, reasonable, logical, solid, weighty, authoritative, convincing, cogent, plausible, credible, reliable.
▷ANTONYMS unsound.
4 *a sound judge of character*: **reliable**, dependable, trustworthy, fair; good, sensible, intelligent, wise, judicious, sagacious, astute, shrewd, perceptive, percipient.
▷ANTONYMS unreliable.
5 *the company is financially sound*: **solvent**, able to pay its debts, debt-free, not in debt, out of debt, in the black, in funds, in credit, creditworthy, of good financial standing, solid, secure; rare unindebted.
▷ANTONYMS insolvent, in debt; bankrupt.
6 *a sound sleep*: **deep**, undisturbed, unbroken, uninterrupted, untroubled, peaceful.
▷ANTONYMS shallow, light, broken, fitful.
7 *such people should be given a sound thrashing*: **thorough**, proper, real, regular, complete, total, veritable, without reserve, unqualified, out-and-out, thoroughgoing, downright, absolute, drastic, severe; informal damn, right, royal, right royal; Austral./NZ informal **fair**.
▷ANTONYMS slight.

Choose the right word **sound, valid, cogent**

See **valid**.

sound[3] verb *he was sounding the depth of the river with a pole*: **measure**, gauge, determine, test, investigate, survey, take a reading of, plumb, fathom, probe.
□ **sound someone out 1** *he sounded people out and found the responses favourable*: **canvass**, test the opinions of, survey, poll, question, interview, sample; test the water, see how the land lies; informal pump. **2** *officials arrived to sound out public opinion*: **investigate**, test, check, examine, probe, carry out an investigation of, conduct a survey of, research, research into, carry out research into, explore, look into, canvass, elicit.

sound[4] noun *he cast off and headed back across the sound*: **channel**, (sea) passage, strait(s), neck, narrows, waterway, stretch of water; **inlet**, branch, arm (of the sea), fjord, creek, bay, voe; estuary, firth.

sour adjective **1** *too much pulp produces a sour wine*: **acid**, acidy, acidic, acidulated, tart, bitter, sharp, acetic, vinegary, pungent, acrid, biting, stinging, burning, smarting, unpleasant, distasteful; N. Amer. acerb; technical acerbic; rare acidulous.
▷ANTONYMS sweet.
2 *milk bottles with traces of sour milk lingering in them*: **(gone) bad**, (gone) off, turned, curdled, fermented, rancid; old, tainted, high, rank, foul, fetid, overripe; N. Amer. clabbered.
▷ANTONYMS fresh.
3 *a sour old man*: **embittered**, **resentful**, nasty, spiteful, sharp-tongued, irritable, irascible, peevish, fractious, fretful, cross, crabbed, crabby, crotchety, cantankerous, curmudgeonly, disagreeable, petulant, pettish; complaining, querulous, bitter, moody, grumpy, huffy, scratchy, bad-tempered, ill-tempered, ill-natured, ill-humoured, sullen, surly, sulky, churlish, touchy, testy, tetchy, snappish, waspish, crusty, bilious, liverish, dyspeptic, splenetic, choleric; informal snappy, chippy, grouchy, cranky, whingeing, whingy; Brit. informal narky, ratty, eggy, stroppy, shirty; N. Amer. informal peckish, sorehead, soreheaded; Austral./NZ informal snaky; informal, dated miffy, waxy.
▷ANTONYMS pleasant, amiable.
▶ **verb 1** *five years of war had soured him*: **embitter**, make bitter, make resentful, anger, exasperate, disillusion, disenchant, poison, envenom, disaffect, dissatisfy, frustrate, alienate.
2 *a dispute soured relations between the two countries for over a year*: **spoil**, mar, damage, harm, impair, be detrimental to, wreck, upset, hurt, worsen, poison, colour, blight, tarnish.
▷ANTONYMS improve.

source noun **1** *the source of the river*: **spring**, origin, head, well head, headspring, headwater(s); S. African eye; literary wellspring.
2 *the source of the rumour*: **origin**, place of origin; birthplace, spring, wellspring, fount; starting point, history, pedigree, provenance, derivation, root, etymology; beginning, genesis, start, rise, cause; author, originator, initiator, creator, inventor, architect, father, mother; N. Amer. provenience; literary fountainhead, begetter; rare radix.
3 *a historian will need to use both primary and secondary sources*: **reference**, authority, informant; documentation.

sourpuss noun informal *Beth, who used to be such a sourpuss, made a very funny card for my birthday*: **misery**, mope, dog in the manger, damper, dampener, spoilsport, pessimist, prophet of doom; **shrew**, curmudgeon, discontent, complainer, grumbler, moaner, fault-finder, carper; N. Amer. crank; informal crosspatch, grouch, grump, virago, grouser, whinger, wet blanket, party-pooper, doom merchant; N. Amer. informal kvetch; rare jade, melancholiac.

souse verb *a crunchy bruschetta soused in green olive oil*: **drench**, soak, steep, douse, saturate, plunge, immerse, dip, submerge, sink, dunk.

soused adjective **1** *a soused herring*: **pickled**, marinated, soaked, steeped.
▷ANTONYMS fresh.
2 informal *he was well and truly soused*. See **drunk**.
▷ANTONYMS sober.

south adjective *the south coast of England | a south wind*: **southern**, southerly, southwardly, meridional, Antarctic, polar; technical austral.
▷ANTONYMS north.
▶ **adverb** *I dawdled around for a while and then headed south*: **to the south**, southward, southwards, southwardly.
▷ANTONYMS north.

souvenir noun *the recording provides a souvenir of a great production*: **memento**, keepsake, reminder, remembrance, token, memorial; testimonial, trophy, relic; (**souvenirs**) memorabilia; archaic memorandum.

sovereign noun **ruler**, monarch, supreme ruler, Crown, crowned head, head of state, potentate, suzerain, overlord, dynast, leader; king, queen, emperor, empress, prince, princess, tsar, royal duke, grand duke, elector, crown prince, princeling, prince regent, mogul, baron, liege (lord), lord, emir, sheikh, sultan, maharaja, raja; historical atheling.
▶ **adjective 1** *he asserted that sovereign power belonged to the people*: **supreme**, absolute, unlimited, unrestricted, unrestrained, unbounded, boundless, infinite, ultimate, total, unconditional, full, utter, paramount; **principal**, chief, dominant, predominant, ruling; **royal**, regal, kingly, monarchical.
2 *the Allies turned the western part of Germany into a sovereign state*: **independent**, self-governing, autonomous, self-determining, self-legislating; non-aligned, free.
3 dated *a sovereign remedy for all ills*. See **effective** (sense 1).

sovereignty noun **1** *the government renewed its claim to sovereignty over the islands*: **jurisdiction**, supremacy, dominion, power, ascendancy, suzerainty, tyranny, hegemony, domination, sway, predominance, authority, control, influence, rule; Indian raj; archaic regiment.
▷ANTONYMS subservience, subjection.
2 *full West German sovereignty was achieved in 1955*: **autonomy**, **independence**, self-government, self-rule, home rule, self-legislation, self-determination, non-alignment, freedom.
▷ANTONYMS hegemony, colonialism.

sow verb **1** *sow the seeds in rows 30cm apart*: **scatter**, spread, broadcast, disperse, strew, disseminate, distribute; drill, dibble, put in the ground; literary bestrew.
2 *large fields were sown with only cabbages or asparagus*: **plant**, seed, reseed.
3 *the new policy has sown confusion and doubt*: **cause**, bring about, occasion, create, give rise to, lead to, produce, engender, generate, induce, invite, implant, plant, lodge, prompt, evoke, elicit, initiate, precipitate, instigate, trigger, spark off, provoke; end in, culminate in, finish in, terminate in, involve, mean, entail, necessitate; promote, foster, foment; formal redound to; literary beget.

space noun **1** *there was not enough space for them all*: **room**, expanse, extent, capacity, area, volume, spaciousness, scope, latitude, expansion, margin, leeway, play, clearance; headroom, legroom, elbow room.
2 *the green spaces in and around London are under constant threat from developers*: **area**, open space, open area, unoccupied area, empty area, expanse, stretch, sweep, tract.
3 *the space between the timbers was filled with mud and straw*: **gap**, interval, opening, aperture, gulf, cavity, cranny, fissure, rift, crack, breach, break, split, flaw, crevasse, interstice, lacuna.
4 *make sure students have written their name in the appropriate space*: **blank**, empty space, gap.
5 *after a space of seven years | within the space of three hours*: **period**, span, time, duration, stretch, course, interval, season, term.
6 *Britain's first woman in space*: **outer space**, deep space, the universe, the cosmos, the galaxy, the solar system, infinity.
▶ **verb** *the chairs should be* **spaced out** *round the table | the teams are spaced only a few metres apart*: **place at intervals**, separate, place, position, arrange, line up, range, order, array, dispose, lay out, deploy, locate, settle, situate, set, stand, station.

Word links **space**

cosmology, **astronomy** study of space

spaceman, spacewoman noun **astronaut**, cosmonaut, space traveller, space cadet; N. Amer. informal jock.

spacious adjective **1** *a spacious house*: **roomy**, commodious, capacious, palatial, airy, voluminous, high-ceilinged, sizeable, open, generous, large, big, vast, immense, rambling, ample.
▷ANTONYMS cramped, poky.
2 *spacious grounds*: **extensive**, broad, wide, wide open, expansive, sweeping, rolling, rambling, open, ample, large, sizeable, substantial, vast, immense.

spadework noun *the politicians coming along have benefited from the spadework done for them*: **preliminary work**, preparations, planning, groundwork, foundations, homework, preliminaries, provision, preparatory measures; hard work, donkey work, labour, drudgery, slog, toil, hard labour, sweated labour, hack work, chores, exertion; informal grind, sweat, elbow grease; Brit. informal graft; archaic travail, moil.

Spain noun

Word links **Spain**

Hispanic relating to Spain
Hispano- related prefix, as in *Hispano-French*
Iberian relating to Spain and Portugal

span noun **1** *gannets have black tipped wings with a six-foot span*: **(full) extent**, length, width, reach, stretch, spread, distance, compass, range.
2 *within the span of one working day*: **period**, space, time, duration, stretch, course, interval, season, term.
▸ verb **1** *a bridge spanned the mountain stream*: **bridge**, cross, traverse, pass over, arch over, vault over.
2 *his career spanned twenty-five years | their interests span almost all the conventional disciplines*: **extend over**, last, stretch across, spread over, cover, range over, comprise, compass.

spank verb *she was spanked for spilling ink on the carpet*: **smack**, slap, slipper, put someone over one's knee, thrash, cane, belt, leather, cuff; informal wallop, whack, lather, give someone a hiding, give someone a hot bottom, warm someone's bottom, give someone a licking; Scottish scud; Scottish & N. English skelp; dated tan, tan/whip someone's hide.

spanner noun
□ **put/throw a spanner in the works (of)** Brit. informal *these divides are threatening to put a spanner in the works of the European constitutional project*: **interfere (with)**, hinder, hamper, obstruct, disrupt, impede, inhibit, retard, baulk, thwart, foil, curb, delay, set back, slow down, hold back, hold up; restrict, restrain, constrain, block, check, curtail, frustrate, cramp, bridle, handicap, cripple, hamstring, shackle, fetter, encumber; informal stymie; N. Amer. informal bork, put/throw a monkey wrench in the works of; rare cumber, trammel.

spar verb *the sight of husband and wife sparring in public*: **quarrel**, argue, have a row/fight, row, fight, disagree, fail to agree, differ, be at odds, have a misunderstanding, be at variance, fall out, dispute, squabble, brawl, bicker, chop logic, wrangle, bandy words, cross swords, lock horns, be at each other's throats, be at loggerheads; informal scrap, argufy, spat, have a spat; archaic altercate.

S

spare adjective **1** *a spare set of keys*: **extra**, supplementary, additional, second, another, alternative, emergency, reserve, backup, relief, fallback, substitute, fresh, auxiliary, ancillary; N. Amer. alternate.
▷ANTONYMS principal.
2 *the company proposes to sell off spare land*: **surplus**, surplus to requirements, superfluous, too much/many, supernumerary, excessive, in excess, going begging; **redundant**, not required, unnecessary, inessential, unessential, needless, unneeded, uncalled for, dispensable, disposable, expendable, unwanted, useless; French de trop.
▷ANTONYMS useful, required.
3 *what do you do in your spare time?* **free**, leisure, unoccupied, own.
▷ANTONYMS occupied.
4 *a spare, bearded figure*: **slender**, lean; willowy, sylphlike, svelte, lissom, graceful, snake-hipped, rangy, clean-limbed, trim, slight, slightly built, without an ounce of fat; thin, as thin as a reed, skinny, size-zero, gaunt, attenuated, lanky, spindly; informal skin and bone; rare gracile, attenuate.
▷ANTONYMS fat.
□ **go spare** Brit. informal *he'll go spare if you're late*: **become very angry**, become enraged, go into a rage, lose one's temper; informal go/get mad, go crazy, go wild, see red, go bananas, hit the roof, go through the roof, go up the wall, go off the deep end, fly off the handle, blow one's top, blow a fuse/gasket, lose one's rag, go ape, flip, flip one's lid, go non-linear, go ballistic, go psycho; Brit. informal go crackers, do one's nut; N. Amer. informal flip one's wig, blow one's lid/stack; vulgar slang go apeshit.
▸ verb **1** *he could not spare any money*: **afford**, do without, manage without, get along without, dispense with, part with, give, let someone have, provide.
2 *animal lovers launched an appeal to spare the dog | few of the men were spared by their captors*: **not harm**, leave uninjured, leave unhurt; **be merciful to**, show mercy to, have mercy on, be lenient to, deal leniently with, have pity on; pardon, grant a pardon to, excuse, leave unpunished, forgive, reprieve, release, free, let off, amnesty; informal go easy on.
□ **to spare** *we still have a few plants to spare*: **left over**, left, over, remaining, unused, unneeded, not required, still available, surplus to requirements; superfluous, surplus, extra; informal going begging.

sparing adjective *he was more sparing with his admiration than with his criticism*: **thrifty**, economical, frugal, canny, careful, prudent, cautious, abstemious, saving, scrimping, parsimonious; **mean**, miserly, niggardly, close-fisted, penny-pinching, cheese-paring, ungenerous, penurious, illiberal, close, grasping, Scrooge-like, stinting; informal stingy, tight-fisted, tight, mingy, money-grubbing, skinflinty; N. Amer. informal cheap; archaic near; Brit. vulgar slang tight-arsed, tight as a duck's arse.
▷ANTONYMS extravagant, lavish.

spark noun **1** *a spark of light*: **flash**, flicker, flare, glint, twinkle, scintillation, streak, spot, pinprick.
2 *there was not a spark of truth in what he said*: **particle**, iota, jot, whit, glimmer, flicker, atom, speck, bit, trace, vestige, ounce, shred, crumb, morsel, fragment, grain, drop, spot, mite, tittle, jot or tittle, modicum, hint, touch, suggestion, whisper, suspicion, scintilla; informal smidgen, smidge, tad; Irish informal stim; archaic scantling, scruple.
3 *we like to get new members for the group as it gives us more spark*: **liveliness**, animation, life, bounce, sparkle, effervescence, fizz, verve, spirit, pep, spiritedness, ebullience, high spirits, enthusiasm, initiative, vitality, vivacity, fire, dash, go, panache, elan, snap, zest, zeal, exuberance; **vigour**, energy, gusto, drive, push, brio, dynamism; informal feistiness, get-up-and-go, gumption, oomph, pizzazz, vim, zing, zip.
▸ verb *the collapse of the trial sparked a furious row last night*: **give rise to**, cause, lead to, set in motion, occasion, bring about, bring on, begin, start, initiate, precipitate, prompt, trigger (off), set off, touch off, provoke, incite, stimulate, stir up.
▷ANTONYMS bring to an end.

sparkle verb **1** *her earrings sparkled as she turned her head*: **glitter**, glint, glisten, twinkle, flicker, flash, blink, wink, shimmer, dance, shine, gleam, glow; literary glister; rare coruscate, fulgurate, effulge.
2 *after a glass of wine, she began to sparkle*: **be lively**, be vivacious, be animated, be ebullient, be exuberant, be bubbly, be effervescent, be sparkling, be witty, be brilliant, be enthusiastic, be full of life.
▸ noun **1** *I swim every day and I love the blue sparkle of the pool*: **glitter**, glint, twinkle, twinkling, flicker, flickering, shimmer, flash, flashing, blinking, winking, dancing, shine, gleam, glow; rare coruscation, fulguration, effulgence.
2 *she reminded Melissa of champagne, full of fizz and sparkle*: **vivacity**, animation, liveliness, vitality, life, verve, high spirits, exuberance, zest, buoyancy, effervescence, enthusiasm, ardour, energy, vigour, go, elan, gusto, brio, bounce, spirit, spiritedness, dynamism, activity, fire, panache, colour, dash, drive; informal oomph, pizzazz, pep, zing, zip, vim, get-up-and-go.

sparkling adjective **1** *sparkling silver jewellery*: **glittering**, glinting, glistening, scintillating, twinkling, flickering, flashing, shimmering, shimmery, bright, brilliant, iridescent, opalescent, lustrous, dancing, shining, gleaming, glowing; literary glistering; rare coruscating, coruscant, fulgurating, effulgent, scintillant.
▷ANTONYMS dull, matte.
2 *sparkling wine*: **effervescent**, fizzy, carbonated, aerated, gassy, bubbly, bubbling, fizzing, foaming, frothy; French mousseux, pétillant; Italian spumante, frizzante; German Schaum-, Perl-.
▷ANTONYMS still, flat.
3 *a sparkling performance*: **brilliant**, dazzling, scintillating, exciting, exhilarating, stimulating, invigorating; vivacious, effervescent, lively, vibrant, animated, ebullient, bright; witty, clever; rare coruscating.
▷ANTONYMS boring, dull, pedestrian.

sparse adjective *areas of sparse population*: **scanty**, scant, scattered, thinly distributed, scarce, infrequent, sporadic, few and far between; meagre, paltry, skimpy, limited, in short supply, at a premium, hard to come by; slight, thin.
▷ANTONYMS abundant, plentiful; thick.

Choose the right word **sparse, scanty, meagre**

See **meagre**.

spartan adjective *a spartan life | spartan but adequate rooms*: **austere**, harsh, hard, frugal, stringent, rigorous, arduous, strict, stern, severe, rigid; **ascetic**, abstemious, self-denying, hair-shirt; bleak, joyless, grim, bare, stark, uncomfortable, simple, plain.
▷ANTONYMS luxurious, opulent.

spasm noun **1** *Lee felt a muscle spasm in her back*: **convulsion**, contraction, throes, cramp; **twitch**, jerk, tic, start, shudder, shiver, tremor, tremble.

2 *a spasm of coughing*: **fit**, paroxysm, attack, burst, bout, seizure, outburst, outbreak, explosion, access; informal splurt; rare ebullition, boutade.

spasmodic adjective *spasmodic fighting continued*: **intermittent**, fitful, irregular, sporadic, erratic, occasional, infrequent, scattered, patchy, isolated, odd, uneven, periodic, periodical, recurring, recurrent, on and off.

spate noun *a spate of burglaries*: **series**, succession, run, cluster, string, outbreak, rash, epidemic, explosion, plague, wave, flurry, rush, flood, deluge, torrent, outpouring.

spatter verb *specks of blood spattered his face*: **splash**, bespatter, splatter, spray, sprinkle, shower, speck, speckle, fleck, mottle, blotch, smear, stain, mark, dirty, soil, daub, cover; informal splotch, splodge; Scottish & Irish informal slabber; literary besprinkle, bedabble.

spawn verb *he wrote in a dry style that spawned hundreds of imitations*: **give rise to**, bring about, occasion, generate, engender, originate, lead to, result in, effect, induce, initiate, start, set off; breed, bear, give birth to; provoke, precipitate, spark off, trigger; contribute to, make for, be conducive to, foster, promote; literary beget.

speak verb **1** *she refused to speak about the incident | he was speaking the truth*: **talk**, say (anything/something); **utter**, state, declare, tell, voice, express, pronounce, articulate, enunciate, vocalize, verbalize; rare enounce.
2 *we spoke the other day*: **have a conversation**, talk, have a talk, have a discussion, converse, communicate, chat, have a chat, pass the time of day, have a word, gossip, make conversation; informal have a confab, chew the fat/rag; Brit. informal natter, have a chinwag; N. Amer. informal shoot the breeze; rare confabulate.
3 *the Minister spoke for two hours*: **give a speech**, give a talk, talk, lecture, give a lecture, deliver an address, give a sermon, hold forth, discourse, expound, expatiate, orate, harangue, sermonize, pontificate; informal spout, spiel, speechify, preachify, jaw, sound off, drone on.
4 *he was **spoken of** as a promising student*: **mention**, make mention of, talk about, discuss, refer to, make reference to, bring in, introduce, remark on, comment on, allude to, advert to, deal with, treat.
5 *his expression spoke disbelief*: **indicate**, mean, suggest, show, denote, display, demonstrate, be evidence of, register, reflect, reveal, betray, evince, disclose, exhibit, manifest; express, convey, signify, impart, bespeak, communicate, bear out, attest, testify to, prove, evidence; literary betoken.
6 *we really must **speak to** him about his rudeness*: **reprimand**, rebuke, admonish, chastise, chide, upbraid, reprove, reproach, scold, remonstrate with, berate, take to task, pull up, castigate, lambaste, read someone the Riot Act, give someone a piece of one's mind, haul over the coals, lecture, criticize, censure; informal tell off, give someone a talking-to, give someone a telling-off, dress down, give someone a dressing-down, give someone an earful, give someone a roasting, give someone a rocket, give someone a rollicking, rap, rap over the knuckles, slap someone's wrist, send someone away with a flea in their ear, let someone have it, bawl out, give someone hell, come down on, blow up, pitch into, lay into, lace into, give someone a caning, put on the mat, slap down, blast, rag, keelhaul; Brit. informal tick off, have a go at, carpet, monster, give someone a mouthful, tear someone off a strip, give someone what for, give someone stick, wig, give someone a wigging, give someone a row, row; N. Amer. informal chew out, ream out; Brit. vulgar slang bollock, give someone a bollocking; N. Amer. vulgar slang chew someone's ass, ream someone's ass; dated call down, rate, give someone a rating, trim; rare reprehend, objurgate.
□ **speak for 1** *the MP who speaks for the Liberal Democrats on education*: **represent**, speak on behalf of, act for, act on behalf of, appear for, intercede for, express the views of, act as spokesman for, act as spokeswoman for, act as spokesperson for. **2** *who would like to speak for the motion?* **advocate**, champion, uphold, defend, stand up for, support, speak in support of, promote, recommend, urge, back, endorse, sponsor, espouse.
▷ANTONYMS speak against, oppose.
□ **speak out/up** *women have been speaking out on this issue for some time*: **speak publicly**, speak openly, speak boldly, speak frankly, speak one's mind, sound off, spout off, go on, stand up and be counted.
□ **speak up** *you'll have to speak up to be heard*: **speak (more) loudly**, speak out, speak clearly, raise one's voice, shout, yell, bellow, call at the top of one's voice; N. Amer. informal holler.

speaker noun *an accomplished speaker*: **speech-maker**, public speaker, lecturer, talker, speechifier, expounder, orator, declaimer, rhetorician, haranguer; spokesman, spokeswoman, spokesperson, mouthpiece; reader, lector, commentator, broadcaster, narrator; informal tub-thumper, spieler, spin doctor; historical demagogue, rhetor; rare prolocutor.

spearhead noun **1** *a Bronze Age spearhead*: **spear tip**, spear point.
2 *the Party became the spearhead of the struggle against Fascism*: **leader(s)**, driving force; forefront, avant-garde, front runner(s), front line, vanguard, van, cutting edge.
▸ verb *she was to spearhead the inner-city campaign*: **lead**, head, front, be the driving force behind; be in the forefront of, be in the front line of, lead the way in/for, be in the van of, be in the vanguard of.

special adjective **1** *they always make a special effort at Christmas | she's a very special person*: **exceptional**, particular, extra special, unusual, marked, singular, uncommon, notable, noteworthy, remarkable, outstanding, unique.
▷ANTONYMS ordinary.
2 *we want to preserve our town's special character*: **distinctive**, distinct, individual, particular, specific, certain, peculiar, definite, express, precise.
▷ANTONYMS general.
3 *a special occasion*: **momentous**, significant, memorable, of moment, signal, important, historic, festive, gala, red-letter.
4 *this is a special tool used for recutting washer seats on taps*: **specific**, particular, purpose-built, tailor-made, custom-built.

specialist noun *a specialist in electronics*: **expert**, authority, pundit, professional, consultant, connoisseur, fancier, master, maestro, adept, virtuoso, old hand, skilled person; informal pro, buff, ace, whizz, wizard, hotshot; Brit. informal dab hand; N. Amer. informal maven, crackerjack; rare proficient.
▷ANTONYMS generalist; amateur; dunce.

speciality noun **1** *his speciality was watercolours*: **forte**, strong point, strength, métier, long suit, strong suit, talent, skill, bent, gift, claim to fame, department, pièce de résistance; informal bag, thing, cup of tea.
2 *funding was agreed for specialities like psychiatry and anaesthesia*: **area of specialization**, specialty, field of study, area, branch of knowledge, medical/surgical field.

species noun *there are several species of spadefoot toad*: **type**, kind, sort; genus, family, order, breed, race, strain, variety, class, category, classification; style, manner, design, shape, form, pattern, group, set, bracket, genre, rank, generation, vintage, make, model, brand.

specific adjective **1** *I use this place for a specific purpose*: **particular**, specified, certain, fixed, set, determined, distinct, separate, definite, single, individual, peculiar, discrete, express, precise.
▷ANTONYMS general.
2 *make sure you give very specific instructions*: **exact**, **accurate**, precise, correct, error-free, pinpoint, detailed, explicit, express, clear-cut, well defined, unambiguous, unequivocal, meticulous, close, strict, definite.
▷ANTONYMS vague.

specification noun **1** *there was no clear specification of objectives*: **statement**, stating, naming, identification, definition, defining, describing, description, setting out, setting down, framing, itemizing, designation, designating, detailing, listing, spelling out, enumeration, enumerating, particularizing, cataloguing, citing, instancing; stipulating, stipulation, prescribing, prescription, commanding, ordaining; rare individuation.
2 (usually **specifications**) *air-raid shelters built to government specifications were death traps*: **instructions**, stipulations, requirements, conditions, provisions, restrictions, provisos, guidelines, parameters, order; description, details, delineation.

specify verb *the manufacturer would not specify the sums involved*: **state**, name, identify, define, describe, set out, set down, draw up, frame, itemize, designate, detail, list, spell out, enumerate, particularize, catalogue, cite, instance, be specific about; stipulate, prescribe, order, command, ordain; rare individuate.

specimen noun *he was asked for a specimen of his handwriting*: **sample**, example, bit, snippet, illustration, demonstration, exemplification, instance, selection, representative piece; model, prototype, pattern, dummy, swatch, test piece, pilot, trailer, trial, indication, foretaste, taste, taster, tester, smear; archaic scantling.

specious adjective *a specious argument*: **plausible but wrong**, seemingly correct, misleading, deceptive, false, fallacious, unsound, casuistic, sophistic.

speck noun **1** *the figure in the distance had become a mere speck*: **dot**, pinprick, spot, fleck, speckle, stain, mark, smudge, blemish.
2 *he brushed a speck of dust from his sleeve*: **particle**, bit, tiny bit, piece, tiny piece, atom, molecule, grain, trace.

speckled adjective *a large speckled brown egg*: **flecked**, speckly, specked, freckled, freckly, spotted, spotty, dotted, stippled, sprinkled, mottled, dappled, blotchy, brindled.
▷ANTONYMS plain.

spectacle noun **1** *the Queen's Birthday Parade is a spectacle fit for a monarch*: **display**, show, performance, presentation, exhibition, pageant, parade, extravaganza.
2 *the four men did present rather an odd spectacle*: **sight**, vision, view, scene, prospect, vista, outlook, picture.
3 *be careful, Your Highness, or you're liable to make a spectacle of yourself*: **exhibition**, laughing stock, fool, curiosity.

spectacles plural noun **glasses**, eyewear; N. Amer. eyeglasses; informal specs.

spectacular adjective **1** *a spectacular victory*: **impressive**, magnificent, splendid, dazzling, sensational, stunning, dramatic, remarkable, outstanding, memorable, unforgettable, never to be forgotten, unique.
▷ANTONYMS unimpressive.
2 *a spectacular view*: **striking**, picturesque, eye-catching, breathtaking, arresting, glorious; informal out of this world.
▷ANTONYMS dull.

▸ **noun** *French history was represented in a spectacular for tourists*: **extravaganza**, display, spectacle, exhibition, performance, presentation, show, pageant.

spectator noun *the game attracted about 40,000 spectators*: **onlooker**, watcher, looker-on, fly on the wall, viewer, observer, witness, eyewitness, bystander, non-participant, sightseer; commentator, reporter, monitor, blogger; informal rubberneck; literary beholder.
▹ANTONYMS participant, player.

spectral adjective *four spectral shapes moved through the thick yellow mist*: **ghostly**, wraithlike, shadowy, phantom, incorporeal, insubstantial, disembodied, unearthly, other-worldly; ghastly, eerie, weird, uncanny; informal spooky; rare phantasmal, phantasmic.

spectre noun 1 *the spectres of the murdered boys*: **ghost**, phantom, apparition, spirit, wraith, shadow, presence, illusion; Scottish & Irish bodach; German doppelgänger; W. Indian duppy; informal spook; literary phantasm, shade, revenant, wight; rare eidolon, manes.
2 *the spectre of a ruinous trade war loomed*: **threat**, menace, shadow, cloud, vision; prospect; danger, peril, fear, dread.

spectrum noun *a broad spectrum of opinion*: **range**, gamut, sweep, scope, span; scale; variety; compass, orbit, ambit.

speculate verb 1 *my colleagues speculate about my private life*: **conjecture**, theorize, form theories, hypothesize, make suppositions, postulate, guess, make guesses, surmise; think, wonder, muse.
2 *investors can make profits from speculating on the stock market*: **gamble**, take a risk/chance, venture, take a venture, wager; invest, play the market; Brit. informal have a flutter, punt.

speculation noun 1 *his resignation fuelled speculation of an imminent cabinet reshuffle*: **conjecture**, theorizing, hypothesizing, supposition, guesswork; talk; theory, hypothesis, thesis, postulation, guess, surmise, opinion, notion; prediction, forecast; informal guesstimate.
2 *a speculation on the stock market*: **gamble**, venture, risk; gambling; investment; informal spec; Brit. informal flutter; archaic adventure.

speculative adjective 1 *any discussion of the question is largely speculative*: **conjectural**, suppositional, theoretical, hypothetical, based on guesswork, putative, academic, notional, abstract; tentative, unproven, untested, unfounded, groundless, unsubstantiated; rare ideational, suppositious, suppositive.
▹ANTONYMS proven.
2 *a speculative investment*: **risky**, hazardous, unsafe, uncertain, unpredictable; informal chancy, dicey, iffy; Brit. informal dodgy.
▹ANTONYMS safe.

speech noun 1 *he was born deaf and without the power of speech*: **speaking**, talking, verbal communication, verbal expression, articulation.
2 *her speech was slurred | Peter's speech was clearly cockney*: **diction**, elocution, manner of speaking, articulation, enunciation, pronunciation; utterance, words, phraseology, talk; rare orthoepy.
3 *an after-dinner speech*: **talk**, address, lecture, discourse, oration, disquisition, peroration, declamation, deliverance, presentation; valedictory; sermon, homily; harangue, diatribe, tirade, rant; monologue, soliloquy, recitation; effusion, outpouring; N. Amer. salutatory; informal spiel; rare allocution, predication, philippic.
4 *Spanish popular speech*: **language**, tongue, parlance, idiom, dialect, idiolect, vernacular, patois; French façon de parler; informal lingo, patter, -speak.

> *Word links* **speech**
>
> **lingual**, **oral**, **phonetic**, **phonic** relating to speech
> **-phone**, **-phasia** related suffixes, as in *Francophone, dysphasia*

S

speechless adjective 1 *she was momentarily speechless*: **lost for words**, at a loss for words, struck dumb, dumbstruck, bereft of speech, tongue-tied, unable to get a word out, inarticulate; mute, dumb, voiceless; dumbfounded, thunderstruck, shocked, astounded, aghast, amazed, dazed; informal flabbergasted, mum, knocked/hit for six; Brit. informal gobsmacked; rare dumbstricken, mumchance, obmutescent.
▹ANTONYMS loquacious, verbose.
2 *Lisa stared back at him in speechless misery*: **silent**, unspoken, unexpressed, wordless, unsaid, unvoiced.
▹ANTONYMS vocal.

speed noun 1 *Lesley grew frustrated at the slow speed of their progress*: **rate**, pace, tempo, momentum.
2 *we were grateful for the speed of the government's response*: **rapidity**, swiftness, speediness, alacrity, quickness, fastness, celerity, velocity, dispatch, promptness, immediacy, expeditiousness, expedition, briskness, sharpness; haste, hurry, hurriedness, precipitateness; acceleration; informal lick, clip; literary fleetness; rare alacritousness.
▹ANTONYMS slowness, dilatoriness.
□ **keep (or bring) someone up to speed on (or with)** informal *she keeps the sales staff up to speed on agronomic issues*: **familiarize**, make conversant, acquaint, get up to date, keep up to date; accustom to, habituate to, instruct in, coach in, train in, teach in, educate in, school in, prime in, indoctrinate in, initiate into, introduce to; informal gen up on, clue in on, clue up on, put in the picture about, put wise to, give the gen about, give the low-down on, give a rundown of, fill in on.
▸ **verb** 1 *I sped back home*: **hurry**, race, run, sprint, dash, bolt, dart, rush, hasten, hurtle, career, streak, shoot, whizz, zoom, go like lightning, go hell for leather, spank along, bowl along, rattle along, whirl, whoosh, buzz, swoop, flash, blast, charge, stampede, gallop, sweep, hare, fly, wing, scurry, scud, scutter, scramble; informal belt, pelt, tear, hotfoot it, leg it, zap, zip, whip, scoot, scorch, burn rubber, go like a bat out of hell; Brit. informal bomb, bucket, shift, put one's foot down, go like the clappers; Scottish informal wheech; N. Amer. informal clip, boogie, hightail, barrel, lay rubber, get the lead out; N. Amer. vulgar slang drag/tear/haul ass; literary fleet; archaic post, hie; rare drive.
▹ANTONYMS amble, stroll.
2 *Cook was over the limit and he was speeding*: **drive too fast**, exceed the speed limit, break the speed limit.
3 *a short holiday will speed his recovery*: **hasten**, expedite, speed up, hurry up, accelerate, step up, advance, further, forward, promote, boost, give a boost to, stimulate, aid, assist, help along, facilitate; informal crank up.
▹ANTONYMS hinder, hold up, set back, slow down.
□ **speed up** *Smith shouted at them to speed up*: **hurry up**, accelerate, move faster, go faster, drive faster, get a move on, put a spurt on, open it up, increase speed, pick up speed, gather speed; Brit. look smart; informal get cracking, get moving, step on it, step on the gas, shake a leg, rattle one's dags; Brit. informal get one's skates on, stir one's stumps; N. Amer. informal get a wiggle on; S. African informal put foot; dated make haste.
▹ANTONYMS slow down.
□ **speed something up** *the episode speeded up the process of political change*. See **speed** (sense 3 of the verb).

> *Word links* **speed**
>
> **tacho-**, **tachy-** related prefixes, as in *tachometer, tachygraphy*
> **tachophobia** fear of speed
> **tachometry**, **velocimetry** measurement of speed

speedily adverb *you should ensure that complaints are handled speedily*: **rapidly**, swiftly, quickly, fast, post-haste, at (full) speed, at the speed of light, at full tilt, as fast as one's legs can carry one, at a gallop; promptly, immediately, briskly; hastily, hurriedly, precipitately; informal p.d.q. (pretty damn quick), double quick, at a lick, hell for leather, pronto, at the double, a mile a minute, like the wind, like a bomb, at warp speed, like a bat out of hell, like a scalded cat, like the deuce, like nobody's business, like (greased) lightning, like a madman/madwoman; Brit. informal like the clappers, at a rate of knots, like billy-o; N. Amer. informal lickety-split; literary apace.
▹ANTONYMS slowly.

speedy adjective 1 *a speedy reply*: **rapid**, swift, quick, fast, prompt, immediate, expeditious, express, brisk, sharp, unhesitating; whirlwind, lightning, meteoric, overnight, fast-track, whistle-stop; hasty, hurried, precipitate, precipitous, breakneck, summary, on-the-spot, rushed; informal p.d.q. (pretty damn quick), snappy, quickie; rare alacritous.
▹ANTONYMS slow, leisurely, dilatory.
2 *a speedy hatchback*: **fast**, fast-moving, high-speed; informal nippy, zippy; literary fleet, fleet of foot, fleet-footed; rare volant.
▹ANTONYMS slow, plodding.

spell[1] verb *the drought could spell disaster for wildlife in some parts of the country*: **lead to**, result in, bring about, bring on, cause, be the cause of; mean, amount to, add up to, constitute, signal, signify, point to; portend, augur, presage, herald, bode, promise; involve; literary betoken, harbinger, foretoken, forebode.
□ **spell something out** *Chapman spelled out his aims for the club*: **explain**, make clear, make plain, elucidate, clarify; **specify**, set out, set forth, state precisely, be specific about, itemize, detail, enumerate, list, unfold, expound, particularize, delineate, catalogue, rehearse.

> *Word links* **spell**
>
> **orthography** spelling system of a language

spell[2] noun 1 *the witch recited a spell*: **incantation**, charm, conjuration, rune, magic formula; abracadabra; (**spells**) **sorcery**, magic, witchcraft, witchery; N. Amer. hex, mojo; NZ makutu.
2 *Margaret surrendered to his spell*: **irresistible influence**, fascination, magnetism, animal magnetism, charisma, allure, lure, charm, attraction, pull, draw, enticement, beguilement; magic, romance, mystique, glamour.
□ **cast a spell on** *everyone froze, as if a wizard had cast a spell on them*: **bewitch**, enchant; curse, jinx, witch; N. Amer. hex; Austral. point the bone at; literary entrance.

spell[3] noun 1 *the current spell of dry weather*: **period**, time, interval, season, stretch, run, course, round, span, streak; snap; Brit. informal patch, spot.
2 *his spells of dizziness*: **bout**, fit, attack; dose.
3 *she did a spell at the tiller*: **stint**, turn, stretch, session, term; shift, tour of duty, watch.

spellbinding adjective *a spellbinding tale*: **fascinating**, enthralling, entrancing, bewitching, captivating, intriguing, riveting, transfixing, engrossing, gripping, very interesting, very exciting, thrilling, absorbing, compelling, compulsive, mesmerizing, mesmeric, hypnotic, magical; informal unputdownable.
▷ANTONYMS boring, dull.

spellbound adjective *the audience was spellbound*: **enthralled**, fascinated, rapt, riveted, transfixed, gripped, entranced, captivated, bewitched, under someone's spell, enraptured, enchanted, mesmerized, hypnotized; informal hooked.
▷ANTONYMS bored, uninterested.

spend verb **1** *she spent £185 on a pair of shoes*: **pay out**, lay out, expend, disburse; squander, go through, run through, waste, fritter away; lavish; informal fork out, shell out, dish out, cough up, blow, splash out, splurge, lash out; Brit. informal stump up, blue; Austral./NZ informal knock down; archaic spring; N. Amer. informal pony up.
▷ANTONYMS save, keep, hoard.
2 *the whole of the morning was spent gardening*: **pass**, occupy, fill, take up, while away, use up.
3 *I've spent hours helping him*: **put in**, devote, employ; waste.
4 *the storm of the previous evening had spent its force*: **use up**, consume, exhaust, deplete, drain.

spendthrift noun *Christopher was a notorious spendthrift*: **profligate**, prodigal, squanderer, waster; informal big spender; archaic wastrel.
▷ANTONYMS miser, skinflint, Scrooge.
▸ adjective *his spendthrift father*: **profligate**, improvident, thriftless, wasteful, extravagant, free-spending, prodigal, squandering; irresponsible.
▷ANTONYMS miserly, thrifty, frugal.

spent adjective **1** *they wrote him off as a spent force*: **used up**, consumed, exhausted, finished, depleted, drained, emptied; informal played out, burnt out.
2 *he stretched his stiff back, feeling old and spent*: **exhausted**, tired, tired out, weary, wearied, worn out, dog-tired, bone-tired, bone-weary, on one's last legs, drained, fatigued, ready to drop, enervated, debilitated, limp; informal done in, all in, dead on one's feet, beat, dead beat, bushed, fagged out, knocked out, wiped out, zonked out, worn to a frazzle, frazzled, bushwhacked; Brit. informal knackered, whacked, jiggered; Scottish informal wabbit; N. Amer. informal pooped, tuckered out, fried, whipped; Austral./NZ informal stonkered; Brit. vulgar slang buggered, shagged out; Austral./NZ vulgar slang rooted; archaic toilworn; rare fordone.

sperm noun **semen**, seminal fluid, spermatic fluid, seed, ejaculate, emission; milt; technical spermatozoa; informal come, cum; vulgar slang jism, jissom, jizz; Brit. vulgar slang spunk.

spew verb **1** *factories and chemical plants were spewing out clouds of yellow smoke*: **emit**, discharge, eject, expel, belch out, pour out, spout, disgorge.
2 *240 million cubic metres of lava spewed out of the volcano*: **pour**, gush, spurt, surge, spout, jet, rush; erupt.
3 informal *he felt faint and nauseous—he had to get out before he spewed*. See **vomit** (sense 1 of the verb).

sphere noun **1** *a glass sphere*: **globe**, ball, orb, spheroid, globule, round; bubble; rare spherule.
2 *Russia's sphere of influence*: **area**, field, compass, orbit; range, scope, extent; jurisdiction, remit; informal bailiwick, turf, patch.
3 *he lacked experience in the sphere of foreign affairs*: **domain**, realm, province, field, area, region, territory, arena, department; area of interest, area of study, discipline, speciality, specialty.

spherical adjective *the electric light bulb hung in a spherical Japanese lantern*: **round**, globular, ball-shaped, globe-shaped, orb-shaped, orb-like, bulbous, bulb-shaped, balloon-like; convex, curved, curvilinear, rounded, rotund; technical cycloidal, discoid, discoidal, spheroid, spheroidal, spheric; rare globate, globose, globoid, orbicular, orbiculate.

spice noun **1** *they use 21 different spices to make their curry powder*: **flavouring**, seasoning, herb; condiment, relish.
2 *the risk of detection had added spice to their affair*: **excitement**, interest, colour, piquancy, spiciness, zest, savour, tang, sharpness, saltiness; bite, edge; informal zip, zing, zap, punch, kick; literary salt.
▸ verb
□ **spice something up** *spice up your life with this new seductive fragrance*: **liven up**, make more exciting, enliven, revitalize, vitalize, perk up, put some/new life into, put some spark into, ginger up, stir up, get going, galvanize, electrify, add some zest to, give a boost to, add some colour to; informal pep up, jazz up, buck up, hot up.

spick and span adjective *the whole place was spick and span*: **neat and tidy**, as neat as a new pin, orderly, well ordered, in (good) order, well kept, shipshape (and Bristol fashion), in apple-pie order, immaculate, uncluttered, straight, trim, spruce; spotless, as fresh as paint; archaic tricksy.
▷ANTONYMS disorderly, untidy.

spicy adjective **1** *a spicy sausage casserole*: **piquant**, tangy, peppery, hot, picante; spiced, seasoned, savoury; tasty, flavoursome, flavourful, well seasoned, strongly flavoured, zesty, strong, sharp, pungent; rare sapid, flavorous.
▷ANTONYMS bland, tasteless.
2 *he regaled them with spicy stories*: **entertaining**, colourful, lively, spirited, exciting, piquant, zesty, zestful; **risqué**, racy, salty, scandalous, ribald, suggestive, titillating, bawdy, naughty, salacious, off colour, indelicate, immodest, dirty, smutty; informal raunchy, juicy; Brit. informal saucy, fruity; N. Amer. informal gamy.
▷ANTONYMS boring, dull, clean.

> *Word toolkit* **spicy**
>
> See **pungent**.

spider noun

> *Word links* **spider**
>
> **arachnophobia** fear of spiders

spiel noun informal *he launched into a big spiel about the merits of the product*: **speech**, line, patter, pitch, sales pitch; **monologue**, rigmarole, story, saga.

spike noun **1** *a metal spike*: **prong**, barb, point, skewer, stake, spit, projection; tine, nail, pin; spur; Mountaineering piton; technical fid; historical pricket.
2 *the prickly spikes of a cactus*: **thorn**, spine, prickle, bristle; technical spicule.
▸ verb **1** *she spiked another oyster*: **impale**, spear, skewer; pierce, penetrate, perforate, stab, run through, stick, spit, transfix; rare transpierce.
2 informal *he claimed his drink had been spiked with drugs*: **adulterate**, contaminate, drug; informal lace, slip a Mickey Finn into, dope, doctor, cut.
3 *the Assembly may well spike his tax-cut proposals*: **put a stop to**, put an end to, put the lid on, scupper, scotch, derail; frustrate, foil, thwart, stymie, baulk, hinder, obstruct; informal put paid to, put the kibosh on, clobber; Brit. informal dish.

spiky adjective *a bed of spiky pineapples*: **jagged**, barbed, serrated, sawtooth, sawtoothed; spiny, pointy, sharp.

Word toolkit

spiky	barbed	jagged
hair	wire	edge
haircut	sutures	rocks
leaves	tail	scar
grass	arrow	metal
fins	whip	glass

spill verb **1** *everyone jumped and Kevin spilled his drink*: **knock over**, tip over, upset, overturn.
2 *some of the wine spilled on to the floor*: **overflow**, flow, pour, run, slop, slosh, splash, splatter; brim, well; leak, escape; Brit. informal splosh; rare overbrim.
3 *students began to spill out of the building*: **stream**, pour, surge, swarm, flood, throng, crowd, mill.
4 *the horse was wrenched off course, spilling his rider*: **unseat**, throw, dislodge, unhorse.
5 informal *she ought not to be spilling out his troubles to you*: **reveal**, disclose, divulge, let out, leak, blurt out, babble, betray, make known, tell; informal let on, blab.
□ **spill the beans** informal *he gave me a look which made me wonder if Mavis had spilled the beans*: **reveal everything**, tell all, give the game away, talk; informal let the cat out of the bag, blab, spill one's guts, come clean; Brit. informal blow the gaff.
▷ANTONYMS keep a secret.
▸ noun **1** *a 25-tonne oil spill*: **spillage**; **leak**, leakage, overspill, overflow, flood; archaic spilth.
2 *he decided to rest following his spill in the opening race*: **fall**, tumble, accident; informal header, cropper, nosedive.

spin verb **1** *the bike lay on the grass, wheels still spinning*: **revolve**, rotate, turn, turn round, go round, whirl, gyrate, circle.
2 *Lisa spun round to face him*: **whirl**, wheel, twirl, turn, swing, twist, swivel, pirouette, pivot, swirl; Scottish birl.
3 *her head was spinning*: **reel**, go round, whirl, be in a whirl, swim, be giddy, be dizzy.
4 *she spun me a yarn about her husband running off to Poland*: **tell**, recount, relate, narrate, unfold, weave; concoct, invent, fabricate, make up.
□ **spin something out** *the longer you can spin out the negotiations the better*: **prolong**, protract, draw out, stretch out, drag out, string out, extend, extend the duration of, carry on, keep going, keep alive, continue; expand, enlarge, fill out, pad out, amplify, lengthen; archaic wire-draw.
▷ANTONYMS cut short, curtail.
▸ noun **1** *a spin of the wheel*: **rotation**, revolution, turn, whirl, twirl, gyration; pirouette, swirl; Scottish birl.
2 *the agency fought hard to put a positive spin on the campaign's progress*:

slant, angle, twist, bias.
3 *he took Lily for a spin in the car*: **trip**, jaunt, outing, excursion, short journey, expedition, sally; **drive**, ride, run, turn, airing; informal tootle, joyride; Scottish informal hurl.
□ **in a flat spin** Brit. informal **agitated**, flustered, in a panic, worked up, beside oneself, overwrought, frantic; informal in a flap, in a fluster, in a state, in a dither, all of a dither, in a tizz/tizzy, in a tiz-woz; Brit. informal having kittens.
▷ANTONYMS calm, relaxed.

spindle noun **pivot**, pin, rod, axle; axis; technical gudgeon, mandrel, arbor, capstan, staff, fusee.

spindly adjective **1** *he was pale, spindly, and ginger-haired*: **tall**, **thin**, skinny, lean, lanky, spare, gangling, gangly, scrawny, scraggy, bony, size-zero, raw-boned, gawky, rangy, angular; informal weedy; dated spindle-shanked.
▷ANTONYMS stocky, fat, thickset.
2 *spindly chairs*: **rickety**, flimsy, wobbly, shaky, fragile, frail, insubstantial.

spine noun **1** *the teenager injured his spine playing rugby*: **backbone**, spinal column, vertebral column, vertebrae; back; technical dorsum, rachis.
2 *players of very high quality who will form the spine of our side*: **mainstay**, backbone, cornerstone, foundation, basis.
3 *he has shown a great deal of spine this year*: **strength of character**, strength of will, firmness of purpose, firmness, resolution, resolve, determination, fortitude, mettle, moral fibre, backbone, steel, nerve, spirit, pluck, pluckiness, courage, courageousness, bravery, braveness, valour, manliness; informal guts, grit, spunk; Brit. informal bottle; vulgar slang balls.
▷ANTONYMS weakness.
4 *the spines of a hedgehog | cactus spines*: **needle**, quill, bristle, barb, spike, prickle; thorn; technical spicule, spicula, spiculum, spinule.

> *Word links* **spine**
>
> **vertebral** relating to the spine

spine-chilling adjective *a spine-chilling ghost story*: **terrifying**, blood-curdling, petrifying, hair-raising, frightening, scaring, chilling, horrifying, fearsome; eerie, sinister; informal spine-tingling, scary, creepy, spooky.
▷ANTONYMS comforting, reassuring.

spineless adjective *Fiona could have smacked him for being so spineless*: **weak**, weak-willed, weak-kneed, feeble, spiritless, soft, ineffectual, inadequate, irresolute, indecisive; **cowardly**, timid, timorous, fearful, faint-hearted, pusillanimous, craven, submissive, unmanly, namby-pamby, lily-livered, chicken-hearted, limp-wristed, afraid of one's shadow; informal wimpish, wimpy, sissy, sissified, chicken, yellow, yellow-bellied, gutless, pathetic; Brit. informal wet; N. Amer. vulgar slang candy-assed, chickenshit; archaic poor-spirited, recreant.
▷ANTONYMS bold, brave, strong-willed.

spiny adjective *spiny clumps of blackthorn*: **prickly**, spiky, thorny, thistly, briary, brambly, bristly, bristled, spiked, barbed, pronged, scratchy, sharp; technical spiculate, spicular, spiniferous, aculeate, barbellate, spinose, spinous, muricate, setaceous.

spiral adjective *a spiral column of smoke*: **coiled**, helical, helix-shaped, corkscrew, curling, winding, twisting, whorled, scrolled; technical cochlear, cochleate, voluted, helicoid, helicoidal.
▸ noun *a spiral of smoke*: **coil**, helix, curl, corkscrew, twist, gyre, whorl, scroll, curlicue, convolution; technical volute, volution.
▸ verb **1** *a wisp of smoke spiralled up from the trees*: **coil**, wind, twirl, swirl, twist, wreathe, snake, gyrate.
2 *inflation continued to spiral*: **soar**, shoot up, rocket, increase rapidly, rise rapidly, leap up, escalate, climb, mount; informal skyrocket, go through the ceiling, go through the roof.
▷ANTONYMS fall.
3 *the economy is **spiralling downward***: **deteriorate**, decline, degenerate, worsen, get worse; informal go downhill, take a nosedive, go to pot, go to the dogs, hit the skids, go down the toilet, go down the tubes.
▷ANTONYMS improve.

spire noun *the spire of a nearby church*: **steeple**, belfry; flèche; Hinduism shikara.

spirit noun **1** *we seek a harmony between body and spirit*: **soul**, psyche, inner self, inner being, essential being; Philosophy **pneuma**; Psychology **anima**, ego, id; in ancient Egypt ka; Hinduism atman.
▷ANTONYMS body, flesh.
2 *the spirit of nature | their spirit lives on*: **life force**, animating principle, vital spark, breath of life; French élan vital.
3 *local people say that his spirit walks among the hills*: **ghost**, phantom, spectre, apparition, wraith, shadow, presence; Scottish & Irish **bodach**; German Doppelgänger; W. Indian duppy; informal spook; literary **phantasm**, shade, revenant, visitant, wight; rare eidolon, manes.
4 *this thought dampened even my optimistic spirit*: **temperament**, disposition, character, nature, personality, temper, make-up, humour, cast/turn of mind, complexion; mind, heart.
5 *she's got the right spirit*: **attitude**, frame of mind, way of thinking, way of looking at it, state of mind, point of view, outlook, thoughts, ideas.
6 *the spirit of the team is high*: **morale**, team spirit; French esprit de corps.
7 *the spirit of the nineteenth century*: **ethos**, prevailing tendency, motivating force, animating principle, dominating characteristic, essence, quintessence; **atmosphere**, mood, feeling, temper, tenor, climate; **attitudes**, beliefs, principles, standards, ethics.
8 *though he was in considerable discomfort, his spirit never failed him*: **courage**, bravery, courageousness, braveness, pluck, pluckiness, valour, strength of character, fortitude, backbone, spine, mettle, stout-heartedness, determination, firmness of purpose, resolution, resoluteness, resolve, fight, gameness; informal guts, grit, spunk; Brit. informal **bottle**; N. Amer. informal sand, moxie.
9 *they played with great spirit | she was full of spirit and raring to go*: **animation**, **enthusiasm**, eagerness, keenness, liveliness, vivacity, vivaciousness, energy, verve, vigour, dynamism, zest, dash, elan, panache, sparkle, exuberance, gusto, brio, pep, go, sap, fervour, zeal, fire, passion; informal pizzazz, oomph, zing, zip, zap, vim, get-up-and-go.
10 *we must be seen to keep to the spirit of the law as well as the letter*: **real/true meaning**, true intention, essence, substance.
▸ verb
□ **spirit someone/something away** *the girl was spirited away before we got anywhere near her*: **abduct**, kidnap, make off with, run away with, whisk away, carry off, steal away with, snatch, seize; abscond with.

spirited adjective *an attractive and spirited young woman | the team produced a spirited performance*: **lively**, vivacious, vibrant, full of life, vital, animated, high-spirited, sparkling, sprightly, energetic, active, vigorous, dynamic, dashing, enthusiastic, passionate, fiery; courageous, brave, plucky, bold, valiant, mettlesome, intrepid, determined, resolute, enterprising; informal feisty, spunky, have-a-go, gutsy, ballsy; N. Amer. informal peppy.
▷ANTONYMS timid, apathetic, lifeless.

spiritless adjective *Lilian was a pallid, spiritless woman | a spiritless performance*: **apathetic**, passive, unenthusiastic, lifeless, listless, lacking in vitality, weak, feeble, spineless, droopy, limp, languid, bloodless, insipid, characterless, submissive, meek, irresolute, indecisive; **lacklustre**, flat, colourless, passionless, uninspiring, uninspired, wooden, dry, desiccated, unimpassioned, anaemic, vapid, dull, boring; informal wishy-washy; Brit. vulgar slang half-arsed.
▷ANTONYMS spirited, lively.

spirits plural noun **1** *she was in good spirits when I left*: **mood**, frame of mind, state of mind, emotional state, humour, temper.
2 *I don't usually drink spirits*: **strong liquor**, liquor, strong drink; gin, vodka, whisky, brandy, rum; informal hard stuff, shorts, firewater, hooch.

spiritual adjective **1** *the spiritual dimension of human experience*: **non-material**, inner, psychic, psychical, psychological; **incorporeal**, intangible, other-worldly, unworldly, ethereal; transcendent, mystic, mystical, numinous, metaphysical; rare extramundane, immaterial.
▷ANTONYMS physical, material, corporeal, mundane.
2 *spiritual music*: **religious**, sacred, divine, holy, non-secular, church, churchly, ecclesiastic, devotional.
▷ANTONYMS secular.

spit[1] verb **1** *Cranston coughed and spat*: **expectorate**, hawk; Brit. informal gob, hoick.
2 *'Go to hell', she spat*: **snap**, say angrily, hiss, rasp, splutter.
3 *the bubbling fat began to spit*: **sizzle**, hiss, crackle, sputter, frizzle, fizz.
4 Brit. *it began to spit*: **rain lightly**, drizzle, spot; N. English mizzle; N. Amer. sprinkle.
▸ noun *he wiped the spit from his face*: **spittle**, saliva, sputum, slaver, slobber, dribble, drool; phlegm; Brit. informal gob.
□ **the (very) spit** informal *Felix is the spit of Rosa's brother*: **exact likeness**, living image, mirror image, very image, double, twin, lookalike, replica, clone, duplicate, copy; German doppelgänger; informal **spitting image**, spit and image, ringer, dead ringer.

spit[2] noun *chicken cooked on a spit*: **skewer**, brochette, rotisserie; rare broach.

spite noun *he'd think I was saying it out of spite*: **malice**, maliciousness, ill will, ill feeling, spitefulness, bitterness, animosity, hostility, antagonism, enmity, resentment, resentfulness, rancour, malevolence, venom, spleen, gall, malignance, malignity, evil intentions, envy, hate, hatred, vengeance, vengefulness, vindictiveness; nastiness, mean-spiritedness, meanness; informal bitchiness, cattiness; literary maleficence.
▷ANTONYMS benevolence, goodwill, affection.
□ **in spite of** *in spite of their mutual dislike, he had helped her*: **despite**, notwithstanding, regardless of, for all; undeterred by, in defiance of, in the face of; even though, although.
▸ verb *I used to worry that you would make trouble, just to spite Martin*: **upset**, hurt, wound, distress, injure; **annoy**, irritate, vex, displease, provoke, gall, peeve, pique, offend, put out; thwart, foil, frustrate; informal aggravate, rile, miff; vulgar slang piss off.
▷ANTONYMS please.

spiteful adjective *the other girls made spiteful remarks about Paula*: **malicious**, mean, nasty, cruel, unkind, unfriendly, snide, hurtful,

S

wounding, barbed, cutting, hateful, ill-natured, bitter, venomous, poisonous, acid, hostile, rancorous, malevolent, evil-intentioned, baleful, vindictive, vengeful, vitriolic, vicious, splenetic, malign, malignant, bilious; defamatory; informal bitchy, catty; literary malefic, maleficent; rare squint-eyed.
▷ANTONYMS benevolent, kind, friendly.

splash verb **1** *splash your face with cool water*: **sprinkle**, spray, shower, splatter, slosh, slop, squirt; daub; wet.
2 *his boots were splashed with mud*: **spatter**, bespatter, splatter, speck, speckle, blotch, smear, stain, mark; informal splotch, splodge; Scottish & Irish informal slabber; literary bedabble.
3 *the Atlantic Ocean splashed against the pier*: **swash**, wash, break, lap; **dash**, beat, lash, batter, crash, buffet, surge; literary plash.
4 *children splashed about gleefully in the shallow water*: **paddle**, wade, slosh; wallow; informal splosh.
5 *the story was splashed across the front pages*: **blazon**, display, spread, plaster, trumpet, publicize, broadcast, headline; informal splatter.
□ **be splashed with** *Lonnie's face was splashed with freckles*: **be flecked with**, be dotted with, be stippled with, be studded with, be scattered with.
□ **splash out** Brit. informal *she splashed out on a Mercedes*: **be extravagant**, go on a spending spree, splurge, spare no expense, spend lavishly, spend a lot of money; informal lash out, push the boat out, go mad, go on a shopping binge, indulge in some retail therapy.
▶ noun **1** *the splash of the water against the rocks*: **splashing**, swashing, dashing, beating, battering; literary plash, plashing; archaic swash.
2 *there was a splash of blood on his forehead*: **spot**, blob, dab, daub, smudge, smear, speck, speckle, fleck; mark, stain; informal splotch, splosh, splodge.
3 *a splash of lemonade*: **drop**, dash, bit, spot, soupçon, dribble, driblet; little, small amount; Scottish informal scoosh.
4 *add a red scarf to give a splash of colour*: **patch**, burst, streak.
5 *a front-page splash*: **feature**, story, article, piece; display; N. Amer. informal screamer.
□ **make a splash** informal **cause a sensation**, cause a stir, attract attention, draw attention to oneself/itself, get noticed, make an impression, make an impact, cut a dash.

spleen noun *obviously you're annoyed but that doesn't give you the right to vent your spleen on me*: **bad temper**, bad mood, ill temper, ill humour, annoyance, anger, wrath, vexation, crossness, irritation, displeasure, dissatisfaction, irritability, irascibility, cantankerousness, peevishness, petulance, pettishness, pique, querulousness, crabbiness, testiness, tetchiness, snappishness, waspishness, touchiness, moodiness, sullenness, resentment, rancour, biliousness, sourness; **spite**, spitefulness, ill feeling, malice, maliciousness, bitterness, animosity, antipathy, hostility, malevolence, venom, gall, malignance, malignity, acrimony, bile, hatred, hate; literary ire, choler.
▷ANTONYMS good humour.

splendid adjective **1** *a splendid palazzo on the Grand Canal | their splendid costumes*: **magnificent**, sumptuous, grand, impressive, imposing, superb, spectacular, resplendent, opulent, luxurious, palatial, de luxe, rich, fine, costly, expensive, lavish, ornate, gorgeous, glorious, dazzling, elegant, handsome, beautiful; stately, majestic, kingly, princely, regal, noble, proud; informal plush, plushy, posh, swanky, ritzy, splendiferous; Brit. informal swish; N. Amer. informal swank; literary brave; rare splendacious, splendorous, magnolious, palatian.
▷ANTONYMS modest, unimpressive, ordinary.
2 *an MP with a splendid reputation*: **distinguished**, glorious, glittering, illustrious, remarkable, outstanding, exceptional, celebrated, renowned, famous, impressive, notable, noted, eminent, noble, lofty, venerable, exemplary.
▷ANTONYMS undistinguished.
3 informal *we had a splendid holiday*: **excellent**, **wonderful**, marvellous, magnificent, superb, glorious, sublime, lovely, delightful, first-class, first-rate; informal super, great, smashing, amazing, fantastic, terrific, tremendous, phenomenal, sensational, incredible, heavenly, stellar, gorgeous, dreamy, grand, fabulous, fab, fabby, fantabulous, awesome, magic, ace, cool, mean, bad, wicked, mega, crucial, mind-blowing, far out, A1, sound, out of this world, marvy, spanking; Brit. informal brilliant, brill, bosting; N. Amer. informal peachy, dandy, jim-dandy, neat, badass, boss, radical, rad, boffo, bully, bitching, bodacious; Austral./NZ informal beaut, bonzer; S. African informal kif, lank; black English dope, def, phat; informal, dated groovy, divine; Brit. informal, dated capital, champion, wizard, corking, ripping, cracking, spiffing, top-hole, topping, beezer; N. Amer. informal, dated swell, keen; archaic goodly.
▷ANTONYMS dreadful, awful, horrible.

splendour noun **1** *a wedding long remembered for its splendour*: **magnificence**, grandeur, sumptuousness, impressiveness, resplendence, opulence, luxury, luxuriousness, richness, fineness, lavishness, ornateness, glory, gloriousness, gorgeousness, splendidness, beauty, elegance; majesty, stateliness, nobility, pomp, pomp and circumstance, panoply, pageantry, spectacle; informal ritziness, poshness, splendiferousness.
▷ANTONYMS ordinariness, modesty.
2 literary *shafts of golden splendour burnished the leaves*: **brightness**, radiance, brilliance, light, gleam, glow, lustre, shine, luminosity, luminousness; rare refulgence, effulgence.

splenetic adjective *he wrote a characteristically splenetic article*: **bad-tempered**, ill-tempered, ill-humoured, angry, wrathful, cross, peevish, petulant, pettish, irritable, irascible, cantankerous, choleric, dyspeptic, testy, tetchy, snappish, waspish, crotchety, crabby, crabbed, querulous, resentful, rancorous, bilious, sour, bitter, acid, liverish; **spiteful**, malicious, ill-natured, hostile, acrimonious, malevolent, malignant, malign; informal bitchy; rare atrabilious, envenomed.
▷ANTONYMS good-humoured.

splice verb *it is easier to splice than any other rope of similar construction | a video splicing together bits from 63 interviews*: **interweave**, braid, plait, entwine, intertwine, interlace, knit, mesh; join, unite, connect, bind, fasten, tie; Nautical marry.
□ **get spliced** informal *they paid £15,000 for a wedding package and ended up getting spliced in a car park*: **get married**, marry, wed, get wed, become man/husband and wife, plight one's troth; informal tie the knot, get hitched, get yoked, take the plunge, say 'I do'; archaic become espoused.
▷ANTONYMS divorce, get divorced.

splinter noun *small splinters of wood | a splinter of glass*: **sliver**, shiver, chip, shard, needle; fragment, piece, bit, shred, spell, spillikin; shaving, paring; (**splinters**) matchwood, flinders; Scottish skelf; technical gallet, spall.
▶ verb *the windscreen splintered*: **shatter**, break into tiny pieces, break into fragments, smash, smash into smithereens, fracture, split, crack, disintegrate, crumble; technical spall; rare shiver.

split verb **1** *the bedside table had been split in two*: **break**, chop, cut, hew, lop, cleave; snap, crack; informal bust.
2 *the ice cracked and split*: **break apart**, fracture, rupture, fissure, snap, come apart, splinter.
3 *not only was her dress covered in mud, it was split*: **tear**, rip, slash, slit; literary rend.
4 *it is an issue which could split the Party*: **divide**, disunite, separate, sever; bisect, partition; literary tear asunder, cleave, rend; archaic sunder, rive; rare dichotomize, factionalize.
▷ANTONYMS unite, unify.
5 *the consortium plan to split the assets between them*: **share (out)**, divide (up), apportion, allocate, allot, distribute, dole out, parcel out, measure out; carve up, slice up; halve; informal divvy up.
6 *soon afterwards the path splits*: **fork**, divide in two, divide, bifurcate, go in different directions, diverge, branch; rare divaricate.
▷ANTONYMS converge, merge.
7 *they split up last year*: **break up**, separate, part, part company, become estranged, reach a parting of the ways; divorce, get a divorce, get divorced; Brit. informal bust up.
▷ANTONYMS get together, marry.
8 informal *as soon as the gig ended, she split*. See **leave**[1] (sense 1).
9 Brit. informal *I told him I wouldn't split on him*: **inform on/against**, tell tales on, give away, sell out, stab in the back; informal tell on, squeal on, blow the whistle on, rat on, peach on, stitch up, do the dirty on, sell down the river; Brit. informal grass on, shop; N. Amer. informal rat out, drop a/the dime on, finger; Austral. informal pimp on, pool, put someone's pot on.
□ **split hairs** See **hair**.
□ **split one's sides** *this movie has its audiences splitting their sides*: **roar with laughter**, laugh, guffaw, roar, laugh loudly, howl with laughter, dissolve into laughter, be creased up, be doubled up; informal fall about, crack up, be in stitches, be rolling in the aisles, laugh fit to bust.
▶ noun **1** *a split in the rock face*: **crack**, fissure, cleft, crevice, break, fracture, breach.
2 *light squeezed through a small split in the curtain*: **rip**, tear, cut, rent, slash, slit.
3 *the accusations caused a split in the Party*: **division**, **rift**, breach, schism, rupture, partition, separation, severance, break-up, alienation, estrangement; rare scission.
4 *he's been living in London since the acrimonious split with his wife*: **break-up**, split-up, separation, parting, estrangement, parting of the ways, rift, rupture, breach; divorce; legal separation, judicial separation; Brit. informal bust-up.
▷ANTONYMS marriage.

> *Word links* **split**
>
> **fissile** easily split
> **schizo-** related prefix, as in *schizocarp*

split-up noun *I was still getting over my split-up with Richard*: **break-up**, separation, split, parting, estrangement, parting of the ways, rift, rupture; divorce; Brit. informal bust-up.

spoil verb **1** *too much sun spoils the complexion*: **mar**, damage, impair, blemish, disfigure, blight, flaw, deface, scar, injure, harm; ruin, destroy, wreck; be a blot on the landscape; rare disfeature.
▷ANTONYMS improve, enhance.
2 *two days of rain spoiled all my plans*: **ruin**, wreck, destroy, upset, undo, mess up, make a mess of, dash, sabotage, scupper, scotch, torpedo, blast, vitiate; cast a shadow over, cast a pall over, cloud, darken, take the shine

S

off, put a damper on, take the enjoyment/pleasure out of, take the edge off; upset someone's apple cart, cook someone's goose; informal foul up, louse up, muck up, queer, screw up, put the kibosh on, banjax, blow a hole in, do for, nix; Brit. informal cock up, dish, muller, queer someone's pitch, throw a spanner in the works of; N. Amer. informal rain on someone's parade, throw a monkey wrench in the works of; Austral. informal cruel, euchre; vulgar slang bugger up, fuck up, balls up; archaic bring to naught.
▷ANTONYMS further, help; enhance.
3 *his sisters spoil him and so does his mother*: **overindulge**, pamper, indulge, mollycoddle, cosset, coddle, baby, spoon-feed, feather-bed, wait on hand and foot, cater to someone's every whim, wrap in cotton wool, kill with kindness; nanny, nursemaid; dote on; archaic cocker.
▷ANTONYMS neglect, treat harshly, be strict with.
4 *I've got some ham that will spoil if we don't eat it tonight*: **go bad**, go off, go rancid, turn, go sour, sour, go mouldy, moulder, become addled, curdle, become rotten, rot, perish, decompose, decay, putrefy.
▷ANTONYMS keep.
□ **spoiling for** *Cooper was spoiling for a fight*: **eager for**, itching for, looking for, keen to have, raring for, after, bent on, set on, on the lookout for, longing for.

spoils plural noun **1** *the looters carried their spoils away*: **booty**, **loot**, stolen goods, plunder, ill-gotten gains, haul, pickings, takings; informal, dated swag, boodle.
2 *he did not have the slightest intention of sharing the spoils of office with Craigbarnet*: **benefits**, advantages, perks; formal perquisites; rare appanages.

spoilsport noun **killjoy**, dog in the manger, misery, damper; informal wet blanket, party-pooper; Austral./NZ informal wowser.

spoken adjective *spoken communication*: **verbal**, **oral**, uttered, voiced, expressed, stated; unwritten; by word of mouth; Latin viva voce.
▷ANTONYMS unspoken, written.
□ **spoken for 1** *some of the villas are already spoken for*: **reserved**, booked, set aside; chosen, selected, claimed; chartered, hired; rare bespoke.
▷ANTONYMS free. **2** *he knows Claudine is spoken for*: **attached**, going out with someone; **engaged**; informal going steady; dated betrothed.
▷ANTONYMS unattached, free.

spokesman, spokeswoman noun **spokesperson**, representative, agent, mouthpiece, voice; negotiator, arbitrator, mediator, intermediary, middleman, go-between, moderator, broker, honest broker; delegate; informal spin doctor; rare prolocutor, fugleman, negotiant.

sponge verb *a boy was **sponging down** the Daimler's windows*: **wash**, clean, wipe, swab; mop, rinse, sluice, swill.
□ **sponge off/on** informal *she could not bear the thought of sponging on her parents*: **scrounge off/from**, live off, be a parasite on, impose on, beg from, borrow from, be dependent on; informal freeload on, cadge from, bum off; N. Amer. informal mooch off; Austral./NZ bludge on.

sponger noun informal *many saw him as an easy touch and he was surrounded by an army of spongers*: **parasite**, hanger-on, leech, scrounger, passenger, drone, beggar; informal freeloader, sponge, cadger, bum, bloodsucker; Brit. informal ligger; N. Amer. informal mooch, moocher, schnorrer; Austral./NZ informal bludger.

spongy adjective **1** *the material has a spongy texture*: **soft**, cushiony, cushioned, squashy, compressible, yielding; springy, resilient, elastic; porous, absorbent, absorptive, permeable, pervious; light; technical spongiform; Brit. informal squidgy; rare spongiose.
▷ANTONYMS hard, solid.
2 *he felt the spongy soil drawing him downwards*: **waterlogged**, wet, soft, heavy, muddy, boggy, marshy, squelchy.
▷ANTONYMS hard, compacted.

S

sponsor noun *the production cost £50,000, most coming from local sponsors*: **backer**, **patron**, promoter, subsidizer, benefactor, benefactress, guarantor, underwriter, supporter, friend; informal angel; rare Maecenas.
▶ verb *Cathay Pacific sponsored the event*: **finance**, put up the money for, fund, subsidize, underwrite, back, promote, lend one's name to, be a patron of, act as guarantor of, support; informal foot the bill for, pick up the tab for; N. Amer. informal bankroll.

sponsorship noun *the team would like to thank the Institute for its sponsorship*: **backing**, support, patronage, funding, financing, promotion; aegis, auspices; help, aid, assistance.

spontaneous adjective **1** *a spontaneous display of affection*: **unforced**, voluntary, unconstrained, unprompted, unbidden, unsolicited, unplanned, unpremeditated, unrehearsed, impulsive, impetuous, unstudied, impromptu, spur-of-the-moment, extempore, extemporaneous; unschooled, untaught, uninstructed; informal off-the-cuff.
▷ANTONYMS planned, forced, calculated.
2 *a spontaneous reaction to danger*: **reflex**, automatic, knee-jerk, involuntary, unthinking, unconscious, instinctive, instinctual; informal gut.
▷ANTONYMS conscious.
3 *she seems friendly and spontaneous*: **natural**, uninhibited, relaxed, unselfconscious, unaffected, easy, free and easy; impulsive, impetuous; open, genuine.
▷ANTONYMS inhibited.

Word toolkit

spontaneous	involuntary	unintentional
applause	manslaughter	injury
reaction	movement	humour
outpouring	unemployment	irony
uprising	servitude	bias
rupture	commitment	death
combustion	treatment	poisoning
mutation	spasm	mistake

spontaneously adverb **1** *the huge crowd spontaneously broke into applause*: **without being asked**, of one's own accord, voluntarily, on impulse, impulsively, on the spur of the moment, extempore, extemporaneously; informal off the cuff.
2 *he'd reacted spontaneously, displaying the full force of his anger*: **without thinking**, automatically, unthinkingly, involuntarily, instinctively.

spoof informal noun **1** *a rather bad Agatha Christie spoof*: **parody**, pastiche, burlesque, take-off, skit, imitation; informal send-up; Brit. vulgar slang piss-take; rare pasquinade, pasticcio.
2 *word got out that the whole thing had been a spoof*: **hoax**, trick, joke, game; informal leg-pull, con; N. Amer. informal dido; archaic quiz.
▶ verb *his quirky personality has been spoofed by several comedians*: **parody**, take off, burlesque, pastiche, make fun of; informal send up; Brit. vulgar slang take the piss out of.

spooky adjective informal *the atmosphere was decidedly spooky*: **eerie**, sinister, ghostly, uncanny, weird, unearthly, mysterious; **frightening**, spine-chilling, hair-raising, scaring, terrifying, petrifying, chilling; informal **creepy**, scary, spine-tingling.

sporadic adjective *we braved the sporadic showers | sporadic fighting broke out*: **occasional**, infrequent, irregular, periodical, periodic, scattered, patchy, isolated, odd, uneven; **intermittent**, spasmodic, on and off, random, fitful, desultory, erratic, unpredictable.
▷ANTONYMS frequent, regular, steady, continuous.

sport noun *he takes part in a variety of sports | we did a lot of sport*: **(competitive) game(s)**, physical recreation, physical activity, physical exercise; pastime.
□ **in sport** *I have assumed the name was given more or less in sport*: **as a joke**, in jest, jokingly, for fun, teasingly, playfully.
▶ verb **1** *he sported a gardenia in his buttonhole*: **wear**, **display**, exhibit, have on show, show off, flourish, parade, flaunt.
2 dated *the children sported in the water*: **play**, have fun, amuse oneself, entertain oneself, enjoy oneself, divert oneself, frolic, gambol, frisk, romp, cavort, caper; informal lark (about/around); archaic or humorous disport oneself; archaic wanton; rare rollick.

sporting adjective *it was jolly sporting of you to let me have first go*: **sportsmanlike**, sportsmanly, generous, gentlemanly, considerate, good; fair, just, honourable; Brit. informal decent.
▷ANTONYMS unsporting, unfair.

sportive adjective archaic *a group of sportive children*. See **playful** (sense 1).

sporty adjective informal **1** *two sporty types wearing jogging suits*: **athletic**, fit, active, energetic, outdoor; hearty; N. Amer. informal outdoorsy.
▷ANTONYMS unfit; lazy.
2 *his spring collection combines a sporty feel with fresh colours*: **stylish**, smart, jaunty; **casual**, informal; informal trendy, sharp, natty, snazzy, snappy; N. Amer. informal sassy, spiffy.
▷ANTONYMS formal, dressy.
3 *the sporty 1.5 litre coupe*: **fast**, speedy; informal nippy, zippy.
▷ANTONYMS slow.

spot noun **1** *the dog was white with black spots | there were a few spots of blood on the pavement*: **mark**, patch, dot, speck, speckle, fleck, smudge, smear, stain, blotch, blot, splash, daub; technical petechia; informal splotch, splosh, splodge; rare macule, macula.
2 *this cream will improve the appearance of wrinkles, brown spots, and uneven skin tone*: **discoloration**; freckle; liver spot, age spot, mole; birthmark, port wine stain, strawberry mark; technical naevus.
3 *he had an angry spot on the side of his nose*: **pimple**, pustule, blemish, blackhead, boil, swelling, eruption, wen, sty; pock, pockmark; **(spots) acne**, rash; technical comedo; informal zit, whitehead; Scottish informal plook; N. Amer. informal hickey; rare papule, bleb, whelk, blain.
4 *there are miles of footpaths and plenty of secluded spots*: **place**, location, site, position, point, situation, scene, setting, locale, locality, area, neighbourhood, region; venue; technical locus.
5 *social policy has a regular spot on the agenda*: **position**, place, niche, slot, space; informal window.
6 Brit. informal *would you like a spot of brandy?* **bit**, little, some, small amount, morsel, modicum, bite; drop, splash; informal smidgen, smidge, tad; Scottish informal scoosh.
7 informal *you're in a **tight spot***: **difficult situation**, awkward situation, tricky situation, predicament, mess, difficulty, trouble, plight, corner, quandary,

dilemma; informal fix, jam, hole, sticky situation, pickle, scrape, pretty/fine kettle of fish, hot water, how-do-you-do.
□ **on the spot** *any official found to be involved in such incidents will be sacked on the spot*: **immediately**, there and then, then and there, straight away, right away, forthwith, instantly, summarily, without delay, without hesitation, at once, that instant, directly; outright; N. Amer. in short order; archaic straight, straightway, instanter, forthright.
▶ **verb 1** *she spotted Iris hovering by the door*: **notice**, see, observe, discern, detect, perceive, make out, pick out, distinguish, recognize, identify, locate; catch sight of, glimpse, sight; mark, remark; Brit. informal clock; literary descry, espy.
2 *her clothes were spotted with grease*: **stain**, mark, fleck, speckle, blotch, mottle, smudge, streak, splash, spatter, bespatter; dirty, soil; informal splotch, splosh, splodge; literary besmirch, smirch.
3 archaic *his soul was spotted with sin*: **sully**, stain, tarnish, blacken, taint, blemish.
4 *it was still spotting with rain*: **rain lightly**, drizzle; Brit. spit; N. English mizzle; N. Amer. sprinkle.

spotless adjective **1** *the kitchen was spotless | a spotless white shirt*: **perfectly clean**, ultra-clean, pristine, immaculate, shining, shiny, gleaming, spick and span; freshly laundered, snowy, snowy-white, snow-white, whiter than white; unsoiled, unmarked, unstained; rare speckless.
▷ANTONYMS dirty, filthy.
2 *a spotless reputation*: **unblemished**, unsullied, untarnished, untainted, unstained, pure, as pure as the driven snow, whiter than white, lily-white, flawless, immaculate, impeccable, faultless, blameless, guiltless, sinless, unimpeachable, irreproachable, above reproach; innocent, untouched, undefiled, uncorrupted; informal squeaky clean.
▷ANTONYMS impure, tarnished.

spotlight noun **(the spotlight)** *she was constantly in the spotlight*: **the public eye**, the glare of publicity, the limelight; the focus of public attention/interest, the focus of media attention/interest.
▶ **verb** *the conference spotlighted the strength of his conservative opponents*: **focus attention on**, highlight, point up, draw/call attention to, foreground, accentuate, accent, make conspicuous, underline, underscore, give prominence to, throw into relief, turn the spotlight on, bring to the fore, bring home; focus on, zero in on, stress, emphasize.
▷ANTONYMS play down.

spot on adjective Brit. informal *Evert's prediction was spot on*: **accurate, correct**, right, perfect, exact, unerring, so as to hit the nail on the head; informal bang on; N. Amer. informal on the money, on the nose.
▷ANTONYMS wrong, incorrect.

spotted adjective **1** *the spotted leaves*: **mottled**, dappled, dapple, pied, piebald, brindled, brindle, speckled, speckly, flecked, specked, stippled; informal splodgy, splotchy; technical macular, maculate, maculated, foxed, guttate.
2 *a black-and-white spotted dress*: **polka-dot**, spotty, dotted; informal dotty.

spotty adjective **1** Brit. *his spotty face*: **pimply**, pimpled, acned, poor-complexioned; pockmarked, pocky; blotchy, blotched; informal zitty; Scottish informal plooky.
▷ANTONYMS clear-complexioned.
2 *a spotty dog | spotty, purply-pink flowers*: **spotted**, mottled, speckled, speckly, flecked, specked, stippled; informal splodgy, splotchy; technical macular, maculate, maculated, foxed, guttate.
3 *a spotty dress*: **polka-dot**, spotted, dotted; informal dotty.
4 *on the whole the standard of football was spotty*: **patchy**, uneven, inconsistent, erratic, fluctuating, irregular, non-uniform.
▷ANTONYMS consistent, uniform.

spouse noun **husband, wife**, partner, mate, consort; informal better half, other half, old man, old woman, old lady, hubby, missis, missus, wifey, WAGs (wives and girlfriends); Brit. informal dutch, trouble and strife, her indoors; dated lady; archaic helpmate, helpmeet.

spout verb **1** *lava was spouting from the crater*: **spurt**, gush, spew, pour, stream, rush, erupt, surge, shoot, pump, squirt, spray, flow, issue; disgorge, discharge, emit, belch forth.
2 *he began to spout off about the decline of the welfare state*: **hold forth**, sound off, go on, talk at length, expatiate, pontificate, declaim, orate, rant, sermonize; informal mouth off, speechify, spiel; rare perorate.
▶ **noun** *a tough metal can with a handy pouring spout*: **nozzle**, lip, rose; technical sparkler, spile.
□ **up the spout** Brit. informal **1** *my computer's up the spout*. See **broken** (sense 3). **2** *his daughter's up the spout*. See **pregnant**.

sprain verb *he sprained his left ankle in a tackle during Saturday's game*: **wrench**, twist, turn, strain, crick; pull, stretch, tear; injure, hurt, damage; Brit. informal rick.
▶ **noun** *a severe ankle sprain*: **wrench**, strain, rick, crick; pull, tear, injury.

sprawl verb **1** *he sprawled on a sofa in the living room*: **stretch out**, lounge, loll, lie, lie down, lie back, recline, drape oneself, be recumbent, be prostrate, be supine, slump, flop, slouch.
2 *gorse and hawthorn sprawled over the hillside*: **spread**, stretch, straggle, ramble, trail, spill.

spray[1] noun **1** *a fine spray of water*: **shower**, sprinkling, sprinkle, jet, mist, drizzle, droplets; spume, spindrift; foam, froth; rare spoondrift.
2 *Mary took a perfume spray from her handbag*: **atomizer**, vaporizer, aerosol, sprinkler; nebulizer; spray gun.
▶ **verb 1** *water was sprayed over the ground | spray the plants with sugar water*: **sprinkle**, shower, spread in droplets, spatter; scatter, disperse, diffuse; mist; douche; literary besprinkle.
2 *water sprayed into the air*: **spout**, jet, gush, spurt, shoot, squirt, stream.

spray[2] noun **1** *a spray of honeysuckle*: **sprig**, small stem, twig, branch; rare branchlet.
2 *a small spray of yellow roses*: **bouquet**, bunch, posy, nosegay, corsage; wreath, garland; buttonhole; flower arrangement; French boutonnière; rare tussie-mussie.

spread verb **1** *he fetched the map and spread it out on the table*: **lay out**, open out, unfurl, unroll, roll out, shake out; straighten out, fan out; stretch out, extend; literary outspread.
▷ANTONYMS fold up.
2 *the spectacular landscape **spread out** below*: **extend**, stretch, open out, be displayed, be exhibited, be on show; sprawl.
3 *Harry gestured at the untidy papers spread all over his desk*: **scatter**, strew, disperse; literary bestrew.
4 *disaffection with his policies is spreading*: **grow**, increase, escalate, advance, develop, broaden, expand, widen, proliferate, mushroom; Medicine metastasize.
5 *Ballard started to spread rumours about him*: **disseminate**, circulate, pass on, put about, communicate, diffuse, make public, make known, purvey, broadcast, publicize, propagate, promulgate; repeat; literary bruit about/abroad.
▷ANTONYMS suppress.
6 *she spread cold cream on her face*: **smear**, daub, plaster, slather, lather, apply, put; smooth, rub.
7 *a thick slice of bread liberally spread with butter*: **cover**, coat, layer, daub, smother; butter.
8 *a row of candles spread a brilliant pool of light*: **cast**, diffuse, shed, radiate.
▶ **noun 1** *the spread of learning*: **expansion**, proliferation, extension, growth, mushrooming, increase, escalation, buildout, advance, advancement, development; dissemination, diffusion, transmission, propagation.
2 *the male's antlers can attain a spread of six feet*: **span**, width, extent, stretch, reach.
3 *the immense spread of the heavens*: **expanse**, area, sweep, stretch.
4 *papers on a wide spread of subjects*: **range**, span, spectrum, sweep; variety.
5 N. Amer. *a patchwork spread*: **bedspread**, bedcover, cover, coverlet, throw, afghan; Brit. eiderdown; N. Amer. comforter; dated counterpane.
6 informal *his mother laid on a huge spread*: **large/elaborate meal**, feast, banquet, repast; informal blowout, nosh.

spree noun **1** *a shopping spree*: **unrestrained bout**, orgy; informal binge, splurge.
2 *it may stop after one or two drinks or it may go on into a spree*: **drinking bout**, debauch; informal binge, bender, session, sesh, booze-up, beer-up, souse, drunk, blind; Scottish informal skite; N. Amer. informal jag, toot; NZ informal boozeroo; Brit. vulgar slang piss-up; literary bacchanal, bacchanalia; archaic wassail, fuddle, potation.

sprig noun *a sprig of lilac*: **small stem**, spray, twig, branch; rare branchlet.

sprightly adjective *she was quite sprightly for her age*: **lively**, spry, energetic, active, full of life, full of energy, vigorous, spirited, animated, vivacious, playful, jaunty, perky, frisky, agile, nimble; informal chipper, sparkly, zippy, zappy, full of vim and vigour, bright-eyed and bushy-tailed, full of beans; N. Amer. informal peppy, peart; N. English informal wick; archaic frolicsome, sportive, as lively/merry as a grig.
▷ANTONYMS doddering, sluggish, lethargic, inactive.

spring verb **1** *Gina sprang to her feet | the cat sprang off her lap*: **leap**, jump, bound, vault, hop.
2 *the branch **sprang back***: **fly back**, recoil; kick back; rare resile.
3 *some of these feelings **spring from** fears about death and ageing*: **originate from**, have its origins in, derive from, arise from, stem from, emanate from, proceed from, start from, issue from, evolve from, come from.
4 *about fifty men sprang from nowhere and surrounded them*: **appear suddenly**, appear unexpectedly, materialize; informal pop up.
5 *I'm sorry to **spring** the news **on** you like this*: **announce suddenly/unexpectedly**, present suddenly/unexpectedly, introduce suddenly/unexpectedly, reveal suddenly/unexpectedly.
6 *hotels are **springing up** all along the coast*: **appear**, develop quickly, shoot up, sprout up, come into being, come into existence; proliferate, mushroom.
▶ **noun 1** *we're getting married next spring*: **springtime**, Eastertide; literary springtide, Maytime.
2 *with a sudden spring he leapt on to the table*: **leap**, jump, bound, vault, hop; pounce; rare saltation.
3 *the mattress has lost its spring*: **springiness**, bounciness, bounce, resilience, elasticity, flexibility, stretch, stretchiness, give; rare tensility.
4 *there was a new spring in his step*: **buoyancy**, bounce, bounciness, energy,

S

liveliness, light-heartedness, jauntiness, sprightliness, confidence.
5 *a mineral spring*: **well head**; source; spa, geyser, hot spring, thermal spring, sulphur spring; literary well, wellspring, fount.
6 *the springs of his own emotions*: **origin**, source, fountainhead, root, roots, basis.
▸ **adjective** *two days of warm spring weather*: **springlike**, vernal.

Word links **spring**
vernal relating to the season of spring

springy **adjective 1** *the turf was springy beneath her feet*: **elastic**, stretchy, whippy, stretchable, tensile; flexible, bouncy, resilient, cushiony, spongy, rubbery; rare tensible.
▷**ANTONYMS** hard, stiff, rigid.
2 *he left the room with a springy step*: **buoyant**, bouncy, lively, light, light-hearted, carefree, jaunty, sprightly, confident.
▷**ANTONYMS** heavy.

sprinkle **verb 1** *he sprinkled water over the towel*: **splash**, trickle, spray, shower; spatter.
2 *sprinkle sesame seeds over the top*: **scatter**, strew; drizzle; literary bestrew.
3 *when the cake is cool, sprinkle it with icing sugar*: **dredge**, dust, powder.
4 *the sky was sprinkled with stars*: **dot**, stipple, stud, bestud, fleck, speckle, bespeckle, spot, pepper; scatter, cover; literary besprinkle.

sprinkling **noun 1** *serve with a sprinkling of nutmeg*: **scattering**, sprinkle, scatter, dusting; pinch, dash.
2 ***a sprinkling of*** *elderly ladies were making their way to church*: **few**, one or two; **handful**, small number, trickle, smattering.

sprint **verb** *she sprinted across the square*: **run**, race, dart, rush, dash, hasten, hurry, scurry, scuttle, scamper, hare, bolt, bound, fly, gallop, career, charge, pound, shoot, hurtle, speed, streak, whizz, zoom, go like lightning, go hell for leather, go like the wind, flash; informal tear, pelt, scoot, hotfoot it, leg it, belt, zip, whip, go like a bat out of hell, step on it, get a move on, get cracking, put on some speed, stir one's stumps; Brit. informal hop it, bomb, go like the clappers; N. Amer. informal boogie, hightail it, barrel, get the lead out; informal, dated cut along; archaic post, hie.
▷**ANTONYMS** walk.

sprite **noun** **fairy**, **elf**, pixie, imp, brownie, puck, peri, goblin, hobgoblin, kelpie, leprechaun; nymph, dryad, sylph, naiad; literary faerie, fay; rare hob, nix, nixie, elfin.

sprout **verb 1** *the weeds began to sprout*: **germinate**, put forth shoots, bud; rare burgeon, vegetate, pullulate.
2 *many black cats sprout a few white hairs*: **grow**, develop; send forth, put forth.
3 *crocuses sprouted up from the grass | forms of nationalism sprouted as the system collapsed*: **spring up**, shoot up, come up, grow, burgeon, develop, appear, mushroom, proliferate.

spruce **adjective** *the Captain appeared on deck looking very spruce*: **neat**, **well groomed**, well turned out, well dressed, besuited, smart, trim, dapper, elegant, chic; French soigné; informal natty, snazzy; N. Amer. informal spiffy; dated as if one had just stepped out of a bandbox; archaic trig.
▷**ANTONYMS** scruffy, untidy, dishevelled.
▸ **verb 1** *the cottage had been* ***spruced up*** *since her last visit*: **smarten up**, make smarter, tidy up, make tidy, make neater, neaten up, put in order, clean up; informal do up; Brit. informal tart up, posh up; N. Amer. informal gussy up.
2 *Sarah had* ***spruced herself up***: **groom oneself**, tidy oneself, smarten oneself up, freshen oneself up, preen oneself, primp oneself, prink oneself, pretty oneself, beautify oneself; Brit. have a wash and brush-up; informal titivate oneself, doll oneself up; Brit. informal tart oneself up; archaic plume oneself, trig oneself.

spry **adjective** *he's remarkably spry for a man of his age*: **sprightly**, lively, energetic, active, full of life, full of energy, vigorous, spirited, animated, vivacious, playful, jaunty, perky, frisky, agile, nimble; informal chipper, sparkly, zippy, zappy, full of vim and vigour, full of beans; N. Amer. informal peppy, peart; N. English informal wick; archaic frolicsome, sportive, as lively as a grig.
▷**ANTONYMS** doddery, inactive.

spume **noun** *the spume of the white-capped waves | the cork popped and Charles caught the spume in a tall glass*: **foam**, froth, surf, spindrift, spray; fizz, effervescence, bubbles, head; lather, suds.

spunk **noun** informal *your sister's got more spunk than you*: **courage**, bravery, pluck, pluckiness, courageousness, braveness, valour, mettle, gameness, daring; **determination**, spirit, backbone, strength of character, fortitude, nerve; informal guts, grit; Brit. informal bottle, ballsiness; N. Amer. informal cojones, sand, moxie; vulgar slang balls.

spur **noun 1** *the outcome of the election added a further spur to the reform movement*: **stimulus**, **incentive**, encouragement, stimulant, stimulation, inducement, impetus, prod, prompt; incitement, goad; fillip; motive, motivation; informal kick up the backside, shot in the arm.
▷**ANTONYMS** disincentive, discouragement.
2 *the doctor took an X-ray which showed a spur of bone on the heel*: **projection**, spike; protuberance, protrusion; technical process.
□ **on the spur of the moment** *his decision had been made on the spur of the moment*: **impulsively**, on impulse, impetuously, without thinking, without planning, without premeditation, unpremeditatedly, impromptu, spontaneously, on the spot; suddenly, all of a sudden, unexpectedly, out of the blue.
▸ **verb** *the confrontation spurred him into writing a letter of resignation | desperation spurred her on*: **stimulate**, give the incentive to, act as a stimulus/incentive to, encourage, prompt, propel, prod, induce, impel, motivate, move, galvanize, inspire, urge, drive, egg on, stir; incite, goad, provoke, prick, sting; N. Amer. informal root on, light a fire under.

spurious **adjective** *it was possible to arrange retirements on spurious medical grounds*: **bogus**, fake, not genuine, specious, false, factitious, counterfeit, fraudulent, trumped-up, sham, mock, feigned, pretended, contrived, fabricated, manufactured, fictitious, make-believe, invalid, fallacious, meretricious; artificial, imitation, simulated, ersatz; informal phoney, pseudo, pretend; Brit. informal cod; rare adulterine.
▷**ANTONYMS** authentic, genuine, real.

spurn **verb** *he spurned the offer of a drink*: **refuse**, decline, say no to, reject, rebuff, scorn, turn down, turn away, repudiate, treat with contempt, disdain, look down one's nose at, despise; snub, slight, disown, jilt, repulse, repel, dismiss, brush off, turn one's back on; give someone the cold shoulder, cold-shoulder, ignore, cut (dead), look right through; informal turn one's nose up at, give someone the brush-off, tell someone where to get off, put down, freeze out, stiff-arm, kick in the teeth; Brit. informal knock back; N. Amer. informal give someone the bum's rush, give someone the brush; Austral. informal snout; informal, dated give someone the go-by.

Choose the right word **spurn, reject, refuse, decline**
See **refuse**[1].

spurt **verb** *he cut his finger, and blood spurted over the sliced potatoes | Mount Pinatubo spurted clouds of steam and ash into the air*: **squirt**, shoot, spray, fountain, jet, erupt; gush, pour, stream, rush, pump, surge, spew, spill, flow, course, well, spring, burst, issue, emanate; disgorge, discharge, emit, belch forth, expel, eject; Brit. informal sloosh.
▸ **noun 1** *the sudden spurt of water scared the bird away*: **squirt**, spray, fountain, jet, spout; gush, outpouring, stream, rush, surge, burst, spill, flow, flood, cascade, torrent.
2 *I felt a spurt of pleasure*: **burst**, outburst, fit, bout, attack, rush, spate, surge, flurry, access.
3 *Daisy put on a spurt to hurry down to the river*: **burst of speed**, turn of speed, increase of speed, burst of energy, sprint, rush.

spy **noun** *the government had planted two spies in the organization*: **secret agent**, undercover agent, enemy agent, foreign agent, secret service agent, intelligence agent, double agent, counterspy, industrial spy, fifth columnist, mole, plant, scout; control, handler; N. Amer. spook; informal snooper; archaic intelligencer; archaic, informal beagle.
▸ **verb 1** *she spied some asparagus on a stall*: **notice**, observe, see, spot, sight, catch sight of, glimpse, catch/get a glimpse of, make out, discern, pick out, detect, have sight of; informal clap/lay/set eyes on; literary espy, behold, descry.
2 *the couple were* ***spied on*** *by reporters*: **observe furtively**, keep under surveillance, watch, keep a watch on, keep an eye on, keep under observation, follow, shadow, trail; informal tail; rare surveil.
3 *he agreed to spy for the West*: **be a spy**, be engaged in spying, gather intelligence, work for the secret service; informal snoop.

spying **noun** *he was charged with spying for a foreign power*: **espionage**, undercover work, cloak-and-dagger activities, surveillance, reconnaissance, intelligence, eavesdropping, infiltration, counter-espionage, counter-intelligence; in Japan ninjutsu; informal bugging, wiretapping, recon.

squabble **noun** *there was a squabble over which way they should go*: **quarrel**, row, argument, fight, contretemps, disagreement, difference of opinion, dissension, falling-out, dispute, disputation, contention, clash, altercation, shouting match, exchange, war of words; tussle, conflict, fracas, affray, wrangle, tangle, passage of/at arms, battle royal; Irish, N. Amer., & Austral. donnybrook; informal tiff, set-to, run-in, shindig, shindy, stand-up, spat, scrap, dust-up; Brit. informal barney, slanging match, bunfight, ding-dong, bust-up, ruck; Scottish informal rammy; N. Amer. informal rhubarb; archaic broil, miff; Scottish archaic threap, collieshangie; French, archaic tracasserie(s).
▸ **verb** *the boys were squabbling over a ball*: **quarrel**, row, argue, bicker, have a row/fight, fight, fall out, disagree, fail to agree, differ, be at odds, have a misunderstanding, be at variance, have words, dispute, spar, wrangle, bandy words, cross swords, lock horns, be at each other's throats, be at loggerheads; informal scrap, go at it hammer and tongs, argufy; archaic altercate, chop logic; Scottish archaic threap.

squad **noun 1** *an assassination squad*: **group**, gang, band, body, crew, team, mob, crowd, outfit, force.
2 *a firing squad*: **detachment**, detail, platoon, battery, troop, patrol, squadron, cadre, commando; unit, formation.

squalid **adjective 1** *the squalid, overcrowded prison*: **dirty**, filthy, grubby, grimy, mucky, slummy, slum-like, foul, vile, low, poor, sorry, wretched,

S

dismal, dingy, miserable, mean, nasty, seedy, shabby, sordid, sleazy, insalubrious, slovenly, repulsive, disgusting; **neglected**, uncared-for, unmaintained, broken-down, run down, down at heel, dilapidated, ramshackle, tumbledown, gone to rack and ruin, crumbling, decaying; informal scruffy, scuzzy, crummy, shambly, grungy, ratty, tacky; Brit. informal grotty; N. Amer. informal shacky.
▷ANTONYMS clean, pleasant.
2 *a squalid attempt to save themselves from electoral embarrassment*: **improper**, **sordid**, unseemly, unsavoury, sleazy, seedy, seamy, shoddy, vile, foul, tawdry, louche, cheap, base, low, low-minded, nasty, debased, degenerate, depraved, corrupt, dishonest, dishonourable, disreputable, despicable, discreditable, disgraceful, contemptible, ignominious, ignoble, shameful, wretched, abhorrent, odious, abominable, disgusting; informal sleazoid.
▷ANTONYMS proper, decent.

squall noun *squalls of driving rain*: **gust**, storm, blast, flurry, shower, gale, blow, rush, puff, scud; windstorm, thunderstorm.

squally adjective *conditions were still wintry with squally showers of rain*: **stormy**, gusty, gusting, blustery, blustering, windy, breezy, blowy; wild, violent, turbulent, tempestuous, rough, boisterous.

squalor noun *they lived in squalor*: **dirt**, dirtiness, squalidness, filth, filthiness, grubbiness, grime, griminess, muck, muckiness, slumminess, foulness, vileness, poverty, wretchedness, dinginess, meanness, nastiness, seediness, shabbiness, sordidness, sleaziness, insalubrity, slovenliness, repulsiveness; **neglect**, decay, dilapidation; informal scruffiness, scuzziness, crumminess, grunge, grunginess, rattiness, tackiness; Brit. informal grottiness.
▷ANTONYMS cleanliness.

squander verb *entrepreneurs squander their profits on expensive cars*: **waste**, misspend, misuse, throw away, dissipate, fritter away, run through, lose, lavish, spend recklessly, spend unwisely, make poor use of, be prodigal with, spend money like water; informal blow, splurge, pour/throw money down the drain, spend money as if it grows on trees, spend money as if there were no tomorrow, spend money as if it were going out of style; Brit. informal blue, splash out.
▷ANTONYMS manage, make good use of; save.

square noun **1** *I got it at a shop in the square*: **marketplace**, close, quadrangle, quad, courtyard; arcade, mall, galleria, precinct, forum; in Spain plaza; in Italy piazza.
2 informal *you're such an old square!* **(old) fogey**, conservative, traditionalist, conventionalist, diehard, conformist, bourgeois, museum piece, fossil, dinosaur, troglodyte; informal stick-in-the-mud, fuddy-duddy, back number, stuffed shirt; N. Amer. informal sobersides.
▸ adjective **1** *a square table*: **quadrilateral**, rectangular, oblong, right-angled, at right angles, perpendicular; straight, straight on, level, parallel, horizontal, upright, vertical, true, plane; cubic.
2 *the sides were square at half-time*: **level**, even, drawn, equal, all square, tied, balanced, on a level, in a position of equality; close together, neck and neck, level pegging, nip and tuck, side by side, on a par, evenly matched, with nothing to choose between them; informal even-steven(s).
▷ANTONYMS uneven.
3 *she'd been as square with him as anybody could be*: **fair**, **honest**, just, equitable, straight, true, upright, above board, ethical, decent, proper, right and proper, honourable, genuine; informal on the level.
▷ANTONYMS underhand.
4 informal *children actually prefer their parents to be square*: **old-fashioned**, behind the times, out of date, conservative, traditionalist, conventional, diehard, conformist, bourgeois, strait-laced, fogeyish, stuffy, unadventurous, boring; informal stick-in-the-mud, fuddy-duddy.
▷ANTONYMS trendy.
▸ verb **1** *do those announcements really square with the facts?* **agree**, tally, be in agreement, be consistent, match up, correspond, fit, coincide, accord, conform, be in harmony, harmonize, be consonant, be compatible, be congruous.
2 *his goal squared the match 1–1*: **level**, even, make equal.
3 *would you **square up** the bill?* **pay**, pay in full, settle, settle up, discharge, clear; defray, liquidate, satisfy, meet, account for, make good.
4 *they were accused of trying to square the press*: **bribe**, buy off, buy, corrupt, suborn, give an inducement to; informal grease someone's palm, give a backhander to, give a sweetener to.
5 *I'd like you to come, if only to square certain things with your dad*: **resolve**, sort out, settle, reach an agreement about, find a solution to, find an answer to, solve, clear up, fix, work out, iron out, smooth over, straighten out, deal with, put right, set right, put to rights, rectify, remedy; informal patch up; archaic compose.

squash verb **1** *wash and squash the cans before depositing them*: **crush**, squeeze, flatten, compress, press, smash, distort, mangle, pound, tamp down, trample (down), stamp on; pulp, mash, cream, liquidize, beat, pulverize, macerate.
2 *she squashed some of her clothes inside the bag*: **force**, ram, thrust, plunge, push, stick, cram, jam, stuff, pack, compress, squeeze, wedge, press, tamp, pound, drive, hammer, bang.
3 *the proposal was immediately squashed by the Heritage Department*: **put an end to**, put a stop to, bring to an end, nip in the bud, scotch, put the lid on; ruin, wreck, scupper, destroy, devastate, smash, shatter, demolish, queer; frustrate, thwart; informal put paid to, blow, put the kibosh on, clobber; Brit. informal dish.
4 *there was no need to squash him in front of his friends*: **humiliate**, humble, mortify, show up, bring down, take down, bring low, demean, expose, show in a bad light, shame, put to shame, make ashamed, discomfit, disgrace, discredit, downgrade, debase, degrade, devalue, dishonour, embarrass, put someone in their place, make a fool of, chasten, subdue, get the better of, have the last laugh on, abash, abase, crush, quash, deflate, flatten, make someone eat humble pie; informal put down, settle someone's hash, cut down to size; N. Amer. informal make someone eat crow.

squashy adjective **1** *a squashy pillow*: **springy**, resilient, spongy, soft, pliant, pliable, yielding, supple, elastic, cushiony, compressible, tender, flexible, ductile, malleable, tensile, plastic.
▷ANTONYMS firm.
2 *the pears have gone a bit squashy*: **mushy**, pulpy, pappy, slushy, sloppy, squelchy, squishy, oozy, doughy, semi-liquid, soft; informal gooey, gloopy; Brit. informal squidgy; rare pulpous.

squat verb *I let my back slide down the pillar until I was squatting on the floor*: **crouch (down)**, hunker (down), sit on one's haunches, sit on one's heels, sit, bend down, bob down, duck down, hunch, cower, cringe; N. Amer. informal scooch.
▸ adjective **1** *he was muscular and squat*: **stocky**, dumpy, stubby, stumpy, short, thickset, heavily built, sturdy, sturdily built, heavyset, chunky, solid; burly, beefy; cobby; technical mesomorphic, pyknic; Austral./NZ nuggety; Brit. informal fubsy.
2 *a two-storey classical building with a squat tower*: **low**, stumpy, short, small, stocky, stunted.

squawk verb **1** *the geese flew upriver, squawking*: **screech**, squeal, shriek, scream, croak, crow, caw, cluck, clack, cackle, hoot, cry, call.
2 informal *he is well known for squawking about price-fixing*: **complain**, protest, object, express disapproval, raise objections, make/take a stand, put up a fight, kick, take exception, grouse, grouch, grumble, whine, wail, moan, carp, squeal; informal kick up a fuss, kick up a stink, gripe, bellyache, bitch, beef, whinge; N. English informal mither.
▸ noun **1** *with a startled squawk the rook flew off*: **screech**, squeal, shriek, scream, croak, crow, caw, cluck, clack, cackle, hoot, cry, call.
2 informal *her plan provoked a loud squawk from her friends*: **complaint**, protest, objection, fuss, grouse, grouch, grumble, whine, wail, moan, carp, squeal; informal stink, gripe, bellyache, bitch, beef, whinge.

squeak noun **1** *the dying squeak of a captured vole or bird*: **peep**, cheep, pipe, piping, squeal, tweet, warble, yelp, whimper.
2 *Clare heard the squeak of the garden gate hinge*: **screech**, creak, scrape, grate, rasp, jar, groan.
▸ verb **1** *the rat squeaked*: **peep**, cheep, pipe, squeal, tweet, yelp, whimper.
2 *the hinges of the gate squeaked as she opened it*: **screech**, creak, scrape, grate, rasp, jar, groan.

squeal noun *they drew up with a squeal of brakes | the harsh squeal of a fox*: **screech**, scream, shriek, squawk, howl, cry, wail, squall, yawp, yelp, shrill.
▸ verb **1** *the taxi squealed to a halt | a dog squealed*: **screech**, scream, shriek, squawk, howl, cry, wail, squall, yawp, yelp, shrill.
2 *the bookies only squealed because we beat them*: **complain**, protest, object, express disapproval, raise objections, make/take a stand, put up a fight, kick, take exception, grouse, grouch, grumble, whine, wail, moan, carp, squawk; informal kick up a fuss, kick up a stink, gripe, bellyache, bitch, beef, whinge; N. English informal mither.
3 informal *who squealed to the police? | drug traffickers get lighter sentences in return for **squealing on** their colleagues*: **inform (on/against)**, act as an informer, tell tales (on), sneak (on), report, give away, be disloyal (to), sell out, stab in the back; informal rat (on), blow the whistle (on), peach (on), snitch (on), put the finger on, sell down the river, stitch up; Brit. informal grass (on), split (on), shop; Scottish informal clype (on); N. Amer. informal rat out, finger, fink on, drop a/the dime on; Austral. informal pimp on, pool, put someone's pot on.

squeamish adjective **1** *some of us ate the monkey, but the squeamish ones had a tin of corned beef | my husband was always squeamish about nappies*: **easily nauseated**, nervous; **(be squeamish about) be put off by**, cannot stand the sight of, ... makes one feel sick.
2 *less squeamish nations will not hesitate to sell them arms*: **scrupulous**, principled, conscientious, fastidious, particular, punctilious, finicky, fussy, prissy, prudish, strait-laced, honourable, upright, upstanding, high-minded, righteous, right-minded, moral, ethical; informal pernickety.

squeeze verb **1** *I squeezed the plastic bottle and sent a jet of water out of it*: **compress**, press, crush, squash, pinch, nip, grasp, grip, clutch, flatten, knead; mash, pulp; wring, screw.
2 *squeeze the juice from both oranges*: **extract**, press, force, express.
3 *Sally squeezed her feet into the sandals*: **force**, thrust, stick, cram, ram, jam, stuff, pack, compress, wedge, press, squash, tamp, drive.
4 *we all squeezed into Steve's van*: **crowd**, crush, cram, pack, jam, squash, wedge oneself, shove, push, jostle, force one's way, thrust.

5 *the headmaster flung his arms round Robert and squeezed him warmly*: **hug**, embrace, cuddle, clasp, crush, clutch, press, enfold, envelop, enclasp, wrap, encircle, fold, take in one's arms, hold tight, hold close, cling to; archaic strain.
6 *councils will want to* **squeeze** *as much money* **out of** *taxpayers as they can*: **extort**, force, extract, wrest, wring, tear from, milk; informal bleed someone of something.
7 informal *she used the opportunity to squeeze him for information*: **pressurize**, pressure, bring pressure to bear on, strong-arm; suck dry, milk, fleece, wring, exploit, impose on; informal put the squeeze on, lean on, bleed, put the screws on; N. Amer. & Austral. informal put the bite on.
▶ **noun 1** *a squeeze of the trigger | he gave her hand a squeeze*: **press**, pinch, nip; grasp, grip, clutch; compression.
2 *Jimmy put an arm around her shoulders and gave her a squeeze*: **hug**, embrace, cuddle, clasp, hold.
3 *it was a tight squeeze in the tiny hall*: **crush**, jam, squash, press, huddle, tightly packed crowd; congestion.
4 *a squeeze of lemon juice*: **drop**, few drops, dash, splash, dribble, trickle, spot, hint, touch, bit.

squint verb **1** *the bright sun made them squint*: **screw up one's eyes**, narrow one's eyes, look with/through narrowed eyes, peer, blink; rare squinny.
2 *he'll need an operation because he squints*: **be cross-eyed**, have a squint; Scottish be skelly; technical suffer from strabismus, be strabismic; Brit. informal be boss-eyed.
▶ **noun 1** informal *we must have another squint at his record card*: **look**, glance, peep, peek, glimpse; view, examination, study, inspection, scan, sight; informal eyeful, dekko, butcher's, gander, look-see, once-over, shufti, recce; Austral./NZ informal geek, squiz.
2 *does he have a squint?* **cross-eyes**; Brit. informal boss-eye; technical strabismus.

squire noun **1** *a country squire*: **landowner**, landholder, landlord, lord of the manor, country gentleman.
2 historical *before him went his squire carrying a banner*: **attendant**, courtier, equerry, aide, companion, steward, page boy, servant boy, serving boy, cupbearer, train-bearer.

squirm verb *I tried to squirm away | he squirmed as he recalled the phrases he had used*: **wriggle**, wiggle, writhe, twist, slide, slither, turn, shift, fidget, jiggle, twitch, thresh, flounder, flail, toss and turn; agonize.

squirrel verb
□ **squirrel something away** *try to squirrel a little cash away for a rainy day*: **save**, put aside, put by, lay by, set aside, lay aside, put to one side, reserve, keep in reserve, preserve, deposit, keep, store, stockpile, accumulate, collect, stock up with/on, heap up, hoard, stow away, cache, garner; informal salt away, stash away.

> *Word links* **squirrel**
>
> **sciurine** relating to squirrels
> **drey** home

squirt verb **1** *this mollusc can squirt a cloud of purple ink into the water | a jet of ink squirted out of the tube*: **spurt**, shoot, spray, fountain, jet, erupt; gush, pour, stream, rush, pump, surge, spew; spill, flow, course, well, spring, burst, issue, emanate; disgorge, discharge, emit, belch forth, expel, eject; Brit. informal sloosh.
2 *she squirted me with scent*: **splash**, wet, spray, shower, spatter, bespatter, splatter, sprinkle; Scottish & Irish informal slabber; literary besprinkle.
▶ **noun 1** *a squirt of water*: **spurt**, jet, spray, fountain, gush, stream, surge, flow.
2 informal *a little squirt called Ollie Bogwhistle sneaked on me*: **impudent person, insignificant person**, gnat, insect; informal **pipsqueak**, twerp; Brit. informal nerd, johnny, squit, whippersnapper, git, plonker; Scottish informal nyaff; N. Amer. informal bozo, picayune, pisher, snip, smart mouth; archaic malapert, quean; archaic, informal dandiprat; N. Amer. vulgar slang pissant; (**squirts**) small fry.

stab verb **1** *he stabbed him in the stomach*: **knife**, run through, skewer, spear, bayonet, gore, spike, stick, impale, transfix, pierce, prick, puncture, penetrate, perforate, gash, slash, cut, tear, scratch, wound, injure; rare transpierce.
2 *she stabbed at the earth with a fork*: **lunge**, thrust, jab, poke, prod, dig.
□ **stab someone in the back betray**, be disloyal to, be unfaithful to, desert, break one's promise to, double-cross, break faith with, sell out, play false, inform on/against; informal tell on, sell down the river, blow the whistle on, squeal on, stitch up, peach on, do the dirty on; Brit. informal grass on, shop; N. Amer. informal rat out, finger, drop a/the dime on; Austral. informal pimp on, pool, put someone's pot on.
▶ **noun 1** *a stab in the leg*: **knife wound**, puncture, gash, slash, incision, prick, cut, perforation, wound, injury.
2 *they gesticulated to us using violent stabs into the air*: **lunge**, thrust, jab, poke, prod, dig, punch.
3 *little stabs of pain shot through her*: **twinge**, pang, ache, throb, spasm, cramp, dart, blaze, prick, flash, thrill, gnawing.
4 informal *Meredith made a feeble stab at joining in*: **attempt**, try, effort, endeavour; guess; informal go, shot, crack, bash, whack; formal essay.

stability noun **1** *parents should check the stability of play equipment*: **firmness**, solidity, steadiness, secureness, strength, fastness, stoutness, sturdiness, security, safety.
2 *doubts were raised regarding his mental stability*: **balance**, balance of mind, mental health, soundness, rationality, reason, lucidity, lucidness, sense, sanity, saneness, right-mindedness.
3 *the stability of their relationship | price stability*: **steadiness**, firmness, sureness, secureness, solidity, strength, durability, lasting nature, enduring nature, constancy, permanence, changelessness, invariability, immutability, indestructibility, reliability, dependability; rare lastingness, perdurability, perenniality, imperishability, inalterability, unchangeableness, unchangeability.

stable adjective **1** *a very stable tent*: **firm**, solid, steady, secure, fixed, strong, fast, stout, sturdy, safe, moored, anchored, stuck down, immovable, well built, well constructed, substantial.
▷ANTONYMS unstable, rickety.
2 *a stable person*: **well balanced**, balanced, sound, mentally sound, of sound mind, sane, normal, right in the head, in possession of all one's faculties, able to think/reason clearly, lucid, clear-headed, rational, coherent, steady, reasonable, sensible, sober, down-to-earth, matter-of-fact, with both one's feet on the ground; Latin compos mentis; informal all there.
▷ANTONYMS unstable, unbalanced.
3 *a stable relationship | prices have remained relatively stable*: **secure**, solid, strong, steady, firm, sure, steadfast, level, unwavering, unvarying, unfaltering, unfluctuating, unswerving; established, long-lasting, long-lived, deep-rooted, well founded, well grounded, abiding, durable, enduring, lasting, constant, permanent, reliable, dependable, true.
▷ANTONYMS unstable, rocky, changeable.

stack noun **1** *a stack of boxes*: **heap**, pile, mound, mountain, pyramid, mass, store, stockpile, hoard, load, tower, drift, clamp, hack; N. Amer. cold deck; Scottish, Irish, & N. English rickle; Scottish bing.
2 *a good stack of hay*: **haystack**, rick, hayrick, stook, mow, haymow, barleymow; rare ruck, shock, cock.
3 *there's a stack of cinemas in Leicester Square | there's stacks of work to be done*: **a great deal**, a lot, a great/large amount, a large quantity, quantities, plenty, abundance, superabundance, plethora, cornucopia, a wealth, profusion, a mountain, reams; informal lots, load, loads, heap, heaps, mass, masses, pile, piles, ocean, oceans, oodles, ton, tons; Brit. informal lashings, shedload; N. Amer. informal slew, gobs, scads; Austral./NZ informal swag; vulgar slang shitload.
▷ANTONYMS few; little.
4 *the main stack belches out clouds of black smoke*: **chimney**, factory chimney, chimney stack, smokestack, funnel, exhaust pipe.
5 *Devil's Chimney is actually a sea stack*: **pillar**, column; tor, dome, plug, stalagmite; French puy.
▶ **verb 1** *Shirley began to stack the plates*: **heap (up)**, pile (up), make a heap/pile/stack of; assemble, put together, collect, hoard, store, stockpile.
2 *he spent most of the time stacking shelves*: **load**, fill (up), lade, pack, charge, stuff, cram; stock.
▷ANTONYMS empty.

stadium noun **arena**, field, ground, pitch; bowl, amphitheatre, coliseum, colosseum, enclosure, ring, dome, astrodome, manège; track, course, racetrack, racecourse, speedway, velodrome; in ancient Rome circus; W. Indian gayelle; rare cirque.

staff noun **1** *there is a reluctance to take on new staff*: **employees**, workers, workforce, personnel, hands, hired hands, labourers, human resources, manpower, labour; office workers, white-collar workers, assistants, secretaries; teachers, lecturers; doctors, nurses; N. Amer. interns; humorous liveware.
2 *a tall man with a cowboy hat and a walking staff*: **stick**, walking stick, cane, crook, crutch, prop.
3 *the miller's wife strikes her husband over the head with a staff*: **club**, stick, cudgel, bludgeon, life preserver, shillelagh, baseball bat; truncheon, baton; N. Amer. blackjack; Indian lathi, danda; S. African kierie, knobkerrie, sjambok; Brit. informal cosh.
4 *a staff of office*: **rod**, tipstaff, mace, wand, sceptre, crozier, verge; Greek Mythology caduceus.
▶ **verb** *the departments are staffed by professional civil servants*: **man**, people, crew, work, operate, occupy.

stage noun **1** *a stage in the development*: **phase**, period, juncture, step, point, time, moment, instant, division, level.
2 *the last stage of a race/journey*: **part**, section, portion, stretch, phase; leg, lap, circuit.
3 *stand on a stage in the theatre*: **platform**, dais, stand, grandstand, staging, apron, rostrum, podium, soapbox, stump; pulpit, box, dock; Indian mandapam; rare tribune.
4 (**the stage**) *she has written for the stage, television, and film*: **(the) theatre**, drama, dramatics, dramatic art, show business, the play, the footlights; informal the boards, rep; rare thespianism.
5 *Britain is playing a leading role on the international stage*: **scene**, setting; context, frame, sphere, field, realm, forum, site, arena, background, backdrop; affairs.

S

▶ **verb 1** *they recently staged 'The Magic Flute' in a car factory*: **put on**, put before the public, present, produce, mount, direct; perform, act, render, give.
2 *the Residents' Association staged a protest march*: **organize**, arrange, make arrangements for, coordinate, lay on, put together, fix up, get together; orchestrate, choreograph, be responsible for, be in charge of, direct, run, manage, stage-manage, conduct, administrate, administer, set up, mastermind, engineer; rare concert.

stagger verb **1** *Sonny took the blow on the temple and staggered sideways*: **lurch**, walk unsteadily, reel, sway, teeter, totter, stumble, wobble, move clumsily, weave, flounder, falter, pitch, roll.
2 *I saw a sight that staggered me*: **astonish**, amaze, nonplus, startle, astound, surprise, bewilder, stun, flabbergast, shock, shake, stop someone in their tracks, stupefy, leave open-mouthed, take someone's breath away, dumbfound, daze, benumb, confound, disconcert, shatter, take aback, jolt, shake up; informal bowl over, knock for six, floor, blow someone's mind, strike dumb.
3 *meetings are staggered throughout the day*: **spread (out)**, space (out), time at intervals, overlap.
4 *stagger the screws at each joint*: **alternate**, step, arrange in a zigzag.

staggered adjective *she was staggered to hear she had a rival*: **astonished**, astounded, amazed, stunned, thunderstruck, shattered, flabbergasted, nonplussed, taken aback, startled, surprised, bewildered, shocked, shaken, stupefied, open-mouthed; dumbfounded, dumbstruck, speechless, at a loss for words; dazed, benumbed, confounded, disconcerted, shaken up; informal bowled over, knocked for six, floored, flummoxed, caught on the hop, caught on the wrong foot, unable to believe one's eyes/ears; Brit. informal gobsmacked.

stagnant adjective **1** *stagnant water*: **still**, motionless, immobile, inert, lifeless, dead, standing, slack, static, stationary; **foul**, stale, dirty, filthy, putrid, putrefied, brackish.
▷ANTONYMS flowing, running; fresh.
2 *a stagnant economy*: **inactive**, sluggish, slow, slow-moving, lethargic, static, flat, depressed, quiet, dull, declining, moribund, dying, dead, dormant, stagnating.
▷ANTONYMS active, vibrant.

stagnate verb **1** *there should be no points in the system where cleaning solutions can stagnate*: **stop flowing**, become stagnant, become trapped; stand; become foul, become stale; fester, putrefy.
▷ANTONYMS flow.
2 *imports rose while exports stagnated*: **become stagnant**, do nothing, stand still, be sluggish, lie dormant, be inert, languish, decline, deteriorate, fall.
▷ANTONYMS rise, boom.

staid adjective *staid old ladies*: **sedate**, respectable, quiet, serious, serious-minded, steady, conventional, traditional, unadventurous, unenterprising, set in one's ways; grave, solemn, severe, sombre, sober, proper, decorous, formal; stuffy, prim, demure, prissy, stiff; informal starchy, uptight, stick-in-the-mud.
▷ANTONYMS frivolous, daring, informal.

stain verb **1** *her clothing was stained with blood*: **discolour**, blemish, soil, mark, muddy, spot, spatter, splatter, smear, splash, smudge, blotch, blacken; dirty, get/make dirty, get/make filthy, sully, spoil, defile, pollute, contaminate, foul, befoul, grime, begrime; literary besmirch.
2 *the awful events would unfairly stain the city's reputation*: **damage**, injure, harm, sully, soil, blacken, tarnish, taint, besmirch, blemish, defile, blot, smear, bring discredit to, dishonour, drag through the mud.
3 *wood can always be stained to a darker shade*: **colour**, tint, dye, tinge, shade, pigment; varnish, paint, colour-wash.
▶ **noun 1** *there were mud stains on my shoes*: **mark**, spot, spatter, splatter, blotch, blemish, smudge, smear; dirt, foxing.
2 *he has been discharged without a stain on his character*: **blemish**, injury, taint, blot, blot on one's escutcheon, slur, smear, discredit, dishonour, stigma; damage.
3 *an exterior type of wood stain*: **tint**, colour, dye, tinge, shade, pigment, colourant; varnish, paint, colour wash.

stake¹ noun *he was replacing broken stakes in a barbed-wire fence*: **post**, pole, stick, spike, upright, support, prop, strut, stave, pale, paling, picket, pile, piling, stanchion, shaft, cane, beanpole, rod, mast; historical palisade.
▶ **verb 1** *the plants have to be staked*: **prop up**, tie up, tether, support, hold up, bolster up, brace, buttress, reinforce, truss, stay.
2 *British governments staked their claim to disputed areas by formalizing imperial control*: **assert**, declare, proclaim, state, make, lay, establish, put on record, put in.
□ **stake something out 1** *the slaves were made to stake out canefields in the rainforest*: **mark off**, mark out, demarcate, mark the boundaries/limits of, outline, measure out, define, delimit, fence off, section off, close off, shut off, cordon off, bound, circumscribe. **2** informal *they'd staked out Culley's flat for half a day*: **observe**, watch, keep an eye on, keep under observation, keep watch on, keep under surveillance, survey, monitor, keep under scrutiny, watch like a hawk, keep a weather eye on, spy on, check out; informal keep tabs on, keep a tab on, case, keep a beady eye on; rare surveil.

stake² noun **1** *if the horse wins, you get five times your stake back*: **bet**, wager, ante, pledge, hazard.
2 *they are racing for record stakes this year*: **prize money**, purse, pot, winnings.
3 *he had just knocked another competitor out of the promotion stakes*: **competition**, contest, battle, challenge, rivalry, race, running, struggle, scramble.
4 *he retains a 40% stake in the business*: **share**, interest, financial interest, investment, involvement, concern.
▶ **verb** *one gambler staked everything he'd got and lost*: **bet**, wager, place a bet of, lay, put on, gamble, pledge, chance, venture, risk, hazard.

stale adjective **1** *stale bread | stale cheese*: **dry**, dried out, hard, hardened, old, past its best, past its sell-by date; off, mouldy, rotten, decayed, unfresh, rancid, rank.
▷ANTONYMS fresh.
2 *stale air*: **stuffy**, close, musty, fusty, unfresh, stagnant, frowzy; Brit. frowsty, fuggy.
3 *stale beer*: **flat**, sour, insipid, tasteless, turned, spoiled, off.
4 *the jokes are a bit stale for real belly laughs*: **hackneyed**, tired, worn out, overworked, threadbare, warmed-up, banal, trite, stock, stereotyped, clichéd, run-of-the-mill, commonplace, platitudinous, unoriginal, derivative, unimaginative, uninspired, flat; out of date, outdated, outmoded, passé, archaic, obsolete, defunct, antiquated; N. Amer. warmed-over; informal old hat, corny, out of the ark, played out, past their sell-by date.
▷ANTONYMS original.

Choose the right word **stale, trite, hackneyed**

See **trite**.

stalemate noun *the talks had reached a stalemate*: **deadlock**, impasse, standstill, dead end, stand-off, draw, tie, dead heat.

stalk¹ noun *the stalk of a plant*: **stem**, shoot, trunk, stock, cane, bine, bent, haulm, straw, reed; branch, bough, twig; technical pedicel, peduncle, petiole, phyllode, scape, seta, stipe, caudex, axis.

Word links **stalk**

cauline relating to stalks

stalk² verb **1** *he noticed a stoat stalking a rabbit*: **creep up on**, trail, follow, shadow, track down, go after, be after, dog, hound, course, hunt, pursue, chase, give chase to, run after; informal tail.
2 *without another word she turned and stalked out*: **strut**, stride, march, flounce, storm, stomp, sweep, swagger, prance.

stall noun **1** *a market stall*: **stand**, table, counter, booth, kiosk, compartment.
2 *he hauled the animal out of the stall*: **pen**, coop, sty, corral, enclosure, compartment, cubicle.
3 (**stalls**) Brit. *they sat in the stalls of the empty theatre*: N. Amer. orchestra, parterre.
▶ **verb 1** *the launching of the agency has been stalled for more than a year*: **obstruct**, impede, interfere with, hinder, hamper, block, interrupt, hold up, hold back, stand in the way of, frustrate, thwart, baulk, inhibit, hamstring, sabotage, encumber, restrain, slow, slow down, retard, delay, stonewall, forestall, arrest, check, stop, halt, stay, derail, restrict, limit, curb, put a brake on, bridle, fetter, shackle; informal stymie; N. Amer. informal bork; rare trammel.
2 *quit stalling and give me the money*: **use delaying tactics**, play for time, temporize, gain time, hang back, hang fire, hold back, procrastinate, hedge, beat about the bush, drag one's feet, delay, filibuster, stonewall.
3 *stall him until I've had time to take a look*: **delay**, divert, distract; **hold off**, stave off, fend off, keep off, ward off, keep at bay, keep at arm's length.

stalwart adjective *a stalwart supporter of the cause*: **staunch**, loyal, faithful, committed, devoted, dedicated, dependable, reliable, steady, constant, trusty, hard-working, vigorous, stable, firm, steadfast, redoubtable, resolute, unswerving, unwavering, unhesitating, unfaltering.
▷ANTONYMS disloyal, unfaithful, unreliable.

stamina noun *rowing is ideal for building stamina*: **endurance**, staying power, indefatigability, tirelessness, resistance, resilience, fortitude, strength, vigour, energy, staunchness, steadfastness, robustness, toughness, determination, tenacity, perseverance; informal grit.

stammer verb *he always began to stammer when he was under pressure*: **stutter**, speak haltingly, stumble over one's words, hesitate, falter, fumble for words, pause, halt, mumble, splutter.
▶ **noun** *a rather insecure young man with a slight stammer*: **stutter**, speech impediment, speech defect.

stamp verb **1** *he threw his cigarette down and stamped on it*: **trample**, step, tread, tramp; **crush**, squash, flatten.
2 *John stamped off, muttering*: **stomp**, stump, clomp, clump, tramp, thunder, lumber, trudge.

3 *the binder would stamp his name on the inside edge of a front or back cover*: **imprint**, print, impress, punch, inscribe, engrave, chase, etch, carve, emboss, brand, frank, mark, label.
4 *the date was stamped indelibly on his memory*: **fix**, inscribe, etch, carve, imprint, impress, register.
5 *his style stamps him as a player to watch*: **identify**, characterize, brand, distinguish, mark out, set apart, single out, designate, categorize, classify.
□ **stamp something out** *urgent action is required to stamp out corruption*: **put an end to**, put a stop to, end, finish, get rid of, crush, put down, check, crack down on, weed out, curb, nip in the bud, scotch, squash, quash, quell, subdue, suppress, repress, quench, extinguish, stifle, abolish, eliminate, eradicate, terminate, beat, overcome, defeat, destroy, demolish, annihilate, wipe out, extirpate; informal squelch, put the kibosh on, clobber.
▷ANTONYMS bring in, introduce.
▸ **noun 1** *the whole project has the stamp of authority*: **mark**, hallmark, indication, label, brand, tag, badge, characteristics, peculiarity, attribute, sign, seal, sure sign, telltale sign, quality, smack, smell, savour, air.
2 *the new prior was of a very different stamp from his predecessor*: **type**, kind, sort, variety, class, category, classification, style, description, condition, calibre, status, quality, nature, manner; design, shape, form, pattern, group, set, bracket, genre, species, rank, genus, family, order, breed, race, strain, generation, vintage, make, model, brand, ilk, kidney, cast, grain, mould; N. Amer. stripe.

stamp collecting noun **philately**; archaic timbrophily, timbromania.

stampede noun *she didn't dare ride fast in case she startled the cows into a stampede*: **charge**, panic, rush, flight, rout, scattering.
▸ **verb** *the nearby sheep stampeded as if they sensed impending danger*: **bolt**, charge, rush, flee, take flight, dash, race, career, sweep, run.

stamping ground noun *activists have turned their attentions north and west of their usual stamping ground*: **hang-out**, haunt, meeting place, territory, domain, purlieu, resort, den, retreat, favourite spot; informal hidey-hole; Brit. informal local, patch, manor.

stance noun **1** *the kick is performed by starting from a natural stance and bringing up the right leg*: **posture**, body position, pose, attitude, bearing.
2 *it is possible for individual teachers to take a more liberal stance*: **attitude**, stand, point of view, viewpoint, opinion, way of thinking, outlook, standpoint, posture, position, angle, perspective, approach, slant, thinking, line, policy, thoughts, ideas, sentiments, feelings.

stand verb **1** *Lionel stood in the doorway*: **be on one's feet**, be upright, be erect, be vertical.
▷ANTONYMS sit, lie.
2 *the two men **stood up** and shook hands*: **rise**, rise to one's feet, get to one's feet, get up, straighten up, pick oneself up, find one's feet, be upstanding; literary arise.
▷ANTONYMS sit down, lie down.
3 *a village once stood there*: **be**, be situated, be located, be positioned, be set, be found, be sited, be established, be perched, sit, perch, nestle.
4 *he stood the book on edge*: **put**, set, set up, erect, upend, place, position, locate, situate, prop, lean, plant, stick, install, arrange, dispose, deposit; informal plonk, park.
5 *my decision stands*: **remain in force**, remain valid, remain effective, remain operative, remain in operation, hold, hold good, obtain, apply, prevail, reign, rule, hold sway, be the case, exist, be in use.
6 *his heart could not stand the strain*: **withstand**, endure, bear, put up with, take, cope with, handle, sustain, resist, stand up to.
7 informal *I can't stand brandy*: **endure**, tolerate, bear, put up with, take, abide, suffer, support, brook, countenance, face; informal stick, swallow, stomach, hack, wear.
□ **stand by** *two battalions were on their way, and a third was standing by*: **wait**, be prepared, be in (a state of) readiness, be ready for action, be on full alert, be at battle stations, wait in the wings.
▷ANTONYMS stand down.
□ **stand by someone/something 1** *she had stood by him during his years in prison*: **remain/be loyal to**, stand up for, support, give one's support to, be supportive of, back, back up, give one's backing to, uphold, defend, come to the defence of, stick up for, champion, take someone's part, take the side of, side with.
▷ANTONYMS abandon.
2 *the government must stand by its pledges*: **abide by**, keep (to), adhere to, hold to, stick to, observe, heed, comply with, act in accordance with.
▷ANTONYMS go back on.
□ **stand down** *no further action was required and all units stood down*: **relax**, stand easy, come off full alert.
▷ANTONYMS stand by.
□ **stand for 1** *BBC stands for British Broadcasting Corporation*: **mean**, be an abbreviation of, represent, signify, denote, indicate, correspond to, be equivalent to, symbolize; literary betoken. **2** informal *I won't stand for any nonsense*: **put up with**, endure, tolerate, allow, accept, take, abide, suffer, support, brook, countenance; informal stick, swallow, stomach, hack, wear.
3 *we stand for animal welfare*: **advocate**, champion, uphold, defend, stand up for, support, be in favour of, promote, recommend, urge, back, endorse, sponsor, espouse, push for, work for, campaign for.
▷ANTONYMS oppose.
□ **stand in** *I'll stand in as coach | Brown **stood in for** the injured Simpson*: **deputize**, act, act as deputy, substitute, act as substitute, act as stand-in, fill in, sit in, do duty, take over, act as understudy, act as locum, do a locum, be a proxy, cover, provide cover, hold the fort, step into the breach; take the place of, do something in someone's place/stead, replace, relieve, take over from, understudy; informal sub, fill someone's shoes/boots, step into someone's shoes/boots; N. Amer. pinch-hit.
□ **stand out 1** *the veins in his neck stood out*: **project**, stick out, bulge (out), protrude, jut out, jut, extend, poke out, obtrude; archaic protuberate.
▷ANTONYMS lie flat.
2 *in that dress she stood out in the crowd*: **be noticeable**, be noticed, be visible, be seen, be obvious, be conspicuous, stick out, be striking, be distinctive, be prominent, attract attention, catch the eye, leap out, show up; informal stick/stand out a mile, stick/stand out like a sore thumb.
▷ANTONYMS be inconspicuous.
□ **stand up** *he has no proof that would stand up in court*: **remain/be valid**, be sound, be plausible, hold water, hold up, stand questioning, survive investigation, bear examination, be verifiable, be provable, ring true, be convincing.
▷ANTONYMS fall down.
□ **stand someone up** *she threw eggs over his car after he stood her up*: **fail to keep a date with**, fail to meet, fail to keep an appointment with, fail to turn up for, jilt, let down.
□ **stand up for someone/something** *we should stand up for our great tradition of parliamentary democracy*: **remain/be loyal to**, stand by, support, give one's support to, be supportive of, back, back up, give one's backing to, uphold, defend, come to the defence of, stick up for, champion, take someone's part, take the side of, side with.
▷ANTONYMS abandon.
□ **stand up to someone/something 1** *she had the courage of her convictions and stood up to her parents*: **defy**, confront, challenge, oppose openly, resist, show resistance to, brave, take on, put up a fight against, take a stand against.
▷ANTONYMS give in to.
2 *the old house has stood up to the war*: **withstand**, survive, come through (unscathed), outlast, outlive, weather, ride out.
▷ANTONYMS succumb to.
▸ **noun 1** *I applaud him for his tough stand on human rights*: **attitude**, stance, point of view, viewpoint, opinion, way of thinking, outlook, standpoint, posture, position, angle, perspective, approach, slant, thinking, policy, line, thoughts, ideas, sentiments, feelings.
2 *he maintained his **stand against** tyranny*: **opposition to**, resistance to, objection to, defensive position against, hostility to, animosity towards, disapproval of.
3 *a large mirror on a stand*: **base**, support, mounting, platform, rest, plinth, bottom; tripod, rack, trivet, bracket, frame, case, shelf, gripper.
4 *a beer stand*: **stall**, booth, kiosk.
5 *a taxi stand*: **rank**, station, park, parking place, place, bay.
6 *the train drew to a stand by the signal box*: **stop**, halt, standstill, dead stop.
7 *a stand of trees*: **copse**, spinney, thicket, grove, coppice, wood; rare boscage.

standard noun **1** *the standard of work is very good*: **quality**, level, grade, degree, worth, calibre, merit, excellence.
2 *half the beaches fail to comply with European standards*: **guideline**, norm, yardstick, benchmark, gauge, measure, criterion, guide, touchstone, model, pattern, example, exemplar, paradigm, ideal, archetype, specification, requirement, rule, principle, law, canon.
3 *offenders against society's standards are punished*: **principle**, rule of living; (**standards**) code of behaviour, code of honour, morals, scruples, ethics, ideals.
4 *the raising of the regiment's standard will be a particularly poignant moment*: **flag**, banner, pennant, pennon, streamer, ensign, colour(s), banderole; Brit. pendant; Nautical burgee; in ancient Rome vexillum; rare gonfalon, guidon, labarum.
▸ **adjective 1** *the standard rate of income tax*: **normal**, usual, typical, stock, common, ordinary, customary, conventional, habitual, accustomed, expected, wonted, everyday, regular, routine, day-to-day, daily, established, settled, set, fixed, traditional, quotidian, prevailing.
▷ANTONYMS unusual, special.
2 *this book will certainly become the standard work on the subject*: **definitive**, established, classic, recognized, approved, accepted, authoritative, most reliable, most complete, exhaustive, official.

> *Word toolkit* **standard**
>
> See **typical**.

standardize verb *they attempted to standardize the names of the plants they were growing*: **systematize**, make consistent, make uniform, make comparable, regulate, normalize, bring into line, equalize; homogenize, assimilate, regiment, mass-produce, stereotype; rare methodize.

stand-in noun *Davies is the obvious stand-in for the injured Cartwright*: **substitute**, replacement, reserve, representative, deputy, surrogate, lieutenant, second, second string, proxy, understudy, double, locum,

S

supply, fill-in, cover, relief, stopgap, standby; informal temp; Latin locum tenens; N. Amer. informal pinch-hitter.

▶ adjective *a stand-in goalkeeper*: **substitute**, replacement, reserve, deputy, second-string, fill-in, stopgap, supply, surrogate, relief, acting, temporary, provisional, caretaker; N. Amer. informal pinch-hitting.

standing noun 1 *his standing in the community*: **status**, rank, ranking, position, social position, station, level, footing, place; repute, reputation, estimation, stature; archaic condition, degree, report.
2 *the departmental records officer was a person of some standing*: **seniority**, rank, eminence, prominence, prestige, reputation, good reputation, repute, stature, esteem, illustriousness, importance, account, consequence, influence, weight, sway, distinction, renown, note, notability, noteworthiness; informal clout; dated mark.
3 *a squabble of long standing*: **duration**, existence, continuance, endurance, length of time, life, validity.

▶ adjective 1 *standing stones*: **upright**, erect, vertical, plumb, upended, on end, rearing, straight (up and down), perpendicular; on one's feet; not yet reaped; Heraldry rampant.
▷ANTONYMS flat, lying down, seated.
2 *standing water*: **stagnant**, still, motionless, immobile, inert, lifeless, dead, slack, static, stationary.
▷ANTONYMS flowing.
3 *a standing invitation*: **permanent**, perpetual, everlasting, continuing, abiding, constant, fixed, indefinite, open-ended; regular, repeated.
▷ANTONYMS temporary, occasional.

stand-off noun *Europe has shown that it is possible to live with a nuclear stand-off*: **deadlock**, stalemate, impasse, standstill, dead end, draw, tie, dead heat.

stand-offish adjective informal *an arrogant, stand-offish prig*: **aloof**, distant, remote, detached, impersonal, withdrawn, reserved, uncommunicative, unforthcoming, unapproachable, unfriendly, unsociable, cool, chilly, cold, haughty, disdainful, uninvolved, unresponsive, indifferent, unconcerned, preoccupied, abstracted; introspective, introvert, introverted; rare Olympian.
▷ANTONYMS friendly, approachable, sociable.

standpoint noun *she writes on religion from the standpoint of a believer*: **point of view**, viewpoint, vantage point, attitude, stance, stand, view, opinion, position, way of thinking, frame of mind, outlook, perspective, angle, slant.

standstill noun *the traffic came to a standstill*: **halt**, stop, dead stop, stand.

staple adjective *rice was the staple crop grown in most villages*: **main**, principal, chief, major, primary, leading, foremost, first, most important, predominant, dominant, (most) prominent, key, crucial, vital, indispensable, essential, basic, fundamental, standard, critical, pivotal, prime, central, premier; informal number-one.

star noun 1 *the sky was full of stars*: **celestial body**, heavenly body, sun; asteroid, planet, planetoid; literary orb.
2 (**stars**) *what do my stars say?* **horoscope**, forecast, augury; dated nativity.
3 *the stars of the film*: **principal**, leading lady, leading man, lead, female lead, male lead, hero, heroine.
▷ANTONYMS extra.
4 *a star of the world of chess*: **celebrity**, superstar, name, big name, famous name, household name, somebody, someone, lion, leading light, celebutante, public figure, important person, VIP, personality, personage, notability, dignitary, worthy, grandee, luminary, panjandrum; informal celeb, bigwig, big shot, big noise, big cheese, big gun, big fish, biggie, heavy, megastar; Brit. informal nob; N. Amer. informal kahuna, macher, high muckamuck, high muckety-muck.
▷ANTONYMS nobody.

▶ adjective 1 *Elinor was a star pupil*: **brilliant**, talented, gifted, able, bright, brainy, clever, masterly, consummate, precocious.
▷ANTONYMS poor.
2 *the star attraction*: **top**, leading, best, greatest, foremost, major, pre-eminent, champion.
▷ANTONYMS insignificant.

Word links **star**

astral, sidereal, stellar relating to stars
astro-, sidero- related prefixes, as in *astrophysics, siderostat*
astronomy study of stars
astrometry measurement of stars
uranography describing and mapping of stars

starchy adjective informal *the chairman of the area board had a rather starchy personality*. See **staid**.

stare verb *he **stared at** her in amazement*: **gaze**, gape, goggle, gawk, glare, ogle, leer, peer, look fixedly, look vacantly; study, survey, observe, watch closely, eyeball, outstare; informal rubberneck; Brit. informal gawp.
□ **stare someone in the face** *the solution was staring him in the face*: **be obvious**, be clear, be plain, be plain to see, be crystal clear, be evident, be apparent, be manifest, be patent, be conspicuous, be prominent, be transparent, be clear-cut, be palpable, be unmistakable, be indisputable, be self-evident, be undeniable, be as plain as a pikestaff, be writ large, be written all over one, be as clear as day, be blinding, be inescapable; informal be as plain as the nose on one's face, be standing/sticking out like a sore thumb, be standing/sticking out a mile, be right under one's nose.

stark adjective 1 *the ridge formed a stark silhouette against the sky | the crisp white shirt was a stark contrast to his weather-beaten tan*: **sharply delineated**, sharp, sharply defined, well focused, crisp, distinct, obvious, evident, clear, clear-cut, graphic, striking.
▷ANTONYMS fuzzy, indistinct.
2 *a stark landscape*: **desolate**, bare, barren, arid, vacant, empty, forsaken, godforsaken, bleak, dreary, gloomy, sombre, depressing, cheerless, joyless, uninviting, miserable, grim, harsh, oppressive, merciless; literary drear.
▷ANTONYMS pleasant.
3 *an upright chair was the only furniture in the stark room*: **austere**, severe, bleak, plain, simple, bare, unadorned, unembellished, undecorated, uncomfortable.
▷ANTONYMS comfortable; ornate.
4 *he came running back in stark terror*: **sheer**, utter, complete, absolute, total, pure, perfect, positive, downright, out-and-out, outright; thorough, thoroughgoing, through and through, consummate, surpassing, veritable, rank, unequivocal, undeniable, unqualified, unmitigated, unalloyed, unadulterated, unmixed.
5 *the stark fact is that the societies simply do not have the funds*: **blunt**, bald, bare, simple, straightforward, basic, plain, unadorned, unembellished, unvarnished, harsh, grim.
▷ANTONYMS disguised.

▶ adverb *he was stark naked | have you gone stark staring mad?* **completely**, totally, utterly, absolutely, downright, dead, entirely, wholly, fully, quite, altogether, simply, thoroughly, truly.

start verb 1 *the meeting starts at 7.45*: **begin**, get under way, go ahead, get going; informal kick off; formal commence.
▷ANTONYMS finish.
2 *this was how her illness had started*: **come into being**, begin, be born, come into existence, appear, arrive, come forth, emerge, erupt, burst out, arise, originate, break, unfold, develop, crop up, first see the light of day; formal commence.
▷ANTONYMS end, clear up.
3 *I'm starting a campaign to get the law changed*: **establish**, set up, found, lay the foundations of, lay the cornerstone of, lay the first stone of, sow the seeds of, create, bring into being, institute, initiate, inaugurate, introduce, open, begin, launch, float, kick-start, put in place, get something off the ground, get something going, get something moving, get something working, get something functioning, activate, originate, pioneer, organize, mastermind, embark on, make a start on, tackle, set about; informal kick something off.
▷ANTONYMS end, wind up.
4 *we had better start now if we are going to finish the job in time*: **make a start**, begin, make a beginning, take the first step, lay the first stone, make the first move, get going, go ahead, set things moving, buckle to/down, turn to, put one's shoulder to the wheel, put one's hand to the plough, start/get/set the ball rolling; informal get moving, get cracking, get stuck in, get down to it, get to it, get down to business, get one's finger out, get the show on the road, take the plunge, kick off, pitch in, get off one's backside, fire away; Brit. informal get weaving; formal commence.
▷ANTONYMS stop; hang about; give up.
5 *Yanto **started out** across the sand at a brisk pace*: **set off**, set out, start out, set forth, begin one's journey, get on the road, depart, leave, get under way, make a start, sally forth, embark, sail; informal hit the road, hit the trail, push off; archaic set forward.
▷ANTONYMS arrive; stay.
6 *you can **start up** the machine with the footswitch*: **activate**, set in motion, switch on, turn on, fire up; energize, actuate, set off, start off, get/set something going/moving, start something functioning, start something operating, kick-start.
▷ANTONYMS stop, close down.
7 *the machine **started up***: **begin working**, start functioning, get going, start operating.
▷ANTONYMS stop.
8 *'Oh my!' she said, starting*: **flinch**, **jerk**, jump, twitch, recoil, shrink, blench, wince, shy.
9 literary *she had seen Meg start suddenly from the thicket*: **jump**, leap, spring, bound, dash, charge, pounce, dive, rush, dart.

▶ noun 1 *we were present at the start of the event*: **beginning**, inception, onset, emergence, (first) appearance, arrival, eruption, dawn, birth; establishment, foundation, institution, origination, inauguration, induction, creation, opening, launch, float, floating; informal kick-off; formal commencement.
2 *that was the start of the trouble*: **origin**, source, root, starting point, germ, seeds, beginning, genesis; **cause**, reason, motivation, motive; Latin fons et origo; literary fountainhead, wellspring, fount.

S

3 *I gave them a quarter of an hour's start*: **lead**, head start, advantage, advantageous position.
4 *they have worked hard to give their children a start in life*: **advantageous beginning**, flying start, opening, opportunity, chance, helping hand, encouragement, lift, assistance, support, boost, kick-start; informal break, leg up.
5 *she awoke with a start*: **jerk**, twitch, flinch, wince, spasm, convulsion, jump.

startle verb *a sudden sound in the doorway startled her | he was startled to see a column of smoke*: **surprise**, **frighten**, scare, alarm, give someone a shock, give someone a fright, give someone a jolt, make someone jump; **perturb**, unsettle, agitate, disturb, disconcert, disquiet; informal give someone a turn, make someone jump out of their skin, flabbergast.
▷ANTONYMS put at ease.

> *Choose the right word* **startle, frighten, scare**
>
> See **frighten**.

startling adjective *startling news awaited him at Naples*: **surprising**, astonishing, amazing, unexpected, unforeseen, staggering, shocking, stunning; extraordinary, remarkable, dramatic; **disturbing**, unsettling, perturbing, disconcerting, disquieting; **frightening**, alarming, scary.
▷ANTONYMS predictable, ordinary.

starvation noun *half of the country's people face starvation as a result of the civil war*: **extreme hunger**, lack of food, famine, want, undernourishment, malnourishment, fasting; deprivation of food; death from lack of food.

starving adjective *she devotes her energies to helping the world's starving children | I'm usually starving by lunchtime*: **dying of hunger**, dying from lack of food, faint from lack of food, deprived of food, undernourished, malnourished, starved, half-starved, unfed; very hungry, ravenous, famished, empty, hollow; fasting; (**be starving**) be hungry; informal could eat a horse.
▷ANTONYMS well fed, full.

stash informal verb *he gathered up his things and stashed them away | he had money stashed away in overseas accounts*: **store**, stow, pack, load, cache, garner, hide, conceal, secrete; hoard, put aside, set aside, put by, lay by, lay aside, save, stockpile, keep in reserve, reserve, deposit, keep, put by for a rainy day; informal salt away, squirrel away.
▸ noun *the thieves had never found my small stash of money*: **cache**, hoard, stock, stockpile, store, supply, accumulation, collection, reserve, fund, pool; rare amassment.

state[1] noun **1** *the current state of the UK economy*: **condition**, shape, situation, circumstances, state of affairs, position; predicament, plight.
2 *she is in no state to make decisions*: **mood**, humour, temper, disposition, spirits, morale, state of mind, emotional state, frame of mind, attitude; condition, shape.
3 *don't get into a state*: **fluster**, flutter, frenzy, fever, fret, panic, state of agitation, state of anxiety, nervous state, distressed state; informal flap, tizzy, tiz-woz, twitter, dither, stew, sweat; N. Amer. informal twit.
4 informal *your room is in a state*: **untidiness**, **mess**, untidy state, chaos, disorder, disarray, disorganization, confusion, clutter, muddle, heap, shambles, tangle, mishmash; turmoil; informal muck.
5 *the states that comprise the EC*: **country**, nation, land, sovereign state, nation state, kingdom, empire, republic, confederation, federation, body politic, commonwealth, power, world power, superpower, polity, domain, territory; fatherland, motherland; Law realm; Latin res publica.
6 *a federation of six states*: **province**, federal state, region, territory, canton, department, county, area, district, sector, zone; Brit. shire.
7 *the power of* **the state** *should not be used to curtail individual liberty*: **government**, parliament, the administration, the regime, the authorities, the council, the Establishment.
▸ adjective *the South African president was on a state visit to Britain*: **ceremonial**, official, formal, governmental, national, public.
▷ANTONYMS unofficial, private, informal.

S

state[2] verb *people will be invited to state their views*: **express**, voice, utter, say, tell, declare, affirm, assert, aver, announce, make known, communicate, reveal, disclose, divulge, give out, give voice to, pronounce, articulate, enunciate, proclaim, present, expound, preach, promulgate, publish, broadcast; set out, set down, frame, formulate, spell out, be specific about; informal come out with; rare asseverate.

stated adjective *routine health checks at stated intervals | the stated aim of the programme*: **set**, fixed, settled, agreed, declared, determined, approved, authorized, accredited, ruled, ordained, designated, laid down; **claimed**, official, supposed, professed, alleged.
▷ANTONYMS undefined, irregular; tacit; actual.

stately adjective *a stately procession*: **dignified**, **majestic**, ceremonious, courtly, imposing, impressive, solemn, awe-inspiring, regal, imperial, elegant, grand, glorious, splendid, magnificent, resplendent, important, august, formal; slow-moving, measured, deliberate.

statement noun *do you agree with this statement?* **declaration**, expression of views/facts, affirmation, assertion, announcement, utterance, communication; revelation, disclosure, divulgence, pronouncement, recitation, articulation, proclamation, presentation, expounding, explanation, promulgation; account, testimony, evidence, report, bulletin, communiqué; rare asseveration, averment.

state-of-the-art adjective *the studio boasted the finest state-of-the-art recording equipment*: **modern**, ultra-modern, futuristic, avant-garde, the latest, new, the newest, up to the minute; advanced, highly developed, innovatory, trailblazing, revolutionary; sophisticated, complex, complicated, elaborate, intricate, subtle, delicate; gimmicky.

statesman, stateswoman noun **senior politician**, respected political figure, elder statesman, political leader, national leader, grand old man, GOM; French éminence grise.

static adjective **1** *they are to keep prices static for the rest of the year*: **unchanged**, fixed, stable, steady, unchanging, changeless, unvarying, invariable, constant, consistent, uniform, undeviating.
▷ANTONYMS variable.
2 *a static display of aircraft*: **stationary**, motionless, immobile, unmoving, still, stock-still, at a standstill, at rest, halted, stopped, parked, immobilized, not moving, not moving a muscle, like a statue, rooted to the spot, unstirring, frozen, inactive, inert, lifeless, inanimate.
▷ANTONYMS mobile, active, dynamic.

station noun **1** *calling at all stations to Oxford*: **stopping place**, stop, halt, station stop, stage; terminus, terminal, depot; railway station, train station, passenger station; bus station, coach station.
2 *a research station in the rainforest | a naval station*: **establishment**, base, base camp, camp; post, depot; mission; site, facility, installation, yard; in India, historical cantonment.
3 *a police station*: **office**, depot, base, headquarters, centre; N. Amer. precinct, station house, substation; Indian kotwali, thana; informal cop shop; Brit. informal nick.
4 *a radio station*: **channel**, broadcasting organization; wavelength.
5 Austral./NZ *as a youngster he was sent out to Australia to work as a jackaroo on a sheep station*: **ranch**, range; farm.
6 *the lookout resumed his station in the bow*: **assigned position**, post, area of duty, place, situation, location.
7 dated *Karen was getting ideas above her station*: **rank**, place, status, position in society, social class, level, grade, standing; caste; archaic condition, degree.
▸ verb *a flagman was stationed at the road crossing*: **put on duty**, post, position, place, set, locate, site; establish, install; deploy, base, garrison.

stationary adjective **1** *a stationary vehicle*: **motionless**, parked, halted, stopped, immobilized, immobile, unmoving, still, static, stock-still, at a standstill, at rest, not moving; like a statue, rooted to the spot, unstirring, frozen, inactive, inert, lifeless, inanimate.
▷ANTONYMS moving.
2 *a stationary population*: **unchanging**, unvarying, invariable, constant, consistent, uniform, unchanged, changeless, fixed, stable, steady, undeviating.
▷ANTONYMS shifting.

> *Easily confused words* **stationary or stationery?**
>
> Owing to their similarity in spelling, **stationary** and **stationery** are often confused; but their meanings have nothing in common. *Stationary* is an adjective meaning 'motionless' (*the car ploughed into a stationary van*). *Stationery* is a noun denoting writing and office materials (*bills for stamps and stationery*).

statue noun **sculpture**, figure, effigy, statuette, figurine, idol; carving, bronze, representation, likeness, image, graven image, model; bust, head.

statuesque adjective *the headmistress was statuesque*: **tall and dignified**, imposing, striking, stately, majestic, noble, magnificent, splendid, impressive, regal, well proportioned, handsome, beautiful.

stature noun **1** *she was small in stature*: **height**, tallness, loftiness; size, build, physical make-up.
2 *an architect of international stature*: **reputation**, repute, standing, status, position, prestige, distinction, illustriousness, eminence, pre-eminence, prominence, importance, import, influence, weight, consequence, account, note, fame, celebrity, renown, acclaim.

status noun **1** *an improvement in the status of women*: **standing**, rank, ranking, position, social position, station, level, footing, place; repute, reputation, estimation, stature; archaic condition, degree, report.
2 *those who enjoy wealth and status*: **prestige**, kudos, cachet, standing, stature, prestigiousness, reputation, repute, (good) name, regard, fame, note, renown, honour, esteem, estimation, image, account, rank, character, celebrity, importance, prominence, consequence, class, distinction, laurels, influence, weight, authority, supremacy, eminence, superiority; NZ mana; Indian izzat; informal clout.

statute noun *the statute in question gave rise to an action for damages*: **law**, regulation, enactment, act, bill, decree, edict, rule, ruling, resolution, promulgation, measure, motion, dictum, command, order, stipulation, commandment, directive, pronouncement, ratification, proclamation, dictate, diktat, fiat, covenant, demand, by-law; N. Amer. **ordinance**; in Tsarist Russia **ukase**; in Spain & Spanish-speaking countries **pronunciamento**.

staunch[1] adjective *a staunch supporter of the cause*: **stalwart**, loyal, faithful, trusty, committed, devoted, dedicated, dependable, reliable, steady, constant, hard-working, vigorous, stable, firm, steadfast, redoubtable, resolute, unswerving, unwavering, unhesitating, unfaltering.
▷ANTONYMS disloyal, unfaithful, unreliable.

Word toolkit

staunch	resolute	determined
supporter	refusal	effort
support	determination	resistance
opposition	declaration	attempt
Republican	conviction	stride

staunch[2] verb *he bound his thigh firmly, staunching the flow of blood*: **stem**; **hold back**, stop, halt, check, block, dam; restrict, restrain, control, contain, curb, slow, lessen, reduce, diminish, retard; N. Amer. stanch; archaic stay.

stave verb **1** *the ship had been driven aground, her hull **staved in***: **break in**, smash in, put a hole in, push in, kick in, cave in, splinter, shiver, fracture.
2 *the government is introducing emergency measures to **stave off** a crisis*: **avert**, prevent, avoid, preclude, rule out, counter, forestall, nip in the bud; ward off, fend off, head off, keep off, keep at bay.

stay[1] verb **1** *the man told her to stay where she was*: **remain (behind)**, stay behind, stay put; **wait**, wait around, linger, stick, continue, be left, hold on, hang on, lodge, rest, delay, pause, stop; informal hang around/round; Brit. informal **hang about**; archaic **bide**, **tarry**.
▷ANTONYMS leave.
2 *we can't stay hidden any longer*: **continue to be**, remain, keep, continue, persist in being, carry on being, go on being, rest.
3 *the girls have come to stay with us*: **visit**; spend some time, put up, stop, stop off, stop over, break one's journey; holiday; lodge, room, board, have rooms, be housed, be accommodated, be quartered, be billeted; take up residence, take a room, settle; N. Amer. vacation; formal sojourn; archaic bide, abide.
4 *legal proceedings in such cases would be either stayed or dropped completely*: **postpone**, put off, delay, defer, put back, hold over/off, carry over, reschedule, do later, shelve, stand over, pigeonhole, put/hold in abeyance, mothball; adjourn, suspend, prorogue; put off the evil day/hour; N. Amer. put over, table, lay on the table, take a rain check on; N. Amer. Law continue; informal put on ice, put on the back burner, put in cold storage; rare remit, respite.
▷ANTONYMS advance.
5 literary *he tries to stay the progress of barbarism*: **delay**, **slow down**, slow up, hold back, set back, keep back, hold up, postpone, put back, detain, decelerate, put a brake on, retard; **hinder**, hamper, obstruct, inhibit, impede, handicap, hamstring, curb, check, restrain, restrict, arrest, interfere with, interrupt, encumber, clog; Brit. informal throw a spanner in the works of; N. Amer. informal throw a monkey wrench in the works of; rare trammel, cumber.
▷ANTONYMS promote.
▸ noun **1** *a brief stay at a hotel*: **visit**, stop, stop-off, stopover, break, holiday, rest; N. Amer. vacation; formal sojourn.
2 *a stay of judgement*: **postponement**, putting off, delay, deferment, deferral, putting back, carrying over, rescheduling, shelving, pigeonholing, mothballing; adjournment, suspension, prorogation; N. Amer. tabling.

stay[2] noun *the mast was raised and the stays rigged*: **strut**, **wire**, brace, tether, prop, beam, rod, support, truss, buttress, pier, shaft, shore, stanchion, stake, stick, spike, post; Nautical shroud.
▸ verb *her masts were stayed with lengths of telephone wire*: **brace**, tether, strut, wire, prop, support, truss, buttress, shore up, stake, stick.

staying power noun informal *she won't have to rough it on this trip, but she still needs staying power*. See **stamina**.

steadfast adjective **1** *he was a steadfast friend*: **loyal**, faithful, committed, devoted, dedicated, dependable, reliable, steady, true, constant, staunch, trusty.
▷ANTONYMS disloyal.
2 *a steadfast policy of internationalism*: **firm**, determined, resolute, steady, staunch, stalwart, stout, relentless, implacable, single-minded; unchanging, unwavering, unhesitating, unfaltering, unswerving, unyielding, unflinching, inflexible, uncompromising.
▷ANTONYMS irresolute.

steady adjective **1** *the base was not steady, and the model fell over*: **stable**, balanced, firm, fixed, secure, secured, fast, safe, immovable, unshakeable, dependable; anchored, moored, jammed, rooted, braced, cemented, riveted, nailed, tied.
▷ANTONYMS unstable, loose.
2 *press the button again, keeping the camcorder as steady as you can*: **motionless**, still, unshaking, static, stationary, unmoving, sure.
▷ANTONYMS shaky.
3 *a steady gaze*: **fixed**, intent, immovable, immobile, unwavering, unfaltering.
▷ANTONYMS darting.
4 *a solid, steady young man*: **sensible**, level-headed, well balanced, balanced, rational, settled, mature, down-to-earth, full of common sense, stolid, calm, equable, imperturbable, reliable, dependable, sound, sober, serious-minded, responsible, serious.
▷ANTONYMS flighty, impulsive, airy-fairy, immature.
5 *a fixed-interest bond is used to provide a steady income*: **constant**, unchanging, changeless, unvarying, invariable, undeviating; uniform, even, regular, consistent; continuous, continual, unceasing, ceaseless, perpetual, unremitting, unwavering, unfaltering, unfluctuating, undying, unending, endless, round-the-clock, all-year-round; reliable, dependable.
▷ANTONYMS fluctuating, intermittent, sporadic.
6 *a steady boyfriend*: **regular**, unchanging, habitual, usual, customary, established, settled, firm, devoted, faithful.
▷ANTONYMS occasional, on-off.
▸ verb **1** *he propped his elbow on his knee to steady the rifle*: **stabilize**, make steady, hold steady; secure, fix, make fast; brace, support; balance, poise.
2 *I took a deep breath to steady my nerves*: **calm**, calm down, soothe, quieten, quiet, compose, settle, pacify, lull; subdue, quell, control, get a grip on; sedate, tranquillize.

steal verb **1** *the raiders stole a fax machine*: **purloin**, thieve, take, take for oneself, help oneself to, loot, pilfer, abscond with, run off with, appropriate, abstract, carry off, shoplift; embezzle, misappropriate; have one's fingers/hand in the till; informal walk off/away with, run away/off with, rob, swipe, nab, rip off, lift, 'liberate', 'borrow', filch, snaffle, snitch, souvenir; Brit. informal nick, pinch, half-inch, whip, knock off, nobble, bone, scrump, blag; N. Amer. informal heist, glom; Austral. informal snavel; W. Indian informal tief; archaic crib, hook; rare peculate, defalcate; **(be stolen)** informal walk, go walkies.
2 *he alleged that his work was stolen by his tutor*: **plagiarize**, copy, pass off as one's own, infringe the copyright of, pirate, poach, borrow, appropriate; informal rip off, lift, pinch, nick, crib.
3 *she was a beauty, and he'd often wanted to steal a kiss*: **snatch**, sneak, obtain stealthily, get surreptitiously.
4 *he stole out of the room*: **creep**, sneak, slink, slip, slither, slide, glide, sidle, slope, edge, move furtively, tiptoe, pussyfoot, pad, prowl.
□ **steal away** *she disobeyed a court order and stole away with the children*: **abscond**, decamp, make off, run off, run away, flee, bolt, take off, take flight, disappear, vanish, slip away, sneak away, beat a hasty retreat, escape, make a run for it, make one's getaway, leave, depart, make oneself scarce; informal split, scram, skedaddle, vamoose, skip, cut and run, make tracks, push off, shove off, clear off, hightail it, hotfoot it, show a clean pair of heels, do a bunk, do a runner, do a moonlight flit, do a disappearing act, head for the hills, fly the coop, take French leave, go AWOL; Brit. informal scarper; N. Amer. informal take a powder, go on the lam, light out, bug out, peel out, cut out; Brit. informal, dated hook it.
□ **steal the show** *she stole the show from her seasoned co-stars*: **be the centre of attention**, get all the attention, attract the most attention, be the focus of attention, be the main attraction, be the outstanding feature, put the others in the shade, be the high point/spot, be the best part, have all eyes on one, be the cynosure; outshine, put in the shade, upstage, overshadow, eclipse, outclass, dwarf, tower above/over, put to shame.
▸ noun **1** N. Amer. *New York's biggest art steal*: **theft**, robbery, raid, ram raid, burglary, larceny, thievery, break-in, hold-up; embezzlement, misappropriation, swindle, fraud; in India or Burma dacoity; informal snatch, pinch, smash-and-grab (raid), stick-up, mugging, job; Brit. informal blag; N. Amer. informal heist; rare peculation, defalcation.
2 informal *at £30 it's a steal*. See **bargain**.

S

Word links **steal**

kleptomania compulsion to steal

stealing noun *he was convicted of stealing*: **theft**, thieving, thievery, robbery, larceny, burglary, shoplifting, pilfering, pilferage, looting, appropriation, misappropriation; embezzlement; rare peculation, defalcation.

Word links **stealing**

kleptomania compulsive stealing
kleptophobia fear of stealing

stealth noun *what they could not accomplish by violence or chicanery they would have to accomplish by stealth*: **furtiveness**, secretiveness, secrecy, surreptitiousness, sneakiness, slyness, covertness, stealthiness, clandestineness.
▷ANTONYMS openness.

stealthy adjective *there was a good deal of stealthy coming and going within the building*: **furtive**, secretive, secret, surreptitious, sneaking, sly,

skulking, slinking, clandestine, hidden, covert, cloaked, conspiratorial, under the table.
▷ANTONYMS open.

steam noun **1** *steam gushed from the spout of the kettle*: **water vapour**, condensation, mist, haze, fog, exhalation, moisture, dampness; rare fume, smoke.
2 *he starts fast but tends to run out of steam*: **energy**, vigour, vigorousness, vitality, stamina, enthusiasm; **momentum**, impetus, power, force, strength, thrust, impulse, push, drive, driving power; speed, pace, velocity.
□ **let off steam** informal **give vent to one's feelings**, speak one's mind, sound off, lose one's inhibitions, let oneself go; use up energy, release surplus energy.
▷ANTONYMS bottle things up.
□ **under one's own steam unaided**, unassisted, without help, without assistance, independently, by oneself, by one's own efforts, on one's own two feet.
▷ANTONYMS with help.
▶ verb informal *he bounced out of the car and steamed into the shop*. See **run**.
□ **get steamed up** informal **1** *he got really steamed up about forgetting his papers*: **become agitated**, get worked up, get overwrought, get flustered, panic, become panic-stricken; informal get het up, get into a state, get into a tizzy, get uptight, get into a stew, get the willies, get the heebie-jeebies, go into a flat spin; Brit. informal have kittens, have an attack of the wobblies.
▷ANTONYMS calm down. **2** *they get steamed up about the media*: **become very angry**, become enraged, go into a rage, lose one's temper; informal go/get mad, go crazy, go wild, see red, go bananas, hit the roof, go through the roof, go up the wall, go off the deep end, fly off the handle, blow one's top, blow a fuse/gasket, lose one's rag, go ape, flip, flip one's lid, go non-linear, go ballistic, go psycho; Brit. informal go crackers, go spare, do one's nut; N. Amer. informal flip one's wig, blow one's lid/stack; vulgar slang go apeshit.
□ **steam up** *glass lenses are more likely to steam up than plastic*: **mist (up)**, fog (up), become misty/misted, become covered with condensation.

steamy adjective **1** *the hot, steamy jungle*: **humid**, muggy, sticky, dripping, moist, damp, clammy, sultry, sweltering, boiling, sweaty, steaming, like a Turkish bath, like a sauna.
2 informal *the steamy love scenes have been cut*: **erotic**, sexy, sexually explicit, suggestive, racy, risqué, provocative, spicy, juicy, bawdy, ribald, uninhibited, unrestrained, earthy; informal raunchy, naughty; Brit. informal saucy, fruity; N. Amer. informal gamy; euphemistic adult.
3 informal *Mac was having this steamy affair with Caroline*: **passionate**, torrid, amorous, ardent, loving, hot-blooded, sexy, lustful, erotic; informal sizzling, zipless, hot, red-hot.

steel verb
□ **steel oneself** *his team were steeling themselves for disappointment*: **brace oneself**, nerve oneself, summon/gather/screw up/muster one's courage, screw one's courage to the sticking place, gear oneself up, prepare oneself, get in the right frame of mind, make up one's mind; fortify oneself, harden oneself, bolster oneself; informal psych oneself up; literary gird (up) one's loins.

steely adjective **1** *the steely predawn light*: **blue-grey**, grey, steel-coloured, steel-grey, iron-grey; harsh.
▷ANTONYMS soft.
2 *his steely pectoral muscles*: **hard**, firm, toned, rigid, stiff, tense, tensed, taut, stretched.
▷ANTONYMS flabby.
3 *he would stare hard at you with steely eyes*: **cruel**, unfeeling, merciless, ruthless, pitiless, heartless, hard-hearted, hard, stony, cold-blooded, cold-hearted, harsh, callous, severe, unmerciful, unrelenting, relentless, unpitying, unsparing, unforgiving, uncaring, unsympathetic, uncharitable, lacking compassion, remorseless, unbending, unmoved, inflexible, inexorable, implacable, unremitting; literary adamantine; rare marble-hearted.
▷ANTONYMS kind.
4 *she had a steely determination that had made her a success in a man's world*: **resolute**, firm, fixed, steadfast, dogged, single-minded; bitter, burning, fiery, ferocious, fierce, fanatical, furious; ruthless, inflexible, iron, granite, stony, grim, gritty, gutsy; unquenchable, unflinching, unswerving, unfaltering, untiring, unwavering, unyielding, undaunted.
▷ANTONYMS half-hearted.

steep[1] adjective **1** *steep limestone cliffs*: **precipitous**, sheer, abrupt, sharp, perpendicular, vertical, bluff, vertiginous, dizzy; rare declivitous, acclivitous, scarped.
▷ANTONYMS gentle.
2 *a steep rise in unemployment*: **sharp**, sudden, precipitate, precipitous, rapid.
▷ANTONYMS gradual.
3 informal *the prices are a bit steep*: **expensive**, dear, costly, high, stiff; unreasonable, excessive, overpriced, exorbitant, extortionate, outrageous, prohibitive; Brit. over the odds; informal pricey, over the top, OTT, criminal.
▷ANTONYMS reasonable.

steep[2] verb **1** *the ham is then steeped in brine for three or four days*: **marinade**, marinate, soak, souse, macerate; pickle, brine.
2 *winding sheets were steeped in mercury sulphate as a disinfectant*: **soak**, saturate, immerse, submerge, wet through, drench; technical ret.
3 *a city* ***steeped in*** *history*: **imbue with**, fill with, permeate with, pervade with, suffuse with, infuse with, perfuse with, impregnate with, soak in; rare stew in.

steeple noun *the steeple of St Bride's church*: **spire**, church tower, tower, bell tower, belfry; minaret; Italian campanile.

steer verb **1** *he steered the boat slowly towards the busy quay*: **guide**, direct, manoeuvre; navigate, pilot, drive, be in the driver's seat of, be at the wheel of; Nautical con, helm.
2 *Luke steered her down the path towards his car*: **guide**, conduct, direct, lead, take, usher, escort, shepherd, marshal, herd.
□ **steer clear of** *you'd best steer clear of him—he's a nasty piece of work*: **keep away from**, keep one's distance from, keep at arm's length, give a wide berth to, avoid, avoid dealing with, have nothing to do with, shun, eschew; sidestep, evade, dodge, skirt round, circumvent, fight shy of; informal duck.
▷ANTONYMS seek out, confront.

stem[1] noun **1** *with any shrub or tree, look for firm healthy roots and a sturdy straight stem*: **trunk**, **stalk**, stock, cane; technical peduncle.
2 *the rose has dark foliage and purplish stems*: **stalk**, shoot, twig; technical bine, pedicel, petiole, peduncle, axis.
▶ verb
□ **stem from** *her depression stems from domestic difficulties*: **have its origins in**, arise from, originate from, spring from, derive from, come from, be rooted in, emanate from, issue from, flow from, proceed from, result from, be consequent on; **be caused by**, be brought on/about by, be produced by.
▷ANTONYMS cause, give rise to; be independent of.

Word links **stem**
cauline relating to stems

stem[2] verb *paramedics tried to stem the flow of blood*: **staunch**, stop, halt, check, hold back, restrain, restrict, control, contain, curb; block, dam; slow, lessen, reduce, diminish, retard; N. Amer. stanch; archaic stay.

stench noun *the stench made me feel sick*: **stink**, bad smell, foul smell, reek, miasma, effluvium; Brit. informal niff, pong, whiff, hum; Scottish informal guff; N. Amer. informal funk; rare mephitis, malodour, fetor, noisomeness.

stentorian adjective *a bulky man was holding forth in stentorian tones*: **loud**, booming, thundering, thunderous, trumpeting, blaring, roaring, ear-splitting, deafening; ringing, resonant, sonorous, carrying, vibrant, powerful, strong, full; strident; rare stentorious.
▷ANTONYMS quiet, soft.

step noun **1** *Frank took another step forward*: **pace**, footstep, stride.
2 *she heard Ellis's step on the stairs*: **footstep**, footfall, tread, tramp.
3 *she left the room with a springy step*: **gait**, walk, way of walking, tread, bearing, carriage.
4 *the market is only a step from the end of the pier*: **short distance**, stone's throw, spitting distance; informal {a hop, skip, and a jump}.
5 *Susan sat on the top step | Maureen ran down the steps*: **stair**, tread, tread board; **(steps) stairs**, staircase, stairway; N. Amer. stoop.
6 *there was a pint of milk on the step*: **doorstep**, sill.
7 *the steps of a ladder*: **rung**, tread.
8 *calling in the bailiffs is a very serious step*: **course of action**, measure, move, act, action, procedure, proceeding, initiative; manoeuvre, tactic, strategy, stratagem, operation; French démarche.
9 *a significant step towards a ceasefire*: **advance**, progression, development, step in the right direction, step forward, move, movement; breakthrough.
10 *the first step on the managerial ladder*: **stage**, level, grade, rank, degree; phase; notch.
□ **in step** *he is utterly in step with mainstream American thinking*: **in accord**, in harmony, in agreement, in tune, in line, in keeping, in conformity, in accordance, in consensus, in consilience.
▷ANTONYMS out of step.
□ **mind/watch one's step be careful**, take care, step carefully/cautiously, walk carefully/cautiously, tread carefully/cautiously, exercise care/caution, mind how one goes, look out, watch out, watch oneself, be wary, be circumspect, be chary, take heed, be attentive, be on one's guard, have/keep one's wits about one, be on the qui vive.
□ **out of step** *the paper was often out of step with public opinion*: **at odds**, at variance, in disagreement, out of tune, out of line, not in keeping, out of harmony, at loggerheads, in opposition, at outs.
▷ANTONYMS in step.
□ **step by step one step at a time**, bit by bit, gradually, in stages, by degrees, slowly, steadily, slowly but surely; rare gradatim.
□ **take steps** *the government must take steps to discourage age discrimination*: **take action**, take measures, act, take the initiative, move.
▶ verb **1** *she stepped off the gangway*: **walk**, move, tread, pace, stride.
2 *the bull had stepped on his hat*: **tread**, stamp, trample, tramp; squash, crush, flatten.

S

□ **step down resign**, stand down, give up one's post/job, bow out; retire, abdicate; informal quit, call it a day.
▷ANTONYMS take up office.
□ **step in intervene**, intercede, become/get involved, act, take action, take measures, take a hand; mediate, arbitrate, intermediate.
□ **step on it** informal **hurry up**, get a move on, speed up, go faster, be quick; informal get cracking, get moving, step on the gas, rattle one's dags; Brit. informal get one's skates on, stir one's stumps; N. Amer. informal get a wiggle on; S. African informal put foot; dated make haste.
□ **step something up 1** *the army stepped up its offensive in the north*: **increase**, intensify, strengthen, augment, escalate, scale up, boost; informal up, crank up. **2** *I stepped up my pace*: **speed up**, increase, accelerate, quicken, hasten.
▷ANTONYMS decrease.

stepmother noun

> *Word links* **stepmother**
>
> **novercal** relating to a stepmother

stereotype noun *the stereotype of the alcoholic as a down-and-out vagrant*: **standard/conventional image**, received idea, cliché, hackneyed idea, formula.
▶ verb *the city is too easily stereotyped as an industrial wasteland*: **typecast**, pigeonhole, conventionalize, standardize, categorize, compartmentalize, label, tag.

stereotyped adjective *stereotyped images of village life*: **stock**, conventional, stereotypical, conventionalized, standardized, standard, formulaic, predictable; hackneyed, clichéd, cliché-ridden, banal, trite, platitudinous, unoriginal, derivative, overused, overworked, well worn, stale, tired; typecast; informal corny, old hat.
▷ANTONYMS unconventional, original, fresh.

sterile adjective **1** *the treatment left her sterile*: **infertile**; childless; technical infecund; archaic barren.
▷ANTONYMS fertile, fecund.
2 *vast tracts of sterile desert land*: **unproductive**, infertile, unfruitful, uncultivatable; arid, dry, barren, lifeless, desert.
▷ANTONYMS rich, fertile, productive.
3 *a sterile debate*: **pointless**, profitless, unproductive, unfruitful, fruitless, unrewarding, abortive, unsuccessful, ineffectual, ineffective, worthless, useless, unprofitable, futile, vain, idle; archaic bootless; rare unfructuous.
▷ANTONYMS fruitful.
4 *sterile academicism*: **unimaginative**, uninspired, uninspiring, unoriginal, derivative, stale, lifeless, musty.
▷ANTONYMS creative, original.
5 *the cells can be propagated in sterile conditions*: **aseptic**, sterilized, germ-free, antiseptic, disinfected, uninfected, uncontaminated, unpolluted, pure, clean; sanitary, hygienic.
▷ANTONYMS septic.

sterility noun **1** *these compounds have successfully been used in the treatment of sterility*: **infertility**; childlessness; technical infecundity; archaic barrenness.
▷ANTONYMS fertility, fecundity.
2 *the sterility of the soil*: **unproductiveness**, unfruitfulness, infertility, sterileness, non-productivity; aridness, aridity, barrenness, lifelessness.
▷ANTONYMS richness, fertility, productiveness.
3 *the sterility of the debate | he contemplated the sterility of his life*: **pointlessness**, unproductiveness, unfruitfulness, fruitlessness, uselessness, futility, profitlessness, worthlessness, abortiveness; emptiness, barrenness, aridity; archaic bootlessness.
▷ANTONYMS fruitfulness.
4 *a temperature of 121°C is the minimum needed to achieve sterility*: **asepsis**, freedom from germs, lack of infection/contamination/pollution, disinfection, purity, cleanliness.
▷ANTONYMS contamination.

sterilize verb **1** *the wards had been thoroughly sterilized*: **disinfect**, purify, fumigate, decontaminate, sanitize; pasteurize; clean, cleanse; technical autoclave; rare depurate, depollute.
▷ANTONYMS contaminate.
2 *in the last half of the year, over 6.5 million people were sterilized*: **vasectomize**, **hysterectomize**; rare ovariectomize, oophorectomize, eunuchize.
3 *she launched a campaign to have France's 30 million cats and dogs sterilized*: **castrate**, geld, neuter, cut, caponize, emasculate; **spay**; N. Amer. & Austral. alter; informal fix, doctor.

sterling adjective Brit. *the sterling work of the social services department*: **excellent**, first-rate, first-class, exceptional, outstanding, splendid, superlative, of the first order, of the highest order, of the first water, magnificent, wonderful, fine, great, praiseworthy, laudable, admirable; informal A1, stellar, top-notch.
▷ANTONYMS poor, unexceptional.

stern[1] adjective **1** *Nick's expression was stern*: **serious**, **unsmiling**, frowning, poker-faced, severe, forbidding, grim, unfriendly, sombre, grave, sober, austere, dour, stony, flinty, steely, unrelenting, unyielding, unforgiving, unbending, unsympathetic, disapproving; rare Rhadamanthine.
▷ANTONYMS genial, friendly.
2 *the stern measures taken by the government added to its unpopularity*: **strict**, severe, stringent, harsh, drastic, hard, tough, fierce, extreme, rigorous, rigid, exacting, demanding, uncompromising, unsparing, inflexible, authoritarian, draconian; Austral./NZ informal solid.
▷ANTONYMS lenient, lax.

stern[2] noun *the stern of the ship*: **rear end**, rear, back, tail, poop.
▷ANTONYMS bow.

stew noun *a beef stew*: **casserole**.
□ **in a stew** informal *she's in a right old stew*: **agitated**, anxious, in a state of nerves, nervous, in a state of agitation, in a panic, worked up, keyed up, overwrought, wrought up, flustered, flurried, in a pother; informal in a flap, in a state, all of a dither, in a sweat, in a tizz/tizzy, in a tiz-woz, all of a lather, het up, in a twitter; Brit. informal strung up, windy, having kittens, all of a doodah; N. Amer. informal in a twit; Austral./NZ informal toey; dated overstrung.
▷ANTONYMS cool, calm, relaxed, laid-back.
▶ verb **1** *stew the meat for an hour or so*: **braise**, casserole, fricassée, simmer, boil; jug; S. African smoor; archaic seethe.
2 informal *there's no point stewing over it*: **worry**, fret, agonize, be anxious, be nervous, be agitated, get in a panic, get worked up, get in a fluster, get overwrought; informal get in a flap, get in a state, get in a tizz/tizzy, get in a tiz-woz, get in a sweat, get steamed up, get in a lather.
3 informal *the girls sat stewing in the heat*: **swelter**, be very hot, perspire, sweat; informal roast, bake, be boiling.

steward noun **1** *an air steward*: **flight attendant**, cabin attendant, member of the cabin staff; stewardess, air hostess; N. Amer. informal stew.
2 *the race stewards did not uphold my protest*: **official**, marshal, organizer.
3 *the steward of the Carewscourt estate*: **(estate) manager**, agent, overseer, custodian, caretaker; Brit. land agent, bailiff; Scottish factor; historical reeve.
4 Brit. historical *the steward of the household*: **major-domo**, seneschal, manciple; butler.

stick[1] noun **1** *he gathered sticks and lit a fire*: **piece of wood**, twig, small branch.
2 *Roger still walked with a stick*: **walking stick**, cane, staff; malacca, alpenstock, blackthorn, ashplant, rattan, thumb stick; crook; crutch; Austral./NZ waddy.
3 *the stems require adequate support—sticks or netting can be used*: **cane**, pole, beanpole, post, stake, upright, rod.
4 *he had beaten her with a stick*: **club**, cudgel, bludgeon, shillelagh; truncheon, baton; cane, birch, switch, rod; Indian lathi, danda; S. African kierie, knobkerrie; Brit. informal cosh.
5 Brit. informal *he's going to get some stick for this*: **criticism**, flak, censure, reproach, reproof, condemnation, castigation, chastisement, blame, abuse; punishment; informal a bashing, a roasting, a caning, an earful, a bawling-out; Brit. informal verbal, a rollicking, a wigging, a rocket, a row; Brit. vulgar slang a bollocking; rare animadversion.
▷ANTONYMS praise, commendation.
□ **the sticks** informal *you should stop living in the sticks and move to London*: **the country**, the countryside, the provinces, rural districts, the backwoods, the back of beyond, the wilds, the hinterland, a backwater; N. Amer. the backcountry, the backland; Austral./NZ the backblocks, the booay; S. African the backveld, the platteland; informal the middle of nowhere; N. Amer. informal the boondocks, the boonies, the tall timbers; Austral./NZ informal Woop Woop, beyond the black stump.

stick[2] verb **1** *he stuck his fork into the sausage*: **thrust**, push, insert, jab, dig, plunge, ram, force; poke, prod.
2 *the bristles* ***stuck into*** *his skin*: **pierce**, penetrate, puncture, prick, spike, stab.
3 *his front teeth* ***stuck out***: **protrude**, jut out, project, stand out, extend, poke out, obtrude; bulge; overhang, beetle; informal be goofy; rare protuberate, impend.
4 *the shabbiness of the surroundings* ***stuck out***: **stand out**, be noticeable, be conspicuous, be obvious, catch the eye, be obtrusive.
5 *the plastic seats stuck to my skin*: **adhere**, cling, be fixed, be glued.
6 *a message was stuck to his computer screen*: **affix**, attach, fasten, fix; paste, glue, gum, tape, sellotape, pin, tack; weld, solder.
7 *he drove into a bog, where his wheels stuck fast*: **become trapped**, become jammed, jam, catch, become wedged, become lodged, become fixed, become embedded, become immobilized, become unable to move, get bogged down.
8 *one particular incident sticks in his mind*: **remain**, stay, linger, dwell, persist, continue, last, endure.
▷ANTONYMS be forgotten.
9 *the authorities couldn't make the charges stick*: **be upheld**, hold, be believed, gain credence, be regarded as valid; informal hold water.
10 informal *just stick that sandwich on my desk*: **put**, place, set, put down, set down, lay, lay down, deposit, situate, position; leave, stow; informal dump,

bung, park, plonk, pop; N. Amer. informal plunk.
11 informal *I don't think I can stick it any longer*: **tolerate**, put up with, take, stand (for), accept, stomach, swallow, endure, bear, support, brook, submit to, take something lying down; Scottish thole; informal abide; Brit. informal wear, be doing with; archaic suffer.
12 archaic *if I had my knife here I would stick him*: **stab**, run through, transfix, impale, spit, spear.
□ **stick at** *if you wish to learn a language, you must stick at it*: **persevere with**, persist with, keep at, work at, continue with, carry on with, go on with, not give up with, hammer away at, stay with, see/follow through, go the distance, stay the course; informal soldier on with, stick it out, hang in there, put one's back into.
▷**ANTONYMS** give up.
□ **stick by** *whatever happens I'll stick by him*: **support**, stand by, be loyal to, remain faithful to, be supportive of, be on someone's side, side with, back, defend.
▷**ANTONYMS** turn against, turn one's back on, let down.
□ **stick it out** *I decided to stick it out for another couple of months*: **put up with it**, grin and bear it, keep at it, keep going, stay with it, see it through, see it through to the end; persevere, persist, carry on, struggle on; informal hang in there, soldier on, tough it out, peg away, plug away, bash on.
▷**ANTONYMS** give up.
□ **stick to** *the government stuck to their election pledges*: **abide by**, keep, adhere to, hold to, fulfil, make good.
▷**ANTONYMS** break.
□ **stick up for** *I don't know anyone else who would stick up for me the way you do*: **support**, give one's support to, take the side of, side with, be on the side of, stand by, stand up for, take someone's part, be supportive of, be loyal to, defend, come to the defence of, champion, speak up for, fight for.
▷**ANTONYMS** turn against, turn one's back on.

stick-in-the-mud noun informal **(old) fogey**, conservative, museum piece, fossil, dinosaur, troglodyte; informal fuddy-duddy, square, back number, stuffed shirt; N. Amer. informal sobersides.

sticky adjective **1** *sticky tape | a sticky label*: **adhesive**, adherent, gummed; rare tenacious.
2 *too much water made the clay sticky and difficult to work*: **glutinous**, viscous, viscid; **gluey**, tacky, gummy, treacly, syrupy; mucilaginous; Brit. claggy; Scottish & N. English clarty; informal gooey, gloopy, cloggy, gungy, icky; N. Amer. informal gloppy; rare viscoid.
▷**ANTONYMS** dry.
3 *an unusually hot and sticky summer*: **humid**, muggy, close, sultry, sweltering, steamy, oppressive, airless, stifling, suffocating, sweaty, soupy, like a Turkish bath, like a sauna.
▷**ANTONYMS** fresh, cool.
4 *thanks for getting me out of a very sticky situation*: **awkward**, difficult, tricky, ticklish, problematic, delicate, touch-and-go, embarrassing, sensitive, uncomfortable; informal hairy.
▷**ANTONYMS** easy.

stiff adjective **1** *a sheet of stiff black cardboard*: **rigid**, hard, firm, hardened, inelastic, non-flexible, inflexible, ungiving; rare impliable, unmalleable.
▷**ANTONYMS** flexible, plastic; limp.
2 *mix to a stiff paste*: **semi-solid**, viscous, viscid, thick, stiffened; firm, compact, dense; rare viscoid.
▷**ANTONYMS** runny.
3 *her muscles were stiff | his stiff legs*: **aching**, achy, painful; arthritic, rheumatic; taut, tight; informal creaky, rheumaticky, rusty; archaic stark.
▷**ANTONYMS** supple, limber.
4 *she greeted him with stiff politeness*: **formal**, reserved, unfriendly, chilly, cold, frigid, icy, austere, unrelaxed, brittle, stand-offish, wooden, forced, constrained, strained, stilted; prim, punctilious, stuffy; informal starchy, uptight.
▷**ANTONYMS** relaxed, informal.
5 *they face stiff fines and a possible jail sentence*: **harsh**, severe, hard, punitive, punishing, stringent, swingeing, crippling, rigorous, drastic, strong, heavy, draconian.
▷**ANTONYMS** lenient, mild.
6 *the army had put up a stiff resistance*: **vigorous**, **determined**, full of determination, strong, spirited, resolute, tenacious, steely, four-square, unflagging, unyielding, dogged, stubborn, obdurate; N. Amer. rock-ribbed.
▷**ANTONYMS** half-hearted.
7 *a long, stiff climb up the bare hillside*: **difficult**, hard, arduous, tough, strenuous, laborious, uphill, exacting, demanding, formidable, challenging, punishing, back-breaking, gruelling, Herculean; tiring, fatiguing, exhausting; informal killing, hellish; Brit. informal knackering; archaic toilsome.
▷**ANTONYMS** easy.
8 *a stiff breeze*: **strong**, vigorous, powerful, brisk, fresh, gusty; howling.
▷**ANTONYMS** gentle.
9 *you need a stiff drink*: **strong**, potent, alcoholic, spirituous, intoxicant.
▷**ANTONYMS** weak.

stiffen verb **1** *stir until the mixture stiffens*: **become stiff**, thicken; set, become solid, solidify, harden, gel, congeal, coagulate, clot.
2 *she stiffened her muscles | without exercise, joints will stiffen*: **make/become stiff/rigid**, tense (up), tighten, tauten; rigidify; technical ankylose.
▷**ANTONYMS** relax.
3 *attempts to intimidate them have only stiffened their resolve*: **strengthen**, harden, toughen, fortify, give strength to, reinforce, brace, steel, give a boost to.
▷**ANTONYMS** weaken.

stiff-necked adjective *he was stiff-necked and argumentative*. See **stubborn** (sense 1).

stifle verb **1** *people in the streets were stifled by the fumes | Hester had stifled her husband with a bolster*: **suffocate**, choke, asphyxiate; smother.
2 *Eleanor stifled a giggle*: **suppress**, smother, restrain, keep back, hold back, hold in, fight back, choke back, gulp back, withhold, check, keep in check, swallow, muffle, quench, curb, silence, contain, bottle up; bite one's lip, cork up.
▷**ANTONYMS** let out.
3 *high taxes were stifling private enterprise | public debate is being stifled*: **constrain**, hinder, hamper, impede, hold back, curb, check, restrain, prevent, inhibit; put an end/stop to, stop, quash, squash, stamp out, destroy, crush, extinguish, deaden, damp down, subdue, suppress, repress; silence, muffle, mute, gag.
▷**ANTONYMS** encourage.

stifling adjective *in summer, Venice is often stifling*: **very hot**, sweltering; **airless**, suffocating, oppressive, humid, close, muggy, sticky, soupy; informal boiling.
▷**ANTONYMS** cold, chilly.

stigma noun *the stigma of bankruptcy*: **shame**, disgrace, dishonour; stain, taint, blot, blot on one's escutcheon, blemish, brand, mark, slur; literary smirch.
▷**ANTONYMS** honour, credit.

stigmatize verb *trade unionism was stigmatized as inimical to the interests of society*: **condemn**, denounce; brand, label, mark out; disparage, vilify, pillory, pour scorn on, cast a slur on, defame, discredit.

still adjective **1** *Polly lay quite still*: **motionless**, unmoving, without moving, without moving a muscle, stock-still, immobile, like a statue, as if turned to stone, as if rooted to the spot, unstirring, stationary; at rest, at a standstill; inert, lifeless.
▷**ANTONYMS** moving, active.
2 *the night was dark and still | the still waters of the lake*: **quiet**, silent, hushed, soundless, noiseless, undisturbed, sound-free; **calm**, tranquil, peaceful, serene, windless, wind-free, halcyon; flat, even, smooth, placid, pacific, waveless, glassy, like a millpond, unruffled; stagnant, standing; literary stilly.
▶ **noun** *the still of the night*: **quietness**, quiet, quietude, silence, stillness, hush, soundlessness, noiselessness; calmness, calm, tranquillity, peace, peacefulness, peace and quiet, serenity.
▷**ANTONYMS** noise, disturbance, hubbub.
▶ **adverb 1** *I understand he's still married to her*: **up to this time**, up to the present time, until now, even now, yet.
▷**ANTONYMS** no longer.
2 *I'm afraid he's crazy. Still, he's harmless*: **nevertheless**, however, in spite of that, despite that, notwithstanding, for all that, all the same, even so, be that as it may, having said that, nonetheless, but; informal still and all; archaic withal, natheless, howbeit.
▶ **verb 1** *he stilled the clamour with a wave of his hand*: **quieten**, quiet, silence, hush; calm, settle, pacify, soothe, lull, allay, assuage, appease, subdue.
▷**ANTONYMS** stir up.
2 *the wind stilled*: **abate**, die down, grow less, lessen, subside, ease up/off, let up, moderate, slacken, weaken, fade away.
▷**ANTONYMS** get stronger, get up.

stilted adjective *after a few minutes of stilted conversation, she retreated*: **strained**, forced, contrived, constrained, laboured, laborious, stiff, self-conscious, awkward, unnatural, wooden, unrelaxed; artificial, mannered.
▷**ANTONYMS** natural, effortless, spontaneous.

stimulant noun **1** *a stimulant that has a direct effect on the nervous system*: **tonic**, restorative, reviver, energizer, refresher; antidepressant; informal pep pill, upper, pick-me-up, bracer; technical excitant, analeptic.
▷**ANTONYMS** sedative, downer.
2 *population growth is a major stimulant to industrial development*: **stimulus**, incentive, encouragement, impetus, inducement, fillip, boost, spur, prompt, prod, jog; provocation, goad, incitement; informal shot in the arm, kick up the backside.
▷**ANTONYMS** deterrent.

Easily confused words **stimulant or stimulus?**

While both these words have meanings relating to something's effect on activity, they are distinct. A **stimulant** is a substance that increases or speeds up bodily activity (*tisanes may appeal to people who find ordinary tea too much of a stimulant | a heart and respiratory stimulant*). **Stimulus**, on the other hand, denotes something that causes a particular physical response (*the syndrome causes bizarre responses to any stimulus to the hemiplegic side*), or something that acts as an incentive to activity or development (*the authorities are convinced of the value of investment as a stimulus to growth*).

stimulate verb *his passionate interest in the music stimulated Mozart to study Bach's fugues | I want to stimulate their imaginations*: **encourage**, act as a stimulus/incentive/impetus/fillip/spur to, prompt, prod, move, motivate, trigger, spark, spur on, galvanize, activate, kindle, fire, fire with enthusiasm, fuel, whet, nourish; inspire, rouse, arouse, excite, animate, quicken, ginger up, pique, electrify; stir up, whip up, instigate, foment, fan, incite, provoke, sting, inflame, goad; N. Amer. light a fire under; literary inspirit, spirit someone up; rare incentivize, fillip.
▷ANTONYMS discourage.

stimulating adjective **1** *plant extracts which have a stimulating effect on the circulation*: **restorative**, tonic, invigorating, bracing, energizing, restoring, reviving, refreshing, vitalizing, revitalizing, vivifying, revivifying; informal pick-me-up; technical analeptic, trophic.
▷ANTONYMS sedative.
2 *a stimulating lecture by Professor Battersby*: **thought-provoking**, interesting, fascinating, inspiring, inspirational, lively, sparkling, entertaining, exhilarating, exciting, stirring, rousing, intriguing, stimulative, giving one food for thought, piquant, refreshing; provocative, challenging; informal sexy; rare exalté.
▷ANTONYMS uninspiring, uninteresting, boring.

Word toolkit **stimulating**

See **bracing**.

stimulus noun *cheap energy provided a major stimulus to economic development in western Europe*: **spur**, stimulant, encouragement, impetus, boost, prompt, prod, incentive, inducement, inspiration, fillip; motive, motivation, impulse; provocation, goad, incitement; informal shot in the arm, kick up the backside; technical precipitant.
▷ANTONYMS deterrent, discouragement.

Easily confused words **stimulus or stimulant?**

See **stimulant**.

sting noun **1** *the herb is said to relieve the pain of wasp and bee stings*: **prick**, wound, injury; bite, nip, puncture.
2 *to soothe the sting of a cut or burn use aloe juice*: **smarting**, smart, stinging, tingling, tingle, pricking; pain, soreness, hurt, irritation.
3 *I recalled the sting of his betrayal*: **heartache**, heartbreak, agony, torture, torment, hurt, pain, anguish, distress, desolation, misery.
4 *she smiled to take the sting out of her words*: **sharpness**, severity, bite, edge, pointedness, asperity, pungency, mordancy, acerbity, acidity, tartness; **sarcasm**, acrimony, malice, spite, venom; rare causticity, mordacity.
5 informal *that little sting netted him the Bentley and a £350,000 house*: **swindle**, fraud, piece of deception, trickery, cheat, bit of sharp practice; informal rip-off, con, con trick, diddle, fiddle; N. Amer. informal bunco.
▸ verb **1** *she was stung by a scorpion*: **prick**, wound, injure, hurt; bite, nip, penetrate; poison; rare urticate.
2 *her eyes were stinging from all the smoke*: **smart**, tingle, burn, be painful, hurt, be irritated, be sore, ache.
3 *in the past she had been stung by his criticism of her*: **upset**, wound, distress, make miserable, cut to the quick, sear, grieve, hurt, pain, torment, mortify.
4 *he was stung into action by an article in the paper*: **provoke**, goad, incite, spur, prick, prod, rouse, stir up, drive, move, motivate, galvanize, stimulate.
▷ANTONYMS deter.
5 informal *an elaborate fraud which stung the bank for thousands*: **swindle**, defraud, cheat, fleece, gull; informal rip off, screw, do, rook, diddle, take for a ride, skin, clip, gyp; N. Amer. informal chisel, gouge, bunco; Brit. informal, dated rush.

stingy adjective informal *Colin was notoriously stingy*: **mean**, miserly, parsimonious, niggardly, close-fisted, penny-pinching, cheese-paring, penurious, Scrooge-like, ungenerous, illiberal, close; informal mingy, tight, tight-fisted; N. Amer. informal cheap; vulgar slang tight-arsed; archaic near.
▷ANTONYMS generous, liberal, magnanimous.

stink verb **1** *his clothes stank of sweat*: **reek**, smell foul/bad/disgusting, stink/smell to high heaven, give off a bad smell.
2 informal *the whole idea stinks*: **be very unpleasant**, be abhorrent, be despicable, be contemptible, be disgusting, be vile, be foul; N. Amer. informal suck.
3 informal *the whole affair stinks of a set-up*: **strongly suggest**, have all the hallmarks of, smack of, give the impression of; reek of, smell of.
▸ noun **1** *the stink of the place hit me as I went in*: **stench**, reek, foul smell, bad smell, fetidness, effluvium, malodour, malodorousness, miasma; Brit. informal pong, niff, hum; Scottish informal guff; Brit. rhyming slang pen and ink; N. Amer. informal funk; rare fetor, mephitis, noisomeness.
2 informal *she kicked up a tremendous stink*: **fuss**, commotion, rumpus, ruckus, trouble, outcry, uproar, brouhaha, furore; informal song and dance, to-do, carry-on, hoo-ha; Brit. informal row, kerfuffle; N. Amer. informal foofaraw.

stinker noun informal **1** *he's a real stinker*: **unpleasant person**; informal swine, beast, pig, rat, creep, bastard, louse, snake, snake in the grass, skunk, dog, weasel, lowlife, scumbag, heel, stinkpot, bad lot, son of a bitch, s.o.b., nasty piece of work; Brit. informal scrote; Irish informal spalpeen; N. Amer. informal rat fink, fink, dirtbag; Austral. informal dingo; NZ informal kuri; informal, dated rotter, hound, bounder, blighter; vulgar slang shit, sod; dated cad; archaic blackguard, dastard, knave, varlet, whoreson.
2 *it's been a stinker of a day*: **nightmare**, horror; informal beast, pig, swine, bummer, bastard, bitch; Austral./NZ informal cow; vulgar slang bugger, sod.

stinking adjective **1** *a mountain of stinking rubbish*: **foul-smelling**, evil-smelling, stinking to high heaven, reeking, fetid, malodorous, pungent, acrid, rank, putrid, noxious; W. Indian fresh; informal smelly, stinky, reeky; Brit. informal niffing, niffy, pongy, whiffy, humming; N. Amer. informal funky; literary noisome, mephitic; rare olid, miasmic, miasmal.
▷ANTONYMS sweet-smelling, aromatic.
2 informal *I've got a stinking cold and a sore throat*: **dreadful**, awful, terrible, frightful, ghastly, nasty, appalling, vile, very bad; Brit. informal rotten, shocking.
▷ANTONYMS mild, slight.

stint verb *he doesn't **stint on** wining and dining*: **skimp on**, scrimp on, be economical with, economize on, be sparing with, hold back on, be frugal with; **be mean with**, be parsimonious with, be niggardly with; limit, restrict; pinch pennies, spoil the ship for a ha'porth of tar; informal be stingy with, be mingy with, be tight-fisted with, be tight with.
▸ noun *his six-month stint on the surgical wards*: **spell**, stretch, period, time, turn, run, session, term; shift, tour of duty, watch.

stipulate verb *he stipulated certain conditions before their marriage*: **specify**, set down, set out, lay down, set forth, state clearly; demand, require, insist on, make a condition of, make a precondition/proviso of, prescribe, impose; Law provide.

stipulation noun *the only stipulation was that Edwards should retain his job as chairman for three years*: **condition**, precondition, proviso, provision, prerequisite, requisite, specification; demand, requirement, non-negotiable point; rider, caveat, qualification; clause; terms.

stir verb **1** *use a wooden spoon to stir the mixture | stir the ingredients together*: **mix**, blend, agitate; beat, whip, whisk, fold in; N. Amer. muddle.
2 *Travis stirred in his sleep*: **move slightly**, change one's position, twitch, quiver, tremble.
3 *a gentle breeze stirred the leaves*: **disturb**, **rustle**, shake, move, flutter, agitate, swish.
4 *when Ruth eventually stirred, it was nearly lunchtime*: **get up**, get out of bed, rouse oneself, bestir oneself, rise, show signs of life, be up and about, be active; **wake up**, awaken, waken; informal be up and doing, rise and shine, surface; literary arise.
▷ANTONYMS go to bed, retire.
5 *you won't even have to **stir out of** your office*: **leave**, depart from, go out of; **move from**, budge from, make a move from, shift from.
▷ANTONYMS stay, stay put.
6 *her imagination was stirred by the thought*: **arouse**, rouse, kindle, inspire, stimulate, excite, awaken, waken, quicken, animate, activate, galvanize, fire, electrify, whet; literary enkindle.
▷ANTONYMS stultify.
7 *the outbreak of the war stirred him to action*: **spur**, drive, rouse, prompt, propel, prod, move, motivate, encourage; urge, impel, induce; provoke, goad, prick, sting, incite, inflame; N. Amer. light a fire under.
□ **stir one's stumps** Brit. informal *'Stir your stumps, girl!' he shouted*: **be quick**, look smart, hurry up, speed up; informal make it snappy, get cracking, get moving, step on it, step on the gas, rattle one's dags; Brit. informal get one's skates on; N. Amer. informal get a wiggle on; S. African informal put foot.
□ **stir something up** *his remarks stirred up a furore*: **whip up**, work up, foment, fan the flames of, trigger, spark off, excite, provoke, instigate, incite; cause, precipitate, produce, generate, give rise to.
▷ANTONYMS stifle, suppress.
▸ noun *the event caused quite a stir*: **commotion**, disturbance, fuss, ado, excitement, flurry, uproar, ferment, brouhaha, furore, turmoil, sensation; informal to-do, hoo-ha, hullabaloo, flap, song and dance, splash; Brit. informal kerfuffle.

stirring adjective *stirring accounts of our heroic history*: **exciting**, thrilling, action-packed, gripping, riveting, dramatic, rousing, spirited, stimulating, moving, inspiring, inspirational, electrifying, passionate, impassioned, emotive, emotional, emotion-charged, heady, soul-stirring; N. Amer. stem-winding; rare inspiriting, anthemic.
▷ANTONYMS boring, pedestrian.

stitch noun *he was panting and had a stitch*: **sharp pain**, stabbing pain, shooting pain, stab of pain, pang, twinge, spasm.
▸ verb *the seam on her skirt needs stitching*: **sew**, baste, tack, seam, hem; **sew up**, repair, mend, darn.
□ **stitch someone up** Brit. informal *I've been stitched up by the Richardson gang*: **falsely incriminate**, get someone into trouble; informal frame, set up; Brit. informal fit someone up, drop someone in it.

S

stock noun **1** *cash-and-carry outlets rely on a rapid turnover of stock*: **merchandise**, **goods**, wares, items/articles for sale, commodities; rare vendibles.
2 *a stock of fuel | he had a good stock of jokes*: **store**, supply, stockpile, reserve, hoard, cache, reservoir, accumulation, quantity, pile, heap, load; fund, bank, pool, mine, repertoire, repertory, inventory; collection, selection, assortment, variety, range; rare amassment.
3 *all the stock were housed and fed in sheds*: **livestock**, **farm animals**, cattle, beasts; cows, sheep, pigs, horses, oxen, goats; flocks, herds.
4 *the railway's in-service stock is being repainted*: **rolling stock**, trains, locomotives, carriages, wagons; machinery, equipment, apparatus, appliances, implements.
5 *the value of the company's stock rose by 86 per cent*: **capital**, funds, assets, property.
6 *stock owned by foreign investors | blue-chip stocks*: **investments**, shares, holdings, securities, equities, bonds; portfolio.
7 *I felt I was right but my stock was low with this establishment*: **reputation**, standing, status, repute, position.
8 *he sighed and threw up his hands in a way that betrayed his French stock*: **descent**, **ancestry**, origin(s), parentage, pedigree, lineage, line, line of descent, heritage, birth, extraction, background, family, blood, bloodline, genealogy, beginnings; rare filiation, stirps.
9 *a pint of chicken stock*: **broth**; French bouillon.
10 *the stock of a tree*: **trunk**, tree trunk, stem, stalk; technical caudex.
11 *the stock of a weapon*: **handle**, butt, haft, grip, shaft, shank, helve.
□ **in stock** *we can order a book for you if we don't have it in stock*: **for sale**, on sale, available, on the shelf.
□ **take stock of** *you need to take stock of the situation first*: **review**, assess, reassess, weigh up, appraise, evaluate, re-evaluate, look carefully at, make an appraisal of; see how the land lies; informal size up.
▸ adjective **1** *the rug comes in six stock sizes*: **standard**, regular, ordinary, average; readily available, widely available; staple.
▷ANTONYMS non-standard.
2 *that has been the stock response to previous economic slowdowns*: **usual**, routine, predictable, set, standard, staple, customary, familiar, conventional, traditional, stereotyped, clichéd, hackneyed, unoriginal, derivative, formulaic, ready-made, well worn, overused, overworked, worn out, banal, trite, platitudinous, tired, run-of-the-mill, commonplace.
▷ANTONYMS original, unusual.
▸ verb **1** *most supermarkets now stock a range of organic produce*: **sell**, market; supply, keep, keep in stock, have, have for sale, carry, handle; offer, provide; trade in, deal in.
2 *the bathroom was stocked with a variety of expensive toilet articles*: **supply**, provide, equip, furnish, provision.
3 *I must **stock up** the fridge*: **fill**, fill up, load, restock, replenish.
4 *you'd better **stock up with** fuel*: **amass supplies of**, obtain a store of, buy up, stockpile, lay in, put away, put aside, put down, store up, collect, gather, accumulate, hoard, cache; informal squirrel away, salt away, stash away.

stockings plural noun **nylons**, stay-ups; tights; hosiery, hose; N. Amer. pantyhose.

stockpile noun *a stockpile of weapons*: **stock**, store, supply, accumulation, collection, reserve, hoard, cache; bank, pool, fund, mine, reservoir; arsenal; rare amassment.
▸ verb *food and ammunition had been stockpiled*: **store up**, amass, accumulate, hoard, cache, collect, gather, pile up, heap up, lay in, put away, put/set aside, put down, put by, put away for a rainy day, stow away, keep, keep in reserve, save; informal squirrel away, salt away, stash away.

stock-still adverb *he stood stock-still*. See **motionless**.

stocky adjective *a short, stocky man*: **thickset**, heavily built, sturdy, sturdily built, heavyset, bull-necked, chunky, solid, dumpy, stubby, stumpy, squat; burly, beefy, meaty, hulking, strapping, hefty; cobby; technical mesomorphic, pyknic; Austral./NZ nuggety; informal hulking; Brit. informal fubsy.
▷ANTONYMS slender, skinny.

stodgy adjective **1** *rich, stodgy puddings*: **indigestible**, starchy, filling, heavy, solid, substantial, lumpy, leaden.
▷ANTONYMS light, fluffy.
2 *a stodgy young man*: **boring**, **dull**, uninteresting, dreary, deadly; prosaic, staid, sedate; **stuffy**, pompous, conventional; informal fuddy-duddy, square.
3 *he used to write rather stodgy plays*: **boring**, **dull**, deadly dull, dull as ditchwater, uninteresting, dreary, turgid, tedious, dry, wearisome, heavy-going, unimaginative, uninspired, unexciting, unoriginal, derivative, monotonous, humdrum; laboured, wooden, ponderous, plodding, pedantic, banal, verbose.
▷ANTONYMS interesting, lively.

stoical adjective *my mother was more stoical and scorned such self-pity*: **long-suffering**, uncomplaining, patient, forbearing, accepting, stoic, with the patience of Job, resigned, impassive, unemotional, phlegmatic, philosophical, fatalistic, imperturbable, calm, cool, unexcitable, stolid; informal unflappable; rare longanimous.

stoicism noun *she accepted her sufferings with remarkable stoicism*: **patience**, forbearance, resignation, lack of protest, lack of complaint, fortitude, endurance, acceptance, acceptance of the inevitable, fatalism, philosophicalness, impassivity, dispassion, phlegm, imperturbability, calmness, coolness, cool; stolidness; informal unflappability; rare longanimity.

stoke verb *Dad returned to his chair while I stoked the fire*: **add fuel to**, mend, keep burning, tend, fuel.

stole noun **shawl**, scarf, wrap, boa, tippet, cape.

stolid adjective *a stolid, slow-speaking man*: **impassive**, phlegmatic, unemotional, calm, placid, unexcitable; apathetic, uninterested, unimaginative, indifferent; dull, bovine, lumpish, wooden, slow, lethargic, torpid, stupid.
▷ANTONYMS emotional, lively, imaginative.

stomach noun **1** *she had pains in her stomach*: **abdomen**, belly, gut, middle; informal tummy, tum, breadbasket, insides; Austral. informal bingy.
2 *his fat stomach*: **paunch**, pot belly, beer belly, girth; informal beer gut, pot, tummy, spare tyre, middle-aged spread; Scottish informal kyte; N. Amer. informal bay window; dated, humorous corporation.
3 *she had no stomach for food | he had little stomach for a fight*: **appetite**, taste, hunger; **inclination**, desire, thirst, liking, fondness, relish, fancy, mind.
▸ verb **1** *if you cannot stomach orange juice, try apple juice*: **digest**, keep down, find palatable, manage to eat/consume, swallow.
2 *I've had just about all I can stomach of your malicious slanders*: **tolerate**, put up with, take, stand, endure, accept, swallow, bear, support, brook, submit to, countenance; Scottish thole; informal stick, hack, abide; Brit. informal wear, be doing with; archaic suffer.

Word links **stomach**

gastric relating to the stomach
gastroenterology branch of medicine concerning the stomach
gastritis inflammation of the stomach
gastroenteritis inflammation of the stomach and intestines
gastrotomy removal of the stomach
gastroplasty repair of the stomach
gastrostomy opening of the stomach
gastrotomy incision of the stomach

stomach ache noun **indigestion**, dyspepsia; colic, gripe; informal bellyache, tummy ache, collywobbles.

stone noun **1** *a gang of youths threw stones and missiles at police officers*: **rock**, pebble, boulder; (**stones**) cobbles, gravel, scree; rare concretion.
2 *a memorial stone had been erected in place of the wooden cross*: **gravestone**, headstone, tombstone; tablet, monument, monolith, obelisk.
3 *cracked paving stones*: **slab**, flagstone, flag, sett.
4 *a gold ring with a small red stone*: **gem**, gemstone, jewel, precious stone, semi-precious stone, brilliant; informal rock, sparkler; archaic bijou.
5 *cut the fruit in half and remove the stones*: **kernel**, seed, pip, pit; technical endocarp.

Word links **stone**

lithic, **lapidary** relating to stone
litho- related prefix, as in *lithography*
gemmology study of precious stones

stony adjective **1** *a stony path*: **rocky**, rock-strewn, pebbly, gravelly, shingly, gritty; rough, hard, rugged.
▷ANTONYMS smooth.
2 *his questions were met with a stony stare*: **unfriendly**, cold, chilly, frosty, icy, frigid; hard, flinty, steely, stern, severe; fixed, expressionless, blank, poker-faced, deadpan; unfeeling, uncaring, unsympathetic, lacking compassion, insensitive, unmoved, indifferent, unresponsive, cold-hearted, callous, heartless, tough, hard-hearted, stony-hearted, inflexible, unbending, unyielding, uncompromising, merciless, pitiless, ruthless, unforgiving, hostile; literary adamantine; rare indurate, marble-hearted, Rhadamanthine.
▷ANTONYMS friendly, sympathetic.

stony broke adjective Brit. informal See **penniless**.

stooge noun **1** *a government stooge*: **underling**, minion, lackey, subordinate, assistant; henchman, myrmidon; **puppet**, pawn, cat's paw, instrument, tool, creature; informal sidekick, skivvy; Brit. informal dogsbody, poodle.
2 *a comedian's stooge*: **butt**, foil, straight man.

stoop verb **1** *Linda stooped to pick up the bottles*: **bend down**, bend, lean over, lean down, kneel, crouch down, squat down, hunker down, hunch down; N. Amer. informal scooch.
2 *he stooped his head*: **lower**, bend, incline, bow, duck.
3 *he tends to stoop when he walks*: **hunch one's shoulders**, walk with a stoop, be round-shouldered.
4 *are you suggesting that I would **stoop to** blackmail?* **lower oneself**, sink, descend, resort; be reduced, go as far as, sink as low as.
▸ noun *a tall, thin man with a stoop*: **hunch**, droop/sag of the shoulders; round-shoulderedness; technical curvature of the spine, kyphosis.

S

stop verb **1** *drastic measures are needed to stop the decline*: **put an end to**, put a stop to, bring to an end, end, bring to a stop, halt, bring to a halt; finish, bring to a close, terminate, bring to a standstill, wind up, discontinue, cut short, interrupt, nip in the bud; immobilize, paralyse, deactivate, shut down.
▷ANTONYMS start, begin; continue.
2 *you really should stop smoking*: **cease**, discontinue, refrain from, desist from, forbear from, break off, call a halt to, call it a day; give up, abandon, abstain from, cut out; Nautical belay; informal quit, leave off, knock off, pack in, lay off, give over, jack in.
3 *the car stopped outside a terraced house*: **pull up**, draw up, come to a stop, come to a halt, come to rest, pull in, pull over; park; Austral. prop.
4 *the music stopped | work stopped at the mine in 1948*: **come to an end**, come to a stop, cease, end, finish, draw to a close, be over, conclude, terminate, come to a standstill; pause, break off; peter out, fade away.
5 *she pressed a pad against his side to stop the flow of blood*: **stem**, staunch, hold back, check, dam, slow, restrict, restrain; N. Amer. stanch; archaic stay.
6 *he tried to stop her leaving the house*: **prevent**, hinder, obstruct, impede, block, bar, preclude; dissuade from.
▷ANTONYMS encourage.
7 *a court action brought by protesters attempting to stop the road plan*: **thwart**, baulk, foil, frustrate, stand in the way of, forestall; scotch, derail; informal put paid to, put the stopper on, put the kibosh on, do for, stymie; Brit. informal scupper.
▷ANTONYMS expedite.
8 *talks broke down, and the employers stopped the strikers' wages*: **withhold**, suspend, keep back, hold back, refuse to pay, cut off, discontinue.
9 *he tried to stop the hole with the heel of his boot*: **block (up)**, plug, close (up), fill (up); seal, caulk; bung up, clog (up), jam (up), choke (up); occlude.
□ **stop off/over** *he decided to stop over in Paris*: **break one's journey**, take a break, pause; stay, remain, put up, lodge, rest; formal sojourn; archaic or literary tarry.
▶ **noun 1** *all business came to a stop*: **halt**, end, finish, close, standstill; cessation, conclusion, termination, stoppage, discontinuation, discontinuance; pause.
▷ANTONYMS start, beginning, continuation.
2 *a brief stop at the small town of Kenora*: **break**, stopover, stop-off, stay, rest; formal sojourn.
3 *she got off the bus at the last stop*: **bus stop**, stopping place, halt; terminus, terminal, depot, station; Brit. fare stage, stage.
4 *a stop at the end of a sentence*: **full stop**, full point, point; punctuation mark; N. Amer. period.
□ **put a stop to** *new legislation could well put a stop to this practice*: **bring to an end**, halt, put an end to, end, bring to a stop, bring to a halt; finish, bring to a close, terminate, bring to a standstill, wind up, discontinue, nip in the bud, put a/the lid on; quell, quash, subdue, suppress, stifle; informal put paid to, put the kibosh on, put the stopper on, do for.

stopgap noun *such tissue transplants are only a stopgap until more sophisticated alternatives can be found*: **temporary solution**, improvisation, expedient, makeshift, last resort; substitute, stand-in.
▶ **adjective** *a stopgap solution | a stopgap prime minister*: **temporary**, provisional, interim, pro tem, short-term, working, makeshift, improvised, emergency, impromptu, rough and ready; caretaker, acting, stand-in, fill-in; Nautical jury-rigged, jury; rare expediential.
▷ANTONYMS permanent.

stopover noun *a brief stopover in the United Kingdom en route to the US*: **stay**, stop, break, stop-off, visit; formal sojourn.

stoppage noun **1** *the stoppage of grain exports*: **discontinuation**, discontinuance, stopping, halting, halt, cessation, termination, end, finish; interruption, suspension, breaking off.
▷ANTONYMS start, beginning, continuation.
2 *a two-day stoppage by workers in the hotel industry*: **strike**, walkout, shutdown, closure; industrial action.
3 *the stoppage of the blood supply*: **obstruction**, blocking; technical occlusion, arrest, stasis, suppression.
4 *a stoppage in the petrol supply*: **blockage**, obstruction, block; airlock.
5 Brit. *she was paid £3.40 an hour before stoppages*: **deduction**, subtraction.

stopper noun *a cologne bottle with a cork and chrome stopper*: **cork**, lid, cap, top; **plug**, bung, spigot, spile; N. Amer. stopple.

store noun **1** *a store of food | her vast store of knowledge*: **supply**, stock, stockpile, reserve, cache, hoard, accumulation, cumulation, quantity, pile, heap, load; fund, bank, pool, mine, wealth, deposit, reservoir, inventory, repertoire, repertory; rare amassment.
2 *a grain store*: **storeroom**, storehouse, warehouse, repository, depository, entrepôt; granary, silo; larder, pantry; arsenal, armoury; Brit. historical still room; archaic garner, spence.
3 (**stores**) *there was a vital need to recruit fresh men and to replenish the stores*: **supplies**, provisions, stocks, rations, food, foodstuffs; formal comestibles, provender.
4 *a DIY store*: **shop**, retail outlet, reseller, department store, chain store, emporium; supermarket, hypermarket, superstore; mart; informal shed; N. Amer. informal big box.
□ **set store by** *Gwen set great store by good manners*: **value**, attach great importance to, put a high value on, put a premium on; **think highly of**, hold in (high) regard, have a high opinion of, admire, appreciate, respect, prize, esteem; informal rate.
▶ **verb 1** *the animals need a place to store food for the winter*: **keep**, keep in reserve, stow, stockpile, lay in/aside, set aside, put away, put down, put to one side, deposit, save, hoard, cache; stock up with/on, get in supplies of, collect, gather, accumulate, cumulate, amass; husband, reserve, preserve; informal put away for a rainy day, squirrel away, salt away, stash.
▷ANTONYMS use.
2 *furniture that had been stored in the attic for thirty years*: **put into storage**, put in store, stow (away), put away; warehouse.
▷ANTONYMS discard.

storehouse noun **warehouse**, depository, repository, store, storeroom, depot, entrepôt; granary, silo; treasury, vault, strongroom; arsenal, armoury; in India & Malaysia godown; archaic garner.

storey noun *a small flat on the second storey*: **floor**, level, tier; flight, deck; piano nobile, mezzanine, entresol.

storm noun **1** *the severe storms that battered Orkney earlier this year*: **tempest**, squall; gale, hurricane, tornado, cyclone, typhoon; thunderstorm, cloudburst, downpour, rainstorm, hailstorm, deluge, monsoon, tropical storm, electrical storm; snowstorm, blizzard; dust storm, dust devil; N. Amer. williwaw, ice storm, windstorm; in central Asia buran.
2 *he's at the centre of a drugs storm in Germany*: **uproar**, commotion, furore, brouhaha, trouble, disturbance, hue and cry, upheaval; controversy, scandal, argument, fracas, fight, war of words; informal to-do, hoo-ha, rumpus, hullabaloo, ballyhoo, ructions, stink; Brit. informal row.
3 *the decision provoked a storm of protest*: **outburst**, outbreak, explosion, eruption, outpouring, surge, upsurge, avalanche, torrent, flood, deluge; blaze, flare-up.
4 *a storm of bullets*: **volley**, salvo, fusillade, barrage, discharge, shower, spray, hail, rain.
5 *an attempt at a storm on the castle was beaten back by defenders*: **assault**, attack, onslaught, offensive, charge, raid, foray, sortie, rush, descent, incursion, thrust, push, blitz, blitzkrieg, aggression; archaic onset.
▶ **verb 1** *she snatched up her coat and stormed out of the kitchen*: **stride angrily**, stomp, march, charge, stalk, flounce, stamp, fling.
2 *police stormed the building*: **attack**, charge, rush, conduct an offensive on, make an onslaught on, make a raid/foray/sortie on, descend on, take by storm, attempt to capture.
3 *his mother stormed at him and ordered him to go to bed*: **rant**, rave, rant and rave, shout, bellow, roar, thunder, rage, explode.

stormy adjective **1** *the weather was wet and stormy | a stormy wind was blowing*: **blustery**, squally, wild, tempestuous, turbulent, windy, gusty, blowy, rainy, thundery, rough, choppy; angry, dirty, foul, nasty, inclement; howling, roaring, raging, furious; rare boisterous.
▷ANTONYMS calm, fine.
2 *the votes came after a long and stormy debate | their relationship had been stormy*: **angry**, heated, fiery, fierce, impassioned, passionate, 'lively'; **tempestuous**, turbulent, tumultuous, explosive, volatile, violent, intense.
▷ANTONYMS peaceful.

story noun **1** *an adventure story*: **tale**, narrative, account, recital; anecdote; chronicle, history; informal yarn, spiel.
2 *the novel has a good story*: **plot**, storyline, scenario, chain of events; technical diegesis.
3 *the story appeared in the papers in the usual tabloid style*: **news item**, news report, article, feature, piece; exclusive, exposé; spoiler; informal scoop.
4 *there have been a lot of stories going round, as you can imagine*: **rumour**, piece of gossip, piece of hearsay, whisper; speculation; French on dit; informal kidology; Austral./NZ informal furphy.
5 *Harper changed his story about how the fire started*: **testimony**, statement, report, account, version, description, representation.
6 *Ellie never told stories—she had always believed in the truth*: **lie**, fib, falsehood, untruth, fabrication, fiction, piece of fiction; white lie; Irish pishogue; W. African nancy story; informal tall story, fairy story, fairy tale, cock and bull story, shaggy-dog story, whopper, terminological inexactitude, fish story; Brit. informal pork pie, porky pie, porky.
▷ANTONYMS the truth.

storyteller noun **narrator**, teller of tales, taleteller, spinner of yarns; raconteur, raconteuse; writer, author, novelist, chronicler, fabulist; in Africa griot; in India kathak; Austral. informal magsman; rare anecdotist, anecdotalist.

stout adjective **1** *a short stout man*: **fat**, fattish, plump, portly, rotund, roly-poly, pot-bellied, round, dumpy, chunky, broad in the beam, overweight, fleshy, paunchy, corpulent; buxom, well upholstered, well covered, well padded, of ample proportions, ample, rounded, well rounded; stocky, burly, bulky, hefty, meaty, heavily built, solidly built, thickset, heavyset, sturdy, well built; informal hulking, tubby, pudgy, beefy, porky, blubbery, poddy; Brit. informal podgy, fubsy; N. Amer. informal zaftig, corn-fed, lard-assed; archaic pursy; rare abdominous.
▷ANTONYMS thin, slender.
2 *Billy had armed himself with a stout stick | stout leather shoes*: **strong**,

S

sturdy, heavy, solid, substantial, robust, tough, strongly made, durable, hard-wearing; thick.
▷ANTONYMS flimsy, fragile.
3 *the garrison put up a stout resistance*: **determined**, full of determination, vigorous, forceful, spirited, stout-hearted; **staunch**, steadfast, stalwart, firm, resolute, unyielding, unbending, unfaltering, unswerving, unwavering, unflinching, stubborn, dogged; **brave**, bold, plucky, courageous, valiant, valorous, gallant, fearless, undaunted, dauntless, doughty, mettlesome, unafraid, intrepid, manly, heroic, lionhearted; N. Amer. rock-ribbed; informal gutsy, spunky.
▷ANTONYMS half-hearted, feeble, cowardly.

stout-hearted adjective *a stout-hearted man who was not easily deterred*: **brave, determined**, full of determination, courageous, bold, plucky, spirited, valiant, valorous, gallant, fearless, undaunted, dauntless, doughty, unafraid, intrepid, manly, heroic, lionhearted; **stalwart**, staunch, steadfast, firm, resolute, unfaltering, unswerving, unwavering, unflinching; N. Amer. rock-ribbed; informal gutsy, spunky.
▷ANTONYMS cowardly, feeble.

stove noun **oven**, range; charcoal burner, furnace; Brit. cooker; Indian tandoor; trademark Aga, Primus.

stow verb *Barney began stowing her luggage into the boot*: **pack**, load, store; place, put, put away, deposit; bundle, cram, jam, wedge, stash; informal stuff, shove.
▷ANTONYMS unload, remove.
□ **stow away** *he stowed away on a ship bound for South Africa*: **hide**, conceal oneself, secrete oneself; travel secretly.

straddle verb 1 *she straddled the motorbike and revved it up*: **sit/stand astride**, bestride, bestraddle; mount, get on.
2 *a mountain range straddling the Franco-Swiss border*: **lie on both sides of**, be situated on both sides of, extend across; span.
3 *a man who had straddled the issue of taxes*: **be equivocal about**, be undecided about, be non-committal about, equivocate about, vacillate about, waver about; Brit. hum and haw; informal sit on the fence.

strafe verb *military aircraft strafed the village*. See **bomb** (sense 1 of the verb).

straggle verb 1 *a few of the men were straggling some half a mile behind the rest*: **trail**, lag, dawdle, amble, wander, walk slowly, meander, drift; fall behind, bring up the rear; be strung out.
2 *his thin grey hair straggled over the collar of his coat*: **grow untidily**, be messy, be dishevelled, be unkempt.
3 *copses of beech and alder straggled along the banks*: **spread irregularly**, sprawl, be scattered, be dispersed.

straggly adjective *a thin woman with straggly hair*: **untidy**, messy, unkempt, straggling, dishevelled, bedraggled; informal ratty.

straight adjective 1 *the aircraft continued on a straight course | a long, straight road*: **unswerving**, undeviating, linear, direct, as straight as an arrow, uncurving, unbending.
▷ANTONYMS winding, zigzag.
2 *one of us must have knocked that picture—it's not straight*: **level**, even, true, in line, aligned, square, plumb, properly positioned; symmetrical; vertical, upright, perpendicular; horizontal.
▷ANTONYMS crooked, askew.
3 *it'll take a long time to get the place straight*: **in order**, tidy, neat and tidy, neat, shipshape (and Bristol fashion), in apple-pie order, orderly, spick and span, organized, arranged, sorted out, straightened out, trim, spruce; informal together.
▷ANTONYMS untidy, messy.
4 *a straight answer*: **honest**, direct, frank, candid, truthful, sincere, forthright, straightforward, plain-spoken, plain-speaking, plain, blunt, downright, outspoken, straight from the shoulder, no-nonsense, unequivocal, unambiguous, unqualified, unvarnished; informal upfront; archaic round, free-spoken.
▷ANTONYMS indirect, evasive.
5 *action is never effective without straight thinking*: **logical**, rational, clear, lucid, sound, coherent, unemotional, dispassionate.
▷ANTONYMS irrational, illogical.
6 *three straight wins*: **successive**, in succession, consecutive, in a row, one after the other; running, uninterrupted, solid, unbroken; informal on the trot.
7 *straight brandy*: **undiluted**, neat, unmixed, unadulterated, pure, unblended, uncut; N. Amer. informal straight up.
▷ANTONYMS diluted.
8 informal *she won't stand for anything like that—she's too straight*: **respectable**, upright, upstanding, honourable, honest, on the level, decent, right-minded, law-abiding; **conventional**, conservative, traditional, conformist, old-fashioned, strait-laced, unadventurous; informal stuffy, square, fuddy-duddy.
▶**adverb** 1 *he looked me straight in the eyes | the ball hit him straight on the head*: **right**, directly, squarely, full, plumb; informal smack, bang, slap bang; N. Amer. informal spang, smack dab.
2 *she drove straight home*: **directly**, right, by a direct route, without deviating, in a beeline; as the crow flies, by the shortest route.
3 *I'll call you straight back*: **right away**, straight away, without delay, immediately, directly, at once, as soon as possible, a.s.a.p.; French tout de suite; informal toot sweet, before you can say Jack Robinson, before you can say knife; archaic straightway, instanter.
▷ANTONYMS later, eventually.
4 *I told her straight that it was over*: **frankly**, directly, straight out, candidly, honestly, forthrightly, outspokenly, plainly, point-blank, bluntly, flatly, roundly, straight from the shoulder, with no holds barred, without beating about the bush, without mincing words, unequivocally, unambiguously, in plain English, to someone's face; informal pulling no punches; Brit. informal straight up.
5 *he's so wound up over you he can't think straight*: **logically**, rationally, clearly, lucidly, coherently, cogently, unemotionally, dispassionately; properly, correctly.
□ **go straight reform**, mend one's ways, turn over a new leaf, make a fresh start; informal get back on the straight and narrow.
▷ANTONYMS reoffend.
□ **straight away** *okay, I'll get on to it straight away*: **at once**, right away, now, right now, this/that (very) minute, this/that instant, immediately, instantly, in/like a flash, directly, on the spot, forthwith, without further/more ado, promptly, quickly, without delay, then and there, there and then, here and now, a.s.a.p., as soon as possible, as quickly as possible, with all speed; N. Amer. in short order; French tout de suite; informal straight off, toot sweet, double quick, in double quick time, p.d.q. (pretty damn quick), pronto, before you can say Jack Robinson, from the word go; N. Amer. informal lickety-split; Indian informal ekdam; archaic straight, straightway, instanter, forthright.
▷ANTONYMS later, eventually.
□ **straight from the shoulder** *he spoke straight from the shoulder*: **frankly**, candidly, honestly, directly, forthrightly, bluntly, plainly, roundly, explicitly, outspokenly, unequivocally, unambiguously, with no holds barred, without beating about the bush, without mincing words, man to man, woman to woman; informal pulling no punches.
▷ANTONYMS evasively.

Word links **straight**

ortho- related prefix
orthodontics straightening of teeth

straighten verb 1 *Rory straightened his tie | she brushed her hair and straightened her clothing*: **make straight**, align; adjust, arrange, rearrange, tidy, make tidy, neaten, spruce up; uncoil, unkink, uncurl.
2 *he didn't know how to* ***straighten*** *things* ***out*** *with Viola*: **put/set right**, sort out, iron out, clear up, settle, resolve, find a solution to, put in order, tidy up, regulate, regularize, rectify, repair, remedy; disentangle, unravel, unsnarl, untangle; informal patch up.
▷ANTONYMS confuse, complicate.
3 *he* ***straightened up****, using the bedside table for support*: **stand up**, stand up straight, stand upright, straighten one's back.
▷ANTONYMS bend over.

straightforward adjective 1 *the process was remarkably straightforward*: **uncomplicated**, simple, easy, effortless, painless, undemanding, unexacting; elementary, plain sailing, a five-finger exercise, child's play; routine; informal as easy as falling off a log, as easy as pie, as easy as ABC, a piece of cake, a cinch, a snip, easy-peasy, no sweat, a doddle, money for old rope, money for jam, kids' stuff, a breeze, a doss, a cakewalk; N. Amer. informal duck soup, a snap; Austral./NZ informal a bludge, a snack; S. African informal a piece of old tackle.
▷ANTONYMS complicated, difficult.
2 *a straightforward man*: **honest, frank**, candid, open, truthful, sincere, on the level, honest-to-goodness; **forthright**, plain-speaking, direct, unambiguous, straight from the shoulder, downright, not afraid to call a spade a spade; informal upfront, on the square; N. Amer. informal two-fisted, on the up and up; archaic free-spoken, round.
▷ANTONYMS evasive, guarded, disingenuous.

strain[1] verb 1 *take care that you don't strain yourself*: **overtax**, overwork, overburden, overextend, overreach, overtask, make too many demands on, run/work oneself into the ground, exert excessively, drive too far, exert to the limit, push to the limit; exhaust, wear out, fatigue, tire, tax; overdo it, work too hard; informal knacker, knock oneself out.
2 *on cold days you are more likely to strain a muscle*: **injure**, hurt, damage, impair; pull, wrench, tear, twist, sprain, rick, crick.
3 *we strained to haul the guns up an almost perpendicular slope*: **struggle**, labour, toil, make a supreme effort, make every effort, spare no effort, strain every nerve, try very hard, strive, break one's back, push/drive oneself to the limit, do one's best; informal pull out all the stops, go all out, give it one's all, bend/lean over backwards, give it one's best shot, bust a gut, break one's neck, do one's damnedest, kill oneself; Austral. informal go for the doctor.
4 *the rapid population growth is straining the supply of usable water*: **make severe demands on**, make excessive demands on, overtax, be too much for; exceed the limits of, drain, sap, use up, exceed the range/scope of, overstep; test, tax, put a strain on, fray.

5 *the bear strained at the chain around its neck*: **pull**, tug, heave, haul, jerk; push; informal yank.
6 *strain the mixture to remove the seeds*: **sieve**, sift, filter, screen, riddle, separate; percolate; leach; rare filtrate, griddle.
▶ **noun 1** *the rope snapped under the strain*: **tension**, tightness, tautness, shear, distension; rare tensity.
2 *a severe stomach muscle strain*: **injury**; sprain, wrench, twist, rick.
3 *the overwhelming strain of her job*: **pressure**, demands, burdens, exertions; stress, tension; informal hassle.
4 *Melissa was showing signs of strain*: **stress**, tension, nervous tension, anxiety; exhaustion, fatigue, tiredness, weariness, pressure of work, overwork, duress.
▷ANTONYMS relaxation.
5 (**strains**) *the soothing strains of Brahms's lullaby*: **sound**, music; melody, tune, air, song.

strain[2] **noun 1** *a different strain of flu | a strain of mice*: **variety**, kind, type, sort; breed, genus.
2 *Hawthorne was of Puritan strain*: **descent**, **ancestry**, stock, origin(s), parentage, pedigree, lineage, line, heritage, birth, extraction, derivation, background, family, blood, bloodline, genealogy, roots; rare filiation, stirps.
3 *there was a* ***strain of*** *insanity on her mother's side of the family*: **tendency to**, susceptibility to, propensity to, proneness to, proclivity to, inclination to; trait, characteristic, disposition.
4 *they have injected a strain of solemnity into a genre of film renowned for its irreverence*: **element**, strand, streak, vein, note, trace, touch, dash, tinge, suggestion, hint, suspicion; French soupçon.
5 archaic *he continued in the same strain for over an hour*: **tone**, spirit, vein, tenor, temper; manner, way, style.

strained adjective 1 *a strained silence | relations between the two countries were strained*: **awkward**, **tense**, uneasy, uncomfortable, fraught, edgy, difficult, troubled, embarrassed, unrelaxed, stilted.
▷ANTONYMS relaxed, friendly.
2 *Jean's pale, strained face*: **drawn**, careworn, worn, pinched, tired, exhausted, weary, fatigued, drained; haggard, hollow-cheeked.
3 *he gave her a strained smile*: **forced**, constrained, laboured, wooden, stiff, self-conscious, hollow, unnatural; **artificial**, insincere, false, affected, put-on.
▷ANTONYMS natural.

strainer noun sieve, colander, filter, sifter, riddle, screen; archaic griddle.

strait noun 1 *the island is separated from the mainland by a strait about six miles wide*: **channel**, sound, narrows, inlet, stretch of water, arm of the sea, sea passage, neck; Scottish kyle.
2 (**straits**) *by Christmas, the company was in* ***desperate straits***: **a bad/difficult situation**, a sorry condition, difficulty, trouble, crisis, a mess, a predicament, a plight, a tight corner; informal a pretty/fine kettle of fish, hot water, deep water, a jam, a hole, a bind, a fix, a scrape.

straitened adjective *he died in 1886, leaving the family* ***in straitened circumstances***: **impoverished**, poverty-stricken, poor, destitute, penniless, on one's beam-ends, as poor as a church mouse, without a sou, dirt poor, in penury, penurious, impecunious, indigent, needy, needful, in need/want, unable to make ends meet, down and out, necessitous, beggarly, moneyless, bankrupt, in reduced circumstances; Brit. on the breadline, without a penny (to one's name); informal broke, flat broke, cleaned out, strapped for cash, strapped, on one's uppers; Brit. informal stony broke, skint, without two pennies/farthings to rub together, in Queer Street; N. Amer. informal stone broke; rare pauperized, beggared.

strait-laced adjective *his strait-laced parents were horrified*: **prim and proper**, prim, proper, prudish, priggish, puritanical, moralistic, prissy, mimsy, niminy-piminy, shockable, Victorian, old-maidish, schoolmistressy, schoolmarmish, governessy; conventional, conservative, old-fashioned, stuffy, staid, of the old school, narrow-minded; informal goody-goody, starchy, square, fuddy-duddy, stick-in-the-mud; rare Grundyish, Pecksniffian.
▷ANTONYMS permissive, broad-minded.

strand[1] **noun 1** *strands of wool*: **thread**, filament, fibre; length, piece, string; ply; technical fibril.
2 *a few strands of blonde hair*: **lock**, tress, wisp, tendril; curl, ringlet.
3 *his introduction draws the ideological strands of this ambitious work together*: **element**, component, factor, ingredient, aspect, feature; theme, strain.

strand[2] **noun** literary *they'd gone for a walk along the strand*: **seashore**, shore, beach, sands, foreshore, shoreline; coast, seaside, seaboard, waterfront, front, waterside, water's edge; technical littoral; French plage.

stranded adjective 1 *the stranded ship*: **beached**, grounded, run aground, high and dry, stuck; shipwrecked, wrecked; marooned, cast away.
2 *she was left stranded in a city she hardly knew*: **helpless**, without help/assistance, without resources, in difficulties; in the lurch, abandoned, forsaken, deserted; trapped, cut off.

strange adjective 1 *suddenly, I heard a strange noise | strange things have been happening round here*: **unusual**, odd, curious, peculiar, funny, bizarre, weird, uncanny, queer, unexpected, unfamiliar, abnormal, atypical, anomalous, untypical, different, out of the ordinary, out of the way, extraordinary, remarkable, puzzling, mystifying, mysterious, perplexing, baffling, unaccountable, inexplicable, incongruous, uncommon, irregular, singular, deviant, aberrant, freak, freakish, surreal; suspicious, dubious, questionable; eerie, unnatural; French outré; Scottish unco; informal fishy, creepy, spooky; Brit. informal rum; N. Amer. informal bizarro.
▷ANTONYMS ordinary, usual.
2 *he's a very strange man | their strange clothes and hairstyles*: **weird**, **eccentric**, odd, peculiar, funny, bizarre, unusual, abnormal; **unconventional**, idiosyncratic, outlandish, offbeat, freakish, quirky, quaint, zany, off-centre; informal wacky, way out, freaky, kooky, kinky, oddball, like nothing on earth, cranky; N. Amer. informal screwy, off the wall, wacko; Austral./NZ informal, dated dilly.
▷ANTONYMS normal, conventional.
3 *when children visit a strange house, they are often a little shy*: **unfamiliar**, unknown, new, alien, previously unencountered.
▷ANTONYMS familiar.
4 *Jean was beginning to feel a little strange*: **ill**, unwell, poorly, indisposed, not (very) well, not oneself, out of sorts, not up to par, under/below par, peaky, liverish, sick, queasy, nauseous; Brit. off, off colour; informal under the weather, not up to snuff, funny, peculiar, crummy, lousy, rough; Brit. informal ropy, grotty; Scottish informal wabbit; Austral./NZ informal crook; dated queer, seedy.
▷ANTONYMS well.
5 *it had been a long time since she'd seen him and she felt strange*: **ill at ease**, uneasy, edgy, uncomfortable, awkward, self-conscious, embarrassed; out of place, like a fish out of water, disorientated.
▷ANTONYMS relaxed.

Choose the right word **strange, odd, curious, peculiar**

These words are all applied to things that are unusual or unfamiliar; they generally also suggest that something is in some way surprising.

Strange is the most neutral term for something that is not expected or is hard to understand or explain (*this is strange behaviour for a left-wing party | he looked at her with a strange expression*). This is the only word of the four that can be used in the expression *strange to say*, as in *I went to see 'Fallen Angels', which, strange to say, is a hit*.

Odd gives a stronger sense that the speaker or writer is perplexed (*do you think it odd that I pay her bills? | they were an odd family*).

Describing something as **curious** implies that one finds it not only strange or puzzling but also interesting or appealing (*the church has a curious history | the room is filled with a curious mixture of people*). It rarely has the connotation of deviance that the other words can have.

Something described as **peculiar** is felt to be very strange, even disturbingly so (*he was struck by the peculiar appearance of a group of birds | whoever thought up that joke has a peculiar sense of humour*).

strangeness noun *the strangeness of Eliot's behaviour*: **oddity**, **eccentricity**, oddness, peculiarity, curiousness, bizarreness, weirdness, queerness, unexpectedness, unusualness, abnormality, atypicality, unfamiliarity, unaccountability, inexplicability, incongruity, incongruousness, outlandishness, irregularity, singularity; freakishness, surrealness.
▷ANTONYMS ordinariness, conventionality.

stranger noun 1 *the man standing beside her was a complete stranger*: **unknown person**; Scottish unco.
2 *he was a stranger in the town*: **newcomer**, new arrival, incomer; visitor; foreigner, outsider, alien; N. English offcomer; Austral. informal blow-in.
□ **a stranger to** *Harker was a stranger to self-doubt*: **unaccustomed to**, unfamiliar with, unused to, unacquainted with, new to, fresh to, inexperienced in, unpractised in, unversed in, unconversant with; archaic strange to.

strangle verb 1 *the victim was strangled with a scarf*: **throttle**, choke, garrotte; asphyxiate, stifle; informal strangulate.
2 *she strangled a sob*: **suppress**, smother, stifle, repress, restrain, hold back, hold in, fight back, bite back, gulp back, swallow, choke back, check.
▷ANTONYMS let out.
3 *too much security is strangling commercial activity in the town*: **hamper**, hinder, impede, restrict, interfere with, inhibit, hold back, curb, check, restrain, constrain; prevent, put an end/stop to, stop, quash, squash, stamp out, destroy, crush, extinguish, deaden, damp down, subdue, suppress, repress; silence, muffle, mute, gag.
▷ANTONYMS encourage, promote.

strap noun *he undid the thick leather straps*: **thong**, tie, cord, band, belt, tape; leash, lead.
▶ **verb 1** *a leather bag was strapped on to the bicycle frame*: **fasten**, secure, tie, bind, make fast, lash; buckle; truss, pinion.
2 *the goalkeeper's knee was* ***strapped up***: **bandage**, bind.
3 *his father had strapped him*: **beat**, flog, whip, leather, belt, thrash, lash, horsewhip, birch, cane, strike, hit, clout; informal wallop, whack, tan someone's hide, give someone a (good) hiding, beat the living daylights out of, lather, larrup; N. Amer. informal whale; archaic stripe, thong.

S

strapping adjective *they had three strapping sons*: **big**, **strong**, well built, sturdily built, sturdy, brawny, burly, broad-shouldered, muscular, muscly, well muscled, robust, rugged, lusty, Herculean; informal hunky, beefy, husky; dated stalwart; literary thewy, stark.
▷ANTONYMS puny, weedy.

stratagem noun *he deployed various cunning stratagems*: **plan**, scheme, tactic, manoeuvre, move, course/line of action, ploy, gambit, device, wile; trick, ruse, plot, machination, subterfuge, artifice, contrivance, expedient, dodge, deception, deceit; Brit. informal wheeze; Austral. informal lurk; archaic shift.

strategic adjective **1** *a strategic move towards their long-term goal of gaining international recognition*: **planned**, calculated, deliberate; tactical, politic, judicious, prudent, clever, shrewd, well thought out.
▷ANTONYMS random.
2 *Russia's retention of strategic bases in the region*: **essential**, key, vital, crucial, critical, important.
▷ANTONYMS unimportant.

strategy noun **1** *the government's economic strategy*: **master plan**, grand design, game plan, plan of action, plan, policy, proposed action, scheme, blueprint, programme, procedure, approach, schedule; tactics, set of tactics.
2 *the process could revolutionize military strategy*: **the art of war**, military science, military tactics; generalship.

Easily confused words **strategy or tactics?**

Both these words denote approaches adopted after reasoning about the best way to achieve one's aims. In military usage, **strategy** denotes the overall planning of operations, while **tactics** applies to the deployment of troops in battle, contributing towards the achievement of a larger *strategy*. More generally, *strategy* denotes planning, usually long-term, towards a major goal (*rethinking sales strategy | the tourist board has launched a major review of its strategy for tourism in Wales*), while *tactics* refers to the adoption of plans in response to a more immediate problem (*the player should be free to concentrate on the tactics of the game*).

stratum noun **1** *a stratum of flint*: **layer**, vein, seam, lode, bed; stratification, thickness, sheet, lamina.
2 *a particular stratum of society*: **level**, class, echelon, rank, grade, station, gradation; group, set, bracket; caste; archaic estate, sphere.

stray verb **1** *a young gazelle which had strayed from the herd*: **wander off**, go astray, drift, get separated; get lost, lose one's way.
2 *we appeared to have strayed a long way from our original topic*: **digress**, deviate, wander, drift, get sidetracked, go off at a tangent; get off the subject, lose the thread; rare divagate.
3 *the younger the men were, the more likely they were to stray*: **be unfaithful**, have affairs, philander; informal play around, carry on, play the field.
4 *he had strayed from the path of righteousness*: **sin**, transgress, err, go astray, go wrong, do wrong, stray from the straight and narrow, go down the primrose path, fall from grace; archaic trespass.
▸ adjective **1** *a stray dog*: **homeless**, lost, strayed, gone astray; abandoned, unclaimed; wandering, vagrant.
2 *she was killed by a stray bullet*: **random**, chance, accidental, freak, unexpected, casual, haphazard; odd, isolated, lone, single; scattered, occasional, incidental.
▸ noun *the council employs two wardens to deal with strays*: **homeless animal**, stray dog/cat; homeless person, waif, foundling; in Asia pye-dog.

Choose the right word **stray, wander, roam, rove, range**

See **wander**.

S

streak noun **1** *a streak of orange light appeared in the east*: **band**, line, strip, stripe, vein, slash, bar; ray, finger, pencil, stroke; trace, touch, fleck, dash; technical stria, striation, lane.
2 *the damp grass had left green streaks on her legs*: **mark**, smear, smudge, stain, blotch; informal splodge, splotch.
3 *a streak of lightning*: **bolt**, shaft, flash, beam.
4 *Tammy had a streak of self-destructiveness*: **element**, vein, trace, touch, dash, strain; trait, characteristic.
5 *I suppose my winning streak had to come to an end eventually*: **period**, spell, stretch, run, time; series; Brit. informal patch.
▸ verb **1** *the sky was streaked with red*: **stripe**, band, bar, fleck; technical striate; archaic freak.
2 *overalls streaked with maroon paint*: **mark**, daub, smear, smudge, stain; informal splodge, splotch.
3 *Miranda streaked across the road*: **race**, dash, rush, run, sprint, bolt, dart, gallop, career, charge, shoot, hurtle, hare, bound, fly, speed, zoom, go hell for leather, plunge, dive, whisk, scurry, scuttle, scamper, scramble; informal tear, belt, pelt, scoot, zap, zip, whip, step on it, get a move on, hotfoot it, leg it, steam, put on some speed, go like a bat out of hell, burn rubber; Brit. informal bomb, go like the clappers, bucket, put one's foot down; Scottish informal wheech; N. Amer. informal boogie, hightail it, clip, barrel, get the lead out; informal, dated cut along; N. Amer. vulgar slang drag/tear/haul ass; literary fleet; archaic post, hie, haste.

streaky adjective *a songbird with streaky brown plumage*: **striped**, stripy, streaked, banded, barred; veined; brindle, brindled; technical striate, striated.

stream noun **1** *a mountain stream*: **brook**, rivulet, rill, runnel, streamlet, freshet; river, watercourse; tributary; Brit. winterbourne; Scottish & N. English burn; N. English beck; S. English bourn; N. Amer. & Austral./NZ creek; Austral. billabong, anabranch; technical influent, confluent; rare rillet, brooklet, runlet.
2 *he was scalded by a stream of boiling water*: **jet**, **flow**, rush, gush, surge, spurt, spout, torrent, flood, cascade, fountain, outpouring, outflux, outflow, effusion; current; technical efflux.
3 *a steady stream of visitors | a stream of questions*: **succession**, series, string, chain; barrage, volley, battery; flood, avalanche, torrent, tide, spate.
▷ANTONYMS trickle.
▸ verb **1** *tears were streaming down her face | rain streamed off the roof*: **flow**, **pour**, course, run, gush, surge, spurt, flood, cascade, sluice; slide, spill, slip, glide, trickle; well.
2 *children streamed out of the classrooms*: **pour**, surge, flood, swarm, pile, crowd, throng.
3 *a flag streamed from the mast*: **flutter**, float, flap, fly, blow, waft; wave, swing, undulate, ripple.
▷ANTONYMS dangle.

streamer noun **pennant**, pennon, flag, banderole, banner, standard, ensign, gonfalon, burgee; ribbon; rare vexillum.

streamlined adjective **1** *streamlined cars*: **aerodynamic**; smooth, sleek, trim, elegant, graceful; technical faired.
2 *a streamlined organization*: **efficient**, smooth-running, well run, well organized, slick; modernized, up to date, rationalized, simplified; time-saving, labour-saving.
▷ANTONYMS inefficient.

street noun *Amsterdam's narrow cobbled streets*: **road**, thoroughfare, way; avenue, drive, row, crescent, terrace, close, parade; side street, side road, lane, alley; French boulevard; N. Amer. highway, strip, blacktop. See also **road**.
□ **the man/woman in the street** **an ordinary person**, an average person, Mr/Mrs Average, John Citizen; Brit. informal Joe Bloggs, Joe Public, the man on the Clapham omnibus; N. Amer. informal John Doe, Joe Sixpack; derogatory pleb, plebeian.
□ **on the streets** *the number of people who are on the streets is growing*: **homeless**, living rough, sleeping rough, without a roof over one's head, of no fixed abode, down and out, vagrant.

strength noun **1** *a man of enormous physical strength*: **power**, brawn, brawniness, muscle, muscularity, burliness, sturdiness, robustness, toughness, hardiness, lustiness; vigour, energy, force, might, forcefulness, mightiness; informal beef; Brit. informal welly; literary thew, thewiness.
▷ANTONYMS weakness, puniness, frailty.
2 *Oliver began to regain his strength*: **health**, fitness, healthiness, vigour; stamina.
▷ANTONYMS infirmity.
3 *she'd always prided herself on her inner strength*: **fortitude**, resilience, backbone, spirit, strength of character, toughness of spirit, firmness, steadfastness, strong-mindedness, stoicism; courage, bravery, pluck, pluckiness, courageousness, braveness; informal guts, grit, spunk.
▷ANTONYMS vulnerability.
4 *they were taking no chances with the strength of the retaining wall*: **robustness**, sturdiness, firmness, toughness, soundness, solidity, solidness, durability, stability; impregnability, resistance.
▷ANTONYMS weakness.
5 *the political and military strength of European governments*: **power**, influence, dominance, ascendancy, supremacy; leverage; informal clout, beef; literary puissance.
▷ANTONYMS weakness, impotence.
6 *street protests demonstrated the strength of feeling against the president*: **intensity**, vehemence, force, forcefulness, depth, ardour, fervour, violence; degree, level; rare fervency, ardency.
▷ANTONYMS half-heartedness.
7 *the strength of the argument for property taxation*: **cogency**, forcefulness, force, weight, power, potency, persuasiveness, effectiveness, efficacy, soundness, validity.
▷ANTONYMS weakness, ineffectiveness.
8 *what do you regard as your strengths?* **strong point**, advantage, asset, forte, strong suit, long suit, aptitude, talent, gift, skill; virtue; speciality, specialty; French métier.
▷ANTONYMS failing, fault, flaw; limitation.
9 literary *he was my closest friend, my strength and shield*: **support**, tower/pillar of strength, rock, mainstay, anchor.
10 *the peacetime strength of the army was 415,000*: **size**, extent, magnitude, largeness, greatness; complement.
□ **on the strength of** *she got into Princeton on the strength of her essays*: **because of**, by virtue of, on account of, on the basis of, based on, on the grounds of.

strengthen verb **1** *calcium helps strengthen growing bones*: **make strong/stronger**, build up, give strength to, make healthy, nourish.
▷ANTONYMS weaken.
2 *engineers strengthened the walls*: **reinforce**, make stronger, buttress, brace, shore up, underpin; rare underprop.
3 *strengthened glass*: **toughen**, temper, anneal.
4 *the wind had strengthened*: **become strong/stronger**, gain strength, intensify, pick up, heighten.
▷ANTONYMS die down, ease off.
5 *his insistence strengthened her determination*: **fortify**, bolster, make stronger, give strength to, give a boost to, boost, reinforce, harden, stiffen, toughen, steel, cement; increase, add to, fuel, add fuel to; renew, vitalize, give new energy to, buoy up, hearten.
▷ANTONYMS sap, weaken.
6 *the organization strengthened its efforts to expand such programmes*: **step up**, increase, heighten, escalate, scale up; informal up, crank up, beef up.
▷ANTONYMS relax, decrease.
7 *the argument is strengthened by evidence from clinical data*: **reinforce**, make more forceful, lend more weight to; support, back up, bolster, confirm, bear out, substantiate, corroborate, authenticate; consolidate.
▷ANTONYMS undermine.

strenuous adjective **1** *it's a pretty strenuous climb*: **arduous**, difficult, hard, tough, taxing, demanding, exacting, uphill, stiff, formidable, heavy, exhausting, tiring, fatiguing, gruelling, back-breaking, murderous, punishing; informal no picnic, killing; Brit. informal knackering; archaic toilsome.
▷ANTONYMS easy, effortless.
2 *the college has made strenuous efforts to attract overseas students*: **vigorous**, energetic, active, enthusiastic, keen, zealous, forceful, strong, Herculean, spirited, dynamic, intense, determined, resolute, tenacious, tireless, stout, indefatigable, unremitting, dogged, pertinacious.
▷ANTONYMS half-hearted, feeble.

stress noun **1** *he's obviously under a lot of stress*: **strain**, pressure, tension, nervous tension, worry, anxiety, nervousness; trouble, difficulty, distress, trauma, suffering, pain, grief; informal hassle.
▷ANTONYMS relaxation.
2 *he has started to lay greater stress on the government's role in education*: **emphasis**, importance, weight, force, insistence.
3 *normally, the stress falls on the first syllable*: **emphasis**, accent, accentuation; beat; Prosody ictus.
4 *the distribution of stress is uniform across the bar*: **pressure**, **tension**, strain, tightness, tautness; rare tensity.
▶ verb **1** *they stressed the need for reform*: **emphasize**, draw attention to, focus attention on, underline, underscore, point up, place emphasis on, lay stress on, highlight, spotlight, turn the spotlight on, bring to the fore, foreground, accentuate, press home, impress on someone, make a point of, dwell on, harp on, belabour, insist on, rub in.
▷ANTONYMS play down, understate.
2 *in French, the last syllable is usually stressed*: **place the emphasis on**, give emphasis to, emphasize, place the accent on.
3 *the staff were stressed by the demands he made upon them*: **overstretch**, overtax, push to the limit, pressurize, pressure, burden, make tense, cause to feel mental/emotional strain; worry, upset, distress, harass; informal hassle.

stressful adjective *he had had a particularly stressful day*: **demanding**, trying, exacting, taxing, difficult, hard, tough; **fraught**, traumatic, pressured, tense, frustrating; worrying, nerve-racking, anxious, anxiety-ridden; wearing, tiring, exhausting, draining.
▷ANTONYMS relaxing, easy.

stretch verb **1** *the material stretches*: **be elastic**, be stretchy, be stretchable, be tensile.
2 *he stretched the elastic until it snapped*: **pull**, pull out, draw out, extend, lengthen, elongate; expand, distend.
3 *stretch your weekend into a mini summer vacation*: **prolong**, lengthen, make longer, extend, extend the duration of, draw out, spin out, protract.
▷ANTONYMS shorten.
4 *my budget won't* **stretch to** *a weekend at a health farm*: **be sufficient for**, be enough for, cover, reach to; afford, have the money for.
5 *the cost of the court case has stretched their finances*: **put a strain on**, put great demands on, overtax, overextend, be too much for; drain, sap.
6 *Owen was stretching the truth a little*: **bend**, strain, distort; exaggerate, overstate, embellish, overdraw; informal lay it on thick.
7 *she* **stretched out** *her hand to him*: **reach out**, hold out, put out, extend, outstretch, thrust out, stick out; proffer, offer; literary outreach.
▷ANTONYMS withdraw.
8 *he stood up and stretched his arms*: **extend**, straighten, straighten out, unbend.
9 *she* **stretched out** *on the sofa*: **lie down**, recline, lean back, be recumbent, be prostrate, be prone, sprawl, drape oneself, lounge, loll.
10 *the desert* **stretches for** *miles*: **extend**, spread, continue, range, unfold, unroll, be unbroken; cover, span.
▶ noun **1** *magnificent stretches of forest*: **expanse**, area, tract, belt, sweep, extent, spread, reach; length, distance.
2 *a four-hour stretch*: **period**, time, spell, term, run, stint, session; tour of duty, shift.
3 informal *he's served six years of a ten-year stretch*: **prison sentence**, sentence, prison term; N. Amer. informal rap.
▶ adjective *today's popular stretch fabrics*: **stretchy**, stretchable, elastic, elasticated.

strew verb *his room was strewn with books and papers*: **scatter**, spread, disperse, distribute, litter, toss, sprinkle, sow, broadcast; literary bestrew, besprinkle.
▷ANTONYMS gather.

stricken adjective *Raymond was stricken with grief* | *she looked at Anne's stricken face*: **troubled**, affected, deeply affected, afflicted, struck, hit, injured, wounded.
▷ANTONYMS unaffected.

strict adjective **1** *a strict interpretation of the new law*: **precise**, exact, literal, close, faithful, true, accurate, unerring, scrupulous, careful, meticulous, rigorous, stringent; conscientious, punctilious, painstaking, thorough; informal spot on, on the mark, on the beam, on the nail, on the button.
▷ANTONYMS imprecise, loose.
2 *strict controls on public spending*: **stringent**, rigorous, severe, harsh, hard, rigid, tough, extreme.
▷ANTONYMS liberal.
3 *their parents were too strict*: **stern**, **severe**, harsh, uncompromising, authoritarian, firm, austere, illiberal, inflexible, unyielding, unbending, no-nonsense; Austral./NZ informal solid.
▷ANTONYMS lenient.
4 *the information will be treated in strict confidence*: **absolute**, utter, complete, total, perfect.
5 *her father was a strict Roman Catholic*: **orthodox**, fundamentalist, conservative, traditional; devout, conscientious, true, religious.
▷ANTONYMS moderate, liberal.

strictness noun **1** *the strictness of the gun control laws*: **severity**, harshness, rigidity, rigidness, stringency, rigorousness, austerity; authoritarianism, sternness.
▷ANTONYMS flexibility.
2 *the provision has been interpreted with some strictness*: **precision**, preciseness, accuracy, exactness, exactitude, correctness, faithfulness, closeness, correspondence; meticulousness, scrupulousness, thoroughness.
▷ANTONYMS imprecision.

stricture noun **1** *guilt was induced by the constant strictures of the nuns*: **criticism**, censure, blame, condemnation, reproof, reproach, admonishment, disparagement, flak; informal knocking; Brit. informal stick, slating.
▷ANTONYMS praise.
2 *the strictures on Victorian women*: **constraint**, restriction, limitation, control, restraint, straitjacket, curb, check, impediment, bar, barrier, obstacle.
▷ANTONYMS freedom.
3 *a small intestinal stricture*: **narrowing**, constriction, strangulation, tightness.
▷ANTONYMS dilatation.

stride verb *she came striding down the garden path*: **march**, stalk, pace, tread, step, walk.
▶ noun *he walked with long swinging strides*: **step**, long step, large step, pace, footstep.
□ **make strides** *they're making strides toward some important answers*: **make progress**, make headway, gain ground, progress, advance, proceed, move, get on, get ahead, come on, come along, shape up, take shape, move forward in leaps and bounds; informal be getting there.
□ **take something in one's stride** **deal with easily**, cope with easily, think nothing of, accept as quite usual/normal, not bat an eyelid.
▷ANTONYMS be fazed by.

strident adjective *a strident voice interrupted the consultation*: **harsh**, raucous, rough, grating, rasping, jarring, loud, stentorian, shrill, screeching, piercing, ear-piercing; unmelodious, unmusical, discordant, dissonant, unharmonious; rare stridulous, stridulant, stridulatory, stentorious.
▷ANTONYMS soft, dulcet.

strife noun *the history of the Empire is full of strife*: **conflict**, friction, discord, disagreement, dissension, variance, dispute, argument, quarrelling, wrangling, bickering, controversy, contention; disharmony, ill feeling, bad feeling, bad blood, hostility, animosity; informal falling-out.
▷ANTONYMS harmony, peace, cooperation.

strike verb **1** *the teacher actually struck and hurt Mary*: **hit**, slap, smack, beat, thrash, spank, thump, thwack, punch, cuff, crack, swat, knock, rap; pummel, pound, batter, pelt, welt, assault, box someone's ears; cane, lash, whip, club, cudgel; Austral./NZ informal quilt; informal **clout**, wallop, belt, whack, bash, clobber, bop, biff, sock, deck, slug, plug, knock about/around, knock into the middle of next week, lay into, do over, rough up; literary smite.
2 *at seven sharp he struck the gong*: **bang**, beat, hit, pound; informal bash, wallop.

S

3 *the stolen car struck a tree*: **crash into**, collide with, be in collision with, hit, run into, knock into, bang into, bump into, smash into, slam into, crack into/against, dash against; N. Amer. impact.
4 *Jennifer struck the ball into the back of the net*: **hit**, drive, propel, force; informal clout, wallop, slam, swipe.
5 *he struck a match and lit the oil lamp*: **ignite**, light.
▷ANTONYMS extinguish.
6 *she was counting the day's takings when the killer struck*: **attack**, make an attack/assault, set upon someone, fall on someone, assault someone.
7 *the disease is striking 3,000 people a year*: **affect**, afflict, attack, hit, come upon, smite.
8 *democratic societies must strike a balance between order and freedom*: **achieve**, reach, arrive at, find, attain, effect, establish.
9 *we have struck a satisfactory bargain*: **agree**, agree on, come to an agreement on, settle on, sign, endorse, ratify, sanction; informal clinch.
10 *the picture showed him striking a heroic pose*: **assume**, adopt, take on, take up, affect, feign, put on; N. Amer. informal cop.
11 *the engineers had struck oil*: **discover**, find, come upon, light on, chance on, happen on, stumble on/across, unearth, uncover, turn up.
12 *a thought suddenly struck her*: **occur to**, come to, dawn on one, hit; come to mind, spring to mind, enter one's head, present itself, come into one's consciousness.
13 *you strike me as an intelligent young woman*: **seem to**, appear to, look to; give someone the impression of being; impress, affect, have an impact on.
14 *our drivers are striking and demanding guarantees of their safety*: **take industrial action**, go on strike, down tools, walk out, work to rule; mutiny, rebel, revolt.
15 *they are about to strike the big tent*: **take down**, pull down, bring down; take apart.
▷ANTONYMS pitch.
16 *Lord Bridport struck his flag*: **lower**, take down, let down, bring down.
▷ANTONYMS hoist.
17 *he ordered the driver to strike south towards the Thames*: **go**, make one's way, set out, head, direct one's footsteps, move towards.
□ **strike back** *the mayor struck back, threatening to sue*: **fight back**, retaliate, hit back, respond, react, reply, reciprocate, counterattack, return fire, return the compliment, put up a fight, take the bait, rise to the bait, return like for like, get back at someone, get, give tit for tat, give as good as one gets, let someone see how it feels, give someone a dose/taste of their own medicine; **have/get/take one's revenge**, take/exact/wreak revenge, be revenged, revenge oneself, avenge oneself, take reprisals, get even, even the score, settle a/the score, settle accounts, pay someone back (in their own coin), pay someone out, repay someone, exact retribution, take an eye for an eye (and a tooth for a tooth); informal give someone their comeuppance; Brit. informal get one's own back; rare give someone a Roland for an Oliver.
□ **strike something out** **delete**, cross out, erase, rub out, obliterate.
□ **strike something up** **1** *the accompanist struck up 'Land of Hope and Glory'*: **begin to play**, start to play, begin/start/commence playing, embark on. **2** *we struck up a friendship*: **begin**, start, embark on, set going, initiate, instigate, establish; formal commence.
▸ **noun 1** *staff held a 48-hour strike*: **industrial action**, walkout.
2 *an imminent military strike*: **attack**, air strike, air attack, assault, bombing, blitz.
3 *a lucky strike in 1848 gave rise to the term 'gold rush'*: **find**, discovery, unearthing, uncovering.

striking adjective **1** *Lizzie bears a striking resemblance to her sister*: **noticeable**, obvious, conspicuous, evident, salient, visible, distinct, prominent, marked, clear-cut, notable, manifest, unmistakable, distinctive, strong; rare, uncommon, out of the ordinary; significant, remarkable, extraordinary, incredible, amazing, astounding, astonishing, surprising, staggering, phenomenal.
▷ANTONYMS inconspicuous; unremarkable.
2 *an opportunity to see Kenya's striking landscape*: **impressive**, imposing, grand, splendid, magnificent, spectacular, breathtaking, superb, marvellous, wonderful, outstanding, dazzling, stunning, staggering, sensational, dramatic, awesome, awe-inspiring, eye-catching, picturesque; informal great, fabulous, fab, smashing; archaic splendent.
▷ANTONYMS ordinary, unimpressive.
3 *a former bunny girl with striking looks*: **stunning**, attractive, good-looking, beautiful, glamorous, gorgeous, prepossessing, comely, captivating, enchanting, arresting, ravishing, alluring, handsome, pretty, bonny; informal drop-dead gorgeous, smashing, fabulous, fab, out of this world, knockout.
▷ANTONYMS unattractive, unremarkable.

string noun **1** *a ball of string*: **twine**, cord, yarn, thread, strand, fibre; rope, cable, line, wire, ligature, thong, hawser; rare fillis.
2 *they lease their pubs to a string of brewers*: **chain**, series, group, firm, company.
3 *a string of convictions*: **series**, succession, chain, sequence, concatenation, run, streak; pattern.
4 *a long winding string of wagons and horses*: **queue**, **procession**, line, row, file, column, rank, convoy, train, cavalcade, stream, succession, sequence; informal crocodile.
5 *a string of priceless pearls*: **strand**, rope, necklace, rosary, chaplet.
6 (**strings**) *an instrumental piece for horns and strings*: **stringed instruments**.
7 (**strings**) *a guaranteed loan with no strings attached*: **conditions**, qualifications, provisions, provisos, caveats, stipulations, riders, contingencies, prerequisites, limitations, limits, constraints, restrictions, reservations, requirements, obligations; informal catches.
▸ **verb 1** *lights were strung across the promenade*: **hang**, suspend, sling, stretch; thread, loop, festoon.
2 *wire mesh was strung from one catwalk to the other*: **stretch**, sling, run, fasten, tie, secure, link.
3 *a necklace of wooden beads strung on a silver chain*: **thread**, loop, link, join.
□ **string along** *with my name I could always* **string along with** *the Irish gang*: **go along**, go too, come too, join in; accompany, join, join up with, take up with.
□ **string someone along** **mislead**, deceive, take in, take advantage of, dupe, hoax, fool, make a fool of, bluff; make use of, play with, toy with, dally with, trifle with, play fast and loose with; informal lead up the garden path, take for a ride, put one over on, kid.
□ **string something out** **1** *these journalists certainly know how to string a story out*: **protract**, spin out, draw out, drag out, lengthen, stretch, stretch out. ▷ANTONYMS shorten.
2 *the mining villages are* **strung out** *along the valleys*: **spread out**, space out, set apart, place at intervals, distribute, extend, fan out, scatter, straggle.
□ **string someone up** informal *he was strung up for murder* **hang**, lynch, gibbet; informal make swing.

stringent adjective *the safety regulations are very stringent*: **strict**, firm, rigid, rigorous, severe, harsh, tough, tight, exacting, demanding, inflexible, stiff, hard and fast, uncompromising, draconian, extreme.
▷ANTONYMS lenient, flexible.

stringy adjective **1** *the girl is small with stringy hair*: **straggly**, straggling, lank, thin.
▷ANTONYMS luxuriant.
2 *a stringy brunette*: **lanky**, gangling, gangly, rangy, wiry, angular, bony, reedy; spindly, spindling, skinny, size-zero, scrawny, thin, thin as a rake, spare, gaunt, emaciated, skeletal, raw-boned.
▷ANTONYMS plump.
3 *he had to chew the stringy meat*: **fibrous**, gristly, sinewy, chewy, ropy, tough, leathery, leather-like, hard.
▷ANTONYMS tender, succulent.

strip[1] verb **1** *he stripped and got into bed*: **undress**, strip off, take one's clothes off, remove one's clothes, shed one's clothes, unclothe, disrobe, strip naked, denude oneself, expose oneself, reveal oneself, uncover oneself; informal peel off; dated divest oneself of one's clothes.
▷ANTONYMS dress.
2 *you'll have to* **strip off** *the paint*: **peel**, remove, take off, flake, scrape, scratch, shave, abrade, rub, clear, clean; pare, skin, flay; technical excoriate, decorticate.
3 *the university stripped him of his doctorate*: **take away from**, dispossess, deprive, confiscate, divest, relieve, deny, rob.
4 *the mechanics are* **stripping down** *my engine*: **dismantle**, disassemble, take to pieces, take to bits, take apart, break up, demolish.
▷ANTONYMS construct, assemble.
5 *the house had been stripped of everything of value*: **empty**, clear, clean out, plunder, rob, burgle, loot, rifle, pillage, ransack, gut, lay bare, devastate, sack, ravage, raid; literary despoil; archaic spoil, reave.
▸ **noun** *he led out an England team sporting a new strip*: **outfit**, clothes, clothing, garments, costume, suit, dress, garb; Brit. **kit**; informal gear, get-up; Brit. informal rig-out.

strip[2] noun *cut a strip of paper 12cm wide*: **narrow piece**, piece, bit, band, belt, ribbon, sash, stripe, bar, swathe, slip, fillet, shred.

stripe noun *green tracksuit bottoms with a yellow stripe on the side*: **line**, band, strip, belt, bar, swathe, streak, striation, vein, thread; chevron, flash, blaze, marking; technical stria.

striped adjective *a blue and white striped shirt*: **banded**, stripy, barred, lined; streaky, striated, variegated.

stripling noun *a thin, blonde boy—a mere stripling*: **youth**, adolescent, youngster, boy, schoolboy, lad, child, teenager, juvenile, minor, junior, young man, whippersnapper, fledgling; Scottish laddie, bairn; informal kid, young 'un, nipper, shaver, tot; derogatory brat, urchin, guttersnipe; archaic hobbledehoy.
▷ANTONYMS old man.

stripy adjective *he wore stripy skintight trousers*: **striped**, barred, lined, banded; streaky, striated, variegated.

strive verb **1** *I shall strive to be virtuous*: **try**, try hard, attempt, endeavour, aim, aspire, venture, undertake, seek, make an effort, make every effort, spare no effort, exert oneself, do one's best, do all one can, do one's utmost, give one's all, labour, work, toil, strain, struggle, apply oneself; have a go at; informal bend/fall/lean over backwards, go all out, give it one's best shot, give

S

it a whirl, have a crack at, have a stab at, pull out all the stops; formal essay.
2 *scholars must strive against this bias*: **struggle**, fight, battle, combat, contend, grapple; campaign, war, crusade.

stroke noun **1** *the rebel Duke had suffered five strokes of the axe*: **blow**, hit, thump, thwack, punch, slap, smack, welt, cuff, box, knock, rap, buffet; informal wallop, clobber, clout, whack, bash, belt, sock, bop, biff, swipe, slug; archaic smite.
2 *Anwar was playing cricket strokes*: **shot**, hit, strike.
3 *Mick swam a couple of strokes*: **movement**, action, motion, move.
4 *it was a stroke of genius by the Prime Minister*: **feat**, accomplishment, achievement, attainment, coup, master stroke, stratagem.
5 *the flat pencil can be used for broad strokes*: **mark**, line, slash, solidus, virgule.
6 *the budget was full of bold strokes*: **detail**, touch, bit, point, item.
7 *I counted the strokes of the church clock*: **peal**, ring, knell, striking, ding-dong, boom.
8 *he had recently suffered a small stroke*: **thrombosis**, embolism, cerebral vascular accident, CVA, cerebral haemorrhage, ictus, seizure; archaic apoplexy.
▸ verb *she reached out and stroked the cat*: **caress**, fondle, pat, pet, touch, brush, rub, massage, knead, soothe; manipulate, finger, handle, feel, maul, tickle; informal paw.

stroll verb *they strolled along the gravelled paths*: **saunter**, amble, wander, meander, ramble, dawdle, promenade, walk, go for a walk, take a walk, roam, traipse, stretch one's legs, get some exercise, get some air, take the air; Scottish & Irish stravaig; informal mosey, tootle; Brit. informal pootle, mooch, swan; N. Amer. informal putter; rare perambulate, peregrinate.
▸ noun *a stroll in the park*: **saunter**, amble, wander, walk, turn, promenade, airing, breather; outing, excursion, jaunt; informal mosey, tootle; Brit. informal pootle; dated constitutional; rare perambulation.

> *Choose the right word* **stroll, saunter, amble**
>
> These words have in common the idea of relaxed and unhurried movement.
>
> People who are **strolling** are typically walking for pleasure, at a relaxed pace which allows them to enjoy their surroundings or company, or both (*a day for lovers to stroll through leafy woods*). They are definitely under no pressure to exert themselves. As a noun, a *stroll* is typically *a gentle stroll*.
>
> **Saunter** can be used in the same way, but it may also suggest a more self-conscious or conspicuous freedom from hurry or anxiety. Someone may saunter to emphasize their lack of concern when they might be expected to be nervous (*Jasper was sauntering past the police station*), or their feeling that they have privileged access to a place (*Dana sauntered into Claudia's office*).
>
> Someone who is **ambling** is walking in a particularly casual way, giving the impression that they have no definite destination or objective (*he ambled down the corridor, whistling*). *Amble* is more commonly used of animals (such as a *bear* or a *horse*) than the other two words are.

strong adjective **1** *a big strong farmer's lad*: **powerful**, **muscular**, brawny, well built, powerfully built, strapping, sturdy, hefty, burly, meaty, robust, fit, athletic, vigorous, tough, rugged; stalwart, staunch, mighty, hardy; lusty, Herculean, strong as an ox/horse/lion; informal beefy, hunky, husky.
▷ANTONYMS weak, puny.
2 *she hasn't been strong since Father's death*: **well**, healthy, in good health, fit, fighting fit, robust, vigorous, blooming, thriving, bursting with health, in rude health, hale, hale and hearty, hearty, in good shape, in excellent shape, in good condition, in good trim, in fine fettle, sound, sound in body and limb; informal in the pink, fit as a fiddle, in tip-top condition.
▷ANTONYMS frail.
3 *a lady of strong character*: **forceful**, determined, spirited, dynamic, self-assertive, tough, tenacious, high-powered, formidable, aggressive, redoubtable, zealous, firm, resolute, strong-minded; informal gutsy, feisty.
▷ANTONYMS weak.
4 *a strong fortress surrounded by a moat*: **secure**, well built, indestructible, well fortified, well defended, well protected, impregnable, impenetrable, inviolable, unassailable; solid.
5 *strong cotton bags*: **durable**, hard-wearing, heavy-duty, tough, sturdy, well made, substantial, solid, rugged; resistant, resilient, imperishable, indestructible, long-lasting, enduring.
▷ANTONYMS weak.
6 *a strong breeze | the current is too strong*: **forceful**, powerful, vigorous, fierce, intense, extreme.
▷ANTONYMS gentle.
7 *a strong interest in literary activities*: **keen**, eager, deep, acute, dedicated, passionate, fervent, zealous.
8 *he still retained strong feelings for the woman*: **intense**, forceful, vehement, passionate, ardent, fervent, profound, deep-seated; consuming, extreme, acute, fierce; rare fervid, perfervid, passional.
9 *a strong supporter of the women's movement*: **keen**, eager, enthusiastic, earnest, dedicated, staunch, loyal, steadfast, passionate, fierce, fervent.
10 *there are strong arguments for introducing grants*: **compelling**, cogent, forceful, powerful, potent, weighty, convincing, plausible, effective, efficacious, sound, valid, well founded, telling; impressive, persuasive, influential, authoritative.
▷ANTONYMS weak, unconvincing.
11 *there was a need to take strong action*: **firm**, forceful, severe, strict, drastic, extreme, draconian.
12 *she bore a very strong resemblance to Vera*: **marked**, noticeable, pronounced, distinct, definite, clear-cut, obvious, evident, unmistakable, notable.
▷ANTONYMS slight.
13 *a strong voice*: **loud**, powerful, forceful, lusty, stentorian, resonant, sonorous, orotund, full, rich, deep, booming, penetrating, carrying, clear; strident; informal fruity; rare canorous.
▷ANTONYMS quiet, weak.
14 *he didn't like strong language*: **bad**, foul, obscene, profane, blasphemous.
15 *strong blues and yellows*: **intense**, deep, rich, warm, bright, brilliant, vivid, striking, colourful, graphic.
▷ANTONYMS pale.
16 *the strong lights of the studio*: **bright**, brilliant, intense, radiant, gleaming, dazzling, glaring.
17 *strong black coffee*: **concentrated**, undiluted, highly flavoured.
▷ANTONYMS weak, mild.
18 *slices of strong cheese*: **highly flavoured**, strongly flavoured, flavourful, flavoursome, savoury, pungent, aromatic, piquant, tangy, sharp, biting, zesty, spicy, hot; rare flavorous, sapid.
▷ANTONYMS mild.
19 *he would have blown his money on horses and strong drink*: **alcoholic**, intoxicating, inebriating, hard, heady, potent, stiff, spirituous, vinous, intoxicant.
▷ANTONYMS non-alcoholic, soft.

> *Choose the right word* **strong, powerful**
>
> See **powerful**.

strong-arm adjective *strong-arm tactics were deployed by both sides*: **aggressive**, forceful, bullying, coercive, oppressive, threatening, intimidatory, terrorizing, thuggish, violent; informal bully-boy.

strongbox noun *she would rob her father's strongbox*: **safe**, safety-deposit box, safe-deposit box, coffer, cash box, money box, money chest, locker, repository; vault, bank.

stronghold noun **1** *they charged towards the enemy stronghold*: **fortress**, fort, castle, citadel, garrison, keep, tower, hold, donjon, bunker; fastness.
2 *the seat appeared to be an impregnable Tory stronghold*: **bastion**, centre, refuge, hotbed.

strong-minded adjective *a strong-minded social reformer*: **determined**, firm, resolute, resolved, purposeful, purposive, sure, self-disciplined, strong-willed, uncompromising, unyielding, unbending, unwavering, unswerving, unfaltering, unshakeable, inexorable, forceful, persistent, persevering, tenacious, dogged, stubborn; dedicated, committed, stalwart; N. Amer. rock-ribbed; informal gutsy, spunky; rare perseverant, indurate.
▷ANTONYMS weak-willed, half-hearted.

strong point noun *arithmetic had never been her strong point*: **strength**, strong suit, long suit, forte, aptitude, bent, speciality, specialty, métier, claim to fame, skill; informal thing, bag, line, cup of tea.
▷ANTONYMS weakness.

strong-willed adjective *he was strong-willed and independent*: **determined**, iron-willed, resolute, stubborn, stubborn as a mule, mulish, obstinate, wilful, headstrong, strong-minded, self-willed, inflexible, unbending, unyielding, intransigent, intractable, obdurate, recalcitrant, refractory; forceful, domineering; informal pushy; rare indurate.
▷ANTONYMS weak-willed, spineless.

stroppy adjective informal *I won't push it unless he gets stroppy*: **bad-tempered**, ill-tempered, irritable, grumpy, cantankerous, truculent, sulky, sullen, awkward, uncooperative, unhelpful, recalcitrant, refractory, difficult, perverse, contrary, confrontational, argumentative, quarrelsome, obstreperous, choleric; Scottish thrawn; informal pig-headed, cussed; Brit. informal shirty, ratty, narky, bolshie, bloody-minded; N. Amer. informal balky, scrappy; archaic contumacious, froward; rare contrarious.

structural adjective *the effects of structural changes in the industry | earth tremors caused structural damage*: **constructional**, organizational, systemic, constitutional, configurational, formational; technical tectonic.

structure noun **1** *a vast Gothic structure with strange ornamental spirelets*: **building**, edifice, construction, erection, pile, complex, assembly.
2 *the structure of local government | the plant's structure is simple*: **construction**, form, formation, shape, composition, fabric, anatomy, make-up, constitution; organization, system, arrangement, layout, design, frame, framework, configuration, conformation, pattern, plan, mould; informal set-up.
▸ verb *the programme is structured around periods of residential study*: **arrange**, organize, order, design, shape, give structure to, assemble, construct, build, put together.

struggle verb **1** *they struggled to make sense of the words*: **strive**, try hard, endeavour, make every effort, spare no effort, exert oneself, do one's best, do all one can, do one's utmost, battle, labour, toil, strain, bend over backwards, put oneself out; informal go all out, give it one's best shot, put one's back into it, plug away, peg away; Brit. informal graft; formal essay.
2 *James was hit in the mouth as he struggled with the raiders*: **fight**, grapple, wrestle, scuffle, brawl, spar, exchange blows, come to blows; informal scrap; Scottish informal swedge.
3 *research teams struggle to be first to the finish*: **compete**, contend, contest, vie, fight, battle, clash, wrangle, jockey, lock horns, cross swords, war, wage war, feud.
4 *she struggled over the dunes*: **scramble**, flounder, stumble; make one's way with difficulty, drag oneself, fight/battle one's way, battle, labour.
▶ **noun 1** *the continuing struggle for justice*: **endeavour**, striving, effort, exertion, labour, work, toiling, pains; **campaign**, battle, crusade, drive, push, movement; Brit. informal graft.
2 *we were able to apprehend the gang without a struggle*: **fight**, scuffle, brawl, tussle, wrestling match, sparring match, wrestling bout, bout, skirmish, fracas, melee, affray, encounter, disturbance, breach of the peace; informal scrap, barney, set-to, dust-up, punch-up, ruction, free-for-all, argy-bargy; Brit. informal bust-up, ding-dong; Scottish informal swedge.
3 *a third of the population perished in the struggle*: **conflict**, fight, battle, armed conflict, combat, confrontation, clash, skirmish, encounter, engagement; **hostilities**, fighting, war, warfare, campaign, crusade.
4 *an unresolved struggle within the leadership*: **contest**, competition, battle, fight, clash, feud; contention, vying, rivalry, strife, friction, feuding, conflict.
5 *life has been a struggle for me*: **effort**, labour, problem, trial, trouble, stress, strain, bother, battle; informal grind, hassle, pain.

strung out adjective *she's so strung out that she starts smoking again.* See **strung up**.

strung up adjective *he was strung up and unable to relax*: **tense**, nervous, on edge, edgy, overwrought, jumpy, keyed up, worked up, agitated, restive; anxious, worried, apprehensive, ill at ease, uneasy, unquiet; Brit. nervy; informal uptight, wound up, twitchy, jittery, wired, a bundle of nerves, like a cat on a hot tin roof.
▷**ANTONYMS** relaxed, laid-back.

strut verb *he strutted around his vast office*: **swagger**, swank, parade, prance, flounce, stride, sweep; walk confidently, walk arrogantly; N. Amer. informal sashay; rare peacock.

> *Choose the right word* **strut, swagger, parade**
>
> These words all refer to types of ostentatious movement.
>
> **Strut** refers to a stiff, erect movement suggesting aggressive self-importance (*he strutted around his vast office like a peacock*). There is often a suggestion that this self-importance is combined with other qualities that the writer or speaker finds obnoxious (*a strutting bully*), or that it is used to conceal feelings of inadequacy (*a small man's strutting arrogance | he strutted angrily and aimlessly off*). It is frequently also used of birds such as *peacocks*, *pheasants*, *cockerels*, and *chickens*.
>
> To **swagger** is to walk with an easier, more expansive and swinging movement, reflecting arrogant self-confidence (*he swaggered around the room in his new uniform*).
>
> Someone who is **parading** is walking in a way that is calculated to draw attention (*I've seen her parading round the village in her fur coat and jewellery*).

stub noun **1** *he ground his cigar stub into the ashtray*: **butt**, end, tail end, remnant; informal dog-end, fag end.
2 *please retain your ticket stub*: **counterfoil**, ticket slip, detachable portion, coupon, tab, receipt.
3 *he found a stub of pencil*: **stump**, remnant, end, tail end, remains.

stubble noun **1** *a field of stubble*: **stalks**, straw.
2 *a weather-beaten face covered in grey stubble*: **bristles**, whiskers, designer stubble, hair, facial hair, beard; informal five o'clock shadow.

stubbly adjective *he scratched his stubbly chin*: **bristly**, unshaven, fuzzy, whiskery, whiskered, hairy, bearded; prickly, rough, coarse, scratchy, spiky.
▷**ANTONYMS** smooth; clean-shaven.

stubborn adjective **1** *you're too stubborn to admit it*: **obstinate**, stubborn as a mule, mulish, headstrong, wilful, strong-willed, self-willed, pig-headed, bull-headed, obdurate, awkward, difficult, contrary, perverse, recalcitrant, refractory; firm, adamant, resolute, dogged, persistent, pertinacious, inflexible, iron-willed, uncompromising, uncooperative, unaccommodating, intractable, unbending, unyielding, unmalleable, unadaptable; N. Amer. rock-ribbed; informal stiff-necked; Brit. informal bolshie, bloody-minded; N. Amer. informal balky; archaic contumacious, froward.
▷**ANTONYMS** compliant, docile.
2 *stubborn stains*: **indelible**, permanent, lingering, persistent, tenacious, fast, resistant.

> *Choose the right word* **stubborn, obstinate, headstrong, wilful**
>
> See **obstinate**.

stubby adjective **1** *a small stubby man with glasses*: **dumpy**, stocky, chunky, chubby, thickset, sturdy, heavyset, squat, solid; **short**, stumpy, dwarfish, diminutive, undersized; Austral./NZ nuggety; Brit. informal **fubsy**; technical mesomorphic, pyknic.
▷**ANTONYMS** slender; tall.
2 *a stubby pencil*: **short**, stumpy, small, little; Scottish wee.

stuck adjective **1** *there was a message stuck to his computer screen*: **fixed**, fastened, attached, glued, pinned.
2 *the iron gate looked rusted and stuck*: **immovable**, stuck fast, jammed, immobile, unbudgeable, fast, stiff, fixed, rooted.
3 *if you get stuck, leave a blank and come back to it*: **baffled**, beaten, lost, at a loss, puzzled, muddled, perplexed, nonplussed, bewildered, at one's wits' end; informal stumped, up against a brick wall, bogged down, clueless, flummoxed, fazed, bamboozled.
□ **get stuck into** Brit. informal *Walsh got stuck into the project*: **get down to**, make a start on, embark on, set about, go about, get to work at, get to grips with, tackle, set one's hand to, throw oneself into; informal have a crack at, have a go at; formal commence.
□ **stuck on** informal *you're still stuck on her, aren't you?* **infatuated with**, besotted with, smitten with, in love with, head over heels in love with, hopelessly in love with, obsessed with, enamoured of, very attracted to, very taken with, devoted to, charmed by, captivated by, enchanted by, enthralled by, bewitched by, beguiled by, under someone's spell; informal bowled over by, swept off one's feet by, struck on, crazy about, mad about, wild about, potty about, very keen on, gone on, sweet on, into, carrying a torch for.
▷**ANTONYMS** indifferent to.
□ **stuck with** *he was stuck with her for two months*: **lumbered with**, left with, made responsible for, hampered by.

stuck-up adjective *a bunch of stuck-up executives*: **conceited**, proud, arrogant, haughty, condescending, disdainful, patronizing, snobbish, snobby, supercilious, imperious, above oneself, self-important, overweening, lordly; informal high and mighty, snooty, uppity, uppish, big-headed, swollen-headed, hoity-toity, la-di-da, too big for one's boots; Brit. informal toffee-nosed, posh; literary vainglorious.
▷**ANTONYMS** modest, unassuming.

studded adjective *a gold cigarette box studded with jewels*: **dotted**, scattered, spotted, sprinkled, covered, flecked, peppered, spangled; literary bespangled, bejewelled.

student noun **1** *a student at Edinburgh University*: **undergraduate**, postgraduate, scholar, tutee; freshman, freshwoman, finalist; N. Amer. sophomore, coed; Brit. informal fresher; N. Amer. informal frosh.
2 *a former student of Whitby School*: **pupil**, schoolchild, schoolboy, schoolgirl, scholar; infant, junior, senior.
3 *a first-year nursing student*: **trainee**, apprentice, probationer, recruit, novice, learner, mentee, beginner; Christianity postulant, novitiate; informal greenhorn, rookie.

studied adjective *the words were said with studied politeness*: **deliberate**, careful, thoughtful, considered, conscious, calculated, intentional, volitional, designed, mannered, measured, studious, knowing, purposeful; guarded, contrived, affected, forced, strained, laboured, feigned, artificial, overworked, overdone, self-conscious.
▷**ANTONYMS** natural, spontaneous.

studio noun *he had worked hard on the dramatic murals in the studio*: **workshop**, workroom, atelier; workplace, place of work, office, study.

studious adjective **1** *a studious and enquiring nature*: **scholarly**, academic, bookish, book-loving, intellectual, erudite, learned, donnish, serious, earnest, thoughtful, cerebral; informal brainy; Brit. informal swotty.
2 *he gave studious attention to the question*: **diligent**, careful, attentive, industrious, assiduous, painstaking, thorough, meticulous, punctilious, zealous, sedulous, heedful; archaic nice.
▷**ANTONYMS** careless, negligent.
3 *they noted his studious absence from public view*: **deliberate**, wilful, conscious, calculated, intentional, volitional, designed, mannered, measured, studied, knowing, purposeful, contrived, artificial.
▷**ANTONYMS** natural, spontaneous.

study noun **1** *two years of study in the sixth form*: **learning**, education, schooling, work, academic work, book work, scholarship, tuition, research; informal swotting, cramming.
2 *a study of manufacturing in the UK*: **investigation**, enquiry, research, examination, analysis, review, survey, scrutiny, evaluation, interpretation.
3 *Father was shut up in his study*: **office**, workroom, workplace, place of work, studio, library; den, cubbyhole, sanctum.
4 *this study concentrates mainly upon attitudes to death*: **essay**, article, piece, work, review, report, paper, dissertation, commentary, discourse,

critique, disquisition.
□ **in a brown study lost in thought**, lost in contemplation, in a reverie, thinking, reflecting, musing, pondering, contemplating, deliberating, ruminating, cogitating, dreaming, daydreaming; informal miles away.
▶ **verb 1** *Anne studied hard at school*: **work**, apply oneself, read up, revise, burn the midnight oil; informal swot, cram, mug up, bone up; archaic con.
2 *he studied electronics and accountancy*: **learn**, read, read up on, work at, be taught, be tutored in; informal mug up on.
3 *Thomas was studying the effects of business re-engineering*: **investigate**, enquire into, research, conduct research into, look into, examine, analyse, explore, probe, monitor, review, appraise, survey, conduct a survey of, scrutinize, dissect, delve into; informal check out, suss out.
4 *she studied her friend thoughtfully*: **scrutinize**, examine, inspect, consider, regard, look at, eye, observe, watch, survey, keep an eye on, keep under surveillance; informal clock, check out; N. Amer. informal eyeball.

Word links **study**

-ology study of something, as in *biology*
-ologist person who studies something, as in *biologist*

stuff noun 1 *suede is tough, resilient stuff*: **material**, fabric, cloth, textile; matter, substance, medium.
2 *the village shop sells first-aid stuff*: **items**, articles, objects, goods; informal **things**, bits and pieces, bits and bobs, odds and ends; Brit. informal odds and sods, gubbins.
3 *we stuck all my stuff in the suitcase*: **belongings**, possessions, personal possessions, effects, property, goods, goods and chattels; paraphernalia, accoutrements, appurtenances, trappings; informal gear, things, tackle, kit; Brit. informal clobber, gubbins.
4 *he knows his stuff*: **facts**, information, data, subject, discipline; informal onions.
□ **stuff and nonsense rubbish**, nonsense, twaddle, balderdash, claptrap, gibberish, drivel; informal poppycock, tripe, bunk, piffle, bosh, bilge, hot air, hogwash, hooey, baloney, mumbo-jumbo; Brit. informal cobblers, codswallop, tosh; Scottish & N. English informal **havers**; Irish informal codology; N. Amer. informal garbage, flapdoodle, blathers, wack, bushwa, applesauce; informal, dated tommyrot, rot, bunkum; vulgar slang bullshit, crap, bollocks, balls; Austral./NZ vulgar slang bulldust.
▶ **verb 1** *flowers were used to stuff pillows and mattresses*: **fill**, pack, pad, line, wad, upholster.
2 *Robyn stuffed clothes frantically into an overnight bag*: **shove**, thrust, push, ram, cram, squeeze, press, force, compress, jam, wedge; pack, crowd, stow, pile, stick.
3 *pregnant mums* ***stuff themselves with*** *such strange food*: **fill**, cram, gorge, overindulge, satiate; gobble, devour, wolf, guzzle; informal pig, pig out, make a pig of oneself, stuff oneself to the gills.
4 *my nose was* ***stuffed up*** *and my throat sore*: **block**, stop, bung; congest, obstruct, choke.
5 Brit. informal *their team got stuffed again on Saturday*. See **trounce**.

stuffing noun 1 *the stuffing is coming out of the armchair*: **padding**, wadding, lining, filling, quilting, cushioning, upholstery, packing, filler; down, duck down, flock, kapok.
2 *sage and onion stuffing*: **filling**, forcemeat, farce, salpicon; N. Amer. dressing.
□ **knock the stuffing out of** *Mike's death knocked the stuffing out of me*: **devastate**, shatter, crush, shock, stun, distress, upset, traumatize; demoralize; informal knock for six, knock sideways.

stuffy adjective 1 *a stuffy atmosphere*: **airless**, close, muggy, sultry, heavy, musty, stale, frowzy; stifling, suffocating, oppressive; Brit. frowsty; Brit. informal fuggy.
▷**ANTONYMS** airy.
2 *a stuffy young man*: **staid**, sedate, sober, stiff, reserved, impersonal, formal, pompous, prim, priggish, fogeyish, strait-laced, conformist, conventional, conservative, old-fashioned, of the old school; stodgy, boring, dull, dreary, uninteresting; informal square, straight, starchy, fuddy-duddy, stick-in-the-mud, uptight.
▷**ANTONYMS** relaxed, informal; modern.
3 *a stuffy nose*: **blocked**, stuffed up, bunged up.
▷**ANTONYMS** clear.

stultify verb 1 *free market forces had been stultified by the welfare state*: **hamper**, impede, obstruct, thwart, frustrate, foil, suppress, smother, repress.
2 *he stultifies her with too much gentleness*: **bore**, make bored, dull, numb, benumb, stupefy, deaden; informal bore rigid, bore stupid, bore to death; rare hebetate.
▷**ANTONYMS** excite.

stumble verb 1 *he stumbled on a brick and fell heavily*: **trip**, trip over, trip up, lose one's balance, lose/miss one's footing, founder, slip, pitch.
2 *he stumbled back to his hotel room*: **stagger**, totter, teeter, dodder, lurch, lumber, blunder, reel, flounder, bumble, shamble, hobble, wobble, move clumsily.
3 *the Consul had stumbled through his speech*: **stammer**, stutter, hesitate, falter, speak haltingly, fumble for words; flounder, blunder, muddle; informal fluff one's lines.
□ **stumble across/on** *the scientists stumbled across the vaccine by chance*: **come across**, come upon, chance on, happen on, light on, hit on, come up with; discover, encounter, find, unearth, uncover, locate, bring to light; informal dig up, put one's finger on.

stumbling block noun *the language problem is a fundamental stumbling block*: **obstacle**, hurdle, barrier, bar, hindrance, impediment, handicap, disadvantage, restriction, limitation; snag, hitch, catch, drawback, difficulty, problem, weakness, defect, pitfall, complication; informal fly in the ointment, hiccup, facer; Brit. informal spanner in the works; N. Amer. informal monkey wrench in the works.
▷**ANTONYMS** advantage, benefit.

stump noun *a tree stump | a stump of candle*: **stub**, end, tail end, remnant, remains, remainder, butt; piece, part, segment; informal fag end, dog end.
▶ **verb 1** *education chiefs were stumped by some of the exam questions*: **baffle**, perplex, puzzle, confuse, confound, bewilder, mystify, nonplus, defeat; be too much for, put at a loss, bring up short; informal flummox, fox, be all Greek to, throw, floor, discombobulate; archaic wilder, gravel, maze; rare obfuscate.
2 *she stumped along the landing to the bathroom*: **stomp**, stamp, clomp, clump, lumber, trudge, plod; thump, thud, bang, thunder.
□ **stump something up** Brit. informal *the banks would be willing to stump up the extra money*: **pay**, pay up, hand over, part with, give, put in, contribute, donate; informal **fork out**, shell out, dish out, lay out, come across with, cough up, chip in; N. Amer. informal ante up, pony up.

stumpy adjective *a little stumpy man | Ben cranked his bike with his stumpy legs*: **short**, stubby, squat, stunted; **stocky**, sturdy, chunky, heavily built, heavyset, solid, thickset, bull-necked; informal beefy; Brit. informal fubsy.
▷**ANTONYMS** long, thin.

stun verb 1 *a glancing blow stunned Gary*: **daze**, stupefy, knock senseless, knock unconscious, knock out, lay out; informal knock for six.
2 *she was quite stunned by her own success*: **astound**, amaze, astonish, startle, take someone's breath away, dumbfound, stupefy, overwhelm, stagger, shock, confound, take aback, shake up; informal flabbergast, knock for six, knock sideways, hit like a ton of bricks, bowl over, floor, blow away.

stunner noun informal *the girl was a stunner*: **beauty**, belle, goddess, Venus, siren, charmer, seductress; dream, vision, sensation; informal looker, good-looker, lovely, knockout, cracker, smasher, bobby-dazzler, dish, sight for sore eyes, eye-catcher, eyeful, peach, honey.

stunning adjective 1 *a stunning 4–0 win in the League Cup final*: **remarkable**, extraordinary, staggering, incredible, impressive, outstanding, amazing, astonishing, marvellous, phenomenal, splendid, imposing, breathtaking, thrilling; informal mind-boggling, mind-blowing, out of this world, fabulous, fab, super, fantastic, tremendous; literary wondrous.
▷**ANTONYMS** ordinary, run-of-the-mill.
2 *she was looking particularly stunning*: **beautiful**, handsome, attractive, lovely, good-looking, comely, pretty, sexy; sensational, radiant, ravishing, striking, dazzling, devastating, wonderful, marvellous, magnificent, glorious, breathtaking, captivating, bewitching, charming, alluring, exquisite, impressive, splendid; Scottish & N. English bonny; informal gorgeous, drop-dead gorgeous, out of this world, fabulous, fab, smashing, super, easy on the eye, knockout; N. Amer. informal bootylicious; literary beauteous; rare pulchritudinous.
▷**ANTONYMS** ordinary, unattractive.

stunt[1] verb *a rare disease that stunts growth*: **inhibit**, impede, hamper, hinder, restrict, retard, slow, curb, arrest, check, stop.
▷**ANTONYMS** promote, encourage.

stunt[2] noun *he performed stunts in circuses*: **feat**, exploit, trick, antic, caper; coup, act, action, deed; French tour de force.

stunted adjective *a clump of stunted trees*: **small**, little, tiny, undersized, undersize, diminutive, dwarf, dwarfish, pygmy; baby; Scottish wee.

stupefaction noun 1 *she has retreated into alcoholic stupefaction*: **oblivion**, obliviousness, unconsciousness, insensibility, senselessness, numbness, lack of sensation/feeling, blankness; stupor, daze, blackout, coma, collapse.
2 *Don shook his head in stupefaction*: **bewilderment**, confusion, perplexity, bafflement, wonder, wonderment, amazement, astonishment; shock, devastation.

stupefy verb 1 *the blow had stupefied her*: **stun**, daze, befuddle, knock senseless, knock unconscious, knock out, lay out, benumb, numb.
2 *they became stupefied by some narcotic*: **drug**, sedate, anaesthetize, give anaesthetic to, tranquillize, narcotize; intoxicate, inebriate; knock out, render unconscious; informal dope.
3 *the amount they spend on clothes would stupefy their grandparents*: **shock**, stun, astound, dumbfound, overwhelm, stagger, amaze, astonish, startle, confound, take aback, shake up, leave open-mouthed, take someone's breath away; informal flabbergast, knock for six, knock sideways, hit like a ton of bricks, bowl over, floor, blow away.

stupendous adjective 1 *truly stupendous achievements*: **amazing**, astounding, astonishing, extraordinary, remarkable, wonderful, prodigious,

S

phenomenal, staggering, breathtaking; informal fantastic, mind-boggling, mind-blowing, great, terrific, awesome, unreal; literary wondrous.
▷ANTONYMS run-of-the-mill, ordinary.
2 *a roc was an imaginary bird of stupendous size*: **colossal**, immense, vast, giant, gigantic, massive, monumental, mammoth, elephantine, gargantuan, prodigious, huge, very large, great, enormous, mighty, titanic, Herculean, Brobdingnagian; informal jumbo, bumper, monster, humongous, whopping, astronomical, mega; Brit. informal ginormous.
▷ANTONYMS minute, tiny.

stupid adjective 1 *they're not as stupid as they look*: **unintelligent**, ignorant, dense, brainless, mindless, foolish, dull-witted, dull, slow-witted, witless, slow, dunce-like, simple-minded, empty-headed, vacuous, vapid, half-witted, idiotic, moronic, imbecilic, imbecile, obtuse, doltish; gullible, naive; informal thick, thick as two short planks, dim, dumb, dopey, dozy, crazy, barmy, cretinous, birdbrained, pea-brained, pig-ignorant, bovine, slow on the uptake, soft in the head, brain-dead, boneheaded, lamebrained, thickheaded, chuckleheaded, dunderheaded, wooden, wooden-headed, fat-headed, muttonheaded; Brit. informal daft, not the full shilling; N. Amer. vulgar slang dumb-ass.
▷ANTONYMS intelligent, clever, astute.
2 *I promised never to make the same stupid mistake again*: **foolish**, silly, unintelligent, idiotic, brainless, mindless, scatterbrained, crackbrained, nonsensical, senseless, irresponsible, unthinking, ill-advised, ill-considered, inept, witless, damfool, unwise, injudicious, indiscreet, short-sighted; inane, absurd, ludicrous, ridiculous, laughable, risible, fatuous, asinine, pointless, meaningless, futile, fruitless, mad, insane, lunatic; informal crazy, dopey, cracked, half-baked, cock-eyed, hare-brained, nutty, potty, dotty, batty, barmy, gormless, cuckoo, loony, loopy, zany, screwy, off one's head, off one's trolley, out to lunch; Brit. informal daft; Scottish & N. English informal glaikit; N. Amer. vulgar slang half-assed.
▷ANTONYMS sensible, prudent.
3 *all he'd do was sit and drink himself stupid*: **into a stupor**, into a daze, into a state of unconsciousness, into oblivion; stupefied, dazed, groggy, sluggish, semi-conscious, unconscious.
▷ANTONYMS alert.

stupidity noun 1 *he cursed the older man's stupidity*: **lack of intelligence**, unintelligence, foolishness, denseness, brainlessness, ignorance, mindlessness, dull-wittedness, dull-headedness, dullness, slow-wittedness, doltishness, slowness, vacancy; gullibility, naivety; informal thickness, dimness, dumbness, dopiness, doziness, craziness.
▷ANTONYMS genius.
2 *she blushed at the stupidity of the question*: **foolishness**, folly, silliness, idiocy, brainlessness, senselessness, irresponsibility, injudiciousness, ineptitude, inaneness, inanity, irrationality, absurdity, ludicrousness, ridiculousness, fatuousness, fatuity, asininity, pointlessness, meaninglessness, futility, fruitlessness, madness, insanity, lunacy; informal craziness; Brit. informal daftness.
▷ANTONYMS sagacity.

stupor noun *they left him slumped in a drunken stupor*: **daze**, state of stupefaction, state of senselessness, state of unconsciousness; inertia, torpor, insensibility, numbness, blankness, oblivion, coma, blackout; Scottish dwam; rare sopor.

sturdy adjective 1 *the boy had grown sturdy and handsome*: **strapping**, well built, well made, muscular, athletic, strong, hefty, brawny, powerfully built, powerful, solidly built, solid, burly, stocky, thickset, rugged, substantial, robust, vigorous, tough, hardy, mighty, lusty, Herculean; fit, able-bodied, healthy, in good health, hale and hearty, hearty, hale, in good shape, in good condition, sound, sound in body and limb; informal husky, beefy, meaty, chunky, fit as a fiddle; dated stalwart; literary thewy, stark.
▷ANTONYMS puny; frail.
2 *the boat was small but it was sturdy*: **robust**, strong, strongly made, well built, well made, solid, substantial, stout, sound, serviceable, stable; tough, resilient, durable, long-lasting, built to last, hard-wearing, imperishable, indestructible, resistant; dated staunch.
▷ANTONYMS weak, ramshackle.
3 *nature is offering a sturdy resistance to man*: **vigorous**, strong, stalwart, firm, determined, resolute, tenacious, staunch, steadfast, unyielding, unwavering, uncompromising.
▷ANTONYMS weak.

Word toolkit **sturdy**

See **burly**.

stutter verb *he stuttered over a word*: **stammer**, stumble, speak haltingly, falter, speak falteringly, flounder, hesitate, pause, halt; blunder, splutter; informal fluff one's lines.
▶noun *the editor had a bad stutter*: **stammer**, speech impediment, speech defect; hesitancy, faltering.

Word links **stutter**

lalophobia fear of stuttering

Stygian adjective literary *Paris was plunged after dark into Stygian gloom*: **dark**, black, pitch-black, pitch-dark, inky, sooty, dusky, dim, murky, shadowy, unlit; gloomy, sombre, dismal, dreary, hellish, infernal, Hadean; literary crepuscular, tenebrous, Cimmerian, Tartarean, caliginous.

style noun 1 *notice the differing styles of these two writers*: **manner**, way, technique, method, methodology, approach, system, mode, form, practice; Latin modus operandi; informal MO.
2 *a non-directive style of counselling*: **type**, kind, manner, variety, sort, nature, genre, vein, species, ilk, vintage, school, brand, quality, calibre, kidney; design, pattern, stamp, model, cast, grain; N. Amer. stripe.
3 *they wear their clothes with style*: **flair**, stylishness, smartness, elegance, grace, gracefulness, poise, polish, suaveness, sophistication, urbanity, chic, dash, finesse, panache, elan, taste; informal class, pizzazz, ritziness, oomph, zing.
4 *Laura travelled in style*: **comfort**, **luxury**, elegance, chic; affluence, wealth, opulence, lavishness.
5 *the groovy styles portrayed in the magazine*: **fashion**, trend, vogue, mode, latest thing; fad, craze, rage.
6 *candidates are asked to criticize both the content and style of the novel*: **phraseology**, mode of expression, wording, language.
▶verb 1 *winter sportswear styled by Karl and Derrick*: **design**, fashion, tailor, make, produce.
2 *by 1300 there were about eighty men styled 'knight'*: **call**, name, title, entitle, dub, designate, term, address, label, tag; christen, baptize, nickname; archaic clepe; rare denominate.

stylish adjective *a stylish gown | they are incredibly stylish people*: **fashionable**, modish, voguish, modern, ultra-modern, contemporary, up to date, up to the minute, trendsetting; smart, sophisticated, elegant, chic, polished, dapper, debonair, dashing, fine, fancy, flashy, designer; French à la mode; informal trendy, with it, all the rage, bang up to date, in, now, hip, cool, big, natty, classy, nifty, dressy, ritzy, snazzy, snappy, flash, sharp, fancy-pants; N. Amer. informal fly, kicky, tony, spiffy.
▷ANTONYMS unfashionable, dowdy.

Word toolkit **stylish**

See **gracious**.

stylus noun **needle**, pointer, probe, style; pen, hand; rare graphium.

stymie verb *NHS changes must not be allowed to stymie new medical treatments*: **impede**, interfere with, hamper, hinder, obstruct, inhibit, frustrate, thwart, foil, spoil, stall, shackle, fetter, stop, check, block, cripple, handicap, scotch; informal put paid to, put the kibosh on, snooker; Brit. informal scupper, throw a spanner in the works of; N. Amer. informal throw a monkey wrench in the works of.
▷ANTONYMS assist, help.

suave adjective *a suave middle-aged man*: **charming**, sophisticated, debonair, urbane, worldly, worldly-wise, polished, refined, poised, self-possessed, dignified, civilized, gentlemanly, gallant; smooth, smooth-talking, smooth-tongued, silver-tongued, glib, bland, polite, well mannered, civil, courteous, affable, tactful, diplomatic, slick; informal cool; dated mannerly.
▷ANTONYMS unsophisticated, rude.

suavity noun *he was somewhat shaken from his confident suavity*: **charm**, sophistication, polish, urbanity, suaveness, worldliness, refinement, confidence, poise, aplomb, dignity, gentility, style; smoothness, politeness, courtesy, courteousness, civility, tact, tactfulness, diplomacy, subtlety; French savoir faire.

subconscious adjective *dreams reflect a person's subconscious desires*: **unconscious**, latent, suppressed, repressed, subliminal, unfulfilled, dormant, hidden, concealed, underlying, innermost, deep, intuitive, instinctive, innate, involuntary; informal bottled up.
▷ANTONYMS conscious, expressed.
▶noun *the creative powers of the subconscious*: **unconscious mind**, mind, imagination, inner self, innermost self, self, inner man/woman, psyche, ego, superego, id, true being, essential nature.
▷ANTONYMS conscious mind.

subdue verb 1 *he is said to have slain or subdued all those who had plotted against him*: **conquer**, defeat, vanquish, get the better of, overpower, overcome, overwhelm, crush, quash, quell, beat, trounce, subjugate, master, suppress, gain the upper hand over, triumph over, tame, bring someone to their knees, hold in check, humble, chasten, cow; informal lick, thrash, wipe the floor with, clobber, demolish, hammer, make mincemeat of, walk all over.
2 *she could not subdue her longing for praise*: **curb**, restrain, hold back, constrain, contain, inhibit, repress, suppress, stifle, smother, check, keep in check, arrest, bridle, rein in; control, govern, master, quash, quell; moderate, tone down, diminish, lessen, damp; informal lick, nip in the bud, keep a/the lid on.

subdued adjective 1 *Lewis's subdued air had changed to one of high good humour*: **sombre**, low-spirited, downcast, sad, dejected, depressed, low, gloomy, despondent, dispirited, disheartened, forlorn, woebegone; restrained, repressed, inactive, spiritless, lifeless, dull, unresponsive,

withdrawn, pensive, thoughtful, preoccupied, quiet; informal down in the mouth, down in the dumps, out of sorts, in the doldrums, with a long face; Brit. informal brassed off, cheesed off, browned off; N. Amer. informal teed off, ticked off.
▷ANTONYMS lively, cheerful.
2 *they chatted in subdued tones*: **hushed**, muted, quiet, low, soft, gentle, whispered, murmured, faint, muffled, indistinct, inaudible; noiseless, soundless, silent, still, calm.
▷ANTONYMS loud, noisy.
3 *the subdued light made Mary appear pale*: **dim**, muted, toned down, softened, soft, lowered, shaded, low-key, subtle, unobtrusive, understated; sombre, dreary, dark.
▷ANTONYMS bright.

subject noun (stress on the first syllable) **1** *the structure of the economy is the subject of this chapter*: **theme**, subject matter, topic, issue, question, concern, text, thesis, content, point, motif, thread; substance, essence, gist, matter.
2 *there were cuts in funding for popular university subjects*: **branch of knowledge**, branch of study, course of study, course, discipline, field, area, specialism, speciality, specialty.
3 *six subjects did trials of the short-term memory tasks*: **participant**, volunteer; case, client, patient; informal guinea pig.
4 *Australians were simultaneously citizens and British subjects until 1984*: **citizen**, national, native, resident, inhabitant; taxpayer, voter.
5 *Santerre is a loyal subject of the king*: **liege**, liegeman, vassal, subordinate, underling; henchman, retainer, follower.
▶ verb (stress on the second syllable) *they have been* ***subjected to*** *physical violence*: **put through**, treat with; expose to, lay open to, submit to.
▶ adjective (stress on the first syllable)
□ **subject to 1** *the position is subject to budgetary approval*: **conditional on**, contingent on, dependent on, depending on, controlled by; hingeing on, resting on, hanging on. **2** *horses are subject to a cough resembling the human common cold*: **susceptible to**, liable to, prone to, vulnerable to, predisposed to, disposed to, apt/likely to suffer from, easily affected by, in danger of, at risk of, open to, wide open to; rare susceptive of. ▷ANTONYMS resistant.
3 *most people were subject to authority for a large part of their lives*: **bound by**, constrained by, answerable to, accountable to, liable to, under the control of, at the mercy of.

Choose the right word **subject, topic, theme**

Subject is the most general term for something that is or could be written, talked, or thought about (*his mind was no longer on the subject of politics | please send questions on any subjects you would like discussed*). A *subject* also means a branch of knowledge studied at school, college, or university (*sixth-form classes in less popular A-level subjects*).

When distinguished from *subject*, **topic** can refer to a smaller and more specific area for discussion (*from this very complex subject, two topics concerning government grants have been selected for discussion in this section*). It is also the most common word for something discussed in speech (*her sole topic of conversation nowadays was the baby*).

A **theme** is typically associated with a relatively long work or discussion and tends to be an underlying idea, recurring throughout it and unifying it (*she deals delicately with the themes of love and jealousy*). A *theme* is generally *developed* or *elaborated* rather than *discussed* or *debated*.

subjection noun *the subjection of aboriginal peoples*: **subjugation**, domination, oppression, control, mastery, repression, suppression, bondage, slavery, enslavement, persecution, exploitation, abuse.

subjective adjective *standards can be judged on quantitative data rather than on subjective opinion*: **personal**, personalized, individual, internal, emotional, instinctive, intuitive, impressionistic; biased, prejudiced, bigoted, idiosyncratic, irrational; informal gut, gut reaction.
▷ANTONYMS objective, impartial.

subjugate verb *Norman leaders had subjugated most of Ireland's Gaelic population*: **conquer**, vanquish, defeat, crush, quell, quash, gain mastery over, gain ascendancy over, gain control of, bring under the yoke, bring to heel, bring someone to their knees, overcome, overpower; enslave, tyrannize, oppress, repress, subdue, colonize, suppress; tame, break, humble; informal lick, clobber, hammer, wipe the floor with, walk all over.
▷ANTONYMS liberate.

sublimate verb *work can serve as a means of sublimating rage*: **channel**, control, divert, transfer, redirect, convert, refine, purify, transmute.

sublime adjective **1** *a sublime vision of human potential*: **exalted**, elevated, noble, lofty, awe-inspiring, awesome, majestic, magnificent, imposing, glorious, supreme; grand, great, outstanding, excellent, first-rate, first-class, superb, perfect, ideal, wonderful, marvellous, splendid, delightful, blissful, rapturous; informal fantastic, fabulous, fab, super, smashing, terrific, stellar, heavenly, divine, mind-blowing, too good to be true, out of this world.
▷ANTONYMS poor, lowly, ordinary.
2 *the sublime confidence of youth*: **supreme**, total, complete, utter, consummate, extreme; arrogant.

subliminal adjective *the screen flashed subliminal messages*: **subconscious**, unconscious; hidden, concealed.
▷ANTONYMS explicit.

submerge verb **1** *the U-boat would have had time to submerge*: **go under water**, dive, sink, plunge, plummet, drop, go down.
▷ANTONYMS surface.
2 *half submerge the bowl in a large saucepan of hot water*: **immerse**, dip, plunge, duck, dunk, sink.
3 *when the farmland was submerged many sheep were lost*: **flood**, inundate, deluge, engulf, swamp, immerse, drown; overflow, pour over.
4 *her husband helped her to resist becoming completely submerged in work*: **overwhelm**, inundate, deluge, swamp, bury, engulf, swallow up, consume, snow under, overload, overburden.
5 *a healthy return to old values which had been submerged*: **hide**, conceal, veil, cloak, repress, suppress.

submission noun **1** *an instinctive submission to authority*: **yielding**, capitulation, agreement, acceptance, consent, accession, compliance.
▷ANTONYMS defiance.
2 *Tim raised his hands in mock submission*: **surrender**, yielding, capitulation, resignation, succumbing, defeat, fall; laying down one's arms, giving in, humbling oneself, knuckling under.
3 *he wanted to gain her total submission*: **compliance**, submissiveness, yielding, malleability, acquiescence, tractability, tractableness, manageability, unassertiveness, non-resistance, passivity, obedience, biddability, dutifulness, duteousness, docility, meekness, tameness, patience, resignation, humility, self-effacement, deference, subservience, servility, subjection, self-abasement, obsequiousness, obeisance; informal bootlicking.
▷ANTONYMS defiance, resistance.
4 *you are required to write a report for submission to the Board*: **presentation**, presenting, proffering, tendering, proposal, proposing, tabling, introduction, suggestion, venturing, broaching, airing, lodgement, positing.
5 *the plan was put forward by Stirling in his original submission*: **proposal**, suggestion, proposition, recommendation, presentation, tender, bid, offer; motion, entry, advance, approach, overture; attempt, try, effort, draft; proffer.
6 *the trial judge rejected his submission*: **argument**, assertion, contention, statement, claim, allegation, protestation, declaration.

submissive adjective *Mary was far from being a timidly submissive woman*: **compliant**, yielding, malleable, acquiescent, accommodating, amenable, tractable, manageable, unassertive, non-resisting, passive, obedient, biddable, dutiful, duteous, docile, ductile, pliant, meek, timid, mild, patient, resigned, forbearing, subdued, humble, self-effacing, spiritless, deferential, obsequious, servile, slavish, self-abasing, spineless, grovelling, lamblike, supine; informal bootlicking, under someone's thumb; archaic resistless; rare longanimous.
▷ANTONYMS domineering, obstinate, intractable.

submissiveness noun *he could exhibit a saint-like submissiveness*: **compliance**, submission, subservience, yielding, acquiescence, deference, assent, meekness, obedience, dutifulness, duteousness, biddableness, malleability, tractableness, tractability, tameness, docility, passiveness, passivity, humility, resignation, forbearance; obsequiousness, sycophancy, servility, self-abasement; informal bootlicking.
▷ANTONYMS assertiveness.

submit verb **1** *the countess had submitted under duress | you are* ***submitting*** *to male domination*: **give in**, yield, give way, back down, cave in, bow, capitulate, relent, defer, agree, consent, accede, conform, acquiesce, comply, accept; surrender, lay down one's arms, raise/show/wave the white flag, knuckle under, humble oneself, bend the knee, kowtow, fall; informal throw in the towel/sponge.
▷ANTONYMS defy.
2 *he refused to* ***submit to*** *censorship*: **be governed by**, abide by, be regulated by, comply with, observe, heed, accept, tolerate, endure, brook, put up with, stomach, adhere to, be subject to, agree to, consent to, conform to; informal keep in step, play by the rules, play it by the book, take it lying down, lump it; Brit. informal wear; archaic suffer.
▷ANTONYMS defy, resist.
3 *we submitted an unopposed bid for the franchise*: **put forward**, present, set forth, offer, proffer, tender, advance, propose, suggest, volunteer, table, lodge, introduce, come up with, raise, air, moot; put in, send in, hand in, enter, register.
▷ANTONYMS withdraw.
4 *the appellant submitted that a community service order was inappropriate*: **contend**, assert, argue, state, claim, aver, propound, posit, postulate, adduce, move, advocate, venture, volunteer; formal opine.

subordinate adjective **1** *she kept her distance from subordinate staff*: **lower-ranking**, junior, lower, lesser, inferior, lowly, minor, supporting; second-fiddle.
▷ANTONYMS superior, senior.
2 *a subordinate rule*: **secondary**, lesser, minor, subsidiary, subservient, ancillary, auxiliary, attendant, peripheral, marginal, of little account/

S

importance; second-class, second-rate, second-fiddle; supplementary, accessory, additional, extra.
▷ANTONYMS central, major, chief.
▶noun *the manager and his or her subordinate jointly review performance*: **junior**, assistant, second, second in command, number two, right-hand man/woman, deputy, aide, adjutant, subaltern, apprentice, underling, flunkey, minion, lackey, mate, inferior; informal sidekick, henchman, second fiddle, man/girl Friday.
▷ANTONYMS superior, senior.

subordination noun *she could not tolerate a life of subordination*: **inferiority**, inferior status/position, secondary status/position, lowliness; **subjection**, subservience, submission, dependence, servitude.
▷ANTONYMS superiority.

sub rosa adverb Latin *the committee is accustomed to operate sub rosa*: **in secret**, secretly, in private, privately, in confidence, confidentially, behind closed doors, surreptitiously, discreetly, furtively, clandestinely, on the quiet, on the sly, unofficially, off the record, between ourselves; Latin in camera; French à huis clos; Italian in petto; informal on the q.t., between you, me, and the gatepost/bedpost; archaic under the rose.
▷ANTONYMS openly, publicly.

subscribe verb **1** *How many magazines do you* ***subscribe to****?* **pay a subscription**, buy regularly, take, take regularly, read, read regularly, contract to buy; be a member of, support.
2 *his release was secured by friends* ***subscribing to*** *a ransom fund*: **donate**, make a donation, make a subscription, give, give money, make a contribution, pay, pledge; contribute towards, sponsor, finance, back, subsidize, underwrite; informal chip into, pitch into; N. Amer. informal kick in.
3 *I'm afraid I can't* ***subscribe to*** *the theory*: **agree with**, be in agreement with, accede to, consent to, accept, believe in, endorse, back, support, advocate, champion.
4 *the names of signatories are subscribed*: **sign**, write, inscribe, initial, autograph, countersign, witness, put one's mark on; add, append; Law set one's hand to; archaic underwrite, style, side-sign; rare chirographate.

subscriber noun *the journal has 10,000 subscribers*: **reader**, regular reader, regular customer, follower, member, patron, supporter, backer, benefactor, sponsor, donor, contributor.

subscription noun **1** *a subscription to a London club*: **membership fee**, dues, annual payment, charge, levy, retainer.
2 *the charity put every penny of your subscription to good use*: **donation**, contribution, offering, gift, present, grant, bestowal, endowment, subsidy, benefaction, handout; historical alms; rare donative.
3 *he wanted to beat up anyone who flaunted their* ***subscription to*** *capitalism*: **agreement with**, subscribing to, acceding to, consent to, acceptance of, belief in, endorsement of, backing for, support of.
4 *the subscription of the document was attested by at least one witness*: **signature**, initials; addition, appendage.

subsequent adjective *he was a caring and stalwart friend to her during the subsequent months*: **following**, ensuing, succeeding, successive, later, future, coming, upcoming, to come, next.
▷ANTONYMS previous, prior, former.
□ **subsequent to** *a record would be published subsequent to the meetings*: **following**, after, in the wake of, at the close/end of, later than; rare posterior to.
▷ANTONYMS prior to.

subsequently adverb *he made a bid for the remaining shares and subsequently acquired them*: **later**, later on, at a later date, at some time/point in the future, at a subsequent time, afterwards, in due course, following this/that, eventually, then, next, by and by; informal after a bit; formal thereafter, thereupon.
▷ANTONYMS previously.

subservient adjective **1** *women were expected to be decorative and subservient*: **submissive**, deferential, acquiescent, compliant, accommodating, obedient, dutiful, duteous, biddable, yielding, meek, docile, ductile, pliant, passive, unassertive, spiritless, subdued, humble, timid, mild, lamblike; servile, slavish, grovelling, truckling, self-effacing, self-abasing, downtrodden, snivelling, cowering, cringing; informal under someone's thumb; archaic resistless; rare longanimous.
▷ANTONYMS domineering; independent.
2 *the rights of the individual are being made* ***subservient to*** *the interests of the state*: **subordinate**, secondary, subsidiary, peripheral, marginal, ancillary, auxiliary, supplementary, inferior, immaterial; less important than, of lesser importance than, lower than.
▷ANTONYMS superior.
3 *the whole narration is* ***subservient to*** *the moral plan of exemplifying twelve virtues*: **ancillary**, subordinate, secondary, supportive; instrumental, contributory, conducive, helpful, useful, advantageous, beneficial, valuable.

subside verb **1** *I'll wait a few minutes until the storm subsides | his anger subsided and he smiled*: **abate**, let up, moderate, quieten down, calm, lull, slacken (off), ease (up), relent, die down, die out, peter out, taper off, recede, lessen, soften, alleviate, attenuate, remit, diminish, decline, dwindle, weaken, fade, wane, ebb, still, cease, come to a stop, come to an end, terminate.
▷ANTONYMS intensify, worsen.
2 *the ground was still waterlogged after the flood had subsided*: **recede**, ebb, fall back, flow back, fall away, fall, go down, get lower, sink, sink lower; abate, diminish; rare retrocede.
▷ANTONYMS rise.
3 *the molten core of a volcano subsides into the earth*: **sink**, sink back, settle, cave in, fall in, collapse, crumple, give way, drop down, sag, slump.
4 *Sarah subsided into a chair*: **slump**, flop, sink, sag, slouch, loll, fall back, collapse, settle; informal flump, plonk oneself, plop oneself.
▷ANTONYMS rise.

subsidence noun *subsidence due to coal mining is a notorious problem*: **collapse**, caving in, falling in, giving way, sinking, settling.

subsidiary adjective *a subsidiary company | monetary policy should be subsidiary to fiscal policy*: **subordinate**, secondary, ancillary, auxiliary, lesser, minor, subservient, supplementary, supplemental, additional, extra, attendant, peripheral; second-fiddle, second-class, lower-level, lower-grade.
▷ANTONYMS central, principal, major.
▶noun *he is a director of the company's two major subsidiaries*: **subordinate company**, wholly owned company; **branch**, division, subdivision, section, part, dependency, peripheral, derivative, satellite, offshoot, wing, attachment, adjunct, appendage; archaic tributary.
▷ANTONYMS parent company.

subsidize verb *they were unwilling to subsidize the poorer southern republics*: **give money to**, pay a subsidy to, give a grant to, contribute to, make a contribution to, invest in, sponsor, fund, finance, provide finance/capital for, capitalize, underwrite; back, support, give support to, keep, help, aid, assist, shore up, prop up, buttress; informal pick up the tab for, foot the bill for, shell out for, fork out for, cough up for, chip in for; N. Amer. informal bankroll, pony up for.

subsidy noun *the theatre receives a subsidy of 1.7 million pounds a year*: **grant**, allowance, endowment, contribution, donation, bursary, gift, present, investment, bestowal, benefaction, allocation, allotment, handout; backing, support, aid, assistance, charity, relief, sponsorship, finance, funding, subvention; informal helping hand, leg up; historical alms; rare donative.

subsist verb **1** *he subsisted on a university pension | the birds cannot subsist on fruit alone*: **survive**, live, stay alive, exist, eke out an existence, endure; **support oneself**, cope, manage, fare, get along, get by, get through, make (both) ends meet, make the grade, keep body and soul together, depend, rely for nourishment, feed; informal keep the wolf from the door, keep one's head above water, make out, hang on.
2 *the tenant's right of occupation subsists*: **continue**, last, persist, endure, prevail, hold out, carry on, live on, live, survive, be in existence, exist, be alive, remain, abide, linger.
3 *the effect of genetic maldevelopment may* ***subsist in*** *chromasomal mutation*: **lie**, reside, have its being, be inherent, rest, dwell, abide, be present, inhere; be attributable to, be ascribable to, be intrinsic to; rare indwell.

subsistence noun **1** *they depend for subsistence on fish and game*: **survival**, existence, living, life; sustenance, nourishment, diet.
2 *he raised a total of £2,000 towards his own travel and subsistence*: **maintenance**, keep, upkeep, support, livelihood, living, board, board and lodging; sustenance, nourishment, nutriment, provisions, supplies, food, food and drink, fare, bread; Scottish vivers; informal eats, nosh, chow, grub, scoff, bread and butter; formal comestibles, provender; archaic meat, vittles, commons, victuals, viands; rare aliment.

substance noun **1** *an organic substance*: **material**, matter, stuff, medium, fabric.
2 *he saw ghostly figures with no substance*: **solidity**, body, corporeality, reality, actuality, materiality, concreteness, tangibility; density, mass, weight, shape, structure.
3 *none of the objections put forward has any substance*: **meaningfulness**, significance, importance, import, moment, power, soundness, validity, content, pith, marrow, core; basis, foundation; informal clout.
4 *the substance of the tale is too thin and familiar by far*: **content**, subject matter, subject, theme, topic, text, message, material, burden, tenor, essence, quintessence, heart, meat, gist, drift, sense, import.
5 *Rangers are a team of substance and skill*: **character**, backbone, mettle, strength of character; consequence, import, importance, significance, moment, magnitude, prominence; informal clout.
6 *the proprietors were independent men of substance*: **wealth**, fortune, riches, affluence, prosperity, money, capital, means, resources, assets, property, estates, possessions.

substandard adjective *children were being educated in substandard buildings*: **inferior**, second-rate, low-quality, low-grade, poor, poor-quality, inadequate, imperfect, faulty, defective, jerry-built, shoddy, shabby, crude, unsound, unacceptable, unsatisfactory, unworthy, disappointing; informal below par, not up to scratch, not up to snuff, tenth-rate, crummy, lousy; Brit. informal **duff**, **ropy**, **rubbish**; vulgar slang **crap**, **crappy**; N. Amer. vulgar slang chickenshit.

S

substantial adjective **1** *spirits are shadowy, human beings substantial*: **real**, true, actual, existing; **physical**, solid, material, concrete, corporeal, tangible, non-spiritual; rare unimaginary.
▷ANTONYMS incorporeal, abstract.
2 *substantial progress had been made*: **considerable**, real, material, weighty, solid, sizeable, meaningful, significant, important, notable, major, marked, valuable, useful, worthwhile.
▷ANTONYMS insubstantial, worthless.
3 *the plaintiff is unlikely to recover substantial damages*: **sizeable**, considerable, significant, large, ample, appreciable, goodly, decent; informal tidy.
4 *a row of substantial Victorian villas*: **sturdy**, solid, stout, strong, well built, well constructed, durable, long-lasting, hard-wearing, imperishable, impervious.
▷ANTONYMS insubstantial, jerry-built.
5 *the food is fit for substantial country gentlemen*: **hefty**, stout, sturdy, strapping, large, big, solid, bulky, burly, well built, weighty, portly, tubby, chubby, beefy.
▷ANTONYMS slight, gaunt.
6 *substantial City companies*: **successful**, buoyant, booming, doing well, profit-making, profitable, prosperous, wealthy, affluent, moneyed, well-to-do, rich, large; informal in the money, rolling in it, loaded, stinking rich, quids in.
▷ANTONYMS paltry.
7 *he is in substantial agreement with Lomax*: **fundamental**, essential, basic.

substantially adverb **1** *the cost of oil imports has fallen substantially*: **considerably**, significantly, greatly, a great deal, to a great extent, to a large extent, to a marked extent, markedly, appreciably.
▷ANTONYMS slightly.
2 *the draft statement was substantially accepted by the executive*: **largely**, for the most part, by and large, on the whole, almost entirely, in the main, mainly, in effect, in essence, essentially, materially, basically, fundamentally, to all intents and purposes, to a great degree.

substantiate verb *none of the allegations were ever substantiated*: **prove**, give proof of, show to be true, give substance to, support, uphold, back up, bear out, justify, vindicate, validate, corroborate, verify, authenticate, confirm, endorse, give credence to, lend weight to, establish, demonstrate; vouch for, attest to, testify to, stand by, bear witness to.
▷ANTONYMS disprove, refute.

substitute noun *the casual workers might be substitutes for agency workers*: **replacement**, deputy, relief, proxy, reserve, surrogate, cover, fill-in, stand-in, standby, locum, locum tenens, understudy, stopgap, alternative, ancillary; informal sub; N. Amer. informal pinch-hitter.
▶ adjective *a substitute teacher*: **acting**, replacement, deputy, relief, reserve, surrogate, fill-in, stand-in, temporary, caretaker, alternative, locum, standby, backup, stopgap, interim, provisional, pro tem, proxy, ancillary; Latin pro tempore; informal second-string; N. Amer. informal pinch-hitting.
▷ANTONYMS permanent.
▶ verb **1** *low-fat cheese can be **substituted for** full-fat cheese*: **exchange**, use as a replacement, switch; replace with, use instead of, use as an alternative to, use in place of, use in preference to; N. Amer. trade; informal swap.
2 *the Senate was empowered to **substitute for** the President*: **deputize**, act as deputy, act as a substitute, fill in, sit in, stand in, act as stand-in, cover, act as locum, be a proxy, hold the fort; take the place of, replace, relieve, understudy, take over from, represent, act in someone's stead; informal sub, fill someone's boots/shoes, step into someone's boots/shoes; N. Amer. informal pinch-hit.

substitution noun *the substitution of a steam locomotive for horsepower*: **exchange**, change, interchange; **replacement**, replacing, swapping, switching; swap, switch, trade-off, barter; N. Amer. trade.

subterfuge noun **1** *journalists should not use subterfuge to gain admission to people's homes*: **trickery**, intrigue, deviousness, evasion, deceit, deception, dishonesty, cheating, duplicity, guile, cunning, craft, craftiness, slyness, chicanery, bluff, pretence, fraud, fraudulence, sophistry, sharp practice; informal monkey business, funny business, hanky-panky, jiggery-pokery, kidology, every trick in the book; Irish informal codology.
▷ANTONYMS honesty, openness.
2 *a disreputable subterfuge*: **trick**, hoax, ruse, wile, ploy, stratagem, artifice, dodge, bluff, manoeuvre, machination, pretext, pretence, expedient, tactic, intrigue, scheme, deception, fraud, masquerade, blind, smokescreen, sleight, stunt, game; informal con, racket, scam, caper; Brit. informal wheeze; Austral. informal lurk; archaic shift.

subtle adjective **1** *the colours are soft and subtle | the dish had a very subtle flavour*: **understated**, low-key, muted, toned down, subdued; **delicate**, faint, pale, soft, indistinct, indefinite, vague, washed out.
▷ANTONYMS lurid; obvious.
2 *subtle distinctions are of little value*: **fine**, fine-drawn, ultra-fine, nice, overnice, minute, precise, narrow, tenuous; **hair-splitting**, indistinct, indefinite, elusive, abstruse; informal minuscule.
▷ANTONYMS crude.
3 *a robust and subtle mind*: **astute**, keen, quick, fine, acute, sharp, razor-like, razor-sharp, rapier-like, canny, shrewd, aware, perceptive, discerning, sensitive, discriminating, penetrating, sagacious, wise, clever, intelligent, skilful, artful; sapient, percipient, perspicacious; informal on the ball, savvy; archaic politic.
▷ANTONYMS slow-witted.
4 *the plan was simple yet subtle*: **ingenious**, clever, skilful, adroit, cunning, crafty, wily, artful, devious.
▷ANTONYMS crude, artless.

subtlety noun **1** *they prefer the cheese for its subtlety and depth of flavour*: **delicacy**, delicateness, subtleness, elusiveness, faintness; **understatedness**, understatement, mutedness, softness.
2 *classification is fraught with subtlety*: **fineness**, subtleness, precision, preciseness, niceness, nicety, nuance, shade, detail, slightness, minuteness, narrowness, tenuousness, indistinctness, indefiniteness, lack of definition, elusiveness.
3 *the subtlety of the human mind*: **astuteness**, keenness, acuteness, fineness, sharpness, razor-sharpness, sharp-wittedness, canniness, shrewdness, perceptiveness, perception, discernment, sensitivity, discrimination, penetration, percipience, perspicacity, perspicuity, acuity, sagacity, wisdom, cleverness, intelligence, skilfulness, skill, artfulness, dexterity, brightness, finesse; informal savvy; rare sapience.
▷ANTONYMS slow-wittedness, dullness.
4 *the employers' tactics varied in their subtlety*: **ingenuity**, cleverness, skilfulness, expertise, adroitness, complexity, intricacy, cunning, guile, craftiness, wiliness, artfulness, deviousness.
▷ANTONYMS crudeness.

subtract verb *the value of their child benefit is subtracted from their total welfare payments*: **take away**, take from, take off, deduct, debit, abstract, discount, dock, remove, withdraw; informal knock off, minus.
▷ANTONYMS add.

suburb noun *a densely populated suburb of Amsterdam*: **outlying district**, residential area, dormitory area/town, commuter belt, conurbation; suburbia, fringes, outskirts, purlieus; Brit. garden suburb; N. Amer. bedroom area; French faubourg, banlieue; Spanish barrio; rare exurb.

suburban adjective **1** *a suburban area*: **residential**, commuter, dormitory; N. Amer. bedroom; rare exurban.
2 *he brought some much-needed glamour to Karen's drab suburban existence*: **dull**, boring, uninteresting, conventional, ordinary, commonplace, average, unremarkable, undistinguished, unexceptional, pedestrian; **provincial**, unsophisticated, small-town, parochial, parish-pump, insular, inward-looking, limited, blinkered, bourgeois, middle-class, conservative; informal bog-standard, nothing to write home about, no great shakes, not up to much; Brit. informal common or garden.
▷ANTONYMS sophisticated, cosmopolitan.

subversive adjective *he was arrested and charged with subversive activities*: **disruptive**, troublemaking, inflammatory, insurgent, insurrectionary, insurrectionist, rabble-rousing; **seditious**, revolutionary, treasonous, treacherous, mutinous, rebellious, rebel, renegade, unpatriotic, dissident, disloyal, perfidious, insubordinate, underground, undermining, corrupting, discrediting, destructive, harmful.
▶ noun *she was designated as a dangerous subversive*: **troublemaker**, dissident, agitator, revolutionary, revolutionist, insurgent, insurrectionist, insurrectionary, renegade, rebel, mutineer, traitor.

subvert verb **1** *a plot to subvert the state*: **destabilize**, unsettle, overthrow, overturn; bring down, bring about the downfall of, topple, depose, oust, supplant, unseat, dethrone, disestablish, dissolve; disrupt, wreak havoc on, sabotage, ruin, upset, destroy, annihilate, demolish, wreck, undo, undermine, undercut, weaken, impair, damage.
2 *he tried to subvert the minds of innocent teenagers*: **corrupt**, pervert, warp, deprave, defile, debase, distort, contaminate, poison, embitter; vitiate.

subway noun **1** *he walked through the subway*: **underpass**, underground passage, pedestrian tunnel, tunnel.
2 *a ride on Tokyo's subway*: **underground railway**, underground, metro; Brit. informal tube.

succeed verb **1** *Darwin succeeded where earlier evolutionists had failed*: **triumph**, be victorious, achieve success, be successful, be a success, do well, make good, prosper, flourish, thrive, advance; informal make it, make the grade, cut it, crack it, make a name for oneself, make one's mark, get somewhere, do all right for oneself, arrive, find a place in the sun.
▷ANTONYMS fail.
2 *the plan would have succeeded but for an important factor*: **be successful**, turn out well, work, work out, go as planned, get results, be effective, be profitable; informal come off, pay off, pan out, do the trick.
▷ANTONYMS fail, flop.
3 *Rosebery had succeeded Gladstone as Prime Minister*: **replace**, take the place of, take over from, come after, follow, supersede, supplant, displace, oust, remove, unseat, usurp; informal step into someone's shoes, fill someone's shoes/boots.
▷ANTONYMS precede.
4 *he succeeded to his title in 1543*: **inherit**, accede to, assume, take over, come into, acquire, attain, be elevated to.
▷ANTONYMS renounce, abdicate.

S

5 *their age of learning was succeeded by an age of superstition*: **follow**, come after, follow after; take the place of, replace.
▷ANTONYMS precede.

succeeding adjective *strands of DNA are reproduced through succeeding generations*: **subsequent**, successive, following, ensuing, later, future, next, coming.
▷ANTONYMS preceding, previous.

success noun **1** *we are very encouraged by the success of the scheme*: **favourable outcome**, successfulness, favourable result, successful outcome, positive result, victory, triumph.
▷ANTONYMS failure.
2 *the modern-day trappings of success*: **prosperity**, prosperousness, successfulness, affluence, wealth, riches, fortune, opulence, luxury, comfort, life of ease, the good life, milk and honey.
▷ANTONYMS failure, poverty.
3 *a West End musical success | the book was a far greater success than I'd expected*: **triumph**, best-seller, box-office success, sell-out, coup, master stroke; informal **hit**, box-office hit, smash hit, smash, crowd-puller, winner, knockout, sensation, wow, biggie.
▷ANTONYMS failure, flop, disaster.
4 *her performance might well have made her a success*: **star**, superstar, celebrity, big name, household name, somebody, important person, VIP, personality, public figure, dignitary, luminary, leading light; informal celeb, bigwig, big shot, big noise, big cheese, big fish, megastar; Brit. informal nob; N. Amer. informal kahuna, macher, high muckamuck.
▷ANTONYMS failure, nobody.

successful adjective **1** *he reported the particulars of his successful campaign to General Cass*: **victorious**, triumphant; fortunate, lucky.
▷ANTONYMS unsuccessful.
2 *she is a very successful designer*: **prosperous**, affluent, wealthy, rich, well-to-do, doing well, moneyed; famous, eminent, at the top, top; informal on the up and up, well heeled, flush, rolling in it, in the money, made of money, loaded, stinking rich, quids in.
▷ANTONYMS unsuccessful.
3 *successful companies know how to handle the occasional failure*: **flourishing**, thriving, booming, buoyant, burgeoning, doing well, profitable, profit-making, moneymaking, lucrative, gainful, fruitful, solvent, bankable; productive, efficient, effective; informal going strong, on the up and up, rolling in it, in the money, loaded, quids in.
▷ANTONYMS unsuccessful, unprofitable, poor.

succession noun **1** *a succession of exciting events*: **sequence**, series, progression, course, chain, cycle, round, string, train, line, line-up, run, continuation, flow, stream; concatenation.
2 *she produced a male heir and thus deprived him of the* ***succession to*** *the throne*: **accession**, elevation; inheritance of, assumption of.
3 *he left behind him a disputed succession between his kinsmen*: **line of descent**, line, descent, ancestral line, blood line, ancestry, dynasty, lineage, genealogy, heritage, pedigree, extraction, derivation, stock, strain, background.
□ **in succession** *he drank six pints of beer in rapid succession*: **one after the other**, in a row, consecutively, one behind the other, successively, in sequence; running, straight, solid, uninterrupted; informal on the trot.

successive adjective *the team have made a great start with three successive wins*: **consecutive**, in a row, straight, solid, sequential, succeeding, in succession, following, serial, running, continuous, unbroken, uninterrupted; informal on the trot; rare seriate.

S

successor noun *Mary was the rightful successor to the English throne*: **heir**, heir apparent, inheritor, next-in-line, descendant, beneficiary; replacement, incomer, substitute.
▷ANTONYMS predecessor.

succinct adjective *he gave a succinct résumé of the economic situation*: **concise**, short, brief, compact, condensed, crisp, laconic, terse, tight, to the point, economic, pithy, thumbnail, summary, short and sweet, in a few well-chosen words, compendious, epigrammatic, synoptic, aphoristic, gnomic.
▷ANTONYMS lengthy, long-winded, verbose.

> *Choose the right word* **succinct, concise**
>
> See **concise**.

succour noun *they provide shelter and succour in times of need*: **aid**, help, a helping hand, assistance; ministration, comfort, ease, relief, support, guidance, backing; rare easement.
▸ verb *the Navy was unable to succour colonies in Africa*: **help**, aid, bring aid to, give help to, give/render assistance to, assist, lend a (helping) hand to, be of service to; **minister to**, care for, comfort, bring comfort to, bring relief to, support, be supportive of, sustain, protect, take care of, look after, attend to, serve, wait on.

succulent adjective *heaps of succulent black grapes | a succulent fillet of beef*: **juicy**, moist, luscious, lush, fleshy, pulpy, soft, tender, fresh, ripe; choice, mouth-watering, appetizing, flavoursome, flavourful, tasty, delicious, delectable, palatable, toothsome; informal scrumptious, scrummy, yummy, moreish, finger-licking, delish; literary **ambrosial**; rare **ambrosian**, nectareous, nectarean, comestible, flavorous, sapid.
▷ANTONYMS dry, shrivelled; unappetizing.

> *Word toolkit* **succulent**
>
> See **ripe**.

succumb verb **1** *she* ***succumbed to*** *temptation*: **yield**, give in, give way, submit, surrender, capitulate, cave in; be overcome by, be overwhelmed by, be conquered by, be beaten by.
▷ANTONYMS resist, conquer.
2 *he* ***succumbed to*** *an obscure lung complaint*: **die from**, die of, pass away as a result of, be a fatality of; catch, develop, contract, pick up, get, become infected with, suffer from, fall victim to, fall ill with; informal come/go down with.
▷ANTONYMS withstand.

suck verb **1** *they sucked mint juleps through straws*: **sip**, sup, siphon, slurp, draw, drink, gulp, lap, guzzle, quaff, swill, swallow, imbibe.
2 *Fran* ***sucked in*** *a deep breath*: **draw**, pull, breathe, gasp, sniff, gulp; inhale, inspire, respire.
3 *the mud had* ***sucked*** *him* ***in*** *up to his waist*: **draw**, pull; engulf, swallow up, swamp.
4 *young children can get* ***sucked into*** *a world of petty crime*: **implicate in**, involve in, draw into; informal mix up in.
5 N. Amer. informal *I love your country but your weather sucks*: **be very bad**, be awful, be terrible, be dreadful, be horrible, be very unpleasant, be abhorrent, be despicable, be contemptible, be vile, be foul; Brit. informal be pants, be a load of pants; informal **stink**.
□ **suck dry** *the country has been sucked dry by state bribery and gangland criminality*: **drain**, exhaust, sap, deplete, deprive, milk, bleed, fleece, empty, reduce, squeeze.
□ **suck up** *they* ***suck up to*** *him, hanging on to his every word*: **grovel**, creep, toady, be obsequious/servile/sycophantic, kowtow, bow and scrape, play up, truckle; fawn on, curry favour with, dance attendance on; informal bootlick, lick someone's boots, be all over, fall all over, butter up, rub up the right way, keep sweet; Brit. vulgar slang lick/kiss someone's arse.

suckle verb *they employed a wet nurse to suckle their babies*: **breastfeed**, feed, nurse; archaic give suck to.

sudden adjective *a sudden downpour took us by surprise*: **unexpected**, unforeseen, unanticipated, unlooked-for, without warning, without notice, not bargained for; immediate, instantaneous, instant, precipitous, precipitate, abrupt, rapid, swift, lightning, quick, hurried, sharp, without delay.
▷ANTONYMS gradual.
□ **all of a sudden** *when you win awards, all of a sudden magazines will call and want your opinion*. See **suddenly**.

suddenly adverb *she suddenly began to laugh*: **immediately**, instantaneously, instantly, in an instant, straight away, all of a sudden, at once, all at once, promptly, abruptly, in a trice, swiftly; **unexpectedly**, without warning, without notice, on the spur of the moment; informal straight off, out of the blue, in a flash, like a shot, before you can say Jack Robinson, before you can say knife, in two shakes (of a lamb's tail).
▷ANTONYMS gradually.

suds plural noun *Aunt Margaret was up to her elbows in suds*: **lather**, foam, froth, bubbles, soap, soapiness; fizz, effervescence; literary spume.

sue verb **1** *he is likely to sue the contractor for negligence*: **take legal action against**, take to court, bring an action against, bring a suit against, proceed against; charge, prosecute, prefer/bring charges against, bring to trial, summons, indict, arraign; N. Amer. impeach; informal have the law on, do.
2 *Richard was in no mood to* ***sue for*** *peace*: **appeal**, petition, ask, beg, plead, entreat, implore, supplicate; solicit, request, seek; rare obtest, impetrate, obsecrate.

suffer verb **1** *I loved him too much to want to see him suffer*: **hurt**, ache, be in pain, feel pain, be racked with pain, endure agony, agonize, be distressed, be in distress, experience hardship, be upset, be miserable, be wretched.
2 *he* ***suffered from*** *asthma for many years*: **be afflicted by**, be affected by, be troubled with, have, have trouble with.
3 *England suffered a humiliating defeat*: **undergo**, experience, be subjected to, receive, encounter, meet with, endure, face, live through, go through, sustain, bear.
4 *the school's reputation has suffered*: **be impaired**, be damaged, deteriorate, fall off, decline, get worse.
5 *he was obliged to suffer intimate proximity with the man he detested*: **tolerate**, put up with, bear, brook, stand, abide, endure, support, accept, weather; informal stick, stomach; Brit. informal wear, hack.
6 *my conscience would not suffer me to accept any more*: **allow**, permit, let, give leave to, give assent to, sanction, give one's blessing to; informal give the green light to, give the go ahead to, give the thumbs up to, give someone/something the nod, OK.

suffering noun *the war caused widespread civilian suffering*: **hardship**, distress, misery, wretchedness, adversity, tribulation; **pain**, agony, anguish, trauma, torment, torture, hurt, hurting, affliction, sadness, unhappiness, sorrow, grief, woe, angst, heartache, heartbreak, stress; informal hell, hell on earth; literary dolour.

suffice verb *their wages only suffice for the necessities | a simple yes or no will suffice*: **be enough**, be sufficient, be adequate, do, serve, meet requirements, satisfy demands, answer/fulfil/meet one's needs, answer/serve the purpose, pass muster; informal fit/fill the bill, make the grade, cut the mustard, hit the spot.

sufficient adjective & determiner *they had secured sufficient evidence to justify a charge*: **enough**, adequate, plenty of, ample, abundant; informal plenty.
▷ANTONYMS insufficient, inadequate.

suffocate verb **1** *she suffocated her victim after a furious row*: **smother**, asphyxiate, stifle; choke; strangle, throttle, strangulate.
2 *two people suffocated in the crowd*: **be smothered**, asphyxiate, be stifled.
3 *she felt as though she was suffocating in the heat*: **be breathless**, be short of air, struggle for air; **be too hot**, swelter; informal roast, bake, boil.

suffrage noun *the congress is elected for five years by universal adult suffrage*: **franchise**, right to vote, voting rights, the vote, enfranchisement, ballot; voice, say, option, choice.

suffuse verb *the room was suffused with soft, pink light | a feeling of relief suffused her*: **permeate**, spread over, spread throughout, cover, bathe, pervade, wash, saturate, imbue, fill, load, charge, impregnate, inform, steep, colour; literary mantle.

sugar noun

> *Word links* **sugar**
>
> **saccharine** relating to sugar
> **glyco-** related prefix, as in *glycogen*

sugary adjective **1** *go easy on sugary snacks*: **sweet**, sugared, oversweet, sickly, sickly sweet.
▷ANTONYMS sour, tart.
2 *a sugary piano score*: **sentimental**, over-sentimental, mawkish, cloying, sickly, sickly sweet, gushing, saccharine, oversweet, syrupy, slushy; informal soppy, schmaltzy, mushy, sloppy, cutesy, drippy, cheesy, corny.
▷ANTONYMS spare, stark.

suggest verb **1** *Ruth suggested a card-playing evening*: **propose**, put forward, submit, recommend, advocate; advise, propound, urge, encourage, counsel; move, table.
2 *evidence suggests that teenagers are more responsive to price increases than adults*: **indicate**, lead to the belief, give the impression, give the idea, argue, point to, demonstrate, show, evince.
3 *government sources suggested that the Prime Minister would not necessarily change his cabinet*: **hint**, insinuate, imply, intimate, drive at, indicate; informal get at.
4 *the seduction scenes have enough ambivalence to suggest his guilt and her loneliness*: **convey**, express, impart, imply, intimate, connote, smack of; put one in mind of, bring to mind, remind one of, evoke, evince, conjure up, summon up, call up; refer to, allude to, signify.

suggestion noun **1** *there are some suggestions for tackling this problem*: **proposal**, proposition, motion, submission, recommendation; advice, counsel, exhortation, hint, tip, clue, tip-off, idea, piece of advice.
2 *I leaned back in my chair with just the suggestion of a smirk on my face*: **hint**, trace, touch, suspicion, tinge, modicum, dash, soupçon; ghost, semblance, shadow, glimmer, impression, breath, whiff, undertone, whisper, nuance, undertone, connotation.
3 *there is no suggestion that the Secretary of State was party to a conspiracy*: **insinuation**, hint, implication, intimation, innuendo, imputation.

> *Choose the right word* **suggestion, hint, innuendo, insinuation**
>
> See **hint**.

suggestive adjective **1** *an odour suggestive of a brewery*: **redolent**, evocative, reminiscent; **characteristic**, indicative, symptomatic, typical; peculiar to, exclusive to.
2 *he was leering and making suggestive remarks*: **indecent**, indelicate, improper, unseemly, titillating, provocative, sexual, sexy, off colour, smutty, dirty, ribald, bawdy, racy, blue, risqué, juicy, lewd, vulgar, coarse, salacious, prurient; informal naughty, near the knuckle, spicy.

suicide noun *she committed suicide*: **self-destruction**, taking one's own life, self-murder, self-slaughter, felo de se; self-immolation; Hinduism, historical suttee; Japanese, historical hara-kiri, suppuku; informal topping oneself, ending it all.

suit noun **1** *a pinstriped suit*: **outfit**, set of clothes, costume, ensemble; clothing, dress, attire, finery; habit, garb, livery; informal get-up, gear, togs, garms, duds; Brit. informal kit, clobber; rhyming slang whistle (and flute); formal apparel; archaic vestments.
2 informal *they hated being messed around by suits in faraway boardrooms*: **businessman, businesswoman**, business person, executive, bureaucrat, administrator, manager, director.
3 *he's been an expert witness in some important medical malpractice suits*: **legal action**, lawsuit, suit at law, case, court case, action, cause, legal proceeding/process, proceedings, judicial proceedings, litigation, trial, legal dispute/contest, bringing to book, bringing of charges, indictment, prosecution.
4 *he could not compete with John in Marian's eyes and his suit came to nothing*: **courtship**, wooing, courting, addresses, attentions, homage, pursuit; respects, blandishments.
▸ verb **1** *blue really suits you*: **look attractive on**, enhance the appearance of, look right on, look good on, become, flatter, show to advantage, set off, enhance, ornament, grace; informal do something for.
2 *we offer savings schemes to suit all pockets*: **be convenient for**, be acceptable to, be suitable for, meet the requirements of, satisfy the demands of, be in line with the wishes of; befit, match, complement, go with; informal fit the bill.
3 *the recipes are ideally **suited to** students*: **make appropriate to/for**, make fitting to/for, tailor, fashion, accommodate, adjust, adapt, modify, fit, gear, equip, design; (**be suited to**) be cut out for.
4 *the best way to construct a healthy diet is to find out which foods suit you*: **be agreeable to**, agree with, be good for, be healthy for.

suitable adjective **1** *there was a dearth of suitable employment opportunities in the islands*: **acceptable**, satisfactory, fit, worthy, fitting; informal right up someone's street.
▷ANTONYMS unsuitable, inappropriate.
2 *a drama serial suitable for all age groups*: **appropriate**, fitting, fit, fitted, acceptable, apt, right.
▷ANTONYMS unsuitable, inappropriate.
3 *the music's more **suitable for** a lively dinner party*: **appropriate to**, suited to, befitting, congruous with, in keeping with, in character with, tailor-made, custom-made; informal cut out for.
▷ANTONYMS unsuitable, unfit.
4 *they treated him with suitable respect*: **proper**, **seemly**, decent, apt, appropriate, fitting, befitting, becoming, right, correct, due, worthy, decorous; French comme il faut.
▷ANTONYMS unsuitable.
5 *suitable candidates are expected to hold a PhD in chemistry*: **well qualified**, well suited, competent, capable, able; right, appropriate, fitting, apt; desirable, preferable, ideal.
▷ANTONYMS unsuitable, unfit.

> *Choose the right word* **suitable, appropriate, proper, fitting**
>
> See **appropriate**.

suitcase noun *he carried a small battered suitcase*: **travelling bag**, travel bag, case, grip, valise, overnight case, portmanteau, vanity case, holdall; briefcase, attaché case, Gladstone bag; trunk, chest; (**suitcases**) luggage, baggage.

suite noun **1** *a penthouse suite*: **apartment**, flat, set of rooms, suite of rooms; living quarters, rooms, chambers.
2 *the Royal Saloon was built for the use of the Queen and her suite*: **retinue**, entourage, train, escort, cortège, royal household, court, company, following, staff; attendants, retainers, followers, companions, servants.

suitor noun **1** *she decided to marry her suitor*: **admirer**, beau, wooer, boyfriend, sweetheart, lover, inamorato, escort; literary swain, follower.
2 *the colonies became rival suitors for the location of the capital of the state*: **petitioner**, supplicant, beseecher, suppliant, plaintiff, pleader, appellant, applicant; rare pretendant.

sulk verb *Dad was sulking in his room*: **mope**, brood, pout, be sullen, have a long face, be in a bad mood, be put out, be out of sorts, be out of humour, be grumpy, be despondent, be moody, be resentful, pine, harbour a grudge, eat one's heart out, moon about/around; informal be in a huff, be down in the dumps, be miffed, glower.
▷ANTONYMS be cheerful.
▸ noun *he sank into a deep sulk and nursed his hurt pride*: **bad mood**, fit of bad humour, fit of ill humour, fit of pique, pet, mood, pout, temper, bad temper, the sulks, the doldrums, the blues; informal huff, grump; Brit. informal strop, paddy.
▷ANTONYMS good mood.

sulky adjective *with sulky faces the students turned to go*: **sullen**, surly, moping, pouting, moody, sour, piqued, petulant, disgruntled, ill-humoured, in a bad mood, having a fit of the sulks, out of humour, fed up, put out, out of sorts, mopey, mopish; bad-tempered, fractious, grumpy, huffy, scowling, glowering, resentful, dark, glum, gloomy, morose; angry, cross, peeved; informal chippy, mumpish, grouchy, stroppy; N. English informal mardy.
▷ANTONYMS cheerful, amiable.

sullen adjective *a bunch of sullen, spoilt brats*: **surly**, sulky, pouting, sour, morose, resentful, glum, moody, gloomy, joyless, frowning, glowering,

grumpy, touchy, peevish, indignant, embittered; bad-tempered, ill-tempered, cross, angry, testy; unresponsive, uncommunicative, unsociable, uncivil, unmannerly, unfriendly; informal stroppy.
▷ANTONYMS cheerful, sociable.

sully verb *he never sullied his lips with swear words*: **taint**, defile, soil, tarnish, stain, blemish, besmirch, befoul, contaminate, pollute, spoil, mar, spot, make impure, disgrace, dishonour, injure, damage.
▷ANTONYMS purify.

sultry adjective **1** *a sultry, sweltering day*: **humid**, close, airless, stuffy, stifling, suffocating, oppressive, muggy, sticky, sweltering, tropical, torrid, steamy, heavy; **hot**, warm, boiling, roasting.
▷ANTONYMS cool, cold, refreshing.
2 *a sultry film star*: **passionate**, **attractive**, sensual, sexy, voluptuous, luscious, erotic, seductive, provocative, alluring, tempting.

sum noun **1** *a large sum of money*: **amount**, quantity, volume.
2 *he handed over a smaller sum to creditors*: **amount of money**, price, charge, fee, cost, tariff.
3 *the sum of two prime numbers*: **total**, sum total, grand total, tally, aggregate, summation, gross; answer.
▷ANTONYMS difference.
4 *a belief in making your own way through life seems to be the sum of his wisdom*: **entirety**, totality, total, whole, aggregate, summation, beginning and end, alpha and omega, be-all and end-all; informal whole shebang, whole caboodle, whole shooting match, {lock, stock, and barrel}.
5 *we did sums at school today*: **arithmetical problem**, problem, calculation, reckoning, tally, question; (**sums**) **arithmetic**, mathematics, figures, numbers, computation; Brit. informal maths; N. Amer. informal math.
□ **in sum** *decentralization, in sum, has profound implications for power relations*: **in short**, briefly, in brief, to put it briefly, to cut a long story short, in a word, to sum up, in a nutshell, to come to the point, in essence, in outline.
▶ verb
□ **sum up** *he was summing up on day two of a historic test case*: **summarize the evidence**, review the evidence, give a summing-up, summarize the argument.
□ **sum someone/something up 1** *one reviewer summed it up as 'the most compelling performance recorded in the past few years'*: **evaluate**, assess, appraise, value, rate, weigh up, gauge, judge, deem, adjudge, estimate, form an opinion of, form an impression of, make one's mind up about, get the measure of, form a judgement of, make something of; informal size up.
2 *in a subsequent article he sums up the reasons for deindustrialization*: **summarize**, make/give a summary of, precis, give an abstract of, encapsulate, outline, give an outline of, recap, recapitulate, review, put in a nutshell, condense, abridge, digest, synopsize, compress, give the gist.
▷ANTONYMS elaborate.

summarily adverb *he was accused of conspiracy and summarily executed*: **immediately**, instantly, right away/off, straight away, at once, on the spot, directly, forthwith, promptly; speedily, swiftly, rapidly, expeditiously, without delay, without hesitation, suddenly, abruptly; **arbitrarily**, without formality, without notice, without warning, peremptorily, without discussion, without due process.

summarize verb *he summarized these ideas in a single phrase*: **sum up**, abridge, condense, encapsulate, outline, give an outline of, put in a nutshell, recap, recapitulate, digest, give/make a summary of, give a synopsis of, synopsize, precis, give a precis of, give a résumé of, give an abstract of, abstract, sketch, give the main points of, give a rundown of, give the gist of, review; rare epitomize.
▷ANTONYMS elaborate, expand on.

summary noun *a summary of the team's findings was released in August*: **synopsis**, precis, résumé, abstract, abridgement, digest, compendium, condensation, encapsulation, abbreviated version; outline, sketch, rundown, review, summing-up, survey, overview, run-through, notes, recapitulation, recap; French tour d'horizon; N. Amer. wrap-up; rare epitome, conspectus, summa.
▶ adjective **1** *a summary financial statement*: **abridged**, abbreviated, shortened, condensed, concise, succinct, thumbnail, compact, terse, short, compressed, cursory, compendious, synoptic; brief, crisp, pithy, to the point.
▷ANTONYMS lengthy, in full.
2 *many collaborators faced summary execution*: **immediate**, instant, instantaneous, on-the-spot, direct, forthwith, prompt; speedy, swift, rapid, expeditious, without delay, without hesitation, sudden, hasty, abrupt; arbitrary, without formality, without notice, without warning, peremptory, without discussion.
▷ANTONYMS dilatory, slow.

summer noun

> *Word links* **summer**
>
> **aestival** relating to summer

summer house noun *one of her favourite haunts as a child was the old summer house on the river bank*: **gazebo**, pavilion, belvedere, arbour, bower, pergola; archaic, Turkey & Iran kiosk.

summit noun **1** *the summit of Mont Blanc*: **top**, peak, crest, crown, apex, vertex, apogee, tip, cap; ridge, brink, brow, needle, crag, tor; mountain top, hilltop; French aiguille, serac.
▷ANTONYMS bottom, base.
2 *they consider the dramas of Aeschylus, Sophocles, and Euripides to form one of the summits of world literature*: **acme**, peak, height, pinnacle, zenith, culmination, climax, high point, high spot, optimum, highlight, crowning glory, crowning point; best, finest, nonpareil; Latin ne plus ultra.
▷ANTONYMS nadir.
3 *it was agreed that the treaty would be signed at the next superpower summit*: **meeting**, negotiation, conference, talk(s), discussion, conclave, consultation, deliberation, dialogue, parley, colloquy; informal confab, powwow; formal confabulation.

summon verb **1** *he was summoned to the American Embassy*: **send for**, call for, ask for, request the presence of, demand the presence of; ask, invite; archaic bid.
2 *the court announced its decision to summon them as witnesses*: **serve with a summons**, summons, cite, serve with a citation, serve with a writ, subpoena.
3 *the official receiver must summon a meeting*: **convene**, assemble, order, call, muster, rally, levy, round up; announce, declare; formal convoke.
4 *he was unable to summon the courage to move closer to where the dogs were tied | people could still* ***summon up*** *energy and enthusiasm*: **muster**, gather, collect, rally, call into action, mobilize, screw up.
5 *emigrants would* ***summon up*** *their memories of home*: **call to mind**, bring to mind, call up/forth, conjure up, evoke, recall, revive, invoke, raise, arouse, kindle, awaken, excite, stir up, spark (off), provoke.
6 *their spirits may be summoned and used for either good or evil*: **conjure up**, call up, invoke, rouse up.

summons noun **1** *the court issued a summons*: **writ**, **subpoena**, warrant, arraignment, indictment, court order, process; N. Amer. citation; Latin subpoena ad testificandum.
2 *she had received a summons to go to the boss's office*: **order**, directive, command, instruction, dictum, demand, decree, injunction, fiat, edict, direction, charge, bidding, call, request, invitation, plea, appeal.
▶ verb *he had been summonsed to appear in court*: **serve with a summons**, summon, cite, serve with a citation, serve with a writ, subpoena.

sumptuous adjective *a sumptuous palace*: **lavish**, luxurious, de luxe, opulent, magnificent, resplendent, gorgeous, splendid, grand, extravagant, lush, lavishly appointed, palatial, princely, rich, costly, expensive, impressive, imposing; informal plush, ritzy, swanky; Brit. informal swish.
▷ANTONYMS humble, plain, cheap.

sun noun **1** *he watched the sun go down over the sea | suns in other galaxies*: **star**; Roman Mythology Sol; Greek Mythology Helios, Phoebus, Apollo; Egyptian Mythology Ra.
2 *she could feel the sun on her face*: **sunshine**, sunlight, daylight, light, warmth; beams, rays.
▶ verb
□ **sun oneself** *he's been sunning himself on the golden shores of Bali*: **sunbathe**, bask, bake, get a tan, tan, brown.

> *Word links* **sun**
>
> **solar** relating to the sun
> **helio-** related prefix, as in *heliograph, heliotrope*
> **heliophobia** fear of the sun

sunbathe verb *she lay sunbathing on the hot sand*: **sun oneself**, bask, bake, get a tan, tan oneself, brown oneself; Austral./NZ sunbake; informal catch some rays.

sunburned, sunburnt adjective **1** *his scarlet, sunburned shoulders*: **burnt**, peeling, inflamed, red, scarlet, blistered, blistering.
2 *a handsome sunburned face*: **tanned**, suntanned, brown, bronzed, bronze, browned, weather-beaten.
▷ANTONYMS pale.

Sunday noun **the Lord's Day**, the Sabbath.

> *Word links* **Sunday**
>
> **dominical** relating to Sunday

sunder verb archaic *his father and he were sundered by religious differences*. See **divide** (sense 5 of the verb).

sundry adjective *wings, radiators, and sundry other items were sent out to various workshops*: **various**, varied, miscellaneous, assorted, mixed, diverse, diversified, motley, random; several, numerous, many, manifold, multifarious, multitudinous, legion; literary divers; rare farraginous.

S

Word toolkit **sundry**

See **diverse**.

sunken adjective **1** *he was very gaunt, with sunken eyes*: **hollowed**, hollow, depressed, deep-set, concave, dented, indented, caved in, drawn, haggard.
2 *a sunken garden*: **below ground level**, at a lower level, lowered, recessed.

sunless adjective **1** *a cold sunless day*: **dark**, overcast, cloudy, grey, gloomy, dismal, dreary, murky, hazy, louring, lowering.
2 *the sunless north-facing side of the house*: **shady**, shadowy, dark, dim, dingy, gloomy, dull, ill-lit.

sunlight noun *the plane was gleaming in the winter sunlight*: **daylight**, sun, sunshine, light of day, sun's rays, sunbeam, natural light, light.

sunny adjective **1** *a sunny spring afternoon*: **bright**, sunshiny, sunlit, brilliant, clear, fine, fair; balmy, summery, clement; cloudless, unclouded, without a cloud in the sky.
▷ANTONYMS dull, shady.
2 *she has a sunny disposition*: **cheerful**, cheery, happy, light-hearted, bright, glad, merry, joyful, bubbly, blithe, jolly, jovial, animated, buoyant, ebullient, upbeat, vivacious, sparky, perky, rosy; warm, friendly, outgoing, genial, benign, agreeable, pleasant; dated gay.
▷ANTONYMS miserable, introverted.
3 *the sunny side of life*: **optimistic**, rosy, bright, cheerful, hopeful, auspicious, favourable, good.
▷ANTONYMS sad, pessimistic.

sunrise noun *the infantry advanced at sunrise*: **dawn**, crack of dawn, daybreak, break of day, first light, first thing in the morning, early morning, cockcrow, morning; N. Amer. sunup; literary peep of day, aurora, dayspring.

sunset noun *strolling along the beach at sunset*: **nightfall**, close of day, twilight, dusk, evening, half-light; N. Amer. sundown; literary eventide, gloaming, vesper.

sunshine noun **1** *we'll relax in the sunshine for a while*: **sunlight**, sun, sun's rays, sunbeams, daylight, light of day, natural light, light.
2 *his smile was all sunshine*: **happiness**, cheerfulness, cheer, gladness, laughter, gaiety, merriment, joy, joyfulness, glee, blitheness, bliss, sparkle, joviality, jollity.

super adjective informal *win a super day out at York*: **excellent**, superb, superlative, first-rate, first-class, superior, outstanding, remarkable, dazzling, marvellous, magnificent, wonderful, splendid, fine, exquisite, exceptional, glorious, sublime, peerless, perfect, of the first water; informal brilliant, great, fantastic, fabulous, terrific, awesome, ace, stellar, divine, smashing, A1, tip-top, top-notch, neat, mega, wicked, cool, banging, crucial; Brit. informal brill, cracking.
▷ANTONYMS rotten, lousy.

superannuated adjective **1** *a superannuated civil servant*: **pensioned off**, retired, pensioned; elderly, old; informal, derogatory over the hill, long in the tooth, past it, put out to grass.
2 *the old terminus was converted into a goods station, a common fate for superannuated passenger stations*: **old**, old-fashioned, antiquated, out of date, outmoded, anachronistic, broken-down, outworn; **obsolete**, disused, fallen into disuse, no longer used, defunct, moribund; informal clapped out.

superb adjective **1** *he scored a superb goal*: **excellent**, superlative, first-rate, first-class, superior, supreme, outstanding, remarkable, dazzling, marvellous, magnificent, wonderful, splendid, admirable, noteworthy, impressive, fine, exquisite, exceptional, glorious, sublime, perfect, of the first order, of the first water; informal great, fantastic, fabulous, stellar, terrific, super, awesome, ace, cool, A1, tip-top; Brit. informal brilliant, brill, smashing, bosting.
▷ANTONYMS poor, inferior.
2 *a superb diamond necklace*: **magnificent**, majestic, splendid, grand, impressive, imposing, awe-inspiring, breathtaking; gorgeous, choice, resplendent, stately; sumptuous, opulent, lavish, luxurious, de luxe; informal plush, ritzy.
▷ANTONYMS poor, inferior.

supercilious adjective *a supercilious young minister*: **arrogant**, haughty, conceited, disdainful, overbearing, pompous, condescending, superior, patronizing, imperious, proud, lofty, lordly, snobbish, snobby, overweening, smug; pretentious, affected; scornful, mocking, sneering, scoffing; informal hoity-toity, high and mighty, uppity, snooty, stuck-up, fancy-pants, toffee-nosed, snotty, jumped up, too big for one's boots.
▷ANTONYMS humble, modest.

superficial adjective **1** *his face was blotched with superficial burns*: **surface**, exterior, external, outer, outside, outermost, peripheral, slight.
▷ANTONYMS deep, thorough.
2 *she made no attempt to be friendly on anything but the most superficial level*: **shallow**, surface, on the surface, skin-deep, minimal, artificial; insignificant, unimportant, empty, hollow, meaningless.
▷ANTONYMS deep, significant.
3 *a superficial investigation*: **cursory**, perfunctory, casual, sketchy, desultory, unconsidered, token, slapdash, slipshod, offhand, inadequate, imperfect, slight; rushed, hasty, hurried, rapid, fleeting, passing.
▷ANTONYMS thorough, comprehensive.
4 *its spines give it a superficial resemblance to a hedgehog*: **apparent**, **specious**, seeming, outward, ostensible, cosmetic, slight.
▷ANTONYMS genuine, authentic.
5 *I think there is too much superficial cricket autobiography available*: **trivial**, lightweight, sketchy, slight, insignificant.
▷ANTONYMS profound.
6 *I suppose Michael was quite a superficial person, but to me he represented excitement*: **facile**, shallow, glib, flippant, thoughtless, empty-headed, trivial, frivolous, silly, inane, without depth, fatuous.
▷ANTONYMS thoughtful.

superficially adverb *some reptiles and amphibians are superficially very alike | superficially, it was an obvious statement to make*: **apparently**, **seemingly**, ostensibly, outwardly, on the surface, on the face of it, to all appearances, to all intents and purposes, at first glance, at face value, to the casual eye; externally, visibly, trivially.

superfluity noun *California has always had a superfluity of fresh crab*: **surplus**, excess, overabundance, glut, surfeit, profusion, plethora, embarrassment, avalanche, deluge, flood, overload.
▷ANTONYMS lack, shortage.

superfluous adjective **1** *a tool for removing superfluous material*: **surplus**, redundant, unneeded, not required, excess, extra, spare, to spare, remaining, unused, left over; useless, unproductive, undue, in excess, surplus to requirements; expendable, disposable, dispensable, unwanted, waste.
▷ANTONYMS necessary, essential.
2 *Charlie gave him a look that made words superfluous*: **unnecessary**, needless, unneeded, inessential, pointless, redundant, uncalled for, unwarranted, unjustified, gratuitous.
▷ANTONYMS necessary, essential.

superhuman adjective **1** *their madness gives them superhuman strength*: **extraordinary**, phenomenal, prodigious, stupendous, exceptional, great, immense, enormous, heroic, godlike, Herculean, remarkable.
▷ANTONYMS average, unremarkable.
2 *the superhuman power which raised Christ from the dead*: **divine**, holy, spiritual, heavenly, godlike.
3 *superhuman agencies and powers*: **supernatural**, preternatural, paranormal, other-worldly, unearthly, extramundane, magical, occult.
▷ANTONYMS mundane.

superintend verb *he was expected to superintend a grand banquet*: **supervise**, oversee, be in charge of, be in control of, preside over, direct, administer, manage, run, look after, be responsible for, govern, operate, conduct, handle, steer, pilot.

superintendent noun **1** *he became superintendent of the university museum*: **manager**, director, administrator, supervisor, overseer, controller, boss, chief, head, governor, organizer, conductor, foreman; informal honcho, gaffer.
2 N. Amer. *the building's superintendent*: **caretaker**, **janitor**, warden, porter, custodian, keeper, watchman, steward.

superior adjective **1** *a superior officer had never apologized to him before*: **higher-ranking**, higher-level, senior, higher, higher-up, upper-level, upper, loftier.
▷ANTONYMS inferior, junior.
2 *the superior candidate*: **better**, more expert, more skilful, more advanced; worthier, fitter, preferred, predominant, prevailing, surpassing.
▷ANTONYMS inferior, worse.
3 *they recognized the value of superior workmanship*: **finer**, better, higher-grade, higher-calibre, surpassing, of higher quality, greater, grander; **supreme**, accomplished, expert, consummate.
▷ANTONYMS inferior, low-quality.
4 *a very superior chocolate*: **good-quality**, high-quality, first-class, first-rate, top-quality, high-grade, of the first water, of the first order; choice, select, exclusive, rare, singular, unique, prime, prize, upmarket, fine, excellent, superb, distinguished, exceptional, outstanding, marvellous, superlative, special; best, choicest, finest, matchless, peerless, unequalled, perfect, flawless; French par excellence.
▷ANTONYMS inferior, low-quality.
5 *a superior hotel*: **high-class**, upper-class, select, exclusive, elite; Brit. upmarket; informal classy, posh, snobby.
▷ANTONYMS inferior, downmarket.
6 *Jake regarded her with superior amusement*: **condescending**, supercilious, patronizing, haughty, disdainful, lofty, lordly, pompous, snobbish, snobby; informal high and mighty, hoity-toity, uppity, snooty, stuck-up, toffee-nosed, fancy-pants, jumped up, too big for one's boots, uppish.
▷ANTONYMS humble, modest.
▶ **noun** *my immediate superior in the department*: **manager**, boss, chief, supervisor, senior, controller, headman, foreman.
▷ANTONYMS inferior, subordinate, assistant.

S

superiority noun *despite the military superiority of the government forces, the rebels continued to hold on to territory in the south*: **supremacy**, advantage, lead, dominance, primacy, ascendancy, leadership, precedence, edge, whip hand, better quality; excellence, eminence, distinction, greatness.
▷ANTONYMS inferiority.

superlative adjective *he is without doubt a superlative photographer*: **excellent**, magnificent, wonderful, glorious, marvellous, brilliant, supreme, consummate, outstanding, prodigious, dazzling, remarkable, formidable, fine, choice, sterling, first-rate, first-class, of the first water, of the first order, of the highest order, premier, prime, unsurpassed, unequalled, unparalleled, unrivalled, unbeatable, peerless, matchless, singular, unique, transcendent, best, greatest, worthiest, pre-eminent, perfect, faultless, flawless; informal crack, ace, stellar, wicked.
▷ANTONYMS poor, unexceptional, mediocre.

supernatural adjective **1** *supernatural powers*: **paranormal**, psychic, magic, magical, occult, mystic, mystical, miraculous, superhuman, supernormal, hypernormal, extramundane; inexplicable, uncanny, unaccountable, unbelievable, non-rational, weird, mysterious, arcane.
▷ANTONYMS natural, normal.
2 *stories about a supernatural hound*: **ghostly**, phantom, spectral, magical, mystic, other-worldly, unearthly, unnatural, unreal, mysterious, fabulous; informal spooky.

supersede verb *I found myself superseded by much younger men | the tutorial has, in most colleges, been superseded by the lecture*: **replace**, supplant, take the place of, take over from, substitute for, displace, oust, overthrow, remove, unseat, override; succeed, come after, step into the shoes of; informal crowd out, fill someone's boots.

> *Choose the right word* **supersede, supplant, replace**
>
> See **replace**.

superstition noun **1** *Mungo remembered the old superstition that seagulls were the souls of dead sailors*: **myth**, belief, old wives' tale, notion; legend, story.
2 *medicine was riddled with superstition and ignorance*: **unfounded belief**, credulity; magic, sorcery, witchcraft; fallacy, delusion, illusion.
▷ANTONYMS science.

superstitious adjective **1** *superstitious beliefs*: **mythical**, irrational, illusory, groundless, unfounded, unprovable; traditional.
▷ANTONYMS rational, factual, scientific.
2 *Joe is incredibly superstitious*: **credulous**, prone to superstition; naive, gullible.
▷ANTONYMS sceptical.

supervise verb **1** *he left early to supervise the loading of the lorries*: **superintend**, oversee, be in charge of, be in control of, preside over, direct, administer, manage, run, look after, be responsible for, govern, operate, conduct, organize, handle, guide, steer, pilot.
2 *you may also need to supervise the patient, in case he forgets what he is doing*: **watch**, oversee, keep an eye on, observe, monitor, inspect, be responsible for, guide, mind.

supervision noun **1** *one of the Bank of England's functions is the supervision of the banking system*: **administration**, management, direction, control, charge; overseeing, superintendence, regulation, government, governance, operation.
2 *there is a sign telling parents to keep their children under supervision*: **observation**, inspection, guidance, custody, charge, safe keeping, care, guardianship, wardship, leadership.

S

supervisor noun *she exchanged a few words with the shift supervisor*: **manager**, director, administrator, overseer, controller, boss, chief, superintendent, inspector, head, governor, superior, organizer, conductor, steward, foreman, ganger; informal honcho, gaffer.

supine adjective **1** *she lay supine on the fine white sand*: **flat on one's back**, prone, recumbent, prostrate, stretched out, spreadeagled; lying, sprawling, horizontal, flat as a pancake.
▷ANTONYMS erect, vertical.
2 *a supine and cowardly press has allowed itself to be intimidated into censoring the truth*: **weak**, spineless, yielding, enervated, effete; docile, acquiescent, pliant, submissive, servile, inactive, passive, inert, spiritless, apathetic, indifferent.
▷ANTONYMS strong, assertive.

supper noun **1** *the Rileys invited me to a formal supper*: **dinner**, evening meal, main meal; feast, banquet, repast; Brit. tea.
2 *a bowl of soup with some crusty bread makes an ideal supper*: **evening snack**; informal bite, bite to eat; formal collation, refection.

supplant verb **1** *vast impersonal motorways supplanted the agreeably irregular network of real roads*: **replace**, displace, supersede, take the place of, take over from, substitute for, undermine, override.
2 *he was asking the man he supplanted as Prime Minister for help*: **oust**, usurp, overthrow, remove, topple, unseat, depose, dethrone, eject, dispel; succeed, come after, step into the shoes of; informal fill someone's boots, crowd out.

> *Choose the right word* **supplant, supersede, replace**
>
> See **replace**.

supple adjective **1** *he watched the movements of her supple body*: **lithe**, limber, nimble, lissom, flexible, loose-limbed, loose-jointed, agile, acrobatic, fit, deft, willowy, graceful, elegant.
▷ANTONYMS stiff, unfit.
2 *supple leather*: **pliant**, pliable, flexible, soft, bendable, workable, malleable, stretchy, stretchable, elastic, springy, yielding, rubbery, plastic, resilient.
▷ANTONYMS rigid, inflexible.

supplement noun **1** *a mouse is not a replacement for a keyboard, merely a supplement*: **addition**, supplementation, additive, extra, companion, add-on, accessory, adjunct, appendage, appurtenance; Computing peripheral.
2 *the single room supplement is £16*: **surcharge**, addition, increase.
3 *a supplement to the essays*: **appendix**, addendum, end matter, tailpiece, codicil, rider, postscript, addition, extension, coda, sequel.
4 *our special supplement is packed with ideas for healthy hair*: **magazine section**, pull-out, insert, special-feature section.
▸ verb *most of the families in the village supplemented their incomes by working in the wool-spinning mills*: **augment**, increase, add to, boost, swell, amplify, enlarge, make larger/bigger/greater; top up, complement, round off, complete; widen, broaden, expand.

supplementary adjective **1** *many MPs feel the need to seek supplementary income*: **additional**, extra, supplemental, increased, further, more; add-on, complementary, subsidiary, accessory, auxiliary, ancillary, supportive, reserve.
2 *a supplementary index*: **appended**, attached, added, extra, accompanying, annexed, adjunct.

suppliant noun *she and the others who addressed high-ranking officials were not mere suppliants*: **petitioner**, pleader, beseecher, supplicant, beggar, appellant, suitor, applicant, claimant.
▸ adjective *the faces around her were suppliant*: **pleading**, begging, beseeching, imploring, entreating, supplicating, craving, on bended knee.

supplicate verb *he supplicated the emperor for the pardon of those who had supported the uprising*: **entreat**, beseech, beg, plead with, implore, petition, appeal to, solicit, call on, urge, enjoin, importune, pray, invoke, sue, ask, request.

supplication noun *she made one last supplication to Sally*: **entreaty**, plea, appeal, petition, solicitation, exhortation, urge, prayer, invocation, suit, request, application; beseeching, begging, pleading; archaic orison; rare imploration, obsecration.

supplies plural noun **1** *next time you go to a supermarket for your supplies, consider your shopping habits*: **provisions**, stores, stocks, rations, food, food and drink, foodstuffs, eatables, subsistence, produce, necessities; informal eats, grub, nosh; formal comestibles, provender; archaic viands, victuals, vittles.
2 *they carried vital supplies to the trenches*: **equipment**, apparatus, paraphernalia, wares, trappings, stuff, tackle, things; Military materiel.

supply verb **1** *they supplied money and professional assistance to rebels at by-elections*: **give**, contribute, provide, furnish, donate, bestow, grant, endow, afford, impart, lay on, come up with, make available, proffer; dispense, allocate, allot, assign, disburse; lavish, shower, regale; informal fork out, shell out; archaic minister.
2 *Lake Cachuma supplies the city of Santa Barbara with water*: **provide**, furnish, endow, serve, confer; equip, kit out, rig out, outfit, clothe, fit, arm; rare endue.
3 *small communities have just a few well-designed windmills to supply all their power needs*: **satisfy**, meet, fulfil, fill, be adequate for, cater for.
▸ noun **1** *we've only a limited supply of food and water*: **stock**, store, reserve, reservoir, stockpile, heap, pile, mass, hoard, cache, collection, storehouse, repository; fund, crop, mine, bank, arsenal.
2 *premises for the sale and supply of alcoholic liquor*: **provision**, providing, supplying, furnishing, dissemination, distribution, laying on, sending out, serving, accommodation.
▸ adjective *a supply teacher*: **substitute**, stand-in, fill-in, locum, temporary, stopgap.

support verb **1** *the roof was supported by massive stone pillars*: **hold up**, bear, carry, prop up, keep up, bolster up, brace, shore up, underpin, buttress, reinforce.
2 *he was struggling to support his family*: **provide for**, provide sustenance for, maintain, sustain, keep, take care of, look after.
3 *Martha lovingly supported him to the end*: **give moral support to**, give strength to, be a source of strength to, comfort, bring comfort to, sustain, encourage, buoy up, hearten, fortify, console, solace, give sympathy to, reassure, succour, soothe; informal buck up.
▷ANTONYMS neglect, abandon.

4 *there seems to be evidence to support both of these arguments*: **substantiate**, back up, give force to, give weight to, bear out, corroborate, confirm, attest to, verify, prove, validate, authenticate, endorse, ratify, document.
▷ANTONYMS contradict, undermine.
5 *all the money we receive will be used to support charitable projects in Africa*: **help**, aid, assist; **contribute to**, give a donation to, give money to, back, underwrite, subsidize, fund, finance, succour; N. Amer. informal bankroll.
6 *he obtained 773 votes as an independent candidate supported by a residents' association*: **back**, champion, give help to, help, assist, aid, be on the side of, side with, favour, prefer, abet, aid and abet, encourage; vote for, ally oneself with, stand behind, fall in with, stand up for, defend, take someone's part, take up the cudgels for; sponsor, vouch for, second, promote, endorse, sanction, approve of, give one's blessing to, smile on; informal stick up for, throw one's weight behind.
▷ANTONYMS oppose.
7 *a bold initiative to support human rights around the world*: **advocate**, **promote**, further, champion, back, be on the side of, espouse, espouse the cause of, be in favour of, recommend, defend, subscribe to.
8 *at work during the day I could support the grief*: **endure**, bear, put up with, tolerate, stand, abide, suffer, stomach, brook, sustain, shoulder, weather.
▶ **noun 1** *one of the bridge supports had developed a six inch crack*: **pillar**, post, prop, underprop, underpinning, base, substructure, foundation; brace, buttress, abutment, bolster, upright, stay, stand, trestle, crutch, plinth.
2 *he can't be forced to pay support for a wife abroad*: **maintenance**, keep, sustenance, subsistence; food and accommodation.
3 *I was lucky to have my family's support during this difficult time*: **moral support**, friendship, strengthening, strength, encouragement, buoying up, heartening, fortification, consolation, solace, succour, relief, easement; informal bucking up.
4 *he was a great support when her father died*: **comfort**, help, assistance, tower of strength, prop, backbone, mainstay.
5 *we will provide support for essential community services*: **contributions**, backing, donations, money, subsidy, funding, funds, finance, capital.
6 *many stars openly voiced their support for one candidate or another*: **backing**, help, assistance, aid, votes, endorsement, sanction, approval, blessing, patronage.
7 *there has been a surge in **support for** decentralization*: **advocacy**, backing, promotion, championship, espousal, defence, recommendation, recommending, argument for, arguing for.

> *Choose the right word* **support, help, aid, assist**
>
> See **help**.

supporter noun **1** *supporters of gun control*: **advocate**, backer, adherent, promoter, champion, defender, upholder, votary, partisan, crusader, proponent, campaigner, believer, apologist.
▷ANTONYMS opponent.
2 *potential Labour supporters*: **backer**, helper, adherent, follower, ally, voter, disciple, comrade, apologist, fanatic; member, card-carrying member, insider.
▷ANTONYMS opponent, adversary.
3 *the society is a charity that relies on its members and supporters for its income*: **contributor**, donor, benefactor, sponsor, backer, patron, subscriber, friend, well-wisher; informal angel.
4 *the end of the match was greeted by cheers from both sets of supporters*: **fan**, follower, enthusiast, devotee, lover, admirer, zealot, aficionado; informal buff, freak, nut.

supportive adjective **1** *a supportive head teacher*: **encouraging**, caring, sympathetic, reassuring, understanding, concerned, helpful, nurturing, sensitive; protective, benevolent, kind, kindly, maternal, paternal.
▷ANTONYMS discouraging.
2 *local societies were largely **supportive of** the proposal*: **in favour**, approving, pro, on the side of; favourable to, sympathetic to, in sympathy with, encouraging of, well disposed to, favourably disposed to, receptive to, responsive to.
▷ANTONYMS opposed to.

suppose verb **1** *I suppose he's used to this kind of work*: **assume**, dare say, take for granted, take as read, presume, expect, take it; believe, think, fancy, be of the opinion, suspect, have a sneaking suspicion, sense, trust; guess, surmise, reckon, conjecture, theorize, deduce, infer, gather, glean, divine; formal opine.
2 *suppose your spacecraft had a two-stage rocket*: **hypothesize**, postulate, theorize, posit, speculate, (let's) say, assume, imagine.
3 *the classical theory supposes rational players*: **require**, presuppose, imply, assume; call for, need.

supposed adjective **1** *we have no viable theory to account for the supposed phenomena*: **apparent**, seeming, alleged, putative, reputed, rumoured, claimed, purported, ostensible, specious; professed, declared, believed, assumed, presumed; French soi-disant.
2 *computers are **supposed to** make their lives easier | I'm **supposed to** meet him at 8.30*: **meant**, intended, expected; ought, required, obliged.

supposition noun *there is a widespread supposition that there is nothing of any value in these techniques*: **belief**, surmise, idea, notion, suspicion, conjecture, speculation, view, inference, theory, thesis, hypothesis, postulation, guess, guesswork, feeling, hunch, assumption, presumption.

suppress verb **1** *the government proved incapable of suppressing the rebellion by force*: **subdue**, defeat, conquer, vanquish, triumph over, repress, crush, quell, quash, squash, stamp out, overpower, extinguish, put down, put out, crack down on, clamp down on, cow, drive underground; end, put an end to, stop, discontinue, terminate, halt, arrest.
▷ANTONYMS incite, encourage.
2 *she only just managed to suppress her irritation*: **conceal**, **restrain**, stifle, smother, bottle up, keep a rein on, hold back, keep back, fight back, choke back, control, keep under control, check, keep in check, curb, contain, bridle, inhibit, put a lid on, deaden, muffle.
3 *the government denied that the report had been suppressed*: **censor**, keep secret, conceal, hide, keep hidden, hush up, gag, keep silent about, withhold, cover up, smother, stifle, muzzle, ban, not disclose, not breathe a word of; mute, proscribe, outlaw, sweep under the carpet.
▷ANTONYMS publicize, disclose.

suppressed adjective *he succumbed to his suppressed passion*: **restrained**, stifled, smothered, muffled, repressed, subdued.

> *Word toolkit* **suppressed**
>
> See **muffled.**

suppression noun **1** *the suppression of subversive activities*: **subduing**, defeat, conquering, vanquishing, repression, crushing, quelling, quashing, squashing, stamping out, crackdown, clampdown, cowing, prevention, extinction; elimination, end, stopping, discontinuation, termination, halting, arrest.
▷ANTONYMS incitement, encouragement.
2 *the British seem to take great pride in the suppression of emotion*: **concealment**, **restraint**, stifling, smothering, holding back, keeping back, choking back, control, keeping under control, checking, curbing, containing, bridling, inhibition, deadening, muffling.
3 *nobody's interest is served by the suppression of the truth*: **censorship**, keeping secret, concealment, hiding, keeping hidden, hushing up, gagging, withholding, covering up, smothering, stifling, muzzling, banning, non-disclosure, proscription, outlawing, restriction.
▷ANTONYMS publication, disclosure.

suppurate verb *a suppurating sore*: **fester**, form pus, swell up, gather, discharge, rot, run, weep, ooze, come to a head; Medicine maturate; rare matter.

supremacy noun **1** *they asserted the supremacy of the people over parliament*: **ascendancy**, predominance, primacy, dominion, hegemony, authority, mastery, control, power, sway, rule, sovereignty, lordship, leadership, influence; rare predomination, paramountcy, prepotence, prepotency, prepollency.
2 *the battle for supremacy in the cellular radio market*: **dominance**, superiority, pre-eminence, ascendancy, advantage; the upper hand, the whip hand, the edge; incomparability, inimitability, matchlessness, peerlessness, greatness, distinction.

supreme adjective **1** *the supreme commander of NATO forces*: **highest ranking**, highest, leading, chief, head, top, foremost, principal, superior, premier, first, cardinal, prime, sovereign; directing, governing; greatest, dominant, predominant, pre-eminent, overriding, prevailing.
▷ANTONYMS subordinate, inferior.
2 *the race makes supreme demands on competitors | a supreme achievement*: **extraordinary**, remarkable, incredible, extreme, intense, great, phenomenal, rare, surpassing, exceptional, outstanding, incomparable, inimitable, unparalleled, unrivalled, peerless, greatest, utmost, uttermost, maximum; severe, acute.
▷ANTONYMS minimum, mild.
3 *he was prepared to make the supreme sacrifice*: **final**, last, ultimate; **utmost**, extreme, total, unconditional, greatest, highest; **fatal**, lethal, mortal.
▷ANTONYMS insignificant.

sure adjective **1** *I am sure that they did not have an affair*: **certain**, positive, convinced, definite, confident, decided, assured, secure, satisfied, persuaded, easy in one's mind, free from doubt; unhesitating, unwavering, unfaltering, unvacillating, unshakeable, unshaken.
▷ANTONYMS unsure, uncertain, doubtful.
2 *he was **sure of** finding a way around the difficulties*: **confident**, certain, assured; with no doubts about.
3 *someone was sure to cop it before the day was out*: **bound**, destined, fated, predestined, very likely.
▷ANTONYMS unlikely.
4 *this is a very attractive way of presenting fruit and is a sure winner with the children*: **guaranteed**, unfailing, infallible, unerring, assured, certain, inevitable, incontestable, irrevocable; informal sure-fire, in the bag, as sure as eggs is eggs.

5 *he could have thrown his servant into the street in the sure knowledge that it would be put down to robust good humour*: **unquestionable**, indisputable, incontestable, irrefutable, incontrovertible, undeniable, indubitable, beyond question, beyond doubt; undoubted, absolute, categorical, true, certain, well grounded, well founded, proven, settled, decided; obvious, evident, plain, clear, conclusive, final, definite, unmistakable, manifest, patent.
6 *he chewed his beard restlessly, a sure sign that he's worried*: **reliable**, dependable, trustworthy, unfailing, infallible, never-failing, certain, unambiguous, tested, tried and true, true, foolproof, established, effective, efficacious; informal sure-fire.
7 *the sure hand of the soloist provides an atmospheric foil for the orchestra*: **firm**, steady, stable, secure, confident, solid, steadfast, unhesitating, unfaltering, unwavering, unswerving.
□ **be sure to** *be sure to send your press releases to the news desk*: **remember to**, don't forget to, make sure to, see that you, mind that you, take care to, be certain to, be careful to.
▷ANTONYMS neglect to, forget to.
□ **for sure** informal *she's guilty for sure*: **definitely**, surely, certainly, without doubt, without question, beyond any doubt, undoubtedly, indubitably, positively, absolutely, undeniably, unmistakably.
□ **make sure** *make sure that the pushchair you choose is covered in easy-clean fabrics*: **check**, confirm, make certain, ensure; assure, verify, corroborate, validate, substantiate, guarantee.
▸ **exclamation** *'Can I ask you something?' 'Sure.'*: **yes**, all right, of course, indeed, certainly, absolutely, agreed; informal OK, yeah, yep, uh-huh, you bet, I'll say, sure thing.

Choose the right word **sure, certain, convinced, positive, definite**

These words are all used to describe a person who is confident that their belief is well founded and, in this sense, are all used after a verb such as *be*, *become*, or *remain*.

Sure, **certain**, and **convinced** all have very similar meanings, but *sure* is the most common in this sense. They can all be followed by *of* (*one thing we were sure of: we couldn't go back*), *about* (*are you absolutely certain about this?*), or a clause, with or without *that* (*he was convinced that his theory was correct*). *Convinced* is the word most typically used with *of* in this sense (*everyone seems very convinced of his guilt*); *sure of* and *certain of* also mean 'confident of receiving or doing something' (*you are always sure of a welcome | he's not certain of his place in the Liverpool line-up*).

Positive is typically used in speech or reported speech, with no following construction (*'Are you sure she won't want to pursue the issue?' 'Positive.'*). It can, however, be followed by a clause (*Columbus was positive that Japan lay just over the horizon*).

If someone is **definite** about something, they are not only confident that it is true but are also stating their belief very firmly (*'Not a chance.' Jean was definite*). *Definite*, in this sense, can be followed by a clause (*Sidney Knowles also saw the body and was quite definite that it was not Crabb*).

surely adverb 1 *surely you remembered to pack a toothbrush?* **it must be the case that**, I believe that, assuredly, without question; informal don't tell me that ... not ....
2 *give me some water, or I shall surely die*: **certainly**, for certain, for sure, to be sure, definitely, undoubtedly, without doubt, doubtless, beyond any/the shadow of a doubt, indubitably, unquestionably, incontestably, irrefutably, incontrovertibly, undeniably, without fail, inevitably, unavoidably; informal sure.
3 *their real achievement lay in slowly but surely creating and manipulating public opinion*: **firmly**, steadily, confidently, solidly, securely, unhesitatingly, unfalteringly, unswervingly, determinedly, doggedly, assuredly.

surety noun 1 *these are all cases in which a wife has become a surety for her husband's obligations*: **guarantor**, sponsor.
2 *he was released on bail of $100,000 with a further $100,000 surety*: **pledge**, **collateral**, guaranty, guarantee, bond, assurance, insurance, bail, deposit; security, indemnity, indemnification; archaic gage, earnest.

surface noun 1 *the paint on the metal surface of the door began to blister*: **outside**, exterior; **top**, **side**, facet, plane, aspect; **finish**, veneer.
▷ANTONYMS inside, interior.
2 *the report managed to get beneath the surface of police culture*: **outward appearance**, superficial appearance, facade.
3 *lightly knead the dough on a floured surface*: **worktop**, top, working top, work surface, counter, table, stand, horizontal surface.
□ **on the surface** *it sounded plausible enough on the surface*: **at first glance**, to the casual eye, outwardly, to all appearances, apparently, ostensibly, superficially, externally, visibly.
▷ANTONYMS at root, fundamentally.
▸ **adjective** *lead news stories are concerned with surface appearances rather than underlying processes*: **superficial**, external, exterior, outward, seeming, ostensible, apparent, cosmetic, skin deep.
▷ANTONYMS fundamental.
▸ **verb 1** *a submarine surfaced in the fjord*: **come to the surface**, come to the top, come up, rise.
▷ANTONYMS dive.
2 *the idea of road pricing first surfaced in the early sixties*: **emerge**, arise, appear, come to light, come up, come into sight, come into view, come out, crop up, materialize, become visible, spring up, loom.
3 informal *our daughter eventually surfaces and has some breakfast*: **get up**, get out of bed, appear, rise, wake, awaken.

surfeit noun *he had tummy trouble resulting from a surfeit of apples and vegetables*: **excess**, surplus, abundance, oversupply, superabundance, superfluity, overdose, glut, avalanche, deluge; too much, more than enough; overindulgence, satiety, satiation; informal bellyful.
▷ANTONYMS lack, dearth.
▸ **verb** *we'll all be surfeited with food and fuddled with wine*: **satiate**, gorge, overfeed, overfill, glut, cram, stuff, overindulge, fill; sicken, nauseate.

surge noun 1 *a surge of water*: **gush**, rush, outpouring, stream, flow, sweep; technical efflux.
2 *a surge in oil production*: **sudden increase**, rise, growth, upswing, upsurge, escalation, jump, leap, boost.
3 *he felt a sudden surge of anger*: **rush**, blast, storm, torrent, blaze, outburst, eruption.
4 *he took one look at the surge of sea and lowered clouds*: **swell**, swelling, heaving, billowing, rolling, roll, bulging, eddying, swirling, tide.
▸ **verb 1** *contaminated water surged into people's homes | the crowd surged forward*: **gush**, rush, stream, flow, burst, pour, cascade, spill, overflow, brim over, well, sweep, spout, spurt, jet, spew, discharge, roll, whirl; seethe, swarm, crowd.
2 *the Dow Jones index surged 47.63 points*: **increase suddenly**, rise, grow, escalate, jump, leap, boost.
3 *the sea surged in the storm*: **rise**, swell, heave, billow, roll, eddy, swirl.

surly adjective *a surly shop assistant*: **bad-tempered**, ill-natured, grumpy, glum, crotchety, prickly, cantankerous, irascible, testy, ill-tempered, short-tempered, ungracious, splenetic, choleric, dyspeptic, bilious, crusty, abrupt, brusque, curt, gruff, blunt, churlish, ill-humoured, crabbed, crabby, uncivil, morose, dour, sullen, sulky, moody, moping, sour, unfriendly, unpleasant, scowling, unsmiling; humourless, disrespectful; informal chippy, grouchy.
▷ANTONYMS good-natured, friendly, pleasant.

surmise verb *she surmised that he was keen to leave*: **guess**, conjecture, suspect, deduce, infer, come to the conclusion, conclude, theorize, speculate, glean, divine; assume, presume, suppose, understand, gather, feel, have a sneaking suspicion, hazard a guess, sense, be of the opinion, think, believe, imagine, judge, fancy, reckon; formal opine.
▷ANTONYMS know.

surmount verb 1 *his reputation is worldwide, and surmounts language barriers*: **overcome**, conquer, get over, prevail over, triumph over, get the better of, beat, vanquish, master; clear, cross, make one's way round/past/over, make it round/past/over, pass over, be unstoppable by; deal with, cope with, resist, endure.
▷ANTONYMS be beaten by.
2 *the four surmount a ridge and see, in the valley below, a deserted city*: **climb to the top of**, climb over, ascend, scale, mount.
▷ANTONYMS descend, climb down.
3 *its copper dome is surmounted by a bronze statue of Justice*: **cap**, top, crown, tip.
4 *a funnel surmounted the structure*: **rise above**, tower above, overtop, dominate.
▷ANTONYMS be dominated by.

surname noun *his surname was Jennings*: **family name**, last name, patronymic.

surpass verb *radio far surpasses the press as a source of news*: **excel**, be better than, be superior to, be greater than, exceed, transcend; **outdo**, outshine, outstrip, outclass, overshadow, put in the shade, eclipse; improve on, top, trump, cap, beat, better, outperform.

Choose the right word **surpass, excel, outdo**

See **excel**.

surpassing adjective *a picture of surpassing beauty*: **exceptional**, extraordinary, remarkable, outstanding, striking, phenomenal, rare, great, supreme, sublime, pre-eminent, consummate, incomparable, inimitable, incredible, unrivalled, unparalleled, matchless, unmatched, unequalled, peerless, unsurpassed, superlative, beyond words, beyond description; informal fabulous, fantastic, stupendous, out of this world, terrific, tremendous, awesome, stellar; literary wondrous.
▷ANTONYMS mediocre; poor.

surplus noun *a surplus of grain*: **excess**, surfeit, overabundance, superabundance, superfluity, oversupply, oversufficiency, glut, profusion, plethora; remainder, residue, remnant; remains, leftovers.
▷ANTONYMS dearth, shortage, lack.

S

▸ **adjective** *clean off any surplus adhesive*: **excess**, excessive, in excess, leftover, left, unused, remaining, extra, additional, reserve, spare; superfluous, redundant, unwanted, unneeded, not required, uncalled for, dispensable, disposable, expendable, useless; French de trop.
▹ANTONYMS necessary; insufficient.

surprise noun 1 *Kate looked at me in surprise*: **astonishment**, amazement, incredulity, bewilderment, stupefaction, wonder, confusion, disbelief; consternation.
2 *the test was supposed to come as a big surprise*: **shock**, bolt from/out of the blue, thunderbolt, bombshell, revelation, source of amazement, rude awakening, eye-opener; informal start; turn up for the books, shocker, whammy.
▸ **verb 1** *I was so surprised when I got the letter telling me about the award that I burst into tears*: **astonish**, amaze, nonplus, startle, astound, stun, flabbergast, stagger, shock, stop someone in their tracks, stupefy, leave open-mouthed, take someone's breath away, dumbfound, daze, benumb, confound, take aback, jolt, shake up; informal bowl over, knock for six, floor, blow someone's mind, strike dumb.
2 *it seems that she surprised a burglar and he attacked her*: **take by surprise**, catch unawares, catch off guard, catch red-handed, catch in the act, catch napping, catch out, burst in on, catch someone with their trousers/pants down, catch in flagrante delicto; Brit. informal catch on the hop.

surprised adjective *he was surprised at the news*: **astonished**, amazed, in amazement, nonplussed, taken aback, startled, astounded, stunned, flabbergasted, staggered, shocked, stupefied, open-mouthed, dumbfounded, dumbstruck, speechless, at a loss for words, thunderstruck, dazed, benumbed, confounded, agape, goggle-eyed, wide-eyed, jolted, shaken up; informal bowled over, knocked for six, floored, flummoxed, caught on the hop, caught on the wrong foot, unable to believe one's eyes/ears.

surprising adjective *he moves with surprising speed*: **unexpected**, unanticipated, unforeseen, unpredictable, unpredicted; **astonishing**, amazing, startling, astounding, striking, staggering, incredible, extraordinary, dazzling, breathtaking, remarkable, wonderful, unusual; informal mind-blowing.
▹ANTONYMS unsurprising, predictable.

surrender verb 1 *the government surrendered to the Allied forces*: **capitulate**, give in, give (oneself) up, yield, concede, submit, climb down, give way, defer, acquiesce, back down, cave in, relent, succumb, quit, crumble; be beaten, be overcome, be overwhelmed, fall victim; lay down one's arms, raise/show the white flag, throw in the towel/sponge, accept defeat, concede defeat.
▹ANTONYMS resist, withstand.
2 *the republics agreed to surrender certain powers to the central government*: **give up**, relinquish, renounce, forgo, forswear, cede, abdicate, waive, forfeit, sacrifice; **hand over**, turn over, deliver (up), yield (up), resign, transfer, commit, grant; part with, let go of; archaic forsake.
▹ANTONYMS seize.
3 *to abandon the past is to surrender all purposeful hope of changing the world*: **abandon**, leave behind, cast aside, turn one's back on, give up, lose.
▸ **noun 1** *the ordeal ended with the peaceful surrender of the hijackers*: **capitulation**, submission, yielding, giving in, succumbing, acquiescence, laying down of arms, quitting; fall, defeat.
2 *a surrender of power to the shop floor*: **relinquishment**, surrendering, renunciation, forgoing, forsaking, ceding, cession, abdication, waiving, resignation; handing over, giving up, yielding up, transfer, abandonment.

surreptitious adjective *Rory tried to sneak a surreptitious glance at Adam's wristwatch*: **secret**, stealthy, clandestine, secretive, sneaky, sly, furtive, concealed, hidden, undercover, covert, veiled, under the table, cloak-and-dagger, backstair, indirect.
▹ANTONYMS blatant, open, honest.

surrogate noun *some argue that modern commerce is a surrogate for warfare*: **substitute**, proxy, replacement; agent, deputy, representative, factor, stand-in, standby, stopgap, fill-in, relief, understudy.

surround verb *the next thing we knew we were surrounded by cops*: **encircle**, enclose, encompass, ring, gird, girdle, go around; fence in, wall in, hedge in, hem in, close in, confine, ring (round), bound, circumscribe, delimit, cut off; besiege, siege, beset, beleaguer, throng, trap; rare environ, enwreathe.
▸ **noun** *a tiled fireplace with a wood surround*: **border**, edging, edge, perimeter, boundary, margin, skirting, skirt, fringe.

surrounding adjective *the surrounding countryside*: **neighbouring**, nearby, near, neighbourhood, local; adjoining, adjacent, bordering, abutting; encircling, encompassing; rare circumambient, circumjacent.

surroundings plural noun *a family-run hotel in exotic surroundings*: **environment**, setting, milieu, background, backdrop, frame, element; conditions, circumstances, situation, context; vicinity, locality, habitat; ambience, atmosphere.

surveillance noun *leading members of the party were to be kept under surveillance*: **observation**, scrutiny, watch, view, inspection, monitoring, supervision, superintendence; **spying**, espionage, intelligence, undercover work, infiltration, reconnaissance; informal bugging, wiretapping, phone-tapping, recon.

survey verb (stress on the second syllable) 1 *Jack stood back to survey his work*: **look at**, look over, take a look at, observe, view, contemplate, regard, see, gaze at, stare at, eye, get a bird's-eye view of; **scrutinize**, examine, inspect, scan, study, consider, review, vet, weigh up, take stock of; informal size up; literary behold.
2 *the BBC surveyed four thousand drug users and their families*: **interview**, question, canvass, poll, cross-examine, investigate, research, study, probe, sample.
3 *a structural engineer should be asked to survey the house*: **make a survey of**, value, carry out a valuation of, estimate the value of; appraise, assess, prospect; triangulate.
▸ **noun** (stress on the first syllable) 1 *there is now a need for a survey of the current literature*: **study**, consideration, review, overview; **scrutiny**, scrutinization, examination, inspection, exploration, appraisal, synopsis, outline, overall picture.
2 *a survey of sexual behaviour*: **poll**, review, investigation, enquiry, study, probe, questionnaire, opinion poll, sampling, census, cross-examination, quiz, research.
3 *make a thorough survey of the property*: **valuation**, **appraisal**, assessment, estimate, estimation, pricing.

survive verb 1 *one passenger survived by escaping through a hole in the fuselage*: **remain alive**, live, sustain oneself, cling to life, pull through, get through, hold on, hold out, make it, keep body and soul together.
2 *they're determined to ensure the theatre survives*: **continue**, remain, last, persist, endure, live on, persevere, abide, go on, keep on, carry on, stay around, linger, be extant, exist, be.
3 *he was survived by Alice and their six sons*: **outlive**, outlast, live (on) after, live longer than, remain alive after.

susceptibility noun 1 *his susceptibility to flattery*: **vulnerability**, sensitivity, openness, defencelessness, receptiveness, responsiveness.
▹ANTONYMS immunity, resistance.
2 *old age brings with it an increased susceptibility to illness*: **liability**, vulnerability, inclination; **predisposition**, proneness, propensity, weakness; likelihood.
▹ANTONYMS immunity, resistance.

susceptible adjective 1 *aggressive TV advertising aimed at susceptible children*: **impressionable**, credulous, gullible, innocent, ingenuous, easily taken in, naive, defenceless, vulnerable, easily led, manageable, acquiescent, adaptable, persuadable, tractable; **sensitive**, responsive, tender, thin-skinned, highly strung, emotional.
▹ANTONYMS sceptical, streetwise.
2 *people **susceptible to** blackmail*: **open to**, receptive to, vulnerable to, defenceless against; an easy target for; rare susceptive to.
3 *some people are more **susceptible to** ulcers than others*: **liable to**, prone to, subject to, inclined to, predisposed to, disposed to, given to, easily affected by, in danger of, at risk of, at the mercy of.
▹ANTONYMS immune, resistant.
4 *the resulting database will be **susceptible of** commercial exploitation*: **capable of**, admitting of, receptive of, open to, responsive to; allowing, permitting; rare susceptive of.
▹ANTONYMS incapable of, not open to.

suspect verb (stress on the second syllable) 1 *I began to suspect that she had made a mistake*: **have a suspicion**, have a feeling, feel, be inclined to think, fancy, reckon, guess, surmise, conjecture, think, think it probable/likely, have a sneaking feeling, have a hunch; be of the opinion, suppose, conclude, expect, presume, consider, deduce, infer, glean, sense, imagine; be afraid, fear, have a foreboding; formal opine.
▹ANTONYMS know.
2 *he is suspected of cheating*: **regard as guilty**, think to be guilty, regard as a wrongdoer.
3 *a broker whose honesty he had no reason to suspect*: **doubt**, distrust, mistrust, have doubts about, harbour suspicions about, have misgivings about, be sceptical about, have qualms about, be suspicious of, be wary of, feel chary about, feel uneasy about, have/harbour reservations about, have a funny feeling about; informal smell a rat about.
▸ **noun** (stress on the first syllable) *a murder suspect*: **suspected person**, accused, defendant.
▸ **adjective** (stress on the first syllable) *a suspect package*: **suspicious**, dubious, untrustworthy, questionable, doubtful, odd, queer, potentially dangerous, potentially false, under suspicion, not quite right; informal fishy, funny, shady, not kosher; Brit. informal dodgy.

suspend verb 1 *protestors had forced the legislative session to be suspended for three hours*: **adjourn**, interrupt, break off, postpone, delay, defer, shelve, arrest, put off, intermit, prorogue, hold over, put aside, pigeonhole, put/hold/keep in abeyance; reschedule; cut short, bring to an end, cease, discontinue, dissolve, disband, terminate, call a halt to; N. Amer. table; informal put on ice, put on the back burner, mothball; N. Amer. informal take a rain check on.
▹ANTONYMS continue, resume.
2 *the treasurer was suspended from his duties pending an external investigation*: **exclude**, debar, shut out, keep out, remove, eliminate, reject, expel, eject, evict, rusticate.

3 *two long fluorescent tubes were suspended from the ceiling*: **hang**, sling, drape, string, put up; swing, dangle.

suspense noun *I can't bear the suspense a moment longer!* **tension**, uncertainty, doubt, doubtfulness, anticipation, expectation, expectancy, excitement, anxiety, nervousness, apprehension, apprehensiveness, strain.
□ **in suspense** *we now wait in suspense for the banker to turn the cards over*: **eagerly**, agog, all agog, with bated breath, on tenterhooks, avid, excited, on edge, open-mouthed, anxious, edgy, jittery, jumpy, keyed up, overwrought, uneasy, worried; informal uptight, waiting for the axe to fall.

suspension noun **1** *the government announced the suspension of army operations*: **adjournment**, interruption, postponement, delay, deferral, deferment, shelving, stay, moratorium, arrest, intermission, interlude, prorogation, tabling, abeyance; rescheduling; hiatus, lacuna, lull, rest, break, pause, respite; armistice; cessation, end, halt, stoppage, cutting short, dissolution, disbandment, termination.
▷ANTONYMS continuation, resumption.
2 *his suspension from school*: **exclusion**, debarment, removal, temporary removal, elimination, rejection, expulsion, ejection, eviction, rustication.

suspicion noun **1** *she had a strong suspicion that he did not like her*: **intuition**, feeling, impression, inkling, surmise, guess, conjecture, speculation, hunch, fancy, notion, supposition, view, belief, idea, conclusion, theory, thesis, hypothesis; presentiment, premonition; informal gut feeling, feeling in one's bones, funny feeling, sixth sense.
▷ANTONYMS certainty.
2 *I confronted him with my suspicions and he admitted everything*: **misgiving**, doubt, qualm, wariness, chariness, reservation, hesitation, scepticism, lack of faith, uncertainty, question, question mark, leeriness, distrust, mistrust.
3 *it tasted like wine with a suspicion of bitters*: **trace**, touch, suggestion, hint, soupçon, tinge, shade, whisper, whiff, bit, trifle, drop, dash, tincture, sprinkling, breath, taste, scent, shadow, glimmer, scintilla, speck, smack, jot, mite, iota, tittle, whit.

suspicious adjective **1** *he was suspicious of all educational innovations | Dolly gave him a suspicious look*: **doubtful**, unsure, dubious, wary, chary, sceptical, distrustful, mistrustful, disbelieving, having reservations, apprehensive, cynical, jaundiced; informal iffy.
▷ANTONYMS trustful, trusting.
2 *I think he's a highly suspicious character*: **disreputable**, unsavoury, dubious, suspect, guilty-looking, dishonest-looking, strange-looking, queer-looking, funny-looking, slippery; informal shifty, shady; Brit. informal dodgy.
▷ANTONYMS upright.
3 *his wife disappeared in suspicious circumstances*: **questionable**, odd, strange, dubious, irregular, queer, funny, doubtful, not quite right, under suspicion, mysterious, murky, dark, criminal, dishonest, corrupt; informal fishy, shady, dodgy.
▷ANTONYMS ordinary, innocent.

sustain verb **1** *they were concerned that the balcony might not be able to sustain the weight*: **bear**, support, carry, stand, keep up, prop up, shore up, bolster, underpin, buttress.
▷ANTONYMS collapse under.
2 *she had lived life to the full, but now had only the memories of such times to sustain her*: **comfort**, help, assist, encourage, succour, support, give strength to, be a source of strength to, be a tower of strength to, buoy up, carry, cheer up, hearten, see someone through; informal buck up.
▷ANTONYMS torment, plague.
3 *they were unable to sustain a coalition*: **continue**, carry on, keep up, keep going, keep alive, keep in existence, keep, maintain, prolong, preserve, conserve, protract, perpetuate, bolster up, prop up, retain, extend.
4 *she had a slab of bread and cheese to sustain her | Britain sustained a much lower population than did Italy*: **maintain**, continue, preserve, keep, keep alive, keep going, provide for; **nourish**, feed, nurture, provide board for.
5 *six Marines sustained slight injuries*: **undergo**, experience, go through, suffer, endure.
6 *the allegation was not sustained by any court*: **uphold**, validate, ratify, vindicate, confirm, endorse, approve; verify, corroborate, substantiate, bear out, prove, authenticate, attest to, back up, evidence, justify.

sustained adjective *a sustained attack on environmentalism*: **continuous**, ongoing, steady, continual, continuing, constant, running, prolonged, persistent, non-stop, perpetual, unfaltering, unremitting, unabating, unrelenting, relentless, unrelieved, unbroken, never-ending, unending, incessant, unceasing, ceaseless, round the clock.
▷ANTONYMS intermittent, sporadic.

sustenance noun **1** *without sustenance the creature will die*: **nourishment**, food, nutriment, nutrition, fare, diet, daily bread, provisions, rations, means of keeping body and soul together; informal grub, chow, scoff; formal comestibles, provender; archaic victuals, vittles, viands, meat; rare aliment.
2 *he kept two or three cows for the sustenance of his family*: **support**, maintenance, keep, means of support, means, living, livelihood, subsistence, income, source of income.

swagger verb **1** *we swaggered into the arena dressed in our costumes*: **strut**, parade, stride, roll, prance; walk confidently, walk arrogantly; N. Amer. informal sashay; archaic swash.
2 *he likes to swagger about his goodness to people*: **boast**, brag, bray, bluster, crow, gloat, parade, strut, posture, pose, blow one's own trumpet, lord it; informal show off, swank, play to the gallery; literary rodomontade.
▶ noun **1** *there was a slight swagger in his stride*: **strut**, parading, roll, prancing; confidence, arrogance, self-assurance, show, ostentation.
2 *Singleton was full of swagger now*: **boasting**, bragging, bluster, bumptiousness, brashness, swashbuckling, vainglory, puffery; informal showing off, swank; literary braggadocio, rodomontade, gasconade.

> *Choose the right word* **swagger, strut, parade**
>
> See **strut**.

swallow verb **1** *she had great difficulty swallowing food*: **eat**, gulp down, consume, devour, eat up, put away, gobble (up), bolt (down), wolf down, stuff down, gorge oneself on, feast on, polish off; ingest, assimilate; informal scoff, get outside of.
2 *he swallowed the last of his drink*: **drink**, gulp down, guzzle, quaff, imbibe, sup, slurp, suck, sip; informal swig, swill down, slug, down, toss off.
3 *I've no intention of swallowing any more of your insults*: **tolerate**, endure, stand, put up with, bear, suffer, abide, submit to, countenance, stomach, brook, take, accept; informal stick, hack; Brit. informal wear.
4 *the magistrate swallowed my story and gave me a year's conditional discharge*: **believe**, credit, accept, trust, put confidence in, give credit to, have faith in; informal fall for, buy, go for, {swallow something hook, line, and sinker}, take as gospel.
5 *last night she had swallowed her pride and rung his flat twice*: **restrain**, repress, hold back, choke back, keep back, hold in, bite back, suppress, fight back; **overcome**, check, conquer, control, keep under control, keep in check, curb, rein in, contain; silence, muffle, stifle, smother, strangle, gag, hide, bottle up, inhibit, frustrate; bite one's lip; informal keep the lid on, button up, cork up.
□ **swallow someone/something up 1** *he watched them till the darkness swallowed them up*: **engulf**, swamp, devour, flood over, overwhelm, overcome, bury, drown, inundate. **2** *a number of art colleges were swallowed up by polytechnics*: **take over**, engulf, absorb, assimilate, incorporate, overrun, overwhelm, swamp.

> *Word links* **swallow**
>
> **phagophobia** fear of swallowing

swamp noun *heavy rain turned the road into a swamp*: **marsh**, bog, quagmire, mire, morass, fen, quag, sump; swampland, marshland, fenland, wetland; saltings; quicksand; N. Amer. salina, bayou, moor.
▶ verb **1** *the rain was driving down with great force, swamping the dry ground*: **flood**, inundate, deluge, wash out, soak, drench, saturate, immerse.
2 *he was swamped by media attention*: **overwhelm**, inundate, flood, deluge, engulf, snow under, bury, overload, overburden, overpower, weigh down, besiege, beset, consume.

swampy adjective *the swampy ground*: **marshy**, boggy, fenny, miry; soft, soggy, muddy, spongy, heavy, squelchy, waterlogged, sodden, slimy, watery, wet, unstable; technical paludal; rare quaggy, uliginose.
▷ANTONYMS firm, dry.

swap verb **1** *I'd swapped some toy cars for a set of dice in a leather case*: **exchange**, interchange, trade, barter, trade off, bargain, traffic; switch, change, replace.
2 *the players swapped jokes and drank pints in the clubhouse*: **bandy**, exchange, trade, reciprocate, pass back and forth, give and take.
▶ noun *he was on the lookout for a job swap*: **exchange**, interchange, trade, barter, switch, trade-off, substitution.

swarm noun **1** *a swarm of bees*: **hive**, flight, flock, covey.
2 *there was the usual swarm of gendarmes rushing around*: **crowd**, multitude, horde, host, mob, gang, throng, stream, mass, body, band, army, troop, legion, flock, herd, pack, drove, sea, array, myriad, pile; knot, cluster, group.
▶ verb *reporters and photographers were swarming all over the place*: **flock**, crowd, throng, stream, surge, flood, seethe, pack, crush.
□ **be swarming with** *the field was swarming with sightseers*: **be crowded with**, be thronged with, be overrun with, be full of, abound in, be teeming with, be bristling with, bristle with, be alive with, be crawling with, be infested with, overflow with, brim with, be prolific in, be abundant in; informal be thick with, be lousy with.

swarthy adjective *the tanned, swarthy skin of his face*: **dark**, dark-coloured, dark-skinned, dark-complexioned, dusky, tanned, black, saturnine, olive-skinned; sallow; rare swart.
▷ANTONYMS pale, fair.

swashbuckling adjective *a band of swashbuckling young crusaders*: **daring**, **romantic**, heroic, daredevil, swaggering, dashing, adventurous, rakish, bold, valiant, valorous, fearless, lionhearted, stout-hearted, dauntless, doughty, devil-may-care, gallant, chivalrous, dazzling, macho, ostentatious.
▷ANTONYMS timid, unadventurous.

S

swathe verb *his hands were swathed in bandages*: **wrap**, envelop, bind, swaddle, bandage, bundle up, muffle up, cover, cloak, shroud, drape, wind, enfold, bedeck, overlay, encase, sheathe.

sway verb **1** *the curtains were swaying in the breeze | they smiled at him and swayed their hips*: **swing**, shake, oscillate, rock, undulate, move from side to side, move to and fro, move back and forth.
2 *she swayed on her feet and the doctor put out a hand to steady her*: **stagger**, wobble, rock, lurch, reel, roll, list, stumble, pitch, keel, veer, swerve.
3 *his thoughts sway constantly between the desire to go on and the desire to settle down*: **waver**, fluctuate, vacillate, oscillate, alternate, vary, see-saw, yo-yo, equivocate, hesitate, shilly-shally, go from one extreme to the other; Brit. hum and haw; informal wobble, blow hot and cold.
4 *a lot of people are swayed by the media*: **influence**, affect, bias, persuade, prevail on, bring round, talk round, win over, convert; manipulate, bend, mould; informal nobble.
5 *she mustn't allow herself to be swayed by emotion*: **rule**, govern, dominate, control, direct, guide.
▶ noun **1** *the slow, easy sway of her hips*: **swing**, sweep, wave, roll, shake, movement, oscillation, undulation.
2 *the province passed under the sway of the Franks*: **jurisdiction**, rule, government, sovereignty, dominion, control, command, power, authority, ascendancy, domination, mastery.
3 *parliament is increasingly under the sway of dogmatists*: **control**, domination, power, authority, supremacy, influence, leadership, direction, leverage; informal pull, clout.
□ **hold sway** *they had held sway in France for a quarter of a century*: **hold power**, wield power, exercise power, rule, be most powerful, be in power, be in control, predominate, have the ascendancy, have the greatest influence, have the upper hand, have the edge, have/hold the whip hand; informal run the show, be in the driving seat, be in the saddle.

swear verb **1** *the godparents will then swear that they believe in the creed and the commandments | they swore to marry each other*: **promise**, vow, promise under oath, solemnly promise, pledge oneself, give one's word, take an oath, swear an oath, swear on the Bible, give an undertaking, undertake, affirm, warrant, state, assert, declare, aver, proclaim, pronounce, profess, attest, guarantee; Law depose, make a deposition, bind oneself; rare asseverate.
2 *she swore that she would never go back to her aunt's house*: **insist**, avow, be emphatic, pronounce, declare, assert, maintain, contend, aver, emphasize, stress.
3 *Kate spilled wine on her jeans and swore*: **curse**, blaspheme, utter profanities, utter oaths, be foul-mouthed, use bad/foul language, be blasphemous, take the Lord's name in vain, swear like a trooper, damn; informal cuss, turn the air blue, eff and blind; archaic execrate.
□ **swear by 1** *I swear by the Blessed Virgin that it fell into the sea*: **invoke**, appeal to, call as one's witness. **2** informal *many of the locals swear by these computers*: **express confidence in**, have faith in, put one's faith in, trust, have every confidence in, believe in; set store by, value; informal rate.
□ **swear in** *he was sworn in as the country's fifteenth Prime Minister*: **install**, instate, induct, invest, inaugurate, introduce, admit into office, institute, initiate; appoint, put in, create; ordain, consecrate, anoint; enthrone, crown.
□ **swear off** *he swore off drink, tobacco, and gambling*: **renounce**, forswear, forgo, abjure, abstain from, go without, shun, avoid, eschew, steer clear of, give a wide berth to, have nothing to do with; **give up**, dispense with, stop, cease, finish, discontinue, break off, drop; informal kick, quit, jack in.
▷**ANTONYMS** take up.

swearing noun *sixty per cent thought there was too much swearing on TV*: **bad language**, foul language, strong language; **profanity**, obscenity, cursing, blaspheming, blasphemy, vilification, imprecation, curses, oaths, expletives, swear words, profanities, insults; technical coprolalia; informal cussing, effing and blinding, four-letter words.

swear word noun *in those days men did not use swear words in front of girls*: **expletive**, obscenity, oath, curse, imprecation, epithet, dirty word, four-letter word; N. Amer. informal cuss word; (**swear words**) bad language, foul language, profanity, blasphemy, swearing.

sweat noun **1** *he was drenched with sweat*: **perspiration**, moisture, dampness, wetness, lather; sweating; informal muck sweat; technical sudor, diaphoresis, hidrosis.
2 informal *I was in a sweat to get away*: **fluster**, flutter, fret, fuss, panic, frenzy, fever, pother, state of anxiety, state of agitation, state of nervousness, nervous state, state of worry; informal state, flap, tizzy, tiz-woz, dither, stew, lather, twitter; N. Amer. informal twit.
3 informal *they made their money from the sweat of the working classes*: **labour**, hard work, toil(s), effort(s), exertion(s), industry, industriousness, drudgery, slog, the sweat of one's brow; back-breaking task, labour of Hercules; informal graft, grind, elbow grease.
▶ verb **1** *the coat had made her so hot that she was sweating heavily*: **perspire**, swelter, exude perspiration, drip with perspiration/sweat, be pouring with sweat, break out in a sweat, glow, be damp, be wet, secrete; informal be in a muck sweat, sweat buckets, sweat like a pig; rare sudate.
2 *I've sweated over this for the last six months, and I'm not going to see that work wasted*: **work hard**, work, work like a Trojan, labour, toil, slog, slave, work one's fingers to the bone, keep one's nose to the grindstone; informal grind, graft, plug away, put one's back into something; archaic drudge.
3 *I sweated over my mistakes*: **worry**, agonize, fuss, panic, fret, dither, lose sleep, be on tenterhooks, be in a state of anxiety, be in a state of agitation, be in a state of nervousness; informal be on pins and needles, be in a state, be in a flap, be in a tiz-woz, be in a stew, be in a lather, bite one's nails, torture oneself, torment oneself.

> *Word links* **sweat**
>
> **sudatory**, **sudorific** relating to sweat

sweaty adjective *he rubbed his sweaty palms on his socks*: **perspiring**, sweating, clammy, sticky, glowing, moist, damp, slimy, soggy, dripping, drenched.
▷**ANTONYMS** dry, cool.

sweep verb **1** *she swept the kitchen floor*: **brush**, clean, scrub, wipe, mop, dust, scour, scrape, rake, buff; vacuum, hoover; informal do.
2 *I swept the crumbs off the floor*: **remove**, wash away, expel, dispose of, eliminate, get rid of; brush, clean, clear, whisk.
3 *he was swept out to sea*: **carry**, pull, drag, drive.
4 *riots swept the country*: **engulf**, overwhelm, flood, flow across, surge over.
5 *he had swept down the stairs with his arm about John's shoulders*: **glide**, sail, stride, breeze, stroll, sally, swagger, drift, flit, flounce.
6 *a flotilla of limousines swept past*: **glide**, sail, dash, charge, rush, streak, speed, fly, zoom, swoop, whizz, hurtle; informal tear.
7 *fire swept through the building*: **race**, hurtle, streak, spread like lightning; informal tear, whip.
8 *police had swept the conference room at 6am and 8am*: **search**, probe, check, explore, hunt through, look through, delve in, go through, sift through, scour, comb, go through with a fine-tooth comb, leave no stone unturned in.
□ **sweep something aside** *they can sweep aside any criticism by declaring that they are rewarding the loyalty of dedicated fans*: **disregard**, ignore, take no notice of, think no more of, dismiss, shrug off, forget about, brush aside.
□ **sweep something under the carpet** *their grievances became clearly visible and could no longer be conveniently swept under the carpet*: **hide**, conceal, keep hidden, suppress, keep quiet about, hush up, not disclose, not breathe a word of, censor, gag, withhold, cover up, smother, stifle, muzzle, ban.
▷**ANTONYMS** disclose, publicize.
▶ noun **1** *with a great sweep of his hand, he bowed*: **gesture**, movement, move, action, stroke, wave.
2 *both men were arrested in a nationwide security sweep*: **search**, hunt, exploration, probe, forage, pursuit, quest.
3 *she looked out into the grey sweep of road*: **curve**, curvature, bend, arc, arch, bow, turn.
4 *this is a modern resort featuring a long sweep of golden sand*: **expanse**, tract, stretch, space, plain, extent, vastness, vista.
5 *the broad sweep of our business interests*: **range**, span, scope, compass, reach, spread, ambit, remit, gamut, orbit, spectrum, sphere, purview, limit, extent.

sweeping adjective **1** *there will be more sweeping changes in education*: **extensive**, wide-ranging, global, broad, wide, comprehensive, all-inclusive, all-embracing, far-reaching, across the board, worldwide, catholic, exhaustive, pervasive; thorough, in-depth, radical; informal wall-to-wall.
▷**ANTONYMS** narrow, restricted, limited.
2 *a sweeping victory for the Republican Party*: **overwhelming**, decisive, thorough, complete, total, absolute, out-and-out, thoroughgoing, unconditional, unlimited, unrestricted, unqualified, plenary.
▷**ANTONYMS** narrow.
3 *there are dangers in making sweeping statements based on this research*: **wholesale**, blanket, over-general, general, inclusive, all-inclusive, unqualified, indiscriminate, universal, oversimplified, imprecise.
▷**ANTONYMS** focused, narrow.
4 *a sweeping curved roof*: **broad**, extensive, expansive, vast, spacious, roomy, boundless, panoramic.
▷**ANTONYMS** small, narrow.

sweet adjective **1** *a packet of sweet biscuits*: **sugary**, **sweetened**, saccharine; sugared, honeyed, candied, glacé; syrupy, treacly, sickly, cloying.
▷**ANTONYMS** sour, sharp; savoury.
2 *the fresh sweet perfume of roses*: **fragrant**, aromatic, sweet-smelling, perfumed, balmy, scented; literary ambrosial, redolent.
3 *she sang the tune in her sweet silvery voice*: **musical**, tuneful, dulcet, melodious, lyrical, mellifluous, soft, harmonious, euphonious, silvery, honeyed, liquid, mellow, rich, smooth, sweet-sounding, sweet-toned, silver-toned, bell-like, golden.
▷**ANTONYMS** harsh, discordant.
4 *life was still sweet, despite Father's mean ways*: **pleasant**, pleasing, agreeable, delightful, nice, satisfying, gratifying, welcome, good, acceptable, to one's liking, entertaining, charming, inviting, attractive, fine;

informal lovely, great.
▷ANTONYMS harsh, disagreeable.
5 *she breathed in the sweet March air*: **pure**, wholesome, fresh, uncontaminated, clean, clear, not sour, not rotten.
▷ANTONYMS harsh, rotten.
6 *she had such a sweet nature*: **likeable**, appealing, engaging, amiable, pleasant, agreeable, genial, friendly, nice, good-natured, kind, kindly, kind-hearted, thoughtful, considerate; charming, winning, enchanting, captivating, delightful, lovely, as nice as pie; Italian & Spanish simpatico; dated taking.
▷ANTONYMS nasty.
7 *she looks quite sweet all tucked up*: **cute**, lovable, adorable, endearing, charming, attractive, dear.
8 *my sweet little sister*: **dear**, dearest, darling, beloved, loved, cherished, precious, treasured, prized, worshipped, idolized.
□ **sweet on** informal *he had been sweet on a couple of local girls*: **fond of**, taken with, attracted to, charmed by, captivated by, enchanted by, in love with, enamoured of, infatuated with, keen on, devoted to, smitten with, head over heels in love with; informal gone on, mad about, struck on, daft about, into, bowled over by, swept off one's feet by.
▷ANTONYMS indifferent to.
▸**noun 1** *I got some sweets for the children*: **piece of confectionery**, chocolate, bonbon, fondant, toffee; N. Amer. candy; informal sweetie; archaic sweetmeat, confection.
2 *you can whip up this delicious sweet in five minutes*: **dessert**, pudding, sweet course, second course, last course; Brit. informal afters, pud.
3 *happy birthday my sweet!* **dear**, darling, dearest, dear one, love, sweetheart, beloved, honey, pet, treasure, angel.

sweeten verb **1** *sweeten the milk with a little sugar*: **make sweet**, add sugar to, sugar, sugar-coat, add honey to, add sweetener to.
2 *he chewed coriander seeds to sweeten his breath*: **freshen**, refresh, fresh, purify, deodorize, perfume.
3 *there is no way to sweeten the bad news*: **soften**, ease, alleviate, make agreeable, relieve, mitigate, make less painful, mellow, temper, cushion; embellish, embroider, dress up.
4 informal *the dividend has been increased to sweeten shareholders*: **mollify**, placate, soothe, soften, soften up, mellow, pacify, appease, win over.

sweetheart noun **1** *you look lovely, sweetheart*: **darling**, dear, dearest, love, beloved, dear one, sweet; informal honey, sweetie, sugar, baby, babe, doll, poppet; archaic sweeting.
2 *my high-school sweetheart*: **girlfriend**, **boyfriend**, lover, beloved, love, significant other, darling, true love, woman friend, man friend, lady friend, lady love, beau, loved one, suitor, admirer, paramour, inamorato, inamorata; informal steady, flame, WAGs (wives and girlfriends); literary swain; dated follower.

swell verb **1** *she felt her top lip **swell up** as she tasted blood*: **expand**, bulge, distend, become distended, inflate, become inflated, dilate, become bloated, bloat, blow up/out, puff up, balloon, fatten, fill out, tumefy, intumesce.
▷ANTONYMS shrink, contract.
2 *peasant hunger grew more acute as the population swelled*: **grow larger**, grow greater, grow, enlarge, increase, expand, rise, wax, mount, escalate, accelerate, step up, accumulate, surge, multiply, proliferate, snowball, mushroom, skyrocket.
▷ANTONYMS decrease, wane.
3 *she felt herself **swell with pride***: **be filled**, be full of, be bursting, brim, overflow, be overcome.
4 *the graduate entry scheme has swelled the numbers entering the profession*: **make larger**, make greater, enlarge, increase, increase in size/scope, expand, augment, boost, top up, build up, accelerate, step up, multiply.
▷ANTONYMS decrease.
5 *he passed a pub, the sound of loud music swelling from inside*: **grow loud**, grow louder, become louder, amplify, intensify, heighten.
▷ANTONYMS quieten.
▸**noun 1** *there was a brief swell in the volume of conversation*: **increase**, rise, growth, expansion, escalation, acceleration, surge, stepping-up, proliferation, snowballing, mushrooming, skyrocketing.
▷ANTONYMS decrease, dip.
2 *a heavy swell on the sea*: **billow**, billowing, undulation, surge, surging, wave, roll, rolling, bulge, bulging, rush, deluge, movement.
▸**adjective** N. Amer. informal, dated *that's a swell idea*. See **excellent**.

swelling noun *he had a great swelling under his eye*: **bump**, lump, bulge, inflammation, protuberance, excrescence, enlargement, distension, prominence, protrusion, tumour, node, nodule; boil, blister, bunion, carbuncle, wen, sty, welt; rare tumescence.

sweltering adjective *a sweltering afternoon*: **hot**, **stifling**, suffocating, humid, steamy, sultry, sticky, muggy, close, stuffy, airless, oppressive, tropical, torrid, burning, searing, parching, like an oven, like a Turkish bath, jungle-like; informal boiling, baking, roasting, blistering, sizzling.
▷ANTONYMS cold, chilly, cool.

swerve verb *a car swerved into her path*: **veer**, change direction, go off course, deviate, skew, diverge, sheer, curve, twist, weave, zigzag, turn aside, branch off, sidetrack; Sailing tack; rare divagate.
▸**noun** *the bowler must regulate his swerve so that the ball hits the wicket*: **curve**, curl, bend, deviation, twist, change of direction; N. Amer., Pool & Billiards English.

swift adjective **1** *Ramsay made a swift decision*: **prompt**, rapid, sudden, immediate, instant, instantaneous, without delay, ready, punctual; abrupt, unhesitating, hasty, hurried, precipitate, headlong; informal p.d.q. (pretty damn quick).
▷ANTONYMS unhurried.
2 *most of them are swift runners*: **fast**, rapid, quick, speedy, fleet-footed, fleet, swift as an arrow, like the wind, like lightning; literary winged, flying; informal nippy, supersonic.
▷ANTONYMS slow, sluggish.
3 *pupils are expected to make swift progress*: **rapid**, quick, brisk, lively, speedy, fast, high-speed, expeditious, express, breakneck, meteoric, whirlwind; informal spanking, nippy.
▷ANTONYMS slow, leisurely.

swiftly adverb **1** *the police reacted swiftly*: **promptly**, immediately, instantly, instantaneously, without delay, post-haste, in a flash, in a trice, in the wink of an eye, in an instant, in no time (at all); readily, punctually, meteorically; suddenly, abruptly, unhesitatingly, hastily, hurriedly, precipitately, headlong; informal before you can say Jack Robinson, before you can say knife, like a shot, like greased lightning, at warp speed, p.d.q. (pretty damn quick), lickety-split, in a jiff/jiffy, pronto, in less than no time.
▷ANTONYMS unhurriedly, in due course.
2 *he went swiftly through the house*: **rapidly**, quickly, fast, speedily, briskly, at high speed, at full tilt, like the wind, like lightning, at breakneck speed, as fast as one's legs can carry one, as swift as an arrow; informal double quick, nippily, like the clappers; literary apace.
▷ANTONYMS slowly.

swiftness noun **1** *the children had the swiftness of weasels*: **speed**, speediness, quickness, velocity, celerity, fleetness, fastness, rapidity, rapidness, liveliness; informal nippiness.
▷ANTONYMS slowness, sluggishness.
2 *bankruptcy can happen with surprising swiftness*: **suddenness**, abruptness, instantaneity, rapidity, rapidness, haste, hastiness, briskness, hurriedness, hurry.
3 *the answer came with unwanted swiftness*: **promptness**, immediateness, immediacy, instantaneousness, rapidity, rapidness, dispatch, punctuality; alacrity, expeditiousness, readiness, willingness.
▷ANTONYMS lateness, tardiness.

swill verb **1** *she was swilling pints of bitter with the lads*: **drink**, quaff, swallow, down, gulp down, drain, guzzle, imbibe, sup, slurp, consume; informal swig, swill (down), slug, knock back, knock off, toss off, put away, get one's laughing gear round, bend one's elbow; Brit. informal bevvy; N. Amer. informal chug, scarf down.
2 *with a clatter of buckets and bowls, we started to **swill down** the yard | she **swilled out** a glass*: **wash**, sluice, clean out, flush, rinse, bathe, cleanse, drench.
▸**noun 1** *he took a noisy swill of coffee*: **gulp**, drink, swallow, draught, mouthful; informal swig, slug.
2 *if a regular source of swill is available, pig keeping can be profitable*: **pigswill**, hogwash, pigwash, wash, mash; **slops**, scraps, refuse, scourings, leftovers, waste matter, waste, remains, detritus.

swim verb **1** *when it rained they played squash or swam in the indoor pool*: **bathe**, go swimming, take a dip, dip, splash around; float, tread water; dive, plunge; snorkel.
2 *Pip's food was **swimming in** gravy*: **be saturated in**, be drenched in, be soaked in, be steeped in, be immersed in, be covered in, be full of.

swimmingly adverb **1** *everything was going swimmingly*: **smoothly**, easily, effortlessly, very well, like clockwork, without a hitch, with no trouble, without difficulty, as planned, to plan; informal like a dream, like magic.
2 *Tommy and I got on swimmingly*: **well**; informal famously, like a house on fire.

swimming pool noun **pool**, baths, leisure pool, lido, piscina; Brit. swimming bath(s); N. Amer. rare natatorium.

swimsuit noun **swimwear**, bathing dress, bathing suit; (swimming) trunks; bikini; Brit. swimming costume, bathing costume; informal swimming togs, cossie; Austral./NZ informal bathers.

swindle verb *the museum has been swindled out of a large sum of money*: **defraud**, cheat, trick, fleece, dupe, deceive, rook, exploit, squeeze, milk, bleed; fool, take advantage of, mislead, delude, hoax, hoodwink, bamboozle, string along; embezzle; informal do, con, sting, diddle, fiddle, swizzle, swizz, rip off, take for a ride, pull a fast one on, pull the wool over someone's eyes, put one over on, sell a pup to, take to the cleaners, bilk, gull, finagle, gazump; N. Amer. informal stiff, euchre, bunco, hornswoggle; archaic cozen, sharp; rare mulct.
▸**noun** *an insurance swindle*: **fraud**, trick, deception, deceit, trickery, chicanery, exploitation, cheat, imposture, sham, sharp practice, artifice; ruse, dodge, racket, wile; informal con trick, con, sting, diddle, rip-off, fiddle, flimflam, swizzle, swizz; N. Amer. informal bunco.

S

swindler noun *more than 10,000 farmers have fallen victim to the swindlers*: **fraudster**, fraud, confidence trickster, confidence man, cheat, trickster, rogue, mountebank, exploiter, charlatan, sham, impostor, hoaxer, embezzler; informal con man, con artist, shark, sharp, hustler, bilker, flimflam man, phoney, chiseller, crook, quack, bunco artist.

swing verb **1** *the basket was swinging in the wind*: **sway**, oscillate, move back and forth, move to and fro, wave, wag, dangle, rock, flutter, flap, vibrate, quiver.
2 *Helen swung the bottle, clubbing Goldman at the base of the skull*: **brandish**, wave, flourish, wield, raise, shake, wag, twirl.
3 *this road swings off to the north*: **curve**, bend, veer, turn, bear, wind, twist, deviate, slew, skew, sheer off, change course, drift, head.
4 *Penny swung down the drive*: **stride**, march, sweep; stroll; N. Amer. informal sashay.
5 *the balance had once more swung from centralization to decentralization*: **change**, fluctuate, oscillate, waver, alternate, see-saw, yo-yo, vary, shift, alter, undulate, ebb and flow, rise and fall, go up and down, go back and forth.
6 *what finally swung it for him was that his family kept writing to the State Governor*: **accomplish**, achieve, obtain, acquire, get, secure, net, win, earn, attain, bag, capture, grab, hook; manoeuvre, sort out; informal wangle, land, fix (up), work, get hold of, nab, collar, pull down, knock off.
□ **swing the lead** Brit. informal *nearly a fifth of working time was wasted through workers swinging the lead*. See **malinger**.
▸ noun **1** *a giant swing of the pendulum | the swing of her hips*: **swaying**, oscillation, undulation; wagging, toing and froing, wobble; Astronomy libration.
2 *the swing to the Conservatives was 6 per cent*: **change**, move; turnaround, turnround, turnabout, reversal, about turn, about face, volte face, change of heart, change of loyalties, U-turn, sea change, swerve, backtracking; rare tergiversation.
3 *there's been a swing towards plain food*: **trend**, tendency, drift, movement, current, course.
4 *there was a sudden swing in her mood*: **fluctuation**, change, shift, switch, variation, oscillation.
▷ANTONYMS stability.
5 *it's all soft swing and mellow music until the chorus*: **rhythm**, beat, pulse, cadence, pace, rhythmical flow/pattern, measure, metre, tempo, lilt; informal groove.

swingeing adjective *swingeing cuts in public expenditure*: **severe**, extreme, serious, substantial, drastic, harsh, punishing, excessive, oppressive, draconian, heavy.
▷ANTONYMS minor, mild.

swipe informal verb **1** *without warning his right hand swiped at her mouth*: **strike**, swing, hit, slap, cuff, lash out; informal belt, wallop, sock, biff, clout.
2 *they're always swiping sweets from the other kids*: **steal**, thieve, take, pilfer, purloin, snatch, help oneself to, appropriate, abstract, shoplift; informal filch, lift, snaffle, rob, nab; Brit. informal nick, pinch, whip, half-inch, blag; N. Amer. glom.
▸ noun *she took a playful swipe at his face*: **strike**, stroke, swing, hit, slap, brush, cuff, clip; informal belt, wallop.

swirl verb *the snow swirled around them | the water swirled over her ankles*: **whirl**, eddy, billow, spiral, wind, churn, swish, agitate, circulate, revolve, spin, twist, gyrate; **flow**, ripple, stream, surge, seethe, foam, froth, boil, ferment.

switch noun **1** *he pressed the switch on top of the telephone console*: **button**, handle, lever, key, control, controller, disc, dial, joystick; circuit-breaker.
2 *we observed a switch from direct to indirect taxation*: **change**, change of direction, move, shift, transition, transformation, diversion; reversal, turnaround, swerve, U-turn, changeover, transfer, conversion, substitution, exchange, interchange; Brit. about-turn.
3 *somebody pulled the old twenty-dollar bill switch on me*: **exchange**, swap, trade, substitution, interchange, replacement, rotation.
4 *a switch of willow*: **branch**, twig, shoot, stick, rod.
▸ verb **1** *people in traditional employment might be encouraged to switch to agency working | he switched sides at the last moment*: **change**, shift, convert, divert, redirect; reverse; informal chop and change.
2 *he managed to switch envelopes so that an empty one was sent instead*: **exchange**, **swap**, interchange, trade, substitute, cause to change places, replace, rotate.
□ **switch something on** *he switched the kettle on*: **turn on**, put on, flick on, activate, power up, start off, set going, get going, trigger off, set in motion, operate, initiate, actuate, boot up, initialize, energize.
□ **switch something off** *she was so shocked she'd switched the TV off*: **turn off**, shut off, flick off, stop working, cut, power down, stop, halt, deactivate; extinguish.

swivel verb *she swivelled round in her seat*: **turn**, spin, swing, rotate, revolve, pivot, twirl, whirl, wheel, gyrate, pirouette.
▸ noun *attached to the wall is a small television on a swivel*: **pivot**, axle, spindle, hinge, axis, fulcrum, pin, hub, kingpin, gudgeon, trunnion.

swollen adjective *swollen glands*: **expanded**, **distended**, bulging, inflamed, inflated, enlarged, dilated, bloated, blown-up, puffed up, puffy, ballooning, protruding, prominent, stretched, tumescent; rare tumid, oedematous, dropsical.
▷ANTONYMS shrunken, shrivelled.

> *Word toolkit* **swollen**
>
> See **puffy**.

swoop verb **1** *the pigeons swooped down after the grain*: **dive**, descend, sweep, pounce, drop, plummet, plunge, pitch, nosedive; rush, dart, speed, zoom.
2 *armed police swooped on a flat in east London*: **raid**, search; pounce, make a raid; attack, assault, assail, charge; N. Amer. informal bust.
▸ noun *police arrested them in an early morning swoop*: **raid**, surprise search; attack, assault; N. Amer. informal bust, takedown.

sword noun *a ceremonial sword*: **blade**, steel; literary brand.
□ **cross swords** See **quarrel** (verb).
□ **put someone to the sword kill**, execute, put to death, murder, butcher, slaughter, annihilate, massacre, cut down, mow down; literary slay.

sybarite noun **hedonist**, sensualist, voluptuary, libertine, pleasure seeker, playboy, epicure, glutton, gourmand, gastronome; French bon vivant, bon viveur.
▷ANTONYMS puritan.

sybaritic adjective *the brothers' opulent and sybaritic lifestyle*: **luxurious**, extravagant, pampered, lavish, self-indulgent, pleasure-seeking, sensual, voluptuous, hedonistic, epicurean, lotus-eating, libertine, debauched, dissolute, decadent, unrestrained.
▷ANTONYMS abstemious, ascetic.

sycophant noun *he was surrounded by flatterers and sycophants*: **toady**, creep, crawler, fawner, flatterer, flunkey, truckler, groveller, doormat, lickspittle, kowtower, obsequious person, minion, hanger-on, leech, puppet, spaniel, Uriah Heep; informal bootlicker, yes-man; vulgar slang arse-licker, arse-kisser, brown-nose; N. Amer. vulgar slang suckhole.

sycophantic adjective *his clique of sycophantic friends*: **obsequious**, servile, subservient, deferential, grovelling, toadying, fawning, flattering, ingratiating, cringing, unctuous, oily, slimy, creeping, crawling, truckling, slavish, bowing and scraping, Uriah Heepish, gushing; informal bootlicking, smarmy; vulgar slang arse-licking, arse-kissing, brown-nosing; N. Amer. vulgar slang suckholing.

syllabus noun *the A-level chemistry syllabus*: **curriculum**, course, course of study, programme of study, educational programme, course outline; timetable, schedule.

symbol noun **1** *the lotus is the symbol of purity*: **emblem**, token, sign, representation, figure, image, type; metaphor, allegory.
2 *the chemical symbol for helium is He*: **sign**, character, mark, letter, hieroglyph, ideogram.
3 *the Red Cross symbol*: **logo**, emblem, badge, stamp, trademark, crest, insignia, coat of arms, seal, figure, device, rune, logotype, logogram, monogram, hallmark, tag, flag, motto, token, motif, colophon, ideogram.

> *Word links* **symbol**
>
> **graphology** study of written symbols

symbolic adjective **1** *few buildings can be as symbolic of the Roman Empire as the mighty Colosseum*: **emblematic**, representative, typical, characteristic, distinctive, symptomatic; meaningful, significant.
2 *religious language is mostly used in symbolic or metaphorical ways*: **figurative**, representative, illustrative, emblematic, allegorical, parabolic, non-literal, allusive, denotative, connotative, suggestive, mnemonic.
▷ANTONYMS literal.

symbolize verb *the wheel symbolizes the power of peaceful change*: **represent**, be a symbol of, stand for, be a sign of, exemplify; denote, signify, mean, communicate, indicate, convey, express, imply, suggest, allude to; embody, epitomize, encapsulate, personify, typify; literary betoken; archaic symbol.

symmetrical adjective **1** *the idea was that the library would be symmetrical, with the entrance and stairs in the centre*: **regular**, uniform, consistent; evenly shaped, aligned, in line, congruous, equal; mirror-image, mirror-like.
▷ANTONYMS asymmetrical, disproportionate.
2 *the sturdy elegance and symmetrical beauty of the viaduct*: **well balanced**, balanced, well proportioned, proportional, in proportion, regular, even, harmonious.
▷ANTONYMS asymmetrical, uneven.

symmetry noun **1** *the garden is neat, laid out with perfect symmetry*: **regularity**, evenness, uniformity, equilibrium, consistency, congruity, conformity, agreement, correspondence, orderliness, equality.
▷ANTONYMS asymmetry, irregularity.

2 *the remarkable symmetry of the poem*: **balance**, proportions, regularity, evenness of form, harmony, harmoniousness, consonance, concord, coordination.
▷ANTONYMS asymmetry.

sympathetic adjective **1** *a sympathetic listener | the dreaded bank manager often turns out to be highly sympathetic*: **commiserating**, commiserative, pitying, condoling, consoling, comforting, supportive, encouraging; **compassionate**, caring, concerned, solicitous, empathetic; considerate, kindly, kind, kind-hearted, soft-hearted, tender-hearted, warm, warm-hearted; understanding, sensitive.
▷ANTONYMS unsympathetic, unfeeling.
2 *Rudy is the most sympathetic male character in the book*: **likeable**, pleasant, agreeable, congenial, friendly, genial, companionable, easy to get along with; Italian & Spanish simpatico.
▷ANTONYMS unsympathetic, unfriendly.
3 *we got along well because I was **sympathetic to** his cause*: **in favour of**, in sympathy with, approving of, pro, on the side of, supportive of, supporting of, favourable, encouraging of; well disposed to, favourably disposed to, receptive to, responsive to.
▷ANTONYMS unsympathetic, indifferent, opposed.

sympathize verb **1** *he **sympathized with** his tearful wife*: **pity**, feel/be sorry for, show sympathy for, be sympathetic towards, show compassion for, be compassionate towards, commiserate, offer condolences to, feel for, show concern, show interest; **console**, offer consolation to, comfort, solace, soothe, succour; be supportive of, support, encourage; **empathize with**, identify with, understand, relate to, be en rapport with, care for, weep for, grieve for, bleed for.
▷ANTONYMS disregard.
2 *they **sympathize with** feminist critiques of traditional theory*: **agree**, support, be in sympathy, be sympathetic towards, be in favour of, go along, favour, be well disposed to, approve of, commend, back, side with, align, encourage.
▷ANTONYMS disapprove.

sympathizer noun *a rebel sympathizer*: **supporter**, advocate, backer, well-wisher, ally, partisan, fellow traveller; collaborator, fraternizer, conspirator, quisling, accomplice.

sympathy noun **1** *Sarah touched his arm in sympathy | he shows commendable sympathy for the world's poor*: **commiseration**, pity, condolence, consolation, comfort, solace, support, encouragement; **compassion**, caring, concern, solicitude, solicitousness, empathy; consideration, kindness, kind-heartedness, tender-heartedness, tenderness, warmth, warm-heartedness.
▷ANTONYMS indifference.
2 *they might publicize John's case out of sympathy with a fellow journalist*: **rapport**, fellow feeling, affinity, empathy, harmony, accord, compatibility; closeness, friendship, fellowship, togetherness, camaraderie, communion.
▷ANTONYMS hostility.
3 *their sympathy with the Republicans*: **agreement**, harmony, favour, approval, approbation, support, encouragement, goodwill, commendation, partiality; association, alignment, affiliation.
▷ANTONYMS disapproval.

symptom noun **1** *he described the symptoms of the disease*: **manifestation**, indication, indicator, sign, mark, feature, trait; Medicine prodrome.
2 *these bookshops are a symptom of the country's present turmoil*: **expression**, sign, indication, mark, token, manifestation; omen, augury, portent, warning, testimony, evidence, proof, clue, hint.

symptomatic adjective *I don't know whether this is something specific to him or possibly symptomatic of a wider societal problem*: **indicative**, signalling, warning, characteristic, suggestive, typical, representative, symbolic; rare indicatory.

synopsis noun *a basic synopsis of the play*: **summary**, precis, résumé, abstract, outline, condensation, digest, summarization, summing-up, rundown, round-up, abridgement, review, sketch, compendium; rare conspectus.

synthesis noun *this painting is a synthesis of elements derived from a variety of different types of ancient art*: **combination**, union, amalgam, blend, mixture, compound, fusion, coalescence, composite, concoction, conglomerate, alloy; combining, unification, uniting, merging, amalgamation, conglomeration, weaving, interweaving, reconciliation, marrying; informal mash-up.

synthetic adjective *synthetic leather*: **artificial**, fake, false, faux, imitation, mock, simulated, ersatz, substitute; pseudo, sham, bogus, spurious, counterfeit, forged, pretended, so-called, plastic; man-made, manufactured, unnatural, fabricated; replica, reproduction, facsimile; informal phoney.
▷ANTONYMS real, genuine, natural.

> *Word toolkit*
>
> See **artificial**.

syrupy adjective **1** *a few teaspoons of syrupy medicine*: **oversweet**, sweet, sickly sweet, sugary, treacly, honeyed, saccharine; **thick**, sticky, slimy, gluey, viscid, glutinous; informal gooey.
2 *syrupy romantic drivel*: **sentimental**, over-sentimental, mawkish, cloying, sickly, sickly sweet, gushing, saccharine, maudlin, emotional, trite; informal soppy, schmaltzy, mushy, slushy, sloppy, weepy, cutesy, lovey-dovey, drippy, cheesy, corny.

system noun **1** *the legal system | a system of canals*: **structure**, organization, order, arrangement, complex, apparatus, network; administration, institution; informal set-up.
2 *a system for regulating medical products*: **method**, methodology, technique, process, procedure, approach, practice, line, line of action, line of attack, attack, means, way, manner, mode, framework, modus operandi; scheme, plan, policy, programme, regimen, set of principles, set of procedures, set of guidelines, formula, routine, tactic, tack.
3 *there was no system at all in the company*: **methodicalness**, orderliness, systematization, planning, logic, routine.
4 (**the system**) *how do you give youngsters who have already been victimized faith in the system?* **the establishment**, the authorities, the powers that be, the ruling class, the regime, bureaucracy, officialdom; the status quo, the prevailing political/social order; archaic the regimen.

systematic adjective *these interviews were conducted in a systematic way*: **structured**, methodical, organized, orderly, well ordered, planned, systematized, regular, routine, standardized, standard, formal, logical, coherent, consistent, efficient, businesslike, practical, careful, fastidious, meticulous; informal joined-up.
▷ANTONYMS disorganized, chaotic.

tab noun **1** *Joe knew it was his jacket, he'd seen his name stencilled on the tab*: **tag**, flap, loop, lappet, label; strap, handle.
2 informal *the company will pick up the tab for any moving expenses*: **bill**, invoice, account, statement, note/list of charges, charge, reckoning, tally; expense, cost; N. Amer. check; archaic score.

table noun **1** *she put the plates on the table*: **bench**, board, work surface, worktop, counter, desk, bar, buffet, stand, workbench, work table, top, horizontal surface, surface.
2 *he was reputed to provide an excellent table*: **meal**, food, fare, diet, board, menu, nourishment, nutriment; eatables, rations, provisions; informal spread, grub, chow, eats, nosh; archaic victuals, vittles, viands.
3 *the text is accompanied by numerous tables*: **list**, chart, diagram, figure, graph, plan; catalogue, inventory, digest, enumeration, tabulation, index, directory, register, itemization, record; Computing graphic.
▶ verb *an opposition MP had tabled a question in parliament*: **submit**, put forward, bring forward, propose, suggest, move, enter, lodge, file, introduce, air, moot, lay.

tableau noun **1** *the sun and moon frequently appear in a symbolic role in mythic tableaux*: **picture**, painting, representation, portrayal, illustration, image.
2 *in the first act the action is represented in a series of tableaux*: **pageant**, tableau vivant, human representation, parade, diorama, scene.
3 *our entrance disturbed the domestic tableau around the fireplace*: **scene**, arrangement, grouping, group; picture, spectacle, image, view, vignette.

tablet noun **1** *a carved stone tablet*: **slab**, panel, plaque, plate, sign; stone, gravestone, headstone, tombstone, memorial.
2 *a headache tablet*: **pill**, capsule, lozenge, caplet, pastille, pellet, drop, ball; informal tab; rare jujube, bolus, troche, pilule.
3 *a tablet of soap*: **bar**, cake, slab, brick, block, chunk, piece.

taboo noun *the taboo against healing on the sabbath*: **prohibition**, proscription, veto, interdiction, interdict, ban, restriction, boycott, non-acceptance, anathema.
▷ANTONYMS acceptance; encouragement.
▶ adjective *drinking, smoking, and gambling in his father's house were all taboo | taboo language*: **forbidden**, prohibited, banned, proscribed, vetoed, ruled out, interdicted, outlawed, not permitted, not allowed, illegal, illicit, unlawful, impermissible, not acceptable, restricted, frowned on, beyond the pale, off limits, out of bounds; unmentionable, unspeakable, unutterable, ineffable, censored; rude, impolite, indecorous, dirty; German verboten; Islam haram; NZ tapu; informal no go; rare non licet.
▷ANTONYMS permitted, acceptable; encouraged.

tabulate verb *the survey results are tabulated in the appendix*: **arrange**, order, organize, set out, chart; systematize, systemize, catalogue, list, sort, index, classify, class, codify, compile, group, range, dispose, file, log, grade, rate; archaic assort.

tacit adjective *the bargaining relies on informal agreements and tacit understandings*: **implicit**, understood, implied, inferred, hinted, suggested, insinuated; **unspoken**, unstated, undeclared, unsaid, unexpressed, unmentioned, unvoiced, silent, mute, wordless, not spelt out; taken for granted, taken as read.
▷ANTONYMS explicit, stated.

> *Choose the right word* **tacit, unspoken, implicit**
>
> See **implicit**.

taciturn adjective *a shy, taciturn man*: **untalkative**, uncommunicative, reticent, unforthcoming, quiet, unresponsive, secretive, silent, tight-lipped, close-mouthed, mute, dumb, inarticulate; reserved, withdrawn, introverted, retiring, antisocial, unsociable, distant, aloof, stand-offish, cold, detached, dour, sullen.
▷ANTONYMS talkative, loquacious.

tack noun **1** *tacks held the carpet to the floor*: **pin**, drawing pin, nail, tin tack, staple, spike, rivet, stud; N. Amer. thumb tack.
2 Sailing *the brig bowled past on the opposite tack*: **heading**, bearing, direction, course, track, path, line.
3 *he changed tack and began to play in a different style*: **approach**, way, method, process; policy, procedure, technique, tactic, plan, strategy, stratagem, programme, line of attack; course of action, line of action, path, line, angle, direction, course.
▶ verb **1** *a photo was tacked to the wall*: **pin**, nail, staple, fix, fasten, attach, secure, affix, put up, put down.
2 *when the dress was roughly tacked together she tried it on*: **stitch**, baste, sew, bind, hem.
3 Sailing *the yachts tacked back and forth across the lake*: **change course**, change direction, change heading; swerve, zigzag; veer off/away; Nautical go about, come about, beat, sail into the wind.
4 *he answered, but she had tacked and was already following a different line of questioning*: **alter one's approach**, change course, change direction, do a U-turn, change one's mind, change one's attitude, have a change of heart; Brit. do an about-turn.
5 *there are some poems **tacked on** at the end of the book*: **attach**, add, append, join, tag, annex.

tackle noun **1** *fishing tackle*: **gear**, equipment, apparatus, outfit, kit, rig, hardware; tools, implements, instruments, accoutrements, paraphernalia, trappings, contrivances, appurtenances, utensils; informal things, stuff, clobber, bits and pieces; archaic equipage.
2 *they attached lifting tackle to it, and hauled it on deck*: **system of pulleys**, hoisting gear, pulley, hoist, block and tackle, crane, winch, davit, windlass, sheave.
3 *his run was brought to a halt by the scrum half's tackle*: **interception**, challenge, block, attack.
▶ verb **1** *we welcome the Government's determination to tackle environmental problems*: **get to grips with**, apply oneself to, address oneself to, address, set about, go about, get to work at, busy oneself with, set one's hand to, grapple with, approach, take on, attend to, see to, throw oneself into, try to solve, try to deal with, try to cope with, try to sort out; deal with, take measures about, take care of, pursue, handle, manage; start on, embark on; informal get stuck into, have a crack at, have a go at, have a shot at.
2 *when I tackled Nina about it, she admitted that she'd bribed one of the chambermaids*: **confront**, speak to, face (up to), initiate a discussion with, discuss something with, interview, question, cross-examine; accost, waylay; remonstrate with.
3 *he was stabbed in the chest after he tackled a masked intruder*: **confront**, face up to, take on, contend with, challenge; **seize**, grab, take hold of, grapple with, obstruct, intercept, block, stop; knock/throw/bring down, floor, fell; informal have a go at.

4 *the winger got tackled*: **intercept**, challenge, block, stop, attack.

tacky[1] adjective *the paint on the frame was still tacky*: **sticky**, wet, gluey, gummy, glutinous, adhesive, viscous, viscid, treacly, syrupy, runny, clinging, sticking; informal gooey.

tacky[2] adjective *a tacky game show*: **tawdry**, tasteless, kitsch, vulgar, crude, garish, gaudy, showy, loud, trashy, cheap, cheap and nasty, nasty, common, second-rate, Brummagem; informal flash, flashy, tatty, naff.
▷ANTONYMS tasteful, refined.

tact noun *the Inspector broke the news to me with tact and consideration*: **sensitivity**, understanding, thoughtfulness, consideration, delicacy, diplomacy, discretion, discernment, judgement, prudence, judiciousness, perception, subtlety, wisdom, tactfulness; etiquette, courtesy, cordiality, politeness, decorum, mannerliness, polish, respect, respectfulness; French savoir faire, politesse; informal savvy.
▷ANTONYMS indiscretion, rudeness, tactlessness.

tactful adjective *a tactful little cough*: **considerate**, sensitive, understanding, thoughtful, delicate, diplomatic, discreet, discerning, judicious, politic, perceptive, subtle, careful, treating someone/something with kid gloves; courteous, cordial, polite, decorous, seemly, respectful; informal savvy; dated mannerly.
▷ANTONYMS tactless, indiscreet, gauche.

tactic noun **1** *tax-saving tactics*: **strategy**, scheme, stratagem, plan, set of tactics, manoeuvre, course/line of action; method, programme, expedient, gambit, move, approach, tack, path, road; device, trick, ploy, dodge, ruse, game, machination, contrivance, stunt; (**tactics**) means, wiles, artifice, subterfuge; informal wangle, caper; archaic shift.
2 (**tactics**) *the larger French fleet was decimated by superior tactics*: **battle plans**, plans, game plans; **moves**, manoeuvres, logistics; strategy, policy, campaign; generalship, military science; organization, planning, arrangement, administration, direction, masterminding, orchestration, handling, running.

> *Easily confused words* **tactics or strategy?**
>
> See **strategy**.

tactical adjective *this appeared to be a tactical move to try to force the CDF to agree to a coalition*: **calculated**, planned, plotted, prudent, strategic, politic, diplomatic, judicious, shrewd, skilful, adroit, clever, smart, cunning, artful, wily; informal foxy.
▷ANTONYMS unwise; spontaneous.

tactless adjective *it was a cruel, tactless thing to say*: **insensitive**, inconsiderate, thoughtless, unthinking, indelicate, undiplomatic, impolitic, indiscreet, unsubtle, clumsy, heavy-handed, graceless, awkward, unpolished, inept, bungling, maladroit, gauche, undiscerning, unsophisticated; blunt, straightforward, frank, plain-spoken, outspoken, abrupt, precipitate; gruff, bluff, rough, crude, coarse, speaking as one finds, calling a spade a spade, like a bull in a china shop; imprudent, injudicious, unwise, foolhardy; rude, impolite, uncouth, discourteous, crass, tasteless, impertinent, disrespectful, ungentlemanly, unladylike, boorish, uncivilized, uncivil; unkind, uncaring, uncalled for, callous, hurtful, thick-skinned, uncharitable, cruel.
▷ANTONYMS tactful, diplomatic, discreet.

tag noun **1** *a price tag*: **label**, ticket, badge, mark, marker, tab, tally, sticker, docket, stub, chit, chitty, counterfoil, flag, stamp.
2 *his jacket was hung up by its tag*: **tab**, flap, loop, lappet, label; strap, handle.
3 *he has vowed to throw off his 'bad boy' tag*: **designation**, denomination, label, description, characterization, identification, identity; nickname, name, epithet, title, soubriquet, pet name, byname; informal handle, moniker; formal appellation, cognomen.
4 *his writing is full of tags from the Bible and Shakespeare*: **quotation**, stock phrase, platitude, cliché, epithet, quote, extract, excerpt, passage, allusion, phrase; saying, proverb, maxim, axiom, adage, saw, aphorism, motto, epigram, epigraph, dictum, formula, truism, slogan, catchphrase; informal, dated gobbet.
▶ verb **1** *the bottles were tagged with colour-coded labels*: **label**, attach tags to, put a label on, mark, ticket, earmark, identify, docket, flag, indicate.
2 *he became tagged as a 'thinking' actor*: **designate**, describe, identify, classify, label, class, categorize, characterize; mark, stamp, brand, pigeonhole, stereotype, typecast, compartmentalize, typify; name, call, nickname, title, entitle, dub, term, style, christen, baptize.
3 *their heads were so large that the rest of their bodies seemed* ***tagged on*** *as an afterthought*: **add**, tack, join; attach, append, affix, annex.
4 *her little boy was* ***tagging along*** *behind her*: **follow**, trail; come after, go after, tread on the heels of, shadow, dog; go with, accompany, attend, escort; informal tail.

tail noun **1** *the dog's tail began to wag frantically*: **hindmost part**, back end, appendage; brush, scut, dock; tailpiece, tail feathers; hind part, hindquarters; technical cauda, uropygium.
▷ANTONYMS front, head.
2 *new items are added on to the tail of the queue*: **rear**, end, back, extremity, conclusion; bottom, lowest part; Brit. informal fag end.
▷ANTONYMS head, front.
3 *the tail of the hunting season*: **close**, end, conclusion, termination, tail end.
▷ANTONYMS beginning, start.
4 informal *I can't put a tail on him, I don't know where he's gone*: **detective**, investigator, private investigator, shadow; informal sleuth, private eye, tec; N. Amer. informal gumshoe, bogey, dick, private dick, shamus.
5 N. Amer. informal *the coach kicked Ryan in his tail*. See **buttocks**.
□ **on someone's tail** *a police car stayed on his tail for half a mile*: **close behind someone**, following someone closely, (hard) on someone's heels, tailing someone.
□ **turn tail** *I was so shocked I just turned tail and ran home as fast as I could*: **run away**, flee, bolt, make off, take to one's heels, show someone a clean pair of heels, cut and run, beat a (hasty) retreat; informal scram, scarper, skedaddle, vamoose.
▷ANTONYMS stand one's ground.
▶ verb informal *a flock of paparazzi had tailed them all over London*: **follow**, shadow, stalk, trail, track, hunt, hound, dog, trace, pursue, chase, give chase to, run after, keep under surveillance.
□ **tail back** *traffic tailed back fourteen miles*: **become congested**, form a tailback, jam.
□ **tail off/away** *the old lady's voice tailed off*: **fade**, wane, ebb, dwindle, decrease, lessen, get less, diminish, decline, subside, abate, drop off, drop away, fall away, peter out, taper off; let up, ease off, die away, die out, die down, go into decline, waste away, recede, relent, desist, weaken, come to an end.
▷ANTONYMS increase, get more intense.

> *Word links* **tail**
>
> **caudal**, **cercal** relating to a tail

tailback noun **traffic jam**, queue, line, file; congestion.

tailor noun **outfitter**, dressmaker, garment-maker, couturier, fashion designer; clothier, costumier, seamstress; dated modiste.
▶ verb *both services can be tailored to customer requirements*: **customize**, adapt, adjust, modify, change, convert, alter, attune, fashion, style, mould, gear, fit, cut, trim, suit, shape, reshape, tune.

> *Word links* **tailor**
>
> **sartorial** relating to tailoring

taint noun *free from the taint of corruption*: **trace**, touch, suggestion, hint, tinge, tincture; **smear**, stain, blot, blemish, slur, stigma, tarnish, scar, black mark, spot, imperfection, flaw, fault, defect, blot on one's escutcheon; discredit, dishonour, disgrace, shame.
▶ verb **1** *the world's last great wilderness is being tainted by pollution*: **contaminate**, pollute, adulterate, infect, blight, befoul, spoil, soil, ruin, destroy.
▷ANTONYMS clean.
2 *fraudulent firms need to be weeded out, lest they taint the reputation of all firms*: **tarnish**, sully, blacken, stain, besmirch, smear, blot, blemish, stigmatize, mar, corrupt, defile, soil, muddy, foul, dirty, damage, injure, harm, hurt, debase, infect, poison, vitiate, drag through the mud, blot one's copybook; brand.
▷ANTONYMS improve.

take verb **1** *Anna smiled as she took his hand*: **lay hold of**, take hold of, get hold of, get into one's hands; grasp, grip, clasp, clutch, grab.
▷ANTONYMS give.
2 *he took an envelope from his inside pocket*: **remove**, pull, draw, withdraw, extract, fish; confiscate, take possession of.
▷ANTONYMS give.
3 *the following passage is taken from my book 'Managing Stress'*: **extract**, quote, cite, excerpt, derive, abstract, reproduce, copy, cull, choose.
4 *she took a little wine with her dinner*: **drink**, imbibe; **consume**, swallow, eat, ingest.
5 *many thousands of prisoners were taken*: **capture**, seize, catch, take captive, arrest, apprehend, take into custody; carry off, abduct, lay hold of; trap, snare.
▷ANTONYMS free, liberate.
6 *these thieving toerags have taken my car*: **steal**, remove, appropriate, misappropriate, make off with, pilfer, purloin, abstract, dispossess someone of; informal filch, pinch, swipe, nick, snaffle, walk off with; rare peculate.
▷ANTONYMS give.
7 *take the bottom number from the total*: **subtract**, deduct, remove, take away/off; discount; informal knock off, minus.
▷ANTONYMS add.
8 *all the seats had been taken*: **occupy**, use, utilize, fill, hold; reserve, engage; informal bag.
9 *I have just taken a room in a nearby house*: **rent**, lease, hire, charter; **reserve**, book, make a reservation for, arrange for, engage.

t

10 *I decided to take the job*: **accept**, take up, take on, undertake.
▷ANTONYMS refuse.
11 *I'd take childbirth today over what my grandmother had to go through*: **pick**, **choose**, select, decide on, settle on, fix on, single out; **prefer**, favour, opt for, plump for, vote for, elect.
▷ANTONYMS refuse, turn down.
12 *take, for instance, the English word 'one'*: **consider**, ponder, contemplate, think about, weigh up, give thought to, mull over, deliberate over, examine, study, cogitate about, chew over, meditate over, ruminate over.
13 *he takes 'The Observer'*: **subscribe to**, pay a subscription to, buy regularly, read regularly, read every day/week/month.
14 *a nurse took his temperature*: **ascertain**, determine, establish, measure, find out, discover; calculate, compute, count, quantify, evaluate, rate, assess, appraise, gauge.
15 *she started to take notes*: **write**, note (down), make a note of, set down, jot (down), scribble, scrawl, take down, record, register, document, minute, put in writing, commit to paper.
16 *I took it back to London with me*: **bring**, **carry**, bear, transport, convey, move, transfer, shift, haul, drag, lug, cart, ferry; informal tote.
17 *she let the priest take her home*: **escort**, accompany, help, assist, show, lead, show someone the way, lead the way, conduct, guide, see, usher, steer, pilot, shepherd, convey.
18 *he took the North London line to Acton*: **travel on**, travel by, journey on, go via; use, make use of, utilize.
19 *the station takes its name from the nearby lake*: **derive**, get, obtain, come by, acquire, pick up, be given.
20 *she took the prize for best individual speaker*: **receive**, obtain, gain, get, acquire, collect, accept, be given, be presented with, be awarded, have conferred on one; secure, procure, come by, win, earn, pick up, walk away/off with, carry off; informal land, bag, net, scoop, cop.
21 *she feared that I might take the chance to postpone the ceremony*: **act on**, take advantage of, capitalize on, use, exploit, make the most of, leap at, jump on, pounce on, seize (on), grasp, grab, snatch, accept, put to advantage, profit from, turn to account, cash in on.
▷ANTONYMS miss, ignore.
22 *he took great pleasure in creating his own individual style*: **derive**, draw, acquire, obtain, get, gain, extract, procure; experience, undergo, feel, encounter, know, come into contact with, face.
23 *Elizabeth took the news of my sacking badly*: **receive**, respond to, react to, meet, greet; deal with, cope with.
24 *do you **take** me **for** a fool?* **regard as**, consider to be, view as, look on as, see as, believe to be, think of as, reckon to be, imagine to be, deem to be, hold to be, judge to be.
25 *I **take** it that you are George Tenison*: **assume**, presume, suppose, imagine, expect, believe, reckon, think, be of the opinion, gather, dare say, trust, surmise, deduce, guess, conjecture, fancy, suspect; take for granted, take as read.
26 *I take your point*: **understand**, grasp, get, comprehend, apprehend, see, follow, take in; **accept**, appreciate, accept/acknowledge/admit the validity of, recognize, sympathize with, agree with.
27 *Shirley was rather taken with this idea*: **captivate**, enchant, charm, delight, attract, win over, fascinate, bewitch, beguile, enthral, entrance, lure, infatuate, seduce, dazzle, hypnotize, mesmerize; please, amuse, divert, entertain, gladden, satisfy, gratify; informal tickle someone pink, tickle someone's fancy.
28 *I can't take much more of this business*: **endure**, bear, suffer, tolerate, stand, put up with, stomach, brook, abide, carry, submit to, accept, permit, allow, admit, countenance, support, shoulder; Scottish thole.
29 *applicants may be asked to take a test*: **perform**, **execute**, effect, discharge, carry out, accomplish, fulfil, complete, conduct, implement, do, make, have; rare effectuate.
30 *I went on to take English, History, and French*: **study**, learn, be taught, have lessons in; read up on, work at, apply oneself to, acquire a knowledge of, gain an understanding of, grasp, master; take up, pursue; Brit. read; informal do.
31 *the journey should take a little over six hours*: **last**, continue for, go on for, carry on for, keep on for, run on for, endure for; require, call for, need, necessitate, entail, involve.
32 *it would take an expert marksman with a high-powered rifle to hit him*: **require**, need, necessitate, demand, call for, entail, involve.
33 *I take size 3 in shoes*: **wear**, habitually wear, use; require, need, be fitted by, fit.
34 *we tried to bring the children up to think this way, but somehow it did not take*: **be effective**, have/take effect, take hold, take root, be efficacious, be productive, be in force, be in operation, be efficient, be effectual, be useful; work, operate, succeed, function.
□ **take after** *Jenny takes after her mother*: **resemble**, look like, be like, be similar to, bear a resemblance to, have the look of; remind one of, put one in mind of, make one think of, cause one to remember, recall, conjure up, suggest, evoke, call up; informal favour, be a chip off the old block, be the spitting image of.
□ **take a chair/seat** *take a seat, I'll be with you in a second*: **sit down**, sit, seat oneself, settle (oneself), install oneself, plant oneself, ensconce oneself, plump oneself down, plop oneself down; flump, perch; informal take a pew, plonk oneself down.
□ **take against** *Bernard soon took against the idea*: **take a dislike to**, feel hostile towards, view with disfavour, look askance on, become unfriendly towards.
□ **take something apart** *we took the machines apart several times*: **dismantle**, pull/take to pieces, pull/take to bits, pull apart, disassemble, break up; tear down, demolish, destroy, pulverize, wreck, smash, shatter.
▷ANTONYMS put together, assemble.
□ **take someone/something apart** informal *she was relishing the sight of me being taken apart by the director*: **criticize**, attack, censure, condemn, denigrate, find fault with, pillory, maul, lambaste, flay, savage; informal knock, slam, pan, bash, crucify, hammer, lay into, roast, skewer.
▷ANTONYMS lavish praise on.
□ **take someone back 1** *a dream which **took me back to** my first year in Vienna*: **evoke**, awaken/evoke one's memories of, remind one of, put one in mind of, conjure up, summon up, call up; echo, suggest, smack of. **2** *if she apologizes I will take her back*: **be reconciled to**, forgive, pardon, excuse, exonerate, absolve; accept back, welcome, receive; let bygones be bygones, forgive and forget, bury the hatchet.
□ **take something back 1** *I take back every word I said*: **retract**, withdraw, renounce, disclaim, disown, unsay, disavow, recant, abjure, repudiate, override; back-pedal. ▷ANTONYMS stand by.
2 *I must take the keys back to the steward*: **return**, carry back, bring back, fetch back, give back, hand back, send back, restore, remit. ▷ANTONYMS keep, hang on to.
3 *I'd damaged the box so the shop wouldn't take it back*: **accept back**, give a refund for, exchange, trade, swap.
4 *the Romans took back the city in the following year*: **regain**, repossess, reclaim, retrieve, recover, recoup, restore, get back; recapture, reconquer.
▷ANTONYMS give away, cede.
□ **take someone by surprise** *executives were taken by surprise when sales dropped off late last year*: **take aback**, surprise, shock, stun, stagger, astound, astonish, startle; dumbfound, daze, nonplus, stop someone in their tracks, stupefy, take someone's breath away; shake (up), jolt, throw, unnerve, disconcert, disturb, disquiet, unsettle, discompose, bewilder; informal flabbergast, knock for six, knock sideways, knock out, floor, strike dumb.
□ **take someone down a peg or two** See **peg**.
□ **take something down 1** *the policeman took down her particulars*: **write down**, note down, make a note of, jot down, set down, mark down, record, put on record, commit to paper, put in black and white, register, draft, document, minute, pen. **2** *we took down the lighting rig at the end of the shoot*: **remove**, dismantle, disassemble, unfasten, separate, take apart, take to pieces, take out, disconnect; demolish, tear down, level, raze.
▷ANTONYMS leave in place. **3** *they insisted he take down the flag*: **pull down**, let down, haul down, move down, lower, drop, let fall, let sink.
▷ANTONYMS pull up, haul up.
□ **take someone in 1** *Mrs Smith took in paying guests*: **accommodate**, board, house, feed, put up, take care of, admit, let in, receive, welcome, take, billet, harbour. ▷ANTONYMS turn someone away. **2** *you were taken in by an elaborate trick*: **deceive**, delude, hoodwink, mislead, trick, dupe, fool, cheat, defraud, swindle, outwit, gull, humbug, bluff, hoax, bamboozle; informal con, bilk, pull the wool over someone's eyes, put one over on; archaic cozen.
□ **take something in 1** *at first she could hardly take in the news*: **comprehend**, understand, grasp, follow, absorb, soak in, assimilate, make out; informal get. **2** *this route takes in some of the most dramatic cliffs in Britain*: **include**, encompass, embrace, contain, comprise, cover, incorporate, embody, comprehend, subsume, envelop; digest, assimilate; admit, hold.
□ **take someone in hand** *someone has to take him in hand*: **control**, have authority over, be in charge of, direct, preside over, lead, dominate, master; **reform**, improve, correct, change, make better, rehabilitate.
□ **take something in hand** *the time has come to take matters in hand*: **deal with**, apply oneself to, address oneself to, get to grips with, get stuck into, busy oneself with, set one's hand to, grapple with, take on, attend to, see to, sort out, take care of, pursue, handle, manage; start on, embark on; formal commence.
□ **take it out of** *I'd had no idea how much hauling one of those things around would take it out of you*: **exhaust**, drain, enervate, tire, fatigue, wear out, weary, debilitate, jade; informal fag out, whack, bush, knacker, poop.
□ **take off 1** *I walked up to the horse, but he took off at a great speed*: **run away**, run off, flee, abscond, take flight, decamp, disappear, leave, go, depart, make off, bolt, make a run/break for it, take to one's heels, beat a hasty retreat, make a quick exit, make one's getaway, escape, head for the hills; informal split, beat it, clear off, clear out, skedaddle, vamoose, hightail it, light out. ▷ANTONYMS stay put.
2 *the plane took off*: **become airborne**, leave the ground, take to the air, take wing; be launched, lift off, blast off. ▷ANTONYMS land, touch down.
3 *the idea really took off*: **succeed**, do well, become popular, catch on, progress, prosper, flourish, thrive, boom, turn out well, work (out).
▷ANTONYMS fail, flop.

□ **take someone off** *he takes off the Prime Minister very well*: **mimic**, impersonate, imitate, ape, parody, mock, caricature, satirize, burlesque, lampoon, ridicule; informal spoof, do, send up.
□ **take oneself off** *I took myself off to the office*: **withdraw**, retire, take one's leave, make one's departure, leave, exit, depart, go away, pull out, quit, make oneself scarce; informal clear off, clear out.
▷ANTONYMS stay put.
□ **take something off 1** *they'd put a tinned steak and kidney pudding in the oven and forgotten to take its lid off*: **detach**, remove, pull off; cut off, clip off, hack off, chop off, prune off, nip off; extract, sever, separate.
▷ANTONYMS leave on. **2** *she took off her clothes and folded them carefully*: **remove**, doff, divest oneself of, shed, strip off, pull off, peel off, climb out of, slip out of, shrug off, throw off, cast off, fling off, fling aside, discard.
▷ANTONYMS put on. **3** *it might help to take a pound or two off the price*: **deduct**, subtract, take away, remove.
□ **take on** Brit. informal *don't take on so!* **get upset**, make a fuss, break down, get excited, go too far, lose one's sense of proportion, overreact; informal lose one's cool, get in a tizzy.
▷ANTONYMS keep calm.
□ **take someone on 1** *they could find no major challenger to take him on*: **compete against**, oppose, challenge, confront, face, fight, pit/match oneself against, vie with, contend with/against, battle with/against, struggle against, take up cudgels against, stand up to, go head to head against. **2** *the Home Office took on extra staff*: **engage**, hire, employ, enrol, enlist, sign up, take into employment, put on the payroll; informal take on board.
▷ANTONYMS fire, dismiss.
□ **take something on 1** *he took on additional responsibility*: **undertake**, accept, take on oneself, tackle, turn one's hand to, adopt, assume, shoulder, embrace, acquire, carry, bear, support; informal have a go at. **2** *in this polarized society, even the narrowest psychological study took on political meaning*: **acquire**, assume, come to have, come by.
▷ANTONYMS abandon, give up.
□ **take someone out** *the very first night he took her out, Frank proposed to her*: **go out with**, escort, partner, accompany, go with; romance, court, woo, go courting with; informal date, see, go steady with.
□ **take someone/something out** informal *they were taken out by a sniper*: **kill**, murder, assassinate, put to death, do away with, put an end to, get rid of, dispatch, execute, finish off, eliminate, exterminate, terminate; **destroy**, obliterate, annihilate; informal do in, bump off, rub out, wipe out, hit, mow down, top; literary slay.
□ **take something out** *that tooth will need to be taken out*: **extract**, remove, pull (out), yank out, tug out, pluck out, prise out, separate, detach, draw; Brit. informal hoick out.
▷ANTONYMS put in.
□ **take something over** *she took over the editorship in 1989*: **assume control of**, take control of, gain control of, take charge of, take command of, assume responsibility for; assume, acquire, gain, appropriate, be elevated to.
□ **take one's time** *he took his time going through the papers*: **go slowly**, not hurry, be leisurely, proceed in a leisurely fashion, dally, dawdle, delay, linger, go at a snail's pace, drag one's feet, waste time, while away time, kill time; informal dilly-dally; archaic or literary tarry.
▷ANTONYMS hurry, rush.
□ **take to 1** *after being mugged a few months back, he had taken to carrying his money in different parts of his clothing*: **make a habit of**, resort to, turn to, have recourse to, begin, start; formal commence. ▷ANTONYMS stop.
2 *Ruth took to Mrs Taylor the moment she opened the door*: **develop a liking for**, like, get on with, become friendly with; informal take a shine to.
▷ANTONYMS dislike.
3 *the dog has really taken to hurdles racing*: **become good at**, develop an ability/aptitude for, be suitable for; develop a liking for, like, enjoy, become interested in.

□ **take something up 1** *we took up our bags and left*: **pick up**, grab, scoop up, gather up, snatch up, swoop up; carry; lift up, raise, uplift, heft, heave, elevate. ▷ANTONYMS put down, drop.
2 *in the thirties he took up abstract painting*: **become involved in**, become interested in, engage in, participate in, take part in, practise, follow; begin, start; formal commence. ▷ANTONYMS give up, drop.
3 *she found that the meetings took up all her time*: **consume**, fill, absorb, use, use up, occupy; cover, extend over; waste, squander, go through.
4 *her cousin took up the story*: **resume**, recommence, restart, begin again, carry on, continue, carry on with, pick up, return to.
5 *he had decided to take up their offer of employment*: **accept**, say yes to, agree to, accede to, adopt, get, gain. ▷ANTONYMS refuse.
6 *you'll need to take the skirt up an inch or two*: **shorten**, make shorter, turn up; raise, lift, make higher.
□ **take up with** *she took up with a middle-aged art historian*: **become friendly with**, become friends with, go around with, go along with, fall in with, join up with, string along with, get involved with, start seeing; informal knock about/around with, hang around/out with; Brit. informal hang about with.

▶noun **1** *the whalers' commercial take*: **catch**, haul, bag, yield, net.
2 *he is determined to increase the state's tax take*: **revenue**, income, gain, profit, money received, payments received; takings, proceeds, returns, receipts, profits, winnings, pickings, earnings, spoils; Sport gate money, purse; Brit. informal bunce.
3 *you need someone with a clapperboard at the start of each take*: **scene**, sequence, filmed sequence, clip, part, segment.
4 *her wry and knowing* **take on** *sex and gender issues*: **view of**, reading of, version of, interpretation of, understanding of, account of, explanation of, analysis of, approach to.

take-off noun **1** *a chartered plane crashed soon after take-off*: **departure**, **lift-off**, launch, blast-off, taking off; leaving, going; ascent, climbing, mounting, flight, flying, soaring.
▷ANTONYMS landing, touchdown.
2 *a take-off of a television talent show*: **parody**, pastiche, mockery, caricature, travesty, satire, lampoon, mimicry, imitation, impersonation, impression, aping; informal send-up, spoof.

takeover noun *the takeover of a building society*: **gaining of control**, change of ownership, purchase, acquisition, buying; buyout, coup, merger, amalgamation, incorporation, combination.

taking adjective dated *he was not a very taking person, she felt*. See **charming**.

takings plural noun *the day's takings*: **proceeds**, returns, receipts, earnings, winnings, pickings, spoils; profit, gain, income, revenue, money received, payments received; Sport gate money, gate, purse.

tale noun **1** *a tale of witches and warlocks*: **story**, short story, narrative, anecdote, report, account, record, history; legend, fable, myth, romance, parable, allegory, epic, saga; informal yarn.
2 *Otto told me some shocking tales about Jean-Claude*: **rumour**, gossip, hearsay, slander, talk, allegation, tittle-tattle, libel, story.
3 *they were exchanging racy stories and tall tales*: **lie**, fib, falsehood, story, untruth, fabrication, fiction, piece of fiction; informal tall story, fairy story/tale, cock and bull story, shaggy-dog story, yarn.

talent noun *she demonstrated her talent for modelling with clay*: **flair**, aptitude, facility, gift, knack, technique, touch, bent, ability, expertise, capacity, power, faculty; strength, strong point, forte, genius, brilliance; dexterity, adroitness, skill, cleverness, virtuosity, artistry.
▷ANTONYMS inability, clumsiness.

talented adjective *a talented musician*: **gifted**, skilful, skilled, accomplished, brilliant, expert, consummate, master, masterly, first-rate, polished, artistic, adroit, dexterous, able, competent, capable, apt, deft, adept, proficient; informal crack, top-notch, top-drawer, ace, wizard.
▷ANTONYMS inept, talentless.

talisman noun **lucky charm**, charm, fetish, amulet, mascot, totem, idol, juju, phylactery; archaic periapt.

talk verb **1** *I was talking to a friend who lives in the next town*: **speak**, give voice, chat; chatter, gossip, prattle, prate, babble, rattle on, blather, blether, orate; informal yak, gab, jaw, go on, chew the fat; Brit. informal natter, rabbit, witter, chunter; N. Amer. informal rap, run off at the mouth; Austral./NZ informal mag.
2 *you're talking rubbish*: **utter**, speak, say, voice, express, articulate, pronounce, enunciate, verbalize, vocalize.
3 *the music was quieter in here, and they were able to talk*: **converse**, communicate, speak to each other, discuss things, have a talk, have a chat, have a tête-à-tête, confer, consult each other; negotiate, have negotiations, parley, palaver; informal have a confab, chew the fat/rag, jaw, rap; formal confabulate.
4 *for all the love that he felt for her, and she him, they had never* **talked of** *marriage*: **mention**, make mention of, refer to, make reference to, speak about, discuss.
5 *I was able to talk English*: **speak**, speak in, talk in, communicate in, converse in, express oneself in, discourse in, use.
6 *nothing would make her talk*: **confess**, speak out, speak up, reveal all, inform, tell tales, tell, divulge information, tell the facts, give the game away, open one's mouth; informal come clean, blab, squeal, let the cat out of the bag, spill the beans, spill one's guts, grass, sing, rat.
7 *we mustn't keep meeting like this—people will talk*: **gossip**, spread rumours, pass comment, make remarks, criticize.
□ **talk back** *he was always talking back to Dad*: **answer back**, answer defiantly, be impertinent, answer impertinently, be cheeky, be rude, contradict, argue with, disagree with.
□ **talk big** informal *Henry was new to the job but he was already talking big*: **brag**, boast, crow, bluster, exaggerate; informal blow one's own trumpet, shoot one's mouth off, swank, show off; Austral./NZ informal skite, big-note oneself.
□ **talk something down 1** *people constantly talk down the coal industry*: **denigrate**, depreciate, deprecate, disparage, belittle, diminish, criticize; informal knock, pan, put down. **2** *the last Lancaster bomber was talked down to safety after the raid*: **give landing instructions to**, bring to land, help to land.
□ **talk down to** *students on the course were talked down to as though they were children*: **condescend to**, patronize, treat condescendingly, speak

condescendingly to, speak haughtily to, look down one's nose at, look down on, put down, be snobbish to.
□ **talk someone into something** *he talked her into parting with an art collection worth £30,000*: **persuade someone to**, convince someone to, argue someone into, cajole someone into, coax someone into, bring someone round to, talk someone round to, inveigle someone into, wheedle someone into, sweet-talk someone into, influence someone to, prevail on someone to; informal hustle, fast-talk.
□ **talk someone out of something** *I quickly talked him out of staying in Britain*: **dissuade from**, persuade against, discourage from, deter from, stop, put off, advise against, urge against, divert from, argue out of.
□ **talk someone round** *he nearly did give up, and it was only mum who talked him round*: **persuade**, prevail on, bring round, win over, influence, sway, convert, affect, bias; manipulate, bend, mould.
□ **talk something up** *the film is being talked up for the awards season*: **promote**, push, boost, hype, merchandise, publicize, advertise, give publicity to, give a puff to, puff, puff up, build up, beat/bang the drum for; informal plug.
▶ **noun 1** *he was bored with all this talk*: **chatter**, chatting, chattering, gossiping, prattling, prating, gibbering, jabbering, babbling, gabbling, rattling on, speaking, talking; informal yakking, gabbing; Brit. informal nattering, rabbiting, wittering.
2 *Polly felt in need of a talk with Vi, the person she turned to in an emergency*: **conversation**, chat, discussion, tête-à-tête, heart-to-heart, dialogue, colloquy, parley, powwow, consultation, conference, meeting; informal confab, jaw, chit-chat, rap, gossip; formal confabulation.
3 (**talks**) *he held peace talks with his United Kingdom counterpart*: **negotiations**, discussions; conference, summit, meeting, consultation, dialogue, symposium, seminar, conclave, colloquy, palaver, parley; bargaining, haggling, wheeling and dealing; mediation, arbitration, intercession, conciliation; informal powwow; formal confabulation.
4 *a firefighter giving a talk on her personal experiences*: **lecture**, speech, address, discourse, oration, presentation, report, sermon, disquisition, dissertation, symposium; informal spiel.
5 *there was talk of a takeover*: **gossip**, rumour, hearsay, tittle-tattle, news, report.
6 *the talk was of what their grandchildren were up to*: **chat**, conversation, discussion, gossip; subject, theme, topic; information, news.
7 *baby talk*: **speech**, language, dialect, jargon, cant, slang, idiom, idiolect, patois, accent; words; informal lingo.

talkative adjective *a talkative cab driver*: **chatty**, **loquacious**, garrulous, voluble, conversational, gossipy, gossiping, chattery, chattering, babbling, blathering, gibbering, communicative; long-winded, wordy, verbose, profuse, prolix, rambling, gushing, effusive; informal gabby, mouthy, big-mouthed, with the gift of the gab, having kissed the blarney stone, yakking, gassy; Brit. informal able to talk the hind legs off a donkey; rare multiloquent, multiloquous.
▷ANTONYMS taciturn, reticent.

Word toolkit

talkative	voluble	garrulous
mood	critics	old fool
nature	crowd	crows
child	public	big shot
fellow	actress	crone
parrot	fans	geezer

talker noun **1** *he's a good and persuasive talker*: **conversationalist**, speaker, communicator.
2 *I think it's better to be a doer than a talker*: **chatterer**, chatterbox, gossip; someone who is all talk.

talking-to noun informal *they gave Peter a talking-to about solving problems with words, not fists*: **reprimand**, lecture, rebuke, scolding, reproof, reproach, rap on the knuckles, slap on the wrists, chiding, remonstration, upbraiding, berating, castigation, tirade, diatribe, admonition, admonishment, lambasting, censure, criticism, obloquy; informal telling-off, ticking-off, wigging, carpeting, tongue-lashing, dressing-down, rocket.
▷ANTONYMS commendation, pat on the back.

tall adjective **1** *a tall, thin man*: **big**, **high**, large, huge, towering; colossal, gigantic, giant, monstrous, giant-size, Brobdingnagian; lanky, rangy, gangling, leggy, long-legged; informal long.
▷ANTONYMS short, small.
2 *tall buildings*: **high**, big, lofty, towering, soaring, elevated, sky-high, sky-scraping; multi-storey.
▷ANTONYMS low.
3 *he's about 5 foot 8 inches tall*: **in height**, high, from head to toe/foot.
▷ANTONYMS wide.
4 *a tall tale*: **unlikely**, improbable, exaggerated, far-fetched, implausible, dubious, overblown, unbelievable, incredible, preposterous, outrageous, absurd; embroidered, dishonest, untrue; informal cock and bull.
▷ANTONYMS believable, credible.
5 *they thought that the deadline was a tall order*: **demanding**, exacting, difficult, unreasonable, exorbitant, impossible.
▷ANTONYMS easy.

tally noun **1** *an officer keeps a tally of the amount due to each man*: **running total**, count, record, reckoning, enumeration, register, account, roll, itemization, listing; census, poll.
2 *his tally of 1,816 wickets is still a county record*: **total**, score, count, sum, result.
3 *the key is so cut as to form a tally with interior machinery*: **counterpart**, match, mate, duplicate.
▶ **verb 1** *these statistics tally fairly well with government figures*: **correspond**, agree, accord, concur, coincide, match, fit, be in agreement, be consistent, conform, equate, harmonize, suit, be in tune, dovetail, correlate, parallel; informal square; N. Amer. informal jibe.
▷ANTONYMS disagree, differ.
2 *votes were being tallied with abacuses*: **count**, calculate, add up, total, enumerate, compute; figure out, work out, reckon, measure, quantify, rate; Brit. tot up.

tame adjective **1** *a tame elephant*: **domesticated**, domestic, not wild, docile, tamed, disciplined, broken, broken-in, trained, not fierce, gentle, mild, used to humans; pet; Brit. house-trained; N. Amer. housebroken.
▷ANTONYMS wild, fierce.
2 *a bunch of demoralized, tame civil servants always looking over their shoulders*: **docile**, submissive, compliant, meek, obedient, tractable, acquiescent, amenable, manageable, unresisting, passive, mild, subdued, under someone's control/thumb, suppressed, unassertive, ineffectual.
▷ANTONYMS independent.
3 *every businessman needs a tame lawyer at his elbow*: **amenable**, biddable, cooperative, available, willing.
▷ANTONYMS uncooperative.
4 *network TV on Saturday night is a pretty tame affair*: **unexciting**, uninteresting, uninspired, uninspiring, dull, bland, flat, insipid, spiritless, pedestrian, vapid, lifeless, dead, colourless, run-of-the-mill, mediocre, ordinary, prosaic, humdrum, boring, tedious, tiresome, wearisome; **harmless**, safe, unobjectionable, inoffensive, mainstream; informal wishy-washy.
▷ANTONYMS exciting, adventurous.
▶ **verb 1** *wild rabbits can be kept in captivity and eventually tamed*: **domesticate**, break, train, master, subdue, subjugate, bring to heel, enslave.
2 *Christine had learned to tame her bad temper*: **subdue**, curb, control, calm, master, bring to heel, tone down, water down, moderate, mitigate, tranquillize, overcome, discipline, suppress, repress, mollify, humble, cow, pacify, mellow, mute, temper, soften, bridle, get the better of, get a grip on; informal lick.

tamper verb **1** *she saw youths* **tampering with** *her neighbour's car*: **interfere**, **monkey around**, meddle, tinker, fiddle (about/around), fool about/around, play about/around, toy, trifle, dabble; do mischief to, doctor, alter, change, adjust, damage, do damage to, harm, deface, vandalize, ruin; informal mess about/around; Brit. informal muck about/around.
2 *there's evidence that the defendant* **tampered with** *the jury*: **influence**, get at, rig, manipulate, bribe, corrupt, bias, pervert; informal fix.

tan adjective *a tan waistcoat*: **yellowish-brown**, brownish-yellow, light brown, pale brown, tawny.
▶ **verb 1** *using a sunscreen means that you won't burn before you tan*: **become suntanned**, take a suntan/tan, brown, go/become brown, bronze.
2 informal *if Mickey so much as touches a fishing net, I'll tan his hide*: **thrash**, beat, wallop, belt, strap, spank, whip, lash, leather, cane, flog, flail, flagellate, horsewhip, birch, switch, flay; informal give someone a hiding, lam, larrup.

tang noun **1** *liven up your cooking with the tang of fresh lemons*: **flavour**, taste, savour; **sharpness**, zest, zestiness, bite, edge, smack, piquancy, spice, spiciness, relish, tastiness; informal zip, punch, ginger, kick, pep.
2 *Caroline could smell the tang of the sea*: **smell**, odour, aroma, fragrance, perfume, redolence.
3 *I wore a tang of aftershave*: **trace**, touch, hint, whiff, suggestion, dab, smack, smattering.

tangible adjective **1** *if you purchase a tangible object, rather than a service, VAT is usually included in the price*: **touchable**, palpable, tactile, material, physical, real, substantial, corporeal, solid, concrete; visible, noticeable.
▷ANTONYMS intangible.
2 *organizations want to see tangible benefits from their investment in technology*: **real**, actual, solid, concrete, substantial, hard, well defined, definite, well documented, clear, clear-cut, distinct, manifest, evident, obvious, striking, indisputable, undoubted, unmistakable, positive, perceptible, verifiable, appreciable, measurable, discernible, intelligible.
▷ANTONYMS abstract, theoretical.

tangle verb **1** *Miles found himself tangled in coils of rope | the wool got* **tangled up** *in a big knot*: **entangle**, snarl, catch, entwine, intertwine, intertwist, twist, ravel, knot, enmesh, coil, mat, jumble, muddle.
▷ANTONYMS untangle, disentangle, unravel.

2 *he was suffering from minor injuries after tangling with his old rival*: **come into conflict**, become involved, have a dispute, dispute, argue, quarrel, fight, row, wrangle, squabble, contend, cross swords, lock horns.
▶ noun 1 *a tangle of branches*: **snarl**, mass, mat, cluster, knot, mesh, disorder, thatch, web.
2 *the home team's defence got into an awful tangle*: **muddle**, jumble, mix-up, confusion, entanglement, mishmash, shambles, scramble.

tangled adjective 1 *her tangled hair*: **ravelled**, entangled, snarled (up), entwined, intertwisted, twisted, knotted, knotty, enmeshed, coiled, matted, tangly, messy, muddled; tousled, uncombed, unkempt, ratty; informal mussed up.
2 *a tangled bureaucratic mess*: **confused**, jumbled, mixed up, messy, chaotic, scrambled, complicated, involved, convoluted, complex, intricate, knotty, tortuous, devious, maze-like, labyrinthine; rare involute, involuted.
▷ANTONYMS simple, straightforward.

tangy adjective *a tangy orange cake*: **sharp-flavoured**, sharp, zesty, acid, acidic, tart, sour, bitter, harsh, biting, piquant, spicy, tasty, flavoursome, pungent.
▷ANTONYMS sweet; bland.

tank noun 1 *a hot water tank*: **container**, receptacle, vat, cistern, barrel, storage chamber, repository, reservoir, holder, basin.
2 *a tank full of small fish*: **aquarium**, bowl.
3 *they made use of tanks, artillery, and heavy weapons*: **armoured vehicle**, armoured car, combat vehicle; German Panzer.

tantalize verb *I was tantalized by the mysterious secrets of her diary*: **tease**, torment, torture, bait; tempt, entice, lure, titillate, intrigue, allure, beguile; flirt with, excite, fascinate, make someone's mouth water, lead on, keep hanging on.
▷ANTONYMS gratify, satisfy.

tantamount adjective
□ **tantamount to** *not taking action would be tantamount to dereliction of duty*: **equivalent to**, equal to, amounting to, as good as, more or less, synonymous with, virtually the same as, much the same as, comparable to, on a par with, commensurate with, along the lines of, as serious as, identical to.

tantrum noun *she throws a tantrum when she can't get the toy she wants*: **fit of temper**, fit of rage, fit of pique, fit, outburst, flare-up, blow-up, pet, paroxysm, frenzy, bad mood, mood, huff, scene; informal paddy, wax, wobbly; Brit. informal, dated bate; N. Amer. informal blowout, hissy fit.

tap[1] noun 1 *she turned the cold tap on full*: **valve**, spout, stopcock, cock, spile; N. Amer. faucet, spigot.
2 *they were found attempting to place a phone tap in the embassy*: **listening device**, wiretap, wire, bug, bugging device, hidden microphone, receiver.
□ **on tap** 1 *there are about half a dozen beers on tap*: **on draught**, cask-conditioned, real-ale, from barrels, not bottled/canned. 2 informal *trained staff are on tap from 9 a.m. to 9 p.m.* **on hand**, to hand, at hand, available, ready, handy, accessible, obtainable, in reserve, standing by.
▶ verb 1 *several barrels had been tapped to celebrate*: **draw liquid from**, drain, bleed, milk; **broach**, open, pierce, puncture.
2 *in the cellar, butlers were tapping ale*: **pour (out)**, draw off, siphon off, pump out, decant, extract, withdraw, remove.
3 *the party leaders say that their telephones are tapped*: **listen in on/to**, wiretap, eavesdrop on, spy on, monitor, overhear; informal **bug**, snoop on, get on record.
4 *its resources were to be tapped for the benefit of all mankind*: **draw on**, exploit, milk, make use of, put to use, use, utilize, open up, mine, turn to account.

tap[2] verb 1 *she tapped on Lucy's door*: **knock**, rap, strike, beat, drum, peck.
2 *Dad leant forward and tapped me on the knee*: **touch**, pat, nudge, strike lightly, slap lightly, jab, poke, dig, shove, hit.
▶ noun 1 *there was a sharp tap at the door*: **knock**, rap, strike, beat, peck; knocking, tapping, rapping, drumming, patter, pattering.
2 *Jack was startled by a tap on the shoulder*: **touch**, pat, nudge, light blow, light slap, jab, poke, dig, shove, pressure.

tape noun 1 *she produced a package wrapped in white linen, tied with tape*: **band**, strip, strap, belt, binding, string, ribbon, stripe, braid.
2 *secure the bandage with tape*: **adhesive tape**, sticky tape, insulating tape, masking tape, parcel tape; trademark Sellotape.
3 *they listened to tapes throughout the journey*: **recording**, **cassette**, tape recording; audiotape, audio cassette; reel, spool; videotape, video cassette, video.
▶ verb 1 *there was a card taped to the box*: **bind**, tie, strap, fasten, stick, seal, secure, fix, join, attach, tether; trademark Sellotape.
2 *they **taped off** an area around the scene of the explosion*: **cordon**, seal, close, shut, mark, fence; form a ring around, put a cordon sanitaire around, isolate, segregate; quarantine.
3 *police taped his confession*: **record**, make a recording of, tape-record, video-record, video, put on tape/video/cassette.
□ **have someone taped** *I had him taped from the start*: **understand fully**, know all about, have all the details of, know the ins and outs of; informal have someone's number.

taper verb 1 *it has roundish leaves which taper at the tip*: **narrow**, thin (out), become narrow, become narrower, become thin, become thinner, come to a point, attenuate.
▷ANTONYMS thicken, swell.
2 *at first there was a flurry of meetings, but these soon tapered off*: **decrease**, lessen, dwindle, diminish, reduce, subside, decline, die off, die away, die down, fade, peter out, wane, ebb, abate, wind down, slacken (off), fall off, drop off, trail off/away, let up, thin out; weaken, wilt, slump, plummet.
▷ANTONYMS increase.
▶ noun *a lighted taper*: **candle**, spill, wick, night light; archaic dip, glim, rushlight, wax light.

tardiness noun *the tardiness of the company's response*: **belatedness**, unpunctuality, lateness, delay, retardation, dilatoriness.
▷ANTONYMS punctuality, timeliness.

tardy adjective *I was fired for being tardy too often*. See **late** (sense 1 of the adjective).

target noun 1 *the competitor must shoot targets at ranges of 75 to 200 yards*: **mark**, bullseye, goal, aim.
2 *eagles can spot their targets from half a mile*: **prey**, quarry, game, kill, bag.
3 *they exceeded their profit target last year*: **objective**, goal, object, aim, end, desired result; plan, purpose, intention, intent, design, aspiration, ambition, ideal, hope, desire, wish, holy grail.
4 *they were the target for a wave of abuse from the press*: **victim**, butt, scapegoat, dupe, recipient, focus, object, subject, fair game, Aunt Sally.
□ **on target** 1 *the Arsenal striker was bang on target*: **accurate**, precise, unerring, sure, true, on the mark; informal spot on. 2 *the project was back on target*: **on schedule**, on time, on track, on course.
▶ verb 1 *the two men were targeted by a gunman*: **pick out**, single out, select, choose, decide on, earmark, fix on; **attack**, aim at, fire at.
2 *each product is targeted at a specific market*: **aim**, direct, level, intend, focus, position.

tariff noun 1 *the reduction of trade barriers and import tariffs*: **tax**, duty, toll, excise, levy, assessment, imposition, impost, charge, rate, fee, exaction; (**tariffs**) customs (duties), dues.
2 *make certain that you understand the tariff for calls*: **price list**, schedule, list of charges, rate.

tarnish verb 1 *gold does not tarnish easily*: **become discoloured**, discolour, stain, rust, oxidize, corrode, deteriorate; become dull, lose its shine, lose its lustre, blacken, become black.
▷ANTONYMS brighten, polish.
2 *detergents and scouring powder can tarnish metal*: **dull**, make dull, dim, blacken, make black, discolour, stain, rust, oxidize, corrode.
▷ANTONYMS brighten, polish.
3 *he thought such rash actions would tarnish his reputation as a scholar*: **sully**, besmirch, blacken, smirch, stain, blemish, blot, taint, soil, befoul, spoil, ruin, dirty, disgrace, mar, damage, defame, calumniate, injure, harm, hurt, undermine, debase, degrade, denigrate, dishonour, stigmatize, vitiate, drag through the mud.
▷ANTONYMS enhance.
▶ noun 1 *he was removing tarnish from the candlesticks*: **discoloration**, oxidation, rust, tarnishing, blackening, film, patina.
2 *this won't overcome the tarnish on Alan's personal reputation*: **smear**, black mark, slur, stain, blemish, blot, taint, stigma, smirch, flaw.

tarry verb archaic or literary *they were not allowed to tarry, but were taken upstairs immediately*. See **linger** (sense 1).

tart[1] noun *a jam tart*: **pastry**, flan, tartlet, quiche, strudel; **pie**, patty, pasty.

tart[2] informal **noun** derogatory *she was a tart I had picked up on a street corner*. See **prostitute**.
▶ verb 1 *she came back to **tart herself up** for the evening*: **dress oneself up**, make oneself up, smarten oneself up, preen oneself, beautify oneself, groom oneself; informal doll oneself up, titivate oneself.
2 *we must **tart** this place **up** a bit*: **decorate**, renovate, refurbish, redecorate, retouch, modernize; smarten up; informal do up, do over, fix up, give something a facelift.

tart[3] adjective 1 *cook a few tart apples*: **sour**, sharp, sharp-tasting, tangy, bitter, acid, acidic, zesty, piquant, pungent, strong, harsh, unsweetened, vinegary, lemony, citrus, burning, acrid, acetic; rare acidulous, acetous.
▷ANTONYMS sweet.
2 *she regretted her rather tart reply*: **acerbic**, sharp, biting, cutting, keen, stinging, mordant, astringent, caustic, trenchant, incisive, pointed, piercing, bitter, barbed, scathing, sarcastic, sardonic, acrimonious, nasty, rude, vicious, spiteful, venomous, wounding.
▷ANTONYMS kind.

task noun *he set himself the daunting task of writing a full-length book*: **job**, duty, chore, charge, labour, piece of work, piece of business, assignment, function, commission, mission, engagement, occupation, undertaking, exercise, business, responsibility, errand, detail, endeavour, enterprise, venture, quest, problem, burden.
□ **take someone to task** *he took some experts to task for their optimistic predictions*: **rebuke**, reprimand, reprove, reproach, remonstrate with,

upbraid, scold, berate, lecture, castigate, censure, criticize, admonish, chide, chasten, lambaste, nag, blame, arraign, call to account, haul over the coals, read someone the Riot Act; informal tell off, give someone a dressing-down, give someone a talking-to; Brit. informal tick off, carpet; N. Amer. informal bawl out, chew out.
▷ANTONYMS praise, commend.

Choose the right word **task, job, chore, duty**

These words all apply to activities that people are obliged to do, whether they want to or not. See also **work**.

Task is the broadest term, meaning 'a piece of work to be done' (*caring for dependent older people can be a daunting task | a new team manager was given the task of harnessing the club's talent*).

A **job** is primarily the occupation by which someone earns their living, in the course of which they may regularly have to perform a number of *tasks* (*Father landed a job as a technical engineer | 200 jobs are at risk*). A single piece of work for which someone is paid may also be referred to as a *job* (*the mechanic quoted him £50 for the job*), as can the responsibility to do something (*it's your job to know what's going on*).

Chores are tedious routine tasks (*help with everyday chores like shopping or housework*) or tasks that are felt to be unpleasant but unavoidable (*financial planning is seen as a nasty chore*).

Duties are tasks that one has to do as part of one's job, especially continuing ones (*your duties will include operating the switchboard*). In the singular, *duty* is usually service performed because of legal or moral obligation (*military duty | I came because I considered it to be my duty*). It can also describe such a feeling of obligation itself (*a sense of filial duty*).

taste noun **1** *a blue cheese with a distinctive sharp taste*: **flavour**, savour, relish, tang, smack.
2 *would you care for a taste of brandy?* **mouthful**, drop, bit, spoonful, sample, sip, nip, swallow, touch, sprinkle, trickle, soupçon; dash, pinch, morsel, bite, nibble, titbit, shred, modicum.
3 *it was a bit sweet for my taste*: **palate**, sense of taste, taste buds, appetite, stomach.
4 *a millionairess with a taste for adventure*: **liking**, love, fondness, fancy, desire, preference, penchant, predilection, inclination, partiality, leaning, bent, disposition, proneness; **hankering**, appetite, thirst, hunger, relish, soft spot, weakness.
▷ANTONYMS dislike.
5 *it was then that I had my first* ***taste of*** *prison*: **experience**, impression, sample; exposure to, contact with, involvement with, familiarity with, participation in.
6 *the house was furnished with taste*: **judgement**, discrimination, discernment, tastefulness, cultivation, culture, refinement, polish, finesse, elegance, grace, style, stylishness.
▷ANTONYMS tastelessness.
7 *we may reject advertisements on grounds of taste*: **decorum**, propriety, correctness, etiquette, politeness, tact, tactfulness, diplomacy, delicacy, nicety, sensitivity, discretion, tastefulness; French politesse.
▸ **verb 1** *Adam tasted the wine and nodded to the waiter*: **sample**, test, try, check, examine, savour; sip, sup, nibble.
2 *he could taste the blood in his mouth*: **perceive**, discern, make out, distinguish, differentiate.
3 *a kind of beer that* ***tasted of*** *cashews*: **have a flavour**, savour, smack, be reminiscent; suggest.
4 *it'll be good to taste real coffee again*: **consume**, drink, eat, partake of, devour.
5 *he tasted defeat for the first time*: **experience**, undergo, encounter, meet, come face to face with, come up against; know, have knowledge of, sample, try.

Word links **taste**

gustative, gustatory relating to the sense of taste

tasteful adjective **1** *the decor throughout the house is simple and tasteful*: **in good taste**, discriminating, fastidious, refined, cultured, cultivated, sensitive, restrained, harmonious, fitting, fit, becoming, pleasing, elegant, graceful, stylish, smart, chic, attractive, beautiful, pretty, charming, handsome, exquisite, aesthetic, artistic.
▷ANTONYMS tasteless, tacky.
2 *this video is artistic, tasteful, but powerfully erotic*: **decorous**, proper, seemly, correct, polite, tactful, respectable, restrained, appropriate, modest; French comme il faut.
▷ANTONYMS improper.

tasteless adjective **1** *the vegetables were watery and tasteless*: **flavourless**, bland, insipid, unappetizing, unflavoured, savourless, watered-down, watery, weak, thin, vapid, uninspired; mild, boring, dull, uninteresting.
▷ANTONYMS tasty, appetizing.
2 *his suite is lined with tasteless leather burgundy panelling*: **vulgar**, crude, tawdry, garish, gaudy, loud, trashy, showy, ostentatious, cheap, cheap and nasty, gross, meretricious, inelegant; informal flash, flashy, tatty, tacky, kitsch, naff.
▷ANTONYMS tasteful, refined.
3 *a tasteless remark*: **crude**, vulgar, low, gross, indelicate, uncouth, crass, tactless, undiplomatic, indiscreet, inappropriate, offensive, unacceptable.
▷ANTONYMS seemly, tasteful.

tasty adjective *a tasty meal*: **delicious**, palatable, luscious, mouth-watering, delectable, toothsome, succulent, juicy, dainty; appetizing, inviting, tempting; piquant, pungent, spicy, flavoursome, flavourful, full-flavoured; informal scrumptious, yummy, scrummy, finger-licking, delish, yum-yum, moreish; dated flavorous; literary ambrosial.
▷ANTONYMS bland, insipid.

tatters plural noun *he was forced to wear tatters a beggar would scorn*: **rags**, scraps, shreds, bits, pieces, bits and pieces, torn pieces, ragged pieces, ribbons, clippings, fragments.
□ **in tatters 1** *his clothes were in tatters*: **ragged**, torn, ripped, frayed, split, tattered, in shreds, in bits, in pieces, worn down, worn out, worn to shreds, moth-eaten, falling to pieces, threadbare. **2** *her marriage was in tatters*: **ruined**, in ruins, on the rocks, destroyed, finished, shattered, demolished, devastated, in disarray; informal kaput, done for, toast.

tattle verb **1** *they were tattling about him over their teacups*: **gossip**, tittle-tattle, chatter, chat, chit-chat, prattle, prate, babble, blabber, jabber, gabble, rattle on, spread rumours, spread gossip, circulate rumours, spread stories; informal chinwag, jaw, yak, gab; Brit. informal natter, rabbit on, witter on; N. Amer. informal run off at the mouth.
2 *I would tattle on her if I had any hard evidence*: **inform**, report, talk, tell all, spill the beans; accuse; informal squeal, sing, let the cat out of the bag.
▸ **noun** *that's a load of tabloid tattle*: **gossip**, rumour, tittle-tattle, hearsay, prattle, scandal, small talk, chit-chat.

taunt noun *he would play truant rather than face the taunts of his classmates*: **jeer**, gibe, sneer, insult, barb, catcall, brickbat, scoff, slap in the face; (**taunts**) teasing, taunting, provocation, goading, ridiculing, derision, mockery, sarcasm; informal dig, put-down.
▸ **verb** *the crowd taunted him about his marriage split*: **jeer at**, gibe at, sneer at, scoff at, poke fun at, make fun of, get at, insult, tease, chaff, torment, provoke, goad, ridicule, deride, mock, heckle; N. Amer. ride; informal rib, needle, put down, hassle, rag, guy; dated make sport of.

taut adjective **1** *the rope went taut*: **tight**, tightly stretched, stretched, rigid, stressed, not slack, not loose.
▷ANTONYMS slack, loose.
2 *his muscles remained hard and taut*: **flexed**, tensed, tightened, hard, solid, firm, rigid, stiff, unyielding.
▷ANTONYMS relaxed.
3 *he glared at her with a taut expression*: **fraught**, strained, stressed, tense, drawn, drained, sapped, fatigued, tired; informal uptight.
4 *a taut, pacy, absorbing tale of gang life*: **concise**, controlled, crisp, pithy, sharp, succinct, compact, terse.
▷ANTONYMS verbose.
5 *he ran a taut ship*: **orderly**, in order, in good order, in good condition, tight, trim, neat, well ordered, well regulated, well disciplined, tidy, spruce, smart, shipshape (and Bristol fashion).

tautology noun *his speeches are notable for tautology, such as 'safe haven'*: **repetition**, repetitiveness, repetitiousness, reiteration, redundancy, superfluity, periphrasis, iteration, duplication; wordiness, long-windedness, prolixity, verbiage, verbosity; rare pleonasm, perissology.

tavern noun archaic See **inn**.

tawdry adjective *she had cheap, tawdry rings on her fingers*: **gaudy**, flashy, showy, garish, loud; **tasteless**, vulgar, brash, crass, rubbishy, trashy, junky, cheap, cheap and nasty, cheapjack, paltry, worthless, shoddy, shabby, meretricious, plastic, tinselly, gimcrack, Brummagem; informal flash, tatty, tacky, kitsch; Brit. informal twopenny-halfpenny.
▷ANTONYMS tasteful, refined.

tax noun **1** *they will have to pay tax on interest earned by savings*: **levy**, tariff, duty, toll, excise, impost, contribution, assessment, tribute, tithe, charge, fee; liability; customs, dues; Scottish, Irish, & Indian cess.
▷ANTONYMS rebate.
2 *a heavy tax on the reader's attention*: **burden**, load, weight, encumbrance, demand, strain, pressure, stress, drain, imposition; responsibility, duty, onus, obligation, care, worry.
▸ **verb 1** *the president pledged to tax foreign companies more harshly*: **levy a tax on**, impose a toll on, charge duty on, exact a tax on, demand a tax on; assess, charge, tithe; rare mulct.
2 *Basil's constant whining and struggling was taxing her strength*: **strain**, stretch, put a strain on, make demands on, weigh heavily on, weigh down; burden, load, overload, encumber, push, push too far; overwhelm, try, task, wear out, exhaust, sap, drain, empty, enervate, fatigue, tire, weary, weaken, overwork.
3 *Curzon taxed him with starting a revolution*: **confront**, accuse, call to account, charge, blame, censure, condemn, denounce; prosecute, bring charges against, indict, arraign, incriminate; N. Amer. impeach; informal point

the finger at.
▷**ANTONYMS** clear, exonerate.

> *Word links* **tax**
>
> **fiscal** relating to tax

taxing adjective *it's quite a taxing job she has*: **demanding**, exacting, challenging, burdensome, arduous, onerous, difficult, hard, tough, heavy, laborious, back-breaking, strenuous, rigorous, uphill, stringent; tiring, exhausting, enervating, draining, sapping, stressful, wearing, trying, punishing, crushing; informal murderous; rare exigent.
▷**ANTONYMS** easy, gentle.

teach verb **1** *she teaches children with special needs | I started teaching in 1961*: **educate**, instruct, school, tutor, give lessons to, coach, train, upskill, ground, enlighten, illuminate, verse, edify, prepare, din something into, indoctrinate, brainwash; drill, discipline, put someone through their paces; N. Amer. teach school.
2 *I was teaching English in a boy's school*: **give lessons in**, lecture in, give instructions in, inform someone about, familiarize someone with, acquaint someone with, instil, inculcate, explicate, explain, expound.
3 *teaching your teenager how to negotiate is implicit in the process of formulating a contract*: **train**, show, guide, instruct, demonstrate to, give someone an idea, make clear; informal learn.

> *Word links* **teach**
>
> **didactic**, **pedagogic**, **educational**, **educative** relating to teaching

teacher noun *a history teacher*: **educator**, tutor, instructor, pedagogue, schoolteacher, schoolmaster, schoolmistress, master, mistress, governess, educationalist, educationist; supply teacher; coach, trainer; lecturer, professor, don, fellow, reader, academic; guide, mentor, guru, counsellor; sophist; Scottish dominie; Indian pandit; N. Amer., chiefly derogatory schoolmarm; informal teach; Brit. informal beak; Austral./NZ informal chalkie, schoolie; archaic doctor, schoolman, usher; rare preceptor.

team noun **1** *the village cricket team | the company's sales team*: **group**, **squad**, side, band, bunch, company, party, gang, selection, crew, troupe, set, line-up, array; body, corps, cadre, partnership, alliance, working party, posse.
2 *a team of horses*: **pair**, span, yoke, duo, set, rig, tandem.
▸ verb **1** *the horses are teamed in pairs*: **harness**, yoke, saddle, bridle, hitch up, couple.
2 *for the long, lean look, team a loose-fitting T-shirt with a pair of matching shorts*: **match**, coordinate, complement, pair up.
3 *you could **team up** with another artist to produce a larger exhibition*: **join (up)**, join forces, collaborate, get together, come together, band together, work together; unite, combine, cooperate, merge, link, ally, associate, amalgamate, integrate, fraternize, form an alliance, pool resources, club together.

tear[1] (rhymes with 'bear') verb **1** *I **tore up** the letter*: **rip up**, rip in two, pull apart, pull to pieces, shred.
2 *her tights were torn by the rough concrete*: **rip**, ladder, snag.
3 *his flesh was torn*: **lacerate**, cut (open), cut to pieces, cut to ribbons, gash, slash, scratch, claw, mangle, mutilate, hack, pierce, stab; injure, wound.
4 *the traumas have **torn her family apart***: **divide**, split, split down the middle, sever, break apart, disunite, rupture; literary rend, rip asunder, cleave; rare sunder, rive, dissever.
▷**ANTONYMS** unite, unify.
5 *Gina tore the book from his hands*: **snatch**, grab, seize, rip, wrench, wrest, pull, pluck; informal yank.
6 *I was torn by guilt*: **torment**, torture, rack, harrow, wring, lacerate; literary rend.
7 informal *Jack tore down the street*: **sprint**, race, run, dart, rush, dash, hasten, hurry, scurry, scuttle, scamper, hare, bolt, bound, fly, gallop, career, charge, pound, shoot, hurtle, speed, streak, flash, whizz, zoom, sweep, go like lightning, go hell for leather, go like the wind; informal pelt, scoot, hotfoot it, leg it, belt, zip, whip, go like a bat out of hell, step on it, get a move on, get cracking, put on some speed, stir one's stumps; Brit. informal go like the clappers, bomb, bucket; Scottish informal wheech; N. Amer. informal boogie, hightail it, barrel, get the lead out; informal, dated cut along; archaic post, hie.
▷**ANTONYMS** stroll, amble.
□ **tear something down** *they tore down the old barn*: **demolish**, knock down, pull down, raze, raze to the ground, flatten, level, bulldoze; take down, dismantle, disassemble.
▷**ANTONYMS** build, erect.
□ **tear into someone** *their tyrannical father tore into all of his sons*: **attack**, assail, hit, strike, let fly at, lay into, lash out at, set about, set upon, fall on, turn on, assault, beat, thrash, pound, pummel, wallop, hammer, pounce on, round on, pelt, drub; **rebuke**, reprimand, reproach, reprove, admonish, remonstrate with, chastise, chide, upbraid, take to task, pull up, castigate, lambaste, read someone the Riot Act, give someone a piece of one's mind, go on at, haul over the coals, criticize, censure; informal lace into, sail into, pitch into, let someone have it, get stuck into, paste, do over, knock about/around, rough up; Brit. informal have a go at.
□ **tear someone off a strip** Brit. informal *we are more at ease tearing our partner off a strip than telling them how much we value them*: **reprimand**, rebuke, scold, admonish, reprove, upbraid, chastise, chide, censure, castigate, lambaste, berate, lecture, criticize, take to task, read the Riot Act to, haul over the coals; informal tell off, give someone a telling-off, dress down, give someone a dressing-down, bawl out, pitch into, lay into, lace into, blow up at, give someone a piece of one's mind, give someone an earful, give someone a roasting, give someone a rocket, give someone a rollicking; Brit. informal have a go at, carpet, give someone what for, let someone have it; N. Amer. informal chew out, ream out; Brit. vulgar slang bollock, give someone a bollocking.
▸ noun *there was a tear in her dress*: **rip**, hole, split, rent, cut, slash, slit; ladder, run, snag.

tear[2] (rhymes with 'fear') noun **1** *tears ran down her cheeks*: **teardrop**.
2 *tears of perspiration*: **drop**, droplet, bead, globule.
□ **in tears** *he was so hurt by her attitude he was nearly in tears*: **crying**, weeping, sobbing, wailing, howling, bawling, whimpering; tearful, upset; Scottish greeting; informal weepy, teary, blubbing, blubbering.

> *Word links* **tear**
>
> **lachrymal** relating to tears
> **lachrymose** inducing tears

tearaway noun **hooligan**, hoodlum, ruffian, lout, rowdy, roughneck; Austral. larrikin; informal tough, bruiser, yahoo; Brit. informal rough, yob, yobbo, bovver boy, lager lout, chav, hoodie; Scottish informal radge; Scottish & N. English informal keelie, ned; Austral./NZ informal roughie, hoon.

tearful adjective **1** *Georgina was tearful*: **in tears**, crying, weeping, sobbing, wailing, snivelling, whimpering; close to tears, on the verge of tears, with tears in one's eyes; emotional, upset, distressed, sad, unhappy; Scottish greeting; informal weepy, teary, blubbering, blubbing; rare lachrymose, larmoyant.
▷**ANTONYMS** happy, smiling, laughing.
2 *a tearful farewell*: **emotional**, upsetting, distressing, sad, heartbreaking, heart-rending, sorrowful; poignant, moving, touching, tear-jerking, affecting, pathetic; literary dolorous.
▷**ANTONYMS** cheerful.

tease verb *the other girls teased her about her accent*: **make fun of**, poke fun at, chaff, make jokes about, rag, mock, laugh at, guy, satirize, be sarcastic about; **deride**, ridicule, scoff at, jeer at, jibe at; taunt, bait, goad, pick on; informal take the mickey out of, send up, rib, josh, wind up, have on, pull someone's leg, make a monkey of; N. Amer. informal goof on, rag on, put on, pull someone's chain, razz, fun, shuck; Austral./NZ informal poke mullock at, poke borak at, sling off at, chiack; Brit. vulgar slang take the piss out of; Brit. informal, dated rot; dated make sport of, twit; archaic quiz, smoke, flout at, rally.

technical adjective **1** *an important technical achievement*: **practical**, scientific, applied, applying science, non-theoretical; technological, high-tech, hi-tech; engineering.
2 *at first sight this might seem very technical*: **specialist**, specialized, scientific; complex, complicated, esoteric.
3 *a technical fault*: **mechanical**.

technique noun **1** *different techniques were developed for dealing with the problem*: **method**, approach, procedure, process, system, method of working, MO, operating procedure, course of action, plan of action, plan of attack, way, manner, mode, fashion, style; means, strategy, tack, tactic, line; routine, practice; Latin modus operandi.
2 *I was very impressed with his technique*: **skill**, skilfulness, ability, capability, proficiency, expertise, expertness, mastery, talent, genius, artistry, art, craftsmanship, craft; aptitude, adroitness, adeptness, deftness, dexterity, dexterousness, knack, facility, competence; execution, performance, delivery; informal know-how; dated address.

tedious adjective *the work was tedious and physically demanding*: **boring**, monotonous, dull, deadly dull, uninteresting, unexciting, unvaried, unvarying, lacking variety, mind-numbing, mindless, soul-destroying, soulless, humdrum, dreary, ho-hum, mundane, wearisome, wearying, tiresome, soporific, dry, as dry as dust, arid, lifeless, colourless, monochrome, uninspired, uninspiring, flat, plodding, slow, banal, vapid, insipid, bland, lacklustre, prosaic, run-of-the-mill, pedestrian, jejune, leaden, heavy; long-drawn-out, overlong, long-winded, prolix, laborious, ponderous, endless, interminable; mechanical, routine; Scottish dreich; informal deadly, draggy; Brit. informal samey; N. Amer. informal dullsville.
▷**ANTONYMS** exciting, interesting.

> *Word toolkit* **tedious**
>
> See **insipid**.

tedium noun *to relieve the tedium of the days, they sang or told stories*: **monotony**, monotonousness, tediousness, dullness, boredom, ennui,

uneventfulness, lack of variety, lack of variation, lack of interest, lack of excitement, sameness, unchangingness, uniformity, routineness, humdrumness, dreariness, mundaneness, wearisomeness, tiresomeness, dryness, aridity, lifelessness, colourlessness, featurelessness, slowness, banality, vapidity, insipidity, blandness, prosaicness, jejuneness; long-windedness, prolixity, laboriousness, ponderousness, endlessness, interminableness; informal deadliness; Brit. informal sameyness.
▷ANTONYMS variety, excitement.

teem[1] verb
□ **teem with** *the pool was teeming with fish*: **be full of**, be filled with, be alive with, be brimming with, be overflowing with, abound in, be swarming with, be bursting at the seams with; be packed with, be crowded with, be thronged with, be crawling with, be overrun by, bristle with, seethe with, be thick with, be crammed with, be cram-full of, be choked with, be congested with; informal be jam-packed with, be chock-a-block with, be chock-full with, be lousy with; rare pullulate with.

teem[2] verb *the rain was teeming down*: **pour (down)**, pelt down, tip down, beat down, lash down, sheet down, come down in torrents/sheets, rain cats and dogs; informal be chucking it down; Brit. informal bucket down, come down in buckets/bucketloads, come down in stair rods, tipple down.

teenage adjective **adolescent**, teenaged, youthful, young, juvenile; informal teen.

teenager noun **adolescent**, youth, young person, boy, girl, minor, juvenile; informal kid, teen, teeny-bopper.

teeny adjective informal *a teeny bedsit*: **tiny**, minuscule, microscopic, very small, little, diminutive; micro, miniature, nanoscopic, baby, toy, midget, dwarf, pygmy, Lilliputian; Scottish wee; informal teeny-weeny, teensy, teensy-weensy, weeny, itsy-bitsy, itty-bitty, eensy, eensy-weensy, tiddly, pint-sized, bite-sized, knee-high to a grasshopper; Brit. informal titchy, ickle; N. Amer. informal little-bitty.
▷ANTONYMS huge, big.

teeter verb **1** *Daisy teetered towards them in her high-heeled boots*: **totter**, walk unsteadily, wobble, toddle; sway, rock, try to keep one's balance; stagger, stumble, reel, roll, lurch, pitch; Scottish stot.
2 *the situation teetered between tragedy and farce*: **see-saw**, veer, fluctuate, oscillate, swing, yo-yo, alternate; waver, wobble; N. Amer. teeter-totter.

teeth plural noun See **tooth**.

teetotal adjective *he's strictly teetotal these days*: **abstinent**, abstemious; sober, avoiding alcohol; informal on the wagon, off the booze, off the sauce, dry.
▷ANTONYMS bibulous, boozy.

teetotalism noun **temperance**, abstinence, abstention, sobriety; rare Rechabitism, nephalism.

teetotaller noun **non-drinker**, abstainer; Austral./NZ informal wowser; rare Rechabite, nephalist, pussyfoot, white ribboner.
▷ANTONYMS drunk, lush.

telegram noun dated **telemessage**, cable, cablegram, telex; radiogram, radio-telegraph; informal wire.

telepathic adjective *as though he were telepathic, he glanced up at her*: **psychic**, clairvoyant, with second sight, with a sixth sense.

telepathy noun **mind-reading**, thought transference; extrasensory perception, ESP; clairvoyance, sixth sense; psychometry.

telephone noun *Sophie picked up the telephone*: **phone**, handset, receiver; informal blower; N. Amer. informal horn.
▸ verb *he telephoned me last night*: **phone**, call, get someone on the phone, get on the phone to, get, reach, dial, make/place a call to; Brit. **ring up**, ring, give someone a ring; informal call up, give someone a call, give someone a buzz, buzz; Brit. informal give someone a bell, bell, give someone a tinkle, get on the blower to; N. Amer. informal get someone on the horn.

telescope noun **spyglass**, glass; informal scope.
▸ verb **1** *the five steel sections telescope into one another*: **slide together**, collapse.
2 *there was a grinding crunch of metal as the front of the car was telescoped*: **crush**, concertina, squash, compact, compress.
3 *less recent employment experience can be telescoped into a short sentence or two*: **condense**, shorten, reduce, abbreviate, abridge, summarize, precis, abstract, boil down, shrink, encapsulate; cut, truncate, curtail, trim; consolidate, conflate; rare capsulize.
▷ANTONYMS amplify.

televise verb *the BBC are televising the Cup Final*: **broadcast**, screen, air, telecast, simulcast; transmit, relay.

television noun **TV**, television set; informal small screen; Brit. informal telly, the box, the gogglebox; N. Amer. informal the tube, the boob tube, the idiot box.

tell verb **1** *why didn't you tell me about this before?* **inform**, let know, notify, apprise, make aware, mention something to, acquaint with, advise, put in the picture, brief, fill in, break the news to; alert, warn, forewarn; informal clue in.
2 *I hope you are telling the truth | she was crying as she told the story*: **speak**, utter, say, voice, state, declare; **communicate**, make known, impart, divulge, announce, proclaim, broadcast; **relate**, recount, narrate, give an account of, set forth, unfold, retail, report, chronicle, recite, rehearse, describe, portray, sketch, delineate, depict, paint, weave, spin.
3 *Corbett told him to leave*: **instruct**, order, give orders, command, direct, charge, enjoin, call on, require; literary bid.
4 *I tell you, I did nothing wrong*: **assure**, promise, give someone one's word, swear, guarantee; dated warrant.
5 *the figures tell a different story*: **reveal**, show, be/give evidence of, disclose, indicate, convey, signify; display, exhibit.
6 *promise you won't tell?* **give the game away**, talk, tell tales, open one's mouth, tattle; informal spill the beans, let the cat out of the bag, blab; Brit. informal blow the gaff.
▷ANTONYMS keep a secret.
7 *he was afraid she would tell on him*: **inform on/against**, tell tales on, give away, denounce, sell out, stab someone in the back; informal split on, blow the whistle on, rat on, peach on, squeal on, squeak on, stitch up, do the dirty on, sell down the river; Brit. informal grass on, sneak on, shop; N. Amer. informal rat out, drop a/the dime on, finger; Austral./NZ informal dob on, pimp on, pool, shelf, put someone's pot on; rare delate.
8 *it was hard to tell what he was thinking*: **ascertain**, decide, determine, work out, make out, deduce, discern, perceive, see, identify, recognize, understand, comprehend; be sure, be certain; informal figure out, get a fix on; Brit. informal suss out.
9 *he didn't look as if he could tell a Renoir from a Renault*: **distinguish**, differentiate, tell apart, discriminate.
10 *the strain of supporting the family was beginning to tell on him*: **take its toll on**, leave its mark on, have an adverse effect on, affect.
□ **tell someone off** informal *my parents told me off for coming home late*: **reprimand**, rebuke, reproach, scold, admonish, reprove, remonstrate with, chastise, chide, upbraid, berate, take to task, pull up, castigate, lambaste, read someone the Riot Act, give someone a piece of one's mind, haul over the coals, criticize, censure; informal give someone a talking-to, give someone a telling-off, dress down, give someone a dressing-down, give someone an earful, give someone a roasting, give someone a rocket, give someone a rollicking, rap, rap someone over the knuckles, slap someone's wrist, let someone have it, bawl out, give someone hell, come down on, blow up, pitch into, lay into, lace into, give someone a caning, blast, rag, keelhaul; Brit. informal tick off, have a go at, carpet, monster, give someone a mouthful, tear someone off a strip, give someone what for, wig, give someone a wigging, give someone a row, row; N. Amer. informal chew out, ream out; Brit. vulgar slang bollock, give someone a bollocking; N. Amer. vulgar slang chew someone's ass, ream someone's ass; dated call down, rate, give someone a rating, trim; rare reprehend, objurgate.
▷ANTONYMS praise.

teller noun **1** *a bank teller*: **cashier**, bank clerk, clerk.
2 *a teller of tales*: **narrator**, raconteur, raconteuse; storyteller; Austral. informal magsman; rare anecdotist, anecdotalist.

telling adjective *a telling critique of the military mind*: **revealing**, significant; **convincing**, persuasive, forceful, striking, potent, powerful, strong, cogent, compelling; trenchant, weighty, important, meaningful, influential; effective, effectual.
▷ANTONYMS unimportant, insignificant.

telling-off noun informal *I've already had one telling off from Dad today*: **reprimand**, rebuke, reproof, admonishment, admonition, reproach, reproval, scolding, remonstration, upbraiding, castigation, lambasting, lecture, criticism, censure; informal rap, rap over the knuckles, slap on the wrist, flea in one's ear, talking-to, dressing-down, earful, roasting, tongue-lashing, bawling-out, caning, blast, blowing up; Brit. informal ticking-off, carpeting, wigging, rollicking, rocket, row; Austral./NZ informal serve; Brit. vulgar slang bollocking; dated rating.

telltale adjective *a telltale blush spread over her face*: **revealing**, revelatory, suggestive, meaningful, significant, meaning, indicative; unmistakable; informal giveaway.
▸ noun *'Steve did it, miss,' said a telltale*: N. Amer. tattletale; informal **blabbermouth**, blabber, loud mouth, snitch, squealer; Brit. informal sneak; Scottish informal clype; Austral./NZ informal pimp; dated talebearer.

temerity noun *I doubt anyone will have the temerity to print these accusations*: **audacity**, boldness, audaciousness, nerve, effrontery, impudence, impertinence, cheek, barefaced cheek, gall, presumption, presumptuousness, brazenness, forwardness, front, rashness; daring; informal face, neck, brass neck, brass; N. Amer. informal chutzpah; informal, dated hide; Brit. informal, dated crust; rare procacity, assumption.
▷ANTONYMS shyness, bashfulness.

temper noun **1** *Drew had walked out in a temper*: **fit of rage**, rage, fury, fit of bad/ill temper, bad temper, tantrum, passion, paroxysm; fit of pique, bad mood, mood, pet, sulk; informal grump, huff, snit; Brit. informal strop, paddy; Brit. informal, dated bate, wax, skid; N. Amer. informal blowout, hissy fit; archaic paddywhack, miff.
2 *an uncharacteristic display of temper*: **anger**, fury, rage, annoyance, vexation, crossness, irascibility, irritation, irritability, ill humour, ill temper, dyspepsia, spleen, pique, petulance, peevishness, pettishness, testiness, tetchiness, snappishness, crabbiness, resentment, surliness,

churlishness; Brit. informal stroppiness; literary ire, choler.
▷ANTONYMS good humour.
3 *she struggled to keep her temper*: **composure**, equanimity, self-control, self-possession, sangfroid, coolness, calm, calmness, tranquillity, good humour; informal cool.
4 *he was of a placid temper*: **temperament**, disposition, nature, character, personality, make-up, constitution, mind, spirit, stamp, mettle, mould; mood, frame of mind, cast of mind, habit of mind, attitude; archaic humour, grain.
□ **lose one's temper** *suddenly, Maria lost her temper*: **become very angry**, fly into a rage, explode, blow up, erupt, lose control, go berserk, breathe fire, begin to rant and rave, flare up, boil over; informal go mad, go crazy, go wild, go bananas, have a fit, see red, fly off the handle, blow one's top, blow a fuse, blow a gasket, do one's nut, hit the roof, go through the roof, go up the wall, go off the deep end, lose one's cool, go ape, flip, flip one's lid, lose one's rag, lose it, freak out, be fit to be tied, be foaming at the mouth, burst a blood vessel, get one's dander up, go non-linear; Brit. informal go spare, go crackers, throw a wobbly, get one's knickers in a twist; N. Amer. informal flip one's wig; Austral./NZ informal go crook; vulgar slang go apeshit.
▶ **verb 1** *the steel is tempered by heat treatment*: **harden**, strengthen, toughen, fortify; technical anneal.
2 *their idealism is tempered with realism*: **moderate**, modify, modulate; tone down, mitigate, palliate, alleviate, allay, assuage, lessen, reduce, weaken, lighten, soften, cushion; qualify.

temperament noun **1** *it was a particularly appealing prospect for a man of his temperament*: **disposition**, nature, character, personality, make-up, constitution, complexion, temper, mind, spirit, stamp, mettle, mould; mood, frame of mind, cast of mind, bent, tendency, attitude, outlook; archaic grain, humour.
2 *he had begun to show signs of temperament*: **volatility**, excitability, emotionalism, mercurialness, capriciousness, hot-headedness, quick-temperedness, hot-temperedness, irritability, impatience, petulance; moodiness, touchiness, sensitivity, oversensitivity, hypersensitivity.
▷ANTONYMS placidity, phlegm.

temperamental adjective **1** *a temperamental chef*: **volatile**, excitable, emotional, overemotional, mercurial, capricious, erratic, unpredictable, changeable, inconsistent, unstable, hot-headed, fiery, explosive, hot-tempered, short-tempered, quick-tempered, irritable, irascible, impatient, petulant, prima donna-ish, melodramatic; touchy, moody, sensitive, oversensitive, hypersensitive, highly strung, neurotic, easily upset; informal on a short fuse.
▷ANTONYMS calm, placid, phlegmatic.
2 *he had a temperamental dislike of all conflict*: **inherent**, innate, natural, inborn, constitutional, deep-rooted, ingrained, congenital.

temperance noun **1** *Davies was a devout Methodist and a strict advocate of temperance*: **teetotalism**, abstinence, abstention, non-drinking, sobriety; prohibition; rare Rechabitism, nephalism.
▷ANTONYMS bibulousness, crapulence.
2 *the temperance of her lifestyle*: **self-restraint**, restraint, moderation, self-control, self-discipline, lack of indulgence; abstemiousness, abstinence, self-denial, austerity, asceticism; rare continence.
▷ANTONYMS intemperance, excess, overindulgence.

temperate adjective **1** *temperate climates*: **mild**, clement, pleasant, agreeable, benign; gentle, balmy, fair.
▷ANTONYMS extreme.
2 *Charles was temperate in his consumption of both food and drink*: **self-restrained**, restrained, moderate, self-controlled, controlled, disciplined; abstemious, self-denying, austere, ascetic; teetotal, abstinent.
▷ANTONYMS intemperate, immoderate.
3 *a lucid and temperate study*: **balanced**, dispassionate, level-headed, sensible, rational, sober, sober-minded; N. Amer. sobersided.

tempest noun **1** *the screaming tempest raged round the house*: **storm**, gale, squall, hurricane, tornado, whirlwind, cyclone, typhoon. See also **storm**.
2 *the tempest of World War II*: **turmoil**, tumult, turbulence, ferment, disturbance, disorder, chaos, upheaval, disruption, commotion, uproar, storm, furore.
▷ANTONYMS tranquillity.

tempestuous adjective **1** *the fine weather had broken and the day was tempestuous*: **stormy**, blustery, squally, wild, turbulent, windy, gusty, blowy, rainy, thundery, rough, choppy; angry, dirty, foul, nasty, inclement; howling, roaring, raging, furious; rare boisterous.
▷ANTONYMS calm, fine.
2 *the increasingly tempestuous political environment*: **turbulent**, stormy, tumultuous, violent, wild, 'lively', heated, explosive, uncontrolled, unrestrained, feverish, hysterical, frenetic, frenzied, frantic.
▷ANTONYMS peaceful.
3 *he was finding it harder and harder to live with such a tempestuous woman*: **emotional**, passionate, intense, impassioned, fiery, temperamental; **volatile**, excitable, mercurial, capricious, unpredictable, erratic, hot-tempered, quick-tempered.
▷ANTONYMS placid, calm.

tempo noun **1** *the tempo of the music quickened*: **cadence**, speed, rhythm, beat, time, pulse; measure, metre.
2 *the tempo of life in Western society*: **pace**, rate, speed, velocity.

temporal adjective **1** *the temporal aspects of church government*: **secular**, non-spiritual, worldly, profane, material, mundane, earthly, terrestrial; non-religious, lay; carnal, fleshly, mortal, corporeal; rare sublunary, terrene.
▷ANTONYMS spiritual.
2 *spatial and temporal boundaries*: **of time**, time-related.

temporarily adverb *the girl was temporarily placed with a foster family*: **for the time being**, for the moment, for now, for the present, in the interim, for the nonce, in/for the meantime, in the meanwhile; for a short time, for a short/little while, briefly, momentarily, fleetingly; provisionally, pro tem; Latin pro tempore, ad interim; French en attendant.
▷ANTONYMS permanently.

temporary adjective **1** *temporary accommodation | the temporary captain*: **non-permanent**, short-term, interim; **provisional**, pro tem, makeshift, stopgap; acting, fill-in, stand-in, caretaker; Latin ad interim, pro tempore.
▷ANTONYMS permanent.
2 *a temporary loss of self-control*: **brief**, short-lived, momentary, fleeting, passing, impermanent, here today and gone tomorrow, transient, transitory, ephemeral, evanescent, fugitive; rare fugacious.
▷ANTONYMS lasting.

temporize verb *he'd been temporizing for weeks, hoping the problem would go away*: **equivocate**, procrastinate, play for time, play a waiting game, stall, use delaying tactics, avoid committing oneself, avoid making a decision, delay, hang back, beat about the bush, be evasive, prevaricate, be indecisive, hesitate; Brit. hum and haw; archaic palter; rare tergiversate, use Fabian tactics.

tempt verb **1** *they were not able to tempt any investors to bankroll the organization*: **entice**, persuade, convince, inveigle, induce, cajole, coax, woo; informal sweet-talk, smooth-talk.
▷ANTONYMS discourage, deter, dissuade.
2 *vegetarian dishes unusual enough to tempt even the staunchest of meat-eaters*: **allure**, attract, appeal to, whet the appetite of, make someone's mouth water; lure, seduce, beguile, tantalize, intrigue, captivate, draw.
▷ANTONYMS repel, put off.
□ **tempt fate** *to bale out at 250 feet was tempting fate*: **run a risk**, live dangerously, play with fire, sail close to the wind, risk it.

Choose the right word **tempt, entice, lure**

All these words are used of persuading someone to do something by offering them the prospect of something attractive.

Tempt can imply that the person being persuaded knows that the attractive thing is wrong or unwise (*a large rucksack could tempt you to carry too much | a wealth of shops, bars, cafes, and restaurants have sprung up to tempt the visitor*). In the passive, it often means simply 'to be inclined' (*looking at the book one is tempted to ask what all the fuss is about*). The participial adjective *tempting* is common (*it's a very tempting offer*).

Entice lacks the sense of persuading somone to do something that they know is wrong, and it typically has the sense of attracting someone in a particular direction (*the new crossing might entice drivers back onto the motorway*). It is often used in commercial or sexual contexts (*rival ferry companies cut fares to entice cross-Channel shoppers | she was busy laying plans to entice him away from his steady girlfriend*). The adjective *enticing* is common (*this is an enticing introduction to the subject*).

To **lure** someone is typically to persuade them to go somewhere (*it would take more than Hollywood stardom to lure him away from his Sussex cottage*), and often with bad intentions (*he twice lured young women into his car*).

temptation noun **1** *Mary resisted the temptation to answer her mother back*: **desire**, urge, itch, impulse, inclination.
2 *he had no intention of exposing her to the temptations of London*: **lure**, allurement, enticement, seduction, attraction, draw, pull, invitation; bait, decoy, snare, trap, siren song; informal come-on.
3 *the temptation of travel to exotic locations*: **allure**, appeal, attraction, attractiveness, fascination.

tempting adjective **1** *the tempting shops of the Via Nazionale*: **enticing**, alluring, attractive, appealing, inviting, captivating, seductive; beguiling, fascinating, intriguing, tantalizing; irresistible.
▷ANTONYMS off-putting, uninviting.
2 *a plate of tempting cakes*: **appetizing**, mouth-watering, delicious, succulent, luscious, toothsome; informal scrummy, scrumptious, yummy, finger-licking, delish; Brit. informal moreish; N. Amer. informal nummy.
▷ANTONYMS unappetizing.
3 *you look very tempting lying there*: **seductive**, sexy, desirable, sexually attractive, provocative; nubile; informal beddable.
▷ANTONYMS undesirable, unattractive.

temptress noun *she'd behaved like a temptress in a fifties movie*: **seductress**, siren, femme fatale, Mata Hari, Delilah, enchantress, sorceress, Circe, Lorelei; **flirt**, coquette, Lolita; N. Amer. informal vamp, mantrap.

ten **cardinal number** **decade**; Music decad, decuplet; rare tensome.

> *Word links* **ten**
>
> **deca-, dec(i)-:** related prefixes, as in *decathlon, decibel*
> **decimal, denary** relating to ten
> **decagon** ten-sided figure
> **decennial** relating to ten years

tenable **adjective** *this politically convenient view is no longer tenable*: **defensible**, justifiable, defendable, supportable, sustainable, maintainable, arguable, able to hold water, reasonable, rational, sound, viable, workable, plausible, credible, believable, conceivable, acceptable, imaginable.
▷ANTONYMS indefensible, untenable.

tenacious **adjective** **1** *he paused for a moment, but without releasing his tenacious grip*: **firm**, tight, fast, clinging; strong, forceful, powerful, unshakeable, immovable, iron.
▷ANTONYMS loose, weak.
2 *he had a reputation for being a tenacious man | a tenacious battle to secure compensation*: **persevering**, **persistent**, pertinacious, determined, dogged, single-minded, strong-willed, tireless, indefatigable, resolute, patient, purposeful, diligent, assiduous, sedulous, unflagging, staunch, steadfast, untiring, unwavering, unswerving, unshakeable, unyielding, uncompromising, insistent, importunate, relentless, unrelenting, inexorable, implacable; stubborn, intransigent, obstinate, obdurate, stiff-necked; N. Amer. rock-ribbed.
▷ANTONYMS irresolute.
3 *he had a tenacious memory*: **retentive**, good; photographic.
4 *she struggled to free herself from the tenacious mud*: **sticky**, adhesive, clinging, gluey, gummy, glutinous, viscid, viscous, mucilaginous; Brit. claggy; Scottish & N. English clarty.

tenacity **noun** *the tenacity with which he stuck to his story*: **persistence**, pertinacity, determination, perseverance, doggedness, tenaciousness, single-mindedness, strength of will, firmness of purpose, strength of purpose, fixity of purpose, bulldog spirit, tirelessness, indefatigability, resolution, resoluteness, resolve, firmness, patience, purposefulness, staunchness, steadfastness, constancy, staying power, application, diligence, assiduity, sedulousness, insistence, relentlessness, inexorability, inexorableness, implacability, inflexibility; stubbornness, intransigence, obstinacy, obduracy, obdurateness; German Sitzfleisch; informal stickability; N. Amer. informal stick-to-it-iveness; rare continuance, perseveration.
▷ANTONYMS irresolution, lack of resolve.

tenancy **noun** *his tenancy of the property*: **occupancy**, period of occupancy, occupation, period of occupation, residence, habitation, holding, possession; **tenure**, lease, rental, leasing, leasehold, renting; rare inhabitance, inhabitancy.
▷ANTONYMS freehold.

tenant **noun** **occupant**, resident, inhabitant; **leaseholder**, lessee, renter, holder; addressee; lodger, boarder; Brit. occupier, sitting tenant; N. Amer. roomer; formal dweller; historical feodary.
▷ANTONYMS owner, freeholder.

tend¹ **verb** **1** *I tend to get very involved in my work*: **be inclined**, be apt, be disposed, be prone, be liable, have/show a tendency, be likely, have a propensity.
2 *younger voters tended towards the tabloid press*: **incline**, lean, swing, veer, gravitate, be drawn, move; favour; show a preference for, be biased; N. Amer. trend.

tend² **verb** *his family had tended the sick for three generations | a well-tended garden*: **look after**, take care of, care for, minister to, attend to, see to, wait on, cater to; watch over, keep an eye on, mind, protect, watch, guard; nurse, nurture, cherish; maintain, cultivate, keep, manage.
▷ANTONYMS neglect.

tendency **noun** **1** *his tendency to take the law into his own hands*: **propensity**, proclivity, proneness, aptness, likelihood, inclination, disposition, predisposition, bent, leaning, penchant, predilection, susceptibility, liability; readiness; habit.
2 *this tendency towards cohabitation*: **trend**, movement, drift, swing, gravitation; orientation, bias; direction, course, tide, turn.

tender¹ **adjective** **1** *he looked a gentle, tender man*: **caring**, kind, kindly, kind-hearted, soft-hearted, tender-hearted, compassionate, sympathetic, warm, warm-hearted, feeling, fatherly, motherly, maternal, gentle, mild, benevolent, generous, giving, humane; susceptible, vulnerable; informal touchy-feely.
▷ANTONYMS hard-hearted, callous, unsympathetic.
2 *he placed a tender kiss on Fabia's brow*: **affectionate**, fond, loving, emotional, warm, gentle, soft; amorous, adoring, amatory; informal lovey-dovey.
3 *tender love songs*: **romantic**, sentimental, emotional, emotive, touching, moving, poignant, evocative; Brit. informal soppy.
4 *simmer for 25–30 minutes until the meat is tender*: **easily chewed**, not tough, chewable, soft, edible, eatable; succulent, juicy, ripe; tenderized.
▷ANTONYMS tough, leathery.
5 *these flowers are tender*: **delicate**, easily damaged, fragile, breakable, frail.
▷ANTONYMS hardy.
6 *her ankle was swollen and tender*: **sore**, painful, sensitive, inflamed, raw, red, chafed; hurting, aching, throbbing, smarting, stinging, burning, irritated, bruised, wounded, injured.
7 *at the tender age of fifteen*: **young**, youthful; early; impressionable, inexperienced, immature, unsophisticated, unseasoned, juvenile, callow, green, raw; informal wet behind the ears.
▷ANTONYMS advanced.
8 *the issue of conscription was a particularly tender one*: **difficult**, delicate, tricky, awkward, problematic, troublesome, ticklish; controversial, emotive; informal sticky.
▷ANTONYMS uncontroversial, straightforward.

tender² **verb** **1** *she tendered her resignation*: **offer**, proffer, present, put forward, propose, suggest, advance, submit, set before someone, extend, give, render; hand in.
2 *firms of interior decorators have been tendering for the work*: **bid**, put in a bid, quote, give an estimate, propose a price.
▸ **noun** *six contractors were invited to submit tenders*: **bid**, offer, quotation, quote, estimate, estimated price, price; proposal, submission.

tender-hearted **adjective** *a loyal and tender-hearted friend*: **kind**, kindly, kind-hearted, tender, caring, compassionate, sympathetic, warm, warm-hearted, feeling, gentle, mild, benevolent, generous, giving, humane; fond, loving, affectionate, sensitive, soft-hearted, sentimental, soft-centred; informal touchy-feely.
▷ANTONYMS hard-hearted, callous, unfeeling.

tenderness **noun** **1** *I felt an enormous tenderness for her*: **affection**, fondness, love, devotion, loving kindness, emotion, sentiment, sentimentality, emotionalism.
▷ANTONYMS dislike.
2 *with unexpected tenderness, Sven told her what had happened*: **kindness**, kindliness, kind-heartedness, soft-heartedness, softness, tender-heartedness, compassion, compassionateness, care, concern, sympathy, warmth, warm-heartedness, fatherliness, motherliness, gentleness, benevolence, generosity, humaneness.
▷ANTONYMS callousness.
3 *meat of great flavour and tenderness*: **succulence**, juiciness, softness.
▷ANTONYMS toughness.
4 *symptoms include abdominal tenderness and a high temperature*: **sensitivity to pain**, soreness, painfulness, inflammation, rawness; ache, aching, smarting, throbbing, irritation, bruising.

tenet **noun** *recycling is a core tenet of the environmental faith*: **principle**, belief, doctrine, precept, creed, credo, article of faith, dogma, canon, rule; theory, component of a theory, thesis, conviction, persuasion, idea, view, opinion, position, hypothesis, postulation, presumption; (**tenets**) ideology, code of belief, teaching(s).

tenor **noun** **1** *the general tenor of his speech*: **sense**, meaning, theme, drift, thread, tendency, import, purport, intent, intention, burden, thrust, significance, message; gist, essence, substance, spirit; mood, character, vein, flavour; archaic strain.
2 *the even tenor of life in the village*: **course**, direction, movement, drift, current, trend.

tense **adjective** **1** *the tense muscles of his neck*: **taut**, stretched tight, tight, rigid, stretched, strained, stiff.
▷ANTONYMS slack, loose.
2 *by five o'clock, Loretta was feeling tense and irritable*: **anxious**, **nervous**, on edge, edgy, strained, stressed, under a strain, under pressure, agitated, ill at ease, unrelaxed, in a state of nerves, in a state of agitation, fretful, uneasy, restless, worked up, keyed up, overwrought, highly strung, wrought up, strung out, jumpy, on tenterhooks, on pins and needles, with one's stomach in knots, fidgety, worried, apprehensive, upset, disturbed, panicky; Brit. nervy; informal with butterflies in one's stomach, a bundle of nerves, jittery, twitchy, in a state, uptight, wired, het up, stressed out, white-knuckled; Brit. informal strung up, windy; N. Amer. informal spooky, squirrelly; Austral./NZ informal toey; dated overstrung.
▷ANTONYMS calm, cool, relaxed.
3 *it was a tense moment for everyone*: **nerve-racking**, stressful, anxious, worrying, fraught, charged, strained, nail-biting, worrisome, difficult, uneasy, uncomfortable; exciting, cliffhanging, knife-edge, dramatic, volatile, explosive; informal hairy, anxious-making, white-knuckle.
▷ANTONYMS relaxing.
▸ **verb** *Hebden tensed his cheek muscles*: **tighten**, tauten, tense up, flex, contract, brace, stiffen; screw up, knot, strain, stretch; N. Amer. squinch up.
▷ANTONYMS relax.

> *Word toolkit* **tense**
>
> See **apprehensive**.

tension **noun** **1** *the tension of the rope*: **tightness**, tautness, tenseness, rigidity; pull, traction, stress, strain, straining, stretching; rare tensity.
▷ANTONYMS slackness, looseness.

2 *the tension was unbearable*: **mental/emotional strain**, stress, anxiety, anxiousness, pressure; worry, apprehensiveness, apprehension, agitation, nerves, nervousness, jumpiness, edginess, restlessness; suspense, uncertainty, anticipation, excitement; informal butterflies (in one's stomach), collywobbles, jitteriness, twitchiness, the jitters, the willies, the heebie-jeebies, the shakes, the jumps, jim-jams, the yips; Brit. informal the (screaming) abdabs/habdabs; Austral. rhyming slang Joe Blakes.
▷ANTONYMS relaxation.
3 *the coup followed months of tension between the military and the government*: **strained relations**, strain, unease; ill feeling, friction, antagonism, antipathy, hostility, enmity.
▷ANTONYMS harmony.

tentative adjective 1 *a tentative arrangement | this can only be a tentative conclusion*: **provisional**, unconfirmed, unsettled, indefinite, pencilled in, preliminary, to be confirmed, TBC, subject to confirmation; **speculative**, conjectural, untried, unproven, unsubstantiated; exploratory, experimental, trial, test, pilot; rare provisory, provisionary.
▷ANTONYMS definite.
2 *he eventually tried a few tentative steps around his hospital room*: **hesitant**, uncertain, cautious, unconfident, timid, hesitating, faltering, shaky, unsteady, halting; wavering, unsure, doubtful, diffident; informal iffy.
▷ANTONYMS confident.

tenterhooks plural noun
□ **on tenterhooks** *she had been on tenterhooks all night, waiting for Joe to return*: **in suspense**, waiting with bated breath; **anxious**, nervous, nervy, apprehensive, worried, worried sick, on edge, edgy, tense, strained, stressed, agitated, in a state of nerves, in a state of agitation, fretful, restless, worked up, keyed up, overwrought, wrought up, strung out, jumpy, with one's stomach in knots, with one's heart in one's mouth, like a cat on a hot tin roof, fidgety, on pins and needles; informal with butterflies in one's stomach, jittery, twitchy, in a state, uptight, wired, in a stew, in a dither, all of a dither, in a sweat, in a flap, in a tizz/tizzy, all of a lather, het up, in a twitter, waiting for the axe to fall; Brit. informal strung up, windy, having kittens, all of a doodah; N. Amer. informal spooky, squirrelly, in a twit; Austral./NZ informal toey; Brit. vulgar slang shitting bricks, bricking oneself; dated overstrung.

tenuous adjective 1 *evidence that greenhouse warming had started was at best tenuous*: **slight**, insubstantial, flimsy, negligible, weak, fragile, shaky, sketchy, doubtful, dubious, questionable, suspect; vague, nebulous, hazy, unspecific, indefinite, indeterminate.
▷ANTONYMS convincing, substantial, strong.
2 *a tenuous thread*: **fine**, thin, slender, attenuated, delicate, gossamer, fragile.
▷ANTONYMS thick.

tenure noun 1 *they have a right to a fair rent and security of tenure*: **tenancy**, occupancy, holding, occupation, residence; possession, title, ownership, proprietorship.
2 *his tenure as Secretary of State for Industry*: **incumbency**, **term of office**, term, period of/in office, time, time in office.

tepid adjective 1 *tepid water*: **lukewarm**, warmish, slightly warm; at room temperature; French chambré.
▷ANTONYMS hot; cold.
2 *his speech received a tepid response*: **unenthusiastic**, apathetic, half-hearted, indifferent, cool, lukewarm, uninterested, unconcerned, offhand, perfunctory, desultory, limp, listless; informal unenthused; Brit. vulgar slang half-arsed.
▷ANTONYMS enthusiastic, passionate.

term noun 1 *a dictionary of current scientific and technical terms*: **word**, expression, phrase, turn of phrase, idiom, locution; name, title, denomination, designation, label; formal appellation.
2 (**terms**) *a protest in the strongest possible terms*: **language**, mode of expression, manner of speaking, phraseology, terminology; words, phrases, expressions.
3 (**terms**) *a legal document which sets out the terms of the contract*: **conditions**, stipulations, specifications, provisions, provisos; restrictions, qualifications; particulars, details, points, clauses, articles.
4 (**terms**) *a policy offering the same cover and benefits on more favourable terms*: **rates**, prices, charges, costs, fees; tariff.
5 *the President is elected for a single four-year term*: **period**, period of time, time, length of time, spell, stint, duration; interval, stretch, run, phase; term of office, period of office, incumbency, administration.
6 *the summer term*: **session**; N. Amer. semester, trimester, quarter.
□ **come to terms** 1 *Charles V and Charles of Navarre came to terms*: **reach (an) agreement/understanding**, come to an agreement/understanding, make a deal, reach a compromise, meet each other halfway, establish a middle ground, be reconciled. 2 *Philippa eventually* ***came to terms with*** *her situation*: **accept**, come to accept, become reconciled to, reconcile oneself to, reach an acceptance (of), get used to, become accustomed to, adjust to, accommodate oneself to, acclimatize oneself to; learn to live with, become resigned to, make the best of; face up to.
□ **in terms of** *replacing the printers is difficult to justify in terms of cost*: **with regard to**, as regards, regarding, concerning, as to, in respect of, with reference to, in the matter of, in connection with.
□ **on ... terms** *the two families were on friendly terms*: **in a ... relationship (with)**, having ... relations (with), on a ... footing (with).
▶verb *he has been termed the father of modern theology*: **call**, name, entitle, title, style, designate, describe as, dub, label, tag; nickname; rare denominate.

terminal adjective 1 *a terminal illness*: **incurable**, untreatable, inoperable; **fatal**, mortal, deadly, lethal, killing.
2 *terminal patients*: **dying**, near death; incurable.
3 *the terminal tip of the probe*: **end**, extreme.
▷ANTONYMS initial, first.
4 *a terminal bonus may be payable when a policy matures*: **final**, last, concluding, closing, ultimate, finishing, terminating.
5 informal *you're making a terminal ass of yourself*: **complete**, utter, absolute, total, real, thorough, out-and-out, downright, consummate, perfect, veritable; Brit. informal right, proper; Austral./NZ informal fair; archaic arrant.
▶noun 1 *a railway terminal*: **station**, last stop, end of the line; depot; Brit. terminus.
2 *the screen of a computer terminal*: **workstation**, VDU, visual display unit, PC, input/output device; monitor, console, keyboard.

terminate verb 1 *treatment was terminated*: **bring to an end**, end, bring to a close/conclusion, close, conclude, finish, stop, put an end to, put a stop to, wind up, discontinue, break off, cease, cut short, bring to an untimely end, abort; axe; informal pull the plug on.
▷ANTONYMS begin, start, commence, continue.
2 *the train will terminate in Stratford*: **end its journey**, finish up, stop.
3 *the consultant assumed I would terminate the pregnancy*: **abort**, end.

termination noun 1 *the termination of a contract*: **ending**, end, closing, close, conclusion, finish, stop, stopping, stoppage, winding up, discontinuance, discontinuation, breaking off, cessation, cutting short; cancellation, dissolution; Law cesser, lapse; informal wind-up.
▷ANTONYMS start, beginning.
2 *she never considered having a termination*: **abortion**; rare feticide.

terminology noun *medical terminology*: **phraseology**, terms, expressions, words, language, parlance, vocabulary, nomenclature; usage, idiom, choice of words; jargon, cant, argot, patter, patois; French façon de parler; informal lingo, -speak, vernacular; rare idiolect.

terminus noun Brit. *the bus terminus*: **station**, last stop, end of the line, terminal; depot, garage.

terrain noun *the rough, rocky terrain*: **land**, ground, territory; topography, landscape, countryside, country.

terrestrial adjective *the idea of terrestrial events being driven by asteroids seems like science fiction*: **earthly**, worldly, mundane, earthbound; rare tellurian, terrene, sublunary, subastral.
▷ANTONYMS cosmic, heavenly.

terrible adjective 1 *a terrible crime | he suffered terrible head injuries*: **dreadful**, awful, appalling, horrific, horrifying, horrible, horrendous, atrocious, abominable, abhorrent, frightful, fearful, shocking, hideous, ghastly, grim, dire, hateful, unspeakable, gruesome, monstrous, sickening, heinous, vile; serious, grave, acute, desperate, grievous, distressing, lamentable; rare egregious.
▷ANTONYMS minor, negligible, insignificant.
2 *there was a terrible smell in the room*: **nasty**, disgusting, very unpleasant, awful, dreadful, ghastly, horrid, horrible, vile, foul, abominable, frightful, loathsome, revolting, repulsive, odious, sickening, nauseating, nauseous, repellent, repugnant, horrendous, hideous, appalling, offensive, objectionable, obnoxious; noxious, evil-smelling, foul-smelling, smelly, stinking, rank, rancid, fetid, malodorous, acrid; informal gruesome, putrid, diabolical, yucky, sick-making, God-awful, gross, from hell, icky, stinky; Brit. informal beastly, grotty, whiffy, pongy, niffy; N. Amer. informal hellacious, lousy, skanky, funky; Austral. informal on the nose; literary noisome, mephitic; archaic disgustful, loathly; rare miasmal, olid.
▷ANTONYMS nice, delightful, lovely, pleasant.
3 *Blake was in terrible pain*: **severe**, extreme, intense, excruciating, agonizing, unbearable, intolerable, unendurable, insufferable.
▷ANTONYMS slight.
4 *that's a terrible thing to say about anyone*: **unkind**, nasty, unpleasant, foul, obnoxious, vile, contemptible, despicable, wretched, shabby; spiteful, mean, malicious, poisonous, mean-spirited, cruel, hateful, hurtful; unfair, uncharitable, uncalled for, below the belt, unacceptable, unwarranted; informal dirty, filthy, dirty rotten, low-down, beastly, off; Brit. informal out of order; vulgar slang shitty.
▷ANTONYMS kind, nice.
5 *I'm terrible at maths | Tom was a terrible father*: **very bad**, dreadful, awful, frightful, atrocious, hopeless, poor, inadequate, inferior, unsatisfactory, laughable, substandard; informal crummy, pathetic, pitiful, useless, lousy, appalling, abysmal, dire; Brit. informal duff, chronic, poxy, rubbish, pants, a load of pants; N. Amer. vulgar slang chickenshit.
▷ANTONYMS brilliant.
6 informal *you're a terrible flirt | the place was in a terrible mess*: **incorrigible**, outrageous, great, extreme; real, awful, dreadful, frightful, shocking;

informal impossible, fearful; Brit. informal right, proper.
▷ANTONYMS a bit of a.
7 *I feel terrible—I've been in bed all day*: **ill**, unwell, poorly, bad, indisposed, sick, queasy, nauseous, nauseated, peaky, liverish, out of sorts, green about the gills; faint, dizzy, giddy, light-headed; Brit. off, off colour; informal under the weather, rough, lousy, awful, dreadful, crummy; Brit. informal grotty, ropy; Scottish informal wabbit, peely-wally; Austral./NZ informal crook; dated queer, seedy; rare peaked, peakish.
▷ANTONYMS well.
8 *he still feels terrible about what he did to John*: **guilty**, conscience-stricken, remorseful, guilt-ridden, ashamed, chastened, contrite, sorry, full of regret, regretful, repentant, penitent, shamefaced, self-reproachful, apologetic.
▷ANTONYMS untroubled, easy in one's mind.

terribly adverb **1** *she's terribly upset | that's terribly good of you*: **very, extremely**, awfully, dreadfully, really, frightfully, exceptionally, exceedingly, immensely, thoroughly, uncommonly, remarkably, eminently, extraordinarily, incredibly, most, positively, decidedly, downright; heartily, profoundly; Scottish unco; N. Amer. quite; informal terrifically, tremendously, fearfully, desperately, seriously, devilishly, hugely, fantastically, madly, ultra, too ... for words, mucho, mega, majorly, oh-so, stinking; Brit. informal jolly, ever so, dead, well, fair, right; N. Amer. informal real, mighty, awful, plumb, powerful, way, bitching; S. African informal lekker; informal, dated devilish; archaic exceeding, sore.
2 *he played terribly*: **very badly**, atrociously, awfully, dismally, dreadfully, appallingly, execrably, poorly, incompetently, inexpertly; informal abysmally, pitifully, crummily, diabolically, rottenly; rare egregiously.
3 *I shall miss you terribly*: **very much**, greatly, a great deal, a lot, mightily; informal loads.

terrific adjective **1** *there was a terrific bang*: **tremendous**, huge, massive, gigantic, colossal, mighty, great, very great, very big, prodigious, formidable, sizeable, considerable; intense, extreme, extraordinary, excessive, inordinate; informal mega, whopping, whopping great, humongous; Brit. informal whacking, whacking great, ginormous.
▷ANTONYMS slight, imperceptible.
2 informal *a terrific game of top-quality football | you look terrific!* **excellent, wonderful**, marvellous, magnificent, superb, splendid, glorious, sublime, lovely, delightful, first-class, first-rate, outstanding; consummate, perfect; informal super, great, smashing, amazing, fantastic, tremendous, phenomenal, sensational, incredible, heavenly, divine, stellar, gorgeous, dreamy, grand, fabulous, fab, fabby, fantabulous, brill, awesome, magic, ace, crack, cool, mean, bad, wicked, mega, crucial, mind-blowing, far out, A1, sound, out of this world, marvy, spanking; Brit. informal brilliant, brill, bosting; N. Amer. informal peachy, dandy, jim-dandy, neat, badass, boss, radical, rad, boffo, bully, bitching, bodacious, crackerjack; Austral./NZ informal beaut, bonzer; S. African informal kif, lank; black English dope, def, phat; informal, dated groovy; Brit. informal, dated capital, champion, wizard, corking, cracking, ripping, spiffing, top-hole, topping, beezer; N. Amer. informal, dated swell, keen; vulgar slang shit-hot; archaic goodly.
▷ANTONYMS dreadful, awful, horrible.
3 archaic *terrific scenes of slaughter and destruction*. See **dreadful** (sense 1).

terrified adjective *it was the worst moment of my life—I was absolutely terrified*: **petrified**, scared stiff, frightened/scared out of one's wits, scared witless, frightened/scared to death, terror-stricken, terror-struck, horror-stricken, horror-struck, paralysed with fear, horrified, panic-stricken, with one's heart in one's mouth, shaking in one's shoes, shaking like a leaf, frantic, hysterical, beside oneself; scared, frightened, afraid; Scottish feart; informal in a cold sweat, in a (blue) funk; Brit. informal funky, windy; N. Amer. informal spooked; vulgar slang scared shitless, shit scared, shitting bricks, bricking oneself; dialect frit; archaic afeared, affrighted.
▷ANTONYMS confident, unafraid.

terrify verb *the unspoken threat terrified her*: **petrify**, scare stiff, scare/frighten someone out of their wits, scare witless, scare/frighten to death, scare/frighten the living daylights out of, scare/frighten the life out of, scare the hell out of, strike terror into, fill with fear, put the fear of God into, make someone's blood run cold, chill someone's blood, paralyse with fear, make someone's flesh creep, give someone goose pimples, make someone's hair stand on end, send into a cold sweat, make someone shake in their shoes; horrify, alarm, appal, panic, throw into a panic; frighten, scare; informal scare the pants off, make someone's hair curl, scarify; Brit. informal throw into a blue funk; Irish informal scare the bejesus out of; N. Amer. informal spook; vulgar slang scare shitless, scare the shit out of; archaic affright.

territory noun **1** *a tiny British territory on the outskirts of eastern Polynesia*: **area of land**, area, region, enclave; country, state, land, dependency, colony, dominion, protectorate, fief, possession, holding; domain, county, district, zone, sector, quarter; soil; archaic demesne.
2 *mountainous territory*: **terrain**, land, tract of land, ground, countryside.
3 *practically everyone else has been muscling in on my territory lately*: **domain**, area of concern/interest/knowledge, province, department, field, preserve, sphere, arena, realm, world; informal bailiwick, turf.
4 *Sheffield was his territory*: **sphere of operations**, area, section, stamping ground; haunts, purlieus; informal turf; Brit. informal patch, manor.

terror noun **1** *Ruth screamed in terror*: **extreme fear**, dread, horror, fear and trembling, fright, trepidation, alarm, panic, shock; informal funk.
2 *she plunged into everyday activity to save herself from the terrors of her own mind*: **demon**, fiend, devil, monster; horror, nightmare.
3 informal *he turned out to be a right little terror*: **rascal**, devil, imp, monkey, wretch, scamp, mischief-maker, troublemaker; informal horror, holy terror; Brit. informal perisher; Irish informal spalpeen; N. English informal tyke, scally; N. Amer. informal varmint, hellion; archaic scapegrace, rapscallion.

terrorist noun **bomber**, arsonist, incendiary; gunman, assassin, desperado; hijacker; revolutionary, radical, guerrilla, urban guerrilla, subversive, anarchist, freedom fighter; rare insurrectionist, insurrectionary.

terrorize verb *families terrorized by racist thugs*: **strike terror in/into**, fill with terror, scare, frighten, terrify, petrify; **persecute**, victimize, torment, tyrannize; **intimidate**, menace, threaten, oppress, bully, browbeat, cow; Brit. informal put the frighteners on, make it/things hot for someone; N. Amer. informal mau-mau.

terse adjective *he issued a terse warning*: **curt**, brusque, abrupt, clipped, blunt, gruff, short, brief, concise, succinct, to the point, compact, crisp, pithy, incisive, short and sweet, economical, laconic, epigrammatic, summary, condensed.
▷ANTONYMS long-winded, verbose, rambling; polite.

> *Choose the right word* **terse, brusque, abrupt, curt**
>
> See **brusque**.

test noun **1** *we'll be conducting a series of scientific tests*: **trial**, experiment, pilot study, try-out; check, examination, assessment, evaluation, appraisal, investigation, inspection, analysis, scrutiny, scrutinization, study, probe, exploration; screening; audition, screen test; technical assay.
2 *candidates may be required to take a test*: **exam**, examination; paper, set of questions; N. Amer. quiz.
3 *the test of a good sparkling wine is the length of time the bubbles last in the glass*: **criterion**, proof, indication, yardstick, touchstone, standard, measure, litmus test, barometer.
▶verb **1** *during the summer, a small-scale prototype was tested | all donated blood is tested for antibodies*: **try out**, trial, carry out trials on, put to the test, put through its paces, experiment with, pilot; **check**, examine, assess, evaluate, appraise, investigate, analyse, scrutinize, study, probe, explore; sample; screen; technical assay.
2 *such behaviour would severely test any marriage*: **put a strain on**, strain, tax, try, make demands on, stretch; drain, sap; challenge.

testament noun *it is a testament to a decade of technological achievement*: **testimony**, witness, evidence, proof, attestation; demonstration, indication, exemplification; **monument**, tribute.

testicles plural noun **gonads**; N. Amer. informal cojones; vulgar slang **balls**, knackers, nuts, rocks; Brit. vulgar slang bollocks, goolies.

testify verb **1** *you may be required to testify in court*: **give evidence**, bear witness, be a witness, give one's testimony, attest; technical make a deposition; Scottish archaic depone.
2 *he testified that he had been threatened by a fellow officer*: **attest**, swear, state on oath, state, declare, assert, affirm, avow, aver, certify; allege, profess, submit, claim; technical depose; rare asseverate.
▷ANTONYMS deny.
3 *the exhibits **testify to** the talents and versatility of the local sculptors*: **be evidence/proof of**, attest to, confirm, evidence, prove, corroborate, substantiate, bear out; show, demonstrate, witness to, establish, indicate, reveal, bespeak; vouch for.
▷ANTONYMS belie.

testimonial noun **1** *Sir Hans drafted a glowing testimonial for him*: **reference**, character reference, recommendation, letter of recommendation, commendation, endorsement, certificate of competence; dated character.
2 *in 1848 Airy received a testimonial from the Royal Astronomical Society*: **tribute**, presentation, gift, trophy; memento, souvenir.

testimony noun **1** *Smith was in court to hear her testimony*: **evidence**, sworn statement, attestation, affidavit; statement, declaration, assertion, affirmation, avowal, protestation; allegation, submission, claim; technical deposition; rare asseveration.
2 *the work is a testimony to his professional commitment*: **testament**, proof, evidence, attestation, witness; confirmation, verification, corroboration; demonstration, indication, manifestation.

testing adjective *it was a particularly testing time for the organization*: **difficult**, challenging, tough, hard; **stressful**, trying, wearing, taxing, demanding, exacting, onerous, arduous.
▷ANTONYMS easy.

testy adjective *he was testy, arrogant, and hard to get on with*: **bad-tempered**, grumpy, ill-tempered, ill-natured, ill-humoured, dyspeptic, irritable, tetchy, irascible, peevish, crotchety, cantankerous, cross, fractious, disagreeable, pettish, crabbed, crabby, waspish, prickly, peppery, impatient, touchy, scratchy, volatile, crusty, liverish, splenetic, short-tempered, hot-tempered,

quick-tempered, choleric; informal snappish, snappy, chippy, grouchy, cranky, on a short fuse; Brit. informal shirty, stroppy, narky, ratty, eggy, like a bear with a sore head; N. Amer. informal peckish, soreheaded; Austral./NZ informal snaky; informal, dated miffy.
▷ANTONYMS good-humoured.

tetchy adjective *he can be very tetchy first thing in the morning*: **irritable**, irascible, peevish, crotchety, cantankerous, cross, fractious, disagreeable, pettish, crabbed, crabby, waspish, prickly, testy, peppery, impatient, grumpy, bad-tempered, ill-tempered, ill-natured, ill-humoured, touchy, scratchy, volatile, crusty, dyspeptic, splenetic, liverish, short-tempered, hot-tempered, quick-tempered, choleric; informal snappish, snappy, chippy, grouchy, cranky, on a short fuse; Brit. informal shirty, narky, ratty, eggy, like a bear with a sore head; N. Amer. informal peckish, soreheaded; Austral./NZ informal snaky; informal, dated miffy.
▷ANTONYMS good-humoured.

tête-à-tête noun **conversation**, chat, cosy chat, talk, heart-to-heart, one-on-one, one-to-one; discussion, dialogue, duologue, consultation, colloquy, parley, powwow; informal confab, jaw, chit-chat, chinwag, gossip; Brit. informal natter; N. Amer. informal rap; formal confabulation.
▸ adverb *his business was conducted tête-à-tête*: **privately**, in private; face to face, heart-to-heart; secretly, in secret, confidentially; French à deux.

tether verb *the horse had been tethered to a post*: **tie**, tie up, hitch, rope, chain; fasten, secure; bind, fetter, shackle, restrain.
▷ANTONYMS unleash, release.
▸ noun **rope**, **chain**, cord, lead, leash; fetter, restraint; halter; archaic lyam.
□ **at the end of one's tether** *the poor man was clearly at the end of his tether*: **at one's wits' end**, desperate, not knowing which way to turn, unable to cope; N. Amer. at the end of one's rope.

text noun **1** *a text which explores pain and grief*: **written work**, book, work, printed work, narrative.
2 *the pictures are clear and relate well to the text*: **words**, wording; subject matter, content, contents, body, main body, main matter.
3 *he sent all enquirers the text of Sir Derek's speech*: **transcript**, script.
4 *academic texts*: **textbook**, book; set book, set text.
5 *the text is taken from the First Book of Samuel*: **passage**, extract, quotation, verse, line; reading, lesson.
6 *he took as his text the fact that Australia is a paradise*: **theme**, subject, topic, issue, point, motif; thesis, argument.

textile noun *hand-printed textiles*: **fabric**, cloth, material.

texture noun *the quality and texture of the fabric*: **feel**, touch; appearance, finish, surface, grain; quality, character; consistency; weave, nap.

thank verb **1** *the superintendent thanked him for his help*: **express (one's) gratitude to**, express one's thanks to, offer/extend thanks to, say thank you to, show appreciation to.
2 *you have only yourself to thank for the plight you are in*: **blame**, hold responsible.

thankful adjective **1** *Merrill closed the door, thankful that the evening was over*: **relieved**, pleased, glad, grateful.
▷ANTONYMS disappointed.
2 *he was really thankful to her for coming to his aid*: **grateful**, filled with gratitude, indebted, obliged, under an obligation, obligated, beholden.
▷ANTONYMS ungrateful.

> *Choose the right word* **thankful, grateful, appreciative**
>
> See **grateful**.

thankless adjective **1** *a thankless task*: **unappreciated**, unrecognized, unrewarded, unacknowledged; unenviable, difficult, unpleasant, unrewarding, unprofitable, profitless, useless, fruitless, vain, futile; archaic bootless.
▷ANTONYMS rewarding, worthwhile.
2 *her thankless children*: **ungrateful**, unappreciative, unthankful.
▷ANTONYMS grateful.

t

thanks plural noun *they expressed their thanks and wished her well*: **gratitude**, gratefulness, appreciation; acknowledgement, recognition, credit.
□ **thanks to** *thanks to foreign loans, the economy was showing signs of recovery*: **as a result of**, owing to, due to, because of, through, by reason of, as a consequence of, in consequence of, on account of, by virtue of, by dint of.
▸ exclamation *thanks for being so helpful*: **thank you**, many thanks, thanks very much, thanks a lot, thank you kindly, much obliged, much appreciated, bless you; informal cheers, thanks a million; Brit. informal ta.

thaw verb **1** *the ice was beginning to thaw*: **melt**, unfreeze, soften, liquefy, dissolve; N. Amer. unthaw.
▷ANTONYMS freeze, solidify.
2 *a frozen turkey may take up to two days to thaw*: **defrost**.
▷ANTONYMS freeze.
3 *since I've been here, he's begun to thaw*: **become friendlier**, become more genial, become more sociable, loosen up, relax, become more relaxed.

theatre noun **1** *there's a good play on at the theatre*: **playhouse**, auditorium, amphitheatre, hippodrome, coliseum.
2 (**the theatre**) *what made you want to go into the theatre?* **acting**, performing; **drama**, the dramatic arts, dramaturgy, the thespian art, stagecraft, theatricals, theatrics; **show business**, the stage; informal the boards, show biz; rare thespianism, histrionics.
3 *the lecture theatre*: **hall**, room, auditorium.
4 *over 200,000 American personnel were in the theatre of war by October*: **scene**, arena, field/sphere/place of action; setting, site.

theatrical adjective **1** *a theatrical career*: **stage**, dramatic, thespian, dramaturgical; **show-business**; informal showbiz; rare histrionic, theatric.
2 *Henry looked over his shoulder with theatrical caution*: **exaggerated**, ostentatious, actressy, stagy, showy, melodramatic, overacted, overdone, histrionic, affected, mannered, artificial, stilted, unreal, forced; informal hammy, ham, campy.
▷ANTONYMS natural, unaffected.

theft noun *he was convicted of theft*: **robbery**, stealing, thieving, larceny, thievery, robbing, pilfering, pilferage, purloining; shoplifting, burglary; raid, hold-up; appropriation, expropriation, misappropriation, embezzlement; in India dacoity; informal rip-off, smash and grab, snatch; N. Amer. informal heist, stick-up; rare peculation, defalcation.

> *Word links* **theft**
>
> **kleptomania** compulsive theft

theme noun **1** *a short speech on a theme of your choice*: **subject**, topic, subject matter; matter, issue, question, concern; idea, concept, thread, motif, keynote, message; thesis, argument, text; gist, essence, core, substance, burden, thrust.
2 *the first violin takes up the theme*: **melody**, tune, air, motif, leitmotif.
3 N. Amer. *students writing themes in French*: **essay**, composition, paper, dissertation.

> *Choose the right word* **theme, subject, topic**
>
> See **subject**.

themselves pronoun
□ **by themselves** See **by oneself** at **by**.

then adverb **1** *I was living in Cairo then*: **at that time**, at that point, in those days; at that point in time, at that moment, on that occasion.
2 *she won the first and then the second game*: **next**, after that, afterwards, subsequently, later.
3 *I'm paid a generous salary, and then there's the money I make at the races*: **in addition**, also, besides, as well, additionally, on top of that, over and above that, moreover, furthermore, what's more, to boot; too.
4 *well, if that's what he wants, then he should leave*: **in that case**, that being the case, that being so, under those circumstances, it follows that.

theological adjective *his theological writings*: **religious**, scriptural, ecclesiastical, doctrinal; divine, holy; rare hierological.

theorem noun **proposition**, hypothesis, postulate, thesis, assumption, deduction, statement; rule, formula, principle.

theoretical adjective **1** *theoretical physics*: **not practical**, conceptual, abstract, pure.
▷ANTONYMS practical, applied.
2 *a theoretical possibility*: **hypothetical**, conjectural, academic, suppositional, speculative, notional, postulatory, conjectured, imagined, assumed, presumed, untested, unproven, unsubstantiated; rare supposititious, suppositive, ideational.
▷ANTONYMS concrete, actual, real.

theorize verb *Darwin theorized that the atolls marked the sites of vanished volcanoes*: **speculate**, conjecture, hypothesize, take as a hypothesis, postulate, form/formulate a theory, propose, posit, surmise, suppose, guess; philosophize; rare hypothecate.

theory noun **1** *I reckon that confirms my theory*: **hypothesis**, thesis, conjecture, supposition, speculation, postulation, postulate, proposition, premise, surmise, assumption, presumption, presupposition, notion, guess, hunch, feeling, suspicion; opinion, view, belief, thinking, thought(s), judgement, contention.
2 *the theory of quantum physics*: **principles**, ideas, concepts; principled explanations; laws; philosophy, ideology, system of ideas, science.
□ **in theory** *in theory this method is ideal—in practice it is unrealistic*: **in principle**, on paper, in the abstract, all things being equal, in an ideal world; hypothetically; French en principe.
▷ANTONYMS in practice, in reality.

therapeutic adjective *the therapeutic effects of acupuncture*: **healing**, curative, curing, remedial, medicinal, restorative, health-giving, tonic, sanative, reparative, corrective, ameliorative, beneficial, good, salubrious, salutary; technical analeptic; rare iatric.
▷ANTONYMS harmful, detrimental.

therapist noun **psychologist**, psychotherapist, analyst, psychoanalyst, psychiatrist, mind doctor, head doctor; counsellor; healer; N. Amer. alienist; informal shrink, trick cyclist, head shrinker.

therapy noun **1** *a wide range of complementary therapies*: **treatment**, remedy, cure, remedial treatment, method of healing.
2 *he's currently in therapy*: **psychotherapy**, psychoanalysis, analysis.

thereabouts adverb **1** *all the land thereabouts was once in possession of the Vachel family*: **near there**, around there, about there.
2 *they sold it for five million or thereabouts*: **approximately (that number/quantity)**, or so, or something like that, give or take a few, plus or minus a few, give or take a bit, in round numbers, not far off; Brit. getting on for; Latin circa; N. Amer. informal in the ballpark of.

thereafter adverb *thereafter their fortunes suffered a steep decline*: **after that (time)**, following that, afterwards, subsequently, then, next.

therefore adverb *he was injured and therefore unable to play*: **for that reason**, **consequently**, so, as a result, as a consequence, hence, thus, accordingly, then, that being so, that being the case, on that account; Latin ergo; formal whence; archaic wherefore, thence.

thesaurus noun **wordfinder**, wordbook, synonym dictionary/lexicon; rare synonymy.

thesis noun **1** *the central thesis of his lecture*: **theory**, contention, argument, line of argument, proposal, proposition, premise, assumption, presumption, hypothesis, postulation, surmise, supposition; belief, idea, notion, opinion, view; theme, subject, topic, text, matter; theorem.
2 *a doctoral thesis*: **dissertation**, essay, paper, treatise, disquisition, composition, monograph, study, piece of writing; N. Amer. theme.

thick adjective **1** *the walls are five feet thick*: **in extent/diameter**, across, wide, broad, deep.
2 *his short, thick legs*: **stocky**, sturdy, chunky, dumpy, hefty, thickset, beefy, meaty, broad, large, big, bulky, solid, substantial; fat, stout, plump.
▸ANTONYMS thin, slender.
3 *a thick Aran sweater*: **chunky**, bulky, heavy, cable-knit, heavyweight; woollen, woolly.
▸ANTONYMS thin, light, lightweight.
4 *the station was thick with people*: **crowded**, filled, packed, teeming, seething, swarming, crawling, crammed, thronged, bursting at the seams, solid, overflowing, choked, jammed, congested; covered; **full of**, cram-full of, overrun by, abounding in; informal jam-packed, chock-a-block, stuffed, chock-full of; Austral./NZ informal chocker; rare pullulating.
5 *the thick summer vegetation*: **plentiful**, abundant, profuse, luxuriant, bushy, rich, riotous, exuberant; rank, rampant; **dense**, close-packed, concentrated, crowded, condensed, compact, impenetrable, impassable; serried; informal jungly.
▸ANTONYMS meagre, sparse.
6 *a thick paste*: **semi-solid**, firm, stiff, stiffened, heavy; clotted, coagulated, viscid, viscous, gelatinous, mucilaginous, ropy; concentrated; rare inspissated, viscoid.
▸ANTONYMS runny.
7 *a motorway pile-up in thick fog*: **dense**, heavy, opaque, impenetrable, soupy, murky, smoggy.
8 informal *he's a bit thick*. See **stupid** (sense 1).
9 *Guy's voice was thick with desire*: **husky**, hoarse, throaty, guttural, gravelly, rough, raspy, rasping, croaky, croaking; indistinct, muffled.
▸ANTONYMS clear, shrill.
10 *a thick Scottish accent*: **obvious**, pronounced, marked, broad, strong, rich, decided, distinct, conspicuous, noticeable, identifiable.
▸ANTONYMS faint, vague.
11 *she's very thick with him*: **friendly**, intimate, familiar, on friendly/good terms, on the best of terms, hand in glove; close to, devoted to, inseparable from; informal pally, palsy-walsy, chummy, matey, buddy-buddy, as thick as thieves, well in.
▸ANTONYMS unfriendly.
□ **a bit thick** Brit. informal *I thought this was a bit thick and tried to defend myself*: **unreasonable**, unfair, unjust, unjustified, uncalled for, unwarranted, unnecessary, excessive; informal below the belt, a bit much, off; Brit. informal out of order; Austral./NZ informal over the fence.
▸ noun *in the thick of the crisis*: **midst**, centre, hub, middle, core, heart; focus.

thicken verb **1** *stir over a gentle heat until the mixture thickens*: **become thick/thicker**, stiffen, become firmer; condense, become more concentrated; solidify, set, gel, congeal, clot, coagulate, cake; rare inspissate, gelatinize.
2 *the plot thickened*: **become more complicated**, become more involved, become more intricate, become more mysterious, deepen.

thicket noun **copse**, coppice, dense growth, grove, brake, covert, tangle, clump; wood; Brit. spinney; archaic hurst.

thickhead noun informal *this is no book for thickheads*. See **fool**.

thickheaded adjective informal *you thickheaded moron!* See **stupid**.

thickness noun **1** *the gateway is several feet in thickness*: **width**, breadth, depth, diameter, extent.
2 *the immense thickness of the walls*: **breadth**, broadness, width, wideness, largeness, bigness, bulkiness, solidness.
▸ANTONYMS thinness.
3 *several thicknesses of limestone*: **layer**, stratum, stratification, seam, vein, band; sheet, film, lamina; ply; coat, coating.
4 *the thickness of the fog*: **density**, denseness, heaviness, opacity, opaqueness, impenetrability, soupiness, murkiness.
5 *Cara could tell by the thickness of Susan's voice that she had been crying*: **huskiness**, hoarseness, throatiness, gravelliness, roughness, raspiness, croakiness, indistinctness.

thickset adjective *a thickset man with a florid complexion*: **heavily built**, stocky, bull-necked, sturdy, sturdily built, well built, chunky, burly, strapping, brawny, muscular, solid, heavy, hefty, beefy, meaty; cobby; Austral./NZ nuggety; technical mesomorphic, pyknic; informal hulking; archaic squabby.
▸ANTONYMS slight, lanky.

thick-skinned adjective *I suppose you have to be pretty thick-skinned to be an MP*: **tough**, impervious, unsusceptible, invulnerable, armour-plated, with a hide like an elephant, hardened, case-hardened, insensitive, unfeeling, uncaring; obtuse, stolid; informal hard-boiled; rare pachydermatous.
▸ANTONYMS sensitive, touchy, thin-skinned.

thief noun **robber**, burglar, housebreaker, cat burglar, shoplifter, pickpocket, sneak thief, mugger, larcenist, stealer, pilferer, poacher; embezzler, swindler; criminal, villain; kleptomaniac; raider, looter, plunderer, pillager, marauder; bandit, brigand, pirate, highwayman; Indian dacoit; informal crook, cracksman, steamer; N. Amer. informal yegg, second-story man/worker; W. Indian informal tief; Brit. rhyming slang tea leaf; archaic cutpurse, pickpurse, footpad, lurcher; rare peculator, defalcator.

thieve verb *he claimed it was the first time he had thieved anything*. See **steal** (sense 1 of the verb).

thievery noun See **thieving**.

thieving noun *some are drawn into a life of crime and petty thieving*: **theft**, **stealing**, thievery, robbery, larceny, pilfering, pilferage; burglary, shoplifting, looting; misappropriation, expropriation, embezzlement; rare peculation, defalcation.
▸ adjective *Harry was a thieving, foul-mouthed old man*: **light-fingered**, thievish, larcenous; dishonest; informal sticky-fingered, crooked, bent; rare furacious, kleptic, theftuous.
▸ANTONYMS honest.

thimbleful noun *a thimbleful of brandy*: **bit**, spot, dram, nip, drop, splash; little, some, small amount; Scottish informal scoosh; rare toothful.

thin adjective **1** *a thin white line*: **narrow**, fine, pencil-thin, thread-like, attenuated; rare attenuate.
▸ANTONYMS thick, broad.
2 *thin, crisp pancakes*: **wafer-thin**, paper-thin, papery.
▸ANTONYMS thick.
3 *the thin cotton of her nightdress*: **lightweight**, light, fine, delicate, floaty, flimsy, diaphanous, gossamer, insubstantial; sheer, gauzy, filmy, chiffony, transparent, see-through, translucent.
▸ANTONYMS heavy, thick.
4 *a tall, thin woman dressed all in black*: **slim**, lean, slender, rangy, willowy, svelte, sylphlike, spare, slight; **skinny**, underweight, scrawny, scraggy, bony, angular, raw-boned, hollow-cheeked, gaunt, as thin as a rake, as thin as a reed, like a matchstick, stick-like, size-zero, skin-and-bones, emaciated, skeletal, cadaverous, like a skeleton, wasted, pinched, undernourished, underfed; lanky, spindly, stringy, gangly, gangling, reedy, weedy; informal looking like a bag of bones, anorexic, anorectic; dated spindle-shanked; rare gracile, starveling, macilent.
▸ANTONYMS fat, plump, overweight.
5 *he ran a hand over his thin grey hair*: **sparse**, scanty, wispy, thinning.
▸ANTONYMS abundant, thick.
6 *attendance on the Conservative back benches was thin to say the least*: **meagre**, paltry, poor, inadequate, insufficient, sparse, scanty, scattered.
7 *a bowl of thin soup*: **watery**, watered down, weak, dilute, diluted, thinned down; runny, sloppy; S. African slap.
▸ANTONYMS thick.
8 *her thin voice trailed off*: **weak**, faint, feeble, small, soft, low; reedy, high-pitched.
▸ANTONYMS strong, loud.
9 *the thin cold air of the mountains*: **rarefied**.
10 *the plot is very thin*: **insubstantial**, flimsy, slight, feeble, lame, poor, weak, shallow, tenuous, threadbare, inadequate, insufficient; **unconvincing**, unbelievable, implausible.
▸ANTONYMS meaty, convincing.
□ **thin on the ground** *breathtaking visual moments are all too thin on the ground*: **rare**, few and far between, scarce, seldom seen/found; uncommon, unusual, infrequent; Brit. out of the common.
▸ verb **1** *some paint must be thinned down before use*: **dilute**, water down, weaken.
2 *the crowds were beginning to thin out*: **become less dense/numerous**, decrease, diminish, dwindle, lessen, become less in number; disperse,

t

dissipate, scatter.
3 *a beautiful shrub which becomes rather dense if not* ***thinned out*** *after flowering*: **prune**, cut back, trim; technical single.

Word toolkit

thin	lean	gaunt
layer	meat	face
line	body	figure
filament	muscle	appearance
slice	beef	features
coating	tissue	cheeks
crust	protein	eyes
blanket	physique	shadow

thing noun **1** *the room was full of strange things*: **object**, article, item, artefact, commodity; device, gadget, contrivance, instrument, utensil, tool, implement; entity, body; informal whatsit, what-d'you-call-it, what's-its-name, what's-it, whatchamacallit, thingummy, thingy, thingamabob, thingamajig, oojamaflip, oojah, gizmo; Brit. informal doodah, doobry, gubbins; N. Amer. informal doodad, doohickey, doojigger, dingus.
2 (**one's things**) *I'll come back tomorrow to collect my things*: **belongings**, possessions, stuff, property, worldly goods, goods, personal effects, effects, paraphernalia, impedimenta, bits and pieces, bits and bobs; luggage, baggage, bags, bags and baggage, chattels, movables, valuables; **clothes**, garments; Law goods and chattels; informal gear, junk, togs, garms, dunnage, traps; Brit. informal clobber; S. African informal trek; vulgar slang shit, crap.
3 (**things**) *her father's gardening things*: **equipment**, apparatus, gear, kit, tackle, stuff; implements, tools, utensils; accoutrements.
4 *I've got several things to do this morning | his asthma stops him from doing things like swimming and running*: **activity**; act, action, deed, undertaking, exploit, feat; task, job, chore, piece of business.
5 *I've got other things on my mind just now*: **thought**, notion, idea, concept, conception; concern, matter, worry, preoccupation.
6 *I keep remembering things he said*: **remark**, statement, comment, utterance, observation, declaration, pronouncement.
7 *quite a few odd things had happened in the last few days*: **incident**, episode, event, happening, occurrence, eventuality, phenomenon.
8 (**things**) *how are things with you?* **matters**, affairs, circumstances, conditions, relations; state of affairs, situation, life.
9 *one of the things I like about you is your optimism*: **characteristic**, quality, attribute, property, trait, feature, point, aspect, facet, element.
10 *there's another thing you should know*: **fact**, piece of information, point, detail, particular, factor.
11 (**the thing**) *the thing is, I'm not sure if it's what I want*: **fact of the matter**, fact, point, issue, problem.
12 *you lucky thing!* **person**, soul, creature, wretch; informal devil, beggar, bunny, bastard; Brit. vulgar slang sod, bugger.
13 *Dora developed a thing about noise*: **phobia**, fear, horror, terror; dislike, aversion, hatred, detestation, loathing; obsession, fixation; complex, neurosis; informal hang-up, bee in one's bonnet.
14 *she had a* ***thing about*** *men who wore glasses*: **penchant for**, preference for, taste for, inclination for, partiality for, predilection for, soft spot for, weakness for, fancy for, fondness for, liking for, love for, passion for; **fetish**, obsession, fixation.
15 (**one's thing**) *books aren't really my thing*: **what one likes**, what interests one; informal one's cup of tea, one's bag, what turns one on, what floats one's boat.
16 (**the thing**) *cosmetic contact lenses are the thing on the catwalk*: **fashionable**, in fashion, in vogue, popular, all the rage; French le dernier cri; informal trendy, cool, in, the in thing, big, with it, hip, happening, now.

t

think verb **1** *do you think Isobel will come? | we thought he must have gone home*: **believe**, be of the opinion, have as one's opinion, be of the view, be under the impression; expect, imagine, anticipate; surmise, suppose, conjecture, guess, fancy; conclude, determine, reason; informal reckon; N. Amer. informal figure; formal opine; archaic ween.
2 *his family was* ***thought to be*** *enormously rich*: **deem**, judge, hold, reckon, consider, presume, estimate; regard as, view as.
3 *Jack thought for a moment*: **ponder**, reflect, deliberate, meditate, contemplate, muse, cogitate, ruminate, be lost in thought, be in a brown study, brood; concentrate, rack one's brains, cudgel one's brains; informal put on one's thinking cap, sleep on it; rare cerebrate.
▷**ANTONYMS** act, leap into action.
4 *he began* ***thinking about*** *a career in politics*: **consider**, contemplate, give thought to, entertain the idea of, deliberate about, weigh up, turn over in one's mind, mull over, chew over, reflect on, ruminate about, muse on; N. Amer. think on.
5 *she* ***thought of*** *all the visits she had made to her father*: **recall**, remember, recollect, call to mind, bring to mind, think back to, review.
6 *she forced herself to think of how he must be feeling*: **imagine**, picture, visualize, envisage, envision; dream about, fantasize about.
□ **think better of** *Lisa was about to say no, but then she thought better of it*: **have second thoughts about**, think twice about, think again about, change one's mind about; reconsider, decide against; informal get cold feet about.
□ **think nothing of** *he thinks nothing of getting up at two or three o'clock in the morning*: **consider normal**, consider usual, consider routine, take in one's stride, not think twice about; have no problems with, have no compunction about, have no hesitation about.
□ **think something over** *she went home to think over his offer*: **consider**, contemplate, deliberate about, weigh up, consider the pros and cons of, mull over, ponder, reflect on, muse on, ruminate on.
□ **think something up** *the idea was thought up by one of my technology students*: **devise**, dream up, come up with, invent, create, concoct, contrive, improvise, make up; hit on.
▸ **noun** *why don't you have a think about it?* **ponder**, muse, spell/period of deliberation/reflection/contemplation.

thinkable adjective *there is no thinkable alternative*: **conceivable**, feasible, reasonable, acceptable, imaginable, possible, within the bounds of possibility; likely; rare cogitable.
▷**ANTONYMS** unthinkable, inconceivable.

thinker noun *one of the most influential economic thinkers of the century*: **theorist**, theoretician, ideologist, philosopher, scholar, savant, sage, intellectual, intellect, mind, learned person, Solomon, Nestor; pundit, expert, mastermind; informal brain.
▷**ANTONYMS** doer, man/woman of action.

thinking adjective *he seemed a thinking man*: **intelligent**, sensible, reasonable, rational, reasoning; logical, analytical; thoughtful, reflective, meditative, contemplative, pensive, philosophical; rare ratiocinative.
▷**ANTONYMS** stupid, irrational.
▸ **noun** *the agency explained the thinking behind the campaign*: **reasoning**, idea(s), theory, thoughts, line of thought, philosophy, beliefs; conclusions; **opinion(s)**, view(s), point(s) of view, viewpoint(s), position, outlook, judgement, assessment, evaluation.

thin-skinned adjective *he was notoriously thin-skinned and disliked criticism*: **sensitive**, oversensitive, hypersensitive, supersensitive, easily offended, quick to take offence, easily hurt, easily upset, touchy, defensive; paranoid, neurotic; rare umbrageous.
▷**ANTONYMS** insensitive, unfeeling, thick-skinned.

third-rate adjective *a third-rate hotel*: **substandard**, below standard, bad, inferior, poor, poor-quality, low-grade; appalling, abysmal, atrocious, abject, awful, terrible, dismal, dreadful, execrable, frightful, miserable, wretched, lamentable, deplorable, pitiful, inadequate, insufficient, unsatisfactory, unacceptable; jerry-built, shoddy, tinny, trashy, rubbishy; Brit. cheap and nasty; N. Amer. cheapjack; informal lousy, not much cop, not up to much, crummy, bum, diabolical, rotten, sad, tatty, tacky, dire, tenth-rate; Brit. informal ropy, duff, naff, rubbish, pants, a load of pants, grotty; vulgar slang crap, crappy, shitty, chickenshit; rare direful, egregious.
▷**ANTONYMS** first-rate, excellent.

thirst noun **1** *I need a drink—I'm dying of thirst*: **thirstiness**, dryness; dehydration; technical polydipsia; archaic drought.
2 *his thirst for knowledge*: **craving**, strong desire, longing, yearning, avidity, hunger, voracity, keenness, eagerness, lust, appetite, passion, love; itch, fancy, hankering; informal yen; archaic appetency, appetence.
▷**ANTONYMS** aversion, distaste.
▸ **verb** *she* ***thirsted for*** *power*: **crave**, want, covet, desire, hunger for/after, lust for/after, hanker for/after, have one's heart set on; wish, long, have a longing, yearn, be hungry, be itching, pant, be desperate, be consumed with desire; informal have a yen, be dying; archaic be athirst.
▷**ANTONYMS** be averse to.

thirsty adjective **1** *the boys were hot and thirsty*: **longing for a drink**, in need of a drink, dry, dehydrated; informal parched, gasping; Brit. informal spitting feathers; Austral./NZ informal spitting chips; rare athirst, thirstful, droughty, sitient.
2 *the thirsty soil*: **dry**, arid, dried up/out, as dry as a bone, parched, baked, desiccated, waterless, moistureless; rare droughty.
▷**ANTONYMS** waterlogged.
3 *his wife was thirsty for power*: **eager**, hungry, greedy, thirsting, consumed with desire, avid, craving, longing, yearning, lusting, burning, desirous, hankering, itching; informal dying.

thong noun *the seals were worn on leather thongs round the owner's neck*: **strip**, band, cord, string, lash, tie, belt, strap, tape, rope, tether.

thorn noun **prickle**, spike, barb, spine, bristle; technical spicule.
□ **thorn in the flesh** (or **in someone's side**) *he has become a thorn in the flesh of any establishment | you're an irritant, a thorn in his side, an embarrassment*: **annoyance**, irritant, irritation, source of irritation, source of vexation, source of annoyance, pinprick, pest, bother, trial, torment, plague, inconvenience, nuisance, menace; informal aggravation, peeve, pain, pain in the neck, bind, bore, headache, hassle; Scottish informal nyaff, skelf; N. Amer. informal pain in the butt, nudnik, burr in/under someone's saddle; Austral./NZ informal nark; Brit. vulgar slang pain in the arse.

thorny adjective **1** *he had to scramble through dense thorny undergrowth*: **prickly**, spiky, barbed, spiny, spined, bristly, briary, sharp, pointed; technical spinose, spinous.

2 *the thorny subject of confidentiality*: **problematic**, tricky, ticklish, delicate, controversial, awkward, prickly; **difficult**, knotty, tough, taxing, trying, troublesome, irksome, vexatious, bothersome, worrying, upsetting; **complicated**, complex, involved, convoluted, intricate, vexed; informal sticky; Brit. informal dodgy.
▷ANTONYMS easy, uncomplicated.

thorough adjective **1** *a thorough investigation*: **rigorous**, in-depth, exhaustive, thoroughgoing, minute, detailed, close, meticulous, scrupulous, assiduous, conscientious, painstaking, methodical, careful, sedulous, complete, comprehensive, elaborate, full, intensive, extensive, widespread, sweeping, searching, all-embracing, all-inclusive.
▷ANTONYMS superficial, cursory, partial.
2 *he is slow but thorough*: **meticulous**, scrupulous, assiduous, conscientious, painstaking, punctilious, methodical, careful, attentive, diligent, industrious, persevering, laborious, hard-working.
▷ANTONYMS careless.
3 *the child is being a thorough nuisance*: **utter**, downright, thoroughgoing, absolute, complete, total, out-and-out, outright, real, perfect, profound, proper, consummate, all-out, wholesale, surpassing, sheer, rank, pure, unqualified, unmitigated; N. Amer. full-bore; Brit. informal right; Austral./NZ informal fair; rare arrant, right-down.

thoroughbred adjective **1** *a thoroughbred horse*: **pure-bred**, pedigree, pure, pure-blooded, full-blooded, pedigreed.
▷ANTONYMS hybrid.
2 informal *with its terrific handling and accurate steering, it feels like a thoroughbred coupé*: **top-quality**, high-quality, first-class, first-rate, high-grade, of the first water, of the first order; choice, select, exclusive, rare, singular, unique, prime, prize, upmarket, fine, excellent, superb, distinguished, exceptional, outstanding, marvellous, superlative, special; best, choicest, finest, matchless, peerless, unequalled, perfect, flawless; French par excellence.

thoroughfare noun **1** *a scheme to stop the park being used as a thoroughfare*: **through route**, access route, way, passage; Brit. informal rat run.
2 *the teeming thoroughfares of central London*: **street**, road, roadway, avenue, boulevard, way; main road, high road, A road, B road, trunk road, arterial road, artery, broadway; Brit. dual carriageway, clearway, motorway; French autoroute; Italian autostrada; German Autobahn; N. Amer. highway, freeway, parkway, crossway, turnpike, pike, throughway, expressway, superhighway, interstate; S. African national road; Austral. beef road; informal main drag.

thoroughly adverb **1** *we will investigate every complaint thoroughly*: **rigorously**, in depth, exhaustively, from top to bottom, minutely, closely, in detail, meticulously, scrupulously, assiduously, conscientiously, painstakingly, methodically, carefully, sedulously, completely, comprehensively, fully, to the fullest extent, intensively, extensively.
2 *she is thoroughly spoilt*: **utterly**, downright, absolutely, completely, totally, entirely, really, perfectly, profoundly, properly, consummately, surpassingly, positively, simply, unconditionally, unreservedly, categorically, incontrovertibly, unquestionably, undeniably, in every respect, through and through, outright; informal plain, clean.

though conjunction *though Scott was not particularly interested in early editions he did own several*: **although**, even though/if, in spite of the fact that, despite the fact that, notwithstanding the fact that, notwithstanding that, for all that, while, whilst, granted that, even supposing, despite the possibility that, albeit, however, yet, but.
▸ adverb *You can't always do that. You can try, though*: **nevertheless**, nonetheless, even so, however, be that as it may, for all that, in spite of that/everything, despite that/everything, after everything, having said that, just the same, all the same, at the same time, in any event, come what may, at any rate, notwithstanding, regardless, anyway, anyhow; informal still and all; archaic howbeit, withal, natheless.

thought noun **1** *a thought came to me as to how we should proceed*: **idea**, notion, line of thinking, belief, concept, conception, conviction, opinion, view, impression, image, perception, mental picture; assumption, presumption, hypothesis, theory, supposition, postulation, abstraction, apprehension, understanding, conceptualization; feeling, funny feeling, suspicion, sneaking suspicion, hunch.
2 *the mere thought of being confined made her breathless*: **anticipation**, expectation, prospect, contemplation, likelihood, possibility, fear.
3 *he gave up any thought of taking a degree*: **hope**, aspiration, ambition, dream; **intention**, idea, plan, design, purpose, aim.
4 *it only took a moment's thought*: **thinking**, reasoning, contemplation, musing, pondering, consideration, reflection, introspection, deliberation, study, rumination, cogitation, meditation, brooding, mulling over, reverie, brown study, concentration, debate, speculation; rare cerebration.
5 *I'll give the matter some thought*: **attention**, consideration, heed, regard, notice, scrutiny, care.
6 *have you no thought for others?* **compassion**, sympathy, caring, concern, regard, solicitude, solicitousness, empathy; consideration, kindness, kindliness, kind-heartedness, tender-heartedness, tenderness, warmth, warm-heartedness; understanding, sensitivity, thoughtfulness, charity, charitableness, benignity, benevolence, philanthropy, altruism, magnanimity.

thoughtful adjective **1** *Uncle Albert paused, looking thoughtful*: **pensive**, thinking, reflective, contemplative, musing, meditative, introspective, prayerful, philosophical, cogitative, ruminative, absorbed, engrossed, rapt, preoccupied, deep/immersed/lost in thought, in a brown study, brooding, broody, serious, studious, solemn, dreamy, dreaming, wistful, melancholy, sad; rare ruminant.
▷ANTONYMS vacant.
2 *how very thoughtful of you!* **considerate**, attentive, caring, understanding, sympathetic, solicitous, concerned, helpful, friendly, obliging, accommodating, neighbourly, unselfish, kind, kindly, compassionate, tender, charitable, benevolent.
▷ANTONYMS inconsiderate, self-centred.
3 *her work is thoughtful and provocative*: **profound**, deep, intelligent, studious, philosophical, sensitive, pithy, serious, meaty, weighty.
▷ANTONYMS superficial.

thoughtless adjective **1** *I'm so sorry—how thoughtless of me*: **inconsiderate**, uncaring, heedless, unmindful, regardless, insensitive, uncharitable, unkind; tactless, undiplomatic, indiscreet, careless, selfish, impolite, rude.
▷ANTONYMS considerate.
2 *to think a few minutes of thoughtless pleasure could end in such a terrible way*: **unthinking**, heedless, careless, unmindful, absent-minded, injudicious, ill-advised, ill-considered, imprudent, unwise, foolish, silly, stupid, reckless, rash, precipitate, negligent, neglectful, remiss.
▷ANTONYMS careful.

> *Choose the right word* **thoughtless, careless, heedless**
>
> See **careless**.

thousand cardinal number informal K, thou; rare chiliad.

> *Word links* **thousand**
>
> **kilo-, milli-:** related prefixes, as in *kilometre, milligram*
> **millenary** relating to a thousand
> **millennium** thousandth anniversary

thrall noun literary *he held us in his evil thrall*: **power**, clutches, hands, control, grip, grasp, yoke; enslavement, bondage, slavery, subjection, subjugation, servitude, tyranny, oppression, domination, hegemony, supremacy.

thrash verb **1** *she thrashed him across the head and shoulders*: **hit**, **beat**, flog, whip, horsewhip, scourge, lash, flagellate, flail, strap, birch, cane, belt, leather; N. Amer. bullwhip; informal give someone a hiding, tan someone's hide, lather, paste, take a strap to, beat the living daylights out of; N. Amer. informal whale; archaic switch, stripe, thong; rare quirt.
2 informal *Newcastle were thrashed 8–1 by the Czech team*: **trounce**, beat hollow, defeat utterly, rout, annihilate, triumph over, win a resounding victory over, be victorious over, crush, overwhelm, best, get the better of, worst, bring someone to their knees; informal lick, hammer, clobber, paste, pound, pulverize, crucify, demolish, destroy, drub, give someone a drubbing, cane, walk all over, wipe the floor with, give someone a hiding, take to the cleaners, blow someone out of the water, make mincemeat of, murder, massacre, slaughter, flatten, turn inside out, tank; Brit. informal stuff, marmalize; N. Amer. informal blow out, cream, shellac, skunk, slam.
3 *he lay on the ground* ***thrashing around*** *in pain*: **flail**, thresh, flounder, toss and turn, jerk, toss, squirm, writhe, twist, wriggle, wiggle, twitch.
□ **thrash something out 1** *it is essential that conflicting views are heard and thrashed out*: **resolve**, settle, sort out, straighten out, iron out, reconcile, disentangle, clarify, clear up, talk through, confer about, debate, exchange views on/about, chew over, air, ventilate, argue out, argue the pros and cons of; go into, deal with, handle, pursue, examine, explore, review, study, scrutinize, analyse, weigh up, sift; informal kick around/about, bat around/about. **2** *they spent much of the weekend trying to thrash out an agreement*: **produce**, come to a decision on, work out, form a resolution about, negotiate, agree on, bring about, complete, accomplish, carry through, effect.

thrashing noun **1** *what he needs is a good thrashing*: **beating**, flogging, whipping, horsewhipping, scourging, lashing, flagellation, caning, belting, leathering; the strap, the birch, the cane, the belt; N. Amer. bullwhipping; informal hiding, tanning, lathering, pasting, going-over.
2 informal *the home side received their biggest thrashing ever*: **crushing defeat**, overwhelming defeat, beating, trouncing, walloping, thumping, battering, rout; informal hiding, licking, pasting, caning, going-over, drubbing, hammering, pounding, clobbering, demolition, slaughter, massacre, annihilation; N. Amer. informal shellacking.

thread noun **1** *he sewed it up with needle and thread*: **yarn**, **cotton**, filament, fibre, strand, string, twine, line; ply.
2 literary *the Thames was a thread of silver below them*: **streak**, strand, stripe, line, striation, strip, seam, vein, belt, bar, swathe.
3 *she lost the thread of the conversation*: **train of thought**, drift, direction, sense, theme, subject matter, motif, tenor, strain, thrust, subject, gist, burden, action; plot, storyline, scenario.

▶ verb 1 *he threaded the rope through a pulley*: **pass**, string, weave, work, ease, inch, move, push, poke, thrust.
2 *a little girl sat threading minute beads*: **string**.
3 *she threaded her way through the tables*: **weave (one's way)**, inch (one's way), wind (one's way), file, work (one's way), push (one's way), squeeze (one's way), shoulder (one's way), elbow (one's way), make one's way; progress, pass.

threadbare adjective 1 *a threadbare carpet*: **worn**, well worn, old, thin, worn out, holey, moth-eaten, mangy, ragged, frayed, tattered, battered; decrepit, shabby, scruffy, unkempt; having seen better days, falling apart at the seams, in shreds, in tatters, falling to pieces; informal tatty, ratty, the worse for wear; N. Amer. informal raggedy, raggedy-ass; Austral. informal warby; rare out at elbows.
▷ANTONYMS pristine.
2 *his threadbare pontifications*: **hackneyed**, trite, banal, vapid, platitudinous, clichéd, cliché-ridden, stock, conventional, unoriginal, derivative, overused, overworked, worn out, tired, stale, dull, pedestrian, run-of-the-mill, routine, humdrum, stereotyped; informal old hat, corny, played out; rare truistic, bromidic.
▷ANTONYMS original, fresh.
3 *their knowledge of pollutants was threadbare*: **limited**, **sketchy**, restricted, basic, rudimentary, patchy, minimal, slight, slender, finite, bounded, narrow, lean, in short supply, short, meagre, scanty, sparse, insubstantial, deficient, lacking, inadequate, insufficient, paltry, poor, miserly, feeble.
▷ANTONYMS impressive, full; adequate.

threat noun 1 *the general had made threats against UN personnel*: **threatening remark**, warning, ultimatum, intimidating remark; rare commination; (**threats**) menaces, menacing.
2 *the ash from the volcano poses a possible threat to aircraft*: **danger**, peril, hazard, menace, risk.
3 *the company faces the threat of liquidation proceedings*: **possibility**, chance, probability, likelihood, risk, danger, peril, menace, fear, prospect.

threaten verb 1 *how dare you threaten me?* **menace**, intimidate, browbeat, bully, cow, pressurize, lean on, terrorize, frighten, scare, alarm; make threats against, issue threats to, threaten to harm/kill.
2 *the rise of nationalism could threaten the stability of Europe*: **endanger**, be a danger to, be a threat to, menace, imperil, put at risk, make vulnerable, expose to danger, put in jeopardy, jeopardize; archaic peril.
3 *the air was raw and threatened rain*: **warn of**, be a warning of, give a warning of, promise, presage, augur, portend, foreshadow, prophesy, be an omen of; **foretell**, herald, bode, announce, be a harbinger of, be an indication of, indicate, point to; **be a sign of**, signal, signify, mean, spell, add up to, amount to, be evidence of; literary betoken, foretoken, forebode, harbinger.
4 *as rain threatened, the party was moved indoors*: **be likely (to happen)**, be imminent, be (close) at hand, be near, be close, be approaching, be on the horizon, be just around the corner, be brewing, be gathering, be looming, be coming (soon), be coming up, be on the way, be expected, be anticipated, be in prospect, be in the wind, be in the air, be forthcoming, be impending; hang over someone; informal be on the cards.

Choose the right word **threaten, menace, intimidate**

When one person **threatens** another they indicate or say that they will do something harmful or unpleasant if that person does not comply with their wishes. They can *threaten* the person (*robbers were threatening the shop assistant with a gun*), or they can *threaten* the thing that will happen (*the general threatened an assault on the city | his attackers threatened to kill him*). *Threaten* can also be used of something that constitutes a danger (*the Amazonian forest is being threatened by a major oil extraction project*) and of undesirable events that are thought to be likely (*the slick threatens to become the world's largest*).

Menace typically occurs as the adjective *menacing* and, compared to *threaten*, is less often used of active threats made by one person to another than of an impression, attitude, or more general danger (*he was a menacing, attacking centre-forward | pristine Amazonian forest is being menaced by an oil extraction project*).

To **intimidate** someone is to behave in such a way as to frighten them into submission or inaction (*one witness had disappeared and two more had been intimidated*). A person or thing may also unintentionally *intimidate* someone by appearing so formidable that the other loses confidence (*I was intimidated by the whole idea of Cambridge*); this sense is often conveyed by the adjectival form *intimidating* (*she was tall, with a most intimidating manner*).

threatening adjective 1 *her mother had received a threatening letter*: **menacing**, intimidating, bullying, frightening, terrifying, scary, fearsome, alarming, forbidding, baleful; warning, admonitory, cautionary; rare minacious, minatory, minatorial, comminatory.
2 *banks of threatening clouds were building up*: **ominous**, glowering, brooding, sinister, menacing, black, thunderous, dark, wintry, gloomy, heavy, dire, ill, evil, baleful, forbidding, doomy, ugly, unpromising, portentous, foreboding, unpropitious, pessimistic, inauspicious, unfavourable, unlucky, ill-fated, dangerous; archaic direful; rare minacious.

three cardinal number **trio**, threesome, triad, troika, triumvirate, trilogy, triptych, trefoil, three-piece, triplets; Poetry **tercet**; Music **triplet**; rare tern, triunity, triune, triplicity.

Word links **three**

ter-, **tri-** related prefixes, as in *tervalent, trimaran*
triple, **treble**, **ternary** relating to three
triangle three-sided figure
triumvirate group of three powerful people
triennial relating to three years
tercentenary three-hundredth anniversary

three-dimensional adjective *a three-dimensional image*: **solid**, concrete, having depth, sculptural, rounded; stereoscopic, stereographic, stereo-, virtual, holographic, perspective, pop-up; technical **axonometric**, orthorhombic.
▷ANTONYMS flat.

threesome noun *we planned excursions as a threesome*: **trio**, triplet(s), triumvirate, triad, trinity, troika, triunity, triangle, triplex; technical trilogy, triptych, tercet; Music terzetto, pas de trois; rare trine.

threnody noun rare *a threnody for Chernobyl*. See **lament** (sense 2 of the noun).

threshold noun 1 *they stood on the threshold of the church*: **doorstep**, sill, doorsill, doorway, entrance, entry, way in, door, gate, gateway, portal, approach.
2 *these young people are at the threshold of their careers*: **start**, starting point, beginning, brink, verge, edge, dawn, birth, origin, inception, conception, opening, launch, inauguration, institution, initiation, debut, creation, day one; informal kick-off; formal commencement.
▷ANTONYMS end.
3 *100 dB is close to the human threshold of pain*: **lower limit**, starting point, minimum, margin; Psychology limen.

Word links **threshold**

liminal relating to a threshold

thrift noun *thrift and hard work led to betterment*: **providence**, prudence, thriftiness, canniness, carefulness, good management, good husbandry, careful budgeting, economy, economizing, saving, scrimping and saving, scrimping, frugality, abstemiousness, parsimony, penny-pinching, miserliness; N. Amer. forehandedness; rare sparingness, frugalness.
▷ANTONYMS profligacy, extravagance.

thriftless adjective *he is a generous, often thriftless fellow*: **extravagant**, profligate, spendthrift, unthrifty, improvident, wasteful, free-spending, prodigal, squandering, lavish; immoderate, excessive, imprudent, reckless, irresponsible.
▷ANTONYMS thrifty.

thrifty adjective *Gran brought me up to be thrifty and never to get into debt*: **careful with money**, **provident**, prudent, canny, economical, frugal, sparing, scrimping, abstemious, parsimonious, penny-pinching, miserly; N. Amer. forehanded.
▷ANTONYMS profligate, extravagant.

thrill noun 1 *the thrill of jumping out of an aeroplane*: **(feeling of) excitement**, thrilling experience, stimulation, sensation, glow, tingle, titillation; fun, enjoyment, amusement, delight, joy, pleasure, treat, adventure; informal buzz, kick; N. Amer. informal charge.
2 *a thrill of excitement ran through her*: **tremor**, wave, rush, surge, flash, flush, blaze, stab, dart, throb, tremble, quiver, flutter, shudder, vibration; flow, gush, stream, flood, torrent.
▶ verb 1 *even though he couldn't read, the sight of books thrilled him*: **excite**, stimulate, arouse, rouse, inspire, give joy to, delight, give pleasure to, stir (up), exhilarate, intoxicate, electrify, galvanize, move, motivate, fire (with enthusiasm), fire someone's imagination, fuel, brighten, animate, lift, quicken; informal give someone a buzz, give someone a kick; N. Amer. informal give someone a charge.
▷ANTONYMS bore.
2 *he thrilled at the sound of her voice*: **be/feel excited**, tingle, feel joy; informal get a buzz out of, get a kick out of; N. Amer. informal get a charge out of.
3 *the shock of alarm thrilled through her*: **rush**, race, surge, cascade, course, flood, flow, gush, wash, well up, sweep, flash, blaze, throb, quiver, shiver, flutter, shudder, vibrate.

thrilling adjective *racegoers are in for a thrilling contest today*: **exciting**, stirring, action-packed, rip-roaring, gripping, riveting, fascinating, dramatic, hair-raising, rousing, lively, animated, spirited, stimulating, moving, inspiring, inspirational, electrifying, passionate, impassioned, emotive, emotional, emotion-charged, heady, soul-stirring; N. Amer. stem-winding; rare inspiriting, anthemic.
▷ANTONYMS boring.

thrive verb *there are several foliage plants that thrive in a window box*: **flourish**, prosper, grow vigorously, develop well, burgeon, bloom, blossom, do well, advance, make strides, succeed; shoot up; boom, profit, expand, go

well, grow rich.
▷ANTONYMS decline, wither, fail, stagnate, die.

Choose the right word **thrive, flourish, prosper**

See **flourish**.

thriving adjective *a thriving business*: **flourishing**, prosperous, prospering, growing, developing, burgeoning, blooming, healthy, successful, advancing, progressing; luxuriant, lush, prolific; booming, profitable, expanding; informal going strong.
▷ANTONYMS moribund, dying, unhealthy.

throat noun **gullet**, oesophagus; windpipe, trachea; crop, craw, maw; neck; technical pharynx, oropharynx, fauces, gorget; informal, dated the red lane; archaic throttle, gorge, gula.

Word links **throat**

guttural, **jugular** relating to the throat
otolaryngology branch of medicine concerning the ears and throat
otorhinolaryngology branch of medicine concerning the ears, nose, and throat

throaty adjective *a low throaty voice*: **gravelly**, husky, rough, guttural, deep, thick, gruff, growly, growling, hoarse, croaky, croaking; rasping, raspy, harsh, grating, jarring, discordant, dissonant, scratchy, creaky; rare stridulant.
▷ANTONYMS high-pitched.

throb verb *her arms and legs throbbed with tiredness*: **pulsate**, beat, pulse, palpitate, pound, thud, thump, hammer, drum, thrum, reverberate, vibrate, pitter-patter, go pit-a-pat, quiver; rare quop.
▶ noun *the throb of the ship's engines*: **pulsation**, beat, beating, pulse, pulsating, palpitation, pounding, thud, thudding, thump, thumping, hammering, drumming, thrum, thrumming, reverberation, vibration, pit-a-pat, pitter-patter, quivering.

throes plural noun *the throes of childbirth*: **agony**, pain, paroxysm, pangs, suffering, torture, torment, anguish, distress, hardship, struggle; archaic travail; rare excruciation.
□ **in the throes of** *she was in the throes of her by-election campaign*: **struggling with**, wrestling with, grappling with, tackling, toiling at/with, labouring at, slaving at, working at/on; **having to cope with**, enduring, living with, weathering, braving, facing, confronting; **in the middle of**, in the process of, in the course of, in the midst of, busy with, occupied in/with, taken up with/by, employed in, involved in, participating in, taking part in, absorbed in, engrossed in, immersed in, preoccupied with, carrying on, conducting, pursuing, following, practising.

thrombosis noun *he died from a thrombosis*: **blood clot**, embolism, embolus, infarction; stroke, ictus, seizure; heart attack, coronary thrombosis, coronary; archaic apoplexy.

throne noun **1** *a golden throne*: **seat of state**, royal seat.
2 *the tsar risked losing his throne*: **sovereign power**, sovereignty, rule, command, dominion.

throng noun *he pushed his way through the throng*: **crowd**, mass, multitude, horde, host, mob, assemblage, gathering, congregation, crush, press, body, band, army, troop, legion, gang, stream, swarm, flock, bevy, herd, pack, drove, array, sea, myriad, pile; knot, cluster, group.
▶ verb **1** *a crowd thronged the station*: **pack (into)**, cram (into), jam, fill, press into, squeeze into; N. Amer. mob.
2 *people thronged to see the play*: **rush**, stream, flock, troop, crowd, swarm, surge, flood, flow, spill, teem.
3 *a large crowd* **thronged round** *to listen | visitors* **thronged around** *him*: **crowd round**, press round, mill around/round; congregate round, converge round, hem in, mob, jostle.

throttle verb **1** *there was a pair of hands round her throat, throttling her*: **choke**, strangle, strangulate, garrotte, asphyxiate, smother, suffocate, stifle.
2 *attempts to throttle the criminal supply of drugs*: **suppress**, inhibit, stifle, control, restrain, check, contain, put a/the lid on; crack down on, clamp down on, drive underground; **stop**, put an end to, bring to an end, end, stamp out, bring to a stop, halt, bring to a halt; informal put paid to, put the kibosh on, put the stopper on, do for.

through preposition **1** *it takes about twenty-five minutes to get through the tunnel | delicious smells wafted through the house*: **into and out of**, to the other/far side of, from one side of ... to the other, from end to end of, between, past, by, down, along, across, by way of, via; throughout, around in, all over.
2 *he got the job through an advertisement*: **by means of**, by way of, by dint of, through the agency of, via, using, with the help of, with the aid of, with the assistance of, thanks to, under the aegis of, by virtue of, as a result of, as a consequence of, on account of, owing to, because of.
3 *he worked through the night*: **throughout**, all through, for the duration of, until/to the end of, during.
4 N. Amer. *the exhibition is open Tuesday through Sunday*: **up to and including**, (from ...) to ... inclusive.
▶ adverb **1** *cosmic rays strike against atoms in the atmosphere as they pass through*: **from one side to the other**, from one end to another, from end to end, from side to side, from top to bottom, in and out the other end/side.
2 *Victoria woke up, but Anthony slept through*: **the whole time**, all the time, from start to finish, without a break, without an interruption, uninterrupted, non-stop, continuously, constantly, throughout.
3 *it was a struggle but we got through*: **to the end**, to the finish, to the termination, to the completion, to the culmination, to a successful conclusion.
□ **through and through** *he was obviously a city kid through and through | I know you through and through*: **in every respect**, to the core; **thoroughly**, utterly, downright, absolutely, completely, totally, wholly, fully, entirely, really, perfectly, profoundly, properly, consummately, surpassingly, positively, simply, unconditionally, unreservedly, categorically, incontrovertibly, unquestionably, undeniably, altogether, out-and-out.
▶ adjective **1** *are you through? | we're* **through with** *you here*: **finished**, done, reached the end, completed, terminated; no longer involved with, no longer wanting anything to do with, tired of.
2 *a through train*: **direct**; non-stop; without changes.

Word links **through**

dia- related prefix, as in *diameter, diachronic*

throughout preposition & adverb **1** *it had repercussions throughout Europe | the house is in good order throughout*: **all over**, all round, in every part (of), everywhere (in), all through, right through, here and there (in), round.
2 *Rose had generally been very fit throughout her life | both MPs retained a smiling dignity throughout*: **all through**, through, for the duration (of), for the whole of, until the end (of), the whole time, all the time.

throw verb **1** *she threw their ball back*: **hurl**, toss, fling, pitch, cast, lob, launch, flip, catapult, shy, dash, aim, direct, project, propel, send, bowl; informal chuck, heave, sling, buzz, whang, bung; N. Amer. informal peg; Austral. informal hoy; NZ informal bish.
▷ANTONYMS catch, hold.
2 *he threw the door open*: **move quickly/suddenly**, push suddenly/violently, thrust, fling, propel, shoot, slam, smack, bang, crash, thump, push, force; informal plonk.
3 *a chandelier threw its bright light over the walls*: **project**, cast, send, give off, emit, radiate.
4 *Cheryl drew back her fist and threw another punch*: **deliver**, give, land.
▷ANTONYMS pull.
5 *she threw him a glance*: **direct**, cast, send, dart, shoot, bestow on, give.
6 *he was thrown twice in the final round*: **fell**, throw to the ground, hurl to the ground, unbalance, bring down, floor, prostrate.
7 *the horse threw his rider*: **unseat**, dislodge, upset, bring down.
8 *his question threw me*: **disconcert**, unnerve, fluster, ruffle, flurry, agitate, harass, upset, disturb, discomfit, put off, put someone off their stroke, throw off balance, make nervous, discompose, discountenance, cause someone to lose their composure; perturb, unsettle, bother, affect, worry, disquiet, trouble, confuse; informal rattle, faze, put into a flap, throw into a tizz, discombobulate, shake up.
9 *if only he could find the switch to throw*: **operate**, switch on, click on, engage, move.
10 *the pots were thrown on a wheel*: **shape**, form, mould, fashion.
11 *he threw a farewell party for them*: **give**, **host**, hold, have, provide, put on, lay on, arrange, organize.
□ **throw something away 1** *he decided to throw away his textbooks and get some practical experience*: **discard**, throw out, dispose of, get rid of, do away with, toss out, scrap, throw on the scrap heap, clear out, remove, dispense with, lose, eliminate, dump, unload, jettison, shed, dismiss, expel, eject, weed out, root out; recycle, break up, demolish, write off; informal chuck (away/out), ditch, bin, junk, get shut of; Brit. informal get shot of, see the back of; N. Amer. informal trash, shuck off, wreck.
▷ANTONYMS keep.
2 *Cambridge threw away a 15–0 lead*: **squander**, waste, fritter away, dissipate, run through, fail to exploit, make poor use of, lose, let slip; informal blow, pour/chuck something down the drain.
▷ANTONYMS exploit.
□ **throw someone off** *she thought she had thrown off her pursuer*: **shake off**, get away from, escape, elude, give someone the slip, leave behind, throw off the scent, dodge, lose, get rid of, rid oneself of; outdistance, outstrip; Brit. informal get shot of.
□ **throw something off** *he shrugged, trying to throw off the pain*: **get rid of**, cast off, discard, shake off, drop, jettison, free/rid oneself of.
□ **throw something on** *she threw on her clothes*: **put on quickly**, pull on, drag on, don quickly, slip into.
□ **throw someone out** *Jim was thrown out when he climbed on to the stage | the government was thrown out after only eight months*: **expel**, eject, evict, drive out, force out, oust, remove; remove from office/power, get rid of, depose, topple, unseat, overthrow, bring down, overturn, put out, drum

out, thrust out, push out, turn out; dismiss, dislodge, displace, supplant, show someone the door; banish, deport, exile; informal boot out, kick out, give someone the boot; Brit. informal turf out.

□ **throw something out 1** *I was continually having to throw out mouldy furniture.* See **throw something away**. **2** *his case was thrown out because an industrial tribunal was not entitled to deal with it*: **reject**, dismiss, turn down, say 'no' to, refuse, disallow, veto, squash; informal give the thumbs down to, give the red light to. **3** *a thermal light bulb throws out a lot of heat*: **radiate**, emit, give off, send out, diffuse, disseminate, disperse.

□ **throw someone over** *he's going to throw you over for your sister*: **abandon**, leave, desert, discard, turn one's back on, cast aside, cast off; **jilt**, break up with, finish with, leave in the lurch, leave high and dry, leave stranded; informal dump, ditch, chuck, drop, walk out on, run out on, rat on, leave flat, give someone the push, give someone the elbow, give someone the big E; archaic forsake.

□ **throw something together** *I'm sorry about the tuna salad, I just sort of threw it together*: **improvise**, contrive, devise, throw together, cobble together, concoct, rig, jury-rig, put together; Brit. informal knock up; informal whip up, fix up, rustle up.

□ **throw up** informal *she threw up in the gutter*: **vomit**, retch; cough up, bring up, regurgitate; heave, gag; Brit. be sick; N. Amer. get sick; informal puke, chunder, chuck up, hurl, spew, do the technicolor yawn, keck; Brit. informal honk, sick up; Scottish informal boke; N. Amer. informal spit up, barf, upchuck, toss one's cookies.

□ **throw something up** *throwing up his career would have meant the end of financial support*: **give up**, abandon, relinquish, resign (from), leave, eschew, abdicate; informal quit, chuck, pack in, jack in.

▶ **noun 1** *we were allowed two throws each*: **lob**, pitch, flip, shy, go; bowl, ball; hurl, toss, fling, cast; informal chuck, heave, sling.

2 informal *drinks are only £1 **a throw***: **each**, apiece, per item, for one.

throwaway adjective **1** *more and more products are displayed without throwaway packaging*: **disposable**, expendable, one-use, non-returnable, one-way, single-trip; cheap, ephemeral, obsolescent; paper, plastic, biodegradable, photodegradable.

2 *a million viewers had heard my throwaway remarks*: **casual**, passing, careless, unthinking, unstudied, unconsidered, ill-considered, parenthetical; nonchalant, offhand.

thrown-together adjective *the production has a thrown-together casualness*: **impromptu**, extempore, extemporary, extemporaneous, expedient, emergency, improvised, ad hoc, rough and ready, makeshift, make-do, cobbled together; Nautical jury-rigged, jury; informal quick and dirty.

thrust verb **1** *she thrust her hands into her pockets | he tried to thrust his way past her*: **shove**, push, propel, impel; send, press, drive, plunge, stick, force, shoot, ram, barge, bump, knock, strike, hit, jolt, butt, prod, poke, nudge, elbow, shoulder; bulldoze, sweep, jostle, bundle, hustle, hurry, rush, manhandle.

2 *he felt that fame had been thrust upon him*: **impose**, force, foist, push, unload, inflict, obtrude, press, urge; (**thrust something on someone**) saddle someone with, land someone with, burden someone with, lumber someone with.

▶ **noun 1** *he gave the gate a hard thrust*: **shove**, push, ram, prod, poke, stab, jab, lunge, drive, barge, bump, bang, jolt, butt, knock, nudge.

2 *a sudden armoured thrust into the city*: **advance**, push, drive, charge, attack, assault, onslaught, onrush, offensive, sortie, foray, raid, sally, invasion, incursion, blitz, campaign; archaic onset.

3 *he countered this verbal attack with some choice thrusts of his own*: **barbed remark**, verbal attack/assault, barb, hostile remark, insult; criticism, censure, vitriol.

4 *only one engine is producing thrust*: **force**, motive force, propulsive force, propulsion, drive, driving force, actuation, impetus, impulse, impulsion, momentum, push, pressure, power.

5 *they failed to grasp the thrust of the speech*: **gist**, substance, drift, implication, intention, burden, meaning, significance, signification, sense, essence, thesis, import, purport, tenor, message, spirit.

thrusting adjective *a thrusting young salesman*: **aggressive**, **ambitious**, assertive, pushy, pushing, insistent, forceful, forward, energetic, determined, obtrusive, bold, brash; bumptious, presumptuous, full of oneself, self-assertive, overbearing, domineering, cocksure, loud, obnoxious; informal full of get-up-and-go; rare pushful.

▷ANTONYMS meek, unambitious.

thud noun *Jean heard the thud of the closing door*: **thump**, clunk, clonk, crash, smash, smack, bang, boom, thunder, wallop; stomp, stamp, clump, clomp; informal wham, whump.

▶ **verb** *bullets thudded into the dusty ground*: **thump**, clunk, clonk, crash, smash, smack, bang, thunder; stomp, stamp, clump, clomp; informal wham, whump.

thug noun **ruffian**, hoodlum, bully boy, bully, bandit, mugger, gangster, terrorist, gunman, murderer, killer, hit man, assassin, hooligan, vandal, Yardie; informal tough, bruiser, hired gun; Brit. informal rough, bovver boy, lager lout, chav, hoodie; Scottish & N. English informal ned; N. Amer. informal hood, goon; Austral./NZ informal roughie, hoon; dated cut-throat, desperado; rare myrmidon.

thumb noun (first) digit, opposable digit; technical pollex.

□ **all thumbs** Brit. informal **clumsy**, awkward, maladroit, inept, bungling, bumbling, incompetent, unskilful, heavy-handed, ungainly, inelegant, inexpert, graceless, ungraceful, gauche, unhandy, uncoordinated, gawky, cloddish, clodhopping; informal butterfingered, cack-handed, ham-fisted, ham-handed; Brit. informal all fingers and thumbs.

▷ANTONYMS dexterous.

□ **thumbs down** informal *moves to demolish a historic former engine shed have been given the thumbs down*: **rejection**, refusal, veto, no, negation, rebuff, disapproval, turning down, turndown, non-acceptance, declining, dismissal, spurning, cold shoulder, cold-shouldering, snub, snubbing; informal red light, knock-back, kick in the teeth, smack in the face/eye.

▷ANTONYMS approval, welcome, thumbs up.

□ **thumbs up** informal *staff gave our police officers a resounding thumbs up*: **approval**, seal of approval, approbation, endorsement, welcome, encouragement; **permission**, liberty, authorization, consent, yes, leave, authority, sanction, ratification, licence, dispensation, nod, assent, acquiescence, agreement, blessing, imprimatur, rubber stamp, clearance, acceptance; informal go-ahead, the OK, green light, say-so; rare permit.

▷ANTONYMS rejection, thumbs down.

▶ **verb 1** *as soon as she thumbed the button, the door slid open*: **press**, push (down), depress, lean on.

2 *the man **thumbed through** his notebook*: **leaf**, flick, flip, skim, browse, glance, look, riffle; read, scan, dip into, run one's eye over, have a look at; peruse.

3 (usually **thumbed**) *his dictionaries were thumbed and ink-stained*: **make dog-eared**, mark, soil, mess up, handle roughly, maul, paw.

4 *thumb a lift | he was thumbing his way across France*: **hitch-hike**, **ask for**, request, signal for; get, obtain; informal hitch, hitch a lift.

□ **thumb one's nose at** *she thumbed her nose at conventional notions of female beauty*: **defy**, go against, rebel against, flout, fly in the face of, disobey, refuse to obey, disregard, ignore, set one's face against, kick against; break, violate, contravene, breach, infringe; informal cock a snook at; archaic set at naught.

thumbnail adjective *a thumbnail sketch of the social and political climate*: **concise**, short, brief, succinct, to the point, compact, terse, curt, summary, outline, crisp, short and sweet, quick, rapid, pithy, epigrammatic, laconic, pointed, abridged, abbreviated, condensed, synoptic, compendious, summarized, contracted, curtailed, truncated, potted.

▷ANTONYMS extensive, prolix.

thump verb **1** *someone thumped him in the back | he thumped on the cottage door*: **hit**, strike, beat, batter, pound, attack, assault, knock, rap, smack, thwack, slap, pummel, punch, rain blows on, belabour, hammer, cudgel, thrash, bang, drub, welt, cuff, crack, buffet, box someone's ears; informal bash, clobber, clout, clip, wallop, beat the living daylights out of, give someone a (good) hiding/beating/drubbing, whack, belt, tan, biff, bop, lay into, pitch into, lace into, let someone have it, knock into the middle of next week, sock, lam, whomp; Brit. informal stick one on, slosh; N. Amer. informal boff, bust, slug, light into, whale; Austral./NZ informal dong, quilt; literary smite, swinge.

2 *her heart thumped with fright*: **throb**, pound, thud, hammer, pulsate, pulse, pump, palpitate, race, beat heavily, go pit-a-pat, pitter-patter, vibrate, drum; literary pant, thrill; rare quop.

▶ **noun 1** *your father would give you a good thump if you did that*: **blow**, hit, punch, smack, thwack, slap, thrashing, bang, hiding, drubbing, lambasting, welt, cuff, box, crack; informal bash, clobber, clout, clip, wallop, whack, belt, tan, biff, bop, sock, lam, whomp; Brit. informal slosh; N. Amer. informal boff, bust, slug, whale; Austral./NZ informal dong; dated **buffet**.

2 *she heard a thump like a ball thrown against a wall*: **thud**, clunk, clonk, crash, smash, smack, bang, boom, thunder, wallop; stomp, stamp, clump, clomp; informal wham, whump.

thumping adjective **1** *he could hear a thumping noise*: **thudding**, pounding, banging, throbbing, hammering, drumming, clunking, clonking, crashing.

2 informal *a thumping majority | his party's thumping victory in the election*: **enormous**, huge, massive, vast, very great, tremendous, substantial, goodly, prodigious, gigantic, giant, terrific, fantastic, colossal, immense, mammoth, monumental, stupendous, gargantuan, elephantine, titanic, mountainous, monstrous; **emphatic**, roaring, decisive, conclusive, striking, impressive, outstanding, unmistakable, notable, noteworthy, memorable, remarkable, extraordinary, resounding, phenomenal; complete, unqualified, out-and-out, thorough; informal whopping, whopping great, thundering, mega, jumbo, humongous, monster, astronomical, dirty great, rip-roaring; Brit. informal whacking, whacking great, ginormous.

▶ **adverb** *a thumping good read*: **extremely**, very, really, thoroughly, exceedingly, immensely, incredibly, amazingly, remarkably, exceptionally, uncommonly, extraordinarily, perfectly, truly, simply, positive, positively, downright; Scottish unco; French très; informal terrifically, tremendously, seriously, majorly, dreadfully, terribly, awfully, fearfully, screamingly, thundering, right, ultra, mega, mucho, stonking, socking, oh-so, madly; Brit. informal damn, damned, blasted, flaming, confoundedly, jolly, hellish, bloody, blooming, dead, well, dirty; N. Amer. informal real, mighty, awful, powerful, way, bitching; S. African informal lekker; informal, dated devilish, frightfully, dashed; vulgar slang fucking, frigging; archaic exceeding, thrice.

thunder noun **1** *thunder and lightning*: **thunderclap**, thunder crack, thunder roll, roll of thunder, peal of thunder, rumble of thunder, crack of thunder, crash of thunder, rumbling, crashing, roar; literary thunderbolt.
2 *she heard the thunder of hooves behind her*: **rumble**, rumbling, boom, booming, roar, roaring, pounding, thud, thudding, thump, thumping, crash, crashing, bang, banging, ring, ringing, grumble, growl, resounding, reverberation, echo; tattoo, drumbeat, rataplan.
▸ verb **1** *below me the surf thrashed and thundered*: **rumble**, **boom**, roar, blast, pound, thud, thump, bang, ring, grumble, growl, resound, reverberate, echo, beat.
2 *he **thundered on about** Italy's invasion of Abyssinia*: **protest strongly at**, make a protest against, fulminate against, inveigh against, rail against, rage against, declaim against, remonstrate about, expostulate about, make a fuss about, speak out against, express disapproval of; object to, raise objections to, take issue with, oppose strongly, complain vociferously/bitterly about, disagree violently with, kick against, take exception to, make/take a stand against, put up a fight against, challenge, curse; **condemn**, criticize severely, denounce, censure; informal kick up a fuss/stink about.
3 *'Answer me,' he thundered*: **roar**, bellow, bark, yell, shout, bawl, howl, cry, clamour, bay, scream, screech; growl, yowl; N. Amer. informal holler; rare vociferate, ululate.

> *Word links* **thunder**
> **brontophobia**, **tonitrophobia**, **keraunophobia** fear of thunder

thundering adjective *he knocked Garber to the floor with two thundering rights to the chin*. See **thumping**.
▸ adverb *a thundering good read*. See **thumping**.

thunderous adjective *thunderous applause*: **very loud**, tumultuous, booming, rumbling, roaring, blaring, resounding, reverberating, reverberant, echoing, vibrant, ringing, carrying, deafening, ear-splitting, ear-piercing, noisy.

thunderstruck adjective *Charles was so thunderstruck that his voice sounded faint*: **astonished**, astounded, amazed, nonplussed, taken aback, startled, bewildered, stunned, flabbergasted, staggered, shocked, stupefied, open-mouthed, dumbfounded, dumbstruck, speechless, at a loss for words, dazed, benumbed, perplexed, confounded, agape, goggle-eyed, wide-eyed, dismayed, disconcerted, jolted, shaken up; informal bowled over, knocked for six, floored, flummoxed, caught on the hop, caught on the wrong foot, unable to believe one's eyes; Brit. informal gobsmacked.

thus adverb **1** *the alloy is highly reflective and was thus widely used for mirrors*: **consequently**, as a consequence, in consequence, so, that being so, therefore, accordingly, hence, as a result, for this/that reason, because of this/that, on this/that account; Latin ergo.
2 *legislation forbids such data being held thus*: **like this/that**, in this/that way, in this/that manner, in this/that fashion, so, like so; as follows, as shown, as demonstrated; informal thusly; archaic in/on this/that wise.
□ **thus far** *thus far they had found nothing*: **so far**, until now/then, up until now/then, till now/then, up to now/then, up to this/that point, hitherto; rare thitherto.

thwack verb *Pedro thwacked the backs of the man's legs with his crutch*: **hit**, strike, beat, batter, pound, attack, assault, knock, rap, smack, slap, pummel, thump, punch, cudgel, thrash, bang, drub, welt, cuff, crack, buffet, box someone's ears; informal bash, clobber, clout, clip, wallop, whack, belt, tan, biff, bop, lay into, pitch into, lace into, let someone have it, knock into the middle of next week, sock, lam, whomp; Brit. informal stick one on, slosh; N. Amer. informal boff, bust, slug, light into, whale; Austral./NZ informal dong, quilt; literary smite, swinge.
▸ noun *he was given a painful thwack with a rolled-up magazine*: **blow**, hit, punch, thump, smack, slap, bang, welt, cuff, box, crack; informal bash, clobber, clout, clip, wallop, whack, belt, tan, biff, bop, sock, lam, whomp; Brit. informal slosh; N. Amer. informal boff, bust, slug, whale; Austral./NZ informal dong; dated buffet.

thwart verb *the move was intended to thwart peace negotiations*: **foil**, frustrate, baulk, stand in the way of, forestall; scotch, derail, smash, dash; stop, check, block, prevent, defeat, impede, obstruct, snooker, oppose, hinder, hamper; upset the apple cart, spike someone's guns; informal put paid to, put the stopper on, put the kibosh on, do for, stymie, cook someone's goose; Brit. informal scupper, put the mockers on, nobble, queer someone's pitch; Austral./NZ & Irish vulgar slang root; archaic traverse.
▹ANTONYMS assist, facilitate.

tic noun *he had a nervous tic around his left eye*: **twitch**, spasm, jerk, convulsion, contraction, tremor, tremble.

tick noun **1** *all that was required was a tick in the 'Yes' or 'No' column*: **mark**, stroke, dash, line; N. Amer. check, check mark.
2 *the tick of his watch*: **clicking**, click, clack, clacking, click-clack, ticking, tick-tock, snick, snicking, plock, plocking, beat, tap, tapping.
3 Brit. informal *I won't be a tick*: **moment**, second, minute, bit, little while, short time, instant, split second; informal sec, jiffy, jiff; Brit. informal mo, two ticks.
▹ANTONYMS a long time.
□ **in a tick** Brit. informal *I'll be with you in a tick*: **(very) soon**, in a second, in a minute, in a moment, in a trice, in a flash, shortly, any second, any minute, any minute now, in a short time, in an instant, in the twinkling of an eye, in (less than) no time, in no time at all, before you know it, before long; N. Amer. momentarily; informal in a jiffy, in two shakes, in two shakes of a lamb's tail, before you can say Jack Robinson, in the blink of an eye, in a blink, in the wink of an eye, in a wink, before you can say knife; Brit. informal in two ticks, in a mo; N. Amer. informal in a snap.
▸ verb **1** *he should have ticked the box for no publicity | make a list of the animals and **tick off** the ones that you see*: **mark**, mark off, check off, indicate.
2 *I could hear the clock ticking*: **click**, clack, tick-tock, snick, plock, beat, tap.
□ **tick someone off 1** Brit. informal *she ticked the children off for being late*. See **reprimand**. **2** N. Amer. *he is seen as an outsider, and that really ticks me off*: **annoy**, irritate, infuriate, anger, incense, inflame, enrage, vex, irk, chagrin, exasperate, madden, pique, provoke, nettle, disturb, upset, perturb, discompose, put out, try, try someone's patience, get on someone's nerves, bother, trouble, worry, agitate, ruffle, hound, rankle with, nag, torment, pain, distress, tease, frustrate, chafe, grate, fret, gall, outrage, displease, offend, disgust, dissatisfy, disquiet; Brit. rub up the wrong way; N. English mither; informal peeve, miff, bug, bite, eat, hassle, aggravate, rile, get to, hack off, make someone's blood boil, make someone see red, get someone's goat, get someone's hackles up, make someone's hackles rise, get someone's back up, get someone's dander up, drive up the wall, drive bananas, needle, be a thorn in someone's side/flesh, be a pain in the neck, ruffle someone's feathers, get in someone's hair, get up someone's nose, get under someone's skin, give someone a hard time; Brit. informal nark, get on someone's wick, give someone the hump, wind up, get across; N. Amer. informal rankle, ride, gravel; vulgar slang piss off; Brit. vulgar slang get on someone's tits.
□ **tick over** *the engine was just ticking over*: **idle**, run slowly in neutral.

ticket noun **1** *a railway ticket*: **pass**, warrant, authorization, licence, permit; token, coupon, voucher; carnet, season ticket, rover, complimentary ticket, chit, slip, card, stub, counterfoil; N. Amer. rain check; informal comp, ducat; Brit. informal chitty; rare laissez-passer, firman.
2 *a parking ticket*: **notice**, notification, warning, certificate.
3 *a price ticket*: **label**, tag, sticker, slip, tally, tab, marker, docket.

tickle verb **1** *he tried to tickle her under the chin*: **stroke**, pet, lightly touch, lightly prod, chuck; archaic titillate.
2 *he found something that tickled his imagination*: **stimulate**, interest, appeal to, excite, arouse, captivate.
3 *he is tickled by the idea*: **amuse**, entertain, divert, please, delight, gladden, cheer up, satisfy, gratify; informal tickle someone pink.
▹ANTONYMS bore.
▸ noun *Dad gave my chin a little tickle*: **stroke**, pet, light prod, chuck; archaic titillation.

ticklish adjective *policy-makers are considering the ticklish question*: **problematic**, tricky, delicate, sensitive, controversial, awkward, prickly, thorny; **difficult**, knotty, tough, taxing, trying, troublesome, irksome, vexatious, bothersome, worrying, upsetting; **complicated**, complex, involved, convoluted, intricate, vexed; informal sticky; Brit. informal dodgy.

tide noun **1** *ships come up the river with the tide*: **tidal flow**, ebb and flow, flood, water, tidewater, tide race, ebb, surge, current, stream, movement.
2 *the whole tide of history seemed to be quickening*: **course**, movement, direction, trend, current, drift, run, turn, tendency, tenor, swing.
▸ verb
□ **tide someone over** *she needed a small loan to tide her over*: **sustain**, keep someone going, keep someone's head above water, see someone through; keep the wolf from the door, bridge the gap, keep someone in funds; **help out**, assist, aid.

tidings plural noun literary *the bearer of good tidings*. See **news**.

tidy adjective **1** *a tidy room*: **neat**, neat and tidy, as neat as a new pin, orderly, well ordered, in (good) order, well kept, shipshape (and Bristol fashion), in apple-pie order, immaculate, spick and span, uncluttered, organized, well organized, well arranged, sorted out, straight, straightened out, trim, spruce; archaic tricksy.
▹ANTONYMS untidy, messy.
2 *he's a very tidy person*: **smart**, spruce, dapper, trim, neat, well groomed, well turned out; organized, well organized, methodical, systematic, efficient, meticulous; fastidious; informal natty; dated as if one had just stepped out of a bandbox; archaic trig.
▹ANTONYMS scruffy; disorganized.
3 informal *a tidy sum*: **large**, sizeable, considerable, substantial, significant, appreciable, handsome, generous, ample, respectable, largish, biggish, fair, decent, decent-sized, healthy; Scottish & N. English bonny; informal not to be sneezed at, serious; archaic goodly.
▹ANTONYMS small, tiny.
▸ verb **1** *I'd better **tidy up** the living room*: **put in order**, clear up, sort out, put to rights, straighten (out), make shipshape, clean, clean up, spruce up; informal dejunk.
2 *she wanted to **tidy herself up** before her appointment*: **groom oneself**, spruce oneself up, freshen oneself up, preen oneself, primp oneself, prink

oneself, pretty oneself, beautify oneself; informal titivate oneself, doll oneself up; Brit. informal tart oneself up; archaic plume oneself, trig oneself.

tie verb **1** *they tied Max to a chair*: **bind**, tie up, tether, hitch, strap, truss, fetter, rope, chain, make fast, moor, lash, attach, fasten, fix, secure, join, connect, link, couple.
▷ANTONYMS untie.
2 *Renwick bent to tie his shoelace*: **do up**; knot, make a knot in, make a bow in, lace.
3 *women who do paid work at home feel themselves tied by childcare responsibilities*: **restrict**, restrain, limit, constrain, confine, cramp; hamper, hinder, impede, tie down, interfere with, slow, obstruct, block, handicap, hamstring, shackle, encumber, inhibit, check, curb; tie someone's hands, cramp someone's style; rare cumber, trammel.
4 *a pay deal tied to a productivity agreement*: **link**, couple, connect, relate, join, marry, wed; make conditional on, bind up with, bundle with.
5 *they tied for second place*: **draw**, be equal, be even, be level, be neck and neck.
□ **tie someone down** *they didn't marry because she was afraid of being tied down*. See **tie** (sense 3 of the verb).
□ **tie in** *you haven't seen how all this ties in with their long-term aims*: **be consistent**, tally, correlate, agree, be in agreement, accord, concur, coincide, conform, fit in, harmonize, be in tune, dovetail; correspond to, match, parallel, reflect, mirror; informal square; N. Amer. informal jibe.
□ **tie something in** *her husband is able to tie in his shifts with hers at the hospital*: **fit in**, harmonize, dovetail, match, mirror, make something consistent, make something correspond, make something tally, make something correlate, make something agree, make something accord, make something coincide, make something conform; informal square.
□ **tie someone/something up 1** *Gabriel tied up his pony*: **bind**, tie, tether, hitch, strap, truss, fetter, rope, chain, make fast, moor, lash, attach, fasten, fix, secure, join, connect, link. ▷ANTONYMS untie. **2** *do not tie your money up if you think you may need it quickly*: **commit**, make unavailable, invest long-term. **3** *he is tied up in meetings all morning*: **occupy**, engage, busy, keep busy, book, reserve, commit. **4** *they were anxious to tie up the contract*: **finalize**, conclude, bring to a conclusion, wind up, wrap up, complete, finish off, seal, set the seal on, settle, secure, clinch.
▶ noun **1** *a sleeveless jacket fastened at the back with ties*: **lace**, string, cord, ligature, wire, bond, fetter, link, fastening, fastener.
2 *he was wearing a collar and tie*: **necktie**; neckwear.
3 *it is important that we keep family ties strong*: **bond**, connection, link, liaison, attachment, association, kinship, affiliation, allegiance, friendship, cords, union, relationship, relatedness, interdependence.
4 *pets can be a tremendous tie*: **restriction**, curb, limitation, constraint, obligation, commitment, restraint, hindrance, check, obstruction, encumbrance, impediment, handicap.
5 *the race ended in a tie for first place*: **draw**, dead heat, deadlock, stalemate.
6 Brit. *Turkey's World Cup tie against Holland*: **contest**, fixture, match, game, event, trial, test, test match, meeting; bout, fight, prizefight, duel; quarter-final, semi-final, final; friendly, derby, local derby; play-off, replay, rematch; Canadian & Scottish playdown; N. Amer. split; archaic tourney.

tie-in noun *there's a tie-in to another case I'm working on*: **connection**, association, link, correlation, correspondence, parallel, tie-up, interrelation, relationship, relation, relatedness, interconnection, interdependence, analogy, similarity.

tier noun **1** *rising tiers of empty seats*: **row**, rank, bank, line; **layer**, level, plane, floor, storey, deck.
2 *the most senior tier of management*: **grade**, gradation, step, echelon, point on the scale, rung on the ladder; archaic degree.

tie-up noun *the Bombay-based firm is contemplating tie-ups with software houses abroad*: **link**, link-up, association, relationship, liaison; deal, bargain, contract, (business) arrangement, covenant, accommodation, understanding, settlement, protocol, accord, entente, compact, bond; alliance, coalition, federation, axis; N. Amer. trust.

tiff noun informal *she had had a tiff with Mr Carson*: **quarrel**, squabble, row, argument, fight, contretemps, disagreement, difference of opinion, dissension, falling-out, dispute, disputation, contention, clash, altercation, shouting match, exchange, war of words; tussle, conflict, fracas, affray, wrangle, tangle; Irish, N. Amer., & Austral. donnybrook; informal set-to, run-in, shindig, shindy, stand-up, spat, scrap, dust-up; Brit. informal barney, slanging match, bunfight, ding-dong, bust-up, ruck; Scottish informal rammy; N. Amer. informal rhubarb; archaic broil, miff; Scottish archaic threap, collieshangie; French, archaic tracasserie(s).

tight adjective **1** *he took a tight grip on her arm*: **firm**, fast, secure, fixed, clenched, clinched.
▷ANTONYMS relaxed, insecure.
2 *the rope was pulled tight*: **taut**, rigid, stiff, tense, stretched, strained, stressed.
▷ANTONYMS slack.
3 *tight jeans*: **tight-fitting**, close-fitting, narrow, figure-hugging, skintight, sheath-like; informal sprayed on.
▷ANTONYMS loose.
4 *a tight mass of fibres*: **compact**, compacted, compressed, dense, hard, unyielding, solid.
▷ANTONYMS loose.
5 *rather a tight space*: **small**, tiny, narrow, compact, poky, limited, restricted, confined, cramped, constricted, uncomfortable, minimal, sparse, inadequate; rare strait, incommodious.
▷ANTONYMS generous, roomy.
6 *the joint will be perfectly tight against petrol leaks*: **impervious**, impenetrable, sealed, sound, hermetic; watertight, waterproof, airtight.
▷ANTONYMS leaking.
7 *security was tight at yesterday's ceremony*: **strict**, rigorous, stringent, tough, rigid, firm, uncompromising, exacting, systematic, meticulous, painstaking, scrupulous.
▷ANTONYMS lax.
8 *he's in a tight spot*: **problematic**, tricky, delicate, sensitive, controversial, awkward, prickly, thorny; **difficult**, knotty, tough, taxing, trying, troublesome, irksome, vexatious, bothersome, worrying, upsetting; informal sticky; Brit. informal dodgy.
▷ANTONYMS problem-free.
9 *there's no substitute for tight writing*: **succinct**, economic, pithy, crisp, straightforward, concise, condensed, well structured, laconic, terse, to the point, summary, short and sweet, in a few well-chosen words; rare compendious, epigrammatic, synoptic, aphoristic, gnomic.
▷ANTONYMS verbose.
10 *it was a tight race*: **close**, even, evenly matched, well matched; hard-fought, neck and neck.
▷ANTONYMS open.
11 *money is a bit tight just now*: **scarce**, scanty, scant, skimpy, meagre, sparse; reduced, depleted, diminished, low, in short supply, limited; deficient, inadequate, insufficient.
▷ANTONYMS plentiful, abundant.
12 *he's tight with his money*: **mean**, miserly, parsimonious, niggardly, close-fisted, penny-pinching, cheese-paring, penurious, Scrooge-like, ungenerous, illiberal, close; informal stingy, mingy, tight-fisted; N. Amer. informal cheap; vulgar slang tight-arsed; archaic near.
▷ANTONYMS generous.
13 informal *he came home tight from the pub*. See **drunk**.

tighten verb **1** *when the structure is flat,* ***tighten up*** *the fixing screws*: **secure**, make fast, make more secure, screw up, give an extra turn to.
▷ANTONYMS loosen.
2 *he tightened his grip on her arm*: **strengthen**, make stronger, reinforce, harden, consolidate.
▷ANTONYMS loosen.
3 *she tightened the rope about his ankles*: **tauten**, make/draw taut, make/draw tight, stretch, strain, extend, make rigid, rigidify, stiffen, tense.
▷ANTONYMS slacken.
4 *my throat tightened | he tightened his lips*: **narrow**, become narrow/narrower, become tight/tighter, become pinched; constrict, contract, brace, draw in, compress, screw up, pucker, purse; N. Amer. squinch; rare constringe.
▷ANTONYMS relax.
5 *councillors have asked supermarkets to* ***tighten up*** *car park security*: **increase**, make stricter, make more rigorous, make more stringent, make more rigid, stiffen, toughen (up), heighten, escalate, scale up; informal up, crank up, beef (up).
▷ANTONYMS relax.
□ **tighten one's belt** *why dip into our savings, if we can tighten our belts instead?* **economize**, cut back, make cutbacks, make cuts, retrench, husband one's resources, budget, be (more) economical, make economies, be thrifty, be sparing, be frugal, buy (more) cheaply, use less, reduce/decrease wastage, scrimp, scrimp and save, scrimp and scrape, cut corners, draw in one's horns, count the/your pennies, watch the/your pennies; save (money), cut expenditure, cut costs; N. Amer. pinch the/your pennies; black English rake and scrape.

tight-fisted adjective *being tight-fisted individuals, we bypassed the fee-paying nature trail*: **mean**, **miserly**, parsimonious, niggardly, close-fisted, penny-pinching, cheese-paring, penurious, Scrooge-like, ungenerous, illiberal, close; informal stingy, mingy, tight; N. Amer. informal **cheap**; vulgar slang tight-arsed; archaic near.
▷ANTONYMS generous, liberal.

tight-lipped adjective *the company remains tight-lipped about the launch date*: **reticent**, taciturn, uncommunicative, unforthcoming, unresponsive, close-mouthed, close-lipped; silent, quiet, unspeaking; guarded, secretive, private, withdrawn, playing one's cards close to one's chest, of few words, untalkative; informal mum.
▷ANTONYMS forthcoming, chatty.

till[1] preposition & conjunction **1** *he stayed in bed till 7 | I will look after you till you die*: **until**, up to, up till, up until, as late as, up to the time of/that, until such time as, pending; N. Amer. through.
▷ANTONYMS beyond, after.
2 *ownership is not transferred till delivery*: **before**, prior to, previous to, up to, until, up until, up till, earlier than, in advance of, ante-, pre-.
▷ANTONYMS after.

till² noun *she counted the money in the till | there were queues at the till*: **cash register**, cash box, cash drawer, strongbox; **checkout**, cash desk, pay desk, counter.
□ **have one's fingers/hand in the till** *he was caught with his fingers in the till and sacked*: **steal**, thieve, rob one's employer, help oneself, embezzle, misappropriate funds; rare peculate, defalcate.

till³ verb *he went back to tilling the land*: **cultivate**, work, farm, plough, dig, spade, turn over, turn up, break up, loosen, harrow, prepare, fertilize, plant; literary delve.

tilt verb **1** *his hat tilted forward a little | they tilted their chairs back on two legs*: **lean**, tip, list, slope, camber, bank, slant, incline, pitch, dip, cant, bevel, angle, cock, heel, careen, bend, be at an angle.
▷ANTONYMS level, right; be/come level, be/come upright.
2 *he tilts at his prey*: **charge**, rush, run; **lunge**, prod, poke, jab, thrust.
3 historical *like a knight tilting at a wayside tournament*: **joust**, tourney, enter the lists; contend, spar, fight, clash.
▶ noun **1** *Mum's cup was on a tilt*: **slope**, list, camber, gradient, bank, slant, incline, pitch, dip, cant, bevel, angle, heel; N. Amer. grade, downgrade, upgrade.
2 *a tilt of the head*: **nod**, dip, tip, inclination, cock, bob.
3 historical *knights would take part in a tilt*: **joust**, tournament, tourney, lists, combat, contest, fight, duel.
4 *a tilt at the European Cup*: **attempt on**, bid for; informal go, crack, shot.
□ **(at) full tilt 1** *they charged full tilt down the side of the dell*: **(at) full speed**, (at) full pelt, as fast as one's legs can carry one, at a gallop, helter-skelter, headlong, hotfoot, post-haste, hurriedly, hastily, wildly, pell-mell, impetuously, recklessly, rashly, at breakneck speed, precipitately, impulsively; informal p.d.q. (pretty damn quick), double quick, at a lick, hell for leather, pronto, at the double, a mile a minute, like the wind, like a bomb, like a bat out of hell, like a scalded cat, like the deuce, like nobody's business, like (greased) lightning, like a madman/madwoman; Brit. informal like the clappers, at a rate of knots, like billy-o; N. Amer. informal lickety-split; literary apace; archaic hurry-scurry. **2** *the marketing blitz has raged at full tilt for some time now*: **with great force**, (with) full force, full blast, with a will, for all one is worth, with might and main, with all the stops out, all out, with a vengeance, vigorously, energetically, strongly, powerfully, madly; informal hammer and tongs, going great guns, like crazy, like mad; Brit. informal like billy-o.

timber noun **1** *tenants had the right to cut standing timber*: **wood**, logs, firewood; planks, wood products; forest, woodland, woods; N. Amer. lumber.
2 *the timbers of wrecked ships*: **(wooden) beam**, spar, pole, plank, batten, lath, board, joist, rafter.

timbre noun *the Czech orchestra have just the right timbre for Smetana*: **tone**, sound, sound quality, voice, voice quality, colour, tone colour, tonality, resonance, ring.

time noun **1** *what time is it?* **hour**; dated o'clock.
2 *late at night was the best time to leave*: **moment**, point, point in time, occasion, hour, minute, second, instant, juncture, stage, phase.
3 *he worked there for a time*: **while**, spell, stretch, stint, span, season, interval, period, period of time, length of time, duration, run, space, phase, stage, term; Brit. informal patch.
4 *in the time of the dinosaurs*: **era**, age, epoch, period, aeon, years, days; generation, date.
5 *I've known a lot of women in my time*: **lifetime**, life, life span, allotted span, days, time on earth, existence, threescore years and ten; this mortal coil; informal born days.
6 *he had been a professional actor in his time*: **heyday**, day, hour, prime, best days/years, youth, vigour, springtime, salad days, maturity.
7 *he would have a hard time in prison*: **situation**, state of affairs, experience, life, way of life; **conditions**, circumstances, affairs, surroundings, environment, context, background, ambience, atmosphere.
8 *tunes in waltz time*: **rhythm**, tempo, beat, pulse, flow; metre, measure, cadence, pattern; accent, stress.
□ **ahead of time** *the bridge was declared ready seven months ahead of time*: **early**, earlier than expected, earlier than required, in good time, with time to spare, timely, in advance, sooner, in readiness, already.
▷ANTONYMS behind time, late.
□ **ahead of one's/its time** *he broke all the rules and achieved an effect that was way ahead of its time*: **revolutionary**, avant-garde, futuristic, innovatory, innovative, innovational, trailblazing, pioneering, groundbreaking; ultra-modern, advanced, highly developed, the latest, new, the newest, up to the minute.
▷ANTONYMS behind the times.
□ **all the time** *he works all the time*: **constantly**, the entire time, around the clock, day and night, night and day, {morning, noon, and night}, {day in, day out}, at all times, always, without a break, ceaselessly, endlessly, incessantly, perpetually, permanently, interminably, unceasingly, continuously, continually, eternally, unremittingly, remorselessly, relentlessly; informal 24-7; archaic without surcease.
▷ANTONYMS never; intermittently.
□ **at one time 1** *she was a nurse at one time*: **formerly**, previously, once, in the past, at one point, at some point, once upon a time, time was when, in days/times gone by, in times past, in the (good) old days, back in the day, long ago; literary in days/times of yore, of yore; archaic sometime, erst, erstwhile, whilom. ▷ANTONYMS never.
2 *several matches were going on at one time*: **simultaneously**, at once, at the same time, at one and the same time, at the same instant/moment, concurrently, concomitantly; together, all together, alongside each other, in unison, in concert, in chorus, as a group; rare synchronously.
▷ANTONYMS separately, consecutively.
□ **at the same time 1** *they arrived at the same time*: **simultaneously**, at the same instant/moment, together, all together, as a group, at once, at one and the same time, at one time, concurrently, concomitantly, alongside each other, in unison, in concert, in chorus; rare synchronously.
▷ANTONYMS separately, consecutively.
2 *I can't really explain it, but at the same time I'm not convinced*: **nevertheless**, nonetheless, even so, however, but, still, yet, though, be that as it may, for all that, in spite of that/everything, despite that/everything, after everything, having said that, just the same, all the same, in any event, come what may, at any rate, notwithstanding, regardless, anyway, anyhow; informal still and all; archaic howbeit, withal, natheless.
□ **at times** *she is at times cruel and ruthless*: **sometimes**, occasionally, from time to time, (every) now and then/again, every so often, (every) once in a while, on occasion, on occasions, on the odd occasion, off and on, at intervals, periodically, sporadically, spasmodically, erratically, irregularly, intermittently, in/by fits and starts, fitfully, discontinuously, piecemeal; rare interruptedly.
▷ANTONYMS constantly.
□ **behind time** *she was behind time and had to rush*: **late**, not on time, behind, behind schedule, behind target, behindhand, delayed, running late, overdue, belated, tardy, unpunctual; slow, dilatory.
▷ANTONYMS ahead of time, early.
□ **behind the times** *the children considered Dad to be behind the times*: **old-fashioned**, outmoded, out of fashion, out of date, unfashionable, frumpish, frumpy, out of style, outdated, dated, out, outworn, old, former, dead, musty, old-time, old-world, behindhand, past, bygone, archaic, obsolescent, obsolete, ancient, antiquated, superannuated; defunct, medieval, prehistoric, antediluvian, old-fogeyish, old-fangled, conservative, backward-looking, quaint, anachronistic, crusted, feudal, fusty, moth-eaten, olde worlde; French démodé, vieux jeu, passé; informal old hat, square, not with it, out of the ark, creaky, mouldy; N. Amer. informal horse-and-buggy, clunky, rinky-dink, mossy; archaic square-toed.
▷ANTONYMS up to date; ahead of one's time.
□ **for the time being** *the sale has been cancelled for the time being, at least until prices recover*: **for now**, for the moment, for the present, in the interim, for the nonce, in/for the meantime, in the meanwhile; for a short time, for a short/little while, briefly, momentarily, fleetingly; temporarily, provisionally, pro tem; informal for the minute; Latin pro tempore, ad interim; French en attendant.
▷ANTONYMS permanently.
□ **from time to time** *all children act up from time to time*: **sometimes**, occasionally, (every) now and then/again, every so often, (every) once in a while, on occasion, on occasions, on the odd occasion, off and on, at times, at intervals, periodically, sporadically, spasmodically, erratically, irregularly, intermittently, in/by fits and starts, fitfully, discontinuously, piecemeal; rare interruptedly.
▷ANTONYMS constantly.
□ **in no time** *you'll have perfect-looking skin in no time | I can run there and back in no time*: **(very) soon**, in a second, in a minute, in a moment, in a trice, in a flash, shortly, any second, any minute, any minute now, in a short time, in an instant, in less than no time, in no time at all, in next to no time, before you know it, before long; **(very) quickly**, rapidly, swiftly, at the speed of light; **suddenly**, immediately, instantly, instantaneously, promptly, without delay, post-haste; N. Amer. momentarily; informal in a jiffy, in two shakes, in two shakes of a lamb's tail, before you can say Jack Robinson, before you can say knife, in the twinkling of an eye, in a twinkling, in the blink of an eye, in a blink, in the wink of an eye, in a wink; Brit. informal in a tick, in two ticks, in a mo; N. Amer. informal in a snap.
▷ANTONYMS not for a while; slowly.
□ **in good time** *we'll be there in good time*: **punctual(ly)**, prompt(ly), on time; early, with time to spare, ahead of time, before the appointed time, ahead of schedule.
▷ANTONYMS late.
□ **in time 1** *I came back in time for Molly's party*: **early enough**, in good time, punctually, promptly, on time, not too late, with time to spare, at the appointed/right time, on schedule. ▷ANTONYMS late.
2 *the attraction of the uniform palled, and, in time, she left the service*: **eventually**, ultimately, finally, in the end, as time goes on/by, by and by, one day, some day, sooner or later, in a while, after a bit, in the long run, in the fullness of time, when all is said and done, at a later time, at a later date, at length, at a future time/date, at some point in the future, in the future, in time to come, in due course. ▷ANTONYMS never.
□ **many a time** *many a time they had gone to bed hungry*: **frequently**, often, repeatedly, again and again, over and over (again), time and (time)

again, time after time, many times, on many occasions, many times over; {day in, day out}, day after day, {week in, week out}, night and day, all the time; persistently, recurrently, constantly, continually, regularly; N. Amer. oftentimes; Latin ad nauseam; literary many a time and oft, oft, oft-times.
▷ANTONYMS occasionally.
□ **on time** *the train was on time | we paid our bills on time*: **punctual(ly)**, prompt(ly), in time, in good time, to/on schedule, when expected, timely, well timed; informal on the dot; Brit. informal bang/spot on time.
▷ANTONYMS late.
□ **time after time** *the camera produces excellent results time after time*: **repeatedly**, again and again, over and over (again), time and (time) again, frequently, often, many times, many a time, on many occasions, many times over; {day in, day out}, day after day, {week in, week out}, night and day, all the time; persistently, recurrently, constantly, continually, regularly; N. Amer. oftentimes; Latin ad nauseam; literary many a time and oft, oft, oft-times.
▷ANTONYMS sporadically, never.
▸ **verb 1** *his meeting had been timed for three o'clock*: **schedule**, set, set up, arrange, organize, fix, fix up, fix a time for, book, line up, slot in, prearrange, timetable, bill, programme, plan; N. Amer. slate.
2 *I had timed my arrival just about perfectly*: **regulate**, adjust, calculate, set, synchronize.
3 *he timed it—it took two minutes and forty-three seconds*: **measure**, put a stopwatch on, meter, count; informal clock.

Word links **time**

chronological, **horological**, **temporal** relating to time
chrono- related prefix, as in *chronograph*
horology study of time
chronometry, **horology** measurement of time
chronophobia fear of time

time-honoured adjective *the barley is spread out and turned by hand in the time-honoured fashion*: **traditional**, established, long-established, long-standing, long-lived, old-time, historic, age-old, folk, old-world, ancestral, enduring, lasting; **respected**, tried and tested, proven; **customary**, conventional, familiar, classic, ritual, ritualistic, habitual, set, fixed, routine, usual, wonted.

timeless adjective *this pretty wall clock has timeless good looks*: **lasting**, **classic**, enduring, ageless, permanent, perpetual, perennial, abiding, unfailing, unchanging, never-changing, changeless, unvarying, unfading, invariable, unending, without end, ceaseless, never dying, undying, deathless, immortal, eternal, everlasting, immutable, indestructible, imperishable; rare sempiternal, perdurable.
▷ANTONYMS ephemeral, fleeting.

timely adjective *a timely warning*: **opportune**, well timed, at the right time, prompt, punctual, convenient, appropriate, suitable, apt, fitting, expedient, felicitous; archaic seasonable.
▷ANTONYMS inopportune, ill-timed, inappropriate, late.

Choose the right word **timely, opportune, auspicious**

See **opportune**.

time-server noun *the party is filling key state posts with its own loyal time-servers*: **equivocator**, trimmer, Vicar of Bray; **hypocrite**, Janus, double-dealer, snake in the grass; **sycophant**, toady, crawler, fawner, truckler, groveller, kowtower, minion, hanger-on, leech, puppet, spaniel; informal bootlicker, yes-man; rare tergiversator.

time-serving adjective *they left the field to their more time-serving and less scrupulous brethren*: **equivocating**, shifting, trimming, temporizing, shuffling; **hypocritical**, two-faced, double-dealing, treacherous, perfidious; **sycophantic**, servile, subservient, deferential, obsequious, grovelling, toadying; rare tergiversating.

timetable noun **1** *a bus timetable | do you have a hectic timetable and feel you just don't have the time to exercise?* **schedule**, programme, agenda, calendar, diary, appointment book/diary, engagement diary, social life; list, rota, roster; itinerary.
2 *there was little place on the timetable for music, dance, and art*: **syllabus**, curriculum, course, programme of instruction, teaching programme.
▸ **verb** *German lessons were timetabled on Wednesday and Friday*: **schedule**, set, set up, arrange, organize, sort out, fix, fix up, fix a time for, time, book, line up, slot in, prearrange, bill, programme, plan; N. Amer. slate.

time-worn adjective **1** *the carpet was old and time-worn*: **worn out**, worn, well worn, old; thin, holey, moth-eaten, mangy, ragged, frayed, tattered, battered, dog-eared; decrepit, shabby, scruffy, unkempt; having seen better days, falling apart at the seams, in shreds, in tatters, falling to pieces, broken-down, ruined, damaged; informal tatty, ratty, the worse for wear; N. Amer. informal raggedy, raggedy-ass; Austral. informal warby; rare out at elbows.
▷ANTONYMS pristine, new.
2 *time-worn faces*: **old**, aged, ancient, weathered, lined, wrinkled, hoary.
▷ANTONYMS unlined, fresh.
3 *unimaginative and time-worn presentations*: **hackneyed**, trite, banal, vapid, platitudinous, clichéd, cliché-ridden, stock, conventional, unoriginal, derivative, overused, overworked, worn out, threadbare, tired, stale, dull, pedestrian, run-of-the-mill, routine, humdrum, stereotyped; informal old hat, corny, played out; rare truistic, bromidic.
▷ANTONYMS imaginative, fresh.

timid adjective *I was too timid to ask for what I wanted*: **easily frightened**, lacking courage, fearful, apprehensive, afraid, frightened, scared, faint-hearted; trembling, quaking, cowering, weak-kneed; **shy**, diffident, bashful, self-effacing, shrinking, unassuming, unassertive, reserved, retiring, reticent, quiet, timorous, nervous, modest, demure, coy, meek, humble; **cowardly**, pusillanimous, lily-livered, pigeon-hearted, spineless, craven; informal wimpish, sissy, yellow, yellow-bellied, chicken, gutless; archaic poor-spirited, recreant.
▷ANTONYMS bold, forthcoming, brazen.

Choose the right word **timid, shy, bashful, diffident**

See **shy**[1].

timorous adjective *she was no helpless, timorous female*: **easily frightened**, lacking courage, fearful, apprehensive, faint-hearted; trembling, quaking, cowering, weak-kneed; **shy**, diffident, bashful, self-effacing, shrinking, unassuming, unassertive, reserved, retiring, reticent, quiet, timid, nervous, modest, demure, coy, meek, humble; informal wimpish, sissy, yellow, yellow-bellied, chicken, gutless, trepidatious; archaic poor-spirited, recreant.
▷ANTONYMS bold, forthcoming, brazen.

tincture noun **1** *tincture of iodine*: **solution**, suspension, infusion, potion, elixir, extract, essence, quintessence, concentrate.
2 *she could not keep a tincture of bitterness out of her voice*: **trace**, note, tinge, touch, dash, suggestion, hint, bit, scintilla, impression, air, savour, flavour, element, strand, streak, vein, overtone, suspicion, soupçon, whisper, whiff.

tinge verb **1** *a mass of white blossom tinged with pink*: **tint**, colour, dye, stain, shade, suffuse, flush, imbue, wash, overlay, bathe, saturate, steep, impregnate, permeate, penetrate, pervade, run through.
2 *his optimism is tinged with realism*: **influence**, affect, touch, flavour, colour, suffuse, imbue, modify, magnify, distort, poison, sour, spice up, enliven.
▸ **noun 1** *the light had a blue tinge to it*: **tint**, colour, shade, tone, hue, tincture, cast, flush, blush.
2 *a tinge of cynicism appeared in his writing*: **trace**, note, touch, dash, suggestion, hint, bit, scintilla, impression, air, savour, flavour, element, strand, streak, vein, overtone, suspicion, soupçon, whisper, whiff, tincture.

tingle verb **1** *her flesh still tingled from the shock*: **prickle**, sting, smart, prick, itch, be itchy, be irritated, have a creeping sensation, have goose pimples, have gooseflesh, have pins and needles; N. Amer. have goosebumps.
2 *she was tingling with excitement*: **tremble**, quiver, quaver, shiver, quake, twitch, wiggle, throb, shudder, pulsate, vibrate.
▸ **noun 1** *she felt a tingle in the back of her neck*: **prickling**, tingling, sting, stinging, smart, smarting, pricking, itch, creeping sensation, goose pimples, gooseflesh, pins and needles; N. Amer. goosebumps.
2 *she felt another tingle of excitement*: **tremor**, wave, rush, surge, flash, flush, blaze, stab, dart, throb, tremble, quiver, shiver, flutter, shudder, vibration; flow, gush, stream, flood, torrent.

tinker verb *he spent hours **tinkering with** the car | these proposals will do no more than **tinker with** the existing laws*: **try to mend/improve**, work amateurishly on, fiddle with, play (about/around) with, toy with, trifle with, dally with, dabble with, potter about with, fool about/around with; tamper with, interfere with, meddle with; tinker at/with the edges of, adjust slightly; informal mess about/around with, rearrange the deckchairs on the Titanic; Brit. informal muck about/around with.

tinkle verb **1** *a bell tinkled as he went into the shop*: **ring**, jingle, jangle, chime, peal, ding, ping, clink, chink; rare tintinnabulate.
2 *cool water tinkled in the stone fountain*: **splash**, purl, babble, burble; literary plash.
▸ **noun 1** *the tinkle of the doorbell*: **ring**, chime, peal, ding, ping, clink, chink, jingle, jangle; rare tintinnabulation.
2 *the faint tinkle of water*: **splash**, purl, babble, burble; literary plash.
3 Brit. informal *I'll give them a tinkle*: **telephone call**, phone call, call; informal buzz; Brit. informal ring, bell.

tinny adjective **1** *tinny music played in the background*: **jangling**, jangly, jingling, jingly, plinky, thin, metallic.
▷ANTONYMS full, round, deep.
2 *a tinny little car*: **flimsy**, thin, insubstantial, cheap, cheapjack, shoddy, poor-quality, inferior, low-grade, tawdry, rubbishy, trashy, gimcrack, jerry-built; informal tacky, tatty.
▷ANTONYMS solid, stout, well made.

tinpot adjective informal *some tinpot little dictatorship*: **inferior**, second-rate, third-rate, gimcrack; informal Mickey Mouse, poxy; Brit. informal twopenny-halfpenny, pathetic; N. Amer. informal two-bit, dime-store; N. Amer. vulgar slang chickenshit.

tinsel noun **1** *fairy lights and tinsel hung from the ceiling*: **spangle**, glitter, metallic yarn; rare clinquant.
2 *his taste for the tinsel of the art world*: **ostentation**, showiness, show, showing off, ostentatiousness, pretentiousness, pretension, vulgarity, conspicuousness, obtrusiveness, display, flamboyance, gaudiness, garishness, tawdriness, meretriciousness, brashness, loudness, extravagance, ornateness, theatricality; kitschness, affectation, bad taste, tastelessness, self-advertisement, exhibitionism, flaunting; informal flashiness, flash, flashness, glitz, glitziness, ritziness, swankiness, swank, splashiness.
▶ **adjective** *Hollywood and its tinsel stardom*: **ostentatious**, pretentious, showy, conspicuous, obtrusive, flamboyant, gaudy, garish, tawdry, meretricious, trashy, brash, vulgar, loud, extravagant, fancy, ornate, affected, theatrical, overdone, over-elaborate; kitsch, tasteless; informal flash, flashy, over the top, OTT, glitzy, ritzy, swanky, splashy; N. Amer. informal superfly, bling-bling, dicty.

tint noun **1** *the sky was taking on an apricot tint*: **shade**, colour, tone, hue, tinge, cast, tincture, flush, blush.
2 *a hair tint*: **dye**, colourant, colouring, wash; streaking, highlights, lowlights.

tiny adjective *a tiny person | a tiny sum*: **minute**, small-scale, scaled-down, mini, baby, toy, pocket, petite, dwarfish, knee-high, miniature, minuscule, microscopic, nanoscopic, infinitesimal, micro, diminutive, pocket-sized, reduced, Lilliputian; trivial, trifling, negligible, insignificant, unimportant, minor, of no account, of no consequence, of no importance, not worth bothering about, not worth mentioning, inconsequential, minimal, inappreciable, imperceptible, nugatory, petty; token, nominal; **paltry**, inadequate, insufficient, meagre, derisory, pitiful, pathetic, miserable; Scottish wee; N. Amer. vest-pocket; informal teeny, teeny-weeny, teensy, teensy-weensy, weeny, itsy-bitsy, itty-bitty, eensy, eensy-weensy, tiddly, pint-sized, bite-sized, piddling, piffling, measly, mingy, poxy; Brit. informal titchy; N. Amer. informal little-bitty, nickel-and-dime.
▷**ANTONYMS** huge, significant.

tip[1] noun **1** *the tip of the spear*: **point**, end, extremity, head, sharp end, spike, prong, tine, nib.
2 *the tips of the Glencoe mountains*: **peak**, point, top, summit, apex, crown, crest, pinnacle, heights, brow, cap; spire; vertex, acme, zenith, apogee.
3 *the sticks have tips fitted to protect them*: **cap**, cover, ferrule.
▶ **verb** *mountains tipped with snow*: **cap**, top, crown, surmount, finish.

tip[2] verb **1** *the hay caught fire when the candle **tipped over** | the boat **tipped over***: **overturn**, turn over, topple (over), fall (over), tumble (over), overbalance; keel over, pitch (over), turn topsy-turvy, capsize, turn turtle; Nautical pitchpole.
▷**ANTONYMS** right itself.
2 *a whale could **tip over** a small boat*: **upset**, overturn, topple over, turn over, throw over, knock over, push over, knock down, upend, invert, capsize, turn topsy-turvy; informal roll; archaic overset.
▷**ANTONYMS** level, right.
3 *I tipped my seat back | the car had tipped to one side*: **lean**, tilt, list, slope, camber, bank, slant, incline, pitch, dip, cant, bevel, angle, cock, heel, careen, bend, be at an angle.
▷**ANTONYMS** level, right; be/become level, be/become upright.
4 *she tipped the contents of the bucket into the trough*: **pour**, empty, drain, unload, dump, discharge, jettison, offload, drop, decant; informal slosh, slop.
▶ **noun** Brit. *you will have to take your own rubbish to the tip*. See **dump** (sense 1 of the noun).

tip[3] noun **1** *he left the waiter a generous tip*: **gratuity**, baksheesh, bonus, little extra, bit extra, present, gift, reward, inducement; French pourboire; S. African bonsella; W. Indian smalls; informal sweetener; Brit. informal dropsy.
2 *lots of useful tips to help you make the right choice*: **hint**, suggestion, piece of advice, word, word of advice, pointer, cue, clue, guideline, recommendation, maxim; warning, word of warning; tip-off, forecast; advice, counsel, guidance, inside information; Brit. nap; informal how-to, wrinkle.
▶ **verb 1** *it was customary to tip taxi drivers*: **give a tip to**, reward, remunerate; informal sweeten.
2 Brit. *she is being tipped as an Oscar nominee*: **predict**, back, recommend, think of, expect; Brit. nap.
□ **tip someone off** informal *the fact that they were so calm should have tipped him off that something was wrong*: **warn**, alert, apprise, give notice, inform, notify, tell, let someone know, make someone aware, give a warning to, give fair warning to, forewarn, put someone on notice/guard, remind; raise/sound the alarm; informal put wise.

tip[4] verb *sometimes the other player will fool you by just tipping a weak shot over your head*: **strike/hit lightly**, touch, tap, flick, flip, lob, kiss, brush, pat, nudge.

tip-off noun informal *arrests came after a tip-off from a member of the public*: **piece of information**, message, alert, prompt, warning, forewarning; hint, idea, cue, clue, lead; information received, evidence, advice, information, notification.

tipple verb **1** *boys discovered tippling were punished*: **drink alcohol**, drink, have a drink; informal indulge, imbibe, booze, take a drop, wet one's whistle, knock something back, hit the bottle, take to the bottle, crack a bottle; Brit. informal bevvy; N. Amer. informal bend one's elbow; archaic wassail, tope.
2 *he tippled some extra rum ration*: **drink**, swallow, gulp (down), guzzle, quaff, attack, down, drink up/down, get down, finish off, polish off, drain, empty, wash something down with, have, take, partake of, ingest, consume, sup, sip, lap; informal sink, kill, imbibe, swig, glug, slug, slurp, swill, hit, knock back, dispose of, toss off, get one's laughing gear round; Brit. informal get outside (of), shift, murder, neck, bevvy; N. Amer. informal snarf, chug, scarf (down); archaic bib.
▶ **noun** informal *their favourite tipple was claret*: **alcoholic drink**, strong drink, drink, liquor, intoxicant; beverage, liquid refreshment; drop, dram, draught, swallow, sip, gulp, nip, tot, bracer, chaser; informal booze, hard stuff, hooch, poison, tincture, libation, swig, slug, glug, swill, snifter; informal, dated quaff.

tippler noun *Londoners are the country's top tipplers, according to official figures*: **drinker**, serious drinker, hard drinker, problem drinker, alcoholic; drunk, drunkard, dipsomaniac, inebriate, sot; informal **boozer**, imbiber, alky, lush, barfly, sponge, souse, dipso, tosspot, wino, soak; Austral./NZ informal hophead; archaic toper; vulgar slang piss artist.
▷**ANTONYMS** teetotaller.

tipsy adjective *Alison had probably been drinking on the plane and was already a bit tipsy*: **merry**, mellow, slightly drunk; Brit. informal tiddly, squiffy.
▷**ANTONYMS** sober.

tirade noun *she rounded on Nathan with a devastating tirade*: **diatribe**, invective, polemic, denunciation, rant, broadside, attack, harangue, verbal onslaught; reviling, railing, decrying, condemnation, brickbats, flak, criticism, censure, lecture, berating, admonishment, admonition, reprimand, rebuke, reproof, reproval, upbraiding, abuse, stream of abuse, battering, stricture, tongue-lashing, vilification, castigation, denouncement, vituperation, obloquy, fulmination; informal knocking, blast; Brit. informal slating; rare philippic.

tire verb **1** *the ascent grew steeper and he began to tire*: **get/grow/become tired**, become fatigued, weaken, grow weak, lose one's strength, flag, droop, drop.
▷**ANTONYMS** stay fresh.
2 *the journey had tired him*: **fatigue**, tire out, wear out, overtire, weary, exhaust, drain, sap, wash out, tax, overtax, enervate, debilitate, enfeeble, jade, incapacitate, devitalize, prostrate; informal whack, shatter, bush, knacker, frazzle, wear to a frazzle, poop, take it out of, fag out, do in, knock out.
▷**ANTONYMS** refresh.
3 *they tired of his difficult behaviour*: **weary**, become/get tired, become/get weary, become/get fed up, become/get fed to death, become/get bored, become/get satiated, become/get jaded, become/get sick, become/get sick to death, sicken; have had a surfeit, have had enough, have had a glut; informal have had something up to here.
4 *their constant boasting tires me*: **bore**, weary, make someone fed up, sicken, nauseate; irk, irritate, exhaust someone's patience, annoy, exasperate, get on someone's nerves; informal get to.
▷**ANTONYMS** stimulate, excite.

tired adjective **1** *you're just tired from travelling*: **worn out**, exhausted, fatigued, tired out, overtired, weary, sleepy, drowsy, wearied, sapped, dog-tired, spent, drained, jet-lagged, played out, debilitated, prostrate, enervated, jaded, low; informal all in, done (in/up), dead, dead beat, dead tired, dead on one's feet, asleep on one's feet, ready to drop, fagged out, bushed, worn to a frazzle, shattered, burnt out; Brit. informal knackered, whacked; N. Amer. informal pooped.
▷**ANTONYMS** energetic, fresh, wide awake.
2 *are you **tired of** having him here?* **fed up with**, bored with/by, weary of, sick of, sick and tired of, jaded with/by, surfeited with/by, satiated by, glutted with/by; (**be tired of**) have had enough of; informal have had a basinful of, have had it up to here with, have had something up to here.
3 *there were tired jokes about buckets and spades*: **hackneyed**, worn out, stale, overworked, threadbare, warmed-up, banal, trite, stock, stereotyped, clichéd, run-of-the-mill, commonplace, platitudinous, unoriginal, unimaginative, uninspired, flat; out of date, outdated, outmoded, passé, archaic, obsolete, defunct, antiquated; N. Amer. warmed-over; informal old hat, corny, out of the ark, played out, past their sell-by date.
▷**ANTONYMS** fresh, lively.

tiredness noun *her eyes were heavy with tiredness*: **fatigue**, weariness, exhaustion, prostration, overtiredness, collapse, jet lag; **sleepiness**, drowsiness, somnolence, doziness; **lethargy**, lassitude, languor, languidness, debility, enervation, listlessness, sluggishness, lifelessness, torpor, inertia.
▷**ANTONYMS** energy, vigour.

tireless adjective *a tireless worker for the party*: **vigorous**, energetic, industrious, determined, resolute, enthusiastic, keen, zealous, forceful, strong, Herculean, spirited, dynamic, intense, dogged, tenacious, persevering, stout, pertinacious; **untiring**, unwearied, unflagging, unremitting, indefatigable, unshakeable, unrelenting, unswerving.
▷**ANTONYMS** lazy, half-hearted.

tiresome adjective **1** *a rather tiresome meeting of the Faculty Committee*: **boring**, dull, tedious, monotonous, humdrum, wearisome, laborious,

wearing, prosaic, unexciting, uninteresting, uneventful, unvarying, unvaried, unremarkable, repetitive, repetitious, routine, ordinary, everyday, day-to-day, quotidian, run-of-the-mill, commonplace, common, workaday, usual, pedestrian; rare banausic.
▷ANTONYMS interesting, exciting.
2 *an exceedingly tiresome man to deal with*: **annoying**, irritating, infuriating, exasperating, maddening, trying, troublesome, bothersome, irksome, vexing, vexatious; informal aggravating, pesky, infernal, pestiferous, plaguy, pestilent.
▷ANTONYMS pleasant.

tiring adjective *it was very tiring work*: **exhausting**, wearying, fatiguing, enervating, draining, sapping, stressful, wearing, trying, crushing; demanding, exacting, taxing, challenging, burdensome, arduous, gruelling, punishing, grinding, onerous, difficult, hard, tough, heavy, laborious, back-breaking, crippling, strenuous, rigorous, uphill, stringent, strict; informal killing, murderous, hellish; rare exigent.

tissue noun **1** *X-rays were accidentally found to penetrate living tissue*: **matter**, material, substance, stuff; flesh, the body.
2 *the flowers are wrapped with tissue and bound with ribbon | a box of tissues*: **tissue paper**, wrapping paper; **paper handkerchief**, disposable handkerchief, facial tissue, toilet tissue, toilet paper, wipe, paper towel, kitchen towel; trademark Kleenex.
3 *modern roofing felt is based on glass tissue reinforced with polyester*: **gauze**, gossamer, chiffon; netting, mesh, lattice, web, webbing, screen, mat; fabric, material, textile, fibre.
4 *a tissue of lies*: **web**, network, nexus, maze, tangle, knot, complex, mass, conglomeration, set, series, chain.

> *Word links* **tissue**
>
> **histo-** relating to organic tissue, as in *histopathology*

titanic adjective *Blackburn Rovers were overcome in a titanic struggle with Liverpool*: **colossal**, gigantic, monumental, massive, enormous, terrific, tremendous, fantastic, towering, immense, vast, giant, mammoth, elephantine, gargantuan, prodigious, huge, very large, great, substantial, mighty, Herculean, Brobdingnagian; informal jumbo, bumper, monster, stupendous, humongous, whopping, whopping great, thumping, thumping great, astronomical, mega; Brit. informal whacking, whacking great, ginormous.

titbit noun **1** *when the puppy comes to you, reward it with a titbit*: **delicacy**, tasty morsel, dainty, fancy, confection, bonne bouche, luxury, treat; snack, nibble, savoury, appetizer; informal goody, bite, little something; N. Amer. tidbit; archaic sweetmeat.
2 *I'll tell you one titbit that should cheer you up*: **piece of gossip**, bit of scandal, juicy bit of gossip, juicy bit of news, scrap of information, morsel of information, item of information.

tit for tat noun *the routine diplomatic tit for tat when countries expel each other's envoys*: **retaliation**, reprisal, counterattack, counterstroke, comeback; revenge, vengeance, retribution, requital, recrimination, an eye for an eye, a tooth for a tooth, as good as one gets, getting even, redress, repayment, payback; Latin lex talionis; informal a taste of someone's own medicine; rare ultion, a Roland for an Oliver.

titillate verb *the lurid sensationalism designed to titillate local audiences*: **arouse**, rouse, excite, stimulate, stir, thrill, interest, attract, please, fascinate; **tantalize**, lead on, seduce, tempt, ravish, inflame, kindle, provoke, quicken; informal turn on, send.
▷ANTONYMS bore, turn off.

> *Easily confused words* **titillate or titivate?**
>
> The verbs **titillate** and **titivate** sound alike but do not have the same meaning. *Titillate*, the commoner word, means 'stimulate or excite', often with sexual overtones, as in *the press are paid to titillate the public* or *a titillating account of the prostitution trade*. *Titivate*, on the other hand, means no more than 'smarten up with small changes', as in *she titivated her hair*.

titillating adjective *he had deliberately chosen a titillating title to help sales*: **sexually arousing**, sexually exciting, sexually stimulating, provocative, salacious, lurid, sexy, sensual, erotic, pornographic; **suggestive**, seductive, tantalizing, tempting, interesting, fascinating, captivating; Brit. informal saucy.
▷ANTONYMS boring, off-putting.

titivate verb informal *she titivated her hair*: **groom**, tidy, arrange, brush, comb, smooth, smarten (up), spruce up, freshen (up), beautify, pretty, preen, primp, prink (up); informal doll up, tart up; N. Amer. informal gussy up; archaic trig, plume.

> *Easily confused words* **titivate or titillate?**
>
> See **titillate**.

title noun **1** *the author and title of the book*: **name**, subtitle; subject.
2 *the cartoon title and ensuing caption*: **caption**, legend, inscription, label, heading, subheading, head, motto, slogan, device, wording, rubric; credit.
3 *the company publishes 400 titles a year*: **publication**, work, offering; book, newspaper, paper, magazine, periodical, organ.
4 *he will inherit the title of Duke of Marlborough*: **designation**, name, denomination, label, rank, status, office, position; **form of address**, epithet, style; informal moniker, handle; formal appellation.
5 *the fifth British woman athlete to win an Olympic title*: **championship**, first place, crown, belt, medal, prize, trophy, cup, shield, plate; laurels, bays, palm, honour, accolade.
6 *the vendor is obliged to prove his* ***title to*** *the land*: **ownership of**, proprietorship of, freehold of, entitlement to, right to, proprietary rights to, claim to; possession of, holding of, hold of, tenure of, control of, keeping of, charge of, custody of, guardianship of.
▸ verb *a policy paper titled 'Law and Order'*: **call**, entitle, name, dub, give something the title of, designate, label, tag, describe something as, style, term, christen, baptize; rare clepe, denominate.

titter verb *several of his class began to titter*: **giggle**, snigger, snicker, tee-hee, give a half-suppressed laugh, chuckle; smirk, sneer, simper.
▸ noun *she caused a few titters*: **giggle**, snigger, snicker, tee-hee, half-suppressed laugh, chuckle; smirk, sneer, simper.

tittle noun *he had passed the night without a tittle of sleep*: **bit**, tiny amount, scrap, shred, speck, iota, particle, ounce, whit, jot, jot or tittle, atom, crumb, morsel, fragment, grain, drop, hint, touch, trace, suggestion, whisper, suspicion, scintilla, spot, mite, modicum; Irish stim; informal smidgen, smidge.

tittle-tattle noun *she would never listen to tittle-tattle*. See **gossip** (sense 1 of the noun).
▸ verb *he was tittle-tattling all over the village*. See **gossip** (sense 1 of the verb).

titular adjective **1** *the chancellor is the titular head of a university*: **nominal**, in title/name only, formal, official, ceremonial; token, puppet; theoretical, purported, supposed, ostensible.
2 *the work's titular song*: **eponymous**, identifying; after whom/which something is named; rare designative, appellative, denominative.

toad noun informal *you're an arrogant little toad*: **wretch**; informal beast, pig, swine, rat, creep, bastard, louse, snake, skunk, dog, weasel, lowlife, scumbag, heel, stinkpot, stinker, bad lot, no-good, son of a bitch, s.o.b., nasty piece of work; Brit. informal scrote; Irish informal spalpeen; N. Amer. informal rat fink, fink, schmuck; Austral. informal dingo; NZ informal kuri; informal, dated rotter, hound, bounder, cad, blighter; black English rass; vulgar slang shit, sod, prick; archaic blackguard, dastard, knave, varlet, whoreson.

> *Word links* **toad**
>
> **batrachian**, **anural** relating to toads

toady noun *a conniving little toady with an eye for the main chance*: **sycophant**, obsequious person, creep, crawler, fawner, flatterer, flunkey, lackey, truckler, groveller, doormat, lickspittle, kowtower, minion, hanger-on, leech, puppet, stooge, spaniel, Uriah Heep; informal bootlicker, yes-man; vulgar slang arse-licker, arse-kisser; Brit. vulgar slang bum-sucker; N. Amer. vulgar slang brown-nose, suckhole.
▷ANTONYMS independent, one's own master.
▸ verb *she imagined him* ***toadying to*** *his rich clients*: **be obsequious towards**, be servile towards, be sycophantic towards, grovel to, kowtow to, abase oneself to, demean oneself to, bow and scrape to, prostrate oneself to, truckle to, make up to, play up to, dance attendance on, fawn on, ingratiate oneself with, rub up the right way, curry favour with, flatter, court; informal suck up to, crawl to, creep to, be all over, lick someone's boots, fall all over, butter up, keep someone sweet; N. Amer. brown-nose; vulgar slang lick/kiss someone's arse.
▷ANTONYMS defy.

toast noun **1** *he raised his glass in a toast*: **tribute**, salute, salutation; honour, health; compliments, best wishes, greetings; archaic pledge.
2 *he was the toast of the West End*: **darling**, **celebrity**, favourite, pet, heroine, hero, talk; apple of someone's eye, the focus of attention; Brit. informal blue-eyed boy/girl; N. Amer. informal fair-haired boy/girl.
▸ verb **1** *meanwhile, split and toast the muffins*: **brown**, crisp (up), grill, barbecue, bake, singe, sear; N. Amer. broil, charbroil.
2 *she toasted her hands in front of the fire*: **warm**, warm up, heat, heat up, roast, bring back to life.
▷ANTONYMS cool down.
3 *we toasted the couple with champagne*: **pay tribute to**, drink (to) the health of, drink to, salute, honour; archaic pledge.

today adverb **1** *the work must be finished today*: **this day**, this very day, before tomorrow, this morning, this afternoon, this evening.
2 *the complex tasks demanded of computers today*: **nowadays**, at the present time, these days, in these times, at this time, in this day and age, now, just now, right now, currently, at present, at the present moment, at this moment in time; in the present climate, in the present circumstances, things being what they are; N. Amer. presently; rare contemporarily.
▸ noun **1** *today is a rest day*: **this day**, this very day.
2 *policies relevant to the society of today*: **the present**, the present day, the present time, now, the here and now, this moment, this time, this period, this age.

Word links **today**

hodiernal relating to today

toddle verb **1** *he watched the child who toddled towards him*: **totter**, teeter, wobble, falter, stagger, dodder, waddle, reel, lurch; shuffle, shamble, drag one's feet, stumble, lumber; rare doddle.
2 informal *every afternoon, Matilda would toddle down to the library*: **amble**, wander, meander, stroll, saunter, maunder; informal mosey, tootle; Brit. informal mooch; N. Amer. informal putter.

to-do noun informal *Sally-Anne thought all this a great to-do about nothing*: **commotion**, fuss, fuss and bother, bother, trouble, ado, disturbance, flurry, excitement, uproar, ferment, tumult, turmoil, hurly-burly, brouhaha, furore, storm, palaver, pantomime, production, hoopla, folderol, hue and cry, bustle, hustle and bustle, pother; informal hoo-ha, hullabaloo, flap, song and dance, business, rumpus, ballyhoo, splash; Brit. informal kerfuffle, carry-on; NZ informal bobsy-die.

toe noun
□ **on one's toes** *unfamiliar situations keep us on our toes*: **alert**, quick-witted, sharp, bright, quick, keen, perceptive, wide awake, responsive, agile, acute, astute; informal on the ball, quick off the mark, quick on the uptake, all there, with it, bright-eyed and bushy-tailed.
▸ verb
□ **toe the line** *the medical community needs to toe the line on informed consent*: **conform**, follow convention, be conventional, follow tradition, follow custom, fit in, adapt, adjust, follow the crowd, run with the pack, swim with the stream; comply, acquiesce, do what one is told, toe the line, obey the rules, comply with the rules, observe the rules, abide by the rules, adhere to the rules, act in accordance with the rules, follow the rules, keep to the rules, stick to the rules; submit, yield; informal play by the rules, keep in step, go with the flow.
▷ANTONYMS rebel.

together adverb **1** *friends who work together*: **with each other**, in conjunction, jointly, conjointly, in cooperation, cooperatively, in collaboration, in partnership, in combination, as one, in unison, in concert, concertedly, with one accord, in league, in alliance, in collusion, side by side, hand in hand, hand in glove, shoulder to shoulder, cheek by jowl; informal in cahoots.
▷ANTONYMS separately.
2 *they both spoke together*: **simultaneously**, at the same time, at the same instant, at the same moment, all together, as a group, at once, at one and the same time, at one time, concurrently, concomitantly, alongside each other, in unison, in concert, in chorus; rare synchronously.
▷ANTONYMS separately, consecutively.
3 *I was not able to get up for days together*: **in succession**, in a row, at a time, successively, consecutively, running, straight, on end, one after the other, continuously, without a break, without interruption; informal on the trot.
▸ adjective informal *she looks a very together young woman*: **level-headed**, well balanced, well adjusted, balanced, sensible, practical, realistic, with one's feet on the ground, prudent, circumspect, pragmatic, wise, reasonable, rational, mature, stable, sane, even-tempered, commonsensical, full of common sense, judicious, sound, sober, businesslike, reliable, dependable; **well organized**, well ordered, orderly, efficient, neat, tidy, methodical, no-nonsense; **calm**, cool, collected, composed, {cool, calm, and collected}, serene, relaxed, at ease, equable, moderate, unworried, unmoved, unemotional, cool-headed, imperturbable; **self-confident**, confident, self-possessed, assured, self-assured, assertive; informal unflappable.
▷ANTONYMS unbalanced, flustered, disorganized.

toil verb **1** *she rolled up her sleeves and toiled all night*: **work hard**, labour, work one's fingers to the bone, work like a Trojan, work like a dog, work day and night, exert oneself, keep at it, keep one's nose to the grindstone, grind away, slave away, grub away, plough away, plod away; informal slog away, peg away, beaver away, plug away, put one's back into something, work one's guts out, work one's socks off, knock oneself out, sweat blood, kill oneself; Brit. informal graft away, fag; Austral./NZ informal bullock; Brit. vulgar slang work one's balls/arse/nuts off; N. Amer. vulgar slang work one's ass/butt off; archaic drudge, travail, moil.
▷ANTONYMS rest, relax, laze.
2 *she began to toil up the cliff path*: **struggle**, move with difficulty, labour, trudge, tramp, traipse, slog, plod, trek, footslog, sweat, drag oneself, fight (one's way), push; Brit. informal trog, yomp; N. Amer. informal schlep.
▸ noun *a life of toil*: **hard work**, toiling, labour, slaving, struggle, effort, exertion, application, industry, grind, slog, {blood, sweat, and tears}, drudgery; informal sweat, elbow grease; Brit. informal graft; Austral./NZ informal (hard) yakka; archaic travail, moil.

Choose the right word **toil, work, labour**

See **work**.

toilet noun **1** *he had to go to the toilet*: **lavatory**, WC, water closet, (public) convenience, facilities, urinal, privy, latrine, outhouse, earth closet, jakes; Brit. cloakroom, the Ladies, the Gents, powder room; N. Amer. restroom, bathroom, washroom, men's room, ladies' room, comfort station; French pissoir; informal little girls' room, little boys' room, smallest room; Brit. informal loo, bog, khazi, lav, throne, thunderbox, cottage; N. English informal netty; N. Amer. informal can, john, honey bucket, tea room; Austral./NZ informal dunny, little house, dyke; vulgar slang pisser, crapper, shithouse, shitter; Nautical head; archaic closet, garderobe, necessary house.
2 *she had always taken a long time over her toilet*: **washing**, bathing, showering; wash, bath, shower; grooming, dressing, make-up; formal or humorous ablutions; dated toilette; rare lavation, lustration.

toils plural noun literary *Henry had become caught in the toils of his own deviousness*. See **trap** (sense 1 of the noun).

token noun **1** *a token of our appreciation*: **symbol**, sign, emblem, badge, representation, indication, mark, index, manifestation, expression, pledge, demonstration, recognition; evidence, attestation, proof.
2 *he kept the menu as a token of their golden wedding*: **memento**, souvenir, keepsake, reminder, record, trophy, relic, remembrance, memorial; archaic memorandum.
3 *a book token*: **voucher**, coupon, chit, docket, stamp, order, credit note, IOU; Brit. informal chitty.
4 *a telephone token*: **counter**, disc, substitute coin, jetton, chip, piece, man.
▸ adjective **1** *the union is balloting its members for a one-day token strike*: **symbolic**, emblematic, indicative; peppercorn.
2 *the practice now meets only token resistance*: **perfunctory**, slight, nominal, minimal, insignificant, minor, trivial, mild, hollow, unimportant, trifling, of no account, of no consequence, of no importance, not worth bothering about, not worth mentioning, inconsequential, superficial, small, tiny, minute, inappreciable, imperceptible, infinitesimal, nugatory, petty; paltry, inadequate, insufficient, meagre, derisory, pitiful, pathetic, miserable; informal minuscule, piddling, piffling, measly, mingy, poxy; N. Amer. informal nickel-and-dime; rare exiguous.

tolerable adjective **1** *did you have a tolerable journey?* **bearable**, endurable, sufferable, supportable, brookable; admissible, manageable, pardonable, excusable, forgivable.
▷ANTONYMS intolerable.
2 *he had a tolerable voice*: **fairly good**, passable, adequate, all right, acceptable, good enough, sufficiently good, sufficient, satisfactory, moderately good, not (too) bad, average, fair, decent, respectable, presentable; admissible, allowable; mediocre, middling, ordinary, run-of-the-mill, workaday, indifferent, unremarkable, undistinguished, unexceptional, amateur, amateurish; informal OK, so-so, fair-to-middling, nothing to write home about, no great shakes, not up to much, not much cop, bog-standard, vanilla, plain vanilla; NZ informal half-pie.
▷ANTONYMS unacceptable; exceptional; appalling.

tolerance noun **1** *an advocate of religious tolerance*: **forbearance**, toleration, sufferance, liberality, open-mindedness, lack of prejudice, lack of bias, broad-mindedness, liberalism; patience, long-suffering, magnanimity, sympathy, understanding, charity, lenience, leniency, lenity, indulgence, clemency, permissiveness, complaisance, laxness.
▷ANTONYMS intolerance.
2 *tolerance to alcohol decreases with age*: **endurance of**, acceptance of; **resistance to**, immunity to, non-susceptibility to, resilience to.
▷ANTONYMS intolerance.
3 *a 1% maximum tolerance in measurement*: **deviation**, fluctuation, variation, allowance, play, clearance, leeway; **inaccuracy**, imprecision, inexactness.

tolerant adjective *a more tolerant attitude towards other religions*: **open-minded**, forbearing, liberal, unprejudiced, unbiased, unbigoted; broad-minded, catholic, patient, long-suffering, magnanimous, sympathetic, understanding, charitable, lenient, indulgent, permissive, free and easy, easy-going, complaisant, lax.
▷ANTONYMS intolerant, narrow-minded.

tolerate verb **1** *their leader would not tolerate serious dissent | how was it that she could tolerate such noise?* **allow**, permit, authorize, sanction, condone, indulge, agree to, accede to, approve of; **endure**, put up with, bear, take, stand, support, submit to, stomach, undergo; **accept**, swallow, brook, countenance, admit of, recognize, acknowledge; **ignore**, turn a blind eye to, wink at; Scottish thole; informal stick, hack, abide; Brit. informal wear, be doing with; archaic suffer.
▷ANTONYMS ban.
2 *his wife could not tolerate eggs*: **consume**, take, stomach, digest, eat, receive, be subjected to, withstand subjection to, be treated with.

toleration noun **1** *scant toleration is shown to individuals who do not conform*: **forbearance**, liberality, open-mindedness, lack of prejudice, lack of bias, broad-mindedness, liberalism; patience, long-suffering, magnanimity, sympathy, charity, lenience, leniency, lenity, indulgence, sufferance, clemency, permissiveness, condoning, condonation, complaisance, laxness.
2 *the church's toleration of the other great religions*: **acceptance**, tolerance, approval, understanding, endurance, putting up with, ignoring.
3 *countries which do not practise religious toleration*: **freedom of worship**, religious freedom, freedom of conscience.

toll[1] noun **1** *a motorway toll*: **charge**, fee, payment, levy, tariff, dues, tax, duty, impost.
2 *the toll of dead and injured mounted*: **number**, count, tally, total, running total, sum total, grand total, sum, score, reckoning, enumeration, register, record, inventory, list, listing, account, roll, roster, index, directory.
3 *the toll of addictive disease is still terrible*: **adverse effect(s)**, undesirable consequence(s), detriment, harm, damage, injury, hurt; cost, price, loss, disadvantage, suffering, penalty.

toll[2] verb *I had heard the bell toll | the old prison bell was tolled when executions took place*: **ring (out)**, chime (out), strike, peal, knell; sound, clash, clang, bong, boom, resound, reverberate.

tomb noun **burial chamber**, burial place, sepulchre, mausoleum, vault, crypt, undercroft, catacomb, pyramid, charnel house, shrine, ossuary, reliquary; last/final resting place, grave, barrow, burial mound, burial pit; monument, memorial, cenotaph, marker; Archaeology mastaba; rare feretory.

> *Word links* **tomb**
>
> **sepulchral** relating to a tomb

tombstone noun **gravestone**, headstone, stone, grave marker, memorial, monument, obelisk.

tome noun **volume**, book, work, opus, writing, publication, title.

tomfool adjective dated *she was destined to take part in some tomfool caper*. See **silly** (sense 1 of the adjective).

tomfoolery noun *the tomfoolery of MPs at question time*: **silliness**, fooling, clowning, capering, capers, antics, pranks, tricks, buffoonery, skylarking, nonsense, horseplay, mischief, foolishness, foolery, stupidity; informal messing about/around, larking about/around, larks, shenanigans; Brit. informal monkey tricks; dated harlequinade.

tone noun **1** *bassoons add considerably to the tone of the tuba*: **timbre**, sound, sound quality, voice, voice quality, colour, tone colour, tonality, resonance, ring.
2 *'So there you are!' he called in a friendly tone*: **intonation**, tone of voice, mode of expression, expression, inflection, pitch, modulation, accentuation.
3 *the somewhat impatient tone of his letter*: **mood**, quality, feel, style, note, air, attitude, character, spirit, flavour, grain, temper, humour, effect; **tenor**, vein, drift, gist.
4 *the dialling tone*: **note**, beep, bleep, whine, buzz, warble, burr, signal.
5 *old-fashioned tones of primrose, lavender, and rose*: **tint**, shade, colour, hue, tinge, cast, tincture.
▸ verb *the rich orange colour of the wood **tones** beautifully **with** the yellow roses*: **harmonize**, go, go well, blend, fit, coordinate, team, accord; match, suit, complement.
□ **tone something down 1** *he has had to tone down his gaudy garments to get them into department stores*: **subdue**, make less garish, soften, lighten, dim, mute. **2** *the newspapers refused to tone down their criticism of the government*: **moderate**, modify, modulate, mitigate, temper, dampen, soften, lighten; subdue, restrain, stifle, bridle, bottle up, contain; qualify; informal keep the lid on.

tongue noun **1** *a foreign tongue*: **language**, dialect, patois, vernacular, mother tongue, native tongue, jargon, argot, cant, pidgin, creole, lingua franca; speech, parlance; informal lingo, patter.
2 *when would she learn to censor her impetuous tongue?* **way/manner of speaking**, way/manner of talking, form/mode of expression, choice of words, verbal expression; conversation, vocabulary, phraseology, style, parlance, speech; French façon de parler.

> *Word links* **tongue**
>
> **lingual**, **glossal** relating to the tongue
> **glossitis** inflammation of the tongue
> **glossectomy** surgical removal of tongue

t

tongue-tied adjective *usually he was tongue-tied with strangers*: **lost for words**, at a loss for words, struck dumb, dumbstruck, bereft of speech, speechless, wordless, unable to get a word out, inarticulate; mute, dumb, voiceless, silent; informal mum; rare dumbstricken, mumchance, obmutescent.
▷ANTONYMS loquacious, articulate.

tonic noun **1** *for over five thousand years ginseng has been used as a natural tonic*: **stimulant**, restorative, refresher, cordial; Medicine analeptic, roborant; informal pick-me-up, bracer, livener.
2 *we found the change of scene a tonic*: **boost**, stimulant, fillip, pleasure; stimulus, spur, push; informal shot in the arm, pick-me-up, reviver.

too adverb **1** *invasion would be too risky*: **excessively**, overly, over, unduly, immoderately, inordinately, unreasonably, ridiculously, to too great an extent/degree, extremely, very; informal too-too.
2 *Simons wanted his coffee black, too*: **also**, as well, in addition, additionally, into the bargain, besides, furthermore, moreover, yet, on top of that, to boot; plus, again, over and above.

tool noun **1** *a set of garden tools*: **implement**, instrument, utensil, device, apparatus, gadget, appliance, machine, contrivance, contraption, mechanism, aid; informal gimmick, gizmo; **(tools)** hardware, equipment, gear, kit, tackle, paraphernalia.
2 *the beautiful Estella is Miss Havisham's tool*: **dupe**, puppet, pawn, minion, lackey, flunkey, instrument, henchman, creature, cat's paw; informal stooge, sucker, poodle.
▸ verb **1** *the book's spine was of red leather, tooled in gold*: **ornament**, embellish, decorate, work, shape, cut, chase, dress, fashion.
2 informal *they tooled around town in their souped up cars*: **drive**, bowl, ride, motor, travel; informal spin.

tooth noun **1** *he clenched his teeth | a huge creature with massive teeth*: **fang**, denticulation; tusk; Zoology denticle; **(teeth)** dentition; informal gnasher; rare tush.
2 *repairs were made to the gearing, including the replacement of several hundred cog teeth*: **prong**, point, tine, cog, ratchet, sprocket.

> *Word links* **tooth**
>
> **dental** relating to teeth
> **dent-**, **odont-** related prefixes, as in *dentine, odontalgia*
> **-odon** related suffix, as in *mastodon*
> **odontology** study of teeth

toothsome adjective *a toothsome delicacy*: **tasty**, delicious, luscious, mouth-watering, delectable, succulent, palatable; tempting, appetizing, inviting; informal scrumptious, yummy, scrummy, finger-licking, delish, yum-yum; Brit. informal moreish.

top noun **1** *we walked along the top of the cliff*: **summit**, peak, pinnacle, crest, crown, brow, brink, ridge, head, highest point/part, tip, apex, vertex, acme, apogee.
▷ANTONYMS bottom, base.
2 *Mike tapped the top of the table with his knuckles*: **upper part**, upper surface, upper layer.
3 *some growers clip off the carrots' green tops in the field*: **leaves**, shoots, stem, stalk.
▷ANTONYMS root.
4 *she couldn't screw the top of the coffee jar on straight*: **lid**, cap, cover, stopper, cork, bung, plug.
5 *United increased their lead at the top of the table*: **high point**, height, peak, pinnacle, zenith, acme, culmination, climax, crowning point, prime, meridian; success.
▷ANTONYMS low point; failure.
6 *she was screaming at the top of her voice*: **highest level**, utmost extent.
□ **on top of that** *the field work was tiring, and there were household duties on top of that*: **as well**, in addition, too, also, besides, into the bargain, to boot; archaic therewithal.
□ **over the top** informal *her reaction had been a bit over the top*: **excessive**, immoderate, inordinate, extreme, over the limit, exaggerated, extravagant, overblown, too much, unreasonable, needless, disproportionate, undue, unwarranted, uncalled for, unnecessary, going too far; informal a bit much, OTT.
▷ANTONYMS moderate, restrained.
▸ adjective **1** *her office is on the top floor*: **highest**, topmost, uppermost, upmost, upper, furthest up, loftiest.
▷ANTONYMS bottom, lowest.
2 *some of the world's top scientists attended the conference*: **foremost**, leading, top-tier, principal, pre-eminent, greatest, finest, worthiest, highest, elite; informal top-notch.
3 *the top management of the organization*: **chief**, principal, main, leading, highest, high, high-ranking, ruling, commanding; most powerful, most important, prominent, eminent, notable, illustrious.
4 *a top Paris hotel*: **prime**, excellent, superb, superior, choice, select, elite, quality, top-quality, top-grade, first-rate, first-class, top-class, high-grade, grade A, best, finest, premier, choicest, superlative, unsurpassed, unexcelled, unparalleled, peerless, second to none; informal A1, top-notch, ace, crack.
▷ANTONYMS inferior, mediocre.
5 *they are travelling at top speed*: **maximum**, maximal, greatest, topmost, utmost.
▷ANTONYMS minimum, lowest.
▸ verb **1** *sales are expected to top £1.3 billion*: **exceed**, surpass, go beyond, transcend, better, best, beat, defeat, excel, outstrip, outdo, outshine, eclipse, surmount, improve on, go one better than, cap, trump, trounce.
2 *their debut CD is currently topping the charts*: **lead**, head, be first in, be at the top of.
3 *they topped a hill and began the run down the other side*: **reach the top of**, crest, climb, scale, ascend, mount, conquer.
4 *chocolate sponge topped with white chocolate mousse*: **cover**, cap, crown, coat, overspread, finish, garnish.
□ **top something up** *he topped up his glass*: **fill**, refill, refresh, freshen, replenish, recharge, resupply; supplement, add to, augment.
▷ANTONYMS empty, finish.

topic noun *he brought the conversation round to the topic of food and drink*: **subject**, subject matter, theme, issue, matter, point, talking point, question, concern, argument, discussion, thesis, text, concept, field, area, keynote, leitmotif.

> *Choose the right word* **topic, subject, theme**
>
> See **subject**.

topical adjective *a forum for the discussion of topical issues*: **current**, up to date, up to the minute, contemporary, recent; newsworthy, in the news; **relevant**, pressing, important, vital, timely, popular; informal trendy.
▷ANTONYMS out of date, outdated.

topmost adjective **1** *the topmost branches of the tree*: **highest**, top, uppermost, upmost, upper, furthest up, loftiest.
2 *the topmost authority on the subject*: **foremost**, **leading**, principal, pre-eminent, greatest, top, finest, worthiest, highest, elite; **chief**, main, highest-ranking, ruling, commanding, powerful, important, prominent, eminent, notable, illustrious; informal top-notch.

top-notch adjective informal *a pub that serves top-notch beer*: **first-rate**, first-class, top-grade, top-level; **excellent**, superb, splendid, fine, outstanding, great, marvellous, brilliant, superlative, sterling, prime, very good, choice, select, superior; informal A1, ace, crack, top-drawer, tip-top, super, out of this world, stellar, wicked, mega, crucial; Brit. informal brill; Brit. informal, dated top-hole, topping, wizard, capital.

topple verb **1** *he banged the table, causing some of the bottles to **topple over***: **fall**, tumble, overturn, overbalance, tip, keel, drop, pitch, plunge, capsize, collapse, founder, plummet, dive, lose one's balance, go head over heels.
2 *protesters toppled a huge statue*: **knock over**, knock down, upset, push over, tip over, upend, capsize; fell, tear down, flatten, level.
3 *a plot to topple the government*: **overthrow**, oust, depose, unseat, overturn, bring down, overcome, bring low, defeat, get rid of, dislodge, eject, supplant, dethrone, defenestrate.

topsy-turvy adverb & adjective **1** *a topsy-turvy flag*: **upside down**, wrong side up, head over heels, inverted, reversed, upset, backwards, vice versa.
▷ANTONYMS right way up.
2 *my emotions are all topsy-turvy*: **in disorder**, disordered, disorderly, in confusion, confused, mixed up, in a muddle, muddled, in a jumble, jumbled, in chaos, chaotic, disorganized, messy, untidy, in disarray, in a mess, awry, askew, upside down, upset, disrupted, at sixes and sevens; informal higgledy-piggledy, every which way.
▷ANTONYMS ordered, neat.

torch noun **1** *he clicked on the torch and a weak beam shone forth*: **lamp**, light, flashlight, beacon; rare illuminant, flambeau.
2 *he held a wolf at bay using a flaming torch*: **firebrand**, brand; lantern, candle, taper; historical link, cresset.
▶ verb informal *one of the shacks had been torched*: **burn**, set fire to, set on fire, set light to, set alight, incinerate, ignite, kindle, put/set a match to, light, start, touch off; reduce to ashes, destroy by fire.

torment noun (stress on the first syllable) **1** *a voice screamed in torment*: **agony**, suffering, torture, pain, anguish, misery, distress, affliction, trauma, wretchedness, woe; hell, purgatory; rare excruciation.
▷ANTONYMS pleasure, joy.
2 *the solitary nights she spent were a torment*: **ordeal**, affliction, scourge, curse, plague, bane, thorn in someone's side/flesh, cross to bear; calamity, sorrow, tribulation, vexation, persecution, trouble, pest, irritation, irritant, annoyance, worry, nuisance, misfortune, bother, discomfort, soreness, harassment; informal pain in the neck.
▶ verb (stress on the second syllable) **1** *she was tormented by shame*: **torture**, afflict, harrow, plague, distress, agonize, cause agony to, cause suffering to, cause pain to, inflict anguish on; excruciate, crucify, rack, pain; mortify, worry, trouble; abuse, maltreat, mistreat, molest.
2 *Maggie began to torment the two younger boys*: **tease**, taunt, victimize, bully, bait, chaff, harass, rib, scorn; irritate, vex, annoy, pester, badger, harry, hector, plague, be a nuisance to, bother, trouble, bedevil, be a pest to, nag, persecute, worry, nettle, chivvy, irk; informal needle, rag, hassle, aggravate.
▷ANTONYMS encourage, support.

torn adjective **1** *a torn shirt*: **ripped**, split, slit, cut, lacerated, rent, separated, severed, cracked, destroyed, ruined, in disrepair; ragged, tattered, in tatters, holey, frayed, shabby, threadbare, in rags, in ribbons; informal tatty.
2 *she was torn between joy and despair*: **divided**, split, wavering, vacillating, irresolute, dithering, uncertain, unsure, undecided, in two minds.
▷ANTONYMS certain, decided.

tornado noun **whirlwind**, windstorm, cyclone, typhoon, tropical storm/cyclone, tempest, dust devil, storm, hurricane, gale, squall; N. Amer. informal twister.

torpid adjective *we lay torpid in the heat*: **lethargic**, sluggish, inert, inactive, slow, slow-moving, lifeless, dull, listless, languid, lazy, idle, indolent, shiftless, slothful, heavy, stagnant, somnolent, sleepy, tired, fatigued, languorous, apathetic, passive, supine, comatose, narcotic.
▷ANTONYMS energetic, active, lively.

torpor noun *he spent most of the journey in a state of torpor*: **lethargy**, torpidity, sluggishness, inertia, inertness, inactivity, inaction, slowness, lifelessness, dullness, heaviness, listlessness, languor, languidness, stagnation, laziness, idleness, indolence, shiftlessness, sloth, slothfulness, apathy, accidie, passivity, weariness, tiredness, lassitude, fatigue, sleepiness, drowsiness, enervation, somnolence, narcosis.
▷ANTONYMS vigour, energy, animation.

torrent noun **1** *they were swept down the hillside in a torrent of water*: **flood**, deluge, inundation, spate, cascade, rush, stream, current, gushing, flow, overflow, tide, fountain.
▷ANTONYMS trickle, drop.
2 *the rain fell in torrents*: **downpour**, deluge, rainstorm, rain, shower.
3 *he directed a torrent of abuse at me*: **outburst**, stream, volley, outpouring, hail, onslaught, avalanche, flow, barrage, battery, tide, spate, effusion, inundation.

torrential adjective *torrential rain caused the game to be stopped*: **copious**, severe, heavy, rapid, relentless, violent; soaking, teeming.

torrid adjective **1** *a torrid summer*: **hot**, sweltering, sultry, scorching, boiling, parching, sizzling, roasting, blazing, burning, blistering, tropical, stifling, suffocating, oppressive; **dry**, arid, barren, parched, waterless, desert.
▷ANTONYMS cold, cool, wet.
2 *a torrid affair*: **passionate**, impassioned, ardent, intense, inflamed, fervent, fervid, lustful, amorous, erotic, sexy; informal steamy, sizzling, hot.
▷ANTONYMS passionless, unemotional.

tortuous adjective **1** *the road follows a tortuous route*: **twisting**, winding, curving, curvy, bending, sinuous, undulating, coiling, looping, meandering, serpentine, snaking, snaky, zigzag, convoluted, spiralling, twisty, circuitous, rambling, wandering, indirect, deviating, devious, labyrinthine, mazy; rare anfractuous, flexuous.
▷ANTONYMS straight.
2 *a tortuous argument*: **convoluted**, roundabout, circuitous, indirect, unstraightforward, involved, complicated, complex, confusing, lengthy, overlong, verbose, difficult to follow.
▷ANTONYMS straightforward.

> *Easily confused words* **tortuous or torturous?**
>
> **Tortuous** and **torturous** have different meanings. *Tortuous* means 'full of twists and turns', as in *a tortuous route*, while *torturous* means 'involving or causing torture', as in *a torturous five days of fitness training*—although something which is *tortuous* in the word's extended sense 'excessively lengthy and complex' may also be *torturous* (*a tortuous piece of bureaucratese*). This overlap has led to *tortuous* being sometimes used where *torturous* would be correct, as in *he would at last draw in a tortuous gasp of air*.

torture noun **1** *the torture of political prisoners*: **infliction of pain**, abuse, torment; **ill-treatment**, maltreatment, harsh treatment, punishment, persecution.
2 *the torture of losing a loved one*: **torment**, agony, suffering, pain; **anguish**, misery, distress, heartbreak, affliction, trauma, wretchedness, woe; hell, purgatory; rare excruciation.
▷ANTONYMS pleasure.
▶ verb **1** *the security forces routinely tortured suspects*: **inflict pain on**, inflict suffering on; **torment**, ill-treat, abuse, mistreat, maltreat, molest, scourge, wound, put someone on the rack, persecute, punish; informal work over, give someone the works.
▷ANTONYMS relieve, comfort.
2 *he was tortured by grief*: **torment**, **afflict**, harrow, plague, distress, agonize, cause agony to, cause suffering to, inflict anguish on; crucify, rack, pain, mortify; worry, trouble, beset.

toss verb **1** *he tossed his tools into the boot*: **throw**, hurl, cast, fling, sling, pitch, shy, lob, propel, launch, project, send, dash, bowl; informal heave, chuck, bung.
2 *he tossed a coin and it landed heads up*: **flip**, flick, spin, twist.
3 *I tossed and turned all night*: **flail**, thrash about, roll, tumble; jerk, twitch, wriggle, writhe, squirm.
4 *the ship tossed about, shaken furiously*: **lurch**, reel, list, keel, veer, labour, flounder, plunge, rock, roll, sway, undulate, pitch, heave, wallow, make heavy weather; Nautical pitchpole.
5 *toss the salad ingredients together gently*: **shake**, stir, turn, churn, mix, combine.
6 *Paula pursed her lips and tossed her head*: **throw back**, jerk, jolt.
□ **toss something off** *Roger tossed off a full glass of wine*: **drink (up/down)**, quaff, swallow, gulp (down), drain, put away, guzzle, sup, sip, finish off; informal down, swill, swig, slug, sink, kill, polish off, knock back; Brit. informal bevvy; N. Amer. informal scarf (down/up), snarf (down/up); rare ingurgitate, bib.
▶ noun *Louise gave a small toss of her head*: **jerk**, jolt, throw; cast, fling, hurl, heave, delivery, lob.

tot[1] noun **1** *the tot looks just like her mum*: **baby**, babe, infant, toddler, newborn, tiny tot, child, little one, mite; Scottish bairn, wean; informal sprog,

young 'un; N. Amer. informal rug rat; technical neonate.
▷ANTONYMS adult.
2 *a tot of rum*: **dram**, small measure, drink, nip, slug, drop, draught, swallow, swig; informal shot, finger, snifter; rare libation.

tot² verb **1** *he picked up the account book and **totted up** some figures*: **add**, total, sum, count, calculate, compute, reckon, enumerate, tally, work something out, figure something out, take stock of something, quantify; dated cast something up.
2 *we've **totted up** 89 victories*: **accumulate**, gather, build up, amass, accrue, stockpile, acquire; mount up.

total adjective **1** *the total number of casualties | the total cost of the funeral*: **entire**, complete, whole, full, comprehensive, combined, aggregate, gross, overall, composite, integral.
2 *they drove home in total silence | a total stranger*: **complete**, **utter**, absolute, thorough, perfect, downright, out-and-out, outright, thoroughgoing, all-out, sheer, positive, prize, rank, pure, dyed-in-the-wool, deep-dyed, real, consummate, veritable, unmitigated, unqualified, unadulterated, unalloyed, unconditional, unequivocal, full, unlimited, limitless, infinite, ultimate, through and through, in-depth; unbroken, undivided, uninterrupted; Brit. informal right, proper; archaic arrant.
▷ANTONYMS partial.
▶noun *lorries and merchandise worth a total of £160,000 were stolen*: **sum**, sum total, grand total, aggregate; whole, entirety, totality, summation, result.
▶verb **1** *the prize money totalled £33,050*: **add up to**, amount to, mount up to, come to, run to, make, correspond to, equal, work out as, number; Brit. tot up to.
2 *my father **totalled up** his score*: **add**, sum, count, reckon, tot, compute, work out, take stock of.
3 informal *he almost totalled the car*: **wreck**, crash, smash, destroy, damage beyond repair, demolish; Brit. **write off**; Brit. informal prang.

totalitarian adjective *a totalitarian state*: **authoritarian**, autocratic, autarchic, dictatorial, tyrannical, oppressive, repressive, one-party, monocratic, absolute, absolutist, undemocratic, illiberal, despotic, fascist, fascistic, Nazi, neo-Nazi, Stalinist; dystopian.
▷ANTONYMS democratic, liberal.
▶noun **authoritarian**, autocrat, dictator, tyrant, absolutist, despot, fascist, Nazi, neo-Nazi, Stalinist.
▷ANTONYMS democrat, liberal.

totality noun **1** *the unifying spiritual whole is by definition difficult to grasp in its totality*: **entirety**, entireness, wholeness, fullness, completeness, inclusiveness, unity.
2 *the conference didn't succeed in the totality of its aims*: **aggregate**, whole, total, sum, sum total, entirety, beginning and end, alpha and omega, be-all and end-all; all, everything.

totally adverb *she was totally deaf*: **completely**, absolutely, entirely, wholly, fully, thoroughly, utterly, quite, altogether, one hundred per cent; downright, unqualifiedly, in all respects, unconditionally, perfectly, unrestrictedly, consummately, undisputedly, unmitigatedly, wholeheartedly, radically, stark, just, to the hilt, all the way, to the maximum extent; informal clean, plumb, dead, bang.
▷ANTONYMS partly, partially, somewhat.

totter verb **1** *she tottered off on her four-inch heels*: **teeter**, walk unsteadily, stagger, wobble, stumble, dodder, shuffle, shamble, falter, reel, toddle, hobble, sway, roll, lurch.
2 *the foundations began to heave and totter*: **shake**, sway, tremble, quiver, teeter, shudder, judder, rock, quake, reel, lurch; vibrate, oscillate.
3 *the Habsburg Empire was tottering*: **be unstable**, be unsteady, be shaky, be insecure, be precarious, be on the point of collapse, falter; informal wobble.

t

touch verb **1** *his shoes were touching the end of the bed*: **be in contact (with)**, come into contact (with), come together (with), meet, join, connect, converge (with), be contiguous (with), border (on), be (up) against, link up (with), adjoin, abut, neighbour.
2 *he reached out and touched her cheek*: **press lightly**, tap, pat, nudge, prod, poke; feel, stroke, rub, rub (up) against, brush, brush (up) against, graze; fondle, caress, pet, tickle, toy with, play about with, fiddle with, finger, thumb, handle; put one's hand on, lay a hand on, lay a finger on.
3 *in June the government touched its lowest point of popularity*: **reach**, attain, arrive at, come to, make; get up to, rise to, soar to; get down to, sink to, plummet to, dive to; informal hit.
4 *nobody can touch him when he's on form*: **compare with**, be on a par with, equal, match, be a match for, be in the same class as, be in the same league as, be on an equal footing with, parallel, rival, come near, get near, approach, come up to, come/get close to, measure up to/against; better, beat; informal hold a candle to.
5 *you're not supposed to touch my typewriter*: **handle**, hold, pick up, move; **meddle with**, play (about/around) with, toy with, fiddle with, interfere with, tamper with, disturb, harm, lay a hand on, lay a finger on; **use**, employ, make use of, put to use, have access to, access, avail oneself of, get (at), take advantage of.
6 *normally he wouldn't touch a job as small as this*: **be associated with**, concern oneself with, involve oneself in/with, get involved with/in, have something to do with, have dealings with, deal with, handle, be a party to; informal touch something with a bargepole.
7 *he wouldn't touch his food*: **taste**, consume, eat, drink, take, partake of.
▷ANTONYMS refrain from.
8 *Germany was comparatively little touched by the Renaissance*: **affect**, have an effect on, concern, involve, have a bearing on, be relevant to, be pertinent to.
9 *Lisa felt touched by the girl's unexpected kindness*: **affect**, move, stir, arouse, make/leave an impression on, impress, have an impact on, have an effect on; influence, impassion; upset, disturb, make sad, arouse sympathy, melt, soften; informal get (to).
10 informal *do you think you can touch him for some more money?* **ask**, approach; beg, borrow from.
□ **touch down** *his plane touched down at Nice airport*: **land**, alight, come in to land, come down, come to earth, come to rest, put down, make a landing, arrive.
▷ANTONYMS take off.
□ **touch something off 1** *he touched off two of the bombs*: **detonate**, set off, trigger, explode, spark (off). **2** *the plan touched off a major political storm*: **initiate**, set off, start, begin, set in motion, instigate, ignite, trigger (off), stir up, provoke, foment, cause, give rise to, lead to, generate, actuate, launch.
□ **touch on/upon 1** *the exhibition did touch on larger issues*: **refer to**, mention, give a mention to, comment on, remark on, bring up, speak of, talk about, write about, deal with, raise, broach, cover, allude to, make an allusion to, hint at, skim over. **2** *a self-confident manner touching on the arrogant*: **come close to**, verge on, border on, incline to, approach, resemble, be tantamount to, be more or less, be not far from/off.
□ **touch someone up** Brit. informal *he was sacked after one of his pupils accused him of touching her up*: **fondle**, molest, feel up; informal grope, paw, maul, goose; N. Amer. informal cop a feel.
□ **touch something up 1** *the flagstaffs were being touched up with gold paint*: **repaint**, patch up, retouch, renovate, refurbish, spruce up, restore, revive, renew, revamp, brush up, rehabilitate, overhaul, recondition, refresh, rejuvenate; enhance, beautify; informal do something up, give something a facelift, titivate. **2** *touch up your CV and improve your interview skills*: **improve**, enhance, gloss, dress up, embellish, embroider; finish off, round off, perfect; update, upgrade; bring up to date, modernize, revamp, revise, redo, polish up, rewrite, edit.
□ **touch wood** *I haven't been caught yet, touch wood!* **hope for the best**; knock on wood, cross one's fingers, keep one's fingers crossed.
▶noun **1** *communicating by touch is the most primitive mode*: **feeling**, feel, sense of touch, contact, tactile sense, tactility; texture.
2 *I gave her a touch on the shoulder*: **press**, tap, pat, nudge, prod, poke, push, glance, flick; stroke, brush, graze; pressure.
3 *she has a lovely touch on the putting greens*: **skill**, skilfulness, expertise, dexterity, deftness, virtuosity, adroitness, adeptness, ability, talent, flair, facility, proficiency; **knack**, technique, approach, style, manner, execution, method; feel, craftsmanship, workmanship, artistry, performance.
4 *she replied with a touch of bravado*: **small amount**, **trace**, bit, suggestion, suspicion, hint, scintilla, tinge, tincture, whiff, whisper, overtone, undertone, nuance, murmur, colouring, breath, vein; dash, taste, spot, drop, dab, pinch, speck, smack, smattering, sprinkling, splash, soupçon.
5 *there were flowers in a vase on the dressing table—a nice touch*: **detail**, feature, fine point, nicety, addition, accessory; **(touches)** minutiae.
6 *visitors put the severity of the house down to the lack of a woman's touch*: **influence**, effect, hand, handling; direction, management, technique, method.
7 *they finished training a few months apart and lost touch | over the next few days I was **in touch** with Eliot by letter and by phone*: **contact**, communication, correspondence, connection, association; having dealings with, up to date with, abreast of, up with, informed about.

Word links **touch**
tactile, **haptic** relating to touch

touch-and-go adjective *it was touch-and-go whether he would be fit enough to play*: **uncertain**, unsure, unclear, dubious, tight, delicate; sticky, tricky, precarious, risky, in jeopardy, in danger, hazardous, dangerous, critical, unsafe, treacherous, suspenseful, cliffhanging, on thin ice, hanging by a thread; informal hairy; Brit. informal dodgy.
▷ANTONYMS certain.

touched adjective **1** *the plumber was so touched by their plight that he waived his fee*: **affected**, **softened**, moved, stirred, swayed, aroused, impressed, influenced, warmed, impassioned, upset, disturbed, distressed.
▷ANTONYMS unmoved, unimpressed.
2 informal *you have to be a little touched to do what I do*. See **mad** (sense 1).

touchiness noun *the visitors' touchiness about defeat*: **sensitivity**, oversensitivity, hypersensitivity; **irritability**, tetchiness, testiness, crotchetiness, irascibility, peevishness, querulousness, bad-temperedness, short-temperedness, hot-temperedness, quick-temperedness, snappiness, captiousness, prickliness, edginess, crossness, surliness, crustiness, curmudgeonliness, cantankerousness, petulance, waspishness, pettishness, quarrelsomeness, spleen, grumpiness, fractiousness, tension; informal grouchiness, crankiness, rattiness, stickiness.

touching adjective *her devotion to him was very touching | at her death Hardy wrote a touching poem entitled 'The Lodging House'*: **moving**, affecting, stirring, warming, heart-warming, impressive; **poignant**, upsetting, saddening, pitiful, piteous, pathetic, plaintive, heartbreaking, heart-rending, tear-jerking, tragic, disturbing, evocative; emotive, emotional, tender, sentimental.
▷ANTONYMS hard-headed.

Choose the right word **touching, moving, affecting**

See **moving**.

touchstone noun *pupil behaviour is a touchstone of the quality of the school system*: **criterion**, standard, yardstick, benchmark, barometer, litmus test, indicator, indication; **measure**, point of reference, norm, gauge, reference, test, guide, guideline, exemplar, model, pattern.

touchy adjective **1** *she's very touchy about her past | anxiety was making her touchy*: **sensitive**, oversensitive, hypersensitive, easily offended, thin-skinned; **irritable**, tetchy, testy, crotchety, irascible, peevish, querulous, bad-tempered, short-tempered, hot-tempered, quick-tempered, temperamental, snappy, captious, crabbed, prickly, edgy, cross, surly, crusty, curmudgeonly, cantankerous, petulant, waspish, pettish, quarrelsome, splenetic, grumpy, fractious, highly strung, tense; informal grouchy, cranky, ratty.
▷ANTONYMS calm, affable, good-humoured.
2 *a touchy subject*: **delicate**, sensitive, tricky, ticklish, thorny, knotty, embarrassing, uncomfortable, uneasy, precarious, chancy, risky, uncertain, contentious, controversial, awkward, difficult; informal sticky.

tough adjective **1** *they had tough leather gloves*: **durable**, strong, resilient, resistant, sturdy, rugged, firm, solid, substantial, sound, stout, indestructible, unbreakable, hard, rigid, stiff, inflexible, toughened; **hard-wearing**, long-lasting, heavy-duty, well built, made to last.
▷ANTONYMS soft, fragile, flimsy.
2 *the hastily prepared steak was tough*: **chewy**, leathery, gristly, stringy, fibrous, sinewy, cartilaginous.
▷ANTONYMS tender.
3 *he must have been a tough little lad to have survived it all*: **resilient**, strong, hardy, gritty, determined, resolute, dogged, stalwart; rugged, fit, robust, powerful, red-blooded, doughty; hardened, cynical, hardbitten; informal hard, (as) tough as old boots.
▷ANTONYMS weak; sentimental.
4 *he conceded the need for tough sentencing | the police will be told to get tough on car theft*: **strict**, stern, severe, hard, harsh, firm, hard-hitting, adamant, inflexible, unyielding, unbending, uncompromising, unsentimental, unsympathetic; **merciless**, ruthless, callous, hard-hearted, uncaring, cold, cool, stony, stony-hearted, flinty; informal hard-nosed, hard-boiled.
▷ANTONYMS soft, light.
5 *a tough area of London*: **rough**, rowdy, unruly, disorderly, violent, wild, lawless, lawbreaking, criminal; vicious, callous, hardened.
6 *my father had a tough job underground*: **arduous**, onerous, difficult, demanding, hard, heavy, taxing, burdensome, tiring, exhausting, punishing, wearying, fatiguing, laborious, strenuous, exacting, troublesome, formidable, stressful, Herculean; rare toilsome, exigent.
▷ANTONYMS easy.
7 *their book raises tough questions for American policy-makers*: **difficult**, hard, knotty, thorny, baffling, tricky, ticklish, prickly, perplexing, puzzling, mystifying, troublesome, bothersome, irksome, intractable.
▷ANTONYMS easy.
8 *the tough way of life of a fisherman*: **harsh**, hard, austere, rigorous, rugged, spartan, bleak, grim, straitened, forbidding, cruel, savage, hostile, unfriendly, dark, dire, rough, taxing, exacting, disagreeable, unpleasant, awful.
▷ANTONYMS easy.
9 informal *they had tough luck when a shot bounced off the crossbar*: **unfortunate**, unlucky, hard, unpleasant, regrettable, distressing; informal too bad.
▷ANTONYMS good, lucky.
▶noun *a gang of toughs*: **ruffian**, rowdy, thug, hoodlum, hooligan, brute, bully, bully boy, rough, gangster, desperado; informal hard man, roughneck, yob, yobbo, heavy, bruiser, tough guy, toughie, gorilla, yahoo; N. Amer. informal hood; Austral./NZ informal hoon.

toughen verb **1** *this process tightens and toughens the wood fibres*: **strengthen**, fortify, reinforce, harden, stiffen, consolidate, temper, season, rigidify, thicken, coarsen; technical indurate, anneal, cement.
▷ANTONYMS soften.
2 *measures to toughen prison discipline*: **make stricter**, make more severe, toughen up, stiffen, tighten; informal beef up.
3 *it is surprising how the army toughens the lads*: **harden**, fortify, strengthen, give strength to, steel, harshen, make resilient; make unfeeling, brutalize, make callous, case-harden, inure.

tour noun **1** *he went on a grand tour of Europe*: **excursion**, journey, expedition, trip, jaunt, outing, day trip, junket, voyage, trek, safari; rare peregrination.
2 *a tour of a car factory*: **visit**, inspection, guided tour, walk round, survey, walkabout, ramble.
3 *they lost all four matches on the tour*: **circuit**, ambit; round, course, beat, leg, lap.
4 *his* ***tour of duty*** *in Ulster was ending*: **stint**, stretch, spell, shift, turn, assignment, duty, period of service, period of enlistment.
▶verb **1** *this hotel is well placed for touring Somerset*: **travel round**, travel through, journey through, go on a trip through, go on an excursion in, explore, voyage around, trek around, sightsee in, holiday in, cruise, range over, roam in, rove through, wander through, globetrot; informal do.
2 *you'll have to tour the client's factory and see how the product is made*: **visit**, go round, go around, walk round, drive round, see, explore, inspect, review, survey, scrutinize, reconnoitre.

tour de force noun *such pictures are by no means simply a technical tour de force*: **triumph**, masterpiece, supreme example, coup, marvellous feat, feather in one's cap, wonder, sensation, master stroke; French coup de maître; informal hit, knockout.

tourist noun *in the summer London is full of tourists*: **holidaymaker**, traveller, sightseer, visitor, excursionist, backpacker, globetrotter, day tripper, tripper; explorer, pilgrim, voyager, journeyer; N. Amer. vacationer, vacationist, out-of-towner; Brit. informal grockle, emmet.
▷ANTONYMS local.

tournament noun **1** *a golf tournament*: **competition**, contest, championship, series, meeting, meet, event, match, trial, bout, fixture.
2 *a knight preparing for a tournament*: **joust**, jousting, tourney, tilt; lists.

tousled adjective *she ran a hand through her tousled hair*: **untidy**, messy, unkempt, disordered, disarranged, messed up, rumpled, dishevelled, bedraggled; uncombed, ungroomed, ruffled, tangled, matted, windblown, wild; informal mussed up.
▷ANTONYMS neat, tidy.

tout verb **1** *he's touting his autobiography*: **peddle**, sell, hawk, offer for sale, market, vend; **promote**, talk up, push, flaunt, advertise, publicize, puff, give a puff to; informal flog, hype, plug.
2 *minicab drivers were* ***touting for*** *business*: **solicit**, seek, drum up; ask, petition, appeal, canvas, beg.
3 *he's being touted as the next Scotland manager*: **commend**, endorse, praise, recommend, support, urge, push, speak of, talk of; Brit. tip.
▶noun **ticket tout**, illegal salesman; N. Amer. informal scalper.

tow verb *a garage man called to tow the car away*: **pull**, draw, drag, haul, tug, trail, lug, heave, trawl, hoist, transport; informal yank.
▶noun *a tow to the garage costs from £95 to £155*: **tug**, towing, haul, pull, drawing, drag, trailing, trawl.
□ **in tow** *they arrived with several young children in tow*: **accompanying**, following, in attendance, in convoy, by one's side, in one's charge, under one's protection.

towards preposition **1** *Henry strode towards her | he was heading towards Manhattan*: **in the direction of**, to, toward, so as to approach, so as to near; on the way to, on the road to, en route for, in the vicinity of.
▷ANTONYMS away from.
2 *they're working towards a drug-free future*: **with the aim of**, in order to obtain, in order to achieve, so as to achieve, for.
▷ANTONYMS away from.
3 *towards evening dark clouds gathered*: **just before**, shortly before, near, nearing, around, approaching, close to, coming to, getting on for, not quite.
4 *it is impossible to be indifferent towards her*: **with regard to**, as regards, regarding, in/with regard to, in/with respect to, respecting, in relation to, concerning, about, in connection with, apropos.
5 *they offered to contribute £2,000 towards a fund to restore the church's organ*: **as a contribution to**, for, as a help to, to help, to assist, supporting, promoting, assisting.

tower noun **1** *a church tower*: **steeple**, spire; column, pillar, obelisk.
2 *much of the land was acquired by later monarchs to increase the tower's defences*: **fortress**, fort, citadel, stronghold, fortification, keep, castle, garrison, bastion, donjon.
▶verb **1** *he* ***towered above*** *her | the wall towered, impossibly high*: **soar**, rise, loom, ascend, mount, rear, reach high, stand high; overshadow, overlook, overhang, hang over, dominate.
2 *tourism* ***towers over*** *all other features of the urban economy*: **surpass**, excel, outshine, outclass, outstrip, overshadow, cap, top, transcend, trump, dominate, eclipse, dwarf, be head and shoulders above, put something in the shade, put something to shame; upstage, beat, better; informal be a cut above, run rings/circles around, leave something standing; archaic outrival, outvie.

towering adjective **1** *a towering skyscraper*: **high**, tall, lofty, elevated, soaring, sky-high, sky-scraping, steep, mountainous, imposing, multi-storey; giant, gigantic, enormous, huge, colossal, vast, immense, massive,

t

monstrous, mammoth, monumental, titanic, Brobdingnagian; informal hulking, whopping, ginormous.
▷ANTONYMS low, short.
2 *a towering rock idol*: **outstanding**, pre-eminent, leading, foremost, finest, chief, excellent, distinguished, prominent, eminent, important, major, star, top, topmost, surpassing, superior, supreme, exceptional, stellar, great, incomparable, unrivalled, unsurpassed, peerless, matchless, unequalled, famous, renowned, celebrated, illustrious, extraordinary.
▷ANTONYMS undistinguished, inferior.
3 *he was in a towering rage*: **extreme**, fierce, terrible, intense, overpowering, mighty, violent, fiery, unrestrained, vehement, passionate, ardent, immoderate, intemperate, inordinate, frenzied, fanatical, zealous, frantic, deep.
▷ANTONYMS minor, half-hearted.

town noun *a small market town*: **urban area**, conurbation, municipality, borough, township, settlement; city, metropolis, megalopolis; American Indian pueblo; Scottish burgh.
▷ANTONYMS country, countryside.

Word links **town**
municipal, **urban** relating to a town

toxic adjective *they were killed by smoke and toxic gases*: **poisonous**, venomous, virulent, noxious, dangerous, destructive, harmful, unsafe, malignant, injurious, pestilential, pernicious; fatal, deadly, lethal, mortal, death-dealing; archaic baneful.
▷ANTONYMS non-toxic, harmless, safe.

toy noun **1** *a cuddly toy*: **plaything**, game.
2 *an executive toy*: **trinket**, bauble, knick-knack, ornament, gewgaw, trifle, gimcrack, bagatelle, triviality; N. Amer. kickshaw; informal whatnot; Brit. informal doodah.
▶adjective **1** *a toy car*: **model**, miniature, imitation, make-believe, fake, simulation, artificial.
▷ANTONYMS real, authentic.
2 *a toy poodle*: **miniature**, small, tiny, diminutive, dwarf, midget, pygmy.
▷ANTONYMS full-size, big.
▶verb
□ **toy with 1** *I was toying with the idea of writing a book*: **think idly about**, play with, flirt with, trifle with, entertain the possibility of, consider, have thoughts about, argue the pros and cons of; informal kick around/about. **2** *he had been toying with her that day on the river*: **flirt with**, dally with, sport with, play with, amuse oneself with, trifle with, fool with. **3** *she could only toy with her food*: **fidget with**, play (about/around) with, fiddle (about/around) with, fool about/around with, tinker with, finger, twiddle (with); nibble, pick at, gnaw (at), peck at, pick over, eat listlessly, eat like a bird; informal mess about/around with.

trace verb **1** *Police hope to trace the owner of the jewellery*: **track down**, find, discover, detect, unearth, uncover, turn up, hunt down, dig up, ferret out, run to ground; follow, pursue, trail, shadow, stalk, dog.
2 *we've traced the call*: **find the source of**, find the origins of, find the roots of, follow to its source, source.
3 *trace a map of the world on to a large piece of paper*: **copy**, reproduce, go over, draw over, draw the lines of; **draw**, draw up, sketch, draft, outline, rough out, mark out, delineate, map, chart, record, indicate, show, depict.
▶noun **1** *in the east wall is the trace of a pointed arch | no trace had been found of the missing plane*: **vestige**, sign, mark, indication, suggestion, evidence, clue; **remains**, remnant, relic, survival; ghost, echo, memory.
2 *she spoke good English with only a trace of an accent*: **bit**, spot, speck, touch, hint, suggestion, suspicion, nuance, intimation; trifle, drop, dash, tinge, tincture, streak, shred, crumb, fragment, shadow, whiff, breath, jot, iota; informal smidgen, tad.
3 *there was enough dust on the floor to have preserved traces of feet*: **trail**, track, spoor, marks, tracks, prints, imprints, footprints, footmarks, footsteps.

track noun **1** *she pedalled her bicycle up the gravel track to the south porch*: **path**, pathway, footpath, lane, trail, route, way, course.
2 *he broke into a run along the track*: **course**, racecourse; running track, racetrack, speedway, velodrome, piste; Brit. circuit.
3 (usually **tracks**) *he followed the tracks of a car*: **traces**, marks, impressions, prints, imprints; footprints, footmarks, footsteps, trail, spoor; scent; wake, slipstream.
4 *Orkney lies on the track of the Atlantic winds*: **course**, path, line, orbit, route, way, trajectory, flight path.
5 *commuters had to leave trains and walk along the tracks*: **rail**, line; railway line, tramlines; metal; N. Amer. railroad.
6 *the title track of their forthcoming album*: **song**, recording, number, piece.
□ **keep track of** *an online diary which allows you to keep track of your appointments*: **monitor**, follow, keep up with, record, keep a record of; supervise, oversee, watch, keep an eye on; keep in touch with, keep up to date with.
▷ANTONYMS lose track of.
□ **lose track of** *he would quite often lose track of the time at work*: **forget about**, forget, be unaware of, lose/cease contact with; lose sight of.
▷ANTONYMS keep track of.
□ **on track** *we're well on track to surpass expectations*: **on course**, on target, on schedule, on time.
▶verb *he tracked a bear for 40 km*: **follow**, trail, trace, pursue, shadow, stalk, dog, spoor, hunt (down), chase, hound, course, keep an eye on, keep in sight; informal tail, keep tabs on, keep a tab on.
□ **track someone/something down** *it took seventeen years to track down the wreck of the ship*: **discover**, **detect**, find (out), hunt down, hunt out, unearth, uncover, disinter, turn up, dig up, seek out, ferret out, root out, nose out, bring to light, expose, recover, capture, catch, smell out, sniff out, run to earth, run to ground, run down; informal suss out.

tract[1] noun *the lords owned large tracts of land*: **area**, region, expanse, span, sweep, stretch, extent, belt, swathe, zone, plot, patch, parcel, portion, section, sector, quarter; territory, estate, acreage, allotment.

tract[2] noun *a great political tract*: **treatise**, essay, article, paper, monograph, disquisition, dissertation, thesis, exposition, study, piece of writing, lecture, homily, sermon, work; **pamphlet**, booklet, leaflet, brochure.

tractable adjective *children are no longer as tractable as they used to be*: **controllable**, manageable, malleable, governable, yielding, amenable, complaisant, compliant; adjustable; **docile**, submissive, obedient, tame, meek, easily handled, biddable, persuadable, persuasible, accommodating, trusting, gullible, dutiful, willing, unassertive, passive, deferential, humble, obsequious, servile, sycophantic.
▷ANTONYMS obstinate, defiant, recalcitrant.

traction noun *the shoes have studs for extra traction*: **grip**, friction, adhesion, purchase, resistance; pull, haulage, propulsion, drag.

trade noun **1** *the illicit trade in stolen cattle*: **commerce**, buying and selling, dealing, traffic, trafficking, business, marketing, merchandising, bargaining; dealings, transactions, negotiations, proceedings.
2 *he left school to learn the glazier's trade*: **craft**, occupation, job, career, profession, business, pursuit, living, livelihood, line, line of work, line of business, vocation, calling, walk of life, province, field; work, employment; French métier.
3 *we'll do a trade—I'll give you Foster if you get me some information*: **swap**, exchange, switch, barter, interchange, substitution, replacement, trade-off; archaic truck.
▶verb **1** *he made his fortune **trading in** beaver pelts*: **deal**, traffic; buy and sell, market, peddle, merchandise, barter; informal hawk, tout, flog, run.
2 *the business is trading at a loss*: **do business**, deal, run, operate.
3 *I traded the old machine for a newer model*: **swap**, exchange, switch, barter, substitute, replace; archaic truck.
□ **trade on** *he trades on his friendship with powerful people*: **exploit**, take advantage of, capitalize on, profit from, use, make use of; milk, abuse, misuse; informal cash in on.

Word links **trade**
mercantile relating to trade

trademark noun **1** *there was a trademark on the back of his jacket*: **logo**, emblem, sign, stamp, symbol, device, badge, crest, insignia, seal, coat of arms, shield, motif, hallmark, mark, figure, monogram, logotype, colophon; trade name, brand name, proprietary name.
2 *long hair was the trademark of the hippy*: **characteristic**, trait, quality, attribute, feature, peculiarity, idiosyncrasy, hallmark, quirk, speciality, sign, telltale sign, penchant, proclivity.

trader noun *a market trader*: **dealer**, merchant, buyer, seller, salesman, saleswoman, buyer and seller, marketeer, merchandiser, broker, agent; businessman, businesswoman, business person, distributor, vendor, purveyor, supplier, trafficker; shopkeeper, retailer, wholesaler; Brit. stockist; informal runner, pusher; dated pedlar, hawker.

tradesman, tradeswoman noun **1** *tradesmen standing nonchalantly outside their stores*: **shopkeeper**, retailer, vendor, merchant, dealer, trader, supplier, stockist; salesman, saleswoman, salesperson, tradesperson, wholesaler; N. Amer. storekeeper; historical chandler, shopman, roundsman.
2 *the installation should be carried out by a qualified tradesman*: **craftsman**, workman, skilled worker, artisan, employee, tradesperson, mechanic.

tradition noun **1** *the Chancellor is, by tradition, allowed to bring alcohol into the House on Budget day*: **historical convention**, unwritten law, oral history, heritage; lore, folklore, old wives' tales.
2 *the hunt maintains a centuries-old tradition*: **custom**, **practice**, convention, ritual, ceremony, observance, wont, routine, way, rule, usage, habit; institution, principle, belief; formal praxis.
3 *a poem in the tradition of Horace's 'Ars Poetica'*: **style**, movement, method.

traditional adjective **1** *Paula always hankered after a traditional white wedding | the traditional nuclear family*: **conventional**, customary, established, long-established, accepted, orthodox, standard, regular, normal, conservative; common, run-of-the-mill, habitual, set, fixed, routine, usual, accustomed; old-fashioned, staid, unadventurous,

t

conformist, stereotyped, clichéd, undistinguished, wonted; old, time-honoured, proven, tried and tested, historic, classical, classic, old-world, folk, familial, ancestral; ritual, ritualistic, ceremonial.
▷ANTONYMS novel, unconventional, modern.
2 *traditional beliefs*: **handed-down**, folk, historical, unwritten, oral.

traditionalist noun *she married an old-guard traditionalist*: **conservative**, right-winger, rightist, reactionary; informal square, stick-in-the-mud, fuddy-duddy.
▸ adjective *a traditionalist splinter group*: **conservative**, traditional, established, accepted, orthodox, conventional, reactionary.

> *Word toolkit* **traditionalist**
>
> See **reactionary**.

traduce verb *it was regarded as respectable political tactics to traduce him on any grounds*: **defame**, slander, speak ill of, speak evil of, gossip about, misrepresent, malign, vilify, calumniate, denigrate, disparage, slur, decry, sully, impugn, smear, besmirch, dishonour, back-bite, revile, run down, blacken the name of, cast aspersions on; informal do a hatchet job on, slag (off), rubbish, knock, drag someone's name through the mud; N. Amer. informal bad-mouth, dump on; rare asperse.

> *Choose the right word* **traduce, malign, slander, libel, defame**
>
> See **malign**.

traducer noun **defamer**, slanderer, calumniator, gossip, vilifier, disparager, denigrator, deprecator, abuser, smearer, detractor; informal mud-slinger, knocker; rare asperser.

traffic noun **1** *the bridge is not open to traffic*: **vehicles**, cars, lorries, trucks.
2 *they might be stuck in traffic*: **congestion**, traffic jam, jam, tailback, hold-up, bottleneck, gridlock, queue, stoppage, obstruction; informal snarl-up.
3 *he owned teams of horses for goods traffic*: **transport**, transportation, movement of goods/people, freight, shipping, conveyancing.
4 *the illegal traffic in stolen art*: **trade**, trading, trafficking, dealing, commerce, business, peddling, buying and selling; smuggling, bootlegging; market, black market; dealings, transactions, negotiations, proceedings.
▸ verb *he confessed to* ***trafficking in*** *gold and ivory*: **trade**, deal, do business, peddle, bargain; buy and sell, market, barter; smuggle, bootleg; informal hawk, tout, flog, push, run.

tragedy noun **1** *the tragedy of his early death | an age of tragedy and conflict*: **disaster**, calamity, catastrophe, cataclysm, devastation, misfortune, misadventure, mishap, reverse, vicissitude, setback, trial, tribulation, affliction, blight, injury, adversity, sad event, serious accident; shock, blow; pain, sorrow, misery, distress, agony, unhappiness, sadness, disappointment; informal bummer.
▷ANTONYMS fortune, joy.
2 *Shakespeare's tragedies*: **tragic drama**, drama, play; literary buskin.
▷ANTONYMS comedy.

> *Word links* **tragedy**
>
> **Melpomene** the Muse of tragedy

tragic adjective **1** *a boy died after a tragic accident*: **disastrous**, calamitous, catastrophic, cataclysmic, devastating, terrible, dreadful, appalling, horrendous, dire, ruinous, gruesome, awful, miserable, wretched, unfortunate; fatal, deadly, mortal, lethal.
▷ANTONYMS fortunate, lucky.
2 *they were a tragic family*: **sad**, unhappy, pathetic, moving, distressing, painful, sorrowful, heart-rending, agonizing, stirring, disturbing, pitiful, piteous; melancholy, doleful, mournful, dejected, despondent, anguished, desolate, dismal, gloomy.
▷ANTONYMS happy, joyful.
3 *a tragic waste of talent*: **dreadful**, terrible, awful, deplorable, lamentable, regrettable, abject, miserable, wretched, grievous, galling, vexatious.

trail noun **1** *he left a trail of clues*: **series**, stream, string, line, chain, row, succession, train.
2 *wolves on the trail of their prey*: **track**, spoor, path, scent; traces, marks, signs, prints, imprints, impressions, footprints, footmarks, footsteps.
3 *the plane was leaving an impressive vapour trail*: **wake**, tail, stream, slipstream.
4 *the torrential rain left a trail of devastation*: **train**, chain, series, sequence, aftermath.
5 *a trail of ants*: **line**, queue, row, train, file, rank, column, procession, string, chain, array, group, following, entourage, convoy.
6 *country parks with nature trails*: **path**, beaten path, pathway, way, footpath, track, course, road, route.
▸ verb **1** *my hands were trailing in the water*: **drag**, sweep, be drawn, draw, stream, dangle, hang (down), tow, droop; archaic depend.
2 *the roses grew wild, their stems trailing over the banks*: **creep**, crawl, slide, slink, slither.
3 *Sharpe suspected that they were trailing him*: **follow**, pursue, track, trace, shadow, stalk, dog, hound, spoor, hunt (down), course, keep an eye on, keep in sight, run to earth, run to ground, run down; informal tail, keep tabs on, keep a tab on.
4 *the defending champions were trailing 10–5 at half time*: **lose**, be down, be behind, lag behind, fall behind, drop behind.
5 *Mark baulked at the idea of trailing around the shops all day | a maid* ***trailed behind*** *them*: **trudge**, plod, drag oneself, wander, amble, meander, drift; dawdle, straggle, loiter, linger, lag; fall behind, take one's time, not keep up, bring up the rear; informal tag along behind.
6 *he let his voice* ***trail off***: **fade**, dwindle, diminish, lessen, wane, ebb, subside, weaken, peter out, melt away, fizzle out, taper off, tail off, grow faint, grow dim, evaporate, disappear, vanish, die, come to nothing, come to a halt, come to an end, run out.
7 *the BBC trailed the series as unsuitable for young people*: **advertise**, publicize, announce, proclaim; **preview**, show excerpts of, call attention to; informal hype.

train verb **1** *the scheme involved workers training their colleagues*: **instruct**, teach, coach, tutor, give lessons to, school, educate, upskill, edify, prime, drill, demonstrate something to, make something clear to; put someone through their paces; inculcate, indoctrinate, condition.
2 *she is now training to be a hairdresser*: **study**, learn, prepare, be taught, take instruction, qualify.
3 *with the Olympics in mind, athletes are training hard*: **exercise**, do exercises, work out, get into shape, practise, prepare.
4 *the race is to include three horses that are trained in Dubai*: **coach**, drill, exercise, prepare, practise, ground, rehearse, make ready, make fit.
5 *she trained the gun on his chest*: **aim**, point, direct, level, line something up, turn something on, fix something on, sight, position, focus; take aim, zero in on.
▸ noun **1** *a minister and his train of attendants*: **retinue**, entourage, cortège, following, staff, household, court, suite; attendants, retainers, followers, bodyguards.
2 *a train of elephants dragging logs*: **procession**, line, file, column, convoy, cavalcade, caravan, queue, rank, string, succession, progression, array.
3 *this set in motion a bizarre train of events*: **chain**, string, series, sequence, succession, set, progression, course, cycle, line, row, order, trail, concatenation.
4 *the bride wore a cream silk dress with a train*: **tail**, appendage.

trainer noun **1** *a fitness trainer*: **instructor**, coach, teacher, mentor, adviser, counsellor, guide, guru, manager, handler, tutor, educator.
2 Brit. *a decent pair of trainers*: **training shoe**, running shoe, sports shoe, tennis shoe, plimsoll; football boot; N. Amer. sneaker.

training noun **1** *he got training in word-processing techniques*: **instruction**, teaching, coaching, tuition, tutoring, tutelage, schooling, education, drilling, priming, preparation, grounding, guidance, indoctrination, inculcation; lessons.
2 *he was overweight when he went back into training*: **exercise**, exercises, physical exercises, working out, bodybuilding; drill, practice, preparation.

traipse verb *I haven't the time to go traipsing around art galleries*: **trudge**, trek, tramp, trail, hike, plod, shuffle, slouch, drag oneself, drag one's feet, clump, slog, wade, footslog.

trait noun *she had an unfortunate trait of bending the truth to suit her*: **characteristic**, attribute, feature, quality, essential quality, property, distinction, idiosyncrasy, peculiarity, quirk, foible, singularity, oddity, eccentricity, abnormality, mark, trademark, hallmark, earmark; mannerism, way, trick, habit, custom, tendency; literary lineament.

traitor noun *he was tried in a military court as a traitor*: **betrayer**, back-stabber, double-crosser, double-dealer, renegade, Judas, quisling, fifth columnist, viper; turncoat, defector, apostate, deserter; collaborator, fraternizer, colluder, informer, double agent; informal snake in the grass, two-timer, rat, scab; rare traditor, tergiversator, renegado.
▷ANTONYMS loyalist, patriot.

traitorous adjective *an agent who had ties with a traitorous party*: **treacherous**, disloyal, treasonous, back-stabbing; double-crossing, double-dealing, faithless, unfaithful, perfidious, two-faced, false-hearted, duplicitous, deceitful, false, untrue, untrustworthy, unreliable, undependable, fickle; informal two-timing.
▷ANTONYMS loyal, faithful, patriotic.

trajectory noun *aerodynamic forces change the trajectory of the ball*: **course**, route, path, track, line, orbit, flight, flight path, ambit, direction, bearing, orientation, way, tack, approach.

trammel literary noun *he made progress towards an ideal which the trammels of tradition never allowed him to attain*: **restraint**, constraint, curb, check, impediment, obstacle, barrier, handicap, bar, block, hindrance, encumbrance, disadvantage, drawback, snag, stumbling block; (**trammels**) shackles, fetters, bonds.
▷ANTONYMS help, assistance.
▸ verb *the narrow skirt trammelled her steps*: **restrict**, restrain, constrain, hamper, confine, curb, check, hinder, handicap, obstruct, impede, interfere

with, forestall, thwart, frustrate; hold back, retard, slow down, cramp, clog, straiten, hem in; hamstring, bridle, encumber, enmesh, ensnare; informal stymie; Brit. informal throw a spanner in the works of; N. Amer. informal throw a monkey wrench in the works of.
▷ANTONYMS help, assist.

tramp[1] verb **1** *men were tramping through the shrubbery*: **trudge**, plod, stamp, trample, lumber, clump, clomp, stump, stomp, stumble, pad, march, thunder; informal traipse, galumph.
2 *he spent ten days tramping through the jungle*: **trek**, trudge, slog, footslog, plod, drag oneself, walk, ramble, hike, march, roam, range, rove, backpack; informal traipse, hoof it, leg it, take Shanks's pony; Brit. informal yomp.
3 *this is one of the few wines still tramped by foot*: **trample**, tread on, step on, stamp on; squash, crush, flatten, pulp.
▶noun **1** *she heard the regular tramp of the sentry's boots*: **footstep**, step, footfall, tread, stamp, stomp, stomping.
2 *Theodora returned from a tramp round Norwich*: **trek**, trudge, slog, hike, march, walk, constitutional, ramble, roam, wander; informal traipse; Brit. informal yomp.

tramp[2] noun **1** *Herbert's eccentricity was to dress as a tramp*: **vagrant**, vagabond, homeless person, derelict, down-and-out; itinerant, traveller, drifter, wanderer, person of no fixed address, beachcomber; ne'er do well, good for nothing; outcast, pariah; beggar, mendicant; N. Amer. hobo, bum; Austral./NZ bagman, sundowner, swagman; informal crusty, bag lady; Brit. informal dosser; Austral./NZ informal derro.
2 N. Amer. informal *he knew she was a tramp, available for any man with enough money*: **slut**, promiscuous woman, prostitute, whore; informal tart, floozie, slag, scrubber, slapper; dated wanton, scarlet woman, loose woman, fallen woman, hussy, trollop, strumpet, slattern.

trample verb **1** *a fence was erected to prevent people* ***trampling on*** *the flowers*: **tread**, tramp, stamp, walk over; squash, crush, flatten, compress, press (down), compact, pound, tamp down, mangle, pulp, mash, pulverize.
2 *we do nothing but* ***trample over*** *their feelings*: **treat with contempt**, ride roughshod over, disregard, set at naught, show no consideration for, treat inconsiderately, treat disrespectfully, take for granted, encroach on, infringe, abuse, do violence to.

trance noun **daze**, stupor, haze, hypnotic state, half-conscious state, dream, daydream, reverie, brown study, suspended animation; Scottish dwam.

tranquil adjective **1** *a wonderfully tranquil village*: **peaceful**, restful, reposeful, calm, quiet, still, serene, placid, relaxing, soothing, undisturbed, idyllic, halcyon, mild, pleasant.
▷ANTONYMS disturbed, busy.
2 *Martha smiled, perfectly tranquil*: **calm**, placid, composed, relaxed, at peace, cool, {cool, calm, and collected}, cool-headed, serene, even-tempered, self-possessed, controlled, unexcitable, unflappable, unruffled, unperturbed, imperturbable, undisturbed, unagitated, dispassionate, stoical, sober, unemotional, untroubled, pacific; informal together, laid-back.
▷ANTONYMS excitable.

Choose the right word **tranquil, serene, calm, placid, peaceful**

See **calm**.

Word toolkit **tranquil**

See **sleepy**.

tranquillity noun **1** *the peace and tranquillity of the Norfolk countryside*: **peace**, peacefulness, restfulness, repose, reposefulness, calm, calmness, quiet, quietness, quietude, silence, hush, noiselessness, stillness, serenity, sedateness, placidity, mildness.
▷ANTONYMS commotion, busyness.
2 *the crash had jolted her out of her tranquillity*: **calm**, calmness, placidity, composure, coolness, cool-headedness, serenity, contentment, content, even-temperedness, self-possession, control, equanimity, unexcitability, unflappability, imperturbability, restraint, self-restraint, stoicism, sobriety, untroubledness; informal togetherness; rare ataraxy, ataraxia.
▷ANTONYMS excitability.

tranquillize verb *as a last resort you may need to tranquillize the horse*: **sedate**, calm (down), soothe, quiet, quieten (down), pacify, settle someone's/something's nerves, mollify, lull, relax; stupefy, anaesthetize, narcotize, knock out, drug; administer a sedative/tranquillizer to; informal dope, zonk.
▷ANTONYMS agitate, disturb, ruffle.

tranquillizer noun **sedative**, calmative, depressant, opiate, neuroleptic, sleeping pill, soporific, drug, narcotic; barbiturate, temazepam, diazepam, chlordiazepoxide, chlorpromazine, meprobamate, benzodiazepine, thioridazine, prochlorperazine; informal downer, trank, sleeper; trademark Valium, Librium; dated bromide.
▷ANTONYMS stimulant.

transact verb *those who transact business in London must know what the rules are*: **negotiate**, **conduct**, carry out, do, perform, execute, enact, manage, handle, organize, take care of, prosecute, work out, thrash out, hammer out, see to, administer, operate; settle, conclude, finish, clinch, discharge, accomplish, reach an agreement on, agree on, come to terms about, reach terms on; informal sort out.

transaction noun **1** *property transactions*: **deal**, business, agreement, undertaking, affair, arrangement, bargain, negotiation, treaty, contract, pact, compact, bond, settlement; (**transactions**) proceedings.
2 (**transactions**) *the transactions of Congress were carefully recorded*: **proceedings**, affairs, concerns, dealings, matters, activities; **records**, report, publication, journal, minutes, annals, log, account, chronicle; informal doings, goings-on.
3 *the transaction of government business*: **negotiation**, **conduct**, conducting, carrying out, performance, execution, enactment, management, handling, organization, prosecution, working out, thrashing out, hammering out, administration, operation; settling, conclusion, clinching, discharge, accomplishment, agreement, settlement.

transcend verb **1** *there were differences of opinion transcending Party lines*: **go beyond**, rise above, cut across.
2 *his latest bout of bad behaviour transcended even his own worst excesses*: **surpass**, excel, exceed, beat, trump, top, cap, outdo, outstrip, leave behind, outrival, outvie, outrank, outshine, eclipse, overstep, overshadow, throw into the shade, upstage.

transcendence, transcendency noun *this novel's theme is the transcendence of human love over the coercions of church and state*: **superiority**, supremacy, predominance, pre-eminence, ascendancy; incomparability, matchlessness, peerlessness; excellence, greatness, magnificence, sublimity, importance; rare paramountcy.

transcendent adjective **1** *a transcendent god*: **supernatural**, preternatural, transcendental, other-worldly, superhuman, mystical, mystic, spiritual, divine, heavenly, exalted, sublime, ethereal, numinous, transmundane, ineffable.
▷ANTONYMS mundane.
2 *a transcendent genius*: **superior**, supreme, consummate, predominant, pre-eminent, ascendant, paramount, superlative, unique, unsurpassed, incomparable, unrivalled, unequalled, unparalleled, matchless, peerless, second to none; excellent, excelling, great, magnificent.
▷ANTONYMS average, mediocre.

transcendental adjective See **transcendent** (sense 1).

transcribe verb **1** *the following passage is transcribed from a tape recording of spontaneous speech*: **write out**, copy out, write/copy in full, put in writing, set down, take down, type out, print out, put on paper, commit to paper, reproduce.
2 *the court was adjourned so that they could transcribe their notes*: **transliterate**, interpret, translate, render, convert, write up, rewrite; Law engross.

transcript noun *a newspaper printed a transcript of the tapes*: **written version**, written copy, copy, printed version, transliteration, reproduction, record, text, script, note, summary, log, documentation.

transfer verb (stress on the second syllable) **1** *the plants should be transferred into a tank*: **move**, convey, shift, remove, take, carry, fetch, lift, bring, bear, conduct, send, pass on, transport, relay, change, relocate, resettle, transplant, uproot.
2 *we will transfer full planning responsibility to local authorities*: **hand over**, pass on, make over, turn over, sign over, transmit, convey, consign, commit, devolve, assign, cede, surrender, relinquish, delegate, entrust, grant, give, refer; divert, channel, redirect.
▷ANTONYMS retain.
▶noun (stress on the first syllable) **1** *he got a free transfer to a Spanish team*: **movement**, **move**, moving, shifting, shift, handover, relocation, repositioning, transplant, redirection, conveyance, transferral, transference, removal, change, changeover, switch, conversion.
2 *she signed the transfer in her maiden name*: **conveyance**, transfer document; papers, deeds, documentation.

transfigure verb *the glow of the sunrise transfigured the whole landscape*: **transform**, change, alter, convert, metamorphose, vary, modify, transmute, mutate; rearrange, reshape, remodel, redo, reconstruct, recast, rebuild, reorganize, renew, revolutionize; humorous transmogrify.

transfix verb **1** *he sat transfixed by the film's sheer beauty*: **mesmerize**, hypnotize, spellbind, bewitch, captivate, entrance, enthral, fascinate, engross, enrapture, stun, stupefy, astound, grip, root someone to the spot, stop someone dead, stop someone in their tracks; paralyse, petrify, immobilize, freeze, rivet; rare gorgonize.
2 *a picture of a nail transfixing a splayed hand*: **impale**, stab, spear, pierce, spike, skewer, stick, gore, pin, bayonet, harpoon, lance, run through, puncture, perforate; rare transpierce.

transform verb *the city has been transformed into a magnet for foreign investment | this development will transform the site*: **change**, alter, modify, convert, metamorphose, transfigure, transmute, mutate; remodel, reshape, remould, redo, reconstruct, rebuild, recast, reorganize, rearrange, reorder, reshuffle, restyle, rejig, rework, renew, revamp, renovate, overhaul, remake; revolutionize, stir up, turn upside down;

humorous transmogrify.
▷ANTONYMS preserve, keep the same.

transformation noun *the food-manufacturing industry underwent a transformation*: **change**, alteration, modification, variation, conversion, revision, amendment, metamorphosis, transfiguration, evolution, mutation, sea change; remodelling, reshaping, remoulding, redoing, reconstruction, rebuilding, recasting, reorganization, rearrangement, reordering, reshuffling, restyling, rejigging, reworking, renewal, renewing, revamping, renovation, overhaul, remaking; revolutionizing, revolution, transmutation; humorous transmogrification.
▷ANTONYMS preservation, conservation.

transgress verb **1** *they must control the impulses which lead them to transgress*: **misbehave**, behave badly, break the law, err, lapse, commit an offence, fall from grace, stray from the straight and narrow, sin, degenerate, do wrong, go astray; informal slip up, be out of order; archaic trespass.
2 *few of us will go through life without transgressing some rule of public law*: **disobey**, defy, infringe, breach, contravene, violate, break, flout, infract, commit a breach of.
▷ANTONYMS obey.

transgression noun **1** *they were granted full amnesty for their transgressions*: **offence**, crime, sin, wrong, wrongdoing, misdemeanour, felony, misdeed, lawbreaking, vice, evil-doing, indiscretion, peccadillo, mischief, mischievousness, wickedness, misbehaviour, bad behaviour; error, lapse, fault; archaic trespass.
2 *Adam's transgression of God's law*: **infringement**, breach, contravention, violation, defiance, infraction, disobedience, breaking, flouting, non-observance, overstepping, exceeding.
▷ANTONYMS obedience.

transgressor noun *a transgressor against human rights*: **offender**, wrongdoer, culprit, lawbreaker, criminal, delinquent, villain, felon, reprobate, outlaw, malefactor, guilty party; sinner, trespasser, evil-doer; Law malfeasant, misfeasor; informal crook; archaic miscreant.

transience noun *the transience of life on earth*: **temporariness**, transitoriness, impermanence, brevity, briefness, shortness, ephemerality, short-livedness, momentariness, mutability, instability, volatility; literary evanescence; rare caducity, fugitiveness.
▷ANTONYMS permanence.

transient adjective *a transient post-war baby boom*: **transitory**, temporary, short-lived, short-term, ephemeral, impermanent, brief, short, momentary; fleeting, flying, evanescent, passing, fugitive, fading, mutable, unstable, volatile, here today and gone tomorrow, fly-by-night; rare fugacious.
▷ANTONYMS permanent, perpetual, constant.

Choose the right word **transient, transitory, ephemeral, fleeting**

None of these words is much used in everyday speech and writing: they are all quite literary, and their shared meaning is 'impermanent' or 'lasting only a short time'.

The basic meaning of **transient** is mainly applied to short-lived phenomena (*a transient upturn in Germany's fortunes*) and often in technical language (*a transient rise in gastric acid output*). The sense of impermanence can derive from the fact that people or animals described as *transient* only stay or work in a place for a short time (*agency workers and their close equivalents form a very transient population | a large proportion of our birds are transient*).

Transitory is very similar but less used in technical contexts (*this transitory life | the report to his school mentioned some transitory emotional difficulties the child was having*) and almost never in relation to the movement of people or animals.

Ephemeral implies that something is not only short-lived but also inconsequential or of limited value (*ephemeral material like leaflets, posters, postcards, etc.*). However, it can be used as a neutral scientific or technical term (*melting coastal snow supports an ephemeral algal flora*).

Fleeting conveys the greatest degree of impermanence and often a note of regret that the phenomenon does not last longer (*she only caught a fleeting glimpse of him all day | Carol was paying a fleeting visit to Paris*).

transit noun *an agreement on the free transit of goods between states*: **movement**; **transport**, transportation, conveyance, shipment, haulage, freightage, carriage; moving, travel, travelling, journeying, passage, passing, transfer, crossing, progress.
□ **in transit** *a painting was damaged in transit*: **en route**, on the journey, during transport, on the way, on the road, on the move, along/on the road, in motion; informal on the go.

transition noun *the transition from school to work*: **change**, move, passage, transformation, conversion, adaptation, adjustment, alteration, changeover, metamorphosis; shift, switch, jump, leap, progression, progress, gradation, development, evolution; transfiguration, flux, mutation, transmutation, vicissitude.

transitional adjective **1** *we will need assistance in the transitional period*: **intermediate**, middle, midway, intervening, interposed; fluid, unsettled; changing, developmental, evolutionary.
▷ANTONYMS initial, final.
2 *the transitional government*: **interim**, temporary, provisional, pro tem, stopgap, short-term, fill-in, make-do, acting, conditional, caretaker, working, contingent, makeshift.
▷ANTONYMS permanent.

transitory adjective *a transitory fashion*: **temporary**, transient, brief, short, short-lived, short-term, impermanent, ephemeral, evanescent, momentary, fleeting, flying, passing, fugitive, flitting, fading, mutable, unstable, volatile, here today and gone tomorrow, fly-by-night; rare fugacious.
▷ANTONYMS permanent, perpetual, lasting.

Choose the right word **transitory, transient, ephemeral, fleeting**

See **transient**.

translate verb **1** *the German original had been translated into English*: **interpret**, render, gloss, put, express, convert, change, construe, transcribe, transliterate.
2 *be prepared to translate the jargon of your profession into normal English*: **render**, paraphrase, reword, rephrase, recast, convert, decipher, decode, gloss, explain, unravel, reveal, elucidate, expound, clarify, spell out.
3 *without some form of supervisory body, their good intentions will not be translated into reality*: **change**, convert, transform, alter, turn, metamorphose, transmute, transfigure, render; humorous transmogrify.
4 *my husband and I, recently translated from California to the North-east, were given similar advice*: **relocate**, transfer, move, remove, shift, convey, transport, transplant.

translation noun **1** *a translation of the 'Odyssey'*: **rendering**, rendition, gloss, conversion, construing, transcription, transliteration, metaphrase.
2 *a modern translation of Hamlet's 'to be, or not to be' speech*: **rendition**, adaptation, version, rendering, paraphrase, paraphrasing, rewording, rephrase, rephrasing, recasting, conversion, deciphering, decoding, gloss, crib, simplification, explanation, elucidation, clarification.
3 *the translation of these policies into practice will vary according to local circumstances*: **change**, conversion, transformation, alteration, adaptation, turning, metamorphosis, transmutation, transfiguration, rendering; humorous transmogrification.
4 *the translation of the Archbishop's remains from London to Canterbury*: **relocation**, transfer, transferral, move, moving, movement, removal, shift, conveyance, conveying, transport, transportation.

translator noun *she worked as a translator at the United Nations*: **interpreter**, transcriber, transliterator, paraphraser, decipherer; **linguist**, polyglot; technical exegete, glossator, glossarist; rare dragoman.

translucent adjective *a mantle of translucent ice*: **semi-transparent**, pellucid, diaphanous, colourless, glassy, glass-like, gossamer, clear, crystalline, see-through, limpid, transparent; rare transpicuous, translucid.
▷ANTONYMS opaque.

Word toolkit **translucent**

See **diaphanous**.

transmission noun **1** *the transmission of the HIV virus | teaching practice aims at transmission of knowledge and culture*: **transference**, transferral, passing on, communication, conveyance, imparting, channelling, carrying, relaying, dispatch, mediation; dissemination, spreading, circulation, diffusion, emanation, scattering, radiation.
2 *after the transmission of the film she received instant celebrity status*: **broadcasting**, relaying, sending out, putting on (the) air, airing, televising, radioing, telecasting, showing, publication, emission.
3 *a live transmission*: **broadcast**, programme, show, presentation, feature, telecast.

transmit verb **1** *modems are used for transmitting data between computers*: **transfer**, pass on, hand on, communicate, convey, impart, channel, carry, bear, relay, dispatch, mediate; disseminate, spread, circulate, diffuse, radiate.
▷ANTONYMS receive.
2 *this programme will be transmitted on Sunday*: **broadcast**, relay, send out, put on (the) air, air, televise, radio, telecast, show, publish, emit, wire, beam, pipe.

transmute verb *these books were transmuted into workable scripts*. See **change** (sense 1 of the verb).

transparency noun **1** *the transparency of the dew on a rose*: **translucency**, lucidity, pellucidity, limpidness, limpidity, glassiness, liquidity, clearness, clarity; rare transpicuousness.
▷ANTONYMS opacity, cloudiness.
2 *the transparency of classical writing*: **clarity**, clearness, lucidity, straightforwardness, plainness, obviousness, explicitness, unambiguity, unambiguousness; rare transpicuousness.
▷ANTONYMS obscurity, ambiguity.

t

3 *the transparency of their predatory motives*: **blatantness**, flagrancy, obviousness, patentness, manifestness, barefacedness, shamelessness, brazenness, boldness, unmistakableness, clearness, clarity, plainness, visibility, distinctness, apparentness, perceptibility, discernibility, palpability.
▷ANTONYMS obscurity.
4 *the report said that the country's economic management lacked transparency*: **frankness**, openness, candidness, honesty, directness, forthrightness, unreservedness, plain-spokenness, straightness, straightforwardness, ingenuousness, innocence, guilelessness, simplicity.
▷ANTONYMS cunning, secrecy.
5 *a colour transparency of the Grand Canyon*: **slide**, diapositive; photograph, photo, picture, snap, image, portrait, print, plate, film, exposure, still.

transparent adjective 1 *a transparent plastic film*: **see-through**, clear, translucent, pellucid, crystal clear, crystalline, limpid, glassy, glass-like, liquid; unclouded, uncloudy; rare transpicuous.
▷ANTONYMS opaque, cloudy.
2 *a transparent dress*: **filmy**, gauzy, fine, sheer, light, lightweight, thin, flimsy, see-through, diaphanous, chiffony, gossamer, delicate.
▷ANTONYMS thick, coarse.
3 *the symbolism of this myth is transparent*: **obvious**, explicit, unambiguous, unequivocal, clear, lucid, straightforward, plain, (as) plain as the nose on your face, apparent, unmistakable, manifest, conspicuous, patent, indisputable, self-evident; rare transpicuous.
▷ANTONYMS obscure, ambiguous.
4 *transparent lies*: **blatant**, flagrant, obvious, patent, manifest, undisguised, unconcealed, barefaced, glaring, shameless, brazen, bold, unmistakable, clear, plain, visible, noticeable, recognizable, distinct, evident, apparent, perceptible, discernible, palpable; archaic arrant.
5 *parliament should render government transparent*: **frank**, open, candid, honest, direct, forthright, unreserved, plain-spoken, straight, straightforward, ingenuous, innocent, guileless, simple, artless; accountable; informal upfront.
▷ANTONYMS cunning, secretive.

Word toolkit **transparent**
See **diaphanous**.

transpire verb 1 *it transpired that Mr. Washington had been in London throughout the period of the robberies*: **become known**, become apparent, be revealed, be disclosed, come to light, emerge, come out, get out, be discovered, be uncovered, materialize, leak out, turn out, be made public.
2 *the visitors explained where they had come from and what had transpired there*: **happen**, occur, take place, come about, come to pass, crop up, turn up, arise, chance, ensue, befall, be realized, take shape; pan out, end up.

transplant verb 1 *the Second Empire style was copied and transplanted to other European capitals*: **transfer**, transport, move, remove, shift, convey, displace, relocate, reposition, resettle, take, carry, fetch, bring.
2 *lift and transplant bulbs when they are becoming overcrowded*: **replant**, repot, relocate; uproot.
3 *the heart valves will be transplanted into local patients*: **graft**, transfer, implant.

transport verb (stress on the second syllable) 1 *the concrete blocks have been transported by lorry*: **convey**, carry, take, transfer, move, shift, bring, fetch, send, deliver, bear, conduct, haul, lug, cart, run, ship, ferry.
2 *he was convicted of theft and transported*: **banish**, exile, deport, drive away, expatriate, extradite.
3 *she was completely transported by the excitement of her passion*: **thrill**, delight, ravish, carry away, enrapture, entrance, enchant, enthral, electrify, captivate, bewitch, fascinate, spellbind, charm, overjoy, elate; informal send.
▸ noun (stress on the first syllable) 1 *this service is used mainly by the elderly who have no access to alternative forms of transport*: **conveyance**, transportation, transfer, transference, transmission, movement; vehicle, car, carriage, carrier.
2 *protect the camera in case it is dropped during transport*: **transit**, transportation, conveyance, traffic, carriage, freight, freightage, shipment, shipping, haulage, delivery, distribution, carrying.
3 *the mother, in a transport of grief, clung to her husband*: **frenzy**, fit, rhapsody; intense feeling, strong emotion, passion, fervour, vehemence.
4 (**transports**) *the transports of passion*: **rapture**, **ecstasy**, elation, exaltation, exhilaration, euphoria, bliss, seventh heaven, heaven, paradise, high; informal cloud nine.

transpose verb 1 *a pair of pictures in which the colours of the flowers and foliage are transposed*: **interchange**, exchange, switch, swap (round), transfer, reverse, invert, rearrange, reorder, turn about/around, change (round), move (around), substitute, trade, alter, convert.
2 *it had been shown that science fiction could be transposed into popular television entertainment*: **shift**, relocate, reposition, transplant, move, displace.

transverse adjective *a transverse bar*: **crosswise**, crossways, cross, diagonal, horizontal, oblique, athwart; technical transversal.

trap noun 1 *it is quite possible that the question was set as a trap*: **trick**, stratagem, ploy, ruse, wile, deception, artifice, subterfuge, device, trickery; informal set-up; archaic toils.
2 *he was fairly certain now that he was walking into a trap, and wished he'd come armed*: **ambush**, lure, decoy, bait; dated ambuscade.
3 *she wrote about what a trap her marriage was*: **snare**, net; cage, prison; encumbrance, burden, problem.
4 informal *shut your trap!* **mouth**, jaws, lips, maw; informal chops, kisser, yap; Brit. informal **gob**, cakehole, mush; N. Amer. informal puss, bazoo.
▸ verb 1 *police trapped the two men, who admitted blackmail*: **snare**, entrap, ensnare, enmesh, lay a trap for; **capture**, catch, bag, land, hook, corner, waylay, ambush; seize, take, lay hold of, run to earth/ground; archaic ambuscade.
2 *a rat trapped in a barn*: **confine**, **catch**, cut off, corner, pin down, drive into a corner, pen, hem in, close in, shut in, hedge in, imprison, hold captive.
3 *he trapped his finger in a spring-loaded hinge*: **get stuck**, catch, get caught.
4 *the politicians had trapped him into a game played by their rules*: **trick**, dupe, deceive, cheat, lure, inveigle, beguile, fool, hoodwink, seduce, cajole, wheedle, gull; catch out, trip up, outwit, outsmart; archaic cozen.

trappings plural noun *some of the appeal of monarchy lay in its ritual and spectacular trappings*: **accessories**, trimmings, frills, accompaniments, extras, ornaments, ornamentation, adornment, decoration; regalia, paraphernalia, apparatus, finery, frippery, livery, fittings, accoutrements; appurtenances, appointments, equipage, equipment, gear, effects, things, panoply; baggage, impedimenta; informal bells and whistles, stuff, bits and pieces, bits and bobs; archaic trumpery.

trash noun 1 N. Amer. *the subway entrance was blocked with trash*: **rubbish**, waste, waste material, refuse, litter, garbage, debris, junk, dross, detritus, sweepings, dregs, remains; vulgar slang crap.
2 *politicians should think and inquire before they speak trash*: **nonsense**, drivel, pap, gibberish, balderdash, bunkum, humbug, rubbish, moonshine; informal bull, poppycock, gobbledegook, hot air, twaddle, rot, tommyrot, bunk, tripe, bilge, piffle, bosh, tosh, hooey; N. Amer. informal garbage, flapdoodle, blathers, wack, bushwa, applesauce; vulgar slang crap, bullshit; Austral./NZ vulgar slang bulldust.
▷ANTONYMS logic, good sense.
3 *get home, you convict trash!* **rabble**, scum, vermin, dregs, good-for-nothings, lowest of the low, underclass, the dregs, untouchables, the hoi polloi; French canaille; informal riff-raff.
▸ verb 1 N. Amer. informal *they trashed their guitars and threw them into the audience*: **wreck**, ruin, damage, destroy; deface, mar, spoil, vandalize; informal total.
2 *his directorial debut had been trashed by the critics*: **criticize**, **lambaste**, censure, attack, insult, abuse, give a bad press to, condemn, flay, savage; informal pan, knock, take to pieces, take/pull apart, crucify, hammer, slam, bash, roast, maul, throw brickbats at; Brit. informal slate, rubbish, slag off; N. Amer. bad-mouth, pummel.

trauma noun 1 *the trauma of divorce*: **shock**, upheaval, distress, stress, strain, pain, anguish, suffering, upset, agony, misery, sorrow, grief, heartache, heartbreak, torture; disturbance, disorder, jolt, ordeal, trial, tribulation, trouble, worry, anxiety, burden, adversity, hardship, nightmare.
2 *the gallstone can be extracted without unnecessary trauma to the liver*: **injury**, damage, hurt, wound, wounding, sore, bruise, cut, laceration, lesion, abrasion, contusion.
▷ANTONYMS healing.

traumatic adjective 1 *they had had traumatic experiences in the war*: **disturbing**, shocking, distressing, disquieting, upsetting, damaging, scarring, injurious, harmful, hurtful, painful, agonizing, awful, chilling, alarming, devastating, harrowing, excruciating, horrifying, terrifying; informal mind-blowing.
▷ANTONYMS soothing, calming.
2 *bankruptcy looked possible after the traumatic first year*: **stressful**, demanding, trying, taxing, terrible, bad, unpleasant, disagreeable, irksome, troublesome, vexatious.
▷ANTONYMS successful, pleasing.

travail literary noun *the travails of austerity in the late 1940s*. See **drudgery**.

travel verb 1 *people seeking an exit visa to travel abroad*: **journey**, **tour**, take a trip, go on a trip, voyage, go on an expedition, go on an excursion, go sightseeing, globetrot, backpack; roam, rove, range, wend one's way, cruise, hike, trek, tramp, ride, roll; cross, traverse, cover, make one's way over, circumnavigate, go round, move round; move, go, proceed; informal gallivant, knock about/around; rare peregrinate.
2 *light travels faster than sound*: **move**, proceed, progress, advance; be transmitted, carry.
3 informal *that lorry's travelling!* **go fast**, go rapidly, drive fast, speed, race, go at breakneck speed, hurry, hurtle, hasten, hotfoot it, whip (along), whizz, go like (greased) lightning; informal go hell for leather, go like a bat out of hell, tear up the miles, steam, belt, tear, zip, get cracking, get a move on, burn rubber; Brit. informal bomb, put one's foot down.
▸ noun *he amassed great wealth during his travels*: **journeys**, expeditions,

trips, tours, excursions, voyages, treks, safaris, odysseys, pilgrimages, jaunts; journeying, travelling, touring, sightseeing, voyaging, cruising, sailing, backpacking, globetrotting, jet-setting, exploration, trekking, wandering, roving, roaming; informal gallivanting; rare peregrinations.

> *Word links* **travel**
>
> **hodophobia** fear of travel

traveller noun **1** *thousands of air travellers were left stranded*: **passenger**, **tourist**, tripper, tourer, journeyer, voyager, excursionist, holidaymaker, sightseer, visitor, globetrotter, jet-setter; backpacker, pilgrim, gadabout; rover, wanderer, explorer, discoverer, scout, surveyor, reconnoitrer, prospector; commuter, fare payer, fare; N. Amer. vacationer, vacationist; informal gallivanter.
2 *a travellers' site*: **gypsy**, Romany, tzigane, didicoi; New Age traveller, New Ager; **nomad**, migrant, wanderer, wayfarer, itinerant, drifter; **tramp**, vagrant, transient, vagabond, tinker; (**travellers**) travelling people, travelling folk.

travelling adjective **1** *a survey of the travelling population*: **nomadic**, itinerant, peripatetic, migratory, migrating, wandering, roaming, roving, wayfaring, rambling, touring, drifting, floating, unsettled, restless, on the move, on the go, on the wing; displaced, homeless; gypsy, Romany, tzigane, didicoi; globetrotting, jet-setting; archaic errant.
▷ANTONYMS fixed, settled.
2 *a travelling circus*: **itinerant**, peripatetic, moving, mobile.
3 *a little travelling clock*: **portable**, mobile, transportable, movable, transferable, easily carried, easy to carry, conveyable, travel, lightweight, compact, handy, convenient, manageable; rare portative.
▷ANTONYMS full-sized.

traverse verb **1** *he traversed the deserts of Persia and Baluchistan*: **travel over/across**, cross, journey over/across, make one's way across, pass over, go across, negotiate; cover; ply; wander, roam, range.
2 *a ditch traversed by a small wooden bridge*: **extend across**, lie across, stretch across, go across, cross, cut across; bridge, span.

travesty noun *he dismissed the proceedings as a travesty of justice*: **misrepresentation**, distortion, perversion, corruption, poor imitation, poor substitute, mockery, parody, caricature; farce, charade, pantomime, sham; apology for, excuse for.
▸ verb *he felt that Michael had betrayed the family by travestying them in his plays*: **misrepresent**, parody, caricature, burlesque, mock, make a mockery of, ridicule, make fun of; distort, pervert.

treacherous adjective **1** *two treacherous Scottish lords betrayed Wallace's whereabouts*: **traitorous**, disloyal, perfidious, faithless, unfaithful, duplicitous, false-hearted, deceitful, false, untrue, back-stabbing, double-crossing, double-dealing, two-faced, untrustworthy, unreliable, undependable, fickle; apostate, renegade, subversive, seditious, rebellious, mutinous, breakaway; treasonable, treasonous; informal two-timing; rare Janus-faced, Punic.
▷ANTONYMS loyal, faithful.
2 *treacherous driving conditions*: **dangerous**, hazardous, perilous, unsafe, precarious, risky, deceptive, unreliable, undependable, unstable; icy, ice-covered, slippery, glassy; informal dicey, hairy, slippy; N. Amer. informal gnarly.
▷ANTONYMS safe, reliable.

treachery noun *the damning evidence of her treachery*: **betrayal**, disloyalty, perfidy, perfidiousness, faithlessness, unfaithfulness, infidelity, bad faith, breach of trust, duplicity, deceit, deceitfulness, deception, false-heartedness, falseness, stab in the back, back-stabbing, double-dealing, untrustworthiness; treason; informal two-timing; rare Punic faith.
▷ANTONYMS loyalty, faithfulness.

tread verb **1** *he trod purposefully down the hall*: **walk**, step, stride, pace, go; march, tramp, plod, stomp, trudge.
2 *the snow had been trodden down by the horses*: **crush**, flatten, press down, squash; **trample on**, tramp on, step on, stamp on, stomp on.
▸ noun *she heard Bryony's heavy tread upstairs*: **step**, footstep, footfall, tramp.

treason noun **treachery**, lese-majesty; disloyalty, betrayal, faithlessness, perfidy, perfidiousness, duplicity, infidelity; sedition, subversion, mutiny, rebellion; high treason; rare Punic faith.
▷ANTONYMS allegiance, loyalty.

treasonable adjective *there was no evidence of treasonable activity*: **traitorous**, treacherous, perfidious, treasonous, disloyal, faithless, duplicitous; seditious, subversive, mutinous, rebellious.
▷ANTONYMS loyal.

treasure noun **1** *a casket of treasure*: **riches**, valuables, jewels, gems, gold, silver, precious metals, money, cash; wealth, fortune; Brit. treasure trove.
2 *art treasures*: **valuable object**, valuable, work of art, objet of virtu, masterpiece.
3 informal *she's been a real treasure—I don't know what I would have done without her*: **paragon**, gem, angel, nonpareil; find, prize; informal star, one of a kind, one in a million, something else, the tops.
4 informal *he was no longer her treasure but a naughty child too old to be smacked*: **darling**, angel, apple of one's eye, pride and joy.
▸ verb *I treasure the photographs I took of Jack*: **cherish**, hold dear, place great value on, prize, set great store by, value greatly, esteem; **adore**, dote on, love dearly, be devoted to, idolize, worship, think very highly of, appreciate greatly; preserve, keep safe.

treasury noun **1** *she transferred billions from the national treasury to her personal bank account*: **exchequer**, purse; bank, coffers; revenues, finances, funds, moneys, resources; archaic fisc.
2 *the area is a treasury of early fossils*: **rich source**, repository, storehouse, store, treasure house, treasure trove; fund, mine, bank.
3 *a treasury of stories*: **anthology**, collection, miscellany, compilation, compendium; archaic garland.

treat verb **1** *Charlotte treated him very badly*: **behave towards**, act towards, conduct oneself towards, use, serve; deal with, handle, manage.
2 *police are treating the fires as arson*: **regard**, consider, view, look on; put down as.
3 *chapter 8 treats topics such as the educational disadvantages of women*: **deal with**, be about, cover, be concerned with, concern itself with, discuss, write/speak/talk about, go into, explore, investigate, tackle, handle; touch on, refer to; consider, study, review, analyse, critique.
4 *Lisa is being treated at Addenbrooke's Hospital*: **attend to**, tend, minister to, nurse, give treatment to; prescribe medicine for, medicate, dose; informal doctor.
5 *the plants may prove useful in treating cancer*: **cure**, heal, remedy, make better.
6 *the wood can be treated with chemical preservative*: **prime**, prepare, process, cover.
7 *he **treated** her **to** a slap-up lunch*: **buy**, take out for, stand, give; pay for, pay/foot the bill for; entertain, wine and dine.
8 *delegates were **treated to** authentic Indonesian dance performances*: **regale with**, entertain with/by, fête with, amuse with/by, divert with/by.
9 formal *propagandists claimed that he was treating with the enemy*: **negotiate**, discuss terms, have talks, consult, parley, talk, confer; make a bargain, bargain.
□ **treat something lightly** *this is a serious matter and he can't treat it lightly*: **minimize**, play down, underplay, make light of, make little of, dismiss, underestimate, undervalue, devalue, laugh off, belittle, trivialize, treat as unimportant, think little of, deprecate, scoff at; informal pooh-pooh; archaic hold cheap; rare misprize, derogate, minify.
▸ noun **1** *a birthday treat*: **celebration**, entertainment, amusement, diversion; surprise; party, excursion, outing.
2 *I bought you some chocolate biscuits as a treat*: **present**, gift; titbit, delicacy, little something, luxury, indulgence, extravagance; informal goodie.
3 *it was a real treat to see them*: **pleasure**, source of pleasure, delight, thrill, joy.

treatise noun *his treatise on medical ethics*: **disquisition**, essay, paper, work, piece of writing, exposition, discourse, dissertation, thesis, monograph, study, critique; tract, pamphlet; rare tractate, institutes.

treatment noun **1** *she accepted his **treatment of** her as if it was no more than she deserved*: **behaviour towards**, conduct towards, action towards, usage of, use of; handling of, management of; dealings with; reception.
2 *she's responding well to treatment*: **therapy**, surgery, medical care/attention, care, ministrations, nursing; therapeutics; (course of) medication, (course of) drugs, medicaments; cure, remedy.
3 *her treatment of the topic*: **presentation**, discussion, coverage, handling, investigation, exploration, consideration, study, analysis, critique.

treaty noun *the two countries signed a peace treaty*: **agreement**, settlement, pact, deal, entente, concordat, accord, concord, protocol, compact, convention, contract, covenant, bargain, pledge; armistice, truce; alliance.

tree noun sapling; conifer, evergreen; bush, shrub.

> *Word links* **tree**
>
> **arboreal** relating to trees
> **dendro-** related prefix, as in *dendrochronology*
> **dendrology** study of trees
> **forestry**, **agroforestry**, **arboriculture**, **silviculture** farming of trees

trek noun *a three-day trek across the desert*: **journey**, trip, expedition, safari, odyssey; hike, march, slog, footslog, tramp, trudge, walk; long haul; Brit. informal yomp, trog.
▸ verb *he's trekked across some of the most inhospitable terrain in the world*: **hike**, tramp, march, slog, footslog, trudge, traipse, walk; travel, journey; Brit. informal yomp, trog.

trellis noun **lattice**, framework, open framework, espalier; network, mesh, tracery; grille, grid, grating; latticework, trelliswork; technical reticulation.

tremble verb **1** *Joe's face was pale and his hands were trembling*: **shake**, shake like a leaf, quiver, twitch, palpitate; quaver, waver; rare tremor, quave.
2 *the entire building trembled*: **shake**, shudder, judder, wobble, rock, vibrate, move, sway, totter, teeter.

3 *she trembled at the thought of what he had in store for her*: **be afraid**, be fearful, be filled with fear, be frightened, be apprehensive, worry, be anxious, be in a state of anxiety, shake in one's shoes; quail, shrink from, blench from, blanch from; informal be in a blue funk, be all of a tremble, be all of a quiver.

▸ **noun** *the slight tremble in her hands*: **tremor**, shake, shakiness, trembling, quiver, twitch, twitchiness.
▹ANTONYMS steadiness.

> *Choose the right word* **tremble, shake, shiver, quiver, quake**
>
> See **shake**.

tremendous adjective **1** *tremendous sums of money*: **very great**, huge, enormous, immense, colossal, massive, prodigious, stupendous, monumental, mammoth, vast, gigantic, giant, mighty, epic, monstrous, titanic, towering, king-sized, king-size, gargantuan, Herculean, Brobdingnagian; substantial; informal whopping, whopping great, thumping, thumping great, astronomical, astronomic, mega, monster, humongous, jumbo, hulking, bumper; Brit. informal whacking, whacking great, ginormous.
▹ANTONYMS tiny, small, slight.
2 *a tremendous explosion*: **very loud**, deafening, ear-splitting, ear-piercing, booming, thundering, thunderous, roaring, resounding, crashing.
▹ANTONYMS soft.
3 informal *I've seen him play and he's tremendous*: **excellent**, **wonderful**, marvellous, magnificent, superb, splendid, glorious, sublime, lovely, delightful, first-class, first-rate, outstanding; consummate, perfect; informal super, great, smashing, amazing, fantastic, terrific, phenomenal, sensational, incredible, heavenly, stellar, gorgeous, dreamy, grand, fabulous, fab, fabby, fantabulous, awesome, magic, ace, crack, cool, mean, bad, wicked, mega, crucial, mind-blowing, far out, A1, sound, out of this world, marvy, spanking; Brit. informal brilliant, brill, bosting; N. Amer. informal peachy, dandy, jim-dandy, neat, badass, boss, radical, rad, boffo, bully, bitching, bodacious, crackerjack; Austral./NZ informal beaut, bonzer; S. African informal kif, lank; black English dope, def, phat; informal, dated groovy, divine; Brit. informal, dated capital, champion, wizard, corking, ripping, cracking, spiffing, top-hole, topping, beezer; N. Amer. informal, dated swell, keen; vulgar slang shit-hot; archaic goodly.
▹ANTONYMS bad, poor.

tremor noun **1** *she tried to still the sudden tremor of her hands*: **trembling**, shaking, shakiness, tremble, shake, quivering, quiver, twitching, twitch, convulsion, vibration, juddering, judder; quavering, quaver; tic.
▹ANTONYMS steadiness.
2 *a tremor of fear ran through her*: **frisson**, shiver, spasm, thrill, tingle, stab, dart, shaft; wave, surge, rush, ripple.
3 *the epicentre of the tremor was 65 miles north of LA*: **earthquake**, earth tremor, shock, foreshock, aftershock; informal quake, shake; N. Amer. informal tremblor.

> *Word links* **tremor**
>
> **seismic** relating to tremors

tremulous adjective **1** *'where?' she asked, in a tremulous voice*: **shaky**, trembling, shaking, unsteady, quavering, wavering, quivering, quivery, quaking; nervous, weak; informal trembly, all of a tremble.
▹ANTONYMS steady.
2 *a tremulous smile*: **timid**, diffident, shy, hesitant, uncertain, timorous, unconfident, fearful, frightened, scared; nervous, anxious, apprehensive.
▹ANTONYMS confident.

trench noun **ditch**, channel, trough, excavation, pit, furrow, rut, conduit, cut, drain, waterway, watercourse; earthwork, entrenchment, moat; technical fosse; historical sap.

trenchant adjective *he made trenchant criticisms of her style of leadership*: **incisive**, cutting, pointed, piercing, penetrating, sharp, keen, acute, razor-sharp, razor-edged, rapier-like; vigorous, forceful, strong, telling, emphatic, forthright, blunt; biting, stinging, mordant, pungent, scathing, caustic, acid, tart, acerbic, astringent, sarcastic; devastating, savage, fierce, searing, blistering, withering; N. Amer. acerb; rare mordacious, acidulous.
▹ANTONYMS woolly, vague.

trend noun **1** *an upward trend in unemployment*: **tendency**, movement, drift, swing, shift, course, current, run, direction, inclination, leaning; bias, bent.
2 *the latest trend in dance music*: **fashion**, vogue, style, mode, craze, mania, rage; informal fad, thing.

▸ **verb** *interest rates are trending up in Japan*: **move**, go, tend, head, drift, gravitate, swing, shift, turn, incline, lean, veer.

trendy adjective informal *trendy clothes*: **fashionable**, in fashion, in vogue, stylish, modish, chic, designer, up to date, up to the minute, latest, contemporary, popular, all the rage; trendsetting; French à la mode, le dernier cri; informal cool, funky, in, the in thing, hot, big, with it, hip, happening, now, smart, sharp, groovy, mod, swinging, snazzy, natty, nifty; N. Amer. informal kicky, tony, fly; Brit. informal, dated all the go, swagger.
▹ANTONYMS unfashionable.

trepidation noun *he sat in the waiting room, full of trepidation*: **fear**, **apprehension**, dread, fearfulness, apprehensiveness, agitation, anxiety, worry, nervousness, tension, misgivings, unease, uneasiness, foreboding, disquiet, disquietude, perturbation, discomposure, dismay, consternation, alarm, panic, trembling, jumpiness; Brit. nerviness; informal butterflies, jitteriness, the jitters, a cold sweat, a blue funk, the heebie-jeebies, the willies, the shakes, the yips, the jim-jams, collywobbles, cold feet; Brit. informal the (screaming) abdabs/habdabs; Austral. rhyming slang Joe Blakes.
▹ANTONYMS calm, equanimity, composure.

trespass verb **1** *there is no excuse for **trespassing on** railway property*: **enter without permission**, intrude on, encroach on, invade, infringe, impinge on; archaic entrench on.
2 *I must not **trespass on** your good nature*: **take advantage of**, impose on, make use of, play on, exploit, abuse, make unfair claims on.
3 archaic *he found it increasingly hard to forgive those who **trespassed against** him*: **wrong**, do wrong to, cause harm to; offend, distress.

▸ **noun 1** *clearly, he is guilty of trespass*: **unlawful entry**, intrusion, encroachment, invasion, infringement, impingement.
2 archaic *he asked forgiveness for his trespasses*. See **sin** (sense 1 of the noun).

trespasser noun *a high stone wall discouraged would-be trespassers*: **intruder**, interloper, unwelcome visitor, encroacher.

tresses plural noun *her long blonde tresses*: **hair**, head of hair, mane, mop of hair, shock of hair; locks, curls, ringlets.

trial noun **1** *the trial is expected to last several weeks*: **court case**, case, lawsuit, suit, hearing, enquiry, tribunal, litigation, judicial proceedings, legal proceedings, proceedings, legal action; court martial; appeal, retrial.
2 *the drug is still undergoing clinical trials*: **test**, try-out, experiment, pilot study; examination, check, assessment, evaluation, appraisal; trial/test period, trial/test run, probation, testing, dummy run; audition, screen test; informal dry run; technical assay.
3 *Eleanor could be a bit of a trial at times*: **nuisance**, pest, bother, irritant, source of irritation/annoyance, worry, problem, inconvenience, vexation, plague, source of aggravation, thorn in one's flesh, the bane of one's life, one's cross to bear; bore; informal pain, pain in the neck, pain in the backside, headache, drag, pill, nightmare; Scottish informal skelf; N. Amer. informal pain in the butt, nudnik, burr under/in someone's saddle; Brit. informal, dated blister; vulgar slang pain in the arse.
4 *a long account of her trials and tribulations*: **trouble**, worry, anxiety, burden, affliction, ordeal, tribulation, adversity, hardship, tragedy, trauma, reverse, setback, difficulty, problem, misfortune, bad luck, stroke of bad luck, ill fortune, mishap, misadventure; suffering, distress, misery, wretchedness, unhappiness, sadness, woe, grief, pain; informal hassle; archaic travails.

▸ **adjective** *a three-month trial period*: **test**, experimental, pilot, exploratory, probationary, provisional.

▸ **verb** *the electronic cash card has been trialled by several banks*: **test**, try out, carry out trials on, put to the test, put through its paces, experiment with; pilot; technical assay.

triangular adjective **three-sided**, three-cornered, triangle-shaped; technical trilateral; rare trigonal, trigonous, trigonic.

tribe noun **1** *the nomadic tribes of the Sahara*: **ethnic group**, people, race, nation; family, dynasty, house; clan, sept; technical gens; archaic folk.
2 *a tribe of children trailed after her*: **group**, crowd, gang, company, body, band, host, bevy, party, pack, army, herd, flock, drove, horde, mob; informal bunch, crew, gaggle, posse, load.

> *Choose the right word* **tribe**
>
> The word **tribe** can cause offence when used to refer to a community living within a traditional society today, and it is better in such cases to use alternative terms such as **community** or **people**. However, if talking about such communities in the past, it is perfectly acceptable to say **tribe**, for example *the area was once inhabited by Slavic tribes.*

tribulation noun *despite his tribulations he maintained a zest for life*: **trouble**, worry, anxiety, burden, cross to bear, affliction, ordeal, trial, adversity, hardship, tragedy, trauma, reverse, setback, blow, difficulty, problem, misfortune, bad luck, stroke of bad luck, ill fortune, mishap, misadventure; suffering, distress, misery, wretchedness, unhappiness, sadness, heartache, woe, grief, pain, anguish, agony; informal hassle; archaic travails.

tribunal noun **1** *a rent tribunal*: **arbitration board/panel**, board, panel, committee; industrial tribunal.
2 *an international war crimes tribunal*: **court**, court of justice, court of law, law court, bar; court of enquiry; N. Amer. forum.

tributary noun *a tributary of the Mississippi*: **headwater**, branch, feeder, side stream; N. Amer. & Austral./NZ creek; technical influent; rare confluent.

tribute noun **1** *tributes flooded in from friends and colleagues*: **accolade**, praise, commendation, acclaim, acclamation, salute, testimonial, paean,

eulogy, panegyric, encomium, homage; celebration, exaltation, extolment, glorification; congratulations, compliments, plaudits; gift, present, offering; informal bouquet; rare laudation.
▷ANTONYMS criticism, condemnation.
2 *it is a* ***tribute to*** *his determination that he ever played again*: **testimony to**, indication of, manifestation of, evidence of, proof of, attestation of.
3 *the Vikings demanded tributes in silver*: **payment**, contribution, dues, levy, tax, duty, impost, tariff, charge; offering, gift; ransom.
□ **pay tribute to** *Mr Turnbull paid tribute to all the staff at the Airedale hospital*: **praise**, sing the praises of, speak highly of, express admiration of, commend, acclaim, take one's hat off to, applaud, salute, honour, show appreciation of, appreciate, recognize, acknowledge, give recognition to, show gratitude to, be grateful for, pay homage to, extol; rare laud.

trice noun
□ **in a trice** *he should be here in a trice*: **in a moment**, in a minute, in a second, shortly, any minute, any minute now, in a short time, (very) soon, in an instant, in the twinkling of an eye, in a flash, in (less than) no time, in no time at all, before you know it, before long; **very quickly**, swiftly, without delay, at once, straight away, right away, directly; N. Amer. momentarily; informal in a jiffy, in two shakes, in two shakes of a lamb's tail, before you can say Jack Robinson, in the blink of an eye, in a blink, in the wink of an eye, in a wink, before you can say knife; Brit. informal in a tick, in two ticks, in a mo; N. Amer. informal in a snap.

trick noun **1** *he's capable of any mean trick*: **stratagem**, ploy, ruse, scheme, device, move, manoeuvre, contrivance, machination, expedient, artifice, wile, dodge; deceit, deception, trickery, subterfuge, chicanery, sharp practice; swindle, hoax, fraud, confidence trick; informal con, con trick, set-up, game, scam, sting, gyp, flimflam; Brit. informal wheeze; N. Amer. informal bunco, grift; Austral. informal lurk, rort; S. African informal schlenter; Brit. informal, dated flanker; archaic shift, fetch, rig.
2 *I think he's playing a trick on us*: **practical joke**, joke, prank, jape, stunt, antic, caper; informal leg-pull, spoof, put-on; Brit. informal cod; N. Amer. informal dido; Austral. informal goak; archaic cutup, quiz; Scottish archaic cantrip.
3 *he entertained the children with conjuring tricks*: **feat**, stunt; (**tricks**) **sleight of hand**, legerdemain, prestidigitation; magic.
4 *it was probably* ***a trick of the light***: **illusion**, optical illusion, deception, figment of the imagination; mirage.
5 *Arthur taught her the tricks of the trade*: **technique**, knack, art, skill; secret; informal know-how.
6 *he sat biting his fingernails, a trick of his when he was excited or angry*: **mannerism**, habit, practice, quirk, idiosyncrasy, peculiarity, foible, eccentricity, way, characteristic, trait.
□ **do the trick** informal *a glass of whisky did the trick—I slept like a log*: **be effective**, work, solve the problem, take care of the problem, achieve the desired result, fill/fit the bill; N. Amer. turn the trick; informal do the necessary.
▶ **verb** *many people have been tricked by villains with false identity cards*: **deceive**, delude, hoodwink, mislead, take in, dupe, fool, double-cross, cheat, defraud, swindle, outwit, outmanoeuvre, catch out, gull, hoax, bamboozle, beguile; entrap; informal con, bilk, diddle, rook, put one over on, pull a fast one on, pull the wool over someone's eyes, take for a ride, lead up the garden path, spoof, shaft, do, have, gyp, flimflam; N. Amer. informal sucker, snooker, goldbrick, give someone a bum steer; Austral. informal pull a swifty on; archaic cozen, chicane, sell; rare illude.
□ **trick someone/something out** *he was tricked out in wide silk trousers, a red sash, and a necklace of silver dollars*: **dress (up)**, array, attire, rig out, garb, get up; **adorn**, decorate, deck (out), embellish, ornament, festoon; literary bedeck, accoutre, apparel, bedizen, caparison, trap out, furbelow.

trickery noun *she looked at me coldly as if suspecting some kind of trickery*: **deception**, deceit, dishonesty, cheating, duplicity, double-dealing, legerdemain, sleight of hand, guile, intrigue, deviousness, cunning, craft, craftiness, artfulness, slyness, subterfuge, skulduggery, chicanery, wiles, fraud, fraudulence, swindling, sophistry, sharp practice, underhandedness; dissimulation, pretence; informal monkey business, funny business, hanky-panky, jiggery-pokery, kidology, shenanigans, flimflam; Irish informal codology; archaic management.
▷ANTONYMS honesty, candour.

trickle verb *blood was trickling from two deep cuts in his bottom lip*: **drip**, dribble, drizzle, flow, run, spill; ooze, leak, seep, exude, percolate.
▷ANTONYMS pour, gush, stream.
▶ **noun** *trickles of water ran down inside his collar*: **dribble**, drip, thin stream, rivulet, runnel.

trickster noun **swindler**, cheat, fraud, fraudster, defrauder, confidence man; charlatan, mountebank, quack, impostor, sham; rogue, villain, scoundrel; deceiver, deluder, dissembler, hoodwinker, hoaxer; joker, practical joker; informal con man, con artist, sharp, phoney, flimflam man, flimflammer; Brit. informal twister; N. Amer. informal grifter, bunco artist, gold brick, chiseller; Austral. informal illywhacker, magsman, shicer; S. African informal schlenter; rare tregetour.

tricky adjective **1** *a tricky situation*: **difficult**, awkward, problematic, delicate, ticklish, sensitive, touchy, risky, uncertain, precarious, touch-and-go; thorny, knotty, involved, complex, complicated, convoluted; vexed; embarrassing; informal sticky, dicey, hairy; N. Amer. informal gnarly.
▷ANTONYMS straightforward, uncomplicated.
2 *a tricky and unscrupulous politician*: **cunning**, crafty, wily, artful, guileful, devious, scheming, sly, slippery, slick, deceitful, deceptive, duplicitous, dishonest, disingenuous, Machiavellian; N. Amer. snide; informal foxy, shifty; Brit. informal fly, dodgy; S. African informal slim; Austral./NZ informal shonky; rare subtle, carny.
▷ANTONYMS honest.

tried adjective *a* ***tried-and-trusted*** *method for solving the problem*: **reliable**, dependable, trustworthy, trusted, certain, sure, true; **proven**, proved, tested, tried out, tried and tested, put to the test, established, fail-safe, time-honoured, classic; reputable.
▷ANTONYMS experimental, novel.

trifle noun **1** *we needn't bother the headmaster over such trifles*: **unimportant thing/matter**, trivial thing/matter, triviality, thing/matter of no consequence, thing/matter of no importance, bagatelle, inessential, nothing; technicality; (**trifles**) trivia, minutiae.
2 *a horse he had bought for a trifle and sold for an incredible sum*: **very small amount**, next to nothing, hardly anything; pittance; informal peanuts, piddling amount; N. Amer. informal chump change.
▷ANTONYMS small fortune.
3 *he went into town to buy a few trifles for Christmas*: **bauble**, trinket, knick-knack, gimcrack, gewgaw, toy; informal whatnot; Brit. informal doodah.
□ **a trifle** *he looked a trifle apprehensive*: **a little**, a bit, somewhat, a touch, a spot, a mite, a whit; informal a tad, ish.
▷ANTONYMS very, extremely.
▶ **verb**
□ **trifle with** *I loathe men who trifle with women's affections*: **treat in a cavalier fashion**, treat lightly, treat frivolously, treat casually, play ducks and drakes with; dally with, play with, amuse oneself with, toy with, flirt with, play fast and loose with; informal mess about/around; archaic sport with, wanton with, palter with.

trifling adjective *a trifling matter* | *trifling sums were awarded in damages*: **trivial**, unimportant, insignificant, inconsequential, petty, minor, of little/no account, of little/no consequence, not worth mentioning, not worth bothering about, light, footling, fiddling, pettifogging, incidental; frivolous, silly, idle, superficial; **small**, tiny, inconsiderable, nominal, negligible, nugatory, minute, minuscule; paltry, derisory, pitiful, pathetic, miserable; informal piffling, piddling, measly, mingy; Brit. informal poxy; N. Amer. informal picayune, nickel-and-dime, small-bore, dinky; rare exiguous.
▷ANTONYMS important, serious; considerable.

trigger verb **1** *the incident triggered an acrimonious debate*: **precipitate**, prompt, trigger off, set off, spark (off), touch off, stimulate, provoke, stir up, fan the flames of; cause, give rise to, lead to, set in motion, occasion, be the cause of, bring about, generate, engender, begin, start, initiate; literary enkindle.
2 *burglars triggered the alarm*: **activate**, set off, set going, trip.

trill verb *a skylark was trilling overhead*: **warble**, sing, chirp, chirrup, tweet, twitter, cheep, peep.

trim verb **1** *his straggly hair had been washed and trimmed*: **cut**, barber, crop, bob, shorten, clip, snip, shear; prune, pollard; mow; neaten, shape, tidy up, even up.
2 *trim off the lower leaves using a sharp knife*: **cut off**, remove, take off, chop off, lop off, shave off, hack off, nip off.
3 *production and labour costs need to be trimmed*: **reduce**, decrease, make reductions in, cut down, cut back on, make cutbacks in, scale down, prune, slim down, pare down, dock, retrench on.
4 *the story was severely trimmed for the film version*: **shorten**, abridge, condense, abbreviate, telescope, truncate, curtail.
5 *a pair of black leather gloves trimmed with fake fur*: **decorate**, adorn, ornament, embellish; edge, pipe, border, hem, fringe; literary bedizen.
▶ **noun 1** *white curtains with a blue trim*: **decoration**, trimming, ornamentation, adornment, embellishment; **border**, edging, piping, purfling, rickrack, hem, fringe, frill.
2 *an unruly mop in desperate need of a trim*: **haircut**, cut, barbering, clip, snip; pruning; tidy-up.
□ **in trim** *she keeps herself in trim with regular visits to the health club*: **fit**, fighting fit, as fit as a fiddle, in good health, in good condition, in fine fettle, aerobicized; **slim**, in shape.
▶ **adjective 1** *a cropped, fitted jacket looks trim with a long-line skirt*: **smart**, stylish, chic, spruce, dapper, elegant, crisp; informal natty, sharp; N. Amer. informal spiffy; archaic trig.
2 *a trim little villa*: **neat**, **tidy**, neat and tidy, as neat as a new pin, orderly, in (good) order, well kept, well looked-after, well maintained, shipshape (and Bristol fashion), in apple-pie order, immaculate, spick and span, uncluttered, straight, spruce; archaic tricksy.
▷ANTONYMS untidy, messy, scruffy.
3 *men find her trim figure and vivacious personality very appealing*: **slim**, slender, lean, clean-limbed, sleek, willowy, lissom, sylphlike, svelte, snake-hipped; streamlined.
▷ANTONYMS fat.

trimming noun **1** *a black party dress with lace trimming*: **decoration**, trim, ornamentation, adornment, passementerie, embroidery, frou-frou; border,

edging, piping, purfling, rickrack, fringes, fringing, frills; rare falbalas, passement, fimbriations.
2 (**trimmings**) *roast turkey with all the trimmings*: **accompaniments**, extras, frills, accessories, accoutrements, trappings, paraphernalia; garnishing, garnish.
3 (**trimmings**) *hedge trimmings*: **cuttings**, clippings, parings, shavings, ends; rare brash.

trinket noun **knick-knack**, bauble, ornament, piece of bric-a-brac, bibelot, curio, trifle, toy, novelty, gimcrack, gewgaw; French objet; informal whatnot, dingle-dangle; Brit. informal doodah; N. Amer. informal tchotchke, tsatske; archaic folderol, furbelow, whim-wham, kickshaw, bijou, gaud.

trio noun **threesome**, three, triumvirate, triad, troika, triplex, trinity, trilogy, triptych, triplets; rare triunity, triune, triplicity.

trip verb **1** *Owen tripped on the loose stones*: **stumble**, lose one's footing, catch one's foot, slip, lose one's balance, stagger, totter, slide; fall, fall down, tumble, topple, take a spill; dated measure one's length.
2 *taxpayers often **trip up** by not declaring taxable income*: **make a mistake**, miscalculate, make a blunder, blunder, go wrong, get something wrong, make an error, err; informal slip up, screw up, make a boo-boo; Brit. informal boob, drop a clanger; N. Amer. informal goof up.
3 *the question was intended to **trip up** the prime minister*: **catch out**, trap, trick, outwit, outsmart; put someone off their stride, throw off balance, disconcert, unsettle, discountenance, discomfit; informal throw, wrong-foot; Brit. informal catch on the hop.
4 *they tripped up the terrace steps*: **run lightly**, skip, dance, prance, waltz, bound, spring, hop, gambol, caper, frisk, scamper.
▷ANTONYMS trudge.
5 *Hoffman tripped the alarm*: **set off**, activate, trigger; turn on, switch on, flip, throw.
6 *when tripping through the Yukon, take time to explore our museums*: **travel**, take a trip, go on a trip/excursion/journey, journey, tour, trek, hike, cruise; rare peregrinate.
▶noun **1** *a four-day trip to Paris*: **excursion**, outing, jaunt; **holiday**, visit, tour, journey, expedition, voyage; drive, run, day out; pilgrimage; informal junket, spin, hop; Scottish informal hurl; rare peregrination.
2 *trips and falls cause nearly half of all such accidents*: **stumble**, slip, misstep, false step; fall, tumble, spill.
3 *an occasional trip in the performance*: **mistake**, error, blunder, gaffe, slip, slip of the tongue/pen, lapse, oversight, indiscretion; French faux pas; Latin lapsus linguae, lapsus calami; informal slip-up, boo-boo, boner, howler; Brit. informal boob, clanger; N. Amer. informal goof, blooper, bloop.

tripe noun informal *you do talk tripe sometimes*. See **nonsense** (sense 1).

triple adjective **1** *a triple alliance*: **three-way**, tripartite; threefold.
2 *they paid him triple the going rate*: **three times**, three times as much as, treble.
▶noun **trio**, threesome, triumvirate, triad, troika; three.
▶verb *the party more than tripled its share of the vote*: **treble**, increase by three.

tripper noun Brit. informal *hordes of trippers flocked into Blackpool*. See **tourist**.

trite adjective *the observation struck me as both trite and irrelevant*: **hackneyed**, banal, clichéd, platitudinous, vapid, commonplace, ordinary, common, stock, conventional, stereotyped, predictable; **stale**, overused, overworked, overdone, worn out, time-worn, tired, threadbare, hoary, hack, unimaginative, unoriginal, derivative, uninspired, dull, pedestrian, run-of-the-mill, routine, humdrum; informal old hat, corny, played out; N. Amer. informal cornball, dime-store; rare truistic, bromidic.
▷ANTONYMS original, fresh, imaginative.

Choose the right word **trite, hackneyed, stale**

All these words suggest a lack of originality, generally springing from laziness on the part of a speaker or writer.

A **trite** remark is intrinsically banal or shallow (*trite stuff about decadence in Tinseltown*). While it is not likely to contain anything that someone could disagree with, it is an easy option, which may cause offence in contexts where one should have made a greater effort (*trite answers for grieving people*).

A **hackneyed** theme or idea has been overused, often because it is an easy trigger for emotion (*hackneyed dramatic devices | the hackneyed image of the poor benighted savage*). There is a sense that a hackneyed phrase, idea, or image is used mindlessly, even to the point of dishonesty: it may well still have some emotional impact, but this may not be justified by the context in which it is used.

Stale expressions and ideas were once telling or valid but have been repeated so often that they have lost their force (*the jokes are a bit stale*).

triumph noun **1** *a garden built to celebrate Napoleon's many triumphs*: **victory**, win, conquest, success; achievement; ascendancy, mastery.
▷ANTONYMS defeat.
2 *his eyes shone with triumph*: **jubilation**, exultation, elation, rejoicing, delight, joy, joyfulness, happiness, glee, pride, satisfaction.
▷ANTONYMS disappointment.
3 *it was a triumph of Victorian engineering*: **tour de force**, masterpiece, supreme example, coup, marvellous feat, feather in one's cap, wonder, sensation, master stroke; French coup de maître; informal hit, knockout.
▷ANTONYMS failure.
▶verb **1** *he triumphed in the British Grand Prix*: **win**, succeed, be successful, come first, be the victor, be victorious, gain a victory, carry the day, carry all before one, prevail, take the honours/prize/crown, come out on top.
▷ANTONYMS lose, fail.
2 *they had no chance of **triumphing over** the Nationalists*: **defeat**, beat, conquer, trounce, vanquish, best, worst, overcome, overpower, overwhelm, get the better of, gain ascendancy over, gain mastery of; bring someone to their knees, prevail against, subdue, subjugate; informal lick.
▷ANTONYMS be defeated by.
3 *'You can't touch me,' she triumphed*: **crow**, gloat, swagger, brag, boast; **exult**, rejoice, celebrate, revel, glory; rare jubilate.

triumphant adjective **1** *the triumphant British team*: **victorious**, successful, winning, prize-winning, conquering; undefeated, unbeaten, unvanquished.
▷ANTONYMS unsuccessful, defeated, losing.
2 *she looked up, a triumphant expression on her face*: **jubilant**, exultant, elated, rejoicing, joyful, joyous, delighted, gleeful, proud, cock-a-hoop; gloating, boastful, swaggering.
▷ANTONYMS despondent, disappointed.

Easily confused words **triumphant, triumphal, or triumphalist?**

A **triumphant** army might march under a **triumphal** arch, possibly uttering *triumphant* cheers. *Triumphant* means 'having won a battle' or 'feeling or expressing elation at victory' (*Simon couldn't suppress a triumphant smile*). *Triumphal*, on the other hand, means 'made or performed to celebrate a victory' (*an imperial triumphal procession*). While these two words are generally neutral, **triumphalist** conveys disapproval of brash and offensive celebration of victory (*they do not want to offend people by appearing triumphalist*).

trivia plural noun *domestic trivia*: **(petty) details**, minutiae, niceties, technicalities, trivialities, trifles, irrelevancies, non-essentials.
▷ANTONYMS essentials, nitty-gritty.

trivial adjective **1** *your problems are trivial in comparison with Peter's*: **unimportant**, insignificant, inconsequential, minor, of no/little account, of no/little consequence, of no/little importance, not worth bothering about, not worth mentioning; incidental, inessential, non-essential, petty, trifling, fiddling, pettifogging, footling, small, slight, little, inconsiderable, negligible, paltry, nugatory; meaningless, pointless, worthless, idle; flimsy, insubstantial; informal piddling, piffling, penny-ante; Brit. informal twopenny-halfpenny; N. Amer. informal nickel-and-dime, small-bore; N. Amer. vulgar slang chickenshit.
▷ANTONYMS important, significant, life-and-death.
2 *I think I used to be quite a trivial person*: **frivolous**, superficial, shallow, unthinking, empty-headed, feather-brained, lightweight, foolish, silly.
▷ANTONYMS serious, profound.

triviality noun **1** *the triviality of the subject matter*: **unimportance**, insignificance, frivolousness, inconsequence, inconsequentiality, pettiness, slightness, paltriness, negligibility; meaninglessness, pointlessness, worthlessness, flimsiness, insubstantiality.
▷ANTONYMS importance, profundity.
2 *he need not concern himself with such trivialities*: **minor detail**, petty detail, mere detail, matter/thing of no importance, matter/thing of no consequence, trifle, non-essential, inessential, nothing; technicality, incidental; (**trivialities**) trivia, minutiae.
▷ANTONYMS essential.

trivialize verb *the problem was either trivialized or ignored by teachers*: **treat as unimportant**, minimize, play down, underplay, make light of, treat lightly, make little of, think little of, laugh off, dismiss, underestimate, undervalue, devalue, belittle, deprecate, scoff at; informal pooh-pooh; archaic hold cheap; rare misprize, derogate, minify.
▷ANTONYMS make a big thing of.

troop noun **1** *a troop of tourists*: **group**, party, band, gang, bevy, body, company, troupe, assemblage, gathering, crowd, throng, horde, pack, drove, flock, swarm, stream, multitude, host, army, cohort; mob; corps, contingent, squad, detachment, unit, detail, patrol; informal bunch, gaggle, crew, posse, load.
2 (**troops**) *British troops were stationed here during the war*: **soldiers**, armed forces, service men, men, service women; the services, the army, the military, soldiery.
▶verb **1** *the children trooped behind him*: **walk**, march, file, straggle; flock, crowd, throng, stream, swarm, surge, spill.
2 *Caroline trooped wearily home from work*: **trudge**, plod, traipse, trail, drag oneself, tramp; N. Amer. informal schlep.

trophy noun **1** *a swimming trophy*: **cup**, medal; **prize**, award; laurels, bays, palm.
2 *tusks from the male are highly coveted as trophies*: **souvenir**, memento, keepsake, reminder, record, relic; spoils, booty.

t

tropical adjective *the tropical weather was debilitating*: **very hot**, sweltering, baking hot, torrid; **humid**, sultry, steamy, sticky, oppressive, stifling, suffocating, heavy; informal boiling.
▷ANTONYMS cold, arctic.

trot verb *Doyle trotted across the patio and into the house*: **run**, jog, jogtrot, dogtrot, lope; scamper, scuttle, scurry, bustle.
□ **trot something out** informal *he trotted out the official Downing Street line*: **recite**, repeat, reiterate, restate, regurgitate, churn out; come out with, produce.
▶ noun
□ **on the trot** Brit. informal *they lost seven matches on the trot*: **in succession**, one after the other, in a row, consecutively, successively, in sequence, one behind the other; running, straight.

troubadour noun historical **minstrel**, singer, balladeer, poet; historical jongleur, trouvère, trouveur, Minnesinger; rare joculator.

trouble noun 1 *it's the least you can do after all the trouble you've caused*: **problems**, difficulty, bother, inconvenience, worry, anxiety, distress, concern, disquiet, unease, irritation, vexation, annoyance, stress, agitation, harassment, unpleasantness; informal hassle.
2 *she ought not to be spilling out her troubles to you*: **problem**, misfortune, difficulty, trial, tribulation, trauma, adversity, hardship, burden, distress, pain, suffering, affliction, torment, woe, grief, unhappiness, sadness, heartache, misery; archaic travails.
3 *he's gone to a lot of trouble to help you*: **bother**, inconvenience, fuss, effort, exertion, work, labour; pains, care, attention, thought; informal hassle.
4 *I wouldn't want to be a trouble to her*: **nuisance**, bother, inconvenience, irritation, irritant, problem, trial, pest, cause of annoyance, source of difficulty, thorn in someone's flesh/side; informal headache, pain in the neck, pain, pain in the backside, drag, bore; N. Amer. informal pain in the butt, burr in/under someone's saddle, nudnik; Brit. vulgar slang pain in the arse.
5 *you're too gullible, that's your trouble*: **shortcoming**, **weakness**, weak point, failing, fault, imperfection, defect, blemish; **problem**, difficulty.
6 *he had a history of heart trouble*: **disease**, illness, sickness, ailment, complaint, problem; **disorder**, disability.
7 *the crash was apparently due to engine trouble*: **malfunction**, dysfunction, failure, breakdown, fault.
8 *there was crowd trouble before the match*: **disturbance**, disorder, unrest, bother, fighting, scuffling, conflict, tumult, commotion, turbulence, uproar, ructions, fracas, rumpus, brouhaha, furore, breach of the peace; Law, dated affray; informal to-do, hoo-ha, hullabaloo; Brit. informal kerfuffle.
▷ANTONYMS order, peace.
□ **in trouble** *by 1995, the firm was in trouble*: **in difficulty**, in difficulties, having problems, in a mess, in a bad way, in a predicament, in dire/desperate straits, heading for disaster, heading for the rocks, with one's back against the wall; informal in shtook, in a tight corner/spot, in a fix, in a hole, in hot water, up the creek (without a paddle), in a jam, in a pickle, in the soup, screwed, up against it; Brit. informal up a gum tree; vulgar slang in the shit, in deep shit, up shit creek.
▶ verb 1 *this matter had been troubling her for some time*: **worry**, bother, cause concern to, concern, disturb, upset, make anxious, make uncomfortable, make uneasy, agitate, distress, grieve, alarm, perturb, annoy, irritate, vex, irk, torment, plague, nag, niggle, gnaw at, prey on someone's mind, weigh/lie heavy on someone's mind, oppress, weigh down, burden, afflict; perplex, puzzle; informal bug.
2 *lately he has **been troubled by** bouts of ill health*: **be afflicted with/by**, be bedevilled by, be beset with/by, be dogged by, be incapacitated with, be racked with, be cursed with; suffer from; informal be a martyr to; archaic ail with.
3 *there is nothing you need trouble about*: **be anxious**, be distressed, be concerned, concern oneself, worry, upset oneself, fret, agonize.
4 *don't trouble to see me out*: **bother**, take the trouble/time, go to the trouble, make the effort, exert oneself, go out of one's way.
5 *I'm sorry to trouble you*: **inconvenience**, cause inconvenience to, bother, impose on, create difficulties for, disturb, put out, disoblige; informal hassle; rare discommode, incommode.

troubled adjective 1 *Joanna looked troubled*: **anxious**, worried, concerned, perturbed, disturbed, bothered, ill at ease, uneasy, unsettled; **distressed**, upset, dismayed, disconcerted, discomposed, agitated, apprehensive.
▷ANTONYMS unworried, unperturbed, carefree.
2 *we live in troubled times*: **difficult**, problematic, full of problems, beset by problems, unsettled, hard, tough, stressful, dark.

troublemaker noun **mischief-maker**, rabble-rouser, firebrand, agitator, ringleader, incendiary, inciter, instigator; demagogue; scandalmonger, gossipmonger, meddler; French agent provocateur; informal stirrer; rare stormy petrel.
▷ANTONYMS peacemaker.

troublesome adjective 1 *a troublesome problem*: **annoying**, irritating, exasperating, maddening, infuriating, irksome, vexatious, vexing, inconvenient, bothersome, tiresome, worrying, worrisome, disturbing, upsetting, distressing, perturbing, niggling, nagging; difficult, awkward, problematic, demanding, taxing, tricky, thorny; informal aggravating, pestiferous, plaguy, pestilential, pestilent; N. Amer. informal pesky.
▷ANTONYMS simple, straightforward.
2 *troublesome adolescents*: **disruptive**, uncooperative, rebellious, unmanageable, unruly, troublemaking, obstreperous, badly behaved, disobedient, naughty, refractory, recalcitrant, difficult, awkward, trying; informal the limit.
▷ANTONYMS cooperative, obedient.

trough noun 1 *a large feeding trough*: **manger**, feeding container, feedbox, feeder, fodder rack, crib.
2 *a thirty-yard trough*: **channel**, conduit, trench, ditch, gully, drain, culvert, cut, flume, gutter, furrow, groove, depression.

trounce verb 1 *Wigan trounced Halifax 32–8*: **defeat utterly**, beat hollow, win a resounding victory over, annihilate, drub, rout, give someone a drubbing, crush, overwhelm, bring someone to their knees; informal hammer, clobber, thrash, paste, give someone a pasting, whip, pound, pulverize, massacre, crucify, demolish, destroy, wipe the floor with, take to the cleaners, make mincemeat of, murder, flatten, turn inside out, run rings around; Brit. informal stuff, marmalize; N. Amer. informal shellac, blow out, cream, skunk.
2 *he should be soundly trounced*: **thrash**, beat, whip, flog, lash, birch, cane, leather, spank, chastise, lambaste; informal belt, wallop, give a hiding to, tan the hide of.

troupe noun **group**, company, band, ensemble, set; cast.

trousers plural noun **slacks**; N. Amer. **pants**; Brit. informal **trews**, **strides**, **kecks**; Austral. informal **daks**; Austral. & S. African informal **rammies**; dated reach-me-downs, unmentionables.

truancy noun **absenteeism**, non-attendance, absence, playing truant, truanting; Brit. informal skiving, bunking off, wagging; N. Amer. informal playing hookey, goofing off, ditching; Austral./NZ informal playing the wag.
▷ANTONYMS attendance.

truant noun **absentee**, non-attender; Brit. informal skiver; Austral./NZ informal wag.
□ **play truant** *it's bad news when youngsters play truant from school*: **stay away from school**, not go to school, be absent, truant; Brit. informal skive (off), bunk off; Irish informal mitch (off); N. Amer. informal play hookey, goof off, ditch; Austral./NZ informal play the wag; rare bag it, hook Jack, mooch, play the hop, hop the wag.
▶ verb *teachers reported on whether pupils had truanted*. See **play truant**.

truce noun *the rebels agreed to a truce*: **ceasefire**, armistice, suspension of hostilities, cessation of hostilities, peace; break, respite, lull, moratorium; treaty, peace treaty; informal let-up.
▷ANTONYMS fighting, hostilities.

truck[1] noun *a succession of heavy trucks rumbled down the street*: **lorry**, articulated lorry, heavy goods vehicle, juggernaut; van, pickup, pickup truck; dumper, dumper truck, tipper, tipper truck; Brit. HGV; N. English bogie; S. African bakkie; dated pantechnicon.

truck[2] noun *members of the agency were advised to have no truck with him*: **dealings**, association, contact, communication, connection, relations, intercourse; business, trade, transactions, traffic.

truckle verb *an ambitious and dauntless woman who **truckled to** no man*: **kowtow**, submit, defer, yield, bend the knee, bow and scrape, make up, be obsequious, pander, toady, prostrate oneself, grovel; fawn on, dance attendance on, curry favour with, ingratiate oneself with, abase oneself before; informal suck up, crawl, lick someone's boots; N. Amer. informal brown-nose; Austral./NZ informal smoodge; vulgar slang kiss/lick someone's arse.
▷ANTONYMS defy, stand up to.

truculent adjective *'what do you want?' he demanded, sounding truculent*: **defiant**, aggressive, antagonistic, belligerent, pugnacious, bellicose, combative, confrontational, ready for a fight, hostile, obstreperous, argumentative, quarrelsome, contentious, uncooperative; bad-tempered, ill-tempered, sullen, surly, cross, ill-natured, rude, discourteous, unpleasant; informal feisty, spoiling for a fight; Brit. informal stroppy, bolshie; N. Amer. informal scrappy.
▷ANTONYMS cooperative, friendly, amiable.

trudge verb *he trudged wearily through the snow*: **plod**, tramp, drag oneself, walk heavily, walk slowly, plough, slog, footslog, toil, trek, clump, clomp, lumber; informal traipse, galumph; Brit. informal yomp, trog.
▷ANTONYMS skip, trip.

true adjective 1 *it may seem hard to believe, but I can assure you it's true*: **accurate**, correct, verifiable, faithful, literal, veracious; in accordance with reality, what actually/really happened, the case, so; unelaborated, unvarnished; informal as true as I'm sitting/standing here.
▷ANTONYMS untrue, false, fallacious.
2 *people are still willing to pay for true craftsmanship*: **genuine**, authentic, real, actual, proper, veritable; Latin bona fide; informal honest-to-goodness, kosher, pukka, legit, the real McCoy, regular; Austral./NZ informal dinkum.
▷ANTONYMS bogus, phoney.
3 *the true owner of the goods*: **rightful**, legitimate, legal, lawful, authorized, recognized, valid; Latin bona fide; Law de jure.
▷ANTONYMS de facto.
4 *the necessity for true repentance*: **sincere**, genuine, real, unfeigned, unpretended, unaffected, heartfelt, from the heart.

t

▷ANTONYMS insincere, feigned.
5 *she was always a true friend to me*: **loyal**, faithful, true-hearted, devoted, dedicated, staunch, true-blue, constant, unswerving, unwavering; trustworthy, trusty, reliable, dependable, firm, steady, dutiful, supportive.
▷ANTONYMS disloyal, faithless.
6 *a true reflection of life in the 50s*: **accurate**, true to life, faithful, telling it like it is, as it really happened, fact-based, realistic, close, lifelike, convincing; correct, unerring, exact, precise, perfect; on target, on the mark; French vérité; Brit. informal spot on; N. Amer. informal on the money; rare verisimilar, veristic.
▷ANTONYMS inaccurate.
□ **true to** *the completed house is remarkably true to the original diagram*: **in keeping with**, consistent with, in harmony with, in accord with, in accordance with, in agreement with, in line with, in character with, compatible with, congruent with, commensurate with; appropriate to, befitting, as befits, suitable for, suited to.
▸ **adverb** literary **1** *I swear I will speak true*: **truthfully**, honestly, sincerely, candidly, frankly, truly, veraciously.
2 *the weapon flew true as an arrow*: **accurately**, unerringly, unswervingly, without deviating.
□ **come true** *seven years later, his dream came true*: **be fulfilled**, be realized, become a reality, happen, occur, take place; literary come to pass.
▸ **noun**
□ **out of (the) true** *the front wheel is a little out of true and a couple of spokes are bent*: **askew**, skew, at an angle, lopsided, crooked, tilting, tilted, atilt, dipping, out of line; at a slant, on the slant, at an angle, not straight, sloping, slanting, slanted, slantwise, slant, oblique, leaning, inclining, inclined, angled, cambered, canted; Scottish squint.

> *Choose the right word* **true, faithful, loyal, constant**
>
> See **faithful**.

true-blue **adjective** *true-blue supporters of the club*: **staunch**, loyal, faithful, stalwart, committed, card-carrying, confirmed, dyed-in-the-wool, devoted, dedicated, firm, steadfast, dependable, reliable, trusty, steady, constant, unswerving, unwavering, unfaltering; informal deep-dyed.
▷ANTONYMS half-hearted.

truism **noun** **platitude**, commonplace, cliché, hackneyed/trite/banal/overworked saying, stock phrase, banality, old chestnut, bromide; maxim, axiom, saw.

truly **adverb** **1** *tell me truly what you want to do*: **truthfully**, honestly, frankly, candidly, openly, to someone's face, without dissembling, laying one's cards on the table; informal with no punches pulled.
2 *I'm truly grateful to them all*: **sincerely**, genuinely, really, indeed, from the bottom of one's heart, heartily, profoundly, veritably; **very**, extremely, awfully, dreadfully, frightfully, exceptionally, exceedingly, immensely, uncommonly, incredibly, most, positively; Scottish unco; N. Amer. quite; informal terribly, terrifically, tremendously, fearfully, desperately, seriously, majorly, hugely, fantastically, madly; Brit. informal jolly, ever so, dead, well, fair, right; N. Amer. informal real, mighty, awful, plumb, powerful, way, bitching; S. African informal lekker; archaic exceeding, sore.
3 *a truly dreadful song*: **really**, absolutely, simply, utterly, totally, perfectly, thoroughly, positively, completely.
4 *this is truly a miracle*: **without (a) doubt**, unquestionably, undoubtedly, certainly, surely, definitely, beyond doubt/question, indubitably, undeniably, beyond the shadow of a doubt; in truth, really, in reality, actually, in fact; archaic forsooth, in sooth, verily.
5 *the streaming system does not truly reflect children's ability*: **accurately**, correctly, exactly, precisely, faithfully, closely, unerringly.

trump **verb** *by wearing the simplest of dresses and no jewellery, she had trumped them all*: **outshine**, outclass, upstage, put in the shade, eclipse, surpass, outdo, outperform; beat, do/be better than, better, top, cap; informal be a cut above, be head and shoulders above, leave standing, walk away from; Brit. informal knock spots off; archaic outrival, outvie.
□ **trump something up** *since her arrest, they've trumped up charges against her*: **invent**, make up, fabricate, concoct, contrive, manufacture, devise, hatch; fake, falsify; informal cook up.

trumped-up **adjective** *the men were arrested on trumped-up charges of espionage*: **bogus**, spurious, specious, false, fabricated, invented, manufactured, made-up, fake, faked, not genuine, factitious, contrived; unfounded, unsubstantiated, unproven, without foundation, groundless, baseless; informal phoney, cooked up.
▷ANTONYMS true, genuine, bona fide.

trumpery archaic **noun** *tables piled with all sorts of trumpery*: **trinkets**, baubles, cheap finery, knick-knacks, ornaments, bibelots, gewgaws, gimcracks.
▸ **adjective** *trumpery jewellery*. See **showy**.

trumpet **noun**
□ **blow one's own trumpet** *he refused to blow his own trumpet and blushingly declined to speak*: **boast**, brag, sing one's own praises, show off, swank, congratulate oneself; N. Amer. informal blow/toot one's own horn; Austral./NZ informal skite; archaic vaunt, rodomontade, gasconade.
▸ **verb** **1** *'come on!' he trumpeted*: **shout**, bellow, roar, yell, cry out, call out; informal holler.
2 *the team of British researchers trumpeted a major medical breakthrough*: **proclaim**, announce, declare, broadcast, promulgate, noise abroad, shout from the rooftops, blazon.

truncate **verb** *the programme may need to be truncated or adapted*: **shorten**, cut, cut short, curtail, dock, prune, trim, lop, abbreviate, telescope; reduce, diminish, decrease.
▷ANTONYMS lengthen, extend.

> *Choose the right word* **truncate, shorten, abbreviate, abridge, curtail**
>
> See **shorten**.

truncheon **noun** Brit. **club**, baton, cudgel, bludgeon; stick, staff; N. Amer. billy, billy club, blackjack, nightstick; Brit. informal life preserver, cosh.

trunk **noun** **1** *the trunk of a cedar tree*: **main stem**, bole, stock.
2 *his powerful trunk*: **torso**, body.
3 *an elephant's trunk*: **proboscis**, nose, snout.
4 *the papers had been stored in an enormous tin trunk*: **chest**, box, storage box, crate, coffer; suitcase, case, portmanteau; S. African kist.
5 N. Amer. *the trunk of his car*: luggage compartment; Brit. **boot**.

truss **noun** **1** *the bridge is supported by three steel trusses*: **support**, buttress, joist, brace, prop, strut, stay, stanchion, shore, pier.
2 *a hernia truss*: **surgical appliance**, support, pad.
▸ **verb** *they* **trussed** *us* **up** *with ropes and chains*: **tie up**, bind, chain up; pinion, fetter, tether, secure, fasten.

trust **noun** **1** *a relationship built on mutual trust and respect*: **confidence**, belief, faith, freedom from suspicion/doubt, sureness, certainty, certitude, assurance, conviction, credence, reliance.
▷ANTONYMS distrust, mistrust, scepticism.
2 *a position of trust*: **responsibility**, duty, obligation.
3 *the money is to be held in trust for his son*: **safe keeping**, keeping, protection, charge, care, custody; trusteeship, guardianship.
▸ **verb** **1** *I should never have trusted her*: **have faith in**, put/place one's trust in, have (every) confidence in, believe in, pin one's hopes/faith on; **rely on**, depend on, bank on, count on, be sure of, be convinced by, swear by; confide in.
▷ANTONYMS distrust, mistrust, doubt.
2 *I trust we shall meet again*: **hope**, expect, think likely, dare say, imagine, believe, assume, presume, suppose, take it; informal guess.
3 *can I trust you with my car?* **entrust**, put in the hands of, allow to look after/use.
4 *they don't like to trust their money to anyone outside the family*: **consign**, commit, give, hand over, turn over, assign, commend.

> *Word links* **trust**
>
> **fiduciary** relating to trust

trustee **noun** **administrator**, agent; custodian, keeper, steward, depositary; executor, executrix; Law fiduciary, feoffee.

trustful **adjective** *she looked up at him with trustful eyes*. See **trusting**.

trusting **adjective** *she was no longer as trusting as she had once been*: **trustful**, unsuspicious, unquestioning, unsuspecting, unguarded, unwary; naive, innocent, childlike, ingenuous, wide-eyed, credulous, gullible, easily taken in, easily deceived.
▷ANTONYMS distrustful, suspicious, cynical.

trustworthy **adjective** *the staff are trustworthy and hard-working*: **reliable**, dependable, honest, full of integrity, worthy of trust, honourable, upright, principled, true, truthful, as good as one's word, ethical, virtuous, incorruptible, unimpeachable, above suspicion; responsible, sensible, level-headed; loyal, faithful, true-blue, staunch, steadfast, trusty, constant, unswerving, unwavering; tried and trusted, tried and true, safe, secure, sound, guaranteed, unfailing, foolproof, never-failing, reputable; informal on the level, sure-fire; N. Amer. informal straight-up.
▷ANTONYMS untrustworthy, unreliable, shifty.

trusty **adjective** *her trusty servant*: **reliable**, dependable, trustworthy, never-failing, unfailing, tried and true, tried and trusted, trusted; loyal, faithful, true, honest, staunch, steadfast, constant, unswerving, unwavering.
▷ANTONYMS unreliable.

truth **noun** **1** *he doubted the truth of her last statement*: **veracity**, truthfulness, verity, sincerity, candour, honesty, genuineness; gospel, gospel truth; accuracy, correctness, rightness, validity, factualness, factuality, authenticity.
▷ANTONYMS dishonesty, falsity.
2 *it's the truth, I swear it*: **the fact of the matter**, what actually/really happened, the case, so; gospel, gospel truth, God's truth, the honest truth.
▷ANTONYMS lies.

3 *truth is stranger than fiction*: **fact(s)**, reality, real life, actuality.
▷ANTONYMS fiction.
4 *scientific truths*: **fact**, verity, certainty, certitude; law, principle.
▷ANTONYMS lie, falsehood, old wives' tale.
□ **in truth** *in truth, she was more than a little unhappy*: **in fact**, in actual fact, in point of fact, as a matter of fact, in reality, really, actually, to tell the truth, if truth be told; archaic in sooth.

truthful adjective **1** *I want a truthful answer*: **honest**, sincere, trustworthy, genuine, meaning what one says; candid, frank, open, forthright, straight, plain-spoken; informal upfront, on the level; N. Amer. informal on the up and up; archaic round, free-spoken.
▷ANTONYMS untruthful, deceptive, deceitful.
2 *a comprehensive and truthful account*: **true**, accurate, correct, true to life, factual, in accordance with the facts, right, exact, faithful, reliable, veracious, verifiable; unvarnished, unembellished, unelaborated; rare veridical.
▷ANTONYMS inaccurate, untrue.

truthfulness noun **honesty**, veracity, sincerity, lack of deceit, trustworthiness, genuineness, candour, candidness, frankness, openness, forthrightness; truth.

try verb **1** *we've got to try to help him*: **attempt**, endeavour, make an effort, exert oneself, seek, strive, struggle, do one's best, do one's utmost, do all one can; undertake, aim, set out, take it on oneself; try one's hand at; informal have a go/shot/crack/stab/bash, give it one's best shot, bend/lean over backwards, bust a gut, do one's damnedest, pull out all the stops, go all out, go for broke, knock oneself out, break one's neck, move heaven and earth; Austral./NZ informal give it a burl, give it a fly; formal essay; archaic assay.
2 *why don't you try it and see what you think?* **test**, try out, check out, put to the test, experiment with; sample, taste, have a taste of; inspect, investigate, examine, appraise, evaluate, assess; informal try something on for size, give something a whirl.
3 *Mary tried everyone's patience to the limit*: **tax**, make severe demands on, strain, put a strain on, test, stretch, sap, drain, exhaust, wear out, tire out, weary.
4 *the case is to be tried by a jury in the Crown Court*: **adjudicate**, consider, hear, pass judgement on, adjudge, examine.
□ **try one's hand** See **hand**.
□ **try something out** *the scheme has been tried out in 20 local authorities*: **test**, trial, experiment with, pilot; put to the test, put through its paces, put into practice; assess, evaluate.
▶ noun *I decided to have one last try*: **attempt**, go, effort, endeavour, bid; informal shot, crack, stab, bash, whack; formal essay.

trying adjective **1** *it had been a particularly trying day*: **stressful**, difficult, taxing, demanding, tough, hard, heavy; pressured, testing, frustrating, fraught, traumatic, arduous, gruelling; tiring, fatiguing, exhausting, wearing; informal hellish, a bitch of a, a stinker of a.
▷ANTONYMS easy, painless.
2 *Steve was turning out to be very trying*: **annoying**, irritating, exasperating, maddening, infuriating; **tiresome**, irksome, troublesome, bothersome, vexatious; informal aggravating.
▷ANTONYMS accommodating.

tub noun **1** *a large wooden tub*: **container**; butt, barrel, cask, drum, keg; rare kid.
2 *a tub of yogurt*: **pot**, carton.
3 N. Amer. *a soak in the tub*: **bath**, bathtub; hot tub.

tubby adjective informal *a tubby little man with a balding head*: **chubby**, **plump**, stout, roly-poly, dumpy, chunky, broad in the beam, portly, rotund; buxom, well upholstered, well covered, well padded, of ample proportions, ample, round, rounded, well rounded; fat, overweight, fleshy, paunchy, pot-bellied, bulky, corpulent; informal pudgy, beefy, porky, blubbery, poddy; Brit. informal podgy, fubsy; N. Amer. informal zaftig, corn-fed, lard-assed; rare pursy, abdominous.
▷ANTONYMS thin, slender, skinny.

tubular adjective *a long tubular structure*: **tube-shaped**, tubiform, pipe-like; rare tubulous, tubulate, tubate, vasiform.

tuck verb **1** *he tucked his shirt into his trousers*: **push**, ease, insert, slip; thrust, stuff, stick, cram; informal pop.
▷ANTONYMS take out, pull out.
2 *the dress was pinned and tucked all over*: **pleat**, gather, fold, ruffle.
3 *he tucked the knife behind his seat*: **hide**, conceal, secrete; store, stow; informal stash.
□ **tuck something away** *I closed my journal and tucked it away under some folders and notebooks*: **hide**, conceal, keep out of sight, keep hidden, secrete; screen, cover, obscure, block out, blot out, disguise, camouflage, mask, cloak, mantle, shroud; put aside, put/lay by, set/lay aside, put to one side, reserve, keep in reserve, deposit, keep, store, stockpile, hoard, stow away, cache; literary enshroud.
□ **tuck someone in/up** *he carried her back to bed and tucked her in*: **make snug**, make comfortable, settle in, cover up; put to bed.
□ **tuck in/into** informal *I tucked into the bacon and scrambled eggs*: **eat heartily**, devour, consume, gobble up, wolf down; informal get stuck into, dig in/into, dispose of, polish off, get outside of, put away, pack away, scoff (down), shovel down, get one's laughing gear round; Brit. informal shift, gollop; N. Amer. informal scarf (down/up), snarf (down/up), inhale; rare ingurgitate.
▶ noun **1** *a dress with tucks along the bodice*: **pleat**, gather, fold, ruffle.
2 Brit. informal *they squabbled and pinched each other's tuck*: **food**; informal eats, grub, nosh, chow, feed; Brit. informal scoff; N. Amer. informal **chuck**; archaic vittles, victuals, viands.

tuft noun *spiky tufts of grass | a tuft of hair*: **clump**, bunch, knot, cluster, tussock, tuffet; lock, wisp; crest, topknot; tassel; technical floccule, flocculus, floccus, byssus, coma, pappus, scopa; rare panache.

tug verb **1** *Benjamin tugged at her sleeve*: **pull**, pluck; tweak, twitch, jerk, wrench, wrest; grab, clutch, catch hold of; informal yank.
2 *she tugged him towards the door*: **drag**, pull, draw, haul, heave, tow, trail; informal lug.
▶ noun *the ropes still held but one good tug would do it*: **pull**, jerk, wrench, heave; informal yank.

tuition noun *private tuition in French*: **teaching**, instruction, coaching, tutoring, lessons, tutorials, education, schooling, tutelage; training, drill, preparation; direction, guidance.

tumble verb **1** *he staggered a step or two and tumbled over*: **fall (over)**, fall down, topple over, lose one's footing, lose one's balance, keel over, pitch over, take a spill, collapse, fall headlong, fall head over heels, fall end over end; trip, trip up, stumble; informal come a cropper; dated measure one's length; archaic grabble.
2 *journalists tumbled from the room, jabbering excitedly*: **hurry**, rush, scramble, pile; scurry, scuttle; jump, spring, bound.
3 *a narrow brook tumbled over the rocks*: **cascade**, fall, stream, flow, pour, spill.
4 *oil prices tumbled*: **fall steeply/sharply**, plummet, plunge, dive, nosedive, take a dive, drop rapidly, slump, slide, fall, decrease, decline; informal crash, go into a tailspin.
▷ANTONYMS rise, soar.
5 *her face was devoid of make-up, and her hair was tumbled*: **tousle**, dishevel, ruffle, rumple, make untidy, disarrange, disorder, mess up; N. Amer. informal muss (up).
6 informal *I finally tumbled to what was happening*: **realize**, understand, grasp, comprehend, take in, apprehend, perceive, see, recognize; see the light; informal latch on to, cotton on to, catch on to, get, get wise to, get one's head around, figure out, get a fix on, get the message, get the picture; Brit. informal twig, suss; N. Amer. informal savvy.
▶ noun **1** *I took a tumble in the nettles*: **fall**, trip, spill; informal nosedive, header, cropper.
2 *a tumble in share prices*: **drop**, fall, plunge, dive, nosedive, slump, decline, collapse; informal crash.
▷ANTONYMS rise.
3 *a tumble of bed linen*: **jumble**, mess, clutter, confusion; chaos, disorder, disarray.

tumbledown adjective *a small tumbledown cottage*: **dilapidated**, ramshackle, crumbling, falling to pieces, disintegrating, decaying, decrepit, broken-down, neglected, run down, in disrepair, uncared-for, badly maintained; ruined, in ruins, derelict, gone to rack and ruin, ruinous; rickety, shaky; N. Amer. informal shacky.
▷ANTONYMS well kept, well maintained.

tumbler noun **glass**, drinking glass, beaker; goblet, wine glass; N. Amer. highball glass; archaic stoup; rare rummer.

tumid rare adjective **1** *her tumid belly*. See **swollen**.
2 *tumid oratory*. See **turgid** (sense 1).

tummy noun informal **stomach**, abdomen, belly, gut, middle; informal tum, breadbasket, insides; Austral. informal bingy.

tumour noun **cancerous growth**, malignant growth, cancer, malignancy; lump, growth, swelling; technical carcinoma, sarcoma, melanoma, lymphoma, myeloma, neoplasm, metastasis, neurofibroma, teratoma, fibroadenoma, meningioma.

Word links **tumour**

onco- related prefix, as in *oncogenic*
-oma related suffix, as in *sarcoma*
oncology branch of medicine concerning tumours
lumpectomy removal of breast tumour

tumult noun **1** *she added her own voice to the tumult*: **din**, loud noise, racket, uproar, commotion, ruckus, rumpus, hubbub, pandemonium, babel, bedlam, brouhaha, fracas, furore, melee, frenzy, ado; shouting, yelling, clamour, clangour; Scottish & N. English stramash; informal **hullabaloo**; Brit. informal row; Law, dated affray.
▷ANTONYMS silence.
2 *years of political tumult*: **turmoil**, confusion, disorder, disarray, disturbance, unrest, chaos, turbulence, mayhem, havoc, upheaval, upset, ferment, agitation, trouble; storms, tempests, maelstroms, convulsions.
▷ANTONYMS peace, tranquillity.

t

tumultuous adjective **1** *he left the stage to tumultuous applause*: **loud**, deafening, thunderous, thundering, ear-shattering, ear-splitting, ear-piercing, uproarious, noisy, clamorous, vociferous.
▷ANTONYMS soft.
2 *their tumultuous relationship*: **tempestuous**, stormy, turbulent, in turmoil, passionate, intense, explosive, violent, volatile, full of upheavals, full of ups and downs, roller-coaster, exciting; hectic, chaotic, confused.
▷ANTONYMS peaceful, uneventful.
3 *a tumultuous crowd*: **disorderly**, unruly, rowdy, uncontrolled, out of control, unrestrained, turbulent, boisterous, excited, agitated, restless, in turmoil, wild, riotous, hysterical, frenzied; Brit. informal rumbustious.
▷ANTONYMS orderly.

tune noun *she left the theatre humming a cheerful tune*: **melody**, air, strain; song, number, jingle, ditty; theme, motif.
▶ verb **1** *the band were still tuning their guitars*: **adjust (to the correct pitch)**, tune up.
2 *like many marine organisms, they have a body clock tuned to the rhythm of the tides*: **attune**, adapt, adjust, fine-tune; regulate, modulate, calibrate.
□ **change one's tune** *by the following week, she had changed her tune*: **change one's mind**, think differently, express a different view/opinion, sing a different song/tune, shift one's ground, do a U-turn, march to the beat of a different drum, have a change of heart; Brit. do an about-turn.
□ **in tune** *their message was in tune with the prevailing intellectual climate*: **in accord**, in keeping, in accordance, in agreement, in harmony, harmonious, in step, in line, in sympathy.
□ **out of tune** *he was out of tune with conventional belief*: **in disagreement**, at odds, at variance, out of step, not in harmony, at outs, out of kilter.

tuneful adjective *a remarkable musical full of tuneful songs*: **melodious**, melodic, musical, mellifluous, sweet-sounding, pleasant-sounding, dulcet, euphonious, harmonious, lyrical, lilting; mellow, smooth, sweet, pleasant, agreeable, easy-listening; catchy, rhythmical; informal easy on the ear, foot-tapping, poppy; rare canorous, euphonic, mellifluent.
▷ANTONYMS discordant, tuneless.

tuneless adjective *tuneless whistling emanated from the kitchen*: **discordant**, unmelodious, unmelodic, unmusical, dissonant, harsh, cacophonous; rare horrisonant.
▷ANTONYMS melodious, tuneful.

tunnel noun *a two-mile tunnel under the Pennine Hills*: **underground passage**, subterranean passage; underpass, subway, hole, burrow; shaft, gallery; historical mine, sap.
▶ verb *he tunnelled under the fence*: **dig**, dig one's way, burrow; excavate, mine, bore, drill.

turbid adjective *the turbid waters of the river*: **murky**, muddy, thick; opaque, cloudy, clouded; N. Amer. riled, roily, roiled; rare feculent.
▷ANTONYMS clear.

turbulence noun **1** *a time of political turbulence*: **turmoil**, instability, conflict, upheaval, tumult, troubles, unrest, ferment, disorder, disruption, disturbance, chaos, confusion; German Sturm und Drang.
▷ANTONYMS peace, calmness.
2 *the plane hit some turbulence*: **rough air currents**, irregular atmospheric motion, uneven air movement.
3 *the turbulence of the seas*: **roughness**, storminess, tempestuousness, heaviness, violence, wildness, choppiness, agitation.
▷ANTONYMS calmness.

turbulent adjective **1** *the country's turbulent past*: **tempestuous**, stormy, unstable, unsettled, tumultuous, explosive, in turmoil, full of upheavals, full of conflict, full of ups and downs, roller-coaster, chaotic, full of confusion; violent, wild, anarchic, lawless.
▷ANTONYMS peaceful.
2 *turbulent seas*: **rough**, stormy, tempestuous, storm-tossed, heavy, violent, wild, angry, raging, boiling, seething, foaming, choppy, bumpy, agitated; squally, blustery; N. Amer. roily; literary weltering; rare boisterous.
▷ANTONYMS calm, quiet, glassy.

turf noun **1** *they walked across the springy turf*: **grass**, lawn, sod; literary sward, greensward.
2 (**the turf**) *they are both devotees of the turf*: **horse racing**, racing, the racing world; racecourses, racetracks.
3 *the vice president was keen to protect his own turf*: **area/sphere of influence**, area/sphere of activity, territory, domain, province, preserve; stamping ground, home ground; informal bailiwick; Brit. informal patch, manor.
▶ verb *the front and rear lawns have been turfed*: **grass over**, lay grass on.
□ **turf someone/something out** Brit. informal *he was turfed out of office after 15 years*: **throw out**, remove, eject, expel, turn out, fling out, force out, drive out, evict, dislodge, oust; dismiss, discharge; informal chuck out, kick out, send packing, boot out, give someone the boot, give someone their marching orders, throw someone out on their ear, show someone the door, sack, fire, give someone the push, give someone the (old) heave-ho; N. Amer. informal give someone the bum's rush.

turgid adjective **1** *his turgid prose*: **bombastic**, pompous, overblown, inflated, high-flown, affected, pretentious, grandiose, florid, flowery, ornate, magniloquent, grandiloquent, rhetorical, oratorical, orotund; stodgy, ponderous, laboured, strained, stilted; informal highfalutin, purple, windy; rare tumid, euphuistic, fustian, sesquipedalian, Ossianic.
▷ANTONYMS simple, plain.
2 *a turgid and fast-moving river*: **swollen**, congested; in spate, in flood.

turmoil noun *a time of great political turmoil*: **confusion**, upheaval(s), turbulence, tumult, disorder, commotion, disturbance, agitation, ferment, unrest, trouble, disruption, upset, convulsions, chaos, mayhem, pandemonium, bedlam, uproar; uncertainty; German Sturm und Drang; N. Amer. informal tohubohu; archaic moil, coil.
▷ANTONYMS calm, peace.
□ **in turmoil** *as he spoke, his mind was in turmoil*: **in confusion**, in a whirl, at sixes and sevens; reeling, spinning, disorientated; informal all over the place, not knowing whether one is coming or going.

turn verb **1** *the wheels were still turning*: **go round**, revolve, rotate, spin, go round and round, go round in circles, roll, circle, wheel, whirl, twirl, gyrate, swivel, spiral, pivot.
2 *I turned and headed back the way I had come*: **change direction**, turn round, change course, make a U-turn, reverse direction; swing round, wheel round, turn about.
3 *the BMW turned the corner and vanished from sight*: **go round**, pass round, sweep round, round; negotiate, take.
4 *a narrow path that turned alternately to right and left*: **bend**, curve, wind, twist, loop, meander, snake, zigzag.
5 *he **turned** his pistol **on** Laidlaw*: **aim at**, point at, level at, direct at, train at, focus on.
6 *Wright turned his ankle in the first minute of the game*: **sprain**, twist, rick, wrench; hurt, injure.
7 *their dream honeymoon **turned into** a nightmare*: **become**, develop into, prove to be, turn out to be; change into, be transformed into, metamorphose into.
8 *Emmeline turned pale*: **become**, go, grow, get, come to be.
9 *he turned the house into three flats*: **convert**, change, transform, make; adapt, modify, rebuild, reconstruct, refashion, remake, make over, restyle.
10 *I've just turned forty*: **reach (the age of)**, get to (the age of), become, pass; informal hit.
11 *the milk had turned*: **go/become sour**, go off, sour, curdle, become rancid, go bad, spoil, taint.
12 *in 1959, he **turned to** politics*: **take up**, become/get involved with, involve oneself in, begin to participate in, go in for, enter, become interested in, start doing, undertake.
▷ANTONYMS give up, drop.
13 *we can now turn to another aspect of the problem*: **move on to**, go on to, begin to consider, turn one's attention to, attend to, address/apply oneself to; pick up, take up, refer to.
14 *she turned a clumsy somersault*: **perform**, execute, do, carry out.
15 *wooden objects turned on a lathe*: **fashion**, make, shape, mould, cast, form.
□ **turn against someone** *people had turned against him*: **become hostile to**, take a dislike to, become unsympathetic to, become disenchanted with, become disillusioned with.
▷ANTONYMS take someone's part, stand up for.
□ **turn someone against someone else** *Helen turned him against his father*: **make hostile to**, set against, cause to dislike, cause to be unfriendly towards, prejudice against, influence against; alienate from, drive a wedge between, estrange from.
▷ANTONYMS reconcile.
□ **turn someone away** *reporters were turned away from the college*: **refuse admittance to**, send away; reject, rebuff, repel, cold-shoulder; informal send packing, give someone the brush-off.
▷ANTONYMS admit.
□ **turn back** *they turned back before reaching the church*: **retrace one's steps**, go back, return; retreat.
▷ANTONYMS continue, carry on.
□ **turn someone/something back** *demonstrators attempted to storm the naval base, but were turned back by police*: **repulse**, drive back, fight back, force back, beat back, beat off, put to flight, repel.
□ **turn someone/something down 1** *his novel was turned down by publisher after publisher*: **reject**, spurn, rebuff, refuse, decline, say no to; informal give the thumbs down to, give the red light to; Brit. informal knock back. ▷ANTONYMS accept.
2 *Pete turned the sound down*: **reduce**, lower, decrease, lessen; muffle, mute. ▷ANTONYMS turn up.
□ **turn in** informal *I think I'll turn in*: **go to bed**, retire, call it a day, go to sleep; informal hit the hay, hit the sack; Brit. informal go up the stairs to Bedfordshire.
□ **turn someone in** *she turned her husband in to the police*: **hand over**, turn over; **betray**, inform on, denounce, sell out, stab someone in the back; informal split on, blow the whistle on, rat on, peach on, squeal on, squeak on; Brit. informal grass on, sneak on, shop; N. Amer. informal rat out, drop a/the dime on, finger; Austral./NZ informal dob on, pimp on, pool, shelf, put someone's pot on; rare delate.
□ **turn something in 1** *the documents must be turned in at a licensing*

office: **hand in/over**, give in, submit, tender, proffer, offer; deliver; return, give back, surrender, give up.
2 *he turned in a score of 199 not out*: **achieve**, attain, reach, make; notch up, chalk up, rack up, register, record.
□ **turn off** *they turned off the main road*: **leave**, branch off; take a side road, take another road; informal make/take a left/right; N. Amer. informal hang a left/right.
▷ANTONYMS join.
□ **turn someone off** informal *most people were turned off by the extreme sentimentality of the film*: **put off**, leave someone cold, repel, disgust, revolt, nauseate, sicken, offend; disenchant, alienate; bore; N. Amer. informal gross out.
▷ANTONYMS attract, arouse.
□ **turn something off** *she turned the light off and lay back on the bed*: **switch off**, turn out, put off, shut off, power down, flick off, extinguish, deactivate, trip; unplug, disconnect; informal kill, cut.
▷ANTONYMS turn on.
□ **turn on** *the decision turned on a principle of civil law*: **depend on**, rest on, hang on, hinge on, be contingent on, be decided by; concern, revolve round, relate to.
□ **turn someone on** informal **arouse**, sexually arouse, excite, stimulate, make someone feel sexually excited, make someone feel sexy, titillate; please, attract; informal give someone a thrill, get someone going, float someone's boat, do it for someone, light someone's fire, tickle someone's fancy.
▷ANTONYMS leave someone cold.
□ **turn something on** *she turned on the TV*: **switch on**, put on, power up, flick on; plug in; start up, boot up, activate, cause to operate.
▷ANTONYMS turn off.
□ **turn on someone** *he turned on her with cold savagery*: **attack**, set on, fall on, launch an attack on, let fly at, lash out at, hit out at; weigh into, round on, lose one's temper with; informal lay into, tear into, lace into, sail into, pitch into, let someone have it, get stuck into, wade into, bite someone's head off, jump down someone's throat; Brit. informal have a go at; N. Amer. informal light into.
□ **turn out 1** *a huge crowd turned out to cheer the home team*: **come**, go, be present, attend, put in an appearance, appear, turn up, arrive; assemble, gather; informal show up. **2** *it turned out that she had been two-timing him*: **transpire**, prove to be the case, emerge, come to light, become known, become apparent, be revealed, be disclosed. **3** *things didn't quite turn out as I'd intended*: **happen**, occur, come about; develop, evolve; work out, come out, end up, result; informal pan out; rare eventuate.
□ **turn someone out** *her father turned her out of the house*: **throw out**, put out, eject, evict; expel, oust, drive out, force out, drum out; deport, banish; informal kick out, chuck out, send packing, boot out, show someone the door, give someone their marching orders, throw someone out on their ear; Brit. informal turf out.
□ **turn something out 1** *he turned out the light*: **switch off**, turn off, put off, shut off, flick off; extinguish; unplug, disconnect. ▷ANTONYMS turn on.
2 *the firm turns out a million meters a year*: **produce**, make, manufacture, fabricate, assemble, put together, process, bring out, put out, churn out.
3 *she had taken it into her head to turn out the kitchen cupboards*: **clear out**, clean out, empty (out).
□ **turn over** *the little dinghy turned over on the lake*: **overturn**, upturn, capsize, keel over, turn turtle, roll over, be upended.
□ **turn something over 1** *I quickly turned over the first few pages*: **flip over**, flick over/through, leaf through. **2** *she turned the proposal over in her mind*: **think about**, think over, consider, weigh up, ponder, contemplate, reflect on, chew over, mull over, muse on, ruminate on, give thought to; archaic pore on. **3** *he turned over the retail side of the business to his brother*: **transfer**, hand over, pass on, give, consign, assign, commit.
□ **turn over a new leaf** See **leaf**.
□ **turn someone's stomach** *the sight of all that blood turned her stomach*: **nauseate**, cause to feel sick, cause to feel nauseous, sicken, make sick, make someone's gorge rise, make someone's stomach rise; informal make someone want to throw up.
□ **turn tail** See **tail**.
□ **turn to someone/something 1** *they turned to the social services*: **seek help from**, have recourse to, approach, apply to, look to, appeal to.
2 *he turned to drink*: **take to**, resort to, have recourse to.
▷ANTONYMS give up, abstain from.
□ **turn up 1** *all the missing documents had turned up*: **be found**, be discovered, be located, come to light; reappear. ▷ANTONYMS disappear, go missing.
2 *a couple of policemen turned up*: **arrive**, put in an appearance, make an appearance, appear, be present, present oneself, turn out; informal show up, show, show one's face. ▷ANTONYMS stay away.
3 *wait and see—something better will turn up*: **present itself**, occur, happen, crop up.
□ **turn something up 1** *she turned up the volume*: **increase**, raise, amplify, make louder, intensify. ▷ANTONYMS turn down.
2 *they turned up a bit of information about his life*: **discover**, uncover, unearth, bring to light, find, hit on, dig up, ferret out, root out, expose. **3** *I had turned up the hem of my skirt*: **take up**, raise; shorten. ▷ANTONYMS let down.
▶ **noun 1** *a turn of the wheel*: **rotation**, revolution, spin, circle, whirl, twirl, gyration, swivel.
2 *the vehicle slowed and made a turn to the left*: **change of direction**, change of course, turning, veer, divergence.
3 *they negotiated the sharp turn at the end of the narrow street*: **bend**, corner, dog-leg, twist, zigzag; Brit. hairpin bend.
4 *slow down, we're approaching the turn*: **turning**, junction, crossroads; N. Amer. turnout.
5 *you'll get your turn in a minute*: **opportunity**, chance, say; stint, spell, time; try, attempt; informal **go**, shot, stab, crack.
6 *a highly entertaining comic turn*: **act**, routine, performance, number, piece; show.
7 *why don't you take a turn around the garden?* **stroll**, walk, saunter, amble, wander, airing, promenade; drive, ride, outing, excursion, jaunt; informal mosey, tootle, spin; Brit. informal poodle; dated constitutional; rare perambulation.
8 *you gave me quite a turn!* **shock**, start, surprise, jolt; fright, scare.
9 *she had done me some good turns over the previous few months*: **service**, deed, act, action; (**a good turn**) **favour**, act of kindness, kindness; (**a bad turn**) **disservice**, wrong, harm, injury.
□ **at every turn** *her name seemed to come up at every turn*: **repeatedly**, recurrently, all the time, always, continually, constantly, on every occasion, again and again, over and over again.
□ **in turn** *let's consider these three points in turn*: **one after the other**, one by one, one at a time, in succession, successively, sequentially, in order; Latin seriatim.
□ **take a turn for the better** *his fortunes took a turn for the better in 1988*: **improve**, get better, pick up, look up, perk up, rally, turn a/the corner; recover, revive.
□ **take a turn for the worse** *Anglo-French relations had taken a turn for the worse*: **deteriorate**, get/grow worse, worsen, decline, retrogress; informal go downhill.
□ **to a turn** *beefburgers done to a turn*: **perfectly**, just right, exactly right, to perfection; informal to a T.
□ **turn of events** *she was utterly unprepared for this turn of events*: **development**, incident, occurrence, happening, circumstance, phenomenon.
□ **turn of mind** *those of us of a less scientific turn of mind*: **bent**, disposition, inclination, tendency, propensity, bias, way of thinking; aptitude, talent, gift, flair.
□ **turn of phrase** *it's not exactly a turn of phrase that trips off the tongue*: **expression**, idiom, choice of words; word, phrase, term, locution.

turncoat **noun** **traitor**, renegade, defector, deserter, betrayer, Judas; fifth columnist, quisling; informal rat; rare tergiversator, renegate, renegado.

turning **noun** *take the first turning on the left*: **turn-off**, turn, side road, exit; N. Amer. turnout.

turning point **noun** *it was a turning point in Jack's life*: **watershed**, critical moment, decisive moment, crossroads, crisis, climacteric, moment of truth; landmark.

turnout **noun 1** *his recent lecture attracted a good turnout*: **attendance**, number of people present, audience, house; **crowd**, gathering, throng, assembly, assemblage, congregation; Sport gate; Austral. informal muster.
2 *his turnout was exceedingly elegant*: **outfit**, clothes, clothing, dress, garb, attire, ensemble, suit; uniform; informal get-up, gear, togs, garms; Brit. informal clobber, kit, rig-out; formal apparel; literary array, raiment, habit.

turnover **noun 1** *a company with an annual turnover of £2.25 million*: **(gross) revenue**, income, yield; volume of business, business; sales.
2 *a high turnover of staff*: **rate of replacement**, coming and going, change, movement.
3 *cash-and-carry outlets rely on a rapid turnover of stock*: **throughput**, rate of buying and selling, movement.

turpitude **noun** *acts of moral turpitude*: **wickedness**, **immorality**, depravity, corruption, corruptness, vice, degeneracy, evil, baseness, iniquity, sinfulness, vileness; rare nefariousness, flagitiousness.
▷ANTONYMS virtue, honour.

tussle **noun 1** *in the ensuing tussle his glasses were smashed*: **scuffle**, fight, struggle, skirmish, brawl, scrimmage, scramble, scrum, fisticuffs, wrestling match, rough and tumble, free-for-all, fracas, fray, rumpus, melee, disturbance; Irish, N. Amer., & Austral. **donnybrook**; Law, dated **affray**; informal **scrap**, dust-up, punch-up, set-to, shindy, shindig, run-in, spat, ruck, ruckus; Brit. informal ding-dong, bust-up, bit of argy-bargy; Scottish informal rammy, swedge; N. Amer. informal **rough house**; Austral./NZ informal stoush; archaic **broil**, **miff**.
2 *an acrimonious tussle between the two departments*: **argument**, quarrel, squabble, contretemps, disagreement, contention, clash, war of words; Brit. informal row.
▶ **verb** *demonstrators tussled with police*: **scuffle**, fight, struggle, exchange blows, come to blows, brawl, grapple, wrestle, clash, scrimmage; informal scrap, have a dust-up, have a punch-up, have a set-to; N. Amer. informal rough-house.

t

tutor noun *my history tutor*: **teacher**, instructor, educator, educationalist, educationist; academic, lecturer, don; coach, trainer; guide, mentor, guru, counsellor; Scottish **dominie**; Indian **pandit**; informal **teach**; archaic **doctor**; rare **pedagogue**, **preceptor**.
▶ verb *he was tutored at home by his father*: **teach**, instruct, give lessons to, educate, school, coach, train, drill, upskill, direct, guide, groom.

tutorial noun **lesson**, class, seminar, period of instruction, period of teaching; informal **tute**.

TV noun **television**; television set; informal **small screen**; Brit. informal **telly**, **the box**, **the goggle-box**; N. Amer. informal **the tube**, **the boob tube**, **the idiot box**.

twaddle noun informal *what a load of absolute twaddle*. See **nonsense** (sense 1).

tweak verb **1** *he tweaked the boy's ear*: **pull sharply**, **twist**, tug, pinch, nip, twitch, squeeze, jerk.
2 informal *the programme can be tweaked to suit your needs*: **adjust**, make adjustments to, modify, alter, make alterations to, change, adapt; refine, improve, make improvements to.
▶ noun **1** *Robin gave her hair a friendly tweak*: **sharp pull**, **twist**, tug, pinch, nip, twitch, squeeze, jerk.
2 informal *a few minor tweaks were required*: **adjustment**, modification, alteration, change, adaptation; refinement, improvement.

twee adjective Brit. **1** *a town full of twee little shops*: **quaint**, sweet, bijou, dainty, pretty, pretty-pretty; informal **cute**, **cutesy**.
2 *the lyrics are stomach-churningly twee in places*: **sentimental**, oversentimental, mawkish, affected, precious; Brit. informal **soppy**.

twelve cardinal number **dozen**, zodiac; Music **dodecuplet**; rare **duodecad**.

> *Word links* **twelve**
>
> **dodeca-** related prefix, as in *dodecahedron*
> **duodecimal, duodenary** relating to twelve
> **dodecagon** twelve-sided figure

twenty cardinal number **score**.

> *Word links* **twenty**
>
> **icos-, eicos-** related prefixes, as in *icosahedron, eicosanoic*
> **vigesimal** relating to twenty

twiddle verb *he twiddled the dials on the radio*: **turn**, twist, swivel, twirl, adjust, move, jiggle; **fiddle with**, play with, toy with, fidget with.
□ **twiddle one's thumbs** *we've been sitting here twiddling our thumbs all afternoon*: **have nothing to do**, kick one's heels, do nothing, be idle, be unoccupied, sit around, kill time, waste time; informal **hang around/round**; Brit. informal **hang about**.

twig[1] noun *she plucked some leafy twigs from the bushes*: **small branch**, shoot, offshoot, stem, scion; **sprig**, spray; stick; withy, withe; rare **branchlet**, **ramulus**.

twig[2] verb Brit. informal *she finally twigged what I was driving at*: **realize**, **understand**, grasp, comprehend, take in, fathom, apprehend, perceive, see, recognize; see the light; informal **latch on to**, **cotton on to**, **catch on to**, **tumble to**, **get**, **get wise to**, **get one's head around**, **wrap one's mind around**, **figure out**, **get a fix on**, **get the message**, **get the picture**; Brit. informal **suss**; N. Amer. informal **savvy**.

twilight noun **1** *we reached the village by twilight*: **dusk**, early evening, evening, close of day; sunset, sundown, nightfall; literary **eventide**, **the gloaming**; rare **owl light**, **crepuscule**, **crepuscle**, **evenfall**.
▷ANTONYMS dawn, daybreak.
2 *it was scarcely visible in the evening twilight*: **half-light**, semi-darkness, dimness, gloom.
3 *he was approaching the twilight of his career*: **decline**, waning, downturn, ebb; autumn, final years, closing years, last years.
▷ANTONYMS peak, height.
▶ adjective *a twilight world*: **shadowy**, dark, twilit, shady, dim, gloomy, obscure; literary **darkling**, **darksome**, **crepuscular**.

> *Word links* **twilight**
>
> **crepuscular** relating to twilight

twin noun **1** *his wife discovered she was expecting twins*: (**twins**) identical twins, non-identical twins, fraternal twins; monozygotic/monozygous twins, dizygotic/dizygous twins; Siamese twins.
2 *he led the way into a sitting room that was the twin of her own*: **exact likeness**, mirror image, double, duplicate, carbon copy, replica, (living) image, lookalike, clone; **counterpart**, match, pair, fellow, mate, partner; German **Doppelgänger**; informal **spitting image**, **spit and image**, **ringer**, **dead ringer**.
▶ adjective **1** *the twin blocks of the stadium*: **matching**, identical, matched, paired.
2 *the need to balance the twin aims of conservation and recreation*: **closely related**, closely linked, closely connected; corresponding, parallel, complementary; equivalent.
3 *the twin blows of the party's electoral losses and its split over partition*: **twofold**, double, dual.
▶ verb *the company twinned its core business of brewing with that of distilling*: **combine**, join, link, couple, pair, yoke, match.

twine noun *a ball of twine*: **string**, cord, strong thread, yarn.
▶ verb **1** *she twined her arms around his neck*: **wind**, entwine; wrap, lace, wreathe.
2 *convolvulus had twined around the stems of the espaliers*: **entwine itself**, coil, loop, twist, spiral, curl, snake.
3 *a spray of jasmine was twined in her hair*: **weave**, interweave, interlace, intertwine, plait, braid, twist.

twinge noun **1** *she's complaining of twinges in her stomach*: **pain**, sharp pain, shooting pain, stab of pain, spasm, ache, throb; cramp, stitch; archaic **throe**.
2 *Kate felt a twinge of guilt*: **pang**, prick, dart; qualm, scruple, misgiving.

twinkle verb **1** *the lights of the city twinkled below me*: **glitter**, sparkle, shine, glimmer, shimmer, glint, gleam, scintillate, glisten, flicker, flash, wink, blink; literary **glister**; rare **coruscate**, **fulgurate**, **effulge**.
2 *his sandalled feet twinkled over the ground*: **run lightly**, dart, dance, skip, flit, glide.
▶ noun *the distant twinkle of the lights*: **glitter**, sparkle, twinkling, glimmer, shimmer, glint, gleam, flicker, dazzle, flash, wink, blink; rare **scintillation**, **coruscation**, **fulguration**.

twinkling adjective *the twinkling lights of the harbour*: **glittering**, sparkling, glimmering, glinting, gleaming, glistening, flickering, winking; bright, shining, brilliant; rare **coruscating**, **scintillating**, **scintillant**, **refulgent**, **effulgent**, **fulgent**, **nitid**, **luculent**.
▶ noun
□ **in a twinkling** *I'll be back in a twinkling*: **(very) soon**, in a second, in a minute, in a moment, in a trice, in a flash, in an instant, in the twinkling of an eye, in (less than) no time, in no time at all, before you know it, before long, shortly, in a very short time, any second (now), any minute (now); N. Amer. **momentarily**; informal **in a jiffy**, **in two shakes (of a lamb's tail)**, **before you can say Jack Robinson**, **in a sec**, **in the blink of an eye**, **in a blink**, **in the wink of an eye**, **in a wink**, **before you can say knife**; Brit. informal **in a tick**, **in two ticks**, **in a mo**, **sharpish**; N. Amer. informal **in a snap**; dated **directly**.

twirl verb **1** *Katy twirled in front of the mirror | she twirled her parasol*: **spin (round)**, pirouette, whirl, turn (round), wheel, gyrate, pivot, swivel; twist, revolve, rotate; Scottish **birl**.
2 *absent-mindedly, Sybil twirled a strand of hair round her fingers*: **wind**, twist, coil, curl, wrap.
▶ noun *she did a quick twirl in the middle of the room*: **pirouette**, spin, whirl, turn; twist, rotation, revolution, gyration; Scottish **birl**.

twist verb **1** *the force of the impact had twisted the chassis*: **crumple**, crush, buckle, mangle, warp, bend out of shape, misshape, deform, distort; N. Amer. informal **pretzel**.
▷ANTONYMS straighten.
2 *her face twisted with rage*: **contort**, screw up, quirk.
3 *Ma was anxiously twisting a handkerchief*: **wring**, squeeze, knead.
4 *Marco twisted round in his seat to look at her*: **turn (round)**, swivel (round), skew (round), spin (round), pivot, rotate, revolve.
5 *she twisted out of his grasp*: **wriggle**, writhe, squirm, worm, wiggle.
6 *he landed awkwardly and twisted his ankle*: **sprain**, wrench, turn, rick, crick.
7 *you are deliberately twisting my words*: **distort**, misrepresent, change, alter, pervert, falsify, warp, skew, put the wrong slant on, misinterpret, misconstrue, misstate, misquote, quote/take out of context, misreport; garble.
8 *he reached for the radio and twisted the knob*: **twiddle**, adjust, turn, rotate, swivel.
9 *she twisted a lock of hair around her finger*: **wind**, twirl, coil, curl, wrap.
10 *cables made up of several wires twisted together*: **intertwine**, twine, entwine, interlace, weave, plait, interweave, braid, wreathe, coil, wind; literary **pleach**.
11 *the road twisted and turned through the hills*: **wind**, bend, curve, turn, meander, weave, zigzag, swerve, loop, corkscrew, snake, worm.
□ **twist someone's arm** informal *don't let him twist your arm if you really don't want to go*: **pressurize**, coerce, bulldoze, force, railroad; persuade; talk someone into something; informal **lean on**, **put the screws on**.
▶ noun **1** *the twist of a dial*: **turn**, twirl, spin, rotation, roll.
2 *the strange twist of his mouth betrayed an inner fury*: **contortion**, contorted/distorted shape.
3 *a slight personality twist which could cause her problems*: **quirk**, idiosyncrasy, foible, eccentricity, peculiarity, oddity, kink; **aberration**, fault, flaw, imperfection, defect, failing, weakness; deviation, perversion.
4 *long twists of black hair*: **ringlet**, curl, corkscrew, coil; lock, hank.
5 *the twists and turns of the mountain road*: **bend**, curve, turn, zigzag, loop, kink, dog-leg; Brit. **hairpin bend**.
6 *the twists and turns of the plot*: **convolution**, complication, complexity, intricacy; surprise, revelation.
7 *Loretta was still trying to take in this curious twist of fate*: **development**,

turn of events, incident, happening, occurrence; turnabout.
8 *a new twist on an old theme*: **interpretation**, slant, outlook, angle, approach, treatment; alteration, variation.

twisted adjective **1** *a tangle of twisted metal*: **crumpled**, bent out of shape, crushed, buckled, warped, misshapen, distorted, deformed; N. Amer. informal pretzeled.
2 *a twisted smile*: **crooked**, wry, lopsided; contorted.
3 *his twisted mind*: **perverted**, warped, deviant, depraved, corrupt, abnormal, unhealthy, aberrant, distorted, corrupted, debauched, debased, degenerate, sadistic, evil, wicked; informal sick, kinky, pervy, sicko.

twisty adjective *a twisty road*: **winding**, windy, twisting, turning, full of twists and turns, bending, bendy, zigzag, zigzagging, meandering, curving, sinuous, snaking, snaky, tortuous; rare anfractuous, flexuous, meandrous, serpentiform.
▷ANTONYMS straight.

twit noun Brit. informal *she must think I'm a real twit*. See **fool**.

twitch verb **1** *his body twitched and then lay still*: **jerk**, move spasmodically/convulsively, spasm, convulse, flutter, quiver, tremble, shiver, quaver, shudder.
2 *he twitched the note out of Ellie's hand*: **snatch**, pluck, pull, tug, tweak; informal yank.
▶ noun **1** *an involuntary twitch of her lips*: **spasm**, convulsive movement, convulsion, jerk, flutter, quiver, tremor, shiver, shudder; tic.
2 *he gave a twitch at his moustache*: **pull**, tug, tweak; informal yank.
3 *he felt a twitch of annoyance*: **twinge**, dart, stab, prick; pang.

twitter verb **1** *sparrows twittered under the eaves*: **chirp**, chirrup, cheep, tweet, peep, chitter, chatter, trill, warble, sing.
2 *oh, for heaven's sake stop twittering about Fabio*: **prattle**, babble, chatter, prate, gabble, jabber, go on, run on, rattle on/away, yap, jibber-jabber, patter, blather, blether, blither, maunder, ramble, drivel; informal yak, yackety-yak, yabber, yatter; Brit. informal witter, rabbit, chunter, natter, waffle; Scottish & Irish informal slabber; Austral./NZ informal mag; archaic twaddle, clack, twattle.
▶ noun **1** *a bird's faint twitter*: **chirp**, chirping, chirrup, chirruping, cheep, cheeping, tweet, tweeting, peep, peeping, chitter, chittering, trill, trilling, warble, warbling; song, cry, call.
2 *her non-stop twitter*: **prattle**, chatter, babble, talk, prating, gabble, jabber, blather, blether, rambling; informal yackety-yak, yabbering, yatter; Brit. informal wittering, nattering, chuntering; archaic clack, twattle.
3 informal *why are you in such a twitter?* **panic**, frenzy, fluster, flutter, flurry, pother; informal tizz/tizzy, tiz-woz, state, sweat, stew, flap, dither; N. Amer. informal twit.

two cardinal number **pair**, duo, duet, dyad, duplet, tandem; archaic twain.

> *Word links* **two**
>
> **bi-** related prefix, as in *bicycle*
> **di-** related prefix, as in *diode, dihedral*
> **duo-** related prefix, as in *duologue, duopoly*
> **binary**, **dual**, **dyadic** relating to two
> **biannual** occurring twice a year
> **biennial** occurring every two years
> **bicentenary** two-hundredth anniversary

two-faced adjective *she's nothing but a two-faced liar*: **deceitful**, **insincere**, double-dealing, hypocritical, back-stabbing, false, untrustworthy, duplicitous, deceiving, dissembling, dishonest; disloyal, treacherous, perfidious, faithless; lying, untruthful, mendacious; rare Janus-faced.
▷ANTONYMS sincere, honest.

twosome noun **couple**, pair, duo.

tycoon noun *a newspaper tycoon*: **magnate**, mogul, big businessman, baron, merchant prince, captain of industry, industrialist, financier, top executive, chief, lord, magnifico, nabob, grandee; entrepreneur; millionaire, billionaire, multimillionaire; informal big shot, big gun, top dog, Big Daddy, Big Chief, bigwig, honcho, zillionaire; Brit. informal supremo; N. Amer. informal big wheel, kahuna, top banana, big enchilada; derogatory fat cat.

type noun **1** *this type of heather grows better in a drier habitat* | *a curate of the old-fashioned type*: **kind**, sort, variety, class, category, classification, group, set, bracket, genre, genus, species, family, order, breed, race, strain; style, description, designation, condition, quality, nature, manner, design, shape, form, pattern, rank; brand, make, model, line, mark, generation, vintage; stamp, ilk, kidney, cast, grain, mould; N. Amer. stripe.
2 informal *two sporty types in tracksuits*: **person**, individual, character, sort; Brit. informal bod.
3 *she characterized his witty sayings as the type of modern wisdom*: **epitome**, quintessence, essence, perfect example, archetype, model, pattern, paradigm, exemplar, embodiment, personification, avatar; prototype.
4 *extracts from the report are set in italic type*: **print**, typeface, face, characters, lettering, letters; font; Brit. fount.

typhoon noun **cyclone**, tropical storm, storm, tornado, hurricane, windstorm, whirlwind; N. Amer. informal twister.

typical adjective **1** *a typical example of 1930s art deco*: **representative**, classic, quintessential, archetypal, model, prototypical, stereotypical; distinctive, distinguishing, particular.
▷ANTONYMS atypical, unusual, abnormal.
2 *the 30th of June had been a fairly typical day*: **normal**, average, ordinary, standard, regular, routine, run-of-the-mill, stock, orthodox, conventional, predictable, unsurprising, unremarkable, unexceptional; informal bog-standard.
▷ANTONYMS exceptional, unusual, atypical.
3 *it's typical of him to forget to tell me*: **characteristic**, in character, in keeping, to be expected, usual, normal, par for the course, predictable, true to form, true to type; customary, habitual; proverbial; informal ... all over.
▷ANTONYMS uncharacteristic, out of keeping.

Word toolkit

typical	**standard**	**common**
example	practice	man
day	procedure	people
response	treatment	theme
fashion	method	sight
family	equipment	belief
male	protocol	complaint
teenager	reference	method
household	format	misconception
style	size	mistake

typify verb **1** *he typified a new breed of civil servant*: **epitomize**, exemplify, be representative of, represent, be characteristic of, characterize; personify, embody, be the embodiment of, be the incarnation of; rare instantiate, incarnate.
2 *the sun typified the Greeks, and the moon the Persians*: **symbolize**, be symbolic of, represent, stand for, be emblematic of; rare emblematize.

tyrannical adjective *a tyrannical government*: **dictatorial**, despotic, autocratic, oppressive, repressive, fascistic, tyrannous, absolute, totalitarian, arbitrary, undemocratic, illiberal; authoritarian, domineering, dominating, overbearing, high-handed, imperious, bullying, harsh, strict, iron-handed, iron-fisted, severe, cruel, brutal, ruthless, unjust; rare Neronian.
▷ANTONYMS democratic, liberal, easy-going.

> *Choose the right word* **tyrannical, autocratic, despotic**
>
> See **autocratic**.

tyrannize verb *she tyrannized her daughter-in-law*: **domineer over**, dominate, order about/around, dictate to, browbeat, intimidate, bully, ride roughshod over, lord it over, keep someone under one's thumb; persecute, victimize, torment; oppress, rule with a rod of iron, rule with an iron hand, rule despotically, suppress, repress, crush, subjugate, hold down, keep down, grind down, trample underfoot, enslave, bring someone to their knees, treat harshly, treat brutally; informal push around.

tyranny noun **despotism**, absolutism, absolute power, autocracy, dictatorship, undemocratic rule, reign of terror, totalitarianism, Fascism; oppression, suppression, repression, subjugation, enslavement; authoritarianism, high-handedness, imperiousness, bullying, harshness, strictness, severity, cruelty, brutality, ruthlessness, injustice, unjustness.
▷ANTONYMS democracy, liberality.

tyrant noun **1** *an evil tyrant who has imprisoned all who oppose his regime*: **dictator**, despot, autocrat, absolute ruler, authoritarian, oppressor.
2 *her boss is an absolute tyrant*: **slave-driver**, martinet, hard taskmaster, scourge; bully.

> *Word links* **tyrant**
>
> **tyrannicide** killing of a tyrant

tyro noun *he first entered parliament in 1977 as a 34-year-old political tyro*. See **novice** (sense 1).

ubiquitous adjective *tracking stray dogs may soon be easier thanks to the ubiquitous microchip*: **omnipresent**, ever-present, present everywhere, everywhere, all-over, all over the place, pervasive, all-pervasive, universal, worldwide, global; rife, prevalent, predominant, very common, popular, extensive, wide-ranging, far-reaching, inescapable.
▷**ANTONYMS** rare, scarce.

UFO noun **flying saucer**, foo fighter.

Word links **UFO**
ufology study of UFOs

ugly adjective **1** *an old man with a horribly ugly face*: **unattractive**, ill-favoured, hideous, plain, plain-featured, plain-looking, unlovely, unprepossessing, unsightly, displeasing, disagreeable; horrible, frightful, awful, ghastly, gruesome, grisly, unpleasant, foul, nasty, grim, vile, shocking, disgusting, revolting, repellent, repugnant, grotesque, monstrous, reptilian, misshapen, deformed, disfigured; N. Amer. **homely**; informal **not much to look at**, **short on looks**, **as plain as a pikestaff**, **as ugly as sin**; Brit. informal **no oil painting**.
▷**ANTONYMS** beautiful, attractive.
2 *a huge fight ensued and things got pretty ugly*: **unpleasant**, nasty, alarming, disagreeable, tense, charged, serious, grave, dangerous, perilous, threatening, menacing, hostile, ominous, sinister; archaic **direful**; rare **minacious**.
▷**ANTONYMS** pleasant, calm, peaceable.
3 *an ugly rumour*: **horrible**, unpleasant, disagreeable, despicable, reprehensible, nasty, horrid, appalling, objectionable, offensive, obnoxious, foul, vile, base, dishonourable, dishonest, rotten, vicious, spiteful, malevolent, evil, wicked.

ulcer noun *most leg ulcers will heal spontaneously*: **sore**, ulceration, open sore, abscess, boil, carbuncle, pustule, blister, cyst, gumboil, wen; N. Amer. **canker sore**; technical **aphtha**, **chancre**, **furuncle**, **vesication**, **noma**; archaic **gathering**, **fester**, **impostume**.

ulcerous adjective *the parasites created ulcerous sores*: **suppurative**, ulcerative, festering, cankerous, cankered; technical **aphthous**, **furunculous**; archaic **ulcerate**.

ulterior adjective *I helped your mother for my own ulterior motives*: **secondary**, underlying, undisclosed, undivulged, unexpressed, unapparent, under wraps, unrevealed, concealed, hidden, covert, secret, personal, private, selfish.
▷**ANTONYMS** primary; overt.

ultimate adjective **1** *the decline and ultimate collapse of the Empire*: **eventual**, last, final, concluding, conclusive, terminal, end, endmost, furthest; resulting, ensuing, consequent, subsequent.
▷**ANTONYMS** immediate.
2 *ultimate truths about human civilization*: **fundamental**, basic, primary, prime, elementary, elemental, absolute, actual, definitive, central, key, crucial, vital, essential, pivotal.
▷**ANTONYMS** peripheral.
3 *the ultimate gift for cat lovers*: **best**, ideal, greatest, supreme, paramount, superlative, highest, unsurpassed, unrivalled, topmost, utmost, optimum, quintessential; rare **apogean**.
▷**ANTONYMS** worst.
▸ noun *a studio apartment offering the ultimate in luxury living*: **utmost**, optimum, last word, very limit, height, epitome, peak, pinnacle, acme, apex, apogee, zenith, culmination, perfection, nonpareil, extreme, extremity; French **crème de la crème**, **dernier cri**, **beau idéal**; Latin **ne plus ultra**; informal **the best thing since sliced bread**, **the bee's knees**, **the cat's pyjamas/whiskers**; archaic **nonsuch**.

ultimately adverb **1** *the cost will ultimately fall on the local authorities*: **eventually**, in the end, in the long run, at length, finally, sooner or later, in time, in the fullness of time, after some time, in the final analysis, when all is said and done, one day, some day, sometime, at last, at long last; informal **when push comes to shove**; Brit. informal **at the end of the day**.
▷**ANTONYMS** immediately.
2 *he gave two ultimately contradictory reasons*: **fundamentally**, basically, primarily, essentially, at heart, deep down.

ultra- combining form *an ultra-conservative politician*: **extremely**, exceedingly, excessively, immensely, especially, exceptionally, unusually, extraordinarily, remarkably, uncommonly, extra; N. English **right**; Scottish **unco**; informal **mega**, **mucho**, **seriously**, **majorly**, **oh-so**; Brit. informal **jolly**, **dead**, **ever so**, **well**, **fair**; N. Amer. informal **real**, **mighty**, **awful**, **plumb**, **powerful**, **way**; S. African informal **lekker**; informal, dated **devilish**, **frightfully**; archaic **exceeding**.
▸ noun (**ultra**) *there is a new school of ultras in the animal rights movement*: **extremist**, radical, fanatic, zealot, diehard, revolutionary, rebel, militant, subversive.

ultra-modern adjective *this computer is a high-performance ultra-modern machine*: **futuristic**, ahead of its/one's time, avant-garde, modernistic, advanced, progressive, forward-looking, up to the minute; informal **way-out**; rare **neoteric**.
▷**ANTONYMS** outdated, old-fashioned.

umbrage noun
□ **take umbrage** *she took umbrage at his remarks*: **take offence**, be offended, take exception, bridle, take something personally, be aggrieved, be affronted, take something amiss, be upset, be annoyed, be angry, be indignant, get one's hackles up, be put out, be insulted, be hurt, be wounded, be piqued, be resentful, be disgruntled, get/go into a huff, get huffy; informal **be miffed**, **have one's nose put out of joint**, **be riled**; Brit. informal **get the hump**.

umbrella noun **1** *they huddled under the umbrella*: parasol, sunshade; Brit. informal **brolly**; N. Amer. informal **bumbershoots**; Brit. informal, dated **gamp**.
2 *television surveys are conducted under the umbrella of two national bodies*: **aegis**, auspices, patronage, championship, protection, safe keeping, protectorship, guardianship, support, guidance, charge, responsibility, care, cover, backing, agency.

umpire noun *the crowd were clamouring for the umpire to reverse the decision*: **referee**, linesman, adjudicator, arbitrator, arbiter, judge, moderator, overseer, supervisor; informal **ref**; N. Amer. informal **ump**.
▸ verb *he umpired boat races on the River Wear*: **referee**, adjudicate, arbitrate, judge, moderate, oversee, supervise; Cricket **stand**; informal **ref**.

umpteen adjective informal *she'd phoned the apartment umpteen times*. See **many** (sense 1).

unabashed adjective *she watched the meeting with unabashed interest*: **unashamed**, shameless, unembarrassed, brazen, audacious, barefaced, blatant, flagrant, bold, bold as brass, confident, immodest, unblushing, unrepentant, undaunted, unconcerned, undismayed, unshrinking,

unflinching, fearless; informal cocky, brass-necked.
▷ANTONYMS abashed, ashamed, sheepish.

unable adjective *he was unable to account for the error*: **not able**, powerless, impotent, not up/equal to, at a loss, inadequate, ineffectual, incompetent, unfit, unfitted, unqualified; incapable of; literary impuissant.
▷ANTONYMS able, capable.

unabridged adjective *each story is unabridged and wholly authentic*: **complete**, entire, whole, intact, full-length, uncut, unshortened, unreduced, uncondensed, unexpurgated.
▷ANTONYMS abridged.

unacceptable adjective *four boys have been suspended for unacceptable behaviour*: **intolerable**, insufferable, unsatisfactory, impermissible, inadmissible, inappropriate, unsuitable, undesirable, unreasonable, objectionable, insupportable; offensive, obnoxious, disagreeable, disgraceful, deplorable, terrible, distasteful, displeasing, improper, unseemly, beyond the pale, bad, poor; informal not on, a bit much, out of order, out, not quite the done thing, too much; Brit. informal a bit thick, a bit off, off, not cricket; Austral./NZ informal over the fence; rare exceptionable, condemnable.
▷ANTONYMS acceptable, satisfactory.

unaccompanied adjective *our parents would not let us go out unaccompanied in the evenings*: **alone**, on one's own, all alone, by oneself, solo, lone, solitary, single, single-handed; **unescorted**, without an escort, unattended, unchaperoned, partnerless, companionless; Latin solus; informal by one's lonesome; Brit. informal on one's tod, on one's lonesome, on one's jack, on one's Jack Jones; Austral./NZ informal on one's pat, on one's Pat Malone.
▷ANTONYMS accompanied.

unaccomplished adjective **1** *the unaccomplished works of Nature's hand*: **uncompleted**, incomplete, unfinished, undone, half-done, unperformed, unexecuted, undeveloped, unfulfilled, neglected.
▷ANTONYMS accomplished, complete.
2 *he was an unaccomplished poet*: **inexpert**, unskilful, unskilled, without finesse, incompetent, incapable, talentless, amateur, amateurish, unqualified, untrained, dilettante, maladroit, blundering; rare dilettantish.
▷ANTONYMS accomplished, expert, skilful.

unaccountable adjective **1** *for some unaccountable reason, the horses drawing the cart stopped short*: **inexplicable**, unexplainable, insoluble, unsolvable, incomprehensible, beyond comprehension, beyond understanding, unfathomable, impenetrable, puzzling, perplexing, baffling, bewildering, mystifying, mysterious, arcane, inscrutable, peculiar, unusual, curious, strange, freak, freakish, unparalleled, queer, odd, bizarre, extraordinary, astonishing, obscure, abstruse, enigmatic; informal weird, fluky, freaky, spooky; Brit. informal rum; N. Amer. informal off the wall; archaic wildering.
2 *the Council is literally unaccountable to anyone*: **not responsible**, unanswerable, not answerable, not liable; free, clear, exempt, immune; out of control, unsupervised.
▷ANTONYMS accountable, liable.

unaccustomed adjective **1** *she was **unaccustomed to** being told what to do*: **unused**, not used, new, fresh, a stranger; unpractised in, unfamiliar with, inexperienced in, unversed in, unconversant with, unacquainted with; archaic strange.
▷ANTONYMS accustomed.
2 *he showed unaccustomed emotion as he spoke*: **unusual**, unfamiliar, uncommon, unwonted, new, exceptional, out of the ordinary, extraordinary, special, remarkable, singular, rare, surprising, strange, abnormal, atypical, out of the way, curious, peculiar.
▷ANTONYMS habitual, usual.

unacquainted adjective *I regret that I am **unacquainted with** the place*: **unfamiliar with**, unaccustomed to, unused to; **new to**, fresh to, a stranger to; inexperienced in, ignorant of, uninformed about, unschooled in, untutored in, unenlightened about, unconversant with; informal in the dark about; archaic strange to; rare nescient of.
▷ANTONYMS acquainted, familiar.

unadorned adjective *they preferred sparse and unadorned church interiors*: **unembellished**, unornamented, undecorated, unelaborate, unvarnished, unfurnished, unpatterned, uncluttered, unostentatious, unfussy, no-nonsense, without frills, plain, penny plain, simple, basic, modest, restrained, straightforward; bare, bald, austere, stark, severe, spartan, ascetic, clinical, clean; informal no-frills.
▷ANTONYMS ornate, fancy.

unadventurous adjective *he led a leisurely, unadventurous life*: **cautious**, careful, prudent, chary, circumspect, wary, hesitant, tentative, timid; conservative, conventional, traditional, unenterprising, unexciting, unimaginative, uncreative, restrained, limited, boring, strait-laced, stuffy, narrow-minded; informal cagey, square, straight, stick-in-the-mud, uptight.
▷ANTONYMS adventurous, enterprising, imaginative.

unaffected adjective **1** *the government's position is **unaffected by** the cabinet reshuffle*: **unchanged**, unaltered, uninfluenced; untouched, unmoved, unimpressed, unstirred; unresponsive to; proof against, impervious to, immune to, not liable to, not subject to.
▷ANTONYMS changed, influenced, affected.
2 *his manner was natural and unaffected*: **unassuming**, unpretentious, down-to-earth, without airs, natural, spontaneous, easy, uninhibited, open, artless, guileless, ingenuous, naive, childlike, innocent, unsophisticated, unworldly, plain, simple.
▷ANTONYMS pretentious, affected.
3 *she was welcomed with unaffected warmth into the family home*: **genuine**, real, sincere, unfeigned, unpretended, unforced, uncontrived, unstilted, honest, earnest, wholehearted, heartfelt, true, bona fide, candid, frank, open, profound; informal upfront; rare full-hearted.
▷ANTONYMS false, feigned.

> *Choose the right word* **unaffected, sincere, genuine, unfeigned**
>
> See **sincere**.

unafraid adjective *these companies are **unafraid of** risks*: **undaunted by**, unabashed by, unalarmed by; **fearless**, brave, courageous, plucky, intrepid, stout-hearted, lionhearted, bold, daring, confident, stout, audacious, doughty, mettlesome, unflinching, unshrinking, unblenching; informal game, gutsy, spunky, ballsy.
▷ANTONYMS afraid, cowardly, timid.

unanimity noun *we have achieved a degree of unanimity*: **agreement**, accord, harmony, concord, unity, union, solidarity, unison, consensus, like-mindedness, assent; uniformity, consistency, congruence, concertedness.
▷ANTONYMS disagreement, division.

unanimous adjective **1** *doctors were unanimous about the effects of lead emission on health*: **united**, in complete agreement, in complete accord, of one mind, like-minded, of the same mind, in harmony, at one, with one voice, concordant, undivided; rare consentient.
▷ANTONYMS divided, at odds.
2 *a unanimous vote of confidence*: **uniform**, consistent, solid, united, concerted, congruent, undivided.

unanimously adverb *a committee of MPs has unanimously agreed to back his bill*: **without opposition, with one accord**, with one mind, to a man, as one, one and all, each and every one, bar none, without exception; in complete agreement, unitedly, concertedly.

unanswerable adjective **1** *an unanswerable case for investment*: **irrefutable**, inarguable, unarguable, indisputable, undeniable, incontestable, incontrovertible; conclusive, absolute, positive; rare irrefragable.
▷ANTONYMS weak, flawed.
2 *it was no use pondering on unanswerable questions*: **insoluble**, unsolvable, insolvable, unresolvable, unexplainable, inexplicable, unascertainable.
▷ANTONYMS obvious.

unanswered adjective *there were a number of unanswered questions*: **unresolved**, undecided, to be decided, unsettled, undetermined, pending, open, open to debate, open to question, up in the air, in doubt, doubtful, disputed; ignored, neglected.

unappetizing adjective *an unappetizing leg of chicken in breadcrumbs*: **unpalatable**, uninviting, unappealing, unpleasant, off-putting, disagreeable, distasteful, unsavoury, insipid, tasteless, flavourless, unattractive, uninteresting, dull; inedible, uneatable, revolting, nauseating, foul, nasty, detestable, loathsome, abhorrent; informal yucky, sick-making, gross.
▷ANTONYMS appetizing, tempting.

unapproachable adjective **1** *unapproachable islands*: **inaccessible**, out of reach, beyond reach, unreachable, remote, out of the way, isolated, far-flung, off the map, in the middle of nowhere, in the hinterlands; informal off the beaten track, in the back of beyond, in the sticks, unget-at-able; N. Amer. informal jerkwater, in the tall timbers; Austral./NZ informal Barcoo, beyond the black stump.
▷ANTONYMS accessible.
2 *her boss appeared fierce and unapproachable*: **aloof**, distant, remote, detached, reserved, withdrawn, uncommunicative, guarded, undemonstrative, unresponsive, unforthcoming, unfriendly, unsympathetic, unsociable, cool, cold, icy, chilly, frosty, frigid, stiff, formal, dispassionate; informal stand-offish, offish, off.
▷ANTONYMS approachable, friendly.

unarmed adjective *troops fired into a crowd of unarmed civilians*: **defenceless**, without arms, without weapons, weaponless, open to attack, wide open, open; **unprotected**, undefended, unguarded, unshielded, vulnerable, exposed, assailable; weak, helpless; rare pregnable.
▷ANTONYMS armed, protected.

unassailable adjective **1** *the world's most unassailable fortress*: **impregnable**, invulnerable, impenetrable, inviolable, invincible,

U

unconquerable, unattackable; secure, safe, safe and sound, well defended, well fortified; strong, stout, indestructible.
▷ANTONYMS assailable; defenceless.
2 *his logic was unassailable*: **indisputable**, undeniable, unquestionable, incontestable, incontrovertible, irrefutable, indubitable, watertight, sound, conclusive, absolute, positive, proven, beyond dispute, beyond question, beyond doubt, beyond a shadow of a doubt, certain, sure, manifest, patent, obvious.

Word toolkit **unassailable**

See **indomitable**.

unassertive adjective *she seemed unassertive and lacking confidence*: **passive**, retiring, submissive, unassuming, self-effacing, modest, humble, meek, unconfident, unforthcoming, diffident, shy, timid, timorous, shrinking, hesitant, insecure, unsure; informal mousy.
▷ANTONYMS assertive, bold.

unassuming adjective *a quiet unassuming man*: **modest**, self-effacing, humble, meek, mild, retiring, demure, restrained, reserved, withdrawn, reticent, diffident, shy, bashful, timid, timorous, shrinking, unconfident, insecure, unassertive; unobtrusive, unostentatious, unpretentious, unaffected, natural, genuine, simple, artless, ingenuous.
▷ANTONYMS bold, boastful, pretentious.

unattached adjective **1** *they were both unattached and deeply attracted to one another*: **unmarried**, **single**, unwed, unwedded; unengaged, unbetrothed; wifeless, husbandless, spouseless, partnerless, without a partner/husband/wife; with no ties, uncommitted, free, available, footloose and fancy free, not going out with anyone, on one's own, by oneself, unescorted, lone, on the shelf, unloved; separated, divorced, widowed; archaic sole.
▷ANTONYMS attached, married, engaged, spoken for.
2 *most of the runners were local people* ***unattached to*** *any organization*: **unaffiliated**, unallied, uncommitted; unassociated with, independent of; autonomous, non-aligned, self-governing, self-ruling, non-partisan, neutral, separate, unconnected, individual, distinct, detached.
▷ANTONYMS attached.

unattainable adjective *an apparently unattainable target*: **unreachable**, unachievable, unobtainable, impossible, unwinnable; unrealistic, implausible.
▷ANTONYMS attainable.

Word toolkit **unattainable**

See **impossible**.

unattended adjective **1** *his cries went quite unattended*: **ignored**, disregarded, neglected, passed over, forgotten, forsaken, abandoned, left.
2 *an unattended vehicle*: **unguarded**, unwatched, by itself, alone, left alone, on its own, solitary, solo.
3 *she had to walk unattended to the drawing room*: **unaccompanied**, unescorted, without an escort, partnerless, companionless, unchaperoned, alone, all alone, lone, on one's own, by oneself, solo; Latin solus; informal by one's lonesome; Brit. informal on one's tod, on one's lonesome, on one's jack, on one's Jack Jones; Austral./NZ on one's pat, on one's Pat Malone.
▷ANTONYMS attended, accompanied.

unattractive adjective *an unattractive little town*: **plain**, **ugly**, plain-looking, ugly-looking, plain-featured, ill-favoured, unappealing, unsightly, unlovely, unprepossessing, displeasing; hideous, monstrous, grotesque, deformed, disfigured; N. Amer. homely; informal not much to look at, short on looks, as plain as a pikestaff, as ugly as sin; Brit. informal no oil painting; Austral./NZ informal drack.
▷ANTONYMS attractive, beautiful.

u

unauthorized adjective *they issued a ban on all unauthorized rallies*: **unofficial**, unsanctioned, uncertified, unaccredited, unlicensed, unwarranted, unapproved; disallowed, prohibited, banned, barred, forbidden, outlawed, illegal, illegitimate, illicit, interdicted, proscribed; informal wildcat.
▷ANTONYMS authorized, official, lawful.

unavailing adjective *persistent calls for justice were unavailing*: **ineffective**, ineffectual, inefficacious, vain, in vain, futile, useless, unsuccessful, non-successful, nugatory, failed, fruitless, unproductive, profitless, unprofitable, pointless, to no avail, to no purpose, to no effect, abortive, inadequate; archaic for nought, bootless; rare Sisyphean.
▷ANTONYMS effective, successful.

unavoidable adjective *workers have been told that redundancies are unavoidable*: **inescapable**, inevitable, bound/sure to happen, inexorable, assured, certain, for sure, sure, fated, predestined, predetermined, preordained, ineluctable, necessary, compulsory, required, obligatory, mandatory, prescribed, out of one's hands; rare ineludible.

unaware adjective *the President was unaware of what was going on*: **ignorant**, unknowing, unconscious, heedless, unmindful, oblivious, unsuspecting, uninformed, unenlightened, unwitting, innocent, inattentive, unobservant, unperceptive, unresponsive, blind, deaf, insensible, insensitive; informal in the dark; rare incognizant, nescient.
▷ANTONYMS aware, conscious.

unawares adverb **1** *a party of brigands caught them unawares*: **by surprise**, unexpectedly, without warning, suddenly, abruptly, unprepared, off-guard, cold; red-handed, in the act, in flagrante delicto; informal with one's trousers/pants down, napping, in flagrante; Brit. informal on the hop.
▷ANTONYMS prepared.
2 *a shoal of young roach approached the pike unawares*: **unknowingly**, unwittingly, unconsciously, without noticing, in all innocence; unintentionally, inadvertently, accidentally, by accident, by mistake, mistakenly.
▷ANTONYMS knowingly; deliberately.

unbalanced adjective **1** *he was considered unbalanced and dangerous*: **unstable**, of unsound mind, mentally ill, deranged, demented, crazed, troubled, disturbed, unhinged, insane, mad, mad as a hatter, mad as a March hare, raving mad, out of one's mind, not in one's right mind, neurotic, psychotic; Latin non compos mentis; informal crazy, loopy, loony, mixed up, nuts, nutty, nutty as a fruitcake, bananas, cracked, crackpot, daft, dippy, screwy, with a screw loose, batty, dotty, cuckoo, bonkers, potty, mental, screwed up, not all there, off one's head, out of one's head, out to lunch, a bit lacking, round the bend, round the twist, away with the fairies; Brit. informal barmy, crackers, barking, barking mad, off one's trolley, off one's rocker, daft as a brush, not the full shilling; N. Amer. informal nutsy, nutso, squirrelly, wacko, buggy; dated touched.
▷ANTONYMS balanced, stable, sane.
2 *a most unbalanced article on a fundamental topic*: **biased**, prejudiced, skewed, one-sided, lopsided, partisan, factional, partial, inequitable, unjust, unfair, uneven, unequal; French parti pris.
▷ANTONYMS balanced, unbiased, fair.

unbearable adjective *the frustration is almost unbearable*: **intolerable**, insufferable, unsupportable, insupportable, unendurable, beyond endurance, unacceptable, unmanageable, impossible, more than flesh and blood can stand, too much to bear, past bearing, not to be borne, overpowering; informal too much, enough to try the patience of Job, enough to try the patience of a saint.
▷ANTONYMS bearable, tolerable.

unbeatable adjective *she has been in unbeatable form since her World Championship triumph*: **invincible**, unstoppable, unassailable, indomitable, unconquerable, invulnerable, unsurpassable, unsurpassed, matchless, unmatched, peerless; excellent, supreme, outstanding.
▷ANTONYMS poor, weak.

unbeaten adjective *Edinburgh are the only unbeaten team in the division | an unbeaten record*: **undefeated**, unconquered, unbowed, unvanquished, unsubdued, unsurpassed, unequalled, unrivalled, unbroken; triumphant, victorious, supreme, matchless, second to none.
▷ANTONYMS beaten, defeated.

unbecoming adjective **1** *a stout lady in an unbecoming striped sundress*: **unflattering**, unattractive, unsightly, plain, ugly, ugly-looking, hideous; unsuitable, unsuited, ill-suited.
▷ANTONYMS becoming, flattering.
2 *they condemned him for conduct* ***unbecoming to*** *the Senate*: **inappropriate**, unfitting, unbefitting, unsuitable, unsuited, ill-suited, inapt, out of keeping, untoward, incorrect, unacceptable; **unworthy of**; improper, lacking in propriety, indecorous, unseemly, unladylike, ungentlemanly, unmannerly, undignified, indelicate, indecent, tasteless.
▷ANTONYMS becoming, proper, appropriate.

unbelief noun *a symptom of unbelief was an inability to pray*: **atheism**, non-belief, agnosticism, heresy, apostasy, irreligion, heathenism, godlessness, nihilism, lack of faith; scepticism, cynicism, disbelief, incredulity, suspicion, distrust, mistrust, doubt, non-conviction, dubiety.
▷ANTONYMS belief, faith.

unbelievable adjective *your audacity is simply unbelievable*: **incredible**, beyond belief, difficult to believe, scarcely credible, inconceivable, unthinkable, unimaginable; unconvincing, far-fetched, implausible, improbable, impossible; informal hard to swallow, mind-boggling, mind-blowing.
▷ANTONYMS believable, credible.

unbeliever noun *a Holy War against the unbelievers*: **infidel**, heretic, heathen, non-believer, atheist, agnostic, pagan, nihilist, apostate, freethinker, dissenter, nonconformist; disbeliever, sceptic, cynic, doubter, doubting Thomas, questioner, scoffer; archaic paynim; rare nullifidian.
▷ANTONYMS believer.

unbelieving adjective *they were to preach to the unbelieving people*: **faithless**, non-believing, agnostic, atheistic, heathen, pagan, infidel, irreligious, unenlightened; disbelieving, doubting, doubtful, sceptical, cynical, unconvinced, incredulous.

▷ANTONYMS believing.

unbend verb **1** *I had trouble unbending my cramped knees*: **straighten**, straighten out, extend, flex, uncurl, flatten.
▷ANTONYMS bend.
2 *you could be fun too, you know, if you'd only unbend a little*: **relax**, become less formal, become informal, unwind, de-stress, loosen up, let oneself go; informal let one's hair down, let up, let it all hang out, hang loose, come down from one's high horse.
▷ANTONYMS tense up.

unbending adjective **1** *the giraffe moves towards me on unbending legs*: **stiff**, rigid, inflexible, unpliable, inelastic, unmalleable; straight, undeviating, linear, unswerving, uncurving, as straight as an arrow.
▷ANTONYMS flexible.
2 *an unbending and somewhat formal man*: **aloof**, formal, stiff, reserved, remote, distant, forbidding, stand-offish, strait-laced, conventional, stuffy, cool, unfeeling, unemotional, unfriendly, austere; informal uptight.
▷ANTONYMS relaxed, informal.
3 *the unbending attitudes of the authorities*: **uncompromising**, inflexible, unyielding, unfaltering, unwavering, hard-line, tough, harsh, strict, stern, severe, firm, resolute, determined, unrelenting, relentless, inexorable, intransigent, immovable.

unbiased adjective *unbiased professional advice*: **impartial**, unprejudiced, non-partisan, neutral, objective, outside, disinterested, without fear or favour, dispassionate, detached, unswayed, even-handed, open-minded, equitable, fair, fair-minded, just; informal on the level, with no axe to grind, sitting on the fence.
▷ANTONYMS biased, partisan, prejudiced.

Word toolkit **unbiased**

See **equitable**.

unbidden adjective **1** *often the unbidden guest proves the best company*: **uninvited**, unasked, unrequested, unsolicited; unwanted, unwelcome.
2 *unbidden excitement grew deep inside her*: **spontaneous**, unprompted, voluntary, unforced, uncompelled, unplanned, unpremeditated, spur-of-the-moment; informal off-the-cuff.

unbind verb *unbind her at once*: **untie**, unchain, unfetter, unshackle, unmanacle, unyoke, unfasten, untether, unknot, unlace, undo, loosen, unloose, disentangle; **release**, emancipate, free, set free/loose, liberate, discharge.
▷ANTONYMS bind, confine.

unblemished adjective *he had an unblemished record as a law-abiding citizen*: **impeccable**, flawless, faultless, without fault, without blemish, perfect, pure, pure as the driven snow, lily-white, whiter than white, clean, spotless, stainless, unsullied, unspoilt, undefiled, untouched, untarnished, uncontaminated, unpolluted, incorrupt, beyond/above reproach, guiltless, sinless, innocent, unimpeachable, blameless; exemplary, ideal, model; informal squeaky clean, A1.
▷ANTONYMS flawed, corrupt.

unborn adjective **1** *German measles can damage your unborn child*: **embryonic**, fetal, expected, awaited; Latin in utero.
2 *the unborn generations which shall follow us on this earth*: **future**, to come, coming, forthcoming, subsequent; formal hereafter.

unbosom verb *he had sat behind him when the chief was* ***unbosoming himself***: **open one's heart**, unburden oneself, confess, tell all, tell one's all; confide in; informal come clean, spill all.

unbounded adjective *I retained my unbounded enthusiasm for work*: **unlimited**, boundless, limitless, without limit, illimitable; unrestrained, unrestricted, unconditional, unconstrained, uncontrolled, unchecked, unbridled; untold, vast, immense; immeasurable, measureless, inestimable; endless, unending, never-ending, interminable, everlasting, infinite, inexhaustible, unflagging; absolute, total, full, utter; informal with no holds barred.
▷ANTONYMS limited, restricted.

unbreakable adjective *a new type of unbreakable plastic bottle*: **shatterproof**, non-breakable, indestructible, imperishable, resistant, durable, everlasting, long-lasting, made to last; toughened, sturdy, stout, hard-wearing, heavy-duty; literary adamantine; rare infrangible.
▷ANTONYMS fragile, flimsy.

unbridled adjective *she strikes the ball with an unbridled enthusiasm*: **unrestrained**, unconstrained, uncontrolled, uninhibited, unrestricted, unchecked, uncurbed, rampant, runaway, irrepressible, unstoppable, uncontainable, unquenchable; excessive, wild, intemperate, immoderate, wanton, self-indulgent.
▷ANTONYMS restrained, controlled.

unbroken adjective **1** *there were no doors or windows left unbroken*: **undamaged**, unimpaired, unharmed, unscathed, unspoilt, untouched, sound, intact, in one piece, whole, complete, entire, perfect.
▷ANTONYMS broken.
2 *an unbroken horse*: **untamed**, unsubdued, wild, undomesticated, feral.
▷ANTONYMS broken.
3 *an unbroken chain of glorious victories*: **uninterrupted**, continuous, ceaseless, unceasing, endless, incessant, constant, unremitting, perpetual, non-stop, without stopping, never-ending, ongoing.
▷ANTONYMS intermittent.
4 *his record of 10.2 seconds is still unbroken*: **unbeaten**, undefeated, unsurpassed, unrivalled, supreme, unmatched, matchless, second to none.
▷ANTONYMS broken, beaten.

unburden verb *he would have liked to* ***unburden himself to*** *somebody*: **open one's heart**, confess, tell all, tell one's all, unbosom oneself; confide in; informal come clean, spill all.
▷ANTONYMS keep it all in, bottle it all up.

uncalled for adjective *I'm ignoring that uncalled-for remark*: **gratuitous**, unnecessary, needless, unneeded, inessential; undeserved, unmerited, unwarranted, unjustified, unreasonable, unfair, inappropriate, pointless; unsought, unasked, unsolicited, unrequested, unprompted, unprovoked, undesired, unwanted, unwelcome.

uncanny adjective **1** *all the clocks had stopped and the silence was uncanny*: **eerie**, unnatural, preternatural, supernatural, unearthly, other-worldly, unreal, ghostly, mysterious, strange, abnormal, odd, curious, queer, weird, bizarre, freakish; Scottish eldritch; informal creepy, spooky, freaky; Brit. informal rum; N. Amer. informal bizarro.
▷ANTONYMS ordinary, normal.
2 *there was an uncanny resemblance between the two pictures*: **striking**, remarkable, extraordinary, out of the ordinary, out of the way, unusual, exceptional, astounding, astonishing, incredible, conspicuous, noteworthy, notable, considerable, distinctive, arresting.
▷ANTONYMS unremarkable, run-of-the-mill.

unceasing adjective *the unceasing efforts of the staff*: **incessant**, ceaseless, unending, endless, never-ending, interminable, non-stop, constant, continuous, continual, uninterrupted, unabated, unabating, unremitting, relentless, unrelenting, unrelieved, sustained, persistent, lasting, eternal, perpetual; unfaltering, unflagging, untiring, unwearied, unwavering, unswerving, undeviating, persevering, dogged, tireless, indefatigable.
▷ANTONYMS intermittent, occasional; half-hearted.

unceremonious adjective **1** *he waved them to an unceremonious halt*: **abrupt**, sudden, hasty, hurried, summary, perfunctory, undignified, rude, impolite, uncivil, discourteous, unmannerly, offhand, dismissive; informal off.
▷ANTONYMS polite.
2 *an affable, unceremonious man*: **informal**, not formal, casual, relaxed; **easy-going**, easy, familiar, natural, unreserved, open, free, loose; informal laid-back, free and easy.
▷ANTONYMS formal.

uncertain adjective **1** *the environmental effects of the project are uncertain*: **unknown**, undetermined, unsettled, unresolved, unsure, pending, in the balance, in limbo, up in the air, debatable, open to question, in doubt; unpredictable, unforeseeable, incalculable, speculative; unreliable, untrustworthy, undependable, risky, chancy; informal dicey, hairy, iffy; Brit. informal dodgy.
▷ANTONYMS certain, settled; predictable.
2 *the uncertain weather meant that passengers needed to pack a pullover or two*: **changeable**, variable, varying, irregular, fitful, unpredictable, unreliable, unsettled, unstable, erratic, fluctuating; rare changeful, fluctuant.
3 *Edward was a little uncertain about the decision*: **unsure**, doubtful, dubious, undecided, unresolved, indecisive, irresolute, hesitant, wavering, vacillating, oscillating, equivocating, vague, hazy, unclear, ambivalent, in two minds, on the horns of a dilemma, torn; informal iffy, blowing hot and cold, on the fence.
▷ANTONYMS certain, sure.
4 *I gave her an uncertain smile*: **hesitant**, hesitating, tentative, halting, faltering, unsure, unconfident, diffident, doubtful.
▷ANTONYMS confident.

uncertainty noun **1** *the uncertainty of the future*: **unpredictability**, unreliability, riskiness, chanciness, precariousness, unsureness; changeability, changeableness, variability, inconstancy, fitfulness, fickleness.
▷ANTONYMS certainty, predictability.
2 *uncertainty about the future is always bad for morale*: **unsureness**, lack of certainty, indecision, irresolution, hesitancy, doubt, doubtfulness, wavering, vacillation, equivocation, vagueness, ambivalence, lack of conviction, disquiet, disquietude, wariness, chariness, scepticism; queries, questions; rare dubiety, incertitude.
▷ANTONYMS certainty.
3 *she pushed the anxious uncertainties out of her mind*: **doubt**, qualm, misgiving, apprehension, quandary, dilemma, reservation, niggle, scruple, second thought, query, question, question mark, suspicion.
4 *there was uncertainty in his voice*: **hesitancy**, tentativeness, unsureness, lack of confidence, diffidence, doubtfulness, doubt.
▷ANTONYMS confidence.

unchangeable adjective *many people think of personality characteristics as virtually unchangeable*: **unalterable**, immutable, invariable, unvarying, invariant, changeless, firm, fixed, hard and fast, cast-iron, set in stone, set, decided, established, permanent, deep-rooted, enduring, abiding, lasting, indestructible, ineradicable, irreversible, unfading, constant, perpetual, eternal, lifelong; rare incommutable, perdurable.
▷ANTONYMS variable, changeable.

unchanging adjective *the unchanging passivity of her face enraged him*: **consistent**, constant, regular, even, uniform, unvarying, predictable, stable, steady, fixed, permanent, perpetual, eternal; sustained, lasting, persistent, uninterrupted, continuous, continual, ceaseless, incessant, unceasing, never-ending, non-stop, interminable, unabating, unabated, unrelieved, unremitting, relentless.
▷ANTONYMS varying, changeable, inconsistent.

uncharitable adjective *I regretted all the uncharitable things I had thought or said*: **unkind**, inconsiderate, thoughtless, insensitive, heedless, selfish, self-centred, mean, mean-spirited, unfriendly, unpleasant; **unsympathetic**, uncaring, lacking compassion, ungenerous, ungracious, unfeeling; unforgiving, merciless, ruthless, harsh, severe, stern, hard, hard-hearted, censorious, uncompromising, inflexible, unfair.
▷ANTONYMS charitable.

uncharted adjective *we ran Borneo's uncharted rapids in canoes*: **unexplored**, untravelled, undiscovered, unresearched, unplumbed, unfamiliar, unknown, strange; **unmapped**, unsurveyed.

uncivil adjective *he'd been short and uncivil with her*: **impolite**, rude, insulting, discourteous, disrespectful, unmannerly, bad-mannered, ill-mannered, impertinent, impudent, ill-bred, ungallant, unchivalrous, ungracious, brusque, tart, sharp, short, curt, offhand, gruff, surly, sullen, churlish, uncouth, ungentlemanly, unladylike, boorish, oafish, loutish, rough, coarse, vulgar; informal off, offish, fresh, flip.
▷ANTONYMS civil, polite.

uncivilized adjective *the human boy is an uncivilized creature*: **uncouth**, coarse, rough, boorish, vulgar, philistine, uneducated, uncultured, uncultivated, benighted, unsophisticated, unrefined, unpolished, ill-bred, ill-mannered, thuggish, loutish; **barbaric**, barbarian, barbarous, primitive, savage, wild, brutish, Neanderthal, in a state of nature; informal yobbish, slobbish; archaic rude.
▷ANTONYMS civilized.

unclean adjective **1** *they were charged with carrying on a food business in unclean premises*: **dirty**, filthy, grubby, grimy, mucky, fouled, foul, impure, adulterated, tainted, tarnished, stained, soiled, begrimed, smeared, unwashed; dusty, sooty, muddy, scummy; polluted, contaminated, infected, insanitary, unhygienic, unhealthy, germ-ridden, germy, disease-ridden, septic; informal yucky, cruddy, icky; Brit. informal manky, grotty, gungy; Austral./NZ informal scungy; archaic uncleanly; literary besmirched; rare feculent.
▷ANTONYMS clean.
2 *sex was considered to be naughty or unclean*: **sinful**, immoral, bad, wicked, evil, corrupt, impure, sullied, unwholesome, sordid, disgusting, debased, degenerate, depraved, licentious, lewd, unchaste, lustful; archaic uncleanly.
▷ANTONYMS pure.
3 *pork is an unclean meat for Muslims*: **impure**; forbidden.
▷ANTONYMS halal, kosher.

unclear adjective *it was unclear how much fluid had leaked out*: **uncertain**, unsure, unsettled, up in the air, debatable, open to question, in doubt, doubtful, unpredictable, unforeseeable, incalculable, speculative; **ambiguous**, inexact, imprecise, inexplicit, ill-defined, equivocal, indefinite, vague, abstruse, puzzling, perplexing, mysterious, arcane, cryptic, obscure, confused, confusing, hazy, misty, foggy, fogged, clouded, lacking definition, nebulous; informal iffy, dicey; Brit. informal dodgy.
▷ANTONYMS clear, evident, certain.

unclothed adjective *she felt awkwardly unclothed in her skimpy bikini*: **naked**, bare, nude, in the nude, stark naked, with nothing on, undressed, disrobed, uncovered, in a state of nature, unclad, undraped, exposed; French au naturel; informal without a stitch on, in one's birthday suit, in the raw, in the altogether, in the buff, as naked as the day one was born, in the nuddy, mother naked; Brit. informal starkers; Scottish informal in the scud, scuddy; N. Amer. informal bare-assed, buck naked; Austral./NZ informal bollocky; Brit. vulgar slang bollock-naked.
▷ANTONYMS clothed, dressed.

U

uncomfortable adjective **1** *a high-backed uncomfortable chair*: **painful**, not comfortable, intolerable, unbearable, disagreeable, excruciating, agonizing, confining, cramped, Spartan.
▷ANTONYMS comfortable.
2 *I have always felt rather uncomfortable in her presence*: **uneasy**, awkward, ill at ease, nervous, tense, edgy, restless, self-conscious, embarrassed, discomfited, disturbed, troubled, upset, worried, anxious, apprehensive; informal rattled, fazed, discombobulated, twitchy; N. Amer. informal antsy; rare unquiet.
▷ANTONYMS relaxed, comfortable.
3 *an uncomfortable silence*: **awkward**, uneasy, unpleasant, disagreeable, distressing, painful, disturbing, embarrassing, embarrassed, tense, strained, charged, worrisome, fraught; informal sticky.
▷ANTONYMS comfortable, pleasant.

uncommitted adjective **1** *ministers were scrambling to woo uncommitted delegates*: **floating**, undecided, non-aligned, non-partisan, unaffiliated, neutral, impartial, independent, undeclared, uncertain, vacillating; informal sitting on the fence.
▷ANTONYMS committed, aligned.
2 *a book about the uncommitted male*: **unmarried**, **unattached**, unwed, unwedded, wifeless, husbandless, partnerless, unengaged, unbetrothed, unpledged, unpromised, free, footloose and fancy free, available, single, lone, not going out with anyone.
▷ANTONYMS committed, attached, married.

uncommon adjective **1** *it is a handsome and relatively uncommon plant*: **unusual**, abnormal, rare, atypical, uncustomary, unconventional, unexpected, unfamiliar, strange, odd, curious, out of the ordinary, extraordinary, out of the way, outlandish, offbeat, irregular, deviant, novel, singular, peculiar, queer, bizarre, freakish, quirky, alien; informal weird, oddball, way out, freaky, something else; N. Amer. informal off the wall.
▷ANTONYMS common.
2 *attempted abductions of children are uncommon*: **rare**, scarce, few and far between, thin on the ground, exceptional, abnormal, isolated, occasional, infrequent, irregular, sporadic; Brit. out of the common; dated seldom.
▷ANTONYMS common.
3 *she displays an uncommon capacity for hard work*: **remarkable**, extraordinary, exceptional, singular, particular, marked, outstanding, notable, noteworthy, distinctive, striking, significant, especial, special, signal, superior, unique, unparalleled, unprecedented, prodigious; informal mind-boggling, mind-blowing.
▷ANTONYMS ordinary, run-of-the-mill.

uncommonly adverb *he is an uncommonly good talker*: **unusually**, remarkably, extraordinarily, extra, exceptionally, outstandingly, singularly, particularly, especially, strikingly, markedly, decidedly, notably, eminently, signally, uniquely, extremely, very, inordinately, incredibly, amazingly, awfully, terribly; N. English right; informal seriously, majorly, ultra; Brit. informal jolly, dead, well; N. Amer. informal powerful; dated devilishly, frightfully.

uncommunicative adjective *he had always been quiet and uncommunicative*: **taciturn**, reserved, shy, retiring, diffident, reticent, laconic, tongue-tied, at a loss for words, mute, quiet, unforthcoming, unconversational, untalkative, silent, tight-lipped, close-mouthed, guarded, secretive, secret, unresponsive, close, private, distant, remote, aloof, withdrawn, stand-offish, unsociable, antisocial, unfriendly, clamlike, playing one's cards close to one's chest; informal mum; archaic mumchance, retired.
▷ANTONYMS communicative, talkative, open.

uncomplicated adjective *an uncomplicated computer interface that is truly easy to use*: **simple**, not difficult, straightforward, clear, accessible, direct, undemanding, unexacting, unchallenging, unsophisticated, trouble-free, painless, effortless, easy, facile, elementary, idiot-proof, plain sailing, a five-finger exercise, nothing; informal easy-peasy, as easy as pie, as easy as falling off a log, as easy as ABC, a piece of cake, child's play, kids' stuff, a cinch, no sweat, a doddle, a breeze, a pushover, money for old rope, money for jam; N. Amer. informal duck soup, a snap; Austral./NZ informal a bludge; S. African informal a piece of old tackle; Brit. vulgar slang a piece of piss; dated a snip.
▷ANTONYMS complicated, difficult, demanding.

uncompromising adjective *her uncompromising attitude led to clashes with the governor*: **inflexible**, unbending, unyielding, unshakeable, unwavering, resolute, unpersuadable, unmalleable, rigid, stiff, hard-line, hard and fast, tough, immovable, intractable, firm, determined, iron-willed, dogged, obstinate, stubborn, not giving an inch, diehard, adamant, obdurate, tenacious, pertinacious, relentless, implacable, inexorable, intransigent, headstrong, pig-headed, bull-headed, single-minded, stiff-necked; Brit. informal bloody-minded; rare indurate.
▷ANTONYMS flexible, compliant.

unconcern noun *I affected a supreme unconcern*: **indifference**, apathy, lack of concern, lack of interest, uninterestedness, nonchalance, equanimity, insouciance, lack of involvement, passivity, dispassionateness, dispassion, detachment, aloofness, remoteness, reserve.
▷ANTONYMS concern, commitment.

unconcerned adjective **1** *readers think that the author is* **unconcerned** *with their responses to the text*: **indifferent about**, unmoved by, apathetic about, uninterested in, incurious about, uninvolved in/with, dispassionate about, deaf to, heedless of, unmindful of, bored by; cool, remote, aloof, detached, lukewarm, unenthusiastic.
▷ANTONYMS concerned, interested, attentive.
2 *Stanley shrugged and tried to look unconcerned*: **untroubled**, unworried, unperturbed, unruffled, unanxious, insouciant, nonchalant, blasé, carefree, blithe, casual, without a care in the world, serene, relaxed, at ease, devil-may-care, happy-go-lucky, {cool, calm, and collected}; informal laid-back,

unflappable; rare poco-curante.
▷ANTONYMS concerned, anxious.

unconditional adjective *he could count on the unconditional support of the president*: **unquestioning**, unqualified, unreserved, unlimited, unrestricted, wholesale, wholehearted; complete, total, entire, full, outright, absolute, downright, out-and-out, utter, all-out, thoroughgoing, unequivocal, positive, express, indubitable, categorical.
▷ANTONYMS conditional.

unconnected adjective **1** *the earth wire was left unconnected*: **detached**, disconnected, unjoined, separate, loose; dangling, hanging, trailing.
▷ANTONYMS connected.
2 *a series of unconnected tasks*: **unrelated**, unassociated, dissociated, separate, independent, distinct, different, disparate, individual, detached, discrete.
▷ANTONYMS related.
3 *there is a tendency to drift off into unconnected chains of thought*: **disjointed**, incoherent, disconnected, rambling, wandering, diffuse, ununified, disorderly, disordered, haphazard, disorganized, garbled, mixed up, muddled, jumbled, scrambled, meaningless, uncoordinated, aimless.
▷ANTONYMS coherent.

unconscionable adjective **1** *the unconscionable use of humans as test animals*: **unethical**, amoral, immoral, unprincipled, indefensible, wrong; unscrupulous, unfair, underhand, dishonourable, dishonest, corrupt, depraved; informal shady.
▷ANTONYMS ethical, acceptable.
2 *we have had to wait an unconscionable time*: **excessive**, unwarranted, uncalled for, unreasonable, unfair, inordinate, disproportionate, immoderate, extreme, undue, outrageous, preposterous, monstrous, inexcusable, unnecessary, needless; informal over the top, OTT.
▷ANTONYMS acceptable, moderate, reasonable.

unconscious adjective **1** *to make sure he stayed unconscious she hit him twice over the head*: **knocked out**, insensible, senseless, insentient, insensate, passed out, comatose, in a coma, inert; stunned, dazed, stupefied, torpid, befuddled, benumbed, numb; collapsed, keeled over, motionless, immobile, prostrate; informal **out cold**, out for the count, blacked out, KO'd, kayoed, out like a light, laid out, flaked out, out, dead to the world; Brit. informal spark out; rare soporose, soporous.
▷ANTONYMS conscious.
2 *she concealed herself in the nettles, **unconscious of** the pain*: **heedless**, unheeding, unmindful, disregardful, disregarding, taking no notice; oblivious to, insensible to, blind to, deaf to, impervious to, unaffected by, unconcerned by, indifferent to, detached from, removed from; **unaware**, ignorant, in ignorance, unknowing, unsuspecting, unenlightened; informal in the dark; rare incognizant, nescient.
▷ANTONYMS conscious, aware.
3 *an unconscious desire for recognition*: **unintentional**, unintended, accidental, unthinking, unwitting, inadvertent, unpremeditated, unplanned; **uncalculating**, chance; **natural**, innate, inherent, unlearned, instinctive, automatic, mechanical, reflex, involuntary, knee-jerk, uncontrolled, spontaneous, subliminal, subconscious, latent, suppressed, sleeping, deep; informal gut, bottled up.
▷ANTONYMS intentional, voluntary; forced.
▶noun *Oedipal fantasies were supposed to be raging in the unconscious*: **subconscious mind**, subconscious, unconscious mind, psyche, ego, superego, id, inner self, innermost self, self, inner man/woman.
▷ANTONYMS conscious mind.

unconsciousness noun *someone gave me a crack across the head and I slipped into unconsciousness*: **insensibility**, senselessness, stupefaction, oblivion, unawareness, blankness, lack of sensation, lack of feeling; blackout, coma, stupor, torpor, trance, sopor, collapse.
▷ANTONYMS consciousness.

uncontrollable adjective **1** *the crowds were fast becoming uncontrollable*: **unmanageable**, out of control, ungovernable, wild, unruly, disorderly, recalcitrant, refractory, obstreperous, turbulent, intractable, incorrigible, disobedient, delinquent, insubordinate, defiant, non-compliant, undisciplined; Brit. informal stroppy, bolshie; archaic contumacious.
▷ANTONYMS under control, obedient, compliant.
2 *his dad flew into an uncontrollable rage*: **ungovernable**, irresistible, irrepressible, unstoppable, unquenchable, uncontainable; wild, violent, forceful, frantic, frenzied, furious, raging, raving, mad, crazed, hysterical, maniacal, manic; informal crazy, hyper; rare fervid, perfervid, passional.
▷ANTONYMS controllable.

uncontrolled adjective *she was horrified by her uncontrolled outburst | the uncontrolled dumping of toxic waste*: **unrestrained**, unconstrained, unrestricted, unchecked, unbridled, uncurbed, unlimited, unfettered, untrammelled, uninhibited, unconfined, unimpeded, unhampered, unbounded, unsuppressed, undisciplined, out of control, out of hand, rampant, wild, runaway, incontinent, immoderate, intemperate.
▷ANTONYMS controlled, restrained.

unconventional adjective *contemporary art employs unconventional techniques and materials*: **unusual**, irregular, unorthodox, unfamiliar, uncommon, uncustomary, unwonted, rare, out of the ordinary, atypical, singular, distinctive, individual, individualistic, alternative, different; new, fresh, novel, newfangled, innovative, groundbreaking, experimental, pioneering, original, unprecedented, unheard of; **eccentric**, idiosyncratic, maverick, quirky, odd, strange, bizarre, weird, outlandish, freakish, funny, quaint, queer, curious, abnormal, anomalous, aberrant, extraordinary, offbeat, radical, esoteric, nonconformist, bohemian; French outré, avant-garde; N. Amer. left-field; informal freaky, way out, far out, oddball, wacky, cranky, kinky, screwy, off the wall, something else, madcap, zany, hippy; Brit. informal rum; N. Amer. informal kooky, wacko, bizarro.
▷ANTONYMS conventional, orthodox, ordinary.

unconvincing adjective *he had a plausible though highly unconvincing story*: **improbable**, unlikely, implausible; incredible, scarcely credible, unbelievable, difficult to believe, beyond belief, questionable, dubious, doubtful; strained, laboured, ponderous, forced, far-fetched, remote, unrealistic, fanciful, fantastic, strange; feeble, weak, unsound, thin, transparent, poor, lame, trifling, shallow, inadequate, unsatisfactory, ineffectual, half-baked, pathetic; informal hard to swallow/take.
▷ANTONYMS convincing, cogent, persuasive.

uncooperative adjective *the authorities were inclined to be uncooperative*: **unhelpful**, awkward, disobliging, unaccommodating, unamenable, unreasonable, unwilling, recalcitrant, perverse, contrary, stubborn, wilful, stiff-necked, unyielding, unbending, inflexible, unadaptable, immovable, obstructive, difficult, obstreperous, troublesome, tiresome, disobedient; Scottish thrawn; N. Amer. rock-ribbed; Brit. informal **bolshie**, **bloody-minded**, stroppy, sticky.
▷ANTONYMS cooperative, obliging.

uncoordinated adjective *as he ran, his uncoordinated limbs flung out in all directions*: **clumsy**, **awkward**, blundering, bumbling, lumbering, shambling; flat-footed, heavy-footed, heavy-handed, graceless; **gawky**, gangling, ungainly, ungraceful, inelegant, clownish, cumbersome, bovine, ponderous; inept, unhandy, unskilful, inexpert, maladroit, bungling; informal butterfingered, cack-handed, ham-fisted, ham-handed, clodhopping, like a bull in a china shop; Brit. informal all thumbs, all fingers and thumbs; N. Amer. informal klutzy; archaic lubberly.
▷ANTONYMS well coordinated, adroit, dexterous.

uncouth adjective *the porters shouted to each other in uncouth tones*: **uncivilized**, uncultured, uncultivated, unrefined, unpolished, unsophisticated, common, low, plebeian, philistine, rough, coarse, provincial, rustic, crude, gross, loutish, hooligan, boorish, oafish; Neanderthal, barbarian, barbarous, barbaric, bearish, primitive, savage; churlish, uncivil, rude, impolite, discourteous, disrespectful, unmannerly, bad-mannered, ill-mannered, ill-bred, indecorous, ungallant, ungentlemanly, unladylike, vulgar, crass, indelicate, offensive; N. Amer. backwoods, hillbilly, hick; informal yobbish, slobbish, clodhopping.
▷ANTONYMS refined, cultivated; polite.

uncover verb **1** *she uncovered the cheese sandwiches*: **lay bare**, bare, expose, expose to view, leave unprotected, reveal, display, put on display, put on show, exhibit; **unwrap**, unveil, strip, denude.
▷ANTONYMS cover, conceal, clothe.
2 *police claim to have uncovered a money-laundering operation*: **detect**, discover, come across, stumble on/across, chance on, hit on, encounter, find, find out, turn up, unearth, dig up, dredge up, root out, hunt out, nose out, ferret out, grub out, disinter, extricate; **expose**, bring to light, bring into the open, unmask, unveil, reveal, lay bare, make known, make public, divulge, disclose, betray, give away, smoke out; informal blow the whistle on, pull the plug on, spill the beans on, let the cat out of the bag, nail; rare uncloak.
▷ANTONYMS conceal, hide, cover up.

unctuous adjective *she sees through his unctuous manners | an unctuous smile*: **sycophantic**, ingratiating, obsequious, fawning, servile, self-abasing, grovelling, subservient, wheedling, cajoling, crawling, cringing, Uriah Heepish, humble, toadying, hypocritical, insincere, flattering, adulatory, honey-tongued, silver-tongued, gushing, effusive, suave, urbane, glib, smooth, smooth-tongued, smooth-spoken, smooth-talking, slick, slippery, saccharine; **oily**, oleaginous, greasy; cloying, nauseating, sickening; informal smarmy, slimy, bootlicking, forelock-tugging, phoney, sucky, soapy; N. Amer. informal brown-nosing, apple-polishing; Brit. vulgar slang arse-licking, bum-sucking; N. Amer. vulgar slang ass-kissing, kiss-ass; rare saponaceous, pinguid.
▷ANTONYMS blunt, no-nonsense.

undaunted adjective *despite the tempest the crews were undaunted*: **unafraid**, undismayed, unalarmed, unflinching, unshrinking, unabashed, unfaltering, unflagging, fearless, dauntless, intrepid, bold, valiant, brave, stout-hearted, lionhearted, courageous, heroic, gallant, doughty, plucky, game, mettlesome, gritty, steely, indomitable, resolute, determined, confident, audacious, daring, daredevil; informal gutsy, spunky, ballsy, feisty, cocky.
▷ANTONYMS afraid, fearful.

undecided adjective **1** *her father's fate was still undecided*: **unresolved**, yet to be decided, uncertain, unsure, unclear, unsettled, indefinite;

undetermined, indeterminate, unknown, unestablished, unascertained, pending, outstanding, in the balance, up in the air, debatable, arguable, disputable, moot, problematic, controversial, open to question, open to doubt, open, doubtful, dubious, borderline, ambiguous, vague; informal iffy, on the back burner, on ice; Brit. informal dodgy.
▷ANTONYMS decided, sealed.
2 *they remained undecided as to the precise role for the EC*: **unsure**, uncertain, doubtful, dubious, unresolved, indecisive, irresolute, hesitant, tentative, wavering, vacillating, oscillating, equivocating, dithering, uncommitted, floating, shilly-shallying, wobbling, vague, hazy, unclear, ambivalent, in two minds, torn, split; in a quandary, in a dilemma, on the horns of a dilemma, in doubt; informal iffy, blowing hot and cold, on the fence.
▷ANTONYMS certain.

undefined adjective 1 *the contract leaves some matters undefined*: **unspecified**, unexplained, non-specific, unspecific, indeterminate, undetermined, unfixed, unsettled; unclear, woolly, imprecise, inexact, indefinite, vague.
▷ANTONYMS specific, definite.
2 *the lights gave a gentle, warm glow with undefined shapes and shadows*: **indistinct**, indefinite, formless, indistinguishable, barely perceptible, vague, hazy, misty, shadowy, nebulous, dim, obscure, blurred, blurry, bleary, out of focus.
▷ANTONYMS distinct, clear.

undemonstrative adjective *my grandmother was an undemonstrative woman*: **unemotional**, unaffectionate, impassive, dispassionate; self-contained, restrained, reserved, unresponsive, unmoved, unloving, unfriendly, unfeeling, passionless, wooden, uncommunicative, unforthcoming, sober, stiff, reticent, guarded, secretive, close, taciturn, aloof, distant, detached, remote, withdrawn; cool, cold, cold-blooded, chilly, frosty, frigid, glacial; informal stand-offish, offish.
▷ANTONYMS demonstrative, gushing.

undeniable adjective *the force of his theory is undeniable*: **indisputable**, indubitable, unquestionable, beyond doubt, beyond question, beyond a shadow of a doubt, inarguable, undebatable, incontrovertible, incontestable, irrefutable, unassailable; **certain**, sure, definite, positive, conclusive, watertight, proven, clear, clear-cut, straightforward, plain, as plain as a pikestaff, transparent, obvious, unmistakable, evident, self-evident, manifest, staring one in the face, patent, marked, pronounced, express, emphatic, categorical, unequivocal, compelling; rare irrefragable, apodictic.
▷ANTONYMS debatable, questionable.

under preposition 1 *they found the baby under a bush*: **beneath**, below, underneath, at the foot/bottom of.
▷ANTONYMS above, over.
2 *the present rent is just under £1200*: **less than**, lower than, smaller than, not so much as, not as much as, below; informal shy of.
▷ANTONYMS more than, over.
3 *all branch managers are under the retail director*: **subordinate to**, junior to, inferior to, secondary to, subservient to, reporting to, answerable to, responsible to, subject to; controlled by, at the mercy of, under the heel of.
▷ANTONYMS above, over.
4 *forty holiday homes are under construction*: **undergoing**, in the process of, receiving.
5 *half of the town was under water*: **flooded by**, immersed in, submerged by, sunk in, engulfed by, inundated by, drowned by.
▷ANTONYMS above.
6 *the finances of the council are under pressure*: **subject to**, liable to, bound by, controlled by, constrained by, under the control of, at the mercy of.
▶adverb *coughing and spluttering she went under*: **down**, downward, lower, below, underneath, beneath; underwater, to the bottom.

underclothes plural noun **underwear**, undergarments, underclothing, lingerie, underlinen, underthings; informal undies, frillies, unmentionables; Brit. informal smalls.

u

undercover adjective *they were arrested after a three-year undercover investigation*: **covert**, secret, clandestine, private, confidential, conspiratorial, underground, surreptitious, furtive, cloak-and-dagger, hole-and-corner, hugger-mugger, back-alley, backstair, stealthy, closet; intelligence; hidden, concealed, masked, veiled, shrouded; informal hush-hush, sneaky.
▷ANTONYMS open, overt.

undercurrent noun 1 *beware the dangerous undercurrents in the cove*: **undertow**, underflow, underswell, underdrift, understream, undertide, underrun; Nautical underset; rare underwork.
2 *she sensed the undercurrent of despair in what he was saying*: **undertone**, overtone, suggestion, connotation, implication, intimation, hint, nuance, trace, suspicion, whisper, murmur, touch, tinge; feeling, atmosphere, aura, tenor, echo, flavour, colouring, vein; vibrations; informal vibes; rare subcurrent.

undercut verb 1 *English cloth manufacturers were able to undercut their continental rivals*: **charge less than**, charge a lower price than, undersell, underbid.
2 *the company denied that his authority was being undercut*: **undermine**, weaken, impair, damage, sap, threaten, subvert, sabotage, ruin, disrupt, undo, destabilize, demolish, wreck, destroy, chip away.

underdog noun *he particularly relished a political battle when he was the underdog*: **weaker party**, victim, prey; loser, scapegoat; informal little fellow, little guy, fall guy, stooge.

underestimate verb 1 *official statistics tend to underestimate the actual volume of economic activity that occurs*: **set too low**, underrate; miscalculate, misjudge, judge incorrectly, estimate wrongly, calculate wrongly, be wrong about, misconstrue, misread; err, be wide of the mark.
▷ANTONYMS overestimate, exaggerate.
2 *his political opponents managed to underestimate his capabilities*: **underrate**, rate too low, undervalue, set little/no store by, not do justice to, do an injustice to, be wrong about, sell short, play down, understate; minimize, de-emphasize, underemphasize, diminish, downgrade, deflate, reduce, lessen, brush aside, gloss over, trivialize; hold cheap, shrug off, belittle; rare misprize, minify.
▷ANTONYMS overestimate, overrate, exaggerate.

undergo verb *she had to undergo a ferocious and lengthy cross-examination*: **go through**, **experience**, engage in, undertake, live through, face, encounter, submit to, be subjected to, come in for, receive, sustain, endure, brave, bear, tolerate, stand, withstand, put up with, weather, support, brook, suffer, cope with; Scottish thole; Brit. informal wear.

underground adjective 1 *they drove up the ramp from the underground car park*: **subterranean**, subterrestrial, below ground, buried, sunken, lower-level, basement; rare hypogean.
▷ANTONYMS surface; overhead.
2 *the underground organizations are designed to spread populist propaganda*: **clandestine**, secret, surreptitious, covert, undercover, private, confidential, closet, hole-and-corner, cloak-and-dagger, hugger-mugger, back-alley, backstair, stealthy, conspiratorial, concealed, hidden, shrouded; sneaky, sly, underhand, shifty, furtive; resistance, subversive, guerrilla, mercenary, revolutionary, rebellious, dissident, insurgent, insurrectionary, renegade, mutinous; informal hush-hush.
3 *the New York underground art scene*: **alternative**, radical, revolutionary, unconventional, unorthodox, avant-garde, experimental, innovative, groundbreaking, pioneering, novel; subversive.
▶adverb 1 *the insects spend years underground as larvae*: **below ground**, below the surface, under the earth, in the earth.
2 *the group went underground and issued calls for national resistance*: **into hiding**, into secrecy, into seclusion, undercover, behind closed doors, out of sight.
▶noun 1 *he took the underground back to his studio apartment*: **underground railway**, metro; N. Amer. subway; Brit. informal tube.
2 *the information had been furnished by the French underground*: **resistance movement**, resistance, illegal opposition; partisans, guerrillas, freedom fighters; in France, historical Maquis.

undergrowth noun *she groped her way through the thick undergrowth*: **shrubbery**, vegetation, greenery, ground cover, underwood, copsewood, brushwood, brush, scrub, underscrub, cover, covert, thicket, copse, coppice, wood, jungle; bushes, plants, weeds, brambles; N. Amer. underbrush, underbush, shin-tangle; SE English frith; archaic rone; rare herbage, verdure.

underhand adjective *he was accused of employing underhand tactics*: **deceitful**, underhanded, dishonest, dishonourable, disreputable, unethical, unprincipled, immoral, unscrupulous, fraudulent, cheating, dubious, dirty, unfair, treacherous, duplicitous, double-dealing, below the belt, two-timing, two-faced, unsporting, unsportsmanlike; devious, calculating, artful, crafty, cunning, conniving, scheming, designing, sly, wily, guileful, tricky; criminal, illegal, unlawful, nefarious; **secret**, secretive, clandestine, surreptitious, sneaky, sneaking, furtive, covert, veiled, shrouded, cloak-and-dagger, hugger-mugger, hole-and-corner, hidden, back-alley, backstairs, under the table, conspiratorial; N. Amer. snide, snidey; informal crooked, shady, bent, low-down, murky, fishy; Brit. informal dodgy; Austral./NZ informal shonky; S. African informal slim.
▷ANTONYMS honest, fair, above board.

underline verb 1 *she underlined the important words*: **underscore**, mark, pick out, emphasize, highlight; italicize.
2 *the programme will underline the health benefits of white meat*: **emphasize**, give emphasis to, stress, put/lay stress on, highlight, accentuate, accent, call/draw attention to, focus (attention) on, zero in on, spotlight, throw into relief, give prominence to, bring to the fore, foreground, bring home, point up, play up, make a feature of; informal rub in.
▷ANTONYMS play down, minimize.

underling noun *he dishes out orders to his underlings*: **subordinate**, inferior, deputy, junior, assistant, adjutant, aide, minion, lackey, flunkey, menial, retainer, vassal, subject, serf, hireling, servant, henchman, myrmidon, right-hand man/woman, girl/man Friday, factotum, stooge; follower, camp follower, hanger-on, disciple; informal sidekick, dogsbody, skivvy; N. Amer. informal gofer, peon; archaic scullion, servitor.
▷ANTONYMS boss, leader.

underlying adjective **1** *he took issue with the underlying aims of the research*: **fundamental**, basic, basal, primary, prime, first, cardinal, central, principal, chief, key, elementary, elemental, rudimentary, root, intrinsic, essential.
▷ANTONYMS subordinate.
2 *she spoke airily despite an underlying feeling of irritation*: **latent**, lurking, repressed, suppressed, unrevealed, undisclosed, unexpressed, undivulged, concealed, hidden, veiled, masked, shrouded, under wraps.
▷ANTONYMS overt.

undermine verb **1** *the integrity of government statistics is being undermined*: **subvert**, sabotage, threaten, weaken, compromise, diminish, reduce, impair, mar, spoil, ruin, impede, hinder, damage, hurt, injure, cripple, disable, enfeeble, sap, shake; whittle away, eat away; informal foul up, botch, put the kibosh on, drag through the mud; Brit. informal throw a spanner in the works of, queer the pitch of; N. Amer. informal throw a monkey wrench in the works of.
▷ANTONYMS enhance, improve, strengthen.
2 *we had no other way to break in but by undermining the building*: **tunnel under**, dig under, burrow under, excavate, sap.
3 *the damp had so undermined the structure that the wall fell down*: **erode**, wear away, eat away at, chip away, undercut.
▷ANTONYMS shore up, support.

underprivileged adjective *the charity arranges holidays for underprivileged children*: **needy**, **deprived**, in need, in want, in distress, disadvantaged, needful, poor, destitute, in reduced circumstances, in straitened circumstances, impoverished, poverty-stricken, penurious, indigent, as poor as a church mouse, unable to keep the wolf from the door; Brit. on the breadline, without two pennies/brass farthings to rub together; informal on one's uppers, on one's beam-ends; rare pauperized, beggared, necessitous.
▷ANTONYMS privileged, wealthy, well off.

underrate verb *most of us have a tendency to underrate our own skills*: **undervalue**, underestimate, set little store by, rate too low, not do justice to, do an injustice to, be wrong about, sell short, play down, understate, minimize, de-emphasize, underemphasize, diminish, downgrade, reduce, lessen, brush aside, gloss over, trivialize; rare misprize, minify.
▷ANTONYMS overrate, exaggerate.

undersized adjective *a skinny, undersized 15-year-old*: **underdeveloped**, **stunted**, small, short, little, tiny, petite, small-boned, slight, compact, minuscule, miniature, mini, diminutive, dwarfish, elfin, bantam, runtish, puny; Scottish wee; informal pint-sized, half-pint, pocket-sized, knee-high to a grasshopper, baby, teeny, teeny-weeny, teensy-weensy, itsy-bitsy; rare homuncular, Lilliputian.
▷ANTONYMS enormous, overgrown.

understand verb **1** *he couldn't understand anything we said to him*: **comprehend**, apprehend, grasp, see, take in, perceive, discern, make out, puzzle out, recognize, keep up with, master, get to know, follow, fathom, get to the bottom of, penetrate, divine, interpret, unravel, decipher, see the light about, envisage; informal get the hang of, get the drift of, catch on to, latch on to, tumble to, crack, make head or tail of, figure out, dig, get, get one's head around, wrap one's mind around, see daylight, get the picture, get the message; Brit. informal twig, suss out, suss; N. Amer. informal savvy; rare cognize.
▷ANTONYMS misunderstand, misinterpret.
2 *Suzanne understood how hard her husband had worked*: **appreciate**, recognize, realize, acknowledge, know, be aware of, be conscious of, be cognizant of, accept; commiserate with, feel compassionate towards, sympathize with, empathize with; informal take on board, be wise to.
▷ANTONYMS ignore.
3 *I understand that you wish to take legal action*: **believe**, be led to believe, be given to understand, think, conclude, come to the conclusion, deduce, infer, draw the inference, assume, surmise, fancy; gather, take it, hear, hear tell, be informed, notice, see, learn, discover.

understandable adjective **1** *he made me rewrite the book to make it understandable to non-scientists*: **comprehensible**, easy to understand, intelligible, penetrable, fathomable, graspable, lucid, coherent, clear, crystal clear, explicit, unambiguous, transparent, plain, straightforward, digestible, user-friendly; perspicuous.
▷ANTONYMS incomprehensible, unfathomable.
2 *parents have a wholly understandable desire for their children to be happy*: **unsurprising**, expected, to be expected, predictable, foreseeable, inevitable; **reasonable**, acceptable, logical, rational, normal, natural, par for the course, explicable, explainable, conceivable, imaginable, thinkable, plausible, tenable; justifiable, justified, admissible, allowable, accountable, defensible, excusable, pardonable, forgivable; informal on the cards.
▷ANTONYMS surprising, mysterious.

understanding noun **1** *the aim of the examination is to test basic understanding of the written language*: **comprehension**, apprehension, grasp, grip, mastery, perception, discernment, appreciation, interpretation, cognizance, ken, conception, digestion, assimilation, absorption; knowledge, awareness, consciousness; insight into, familiarity with, acquaintance with; skill in, expertise in, proficiency in; informal know-how.
▷ANTONYMS ignorance; misunderstanding.
2 *a young man of brilliant understanding and great eloquence*: **intellect**, intelligence, mind, brainpower, capability, insight, judgement, sense, reason, reasoning; intuition, shrewdness, sharpness, quickness, acumen, sagacity, perspicacity, wisdom, wit; thought, mentality; brains, powers of reasoning/intuition; French savoir faire; informal grey matter, nous, savvy, know-how.
3 *it was my understanding that because of the war there would be no ceremonies*: **belief**, perception, view, notion, idea, conclusion, conviction, feeling, opinion, intuition, impression, assumption, supposition, postulation, way of thinking, point of view; suspicion, sneaking suspicion, hunch, funny feeling.
4 *he always treated me with great kindness and understanding*: **compassion**, sympathy, pity, empathy, feeling, concern, considerateness, consideration, tenderness, tender-heartedness, kindness, kind-heartedness, sensitivity, insight, fellow feeling, brotherly love, neighbourliness, decency, humanity, humanitarianism, humaneness, charity, goodwill, mercy, mercifulness, gentleness, tolerance, lenience, leniency, warmth, warm-heartedness, affection, love.
▷ANTONYMS ignorance, indifference.
5 *we had a tacit understanding that we would keep it secret*: **agreement**, gentleman's agreement, arrangement, deal, bargain, settlement, pledge, promise, pact, compact, contract, concord, treaty, covenant, bond.
▶ adjective *he's a very good and understanding friend*: **compassionate**, sympathetic, sensitive, considerate, tender, kind, kindly, kind-hearted, thoughtful, tolerant, patient, forbearing, lenient, merciful, forgiving, humane, human, good-natured, approachable, supportive, reassuring; tactful, diplomatic, perceptive, subtle, prudent.

understate verb *we have been guilty of understating the size of the problem*: **play down**, downplay, make light of, underrate, rate too low, not do justice to, do an injustice to, underplay, de-emphasize, underemphasize, trivialize, minimize, diminish, downgrade, reduce, lessen, brush aside, gloss over, shrug off; informal soft-pedal, sell short; rare misprize, minify.
▷ANTONYMS overstate, exaggerate, emphasize.

understatement noun *to say I am delighted is an understatement* | *he spoke with a delightful degree of understatement*: **minimization**, trivialization, euphemism; understatedness, restraint, reserve, underplaying, underemphasis; subtlety, delicacy; technical litotes, meiosis.
▷ANTONYMS overstatement, exaggeration.

understudy noun *he muffed his lines and was often replaced by an understudy*: **stand-in**, substitute, replacement, reserve, fill-in, locum, proxy, backup, relief, standby, supply, surrogate, stopgap, second, alternative, ancillary; Latin locum tenens; informal sub; N. Amer. informal pinch-hitter.

undertake verb *the team were asked to undertake a further project*: **tackle**, take on, take on oneself, take up, accept, shoulder, handle, assume, manage, deal with, take responsibility for, be responsible for; engage in, become involved in, take part in, participate in, devote oneself to, concentrate on, address oneself to, turn one's hand to, go about, set about, approach, get down to, get to grips with; launch into, enter on, begin, start, embark on, venture on; attempt, try, endeavour; informal get cracking on, have a crack/go/shot/stab at, give something a whirl; formal commence, essay.
▷ANTONYMS neglect, forgo.

undertaker noun *the undertaker brought the coffin to our house*: **funeral director**; N. Amer. **mortician**; archaic upholder, blackmaster, cold cook, death-hunter; rare thanatologist.

undertaking noun **1** *why did you get involved in such a risky undertaking?* **enterprise**, venture, project, campaign, scheme, plan, operation, endeavour, effort, task, assignment, charge, activity, pursuit, exploit, job, business, affair, procedure, proceeding, process, transaction; mission, quest, exploration, expedition.
2 *all students shall sign an undertaking to comply with the regulations of the university*: **pledge**, agreement, promise, oath, covenant, vow, word, word of honour, solemn word, bond, commitment, guarantee, assurance, warrant, contract, compact.

undertone noun **1** *he said something in an undertone to the woman at his side*: **low voice**, murmur, whisper, mutter; low tones, hushed tones.
▷ANTONYMS shout.
2 *she was deeply affected by the story's dark undertones*: **undercurrent**, hint, overtone, suggestion; **connotation**, nuance, intimation, inkling, insinuation, implication, trace, suspicion, tinge, touch, vein, breath, whiff, whisper, glimmer, atmosphere, aura, tenor, flavour, colouring, shade, smack; rare subcurrent.

undervalue verb *the enthusiasm and initiative of youth was often undervalued by the older generation*: **underrate**, set little store by, rate too low, think too little of, underestimate, not do justice to, do an injustice to, play down, understate, underemphasize, de-emphasize, diminish, minimize, downgrade, reduce, lessen, brush aside, gloss over, shrug off,

trivialize; belittle, hold cheap; informal sell short; rare misprize, minify.
▷ANTONYMS overrate.

underwater adjective *there are some underwater caves nearby*: **undersea**, submarine, sub-aquatic, subaqueous; **submerged**, immersed, sunken.

underworld noun **1** *vagrants were forced into the violent underworld of Southwark*: **criminal world**, world of crime, organized crime; criminals, gangsters; informal gangland, mob, mobsters.
2 *Osiris, the god of the underworld*: **the netherworld**, the land/abode of the dead, the infernal regions, the nether regions, hell, the abyss; the abode of the damned, eternal damnation, eternal punishment, perdition; Biblical Gehenna, Tophet, Abaddon; Judaism Sheol; Greek Mythology Hades, Tartarus, Acheron; Roman Mythology Avernus; Scandinavian Mythology Niflheim; Brit. the other place; literary the pit, the shades; archaic the lower world.
▷ANTONYMS heaven, paradise.

Word links **underworld**

Plutonic relating to the underworld

underwrite verb *the London-based company which underwrote the deal has crashed*: **sponsor**, support, back, insure, indemnify, provide security for, take the risk for, subsidize, contribute to, pay for, provide capital for, finance, fund; **sanction**, agree to, approve, confirm, ratify, validate, authenticate, certify, seal, guarantee, warrant, accredit; informal foot the bill for, pick up the tab for; N. Amer. informal bankroll.

undesirable adjective **1** *a mix of medicines may result in undesirable side effects*: **unpleasant**, disagreeable, nasty, unacceptable, unwelcome, unwanted, unwished-for, unenviable, unappealing; unfortunate, infelicitous.
▷ANTONYMS desirable, pleasant, preferable.
2 *William had been involved with some very undesirable people*: **unpleasant**, disagreeable, distasteful, displeasing, unacceptable, off-putting, obnoxious; **nasty**, disgusting, awful, terrible, dreadful, frightful, repulsive, repellent, repugnant, revolting, abhorrent, loathsome, hateful, detestable, reprehensible, deplorable, appalling, insufferable, intolerable, despicable, contemptible, beyond the pale, odious, vile, obscene, foul, unsavoury, unpalatable, sickening, nauseating, nauseous, noxious; informal ghastly, horrible, horrid; Brit. informal beastly; archaic disgustful, loathly; rare exceptionable, rebarbative.
▷ANTONYMS pleasant, agreeable, acceptable.

undetectable adjective *there may have been an undetectable amount of poison in the tea*: **unnoticeable**, imperceptible, invisible, inaudible, odorless, subtle, faint, obscure; tiny, minute, infinitesimal.

Word toolkit **undetectable**

See **invisible**.

undignified adjective *there was an undignified scramble for seats on the train*: **unseemly**, demeaning, unbecoming, ungentlemanly, unladylike, unworthy, unfitting, unbefitting, degrading, debasing, cheapening, belittling, lowering, shaming, shameful, humiliating, mortifying, dishonourable, ignominious, discreditable, ignoble, inglorious, unceremonious, scandalous, disgraceful, indecent, untoward, unsuitable, abject, sorry, low, base, wretched; informal infra dig.
▷ANTONYMS dignified, seemly.

undisciplined adjective **1** *the school said that his kid was lazy and undisciplined*: **unruly**, disorderly, disobedient, badly behaved, obstreperous, recalcitrant, refractory, intractable, wilful, wayward, delinquent, perverse, naughty, contrary, rebellious, mutinous, insubordinate, disruptive, turbulent, errant, out of hand, out of control; uncontrolled, uncontrollable, unrestrained, ungovernable, wild, capricious, unsteady, untrained, unschooled; Brit. informal stroppy, bolshie; archaic contumacious.
▷ANTONYMS disciplined, well behaved.
2 *nobody knew how undisciplined she had been with her money*: **disorganized**, unorganized, erratic, unsystematic, unmethodical, disorderly, chaotic, random, irregular, haphazard, in disarray, confused, muddled, jumbled; lax, slapdash, slipshod, sloppy; informal all over the place; Brit. informal shambolic, all over the shop; N. Amer. informal all over the map, all over the lot.
▷ANTONYMS orderly, organized.

undisguised adjective *he regarded her with undisguised affection*: **obvious**, evident, patent, manifest, transparent, open, overt, unconcealed, unhidden, unrestrained, unmistakable, undeniable, plain, plain to see, as plain as a pikestaff, straightforward, frank, clear, clear-cut, as clear as day, explicit, naked, palpable, visible, recognizable, observable, writ large; blatant, barefaced, flagrant, glaring, bold, bald, stark, pointed, out-and-out, brazen, shameless, audacious; informal as plain as the nose on one's face, standing/sticking out like a sore thumb, standing/sticking out a mile, right under one's nose.
▷ANTONYMS disguised, hidden, imperceptible.

undisputed adjective *his military pre-eminence was undisputed*: **undoubted**, uncontested, unchallenged, unquestioned, not in question, unquestionable, indubitable, not in doubt, incontrovertible, incontestable, unequivocal, undeniable, irrefutable, unmistakable, sure, certain, clear, clear-cut, manifest, decided, definite, confirmed, absolute, accepted, acknowledged, recognized, positive.
▷ANTONYMS disputed, doubtful.

undistinguished adjective *he had an undistinguished career as a lecturer in mathematics*: **run-of-the-mill**, ordinary, middle-of-the-road, average, common, commonplace, everyday, workaday, quotidian, pedestrian, suburban, mundane, mediocre, humdrum, prosaic, lacklustre, unexceptional, indifferent, forgettable, unmemorable, uninspired, unimpressive, unexciting, unspectacular, uneventful, unremarkable, inconsequential, unnoticeable, inconspicuous, characterless, featureless, nondescript, plain, simple, fair, not bad, passable, all right, middling, moderate; hackneyed, trite, jejune; N. Amer. garden-variety; informal nothing special, no big deal, no great shakes, nothing to write home about, nothing to get excited about, not so hot, not up to much, not much cop, OK, okay, so-so, bog standard, (plain) vanilla, fair-to-middling, a dime a dozen; Brit. informal common or garden; N. Amer. informal ornery, bush-league; Austral./NZ informal half-pie.
▷ANTONYMS distinguished, remarkable, extraordinary.

undivided adjective *they need the undivided attention of a sympathetic listener*: **complete**, full, total, whole, entire, out-and-out, absolute, unqualified, unadulterated, unalloyed, unreserved, unmitigated, unshared, unbroken, solid, consistent, thorough, concentrated, exclusive, dedicated, wholehearted, sincere, consummate; undistracted, focused, engrossed, absorbed, attentive, committed.
▷ANTONYMS divided, distracted.

undo verb **1** *Gerald undid another button of his waistcoat*: **unfasten**, unbutton, unhook, untie, unlace; unbind, unfetter, unshackle, unmanacle, unbridle, unlock, unbolt, uncouple, unhitch, unlink, loosen, loose, disentangle, disentwine, extricate, release, detach, free, set free, liberate, open, unseal, unwrap, let out; disconnect, disjoin, disengage, disunite, separate.
▷ANTONYMS fasten, do up.
2 *the British government has just refused to undo a decision by the law lords*: **revoke**, overrule, overturn, repeal, rescind, reverse, retract, take back, rule against, disallow, veto, countermand, cancel, annul, nullify, render null and void, invalidate, render invalid, negate, abrogate, disestablish, make ineffective, set aside, do away with, wipe out, bring to an end; Law avoid, vacate; archaic recall; rare disannul.
▷ANTONYMS ratify.
3 *the action of one individual can undo much of the good work done by others*: **ruin**, undermine, put an end to, put at risk, subvert, overturn, topple, scupper, scotch, sabotage, spoil, mess up, make a mess of, quash, squelch, crush, harm, cripple, impair, mar, destroy, devastate, play havoc with, wreck, smash, shatter, annihilate, eradicate, obliterate, defeat; cancel out, neutralize, render ineffective; thwart, upset, foil, frustrate, hamper, hinder, obstruct; informal botch, blow, put the kibosh on, foul up, muck up, louse up, blow a hole in, do for; Brit. informal cock up, throw a spanner in the works of; N. Amer. informal rain on someone's parade, throw a monkey wrench in the works of; vulgar slang bugger up, fuck up, balls up; archaic bring to naught.
▷ANTONYMS further, enhance, help.

undoing noun **1** *she was constantly plotting the king's undoing*: **downfall**, defeat, conquest, vanquishing, toppling, deposition, ousting, unseating, overthrow, ruin, ruination, destruction, annihilation, elimination, end, collapse, failure, loss of power, debasement; nemesis, Waterloo; rare labefaction.
▷ANTONYMS betterment, preferment.
2 *their complacency was to be their undoing*: **fatal flaw**, Achilles heel, weakness, weak point/spot, (soft) underbelly, failing, blight, misfortune, affliction, trouble, curse.
▷ANTONYMS making.

undone adjective **1** *some improvement work was to be left undone due to the cost*: **unfinished**, incomplete, half-done; not started, not done, unaccomplished, unperformed, unexecuted, unfulfilled, unconcluded, unattended to, omitted, neglected, passed over, disregarded, ignored, left, remaining, outstanding, deferred, pending, on ice, awaiting attention, (up) in the air; informal on the back burner.
▷ANTONYMS finished, complete.
2 *she had lost her one advantage and would be utterly undone*: **defeated**, beaten, foiled, frustrated, thwarted; finished, ruined, destroyed, doomed, lost; informal washed up, done for, toast.
▷ANTONYMS successful, established.

undoubted adjective *there has been an undoubted improvement in VDU design*: **undisputed**, uncontested, unchallenged, unquestioned, not in question, unquestionable, indubitable, not in doubt, incontrovertible, irrefutable, incontestable, unequivocal, sure, certain, obvious, evident,

unmistakable, transparent, manifest, patent; **definite**, confirmed, accepted, acknowledged, recognized, positive, clear-cut.
▷ANTONYMS doubtful, possible.

undoubtedly adverb *they are undoubtedly guilty*: **doubtless**, indubitably, doubtlessly, no doubt, without (a) doubt, beyond (a) doubt, beyond the shadow of a doubt; unquestionably, beyond question, indisputably, undeniably, incontrovertibly, irrefutably; unequivocally, clearly, plainly, obviously, patently, positively, absolutely, certainly, with certainty; decidedly, definitely, surely, assuredly, of course, indeed.
▷ANTONYMS possibly.

undreamed of, undreamt of (Brit.) adjective *he raised the party's profile to undreamed-of heights*: **unexpected**, unforeseen, unanticipated, not bargained for, unhoped-for, unsought, unlooked-for, unpredicted; unintentional, unintended, inadvertent, unplanned, unpremeditated, unwitting, fortuitous, chance, coincidental, serendipitous, random, fluky; sudden, abrupt, surprise, surprising, without warning, without notice, startling, astonishing, out of the blue.
▷ANTONYMS deliberate, planned.

undress verb **1** *he undressed and got into bed*: **take one's clothes off**, strip, strip naked, disrobe, remove one's clothes, doff one's clothes, shed one's clothes, uncover oneself; informal peel off; dated divest oneself of one's clothes.
2 *she undressed the little boy*: **take someone's clothes off**, strip, unclothe, disrobe; dated divest someone of their clothes; literary disarray.
▶ noun *she was wandering about her bedroom in a state of undress*: **nudity**, nakedness, bareness; French déshabillé; informal one's birthday suit.

undressed adjective **1** *he was undressed and ready for bed*: **naked**, nude, stark naked, bare, unclothed, unclad, stripped, denuded, disrobed, undraped, with nothing on, exposed; French au naturel; informal in one's birthday suit, without a stitch on, in the raw, in the altogether, in the buff, in the nuddy, mother naked; Brit. informal starkers; N. Amer. informal bare-assed, buck naked; Brit. vulgar slang bollock-naked.
▷ANTONYMS dressed, clothed.
2 *a rough undressed stone slab*: **untreated**, unprocessed, unprepared, unfinished, raw, rough, natural.

undue adjective *make sure that you can afford the repayments without putting undue strain on your finances*: **excessive**, extreme, immoderate, intemperate, disproportionate, inordinate; fulsome, superfluous, too much, too great; uncalled for, unneeded, unnecessary, non-essential, not required, needless; unwarranted, unjustified, unreasonable; inappropriate, unmerited, unsuitable, unseemly, unbecoming, improper, ill-advised.
▷ANTONYMS due, appropriate, proper.

undulate verb *the land undulates between 200 and 250 feet above sea level* | *dark shapes undulated through the jungle*: **rise and fall**, surge, wave, billow, roll, swell, ripple, heave, flow, wind, swing, whirl, wobble, oscillate.

unduly adverb *that may seem an unduly harsh judgement*: **excessively**, immoderately, intemperately, disproportionately, out of all proportion, inordinately; superfluously, too, overly, overmuch; unnecessarily, needlessly; unwarrantedly, unjustifiably, unreasonably; inappropriately, unsuitably, improperly, ill-advisedly.
▷ANTONYMS duly, appropriately.

undying adjective *his undying devotion to the club*: **abiding**, lasting, enduring, permanent, continuing, constant, perennial, infinite; unceasing, perpetual, ceaseless, incessant, unending, never-ending, unfading; immortal, eternal, deathless, never-dying; indestructible, imperishable, inextinguishable; undiminished, undestroyed; rare sempiternal.
▷ANTONYMS transient, ephemeral; mortal.

unearth verb **1** *workmen unearthed an ancient artillery shell*: **dig up**, excavate, exhume, disinter, bring to the surface, mine, quarry, pull out, root out, scoop out, disentomb, unbury.
▷ANTONYMS bury.
2 *some recent research has unearthed an interesting fact*: **discover**, uncover, find, come across, hit on, strike on, encounter, track down, bring to light, reveal, expose, elicit, turn up, dredge up, ferret out, hunt out, fish out, nose out, sniff out, smell out, take the wraps off.
▷ANTONYMS cover up.

unearthly adjective **1** *there was an unearthly chill in that ghastly chamber*: **other-worldly**, not of this world, supernatural, preternatural, extraterrestrial, alien; ghostly, spectral, phantom, mysterious, haunted, chilling, spine-chilling, hair-raising, blood-curdling; uncanny, eerie, macabre, strange, weird, unnatural, bizarre; Scottish eldritch; informal spooky, creepy, scary; rare phantasmal, phantasmic.
▷ANTONYMS normal, mundane.
2 informal *they rise at some unearthly hour for the long drive*: **unreasonable**, preposterous, abnormal, extraordinary, absurd, ridiculous, horrendous, outrageous, unheard of, out of the ordinary; informal ungodly, unholy, God-awful.
▷ANTONYMS reasonable.

uneasy adjective **1** *the doctor made him feel uneasy*: **worried**, anxious, ill at ease, troubled, disturbed, agitated, nervous, tense, overwrought, keyed up, on edge, edgy, apprehensive, restive, restless, fidgety, discomposed, discomfited, perturbed, alarmed, fearful, fraught, upset; uncomfortable, self-conscious, embarrassed, unsettled; Brit. nervy; informal jittery.
▷ANTONYMS calm, at ease.
2 *he had an uneasy feeling that it was going to cause trouble*: **worrying**, disturbing, troubling, agitating, alarming, dismaying, perturbing, disquieting, unsettling, disconcerting, upsetting.
3 *this victory ensured an uneasy peace for nearly three years*: **tense**, awkward, strained, constrained, forced, fraught, precarious, unstable, insecure.
▷ANTONYMS stable.

uneconomic adjective *it was uneconomic for landlords to maintain rent-controlled housing*: **unprofitable**, uncommercial, unremunerative, non-viable; loss-making, non-paying, non-profit-making, worthless; wasteful, inefficient, unfrugal, improvident, squandering.
▷ANTONYMS economic, profitable.

uneducated adjective *the workforce remains largely uneducated and unskilled*: **untaught**, unschooled, ill-educated, untutored, untrained, unread, unscholarly, illiterate, unlettered, ignorant, ill-informed, uninformed, lowbrow; uncouth, unsophisticated, uncultivated, uncultured, unaccomplished, unenlightened, philistine, benighted, backward, vulgar, simple; archaic rude.
▷ANTONYMS educated, learned.

unemotional adjective *professionals should remain detached and unemotional*: **reserved**, controlled, undemonstrative, restrained, self-controlled, impersonal, clinical, passionless, emotionless, cold, frigid, cool, calm, composed, collected, {cool, calm, and collected}, cool-headed, level-headed, hard-headed, businesslike, rational, sober, unsentimental, unfeeling, unresponsive, unexcitable, unmoved, unagitated, unruffled, serene, impassive, tranquil, indifferent, apathetic, phlegmatic, stoical, equable, detached, distant, remote, aloof, disinterested, unconcerned.
▷ANTONYMS emotional, expressive.

unemployed adjective *he lost his job in February and is still unemployed*: **jobless**, out of work, out of a job, not working, between jobs, workless, unwaged, unoccupied, idle; redundant, laid off, sacked, dismissed; on benefit; Brit. signing on; N. Amer. on welfare, collecting unemployment; Brit. informal on the dole, 'resting'; Austral./NZ informal on the wallaby track.
▷ANTONYMS employed, in work.

unending adjective *she toiled at unending tasks*: **endless**, never-ending, without end; **interminable**, perpetual, eternal, infinite, undying, ceaseless, incessant, unceasing, non-stop, uninterrupted, continuous, continual, constant, persistent, unbroken, abiding, unabating, unremitting, unrelenting, relentless, limitless, boundless.
▷ANTONYMS finite, intermittent.

unendurable adjective *the heat of the stoves made the kitchen almost unendurable*: **intolerable**, unbearable, unacceptable, insufferable, insupportable, not to be borne, more than flesh and blood can stand; oppressive, overwhelming, overpowering, impossible; informal too much.
▷ANTONYMS endurable, bearable.

unenthusiastic adjective *he was unenthusiastic about the proposal*: **indifferent**, apathetic, uninvolved, passive, phlegmatic, half-hearted, lukewarm, tepid, casual, cool, listless, lacklustre, languid, lethargic, offhand, emotionless, cursory, perfunctory, unmoved; informal unenthused; rare Laodicean.
▷ANTONYMS enthusiastic, keen.

Word toolkit **unenthusiastic**

See **unwilling**.

unenviable adjective *he had the unenviable task of trying to reconcile their disparate interests*: **disagreeable**, unpleasant, undesirable, difficult, nasty, horrible, painful, thankless; unwanted, uncoveted, unwished-for.
▷ANTONYMS enviable, desirable.

unequal adjective **1** *they are unequal in length*: **different**, differing, dissimilar, unlike, unalike, unidentical, disparate, not uniform, unmatched, not matching; uneven, unbalanced, asymmetrical, unsymmetrical, lopsided, irregular, random, fluctuating, varying, variable.
▷ANTONYMS equal, identical.
2 *the unequal distribution of wealth*: **unfair**, unjust, random, disproportionate, inequitable, biased, prejudiced.
▷ANTONYMS fair.
3 *the interlopers soon gave up the unequal contest*: **one-sided**, uneven, unfair, unjust, inequitable, ill-matched, unbalanced, lopsided.
▷ANTONYMS equal, fair, evenly balanced, neck and neck.
4 *she suddenly felt* **unequal to** *the task she had set herself*: **inadequate for**, insufficient for, incapable of, unqualified for, unsuited to, unfitted for, incompetent at, not up to, found wanting in; informal not cut out for.
▷ANTONYMS equal, competent.

U

unequalled adjective *an unequalled record of five World Cup victories*: **unbeaten**, unmatched, matchless, unrivalled, without equal, unsurpassed, unparalleled, without parallel, peerless, incomparable, beyond compare, inimitable, second to none, record, best ever, nonpareil, unique; French par excellence.

unequivocal adjective *the report's advice was unequivocal*: **unambiguous**, unmistakable, indisputable, incontrovertible, indubitable, undeniable; clear, clear-cut, crystal clear, plain, well defined, explicit, specific, unqualified, unreserved, categorical, outright, downright, direct, straightforward, blunt, outspoken, candid, point-blank, straight from the shoulder, black and white, positive, certain, decisive, emphatic, absolute, manifest, distinct.
▷ANTONYMS equivocal, ambiguous, vague.

unerring adjective *with unerring accuracy he hit the gold*: **unfailing**, infallible, unswerving, perfect, flawless, faultless, error-free, impeccable, unimpeachable, sure, true, inevitable, assured, certain, uncanny, deadly, scrupulous, meticulous; informal sure-fire, spot on, dead.
▷ANTONYMS fallible, imperfect.

unethical adjective *it is unethical to produce and market a drug which would harm the patient*: **immoral**, amoral, unprincipled, unscrupulous, dishonourable, wrong, dishonest, deceitful, disreputable, unconscionable, fraudulent, dirty, unfair, underhand, devious, slippery, bad, wicked, evil, sinful, iniquitous, corrupt, depraved, villainous; unprofessional, improper, unseemly, unworthy, negligent; informal shady, crooked, not cricket; Brit. informal dodgy.
▷ANTONYMS ethical, acceptable.

uneven adjective **1** *they stumbled over the uneven ground*: **bumpy**, rough, lumpy, stony, rocky, potholed, holey, rutted, rutty, pitted, jagged, cragged, craggy, dented, indented, knobby.
▷ANTONYMS even, flat, smooth.
2 *her uneven yellow teeth*: **irregular**, unequal, differing, dissimilar, unlike, unalike, unidentical, unbalanced, lopsided, awry, askew, crooked, asymmetrical, unsymmetrical, disproportionate, not matching.
▷ANTONYMS even, regular.
3 *an uneven double album*: **inconsistent**, variable, varying, changeable, fluctuating, intermittent, wavering, irregular, erratic, patchy, bitty.
▷ANTONYMS consistent.
4 *an uneven contest | the uneven distribution of land*: **one-sided**, unequal, unfair, unjust, inequitable, ill-matched, unbalanced, lopsided; biased, prejudiced, skewed.
▷ANTONYMS equal, fair.
5 *an uneven number*: **odd**, not divisible by two.
▷ANTONYMS even.

uneventful adjective *a place where dull people live uneventful lives*: **unexciting**, uninteresting, monotonous, unchanging, boring, dull, tedious, slow, flat, humdrum, routine, bland, insipid, unvaried, ordinary, run-of-the-mill, pedestrian, commonplace, everyday, mundane, predictable, unexceptional, unremarkable, uninspiring, unmemorable.
▷ANTONYMS eventful, exciting.

Word toolkit **uneventful**

See **insipid**.

unexceptional adjective *an adequate but unexceptional hotel*: **ordinary**, average, typical, common, everyday, run-of-the-mill, middle-of-the-road, stock, mediocre, so-so, pedestrian, unremarkable, undistinguished, indifferent, unimpressive; adequate, acceptable, tolerable, decent, unpretentious; informal OK, nothing special, nothing to write home about, no great shakes, not much cop, fair-to-middling, bog standard.
▷ANTONYMS exceptional, noteworthy.

Easily confused words **unexceptional or unexceptionable?**

The clear distinction in meaning between *exceptionable* ('open to objection') and *exceptional* ('out of the ordinary; very good') has become blurred in the negative forms **unexceptionable** and **unexceptional**. Strictly speaking, *unexceptionable* means 'not open to objection', as in *this view is unexceptionable in itself*, while *unexceptional* means 'not outstanding', as in *the hotel was adequate but unexceptional*. However, *unexceptionable* is often used in contexts where it could equally well mean 'ordinary', as in *the food was bland and unexceptionable*.

unexpected adjective *he received an unexpected invitation from Professor Dobson*: **unforeseen**, unanticipated, unpredicted, not bargained for, unlooked for, unhoped for, out of the blue, without warning, without notice; chance, fortuitous, unplanned, serendipitous, adventitious; sudden, abrupt, surprising, startling, astonishing, uncommon, abnormal, extraordinary.
▷ANTONYMS expected, predictable.

unexpressive adjective *his big brown eyes were dull and unexpressive*: **emotionless**, expressionless, inexpressive, blank, vacant, impassive, inscrutable, deadpan.
▷ANTONYMS expressive.

unfailing adjective *he was remembered for his modesty and his unfailing good humour*: **constant**, reliable, dependable, steadfast, steady, sure; endless, undying, unfading, inexhaustible, boundless, ceaseless, never-failing, infallible.
▷ANTONYMS ephemeral; unreliable.

unfair adjective **1** *an unfair trial*: **unjust**, inequitable, prejudiced, biased, discriminatory; preferential, one-sided, unequal, uneven, unbalanced, non-objective, partisan, partial, intolerant, bigoted, coloured, distorted, warped, loaded, weighted, slanted.
▷ANTONYMS fair, just.
2 *his comments were excessive and unfair*: **undeserved**, unmerited, uncalled for, unreasonable, unjustified, unjustifiable, unwarrantable, out of proportion, disproportionate, excessive, extreme, immoderate; informal a bit much; Brit. informal off, a bit thick.
▷ANTONYMS fair, justified.
3 *unfair play*: **unsporting**, foul, unsportsmanlike, dirty, below the belt, illegal, illegitimate, illicit, underhand, unscrupulous, dishonourable; informal crooked, low-down.
▷ANTONYMS fair, sporting.
4 *I'm being unfair, prattling on like this when you need your rest*: **inconsiderate**, thoughtless, insensitive, selfish, mean, unkind, unreasonable, uncharitable, unfeeling, callous.

unfaithful adjective **1** *she found out that her husband had been unfaithful*: **adulterous**, faithless, fickle, untrue, inconstant, flighty; informal cheating, two-timing.
▷ANTONYMS faithful.
2 *you have proved to be an unfaithful member of this community*: **disloyal**, treacherous, traitorous, untrustworthy, unreliable, undependable, false, false-hearted, faithless, perfidious, insincere, two-faced, back-stabbing, double-crossing, double-dealing, deceitful; archaic recreant.
▷ANTONYMS loyal.

Word toolkit

unfaithful	disloyal	seditious
wife/husband	subject	conspiracy
boyfriend/girlfriend	friend	act
lover	citizen	literature
partner	employee	ideas

unfaltering adjective *he moved with an unfaltering step*: **steady**, resolute, resolved, firm, steadfast, fixed, decided, unswerving, unfluctuating, unhesitating, unwavering, unvacillating, untiring, tireless, unflagging, indefatigable, persistent, unyielding, relentless, unremitting, unrelenting, sustained, inexorable, unshakeable.
▷ANTONYMS faltering, unsteady.

unfamiliar adjective **1** *a part of the city unfamiliar to him*: **unknown**, new, strange, queer, foreign, alien, unheard of, beyond someone's ken.
▷ANTONYMS familiar.
2 *the unfamiliar sound of a Scottish dance band*: **unusual**, uncommon, unconventional, novel, different, exotic, alternative, unorthodox, odd, peculiar, curious, atypical, uncharacteristic, unwonted, abnormal, anomalous, aberrant, out of the ordinary.
▷ANTONYMS common.
3 *the aim is to encourage investors* ***unfamiliar with*** *the stock market to trade more freely*: **unacquainted with**, unused to, unaccustomed to, unconversant with, unpractised in, inexperienced in, unskilled in, unversed in, uninformed about, unenlightened about, ignorant of, uninitiated in, new to, fresh to, strange to, a stranger to, unaware of; informal in the dark about; rare nescient of.
▷ANTONYMS conversant.

Word toolkit

unfamiliar	novel	exotic
territory	idea	species
voice	approach	plants
surroundings	method	places
faces	solution	birds
situation	use	destinations
feeling	technique	fruit
language	technology	pets
landscape	insight	lands
streets	treatment	spices
sounds	theory	diseases

unfashionable adjective *unfashionable clothes*: **out of fashion**, out of date, outdated, old-fashioned, outmoded, out of style, dated, behind the times, last year's, yesterday's, unpopular, unstylish, superseded, archaic,

obsolete, antiquated; bygone, old-fangled, crusty, olde worlde, prehistoric, antediluvian; French passé, démodé; informal old hat, out, square, out of the ark.
▷ANTONYMS fashionable.

unfasten verb *Ron unfastened his seat belt*: **undo**, open, detach, disconnect, remove, untie, unbutton, unzip, loose, loosen, free, separate, disengage, disjoin, uncouple, unwrap, unbind, unhook, unlace, unhitch, untether, unlock, unbolt.
▷ANTONYMS fasten, do something up, lock.

unfathomable adjective **1** *the dark unfathomable eyes of a stranger*: **inscrutable**, incomprehensible, enigmatic, incalculable, indecipherable, obscure, esoteric, abstruse, puzzling, cryptic, mysterious, mystifying, baffling, deep, profound, secretive.
▷ANTONYMS comprehensible, penetrable.
2 *a pool of dark, unfathomable water*: **deep**, immeasurable, fathomless, unfathomed, unplumbed, unplumbable, bottomless, unsounded, profound.
▷ANTONYMS shallow.

unfavourable adjective **1** *his poor turnout received unfavourable comment*: **adverse**, critical, hostile, inimical, unfriendly, antagonistic, unsympathetic, negative; opposing, ill-disposed, contrary, discouraging, disapproving, uncomplimentary, unflattering, damaging, injurious, poor, low, bad, antipathetic.
▷ANTONYMS favourable, positive.
2 *the unfavourable economic climate*: **disadvantageous**, adverse, inauspicious, unpropitious, unfortunate, unlucky, unhappy, detrimental, bad, gloomy; unsuitable, inappropriate, inconvenient, inopportune, inapt.
▷ANTONYMS favourable, advantageous.

unfeeling adjective *my mother is a cold, unfeeling, and unresponsive woman*: **uncaring**, unsympathetic, unemotional, unfriendly, uncharitable; hard-hearted, stony-hearted, with a heart of stone, heartless, hard, harsh, austere, cold, cold-blooded, cold-hearted, callous, cruel, severe, pitiless, ruthless, unforgiving, unpitying, inhumane, brutal, sadistic, inhuman; informal hard-boiled, hard-nosed, thick-skinned.
▷ANTONYMS sympathetic, compassionate.

unfeigned adjective *he looked at his wife with unfeigned admiration*: **sincere**, genuine, real, true, honest, authentic, unaffected, unpretended, unforced, uncontrived, artless, candid, frank, bona fide, earnest, heartfelt, wholehearted, deep, from the heart; informal pukka, upfront, on the level; rare full-hearted.
▷ANTONYMS insincere, feigned, pretended.

> *Choose the right word* **unfeigned, sincere, genuine, unaffected**
>
> See **sincere**.

unfettered adjective *the choice between a planned economy and an unfettered market*: **unrestrained**, unrestricted, unconstrained, free, unbridled, untrammelled, unchecked, unconfined, unimpeded, unhampered, uncontrolled, unbound, untied, unchained, unshackled, loose.
▷ANTONYMS restricted, fettered.

unfinished adjective **1** *an unfinished essay*: **incomplete**, uncompleted, truncated, aborted; partial, undone, half-done, unexecuted, undeveloped, deferred, put off, abandoned; imperfect, unaccomplished, immature, defective, deficient, lacking, wanting, unpolished, unrefined, sketchy, fragmentary, patchy, rough, crude.
▷ANTONYMS finished, complete.
2 *the door can be supplied unfinished for you to paint yourself*: **unpainted**, unvarnished, undressed, untreated, unprocessed, unprepared, raw, rough, natural.
▷ANTONYMS finished, painted.

unfit adjective **1** *the video has been deemed* ***unfit for*** *broadcast | a medical board found him* ***unfit for*** *duty*: **unsuitable for**, unsuited to, inappropriate to, ill-suited to, ill-adapted to, unequipped for, inadequate for, unprepared for, unfitted for, not designed for, ineligible for, unworthy of; **incapable of**, incompetent at, unable to do something, not up to, not equal to, not good enough for; unqualified for, untrained for; improper, unbecoming; informal not cut out for, not up to scratch.
▷ANTONYMS fit, suitable, capable.
2 *unfit and overweight children*: **unhealthy**, out of condition, out of shape, in poor condition, in poor shape, flabby, debilitated, weak, infirm, decrepit.
▷ANTONYMS fit.

unflagging adjective *an unflagging commitment to the ideals of peace*: **tireless**, persistent, dogged, tenacious, determined, resolute, staunch, single-minded, unremitting, unrelenting, unswerving, unfaltering, unfailing, unending, zealous.
▷ANTONYMS flagging, inconstant.

unflappable adjective informal *I prided myself on being unflappable even in the most chaotic circumstances*: **imperturbable**, unexcitable, cool, calm, collected, {cool, calm, and collected}, controlled, self-controlled, self-possessed, cool-headed, level-headed, relaxed, insouciant, serene, stoical, phlegmatic, unmoved; informal laid-back, together.
▷ANTONYMS excitable.

unflattering adjective **1** *an unflattering review of his new book*: **unfavourable**, uncomplimentary, harsh, unsympathetic, critical, attacking, hostile, disapproving, scathing, biting; blunt, candid, honest, stark, realistic, straightforward, outspoken, straight from the shoulder; informal warts and all.
▷ANTONYMS flattering, complimentary.
2 *I wore an unflattering dress*: **unattractive**, unbecoming, unsightly, ugly, ugly-looking, plain, hideous; ill-fitting, unsuitable, unsuited, ill-suited.
▷ANTONYMS flattering, becoming.

unflinching adjective *they stood together in unflinching determination to win*: **resolute**, determined, single-minded, dogged, decided, resolved, firm, persistent, persevering, committed, unshrinking, unshakeable, steady, unwavering, unblinking, immoveable, unflagging, unswerving, unfaltering, untiring, undaunted, fearless, courageous, stalwart.
▷ANTONYMS unsteady, wavering.

unfold verb **1** *Ma unfolded the evening paper*: **open out**, spread out, stretch out, flatten, straighten out, unfurl, unroll, unravel, uncoil, unwind, extend.
▷ANTONYMS fold up.
2 *as she unfolded her tale Joanna's face fell*: **narrate**, relate, recount, tell, reveal, make known, disclose, divulge, present, communicate, report, recite, portray, elaborate, spell out, give an account of, set forth, set out.
3 *I watched the events unfold*: **develop**, evolve, happen, take place, occur, transpire, unroll, emerge, grow, progress, mature, work out, untangle, bear fruit, blossom.

unforeseen adjective *due to unforeseen circumstances*: **unpredicted**, unexpected, unanticipated, unplanned, accidental, unlooked for, unsought, not bargained for, unthought of; sudden, abrupt, surprising, startling, astonishing, abnormal, out of the blue.
▷ANTONYMS expected, predictable.

unforgettable adjective *a visit to Morocco is a truly unforgettable experience*: **memorable**, indelible, not/never to be forgotten, fixed in the mind, haunting, catchy, persistent; striking, impressive, distinctive, significant, special, outstanding, spectacular, extraordinary, exceptional, remarkable, arresting, singular, signal.
▷ANTONYMS forgettable, unexceptional.

unforgivable adjective *he had committed the unforgivable sin—he had informed on his friends*: **inexcusable**, unpardonable, unjustifiable, indefensible, reprehensible, outrageous, deplorable, insupportable, despicable, contemptible, disgraceful, shameful; inexpiable, irremissible, unwarrantable, condemnable; mortal, deadly.
▷ANTONYMS forgivable, unserious; venial.

unfortunate adjective **1** *today, many unfortunate people have too much enforced leisure*: **unlucky**, hapless, out of luck, down on one's luck, luckless, wretched, miserable, forlorn, unhappy, poor, pitiful; ill-starred, ill-fated, ill-omened, star-crossed, jinxed, cursed, doomed.
▷ANTONYMS fortunate, lucky.
2 *it was a very unfortunate chain of circumstances*: **adverse**, disadvantageous, unadvantageous, unfavourable, unlucky, untoward, unwelcome; untimely, unpromising, inauspicious, unpropitious, hostile, tough, hard, inimical, harmful, detrimental, injurious, ruinous, disastrous, calamitous, dire, miserable, distressing, grievous, black, lamentable, tragic, terrible, awful, wretched.
▷ANTONYMS fortunate, auspicious.
3 *an unfortunate remark*: **regrettable**, inappropriate, unsuitable, inapt, infelicitous, tactless, untoward, injudicious.
▷ANTONYMS tactful, appropriate.

> *Choose the right word* **unfortunate, unlucky, ill-starred, hapless**
>
> These words all express a recognition that something undesirable and probably undeserved has happened to someone, with some degree of sympathy for them. All but *hapless* can describe the event, as well as the person to whom it happens.
>
> **Unfortunate** is used to acknowledge the unpleasantness of a situation (*the unfortunate Cunningham was sacked | we are just glad the whole unfortunate episode has had a happy ending*). *Unfortunate* can also be used of a regrettable event or situation, often euphemistically ascribing blame (*the Judge was severely reprimanded for a number of unfortunate remarks made by him*).
>
> Describing someone as **unlucky** lays some emphasis on the element of chance involved in their misfortune (*John and Alison were one of the unlucky couples to have their wedding cancelled | a series of unlucky breakdowns curtailed his career*). *Unlucky* is often used of people who are unsuccessful despite their best efforts (*Cooper was unlucky, coming 11th*).
>
> **Ill-starred** is seldom found outside self-consciously literary writing and is the only one of these four words to retain any significant sense of fate, with which

the stars are often associated; it means 'doomed from the outset' (*Scott's ill-starred Polar expedition | none of my ill-starred relations has ever died by the gun*).

The pity expressed for a **hapless** person is sometimes tinged with amusement or exasperation. It is strongly hinted that they have contributed to their own misfortune through incompetence or weakness (*a powerful cross which the hapless Robinson diverted into his own net | some documents were lost by hapless temps*). The similarity in sound of 'hopeless' and 'helpless' may have played a part in the development of this implication. Often, the victim's inability to improve their plight is emphasized (*the hapless victims of some depraved international conspiracy*).

unfortunately adverb *unfortunately, when my husband mentioned this to his mother all hell broke loose*: **unluckily**, sadly, regrettably, unhappily, woefully, lamentably, alas, sad to say, sad to relate; informal worse luck.
▷ANTONYMS luckily.

unfounded adjective *the article was a piece of unfounded speculation*: **groundless**, baseless, unsubstantiated, unproven, unsupported, uncorroborated, untested, unconfirmed, unverified, unattested, unjustified, unwarranted, foundationless, ill-founded, without basis, without foundation, not backed up by evidence; speculative, conjectural, idle, vain, unsound, unreliable, questionable, misinformed, misguided, spurious, specious, fallacious, erroneous, fabricated, untrue, trumped-up.
▷ANTONYMS well founded, proven, substantiated.

unfriendly adjective **1** *she directed an unfriendly look at Harold*: **hostile**, disagreeable, misanthropic, antagonistic, aggressive; ill-natured, unpleasant, surly, sour, inimical, unamicable, uncongenial; inhospitable, unneighbourly, unwelcoming, unkind, unsympathetic, unaffable; unsociable, unsocial, antisocial; aloof, cold, cool, chilly, frigid, frosty, distant, stand-offish, unapproachable; withdrawn, reserved, unforthcoming, uncommunicative, impersonal, haughty, supercilious, disdainful, indifferent; stiff, stern, severe; ungracious, obnoxious, menacing, nasty; quarrelsome; rude, discourteous, uncivil, impolite, unmannerly, cross; informal starchy; rare Olympian.
▷ANTONYMS friendly, amiable.
2 *Mesopotamia was discovered to be unfriendly terrain for military manoeuvres*: **unfavourable**, disadvantageous, unpropitious, inauspicious, hostile, inimical, uncongenial, negative, alien, damaging, destructive.
▷ANTONYMS friendly, favourable.

ungainly adjective *an uncouth man with an ungainly walk*: **awkward**, **clumsy**, ungraceful, graceless, inelegant, gawky, gangling, maladroit, gauche, inept, blundering, bungling, bumbling, lumbering, uncoordinated; inexpert, unskilful, unhandy, oafish, bovine, like a bull in a china shop; informal cack-handed, ham-fisted, ham-handed, butterfingered, all thumbs, hulking; archaic lubberly.
▷ANTONYMS graceful, elegant.

ungodly adjective **1** *blasphemy, whoredom, drunkenness, and other ungodly behaviour*: **unholy**, godless, irreligious, impious, blasphemous, sacrilegious, profane, heathen, pagan, atheistic, irreverent; immoral, corrupt, depraved, sinful, wicked, evil, iniquitous, devilish, fiendish, demonic, diabolical, satanic, infernal.
▷ANTONYMS godly, holy.
2 informal *he wasn't expecting her at this ungodly hour*: **unreasonable**, preposterous, abnormal, extraordinary, absurd, ridiculous, horrendous, outrageous, unheard of; unsocial, antisocial; informal unholy, unearthly, God-awful.
▷ANTONYMS reasonable.

ungovernable adjective *the country had become ungovernable*: **uncontrollable**, unmanageable, anarchic, chaotic, intractable; unruly, disorderly, rebellious, riotous, wild, mutinous, obstreperous, recalcitrant, refractory, undisciplined, disobedient; without law and order.
▷ANTONYMS orderly, tractable.

ungracious adjective *it was ungracious not to thank them*: **rude**, impolite, uncivil, discourteous, ill-mannered, bad-mannered, unmannerly, uncouth, disrespectful, ungallant, insolent, impertinent, impudent, churlish, boorish, gauche, cavalier, offhand, unladylike, ungentlemanly, blunt, gruff, curt, terse, sharp, short, surly, unfriendly, hostile, unkind, inconsiderate, insensitive.
▷ANTONYMS gracious, polite.

ungrateful adjective *she's so rude and ungrateful for everything we do*: **unappreciative**, unthankful, thankless, ungracious.
▷ANTONYMS grateful, thankful.

unguarded adjective **1** *an unguarded frontier*: **undefended**, unprotected, defenceless, unfortified, unshielded, unarmed; vulnerable, insecure, assailable, open to attack, wide open, exposed, in danger, endangered; unpatrolled, unattended, unwatched; rare pregnable.
▷ANTONYMS guarded, secure.
2 *an unguarded remark*: **careless**, ill-advised, ill-considered, incautious, thoughtless, unthinking, rash, foolhardy, foolish, indiscreet, imprudent, injudicious, ill-judged, ill-thought-out, unthought-out, unwise; undiplomatic, misguided, hasty, spur-of-the-moment, hare-brained, inadvertent, insensitive; rare temerarious.
3 *in an unguarded moment, Iris had let drop that she was receiving no fee to run the course*: **unwary**, inattentive, unobservant, off guard, unmindful, unwatchful, unheeding, heedless, distracted, absent-minded.

unhappiness noun *I've seen too much unhappiness caused by broken marriages*: **sadness**, sorrow, dejection, depression, misery, cheerlessness, downheartedness, despondency, despair, desolation, wretchedness, malaise, glumness, gloom, gloominess, dolefulness; regret, melancholy, low spirits, mournfulness, woe, broken-heartedness, heartache, distress, chagrin, grief, pain, agony, mortification; informal the blues, down; rare disconsolateness, disconsolation.

unhappy adjective **1** *an unhappy childhood | she looked tired and unhappy*: **sad**, miserable, sorrowful, dejected, despondent, disconsolate, morose, regretful, broken-hearted, heartbroken, down, downcast, dispirited, downhearted, heavy-hearted, crestfallen, depressed, melancholy, blue, gloomy, glum, mournful, despairing, doleful, forlorn, woebegone, woeful, tearful, long-faced, joyless, cheerless, out of sorts; informal down in the mouth, down in the dumps, fed up, grumpy; rare lachrymose.
▷ANTONYMS happy, cheerful.
2 *in the unhappy event of litigation*: **unfortunate**, unlucky, luckless, hapless, ill-starred, ill-fated, star-crossed, ill-omened, doomed, blighted, wretched, miserable; disadvantageous, adverse; informal jinxed.
3 *if you are **unhappy with** a new hairstyle, complain to your hairdresser while you are still in the salon*: **dissatisfied**, displeased, discontented, disappointed, disgruntled; disapproving of.
4 *indeed, 'disorganized capitalism' seems an unhappy term for conveying what they are dealing with*: **inappropriate**, unsuitable, inapt, unfortunate; regrettable, ill-chosen, tactless, ill-advised, injudicious; awkward, clumsy.

unharmed adjective **1** *negotiators persuaded the man to release his hostage unharmed*: **uninjured**, unhurt, unscathed, safe, safe and sound, alive and well, all right, fine, in one piece, without a scratch; informal OK.
▷ANTONYMS harmed, injured.
2 *the saint's tomb was a grey and time-worn block unharmed by the Reformation*: **undamaged**, unbroken, unmarred, unspoilt, unsullied, unmarked, unmutilated; sound, intact, perfect, unimpaired, unblemished, unflawed, pristine.
▷ANTONYMS harmed, damaged.

unhealthy adjective **1** *she was leading a very unhealthy lifestyle*: **harmful**, detrimental, destructive, injurious, damaging, deleterious, ruinous, malign, noxious, poisonous, insalubrious, baleful; risky, dangerous, perilous.
2 *he had a bony face and an unhealthy pallor*: **ill-looking**, ill, unwell, in poor health, ailing, sick, sickly, poorly, indisposed, unsound, unfit, weak, feeble, frail, delicate, debilitated, infirm, valetudinarian, washed out, run down, peaky, out of condition/shape, in poor condition/shape.
3 *he had an unhealthy obsession with drugs*: **unwholesome**, undesirable, morbid, macabre, ghoulish, twisted, warped, depraved, abnormal, unnatural; informal sick.

unheard of adjective **1** *in those days it was unheard of for a girl to leave her family and become independent*: **unprecedented**, exceptional, extraordinary, out of the ordinary, uncommon, unusual, unparalleled, unrivalled, unmatched, unequalled, singular, unique; unthought of, undreamt of, unbelievable, inconceivable, unimagined, unimaginable, unthinkable, implausible, shocking, outrageous; rare unexampled.
▷ANTONYMS common.
2 *we were to play a game unheard of in the UK*: **unknown**, unfamiliar, new, little known, undiscovered, obscure, nameless, unsung, unheralded, groundbreaking.
▷ANTONYMS famous, well known.

unheeded adjective *my protest went unheeded*: **disregarded**, ignored, neglected, overlooked, unobserved, unnoted, unrecognized, disobeyed, unnoticed, passed over, spurned.
▷ANTONYMS heeded, noted.

unhinged adjective *Lydia was unhinged with the shock of bereavement*: **deranged**, demented, unbalanced, out of one's mind, crazed, mad, insane; lunatic, manic, maniac, berserk, disturbed, distracted, confused; informal crazy, mental, potty, bonkers, bats, batty, loopy, bananas, touched, out to lunch, off one's head, off one's rocker.
▷ANTONYMS sane, stable.

unholy adjective **1** *a grin of unholy amusement spread across his face*: **ungodly**, godless, irreligious, impious, blasphemous, sacrilegious, profane, heathen, pagan, atheistic, irreverent; **wicked**, evil, iniquitous, immoral, corrupt, depraved, sinful, devilish, fiendish, demonic, diabolical, satanic, infernal.
▷ANTONYMS righteous, holy.
2 *she'd had an unholy row with Mama*: **shocking**, dreadful, outrageous, appalling, terrible, horrifying, horrendous, horrific, frightful; informal ungodly.
▷ANTONYMS mild.

3 *an unholy alliance between art and commerce had sprung up*: **unnatural**, discordant, incompatible, unusual, improbable; hellish, made in hell.

unhoped for adjective *he had given her an unhoped-for opportunity to go on in a big part*: **unexpected**, unanticipated, unforeseen, unpredicted, unlooked-for, unplanned, not bargained for, without warning, without notice; **undreamed of**, out of the blue, beyond one's wildest dreams, like a dream come true; startling, astonishing, surprising, unbelievable.
▷ANTONYMS expected; unwanted.

unhurried adjective *he began opening the drawers of his desk in an unhurried way*: **leisurely**, unhasty, leisured, easy, easy-going, relaxed, unrushed, slow, slow-moving, slow-going, slow and steady; deliberate, careful, cautious, sedate, measured, calm; gradual, lingering, loitering.
▷ANTONYMS hurried, hasty.

unhygienic adjective *animals are kept in cramped and often unhygienic conditions*: **insanitary**, unsanitary, dirty, filthy, unclean, impure, contaminated, unhealthy, deleterious, detrimental, harmful, unwholesome, germ-ridden, germy, disease-ridden, infested, insalubrious, noxious, polluted, foul, septic.
▷ANTONYMS hygienic, sanitary.

unidentified adjective *he had been followed by unidentified armed men*: **unknown**, unnamed, anonymous, incognito, nameless; obscure, unfamiliar, strange, mysterious, unspecified, unmarked, undesignated, unclassified; rare innominate.
▷ANTONYMS identified, known.

unification noun *the costs of German unification*: **union**, merger, fusion, fusing, amalgamation, integration, coalition, junction, combination, consolidation, confederation, federation; synthesis, joining, marrying, marriage; Greek enosis.

uniform adjective 1 *a uniform temperature of between 18 and 21 degrees*: **constant**, consistent, steady, invariable, unvarying, unfluctuating, unvaried, unchanging, unwavering, undeviating, stable, static, sustained, regular, fixed, even, equal, equable, monotonous.
▷ANTONYMS changeable, variable.
2 *cut the vegetables into pieces of uniform size*: **identical**, matching, similar, equal; **same**, alike, like, selfsame, homogeneous, consistent, corresponding, equivalent.
▷ANTONYMS varied, different.
▶ noun *a soldier in uniform*: **costume**, livery, regalia, habit, suit, dress, garb, attire, ensemble, outfit; regimentals, colours, garments, trappings; informal get-up, rig, gear, togs; formal apparel; literary raiment; archaic vestments.

uniformity noun 1 *Philip moved to establish greater uniformity in urban law*: **constancy**, consistency, conformity, steadiness, invariability, invariableness, stability, regularity, evenness, lack of variation, lack of change, equality, equability.
▷ANTONYMS variation, changeableness.
2 *there seems to be no uniformity in the size of clothes in shops*: **sameness**, likeness, resemblance, alikeness, identicalness, similarity, equality, equalness, homogeneity, homogeneousness, consistency, equivalence, comparability, compatibility, correspondence, agreement, concord, accord, interchangeability, parallelism, symmetry.
▷ANTONYMS variety, difference.
3 *there was a dull uniformity about the place*: **monotony**, tedium, tediousness, lack of variety, dullness, drabness, dreariness, colourlessness, flatness, featurelessness, sameness, humdrumness; Brit. informal sameyness.
▷ANTONYMS diversity, variety.

unify verb *he unified the confederacy into a powerful entity*: **unite**, bring together, join (together), merge, fuse, amalgamate, coalesce, combine, blend, mix, bind, link up, consolidate, integrate, marry, synthesize, federate, weld together.
▷ANTONYMS separate, split, disunite.

unimaginable adjective *unimaginable riches*: **unthinkable**, inconceivable, incredible, unbelievable, unheard of, unthought of, unspeakable, unutterable, untold, ineffable, implausible, improbable, unlikely, impossible, undreamed of, beyond one's wildest dreams, beyond the realm of reason; astounding, amazing, astonishing, fantastic, fabulous, breathtaking, overwhelming, staggering; informal mind-boggling, mind-blowing.

unimaginative adjective *the production was plodding and unimaginative*: **uninspired**, uninventive, unoriginal, uncreative, unartistic, commonplace, pedestrian, mundane, matter-of-fact, ordinary, usual, routine, humdrum, prosaic, workaday, run of the mill, (plain) vanilla; stale, hackneyed, trite, derived, derivative, conventional, unadventurous, dull, banal, monotonous, lifeless, lacklustre, sterile, uninspiring, spiritless, vapid, insipid, bland, dry, barren, flat, stodgy; informal common or garden.
▷ANTONYMS imaginative, creative, original.

unimpeachable adjective *this was information that I got from an unimpeachable source*: **trustworthy**, reliable, dependable, unquestionable, unassailable, unchallengeable, above suspicion, beyond suspicion; perfect, faultless, blameless, impeccable, irreproachable, unblemished.
▷ANTONYMS dubious, unreliable.

unimpeded adjective *he had an unimpeded view of them*: **unrestricted**, unconstrained, unhindered, unblocked, unhampered, free, open, clear, unchecked, uninhibited, untrammelled, unlimited.
▷ANTONYMS impeded, obstructed.

unimportant adjective *the details are unimportant at this stage*: **insignificant**, inconsequential, trivial, minor, slight, trifling, of little/no importance, of little/no consequence, of no account, of no moment, non-essential, immaterial, irrelevant, peripheral, extraneous, not worth mentioning, not worth speaking of, petty, paltry, insubstantial, light, inconsiderable, superficial, inferior, worthless, nugatory, pointless, frivolous; informal small-time, piddling, small-fry, no great shakes; Brit. informal twopenny-halfpenny, tinpot; N. Amer. informal dinky, picayune.
▷ANTONYMS important.

> *Word toolkit* **unimportant**
>
> See **minor**.

uninformed adjective *they prey upon uninformed buyers*: **unenlightened**, uneducated, unknowledgeable, untaught, unlearned, unread, ignorant.
▷ANTONYMS enlightened.

> *Word toolkit* **uninformed**
>
> See **ignorant**.

uninhabited adjective 1 *much of this land was uninhabited*: **unpopulated**, unpeopled, unsettled, unfrequented, unoccupied; barren, desert, desolate, lonely, deserted, depopulated, bare, wild.
2 *an uninhabited hut*: **vacant**, empty, unoccupied, untenanted, tenantless, unfilled, to let, free; abandoned, deserted, forsaken.

uninhibited adjective 1 *the uninhibited dancing of the local people*: **unrestrained**, unrepressed, abandoned, wild, impetuous, carefree, reckless; unrestricted, unconstrained, uncontrolled, uncurbed, unchecked, unbridled, intemperate, boisterous, wanton.
▷ANTONYMS inhibited, controlled.
2 *I'm a pretty uninhibited sort of person*: **unreserved**, unrepressed, liberated, unconstrained, unselfconscious, free and easy, relaxed, informal, open, outgoing, extrovert, candid, outspoken, frank, forthright, spontaneous, instinctive, shameless; informal upfront.
▷ANTONYMS inhibited, reserved, repressed.

uninspired adjective *an album full of uninspired love songs*: **unimaginative**, uninventive, pedestrian, mundane, unoriginal, prosaic, commonplace, ordinary, routine, second-rate, undistinguished, unexceptional, indifferent, humdrum, matter-of-fact, run of the mill, workaday, everyday, quotidian, (plain) vanilla; **spiritless**, colourless, passionless, anaemic, stale, hackneyed, trite, derived, derivative, conventional, unadventurous, dull, banal, monotonous, lifeless, lacklustre, sterile, uninspiring, vapid, insipid, bland, dry, barren, flat, stodgy; informal common or garden.
▷ANTONYMS inspired.

uninspiring adjective *they remained a weak and uninspiring political force*: **boring**, dull, dreary, drab, unexciting, unstimulating; dry, insipid, colourless, grey, bland, anaemic, watery, tame, flat, lifeless, lacklustre, tedious, vapid, humdrum, run of the mill, unromantic, jejune, dull as ditchwater, as dry as dust.
▷ANTONYMS inspiring, exciting.

unintelligent adjective *he treated me like an erring and somewhat unintelligent son*: **stupid**, ignorant, dense, brainless, mindless, foolish, dull-witted, witless, slow, dunce-like, simple-minded, empty-headed, vacuous, vapid, half-witted, idiotic, moronic, imbecilic, imbecile, obtuse; informal thick, thick as two short planks, dim, dumb, dopey, dozy, cretinous, birdbrained, pea-brained, wooden-headed, fat-headed.
▷ANTONYMS intelligent.

unintelligible adjective 1 *jargon words usually sound ugly and unintelligible to outsiders*: **incomprehensible**, indiscernible, meaningless, unfathomable, obscure, cryptic, inscrutable, enigmatic, mumbled, indistinct, unclear, slurred, inarticulate, incoherent, confused, garbled, scrambled, muddled, jumbled, senseless; informal all Greek to me.
2 *unintelligible graffiti*: **illegible**, indecipherable, unreadable, hard to read, scrawled, scribbled, crabbed.

unintentional adjective *I assure you, the insult was unintentional*: **unintended**, accidental, inadvertent, involuntary, unwitting, unthinking, unmeant, unplanned, unpremeditated, unexpected, unforeseen, fortuitous, chance, coincidental, serendipitous, unconscious, subconscious.
▷ANTONYMS intentional, deliberate.

> *Word toolkit* **unintentional**
>
> See **spontaneous**.

U

uninterested adjective *Derek was uninterested in politics*: **indifferent to**, unconcerned about, uninvolved in/with, incurious about, apathetic towards, bored by, unmoved by, unresponsive to, blasé about, nonchalant about, offhand about, lukewarm about, unenthusiastic about, phlegmatic about; impassive, dispassionate; aloof from, detached from, distant from.
▶ANTONYMS interested.

Easily confused words **uninterested or disinterested?**

See **disinterested**.

uninteresting adjective *an uninteresting book about genealogy*: **unexciting**, boring, dull, tiresome, wearisome, tedious, dreary, tiring, flat, lifeless, monotonous, humdrum, uneventful, slow, unvaried, repetitious, commonplace, colourless, bland, insipid, banal, dry, pedestrian, prosaic, hackneyed, trite, clichéd, stale; informal samey, mind-numbing.
▶ANTONYMS interesting, exciting.

uninterrupted adjective *ten hours of uninterrupted sleep*: **unbroken**, continuous, continual, undisturbed, steady, constant, sustained, consecutive, successive, in succession, non-stop, without stopping, unceasing, incessant, untroubled, smooth, peaceful; running, solid, straight.
▶ANTONYMS interrupted, intermittent.

uninvited adjective **1** *an uninvited guest*: **unasked**, unbidden, unwelcome, unwanted, unexpected.
▶ANTONYMS invited.
2 *uninvited suggestions*: **unsolicited**, unrequested, unwanted, not required, unprompted, unsought.
▶ANTONYMS solicited.

uninviting adjective *the bed looked cold and uninviting*: **unappealing**, untempting, undesirable, unattractive, unappetizing; bleak, cheerless, joyless, dreary, dismal, depressing, grim, comfortless, inhospitable; unpleasant, disagreeable, distasteful, objectionable, offensive, unpalatable, sickening, nauseating, foul; repellent, revolting, repugnant; informal off-putting.
▶ANTONYMS inviting, tempting.

union noun **1** *the gardens are an example of the union of art and nature*: **unification**, uniting, joining, merging, merger, fusion, fusing, amalgamating, amalgamation, junction, coalition, combining, combination, consolidation, conjunction, confederation, federation, integration, synthesis, blend, blending, mixture, mingling, commingling; informal mash-up.
▶ANTONYMS separation, parting.
2 *the crowd moved in union to the beat*: **unity**, accord, unison, unanimity, harmony, concord, agreement, concurrence, undividedness.
3 *his daughter's union with the prince*: **marriage**, wedding, partnership, pairing, alliance, match, compact, affiliation, civil partnership; **coupling**, intercourse, mating; formal coition, coitus, copulation.
▶ANTONYMS divorce, annulment.
4 *all employees should have the right to be represented by a union*: **association**, trade union, alliance, league, guild; coalition, consortium, combine, syndicate, confederation, federation, confederacy, partnership, fraternity, brotherhood, sorority, society, club, group, organization.

unique adjective **1** *each archaeological site is unique*: **distinctive**, individual, special, especial, idiosyncratic, quirky, eccentric, isolated; **single**, sole, lone, unrepeated, unrepeatable, solitary, exclusive, only, one and only, in a class by itself; rare, uncommon, unusual, peculiar, novel, strange, odd; Latin sui generis; informal one-off.
▶ANTONYMS common, ordinary.
2 *a unique insight into the history of this beautiful region*: **remarkable**, special, singular, noteworthy, notable, signal, outstanding, extraordinary; **unequalled**, without equal, unparalleled, unmatched, matchless, peerless, nonpareil, unsurpassed, unexcelled, incomparable, beyond compare, superior, inimitable, second to none; rare unexampled.
▶ANTONYMS unremarkable.
3 *the two species are **unique to** the island*: **peculiar**, specific, particular, found only in; characteristic of, typical of.

Word toolkit **unique**

See **exceptional**.

unison noun
□ **in unison 1** *they lifted their arms in unison*: **simultaneously**, at (one and) the same time, (all) at once, at the same moment, (all) together, as one, in concert, in chorus. **2** *both ministers have spoken in complete unison on this*: **in agreement**, in accord, in rapport, in harmony, in unity, in concord, in concert, unanimously, in sympathy, in cooperation, as one, identically; in partnership, shoulder to shoulder, side by side, arm in arm, hand in hand.

unit noun **1** *the family is the fundamental unit of British society*: **component**, part, section, element, constituent, subdivision, portion, segment, module, item, member, ingredient, factor, feature, piece, fragment; entity, whole, discrete item.
2 *the farthing was still a useful unit of currency*: **quantity**, measure, measurement, denomination, value.
3 *a guerrilla unit*: **detachment**, contingent, outfit, section, division, company, squadron, corps, regiment, brigade, platoon, battalion, force, garrison, legion, formation, crew, squad, detail; cell, faction.

unite verb **1** *what the land needs is a champion, someone to unite the people and restore order*: **unify**, join, link, connect, combine, amalgamate, fuse, integrate, weld, bond, stick together, bring together, knit together; glue, cement, coalesce.
▶ANTONYMS divide, separate.
2 *environmentalists and union activists united to demand changes*: **join together**, join forces, combine, associate, band together, club together, ally, cooperate, collaborate, work together, act together, pull together, get together, team up, go into partnership, work side by side, pool resources; informal gang up.
▶ANTONYMS split.
3 *in his designs he sought to unite comfort with elegance*: **merge**, mix, blend, mingle, combine, synthesize, commix, admix, intermix, commingle, homogenize.

united adjective **1** *a united Germany*: **unified**, integrated, consolidated, amalgamated, joined, merged, banded together; federal, federated, confederate.
▶ANTONYMS divided, separated.
2 *the parties must decide on a united response to the proposals*: **common**, shared, joint, combined, corporate, mutual, communal, allied, cooperative, collective, collaborative, aggregate, undivided, solid, consistent, concerted, pooled, cross-party.
▶ANTONYMS different.
3 *they were united in their views*: **in agreement**, agreed, in unison, of the same opinion, of the same mind, of like mind, like-minded, at one, as one, in accord, in concord, unanimous, in sympathy, in rapport, in harmony, in unity, shoulder to shoulder.
▶ANTONYMS disagreeing, differing.

United States of America noun **the States**, the land of the free, God's own country; informal the US of A; literary **Columbia**.

unity noun **1** *some officials saw European unity as the solution*: **union**, unification, integration, amalgamation; coalition, federation, confederation.
▶ANTONYMS division, disunity.
2 *their leaders called for unity between opposing factions*: **harmony**, accord, concord, concurrence, cooperation, collaboration, agreement, unanimity, consensus, assent, concert, togetherness, solidarity, like-mindedness, peace, synthesis.
▶ANTONYMS discord, strife.
3 *they believed in the organic unity of the whole universe*: **oneness**, singleness, wholeness, entity, integrity, undividedness, cohesion, coherence, congruity, congruence, uniformity, homogeneity, identity, sameness.
▶ANTONYMS disunity.

universal adjective *the universal features of language*: **general**, **ubiquitous**, comprehensive, common, omnipresent, all-embracing, all-inclusive, all-round, across the board; global, worldwide, international, widespread, blanket, sweeping, rampant, catholic, inescapable, pervading, pervasive, permeating.
▶ANTONYMS particular, restricted, local.

universally adverb *it was universally accepted that no man married merely for love*: **invariably**, always, without exception, in all instances, in all cases, in every case, in every instance; **everywhere**, worldwide, globally, internationally; broadly, widely, commonly, generally.

universe noun **1** *the laws of the physical universe*: **cosmos**, macrocosm, totality, whole world, Creation, (outer) space, the heavens, the firmament; infinity, all existence.
2 *the ROM chip clearly belongs to the universe of hardware*: **province**, world, sphere, preserve, domain, circle, milieu, territory, quarter.

Word links **universe**

cosmic relating to the universe
cosmology, **astronomy**, **cosmogony** study of the universe

university noun **college**, academy, educational establishment/institution, institute, varsity; N. Amer. school; historical polytechnic.

unjust adjective **1** *several groups have attacked the report as unjust*: **biased**, prejudiced, unfair, inequitable, discriminatory, partisan, preferential, weighted, partial, one-sided, influenced, slanted, bigoted.
▶ANTONYMS just, fair, balanced.

2 *an unjust law*: **wrongful**, wrong, unfair, undue, undeserved, unmerited, unwarranted, uncalled for, unreasonable, gratuitous, unjustifiable, indefensible, groundless, inappropriate.
▷ANTONYMS just, fair, reasonable.

unjustifiable adjective **1** *an unjustifiable extravagance*: **indefensible**, inexcusable, unforgivable, unpardonable; uncalled for, unprovoked, without justification, without cause, without reason, unreasonable; regrettable, unacceptable, unworthy, remiss, blameworthy, culpable, unwarrantable; excessive, immoderate, unconscionable, outrageous.
▷ANTONYMS justifiable, reasonable.
2 *an unjustifiable slur on his character*: **groundless**, unfounded, without foundation, foundationless, baseless, without basis, unsupported, unsubstantiated, unconfirmed, uncorroborated, invalid, untenable, weak, shaky, flawed, defective.
▷ANTONYMS justifiable, true.

unkempt adjective *a rough-looking youth with long unkempt hair*: **untidy**, messy, scruffy, disordered, dishevelled, disarranged, rumpled, windblown, ungroomed, bedraggled, in a mess, messed up, shabby, slovenly, shaggy; tousled, uncombed, knotted, matted; informal sloppy, tatty, the worse for wear; Brit. informal grotty; N. Amer. informal mussed up.
▷ANTONYMS tidy, neat.

unkind adjective **1** *everyone was being rude and unkind to him*: **uncharitable**, unpleasant, disagreeable, nasty, mean, mean-spirited, cruel, vicious, spiteful, malicious, malevolent, harsh, callous, pitiless, ruthless, unsympathetic, unfeeling, compassionless, uncaring, snide, shabby, hurtful, wounding, upsetting, ill-natured, hard-hearted, heartless, cold-hearted, merciless, brutal, savage, inhuman; unfriendly, unamiable, uncivil, inconsiderate, insensitive, ungenerous, inhospitable, unkindly, hostile; informal beastly, bitchy, catty.
▷ANTONYMS kind.
2 *we were unlucky to have such unkind weather*: **inclement**, harsh, intemperate, rough, severe, bitter, filthy.
▷ANTONYMS fine.

unkindness noun *she had had enough of her father's unkindness*: **nastiness**, unpleasantness, disagreeableness, cruelty, spite, malice, meanness, mean-spiritedness, viciousness, malevolence, uncharitableness; harshness, callousness, pitilessness, ruthlessness, unfeelingness, compassionlessness, shabbiness, hard-heartedness, heartlessness, cold-heartedness, mercilessness, brutality, savagery, savageness, inhumanity; unfriendliness, inconsiderateness, insensitivity, ungenerousness, inhospitality, unkindliness, hostility; informal beastliness, bitchiness, cattiness.
▷ANTONYMS kindness.

unknown adjective **1** *the ultimate outcome of their dispute was unknown*: **undisclosed**, unrevealed, undivulged, untold, unspecified, secret, mysterious, dark, hidden, concealed; **undetermined**, undecided, unresolved, unfixed, unestablished, unsettled, unsure; pending, unascertained, undefined, indefinite, inconclusive, in the balance, in limbo, up in the air.
▷ANTONYMS known, decided.
2 *all his instincts were warning him of the dangers in the unknown country ahead*: **unexplored**, uncharted, unmapped, untravelled, undiscovered, virgin; remote, exotic, outlandish.
▷ANTONYMS familiar, well travelled.
3 *he was murdered by a person or persons unknown*: **unidentified**, unnamed, nameless, anonymous, undesignated, incognito, mysterious; rare innominate.
▷ANTONYMS identified, named.
4 *firearms were unknown to the Indians at the time of the conquest*: **unfamiliar**, unheard of, unprecedented, new, novel, strange, exotic.
▷ANTONYMS familiar.
5 *unknown artists of the avant-garde*: **obscure**, unheard of, little known, unsung, minor, insignificant, unimportant, undistinguished, unrenowned, inconsequential, lowly, unhonoured, forgotten.
▷ANTONYMS famous, celebrated.

unlawful adjective *unlawful imports of recreational drugs*: **illegal**, illicit, lawbreaking, illegitimate, against the law; **criminal**, felonious, indictable, actionable, delinquent, culpable; prohibited, banned, outlawed, proscribed, forbidden, unauthorized, unsanctioned, unwarranted, unlicensed, contraband, black-market, under the counter/table; villainous, corrupt, dishonest, fraudulent, nefarious; German verboten; informal crooked, shady, bent; archaic miscreant.
▷ANTONYMS lawful, legal.

Choose the right word **unlawful, illegal, illicit**

See **illegal**.

unleash verb *we unleashed the dog*: **let loose**, release, free, set free, loose, unloose, unbridle, untie, untether, unchain, unbind, unshackle, unmanacle; discharge, let go of, let fly.
▷ANTONYMS restrain.

unlettered adjective *the unwashed, unlettered people who worked in the foundry*: **illiterate**, **uneducated**, poorly educated, untaught, unschooled, untutored, untrained, uninstructed, unlearned, unread, uninformed, ignorant, unenlightened, unsophisticated, uncultivated, uncultured, philistine, benighted, vulgar, simple; rare nescient.
▷ANTONYMS lettered, educated.

unlike preposition **1** *England was totally unlike Jamaica*: **different from**, unalike, dissimilar to, not like, not similar to, not resembling, far from, far apart from, distant from.
▷ANTONYMS like, similar to.
2 *unlike Linda, Chrissy was a bit of a radical*: **in contrast to/with**, differently from, in contradistinction to, as opposed to, not like, not typical of, uncharacteristic of.
▷ANTONYMS like, similarly to.
▶ adjective *a meeting of unlike minds*: **dissimilar**, unalike, disparate, contrastive, contrasting, contrasted, contrary, antithetical, different, distinct, non-identical, diverse, heterogeneous, divergent, distinguishable, incompatible, inconsistent, opposed, at variance, varying, variant, at odds, clashing, conflicting, discrepant, ill-matched, incongruous; informal like chalk and cheese.
▷ANTONYMS like, identical.

unlikely adjective **1** *it is unlikely that the band will play here again this year*: **improbable**, not likely, doubtful, dubious, unexpected, beyond belief, implausible.
▷ANTONYMS likely, certain.
2 *they laughed at themselves for believing such an unlikely story*: **implausible**, improbable, questionable, unconvincing, remote, far-fetched, strained, laboured, unrealistic, incredible, unbelievable, inconceivable, unimaginable, fantastic, fabulous, fanciful, ridiculous, absurd, preposterous; informal tall, cock and bull, hard to swallow/take.
▷ANTONYMS likely, believable.

unlimited adjective **1** *the land has unlimited supplies of water*: **inexhaustible**, limitless, illimitable, boundless, unbounded, immense, vast, great, extensive, immeasurable, incalculable, untold, unfailing, everlasting, infinite, endless, never-ending, bottomless, measureless, inestimable.
▷ANTONYMS limited, finite.
2 *the ticket gives unlimited travel on city buses for as little as £5*: **unrestricted**, unconstrained, uncontrolled, unrestrained, unchecked, unhindered, unhampered, unimpeded, unfettered, untrammelled, unbridled, uncurbed.
▷ANTONYMS limited, restricted.
3 *the unit will be given unlimited power to curb all environmentally destructive activities*: **total**, unqualified, unconditional, unrestricted, absolute, full, utter, ultimate, supreme, sovereign, omnipotent.
▷ANTONYMS limited.

unload verb **1** *we unloaded the van*: **unpack**, empty, unburden, disburden; rare unlade.
▷ANTONYMS load.
2 *they began to unload the cases from the lorry*: **remove**, offload, discharge, jettison, drop, deliver, deposit, set down, leave, put off, tip out, pour out.
▷ANTONYMS load.
3 *the state will unload its 25 per cent stake in a few weeks*: **sell**, **discard**, jettison, offload, eject, get rid of, dispose of, pass off, throw out/away, clear out, scrap, destroy; palm something off on someone, foist something on someone, fob something off on someone; informal dump, lose, junk, get shot/shut of, see the back of.
▷ANTONYMS buy, acquire.

unlock verb *I unlocked the door and led the way in*: **unbolt**, unlatch, unbar, undo, unfasten, unpick, unseal, unclose, open, free, throw open/wide.
▷ANTONYMS lock.

unlooked-for adjective *the unlooked-for publicity made his work more saleable*: **unexpected**, unforeseen, unanticipated, not bargained for, unhoped-for, unsought, undreamed of, unpredicted; unintentional, unintended, inadvertent, unplanned, unpremeditated, unwitting, fortuitous, chance, coincidental, serendipitous, random, fluky; sudden, abrupt, surprise, surprising, without warning, without notice, startling, astonishing, out of the blue.
▷ANTONYMS deliberate, planned.

unloved adjective *Melanie felt lonely and unloved*: **uncared-for**, unwanted, friendless, unbeloved, uncherished, unvalued; unpopular, disliked, hated, detested, loathed; forsaken, rejected, unwelcome, jilted, shunned, spurned, neglected, outcast, abandoned.
▷ANTONYMS loved, popular.

unlucky adjective **1** *he was unlucky not to score*: **unfortunate**, luckless, out of luck, down on one's luck, hapless, ill-fated, ill-starred, star-crossed, blighted, unhappy, unsuccessful, wretched, miserable, poor, pitiful; accident-prone.
▷ANTONYMS lucky, fortunate.
2 *three can be an unlucky number*: **unfavourable**, unpromising, inauspicious, unpropitious, ominous, doomed, jinxed, damned, cursed,

ill-fated, ill-omened, bringing bad luck, adverse, disadvantageous, unfortunate, detrimental, deleterious, ruinous.
▷ANTONYMS lucky, favourable.

> *Choose the right word* **unlucky, unfortunate, ill-starred, hapless**
>
> See **unfortunate**.

unmanageable adjective **1** *the huge Victorian house was unmanageable and uneconomic*: **troublesome**, demanding, awkward, inconvenient; cumbersome, bulky, unmanoeuvrable, unwieldy, incommodious.
▷ANTONYMS manageable.
2 *his behaviour was becoming unmanageable at home*: **uncontrollable**, ungovernable, irrepressible, unruly, disorderly, rowdy, out of hand, wild, boisterous, difficult, disruptive, ill-disciplined, undisciplined, refractory, recalcitrant, intractable, impossible, obstreperous, fractious, wayward, incorrigible; informal stroppy; archaic contumacious.
▷ANTONYMS manageable, controllable.

unmanly adjective *he was on the verge of tears, but did not wish to appear unmanly*: **effeminate**, effete, unmasculine; womanish, girlish, feminine; **weak**, soft, timid, timorous, fearful, cowardly, lily-livered, limp-wristed, spineless, craven, milksoppish, pusillanimous, chicken-hearted, weak-kneed; informal sissy, wimpish, wimpy, pansy-like, queeny.
▷ANTONYMS manly, virile.

unmannerly adjective *a rough, unmannerly soldier*: **rude**, impolite, uncivil, discourteous, bad-mannered, ill-mannered, mannerless, disrespectful, impertinent, impudent, insolent, badly behaved, abusive, blunt; uncouth, ungallant, ungracious, graceless, ungentlemanly, unladylike, unchivalrous, boorish, oafish, loutish, ill-bred, low-bred, coarse, rough, vulgar.
▷ANTONYMS mannerly, polite.

unmarried adjective *an unmarried woman*: **unwed**, unwedded, single, spouseless, partnerless, husbandless, wifeless; spinster, bachelor; celibate, chaste, maiden, virgin; unattached, available, eligible, free, {young, free, and single}, footloose and fancy free; separated, divorced, widowed; left on the shelf.
▷ANTONYMS married.

unmatched adjective **1** *he had a talent for publicity unmatched by any other politician of this century*: **unequalled**, unrivalled, unparalleled, unbeaten, unsurpassed.
2 *they have captured all the subtleties of Beethoven with unmatched clarity, depth, and balance*: **peerless**, matchless, without equal, without parallel, incomparable, beyond compare, inimitable, superlative, extraordinary, supreme, top, paramount, outstanding, second to none, in a class of its own, consummate, record, best ever, nonpareil, unique, singular, rare, perfect; French par excellence.

unmentionable adjective *sex was the unmentionable subject*: **taboo**, censored, forbidden, banned, interdicted, proscribed, prohibited, not to be spoken of, ineffable, unspeakable, unutterable, unprintable, indescribable, out of bounds, beyond the pale, off limits, that dare not speak its name, disapproved of, frowned on; offensive, embarrassing, shocking; indecent, indecorous, rude, immodest, impolite; scandalous, disgraceful, appalling, shameful, obscene, filthy; informal no go.

unmerciful adjective *he gave me an unmerciful thrashing*: **ruthless**, **cruel**, harsh, merciless, pitiless, unpitying, remorseless, cold-blooded, hard-hearted, hard, callous, brutal, brutish, severe, rigorous, draconian, unrelenting, unforgiving, unsparing, barbarous, savage, inhumane, inhuman, stony, heartless, cut-throat, unsympathetic, unfeeling, illiberal, uncharitable, inflexible, intolerant, rigid, stern, strict, punishing, sadistic.
▷ANTONYMS merciful.

unmindful adjective *he is **unmindful of** the peril he is courting*: **heedless of**, taking no notice of, paying no heed to, careless of, disregardful of, regardless of, unheeding of, neglectful of, unconscious of, oblivious to, inattentive to, blind to, deaf to; incautious, imprudent, rash, reckless, foolhardy, blithe, precipitate, unthinking, thoughtless, improvident, unwary, unobservant, unwatchful.

unmistakable adjective *there was the unmistakable odour of whisky on his breath*: **distinctive**, distinct, telltale, well defined; indisputable, indubitable, undoubted, beyond a doubt, unquestionable, beyond question, undeniable; **plain**, clear, clear-cut, sure, definite, obvious, evident, self-evident, manifest, apparent, patent, unambiguous, unequivocal, categorical, palpable, conspicuous, noticeable, pronounced, striking, glaring, blatant, obtrusive, as plain as the nose on your face, as plain as daylight.
▷ANTONYMS unclear, uncertain.

unmitigated adjective *the raid was an unmitigated disaster*: **absolute**, unqualified, unconditional, categorical, complete, total, thoroughgoing, downright, outright, utter, out-and-out, unadulterated, unalloyed, undiluted, unmixed, untempered, unmoderated, unmodified, unabated, undiminished, unmollified, unsoftened, unredeemed, unambiguous, unequivocal, veritable, perfect, consummate, pure, sheer, rank, in every way, positive, real, deep-dyed; archaic arrant.
▷ANTONYMS partial.

unmoved adjective **1** *he was totally **unmoved by** her outburst*: **unaffected**, untouched, unstirred, unimpressed, unperturbed, unruffled, untroubled, undismayed, unworried; aloof, cool, cold, stolid, stony, stony-hearted, hard-hearted, dry-eyed; unconcerned, uncaring, indifferent, uninterested, unflappable, apathetic; impassive, unfeeling, unemotional, unresponsive, stoical, phlegmatic, equable; impervious (to), oblivious (to), heedless (of), immune (to), unmindful (of), proof against, deaf to.
2 *the American negotiator remained unmoved on the crucial issues*: **steadfast**, firm, unshaken, staunch, unwavering, unswerving, undeviating, uninfluenced, determined, resolute, decided, resolved, inflexible, unbending, implacable, adamant.

unnatural adjective **1** *the life of a battery hen is completely unnatural*: **abnormal**, unusual, uncommon, extraordinary, strange, freakish, freak, queer, odd, peculiar, weird, unorthodox, exceptional, irregular, atypical, untypical, non-typical, anomalous, divergent, aberrant, bizarre, preternatural.
▷ANTONYMS natural, normal.
2 *the tractor passed in a flash of unnatural colour*: **artificial**, man-made, synthetic, manufactured, fabricated, fake, false, faux, simulated, not found/existing in nature.
▷ANTONYMS natural, genuine.
3 *he was beheaded for unnatural vice*: **perverted**, warped, twisted, deviant, depraved, degenerate, bestial, unhealthy, immoral, abnormal, decadent; informal kinky, pervy, sick, sicko; rare deviative.
4 *her voice sounded unnatural*: **affected**, artificial, stilted, self-conscious, contrived, forced, laboured, studied, strained, stiff, wooden; assumed, feigned, false, bogus, fake, insincere, pretended, unspontaneous, theatrical, stagy, mannered, pretentious; informal put on, phoney.
5 *they condemned her as an unnatural woman*: **uncaring**, unconcerned, unfeeling, inhuman, soulless, heartless, cold, cold-blooded, hard, hard-hearted, callous, cruel, brutal, merciless, pitiless, remorseless, inhumane, evil, wicked, monstrous.
▷ANTONYMS caring.

unnecessary adjective *many people feel that holiday insurance is unnecessary for travel in Britain*: **unneeded**, needless, inessential, non-essential, not required, uncalled for, gratuitous, useless, unmerited, unwarranted, unwanted, undesired, dispensable, avoidable, peripheral, cosmetic, unimportant, trivial, incidental, optional, extraneous, expendable, disposable, redundant, pointless, purposeless, to no purpose, to no avail; wasted, wasteful, wanton; superfluous, excess, excessive, too much, disproportionate, surplus (to requirements); French de trop; rare supererogatory.
▷ANTONYMS necessary, essential, useful.

unnerve verb *the bleakness of his gaze unnerved her*: **demoralize**, discourage, dishearten, dispirit, deject, daunt, cow, alarm, frighten, unman, dismay, distress, disconcert, discompose, perturb, upset, discomfit, take aback, unsettle, disquiet, jolt, startle, fluster, agitate, shake, ruffle, throw, throw off balance, put someone off their stroke, cause someone to lose their composure, confound, panic, stupefy, stun; informal rattle, faze, put into a flap, throw into a tizz, discombobulate, shake up; Brit. informal put the wind up.
▷ANTONYMS encourage, hearten.

unobtrusive adjective **1** *she was unobtrusive and shy*: **self-effacing**, retiring, unassuming, modest, demure, quiet, meek, humble; shy, bashful, unconfident, timid, timorous, shrinking, diffident, insecure, reserved, withdrawn, introvert, introverted, reticent, unforthcoming, unpresuming, unpretentious, unaggressive, unassertive, mousy, low-profile.
▷ANTONYMS bold, extrovert.
2 *our staff offer efficient, unobtrusive service*: **inconspicuous**, unnoticeable, restrained, subdued, quiet, low-key, discreet, circumspect, understated, muted, subtle, played down, toned down, unostentatious, unshowy, relaxed, downbeat, out of sight, in the background.
▷ANTONYMS obtrusive, conspicuous.

unoccupied adjective **1** *an unoccupied house*: **vacant**, empty, uninhabited, untenanted, tenantless, vacated, unused; free, untaken, available, to let.
▷ANTONYMS occupied, inhabited.
2 *an unoccupied territory*: **uninhabited**, unpopulated, unpeopled, unsettled, unfrequented; deserted, evacuated, depopulated, abandoned, forsaken; desolate, bare, barren, wild, godforsaken.
▷ANTONYMS occupied, populated.
3 *at weekends the young people were unoccupied*: **at leisure**, idle, free, inactive, not at work, not busy, not tied up, unengaged, with time on one's hands, with time to spare, at a loose end; **unemployed**, jobless, out of work, without work, workless.
▷ANTONYMS occupied, busy, employed.

unofficial adjective **1** *unofficial figures put the death toll at over 300*: **unauthenticated**, unconfirmed, uncorroborated, unsubstantiated, unratified; undocumented, off the record; unauthorized, unsanctioned, uncertified.

u

▷ANTONYMS official, confirmed.
2 *he took it on himself to act as chairman of an unofficial committee*: **informal**, casual; unauthorized, unsanctioned, unaccredited; wildcat.
▷ANTONYMS official, formal.

unorthodox adjective **1** *Hobson's unorthodox views denied him an academic career*: **unconventional**, unusual, uncommon, unwonted, out of the ordinary, radical, revolutionary, nonconformist, irregular, offbeat, avant-garde, original, new, novel, fresh, eccentric, exotic, Bohemian, alternative, idiosyncratic, abnormal, extreme, divergent, aberrant, anomalous, bizarre, outlandish, perverse; informal off the wall, oddball, way out, cranky, zany; rare heteroclite.
▷ANTONYMS orthodox, conventional.
2 *unorthodox religious views*: **heterodox**, uncanonical, heretical, nonconformist, dissenting, dissentient, renegade.
▷ANTONYMS orthodox.

unpaid adjective **1** *a string of unpaid bills*: **unsettled**, outstanding, unresolved, unattended to, due, overdue, owing, owed, receivable, to be paid, payable, undischarged, in arrears, in the red; N. Amer. delinquent, past due.
▷ANTONYMS paid, settled.
2 *unpaid charity work*: **voluntary**, volunteer, honorary, unrewarded, unremunerative, unsalaried, gratuitous, free; Law pro bono (publico).
▷ANTONYMS paid, professional.

unpalatable adjective **1** *scraps of unpalatable food*: **unappetizing**, uninviting, unappealing, unsavoury, off-putting, inedible, uneatable; bitter, sour, rancid; disgusting, revolting, nauseating, sickening, horrible, tasteless, flavourless, bland, insipid; informal yucky, sick-making, gross.
▷ANTONYMS palatable, tasty.
2 *he had been bold enough to speak the unpalatable truth*: **disagreeable**, unpleasant, displeasing, unattractive, regrettable, unwelcome, upsetting, distressing, lamentable, repugnant, nasty, horrible, dreadful, hateful, distasteful, offensive, objectionable, obnoxious, repulsive, repellent, vile, foul.
▷ANTONYMS palatable.

unparalleled adjective *an unparalleled opportunity to change society*: **exceptional**, unique, singular, rare, unprecedented, without parallel, without equal, unequalled; matchless, unmatched, peerless, unrivalled, unsurpassed, unsurpassable, unexcelled, superlative, incomparable, beyond compare, nonpareil, inimitable, second to none, in a league of its own, supreme; unheard of, unusual, aberrant, freak; French hors concours; rare unexampled.
▷ANTONYMS ordinary, unexceptional.

unperturbed adjective *Daniel was unperturbed by the outburst*: **untroubled**, undisturbed, unworried, unconcerned, unmoved, unflustered, unruffled, unshaken, undismayed; calm, composed, cool, collected, controlled, unemotional, serene, tranquil, self-possessed, self-assured, poised, level-headed, at ease, placid, {cool, calm, and collected}, unflappable, unflinching, as cool as a cucumber; unfazed, laid-back, together.
▷ANTONYMS perturbed, anxious.

unpleasant adjective **1** *a very unpleasant situation*: **disagreeable**, irksome, troublesome, annoying, irritating, vexatious, displeasing, uncomfortable, distressing, nasty, horrible, appalling, terrible, awful, dreadful, hateful, detestable, miserable, abominable, execrable, odious, invidious, objectionable, offensive, obnoxious, repugnant, repulsive, repellent, revolting, disgusting, distasteful, nauseating, unsavoury, unpalatable, ugly.
▷ANTONYMS pleasant, agreeable.
2 *he was the most unpleasant man I knew*: **unlikable**, unlovable, unattractive, disagreeable; unfriendly, inconsiderate, rude, impolite, obnoxious, nasty, spiteful, cruel, malicious, mean, mean-spirited, vicious, poisonous, venomous, vindictive, malign; frightful, ghastly, insufferable, unbearable, annoying, irritating; churlish, ill-natured, ill-humoured, ill-tempered, cross, bad-tempered.
▷ANTONYMS pleasant, likeable.
3 *an unpleasant burnt sugar taste*: **unappetizing**, unpalatable, unsavoury, uninviting, unappealing, off-putting, inedible, uneatable, bitter, sour, rancid; disgusting, repugnant, revolting, nauseating, sickening, offensive, foul, rotten, vile.
▷ANTONYMS pleasant, palatable.

unpolished adjective **1** *the floor was of pale unpolished wood*: **unvarnished**, unlacquered, unfinished, unprocessed, untreated, unworked, plain, raw, unrefined, natural, coarse, rough; stripped.
▷ANTONYMS polished, varnished.
2 *you must not mind his unpolished ways*: **unsophisticated**, unrefined, uncouth, uncultured, uncultivated, coarse, inelegant, crude, crass, raw, rough, rough and ready, awkward, clumsy, gauche, graceless, tactless, insensitive, vulgar, philistine, uneducated; provincial, parochial, rustic.
▷ANTONYMS polished, sophisticated.
3 *it was an unpolished performance lacking spark*: **slipshod**, rough, crude, untidy, uneven, incoherent, defective, deficient, scrappy, sketchy, bitty.
▷ANTONYMS polished.

unpopular adjective *he was unpopular at school*: **disliked**, friendless, unliked, unloved, unbefriended, uncherished, hated, detested, despised, loathed; unwanted, unwelcome, avoided, ignored, rejected, shunned, spurned, unsought after, out in the cold, cold-shouldered, out of favour, not in the swim, in bad odour; Brit. sent to Coventry.
▷ANTONYMS popular, liked.

unprecedented adjective *an era of warfare on an unprecedented scale*: **unparalleled**, unequalled, unmatched, unrivalled, without parallel, without equal; extraordinary, uncommon, out of the ordinary, unusual, outstanding, striking, exceptional, prodigious, abnormal, singular, remarkable, unique, anomalous, atypical, untypical, freakish; unheard of, unknown, novel, original, new, groundbreaking, revolutionary, pioneering; informal one of a kind; rare unexampled.
▷ANTONYMS normal, common.

unpredictable adjective **1** *the unpredictable results of the first-past-the-post system*: **unforeseeable**, undivinable, incalculable, uncertain, unsure, doubtful, dubious, in the balance, up in the air, random, arbitrary; informal iffy, hit and miss.
▷ANTONYMS predictable.
2 *the men in here are unpredictable, violent, and dangerous*: **erratic**, moody, volatile, unstable, fickle, capricious, whimsical, temperamental, mercurial, changeable, variable, inconstant, undependable, unreliable, unmanageable, impulsive.
▷ANTONYMS predictable, reliable.

unprejudiced adjective **1** *science must start with unprejudiced observation*: **objective**, impartial, unbiased, fair, neutral, even-handed, non-partisan, detached, uninvolved, disinterested.
▷ANTONYMS prejudiced, partisan.
2 *we need unprejudiced support for lesbians and gay men*: **unbiased**, non-discriminatory, tolerant, liberal, broad-minded, open-minded, unbigoted, just, freethinking, progressive, enlightened.
▷ANTONYMS prejudiced, intolerant.

unpremeditated adjective *her unpremeditated reply*: **unplanned**, spontaneous, unprepared, unarranged, uncontrolled, unintentional, unintended, extempore, extemporary, extemporized, extemporaneous, impromptu, ad lib; spur-of-the-moment, on-the-spot, improvised, improvisatory, unrehearsed, unscripted, unstudied, uncontrived, casual; impulsive, hasty, unthinking, natural, involuntary, automatic; Latin ad libitum; informal off-the-cuff.
▷ANTONYMS premeditated, planned.

unprepared adjective **1** *four out of ten companies were unprepared for the new VAT regime*: **not ready**, unready, off (one's) guard, surprised, taken aback, unsuspecting; unrehearsed, unwatchful, unqualified, ineligible, unfit, incompetent, incapable, ill-equipped, unequipped, not equal/up to; informal caught napping, caught on the hop.
▷ANTONYMS prepared, ready.
2 *the Whigs showed themselves unprepared to support the reforms*: **unwilling**, disinclined, averse, loath, reluctant, indisposed, resistant, opposed.
▷ANTONYMS prepared, willing.

unpretentious adjective **1** *in spite of his fame he was thoroughly unpretentious*: **unaffected**, modest, unassuming, without airs, natural, straightforward, open, honest, sincere, frank, ingenuous, artless, guileless, honest-to-goodness.
▷ANTONYMS pretentious.
2 *a friendly and unpretentious hotel*: **simple**, plain, modest, ordinary, humble, unostentatious, unshowy, restrained, unfussy, unimposing, homely, unsophisticated, unspoilt.
▷ANTONYMS pretentious, showy.

unprincipled adjective *he is an unprincipled opportunist*: **immoral**, unethical, unscrupulous, amoral, dishonourable, reprobate, dishonest, unprofessional, deceitful, devious, corrupt, corrupted, dissolute, underhand, crooked, bad, wicked, evil, villainous, roguish, shameless, sinful, ignoble, base, low, degenerate, sordid; archaic dastardly.
▷ANTONYMS principled, ethical.

unproductive adjective **1** *acidic, unproductive soil*: **sterile**, barren, infertile, uncultivatable, unfruitful, poor, lifeless, lean, arid.
▷ANTONYMS productive, fruitful.
2 *a costly and unproductive bureaucracy*: **fruitless**, futile, vain, idle, useless, worthless, valueless, pointless, ineffective, ineffectual, to no effect, impotent, inefficacious, unprofitable, unremunerative, unrewarding; rare otiose.
▷ANTONYMS productive, efficient.

unprofessional adjective **1** *she was reprimanded for unprofessional conduct*: **improper**, unethical, unprincipled, unscrupulous, dishonourable, disreputable, unseemly, unbecoming, unbefitting, indecorous, unworthy, lax, negligent; informal shady, crooked, not cricket; Brit. informal dodgy.
2 *he accused the detectives of being unprofessional and incompetent*: **amateurish**, amateur, unskilled, unskilful, inexpert, untrained, unqualified, inexperienced, unpractised, incompetent, sloppy, careless,

slapdash, slipshod, shoddy, bungling, bumbling, blundering, second-rate, clumsy, crude, inefficient; informal cack-handed, cowboy.

unpromising adjective *they were not deterred by this unpromising start*: **inauspicious**, unfavourable, adverse, disadvantageous, unpropitious, uninviting, discouraging, disheartening, gloomy, bleak, black, portentous, foreboding, hopeless, ominous, creepy, baleful, doomed, jinxed, damned, cursed, ill-fated, ill-omened.
▷ANTONYMS promising, auspicious.

unqualified adjective **1** *no company would permit an unqualified accountant to audit its books*: **uncertificated**, unlicensed, unchartered, untrained, inexperienced.
▷ANTONYMS qualified.
2 *we cannot leave children in the hands of those unqualified to look after them*: **unsuitable**, unfit, ineligible, incompetent, unable, inadequate, incapable, unequipped, ill-equipped, unprepared, unfitted, inapt, not equal/up to, not cut out, insufficient.
▷ANTONYMS fit, qualified.
3 *the chairman gave the manager his unqualified support*: **unconditional**, unreserved, unlimited, without reservations, categorical, unequivocal, unambiguous, unrestricted, wholehearted, positive, unmitigated, unadulterated, undiluted, unalloyed, unvarnished, unstinting; complete, absolute, downright, entire, undivided, solid, thorough, thoroughgoing, total, utter, outright, out-and-out; archaic arrant.
▷ANTONYMS limited, qualified.

unquestionable adjective *the sincerity of his beliefs is unquestionable*: **indubitable**, undoubted, beyond question, beyond doubt, indisputable, undeniable, irrefutable, incontestable, incontrovertible, unimpeachable, unambiguous, unequivocal, unassailable; certain, sure, definite, positive, dependable, conclusive, self-evident, evident, manifest, obvious, apparent, patent, proven, settled, decided; rare undoubtable.

unravel verb **1** *he cut the rope and started to unravel its strands*: **untangle**, disentangle, straighten out, separate out, unsnarl, unknot, unwind, untwist, undo, untie, unkink, unjumble.
▷ANTONYMS entangle, tangle.
2 *detectives are still trying to unravel the mystery surrounding the death of a wealthy farmer*: **solve**, resolve, work out, clear up, puzzle out, find an answer to, get to the bottom of, explain, elucidate, fathom, decipher, decode, crack, penetrate, untangle, unfold, settle, reveal, clarify, sort out, make head or tail of; informal figure out, suss (out).
▷ANTONYMS complicate.
3 *a society that does not shelter its young is a society starting to unravel*: **fall apart**, come apart (at the seams), fail, collapse, go wrong.
▷ANTONYMS succeed.

unreadable adjective **1** *an almost unreadable photocopy*: **illegible**, hard to read, indecipherable, unintelligible; faint, faded, pale, indistinct, obscure, scrawled, scribbled, hieroglyphic, squiggly, crabbed; informal clear as mud.
▷ANTONYMS clear, legible.
2 *the heavy, unreadable novels which so often win prizes*: **dull**, tedious, boring, uninteresting, dry, (as) dry as dust, wearisome, difficult, heavy-going, heavy, turgid; incoherent, inarticulate, incomprehensible.
▷ANTONYMS readable, accessible.
3 *Nathan's expression was unreadable*: **inscrutable**, enigmatic, impenetrable, cryptic, impossible to interpret, mysterious, puzzling, deadpan; informal poker-faced.
▷ANTONYMS transparent.

unreal adjective *the unreal world of art*: **imaginary**, imagined, fictitious, pretend, make-believe, made-up, dreamed-up, non-existent, mock, false, invented, illusory, mythical, fanciful, fancied, fantastic, fabulous, legendary, chimerical, fairy-tale, phantasmagoric; hypothetical, theoretical, ideal; informal phoney.
▷ANTONYMS real.

unrealistic adjective **1** *it is unrealistic to expect a government minister to know all about administration*: **impractical**, impracticable, unworkable, unfeasible, non-viable; unreasonable, irrational, illogical, senseless, silly, improbable, impossible, foolish, fanciful, wild, absurd, delusory, quixotic; idealistic, Utopian, far-fetched, perfectionist, unworldly, romantic, starry-eyed, visionary; informal half-baked, crazy, potty.
▷ANTONYMS realistic, pragmatic.
2 *manga comics are deliberately stylized and unrealistic*: **unlifelike**, non-realistic, unreal-looking, non-naturalistic, unnatural, non-representational, unrepresentative, abstract.
▷ANTONYMS realistic, lifelike.

unreasonable adjective **1** *an unreasonable old woman*: **uncooperative**, obstructive, unhelpful, disobliging, unaccommodating, troublesome, awkward, contrary, difficult, tiresome, annoying, vexatious; **obstinate**, obdurate, wilful, headstrong, pig-headed, bull-headed, intractable, intransigent, inflexible, mulish; **irrational**, illogical, opinionated, biased, prejudiced, intolerant, blinkered.
2 *the bill placed unreasonable demands on industry*: **unacceptable**, preposterous, outrageous, ludicrous, absurd, senseless, nonsensical, irrational, illogical; excessive, immoderate, extreme, disproportionate, undue, inordinate, exorbitant, extortionate, extravagant, intolerable, unconscionable; unnecessary, unjustified, unwarranted, uncalled for; informal over the top, OTT, steep.

unrecognizable adjective *with his moustache and beard he is practically unrecognizable*: **unidentifiable**, unknowable; disguised, incognito; changed, altered.
▷ANTONYMS recognizable.

unrefined adjective **1** *unrefined clay*: **unprocessed**, untreated, unpurified, crude, raw, natural, plain, coarse, rough, unworked, unprepared, unmilled, unfinished.
▷ANTONYMS refined, processed.
2 *the miners were hard, unrefined men*: **uncultured**, uncultivated, uncivilized, philistine, uneducated, unsophisticated, unpolished, indelicate, inelegant, ungraceful; boorish, oafish, loutish, barbarian, coarse, vulgar, rude, uncouth, crude, ill-bred, ill-mannered, crass, raw, rough, rough and ready; provincial, parochial, rustic.
▷ANTONYMS refined, cultured; effete.

unrelated adjective **1** *two men had been arrested in unrelated incidents*: **separate**, unconnected, independent, unattached, unassociated, unlinked, unallied, distinct, discrete, individual, uncoupled; unlike, varying, variant, disparate.
▷ANTONYMS related, similar.
2 *I chose London for another reason, unrelated to my work*: **irrelevant**, immaterial, inapplicable, unconcerned, inapt, foreign, alien, extraneous, extrinsic, peripheral, off the subject, beside/off the point, wide of the mark, not pertinent, not germane; informal neither here nor there.
▷ANTONYMS relevant.

unrelenting adjective **1** *a vicious, unrelenting guerrilla war*: **continual**, constant, continuous, relentless, unremitting, unabating, unrelieved, sustained, incessant, unceasing, ceaseless, steady, unbroken, non-stop, endless, unending, persistent, perpetual.
▷ANTONYMS intermittent, spasmodic.
2 *he was an unrelenting opponent of the Jacobite cause*: **implacable**, inflexible, uncompromising, unyielding, unbending, inexorable, relentless, resolute, determined, unstoppable, dogged, tireless, unflagging, unshakeable, unswerving, unwavering, assiduous, sedulous; intransigent, merciless, pitiless, unforgiving, unsparing, ruthless, cruel, rigid, rigorous, hard, strict, harsh, stern, adamant, steely, tough.

unreliable adjective **1** *an unreliable group of volunteers*: **undependable**, untrustworthy, irresponsible, reckless, fickle, capricious, irregular, erratic, unpredictable, inconstant, mutable, faithless, untrue, flighty, slippery.
▷ANTONYMS reliable, steadfast.
2 *unemployment can be an unreliable indicator of the tightness of labour markets*: **questionable**, open to question, open to doubt, doubtful, dubious, suspect, unsound, tenuous, flimsy, weak, unsubstantial, implausible, unconvincing, unsupported, unsubstantiated, fallible, shaky, rocky; risky, chancy, disreputable, specious, defective; inaccurate, vague, untrue, incorrect, wide of the mark, off-target, wrong; informal iffy, dicey; Brit. informal dodgy.
▷ANTONYMS reliable, accurate.

unremitting adjective *their lives were little more than unremitting toil*: **relentless**, unrelenting, continual, constant, continuous, unabating, unrelieved, sustained, incessant, unceasing, ceaseless, steady, unbroken, non-stop, endless, unending, persistent, perpetual, interminable, unyielding, inexorable, unsparing, without respite; hard, harsh, stern.
▷ANTONYMS intermittent, spasmodic.

unrepentant adjective *an unrepentant sinner*: **impenitent**, unrepenting, uncontrite, remorseless, unremorseful, shameless, unashamed, unblushing, unapologetic, unregenerate, obdurate, unabashed; incorrigible, incurable, confirmed, inveterate, irredeemable, unreformable, brazen, hardened, callous, abandoned, conscienceless.
▷ANTONYMS repentant, regretful.

unreserved adjective **1** *the Prime Minister has had the unreserved support of the Opposition*: **unconditional**, unqualified, without reservations, unlimited, unrestricted, categorical, unequivocal, unambiguous, positive, unadulterated, undiluted, unalloyed, unvarnished, unstinting; absolute, complete, thorough, thoroughgoing, through and through, wholehearted, total, utter, outright, out-and-out, downright, entire, undivided, solid, sheer, deep-dyed, perfect, consummate; archaic arrant.
▷ANTONYMS qualified, tentative.
2 *an unreserved young man*: **uninhibited**, liberated, extrovert, outgoing, unrestrained, expressive, open, affable, talkative, effusive, demonstrative, unconstrained, unselfconscious, bold, communicative, expansive, ebullient, exuberant, gushing, outspoken, frank, candid, warm.
▷ANTONYMS reserved, reticent.
3 *unreserved seats*: **unbooked**, unhired, unallocated, unchartered, unoccupied, untaken, free, empty, vacant, spare.
▷ANTONYMS reserved, booked.

unresolved adjective *the judge said that some questions remained unresolved*: **undecided**, to be decided, unsettled, undetermined, uncertain,

u

open, arguable, debatable, unsolved, unanswered, pending, open to debate, open to question, doubtful, in doubt, borderline, moot, up in the air, indefinite, inconclusive, unconfirmed, confused, problematic, vexed, ambiguous, equivocal, vague, in (a state of) limbo, in a state of uncertainty, ongoing, incomplete; informal iffy.
▷ANTONYMS resolved, decided.

unrest noun *the government was clearly fearful of social unrest*: **disruption**, disturbance, agitation, upset, trouble, turmoil, tumult, disorder, chaos, anarchy, turbulence, uproar; **discord**, dissension, dissent, strife, protest, sedition, rebellion, uprising, rioting; **dissatisfaction**, discontent, discontentment, disaffection, unease, anxiety, anguish, disquiet; informal ructions.
▷ANTONYMS calm, peace.

unrestrained adjective *this was a period of unrestrained corruption*: **uncontrolled**, unconstrained, unrestricted, unchecked, unbridled, unlimited, unfettered, unshackled, untrammelled, uninhibited, unconfined, unimpeded, unhampered, unbounded, boundless, unsuppressed, undisciplined, uncontrollable, out of control, out of hand; outrageous, rampant, reckless, wild, wanton, free, runaway, irrepressible, unstoppable, uncontainable, unquenchable, immoderate, intemperate, inordinate.
▷ANTONYMS restrained, restricted.

unrestricted adjective *open drives provide unrestricted access to the rear of the property*: **unlimited**, open, free, clear, unhindered, unimpeded, unhampered, unchecked, unopposed, unbridled, unrestrained, unconstrained, unblocked, untrammelled, unbounded, unconfined, uncurbed, unconditional, unqualified, absolute, total; informal free for all, with no holds barred.
▷ANTONYMS restricted, limited.

unripe adjective *unripe fruit*: **immature**, unready, not ripe, undeveloped, unfinished, incomplete, half-grown, unmellowed, green, sour.
▷ANTONYMS ripe, mature.

unrivalled adjective *an unrivalled collection of rare coins*: **unequalled**, without equal, unparalleled, without parallel, matchless, unmatched, peerless, without peer, unsurpassed, unbeaten, unexcelled, incomparable, beyond compare, inimitable; superlative, extraordinary, supreme, top, paramount, outstanding, singular, unique, rare, perfect, second to none, in a class of its own, consummate, record, best ever, nonpareil; French par excellence.
▷ANTONYMS average.

unruffled adjective **1** *Julius replied in an unruffled tone*: **calm**, composed, undisturbed, unagitated, unmoved, controlled, self-controlled, self-possessed, untroubled, undismayed, unperturbed, at ease, tranquil, relaxed, serene, cool, {cool, calm, and collected}, cool-headed, unshaken, unbothered, unexcitable, unemotional, equanimous, unflappable, imperturbable, equable, stoical, urbane; informal together, unfazed.
▷ANTONYMS frantic, nervous.
2 *an unruffled sea*: **tranquil**, calm, smooth, still, flat, even, motionless, placid, waveless, pacific, undisturbed, unagitated, unbroken, like a millpond.
▷ANTONYMS choppy, stormy.

unruly adjective *she was scolding some unruly children*: **disorderly**, rowdy, wild, unmanageable, uncontrollable, disobedient, disruptive, undisciplined, troublemaking, rebellious, mutinous, anarchic, chaotic, lawless, insubordinate, defiant, wayward, wilful, headstrong, irrepressible, unrestrained, obstreperous, difficult, intractable, out of hand, refractory, recalcitrant; boisterous, lively, loud, noisy, rollicking, romping, rumbustious, reckless, heedless; archaic contumacious.
▷ANTONYMS disciplined, obedient.

Word toolkit

unruly	rebellious	defiant
child	spirit	stance
students	nature	look
passengers	teenager	message
mob	stage	tone
fans	colonies	gesture
customers	slaves	voice

unsafe adjective **1** *the building was becoming unsafe | many women feel that it is unsafe to go out alone*: **dangerous**, risky, perilous, hazardous, precarious, life-threatening, high-risk, treacherous, insecure, unsound, vulnerable, exposed, defenceless; destructive, harmful, injurious, malignant, toxic; threatening, menacing; informal hairy, chancy; Brit. informal dodgy.
▷ANTONYMS safe, harmless, secure.
2 *the verdict was unsafe*: **unreliable**, insecure, unsound, questionable, open to question, doubtful, open to doubt, dubious, uncertain, suspect, shaky, flimsy, weak, unconvincing, unsupported, unsubstantiated, fallible; informal iffy, dodgy, dicey.
▷ANTONYMS safe, reliable.

unsaid adjective *you've made me say things much better left unsaid*: **unspoken**, unuttered, unstated, unmentioned, untold, unarticulated, unexpressed, unvoiced, unpronounced, untalked-of, suppressed, unrevealed, undeclared, unavowed; **tacit**, implicit, understood, not spelt out, taken for granted, taken as read, inferred, implied, hinted, suggested, insinuated, left to the/someone's imagination.
▷ANTONYMS said, spoken; explicit.

unsanitary adjective *the houses themselves are overcrowded and unsanitary*: **unhygienic**, insanitary, dirty, filthy, unclean, impure, contaminated, unhealthy, unwholesome, germ-ridden, germy, disease-ridden, infested; insalubrious, noxious, polluted, foul, septic, harmful.
▷ANTONYMS sanitary, hygienic, clean.

unsatisfactory adjective *this was a most unsatisfactory outcome*: **disappointing**, dissatisfying, undesirable, disagreeable, displeasing, deplorable; inadequate, unacceptable, unworthy, poor, bad, substandard, weak, mediocre, lacking, not good enough, defective, deficient, insufficient, faulty, imperfect, inferior; terrible, intolerable, insufferable; impermissible, inadmissible, inappropriate, unsuitable; informal lousy, sad, leaving a lot to be desired, no great shakes, not much cop, not up to par, not up to scratch.
▷ANTONYMS satisfactory, good.

unsavoury adjective **1** *the scanty, unsavoury portions of food doled out to them*: **unpalatable**, unappetizing, unpleasant, distasteful, disagreeable, uninviting, unappealing, unattractive; inedible, uneatable, disgusting, loathsome, repugnant, revolting, nauseating, sickening, foul, nasty, vile; insipid, tasteless, bland, flavourless, dull, uninteresting; informal yucky, sick-making, gross; literary noisome.
▷ANTONYMS tasty, appetizing.
2 *the unsavoury characters lurking about*: **disreputable**, unpleasant, disagreeable, nasty, mean, rough, seedy, sleazy, seamy, unwholesome, objectionable, offensive, obnoxious, repellent, repulsive, immoral; degenerate, dishonourable, dishonest, unprincipled, unscrupulous, villainous, notorious, suspicious, suspect, dubious, base, low, rascally, despicable, coarse, gross, vulgar, boorish, churlish, rude, uncouth; informal shady, crooked, funny, iffy; Brit. informal dodgy; literary noisome.
▷ANTONYMS reputable.

unscathed adjective *his wife and son were fortunate to escape unscathed*: **unharmed**, unhurt, uninjured, undamaged, in one piece, intact, safe, safe and sound, unmarked, untouched, unscarred, unscratched, secure, well, as (good as) new; informal like new; rare scatheless.
▷ANTONYMS harmed, injured.

unscrupulous adjective *a crackdown on unscrupulous landlords*: **unprincipled**, unethical, immoral, amoral, conscienceless, untrustworthy, shameless, reprobate, exploitative, corrupt, corrupted, dishonest, fraudulent, cheating, dishonourable, deceitful, devious, underhand, guileful, cunning, furtive, sly, wrongdoing, unsavoury, disreputable, improper, bad, evil, wicked, villainous, roguish, sinful, ignoble, degenerate, venal; informal crooked, shady, shifty, slippery; Brit. informal dodgy; archaic dastardly.
▷ANTONYMS ethical, honest.

unseat verb **1** *the favourite unseated his rider at the start*: **dislodge**, throw, dismount, spill, upset, unhorse.
2 *an attempt to unseat the party leader*: **depose**, oust, remove from office, topple, overthrow, bring down, dislodge, discharge, dethrone, displace, supplant, usurp, overturn, dismiss, eject, evict; informal drum out.

unseemly adjective *an unseemly squabble*: **indecorous**, improper, inappropriate, unbecoming, unfitting, unbefitting, unsuitable, unworthy, undignified, unrefined, indiscreet, indelicate, ungentlemanly, unladylike, impolite; ill-advised, out of place/keeping, tasteless, in poor/bad taste, disreputable, coarse, crass, shameful.
▷ANTONYMS seemly, decorous.

unseen adjective *an unseen sniper*: **hidden**, concealed, obscured, camouflaged, unrevealed, out of sight, invisible, not visible, imperceptible, undetectable, unnoticeable, unnoticed, unobserved, covered, masked, shrouded, veiled.
▷ANTONYMS seen, spotted.

unselfish adjective *he always acted from unselfish motives*: **altruistic**, disinterested, selfless, self-denying, self-forgetting, self-sacrificing; generous, philanthropic, public-spirited, humanitarian, humane, charitable, compassionate, benevolent, caring, kind, considerate, open-handed, magnanimous, liberal, unsparing, ungrudging, unstinting, decent, noble.
▷ANTONYMS selfish, greedy.

Word toolkit **unselfish**

See **generous**.

U

unsettle verb *all this talk of death was unsettling him*: **discompose**, unnerve, upset, disturb, disquiet, make anxious, make uneasy, perturb, discomfit, disconcert, alarm, confuse, nonplus, bewilder, confound, perplex; daunt, dismay, trouble, bother, agitate, fluster, ruffle, jolt, shake (up), throw, put off, take aback, unbalance, destabilize, throw off balance, put someone off their stroke, pull the rug (out) from under; informal rattle, faze, psych out.

unsettled adjective **1** *an unsettled, unsatisfied life*: **aimless**, directionless, purposeless, without purpose, without a goal; rootless, moving, wandering, nomadic, travelling, transient.
▷ANTONYMS settled, purposeful.
2 *I was an unsettled child*: **restless**, restive, fidgety, anxious, worried, troubled, fretful; disquieted, flustered, agitated, ruffled, uneasy, disconcerted, discomposed, unnerved, ill at ease, uncomfortable, edgy, on edge, tense, nervous, apprehensive, alarmed, concerned, dismayed, disturbed, turbulent, perturbed, shaken, upset, bothered, distressed; informal thrown, rattled, fazed, twitchy, shaky, wired.
▷ANTONYMS settled, composed.
3 *more unsettled weather is forecast*: **changeable**, changing, variable, varying, inconstant, inconsistent, ever-changing, erratic, unstable, unsteady, shifting, fluid, undependable, unreliable, uncertain, unpredictable, mercurial, quicksilver, kaleidoscopic, chameleon-like; rare protean.
▷ANTONYMS settled, unchanging, predictable.
4 *the question remains unsettled*: **undecided**, to be decided, unresolved, undetermined, uncertain, open, arguable, debatable, disputed, unanswered, open to debate, doubtful, in doubt, moot, up in the air, in (a state of) limbo, in a state of uncertainty, indefinite, inconclusive, unconfirmed, unsolved, ongoing, pending; confused, problematic, vexed, ambiguous, equivocal, vague, borderline; informal iffy.
▷ANTONYMS settled.
5 *they charge interest on debts that remain unsettled after 30 days*: **unpaid**, payable, outstanding, owing, owed, to be paid, due, overdue, undischarged, in arrears, in the red, receivable; N. Amer. delinquent, past due.
▷ANTONYMS settled, paid.
6 *unsettled or thinly populated areas*: **uninhabited**, unpopulated, unpeopled, unoccupied, unfrequented; empty, vacant, abandoned, deserted, depopulated, forsaken, desolate, lonely.
▷ANTONYMS settled, populated.

unshakeable adjective *they both have an unshakeable confidence in the rightness of their own opinions*: **steadfast**, resolute, staunch, firm, constant, decided, determined, fixed, ingrained, unswerving, unwavering, unvacillating, unfaltering, unflinching; unyielding, inflexible, dogged, obstinate, persistent, unassailable, immovable, irremovable, indelible, iron, adamant, deep-dyed, indefatigable, tireless, unflagging, unremitting, unrelenting, relentless.
▷ANTONYMS weak, half-hearted.

unsightly adjective *an unsightly concrete church*: **ugly**, unattractive, unprepossessing, unlovely, ill-favoured, disagreeable, displeasing, awful-looking, frightful-looking, hideous, horrible, repulsive, revolting, repellent, disgusting, offensive, grotesque, monstrous, gruesome, ghastly.
▷ANTONYMS beautiful, attractive.

unskilful adjective *the furniture had been repaired by an unskilful hand*: **inexpert**, incompetent, inept, unskilled, clumsy, awkward, maladroit, unhandy, amateur, amateurish, unprofessional, inexperienced, untrained, unpractised, crude, rude, unsophisticated, gauche, fumbling, bungling, blundering, botching; informal ham-fisted, ham-handed, cack-handed, cowboy, not up to scratch.
▷ANTONYMS skilful.

unskilled adjective *unskilled manual workers*: **untrained**, unqualified, untaught, unschooled; manual, blue-collar, labouring, menial; inexpert, inexperienced, unpractised, unequipped, unversed, unaccomplished, uneducated, amateur, amateurish, unprofessional.
▷ANTONYMS skilled.

unsociable adjective *he was grumpy and unsociable*: **unfriendly**, unamiable, unaffable, uncongenial, unneighbourly, inhospitable, hostile, unapproachable, reclusive, introverted, solitary, private, misanthropic, uncommunicative, unforthcoming, reticent, reserved, withdrawn, aloof, distant, remote, detached, stand-offish, unsocial, antisocial, taciturn, silent, quiet, sulky, mopey, mopish, uncivil, rude, cold, cool, chilly, frigid, haughty, suspicious, distrustful, scowling, glowering.
▷ANTONYMS sociable, friendly.

Easily confused words **unsociable, unsocial, or antisocial?**

There is some overlap in the use of the adjectives **unsociable**, **unsocial**, and **antisocial**, but they have distinct core meanings. *Unsociable* means 'not enjoying the company of others', as in *Terry was grumpy and unsociable*. *Antisocial* means 'contrary to the laws and customs of a society', as in *aggressive and antisocial behaviour*. *Unsocial* is usually restricted to the sense '(of hours) falling outside the normal working day', as in *employees were expected to work unsocial hours*.

unsolicited adjective *he did not take easily to unsolicited advice*: **uninvited**, unsought, unasked for, unrequested, undemanded, uncalled for, not required, unprompted, unbidden, unwelcome, gratuitous, volunteered, voluntary, spontaneous.
▷ANTONYMS requested, invited.

unsophisticated adjective **1** *she seemed terribly unsophisticated*: **unworldly**, naive, simple, innocent, ignorant, green, immature, callow, inexperienced, childlike, artless, guileless, ingenuous, down-to-earth, natural, unaffected, unassuming, unpretentious, modest, without airs; unrefined, unpolished, gauche, provincial, parochial, rustic.
▷ANTONYMS sophisticated, worldly.
2 *unsophisticated computer software*: **simple**, **crude**, unrefined, basic, rudimentary, primitive, rough and ready, rough-hewn, make-do, cobbled together, undeveloped, homespun; straightforward, uncomplicated, uninvolved, unspecialized; dated rude.
▷ANTONYMS sophisticated, complex.

unsound adjective **1** *the tower is structurally unsound*: **rickety**, flimsy, shaky, wobbly, unstable, tottery, defective, disintegrating, crumbling, decaying, broken, broken-down, damaged, rotten, ramshackle, insubstantial, jerry-built, unsafe, unreliable, dangerous.
▷ANTONYMS sound, strong.
2 *this submission appears to us unsound on several grounds*: **untenable**, flawed, defective, faulty, ill-founded, flimsy, weak, shaky, unreliable, questionable, dubious, tenuous, suspect, illogical, irrational, unfounded, ungrounded, unsubstantiated, unsupported, specious, hollow, spurious, false, fallacious, fallible, erroneous, wrong, sophistic, casuistic; informal iffy; Brit. informal dodgy.
▷ANTONYMS sound, strong.
3 *of unsound mind*: **disordered**, diseased, deranged, disturbed, troubled, demented, unstable, unbalanced, unhinged, insane, crazed, distracted; informal touched.
▷ANTONYMS sane.

unsparing adjective **1** *an unsparing analysis of the way the two parties collude to stay in power*: **merciless**, pitiless, unpitying, ruthless, relentless, remorseless, unmerciful, unforgiving, implacable, uncompromising; stern, strict, severe, stringent, harsh, tough, rigorous, exacting, demanding, inflexible, draconian; Austral./NZ informal solid.
▷ANTONYMS merciful, gentle, mild.
2 *she had won her mother's unsparing approval*: **ungrudging**, unstinting, willingly given, free, free-handed, ready, beneficent, benevolent, big-hearted, kind-hearted, kind, unselfish; **lavish**, liberal, generous, magnanimous, open-handed, munificent, bountiful; profuse, abundant; literary bounteous, plenteous.
▷ANTONYMS grudging, mean.

unspeakable adjective **1** *the book is a treasure trove of unspeakable delights*: **indescribable**, beyond words, beyond description, inexpressible, unutterable, indefinable, beggaring description, ineffable, unimaginable, inconceivable, unthinkable, unheard of, marvellous, wonderful.
2 *an unspeakable crime*: **dreadful**, awful, appalling, horrific, horrifying, horrible, terrible, horrendous, atrocious, insufferable, abominable, abhorrent, repellent, repulsive, repugnant, revolting, sickening, frightful, fearful, shocking, hideous, ghastly, grim, dire, hateful, odious, loathsome, gruesome, monstrous, outrageous, heinous, deplorable, despicable, contemptible, execrable, vile, indescribable, indescribably bad/wicked/evil; rare egregious.
▷ANTONYMS commendable.

unspecified adjective *he proposed to resign at an unspecified date*: **unnamed**, unstated, unidentified, unquantified, undesignated, undefined, unfixed, undecided, undetermined, uncertain, uncounted; nameless, anonymous, mystery, mysterious, incognito, unknown; indefinite, indeterminate, vague, obscure, arbitrary, such-and-such a ..., some, any; informal this, nth, x number of ...; rare innominate.
▷ANTONYMS specified, fixed, known.

unspectacular adjective *he had a steady, unspectacular career*: **unremarkable**, unexceptional, undistinguished, uneventful, unmemorable, inconspicuous; **ordinary**, average, normal, commonplace, nothing out of the ordinary; **mediocre**, middling, run-of-the-mill, workaday, indifferent, amateur, amateurish, dull, boring, plodding.
▷ANTONYMS spectacular, remarkable.

unspoilt adjective **1** *unspoilt countryside*: **unimpaired**, preserved, intact, as good as new/before, perfect, spotless, pristine, immaculate, virgin, unblemished, unharmed, unbroken, unflawed, undamaged, unmutilated, untouched, unmarked, untainted, unaffected, unchanged.
▷ANTONYMS spoilt, devastated, overdeveloped.
2 *a noble and unspoilt man*: **innocent**, wholesome, natural, simple, artless, unaffected, pure, uncorrupted, unsullied, undefiled, unblemished, untarnished, stainless, spotless, impeccable.
▷ANTONYMS spoilt, corrupt.

unspoken adjective *there was an unspoken contract between them*: **unstated**, unexpressed, unuttered, unsaid, unmentioned, unvoiced,

unarticulated, undeclared, unavowed, not spelt out, mute, silent, wordless, voiceless; **tacit**, implicit, implied, understood, taken for granted, taken as read, inferred, hinted (at), suggested, insinuated.
▷ANTONYMS stated, explicit.

Choose the right word **unspoken, implicit, tacit**

See **implicit**.

unstable adjective **1** *icebergs are notoriously unstable and may flip over*: **unsteady**, rocky, wobbly, wobbling, rickety, shaky, tottery, tottering, teetering, doddery, unsafe, unbalanced, unreliable, insecure, not secure, unfastened, unsecured, movable, precarious; Irish bockety.
▷ANTONYMS stable, steady.
2 *the country suffered from unstable coffee prices*: **changeable**, volatile, variable, unsettled, fluctuating, inconstant, inconsistent, irregular, fitful, unpredictable, unreliable, fickle, capricious, mercurial, erratic, uncertain, wavering.
▷ANTONYMS stable, firm.
3 *he was mentally unstable*: **unbalanced**, of unsound mind, mentally ill, deranged, demented, crazed, distracted, troubled, disturbed, unhinged, insane, mad, mad as a hatter, mad as a March hare, raving mad, lunatic, out of one's mind/head, not in one's right mind, neurotic, psychotic; Latin non compos mentis; informal crazy, loopy, loony, mixed up, nuts, nutty, nutty as a fruitcake, bananas, cracked, crackpot, daft, dippy, screwy, bats, batty, dotty, cuckoo, bonkers, potty, mental, screwed up, not all there, off one's head, out to lunch, a bit lacking, round the bend/twist, away with the fairies; Brit. informal barmy, crackers, barking, barking mad, off one's trolley/rocker, daft as a brush, not the full shilling; N. Amer. informal nutsy, nutso, squirrelly, wacko, buggy; dated touched.
▷ANTONYMS stable, balanced.

Word toolkit **unstable**

See **variable**.

unsteady adjective **1** *she was unsteady on her feet*: **unstable**, rocky, wobbly, wobbling, rickety, shaky, shaking, tottery, tottering, teetering, unsafe, unbalanced, unreliable, insecure, not secure, unfastened, unsecured, movable, precarious; dizzy, light-headed, faint, weak-kneed, weak at the knees, groggy, punch-drunk; feeble, faltering, doddery, doddering; tentative, nervous, timid, hesitant; informal trembly, all of a quiver, teetery, (with legs) like jelly; rare vertiginous.
▷ANTONYMS steady, stable.
2 *the baby poured tea in an unsteady stream on to the pink carpet*: **irregular**, uneven, varying, variable, erratic, jerky, unreliable, volatile, spasmodic, sporadic, changeable, changing, fluctuating, wavering, vacillating, inconstant, intermittent, fitful, desultory, occasional, unsystematic; flickering, flashing, trembling; technical aperiodic.

unstinted adjective *Gina gave him the unstinted praise he deserved*: **lavish**, liberal, generous, magnanimous, open-handed, munificent, bountiful; **ungrudging**, unsparing, willingly given, ready, beneficent, benevolent, kind, unselfish; profuse, abundant, ample; literary bounteous, plenteous.

unstinting adjective *her unstinting charity work*: **ungrudging**, unsparing, willingly given, free, free-handed, ready, beneficent, benevolent, big-hearted, kind-hearted, kind, unselfish; lavish, liberal, generous, magnanimous, open-handed, munificent, bountiful; profuse, abundant, ample; literary bounteous, plenteous.

unstudied adjective *he always does it with unstudied grace | she writes a seemingly unstudied prose*: **natural**, unlaboured, easy, unaffected, unforced, uncontrived, unmannered, unstilted, unpretentious, without airs, artless, guileless, informal, casual, nonchalant, spontaneous, impromptu, ad lib; unrehearsed, improvised, unscripted, unpremeditated, extempore, extemporized; Latin ad libitum; rare extemporary, extemporaneous.
▷ANTONYMS studied, stilted, prepared.

unsubstantiated adjective *there were unsubstantiated allegations of serious misbehaviour*: **unconfirmed**, unsupported, uncorroborated, not backed up by evidence, unverified, unattested, unproven, not validated, untested; unfounded, ill-founded, groundless, baseless, without basis, without foundation, unjustified, unwarranted, unjustifiable, unreasonable; speculative, conjectural, assumed, presumed; questionable, open to question, disputable, debatable; unreliable, untrustworthy, dubious, doubtful, tenuous, spurious, suspect, flimsy, weak, nebulous, unsound, undependable; informal iffy; Brit. informal dodgy; rare unestablished, suppositious, suppositive.
▷ANTONYMS well founded, undeniable.

unsuccessful adjective **1** *an unsuccessful attempt*: **failed**, without success, abortive, misfired; vain, in vain, futile, useless, pointless, worthless, nugatory; ineffective, ineffectual, inefficacious, unavailing, fruitless, profitless, unproductive; thwarted, baulked, frustrated, foiled; archaic bootless.
▷ANTONYMS successful.
2 *an unsuccessful business venture | an unsuccessful candidate*: **unprofitable**, unprosperous, loss-making; **failed**, losing, beaten; unlucky, luckless, out of luck, unfortunate, ill-starred, fated, ill-fated, ill-omened.
▷ANTONYMS profitable; winning.

unsuitable adjective **1** *they had been sold an unsuitable product*: **inappropriate**, unsuited, ill-suited, inapt, inapposite, unfitting, unbefitting, undue, incompatible, out of place, out of keeping, out of character, incongruous; unacceptable, ineligible, not good enough.
▷ANTONYMS suitable.
2 *unsuitable reading matter for a young lady*: **unbecoming**, unseemly, indecorous, improper.
▷ANTONYMS becoming.
3 *her comment came at an unsuitable moment*: **inopportune**, infelicitous, malapropos; badly chosen; archaic unseasonable.
▷ANTONYMS opportune.

unsullied adjective *he came with an unsullied reputation*: **spotless**, untarnished, unblemished, untainted, impeccable, undamaged, unspoilt, unimpaired, undefiled, stainless, intact, perfect, pristine, immaculate, virgin, unharmed, unbroken, unflawed, unmutilated, untouched, unmarked, unaffected.
▷ANTONYMS sullied, tarnished.

unsung adjective *one of the finest unsung heroes of the last war*: **unacknowledged**, uncelebrated, unacclaimed, unapplauded, unpraised, unhailed, unlauded, unhonoured, unrenowned, untrumpeted, unbemoaned; **neglected**, disregarded, unrecognized, overlooked, forgotten; unknown, anonymous, nameless, unnamed, obscure, unmissed.
▷ANTONYMS famous, celebrated.

unsure adjective **1** *she felt very unsure*: **unconfident**, not confident, lacking confidence, lacking self-confidence, not self-assured, lacking assurance, unassertive; **insecure**, hesitant, diffident, timid, timorous, anxious, apprehensive, fearful.
▷ANTONYMS confident, assertive.
2 *Sally was unsure whether to be pleased*: **undecided**, irresolute, dithering, equivocating, in two minds, in a dilemma, in a quandary, ambivalent, vague.
▷ANTONYMS decided.
3 *some teachers are unsure about the proposed strike*: **dubious**, doubtful, sceptical, distrustful, suspicious, mistrustful, uncertain, unconvinced; informal iffy.
▷ANTONYMS happy, convinced.
4 *the date is unsure*: **not fixed**, not settled, undecided, indeterminate, uncertain, unknown.
▷ANTONYMS fixed.

unsurpassed adjective *Beethoven's nine unsurpassed masterpieces*: **unmatched**, unrivalled, unparalleled, unequalled, matchless, peerless, without peer, without equal, in a class of its own, all-time best, inimitable, incomparable, beyond compare, beyond comparison, second to none, unsurpassable, surpassing, nonpareil; unique, consummate, perfect, rare, exquisite, transcendent, superlative, supreme, outstanding, pre-eminent, top, towering, leading, foremost, premier, the best; rare unexampled; French hors concours; (**be unsurpassed**) stand alone.
▷ANTONYMS inferior; eclipsed.

unsurprising adjective *his failure to win the leadership of the party was unsurprising*: **predictable**, foreseeable, (only) to be expected, what one would expect, not unexpected, predicted, foreseen, forecast, anticipated, awaited; probable, likely, par for the course, normal; logical, understandable, plausible, obvious; informal inevitable, on the cards.
▷ANTONYMS surprising, unpredictable.

unsuspecting adjective *this is a very nasty trick to play on the unsuspecting public*: **unsuspicious**, unwary, unaware, unconscious, off guard, ignorant, unknowing, unwitting, oblivious, heedless, unmindful; **trusting**, trustful; gullible, credulous, ingenuous, naive, innocent, dupable, easily deceived, easily taken in, exploitable; rare incognizant, nescient.
▷ANTONYMS suspicious, knowing, wary.

unswerving adjective *she has always demanded unswerving loyalty*: **unwavering**, unfaltering, unhesitating, unflinching, steadfast, unshakeable, undaunted, staunch, firm, resolute, stalwart, dedicated, committed, constant, single-minded, earnest; stubborn, tenacious, bulldog, strong-minded, strong-willed, dogged, indefatigable, unyielding, unbending, immovable, unrelenting; spirited, brave, bold, courageous, plucky, stout, stout-hearted, mettlesome, indomitable, strenuous, vigorous, gritty, stiff; N. Amer. rock-ribbed.
▷ANTONYMS half-hearted, ambiguous, unreliable.

unsympathetic adjective **1** *benefit claimants often encounter unsympathetic staff*: **uncaring**, unconcerned, unfeeling, insensitive, unkind, compassionless, uncharitable, unpitying, pitiless, uncommiserating, indifferent, unresponsive, apathetic, unmoved, untouched, heartless, cold, hard-hearted, stony-hearted, hard, harsh, callous, cruel, inhuman.

U

▷ANTONYMS sympathetic, caring.
2 *the new Assembly was quite unsympathetic to these views*: **opposed to**, against, (dead) set against, antagonistic towards, inimical to, anti, ill-disposed towards, disapproving of.
▷ANTONYMS sympathetic, in agreement with.
3 *he is a totally unsympathetic character*: **unlikeable**, disagreeable, unpleasant, objectionable, obnoxious, unsavoury, unattractive; unsociable, uncongenial, unfriendly, inhospitable, unneighbourly, unapproachable, aloof, cool, cold, distant; **nasty**, ill-natured, cross, bad-tempered.
▷ANTONYMS likeable.

unsystematic adjective *the burial mound was excavated in an unsystematic way*: **unmethodical**, uncoordinated, undirected, disorganized, unarranged, unplanned, unpremeditated, indiscriminate; random, inconsistent, desultory, patchy, fragmentary, sketchy, sporadic, spasmodic, fitful, inconstant, intermittent, irregular, erratic, stray, spot, casual, occasional, haphazard; chaotic, non-linear, entropic, fractal.
▷ANTONYMS systematic, well planned.

untamed adjective *the untamed wildlife which proliferates in the region*: **wild**, savage, feral, natural, free, uncontrollable; **undomesticated**, unbroken, not broken in, untrained, unused to humans; rare brutish, bestial.
▷ANTONYMS tame, domesticated.

untangle verb 1 *I untangled the fishing tackle*: **disentangle**, unravel, unsnarl, unjumble, straighten out, sort out, untwist, untwine, untie, unknot, undo.
▷ANTONYMS tangle, jumble.
2 *I started to try and untangle the mystery*: **solve**, find the/an answer to, answer, find a/the solution to, resolve, work out, puzzle out, fathom, understand, find the key to, find the answer to, decipher, clear up, make easier to understand, make simpler, make plainer, clarify, make more comprehensible, make more intelligible, remove the complexities from, straighten out, sort out, get to the bottom of, make head or tail of, unravel, disentangle, unfold, piece together, simplify, explain, expound, elucidate, illuminate; informal figure out, suss out, crack.
▷ANTONYMS complicate, confuse, cloud.

untarnished adjective *the reputation of the school was untarnished*: **unsullied**, unblemished, untainted, impeccable, undamaged, unspoilt, unimpaired, undefiled, spotless, stainless, intact, perfect, pristine, immaculate, virgin, unharmed, unbroken, unflawed, untouched, unmarked, unaffected.
▷ANTONYMS tarnished.

untenable adjective *the Government's position is untenable*: **indefensible**, undefendable, unarguable, insupportable, refutable, unsustainable, unjustified, unwarranted, unjustifiable, inadmissible, unsound, ill-founded, flimsy, weak, shaky, flawed, defective, faulty, implausible, specious, groundless, unfounded, baseless, invalid, absurd, illogical, irrational, preposterous, senseless, unacceptable.
▷ANTONYMS tenable, defensible.

unthinkable adjective 1 *Beethoven is unthinkable without the tradition of western music*: **unimaginable**, inconceivable, unbelievable, incredible, beyond belief, highly unlikely, unheard of, implausible, illogical, impossible, beyond the bounds of possibility.
▷ANTONYMS likely, imaginable, plausible.
2 *to me a lentil soup is unthinkable without lemon and olive oil*: **highly undesirable**, not to be considered, unconscionable, out of the question, absurd, unreasonable, preposterous, ludicrous, outrageous, shocking; informal not on.
▷ANTONYMS desirable.

unthinking adjective 1 *Dorothea was often an unthinking woman*: **thoughtless**, inconsiderate, uncaring, heedless, unmindful, regardless, insensitive, injudicious, blundering, uncharitable, unkind; tactless, undiplomatic, indiscreet, careless, selfish, impolite, rude.
▷ANTONYMS thoughtful, careful.
2 *don't encourage the unthinking sprinkling of salt over food*: **absent-minded**, heedless, thoughtless, unmindful, careless, injudicious, ill-advised, ill-considered, imprudent, unwise, foolish, silly, stupid, reckless, rash, precipitate, negligent, neglectful, remiss; involuntary, inadvertent, unintentional, unintended, mechanical, automatic, reflex, spontaneous, instinctive, impulsive, intuitive, unpremeditated, unconscious.
▷ANTONYMS intentional, planned.

unthought of adjective *what we have today was once unthought of and in most cases seemed impossible*: **unpredicted**, unforeseen, unanticipated, unplanned, accidental, unlooked for, unsought, unexpected, not bargained for; sudden, abrupt, surprising, startling, astonishing, abnormal, out of the blue.
▷ANTONYMS expected, predictable.

untidy adjective 1 *Fran smoothed her untidy hair*: **scruffy**, tousled, dishevelled, unkempt, messy, disordered, disarranged, messed up, rumpled, bedraggled, uncombed, ungroomed, straggly, ruffled, tangled, matted, windblown, wild; frowzy, dirty, sleazy, seedy, slovenly, slatternly, sloppy; informal ratty, mussed up, slobbish, slobby; N. Amer. informal raggedy, schlumpy, raunchy; archaic draggle-tailed.
▷ANTONYMS tidy, neat.
2 *the place was dreadfully untidy*: **disordered**, messy, in a mess, disorderly, disorganized, in disorder, in confusion, confused, cluttered, in a clutter, mixed up, in a muddle, muddled, in a jumble, jumbled, in chaos, chaotic, haywire, topsy-turvy, in disarray, awry, askew, upside down, upset, disrupted, at sixes and sevens; informal higgledy-piggledy, every which way; Brit. informal shambolic, like a dog's dinner/breakfast.
▷ANTONYMS tidy, orderly.

untie verb *she knelt to untie her laces | he hung over the bank and untied the boat*: **undo**, unknot, unbind, unfasten, unwrap, unlace, untether, unfetter, unhitch, unmoor; **loose**, detach, free, set free, release, let go, set adrift, cast off.
▷ANTONYMS tie up.

until preposition & conjunction 1 *I was working away until midnight | young trees should be staked until they are well established*: **till**, up to, up till, up until, as late as, up to the time of/that, until such time as, pending; N. Amer. through.
▷ANTONYMS beyond, after.
2 *this did not happen until 1998*: **before**, prior to, previous to, up to, up until, till, up till, earlier than, in advance of, ante-, pre-.
▷ANTONYMS after.

untimely adjective 1 *I would like to explain the untimely interruption you heard a few minutes ago*: **ill-timed**, badly timed, mistimed; inopportune, inappropriate; inconvenient, awkward, unwelcome, unfavourable, unfortunate, infelicitous, inapt, unsuitable; rare malapropos; archaic unseasonable.
▷ANTONYMS timely, opportune.
2 *his untimely death*: **premature**, early, too early, too soon, before time; archaic unseasonable.
▷ANTONYMS expected.

untiring adjective *an untiring advocate of political and economic reform*: **vigorous**, energetic, industrious, determined, resolute, enthusiastic, keen, zealous, forceful, strong, Herculean, spirited, dynamic, intense, dogged, tenacious, persistent, persevering, constant, incessant, unceasing, steady, stout, staunch, pertinacious; **tireless**, unwearied, unflagging, unfailing, unfaltering, unwavering, indefatigable, unshakeable, unrelenting, unremitting, unswerving.
▷ANTONYMS lazy, half-hearted.

untold adjective 1 *thieves caused untold damage*: **boundless**, measureless, limitless, without limit, unlimited, unbounded, immense, vast, great, endless, unending, never-ending, without end, inexhaustible, infinite, interminable, unceasing, everlasting, immeasurable, incalculable.
▷ANTONYMS limited.
2 *untold billions have been poured into research*: **countless**, innumerable, unlimited, endless, limitless, numberless, an infinite number of, an incalculable number of, more than one can count, too many to be counted, without number, uncountable, uncounted; numerous, many, multiple, manifold, legion; informal more … than one can shake a stick at; literary multitudinous, myriad; rare unnumbered, unnumberable, innumerous, unsummed.
3 *a £300,000 docudrama will reveal the untold story that led to his acquittal*: **unreported**, unrecounted, unrelated, unrevealed, undisclosed, undivulged, unpublished, secret, suppressed, unnarrated, unmentioned, unstated, unspoken.

untouched adjective 1 *the food sat on their plates untouched*: **uneaten**, unconsumed, undrunk; left over, surplus, unwanted.
2 *one of the few untouched areas left on this fast developing island*: **unspoilt**, unmarked, unblemished, untarnished, unsullied, undefiled, undamaged, unharmed, unscathed, unmarred, unpolluted; **pristine**, intact, natural, immaculate, in perfect condition, perfect, spotless, flawless, clean, fresh, virgin, pure; unaffected, unchanged, unaltered, uninfluenced.
▷ANTONYMS developed, built-up, industrialized.

untoward adjective *Tom had noticed nothing untoward*: **unexpected**, unanticipated, unforeseen, unpredictable, unpredicted; surprising, unusual; inopportune, untimely, ill-timed, badly timed, mistimed; inconvenient, awkward, unwelcome, unfavourable, adverse, unfortunate, infelicitous; inappropriate, unsuitable, inapt; rare malapropos; archaic unseasonable.
▷ANTONYMS expected, timely, appropriate.

untrained adjective *the system can be utilized quickly by untrained users*: **unskilled**, untaught, non-technical, unschooled, untutored, unpractised, inexperienced, unequipped, unversed, uninformed, unacquainted; unqualified, unlicensed, uncertificated, unchartered; incompetent, incapable, inexpert, ignorant, green, raw; amateur, non-professional, lay, dilettante.
▷ANTONYMS trained, professional.

untried adjective *he chose two untried actors for leading roles | dealers used their clients as guinea pigs for their untried techniques*: **untested**,

unestablished, new; **experimental**, exploratory, unattempted, prototype, trial, test, pilot; speculative, conjectural, unproven, unsubstantiated.
▷ANTONYMS established, well tried.

untroubled adjective *a man untroubled by a guilty conscience*: **unworried**, unperturbed, unconcerned, unruffled, undisturbed, undismayed, unbothered, unagitated, unflustered; unanxious, insouciant, nonchalant, blasé, carefree, blithe, casual, without a care in the world; serene, composed, relaxed, peaceful, tranquil, at ease, devil-may-care, happy-go-lucky, {cool, calm, and collected}; trouble-free, unbroken, uninterrupted; informal laid-back, unflappable.
▷ANTONYMS troubled, anxious.

untrue adjective **1** *these suggestions are totally untrue*: **false**, untruthful, fabricated, made up, invented, concocted, trumped up; erroneous, in error, wrong, incorrect, inaccurate, inexact; flawed, specious, fallacious, unsound, unfounded, misguided, distorted, out, misleading; fictitious, fabulous, mythical, mythological; humorous economical with the truth.
▷ANTONYMS true, correct.
2 *he was untrue to himself*: **unfaithful**, disloyal, faithless, false, false-hearted, treacherous, traitorous, perfidious, deceitful, deceiving, untrustworthy, duplicitous, double-dealing, insincere, unreliable, undependable, inconstant; adulterous; informal two-timing.
▷ANTONYMS true, faithful.

untrustworthy adjective *the clubs are vulnerable to untrustworthy treasurers*: **dishonest**, deceitful, not to be trusted, double-dealing, treacherous, traitorous, two-faced, unfaithful, duplicitous, dishonourable, unprincipled, unscrupulous, corrupt, shady, shifty, underhand; **unreliable**, undependable, capricious, fickle, slippery; informal iffy; Brit. informal dodgy; Austral./NZ informal shonky; rare Janus-faced.
▷ANTONYMS trustworthy, reliable.

untruth noun **1** *her account of what had happened was a patent untruth*: **lie**, falsehood, fib, fabrication, deception, made-up story, trumped-up story, invention, fiction, piece of fiction, falsification, falsity, cock and bull story, barefaced lie; (little) white lie, half-truth, exaggeration, prevarication, departure from the truth; yarn, story, red herring, rumour, fable, myth, flight of fancy, figment of the imagination; pretence, pretext, sham, ruse, wile, stratagem; (**untruths**) misinformation, disinformation, trickery, perjury, dissimulation, gossip, propaganda; informal tall story, tall tale, fairy story, fairy tale, whopper; Brit. informal porky, pork pie, porky pie; humorous terminological inexactitude, economy with the truth; vulgar slang bullshit; Austral./NZ vulgar slang bulldust.
2 *he was livid at the total untruth of the story*: **falsity**, falsehood, falseness, untruthfulness, fallaciousness, fiction, fictitiousness, inaccuracy, hollowness; **mendacity**, fabrication, dishonesty, deceit, deceitfulness, deception, duplicity, disingenuousness, hypocrisy, fraud, fraudulence; informal kidology; rare unveracity.

untruthful adjective **1** *the answers may be untruthful*: **false**, untrue, fabricated, made up, invented, concocted, trumped up; erroneous, in error, wrong, incorrect, inaccurate, inexact; flawed, specious, fallacious, unsound, unfounded, misguided, distorted, out, misleading; fictitious, fabulous, mythical, mythological; humorous economical with the truth.
2 *an untruthful person*: **lying**, mendacious, perfidious, dishonest, deceitful, deceiving, deceptive, duplicitous, dissimulating, dissembling, false, double-dealing, two-faced, guileful, underhand, sneaky, disingenuous; informal crooked, bent, tricky; archaic hollow-hearted.
▷ANTONYMS honest, truthful.

untutored adjective *such articles will make little sense to an untutored reader*: **uneducated**, untaught, unschooled, ill-educated, untrained; illiterate, unlettered, ignorant, ill-informed, uninformed, lowbrow; uncouth, unsophisticated, uncultivated, uncultured, unaccomplished, unenlightened, philistine, benighted, backward, vulgar, simple; archaic rude.
▷ANTONYMS tutored, educated.

untwine verb *Robyn untwined her fingers*: **untwist**, disentwine, disentangle, unravel, unsnarl, unwind, unroll, uncoil, unreel, undo, spread out, unfurl, open (out), lay out, straighten (out), unkink; Nautical unlay.
▷ANTONYMS twine.

untwist verb *he untwisted the wire and straightened it out*: **untwine**, disentwine, disentangle, unravel, unsnarl, unwind, unroll, uncoil, unreel, undo, spread out, unfurl, open (out), lay out, straighten (out), unkink; Nautical unlay.
▷ANTONYMS twist.

unused adjective **1** *the new operating theatre will stand unused until next April | a charitable organization collects unused food*: **unutilized**, not made use of, unemployed, unexploited, not in service, non-functioning; **left over**, remaining, uneaten, unconsumed, untouched, unneeded, not required, still available, surplus to requirements, to spare, superfluous, surplus, extra; **pristine**, immaculate, as new, unspoilt, spotless, flawless, clean, fresh, blank, new, virgin, pure, untouched, unopened, unmarked, unblemished, untarnished, unsullied, undefiled, unworn; informal going begging.
▷ANTONYMS used, in use.
2 *he was unused to such directness*: **unaccustomed**, not used, new, fresh, a stranger; unfamiliar with, unconversant with, unacquainted with; unpractised in, inexperienced in, unversed in; archaic strange.
▷ANTONYMS used, accustomed.

unusual adjective **1** *the unusual sight of a golden eagle flying over Regents Park*: **uncommon**, abnormal, atypical, unexpected, surprising, unfamiliar, unwonted, different; strange, odd, curious, out of the ordinary, extraordinary, out of the way, unorthodox, uncustomary, unconventional, outlandish, offbeat, deviant, novel, singular, peculiar, queer, bizarre, freakish, quirky, alien; **rare**, scarce, few and far between, thin on the ground, exceptional, isolated, occasional, infrequent, irregular, sporadic; Brit. out of the common; informal weird, oddball, way out, freaky, something else; N. Amer. informal off the wall; dated seldom.
▷ANTONYMS common, everyday.
2 *a man of unusual talent*: **remarkable**, extraordinary, exceptional, singular, particular, marked, outstanding, notable, noteworthy, distinctive, striking, significant, especial, special, signal, superior, unique, unparalleled, unprecedented, prodigious; informal mind-boggling, mind-blowing.
▷ANTONYMS unremarkable.

unutterable adjective **1** *an existence of unutterable boredom*: **indescribable**, beyond words, beyond description, inexpressible, unspeakable, undefinable, beggaring description, inconceivable, unthinkable, unheard of; **extreme**, intense, great, overwhelming; **dreadful**, awful, appalling, horrible, terrible, insufferable.
2 *unutterable joy suffused her whole being*: **marvellous**, wonderful, superb, splendid, ineffable, unimaginable, profound, deep, ecstatic.
▷ANTONYMS mild.

unvarnished adjective **1** *the unvarnished wood panelling*: **bare**, plain, unpainted, unlacquered, unpolished, unfinished, untreated, raw, natural, matt; stripped.
▷ANTONYMS varnished.
2 *the programme gives an unvarnished account of the proceedings of the House*: **straightforward**, plain, simple, stark, naked, bald; truthful, realistic, true to life; candid, honest, frank, outspoken, forthright, plain-spoken, direct, blunt, downright, brutal, harsh, straight from the shoulder, explicit, unequivocal, unambiguous, unexaggerated, unadorned, undisguised, unveiled, unqualified; informal upfront, warts and all.
▷ANTONYMS qualified.

unveil verb *the club has unveiled plans for a new 1600-seat stand*: **reveal**, present, disclose, divulge, make known, make public, air, communicate, publish, broadcast; display, show, exhibit, demonstrate, put on show, put on display, put on view, expose to view, parade, flaunt; release, bring out, launch, introduce.

unwanted adjective **1** *the Council said the plan was an unwanted development*: **unwelcome**, undesirable, undesired, unpopular, unfortunate, unlucky, unfavourable, untoward, too bad; unpleasant, disagreeable, displeasing, unpalatable, distasteful, objectionable, offensive, upsetting, disappointing, distressing; regrettable, deplorable, lamentable, reprehensible, blameworthy, ill-advised; unacceptable, intolerable, awful, terrible, wretched, sad, dire, disastrous, appalling; ignominious, pitiful, disgraceful, shameful.
▷ANTONYMS wanted, welcome, desirable.
2 *a Darlington couple are collecting tins of unwanted pet food for an animal rescue centre*: **unused**, left over, surplus, superfluous, redundant; uneaten, unconsumed, untouched.
3 *any unwanted guest soon found himself bundled out*: **uninvited**, intruding, gatecrashing, unbidden, unasked, unrequested, unsolicited.
▷ANTONYMS invited.
4 *many ageing people feel unwanted*: **friendless**, unloved, uncared-for, uncherished, unpopular, forsaken, rejected, shunned, disliked; superfluous, useless, unnecessary; French de trop.
▷ANTONYMS loved.

unwarranted adjective **1** *they feel the criticism is unwarranted*: **unjustified**, unjustifiable, indefensible, inexcusable, unforgivable, unpardonable, uncalled for, gratuitous, unnecessary, undue, unreasonable, unjust, groundless, inappropriate, unsuitable, unseemly, unbecoming, improper, ill-advised, excessive, immoderate, disproportionate, inordinate.
▷ANTONYMS justified.
2 *the judge decided that the owner used unwarranted force*: **unauthorized**, unsanctioned, unapproved, uncertified, unaccredited, unlicensed; illegal, unlawful, illicit, illegitimate, criminal, punishable, felonious, actionable, prohibited.
▷ANTONYMS permitted, legal.

unwary adjective *accidents can happen to the unwary traveller*: **incautious**, careless, thoughtless, unthinking, heedless, inattentive, unwatchful, unobservant, off-guard, off one's guard, absent-minded; informal napping; Brit. informal dozy.

unwavering adjective *she fixed him with an unwavering stare*: **steady**, fixed, resolute, resolved, firm, steadfast, decided, unswerving,

unfluctuating, unhesitating, unfaltering, unvacillating, untiring, tireless, unflagging, indefatigable, persistent, unyielding, relentless, unremitting, unrelenting, sustained, inexorable, unshakeable.
▷ANTONYMS wavering, unsteady.

unwelcome adjective **1** *I did not mean to make you feel unwelcome*: **unwanted**, uninvited, unbidden, unasked, unrequested, unsolicited; French de trop.
▷ANTONYMS welcome.
2 *even a small increase in unemployment is unwelcome*: **undesirable**, undesired, unpopular, unfortunate, unlucky, too bad; disappointing, upsetting, distressing, unpleasant, disagreeable, displeasing, unpalatable, distasteful; **regrettable**, deplorable, lamentable, reprehensible, blameworthy, ill-advised.
▷ANTONYMS welcome, desirable.

unwell adjective *he had been unwell for some time*: **ill**, sick, poorly, indisposed, ailing, not (very) well, not oneself, not in good shape, in a bad way, out of sorts, not up to par, under/below par, peaky, liverish, queasy, nauseous; Brit. off, off colour; informal under the weather, not up to snuff, funny, peculiar, crummy, lousy, rough; Brit. informal ropy, grotty; Scottish informal wabbit; Austral./NZ informal crook; dated queer, seedy.
▷ANTONYMS well, in good health.

unwholesome adjective **1** *the unwholesome smoke-filled air*: **unhealthy**, noxious, poisonous; unnourishing, innutritious; **insalubrious**, unhygienic, insanitary; harmful, injurious, detrimental, destructive, damaging, deleterious, ruinous, malign, baleful.
▷ANTONYMS wholesome, healthy, beneficial.
2 *the application allows parents to limit children's access to unwholesome Web pages*: **improper**, immoral, indecent, corrupting, depraving, salacious, subversive, exploitative.
▷ANTONYMS proper, seemly.

unwieldy adjective *he dragged his big unwieldy sword out of its scabbard*: **cumbersome**, unmanageable, unhandy, unmanoeuvrable; awkward, difficult, clumsy, ungainly; massive, heavy, hefty, bulky, weighty, ponderous; informal hulking, clunky.
▷ANTONYMS manageable, dainty.

unwilling adjective **1** *unwilling conscripts*: **reluctant**, unenthusiastic, hesitant, afraid, resistant, grudging, involuntary, forced, enforced.
▷ANTONYMS willing, keen.
2 *he was unwilling to take on that responsibility*: **disinclined**, reluctant, averse, loath, indisposed, not in the mood, slow, not about; (**be unwilling to do something**) not have the heart to, baulk at, jib at, demur at, shy away from, flinch from, recoil from, shrink from, mind, have qualms about, have scruples about, have misgivings about, have reservations about, stick at, think twice about, waver about, vacillate about, drag one's feet/heels over, can't be bothered doing something; informal be cagey about, boggle at; archaic sweer, disrelish something.
▷ANTONYMS willing, keen.

Word toolkit

unwilling	unenthusiastic	hesitant
participant	applause	step
victim	reception	pause
addict	tone	knock
accomplice	response	approach

unwillingness adjective *he deplored the Government's unwillingness to provide adequate funds*: **disinclination**, **reluctance**, slowness, lack of enthusiasm; hesitation, hesitance, hesitancy, diffidence, coyness, timidity, timorousness, trepidation, backwardness (in coming forward); aversion to, dislike for, distaste for; demurral, wavering, vacillation, foot-dragging; resistance to, objection to, opposition to; doubts, second thoughts, scruples, qualms, pangs of conscience, misgivings; archaic disrelish; rare indisposedness, nolence, nolition, sweerness.

unwind verb **1** *Ella unwound the long woollen scarf from her neck*: **unroll**, uncoil, unreel, undo, unravel, untwine, untwist, disentangle, spread out, unfurl, open (out), lay out, straighten (out), unkink.
2 *it's a good place to unwind after work*: **relax**, loosen up, ease up/off, let up, slow down, de-stress, unbend, rest, repose; laze, idle, loaf, do nothing, sit back, stand down, lounge, loll, slump, flop, put one's feet up, take it easy, luxuriate, take time off, slack off, be at leisure, take one's leisure, take one's ease, enjoy oneself, amuse oneself, play, entertain oneself; informal wind down, let it all hang out, let one's hair down, unbutton, veg out; N. Amer. informal hang loose, stay loose, chill out, kick back.

unwise adjective *it would have been unwise to argue*: **injudicious**, ill-advised, imprudent; **foolish**, silly, ill-considered, ill-judged, inadvisable, impolitic, incautious, indiscreet, short-sighted, misguided, foolhardy, wrong-headed, irresponsible, rash, hasty, overhasty, reckless, thoughtless.
▷ANTONYMS wise, sensible.

Choose the right word **unwise, imprudent, injudicious, ill-advised**

These terms are all used to criticize a person or their behaviour as foolish; they generally suggest that the person should have been capable of taking a more sensible decision, if they had been prepared to think more carefully.

Unwise is typically used with an impersonal *it* and followed by an infinitive (*it would be unwise to try and fight*). Besides indicating foolishness, it may be applied to an intellectual judgement that is merely not justified (*it would be unwise to see the Jacobite unrest as typical of public opinion at the time*).

Imprudent emphasizes a person's failure to think of the future, and it is often used in financial contexts (*it would be imprudent to leave her winter coat behind | the banks made hundreds of imprudent loans in the 1970s*).

Injudicious is a relatively formal word. It is typically used of an action, rather than the person performing it, and not followed by an infinitive (*he will probably pay dearly for his injudicious comments*).

Ill-advised is typically used to describe an action and implies that others could have warned the perpetrator of the consequences of their folly (*the strike was ill-advised and would play into the hands of the management | you would be ill-advised to go on your own*).

unwitting adjective **1** *an unwitting accomplice*: **unknowing**, unconscious, unsuspecting, oblivious, unaware, innocent; unmindful, uninformed, ignorant, unenlightened; informal in the dark; rare incognizant, nescient.
▷ANTONYMS witting, knowing.
2 *an unwitting mistake*: **unintentional**, unintended, inadvertent, involuntary, unmeant, unthinking, unplanned, unpremeditated, unconscious, accidental, chance.
▷ANTONYMS deliberate, conscious.

unwonted adjective *they came running with unwonted energy*: **unusual**, uncommon, unaccustomed, uncustomary, unfamiliar, unprecedented, atypical, untypical, abnormal, strange, peculiar, curious, out of the way, irregular, anomalous, exceptional, extraordinary, special, remarkable, singular, rare, surprising.
▷ANTONYMS usual, customary, habitual.

unworldly adjective **1** *the transformation from gauche, unworldly girl to dignified lady*: **naive**, simple, inexperienced, innocent, green, raw, callow, immature, uninitiated, natural, unaffected, unsophisticated, gullible, born yesterday, ingenuous, artless, guileless, childlike, trusting, credulous, idealistic.
2 *the region has a stark, unworldly beauty*: **unearthly**, other-worldly, extraterrestrial, ethereal, ghostly, spectral, phantom, preternatural, supernatural, paranormal, mystical, transcendent, numinous; rare extramundane.
3 *a completely unworldly religious order*: **non-materialistic**, non-material, immaterial; spiritual, spiritualistic, religious.

unworthy adjective **1** *he was unworthy of trust*: **undeserving**, not worthy, not good enough for, ineligible for, unqualified for, unfit for.
▷ANTONYMS worthy, deserving.
2 *he despised such unworthy behaviour*: **unbecoming**, unsuitable, inappropriate, unbefitting, unfitting, unseemly, improper, incongruous; inconsistent, incompatible, out of keeping, out of character, out of place; degrading, discreditable, shameful, dishonourable, despicable, ignoble, contemptible, reprehensible, inexcusable, unforgivable.
▷ANTONYMS worthy, becoming.

unwritten adjective *there are unwritten rules about what is acceptable dress*: **tacit**, implicit, unvoiced, silent, implied, taken for granted, accepted, recognized, understood, unrecorded; traditional, customary, conventional, folk, handed down; oral, verbal, spoken, vocal, word-of-mouth, by mouth, by word of mouth; Latin viva voce.
▷ANTONYMS written.

unyielding adjective **1** *a basket made from unyielding spikes of cane*: **stiff**, inflexible, unpliable, non-flexible, unbending, inelastic, firm, hard, solid, tough, tight, taut, compact, compacted, compressed, dense; rare impliable, unmalleable, renitent.
2 *an unyielding policy on inflation*: **resolute**, inflexible, uncompromising, unbending, unshakeable, unwavering; unpersuadable, uncooperative, immovable, intractable, intransigent, rigid, stiff, hard-line, hard and fast, tough, firm, determined, iron-willed, dogged, obstinate, stubborn, not giving an inch, diehard, adamant, obdurate, tenacious, pertinacious, relentless, implacable, inexorable, single-minded, stiff-necked; Brit. informal bloody-minded; rare indurate, renitent, unmalleable.

up-and-coming adjective *up-and-coming young players*: **promising**, budding, rising, coming, on the up and up, in the making, with potential, likely to succeed; talented, gifted, able, apt.
▷ANTONYMS on the way out.

upbeat adjective informal *the share price rose 13p after an upbeat presentation to brokers*. See **optimistic** (sense 1).

U

upbraid verb *she had upbraided him firmly for his deception*: **reprimand**, rebuke, reproach, scold, admonish, reprove, remonstrate with, chastise, chide, berate, take to task, pull up, castigate, lambaste, read someone the Riot Act, give someone a piece of one's mind, haul over the coals, criticize, censure; informal tell off, give someone a talking-to, give someone a telling-off, dress down, give someone a dressing-down, give someone an earful, give someone a roasting, give someone a rocket, give someone a rollicking, rap, rap someone over the knuckles, slap someone's wrist, let someone have it, bawl out, give someone hell, come down on, blow up, pitch into, lay into, lace into, give someone a caning, blast, rag, keelhaul; Brit. informal tick off, have a go at, carpet, monster, give someone a mouthful, tear someone off a strip, give someone what for, wig, give someone a wigging, row, give someone a row; N. Amer. informal chew out, ream out; Brit. vulgar slang bollock, give someone a bollocking; N. Amer. vulgar slang chew someone's ass, ream someone's ass; dated call down, rate, give someone a rating, trim; rare reprehend, objurgate.
▷**ANTONYMS** congratulate.

upbringing noun *her upbringing had not prepared her for that*: **bringing up**, rearing, raising, breeding, care, upkeep, cultivation, fostering, tending; **nurture**, training, teaching, education; childhood, early life, family history, background; nature, character; in ancient Greece paideia.

update verb **1** *security measures are continually updated*: **modernize**, bring up to date, bring into the twenty-first century, renovate, refurbish, recondition, overhaul, re-equip, improve, better, upgrade, streamline, rationalize, reform, revise, correct, amend; N. Amer. bring up to code.
2 *I'm going to update the Colonel on today's developments*: **brief**, bring up to date, inform, fill in, advise, notify, apprise, report to, give details to, explain the situation to, give information to, give someone the latest information, refresh, explain the circumstances to, describe the state of affairs to; keep someone informed, keep someone posted, keep someone briefed, keep someone in the picture, keep someone up to date; informal clue in, give a sitrep to, bring up to speed, keep someone up to speed.

upgrade verb **1** *there are also plans to upgrade the rail system*: **improve**, better, make better, ameliorate, reform, enhance, add to, customize, touch up; rehabilitate, refurbish, recondition, modernize, update, bring up to date, renovate, redecorate, revamp, restore, remodel, redo, brighten up, spruce up; N. Amer. bring up to code; informal do up, fix up.
▷**ANTONYMS** degrade.
2 *some primary school teachers were upgraded to teach in secondary schools*: **promote**, give a higher rank to, place in a higher rank, give promotion to, give a higher position to, elevate, advance, move up, raise, lift, boost, improve the position/status of, aggrandize, exalt; informal kick upstairs; archaic prefer.
▷**ANTONYMS** downgrade, demote.

upheaval noun *the upheaval caused by wartime evacuation*: **disruption**, upset, disturbance, trouble, turbulence; disorder, disorganization, confusion, turmoil, pandemonium, bedlam, furore, uproar, disarray, chaos, mayhem, cataclysm; revolution, violent change, sudden change.
▷**ANTONYMS** stability, tranquillity.

uphill adjective **1** *an uphill path*: **upward**, rising, ascending, climbing, mounting; rare acclivitous, upsloping.
▷**ANTONYMS** downhill.
2 *an uphill job*: **arduous**, difficult, hard, tough, taxing, demanding, exacting, stiff, formidable, heavy, exhausting, tiring, wearying, wearisome, fatiguing, laborious, gruelling, back-breaking, murderous, punishing, burdensome, onerous, Herculean; informal no picnic, killing; Brit. informal knackering; archaic toilsome.
▷**ANTONYMS** easy.

uphold verb **1** *the court upheld his claim for damages*: **confirm**, endorse, sustain, validate, ratify, verify, vindicate, justify, approve; support, give one's support to, be supportive of, back, back up, give one's backing to, stand by, champion, defend, come to the defence of, stick up for.
▷**ANTONYMS** overturn, oppose.
2 *they've a tradition to uphold*: **maintain**, sustain, continue, preserve, protect, keep, hold to, keep alive, keep going, strengthen, nurture.
▷**ANTONYMS** abandon.

upkeep noun **1** *we will be responsible for the upkeep of the access road*: **maintenance**, repair(s), service, servicing, care, aftercare, preservation, conservation, running.
2 *Casey paid a monthly sum for the child's upkeep*: **subsistence**, care, upbringing, support, keep, maintenance, sustenance, welfare.

uplift verb *this is the kind of music that uplifts him*: **boost**, raise, buoy up, elevate, edify, inspire, lift, give a lift to, cheer up, perk up, enliven, brighten up, lighten, ginger up, gladden, encourage, stimulate, arouse, revive, restore; informal buck up.

uplifted adjective *his uplifted hand shot to his face*: **raised**, elevated, hoisted, upraised, upthrust, reared, hitched up, held high, erect, proud; rare upheaved, upreared.
▷**ANTONYMS** lowered.

uplifting adjective *it's a sweet, uplifting story about an English girl at a mission in India*: **inspiring**, stirring, moving, touching, affecting, warming, cheering, cheerful, gladdening, encouraging; emotional, profound, fervent, heartfelt, sincere, passionate; meaningful, significant, eloquent, expressive; sad, soulful, mournful, doleful.

upper adjective **1** *he made his way to the upper floor*: **higher**, further-up, loftier; overlying, superior; top.
▷**ANTONYMS** lower.
2 *the upper echelons of the party*: **senior**, superior, higher-level, higher-ranking, highest-ranking, top, chief, more/most important, elevated, eminent.
▷**ANTONYMS** junior, inferior.
□ **the upper hand** *I decided to gain the upper hand by launching a surprise attack*: **an advantage**, a commanding position, an/the edge, the whip hand, a lead, a head start, ascendancy, superiority, supremacy, sway, control, predominance, power, mastery, dominance, command; rare prepotence, prepotency, paramountcy, prepollency.
▶ **noun**
□ **on one's uppers** informal *far from being on their uppers, people approaching retirement today are better off than their parents' generation*: **penniless**, impoverished, poverty-stricken, poor, destitute, impecunious, indigent, down and out, pauperized, without a penny to one's name, without two farthings/pennies to rub together; insolvent, ruined; needy, in need, in want, hard up, on the breadline, hard-pressed, in reduced/straitened circumstances, deprived, disadvantaged, distressed, badly off; beggarly, beggared; informal up against it, broke, flat broke, strapped (for cash), without a brass farthing, without a bean, without a sou, as poor as a church mouse, on one's beam-ends; Brit. informal stony broke, skint, boracic (lint); N. Amer. informal stone broke, without a red cent, on skid row; formal penurious.

upper-class adjective *she was born into an upper-class family*: **aristocratic**, noble, noble-born, of noble birth, patrician, titled, blue-blooded, high-born, well born, elite, upper-crust, landowning, landed, born with a silver spoon in one's mouth; high-class, select, exclusive; Brit. county, upmarket; informal top-drawer, top-people's, {huntin', shootin', and fishin'}, classy, posh, snobby; archaic gentle, of gentle birth.

uppermost adjective **1** *she gazed at the uppermost branches*: **highest**, furthest up, loftiest, top, topmost, most elevated.
2 *their own problems remained uppermost in their minds*: **predominant**, most important, of greatest importance, to the fore, foremost, top, dominant, preponderant, principal, leading, greatest, chief, main, paramount, major.

uppish adjective informal *she sensed that her accent made her sound uppish*. See **arrogant**.

upright adjective **1** *check that the posts are upright*: **vertical**, perpendicular, plumb, straight (up), straight up and down, bolt upright, erect, on end, standing up, rearing, rampant; on one's feet.
▷**ANTONYMS** horizontal.
2 *an upright member of the community*: **honest**, **honourable**, upstanding, respectable, reputable, high-minded, law-abiding, right-minded, worthy, moral, ethical, righteous, decent, good, virtuous, principled, high-principled, of principle, proper, correct, just, noble, incorruptible, conscientious.
▷**ANTONYMS** dishonourable, crooked.
▶ **noun** *he peered between the uprights of the gate*: **column**, standard, stanchion, post, pole.

uprightness noun *there is a general lack of uprightness in these postmodern times*: **rectitude**, decency, integrity, principle, honesty, honour, honourableness, upstandingness, respectability, high-mindedness, right-mindedness, worthiness, morality, righteousness, goodness, virtue, moral virtue, ethics, principles, correctness, probity, trustworthiness, truthfulness, good character, scrupulousness, nobility, conscientiousness, incorruptibility, fairness, equity, justice.

uprising noun *the uprising was put down by the action of the police and the army*: **rebellion**, revolt, insurrection, mutiny, revolution, insurgence, insurgency, rising, rioting, riot; civil disobedience, civil disorder, unrest, anarchy, fighting in the streets; coup, regime change; French coup d'état, jacquerie; German putsch.

uproar noun **1** *the headmistress found the class in uproar | Joseph's voice rose above the uproar*: **turmoil**, disorder, confusion, chaos, commotion, disturbance, tumult, turbulence, mayhem, pandemonium, havoc, bedlam, all hell broken loose; **noise**, din, clamour, hubbub, racket, row, clangour; babble, shouting, yelling, babel; W. Indian bangarang; informal hullabaloo, rumpus.
▷**ANTONYMS** calm.
2 *there was an uproar when he was dismissed*: **outcry**, furore, outrage, howl of protest, protest, protestation, complaint, objection; clamour, fuss, commotion, hue and cry, row, ruckus, brouhaha; opposition, dissent, vociferation, indignation; informal hullabaloo, rumpus, ballyhoo, stink, ruction.
▷**ANTONYMS** acquiescence.

uproarious adjective **1** *an uproarious party*: **disorderly**, tumultuous, riotous, unruly, wild, unrestrained, rip-roaring, rollicking, boisterous, roisterous; noisy, loud, rowdy, rackety, clamorous; Brit. informal **rumbustious**; N. Amer. informal **rambunctious**; archaic **robustious**.
▷ANTONYMS quiet, tame.
2 *they were laughing as if at some uproarious joke*: **hilarious**, extremely amusing, very funny, comic, riotous, screamingly/hysterically funny, too funny for words, side-splitting, rib-tickling, comical, absurd, ridiculous; informal **priceless**, **a scream**, **a hoot**; dated **killing**, **killingly funny**.
▷ANTONYMS solemn; unfunny.

uproot verb **1** *don't pick or uproot wild flowers*: **pull up**, root out, take out, rip out/up, tear up by the roots, grub out/up; rare **deracinate**.
▷ANTONYMS plant.
2 *a revolution is necessary to uproot the social order*: **eradicate**, get rid of, eliminate, root out, weed out, remove, destroy, put an end to, do away with, wipe out, stamp out, extirpate, abolish, extinguish.
▷ANTONYMS establish.

ups and downs plural noun *the ups and downs of life are all tied together with the ups and downs of the farm*: **vicissitudes**, uncertainties, inconstancy, instability, unpredictability, chanciness, fickleness, variability, changeability, fluctuation, vacillation, alteration, changes; reversal, reverse, downturn.

upset verb (stress on the second syllable) **1** *the accusation upset her*: **distress**, trouble, perturb, disturb, discompose, unsettle, disconcert, discountenance, dismay, disquiet, worry, bother, inconvenience, agitate, fluster, throw, ruffle, unnerve, shake, frighten, alarm, anger, annoy, irritate, vex, irk, fret, pester, harass, torment, plague, hurt, grieve; informal **hassle**.
▷ANTONYMS put at ease.
2 *he upset a tureen of soup*: **knock over**, overturn, upend, tip over, push over, topple (over), capsize, turn topsy-turvy; spill, slop, slosh; archaic **overset**.
▷ANTONYMS right.
3 *the dam will upset the ecological balance*: **disrupt**, interfere with, disturb, throw out, turn topsy-turvy, disorder, unsettle, confuse, throw into confusion, throw into chaos, throw into disorder, disorganize, disarrange, mix up, jumble, mess up, wreck, ruin.
▷ANTONYMS maintain.
4 *his side were upset 2-1 by Sheffield United*: **defeat**, beat, conquer, vanquish, rout, overthrow, overcome, triumph over, be victorious over, get the better of, worst, thrash, trounce, topple.
▶noun **1** (stress on the first syllable) *a legal dispute will cause worry and upset*: **distress**, trouble, perturbation, disturbance, discomposure, dismay, disquiet, worry, bother, inconvenience, agitation, fluster, alarm, fright, anger, annoyance, irritation, vexation, harassment, torment, hurt, grief.
▷ANTONYMS calm, ease.
2 *they nearly pulled off one of motor sport's biggest upsets*: **unexpected result**; **major defeat**, rout, trouncing, thrashing, drubbing, toppling; **surprise victory**, coup, tour de force, feat, master stroke; informal **hammering**.
▷ANTONYMS walkover.
3 *a stomach upset*: **disorder**, complaint, ailment, illness, sickness, disease, malady, affliction, indisposition, infirmity; informal **lurgy**, **bug**; Austral. informal **wog**.
▶adjective **1** *I was upset by Sheila's illness*: **distressed**, troubled, perturbed, disturbed, discomposed, unsettled, disconcerted, discountenanced, dismayed, disquieted, worried, bothered, inconvenienced, anxious, agitated, flustered, ruffled, unnerved, shaken, frightened, alarmed, angered, annoyed, irritated, vexed, irked, fretted, hurt, saddened, grieved; informal **cut up**, **choked**; Brit. informal **gutted**.
▷ANTONYMS unperturbed, calm about.
2 *an upset stomach*: **disordered**, disturbed, unsettled, queasy, bad, poorly, ill, sick; informal **gippy**, **holiday**.
▷ANTONYMS settled.

upshot noun *the upshot of this conflict of interests was a compromise*: **result**, consequence, outcome, out-turn, sequel, effect, reaction, repercussion, reverberations, ramification, end, end result, conclusion, termination, culmination, denouement, corollary, concomitant, aftermath, fruit(s), product, produce, by-product; Medicine **sequelae**; informal **pay-off**; dated **issue**; archaic **success**.
▷ANTONYMS cause, origin.

upside down adjective **1** *the mangled remains of a vehicle were found hanging upside down in a tree*: **upturned**, upended, bottom up, wrong side up, head over heels, inverted, reversed, overturned, capsized, upset, flipped.
▷ANTONYMS upright, the right way up.
2 *they left the flat upside down | my world was thrown upside down*: **in/into disarray**, in/into disorder, jumbled up, in/into a jumble, in/into a muddle, untidy, disorganized, chaotic, all over the place, in/into chaos, in/into confusion, topsy-turvy, at sixes and sevens; informal **messed up**, **higgledy-piggledy**.
▷ANTONYMS tidy.
□ **turn something upside down** *the burglars have turned our house upside down*: **throw into disarray**, throw into disorder, make disorderly, disorder, untidy, make untidy, disorganize, disturb, jumble, mix up, muddle, upset, turn something topsy-turvy; informal **mess up**; N. Amer. informal **muss up**.
▷ANTONYMS tidy.

upstanding adjective **1** *an upstanding member of the community*: **honest**, **honourable**, upright, respectable, reputable, high-minded, law-abiding, right-minded, worthy, moral, ethical, righteous, decent, good, virtuous, principled, high-principled, of principle, proper, correct, just, noble, incorruptible, conscientious.
▷ANTONYMS dishonourable, crooked.
2 *a strong breeze caught the upstanding feathered plumes*: **upright**, erect, vertical, plumb, upended, on end, rearing, straight (up and down), perpendicular; on one's feet, standing, in a standing position; Heraldry **rampant**.
▷ANTONYMS flat, lying down, seated.

upstart noun *these upstarts, they don't know their place*: **parvenu(e)**, arriviste, nouveau riche, vulgarian; status seeker, social climber; (**upstarts**) the new rich, new money; informal **would-be**, **wannabe**.

up to date adjective **1** *the Unit is trying to raise £40,000 to buy an up-to-date scanner*: **modern**, contemporary, the latest, up to the minute, recent, new, the newest, newfangled, new-fashioned, ultra-modern, fresh, current, prevalent, prevailing, present-day; **fashionable**, in fashion, in vogue, voguish, trendsetting; French **à la mode**; informal **bang up to date**, **in the swim**, **all the rage**, **trendy**, **with it**, **mod**, **cool**, **now**, **in**, **hip**, **big**.
▷ANTONYMS out of date, old-fashioned.
2 *the monthly bulletin keeps staff* ***up to date on*** *topical issues*: **informed about**, conversant with, au fait with, up to speed on, in touch with, up with, au courant with, plugged into, familiar with, knowledgeable about, acquainted with, aware of.

upturn noun **1** *there was a general upturn in beer consumption*: **increase**, rise, jump, leap, surge, upswing, upsurge, boost, acceleration, escalation, soaring, step up.
▷ANTONYMS fall.
2 *an upturn in the economy*: **improvement**, recovery, revival, rally, pickup, comeback, resurgence, renewal, reinvigoration, upswing, advancement, betterment, a turn for the better.
▷ANTONYMS slump, downturn.

upward adjective *an upward trend in nickel prices*: **rising**, ascending, climbing, mounting; skyward, heavenward; uphill; rare **acclivitous**, **upsloping**.
▷ANTONYMS downward.
▶adverb See **upwards**.

upwards adverb *the taxi went on ever upwards | she peered upwards at the sky*: **up**, upward, uphill, towards a higher level, to the top; skywards, heavenwards.
▷ANTONYMS downward.
□ **upward(s) of** *it will cost upwards of a million dollars*: **more than**, above, over, in excess of, exceeding, beyond, greater than.
▷ANTONYMS less than.

urban adjective *crime rates are significantly higher in urban areas*: **built-up**, town, city, inner-city, densely populated, townified, citified, metropolitan, suburban, non-rural; municipal, civic, borough; informal **towny**, **townish**; rare **oppidan**.
▷ANTONYMS rural.

urbane adjective *the urbane and scholarly former information minister*: **suave**, sophisticated, debonair, worldly, elegant, cultivated, cultured, civilized, well bred, worldly-wise; **glib**, smooth, slick, polished, refined, poised, self-possessed, dignified; **courteous**, polite, civil, well mannered, gentlemanly, gallant, courtly, charming, affable, tactful, diplomatic; informal **cool**; dated **mannerly**.
▷ANTONYMS uncouth, unsophisticated, boorish.

> *Choose the right word* **urbane, glib, slick, smooth**
>
> See **glib**.

urbanity noun *she could see him growing quite testy beneath that polished urbanity of his*: **suaveness**, sophistication, worldliness, elegance, cultivation, culture, civilization, breeding, smoothness, polish, refinement, poise, self-possession, dignity; courtesy, politeness, civility, mannerliness, manners, gentlemanliness, gallantry, courtliness, graciousness, charm, affability, tact, diplomacy; informal **cool**.

urchin noun *he was surrounded by a dozen urchins imploring him to be generous*: **mischievous child**, imp, monkey, Puck, rascal, rogue, minx, mischief-maker, prankster, tearaway; ragamuffin, guttersnipe, waif, stray; informal **scamp**, **scallywag**, **brat**, **whippersnapper**, **horror**, **varmint**, **scarecrow**; Brit. informal **perisher**, **pickle**, **tinker**; N. Amer. informal **hellion**; dated **jackanapes**, rip, gamin, gamine; historical mudlark; archaic scapegrace, street Arab, wastrel, tatterdemalion.

urge verb **1** *she urged him to buy a boat*: **encourage**, try to persuade, enjoin, adjure, admonish, press, prompt, prod, goad, egg on, spur, push, pressure, put pressure on, use pressure on, pressurize, lean on; dragoon, constrain; entreat, exhort, implore, call on, appeal, beg, beseech, plead, nag; informal psych up, put the heat on, put the screws on, twist someone's arm, railroad into, bulldoze into.
▷ANTONYMS discourage.
2 *she urged her horse down the rutted lane*: **impel**, spur (on), force, drive, coerce, goad.
3 *I urge caution in interpreting these results*: **advise**, counsel, advocate, recommend, suggest; support, endorse, back, champion.
▶ **noun** *I also have this urge to travel*: **desire**, wish, need, impulse, compulsion, longing, yearning, hankering, craving, appetite, hunger, thirst, lust, fancy; informal yen, itch.

urgency noun **1** *the discovery of the ozone hole gave urgency to the issue of CFCs*: **importance**, top priority, imperativeness, weight, weightiness, gravity, necessity, exigency, seriousness, momentousness, cruciality, extremity, hurry, haste.
2 *Emilia heard the urgency in his voice*: **insistence**, persistence, determination, resolution, tenacity, obstinacy, doggedness; importunateness, clamour, clamorousness, earnestness, pleading, begging.

urgent adjective **1** *an urgent need for better storage*: **acute**, grave, pressing, dire, desperate, critical, crucial, sore, serious, intense, crying, burning, compelling, drastic, extreme; life-and-death, great, very great, terrible; archaic or humorous parlous.
▷ANTONYMS trivial.
2 *she needs urgent treatment*: **emergency**, high-priority, top-priority, important, vital, crucial; hurried, rushed, hasty, fast, quick, rapid, swift; N. Amer. informal hurry-up.
▷ANTONYMS non-urgent, elective.
3 *'In here!' came an urgent whisper*: **insistent**, persistent, determined, resolute, tenacious, obstinate, dogged, pressing, unrelenting; importunate, demanding, earnest, entreating, pleading, begging, clamorous; repeated, unremitting, continuous, incessant; rare exigent.
▷ANTONYMS casual.

urinate verb **pass water**, go to the loo, go to the toilet, go to the lavatory, relieve oneself; wet one's bed/pants, wet oneself; cock/lift its leg; informal go, do it, spend a penny, have/take a leak, shake hands with an old friend, answer the call of nature, pee, pee oneself, pee one's pants, piddle, have a piddle, widdle, have a widdle, tinkle, have a tinkle; Brit. informal wee, have a wee, wee-wee, have a Jimmy (Riddle), have a slash, have a wazz; N. Amer. informal whizz, take a whizz; vulgar slang piss, have a piss; technical micturate.

usable adjective **1** *his family owned about one sixth of the usable land in the country*: **available for use**, utilizable, disposable, at someone's disposal, ready for use, fit for use; working, in working order, functioning, functional, serviceable, workable, operational, operative, running, up and running; viable, feasible, practicable.
2 *a usable waterway*: **negotiable**, passable, navigable.
▷ANTONYMS unusable.

usage noun **1** *the increased usage of private cars | significant increases in energy usage*: **utilization**, use, employment, consumption, operation, manipulation, running, handling.
2 *the intricacies of English usage*: **phraseology**, phrasing, diction, parlance, idiom, choice of words, terminology; way of speaking/writing, manner of speaking/writing, style (of speaking/writing), mode of speaking/writing, mode of expression; French façon de parler; technical idiolect, sociolect.
3 *the dictates and usages of polite society*: **custom**, practice, habit, tradition, convention, routine, rule, rite, ritual, observance, ordinance, ceremony, ceremonial; way, procedure, method, mode, form, formality, wont; formal praxis; (**usages**) Latin mores; French moeurs.

use verb **1** *she used her key to open the front door*: **utilize**, make use of, avail oneself of, employ, work, operate, wield, ply, apply, manoeuvre, manipulate, put to use, put into service, find a use for, resort to.
2 *the court will use its discretion in making an order*: **exercise**, employ, apply, exert, bring into play, practise, implement, draw on.
3 *use your troops well and they will not let you down*: **manage**, handle, treat, behave towards, act towards, conduct oneself towards, deal with.
4 *he may be innocent, but his sort use people like us*: **take advantage of**, exploit, make use of, manipulate, take liberties with, capitalize on, profit from, trade on, milk, impose on, abuse, misuse, mistreat, maltreat, treat lightly, trifle with, play with; informal cash in on, bleed, walk all over, play someone for a sucker.
5 *I'm afraid I've* **used up** *all the eggs*: **consume**, get through, go through, exhaust, deplete, expend, spend, waste, fritter away, squander, dissipate.
▶ **noun 1** *they renounced the use of such weapons*: **utilization**, application, usage, employment, operation, manipulation, manoeuvring.
2 *his use of other people for his own ends*: **exploitation**, manipulation; abuse, misuse, mistreatment, maltreatment.
3 *what is the use of that?* **usefulness**, advantage, benefit, service, utility, help, good, gain, avail, profit, value, worth, point, object, motive, aim, goal, purpose, sense, reason.
4 *composers do not seem to have found much use for the device*: **need**, necessity, call, demand, occasion, purpose, reason, cause, grounds, justification, requirement, excuse.

used adjective *a used car*: **second-hand**, old, nearly new, worn, pre-owned, handed-down, cast-off; informal hand-me-down, reach-me-down.
▷ANTONYMS unused, new.
□ **used to** *I'm used to hard work*: **accustomed to**, not new to, no stranger to; practised in, familiar with, at home with, in the habit of, experienced in, versed in, conversant with, acquainted with; given to, prone to, wont to; habituated to, addicted to.
▷ANTONYMS unused, unaccustomed.

useful adjective **1** *it is such a useful box*: **functional**, practical, handy, neat, convenient, utilitarian, utility, helpful, applicable, serviceable, of use, of service; informal nifty.
▷ANTONYMS useless.
2 *they found watching the court proceedings a useful experience*: **beneficial**, advantageous, helpful, worthwhile, profitable, gainful, rewarding, productive, constructive, effective, efficacious, valuable, fruitful, of help, of assistance.
▷ANTONYMS disadvantageous.
3 *they had some very useful players*: **competent**, capable, able, expert, skilful, skilled, proficient, practised, experienced, effective, handy.
▷ANTONYMS incompetent.

usefulness noun *faults that affect the book's usefulness*: **functionality**, practicality, serviceability, fitness, adequacy, handiness, neatness, convenience, utility, use, effectiveness, efficacy; value, worth, merit, success; benefits, advantages, helpfulness, good, avail, help, assistance; informal niftiness.
▷ANTONYMS uselessness, disadvantage.

useless adjective **1** *it was useless to try | a piece of useless knowledge*: **futile**, pointless, purposeless, impractical, vain, in vain, to no purpose, to no avail, unavailing, bootless, nugatory, hopeless, unusable, ineffectual, inefficacious, impotent, fruitless, unprofitable, profitless, unproductive, unachievable, Sisyphean; unworkable, broken, kaput, unserviceable; informal junky; rare inutile.
▷ANTONYMS useful, beneficial.
2 informal *he was useless at his job*: **incompetent**, ineffective, worthless, ineffectual, incapable, inept, inadequate, hopeless, weak, bad, no good; informal bum, a dead loss.
▷ANTONYMS competent, effective.

usher verb *he ushered him to a window seat*: **escort**, accompany, help, assist, take, show, see, lead, show someone the way, lead the way, conduct, guide, steer, pilot, shepherd, convoy.
□ **usher in** *the railways* **ushered in** *an era of cheap mass travel*: **herald**, mark the start of, signal, announce, give notice of, ring in, show in, set the scene for, pave the way for, clear the way for, open the way for, smooth the path of; portend, foreshadow; start, begin, initiate, introduce, put in place, open the door to, allow to happen, inaugurate, get going, get off the ground, set in motion, get under way, kick off, launch, cause; precede, antecede.
▶ **noun attendant**, escort, guide; doorkeeper, commissionaire, aide, lackey, flunkey.

usual adjective *his usual route to work*: **habitual**, customary, accustomed, wonted, normal, routine, regular, constant, standard, typical, established, recognized, set, fixed, settled, stock, conventional, traditional, orthodox, accepted, expected, predictable, familiar, average, general, ordinary, everyday, daily, quotidian.
▷ANTONYMS unusual, strange, exceptional.

usually adverb *he usually arrived home about one o'clock*: **normally**, generally, habitually, customarily, standardly, routinely, regularly, typically, ordinarily, commonly, conventionally, traditionally, historically; as a rule, as a general rule, in general, in the general run of things, by and large, more often than not, almost always, in the main, mainly, mostly, for the most part, most of the time, on the whole.
▷ANTONYMS exceptionally.

usurer noun **extortionate moneylender**, Shylock; Irish gombeen man; informal loan shark.

usurp verb **1** *Richard usurped the throne*: **seize**, take over, expropriate, take possession of, take, appropriate, steal, wrest, arrogate, commandeer, annex, assume, lay claim to.
2 *the Hanoverian dynasty had usurped the Stuarts*: **oust**, overthrow, remove, topple, unseat, depose, dethrone, eject, dispel; succeed, come after, step into the shoes of, supplant, replace; informal fill someone's boots, crowd out; archaic deprive.

usury noun **extortionate moneylending**, shylocking; informal loan-sharking.

utensil noun *kitchen utensils*: **implement**, tool, instrument, device, apparatus, gadget, appliance, machine, contrivance, contraption, mechanism, aid; informal gimmick, gizmo; (**utensils**) hardware, equipment, gear, kit, tackle, paraphernalia, things, bits.

utilitarian adjective *coal-burning fires have been replaced with utilitarian heaters and radiators*: **practical**, functional, serviceable, useful, sensible, effective, efficient, (suited) to the purpose, pragmatic, realistic, utility, working, workaday, handy, neat, ordinary, down-to-earth; plain, unadorned, undecorative, unpretentious, unsentimental, soulless; hard-wearing, durable, lasting, long-lasting, tough, strong, robust, wear-resistant.
▷ANTONYMS decorative.

utility noun *a study that looks at the utility of using sled dogs rather than snowmobiles*: **usefulness**, use, advantage, benefit, value, help, helpfulness, profitability, convenience, practicality, effectiveness, efficacy, avail, service, serviceableness, advantageousness; **feasibility**, viability, workability, practicability, possibility; informal mileage.

utilize verb *concrete had long been utilized as a bonding and covering material*: **make use of**, put to use, use, employ, avail oneself of, have recourse to, resort to, look to, bring into service, press into service, take advantage of, exploit, milk, tap, turn to account, bring into play, bring into effective action, deploy.

utmost adjective **1** *a matter of* ***the utmost*** *importance*: **greatest**, maximum, greatest possible, highest, most, most extreme, greatest amount of, uttermost; maximal, extreme, supreme, paramount, superlative, enormous, major.
▷ANTONYMS least possible, very little.
2 *the utmost tip of Shetland*: **furthest**, farthest, furthermost, farthermost, furthest/farthest away, extreme, very, uttermost, outermost, aftermost, endmost, ultimate, final, last, terminal, remotest; rare outmost.
▷ANTONYMS nearest.
▶noun *we will do our utmost to help you*: **best**, uttermost, hardest, maximum, greatest possible extent.
▷ANTONYMS least.

> *Word toolkit* **utmost**
>
> See **vital**.

Utopia noun *it may be your idea of Utopia, but it's not mine*: **ideal place**, paradise, heaven, heaven on earth, Eden, Garden of Eden, Shangri-La, Elysium, the Elysian Fields, Happy Valley, seventh heaven, idyll, nirvana, bliss; literary Arcadia, Arcady, Erewhon.
▷ANTONYMS hell on earth.

Utopian adjective **1** *a Utopian community of farmers and skilled craftsmen*: **unworldly**, non-materialistic, non-material, immaterial; progressive, reforming, socialist; ideal, paradisal, heavenly, idyllic, blissful, divine, sublime, Elysian, perfect; literary Arcadian, Erewhonian; rare Edenic, paradisiacal, paradisaical, paradisical.
▷ANTONYMS materialistic, real-life.
2 *a Utopian vision of gender equality*: **idealistic**, visionary, perfectionist, romantic, idealized, fairy-tale, quixotic, starry-eyed, fanciful, unrealistic, impracticable.
▷ANTONYMS realistic, practicable, down-to-earth.

utter¹ adjective *Charlotte stared at her in utter amazement*: **complete**, total, absolute, thorough, perfect, downright, out-and-out, outright, thoroughgoing, all-out, sheer, positive, prize, rank, pure, dyed-in-the-wool, deep-dyed, real, veritable, consummate, categorical, unmitigated, unqualified, unadulterated, unalloyed, unconditional, unequivocal, full, unlimited, limitless, infinite, ultimate; Brit. informal right, proper; archaic arrant.
▷ANTONYMS partial.

utter² verb **1** *he uttered an exasperated snort*: **emit**, let out, give, produce, give vent to, issue, come out with, breathe.
2 *Alan uttered an impatient curse*: **voice**, express, put into words, speak, say, deliver, sound, mouth, breathe, articulate, pronounce, enunciate, verbalize, vocalize, state, declare.

utterance noun **1** *the victory was soured by the jingoistic utterances of the commentators*: **remark**, comment, word, expression, statement, observation, declaration, pronouncement; reflection, thought, opinion.
2 *there was a gasp at this public utterance of the forbidden word*: **voicing**, saying, speaking, expression, delivery, sounding, mouthing, breathing, articulation, enunciation, verbalization, vocalization.

utterly adverb *he looked utterly ridiculous*: **completely**, totally, absolutely, entirely, wholly, fully, thoroughly, quite, altogether, one hundred per cent, downright, outright, unqualifiedly, in all respects, unconditionally, perfectly, implicitly, unrestrictedly, really, veritably, categorically, consummately, undisputedly, unmitigatedly, wholeheartedly, radically, stark, just, to the hilt, to the core, all the way, to the maximum extent, extremely, infinitely, unlimitedly, limitlessly, ultimately; informal clean, plumb, dead, bang.
▷ANTONYMS partly, partially, somewhat.

uttermost adjective **1** *he changed from one character to another with* ***the uttermost*** *rapidity*: **greatest**, maximum, greatest possible, highest, most, most extreme, greatest amount of; maximal, extreme, supreme, paramount, superlative, enormous, major.
▷ANTONYMS least possible, very little.
2 *New Zealand's uttermost southern extremity*: **furthest**, farthest, furthermost, farthermost, furthest/farthest away, extreme, very, utmost, outermost, aftermost, endmost, ultimate, final, last, terminal, remotest; rare outmost.
▷ANTONYMS nearest.
▶noun **1** *I will do my uttermost against him*: **best**, utmost, hardest.
▷ANTONYMS least.
2 *a desire to use every instant to the uttermost*: **utmost**, maximum, greatest possible extent.

U-turn noun **1** *he did an angry U-turn then roared up the drive*: **one-eighty**; Brit. about-turn; N. Amer. about-face; informal U-ey.
2 *a complete U-turn in economic policy*: **reversal**, reversal of policy, volte-face, about-face, sea change, shift, change of heart, change of mind, turnaround, turnround, turnabout, backtracking, retraction, eating one's words, change of plan; informal one-eighty; Brit. about-turn.

vacancy noun 1 *there are vacancies for computer technicians*: **opening**, position, vacant position, situation, situation vacant, post, job, opportunity, job opportunity, placement, place, niche, slot; informal berth.
2 *every seaside guest house had a 'No Vacancies' sign hanging in the window*: **unoccupied room**, room; **(vacancies)** accommodation available.
3 *Cathy stared into vacancy, seeing nothing*: **empty space**, emptiness, vacuity, nothingness, void, vacantness, nullity, oblivion; rare voidness.
4 *impartiality is nothing more than a vacancy of mind*: **empty-headedness**, lack of thought, lack of intelligence, brainlessness, denseness, thickness, vacuousness, vacuity, inaneness, inanity, stupidity.
▷ANTONYMS intelligence.

vacant adjective 1 *a vacant house*: **empty**, unoccupied, unfilled, free, available, not in use, unused, unengaged, uninhabited, untenanted, tenantless, to let, for sale, on the market, abandoned, deserted; informal up for grabs.
▷ANTONYMS full, occupied, open.
2 *an oddly vacant look had come over her features*: **blank**, expressionless, deadpan, inscrutable, inexpressive, poker-faced, emotionless, impassive, absent, absent-minded, uninterested, vacuous, empty, glassy, stony, wooden, motionless, lifeless, inanimate.
▷ANTONYMS expressive, meaningful.
3 *he continued to look vacant*: **empty-headed**, unintelligent, without thought, brainless, dense, dull-witted, thick, vacuous, inane, stupid; informal brain-dead.
▷ANTONYMS thinking, intelligent.

vacate verb 1 *guests are requested to vacate their rooms by 12 noon*: **leave**, get out of, move out of, evacuate, quit, go away from, depart from, exit from, withdraw from, pull out of; abandon, desert, relinquish; archaic forsake.
▷ANTONYMS occupy, inhabit.
2 *he will be vacating his post next year*: **resign from**, leave, stand down from, give up, bow out of, relinquish, depart from, walk out on, retire from, abdicate; informal quit, chuck, pack in.
▷ANTONYMS take up.

vacation noun 1 *he is on vacation*: **holiday**, holidays, trip, tour, break, mini-break, stopover; day off, recess, adjournment, furlough, rest, respite, leave of absence; leave, time off; informal hols, vac; formal sojourn.
▷ANTONYMS work; term.
2 *he insisted on the squatters' vacation of the occupied land*: **quitting**, evacuation, abandonment, desertion, relinquishment, leaving; departure from, exit from, withdrawal from.
▷ANTONYMS occupation.
▸ verb N. Amer. *I was vacationing in Europe with my family*: **holiday**, take a holiday, be on holiday, take a break, travel, tour, stay, visit, stop over; formal sojourn.

> *Choose the right word* **vacation, holiday, break**
>
> See **holiday**.

vacillate verb *I had for a time vacillated between teaching and journalism*: **dither**, be indecisive, be irresolute, be undecided, be uncertain, be unsure, be doubtful, waver, teeter, temporize, hesitate, oscillate, fluctuate, keep changing one's mind; Brit. haver, hum and haw; Scottish swither; informal dilly-dally, shilly-shally, blow hot and cold.

vacillating adjective *he became the target for accusations of vacillating leadership*: **irresolute**, hesitant, tentative, dithering, wavering, teetering, fluctuating, ambivalent, divided, doubtful, unsure, uncertain, in two minds, undecided, indefinite, unresolved, undetermined; informal dilly-dallying, shilly-shallying, iffy, blowing hot and cold.
▷ANTONYMS resolute.

vacillation noun *a decision is always easier to defend than vacillation*: **dithering**, indecision, indecisiveness, irresoluteness, uncertainty, unsureness, doubt, wavering, teetering, temporization, hesitation, oscillation, fluctuation, inconstancy; Brit. havering, humming and hawing; Scottish swither; informal dilly-dallying, shilly-shallying, blowing hot and cold.

vacuity noun *the book's principal defect remains the vacuity of its protagonist*: **empty-headedness**, lack of thought, lack of intelligence, brainlessness, denseness, thickness, vacuousness, vacancy, inaneness, inanity, stupidity.
▷ANTONYMS intelligence, depth.

vacuous adjective 1 *he had a vacuous expression on his face*: **blank**, vacant, expressionless, deadpan, inscrutable, inexpressive, poker-faced, emotionless, impassive, absent, absent-minded, uninterested, empty, glassy, stony, wooden, motionless, lifeless, inanimate.
▷ANTONYMS expressive, meaningful.
2 *an elite clique of vacuous High School beauties*: **empty-headed**, unintelligent, without thought, brainless, dense, dull-witted, thick, vacant, inane, stupid; informal brain-dead.
▷ANTONYMS thinking, intelligent.

> *Word toolkit* **vacuous**
>
> See **foolish**.

vacuum noun 1 *the experiment has to be conducted in a vacuum*: **empty space**, emptiness, void, nothingness, vacuity, vacancy; rare voidness, nihility.
2 *his exit would leave a power vacuum*: **gap**, space, absence, lack, deficiency, blank, lacuna.
▷ANTONYMS continuity.
3 *if you just clear your bits off the floor I can get round with the vacuum*: **vacuum cleaner**; Brit. informal vac; trademark Hoover.
▸ verb *the carpets must be vacuumed*: **vacuum-clean**; Brit. hoover.

vade mecum noun Latin *this impressive publication should become a vade mecum to all those interested in Scottish history*: **handbook**, companion, manual, guide, guidebook, reference book, instruction book, ABC, primer; informal bible; rare enchiridion.

vagabond noun *the police had hauled him up as a vagabond*: **itinerant**, wanderer, nomad, wayfarer, traveller, gypsy, rover, tramp, vagrant, drifter, transient, migrant, homeless person, derelict, beachcomber, down-and-out, beggar, person of no fixed address/abode, knight of the road, bird of passage, rolling stone; N. Amer. hobo; Austral. bagman, knockabout, overlander, sundowner, whaler; informal bag lady; N. Amer. informal bum, bindlestiff; S. African informal outie; Austral./NZ informal derro.
▸ adjective *a vagabond poacher*: **itinerant**, wandering, nomadic, travelling, ambulatory, mobile, on the move, journeying, roving, roaming, vagrant, transient, floating, migrant, migrating, migratory; refugee, displaced, homeless, rootless; drifting, unsettled, footloose; of no fixed address/abode; archaic errant.

vagary noun *the vagaries of the weather*: **quirk**, idiosyncrasy, peculiarity, oddity, eccentricity, unpredictability, fluctuation, foible, whim, whimsy, notion, conceit, caprice, fancy, kink, crotchet; informal hang-up, thing; rare megrim, singularity.

vagina noun **vulva**; children's word front bottom; black slang punani; vulgar slang cunt, pussy, twat, snatch, honeypot, muff, tail; Brit. vulgar slang fanny, quim, minge; N. Amer. vulgar slang box, beaver, jelly roll; W. Indian vulgar slang pum-pum.

vagrancy noun *sleeping in parks constituted vagrancy*: **homelessness**, drifting, roving, roaming, wandering, travelling, itinerancy, migrancy, nomadism, vagabondism.

vagrant noun *the old car was a welcome shelter for the occasional vagrant*: **tramp**, drifter, down-and-out, derelict, beggar, itinerant, wanderer, nomad, wayfarer, traveller, gypsy, rover, vagabond, transient, migrant, homeless person, beachcomber, person of no fixed address/abode, knight of the road, bird of passage, rolling stone; N. Amer. hobo; Austral. bagman, knockabout, overlander, sundowner, whaler; informal bag lady; N. Amer. informal bum, bindlestiff; S. African informal outie; Austral./NZ informal derro.
▶ adjective *the Council provides facilities for vagrant alcoholics*: **homeless**, drifting, transient, roving, roaming, floating, unsettled, footloose, itinerant, wandering, nomadic, travelling, ambulatory, mobile, on the move, journeying, rambling, touring, vagabond, migrant, migrating, migratory, rootless; of no fixed address/abode; archaic errant.

vague adjective **1** *they could just make out the vague shape of a ship in the mist*: **indistinct**, indefinite, indeterminate, unclear; **hazy**, cloudy, fuzzy, misty, lacking definition, blurred, blurry, out of focus, murky, foggy, faint, shadowy, dim, obscure, nebulous, shapeless, formless, unformed, amorphous; rare nebulose.
▷ANTONYMS clear, precise.
2 *a vague description*: **imprecise**, inexact, rough, approximate, inexplicit, non-specific, loose, ill-defined, generalized, ambiguous, equivocal, hazy, woolly; **sketchy**, incomplete, inadequate, imperfect; superficial, cursory, perfunctory.
3 *I'm a little vague about the details*: **unclear**, hazy, uncertain, unsure, undecided; **puzzled**, baffled, mystified, bemused, bewildered, confused, nonplussed; indecisive, irresolute, hesitant, tentative, wavering, vacillating; informal iffy.
▷ANTONYMS clear, certain.
4 *they had only vague plans*: **uncertain**, undecided, yet to be decided, unsure, unclear, unsettled, indefinite, indeterminate, unknown, unestablished, unconfirmed, unresolved, unascertained, pending, outstanding, in the balance, up in the air, speculative.
▷ANTONYMS firm.
5 *she was so vague in everyday life*: **absent-minded**, forgetful, with a mind like a sieve, disorganized, unsystematic, unreliable, undependable; dreamy, inattentive, abstracted, with one's head in the clouds, scatterbrained, feather-brained, feather-headed, birdbrained, empty-headed, erratic, giddy; informal scatty, dizzy, dippy, not with it.
▷ANTONYMS organized, together.

> *Word toolkit* **vague**
>
> See **incomplete**.

vaguely adverb **1** *she looks vaguely familiar*: **slightly**, a little, a bit, somewhat, rather, moderately, to some degree, to a certain extent, in a way, to a slight extent, faintly, obscurely, dimly; marginally, a shade; informal sort of, kind of, kinda, ish.
▷ANTONYMS very.
2 *he fired his rifle vaguely in our direction*: **roughly**, more or less, approximately, nearly, just about, practically, virtually, as near as dammit, for all practical purposes, to all intents and purposes; S. African plus-minus; informal pretty much.
▷ANTONYMS exactly.
3 *he just smiles vaguely*: **absent-mindedly**, abstractedly, inattentively, with one's head in the clouds, vacantly, vacuously, giddily, forgetfully; informal scattily, dizzily, dippily.

V

vagueness noun **1** *she used the vagueness and flexibility of the constitution to her own ends*: **impreciseness**, inexactness, lack of precision, ambiguity, woolliness, looseness, unclearness, obscurity, indistinctness, generality, indefiniteness, indeterminateness, haziness, cloudiness, fuzziness, mistiness, lack of definition.
▷ANTONYMS precision.
2 *the scene had the swirling vagueness of a painting by Turner*: **fuzziness**, blurriness, indeterminateness, indefiniteness, lack of focus, lack of definition, obscurity, haziness, cloudiness, mistiness, murkiness, fogginess, faintness, shadowiness, dimness, nebulosity, nebulousness, shapelessness, formlessness, amorphousness.
▷ANTONYMS sharpness.
3 *an amiable eccentric whose vagueness probably results from constant imbibing*: **absent-mindedness**, forgetfulness, disorganization, dreaminess, inattention, abstraction, wool-gathering, empty-headedness, giddiness, confusion, befuddlement.
▷ANTONYMS sharpness.

vain adjective **1** *he was vain about his looks*: **conceited**, narcissistic, self-loving, in love with oneself, self-admiring, self-regarding, wrapped up in oneself, self-absorbed, self-obsessed, self-centred, egotistic, egotistical, egoistic, egocentric, egomaniac; proud, haughty, arrogant, boastful, swaggering, imperious, overweening, cocky, affected; literary vainglorious; rare peacockish; (**be vain**) have an excessively high opinion of oneself, think too highly of oneself, think a lot of oneself; informal think one is the cat's whiskers/pyjamas, think one is God's gift (to women).
▷ANTONYMS modest.
2 *a vain attempt to tidy up the room*: **futile**, useless, pointless, worthless, nugatory, to no purpose, in vain; **ineffective**, ineffectual, inefficacious, impotent, powerless, unavailing, to no avail, fruitless, profitless, unproductive; unsuccessful, failed, without success, abortive, misfired; thwarted, baulked, frustrated, foiled; archaic bootless.
▷ANTONYMS successful, productive.
□ **in vain 1** *they waited in vain for a response*: **unsuccessfully**, vainly, without success, to no avail, to no purpose, ineffectually, with no result, fruitlessly, profitlessly, unproductively.
▷ANTONYMS successfully.
2 *his efforts were in vain*: **futile**, useless, pointless, to no purpose, worthless, nugatory; **ineffective**, ineffectual, inefficacious, impotent, powerless, unavailing, to no avail, fruitless, profitless, unproductive; unsuccessful, without success, abortive; thwarted, baulked, frustrated, foiled; archaic bootless.
▷ANTONYMS successful, productive.

> *Choose the right word* **vain, futile, fruitless, pointless**
>
> See **futile**.

valediction noun *he left her without a valediction*: **farewell**, goodbye, adieu, leave-taking, parting, send-off; Latin vale.
▷ANTONYMS salutation, welcome.

valedictory adjective *a valedictory message from the retiring ambassador*: **farewell**, goodbye, leaving, parting, departing, going away, last, final.
▷ANTONYMS welcome, salutatory.

valet noun **manservant**, man, personal attendant, gentleman's gentleman, Jeeves; French valet de chambre; Brit. dated batman.

valetudinarian noun *an elderly valetudinarian in search of medical advice*: **hypochondriac**, neurotic, invalid, valetudinary; French malade imaginaire; archaic melancholico.
▶ adjective *the valetudinarian English*: **hypochondriac**, self-obsessed, neurotic, obsessed with one's health; sickly, ailing, poorly, in poor health, weak, feeble, frail, delicate, debilitated, invalid, bedridden, infirm, washed out, run down, valetudinary; archaic splenetic; rare hipped, hippish.

valiant adjective *a valiant warrior | a valiant attempt*: **brave**, fearless, courageous, valorous, plucky, intrepid, heroic, stout-hearted, lionhearted, manly, manful, bold, daring, audacious, gallant, confident, spirited, stout, undaunted, dauntless, doughty, mettlesome, unalarmed, unflinching, unshrinking, unblenching, unabashed, undismayed; **determined**, stalwart, staunch, indomitable, resolute, steadfast, firm, unyielding, unbending, unfaltering, unswerving, unwavering, stubborn, dogged; N. Amer. rock-ribbed; informal game, gutsy, spunky, ballsy.
▷ANTONYMS cowardly, irresolute.

valid adjective **1** *a valid criticism*: **well founded**, sound, well grounded, reasonable, rational, logical, justifiable, defensible, defendable, supportable, sustainable, maintainable, workable, arguable, able to hold water, plausible, telling, viable, bona fide; cogent, effective, powerful, convincing, credible, believable, substantial, forceful, strong, weighty, authoritative, reliable; rare vindicable.
2 *only one valid nomination was received*: **correct**, authentic, legally acceptable, proper, bona fide, genuine, official, signed and sealed; lawful, legal, licit, legitimate, legally binding, binding, contractual; in force, in effect, effective.
▷ANTONYMS invalid, illegal, void.

> *Choose the right word* **valid, sound, cogent**
>
> When applied to reasoning, **valid** indicates that something has the power to convince: a *valid argument* contains no errors of logic, and a *valid conclusion* follows logically from the argument in its favour. *Valid* can also refer to things that are legally binding or acceptable (*a valid passport is essential when you travel abroad*).
>
> **Sound** can have the sense 'solid' or 'dependable'. An argument or position that is *sound* is secure against objections because it is based on good evidence and accurate reasoning (*scientifically sound papers*).
>
> **Cogent** denotes arguments that are clear, logical, and likely to influence the opinions of others (*it was Williams who marshalled the evidence, and he did so in cogent terms | an impassioned and cogent plea for judicial reform*).

validate verb **1** *clinical trials now exist to validate this claim*: **prove**, give proof of, show to be true, give substance to; **uphold**, support, back up, bear out, justify, vindicate, substantiate, corroborate, verify, demonstrate, authenticate, confirm, endorse, give credence to, lend weight to; vouch for, attest to, testify to, stand by, bear witness to.
▷ANTONYMS invalidate, disprove.
2 *the board refused to validate the aircraft's US certificate of airworthiness*: **ratify**, endorse, confirm, approve, agree to, accept, consent to, assent to, affirm, authorize, make valid, sanction, formalize, recognize, legalize, legitimize, warrant, license, certify; sign, countersign, put one's name to, set one's seal to.
▷ANTONYMS invalidate, reject, revoke.

validity noun **1** *it is time to examine the validity of this argument*: **soundness**, reasonableness, rationality, logic, justifiability, defensibility, sustainability, plausibility, viability, bona fides, effectiveness, cogency, power, credibility, believability, force, strength, weight, foundation, substance, substantiality, authority, reliability.
▷ANTONYMS invalidity.
2 *the judges have recognized the validity of the contract*: **legal acceptability**, authenticity, correctness, bona fides, genuineness; lawfulness, legality, legitimacy, binding nature, contractual nature; force, effect, effectiveness.

valley noun **dale**, vale; hollow, depression, hole, basin, gully, gorge, pass, ravine, canyon, rift, gap; Brit. **combe**, slade, dene; N. English **clough**; Scottish glen, strath; Indian **nullah**; S. African **kloof**; Spanish **vega**; in Arabic-speaking countries wadi; literary **dell**, dingle.

valour noun *the medals are awarded for acts of valour*: **bravery**, courage, fearlessness, courageousness, braveness, intrepidity, intrepidness, pluck, pluckiness, nerve, backbone, spine, heroism, stout-heartedness, manliness, manfulness, audacity, boldness, gallantry, daring, spirit, fortitude, mettle, dauntlessness, doughtiness, hardihood; informal **guts**, **spunk**; Brit. informal **bottle**, ballsiness; N. Amer. informal **cojones**, sand, moxie; vulgar slang **balls**.
▷ANTONYMS cowardice.

valuable adjective **1** *a valuable watch*: **precious**, **costly**, high-priced, high-cost, expensive, dear, worth its weight in gold, worth a king's ransom, priceless, beyond price, without price, of incalculable value/worth, of inestimable value/worth, of immeasurable value/worth, invaluable, irreplaceable, inestimable; prized, cherished, valued, treasured.
▷ANTONYMS cheap, worthless.
2 *a valuable contribution*: **useful**, helpful, of use, of help, of assistance, practical, beneficial, invaluable, productive, constructive, effective, handy, advantageous, worthwhile, profitable, rewarding, gainful, fruitful, worthy, important.
▷ANTONYMS useless.

valuables plural noun *valuables may be left in the hotel safe*: **precious items**, costly articles, prized possessions, personal effects, treasures.

valuation noun *you should obtain an insurance valuation on the painting*: **price**, value, evaluation, costing, quotation, estimate.

value noun **1** *houses exceeding £250,000 in value*: **price**, **cost**, worth; market price, selling price, asking price, monetary value, face value.
2 *the value of adequate preparation cannot be understated*: **merit**, worth, usefulness, use, utility, practicality, advantage, desirability, benefit, gain, profit, good, service, help, helpfulness, assistance, effectiveness, efficacy, avail, importance, significance, point, sense; informal **mileage**.
3 (**values**) *society's values are passed on to us as children*: **principles**, moral principles, ethics, moral code, morals, moral values, standards, moral standards, code of behaviour, rules of conduct, standards of behaviour.
▸ verb **1** *his estate was valued at £45,000*: **evaluate**, assess, estimate, appraise, assay, rate, price, put/set a price on, cost (out).
2 *teachers must value the child's contribution*: **appreciate**, rate (highly), esteem, hold in high esteem, hold in high regard, hold dear, have a high opinion of, think highly of, think much of, set (great) store by, attach importance to, respect, admire, prize, cherish, treasure.

valued adjective *a valued friend*: **cherished**, treasured, dear, prized, favourite, precious, worth its/one's weight in gold; special, appreciated, esteemed, respected, highly regarded, well thought of.

valueless adjective **1** *the watercolours turned out to be valueless*: **worthless**, of no (financial) value, of little/negligible value, trifling; **inferior**, substandard, second-rate, third-rate, poor-quality, low-quality, low-grade, cheap, shoddy, trashy, rubbishy, tawdry, gimcrack, twopenny-halfpenny, Brummagem; (**be valueless**) would fetch nothing.
2 *their efforts were valueless*: **pointless**, useless, to no purpose, (of) no use, unprofitable, profitless, futile, vain, in vain, to no avail, to no effect, fruitless, senseless, unproductive, purposeless, idle, worthless, ineffective, unavailing, nugatory, unrewarding, thankless; archaic **bootless**.

vamp[1] verb informal *a newly vamped museum*: **refurbish**, renovate, modernize, redecorate, revamp, make over, restore, recondition, rehabilitate, overhaul, repair, redevelop, rebuild, reconstruct, remodel; update, bring up to date, improve; upgrade; refit, re-equip, refurnish; N. Amer. **bring something up to code**; informal **do up**, **fix up**, **give something a facelift**, **tart up**, **vamp up**, **patch up**; N. Amer. informal **rehab**.

vamp[2] N. Amer. informal noun *she portrayed man-devouring vamps in a succession of films*: **seductress**, temptress, siren, femme fatale, enchantress, Delilah, Circe, Lorelei, Mata Hari; **flirt**, coquette, tease, Lolita; informal **tart**, mantrap.
▸ verb *will you promise you won't vamp him?* **seduce**, tempt, lure, beguile, entice; **flirt with**, make up to, make eyes at, lead on, toy with, trifle with, philander with; informal **pull**, **chat up**.

van noun *he was in the van of the movement*. See **vanguard**.

vanguard noun *women are often in the vanguard of linguistic change*: **forefront**, van, advance guard, avant-garde, spearhead, front, front line, front rank, fore, lead, leading position, cutting edge, driving force; leaders, founders, founding fathers, pioneers, architects, creators, instigators, trailblazers, pathfinders, avant-gardists, trendsetters, innovators, groundbreakers.
▷ANTONYMS rear; followers.

vanish verb **1** *she caught Archie trying to vanish upstairs*: **disappear**, vanish into thin air, be lost to sight/view, be/become invisible, evaporate, dissipate, disperse, fade, fade away, melt away, evanesce, recede from view, withdraw, depart, leave, go away.
▷ANTONYMS appear, materialize.
2 *all hope of freedom vanished*: **come to an end**, end, cease to exist/be, pass away, pass, die out, be no more, become extinct/obsolete, evaporate; **dwindle**, fizzle out, peter out, wear off, become/grow less, become/grow smaller, decrease, lessen, diminish, shrink, contract, fade, wane.
▷ANTONYMS materialize; last.

vanity noun **1** *she had none of the vanity so often associated with beautiful women*: **conceit**, conceitedness, self-conceit, narcissism, self-love, self-admiration, self-regard, self-absorption, self-obsession, self-centredness, egotism, egoism, egocentrism, egomania; pride, haughtiness, arrogance, boastfulness, swagger, imperiousness, cockiness, pretension, affectation, airs, show, ostentation; literary **vainglory**, **braggadocio**.
▷ANTONYMS modesty.
2 *the vanity of all desires of the will*: **futility**, uselessness, pointlessness, worthlessness, purposelessness, idleness, fruitlessness, profitlessness.

vanquish verb *after five weeks, government troops vanquished the rebels*: **conquer**, defeat (utterly), beat (hollow), trounce, annihilate, triumph over, win a resounding victory over, be victorious over, best, get the better of, worst, bring someone to their knees, overcome, overwhelm, subdue, subjugate, put down, quell, quash, crush, repress, rout; informal **lick**, **hammer**, **clobber**, **thrash**, **paste**, **pound**, **pulverize**, **crucify**, **demolish**, **destroy**, **drub**, **give someone a drubbing**, **cane**, **wipe the floor with**, **walk all over**, **give someone a hiding**, **take to the cleaners**, **blow someone out of the water**, **make mincemeat of**, **murder**, **massacre**, **slaughter**, **flatten**, **turn inside out**, **tank**; Brit. informal **stuff**; N. Amer. informal **blow out**, **cream**, **shellac**, **skunk**, **slam**.

vantage point noun *from our vantage point it remains a pretty hot issue*: **point of view**, viewpoint, standpoint, stance, stand, view, opinion, position, way of thinking, frame of mind, outlook, perspective, angle, slant.

vapid adjective *tuneful but vapid musical comedies*: **insipid**, uninspired, colourless, uninteresting, feeble, flat, dead, dull, boring, tedious, tired, unexciting, uninspiring, unimaginative, lifeless, zestless, spiritless, sterile, anaemic, tame, bloodless, jejune, vacuous, bland, stale, trite, pallid, wishy-washy, watery, tasteless, milk-and-water, flavourless.
▷ANTONYMS lively, colourful, exciting.

vapour noun **haze**, mist, spray, steam, water vapour, condensation, smoke, fumes, exhalation, fog, smog, murk, cloud, cloudiness, drizzle, dampness, humidity, mistiness, Scotch mist.

variable adjective *the wind was variable in direction and strength*: **changeable**, changing, varying, shifting, fluctuating, irregular, wavering, vacillating, inconstant, inconsistent, fluid, floating, unsteady, uneven, unstable, unsettled, movable, mutable, protean, chameleonic, unfixed, fitful, capricious, temperamental, fickle, kaleidoscopic, volatile, unpredictable, undependable, unreliable; informal **up and down**, **blowing hot and cold**; rare **changeful**, **variational**.
▷ANTONYMS constant, uniform.

Word toolkit

variable	unstable	mercurial
rate	situation	nature
length	world	talent
speed	region	temperament
size	environment	personality
results	condition	moods
effects	economy	shifts
frequency	government	energy

variance noun *data indicate no variance in church attendance between blue- and white-collar workers*: **difference**, variation, discrepancy, dissimilarity,

V

disagreement, conflict, divergence, deviation, contrast, distinction, contradiction, imbalance, incongruity.
□ **at variance 1** *his recollections were at variance with documentary evidence*: **inconsistent**, at odds, not in keeping, out of keeping, out of line, out of step, in opposition, conflicting, clashing, disagreeing, in disagreement, differing, contrary, incompatible, contradictory, irreconcilable, incongruous, discrepant. **2** *science and religion do not need to be at variance*: **conflicting**, in conflict, contrasting, incompatible, irreconcilable, antithetical, contradictory, clashing, contrary, different, differing, divergent, dissimilar, disagreeing, in disagreement, at odds, at cross purposes, at loggerheads, opposed, opposing, opposite, in opposition, poles apart, polar, at outs; N. Amer. on the outs; rare oppugnant.

variant noun *there are a number of variants of the same idea*: **variation**, form, alternative, alternative form, other form, different form, derived form, development, adaptation, alteration, modification, revision, revised version, transformation, permutation, transfiguration, metamorphosis, mutant, deviant, rogue, aberration.
▷ANTONYMS standard form; identical form.
▸ adjective *a variant spelling*: **alternative**, other, different, divergent, disparate, derived, adapted, modified, revised, altered, mutant, deviant, rogue, aberrant.
▷ANTONYMS standard; identical.

variation noun **1** *regional variations in farming practice*: **difference**, dissimilarity, disparity, inequality, contrast, discrepancy, imbalance, dissimilitude, differential, distinction.
▷ANTONYMS constant.
2 *opening times are likely to be subject to variation*: **change**, alteration, modification, varying, variety, variability, diversification.
▷ANTONYMS uniformity, standardization.
3 *there was very little variation from an understood pattern*: **deviation**, variance, divergence, departure, fluctuation, tolerance.
4 *he was wearing a variation of court dress*: **variant**, form, alternative, alternative form, other form, different form, derived form, development, adaptation, alteration, modification, revision, revised version.
▷ANTONYMS standard form.

varied adjective *a varied selection*: **diverse**, assorted, diversified, differing, miscellaneous, mixed, motley, sundry, jumbled, haphazard, heterogeneous, manifold, wide-ranging, disparate, variegated, multifarious.
▷ANTONYMS uniform.

variegated adjective *evergreen shrubs with variegated foliage*: **multicoloured**, particoloured, varicoloured, multicolour, many-coloured, many-hued, polychromatic, colourful, prismatic, rainbow-like, rainbow, kaleidoscopic, psychedelic, jazzy, harlequin, motley; **mottled**, marbled, striated, streaked, speckled, flecked, patchy, blotchy, blotched, dappled; informal splotchy, splodgy; technical poikilo-; rare marled, jaspé.
▷ANTONYMS plain, monochrome.

variety noun **1** *his mother introduced more variety into his diet*: **diversity**, variation, diversification, multifariousness, heterogeneity, variegation, many-sidedness, change, difference.
▷ANTONYMS uniformity.
2 *there was a variety of wildfowl*: **assortment**, miscellany, range, array, collection, selection, line-up, mixture, medley, mixed bag, mix, diversity, multiplicity, motley, motley collection, pot-pourri; rare omnium gatherum.
3 *fifty varieties of fresh and frozen pasta*: **sort**, kind, type, class, category, classification, style, description, status, quality, nature, manner, design, shape, form, pattern, group, set, bracket, genre, species, rank, genus, family, order, breed, race, strain, generation, vintage, make, model, brand, stamp, ilk, kidney, cast, grain, mould; N. Amer. stripe.

various adjective **1** *there are various kinds of evidence for this*: **diverse**, different, differing, varied, varying, a variety of, dissimilar, disparate, assorted, mixed, sundry, miscellaneous, variegated, heterogeneous; literary divers.
2 *he needed somewhere to store the various artefacts he had collected*: **numerous**, many, several, copious, abundant, profuse, countless, innumerable, large number of, multiplicity of.

varnish noun *several coats of varnish*: **lacquer**, lac, shellac, japan, enamel, glaze, polish, oil, resin, wax.
▸ verb *we stripped the floor and varnished it*: **lacquer**, shellac, japan, enamel, glaze, polish, oil, resin, wax.

vary verb **1** *estimates of the development cost vary greatly*: **differ**, be different, be unlike, be dissimilar.
▷ANTONYMS agree.
2 *rates vary from £50 to £90 per hour*: **range**, extend, stretch, reach, cover, go, run, pass.
3 *rates of interest vary over time*: **fluctuate**, rise and fall, go up and down, change, alter, shift, swing, waver, oscillate, see-saw, yo-yo.
▷ANTONYMS be static.
4 *the diaphragm is used for varying the aperture of the lens*: **modify**, change, alter, adjust, make adjustments to, regulate, control, set.
5 *he tried to vary his diet*: **diversify**, variegate, bring variety to, assort, mix, enlarge, expand, widen, broaden, increase, proliferate, extend; reorder; rare permutate.
6 *the routine never varied*: **change**, alter, deviate, diverge, depart, differ, fluctuate, move on.

varying adjective *varying degrees of difficulty*: **varied**, differing, different; diverse, diversified, assorted.

> *Word toolkit* **varying**
> See **divergent**.

vassal noun historical **villein**, liege, liegeman, man, bondsman, vavasour, serf, helot, slave, thrall, subject.
▷ANTONYMS freeman; lord.

vast adjective *a vast plain full of orchards*: **huge**, extensive, expansive, broad, wide, boundless, immeasurable, limitless, infinite, enormous, gigantic, very big, very large, great, giant, massive, colossal, mammoth, immense, tremendous, mighty, stupendous, monumental, epic, prodigious, mountainous, monstrous, titanic, towering, elephantine, king-sized, king-size, gargantuan, Herculean, Brobdingnagian; substantial, hefty, bulky, weighty, heavy, gross; informal mega, monster, whopping, whopping great, thumping, thumping great, humongous, jumbo, hulking, bumper, astronomical, astronomic; Brit. informal whacking, whacking great, ginormous.
▷ANTONYMS tiny.

vat noun **tub**, tank, cistern, bin, drum, canister, basin, steeper, boiler; vessel, receptacle, container, holder, storage chamber, repository, reservoir; barrel, butt, cask, keg, tun; rare kid, kier, keeve.

vault[1] noun **1** *the vault was supported on eight massive stone piers*: **arched roof**, arched ceiling, dome, arch.
2 *the vault under the church*: **cellar**, basement, underground chamber, crypt, undercroft, catacomb, cavern; burial chamber, tomb, sepulchre.
3 *valuables stored in the vault*: **strongroom**, safe deposit, safety deposit, safe, repository, depository, treasury.

vault[2] verb *he vaulted over the gate | I vaulted the fence*: **jump (over)**, leap (over), skip (over), leapfrog (over), spring over, bound over, sail over, hurdle, clear, pole-vault.
▸ noun *the barman was quickly back with a practised vault of the bar*: **jump**, leap, spring, bound, skip, hurdle, clearance, leapfrog, pole vault.

vaulted adjective *a high vaulted ceiling*: **arched**, curved, rounded, bowed, domed, humped; literary embowed.

vaunt verb (usually **vaunted**) *the much vaunted health-care system*: **boast about**, brag about, make much of, crow about, gloat over, give oneself airs about, exult in, parade, flaunt, show off, flourish; **acclaim**, esteem, revere, extol, celebrate; informal show off about, flash; rare laud.

veer verb *the car veered to the left and crashed into the van*: **swerve**, career, skew, swing, sheer, weave, wheel; change direction, change course, go off course, deviate, be deflected, diverge; turn (aside), branch off, curve, twist, bend, curl, incline, swivel, zigzag; Sailing tack; rare divagate.

vegetate verb *it is important not to let him vegetate in front of the television*: **do nothing**, idle, be inactive, languish, laze (around/about), lounge (around/about), loll (around/about), loaf (around/about), slouch (around/about); go to seed, degenerate, moulder, stagnate; informal hang around/round, veg out; Brit. informal hang about, mooch about/around, slummock; N. Amer. informal bum around, bat around/about, lollygag.

vegetation noun **plants**, plant life, flora; greenery, foliage; rare herbage, verdure.

> *Word links* **vegetation**
> **herbicide** substance used to kill vegetation

vehemence noun *the vehemence of her answer surprised both of them*: **passion**, force, forcefulness, ardour, fervour, spirit, spiritedness, urgency, strength, forcibleness, emphasis, vigour, intensity, violence, earnestness, eagerness, keenness, enthusiasm, zeal, zealousness, fanaticism; vociferousness, outspokenness, forthrightness, insistence.
▷ANTONYMS mildness, apathy.

vehement adjective *parents are vehement in their support for the school*: **passionate**, forceful, ardent, impassioned, heated, spirited, urgent, fervent, fervid, strong, forcible, powerful, emphatic, vigorous, animated, intense, violent, fierce, earnest, eager, keen, enthusiastic, zealous, fanatical; loud, noisy, clamorous, vocal, vociferous, outspoken, strident, forthright, insistent.
▷ANTONYMS mild, apathetic.

vehicle noun **1** *they were hit by a stolen vehicle*: **automobile**, motor vehicle, motorized vehicle, means of transport, conveyance, machine; informal wheels, heap, crate, jalopy; N. Amer. informal **auto**; US informal **hooptie**.
2 *education was a vehicle for the cultural assimilation of colonized peoples*: **channel**, medium, means, means of expression, agency, agent, instrument,

mechanism, organ, apparatus, structure, machine, machinery; force, catalyst; route, avenue, course, technique, method, approach.

> *Word links* **vehicle**
>
> **automotive** relating to vehicles

veil noun **1** *her face was hidden behind a black veil*: **face covering**, veiling; in Spanish-speaking countries mantilla; in Muslim & Hindu societies yashmak, purdah.
2 *a thin veil of high cloud made the sun hazy*: **covering**, cover, screen, shield, curtain, layer, film, mantle, cloak, mask, blanket, shroud, canopy, cloud, blur, haze, mist, pall.
▸ verb *the peak was often veiled in mist*: **envelop**, surround, swathe, enfold, cover, cover up, conceal, hide, secrete, camouflage, disguise, mask, screen, shield, cloak, blanket, shroud, enwrap, canopy, overlay; obscure, shade, shadow, eclipse, cloud, blot out, block out, blank out, obliterate, overshadow; literary enshroud, mantle, bedim, benight, becloud, befog; rare obnubilate.
▷ANTONYMS unveil, expose, uncover.

veiled adjective *they backed up their demands with veiled threats*: **covert**, surreptitious, hidden, concealed, disguised, camouflaged, masked, suppressed, underlying, unrevealed, implied, indirect, hinted at; ill-defined, indistinct, vague, obscure, unclear.
▷ANTONYMS overt, blatant.

> *Word toolkit* **veiled**
>
> See **invisible**.

vein noun **1** *the mineral veins in the rock vary in thickness*: **layer**, lode, seam, stratum, stratification, bed, deposit, accumulation.
2 *the floor was made of cold, white marble with grey veins*: **streak**, marking, mark, line, stripe, strip, band, thread, fleck, dash, flash, swathe, strand; technical stria, striation, lane.
3 *drinking produced a vein of brilliance in him*: **streak**, strain, trait, element, dash, dab, smattering, sprinkling, trace, hint, sign, suggestion, suspicion, indication, nuance.
4 *he closes the article in a somewhat humorous vein*: **mood**, humour, temper, temperament, disposition, frame of mind, state of mind, attitude, inclination, tendency, tenor, tone, key, spirit, character, stamp, feel, feeling, flavour, quality, atmosphere; manner, way, style.

> *Word links* **vein**
>
> **vascular**, **venous** relating to veins
> **angio-** relating to blood vessels, as in *angioplasty*
> **phlebotomy** incision into a vein

velocity noun *light always travels at the same constant velocity*: **speed**, pace, rate, tempo, momentum, impetus; swiftness, swift/fast pace, fastness, quickness, speediness, rapidity, briskness, expeditiousness, expedition, dispatch; acceleration; informal clip, fair old rate, fair lick, steam, nippiness; literary fleetness, celerity.

venal adjective *the law courts are venal and can take decades to decide a case*: **corrupt**, corruptible, bribable, open to bribery, purchasable, buyable, grafting; dishonest, fraudulent, dishonourable, untrustworthy, unscrupulous, unprincipled; mercenary, avaricious, grasping, rapacious; informal bent, crooked, warped, shady; rare simoniacal, simoniac.
▷ANTONYMS honourable, honest.

> *Easily confused words* **venal or venial?**
>
> See **venial**.

vendetta noun *he was the victim of a political vendetta*: **feud**, blood feud, quarrel, argument, falling-out, wrangle, clash, altercation, dispute, fight, war; bad blood, bitterness, enmity, rivalry, conflict, discord, strife; informal tiff, scrap, spat, ruction, bust-up.

vendor noun *the ice-cream vendors were doing a brisk trade*: **seller**, salesperson, salesman, saleswoman, dealer, trader, tradesman, retailer, shopkeeper, shopman, shop girl, shop boy, sales assistant, assistant, wholesaler, merchant, trafficker, purveyor, supplier, stockist, marketer, marketeer, sales representative, door-to-door salesman, travelling salesman, commercial traveller; tout, barrow boy; broker, agent, representative, negotiator; N. Amer. sales clerk, clerk, storekeeper; informal counter-jumper, rep, knight of the road, runner, pusher; dated chandler, pedlar, hawker; rare huckster, crier, colporteur.

veneer noun **1** *the boxes are made from American cherry wood with maple veneer*: **surface**, **lamination**, overlay, facing, covering, coat, finish, finishing coat, layer, decorative/protective layer, cladding, exterior; patina, varnish, polish, glaze, film, membrane, skin, sheet.
2 *a rigid veneer of courtesy hid her mounting fury*: **facade**, front, false front, show, outward display, appearance, false appearance, outward appearance, impression, image, semblance, posture, pose, guise, disguise, mask, masquerade, pretence, charade, illusion, gloss, camouflage, false colours, smokescreen, cover, cloak; archaic snivel.

venerable adjective *he was a venerable and most pious king*: **respected**, venerated, revered, reverenced, worshipped, honoured, esteemed, hallowed, august, distinguished, acclaimed, celebrated, lionized; renowned, illustrious, glorious, legendary, famed, eminent, pre-eminent, great, elevated, prominent, notable, noted; respectable, reputable, decent, honourable, worthy, exemplary.
▷ANTONYMS disreputable, dishonourable.

venerate verb *the Hindus venerate oxen*: **revere**, reverence, respect, worship, adulate, hallow, deify, idolize, hold sacred, exalt, honour, esteem, look up to, think highly of, pay homage to, pay tribute to; adore, praise, extol, aggrandize, lionize, hold in awe, stand in awe of, marvel at, value; informal put on a pedestal; rare magnify, laud.
▷ANTONYMS despise.

venerated adjective *one of the most venerated shrines in the Himalayan world*: **revered**, respected, esteemed, honoured; hallowed, holy, sacred.

veneration noun *in parts of India the snake is an object of veneration*: **reverence**, respect, worship, adoration, homage, exaltation, adulation, glorification, extolment, idolization, devotion; honour, esteem, regard, high regard, praise; respectfulness, worshipfulness, obeisance, submission, deference, awe; rare laudation, magnification.
▷ANTONYMS disrespect.

vengeance noun *he demanded vengeance for the murder of his father*: **revenge**, avengement, retribution, retributive justice, retaliation, requital, reprisal; counterstroke, comeback, nemesis, satisfaction, an eye for an eye (and a tooth for a tooth), tit for tat, measure for measure, blow for blow; Latin quid pro quo, lex talionis; informal comeuppance, a taste of one's own medicine; rare ultion, a Roland for an Oliver.
□ **with a vengeance** *she set to work with a vengeance*: **vigorously**, strenuously, energetically, with a will, with might and main, with all the stops out, for all one is worth, to the utmost, to the greatest extreme, to the full, to the limit, all out, flat out, at full tilt; powerfully, strongly, forcefully, violently, vehemently, furiously, wildly, madly; informal hammer and tongs, like crazy, like mad; Brit. informal like billy-o.

vengeful adjective *he was such a vengeful man that he had wanted his attacker dead*: **vindictive**, revengeful, out for revenge, avenging, unforgiving, resentful, grudge-bearing, bitter, acrimonious; literary malefic, maleficent.
▷ANTONYMS forgiving, benevolent.

venial adjective *he had compounded a number of venial failings with the mortal sin of adultery*: **pardonable**, forgivable, excusable, condonable, tolerable, permissible, allowable, understandable, justifiable; slight, minor, unimportant, insignificant, trivial, trifling, not serious, all right, within accepted bounds.
▷ANTONYMS unforgivable, unpardonable, mortal.

> *Easily confused words* **venial or venal?**
>
> There is only one letter's difference in the spelling of these words; but it marks the difference between a word used to excuse a minor transgression and one denoting something far worse. **Venial** is a Christian theological term for a sin that is less serious than a mortal sin; more loosely, it denotes faults or offences that are regarded as slight and pardonable (*smoking cigarettes became a venial sin in suburban high schools*). **Venal**, on the other hand, means 'susceptible to bribery' (*drug traffickers flourish where policemen are venal or lazy*).

venom noun **1** *vipers kill their victims by injecting them with venom*: **poison**, toxin; archaic bane; rare toxicant.
2 *the venom in his voice was shocking*: **rancour**, **malevolence**, vitriol, spite, spitefulness, vindictiveness, malice, maliciousness, malignity, malignancy, viciousness, nastiness, ill will, ill feeling, animosity, animus, acrimony, acrimoniousness, bitterness, embitterment, embitteredness, sourness, resentment, grudgingness, virulence, antagonism, hostility, bad blood, bile, spleen, gall, enmity, hate, hatred, dislike, antipathy, aversion; informal bitchiness, cattiness; rare maleficence, causticity, mordacity.
▷ANTONYMS love, goodwill.

V

venomous adjective **1** *black mambas are among the most venomous snakes in the world*: **poisonous**, toxic, noxious, dangerous, harmful; **deadly**, lethal, death-dealing, life-threatening, fatal, mortal, terminal, killing; literary deathly, nocuous, mephitic; archaic baneful.
▷ANTONYMS harmless, innocuous.
2 *the porter threw a venomous look at Ralf*: **vicious**, spiteful; **rancorous**, **malevolent**, vitriolic, vindictive, malicious, malignant, malign, poisonous, baleful, bitter, acrimonious, resentful, grudging, virulent, pernicious, antagonistic, hostile, hate-filled, menacing, nasty, evil, evil-intentioned, unfriendly, cruel, unkind, unpleasant; acerbic, sharp, acid, tart, caustic, astringent, cutting, biting, razor-edged, waspish, wounding, barbed; informal bitchy, catty; literary malefic, maleficent.
▷ANTONYMS friendly, benevolent, kind.

vent noun *inside the tent are two funnel-shaped air vents*: **outlet**, **inlet**, opening, aperture, vent hole, hole, gap, orifice, space, cavity, cleft, slit, pore, port; duct, flue, shaft, channel, well, passage, air passage, airway, blowhole, breather.
▸ verb *the crowd vented their fury by pelting him with rotten eggs*: **let out**, give vent to, give free rein to, release, pour out, emit, discharge; reveal, bring into the open, come out with, express, give expression to, air, communicate, utter, voice, give voice to, verbalize, articulate, broadcast, make public, proclaim, assert, ventilate, find an outlet for.

ventilate verb **1** *the conservatory will become stiflingly hot if not properly ventilated*: **aerate**, air, oxygenate, air-condition, fan, freshen, refresh, cool.
2 *the workers ventilated their discontent*: **express**, give expression to, air, give an airing to, bring into the open, raise, register, lodge, bring up, come out with, reveal, assert, declare, communicate, utter, voice, give voice to, put into words, verbalize, talk about, discuss, debate, talk over.

venture noun *their fortune was wiped out by an unsuccessful business venture*: **enterprise**, undertaking, project, scheme, pursuit, operation, endeavour, campaign, activity, act, deed, move, measure, task, exploit, mission, adventure, trial; speculation, plunge, gamble, leap in the dark, experiment, crusade; formal essay.
▸ verb **1** *some villagers rarely ventured beyond their nearest market town*: **travel**, journey, go, move, proceed, progress, set out, set forth, rove; wander, stray, drift, migrate.
2 *he ventured the opinion that Peter was dangerously insane*: **put forward**, volunteer, advance, submit, proffer, offer, air, bring up, suggest, propound, posit, propose, moot, ventilate, table, broach, lodge, introduce, put up, present; conjecture, speculate, postulate; formal opine, essay.
3 *I ventured to ask her to come and dine with me*: **dare**, make so bold as, be so bold as, presume, have the temerity, have the effrontery, have the audacity, have the nerve, be brave enough, have the courage, go so far as; take the liberty of; informal stick one's neck out, go out on a limb; N. Amer. informal take a flyer.

veracious adjective *the manuscripts contain veracious accounts of the event*: **true**, accurate, veritable, correct, errorless, unerring, exact, precise, factual, literal, realistic, authentic, faithful, close, strict, just, unelaborated, unvarnished; truthful, honest, sincere, frank, candid, honourable, reputable, trustworthy, trusty, reliable, dependable, scrupulous, upright, upstanding, ethical, moral, righteous, virtuous, decent, good; informal on the nail, spot on, as true as I'm sitting/standing here.
▷ANTONYMS untrue; dishonest.

veracity noun *they expressed doubts about the veracity of the story*: **truthfulness**, truth, accuracy, accurateness, correctness, exactness, precision, preciseness, realism, authenticity, faithfulness, fidelity; reputability, honesty, sincerity, trustworthiness, reliability, dependability, scrupulousness, ethics, morality, righteousness, virtuousness, decency, goodness, probity.
▷ANTONYMS falsity.

verbal adjective *he was given a verbal assurance that his application would be approved*: **oral**, spoken, said, uttered, articulated, expressed, stated, verbalized, vocal, unwritten, by mouth, word-of-mouth; Latin viva voce.
▷ANTONYMS non-verbal, unspoken; written.
▸ noun Brit. informal *I'd go out on the pitch and get a load of verbal from the crowd*: **abuse**, stream/torrent of abuse, teasing, hectoring, jeering, barracking, cursing, scolding, upbraiding, rebuke, reproval, castigation, revilement, vilification, vituperation, defamation, slander, flak; insults, curses, aspersions; informal mud-slinging, bad-mouthing, tongue-lashing, a lashing, a roasting, a caning; Brit. informal stick, slagging off, slating, a rollicking, a wigging, a rocket; Brit. vulgar slang a bollocking.
▷ANTONYMS praise.

verbatim adverb *their stories were taped and then transcribed verbatim*: **word for word**, letter for letter, line for line, to the letter, literally, exactly, precisely, in every detail, closely, faithfully, religiously, rigorously, punctiliously, with strict attention to detail, strictly; rare literatim.
▷ANTONYMS loosely, imprecisely.
▸ adjective *a verbatim record of the proceedings*: **word for word**, letter for letter, line for line, literal, exact, direct, precise, close, faithful, undeviating, strict; unadulterated, unabridged, unvarnished, unembellished.
▷ANTONYMS loose, imprecise.

V

verbiage noun *there is plenty of irrelevant verbiage but no real information*: **verbosity**, verboseness, padding, wordiness, prolixity, prolixness, superfluity, redundancy, long-windedness, lengthiness, protractedness, discursiveness, expansiveness, digressiveness, convolution, circumlocution, circuitousness, rambling, wandering, meandering; Brit. informal waffle, waffling, wittering, flannel; rare logorrhoea.

verbose adjective *verbose articles from amateur authors*: **wordy**, loquacious, garrulous, talkative, voluble, orotund, expansive, babbling, blathering, prattling, prating, jabbering, gushing, effusive; long-winded, lengthy, protracted, prolix, periphrastic, circumlocutory, circuitous, tautological, repetitious, redundant, tortuous, indirect, convoluted; diffuse, discursive, digressive, rambling, wandering, meandering; informal mouthy, gabby, windy, gassy, with the gift of the gab, having kissed the Blarney stone, yakking, big-mouthed; Brit. informal wittering; rare multiloquent, multiloquous, ambagious, logorrhoeic, pleonastic.
▷ANTONYMS succinct, laconic.

verbosity noun *the dialogue is a reasonable compromise between clarity and verbosity*: **wordiness**, verboseness, loquacity, garrulity, talkativeness, volubility, expansiveness, babbling, blathering, waffling, prattling, prating, jabbering, gushing; long-windedness, lengthiness, protractedness, verbiage, prolixity, periphrasis, tautology, circumlocution, convolution, redundancy; diffuseness, discursiveness, digressiveness; informal the gift of the gab, big mouth, mouthiness, gassiness, gabbiness, windiness, blah-blah, gobbledegook; Brit. informal wittering; rare orotundity, logorrhoea, multiloquence, pleonasm, perissology.
▷ANTONYMS brevity, taciturnity.

verdant adjective *the verdant forests of southern Vermont*: **green**, leafy, grassy, grass-covered; **lush**, rich, flourishing, thriving, teeming, prolific, rampant, overgrown, dense, thick, jungle-like; informal jungly; rare verdurous, viridescent, virid, graminaceous, gramineous.

verdict noun *the coroner recorded a verdict of death by misadventure*: **judgement**, adjudication, adjudgement, decision, finding, ruling, resolution, pronouncement, decree, order, settlement, result, conclusion, opinion, prognosis, conviction, assumption, presumption; sentence, punishment; N. Amer. resolve; Law determination.

verge noun **1** *park your car on the road verge*: **edge**, border, margin, side, brink, rim, lip, limit, boundary, outskirts, perimeter, periphery, borderline, frontier; end, extremity, termination; fringes, bounds, limits, confines; literary bourn, marge, skirt.
▷ANTONYMS centre, middle.
2 *Spain was on the verge of a major economic crisis*: **brink**, threshold, edge, point, dawn; starting point, start.
▷ANTONYMS middle.
▸ verb *she showed a degree of caution that* **verged on** *the obsessive*: **tend towards**, incline to, incline towards, border on, approach, near, come near, be close/near to, touch on, be tantamount to, be more or less, be not far from, approximate to, resemble, be similar to.

verification noun *the banking software has an array of functions including signature verification*: **confirmation**, substantiation, corroboration, attestation, affirmation, validation, authentication, endorsement, accreditation, ratification, establishment, certification; evidence, proof, support, witness, testament, documentation.

verify verb *reports of the massacre could not be verified*: **substantiate**, confirm, prove, show to be true, corroborate, back up, support, uphold, evidence, establish, demonstrate, demonstrate the truth of, show, show beyond doubt, attest to, testify to, validate, authenticate, endorse, certify, accredit, ratify, warrant, vouch for, bear out, bear witness to, give credence to, give force to, give/lend weight to, justify, vindicate; make sure, make certain, check; informal pin down; Brit. informal suss out.
▷ANTONYMS refute.

vernacular noun *he wrote in the vernacular and adopted a non-academic style accessible to the public*: **everyday language**, spoken language, colloquial speech, native speech, conversational language, common parlance, non-standard language, jargon, -speak, cant, slang, idiom, argot, patois, dialect; regional language, local tongue, regionalism, localism, provincialism; informal lingo, local lingo, patter; rare idiolect.
▷ANTONYMS formal language; Latin.

versatile adjective *he was versatile enough to play on either wing*: **adaptable**, flexible, all-round, multifaceted, multitalented, many-sided, resourceful, protean; adjustable, variable, convertible, alterable, modifiable, multi-purpose, all-purpose, handy; rare polytropic, flexile.
▷ANTONYMS inflexible, limited.

verse noun **1** *she provides written commentary in prose and verse*: **poetry**, versification, metrical composition, rhythmical composition, rhyme, rhyming, balladry, doggerel; poems, lyrics, rhymes; literary poesy, Parnassus.
▷ANTONYMS prose.
2 *he sent me a verse he'd composed especially to mark my anniversary*: **poem**, piece of poetry, lyric, sonnet, ode, limerick, rhyme, composition, metrical composition, piece of doggerel; ditty, song, jingle, lay, ballad; rare tenson, verselet.
3 *a poem with sixty verses*: **stanza**, strophe, stave, canto; couplet, distich, triplet, tercet, tetrastich; part, section, portion.
▸ verb *the author does not seem thoroughly* **versed in** *the scholarship of her field*: **acquainted with**, conversant with, familiar with, informed about, knowledgeable about, well informed about, instructed in, skilled in, proficient in; at home with, no stranger to, au fait with, au courant with, apprised of, abreast of, up to date with, in touch with; informal well up on, in the know about, genned up on, clued in on, clued up on, plugged into; Brit. informal switched on to.
▷ANTONYMS unfamiliar with.

version noun **1** *the court accepted the policeman's version of events*: **report**, statement, description, record, account, story, tale, history, chronicle, narrative, narration, rendition, rendering, interpretation, explanation, construction, construal, analysis, understanding, reading, impression, side, view; informal take (on).
2 *he published a German version of his book*: **edition**, **translation**, adaptation, rendering, interpretation, variant, variation, form, copy, reproduction, impression, issue, release, instalment, revision.
3 *they have replaced coal-burning fires with gas versions*: **sort**, kind, type, variety, genre, class, category, style, form, brand, make, model, design.

vertex noun *a line was drawn from the vertex of the figure to the middle of the base*: **apex**, peak, tip, top, summit, pinnacle, crest, brow, crown, height, highest point; technical acme, zenith, apogee.

vertical adjective *in this exercise the legs are raised to an almost vertical position | the manhole lid conceals a vertical shaft*: **upright**, erect, perpendicular, plumb, straight (up and down), on end, standing, upstanding, bolt upright, upended; sheer, steep, sharp, precipitous, bluff, vertiginous; Heraldry rampant; rare acclivitous, declivitous, scarped.
▷ANTONYMS horizontal, flat.

vertigo noun *she kept well away from the edge and steeled herself against a spasm of vertigo*: **dizziness**, giddiness, light-headedness, loss of balance, loss of equilibrium, spinning/swimming of the head; fear of heights, acrophobia; Scottish mirligoes; informal wooziness; technical sturdy; rare turnsick, vertiginousness.

verve noun *I played most sports with schoolboy verve*: **enthusiasm**, vigour, energy, pep, dynamism, go, elan, vitality, vivacity, buoyancy, liveliness, animation, sprightliness, zest, sparkle, effervescence, fizz, spirit, spiritedness, ebullience, life, dash, brio, fervour, gusto, eagerness, keenness, passion, zeal, relish, feeling, ardour, fire, fieriness, drive, forcefulness, force, strength, determination, motivation, push, vehemence, fanaticism; informal zing, zip, vim, punch, get-up-and-go, pizzazz, oomph, feistiness.

> *Choose the right word* **verve, zest, gusto**
>
> See **zest**.

very adverb *I'm not very brave | read each question very carefully*: **extremely**, exceedingly, exceptionally, especially, tremendously, immensely, vastly, hugely; extraordinarily, extra, excessively, overly, over, abundantly, inordinately, singularly, significantly, distinctly, outstandingly, uncommonly, unusually, decidedly, particularly, eminently, supremely, highly, remarkably, really, truly, mightily, thoroughly; all that, to a great extent, most, so, too; Scottish unco; French très; N. English right; informal terrifically, awfully, terribly, devilishly, madly, majorly, seriously, desperately, mega, ultra, oh-so, too-too, stinking, mucho, damn, damned, too ... for words; informal, dated devilish, hellish, frightfully; Brit. informal ever so, well, bloody, dead, dirty, jolly, fair; N. Amer. informal real, mighty, powerful, awful, plumb, darned, way, bitching; S. African informal lekker; archaic exceeding, sore.
▷ANTONYMS slightly, sort of, not particularly.
▸ adjective **1** *that is the very thing I was thinking of myself*: **exact**, actual, precise, particular, specific, distinct.
2 *this boy's a gold mine—he's the very thing I need*: **ideal**, perfect, appropriate, suitable, apt, fitting, fit, right, just right, made to order, tailor-made; Brit. informal spot on, just the job.
3 *the very word 'modern' was exciting to them*: **mere**, simple, pure, pure and simple, plain, basic; sheer, utter.

vessel noun **1** *the lifeboat was called to the aid of a fishing vessel*: **boat**, sailing boat, ship, yacht, craft, watercraft; literary barque, keel.
2 *pour the decoction into a heatproof vessel*: **container**, receptacle, repository, holder, carrier; basin, bowl, dish, pan, pot, can, tin, jar, jug, pitcher, carafe, flask, decanter; urn, tub, bin, tank, drum, canister, butt, vat, cask, barrel; box, case, chest, casket; archaic reservatory.
3 *he burst a blood vessel during a fit of coughing*: **duct**, tube, channel, passage, pipe; artery, vein; technical vas, trachea.

vest verb *the executive power of the state is **vested in** the Governor*: **entrust to**, invest in, bestow on, confer on, grant to, give to; endow, lodge, lay, place; put in the hands of.

vestibule noun *we sat in a high vestibule between the street and the courtyard*: **entrance hall**, hall, hallway, entrance, porch, portico, foyer, reception area, lobby, anteroom, antechamber, outer room, waiting room.

vestige noun **1** *vestiges of England's Tudor past were still evident*: **remnant**, remainder, fragment, relic, echo, indication, sign, trace, mark, print, imprint, impression, legacy, reminder, memento, souvenir, token, trophy; remains, leftovers, leavings, evidence, residue; archaic memorandum, memory, remembrancer.
2 *she showed no vestige of emotion*: **trace**, scrap, touch, tinge, hint, suggestion, suspicion, soupçon, inkling, whisper, scintilla, whit, spark, glimmer, flicker, atom, speck, bit, ounce, drop, dash, jot, iota, shred, crumb, morsel, fragment, grain, spot, mite, modicum; informal smidgen, smidge, tad; Irish informal stim; archaic scantling, scruple.

vestigial adjective **1** *vestigial limbs enabled the fish to crawl on to the land*: **rudimentary**, undeveloped, incomplete, embryonic, immature; non-functional; technical abortive, primitive, obsolete.
▷ANTONYMS well developed.
2 *he feels a vestigial flicker of anger from last night*: **remaining**, surviving, residual, leftover, lingering; persisting, abiding, lasting, enduring.

vet verb *they try to vet all the publications they sell*: **screen**, assess, evaluate, appraise, weigh up, examine, look over, review, consider, scrutinize, study, inspect; **investigate**, **censor**, check, check out, check up on; probe, research, look into, delve into, dig into, search into; informal give something a/the once-over, size up.
▸ noun *I took the cat to the vet*: **animal doctor**, veterinary surgeon, VS, horse doctor; N. Amer. **veterinarian**, doctor; dated veterinary.

veteran noun *an army veteran*: **retired soldier**; **old hand**, old-timer, old stager; past master, doyen, authority, master, grandmaster, master hand, expert, virtuoso, maestro; informal pro, ace, hotshot, old warhorse.
▷ANTONYMS novice, apprentice, recruit.
▸ adjective *a veteran diplomat specializing in US affairs*: **long-serving**, seasoned, mature, old, established; hardened; adept, master, expert, consummate, well versed, well trained, practised, experienced, worldly-wise, qualified, proficient, professional; informal battle-scarred, crack, ace, mean.

veto noun *the president still has the power of veto over Congressional legislation*: **rejection**, vetoing, dismissal, denial, declination, turndown; **prohibition**, prohibiting, proscription, preclusion, restriction, suppression, stoppage; embargo, ban, boycott, bar, interdict; informal thumbs down, red light, knock-back.
▷ANTONYMS approval, OK.
▸ verb *the president carried out his threat to veto the bill*: **reject**, turn down, throw out, dismiss, say 'no' to, rule against, overrule, rule out, quash; **prohibit**, forbid, interdict, proscribe, disallow, outlaw, embargo, place an embargo on, ban, bar, block, preclude, put a stop to, put an end to, stop, nullify, declare null and void; informal kill, squash, put the kibosh on, give the thumbs down to, give the red light to.
▷ANTONYMS approve, authorize.

vex verb *Alice was vexed by his remarks*: **annoy**, irritate, infuriate, anger, incense, inflame, enrage, irk, chagrin, exasperate, madden, pique, provoke, nettle, disturb, upset, perturb, discompose, put out; try, try someone's patience, get on someone's nerves, bother, trouble, worry, agitate, harass, harry, fuss, fluster, ruffle, hound; rankle with, nag, torment, pain, distress, tease, frustrate, chafe, grate, fret, gall, outrage, displease, offend, disgust, dissatisfy, disquiet; Brit. rub up the wrong way; N. English mither; informal peeve, aggravate, miff, bug, bite, eat, hassle, rile, get to, hack off, make someone's blood boil, make someone see red, get someone's goat, get someone's hackles up, make someone's hackles rise, get someone's back up, get someone's dander up, drive up the wall, drive bananas, needle, be a thorn in someone's side/flesh, be a pain in the neck, ruffle someone's feathers, get in someone's hair, get up someone's nose, get under someone's skin, give someone a hard time; Brit. informal nark, get on someone's wick, give someone the hump, wind up, get across; N. Amer. informal tick off, ride, rankle, gravel; vulgar slang piss off, get on someone's tits.
▷ANTONYMS mollify, appease.

> *Choose the right word* **vex, annoy, irritate, aggravate, peeve**
>
> See **annoy**.

vexation noun *Erica stamped her foot in vexation*: **annoyance**, irritation, irritability, exasperation, anger, rage, fury, temper, bad temper, hot temper, wrath, spleen, chagrin, pique, crossness, indignation, displeasure, discontent, dissatisfaction, disgruntlement, ill humour, peevishness, petulance, testiness, tetchiness, gall, resentment, umbrage; perturbation, discomposure, worry, agitation, harassment; informal needling, aggravation, being rubbed up the wrong way, crabbiness; Brit. informal stroppiness; literary ire, choler.

vexatious adjective *he had been left in a very vexatious position*: **annoying**, vexing, irritating, irksome, displeasing, infuriating, maddening, exasperating, provoking, galling, rankling, grating, jarring, harassing, harrying, bothersome, tiresome, troublesome, niggling; upsetting, perturbing, worrying, worrisome, trying, taxing, distressing, traumatic, unsettling, unpleasant; difficult, awkward, problematic, inconvenient, lamentable, deplorable; informal aggravating.

vexed adjective **1** *a vexed expression crossed Louise's face*: **annoyed**, irritated, angry, irate, furious, incensed, inflamed, enraged, infuriated, maddened, fuming, wrathful, choleric, exasperated, piqued, irked, nettled, ill-humoured, hot-tempered, testy, cross, in a bad mood, in a temper, in high dudgeon, huffy, in a huff, put out, fed up, disgruntled, displeased, dissatisfied, frustrated, resentful; upset, perturbed, fretted, bothered,

troubled, worried, agitated, harassed, harried, flustered, distressed; informal aggravated, peeved, miffed, miffy, mad, riled, hacked off, peed off, hot under the collar, foaming at the mouth; Brit. informal browned off, cheesed off, brassed off, narked, eggy; N. Amer. informal teed off, ticked off, sore, steamed; W. Indian informal vex; vulgar slang pissed off; N. Amer. vulgar slang pissed; literary ireful; archaic snuffy, wrath.
▷ANTONYMS calm, content.
2 *first, there is the vexed issue of what independence means*: **disputed**, in dispute, contested, in contention, contentious, debated, debatable, open to debate, open to question, questionable, at issue, open to doubt, controversial, moot, unresolved, unsettled, up in the air, undecided, yet to be decided, undetermined, unconcluded, ongoing; problematic, problematical, taxing, knotty, thorny, ticklish, delicate; informal sticky, dicey, hairy, iffy; Brit. informal dodgy.
▷ANTONYMS undisputed, resolved.

viable adjective *the committee came forward with the only viable solution*: **workable**, feasible, practicable, practical, applicable, usable, manageable, operable, operational, possible, within the bounds/realms of possibility, within reach, within reason, likely, achievable, attainable, accomplishable, realizable, reasonable, sensible, realistic, logical, useful, of use, serviceable, suitable, expedient, effective, valid, tenable; sound, well advised, well thought out, well grounded, judicious, level-headed, wise; informal doable.
▷ANTONYMS impracticable.

vibrant adjective **1** *they listened to vibrant tunes in the open air*: **resonant**, sonorous, throbbing, pulsating, reverberating, reverberant, resounding, ringing, echoing, carrying, booming, blaring, thunderous, strident; rich, full, full-bodied, strong, fruity, lively; rare canorous.
▷ANTONYMS soft, mellow.
2 *she was a vibrant and passionate woman*: **spirited**, lively, full of life, full of spirit, high-spirited, energetic, sprightly, vigorous, vital, full of vim and vigour, animated, sparkling, effervescent, vivacious, dynamic, flamboyant, electrifying, dazzling, stimulating, exciting, dashing, passionate, fiery, determined; informal peppy, zippy, full of beans, feisty, spunky, have-a-go, ballsy; rare coruscating.
▷ANTONYMS spiritless, listless, dull.
3 *in spring the flower fields burst into vibrant colour*: **vivid**, striking, intense, brilliant, bright, strong, rich, deep, warm, full; psychedelic, flamboyant, luminous; informal jazzy.
▷ANTONYMS pale, washed out.
4 *she was vibrant with excitement*: **quivering**, trembling, shaking, shaky, shivering, shivery, shuddering, shuddery, quavering, quavery, quaking; informal trembly.

vibrate verb **1** *the ground beneath their feet began to vibrate*: **quiver**, shake, tremble, quaver, waver, shiver, shudder, judder, jiggle, wobble; rock, undulate, move, heave, convulse, jerk, jolt, jar; **oscillate**, vacillate, swing, sway, move to and fro, swing back and forth, swing backwards and forwards, wave, agitate, waggle, wag; N. Amer. wigwag.
2 *a low rumbling sound began to vibrate through the car*: **throb**, reverberate, pulsate, pulse, palpitate, resonate, resound, ring, echo, re-echo, boom, thunder, thump, pound, beat, drum, thud, thrum, hammer; ripple, murmur, hum, drone; rare quop.

vibration noun **1** *the slightest vibration of the water's surface is detected by the beetle*: **quiver**, quivering, shake, shaking, shaking movement, quaver, quavering, quake, quaking, tremble, trembling, tremor, judder, shiver, shivering, shudder, shuddering; oscillation, vacillation.
2 *the room shakes with the vibration of rock rhythms*: **reverberation**, resonance, throbbing, throb, vibrating, pulsation, pulsing, rumbling, rumble, beating, beat, drumming, drum, thumping, thump, thrumming, thrum, pounding, pound, palpitating, palpitation; hum, humming, murmur, murmuring, drone, droning, buzz, buzzing.

vicar noun *as vicar of a large parish he had many and constant duties*: **minister**, rector, priest, parson, minister of religion, clergyman, clergywoman, cleric, churchman, churchwoman, ecclesiastic, pastor, father, man/woman of the cloth, man/woman of god, curate, chaplain, curé, presbyter, preacher, lay preacher, evangelist, divine; Scottish kirkman; N. Amer. dominie; informal reverend, padre, Holy Joe, sky pilot; Austral. informal josser.

V

vicarious adjective *my friend was going to Italy and I was in a fever of vicarious excitement*: **indirect**, second-hand, secondary, derivative, derived, at one remove, surrogate, substitute, substituted, by proxy; empathetic, empathic.

vice noun **1** *people may be driven to vice by cruel social circumstances*: **immorality**, wrongdoing, wrong, wickedness, badness, evil-doing, evil, iniquity, villainy, venality, impurity, corruption, corruptness, misconduct; sin, sinfulness, ungodliness, godlessness, unholiness, unrighteousness, profanity; **depravity**, degeneracy, turpitude, sordidity, perversion, pervertedness, dissolution, dissipation, debauchery, decadence, lasciviousness, lewdness, lechery, lecherousness, degradation; crime, transgression, offence, immoral act, evil act, act of wickedness, fall from grace; archaic trespass; rare peccability, peccancy.
▷ANTONYMS virtue, righteousness.
2 *smoking is my only vice*: **shortcoming**, failing, flaw, fault, defect, weakness, weak point, deficiency, limitation, imperfection, blemish, foible, fallibility, frailty, infirmity.
▷ANTONYMS virtue, strong point.

vice versa adverb *dancers can teach actors a lot and vice versa*: **conversely**, inversely, the other way round, contrariwise, oppositely, in reverse, reciprocally.

vicinity noun **1** *many famous writers made their homes in the vicinity*: **surrounding district**, surrounding area, neighbourhood, locality, locale, local area, area, district, region, quarter, sector, territory, domain, place, zone; environs, surroundings, surrounds, precincts, purlieus; informal this neck of the woods; technical locus; rare vicinage.
2 *the forest's vicinity to the dockyards made it a vital source of timber*: **nearness**, closeness, proximity, propinquity, adjacency, juxtaposition; accessibility, handiness; rare contiguity, contiguousness, vicinage.
□ **in the vicinity** *his fortune is* **in the vicinity of** *three million pounds*: **around**, about, nearly, approaching, just about, just over, just under, roughly, something like, more or less; in the region of, in the neighbourhood of, near to, close to, close on; Brit. getting on for; Latin circa; N. Amer. informal in the ballpark of.

vicious adjective **1** *there was a vicious killer at large*: **brutal**, ferocious, savage, violent, dangerous, ruthless, remorseless, merciless, heartless, callous, cruel, harsh, cold-blooded, inhuman, fierce, barbarous, barbaric, brutish, bestial, bloodthirsty, bloody, fiendish, sadistic, monstrous, villainous, murderous, homicidal, heinous, atrocious, diabolical, terrible, dreadful, awful, grim; Brit. informal beastly; archaic fell, sanguinary.
▷ANTONYMS gentle.
2 *the MP was the victim of a vicious hate campaign*: **malicious**, malevolent, malignant, malign, spiteful, vindictive, venomous, poisonous, baleful, virulent, pernicious, backbiting, rancorous, caustic, mean, cruel, bitter, acrimonious, hostile, hate-filled, menacing, nasty, unpleasant, evil; defamatory, slanderous; informal bitchy, catty; literary malefic, maleficent.
▷ANTONYMS kindly, benevolent.

vicissitude noun *he maintains his sunny disposition despite life's vicissitudes*: **change**, alteration, alternation, transformation, metamorphosis, transmutation, mutation, modification, transition, development, shift, switch, turn; **reversal**, reverse, downturn; inconstancy, instability, uncertainty, unpredictability, chanciness, fickleness, variability, changeability, fluctuation, vacillation; ups and downs.

victim noun **1** *a victim of violent crime*: **sufferer**, injured party, casualty, injured person, wounded person; dead person, fatality, loss; loser.
▷ANTONYMS attacker, assailant.
2 *they intended me to be the victim of a confidence trick*: **dupe**, easy target, easy prey, fair game, sitting target, everybody's fool, stooge, gull, fool, Aunt Sally; **target**, prey, quarry, object, subject, recipient, focus; informal sitting duck, sucker, fall guy, pushover, soft touch, easy touch, chump, muggins, charlie; N. Amer. informal patsy, pigeon, sap, schlemiel, mark; Austral./NZ informal dill.
3 *he offered himself as a sacrificial victim*: **sacrifice**, offering, burnt offering, scapegoat.
□ **fall victim to** *the girls had fallen victim to a flu epidemic*: **fall ill with**, be stricken with, become infected with, catch, develop, contract, pick up; succumb to, be overcome by, be overwhelmed by; informal come/go down with.
▷ANTONYMS resist.

victimize verb *he was victimized by cruel practical jokers*: **exploit**, prey on, take advantage of, swindle, dupe, cheat, trick, hoodwink, double-cross, defraud; **persecute**, pick on, push around, lean on, bully, abuse, discriminate against, ill-treat, mistreat, maltreat, harass, hound, torment, terrorize, torture, punish unfairly; informal get at, have it in for, have a down on, be down on, give someone a hard time, hassle, needle, get on someone's back, make things hot for someone, take for a ride, con, diddle, rip off, fleece.

victor verb *a disastrous civil war from which no victor can emerge*: **winner**, champion, conqueror, vanquisher, conquering hero, hero; prizewinner, medallist, cup winner, prizeman; Spanish conquistador; Latin victor ludorum; informal champ, top dog, number one.
▷ANTONYMS loser, vanquished.

victorious adjective *the victorious British team brought the trophy back from Paris*: **triumphant**, conquering, vanquishing, winning, champion, successful, top, first, second to none; prizewinning, cup-winning; undefeated, unbeaten, unconquered, unvanquished, unsubdued.
▷ANTONYMS unsuccessful, defeated.

victory noun *they had won a tremendous victory*: **success**, triumph, conquest, win, successful outcome, positive result, favourable result, landslide, achievement, coup; conquering, beating, overpowering, vanquishment, crushing, mastery, superiority, supremacy, pre-eminence, the upper hand; informal walkover, thrashing, trouncing.
▷ANTONYMS defeat.

victuals plural noun archaic *visitors were offered fine victuals*. See **food** (sense 1).

vie verb *restaurants vied with each other to attract custom*: **compete**, contend, contest, struggle, fight, battle, cross swords, lock horns, jockey, jostle, grapple, wrestle; war, wage war, feud.

view noun **1** *the view from her top-floor flat never failed to please her*: **outlook**, prospect, panorama, vista, scene, aspect, perspective, spectacle, sight; scenery, landscape, seascape, riverscape, cityscape, townscape, snowscape; archaic lookout.
2 *not all adolescents agree with this view*: **opinion**, point of view, viewpoint, belief, judgement, reckoning, way of thinking, thinking, thought, notion, idea, conviction, persuasion, attitude, feeling, sentiment, impression, concept, conception, hypothesis, theory, thesis, estimate, estimation, conclusion, verdict; statement, observation, remark, point; angle, slant, stance, posture, standpoint, approach.
3 *as one walks down the lane, the parish church comes into view*: **sight**, perspective, field of vision, range of vision, vision, visibility, eyeshot.
□ **in view of** *in view of its location, no removal of the tumour was attempted*: **considering**, taking into consideration, bearing in mind, keeping in mind, mindful of, taking into account, on account of, taking note of, in the light of, owing to, because of, as a result of.
□ **on view** *over one hundred of Van Gogh's paintings are on view in Amsterdam*: **on display**, on exhibition, on show; displayed, showing.
▸ verb **1** *they viewed the passing landscape from their carriages*: **look at**, gaze at, stare at, peer at, eye, observe, ogle, contemplate, regard, scan, survey, watch; look over, see over, be shown over, examine, inspect, scrutinize; catch sight of, glimpse, lay eyes on, spy, spot; N. Amer. check something out; informal get a load of, gawp at, rubberneck at, give something a/the once-over, have a look-see at, have/take a gander at, have a squint at, clap eyes on; Brit. informal have/take a dekko at, have/take a butcher's at, take a shufti at, clock; N. Amer. informal eyeball; literary espy, behold, descry.
2 *the law was often viewed as a last resort*: **consider**, regard, look on, see, perceive, judge, adjudge, estimate, deem, reckon, think of, treat.

viewer noun *the new television series has been a smash hit with viewers*: **watcher**, television watcher, spectator, onlooker, observer, non-participant; witness, eyewitness, looker-on; (**viewers**) audience, crowd; informal couch potato; literary beholder.

viewpoint noun *you seem to have adopted a very cynical viewpoint*: **way of thinking**, point of view, view, frame of reference, outlook, perspective, angle, slant, standpoint, position, posture, stance, stand, attitude, opinion, belief, judgement, interpretation, thought, school of thought, mind, line, policy; ideas, thoughts, sentiments, feelings.

vigilance noun *his security duties demand long hours of vigilance*: **watchfulness**, careful observation, surveillance, attentiveness, attention, alertness, guardedness, carefulness, care, caution, cautiousness, wariness, chariness, circumspection, prudence, heedfulness, heed, mindfulness.
▹ANTONYMS inattentiveness.

vigilant adjective *there had been a rash of petty thefts and we were warned to be vigilant*: **watchful**, on the lookout, observant, sharp-eyed, keen-eyed, gimlet-eyed, eagle-eyed, hawk-eyed, with eyes like a hawk, with one's eyes open, keeping one's eyes peeled/skinned, attentive, paying attention, alert, on the alert, on one's toes, on the qui vive; awake, wide awake, unsleeping, on one's guard, on guard, concentrating, careful, cautious, wary, chary, circumspect, prudent, heedful, mindful; prepared, ready; informal beady-eyed, not missing a trick, on the ball, keeping a weather eye on things, leery; rare regardful, Argus-eyed.
▹ANTONYMS negligent, inattentive.

vigorous adjective **1** *the child was strong and vigorous*: **robust**, healthy, in good health, hale and hearty, strong, strong as an ox/horse/lion, sturdy, fine, fit, in good condition, in tip-top condition, in good shape, in good trim, in good kilter; hardy, tough, athletic, strapping, able-bodied; bouncing, thriving, flourishing, blooming; **energetic**, lively, active, spry, sprightly, perky, playful, jaunty, vivacious, animated, spirited, high-spirited, dynamic, vibrant, full of life, vital, sparkling, effervescent, zestful, buoyant, tireless, indefatigable; informal go-getting, zippy, peppy, bouncy, upbeat, full of vim, full of beans, raring to go, bright-eyed and bushy-tailed, in the pink, fit as a fiddle; N. English informal wick; N. Amer. informal chipper.
▹ANTONYMS frail, weak.
2 *a vigorous defence of government policy*: **strenuous**, powerful, potent, forceful, forcible, spirited, mettlesome, determined, resolute, aggressive, eager, keen, active, enthusiastic, zealous, ardent, fervent, vehement, intense, intensive, passionate, fiery, wild, unrestrained, uncontrolled, unbridled; tough, blunt, hard-hitting, pulling no punches; informal all-out, punchy, in-your-face.
▹ANTONYMS weak, feeble.

vigorously adverb *she pedalled vigorously down the farm track*: **strenuously**, with great vigour, strongly, powerfully, potently, forcefully, with force, forcibly, energetically, aggressively, heartily, eagerly, with eagerness, enthusiastically, with enthusiasm, with great effort, with all one's might, with might and main, with a will, for dear life, for all one is worth, to the best of one's abilities, as best one can, all out, with a vengeance, fiercely, intensely, hard, as hard as possible, as hard as one can, with all the stops out, like the devil, like the deuce, at full tilt; informal like mad, like crazy, like nobody's business, like it's going out of style, like billy-o, hammer and tongs, going great guns.

vigour noun *they ran with great vigour*: **robustness**, healthiness, good health, hardiness, strength, stamina, sturdiness, fitness, good shape, good trim, good condition, fine fettle, toughness, ruggedness, muscle, power; bloom, radiance, sap; **energy**, activity, liveliness, life, spryness, sprightliness, vitality, vivacity, vivaciousness, verve, animation, spiritedness, spirit, enthusiasm, fire, fieriness, fervour, ardour, zeal, passion, might, forcefulness, determination, intensity, dynamism, sparkle, effervescence, zest, dash, snap, spark, gusto, pep, bounce, exuberance, drive, push, elan; informal zip, zing, oomph, vim, go, get-up-and-go, punch; Brit. informal welly; literary thew, thewiness.
▹ANTONYMS weakness, listlessness, lethargy.

vile adjective *a vile smell | he shouldn't be allowed to get away with such vile behaviour*: **foul**, nasty, unpleasant, bad, disagreeable, horrid, horrible, dreadful, abominable, atrocious, offensive, obnoxious, odious, unsavoury, repulsive, off-putting, repellent, revolting, repugnant, disgusting, distasteful, loathsome, hateful, nauseating, sickening; base, low, mean, wretched, disgraceful, appalling, shocking, ugly, vulgar, sorry, shabby, shameful, dishonourable, execrable, heinous, abhorrent, deplorable, monstrous, wicked, evil, dark, dirty, vicious, iniquitous, sinful, corrupt, sordid, depraved, perverted, debased, reprobate, degenerate, debauched, dissolute, contemptible, despicable, reprehensible, diabolical, diabolic, devilish, fiendish, hellish, damnable; informal yucky, sick-making, gut-churning, icky, gross, God-awful, low-down, rotten, sick; Brit. informal beastly; N. Amer. informal lousy, vomitous; vulgar slang shitty; literary noisome; archaic scurvy, disgustful, loathly; rare egregious, flagitious.
▹ANTONYMS pleasant.

vilification noun *he was singled out for vilification in a sermon*: **condemnation**, criticism, censure, castigation, denunciation, vituperation, abuse, flak, defamation, denigration, disparagement, obloquy, opprobrium, derogation, slander, revilement, reviling, calumny, calumniation, execration, excoriation, lambasting, upbraiding, a bad press, character assassination, attack, invective, libel, insults, aspersions; informal mud-slinging, bad-mouthing, tongue-lashing; Brit. informal stick, verbal, slagging off; archaic contumely; rare animadversion, objurgation.
▹ANTONYMS praise.

vilify verb *the media vilified several of the election candidates*: **disparage**, denigrate, defame, run down, revile, berate, belittle, abuse, insult, slight, attack, speak ill of, speak evil of, pour scorn on, cast aspersions on, criticize, censure, condemn, decry, denounce, pillory, lambaste; fulminate against, rail against, inveigh against, malign, slander, libel, conduct a smear campaign against, spread lies about, blacken the name/reputation of, sully the reputation of, give someone a bad name, bring someone into disrepute, discredit, stigmatize, traduce, calumniate, impugn; N. Amer. slur; informal do down, do a hatchet job on, take to pieces, pull apart, throw mud at, drag through the mud, slate, have a go at, hit out at, jump on, lay into, tear into, knock, slam, pan, bash, hammer, roast, skewer, bad-mouth, throw brickbats at; Brit. informal rubbish, slag off, monster; N. Amer. informal pummel, dump on; Austral./NZ informal bag; archaic contemn; rare derogate, vituperate, asperse, vilipend.
▹ANTONYMS commend, lionize.

villain noun *an evil villain bent on destroying and dominating the world*: **criminal**, lawbreaker, outlaw, offender, felon, convict, jailbird, malefactor, wrongdoer; transgressor, sinner; gangster, gunman, bandit, brigand, desperado, thief, robber, mugger, swindler, fraudster, racketeer, terrorist, pirate; **rogue**, scoundrel, wretch, heel, reprobate, charlatan, evil-doer, ruffian, hoodlum, hooligan, thug, delinquent, ne'er-do-well, good-for-nothing; informal **crook**, con, crim, baddy, shark, rat, snake, snake in the grass, dog, hound, louse, swine, scumbag, wrong 'un; Brit. informal, dated rotter, bounder, bad egg, stinker; Law malfeasant, misfeasor, infractor; dated cad, knave, rake; archaic miscreant, blackguard.

villainous adjective *Captain Mason led the villainous attack on the sleeping village*: **wicked**, evil, iniquitous, sinful, nefarious, vile, foul, monstrous, shocking, outrageous, atrocious, abominable, reprehensible, hateful, detestable, despicable, odious, contemptible, horrible, heinous, execrable, diabolical, diabolic, fiendish, vicious, murderous, barbarous, black, dark, rotten; criminal, illicit, unlawful, illegal, illegitimate, lawless, felonious, indictable, transgressing, wrong, immoral, corrupt, degenerate, reprobate, sordid, depraved, dissolute, bad, base, dishonourable, dishonest, unscrupulous, unprincipled, underhand, roguish; informal crooked, bent, warped, low-down, stinking, dirty, shady, rascally, scoundrelly; Brit. informal beastly, not cricket; Law malfeasant; archaic dastardly; rare egregious, flagitious.
▹ANTONYMS good, virtuous.

villainy noun *the potential to degenerate into villainy lies within even a nobleman*: **wickedness**, badness, evil, evil-doing, sin, sinfulness, iniquity, vileness, baseness, wrong, wrongdoing, dishonesty, double-dealing, unscrupulousness, roguery, rascality, delinquency, disgrace, viciousness, degeneracy, depravity, dissolution, dissipation, immorality, turpitude, devilry, devilishness, heinousness; **crime**, vice, criminality, lawlessness, lawbreaking, corruption, venality; offence, misdeed, misconduct, transgression; informal crookedness, shadiness; Law malfeasance; archaic knavery, deviltry.

vindicate verb **1** *he maintained his innocence throughout the trial and has been fully vindicated by the jury*: **acquit**, clear, absolve, free from blame, declare innocent, exonerate, exculpate, discharge, liberate, free, deliver, redeem; informal let off, let off the hook.
▷ANTONYMS convict, blame, incriminate.
2 *I felt I had fully vindicated my request*: **justify**, warrant, substantiate, establish, demonstrate, ratify, authenticate, verify, confirm, corroborate, prove, defend, offer grounds for, support, back, evidence, bear out, bear witness to, endorse, give credence to, lend weight to; rare extenuate.
▷ANTONYMS disprove.

vindictive adjective *he never destroyed a person simply on the say-so of vindictive enemies*: **vengeful**, out for revenge, revengeful, avenging, unforgiving, grudge-bearing, resentful, ill-disposed, implacable, unrelenting, acrimonious, bitter; **spiteful**, mean, mean-spirited, rancorous, venomous, poisonous, malicious, malevolent, malignant, malign, evil, evil-intentioned, nasty, cruel, unkind, ill-natured, baleful; informal catty, bitchy; literary malefic, maleficent.
▷ANTONYMS forgiving.

vintage noun **1** *1986 was a classic vintage for the Cabernet Sauvignon grape*: **year**.
2 *he never lost a vintage through frost*: **grape harvest**, grape gathering, grape crop, harvest, crop, yield, year's growth.
3 *the hotel was furnished with some choice pieces of Louis XV vintage*: **period**, era, epoch, time, origin; genre, style, kind, sort, type, cast, stamp, school, ilk.
▶ adjective **1** *vintage French wine*: **high-quality**, quality, prime, choice, select, superior, best.
2 *a vintage Sherlock Holmes adventure | vintage motor vehicles*: **classic**, ageless, timeless, enduring; old, antique, veteran, heritage, historic, old-world, age-old.
3 *his reaction to her letter was vintage Francis*: **characteristic**, typical, most typical, supreme, absolute, at his/her/its best.

violate verb **1** *the directive violates fundamental human rights*: **contravene**, breach, commit a breach of, infringe, infract, break, transgress, overstep, not comply with, disobey, defy, flout, fly in the face of, rebel against; disregard, ignore, pay no heed to, take no notice of; archaic set at naught.
▷ANTONYMS comply with.
2 *her daughter's tomb had been violated*: **desecrate**, profane, treat sacrilegiously, treat with disrespect, blaspheme, defile, degrade, debase; damage, vandalize, deface, destroy; N. Amer. informal trash.
▷ANTONYMS respect.
3 *she did not like having her personal space violated*: **invade**, intrude on, encroach on, impinge on, trespass on, obtrude on, break into, interfere with, disturb, disrupt, upset, shatter.
4 *he drugged her and then violated her*: **rape**, indecently assault, sexually assault, assault, force oneself on, force, sexually abuse, abuse, molest, interfere with, seduce; informal pop someone's cherry, bed; euphemistic have one's (evil) way with, take advantage of; dated ravish, deflower, defile, dishonour, ruin, take away someone's innocence.

violation noun **1** *a flagrant violation of human rights*: **contravention**, breach, infringement, infraction, breaking, transgression, non-observance, lack of compliance with, disobeying, disobedience, defiance, defying, flouting, flying in the face of, rebelling against; neglect, ignoring, paying no heed to, taking no notice of.
2 *the wiretaps were a severe violation of the victims' private lives*: **invasion**, interruption, breach, infraction; trespass, intrusion, encroachment, disruption, disturbance, upset.
3 *his daughter was threatened with violation*: **rape**, sexual assault, indecent assault, sexual abuse, abuse, molestation, molesting, interference, interfering, seduction, seducing; informal bedding; dated ravishing, ravishment, deflowering, defloration, defilement, dishonour, ruin, ruination.

violence noun **1** *there had been widespread fears of police violence*: **brutality**, brute force, roughness, ferocity, fierceness, savagery, cruelty, sadism, barbarity, barbarousness, brutishness, murderousness, bloodthirstiness, ruthlessness, inhumanity, heartlessness, pitilessness, mercilessness; strong-arm tactics; rare ferity.
▷ANTONYMS gentleness, kindness.
2 *the violence of the blow*: **forcefulness**, force, full force, power, powerfulness, strength, might, savagery, ferocity, brutality, destructiveness.
▷ANTONYMS weakness.
3 *the violence of his passion*: **intensity**, severity, strength, force, great force, vehemence, powerfulness, power, potency, ferocity, forcefulness, wildness, frenziedness, fury, storminess, tempestuousness, turbulence; lack of control, lack of restraint, passionateness; rare fervency, ardency.
▷ANTONYMS mildness.

violent adjective **1** *I was married to a violent alcoholic*: **brutal**, vicious, savage, harsh, rough, aggressive, bullying, threatening, terrorizing, fierce, wild, intemperate, hot-headed, hot-tempered, bloodthirsty, ferocious, berserk, frenzied; in a frenzy, out of control, barbarous, barbaric, thuggish, cut-throat, homicidal, murderous, maniacal, rabid, inhuman, heartless, callous, ruthless, merciless, pitiless, cruel; Scottish informal radge.
▷ANTONYMS gentle.
2 *she killed him with one violent blow*: **powerful**, forceful, hard, sharp, smart, strong, vigorous, mighty, hefty, harsh, thunderous, savage, ferocious, fierce, brutal, vicious, destructive, damaging, painful; lethal, deadly, fatal, mortal, death-dealing.
▷ANTONYMS weak.
3 *a rush of violent jealousy swept through her*: **intense**, extreme, strong, powerful, forceful, great, vehement, wild, frenzied, raging, riotous, rampaging, rampant, out of control, stormy, tempestuous, turbulent, tumultuous, intemperate, uncontrolled, unrestrained, uncurbed, unchecked, unbridled, unfettered, uncontrollable, unmanageable, ungovernable, inordinate, excessive, consuming, passionate, overwhelming, immoderate.
▷ANTONYMS mild.

VIP noun *even the most humble visitors are treated like VIPs*: **celebrity**, famous person, very important person, personality, name, big name, famous name, household name, star, superstar, celebutante, leading light, mogul, giant, great, master, king, guru; **dignitary**, luminary, worthy, grandee, lion, public figure, pillar of society, notable, notability, personage, panjandrum; informal heavyweight, celeb, somebody, someone, bigwig, biggie, big shot, big noise, big gun, big cheese, big chief, nob, lady muck, lord muck, top brass, honcho, head honcho, top dog, supremo, megastar, heavy, fat cat; N. Amer. informal big wheel, big kahuna, kahuna, top banana, big enchilada, macher, high muckamuck, high muckety-muck.
▷ANTONYMS nobody, nonentity.

virago noun **harridan**, shrew, dragon, termagant, vixen; fishwife, witch, hellcat, she-devil, tartar, martinet, spitfire, hag, gorgon, fury, ogress, harpy, nag, trout; informal battleaxe, old bag, old bat, cow, old cow, bitch; archaic scold; rare Xanthippe.

virgin noun *she wished to remain a virgin*: **maiden**, unmarried girl, maid, vestal virgin, chaste woman, celibate; Latin virgo intacta; literary vestal.
▶ adjective **1** *extensive tracts of virgin forest*: **untouched**, unspoilt, untainted, untarnished, unadulterated, pure, immaculate, pristine, flawless; **unmarked**, unblemished, spotless, stainless, unsullied, unpolluted, undefiled, unaffected, unchanged, intact, inviolate, preserved; unused, in mint condition, perfect, in perfect condition; unexplored, uncharted, unmapped.
2 *virgin teenage girls*: **chaste**, virginal, celibate, abstinent, self-restrained, self-denying; unmarried, unwed, maiden, maidenly; **pure**, pure as the driven snow, virtuous, uncorrupted, incorrupt, undefiled, unblemished, unsullied, innocent, sinless, moral, decent, demure; literary vestal.

virginal adjective *the vampire sucks the blood from a virginal girl*. See **virgin** (sense 2 of the adjective).

virginity noun *I managed to graduate from high school with my virginity intact*: **chastity**, **maidenhood**, chasteness, virtue, honour, purity, pureness; innocence, decency, virtuousness, respectability, dignity, modesty; lack of sin, sinlessness, spotlessness; celibacy, abstinence, self-restraint, self-denial; informal cherry; Theology immaculateness.

virile adjective *she liked to read about strong, virile heroes*: **manly**, masculine, male, all-male; gallant, chivalrous, swashbuckling, valiant, valorous, courageous, brave, intrepid, fearless, stout-hearted, lionhearted, bold, heroic, daring; strong, tough, vigorous, robust, powerfully built, well made, well built, muscular, muscly, brawny, rugged, strapping, sturdy, hefty, husky, burly, solid, substantial; red-blooded, sexually potent, fertile, fecund; informal macho, laddish, butch, beefy, hunky, studly.
▷ANTONYMS unmanly, effeminate, weak.

virility noun *there was a virility about him that showed in his every movement*: **manliness**, masculinity, maleness, manfulness, manhood, machismo, gallantry, chivalry, valour, valiance, fearlessness, bravery, intrepidity, stout-heartedness, lionheartedness, boldness, daring, heroism, mettle, spirit; strength, vigour, toughness, robustness, powerful build, muscularity, muscle, brawniness, sturdiness, ruggedness, heftiness, huskiness; red-bloodedness, sexual potency, potency, sexuality, fertility, fecundity; informal laddishness, hunkiness, beefiness.

virtual adjective *we drove to the cottage in virtual silence*: **effective**, in effect, near, near enough, essential, practical, for all practical purposes, to all intents and purposes, in all but name, indirect, implied, implicit, unacknowledged, tacit.

virtually adverb *the huge building was virtually empty*: **in effect**, effectively, all but, more or less, practically, almost, nearly, close to, approaching, not far from, nearing, verging on, bordering on, well nigh, nigh on, just about, as good as, essentially, in essence, in practical terms, for all practical purposes, to all intents and purposes, in all but name, as near as dammit; roughly, approximately, not quite; S. African plus-minus; informal pretty much, pretty nearly, pretty well.

virtue noun **1** *the simple virtue and integrity of peasant life*: **goodness**, virtuousness, righteousness, morality, ethicalness, uprightness,

V

upstandingness, integrity, dignity, rectitude, honesty, honourableness, honourability, honour, incorruptibility, probity, propriety, decency, respectability, nobility, nobility of soul/spirit, nobleness, worthiness, worth, good, trustworthiness, meritoriousness, irreproachableness, blamelessness, purity, pureness, lack of corruption, merit; principles, high principles, ethics.
▷ANTONYMS vice, iniquity.
2 *promptness was not one of his virtues*: **good point**, good quality, strong point, strong suit, long suit, asset, forte, attribute, advantage, benefit, strength, talent; informal plus.
▷ANTONYMS failing.
3 dated *she lost her wealth and her virtue in the great city*. See **virginity**.
4 *I can see no virtue in such an arrangement*: **merit**, advantage, benefit, usefulness, efficacy, efficaciousness, power, potency, force, strength.
▷ANTONYMS disadvantage.
□ **by virtue of** *they hold the posts by virtue of family connections*: **because of**, on account of, by reason of, by dint of, by means of, by way of, via, through, as a result of, as a consequence of, on the strength of, owing to, thanks to, due to, based on; with the help of, with the aid of, with the assistance of.

virtuosity noun *the singer has to display extreme virtuosity*: **skill**, skilfulness, mastery, expertise, expertness, prowess, proficiency, ability, aptitude, adroitness, dexterity, deftness, excellence, brilliance, talent, genius, artistry, technique, art, creativity, flair, finish, polish, panache, finesse, wizardry, calibre, quality, professionalism; craftsmanship, handiness, workmanship, musicianship; French éclat; informal know-how.
▷ANTONYMS lack of skill.

virtuoso noun *the piano player is clearly a virtuoso of the first order*: **genius**, expert, master, master hand, artist, maestro, prodigy, marvel, adept, past master, specialist, skilled person, professional, doyen, authority, veteran; star, champion; German wunderkind; informal hotshot, wizard, wiz, whizz, whizz-kid, buff, pro, ace, something else, something to shout about, something to write home about; Brit. informal dab hand; N. Amer. informal maven, crackerjack; rare proficient.
▷ANTONYMS beginner, amateur, duffer.
▶ adjective *a virtuoso violinist*: **skilful**, expert, accomplished, masterly, master, consummate, proficient, talented, gifted, adept, adroit, dexterous, deft, able, good, competent, capable, efficient, experienced, professional, polished, well versed, smart, clever, artful, impressive, outstanding, exceptional, exceptionally good, magnificent, supreme, first-rate, first-class, fine, brilliant, excellent, dazzling, bravura; informal superb, out of this world, stellar, mean, ace, crack, A1; vulgar slang shit-hot.
▷ANTONYMS inexpert, incompetent.

virtuous adjective **1** *they were entirely virtuous in their endeavours*: **righteous**, good, moral, morally correct, ethical, upright, upstanding, high-minded, right-minded, right-thinking, principled, exemplary, clean, law-abiding, lawful, irreproachable, blameless, guiltless, unimpeachable, just, honest, honourable, unbribable, incorruptible; scrupulous, reputable, decent, respectable, noble, lofty, elevated, worthy, trustworthy, meritorious, praiseworthy, commendable, admirable, laudable; pure, pure as the driven snow, whiter than white, sinless, saintly, saintlike, godly, angelic; Christianity immaculate, impeccable; informal squeaky clean.
▷ANTONYMS bad, sinful.
2 *his virtuous sister had been threatened with seduction*: **virginal**, virgin, chaste, maidenly, vestal, celibate, abstinent; **pure**, pure as the driven snow, sinless, free from sin, flawless, spotless, undefiled, untainted, unsullied, uncorrupted, intact, innocent, demure, modest, decent, seemly, decorous, wholesome.
▷ANTONYMS promiscuous, sinful.

virulent adjective **1** *some plant varieties can withstand being sprayed by the most virulent herbicides*: **poisonous**, toxic, venomous, noxious, deadly, lethal, fatal, mortal, terminal, death-dealing, life-threatening, dangerous, harmful, injurious, pernicious, damaging, destructive, unsafe; contaminating, polluting; literary deathly, nocuous, mephitic; archaic baneful.
▷ANTONYMS non-toxic, harmless, safe.
2 *a virulent epidemic of cholera swept through London*: **highly infectious**, highly infective, highly contagious, infectious, infective, contagious, rapidly spreading, communicable, transmittable, transmissible, spreading, malignant, uncontrollable, pernicious, pestilential; severe, extreme, violent, dangerous, harmful, lethal, life-threatening; informal catching; literary pestiferous.
▷ANTONYMS non-contagious.
3 *a virulent attack on contemporary morals*: **vitriolic**, malicious, malevolent, malignant, malign, evil-intentioned, resentful, hostile, spiteful, venomous, vicious, vindictive, bitter, rancorous, acrimonious, mordant, astringent, incisive, cutting, biting, scathing, caustic, stinging, blistering, searing, withering, abusive, mean, nasty, aggressive, savage, harsh, devastating; informal bitchy, catty; literary malefic, maleficent.
▷ANTONYMS amicable, benevolent.

virus noun

> *Word links* **virus**
>
> **virology** study of viruses

viscous adjective *pools of viscous liquid had started to spread across the floor*: **sticky**, gummy, glue-like, gluey, adhesive, tacky, adhering, adherent, sticking, clinging, treacly, syrupy; **glutinous**, gelatinous, thick, viscid, pasty, mucous, mucoid, mucilaginous, jelly-like, slimy; informal gooey, gunky, gloopy, cloggy, icky; N. Amer. informal gloppy; rare viscoid.
▷ANTONYMS watery.

visible adjective *light from the fires was visible for many miles | he made a visible effort to control himself*: **perceptible**, perceivable, seeable, observable, noticeable, easily seen, detectable, discernible, recognizable, in view, in sight, on view, on display; evident, self-evident, in evidence, apparent, manifest, transparent, plain, plain to see, clear, clear-cut, conspicuous, obvious, patent, palpable, tangible, unmistakable, unconcealed, undisguised, distinct, distinguishable, prominent, salient, striking, arresting, blatant, glaring, writ large; informal as plain as the nose on your face, as plain as a pikestaff, sticking out like a sore thumb, standing out a mile, right under one's nose, staring someone in the face, written all over someone; archaic sensible.
▷ANTONYMS invisible, hidden.

vision noun **1** *her vision was blurred by tears*: **eyesight**, sight, power of sight, faculty of sight, ability to see, power of seeing, powers of observation, observation, perception, visual perception; eyes; field of vision, view, perspective.
2 *he gazes into the fire seeing visions of the ancestral pilgrims*: **apparition**, spectre, phantom, hallucination, ghost, wraith, shadow, manifestation, chimera, illusion, mirage, image; Scottish & Irish bodach; W. Indian duppy; informal spook; literary phantasm, shade, revenant, wight, visitant; rare eidolon, manes.
3 *they have visions of a more hopeful future*: **dream**, daydream, reverie, mental picture, conceptualization; plans, hopes; fantasy, fancy, flight of fancy, fanciful notion, pipe dream, delusion, figment of the imagination, prospect.
4 *his conference speech was a little lacking in vision*: **imagination**, creativity, creative power, inventiveness, innovation, inspiration, intuition, perceptiveness, perception, breadth of view, foresight, insight, far-sightedness, prescience, discernment, awareness, penetration, shrewdness, sharpness, cleverness.
5 *Melissa was a vision in pale lilac*: **beautiful sight**, vision of loveliness, feast for the eyes, pleasure to behold, delight, dream, beauty, spectacle, picture, joy, marvel, sensation; informal sight for sore eyes, eyeful, stunner, cracker, smasher, knockout, looker, good-looker, bobby-dazzler, peach, honey.

> *Word links* **vision**
>
> **visual**, **optical** relating to vision
> **perimetry** measurement of field of vision

visionary adjective *a visionary leader*: **inspired**, imaginative, creative, inventive, insightful, ingenious, enterprising, innovative, perceptive, intuitive, far-sighted, prescient, discerning, penetrating, sharp, shrewd, wise, clever, talented, gifted, resourceful; idealistic, idealized, utopian, romantic, quixotic, impractical, unrealistic, unworkable, unfeasible, out of touch with reality, fairy-tale, fanciful, dreamy, ivory-towered, theoretical, hypothetical; informal starry-eyed, head-in-the-clouds.
▶ noun **1** *a contemporary visionary pictured him in hell*: **seer**, mystic, oracle, prophet, prophetess, soothsayer, sibyl, augur, diviner, prognosticator, clairvoyant, psychic, crystal-gazer; dreamer; Scottish spaeman, spaewife; rare oracler, vaticinator.
2 *he was too much of a visionary to run a business effectively*: **dreamer**, daydreamer, idealist, romantic, romanticist, fantasist, theorist, utopian.

> *Word toolkit* **visionary**
>
> See **quixotic**.

visit verb **1** *I was away visiting a dear uncle of mine*: **call on**, call in on, pay a call on, pay a visit to, pay someone a call, pay someone a visit, go to see, come to see, look in on; stay with, spend time with, be the guest of, holiday with; stop by, drop by, pay a call, pay a visit, come to stay; N. Amer. visit with, go see; informal pop in on, drop in on, blow in on, drop round to see, look up.
2 *Alex was visiting America on a hectic tour*: **stay in**, stop over in, spend time in, holiday in; tour, drive round, go round, explore; see, view, inspect, survey, examine; N. Amer. vacation in.
3 *the citizens were visited with repeated epidemics of a strange disease*: **afflict**, attack, assail, trouble, harrow, torment, torture; descend on; archaic smite.
□ **be visited on someone** *it is hard to imagine a greater psychological cruelty visited on a child*: **happen to**, overtake, befall, come upon, fall upon, hit, strike.

▸ **noun 1** *after reading the play she paid a visit to the poet*: **social call**, call.
2 *a school visit to the Ashmolean Museum*: **trip to**, tour of, look around/round; stopover, stop-off, stay, stop; holiday, break; N. Amer. vacation, sojourn.

visitation noun **1** *the bishop conducted a busy schedule of pastoral visitations*: **official visit**, visit, inspection, tour of inspection, survey, review, scrutiny, examination.
2 *the blinding light had signified a visitation from God*: **apparition**, appearance, manifestation, materialization, emergence, vision.
3 *Jehovah was considered as punishing sinners by providential visitations*: **affliction**, scourge, bane, curse, ordeal, plague, pestilence, blight, disaster, tragedy, calamity, catastrophe, cataclysm; punishment, retribution, penalty, vengeance.
▷ANTONYMS blessing.

visitor noun **1** *I am expecting a visitor*: **guest**, caller; company; archaic visitant.
2 *the monument attracts visitors from all over the world*: **tourist**, traveller, holidaymaker, day tripper, tripper, sightseer, globetrotter, jet-setter, backpacker, voyager, tourer, explorer, pilgrim; foreigner, outsider, stranger, alien; N. Amer. vacationer, vacationist, out-of-towner; Brit. informal emmet, grockle; rare excursionist.

vista noun *there's a marvellous vista from the hotel balcony*: **view**, prospect, panorama, aspect, perspective, spectacle, sight; scenery, landscape, seascape, riverscape, townscape, cityscape, snowscape; archaic outlook.

visual adjective **1** *the child has visual defects*: **optical**, seeing, optic, ocular, eye; vision, sight.
2 *many cheap car alarms have no visual indication that they are in operation*: **visible**, perceptible, perceivable, seeable, to be seen, discernible.

visualize verb *it is not easy to visualize the future*: **envisage**, envision, conjure up, conjure up an image/picture of, picture in the mind's eye, picture, call to mind, see, imagine, evoke, fancy, dream about, dream up, fantasize about, conceptualize, conceive of, think about, contemplate; foresee, predict, forecast, anticipate.

vital adjective **1** *it is vital that action is taken to protect jobs*: **essential**, indispensable, crucial, key, necessary, needed, required, requisite, important, all-important, of the utmost importance, of great consequence, of the essence, critical, life-and-death, imperative, mandatory, urgent, pressing, burning, compelling, acute, paramount, pre-eminent, high-priority, significant, consequential; informal earth-shattering, world-shaking.
▷ANTONYMS unimportant, peripheral, secondary.
2 *a layer of fat protects the vital organs*: **life-preserving**, life-sustaining, basic, fundamental, essential, necessary; major, main, chief, key, prime.
▷ANTONYMS minor, dispensable.
3 *the new president appeared young and vital*: **lively**, energetic, active, sprightly, spry, animated, spirited, high-spirited, vivacious, exuberant, bouncy, enthusiastic, vibrant, zestful, sparkling, dynamic, vigorous, full of vim and vigour, forceful, fiery, lusty, hale and hearty, in fine fettle; informal go-getting, zippy, peppy, feisty, spunky, raring to go, full of beans, bright-eyed and bushy-tailed; N. Amer. chipper.
▷ANTONYMS listless.

Word toolkit

vital	crucial	utmost
information	role	importance
service	part	respect
work	question	care
ingredient	factor	concern
support	moment	caution
resources	step	attention
funds	stage	urgency
equipment	evidence	secrecy

vitality noun *everything about Nicola shone with vitality*: **liveliness**, life, energy, animation, spirit, spiritedness, high-spiritedness, vivacity, exuberance, buoyancy, bounce, vibrancy, verve, vim, pep, brio, zest, zestfulness, sparkle, spark, effervescence, dynamism, passion, fire, vigour, forcefulness, ardour, zeal, relish, gusto, push, drive, punch, elan; informal zip, zing, fizz, get-up-and-go, oomph, pizzazz, feistiness.

V

vitriolic adjective *he launched a vitriolic attack on the government*: **acrimonious**, rancorous, bitter, caustic, mordant, acerbic, astringent, acid, acrid, trenchant, virulent, spiteful, crabbed, savage, venomous, poisonous, malicious, malignant, malign, pernicious, splenetic; nasty, mean, cruel, unkind, harsh, ill-natured, evil-intentioned, vindictive, scathing, searing, biting, barbed, wounding, stinging, tart, sharp, rapier-like, razor-edged, cutting, withering, sarcastic, sardonic, irascible; informal bitchy, catty, slashing; literary malefic, maleficent; rare acidulous, mordacious, squint-eyed.
▷ANTONYMS pleasant, kind.

vituperate verb *he **vituperated against** all presidents with equal gusto*: **revile**, rail against, inveigh against, fulminate against, attack, upbraid, berate, harangue, lambaste, reprimand, castigate, chastise, rebuke, scold, chide, censure, condemn, damn, denounce, find fault with, run down, take to task, vilify, denigrate, calumniate, insult, abuse, curse, slander, smear; informal slate, slam, knock, hammer, carpet, roast, skewer, crucify, read someone the Riot Act, lay into, tear a strip off, bawl out, give someone a dressing-down, tell off, bad-mouth; Brit. informal rubbish, slag off; archaic contemn; rare asperse, excoriate, vilipend.
▷ANTONYMS praise.

vituperation noun *they were unprepared for the hate and vituperation which descended on them*: **revilement**, invective, condemnation, castigation, chastisement, opprobrium, rebuke, scolding, criticism, flak, disapprobation, fault-finding; blame, reprimand, upbraiding, admonition; abuse, insults, curses, tongue-lashing, harangue, vilification, denunciation, obloquy, denouncement, denigration, disparagement, slander, slandering, libel, defamation, calumny, calumniation, evil-speaking, backbiting, malice, spite, spitefulness, vitriol, venom; slurs, aspersions, fulminations; informal slamming, knocking, bashing, mud-slinging, cattiness, bitchiness, bitching, bad-mouthing; Brit. informal rubbishing, slagging off, slating, stick, verbal; archaic contumely; rare objurgation, animadversion, derogation.
▷ANTONYMS praise.

vivacious adjective *she was a pretty and vivacious brunette*: **lively**, animated, full of life, spirited, high-spirited, effervescent, bubbling, bubbly, ebullient, buoyant, sparkling, scintillating, light-hearted, carefree, happy-go-lucky, jaunty, merry, happy, jolly, joyful, full of fun, full of the joys of spring, cheery, cheerful, perky, sunny, airy, breezy, bright, enthusiastic, irrepressible, vibrant, vivid, vital, zestful, energetic, dynamic, vigorous, full of vim and vigour, lusty; informal bright-eyed and bushy-tailed, bright and breezy, peppy, zingy, zippy, bouncy, upbeat, chirpy, full of beans, chipper; N. Amer. informal peart; dated gay.
▷ANTONYMS dull, listless.

vivacity noun *she had none of her mother's vivacity*: **liveliness**, animation, effervescence, ebullience, sparkle, scintillation, spirit, spiritedness, high-spiritedness, high spirits, sprightliness, jauntiness, light-heartedness, gaiety, merriment, jollity, happiness, cheerfulness, perkiness, breeziness, brightness, enthusiasm, irrepressibility, vibrancy, vividness, vitality, life, verve, zeal, gusto, relish, zest, energy, dynamism, spark, fire, fieriness, vigour, vim, brio, dash; French joie de vivre, elan, éclat; informal pep, zing, zip, bounce, chirpiness, go, get-up-and-go, oomph, pizzazz.
▷ANTONYMS listlessness.

vivid adjective **1** *a vivid blue Mediterranean sea*: **bright**, bright-coloured, colourful, deep-coloured, brilliant, glowing, radiant, vibrant, strong, bold, deep, intense, rich, warm, flaming, flamboyant, glaring, eye-catching; informal jazzy.
▷ANTONYMS dull, washed out.
2 *Dickens provides us with a vivid account of nineteenth-century urban poverty*: **graphic**, evocative, realistic, true to life, lifelike, faithful, authentic, clear, crystal clear, detailed, lucid, striking, arresting, impressive, colourful, highly coloured, rich, dramatic, picturesque, lively, stimulating, interesting, fascinating, scintillating; memorable, unforgettable, powerful, stirring, affecting, emotive, moving, haunting.
▷ANTONYMS vague; boring.
3 *she had a deep voice and a strikingly vivid personality*: **dynamic**, flamboyant, striking, strong, powerful, fiery, lively, animated, spirited, vibrant, vital, vigorous, energetic, vivacious, zestful.

Word toolkit **vivid**

See **graphic**.

vixen noun *Margaret proved to be a fiery little vixen*: **virago**, harridan, shrew, dragon, termagant, cat, witch, hellcat, she-devil, tartar, martinet, spitfire, hag, gorgon, fury, ogress, harpy, nag; informal bitch; archaic scold; rare Xanthippe.

viz. adverb *article one sets out its purpose, viz. to ensure the continuation of farming*: **namely**, that is to say, that is, to wit, to be specific, specifically, in other words, to put it another way; such as, as, like, for instance, for example; Latin videlicet, scilicet, sc., id est.

vocabulary noun **1** *they are intelligent people with an extensive vocabulary*: **lexicon**, word stock, lexis.
2 *we listed the acceptable terms in a vocabulary*: **wordbook**, dictionary, word list, wordfinder, glossary, lexicon, concordance, thesaurus.

vocal adjective **1** *Neanderthal man could produce a reasonable range of vocal sounds*: **vocalized**, voiced, spoken, said, uttered, expressed, articulated, oral, by mouth.
2 *he is a vocal critic of the government*: **vociferous**, outspoken, forthright, plain-spoken, blunt, frank, direct, candid, open, uninhibited; vehement, vigorous, emphatic, insistent, forceful, keen, zealous, enthusiastic; clamorous, strident, loud, noisy; archaic free-spoken.
▷ANTONYMS taciturn, reticent.

vocation noun *his vocation as a clergyman was not eclipsed by his scientific career*: **calling**, life's work, mission, purpose, function, position, niche; **profession**, occupation, career, job, work, employment, pursuit, trade, craft, business, line, line of work, speciality, specialty, province, sphere, walk of life; French métier; informal line of country, game, thing, bag, racket.

vociferous adjective *a vociferous champion of equal rights*: **vehement**, outspoken, vocal, forthright, plain-spoken, frank, candid, open, uninhibited, direct, earnest, eager, enthusiastic, vigorous, insistent, emphatic, demanding; clamorous, strident, loud, loud-mouthed, raucous, noisy, rowdy.
▷ANTONYMS silent, quiet.

vogue noun *utility furniture is now enjoying a new vogue*: **fashion**, mode, style, trend, taste, fad, fancy, passing fancy, craze, rage, enthusiasm, passion, infatuation, obsession, mania, fascination; fashionableness, modishness, popularity, currency, prevalence, favour; French dernier cri; informal thing, trendiness, coolness, snazziness.
□ **in vogue** *crochet garments were in vogue*: **fashionable**, in fashion, voguish, stylish, in style, modish, up to date, up to the minute, modern, ultra-modern, current, prevalent, popular, in favour, in demand, desired, sought-after, all the rage, trendsetting, chic, smart; the latest thing, the big thing, the last word; French à la mode, le dernier cri; informal trendy, hip, cool, big, happening, now, in, with it, ritzy, flash, snazzy, natty, nifty, swinging, bang up to date; N. Amer. informal tony, kicky.
▷ANTONYMS unfashionable, out of date.

voice noun **1** *there was great dismay when the starlet lost her voice*: **power of speech**; powers of articulation.
2 *he gave voice to the anger and frustration of urban youth*: **expression**, utterance, verbalization, vocalization, airing.
3 *the government promised to listen to the voice of the people*: **opinion**, view, comment, feeling, wish, desire, vote, input; one's say; informal one's twopence worth, one's twopenn'orth.
4 *the body could be a powerful voice for conservation*: **mouthpiece**, forum, organ, agency, agent, representative, spokesperson, spokesman, spokeswoman, intermediary, medium, vehicle, instrument, channel, means of expression.
▶ verb *councillors voiced their opposition to the proposal*: **express**, give expression to, vocalize, give voice to, put in words, give utterance to, communicate, declare, state, set forth, bring into the open, make public, assert, divulge, reveal, proclaim, announce, raise, table, air, ventilate, vent, give vent to, pour out, mention, talk of, point out, go into; utter, say, speak, articulate, enunciate, pronounce, mouth; informal come out with.

void noun *the black void of space*: **gap**, empty space, space, blank space, blank, vacuum, lacuna, hole, cavity, chasm, abyss, gulf, pit, hiatus; emptiness, nothingness, blankness, vacancy, vacuity, oblivion, nullity; rare voidness, nihility.
▶ verb **1** *the contract was voided*: **invalidate**, render invalid, annul, nullify; negate, disallow, quash, cancel, countermand, repeal, revoke, rescind, retract, withdraw, reverse, abrogate, undo, abolish, obliterate, terminate, repudiate; Law avoid, vacate.
▷ANTONYMS validate, ratify.
2 *the patients had difficulty in voiding their bladders*: **evacuate**, empty, empty out, drain, clear, unload, unburden, purge.
▷ANTONYMS fill.
3 *the bacteria are present in the kidneys of the rat and are voided in the urine*: **eject**, expel, emit, discharge, pass, excrete, egest, let out, send out, release, exude, eliminate; rare disembogue.
▷ANTONYMS take in.
▶ adjective **1** *the cathedral has vast void spaces*: **empty**, emptied, vacant, without contents, containing nothing, blank, bare, clear, free, unfilled, unoccupied, uninhabited, desolate, barren.
▷ANTONYMS full.
2 *a populous country suddenly left **void of** man or beast*: **devoid of**, empty of, vacant of, bare of, destitute of, bereft of, denuded of, deficient in, free from; lacking, wanting, without.
▷ANTONYMS occupied.
3 *the election had been declared void*: **invalid**, null and void, null, nullified, cancelled, revoked, rescinded, abolished, inoperative, ineffective, not binding, not in force, non-viable, useless, worthless, nugatory; lapsed, expired, out of date, terminated, discontinued, unrenewed.
▷ANTONYMS valid.

volatile adjective **1** *her sister was headstrong and volatile*: **unpredictable**, **changeable**, variable, inconstant, inconsistent, uncertain, erratic, irregular, unstable, turbulent, unsteady, unsettled, unreliable, undependable, changing, ever-changing, varying, shifting, fluctuating, fluid, mutable, protean, fitful, wavering, full of ups and downs; mercurial, capricious, whimsical, fickle, flighty, giddy, impulsive, wayward, temperamental, highly strung, excitable, emotional, overemotional, fiery, moody, choleric, stormy, tempestuous, volcanic; informal blowing hot and cold; technical labile; rare fluctuant, changeful.
▷ANTONYMS stable, constant.
2 *the atmosphere in the capital seems far too volatile for any talk of elections*: **tense**, strained, fraught, uneasy, uncomfortable, charged, explosive, eruptive, inflammatory, turbulent, in turmoil, full of upheavals; informal hairy, nail-biting, white-knuckle; Brit. informal dodgy.
▷ANTONYMS stable, calm.
3 *a plume of pollution caused by a volatile organic compound*: **evaporative**, vaporous, vaporescent; explosive, eruptive, inflammable; unstable; technical labile.

volition noun
□ **of one's own volition** *they chose to leave early of their own volition*: **of one's own free will**, of one's own accord, of one's own choice, of one's own choosing, by choice, by preference, by one's own preference; voluntarily, willingly, readily, freely, intentionally, consciously, deliberately, on purpose, purposely, spontaneously, without being asked, without hesitation, without reluctance; gladly, with pleasure, with good grace, eagerly, enthusiastically.
▷ANTONYMS reluctantly.

volley noun *he fired off a volley of shots from his semi-automatic rifle*: **barrage**, cannonade, battery, blast, bombardment, broadside, salvo, fusillade; storm, hail, shower, cascade, rain, stream, deluge, torrent, avalanche, blitz; wall/curtain/barrier of fire.

volubility noun *he is a figure of magnetic charm and great volubility*: **talkativeness**, loquaciousness, loquacity, garrulousness, garrulity, verboseness, long-windedness, wordiness, chattiness, effusiveness, profuseness, communicativeness, expansiveness, openness, lack of reserve; articulacy, articulateness, eloquence, fluency, glibness; informal mouthiness, gabbiness, windiness, gassiness, big mouth, gift of the gab; Brit. informal wittering; rare logorrhoea, multiloquence.
▷ANTONYMS taciturnity.

voluble adjective *Mrs Maddox was as voluble as her husband was silent*: **talkative**, loquacious, garrulous, verbose, long-winded, wordy, chatty, chattery, gossipy, chattering, babbling, blathering, prattling, jabbering, effusive, gushing, forthcoming, conversational, communicative, expansive, open, unreserved; articulate, eloquent, fluent, glib, silver-tongued; informal mouthy, gabby, gassy, windy, yakking, big-mouthed, with the gift of the gab, having kissed the Blarney Stone; Brit. informal wittering, able to talk the hind legs off a donkey; rare multiloquent, multiloquous.
▷ANTONYMS taciturn, uncommunicative, mute.

> *Word toolkit* **voluble**
>
> See **talkative**.

volume noun **1** *this volume could stand in pride of place in any library*: **book**, publication, tome, hardback, paperback, softback, work, opus, title, treatise, manual, almanac, compendium.
2 *a large glass syringe of known volume is weighed with and without the gas*: **capacity**, cubic measure, size, magnitude, largeness, bigness, mass, bulk, extent, extensiveness; dimensions, proportions, measurements.
3 *a huge volume of water is released from the dam*: **quantity**, amount, proportion, portion, measure, mass, bulk; level, degree.
4 *she leaned forward to turn the volume down*: **loudness**, sound, amplification.

voluminous adjective *he folded his arms into the voluminous sleeves of his robe*: **capacious**, commodious, roomy, spacious, ample, full, big, large, sizeable, immense, vast, generous; billowing, baggy, loose-fitting; rare spacey.
▷ANTONYMS tiny; tight-fitting.

voluntarily adverb *they signed a paper agreeing to leave the country voluntarily*: **of one's own free will**, of one's own accord, of one's own volition, of one's own choice, of one's own choosing, by choice, by preference; willingly, readily, freely, intentionally, deliberately, on purpose, purposely, spontaneously, without being asked, without being forced, without hesitation, without reluctance; gladly, with pleasure, with good grace, eagerly, enthusiastically.
▷ANTONYMS under duress.

voluntary adjective **1** *attendance at lectures is voluntary*: **optional**, discretionary, at one's discretion, elective, non-compulsory, non-mandatory, not required, open, open to choice, volitional, up to the individual; Law permissive; rare discretional.
▷ANTONYMS compulsory, obligatory.
2 *she spent some time doing voluntary work*: **unpaid**, unsalaried, without pay, without payment, free of charge, without charge, for nothing, for free; honorary, volunteer, unrewarded; Law pro bono (publico).
▷ANTONYMS paid.

volunteer verb **1** *I volunteered my services as a school governor*: **offer**, tender, proffer, present, put forward, put up, venture.
▷ANTONYMS refuse, withdraw.
2 *he volunteered as an ambulance driver on the Italian front*: **offer one's services**, present oneself, step forward, come forward, make oneself available.
▷ANTONYMS be conscripted.
▶ noun *during the investigation, each volunteer was studied three times*: **subject**, participant, case, client, patient; informal guinea pig.

voluptuous adjective **1** *a voluptuous girl with black hair*: **curvaceous**, shapely, opulent, full-figured, well formed, well proportioned, Junoesque, ample, Rubensesque, buxom, full-bosomed, lush, luscious; seductive, alluring, sultry, sensuous, sexually attractive; informal curvy, busty, sexy, slinky, beddable; archaic well turned, gainly, comely.
▷ANTONYMS scrawny, plain.
2 *the voluptuous charms of a luscious pudding*: **hedonistic**, sybaritic, epicurean, pleasure-loving, pleasure-seeking, self-indulgent, indulgent; lotus-eating, decadent, intemperate, immoderate, dissipated, dissolute, abandoned; sensual, carnal, licentious, lascivious, salacious.
▷ANTONYMS ascetic.

vomit verb **1** *he desperately wanted to vomit*: **be sick**, spew, spew up, fetch up; heave, retch, reach, gag; N. Amer. get sick; informal throw up, puke, chunder, chuck up, hurl, pray to the porcelain god, do the technicolor yawn, keck, ralph; Brit. informal honk, shoot the cat; Scottish informal boke; N. Amer. informal barf, spit up, upchuck, blow chunks, toss one's cookies; Austral./NZ informal go for the big spit, play the whale, yodel, perk; archaic regorge, purge, brake, cascade; rare egurgitate.
2 *I vomited my breakfast all over the car*: **regurgitate**, bring up, spew up, heave up, cough up; Medicine reject, lose; informal chuck up, throw up, puke; Brit. informal sick up; N. Amer. informal spit up; archaic regorge, void.
3 *the printer is vomiting folds of perforated paper*: **eject**, issue, emit, expel, send forth, discharge, disgorge, spout, throw out, cast out, spew out, belch; rare disembogue, eruct.
▸ noun *the front of his jacket was stained with vomit*: **sick**; technical vomitus, ejecta; informal chunder, puke, spew, pavement pizza, technicolor yawn, liquid laugh; N. Amer. informal barf, upchuck; archaic purge, parbreak.

Word links **vomit**

emetophobia fear of vomiting

voracious adjective *boxer dogs have voracious appetites*: **insatiable**, unquenchable, unappeasable, prodigious, uncontrollable, uncontrolled, omnivorous, compulsive, gluttonous, greedy, rapacious; enthusiastic, eager, keen, avid, desirous, craving, hungry, ravenous, ravening, wolfish; informal piggish, hoggish, swinish, gutsy; Brit. informal gannet-like; rare insatiate, edacious, esurient.

vortex noun *a whirling vortex of buff-coloured smoke*: **whirlwind**, **whirlpool**, gyre, maelstrom, eddy, swirl, swirling, countercurrent, counterflow; literary Charybdis.

vote noun **1** *she was elected in a rigged vote*: **ballot**, poll, election, referendum, plebiscite, public vote, general election, local election, popular vote, straw poll, show of hands; voting, polling.
2 *in 1918 women over thirty got the vote in Britain*: **suffrage**, franchise, enfranchisement, right to vote, voting rights; voice, say, option, choice.
▷ANTONYMS disenfranchisement.
▸ verb **1** *only 28 per cent of the electorate voted in the referendum*: **go to the polls**, cast one's vote, mark one's ballot paper.
2 *I vote we have one more game*: **suggest**, propose, recommend, advocate, move, table, submit.
□ **vote someone in** *he was voted in as honorary secretary*: **elect**, return, put in power, select, choose, pick, adopt, appoint, designate, opt for, plump for, decide on, settle on, fix on.
□ **vote someone out** *he persuaded delegates to vote out the prime minister*: **depose**, oust, push out, turn out, remove from office, remove from power, unseat, dethrone, displace, dismiss, discharge, dislodge, eject, cashier; informal boot out, kick out, drum out, give someone the boot; Brit. informal turf out; dated out.

Word links **vote**

psephology study of elections and voting

vouch verb
□ **vouch for** *I can vouch for the veracity of his story*: **attest to**, confirm, affirm, verify, swear to, testify to, bear witness to, bear out, back up, support, corroborate, substantiate, prove, uphold, show the truth of, give substance to, give credence to, second, endorse, certify, warrant, validate, give assurance of; answer for, be responsible for, be liable for, go/stand bail for; informal stick up for, throw one's weight behind.

voucher noun *a free travel voucher*: **coupon**, token, ticket, document, certificate, licence, permit, carnet, pass, paper, card, form, deed; chit, slip, stub, docket; Brit. informal chitty; N. Amer. informal ducat, comp.

vouchsafe verb **1** *he gave thanks for the grace which had been vouchsafed to him*: **grant**, give, accord, award, offer, hand; confer on, bestow on, yield to, cede to, favour with.
▷ANTONYMS withhold, refuse.
2 *you'd never vouchsafed that titbit of information before*: **disclose**, reveal, divulge, impart, pass on, tell, let out, let slip, give away, bring into the open, make public, make known, broadcast, air, circulate; informal blab, spill, come clean about; Brit. informal cough, blow the gaff on.
▷ANTONYMS withhold, conceal.
3 *if he would vouchsafe to talk with them he might hear some unexpected revelations*: **deign**, condescend, stoop, unbend, sink, lower oneself, humble oneself, demean oneself; informal come down from one's high horse.

vow noun *the monks had taken a vow of silence*: **oath**, pledge, promise, bond, covenant, commitment, avowal, profession, sworn statement, affirmation, attestation, assurance, word, word of honour, guarantee; archaic troth; rare asseveration, averment.
▸ verb *I vowed to do better*: **swear**, swear/state under oath, swear on the Bible, take an oath, pledge, promise, affirm, avow, undertake, give an undertaking, engage, commit, commit oneself, make a commitment, give one's word, give one's word of honour, give an assurance, guarantee; Law depose, make a deposition, bind oneself; archaic plight, asseverate.

Word links **vow**

votive relating to a vow

voyage noun *the voyage lasted some eighteen days*: **journey**, trip, expedition, excursion, tour, hike, trek, tramp, safari, pilgrimage, quest, crusade, odyssey; crossing, cruise, sail, sailing, passage, flight, drive; travels, globetrotting, journeying, wandering; rare peregrination, itineration.
▸ verb *he voyaged through Venezuela and Peru*: **travel**, journey, take a trip, go on a trip, go on an expedition, go on an excursion, tour, globetrot; sail, steam, cruise, fly, drive; informal gallivant, do, knock about/around; rare peregrinate, itinerate.

vulgar adjective **1** *a vulgar seaside postcard | vulgar verbal abuse*: **rude**, indecent, indelicate, offensive, distasteful, obnoxious, risqué, suggestive, racy, earthy, off colour, colourful, coarse, crude, ribald, Rabelaisian, bawdy, obscene, lewd, salacious, licentious, vile, depraved, sordid, smutty, dirty, filthy, pornographic, X-rated, scatological; profane, foul, foul-mouthed, blasphemous, abusive, scurrilous; informal sleazy, porno, porn, raunchy, naughty, blue, steamy, spicy, locker-room; Brit. informal fruity, saucy, near the knuckle, close to the bone; N. Amer. informal gamy; euphemistic adult; rare concupiscent.
▷ANTONYMS decent, wholesome, inoffensive.
2 *the decor showed that one could be lavish without being vulgar*: **tasteless**, gross, crass, unrefined, tawdry, ostentatious, flamboyant, over-elaborate, overdone, showy, flashy, gaudy, garish, brassy, kitsch, tinselly, flaunting, glaring, brash, loud, harsh; informal flash, tacky, over the top, OTT, glitzy, swanky.
▷ANTONYMS tasteful, restrained.
3 *it was considered vulgar for a woman to whistle*: **impolite**, ill-mannered, unmannerly, indecorous, unseemly, ill-bred, boorish, low, low-minded, gross, uncouth, crude, rough; uncultured, uncultivated, unsophisticated, unrefined; illiterate, uneducated, philistine; common, ordinary, low-born, plebeian; informal yobbish, loutish, plebby, ignorant; archaic baseborn.
▷ANTONYMS genteel, decorous.

vulgarity noun **1** *he avoided vulgarity and innuendo*: **rudeness**, crudity, indecency, indelicacy, offensiveness, suggestiveness, bawdiness, ribaldry, obscenity, lewdness, salaciousness, licentiousness, depravity, sordidness, smuttiness, dirtiness, filthiness, smut, dirt, filth, pornography; profanity, blasphemy, swearing, bad language, strong language, foulness, abusiveness, scurrilousness; informal raunchiness, raunch, sleaziness, sleaze, porn, blueness; Brit. informal fruitiness, sauciness; rare concupiscence, bawdry, salacity.
▷ANTONYMS decency.
2 *she thought the quantities of gilt were evidence of shocking vulgarity*: **tastelessness**, bad taste, grossness, crassness, lack of refinement, tawdriness, flamboyance, flamboyancy, ostentation, excess, gaudiness, garishness, showiness, flashiness, brassiness, tinsel, kitsch, loudness, harshness; informal tackiness, swankiness, swank, glitziness.
▷ANTONYMS tastefulness, restraint.
3 *her mother was free from any trace of vulgarity*: **impoliteness**, ill manners, bad manners, impropriety, grossness, indecorousness, uncouthness, crudeness, coarseness, roughness; commonness, lowness, unsophisticatedness, lack of refinement, lack of sophistication; informal ignorance.
▷ANTONYMS gentility, decorum.

vulnerable adjective **1** *they evacuated children from the most vulnerable cities*: **in danger**, in peril, in jeopardy, at risk, endangered, unsafe, unprotected, ill-protected, unguarded; open to attack, attackable, assailable, exposed, wide open; undefended, unshielded, unfortified, unarmed, without arms, without weapons, defenceless, easily hurt/wounded/damaged, powerless, helpless; rare pregnable, impuissant, resistless.
▷ANTONYMS well protected, invulnerable, resilient.
2 *he is extremely sensible and less* ***vulnerable to*** *criticism than most*: **exposed to**, open to, wide open to, liable to, prone to, prey to, susceptible to, subject to, not above, in danger of, at risk of, at the mercy of, an easy target for, easily affected by; in the firing line; rare susceptive of.
▷ANTONYMS immune to, above.

wacky adjective informal *a wacky movie spoof*: **zany**, madcap, offbeat, quirky, outlandish, eccentric, idiosyncratic, surreal, ridiculous, nonsensical, crazy, absurd, insane, far out, fantastic, bizarre, peculiar, weird, odd, strange, cranky, freakish; **funny**, amusing, comic, clownish; informal loopy, loony, mad, dotty, nutty, nuts, freaky, batty, potty, goofy, bonkers, crackpot, screwy, screwball, oddball, way-out, off-centre, off the wall, dippy, cuckoo, kinky; Brit. informal barmy, daft; N. Amer. informal kooky, wacko; bizarro.
▷ANTONYMS conventional; sensible.

wad noun **1** *a wad of cotton wool | a wad of sealing wax*: **lump**, mass, chunk, hunk, wedge, ball, clump, block, pat, brick, cube, bar, cake, slab, nugget, plug, pad, knob, gobbet, glob, dollop, cluster, nub; bit, piece, portion, segment; Brit. informal wodge, gob.
2 *Mike pulled out a wad of hundred-dollar bills*: **bundle**, roll, bankroll, pile, stack, sheaf, pocketful, load.
3 *a huge wad of tobacco*: **quid**, twist, plug, chew; N. Amer. informal chaw; rare pigtail, cud, cake.
▸ verb *the teddy bear had huge empty eye sockets wadded with cotton*: **stuff**, pad, fill, pack, line; wrap, cover, encase, cushion, protect.

wadding noun **stuffing**, filling, filler, packing, padding, lining, cushioning, quilting; reinforcement, buffer, protection, guard.

waddle verb *he waddled forward to greet her*: **toddle**, dodder, wobble, totter, shamble; sway, rock, lurch, limp, shuffle, stumble, reel, stagger; duckwalk, walk like a duck; informal waggle.

wade verb **1** *five or six men were wading in the icy water*: **paddle**, wallow, dabble, slop, squelch, trudge, plod; informal splosh.
2 *Tony waded across the stream*: **ford**, cross, traverse, walk across, make one's way across.
3 *they could just click it up on screen, rather than having to **wade through** some hefty document*: **work one's way**, plough, plod, trawl, proceed with difficulty, labour, toil away at, plug away at; peruse, study; browse, leaf, flick, skim, look, thumb; informal slog.
□ **wade in** informal *police with truncheons waded in*: **move in**, set to, set to work, pitch in, buckle down, go to it, put one's shoulder to the wheel; informal plunge in, dive in, get stuck in, get cracking.
□ **wade into someone** informal *I waded into those skinheads*: **attack**, set upon, assault, launch oneself at, weigh into, fly at, let fly at, turn on, round on, lash out at, hit out at, fall on, jump on/at, lunge at, charge, rush, storm; informal lay into, light into, tear into, lace into, pitch into, beat up; Brit. informal have a go at.
□ **wade into something** informal *Flynn would gladly wade into the attack*: **get involved in**, intervene in, get to work on, set to work on, tackle.

waffle Brit. informal verb *they were waffling on about the baby*: **prattle**, chatter, babble, ramble, jabber, gibber, gabble, gab, burble, flannel, run on, mutter, mumble, prate, drivel, bleat, cackle; Brit. hum and haw; informal blather; Brit. informal rabbit, witter, natter.
▸ noun *my panic reduced the interview to waffle*: **prattle**, jabbering, verbiage, drivel, meaningless talk, nonsense, twaddle, gibberish, stuff and nonsense, bunkum, mumbo-jumbo, padding, flannel, verbosity, prolixity; informal hot air, poppycock, tripe, bosh, bunk, blah, hogwash, eyewash, gobbledegook, rot, tommyrot, guff; Brit. informal wittering; rare logorrhoea.

waft verb **1** *spicy smells wafted through the air*: **drift**, float, glide, whirl, travel, be carried, be borne, be conveyed, be transported.
2 *a breeze wafted the smell of barbecued lamb kebabs towards us*: **convey**, transport, transmit, carry, bear; blow, puff.

wag[1] verb **1** *the dog's tail began to wag frantically*: **swing**, sway, shake, move to and fro, swish, switch, quiver, twitch, flutter, waver, whip; oscillate, vibrate, undulate.
2 *he shouted and wagged his finger*: **shake**, wave, waggle, wiggle, wobble, flourish, brandish, raise.
▸ noun **1** *Flossie managed a feeble wag of her tail*: **swing**, sway, shake, swish, switch, quiver, twitch, flutter, waver, whip, oscillation, vibration, undulation.
2 *a wag of the finger*: **waggle**, wiggle, wobble, wave, shake, flourish, brandish.

wag[2] noun dated *he's a bit of a wag*. See **joker**.

wage noun **1** (usually **wages**) *the wages of farm workers are determined by the local labour market | a fair wage*: **pay**, payment, remuneration, salary, emolument, stipend, fee, allowance, honorarium; income, revenue; yield, profit, gain, reward; compensation, recompense, reimbursement; (**wages**) earnings, takings, proceeds.
2 (**wages**) *the wages of sin is death*: **reward**, recompense, requital, retribution; returns, deserts.
▸ verb *the government continued to wage war on the guerrillas*: **engage in**, carry on, conduct, execute, pursue, undertake, prosecute, practise, proceed with, devote oneself to, go on with.

wager noun **bet**, gamble, speculation, venture, game of chance; stake, pledge, hazard, ante; Brit. informal flutter.
▸ verb *I'll wager that there will be no trace of them | I'll wager a pound or two on the home team*: **bet**, gamble, lay a wager, place/make/lay a bet, lay odds, put money on; stake, pledge, risk, venture, hazard, chance, speculate; informal punt; Brit. informal put one's shirt on.

waggish adjective dated *a waggish riposte*. See **playful**.

waggle verb informal *Jonathan waggled his finger at Rex*: **wag**, shake, wiggle, wobble, wave, quiver, jerk, twitch, flutter, jiggle, joggle, bobble, brandish, flourish, flail about.

waif noun **ragamuffin**, street urchin, guttersnipe; abandoned infant, foundling, orphan, stray, outcast; archaic gamin, mudlark.

wail noun *I heard a wail of anguish*: **howl**, bawl, yowl, keening; cry, cry of grief, cry of pain, lament, lamentation, sob, moan, groan; shriek, scream, yelp, bellow, roar, caterwaul; whine, complaint, whimper; rare ululation.
▸ verb *the children immediately began to wail*: **howl**, weep, cry, sob, moan, groan, keen, lament, yowl, blubber, snivel, whimper, whine, squall, bawl, shriek, scream, yelp, caterwaul, waul; complain, grumble, carp, sorrow, beat one's breast; Scottish greet; rare ululate.

wait verb **1** *they waited in the airport for two hours*: **stay**, remain, rest, linger, loiter, dally, stop, stay put; informal stick around, kick around/about; archaic bide, tarry.
▷ANTONYMS leave.
2 *she had to wait until her passport came through*: **stand by**, hold back, be patient, bide one's time, hang fire, mark time, kill time, waste time, cool one's heels, kick one's heels, twiddle one's thumbs; pause, stop, cease, halt, discontinue, rest; informal hold on, hang around, sit tight, hold one's horses, sweat it out; Brit. informal hang about.
3 *they were **waiting for** the kettle to boil*: **await**, look/watch out; **anticipate**, expect, be ready, be in readiness; long for, hope for, count the days until.
4 *it will have to wait until we've got some money*: **be postponed**, be delayed, be put off, be held back, be deferred; informal be put on the back burner, be put on ice.

5 informal *we've waited dinner for forty minutes*: **delay**, postpone, put off, hold off, hold back, defer.
□ **wait on** *the men ate in silence, waited on by the two girls*: **serve**, attend to, tend, cater for/to, act as a waitress/waiter to; accommodate, minister to, take care of, look after, see to, succour, pander to.
□ **wait up** *I'll be back late—don't wait up for me*: **stay awake**, stay up, keep vigil.
▶ **noun** *we resigned ourselves to a long wait*: **delay**, hold-up, period of waiting, interval, interlude, intermission, pause, break, stay, cessation, suspension, detention, check, stoppage, halt, interruption, lull, respite, recess, postponement, discontinuation, moratorium, hiatus, gap, lapse, rest, entr'acte.

waiter, waitress noun *the waitress came to take their order*: **server**, stewardess, steward, attendant; head waitress/waiter, hostess, host; wine steward, wine waiter; butler, servant, page, flunkey; N. Amer. waitperson, carhop; French garçon, maître d'hôtel, sommelier (des vins).

waive verb **1** *an individual can waive his right to a hearing*: **relinquish**, renounce, give up, abandon, reject, surrender, yield, cede, do without, dispense with, set/put aside, abdicate, abjure, sacrifice, refuse, turn down, spurn, sign away.
▷ANTONYMS claim; pursue.
2 *the manager waived the rules and let us in*: **disregard**, ignore, overlook, set aside, forgo, drop, omit, cast aside, brush aside.
▷ANTONYMS uphold; follow.

waiver noun *a waiver of one's rights*: **renunciation**, surrender, repudiation, rejection, relinquishment, abdication, disavowal, refusal, disaffirmation, dispensation, abandonment, deferral; disclaimer; rare abjuration.

wake[1] verb **1** *if Gran wakes she'll want a glass of water | at 4.30 a.m. Mark* ***woke up***: **awake**, awaken, waken (up), rouse, stir, come to, come around; get up, get out of bed, bestir oneself, get going, come alive, show signs of life; literary arise.
▷ANTONYMS sleep; fall asleep.
2 *she opened the door before waking her husband | he* ***woke*** *her* ***up*** *with a cup of tea*: **waken**, rouse, arouse, bring to, bring around; Brit. informal knock up.
3 *a clip round the ear might wake him up a bit*: **stir up**, activate, stimulate, spur, prod, galvanize, enliven, give a lift/boost to, ginger up, buoy up, refresh, invigorate, revitalize, inspire; informal perk up, pep up.
4 *they finally* ***woke up to*** *what we have been saying*: **realize**, become aware of, become conscious of, become mindful of, become heedful of, become alert to.
5 *the name woke a forgotten and embarrassing memory*: **evoke**, call up, conjure up, rouse, stir, revive, awaken, refresh, renew, resuscitate, revivify, rekindle, reignite, rejuvenate, stimulate.
▶ **noun** *a mourner at a wake*: **vigil**, death-watch, watch; funeral.

wake[2] noun **1** *a flotilla of rafts followed in the wake of the cruiser*: **backwash**, wash, slipstream, turbulence; trail, path, track.
2 *share prices tumbled* ***in the wake of*** *the interest-rate rise*: **aftermath**; as a result of, as a consequence of, on account of, because of, owing to, after, subsequent to, following, behind.

wakeful adjective **1** *he had been wakeful all night*: **unsleeping**, awake, restless, restive, tossing and turning, without sleep, wide awake, insomniac; archaic watchful.
▷ANTONYMS sleeping, asleep.
2 *I was suddenly wakeful*: **alert**, on the alert, vigilant, on the lookout, on one's guard, on one's toes, on the qui vive, watchful, observant, attentive, sharp, heedful, wary.
▷ANTONYMS inattentive.

waken verb See **wake**[1].

Wales noun Welsh Cymru; Brit. the Principality; Latin Cambria; informal the Land of Song.

walk verb **1** *the two men walked along the road deep in conversation*: **stroll**, saunter, amble, wend one's way, trudge, plod, hike, tramp, trek, march, stride, troop, patrol, step out, wander, ramble, tread, prowl, footslog, promenade, roam, traipse; stretch one's legs, go for a walk, take the air; advance, proceed, move, go, make one's way; informal mosey, pootle; Brit. informal yomp; rare perambulate.
2 *he walked the five miles into town*: **go by/on foot**, travel on foot, foot it, be a pedestrian; informal go by/on Shanks's pony, hoof it.
3 *she thanked him for walking her home*: **accompany**, escort, guide, show, see, convoy, conduct, usher, marshal, lead, take, attend, chaperone, steer, herd, shepherd.
□ **walk all over someone** informal **1** *be a bit firmer with the kids or they'll walk all over you*: **take advantage of**, impose on, exploit, make use of, use, abuse, misuse, manipulate, take liberties with, trifle with, play with; informal walk over, take for a ride, put one over on, play for a sucker, run rings around. **2** *Kelburne looked as though they were going to walk all over the home team*: **trounce**, beat hollow, defeat utterly, rout, annihilate, triumph over, win a resounding victory over, be victorious over, crush, overwhelm, best, get the better of, worst, bring someone to their knees; informal thrash, lick, hammer, clobber, paste, pound, pulverize, crucify, demolish, destroy, drub, give someone a drubbing, cane, wipe the floor with, give someone a hiding, take to the cleaners, blow someone out of the water, make mincemeat of, murder, massacre, slaughter, flatten, turn inside out, tank; Brit. informal stuff, marmalize; N. Amer. informal blow out, cream, shellac, skunk, slam.
□ **walk off/away with 1** informal *someone's walked off with my car keys*: **steal**, thieve, make/run off with, carry off, help oneself to, rob, pilfer, purloin, pocket, snatch, take, appropriate, abstract; informal filch, swipe, nab, snaffle, blag, 'borrow', 'liberate', rip something off; Brit. informal pinch, nick, half-inch, whip, knock off, trouser. **2** *he walked off with four awards*: **win easily**, win hands down, achieve, attain, earn, gain, receive, obtain, acquire, secure, collect, pick up, come away with, net; informal bag.
□ **walk out 1** *he had walked out in a temper*: **leave suddenly**, make a sudden departure, get up and go, storm off/out, flounce out, push off, depart, leave, get out, absent oneself, take wing; informal take off. **2** *teachers are ready to walk out in a protest over class sizes*: **go on strike**, call a strike, strike, withdraw one's labour, stop work, take industrial action; protest, mutiny, revolt; Brit. informal down tools.
□ **walk out on** *he walked out on his pregnant girlfriend*: **desert**, abandon, leave, leave in the lurch, betray, run away from, throw over, jilt, run out on, rat on; informal chuck, dump, ditch, leave someone holding the baby; archaic forsake.
▶ **noun 1** *country walks*: **stroll**, saunter, amble, promenade; **ramble**, hike, tramp, march; constitutional, turn, airing, excursion, outing, breather.
2 *he admired her elegant walk*: **gait**, manner of walking, pace, step, stride, tread, carriage, bearing.
3 *street lamps illuminated the riverside walk*: **pathway**, path, footpath, track, lane, alley, alleyway, walkway, promenade, footway, pavement, trail, trackway, ride, towpath; road, avenue, drive.
4 *the first job is to sort the post into different walks*: **route**, beat, round, run, circuit.
□ **walk of life** *people from all walks of life*: **class**, status, rank, caste, station, sphere, arena, area, domain, realm; line of work, line, profession, career, vocation, calling, job, occupation, employment, business, trade, craft, pursuit, work, province, field; French métier.
□ **walk in the park** informal *the second movement is consequently a little easier, though still no walk in the park*: **easy task**, easy job, child's play, nothing, five-finger exercise, gift, walkover, sinecure; informal doddle, breeze, piece of cake, picnic, money for old rope, money for jam, cinch, sitter, kids' stuff, cushy job/number, doss, cakewalk, pushover; N. Amer. informal duck soup, snap; Austral./NZ informal bludge, snack; S. African informal a piece of old tackie; Brit. vulgar slang a piece of piss; dated snip.

walker noun **hiker**, rambler, wayfarer, traveller, roamer, rover, footslogger; pedestrian, person on foot, foot traveller, stroller.

walkout noun **strike**, industrial action, stoppage, withdrawal of labour, go-slow, protest; revolt, mutiny, rebellion.

walkover noun *away games are never a walkover*: **easy victory**, runaway victory, rout, landslide, triumph, gift; informal piece of cake, kid's stuff, child's play, doddle, pushover, cinch, breeze, sitter, picnic, like taking candy from a baby, thrashing, whitewash; N. Amer. informal shoo-in, cake walk, duck soup; dated snip; Brit. vulgar slang piece of piss.
▷ANTONYMS struggle.

wall noun **1** *solid brick walls*: **barrier**, partition, room divider, enclosure, screen, panel, separator; palisade; dam, dyke.
2 *an ancient city wall*: **fortification**, rampart, barricade, parapet, bulwark, stockade, bailey, breastwork.
3 *we will work to break down the walls that stop world trade*: **obstacle**, barrier, barricade, fence; impediment, hindrance, block, check.
□ **drive someone up the wall** *each one had some irritating habit that drove him up the wall*: **enrage**, incense, anger, infuriate, madden, inflame, antagonize, make someone's blood boil, make someone's hackles rise, rub up the wrong way, ruffle someone's feathers, ruffle, peeve; annoy, irritate, exasperate, irk, vex, put out, provoke, pique, gall, displease; informal drive mad/crazy, make someone see red, get someone's back up, get someone's dander up, get someone's goat, get under someone's skin, get up someone's nose, rattle someone's cage; aggravate, get someone, needle, bug, nettle, rile, miff, hack off; Brit. informal wind up, get at, nark, get across, get on someone's wick; N. Amer. informal tee off, tick off, burn up, gravel; vulgar slang piss off; informal, dated give someone the pip; rare empurple.
□ **go to the wall** informal *thousands of businesses are expected to go to the wall this year*: **fail**, collapse, go bankrupt, become insolvent, go into receivership, go into liquidation, crash, fold (up), go under, founder, be ruined, cave in; informal go broke, go bust, go bump, go belly up, come a cropper, flop.
□ **go up the wall** informal *this causes the dog to go up the wall and bark his head off*: **lose one's temper**, lose control, become enraged, go into a rage, fly into a temper/passion, boil over, boil over with rage, flare up, fire up, go berserk, throw a tantrum, explode; informal blow one's top, fly off the handle, lose one's cool, get mad, go crazy, go wild, go bananas, hit the roof, go through the roof, see red, go off the deep end, blow a fuse/gasket, lose one's rag, go ape, burst a blood vessel, flip, flip one's lid, foam at the mouth, get all steamed up, get worked up, have a fit; Brit. informal go spare, go

crackers, do one's nut, get one's knickers in a twist, throw a wobbly; N. Amer. informal flip one's wig, blow one's lid/stack, have a cow, go postal, have a conniption fit; vulgar slang go apeshit.
□ **off the wall** N. Amer. informal *an off-the-wall cable television programme*: **eccentric**, zany, far out, freakish, quirky, idiosyncratic, unconventional, unorthodox, weird, outlandish, offbeat, bizarre, strange, unfamiliar; French outré; informal way-out, wacky, freaky, kooky, screwy, kinky, oddball, cranky; N. Amer. informal in left field.
▷ANTONYMS conventional.
▸ **verb 1** *the tenements **walled in** the space completely*: **enclose**, bound, encircle, confine, hem, circumscribe, close, shut, fence; separate, partition.
2 *one doorway had been **walled up***: **block**, seal, close, brick up.

Word links **wall**

mural relating to a wall

wallet noun *he pulled out a wallet and took a photograph from it*: **notecase**, purse, pouch, pochette; N. Amer. billfold, pocketbook.

wallop verb informal *Grandma walloped him with her stick*. See **thump**.

wallow verb **1** *a pond in which water buffalo wallowed*: **loll about/around**, lie about/around, tumble about/around, splash about/around; slosh, wade, paddle, slop, squelch, welter; informal splosh.
2 *a ship wallowing in stormy seas*: **roll**, lurch, toss (about), plunge, reel, sway, rock, flounder, keel, list; labour, make heavy weather.
3 *she seems to **wallow in** her self-pity*: **luxuriate**, bask, take pleasure, take satisfaction, indulge (oneself), delight, revel, glory; give oneself up to, take to; enjoy, like, love, relish, savour, rejoice in, exult in; informal get a kick/buzz out of, get a kick/buzz from; N. Amer. informal get a bang from, get a charge out of.
▷ANTONYMS eschew.

wan adjective **1** *she looked so wan and frail*: **pale**, pallid, ashen, white, white as a sheet, grey; anaemic, jaundiced, colourless, bloodless, waxen, chalky, milky, pasty, pasty-faced, whey-faced, peaky, sickly, tired-looking, washed out, sallow, drained, drawn, sapped, ghostly, deathly, deathlike, bleached; rare etiolated.
▷ANTONYMS flushed, ruddy.
2 *the wan light of the moon*: **dim**, faint, weak, feeble, pale, watery, wishy-washy.
▷ANTONYMS bright.

wand noun *a magic wand*: **baton**, stick, staff, pole, bar, dowel, rod, stake; club, truncheon, mace, sceptre; twig, cane, birch, switch, sprig, withe, withy; Greek & Roman Mythology caduceus.

wander verb **1** *you can spend the afternoon wandering around the estate*: **stroll**, amble, saunter, walk, dawdle, potter, ramble, maunder, meander; **roam**, rove, range, knock about/around, drift, coast, gallivant, gad about, prowl, mill about/around/round; trek, trudge, stretch one's legs; Scottish & Irish stravaig; informal traipse, mosey, tootle; Brit. informal mooch; rare peregrinate.
2 *he had **wandered away** from his mates | we are wandering from the point*: **stray**, depart, diverge, veer, swerve, deviate, digress, vary, drift, get separated, get sidetracked, go wool-gathering; rare divagate.
3 *the child **wandered off** when we weren't looking*: **get lost**, lose one's way, go off course, lose one's bearings, go astray, go off at a tangent.
4 *the narrow road wanders along the foreshore*: **meander**, wind, twist, turn, curve, zigzag, bend, snake, worm.
5 *he was wandering now, his voice had dropped as he struggled to keep his thread*: **be incoherent**, ramble, babble, talk nonsense, rave, be delirious.
▸ **noun stroll**, amble, saunter, walk, roam, meander, dawdle, potter, ramble; gallivant, prowl, drift, maunder, promenade, constitutional; turn, breather, airing, trek, trudge; informal traipse, mosey, tootle; Brit. informal mooch; rare perambulation, peregrination.

Choose the right word **wander, roam, rove, range, stray**

These words all denote walking or moving in some way that is not a direct line. Some imply more energy and purpose than others.

Wandering denotes movement that is not purposefully directed towards a particular goal. This lack of purpose may result from indecision or lack of energy, or may simply indicate that someone is not in a hurry (*she wandered aimlessly about the living room | wandering around looking at different displays*).

Those who **roam** move around with little forward planning but generally show more energy than the wanderer (*packs of savage dogs roamed the streets | dark lanes where gangs roamed*).

Rove is a rather old-fashioned word meaning 'travel constantly without a fixed long-term destination' (*he had roved the district in search of cinematic distraction*) but is now most commonly used as *roving*, which conveys quite a strong sense of purpose (*a roving busload of activists who went all over Europe*). *Roving* often means 'employed to work in many different places' (*communication with a roving agent was always fraught with difficulties*).

Range is a less common word, indicating movement that is free from restrictions or constraints and is usually over a wide area but is nevertheless purposeful (*railway entrepreneurs ranged the globe in search of trade | they ranged over the Pacific in outriggers*).

Stray denotes movement away from where one should be (*if you stray off the route it's almost impossible to get back | for an instant her tired mind strayed*), or into a wrong or inappropriate place (*the military arrested anyone who strayed into the exclusion zone*).

wanderer noun *a wanderer in the wilderness*: **traveller**, rambler, hiker, wayfarer, migrant, globetrotter, roamer, rover; itinerant, rolling stone; nomad, gypsy, Romany; tramp, drifter, tinker, vagabond, vagrant; homeless person, displaced person, person of no fixed address/abode; informal dosser, bag lady; N. Amer. informal hobo, bum; dated bird of passage.

wandering adjective *a wandering minstrel*: **travelling**, rambling, roaming, roving, journeying, drifting, itinerant, floating, wayfaring, voyaging, touring; peripatetic, unsettled, rootless, restless, on the move, on the go, on the wing; nomadic, gypsy, Romany; vagabond, vagrant, migrant, migratory, migrating, transient, homeless, displaced; archaic errant.

wane verb **1** *the moon is waning*: **disappear**, decrease, diminish, dwindle.
▷ANTONYMS wax.
2 *support for the strike was waning*: **decrease**, decline, diminish, dwindle, shrink, contract, taper off, tail off, subside, slacken, droop, sink, ebb, dim, fade (away), grow faint, lessen, dissolve, peter out, wind down, fall off, attenuate, be on the way out, abate, fail, recede, slump, flag, atrophy, become weak, weaken, give in, give way, melt away, deteriorate, crumble, wither, disintegrate, degenerate, evaporate, collapse, go downhill, draw to a close, vanish, die out; rare evanesce, remit.
▷ANTONYMS increase, grow.
▸ **noun**
□ **on the wane** *the popularity of these films may be on the wane*: **declining**, on the decline, decreasing, diminishing, dwindling, shrinking, contracting, tapering off, tailing off, subsiding, slackening, drooping, sinking, ebbing, dimming, fading away, growing faint, lessening, dissolving, petering out, winding down, falling off, attenuating, on the way out, abating, failing, receding, slumping, in a slump, in remission, flagging, atrophying, weakening, giving way, melting away, deteriorating, in a state of deterioration, crumbling, withering, disintegrating, degenerating, evaporating, collapsing, drawing to a close, vanishing, dying out, obsolescent, moribund; informal on one's last legs; rare evanescing.
▷ANTONYMS increasing, growing.

wangle verb informal *I think we should be able to wangle it so that you can start tomorrow | I wangled an invitation to her flat*: **contrive**, manipulate, manoeuvre, engineer, devise, orchestrate, fix, arrange, direct, conduct, handle, work, pull off, scheme, plot; acquire, attain, achieve, bring about, net, win, grab, hook; informal fiddle, finagle, swing.

want verb **1** *do you want more coffee? | he wants a place in the squad*: **desire**, wish for, hope for, fancy, have a fancy for, take a fancy to, have an inclination for, care for, like, set one's heart on; long for, yearn for, pine for, sigh for, crave, hanker after, hunger for, thirst for, lust after, cry out for, be desperate for, itch for, covet, need, be bent on; informal have a yen for, be dying for.
2 informal *his toaster wants repairing*: **need**, be/stand in need of, require, demand, cry out for.
3 informal *you **want to** be more careful*: **should**, ought, need, must.
▸ **noun 1** *millions perished for want of a safe haven | his want of vigilance*: **lack**, absence, non-existence, unavailability; dearth, deficiency, inadequacy, insufficiency, paucity, shortage, shortfall, shortness, scarcity, scarceness, scantiness, undersupply, deficit; rare exiguity.
▷ANTONYMS abundance; presence.
2 archaic *a time of want*: **need**, neediness, austerity, privation, deprivation, poverty, impoverishment, impecuniousness, impecuniosity, pennilessness, pauperism, penury, destitution, famine, drought, indigence.
▷ANTONYMS wealth, plenty.
3 *she had faith that all her wants would be taken care of*: **wish**, desire, demand, longing, yearning, fancy, craving, hankering; **need**, requirement, necessity, essential, requisite; informal yen.

wanting adjective **1** *when they came under siege the defences were found wanting*: **deficient**, inadequate, lacking, insufficient, imperfect, not up to standard/par, not good enough, disappointing, unsatisfying, unacceptable, not acceptable, not up to expectations, leaving much to be desired, flawed, faulty, defective, impaired, unsound, substandard, inferior, second-rate, poor, shabby, shoddy, patchy, sketchy, limited, restricted, incomplete, unfinished, unpolished, unrefined; Brit. informal not much cop.

▷ANTONYMS sufficient, acceptable.
2 *the kneecap is wanting in amphibians and reptiles*: **absent**, missing, lacking, not there, not present, non-existent, not to be found, unavailable, short.
▷ANTONYMS present.
3 *millions were left **wanting for** food | we will not be **wanting in** confidence*: **without**, lacking, devoid of, bereft of, bankrupt of, destitute of, empty of,

deprived of, free from/of, in need of; deficient in, low on, short on; informal minus, sans.

wanton adjective **1** *wanton destruction*: **deliberate**, wilful, malicious, malevolent, spiteful, vicious, wicked, evil, cruel; **unprovoked**, unmotivated, motiveless, arbitrary, groundless, unjustifiable, unjustified, needless, unnecessary, uncalled for, gratuitous, senseless, pointless, purposeless, aimless, useless, meaningless, empty, vacuous.
▷ANTONYMS justifiable.
2 *a wanton seductress*: **promiscuous**, immoral, loose, immodest, indecent, shameless, unblushing, unchaste, unvirtuous, fast, of easy virtue, impure, abandoned, lustful, lecherous, lascivious, salacious, lubricious, libidinous, licentious, libertine, profligate, dissolute, dissipated, debauched, degenerate, reprobate, corrupt, sinful, whorish, disreputable.
▷ANTONYMS chaste, moral.
3 literary *a wanton fawn*. See **playful** (sense 1).

war noun **1** *the Napoleonic wars | the outbreak of war*: **conflict**, warfare, combat, fighting, struggle, armed conflict, action, military action, bloodshed, contest, tussle; battle, skirmish, fight, clash, confrontation, engagement, affray, encounter, collision, offensive, attack, blitz, siege; campaign, crusade, feud, vendetta; strife, hostility, enmity, antagonism, discord, disunity, animus, ill will, bad blood; hostilities.
▷ANTONYMS peace; truce, ceasefire; harmony.
2 *the war against drugs*: **campaign**, crusade, battle, fight, struggle, movement, drive, mission.
▶ verb *rival Emperors **warred against** each other*: **fight**, battle, combat, wage war, make war, be at war, be in conflict, conduct a war, do battle, join battle, take the field, take up arms; feud, quarrel, struggle, strive, contend, grapple, wrangle, tilt, cross swords, lock horns, come to blows; attack, engage, clash with, encounter, take on, set to, skirmish with, grapple with; informal be at each other's throats, fight like cat and dog.
▷ANTONYMS make peace.

> *Word links* **war**
>
> **belligerent, martial** relating to war

warble verb *larks warbled in the blue sky*: **trill**, sing, chirp, chirrup, chirr, cheep, twitter, tweet, whistle, chatter, squeak, pipe, peep.
▶ noun *a solitary warble pierces the air*: **trill**, trilling, song, birdsong, cry, warbling, chirp, chirping, chirrup, chirruping, chirr, chirring, cheep, cheeping, twitter, twittering, tweet, tweeting, whistle, whistling, chatter, chattering, squeak, squeaking, pipe, piping, peep, peeping, call, calling.

war cry noun **battle cry**, war whoop, rallying call.

ward noun **1** *the men's surgical ward*: **room**, compartment, department, unit, area.
2 *the second most marginal ward in Westminster*: **district**, constituency, division, quarter, zone, parish, community, department, canton.
3 *for the last three years the boy has been my ward*: **dependant**, charge, protégé, pupil, trainee, apprentice; minor.
▷ANTONYMS guardian.
▶ verb *the last of the accident victims was warded*: **admit to hospital**, admit, take in, let in, accept, receive, give entry to.
▷ANTONYMS discharge.
□ **ward someone off** *Kelly held out a hand to ward him off*: **fend off**, drive back, keep off, stave off, repel, repulse, beat back, rout, put to flight, chase away; informal send packing.
□ **ward something off 1** *Candy held up her hands as though warding off a blow*: **parry**, avert, deflect, block, turn aside, defend oneself against, guard against, evade, avoid, dodge. **2** *garlands of turmeric and garlic are worn to ward off evil spirits*: **avert**, **rebuff**, rebut, keep at bay, keep at arm's length, fend off, stave off, oppose, resist, prevent, hinder, obstruct, impede, foil, frustrate, thwart, check, baulk, stop, head off.

warden noun **1** *a group of self-contained flats with a resident warden*: **superintendent**, supervisor, steward, overseer, caretaker, janitor, porter, custodian, watchman, concierge, doorman.
2 *the chief game warden*: **ranger**, custodian, keeper, guardian, protector, preserver, curator.
3 *handcuffed to a warden, he was led to his cell*: **prison officer**, guard, jailer, (prison) warder, (prison) wardress, keeper, sentry, captor; informal screw.
4 Brit. *the Warden of All Souls College*: **principal**, head, governor, master, mistress, rector, provost, president, chief, director, chancellor, vice-chancellor; N. Amer. informal prexy, prex.

warder, wardress noun **prison officer**, guard, jailer, (prison) warden, keeper, sentry, captor; informal screw; archaic turnkey.

wardrobe noun **1** *she left the doors of the wardrobe open*: **clothes cupboard**, cupboard, cabinet, locker, storage room; N. Amer. closet.
2 *her wardrobe is extensive, with an outfit to match every mood*: **collection of clothes**; clothes, garments, attire, outfits, wear; trousseau.

warehouse noun *a furniture warehouse*: **storeroom**, storehouse, store, depot, depository, repository, stockroom; magazine; granary, silo; in India & Malaysia godown; informal lock-up; archaic garner.

wares plural noun **merchandise**, goods, products, produce, stock, commodities, items/articles for sale, lines, range; rare vendibles.

warfare noun *the reality of modern warfare*: **fighting**, war, combat, conflict, armed conflict, struggle, military action, hostilities; bloodshed, battles, skirmishes, campaigning, passage of/at arms; strife, hostility, enmity, antagonism, discord.
▷ANTONYMS peace; harmony.

warily adverb **1** *he walked towards it, treading warily to avoid the puddles*: **carefully**, with care, cautiously, gingerly, circumspectly, charily, guardedly, on one's guard, on the alert, on the lookout, on the qui vive, attentively, heedfully, watchfully, vigilantly, observantly, alertly, cannily; hesitantly, timidly, timorously.
▷ANTONYMS recklessly.
2 *the little boy eyed her warily*: **suspiciously**, distrustfully, mistrustfully, charily, cautiously, uneasily; informal cagily.
▷ANTONYMS trustingly.

wariness noun **1** *the issue should be treated with a degree of wariness*: **caution**, carefulness, care, circumspection, prudence, guardedness, alertness, attention, heed, heedfulness, watchfulness, vigilance, observance, awareness, mindfulness, canniness; hesitance, hesitancy, hesitation, timidness, timidity, timorousness.
▷ANTONYMS recklessness.
2 *they have the same wariness of strangers as everyone else*: **suspicion**, distrust, mistrust, caution, unease, scepticism, doubt, chariness; informal caginess.
▷ANTONYMS trust.

warlike adjective *a warlike ruler*: **aggressive**, belligerent, warmongering, warring, bellicose, pugnacious, combative, bloodthirsty, hawkish, gung-ho, jingoistic, sabre-rattling; hostile, threatening, inimical, violent, quarrelsome; militaristic, militant, martial, soldierly; archaic sanguinary.
▷ANTONYMS peaceable.

warlock noun **sorcerer**, wizard, male witch, (black) magician, diviner, occultist, enchanter, necromancer, spell-caster, thaumaturge; Irish pishogue; literary magus, mage.

warm adjective **1** *Patsy was in the big, warm kitchen*: **hot**, warming; cosy, snug, comfortable, homely, mellow; informal comfy, toasty.
▷ANTONYMS cold, cool.
2 *the first really warm day of spring*: **balmy**, summery, sultry, hot, mild, temperate, pleasant, agreeable; sunny, bright, fine.
▷ANTONYMS cold, chilly.
3 *a tumbler of warm water*: **heated**, tepid, lukewarm; French chambré.
▷ANTONYMS cold, chilled.
4 *she dressed in jeans and a warm sweater*: **thick**, chunky, thermal, winter, woolly.
▷ANTONYMS light, summery.
5 *he gave her a warm smile | a warm welcome*: **friendly**, comradely, affable, amiable, genial, cordial, kindly, kind, pleasant, sympathetic, affectionate, warm-hearted, good-natured, loving, tender, fond; welcoming, hospitable, liberal; caring, benevolent, benign, fatherly, motherly, paternal, maternal, comforting, charitable, solicitous; sincere, genuine, earnest, wholehearted, heartfelt, enthusiastic, eager, hearty.
▷ANTONYMS unfriendly, hostile, cold.
6 informal *they haven't found it yet, but they're getting warm*: **close**, near, about to make a discovery, on the brink of making a discovery; informal hot.
▷ANTONYMS cold; distant.
▶ verb *she sat by the fire, warming her hands and feet | can you **warm** the soup up for me?* **heat (up)**, make/become warm, make/become hot, raise the temperature of, increase in temperature, thaw (out), melt; reheat, cook; N. Amer. warm over; informal hot (up), zap.
▷ANTONYMS cool, chill.
□ **warm to/towards 1** *everyone immediately warmed to him*: **like**, **take to**, get on (well) with, feel a fondness for, feel attracted to, feel well disposed towards, hit it off with, be on good terms with, feel sympathetic to.
▷ANTONYMS dislike. **2** *he couldn't warm to the notion*: **become enthusiastic about**, become supportive of, become excited about/over, become animated over/about.
□ **warm up** *if you don't warm up first you can easily pull a muscle*: **limber up**, loosen up, stretch, work out, exercise, get into condition, get into shape, practise, prepare, get ready; rehearse.
□ **warm someone/something up** *on stage, Miles was warming up the crowd*: **enliven**, liven (up), stimulate, animate, rouse, put some life into, stir (up), move, excite, cheer up; informal get going.
▷ANTONYMS calm down.

warm-blooded adjective **1** *birds, like mammals, are warm-blooded*: technical **homeothermic**, homeothermal.
▷ANTONYMS cold-blooded, poikilothermic.
2 *a warm-blooded young Latin lady*: **passionate**, ardent, red-blooded, hot-blooded, fervid, impetuous, emotional, intense, lively, spirited, fiery, tempestuous, hot, sultry, torrid.
▷ANTONYMS cool, reserved.

warmed-up adjective **1** *a warmed-up pasty*: **reheated**, heated up; N. Amer. warmed-over.
▷ANTONYMS fresh.
2 *the proposal is a mishmash of warmed-up ideas*: **unoriginal**, derivative, imitative, uninventive, copied, plagiarized, plagiaristic, second-hand, rehashed; trite, hackneyed, stale, tired, worn out, flat, stock, banal, uninspired; informal old hat.
▷ANTONYMS original, innovative.

warm-hearted adjective *they are perhaps the most generous, warm-hearted people in the universe*: **kind**, warm, kind-hearted, kindly, soft-hearted, good-hearted, big-hearted, tender-hearted, tender, loving, caring, feeling, unselfish, selfless, benevolent, humane, good-natured, affectionate; gentle, mild, indulgent, friendly, open, sympathetic, understanding, compassionate, charitable, generous, magnanimous.
▷ANTONYMS unkind, unfriendly.

warmonger noun *a trigger-happy warmonger*: **militarist**, hawk, jingoist, sabre-rattler, aggressor, provoker, belligerent.
▷ANTONYMS pacifist.

warmth noun **1** *the warmth of the fire*: **heat**, warmness, hotness; cosiness, snugness, comfort, homeliness, mellowness.
▷ANTONYMS cool, chill.
2 *she was surprised by the warmth of his smile | the warmth of their welcome*: **friendliness**, affability, amiability, geniality, cordiality, kindliness, kindness, sympathy, understanding, affection, warm-heartedness, good-naturedness, love, tenderness, fondness; welcomingness, hospitality, liberality; care, benevolence, benignity, charity, charitableness; wholeheartedness, enthusiasm, eagerness, heartiness, ardour, vehemence, passion, intensity, fervour, zeal, zest, effusiveness, spiritedness.
▷ANTONYMS hostility, half-heartedness.

warn verb **1** *David had warned her that it would be late when he returned*: **notify**, alert, apprise, give notice, inform, tell, let someone know, make someone aware, give a warning to, give fair warning to, forewarn, put someone on notice/guard, remind; raise/sound the alarm; informal tip off, put wise.
2 *police are warning museums and galleries to take extra precautions*: **advise**, exhort, urge, counsel, caution; put on the alert, put someone on guard.

warning noun **1** *the earthquake came without warning*: **notice**, advance notice, a word of warning, forewarning, alert; hint, signal, sign, alarm bells; informal a tip-off.
2 *cigarette packets are required to carry a health warning*: **caution**, piece of advice, notification, information; exhortation, injunction, a (warning) shot across the bows; advice, counselling; informal a word to the wise.
3 *a warning of things to come*: **omen**, premonition, foreboding, prophecy, prediction, forecast, token, portent, augury, signal, sign, threat; literary foretoken.
4 *he was considering locking Lenny up as a warning to other young drivers*: **example**, deterrent, lesson, caution, exemplar, message, moral.
5 *a further complaint may lead to a written warning*: **admonition**, caution, remonstrance, injunction, reprimand, censure, caveat; informal dressing-down, talking-to, ticking-off, telling-off; Brit. informal carpeting.

warp verb **1** *timber which is too dry will warp and lose its strength*: **buckle**, twist, bend, distort, deform, misshape, malform, curve, make/become crooked/curved, flex, bow, arch, contort, gnarl, kink, wrinkle.
▷ANTONYMS straighten; keep shape.
2 *a fanatic who warped the mind of her only child*: **corrupt**, twist, pervert, deprave, bend, skew.

warrant noun **1** *a judge has now issued a warrant for his arrest*: **authorization**, written order, licence, permit, official document; writ, order, summons, subpoena; mandate, decree, fiat, edict; papers.
2 *a travel warrant*: **voucher**, chit, slip, paper, ticket, coupon, pass.
3 *the legislation gives no warrant for this assumption*: **justification**, grounds, cause, rationale, basis, assurance; authority, licence, authorization, sanction, vindication.
▸ verb **1** *the charges warranted a severe sentence*: **justify**, vindicate, call for, sanction, validate, be a justification/reason for; permit, authorize, entitle, empower; uphold, condone, endorse, deserve, excuse, be a defence of, explain away, account for, offer grounds for, legitimize; support, consent to, license, approve of; merit, qualify for, rate, be worthy of, be worth, be entitled to, be deserving of.
2 *the authors warrant that their texts do not infringe any copyright*: **guarantee**, affirm, swear, promise, vow, pledge, give an undertaking, undertake, state, assert, declare, aver, proclaim, pronounce, profess, attest; vouch, testify, bear witness; support, endorse, underwrite, back up, stand by.

warrantable adjective *his interference was scarcely warrantable*: **justifiable**, vindicable, excusable, explainable, explicable, reasonable, supportable.

warranty noun *a three-year warranty*: **guarantee**, assurance, promise, commitment, covenant, undertaking, agreement.

warring adjective *envoys for peace are trying to bring the warring factions together*: **opposing**, conflicting, clashing, at war, contending, fighting, battling, quarrelling; pugnacious, quarrelsome, aggressive, belligerent, militant, martial, warlike, warmongering; competing, hostile, rival, at loggerheads, at daggers drawn; informal at each other's throats.

warrior noun *fearsome warriors*: **fighter**, soldier, fighting man, serviceman, combatant; brave.

wart noun *she had a wart on her cheek*: **growth**, lump, swelling, protuberance, carbuncle, boil, blister, verruca, corn, tumour, excrescence; rare tumescence.
□ **warts and all** informal *my gosh, you showed us warts and all*: **unvarnished**, truthful, realistic, true to life; straightforward, plain, simple, stark, naked, bald; candid, honest, frank, outspoken, forthright, plain-spoken, direct, blunt, downright, brutal, harsh, straight from the shoulder, explicit, unequivocal, unambiguous, unexaggerated, unadorned, undisguised, unveiled, unqualified; informal upfront.

wary adjective **1** *as a soldier, he was trained to be wary*: **cautious**, careful, circumspect, on one's guard, chary, alert, on the alert, on the lookout, on the qui vive, prudent; attentive, heedful, watchful, vigilant, observant; informal wide awake, on one's toes, cagey.
▷ANTONYMS unwary, inattentive.
2 *we are wary of strangers in the city these days*: **suspicious**, chary, careful, distrustful, mistrustful, sceptical, doubtful, dubious; guarded, on one's guard; informal leery.
▷ANTONYMS unwary, trustful.

Word toolkit

wary	watchful	circumspect
investor	eye	approach
consumer	gaze	manner
rabbit	supervision	dissimulation
owners	parents	lawyer

wash verb **1** *he reached for the soap and began to wash*: **clean oneself**, have a wash, wash oneself; bathe, bath, shower, have a bath/shower, take a bath/shower, soak, douche, freshen up; formal or humorous perform one's ablutions; dated make one's toilet.
2 *Melissa slipped indoors to wash her face and hands*: **clean**, cleanse, sponge, scrub, wipe, scour; literary lave.
▷ANTONYMS dirty, soil.
3 *I washed and waxed the floor*: **clean**, cleanse, sponge, scrub, mop, hose down, squeegee, sluice (down), swill (down), douse, swab (down), flush, disinfect.
▷ANTONYMS dirty, soil.
4 *she **washed off** the dried blood*: **remove by washing**, sponge off, scrub off, wipe off, rinse off, remove, flush out/away, expunge, eradicate.
5 *a few women were washing clothes beside the shore*: **launder**, clean, rinse (out); dry-clean; literary lave.
6 *I must shower and wash my hair*: **shampoo**, lather, clean.
7 *gentle waves were washing against the hull*: **splash**, lap, splosh, dash, break, beat, strike, sweep, move, surge, ripple, roll, flow; literary plash, lave.
8 *wreckage was **washed up** on the coast of Alaska*: **sweep**, carry, convey, transport, move, deliver, deposit, drive.
9 *a wave of guilt **washed over** her*: **affect**, rush over/through, thrill through, race over, surge through, course through, flood over, flow over, sweep over, flutter through.
10 *the stonework was washed with water-based paint*: **paint**, colour, apply paint to, tint, highlight, shade, dye, stain, distemper; coat, cover.
11 *copper washed with silver*: **plate**, cover, coat, overlay, laminate, veneer, glaze, gild, silver.
12 informal *people will see that this budget is merely an election bribe and it won't wash*: **be accepted**, be acceptable, be plausible, be convincing, hold up, hold water, stand up, bear scrutiny, stand the test of time, be believable/credible, pass muster, prove true, make sense; informal stick.
□ **wash something away** *about two acres of land has been washed away*: **erode**, abrade, wear away, corrode, eat away, eat into, denude, grind down, undermine.
□ **wash one's hands of** *I'm going to wash my hands of the whole business*: **disown**, disclaim, renounce, reject, abjure, forswear, disavow, have nothing to do with, have done with, be finished/through with, give up on, turn one's back on, cast aside, end relations with, abandon; Law disaffirm.
□ **wash up** *I cook for him, but he usually washes up*: **wash the dishes**, wash the crockery, do the dishes, do the washing-up.
□ **wash something up** *he washed up the dishes*: **clean**, rinse, do, scrub, scour.
▸ noun **1** *her hair needs a wash | he had a quick wash and shave*: **clean**, cleaning, cleansing; shower, douche, dip, bath, soak; formal or humorous ablutions; rare lavation.
2 *that shirt should really go in the wash straight away*: **laundry**, washing; dirty washing, dirty clothes, soiled linen; Brit. dated bagwash.

3 *an antiseptic skin wash*: **lotion**, salve, application, preparation, rinse, liquid, liniment, embrocation, emulsion.
4 *his jet ski ploughed into the wash of a motor boat*: **backwash**, backflow, wake, trail, train, path; churning, disturbance.
5 *the wash of the waves on the pebbled beach*: **surge**, flow, swell, welling, sweep, undulation, rise and fall, ebb and flow, roll, splash.
6 *water was applied to thin out the crayon into a wash*: **paint**, stain, varnish, coat, layer, film, overlay.

washed out adjective 1 *a washed-out denim jacket*: **faded**, blanched, bleached, lightened, decolorized; stonewashed.
▷ANTONYMS bold.
2 *wooden shutters of washed-out blue and green*: **pale**, light, flat, drab, grey, muted, lacklustre, lustreless, watery.
▷ANTONYMS vivid.
3 *a woman with a worn, washed-out face*: **wan**, pallid, pale, white, grey, pasty, pasty-faced, anaemic, colourless, bloodless, drawn, haggard, blanched, drained, pinched, peaky, peakish, ashen, ashen-faced, chalky, chalk-white, waxy, waxen, sickly, sallow, whey-faced, ghostly, deathlike, deathly pale, as white as a sheet, looking as if one has seen a ghost; rare lymphatic.
▷ANTONYMS ruddy, flushed.
4 *he was looking washed out after his exams*: **exhausted**, tired (out), worn out, weary, fatigued, spent, drained, enfeebled, enervated, run down; informal all in, done in, dead on one's feet, dead, dog-tired, played out, knocked out, bushed, fagged (out), beat, zonked, like death warmed up; Brit. informal knackered, whacked; N. Amer. informal pooped, tuckered out; rare etiolated.
▷ANTONYMS energetic, perky.

washout noun informal *I was a bit of a washout at school | the last dance was a total washout financially speaking*: **failure**, disappointment, let-down, loser, non-achiever, ne'er-do-well; fiasco, setback, blow, misfortune, disaster, catastrophe, mess, debacle, damp squib; informal flop, dud, non-starter, no-hoper, lead balloon; N. Amer. clinker.
▷ANTONYMS success, triumph.

waspish adjective *she sounded waspish and impatient*: **irritable**, touchy, testy, irascible, cross, snappish, cantankerous, splenetic, short-tempered, ill-tempered, bad-tempered, foul-tempered, moody, crabbed, crotchety, grumpy, huffy, ratty, petulant, peevish, querulous, angry, sharp; informal grouchy; N. English informal mardy.

waste verb 1 *he doesn't like to waste money on bus fares*: **squander**, fritter away, misspend, misuse, spend recklessly, throw away, lavish, be wasteful with, dissipate, spend like water, throw around like confetti; go through, run through, exhaust, drain, deplete, burn up, use up, consume; informal blow, splurge.
▷ANTONYMS conserve.
2 *junkies **wasting away** in the streets*: **grow weak**, wither, atrophy, become emaciated, shrivel up, shrink, decay; decline, wilt, fade, flag, deteriorate, degenerate, rot, moulder, languish, be abandoned, be neglected, be forgotten, be disregarded.
▷ANTONYMS flourish, thrive.
3 *the disease had wasted his legs*: **emaciate**, **atrophy**, wither, debilitate, shrivel, shrink, weaken, enfeeble, sap the strength of.
4 N. Amer. informal *I saw them waste the guy I worked for*: **murder**, kill, do away with, assassinate, liquidate, do to death, eliminate, terminate, dispatch, finish off, put to death, execute; slaughter, butcher, massacre, wipe out, destroy, annihilate, eradicate, exterminate, extirpate, decimate, mow down, shoot down, cut down, cut to pieces; informal bump off, polish off, do in, knock off, top, take out, croak, stiff; N. Amer. informal ice, off, rub out, whack, smoke; literary slay.
▶ adjective 1 *I collected two bags containing waste material*: **unwanted**, excess, superfluous, left over, scrap, extra, unused, useless, worthless; unproductive, unusable, unprofitable.
▷ANTONYMS useful.
2 *she took a short cut across waste ground*: **uncultivated**, barren, desert, unproductive, infertile, unfruitful, arid, bare; desolate, solitary, lonely, empty, void, uninhabited, unpopulated; wild.
▷ANTONYMS cultivated.
▶ noun 1 *what a waste of money*: **squandering**, dissipation, frittering away, misspending, misuse, misapplication, misemployment, abuse; prodigality, extravagance, wastefulness, lavishness, unthriftiness.
2 *household waste*: **rubbish**, refuse, litter, debris, dross, junk, detritus, scrap; dregs, leavings, remains, scraps, offscourings; sewage, effluent, effluvium; N. Amer. garbage, trash.
3 (usually **wastes**) *the frozen wastes of the South Pole*: **desert**, wasteland, wilderness, barrenness, emptiness, vastness, wilds.
□ **lay waste** See **lay**[1].

wasted adjective 1 *it was a wasted effort*: **squandered**, misspent, misdirected, misused, dissipated, frittered away; pointless, useless, unnecessary, needless, not needed; informal blown, splurged.
2 *a wasted opportunity*: **missed**, lost, past, forfeited, neglected, squandered, bungled, gone, gone by the board; informal down the drain.
3 *I'm wasted in this job*: **underemployed**, underused, too good for; abandoned, neglected, forgotten, disregarded, languishing.
4 *his skinny wasted legs*: **emaciated**, **atrophied**, withered, shrivelled, weak, weakened, frail, shrunken, skeletal, rickety, scrawny, cadaverous, wilted, faded, flagging, deteriorating, degenerative; gaunt, haggard, wizened, undernourished, starved, half-starved.
5 informal *everybody at the party was pretty wasted*. See **drunk** (adjective).

wasteful adjective *wasteful use of energy in the home*: **prodigal**, profligate, uneconomical, extravagant, lavish, excessive, careless, imprudent, improvident, reckless; thriftless, spendthrift, squandering; needless, useless, not needed, squandered.
▷ANTONYMS thrifty, frugal.

wasteland noun *he turned the land into a desolate wasteland*: **wilderness**, desert, waste, barren land, dust bowl; wilds, badlands.

waster noun informal *all her friends are drunks or wasters*: **idler**, loafer, good-for-nothing, drone, ne'er-do-well, do-nothing, slob, lounger, shirker, sluggard, laggard, slugabed; informal loser, skiver, slacker, lazybones; N. Amer. informal bum, gold brick; literary wastrel.

wastrel noun literary 1 *her money was gambled away by her wastrel of a husband*: **spendthrift**, prodigal, profligate, squanderer; informal big spender.
2 *he was mixing with thieves and wastrels when he ought to have been studying*: **idler**, loafer, good-for-nothing, drone, ne'er-do-well, do-nothing, layabout, slob, lounger, shirker, sluggard, laggard, slugabed; informal waster, loser, slacker, lazybones; Brit. informal skiver.

watch verb 1 *Philippa continued to watch him as he spoke*: **observe**, view, look at, eye, gaze at, stare at, gape at, peer at; contemplate, survey, feast one's eyes on, watch like a hawk, keep a weather eye on; inspect, scrutinize, scan, examine, study, take in, take stock of, glance at; see, notice, spot, glimpse, spy, catch sight of, lay one's eyes on, perceive, witness; ogle, leer at, make eyes at; pay attention to, regard, attend, take note of, mark; informal check out, get a load of, recce, eyeball, not take one's eyes off; Brit. informal take a dekko at, take a butcher's at; literary behold.
▷ANTONYMS ignore, disregard.
2 *he was being watched by plain-clothes police*: **spy on**, keep watch on, keep an eye on, keep in sight, keep track of, track, monitor, survey, follow, keep under observation, keep under surveillance; informal keep tabs on, keep a beady eye on, stake out; rare surveil.
3 *we need to find a trustworthy person to watch the kids*: **look after**, mind, take care of, care for, supervise, superintend, tend, attend to, minister to, foster, nurse, guard, safeguard, protect; informal keep an eye on.
▷ANTONYMS neglect.
4 *they came to a large set of steel doors, **watched over** by a single guard | two men stayed to watch the boat*: **guard**, stand guard over, keep guard on, protect, shield, preserve, defend, safeguard, screen, shelter; cover, patrol, police, picket, keep a lookout at.
5 *most women watch their diet during pregnancy | watch what you say to him*: **be careful about/of**, exercise care/caution/restraint about; be aware of, pay attention to, consider, take into account/consideration, bear in mind, keep in mind; mind, attend to, pay heed to.
□ **watch out/it/yourself** *'Watch out' he yelled | watch it, Bob, or you'll go over the edge*: **be careful**, be watchful, beware, be on the watch, be wary, be cautious, be on your guard, mind out, look out, pay attention, take heed/care, have a care, be on the alert/lookout, keep a sharp lookout, be vigilant, be on the qui vive; informal keep an eye open/out, keep one's eyes peeled/skinned.
□ **watch (out) for** *he made idle banter as they watched for the van*: **look out for**, wait for, await, stand by for, hold back for; anticipate, expect; informal keep an eye open for.
▶ noun 1 *Harvey looked at his watch and said 'Time to get ready'*: **timepiece**, chronometer, small clock, timer; wristwatch, pocket watch, fob watch, digital watch, stopwatch.
2 *we kept watch on the yacht*: **guard**, vigil, lookout, an eye; observance, observation, surveillance, vigilance, view, notice.
3 *Ratagan took the first watch while the rest slept*: **shift**, stint, spell, stretch, turn.

watchdog noun 1 *they use watchdogs and armed guards to ward off trespassers*: **guard dog**, house dog.
2 *the department acts as a watchdog over life assurance companies | a consumer watchdog*: **ombudsman**, monitor, scrutineer, inspector, observer, supervisor; custodian, guardian, guard, protector.

watcher noun **onlooker**, spectator, observer, viewer, looker-on, witness, eyewitness, fly on the wall, sightseer; bystander, passer-by, non-participant; spy; informal rubberneck; literary beholder.

watchful adjective *her mother kept a watchful eye on her*: **observant**, alert, vigilant, attentive, perceptive; awake, wakeful, aware, heedful, sharp; sharp-eyed, keen-eyed, eagle-eyed, hawk-eyed, gimlet-eyed, with one's eyes open; on the lookout, on the qui vive, wary, cautious, careful, suspicious, circumspect, chary; informal with one's eyes skinned/peeled.
▷ANTONYMS inattentive, careless.

> *Word toolkit* **watchful**
> See **wary**.

watchman noun *a night watchman*: **security guard**, security man, guard, custodian, doorman; caretaker, janitor, superintendent, warden, steward, curator.

watchword noun *efficiency in all things was the watchword*: **guiding principle**, **slogan**, motto, maxim, axiom, mantra, truism, catchword, catchphrase, catchline, sound bite, byword, battle/rallying cry, formula, refrain, saying; informal buzzword.

water noun **1** *a glass of water*: Latin aqua; technical H_2O; rare Adam's ale.
2 *he had a house down by the water*: **sea**, ocean; **lake**, loch, pond, pool, reservoir; **river**.
▷ANTONYMS land.
□ **get into hot/deep water** informal *whenever we spoke out, we got into hot water*: **be severely reprimanded**, be upbraided, be scolded, get a scolding, be admonished, be castigated, be rebuked, be chastised, be censured, be criticized severely, be taken to task, get into trouble, be hauled over the coals; informal catch it, get what for, be told off, get hell, get into shtook, get a dressing-down, get an earful, get a roasting, get a rocket, get a rollicking, get a rap over the knuckles, get a slap on the wrist.
□ **hold water** *there are times when this theory just does not hold water*: **be tenable**, ring true, bear examination/scrutiny, survive investigation, make sense, work out, stand up, hold up, be convincing, be plausible, be verifiable, be provable, be sound.
▷ANTONYMS fall down.
▶ verb **1** *he told me to water the plants*: **sprinkle**, moisten, dampen, wet, spray, splash; soak, douse, souse, drench, saturate, flood, waterlog; hose (down), water down; archaic sodden.
▷ANTONYMS dry out, parch.
2 *Ralph's eyes were watering | my mouth watered as I looked at the strawberries*: **moisten**, exude water, become wet, leak; cry, weep; salivate.
3 *he was accused of watering the claret*. See **water something down** (sense 1).
□ **water something down 1** *staff at the club had watered down the drinks*: **dilute**, add water to, water, thin (out), make thin/thinner, weaken, make weak/weaker; adulterate, doctor, taint, mix; informal cut. **2** *in the end the proposals were considerably watered down*: **moderate**, temper, qualify, mitigate, mute, mellow, tone down, soften; subdue, curb, tame, calm, bridle; understate, underemphasize, play down, soft-pedal, downplay.
▷ANTONYMS enhance, strengthen.

> *Word links* **water**
> **aqueous** relating to water
> **aqua-**, **hydro-** related prefixes, as in *aquaculture, hydroelectric*
> **hydrophobia** fear of water

waterfall noun **cascade**, cataract, shower, torrent, outpouring, white water, chute; falls, rapids; N. English **force**; Scottish archaic **linn**.

waterproof adjective *a warm waterproof jacket*: **watertight**, water-repellent, water-resistant, weatherproof; damp-proof; impermeable, impervious; coated, proofed, rubberized, waxed.
▷ANTONYMS leaky.
▶ noun Brit. *she put on boots and a waterproof*: **raincoat**, anorak, mackintosh, sou'wester, oilskin, cagoule, cape; Brit. informal mac.

watertight adjective **1** *a watertight container*: **waterproof**, water-repellent, water-resistant, weatherproof; damp-proof; **impermeable**, impervious, sealed, hermetically sealed, coated, proofed, rubberized.
▷ANTONYMS leaky.
2 *Sam had arranged a watertight alibi*: **indisputable**, unquestionable, incontrovertible, undeniable, irrefutable, unassailable, impregnable, beyond dispute, beyond question, beyond doubt, indubitable; foolproof, sound, flawless, airtight, conclusive, perfect, without loopholes.
▷ANTONYMS flawed.

watery adjective **1** *the patient's nose may be streaming with a watery discharge*: **liquid**, fluid, liquefied; technical aqueous, hydrous.
▷ANTONYMS solid.
2 *a watery meadow*: **wet**, damp, moist, sodden, soggy, squelchy, soft; saturated, waterlogged; marshy, boggy, swampy, fenny, miry, muddy, oozy.
▷ANTONYMS dry.
3 *a bowl of watery porridge*: **thin**, runny, weak, sloppy, dilute, diluted, watered down, thinned down, adulterated; tasteless, flavourless, insipid, bland; informal wishy-washy.
▷ANTONYMS thick, concentrated.
4 *the light was watery and grey*: **pale**, wan, thin, faint, weak, feeble, washed out, anaemic, colourless, insipid; informal wishy-washy.
▷ANTONYMS bright.
5 *she dabbed at a watery eye*: **tearful**, teary, weeping, weepy, moist, rheumy, dewy-eyed; formal lachrymose.
▷ANTONYMS dry.

> *Word toolkit* **watery**
> See **runny**.

wave verb **1** *Farrell waved a hand dismissively | the linesman waved his flag furiously*: **move to and fro**, move up and down, wag, waggle; swing, shake, swish, sweep, swipe, brandish, flourish, flaunt, wield, flick, flutter.
2 *the grass waved in the morning breeze*: **ripple**, flutter, undulate, stir, flap, sway, swing, waft, shake, quiver, oscillate, move; blow.
3 *the waiter was waving to them to sit closer*: **gesture**, gesticulate, signal, sign, beckon, indicate, motion, nod, bid.
4 *her thick dark hair fell in a waving mass to her shoulders*: **curl**, kink, coil, undulate; crimp, frizz, frizzle.
□ **wave something aside** *he waved aside her protest*: **dismiss**, reject, set/put/brush aside, shrug off, disregard, ignore, spurn, rebuff, discount, repudiate, put out of one's mind, play down, treat with contempt; informal pooh-pooh, pour cold water on.
□ **wave something down** *he waved down a taxi and drove off*: **flag down**, hail, signal to stop, stop, signal, summon, call, shout to, accost.
▶ noun **1** *Whitlock gave him a friendly wave as he drove past*: **gesture**, gesticulation, hand movement; signal, sign, motion, indication.
2 *he loves surfing the big waves*: **breaker**, billow, roller, comber, ripple, white horse, white cap; (**waves**) swell, surf, froth; Austral./NZ bombora; informal boomer; N. Amer. informal **kahuna**.
3 *the wave of emigration to Israel*: **flow**, rush, surge, flood, stream, swell, tide, deluge, torrent, spate, billow.
4 *Lee felt a wave of self-pity | a crime wave*: **surge**, rush, ripple, spasm, thrill, frisson, shiver, tingle, stab, dart; upsurge, welling up, outbreak, rash; feeling.
5 *he had dark hair that sprang in thick waves from his forehead*: **curl**, kink, corkscrew, crimp, twist, twirl, ringlet, frizz, coil, loop, undulation.
6 *electromagnetic waves | light waves*: **ripple**, vibration, oscillation, undulation.
□ **make waves** informal *plenty of backbenchers continue to make waves*: **cause trouble**, be disruptive, be troublesome, cause a disturbance; make an impression, be noticed.

waver verb **1** *the candlelight in the room wavered in a warm draught*: **flicker**, quiver, tremble, twinkle, glimmer, wink, blink.
2 *his voice wavered with a hint of uncertainty*: **become unsteady**, falter, wobble, tremble, hesitate.
3 *he had wavered between the Church of Ireland and Catholicism*: **be undecided**, be irresolute, be indecisive, hesitate, dither, equivocate, vacillate, fluctuate, see-saw, yo-yo; think twice, change one's mind, get cold feet, dally, stall; Brit. haver, hum and haw; informal dilly-dally, shilly-shally, pussyfoot around, blow hot and cold, sit on the fence; rare tergiversate.

wavy adjective *the leaf has a wavy edge*: **curling**, curly, curvy, curving, curved, undulating, meandering, winding, squiggly, rippled, crinkly, kinked, zigzag.
▷ANTONYMS straight.

wax verb **1** *the moon is waxing*: **approach full moon**, get bigger, increase in size, enlarge.
▷ANTONYMS wane.
2 literary *price sensitivity is waxing and brand loyalty waning*: **increase**, grow, develop, rise, expand, swell, enlarge, magnify, extend, escalate, deepen, intensify, widen, broaden, spread, mushroom, snowball.
▷ANTONYMS decrease, wane.
3 *Jimmy seldom waxed enthusiastic about anything*: **become**, grow, get, come to be, turn.
□ **wax lyrical** *he waxed lyrical about how he would spend his earnings*: **become enthusiastic**, enthuse, rave, gush, get carried away.

waxen adjective *the waxen pallor of a corpse*: **pallid**, pale, pasty, wan, ashen, colourless, anaemic, bloodless, washed out, ashy, chalky, chalk-white, white, grey, whitish, waxy, blanched, drained, ghastly, sickly, sallow, as white as a sheet/ghost, deathly pale; milky, creamy, cream, ivory, milk-white, alabaster.
▷ANTONYMS ruddy.

way noun **1** *a way of reducing environmental damage*: **method**, course of action, process, procedure, technique, system; plan, strategy, scheme; means, mechanism, routine, manner, approach, route, road; Latin modus operandi.
2 *she kissed him in her brisk way*: **manner**, style, fashion, mode, method.
3 *I've learned my lesson and changed my ways*: **practice**, wont, habit, custom, characteristic, policy, procedure, convention, fashion, use, routine, rule; trait, attribute, mannerism, peculiarity, idiosyncrasy, oddity; **conduct**, behaviour, manner, style, nature, personality, temperament, disposition, character; Latin modus operandi, modus vivendi; formal praxis.
4 *he tried to remember which way led home*: **road**, roadway, street, thoroughfare, track, path, pathway, lane, avenue, drive, channel; **route**, course, direction.

5 *I'll go out the back way*: **door**, doorway, gate, exit, entrance, entry, portal; route.
6 *the mill stands a short way downstream*: **distance**, length, stretch, journey, extent; space, interval, span, gap, separation.
7 *April seems a long way away*: **period of time**, time, stretch, term, span, duration.
8 *she swerved to miss a car coming the other way*: **direction**, bearing, course, orientation, line, run, tack.
9 informal *what do they call a missel thrush down your way?* **locality**, neighbourhood, area, district, locale, quarter, community, region, zone, part; informal neck of the woods, parts; Brit. informal manor; N. Amer. informal hood, nabe.
10 *in some ways, he may be better off in Birmingham*: **aspect**, regard, facet, respect; sense, feature, detail, point, particular, characteristic, question, connection.
11 *I hear that the country is in a bad way*: **state**, condition, situation, circumstances, position; predicament, plight; informal shape.
□ **by the way** *oh, by the way Katie, you had a call*: **incidentally**, by the by, in passing, en passant.
□ **give way 1** *the government finally gave way and passed the bill*: **yield**, back down, make concessions, surrender, concede/admit defeat, give up/in, submit, succumb, raise/show the white flag; acquiesce, agree, concur, approve, assent; informal throw in the towel/sponge, cave in. **2** *he crashed into the door and it gave way*: **collapse**, give, fall to pieces, come apart, crumple, crumble, cave in, fall in, disintegrate, go to pieces. **3** *she never gave way to anger*: **succumb**, yield, give in, submit, surrender, fall victim; be overcome by, be overwhelmed by, be conquered by. **4** *grief* ***gave way*** *to a feeling of guilt*: **be replaced by**, be succeeded by, be followed by, be superseded by, be supplanted by, be ousted by.
□ **make way** See **make**.
□ **on the/one's way** *the doctor's on his way*: **coming**, imminent, forthcoming, approaching, impending, close, near, on us; proceeding, journeying, travelling, en route, in transit.
□ **way of life 1** *war in the region is hindering this traditional way of life*: **culture**, civilization, society, lifestyle; customs, traditions, heritage, habits, ways, mores, values. **2** *I aim only for a society that offers a decent way of life to all*: **lifestyle**, way of living, manner of living, life, situation, position, state, station, condition, set of circumstances, fate, lot.

wayfarer noun **traveller**, journeyer, nomad, migrant, gypsy, vagabond, vagrant, itinerant, drifter; **walker**, hiker, rambler, wanderer, roamer, rover, backpacker, footslogger.

wayfaring adjective *a wayfaring man*: **travelling**, journeying, walking, hiking, rambling, touring; wandering, roaming, roving, drifting, nomadic, itinerant, peripatetic, migratory, migrating, floating, on the move/go/wing.

waylay verb **1** *we were on our way to Winchester when we were waylaid and robbed*: **ambush**, hold up, attack, assail, rob; lie in wait for, lay a trap for, trap, entrap; informal mug, stick up.
2 *a series of people waylaid her to chat before she was out of the room*: **accost**, detain, intercept, take aside, stop and talk to, pounce on, swoop down on, importune; informal buttonhole.

way-out adjective informal *a way-out ideology*: **unconventional**, offbeat, outlandish, eccentric, quirky, aberrant, unusual, crazy, absurd, bizarre, mad, strange, weird, freakish, peculiar, odd, uncommon, avant-garde; informal far out, oddball, wacky, screwy, nutty, batty; Brit. informal rum; N. Amer. informal bizarro, off the wall.
▷ANTONYMS normal, ordinary.

wayward adjective *a wayward child | wayward behaviour*: **wilful**, self-willed, headstrong, stubborn, obstinate, obdurate, perverse, contrary, rebellious, defiant, uncooperative, refractory, recalcitrant, unruly, wild, ungovernable, unmanageable, unpredictable, capricious, whimsical, fickle, inconstant, changeable, erratic, intractable, difficult, impossible, intolerable, unbearable, fractious, disobedient, insubordinate, undisciplined; archaic contumacious.
▷ANTONYMS well behaved, docile.

weak adjective **1** *they are too weak to move*: **frail**, feeble, puny, fragile, delicate, weakly; infirm, sick, sickly, shaky, debilitated, incapacitated, ailing, indisposed, decrepit, enervated, tired, fatigued, exhausted, spent, worn out; informal weedy.
▷ANTONYMS strong.

2 *bats have very weak eyes*: **inadequate**, poor, feeble; defective, faulty, flawed, deficient, imperfect, substandard, lacking, wanting.
▷ANTONYMS strong, powerful, keen.
3 *she made some weak excuse to break the appointment*: **unconvincing**, untenable, tenuous, implausible, unsatisfactory, slight, poor, inadequate, thin, transparent; unsound, feeble, flimsy, lame, hollow; informal pathetic.
▷ANTONYMS convincing.
4 *I was too weak to be a rebel*: **irresolute**, **spineless**, craven, cowardly, pusillanimous, timorous, timid, indecisive, ineffectual, useless, inept, effete, meek, tame, powerless, ineffective, impotent, namby-pamby, soft, lily-livered, faint-hearted; informal yellow, weak-kneed, gutless, yellow-bellied, chicken-hearted, chicken.
▷ANTONYMS strong, resolute.
5 *he had only a weak light to work by*: **dim**, pale, wan, faint, dull, feeble, muted.
▷ANTONYMS strong, bright.
6 *'you did this to her,' he said in a weak voice | a weak signal*: **indistinct**, muffled, stifled, muted, hushed, faint, low, scarcely audible.
▷ANTONYMS strong, loud.
7 *they drank weak coffee*: **watery**, diluted, dilute, watered down, thinned down, thin, adulterated, tasteless, flavourless, bland, insipid, mild, under-strength; informal wishy-washy.
▷ANTONYMS strong, powerful.
8 *a weak smile*: **unenthusiastic**, feeble, half-hearted, limp, lame.
□ **weak at the knees** *she has accepted a challenge that would make the bravest man go weak at the knees*: **faint**, dizzy, light-headed, giddy, shaky; weak-kneed, wobbly, quivery, unsteady, groggy, muzzy; informal trembly, all of a tremble, all of a quiver, with rubbery legs, woozy; rare vertiginous.

Word toolkit

weak	feeble	frail
link	attempt	body
signal	excuse	patient
support	effort	voice
pound	response	frame
economy	protest	creature
market	apology	child
tea	explanation	grandparents

weaken verb **1** *the virus has weakened him terribly*: **enfeeble**, debilitate, incapacitate, sap one's strength, enervate, tire, exhaust, wear out; wither, erode, diminish, destroy.
▷ANTONYMS strengthen.
2 *she tried to weaken the impact of what she'd just said*: **reduce**, decrease, diminish, lessen, moderate, temper, sap, dilute, water down, thin, blunt, mitigate, deplete, soften (up).
▷ANTONYMS increase, boost.
3 *our morale weakened*: **abate**, lessen, decrease, dwindle, diminish, ease up, let up, trail off, wane, ebb, subside, peter out, melt away, fizzle out, taper off, tail off, grow dim, grow faint; decline, deteriorate, degenerate, shrivel, wilt, tire, languish, falter.
▷ANTONYMS strengthen, intensify.
4 *the move weakened her authority*: **impair**, undermine, compromise; invalidate, refute, rebut, negate, discredit.
▷ANTONYMS strengthen, bolster.
5 *when she wept and begged him not to turn her out he weakened*: **relent**, give in, acquiesce, yield, give way, accede, succumb, come round; consent, assent, agree; soften, bend, ease up, ease off.
▷ANTONYMS stand firm.

weakling noun *a nine-stone weakling*: **milksop**, namby-pamby, weak person, coward, pushover, mouse; informal wimp, weed, sissy, drip, wet, ninny, mummy's boy, pansy, softie, doormat, runt, chicken, yellow-belly, fraidy-cat, scaredy-cat; N. Amer. informal wuss, pussy; archaic poltroon.
▷ANTONYMS strongman, hero.

weak-minded adjective *he is just a weak-minded fool*: **irresolute**, weak-willed, weak, impressionable, spineless, indecisive, unassertive, persuadable, persuasible, submissive, compliant, pusillanimous; foolish, simple, feeble-minded, witless, mindless, brainless, stupid, idiotic.
▷ANTONYMS strong-willed; intelligent.

weakness noun **1** *his illness resulted in weakness for the rest of his life*: **frailty**, feebleness, enfeeblement, puniness, fragility, delicateness, delicacy, weakliness; infirmity, sickness, sickliness, shakiness, debility, incapacity, indisposition, decrepitude, enervation, fatigue, exhaustion, tiredness; informal weediness.
▷ANTONYMS strength, vigour.
2 *he has worked on his weaknesses and his form has improved*: **fault**, flaw, defect, deficiency, weak point/spot, failing, foible, shortcoming, imperfection, blemish, Achilles heel, chink in one's armour.
▷ANTONYMS strength, forte.
3 *he had a weakness for champagne*: **fondness**, liking, love, passion, partiality, preference, penchant, soft spot, bent, predisposition, predilection, leaning, inclination, proneness, proclivity, disposition, taste, eye; relish, zeal, enthusiasm, appetite.
▷ANTONYMS dislike.
4 *the President's public changes of mind led to accusations of indecision and weakness*: **spinelessness, timidity**, cravenness, cowardliness, pusillanimity, timorousness, indecisiveness, indecision, irresolution, ineffectuality, uselessness, ineptness, ineptitude, effeteness, meekness, tameness, powerlessness, ineffectiveness, impotence, faint-heartedness; informal chicken-heartedness.
▷ANTONYMS strength, resolve.
5 *the symptoms include weakness of the eyes*: **inadequacy**, defectiveness,

faultiness, deficiency, imperfection.
▷ANTONYMS strength, power.
6 *the weakness of this argument was soon shown up*: **unconvincingness**, untenability, tenuousness, implausibility, unsatisfactoriness, slightness, poverty, inadequacy, thinness, transparency; unsoundness, flimsiness, lameness, hollowness.
▷ANTONYMS strength.
7 *the weakness of the sound | the weakness of the street lamps*: **indistinctness**, muffledness, mutedness, faintness, lowness, low intensity; **dimness**, paleness, wanness, dullness, feebleness.
▷ANTONYMS strength.

Word links **weakness**
asthenophobia fear of weakness

weak-willed adjective *I was too weak-willed to give up*: **irresolute**, **spineless**, weak, weak-minded, impressionable, indecisive, doubtful, unassertive, persuadable, persuasible, submissive, compliant, pusillanimous, weak-kneed; informal wimpish, chicken.
▷ANTONYMS strong-willed, resolute.

weal noun *blood dripped from a weal on his shoulders*: **welt**, wound, lesion, swelling; scar, cicatrix, mark, blemish, discoloration, pockmark.

wealth noun 1 *a gentleman of wealth and distinction*: **affluence**, prosperity, opulence, riches, means, substance, luxury, well-being, plenty; Mammon; money, cash, lucre, capital, principal, treasure, fortune, finance; assets, possessions, resources, effects, goods, funds, valuables; property, stock, reserves, securities, holdings, belongings, chattels; ill-gotten gains; informal wherewithal, dough, bread; archaic pelf.
▷ANTONYMS poverty, privation.
2 *the coastline has a wealth of bird life | a wealth of information*: **abundance**, profusion, plethora, mine, store, treasury, copiousness, plenitude, amplitude, bounty, cornucopia; informal lot, load, heap, mass, pile, mountain, ocean, sea, stack, ton; Brit. informal **shedload**; Austral./NZ informal **swag**; vulgar slang shitload.
▷ANTONYMS dearth, lack.

wealthy adjective *he enjoyed the company of wealthy people*: **rich**, affluent, moneyed, well off, with deep pockets, well-to-do, prosperous, comfortable, opulent, propertied, of means, of substance, in clover, plutocratic; N. Amer. silk-stocking; informal well heeled, rolling in it/money, in the money, made of money, filthy rich, stinking rich, loaded, flush, on easy street, quids in, worth a packet/bundle; Austral./NZ informal financial; informal, dated oofy.
▷ANTONYMS poor, impoverished.

wear verb 1 *he was wearing a dark green suit*: **be dressed in**, be clothed in, have on, sport; dress in, clothe oneself in, put on, don.
2 *Barbara wore a sweet smile*: **have (on one's face)**, present, show, display, exhibit, bear; give, put on, assume, form one's face into, make one's face into, compose one's face into, rearrange one's face into, ease one's face into, smooth one's face into, draw one's face into, twist one's face into, tug one's face into, pull one's face into, pinch one's face into, crease one's face into, crack one's face into, screw (up) one's face into.
3 *the bricks have been **worn down** by centuries of knife-sharpening | the waterproofing coating soon starts to **wear away***: **erode**, abrade, scour, scratch, scrape, rasp, rub away, rub down, grind away, fret, waste away, wash away, crumble (away), wear down; corrode, eat away (at), gnaw away (at), dissolve, bite into.
4 *the tyres are wearing well*: **last**, endure, hold up, survive, bear up, keep going, carry on, prove durable, stand/withstand/resist wear, stand up to wear, do; informal hang in there.
5 Brit. informal *I've asked him to keep the bar open an hour later, but he won't wear it*: **allow**, permit, authorize, sanction, condone, indulge, agree to, accede to, approve of; endure, put up with, bear, take, stand, support, submit to, undergo; **accept**, swallow, tolerate, brook, countenance, admit of; Scottish thole; informal stick, hack, abide, stomach; Brit. informal be doing with; archaic suffer.
□ **wear something down** *she protested, but he wore down her resistance*: **gradually overcome**, slowly reduce/diminish/lessen, drain, erode, wear away, exhaust, undermine, chip away at.
□ **wear off** *the novelty soon wore off*: **fade**, dwindle, diminish, lessen, decrease, wane, ebb, subside, weaken, lose intensity, lose strength, peter out, melt away, fizzle out, pall, taper off, tail off, grow faint, grow dim, evaporate, disappear, vanish, die, come to nothing, come to a halt, come to an end, run out; lose its effectiveness/effect.
□ **wear on** *as the afternoon wore on he began to look unhappy*: **pass**, elapse, proceed, progress, advance, move on, run its course, go by/past/on, roll by/past/on, march on, glide by/past, slide by/past, slip by/away/past, fly by/past, steal by/past, tick by/past.
□ **wear out** *a cheap bed will wear out faster than a quality one*: **deteriorate**, become worn, show signs of wear, come to the end of its life, become useless, wear thin, fray, become threadbare, go into holes, go through, wear through.
□ **wear something out** *he wore out six pairs of walking boots*: **use up**, consume, go through, wear holes in, make threadbare, make worn.
□ **wear someone out** *eventually her exertions wore her out*: **fatigue**, tire out, overtire, weary, exhaust, drain, sap, wash out, tax, overtax, enervate, debilitate, enfeeble, jade, incapacitate, devitalize, prostrate; informal whack, bush, shatter, frazzle, wear to a frazzle, poop, take it out of, fag out, do in; Brit. informal knacker.
▸ noun 1 *you won't get much wear out of something so cheap*: **use**, wearing, service, employment, utility, value; informal mileage.
2 *the band were dressed in evening wear*: **clothes**, dress, clothing, attire, garb, finery, garments, outfits, wardrobe; Brit. kit, strip; informal get-up, gear, togs, clobber; formal apparel; literary array, raiment, habiliments.
3 *choose a varnish which will withstand wear*: **damage**, wear and tear, battering, friction, erosion, attrition, corrosion, abrasion, deterioration, degeneration; informal a few knocks; rare detrition.

weariness noun *stumbling with weariness, she forced herself on*: **tiredness**, fatigue, exhaustion, prostration, overtiredness, collapse; jet lag; sleepiness, drowsiness, somnolence, doziness; **lethargy**, lassitude, languor, languidness, debility, enervation, listlessness, sluggishness, lifelessness, torpor, inertia.

wearing adjective *it had been a rather wearing day*: **tiring**, exhausting, wearying, fatiguing, enervating, draining, sapping, stressful, weary, crushing; demanding, exacting, taxing, trying, challenging, burdensome, arduous, gruelling, punishing, grinding, onerous, difficult, hard, tough, heavy, laborious, back-breaking, crippling, strenuous, rigorous, uphill.
▷ANTONYMS refreshing, relaxing.

wearisome adjective *I can't think of anything more wearisome than traipsing round a factory all day*: **tiring**, exhausting, wearying, fatiguing, enervating, draining, sapping, stressful, wearing, crushing; demanding, exacting, taxing, trying, challenging, burdensome, arduous, gruelling, punishing, grinding, onerous, difficult, hard, tough, heavy, laborious, back-breaking, crippling, strenuous, rigorous, uphill; tiresome, irksome, weary, boring, dull, tedious, monotonous, humdrum, prosaic, unexciting, uninteresting.
▷ANTONYMS refreshing; interesting, enjoyable.

weary adjective 1 *he arrived home weary after cycling several miles*: **tired**, tired out, worn out, exhausted, fatigued, overtired, sleepy, drowsy, wearied, sapped, dog-tired, spent, drained, jet-lagged, played out, debilitated, prostrate, enervated, jaded, low; informal all in, done (in/up), dead, dead beat, dead tired, dead on one's feet, asleep on one's feet, ready to drop, fagged out, burnt out, bushed, worn to a frazzle, shattered; Brit. informal knackered, whacked; N. Amer. informal pooped, tuckered out.
▷ANTONYMS energetic, fresh.
2 *she was **weary of** their constant arguments*: **tired of**, fed up with, bored with/by, sick of, sick and tired of, jaded with/by, surfeited with/by, satiated by, glutted with/by; (**be weary of**) have had enough of; informal have had a basinful of, have had it up to here with, have had something up to here.
▷ANTONYMS enthusiastic.
3 *the weary journey began*: **tiring**, exhausting, wearying, fatiguing, enervating, draining, sapping, stressful, wearing, trying, crushing; demanding, exacting, taxing, challenging, burdensome, arduous, gruelling, punishing, grinding, onerous, difficult, hard, tough, heavy, laborious, back-breaking, crippling, strenuous, rigorous, uphill.
▷ANTONYMS refreshing, enjoyable.
▸ verb 1 *she was wearied by her persistent cough*: **tire**, tire out, fatigue, wear out, overtire, exhaust, drain, sap, wash out, tax, overtax, enervate, debilitate, enfeeble, jade, incapacitate, devitalize, prostrate; informal whack, bush, shatter, frazzle, wear to a frazzle, poop, take it out of, fag out, do in, knock out; Brit. informal knacker.
▷ANTONYMS refresh.
2 *this must be stated again at the risk of wearying the reader*: **bore**, tire, make fed up; irk, irritate, exhaust someone's patience, annoy, exasperate, get on someone's nerves; informal get to.
▷ANTONYMS interest.
3 *her friend had also **wearied of** the struggle*: **tire of**, become/get weary of, become/get tired of, become/get fed up with, become/get fed to death with, become/get bored with/by, become/get satiated with, become/get jaded with, become/get sick of, become/get sick to death of, sicken of; have had enough of, have had a surfeit of, have had a glut of; informal become/get bored of, have had something up to here.

wearying adjective *it will be a long and wearying discussion*: **tiring**, exhausting, wearing, trying, fatiguing, enervating, draining, sapping, stressful, weary, crushing; demanding, exacting, taxing, challenging, burdensome, arduous, gruelling, punishing, grinding, onerous, difficult, hard, tough, heavy, laborious, back-breaking, crippling, strenuous, rigorous, uphill; tiresome, irksome, wearisome, boring, dull, tedious, monotonous, humdrum, prosaic, unexciting, uninteresting.
▷ANTONYMS refreshing.

weasel noun *he was a double-crossing weasel*: **scoundrel**, wretch, rogue; informal swine, bastard, creep, louse, rat, toad, snake, snake in the grass, serpent, viper, skunk, dog, cur, scumbag, heel, bad lot, nasty piece of work; N. Amer. informal **rat fink**; Irish informal **sleeveen**; Austral. informal **dingo**; vulgar slang shit, sod, son of a bitch, s.o.b.; Brit. dated informal rotter, hound, bounder; dated cad; archaic blackguard, dastard, knave, varlet.

> *Word links* **weasel**
>
> **musteline** relating to weasels

weather noun *what's the weather like?* **meteorological conditions**, atmospheric conditions, meteorology, climate; temperature, humidity, cloud cover, wind speed, atmospheric pressure; elements; **forecast**, outlook; informal met, met report.
□ **under the weather** *I feel a bit under the weather—I haven't eaten all day*: **ill**, unwell, indisposed, ailing, poorly, not (very) well, not oneself, not in good shape, out of sorts, not up to par, under/below par, peaky, liverish; sick, queasy, nauseous; Brit. off colour; informal not up to snuff, funny, peculiar, crummy, lousy, rough; Brit. informal ropy, grotty; Scottish informal wabbit; Austral./NZ informal crook; dated queer, seedy.
▸ verb *most member companies weathered the recession*: **survive**, come/get through, ride out, live through, pull through, come through (unscathed), outlast, outlive; **withstand**, stand up to, bear up against, stand, endure, rise above, surmount, overcome, resist; informal stick out.

weathered adjective *a weathered stone urn | his weathered face*: **weather-beaten**, eroded, worn, disintegrating, crumbling; bleached, discoloured, tanned, bronzed; lined, creased, wrinkled, wizened, shrivelled, gnarled.

weave[1] verb **1** *grass and twigs were woven into their uniforms to break up their silhouettes*: **entwine**, lace, work, twist, knit, interlace, intertwine, interwork, intertwist, interknit, twist together, criss-cross, braid, twine, plait.
2 *he weaves colourful, cinematic plots*: **invent**, make up, fabricate, put together, construct, create, contrive, spin; tell, recount, relate, narrate, unfold.

weave[2] verb *he had to* ***weave his way*** *through the crowds*: **thread (one's way)**, wind (one's way), work (one's way), dodge, move in and out, swerve, zigzag, criss-cross.

web noun **1** *a spider's web | a fine-spun cotton web*: **mesh**, netting, net, lattice; latticework, lacework, interlacing, webbing; tissue, gauze, gossamer, chiffon; fabric, material, textile, fibre.
2 *a web of friendships*: **network**, nexus, tangle, knot, complex, mass, conglomeration, set, series, chain, maze, snare, trap.

wed verb **1** *they are old enough to wed*: **marry**, get/be married, be wed, become husband and wife, become man and wife, plight/pledge one's troth; informal tie the knot, walk down the aisle, take the plunge, get spliced, get hitched, get yoked, say 'I do'; archaic become espoused.
▷ANTONYMS divorce, separate.
2 *he's planning to wed his long-term girlfriend*: **get/be married to**, marry, be wed to, take as one's wife/husband, lead to the altar; informal get hitched to, get spliced to, tie the knot with, make an honest woman of; archaic espouse, wive.
▷ANTONYMS divorce; jilt.
3 *she wedded the old and new forms of spirituality*: **unite**, unify, join, link, connect, combine, amalgamate, fuse, integrate, weld, bond, stick together, bring together, knit together, glue, cement, coalesce, merge.

wedded adjective **1** *wedded bliss*: **married**, matrimonial, marital, conjugal, connubial, nuptial, marriage, wedding; Law spousal; literary hymeneal, epithalamic.
2 *the company became* ***wedded to*** *the project*: **dedicated to**, devoted to, attached to, fixated on, obsessive about, fanatical about, single-minded about, addicted to, hell-bent on; (**be wedded to**) stick to, refuse to give up.

wedding noun **marriage**, marriage ceremony, wedding ceremony, nuptial ceremony, marriage service, wedding service, marriage rites, wedding rites, nuptials, union; archaic espousal(s).

> *Word links* **wedding**
>
> **nuptial** relating to a wedding

wedge noun **1** *the door was secured by a wedge*: **tapered block**, chock, door stop.
2 *a wedge of cheese*: **triangle**, tapered piece, segment, slice, section; **chunk**, lump, slab, hunk, block; Brit. informal wodge.
▸ verb *she wedged her holdall between two bags*: **squeeze**, cram, jam, crush, pack, thrust, ram, force, push, stow; informal stuff, shove, bung.

wedlock noun **marriage**, matrimony, holy matrimony, married state, union, conjugal bond.

wee adjective Scottish *a wee boy | it was all just a wee misunderstanding*: **little**, small, tiny, minute, miniature, small-scale, compact, mini, undersized, diminutive, dwarf, midget, Lilliputian, infinitesimal, microscopic, nanoscopic, minuscule, bijou, toy; **trivial**, trifling, negligible, insignificant, unimportant, minor, of no account, of no consequence, of no importance, not worth bothering about, not worth mentioning, inconsequential, minimal, inappreciable, imperceptible, nugatory, petty; informal teeny, teeny-weeny, teensy, teensy-weensy, itsy-bitsy, half-pint, dinky, piddling, piffling; Brit. informal titchy; N. Amer. informal little-bitty, vest-pocket.
▷ANTONYMS big; major.

weed verb
□ **weed something/someone out** *a good agency will weed out those unsuitable candidates*: **isolate**, separate out, set apart, put to one side, divide, segregate, sort out, sift out, winnow out, filter out, sieve; eliminate, get rid of, remove, dispense with, shed; informal dump, lose.

weedy adjective informal *a weedy little man*: **puny**, feeble, weak, frail, delicate, underdeveloped, thin, undersized, slight, slightly built, skinny, scrawny, a slip of a ...; informal pint-sized.
▷ANTONYMS burly.

weekly adjective *he was paying off his debt in weekly instalments*: **once a week**, seven-day; lasting a week; rare hebdomadal, hebdomadary.
▸ adverb *the directors meet weekly*: **once a week**, every week, each week, on a weekly basis; by the week, per week, a week; rare hebdomadally.

weep verb *I've seen the toughest soldiers break down and weep*: **cry**, shed tears, sob, snivel, whimper, whine, mewl, bawl, lament, grieve, mourn, keen, wail; Scottish greet; informal boohoo, blub, blubber; literary pule.
▷ANTONYMS laugh, rejoice.
▸ noun *you sit and have a weep*: **cry**, sob, snivel, whimper, mewl, bawl, lament; flood of tears; informal blub, blubber; Brit. informal grizzle; literary pule.

> *Word links* **weep**
>
> **lachrymal** relating to weeping
> **lachrymose** given to weeping

weepy adjective *she was weepy when her husband was first admitted to hospital*: **tearful**, in tears, crying, weeping, sobbing, wailing, snivelling, whimpering; close to tears, on the verge of tears, with tears in one's eyes; emotional, upset, distressed, sad, unhappy; Scottish greeting; informal teary, blubbing, blubbering; rare lachrymose, larmoyant.

weigh verb **1** *the vendor at our market weighs the vegetables carefully*: **measure the weight of**, measure how heavy someone/something is, put someone/something on the scales.
2 *he weighed 118 kg*: **tip/turn the scales at**, come to.
3 *the destructive family situation* ***weighed*** *heavily* ***on*** *him*: **oppress**, lie heavy on, press down on, burden, be a burden on/to, weigh down, cast down, hang over, gnaw at, prey on, prey on someone's mind; **trouble**, worry, beset, bother, disturb, upset, get someone down, depress, distress, grieve, haunt, nag, torment, afflict, perturb; plague, obsess, take over, take control of.
4 *the consequences of the move would need to be very carefully weighed | he has to* ***weigh up*** *the possibility of a conviction*: **consider**, contemplate, think about, give thought to, entertain the idea of, deliberate about, turn over in one's mind, mull over, chew over, reflect on, ruminate about, muse on; **assess**, appraise, analyse, investigate, enquire into, look into, make enquiries into, examine, scrutinize, research, review, explore, probe, study, survey, inspect, take stock of; N. Amer. think on.
▷ANTONYMS ignore, take on trust.
5 *they need to* ***weigh*** *benefit* ***against*** *risk*: **balance**; compare with, evaluate, juxtapose with, place side by side (with), contrast with.
6 *the opinions of chief fire officers will obviously* ***weigh with*** *the Government*: **influence**, have influence with, be influential to, carry weight with, count with, tell with, matter to, be important to, be significant to, mean something to, make an impression on, get to, register with.
□ **weigh someone down 1** *my waders and fishing gear weighed me down*: **burden**, weight, saddle, charge; overload, overburden, overwhelm, encumber, hamper, handicap, tax, strain; literary trammel. **2** *the awful silence of the terrible prison weighed me down*: **oppress**, **depress**, lie heavy on, weigh on, press down on, burden, be a burden on/to, cast down, hang over, gnaw at, prey on, prey on someone's mind; **trouble**, worry, beset, bother, disturb, upset, get someone down, distress, grieve, haunt, nag, torment, afflict, perturb; plague, obsess, take over, take control of.
□ **weigh into someone** *he weighs into the tribunes with unmasked contempt*: **attack**, turn on, lash out at, set upon, assault, fly at, lunge at, let fly at, tear into, pitch into, belabour; informal lay into, sail into, lace into, let someone have it, take a pop at; N. Amer. informal light into.

weight noun **1** *she misjudged the weight of the book*: **heaviness**, mass, load, burden, pressure, force; poundage, tonnage; informal avoirdupois.
2 *a recommendation by the committee will carry great weight*: **influence**, force, leverage, sway, muscle, teeth, importance, significance, consequence, value, substance, power, authority, prestige; informal clout, beef, pull.
3 *that will take a weight off his mind*: **burden**, load, onus, millstone, millstone round one's neck, albatross, cross to bear, encumbrance; oppression, trouble, worry, strain; obligation, responsibility, liability.
4 *the weight of the evidence is against him*: **preponderance**, majority, bulk, mass, greater quantity/number, larger part/number, best/better part,

main part, most, almost all, more than half, (main) body, lion's share, predominance, generality.

Word links **weight**

gravimetry measurement of weight

weighty adjective **1** *a weighty tome of rules and regulations*: **heavy**, massive, thick, bulky, hefty, cumbersome, clumsy, ponderous, overweight.
▷ANTONYMS light.
2 *a weighty subject*: **important**, of great import/importance, significant, of significance, momentous, of moment, consequential, of consequence, far-reaching, key, major, vital, critical, crucial, life-and-death, high-priority, decisive, serious, grave, solemn; no joke, no laughing matter.
▷ANTONYMS unimportant, trivial.
3 *it is a rather weighty responsibility to shoulder*: **burdensome**, onerous, heavy, oppressive, stressful, taxing, troublesome, worrisome, vexatious.
4 *weighty arguments*: **compelling**, cogent, strong, forceful, powerful, potent, convincing, plausible, effective, efficacious, effectual, sound, valid, well founded, telling; impressive, persuasive, influential, authoritative.
▷ANTONYMS weak.

weird adjective **1** *they have experienced all sorts of weird events*: **uncanny**, eerie, unnatural, preternatural, supernatural, unearthly, other-worldly, unreal, ghostly, mysterious, mystifying, strange, abnormal, unusual; Scottish eldritch; informal creepy, spooky, freaky; Brit. informal rum.
▷ANTONYMS normal, ordinary.
2 *some people have a weird sense of humour*: **bizarre**, offbeat, quirky, outlandish, eccentric, unconventional, unorthodox, idiosyncratic, surreal, crazy, absurd, grotesque, peculiar, odd, curious, strange, queer, cranky, freakish, insane, zany, madcap, off-centre, far out, alternative; French outré; informal wacky, freaky, way-out, rum; N. Amer. informal wacko, off the wall, in left field, bizarro.
▷ANTONYMS conventional.

weirdo noun informal *he's a real weirdo*: **eccentric**, oddity, unorthodox person, individualist, individual, nonconformist, free spirit, bohemian, maverick, deviant, pervert, misfit, dropout; informal oddball, odd/queer fish, freak, character, weirdie, crackpot, loony, nut, nutter, nutcase, head case, sicko, perv; Brit. informal one-off, odd bod; N. Amer. informal wacko, wack, screwball, kook; informal, dated case, card.

welcome noun *the festival starts at 6.30 p.m. with a welcome from the vicar*: **greeting**, salutation, hail, welcoming; reception, warm reception, favourable reception, acceptance, hospitality, red carpet; Scottish & Irish fáilte.
▷ANTONYMS farewell; rebuff.
▶verb **1** *hotels should welcome guests in their own language*: **greet**, say hello to, salute, bid someone welcome, play host/hostess to, show hospitality to, receive, meet, embrace, receive with open arms, roll out the red carpet for, fête; usher in.
▷ANTONYMS shun, spurn.
2 *we welcomed the bank's decision to cut its rates*: **express pleasure/satisfaction at**, be pleased by, be glad about, take pleasure in, approve of, appreciate, accept, embrace; informal give the thumbs up to.
▷ANTONYMS reject, disapprove of.
▶adjective **1** *I'm pleased to see you, lad—you're welcome*: **gladly received**, wanted, appreciated, popular, desirable, acceptable, accepted.
▷ANTONYMS unwelcome.
2 *that is very welcome news*: **pleasing**, agreeable, encouraging, gratifying, heartening, promising, refreshing, favourable, propitious, cheering, much needed, pleasant, to one's liking, to one's taste.
▷ANTONYMS unpleasant, disappointing.

weld verb *they simply welded sheets of metal together*: **fuse**, unite, bond, connect, stick, join, link, attach, bind, seal, amalgamate, knit, splice, meld, melt, blend, solder, cement, glue, gum, paste.
▷ANTONYMS separate.

welfare noun **1** *local authorities have a duty to promote the welfare of children*: **well-being**, health, good health, happiness, comfort, security, safety, protection, prosperity, profit, good, success, fortune, good fortune, advantage, interest, prosperousness, successfulness.
▷ANTONYMS hardship.
2 *youngsters cannot claim welfare*: **social security**, benefit, state benefit, benefit payment, public assistance; allowance, pension, credit, support; sick pay, sickness benefit, unemployment benefit/pay.

well[1] adverb **1** *I am sure you will behave well*: **satisfactorily**, in a satisfactory manner/way, nicely, correctly, rightly, properly, fittingly, suitably, aptly, appropriately.
▷ANTONYMS badly.
2 *they get on well together*: **harmoniously**, agreeably, pleasantly, nicely, happily, politely, amicably, amiably, affably, genially, peaceably; informal famously.
▷ANTONYMS badly.
3 *he plays the piano well*: **skilfully**, with skill, ably, competently, proficiently, adeptly, adroitly, deftly, dexterously, effectively, expertly, with expertise, admirably, excellently, consummately, professionally.
▷ANTONYMS poorly.
4 *treating employees well makes good business sense*: **decently**, **fairly**, civilly, politely, genially, kindly, in a kind/kindly way, generously, hospitably; respectably, honestly.
▷ANTONYMS harshly.
5 *mix the ingredients well*: **thoroughly**, completely, efficiently, rigorously, effectively, conscientiously, industriously, carefully.
6 *I know her quite well*: **intimately**, thoroughly, fully, deeply, profoundly, personally.
7 *the company has obviously studied the car market well*: **carefully**, closely, attentively, rigorously, in depth, exhaustively, from top to bottom, minutely, in detail, meticulously, scrupulously, assiduously, conscientiously, painstakingly, methodically, completely, comprehensively, fully, to the fullest extent, intensively, extensively.
▷ANTONYMS casually, negligently.
8 *they all speak well of him*: **admiringly**, highly, approvingly, favourably, appreciatively, warmly, enthusiastically, glowingly, with admiration, with praise, with approbation.
▷ANTONYMS scornfully.
9 *she hopes to make enough money to live well*: **comfortably**, in comfort, in (the lap of) luxury, in ease, splendidly, prosperously, without hardship.
10 *you may well be right*: **quite possibly**, conceivably, quite likely, probably; undoubtedly, certainly, unquestionably; justifiably, reasonably.
11 *he is well over forty*: **considerably**, very much, greatly, to a great/marked extent/degree, a great deal, markedly, decidedly, substantially, easily, comfortably, materially, significantly, signally; informal seriously.
▷ANTONYMS barely, little.
12 *she could well afford it*: **easily**, comfortably, readily, with ease, without difficulty, effortlessly.
▷ANTONYMS barely.
□ **as well** *ducks eat waterweed and tadpoles as well*: **too**, also, in addition, additionally, into the bargain, besides, furthermore, moreover, to boot.
□ **as well as** *we sell books as well as newspapers*: **together with**, in addition to, along with, besides, plus, and, coupled with, with, over and above, on top of, over and beyond, not to mention, to say nothing of, let alone.
□ **well up on** *I thought I was pretty well up on my internet jargon but I'm stumped on that one*: **well versed in**, well informed about, conversant with, knowledgeable about, informed about, abreast of, apprised of, up to date on, au courant with; familiar with, acquainted with, au fait with, at home with, no stranger to; experienced in, proficient in, practised in, skilled in; informal up to speed on, clued up on, genned up on, plugged into; formal cognizant of; dated perfect in.
▷ANTONYMS ignorant of; unfamiliar with.
▶adjective **1** *it would be some time before she was completely well*: **healthy**, in good health, all right, fine, fit, fighting fit, as fit as a fiddle, as fit as a flea, robust, strong, vigorous, blooming, thriving, bursting with health, in rude health, hale, hale and hearty, hearty, in good shape, in excellent shape, in good condition, in tip-top condition, in good trim, in fine fettle, sound, sound in body and limb; informal in the pink, up to snuff.
▷ANTONYMS poorly.
2 *all is not well in further education*: **satisfactory**, all right, fine, in order, as it should be, acceptable; informal OK, fine and dandy, hunky-dory; N. Amer. & Austral./NZ informal jake; Brit. informal, dated tickety-boo.
▷ANTONYMS unsatisfactory.
3 *it would be well to know just what this suggestion entails*: **advisable**, sensible, prudent, politic, commonsensical, wise, canny, judicious, shrewd, expedient, provident, recommended, advantageous, beneficial, profitable, gainful, desirable; a good idea.
▷ANTONYMS inadvisable.

well[2] noun **1** **borehole**, spring, waterhole, bore, shaft.
2 *it is not a priest's function to be a bottomless well of uncritical forgiveness*: **source**, **supply**, wellspring, fount, fountainhead, reservoir, mine, fund, bank, repository, storehouse, treasury.
▶verb *tears were beginning to well from her eyes*: **flow**, stream, run, rush, gush, course, roll, cascade, flood, surge, rise, spurt, spout, squirt, jet; ooze, seep, trickle; burst, issue, discharge; spill, overflow, brim over; rare disembogue.

well advised adjective *you would be well advised to take your time*: **wise**, prudent, sensible, advised.
▷ANTONYMS unwise.

well balanced adjective **1** *stick to a diet that is well balanced*: **mixed**, varied; sensible, balanced; healthy.
▷ANTONYMS unbalanced; unhealthy.
2 *they created a well-balanced Palladian house*: **graceful**, elegant; harmonious, balanced, well proportioned, proportional, in proportion, well arranged; regular, even; symmetrical.
▷ANTONYMS uneven, out of proportion.
3 *a well-balanced young woman*: **sensible**, well adjusted, reasonable, rational, level-headed, sound, practical, discerning, logical, able to think clearly, lucid, clear-headed, coherent; steady, stable, responsible, equable, self-controlled, even-tempered, sober, down-to-earth, matter-of-fact, with

both one's feet on the ground, in one's right mind, in possession of all one's faculties, mentally sound, of sound mind, sane, normal, right in the head; Latin compos mentis; informal all there.
▷ANTONYMS silly.

well behaved adjective *well-behaved children*: **well mannered**, polite, civil, courteous, respectful, deferential, obedient, gentlemanly, chivalrous, gallant, ladylike, genteel, cultivated, gracious, obliging, considerate, thoughtful, urbane, civilized, well spoken, formal, proper, decorous, refined, polished, well brought up; **orderly**, law-abiding, disciplined, peaceful, peaceable, non-violent, tranquil, docile, controlled, restrained, cooperative, compliant; dated mannerly; archaic well conducted, ruly.
▷ANTONYMS naughty; rude; disorderly.

well-being noun *the nurse's prime concern is the well-being of the patient*: **welfare**, health, good health, happiness, comfort, security, safety, protection, prosperity, profit, good, success, fortune, good fortune, advantage, interest, prosperousness, successfulness.

well bred adjective *she is too well bred to say anything*: **well brought up**, **well mannered**, well behaved, polite, civil, courteous, respectful, deferential; ladylike, gentlemanly, chivalrous, gallant, genteel, cultivated, gracious, obliging, considerate, thoughtful, urbane, formal, proper, refined, polished; dated mannerly.
▷ANTONYMS rude, discourteous, ill-bred.

well built adjective *he was about six feet tall and well built*: **sturdy**, sturdily built, strapping, brawny, burly, hefty, broad-shouldered, muscular, muscly, well muscled, strong, robust, rugged, lusty, Herculean; informal hunky, beefy, husky, hulking; dated stalwart; literary thewy, stark.
▷ANTONYMS puny, slight.

well dressed adjective *he was always well dressed, regardless of the time of day*: **smart**, fashionable, stylish, well turned out, besuited, fashionably dressed, chic, modish, elegant, neat, spruce, trim, dapper, debonair; French soigné(e); informal snazzy, natty, snappy, sharp, nifty, cool, with it; N. Amer. informal sassy, spiffy, fly, kicky; dated as if one had just stepped out of a bandbox; archaic trig.
▷ANTONYMS scruffy.

well founded adjective *they have a well-founded fear of persecution if they are deported*: **justifiable**, justified, warranted, legitimate, defensible, supportable, sustainable, tenable, well grounded, valid, admissible, allowable, understandable, excusable, warrantable, acceptable, reasonable, logical, sensible, sound, just, bona fide, genuine, plausible, credible, believable.
▷ANTONYMS unjustified, groundless.

well groomed adjective *she always appeared well groomed at her golf club*: **neat**, **smart**, well turned out, well dressed, neatly dressed, besuited, trim, dapper, elegant, chic, with not a hair out of place; French soigné(e); informal natty, snazzy; N. Amer. informal spiffy; dated as if one had just stepped out of a bandbox; archaic trig.
▷ANTONYMS untidy, unkempt.

well heeled adjective informal *a group of well-heeled tourists*: **wealthy**, rich, well off, affluent, moneyed, with deep pockets, well-to-do, prosperous, opulent, substantial, comfortable, propertied; of means, of substance; informal rolling in money, rolling in it, in the money, loaded, stinking rich, filthy rich, flush, made of money, quids in, worth a packet, worth a bundle, on easy street; informal, dated oofy.
▷ANTONYMS poor.

well known adjective **1** *their behaviour conforms to fairly well-known principles*: **familiar**, widely known, popular, common, usual, everyday, customary, conventional, established.
▷ANTONYMS unknown, abstruse.
2 *Wyatt was a member of a well-known family of architects*: **famous**, noted, notable, famed, prominent, renowned; distinguished, leading, eminent, illustrious, great, celebrated, acclaimed, esteemed, august, recognized, pre-eminent, important, of high standing, of distinction, of repute, considerable.
▷ANTONYMS obscure, unimportant; unsung.

> *Choose the right word* **well known, famous, celebrated, renowned**
>
> See **famous**.

W

well mannered adjective *they were well mannered and eager to please*: **polite**, courteous, well behaved, civil, gentlemanly, ladylike, genteel, decorous, respectful, refined, polished, civilized, cultivated, gracious, chivalrous, urbane, well bred, well brought up; dated mannerly.
▷ANTONYMS rude.

well-nigh adverb *policing the coastline all the time was well-nigh impossible*: **almost**, nearly, just about, about, more or less, practically, virtually, all but, as good as, next to, close to, near, nigh on, to all intents and purposes, approaching, bordering on, verging on, nearing; roughly, approximately; not quite; informal pretty nearly, pretty much, pretty well.

well off adjective **1** See **well-to-do**.
2 *the Basque shepherds were just as well off with their little woodstoves*: **fortunate**, lucky, comfortable, well placed, in a fortunate position, in a privileged position, thriving, successful, flourishing; informal sitting pretty.
▷ANTONYMS unfortunate.
3 *central Greece is not **well off for** harbours*: **well supplied with**, well stocked with, well furnished with, well equipped with; (**be well off for**) have plenty of, have enough of.
▷ANTONYMS badly off.

well read adjective *he was very **well read in** this field*: **knowledgeable (about)**, well informed (about), well versed in, widely read; erudite, scholarly, literate, educated, cultured, literary, bookish, studious; dated lettered.
▷ANTONYMS ignorant.

well spoken adjective **articulate**, nicely spoken, speaking correctly, with a nice/standard accent; refined, polite, elegant; Brit. informal posh, posh-sounding, with a posh accent.

well thought of adjective *Joe was well thought of by his employers*: **esteemed**, highly thought of, highly regarded, (well) respected, looked up to, acclaimed, admired, honoured, revered, venerated, with a good reputation, reputable, of good repute, of high standing; archaic of good report.
▷ANTONYMS disdained.

well-to-do adjective **wealthy**, rich, affluent, moneyed, with deep pockets, well off, prosperous, opulent, substantial, comfortable, propertied; of means, of substance; informal rolling in money, rolling in it, in the money, loaded, stinking rich, filthy rich, well heeled, flush, made of money, quids in, worth a packet, worth a bundle, on easy street; informal, dated oofy.

well worn adjective **1** *a well-worn leather armchair*: **shabby**, scruffy, battered, worn, old, thin, threadbare, worn out, holey, moth-eaten, mangy, ragged, frayed, tattered, falling apart at the seams, in shreds, in tatters, falling to pieces, decrepit, having seen better days; informal tatty, ratty, the worse for wear; N. Amer. informal raggedy, raggedy-ass; Austral. informal warby; rare out at elbows.
▷ANTONYMS pristine.
2 *a well-worn argument*: **stale**, hackneyed, clichéd, stock, trite, banal, worn out, time-worn, threadbare, hoary, tired, overused, obsolete, antiquated, old; informal played out, clapped out, old hat.
▷ANTONYMS novel.

welter noun *a welter of confused sounds*: **confusion**, jumble, tangle, clutter, mess, hotchpotch, mishmash, flurry, rush, mass.

wend verb *they **wended their way** across the city*: **meander**, make one's way, wind one's way, find one's way, pick one's way; wander, potter, amble, stroll, saunter, drift, roam, breeze, float, cruise, swan, waltz, traipse, trog; go, proceed, travel, move, pass, walk, journey; perambulate; informal mosey, toddle, truck, bat.

west noun (**the West**) **the Occident**.
▷ANTONYMS the East.
▶ adjective *the Scottish west coast | a west wind*: **western**, westerly, westwardly, occidental.
▷ANTONYMS east.
▶ adverb *the Great Black cockatoo never ventures further west than New Guinea and northern Queensland*: **to the west**, westward, westwards, westwardly.
▷ANTONYMS east.

wet adjective **1** *he draped his wet clothes in front of the stove | their feet sank into the wet ground*: **damp**, dampened, moist, moistened; **soaked**, drenched, saturated, wet through, sopping/dripping/wringing wet, sopping, dripping, soggy; waterlogged, squelchy, marshy, boggy, swampy, miry.
▷ANTONYMS dry.
2 *it was cold and wet that day*: **rainy**, raining, pouring, teeming, showery, drizzly, drizzling; damp, humid, dank, misty.
▷ANTONYMS dry, fine.
3 *the paint is still wet*: **sticky**, not set, not hardened, not hard, tacky; fresh.
▷ANTONYMS dry, set, hard.
4 *a wet mortar mix*: **aqueous**, watery, sloppy.
▷ANTONYMS dry.
5 Brit. informal *they thought the cadets were a bit wet*: **feeble**, **silly**, weak, foolish, inept, ineffective, ineffectual, effete, soft, namby-pamby, timid, timorous, spiritless, cowardly, spineless; informal sissy, sissified, pathetic, drippy, wimpish, wimpy, weedy, daft, chicken, yellow-bellied.
▷ANTONYMS strong; brave.
▶ verb *wet the clothes before ironing them*: **dampen**, damp, moisten, humidify; sprinkle, spray, splash; **soak**, saturate, waterlog, flood, deluge, douse, souse, drench; hose down, water, irrigate; technical ret; Scottish & N. English drouk; archaic sop.
▷ANTONYMS dry.
▶ noun **1** *I could feel the wet of his tears*: **wetness**, damp, dampness, moisture, moistness; clamminess, sogginess; wateriness, water, liquid.
2 *the race was held in the wet*: **rain**, rains, drizzle, wet/rainy/showery/damp

weather, precipitation, spray, dew, damp.
3 Brit. informal *come on, don't be such a wet*: **namby-pamby**, weakling, milksop, Milquetoast, baby; coward, mouse; informal wimp, weed, drip, mummy's boy, mollycoddle, sissy, softie, jellyfish, chicken, yellow-belly, fraidy-cat, scaredy-cat; Brit. informal big girl's blouse, jessie; N. Amer. informal candy-ass, cupcake, pantywaist, pussy; Austral./NZ informal sook; archaic poltroon.

Word toolkit

wet	damp	moist
weather	cloth	eyes
grass	basement	skin
sand	cave	towelette
snow	climate	gauze
dog	walls	breath

wetness noun **moisture**, moistness, dampness, damp; condensation, steam, vapour, humidity, mugginess, clamminess, dankness, sogginess; wateriness, wet, water, liquid.
▷ANTONYMS dryness.

whack informal verb *his attacker whacked him on the head*: **hit**, beat, strike, punch, knock, rap, smack, slap, thump, thwack, crack, cudgel, thrash, bang, drub, welt, cuff, buffet, pummel, box someone's ears; informal bash, clobber, clout, clip, wallop, belt, tan, biff, bop, lay into, pitch into, lace into, let someone have it, knock into the middle of next week, sock, lam, whomp; Brit. informal stick one on, slosh; N. Amer. informal boff, bust, slug, light into, whale; Austral./NZ informal dong, quilt; literary smite, swinge.
▶noun **1** *one of his mates got a whack with a stick*: **blow**, hit, punch, thump, thwack, crack, smack, slap, bang, welt, cuff, box; informal bash, clobber, clout, clip, wallop, belt, biff, bop, sock, lam, whomp; Brit. informal slosh; N. Amer. informal boff, bust, slug, whale; Austral./NZ informal dong; dated buffet.
2 Brit. informal *everyone will get their whack*: **share**, quota, portion, slice, part, allocation, ration, allowance, allotment, amount, quantity, bit, piece, percentage, proportion, section, segment, division, fraction, measure, due; informal cut, piece/slice of the cake, piece of the action, rake-off; Brit. informal divvy; rare apportionment, quantum, moiety.

whacking adjective Brit. informal *we weren't prepared to pay a whacking salary*: **huge**, massive, enormous, gigantic, very big, very large, great, giant, colossal, mammoth, vast, immense, tremendous, mighty, stupendous, monumental, epic, prodigious, mountainous, monstrous, titanic, towering, elephantine, king-sized, king-size, gargantuan, Herculean, Brobdingnagian, substantial, extensive, hefty, bulky, weighty, heavy, gross; informal mega, monster, whopping, whopping great, thumping, thumping great, humongous, jumbo, hulking, bumper, astronomical, astronomic; Brit. informal whacking great, ginormous.

whale noun **cetacean**, leviathan.

Word links **whale**

bull male
cow female
calf young
school, pod collective noun

wharf noun **quay**, pier, dock, berth, landing stage, landing place, landing, jetty; harbour, dockyard, yard, marina; waterfront.

whatsit noun informal **thing**, so-and-so, whatever it is, whatever it is called; informal whatnot, what-d'you-call-it, what's-its-name, whatchamacallit, thingummy, thingy, thingamabob, thingamajig, oojamaflip, oojah, gizmo; Brit. informal gubbins, doings, doodah, doobry; N. Amer. informal doodad, doohickey, doojigger, dingus, hootenanny.

wheedle verb *she had wheedled us into employing her brother*: **coax**, cajole, inveigle, lure, induce, blarney, entice, charm, tempt, beguile, flatter, persuade, influence, sway, win someone over, bring someone round, prod, talk, convince, make, get, press, prevail on, get round, argue, reason, urge, pressure, pressurize, bring pressure to bear on, coerce; informal sweet-talk, soft-soap, twist someone's arm, smooth-talk, butter someone up.

wheel noun **1** *a wagon wheel*: **disc**, hoop, ring, circle.
2 *a right wheel*: **turn**, rotation, pivot, swivel, gyration.
□ **at the wheel/behind the wheel** *he was at the wheel of his Mercedes*: **driving**, steering, in the driving seat, in the driver's seat, in charge of.
▶verb **1** *she wheeled the trolley into the kitchen*: **push**, trundle, roll.
2 *a flock of doves rose up into the air, wheeled round, and flew off*: **turn**, turn round, go round, rotate, revolve, circle, orbit.

wheeze verb *the illness often leaves her wheezing*: **breathe audibly/noisily**, gasp, whistle, hiss, rasp, croak, pant, cough.
▶noun **1** *she still had a slight wheeze*: **constricted breathing**, gasp, whistle, hiss, rasp, croak, pant, cough.
2 Brit. informal *a brilliant wheeze dreamed up by the fashion industry*: **scheme**, plan, idea, tactic, move, stratagem, ploy, gambit, device, manoeuvre, contrivance, expedient; trick, dodge, subterfuge, game, wile, ruse, joke, prank, stunt; archaic shift.

whereabouts noun *his whereabouts remain secret*: **location**, position, site, place, situation, locality, spot, point, placement, locale, neighbourhood, vicinity; home, address; bearings, orientation; technical locus.

wherewithal noun *she had the wherewithal to buy anything which took her fancy*: **money**, ready money, cash, capital, finance(s), resources, funds, reserves; **means**, ability, capability; informal dough, bread, loot, the ready, readies, shekels, moolah, the necessary, wad, boodle, dibs, gelt, ducats, rhino, gravy, scratch, stuff, oof; Brit. informal dosh, brass, lolly, spondulicks, wonga, ackers; N. Amer. informal dinero, greenbacks, simoleons, bucks, jack, mazuma; Austral./NZ informal Oscar; informal, dated splosh, green, tin; Brit. dated l.s.d.; N. Amer. informal, dated kale, rocks, shinplasters; archaic pelf.

whet verb **1** *he whetted his knife on a stone*: **sharpen**, hone, put an edge on, strop, grind, file; rare edge, acuminate.
▷ANTONYMS blunt.
2 *is that enough to whet your appetite?* **stimulate**, excite, arouse, rouse, kindle, trigger, spark, quicken, waken, stir, inspire, animate, fan, fuel, fire, activate, incite, titillate, tempt, galvanize, prompt, strengthen, intensify.
▷ANTONYMS dull, spoil.

whiff noun **1** *I caught a whiff of peachy perfume*: **faint smell**, brief smell, trace, sniff, scent, odour, aroma.
2 Brit. informal *there's a terrible whiff in here*: **stench**, stink, foul smell, reek, fetidness, effluvium, miasma; Brit. informal pong, niff, hum; Brit. rhyming slang pen and ink; Scottish informal guff; N. Amer. informal funk; rare fetor, malodour, mephitis, noisomeness.
3 *there was the faintest whiff of irony in his letter*: **trace**, hint, note, suggestion, impression, suspicion, soupçon, touch, nuance, intimation, trifle, drop, dash, tinge, tincture, streak, vein, shred, crumb, shadow, breath, whisper, air, savour, flavour, element, overtone, scintilla, jot, bit, spot, speck, iota; informal smidgen, tad.
4 *whiffs of smoke emerged from the boiler*: **puff**, gust, blast, rush, flurry, gale, breath, draught, waft.

while noun *we chatted for a while*: **time**, spell, stretch, stint, span, season, interval, period, period of time, length of time, duration, run, phase, stage, term; Brit. informal patch.
▶verb *tennis and quoits helped to* ***while away*** *the time during the voyage*: **pass**, spend, occupy, use up, kill, beguile.

whim noun **1** *she bought it on a whim*: **impulse**, urge, notion, fancy, whimsy, foible, idea, caprice, conceit, vagary, kink, megrim, crotchet, craze, fad, passion, inclination, bent; archaic freak, maggot, humour, whim-wham.
2 *success depends upon something as arbitrary as human whim*: **capriciousness**, whimsy, caprice, volatility, fickleness, idiosyncrasy, eccentricity, unpredictability.

whimper verb *he fell to his knees, whimpering in pain*: **whine**, cry, sniffle, snivel, sob, moan, bleat, mewl, wail, groan; informal grizzle.
▶noun *she gave a whimper of protest*: **whine**, cry, sniffle, snivel, sob, moan, bleat, mewl, wail, groan; informal grizzle.

whimsical adjective **1** *a whimsical sense of humour*: **fanciful**, playful, mischievous, waggish, quaint, fantastic, unusual, curious, droll; eccentric, quirky, offbeat, idiosyncratic, unconventional, outlandish, peculiar, queer, bizarre, weird, odd, freakish; informal dotty, freaky.
2 *the whimsical arbitrariness of autocracy*: **volatile**, capricious, temperamental, impulsive, excitable, fickle, changeable, unpredictable, variable, erratic, quicksilver, mercurial, mutable, inconstant, inconsistent, unstable, unsteady, fluctuating, ever-changing, protean, kaleidoscopic, fluid, wavering, vacillating, wayward; technical labile.

whine noun **1** *the dog gave a small whine*: **whimper**, wail, cry, mewl, groan, moan, howl, yowl.
2 *the whine of an electric motor*: **hum**, drone, singing, note.
3 *a constant whine about the quality of public services*: **complaint**, complaining, grouse, grousing, moan, moaning, moans and groans, grouch, grouching, grumble, whining, carping, muttering, murmur, murmuring, whispering; informal gripe, griping, whinge, whingeing, bellyache, bitch, beef, beefing; N. English informal mithering.
▶verb **1** *a child was whining*: **wail**, whimper, cry, sob, mewl, groan, moan, howl, yowl.
2 *the lift began to whine*: **hum**, drone, sing.
3 *he's always whining about the state of the country*: **complain**, grouse, grouch, grumble, moan, carp, mutter, murmur, whisper; informal gripe, bellyache, bitch, beef, whinge; N. English informal mither.

whinge informal verb *I am not going to whinge about the weather*: **complain**, grouse, grouch, grumble, whine, moan, carp, mutter, murmur, whisper; informal gripe, bellyache, bitch, beef; N. English informal mither.
▶noun *his sorry tale is one long whinge about his own suffering*: **complaint**, grouse, moan, grouch, grumble, whine, carp, mutter, murmur, whisper; informal gripe, bellyache, bitch, beef; N. English informal mither.

whip noun *he would use a whip on anyone trespassing on his property*: **lash**, scourge, thong, strap, belt; crop, switch, birch, cane; historical cat-o'-nine-tails, cat, knout.

□ **the whip hand** *life became a battle over who would gain the whip hand*: **the upper hand**, a commanding position, an/the edge, an advantage, a lead, a head start, ascendancy, superiority, supremacy, sway, control, predominance, power, mastery, dominance, command; rare prepotence, prepotency, paramountcy, prepollency.

▶ **verb 1** *Lewis whipped the boy twenty times*: **flog**, scourge, flagellate, lash, birch, switch, tan, strap, belt, cane, thrash, beat, leather, tan/whip someone's hide, give someone a hiding, beat the living daylights out of.
2 *whip the cream until it forms soft peaks*: **whisk**, beat, mix, stir.
3 *the radio host whipped his listeners into a frenzy*: **rouse**, stir up, excite, galvanize, electrify, stimulate, inspire, move, fire up, fire the enthusiasm of, fire the imagination of, get someone going, inflame, agitate, goad, provoke; incite, egg on, spur on; N. Amer. light a fire under; rare inspirit.
4 informal *Cleveland whipped Los Angeles 28–16 in the third game of last season*. See **trounce** (sense 1).
5 informal *he whipped round the corner*. See **dash** (sense 1 of the verb).
6 informal *he whipped out a revolver*: **pull**, whisk, snatch, pluck, tug, jerk, remove, take; produce; informal yank.
7 Brit. informal *they whipped the cones from a building site*. See **steal** (sense 1 of the verb).
□ **whip something up** *we tried hard to whip up interest in the products*: **stimulate, rouse**, arouse, stir up, work up, wake, waken, awaken, quicken, inspire, call forth, call/bring into being, draw forth, bring out, excite, evoke, whet, stir, provoke, spur, fire, inflame, trigger, prompt, induce, encourage, actuate, activate, touch off, spark off, set off, set going, incite, promote, engender, generate; literary enkindle.

whippersnapper noun Brit. informal **young upstart**; informal pipsqueak, squirt, stripling, brat, minx, slip of a ...; Brit. informal squit; N. Amer. informal snip; dated puppy, pup; archaic malapert.
▷**ANTONYMS** old hand.

whipping noun *whipping was to be abolished as a punishment*: **lashing**, flogging, scourging, flagellation, switching, birching, strapping, belting, caning, thrashing, tanning, hiding, beating, leathering; the lash, the scourge, the birch, the switch, the cane.

whirl verb **1** *leaves whirled in eddies of wind*: **rotate**, turn, turn round, go round, revolve, circle, wheel, orbit, pivot, swivel, gyrate, spin, roll, twirl, pirouette; Scottish birl.
2 *Sybil stood waving as they whirled past*: **hurry**, speed, race, run, sprint, dash, bolt, dart, rush, hasten, hurtle, career, streak, shoot, whizz, zoom, go like lightning, go hell for leather, spank along, bowl along, rattle along, whoosh, buzz, swoop, flash, blast, charge, stampede, gallop, sweep, hare, fly, wing, scurry, scud, scutter, scramble; informal belt, pelt, tear, hotfoot it, leg it, zap, zip, whip, scoot, go like a bat out of hell; Brit. informal bomb, bucket, shift, go like the clappers; Scottish informal wheech; N. Amer. informal clip, boogie, hightail, barrel; N. Amer. vulgar slang drag/tear/haul ass; literary fleet; archaic post, hie.
3 *his mind was whirling*: **spin**, reel, go round, be in a whirl, swim, be/feel giddy, be/feel dizzy.
▶ **noun 1** *he was gone in a whirl of dust*: **swirl**, flurry, eddy.
2 *all part of the mad social whirl*: **hurly-burly**, hectic activity, bustle, rush, flurry, to-do, fuss, panic, turmoil; archaic hurry scurry.
3 *her life was a whirl of parties*: **succession**, series, sequence, progression, string, chain, cycle, round, merry-go-round.
4 *Laura's mind was in a whirl*: **spin**, daze, stupor, muddle, jumble; confusion; informal dither.
5 *the only way to find out was to give it a whirl*: **try**, try-out, test; informal go, shot, bash, stab.

whirlpool noun **1** *there was a whirlpool which appeared without warning and sucked ships down*: **eddy**, vortex, maelstrom, swirl, whirl; N. Amer. informal suckhole; literary Charybdis.
2 *we also have a sauna, Turkish bath, whirlpool, and solarium*: **spa bath**, hot tub; trademark jacuzzi.

whirlwind noun **1** *the building was hit by a hellish whirlwind*: **tornado**, hurricane, typhoon, cyclone, tropical storm, tropical cyclone, vortex; dust devil, waterspout; N. Amer. informal twister; Austral./NZ informal willy-willy.
2 *a hectic whirlwind of activity*: **bedlam**, madhouse, mayhem, maelstrom, babel, chaos, pandemonium, uproar, turmoil, turbulence, swirl, tumult, hurly-burly, commotion, disorder, jumble, disarray, confusion, seething mass, welter; informal all hell broken loose; N. Amer. three-ring circus.
▶ **adjective** *a whirlwind romance*: **rapid**, lightning, overnight, instant, headlong, impulsive, breakneck, whistle-stop, fast-track, accelerated, meteoric, sudden, swift, fast, quick, speedy; informal quickie.

whisk verb **1** *the cable car will whisk you to the top of the mountain*: **speed**, hurry, rush, catapult; sweep, hurtle, shoot.
2 *she did not have the audacity to simply whisk the cloth away*: **pull**, snatch, pluck, tug, jerk, take; remove; informal whip, yank.
3 *they just recognized him before he whisked out of sight*: **dash**, rush, tear, dart, hasten, hurry, scurry, scuttle, scamper, sprint, race, run, hare, bolt, bound, fly, gallop, career, charge, pound, shoot, hurtle, speed, streak, whizz, zoom, sweep, go like lightning, go hell for leather, go like the wind, flash, double; informal pelt, scoot, hotfoot it, leg it, belt, zip, whip, go like a bat out of hell; Brit. informal go like the clappers, bomb, bucket; Scottish informal wheech; N. Amer. informal boogie, hightail it, barrel, get the lead out; informal, dated cut along; archaic post, hie.
4 *horses whisk their tails for various purposes*: **flick**, twitch, wave, brandish.
5 *whisk the yolks with half the sugar*: **whip**, beat, stir/mix vigorously.
▶ **noun 1** *the horse gave a whisk of its tail*: **flick**, twitch, wave, sweep, swipe.
2 *combine the eggs and milk with a whisk*: **beater**, mixer, blender, swizzle stick.

whisky noun the water of life; Irish & Scottish usquebaugh; Scottish usque, screigh; informal screech; N. Amer. informal red-eye.

whisper verb **1** *Alison was whispering in his ear*: **murmur**, mutter, mumble, speak/say softly, speak/say in muted tones, speak/say in hushed tones, speak/say sotto voce; breathe, purr, say under one's breath.
▷**ANTONYMS** shout.
2 literary *the wind and the mist whispered in the grass*: **rustle**, murmur, sigh, moan, sough, whoosh, whirr, swish, blow, breathe; rare susurrate.
▷**ANTONYMS** howl, roar.
▶ **noun 1** *she spoke in a whisper*: **murmur**, mutter, mumble, low voice, hushed tone, undertone.
▷**ANTONYMS** shout.
2 literary *the hot desert wind died to a whisper*: **rustle**, murmur, sigh, moan, sough, whoosh, whirr, swish; rare susurration.
▷**ANTONYMS** howl, roar.
3 literary *the whisper of falling water*: **babble**, burble, purl, lap; literary plash.
▷**ANTONYMS** roar, thunder.
4 *I heard a whisper that he's been selling coins lately*: **rumour**, story, report, speculation, insinuation, suggestion, hint; **(whispers)** gossip, hearsay, word, scandal, tittle-tattle, idle talk; French on dit, bavardage; German Kaffeeklatsch; W. Indian labrish, shu-shu; informal buzz; Brit. informal goss; N. Amer. informal scuttlebutt; Austral./NZ informal furphy; S. African informal skinder; rare bruit.
5 *he didn't even show a whisper of interest*. See **trace** (sense 2 of the noun).

whit noun *his death wouldn't have made a whit of difference*: **scrap**, bit, tiny amount, speck, iota, particle, ounce, jot, atom, crumb, shred, morsel, trifle, fragment, grain, drop, touch, trace, shadow, suggestion, whisper, suspicion, scintilla, spot, mite, tittle, jot or tittle, modicum; Irish stim; informal smidgen, smidge; archaic scantling, scruple.

white adjective **1** *a clean white bandage*: **colourless**, unpigmented, undyed, bleached, natural; snowy, milky, chalky, snow-white, snowy-white, milk-white, milky-white, chalk-white, chalky-white, ivory; pale, clear, transparent.
▷**ANTONYMS** black.
2 *her face was white with fear*: **pale**, pallid, wan, ashen, white as a ghost/sheet, grey, anaemic, jaundiced, colourless, bloodless, waxen, chalky, chalk-white, milky, pasty, pasty-faced, whey-faced, peaky, sickly, tired-looking, washed out, sallow, drained, drawn, sapped, ghostly, deathly, deathlike, bleached; rare etiolated.
▷**ANTONYMS** healthy; ruddy; tanned.
3 *he had a mane of white hair*: **snowy**, snowy-white, grey, silver, silvery, hoary, grizzled; albino.
4 *the early white settlers of Australia*: **Caucasian**, European, non-black.
5 *a whiter than white, no-sleaze government*: **virtuous**, moral, ethical, good, righteous, angelic, saintly, pious, honourable, reputable, wholesome, clean, honest, upright, upstanding, exemplary, beyond/above reproach, irreproachable, innocent; decent, worthy, noble; blameless, guiltless, sinless, stainless, spotless, immaculate, impeccable, unsullied, unblemished, unspoilt, unaffected, uncorrupted, untainted, undefiled; informal squeaky clean.
▷**ANTONYMS** immoral.

> *Word links* **white**
>
> **leuc-, leuk-** related prefixes, as in *leucocyte, leukaemia*

white-collar adjective *white-collar workers*: **non-manual**, office, clerical, professional, executive, salaried; technical ABC1.

whiten verb *snow whitened the mountain tops | her knuckles whitened*: **make/become white**, make/become pale, bleach, blanch, lighten, fade, wash out, be washed out, etiolate; Brit. Military blanco; archaic white.
▷**ANTONYMS** blacken, darken, colour.

whitewash noun *the report was dismissed as a whitewash*: **cover-up**, -gate, camouflage, disguise, mask, concealment, suppression, deception, false front, facade, veneer, pretext.
▷**ANTONYMS** exposé.
▶ **verb** *I just want to make sure they don't whitewash what happened*: **cover up**, sweep under the carpet, hush up, suppress, draw/pull a veil over, conceal, camouflage, keep secret, keep dark, cloak, screen, veil, obscure; gloss over, deal rapidly with, downplay, make light of, soft-pedal, minimize, de-emphasize, treat as unimportant.
▷**ANTONYMS** expose.

whittle verb **1** *he sat whittling a piece of wood with a knife*: **pare**, shave, peel, cut, hew, trim, carve, shape, model.
2 *the powers of the papacy were gradually* ***whittled away***: **erode**, wear away, eat away, consume, use up, reduce, diminish, undermine, weaken, threaten, sabotage, subvert, compromise, destroy, impair, mar, spoil, ruin, impede, hinder, damage, hurt, injure, cripple, disable, enfeeble, emasculate, sap, shake, break, crush.
▷ANTONYMS increase.
3 *the ten teams in contention have been* ***whittled down*** *to six*: **reduce**, cut down, cut back, cut, prune, trim, slim down, pare down, shrink, make cutbacks in, lessen, decrease, diminish, make reductions in, scale down.
▷ANTONYMS augment.

whole adjective **1** *they refused to publish the whole report*: **entire**, complete, full, total; unabridged, full-length, uncut, uncondensed, unexpurgated, unreduced, undivided.
▷ANTONYMS partial, incomplete.
2 *they discovered a whole marble mantelpiece*: **intact**, in one piece, sound, unbroken; unimpaired, undamaged, unharmed, unhurt, untouched, uninjured, unscathed, unmutilated, inviolate, flawless, faultless, unmarked, unspoilt, perfect, mint, pristine.
▷ANTONYMS in pieces, broken.
▸ noun **1** *the two movements had been fused into a single whole*: **entity**, unit, body, piece, discrete item, ensemble, combination, package, conglomeration, object; totality, entirety, unity.
2 *it may take* ***the whole*** *of the year*: **all**, every part, everything, the lot, the sum, the sum total, the aggregate.
□ **on the whole** *on the whole they lived peaceably*: **overall**, all in all, all things considered, altogether, taking everything into consideration/account, on balance, on average, for the most part, mostly, mainly, in the main, chiefly, principally, predominantly, largely, in general, generally, generally speaking, as a rule, as a general rule, in the general run of things, by and large, to a large extent, to a great degree, basically, substantially, effectively, virtually, to all intents and purposes; **normally**, usually, more often than not, almost always, most of the time, habitually, customarily, regularly, typically, ordinarily, commonly.

Word links **whole**

holo- related prefix, as in *holocaust, Holocene*

wholehearted adjective *you have my wholehearted support*: **committed**, positive, emphatic, devoted, dedicated, enthusiastic, unshakeable, unflinching, unswerving, constant, staunch, loyal, stalwart; **unqualified**, unreserved, unlimited, without reservations, unconditional, categorical, unequivocal, unambiguous, unrestricted, unmitigated, unadulterated, undiluted, unalloyed, unstinting; complete, full, total, absolute, undivided, entire, solid, thorough, thoroughgoing, utter, outright, out-and-out.
▷ANTONYMS half-hearted, qualified, partial.

wholesale adverb *images were removed from churches wholesale*: **extensively**, on a large scale, comprehensively, thoroughly; **indiscriminately**, undiscriminatingly, without exception, across the board.
▷ANTONYMS partially, selectively.
▸ adjective *the wholesale destruction of a city*: **extensive**, widespread, large-scale, wide-ranging, far-reaching, comprehensive, all-inclusive, total, outright, thorough, sweeping, blanket, broad, mass; indiscriminate.
▷ANTONYMS partial, selective.

wholesome adjective **1** *wholesome food*: **healthy**, health-giving, healthful, good, good for one, beneficial, sustaining, strengthening, nutritious, nourishing, full of nourishment, full of nutrients, nutritive, unrefined; natural, uncontaminated, organic, additive-free; rare nutrimental, nutrient, alimentary, alible.
2 *good wholesome fun*: **moral**, ethical, good, nice, clean, virtuous, pure, innocent, chaste; uplifting, edifying, improving, non-erotic, non-violent, righteous, upright, upstanding, high-minded, right-minded, proper, correct, honourable, honest, just, noble, respectable, decent, simple; informal squeaky clean.

wholly adverb **1** *the budget measures were wholly inadequate*: **completely**, totally, absolutely, entirely, fully, thoroughly, utterly, quite, perfectly, altogether, downright, without qualification, without reservation, unreservedly, in every respect, in all respects, unconditionally, unconstrainedly, unrestrictedly, consummately, undisputedly, unmitigatedly, wholeheartedly, radically, stark, just, to the hilt, all the way, to the maximum extent; informal one hundred per cent.
2 *they still rely wholly on you*: **exclusively**, only, solely, purely, simply, merely, alone, to the exclusion of everything/everyone else.

whoop noun *whoops of delight*: **shout**, cry, call, yell, roar, scream, shriek, screech, hoot, hoop, cheer, hurrah; informal holler; archaic huzza.
▸ verb *he whooped for joy*: **shout**, cry, call, yell, roar, scream, shriek, screech, hoot, hoop, cheer, hurrah; informal holler; archaic huzza.
□ **whoop it up** informal *the fans started to cheer and whoop it up*: **celebrate**, rejoice, enjoy oneself, make merry, have fun, have a good/wild time, rave, party, have a party, revel, roister, carouse, kill the fatted calf, put the flag(s) out; N. Amer. step out; informal go out on the town, paint the town red, make whoopee, junket, have a night on the tiles, live it up, have a ball; Brit. informal push the boat out.

whopper noun informal **1** *the largest salmon ever caught was a 64-pound whopper*: **monster**, brute, beast, giant, colossus, mountain, behemoth, leviathan, mammoth, monstrosity; informal jumbo.
2 *Joseph's story is turning out to be a whopper*: **lie**, untruth, falsehood, fib, fabrication, deception, made-up story, trumped-up story, invention, piece of fiction, fiction, falsification, falsity, fairy story/tale, cock and bull story, barefaced lie; (little) white lie, half-truth, exaggeration, prevarication, departure from the truth; yarn, story, red herring, rumour, fable, myth, flight of fancy, figment of the imagination; pretence, pretext, sham, ruse, wile, trickery, stratagem; informal tall story, tall tale; Brit. rhyming slang pork pie, porky, porky pie; humorous terminological inexactitude.

whopping adjective informal *they made a whopping £74 million loss*: **huge**, massive, enormous, gigantic, very big, very large, great, giant, colossal, mammoth, vast, immense, tremendous, mighty, stupendous, monumental, epic, prodigious, mountainous, monstrous, titanic, towering, elephantine, king-sized, king-size, gargantuan, Herculean, Brobdingnagian, substantial, extensive, hefty, bulky, weighty, heavy, gross; informal mega, monster, whopping great, thumping, thumping great, humongous, jumbo, hulking, bumper, astronomical, astronomic; Brit. informal whacking, whacking great, ginormous.

whore noun **prostitute**, promiscuous woman, slut, sex worker, call girl, white slave; French fille de joie, demi-mondaine, grande horizontale; Spanish puta; informal tart, pro, moll, brass nail, tom, woman on the game, working girl, member of the oldest profession, tramp, floozie, scrubber, slapper; Brit. informal slag; N. Amer. informal hooker, hustler, roundheel; black English, informal ho; euphemistic model, escort, masseuse; dated streetwalker, woman of the streets, lady/woman of the night, scarlet woman, fallen woman, woman of easy virtue, cocotte, wanton, loose woman; archaic courtesan, strumpet, harlot, trollop, woman of ill repute, lady of pleasure, Cyprian, doxy, drab, quean, trull, wench.
▸ verb **1** *she spent her life whoring*: **work as a prostitute**, prostitute oneself, sell one's body, sell oneself, walk the streets, be on the streets, solicit, work in the sex industry; informal be on the game, tom, practise the oldest profession.
2 *the pilots whored and drank like madmen*: **use prostitutes**; archaic wench.

whorehouse noun informal **brothel**, bordello, house of ill repute; Law disorderly house; informal cathouse, drum; Brit. informal knocking shop; N. Amer. informal creepjoint; Austral./NZ informal crib; euphemistic massage parlour; archaic bawdy house, house of ill fame, bagnio, stew.

whorl noun *elegant whorls of wrought iron*: **loop**, coil, hoop, ring, turn, curl, twirl, twist, spiral, helix, lap, tier, lock, convolution.

wicked adjective **1** *a wicked man | a wicked deed*: **evil**, sinful, immoral, wrong, morally wrong, wrongful, bad, iniquitous, corrupt, black-hearted, ungodly, unholy, irreligious, unrighteous, sacrilegious, profane, blasphemous, impious, base, mean, vile; irreverent, villainous, nefarious, erring, fallen, impure, sullied, tainted, foul, monstrous, shocking, outrageous, atrocious, abominable, reprehensible, hateful, detestable, despicable, odious, contemptible, horrible, heinous, execrable, godless, diabolical, diabolic, fiendish, vicious, murderous, barbarous, black, dark, rotten; criminal, illicit, unlawful, illegal, illegitimate, lawless, felonious, indictable; perverted, reprobate, sordid, depraved, degenerate, dissolute, dishonourable, dishonest, unscrupulous, unprincipled, underhand, roguish; informal crooked, warped, low-down, stinking, dirty, shady, rascally, scoundrelly; Brit. informal beastly, bent, not cricket; Law malfeasant; archaic dastardly; rare peccable, egregious, flagitious.
▷ANTONYMS virtuous.
2 *the wind outside was wicked*: **disagreeable**, unpleasant, foul, fierce, bad, nasty, irksome, troublesome, annoying, irritating, vexatious, displeasing, uncomfortable, distressing, hateful, detestable, miserable, abominable, execrable, odious, invidious, objectionable.
▷ANTONYMS agreeable.
3 *a wicked sense of humour*: **mischievous**, playful, naughty, impish, roguish, arch, rascally, rakish, puckish, waggish, devilish, tricksy, cheeky, raffish, teasing.
4 informal *Sophie makes wicked cakes*: **excellent**, superb, superlative, first-rate, first-class, superior, outstanding, remarkable, dazzling, marvellous, magnificent, wonderful, splendid, admirable, noteworthy, impressive, fine, exquisite, exceptional, glorious, sublime, peerless, perfect, of the first water; informal great, fantastic, fabulous, terrific, awesome, heavenly, stellar, ace, smashing, A1, tip-top, top-notch, neat, mega, cool, banging, cracking, crucial; Brit. informal brilliant, brill, bosting; informal, dated divine.
▷ANTONYMS lousy.

wickedness noun *they had been punished for their wickedness*: **evil-doing**, evil, evilness, sin, sinfulness, iniquity, iniquitousness, vileness, foulness, baseness, badness, wrong, wrongdoing, dishonesty, double-dealing, unscrupulousness, roguery, villainy, rascality, delinquency, viciousness, degeneracy, depravity, dissolution, dissipation, immorality, vice, perversion, pervertedness, corruption, corruptness, turpitude, devilry, devilishness, fiendishness; ungodliness, godlessness, unholiness, irreligiousness, sacrilegiousness, profanity, blasphemy, impiety, impiousness, irreverence, impurity, heinousness; informal crookedness, shadiness; Law malfeasance; archaic knavery, deviltry; rare peccability, peccancy.

wide adjective **1** *a wide river | a wide road*: **broad**, extensive, spacious, open, vast, spread out, outspread.
▷ANTONYMS narrow.
2 *their mouths were wide with shock*: **fully open**, gaping, agape, wide open, yawning.
▷ANTONYMS closed.
3 *a wide range of opinion*: **comprehensive**, ample, broad, extensive, large, large-scale, vast, immense, far-ranging, wide-ranging, expansive, sweeping, encyclopedic, exhaustive, general, all-inclusive, all-embracing, universal, catholic, compendious.
▷ANTONYMS restricted, limited.
4 *wide trousers*: **baggy**, loose, capacious, roomy, ample, full, generous, generously cut, commodious, voluminous, oversize; slack, sloppy, shapeless, sack-like, ill-fitting, ballooning, billowing, floppy.
▷ANTONYMS tight.
5 *his shot was wide*: **off target**, off the mark, wide of the mark/target, inaccurate, off course, astray, nowhere near, out; informal off beam.
▷ANTONYMS on target, accurate.
▶ adverb **1** *he opened his eyes wide*: **fully**, to the fullest/furthest extent, as far/much as possible, all the way, completely.
▷ANTONYMS partly.
2 *he shot wide*: **off target**, wide of the mark/target, off course, inaccurately, astray; informal off beam.
▷ANTONYMS accurately.

wide awake adjective **fully awake**, conscious, open-eyed, not asleep, sleepless, unsleeping, insomniac; archaic watchful.
▷ANTONYMS asleep; tired.

wide-eyed adjective **1** *the whole class was wide-eyed, glued to the television*: **staring in amazement**, goggle-eyed; agape, open-mouthed, tongue-tied, at a loss for words, speechless, dumbfounded, dumbstruck; surprised, amazed, astonished, astounded, stunned, staggered, thunderstruck, aghast, stupefied, dazed, taken aback, shocked, in shock, nonplussed; informal flabbergasted, bowled over; Brit. informal gobsmacked.
2 *locals with tales to tell latch on to the wide-eyed visitor*: **innocent**, naive, impressionable, ingenuous, childlike, credulous, trusting, over-trusting, trustful, unsuspicious, unquestioning, unsuspecting, unguarded, unwary, simple, unsophisticated, inexperienced, raw, green, green as grass, jejune, gullible, easily taken in, easily deceived; informal wet behind the ears, born yesterday.
▷ANTONYMS knowing, sophisticated.

widen verb **1** *a proposal to widen the motorway | his grin widened*: **broaden**, make/become wider, open up, open out, spread, expand, extend, enlarge, stretch; fatten, distend, dilate.
▷ANTONYMS narrow.
2 *the Party must widen its support*: **increase**, augment, add to, develop, boost, swell, supplement, amplify, enlarge, make larger/bigger/greater.
▷ANTONYMS restrict, limit.

wide open adjective **1** *his eyes were wide open*: **fully open**, open wide, gaping, agape, yawning, cavernous.
▷ANTONYMS shut.
2 *the championship race is wide open*: **unpredictable**, **uncertain**, unsure, indeterminate, undetermined, unsettled, unforeseeable, in the balance, up in the air; informal anyone's guess.
▷ANTONYMS settled.
3 *they were* ***wide open to*** *fighter attacks*: **vulnerable**, exposed; unprotected, unguarded, defenceless, undefended, at risk, in danger, endangered; rare pregnable.
▷ANTONYMS well protected.

widespread adjective *there is widespread concern about the outcome*: **general**, extensive, universal, common, global, worldwide, international, omnipresent, ubiquitous, wholesale, all-embracing, all-inclusive, all-round, across the board, far-reaching, predominant, prevalent, rife, broad, blanket, sweeping, rampant, catholic, inescapable, pervading, pervasive, permeating, epidemic; rare preponderate.
▷ANTONYMS local; limited.

width noun **1** *the width of the river*: **wideness**, breadth, broadness, thickness, spread, span, diameter, girth; technical calibre, gauge; Nautical beam.
▷ANTONYMS length.
2 *candidates under the age of 30 are unlikely to have the width of experience required*: **range**, breadth, compass, scope, span, scale, sweep, extent, extensiveness, vastness, immensity, immenseness, expansiveness, comprehensiveness, compendiousness; rare catholicity.
▷ANTONYMS narrowness.

wield verb **1** *one of our assailants was wielding a sword*: **brandish**, flourish, wave, twirl, display, flaunt, hold aloft, show off, swing, shake; use, put to use, employ, handle, ply, manipulate, operate.
2 *he had wielded power since the coup in 1972*: **exercise**, exert, be possessed of, have, have at one's disposal, hold, maintain, command, control, manage, be in charge of.

wife noun **spouse**, partner, mate, consort, woman, bride; informal old lady, wifey, one's better half, the missus, the little woman, WAGs (wives and girlfriends); Brit. informal one's other half, her indoors, (old) dutch; Brit. rhyming slang trouble and strife; dated lady, memsahib; archaic helpmate, helpmeet.

> *Word links* **wife**
>
> **uxorial** relating to a wife
> **uxoricide** killing of one's wife

wiggle verb *she wiggled her toes*: **jiggle**, wriggle, twitch, flutter, shimmy, joggle, wag, wobble, shake, twist, squirm, writhe, wave, quiver, jerk, bobble; informal waggle.

wild adjective **1** *wild animals*: **untamed**, undomesticated, feral; unbroken; fierce, ferocious, savage.
▷ANTONYMS tame.
2 *wild flowers*: **uncultivated**, natural; native, indigenous; technical agrestal.
▷ANTONYMS cultivated, hothouse.
3 *a wild tribe*: **primitive**, uncivilized, uncultured, uncultivated, uneducated, ignorant; savage, barbarous, barbaric, brutish, ferocious, fierce; Indian jungli; archaic rude.
▷ANTONYMS civilized.
4 *a tract of wild hill country*: **uninhabited**, unpopulated, uncultivated, unfarmed, unmanaged, virgin; **rugged**, rough, inhospitable, desolate, empty, deserted, trackless, waste, barren.
5 *a wild night | the wild sea*: **stormy**, squally, tempestuous, turbulent, blustery, windy, howling, raging, roaring, furious, violent; angry, dirty, foul, nasty, inclement; rough, storm-tossed, choppy, boiling; rare boisterous.
▷ANTONYMS calm.
6 *her wild black hair*: **dishevelled**, tousled, tangled, windswept; windblown, untidy, messy, disordered, disarranged; uncombed, unkempt; N. Amer. mussed up.
▷ANTONYMS tidy, sleek.
7 *he had a reputation for wild behaviour*: **uncontrolled**, unrestrained, out of control, undisciplined, unconstrained, uncurbed, unbridled, unchecked, chaotic; uninhibited, extrovert, unconventional; wayward, self-willed, ungovernable, unmanageable, unruly, rowdy, disorderly, riotous, lawless; rare corybantic.
▷ANTONYMS self-disciplined.
8 *the crowd was wild with excitement*: **very excited**, jumping up and down, on fire, delirious, in a frenzy, frantic; uproarious, tumultuous, passionate, vehement, eager, unrestrained, untrammelled.
▷ANTONYMS calm.
9 informal *I was wild with jealousy*: **distraught**, frantic, beside oneself, not knowing what to do with oneself, frenzied, in a frenzy, hysterical, crazed, deranged, berserk; informal mad, crazy.
10 informal *Hank's going to be wild when he finds out*: **furious**, very angry, infuriated, incensed, enraged, beside oneself, irate, fuming, in a rage, raging, seething, maddened, exasperated; informal livid, mad, hopping mad, seeing red, hot under the collar, up in arms, foaming at the mouth, on the warpath, steamed up, fit to be tied; Brit. informal spare; Scottish informal radge.
▷ANTONYMS pleased.
11 informal *his family weren't exactly* ***wild about*** *me*: **very keen on**, very enthusiastic about, passionate about, enamoured of, infatuated with, smitten with; informal crazy about, mad about, nutty/nuts about, potty about, gone on.
▷ANTONYMS unenthusiastic, indifferent.
12 *Bill's wild schemes*: **madcap**, ridiculous, ludicrous, foolish, stupid, lunatic, foolhardy, idiotic, absurd, silly, asinine, unwise, ill-advised, ill-considered, ill-conceived, illogical, senseless, nonsensical; impractical, impracticable, unpractical, unworkable, imprudent, reckless, preposterous, outrageous; extravagant, fantastical, fantastic, fanciful; informal crazy, crackpot, crackbrained, cock-eyed; Brit. informal daft.
▷ANTONYMS sensible, practical.
13 *a wild guess*: **random**, arbitrary, hit-or-miss, haphazard, uninformed; informal shot-in-the-dark.
▷ANTONYMS considered.
□ **run wild 1** *the vegetable garden had been allowed to run wild*: **grow unchecked**, grow profusely, run riot, spread like wildfire, ramble, straggle.
2 *children in the city are running wild*: **run free**, **run amok**, run riot, get out of control, cut loose, be undisciplined, go on the rampage; Austral. go bush; informal raise hell; N. Amer. informal go postal.

wilderness noun **1** *the Siberian wilderness of Kamchatka*: **wilds**, wastes, uninhabited region, inhospitable region, uncultivated region, badlands; jungle; desert; S. African bundu.
2 *a litter-strewn north London wilderness*: **wasteland**, neglected area, abandoned area, no-man's-land.
3 *a wilderness of boxes, suitcases, and trunks*: **jumble**, muddle, clutter, confusion.

wildlife noun (wild) animals, fauna; flora and fauna.

wilds plural noun *he spent a year in the wilds of Canada*: **remote areas**, wilderness; backwoods, hinterlands; N. Amer. backcountry, backland; Austral./NZ outback, bush, backblocks, booay; S. African backveld, platteland; N. Amer. informal boondocks, boonies, tall timbers; Austral./NZ informal Woop Woop, beyond the black stump.

wiles plural noun *feminine wiles*: **tricks**, ruses, ploys, schemes, dodges, manoeuvres, gambits, subterfuges, cunning stratagems, artifices, devices, contrivances; guile, artfulness, art, cunning, craftiness.

wilful adjective **1** *the wilful destruction of property*: **deliberate**, intentional, intended, done on purpose, premeditated, planned, calculated, purposeful, conscious, knowing; voluntary, volitional.
▷ANTONYMS accidental, unintentional.
2 *a spoiled and wilful child*: **headstrong**, self-willed, strong-willed, with a will of one's own, determined to have one's own way; **obstinate**, stubborn, as stubborn as a mule, mulish, pig-headed, bull-headed, refractory, recalcitrant, uncooperative, intractable, obstreperous, contrary, perverse, wayward, defiant, disobedient, ungovernable, unmanageable, rebellious, mutinous, insubordinate; Scottish thrawn; informal cussed; Brit. informal bloody-minded, bolshie; N. Amer. informal balky; archaic froward, contumacious; rare contrarious, renitent, pervicacious.
▷ANTONYMS biddable, amenable.

> *Choose the right word* **wilful, obstinate, stubborn, headstrong**
>
> See **obstinate**.

will¹ verb *accidents will happen*: **have a tendency to**, are bound to, have a habit of, do.

will² noun **1** *she has the will to succeed | a stupendous effort of will*: **determination**, firmness of purpose, fixity of purpose, will power, strength of character, resolution, resolve, resoluteness, purposefulness, single-mindedness, drive, commitment, dedication, doggedness, tenacity, tenaciousness, staying power, backbone, spine; self-control, self-restraint, self-discipline, self-mastery; volition; German Sitzfleisch; informal stickability; N. Amer. informal stick-to-it-iveness; rare perseveration.
2 *Jane had not wanted them to stay against their will | the political will of the electorate*: **desire**, wish, preference, inclination, mind, disposition; intention, intent.
3 *they believed it to be God's will*: **wish**, desire, decision, choice, intention; decree, ordinance, command, dictate.
4 *freedom of the will*: **volition**, choice, option, decision, discretion, prerogative.
5 *his late father's will*: **testament**, last will and testament, last wishes; bequest(s).
□ **at will** *he seemed to think he could walk in and out of my life at will*: **as one pleases**, as one wishes, as one thinks fit, to suit oneself, at one's pleasure, at one's inclination/discretion, at whim.
▸ verb **1** *do what you will—it makes no difference to me*: **want**, wish, desire, please, see/think fit, think best, like, feel like; choose, prefer.
2 *God willed it*: **decree**, order, ordain, command, direct; intend, wish, want.
3 *she willed the money to her husband*: **bequeath**, leave, give, hand down, hand on, pass on, settle on, make over, transfer, gift; Law devise.

willing adjective **1** *I'm perfectly willing to give it a try | a crowd of willing helpers*: **ready**, **prepared**, disposed, inclined, nothing loath, of a mind, so minded, minded, in the mood; happy, glad, pleased; eager, keen, enthusiastic; consenting, agreeable, amenable, accommodating, obliging, compliant, acquiescent; informal game.
▷ANTONYMS unwilling, reluctant, disinclined.
2 *there was no lack of willing help*: **readily given**, gladly given, willingly given, promptly given, ungrudging.
▷ANTONYMS grudging.

willingly adverb *Joe had gone with her willingly | those who willingly gave their time to help us*: **voluntarily**, of one's own free will, of one's own accord, of one's own volition, by choice; readily, without hesitation, without reluctance, ungrudgingly, cheerfully, happily, gladly, with pleasure, with good grace, eagerly, enthusiastically; freely, spontaneously, unforced; informal at the drop of a hat, like a shot.
▷ANTONYMS reluctantly, unwillingly.

willingness noun *many people have expressed a willingness to help*: **readiness**, preparedness, disposition, inclination, will, wish, desire; eagerness, keenness, enthusiasm.
▷ANTONYMS reluctance, unwillingness.

willowy adjective *a willowy blonde*: **tall**, **slim**, slender, lean, svelte, lissom, sylphlike, snake-hipped, rangy, long-limbed, clean-limbed, graceful, lithe, loose-limbed; informal slinky; rare gracile, attenuate.
▷ANTONYMS short, fat.

will power noun *it took every ounce of will power she possessed not to give in*: **determination**, strength of will, strength of character, firmness of purpose, fixity of purpose, resolution, resolve, resoluteness, purposefulness, single-mindedness, drive, commitment, dedication, doggedness, tenacity, tenaciousness, staying power, backbone, spine; self-control, self-restraint, self-discipline, self-mastery; German Sitzfleisch; informal stickability; N. Amer. informal stick-to-it-iveness; rare perseveration.

willy-nilly adverb **1** *cars and trucks were parked willy-nilly*: **haphazardly**, at random, randomly, without planning, without method.
2 *it is becoming painfully obvious that we are, willy-nilly, in a totally new situation*: **whether one likes it or not**, of necessity, necessarily; one way or the other; Latin nolens volens; informal like it or not, like it or lump it; formal perforce.

wilt verb **1** *the roses had begun to wilt*: **droop**, sag, become limp, become flaccid, flop; wither, shrivel (up).
▷ANTONYMS thrive, flourish.
2 *people were wilting in the heat*: **languish**, flag, lose energy, become listless, feel weak/faint; droop, sag.
▷ANTONYMS perk up.
3 *Shelley's happy mood wilted*: **diminish**, dwindle, lessen, grow less, fade, ebb, wane, weaken; evaporate, melt away, disappear.

wily adjective *a wily old rascal*: **shrewd**, clever, sharp, sharp-witted, astute, canny, smart; **crafty**, cunning, artful, sly, scheming, calculating, guileful, disingenuous, devious, Machiavellian; deceitful, deceptive, dishonest, cheating, double-dealing; informal tricky, foxy; Brit. informal fly; Scottish & N. English informal pawky; N. Amer. informal heads-up; S. African informal slim; archaic subtle; rare vulpine, carny.
▷ANTONYMS naive, guileless.

wimp noun informal **coward**, namby-pamby, milksop, Milquetoast, mouse, weakling; informal drip, sissy, weed, doormat, wuss, pansy, jellyfish, crybaby, scaredy-cat, chicken; Brit. informal wet, mummy's boy, big girl's blouse, jessie, chinless wonder, cream puff, yellow-belly; N. Amer. informal candy-ass, cupcake, pantywaist, nebbish, pussy; Austral./NZ informal sook; S. African informal moffie; archaic poltroon.

win verb **1** *Steve has won the Isle of Man race three times*: **come first in**, finish first in, be victorious in, triumph in, take first prize in, achieve success in, be successful in, prevail in; informal wrap up.
▷ANTONYMS lose.
2 *she was determined to win*: **come first**, finish first, be the winner, be victorious, be the victor, carry/win the day, carry all before one, defeat/overcome the opposition, take the honours/crown, gain the palm, come out ahead, come out on top, succeed, triumph, prevail, achieve mastery; sweep the board, make a clean sweep; informal win out, clean up.
▷ANTONYMS lose, be beaten.
3 *he won a £20,000 cash prize*: **secure**, gain, achieve, attain, earn, obtain, acquire, procure, get, collect, pick up, walk away/off with, come away with, carry off; receive; informal land, net, bag, bank, pot, scoop.
4 *Ilona seems to have won his heart*: **captivate**, steal, gain.
□ **win someone round/over** *Daisy made heroic efforts to win him round*: **persuade**, talk round, bring round, convince, induce, sway, prevail on.
▸ noun *a 3–0 win over Birmingham*: **victory**, triumph, conquest, success.
▷ANTONYMS defeat.

wince verb *he winced as she dabbed disinfectant on the cut*: **grimace**, pull a face; **flinch**, blench, start, draw back, shrink away, recoil, cringe, squirm.
▸ noun *a wince of pain*: **grimace**; flinch, start.

winch noun *the winch was once used to haul goods and furniture into the building*: **crane**, derrick, hoist, davit, windlass, tackle, block and tackle, lifting gear, hoisting gear, system of pulleys, sheave; Nautical sheer legs.
▸ verb *the crew were winched to safety along the rope*: **haul**, pull, drag, hoist, crane, lift, tug, heave, trail, draw, tow, manhandle; archaic hale.

wind¹ (rhymes with 'tinned') noun **1** *the slender pine trees were swaying in the wind*: **breeze**; air current, current of air; gale, hurricane; draught; informal blow; literary zephyr.
2 *he waited while Jez got his wind back*: **breath**; informal puff.
3 *you do talk a lot of wind*: **nonsense**, balderdash, gibberish, claptrap, blarney, blather, blether; informal hogwash, baloney, tripe, drivel, bilge, bosh, bull, bunk, rot, hot air, eyewash, piffle, poppycock, phooey, hooey, malarkey, twaddle, guff; boastful talk, bombast, bluster, fanfaronade; Brit. informal codswallop, cobblers, stuff and nonsense, tosh, taradiddle, cock, cack; Scottish & N. English informal havers; Irish informal codology; N. Amer. informal garbage, flapdoodle, blathers, wack, bushwa; informal, dated bunkum, tommyrot; literary rodomontade, braggadocio; vulgar slang shit, crap, bullshit, bollocks, balls; Austral./NZ vulgar slang bulldust.
4 **flatulence**, flatus, gas; technical borborygmus.
5 *a concerto for piano, violin, and wind*: **wind instruments**..
□ **get wind of** informal *White House officials got wind of the plan*: **hear about/of**, learn of, find out about, become aware of, be made aware of, be told about, be informed of, hear tell of, have brought to one's notice; informal hear something on the grapevine.
□ **in the wind** *there is trouble in the wind*: **on the way**, coming, about to happen, in the offing, in the air, close at hand, on the horizon, approaching, imminent, impending, looming, brewing, afoot; likely, probable; informal on the cards.

□ **put the wind up someone** Brit. informal *stop playing silly buggers—you're putting the wind up me*: **scare**, frighten, make afraid, make nervous, throw into a panic, panic, alarm, unnerve; informal give someone the heebie-jeebies; N. Amer. informal spook.
▷ANTONYMS reassure.

> *Word links* **wind**
>
> **aeolian** relating to the wind
> **anemo-** related prefix, as in *anemotropic*
> **anemometer** instrument for measuring wind speed

wind² (rhymes with 'mind') **verb 1** *the road winds up through the mountainside to the village*: **twist and turn**, twist, turn, bend, curve, loop, zigzag, weave, snake, meander, ramble; swerve, veer.
2 *he wound a towel around his midriff* | *he wound a lock of her hair round his fingers*: **wrap**, furl, fold; entwine, lace, wreathe.
3 *Anne wound the wool into a ball*: **coil**, roll, twist, twine; reel.
□ **wind down 1** informal *he needed to wind down after the spiralling tensions of the day*: **relax**, unwind, calm down, cool down/off, ease up/off, take it easy, rest, put one's feet up; informal de-stress, let it all hang out, unbutton; N. Amer. informal hang loose, stay loose, chill out, chill, kick back. **2** *the campaign was winding down*: **draw to a close**, come to an end, tail off, taper off, diminish, lessen, dwindle, decline; **slacken off**, slack off, slow down.
▷ANTONYMS escalate.
□ **wind something down** *a decision was taken to wind down the property development business*: **bring to a close/end**, wind up, run down, close down, phase out; N. Amer. close out.
▷ANTONYMS expand.
□ **wind up** informal *it's no wonder he wound up in hospital*: **end up**, finish up, find oneself, land up, land oneself; informal fetch up.
□ **wind someone up 1** Brit. informal *I knew Katie was just winding me up*: **tease**, make fun of, chaff; annoy, vex; informal take the mickey out of, send up, rib, josh, kid, have on, pull someone's leg, rag; N. Amer. informal goof on, rag on, put on, pull someone's chain, razz, fun, shuck; Austral./NZ informal poke mullock at, poke borak at, sling off at; Brit. vulgar slang take the piss out of; dated make sport of, twit. **2** *Alan was getting hot under the collar—David seemed to be winding him up on purpose*: **annoy**, anger, irritate, exasperate, get/put someone's back up, nettle, pique, get on someone's nerves, ruffle someone's feathers; provoke, goad, work up, make tense; informal aggravate, rile, niggle, get in someone's hair, get to, bug, miff, peeve, get under someone's skin, get up someone's nose, hack off; Brit. informal rub up the wrong way, nark, get across; N. Amer. informal ride; vulgar slang piss off.
□ **wind something up 1** *Richard wound up the meeting just before noon*: **conclude**, bring to an end/close, end, terminate, finish; tie up, tie up the loose ends of; informal wrap up. ▷ANTONYMS open, begin. **2** *the company has since been wound up*: **close (down)**, dissolve, liquidate, put into liquidation.

winded adjective *he lay there for a moment, winded*: **out of breath**, breathless, gasping for breath, panting, puffing, huffing and puffing, puffing and blowing; informal puffed out, out of puff.

windfall noun *a £43,000 windfall*: **bonanza**, jackpot, pennies from heaven, unexpected gain; piece/stroke of good luck, godsend, manna from heaven.

winding noun *the windings of the stream*: **twist**, turn, turning, bend, loop, curve, zigzag, convolution, meander, meandering; oxbow; rare anfractuosity, flexuosity.
▶ **adjective** *the winding country roads*: **twisting and turning**, full of twists and turns, meandering, windy, twisty, bending, curving, looping, zigzag, zigzagging, serpentine, sinuous, snaking, snaky, tortuous, convoluted; circuitous, roundabout, indirect; rare anfractuous, flexuous, meandrous, serpentiform.
▷ANTONYMS straight.

> *Word toolkit* **winding**
>
> See **serpentine**.

window noun casement, opening, aperture.

windpipe noun trachea, pharynx; throat; archaic weasand.

> *Word links* **windpipe**
>
> **tracheal** relating to the windpipe

windswept adjective 1 *the windswept moors*: **exposed**, unprotected, bleak, bare, desolate; windy, blowy.
▷ANTONYMS sheltered.
2 *his windswept hair*: **dishevelled**, tousled, unkempt, windblown, untidy, messy, disordered, disarranged; N. Amer. mussed up.
▷ANTONYMS tidy, sleek.

windy adjective 1 *a windy day*: **breezy**, blowy, fresh, blustery, gusty; wild, stormy, squally, tempestuous, turbulent; rare boisterous, blusterous.
▷ANTONYMS still, windless.
2 *the cold windy hills*: **windswept**, exposed, unprotected, open to the elements, bare, bleak.
▷ANTONYMS sheltered.
3 informal *a series of windy speeches*: **verbose**, long-winded, wordy, prolix, lengthy, overlong, prolonged, protracted, long-drawn-out, tedious; talkative, garrulous, voluble, loquacious; rambling, meandering, repetitious, tautological, periphrastic, circumlocutory, tortuous; rare pleonastic.
▷ANTONYMS concise, succinct.
4 Brit. informal *she felt a bit windy about his visit*: **nervous**, **anxious**, worried, apprehensive, on edge, edgy, tense, stressed, fretful, uneasy, jumpy, with one's stomach in knots; frightened, scared, afraid, fearful; informal with butterflies in one's stomach, jittery, twitchy, trepidatious, in a state, uptight, in a stew, in a dither, all of a dither, in a sweat, in a flap, in a tizz/tizzy, all of a lather, het up, in a twitter; Brit. informal strung up, all of a doodah; N. Amer. informal spooky, squirrelly, in a twit; Austral./NZ informal toey; dated overstrung.
▷ANTONYMS calm, unperturbed.

wine noun French vin de table, vin ordinaire, vin du pays; informal plonk, vino, the grape.

> *Word links* **wine**
>
> **vinous** relating to wine
> **oeno-** related prefix, as in *oenophile*
> **viniculture** wine production
> **oenology** study of wine

wing noun 1 *a bird's wings*: literary pinion, van; rare pennon.
2 *the east wing of the house*: **part**, section, side; annexe, extension; N. Amer. ell.
3 *the radical wing of the party*: **faction**, camp, caucus, arm, side, branch, group, grouping, section, set, clique, coterie, cabal; fringe movement; lobby.
▶ **verb 1** *a solitary seagull **winged its way** over the sea*: **fly**, glide, soar; take wing.
2 *there was a high-pitched whistle as the bomb winged along its trajectory*: **hurtle**, speed, shoot, whizz, zoom, streak, sweep, fly, race; sail.
3 *she was shot at and winged by border guards*: **wound**, graze, hit, clip.
□ **wing it** informal *there were no guidelines—I just had to wing it*: **improvise**, play it by ear, extemporize, ad lib; informal busk it.

> *Word links* **wing**
>
> **ptero-** related prefix, as in *pterosaur*

wink verb 1 *he winked an eye at his companion*: **blink**, flutter, bat; technical nictate, nictitate.
2 *the diamond on her finger winked in the moonlight*: **sparkle**, twinkle, flash, flicker, glitter, gleam, shimmer, shine; blink; rare scintillate.
□ **wink at** *the authorities winked at their illegal trade*: **turn a blind eye to**, close/shut one's eyes to, ignore, overlook, disregard, pretend not to notice; look the other way; connive at, condone, tolerate.
▶ **noun** *he noticed a wink of light in the west*: **glimmer**, glimmering, gleam, glint, flash, flicker, twinkle, sparkle; blink.
□ **in the wink of an eye** informal **very soon/quickly**, in a second, in a minute, in a moment, in a trice, in a flash, in an instant, in the twinkling of an eye, in (less than) no time, in no time at all, before you know it, in a very short time; N. Amer. momentarily; informal in a jiffy, in two shakes (of a lamb's tail), before you can say Jack Robinson, in a sec, in the blink of an eye, in a blink, before you can say knife; Brit. informal in a tick, in two ticks, in a mo; N. Amer. informal in a snap.

winkle verb
□ **winkle something/someone out 1** *Ewan managed to winkle the details out of him*: **worm out**, prise out, dig out, extract with difficulty, draw out.
2 *there were huge profits to be made from winkling out sitting tenants*: **force out**, dislodge, displace, remove, evict, uproot.

winner noun victor, champion, conqueror, vanquisher, defeater, conquering hero, hero; gold medallist, cup winner, prizewinner, prizeman; Spanish conquistador; Latin victor ludorum; informal champ, top dog, number one.
▷ANTONYMS loser.

winning adjective 1 *the winning team*: **victorious**, successful, triumphant, vanquishing, conquering; first, top, top-scoring; unbeaten, undefeated, unvanquished.
▷ANTONYMS losing.
2 *a winning smile*: **engaging**, charming, appealing, endearing, sweet, cute, winsome, attractive, pretty, prepossessing, fetching, lovely, adorable, lovable, delightful, disarming, captivating, enchanting, beguiling, persuasive, irresistible; dated taking.
▷ANTONYMS off-putting, unattractive.

winnings plural noun *Sanchez collected his winnings*: **prize money**, money won, gains; prize(s), booty, spoils; proceeds, profits, takings; Sport purse.
▷ANTONYMS losses.

winnow verb **1** *the dust and chaff is winnowed from the grain*: **separate**, divide, sort out; remove, get rid of.
2 *it's difficult to* ***winnow out*** *the truth*: **separate out**, sift out, filter out, isolate, sort out, find, identify, ferret out; separate the wheat from the chaff.

winsome adjective *his winsome daughter* | *a winsome smile*: **appealing**, engaging, charming, winning, attractive, pretty, sweet, cute, endearing, darling, dear, lovable, adorable, lovely, delightful, enchanting, captivating, fetching; dated taking.

winter noun

Word links **winter**

hibernal relating to winter

wintry adjective **1** *wintry weather*: **bleak**, **cold**, chilly, frosty, freezing, icy, snowy, icy-cold, arctic, glacial, frigid, bitter, biting, piercing, sharp, raw; informal nippy; Brit. informal parky; literary chill; rare hyperborean, hibernal, hiemal, brumal.
▷ANTONYMS summery, balmy, hot.
2 *his wintry smile*: **unfriendly**, cool, chilly, cold, frosty, frigid, glacial, bleak, distant, remote.
▷ANTONYMS friendly, warm.

wipe verb **1** *Beth wiped the kitchen table with a damp cloth*: **rub**, **clean**, mop, sponge, swab; dry, polish; Scottish & N. English dight.
2 *he* ***wiped*** *the marks* ***off*** *the window*: **rub off**, clean off, sponge off, polish off; remove, get rid of, dispose of, take off, erase, efface.
3 *they* ***wiped up*** *the mess*: **clean up**, clear up, mop up, sponge up; remove, get rid of.
4 *she wiped the unpleasant memory from her mind*: **obliterate**, expunge, erase, blot out, remove, remove all traces of, blank out.
□ **wipe someone/something out** *soldiers wiped out an entire village in Lampung province*: **destroy**, annihilate, eradicate, eliminate, extirpate; slaughter, massacre, kill, kill off, exterminate; demolish, raze to the ground, level; informal wipe off the face of the earth, wipe off the map, take out, liquidate, zap; N. Amer. informal waste; literary slay.
▶ noun *Bert gave the table a final wipe*: **rub**, clean, mop, sponge, swab, polish.

wire noun **cable**, lead, flex.

wiry adjective **1** *a small, wiry man*: **sinewy**, strong, tough, athletic; **lean**, spare, thin, stringy, skinny; literary thewy.
▷ANTONYMS frail; flabby.
2 *his wiry black hair*: **coarse**, rough, stiff, tough, strong; curly, wavy.
▷ANTONYMS straight, smooth.

wisdom noun **1** *a number of senior politicians questioned the wisdom of the decision*: **sagacity**, sageness, intelligence, understanding, insight, perception, perceptiveness, percipience, penetration, perspicuity, acuity, discernment, sense, good sense, common sense, shrewdness, astuteness, acumen, smartness, judiciousness, judgement, foresight, clear-sightedness, prudence, circumspection; logic, rationale, rationality, soundness, saneness, advisability; informal sharpness; N. Amer. informal savvy, smarts; rare sapience, arguteness.
▷ANTONYMS stupidity, folly.
2 *the wisdom of the ancients*: **knowledge**, learning, erudition, scholarship, philosophy; lore.

wise adjective *a wise old man* | *a wise decision*: **sage**, sagacious, intelligent, clever, learned, with/showing great knowledge, knowledgeable, informed, enlightened; astute, shrewd, acute, sharp, sharp-witted, canny, knowing, sensible, prudent, discerning, judicious, penetrating, perceptive, full of insight, insightful, clear-sighted, percipient, perspicacious, perspicuous, owlish; well advised, well thought out, well judged, politic, expedient, strategic, tactical, far-sighted; rational, logical, sound, sane; informal smart; Brit. informal fly; dated long-headed; rare sapient, argute.
▷ANTONYMS stupid, silly, foolish.
□ **put someone wise** informal *I suppose Lucy put you wise*: **tell**, inform, notify, apprise, make aware, put in the picture, fill in, break the news to; warn, forewarn, alert; informal clue in/up, tip off, tip someone the wink.
□ **wise to** informal *Alpine climbers have been wise to these techniques for years*: **aware of**, familiar with, acquainted with, cognizant of.

wisecrack noun informal **joke**, **witticism**, quip, witty remark, flash of wit, jest, rejoinder, sally; pun; barb, gibe; French bon mot; informal crack, gag, funny, one-liner, comeback.

wish verb **1** *I have never* ***wished for*** *power*: **desire**, want, hope for, long for, yearn for, crave, hunger for, thirst for, lust after, covet, sigh for, pine for, dream of; aspire to, set one's heart on, have as one's goal/aim, seek, be bent on; informal fancy, hanker after, have a yen for, itch for; archaic be desirous of; rare desiderate.
2 *if you wish to leave a message, please speak after the tone* | *they can do as they wish*: **want**, desire, have an inclination, feel/be inclined, feel like, care; choose, please, think fit.
3 *I wish you to send them a message*: **want**, desire, require.
4 *I wished him farewell*: **bid**.
▶ noun **1** *he had never expressed a wish to own a Mercedes*: **desire**, longing, hope, yearning, inclination, urge, whim, craving, hunger, thirst, lust; aspiration, aim, ambition, dream; informal fancy, hankering, yen, itch.
2 *she was unwilling to go against her parents' wishes*: **request**, requirement, bidding, instruction, direction, demand, order, command; want, desire; will; literary behest.

Word links **wish**

precatorial relating to a wish

wishy-washy adjective **1** *I feel like an idiot for being so wishy-washy*: **feeble**, ineffectual, weak, vapid, milk-and-water, effete, spineless, limp, limp-wristed, namby-pamby, half-hearted, spiritless, irresolute, indecisive; informal wet, pathetic, weak-kneed; Brit. informal **half-arsed**.
▷ANTONYMS strong, firm, decisive.
2 *wishy-washy soup*: **watery**, weak, watered down, thin; tasteless, flavourless, insipid.
▷ANTONYMS thick; flavoursome.
3 *a wishy-washy colour*: **pale**, insipid; pallid, wan, sickly.

wisp noun *a stray wisp of hair*: **strand**, tendril, lock; piece, scrap, shred, thread.

wispy adjective *her wispy blonde hair*: **thin**, fine, feathery, flyaway, straggly.

wistful adjective *his wistful expression*: **regretful**, **nostalgic**, yearning, longing; plaintive, rueful, melancholy, sad, mournful, forlorn, disconsolate, woebegone, doleful; pensive, reflective, contemplative, meditative, dreamy, daydreaming, in a reverie.

Word toolkit

wistful	plaintive	pensive
glance	cry	mood
memory	plea	state
lyrics	question	frown
sigh	refrain	look
nostalgia	call	silence
longing	letter	moment

wit noun **1** (also **wits**) *Eleanor was possessed of a great deal of native wit* | *he needed all his wits to figure out the way back*: **intelligence**, shrewdness, astuteness, cleverness, canniness, acuteness, acuity, sharpness, sharp-wittedness, sense, good sense, common sense, wisdom, sagacity, judgement, understanding, acumen, discernment, perception, insight, percipience, perspicacity; brains, mind; informal nous, gumption, horse sense; Brit. informal common; N. Amer. informal savvy, smarts.
▷ANTONYMS stupidity.
2 *I wanted to bowl him over with my sparkling wit*: **wittiness**, humour, funniness, facetiousness, drollery, waggishness; **repartee**, badinage, banter, wordplay, raillery, jokes, witticisms, quips, puns.
▷ANTONYMS humourlessness.
3 *she's such a wit*: **wag**, comedian, humorist, funny person, comic, joker, jokester; French farceur; informal character; informal, dated card, caution; rare punster.

witch noun **1** **sorceress**, enchantress, occultist, necromancer, Wiccan; archaic beldam; rare hex, pythoness.
2 informal *she's a right old witch*: **hag**, crone, harpy, harridan, termagant, she-devil; informal battleaxe, old bag; archaic scold.

witchcraft noun **sorcery**, black magic, the black arts, the occult, occultism, wizardry, witching, necromancy, voodooism, voodoo, hoodoo, wonder-working, divination; Wicca, white magic, natural magic; NZ makutu; rare thaumaturgy, theurgy, the old religion, witchery, demonry, diablerie, sortilege.

witch doctor noun **medicine man**, shaman, healer; Austral. boyla; in southern Africa sangoma; in Hawaii kahuna; in Greenland angekok.

with preposition *she's gone out with her boyfriend*: **accompanied by**, in the company of, escorted by.

withdraw verb **1** *he withdrew a roll of banknotes from his pocket* | *Ruth withdrew her hand from his*: **remove**, extract, draw out, pull out, take out; take back, pull back, take away.
▷ANTONYMS insert.
2 *the ban on advertising was withdrawn*: **abolish**, **cancel**, lift, raise, set aside, discontinue, end, stop, terminate, remove, reverse, revoke, rescind, repeal, countermand, annul, void.
▷ANTONYMS introduce, bring in.
3 *she withdrew all her money from the bank*: **take out**, draw out.
▷ANTONYMS deposit.

4 *she later withdrew the allegation*: **retract**, take back, unsay, go back on, recall, recant, disavow, disclaim, abjure, repudiate, renounce; back down, climb down, backtrack, back-pedal, do a U-turn, eat one's words; Brit. do an about-turn.
▷ANTONYMS put forward.
5 *government troops **withdrew from** the city*: **leave**, pull out of, move out of, evacuate, quit, retire from, retreat from, pull back from; disengage from.
▷ANTONYMS enter.
6 *at the last minute, his co-partner withdrew from the project*: **pull out of**, back out of, beg off, bow out of, scratch from; get cold feet; N. Amer. informal crap out; Austral./NZ informal pike on; archaic recede from.
7 *they withdrew to their rooms*: **go**, retire, retreat, take oneself, leave, depart, absent oneself, adjourn, decamp, beat a retreat; shut oneself away; formal repair, remove; literary betake oneself; rare abstract oneself.
8 *Mrs Reynolds withdrew into the shadows*: **draw back**, retreat, shrink back.

withdrawal noun **1** *the withdrawal of state subsidies*: **removal**, taking away; abolition, cancellation, discontinuation, ending, stopping, termination, elimination.
▷ANTONYMS introduction.
2 *the withdrawal of the troops*: **departure**, pull-out, exit, exodus, evacuation, retirement, retreat, disengagement.

withdrawn adjective *over the last few months he had become very withdrawn*: **introverted**, inward-looking, unsociable, socially inhibited; **uncommunicative**, unforthcoming, taciturn, silent, quiet, reticent, reserved, retiring, distant, remote, private, reclusive; shy, timid, diffident, shrinking, timorous; stand-offish, aloof.
▷ANTONYMS outgoing, extrovert, sociable.

wither verb **1** *the flowers had withered in the hot summer sun*: **wilt**, become limp, droop, fade; **shrivel (up)**, dry up; die, perish; technical become marcescent.
▷ANTONYMS thrive, flourish.
2 *the muscles in his leg had withered*: **waste (away)**, become shrunken, shrivel (up), atrophy, decay.
▷ANTONYMS strengthen.
3 *her confidence **withered away***: **diminish**, dwindle, shrink, lessen, fade, ebb (away), wane, weaken, languish; evaporate, melt away, disappear.
▷ANTONYMS grow.

withering adjective *a withering look | withering remarks*: **scornful**, contemptuous, full of contempt, mocking, sneering; scathing, stinging, searing, blistering, biting, devastating; supercilious, disdainful, superior, dismissive; humiliating, mortifying.
▷ANTONYMS encouraging, admiring.

withhold verb **1** *the council withheld payments to some contractors | he deliberately withheld the information*: **refuse to give**, hold back, keep back, stop; retain, keep hold of, hold on to; fail to disclose, hide, conceal, keep secret; informal sit on, keep under one's hat.
2 *Elizabeth could no longer withhold her tears*: **suppress**, repress, hold back, keep back, fight back, choke back, swallow, control, keep in check, check, restrain, contain, curb.

within preposition **1** *within the walls of the prison*: **inside**, in, within the bounds/confines of, enclosed by, surrounded by.
▷ANTONYMS outside.
2 *within the speed limit*: **inside**, inside the range/limits of, within the bounds of.
▷ANTONYMS outside.
3 *within a few hours*: **in less than**, in under, in no more than, after only.

with it adjective informal See **fashionable**.

without preposition **1** *thousands were left homeless and without food*: **lacking**, in need of, wanting for, needing, requiring, short of; deprived of, destitute of.
▷ANTONYMS with.
2 *I don't want to go without you*: **unaccompanied by**, unescorted by; in the absence of.
▷ANTONYMS with.

withstand verb *the company was able to withstand the rigours of the recession*: **resist**, hold out against, stand firm against, stand/hold one's ground against, bear up against, hold the line against, persevere in the face of, stand up to, fight, combat, grapple with, oppose, face, confront, defy, brave; weather, survive, live through, ride out, endure, take, cope with, stand, tolerate, bear, put up with; informal go the distance against.
▷ANTONYMS give in, surrender, yield.

witless adjective **1** *a witless youth*: **foolish**, **stupid**, unintelligent, idiotic, brainless, mindless, imbecilic, imbecile; fatuous, inane, immature, childish, puerile, half-baked, empty-headed, half-witted, slow-witted, weak-minded, doltish; informal crazy, dotty, scatty, loopy, brain-dead, cretinous, thick, thickheaded, birdbrained, pea-brained, pinheaded, dopey, dim, dim-witted, dippy, blockheaded, boneheaded, lamebrained, chuckleheaded, dunderheaded, wooden-headed, muttonheaded, damfool; Brit. informal daft, divvy; Scottish & N. English informal glaikit; N. Amer. informal dumb-ass, chowderheaded; S. African informal dof; W. Indian informal dotish.
2 *I was bored witless*: **out of one's mind**, to death, to tears, silly, stupid, sick.

witness noun **1** *several witnesses claimed that Slater started the fight*: **observer**, onlooker, looker-on, eyewitness, spectator, viewer, watcher; bystander, passer-by; N. Amer. earwitness.
2 *a key witness at the trial*: **attestor**, testifier; Law deponent.
3 *a bottle of whisky was the only witness of his low mood*: **evidence**, indication, proof, testimony.
□ **bear/stand/give witness** *the surviving letters **bear witness to** the extent of his involvement*: **attest to**, be evidence/proof of, testify to, confirm, evidence, prove, corroborate, verify, substantiate, bear out; show, demonstrate, establish, be a monument to, indicate, reveal, bespeak.
▷ANTONYMS belie.
▶ verb **1** *police are anxious to hear from anyone who witnessed the incident*: **see**, observe, watch, look on at, be a witness to, view, note, notice, spot; be present at, attend; literary behold.
2 *it is important to ensure that a will is correctly witnessed*: **countersign**, sign, endorse, validate; certificate, document; N. Amer. notarize.
3 *his writings witness to an inner toughness*: **attest to**, be evidence/proof of, testify to, bear witness to, confirm, evidence, prove, verify, corroborate, substantiate, bear out; show, demonstrate, establish, be a monument to, indicate, reveal; literary bespeak.

witter verb Brit. informal *she smiled and nodded as he wittered on*: **prattle**, babble, chatter, prate, gabble, jabber, go on, run on, rattle on/away, yap, jibber-jabber, patter, blather, blether, blither, maunder, ramble, drivel; informal yak, yackety-yak, yabber, yatter; Brit. informal rabbit, chunter, natter, waffle; Scottish & Irish informal slabber; Austral./NZ informal mag; archaic twaddle, clack, twattle.

witticism noun **joke**, quip, witty remark, flash of wit, jest, pun, play on words, double entendre, sally, riposte, pleasantry; epigram; (**witticisms**) repartee, banter, badinage; French bon mot; informal one-liner, gag, funny, crack, wisecrack, comeback; rare paronomasia, equivoque, Atticism.

witty adjective *his witty conversation*: **humorous**, amusing, droll, funny, comic, comical, chucklesome; sparkling, scintillating, lively, entertaining; **clever**, quick-witted, sharp-witted, piquant, original, ingenious; jocular, facetious, waggish; epigrammatic.
▷ANTONYMS boring, dull.

Word toolkit

witty	clever	droll
banter	idea	sense of humour
dialogue	use	wit
repartee	ways	comedy
lyrics	strategy	voice
comeback	ploy	delivery
commentary	wordplay	manner
one-liner	twist	humour

wizard noun **1** *the wizard had cast a spell over them*: **sorcerer**, warlock, male witch, magus, (black) magician, necromancer, occultist, enchanter; Irish pishogue; archaic mage; rare thaumaturge, thaumaturgist.
2 *a financial wizard*: **genius**, expert, master, adept, virtuoso, maestro, past master, marvel, prodigy; star; German wunderkind; informal hotshot, demon, wiz, whizz, whizz-kid, buff, old hand, pro, ace, something else, something to shout about, something to write home about; Brit. informal dab hand; N. Amer. informal maven, crackerjack; rare proficient.
▷ANTONYMS beginner, amateur; duffer.

wizened adjective *his wizened face*: **wrinkled**, lined, creased, shrivelled (up), withered, weather-beaten, thin, shrunken, gnarled, dried up, worn, wasted; literary sear.

wobble verb **1** *the table wobbled and milk spilled over the edge of her bowl*: **rock**, move unsteadily, jiggle, sway, see-saw, teeter; shake, vibrate.
2 *he got up and wobbled across to the door*: **teeter**, totter, stagger, walk unsteadily, lurch.
3 *her voice wobbled and she felt close to tears*: **tremble**, shake, quiver, quaver, waver; rare quave.
4 *for a few days the prime minister wobbled*: **waver**, **hesitate**, vacillate, dither, shilly-shally, be undecided, be uncertain, be indecisive, be unable to make up one's mind, keep changing one's mind, yo-yo; Scottish swither; informal blow hot and cold.
▶ noun **1** *Mimi stood up with a slight wobble*: **unsteady movement**, totter, teeter, sway; rocking, swaying, shaking.
2 *the operatic wobble in her voice*: **tremor**, quiver, quaver, shaking, trembling; technical vibrato.

wobbly adjective **1** *a wobbly table*: **unsteady**, unstable, shaky, rocky, rickety; flimsy, frail, spindly, unsafe, precarious, insecure; uneven, unbalanced; informal teetery; Brit. informal wonky, dicky.
▷ANTONYMS stable, steady.

2 *her legs were still a bit wobbly*: **shaky**, trembling, shaking, tremulous, quivering, quivery, doddery, unsteady; informal trembly.
3 *I must sit down—I feel so wobbly*: **faint**, **dizzy**, light-headed, giddy; weak, weak-kneed, weak at the knees, quivery, unsteady, groggy, muzzy; informal trembly, all of a tremble, all of a quiver, like jelly, with rubbery legs, woozy; rare vertiginous.

woe noun **1** *she launched into another tale of woe*: **misery**, sorrow, distress, wretchedness, sadness, unhappiness, heartache, heartbreak, despondency, desolation, despair, dejection, depression, gloom, melancholy; **adversity**, misfortune, disaster, affliction, suffering, hardship, pain, agony, grief, anguish, torment; literary dolour.
▷ANTONYMS happiness, joy.
2 *the company's recent financial woes*: **trouble**, difficulty, problem, trial, tribulation, burden, cross to bear, misfortune, stroke of bad luck, setback, reverse, blow, misadventure, mishap, vicissitude, failure, accident, disaster, tragedy, catastrophe, calamity, adversity, affliction.

woebegone adjective *her woebegone expression*: **sad**, unhappy, miserable, dejected, disconsolate, forlorn, crestfallen, sorry for oneself, hangdog, abject, downcast, glum, gloomy, doleful, downhearted, despondent, melancholy, sorrowful, mournful, woeful, lugubrious, long-faced, depressed, despairing, desolate, wretched; tearful; informal down in the mouth, down in the dumps, blue; literary dolorous; archaic chap-fallen.
▷ANTONYMS cheerful, happy.

woeful adjective **1** *her face was woeful*: **sad**, unhappy, miserable, woebegone, doleful, forlorn, crestfallen, glum, gloomy, dejected, downcast, disconsolate, downhearted, despondent, depressed, despairing, dismal, melancholy, broken-hearted, heartbroken, inconsolable, grief-stricken; informal blue, down in the mouth, down in the dumps.
▷ANTONYMS happy, cheerful.
2 *a woeful tale of broken romance*: **tragic**, sad, saddening, unhappy, sorrowful, miserable, cheerless, wretched, sorry, pitiful, pathetic, pitiable, gloomy, grievous, traumatic, upsetting, depressing, distressing, heartbreaking, heart-rending, tear-jerking, agonizing, harrowing; rare distressful.
▷ANTONYMS uplifting, cheerful.
3 *the team's woeful midweek performance*: **dreadful**, very bad, awful, terrible, frightful, atrocious, disgraceful, deplorable, shameful, hopeless, lamentable, laughable, substandard, poor, inadequate, inferior, unsatisfactory; informal rotten, appalling, crummy, pathetic, pitiful, useless, lousy, shocking, abysmal, dire, the pits; Brit. informal duff, chronic, rubbish, pants, a load of pants, poxy; N. Amer. vulgar slang chickenshit.
▷ANTONYMS excellent.

wolf noun informal *he's a bit of a wolf*: **womanizer**, Casanova, Romeo, Don Juan, Lothario, flirt, ladies' man, playboy, philanderer, seducer, rake, roué, libertine, debauchee; informal skirt-chaser, ladykiller, goat; informal, dated gay dog.
▸ verb *he* **wolfed down** *his breakfast*: **devour greedily**, gobble (up), guzzle, gulp down, bolt, cram down, gorge oneself with; informal pack away, demolish, shovel down, stuff one's face with, stuff oneself with, pig oneself on, pig out on, sink, scoff (down), put away, get outside of; Brit. informal gollop, shift; N. Amer. informal scarf (down/up), snarf (down/up), inhale; rare ingurgitate.
▷ANTONYMS nibble, pick at.

Word links **wolf**

dog male
bitch female
cub young
lupine relating to wolves
pack collective noun

wolfish adjective *he gave her a wolfish grin*: **lascivious**, lecherous, lustful, leering; **predatory**, greedy, rapacious.

woman noun **1** *a car drew up and two women got out*: **lady**, girl, member of the fair/gentle sex, female; matron, dowager; Scottish & N. English lass, lassie; Irish colleen; informal chick, girlie, filly, biddy; Brit. informal bird, bint, popsy; Scottish & N. English informal besom, wifie; N. Amer. informal dame, broad, gal, jane; Austral./NZ informal sheila; black English bitch, sister; Brit. informal, dated Judy; N. Amer. informal, dated frail; derogatory piece, bit, mare, baggage; literary maid, maiden, damsel, demoiselle; archaic or humorous wench; archaic gentlewoman, petticoat.
2 *apparently he's found himself a new woman*: **girlfriend**, girl, sweetheart, partner, significant other, inamorata, fiancée; wife, spouse, helpmate, helpmeet, consort; lover, mistress, paramour; informal bird, fancy woman, old lady, missus, missis, better half, other half, WAGs (wives and girlfriends), POSSLQ (person of the opposite sex sharing living quarters), queen; Brit. informal Dutch, her indoors; Irish informal mot; N. Amer. informal squeeze, patootie; Austral. informal dona; Indian informal bibi; Brit. rhyming slang trouble and strife; dated lady friend, lady love, young lady, lady, lady wife; archaic leman, doxy, concubine.
3 *her daily woman was due to arrive any minute*: **cleaning woman**, cleaner, domestic help, domestic, maid; Brit. dated charwoman, char; Brit. informal daily, Mrs Mop.

Word links **woman**

female, **feminine** relating to women
gyn(o)-, **gynaeco-** related prefixes, as in *gynocentric*
gynaecology branch of medicine concerning women
gynophobia fear of women
misogyny hatred of women
gynaecocracy, **gynarchy** rule by women

Choose the right word **woman, girl, lady**

Woman is the most commonly neutral word for an adult female person, but can be insulting when used to address a woman directly (*don't be daft, woman!*) or when referring to a man's girlfriend or wife (*he wondered whether Billy had his woman with him*).

Girl is considered by some women to be patronizing when used by a man to describe a grown woman, especially in a role that could equally be taken by a man (*the girl in the ticket office*). On the other hand, it can be used acceptably by other women, in certain phrases (*a girls' night out*), or of a man's girlfriend (*you're my girl now, aren't you?*).

Lady used to be the standard polite word but is now slightly formal or dated, as in *the lady at the travel agency* or when used of a man's wife (*the Colonel and his lady*). It can be complimentary, meaning a courteous, decorous, or genteel woman (*his wife was a real lady, with such nice manners*).

womanhood noun **1** *she was on the brink of womanhood*: **adulthood**, maturity; rare muliebrity.
2 *Mary was considered to be an ideal of womanhood*: **womanliness**, femininity, feminineness, womanly/feminine qualities.
3 *the changing social status of Britain's womanhood*: **women**, womenfolk; womankind, womenkind, woman; the female sex.

womanish adjective *his high womanish voice*: **effeminate**, effete, unmanly, unmasculine, girlish, namby-pamby; informal sissy, girly, camp, limp-wristed, queeny; rare epicene, emasculate.
▷ANTONYMS manly, macho.

womanizer noun **philanderer**, Casanova, Don Juan, Romeo, Lothario, flirt, ladies' man, playboy, seducer, rake, roué, libertine, debauchee, lecher; informal skirt-chaser, ladykiller, wolf, goat, lech; informal, dated gay dog.

womankind noun **women**, the female sex, womenkind, womanhood, womenfolk, woman.

womanly adjective **1** *her womanly virtues*: **feminine**, female; archaic feminal.
▷ANTONYMS masculine.
2 *the womanly curves of her hips and thighs*: **voluptuous**, curvaceous, shapely, ample, opulent, full-figured, well formed, well proportioned, Junoesque, Rubensesque, buxom, full-bosomed, lush, luscious; informal curvy, busty.
▷ANTONYMS boyish.

womb noun

Word links **womb**

hyster(o)- related prefix
hysterectomy surgical removal of womb

wonder noun **1** *the sight left her speechless with wonder*: **awe**, admiration, wonderment, fascination; surprise, astonishment, amazement.
2 *the wonders of nature*: **marvel**, miracle, phenomenon, wonderful thing, sensation, sight, spectacle, beauty; curiosity, rarity, nonpareil.
▸ verb **1** *I began to wonder what was going through her mind*: **ponder**, ask oneself, think about, meditate on, reflect on, deliberate about, muse on, speculate about, conjecture; puzzle about, be curious about, be inquisitive about; informal cudgel one's brains about.
2 *I wonder you were so patient with him*: **be surprised**, express surprise, find it surprising, be astonished/amazed.
3 *people stood by and wondered at such bravery*: **marvel**, be amazed, be filled with amazement, be filled with admiration, be astonished, be surprised, be awed, stand in awe, be full of wonder, be lost for words, not believe one's eyes/ears, not know what to say, be dumbfounded, gape, goggle, gawk; informal be flabbergasted, boggle.

wonderful adjective *I've had a wonderful evening*: **marvellous**, magnificent, superb, glorious, sublime, lovely, delightful, first-class, first-rate; informal super, great, smashing, amazing, fantastic, terrific, tremendous, sensational, incredible, heavenly, gorgeous, dreamy, grand, fabulous, fab, fabby, fantabulous, awesome, magic, ace, cool, mean, bad, wicked, mega, crucial, mind-blowing, far out, A1, sound, out of this world, marvy, spanking; Brit. informal brilliant, brill; N. Amer. informal peachy, dandy,

jim-dandy, neat, badass, boss, radical, rad, boffo, bully, bitching, bodacious; Austral./NZ informal **beaut**, **bonzer**; S. African informal **kif**, **lank**; black English **dope**, **def**, **phat**; informal, dated **groovy**, **divine**; Brit. informal, dated **capital**, **champion**, **wizard**, **corking**, **cracking**, **ripping**, **spiffing**, **top-hole**, **topping**, **beezer**; N. Amer. informal, dated **swell**, **keen**; literary **wondrous**; archaic **goodly**.
▷ANTONYMS awful, dreadful.

wonky adjective Brit. informal **1** *a wonky nose*: **crooked**, off-centre, lopsided, askew, skew; Brit. informal skew-whiff.
▷ANTONYMS straight.
2 *wonky stools*: **wobbly**, unsteady, unstable, shaky, rocky; Irish bockety.
▷ANTONYMS stable.

wont adjective *he was wont to arise at 5.30 every morning*: **accustomed**, used, given, inclined; in the habit of.
▶ noun *Paul, as was his wont, was driving far too fast*: **custom**, habit, way, practice, convention, routine, use, rule.

wonted adjective *McTeague had relapsed into his wonted stolidity*: **customary**, habitual, usual, accustomed, familiar, normal, conventional, traditional; routine, regular, common, frequent, daily.

woo verb **1** *Richard wooed Joan with single-minded persistence*: **court**, pay court to, pursue, chase, chase after, run after; dated romance, seek the hand of, press one's suit with, set one's cap at, make love to; archaic spark.
2 *the party wooed voters with promises of electoral reform*: **seek the support of**, seek the favour of, try to win, try to attract, try to cultivate, chase, pursue, try to ingratiate oneself with, curry favour with.
3 *an attempt to woo Green out of his semi-retirement*: **entice**, tempt, coax, persuade, wheedle; informal sweet-talk, smooth-talk.

wood noun **1** *a table made of dark polished wood*: **timber**, planks, planking; N. Amer. lumber.
2 *Bob fetched wood and lit a fire*: **firewood**, kindling, logs; fuel.
3 *a short walk through the pine woods*: **forest**, woodland, trees; copse, thicket, coppice, grove, brake; plantation; Brit. spinney; archaic holt, greenwood; rare boscage.

> *Word links* **wood**
>
> **ligneous** relating to wood
> **agroforestry**, **arboriculture**, **forestry**, **silviculture** farming of wood

wooded adjective *a wooded valley*: **forested**, afforested, tree-covered, woody; literary sylvan, bosky, tree-clad; rare timbered.

wooden adjective **1** *the heavy wooden door*: **made of wood**, wood, timber, woody; ligneous; rare treen.
2 *wooden acting*: **stilted**, stiff, unnatural, clumsy, awkward, graceless, inelegant, ungainly, leaden; dry, flat, stodgy, lifeless, lacking vitality, passionless, unimpassioned, spiritless, soulless.
▷ANTONYMS lively, flowing.
3 *her eyes were hard and her face wooden*: **expressionless**, impassive, poker-faced, devoid of emotion, emotionless, blank, empty, vacant, unresponsive.

woodland noun *1000 acres of natural woodland*: **woods**, wood, forest, trees; archaic greenwood; rare boscage.

woodwork noun **carpentry**, joinery.

wool noun *tufts of sheep's wool*: **fleece**, hair, coat; rare floccus.
□ **pull the wool over someone's eyes** informal **deceive**, fool, trick, take in, hoodwink, dupe, delude; informal lead up the garden path, pull a fast one on, put one over on, bamboozle, con.

> *Word links* **wool**
>
> **lanate** relating to wool

wool-gathering noun **daydreaming**, dreaming, building castles in the air, building castles in Spain, reverie, musing, abstraction, preoccupation, brown study, distraction, inattention; absent-mindedness, forgetfulness.
▷ANTONYMS concentration, attentiveness.

woolly adjective **1** *a woolly hat*: **woollen**, made of wool, wool, fleecy.
2 *a sheep's woolly coat*: **fleecy**, shaggy, hairy, fluffy; wool-bearing; rare flocculent, laniferous, lanigerous.
3 *woolly grey-green foliage*: **downy**; technical floccose, lanate.
4 *woolly generalizations about economic growth*: **vague**, ill-defined, hazy, unclear, unfocused, fuzzy, blurry, foggy, nebulous, imprecise, inexact, indefinite; **confused**, muddled, muddle-headed, disorganized.
▷ANTONYMS clear.

woozy adjective informal *I still felt woozy from all the pills*: **light-headed**, dizzy, giddy, faint; unsteady, groggy, wobbly, weak; muzzy, dazed, confused; informal dopey, not with it; rare vertiginous.
▷ANTONYMS clear-headed.

word noun **1** *the Italian word for 'ham'*: **term**, name, expression, designation, locution; turn of phrase, idiom; formal appellation; rare vocable.
2 (usually **words**) *his grandfather's words had been meant kindly*: **remark**, comment, statement, utterance, observation, pronouncement, declaration.
3 (**words**) *I've only got three weeks to learn the words*: **script**, text; **lyrics**, libretto.
4 *everything will be taken care of—I give you my word*: **promise**, word of honour, assurance, guarantee, undertaking; pledge, vow, oath, bond; archaic troth, parole.
5 *I want a word with you in private*: **talk**, conversation, chat, tête-à-tête, heart-to-heart, one-on-one, one-to-one, head-to-head; discussion, consultation, exchange of views, colloquy; informal confab, powwow; formal confabulation.
6 *apparently there's no word from the hospital yet*: **news**, information, communication, intelligence, notice; message, report, communiqué, dispatch, bulletin, account; data, facts; informal info, the gen, the low-down; N. Amer. informal the dope, the poop; literary tidings; archaic advices.
7 *word has it he's turned over a new leaf*: **rumour**, hearsay, talk, gossip; informal the grapevine, the word on the street; N. Amer. informal the scuttlebutt.
8 *I'm waiting for the word from the Department of Justice*: **instruction**, order, command; signal, prompt, cue, tip-off; informal go-ahead, thumbs up, green light; N. Amer. informal high sign.
9 *he was a strict disciplinarian whose word was law*: **command**, order, decree, edict, mandate; bidding, will.
10 *our word now must be success*: **motto**, slogan, watchword, password, catchword; buzz word.
□ **have words** *it's obvious the two of you have had words*: **quarrel**, argue, disagree, row, squabble, bicker, fight, wrangle, dispute, feud, have a row, cross swords, lock horns, clash, be at each other's throats; informal fall out, have a tiff, have a spat; Brit. informal have a barney; archaic altercate.
□ **in a word** *the answer, in a word, is yes*: **to put it briefly**, to be brief, briefly, in short, in a nutshell, succinctly, concisely, to come to the point, to cut a long story short, not to mince words, not to beat about the bush, not to put too fine a point on it; to sum up, to summarize, in sum, in summary.
□ **word for word 1** *reporters took down the speeches word for word*: **verbatim**, line for line, letter for letter, to the letter; exactly, precisely, faithfully; rare literatim. **2** *a word-for-word translation*: **verbatim**, literal, exact, direct, precise, accurate, faithful, strict, undeviating; unadulterated, unabridged, unvarnished, unembellished.
▷ANTONYMS loose.
▶ verb *the question had been carefully worded*: **phrase**, express, put, couch, frame, set forth, formulate, style; say, utter, state.

> *Word links* **word**
>
> **verbal**, **lexical** relating to words
> **lexicology** study of words

wording noun *the wording of the question was ambiguous*: **phrasing**, phraseology, choice of words, words, language, mode of expression, expression, terminology, diction.

wordplay noun **punning**, puns, double entendres, play on words; wit, witticisms, repartee; rare paronomasia.

wordy adjective *a wordy speech*: **long-winded**, **verbose**, prolix, full of verbiage, lengthy, protracted, long-drawn-out, diffuse, discursive, rambling, digressive, maundering, circumlocutory, periphrastic, repetitious, tautological, tortuous; loquacious, garrulous, voluble; informal windy; Brit. informal waffly; rare pleonastic, logorrhoeic, ambagious.
▷ANTONYMS concise, succinct.

work noun **1** *he was tired after a day's work in the fields*: **labour**, toil, exertion, effort, slog, drudgery, the sweat of one's brow; industry; service; informal grind, sweat, donkey work, spadework, elbow grease; Brit. informal graft, fag; Austral./NZ informal yakka; archaic travail, moil.
▷ANTONYMS leisure, rest.
2 *I'm still looking for work* | *his work takes him to France, Spain, and Germany*: **employment**, a job, a post, a position, a situation, a means of earning one's living; occupation, profession, career, business, trade, line; vocation, calling; archaic employ.
3 *haven't you got any work to do?* **tasks**, jobs, duties, assignments, commissions, projects; chores.
4 *one of the best works of modern English literature*: **composition**, piece, creation, achievement, accomplishment; work of art, opus, oeuvre.
5 *the shooting was the work of a radical left-wing group*: **handiwork**, doing, act, deed, feat, performance.
6 (**works**) *a lifetime spent doing good works*: **deeds**, acts, actions.
7 (**works**) *the complete works of Shakespeare*: **writings**, oeuvre, canon, output.
8 (**works**) *the site of a former car works*: **factory**, plant, manufacturing complex, mill, foundry, yard, industrial unit; workshop, shop.
9 (**works**) *the works of a clock*: **mechanism**, machinery, workings, working parts, parts, movement, action; informal innards, insides.
10 (**the works**) informal *for only $60 you can get the works*: **everything**, the full treatment; informal everything but the kitchen sink, the lot, the whole shooting match, the whole (kit and) caboodle, the whole shebang, the whole nine yards; Brit. informal the full monty; N. Amer. informal the whole ball of wax.

▶ **verb 1** *staff worked late into the night to make the necessary repairs*: **toil**, labour, exert oneself, slave (away), plod away; work one's fingers to the bone, work like a Trojan/dog, work day and night, keep at it, keep one's nose to the grindstone; informal slog (away), beaver away, plug away, peg away, put one's back into something, work one's guts out, work one's socks off, knock oneself out, sweat blood, kill oneself; Brit. informal graft, fag; Austral./NZ informal **bullock**; Brit. vulgar slang **work one's balls/arse off**; N. Amer. vulgar slang work one's ass/butt off; archaic drudge, travail, moil.
▷ANTONYMS rest, play.
2 *Taylor has worked in education for 17 years*: **be employed**, have a job, earn one's living, hold down a job, do business, follow/ply one's trade.
3 *many farmers had given up working the land*: **cultivate**, farm, till, plough; exploit.
4 *Dino's car was now working perfectly*: **function**, go, run, operate, perform; be in working order; informal behave.
5 *she showed me how to work the ice-cream machine*: **operate**, use, handle, control, manipulate, manoeuvre, drive, run, direct; ply, wield.
6 *their desperate ploy had worked*: **succeed**, be successful, work out, turn out well, go as planned, have the desired result, get results; be effective, take effect, be efficacious; informal come off, pay off, do the trick, do the business; N. Amer. informal turn the trick.
▷ANTONYMS fail.
7 *with a dash of blusher you can work miracles*: **bring about**, accomplish, achieve, produce, do, perform, carry out, implement, execute, create, engender, contrive, effect.
8 informal *the chairman was prepared to work it for Philip if he was interested*: **arrange**, manipulate, manoeuvre, contrive; pull strings; N. Amer. pull wires; informal fix, swing, wangle, fiddle.
9 *he worked the crowd into a frenzy*: **stir (up)**, excite, drive, move, spur, rouse, fire, galvanize; whip up, inflame, incite, agitate.
10 *work the mixture into a paste*: **knead**, squeeze, form, shape, fashion, mould, model; mix, stir, blend.
11 *he worked the blade into the padlock*: **manoeuvre**, manipulate, negotiate, guide, edge.
12 *Bella's mouth worked furiously for a few seconds*: **twitch**, quiver, twist, move spasmodically, convulse.
13 *John had worked his way through the crowd*: **manoeuvre**, make, thread, wind, weave.
□ **work on someone** *leave him to me—I'll work on him*: **persuade**, **manipulate**, influence, sway, put pressure on, lean on; coax, cajole, wheedle, soften up; informal twist someone's arm, put the squeeze on.
□ **work out 1** *the bill works out at £50*: **amount to**, add up to, come to, total; Brit. tot up to. **2** *I'm glad my idea worked out*: **succeed**, be successful, work, turn out well, go as planned, get results, be effective; informal come off, pay off, do the trick, do the business. ▷ANTONYMS fail. **3** *things didn't quite work out the way she had planned*: **end up**, turn out, go, come out, develop, evolve, result; happen, occur; informal pan out. **4** *Bob keeps in shape by working out at the local gym*: **exercise**, do exercises, train.
□ **work something out 1** *work out how much you can afford to spend*: **calculate**, compute, reckon up, determine. **2** *I'm still trying to work out what she meant*: **understand**, comprehend, puzzle out, sort out, reason out, make sense of, think out, think through, get to the bottom of, make head or tail of, solve, find an answer/solution to, unravel, untangle, decipher, decode, find the key to, piece together; informal figure out, crack; Brit. informal suss out. **3** *they worked out a plan of action*: **devise**, formulate, draw up, put together, develop, prepare, construct, arrange, organize, plan, think up, contrive, concoct; hammer out, thrash out, reach an agreement on, negotiate.
□ **work someone over** *it looked like someone had worked him over to get him to say what they wanted him to say*: **beat up**, beat, attack, assault, knock about/around, maltreat, mistreat, abuse, batter, manhandle; informal do over, bash up, rough up, beat the living daylights out of; Brit. informal duff up; N. Amer. informal beat up on.
□ **work something up** *he couldn't seem to work up any enthusiasm*: **stimulate**, rouse, raise, arouse, awaken, excite, build up, whet; develop, produce.

Word links **work**

ergophobia fear of work

Choose the right word **work, labour, toil**

Work is the general term for things that one has to do in order to earn a living or to achieve a particular aim (*she did clerical work before she married | work on landscaping the disused railway line was started in 1980*). When applied to the actual doing of these things, *work* implies that effort is involved (*thank you for your hard work on the project*). As a verb, the word means simply to carry out any kind of such activity (*a man was working in the garden*).

Labour typically denotes physical work, especially when this is hard and exhausting (*manual labour | exhausted by labour in the fields*). To *labour* is to work hard (*they laboured from dawn to dusk*) or to have difficulty in doing something in spite of working hard (*the media group is currently labouring to reduce its debt mountain*).

Toil, as a noun or a verb, refers to exhausting, tedious, and seemingly unending hard work (*most of the poet's life was spent in toil on the farm | the clerks sat toiling into the night over some urgent piece of business*). To *toil* in a stated direction means to struggle to move somewhere (*she toiled up the path with her packages*).

workable adjective *a workable solution to the problem*: **practicable**, **feasible**, viable, possible, within the bounds/realms of possibility, achievable, accomplishable; realistic, reasonable, sensible, practical; informal doable.
▷ANTONYMS unworkable, impracticable, impossible.

workaday adjective *workaday prose | her workaday life*: **ordinary**, average, run-of-the-mill, middle-of-the-road, mainstream, conventional, unremarkable, unexceptional, unpretentious, plain, simple, undistinguished, nondescript, characterless, colourless, commonplace, humdrum, mundane, unmemorable, unspectacular, pedestrian, prosaic; routine, everyday, day-to-day, quotidian; N. Amer. garden-variety; informal bog-standard, vanilla, plain vanilla, nothing to write home about, a dime a dozen; Brit. informal common or garden, two a penny; N. Amer. informal ornery.
▷ANTONYMS extraordinary, exceptional.

worker noun **1** *an unofficial strike by 500 workers at the factory*: **employee**, member of staff, working man, working woman, workman, labourer, hand, operative, operator; blue-collar worker, white-collar worker; proletarian; artisan, journeyman, craftsman, craftswoman; wage-earner, breadwinner; archaic mechanical.
2 informal *I got a reputation for being a worker*: **hard worker**, toiler, workhorse, Stakhanovite; informal busy bee, eager beaver, workaholic; N. Amer. informal wheel horse, wonk.

workforce noun **employees**, staff, personnel, human resources; **workers**, labour force, manpower; humorous liveware.

working adjective **1** *childcare for working mothers*: **employed**, in work, in a job, waged, in gainful employment.
▷ANTONYMS unemployed, out of work.
2 *the mill still has a working waterwheel*: **functioning**, operating, going, running, active; in working order, operational, functional, able to function, usable, serviceable; informal up and running.
▷ANTONYMS broken, faulty.
3 *a working knowledge of contract law*: **sufficient**, adequate, good enough, viable; useful, effective.
▶ **noun 1** *the working of a carburettor*: **functioning**, operation, running, action, performance.
2 (**workings**) *the workings of a pocket watch*: **mechanism**, machinery, working/moving parts, movement, action, works; informal innards, insides.

workman noun **worker**, manual worker, labourer, hand, operative, operator; employee; journeyman, artisan; Indian maistry.

workmanlike adjective *the team put up a good, workmanlike performance*: **efficient**, competent, satisfactory; professional, proficient, skilled, skilful, adept, masterly.
▷ANTONYMS amateurish.

workmanship noun **craftsmanship**, artistry, craft, art, artisanship, handiwork, work; **skill**, skilfulness, technique, expertise.

workout noun **exercise session**, keep-fit session, physical training session, drill; warm-up, limbering up; exercises, aerobics, isometrics, gymnastics, callisthenics; informal, dated daily dozen.

workshop noun **1** *a car repair workshop*: **factory**, works, plant; shop, industrial unit; garage.
2 *the craftsmen worked in a freezing cold workshop*: **workroom**, studio, atelier.
3 *a workshop on 'Combating Job Stress'*: **study group**, discussion group, seminar, class.

world noun **1** *he travelled the world with the army*: **earth**, globe, planet, sphere.
2 *he was convinced of the possibility of life on other worlds*: **planet**, satellite, moon, star, heavenly body, orb.
3 *the academic world | the world of work is not where all her life ambitions lie*: **sphere**, society, circle, arena, milieu, province, domain, territory, orbit, preserve, realm, field, discipline, area, department, sector, section, group, division.

4 (**the world**) *she would show the world that she was no weak-kneed lady of leisure*: **everyone**, everybody, each and every one, people, mankind, humankind, humanity, people everywhere, the whole world, the world at large, the public, the general public, the population, the populace, all and sundry, every mother's son, {every Tom, Dick, and Harry}, every man jack.
5 *there's a world of difference between the two men*: **huge amount**, vast amount, enormous amount, good deal, great deal, abundance, wealth, profusion, mountain, immensity; many, much, plenty, reams; informal heap, pile, lot, load, stack, ton, masses; Brit. informal shedload, lashings; Austral./NZ informal swag.
▷ANTONYMS very little.

6 *she renounced the world and became a nun*: **society**, high society; secular interests, temporal concerns, earthly concerns; human existence.
□ **in a world of one's own** *he is in a world of his own and is frequently carried away by his own flights of fancy*: **absent-minded**, preoccupied, absorbed, engrossed, far away, somewhere else, not there, not with us, abstracted, with one's head in the clouds, daydreaming, dreamy, inattentive, distracted, thoughtful, pensive, lost in thought, deep in thought, immersed in thought, wool-gathering, in a brown study, musing, brooding, absent, distrait, heedless, oblivious; informal miles away.
□ **on top of the world** informal See **overjoyed**.
□ **out of this world** informal *her breakfasts are out of this world*. See **wonderful**.

Word links **world**
mondial relating to the whole world

worldly adjective **1** *his youth was being wasted on worldly and dissolute pursuits*: **earthly**, terrestrial, temporal, mundane, mortal, human, non-spiritual, unspiritual, material, materialistic, physical, tangible, carnal, fleshly, bodily, corporeal, gross, sensual, base, sordid, vile, profane; secular, lay, non-church, non-religious; rare sublunary, terrene, laic.
▷ANTONYMS spiritual.
2 *a charming worldly man*: **sophisticated**, experienced, worldly-wise, knowledgeable, knowing, aware, enlightened, shrewd, astute, perceptive, mature, seasoned, cosmopolitan, urbane, cultivated, cultured, unprovincial; informal having been around.
▷ANTONYMS naive, unsophisticated.

worldly-wise adjective *Lisa was sufficiently worldly-wise to understand the situation*: **sophisticated**, **experienced**, worldly, knowledgeable, knowing, aware, enlightened, shrewd, astute, perceptive, mature, seasoned, cosmopolitan, urbane, cultivated, cultured, unprovincial; informal having been around.
▷ANTONYMS naive, unsophisticated.

worldwide adjective *a worldwide effort to stop the spread of AIDS*: **global**, international, intercontinental, world, universal, planetary, pandemic; general, common, ubiquitous, extensive, widespread, far-reaching, wide-ranging, all-embracing, across the board.
▷ANTONYMS local, restricted.

worm noun

Word links **worm**
vermian relating to a worm
vermi- related prefix
vermiform worm-shaped
vermivorous worm-eating
vermicide substance used to kill worms
helminthophobia fear of worms

worn adjective **1** *his hat was old and worn*: **shabby**, well worn, worn out, worn to shreds, threadbare, tattered, in tatters, in ribbons, in rags, in holes, holey, falling to pieces, falling apart at the seams, ragged, frayed, patched, moth-eaten, faded, seedy, shoddy, sorry, scruffy, dilapidated, crumbling, broken-down, run down, tumbledown, decrepit, deteriorated, on its last legs, having seen better days, time-worn; informal tatty, ratty, the worse for wear, clapped out; Brit. informal grotty; N. Amer. informal raggedy, raggedy-ass; Austral./NZ informal warby; literary rent.
▷ANTONYMS new, smart.
2 *her face looked tired and worn*: **strained**, drawn, drained, worn out, fatigued, tired, tired out, exhausted, weary, wearied, wan, sapped, spent, careworn, haggard, hollow-cheeked, hollow-eyed, gaunt, pinched, pale, peaky, pasty-faced, washed out, ashen, blanched; informal worn to a frazzle, all in, done in, dog-tired, dead on one's feet, dead beat, fit to drop, played out, fagged out, shattered, bushed; Brit. informal knackered, whacked; N. Amer. informal pooped, tuckered out.
▷ANTONYMS fresh, energetic.

worn out adjective **1** *he wore old jeans and a worn-out shirt*: **shabby**, well worn, worn, worn to shreds, threadbare, tattered, in tatters, in ribbons, in rags, in holes, holey, falling to pieces, falling apart at the seams, ragged, frayed, patched, moth-eaten, faded, seedy, shoddy, sorry, scruffy, dilapidated, crumbling, broken-down, run down, tumbledown, decrepit, deteriorated, on its last legs, having seen better days, time-worn; informal tatty, ratty, the worse for wear, clapped out; Brit. informal grotty; N. Amer. informal raggedy, raggedy-ass; Austral./NZ informal warby; literary rent.
▷ANTONYMS new, smart.
2 *they were slogging away and looked pretty well worn out*: **exhausted**, fatigued, tired, tired out, weary, wearied, strained, drained, worn, drawn, wan, sapped, spent, careworn, haggard, hollow-cheeked, hollow-eyed, gaunt, pinched, pale, peaky, pasty-faced, washed out, ashen, blanched; informal worn to a frazzle, all in, done in, dog-tired, dead on one's feet, dead beat, fit to drop, played out, fagged out, shattered, bushed; Brit. informal knackered, whacked, jiggered; N. Amer. informal pooped, tuckered out; rare fordone.
▷ANTONYMS fresh, energetic.
3 *they portrayed the opposition as the party of worn-out ideas*: **obsolete**, antiquated, old, well worn, stale, time-worn, hackneyed, banal, trite, overused, overworked, stereotyped, clichéd, unoriginal, derivative, unimaginative, commonplace, common, pedestrian, prosaic, run-of-the-mill, stock, conventional; informal played out, corny, old hat.
▷ANTONYMS fresh.

worried adjective *they kept their fingers crossed but they weren't too worried*: **anxious**, disturbed, perturbed, troubled, bothered, distressed, concerned, upset, distraught, worried sick, disquieted, uneasy, ill at ease, fretful, fretting, agitated, in a state of agitation, nervous, edgy, on edge, like a cat on a hot tin roof, tense, overwrought, worked up, keyed up, strung out, jumpy, with one's stomach in knots, stressed, under stress; distracted, apprehensive, fearful, afraid, frightened, scared, with one's heart in one's mouth, quaking, trembling, shaking in one's shoes, in a cold sweat; informal uptight, a bundle of nerves, on tenterhooks, with butterflies in one's stomach, hassled, jittery, twitchy, in a state, wired, in a stew, in a dither, all of a dither, in a flap, in a sweat, in a tizz/tizzy, all of a lather, het up, in a twitter, rattled; Brit. informal strung up, windy, having kittens; N. Amer. informal antsy, spooky, spooked, squirrelly, in a twit; Austral./NZ informal toey; Brit. vulgar slang shitting bricks, bricking oneself; dated overstrung, unquiet.
▷ANTONYMS carefree, calm, unconcerned.

worrisome adjective *the most worrisome of all environmental threats*: **worrying**, daunting, alarming, perturbing, trying, taxing, vexatious, niggling, bothersome, troublesome, unsettling, harassing, harrying, harrowing, nerve-racking, distressing, dismaying, disquieting, upsetting, traumatic, unpleasant, awkward, difficult, tricky, thorny, problematic, grave; informal scary, hairy, sticky, prickly, anxious-making.

worry verb **1** *she worries about his blood pressure*: **fret**, be worried, be concerned, be anxious, agonize, brood, dwell on, panic, get in a panic, lose sleep, get worked up, get in a fluster, get overwrought, be on tenterhooks; informal have butterflies in one's stomach, get stressed, get in a flap, get in a state, get in a tizz/tizzy, get in a sweat, sweat, get steamed up, get in a lather, stew, torture oneself, torment oneself; Brit. informal be in a blue funk.
2 *I can see that something is worrying you*: **trouble**, bother, cause anxiety, make anxious, disturb, distress, upset, concern, disquiet, discompose, fret, agitate, unsettle, perturb, frighten, alarm, scare, fluster, flurry, stress, strain, tax, harass, torment, plague, bedevil, besiege, irk, vex; prey on one's mind, weigh heavily on one's mind, weigh down, oppress, burden, be a great weight on, lie heavy on, gnaw at; informal hassle, give someone a hard time, throw, faze, rattle, bug, get to, do someone's head in, discombobulate; N. Amer. informal mess with someone's head.
3 *a dog was worrying his sheep*: **attack**, savage, maul, mutilate, mangle, go for, tear at, tear to pieces, claw, bite, gnaw at, lacerate, shake, pull at; molest, torment, persecute.
▸ noun **1** *I'm beside myself with worry*: **anxiety**, disturbance, perturbation, trouble, bother, distress, concern, care, upset, uneasiness, unease, disquiet, disquietude, disconcertment, fretfulness, restlessness, nervousness, nerves, agitation, edginess, tension, tenseness, stress, strain; apprehension, fear, fearfulness, dread, foreboding, trepidation, misgiving, angst; informal butterflies (in the stomach), the willies, the heebie-jeebies, the shakes, the jumps, jitteriness, twitchiness.
2 *the rats are a worry because they can contaminate food*: **problem**, cause for concern; nuisance, pest, plague, trial, tribulation, trouble, irritation, irritant, vexation, bane, bugbear, thorn in one's flesh/side, burden, cross, cross to bear; informal pain, pain in the neck, headache, hassle, stress.

worrying adjective *their financial situation was very worrying*: **alarming**, worrisome, daunting, perturbing, trying, taxing, vexatious, niggling, bothersome, troublesome, unsettling, harassing, harrying, harrowing, nerve-racking; distressing, dismaying, disquieting, upsetting, traumatic, unpleasant, awkward, difficult, tricky, thorny, problematic, grave; informal scary, hairy, sticky, prickly, anxious-making.

worse adjective
□ **the worse for wear** *the bright paint was looking somewhat the worse for wear*: **shabby**, run down, worn out, falling to pieces, falling apart, dilapidated, rickety, ramshackle, crumbling, decayed, antiquated, superannuated, decrepit, on its last legs, battered; untidy, unkempt, bedraggled, messy, dishevelled, ungroomed, ill-groomed.

worsen verb **1** *insomnia can considerably worsen a patient's distress*: **aggravate**, **exacerbate**, make worse, compound, add to, intensify, increase, magnify, heighten, inflame, augment; informal add fuel to the fire/flames, put salt on the wound.
▷ANTONYMS improve, ameliorate.
2 *the economic recession continued to worsen*: **deteriorate**, degenerate, decline, get/grow/become worse, take a turn for the worse, weaken; sink, slip, slide, slump, fall off, ebb, wane, lapse, regress, retrogress; informal go downhill, go to pot, go to the dogs, go down the toilet, go down the tubes, hit the skids, nosedive, take a nosedive.
▷ANTONYMS improve, recover.

worship noun **1** *the new Church rejected the worship of saints and relics*: **reverence**, revering, worshipping, veneration, venerating, adoration, adoring, -olatry, devotion, praise, thanksgiving, praising, praying to, glorification, glorifying, glory, exaltation, exalting, extolment, extolling, homage, respect, honour, honouring, esteem; Roman Catholic Church dulia, latria; rare laudation, magnification.
2 *morning worship*: **service**, church service, religious rite, religious act, prayer, prayer meeting, praise, devotion, religious observance; matins, morning prayer, vespers, evening prayer, evensong.
3 *he contemplated the pin-up with worship*: **admiration**, adulation, idolization, deification, lionization, hero-worship.
▸ verb *they do not worship pagan gods | the ladies worshipped their brother*: **revere**, reverence, venerate, pay homage to, honour, adore, praise, pray to, bow down before, glorify, exalt, extol; **be devoted to**, dote on, love, hold dear, cherish, treasure, admire, esteem, adulate, idolize, deify, hero-worship, lionize, have a high regard for, hold in high regard, hold in esteem, hold in awe, look up to; informal be wild about, put on a pedestal; archaic magnify; rare laud.
▷ANTONYMS loathe, despise.

worst verb *they were worsted by a large and desperate band of armed malefactors*: **defeat**, beat, best, get the better of, gain the advantage over, prevail over, triumph over, gain a victory over, trounce, rout, thrash, drub, vanquish, conquer, master, overcome, overwhelm, overpower, overthrow, crush, subdue, subjugate; outdo, outclass, outstrip, surpass, outwit, outsmart, score points off, make a fool of, humiliate; informal lick, clobber, whip, hammer, beat hollow, slaughter, murder, kill, wipe out, do in, crucify, demolish, wipe the floor with, take to the cleaners, walk all over, run rings around, make mincemeat of, blow out of the water, give someone a hiding, get one up on, get one over on; Brit. informal stuff; N. Amer. informal shellac, blow out, cream, skunk, slam.

worth noun **1** *a buyer may require independent evidence of the rug's worth*: **value**, financial value, monetary value, price, asking price, selling price, cost; valuation, quotation, estimate, assessment.
2 *the intrinsic worth of education*: **benefit**, advantage, use, value, virtue, usefulness, utility, service, gain, profit, avail, validity, help, assistance, aid; desirability, attractiveness, allure, appeal; significance, point, sense; informal mileage, percentage; archaic behoof.
3 *club members have a sense of belonging and personal worth*: **worthiness**, merit, meritoriousness, credit, value, excellence, calibre, quality, stature, eminence, greatness, consequence, importance, significance, distinction, superiority; gifts, talents, strengths, endowments.

worthless adjective **1** *the icon turns out to be worthless*: **valueless**, of little/no value, of little/no worth, without value, of little/no financial value; rubbishy, trashy, paltry, (of) poor quality, (of) low quality, inferior, second-rate, third-rate, low-grade, cheap, cheap and nasty, shoddy, tawdry, gimcrack; informal crummy; Brit. informal two a penny, ten a penny, twopenny-halfpenny; N. Amer. informal nickel-and-dime.
▷ANTONYMS valuable, precious.
2 *your conclusions are utterly worthless*: **useless**, no use, of no benefit, to no avail, futile, ineffective, ineffectual, fruitless, unproductive, unavailing, pointless, nugatory, valueless, inadequate, deficient, defective, inferior, unsatisfactory, meaningless, senseless, insubstantial, empty, hollow, silly, banal, trifling, petty, inconsequential, lame, paltry, pathetic, piddling; informal a dead loss; archaic bootless; rare unfructuous.
▷ANTONYMS useful.
3 *he was destroyed by his loyalty to his worthless son*: **good-for-nothing**, ne'er-do-well, useless, despicable, contemptible, base, low, vile, abject, debased, degraded, ignominious, mean, corrupt, villainous, depraved, degenerate, wretched, miserable, sorry, shiftless, feckless, incompetent; informal no-good, no-account, lousy.

worthwhile adjective *everyone felt that the campaign had been worthwhile | a worthwhile job*: **valuable**, of value, worth it, worth the effort, useful, of use, usable, of service, beneficial, rewarding, advantageous, positive, helpful, of help, of assistance, purposeful, profitable, gainful, fruitful, productive, constructive, effective, efficacious, effectual, justifiable, significant, important, substantial, meaningful, worthy; excellent, exemplary, good.
▷ANTONYMS worthless, useless.

worthy adjective *Samuel was a worthy and responsible citizen | a worthy cause*: **virtuous**, good, moral, ethical, principled, high-principled, high-minded, right-thinking, noble, upright, upstanding, righteous, solid, decent, law-abiding, honest, honourable, respectable, respected, venerable, reputable, trustworthy, trusty, trusted, reliable, dependable, conscientious, irreproachable, blameless, unimpeachable, exemplary, admirable, praiseworthy, laudable, commendable, estimable, deserving, meritorious, creditable, sterling; informal squeaky clean; archaic of good report; rare applaudable.
▷ANTONYMS disreputable, unworthy.
□ **be worthy of** *he believes everyone has ideas that are worthy of attention*: **deserve**, be deserving of, merit, warrant, rate, justify, earn, be entitled to, have a right to, have a claim to/on, be qualified for, qualify for.
▷ANTONYMS be unworthy of, be undeserving of.
▸ noun *the candidate gained the support of some significant local worthies*: **dignitary**, notable, notability, celebrity, personage, famous person, important person, person of note, luminary, public figure, official, pillar of society, grandee, panjandrum, leading light, name, big name, somebody, someone; informal VIP, top brass, Mr Big, big Daddy, big shot, bigwig, big cheese, big fish, big gun, big noise, celeb, biggie, heavy, hotshot; Brit. informal Lady Muck, Lord Muck, nob; N. Amer. informal big wheel, kahuna, big kahuna, macher, high muckamuck, high muckety-muck.
▷ANTONYMS nobody.

would-be adjective *would-be actors*: **aspiring**, budding, promising, prospective, potential, striving, hopeful, optimistic, keen, eager, ambitious, enterprising, wishful, longing; informal wannabe.

wound noun **1** *he had a large wound in his chest*: **injury**, **lesion**, cut, gash, laceration, tear, rent, puncture, slash; sore, graze, scratch, scrape, abrasion; bruise, contusion; Medicine trauma, traumatism.
2 *the wounds inflicted by the media will take a long time to heal*: **insult**, blow, slight, offence, affront; hurt, harm, damage, injury, pain, pang, ache, distress, grief, trauma, anguish, torment, torture.
▸ verb **1** *he was critically wounded in the battle and nearly died | they were wounded by shrapnel*: **injure**, hurt, damage, harm, maim, mutilate, disable, incapacitate, scar; lacerate, cut, cut to ribbons, graze, scratch, gash, tear, tear apart, hack, rip, puncture, pierce, stab, slash; informal zap, plug, blast.
▷ANTONYMS heal.
2 *she could see that her words had wounded him*: **hurt**, hurt the feelings of, scar, damage, harm, injure, insult, slight, offend, give offence to, affront, distress, disturb, upset, make miserable, trouble, discomfort; grieve, sadden, mortify, anguish, pain, sting, cut to the quick, shock, traumatize, cause suffering to, torment, torture, crucify, tear to pieces, gnaw at.
▷ANTONYMS boost.

wraith noun **ghost**, spectre, spirit, phantom, apparition, manifestation, vision, shadow, presence, poltergeist, supernatural being; Scottish & Irish bodach; W. Indian duppy; informal spook; literary shade, visitant, revenant, phantasm, wight; rare eidolon, manes, lemures.

wrangle noun *a demeaning wrangle over a small amount of money*: **argument**, **dispute**, disagreement, quarrel, row, fight, squabble, difference of opinion, altercation, angry exchange, war of words, shouting match, tiff; tussle, brouhaha, fracas, rumpus, brawl, clash, scuffle, battle, war, feud; controversy, uproar; Irish, N. Amer., & Austral. donnybrook; informal falling-out, set-to, run-in, shindig, shindy, dust-up, punch-up, scrap, spat, free-for-all, argy-bargy, ruckus, fisticuffs, ruction; Brit. informal barney, bunfight, ding-dong, bust-up, ruck, slanging match; Scottish informal rammy; N. Amer. informal rhubarb; archaic broil, miff.
▷ANTONYMS agreement.
▸ verb *negotiators had wrangled over details of the agreement*: **argue**, quarrel, row, have a row, bicker, squabble, have words, debate, disagree, have a disagreement, have an altercation, be at odds, bandy words; contend, fight, have a fight, war, battle, feud, clash, grapple, brawl, spar, wrestle, tilt, come to blows, cross swords, lock horns, be at each other's throats, be at loggerheads; informal fall out, scrap, go at it hammer and tongs, fight like cat and dog; rare altercate, chop logic; Scottish archaic threap.
▷ANTONYMS agree.

Choose the right word **wrangle, quarrel, argue, dispute, bicker**

See **quarrel**.

wrap verb **1** *Flora got out of the bath and wrapped herself in a towel*: **swathe**, bundle up, swaddle, sheathe, muffle, cloak, enfold, envelop, encase, enclose, cover, fold, wind; literary lap.
2 *I wrapped the vase carefully in newspaper | he* **wrapped** *the book* **up** *as a present for her*: **parcel up**, parcel, package, pack, pack up, bundle, bundle up, do up, tie up, gift-wrap.
□ **wrap up 1** *wrap up well before you go into that garden*: **dress warmly**, wear warm clothes, put on more clothes, muffle up. **2** Brit. informal *tell that child to wrap up*: **be quiet**, quieten down, be silent, fall silent, stop talking, hold one's tongue, keep one's lips sealed; informal shut up, shut one's mouth, shut one's face, shut one's trap, button one's lip, put a sock in it, pipe down, belt up, cut the cackle, give it a rest; Brit. informal shut one's gob, wrap it up; N. Amer. informal save it.

□ **wrap something up** *it was time to wrap up the conference*: **conclude**, finish, end, bring to an end, bring to a close, bring to a conclusion, round off, terminate, stop, cease, finalize, complete, settle, tie up, put the finishing touches to; informal wind up, sew up, polish off.
▸ noun *he put a wrap round her shoulders*: **shawl**, stole, cloak, cape, mantle, scarf; S. American poncho, serape; rare pelisse, pelerine, mantlet.
□ **under wraps** *latest developments are still under wraps while they make their way through the budgeting process*: **secret**, top secret, confidential, strictly confidential, classified, restricted, hush-hush, off the record, not for publication/circulation, not to be made public, not to be disclosed; unrevealed, undisclosed, unpublished, untold, unknown; Latin sub rosa.

wrapper noun **1** *a sweet wrapper*: **cover**, wrapping, covering, packaging, paper; jacket, dust jacket, binding, sheath, sheathing.
2 N. Amer. *she was lying down in her cotton wrapper*: **housecoat**, bathrobe, dressing gown, robe, negligee, kimono; French peignoir, robe de chambre.

wrath noun *he hadn't the nerve to face his mother's wrath*: **anger**, rage, fury, annoyance, indignation, outrage, pique, spleen, chagrin, vexation, exasperation, dudgeon, high dudgeon, hot temper, bad temper, bad mood, ill humour, irritation, irritability, crossness, displeasure, discontentment, disgruntlement, irascibility, cantankerousness, peevishness, querulousness, crabbiness, testiness, tetchiness, snappishness; literary ire, choler.
▷ANTONYMS happiness, good humour.

wrathful adjective *all at once he grew wrathful, his face purpling*: **angry**, irate, raging, enraged, incensed, infuriated, furious, choleric, fuming, ranting, raving, seething, frenzied, in a frenzy, beside oneself, indignant, outraged, vexed, in high dudgeon, exasperated, in a temper, irritated, provoked, piqued, cross, displeased; bad-tempered, hot-tempered, ill-humoured, irascible; informal mad, wild, livid, boiling, spare, aerated, hot under the collar, on the warpath, up in arms, with all guns blazing, foaming at the mouth, seeing red, steamed up, fit to be tied; N. Amer. informal sore; literary ireful.
▷ANTONYMS calm, good-humoured.

wreak verb *these policies would wreak havoc on the British economy*: **inflict**, create, cause, result in, effect, engender, bring about, perpetrate, unleash, vent, bestow, deal out, mete out, serve out, administer, carry out, deliver, apply, lay on, impose, exact; rare effectuate.

wreath noun *a delicate wreath of roses*: **garland**, chaplet, circlet, coronet, crown, diadem, festoon, lei, swathe, fillet; ring, loop, circle.

wreathe verb **1** *the pulpit had been wreathed in holly | their faces were wreathed in ecstatic smiles*: **festoon**, garland, drape, cover, envelop, array, bedeck, deck, decorate, ornament, adorn.
2 *blue smoke wreathed upwards*: **spiral**, coil, loop, gyrate, wind, curl, twist, twist and turn, corkscrew, snake, curve, meander, zigzag.

wreck noun **1** *heavy seas prevented salvage teams from landing on the wreck*: **shipwreck**, sunken ship, sunken vessel, derelict, hulk; shell, skeleton, hull, frame.
2 *the wreck of a stolen car*: **wreckage**, debris, detritus, remainder; ruins, remains, remnants, fragments, pieces, relics.
3 *his voyage ended in the wreck of his ship off Greece*: **destruction**, **sinking**, wrecking; devastation, ruination, ruin, demolition, smashing, shattering, disintegration.
▸ verb **1** *she knew who had wrecked her car*: **demolish**, **crash**, smash, smash up, ruin, damage, damage beyond repair, destroy, break up, dismantle, vandalize, deface, desecrate, sabotage, leave in ruins; informal write off; Brit. informal prang; N. Amer. informal trash, total.
2 *he was drowned when his ship was wrecked*: **shipwreck**, sink, capsize, run aground, break up.
3 *the crisis had wrecked his plans for the week*: **ruin**, spoil, disrupt, undo, mar, play havoc with, make a mess of, put an end to, end, bring to an end, put a stop to, prevent, frustrate, blight, crush, quell, quash, dash, destroy, scotch, shatter, devastate, demolish, sabotage; informal mess up, screw up, louse up, foul up, make a hash of, do in, put paid to, put the lid on, put the kibosh on, stymie, queer, nix, banjax, blow a hole in; Brit. informal scupper, dish, throw a spanner in the works of; N. Amer. informal throw a monkey wrench in the works of; Austral. informal euchre, cruel; archaic bring to naught.
▷ANTONYMS facilitate.

wreckage noun *the wreckage of a crashed aircraft*: **wreck**, debris, detritus, remainder; hulk, shell, skeleton, hull, frame; ruins, remains, remnants, relics, fragments, pieces.

wrench noun **1** *she felt a terrific wrench on her shoulders as he tried to haul her back*: **tug**, pull, jerk, jolt, wrest, heave, twist; informal **yank**.
2 *hold the piston with a wrench and unscrew the washer*: Brit. **spanner**, adjustable spanner; N. Amer. monkey wrench.
3 *he had no injury other than a wrench in his arm*: **sprain**, twist, strain, rick, crick, dislocation.
4 *leaving Africa was an immense wrench*: **painful parting**, distressing separation, traumatic event; pain, ache, pang, trauma.
▸ verb **1** *he wrenched the gun from her hand*: **tug**, pull, jerk, wrest, heave, twist, tear, rip, pluck, grab, seize, snatch, force, take by force, remove by force, prise, peel; N. Amer. pry; informal **yank**.
2 *Ruth had slipped and wrenched her ankle*: **sprain**, twist, turn, strain, rick, crick, pull, dislocate, put out of joint; damage, injure, hurt.

wrest verb *he tried to wrest the broom from Angela's grasp*: **wrench**, snatch, seize, grab, take by force, remove by force, force, prise, peel, pluck, tear, rip, heave, twist, tug, pull, jerk, dislodge; N. Amer. pry; informal yank.

wrestle verb *the two men wrestled each other in deadly silence | she wrestled with her conscience*: **grapple**, **fight**, struggle, wrangle, contend, vie, battle, combat; scuffle, tussle, jostle, brawl, clash; get to grips, come to grips; informal scrap.

wretch noun **1** *the unfortunate wretches were driven to kill themselves*: **poor creature**, poor soul, poor thing, miserable creature, sad case, unfortunate, poor unfortunate; informal poor devil, poor beggar, poor bastard, poor bunny; Brit. vulgar slang sod, bugger.
2 *I wouldn't trust the old wretch an inch*: **scoundrel**, villain, ruffian, rogue, rascal, reprobate, criminal, delinquent, good-for-nothing, cad; informal heel, creep, jerk, louse, rat, swine, pig, skunk, dog, hound, weasel, toad, snake, snake in the grass, lowlife, scumbag, bad egg, stinker, bad lot, nasty piece of work; Brit. informal scrote; Irish informal sleeveen, spalpeen; N. Amer. informal rat fink, varmint; informal, dated rotter, bounder, blighter; vulgar slang shit, bugger, bastard, son of a bitch, s.o.b.; archaic blackguard, miscreant, knave, dastard, varlet, wastrel, rapscallion, whoreson.

wretched adjective **1** *I felt so wretched because I thought I might never see you again*: **miserable**, unhappy, sad, broken-hearted, heartbroken, grief-stricken, grieving, sorrowful, sorrowing, mourning, anguished, distressed, desolate, devastated, despairing, inconsolable, disconsolate, downcast, down, downhearted, dejected, crestfallen, cheerless, depressed, melancholy, morose, gloomy, glum, mournful, doleful, dismal, forlorn, woeful, woebegone, abject, low-spirited, long-faced; informal blue, down in the mouth, down in the dumps, choked, cut up; Brit. informal gutted; literary dolorous; archaic chap-fallen.
▷ANTONYMS cheerful.
2 *I feel wretched*: **ill**, unwell, poorly, sick, sickly, ailing, below par; Brit. off colour; informal under the weather, out of sorts.
▷ANTONYMS well.
3 *their living conditions are particularly wretched*: **harsh**, hard, grim, stark, difficult; poor, poverty-stricken, run down, down at heel, impoverished; pitiful, piteous, pathetic, tragic, miserable, bleak, cheerless, hopeless, sorry, sordid, shabby, seedy, dilapidated, shoddy, godforsaken; informal scummy, crummy; Brit. informal grotty.
▷ANTONYMS comfortable, luxurious.
4 *the wretched dweller in the shanty town doesn't choose to live there*: **unfortunate**, unlucky, luckless, down on one's luck, ill-starred, star-crossed, damned, blighted, hapless, poor, pitiable, distressed, downtrodden, oppressed, powerless, helpless.
▷ANTONYMS fortunate.
5 *he's a wretched coward*: **despicable**, contemptible, beyond contempt, reprehensible, base, low, vile, mean, scurvy, abominable, loathsome, hateful, detestable, odious, disreputable, depraved, debased, infamous, villainous, ignoble, shameful, shabby, worthless; informal dirty, filthy, dirty rotten, rotten, low-down, no-good, lousy; Brit. informal beastly.
▷ANTONYMS worthy, admirable.
6 *they had several days of wretched weather*: **terrible**, awful, dire, dreadful, atrocious, unspeakable, dismal, bad, poor, lamentable, deplorable, unsatisfactory, substandard, low-quality, inferior; informal yucky, God-awful; Brit. informal beastly, pants, a load of pants.
▷ANTONYMS excellent.
7 *I keep telling you, I don't want the wretched money*: informal **damn**, damned, blasted, blessed, flaming, precious, confounded, rotten; Brit. informal flipping, blinking, blooming, bloody, bleeding, effing, naffing, chuffing; N. Amer. informal goddam; Austral./NZ informal plurry; Brit. informal, dated bally, ruddy, deuced; vulgar slang fucking, frigging; Brit. vulgar slang sodding; Irish vulgar slang fecking.

wriggle verb **1** *she tried to hug him but he fought and wriggled*: **squirm**, writhe, wiggle, jiggle, jerk, thresh, flounder, flail, twitch, turn, twist, twist and turn, zigzag; snake, worm, slither, slink, crawl, creep.
2 *he tried to **wriggle out of** his responsibilities*: **avoid**, **shirk**, dodge, evade, elude, sidestep, circumvent, eschew; hide from, escape from, extricate oneself from, steer clear of; informal duck; archaic bilk.
▷ANTONYMS face up to.
▸ noun **squirm**, jiggle, wiggle, jerk, twist, turn.

wring verb **1** *she showed me how to **wring out** the clothes*: **twist**, squeeze, screw, scrunch, knead, press, mangle; dry, squeeze dry, screw the water out of.
2 *a few concessions were wrung from the government*: **extract**, elicit, force, coerce, exact, extort, wrest, wrench, screw, squeeze, milk; informal bleed.
3 *the expression she saw in his eyes wrung her heart*: **rend**, tear at, harrow, pierce, stab, wound, lacerate, rack; **distress**, pain, hurt, torment, torture.

wrinkle noun **1** *there were fine wrinkles about her mouth | she smoothed out the wrinkles in his coat*: **crease**, fold, pucker, gather, furrow, ridge, line, corrugation, groove, crinkle, crumple, rumple; informal crow's feet.
2 informal *learning the wrinkles from someone more experienced saves time*: **guideline**, hint, tip, pointer, clue, cue, suggestion, piece of advice, word of advice; (**wrinkles**) **inside information**, guidance, advice, help, counsel.
▸ verb *overexposed skin will age and wrinkle prematurely | his coat sleeve wrinkled up*: **crease**, pucker, gather, furrow, line, cover with lines, corrugate, crinkle, crimp, crumple, rumple, ruck up, scrunch up; Brit. rare ruckle.

wrinkled adjective *an elderly man with a deeply wrinkled face*: **creased**, wrinkly, lined, covered with lines, crinkled, crinkly, furrowed, grooved, ridged, crumpled, puckered, shrivelled, wizened; weather-beaten, time-

worn, worn, leathery.
▷**ANTONYMS** smooth.

writ noun *they were served with a High Court writ*: **summons**, subpoena, warrant, arraignment, indictment, court order, process, decree; N. Amer. citation; Latin subpoena ad testificandum.

write verb **1** *he wrote her name in the school jotter | Oliver **wrote down** the address for me*: **put in writing**, write down, put down, put in black and white, commit to paper, jot down, note, note down, make a note of, set down, take down, mark down, record, register, log, list, make a list of, inscribe, sign, scribble, scrawl, pencil.
2 *I'll go and write a poem*: **compose**, draft, create, invent, think up, draw up, formulate, compile, put together, pen, dash off, produce.
3 *he had her address and was going to write*: **correspond**, write a letter, communicate, get in touch, keep in touch, keep in contact; informal drop someone a line, drop someone a note.
□ **write someone/something off 1** *they have had to write off loans and lose their investments*: **forget about**, disregard, give up on, give up for lost, cancel, annul, nullify, wipe out, cross out, score out. **2** *he drove off the road and wrote off his new car*: **wreck**, damage beyond repair, smash, smash up, crash, destroy, demolish, ruin; Brit. informal prang; N. Amer. informal total.
3 *who would write off a player of his stature?* **disregard**, regard as finished, consider unimportant, dismiss, ignore.

writer noun **author**, wordsmith, man/woman of letters, penman, creative writer; informal scribbler, scribe, pen-pusher, hack, potboiler.

writhe verb *she writhed about on the floor in agony*: **squirm**, wriggle, thrash, flounder, flail, toss, toss and turn, twitch, twist, twist and turn, roll, jiggle, wiggle, jerk, jolt.

writing noun **1** *his writing is much larger than mine*: **handwriting**, hand, script, penmanship, pen, print, printing, longhand, calligraphy, chirography; letters; informal scribble, scrawl, fist.
2 (**writings**) *she has had published various writings on comparative education*: **compositions**, works, oeuvre, opus, books, volumes, publications, titles, tomes; papers, articles, essays.
□ **the writing on the wall omen**, ill omen, bad omen, portent, sign, indication, presage, warning, forewarning, foreshadowing, forecast, harbinger, augury, threat, menace, signal, hint, straw in the wind; literary foretoken.

> *Word links* **writing**
>
> **scriptorial** relating to writing
> **graphology** study of handwriting
> **palaeography** study of ancient writing systems
> **graphophobia** fear of writing

wrong adjective **1** *there were no right or wrong answers | in my opinion the judge was wrong*: **incorrect**, **mistaken**, in error, erroneous, inaccurate, not accurate, inexact, not exact, imprecise, invalid, untrue, false, fallacious, wide of the mark, off target; misleading, illogical, unsound, unfounded, without foundation, faulty, flawed; informal off beam, bogus, phoney, out, way out, full of holes, dicey, iffy; Brit. informal dodgy; archaic abroad.
▷**ANTONYMS** right, correct, spot on.
2 *he knew at once that he had said the wrong thing*: **inappropriate**, unsuitable, inapt, inapposite, undesirable; ill-advised, ill-considered, ill-judged, impolitic, injudicious, infelicitous, unacceptable, beyond the pale, unwarranted, unfitting, out of keeping, improper, unseemly, unbecoming, indecorous, lacking in propriety; informal out of order.
▷**ANTONYMS** appropriate.
3 *driving while drunk is wrong*: **illegal**, unlawful, illicit, indictable, lawless, lawbreaking, criminal, delinquent, felonious, dishonest, dishonourable, corrupt; **unethical**, immoral, morally wrong, bad, wicked, base, evil, sinful, foul, despicable, iniquitous, nefarious, blameworthy, condemnable, culpable; informal crooked, shady; Brit. informal bent, not cricket.
▷**ANTONYMS** legal; ethical.
4 *there is no sign of anything wrong with your heart*: **amiss**, awry, out of order, not right, faulty, defective, unsatisfactory, incorrect, inappropriate.
5 *lay the curtain out flat with the wrong side uppermost*: **reverse**, inside, opposite, inverse.
▸ adverb *the government might do its sums wrong*: **incorrectly**, wrongly, inaccurately, erroneously, mistakenly; inexactly, imprecisely, falsely.
□ **get someone/something wrong** *don't get me wrong, motorways aren't always a bad thing*: **misunderstand**, misinterpret, misapprehend, misconstrue, misconceive, mistake, misread, take amiss; get the wrong idea, receive a false impression, be under a delusion, be at cross purposes; informal be barking up the wrong tree, get the wrong end of the stick.
□ **go wrong 1** *there's no need to beat yourself up if you go wrong*: **make a mistake**, make an error, err, make a blunder, blunder, go astray, miscalculate, be incorrect, be wide of the mark, trip up; informal slip up, screw up, make a boo-boo, make a bloomer; Brit. informal boob, drop a clanger.
2 *their plans to poison him went wrong*: **go awry**, go amiss, go adrift, go off course, fail, not succeed, be unsuccessful, go badly, be ruined, fall through, fall flat, fall apart, come apart at the seams, break down, come to nothing, flounder, collapse, meet with disaster, backfire, rebound, boomerang, misfire, miscarry, abort; informal come to grief, flop, come a cropper, go haywire, bite the dust, go up in smoke. **3** *the new television sets will contain fewer components to go wrong*: **break down**, malfunction, fail, stop working, stop functioning, cease to function, crash, give out, go out of control, develop a fault, act up, be defective; informal be on the blink, conk out, go kaput, go phut, go haywire, bite the dust, have had it; Brit. informal play up, pack up. **4** *young people who go wrong*: **go astray**, err, do wrong, commit a crime, commit a sin, fall into a life of crime, get into bad ways, stray from the straight and narrow, fall from grace; informal go to the dogs.
▸ noun **1** *they knew the difference between right and wrong*: **immorality**, **badness**, sin, sinfulness, wickedness, evil, vice, depravity, vileness, iniquity; unlawfulness, crime, corruption, villainy, dishonesty, injustice, wrongdoing, misconduct, transgression; informal crookedness.
▷**ANTONYMS** right, virtue, honour.
2 *no one is entitled to profit from his own wrong | the fellow had really done him a wrong*: **misdeed**, bad deed, bad act/action, offence, injury, crime, unlawful act, illegal act, violation, infringement, infraction, transgression, peccadillo, sin; **injustice**, unfairness, unjust act, grievance, outrage, atrocity; Law malfeasance, tort; archaic trespass; rare malefaction.
□ **in the wrong 1** *he was ashamed to admit that he was in the wrong*: **mistaken**, **in error**, erring, errant, off course, off target, wide of the mark; informal off beam. ▷**ANTONYMS** right.
2 *the law considers you to be in the wrong*: **to blame**, blameworthy, at fault, condemnable, censurable, reproachable, reprehensible, responsible, culpable, answerable, guilty; archaic peccant. ▷**ANTONYMS** blameless.
▸ verb *when you have wronged someone admit it and apologize*: **malign**, misrepresent, do a disservice to, do an injustice to, dishonour, impugn, vilify, defame, slander, libel, denigrate, insult; **mistreat**, do wrong to, abuse, maltreat, ill-treat, ill-use, harm, hurt, injure, do injury to, offend against, oppress; informal bad mouth, kick in the teeth, do the dirty on.

wrongdoer noun **offender**, lawbreaker, criminal, felon, convict, jailbird, delinquent, villain, culprit, guilty party, evil-doer, sinner, transgressor, malefactor, reprobate, rogue, scoundrel, rascal, outlaw; informal crook, con, crim, wrong 'un, baddy, bad guy, bad egg; Law malfeasant, misfeasor, infractor; archaic miscreant, trespasser.
▷**ANTONYMS** law-abiding citizen.

wrongdoing noun *good journalism can expose wrongdoing | he had admitted his wrongdoings*: **crime**, lawbreaking, lawlessness, criminality, misconduct, malpractice, corruption, unethical behaviour, immorality, sin, sinfulness, wickedness, badness, evil, vice, iniquity, villainy, delinquency, misbehaviour, mischief, naughtiness; offence, felony, criminal act, wrong, misdeed, misdemeanour, fault, error, lapse, peccadillo, transgression, immoral act, evil act; Law malfeasance, tort; archaic trespass; rare maleficence, malefaction, malversation.

wrongful adjective *she's suing the police for wrongful arrest*: **unjustified**, unwarranted, unjust, unfair, undue, undeserved, uncalled for, unreasonable, unnecessary, groundless, indefensible, inappropriate, improper, unlawful, illegal, illegitimate, illicit.
▷**ANTONYMS** rightful, fair.

wrongly adverb *the two women were wrongly accused of kidnapping*: **incorrectly**, mistakenly, by mistake, erroneously, in error, falsely, fallaciously, inaccurately, imprecisely, inappropriately.
▷**ANTONYMS** rightly, correctly.

wrought up adjective *it was easy to see that she was wrought up over something*: **agitated**, in a state of agitation, tense, stressed, overwrought, nervous, in a state of nerves, on edge, edgy, keyed up, strung out, jumpy, on tenterhooks, ruffled, flustered, flurried, perturbed, disquieted, fretful, fearful, frightened, scared, with one's heart in one's mouth, with one's stomach in knots, like a cat on a hot tin roof, shaking in one's shoes, on pins and needles, in a cold sweat; Brit. nervy; informal with butterflies in one's stomach, jittery, twitchy, in a state, in a stew, in a sweat, in a flap, in a twitter, in a dither, all of a dither, all of a lather, het up, wired, uptight; Brit. informal strung up, windy, having kittens; N. Amer. informal spooky, squirrelly, in a twit.

wry adjective **1** *his wry humour made her laugh*: **ironic**, sardonic, satirical, mocking, scoffing, sneering, derisive, scornful, sarcastic, double-edged, dry, droll, witty, humorous; Brit. informal sarky.
2 *he sipped his cold coffee and made a wry face*: **disgusted**, displeased, discontented, offended, unimpressed, annoyed, irritated, irked, vexed, piqued, nettled, put out, disgruntled; informal peeved, narked, hacked off; Brit. informal cheesed off; N. Amer. informal sore, ticked off, teed off; vulgar slang pissed off.

xenophobia noun *there must be no room for xenophobia in today's Europe*: **racism**, racialism, racial hatred, ethnocentrism, ethnocentricity; nationalism, jingoism, isolationism; prejudice, intolerance, bigotry, bias; in S. Africa, historical apartheid; rare xenophoby.
▷ANTONYMS xenomania.

xenophobic adjective *an unadventurous and xenophobic nation*: **racist**, racialist, ethnocentric, ethnocentrist; nationalist, nationalistic, jingoistic, jingo, isolationist; prejudiced, intolerant, bigoted, parochial, insular.
▷ANTONYMS xenomaniac.

xerox verb *he xeroxed the printout and faxed it to his agent*: **photocopy**, copy, duplicate, replicate, make a replica of, make a facsimile of, reproduce, photostat, mimeograph, mimeo, print, run off; trademark make a Xerox of.
▶ noun (**Xerox**) trademark *in case you haven't read the article I enclose a Xerox*: **photocopy**, copy, carbon copy, duplicate, replica, reproduction, reprint, facsimile, mimeograph, mimeo; transcript; trademark **photostat**; informal **dupe**.

Xmas noun informal *an Xmas panto*: **Christmas**, Christmastime, Christmastide, festive season; Nativity; Indian Burra Din; Brit. informal Chrimbo, Crimbo, Chrissie, Chrissy; literary Yuletide, Yule, Noel.

X-ray noun *an X-ray of her left knee*: **radiogram**, radiograph, X-ray image; technical roentgenogram; Medicine angiogram, lymphangiogram, mammogram, pyelogram, cholangiogram.

Word links **X-ray**

radiography making images using X-rays
radiology study of X-rays

yahoo noun *you're no yahoo; you're too smart*: **barbarian**, philistine, vulgarian, savage, brute, beast, boor, oaf, ruffian, thug, lout, hoodlum, hooligan, vandal, rowdy, bully boy, brawler; informal clod, clodhopper, tough, toughie, roughneck, bruiser, hard man; Brit. informal yobbo, yob, bovver boy, lager lout, chav, oik, ape, gorilla, bear, lump; Scottish informal radge; N. Amer. informal lummox; Austral./NZ informal hoon.

yak, yack verb *she was yakking about her passion for antiques*: **prattle**, blather, blether, blither, babble (on), gabble, prate, drivel, rattle on/away, ramble, maunder, go on, run on, talk at length, talk incessantly, talk a lot, chatter, yap, gossip; Brit. talk nineteen to the dozen; Scottish & Irish slabber on; informal jabber, blabber, yatter, jaw, gab, gas, chit-chat, yackety-yak; Brit. informal rabbit, witter, waffle, natter, chunter, talk the hind legs off a donkey; N. Amer. informal run off at the mouth; Austral./NZ informal mag; archaic twaddle, twattle, claver, clack.

yank informal verb *Gilbert yanked open the door to the office*: **jerk**, pull, tug, wrench, heave, haul, drag, tweak, twitch, pluck, snatch, seize, rip, tear, whisk, jolt, force; informal whip.
▸ **noun** *she gave his hat a sharp yank*: **jerk**, pull, tug, jolt, wrench, heave, tweak, twitch.

yap verb **1** *the dogs yapped about his heels*: **yelp**, bark, woof, bay.
2 *the presenter was **yapping away** on the television*: **chatter**, prattle, prate, gibber, babble, blather, blether, blither, gabble, gossip, rattle, ramble, maunder; go on, run on, talk at length, talk incessantly, talk a lot; Brit. talk nineteen to the dozen; Scottish & Irish slabber on; informal jabber, blabber, yatter, jaw, gab, gas, chit-chat, yackety-yak; Brit. informal rabbit, witter, waffle, natter, chunter, talk the hind legs off a donkey; N. Amer. informal run off at the mouth; Austral./NZ informal mag; archaic twaddle, twattle, claver, clack.
▸ **noun 1** *her dog greeted her with excited yaps*: **yelp**, bark, woof.
2 N. Amer. informal *will you kindly keep your yap shut for a minute?* See **mouth**.

yard noun **1** *they kicked a football about the yard*: **backyard**, garden; courtyard, court, quadrangle, enclosure, cloister, close; informal quad.
2 *we took over the management of a boatbuilding yard*: **workshop**, works, factory, garage, plant, foundry, mill, industrial unit; shipyard; archaic manufactory.

yardstick noun *they ought to appraise their investments against a more realistic yardstick*: **standard**, measure, gauge, scale, guide, guideline, indicator, test, touchstone, barometer, specification, criterion, norm, average, benchmark, point of reference, model, pattern, rule, principle, paradigm, convention, ideal.

yarn noun **1** *you need to use a fine yarn*: **thread**, cotton, wool, fibre, filament, strand; ply; cord, twine, string, line.
2 *he told a rather tedious yarn about two Italian peasants*: **story**, tale, anecdote, fable, parable, traveller's tale, fairy story, rigmarole, saga, sketch, narrative, reminiscence, account, report, history; informal tall tale, tall story, cock and bull story, shaggy-dog story, spiel.

yawning adjective *there was a yawning hole where the door had been wrenched off*: **gaping**, wide open, wide, cavernous, deep; large, huge, great, big; rare chasmal.

year noun *he become Head of Campaigns for one year*: **twelve-month period**, twelve-month session; calendar year, tax year, financial year, fiscal year, FY; literary sun, summer, winter; archaic twelvemonth.
□ **year in, year out** *we pay the same fixed sum year in, year out*: **repeatedly**, again and again, time and (time) again, time after time, over and over (again), {week in, week out}, {day in, day out}, recurrently, continuously, continually, constantly, habitually, regularly, without a break, persistently, unfailingly, always.
▹**ANTONYMS** occasionally.

> *Word links* **year**
>
> **annual** occurring once a year or lasting a year

yearly adjective *a yearly payment of £5*: **annual**, once a year, every year, each year.
▸ **adverb** *the guide is published yearly*: **annually**, once a year, by the year, per annum, every year, each year.

yearn verb *she yearned to be with him*: **long**, pine, crave, desire, want, want badly, wish, have/feel a longing, covet, lust, pant, hunger, thirst, ache, be aching, itch, be itching; hanker after, dream of, fancy, have one's heart set on, be bent on, eat one's heart out over; informal have a yen, yen, be dying; archaic be athirst for, be desirous; rare suspire for.

> *Choose the right word* **yearn, long, pine, hanker**
>
> To **yearn** for something is to desire it intensely, even though it is difficult or impossible to obtain; recognition of this means that the desire tends to be mixed with sorrow or melancholy (*she yearned for her missing father | his ambition was always yearning after the impossible | I yearned to live a semi-bohemian lifestyle*).
>
> To **long** is also to feel a deep desire (*she'd longed to hear him whisper that he loved her*), but it may also be used more trivially to say that one very much wants something, especially food or drink, that one is quite likely to get soon (*I'm longing for a cup of tea*).
>
> To **pine** is to long for someone or something that one has lost (*even though he had a new girlfriend she still pined for him*), and is often used of animals who lose their owners. When used without *for*, it means to decline mentally or physically as a result of such longing (*she was the Major's gundog and had pined badly when her master died*).
>
> **Hanker** is a less formal word than *yearn* and, compared with *long*, implies a vaguer, more wistful, or more forlorn desire (*it may be that you hanker after some lost love | she had always hankered for a job in uniform | I've been hankering to play country music again*).

yearning noun *they sometimes feel a yearning for the mountains and the sea*: **longing**, pining, craving, desire, want, wish, hankering, urge, need, hunger, hungering, thirst, appetite, greed, lust, ache, burning, fancy, inclination, eagerness, fervour; informal yen, itch; rare cacoethes.

yell noun *the creature gave an unearthly yell*: **cry**, yelp, call, shout, howl, yowl, wail, scream, shriek, screech, squawk, squeal; bay, roar, bawl, yawp, whoop, caterwaul; informal holler.
▹**ANTONYMS** whisper, murmur.
▸ **verb** *he yelled in agony*: **cry out**, call out, call at the top of one's voice, yelp, shout, howl, yowl, wail, scream, shriek, screech, squawk, squeal; bay, roar, bawl, yawp, whoop, caterwaul; informal holler; rare ululate.
▹**ANTONYMS** whisper, murmur.

yellow adjective **1** *bright yellow flowers | the man with the yellow hair*: yellowish, yellowy, lemon, lemony, amber, gold, golden; blonde, light

brown, fair, flaxen.
2 informal *he'd better get back there quick and prove he's not yellow*: **cowardly**, lily-livered, faint-hearted, chicken-hearted, pigeon-hearted, craven, spiritless, spineless, timid, timorous, fearful, trembling, quaking, shrinking, cowering, afraid of one's own shadow, pusillanimous, weak, feeble, soft; informal **chicken**, weak-kneed, gutless, yellow-bellied, wimpish, wimpy, sissy, sissified; Brit. informal **wet**; N. Amer. informal **candy-assed**; N. Amer. vulgar slang **chickenshit**; archaic **poltroon**, recreant, poor-spirited.
▷ANTONYMS brave, courageous.

yelp verb *he yelped in pain | the red setter yelped and skittered across the floor*: **squeal**, squawk, screech, shriek, scream, howl, yowl, wail, yell, cry out, call out, shout, bawl, yawp; yap, bark, woof, bay; informal **holler**.
▶ noun *she gave an involuntary yelp | her dog gave a loud, happy yelp*: **squeal**, squawk, screech, shriek, scream, howl, yowl, wail, yell, cry, call, shout, bawl, yawl, whoop; yap, bark, woof, bay; informal **holler**.

yen noun informal *he had a yen for foreign travel*: **hankering**, yearning, longing, craving, urge, desire, want, wish, hunger, thirst, lust, appetite, greed, ache, burning, eagerness, fervour; fancy, inclination; informal **itch**.

yes adverb *yes, I'll come to your party*: **all right**, alright, very well, of course, by all means, sure, certainly, absolutely, indeed, affirmative, in the affirmative, agreed, roger; Scottish, N. English, & archaic **aye**; Nautical **aye aye**; informal **yeah**, yah, yep, yup, uh-huh, okay, OK, okey-dokey, okey-doke; Brit. informal **righto**, righty-ho; N. Amer. informal **surely**; Indian informal **acha**; archaic or formal **yea**.
▷ANTONYMS no.

yes-man noun informal *a Hollywood yes-man*: **sycophant**, toady, lackey, flunkey, minion, stooge, kowtower, truckler, groveller, crawler, creep, fawner, flatterer, lickspittle, Uriah Heep, puppet, cat's paw, instrument, pawn, underling, hanger-on, camp follower, doormat, spaniel; informal **bootlicker**; Brit. informal **poodle**, dogsbody; N. Amer. informal **suck-up**; Indian informal **chamcha**; Brit. vulgar slang **arse-licker**, bum-sucker; N. Amer. vulgar slang **brown-nose**, ass-kisser, suckhole; archaic **toad-eater**.

yet adverb **1** *he has not made up his mind yet*: **so far**, thus far, as yet, still, even now, up till now, up to now, until now, up to the present time.
2 *don't celebrate just yet*: **now**, right now, at this time, at this moment in time; already, so soon.
3 *he was doing nothing, yet he appeared purposeful*: **nevertheless**, nonetheless, even so, but, however, still, notwithstanding, despite that, in spite of that, for all that, all the same, just the same, at the same time, be that as it may; though, although; archaic **natheless**.
4 *he supplied yet more unsolicited advice*: **even**, still, further, in addition, additionally, besides, into the bargain, to boot.

yield verb **1** *too many projects yield poor returns*: **produce**, bear, give, supply, provide, afford, return, bring in, pull in, haul in, gather in, fetch, earn, net, realize, generate, furnish, bestow, pay out, contribute; informal **rake in**.
2 *she yielded her seat to the doctor*: **relinquish**, surrender, part with, deliver up, hand over, turn over, give over; make over, bequeath, remit, cede, leave, sacrifice.
▷ANTONYMS retain.
3 *the younger child was forced to yield*: **surrender**, capitulate, submit, relent, admit defeat, accept defeat, concede defeat, back down, climb down, quit, give in, give up the struggle, lay down one's arms, raise/show the white flag, knuckle under; be overcome, be overwhelmed, be conquered, be beaten, fall victim; informal **throw in the towel**, throw in the sponge, cave in.
4 *he yielded to the plea of his dying godson*: **accede to**, submit to, bow down to, defer to, comply with, conform to, agree to, consent to, go along with, be guided by, heed, note, pay attention to; grant, permit, allow, sanction, warrant.
▷ANTONYMS resist, defy.
5 *the floorboards yielded underfoot*: **bend**, give, flex, be flexible, be pliant.
▶ noun *risky investments usually have higher yields*: **profit**, gain, return, reward, revenue, dividend, proceeds, receipts, earnings, takings; product, production, produce, output, crop, harvest; N. Amer. **take**; informal **pickings**; Brit. informal **bunce**.

yob, yobbo noun Brit. informal *yobs showered the police with broken bottles*. See **hooligan**.

yoke noun **1** *the horses were loosened from the yoke*: **harness**, collar, coupling, tackle, tack, equipage.
2 *these countries were struggling under the yoke of imperialism*: **tyranny**, oppression, domination, hegemony, enslavement, slavery, servitude, subjugation, subjection, bondage, serfdom, vassalage; bonds, chains, fetters, shackles; literary **thrall**, thraldom.
3 *the yoke of marriage*: **bond**, tie, link.
▶ verb **1** *I yoke my oxen to the plough*: **harness**, hitch, hitch up, couple, tether, fasten, attach, join, join up, team.
▷ANTONYMS unhitch.
2 *Mariana is yoked in an arranged marriage to her cousin*: **unite**, join, link, connect, bond, tie, bind.

yokel noun *the yokels drank cider and pronounced it 'zyder'*: **bumpkin**, country bumpkin, country cousin, rustic, countryman, countrywoman, country dweller, son/daughter of the soil, peasant, provincial, oaf, lout, boor, barbarian; French **paysan**; Spanish **campesino**; Italian **contadino**, contadina, paisano; Russian **muzhik**, kulak; Egyptian **fellah**; Indian **ryot**; informal **clod**, clodhopper, yahoo, yob, yobbo; Irish informal **culchie**, bogman; N. Amer. informal **hayseed**, hillbilly, hick, rube, schlub; Austral. informal **bushy**; archaic **carl**, churl, hind, kern; rare **bucolic**.

young adjective **1** *I hate to see a young man throwing his life away*: **youthful**, juvenile; junior, adolescent, teenage, teenaged; immature, childlike, babyish, boyish, girlish; in the springtime of life, in one's salad days; informal **teen**.
▷ANTONYMS old, elderly; mature.
2 *a very agreeable young wine*: **new**, recent, fresh, immature, undeveloped, developing, in the making, in its infancy.
▷ANTONYMS mature.
▶ noun **1** *female flycatchers usually raise five or six young*: **offspring**, progeny, family, children, issue, little ones, youngsters, babies; sons, daughters, heirs, descendants, successors, scions; informal **kids**, kiddies, nippers, tots, tinies; Brit. informal **sprogs**; N. Amer. informal **rug rats**; Austral./NZ informal **ankle-biters**; literary **babes**, the fruit of one's loins; rare **progeniture**.
2 (**the young**) **young people**, youths, children, boys and girls, youngsters, young ones, the younger generation, the next generation, juveniles, minors, schoolboys, schoolgirls, whippersnappers, striplings; informal **kids**, kiddies, young 'uns, lads, lasses.

youngster noun *a new magazine for youngsters*: **young person**, young adult, young man/woman, youth, juvenile, teenager, adolescent, junior, stripling, whippersnapper, young one, little one, child; lad, boy, schoolboy, lass, girl, schoolgirl; Scottish & N. English **bairn**, wean; derogatory **brat**, chit; informal **kid**, kiddie, kiddiewink, shaver, nipper, young 'un, teen; Brit. informal **sprog**; N. Amer. informal **rug rat**; Austral./NZ informal **ankle-biter**; Law **minor**.

yourself, yourselves pronoun
□ **by yourself/yourselves** See **by oneself** at **by**.

youth noun **1** *he had been a keen sportsman in his youth*: **early years**, early life, young days, teens, teenage years, adolescence, young adulthood, boyhood, girlhood, childhood; immaturity; prime, heyday, day, hour, time, springtime, salad days, bloom, peak, pinnacle, height; Law **minority**; rare **juvenility**, juvenescence.
▷ANTONYMS adulthood, old age.
2 *she had kept her youth and beauty*: **youthfulness**, youngness, freshness, bloom.
▷ANTONYMS maturity.
3 *the problem of unemployment among local youths*: **young man**, boy, lad, youngster, juvenile, teenager, adolescent, junior, minor, young one; stripling, whippersnapper, fledgling; Scottish & N. English **bairn**; informal **kid**, chav, hoodie, teen, shaver.
▷ANTONYMS old man.
4 *the youth of the nation are looking for a hero*: **young people**, young, younger generation, rising generation, next generation; informal **kids**.
▷ANTONYMS elderly.

youthful adjective *the party had a youthful new leader*: **young-looking**, spry, sprightly, vigorous, active; young, juvenile, boyish, girlish, childlike; fresh-faced, in the springtime of life, in one's salad days.
▷ANTONYMS old, elderly, doddering.

Word toolkit

youthful	immature	juvenile
exuberance	cell	delinquent
enthusiasm	tissue	offender
indiscretion	seed	court
appearance	fruit	crime
passion	leaf	nuisance
idealism	stage	diabetes
innocence	male	arthritis

yo-yo verb *the industry yo-yos between boom and bust*: **oscillate**, swing, fluctuate, alternate, see-saw, veer, waver, sway, go from one extreme to the other, vary, vacillate, teeter, hover; informal **wobble**, blow hot and cold.

Zz

zany adjective *the film has a zany plot and some peculiar characters*: **eccentric**, bizarre, weird, peculiar, odd, quirky, avant-garde, unconventional, strange, outlandish, ridiculous, ludicrous; mad, insane, crazy, absurd, comic, comical, clownish, farcical, madcap, silly, light-hearted, funny, amusing, chucklesome, diverting, waggish, hilarious; informal wacky, screwy, nutty, nuts, crackpot, cracked, oddball, cranky, kinky, off the wall, way out, dippy, cuckoo; Brit. informal **daft**; N. Amer. informal kooky, wacko, in left field; Austral./NZ informal, dated dilly.
▷ANTONYMS conventional, sensible, serious.

zap verb informal **1** *the monster gets zapped by a flying saucer*. See **kill**, **destroy**. **2** *racing cars zapped past on the track below*. See **speed**.

zeal noun *his zeal for football*: **passion**, zealousness, committedness, ardour, love, fervour, fire, avidity, fondness, devotion, devotedness, enthusiasm, eagerness, keenness, appetite, taste, relish, gusto; vigour, energy, verve, zest; rare fervency, ardency.
▷ANTONYMS apathy, indifference.

zealot noun *reforming zealots destroyed a vast collection of papers*: **fanatic**, enthusiast, extremist, radical, Young Turk, diehard, activist, militant; bigot, dogmatist, sectarian, partisan; informal fiend, maniac, ultra, nut.
▷ANTONYMS moderate.

zealotry noun *religious zealotry could lead to communal tension*: **fanaticism**, zeal, zealousness, extremism, radicalism, militancy, dogmatism, bigotry, single-mindedness; vehemence, forcefulness.
▷ANTONYMS apathy.

zealous adjective *he is a zealous worker*: **fervent**, ardent, fervid, fiery, passionate, impassioned, devout, devoted; **committed**, dedicated, enthusiastic, eager, keen, avid, sincere, wholehearted, hearty, earnest, vigorous, energetic, zestful, purposeful, forceful, intense, fierce, single-minded; informal go-ahead, pushy; rare perfervid.
▷ANTONYMS apathetic, indifferent.

Word toolkit

zealous	**fervent**	**fanatical**
fan	hope	devotion
pursuit	appeal	support
nationalism	imagination	groups
missionary	embrace	hatred

zenith noun *the king was at the zenith of his power*: **highest point**, high point, crowning point, height, top, acme, peak, pinnacle, apex, apogee, vertex, tip, crown, crest, summit, climax, culmination, maximum, optimum, prime, meridian, flower; informal high noon.
▷ANTONYMS nadir, bottom.

zero noun **1** *the sum's wrong—you've left off a zero*: **nought**, nothing, cipher, nil, o; Computing null character; archaic naught.
2 *the allowable dolphin kill will be gradually reduced each year to zero*: **nothing**, nil, nothing at all, not a single thing, not anything, none; N. English nowt; informal zilch, nix, sweet Fanny Adams, sweet FA, not a dicky bird; Brit. informal damn all, not a sausage; N. Amer. informal zip, zippo, nada, diddly-squat, a goose egg, bupkis; Brit. vulgar slang bugger all, fuck all, sod all; archaic naught, nought.
3 *his energy levels were at zero*: **rock bottom**, the bottom, the lowest point, the all-time low, as low as one can get, low-water mark, the depths, the nadir; informal the pits.
▶verb *zero the counter at the end point of the tape*: **return to nought**, return to zero, adjust to zero point.
□ **zero in on** *different scientists chose to zero in on different diseases*: **focus on**, focus attention on, centre on, concentrate on, home in on, fix on, pinpoint, give prominence to, highlight, spotlight, underline, emphasize; informal zoom in on.

zero hour noun *as zero hour approached, thirty ships swung into position*: **the appointed time**, the appointed hour, the crucial moment, the vital moment, the critical moment, the moment of truth, the point/moment of decision, the Rubicon, the critical point, the crux; informal the crunch.

zest noun **1** *she had a great zest for life*: **enthusiasm**, **gusto**, relish, zestfulness, appetite, eagerness, keenness, avidity, zeal, fervour, ardour, passion, love, enjoyment, joy, delight, excitement; verve, vigour, liveliness, sparkle, fizz, effervescence, fire, animation, vitality, dynamism, energy, buoyancy, brio, bounce, pep, spirit, spiritedness, exuberance, high spirits, high-spiritedness; informal zing, zip, oomph, vim, pizzazz, get-up-and-go.
▷ANTONYMS apathy, indifference; distaste.
2 *the slice of lemon in a gin and tonic is there to add zest*: **piquancy**, tang, sharpness, tartness, flavour, flavouring, savour, taste, tastiness, pungency, spice, spiciness, relish, bite; interest, an edge, effect, potency; informal kick, punch, zing, oomph.
▷ANTONYMS blandness.
3 *add the finely grated zest of an orange*: **rind**, peel, skin, covering, outer layer; technical epicarp, pericarp, exocarp.

Choose the right word **zest, gusto, verve**

Zest originally denoted the grated outer rind of a lemon, orange, or lime; hence it has also come to refer to a quality of excitement or piquancy (*I try to beat previous records in order to give zest to an otherwise monotonous job*). It also describes the eager enthusiasm inspired by such a quality (*the grass court season has given him renewed zest, and he is playing the best tennis of his career | she had a zest for life and boundless energy*).

To do something with **gusto** is to do it with obvious enthusiasm, enjoyment, and energy (*the crowd sang the anthem with gusto | I was attacking a delicious crême brûlée with great gusto*).

Verve also denotes energy and liveliness, but additionally suggests stylishness and expertise (*performances of undeniable verve and grace | he drove with assurance and verve*).

zigzag adjective *I steered a zigzag course between the trees*: **meandering**, zigzagging, snaking, snaky, winding, wiggly, squiggly, crooked, tacking, twisting, twisty, full of twists and turns, curving, curvy, wavy, deviating, undulating, sinuous, serpentine, tortuous, irregular; technical sinuate, ogee; rare anfractuous, flexuous, meandrous, serpentiform.
▷ANTONYMS straight.
▶verb *a narrow path zigzagged steeply down from the house*: **meander**, snake, twist, twist and turn, tack, wind, weave, wander, wiggle, squiggle, undulate.

zing noun informal **1** *he had a real zing in his sprightly voice*: **enthusiasm**, zest, zestfulness, appetite, relish, gusto, eagerness, keenness, avidity, zeal, fervour, ardour, passion, love, enjoyment, joy, delight, pleasure, excitement; **vigour**, verve, liveliness, sparkle, fizz, effervescence, fire, animation, vitality, dynamism, energy, buoyancy, brio, bounce, pep, spirit, spiritedness, exuberance, high spirits, high-spiritedness; informal zip, oomph, vim, pizzazz, get-up-and-go.

2 *sprinkle Cajun seasoning on chops to give them zing*: **piquancy**, pungency, spice, spiciness, saltiness, pepperiness, flavour, flavouring, savour, taste, tastiness, relish, bite, tang, zest, sharpness, tartness; interest, edge, effect, potency; informal kick, punch, oomph.

zip informal **noun** *we were full of vim and zip*. See **zing**.
▸ **verb** *house martins zipped back and forth over the lake*. See **speed**.

zone noun *the immediate vicinity of a radar mast is a dangerous zone*: **area**, sector, section, belt, region, territory, tract, stretch, expanse, district, quarter, precinct, locality, neighbourhood, province, land.

zoom verb informal *a motorbike zoomed across their path*. See **speed**.